Y0-BDH-823
MORTON & LACY

MARTINDALE-HUBBELL®

BAR REGISTER OF PREEMINENT LAWYERS™ 1995

SEVENTY-NINTH EDITION

MARTINDALE-HUBBELL
A Reed Reference Publishing Company
121 Chanlon Road
New Providence, New Jersey 07974
(908) 464-6800

Published by Martindale-Hubbell®, a Reed Reference Publishing Company

Ira Siegel, President, CEO
Andrew W. Meyer, Executive Vice President
Peter E. Simon, Senior Vice President, Database Publishing
Stanley Walker, Senior Vice President, Marketing
Edward J. Roycroft, Senior Vice President, Sales

Lawyers providing information regarding themselves and their practices for inclusion in the Martindale-Hubbell® Bar Register of Preeminent Lawyers are responsible for the accuracy of the information submitted and compliance with local law and bar regulations.

International Standard Book Number: 1-56160-138-1

Printed and Bound in the United States of America
by Rand McNally Book Manufacturing Company
Taunton, Massachusetts

ISBN 1-56160-138-1

9 781561 601387

TABLE OF CONTENTS

FOREWORD

This year, we are pleased to publish the 79th edition of the **Martindale-Hubbell® Bar Register of Preeminent Lawyers**, which includes over 23,000 listings of the legal community's most highly-regarded professionals.

The **Bar Register** lists only those sole practitioners and law firms who have received the highest (AV) rating in the *Martindale-Hubbell® Law Directory*. These ratings result from confidential questionnaires sent to other practicing attorneys and members of the judiciary. The "A" rating is the highest legal ability rating, while the "V" signifies adherence to professional standards of conduct, ethics, reliability, and diligence.

The 1995 **Bar Register** provides information on firms excelling in general practice and 34 specific areas of practice, including new sections on Public Utilities, Product Liability, and Appellate Practice.

Organized by areas of practice then alphabetically by state and city, each entry in the **Bar Register** features complete contact information, names of associates and "of counsel", representative clients, and branch office locations.

I'm certain you will find this edition valuable as a source of information on the finest legal representation available, and I welcome any comments you may have concerning the **Martindale-Hubbell Bar Register of Preeminent Lawyers**.

Ira Siegel
President, CEO

MARTINDALE-HUBBELL® LEGAL ADVISORY BOARD

The Martindale-Hubbell Legal Advisory Board was formed to insure that the Martindale-Hubbell Law Directory is responsive to the constantly changing needs of the legal profession.

The following lawyers selected from the private, corporate and International sectors of the profession, as well as the legal academic community, comprise the 1994-1995 Board.

Vincent J. Apruzzese
Apruzzese, McDermott, Mastro & Murphy
Liberty Corner, New Jersey

Richard G. Baker
U.K. Legal Director and Company Secretary
Reed Elsevier p l c
London, England

Martha W. Barnett
Holland & Knight
Tallahassee, Florida

Allen E. Brennecke
Welp, Harrison, Brennecke & Moore
Marshalltown, Iowa

Benjamin R. Civiletti
Venable, Baetjer and Howard
Baltimore, Maryland

James W. Hewitt
Attorney at Law
Lincoln, Nebraska

Thomas J. Klitgaard
Senior Vice President and General Counsel
Sega of America, Inc.
Redwood City, California

Ralph I. Lancaster, Jr.
Pierce, Atwood, Scribner, Allen, Smith & Lancaster
Portland, Maine

Judge William B. Lawless
President
Judges Mediation Network
Newport Beach, California

William G. Paul
Senior Vice President and General Counsel
Phillips Petroleum Company
Bartlesville, Oklahoma

Wm. Reece Smith, Jr.
Carlton, Fields, Ward, Emmanuel, Smith & Cutler
Tampa, Florida

Sir David Williams
Vice Chancellor
Cambridge University
Cambridge, England

USER'S GUIDE

The **MARTINDALE-HUBBELL® BAR REGISTER OF PREEMINENT LAWYERS** is a single volume registry of firms and attorneys of significant stature. The 1995 Edition presents thirty-five alphabetically sequenced practice area sections and an index to the firms listed in each practice area.

This **Subscribers Index**, arranged alphabetically by subscriber name, will assist the user in identifying those practice areas and geographic location(s) where the subscriber lists.

A typical entry appears as follows:

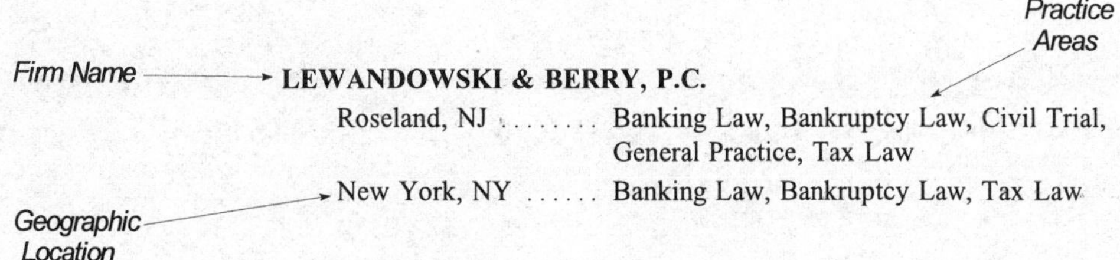

The **Practice Area Section** clearly lists the practice area at the top of the page, along with the geographic location. Listings for the United States and Canada are arranged in alphabetic sequence by state (or Canadian province) and within state (or Canadian province) by city name and finally by listee name. For countries other than the United States and Canada, alphabetic country name is the major sequence, followed by city and then listee name.

A typical section entry appears as follows:

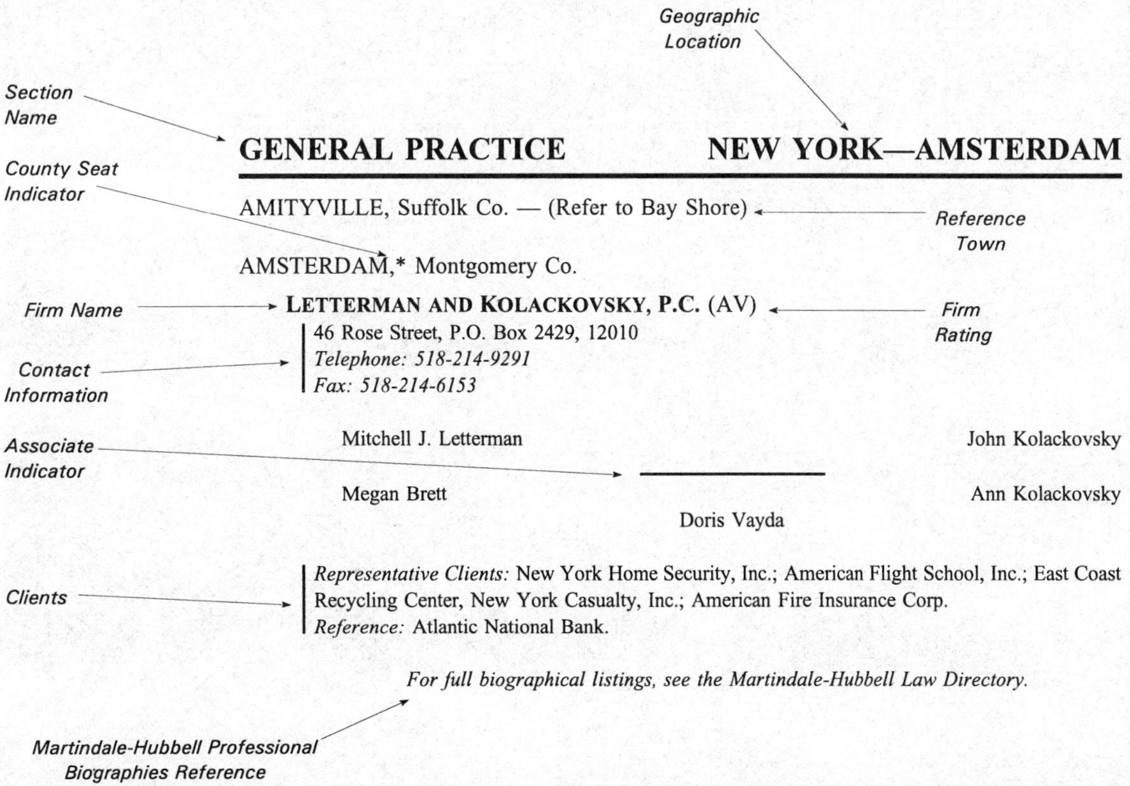

For additional help or explanation, please call Martindale-Hubbell Customer Service, at (800) 526-4902.

INDEX SECTION

AABY, PUTNAM, ALBO & CAUSEY, A PROFESSIONAL SERVICES CORPORATION
Seattle, WA ..... Personal Injury Law

AARONSON & AARONSON
Encino, CA ..... Real Estate Law

ABADIE, JAMES F.
Baton Rouge, LA ..... Personal Injury Law

ABBEY, JOE B.
Dallas, TX ..... Appellate Practice, Banking Law, Civil Trial Practice, Natural Resources Law

ABBOTT, C. MICHAEL, P.C.
Atlanta, GA ..... Criminal Trial Practice

ABBOTT, NICHOLSON, QUILTER, ESSHAKI & YOUNGBLOOD, P.C.
Detroit, MI ..... Business Law, Civil Trial Practice, Employment Benefits Law, Labor and Employment Law, Probate and Estate Planning Law, Real Estate Law

ABDO AND ABDO, P.A.
Minneapolis, MN ..... Business Law, General Practice, Probate and Estate Planning Law, Real Estate Law, Securities Law

ABEL, BAND, RUSSELL, COLLIER, PITCHFORD & GORDON, CHARTERED
Sarasota, FL ..... Banking Law, Bankruptcy Law, Business Law, Civil Trial Practice, Environmental Law, Probate and Estate Planning Law

ABEL, MUSSER, SOKOLOSKY, MARES, HAUBRICH, BURCH & KOURI
Oklahoma City, OK ..... Civil Trial Practice, Insurance Defense Law, Personal Injury Law

ABELSON LAW FIRM, THE
Washington, DC ..... Civil Trial Practice, Medical Malpractice Law, Personal Injury Law

ABEYTA-NELSON, P.C.
Yakima, WA ..... Personal Injury Law

ABOWITZ, WELCH AND RHODES
Oklahoma City, OK ..... Civil Trial Practice, Insurance Defense Law, Personal Injury Law, Securities Law

ABRAHAMS, SEYMOUR J.
San Jose, CA ..... Bankruptcy Law

ABRAHAMS, KASLOW & CASSMAN
Omaha, NE ..... General Practice

ABRAHAMSON, REED & ADLEY
Hammond, IN ..... Civil Trial Practice, Insurance Defense Law, Transportation Law

ABRAMS, BYRON, HENDERSON & RICHMOND
Beckley, WV ..... General Practice

ABRAMS & MARTIN, P.C.
New York, NY ..... Administrative Law, Insurance Defense Law

ABRAMSON & FOX
Chicago, IL ..... Civil Trial Practice

ABRAMSON, FREEDMAN & THALL
Philadelphia, PA ..... Administrative Law, Civil Trial Practice, Commercial Law

ABRAMSON, REIS AND BROWN
Manchester, NH ..... Medical Malpractice Law, Personal Injury Law

ACHOR, MILLER, CULVER & MAILLIARD
Santa Rosa, CA ..... Civil Trial Practice, General Practice

ACKERMAN, JAMES H. LAW OFFICES OF
Long Beach, CA ..... Admiralty/Maritime Law, General Practice

ACKMAN, MAREK, BOYD & SIMUTIS, LTD.
Kankakee, IL ..... Civil Trial Practice, General Practice, Insurance Defense Law
Watseka, IL ..... General Practice

ACTON AND SNYDER
Danville, IL ..... General Practice

ADAMO & NEWMAN
Westerly, RI ..... Criminal Trial Practice, Family Law, Personal Injury Law

ADAMS, WESTON
Columbia, SC ..... General Practice

ADAMS & ADAMS
Miami, FL ..... Civil Trial Practice, General Practice
Somerset, KY ..... General Practice

ADAMS, BARFIELD, DUNAWAY & HANKINSON
Thomaston, GA ..... General Practice

ADAMS, BROOKING, STEPNER, WOLTERMANN & DUSING
Covington, KY ..... Civil Trial Practice, General Practice, Insurance Defense Law, Personal Injury Law, Probate and Estate Planning Law
Florence, KY ..... Civil Trial Practice, General Practice, Insurance Defense Law, Personal Injury Law, Probate and Estate Planning Law

ADAMS, COFFEY & DUESLER, L.L.P.
Beaumont, TX ..... Insurance Defense Law

ADAMS, COOGLER, WATSON & MERKEL, P.A.
West Palm Beach, FL ..... Civil Trial Practice

ADAMS & CRAMER
Shelbyville, IN ..... General Practice

ADAMS, DUQUE & HAZELTINE
Los Angeles, CA ..... Antitrust Law, Bankruptcy Law, Civil Trial Practice, General Practice, Insurance Defense Law, Labor and Employment Law, Real Estate Law, Tax Law
San Francisco, CA ..... Environmental Law, General Practice, Insurance Defense Law, Real Estate Law

ADAMS & ELLIS, A PROFESSIONAL CORPORATION
Savannah, GA ..... General Practice

ADAMS, GILBERT T., A PROF. CORP., LAW OFFICES OF
Beaumont, TX ..... Civil Trial Practice, Personal Injury Law

ADAMS AND GRAHAM, L.L.P.
Harlingen, TX ..... General Practice

ADAMS AND JOHNSTON
New Orleans, LA ..... Insurance Defense Law

ADAMS, JONES, ROBINSON AND MALONE, CHARTERED
Wichita, KS ..... General Practice, Natural Resources Law

ADAMS KLEEMEIER HAGAN HANNAH & FOUTS
Greensboro, NC ..... Civil Trial Practice, General Practice, Labor and Employment Law, Tax Law

ADAMS, NICHOLS AND EVANS, P.A.
Harrison, AR ..... General Practice

ADAMS, QUACKENBUSH, HERRING & STUART, P.A.
Columbia, SC ..... Civil Trial Practice, Real Estate Law

ADAMS & WHITEAKER, P.C.
Nashville, TN ..... Commercial Law, Probate and Estate Planning Law

ADANG, PETER J., P.C.
Albuquerque, NM ..... Civil Trial Practice, Labor and Employment Law

ADDISON, MICHAEL C.
Tampa, FL ..... Antitrust Law, Construction Law, Product Liability Law, Securities Law

ADDUCI, MASTRIANI, SCHAUMBERG & SCHILL
Washington, DC ..... International Business Law

ADELMAN, GETTLEMAN & MERENS, LTD.
Chicago, IL ..... Bankruptcy Law

ADELMAN LAVINE GOLD AND LEVIN, A PROFESSIONAL CORPORATION
Philadelphia, PA ..... Bankruptcy Law

ADERSON, FRANK & STEINER, A PROFESSIONAL CORPORATION
Pittsburgh, PA ..... Administrative Law, Bankruptcy Law, Civil Trial Practice, Commercial Law, Family Law, Personal Injury Law, Probate and Estate Planning Law, Product Liability Law

ADINOLFI, O'BRIEN & HAYES, P.C.
West Hartford, CT ..... Civil Trial Practice, General Practice

ADKINS & ADKINS
Catlettsburg, KY ..... Probate and Estate Planning Law, Real Estate Law

ADKINS & KISE, P.A.
Tampa, FL ..... Civil Trial Practice, Construction Law, Patent, Trademark, Copyright and Unfair Competition Law

ADKINS, POTTS & SMETHURST
Ocean City, MD ..... General Practice
Salisbury, MD ..... General Practice

ADLER, DAVID W.
Phoenix, AZ ..... Family Law

ADVICE & COUNSEL INCORPORATED
San Francisco, CA ..... Probate and Estate Planning Law

AGAPAY, LEVYN & HALLING, A PROFESSIONAL CORPORATION
Los Angeles, CA ..... Civil Trial Practice

AGNEW & BRUSAVICH
Los Angeles, CA ..... Personal Injury Law

Torrance, CA....Personal Injury Law

AHLERS, COONEY, DORWEILER, HAYNIE, SMITH & ALLBEE, P.C.
Des Moines, IA....Banking Law, Civil Trial Practice, General Practice, Labor and Employment Law, Municipal Bond/Public Authority Financing Law, Tax Law

AIKINS, MACAULAY & THORVALDSON
Winnipeg, MB, Canada....Business Law, Civil Trial Practice, General Practice, Insurance Defense Law, Personal Injury Law, Probate and Estate Planning Law, Tax Law

AINSLIE & BRONSON
Philadelphia, PA....Criminal Trial Practice

AINSWORTH, SULLIVAN, TRACY, KNAUF, WARNER & RUSLANDER
Albany, NY....General Practice

AIRD & BERLIS
Toronto, ON, Canada....General Practice

AITKEN, SCHAUBLE, PATRICK, NEILL & RUFF
Pullman, WA....General Practice

AITKEN, WYLIE A., A LAW CORPORATION, LAW OFFICES OF
Santa Ana, CA....Personal Injury Law

AJALAT, POLLEY & AYOOB
Los Angeles, CA....Tax Law

AKIN, GUMP, STRAUSS, HAUER & FELD, L.L.P.
Washington, DC....General Practice
Austin, TX....General Practice
Dallas, TX....General Practice
Houston, TX....General Practice
San Antonio, TX....General Practice

AKIN, GUMP, STRAUSS, HAUER, FELD & DASSESSE
Brussels, Belgium....General Practice

AKIN, WARREN & WM. MORGAN, P.C., LAW OFFICES
Cartersville, GA....General Practice

AL-AIBAN, MOSAAD M., DR., LEGAL ADVISORS
Riyadh, Saudi Arabia....General Practice

ALALA MULLEN HOLLAND & COOPER, P.A.
Gastonia, NC....General Practice

ALBANESE, ALBANESE & FIORE, LLP
Garden City, NY....Banking Law, Civil Trial Practice, General Practice, Probate and Estate Planning Law

ALBERT, WARD & JOHNSON, P.C.
Greenwich, CT....Civil Trial Practice, Construction Law, General Practice, Municipal and Zoning Law, Probate and Estate Planning Law, Real Estate Law

ALBRECHT, MAGUIRE, HEFFERN & GREGG, P.C.
Buffalo, NY....Civil Trial Practice, Employment Benefits Law, General Practice, Probate and Estate Planning Law, Tax Law

ALBRIGHT, STODDARD, WARNICK & ALBRIGHT, A PROFESSIONAL CORPORATION
Las Vegas, NV....Bankruptcy Law, Commercial Law, Construction Law, Insurance Defense Law, Personal Injury Law, Real Estate Law

ALCANTARA & FRAME, ATTORNEYS AT LAW, A LAW CORPORATION
Honolulu, HI....Admiralty/Maritime Law, Insurance Defense Law

ALDERMAN & AHLBRAND, P.A.
Fort Myers, FL....Civil Trial Practice, Criminal Trial Practice, General Practice

ALDERSON, ONDOV, LEONARD, SWEEN & RIZZI, P.A.
Austin, MN....General Practice

ALEMBIK, FINE & CALLNER, P.A.
Atlanta, GA....Business Law, Civil Trial Practice, Family Law, General Practice, Insurance Defense Law, Real Estate Law

ALEXANDER, GEBHARDT, APONTE & MARKS, L.L.C.
Silver Spring, MD....Administrative Law, Banking Law, Bankruptcy Law, Business Law, Civil Trial Practice, Commercial Law, Communications Law, Employment Benefits Law, Environmental Law, Immigration and Naturalization Law, Labor and Employment Law, Municipal Bond/Public Authority Financing Law, Municipal and Zoning Law, Real Estate Law, Tax Law, Trademark, Copyright and Unfair Competition Law

ALEXANDER, HOLBURN, BEAUDIN & LANG
Vancouver, BC, Canada....General Practice, Insurance Defense Law, Labor and Employment Law

ALEXANDER LAW FIRM, P.C.
Denver, CO....Civil Trial Practice, Commercial Law, Insurance Defense Law

ALEXANDER LAW FIRM, THE
San Jose, CA....Civil Trial Practice, Environmental Law, Personal Injury Law, Product Liability Law

ALEXANDER & MCEVILY
Houston, TX....Civil Trial Practice, Family Law

ALEXANDER & VANN
Thomasville, GA....General Practice

ALFORD, E. GREGORY
San Diego, CA....Family Law

ALFRED, JEAN-ROBERT
Christiansted, St. Croix, VI....Civil Trial Practice, General Practice, Insurance Defense Law, Real Estate Law

ALLABEN, MASSIE, VANDER WEYDEN & TIMMER
Grand Rapids, MI....Civil Trial Practice, General Practice, Insurance Defense Law

ALLAIN & LIBERTO, R.L.L.P.
New Orleans, LA....Immigration and Naturalization Law

ALLARD & FISH, A PROFESSIONAL CORPORATION
Detroit, MI....Bankruptcy Law, Commercial Law

ALLEGRETTI & WITCOFF, LTD.
Chicago, IL....Patent, Trademark, Copyright and Unfair Competition Law

ALLEN, RICHARD E.
Augusta, GA....Civil Trial Practice, Criminal Trial Practice

ALLEN, BRINTON & SIMMONS, P.A.
Jacksonville, FL....Civil Trial Practice, General Practice

ALLEN & CARWILE, P.C.
Waynesboro, VA....General Practice

ALLEN & CLASSENS
Statesboro, GA....General Practice

ALLEN, COOLEY & ALLEN
Lawrence, KS....General Practice

ALLEN, DELL, FRANK & TRINKLE
Tampa, FL....Civil Trial Practice, General Practice

ALLEN, DIXON & BELL
Fredericton, NB, Canada....General Practice

ALLEN, DYER, DOPPELT, FRANJOLA & MILBRATH
Orlando, FL....Patent, Trademark, Copyright and Unfair Competition Law

ALLEN & HAROLD, P.L.C.
Manassas, VA....Business Law, Commercial Law, Communications Law

ALLEN, JOHN T., JR., P.A.
St. Petersburg, FL....General Practice

ALLEN, JOHNSON, ALEXANDER & KARP, P.A.
Washington, DC....General Practice
Baltimore, MD....Civil Trial Practice, Family Law, General Practice, Insurance Defense Law

ALLEN AND KIMBELL
Santa Barbara, CA....General Practice

ALLEN LAW FIRM, A PROFESSIONAL CORPORATION
Little Rock, AR....Banking Law, Civil Trial Practice, Insurance Defense Law, Securities Law

ALLEN, MATKINS, LECK, GAMBLE & MALLORY
Irvine, CA....General Practice
Los Angeles, CA....General Practice
San Diego, CA....General Practice

ALLEN, NELSON & BOWERS
Elizabethton, TN....Civil Trial Practice, General Practice

ALLEN AND PINNIX
Raleigh, NC....Antitrust Law, Immigration and Naturalization Law, International Business Law

ALLEN, POLGAR, PROIETTI & FAGALDE
Merced, CA....General Practice

ALLEN, RHODES & SOBELSOHN
Los Angeles, CA....Insurance Defense Law
Ontario, CA....Insurance Defense Law
Palm Desert, CA....Insurance Defense Law
Santa Ana, CA....Insurance Defense Law
Santa Barbara, CA....Insurance Defense Law

ALLEN, ROGERS, METCALF AND VAHRENWALD
Fort Collins, CO....General Practice

ALLEN, VAUGHN, COBB & HOOD, P.A.
Gulfport, MS..........Civil Trial Practice, Insurance Defense Law

ALLEN, YAZBECK & O'HALLORAN, P.C.
Portland, OR..........Construction Law

ALLEN, YURASEK & MERKLIN
Marysville, OH..........General Practice

ALLEY AND ALLEY, CHARTERED
Miami, FL..........Labor and Employment Law
Tampa, FL..........Civil Trial Practice, Labor and Employment Law

ALLEY, RAYMOND A., JR., P.A.
Tampa, FL..........Family Law

ALLFORD, ASHMORE, IVESTER, ZELLMER & GREEN
Mc Alester, OK..........General Practice

ALLISON, MACKENZIE, HARTMAN, SOUMBENIOTIS & RUSSELL, LTD.
Carson City, NV..........General Practice

ALLMAN SPRY HUMPHREYS & LEGGETT, P.A.
Winston-Salem, NC..........General Practice

ALLOTT, ENGINEER & MAKAR, A PROFESSIONAL CORPORATION
Denver, CO..........Immigration and Naturalization Law

ALLRED & DONALDSON
Jackson, MS..........Banking Law, Civil Trial Practice, Commercial Law, Environmental Law, Insurance Defense Law, Personal Injury Law, Product Liability Law

ALLRED, JOEL M., P.C.
Salt Lake City, UT..........Civil Trial Practice, Family Law, Personal Injury Law

ALLSHOUSE, J. D. BUCKY, A PROFESSIONAL CORPORATION
Houston, TX..........Family Law

ALPERT, JOSEY & HUGHES, P.A.
Tampa, FL..........Civil Trial Practice, Insurance Defense Law

ALSCHULER, GROSSMAN & PINES
Los Angeles, CA..........General Practice

ALSTON & BIRD
Atlanta, GA..........Antitrust Law, Banking Law, Civil Trial Practice, Communications Law, Environmental Law, General Practice, Immigration and Naturalization Law, Labor and Employment Law, Municipal Bond/Public Authority Financing Law, Real Estate Law, Tax Law, Trademark, Copyright and Unfair Competition Law

ALSTON, HUNT, FLOYD & ING, ATTORNEYS AT LAW, A LAW CORPORATION
Honolulu, HI..........General Practice

ALSTON, RUTHERFORD, TARDY & VAN SLYKE
Jackson, MS..........Antitrust Law, Civil Trial Practice, Communications Law, General Practice, Natural Resources Law, Patent, Trademark, Copyright and Unfair Competition Law, Tax Law

ALSUP BEVIS & PETTY
Houston, TX..........Civil Trial Practice, Natural Resources Law, Public Utilities Law

ALTHEIMER & GRAY
Chicago, IL..........General Practice

ALTHOUSE & BAMBER
Upland, CA..........Civil Trial Practice, General Practice

ALTICK & CORWIN
Dayton, OH..........Bankruptcy Law, General Practice, Probate and Estate Planning Law

ALTMAN, JAMES J.
New Port Richey, FL..........General Practice

ALTMAN & CALARDO CO., A LEGAL PROFESSIONAL ASSOCIATION
Cincinnati, OH..........Civil Trial Practice, Environmental Law, Personal Injury Law

ALTMAN & GREER
Lake Worth, FL..........Probate and Estate Planning Law, Real Estate Law

ALTMAN, KRITZER & LEVICK, P.C.
Atlanta, GA..........Employment Benefits Law, Real Estate Law, Securities Law

ALTSHULER, BERZON, NUSSBAUM, BERZON & RUBIN
San Francisco, CA..........Labor and Employment Law

ALVAREZ, EDNA R.S.
Los Angeles, CA..........Probate and Estate Planning Law

ALVERSON, TAYLOR, MORTENSEN & NELSON
Las Vegas, NV..........Administrative Law, Banking Law, Bankruptcy Law, Business Law, Civil Trial Practice, Commercial Law, Construction Law, Insurance Defense Law, Medical Malpractice Law, Municipal Bond/Public Authority Financing Law, Real Estate Law

AMELUNG, WULFF & WILLENBROCK, P.C.
St. Louis, MO..........Insurance Defense Law

AMENT, JOHN S. III
Jacksonville, TX..........Civil Trial Practice

AMERLING & BURNS, A PROFESSIONAL ASSOCIATION
Portland, ME..........Civil Trial Practice, Commercial Law, Construction Law, Environmental Law, General Practice, Insurance Defense Law, Product Liability Law

AMES, MORGAN P.
Stamford, CT..........Personal Injury Law

AMES & AMES
Onancock, VA..........General Practice

ANAPOL, SCHWARTZ, WEISS AND COHAN, A PROFESSIONAL CORPORATION
Philadelphia, PA..........Civil Trial Practice, Personal Injury Law

ANCEL & DUNLAP
Indianapolis, IN..........Bankruptcy Law

ANCHORS, FOSTER, MCINNIS & KEEFE, P.A.
Destin, FL..........General Practice
Fort Walton Beach, FL..........General Practice

ANDERLINI, GUHEEN, FINKELSTEIN, EMERICK & MCSWEENEY, A PROFESSIONAL CORPORATION
San Mateo, CA..........Civil Trial Practice, Criminal Trial Practice, General Practice, Personal Injury Law, Probate and Estate Planning Law, Real Estate Law, Tax Law

ANDERSEN, BERKSHIRE, LAURITSEN & BROWER
Omaha, NE..........General Practice, Labor and Employment Law

ANDERSEN, DAVIDSON & TATE, P.C.
Lawrenceville, GA..........Banking Law, Business Law, Civil Trial Practice, General Practice

ANDERSON, KENNETH G.
Jacksonville, FL..........Tax Law

ANDERSON, LLOYD V.
Anchorage, AK..........Product Liability Law

ANDERSON, THOMAS T. & ASSOCIATES
Indio, CA..........General Practice

ANDERSON, ALDEN, HAYES & ZIOGAS, L.L.C.
Bristol, CT..........General Practice

ANDERSON, BANKS, CURRAN & DONOGHUE
Mount Kisco, NY..........General Practice, Labor and Employment Law, Real Estate Law

ANDERSON, BYRD, RICHESON & FLAHERTY
Ottawa, KS..........General Practice
Wellsville, KS..........General Practice

ANDERSON, COE & KING
Baltimore, MD..........General Practice

ANDERSON, COX & ENNIS
Wilmington, NC..........Insurance Defense Law

ANDERSON, GALLOWAY & LUCCHESE, A PROFESSIONAL CORPORATION
Walnut Creek, CA..........Insurance Defense Law, Medical Malpractice Law, Product Liability Law

ANDERSON & GILBERT
St. Louis, MO..........Civil Trial Practice, General Practice

ANDERSON GREENFIELD & DOUGHERTY
Philadelphia, PA..........Banking Law, Business Law, Commercial Law, Insurance Defense Law, Labor and Employment Law

ANDERSON KILL OLICK & OSHINSKY
Washington, DC..........Civil Trial Practice, General Practice
New York, NY..........Antitrust Law, Civil Trial Practice

ANDERSON & KILPATRICK
Little Rock, AR..........Civil Trial Practice, Insurance Defense Law, Personal Injury Law

ANDERSON, MCPHARLIN & CONNERS
Los Angeles, CA..........Insurance Defense Law

ANDERSON, NELSON & HALL
Idaho Falls, ID..........General Practice

ANDERSON & QUINN
Washington, DC..........Civil Trial Practice, General Practice, Insurance Defense Law, Personal Injury Law
Rockville, MD..........Civil Trial Practice, General Practice, Insurance Defense Law, Personal Injury Law

ANDERSON & SALISBURY, A PROFESSIONAL CORPORATION
Pasadena, CA....Family Law

ANDERSON, SHANNON, O'BRIEN, RICE & BERTZ
Stevens Point, WI....General Practice

ANDERSON, SMITH, NULL, STOFER & MURPHREE, L.L.P.
Victoria, TX....General Practice

ANDERSON, WALKER & REICHERT
Macon, GA....General Practice, Insurance Defense Law, Labor and Employment Law, Tax Law

ANDERSON, ZEIGLER, DISHAROON, GALLAGHER & GRAY, PROFESSIONAL CORPORATION
Santa Rosa, CA....General Practice

ANDORA, PALMISANO & GEANEY, A PROFESSIONAL CORPORATION
Elmwood Park, NJ....Banking Law, Commercial Law, General Practice, Municipal and Zoning Law, Public Utilities Law, Tax Law

ANDRADE & ASSOCIATES
Irvine, CA....Admiralty/Maritime Law, Construction Law, Insurance Defense Law, Labor and Employment Law

ANDREOS, GEORGE P., A PROFESSIONAL LAW CORPORATION
San Diego, CA....Personal Injury Law

ANDREWS, ANGUS G.
De Funiak Springs, FL....General Practice

ANDREWS DAVIS LEGG BIXLER MILSTEN & PRICE, A PROFESSIONAL CORPORATION
Oklahoma City, OK....Antitrust Law, Banking Law, Civil Trial Practice, Communications Law, Employment Benefits Law, Environmental Law, General Practice, Health Care Law, Insurance Defense Law, Labor and Employment Law, Natural Resources Law, Probate and Estate Planning Law, Real Estate Law, Securities Law, Tax Law, Trademark, Copyright and Unfair Competition Law, Transportation Law

ANDREWS & KURTH, L.L.P.
Los Angeles, CA....General Practice
Washington, DC....General Practice
New York, NY....General Practice
Dallas, TX....General Practice
Houston, TX....General Practice

ANDRUS, SCEALES, STARKE & SAWALL
Milwaukee, WI....Patent, Trademark, Copyright and Unfair Competition Law

ANESI, FRANK J.
Durango, CO....Commercial Law, General Practice, Real Estate Law

ANESI, OZMON & RODIN, LTD.
Chicago, IL....Civil Trial Practice, Personal Injury Law

ANGINO & ROVNER, P.C.
Harrisburg, PA....Appellate Practice, Civil Trial Practice, Medical Malpractice Law, Personal Injury Law, Product Liability Law

ANGLE, MURPHY, VALENTINO & CAMPBELL, P.C.
York, NE....General Practice

ANGONES, HUNTER, MCCLURE, LYNCH & WILLIAMS, P.A.
Miami, FL....Civil Trial Practice, General Practice, Insurance Defense Law, Medical Malpractice Law

ANNINO, DRAPER & MOORE, P.C.
Springfield, MA....Construction Law, Environmental Law, Health Care Law

ANSELL ZARO BENNETT & GRIMM, A PROFESSIONAL CORPORATION
Eatontown, NJ....General Practice

ANSPACH, ROBERT M., ASSOCIATES
Toledo, OH....Civil Trial Practice, Insurance Defense Law, Labor and Employment Law, Medical Malpractice Law, Product Liability Law

ANSTANDIG, LEVICOFF & MCDYER, A PROFESSIONAL CORPORATION
Pittsburgh, PA....Civil Trial Practice, General Practice, Insurance Defense Law

ANTHEIL NICHOLAS MASLOW & MACMINN
Doylestown, PA....Business Law

ANTIN & TAYLOR
Los Angeles, CA....Employment Benefits Law, Probate and Estate Planning Law, Tax Law

ANTON, BRUCE
Dallas, TX....Criminal Trial Practice

APFELBAUM, APFELBAUM & APFELBAUM
Sunbury, PA....General Practice

APKER, APKER, HAGGARD & KURTZ, P.C.
Phoenix, AZ....Civil Trial Practice, General Practice, Natural Resources Law, Real Estate Law

APPELBAUM, EISENBERG, BAUMAN & APPELBAUM
Liberty, NY....Civil Trial Practice, General Practice

APPEL & YOST
Lancaster, PA....Business Law, Real Estate Law, Tax Law

APPLE AND APPLE, A PROFESSIONAL CORPORATION
Pittsburgh, PA....Bankruptcy Law, Commercial Law

APRUZZESE, MCDERMOTT, MASTRO & MURPHY, A PROFESSIONAL CORPORATION
Liberty Corner, NJ....Commercial Law, Labor and Employment Law
Newark, NJ....Commercial Law, Labor and Employment Law
Springfield, NJ....Commercial Law, Labor and Employment Law

ARAGON, MARTIN, BURLINGTON & CROCKETT, P.A.
Miami, FL....Civil Trial Practice

ARANSON & ASSOCIATES
Dallas, TX....Civil Trial Practice, Criminal Trial Practice, Family Law, General Practice

ARBES, JAKE
Atlanta, GA....Criminal Trial Practice

ARCHBALD & SPRAY
Santa Barbara, CA....Civil Trial Practice, General Practice

ARENSTEIN, ROBERT D.
Teaneck, NJ....Family Law
New York, NY....Family Law

ARENT FOX KINTNER PLOTKIN & KAHN
Washington, DC....General Practice

ARESTY INTERNATIONAL LAW OFFICES
Boston, MA....International Business Law

ARGUE PEARSON HARBISON & MYERS
Los Angeles, CA....Real Estate Law

ARIANO, ANDERSON, BAZOS, HARDY & CASTILLO
Elgin, IL....General Practice

ARKIN, HARRY L. & ASSOCIATES
Denver, CO....International Business Law, Probate and Estate Planning Law

ARKIN SCHAFFER & SUPINO
New York, NY....Appellate Practice, Civil Trial Practice, Criminal Trial Practice

ARLEN, ROBERT M., P.A.
Boynton Beach, FL....Probate and Estate Planning Law, Tax Law

ARMBRECHT, JACKSON, DEMOUY, CROWE, HOLMES & REEVES
Mobile, AL....Administrative Law, Admiralty/Maritime Law, Civil Trial Practice, General Practice, Insurance Defense Law, Labor and Employment Law, Natural Resources Law, Tax Law

ARMENTOR & WATTIGNY, A PROFESSIONAL LAW CORPORATION
New Iberia, LA....General Practice

ARMOR, G. W.
Laverne, OK....Civil Trial Practice, Environmental Law, Probate and Estate Planning Law

ARMSTRONG, E. ALAN
Atlanta, GA....Civil Trial Practice

ARMSTRONG ALLEN PREWITT GENTRY JOHNSTON & HOLMES
Memphis, TN....Antitrust Law, Banking Law, Bankruptcy Law, Civil Trial Practice, Commercial Law, Communications Law, Environmental Law, General Practice, Insurance Defense Law, Labor and Employment Law, Municipal Bond/Public Authority Financing Law, Personal Injury Law, Probate and Estate Planning Law, Real Estate Law, Tax Law, Trademark, Copyright and Unfair Competition Law

ARMSTRONG & ARMSTRONG, P.A.
Smithfield, NC....Family Law, Medical Malpractice Law, Personal Injury Law

ARMSTRONG, DONOHUE & CEPPOS, CHARTERED
Rockville, MD....Civil Trial Practice, Criminal Trial Practice, Insurance Defense Law, Medical Malpractice Law, Personal Injury Law

ARMSTRONG, GARRISON R., LAW CORPORATION
San Diego, CA....Employment Benefits Law, Probate and Estate Planning Law, Tax Law

ARMSTRONG, PATTEN, THOMAS & LEACH
Hazlehurst, MS....General Practice

ARMSTRONG & PRAUSER
Columbus, KS....General Practice

ARMSTRONG & STRAHAN, A PROFESSIONAL CORPORATION
El Paso, TX....Personal Injury Law

ARMSTRONG, TEASDALE, SCHLAFLY & DAVIS
Kansas City, MO....General Practice
St. Louis, MO....Antitrust Law, Civil Trial Practice, Environmental Law, General Practice, Labor and Employment Law, Tax Law

ARNETT, DRAPER & HAGOOD
Knoxville, TN....Civil Trial Practice, General Practice, Labor and Employment Law

ARNOLD, LYNWOOD F. JR.
Tampa, FL....Probate and Estate Planning Law, Real Estate Law

ARNOLD & ANDERSON
Atlanta, GA....Labor and Employment Law

ARNOLD, GROBMYER & HALEY, A PROFESSIONAL ASSOCIATION
Little Rock, AR....Banking Law, Bankruptcy Law, Civil Trial Practice, Commercial Law, General Practice, Probate and Estate Planning Law, Real Estate Law, Tax Law

ARNOLD & MCDOWELL
Minneapolis, MN....Business Law, Civil Trial Practice, Family Law, General Practice, Personal Injury Law, Real Estate Law

ARNOLD & PORTER
Washington, DC....General Practice

ARNOLD, WHITE & DURKEE, A PROFESSIONAL CORPORATION
Palo Alto, CA....Patent, Trademark, Copyright and Unfair Competition Law
Chicago, IL....Patent, Trademark, Copyright and Unfair Competition Law
Austin, TX....Patent, Trademark, Copyright and Unfair Competition Law
Houston, TX....Patent, Trademark, Copyright and Unfair Competition Law
Arlington, VA....Patent, Trademark, Copyright and Unfair Competition Law

ARONBERG GOLDGEHN DAVIS & GARMISA
Chicago, IL....Banking Law, General Practice, Insurance Defense Law, Probate and Estate Planning Law, Real Estate Law

ARONSOHN & WEINER
Hackensack, NJ....Family Law

ARONSON, ROBERT
Springfield, MA....Civil Trial Practice

ARSENEAULT, DONOHUE, SORRENTINO & FASSETT
Chatham, NJ....Appellate Practice, Civil Trial Practice, Criminal Trial Practice

ARTER & HADDEN
Los Angeles, CA....General Practice
Washington, DC....General Practice
Cleveland, OH....Antitrust Law, General Practice, Labor and Employment Law, Tax Law
Columbus, OH....General Practice

ARTHUR, CHAPMAN, MCDONOUGH, KETTERING & SMETAK, P.A.
Minneapolis, MN....Civil Trial Practice, Environmental Law, General Practice, Insurance Defense Law, Labor and Employment Law, Personal Injury Law

ARTHUR, PEARSON & MARTIN, LTD.
Arlington, VA....Civil Trial Practice

ARTZ, WILLIAM E., A PROFESSIONAL CORPORATION
Arlington, VA....Medical Malpractice Law, Personal Injury Law

ASBILL, JUNKIN & MYERS, CHTD.
Washington, DC....Civil Trial Practice, Criminal Trial Practice, General Practice

ASHBY & GEDDES
Wilmington, DE....Civil Trial Practice, General Practice

ASHFORD & NAKAMURA
Honolulu, HI....Admiralty/Maritime Law, Civil Trial Practice, Commercial Law, Insurance Defense Law, Personal Injury Law, Product Liability Law

ASHFORD & WRISTON
Honolulu, HI....General Practice

ASHLEY, ASHLEY & ARNOLD
Dyersburg, TN....Civil Trial Practice, Environmental Law, General Practice, Insurance Defense Law

ASHMORE, JOSEPH E., JR., P.C.
Dallas, TX....Banking Law, General Practice, Health Care Law, Probate and Estate Planning Law

ASHTON, ASHTON, WISENER AND MUNKACSY, INC.
Lawton, OK....General Practice, Personal Injury Law

ASPEY, WATKINS & DIESEL
Cottonwood, AZ....General Practice
Flagstaff, AZ....Business Law, Civil Trial Practice, Commercial Law, Construction Law, Criminal Trial Practice, Family Law, General Practice, Insurance Defense Law, Medical Malpractice Law, Personal Injury Law, Probate and Estate Planning Law, Real Estate Law
Page, AZ....General Practice
Sedona, AZ....General Practice
Winslow, AZ....General Practice

ASQUITH, MAHONEY & ROBINSON
Providence, RI....General Practice

ASTOR WEISS KAPLAN & ROSENBLUM
Philadelphia, PA....Bankruptcy Law, Business Law, Family Law, General Practice, Insurance Defense Law, Probate and Estate Planning Law, Real Estate Law

ASWAD & INGRAHAM
Binghamton, NY....General Practice

ATCHISON, ANDERSON, HURLEY & BARISONE, A PROFESSIONAL CORPORATION
Santa Cruz, CA....Civil Trial Practice, General Practice, Insurance Defense Law, Municipal and Zoning Law, Personal Injury Law, Probate and Estate Planning Law, Real Estate Law

ATCHLEY, RUSSELL, WALDROP & HLAVINKA, L.L.P.
Texarkana, TX....Civil Trial Practice, General Practice

ATER WYNNE HEWITT DODSON & SKERRITT
Portland, OR....General Practice

ATHERTON & ATHERTON
Emporia, KS....General Practice

ATKINSON & ATKINSON
Evanston, IL....Health Care Law

ATKINSON, HASKINS, NELLIS, BOUDREAUX, HOLEMAN, PHIPPS & BRITTINGHAM
Tulsa, OK....Civil Trial Practice, Insurance Defense Law, Medical Malpractice Law, Personal Injury Law

ATKINSON & KELSEY, P.A.
Albuquerque, NM....Family Law

ATKINSON MILVAIN
Calgary, AB, Canada....General Practice

ATLAS & HALL, L.L.P.
McAllen, TX....General Practice

ATLAS, PEARLMAN, TROP & BORKSON, P.A.
Fort Lauderdale, FL....General Practice

ATLASS PROFESSIONAL CORPORATION
Denver, CO....Probate and Estate Planning Law, Tax Law

ATLEE & HALL
Lancaster, PA....Medical Malpractice Law, Product Liability Law

ATWOOD & CHERNY
Boston, MA....Civil Trial Practice, Family Law

ATWOOD, MALONE, MANN & TURNER, A PROFESSIONAL ASSOCIATION
Roswell, NM....General Practice

AUBRY, MEYER, WALSH & POMMERANZ
Toledo, OH....Family Law, Immigration and Naturalization Law

AUERBACH, MARSHALL J., & ASSOCIATES, LTD.
Chicago, IL....Family Law

AUERBACH, PHILIP G., A PROFESSIONAL CORPORATION
Red Bank, NJ....Civil Trial Practice, General Practice, Medical Malpractice Law, Personal Injury Law, Product Liability Law

AUGUST, COMITER, KULUNAS & SCHEPPS, P.A.
Washington, DC....Tax Law
West Palm Beach, FL....Probate and Estate Planning Law, Tax Law

AULTMAN, TYNER, MCNEESE & RUFFIN, LTD., A PROFESSIONAL LAW CORPORATION
Columbia, MS....Admiralty/Maritime Law, Civil Trial Practice, Commercial Law, Environmental Law, General Practice, Insurance Defense Law
Gulfport, MS....Admiralty/Maritime Law, Civil Trial Practice, Commercial Law, Environmental Law, General Practice, Insurance Defense Law

Hattiesburg, MS....................Admiralty/Maritime Law, Civil Trial Practice, Commercial Law, Environmental Law, General Practice, Insurance Defense Law

AUSLEY, THOMAS L., A PROFESSIONAL CORPORATION
Austin, TX....................Family Law

AUSTIN & ABRAMS, A PROFESSIONAL ASSOCIATION
Minneapolis, MN....................Civil Trial Practice, General Practice, Personal Injury Law

AUSTIN, HINDERAKER, HOPPER & STRAIT
Watertown, SD....................General Practice

AUSTIN, PEIRCE & SMITH, P.C.
Aspen, CO....................Appellate Practice, Civil Trial Practice, Environmental Law, General Practice, Municipal and Zoning Law, Natural Resources Law, Real Estate Law

AUSTIN & PEPPERMAN
Leesburg, FL....................Civil Trial Practice, General Practice

AVERY & ASSOCIATES
San Francisco, CA....................Probate and Estate Planning Law, Tax Law

AVERY, WHIGHAM & WINESETT, P.A.
Fort Myers, FL....................Civil Trial Practice, Probate and Estate Planning Law, Real Estate Law

AWTREY AND PARKER, P.C.
Marietta, GA....................Civil Trial Practice, General Practice, Municipal Bond/Public Authority Financing Law, Personal Injury Law, Probate and Estate Planning Law

AXE, JOHN R. AND ASSOCIATES
Grosse Pointe Farms, MI....................Municipal Bond/Public Authority Financing Law

AXLEY BRYNELSON
Madison, WI....................Civil Trial Practice, Commercial Law, General Practice, Personal Injury Law

AYABE, CHONG, NISHIMOTO, SIA & NAKAMURA
Honolulu, HI....................Civil Trial Practice, Construction Law, General Practice, Insurance Defense Law, Medical Malpractice Law, Personal Injury Law, Real Estate Law

AYRES, CLUSTER, CURRY, MCCALL & BRIGGS, P.A.
Ocala, FL....................General Practice

AYRES & HARTNETT, P.C.
Accomac, VA....................General Practice

BABB & BRADSHAW, P.C.
Austin, TX....................General Practice

BABBITT, HAZOURI AND JOHNSON, P.A.
West Palm Beach, FL....................Civil Trial Practice, Medical Malpractice Law, Personal Injury Law

BABST, CALLAND, CLEMENTS AND ZOMNIR, A PROFESSIONAL CORPORATION
Pittsburgh, PA....................Commercial Law, Construction Law, Environmental Law

BACHMAN & LAPOINTE, P.C.
New Haven, CT....................Patent, Trademark, Copyright and Unfair Competition Law

BACHMANN, HESS, BACHMANN & GARDEN
Wheeling, WV....................General Practice, Insurance Defense Law, Personal Injury Law

BACKER, GLENN
New York, NY....................Civil Trial Practice

BACKER & BACKER, A PROFESSIONAL CORPORATION
Indianapolis, IN....................Commercial Law, Construction Law, Probate and Estate Planning Law, Real Estate Law

BACKES & HILL
Trenton, NJ....................Banking Law, Civil Trial Practice, General Practice, Health Care Law

BADER & VILLANUEVA, P.C.
Denver, CO....................Civil Trial Practice

BADGER, DAVID R., P.A.
Charlotte, NC....................Bankruptcy Law

BADGER, DOLAN, PARKER & COHEN
Boston, MA....................Insurance Defense Law

BADIAK WILL & MALOOF
New York, NY....................Admiralty/Maritime Law, General Practice

BAER MARKS & UPHAM
New York, NY....................Civil Trial Practice, General Practice

BAGBY, WILLIAM R.
Lexington, KY....................Tax Law

BAGGETT, MCCALL & BURGESS, A PROFESSIONAL LAW CORPORATION
Lake Charles, LA....................Admiralty/Maritime Law, General Practice

BAI, POLLOCK AND DUNNIGAN, P.C.
Bridgeport, CT....................Civil Trial Practice

BAILEY, CHARLES T.
Logan, WV....................Real Estate Law

BAILEY, BORLACK, NADELHOFFER & CARROLL
Chicago, IL....................Civil Trial Practice, Patent, Trademark, Copyright and Unfair Competition Law, Real Estate Law

BAILEY & DIXON
Raleigh, NC....................Civil Trial Practice, Insurance Defense Law, Personal Injury Law

BAILEY, NEGEM & PATTERSON, L.L.P.
Tyler, TX....................Personal Injury Law

BAILEY, PATTERSON, CADDELL, HART & BAILEY, P.A.
Charlotte, NC....................Civil Trial Practice, Personal Injury Law

BAILEY, RALPH, P.A.
Greenville, SC....................Patent, Trademark, Copyright and Unfair Competition Law

BAILEY AND WILLIAMS
Dallas, TX....................General Practice, Insurance Defense Law

BAILEY, WORRELL, VIERS & BROWNING
Pineville, WV....................General Practice

BAIN, TROY E.
Shreveport, LA....................Civil Trial Practice, Personal Injury Law

BAIN FILES ALLEN AND WORTHEN, A PROFESSIONAL CORPORATION
Tyler, TX....................General Practice

BAIN & MCRAE
Lillington, NC....................General Practice

BAINBRIDGE, MIMS & ROGERS
Birmingham, AL....................Civil Trial Practice, General Practice

BAIR, KAUTZMANN & BAIR
Mandan, ND....................Civil Trial Practice, General Practice

BAIRD, BAIRD, BAIRD AND JONES, P.S.C.
Pikeville, KY....................General Practice

BAKER, J. NORMAN
Mountain View, CA....................Family Law

BAKER & BOTTS, L.L.P.
Washington, DC....................Administrative Law, Business Law, Civil Trial Practice, Commercial Law, Environmental Law, General Practice, Natural Resources Law, Patent, Trademark, Copyright and Unfair Competition Law, Tax Law, Trademark, Copyright and Unfair Competition Law
New York, NY....................Business Law, Civil Trial Practice, Commercial Law, General Practice, Tax Law
Austin, TX....................Administrative Law, Banking Law, Bankruptcy Law, Business Law, Civil Trial Practice, Commercial Law, Environmental Law, General Practice, Patent, Trademark, Copyright and Unfair Competition Law, Real Estate Law, Trademark, Copyright and Unfair Competition Law
Dallas, TX....................Administrative Law, Antitrust Law, Banking Law, Bankruptcy Law, Business Law, Civil Trial Practice, Commercial Law, General Practice, Labor and Employment Law, Patent, Trademark, Copyright and Unfair Competition Law, Personal Injury Law, Real Estate Law, Trademark, Copyright and Unfair Competition Law
Houston, TX....................Administrative Law, Admiralty/Maritime Law, Antitrust Law, Banking Law, Bankruptcy Law, Business Law, Civil Trial Practice, Commercial Law, Environmental Law, General Practice, Labor and Employment Law, Patent, Trademark, Copyright and Unfair Competition Law, Personal Injury Law, Probate and Estate Planning Law, Real Estate Law, Tax Law

BAKER, CAMPBELL & PARSONS
Nashville, TN....................General Practice

BAKER & DANIELS
Fort Wayne, IN....................General Practice, Patent, Trademark, Copyright and Unfair Competition Law
Indianapolis, IN....................Bankruptcy Law, Civil Trial Practice, Environmental Law, General Practice, Labor and Employment Law, Municipal Bond/Public Authority Financing Law, Patent, Trademark, Copyright and Unfair Competition Law, Real Estate Law, Tax Law
South Bend, IN....................General Practice, Patent, Trademark, Copyright and Unfair Competition Law

BAKER, DONELSON, BEARMAN & CALDWELL
Chattanooga, TN .... General Practice, Health Care Law, Tax Law
Huntsville, TN .... General Practice
Johnson City, TN .... General Practice, Natural Resources Law
Knoxville, TN .... Civil Trial Practice, Environmental Law, General Practice, Tax Law
Memphis, TN .... Banking Law, Bankruptcy Law, Civil Trial Practice, Environmental Law, General Practice, Insurance Defense Law, Labor and Employment Law, Municipal Bond/Public Authority Financing Law, Patent, Trademark, Copyright and Unfair Competition Law, Tax Law
Nashville, TN .... Civil Trial Practice, General Practice, Health Care Law, Tax Law

BAKER, HACKENBERG & COLLINS CO., L.P.A.
Painesville, OH .... General Practice, Insurance Defense Law

BAKER & HOSTETLER
Long Beach, CA .... Admiralty/Maritime Law, General Practice
Los Angeles, CA .... Admiralty/Maritime Law, Bankruptcy Law, Civil Trial Practice, Environmental Law, General Practice, Labor and Employment Law, Real Estate Law, Trademark, Copyright and Unfair Competition Law
Denver, CO .... Civil Trial Practice, Environmental Law, General Practice
Washington, DC .... Administrative Law, Antitrust Law, Banking Law, Civil Trial Practice, Communications Law, Environmental Law, General Practice, Labor and Employment Law, Tax Law, Trademark, Copyright and Unfair Competition Law, Transportation Law
Orlando, FL .... Civil Trial Practice, Construction Law, General Practice, Municipal Bond/Public Authority Financing Law, Real Estate Law, Tax Law
Cleveland, OH .... Antitrust Law, Banking Law, Bankruptcy Law, Civil Trial Practice, Communications Law, Construction Law, Employment Benefits Law, Environmental Law, General Practice, Immigration and Naturalization Law, Labor and Employment Law, Municipal Bond/Public Authority Financing Law, Probate and Estate Planning Law, Real Estate Law, Tax Law, Trademark, Copyright and Unfair Competition Law
Columbus, OH .... Bankruptcy Law, Civil Trial Practice, Employment Benefits Law, General Practice, Labor and Employment Law, Tax Law, Transportation Law
Houston, TX .... Civil Trial Practice, General Practice

BAKER, KINSMAN & HOLLIS, P.C.
Chattanooga, TN .... Insurance Defense Law

BAKER, MANOCK & JENSEN, A PROFESSIONAL CORPORATION
Fresno, CA .... General Practice

BAKER, MAXHAM, JESTER & MEADOR, A PROFESSIONAL CORPORATION
San Diego, CA .... Patent, Trademark, Copyright and Unfair Competition Law

BAKER & MCKENZIE
Palo Alto, CA .... General Practice
San Diego, CA .... General Practice
San Francisco, CA .... General Practice
Washington, DC .... General Practice
Miami, FL .... General Practice
Chicago, IL .... General Practice
New York, NY .... General Practice
Dallas, TX .... General Practice
Toronto, ON, Canada .... General Practice
Buenos Aires, Argentina .... General Practice
Melbourne, Victoria, Australia .... General Practice
Sydney, New South Wales, Australia .... General Practice
Brussels, Belgium .... General Practice
Beijing (Peking), People's Republic of China .... General Practice
Prague, Czech Republic .... General Practice
Cairo, Egypt .... General Practice
Paris, France .... General Practice
Hong Kong, Hong Kong (British Crown Colony) .... General Practice
Budapest, Hungary .... General Practice
Milan, Italy .... General Practice
Rome, Italy .... General Practice
Mexico, D.F., Mexico .... General Practice
Moscow, Russia .... General Practice
St. Petersburg, Russia .... General Practice
Singapore, Singapore .... General Practice
Barcelona, Spain .... General Practice
Madrid, Spain .... General Practice
Zürich, Switzerland .... General Practice
Taipei, Taiwan .... General Practice
Bangkok, Thailand .... General Practice
Kiev, Ukraine .... General Practice
Caracas, Venezuela .... General Practice
Valencia, Venezuela .... General Practice
Hanoi, Vietnam .... General Practice
Ho Chi Minh City, Vietnam .... General Practice
Monterrey, Nuevo León, Mexico .... General Practice
Ciudad Juarez, Chihuahua, Mexico .... General Practice
Tijuana, Baja California, Mexico .... General Practice
Stockholm, Sweden .... General Practice
Almaty, Kazakhstan .... General Practice
Warsaw, Poland .... General Practice

BAKER, MCREYNOLDS, BYRNE, BRACKETT, O'KANE & SHEA
Knoxville, TN .... Civil Trial Practice, General Practice

BAKER, MEEKISON & DUBLIKAR
Canton, OH .... Civil Trial Practice

BAKER, STERCHI & COWDEN
Kansas City, MO .... Bankruptcy Law, Civil Trial Practice, Commercial Law, Construction Law, Environmental Law, Insurance Defense Law, Labor and Employment Law

BAKKE, JOHN E. III
San Antonio, TX .... Probate and Estate Planning Law

BALCH & BINGHAM
Birmingham, AL .... Administrative Law, Antitrust Law, Banking Law, Bankruptcy Law, Business Law, Civil Trial Practice, Commercial Law, Construction Law, Employment Benefits Law, Environmental Law, General Practice, Health Care Law, Insurance Defense Law, Labor and Employment Law, Municipal Bond/Public Authority Financing Law, Natural Resources Law, Patent, Trademark, Copyright and Unfair Competition Law, Personal Injury Law, Probate and Estate Planning Law, Real Estate Law, Securities Law, Tax Law, Trademark, Copyright and Unfair Competition Law
Huntsville, AL .... Banking Law, Business Law, Commercial Law, General Practice, Patent, Trademark, Copyright and Unfair Competition Law, Trademark, Copyright and Unfair Competition Law
Montgomery, AL .... Banking Law, Bankruptcy Law, Business Law, Civil Trial Practice, Commercial Law, Communications Law, Environmental Law, General Practice, Labor and Employment Law, Natural Resources Law, Probate and Estate Planning Law, Real Estate Law, Tax Law
Washington, DC .... Environmental Law, General Practice, Natural Resources Law

BALDWIN RENNER & CLARK
Philadelphia, PA .... Business Law
Wayne, PA .... Business Law, Securities Law

BALFOUR MACDONALD TALBOT MIJUSKOVIC & OLMSTED, A PROFESSIONAL CORPORATION
Costa Mesa, CA .... Business Law, Civil Trial Practice, General Practice, Probate and Estate Planning Law, Real Estate Law

BALFOUR MOSS
Regina, SK, Canada .... Civil Trial Practice, Commercial Law, General Practice

BALISLE & ROBERSON, S.C.
Madison, WI .... Appellate Practice, Family Law, Probate and Estate Planning Law

BALLARD SPAHR ANDREWS & INGERSOLL
Denver, CO .... Bankruptcy Law, General Practice, Municipal Bond/Public Authority Financing Law, Tax Law
Washington, DC .... General Practice, Municipal Bond/Public Authority Financing Law, Tax Law
Baltimore, MD .... Real Estate Law
Philadelphia, PA .... Antitrust Law, Banking Law, Bankruptcy Law, Civil Trial Practice, Commercial Law, Employment Benefits Law, Environmental Law, General Practice, Health Care Law, Labor and Employment Law, Municipal Bond/Public Authority Financing Law, Probate and Estate Planning Law, Real Estate Law, Tax Law
Salt Lake City, UT .... Municipal Bond/Public Authority Financing Law

BALL, BALL, MATTHEWS & NOVAK, P.A.
Montgomery, AL .... Civil Trial Practice, General Practice

BALL, BARTON & HOFFMAN
Monticello, AR .... General Practice

BALL, EGGLESTON, BUMBLEBURG & MCBRIDE
Lafayette, IN .... General Practice, Insurance Defense Law, Municipal and Zoning Law, Personal Injury Law

BALL & MOURTON, LTD. A PROFESSIONAL CORPORATION
Fayetteville, AR .... General Practice

BALZARINI, CAREY & WATSON
Pittsburgh, PA ....Civil Trial Practice, General Practice, Personal Injury Law

BAMBERGER & ABSHIER
Owensboro, KY ....Bankruptcy Law, General Practice

BAMBERGER, FOREMAN, OSWALD AND HAHN
Evansville, IN........................Banking Law, Bankruptcy Law, Civil Trial Practice, General Practice

BANDY, ROBERT M., P.C.
Tyler, TX........................Bankruptcy Law, Probate and Estate Planning Law, Tax Law

BANGEL, BANGEL & BANGEL
Portsmouth, VA........................Personal Injury Law

BANGS, MCCULLEN, BUTLER, FOYE & SIMMONS
Rapid City, SD........................Civil Trial Practice, General Practice, Labor and Employment Law

BANGSER KLEIN ROCCA & BLUM
New York, NY........................General Practice

BANNER, BIRCH, MCKIE & BECKETT
Washington, DC........................Patent, Trademark, Copyright and Unfair Competition Law, Trademark, Copyright and Unfair Competition Law

BANNER, BRILEY & WHITE, L.L.P.
Wichita Falls, TX........................Civil Trial Practice, General Practice

BANNIGAN & KELLY, P.A.
St. Paul, MN........................Civil Trial Practice, Municipal and Zoning Law, Personal Injury Law

BANTA, HOYT, GREENE & EVERALL, P.C.
Englewood, CO........................Civil Trial Practice, General Practice, Real Estate Law

BANTZ, GOSCH, CREMER, PETERSON & SOMMERS
Aberdeen, SD........................Banking Law, Business Law, Insurance Defense Law

BANZET, BANZET & THOMPSON
Warrenton, NC........................General Practice

BARASH, STOERZBACH & HENSON, P.C.
Galesburg, IL........................General Practice

BARBAS, WEED, GLENN, MORGAN & WHEELEY
Tampa, FL........................Medical Malpractice Law

BARBEAU & COMPANY
Vancouver, BC, Canada..........Tax Law

BARBER, EMERSON, SPRINGER, ZINN & MURRAY, L.C.
Lawrence, KS........................General Practice

BARBER, HART & O'DELL, L.L.P.
Dallas, TX........................Medical Malpractice Law, Personal Injury Law

BARBER, MCCASKILL, AMSLER, JONES & HALE, P.A.
Little Rock, AR........................Commercial Law, General Practice, Health Care Law, Insurance Defense Law

BARBER, WILL
Austin, TX........................Civil Trial Practice, Insurance Defense Law

BARBERA, CLAPPER, BEENER, RULLO & MELVIN
Somerset, PA........................General Practice

BARBIER & BARBIER, P.C.
Grosse Pointe Woods, MI.......Civil Trial Practice, Insurance Defense Law

BARCE & RYAN
Fowler, IN........................Civil Trial Practice, General Practice
Kentland, IN........................Civil Trial Practice, General Practice

BARISH, MARVIN I., LAW OFFICES, A PROFESSIONAL CORPORATION
Philadelphia, PA........................Admiralty/Maritime Law, Civil Trial Practice, Personal Injury Law

BARKAN AND ROBON
Toledo, OH........................Banking Law, Bankruptcy Law, Real Estate Law

BARKER & ASSOCIATES, A PROFESSIONAL CORPORATION
Pasadena, CA........................Civil Trial Practice, Real Estate Law

BARKER, GILLOCK, KONING & BROWN, A PROFESSIONAL CORPORATION
Las Vegas, NV........................Civil Trial Practice, Insurance Defense Law

BARLEY, SNYDER, SENFT & COHEN
Harrisburg, PA........................General Practice
Lancaster, PA........................General Practice
York, PA........................General Practice

BARLOW & BARLOW, LTD.
Providence, RI........................Patent, Trademark, Copyright and Unfair Competition Law

BARLOW AND HARDTNER, L.C.
Shreveport, LA........................Administrative Law, Antitrust Law, Appellate Practice, Banking Law, Business Law, Civil Trial Practice, Commercial Law, Communications Law, Construction Law, Environmental Law, General Practice, Insurance Defense Law, Labor and Employment Law, Natural Resources Law, Probate and Estate Planning Law, Product Liability Law, Public Utilities Law, Real Estate Law, Securities Law, Tax Law, Transportation Law

BARLOW, JOHNSON, FLODMAN, SUTTER, GUENZEL & ESKE
Lincoln, NE........................Civil Trial Practice, Family Law, General Practice, Insurance Defense Law, Labor and Employment Law, Probate and Estate Planning Law

BARLOW & LANGE, P.C.
Troy, MI........................Business Law, Health Care Law, Labor and Employment Law

BARNES, ALFORD, STORK & JOHNSON, L.L.P.
Columbia, SC........................Banking Law, General Practice, Insurance Defense Law, Medical Malpractice Law, Product Liability Law, Real Estate Law, Tax Law

BARNES, BROWNING, TANKSLEY & CASURELLA
Marietta, GA........................Banking Law, Family Law, Insurance Defense Law, Medical Malpractice Law, Personal Injury Law, Product Liability Law

BARNES, KISSELLE, RAISCH, CHOATE, WHITTEMORE & HULBERT, P.C.
Detroit, MI........................Patent, Trademark, Copyright and Unfair Competition Law

BARNETT, NOBLE, HANES, O'NEAL & DUFFEE
Birmingham, AL........................Civil Trial Practice, Family Law

BARNETT & RICH, P.C.
Ann Arbor, MI........................General Practice

BARNEY, GROSSMAN, ROTH & DUBOW
Ithaca, NY........................General Practice

BARNHART, KATHERINE L., P.C.
Royal Oak, MI........................Family Law

BARNHART, STURGEON & SPENCER
Bloomington, IN........................Civil Trial Practice, General Practice

BARNHORST, SCHREINER & GOONAN, A PROFESSIONAL CORPORATION
San Diego, CA........................Business Law, Commercial Law

BARNWELL WHALEY PATTERSON & HELMS
Charleston, SC........................Civil Trial Practice, Construction Law, General Practice, Insurance Defense Law

BARON, GALLAGHER, HERTZBERG & PERZLEY
Parsippany, NJ........................Banking Law, Real Estate Law

BARR, BARR AND MCINTOSH
Charleston, SC........................Civil Trial Practice, Criminal Trial Practice

BARR, SINCLAIR & HILL, A PROFESSIONAL CORPORATION
Redding, CA........................General Practice

BARRACK, RODOS & BACINE
Philadelphia, PA........................Antitrust Law, Securities Law

BARRANGER, GARIC KENNETH
Covington, LA........................General Practice

BARRET, HAYNES, MAY, CARTER AND ROARK, P.S.C.
Hazard, KY........................General Practice

BARRETT BURKE WILSON CASTLE DAFFIN & FRAPPIER, L.L.P.
Dallas, TX........................Banking Law, Civil Trial Practice, Real Estate Law

BARRETT & DEACON
Jonesboro, AR........................Civil Trial Practice, General Practice, Insurance Defense Law

BARRETT & MCNAGNY
Fort Wayne, IN........................Banking Law, Bankruptcy Law, Civil Trial Practice, Environmental Law, General Practice

BARRETT & WEBER, A LEGAL PROFESSIONAL ASSOCIATION
Cincinnati, OH........................Administrative Law, Municipal and Zoning Law, Probate and Estate Planning Law, Real Estate Law

BARRICK & MCKAY
Charlottesville, VA........................General Practice

BARRIGAR MOSS HAMMOND MCGRUDER CASSAN & MACLEAN
Ottawa, ON, Canada........................Patent, Trademark, Copyright and Unfair Competition Law

BARRIS, SOTT, DENN & DRIKER, P.L.L.C.
Detroit, MI........................Civil Trial Practice, Real Estate Law, Tax Law

BARRON, VANCE JR.
Greensboro, NC........................Commercial Law, Medical Malpractice Law, Personal Injury Law

BARRON, ORENDAIN, MALANY & FLANAGAN
McAllen, TX .... General Practice

BARRON & STADFELD, P.C.
Boston, MA .... Banking Law, Civil Trial Practice, Environmental Law, General Practice, Personal Injury Law, Real Estate Law

BARROS, MCNAMARA, SCANLON, MALKIEWICZ & TAYLOR, PROFESSIONAL ASSOCIATION
Dover, DE .... Civil Trial Practice

BARROW, SIMS, MORROW & LEE, A PROFESSIONAL CORPORATION
Savannah, GA .... Insurance Defense Law

BARRY & MCMORAN, A PROFESSIONAL CORPORATION
Newark, NJ .... Appellate Practice, Civil Trial Practice, Criminal Trial Practice, Labor and Employment Law

BARRY, RICHARD, AND SHARON MAH
San Rafael, CA .... Family Law

BARTHOLIC, ROBERT L.
Denver, CO .... Construction Law, Natural Resources Law, Probate and Estate Planning Law, Real Estate Law, Transportation Law

BARTHOLOMEW & WASZNICKY
Sacramento, CA .... Family Law

BARTIMUS, KAVANAUGH & FRICKLETON, A PROFESSIONAL CORPORATION
Kansas City, MO .... Medical Malpractice Law, Personal Injury Law, Product Liability Law

BARTLET & RICHARDES
Windsor, ON, Canada .... General Practice

BARTLETT AND BARTLETT
Walden, NY .... General Practice

BARTON, KLUGMAN & OETTING
Los Angeles, CA .... General Practice
Newport Beach, CA .... General Practice

BARTON & SCHNEIDER, L.L.P.
San Antonio, TX .... Real Estate Law

BARTON AND STREVER, P.C.
Newport, OR .... Personal Injury Law

BARTRON, WILES, RYLANCE & HOLGERSON
Watertown, SD .... Criminal Trial Practice, General Practice, Real Estate Law

BASILE, PAUL L. JR.
Los Angeles, CA .... Tax Law

BASILE, TESTA & TESTA, A PROFESSIONAL CORPORATION
Vineland, NJ .... General Practice

BASKIN, H. H., JR., P.A.
Clearwater, FL .... Probate and Estate Planning Law

BASKIN, JACKSON & HANSBARGER, A PROFESSIONAL CORPORATION
Falls Church, VA .... General Practice

BASKINS & ROEDER
North Platte, NE .... General Practice

BASON, GEORGE FRANCIS JR.
Washington, DC .... Bankruptcy Law

BASS, BERRY & SIMS
Nashville, TN .... Antitrust Law, Environmental Law, Health Care Law, Labor and Employment Law, Municipal Bond/Public Authority Financing Law, Securities Law, Tax Law, Trademark, Copyright and Unfair Competition Law

BASSETT LAW FIRM
Fayetteville, AR .... Civil Trial Practice, General Practice

BASSEY AND SELESKO, P.C.
Southfield, MI .... Business Law

BASSFORD, LOCKHART, TRUESDELL & BRIGGS, P.A.
Minneapolis, MN .... Civil Trial Practice, Environmental Law, General Practice, Insurance Defense Law, Personal Injury Law

BASTEDO SHELDON MCGIVNEY & PECK
Toronto, ON, Canada .... General Practice

BASYE & GOLDEN
San Mateo, CA .... Probate and Estate Planning Law

BATCHELOR, JAMES K., A PROFESSIONAL CORPORATION
Orange, CA .... Family Law

BATEMAN & CHILDERS
Memphis, TN .... Admiralty/Maritime Law, General Practice, Insurance Defense Law

BATES MECKLER BULGER & TILSON
Chicago, IL .... Civil Trial Practice, Labor and Employment Law

BATHGATE, WEGENER, DUGAN & WOLF, P.C.
Lakewood, NJ .... General Practice
Newark, NJ .... General Practice, Municipal Bond/Public Authority Financing Law

BATISTA, PAUL A., A PROFESSIONAL CORPORATION
New York, NY .... Civil Trial Practice, General Practice

BATJER, ROBERT D. JR.
Abilene, TX .... General Practice, Insurance Defense Law

BATTLE FOWLER LLP
New York, NY .... General Practice

BATZAR & WEINBERG, A PROFESSIONAL CORPORATION
Rockville Centre, NY .... Bankruptcy Law, Commercial Law

BAUDLER, BAUDLER, MAUS & BLAHNIK
Austin, MN .... General Practice
Spring Valley, MN .... General Practice

BAUER, BERNARD K., CO., L.P.A.
Findlay, OH .... Personal Injury Law

BAUGHER, METTLER & SHELTON
Palm Beach, FL .... Probate and Estate Planning Law, Real Estate Law, Tax Law

BAUMAN & KUNKIS, P.C.
New York, NY .... Personal Injury Law

BAUMANN, RIECKE
Houston, TX .... Bankruptcy Law

BAUM & ASSOCIATES
Bloomfield Hills, MI .... Civil Trial Practice, Criminal Trial Practice, Personal Injury Law, Product Liability Law
Detroit, MI .... Criminal Trial Practice, Personal Injury Law

BAXLEY, DILLARD, DAUPHIN & MCKNIGHT
Birmingham, AL .... Criminal Trial Practice

BAYLESS & STOKES
Houston, TX .... Civil Trial Practice, Probate and Estate Planning Law

BAYLIFF, HARRIGAN, CORD & MAUGANS, P.C.
Kokomo, IN .... Civil Trial Practice, General Practice, Personal Injury Law

BAYLOR, EVNEN, CURTISS, GRIMIT & WITT
Lincoln, NE .... General Practice

BAZELIDES, PAUL P.
Houston, TX .... International Business Law

BEALE & HUMPHREY, P.S.C.
Louisville, KY .... General Practice

BEALL & JOHNSON LAW OFFICE, INC.
Kingfisher, OK .... General Practice, Probate and Estate Planning Law, Real Estate Law

BEAL, PRATT AND PRATT
Monmouth, IL .... General Practice

BEAM, STEPHEN D.
Weatherford, OK .... General Practice

BEAM, BROBECK & WEST
Santa Ana, CA .... General Practice

BEAN & GENTRY
Olympia, WA .... Business Law, Insurance Defense Law, Personal Injury Law

BEAN, KINNEY & KORMAN, A PROFESSIONAL CORPORATION
Arlington, VA .... Banking Law, Family Law, Personal Injury Law

BEARD, STEVEN L., P.C.
Marietta, GA .... Personal Injury Law

BEARMAN TALESNICK & CLOWDUS, PROFESSIONAL CORPORATION
Denver, CO .... Real Estate Law, Securities Law

BEASLEY, CASEY, COLLERAN, ERBSTEIN, THISTLE & KLINE
Philadelphia, PA .... General Practice

BEASLEY, WILSON, ALLEN, MAIN & CROW, P.C.
Montgomery, AL .... Personal Injury Law, Product Liability Law

BEATIE, KING & ABATE
New York, NY .... Civil Trial Practice, Commercial Law, Environmental Law, Insurance Defense Law, Securities Law

BEATTIE PADOVANO
Montvale, NJ....................Appellate Practice, Banking Law, Civil Trial Practice, Criminal Trial Practice, Family Law, General Practice, Insurance Defense Law, Personal Injury Law, Real Estate Law

BEATTY, THOMAS D.
Las Vegas, NV....................Civil Trial Practice, Criminal Trial Practice

BEATTY, YOUNG, OTIS & LINCKE
Media, PA....................General Practice, Medical Malpractice Law, Municipal and Zoning Law, Probate and Estate Planning Law

BEAUREGARD & BURKE
New Bedford, MA....................Civil Trial Practice

BECKER, GLYNN, MELAMED & MUFFLY
New York, NY....................General Practice

BECKER LAW OFFICE
San Francisco, CA....................Bankruptcy Law

BECKER, STEVEN A., A PROFESSIONAL LAW CORPORATION
San Bernardino, CA....................Family Law

BECKER, THEODORE M., P.C., LAW OFFICES OF
Chicago, IL....................Civil Trial Practice

BECKERMAN & BECKERMAN
Rochester, NY....................General Practice

BECK & HALBERG
New York, NY....................Admiralty/Maritime Law

BECKHAM & BECKHAM, P.A.
North Miami Beach, FL....................Appellate Practice, Transportation Law

BECKLEY, JAMES E., & ASSOCIATES, P.C.
Wheaton, IL....................Securities Law

BECKLEY & MADDEN
Harrisburg, PA....................Construction Law, Labor and Employment Law

BECKLEY, SINGLETON, DE LANOY, JEMISON & LIST, CHARTERED, A PROFESSIONAL LAW CORPORATION
Las Vegas, NV....................Civil Trial Practice, General Practice, Insurance Defense Law
Reno, NV....................General Practice

BECKMAN, KELLY & SMITH
Hammond, IN....................Civil Trial Practice, Commercial Law, Environmental Law

BECKMAN, LAWSON, SANDLER, SNYDER & FEDEROFF
Fort Wayne, IN....................General Practice

BECKMAN & MILLMAN, P.C.
New York, NY....................Business Law, Civil Trial Practice, General Practice

BECK, OWEN & MURRAY
Griffin, GA....................Insurance Defense Law

BEDFORD, KIRSCHNER AND VENKER, P.C.
Atlanta, GA....................Criminal Trial Practice, Medical Malpractice Law, Personal Injury Law

BEECHER, RATHERT, ROBERTS, FIELD, WALKER & MORRIS, P.C.
Waterloo, IA....................General Practice

BEECHER, WAGNER, ROSE & KLEMEYER
Milford, PA....................General Practice

BEELER, JOSEPH, P.A.
Miami, FL....................Criminal Trial Practice

BEEMER & BEEMER
Clarks Summit, PA....................Civil Trial Practice

BEGAM, LEWIS, MARKS, WOLFE & DASSE, A PROFESSIONAL ASSOC. OF LAWYERS
Phoenix, AZ....................Civil Trial Practice, Medical Malpractice Law, Personal Injury Law, Product Liability Law

BEGGS & LANE
Pensacola, FL....................General Practice

BEGIER, HARRY P., JR., LTD.
Philadelphia, PA....................Civil Trial Practice

BEGLEY, CARLIN & MANDIO
Bristol, PA....................Civil Trial Practice, General Practice
Langhorne, PA....................Civil Trial Practice, General Practice

BEGLEY & FERRITER, P.C.
Holyoke, MA....................General Practice

BEHRENDS & GENTRY
Peoria, IL....................Business Law

BEHRENFELD, WILLIAM H.
Sarasota, FL....................General Practice

BEIL, JACOB
Columbus, GA....................Commercial Law

BEIRNE, MAYNARD & PARSONS, L.L.P.
Houston, TX....................Civil Trial Practice, General Practice

BELANGER & PLIMPTON
Lovelock, NV....................General Practice

BÉLANGER, SAUVÉ
Montreal, QU, Canada....................General Practice

BELCHER, HENZIE & BIEGENZAHN, A PROFESSIONAL CORPORATION
Los Angeles, CA....................General Practice

BELDEN, ABBEY, WEITZENBERG & KELLY, A PROFESSIONAL CORPORATION
Santa Rosa, CA....................Banking Law, Bankruptcy Law, Business Law, Civil Trial Practice, Commercial Law, Construction Law, General Practice, Insurance Defense Law, Labor and Employment Law, Medical Malpractice Law, Personal Injury Law, Probate and Estate Planning Law, Real Estate Law

BELDEN, BELDEN, PERSIN, JOHNSTON & ZUZIK
Greensburg, PA....................General Practice

BELDOCK LEVINE & HOFFMAN
New York, NY....................Civil Trial Practice, Criminal Trial Practice, Family Law

BELES GROUP, THE
Seattle, WA....................International Business Law

BELGRADE AND O'DONNELL, A PROFESSIONAL CORPORATION
Chicago, IL....................Admiralty/Maritime Law, Insurance Defense Law, Transportation Law

BELIN HARRIS LAMSON MCCORMICK, A PROFESSIONAL CORPORATION
Des Moines, IA....................Civil Trial Practice, General Practice

BELINKIE & LAX
Bridgeport, CT....................Family Law

BELKIN & HARROLD CO., L.P.A.
Cleveland, OH....................Labor and Employment Law

BELLAMY, RUTENBERG, COPELAND, EPPS, GRAVELY & BOWERS, P.A.
Myrtle Beach, SC....................Civil Trial Practice, General Practice

BELL AND ASSOCIATES, P.C.
Cleveland, TN....................Civil Trial Practice, General Practice, Insurance Defense Law

BELLATTI, FAY, BELLATTI & BEARD
Jacksonville, IL....................General Practice

BELL, BOYD & LLOYD
Washington, DC....................Antitrust Law, Banking Law, Civil Trial Practice, Communications Law, Construction Law, Environmental Law, General Practice
Chicago, IL....................Antitrust Law, Banking Law, Civil Trial Practice, Environmental Law, General Practice, Health Care Law, Labor and Employment Law, Municipal Bond/Public Authority Financing Law, Real Estate Law, Securities Law, Tax Law

BELL, DAVIDSON & MYERS
Las Vegas, NV....................Civil Trial Practice, Criminal Trial Practice

BELL, DAVIS & PITT, P.A.
Winston-Salem, NC....................General Practice

BELLER & KELLER
New York, NY....................Banking Law, International Business Law

BELL, FALK & NORTON, P.A.
Keene, NH....................Civil Trial Practice, General Practice, Municipal and Zoning Law, Probate and Estate Planning Law

BELL, METZNER, GIERHART & MOORE, S.C.
Madison, WI....................Civil Trial Practice, General Practice, Insurance Defense Law

BELL AND ODOM
Birmingham, AL....................General Practice
Sylacauga, AL....................General Practice

BELL, ORR, AYERS & MOORE, P.S.C.
Bowling Green, KY....................Banking Law, Civil Trial Practice, General Practice, Product Liability Law, Tax Law

BELLOWS AND BELLOWS, A PROFESSIONAL CORPORATION
Chicago, IL....................Securities Law

BELL & PANNELL
Augusta, GA....................Civil Trial Practice

BELL, SCHUSTER & WHEELER, P.A.
Pensacola, FL....Insurance Defense Law, Medical Malpractice Law

BELL, SELTZER, PARK & GIBSON, PROFESSIONAL ASSOCIATION
Charlotte, NC....Patent, Trademark, Copyright and Unfair Competition Law
Raleigh, NC....Patent, Trademark, Copyright and Unfair Competition Law

BELSKY & ASSOCIATES
San Diego, CA....Insurance Defense Law, Medical Malpractice Law

BELTRAN & ASSOCIATES
Atlanta, GA....Civil Trial Practice, Personal Injury Law

BELTZ & ASSOCIATES
Flint, MI....Personal Injury Law, Product Liability Law

BENCKENSTEIN, NORVELL & NATHAN, L.L.P.
Beaumont, TX....General Practice, Insurance Defense Law

BENCKENSTEIN & OXFORD, L.L.P.
Beaumont, TX....Admiralty/Maritime Law, Civil Trial Practice, Environmental Law, General Practice, Natural Resources Law

BENDER, LEVI & BUSS, S.C.
Watertown, WI....General Practice

BENDER, MICHAEL L., P.C.
Denver, CO....Criminal Trial Practice

BENDURE & THOMAS
Detroit, MI....Appellate Practice, Civil Trial Practice

BENESCH, FRIEDLANDER, COPLAN & ARONOFF
Cleveland, OH....Civil Trial Practice, General Practice, Labor and Employment Law, Tax Law
Columbus, OH....Civil Trial Practice, General Practice, Labor and Employment Law

BENETAR BERNSTEIN SCHAIR & STEIN
New York, NY....Labor and Employment Law

BENJAMIN & BENSON
Cambridge, MA....Family Law

BENJAMIN, YOCUM & HEATHER
Cincinnati, OH....Construction Law, Insurance Defense Law, Probate and Estate Planning Law

BENNETT & BENNETT
Eaton, OH....Civil Trial Practice, Criminal Trial Practice, General Practice, Probate and Estate Planning Law

BENNETT & BLANCATO, L.L.P.
Winston-Salem, NC....Insurance Defense Law, Medical Malpractice Law

BENNETT, BOEHNING, POYNTER & CLARY
Lafayette, IN....General Practice

BENNETT, BOWMAN, TRIPLETT & VITTITOW
Louisville, KY....General Practice, Insurance Defense Law

BENNETT, BROOCKS, BAKER & LANGE, L.L.P.
Houston, TX....Civil Trial Practice, Criminal Trial Practice, Personal Injury Law

BENNETT & DILLON
Topeka, KS....Civil Trial Practice, Criminal Trial Practice, General Practice

BENNETT & HARTMAN
Portland, OR....Civil Trial Practice

BENNETT, HERBERT H., AND ASSOCIATES, P.A.
Portland, ME....Civil Trial Practice, General Practice, Labor and Employment Law, Personal Injury Law

BENNETT, INGVALDSON & COATY, P.A.
Minneapolis, MN....Civil Trial Practice, Real Estate Law

BENNETT JONES VERCHERE
Calgary, AB, Canada....Appellate Practice, Banking Law, Business Law, Civil Trial Practice, Commercial Law, Employment Benefits Law, Environmental Law, General Practice, Health Care Law, International Business Law, Medical Malpractice Law, Natural Resources Law, Probate and Estate Planning Law, Public Utilities Law, Real Estate Law, Securities Law
Edmonton, AB, Canada....General Practice
Ottawa, ON, Canada....General Practice, Patent, Trademark, Copyright and Unfair Competition Law, Trademark, Copyright and Unfair Competition Law
Toronto, ON, Canada....General Practice
Montreal, QU, Canada....General Practice

BENNETT & KISTNER
Long Beach, CA....Business Law, Civil Trial Practice, Insurance Defense Law, Medical Malpractice Law, Personal Injury Law, Product Liability Law, Transportation Law

BENNETT, LYTLE, WETZLER, MARTIN & PISHNY, L.C.
Prairie Village, KS....General Practice

BENNETT, MAIN & FREDERICKSON, A PROFESSIONAL CORPORATION
Belle Fourche, SD....Environmental Law, General Practice, Natural Resources Law, Probate and Estate Planning Law

BENNETT, MCCONKEY, THOMPSON & MARQUARDT, P.A.
Morehead City, NC....Business Law, Civil Trial Practice, General Practice, Personal Injury Law, Probate and Estate Planning Law, Real Estate Law

BENNETT, SAMUELSEN, REYNOLDS AND ALLARD, A PROFESSIONAL CORPORATION
Oakland, CA....Insurance Defense Law

BENNINGTON JOHNSON RUTTUM & REEVE, A PROFESSIONAL CORPORATION
Denver, CO....Commercial Law

BENOIT LAW CORPORATION
Los Angeles, CA....General Practice

BENSINGER, COTANT, MENKES & AARDEMA, P.C.
Gaylord, MI....Civil Trial Practice, Insurance Defense Law
Grand Rapids, MI....Insurance Defense Law
Marquette, MI....Insurance Defense Law

BENTON, ORR, DUVAL & BUCKINGHAM, A PROFESSIONAL CORPORATION
Ventura, CA....Civil Trial Practice, General Practice

BERCHEM, MOSES & DEVLIN, A PROFESSIONAL CORPORATION
Milford, CT....General Practice, Labor and Employment Law

BERENBAUM, WEINSHIENK & EASON, P.C.
Denver, CO....General Practice

BERENS & TATE, P.C.
Omaha, NE....General Practice, Labor and Employment Law

BERENSTEIN VRIEZELAAR MOORE MOSER & TIGGES
Sioux City, IA....General Practice, Tax Law

BERESKIN & PARR
Toronto, ON, Canada....Patent, Trademark, Copyright and Unfair Competition Law

BERG & ANDROPHY
Houston, TX....Criminal Trial Practice

BERG, ZIEGLER, ANDERSON & PARKER
San Francisco, CA....Civil Trial Practice, Real Estate Law

BERGER, GARY D. LAW OFFICES OF
San Francisco, CA....Probate and Estate Planning Law

BERGER AND BERGER
Evansville, IN....Civil Trial Practice, Criminal Trial Practice, Labor and Employment Law, Personal Injury Law

BERGER, FRIEDMAN & CHRISTIANA, P.C.
Ellenville, NY....General Practice

BERGER KAPETAN MEYERS ROSEN LOUIK & RAIZMAN, P.C.
Pittsburgh, PA....Medical Malpractice Law, Personal Injury Law, Product Liability Law

BERGER & MONTAGUE, P.C.
Philadelphia, PA....Antitrust Law, General Practice

BERGER, SHAPIRO & DAVIS, P.A.
Fort Lauderdale, FL....Business Law, Civil Trial Practice, Real Estate Law, Tax Law

BERGESON, ELIOPOULOS, GRADY & GRAY
San Jose, CA....General Practice

BERGMAN & BARRETT
Princeton, NJ....Civil Trial Practice, Family Law

BERGMAN, HOROWITZ & REYNOLDS, P.C.
New Haven, CT....Bankruptcy Law, Commercial Law, General Practice, Probate and Estate Planning Law, Real Estate Law, Tax Law

BERGMAN & WEDNER, INC.
Los Angeles, CA....Business Law, Real Estate Law

BERGSTEDT & MOUNT
Lake Charles, LA....Admiralty/Maritime Law, Banking Law, Civil Trial Practice, General Practice, Insurance Defense Law, Real Estate Law

BERICK, PEARLMAN & MILLS, A LEGAL PROFESSIONAL ASSOCIATION
Cleveland, OH....Banking Law, Business Law, General Practice, Real Estate Law, Securities Law, Tax Law

BERKEY, JON H., P.C.
Bloomfield Hills, MI....Commercial Law, Real Estate Law

BERKMAN, GORDON, MURRAY, PALDA & DEVAN
Cleveland, OH....Civil Trial Practice, Criminal Trial Practice

BERKOWITZ, LEFKOVITS, ISOM & KUSHNER, A PROFESSIONAL CORPORATION
Birmingham, AL....Antitrust Law, Business Law, Civil Trial Practice, General Practice, Health Care Law, Labor and Employment Law, Probate and Estate Planning Law, Real Estate Law, Securities Law, Tax Law

BERLAND, ALLAN M.
San Francisco, CA....Real Estate Law

BERLINER, CORCORAN & ROWE
Washington, DC....International Business Law

BERLINER ZISSER WALTER & GALLEGOS, P.C.
Denver, CO....Securities Law

BERMAN, DAVID
Medford, MA....Civil Trial Practice

BERMAN, HAROLD B.
Dallas, TX....General Practice, Probate and Estate Planning Law

BERMAN, BLANCHARD, MAUSNER & KINDEM, A LAW CORPORATION
Los Angeles, CA....Civil Trial Practice, Trademark, Copyright and Unfair Competition Law

BERMAN, BOURNS & CURRIE
West Hartford, CT....Family Law, General Practice, Probate and Estate Planning Law, Real Estate Law

BERMAN, GAUFIN & TOMSIC, A PROFESSIONAL CORPORATION
Salt Lake City, UT....Civil Trial Practice, Criminal Trial Practice

BERMAN, PALEY, GOLDSTEIN & KANNRY
New York, NY....Construction Law

BERMAN & SIMMONS, P.A.
Bridgton, ME....Civil Trial Practice, Criminal Trial Practice, Personal Injury Law
Lewiston, ME....Appellate Practice, Civil Trial Practice, Criminal Trial Practice, Personal Injury Law, Product Liability Law
Portland, ME....Civil Trial Practice, Criminal Trial Practice, Personal Injury Law
South Paris, ME....Civil Trial Practice, Criminal Trial Practice, Personal Injury Law

BERMAN AND TRACHTMAN, P.C.
Chicago, IL....Personal Injury Law

BERMINGHAM & COOK, P.C.
Buffalo, NY....General Practice

BERNARD, JACK M.
Philadelphia, PA....Civil Trial Practice

BERNARD, CASSISA & ELLIOTT, A PROFESSIONAL LAW CORPORATION
Metairie, LA....General Practice

BERNARD & DAVIDSON
Granite City, IL....Civil Trial Practice, General Practice

BERNARDINI, PAUL A. LAW OFFICE OF
Daytona Beach, FL....Personal Injury Law

BERNAUER, THOMAS A., A PROFESSIONAL CORPORATION
Newport Beach, CA....Family Law

BERNHOLZ & HERMAN
Chapel Hill, NC....Civil Trial Practice, Criminal Trial Practice, General Practice, Personal Injury Law

BERNICK AND LIFSON, P.A.
Minneapolis, MN....Securities Law, Tax Law

BERNSTEIN, EUGENE SR.
Memphis, TN....Business Law, General Practice, Tax Law

BERNSTEIN AND BERNSTEIN, A PROFESSIONAL CORPORATION
Pittsburgh, PA....Bankruptcy Law, Commercial Law, Real Estate Law

BERNSTEIN & BERNSTEIN, P.A.
Charleston, SC....Bankruptcy Law, Civil Trial Practice, Commercial Law

BERNSTEIN, SHUR, SAWYER AND NELSON, A PROFESSIONAL CORPORATION
Portland, ME....General Practice

BERNSTEIN, STAIR & MCADAMS
Knoxville, TN....Civil Trial Practice, General Practice

BERRY, THOMAS A. & ASSOCIATES
Bloomington, IN....Civil Trial Practice

BERRY, THOMAS E. & ASSOCIATES
Houston, TX....Probate and Estate Planning Law, Tax Law

BERRY, ABLES, TATUM, LITTLE & BAXTER, P.C.
Huntsville, AL....Bankruptcy Law, Business Law, Family Law, General Practice, Labor and Employment Law, Personal Injury Law, Probate and Estate Planning Law, Real Estate Law

BERRY & BERRY, A PROFESSIONAL CORPORATION
Oakland, CA....General Practice

BERRY & BYRD
Fayetteville, NC....Personal Injury Law

BERRY, CAPPER & TULLEY
Crawfordsville, IN....General Practice

BERRY, DUNBAR, DANIEL, O'CONNOR & JORDAN
Columbia, SC....General Practice, Immigration and Naturalization Law, International Business Law, Real Estate Law

BERRY & FLOYD, P.S.C.
New Castle, KY....Banking Law

BERRY, JOHN STEVENS, P.C.
Lincoln, NE....Appellate Practice, Criminal Trial Practice

BERRY, KAGAN AND SAHRADNIK, A PROFESSIONAL CORPORATION
Toms River, NJ....General Practice

BERRY AND OGLESBY
Franklin, TN....General Practice

BERRY & SHOEMAKER
Columbus, OH....Civil Trial Practice, Family Law, Personal Injury Law

BERRYHILL, WILLIAMS & JORDAN, P.A.
Fort Lauderdale, FL....General Practice

BERSCH & RHODES, P.C.
Roanoke, VA....Business Law, Employment Benefits Law, Probate and Estate Planning Law

BERTIN, EMANUEL A., P.C.
Norristown, PA....Family Law

BERTZ, MICHAEL A.
Los Angeles, CA....Securities Law

BESLOW, WILLIAM S. LAW OFFICE OF
New York, NY....Family Law

BESS & DYSART, P.C.
Phoenix, AZ....Civil Trial Practice, Environmental Law, Insurance Defense Law, Personal Injury Law

BESSEY, JOHN D.
Sacramento, CA....Bankruptcy Law

BEST & ANDERSON, P.A.
Crystal River, FL....Civil Trial Practice, Medical Malpractice Law, Personal Injury Law
Orlando, FL....Civil Trial Practice, Medical Malpractice Law, Personal Injury Law

BEST, BEST & KRIEGER
Riverside, CA....General Practice

BEST & FLANAGAN
Minneapolis, MN....General Practice

BEST, SHARP, HOLDEN, SHERIDAN, BEST & SULLIVAN, A PROFESSIONAL CORPORATION
Tulsa, OK....Civil Trial Practice, Insurance Defense Law, Medical Malpractice Law, Personal Injury Law

BETHEA, JORDAN & GRIFFIN, P.A.
Hilton Head Island, SC....Probate and Estate Planning Law, Tax Law

BETHELL, CALLAWAY, ROBERTSON, BEASLEY & COWAN
Fort Smith, AR....Civil Trial Practice, General Practice

BETTS, PATTERSON & MINES, P.S.
Seattle, WA....Bankruptcy Law, Business Law, Civil Trial Practice, Environmental Law, Insurance Defense Law, Product Liability Law, Real Estate Law

BEVER, DYE, MUSTARD & BELIN
Wichita, KS....Tax Law

BEVERIDGE, DEGRANDI, WEILACHER & YOUNG
Washington, DC....Patent, Trademark, Copyright and Unfair Competition Law

BEVERIDGE & DIAMOND
San Francisco, CA....General Practice
Washington, DC....General Practice
New York, NY....General Practice

BEVERLY & TITTLE, P.A.
West Palm Beach, FL.............Civil Trial Practice, General Practice

BEWLEY, LASSLEBEN & MILLER
Whittier, CA............................Civil Trial Practice, General Practice, Probate and Estate Planning Law

BIBBY & GOOD
Charleston, WV.....................Probate and Estate Planning Law

BIBLE, HOY, TRACHOK, WADHAMS & ZIVE, A PROFESSIONAL CORPORATION
Reno, NV ....Civil Trial Practice

BICKEL & ASSOCIATES
San Francisco, CA..................Real Estate Law

BICKFORD, PASLEY & FARABOUGH
Ardmore, OK..........................General Practice

BIEBEL & FRENCH, A LEGAL PROFESSIONAL ASSOCIATION
Columbus, OH.........................Patent, Trademark, Copyright and Unfair Competition Law
Dayton, OH.............................Patent, Trademark, Copyright and Unfair Competition Law

BIEN, ELLIOT L. LAW OFFICES OF
San Francisco, CA..................Appellate Practice

BIENSTOCK & CLARK
Santa Monica, CA...................Civil Trial Practice

BIERI & BERNSTEIN
Detroit, MI..............................Real Estate Law

BIERMAN, SHOHAT, LOEWY & PERRY, PROFESSIONAL ASSOCIATION
Miami, FL................................Appellate Practice, Criminal Trial Practice, General Practice, International Business Law

BIESER, GREER & LANDIS
Dayton, OH.............................Civil Trial Practice, General Practice

BIGGS AND BATTAGLIA
Wilmington, DE.......................Civil Trial Practice, Criminal Trial Practice, General Practice

BIGHAM ENGLAR JONES & HOUSTON
New York, NY.........................Admiralty/Maritime Law, Civil Trial Practice, General Practice, Insurance Defense Law
London, England.....................General Practice

BILLINGS & SOLOMON, P.C.
Houston, TX............................Admiralty/Maritime Law

BINGAMAN, HESS, COBLENTZ & BELL, A PROFESSIONAL CORPORATION
Reading, PA.............................Banking Law, Bankruptcy Law, Civil Trial Practice, General Practice

BINGHAM, DANA & GOULD
Hartford, CT...........................General Practice
Washington, DC......................General Practice
Boston, MA.............................Admiralty/Maritime Law, Bankruptcy Law, General Practice, Municipal Bond/Public Authority Financing Law, Tax Law
London, England.....................General Practice

BINNING, J. BOYD
Columbus, OH.........................Personal Injury Law

BINSTOCK, SHELTON M. THE LAW OFFICES OF
Washington, DC......................Probate and Estate Planning Law

BIRCH, DE JONGH & HINDELS
Charlotte Amalie, St. Thomas, VI.............................Banking Law, General Practice, Real Estate Law

BIRCH, STEWART, KOLASCH & BIRCH
Falls Church, VA....................Patent, Trademark, Copyright and Unfair Competition Law

BIRD, FRANCIS M. JR.
Atlanta, GA.............................Bankruptcy Law, General Practice, Probate and Estate Planning Law

BIRD, BALLARD & STILL
Atlanta, GA.............................Medical Malpractice Law, Personal Injury Law, Product Liability Law

BIRD, MARTIN & SALOMON, S.C.
Milwaukee, WI........................Bankruptcy Law, Civil Trial Practice, Commercial Law, General Practice

BIRDWELL, WILLIAM A. & ASSOCIATES
Portland, OR...........................Patent, Trademark, Copyright and Unfair Competition Law

BIREN, MATTHEW B. F. & ASSOCIATES
Los Angeles, CA.....................Personal Injury Law, Product Liability Law

BIRNBAUM, IRWIN
Syracuse, NY..........................Civil Trial Practice

BISHINS, LARRY V., P.A.
Fort Lauderdale, FL................Business Law, Tax Law

BISHOP, JAMES A. LAW OFFICES OF
Brunswick, GA........................General Practice

BISHOP & BISHOP
Ashdown, AR..........................General Practice

BISHOP, COLVIN, JOHNSON & KENT
Birmingham, AL......................General Practice

BISHOP, E. THOMAS, P.C.
Dallas, TX...............................Insurance Defense Law

BISHOP, PAYNE, WILLIAMS & WERLEY, L.L.P.
Fort Worth, TX.......................Civil Trial Practice

BITTMAN, HOWARD
Boulder, CO............................Civil Trial Practice, Criminal Trial Practice, General Practice

BIVENS, HOFFMAN & FOWLER
Atlanta, GA.............................Business Law, Family Law, Probate and Estate Planning Law, Tax Law

BIXBY, LECHNER & POTRATZ, P.C. A PROFESSIONAL CORPORATION
Chicago, IL.............................Insurance Defense Law

BLACHLY, TABOR, BOZIK & HARTMAN
Valparaiso, IN.........................Civil Trial Practice, General Practice, Personal Injury Law, Probate and Estate Planning Law, Real Estate Law

BLACK & BLACK
Port Arthur, TX.......................General Practice

BLACK & GOTTLIEB
Phoenix, AZ............................Criminal Trial Practice

BLACK HELTERLINE
Portland, OR...........................Banking Law, Bankruptcy Law, Civil Trial Practice, Commercial Law, Environmental Law, General Practice, Immigration and Naturalization Law, Natural Resources Law, Real Estate Law, Tax Law

BLACKHURST, HORNECKER, HASSEN & ERVIN B. HOGAN
Medford, OR...........................General Practice

BLACK, MCCARTHY & ANEWALT, P.C.
Allentown, PA.........................General Practice

BLACKMON & DROZD
Sacramento, CA......................Criminal Trial Practice

BLACKMUN, BOMBERGER & MORAN
Highland, IN............................General Practice, Insurance Defense Law

BLACK, NOLAND & READ
Staunton, VA..........................General Practice

BLACKWELL SANDERS MATHENY WEARY & LOMBARDI L.C.
Overland Park, KS..................General Practice
Kansas City, MO.....................Antitrust Law, Civil Trial Practice, General Practice, Insurance Defense Law, Labor and Employment Law, Tax Law

BLACKWELL & WALKER, ATTYS. AT LAW, A PROF. ASSN.
Miami, FL................................General Practice

BLACKWOOD & MATTHEWS
Atlanta, GA.............................Civil Trial Practice, Personal Injury Law, Product Liability Law

BLAIR, HOLLADAY AND PARSONS
Pell City, AL...........................Civil Trial Practice, General Practice, Insurance Defense Law

BLAIR, SCHAEFER, HUTCHISON & WOLFE
Vancouver, WA.......................General Practice

BLAIR & STROUD
Batesville, AR.........................General Practice

BLAKE, CASSELS & GRAYDON
Calgary, AB, Canada..............General Practice
Vancouver, BC, Canada..........General Practice
Ottawa, ON, Canada...............General Practice
Toronto, ON, Canada..............General Practice
London, England.....................General Practice

BLAKENEY & ALEXANDER
Charlotte, NC..........................Civil Trial Practice, General Practice, Labor and Employment Law

BLANCHARD, TWIGGS, ABRAMS & STRICKLAND, P.A.
Raleigh, NC............................Civil Trial Practice, Personal Injury Law, Product Liability Law

BLANCHARD, VAN FLEET, MARTIN, ROBERTSON & DERMOTT
Joplin, MO .... General Practice, Insurance Defense Law

BLANCHFIELD AND MOORE, A PROFESSIONAL CORPORATION
Charlotte, NC .... Tax Law

BLANCO TACKABERY COMBS & MATAMOROS, P.A.
Winston-Salem, NC .... Bankruptcy Law, Commercial Law

BLANEY, MCMURTRY, STAPELLS
Toronto, ON, Canada .... General Practice

BLANKE, NORDEN, BARMANN, KRAMER & BOHLEN, P.C.
Kankakee, IL .... Commercial Law, General Practice, Health Care Law

BLANKENSHIP AND RHODES, ATTORNEYS-AT-LAW, P.C.
Huntsville, AL .... Family Law

BLANTON, RICE, SIDWELL & OTTINGER
Sikeston, MO .... General Practice, Insurance Defense Law

BLASE, VALENTINE & KLEIN, A PROFESSIONAL CORPORATION
Palo Alto, CA .... Civil Trial Practice, General Practice

BLASINGAME, BURCH, GARRARD & BRYANT, P.C.
Athens, GA .... Civil Trial Practice, General Practice

BLASKE AND BLASKE
Ann Arbor, MI .... Civil Trial Practice, Personal Injury Law
Battle Creek, MI .... Civil Trial Practice, Personal Injury Law

BLAU, KRAMER, WACTLAR & LIEBERMAN, P.C.
Jericho, NY .... Securities Law

BLAZZARD, GRODD & HASENAUER, P.C.
Westport, CT .... General Practice, Probate and Estate Planning Law, Securities Law, Tax Law

BLEAKLEY PLATT & SCHMIDT
White Plains, NY .... Civil Trial Practice, General Practice

BLECHER & COLLINS, A PROFESSIONAL CORPORATION
Los Angeles, CA .... Antitrust Law, Civil Trial Practice

BLEDSOE, LOUIS A., JR., PROFESSIONAL ASSOCIATION
Charlotte, NC .... General Practice

BLEDSOE, SCHMIDT, LIPPES & ADAMS, P.A.
Jacksonville, FL .... Civil Trial Practice

BLEIMAIER, JOHN KUHN
Princeton, NJ .... Immigration and Naturalization Law, International Business Law

BLETHEN, GAGE & KRAUSE
Mankato, MN .... Civil Trial Practice, Criminal Trial Practice, General Practice

BLISH & CAVANAGH
Providence, RI .... Antitrust Law, Civil Trial Practice, Commercial Law, Construction Law, Environmental Law, General Practice, Labor and Employment Law

BLITMAN AND KING
Syracuse, NY .... Labor and Employment Law

BLOCK & COLUCCI, P.C.
Buffalo, NY .... Banking Law, General Practice, Real Estate Law

BLODNICK ABRAMOWITZ & BLODNICK
Roslyn Heights, NY .... General Practice

BLOND, BARTON S., P.C., LAW OFFICES OF
Kansas City, MO .... Family Law

BLOODWORTH & BLOODWORTH
Poplar Bluff, MO .... General Practice

BLOOM, DAVID B., A PROFESSIONAL CORPORATION, LAW OFFICES OF
Los Angeles, CA .... Banking Law, Bankruptcy Law, Business Law, Civil Trial Practice, Commercial Law, Construction Law, General Practice, Real Estate Law

BLOUNT, MARVIN K. JR.
Greenville, NC .... Environmental Law, Medical Malpractice Law, Personal Injury Law

BLUM, EDWARD L.
Oakland, CA .... Commercial Law

BLUT, JEROME L., CHARTERED
Las Vegas, NV .... Probate and Estate Planning Law, Tax Law

BLUTRICH, HERMAN & MILLER, LLP.
New York, NY .... Commercial Law

BLYLER, WILLIAM E.
Coral Springs, FL .... General Practice

BOARD, JOHN
Guymon, OK .... General Practice

BOARDMAN, SUHR, CURRY & FIELD
Madison, WI .... Civil Trial Practice, General Practice, Personal Injury Law

BOBERSCHMIDT, MILLER, O'BRYAN, TURNER & ABBOTT, A PROFESSIONAL ASSOCIATION
Indianapolis, IN .... Civil Trial Practice, Family Law, General Practice, Probate and Estate Planning Law

BOBO, SPICER, CIOTOLI, FULFORD, BOCCHINO, DEBEVOISE & LE CLAINCHE, P.A.
Orlando, FL .... Civil Trial Practice, General Practice, Health Care Law
West Palm Beach, FL .... Civil Trial Practice, General Practice, Health Care Law

BOBROW GREENAPPLE SKOLNIK & SHAKARCHY, P.C.
New York, NY .... General Practice

BOCCARDO LAW FIRM, THE
San Jose, CA .... Medical Malpractice Law, Personal Injury Law, Product Liability Law

BOCK, JOHN GORDON
Houston, TX .... Civil Trial Practice, Family Law

BOCKOL, RICHARD MAX
Bala Cynwyd, PA .... Civil Trial Practice

BODDINGTON & BROWN, CHTD.
Kansas City, KS .... General Practice

BODENHEIMER, BUSBEE, HUNTER & GRIFFITH
Aiken, SC .... Civil Trial Practice, General Practice, Personal Injury Law

BODENHEIMER, JONES, KLOTZ & SIMMONS
Shreveport, LA .... Banking Law, Bankruptcy Law, Civil Trial Practice, Commercial Law, Insurance Defense Law, Natural Resources Law, Personal Injury Law, Probate and Estate Planning Law, Real Estate Law

BODKIN, MCCARTHY, SARGENT & SMITH
Los Angeles, CA .... Civil Trial Practice, General Practice, Real Estate Law

BODMAN, LONGLEY & DAHLING
Ann Arbor, MI .... Patent, Trademark, Copyright and Unfair Competition Law, Probate and Estate Planning Law, Real Estate Law
Cheboygan, MI .... Banking Law
Detroit, MI .... Administrative Law, Antitrust Law, Appellate Practice, Banking Law, Bankruptcy Law, Business Law, Civil Trial Practice, Commercial Law, Communications Law, Construction Law, Environmental Law, General Practice, Labor and Employment Law, Municipal Bond/Public Authority Financing Law, Municipal and Zoning Law, Natural Resources Law, Patent, Trademark, Copyright and Unfair Competition Law, Probate and Estate Planning Law, Product Liability Law, Real Estate Law, Securities Law, Tax Law, Trademark, Copyright and Unfair Competition Law

BODYFELT, MOUNT, STROUP & CHAMBERLAIN
Portland, OR .... Civil Trial Practice, Insurance Defense Law

BOEHL STOPHER & GRAVES
Lexington, KY .... Civil Trial Practice, General Practice
Louisville, KY .... Civil Trial Practice, General Practice
Paducah, KY .... Civil Trial Practice, General Practice

BOEHM, KURTZ & LOWRY
Cincinnati, OH .... Public Utilities Law

BOESCHE, MCDERMOTT & ESKRIDGE
Tulsa, OK .... Banking Law, Bankruptcy Law, General Practice, International Business Law, Natural Resources Law

BOGART, SUSAN
Chicago, IL .... Criminal Trial Practice, Labor and Employment Law

BOGATIN LAW FIRM, THE
Memphis, TN .... Civil Trial Practice, Criminal Trial Practice, General Practice, International Business Law, Probate and Estate Planning Law, Tax Law

BOGENSCHUTZ & DUTKO, P.A.
Fort Lauderdale, FL .... Criminal Trial Practice

BOGGS, LOEHN & RODRIGUE
New Orleans, LA .... Environmental Law, Health Care Law, Insurance Defense Law, Medical Malpractice Law

BOGIN, PATTERSON & BOHMAN
Dayton, OH .... Bankruptcy Law, Business Law, Civil Trial Practice

BOGOSLOW & JONES, P.A.
Walterboro, SC....................General Practice

BOGUTZ & GORDON, P.C.
Tucson, AZ....................Probate and Estate Planning Law

BOIVIN, JONES, UERLINGS, DIIACONI & ODEN
Klamath Falls, OR....................General Practice

BOLDING, EDWARD P.
Tucson, AZ....................Civil Trial Practice, Criminal Trial Practice

BOLGER PICKER HANKIN & TANNENBAUM
Philadelphia, PA....................Commercial Law, General Practice

BOLING, RICE, BETTIS, BOTTOMS & BAGLEY
Cumming, GA....................General Practice

BOLLING, WALTER & GAWTHROP, A PROFESSIONAL CORPORATION
Sacramento, CA....................Civil Trial Practice

BOMAR, SHOFNER, IRION & RAMBO
Shelbyville, TN....................General Practice

BONAPARTE & MIYAMOTO, A PROFESSIONAL LAW CORPORATION
Los Angeles, CA....................Immigration and Naturalization Law

BOND & BALMAN
Tulsa, OK....................Business Law

BOND, SCHOENECK & KING
Boca Raton, FL....................General Practice
Naples, FL....................General Practice
Albany, NY....................General Practice
Oswego, NY....................General Practice
Syracuse, NY....................Antitrust Law, Civil Trial Practice, Environmental Law, General Practice, Insurance Defense Law, Labor and Employment Law, Municipal Bond/Public Authority Financing Law, Personal Injury Law, Tax Law

BONDURANT, MIXSON & ELMORE
Atlanta, GA....................Antitrust Law, Bankruptcy Law, Civil Trial Practice, Criminal Trial Practice, Environmental Law, General Practice, Trademark, Copyright and Unfair Competition Law

BONDY & SCHLOSS
New York, NY....................General Practice

BONICA, JOHN R., P.C.
Houston, TX....................Natural Resources Law

BONINA & BONINA, P.C.
Brooklyn, NY....................Civil Trial Practice, Medical Malpractice Law

BONN, LUSCHER, PADDEN & WILKINS, CHARTERED
Phoenix, AZ....................Business Law, Civil Trial Practice, Commercial Law, Construction Law, Health Care Law, Real Estate Law

BONNE, BRIDGES, MUELLER, O'KEEFE & NICHOLS, PROFESSIONAL CORPORATION
Los Angeles, CA....................Medical Malpractice Law

BONNER, HOGAN & COLEMAN, P.A.
Clearwater, FL....................General Practice

BONNER, RICHARD W., A PROFESSIONAL CORPORATION
Newport Beach, CA....................Criminal Trial Practice

BONNETT, FAIRBOURN, FRIEDMAN, HIENTON, MINER & FRY, P.C.
Phoenix, AZ....................Civil Trial Practice, Insurance Defense Law, Personal Injury Law

BONNEY, WEAVER, CORLEY, BENEFIELD & GOSSETT
Duncan, OK....................General Practice

BONYA AND DOUGLASS
Indiana, PA....................Business Law, Environmental Law, General Practice

BOONE, DAVID WM., P.C.
Atlanta, GA....................Medical Malpractice Law, Personal Injury Law

BOONE, KARLBERG AND HADDON
Missoula, MT....................General Practice

BOONE, SMITH, DAVIS, HURST & DICKMAN, A PROFESSIONAL CORPORATION
Tulsa, OK....................Banking Law, Employment Benefits Law, General Practice, Health Care Law, Securities Law

BOOTH, MITCHELL B.
New York, NY....................Probate and Estate Planning Law

BOOTH, BATE, GRIECO AND BRIODY
Montclair, NJ....................Probate and Estate Planning Law

BOOTH, MITCHEL & STRANGE
Los Angeles, CA....................Insurance Defense Law

BOOTH, PATTERSON, LEE, NEED & ADKISON, P.C.
Pontiac, MI....................Business Law, Civil Trial Practice, General Practice, Municipal and Zoning Law, Personal Injury Law, Probate and Estate Planning Law, Real Estate Law

BOOTH, WADE & CAMPBELL
Atlanta, GA....................General Practice, International Business Law

BOOTHBY & YINGST
Washington, DC....................Civil Trial Practice
Berrien Springs, MI....................Civil Trial Practice

BOOTHMAN, HEBERT & ELLER, P.C.
Ann Arbor, MI....................Civil Trial Practice, General Practice, Medical Malpractice Law
Detroit, MI....................Civil Trial Practice, General Practice, Medical Malpractice Law

BORDEN & ELLIOT
Toronto, ON, Canada....................Administrative Law, Admiralty/Maritime Law, Antitrust Law, Banking Law, Bankruptcy Law, Business Law, Civil Trial Practice, Commercial Law, Communications Law, Construction Law, Criminal Trial Practice, Employment Benefits Law, Environmental Law, Family Law, General Practice, Health Care Law, Immigration and Naturalization Law, Insurance Defense Law, International Business Law, Labor and Employment Law, Medical Malpractice Law, Municipal and Zoning Law, Natural Resources Law, Patent, Trademark, Copyright and Unfair Competition Law, Personal Injury Law, Probate and Estate Planning Law, Real Estate Law, Securities Law, Tax Law

BORING, PARROTT & PILGER, P.C.
Vienna, VA....................Business Law, Civil Trial Practice, Commercial Law, Employment Benefits Law, Labor and Employment Law, Probate and Estate Planning Law, Real Estate Law, Tax Law

BORNN BORNN HANDY
Charlotte Amalie, St. Thomas, VI....................Civil Trial Practice, Commercial Law, Family Law, General Practice, Labor and Employment Law, Real Estate Law, Tax Law

BOROD & KRAMER, P.C.
Memphis, TN....................Bankruptcy Law, Civil Trial Practice, General Practice, Securities Law

BOROUGHS, GRIMM, BENNETT & MORLAN, P.A.
Orlando, FL....................Commercial Law, General Practice, International Business Law

BORRE, PETERSON, FOWLER & REENS, P.C.
Grand Rapids, MI....................Bankruptcy Law, Civil Trial Practice, General Practice, Real Estate Law, Tax Law

BORRON, DELAHAYE, EDWARDS & DORÉ
Plaquemine, LA....................General Practice, Medical Malpractice Law

BORRUS, GOLDIN & FOLEY, A PROFESSIONAL CORPORATION
New Brunswick, NJ....................General Practice

BORRUS, GOLDIN, FOLEY, VIGNUOLO, HYMAN & STAHL, A PROFESSIONAL CORPORATION
North Brunswick, NJ....................Civil Trial Practice, Criminal Trial Practice, Family Law, General Practice, Probate and Estate Planning Law, Real Estate Law

BORTON, PETRINI & CONRON
Bakersfield, CA....................General Practice, Tax Law

BOSE MCKINNEY & EVANS
Indianapolis, IN....................Antitrust Law, Banking Law, Bankruptcy Law, Civil Trial Practice, Communications Law, Environmental Law, General Practice, Labor and Employment Law, Municipal Bond/Public Authority Financing Law, Public Utilities Law, Real Estate Law, Tax Law

BOSSIN, PHYLLIS G., CO., L.P.A.
Cincinnati, OH....................Family Law

BOSSO, WILLIAMS, LEVIN, SACHS & BOOK, A PROFESSIONAL CORPORATION
Santa Cruz, CA....................General Practice

BOSTON, WILLIAM C. & ASSOCIATES
Oklahoma City, OK....................Commercial Law, Transportation Law

BOSTON, JAMES R., & ASSOCIATES, P.C.
Houston, TX....................Medical Malpractice Law

BOSTWICK & TEHIN
San Francisco, CA....................Admiralty/Maritime Law, Civil Trial Practice, Medical Malpractice Law, Personal Injury Law, Product Liability Law

BOSWELL & HALLMARK, A PROFESSIONAL CORPORATION
Houston, TX....................Civil Trial Practice, Insurance Defense Law

BOSWELL, SNYDER, TINTNER & PICCOLA
Harrisburg, PA.....Business Law, Civil Trial Practice, Labor and Employment Law, Real Estate Law

BOSWELL, STIDHAM, PURCELL, CONNER, WILSON & BREWER, P.A.
Bartow, FL.....Civil Trial Practice, Criminal Trial Practice

BOSWORTH, ARTHUR, & ASSOCIATES, P.C.
Denver, CO.....Civil Trial Practice

BOTTI, MARINACCIO & TAMELING, LTD.
Oak Brook, IL.....Civil Trial Practice, Criminal Trial Practice, Family Law

BOTTS, R. DAVID
Atlanta, GA.....Criminal Trial Practice, General Practice, Personal Injury Law

BOUCHARD & MALLORY, P.A.
Manchester, NH.....Insurance Defense Law, Personal Injury Law, Product Liability Law

BOUDREAU & TRENTACOSTA, A PROFESSIONAL LAW CORPORATION
San Diego, CA.....Personal Injury Law

BOUGHEY, GARVIE & BUSHNER
San Francisco, CA.....Admiralty/Maritime Law, Insurance Defense Law

BOUHAN, WILLIAMS & LEVY
Savannah, GA.....General Practice

BOULT, CUMMINGS, CONNERS & BERRY
Nashville, TN.....General Practice

BOURDEAUX AND JONES
Meridian, MS.....Civil Trial Practice, General Practice, Insurance Defense Law

BOURLAND, HEFLIN, ALVAREZ, HOLLEY & MINOR
Memphis, TN.....Civil Trial Practice, General Practice

BOURNE, NOLL & KENYON, A PROFESSIONAL CORPORATION
Summit, NJ.....Banking Law, Commercial Law, General Practice, Probate and Estate Planning Law, Real Estate Law

BOUTIN • GIBSON
Sacramento, CA.....Civil Trial Practice

BOVIS, KYLE & BURCH
Atlanta, GA.....Construction Law, Environmental Law, Insurance Defense Law

BOWEN & SIEGEL
Northampton, MA.....Real Estate Law

BOWEN, WILLIAM M., P.A.
Hilton Head Island, SC.....General Practice

BOWERMAN, DONALD B.
Oregon City, OR.....Civil Trial Practice, Personal Injury Law

BOWERS, HARRISON, KENT & MILLER
Evansville, IN.....Appellate Practice, Banking Law, Bankruptcy Law, Business Law, Civil Trial Practice, Commercial Law, General Practice, Labor and Employment Law, Real Estate Law

BOWERS ORR & ROBERTSON
Columbia, SC.....Civil Trial Practice, Construction Law, Environmental Law, Insurance Defense Law, Product Liability Law

BOWLES, KEATING, HERING & LOWE, CHARTERED
Chicago, IL.....Business Law, Civil Trial Practice, General Practice, International Business Law

BOWLES RICE MCDAVID GRAFF & LOVE
Charleston, WV.....Civil Trial Practice, General Practice
Martinsburg, WV.....Civil Trial Practice, General Practice
Morgantown, WV.....Civil Trial Practice, General Practice
Parkersburg, WV.....Civil Trial Practice, General Practice

BOWLING, BOWLING & ASSOCIATES
Memphis, TN.....Labor and Employment Law

BOWMAN, ANDREW B.
Westport, CT.....Appellate Practice, Civil Trial Practice, Criminal Trial Practice

BOWMAN, ALAN DEXTER, P.A.
Newark, NJ.....Civil Trial Practice

BOWMAN AND BROOKE
Minneapolis, MN.....Civil Trial Practice, Product Liability Law

BOWMER, COURTNEY, BURLESON, NORMAND & MOORE
Temple, TX.....General Practice

BOXER, SANDOR T.
Los Angeles, CA.....Commercial Law

BOYAJIAN, HARRINGTON & RICHARDSON
Providence, RI.....General Practice

BOYCE & BOYCE, A PROFESSIONAL ASSOCIATION
Newport, AR.....General Practice

BOYCE LAW FIRM
Newport, AR.....General Practice

BOYCE, MURPHY, MCDOWELL & GREENFIELD
Sioux Falls, SD.....General Practice

BOYD & BOYD, P.C.
Weston, MA.....Probate and Estate Planning Law
Norfolk, VA.....Business Law

BOYER, REYNOLDS & DEMARCO, LTD.
Providence, RI.....Civil Trial Practice, Insurance Defense Law

BOYER, TANZLER & BOYER
Jacksonville, FL.....Civil Trial Practice

BOYER, WAYNE J., P.A.
Clearwater, FL.....Family Law

BOYLE & ANDERSON, P.C.
Auburn, NY.....General Practice, Immigration and Naturalization Law

BOYLE, CARTER & GAINES
Wilmington, NC.....Personal Injury Law

BOYLE, CHARLES A., & ASSOCIATES, LTD.
Chicago, IL.....Personal Injury Law

BOYLE, CORDES AND BROWN
De Kalb, IL.....General Practice

BOYLE, GOLDSMITH & BOLIN
Hennepin, IL.....General Practice

BRACH, EICHLER, ROSENBERG, SILVER, BERNSTEIN, HAMMER & GLADSTONE, A PROFESSIONAL CORPORATION
Roseland, NJ.....Banking Law, Civil Trial Practice, General Practice, Health Care Law, Insurance Defense Law, Personal Injury Law, Real Estate Law, Tax Law

BRACKEN & MARGOLIN
Islandia, NY.....General Practice

BRADEN & OLSON
Lake Geneva, WI.....Civil Trial Practice, Personal Injury Law, Probate and Estate Planning Law, Real Estate Law

BRADFORD, MICHAEL E.
Phoenix, AZ.....Medical Malpractice Law, Personal Injury Law

BRADFORD, PETER C.
Newport Beach, CA.....Probate and Estate Planning Law

BRADLEY, JOSEPH D.
South Bend, IN.....Bankruptcy Law

BRADLEY, ARANT, ROSE & WHITE
Birmingham, AL.....Antitrust Law, Banking Law, Bankruptcy Law, Business Law, Civil Trial Practice, Commercial Law, Communications Law, Construction Law, Employment Benefits Law, Environmental Law, General Practice, Health Care Law, Insurance Defense Law, International Business Law, Labor and Employment Law, Municipal Bond/Public Authority Financing Law, Municipal and Zoning Law, Natural Resources Law, Patent, Trademark, Copyright and Unfair Competition Law, Personal Injury Law, Probate and Estate Planning Law, Real Estate Law, Securities Law, Tax Law, Trademark, Copyright and Unfair Competition Law, Transportation Law
Huntsville, AL.....Civil Trial Practice, Communications Law, Environmental Law, General Practice, Insurance Defense Law, Labor and Employment Law, Personal Injury Law, Probate and Estate Planning Law, Real Estate Law, Tax Law

BRADLEY & BRADLEY
Georgetown, KY.....General Practice, Probate and Estate Planning Law

BRADLEY, CAMPBELL, CARNEY & MADSEN, PROFESSIONAL CORPORATION
Golden, CO.....Civil Trial Practice, General Practice, Labor and Employment Law, Real Estate Law

BRADSHAW, JOHN H.
Eden Valley, MN.....Criminal Trial Practice, Personal Injury Law

BRADY HATHAWAY, PROFESSIONAL CORPORATION
Detroit, MI.....Administrative Law, Admiralty/Maritime Law, Civil Trial Practice, General Practice, Labor and Employment Law

BRADY, MCQUEEN, MARTIN, COLLINS & JENSEN
Elgin, IL .... General Practice

BRAFMAN GILBERT & ROSS, P.C.
New York, NY .... Criminal Trial Practice

BRAGG & BAKER, P.C.
Denver, CO .... Personal Injury Law

BRAINARD, BOWER & KRAMER
Charleston, IL .... General Practice

BRAMBLETT & PRATT
Camden, AR .... General Practice

BRAME, BERGSTEDT & BRAME
Lake Charles, LA .... General Practice

BRANAGAN, JAMES J.
Cleveland, OH .... Business Law

BRANDLEY AND KLEPPE
Caldwell, NJ .... Probate and Estate Planning Law

BRANDON, SCHMIDT & PALMER
Carbondale, IL .... General Practice

BRANDT & BEESON
Johnson City, TN .... General Practice

BRANDT, HAUGHEY, PENBERTHY, LEWIS, HYLAND & CLAYPOOLE, A PROFESSIONAL CORPORATION
Moorestown, NJ .... Banking Law, Probate and Estate Planning Law, Real Estate Law

BRANDT, LARRY C., P.A.
Walhalla, SC .... Appellate Practice, Civil Trial Practice, General Practice, Medical Malpractice Law, Personal Injury Law, Product Liability Law

BRANN & ISAACSON
Lewiston, ME .... General Practice, Tax Law

BRANNEN, SEARCY & SMITH
Savannah, GA .... Civil Trial Practice, General Practice, Insurance Defense Law

BRANNON, BROWN, HALEY, ROBINSON & COLE, P.A.
Lake City, FL .... General Practice

BRANSON, FRANK L., P.C., LAW OFFICES OF
Dallas, TX .... Business Law, Civil Trial Practice, Medical Malpractice Law, Personal Injury Law

BRANTON & HALL, P.C.
San Antonio, TX .... Personal Injury Law

BRASHEAR & GINN
Omaha, NE .... Bankruptcy Law, Business Law, Civil Trial Practice, Commercial Law, General Practice

BRAUDE & MARGULIES, P.C.
Washington, DC .... Civil Trial Practice, Construction Law
Baltimore, MD .... Civil Trial Practice, Construction Law

BRAULT, GRAHAM, SCOTT & BRAULT
Washington, DC .... Civil Trial Practice, General Practice, Medical Malpractice Law, Personal Injury Law
Rockville, MD .... Civil Trial Practice, General Practice, Medical Malpractice Law, Personal Injury Law

BRAULT, PALMER, GROVE, ZIMMERMAN, WHITE & MIMS
Fairfax, VA .... Civil Trial Practice, General Practice

BRAUN KENDRICK FINKBEINER
Bay City, MI .... Banking Law, Bankruptcy Law, Environmental Law, General Practice, Labor and Employment Law, Natural Resources Law, Real Estate Law, Tax Law
Saginaw, MI .... Banking Law, Bankruptcy Law, Commercial Law, Environmental Law, General Practice, Insurance Defense Law, Labor and Employment Law, Natural Resources Law, Personal Injury Law, Probate and Estate Planning Law, Real Estate Law, Tax Law

BRAUNLICH, RUSSOW & BRAUNLICH, A PROFESSIONAL CORPORATION
Monroe, MI .... Insurance Defense Law, Municipal and Zoning Law, Probate and Estate Planning Law

BRAUNSCHWEIG RACHLIS FISHMAN & RAYMOND, P.C.
New York, NY .... Antitrust Law, Commercial Law, General Practice, International Business Law

BRAUNSTEIN AND TODISCO, PROFESSIONAL CORPORATION
Trumbull, CT .... Probate and Estate Planning Law, Tax Law

BRAUWERMAN & BRAUWERMAN, P.A.
Miami, FL .... Immigration and Naturalization Law

BRAWER, MARC H.
Fort Lauderdale, FL .... Family Law

BRAY, GEIGER, RUDQUIST & NUSS
Stockton, CA .... General Practice

BRAYTON, THOMAS L., P.C.
Waterbury, CT .... Medical Malpractice Law

BREAZEALE, SACHSE & WILSON, L.L.P.
Baton Rouge, LA .... Antitrust Law, Civil Trial Practice, General Practice, Labor and Employment Law, Municipal Bond/Public Authority Financing Law, Natural Resources Law
New Orleans, LA .... General Practice

BREEDEN, HUBBARD, TERRY & BREEDEN, A PROFESSIONAL CORPORATION
Irvington, VA .... General Practice

BREEDEN, MACMILLAN & GREEN, P.L.C.
Norfolk, VA .... General Practice

BREGA & WINTERS, P.C.
Denver, CO .... Civil Trial Practice, Criminal Trial Practice, General Practice, Securities Law
Greeley, CO .... Business Law, Civil Trial Practice, Probate and Estate Planning Law, Real Estate Law

BREIER AND SEIF, P.A.
Miami, FL .... Business Law, Probate and Estate Planning Law, Tax Law

BREMER, WADE, NELSON, LOHR & COREY
Grand Rapids, MI .... Civil Trial Practice, Insurance Defense Law, Medical Malpractice Law, Personal Injury Law

BREMYER & WISE, P.A.
McPherson, KS .... General Practice

BRENNAN, DAVID C.
Orlando, FL .... Probate and Estate Planning Law

BRENNAN, HAYSKAR, JEFFERSON, GORMAN, WALKER & SCHWERER, PROFESSIONAL ASSOCIATION
Fort Pierce, FL .... Civil Trial Practice, General Practice

BRENNAN, ROBINS & DALEY
Pittsburgh, PA .... Civil Trial Practice, Real Estate Law

BRENNAN, STEIL, BASTING & MACDOUGALL, S.C.
Janesville, WI .... General Practice

BRENNER & GLASSMAN, LTD. A PROFESSIONAL ASSOCIATION
Minneapolis, MN .... Business Law, General Practice, Real Estate Law

BRENNER, SALTZMAN & WALLMAN
New Haven, CT .... General Practice, Real Estate Law, Securities Law, Tax Law

BREON, O'DONNELL, MILLER, BROWN & DANNIS
San Francisco, CA .... Construction Law, Labor and Employment Law

BRESLIN AND BRESLIN, P.A.
Hackensack, NJ .... Civil Trial Practice, Criminal Trial Practice, General Practice, Medical Malpractice Law, Personal Injury Law, Real Estate Law

BRESLIN & TROVINI
Hackensack, NJ .... Antitrust Law, Insurance Defense Law

BRESLOW & WALKER
New York, NY .... Business Law, Securities Law

BRETT & DAUGERT
Bellingham, WA .... General Practice, Personal Injury Law

BREW, RICHARD DOUGLAS, A PROFESSIONAL LAW CORPORATION
Modesto, CA .... Business Law, International Business Law, Real Estate Law

BREWER, R. KENT
Walnut Creek, CA .... Family Law

BREWER, CHARLES M., LTD.
Phoenix, AZ .... Civil Trial Practice, Personal Injury Law

BREWER, WORTEN, ROBINETT, JOHNSON, WORTEN & KING
Bartlesville, OK .... General Practice

BREWSTER, MORHOUS & CAMERON
Bluefield, WV .... General Practice

BRICE-RIDDLE GROUP, THE, P.C.
Dallas, TX .... Civil Trial Practice

BRICKER & ECKLER
Columbus, OH .... Banking Law, Civil Trial Practice, Commercial Law, Environmental Law, General Practice, Labor and Employment Law, Municipal Bond/Public Authority Financing Law, Real Estate Law, Tax Law

BRICKFIELD, BURCHETTE & RITTS, P.C.
Washington, DC....................Administrative Law, Natural Resources Law, Public Utilities Law

BRIDGES, YOUNG, MATTHEWS & DRAKE, PLC
Pine Bluff, AR....................General Practice

BRIDGFORTH & BUNTIN
Southaven, MS....................General Practice, Real Estate Law

BRIERLY LAW OFFICE
Newton, IA....................General Practice

BRIGDEN & PETAJAN, S.C.
Milwaukee, WI....................Labor and Employment Law

BRIGGS AND MORGAN, PROFESSIONAL ASSOCIATION
Minneapolis, MN....................General Practice
St. Paul, MN....................Civil Trial Practice, Environmental Law, General Practice, Labor and Employment Law, Municipal Bond/Public Authority Financing Law

BRIGHT AND BROWN
Glendale, CA....................Environmental Law

BRIGHT & LORIG, A PROFESSIONAL CORPORATION
Los Angeles, CA....................Patent, Trademark, Copyright and Unfair Competition Law

BRILL, MOORE & WAGONER, P.C.
West Plains, MO....................General Practice

BRIN & BRIN, P.C.
Corpus Christi, TX....................Civil Trial Practice, Insurance Defense Law

BRINKER, DOYEN & KOVACS, P.C.
St. Louis, MO....................Insurance Defense Law

BRINKLEY AND BRINKLEY
Columbus, GA....................Personal Injury Law, Probate and Estate Planning Law

BRINKLEY, MCNERNEY, MORGAN, SOLOMON & TATUM
Fort Lauderdale, FL....................Real Estate Law

BRINK, SOBOLIK, SEVERSON, VROOM & MALM, P.A.
Hallock, MN....................Civil Trial Practice, General Practice, Personal Injury Law

BRINSON, ASKEW, BERRY, SEIGLER, RICHARDSON & DAVIS
Rome, GA....................Civil Trial Practice, General Practice

BRINTON & FEDOTA
Chicago, IL....................Insurance Defense Law, Medical Malpractice Law

BRIONES LAW FIRM, A PROFESSIONAL ASSOCIATION
Farmington, NM....................General Practice

BRISKMAN & BINION, P.C.
Mobile, AL....................Civil Trial Practice, Criminal Trial Practice, Family Law, Insurance Defense Law, Personal Injury Law

BRITTON AND ADCOCK
Oklahoma City, OK....................Banking Law, Business Law, Civil Trial Practice, Securities Law

BROBECK, PHLEGER & HARRISON
Los Angeles, CA....................General Practice
Newport Beach, CA....................General Practice
Palo Alto, CA....................General Practice
San Diego, CA....................General Practice
San Francisco, CA....................General Practice
New York, NY....................General Practice

BROCATO, ANTHONY G. LAW OFFICES OF
Beaumont, TX....................Civil Trial Practice

BROCK, BROCK & BAGBY
Lexington, KY....................Civil Trial Practice, Family Law, General Practice, Probate and Estate Planning Law

BROCKERMEYER & ASSOCIATES
Fort Worth, TX....................Product Liability Law

BROCKINTON, BROCKINTON & KERR, P.A.
Charleston, SC....................General Practice

BROCK, MARKWALDER, SUNDERLAND, MURPHY & SPENN
Watseka, IL....................General Practice

BRODERICK, NEWMARK & GRATHER, A PROFESSIONAL CORPORATION
Morristown, NJ....................Family Law, Labor and Employment Law

BRODERICK, THORNTON & PIERCE
Bowling Green, KY....................General Practice, Insurance Defense Law

BRODIE & PAWLUC
Stuart, FL....................Probate and Estate Planning Law

BRODY, MARVIN D., PROFESSIONAL CORPORATION
Phoenix, AZ....................Tax Law

BRODY AND OBER, P.C.
Southport, CT....................Business Law, Civil Trial Practice, Probate and Estate Planning Law, Real Estate Law

BROENING, OBERG & WOODS, P.C.
Phoenix, AZ....................Civil Trial Practice, Insurance Defense Law

BROGAN & STAFFORD, P.C.
Norfolk, NE....................General Practice

BRONSON, BRONSON & MCKINNON
Los Angeles, CA....................Civil Trial Practice, General Practice
San Francisco, CA....................General Practice, Labor and Employment Law
Santa Rosa, CA....................General Practice

BRONSTEIN, VAN VEEN & BRONSTEIN, P.C.
New York, NY....................Family Law

BROOKES, LAWRENCE V.
San Francisco, CA....................Tax Law

BROOKS, GARY L.
Oklahoma City, OK....................Civil Trial Practice, Medical Malpractice Law, Personal Injury Law, Product Liability Law

BROOKS, PIERCE, MCLENDON, HUMPHREY & LEONARD, L.L.P.
Greensboro, NC....................Civil Trial Practice, General Practice

BROOTEN, KENNETH E., JR., CHARTERED
Winter Park, FL....................Health Care Law

BROPHY, MILLS, SCHMOR, GERKING & BROPHY
Medford, OR....................General Practice

BROSE, POSWISTILO & ELLIOTT
Easton, PA....................Business Law

BROSNAHAN, JOSEPH, LOCKHART & SUGGS
Minneapolis, MN....................Personal Injury Law

BROWN, DOUGLAS C.
San Diego, CA....................Criminal Trial Practice

BROWN AND AMODIO, A LEGAL PROFESSIONAL ASSOCIATION
Medina, OH....................General Practice

BROWN, ANDREW, HALLENBECK, SIGNORELLI & ZALLAR, P.A.
Duluth, MN....................Insurance Defense Law, Personal Injury Law, Probate and Estate Planning Law

BROWN & BAIN
Palo Alto, CA....................General Practice, Patent, Trademark, Copyright and Unfair Competition Law
Phoenix, AZ....................Antitrust Law, Appellate Practice, Banking Law, Civil Trial Practice, Commercial Law, Communications Law, Environmental Law, General Practice, Labor and Employment Law, Patent, Trademark, Copyright and Unfair Competition Law, Product Liability Law, Public Utilities Law, Real Estate Law
Tucson, AZ....................General Practice

BROWN, BEMILLER, MURRAY & MCINTYRE
Mansfield, OH....................General Practice, Insurance Defense Law

BROWN AND BROWN
St. Ignace, MI....................General Practice

BROWN & BROWN, P.C.
Newark, NJ....................Civil Trial Practice, Criminal Trial Practice, General Practice, Medical Malpractice Law, Personal Injury Law

BROWN, BROWN & BROWN, A PROFESSIONAL ASSOCIATION
Bel Air, MD....................General Practice

BROWN, BROWN, BROWN AND STOKES
Albemarle, NC....................General Practice

BROWN & BRYANT, P.C.
Chicago, IL....................Environmental Law

BROWN & CONNERY
Camden, NJ....................Admiralty/Maritime Law, Civil Trial Practice, General Practice, Insurance Defense Law
Westmont, NJ....................Admiralty/Maritime Law, Civil Trial Practice, General Practice, Insurance Defense Law

BROWN, CRAIG M., INC.
San Jose, CA....................Civil Trial Practice, Criminal Trial Practice

BROWN, CUMMINS & BROWN CO., L.P.A.
Cincinnati, OH....................Business Law, Civil Trial Practice, Health Care Law, Labor and Employment Law, Securities Law

BROWN, DOBSON, BURNETTE & KESLER
Chattanooga, TN....................Bankruptcy Law, Labor and Employment Law

BROWN, DOUGLAS & BROWN
St. Joseph, MO........................General Practice

BROWN & DREW
Casper, WY............................Administrative Law, Appellate Practice, Banking Law, Bankruptcy Law, Business Law, Civil Trial Practice, Commercial Law, Construction Law, Environmental Law, Family Law, General Practice, Insurance Defense Law, Labor and Employment Law, Natural Resources Law, Probate and Estate Planning Law, Public Utilities Law, Real Estate Law, Tax Law

BROWN, GERBASE, CEBULL, FULTON, HARMAN & ROSS, P.C.
Billings, MT............................General Practice

BROWN, HAY & STEPHENS
Springfield, IL.........................General Practice

BROWN, JACOBSON, TILLINGHAST, LAHAN & KING, P.C.
Groton, CT..............................General Practice
Norwich, CT............................General Practice, Insurance Defense Law

BROWN, JEFFERIES AND BOULWARE
Barnwell, SC............................General Practice

BROWN, KELLEHER, ZWICKEL & WILHELM
Windham, NY...........................Civil Trial Practice, Patent, Trademark, Copyright and Unfair Competition Law, Real Estate Law

BROWN & KELLY
Buffalo, NY.............................Civil Trial Practice, Construction Law, General Practice

BROWN, MALCOLM H., P.C.
Bismarck, ND..........................Commercial Law

BROWN, PAINDIRIS & ZARELLA
Hartford, CT...........................Criminal Trial Practice, General Practice

BROWN, PISTONE, HURLEY, VAN VLEAR & SELTZER, A PROFESSIONAL CORPORATION
Irvine, CA...............................Construction Law, Environmental Law, International Business Law, Natural Resources Law

BROWN RAYSMAN & MILLSTEIN
New York, NY.........................Civil Trial Practice, General Practice

BROWN, ROSETA, LONG & MCCONVILLE
Eugene, OR.............................Insurance Defense Law

BROWN, SCHLAGETER, CRAIG & SHINDLER
Toledo, OH..............................General Practice

BROWN, SHIELS & CHASANOV
Dover, DE................................General Practice
Georgetown, DE.......................General Practice

BROWN, SIMS, WISE & WHITE, A PROFESSIONAL CORPORATION
Houston, TX............................Admiralty/Maritime Law, Insurance Defense Law

BROWN & STADFELD
Boston, MA.............................Antitrust Law, General Practice

BROWN, TERRELL, HOGAN, ELLIS, MCCLAMMA & YEGELWEL, P.A.
Jacksonville, FL.......................Civil Trial Practice

BROWN & TIGHE
Washington, DC.......................General Practice

BROWN, WALDRON & CARLTON
Arcadia, FL.............................General Practice

BROWN, WARD, HAYNES, GRIFFIN & SEAGO, P.A.
Waynesville, NC.......................General Practice

BROWN & WATT, P.A.
Biloxi, MS...............................Environmental Law, Product Liability Law, Transportation Law
Pascagoula, MS.......................Environmental Law, Product Liability Law, Transportation Law

BROWN & WELSH, P.C.
Meriden, CT............................Business Law

BROWN, WINICK, GRAVES, BASKERVILLE AND SCHOENEBAUM, P.L.C.
Des Moines, IA........................General Practice

BROWN & WOOD
Washington, DC.......................General Practice
New York, NY.........................General Practice

BROWNE, SPITZER, HERRIMAN, STEPHENSON, HOLDEREAD & MUSSER
Marion, IN..............................Civil Trial Practice, General Practice, Insurance Defense Law

BROWNING, BUSHMAN, ANDERSON & BROOKHART, A PROFESSIONAL CORPORATION
Houston, TX............................Patent, Trademark, Copyright and Unfair Competition Law

BROWNING, KALECZYC, BERRY & HOVEN, P.C.
Helena, MT..............................Business Law, Environmental Law, General Practice

BROWNSTEIN HYATT FARBER & STRICKLAND, P.C.
Denver, CO.............................Administrative Law, Business Law, Civil Trial Practice, Environmental Law, General Practice, Municipal Bond/Public Authority Financing Law, Real Estate Law, Tax Law

BRUCKER, ALEX M., A LAW CORPORATION
Los Angeles, CA......................Employment Benefits Law

BRUCKNER & SYKES, L.L.P.
Houston, TX............................Labor and Employment Law

BRUDER, GENTILE & MARCOUX
Washington, DC.......................Public Utilities Law

BRUMBAUGH, GRAVES, DONOHUE & RAYMOND
New York, NY.........................Patent, Trademark, Copyright and Unfair Competition Law, Trademark, Copyright and Unfair Competition Law

BRUNER & BRUNER
Carroll, IA...............................General Practice

BRUNN & FLYNN, A PROFESSIONAL CORPORATION
Modesto, CA...........................Civil Trial Practice, Insurance Defense Law, Probate and Estate Planning Law, Real Estate Law

BRUNO, FREDERIC & ASSOCIATES
Minneapolis, MN.....................Criminal Trial Practice

BRYAN, NELSON, SCHROEDER, CASTIGLIOLA & BANAHAN
Pascagoula, MS.......................Civil Trial Practice

BRYANT, BLACKSHER & LESTER
Mobile, AL...............................Personal Injury Law, Probate and Estate Planning Law

BRYANT AND HIGBY, CHARTERED
Panama City, FL......................General Practice

BRYCE, WILLIAM D.
Georgetown, TX.......................General Practice

BRYDGES & MAHAN
Virginia Beach, VA..................Civil Trial Practice, Criminal Trial Practice, Personal Injury Law

BRYDON, SWEARENGEN & ENGLAND, PROFESSIONAL CORPORATION
Jefferson City, MO..................General Practice

BUCHALTER, NEMER, FIELDS & YOUNGER, A PROFESSIONAL CORPORATION
Los Angeles, CA......................Bankruptcy Law, Civil Trial Practice, Commercial Law, General Practice, Insurance Defense Law, Labor and Employment Law, Real Estate Law, Tax Law
Newport Beach, CA..................Bankruptcy Law, Civil Trial Practice, General Practice
San Francisco, CA...................Civil Trial Practice, General Practice
San Jose, CA...........................Commercial Law, General Practice

BUCHANAN & BOS
Grand Rapids, MI.....................Civil Trial Practice, Insurance Defense Law, Medical Malpractice Law, Personal Injury Law, Product Liability Law

BUCHANAN INGERSOLL
Princeton, NJ...........................Business Law, Commercial Law, General Practice, Patent, Trademark, Copyright and Unfair Competition Law, Trademark, Copyright and Unfair Competition Law
North Miami Beach, FL............Bankruptcy Law, Civil Trial Practice, Commercial Law, Construction Law, General Practice, Insurance Defense Law, Probate and Estate Planning Law, Real Estate Law, Tax Law
Tampa, FL...............................Civil Trial Practice, General Practice, Health Care Law
Lexington, KY..........................Environmental Law, General Practice, Natural Resources Law
Harrisburg, PA.........................Administrative Law, Business Law, Civil Trial Practice, Commercial Law, Construction Law, Environmental Law, General Practice, Health Care Law, Insurance Defense Law, Labor and Employment Law, Natural Resources Law, Personal Injury Law, Probate and Estate Planning Law, Real Estate Law, Tax Law
Philadelphia, PA......................Administrative Law, Antitrust Law, Banking Law, Bankruptcy Law, Business Law, Commercial Law, Construction Law, Criminal Trial Practice, Environmental Law, General Practice, Labor and Employment Law, Natural Resources Law, Real Estate Law, Tax Law
Pittsburgh, PA..........................Administrative Law, Admiralty/Maritime Law, Antitrust Law, Banking Law, Bankruptcy Law, Business Law, Civil Trial Practice, Commercial Law, Communications Law, Construction Law, Employment Benefits Law, Environmental Law, Family Law, General Practice, Health Care Law, Immigration and Naturalization Law, Insurance Defense Law, Labor and Employment Law, Municipal Bond/Public Authority Financing Law, Municipal and Zoning Law, Natural Resources Law, Patent, Trademark, Copyright and Unfair Competition Law, Personal Injury Law, Probate and Estate Planning Law, Real Estate Law, Tax Law, Trademark, Copyright and Unfair Competition Law

BUCK & GORDON
Seattle, WA ....Environmental Law, Municipal and Zoning Law, Real Estate Law

BUCKINGHAM, HOLZAPFEL, ZEIHER, WALDOCK & SCHELL CO., L.P.A.
Sandusky, OH ....General Practice

BUCKLEY & JENSEN
St. Paul, MN ....Bankruptcy Law

BUCKLEY KING & BLUSO, A LEGAL PROFESSIONAL ASSOCIATION
Cleveland, OH..........................Civil Trial Practice

BUCKLEY, MILLER & WRIGHT
Wilmington, OH.......................General Practice, Insurance Defense Law, Probate and Estate Planning Law

BUCKLEY, NAGLE, GENTRY, MCGUIRE & MORRIS
West Chester, PA.....................Business Law, Family Law, General Practice, Personal Injury Law, Real Estate Law

BUELL & BERNER
San Francisco, CA ....Civil Trial Practice, Labor and Employment Law, Tax Law

BUESSER, BUESSER, BLACK, LYNCH, FRYHOFF & GRAHAM, P.C.
Detroit, MI..............................General Practice

BUIST, MOORE, SMYTHE & MCGEE, P.A.
Charleston, SC ....Admiralty/Maritime Law, Bankruptcy Law, Civil Trial Practice, Commercial Law, Environmental Law, General Practice, Insurance Defense Law, Real Estate Law

BULLEN, MOILANEN, KLAASEN & SWAN, P.C.
Jackson, MI ....General Practice, Insurance Defense Law

BULL, HOUSSER & TUPPER
Vancouver, BC, Canada..........General Practice

BULLIVANT, HOUSER, BAILEY, PENDERGRASS & HOFFMAN, A PROFESSIONAL CORPORATION
Portland, OR...........................General Practice

BUMGARDNER, HARDIN & ELLIS, A PROFESSIONAL CORPORATION
Springfield, NJ ....Civil Trial Practice, Product Liability Law

BUMP AND BUMP
Chadron, NE............................General Practice

BUNCH & BROCK
Lexington, KY ....Bankruptcy Law

BUNDA STUTZ & DEWITT
Toledo, OH ....Civil Trial Practice, Product Liability Law

BUNGER & ROBERTSON
Bloomington, IN......................Banking Law, Business Law, Civil Trial Practice, General Practice, Health Care Law, Insurance Defense Law, Personal Injury Law, Probate and Estate Planning Law, Real Estate Law

BUNKER, SAGHATELIAN & GIBBS
Bakersfield, CA ....Civil Trial Practice, General Practice, Probate and Estate Planning Law

BUONAURO, ROBERT J., P.A.
Orlando, FL ....Criminal Trial Practice

BURAK & ANDERSON
Burlington, VT ....Administrative Law, Appellate Practice, Banking Law, Bankruptcy Law, Business Law, Commercial Law, Environmental Law, General Practice, Municipal Bond/Public Authority Financing Law, Municipal and Zoning Law, Public Utilities Law, Real Estate Law, Securities Law

BURBIDGE AND MITCHELL
Salt Lake City, UT..................Antitrust Law, Civil Trial Practice

BURCH & CRACCHIOLO, P.A.
Phoenix, AZ ....Appellate Practice, Bankruptcy Law, Civil Trial Practice, Commercial Law, Criminal Trial Practice, Environmental Law, Family Law, General Practice, Insurance Defense Law, Medical Malpractice Law, Personal Injury Law, Probate and Estate Planning Law, Product Liability Law, Real Estate Law, Tax Law

BURCH, PORTER & JOHNSON
Memphis, TN...........................General Practice

BURCHELL MACDOUGALL
Truro, NS, Canada...................General Practice

BURCHFIELD, PARK, & ASSOCIATES, P.C.
Brighton, MI ....Business Law, Civil Trial Practice

BURD, WILLIAM M. LAW OFFICES OF
Santa Ana, CA.........................Bankruptcy Law

BURESH, KAPLAN, JANG, FELLER & AUSTIN
Berkeley, CA ....Insurance Defense Law

BURG & ELDREDGE, P.C.
Denver, CO ....Civil Trial Practice, Commercial Law, Insurance Defense Law

BURGER, WILLIAM KENNERLY
Murfreesboro, TN....................Civil Trial Practice

BURGETT & ROBBINS
Jamestown, NY........................General Practice

BURGE & WETTERMARK, P.C.
Birmingham, AL ....Personal Injury Law, Transportation Law

BURKE, PATRICK J.
Denver, CO ....Criminal Trial Practice

BURKE HORAN & MACRI
New York, NY.........................Labor and Employment Law

BURKE, MURPHY, COSTANZA & CUPPY
East Chicago, IN.....................General Practice
Merrillville, IN ....Civil Trial Practice, Commercial Law, Environmental Law, General Practice, Insurance Defense Law, Real Estate Law

BURKE, SAKAI, MCPHEETERS & BORDNER, ATTORNEYS AT LAW, A LAW CORPORATION
Honolulu, HI...........................General Practice

BURKE, THOMAS M., P.C., LAW OFFICES
St. Louis, MO..........................Personal Injury Law

BURKERT & HART
Fort Myers, FL ....Personal Injury Law

BURKET, SMITH, BOWMAN & GEORGE
Sarasota, FL............................General Practice, Probate and Estate Planning Law

BURKETT AND ROSS
Dimmitt, TX ....General Practice

BURNETT, LOUIS J., P.C.
Birmingham, MI......................Business Law, Commercial Law, Real Estate Law

BURNHAM, KLINEFELTER, HALSEY, JONES & CATER, P.C.
Anniston, AL ....Civil Trial Practice, General Practice

BURNS, AMMIRATO, PALUMBO, MILAM & BARONIAN, A PROFESSIONAL LAW CORPORATION
Long Beach, CA.......................General Practice, Insurance Defense Law, Medical Malpractice Law, Personal Injury Law
Pasadena, CA ....General Practice, Insurance Defense Law, Medical Malpractice Law, Personal Injury Law

BURNS, BRYANT, HINCHEY, COX & ROCKEFELLER, P.A.
Dover, NH ....General Practice

BURNS, CUNNINGHAM & MACKEY, P.C.
Mobile, AL..............................Civil Trial Practice, Personal Injury Law, Product Liability Law

BURNS, DAY & PRESNELL, P.A.
Raleigh, NC.............................Commercial Law, General Practice, Personal Injury Law

BURNS, DOANE, SWECKER & MATHIS
Alexandria, VA ....Patent, Trademark, Copyright and Unfair Competition Law, Trademark, Copyright and Unfair Competition Law

BURNS & LEVINSON
Boston, MA..............................Civil Trial Practice, General Practice, Tax Law

BURNS, MCDONALD, BRADFORD, PATRICK & TINSLEY, L.L.P.
Greenwood, SC ....General Practice

BURNS WALL SMITH AND MUELLER, A PROFESSIONAL CORPORATION
Denver, CO ....Business Law, General Practice, Natural Resources Law

BURNSIDE DEES JOHNSTON & CHOISSER
Vandalia, IL ....Civil Trial Practice, General Practice

BURNSIDE, WALL, DANIEL, ELLISON & REVELL
Augusta, GA ....Civil Trial Practice, General Practice

BURR & FORMAN
Birmingham, AL ....Antitrust Law, Banking Law, Business Law, Civil Trial Practice, Communications Law, Environmental Law, General Practice, Labor and Employment Law, Municipal Bond/Public Authority Financing Law, Probate and Estate Planning Law, Real Estate Law, Tax Law
Huntsville, AL.........................Banking Law, Business Law, Probate and Estate Planning Law, Real Estate Law

BURROUGHS, HEPLER, BROOM, MACDONALD & HEBRANK
Edwardsville, IL......................General Practice

BURSIK, KURITSKY & GIASULLO
West Orange, NJ — Business Law, Civil Trial Practice, General Practice

BURSTEIN, FRED, & ASSOCIATES, P.A.
Minneapolis, MN — Civil Trial Practice, General Practice, Personal Injury Law, Probate and Estate Planning Law, Real Estate Law

BURT & BURT
Wilmington, DE — Environmental Law, Insurance Defense Law, Medical Malpractice Law, Product Liability Law

BURT & PUCILLO
West Palm Beach, FL — Commercial Law, Environmental Law, Securities Law

BURT & VETTERLEIN, P.C.
Portland, OR — General Practice, Tax Law

BUSBY, A. JERRY, P.C.
Phoenix, AZ — Family Law, Probate and Estate Planning Law, Tax Law

BUSCH AND BUSCH
North Brunswick, NJ — General Practice, Insurance Defense Law, Personal Injury Law

BUSCH AND COHEN, P.C.
Lakewood, CO — Criminal Trial Practice, Medical Malpractice Law, Personal Injury Law

BUSCH & TALBOTT, L.C.
Elkins, WV — Civil Trial Practice, Criminal Trial Practice, General Practice

BUSCHMANN, CARR & SHANKS, PROFESSIONAL CORPORATION
Indianapolis, IN — Bankruptcy Law, Civil Trial Practice, Commercial Law, General Practice

BUSH ROSS GARDNER WARREN & RUDY, P.A.
Tampa, FL — General Practice

BUSSART, WEST, ROSSETTI, PIAIA & TYLER, P.C.
Rock Springs, WY — Civil Trial Practice, General Practice

BUTCH, QUINN, ROSEMURGY, JARDIS, BUSH, BURKHART & STROM, P.C.
Escanaba, MI — Banking Law, Business Law, Civil Trial Practice, Family Law, General Practice, Labor and Employment Law, Real Estate Law

BUTLER & BINION, L.L.P.
Washington, DC — General Practice
Dallas, TX — General Practice
Houston, TX — General Practice
San Antonio, TX — General Practice

BUTLER, CINCIONE, DICUCCIO & DRITZ
Columbus, OH — Civil Trial Practice, Medical Malpractice Law, Personal Injury Law

BUTLER, HICKY & LONG
Forrest City, AR — General Practice

BUTLER, SNOW, O'MARA, STEVENS & CANNADA
Jackson, MS — General Practice

BUTLER, VINES AND BABB
Knoxville, TN — Civil Trial Practice, Environmental Law, General Practice, Insurance Defense Law, Medical Malpractice Law, Personal Injury Law

BUTLER, WOOTEN, OVERBY & CHEELEY
Atlanta, GA — Civil Trial Practice, Medical Malpractice Law, Personal Injury Law
Columbus, GA — Civil Trial Practice, Medical Malpractice Law, Personal Injury Law

BUTSAVAGE & ASSOCIATES, P.C.
Washington, DC — Civil Trial Practice, Labor and Employment Law

BUTT, THORNTON & BAEHR, P.C.
Albuquerque, NM — Civil Trial Practice, General Practice

BUTTERMORE, MULLEN, JEREMIAH AND PHILLIPS
Westfield, NJ — General Practice, Probate and Estate Planning Law

BUTTERWICK, BRIGHT & O'LAUGHLIN, INC., A PROFESSIONAL LAW CORPORATION
Riverside, CA — General Practice

BUTTS & LENORA
Chandler, OK — General Practice

BUTZ, LUCAS, DUNN & ENRIGHT, A PROFESSIONAL CORPORATION
San Diego, CA — Civil Trial Practice

BUTZBAUGH & DEWANE
St. Joseph, MI — General Practice

BUTZEL LONG, A PROFESSIONAL CORPORATION
Ann Arbor, MI — Administrative Law, General Practice
Birmingham, MI — Administrative Law, Family Law, General Practice
Detroit, MI — Administrative Law, Admiralty/Maritime Law, Antitrust Law, Banking Law, Bankruptcy Law, Business Law, Civil Trial Practice, Commercial Law, Communications Law, Construction Law, Employment Benefits Law, Environmental Law, General Practice, Health Care Law, Immigration and Naturalization Law, Insurance Defense Law, International Business Law, Labor and Employment Law, Municipal Bond/Public Authority Financing Law, Probate and Estate Planning Law, Product Liability Law, Real Estate Law, Securities Law, Tax Law, Trademark, Copyright and Unfair Competition Law, Transportation Law
Grosse Pointe Farms, MI — General Practice
Lansing, MI — Administrative Law, General Practice

BUZAK, EDWARD J.
Montville, NJ — Environmental Law, Municipal and Zoning Law

BUZARD, A. VINCENT LAW OFFICES OF
Rochester, NY — Civil Trial Practice, General Practice

BYE BOYD AGNEW, LTD.
Duluth, MN — General Practice

BYERS, FRITZ
Toledo, OH — Civil Trial Practice, Communications Law

BYERS CASGRAIN
Montreal, QU, Canada — Banking Law, Civil Trial Practice, Environmental Law, General Practice, Labor and Employment Law, Natural Resources Law, Real Estate Law, Securities Law, Tax Law

BYNUM, ARLEN DEAN SPIDER, P.C., LAW OFFICES OF
Dallas, TX — Insurance Defense Law

BYRD, BYRD, ERVIN, WHISNANT, MCMAHON & ERVIN, P.A.
Morganton, NC — General Practice

BYRD & MURPHY
Fort Lauderdale, FL — Civil Trial Practice, Commercial Law, General Practice, Personal Injury Law

BYRNE & BENESCH, P.C.
Yuma, AZ — General Practice, Real Estate Law

BYRNE, JAMES B., JR., P.A.
Longwood, FL — Civil Trial Practice

BYRON & ROBERTS
Owingsville, KY — Civil Trial Practice, Probate and Estate Planning Law, Real Estate Law

BYSSHE, FREDERICK H. JR., LAW OFFICES OF
Ventura, CA — General Practice, Medical Malpractice Law, Personal Injury Law

CABANISS, JOHNSTON, GARDNER, DUMAS & O'NEAL
Birmingham, AL — Admiralty/Maritime Law, Civil Trial Practice, General Practice
Mobile, AL — Civil Trial Practice, General Practice

CABLE HUSTON BENEDICT HAAGENSEN & FERRIS
Portland, OR — Probate and Estate Planning Law

CACCIATORE, RONALD K., P.A.
Tampa, FL — Criminal Trial Practice

CACHERIS & TREANOR
Washington, DC — Criminal Trial Practice
Alexandria, VA — Criminal Trial Practice

CADES SCHUTTE FLEMING & WRIGHT
Honolulu, HI — Banking Law, Civil Trial Practice, General Practice, Patent, Trademark, Copyright and Unfair Competition Law, Probate and Estate Planning Law, Real Estate Law
Kailua-Kona, HI — Civil Trial Practice, General Practice

CAESAR, RIVISE, BERNSTEIN, COHEN & POKOTILOW, LTD.
Philadelphia, PA — Patent, Trademark, Copyright and Unfair Competition Law, Trademark, Copyright and Unfair Competition Law

CAHALANE, VINCENT P., P.C.
Brockton, MA — Civil Trial Practice, Insurance Defense Law, Personal Injury Law, Product Liability Law

CAHILL GORDON & REINDEL
Washington, DC — General Practice
New York, NY — General Practice, Municipal Bond/Public Authority Financing Law
Paris, France — General Practice

CAHN WISHOD & LAMB, L.L.P.
Melville, NY — General Practice

CAIN, HIBBARD, MYERS & COOK, A PROFESSIONAL CORPORATION
Pittsfield, MA....General Practice

CAIRNS, DOYLE, LANS, NICHOLAS & SONI, A LAW CORPORATION
Pasadena, CA....Banking Law, Bankruptcy Law, Insurance Defense Law

CALAFELL, RAY, JR., P.A.
Tampa, FL....Civil Trial Practice

CALAWAY, STEPHEN G.
Winston-Salem, NC....Real Estate Law

CALBERT, J. D.
Greencastle, IN....General Practice

CALBOM & SCHWAB, P.S.C.
Moses Lake, WA....Personal Injury Law

CALDWELL, J. THOMAS LAW OFFICES OF
Ripley, TN....General Practice

CALDWELL, BERNER & CALDWELL
Woodstock, IL....General Practice

CALDWELL & KEARNS, A PROFESSIONAL CORPORATION
Harrisburg, PA....Civil Trial Practice, Medical Malpractice Law

CALDWELL & PACETTI
Palm Beach, FL....General Practice, Municipal Bond/Public Authority Financing Law

CALFAS, JOHN A., A PROFESSIONAL CORPORATION
Los Angeles, CA....Probate and Estate Planning Law, Securities Law, Tax Law

CALFEE, HALTER & GRISWOLD
Cleveland, OH....General Practice, Trademark, Copyright and Unfair Competition Law
Columbus, OH....General Practice

CALHOUN, FAULK, WATKINS & CLOWER
Troy, AL....Civil Trial Practice, General Practice

CALHOUN & STACY
Dallas, TX....Banking Law, Bankruptcy Law, Business Law, Civil Trial Practice, Commercial Law, Communications Law, Construction Law, Environmental Law, General Practice, Health Care Law, Insurance Defense Law, Labor and Employment Law, Medical Malpractice Law, Municipal and Zoning Law, Patent, Trademark, Copyright and Unfair Competition Law, Personal Injury Law, Probate and Estate Planning Law, Product Liability Law, Real Estate Law, Transportation Law

CALKINS & CALKINS
Eugene, OR....General Practice

CALLAGHAN & RUCKMAN
Summersville, WV....General Practice

CALLAHAN & CALLAHAN
Wray, CO....Probate and Estate Planning Law

CALLAHAN & GAUNTLETT
Irvine, CA....Business Law, Environmental Law, General Practice, Trademark, Copyright and Unfair Competition Law

CALLAN, REGENSTREICH, KOSTER & BRADY
New York, NY....Civil Trial Practice, Insurance Defense Law

CALL, BARRETT & BURBANK, A PROFESSIONAL CORPORATION
Fairbanks, AK....General Practice

CALL, CLAYTON & JENSEN, A PROFESSIONAL CORPORATION
Newport Beach, CA....Civil Trial Practice, Real Estate Law

CALLENDER, JOHN F.
Jacksonville, FL....Civil Trial Practice

CALLISTER, NEBEKER & MCCULLOUGH, A PROFESSIONAL CORPORATION
Salt Lake City, UT....Antitrust Law, Banking Law, Bankruptcy Law, Business Law, Civil Trial Practice, Commercial Law, Employment Benefits Law, Environmental Law, General Practice, Municipal Bond/Public Authority Financing Law, Natural Resources Law, Personal Injury Law, Probate and Estate Planning Law, Real Estate Law, Securities Law, Tax Law

CAMBRIDGE, FEILMEYER, LANDSNESS, CHASE & JONES
Atlantic, IA....General Practice

CAMERON & HORNBOSTEL
Washington, DC....Banking Law, International Business Law

CAMERON, MADDEN, PEARLSON, GALE & SELLARS
Long Beach, CA....Civil Trial Practice, General Practice, Real Estate Law, Tax Law

CAMP CHURCH & ASSOCIATES
Vancouver, BC, Canada....Appellate Practice, Civil Trial Practice, Product Liability Law

CAMPBELL, DONALD J. & ASSOCIATES
Las Vegas, NV....Criminal Trial Practice

CAMPBELL, ANDERSON, CASEY, SINK & JOHNSON, A PROFESSIONAL CORPORATION, THE LAW OFFICES OF
Santa Rosa, CA....Insurance Defense Law

CAMPBELL, BLACK, CARNINE & HEDIN, P.C.
Mount Vernon, IL....Civil Trial Practice, General Practice

CAMPBELL & CAMPBELL
Chattanooga, TN....Civil Trial Practice, Insurance Defense Law, Personal Injury Law

CAMPBELL, CARR, BERGE & SHERIDAN, P.A.
Santa Fe, NM....Antitrust Law, Civil Trial Practice, Environmental Law, General Practice, Labor and Employment Law, Natural Resources Law

CAMPBELL, DELONG, HAGWOOD & WADE
Greenville, MS....General Practice

CAMPBELL, DILLE AND BARNETT
Puyallup, WA....Civil Trial Practice

CAMPBELL, GEORGE W., JR., & ASSOC., A P.C., LAW OFFICES OF
Arlington, VA....Insurance Defense Law

CAMPBELL, KERRICK & GRISE
Bowling Green, KY....Appellate Practice, Business Law, Civil Trial Practice, Commercial Law, General Practice, Health Care Law, Insurance Defense Law, Labor and Employment Law, Medical Malpractice Law, Personal Injury Law, Probate and Estate Planning Law, Product Liability Law, Real Estate Law

CAMPBELL KYLE PROFFITT
Carmel, IN....General Practice
Noblesville, IN....General Practice

CAMPBELL, LEA, MICHAEL, MCCONNELL & PIGOT
Charlottetown, PE, Canada....Administrative Law, Business Law, Civil Trial Practice, General Practice, Insurance Defense Law, Personal Injury Law

CAMPBELL & LEVINE
Pittsburgh, PA....Bankruptcy Law, Commercial Law

CAMPBELL MAACK & SESSIONS, A PROFESSIONAL CORPORATION
Salt Lake City, UT....Civil Trial Practice, General Practice

CAMPBELL, O'BRIEN & MISTELE, P.C.
Troy, MI....Business Law, General Practice

CAMPBELL, PICA, OLSON & SEEGMILLER
Albuquerque, NM....Administrative Law, Business Law, Civil Trial Practice, Commercial Law, Probate and Estate Planning Law, Real Estate Law

CAMPBELL, WARBURTON, BRITTON, FITZSIMMONS & SMITH, A PROFESSIONAL CORPORATION
San Jose, CA....General Practice, Insurance Defense Law, Medical Malpractice Law

CAMPBELL, WOODS, BAGLEY, EMERSON, MCNEER & HERNDON
Charleston, WV....General Practice
Huntington, WV....General Practice

CAMPEAU & THOMAS, A LAW CORPORATION
San Jose, CA....Bankruptcy Law, Commercial Law

CAMPNEY & MURPHY
Vancouver, BC, Canada....General Practice

CANDOR, YOUNGMAN, GIBSON AND GAULT
Williamsport, PA....General Practice, Probate and Estate Planning Law

CANGES, IWASHKO & BETHKE, A PROFESSIONAL CORPORATION
Denver, CO....Civil Trial Practice, Criminal Trial Practice, Family Law

CANNIZZARO, FRASER & BRIDGES
Marysville, OH....Civil Trial Practice, Personal Injury Law

CANNON & DUNPHY, S.C.
Milwaukee, WI....Personal Injury Law

CANNON, MEYER VON BREMEN & MEIER
Albany, GA....Civil Trial Practice, Personal Injury Law, Real Estate Law

CANNON, WILLIAM T., P.C.
Philadelphia, PA....Criminal Trial Practice

CANO, KRISTIN M.
Newport Beach, CA....Securities Law

CANSLER LOCKHART & EVANS, P.A.
Charlotte, NC........................Insurance Defense Law

CANTERBURY, STUBER, PRATT, ELDER & GOOCH, A PROFESSIONAL CORPORATION
Dallas, TX...............................Construction Law, Labor and Employment Law

CANTEY & HANGER
Dallas, TX...............................General Practice
Fort Worth, TX.......................General Practice, Labor and Employment Law, Tax Law

CANTRILL, SKINNER, SULLIVAN & KING
Boise, ID.................................General Practice

CAPELL, HOWARD, KNABE & COBBS, P.A.
Montgomery, AL.....................Construction Law, General Practice, Labor and Employment Law, Municipal Bond/Public Authority Financing Law, Probate and Estate Planning Law, Real Estate Law, Tax Law

CAPERS, DUNBAR, SANDERS & BRUCKNER
Augusta, GA...........................Civil Trial Practice, General Practice, Insurance Defense Law, Real Estate Law

CAPITELLI & WICKER
New Orleans, LA.....................Admiralty/Maritime Law, Criminal Trial Practice, Personal Injury Law

CAPLIN & DRYSDALE, CHARTERED
Washington, DC......................Business Law, Civil Trial Practice, Criminal Trial Practice, Probate and Estate Planning Law, Tax Law
New York, NY........................Business Law, Civil Trial Practice, Criminal Trial Practice, Probate and Estate Planning Law

CAPOUANO, WAMPOLD, PRESTWOOD & SANSONE, P.A.
Montgomery, AL.....................Administrative Law, Appellate Practice, Banking Law, Business Law, Civil Trial Practice, Commercial Law, General Practice, Labor and Employment Law, Probate and Estate Planning Law, Real Estate Law, Tax Law

CAPRETZ & RADCLIFFE
Newport Beach, CA................Business Law, Civil Trial Practice, International Business Law

CAPUTO, JOHN A. & ASSOCIATES
Pittsburgh, PA........................Medical Malpractice Law, Personal Injury Law, Product Liability Law

CAPUTO, ANTHONY J., P.C.
White Plains, NY...................Civil Trial Practice

CAPWELL AND BERTHELSEN
Racine, WI.............................General Practice

CARDELLI, SCHAEFER & MASON, P.C.
Royal Oak, MI........................Civil Trial Practice, Commercial Law, Insurance Defense Law

CARDENAS, WHITIS & STEPHEN, L.L.P.
McAllen, TX..........................General Practice, Real Estate Law

CARELLA, BYRNE, BAIN, GILFILLAN, CECCHI, STEWART & OLSTEIN, A PROFESSIONAL CORPORATION
Roseland, NJ..........................General Practice, Municipal Bond/Public Authority Financing Law, Patent, Trademark, Copyright and Unfair Competition Law

CAREY, AUSTIN, JR., P.C.
Hartford, CT..........................Environmental Law

CAREY, O'MALLEY, WHITAKER & LINS, P.A.
Tampa, FL..............................Commercial Law, Construction Law

CARLIN, HELLSTROM & BITTNER
Davenport, IA........................General Practice

CARLIN, MADDOCK, FAY & CERBONE, P.C.
Florham Park, NJ...................Environmental Law, General Practice

CARLISLE, RUSSELL E., P.A., LAW OFFICES OF
Campton, NH.........................Probate and Estate Planning Law

CARLOCK, DAVID, P.C.
Dallas, TX..............................Family Law

CARLSMITH BALL WICHMAN MURRAY CASE & ICHIKI
Long Beach, CA.....................General Practice
Los Angeles, CA....................General Practice
Washington, DC.....................General Practice
Hilo, HI..................................General Practice
Honolulu, HI..........................General Practice
Kailua-Kona, HI....................General Practice
Wailuku, HI...........................General Practice
Agana, GU.............................General Practice
Saipan, TT.............................General Practice
Mexico, D.F., Mexico............General Practice

CARLSON, HAMMOND & PADDOCK
Denver, CO............................Environmental Law

CARLSON WENDLER, & ASSOCIATES, P.C.
Edwardsville, IL....................Personal Injury Law

CARLTON, FIELDS, WARD, EMMANUEL, SMITH & CUTLER, P.A.
Orlando, FL...........................General Practice
Pensacola, FL........................General Practice
St. Petersburg, FL..................General Practice
Tallahassee, FL......................General Practice
Tampa, FL..............................General Practice
West Palm Beach, FL.............General Practice

CARMICHAEL, R. CARTWRIGHT JR.
Charlotte, NC........................General Practice

CARMICHAEL & POWELL, PROFESSIONAL CORPORATION
Phoenix, AZ...........................Administrative Law, Bankruptcy Law, Real Estate Law

CARMICHAEL & TILKER
Scottsdale, AZ.......................Business Law, Civil Trial Practice, Personal Injury Law

CARMODY & TORRANCE
New Haven, CT......................General Practice
Waterbury, CT.......................General Practice

CARNAHAN, EVANS, CANTWELL & BROWN, P.C.
Springfield, MO.....................General Practice

CARNEY BADLEY SMITH & SPELLMAN, A PROFESSIONAL SERVICES CORPORATION
Seattle, WA...........................General Practice

CARON & STEVENS
Amsterdam, The Netherlands....General Practice

CARP, TED
Eugene, OR............................Criminal Trial Practice, Personal Injury Law

CARPENTER, BENNETT & MORRISSEY
Newark, NJ............................Admiralty/Maritime Law, Antitrust Law, Banking Law, Civil Trial Practice, Commercial Law, General Practice, Immigration and Naturalization Law, Labor and Employment Law, Natural Resources Law, Personal Injury Law, Probate and Estate Planning Law, Real Estate Law, Tax Law

CARPENTER & CHÁVEZ, LTD.
Albuquerque, NM...................Civil Trial Practice, Personal Injury Law, Product Liability Law

CARPENTER, COMEAU, MALDEGEN, BRENNAN, NIXON & TEMPLEMAN
Santa Fe, NM.........................Civil Trial Practice, Commercial Law, General Practice, Insurance Defense Law, Natural Resources Law

CARPENTER & KLATSKIN, P.C.
Denver, CO............................Commercial Law, Real Estate Law

CARPENTER & O'CONNOR
Knoxville, TN........................General Practice, Insurance Defense Law

CARPENTER, PAFFENBARGER & MCGIMPSEY
Norwalk, OH..........................General Practice

CARR, FOUTS, HUNT, CRAIG, TERRILL & WOLFE, L.L.P.
Lubbock, TX..........................General Practice, Insurance Defense Law

CARR, GOODSON & LEE, P.C.
Washington, DC.....................Environmental Law, General Practice, Insurance Defense Law

CARR, KENNEDY, PETERSON & FROST, A LAW CORPORATION
Redding, CA...........................General Practice

CARR & KESSLER
Atlanta, GA...........................Medical Malpractice Law, Personal Injury Law

CARR, KOREIN, TILLERY, KUNIN, MONTROY & GLASS
East St. Louis, IL..................Admiralty/Maritime Law, General Practice, Medical Malpractice Law

CARR, MCCLELLAN, INGERSOLL, THOMPSON & HORN, PROFESSIONAL CORPORATION
Burlingame, CA......................General Practice

CARR & MUSSMAN, A PROFESSIONAL CORPORATION
San Francisco, CA.................Antitrust Law, Civil Trial Practice

CARRICO, JOHN B.
Charleston, WV......................General Practice

CARRINGTON, COLEMAN, SLOMAN & BLUMENTHAL, L.L.P.
Dallas, TX..............................Antitrust Law, General Practice, Tax Law

CARROLL, GEORGE & PRATT
Rutland, VT .... Banking Law, Bankruptcy Law, Business Law, Criminal Trial Practice, Environmental Law, Family Law, General Practice, Health Care Law, Personal Injury Law, Probate and Estate Planning Law, Real Estate Law, Securities Law

CARROLL, HEYD
Barrie, ON, Canada .... General Practice

CARROLL, KELLY & MURPHY
Providence, RI .... Civil Trial Practice, General Practice

CARROLL, POSTLEWAITE, GRAHAM & PENDERGAST, S.C.
Eau Claire, WI .... Civil Trial Practice, General Practice, Insurance Defense Law

CARRUTHERS & ROTH, P.A.
Greensboro, NC .... Civil Trial Practice, General Practice

CARSON, LESLIE J. JR.
Philadelphia, PA .... Bankruptcy Law, General Practice, Probate and Estate Planning Law, Real Estate Law

CARSON FISCHER, P.L.C.
Birmingham, MI .... Bankruptcy Law, Business Law, Civil Trial Practice, Commercial Law, Construction Law, Environmental Law, Family Law, Medical Malpractice Law, Municipal and Zoning Law, Personal Injury Law, Probate and Estate Planning Law, Real Estate Law, Securities Law, Tax Law

CARTER, BENJAMIN E.
Riverhead, NY .... Civil Trial Practice, Family Law, Real Estate Law

CARTER, LOUIS J.
Philadelphia, PA .... General Practice, Public Utilities Law, Real Estate Law, Transportation Law

CARTER & ANSLEY
Atlanta, GA .... Business Law, Civil Trial Practice, General Practice

CARTER, CONBOY, CASE, BLACKMORE, NAPIERSKI AND MALONEY, P.C.
Albany, NY .... Civil Trial Practice, General Practice, Insurance Defense Law

CARTER & CONNOLLY, P.A.
Boca Raton, FL .... Civil Trial Practice, General Practice, Personal Injury Law, Probate and Estate Planning Law

CARTER, CRAIG, BASS, BLAIR & KUSHNER, P.C.
Danville, VA .... Civil Trial Practice, Personal Injury Law, Real Estate Law

CARTER, HARROD & CUNNINGHAM
Athens, TN .... Civil Trial Practice, General Practice, Insurance Defense Law

CARTER, LEDYARD & MILBURN
New York, NY .... General Practice

CARTER, STEIN, SCHAAF & TOWZEY
St. Petersburg, FL .... Appellate Practice, Civil Trial Practice, Real Estate Law

CARTON, WITT, ARVANITIS & BARISCILLO
Asbury Park, NJ .... General Practice
Manasquan, NJ .... General Practice

CARTWRIGHT, DRUKER & RYDEN
Marshalltown, IA .... General Practice

CARTWRIGHT, SLOBODIN, BOKELMAN, BOROWSKY, WARTNICK, MOORE & HARRIS, INC.
San Francisco, CA .... Personal Injury Law

CARUSO, JAMES D.
Toledo, OH .... Personal Injury Law

CARUSO, BURLINGTON, BOHN & COMPIANI, P.A.
West Palm Beach, FL .... Civil Trial Practice

CASARINO, CHRISTMAN & SHALK
Wilmington, DE .... Civil Trial Practice, Insurance Defense Law, Personal Injury Law

CASASSA AND RYAN
Hampton, NH .... General Practice, Probate and Estate Planning Law

CASE & LYNCH
Hilo, HI .... General Practice
Honolulu, HI .... Civil Trial Practice, General Practice
Kahului, HI .... General Practice
Kailua-Kona, HI .... General Practice
Kilauea, HI .... General Practice
Lihue, HI .... General Practice

CASEY, GERRY, CASEY, WESTBROOK, REED & SCHENK
San Diego, CA .... Civil Trial Practice, Personal Injury Law

CASEY, PATRICK A., P.A.
Santa Fe, NM .... Civil Trial Practice, Personal Injury Law

CASH, CASH, EAGEN & KESSEL
Cincinnati, OH .... Business Law, Insurance Defense Law, Real Estate Law

CASHIN, MORTON & MULLINS
Atlanta, GA .... Business Law, Family Law, General Practice

CASKIE & FROST, A PROFESSIONAL CORPORATION
Lynchburg, VA .... General Practice

CASNER & EDWARDS
Boston, MA .... General Practice

CASPER & DE TOLEDO
Stamford, CT .... Labor and Employment Law, Personal Injury Law

CASSADY, FULLER & MARSH
Enterprise, AL .... Civil Trial Practice, General Practice

CASSEBAUM, MCFALL & LAYMAN, A PROFESSIONAL CORPORATION
Bangor, PA .... General Practice

CASSELBERRY, STEVEN
Irvine, CA .... Banking Law, Bankruptcy Law

CASSELS BROCK & BLACKWELL
Toronto, ON, Canada .... General Practice

CASSEM, TIERNEY, ADAMS, GOTCH & DOUGLAS
Omaha, NE .... Civil Trial Practice, General Practice, Insurance Defense Law

CASSIDAY, BENJAMIN B. III
Honolulu, HI .... Criminal Trial Practice

CASSIDAY, SCHADE & GLOOR
Chicago, IL .... General Practice

CASSIDY, SEAN
Greensburg, PA .... Natural Resources Law

CASSIDY, BRUCE G., & ASSOCIATES, P.A.
Philadelphia, PA .... Civil Trial Practice, Criminal Trial Practice, International Business Law

CASSIDY & MUELLER
Peoria, IL .... Civil Trial Practice, General Practice

CASSIDY, WARNER, BROWN, COMBS & THURBER, A PROFESSIONAL CORPORATION
Santa Ana, CA .... Insurance Defense Law, Product Liability Law

CASSTEVENS, HANNER, GUNTER & GORDON, P.A.
Charlotte, NC .... General Practice

CASTELLOE, PAUL E., THE LAW OFFICES OF
Raleigh, NC .... Business Law

CATAFAGO, JACQUES
New York, NY .... Civil Trial Practice

CATALANO, FISHER, GREGORY, CROWN & SULLIVAN, CHARTERED
Naples, FL .... General Practice, Tax Law

CATES & HOLLOWAY
Scottsdale, AZ .... Patent, Trademark, Copyright and Unfair Competition Law

CATHEY & STRAIN
Cornelia, GA .... Civil Trial Practice

CATLETT & YANCEY
Little Rock, AR .... Tax Law

CATRON, CATRON & SAWTELL, A PROFESSIONAL ASSOCIATION
Santa Fe, NM .... Appellate Practice, Banking Law, Civil Trial Practice, Commercial Law, Family Law, General Practice, Probate and Estate Planning Law, Real Estate Law, Tax Law

CATRON, KILGORE & BEGLEY
Bowling Green, KY .... Banking Law, Business Law, Civil Trial Practice, Commercial Law, Health Care Law, Insurance Defense Law, Labor and Employment Law, Municipal and Zoning Law, Probate and Estate Planning Law, Real Estate Law, Tax Law

CATTERTON & KEMP
Rockville, MD .... Criminal Trial Practice

CAUDLE & SPEARS, P.A.
Charlotte, NC .... Civil Trial Practice, General Practice, Insurance Defense Law, Personal Injury Law

CAULFIELD, DAVIES & DONAHUE
Sacramento, CA .... Construction Law, Insurance Defense Law, Personal Injury Law, Product Liability Law

CAUSEY, CAYWOOD, TAYLOR & MCMANUS
Memphis, TN..........Criminal Trial Practice, Family Law, General Practice, Probate and Estate Planning Law

CAUTHEN AND OLDHAM, P.A.
Tavares, FL..........General Practice

CAYER, KILSTOFTE & CRATON, A PROFESSIONAL LAW CORPORATION
Long Beach, CA..........Banking Law, Civil Trial Practice, General Practice

CEARLEY LAW FIRM
Little Rock, AR..........Civil Trial Practice, General Practice

CELENTANO, STADTMAUER & WALENTOWICZ
Clifton, NJ..........Civil Trial Practice, Health Care Law, Real Estate Law

CENTER FOR EMPLOYMENT LAW, THE, P.C.
Roanoke, VA..........Labor and Employment Law

CERRATO, DAWES, COLLINS, SAKER & BROWN, A PROFESSIONAL CORPORATION
Freehold, NJ..........General Practice

CERTILMAN BALIN ADLER & HYMAN, LLP
East Meadow, NY..........Bankruptcy Law, Civil Trial Practice, General Practice, Municipal and Zoning Law, Probate and Estate Planning Law, Real Estate Law, Securities Law, Tax Law

CERUSSI & SPRING, A PROFESSIONAL CORPORATION
White Plains, NY..........Civil Trial Practice, Insurance Defense Law, Personal Injury Law

CESARI AND MCKENNA
Boston, MA..........Patent, Trademark, Copyright and Unfair Competition Law

CETRULO, ROBERT C., P.S.C.
Covington, KY..........Civil Trial Practice, Insurance Defense Law, Personal Injury Law

CHADBOURNE & PARKE
Los Angeles, CA..........General Practice
Washington, DC..........General Practice
New York, NY..........General Practice
London, England..........General Practice
Hong Kong, Hong Kong (British Crown Colony)..........General Practice
Moscow, Russia..........General Practice
New Delhi, India..........General Practice

CHAFFE, MCCALL, PHILLIPS, TOLER & SARPY
New Orleans, LA..........Admiralty/Maritime Law, General Practice, Labor and Employment Law, Natural Resources Law

CHAIT AMYOT
Montreal, QU, Canada..........General Practice, Real Estate Law

CHALEFF, ENGLISH AND CATALANO
Santa Monica, CA..........Criminal Trial Practice, General Practice

CHALFIE, JAMES J., CO., L.P.A.
Cincinnati, OH..........Family Law, General Practice, Personal Injury Law, Probate and Estate Planning Law

CHALOS & BROWN, P.C.
New York, NY..........Admiralty/Maritime Law, Environmental Law, Insurance Defense Law, Transportation Law

CHAMBERLAIN, D'AMANDA, OPPENHEIMER & GREENFIELD
Rochester, NY..........Civil Trial Practice, Commercial Law, Environmental Law, General Practice

CHAMBERLAIN & HIGBEE
Cedar City, UT..........General Practice

CHAMBERLAIN, NEATON & JOHNSON
Wayzata, MN..........Civil Trial Practice

CHAMBERS, MABRY, MCCLELLAND & BROOKS
Atlanta, GA..........Insurance Defense Law, Medical Malpractice Law, Personal Injury Law, Probate and Estate Planning Law, Product Liability Law

CHAMBERS, SALZMAN & BANNON, PROFESSIONAL ASSOCIATION
St. Petersburg, FL..........Personal Injury Law

CHAMBLESS, HIGDON & CARSON
Macon, GA..........Civil Trial Practice, General Practice, Insurance Defense Law, Medical Malpractice Law, Personal Injury Law, Product Liability Law

CHAMBLISS & BAHNER
Chattanooga, TN..........Bankruptcy Law, Civil Trial Practice, Commercial Law, General Practice, Labor and Employment Law, Municipal Bond/Public Authority Financing Law, Probate and Estate Planning Law, Real Estate Law, Tax Law

CHAMLEE, DUBUS & SIPPLE
Savannah, GA..........Admiralty/Maritime Law, General Practice

CHAMPION, JAN
San Jose, CA..........Civil Trial Practice, Personal Injury Law

CHANCE, MADDOX & SMITH
Calhoun, GA..........General Practice

CHANDLER, LAWRENCE U. L.
West Palm Beach, FL..........Civil Trial Practice, Personal Injury Law

CHANDLER, BUJOLD & CHANDLER
Troy, MI..........General Practice, Labor and Employment Law

CHANDLER, GEORGE, LAW OFFICES OF
Lufkin, TX..........Personal Injury Law

CHANDLER, TULLAR, UDALL & REDHAIR
Tucson, AZ..........Civil Trial Practice, General Practice, Insurance Defense Law, Natural Resources Law, Real Estate Law

CHANFRAU & CHANFRAU
Daytona Beach, FL..........Personal Injury Law

CHAPIN, FLEMING & WINET, A PROFESSIONAL CORPORATION
San Diego, CA..........Civil Trial Practice, Commercial Law, Insurance Defense Law

CHAPLIN, ANSEL B., LAW OFFICES OF
Boston, MA..........General Practice
Truro, MA..........General Practice

CHAPMAN AND CUTLER
Chicago, IL..........General Practice, Municipal Bond/Public Authority Financing Law, Tax Law
Salt Lake City, UT..........General Practice

CHAPMAN & FENNELL
Stamford, CT..........Banking Law, Civil Trial Practice, Communications Law, Patent, Trademark, Copyright and Unfair Competition Law, Real Estate Law, Securities Law
New York, NY..........Banking Law, Communications Law, Patent, Trademark, Copyright and Unfair Competition Law, Securities Law

CHAPMAN, FULLER & BOLLARD
Irvine, CA..........Civil Trial Practice

CHAPMAN, HENKOFF, KESSLER, PEDUTO & SAFFER
Roseland, NJ..........General Practice

CHAPMAN, LEWIS & SWAN
Clarksdale, MS..........General Practice, Personal Injury Law

CHAPPELL, E. HUGH, JR., P.A.
Fort Lauderdale, FL..........Personal Injury Law

CHAPPELL & MCGARTLAND, L.L.P.
Fort Worth, TX..........Civil Trial Practice, General Practice

CHAR SAKAMOTO ISHII & LUM
Honolulu, HI..........General Practice

CHARFOOS, REITER, PETERSON, HOLMQUIST & PILCHAK, P.C.
Detroit, MI..........Labor and Employment Law
Farmington Hills, MI..........Labor and Employment Law

CHARITON & KEISER
Scranton, PA..........Civil Trial Practice, Commercial Law
Wilkes-Barre, PA..........Civil Trial Practice, Commercial Law

CHARLSON, MARBEN & JORGENSON, P.A.
Thief River Falls, MN..........General Practice

CHARTIER, OGAN, BRADY & LUKAKIS
Holyoke, MA..........General Practice

CHARTRAND & BADGLEY
Pontiac, MI..........Civil Trial Practice

CHASE, HAYES & KALAMON, P.S.
Spokane, WA..........Business Law, General Practice, Health Care Law, Personal Injury Law, Probate and Estate Planning Law

CHATHAM, GERALD W. SR.
Hernando, MS..........General Practice, Medical Malpractice Law

CHATTMAN, SUTULA, FRIEDLANDER & PAUL, A LEGAL PROFESSIONAL ASSOCIATION
Cleveland, OH..........Civil Trial Practice, Labor and Employment Law

CHAUVIN & CHAUVIN
Louisville, KY..........General Practice

CHAVIANO & ASSOCIATES, LTD.
Chicago, IL..........Insurance Defense Law

CHAZEN & CHAZEN
Englewood, NJ..........Civil Trial Practice, General Practice

CHEATHAM ACKER & SHARP, P.C.
West Bloomfield, MI..........Civil Trial Practice, Insurance Defense Law, Medical Malpractice Law

CHEEK, MICHAEL C.
Clearwater, FL..........Criminal Trial Practice

CHEN, WALSH, TECLER & MCCABE
Rockville, MD..........General Practice, Real Estate Law

CHERNOFF, VILHAUER, MCCLUNG & STENZEL
Portland, OR..........Patent, Trademark, Copyright and Unfair Competition Law

CHERPELIS & ASSOCIATES, P.A.
Albuquerque, NM..........Labor and Employment Law

CHERRY, DAVIS, HARRISON, MONTEZ, WILLIAMS & BAIRD, P.C.
Waco, TX..........General Practice

CHERWIN & GLICKMAN
Boston, MA..........Business Law, General Practice

CHESTER, PFAFF & BROTHERSON
Elkhart, IN..........Business Law, Civil Trial Practice, Commercial Law, General Practice, Personal Injury Law, Probate and Estate Planning Law, Real Estate Law

CHESTER, WILLCOX AND SAXBE
Columbus, OH..........Civil Trial Practice, General Practice, Real Estate Law

CHESTNUT & BROOKS, PROFESSIONAL ASSOCIATION
Minneapolis, MN..........Civil Trial Practice, Personal Injury Law

CHICOINE & HALLETT, P.S.
Seattle, WA..........Tax Law

CHIERICI & WRIGHT, A PROFESSIONAL CORPORATION
Moorestown, NJ..........Appellate Practice, Civil Trial Practice, Medical Malpractice Law, Personal Injury Law, Product Liability Law

CHILDS, EMERSON, RUNDLETT, FIFIELD & CHILDS
Portland, ME..........Personal Injury Law

CHILIVIS & GRINDLER
Atlanta, GA..........Administrative Law, Criminal Trial Practice

CHINNERY, CARL, & ASSOCIATES, P.C.
Lee's Summit, MO..........Business Law, Probate and Estate Planning Law, Real Estate Law

CHISHOLM AND FELDMAN
Providence, RI..........Civil Trial Practice, Personal Injury Law

CHISM, JACOBSON & JOHNSON
Seattle, WA..........Commercial Law, Construction Law

CHOATE, HALL & STEWART
Boston, MA..........General Practice

CHOLETTE, PERKINS & BUCHANAN
Grand Rapids, MI..........Civil Trial Practice, General Practice, Insurance Defense Law, Product Liability Law

CHORCHES & NOVAK, P.C.
Wethersfield, CT..........Bankruptcy Law

CHRISTENSEN LAW OFFICES
Deadwood, SD..........General Practice

CHRISTENSEN, O'CONNOR, JOHNSON & KINDNESS
Seattle, WA..........Patent, Trademark, Copyright and Unfair Competition Law

CHRISTIAN, SPARTZ, KEOGH & CHRISTIAN
Le Center, MN..........General Practice

CHRISTIANSEN & JACKNIN
West Palm Beach, FL..........Civil Trial Practice

CHRISTIANSEN, JUBE & KEEGAN, A PROFESSIONAL CORPORATION
Shrewsbury, NJ..........General Practice

CHRISTISON & MARTIN
San Diego, CA..........Bankruptcy Law, Commercial Law

CHRISTOPHER & LEDOUX
Worcester, MA..........Civil Trial Practice, Environmental Law, Health Care Law

CHRISTOVICH AND KEARNEY, L.L.P.
New Orleans, LA..........Admiralty/Maritime Law, General Practice, Insurance Defense Law

CHUHAK & TECSON, P.C.
Chicago, IL..........Health Care Law, Probate and Estate Planning Law

CHUN, KERR, DODD & KANESHIGE
Honolulu, HI..........General Practice

CHURCH, CHURCH, HITTLE & ANTRIM
Noblesville, IN..........General Practice, Municipal Bond/Public Authority Financing Law, Personal Injury Law

CHURCH, KRITSELIS, WYBLE & ROBINSON, P.C.
Lansing, MI..........Civil Trial Practice, Medical Malpractice Law, Municipal and Zoning Law, Personal Injury Law, Product Liability Law, Real Estate Law

CHURCHILL, MANOLIS, FREEMAN, KLUDT & KAUFMAN
Huron, SD..........General Practice

CIARDI & DIDONATO, P.C.
Philadelphia, PA..........Bankruptcy Law

CICCARELLO, DEL GIUDICE & LAFON
Charleston, WV..........Civil Trial Practice, Medical Malpractice Law, Personal Injury Law

CIVEROLO, WOLF, GRALOW & HILL, A PROFESSIONAL ASSOCIATION
Albuquerque, NM..........Civil Trial Practice, General Practice, Insurance Defense Law

CLAIRE, COLLEEN M.
Newport Beach, CA..........Probate and Estate Planning Law

CLANAHAN, TANNER, DOWNING AND KNOWLTON, P.C.
Denver, CO..........Civil Trial Practice, General Practice, Natural Resources Law

CLANCY, CALLAHAN & SMITH
Roseland, NJ..........Business Law, Commercial Law, Construction Law

CLAPHAM, E. GEOFFREY
Columbus, OH..........Real Estate Law

CLARK, BEVERLY
Detroit, MI..........Family Law

CLARK, CHARLTON & MARTINO, A PROFESSIONAL ASSOCIATION
Tampa, FL..........Civil Trial Practice

CLARK, DRUMMIE & COMPANY
Saint John, NB, Canada..........Administrative Law, Admiralty/Maritime Law, Banking Law, Bankruptcy Law, Civil Trial Practice, Commercial Law, Environmental Law, Family Law, General Practice, Insurance Defense Law, Labor and Employment Law, Municipal and Zoning Law, Personal Injury Law, Probate and Estate Planning Law, Real Estate Law, Transportation Law

CLARKE, JON B., P.C.
Denver, CO..........Bankruptcy Law, Real Estate Law

CLARKE & LEARY
North Hollywood, CA..........Probate and Estate Planning Law

CLARKE & SILVERGLATE, PROFESSIONAL ASSOCIATION
Miami, FL..........Admiralty/Maritime Law, Commercial Law, Labor and Employment Law, Personal Injury Law, Product Liability Law

CLARK, GAGLIARDI & MILLER, P.C.
White Plains, NY..........Civil Trial Practice, General Practice, Personal Injury Law

CLARK, GLEN B., JR., P.C.
Denver, CO..........Banking Law, Business Law, Real Estate Law

CLARK, KLEIN & BEAUMONT
Bloomfield Hills, MI..........Business Law, Environmental Law, General Practice, Real Estate Law, Tax Law
Detroit, MI..........Administrative Law, Antitrust Law, Bankruptcy Law, Business Law, Civil Trial Practice, Commercial Law, Communications Law, Construction Law, Employment Benefits Law, Environmental Law, General Practice, Immigration and Naturalization Law, Labor and Employment Law, Probate and Estate Planning Law, Product Liability Law, Real Estate Law, Securities Law, Tax Law, Transportation Law

CLARK, LADNER, FORTENBAUGH & YOUNG
Philadelphia, PA..........Admiralty/Maritime Law, General Practice

CLARK, LINDAUER, MCCLINTON, FETHERSTON, EDMONDS & LIPPOLD
Salem, OR..........General Practice

CLARK, MIZE & LINVILLE, CHARTERED
Salina, KS..........General Practice

CLARK, NEWTON, HINSON & MCLEAN, L.L.P.
Wilmington, NC..........Admiralty/Maritime Law, Civil Trial Practice, General Practice

CLARK, PAUL, HOOVER & MALLARD
Atlanta, GA..........Employment Benefits Law, Labor and Employment Law

CLARK, PERDUE, ROBERTS & SCOTT CO., L.P.A.
Columbus, OH ....Civil Trial Practice, Medical Malpractice Law, Personal Injury Law, Product Liability Law, Transportation Law

CLARK, QUINN, MOSES & CLARK
Indianapolis, IN ....Municipal and Zoning Law, Real Estate Law

CLARK & SCHOLNIK
Fort Lauderdale, FL ....General Practice, Real Estate Law

CLARK, SPARKMAN, ROBB, NELSON & MASON
Miami, FL ....Civil Trial Practice, Insurance Defense Law

CLARK & STANT, P.C.
Virginia Beach, VA ....Civil Trial Practice, General Practice, Tax Law

CLARK, THOMAS & WINTERS, A PROFESSIONAL CORPORATION
Austin, TX ....Civil Trial Practice, General Practice

CLARK & TREVITHICK, A PROFESSIONAL CORPORATION
Los Angeles, CA ....Banking Law, Bankruptcy Law, Business Law, Civil Trial Practice, Commercial Law, Environmental Law, General Practice, Insurance Defense Law, Labor and Employment Law, Probate and Estate Planning Law, Product Liability Law, Real Estate Law, Securities Law, Tax Law

CLARK WHARTON & BERRY
Greensboro, NC ....Civil Trial Practice, General Practice

CLARK & WILLIAMS
Tulsa, OK ....Family Law, General Practice

CLARK, WILSON
Vancouver, BC, Canada ....Family Law, Patent, Trademark, Copyright and Unfair Competition Law

CLARY, NANTZ, WOOD, HOFFIUS, RANKIN & COOPER
Grand Rapids, MI ....Bankruptcy Law, Business Law, Civil Trial Practice, Environmental Law, General Practice, Insurance Defense Law, Labor and Employment Law, Municipal Bond/Public Authority Financing Law, Natural Resources Law, Personal Injury Law, Real Estate Law, Tax Law

CLAUSEN MILLER GORMAN CAFFREY & WITOUS, P.C.
Chicago, IL ....General Practice
Wheaton, IL ....General Practice

CLAWSON & STAUBES
Charleston, SC ....Civil Trial Practice

CLAYSON, MANN, AREND & YAEGER, A PROFESSIONAL LAW CORPORATION
Corona, CA ....Business Law, General Practice

CLEARY, DAVID L., ASSOCIATES, A PROFESSIONAL CORPORATION
Rutland, VT ....Civil Trial Practice, General Practice, Insurance Defense Law, Medical Malpractice Law, Personal Injury Law, Product Liability Law

CLEARY, GOTTLIEB, STEEN & HAMILTON
Washington, DC ....General Practice
New York, NY ....General Practice
Brussels, Belgium ....General Practice
London, England ....General Practice
Paris, France ....General Practice
Frankfurt/Main, Germany ....General Practice
Hong Kong, Hong Kong (British Crown Colony) ....General Practice
Tokyo, Japan ....General Practice

CLEMENS, KORHN & LIMING
Defiance, OH ....Insurance Defense Law
Hicksville, OH ....Insurance Defense Law

CLEMENT, BRUCE
Federal Way, WA ....Personal Injury Law

CLEMENT, CHARLES E.
Boone, NC ....Civil Trial Practice, Commercial Law, General Practice, Real Estate Law

CLEMENT, FITZPATRICK & KENWORTHY, INCORPORATED
Santa Rosa, CA ....Civil Trial Practice, Real Estate Law

CLEMENT & WHEATLEY, A PROFESSIONAL CORPORATION
Danville, VA ....General Practice

CLEMENTE, DICKSON & MUELLER, P.A.
Morristown, NJ ....Civil Trial Practice, General Practice

CLEM, POLACKWICH & VOCELLE
Vero Beach, FL ....Civil Trial Practice, Personal Injury Law, Real Estate Law

CLENDENEN, WILLIAM H., JR., A PROFESSIONAL CORPORATION
New Haven, CT ....Civil Trial Practice, General Practice

CLONTZ & COX
Mount Vernon, KY ....Criminal Trial Practice, General Practice

CLOPPERT, PORTMAN, SAUTER, LATANICK & FOLEY
Columbus, OH ....Civil Trial Practice, Labor and Employment Law, Personal Injury Law

CLUNE, HAYES, FREY, BENTZEN & CLUNE, P.C.
Harrison, NY ....Civil Trial Practice, General Practice

CLURE, EATON, BUTLER, MICHELSON, FERGUSON & MUNGER, P.A.
Duluth, MN ....Civil Trial Practice

COATES, HATFIELD, CALKINS & WELLNITZ
Indianapolis, IN ....Probate and Estate Planning Law

COBB, SAM B. JR.
Tyler, TX ....Natural Resources Law

COBB COLE & BELL
Daytona Beach, FL ....General Practice
Orlando, FL ....Civil Trial Practice, General Practice

COBB & SHEALY, P.A.
Dothan, AL ....Civil Trial Practice, General Practice

COBLENTZ, CAHEN, MCCABE & BREYER
San Francisco, CA ....General Practice

COBRIN GITTES & SAMUEL
New York, NY ....Patent, Trademark, Copyright and Unfair Competition Law

COBURN, GEORGE M.
Washington, DC ....Administrative Law

COBURN & CROFT
St. Louis, MO ....General Practice

COCKRELL & WEED
Dallas, TX ....Civil Trial Practice, Natural Resources Law

CODDINGTON, HICKS & DANFORTH, A PROFESSIONAL CORPORATION
Redwood City, CA ....Civil Trial Practice

CODE HUNTER WITTMANN
Calgary, AB, Canada ....General Practice

COFER, WILLIAM L., P.A.
Winston-Salem, NC ....Criminal Trial Practice

COFFEE, MELVIN A., & ASSOCIATES, P.C.
Denver, CO ....Tax Law

COFFMAN, COLEMAN, ANDREWS & GROGAN, PROFESSIONAL ASSOCIATION
Jacksonville, FL ....Labor and Employment Law

COFFMAN, DEFRIES & NOTHERN, A PROFESSIONAL ASSOCIATION
Topeka, KS ....Tax Law

COGAVIN AND WAYSTACK
Boston, MA ....Civil Trial Practice, Insurance Defense Law

COGBURN, JOHN M. JR.
Griffin, GA ....Business Law, General Practice, Probate and Estate Planning Law, Real Estate Law

COGGIN & ASSOCIATES
Birmingham, AL ....General Practice

COGSWELL, WILTON W. III
Colorado Springs, CO ....Probate and Estate Planning Law, Tax Law

COHEN, DAVID LAW OFFICE OF
Austin, TX ....General Practice

COHEN, ERNEST ALLEN
Tucson, AZ ....Labor and Employment Law

COHEN, ROBERT A.
Pittsburgh, PA ....Civil Trial Practice, General Practice, Personal Injury Law, Product Liability Law

COHEN, BARRY A., P.A., THE LAW FIRM OF
Tampa, FL ....Criminal Trial Practice

COHEN AND COTTON, A PROFESSIONAL CORPORATION
Phoenix, AZ ....Civil Trial Practice, Real Estate Law

COHEN, GETTINGS, DUNHAM & HARRISON, P.C.
Arlington, VA ....Civil Trial Practice

COHEN & GRIGSBY, P.C.
Pittsburgh, PA ....General Practice, Securities Law

COHEN, HENNESSEY & BIENSTOCK, P.C.
New York, NY ....Family Law

COHEN, JULES S., P.A.
Orlando, FL ....Bankruptcy Law

COHEN & LOMBARDO, P.C.
Buffalo, NY ....Insurance Defense Law

COHEN, MARK A., & ASSOCIATES, P.A.
Miami, FL ....Civil Trial Practice

COHEN, MARK A., & ASSOCIATES, P.C.
Washington, DC....................Civil Trial Practice

COHEN & MARLOW
Greenwich, CT ....Family Law
New Haven, CT ....Family Law

COHEN MCGOVERN SHORALL & STEVENS, P.C.
Phoenix, AZ ....Insurance Defense Law

COHEN, PETER A., P.A.
Miami, FL ....Civil Trial Practice

COHEN AND WOLF, P.C.
Bridgeport, CT ....General Practice

COHEN/DAVID & ASSOCIATES, P.C.
Atlanta, GA ....Real Estate Law

COHN, CLIFFORD B.
Philadelphia, PA ....Civil Trial Practice, Personal Injury Law

COKER, JEAN C., P.A.
Jacksonville, FL ....Probate and Estate Planning Law

COLBY, MONET, DEMERS, DELAGE & CREVIER
Montreal, QU, Canada ....General Practice

COLE, DOROTHY A.
Escondido, CA ....Probate and Estate Planning Law

COLE ACTON HARMON DUNN, A LEGAL PROFESSIONAL ASSOCIATION
Springfield, OH ....General Practice, Personal Injury Law, Real Estate Law

COLELLA, TRIGILIO & STEPHENSON
Lorain, OH....................Commercial Law

COLEMAN, JOSEPH C.
Columbia, SC ....Civil Trial Practice

COLEMAN, REFORD H. AND ASSOCIATES
Elizabethtown, KY ....General Practice

COLEMAN, GLEDHILL & HARGRAVE, P.C.
Hillsborough, NC....................Civil Trial Practice, Criminal Trial Practice, General Practice, Personal Injury Law

COLEMAN & MARCUS, A PROFESSIONAL CORPORATION
Los Angeles, CA....................Civil Trial Practice, Criminal Trial Practice

COLEMAN, RITCHIE & ROBERTSON
Twin Falls, ID....................General Practice

COLE, MOORE & MCCRACKEN
Bowling Green, KY ....Banking Law, Civil Trial Practice, General Practice

COLE, RAYWID & BRAVERMAN, L.L.P.
Washington, DC....................Communications Law

COLFER, WOOD, LYONS & WOOD
Mc Cook, NE....................General Practice

COLINGO, WILLIAMS, HEIDELBERG, STEINBERGER & MCELHANEY, P.A.
Pascagoula, MS ....Environmental Law, General Practice, Insurance Defense Law, Medical Malpractice Law, Personal Injury Law

COLLARD & ROE, P.C.
Roslyn, NY ....Patent, Trademark, Copyright and Unfair Competition Law

COLLERAN, O'HARA & MILLS
Garden City, NY ....General Practice, Labor and Employment Law

COLLEY, MICHAEL F., CO., L.P.A.
Columbus, OH ....Civil Trial Practice, General Practice, Medical Malpractice Law, Personal Injury Law, Product Liability Law

COLLIER, ARNETT, QUICK & COLEMAN
Elizabethtown, KY ....General Practice, Insurance Defense Law

COLLIER & COLLIER
Ironton, OH ....Probate and Estate Planning Law, Real Estate Law

COLLINS, BROWN & CALDWELL, CHARTERED
Vero Beach, FL....................Civil Trial Practice, Environmental Law, General Practice, Real Estate Law

COLLINS, BUCKLEY, SAUNTRY AND HAUGH
St. Paul, MN....................Family Law, General Practice, Insurance Defense Law, Personal Injury Law

COLLINS, COLLINS, MUIR & TRAVER
Pasadena, CA ....Civil Trial Practice, Construction Law, Insurance Defense Law, Personal Injury Law

COLLINS, GEORGE W., INC., A PROFESSIONAL CORPORATION
Santa Monica, CA....................General Practice

COLLINS AND GRIMM, A PROFESSIONAL CORPORATION
Macon, MO ....General Practice

COLLINS & LACY
Columbia, SC ....Civil Trial Practice, General Practice

COLLINS & SCHLOTHAUER
San Jose, CA ....Insurance Defense Law, Medical Malpractice Law, Personal Injury Law

COLLINS & TRUETT, P.A.
Tallahassee, FL ....Appellate Practice, Civil Trial Practice, General Practice, Insurance Defense Law, Medical Malpractice Law, Product Liability Law, Public Utilities Law, Real Estate Law

COLMAN-SCHWIMMER, ARLENE, A PROFESSIONAL CORPORATION
Beverly Hills, CA....................Family Law

COLSON, HICKS, EIDSON, COLSON, MATTHEWS & GAMBA
Miami, FL ....Commercial Law, General Practice, Personal Injury Law

COMBS AND STEVENS
Prestonsburg, KY ....General Practice, Natural Resources Law

COMPTON & DULING, L.C.
Woodbridge, VA ....General Practice

COMPTON, PREWETT, THOMAS & HICKEY, P.A.
El Dorado, AR ....General Practice

CONANT WHITTENBURG WHITTENBURG & SCHACHTER, P.C.
Amarillo, TX....................Bankruptcy Law, Civil Trial Practice, General Practice
Dallas, TX....................Civil Trial Practice, General Practice

CONBOY, MCKAY, BACHMAN & KENDALL
Carthage, NY ....General Practice
Watertown, NY....................General Practice, Insurance Defense Law

CONDE, STONER & KILLOREN
Rockford, IL ....General Practice, Probate and Estate Planning Law, Tax Law

CONDO, JOSEPH A., & ASSOCIATES, P.C.
Vienna, VA....................Family Law

CONGALTON, JOHN S.
Seattle, WA ....Admiralty/Maritime Law

CONGER, J. HILTON
Smithville, TN....................General Practice

CONGER & ELLIOTT, PROF. CORP.
Carmi, IL....................General Practice, Probate and Estate Planning Law

CONKLIN, BENHAM, DUCEY, LISTMAN & CHUHRAN, P.C.
Detroit, MI....................Labor and Employment Law

CONKLIN, NYBO, LEVEQUE & MURPHY, P.C.
Great Falls, MT ....Insurance Defense Law, Personal Injury Law

CONLEY & FOOTE
Middlebury, VT ....Administrative Law, Civil Trial Practice, Family Law, General Practice, Insurance Defense Law, Personal Injury Law, Probate and Estate Planning Law, Real Estate Law

CONLEY, HALEY & O'NEIL
Bath, ME....................Civil Trial Practice, Environmental Law, General Practice, Labor and Employment Law, Personal Injury Law, Public Utilities Law

CONLEY & HAUSHALTER
Princeton, NJ ....Tax Law

CONLIFFE, SANDMANN & SULLIVAN
Louisville, KY ....General Practice, Probate and Estate Planning Law

CONLIN, MCKENNEY & PHILBRICK, P.C.
Ann Arbor, MI ....Banking Law, Bankruptcy Law, General Practice, Real Estate Law

CONLIN, ROXANNE B., AND ASSOCIATES, P.C.
Des Moines, IA....................Business Law, Medical Malpractice Law, Personal Injury Law

CONMY, FESTE, BOSSART, HUBBARD & CORWIN, LTD.
Fargo, ND ....Banking Law, Civil Trial Practice, General Practice, Personal Injury Law, Probate and Estate Planning Law, Real Estate Law

CONNELL, FOLEY & GEISER
Roseland, NJ........Civil Trial Practice, General Practice, Insurance Defense Law

CONNELL LIGHTBODY
Vancouver, BC, Canada........General Practice

CONNELLY, SOUTAR & JACKSON
Toledo, OH........Civil Trial Practice, Medical Malpractice Law, Personal Injury Law

CONNER, LESLIE L. JR.
Oklahoma City, OK........Probate and Estate Planning Law

CONNER, CANTEY & CLOVER
Sealy, TX........Civil Trial Practice

CONNER & OPIE
Great Bend, KS........General Practice

CONNER & RILEY
Erie, PA........Personal Injury Law

CONNER & WINTERS, A PROFESSIONAL CORPORATION
Oklahoma City, OK........Antitrust Law, Civil Trial Practice, General Practice
Tulsa, OK........Civil Trial Practice, General Practice, Natural Resources Law, Securities Law, Tax Law

CONNOLLY, BOVE, LODGE & HUTZ
Wilmington, DE........Business Law, Commercial Law, General Practice, Patent, Trademark, Copyright and Unfair Competition Law, Probate and Estate Planning Law

CONNOLLY, O'MALLEY, LILLIS, HANSEN & OLSON
Des Moines, IA........General Practice, Probate and Estate Planning Law, Real Estate Law

CONNOR, BUNN, ROGERSON & WOODARD, P.A.
Wilson, NC........General Practice

CONNOR, CURRAN & SCHRAM, P.C.
Hudson, NY........General Practice

CONNOR, NEAL & STEVENSON
Owensboro, KY........Business Law, Probate and Estate Planning Law, Real Estate Law

CONNOR & WEBER, P.C.
Philadelphia, PA........Insurance Defense Law

CONNORS & CORCORAN
Rochester, NY........General Practice

CONNORS & VILARDO
Buffalo, NY........Civil Trial Practice, Criminal Trial Practice

CONOUR • DOEHRMAN
Indianapolis, IN........Civil Trial Practice, Medical Malpractice Law, Personal Injury Law

CONRAD, SCHERER, JAMES & JENNE
Fort Lauderdale, FL........Civil Trial Practice, General Practice, Insurance Defense Law, Personal Injury Law

CONROY, BALLMAN & DAMERON, CHARTERED
Bethesda, MD........General Practice
Bowie, MD........General Practice
Gaithersburg, MD........General Practice
Rockville, MD........General Practice

CONSTANCE, STEWART & COOK
Independence, MO........General Practice

CONSTANGY, BROOKS & SMITH
Birmingham, AL........Labor and Employment Law
Washington, DC........Labor and Employment Law
Atlanta, GA........Labor and Employment Law
Winston-Salem, NC........Labor and Employment Law
Columbia, SC........Labor and Employment Law
Nashville, TN........Labor and Employment Law

CONTANT, SCHERBY & ATKINS
Hackensack, NJ........Banking Law, Commercial Law

CONTIGUGLIA & GIACONA
Auburn, NY........General Practice

CONWAY, JACK K.
San Marino, CA........Personal Injury Law

CONWAY, JOSEPH WM.
Pittsburgh, PA........Civil Trial Practice

CONWAY & HALL, A LEGAL PROFESSIONAL ASSOCIATION
Dayton, OH........General Practice

COOGAN, SMITH, BENNETT, MCGAHAN, LORINCZ & JACOBI
Attleboro, MA........General Practice

COOK, H. CLAYTON JR.
Washington, DC........Admiralty/Maritime Law, General Practice, Tax Law
McLean, VA........Admiralty/Maritime Law, General Practice, Tax Law

COOK AND BATISTA CO., L.P.A.
Lorain, OH........General Practice

COOKE & COOKE
Greensboro, NC........General Practice

COOK, EGAN, MCFARRON & MANZO, LTD., A PROFESSIONAL CORPORATION
Chicago, IL........Patent, Trademark, Copyright and Unfair Competition Law

COOK & FRANKE, S.C.
Milwaukee, WI........Admiralty/Maritime Law, General Practice, Tax Law

COOK & LEE, P.C.
Boulder, CO........Civil Trial Practice, General Practice, Personal Injury Law
Denver, CO........Civil Trial Practice, General Practice, Personal Injury Law

COOK, MEDA AND LANDE, A PROFESSIONAL CORPORATION
Phoenix, AZ........Bankruptcy Law, Commercial Law

COOK, NOELL, TOLLEY & WIGGINS
Athens, GA........Criminal Trial Practice

COOK & PALMOUR
Summerville, GA........Civil Trial Practice, Criminal Trial Practice

COOK, TUCKER, NETTER & CLOONAN, P.C.
Kingston, NY........General Practice

COOK, YANCEY, KING & GALLOWAY, A PROFESSIONAL LAW CORPORATION
Shreveport, LA........Banking Law, Bankruptcy Law, Civil Trial Practice, Commercial Law, Environmental Law, General Practice, Insurance Defense Law, Labor and Employment Law, Natural Resources Law, Probate and Estate Planning Law, Real Estate Law, Tax Law

COOLEY GODWARD CASTRO HUDDLESON & TATUM
Palo Alto, CA........General Practice
San Francisco, CA........General Practice

COOLEY, SHRAIR, P.C.
Springfield, MA........General Practice, Labor and Employment Law

COOMBS & DUNLAP
Napa, CA........General Practice

COONEY & CREW, P.C.
Portland, OR........Business Law, Civil Trial Practice, Health Care Law, Insurance Defense Law, Labor and Employment Law, Medical Malpractice Law, Transportation Law

COONEY, HALICZER, MATTSON, LANCE, BLACKBURN, PETTIS & RICHARDS, P.A.
Fort Lauderdale, FL........Medical Malpractice Law, Personal Injury Law

COONEY, SCULLY AND DOWLING
Hartford, CT........General Practice, Insurance Defense Law

COOPER, C. JAMES JR.
Denver, CO........Immigration and Naturalization Law

COOPER, HAROLD J.
Dallas, TX........Personal Injury Law

COOPER & COOPER
New Rochelle, NY........Construction Law, General Practice

COOPER, COPPINS & MONROE, P.A.
Tallahassee, FL........Civil Trial Practice

COOPER, COX, BARLOW AND JACOBS
Madison, IN........General Practice

COOPER & DUNHAM
New York, NY........General Practice, Patent, Trademark, Copyright and Unfair Competition Law, Trademark, Copyright and Unfair Competition Law

COOPER, FINK & ZAUSMER, P.C.
Farmington Hills, MI........Environmental Law, Municipal and Zoning Law

COOPER, HALL, WHITTUM AND SHILLABER, P.C.
Rochester, NH........General Practice

COOPER, HEWITT & KATZ
Atlanta, GA........Civil Trial Practice

COOPER, MITCH, CRAWFORD, KUYKENDALL & WHATLEY
Birmingham, AL .... Civil Trial Practice, Environmental Law, General Practice, Labor and Employment Law

COOPER PERSKIE APRIL NIEDELMAN WAGENHEIM & LEVENSON, A PROFESSIONAL ASSOCIATION
Atlantic City, NJ .... Bankruptcy Law, General Practice

COOPER ROSE & ENGLISH
Summit, NJ .... Civil Trial Practice, Environmental Law, Family Law, General Practice, Probate and Estate Planning Law, Real Estate Law, Tax Law

COOPER, SPONG & DAVIS, P.C.
Portsmouth, VA .... General Practice

COOTS, HENKE & WHEELER, PROFESSIONAL CORPORATION
Carmel, IN .... Civil Trial Practice, Family Law, General Practice, Insurance Defense Law, Personal Injury Law, Probate and Estate Planning Law, Real Estate Law

COPELAND, DONALD F.
Norristown, PA .... Probate and Estate Planning Law

COPELAND COOK TAYLOR & BUSH
Jackson, MS .... Civil Trial Practice, Insurance Defense Law

COPELAND, LANDYE, BENNETT AND WOLF
Portland, OR .... General Practice

COPP & BERALL
Hartford, CT .... Probate and Estate Planning Law, Tax Law

CORBALLY, GARTLAND AND RAPPLEYEA
Poughkeepsie, NY .... Banking Law, Civil Trial Practice, General Practice, Municipal and Zoning Law, Real Estate Law

CORBAN & GUNN
Biloxi, MS .... General Practice

CORBETT, ANDERSON, CORBETT, POULSON, FLOM & VELLINGA
Sioux City, IA .... General Practice

CORBETT & KANE, A PROFESSIONAL CORPORATION
Oakland, CA .... Labor and Employment Law
San Francisco, CA .... Labor and Employment Law

CORBIN, DICKINSON, DUVALL & MARGULIES
Jacksonville, FL .... General Practice, Labor and Employment Law

CORBIN, ROBERT L., P.C., LAW OFFICES OF
Los Angeles, CA .... Civil Trial Practice, Criminal Trial Practice

CORBOY • DEMETRIO • CLIFFORD, P.C.
Chicago, IL .... Civil Trial Practice, Medical Malpractice Law, Personal Injury Law

CORBYN & HAMPTON
Oklahoma City, OK .... Civil Trial Practice

CORCORAN, PECKHAM & HAYES, P.C.
Newport, RI .... General Practice

CORETTE POHLMAN ALLEN BLACK & CARLSON, A PROFESSIONAL CORPORATION
Butte, MT .... General Practice

COREY, BYLER, REW, LORENZEN & HOJEM
Pendleton, OR .... General Practice

COREY & FARRELL, P.C.
Tucson, AZ .... Administrative Law, Civil Trial Practice, Commercial Law, Labor and Employment Law, Personal Injury Law, Probate and Estate Planning Law, Real Estate Law

CORINBLIT & SELTZER, A PROFESSIONAL CORPORATION
Los Angeles, CA .... Antitrust Law, Business Law, Civil Trial Practice, General Practice, Securities Law

CORLETT KILLIAN, A PROFESSIONAL ASSOCIATION
Miami, FL .... Civil Trial Practice

CORLEY, MONCUS & WARD, P.C.
Birmingham, AL .... Bankruptcy Law, General Practice, Probate and Estate Planning Law, Real Estate Law, Securities Law

CORNELIUS & COLLINS
Nashville, TN .... Civil Trial Practice, General Practice

CORNELLA, DOMINIC J., ASSOCIATES, P.C.
Mineola, NY .... Insurance Defense Law, Product Liability Law

CORNELL AND GOLLUB
Boston, MA .... Civil Trial Practice, General Practice, Insurance Defense Law, Medical Malpractice Law

CORNWELL, GARY T.
The Woodlands, TX .... Civil Trial Practice

CORS & BASSETT
Cincinnati, OH .... General Practice, Labor and Employment Law

CORSI, MARIO D.
Dover, OH .... General Practice

CORSON, GETSON & SCHATZ
Philadelphia, PA .... Civil Trial Practice, Immigration and Naturalization Law, International Business Law

CORWIN, GREGG M. & ASSOCIATES
Minneapolis, MN .... Labor and Employment Law

CORWIN & MATTHEWS
Huntington, NY .... General Practice

CORY, MEREDITH, WITTER, ROUSH & CHENEY, A LEGAL PROFESSIONAL ASSOCIATION
Lima, OH .... General Practice

COSGRAVE, VERGEER & KESTER
Portland, OR .... General Practice

COSGROVE, FLYNN & GASKINS
Minneapolis, MN .... Civil Trial Practice, Insurance Defense Law, Product Liability Law

COSGROVE, MICHELIZZI, SCHWABACHER, WARD & BIANCHI, A PROFESSIONAL CORPORATION
Lancaster, CA .... General Practice

COSGROVE, WEBB & OMAN
Topeka, KS .... General Practice

COSKEY & BALDRIDGE
Los Angeles, CA .... Commercial Law

COSTELLO COONEY & FEARON
Syracuse, NY .... Civil Trial Practice, General Practice

COSTELLO, MARSH & WARD
Greensburg, PA .... General Practice

COSTELLO, PORTER, HILL, HEISTERKAMP & BUSHNELL
Rapid City, SD .... Civil Trial Practice, General Practice

COSTELLO, SHEA & GAFFNEY
New York, NY .... Civil Trial Practice, Medical Malpractice Law, Personal Injury Law

COSTENBADER, FRANCIS J.
Nutley, NJ .... Probate and Estate Planning Law, Tax Law

COSTIGAN & WOLLRAB, P.C.
Bloomington, IL .... General Practice

COTICCHIO, ZOTTER, SULLIVAN, MOLTER, SKUPIN & TURNER, PROFESSIONAL CORPORATION
Detroit, MI .... Medical Malpractice Law, Personal Injury Law

COTKIN & COLLINS, A PROFESSIONAL CORPORATION
Los Angeles, CA .... General Practice
Santa Ana, CA .... General Practice

COTSIRILOS, JOHN G.
San Diego, CA .... Criminal Trial Practice

COTTINGHAM & PORTER, P.C.
Douglas, GA .... General Practice

COUCH, WHITE, BRENNER, HOWARD & FEIGENBAUM
Albany, NY .... General Practice

COUDERT BROTHERS
Washington, DC .... General Practice
New York, NY .... General Practice
Brussels, Belgium .... General Practice
London, England .... General Practice
Hong Kong, Hong Kong (British Crown Colony) .... General Practice
Tokyo, Japan .... General Practice
Singapore, Singapore .... General Practice

COUDERT FRÈRES
Paris, France .... General Practice

COUGHLAN, SEMMER & LIPMAN
San Diego, CA .... Civil Trial Practice, Criminal Trial Practice

COUGHLIN & GERHART
Binghamton, NY .... General Practice

COULOMBE KOTTKE & KING, A PROFESSIONAL CORPORATION
Costa Mesa, CA .... Appellate Practice, Banking Law, Business Law, Civil Trial Practice, Commercial Law, Construction Law, Real Estate Law, Securities Law

COULTER, FRASER, BOLTON, BIRD & VENTRE
Syracuse, NY .... General Practice

COUNCIL, BARADEL, KOSMERL & NOLAN, P.A.
Annapolis, MD ....General Practice

COURNOYER & ASSOCIATES, P.C.
Sudbury, MA ....Real Estate Law

COURTADE, A. DAVID, ATTY. AND COUN. AT LAW, A P.C.
Fort Worth, TX ....Family Law

COURTER, KOBERT, LAUFER & COHEN, P.A.
Hackettstown, NJ ....General Practice

COURTNEY, ROBIN S.
Columbia, TN ....Banking Law, Bankruptcy Law, Real Estate Law

COUSINEAU, MCGUIRE & ANDERSON, CHARTERED
Minneapolis, MN ....Insurance Defense Law

COUSINS AND JOHNSON
Stratford, CT ....Personal Injury Law

COUZENS, LANSKY, FEALK, ELLIS, ROEDER & LAZAR, P.C.
Farmington Hills, MI ....Bankruptcy Law, Business Law, Civil Trial Practice, Commercial Law, Tax Law

COVEY, ROBERTS, BUCHANAN & LONERGAN
Katonah, NY ....General Practice, Probate and Estate Planning Law

COVINGTON & CROWE
Ontario, CA ....General Practice

COWAN, DENNIS K.
Redding, CA ....Bankruptcy Law

COWAN, STUART M. LAW OFFICES OF
Honolulu, HI ....Product Liability Law

COWAN & OWEN, P.C.
Richmond, VA ....Civil Trial Practice, Insurance Defense Law

COWART, ROY N., P.C.
Warner Robins, GA ....General Practice

COWDREY, THOMPSON & KARSTEN, P.A.
Easton, MD ....General Practice

COWEN, CROWLEY & NORD, P.C.
Chicago, IL ....Business Law, Civil Trial Practice, Probate and Estate Planning Law

COWPERTHWAIT, LINDLEY M., JR., P.C.
Norristown, PA ....Civil Trial Practice, Commercial Law, Medical Malpractice Law, Personal Injury Law, Product Liability Law

COX, JAMES S. & ASSOCIATES
Memphis, TN ....Civil Trial Practice, Family Law, Personal Injury Law

COX & COX
Hemet, CA ....General Practice

COX, COX & STOKES, P.C.
Wellsboro, PA ....General Practice, Probate and Estate Planning Law

COX DOWNIE
Halifax, NS, Canada ....General Practice

COX & GOUDY
Minneapolis, MN ....Civil Trial Practice, Commercial Law, Personal Injury Law

COX, MUSTAIN-WOOD AND WALKER
Littleton, CO ....Family Law

COX & SMITH, INCORPORATED
San Antonio, TX ....Antitrust Law, Civil Trial Practice, General Practice, Labor and Employment Law, Natural Resources Law, Patent, Trademark, Copyright and Unfair Competition Law, Tax Law

COX, TAYLOR
Victoria, BC, Canada ....General Practice

COX, ZWERNER, GAMBILL & SULLIVAN
Terre Haute, IN ....Banking Law, Civil Trial Practice, General Practice, Insurance Defense Law, Probate and Estate Planning Law, Real Estate Law

COY, GILBERT & GILBERT
Richmond, KY ....Banking Law, General Practice, Personal Injury Law, Real Estate Law

COYLE, JOHN J., JR., P.C.
Phillipsburg, NJ ....Civil Trial Practice, Personal Injury Law, Product Liability Law

COZEN AND O'CONNOR, A PROFESSIONAL CORPORATION
Philadelphia, PA ....Civil Trial Practice, Commercial Law, General Practice, Insurance Defense Law, Personal Injury Law

CRABBE, BROWN, JONES, POTTS & SCHMIDT
Columbus, OH ....Civil Trial Practice, General Practice, Insurance Defense Law

CRABTREE & GOFORTH
London, KY ....General Practice, Insurance Defense Law

CRABTREE, SCHMIDT, ZEFF & JACOBS
Modesto, CA ....General Practice

CRAFT & MCGHEE, P.C.
Christiansburg, VA ....General Practice

CRAIG, RANDALL K. LAW OFFICES OF
Evansville, IN ....Business Law, Probate and Estate Planning Law, Tax Law

CRAIG & CRAIG
Mattoon, IL ....Civil Trial Practice, General Practice

CRAIG AND MACAULEY, PROFESSIONAL CORPORATION
Boston, MA ....Banking Law, Bankruptcy Law, Business Law, General Practice

CRAIGE, BRAWLEY, LIIPFERT, WALKER & SEARCY
Winston-Salem, NC ....General Practice, Probate and Estate Planning Law

CRAIGHILL & SMITH, P.A.
Charlotte, NC ....Insurance Defense Law

CRAMER & ANDERSON
Litchfield, CT ....General Practice
New Milford, CT ....General Practice

CRAMER, MULTHAUF & HAMMES
Waukesha, WI ....Civil Trial Practice, Commercial Law, General Practice, Personal Injury Law, Probate and Estate Planning Law, Real Estate Law, Tax Law

CRAMP, D'IORIO, MCCONCHIE AND FORBES, P.C.
Media, PA ....Commercial Law, General Practice, Personal Injury Law

CRANDALL & TRAVER
Palm Desert, CA ....Municipal and Zoning Law, Real Estate Law

CRANE, PAUL N.
Los Angeles, CA ....Real Estate Law

CRANE & KAHN
New Haven, CT ....Family Law

CRANE & MCCANN
Santa Monica, CA ....Business Law, Civil Trial Practice, Criminal Trial Practice, General Practice

CRANFILL, SUMNER & HARTZOG
Raleigh, NC ....Insurance Defense Law, Personal Injury Law

CRASSWELLER, MAGIE, ANDRESEN, HAAG & PACIOTTI, P.A.
Duluth, MN ....Banking Law, Civil Trial Practice, General Practice, Insurance Defense Law, Real Estate Law

CRAVATH, SWAINE & MOORE
New York, NY ....General Practice
London, England ....General Practice
Hong Kong, Hong Kong (British Crown Colony) ....General Practice

CRAWFORD, BACON, BANGS & BRIESEMEISTER, A PROFESSIONAL CORPORATION
West Covina, CA ....Construction Law

CRAWFORD, CRAWFORD & HUGHES
Uvalde, TX ....General Practice

CRAWFORD, CROWE & BAINBRIDGE, P.A.
Tulsa, OK ....Antitrust Law, Civil Trial Practice, Family Law, General Practice, Securities Law

CRAWFORD & MCKINNEY
Houston, TX ....Personal Injury Law

CRAWFORD, THOMAS M., P.S.C.
Louisville, KY ....General Practice

CRAWFORD, WILSON, RYAN & AGULNICK, P.C.
West Chester, PA ....Business Law, Civil Trial Practice, General Practice, Municipal and Zoning Law, Real Estate Law, Tax Law

CREEL & ATWOOD, A PROFESSIONAL CORPORATION
Dallas, TX ....Bankruptcy Law

CREMEN, FRANK J.
Las Vegas, NV ....Criminal Trial Practice

CRENSHAW, DUPREE & MILAM, L.L.P.
Lubbock, TX ....General Practice, Insurance Defense Law, Probate and Estate Planning Law

CRENSHAW, WARE AND MARTIN, P.L.C.
Norfolk, VA ....Admiralty/Maritime Law, Banking Law, Civil Trial Practice, General Practice, Real Estate Law

CREUTZ AND CREUTZ
Los Angeles, CA ....Probate and Estate Planning Law

CREW, BUCHANAN & LOWE
Dayton, OH ....Civil Trial Practice, Family Law, General Practice, Personal Injury Law, Real Estate Law

CRIBBS & MCFARLAND, A PROFESSIONAL CORPORATION
Arlington, TX ....General Practice

CRIDER, RONNIE G., P.A.
Clearwater, FL ....Criminal Trial Practice

CRISLIP, PHILIP, & ASSOCIATES
Memphis, TN ....General Practice

CRISPE & CRISPE
Brattleboro, VT ....Civil Trial Practice, General Practice, Personal Injury Law

CRISTE, VIRGINIA S. LAW OFFICES OF
Palm Desert, CA ....Family Law

CRISWELL & CRISWELL, INC. A PROFESSIONAL CORPORATION
Durant, OK ....General Practice

CRITCHFIELD, CRITCHFIELD & JOHNSTON
Wooster, OH ....General Practice

CRITELLI, NICHOLAS, ASSOCIATES, P.C.
Des Moines, IA ....Civil Trial Practice, Criminal Trial Practice, Personal Injury Law

CRITTENDEN & CRITTENDEN, P.A.
Winter Haven, FL ....General Practice

CROCKETT, DAVID G., P.C.
Atlanta, GA ....Bankruptcy Law, Civil Trial Practice, Commercial Law, Real Estate Law

CROCKETT & MYERS, LTD. A PROFESSIONAL CORPORATION
Las Vegas, NV ....Business Law, Criminal Trial Practice, General Practice, Personal Injury Law, Probate and Estate Planning Law

CROLEY, DAVIDSON & HUIE
Knoxville, TN ....Real Estate Law

CROMAN • GIBBS • SCHWARTZMAN
San Antonio, TX ....Probate and Estate Planning Law, Tax Law

CROMER, EAGLESFIELD & MAHER
Indianapolis, IN ....Environmental Law, Insurance Defense Law

CRONIN, FRIED, SEKIYA, KEKINA & FAIRBANKS, ATTORNEYS AT LAW, A LAW CORPORATION
Honolulu, HI ....Admiralty/Maritime Law, Medical Malpractice Law, Personal Injury Law, Product Liability Law

CRONIN & STANEWICH
Phoenix, AZ ....Insurance Defense Law, Personal Injury Law

CROSBY, GUENZEL, DAVIS, KESSNER & KUESTER
Lincoln, NE ....General Practice

CROSS, GADDIS, KIN, HERD & KELLY, P.C.
Colorado Springs, CO ....Civil Trial Practice, Family Law, Personal Injury Law, Probate and Estate Planning Law, Real Estate Law

CROSS, HARRY M., JR.
Missoula, MT ....Patent, Trademark, Copyright and Unfair Competition Law

CROSS, JENKS, MERCER AND MAFFEI
Baraboo, WI ....General Practice

CROSS, MURPHY, SMUCK & HOUSTON
Washington, DC ....Probate and Estate Planning Law, Tax Law

CROSSETT, EDGAR L., III, P.C.
Atlanta, GA ....Personal Injury Law

CROUCH, RICHARD E.
Arlington, VA ....Family Law

CROW AND CROW
Pomeroy, OH ....Civil Trial Practice, Criminal Trial Practice

CROW, REYNOLDS, PREYER AND SHETLEY
Kennett, MO ....General Practice, Insurance Defense Law

CROWDER & SCOGGINS, LTD.
Columbia, IL ....General Practice

CROWE & DUNLEVY, A PROFESSIONAL CORPORATION
Oklahoma City, OK ....Antitrust Law, Civil Trial Practice, General Practice, Labor and Employment Law, Municipal Bond/Public Authority Financing Law, Natural Resources Law, Tax Law

CROWE & SCOTT, A PROFESSIONAL ASSOCIATION
Phoenix, AZ ....Criminal Trial Practice

CROWELL & MORING
Irvine, CA ....General Practice
Washington, DC ....General Practice
London, England ....General Practice

CROWELL & OWENS
Alexandria, LA ....Business Law

CROWLEY, HAUGHEY, HANSON, TOOLE & DIETRICH
Billings, MT ....Administrative Law, Banking Law, Bankruptcy Law, Business Law, Civil Trial Practice, Commercial Law, Criminal Trial Practice, Employment Benefits Law, Environmental Law, Family Law, General Practice, Health Care Law, Immigration and Naturalization Law, Insurance Defense Law, Labor and Employment Law, Medical Malpractice Law, Municipal Bond/Public Authority Financing Law, Natural Resources Law, Personal Injury Law, Probate and Estate Planning Law, Product Liability Law, Public Utilities Law, Real Estate Law, Securities Law, Tax Law, Trademark, Copyright and Unfair Competition Law

CRUMLEY, JOHN W., P.C.
Fort Worth, TX ....General Practice, Probate and Estate Planning Law, Real Estate Law

CRUMMY, DEL DEO, DOLAN, GRIFFINGER & VECCHIONE
Brussels, Belgium ....General Practice
Newark, NJ ....Antitrust Law, Civil Trial Practice, Environmental Law, General Practice, Insurance Defense Law, Labor and Employment Law

CRUMPLER O'CONNOR & WYNNE
El Dorado, AR ....General Practice

CRUSE, SCOTT, HENDERSON & ALLEN, L.L.P.
Houston, TX ....Civil Trial Practice, Medical Malpractice Law

CUBBAGE, BENJAMIN C.
Henderson, KY ....Natural Resources Law

CUCCIO AND CUCCIO
Hackensack, NJ ....Civil Trial Practice, Commercial Law, Criminal Trial Practice, General Practice, Personal Injury Law

CUDDY BIXBY
Boston, MA ....Business Law, Civil Trial Practice, Family Law, General Practice, Labor and Employment Law, Probate and Estate Planning Law

CUDDY & FEDER
New York, NY ....Real Estate Law
White Plains, NY ....General Practice, Real Estate Law

CULBERTSON, THOMAS A.
Santa Ana, CA ....Civil Trial Practice

CULLEN, CARSNER, SEERDEN & CULLEN, L.L.P.
Victoria, TX ....General Practice, Insurance Defense Law, Medical Malpractice Law

CULLEN AND DYKMAN
Brooklyn, NY ....General Practice, Probate and Estate Planning Law
Garden City, NY ....Banking Law, General Practice

CULLEN LAW FIRM, LTD.
Minneapolis, MN ....Civil Trial Practice

CULP ELLIOTT & CARPENTER, P.L.L.C.
Charlotte, NC ....Business Law, Real Estate Law, Tax Law

CULP, GUTERSON & GRADER
Seattle, WA ....General Practice

CULVER, KNOWLTON, EVEN & FRANKS
Muskegon, MI ....General Practice

CUMMING, CUMMING & ESARY
Griffin, GA ....General Practice, Real Estate Law

CUMMING, HATCHETT, MOSCHEL, PATRICK & CLANCY, A PROFESSIONAL CORPORATION
Hampton, VA ....General Practice

CUMMINS, BERNARD F.
Martinez, CA ....General Practice

CUNNINGHAM, JOSEPH FRANCIS & ASSOCIATES
Washington, DC ....Civil Trial Practice

CUNNINGHAM, BLACKBURN, FRANCIS, BROCK & CUNNINGHAM
Grand Island, NE ....General Practice

CUNNINGHAM, BOUNDS, YANCE, CROWDER & BROWN
Mobile, AL ....Admiralty/Maritime Law, Civil Trial Practice, General Practice, Personal Injury Law, Product Liability Law

CUNNINGHAM DALMAN, P.C.
Holland, MI ....General Practice

CUNNINGHAM, JAMES P., P.C.
Phoenix, AZ ....Personal Injury Law

CUNNINGHAM LAW GROUP, P.A.
Tampa, FL ....Civil Trial Practice, General Practice, Personal Injury Law, Product Liability Law

CUNNINGHAM & MORGAN, PROFESSIONAL ASSOCIATION
Orlando, FL ....Personal Injury Law

CURRAN, DENNIS J.
Boston, MA....Civil Trial Practice, Personal Injury Law

CURRIE & KENDALL, P.C.
Midland, MI....Banking Law, Civil Trial Practice, General Practice, Real Estate Law, Tax Law

CURRY & SALZER
Toms River, NJ....General Practice

CURTIS, BRINCKERHOFF & BARRETT, P.C.
Stamford, CT....General Practice

CURTIS, MALLET-PREVOST, COLT & MOSLE
Washington, DC....General Practice
New York, NY....Civil Trial Practice, Criminal Trial Practice, General Practice, Tax Law
London, England ....General Practice
Paris, France....General Practice

CURTIS, MORRIS & SAFFORD, P.C.
New York, NY....Patent, Trademark, Copyright and Unfair Competition Law

CURTIS WILDE & NEAL LAW OFFICES
Oshkosh, WI....Civil Trial Practice, Labor and Employment Law, Personal Injury Law

CURTIS, ZAKLUKIEWICZ, VASILE, DEVINE & MCELHENNY
Merrick, NY....Civil Trial Practice
Riverhead, NY....Civil Trial Practice

CUSHMAN DARBY & CUSHMAN, L.L.P.
Washington, DC....Patent, Trademark, Copyright and Unfair Competition Law, Trademark, Copyright and Unfair Competition Law

CUSICK, MADDEN, JOYCE AND MCKAY
Sharon, PA ....General Practice, Insurance Defense Law

CUSTER & HILL, P.C.
Marietta, GA....Family Law, General Practice

CUTHBERT LAW OFFICES, A PROFESSIONAL CORPORATION
Petersburg, VA....Personal Injury Law

CUTLER, LAURENCE J.
Morristown, NJ....Family Law

CUTLER & STANFIELD
Washington, DC....Environmental Law

CUTRIGHT & CUTRIGHT
Chillicothe, OH ....General Practice, Probate and Estate Planning Law

CUYLER, BURK & MATTHEWS
Parsippany, NJ ....Civil Trial Practice, Insurance Defense Law

CYPERT, CROUCH, CLARK & HARWELL
Springdale, AR....Civil Trial Practice, General Practice

CYRIL & CROWLEY
San Francisco, CA ....Civil Trial Practice

DAAR & NEWMAN, PROFESSIONAL CORPORATION
Los Angeles, CA....General Practice

DAERR-BANNON, KATHLEEN L.
Philadelphia, PA ....Civil Trial Practice, Personal Injury Law

DAGUANNO AND ACCETTURA
Farmington Hills, MI....Business Law, Employment Benefits Law, Probate and Estate Planning Law, Tax Law

DAILEY, GARRETT C.
Oakland, CA ....Family Law

DAILY, WEST, CORE, COFFMAN & CANFIELD
Fort Smith, AR....Civil Trial Practice, General Practice, Insurance Defense Law

DALE & EKE, PROFESSIONAL CORPORATION
Indianapolis, IN ....Civil Trial Practice, Probate and Estate Planning Law, Real Estate Law, Tax Law

DALEIDEN, THOMPSON & TREMAINE, LTD.
Chicago, IL....General Practice

DALE & KLEIN, L.L.P.
McAllen, TX ....Civil Trial Practice, Insurance Defense Law

D'ALESSANDRO & JACOVINO
Florham Park, NJ ....General Practice

DALEY, BLACK & MOREIRA
Halifax, NS, Canada ....General Practice

DALEY, ERISMAN & VAN OGTROP
Wilmington, DE....Medical Malpractice Law, Personal Injury Law, Probate and Estate Planning Law, Real Estate Law

DALLER GREENBERG & DIETRICH
Fort Washington, PA....Civil Trial Practice, Insurance Defense Law, Product Liability Law

DALTON, TREASURE & MOWRER
Kennett, MO ....General Practice

DALY & LAVERY
Ossining, NY ....General Practice

D'AMATO & LYNCH
New York, NY....Civil Trial Practice, Insurance Defense Law

DAMON KEY BOCKEN LEONG KUPCHAK, ATTORNEYS AT LAW, A LAW CORPORATION
Honolulu, HI....General Practice, Immigration and Naturalization Law

DAMON & MOREY
Buffalo, NY ....General Practice

DAMRELL, NELSON, SCHRIMP, PALLIOS & LADINE, A PROFESSIONAL CORPORATION
Modesto, CA ....Civil Trial Practice, General Practice

DAMSEL & GELSTON, P.A.
West Palm Beach, FL ....Civil Trial Practice

DANAHER, JAMES T.
Palo Alto, CA ....Family Law

DANE, HENRY J. LAW OFFICE OF
Concord, MA ....Business Law, General Practice, Real Estate Law

DANFORTH, MEIERHENRY & MEIERHENRY
Sioux Falls, SD....Civil Trial Practice, Real Estate Law

D'ANGELO AND EURELL
Philadelphia, PA ....Civil Trial Practice, General Practice, Probate and Estate Planning Law

DANIEL & DANIEL
Columbia, SC ....General Practice

DANIEL, HARVILL, BATSON & NOLAN
Clarksville, TN....General Practice

DANIEL & KOMAREK, CHARTERED
Panama City, FL....Criminal Trial Practice

DANIEL, MCCAIN, BROWN, WALLACE & BRUBAKER, LLC
Brighton, CO....General Practice

DANIELS, BARATTA & FINE
Los Angeles, CA ....Appellate Practice, Civil Trial Practice, Construction Law, Insurance Defense Law

DANIELS, KASHTAN & FORNARIS, P.A.
Miami, FL ....Construction Law, Insurance Defense Law

DANN, DORFMAN, HERRELL AND SKILLMAN, A PROFESSIONAL CORPORATION
Philadelphia, PA ....Patent, Trademark, Copyright and Unfair Competition Law

DANNING, GILL, DIAMOND & KOLLITZ
Los Angeles, CA....Bankruptcy Law

DANO * MILLER * RIES
Moses Lake, WA....General Practice, Probate and Estate Planning Law

DANTIN & DANTIN
Columbia, MS ....General Practice

DANZIGER & MARKHOFF
White Plains, NY ....Probate and Estate Planning Law, Tax Law

DARBY & DARBY, PROFESSIONAL CORPORATION
New York, NY....Patent, Trademark, Copyright and Unfair Competition Law

DARBY, PEELE, BOWDOIN & PAYNE
Lake City, FL....General Practice

DARLING, HALL & RAE
Los Angeles, CA ....Probate and Estate Planning Law, Real Estate Law

DART, ADAMSON & DONOVAN
Salt Lake City, UT................Family Law

DASCHBACH, KELLY & COOPER, PROFESSIONAL ASSOCIATION
Lebanon, NH................General Practice

DASILVA & KEIDEL
Garden City, NY................Family Law

DAUGHERTY, FOWLER & PEREGRIN, A PROFESSIONAL CORPORATION
Oklahoma City, OK................Civil Trial Practice, Commercial Law

DAUGHTON, HAWKINS, BROCKELMAN, GUINAN & PATTERSON
Phoenix, AZ................Environmental Law, General Practice, Labor and Employment Law

DAUZAT, FALGOUST, CAVINESS, BIENVENU & STIPE
Opelousas, LA................Civil Trial Practice, General Practice, Insurance Defense Law, Product Liability Law, Real Estate Law

DAVENPORT, EVANS, HURWITZ & SMITH
Sioux Falls, SD................Banking Law, Bankruptcy Law, Business Law, Civil Trial Practice, General Practice, Insurance Defense Law, Personal Injury Law, Real Estate Law, Tax Law

DAVENPORT, FILES & KELLY
Monroe, LA................Criminal Trial Practice, General Practice, Insurance Defense Law

DAVID & HAGNER, P.C.
Washington, DC................General Practice

DAVIDSON, CALHOUN & MILLER, P.C.
Columbus, GA................Banking Law, General Practice, Probate and Estate Planning Law, Tax Law

DAVIDSON, HORNE & HOLLINGSWORTH, A PROFESSIONAL ASSOCIATION
Little Rock, AR................Civil Trial Practice, General Practice

DAVIDSON, MEAUX, SONNIER, MCELLIGOTT & SWIFT
Lafayette, LA................Civil Trial Practice, General Practice, Insurance Defense Law

DAVIDSON & TROILO, A PROFESSIONAL CORPORATION
San Antonio, TX................General Practice

DAVIDSON, WIGGINS & CROWDER, P.C.
Tuscaloosa, AL................Civil Trial Practice, General Practice, Insurance Defense Law

DAVID, THOMAS L., P.A.
Miami, FL................General Practice

DAVIES, CANTRELL, HUMPHREYS & MCCOY
Nashville, TN................General Practice

DAVIES MCFARLAND & CARROLL, P.C.
Pittsburgh, PA................Civil Trial Practice, General Practice, Insurance Defense Law, Medical Malpractice Law

DAVIES, WARD & BECK
Toronto, ON, Canada................General Practice, Tax Law

DAVIS, STEPHEN J.
Minneapolis, MN................Real Estate Law

DAVIS, ARNEIL, DORSEY, KIGHT & PARLETTE
Wenatchee, WA................General Practice

DAVIS, BEALL, MCGUIRE & THOMPSON, CHARTERED
Leavenworth, KS................General Practice

DAVIS, BROWNING & SCHNITKER
Madison, FL................General Practice

DAVIS, BUJOLD & STRECK, PROFESSIONAL ASSOCIATION
Manchester, NH................Patent, Trademark, Copyright and Unfair Competition Law

DAVIS AND CANNON
Cheyenne, WY................General Practice
Sheridan, WY................Civil Trial Practice, General Practice, Insurance Defense Law, Natural Resources Law

DAVIS & COMPANY
Vancouver, BC, Canada................General Practice

DAVIS, COX & WRIGHT
Fayetteville, AR................Civil Trial Practice, General Practice

DAVIS & DAVIS, P.C.
Austin, TX................Administrative Law, Business Law, General Practice, Health Care Law, Insurance Defense Law, Labor and Employment Law, Medical Malpractice Law, Probate and Estate Planning Law, Real Estate Law

DAVIS, DAVIS & KAAR
Milton, PA................General Practice

DAVIS, DONNELL, WORRALL & BANCROFT, P.C.
Worland, WY................Business Law

DAVIS AND FAJEN, P.C.
Ann Arbor, MI................Civil Trial Practice, General Practice, Medical Malpractice Law, Personal Injury Law, Product Liability Law

DAVIS, GRAHAM & STUBBS, L.L.C.
Denver, CO................General Practice
Washington, DC................General Practice

DAVIS, GREGORY, CHRISTY & FOREHAND
Cordele, GA................General Practice
Vienna, GA................General Practice

DAVIS & HARMAN
Washington, DC................Administrative Law

DAVIS, HOCKENBERG, WINE, BROWN, KOEHN & SHORS, P.C.
Des Moines, IA................General Practice, Patent, Trademark, Copyright and Unfair Competition Law, Tax Law

DAVIS, HOWARD M., P.C.
West Orange, NJ................General Practice

DAVIS HOXIE FAITHFULL & HAPGOOD
New York, NY................International Business Law, Patent, Trademark, Copyright and Unfair Competition Law

DAVIS & KUELTHAU, S.C.
Milwaukee, WI................Admiralty/Maritime Law, Business Law, Environmental Law, Labor and Employment Law, Municipal Bond/Public Authority Financing Law, Probate and Estate Planning Law, Real Estate Law, Tax Law

DAVIS & LOWE, P.C.
Phoenix, AZ................Bankruptcy Law

DAVIS, MATTHEWS & QUIGLEY, P.C.
Atlanta, GA................Civil Trial Practice, Family Law, General Practice, Real Estate Law, Tax Law

DAVIS & MURPHY
Westminster, MD................General Practice

DAVIS, MURRELLE & LUMSDEN, P.A.
Beaufort, NC................Admiralty/Maritime Law, Civil Trial Practice, Personal Injury Law

DAVIS POLK & WARDWELL
Washington, DC................General Practice
New York, NY................General Practice
London, England................General Practice
Paris, France................General Practice

DAVIS, PUNELLI, KEATHLEY & WILLARD
Newport Beach, CA................Business Law, Civil Trial Practice, Environmental Law, General Practice, Real Estate Law

DAVIS, REBERKENNY & ABRAMOWITZ, A PROFESSIONAL CORPORATION
Cherry Hill, NJ................Bankruptcy Law, Public Utilities Law

DAVIS, STURGES & TOMLINSON
Louisburg, NC................General Practice

DAVIS & TAFF
Tallahassee, FL................Banking Law, Civil Trial Practice, Personal Injury Law

DAVIS, TUPPER, GRIMSLEY & SEELHOFF
Beaufort, SC................Insurance Defense Law, Medical Malpractice Law, Product Liability Law, Real Estate Law

DAVIS, UNREIN, HUMMER, MCCALLISTER & BUCK
Topeka, KS................Civil Trial Practice, General Practice, Insurance Defense Law, Personal Injury Law

DAVIS & WEINSTEIN
Denver, CO................Construction Law, Family Law, Real Estate Law

DAVIS & WILKERSON, P.C.
Austin, TX................Civil Trial Practice, Health Care Law, Insurance Defense Law, Labor and Employment Law, Medical Malpractice Law

DAVIS WRIGHT TREMAINE
Bellevue, WA................General Practice
Seattle, WA................General Practice

DAVIS AND YOUNG CO., L.P.A.
Cleveland, OH................General Practice, Insurance Defense Law

DAY, DAVID F.
Honolulu, HI................Business Law, International Business Law

DAY, BERRY & HOWARD
Hartford, CT..........Antitrust Law, General Practice
Stamford, CT..........General Practice
Boston, MA..........General Practice

DAY, EDWARDS, FEDERMAN, PROPESTER & CHRISTENSEN, P.C.
Oklahoma City, OK..........Banking Law, Bankruptcy Law, Business Law, Civil Trial Practice, Commercial Law, Construction Law, Environmental Law, General Practice, Health Care Law, Insurance Defense Law, International Business Law, Labor and Employment Law, Natural Resources Law, Real Estate Law, Securities Law

DAY, KETTERER, RALEY, WRIGHT & RYBOLT
Canton, OH..........Business Law, General Practice, Insurance Defense Law

DAY & SAWDEY, A PROFESSIONAL CORPORATION
Grand Rapids, MI..........Bankruptcy Law, Civil Trial Practice, Commercial Law, Construction Law, Environmental Law, Real Estate Law

DAY SWANGO BRATTAIN & NATTKEMPER
Terre Haute, IN..........General Practice

DEAN, DEAN, SEGAR, HART & SHULMAN, P.C.
Flint, MI..........Civil Trial Practice, General Practice, Labor and Employment Law

DEAN & GIBSON
Charlotte, NC..........Insurance Defense Law

DEAN, GIBSON, II, P.C.
Buford, GA..........General Practice

DEANER, DEANER, SCANN, CURTAS & MALAN
Las Vegas, NV..........General Practice, Real Estate Law

DEARTH, MARKHAM & JACK, CHARTERED
Parsons, KS..........General Practice

DEASEY, MAHONEY, BENDER & MCKENNA, LTD.
Philadelphia, PA..........Insurance Defense Law

DEASON, CHARLES A. JR.
El Paso, TX..........Medical Malpractice Law, Personal Injury Law

DEATON & DAVISON, INC.
Ada, OK..........General Practice, Insurance Defense Law

DEBEVOISE & PLIMPTON
Los Angeles, CA..........General Practice
Washington, DC..........General Practice
New York, NY..........Banking Law, Civil Trial Practice, General Practice, Tax Law, Trademark, Copyright and Unfair Competition Law
London, England..........General Practice
Paris, France..........General Practice
Hong Kong, Hong Kong (British Crown Colony)..........General Practice
Budapest, Hungary..........General Practice

DEBLASIO & ALTON, P.C.
New York, NY..........Civil Trial Practice, Medical Malpractice Law, Personal Injury Law

DEBRUYN, JOHN LAW OFFICES
Denver, CO..........Probate and Estate Planning Law, Tax Law

DEBUS & KAZAN, LTD.
Phoenix, AZ..........Criminal Trial Practice, Personal Injury Law

DECHERT PRICE & RHOADS
Washington, DC..........General Practice
Boston, MA..........General Practice
Princeton, NJ..........General Practice
New York, NY..........General Practice
Harrisburg, PA..........General Practice
Philadelphia, PA..........General Practice
Brussels, Belgium..........General Practice
London, England..........General Practice

DECKELBAUM OGENS & FISCHER, CHARTERED
Washington, DC..........Bankruptcy Law, Civil Trial Practice, Family Law
Bethesda, MD..........Bankruptcy Law, Civil Trial Practice, Family Law

DECKER & GUNTA, S.C.
Milwaukee, WI..........Construction Law

DECOCQ, PAUL L.
Howell, MI..........General Practice

DECOF & GRIMM, A PROFESSIONAL CORPORATION
Providence, RI..........Commercial Law, Medical Malpractice Law, Personal Injury Law

DEEGAN, DONALD E., LAW FIRM OF
Hempstead, NY..........General Practice

DEENER, FEINGOLD & STERN, A PROFESSIONAL CORPORATION
Hackensack, NJ..........Administrative Law, Business Law, General Practice, Probate and Estate Planning Law, Tax Law

DEEP & WOMACK
Henderson, KY..........Civil Trial Practice, General Practice, Insurance Defense Law

DEETH WILLIAMS WALL
Toronto, ON, Canada..........Patent, Trademark, Copyright and Unfair Competition Law

DEFINO, MICHAEL G.
Media, PA..........Civil Trial Practice

DEFOREST & KOSCELNIK
Pittsburgh, PA..........Civil Trial Practice, Commercial Law, Labor and Employment Law

DE GRANDPRÉ, GODIN
Montreal, QU, Canada..........General Practice

DE GROOT, KELLER & VINCENT
Grand Rapids, MI..........Bankruptcy Law, Commercial Law, Personal Injury Law

DEGUERIN & DICKSON
Houston, TX..........Criminal Trial Practice

DEHNER & ELLIS
Morehead, KY..........Banking Law, Insurance Defense Law, Probate and Estate Planning Law

DEITCH & HAMILTON, A PROFESSIONAL CORPORATION
Austin, TX..........Civil Trial Practice, Commercial Law

DEKLE, PATRICK H., P.A.
Tampa, FL..........Civil Trial Practice, Personal Injury Law

DE LA GARZA, BILL, & ASSOCIATES, P.C.
Houston, TX..........Family Law, Real Estate Law

DELANEY, FRANK G.
Corpus Christi, TX..........Real Estate Law

DELANEY & BALCOMB, P.C.
Glenwood Springs, CO..........General Practice

DELANEY, WILES, HAYES, REITMAN & BRUBAKER, INC.
Anchorage, AK..........General Practice

DE LA PARTE, GILBERT & BALES, PROFESSIONAL ASSOCIATION
Tampa, FL..........Environmental Law

DEL SOLE & DEL SOLE
New Haven, CT..........Civil Trial Practice

DEL TORO & SANTANA
San Juan, PR..........Commercial Law, General Practice

DEMARIA, ELLIS, HUNT, SALSBERG & FRIEDMAN
Newark, NJ..........Bankruptcy Law, Civil Trial Practice, Commercial Law, Environmental Law, General Practice, Labor and Employment Law

DEMARS, GORDON, OLSON, RECKNOR & SHIVELY
Lincoln, NE..........Business Law, General Practice, Insurance Defense Law

DE MARTINO FINKELSTEIN ROSEN & VIRGA
Washington, DC..........Business Law, Securities Law

DEMERSSEMAN JENSEN
Rapid City, SD..........General Practice

DEMETRIOU, DEL GUERCIO, SPRINGER & MOYER
Los Angeles, CA..........Business Law, Civil Trial Practice, Environmental Law, Natural Resources Law, Probate and Estate Planning Law, Real Estate Law

DEMING, HUGHEY, LEWIS, ALLEN & CHAPMAN, P.C.
Kalamazoo, MI..........Business Law, Commercial Law, Environmental Law, General Practice, Personal Injury Law, Probate and Estate Planning Law, Real Estate Law

DEMPSEY & ASSOCIATES, P.A.
Orlando, FL..........Antitrust Law, Civil Trial Practice, Construction Law, Criminal Trial Practice, Labor and Employment Law

DEMUTH & KEMP
Denver, CO..........General Practice

DENARDIS, MCCANDLESS & MULLER, P.C.
Detroit, MI..........Business Law, Civil Trial Practice, Medical Malpractice Law, Personal Injury Law, Product Liability Law

DENFIELD, TIMMER, JAMO & O'LEARY
Lansing, MI..........Civil Trial Practice, General Practice, Insurance Defense Law, Medical Malpractice Law, Personal Injury Law

DENISSEN, KRANZUSH, MAHONEY & EWALD, S.C.
Green Bay, WI ....Civil Trial Practice, Insurance Defense Law

DENIUS, FRANKLIN W.
Austin, TX ....Civil Trial Practice

DENLINGER, ROSENTHAL & GREENBERG
Cincinnati, OH ....Labor and Employment Law

DENMEAD & MALONEY
Columbus, OH ....Civil Trial Practice, General Practice, Personal Injury Law

DENNIS, DAN E.
Anchorage, AK ....Criminal Trial Practice

DENNIS, CORRY, PORTER & GRAY
Atlanta, GA ....Civil Trial Practice, Insurance Defense Law, Personal Injury Law, Transportation Law

DENTON & AXLEY, A PROFESSIONAL CORPORATION
Dallas, TX...............................Real Estate Law

DENTON & CARY
Bolivar, TN ....General Practice

DENTON & DENTON, LTD.
Las Vegas, NV ....Civil Trial Practice

DE ORCHIS & PARTNERS
New York, NY........................Admiralty/Maritime Law

DEPEW & GILLEN
Wichita, KS ....Civil Trial Practice, Environmental Law, General Practice, Insurance Defense Law, Personal Injury Law

DERR, DAILEY J., P.A.
Durham, NC ....Construction Law

DESHAZO, GARY F. & ASSOCIATES
Austin, TX ....Civil Trial Practice

DESJARDINS DUCHARME STEIN MONAST
Montreal, QU, Canada ....General Practice
Quebec, QU, Canada ....General Practice

DESTEFANO & WARREN, P.C.
Philadelphia, PA ....Civil Trial Practice, Criminal Trial Practice

DESTRIBATS, CAMPBELL, DESANTIS & MAGEE
Trenton, NJ ....Civil Trial Practice, Medical Malpractice Law

DETISCH, CHRISTENSEN & WOOD
San Diego, CA ....Business Law, Civil Trial Practice, Construction Law, Real Estate Law

DETWEILER, ROBERT A.
Swarthmore, PA......................Civil Trial Practice, Probate and Estate Planning Law

DEUSCHLE AND ASSOCIATES, P.A.
Fort Lauderdale, FL ....General Practice

DEUTSCH & BLUMBERG, P.A.
Miami, FL...............................Civil Trial Practice, Medical Malpractice Law, Personal Injury Law, Product Liability Law

DEUTSCH, KERRIGAN & STILES
New Orleans, LA.....................Admiralty/Maritime Law, Antitrust Law, Commercial Law, Construction Law, Environmental Law, General Practice, Insurance Defense Law, Labor and Employment Law, Tax Law

DEUTSCH, LEVY & ENGEL, CHARTERED
Chicago, IL.............................Civil Trial Practice, General Practice, Probate and Estate Planning Law, Real Estate Law, Tax Law

DEUTSCH & RUBIN
Los Angeles, CA ....Family Law

DEUTSCH WILLIAMS BROOKS DERENSIS HOLLAND & DRACHMAN, P.C.
Boston, MA.............................Civil Trial Practice
Nantucket, MA........................Civil Trial Practice

DEVEAU, COLTON & MARQUIS
Atlanta, GA ....Patent, Trademark, Copyright and Unfair Competition Law

DE VINE & KOHN
Southfield, MI ....Business Law, Construction Law, Tax Law

DEVINE, MILLIMET & BRANCH, PROFESSIONAL ASSOCIATION
Manchester, NH......................General Practice

DEVITT & THISTLE, P.A.
Delray Beach, FL....................Probate and Estate Planning Law

DEVLIN, CITTADINO & SHAW, P.C.
Trenton, NJ ....Medical Malpractice Law, Personal Injury Law

DEVLIN, JOHN GERARD, & ASSOCIATES, P.C.
Philadelphia, PA ....Environmental Law, Insurance Defense Law, Transportation Law

DEWEY BALLANTINE
Washington, DC.....................General Practice
New York, NY........................General Practice, Municipal Bond/Public Authority Financing Law

DEWITT ROSS & STEVENS, S.C.
Madison, WI ....General Practice, Patent, Trademark, Copyright and Unfair Competition Law

DEWOLF, WARD, O'DONNELL & HOOFMAN, P.A.
Orlando, FL ....Civil Trial Practice, General Practice

DEYOE, HEISSENBUTTEL & MATTIA
Wayne, NJ...............................Civil Trial Practice, Environmental Law, Family Law, General Practice, Insurance Defense Law, Medical Malpractice Law, Personal Injury Law, Product Liability Law

DIAMOND AND DIAMOND
South Bend, IN ....Business Law, General Practice

DIAMOND, HASSER & FROST
Mobile, AL..............................Admiralty/Maritime Law, Personal Injury Law, Product Liability Law

DIAMOND RASH GORDON & JACKSON, P.C.
El Paso, TX.............................General Practice, Municipal Bond/Public Authority Financing Law, Public Utilities Law

DIAMOND, STUART & CLOVER
Shawnee, OK ....Banking Law, General Practice

DICE, MICHAEL R., AND COMPANY, L.L.C.
Denver, CO ....Probate and Estate Planning Law

DICK & DICK
The Dalles, OR ....General Practice

DICKENSON, MURDOCH, REX AND SLOAN, CHARTERED
Boca Raton, FL ....Probate and Estate Planning Law, Real Estate Law

DICKERSON, DICKERSON, LIEBERMAN & CONSUL
Las Vegas, NV ....Civil Trial Practice, Family Law

DICKERSON, RICE, SPAETH, HEISSERER & SUMMERS, L.C.
Cape Girardeau, MO ....Business Law, Civil Trial Practice

DICKEY, H. ELDRIDGE JR.
Fort Worth, TX ....Business Law, Probate and Estate Planning Law, Tax Law

DICK AND HARRIS
Chicago, IL..............................Patent, Trademark, Copyright and Unfair Competition Law, Trademark, Copyright and Unfair Competition Law

DICKIE, MCCAMEY & CHILCOTE, A PROFESSIONAL CORPORATION
Pittsburgh, PA ....Antitrust Law, Business Law, Civil Trial Practice, Criminal Trial Practice, Environmental Law, General Practice, Insurance Defense Law, International Business Law, Medical Malpractice Law, Patent, Trademark, Copyright and Unfair Competition Law, Probate and Estate Planning Law, Securities Law, Tax Law

DICKINSON & GIBBONS, P.A.
Sarasota, FL ....Civil Trial Practice, General Practice, Insurance Defense Law, Medical Malpractice Law

DICKINSON, MACKAMAN, TYLER & HAGEN, P.C.
Des Moines, IA ....Antitrust Law, Banking Law, General Practice, Labor and Employment Law, Probate and Estate Planning Law, Real Estate Law, Tax Law

DICKINSON, WRIGHT, MOON, VAN DUSEN & FREEMAN
Washington, DC......................General Practice, Patent, Trademark, Copyright and Unfair Competition Law
Chicago, IL..............................General Practice
Bloomfield Hills, MI ....General Practice
Detroit, MI..............................Antitrust Law, Banking Law, Bankruptcy Law, Civil Trial Practice, Environmental Law, General Practice, Immigration and Naturalization Law, Insurance Defense Law, International Business Law, Labor and Employment Law, Municipal Bond/Public Authority Financing Law, Patent, Trademark, Copyright and Unfair Competition Law, Probate and Estate Planning Law, Product Liability Law, Real Estate Law, Tax Law
Grand Rapids, MI ....General Practice, Labor and Employment Law
Lansing, MI.............................General Practice

DICKSON, CARLSON & CAMPILLO
Santa Monica, CA...................Civil Trial Practice, Construction Law, General Practice, Insurance Defense Law, Medical Malpractice Law, Personal Injury Law

DIEHL & CLAYTON
Newton, IA ....General Practice

DIEHL, STEINHEIMER, RIGGIO, HAYDEL & MORDAUNT, A PROFESSIONAL LAW CORPORATION
Stockton, CA..........................Civil Trial Practice, General Practice

DIEPENBROCK & COSTA
Sacramento, CA......................Environmental Law, Insurance Defense Law

DIEPENBROCK LAW FIRM, THE, A PROFESSIONAL CORPORATION
Sacramento, CA......................General Practice

DIEPENBROCK, WULFF, PLANT & HANNEGAN
Sacramento, CA......................Business Law, Civil Trial Practice

DIETRICH, ZODY, HOWARD & VANDERROEST, P.C.
Kalamazoo, MI........................Civil Trial Practice, Commercial Law, Insurance Defense Law, Probate and Estate Planning Law

DIKE, BRONSTEIN, ROBERTS & CUSHMAN
Boston, MA.............................Patent, Trademark, Copyright and Unfair Competition Law, Trademark, Copyright and Unfair Competition Law

DIKMAN AND DIKMAN
Jamaica, NY............................Family Law

DILLARD AND KATONA
Tappahannock, VA.................General Practice

DILLON, MCCANDLESS & KING
Butler, PA...............................General Practice

DILL & SHOWLER
Redlands, CA..........................General Practice

DILWORTH, PAXSON, KALISH & KAUFFMAN
Harrisburg, PA.......................General Practice
Philadelphia, PA.....................General Practice, Municipal Bond/Public Authority Financing Law, Tax Law

DIMOCK & ASSOCIATES
Toronto, ON, Canada.............Patent, Trademark, Copyright and Unfair Competition Law

DINSE, ERDMANN & CLAPP
Burlington, VT.......................General Practice

DINSMORE & SHOHL
Cincinnati, OH........................Administrative Law, Admiralty/Maritime Law, Antitrust Law, Banking Law, Bankruptcy Law, Business Law, Civil Trial Practice, Construction Law, Criminal Trial Practice, Employment Benefits Law, Environmental Law, General Practice, Health Care Law, Immigration and Naturalization Law, Insurance Defense Law, Labor and Employment Law, Medical Malpractice Law, Municipal and Zoning Law, Patent, Trademark, Copyright and Unfair Competition Law, Personal Injury Law, Probate and Estate Planning Law, Product Liability Law, Real Estate Law, Tax Law

DIORIO & FALZONE
Media, PA...............................Civil Trial Practice, Personal Injury Law

DIPPEL, C. CHARLES
Houston, TX...........................Appellate Practice, Civil Trial Practice

DI RENZO AND BOMIER
Neenah, WI.............................Business Law, General Practice, Insurance Defense Law

DISE & GUREWITZ, P.C.
Detroit, MI.............................Appellate Practice, Civil Trial Practice, Criminal Trial Practice, Insurance Defense Law

DITTMER, WOHLUST & WILKINS, P.A.
Maitland, FL..........................Probate and Estate Planning Law

DIVER, GRACH, QUADE & MASINI
Waukegan, IL..........................Civil Trial Practice, General Practice, Personal Injury Law

DIVINE, WILKIN, RAULERSON & FIELDS
Albany, GA.............................General Practice

DIXON, SMITH & STAHL
Fairfax, VA............................Construction Law, Real Estate Law

DOAR, DRILL & SKOW, S.C.
New Richmond, WI................Civil Trial Practice, Personal Injury Law

DOBKIN, JOSEPH MARTIN
Miami, FL..............................Criminal Trial Practice

DOBSON, CHRISTENSEN & BROWN, P.A.
St. Augustine, FL...................Commercial Law

DODD, LESSACK, RANANDO & DALTON, L.L.C.
Cheshire, CT..........................Civil Trial Practice, Personal Injury Law

DODDS, KIDD, RYAN & MOORE
Little Rock, AR......................Personal Injury Law

DODD & TURNER, P.C.
Valdosta, GA..........................Civil Trial Practice, Criminal Trial Practice

DODGE, DAVID A., P.C.
Grand Rapids, MI..................Criminal Trial Practice

DOERING, STEVEN B.
Garnett, KS............................General Practice

DOERNER, STUART, SAUNDERS, DANIEL & ANDERSON
Tulsa, OK...............................General Practice, Labor and Employment Law, Natural Resources Law, Securities Law

DOHENY & DOHENY
St. Louis, MO.........................General Practice

DOHERTY, MARY CUSHING
Norristown, PA.......................Family Law

DOHERTY, SHERIDAN & GRIMALDI, L.L.P.
Fairfax, VA............................Insurance Defense Law

DOHERTY, WALLACE, PILLSBURY AND MURPHY, P.C.
Springfield, MA......................General Practice

DOLACK HANSLER FIRM, THE, A PROFESSIONAL SERVICES CORPORATION
Tacoma, WA...........................General Practice

DOLD, SPATH & MCKELVIE, P.C.
Grosse Pointe, MI..................General Practice
Troy, MI.................................General Practice

DOLE, COALWELL, CLARK & WELLS, P.C.
Roseburg, OR.........................Civil Trial Practice, General Practice

DOLIN, NORMAN M.
Los Angeles, CA.....................Family Law

DOLLINGER, GONSKI, GROSSMAN, PERMUT & HIRSCHHORN
Carle Place, NY.....................Civil Trial Practice, General Practice, Real Estate Law

DOMENGEAUX, WRIGHT, MOROUX & ROY, A PROFESSIONAL LAW CORPORATION
Lafayette, LA.........................Admiralty/Maritime Law, Antitrust Law, Civil Trial Practice, Personal Injury Law, Product Liability Law

DOMINA & COPPLE, P.C.
Norfolk, NE...........................Banking Law, Civil Trial Practice, Insurance Defense Law, Personal Injury Law

DOMINICK, FLETCHER, YEILDING, WOOD & LLOYD, P.A.
Birmingham, AL.....................Civil Trial Practice, General Practice, Real Estate Law, Tax Law

DOMINIK, STEIN, SACCOCIO, REESE, COLITZ & VAN DER WALL
Miami, FL..............................Patent, Trademark, Copyright and Unfair Competition Law
Tampa, FL..............................Patent, Trademark, Copyright and Unfair Competition Law

DONAHOO, DONAHOO & BALL, P.A.
Jacksonville, FL.....................Real Estate Law, Tax Law

DONAHUE & DONAHUE, ATTORNEYS, P.C.
Lowell, MA............................General Practice, Insurance Defense Law

DONAHUE LAMBERT & WOOD
Sacramento, CA.....................Civil Trial Practice

DONAU & BOLT
Tucson, AZ............................Criminal Trial Practice, Family Law

DONNELLY, DANIEL
New York, NY.......................Civil Trial Practice, Personal Injury Law, Product Liability Law

DONNELLY, BALDWIN AND WILHITE, P.C.
Lebanon, MO.........................General Practice

DONOHUE, SABO, VARLEY & ARMSTRONG, P.C.
Albany, NY............................Civil Trial Practice, Construction Law, General Practice, Insurance Defense Law

DONOVAN, MARTIN K.
Providence, RI.......................Civil Trial Practice, General Practice, Insurance Defense Law, Personal Injury Law

DONOVAN & DESJARDINS, P.C.
Lancaster, NH........................General Practice

DONOVAN LEISURE NEWTON & IRVINE
Washington, DC.....................General Practice
New York, NY........................General Practice
Paris, France..........................General Practice

DONOVAN & ROBERTS, P.C.
Wheaton, IL .... Civil Trial Practice, General Practice, Personal Injury Law

DONOVAN, ROSE, NESTER & SZEWCZYK, P.C.
Belleville, IL .... Civil Trial Practice, General Practice, Insurance Defense Law

DORAMUS & TRAUGER
Nashville, TN .... Business Law, Civil Trial Practice

DORAN BLACKMOND READY HAMILTON & WILLIAMS
South Bend, IN .... Civil Trial Practice, Commercial Law, Environmental Law, Insurance Defense Law

DOREMUS, JONES AND SMITH, P.C.
Metter, GA .... General Practice

DORF & DORF, A PROFESSIONAL CORPORATION
Rahway, NJ .... Labor and Employment Law

DORITY & MANNING, P.A.
Greenville, SC .... Patent, Trademark, Copyright and Unfair Competition Law

DORN, MCEACHRAN, JAMBOR & KEATING
Chicago, IL .... Patent, Trademark, Copyright and Unfair Competition Law

DORR, BAIRD AND LIGHTNER, A PROFESSIONAL CORPORATION
Springfield, MO .... Civil Trial Practice, Insurance Defense Law

DORR, CARSON, SLOAN & PETERSON, P.C.
Denver, CO .... Patent, Trademark, Copyright and Unfair Competition Law, Trademark, Copyright and Unfair Competition Law

DORSEY & WHITNEY
Minneapolis, MN .... General Practice

DORTCH, WRIGHT & WRIGHT
Gadsden, AL .... Civil Trial Practice, General Practice

DÖSER AMERELLER NOACK
Berlin, Germany .... General Practice
Frankfurt/Main, Germany .... General Practice

DOSLAND, NORDHOUGEN, LILLEHAUG & JOHNSON, P.A.
Moorhead, MN .... Commercial Law, General Practice, Insurance Defense Law, Real Estate Law

DOSS, OWEN L., P.C.
Chicago, IL .... Family Law

DOTY & SHAPIRO, P.C.
Boulder, CO .... Business Law, Probate and Estate Planning Law

DOUGHERTY, HESSIN, BEAVERS & GILBERT, A PROFESSIONAL CORPORATION
Oklahoma City, OK .... Patent, Trademark, Copyright and Unfair Competition Law

DOUGHERTY & HILDRE
San Diego, CA .... Admiralty/Maritime Law, Personal Injury Law, Product Liability Law

DOUGLAS, ALEXA, KOEPPEN & HURLEY
Valparaiso, IN .... Civil Trial Practice, General Practice, Personal Injury Law, Probate and Estate Planning Law, Real Estate Law

DOUGLAS & DOUGLAS
Concord, NH .... Civil Trial Practice

DOUGLAS, DOUGLAS & DOUGLAS
Carlisle, PA .... Civil Trial Practice, General Practice, Insurance Defense Law, Personal Injury Law

DOUMAR, CURTIS, CROSS, LAYSTROM & PERLOFF
Fort Lauderdale, FL .... Commercial Law, General Practice, Municipal Bond/Public Authority Financing Law

DOVER & DIXON, P.A.
Little Rock, AR .... General Practice

DOW, COGBURN & FRIEDMAN, P.C.
Houston, TX .... Real Estate Law

DOW, LOHNES & ALBERTSON
Washington, DC .... Antitrust Law, Communications Law, General Practice, Tax Law

DOWD & DOWD, LTD.
Chicago, IL .... Appellate Practice, Civil Trial Practice, Insurance Defense Law, Product Liability Law

DOWDING, PHILLIPS M.
Newport News, VA .... Civil Trial Practice, Insurance Defense Law, Personal Injury Law

DOWDY, T. WILLIAM
Springfield, VA .... Real Estate Law

DOWLING LAW FIRM, P.A.
Beaufort, SC .... Civil Trial Practice, General Practice

DOWLING, MAGARIAN, AARON & HEYMAN, INCORPORATED
Fresno, CA .... Bankruptcy Law, Business Law, Civil Trial Practice, Commercial Law, Employment Benefits Law, Environmental Law, Family Law, General Practice, Health Care Law, Insurance Defense Law, Labor and Employment Law, Probate and Estate Planning Law, Real Estate Law, Tax Law

DOWNEY, BRAND, SEYMOUR & ROHWER
Sacramento, CA .... Bankruptcy Law, Environmental Law, General Practice, Natural Resources Law

DOWNEY & CLEVELAND
Marietta, GA .... Civil Trial Practice, General Practice, Insurance Defense Law, Medical Malpractice Law, Personal Injury Law

DOWNING & MEHRTENS, P.C.
New York, NY .... Insurance Defense Law

DOWNING, RICHARD C., P.A.
Little Rock, AR .... Business Law, Real Estate Law, Securities Law

DOYLE, GARTLAND, NELSON & MCCLEERY, P.C.
Eugene, OR .... General Practice

DOYLE & HARRIS, A PROFESSIONAL CORPORATION
Tulsa, OK .... Antitrust Law, Civil Trial Practice, Securities Law

DOYLE, LEWIS & WARNER
Toledo, OH .... Civil Trial Practice, General Practice, Insurance Defense Law, Probate and Estate Planning Law, Real Estate Law, Transportation Law

DOYLE & NELSON
Augusta, ME .... General Practice

DRAGER, O'BRIEN, ANDERSON, BURGY & GARBOWICZ
Eagle River, WI .... General Practice

DRANOFF & JOHNSON
New York, NY .... Family Law, General Practice
Pearl River, NY .... Family Law, General Practice

DRANOFF-PERLSTEIN ASSOCIATES
Philadelphia, PA .... Personal Injury Law

DRAUGELIS & ASHTON
Plymouth, MI .... Civil Trial Practice, Insurance Defense Law, Personal Injury Law

DRAZIN AND WARSHAW
Red Bank, NJ .... General Practice

DREILING, BIEKER & HOFFMAN
Hays, KS .... General Practice

DRENDEL, TATNALL, HOFFMAN & MCCRACKEN, A PROFESSIONAL CORPORATION
Batavia, IL .... General Practice

DRENNAN, J. C.
Medford, OK .... General Practice

DRESSER LAW OFFICE, P.C.
Sturgis, MI .... General Practice

DRESSLER, GOLDSMITH, SHORE & MILNAMOW, LTD.
Chicago, IL .... Patent, Trademark, Copyright and Unfair Competition Law

DREW ECKL & FARNHAM
Atlanta, GA .... Civil Trial Practice, Commercial Law, General Practice, Medical Malpractice Law

DREW, WARD, GRAF, COOGAN & GOEDDEL, A LEGAL PROFESSIONAL ASSOCIATION
Cincinnati, OH .... Civil Trial Practice, Family Law, Probate and Estate Planning Law

DREYER, BABICH, BUCCOLA & CALLAHAM
Sacramento, CA .... Personal Injury Law, Product Liability Law

DREYER, BOYAJIAN & TUTTLE
Albany, NY .... Civil Trial Practice, Criminal Trial Practice, Labor and Employment Law

DRIEBE & DRIEBE, P.C.
Jonesboro, GA .... Civil Trial Practice, General Practice, Personal Injury Law

DRIGGERS, SCHULTZ, HERBST & PATERSON, A PROFESSIONAL CORPORATION
Troy, MI .... Business Law

DRINKER BIDDLE & REATH
Washington, DC....................General Practice
Philadelphia, PA....................General Practice

DRISCOLL, JAMES O., P.A.
Orlando, FL....................General Practice

DRISDALE & LINDSTROM, P.A.
Jackson, MS....................Business Law, Probate and Estate Planning Law

DRUCKER & SOMMERS
Beverly Hills, CA....................Patent, Trademark, Copyright and Unfair Competition Law

DRUMMOND & DRUMMOND
Portland, ME....................General Practice

DRUMM, WINCHESTER & GLEASON
Sikeston, MO....................Civil Trial Practice, General Practice

DRUMMY KING & WHITE, A PROFESSIONAL CORPORATION
Costa Mesa, CA....................General Practice, Real Estate Law

DRYDEN, GROSSHEIM & SUTTON
Beaumont, TX....................Personal Injury Law

DUANE, MORRIS & HECKSCHER
Wilmington, DE....................General Practice
New York, NY....................General Practice
Allentown, PA....................General Practice
Harrisburg, PA....................General Practice
Philadelphia, PA....................Administrative Law, Bankruptcy Law, Environmental Law, General Practice, Health Care Law, Labor and Employment Law, Patent, Trademark, Copyright and Unfair Competition Law, Tax Law
Wayne, PA....................General Practice

DUANE AND SHANNON, P.C.
Richmond, VA....................Civil Trial Practice, Criminal Trial Practice, Insurance Defense Law, Personal Injury Law

DUBÉ AND WRIGHT, P.A., LAW OFFICES OF
Miami, FL....................Civil Trial Practice, General Practice

DUBITSKY, IRA L., P.A.
Miami, FL....................Family Law

DUBUISSON AND DUBUISSON
Opelousas, LA....................General Practice

DUCEY LAW FIRM, THE, P.C.
Belleville, IL....................Civil Trial Practice, General Practice

DUCKER, DEWEY & SEAWELL, P.C.
Denver, CO....................Bankruptcy Law, Business Law, Commercial Law, Real Estate Law

DUDLEY, DUDLEY, WINDLE & STEVENS
El Paso, TX....................Insurance Defense Law, Personal Injury Law

DUEL AND HOLLAND
Greenwich, CT....................General Practice

DUFFIELD, MILLER, YOUNG, ADAMSON & ALFRED, P.C.
Green Valley, AZ....................Civil Trial Practice, General Practice
Tucson, AZ....................General Practice

DUFFORD & BROWN, P.C.
Denver, CO....................Antitrust Law, Bankruptcy Law, Business Law, Civil Trial Practice, Commercial Law, Environmental Law, General Practice, Labor and Employment Law, Natural Resources Law, Real Estate Law, Trademark, Copyright and Unfair Competition Law

DUFFY & GREEN
West Chester, PA....................Criminal Trial Practice, General Practice, Personal Injury Law

DUKE, GERSTEL, SHEARER & BREGANTE
San Diego, CA....................Construction Law

DUKER & BARRETT
New York, NY....................Appellate Practice, Civil Trial Practice, Criminal Trial Practice

DUKES, DUKES, KEATING AND FANECA, P.A.
Gulfport, MS....................Administrative Law, Admiralty/Maritime Law, Bankruptcy Law, Business Law, Civil Trial Practice, Commercial Law, Construction Law, Environmental Law, Insurance Defense Law, Labor and Employment Law, Municipal and Zoning Law, Product Liability Law, Real Estate Law, Transportation Law

DULANY & LEAHY
Westminster, MD....................General Practice

DUMOUCHEL, DAVID F., P.C.
Detroit, MI....................Criminal Trial Practice

DUNAWAY & CROSS, A PROFESSIONAL CORPORATION
Washington, DC....................Administrative Law, Antitrust Law

DUNCAN & ALLEN
Washington, DC....................General Practice

DUNCAN & CRAIG
Edmonton, AB, Canada....................General Practice

DUNCAN, GREEN, BROWN, LANGENESS & ECKLEY, A PROFESSIONAL CORPORATION
Des Moines, IA....................General Practice

DUNCAN & KOFAKIS
Casper, WY....................Civil Trial Practice, Medical Malpractice Law, Personal Injury Law

DUNCAN & RAINWATER, TRIAL LAWYERS, A PROF. ASSOC.
Little Rock, AR....................Civil Trial Practice, Personal Injury Law

DUNCAN, THOMASSON & ACREE
La Grange, GA....................General Practice

DUNHAM, BOMAN & LESKERA
Collinsville, IL....................General Practice
East St. Louis, IL....................General Practice

DUNKLEY, BENNETT & CHRISTENSEN, P.A.
Minneapolis, MN....................Civil Trial Practice, Personal Injury Law

DUNLAP, CALVIN R. X.
Reno, NV....................Criminal Trial Practice, Personal Injury Law

DUNLAP, BURDICK AND MCCORMACK, A PROFESSIONAL LAW CORPORATION
Santa Cruz, CA....................Civil Trial Practice, Medical Malpractice Law, Personal Injury Law, Product Liability Law, Real Estate Law

DUNLAP, CODDING & LEE, P.C.
Oklahoma City, OK....................Patent, Trademark, Copyright and Unfair Competition Law

DUNLAP & SEEGER, P.A.
Rochester, MN....................General Practice

DUNN, ABPLANALP & CHRISTENSEN, P.C.
Vail, CO....................Civil Trial Practice, General Practice, Real Estate Law

DUNN, CARNEY, ALLEN, HIGGINS & TONGUE
Portland, OR....................General Practice

DUNN, HAASE, SULLIVAN, MALLON, CHERNER & BROADT
Media, PA....................General Practice

DUNN, KACAL, ADAMS, PAPPAS & LAW, A PROFESSIONAL CORPORATION
Houston, TX....................Civil Trial Practice

DUNN, LODISH & WIDOM, P.A.
Miami, FL....................Civil Trial Practice

DUNN, PASHMAN, SPONZILLI, SWICK & FINNERTY
Hackensack, NJ....................Civil Trial Practice, Commercial Law, Family Law, General Practice, Probate and Estate Planning Law, Real Estate Law, Tax Law

DUNN, ROGASKI, PREOVOLOS & WEBER
Vallejo, CA....................General Practice

DUNN, ULBRICH, HUNDMAN, STANCZAK & OGAR
Bloomington, IL....................General Practice

DUNN & WEATHERED, P.C.
Corpus Christi, TX....................Insurance Defense Law, Product Liability Law

DUNNAM & DUNNAM, L.L.P.
Waco, TX....................Civil Trial Practice, Criminal Trial Practice, Family Law, General Practice

DUNNINGS & FRAWLEY, P.C.
Lansing, MI....................Administrative Law, Civil Trial Practice, Criminal Trial Practice, Family Law, General Practice, Labor and Employment Law, Personal Injury Law

DUNTON, RAINVILLE, TOUPIN, PERRAULT
Montreal, QU, Canada....................General Practice

DUNTON, SIMMONS & DUNTON
White Stone, VA....................General Practice

DURANT & DURANT
Philadelphia, PA....................Civil Trial Practice, Criminal Trial Practice

DURHAM, EDWARD D.
Montrose, CO....................Civil Trial Practice, Criminal Trial Practice, Family Law

DURHAM, EVANS, JONES & PINEGAR
Salt Lake City, UT....................Business Law, Civil Trial Practice, Real Estate Law

DURIE, JACK F. (JAY), JR., LAW OFFICES OF
Orlando, FL....................Civil Trial Practice, Medical Malpractice Law, Personal Injury Law

DURLAND & DURLAND
Oklahoma City, OK....................Commercial Law, Medical Malpractice Law, Personal Injury Law, Securities Law

DURR AND KEINZ
Utica, NY....................General Practice, Personal Injury Law

DURRETT, CHARLES W., A PROFESSIONAL CORPORATION
Alamogordo, NM....................General Practice

DUSHOFF MCCALL, A PROFESSIONAL CORPORATION
Phoenix, AZ....................Civil Trial Practice, Municipal and Zoning Law, Real Estate Law

DUTHIE & TATE
Durango, CO....................General Practice

DUTTON, BRAUN, STAACK, HELLMAN & IVERSEN, P.L.C.
Waterloo, IA....................General Practice

DUTTON OVERMAN GOLDSTEIN PINKUS, A PROFESSIONAL CORPORATION
Indianapolis, IN....................Business Law, Civil Trial Practice, Construction Law, Employment Benefits Law

DUVALL & DUVALL
Salisbury, MD....................General Practice

DUVIN, CAHN & BARNARD, A LEGAL PROFESSIONAL ASSOCIATION
Cleveland, OH....................Civil Trial Practice, Criminal Trial Practice, Employment Benefits Law, Labor and Employment Law

DWIGHT, ROYALL, HARRIS, KOEGEL & CASKEY
Washington, DC....................General Practice
New York, NY....................General Practice

DWYER & CANELLIS, P.A.
Westfield, NJ....................Civil Trial Practice, Commercial Law, Health Care Law

DWYER IMANAKA SCHRAFF KUDO MEYER & FUJIMOTO, ATTORNEYS AT LAW, A LAW CORPORATION
Honolulu, HI....................Administrative Law, Banking Law, Bankruptcy Law, Civil Trial Practice, Commercial Law, Construction Law, Environmental Law, Health Care Law, Labor and Employment Law, Municipal and Zoning Law, Natural Resources Law, Real Estate Law

DWYER, POHREN, WOOD, HEAVEY, GRIMM, GOODALL & LAZER
Omaha, NE....................Bankruptcy Law, Civil Trial Practice, General Practice, Health Care Law, Personal Injury Law, Tax Law

DWYER & WHITE
Atlanta, GA....................Medical Malpractice Law, Personal Injury Law

DYE, TUCKER, EVERITT, WHEALE & LONG, A PROFESSIONAL ASSOCIATION
Augusta, GA....................Civil Trial Practice, General Practice

DYER, DYER, JONES & DANIELS, A PROFESSIONAL ASSOCIATION
Greenville, MS....................Personal Injury Law

DYER, GAROFALO, MANN & SCHULTZ, A LEGAL PROFESSIONAL ASSOCIATION
Dayton, OH....................Personal Injury Law

DYKEMA GOSSETT
Ann Arbor, MI....................General Practice
Bloomfield Hills, MI....................General Practice, Patent, Trademark, Copyright and Unfair Competition Law
Detroit, MI....................Antitrust Law, Civil Trial Practice, Environmental Law, General Practice, Health Care Law, International Business Law, Labor and Employment Law, Municipal Bond/Public Authority Financing Law, Personal Injury Law, Real Estate Law, Tax Law
Grand Rapids, MI....................General Practice
Lansing, MI....................General Practice
Washington, DC....................General Practice

DYMOND, LEWIS W., JR., A PROFESSIONAL CORPORATION
Aurora, CO....................Family Law, Personal Injury Law

EAGLETON, EAGLETON AND HARRISON, INC.
Tulsa, OK....................Tax Law

EAMES & STERNS
Skowhegan, ME....................General Practice

EAMES, WILCOX, MASTEJ, BRYANT, SWIFT & RIDDELL
Detroit, MI....................Administrative Law, Bankruptcy Law, Civil Trial Practice, Commercial Law, Personal Injury Law, Probate and Estate Planning Law, Transportation Law

EARL, BLANK, KAVANAUGH & STOTTS, PROFESSIONAL ASSOCIATION
Miami, FL....................Natural Resources Law
Sarasota, FL....................Natural Resources Law
Tallahassee, FL....................Natural Resources Law

EARLEY & KELLER
Irvine, CA....................Criminal Trial Practice

EARLY, LENNON, PETERS & CROCKER, P.C.
Kalamazoo, MI....................Business Law, General Practice, Insurance Defense Law, Probate and Estate Planning Law, Real Estate Law, Tax Law

EARNEST, FOSTER, EDER, LEVI & NORTHAM
Rushville, IN....................General Practice

EASLEY & WILLITS, P.A.
West Palm Beach, FL....................Civil Trial Practice, General Practice

EASTMAN & SMITH
Toledo, OH....................Banking Law, Business Law, Civil Trial Practice, Environmental Law, General Practice, Health Care Law, Labor and Employment Law, Municipal and Zoning Law, Probate and Estate Planning Law, Tax Law

EASTON, W. DOUGLAS LAW OFFICES OF
Costa Mesa, CA....................Medical Malpractice Law, Personal Injury Law

EATON AND COTTRELL, P.A.
Gulfport, MS....................General Practice

EATON, PEABODY, BRADFORD & VEAGUE, P.A.
Bangor, ME....................Antitrust Law, Banking Law, Business Law, Civil Trial Practice, Environmental Law, General Practice, Health Care Law, Insurance Defense Law, Labor and Employment Law, Municipal Bond/Public Authority Financing Law, Personal Injury Law, Probate and Estate Planning Law, Real Estate Law

EATON & ROMWEBER
Batesville, IN....................General Practice
Versailles, IN....................Civil Trial Practice, General Practice, Insurance Defense Law

EAVES, BARDACKE & BAUGH, P.A.
Albuquerque, NM....................Antitrust Law, Civil Trial Practice, Environmental Law

EBERLE, BERLIN, KADING, TURNBOW & MCKLVEEN, CHARTERED
Boise, ID....................Antitrust Law, Civil Trial Practice, General Practice, Natural Resources Law, Securities Law, Tax Law

ECKARDT & KHOURY
Los Angeles, CA....................Business Law, Civil Trial Practice

ECKBERG, LAMMERS, BRIGGS, WOLFF & VIERLING
Stillwater, MN....................General Practice

ECKERT SEAMANS CHERIN & MELLOTT
Washington, DC....................General Practice
Allentown, PA....................Patent, Trademark, Copyright and Unfair Competition Law
Harrisburg, PA....................General Practice
Philadelphia, PA....................Patent, Trademark, Copyright and Unfair Competition Law
Pittsburgh, PA....................General Practice, Patent, Trademark, Copyright and Unfair Competition Law

ECKERT & STINGL
Rhinelander, WI....................Appellate Practice, Civil Trial Practice, General Practice, Insurance Defense Law

EDENFIELD, STONE & COX
Statesboro, GA....................Civil Trial Practice

EDGARTON, ST. PETER, PETAK, MASSEY & BULLON
Fond du Lac, WI....................General Practice

EDMONDS & BEIER, P.C.
New York, NY....................Business Law

EDMUNDS, JAMES E.
Halifax, VA....................Civil Trial Practice, Criminal Trial Practice, Personal Injury Law

EDMUNDS & WILLIAMS, P.C.
Lynchburg, VA....................General Practice

EDWARDS, CHARLES W.
Spencer, IN....................General Practice

EDWARDS & ANGELL
Providence, RI....................Antitrust Law, Civil Trial Practice, Communications Law, Environmental Law, General Practice, Labor and Employment Law, Municipal Bond/Public Authority Financing Law, Natural Resources Law, Tax Law, Trademark, Copyright and Unfair Competition Law

EDWARDS & ANTHOLIS
Morristown, NJ........................Tax Law

EDWARDS, BELK, HUNTER & KERR
El Paso, TX............................Banking Law

EDWARDS, DANIEL P., P.C.
Colorado Springs, CO.............Business Law, General Practice, Probate and Estate Planning Law, Real Estate Law

EDWARDS & HALE, LTD.
Las Vegas, NV........................Insurance Defense Law

EDWARDS & KLEIN, CO., L.P.A.
Ironton, OH............................Insurance Defense Law

EDWARDS LAW FIRM
Billings, MT............................Business Law, Personal Injury Law

EDWARDS, RICK, INC.
Los Angeles, CA......................Civil Trial Practice

EDWARDS, TERRY, BAIAMONTE & EDWARDS
Corpus Christi, TX.................Civil Trial Practice, Personal Injury Law

EDWARDS, WHITE & SOOY, A PROFESSIONAL CORPORATION
San Diego, CA........................Civil Trial Practice

EGAN, FLANAGAN AND COHEN, P.C.
Springfield, MA......................General Practice

EGERTON, MCAFEE, ARMISTEAD & DAVIS, P.C.
Knoxville, TN........................Banking Law, Civil Trial Practice, General Practice, Patent, Trademark, Copyright and Unfair Competition Law, Probate and Estate Planning Law, Tax Law

EGGENBERGER, EGGENBERGER, MCKINNEY, WEBER & HOFMEISTER, P.C.
Detroit, MI.............................Business Law, Civil Trial Practice, Insurance Defense Law, Personal Injury Law

EGGERS, EGGERS & EGGERS
Boone, NC..............................General Practice

EGITO COELHO, TRENCH E VEIRANO ADVOGADOS
Brasília, Brazil........................General Practice

EHLINGER & KRILL, S.C.
Milwaukee, WI........................Business Law, Civil Trial Practice, Health Care Law

EHMANN & HILLER, P.C.
Phoenix, AZ............................Probate and Estate Planning Law, Tax Law

EHRENPREIS, RALPH, A PROFESSIONAL LAW CORPORATION
Los Angeles, CA......................Immigration and Naturalization Law

EHRLICH, FRAZER & FELDMAN
Garden City, NY......................Labor and Employment Law

EIBERGER, STACY, SMITH & MARTIN
Denver, CO.............................Civil Trial Practice, Labor and Employment Law

EICH & FRANKLIN
Chicago, IL.............................Insurance Defense Law

EICHELBERGER & PERROTTA
Atlanta, GA............................Medical Malpractice Law, Personal Injury Law

EICHEL & KRONE CO., L.P.A.
Cincinnati, OH........................Business Law, Probate and Estate Planning Law, Real Estate Law

EICHENBAUM, SCOTT, MILLER, LILES & HEISTER, P.A.
Little Rock, AR......................General Practice

EICHLER, FORGOSH, GOTTILLA AND RUDNICK, A PROFESSIONAL CORPORATION
Chatham, NJ............................Commercial Law, General Practice

EIDSMOE, HEIDMAN, REDMOND, FREDREGILL, PATTERSON & SCHATZ
Sioux City, IA.........................Civil Trial Practice, General Practice, Insurance Defense Law

EIDSON & ASSOCIATES, P.C.
Atlanta, GA............................Civil Trial Practice

EIKENBURG & STILES
Houston, TX...........................Commercial Law

EILAND & BENNETT
Logan, WV.............................General Practice

EINHORN, HARRIS, ASCHER & BARBARITO, A PROFESSIONAL CORPORATION
Denville, NJ............................General Practice, Health Care Law

EISEN & JOHNSTON
Sacramento, CA......................Appellate Practice

EISENBERG, ANDERSON, MICHALIK & LYNCH
New Britain, CT......................Labor and Employment Law

EISENHART & EISENHART
Cambridge, NE........................General Practice

EISENHOWER & CARLSON
Tacoma, WA...........................General Practice

EISENSTAT, GABAGE, BERMAN & FURMAN, A PROFESSIONAL CORPORATION
Vineland, NJ...........................Civil Trial Practice, General Practice

EISENSTEIN, GWEN M., P.C.
Dallas, TX..............................Real Estate Law

EISNAUGLE & GRAHAM CO., L.P.A.
Columbus, OH.........................Tax Law

EISNER & LEVY
Elmsford, NY..........................Banking Law

EKMAN & BOHRER, P.S.
Seattle, WA............................Employment Benefits Law

ELAM & BURKE, A PROFESSIONAL ASSOCIATION
Boise, ID................................Antitrust Law, Civil Trial Practice, Commercial Law, Environmental Law, General Practice, Labor and Employment Law, Municipal Bond/Public Authority Financing Law, Natural Resources Law, Securities Law, Tax Law

ELAM, GLASGOW & ACREE
Union City, TN.......................General Practice, Insurance Defense Law

ELARBEE, THOMPSON & TRAPNELL
Atlanta, GA............................Employment Benefits Law, Labor and Employment Law

ELDEN, DOUGLAS L. & ASSOCIATES
Chicago, IL.............................Health Care Law

ELDERKIN, MARTIN, KELLY & MESSINA, P.C.
Erie, PA..................................General Practice, Labor and Employment Law

ELDER & PHILLIPS, P.C.
Grand Junction, CO.................General Practice

ELGIN, CLOGG & PATIN
Indianola, IA..........................General Practice

ELKINS, JAMES W., P.A.
Naples, FL..............................General Practice, Tax Law

ELLENBOGEN & GOLDSTEIN, P.C.
New York, NY.........................Family Law

ELLIN AND BAKER
Baltimore, MD........................Civil Trial Practice, Medical Malpractice Law

ELLIOTT, TYRON C.
Manchester, GA.......................Personal Injury Law

ELLIOTT, EDNA, J.D., P.A.
Tampa, FL..............................Construction Law, Family Law

ELLIOTT LAW OFFICES, THE
Arvada, CO.............................Civil Trial Practice, Criminal Trial Practice, Personal Injury Law

ELLIOTT LAWSON & POMRENKE
Bristol, VA.............................Civil Trial Practice, Construction Law, Environmental Law, General Practice, Labor and Employment Law

ELLIOTT, REIHNER, SIEDZIKOWSKI, NORTH & EGAN, P.C.
Blue Bell, PA..........................Commercial Law

ELLIS, RONALD D.
Los Angeles, CA......................Commercial Law

ELLIS & EASTERLIN, A PROFESSIONAL CORPORATION
Americus, GA..........................General Practice

ELLIS, HOOPER, WARLICK, MORGAN & HENRY
Jacksonville, NC......................General Practice

ELLIS LAW FIRM
Benton, AR.............................Civil Trial Practice, Insurance Defense Law

ELLIS, LEONARD & BUCKHOLTS
Duncan, OK............................Banking Law, Family Law, Insurance Defense Law

ELLIS, SPENCER AND BUTLER
Hollywood, FL.........................Civil Trial Practice, General Practice

ELLISON, HINKLE & BAYER, A PROFESSIONAL LAW CORPORATION
Ventura, CA............................Personal Injury Law

ELMAN & EHARDT, LTD.
Harvard, IL .... General Practice

ELMAN WILF & FRIED, A PROFESSIONAL CORPORATION
Media, PA .... Patent, Trademark, Copyright and Unfair Competition Law

ELMORE & ELMORE, P.A.
Asheville, NC .... Civil Trial Practice, Criminal Trial Practice, Family Law, Personal Injury Law

ELROD LAW FIRM
Siloam Springs, AR .... Civil Trial Practice

ELSENER & CADENHEAD
Seminole, OK .... Civil Trial Practice, General Practice

ELSER, GREENE, HODOR & FABAR
Miami, FL .... Family Law

ELSTEIN AND ELSTEIN, P.C.
Bridgeport, CT .... Business Law, Communications Law, Real Estate Law

ELWOOD, O'DONOHOE, O'CONNOR & STOCHL
Cresco, IA .... General Practice
New Hampton, IA .... General Practice

ELY, CARY, WELCH & HICKMAN
Hannibal, MO .... General Practice

ELY & KING
Springfield, MA .... Appellate Practice, Business Law, Civil Trial Practice, Employment Benefits Law, General Practice, Insurance Defense Law, Labor and Employment Law, Medical Malpractice Law, Personal Injury Law, Product Liability Law, Real Estate Law

ELY AND TRUE
Batavia, OH .... General Practice

EMENS, KEGLER, BROWN, HILL & RITTER
Columbus, OH .... Administrative Law, Banking Law, Bankruptcy Law, Business Law, Civil Trial Practice, Construction Law, Employment Benefits Law, Environmental Law, General Practice, Health Care Law, Immigration and Naturalization Law, Labor and Employment Law, Municipal and Zoning Law, Natural Resources Law, Patent, Trademark, Copyright and Unfair Competition Law, Probate and Estate Planning Law, Real Estate Law, Tax Law, Trademark, Copyright and Unfair Competition Law

EMERICK & DIGGINS, P.C.
Kendallville, IN .... General Practice

EMERSON & EMERSON, P.A.
Naples, FL .... Commercial Law

EMERY JAMIESON
Edmonton, AB, Canada .... Civil Trial Practice, General Practice, Patent, Trademark, Copyright and Unfair Competition Law

EMISON, DOOLITTLE, KOLB & ROELLGEN
Vincennes, IN .... General Practice, Insurance Defense Law

EMISON AND EMISON, P.C.
Alamo, TN .... General Practice

EMMET, MARVIN & MARTIN, LLP
New York, NY .... Banking Law, Civil Trial Practice, General Practice, Securities Law, Tax Law

EMORY, CAROL A.
Portland, OR .... International Business Law

ENFIELD, GUIMOND, BROWN & COLLINS
Salem, OR .... General Practice

ENGEL & RUDMAN, P.C.
Denver, CO .... International Business Law, Probate and Estate Planning Law

ENGLAND & MCKNIGHT
Atlanta, GA .... Civil Trial Practice, Criminal Trial Practice, Insurance Defense Law, Medical Malpractice Law, Personal Injury Law, Product Liability Law

ENGLAND, WHITFIELD, SCHRÖEDER & TREDWAY
Oxnard, CA .... General Practice, Real Estate Law, Tax Law
Thousand Oaks, CA .... General Practice

ENGLE & BRIDE
Ventura, CA .... General Practice, Insurance Defense Law, Medical Malpractice Law

ENGLISH, LUCAS, PRIEST & OWSLEY
Bowling Green, KY .... Banking Law, Bankruptcy Law, Civil Trial Practice, Commercial Law, Criminal Trial Practice, Environmental Law, Family Law, General Practice, Immigration and Naturalization Law, Labor and Employment Law, Medical Malpractice Law, Municipal Bond/Public Authority Financing Law, Natural Resources Law, Personal Injury Law, Probate and Estate Planning Law, Real Estate Law, Tax Law

ENGLISH & VAN HORNE, P.C.
Detroit, MI .... Immigration and Naturalization Law

ENWALL, MICHAEL R. LAW OFFICES OF
Boulder, CO .... Civil Trial Practice, Criminal Trial Practice

ENZ, JONES & LEGRAND
Columbus, OH .... General Practice

EPPES, WATTS & SHANNON
Meridian, MS .... Civil Trial Practice, General Practice, Insurance Defense Law

EPPS AND EPPS, LAW OFFICE OF
Johnson City, TN .... General Practice

EPSTEIN, SHERWIN L. & ASSOCIATES
Kansas City, MO .... Appellate Practice, Business Law, Civil Trial Practice, Municipal and Zoning Law, Real Estate Law

EPSTEIN, BARRY D., P.A.
Rochelle Park, NJ .... Civil Trial Practice

EPSTEIN, EDNA SELAN, THE LAW OFFICES OF
Chicago, IL .... Civil Trial Practice, Labor and Employment Law

EPSTEIN, ZAIDEMAN & ESRIG, P.C.
Chicago, IL .... Construction Law, Criminal Trial Practice, Medical Malpractice Law, Personal Injury Law, Product Liability Law

ERICKSON, DAVIS, MURPHY, GRIFFITH & WALSH, LTD.
Decatur, IL .... Civil Trial Practice, General Practice

ERICKSON, LEWAYNE M., P.C.
Brookings, SD .... Business Law, Civil Trial Practice, Probate and Estate Planning Law, Tax Law

ERICKSON & SEDERSTROM, P.C.
Lincoln, NE .... Civil Trial Practice, General Practice, Insurance Defense Law, Labor and Employment Law, Personal Injury Law, Probate and Estate Planning Law, Tax Law
Omaha, NE .... Civil Trial Practice, General Practice, Insurance Defense Law, Labor and Employment Law, Personal Injury Law, Probate and Estate Planning Law, Tax Law

ERICKSON, THORPE & SWAINSTON, LTD.
Reno, NV .... Civil Trial Practice, Construction Law, General Practice, Insurance Defense Law, Personal Injury Law

ERICKSON, WEBB & SCOLTON
Jamestown, NY .... General Practice

ERLACH & ERLACH
San Francisco, CA .... Business Law, Civil Trial Practice, Health Care Law

ERNSTROM & DRESTE
Rochester, NY .... General Practice

ERVIN, COHEN & JESSUP
Beverly Hills, CA .... General Practice, Probate and Estate Planning Law, Securities Law, Tax Law

ERVIN, VARN, JACOBS, ODOM & ERVIN
Tallahassee, FL .... General Practice

ERWIN, OTT, CLARK & CAMPBELL
York, ME .... Bankruptcy Law, Civil Trial Practice, Environmental Law, Real Estate Law

ESDAILE, BARRETT & ESDAILE
Boston, MA .... General Practice

ESKIN & JACKSON
Santa Barbara, CA .... Criminal Trial Practice
Ventura, CA .... Criminal Trial Practice

ESLER PETRIE & SALKIN, P.A.
Fort Lauderdale, FL .... Civil Trial Practice, General Practice, Insurance Defense Law, Personal Injury Law

ESSEN & ESSEN, P.A.
Miami, FL .... Criminal Trial Practice

ESTES, LEE LAW OFFICES OF
West Bloomfield, MI .... Insurance Defense Law

ETHEREDGE, EDWARD D. LAW OFFICES
Northampton, MA .... General Practice

ETHERIDGE, MOSER, GARNER AND BRUNER, P.A.
Laurinburg, NC .... General Practice

ETIENNE, BLUM, STEHLÉ, MANFRINI ET ASSOCIÉS, ETUDE
Geneva, Switzerland .... General Practice

ETNIRE, GEOFFREY C.
Pleasanton, CA....Real Estate Law

ETTINGER, JACK A., P.C.
Tucson, AZ....Civil Trial Practice, Personal Injury Law

EUBANK, HASSELL & LEWIS
Daytona Beach, FL....Insurance Defense Law, Medical Malpractice Law, Product Liability Law

EUBANKS, GARY, & ASSOCIATES, P.A.
Little Rock, AR....Personal Injury Law

EUBANKS, HILYARD, RUMBLEY, MEIER & LENGAUER, A PROFESSIONAL ASSOCIATION
Orlando, FL....General Practice

EULER & MCQUILLAN
Troy, KS....General Practice

EVANS, JOHN F. Q.C.
Hamilton, ON, Canada....General Practice

EVANS, CARTER, KUNES & BENNETT, P.A.
Charleston, SC....Probate and Estate Planning Law, Tax Law

EVANS & DIXON
St. Louis, MO....Admiralty/Maritime Law, General Practice, Insurance Defense Law

EVANS, GANDY, DANIEL & MOORE
Fort Worth, TX....Criminal Trial Practice

EVANS HAND
West Paterson, NJ....Banking Law, Civil Trial Practice, Environmental Law, General Practice, Real Estate Law

EVANS, IVORY, P.C.
Pittsburgh, PA....Medical Malpractice Law, Personal Injury Law

EVANS, JONES & REYNOLDS, A PROFESSIONAL CORPORATION
Nashville, TN....General Practice

EVANS, KEANE
Boise, ID....General Practice
Kellogg, ID....General Practice

EVANS, ORR, LAFFAN, TORRES & DEMAGGIO, P.C.
New York, NY....Civil Trial Practice, Medical Malpractice Law, Personal Injury Law

EVANS, OSBORNE, KREIZMAN & BONNEY
Red Bank, NJ....General Practice

EVANS & PETREE
Memphis, TN....General Practice, Insurance Defense Law

EVANS, PORTNOY & QUINN
Pittsburgh, PA....Medical Malpractice Law, Personal Injury Law

EVANS, WILLIAM D., A PROFESSIONAL CORPORATION, LAW OFFICES OF
Long Beach, CA....Civil Trial Practice

EVERETT, EVERETT, WARREN & HARPER
Greenville, NC....General Practice

EVERETT, GASKINS, HANCOCK & STEVENS
Raleigh, NC....Administrative Law, Bankruptcy Law, Civil Trial Practice, Commercial Law, Communications Law, General Practice

EVERETT & LUYMES, P.C.
Galva, IL....General Practice

EVERITT, THOMAS E., P.C.
Scottsburg, IN....General Practice

EVERSON, WHITNEY, EVERSON & BREHM, S.C.
Green Bay, WI....General Practice

EWELL & LEVY
San Francisco, CA....Civil Trial Practice, Environmental Law, Real Estate Law, Securities Law

EWEN, HILLIARD & BUSH
Louisville, KY....Civil Trial Practice, General Practice, Insurance Defense Law

EWING & JOHNSON, A PROFESSIONAL LAW CORPORATION
El Centro, CA....General Practice

EWING, SMITH & HOBEROCK
Nevada, MO....General Practice

EYSTER, KEY, TUBB, WEAVER & ROTH
Decatur, AL....General Practice, Insurance Defense Law

EZER & WILLIAMSON
Los Angeles, CA....Construction Law, Real Estate Law

FABRIS, BURGESS & RING, A PROFESSIONAL CORPORATION
San Francisco, CA....General Practice

FADEL & BEYER
Cleveland, OH....General Practice

FAEGRE & BENSON
Denver, CO....General Practice
Minneapolis, MN....General Practice
London, England....General Practice

FAIN, HARRY M.
Beverly Hills, CA....Family Law

FAIN, MAJOR & WILEY, P.C.
Atlanta, GA....General Practice, Insurance Defense Law, Labor and Employment Law

FAIRCHILD, PRICE, THOMAS & HALEY
Center, TX....General Practice

FAIRFIELD AND WOODS, P.C.
Denver, CO....Civil Trial Practice, General Practice, Real Estate Law

FAISANT, ROBIN D.
Menlo Park, CA....Probate and Estate Planning Law

FAISON & FLETCHER
Durham, NC....General Practice
Wilmington, NC....General Practice

FAKES, ARTHUR, P.C.
Lombard, IL....International Business Law

FALCIANI, ANGELO J., P.A., A PROFESSIONAL CORPORATION
Woodbury, NJ....Civil Trial Practice, General Practice

FALK LAW FIRM, THE, A PROFESSIONAL LIMITED COMPANY
Washington, DC....Civil Trial Practice, Health Care Law, Labor and Employment Law, Medical Malpractice Law, Probate and Estate Planning Law

FANNIN, TYLER & HAMILTON, P.A.
Jacksonville, FL....Civil Trial Practice, General Practice

FANT, PHILIP A.
San Francisco, CA....Admiralty/Maritime Law

FARAGE AND MCBRIDE
Philadelphia, PA....Medical Malpractice Law

FARBER, STEVEN G.
Santa Fe, NM....Criminal Trial Practice, Personal Injury Law

FARESE, FARESE & FARESE, P.A.
Ashland, MS....Criminal Trial Practice, Personal Injury Law

FARHAT, STORY & KRAUS, P.C.
East Lansing, MI....Appellate Practice, Business Law, Civil Trial Practice, Commercial Law, Criminal Trial Practice, Environmental Law, Family Law, General Practice, Health Care Law, Medical Malpractice Law, Personal Injury Law, Probate and Estate Planning Law, Real Estate Law, Tax Law

FARISH, FARISH & ROMANI
West Palm Beach, FL....Civil Trial Practice, General Practice, Personal Injury Law

FARKAS, LEDFORD AND PERRY
Albany, GA....General Practice

FARLOW LAW FIRM, THE
Albuquerque, NM....Civil Trial Practice, Insurance Defense Law, Personal Injury Law

FARMER, KELLEY & FARMER
London, KY....Civil Trial Practice, General Practice, Insurance Defense Law, Medical Malpractice Law, Product Liability Law

FARMER, PRICE, HORNSBY & WEATHERFORD
Dothan, AL....Personal Injury Law

FARMER & WATLINGTON
Yanceyville, NC....General Practice

FARNSWORTH & VONBERG
Houston, TX....Business Law, Commercial Law, Labor and Employment Law, Natural Resources Law

FARR, DAVIS & FITZE
Tunkhannock, PA....Civil Trial Practice, General Practice

FARR & OOSTERHOUSE
Grand Rapids, MI....Civil Trial Practice, General Practice, Insurance Defense Law, Personal Injury Law

FARRELL, FARRELL & GINSBACH
Hot Springs, SD....................General Practice

FARRELL, FRITZ, CAEMMERER, CLEARY, BARNOSKY & ARMENTANO, PROFESSIONAL CORPORATION
Uniondale, NY....................Civil Trial Practice, General Practice

FARRELL, GERALD E., P.C.
Wallingford, CT....................Criminal Trial Practice, General Practice, Personal Injury Law

FARRINGTON & CURTIS, P.C.
Springfield, MO....................Civil Trial Practice, General Practice

FARRIS & GREEN
Austin, TX....................Family Law

FARRIS, HANCOCK, GILMAN, BRANAN & HELLEN
Memphis, TN....................Admiralty/Maritime Law, Civil Trial Practice, General Practice, Insurance Defense Law, Municipal and Zoning Law

FARRIS, VAUGHAN, WILLS & MURPHY
Vancouver, BC, Canada....................General Practice

FARRIS, WARFIELD & KANADAY
Nashville, TN....................General Practice

FARRISH, JOHNSON & MASCHKA
Mankato, MN....................Civil Trial Practice, General Practice, Insurance Defense Law

FARUKI GILLIAM & IRELAND
Dayton, OH....................Civil Trial Practice, Criminal Trial Practice, Environmental Law

FASKEN CAMPBELL GODFREY
Toronto, ON, Canada....................General Practice, Trademark, Copyright and Unfair Competition Law

FASKEN MARTINEAU
Brussels, Belgium....................General Practice
London, England....................General Practice

FAULKNER, BANFIELD, DOOGAN & HOLMES, A PROFESSIONAL CORPORATION
Anchorage, AK....................General Practice
Juneau, AK....................General Practice
Seattle, WA....................General Practice

FAULKNER & BOYCE, P.C.
New London, CT....................Civil Trial Practice, Personal Injury Law

FAULKNER, PLAUT, HANNA, FREUND & WORTHEN, P.C.
Keene, NH....................General Practice

FAULKNER & TEPE
Cincinnati, OH....................Bankruptcy Law, Civil Trial Practice, Insurance Defense Law

FAUST, HARRELSON, FULKER, MCCARTHY & SCHLEMMER
Troy, OH....................General Practice

FAVARO, LAVEZZO, GILL, CARETTI & HEPPELL, A PROFESSIONAL CORPORATION
Vallejo, CA....................General Practice

FAVOUR, MOORE, WILHELMSEN & SCHUYLER, A PROFESSIONAL ASSOCIATION
Prescott, AZ....................Civil Trial Practice, Commercial Law, Family Law, General Practice, Insurance Defense Law, Probate and Estate Planning Law, Real Estate Law

FAW, FOLGER, JOHNSON & BELL
Mount Airy, NC....................General Practice

FAY, SHARPE, BEALL, FAGAN, MINNICH & MCKEE
Cleveland, OH....................Patent, Trademark, Copyright and Unfair Competition Law

FEARER, NYE, AHLBERG & CHADWICK
Rochelle, IL....................General Practice

FECZKO AND SEYMOUR
Pittsburgh, PA....................Civil Trial Practice, Personal Injury Law, Probate and Estate Planning Law

FEDER, MORRIS, TAMBLYN & GOLDSTEIN, P.C.
Denver, CO....................Civil Trial Practice, Commercial Law, Construction Law, Family Law, Medical Malpractice Law, Personal Injury Law, Probate and Estate Planning Law

FEDOR & FEDOR
Largo, FL....................Securities Law

FEE, BRYAN & KOBLEGARD, P.A.
Fort Pierce, FL....................Civil Trial Practice, Criminal Trial Practice, Family Law, General Practice

FEENEY, DENA C., P.A.
Silver Spring, MD....................Probate and Estate Planning Law

FEENEY KELLETT & WIENNER, PROFESSIONAL CORPORATION
Bloomfield Hills, MI....................Civil Trial Practice, Commercial Law, General Practice, Personal Injury Law, Product Liability Law

FEIBELMAN, SHULMAN AND TERRY
Mobile, AL....................Bankruptcy Law, Commercial Law

FEIKENS, VANDER MALE, STEVENS, BELLAMY & GILCHRIST, P.C.
Detroit, MI....................Civil Trial Practice, General Practice, Health Care Law, Medical Malpractice Law

FEINBERG, KENNETH R. & ASSOCIATES
Washington, DC....................Business Law, Civil Trial Practice, Commercial Law, Construction Law, Employment Benefits Law, General Practice, Insurance Defense Law, Labor and Employment Law, Medical Malpractice Law, Patent, Trademark, Copyright and Unfair Competition Law, Product Liability Law

FEINGOLD, EUGENE M. LAW OFFICES OF
Munster, IN....................Civil Trial Practice, General Practice, Municipal and Zoning Law

FEINGOLD & NAPOLI
New York, NY....................Tax Law

FEIRICH/SCHOEN/MAGER/GREEN
Carbondale, IL....................General Practice

FEIWELL & ASSOCIATES
Indianapolis, IN....................Bankruptcy Law, Commercial Law, Real Estate Law

FELDER, RAOUL LIONEL, P.C., THE FIRM OF
New York, NY....................Family Law

FELDMAN & FIORELLO
Wayne, NJ....................Civil Trial Practice, Construction Law, Family Law

FELDMAN, HALL, FRANDEN, WOODARD & FARRIS
Tulsa, OK....................Civil Trial Practice, Medical Malpractice Law, Securities Law

FELDMAN, JOEL H., P.A.
Boca Raton, FL....................Family Law, Real Estate Law

FELDMAN, KARP & FELDMAN, A PROFESSIONAL CORPORATION
Woodland Hills, CA....................Business Law, Civil Trial Practice, Real Estate Law

FELDMAN, WALDMAN & KLINE, A PROFESSIONAL CORPORATION
San Francisco, CA....................Bankruptcy Law, Business Law, Civil Trial Practice, Construction Law, General Practice, Probate and Estate Planning Law, Real Estate Law, Tax Law

FELDSTEIN GRINBERG STEIN & MCKEE, A PROFESSIONAL CORPORATION
Pittsburgh, PA....................Business Law, Civil Trial Practice, Employment Benefits Law, Family Law, Health Care Law, Insurance Defense Law, Personal Injury Law

FELHABER, LARSON, FENLON AND VOGT, PROFESSIONAL ASSOCIATION
Minneapolis, MN....................General Practice, Labor and Employment Law
St. Paul, MN....................General Practice

FELLERS, SNIDER, BLANKENSHIP, BAILEY & TIPPENS, A PROFESSIONAL CORPORATION
Oklahoma City, OK....................General Practice

FELLHEIMER EICHEN BRAVERMAN & KASKEY, A PROFESSIONAL CORPORATION
Philadelphia, PA....................Banking Law, Bankruptcy Law, Business Law, Civil Trial Practice, General Practice, Real Estate Law, Securities Law, Tax Law

FELL, MCGARVEY, TRAURING & WILSON
Kokomo, IN....................General Practice, Insurance Defense Law, Probate and Estate Planning Law, Real Estate Law

FENDIG, MCLEMORE, TAYLOR & WHITWORTH, P.C.
Brunswick, GA....................Civil Trial Practice, General Practice

FENNEBRESQUE, CLARK, SWINDELL & HAY
Charlotte, NC....................Banking Law, Real Estate Law

FENNEMORE CRAIG, A PROFESSIONAL CORPORATION
Phoenix, AZ....................Administrative Law, Antitrust Law, Banking Law, Bankruptcy Law, Business Law, Civil Trial Practice, Commercial Law, Construction Law, Employment Benefits Law, Environmental Law, General Practice, Health Care Law, Insurance Defense Law, Labor and Employment Law, Medical Malpractice Law, Municipal and Zoning Law, Natural Resources Law, Patent, Trademark, Copyright and Unfair Competition Law, Personal Injury Law, Probate and Estate Planning Law, Real Estate Law, Securities Law, Tax Law, Transportation Law
Scottsdale, AZ....................General Practice, Real Estate Law
Tucson, AZ....................General Practice, Labor and Employment Law

FENSTER AND FAERBER, PROFESSIONAL ASSOCIATION
Plantation, FL .... Civil Trial Practice, Personal Injury Law

FENTON, CHAPMAN, FENTON, SMITH & KANE, P.A.
Bar Harbor, ME .... Civil Trial Practice, Environmental Law, General Practice, International Business Law, Patent, Trademark, Copyright and Unfair Competition Law, Personal Injury Law, Real Estate Law

FENTON, FENTON, SMITH, RENEAU & MOON, A PROFESSIONAL CORPORATION
Oklahoma City, OK .... General Practice, Insurance Defense Law, Medical Malpractice Law

FERGUSON, CASE, ORR, PATERSON & CUNNINGHAM
Ventura, CA .... Civil Trial Practice, General Practice

FERGUSON, NEWBURN & WESTON, A PROFESSIONAL CORPORATION
La Jolla, CA .... Probate and Estate Planning Law

FERGUSON, STEIN, WALLAS, ADKINS, GRESHAM & SUMTER, P.A.
Charlotte, NC .... Criminal Trial Practice

FERGUSON & WIDMAYER, P.C.
Ann Arbor, MI .... Employment Benefits Law

FERNANDEZ, JOHN D., P.A.
Clearwater, FL .... Personal Injury Law

FERRARA, FIORENZA, LARRISON, BARRETT & REITZ, P.C.
East Syracuse, NY .... Labor and Employment Law

FERRARI, ALVAREZ, OLSEN & OTTOBONI, A PROFESSIONAL CORPORATION
San Jose, CA .... Business Law, Civil Trial Practice, Environmental Law, Health Care Law, Labor and Employment Law, Probate and Estate Planning Law, Real Estate Law, Tax Law

FERRELL & FERTEL, P.A.
Miami, FL .... Civil Trial Practice, Criminal Trial Practice, Municipal and Zoning Law

FERRELL & HUBBARD
Jackson, MS .... Commercial Law, Environmental Law, Personal Injury Law

FERRERI & FOGLE
Lexington, KY .... General Practice
Louisville, KY .... General Practice

FERRERO & MIDDLEBROOKS, P.A.
Fort Lauderdale, FL .... Personal Injury Law

FERRIS & BRITTON, A PROFESSIONAL CORPORATION
San Diego, CA .... Antitrust Law, Banking Law, Business Law, Civil Trial Practice, Commercial Law, Communications Law, General Practice, Insurance Defense Law, Labor and Employment Law, Real Estate Law, Securities Law, Tax Law, Trademark, Copyright and Unfair Competition Law

FERRITER, SCOBBO, SIKORA, SINGAL, CARUSO & RODOPHELE, P.C.
Boston, MA .... General Practice

FERRO LABELLA LOGERFO & ZUCKER, A PROFESSIONAL CORPORATION
Hackensack, NJ .... Commercial Law

FETTER, KESSLER AND PERSING
Lewisburg, PA .... General Practice

FETTERLY & GORDON, P.A.
Minneapolis, MN .... Civil Trial Practice, Insurance Defense Law, Personal Injury Law

FEULNER, GEORGE J., P.C., LAW OFFICES OF
Tucson, AZ .... Commercial Law, Real Estate Law

FEW & FEW, P.A.
Greenville, SC .... Civil Trial Practice, Environmental Law, Personal Injury Law, Product Liability Law, Securities Law

FIDDLER, GONZÁLEZ & RODRÍGUEZ
San Juan, PR .... Antitrust Law, Banking Law, Bankruptcy Law, Civil Trial Practice, Commercial Law, Environmental Law, General Practice, Immigration and Naturalization Law, Insurance Defense Law, Labor and Employment Law, Municipal Bond/Public Authority Financing Law, Real Estate Law, Tax Law, Trademark, Copyright and Unfair Competition Law

FIEGER, FIEGER & SCHWARTZ, A PROFESSIONAL CORPORATION
Southfield, MI .... Civil Trial Practice, Criminal Trial Practice, Medical Malpractice Law, Personal Injury Law

FIELD, BAKER & RICHARDSON
Walnut Creek, CA .... Construction Law, Real Estate Law

FIELD & FIELD PERRATON
Calgary, AB, Canada .... General Practice
Edmonton, AB, Canada .... General Practice

FIELD, GENTRY & BENJAMIN, P.C.
Kansas City, MO .... General Practice

FIELD & OLESNYCKY
Maplewood, NJ .... General Practice

FIELDS AND CREASON
Santa Ana, CA .... Construction Law

FIGARI & DAVENPORT
Dallas, TX .... Civil Trial Practice, General Practice

FIKE, CASCIO & BOOSE
Somerset, PA .... General Practice

FILDEW, HINKS, MILLER, TODD & WANGEN
Detroit, MI .... Civil Trial Practice, General Practice, Real Estate Law, Tax Law

FILE, PAYNE, SCHERER & FILE
Beckley, WV .... General Practice, Insurance Defense Law

FILLEY, G. WILLIAM
San Francisco, CA .... Family Law

FINCH, BRADSHAW, STROM & STEELE, L.C.
Cape Girardeau, MO .... General Practice

FINCH, MONTGOMERY & WRIGHT
Palo Alto, CA .... Probate and Estate Planning Law

FINCK, KEVIN W. LAW OFFICE OF
San Francisco, CA .... Business Law, Commercial Law, International Business Law

FINE, FINE, LEGUM & FINE, PROFESSIONAL ASSOCIATION
Virginia Beach, VA .... Civil Trial Practice

FINE & HATFIELD
Evansville, IN .... Appellate Practice, Bankruptcy Law, Business Law, Civil Trial Practice, Environmental Law, General Practice, Health Care Law, Insurance Defense Law, Labor and Employment Law, Probate and Estate Planning Law, Product Liability Law, Real Estate Law, Tax Law

FINE & MCDOWELL
Russellville, AL .... General Practice, Insurance Defense Law

FINE, RICHARD I., & ASSOCIATES, A PROFESSIONAL CORPORATION, LAW OFFICES OF
Los Angeles, CA .... Antitrust Law, International Business Law

FINEMAN & BACH, P.C.
Philadelphia, PA .... Civil Trial Practice, General Practice, Insurance Defense Law

FINER, KIM & STEARNS
Torrance, CA .... Bankruptcy Law, Environmental Law, General Practice, Probate and Estate Planning Law, Real Estate Law

FINKBOHNER AND LAWLER
Mobile, AL .... Bankruptcy Law, Civil Trial Practice, Commercial Law, General Practice, Municipal and Zoning Law, Personal Injury Law, Product Liability Law

FINKEL, GOLDBERG, SHEFTMAN & ALTMAN, P.A.
Columbia, SC .... Bankruptcy Law, Civil Trial Practice, Commercial Law, Insurance Defense Law, Personal Injury Law

FINKELSTEIN BRUCKMAN WOHL MOST & ROTHMAN
New York, NY .... Family Law, General Practice, Health Care Law, Medical Malpractice Law

FINK & SWEET
Daytona Beach, FL .... Civil Trial Practice, General Practice

FINLEY, ALT, SMITH, SCHARNBERG, MAY & CRAIG, P.C.
Des Moines, IA .... Business Law, Civil Trial Practice, General Practice, Health Care Law, Medical Malpractice Law

FINMAN, SHELDON E., P.A.
Fort Myers, FL .... Family Law

FINNEGAN, HENDERSON, FARABOW, GARRETT & DUNNER
Washington, DC .... Patent, Trademark, Copyright and Unfair Competition Law, Trademark, Copyright and Unfair Competition Law

FIORE, OWEN G.
San Jose, CA .... Probate and Estate Planning Law, Tax Law

FIORENZA & HAYES, S.C.
Milwaukee, WI .... Business Law, Civil Trial Practice, General Practice

FIORETTI, MICHAEL D.
Cherry Hill, NJ .... Family Law
Philadelphia, PA .... Family Law

FISCHER, BESSETTE & MULDOWNEY
Malone, NY....General Practice

FISCHER, BROWN, HUDDLESON & GUNN, P.C.
Fort Collins, CO....General Practice

FISCHER, HOWARD & FRANCIS
Fort Collins, CO....Commercial Law, General Practice, Real Estate Law

FISCHETTE, OWEN & HELD
Jacksonville, FL....Bankruptcy Law

FISCHETTI & RUSSO
New York, NY....Criminal Trial Practice

FISCHL CULP MCMILLIN CHAFFIN BAHNER & BROWN
Ardmore, OK....General Practice

FISCHOFF, GELBERG & DIRECTOR
Garden City, NY....Bankruptcy Law, Civil Trial Practice, Commercial Law, Real Estate Law

FISH & NEAVE
New York, NY....Patent, Trademark, Copyright and Unfair Competition Law

FISH & RICHARDSON
Washington, DC....Patent, Trademark, Copyright and Unfair Competition Law
Boston, MA....Patent, Trademark, Copyright and Unfair Competition Law
Menlo Park, CA....Patent, Trademark, Copyright and Unfair Competition Law
Houston, TX....Patent, Trademark, Copyright and Unfair Competition Law

FISHER & DONOVAN
New York, NY....Real Estate Law

FISHER FISHER GAYLE CLINARD & CRAIG, P.A.
High Point, NC....General Practice

FISHER, GALE, P.C.
Sioux Falls, SD....General Practice

FISHER LAW OFFICE
St. Joseph, MI....General Practice, Probate and Estate Planning Law

FISHER, PATTERSON, SAYLER & SMITH
Overland Park, KS....Civil Trial Practice, Insurance Defense Law, Medical Malpractice Law, Product Liability Law
Topeka, KS....Civil Trial Practice, General Practice, Insurance Defense Law, Personal Injury Law

FISHER & PHILLIPS
Newport Beach, CA....Labor and Employment Law
Redwood City, CA....Labor and Employment Law
Fort Lauderdale, FL....Labor and Employment Law
Atlanta, GA....Employment Benefits Law, Labor and Employment Law

FISHER & PORTER, A LAW CORPORATION
Long Beach, CA....Admiralty/Maritime Law, Environmental Law, General Practice, Transportation Law

FISHER, ROBERT A., INC.
Irvine, CA....Bankruptcy Law

FISHER, ROBERT W., P.C.
Atlanta, GA....Tax Law

FISHER WAYLAND COOPER LEADER & ZARAGOZA, L.L.P.
Washington, DC....Communications Law, General Practice

FITCH, EVEN, TABIN & FLANNERY
San Diego, CA....Patent, Trademark, Copyright and Unfair Competition Law
Chicago, IL....Patent, Trademark, Copyright and Unfair Competition Law

FITE, DAVIS, ATKINSON, GUYTON & BENTLEY, P.C.
Hamilton, AL....General Practice, Personal Injury Law

FITZGERALD, ABBOTT & BEARDSLEY
Oakland, CA....General Practice

FITZGERALD LAW OFFICES
Cheyenne, WY....Civil Trial Practice
Laramie, WY....Civil Trial Practice

FITZGIBBONS, JOHN M.
Sarasota, FL....Criminal Trial Practice
Tampa, FL....Criminal Trial Practice

FITZGIBBONS BROTHERS
Estherville, IA....General Practice

FITZGIBBONS LAW OFFICES
Casa Grande, AZ....General Practice, Personal Injury Law, Probate and Estate Planning Law

FITZPATRICK, CELLA, HARPER & SCINTO
Washington, DC....Patent, Trademark, Copyright and Unfair Competition Law
New York, NY....Patent, Trademark, Copyright and Unfair Competition Law

FITZPATRICK, F. EMMETT, P.C.
Philadelphia, PA....Appellate Practice, Civil Trial Practice, Criminal Trial Practice, General Practice

FITZPATRICK & WATERMAN
Bayonne, NJ....Environmental Law, General Practice, Municipal Bond/Public Authority Financing Law
Secaucus, NJ....Environmental Law, General Practice, Municipal Bond/Public Authority Financing Law

FIX, SPINDELMAN, BROVITZ, TURK, HIMELEIN & SHUKOFF
Rochester, NY....General Practice

FIXEL & MAGUIRE, P.A.
Orlando, FL....Real Estate Law

FLACK, MCRAVEN & STEPHENS
Macomb, IL....General Practice

FLAHERTY, COHEN, GRANDE, RANDAZZO & DOREN, P.C.
Buffalo, NY....Labor and Employment Law

FLAHERTY, MEISLER & COURTNEY
Vernon, CT....General Practice

FLANAGAN, BOOTH, UNGER & MOSES
Glendale, CA....Criminal Trial Practice, Personal Injury Law

FLANAGAN, LIEBERMAN, HOFFMAN & SWAIM
Dayton, OH....Criminal Trial Practice, General Practice

FLANDERS + MEDEIROS INC.
Providence, RI....Antitrust Law, Civil Trial Practice, General Practice, Labor and Employment Law

FLANDERS, SONNESYN & STOVER
Longmont, CO....General Practice

FLANIGAN, MCCANSE & LASLEY
Carthage, MO....General Practice

FLASTER, GREENBERG, WALLENSTEIN, RODERICK, SPIRGEL, ZUCKERMAN, SKINNER & KIRCHNER, P.C.
Marlton, NJ....Business Law, Tax Law

FLECK, MATHER & STRUTZ, LTD.
Bismarck, ND....Civil Trial Practice, Environmental Law, General Practice, Insurance Defense Law, Labor and Employment Law, Natural Resources Law, Personal Injury Law, Tax Law

FLEESON, GOOING, COULSON & KITCH, L.L.C.
Wichita, KS....Antitrust Law, Civil Trial Practice, Communications Law, Environmental Law, General Practice, Labor and Employment Law, Natural Resources Law, Probate and Estate Planning Law, Tax Law

FLEHR, HOHBACH, TEST, ALBRITTON & HERBERT
Palo Alto, CA....Patent, Trademark, Copyright and Unfair Competition Law
San Francisco, CA....Patent, Trademark, Copyright and Unfair Competition Law

FLEISCHMANN & FLEISCHMANN
San Francisco, CA....Business Law, Civil Trial Practice, Commercial Law, Health Care Law, International Business Law, Securities Law

FLEISSNER, COOPER, MARCUS & QUINN
Chattanooga, TN....Civil Trial Practice, Insurance Defense Law, Labor and Employment Law, Product Liability Law

FLEMING, DAVID W., P.C.
Universal City, CA....Business Law, Probate and Estate Planning Law

FLEMING, DONALD D., P.S.
Bellevue, WA....General Practice, Probate and Estate Planning Law, Real Estate Law

FLEMING, JOSEPH Z., P.A.
Miami, FL....Communications Law, Environmental Law, Labor and Employment Law, Natural Resources Law

FLEMING, PATTRIDGE & RUNNERSTROM, P.C.
Golden, CO....General Practice

FLETCHER, HARLEY & FLETCHER
Augusta, GA....General Practice

FLETCHER, HEALD & HILDRETH, P.L.C.
Washington, DC....Communications Law

FLETCHER, PAUL G., P.A.
Miami, FL....Family Law, Real Estate Law

FLETCHER, SIBELL, MIGATZ & BURNS, P.C.
Manhasset, NY .... General Practice

FLETCHER, TILTON & WHIPPLE, P.C.
Worcester, MA .... General Practice

FLEURIET & SCHELL
Harlingen, TX .... Civil Trial Practice

FLICKER & KERIN
Palo Alto, CA .... Business Law, Family Law

FLINN MERRICK
Halifax, NS, Canada .... General Practice

FLIPPIN, COLLINS, HUEY & WEBB
Milan, TN .... General Practice

FLORANCE, GORDON AND BROWN, A PROFESSIONAL CORPORATION
Richmond, VA .... Civil Trial Practice, Probate and Estate Planning Law, Real Estate Law

FLORES, CASSO, ROMERO & PETTITT
McAllen, TX .... General Practice

FLOYD, KEENER, CUSIMANO & ROBERTS, P.C.
Gadsden, AL .... Civil Trial Practice, Criminal Trial Practice, General Practice

FLOYD LAW FIRM PC, THE
Surfside Beach, SC .... General Practice

FLOYD PEARSON RICHMAN GREER WEIL BRUMBAUGH & RUSSOMANNO, P.A.
Miami, FL .... Civil Trial Practice, General Practice

FLOYD, TAYLOR & RILEY, L.L.P.
Houston, TX .... Civil Trial Practice, Personal Injury Law

FLUEGEL, HELSETH, MCLAUGHLIN, ANDERSON & BRUTLAG, CHARTERED
Elbow Lake, MN .... General Practice

FLYNN, DELICH & WISE
Long Beach, CA .... Admiralty/Maritime Law, Civil Trial Practice, Insurance Defense Law, International Business Law
San Francisco, CA .... Admiralty/Maritime Law, Civil Trial Practice, Insurance Defense Law, International Business Law, Patent, Trademark, Copyright and Unfair Competition Law

FLYNN, HARDY & COHN
Waltham, MA .... General Practice

FLYNN MCKENNA & WRIGHT, LIMITED LIABILITY COMPANY
Colorado Springs, CO .... Banking Law, Commercial Law, Real Estate Law

FLYNN, PALMER & TAGUE
Champaign, IL .... General Practice

FLYNN, PY & KRUSE, A LEGAL PROFESSIONAL ASSOCIATION
Sandusky, OH .... General Practice

FOGEL, FELDMAN, OSTROV, RINGLER & KLEVENS, A LAW CORPORATION
Santa Monica, CA .... Civil Trial Practice, Labor and Employment Law, Personal Injury Law

FOGG, FOGG & HANDLEY
El Reno, OK .... General Practice
Oklahoma City, OK .... General Practice

FOLEY, HOAG & ELIOT
Washington, DC .... General Practice
Boston, MA .... General Practice, Labor and Employment Law, Tax Law

FOLEY & LARDNER
Washington, DC .... General Practice
Jacksonville, FL .... General Practice
Orlando, FL .... General Practice, Labor and Employment Law
Tallahassee, FL .... General Practice
Tampa, FL .... General Practice
West Palm Beach, FL .... General Practice
Chicago, IL .... General Practice
Annapolis, MD .... General Practice
Madison, WI .... General Practice
Milwaukee, WI .... Antitrust Law, General Practice, Tax Law

FOLEY MAEHARA NIP & CHANG
Honolulu, HI .... Business Law, Commercial Law, Immigration and Naturalization Law, International Business Law, Municipal and Zoning Law, Probate and Estate Planning Law, Real Estate Law

FOLEY, MCLANE, NEALON, FOLEY & MCDONALD
Scranton, PA .... Civil Trial Practice, Medical Malpractice Law, Personal Injury Law

FOLGER & LEVIN
San Francisco, CA .... General Practice

FOLGER, TUCKER & HOWE
Madison, NC .... General Practice

FOLIART, HUFF, OTTAWAY & CALDWELL, A PROFESSIONAL CORPORATION
Oklahoma City, OK .... Civil Trial Practice, Insurance Defense Law, Medical Malpractice Law, Personal Injury Law

FOLKESTAD, KOKISH & FAZEKAS, P.C.
Castle Rock, CO .... General Practice, Municipal and Zoning Law, Real Estate Law

FOLKS, KHOURY & DEVENNY
Lancaster, SC .... General Practice

FOLTZ, JOHN R.
St. Petersburg, FL .... General Practice

FONVIELLE & HINKLE
Tallahassee, FL .... Medical Malpractice Law, Personal Injury Law, Product Liability Law

FORBES, THOMAS A.
Austin, TX .... Administrative Law, General Practice

FORBES & BOWMAN
Savannah, GA .... Insurance Defense Law, Product Liability Law

FORBES & POHL
Eureka, KS .... General Practice

FORCENO & HANNON
Philadelphia, PA .... Personal Injury Law, Product Liability Law

FORD, HULEN
Dallas, TX .... Personal Injury Law

FORD & DOYLE, L.L.P.
Dallas, TX .... Civil Trial Practice

FORD & FERRARO, L.L.P.
Austin, TX .... Banking Law, Civil Trial Practice, Health Care Law, Insurance Defense Law

FORD & HARRISON
Los Angeles, CA .... Labor and Employment Law
Atlanta, GA .... Labor and Employment Law

FORD & HUNTER, P.C.
Gadsden, AL .... Banking Law, Bankruptcy Law, Civil Trial Practice, Commercial Law, General Practice, Insurance Defense Law

FORD MARRIN ESPOSITO WITMEYER & GLESER
New York, NY .... General Practice

FORDNEY, DUST & PRINE
Saginaw, MI .... Insurance Defense Law, Medical Malpractice Law

FORD, WALKER, HAGGERTY & BEHAR, PROFESSIONAL LAW CORPORATION
Long Beach, CA .... Civil Trial Practice, General Practice, Insurance Defense Law

FOREMAN & ARCH, P.S.
Wenatchee, WA .... Civil Trial Practice

FORET & THOMPSON
Washington, DC .... Civil Trial Practice, Personal Injury Law

FORKIN, MCSHANE & ROTZ, A PROFESSIONAL ASSOCIATION
Cherry Hill, NJ .... Civil Trial Practice, Family Law, General Practice

FORMAN, CHARLES M. & ASSOCIATES
Newark, NJ .... Bankruptcy Law

FORMAN, MARTH, BLACK & ANGLE, P.A.
Greensboro, NC .... Business Law, Probate and Estate Planning Law, Tax Law

FORRESTER & BRIM
Gainesville, GA .... Insurance Defense Law, Medical Malpractice Law

FORSYTH, HOWE, O'DWYER & KALB, P.C.
Rochester, NY .... Commercial Law, General Practice

FORTINO, PLAXTON & MOSKAL
Alma, MI .... General Practice

FORTUNE, JOHNNY, P.A.
Fort Walton Beach, FL .... General Practice

FOSS, WHITTY, LITTLEFIELD & MCDANIEL
Coos Bay, OR .... General Practice

FOSSETT & BRUGGER, CHARTERED
Seabrook, MD .... Civil Trial Practice, General Practice, Real Estate Law

FOSTER, WILLIAM D. & ASSOCIATES
Minneapolis, MN....................Civil Trial Practice, Personal Injury Law

FOSTER, FOSTER, ALLEN & DURRENCE
Chattanooga, TN....................Civil Trial Practice, Construction Law, Environmental Law, General Practice, Insurance Defense Law, Medical Malpractice Law, Personal Injury Law, Real Estate Law, Securities Law

FOSTER, HELLER & KILGORE, P.C.
San Antonio, TX....................Labor and Employment Law

FOSTER LAW FIRM, THE, P.A.
Fairhope, AL....................Civil Trial Practice

FOSTER, LEWIS, LANGLEY, GARDNER & BANACK, INCORPORATED
San Antonio, TX....................General Practice

FOSTER, MEADOWS & BALLARD, P.C.
Detroit, MI....................Admiralty/Maritime Law, General Practice, Insurance Defense Law, Probate and Estate Planning Law, Product Liability Law, Real Estate Law, Transportation Law

FOSTER PEPPER & SHEFELMAN
Seattle, WA....................General Practice

FOSTER, PURDY, ALLAN, PETERSON & DAHLIN
Medford, OR....................General Practice

FOSTER & SULLIVAN
Greenville, SC....................Civil Trial Practice, General Practice

FOSTER, SWIFT, COLLINS & SMITH, P.C.
Farmington Hills, MI....................Transportation Law
Lansing, MI....................Banking Law, Civil Trial Practice, Employment Benefits Law, Environmental Law, General Practice, Health Care Law, Immigration and Naturalization Law, Insurance Defense Law, International Business Law, Labor and Employment Law, Patent, Trademark, Copyright and Unfair Competition Law, Personal Injury Law, Probate and Estate Planning Law, Real Estate Law, Transportation Law

FOSTER, WALDECK, LIND & GRIES, LTD.
Minneapolis, MN....................Appellate Practice, Business Law, Civil Trial Practice, General Practice, Insurance Defense Law

FOULSTON & SIEFKIN
Topeka, KS....................Administrative Law, Business Law, Employment Benefits Law, Tax Law, Transportation Law
Wichita, KS....................Administrative Law, Antitrust Law, Banking Law, Bankruptcy Law, Business Law, Civil Trial Practice, Commercial Law, Construction Law, Employment Benefits Law, Environmental Law, General Practice, Health Care Law, Insurance Defense Law, International Business Law, Labor and Employment Law, Medical Malpractice Law, Natural Resources Law, Personal Injury Law, Probate and Estate Planning Law, Real Estate Law, Securities Law, Tax Law, Trademark, Copyright and Unfair Competition Law

FOWLER, MEASLE & BELL
Lexington, KY....................Banking Law, Bankruptcy Law, Civil Trial Practice, General Practice, Real Estate Law

FOWLER, WHITE, BURNETT, HURLEY, BANICK & STRICKROOT, A PROFESSIONAL ASSOCIATION
Miami, FL....................Admiralty/Maritime Law, General Practice, Tax Law

FOX, WAYNE C.
Houston, TX....................Business Law, Civil Trial Practice, Real Estate Law

FOX AND FOX
Newark, NJ....................Administrative Law, Banking Law, Commercial Law, General Practice, Probate and Estate Planning Law, Real Estate Law, Tax Law

FOX & GROVE, CHARTERED
Chicago, IL....................Civil Trial Practice, Commercial Law, Labor and Employment Law

FOX, OLDT & BROWN
Easton, PA....................General Practice, Personal Injury Law

FOX, ROTHSCHILD, O'BRIEN & FRANKEL
Trenton, NJ....................Banking Law, General Practice
Philadelphia, PA....................General Practice, Real Estate Law, Tax Law

FOYEN & PARTNERS
Maplewood, NJ....................Banking Law, Commercial Law, International Business Law

FRANCIS, KAZEE & FRANCIS
Prestonsburg, KY....................General Practice, Insurance Defense Law, Natural Resources Law

FRANCIS & STARZYNSKI, P.A.
Albuquerque, NM....................Bankruptcy Law

FRANCO BRADLEY & MARTORELLA
San Diego, CA....................Civil Trial Practice, Environmental Law, Insurance Defense Law

FRANKE, RAINEY & SALLOUM
Gulfport, MS....................Admiralty/Maritime Law, Civil Trial Practice, Insurance Defense Law, Probate and Estate Planning Law, Real Estate Law

FRANKEL, HARDWICK, TANENBAUM & FINK, P.C.
Atlanta, GA....................Business Law, Civil Trial Practice, Commercial Law, Construction Law, Employment Benefits Law, Family Law, General Practice, Probate and Estate Planning Law, Real Estate Law

FRANKEL, SANDOR, P.C.
New York, NY....................Civil Trial Practice, Criminal Trial Practice

FRANK, JOHN J., PARTNERSHIP, THE
St. Louis, MO....................Personal Injury Law

FRANKLIN AND HANCE, P.S.C.
Louisville, KY....................Civil Trial Practice, Medical Malpractice Law, Personal Injury Law

FRANK & MILCHEN
San Diego, CA....................Criminal Trial Practice, General Practice

FRANKOVITCH & ANETAKIS
Weirton, WV....................General Practice

FRANKS, JON MICHAEL
Fort Worth, TX....................Family Law

FRANSCELL, STRICKLAND, ROBERTS & LAWRENCE, A PROFESSIONAL CORPORATION
Pasadena, CA....................Civil Trial Practice, General Practice, Personal Injury Law

FRANTZ, MCCONNELL & SEYMOUR
Knoxville, TN....................Civil Trial Practice, General Practice

FRASCOGNA, COURTNEY, WRIGHT, BIEDENHARN & SMITH
Jackson, MS....................General Practice

FRASER & BEATTY
Vancouver, BC, Canada....................General Practice
North York, ON, Canada....................General Practice
Ottawa, ON, Canada....................General Practice
Toronto, ON, Canada....................General Practice

FRASER, STRYKER, VAUGHN, MEUSEY, OLSON, BOYER & BLOCH, P.C.
Omaha, NE....................Banking Law, Commercial Law, Environmental Law, General Practice, Insurance Defense Law, Labor and Employment Law, Real Estate Law, Tax Law

FRASER TREBILCOCK DAVIS & FOSTER, P.C.
Lansing, MI....................Banking Law, Civil Trial Practice, Employment Benefits Law, Environmental Law, General Practice, Health Care Law, Insurance Defense Law, Labor and Employment Law, Medical Malpractice Law, Probate and Estate Planning Law, Product Liability Law, Real Estate Law

FRASER, WHITE & DES ROCHES
New Orleans, LA....................General Practice

FRASSINETI AND GLOVER
Greensboro, NC....................Probate and Estate Planning Law, Real Estate Law

FRAZER, S. STEWART
Dallas, TX....................Civil Trial Practice

FRAZIER & FRAZIER, ATTORNEYS AT LAW, P.A.
Jacksonville, FL....................Tax Law

FRAZIER & OXLEY, L.C.
Huntington, WV....................Banking Law, Probate and Estate Planning Law, Tax Law

FREDERICKSON & HEINTSCHEL, CO., L.P.A.
Toledo, OH....................Bankruptcy Law, Civil Trial Practice, Probate and Estate Planning Law

FREDRICKSON & JOHNSON, P.C.
Canon City, CO....................General Practice

FREDRIKSON & BYRON, P.A.
Minneapolis, MN....................Antitrust Law, General Practice, Labor and Employment Law

FREEBURG, JUDY, MACCHIAGODENA & NETTELS
Pasadena, CA....................Civil Trial Practice, Environmental Law, Insurance Defense Law, Medical Malpractice Law

FREEDMAN & ASSOCIATES
Philadelphia, PA....................Employment Benefits Law, Tax Law

FREEDMAN, BOYD, DANIELS, PEIFER, HOLLANDER, GUTTMANN & GOLDBERG, P.A.
Albuquerque, NM....................Civil Trial Practice, Criminal Trial Practice

FREEDMAN, GARY, LAW OFFICES OF
Santa Monica, CA....................Business Law, Civil Trial Practice

FREEDMAN, LEVY, KROLL & SIMONDS
Washington, DC....................Environmental Law, General Practice, Natural Resources Law

FREELAND & FREELAND
Oxford, MS....................Banking Law, Bankruptcy Law, Civil Trial Practice, Commercial Law, Insurance Defense Law, Product Liability Law, Real Estate Law

FREEMAN, FREEMAN & SALZMAN, P.C.
Chicago, IL....................Antitrust Law, Commercial Law, Securities Law

FREEMAN & HAWKINS
Atlanta, GA....................Civil Trial Practice, Environmental Law, General Practice, Municipal and Zoning Law, Product Liability Law

FREEMAN & JENNER, P.C.
Aspen, CO....................Medical Malpractice Law, Patent, Trademark, Copyright and Unfair Competition Law, Personal Injury Law
Bethesda, MD....................Medical Malpractice Law, Patent, Trademark, Copyright and Unfair Competition Law, Personal Injury Law

FREEMAN & LOFTUS
New City, NY....................Probate and Estate Planning Law, Real Estate Law

FREEMAN, MINTZ, HAGNER & DEICHES, P.A.
Haddonfield, NJ....................General Practice

FREEMAN & ROSS, P.A.
West Palm Beach, FL....................Civil Trial Practice, Medical Malpractice Law, Personal Injury Law

FREISHTAT & SANDLER
Baltimore, MD....................Civil Trial Practice, Criminal Trial Practice

FREITAS, MCCARTHY, MACMAHON & KEATING
San Rafael, CA....................General Practice

FRENCH, WEST & BROWN, P.C.
Breckenridge, CO....................General Practice

FRENSLEY & TOWERMAN, P.C.
Kansas City, MO....................General Practice

FREUND, FREEZE & ARNOLD, A LEGAL PROFESSIONAL ASSOCIATION
Dayton, OH....................Appellate Practice, Civil Trial Practice, Construction Law, Insurance Defense Law, Medical Malpractice Law, Product Liability Law

FREUND, MARK, P.A.
Tallahassee, FL....................Bankruptcy Law, Probate and Estate Planning Law

FRIDAY, ELDREDGE & CLARK
Little Rock, AR....................Antitrust Law, Banking Law, Civil Trial Practice, General Practice, Insurance Defense Law, Labor and Employment Law, Municipal Bond/Public Authority Financing Law, Personal Injury Law, Securities Law, Tax Law

FRIED & ASSOCIATES, P.C.
Livonia, MI....................Tax Law

FRIEDBERG, JOSEPH S., CHARTERED
Minneapolis, MN....................Criminal Trial Practice

FRIED, BIRD & CRUMPACKER, A PROFESSIONAL CORPORATION
Los Angeles, CA....................Banking Law, Real Estate Law

FRIED, FRANK, HARRIS, SHRIVER & JACOBSON
Washington, DC....................General Practice, Real Estate Law, Tax Law
New York, NY....................General Practice
London, England....................General Practice
Paris, France....................General Practice

FRIEDLANDER, MISLER, FRIEDLANDER, SLOAN & HERZ
Washington, DC....................Banking Law, General Practice

FRIEDLOB SANDERSON RASKIN PAULSON & TOURTILLOTT
Denver, CO....................Business Law, Civil Trial Practice, Securities Law

FRIEDL, RICHTER & BURI
Phoenix, AZ....................Criminal Trial Practice, Family Law, Medical Malpractice Law, Personal Injury Law

FRIEDMAN & ATHERTON
Boston, MA....................Civil Trial Practice, General Practice

FRIEDMAN & BABBITT CO., L.P.A.
Columbus, OH....................Family Law

FRIEDMAN & BABCOCK
Portland, ME....................Civil Trial Practice, Environmental Law, Insurance Defense Law, Personal Injury Law, Product Liability Law

FRIEDMAN, C. MARSHALL, A PROFESSIONAL CORPORATION
St. Louis, MO....................Civil Trial Practice

FRIEDMAN AND COLLARD, PROFESSIONAL CORPORATIONS
Sacramento, CA....................General Practice, Personal Injury Law

FRIEDMAN, DOMIANO & SMITH CO., L.P.A.
Cleveland, OH....................Personal Injury Law, Product Liability Law

FRIEDMAN & FRIEDMAN
Beverly Hills, CA....................Civil Trial Practice, Family Law

FRIEDMAN & KAPLAN
New York, NY....................Civil Trial Practice, Securities Law

FRIEDMAN, ROSS & HERSH, A PROFESSIONAL CORPORATION
San Francisco, CA....................Civil Trial Practice

FRIEDRICH & FRIEDRICH, P.A.
Fort Lauderdale, FL....................Probate and Estate Planning Law

FRIEND, KARL E.
Allentown, PA....................Bankruptcy Law
Reading, PA....................Bankruptcy Law

FRIJOUF, RUST & PYLE, P.A.
Tampa, FL....................Patent, Trademark, Copyright and Unfair Competition Law

FRIMET & MICHALSEN, P.C.
Southfield, MI....................Health Care Law

FRINK, FOY, GAINEY & YOUNT, P.A.
Shallotte, NC....................General Practice
Southport, NC....................General Practice

FRISK, FRANK W., JR., P.C.
Washington, DC....................Administrative Law, Environmental Law, Municipal and Zoning Law, Natural Resources Law

FRITH, DOUGLAS K., & ASSOCIATES, P.C.
Martinsville, VA....................Civil Trial Practice, Criminal Trial Practice, Family Law, Personal Injury Law

FRITH, STUMP & STOREY, P.A.
Orlando, FL....................Commercial Law

FROHNMAYER, DEATHERAGE, PRATT JAMIESON & CLARKE, P.C.
Medford, OR....................General Practice

FROIMSON, JEROME L.
Phoenix, AZ....................Labor and Employment Law

FROMMELT & EIDE, LTD.
Minneapolis, MN....................Business Law, Real Estate Law, Securities Law

FRONEFIELD AND DE FURIA
Media, PA....................General Practice, Insurance Defense Law, Labor and Employment Law, Probate and Estate Planning Law

FROST & JACOBS
Cincinnati, OH....................Antitrust Law, Banking Law, Bankruptcy Law, Civil Trial Practice, Commercial Law, Communications Law, Environmental Law, General Practice, Labor and Employment Law, Patent, Trademark, Copyright and Unfair Competition Law, Real Estate Law, Tax Law
Middletown, OH....................General Practice

FROST, O'TOOLE & SAUNDERS, P.A.
Bartow, FL....................Civil Trial Practice, General Practice, Medical Malpractice Law, Personal Injury Law

FRUMENTO, AEGIS J.
New York, NY....................Civil Trial Practice

FRUMKES, MELVYN B., & ASSOCIATES, P.A.
Miami, FL....................Family Law

FRYBERGER, BUCHANAN, SMITH & FREDERICK, P.A.
Duluth, MN....................Banking Law, Bankruptcy Law, Civil Trial Practice, Employment Benefits Law, General Practice, Personal Injury Law

FTHENAKIS & VOLK
Palo Alto, CA....................Antitrust Law, Civil Trial Practice, General Practice, Securities Law

FUENTES AND KREISCHER
Tampa, FL....................Personal Injury Law, Probate and Estate Planning Law, Real Estate Law

FUGATE, IVAN D.
Denver, CO....................Banking Law

FUGATE, LEE
Clearwater, FL.......................Criminal Trial Practice

FUJIYAMA, DUFFY & FUJIYAMA, ATTORNEYS AT LAW, A LAW CORPORATION
Honolulu, HI.......................General Practice

FULCHER, HAGLER, REED, HANKS & HARPER
Augusta, GA.......................Civil Trial Practice, General Practice, Insurance Defense Law

FULLER, W. SIDNEY
Andalusia, AL.......................General Practice

FULLER, BECTON, BILLINGS, SLIFKIN & BELL, P.A.
Raleigh, NC.......................Medical Malpractice Law, Personal Injury Law

FULLER AND EVANS
Denver, CO.......................General Practice

FULLER & HENRY
Toledo, OH.......................Civil Trial Practice, Environmental Law, General Practice, Health Care Law, Insurance Defense Law, Labor and Employment Law, Natural Resources Law, Probate and Estate Planning Law, Real Estate Law, Tax Law

FULLER, JOHNSON & FARRELL, P.A.
Pensacola, FL.......................Civil Trial Practice, Product Liability Law
Tallahassee, FL.......................Civil Trial Practice, Product Liability Law

FULLER, ROSENBERG, PALMER & BELIVEAU
Worcester, MA.......................Civil Trial Practice, Insurance Defense Law, Personal Injury Law, Product Liability Law

FULLER & TELLINGHUISEN
Lead, SD.......................General Practice

FULLER, TUBB & POMEROY
Oklahoma City, OK.......................Bankruptcy Law, Commercial Law, General Practice, Probate and Estate Planning Law

FULTON, THEODORE H. JR.
Fort Lauderdale, FL.......................Probate and Estate Planning Law

FULWIDER, PATTON, LEE & UTECHT
Los Angeles, CA.......................Patent, Trademark, Copyright and Unfair Competition Law

FUNDERBURK & FUNDERBURK, L.L.P.
Houston, TX.......................Civil Trial Practice, Insurance Defense Law, Product Liability Law

FURBEE, AMOS, WEBB & CRITCHFIELD
Fairmont, WV.......................General Practice
Morgantown, WV.......................General Practice

FUREY, FUREY, LAPPING, DEMARIA & PETROZZO, P.C.
Hempstead, NY.......................Civil Trial Practice, General Practice

FURGANG, PHILIP LAW OFFICES OF
New York, NY.......................Patent, Trademark, Copyright and Unfair Competition Law

FURMAN & HALPERN, P.C.
Bala Cynwyd, PA.......................Civil Trial Practice, Health Care Law, Tax Law

FURNESS, MIDDLEBROOK, KAISER & HIGGINS, A PROFESSIONAL CORPORATION
San Bernardino, CA.......................Civil Trial Practice, Insurance Defense Law

FURR AND HENSHAW
Columbia, SC.......................Civil Trial Practice, Medical Malpractice Law, Personal Injury Law

FURTH, FAHRNER & MASON
San Francisco, CA.......................Antitrust Law, Business Law

FUSCO & NEWBRAUGH
Morgantown, WV.......................Antitrust Law, Civil Trial Practice, General Practice

GABEL & HAIR
Jacksonville, FL.......................Admiralty/Maritime Law, Civil Trial Practice, Communications Law, General Practice

GABERMAN & PARISH, P.C.
Springfield, MA.......................Business Law, Employment Benefits Law, Probate and Estate Planning Law, Real Estate Law, Tax Law

GABLE & GOTWALS
Tulsa, OK.......................Antitrust Law, Banking Law, Bankruptcy Law, Business Law, Civil Trial Practice, Commercial Law, Communications Law, Employment Benefits Law, Environmental Law, Family Law, General Practice, Insurance Defense Law, Labor and Employment Law, Natural Resources Law, Probate and Estate Planning Law, Real Estate Law, Securities Law, Tax Law, Trademark, Copyright and Unfair Competition Law

GABLER & ASSOCIATES, P.C.
Pittsburgh, PA.......................Employment Benefits Law

GABROY, ROLLMAN & BOSSÉ, P.C.
Tucson, AZ.......................Civil Trial Practice, General Practice, Tax Law

GACA, MATIS & HAMILTON, A PROFESSIONAL CORPORATION
Pittsburgh, PA.......................Admiralty/Maritime Law, Banking Law, Civil Trial Practice, Commercial Law, Construction Law, Environmental Law, Health Care Law, Insurance Defense Law, Labor and Employment Law, Patent, Trademark, Copyright and Unfair Competition Law, Personal Injury Law

GADSBY & HANNAH
Boston, MA.......................Civil Trial Practice, General Practice

GAGER & HENRY
Waterbury, CT.......................General Practice

GAGNON & DIEHL, ATTORNEYS AT LAW, A PROF. ASSN.
Indianapolis, IN.......................Insurance Defense Law

GAHARAN & WILSON
Jena, LA.......................General Practice

GAIMS, WEIL, WEST & EPSTEIN
Los Angeles, CA.......................Civil Trial Practice

GAINSBURGH, BENJAMIN, FALLON, DAVID & ATES
New Orleans, LA.......................Admiralty/Maritime Law, Criminal Trial Practice, Environmental Law, International Business Law, Medical Malpractice Law, Personal Injury Law

GAIR, GAIR, CONASON, STEIGMAN & MACKAUF
New York, NY.......................Civil Trial Practice, Medical Malpractice Law, Personal Injury Law

GAITÁN & CUSACK
Seattle, WA.......................Administrative Law, Banking Law, Business Law, Civil Trial Practice, Commercial Law, Construction Law, Environmental Law, General Practice, Immigration and Naturalization Law, Insurance Defense Law, International Business Law, Labor and Employment Law, Medical Malpractice Law, Real Estate Law

GAITENS, TUCCERI & NICHOLAS, A PROFESSIONAL CORPORATION
Pittsburgh, PA.......................Civil Trial Practice, Criminal Trial Practice, General Practice, Insurance Defense Law, Medical Malpractice Law, Personal Injury Law

GALATZ, EARL & BULLA
Las Vegas, NV.......................Medical Malpractice Law, Personal Injury Law

GALBUT & ASSOCIATES, A PROFESSIONAL CORPORATION
Phoenix, AZ.......................Civil Trial Practice, Securities Law

GALLAGHER & ARCHAMBEAULT, A PROFESSIONAL CORPORATION
Glasgow, MT.......................General Practice

GALLAGHER, BRENNAN & GILL
Wilkes-Barre, PA.......................Civil Trial Practice, Probate and Estate Planning Law, Real Estate Law

GALLAGHER, CASADOS & MANN, P.C.
Albuquerque, NM.......................Bankruptcy Law, Civil Trial Practice, Commercial Law, Insurance Defense Law

GALLAGHER, EVELIUS & JONES
Baltimore, MD.......................Real Estate Law

GALLAGHER GALLAGHER & CALISTRO
New Haven, CT.......................Civil Trial Practice, General Practice

GALLAGHER GOSSEEN & FALLER
Garden City, NY.......................Civil Trial Practice, Employment Benefits Law, General Practice, Insurance Defense Law, Labor and Employment Law, Personal Injury Law, Product Liability Law

GALLAGHER, LANGLAS & GALLAGHER, P.C.
Waterloo, IA.......................Civil Trial Practice, General Practice

GALLAGHER, REILLY AND LACHAT, P.C.
Philadelphia, PA.......................Business Law, Civil Trial Practice, General Practice, Insurance Defense Law, Medical Malpractice Law, Personal Injury Law, Product Liability Law, Transportation Law

GALLAGHER, THOMAS A., A PROFESSIONAL CORPORATION
San Francisco, CA.......................Patent, Trademark, Copyright and Unfair Competition Law

GALLEGOS LAW FIRM, P.C.
Santa Fe, NM.......................Antitrust Law, Civil Trial Practice, Commercial Law, Natural Resources Law

GALLIGAN & NEWMAN
McMinnville, TN.......................Civil Trial Practice, General Practice

GALLON, E. S., & ASSOCIATES
Dayton, OH............................Civil Trial Practice, Personal Injury Law

GALLOP, JOHNSON & NEUMAN, L.C.
St. Louis, MO.........................Civil Trial Practice, General Practice

GALLOWAY & GALLOWAY, P.A.
Gulfport, MS..........................General Practice

GALLOWAY, WIEGERS & HEENEY
Marysville, KS........................General Practice

GALLUCCI, HOPKINS & THEISEN, P.C.
Fort Wayne, IN........................Civil Trial Practice, Environmental Law, Labor and Employment Law

GALTON & HELM
Los Angeles, CA.......................Civil Trial Practice, Health Care Law, Insurance Defense Law

GALUMBECK SIMMONS AND REASOR
Tazewell, VA..........................Civil Trial Practice, Criminal Trial Practice, Personal Injury Law

GALVIN, GALVIN & LEENEY
Hammond, IN...........................Banking Law, Civil Trial Practice, General Practice, Health Care Law, Insurance Defense Law

GAMBLE HARTSHORN ALDEN
Columbus, OH..........................Civil Trial Practice, Transportation Law

GAMMAGE & BURNHAM
Phoenix, AZ...........................Bankruptcy Law, General Practice, Health Care Law, Municipal and Zoning Law, Real Estate Law

GAMMON & GRANGE, P.C.
McLean, VA............................Civil Trial Practice, Communications Law

GANDELOT, JON B., P.C.
Grosse Pointe Woods, MI.......Probate and Estate Planning Law

GANDIN, SCHOTSKY & RAPPAPORT, P.C.
Melville, NY..........................Personal Injury Law, Product Liability Law

GANDY, FRANCIS I. JR.
Corpus Christi, TX...................Civil Trial Practice

GANNON, COTTRELL & WARD, P.C.
Alexandria, VA........................Family Law
Fairfax, VA...........................Family Law

GANZ, HOLLINGER & TOWE
New York, NY..........................Employment Benefits Law, Labor and Employment Law, Personal Injury Law, Real Estate Law

GARAN, LUCOW, MILLER, SEWARD, COOPER & BECKER, P.C.
Ann Arbor, MI.........................General Practice
Detroit, MI...........................Civil Trial Practice, General Practice, Insurance Defense Law
Grand Blanc, MI.......................General Practice
Mount Clemens, MI.....................General Practice
Port Huron, MI........................General Practice
Troy, MI..............................General Practice

GARBARINI & SCHER, P.C.
New York, NY..........................Insurance Defense Law, Medical Malpractice Law

GARCIA, JULIO A.
Laredo, TX............................General Practice

GARCIA & FIELDS, P.A.
Tampa, FL.............................Family Law, Real Estate Law

GARDENAL, JOHN, A PROFESSIONAL CORPORATION
San Francisco, CA.....................Medical Malpractice Law, Personal Injury Law, Product Liability Law

GARDERE & WYNNE, L.L.P.
Dallas, TX............................General Practice, Labor and Employment Law

GARDINER, ROBERTS
Toronto, ON, Canada...................General Practice

GARDNER, EWING & SOUZA
Louisville, KY........................Medical Malpractice Law

GARDNER & FERGUSON, INC., A PROFESSIONAL CORPORATION
San Antonio, TX.......................Administrative Law, Construction Law

GARDNER, GARDNER & GARDNER
Sedalia, MO...........................General Practice

GARDNER, MIDDLEBROOKS & FLEMING, P.C.
Mobile, AL............................Insurance Defense Law, Labor and Employment Law

GARGARO, WILLIAM J., JR., A PROFESSIONAL CORPORATION
Los Angeles, CA.......................Medical Malpractice Law, Personal Injury Law, Product Liability Law

GARIPPA AND DAVENPORT, A PROFESSIONAL CORPORATION
Montclair, NJ.........................Tax Law

GARLAND, SAMUEL & LOEB, P.C.
Atlanta, GA...........................Civil Trial Practice, Criminal Trial Practice, Medical Malpractice Law, Personal Injury Law, Product Liability Law

GARLINGTON, LOHN & ROBINSON
Missoula, MT..........................General Practice

GARMON & GOODMAN
Glasgow, KY...........................Bankruptcy Law, General Practice, Real Estate Law

GARNER, LOVELL & STEIN, P.C.
Amarillo, TX..........................Civil Trial Practice, Commercial Law, Personal Injury Law

GARNIER & GARNIER, P.C.
Falls Church, VA......................Civil Trial Practice

GARRETT & GARRETT, A PROF. CORP., LAW OFFICES
Bedford, VA...........................General Practice

GARRETT & JENSEN
Santa Ana, CA.........................Insurance Defense Law

GARRIGLE & PALM
Cherry Hill, NJ.......................Civil Trial Practice, Environmental Law, Insurance Defense Law, Personal Injury Law

GARTNER & YOUNG, A PROFESSIONAL CORPORATION
Los Angeles, CA.......................Labor and Employment Law

GARTRELL & ASSOCIATES
Silver Spring, MD.....................Civil Trial Practice

GARVEY, ANDERSON, JOHNSON, GABLER & GERACI, S.C.
Eau Claire, WI........................General Practice, Insurance Defense Law

GARVEY, SCHUBERT & BARER
Portland, OR..........................General Practice
Seattle, WA...........................Admiralty/Maritime Law, General Practice

GARVIN & TRIPP, A PROFESSIONAL ASSOCIATION
Fort Myers, FL........................Personal Injury Law

GARY, ANDREW
San Marcos, TX........................General Practice

GASKINS, JOHNNY S.
Raleigh, NC...........................Criminal Trial Practice, Personal Injury Law

GASSMAN FISHER & FASS
Garden City, NY.......................Family Law

GATES & GATES
Columbia City, IN.....................Probate and Estate Planning Law, Real Estate Law

GATHRIGHT AND LEONARD
Doylestown, PA........................General Practice, Probate and Estate Planning Law

GATLIN, WOODS, CARLSON & COWDERY
Tallahassee, FL.......................Administrative Law, Public Utilities Law

GATTIS, HALLOWES & CARPENTER, PROFESSIONAL ASSOCIATION
Orlando, FL...........................Civil Trial Practice, General Practice

GATZKE, MISPAGEL & DILLON
Carlsbad, CA..........................Civil Trial Practice, Environmental Law

GAULEY & CO.
Saskatoon, SK, Canada.................Civil Trial Practice, Commercial Law, General Practice

GAULT DAVISON
Flint, MI.............................General Practice

GAWTHROP, GREENWOOD & HALSTED, A PROFESSIONAL CORPORATION
West Chester, PA......................General Practice

GAY & CHACKER, A PROFESSIONAL CORPORATION
Philadelphia, PA......................Personal Injury Law

GAYLORD, SINGLETON, MCNALLY, STRICKLAND AND SNYDER
Greenville, NC........................General Practice

GEARHISER, PETERS & HORTON
Chattanooga, TN.......................Business Law, Civil Trial Practice, General Practice, Probate and Estate Planning Law, Tax Law

GEBHARDT & KIEFER, P.C.
Clinton, NJ...........................General Practice

GEDNEY, SEAMAN & HILGENDORFF
Florham Park, NJ......................General Practice, Probate and Estate Planning Law

GEHLHAUSEN, JOHN, P.C.
Lamar, CO.............................Civil Trial Practice, Personal Injury Law

GEIGER AND ROTHENBERG
Rochester, NY..........Civil Trial Practice

GEIGER, TEEPLE, SMITH & HAHN
Alliance, OH..........Natural Resources Law, Real Estate Law, Securities Law

GELB & GELB
Boston, MA..........Family Law, Securities Law

GELERMAN & CASHMAN
Dedham, MA..........General Practice

GELMAN, NORRIS E.
Philadelphia, PA..........Appellate Practice, Criminal Trial Practice

GENERAUX, ARTHUR P., A LAW CORPORATION
Newport Beach, CA..........Tax Law

GENNET, KALLMANN, ANTIN & ROBINSON, A PROFESSIONAL CORPORATION
Parsippany, NJ..........Appellate Practice, Civil Trial Practice, Insurance Defense Law

GENOVA, BURNS, TRIMBOLI & VERNOIA
Livingston, NJ..........Administrative Law, Civil Trial Practice, Environmental Law, Health Care Law, Labor and Employment Law

GENSBURG, ROBERT A.
St. Johnsbury, VT..........Commercial Law

GENT, GENT AND SNYDER
Franklin, PA..........General Practice

GENTRY, ELVIN L., P.C.
Colorado Springs, CO..........Criminal Trial Practice

GENTRY, TIPTON, KIZER & LITTLE, P.C.
Knoxville, TN..........Bankruptcy Law, General Practice, Tax Law

GEORGE, EDWARD P., JR., INC., A PROF. CORP.
Long Beach, CA..........Civil Trial Practice, Criminal Trial Practice

GEORGE, GALLO & SULLIVAN, A LAW CORPORATION
Los Osos, CA..........Civil Trial Practice, Probate and Estate Planning Law
San Luis Obispo, CA..........Civil Trial Practice, Probate and Estate Planning Law

GEORGE AND GEORGE, LTD., A PROFESSIONAL LAW CORPORATION
Baton Rouge, LA..........Admiralty/Maritime Law, Personal Injury Law

GEORGE, HARTZ, LUNDEEN, FLAGG & FULMER
Miami, FL..........Insurance Defense Law, Medical Malpractice Law

GEORGESON, MCQUAID, THOMPSON & ANGARAN, CHARTERED
Reno, NV..........Insurance Defense Law

GERAGHTY, O'LOUGHLIN & KENNEY, PROFESSIONAL ASSOCIATION
St. Paul, MN..........Civil Trial Practice, Construction Law, Insurance Defense Law, Labor and Employment Law, Medical Malpractice Law

GERALDS, MOLONEY & JONES
Lexington, KY..........General Practice, Insurance Defense Law, Real Estate Law

GERBER & GERBER
Norristown, PA..........Business Law, Civil Trial Practice, Criminal Trial Practice, General Practice, Personal Injury Law

GERBER, RITCHEY & O'BANION
Sacramento, CA..........Patent, Trademark, Copyright and Unfair Competition Law

GERLING LAW OFFICES, PROFESSIONAL CORPORATION
Evansville, IN..........Civil Trial Practice, Personal Injury Law

GERMAN, GALLAGHER & MURTAGH, A PROFESSIONAL CORPORATION
Philadelphia, PA..........Antitrust Law, Civil Trial Practice, Environmental Law, General Practice, Insurance Defense Law, Medical Malpractice Law, Transportation Law

GERMER & GERTZ, L.L.P.
Beaumont, TX..........Business Law, Personal Injury Law

GERRISH & MCCREARY, P.C.
Memphis, TN..........Banking Law

GERRITY, TIMOTHY D.
Columbus, OH..........Family Law, Personal Injury Law

GERSON GREKIN WYNHOFF & THIELEN, ATTORNEYS AT LAW, A LAW CORPORATION
Honolulu, HI..........Probate and Estate Planning Law

GERSTEIN, COHEN & GRAYSON
Haddonfield, NJ..........General Practice

GERSTEIN, JOE W., P.C.
Doraville, GA..........General Practice

GERSTEN & GERSTEN
Hartford, CT..........General Practice

GERTNER & GERTNER
Columbus, OH..........Civil Trial Practice

GESS MATTINGLY & ATCHISON, P.S.C.
Lexington, KY..........General Practice

GESSLER, FLYNN, FLEISCHMANN, HUGHES & SOCOL, LTD.
Chicago, IL..........Civil Trial Practice, Immigration and Naturalization Law, Insurance Defense Law, Labor and Employment Law, Personal Injury Law

GETMAN, FRANK W.
Oneonta, NY..........General Practice

GEX, LUCIEN M. JR.
Waveland, MS..........Civil Trial Practice, Construction Law

GHOLSON, HICKS, NICHOLS & WARD, A PROFESSIONAL ASSOCIATION
Columbus, MS..........General Practice
Starkville, MS..........General Practice

GIACOMINI & KNIEPS
Klamath Falls, OR..........General Practice

GIANAS, PETER T., P.C.
Tucson, AZ..........Business Law, General Practice, Probate and Estate Planning Law, Real Estate Law

GIANELLI & FORES, A PROFESSIONAL LAW CORPORATION
Modesto, CA..........General Practice

GIAUQUE, CROCKETT, BENDINGER & PETERSON, A PROFESSIONAL CORPORATION
Salt Lake City, UT..........General Practice

GIBBES GRAVES MULLINS BULLOCK & FERRIS
Laurel, MS..........General Practice

GIBBINS, WINCKLER & HARVEY, L.L.P.
Austin, TX..........Civil Trial Practice, Medical Malpractice Law, Personal Injury Law

GIBBONS, BUCKLEY, SMITH, PALMER & PROUD, P.C.
Media, PA..........Insurance Defense Law

GIBBONS, SMITH, COHN & ARNETT, A PROFESSIONAL ASSOCIATION
Tampa, FL..........General Practice

GIBBS & BRUNS, L.L.P.
Houston, TX..........Civil Trial Practice, Commercial Law

GIBBS & HOLMES
Charleston, SC..........Labor and Employment Law

GIBBS, ROPER, LOOTS & WILLIAMS, S.C.
Milwaukee, WI..........Antitrust Law, Civil Trial Practice, Commercial Law, General Practice, Insurance Defense Law, Probate and Estate Planning Law, Real Estate Law, Tax Law

GIBNEY, ANTHONY & FLAHERTY, L.L.P.
New York, NY..........General Practice

GIBSON & ASSOCIATES
Princeton, WV..........Banking Law, Civil Trial Practice, Criminal Trial Practice, Medical Malpractice Law, Personal Injury Law, Product Liability Law

GIBSON, EVERETT B., LAW FIRM
Memphis, TN..........Civil Trial Practice

GIDLEY, SARLI & MARUSAK
Providence, RI..........General Practice, Health Care Law, Insurance Defense Law, Labor and Employment Law, Medical Malpractice Law, Municipal and Zoning Law, Personal Injury Law

GIFFEN, LEE, WAGNER, MORLEY & GARBUTT
Kitchener, ON, Canada..........Appellate Practice, Bankruptcy Law, Business Law, Civil Trial Practice, Commercial Law, Employment Benefits Law, Family Law, Insurance Defense Law, Personal Injury Law, Probate and Estate Planning Law, Product Liability Law

GIFFIN, WINNING, COHEN & BODEWES, P.C.
Springfield, IL..........Civil Trial Practice, General Practice, Insurance Defense Law

GIGNAC, SUTTS
Windsor, ON, Canada..........Civil Trial Practice, Commercial Law, General Practice

GIGRAY, MILLER, DOWNEN & WILPER
Caldwell, ID..........General Practice

GILARDI & COOPER, P.A.
Pittsburgh, PA ....Civil Trial Practice

GILBERT, HARRELL, GILBERT, SUMERFORD & MARTIN, P.C.
Brunswick, GA........................Civil Trial Practice, General Practice

GILBERT, MCGLOAN, GILLIS
Saint John, NB, Canada ....Business Law, Civil Trial Practice, General Practice, Insurance Defense Law

GILES, GERALD F.
Portsmouth, NH ....Civil Trial Practice

GILES AND GILES
Sioux City, IA ....Bankruptcy Law, Family Law, General Practice

GILL AND BALDWIN
Glendale, CA...........................Construction Law

GILLESPIE AND GILLESPIE, P.A.
New Smyrna Beach, FL..........General Practice

GILLESPIE, HART, ALTIZER & WHITESELL, P.C.
Tazewell, VA ....General Practice

GILLESPIE, JAMES R., P.A.
Boise, ID.................................General Practice

GILLIGAN & PEPPELMAN
Philadelphia, PA ....Civil Trial Practice

GILLILAND, JOHN C. II, THE LAW OFFICE OF
Crestview Hills, KY................Health Care Law

GILLILAND & HAYES, P.A. A PROFESSIONAL CORPORATION
Hutchinson, KS.......................General Practice

GILLIN, JACOBSON, ELLIS, LARSEN & DOYLE
Berkeley, CA ....Civil Trial Practice, Personal Injury Law

GILLIS & ANGLEY
Hingham, MA..........................General Practice

GILL LAW FIRM
Little Rock, AR.......................Business Law, General Practice, Municipal Bond/Public Authority Financing Law

GILMAN, MCLAUGHLIN & HANRAHAN
Boston, MA..............................General Practice

GILMARTIN, POSTER & SHAFTO
New York, NY.........................Admiralty/Maritime Law, Real Estate Law

GILMER, SADLER, INGRAM, SUTHERLAND & HUTTON
Blacksburg, VA.......................Criminal Trial Practice, General Practice, Probate and Estate Planning Law
Pulaski, VA ....Civil Trial Practice, Commercial Law, Criminal Trial Practice, General Practice, Insurance Defense Law

GILMORE, R. PATRICK
Chandler, OK..........................Civil Trial Practice

GILMORE, AAFEDT, FORDE, ANDERSON & GRAY, P.A.
Minneapolis, MN....................Civil Trial Practice, General Practice, Insurance Defense Law, Personal Injury Law, Product Liability Law

GILMORE, REES & CARLSON, P.C.
Franklin, MA ....Probate and Estate Planning Law

GILPIN, PAXSON & BERSCH
Houston, TX ....Banking Law, Civil Trial Practice, Commercial Law, General Practice, Insurance Defense Law, Real Estate Law

GILREATH & ASSOCIATES
Knoxville, TN ....Environmental Law, Medical Malpractice Law, Personal Injury Law

GILREATH, JAMES R., P.A.
Greenville, SC.........................Civil Trial Practice, Probate and Estate Planning Law, Tax Law

GINGELL & JENKINS
Silver Spring, MD ....General Practice

GINNINGS, C. MICHAEL
El Paso, TX.............................Business Law

GINSBERG & BROOME
New York, NY.........................Civil Trial Practice, Medical Malpractice Law, Personal Injury Law

GINSBERG AND BRUSILOW, P.C.
Dallas, TX...............................Tax Law

GIOFFRE, GIOFFRE AND MASCALI, P.C.
Port Chester, NY ....General Practice

GIORDANO, HALLERAN & CIESLA, A PROFESSIONAL CORPORATION
Middletown, NJ ....General Practice

GISLASON, DOSLAND, HUNTER AND MALECKI
Mankato, MN ....Civil Trial Practice
Minneapolis, MN....................Civil Trial Practice
New Ulm, MN.........................Civil Trial Practice, General Practice

GITLIN & GITLIN
Woodstock, IL ....Family Law

GIULIANO, FRANCIS T.
Ramsey, NJ ....Civil Trial Practice, Commercial Law, General Practice

GLADSTONE, SCHWARTZ, BLUM, WOODS, L.L.C.
Bridgeport, CT ....Civil Trial Practice, Family Law, General Practice

GLANKLER BROWN
Memphis, TN ....General Practice

GLASS, JOSEPH G.
Louisville, KY ....General Practice

GLASS, MCCULLOUGH, SHERRILL & HARROLD
Atlanta, GA ....Business Law, Civil Trial Practice, General Practice, Immigration and Naturalization Law, International Business Law, Real Estate Law

GLASSCOCK, GARDY AND SAVAGE
Suffolk, VA.............................Civil Trial Practice, General Practice, Insurance Defense Law, Personal Injury Law

GLASSMAN, JETER, EDWARDS & WADE, P.C.
Memphis, TN ....Civil Trial Practice, Construction Law, Insurance Defense Law, Product Liability Law

GLAZER, LEONARD, P.C. & ASSOCIATES, LAW OFFICES OF
Boston, MA.............................Medical Malpractice Law

GLEASON, BARLOW & BOHNE, P.A.
Melbourne, FL ....Civil Trial Practice, Real Estate Law

GLEASON, MCGUIRE & SHREFFLER
Chicago, IL..............................Civil Trial Practice, Insurance Defense Law

GLEAVES SWEARINGEN LARSEN POTTER SCOTT & SMITH
Eugene, OR.............................General Practice

GLEISS, LOCANTE & GLEISS
Sparta, WI ....General Practice

GLENN, FLIPPIN, FELDMANN & DARBY, A PROFESSIONAL CORPORATION
Roanoke, VA...........................Business Law, General Practice

GLENN, IRVIN, MURPHY, GRAY & STEPP
Columbia, SC ....Civil Trial Practice, Criminal Trial Practice, General Practice, Personal Injury Law, Product Liability Law

GLENN, MILLS & FISHER, P.A.
Durham, NC ....Civil Trial Practice, Personal Injury Law

GLENN RASMUSSEN & FOGARTY
Tampa, FL ....Banking Law, Civil Trial Practice, General Practice

GLENNON, GOODMAN & LUBELEY
Reston, VA..............................General Practice

GLICKMAN, SUGARMAN & KNEELAND
Worcester, MA........................Civil Trial Practice, General Practice

GLICK, PAUL M., CHARTERED
Chicago, IL..............................Employment Benefits Law

GLINSKI, HAFERMAN, ILTEN & KLEIN, S.C.
Stevens Point, WI....................General Practice

GLOBENSKY, GLEISS, BITTNER & HYRNS, P.C.
St. Joseph, MI ....Civil Trial Practice, Medical Malpractice Law, Municipal and Zoning Law

GLOVER, THOMAS H.
Lexington, KY ....Construction Law

GLOVER & BLOUNT, P.C.
Augusta, GA ....Insurance Defense Law

GLOVER & DAVIS, P.A.
Newnan, GA ....Business Law, Civil Trial Practice, Construction Law, General Practice, Municipal and Zoning Law, Real Estate Law

GLOVSKY & ASSOCIATES
Boston, MA.............................Civil Trial Practice, Labor and Employment Law

GLOVSKY & GLOVSKY
Beverly, MA ....Business Law, General Practice

GOCIO, DOSSEY & REEVES
Bentonville, AR........................Probate and Estate Planning Law

GODARD, WEST & ADELMAN, P.C.
Fairfax, VA ....Insurance Defense Law, Medical Malpractice Law

GODDARD & GODDARD, P.C.
Denver, CO ....Probate and Estate Planning Law

GODFREY FIRM, THE, A PROFESSIONAL LAW CORPORATION
New Orleans, LA....................Civil Trial Practice, Employment Benefits Law, Municipal Bond/Public Authority Financing Law, Tax Law

GODFREY & KAHN, S.C.
Green Bay, WI ....General Practice
Madison, WI ....General Practice
Milwaukee, WI........................General Practice
Oshkosh, WI............................General Practice
Sheboygan, WI ....General Practice

GODFREY, NESHEK, WORTH & LEIBSLE, S.C.
Elkhorn, WI ....General Practice

GODLOVE, JOYNER, MAYHALL, DZIALO, DUTCHER & ERWIN, A PROFESSIONAL CORPORATION
Lawton, OK ....General Practice

GODWIN & CARLTON, A PROFESSIONAL CORPORATION
Dallas, TX...............................Banking Law, Bankruptcy Law, Civil Trial Practice, Commercial Law, General Practice, Insurance Defense Law, Labor and Employment Law, Probate and Estate Planning Law, Real Estate Law, Tax Law

GOEBEL, LOUIS E., P.C., LAW OFFICES OF
San Diego, CA ....Civil Trial Practice, General Practice

GOETZ, FITZPATRICK & FLYNN
New York, NY.........................Construction Law, Real Estate Law

GOETZ, HIRSCH & KLIMISCH
Yankton, SD............................General Practice

GOFF AND GOFF
Ruston, LA ....General Practice

GOFF, KAPLAN & WOLF, PROFESSIONAL ASSOCIATION
St. Paul, MN ....Family Law, Personal Injury Law

GOICOECHEA & DI GRAZIA, LTD., LAW OFFICES, A PROF. CORP.
Elko, NV ....Business Law, Civil Trial Practice, General Practice

GOLANT, JOSEPH H.
Los Angeles, CA ....Patent, Trademark, Copyright and Unfair Competition Law

GOLBERT KIMBALL & WEINER
Los Angeles, CA ....International Business Law, Securities Law, Tax Law

GOLD, ESTELLA S.
Moorestown, NJ......................Civil Trial Practice

GOLD & BENNETT, A PROFESSIONAL LAW CORPORATION
San Francisco, CA ....Antitrust Law, Securities Law

GOLDBERG BROWN, L.L.P.
Houston, TX ....Real Estate Law

GOLDBERG & COHN
Brooklyn, NY..........................Family Law

GOLDBERG & EASTERLING, P.A.
Bennettsville, SC ....General Practice

GOLDBERG, EVANS, MALCOLM, HERALD, DONATONI & ROHLFS
West Chester, PA....................Civil Trial Practice, General Practice

GOLDBERG, GOLDSTEIN & BUCKLEY, P.A.
Fort Myers, FL ....Commercial Law, Construction Law, General Practice, Personal Injury Law

GOLDBERG, GRUENER, GENTILE, VOELKER & HOROHO, P.C.
Pittsburgh, PA ....Family Law

GOLDBERG & HALL
San Diego, CA ....Criminal Trial Practice

GOLDBERG, KATZMAN & SHIPMAN, P.C.
Harrisburg, PA........................Antitrust Law, Business Law, Civil Trial Practice, Commercial Law, Criminal Trial Practice, Family Law, General Practice, Insurance Defense Law, Medical Malpractice Law, Municipal Bond/Public Authority Financing Law, Municipal and Zoning Law, Personal Injury Law, Probate and Estate Planning Law, Product Liability Law, Real Estate Law, Tax Law

GOLDBERG, KOHN, BELL, BLACK, ROSENBLOOM & MORITZ, LTD.
Chicago, IL..............................Real Estate Law

GOLDBERG, MUFSON & SPAR, A PROFESSIONAL CORPORATION
West Orange, NJ......................General Practice, Probate and Estate Planning Law, Tax Law

GOLDBERG & SIMPSON, P.S.C.
Louisville, KY ....Civil Trial Practice, General Practice, Insurance Defense Law

GOLDBERG, STINNETT, MEYERS & DAVIS, A PROFESSIONAL CORPORATION
San Francisco, CA ....Bankruptcy Law

GOLDBERG, WEPRIN & USTIN
New York, NY.........................Real Estate Law

GOLDBERG & YOUNG, P.A., LAW OFFICES
Fort Lauderdale, FL...............General Practice

GOLDBERGER AND DUBIN, P.C.
New York, NY.........................Criminal Trial Practice

GOLDBLATT, LIPKIN & COHEN, P.C.
Norfolk, VA ....Bankruptcy Law, Commercial Law, Family Law, Personal Injury Law

GOLD, DAVID R., P.C.
Greensburg, PA.......................General Practice

GOLDENBERG & MURI
Providence, RI........................Banking Law, Business Law, Civil Trial Practice, Environmental Law

GOLDEN, TAYLOR & POTTERFIELD
Columbia, SC ....Civil Trial Practice, Family Law

GOLDEN, WEXLER & SARNESE, P.C.
Garden City, NY ....General Practice

GOLDFARB & REZNICK
Cleveland, OH.........................Business Law, Labor and Employment Law

GOLDFEIN & JOSEPH, A PROFESSIONAL CORPORATION
Philadelphia, PA ....Civil Trial Practice, Insurance Defense Law, Medical Malpractice Law, Product Liability Law

GOLDING, MEEKINS, HOLDEN, COSPER & STILES
Charlotte, NC..........................Civil Trial Practice

GOLDMAN, WILLIAM L.
Doylestown, PA.......................Family Law, Personal Injury Law

GOLDMAN ANTONETTI & CÓRDOVA
San Juan, PR...........................Banking Law, Civil Trial Practice, Commercial Law, Environmental Law, General Practice, Labor and Employment Law, Municipal Bond/Public Authority Financing Law, Natural Resources Law, Real Estate Law, Tax Law

GOLDMAN & CURTIS
Lowell, MA ....General Practice

GOLDMAN, GORDON & LIPSTONE
Los Angeles, CA......................Bankruptcy Law, Civil Trial Practice, Commercial Law, Real Estate Law

GOLDMAN & HAFETZ
New York, NY.........................Criminal Trial Practice

GOLDMAN, JACOBSON, KRAMER, FRADKIN & STARR, A PROFESSIONAL CORPORATION
Roseland, NJ...........................Appellate Practice, Probate and Estate Planning Law, Tax Law

GOLDMAN & KAGON, LAW CORPORATION
Los Angeles, CA......................Family Law, General Practice, Probate and Estate Planning Law

GOLDNER, SOMMERS, SCRUDDER & BASS
Atlanta, GA ....Civil Trial Practice, Commercial Law, General Practice, Health Care Law, Insurance Defense Law, Medical Malpractice Law, Personal Injury Law, Product Liability Law

GOLD, RESNICK & SEGALL, P.A.
Tampa, FL ....Business Law, Labor and Employment Law, Probate and Estate Planning Law, Real Estate Law

GOLD, ROTATORI & SCHWARTZ, L.P.A.
Cleveland, OH.........................Criminal Trial Practice, General Practice

GOLD & STANLEY, P.C. A PROFESSIONAL CORPORATION
Washington, DC.......................General Practice

GOLD & STANLEY, P.C. PROFESSIONAL CORPORATION
Alexandria, VA ....General Practice

GOLDSTEIN, RICHARD S. LAW OFFICES OF
New York, NY.........................Immigration and Naturalization Law

GOLDSTEIN, BERSHAD AND FRIED, PROFESSIONAL CORPORATION
Southfield, MI .... Bankruptcy Law

GOLDSTEIN, FLANZ & FISHMAN
Montreal, QU, Canada .... Banking Law, Bankruptcy Law

GOLDSTEIN, KINGSLEY & MCGRODER, LTD. A PROFESSIONAL CORPORATION
Phoenix, AZ .... Civil Trial Practice, Criminal Trial Practice, Personal Injury Law

GOLDSTEIN, NAVAGH, BULAN & CHIARI
Buffalo, NY .... General Practice

GOLDSTEIN AND PECK, P.C.
Bridgeport, CT .... General Practice
Westport, CT .... General Practice

GOLDSTEIN AND PRICE, L.C.
St. Louis, MO .... Admiralty/Maritime Law

GOLDSTEIN & RUBINTON, P.C.
Huntington, NY .... Family Law, Municipal and Zoning Law, Personal Injury Law, Real Estate Law

GOLDSTEIN, STUART
Phoenix, AZ .... Personal Injury Law

GOLDSTEIN TILL & LITE
Newark, NJ .... Admiralty/Maritime Law, Civil Trial Practice, Commercial Law, Criminal Trial Practice, Family Law, Personal Injury Law

GOLDSTICK, WEINBERGER, FELDMAN & GROSSMAN, P.C.
New York, NY .... Real Estate Law

GOLD, WEEMS, BRUSER, SUES & RUNDELL, A PROFESSIONAL LAW CORPORATION
Alexandria, LA .... General Practice, Tax Law

GOLENBOCK, EISEMAN, ASSOR & BELL
New York, NY .... Commercial Law, General Practice

GOLLAHER & CHAMBERS, A PROFESSIONAL CORPORATION
Dallas, TX .... Insurance Defense Law

GOLOB, MICHAEL H.
Farmington Hills, MI .... Civil Trial Practice, Commercial Law, Family Law

GOMEL & DAVIS
Atlanta, GA .... Business Law, Tax Law

GOMEZ, DAVID F., A PROFESSIONAL CORPORATION
Phoenix, AZ .... Labor and Employment Law

GOMPERS, BUCH, MCCARTHY & MCCLURE
Wheeling, WV .... Civil Trial Practice, General Practice, Personal Injury Law

GONANO & HARRELL, CHARTERED
Fort Pierce, FL .... Real Estate Law

GONDELMAN, HAROLD
Pittsburgh, PA .... Civil Trial Practice, Criminal Trial Practice, Personal Injury Law

GONZALEZ & BENNAZAR
San Juan, PR .... Banking Law, Bankruptcy Law, Civil Trial Practice, General Practice, Insurance Defense Law, Real Estate Law, Trademark, Copyright and Unfair Competition Law

GOOD, JOHN E.
West Chester, PA .... Municipal and Zoning Law, Probate and Estate Planning Law, Real Estate Law

GOODELL, STRATTON, EDMONDS & PALMER
Topeka, KS .... Civil Trial Practice, Communications Law, Environmental Law, General Practice, Insurance Defense Law, Labor and Employment Law, Probate and Estate Planning Law, Securities Law, Tax Law

GOODIN & KRAEGE
Indianapolis, IN .... Business Law, Insurance Defense Law, Real Estate Law

GOODING & DODSON
Texarkana, TX .... Civil Trial Practice, Insurance Defense Law

GOODING, HUFFMAN, KELLEY & BECKER
Lima, OH .... Civil Trial Practice, Insurance Defense Law

GOODMAN, EARLE GARY
Los Angeles, CA .... Real Estate Law

GOODMAN & BOLLAR, CHARTERED
Rupert, ID .... General Practice

GOODMAN BREEN LILE & GOLDMAN
Naples, FL .... Probate and Estate Planning Law

GOODMAN & CHESNOFF, A PROFESSIONAL CORPORATION
Las Vegas, NV .... Criminal Trial Practice, Personal Injury Law

GOODMAN & CLARK
Arlington, TX .... Family Law

GOODMAN, GLAZER, GREENER & KREMER, P.C.
Memphis, TN .... General Practice

GOODMAN & GOODMAN, A LEGAL PROFESSIONAL ASSOCIATION
Cincinnati, OH .... Administrative Law, Health Care Law

GOODMAN PHILLIPS & VINEBERG
Montreal, QU, Canada .... General Practice
Hong Kong, Hong Kong (British Crown Colony) .... General Practice

GOODMAN, ROBERT U., P.L.C.
Shreveport, LA .... Business Law, Civil Trial Practice

GOODMAN WEISS MILLER FREEDMAN
Cleveland, OH .... Business Law, Civil Trial Practice, Securities Law

GOODSILL ANDERSON QUINN & STIFEL
Honolulu, HI .... General Practice
Kailua-Kona, HI .... General Practice

GOODSON & MANLEY, P.C.
Phoenix, AZ .... Business Law, General Practice, Probate and Estate Planning Law

GOODSTEIN, WILLIAM
New York, NY .... General Practice

GOODWIN & GOODWIN
Charleston, WV .... Civil Trial Practice, General Practice, Insurance Defense Law, Municipal Bond/Public Authority Financing Law, Personal Injury Law
Parkersburg, WV .... General Practice
Ripley, WV .... General Practice

GOODWIN, PROCTER & HOAR
Boston, MA .... Antitrust Law, Environmental Law, General Practice, Labor and Employment Law, Municipal Bond/Public Authority Financing Law, Tax Law

GOOGASIAN, HOPKINS, HOHAUSER & FORHAN, P.C.
Bloomfield Hills, MI .... Business Law, Personal Injury Law

GOOLD, PATTERSON, DEVORE & RONDEAU
Las Vegas, NV .... Commercial Law, General Practice, International Business Law, Real Estate Law

GORDON, J. HOUSTON
Covington, TN .... General Practice

GORDON, WALTER JAMES
Hartwell, GA .... Civil Trial Practice, General Practice, Real Estate Law

GORDON, ARATA, MCCOLLAM & DUPLANTIS, L.L.P.
Baton Rouge, LA .... Natural Resources Law
Lafayette, LA .... Natural Resources Law
New Orleans, LA .... Environmental Law, General Practice, Natural Resources Law

GORDON BENDALL BRANHAM MCNEELY & DELANEY
Huntington, IN .... General Practice

GORDON, CUTLER AND HOFFMAN, P.C.
Southfield, MI .... Civil Trial Practice, Personal Injury Law, Product Liability Law

GORDON & EINSTEIN, LTD.
Chicago, IL .... Business Law, Real Estate Law, Tax Law

GORDON, FEINBLATT, ROTHMAN, HOFFBERGER & HOLLANDER
Baltimore, MD .... Bankruptcy Law, Civil Trial Practice, Environmental Law, General Practice, Health Care Law, Labor and Employment Law, Real Estate Law

GORDON & GLICKSON, P.C.
Chicago, IL .... Business Law, Commercial Law, Trademark, Copyright and Unfair Competition Law

GORDON, MUIR AND FOLEY
Hartford, CT .... Banking Law, Civil Trial Practice, Commercial Law, Construction Law, General Practice, Insurance Defense Law, Medical Malpractice Law, Probate and Estate Planning Law, Real Estate Law

GORDON, SILBERMAN, WIGGINS & CHILDS, A PROFESSIONAL CORPORATION
Birmingham, AL .... Banking Law, Bankruptcy Law, Business Law, Employment Benefits Law, General Practice, Labor and Employment Law, Tax Law

GORDON, WILLIAM C., A PROFESSIONAL CORPORATION
Sausalito, CA .... Personal Injury Law

GORDON & WOLF, A PROFESSIONAL CORPORATION
Newport Beach, CA................Banking Law, Bankruptcy Law

GOREN & GOREN, P.C.
Birmingham, MI......................Health Care Law, Medical Malpractice Law, Personal Injury Law

GORHAM, STEWART, KENDRICK, BRYANT & BATTLE, P.C.
Birmingham, AL......................General Practice, Real Estate Law, Tax Law

GORMAN & ENRIGHT, P.C.
New Haven, CT......................Commercial Law, Real Estate Law

GORMAN, VESKAUF, HENSON & WINEBERG
Springfield, OH......................Probate and Estate Planning Law

GORMAN, WASZKIEWICZ, GORMAN & SCHMITT
Utica, NY..............................General Practice

GORMLEY, GEORGE F., P.C.
Cambridge, MA......................Criminal Trial Practice, General Practice, Insurance Defense Law

GOSNELL, BORDEN & ENLOE, LTD.
Lawrenceville, IL....................Civil Trial Practice, General Practice

GOTHA, FREDERICK
Pasadena, CA.........................Patent, Trademark, Copyright and Unfair Competition Law

GOTT, YOUNG & BOGLE, P.A.
Wichita, KS............................General Practice

GOUBEAUX & GOUBEAUX
Greenville, OH.......................General Practice

GOUGH, SHANAHAN, JOHNSON & WATERMAN
Helena, MT.............................General Practice

GOUGH, SKIPWORTH, SUMMERS, EVES & TREVETT, P.C.
Rochester, NY.........................Insurance Defense Law

GOULD, COOKSEY, FENNELL, BARKETT, O'NEILL & MARINE, PROFESSIONAL ASSOCIATION
Vero Beach, FL.......................Civil Trial Practice, General Practice

GOULD, KILLIAN & WYNNE
Hartford, CT...........................General Practice

GOULSTON & STORRS, A PROFESSIONAL CORPORATION
Boston, MA.............................General Practice

GOURVITZ, ELLIOT H., P.A.
Springfield, NJ........................Appellate Practice, Family Law

GOZIGIAN, WASHBURN & CLINTON
Cooperstown, NY.....................General Practice

GRACE, JOHN PHILIP, P.C.
Phoenix, AZ............................Personal Injury Law

GRACEY, RUTH, HOWARD, TATE & SOWELL
Nashville, TN..........................General Practice

GRAD, LOGAN & KLEWANS, P.C.
Alexandria, VA.......................Business Law, Civil Trial Practice, Commercial Law, Health Care Law, Labor and Employment Law, Probate and Estate Planning Law

GRAHAM, CLARK, JONES, PRATT & MARKS
Winter Park, FL......................Civil Trial Practice, Real Estate Law

GRAHAM & DUNN, A PROFESSIONAL SERVICE CORPORATION
Seattle, WA.............................Communications Law, General Practice

GRAHAM AND GRAHAM
Springfield, IL.........................General Practice

GRAHAM & JAMES
Los Angeles, CA......................General Practice
Palo Alto, CA..........................General Practice
San Francisco, CA...................Admiralty/Maritime Law, General Practice
Washington, DC......................General Practice
Milan, Italy..............................General Practice

GRAHAM, MARJORIE GADARIAN, P.A.
Palm Beach Gardens, FL.........Civil Trial Practice

GRANIK SILVERMAN SANDBERG CAMPBELL NOWICKI RESNIK HEKKER
New City, NY..........................Banking Law, Employment Benefits Law, Municipal and Zoning Law, Real Estate Law

GRANNAN & MALOY, P.C.
Arlington, MA.........................Probate and Estate Planning Law, Real Estate Law

GRANT, BERNARD, LYONS & GADDIS, A PROFESSIONAL CORPORATION
Longmont, CO.........................General Practice

GRANT, KONVALINKA & HARRISON, PROFESSIONAL CORPORATION
Chattanooga, TN.....................Probate and Estate Planning Law

GRANT, LEATHERWOOD & STERN, P.A.
Greenville, SC.........................Civil Trial Practice

GRANT, ROGERS, MAUL & GRANT
Columbus, NE.........................General Practice

GRAVEL AND SHEA, A PROFESSIONAL CORPORATION
Burlington, VT.........................Appellate Practice, Civil Trial Practice, Commercial Law, Environmental Law, General Practice, Municipal and Zoning Law, Probate and Estate Planning Law, Real Estate Law, Tax Law

GRAVES, ALLEN, CORNELIUS & CELESTRE
Oakland, CA............................Real Estate Law

GRAVES AND ASSOCIATES
St. Catharines, ON, Canada....Civil Trial Practice

GRAVES, DOUGHERTY, HEARON & MOODY, A PROFESSIONAL CORPORATION
Austin, TX..............................Administrative Law, General Practice

GRAY, PAUL BRYAN
Claremont, CA........................General Practice

GRAY CARY WARE & FREIDENRICH, A PROFESSIONAL CORPORATION
El Centro, CA..........................General Practice
La Jolla, CA............................General Practice
Palo Alto, CA..........................Antitrust Law, Commercial Law, General Practice
San Diego, CA.........................Admiralty/Maritime Law, Antitrust Law, Banking Law, Environmental Law, General Practice, Labor and Employment Law, Patent, Trademark, Copyright and Unfair Competition Law, Tax Law, Trademark, Copyright and Unfair Competition Law

GRAY, HARRIS AND ROBINSON, PROFESSIONAL ASSOCIATION
Orlando, FL............................Civil Trial Practice, General Practice

GRAY, HENRY L., JR., P.A.
Gainesville, FL.......................General Practice

GRAY, SOWLE & IACCO, A PROFESSIONAL CORPORATION
Mount Pleasant, MI.................Medical Malpractice Law, Personal Injury Law

GRAY, YORK, DUFFY & RATTET
Los Angeles, CA......................Civil Trial Practice, General Practice

GRECO, MOLLIS & O'HARA, A PROFESSIONAL CORPORATION
Irvine, CA...............................Tax Law

GREELEY WALKER & KOWEN
Honolulu, HI...........................Civil Trial Practice, Insurance Defense Law

GREEMAN, KELLERMAN & KOEPCKE
Batesville, IN..........................General Practice

GREEN, CHENEY AND HUGHES
Jackson, MS...........................General Practice

GREEN, LUNDGREN & RYAN, A PROFESSIONAL CORPORATION
Haddonfield, NJ.......................General Practice

GREEN, MILES, LIPTON, WHITE & FITZ-GIBBON
Northampton, MA....................Civil Trial Practice

GREEN PARISH
Halifax, NS, Canada...............Civil Trial Practice, Commercial Law

GREEN, SCHULZ, ROBY, OVIATT & CUMMINGS
Watertown, SD........................General Practice

GREENBAUM, ROWE, SMITH, RAVIN AND DAVIS
Woodbridge, NJ......................Bankruptcy Law, Civil Trial Practice, General Practice, Real Estate Law, Tax Law

GREENBERG DAUBER AND EPSTEIN, A PROFESSIONAL CORPORATION
Newark, NJ.............................Banking Law, Civil Trial Practice, Commercial Law, Criminal Trial Practice, General Practice, Tax Law

GREENBERG, GLUSKER, FIELDS, CLAMAN & MACHTINGER
Los Angeles, CA......................General Practice, Probate and Estate Planning Law, Tax Law

GREENBERG, MAX E., TRAGER, TOPLITZ & HERBST
New York, NY.........................Civil Trial Practice, Construction Law, Real Estate Law

GREENBERG & PARENTEAU, P.C.
New London, CT.....................General Practice

GREENBERG & PLEBAN
St. Louis, MO..........................Criminal Trial Practice, Medical Malpractice Law, Personal Injury Law, Product Liability Law

GREENBERG, WANDERMAN & FROMSON
Spring Valley, NY...................General Practice

GREENBLATT, JAY H., & ASSOCIATES, A PROF. CORP.
Vineland, NJ............................Civil Trial Practice, Insurance Defense Law, Personal Injury Law

GREENBURG & POSNER
White Plains, NY....................Commercial Law, Environmental Law, Real Estate Law

GREENE & BELL, P.A.
Miami, FL...............................Labor and Employment Law

GREENE, BROILLET, TAYLOR & WHEELER
Santa Monica, CA.....................Personal Injury Law

GREENE, BUCKLEY, JONES & MCQUEEN
Atlanta, GA.............................Civil Trial Practice, Commercial Law

GREENE & MCQUILLAN CO., L.P.A.
Cleveland, OH.........................Personal Injury Law

GREENE AND REID
Syracuse, NY..........................Personal Injury Law

GREENE & ZINNER, P.C.
White Plains, NY....................Business Law, Civil Trial Practice

GREENEBAUM DOLL & MCDONALD
Covington, KY.........................Administrative Law, Business Law, Civil Trial Practice, Commercial Law, General Practice, Health Care Law, Insurance Defense Law, Municipal and Zoning Law, Personal Injury Law
Lexington, KY.........................Administrative Law, Business Law, Civil Trial Practice, Commercial Law, Construction Law, Environmental Law, Family Law, General Practice, Health Care Law, Municipal and Zoning Law, Natural Resources Law, Probate and Estate Planning Law, Real Estate Law
Louisville, KY.........................Administrative Law, Antitrust Law, Banking Law, Bankruptcy Law, Business Law, Civil Trial Practice, Commercial Law, Construction Law, Employment Benefits Law, Family Law, General Practice, Health Care Law, Insurance Defense Law, Municipal and Zoning Law, Personal Injury Law, Probate and Estate Planning Law, Real Estate Law, Tax Law

GREENEBAUM, JOHN S., P.S.C.
Louisville, KY.........................Banking Law, Labor and Employment Law

GREENFELDER, MANDER, HANSON, MURPHY & DWYER
Dade City, FL..........................Criminal Trial Practice, Personal Injury Law

GREENFIELD AND MURPHY
New Haven, CT........................Civil Trial Practice, Family Law, General Practice

GREENFIELD, STANLEY, & ASSOCIATES
Pittsburgh, PA........................Civil Trial Practice, Criminal Trial Practice

GREENHAW & GREENHAW
Fayetteville, AR......................General Practice

GREENLEE, DERRICO, POSA & RODGERS
Washington, PA.......................Business Law, Probate and Estate Planning Law, Real Estate Law

GREENLEE AND WINNER, P.C.
Boulder, CO............................Patent, Trademark, Copyright and Unfair Competition Law

GREENMAN, GOLDBERG, RABY & MARTINEZ, PROFESSIONAL CORPORATION
Las Vegas, NV.........................Civil Trial Practice, Personal Injury Law

GREENSPAN, BERK & GABER, P.C.
Philadelphia, PA.....................Personal Injury Law

GREENSPAN & GREENSPAN
White Plains, NY....................Civil Trial Practice, Criminal Trial Practice, Securities Law, Tax Law

GREENWALD, GREENWALD & POWERS
Westborough, MA....................Civil Trial Practice, Personal Injury Law, Real Estate Law

GREENWALD, HOFFMAN & MEYER
Glendale, CA..........................Probate and Estate Planning Law

GREESON, GRIFFIN & ASSOCIATES
Greensboro, NC.......................Civil Trial Practice, Personal Injury Law

GREFE & SIDNEY
Des Moines, IA.......................Civil Trial Practice, General Practice, Insurance Defense Law, Probate and Estate Planning Law, Tax Law

GREGG, HART & FARRIS
Batesville, AR.........................General Practice

GREGG & MIESZKUC, P.C.
Houston, TX............................Civil Trial Practice, General Practice, Municipal and Zoning Law, Probate and Estate Planning Law, Real Estate Law

GREGORY AND ADAMS, P.C.
Wilton, CT..............................General Practice

GREGORY, EASLEY AND BLANKENSHIP
Murray, KY.............................General Practice

GREGSON LAW OFFICES, P.C.
Denver, CO.............................Labor and Employment Law

GRENADIER, DAVIS & SIMPSON
Alexandria, VA........................Family Law

GRENLEY, ROTENBERG EVANS & BRAGG, P.C.
Portland, OR...........................Business Law, Civil Trial Practice, Probate and Estate Planning Law, Real Estate Law, Securities Law, Tax Law

GRESHAM, DAVIS, GREGORY, WORTHY & MOORE, A PROFESSIONAL CORPORATION
San Antonio, TX......................General Practice

GRESHAM, VARNER, SAVAGE, NOLAN & TILDEN
San Bernardino, CA.................Civil Trial Practice, Environmental Law, General Practice, Labor and Employment Law, Probate and Estate Planning Law, Real Estate Law, Tax Law

GRESHIN, ZIEGLER & PRUZANSKY
Smithtown, NY........................Civil Trial Practice, General Practice, Personal Injury Law, Probate and Estate Planning Law

GREVE, CLIFFORD, WENGEL & PARAS
Sacramento, CA.......................General Practice

GRIBBIN, BURNS & EIDE
Watertown, SD.........................General Practice

GRIBOW, DALE S., A PROFESSIONAL CORPORATION
Beverly Hills, CA.....................Criminal Trial Practice, Personal Injury Law

GRIDER, HAL L.
Altus, OK................................Civil Trial Practice

GRIEM, DAVID
Detroit, MI..............................Criminal Trial Practice
Mount Clemens, MI.................Criminal Trial Practice

GRIER AND GRIER, P.A.
Charlotte, NC..........................Bankruptcy Law, Environmental Law

GRIFFIN, CALDWELL, HELDER, LEE & HELMS, P.A.
Monroe, NC.............................General Practice

GRIFFIN COCHRANE & MARSHALL, A PROFESSIONAL CORPORATION
Atlanta, GA.............................Construction Law

GRIFFIN, COOGAN & VENERUSO, P.C.
Bronxville, NY.........................General Practice, Tax Law

GRIFFIN & FLETCHER
Cincinnati, OH.........................Real Estate Law

GRIFFIN & GOULKA
Boston, MA.............................Insurance Defense Law

GRIFFIN, RAINWATER & DRAPER, P.A.
Crossett, AR............................General Practice

GRIFFINGER, FREED, HEINEMANN, COOK & FOREMAN
San Francisco, CA...................Bankruptcy Law, Business Law, Civil Trial Practice, Real Estate Law, Tax Law

GRIFFITH LAW OFFICES
Rome, NY................................General Practice, Probate and Estate Planning Law

GRIJALVA, J. ERNESTO LAW OFFICES OF
San Diego, CA.........................International Business Law

GRIMBALL & CABANISS
Charleston, SC........................Civil Trial Practice, General Practice, Medical Malpractice Law

GRIMES, GOEBEL, GRIMES & HAWKINS, P.A.
Bradenton, FL.........................Environmental Law, General Practice, Probate and Estate Planning Law, Real Estate Law, Tax Law

GRIMES & WARWICK
San Diego, CA.........................Criminal Trial Practice

GROBEN, GILROY, OSTER & SAUNDERS
Utica, NY................................General Practice, Probate and Estate Planning Law

GROCE, LOCKE & HEBDON, A PROFESSIONAL CORPORATION
San Antonio, TX......................General Practice

GROGAN, GRAFFAM, MCGINLEY & LUCCHINO, P.C.
Pittsburgh, PA........................General Practice

GROH, EGGERS & PRICE
Anchorage, AK........................Commercial Law

GRONER AND GRONER, CHARTERED
Bethesda, MD ....Family Law

GROSMAN & GROSMAN
Millburn, NJ ....Family Law

GROSS AND KWALL, P.A.
Clearwater, FL ....Criminal Trial Practice, General Practice

GROSS, MCGINLEY, LABARRE & EATON
Allentown, PA ....Civil Trial Practice, Commercial Law, Communications Law, Family Law

GROSS, MINSKY, MOGUL & SINGAL, P.A.
Bangor, ME ....Banking Law, Bankruptcy Law, Civil Trial Practice, Criminal Trial Practice, General Practice, Real Estate Law

GROSS, NEMETH & SILVERMAN, P.L.C.
Detroit, MI ....Appellate Practice, Environmental Law

GROSS SHUMAN BRIZDLE & GILFILLAN, P.C.
Buffalo, NY ....General Practice

GROSSMAN, ALLAN F.
Encino, CA ....Appellate Practice, Civil Trial Practice

GROSSMAN, JEFFREY A., CO., L.P.A.
Columbus, OH ....Family Law

GROSSMAN KINNEY DWYER & HARRIGAN, P.C.
Syracuse, NY ....Civil Trial Practice, Criminal Trial Practice, General Practice, Labor and Employment Law, Natural Resources Law, Real Estate Law

GROVE, JASKIEWICZ AND COBERT
Washington, DC ....Antitrust Law, General Practice, Transportation Law

GROVES, DECKER & WYATT, PROFESSIONAL CORPORATION
Flint, MI ....Civil Trial Practice, Insurance Defense Law, Labor and Employment Law, Product Liability Law

GROWHOSKI, CALLAHAN, KUNDL & KUZMESKI
Northampton, MA ....General Practice

GRUCCIO, PEPPER, GIOVINAZZI, DESANTO & FARNOLY, P.A., A PROFESSIONAL CORPORATION
Vineland, NJ ....Civil Trial Practice, General Practice, Insurance Defense Law, Labor and Employment Law

GRUEL, MILLS, NIMS AND PYLMAN
Grand Rapids, MI ....Civil Trial Practice, Commercial Law, Environmental Law, General Practice, Health Care Law, Medical Malpractice Law, Personal Injury Law

GRUND & STARKOPF, A PROFESSIONAL CORPORATION
Chicago, IL ....Family Law

GRUNERT STOUT BRUCH & MOORE
Charlotte Amalie, St. Thomas, VI ....Banking Law, Business Law, Civil Trial Practice, Commercial Law, Criminal Trial Practice, General Practice, International Business Law, Personal Injury Law, Real Estate Law, Tax Law

GUDMUNDSON, SIGGINS, STONE & SKINNER
San Francisco, CA ....Insurance Defense Law

GUEBERT & YEOMANS, P.C.
Albuquerque, NM ....Civil Trial Practice

GUERNSEY BUTTS OSTERTAG & O'LEARY
Poughkeepsie, NY ....General Practice, Tax Law

GUEVARA, REBE, BAUMANN, COLDWELL & GARAY
El Paso, TX ....Civil Trial Practice, Probate and Estate Planning Law

GUILD, RUSSELL, GALLAGHER & FULLER, LTD.
Reno, NV ....Civil Trial Practice, General Practice, Insurance Defense Law

GUION, STEVENS & RYBAK
Litchfield, CT ....General Practice

GULICK, ROBIN C., P.C.
Warrenton, VA ....Criminal Trial Practice, Family Law, Probate and Estate Planning Law

GULLAHORN & HARE, P.C.
Albertville, AL ....Banking Law, Civil Trial Practice, General Practice, Municipal Bond/Public Authority Financing Law

GULLETT & COMBS
Hazard, KY ....General Practice, Natural Resources Law

GULLEY KUHN & TAYLOR, L.L.P.
Raleigh, NC ....Civil Trial Practice, Family Law, General Practice

GUNDERSON, PALMER, GOODSELL & NELSON
Rapid City, SD ....Business Law, Civil Trial Practice, General Practice

GUNDLACH, LEE, EGGMANN, BOYLE & ROESSLER
Belleville, IL ....General Practice

GUNHUS, GRINNELL, KLINGER, SWENSON & GUY, LTD.
Moorhead, MN ....Civil Trial Practice, General Practice
Fargo, ND ....General Practice

GUNN & HICKMAN, P.C.
Danville, IL ....Civil Trial Practice, General Practice

GUNN, OGDEN & SULLIVAN, PROFESSIONAL ASSOCIATION
Tampa, FL ....Civil Trial Practice, Insurance Defense Law, Medical Malpractice Law, Product Liability Law

GUNTHER & WHITAKER, P.A.
Fort Lauderdale, FL ....General Practice, Personal Injury Law

GURMAN, KURTIS, BLASK & FREEDMAN, CHARTERED
Washington, DC ....Communications Law

GURMANKIN, JAY D.
Salt Lake City, UT ....Civil Trial Practice

GURNEY & HANDLEY, P.A.
Orlando, FL ....Civil Trial Practice, General Practice

GUSRAE, KAPLAN & BRUNO
New York, NY ....Civil Trial Practice, Securities Law

GUSTE, BARNETT & SHUSHAN, L.L.P.
New Orleans, LA ....General Practice

GUTGLASS ERICKSON & BONVILLE, S.C.
Milwaukee, WI ....Insurance Defense Law

GUTHERY & RICKLES, P.C.
Denver, CO ....General Practice, Tax Law

GUTHRIE, DAN
Dallas, TX ....Criminal Trial Practice

GUTHRIE, WILLIAM W., & ASSOCIATES, A PROF. CORP.
Pittsburgh, PA ....Civil Trial Practice, Insurance Defense Law, Personal Injury Law, Product Liability Law

GUY & GILBERT
Montreal, QU, Canada ....General Practice

GWIN, LEWIS & PUNCHES
Natchez, MS ....General Practice, Insurance Defense Law
Woodville, MS ....General Practice

HAAS, THOMAS M.
Mobile, AL ....Criminal Trial Practice

HAASIS, POPE & CORRELL, A PROFESSIONAL CORPORATION
San Diego, CA ....Civil Trial Practice, Construction Law, Environmental Law, Insurance Defense Law, Personal Injury Law

HABANS, BOLOGNA & CARRIERE, A PROFESSIONAL LAW CORPORATION
New Orleans, LA ....Criminal Trial Practice, Environmental Law, Insurance Defense Law

HABEDANK, CUMMING, BEST & SAVAGE
Sidney, MT ....General Practice

HABUSH, HABUSH, DAVIS & ROTTIER, S.C.
Madison, WI ....Personal Injury Law
Milwaukee, WI ....Personal Injury Law

HACKETT, MAXWELL & PHILLIPS, P.L.L.C.
Pontiac, MI ....Civil Trial Practice, Transportation Law

HACKMAN MCCLARNON HULETT & CRACRAFT
Indianapolis, IN ....Administrative Law, General Practice, Real Estate Law

HACK, PIRO, O'DAY, MERKLINGER, WALLACE & MCKENNA, P.A.
Florham Park, NJ ....Bankruptcy Law, Civil Trial Practice, Environmental Law, General Practice, Insurance Defense Law, Personal Injury Law, Probate and Estate Planning Law, Product Liability Law, Real Estate Law

HADDAD, FRANK E. JR.
Louisville, KY ....Civil Trial Practice, Criminal Trial Practice, Personal Injury Law

HADDAD, SUSAN CHRISTINE
Chicago, IL ....Family Law

HADDAD, JOSEPHS, JACK, GAEBE & MARKARIAN
Miami, FL ....Civil Trial Practice, General Practice, Insurance Defense Law, Medical Malpractice Law, Product Liability Law

HADDEN CO., L.P.A.
Columbus, OH ....Civil Trial Practice

HADDLETON & COLLINS, P.C.
Hyannis, MA........................Probate and Estate Planning Law

HADIPUTRANTO, HADINOTO & PARTNERS
Jakarta, Indonesia ....General Practice

HADSELL, LANDGRAF & LYNCH
Niles, MI ....General Practice

HAGEN, DYE, HIRSCHY & DILORENZO, P.C.
Portland, OR..........................Business Law, Commercial Law, Probate and Estate Planning Law, Real Estate Law, Tax Law

HAGEN, LEE, LAW OFFICE, LTD.
Fargo, ND................................Personal Injury Law

HAGGERTY, DONOHUE & MONAGHAN, A PROFESSIONAL ASSOCIATION
Summit, NJ ....Civil Trial Practice, Criminal Trial Practice, General Practice, Insurance Defense Law, Personal Injury Law, Product Liability Law

HAGGERTY, MCDONNELL, O'BRIEN & WRIGHT
Scranton, PA..........................General Practice

HAHN & HAHN
Pasadena, CA ....General Practice

HAHN, MCCLURG, WATSON, GRIFFITH & BUSH, P.A.
Lakeland, FL..........................General Practice, Real Estate Law

HAIGHT, BROWN & BONESTEEL
Santa Ana, CA........................Civil Trial Practice, General Practice, Insurance Defense Law, Personal Injury Law
Santa Monica, CA....................Banking Law, Civil Trial Practice, Commercial Law, Environmental Law, General Practice, Insurance Defense Law, Labor and Employment Law, Personal Injury Law

HAIGHT, TRAMONTE, SICILIANO & FLASK, P.C.
Vienna, VA ....Civil Trial Practice, Real Estate Law

HAILEY, MCNAMARA, HALL, LARMANN & PAPALE
Metairie, LA...........................Admiralty/Maritime Law, General Practice, Insurance Defense Law

HAIMS, JOHNSON, MACGOWAN & MCINERNEY
Oakland, CA ....Civil Trial Practice, Construction Law, Environmental Law, Health Care Law, Insurance Defense Law, Personal Injury Law, Product Liability Law

HAINER & DEMOREST, P.C.
Troy, MI.................................Business Law, Environmental Law

HAISCH & BOYDA
Detroit, MI.............................Civil Trial Practice, Commercial Law, Labor and Employment Law, Real Estate Law

HALDEMAN & ASSOCIATES
Rockford, IL ....Civil Trial Practice

HALE AND DORR
Washington, DC......................General Practice
Boston, MA............................General Practice
Manchester, NH......................General Practice

HALE, FOGLEMAN & ROGERS
West Memphis, AR ....General Practice

HALE & HAMLIN
Ellsworth, ME........................Civil Trial Practice, General Practice

HALE, KINCAID & SKINNER, P.C.
Liberty, MO ....General Practice

HALE, LANE, PEEK, DENNISON AND HOWARD
Las Vegas, NV ....Bankruptcy Law, Civil Trial Practice, Commercial Law, General Practice, Probate and Estate Planning Law, Real Estate Law
Reno, NV ....Bankruptcy Law, Civil Trial Practice, Commercial Law, Environmental Law, General Practice, Natural Resources Law, Probate and Estate Planning Law, Real Estate Law, Tax Law

HALE, SKEMP, HANSON & SKEMP
La Crosse, WI ....General Practice

HALEY, BADER & POTTS
Arlington, VA ....Communications Law, Trademark, Copyright and Unfair Competition Law

HALEY, PURCHIO, SAKAI & SMITH
Hayward, CA..........................General Practice

HALFPENNY, HAHN, ROCHE & MARCHESE
Chicago, IL.............................Antitrust Law

HALIO & HALIO
Charleston, SC ....Civil Trial Practice

HALKIDES & MORGAN, A PROFESSIONAL CORPORATION
Redding, CA ....Insurance Defense Law

HALL, BLOCH, GARLAND & MEYER
Macon, GA ....Banking Law, Business Law, Civil Trial Practice, General Practice, Insurance Defense Law, Personal Injury Law, Tax Law

HALL, DAVID W., ATTORNEY AT LAW, A LAW CORPORATION
Honolulu, HI...........................Civil Trial Practice, Criminal Trial Practice

HALLENBECK, LASCELL, NORRIS & ZORN
Rochester, NY.........................Insurance Defense Law

HALL, ESTILL, HARDWICK, GABLE, GOLDEN & NELSON, A PROFESSIONAL CORPORATION
Tulsa, OK...............................General Practice

HALL & EVANS, L.L.C.
Colorado Springs, CO............General Practice
Denver, CO ....General Practice

HALL, FARLEY, OBERRECHT & BLANTON
Boise, ID................................Banking Law, Civil Trial Practice, Commercial Law, Construction Law, Employment Benefits Law, General Practice, Health Care Law, Insurance Defense Law, Medical Malpractice Law, Probate and Estate Planning Law

HALL, FOX, ATLEE AND ROBINSON, P.C.
Newport News, VA ....Civil Trial Practice, Family Law

HALLIDAY, SHEETS & SAUNDERS
Gallipolis, OH ....Personal Injury Law

HALL LAW OFFICE, THE
Rockwall, TX..........................General Practice

HALL, LESTAGE & LANDRENEAU
De Ridder, LA ....General Practice, Insurance Defense Law

HALL AND LEWIS
Mount Pleasant, MI................General Practice

HALLMARK, KEATING & ABBOTT, P.C.
Portland, OR..........................Insurance Defense Law

HALL, MARKLE, SICKELS & FUDALA, P.C.
Fairfax, VA ....Personal Injury Law

HALL, MONAHAN, ENGLE, MAHAN & MITCHELL
Leesburg, VA ....Civil Trial Practice, General Practice

HALL AND O'BRIEN, P.A.
Miami, FL ....Civil Trial Practice, Commercial Law, Family Law, Personal Injury Law

HALLOCK, MARCY M., P.A., LAW OFFICES OF
Baltimore, MD ....Labor and Employment Law

HALLORAN & SAGE
Hartford, CT ....General Practice
Middletown, CT......................General Practice

HALL, PARTENHEIMER & KINKLE
Princeton, IN..........................General Practice, Natural Resources Law, Real Estate Law

HALL, RENDER, KILLIAN, HEATH & LYMAN, PROFESSIONAL CORPORATION
Indianapolis, IN ....General Practice, Health Care Law, Medical Malpractice Law, Probate and Estate Planning Law

HALL, ROACH, JOHNSTON, FISHER & BOLLMAN
Waukegan, IL.........................General Practice

HALPERIN & HALPERIN, P.C.
New York, NY........................General Practice

HALSTEAD, BAKER & OLSON
Los Angeles, CA ....Civil Trial Practice, General Practice, Real Estate Law, Tax Law

HALVERSON, LOWELL K. LAW OFFICES OF
Mercer Island, WA ....Family Law

HALVERSON & APPLEGATE, P.S.
Yakima, WA...........................General Practice

HALVERSON, WATTERS, BYE, DOWNS, REYELTS & BATEMAN, LTD.
Duluth, MN ....General Practice, Insurance Defense Law, Real Estate Law

HAMB & POFFENBARGER
Charleston, WV......................General Practice, Municipal Bond/Public Authority Financing Law, Real Estate Law

HAMEL, DESHAIES & GAGLIARDI
Amesbury, MA ....Business Law, Commercial Law, General Practice, Probate and Estate Planning Law

HAMILTON AND FAATZ, A PROFESSIONAL CORPORATION
Denver, CO ....Business Law, Civil Trial Practice, General Practice

HAMILTON, GIBSON, NICKELSEN, RUSH & MOORE
Honolulu, HI..................General Practice

HAMILTON & LINDER
Meridian, MS ....General Practice, Personal Injury Law

HAMMER JACOBS & THROGMORTON
San Jose, CA ....Family Law

HAMM, MILBY & RIDINGS
London, KY..................General Practice, Insurance Defense Law

HAMMOND, CLARK AND WHITE
Loveland, CO..................General Practice

HAMMOND LAW OFFICE
Columbus, OH ....Insurance Defense Law

HAMPTON & HAMPTON
Pratt, KS..................General Practice

HAMPTON, ROYCE, ENGLEMAN & NELSON
Salina, KS..................General Practice

HAMRICK, BOWEN, NANNEY & DALTON
Rutherfordton, NC ....General Practice

HAMRICK, GARROTTO, BRISKIN & PENE, A PROFESSIONAL CORPORATION
Los Angeles, CA ....Civil Trial Practice, Medical Malpractice Law, Personal Injury Law

HANCOCK & ESTABROOK
Syracuse, NY..................General Practice, Municipal Bond/Public Authority Financing Law, Tax Law

HANCOCK, ROTHERT & BUNSHOFT
San Francisco, CA ....General Practice

HAND, ARENDALL, BEDSOLE, GREAVES & JOHNSTON
Mobile, AL..................Admiralty/Maritime Law, Environmental Law, General Practice, Health Care Law, Insurance Defense Law, Labor and Employment Law, Product Liability Law, Tax Law

HANDLON, EASTMAN & DEWITT, P.C.
Midland, MI..................General Practice

HANES & SCHUTZ, P.C.
Colorado Springs, CO..................Civil Trial Practice, Patent, Trademark, Copyright and Unfair Competition Law

HANES, SEVILA, SAUNDERS & MCCAHILL, A PROFESSIONAL CORPORATION
Leesburg, VA ....Family Law, General Practice, Personal Injury Law

HANFT, FRIDE, O'BRIEN, HARRIES, SWELBAR & BURNS, P.A.
Duluth, MN ....Civil Trial Practice, General Practice, Insurance Defense Law, Probate and Estate Planning Law

HANGER, ENGEBRETSON, MAYER & VOGT
Clarksville, IN..................Civil Trial Practice, General Practice, Personal Injury Law, Probate and Estate Planning Law, Real Estate Law

HANIFY & KING, PROFESSIONAL CORPORATION
Boston, MA..................Antitrust Law, Bankruptcy Law, Civil Trial Practice, Commercial Law, Labor and Employment Law, Product Liability Law

HANKINS, MOODY & HAYS, L.L.P.
Lubbock, TX..................General Practice

HANLEY, BRUCE H., P.A.
Minneapolis, MN..................Criminal Trial Practice

HANNA, GERDE & BURNS
Lafayette, IN ....Civil Trial Practice, Personal Injury Law

HANNA, KERNS & STRADER, A PROFESSIONAL CORPORATION
Portland, OR..................Real Estate Law, Tax Law

HANNA AND MORTON
Los Angeles, CA..................Civil Trial Practice, Environmental Law, General Practice, Natural Resources Law, Probate and Estate Planning Law, Real Estate Law, Tax Law

HANNA & VAN ATTA
Palo Alto, CA ....Real Estate Law

HANNA, YOUNG, UPRIGHT & PAZUHANICH
Stroudsburg, PA..................Probate and Estate Planning Law, Tax Law

HANNAFAN, MICHAEL T., & ASSOCIATES, LTD.
Chicago, IL..................Civil Trial Practice

HANNOCH WEISMAN, A PROFESSIONAL CORPORATION
Roseland, NJ..................Banking Law, Civil Trial Practice, Commercial Law, Criminal Trial Practice, Environmental Law, Family Law, General Practice, Labor and Employment Law, Real Estate Law, Tax Law

HANOVER & SCHNITZER
San Bernardino, CA..................Bankruptcy Law

HANOVER & TURNER
Kansas City, MO..................Medical Malpractice Law, Personal Injury Law, Product Liability Law

HANOVER, WALSH, JALENAK & BLAIR
Memphis, TN..................Bankruptcy Law, Civil Trial Practice, General Practice, Immigration and Naturalization Law, Real Estate Law

HANSEN, BOYD, CULHANE & WATSON
Sacramento, CA..................Appellate Practice, Business Law, Civil Trial Practice, Insurance Defense Law, Real Estate Law

HANSEN, ENGLES & LOCHER, P.C.
Omaha, NE ....General Practice

HANSEN AND HOLMES, A PROFESSIONAL CORPORATION
Denver, CO ....Civil Trial Practice

HANSEN, MCCLINTOCK & RILEY
Des Moines, IA..................General Practice

HANSON, BRIDGETT, MARCUS, VLAHOS & RUDY
San Francisco, CA ....General Practice

HANSON, CURRAN, PARKS & WHITMAN
Providence, RI..................Admiralty/Maritime Law, Appellate Practice, Civil Trial Practice, Environmental Law, General Practice, Insurance Defense Law, Labor and Employment Law

HANSON, EPPERSON & SMITH, A PROFESSIONAL CORPORATION
Salt Lake City, UT..................General Practice, Insurance Defense Law, Medical Malpractice Law

HANSON & HANSON
Mc Cook, NE..................General Practice

HANSON, HASHEY
Fredericton, NB, Canada..................Civil Trial Practice, General Practice
Saint John, NB, Canada ....Tax Law

HANSON & NORRIS
San Mateo, CA..................Family Law

HARALSON, KINERK & MOREY, P.C.
Tucson, AZ ....Civil Trial Practice, Personal Injury Law

HARBEN & HARTLEY
Gainesville, GA..................General Practice, Labor and Employment Law

HARBISON, KESSINGER, LISLE & BUSH
Lexington, KY..................General Practice

HARBOLD, R. CHRIS
Columbus, OH..................Family Law

HARDAWAY LAW FIRM, P.A.
Greenville, SC..................Patent, Trademark, Copyright and Unfair Competition Law

HARDIG, LEE AND GROVES, PROFESSIONAL ASSOCIATION
South Bend, IN..................Civil Trial Practice, Medical Malpractice Law, Personal Injury Law, Product Liability Law

HARDIG & PARSONS
Bloomfield Hills, MI..................Business Law, Civil Trial Practice, Commercial Law, Family Law

HARDIMAN, HA & OLSON, A LAW PARTNERSHIP
San Francisco, CA ....Insurance Defense Law
Torrance, CA..................Insurance Defense Law

HARDIN, COOK, LOPER, ENGEL & BERGEZ
Oakland, CA ....Civil Trial Practice, Environmental Law, General Practice, Insurance Defense Law, Probate and Estate Planning Law

HARDIN & HAWKINS
Birmingham, AL..................Civil Trial Practice, Personal Injury Law

HARDIN, JESSON, DAWSON & TERRY
Fort Smith, AR..................General Practice, Insurance Defense Law

HARDING, BASS, FARGASON & BOOTH, L.L.P.
Lubbock, TX..................General Practice

HARDT, FREDERICK W.
Moorestown, NJ..................Municipal and Zoning Law

HARDT & STEWART
Naples, FL....Civil Trial Practice, Insurance Defense Law, Personal Injury Law

HARDY, BISSETT & LIPTON, P.A.
Miami, FL....Civil Trial Practice, General Practice, Personal Injury Law, Product Liability Law

HARDY JACOBSON GAZDA & JACOBSON, P.C.
San Antonio, TX....Municipal Bond/Public Authority Financing Law

HARDY & JOHNS
Houston, TX....Civil Trial Practice, Commercial Law, Personal Injury Law

HARDY, TERRELL, BOSWELL & SIMS
Paducah, KY....General Practice

HARGADON, LENIHAN, HARBOLT, & HERRINGTON
Louisville, KY....Medical Malpractice Law

HARGIS, WOOD & LOCKHART, A PROFESSIONAL ASSOCIATION
Little Rock, AR....General Practice

HARGRAVES, KARB, WILCOX & GALVANI
Framingham, MA....General Practice

HARHAI, STEPHEN J.
Denver, CO....Family Law

HARKAVY, SHAINBERG, KOSTEN & PINSTEIN
Memphis, TN....General Practice, Labor and Employment Law, Real Estate Law

HARKINS CUNNINGHAM
Washington, DC....Transportation Law
Philadelphia, PA....Civil Trial Practice

HARKLEROAD & HERMANCE, A PROFESSIONAL CORPORATION
Atlanta, GA....Administrative Law, International Business Law

HARLAN, THOMAS J., JR., P.C.
Norfolk, VA....Antitrust Law, Civil Trial Practice, General Practice, Medical Malpractice Law, Personal Injury Law

HARLAND LAW FIRM
Eureka, CA....Business Law, Probate and Estate Planning Law

HARLEM, ROBERT A., INC. & ASSOCIATES, A PROFESSIONAL CORPORATION
San Francisco, CA....Civil Trial Practice, Insurance Defense Law, Medical Malpractice Law, Personal Injury Law, Product Liability Law

HARLEY & BROWNE
New York, NY....Civil Trial Practice, Medical Malpractice Law

HARLIN & PARKER, P.S.C.
Bowling Green, KY....Appellate Practice, Banking Law, Bankruptcy Law, Civil Trial Practice, Construction Law, General Practice, Insurance Defense Law, Medical Malpractice Law, Personal Injury Law, Probate and Estate Planning Law, Product Liability Law, Real Estate Law
Smiths Grove, KY....General Practice

HARLOW, ADAMS & FRIEDMAN, P.C.
Milford, CT....General Practice, Real Estate Law

HARMAN, OWEN, SAUNDERS & SWEENEY, A PROFESSIONAL CORPORATION
Atlanta, GA....Business Law, Insurance Defense Law

HARMATA LAW OFFICES
Sacramento, CA....Administrative Law, Construction Law, General Practice

HARMON, STEVEN L.
Riverside, CA....Criminal Trial Practice

HARMON, SMITH, BRIDGES & WILBANKS
Atlanta, GA....Civil Trial Practice

HARNED & MCMEEN
Marengo, IA....Civil Trial Practice, General Practice

HARNESS, DICKEY & PIERCE
Newport Beach, CA....Patent, Trademark, Copyright and Unfair Competition Law
San Diego, CA....Patent, Trademark, Copyright and Unfair Competition Law
Ann Arbor, MI....Patent, Trademark, Copyright and Unfair Competition Law
Troy, MI....Patent, Trademark, Copyright and Unfair Competition Law

HARNEY, DAVID M. LAW OFFICES OF
Los Angeles, CA....Civil Trial Practice, Medical Malpractice Law, Personal Injury Law

HARNISH, JENNEY, MITCHELL AND RESH
Waltham, MA....General Practice

HARP & JOHNSON, P.C.
Columbus, GA....Family Law

HARPER, FERGUSON & DAVIS
Louisville, KY....Municipal Bond/Public Authority Financing Law

HARPER GREY EASTON
Vancouver, BC, Canada....Civil Trial Practice, Criminal Trial Practice, General Practice, Insurance Defense Law

HARPER, HORNBAKER, ALTENHOFEN & OPAT, CHARTERED
Junction City, KS....General Practice

HARPER, YOUNG, SMITH & MAURRAS, P.L.C.
Fort Smith, AR....General Practice

HARRANG LONG GARY RUDNICK, P.C.
Eugene, OR....General Practice

HARRAY, PIERCE & MASUDA
Monterey, CA....Civil Trial Practice, Insurance Defense Law

HARRELL AND HARRELL
Trenton, TN....Criminal Trial Practice, Personal Injury Law

HARRINGTON HUXLEY SMITH MITCHELL & REED
Youngstown, OH....Banking Law, Bankruptcy Law, General Practice

HARRINGTON, PORTER & WINKEL
Champaign, IL....Commercial Law

HARRINGTON & STULTZ
Eden, NC....General Practice
Wentworth, NC....General Practice

HARRIS BEACH & WILCOX
Hamburg, NY....Environmental Law
Ithaca, NY....General Practice

HARRIS, CADDELL & SHANKS, P.C.
Decatur, AL....General Practice

HARRIS, CARTER & MAHOTA
Columbus, OH....Civil Trial Practice, International Business Law

HARRIS & CHESWORTH
Rochester, NY....Business Law, Environmental Law, Probate and Estate Planning Law, Real Estate Law

HARRIS & COMPANY
Vancouver, BC, Canada....Labor and Employment Law

HARRIS, EVANS, BERG, MORRIS & ROGERS, P.C.
Birmingham, AL....Civil Trial Practice, Insurance Defense Law, Medical Malpractice Law

HARRIS & HARRIS
Warsaw, IN....General Practice, Probate and Estate Planning Law

HARRIS & JAMES
Macon, GA....General Practice

HARRIS, LAMBERT, HOWERTON & DORRIS
Marion, IL....Criminal Trial Practice, Personal Injury Law

HARRIS, MIDYETTE & GEARY, P.A.
Lakeland, FL....General Practice

HARRIS & PALUMBO, A PROFESSIONAL CORPORATION
Phoenix, AZ....Medical Malpractice Law, Personal Injury Law

HARRIS, SHELTON, DUNLAP AND COBB
Memphis, TN....General Practice

HARRIS, SHIELDS AND CREECH, P.A.
New Bern, NC....Civil Trial Practice

HARRIS & SMITH
Media, PA....Criminal Trial Practice, General Practice, Personal Injury Law

HARRIS & THOMAS
Corpus Christi, TX....Civil Trial Practice

HARRIS, TIM L., AND ASSOCIATES
Charlotte, NC....Medical Malpractice Law, Personal Injury Law
Gastonia, NC....General Practice, Medical Malpractice Law, Personal Injury Law

HARRIS, TUCKER & HARDIN, P.C.
Dallas, TX....Patent, Trademark, Copyright and Unfair Competition Law

HARRIS, WALLEN, MACDERMOTT & TINSLEY
Los Angeles, CA....Patent, Trademark, Copyright and Unfair Competition Law

HARRIS, WELSH & LUKMANN
Chesterton, IN .... General Practice

HARRISON, HARRISON & LLOP
Eastman, GA .... General Practice

HARRISON & HAYES
Spartanburg, SC .... Civil Trial Practice, Family Law, Personal Injury Law

HARRISON & JOHNSTON
Winchester, VA .... General Practice

HART, BELL, DEEM, EWING & STUCKEY
Vincennes, IN .... General Practice

HART AND HART
Benton, IL .... Civil Trial Practice, General Practice

HART & MCINTYRE
Atlanta, GA .... Medical Malpractice Law, Personal Injury Law

HART & WOLFF, ATTORNEYS AT LAW, A LAW CORPORATION
Honolulu, HI .... Criminal Trial Practice

HARTER, SECREST & EMERY
Rochester, NY .... Banking Law, Civil Trial Practice, Employment Benefits Law, General Practice, Health Care Law, Immigration and Naturalization Law, Labor and Employment Law, Real Estate Law, Securities Law, Tax Law

HARTE, WILLIAM J., LTD.
Chicago, IL .... Civil Trial Practice, Securities Law

HARTLEY, DENNIS W., P.C., PROFESSIONAL CORPORATION
Colorado Springs, CO .... Criminal Trial Practice

HARTLEY & WALL
Orlando, FL .... Civil Trial Practice

HARTMAN, LAPHAM & SMITH, L.L.P.
Victoria, TX .... Civil Trial Practice, Personal Injury Law

HARTNETT LAW OFFICE
Syracuse, NY .... General Practice, Personal Injury Law

HARTSELL, HARTSELL & MILLS, P.A.
Concord, NC .... General Practice

HARTUNIAN, ARAM A., AND ASSOCIATES
Chicago, IL .... Antitrust Law, Business Law

HARTZELL, GLIDDEN, TUCKER AND HARTZELL
Carthage, IL .... General Practice

HARTZOG CONGER & CASON, A PROFESSIONAL CORPORATION
Oklahoma City, OK .... Banking Law, Bankruptcy Law, Civil Trial Practice, Commercial Law, General Practice, Health Care Law, Labor and Employment Law, Natural Resources Law, Probate and Estate Planning Law, Real Estate Law, Securities Law, Tax Law

HARTZOG, SILVA & DAVIES
Franklin, TN .... General Practice

HARVEY & BATTEY, P.A.
Beaufort, SC .... General Practice

HARVEY AND HARVEY, HARVEY & MUMFORD
Albany, NY .... Civil Trial Practice

HARVEY, PENNINGTON, HERTING & RENNEISEN, LTD.
Philadelphia, PA .... General Practice

HARWICK, MAURICE
Santa Monica, CA .... Civil Trial Practice

HARWOOD LLOYD
Hackensack, NJ .... Civil Trial Practice, General Practice, Insurance Defense Law, Personal Injury Law
Ridgewood, NJ .... General Practice

HASH, O'BRIEN & BARTLETT
Kalispell, MT .... General Practice, Insurance Defense Law, Real Estate Law, Tax Law

HASKEL, HAND & LANCASTER
Mineola, NY .... Probate and Estate Planning Law

HASKELL & PERRIN
Chicago, IL .... Insurance Defense Law

HASKELL SLAUGHTER YOUNG & JOHNSTON, PROFESSIONAL ASSOCIATION
Birmingham, AL .... Business Law, Civil Trial Practice, Commercial Law, General Practice, Health Care Law, Labor and Employment Law, Municipal Bond/Public Authority Financing Law

HASKELL SLAUGHTER YOUNG JOHNSTON & GALLION, PROFESSIONAL ASSOCIATION
Montgomery, AL .... Civil Trial Practice, General Practice, Labor and Employment Law

HASSENFELD, MERRILL I.
Boston, MA .... Commercial Law

HASTIE AND KIRSCHNER, A PROFESSIONAL CORPORATION
Oklahoma City, OK .... Banking Law, Bankruptcy Law, General Practice, Securities Law

HASTINGS AND ESTREICHER, P.A.
St. Petersburg, FL .... Family Law

HATCHER, STUBBS, LAND, HOLLIS & ROTHSCHILD
Columbus, GA .... Banking Law, Commercial Law, Employment Benefits Law, General Practice, Insurance Defense Law, Municipal Bond/Public Authority Financing Law, Probate and Estate Planning Law, Real Estate Law, Tax Law

HATHAWAY, SPEIGHT & KUNZ
Cheyenne, WY .... Civil Trial Practice, General Practice

HATTERY, SIMPSON & WEST
Galesburg, IL .... General Practice

HAUGEN AND NIKOLAI, P.A.
Minneapolis, MN .... International Business Law, Patent, Trademark, Copyright and Unfair Competition Law

HAUGH & HAUGH, P.C.
Charlottesville, VA .... Civil Trial Practice, Criminal Trial Practice

HAVERSTOCK, MEDLEN & CARROLL
San Francisco, CA .... Patent, Trademark, Copyright and Unfair Competition Law

HAWKINS, BLICK & FITZPATRICK
San Jose, CA .... Personal Injury Law

HAWKINS, DELAFIELD & WOOD
New York, NY .... General Practice

HAWKINS, SCHNABEL, LINDAHL & BECK
Los Angeles, CA .... Admiralty/Maritime Law, Civil Trial Practice, Insurance Defense Law, Labor and Employment Law, Personal Injury Law, Product Liability Law

HAWLEY, HUDSON & ALMON
Mt. Vernon, IN .... General Practice, Natural Resources Law

HAWLEY, NYSTEDT & FLETCHER, P.C.
Tucson, AZ .... Probate and Estate Planning Law, Tax Law

HAWORTH, RIGGS, KUHN & HAWORTH
High Point, NC .... General Practice

HAWTHORNE, ACKERLY & DORRANCE
New Canaan, CT .... General Practice

HAYDEN AND MILLIKEN, P.A.
Miami, FL .... Admiralty/Maritime Law, Insurance Defense Law
Tampa, FL .... Admiralty/Maritime Law, Insurance Defense Law

HAYDEN, THOMAS C., JR., P.A.
La Plata, MD .... General Practice

HAYDUK, ANDREWS & HYPNAR, P.C.
Detroit, MI .... Civil Trial Practice, Insurance Defense Law, Product Liability Law

HAYES, J. MICHAEL
Buffalo, NY .... Civil Trial Practice, Personal Injury Law

HAYES, C. W. & H. M., P.A.
Dover-Foxcroft, ME .... General Practice

HAYES, HARKEY, SMITH & CASCIO, L.L.P.
Monroe, LA .... Civil Trial Practice, General Practice

HAYES & HAYES
Fort Wayne, IN .... Family Law

HAYES, PHILLIPS & MALONEY, P.C.
Denver, CO .... Municipal and Zoning Law

HAYES & REINSMITH
Hartford, CT .... Patent, Trademark, Copyright and Unfair Competition Law

HAYGOOD, LYNCH, HARRIS & MELTON
Forsyth, GA .... General Practice
Monticello, GA .... General Practice

HAYNER, WILLIAM M. & ASSOCIATES
Dallas, TX .... Personal Injury Law

HAYNES AND BOONE, L.L.P.
Fort Worth, TX .... Municipal Bond/Public Authority Financing Law, Securities Law

HAYNES, FORD AND ROWE
Lewisburg, WV .... General Practice

HAYNES, HULL & RIEDER, P.A.
Tullahoma, TN .... General Practice

HAYNSWORTH, BALDWIN, JOHNSON AND GREAVES, P.A.
Charlotte, NC .... Labor and Employment Law
Greensboro, NC .... Labor and Employment Law
Raleigh, NC .... Labor and Employment Law
Columbia, SC .... Labor and Employment Law
Greenville, SC .... Labor and Employment Law

HAYNSWORTH, BALDWIN, JOHNSON AND HARPER
Jacksonville, FL .... Labor and Employment Law
Tampa, FL .... Labor and Employment Law
Macon, GA .... Labor and Employment Law

HAYNSWORTH, MARION, MCKAY & GUÉRARD, L.L.P
Charleston, SC .... Administrative Law, Bankruptcy Law, Business Law, Civil Trial Practice, Construction Law, Employment Benefits Law, General Practice, Health Care Law, Medical Malpractice Law, Municipal Bond/Public Authority Financing Law, Product Liability Law, Public Utilities Law, Real Estate Law, Securities Law, Tax Law
Columbia, SC .... Administrative Law, Banking Law, Bankruptcy Law, Business Law, Civil Trial Practice, Construction Law, General Practice, Insurance Defense Law, Medical Malpractice Law, Municipal Bond/Public Authority Financing Law, Product Liability Law, Public Utilities Law, Real Estate Law, Securities Law
Greenville, SC .... Administrative Law, Banking Law, Bankruptcy Law, Business Law, Civil Trial Practice, Construction Law, Employment Benefits Law, Environmental Law, General Practice, Health Care Law, Insurance Defense Law, Medical Malpractice Law, Patent, Trademark, Copyright and Unfair Competition Law, Probate and Estate Planning Law, Product Liability Law, Public Utilities Law, Real Estate Law, Securities Law, Tax Law

HAYNSWORTH, PERRY, BRYANT, MARION & JOHNSTONE
Greenville, SC .... General Practice

HAYS & DABNEY, P.C.
Chickasha, OK .... General Practice

HAYS, MCCONN, RICE & PICKERING
Houston, TX .... Banking Law, Civil Trial Practice

HAYTHE & CURLEY
New York, NY .... Business Law

HAZEL & THOMAS, A PROFESSIONAL CORPORATION
Alexandria, VA .... General Practice
Falls Church, VA .... General Practice
Leesburg, VA .... General Practice
Manassas, VA .... General Practice
Richmond, VA .... General Practice

HAZLETT & WILKES
Tucson, AZ .... General Practice, Insurance Defense Law

HEAD, SMITH, METCALF, AGUILAR, MOSS & SIERON, P.A.
Orange Park, FL .... Civil Trial Practice, Criminal Trial Practice, Family Law, Personal Injury Law, Probate and Estate Planning Law, Real Estate Law, Tax Law

HEAGNEY, LENNON & SLANE
Greenwich, CT .... General Practice

HEALY, JOHN PATRICK
Chicago, IL .... Civil Trial Practice, Personal Injury Law

HEALY & BAILLIE
New York, NY .... Admiralty/Maritime Law

HEALY AND BEAL, P.C.
Tucson, AZ .... Medical Malpractice Law, Personal Injury Law

HEARD, LEVERETT, PHELPS, WEAVER & CAMPBELL
Elberton, GA .... General Practice

HEATH & MARTIN
Holley, NY .... General Practice

HEBB & GITLIN, A PROFESSIONAL CORPORATION
Hartford, CT .... Bankruptcy Law, General Practice

HEBERT, MOULEDOUX & BLAND, A PROFESSIONAL LAW CORPORATION
New Orleans, LA .... Admiralty/Maritime Law, Commercial Law, General Practice

HECKENKAMP, SIMHAUSER & LABARRE, P.C.
Springfield, IL .... General Practice

HECOX, TOLLEY, KEENE & BELTZ, P.C.
Colorado Springs, CO .... General Practice

HEDEEN, HUGHES & WETERING
Adrian, MN .... General Practice
Worthington, MN .... General Practice

HEENAN BLAIKIE
Montreal, QU, Canada .... General Practice

HEIDELL, PITTONI, MURPHY & BACH, P.C.
New York, NY .... Insurance Defense Law, Medical Malpractice Law

HEIDEPRIEM, WIDMAYER, ZELL & JONES
Miller, SD .... General Practice

HEILIG, MCKENRY, FRAIM & LOLLAR, A PROFESSIONAL CORPORATION
Norfolk, VA .... Civil Trial Practice, Labor and Employment Law, Medical Malpractice Law

HEILIGENSTEIN & BADGLEY, PROFESSIONAL CORPORATION
Belleville, IL .... General Practice

HEIMERL, KEENAN & LONGO
Buffalo, NY .... General Practice

HEIN, SMITH, BEREZIN, MALOOF & ROGERS
Hackensack, NJ .... Business Law, Civil Trial Practice, Commercial Law, Employment Benefits Law, General Practice, Insurance Defense Law, Medical Malpractice Law, Personal Injury Law, Probate and Estate Planning Law, Real Estate Law, Tax Law

HEINRICH GORDON BATCHELDER HARGROVE & WEIHE
Fort Lauderdale, FL .... Civil Trial Practice, General Practice, Personal Injury Law, Real Estate Law

HEINTZMAN, WARREN & WISE
Pittsburgh, PA .... Civil Trial Practice, Insurance Defense Law, Medical Malpractice Law, Product Liability Law

HEINZEN, BERNARD G., LTD.
Philadelphia, PA .... Commercial Law, International Business Law

HEISERMAN, ROBERT G., P.C.
Denver, CO .... Immigration and Naturalization Law

HELLER, HOLMES, & ASSOCIATES, P.C.
Mattoon, IL .... Civil Trial Practice, General Practice

HELLRING LINDEMAN GOLDSTEIN & SIEGAL
Newark, NJ .... Antitrust Law, Bankruptcy Law, Civil Trial Practice, Commercial Law, Criminal Trial Practice, Environmental Law, Family Law, General Practice, Natural Resources Law, Real Estate Law, Securities Law, Tax Law

HELMKE, BEAMS, BOYER & WAGNER
Fort Wayne, IN .... General Practice, Municipal and Zoning Law, Probate and Estate Planning Law

HELMS, HANRAHAN & MYERS
Arcadia, CA .... Family Law, General Practice, Probate and Estate Planning Law

HELMSING, LYONS, SIMS & LEACH, P.C.
Mobile, AL .... Civil Trial Practice, General Practice, Insurance Defense Law, Personal Injury Law

HELSELL, FETTERMAN, MARTIN, TODD & HOKANSON
Seattle, WA .... General Practice

HEMENWAY & BARNES
Boston, MA .... Business Law, General Practice, Probate and Estate Planning Law

HEMRY & HEMRY, P.C., THE LAW OFFICES OF
Oklahoma City, OK .... Probate and Estate Planning Law, Real Estate Law

HENDEL, COLLINS & NEWTON, P.C.
Springfield, MA .... Banking Law, Bankruptcy Law, Commercial Law, Real Estate Law

HENDERSON, FRANKLIN, STARNES & HOLT, PROFESSIONAL ASSOCIATION
Fort Myers, FL .... Civil Trial Practice, General Practice, Insurance Defense Law, Personal Injury Law, Probate and Estate Planning Law, Real Estate Law, Tax Law

HENDERSON & SALLEY
Aiken, SC .... Civil Trial Practice, General Practice, Insurance Defense Law, Personal Injury Law

HENDERSON & STURM
Washington, DC .... Patent, Trademark, Copyright and Unfair Competition Law
Davenport, IA .... Patent, Trademark, Copyright and Unfair Competition Law

Des Moines, IA .... Patent, Trademark, Copyright and Unfair Competition Law
Omaha, NE .... Patent, Trademark, Copyright and Unfair Competition Law

HENDREN AND ANDRAE
Jefferson City, MO .... General Practice

HENDREN LAW OFFICES
Oroville, CA .... Civil Trial Practice

HENDRICK, PHILLIPS, SCHEMM & SALZMAN, A PROFESSIONAL CORPORATION
Atlanta, GA .... Construction Law

HENDRICKS, LEWIS S.
Rockwell City, IA .... General Practice

HENDRICKS & HENDRICKS
Coral Gables, FL .... Probate and Estate Planning Law

HENDRICKSON, RAY
Irvine, CA .... Family Law

HENDRY, LLOYD G., P.A., LAW OFFICES OF
Fort Myers, FL .... General Practice, Real Estate Law

HENINGER AND HENINGER, PROFESSIONAL CORPORATION
Davenport, IA .... General Practice

HENNENHOEFER, JAMES A., A PROFESSIONAL CORPORATION
Vista, CA .... Family Law

HENRY & BEAVER
Lebanon, PA .... Civil Trial Practice, General Practice

HENRY, BUCHANAN, MICK, HUDSON & SUBER, P.A.
Tallahassee, FL .... Civil Trial Practice, General Practice, Insurance Defense Law

HENRY & HENRY
Conway, AR .... General Practice

HENRY, MCCORD & BEAN
Tullahoma, TN .... General Practice

HENSHALL, PENNINGTON & BRAKE
Chanute, KS .... General Practice

HENSLEY, DUNN, ROSS & HOWARD
Horse Cave, KY .... General Practice

HENSON, JOHN P.
Greenwood, MS .... Business Law, General Practice, Real Estate Law

HENSON, RICHARD W.
San Carlos, CA .... Probate and Estate Planning Law

HENSON & EFRON, P.A.
Minneapolis, MN .... Environmental Law, Family Law, General Practice, Securities Law

HENSON HENSON BAYLISS & SUE
Greensboro, NC .... Civil Trial Practice, Insurance Defense Law, Personal Injury Law

HENSON, HENSON, HENSON, MARSHALL & MILBURN
Shawnee, OK .... General Practice

HENTHORN, HARRIS AND TAYLOR, P.C.
Crawfordsville, IN .... General Practice

HEPBURN WILLCOX HAMILTON & PUTNAM
Philadelphia, PA .... General Practice

HEPFORD, SWARTZ & MORGAN
Harrisburg, PA .... Administrative Law, Appellate Practice, Business Law, Civil Trial Practice, Criminal Trial Practice, Family Law, General Practice, Insurance Defense Law, Medical Malpractice Law, Personal Injury Law, Probate and Estate Planning Law, Product Liability Law, Real Estate Law

HERBERT & HERBERT
Glasgow, KY .... Civil Trial Practice, Family Law, General Practice, Real Estate Law

HERBOLSHEIMER, LANNON, HENSON, DUNCAN AND REAGAN, P.C.
La Salle, IL .... General Practice, Insurance Defense Law, Real Estate Law

HEREFORD & HEREFORD
Charleston, WV .... General Practice

HERMANIES, MAJOR, CASTELLI & GOODMAN
Cincinnati, OH .... Civil Trial Practice, Medical Malpractice Law, Personal Injury Law

HERMANN, CAHN & SCHNEIDER
Cleveland, OH .... Civil Trial Practice, Family Law, Insurance Defense Law, Personal Injury Law, Product Liability Law

HERNDON, COLEMAN, BRADING & MCKEE
Johnson City, TN .... General Practice

HERRICK, ARY, COOK, COOK, COOK & COOK
Cherokee, IA .... General Practice

HERRICK, LANGDON & LANGDON
Des Moines, IA .... Civil Trial Practice, General Practice

HERRIG & VOGT
Sacramento, CA .... Construction Law
Kennewick, WA .... Construction Law

HERRIN & HERRIN
Johnson City, TN .... Civil Trial Practice, General Practice

HERRMANN, LAWRENCE M.
Jackson Heights, NY .... Criminal Trial Practice

HERSCHBACH, TRACY, JOHNSON, BERTANI & WILSON
Joliet, IL .... Commercial Law, General Practice, Municipal and Zoning Law, Real Estate Law

HERSHBERGER, PATTERSON, JONES & ROTH, L.C.
Wichita, KS .... Civil Trial Practice, Commercial Law, General Practice, Insurance Defense Law, Natural Resources Law

HERSHNER, HUNTER, MOULTON, ANDREWS & NEILL
Eugene, OR .... General Practice

HERSTER, NEWTON & MURPHY
Easton, PA .... Banking Law, Business Law, Commercial Law, Family Law, General Practice, Municipal and Zoning Law, Probate and Estate Planning Law, Real Estate Law

HERT & BAKER, A PROFESSIONAL CORPORATION
Stillwater, OK .... General Practice

HERTZBERG, RICHARD J.
Phoenix, AZ .... Criminal Trial Practice

HERZFELD & RUBIN, P.C.
New York, NY .... General Practice

HERZOG, ENGSTROM & KOPLOVITZ, P.C.
Albany, NY .... General Practice

HESLIN, THOMAS P.
Hartford, CT .... Civil Trial Practice

HESLIN & ROTHENBERG, P.C.
Albany, NY .... Patent, Trademark, Copyright and Unfair Competition Law

HESTER, GRADY, HESTER & GREENE
Elizabethtown, NC .... General Practice

HESTER, JON L., P.C., A PROFESSIONAL CORPORATION
Oklahoma City, OK .... Family Law

HETTINGER & LEEDY
Riverton, WY .... General Practice

HEWITT, JAMES W.
Lincoln, NE .... General Practice

HEWLETT, COLLINS AND ALLARD
Wilmington, NC .... Criminal Trial Practice

HEYL, ROYSTER, VOELKER & ALLEN, PROFESSIONAL CORPORATION
Edwardsville, IL .... General Practice
Peoria, IL .... General Practice
Rockford, IL .... General Practice
Springfield, IL .... General Practice
Urbana, IL .... General Practice

HIBBARD, CALDWELL & SCHULTZ, A PROFESSIONAL CORPORATION
Oregon City, OR .... General Practice

HICKEY & HICKEY
Kingston, ON, Canada .... General Practice

HICKEY, MACKEY, EVANS, WALKER & STEWART
Cheyenne, WY .... Banking Law, Civil Trial Practice, Commercial Law, Communications Law, Criminal Trial Practice, General Practice, Personal Injury Law

HICKS, ANDERSON & BLUM, P.A.
Miami, FL .... Appellate Practice, General Practice

HICKS, MALOOF & CAMPBELL, A PROFESSIONAL CORPORATION
Atlanta, GA .... Business Law

HICKS, SCHMIDLIN & BANCROFT, P.C.
Flint, MI .... Business Law, Probate and Estate Planning Law

HICKSON, DAVID L.
San Diego, CA........................Probate and Estate Planning Law

HIERING & DUPIGNAC, A PROFESSIONAL CORPORATION
Toms River, NJ........................General Practice

HIERONYMUS, HODGDEN & HALLREN
Woodward, OK........................General Practice

HIGGINS, CAVANAGH & COONEY
Providence, RI........................Civil Trial Practice, General Practice

HIGGINS, ROBERTS, BEYERL & COAN, P.C.
Schenectady, NY........................General Practice

HIGGINS & SLATTERY
Providence, RI........................General Practice, Probate and Estate Planning Law

HIGGS, FLETCHER & MACK
Escondido, CA........................General Practice
San Diego, CA........................Banking Law, Civil Trial Practice, General Practice

HIGGS LAW OFFICES
Bay City, MI........................General Practice

HIGH, STACK, LAZENBY, PALAHACH & DEL AMO
Miami, FL........................General Practice

HIGH, SWARTZ, ROBERTS & SEIDEL
Norristown, PA........................General Practice

HIGHLAND & ZANETTI
Southfield, MI........................Medical Malpractice Law, Personal Injury Law, Product Liability Law

HIGHSAW, MAHONEY & CLARKE, P.C.
Washington, DC........................Labor and Employment Law

HILBRECHT & ASSOCIATES, CHARTERED
Las Vegas, NV........................Administrative Law, General Practice

HILBURN, CALHOON, HARPER, PRUNISKI & CALHOUN, LTD.
Little Rock, AR........................Civil Trial Practice, General Practice, Labor and Employment Law, Securities Law, Tax Law, Transportation Law

HILL & BARLOW, A PROFESSIONAL CORPORATION
Boston, MA........................General Practice

HILL & BEYER, A PROFESSIONAL LAW CORPORATION
Lafayette, LA........................Admiralty/Maritime Law, Business Law, Civil Trial Practice, Environmental Law, Insurance Defense Law, Labor and Employment Law, Product Liability Law

HILL AND BLEIBERG
Atlanta, GA........................Medical Malpractice Law, Personal Injury Law, Product Liability Law

HILLER, BENJAMIN, & ASSOCIATES
Idaho Falls, ID........................General Practice

HILL, FARRER & BURRILL
Los Angeles, CA........................General Practice, Labor and Employment Law, Tax Law

HILL & HILL, ATTYS. AT LAW, A PROF. CORP.
Houston, TX........................General Practice

HILL, HILL, CARTER, FRANCO, COLE & BLACK, P.C.
Montgomery, AL........................Civil Trial Practice, General Practice

HILLIS CLARK MARTIN & PETERSON, A PROFESSIONAL SERVICE CORPORATION
Seattle, WA........................General Practice

HILLIX, BREWER, HOFFHAUS, WHITTAKER & WRIGHT, L.L.C.
Kansas City, MO........................General Practice

HILL, PARKER & JOHNSON, A PROFESSIONAL CORPORATION
Houston, TX........................Civil Trial Practice

HILL AND PONTON, PROFESSIONAL ASSOCIATION
Orlando, FL........................Civil Trial Practice

HILL, SAM, INC.
San Clemente, CA........................Business Law

HILL, WARD & HENDERSON, A PROFESSIONAL ASSOCIATION
Tampa, FL........................Civil Trial Practice, Real Estate Law

HILLYER & IRWIN, A PROFESSIONAL CORPORATION
San Diego, CA........................Business Law, Civil Trial Practice, Commercial Law, Construction Law, Environmental Law, Insurance Defense Law, Probate and Estate Planning Law, Real Estate Law

HINCKLEY, ALLEN & SNYDER
Boston, MA........................General Practice
Providence, RI........................General Practice

HINDS, COWAN, STRANGE, GEER & LUMPKIN
Georgetown, SC........................General Practice

HINDS, ROBERT T., JR. AND ASSOCIATES, P.C.
Denver, CO........................Family Law

HINES & THOMAS
San Francisco, CA........................Civil Trial Practice

HINKLE, COX, EATON, COFFIELD & HENSLEY
Albuquerque, NM........................Antitrust Law, Banking Law, Bankruptcy Law, Business Law, Civil Trial Practice, Commercial Law, Communications Law, Employment Benefits Law, General Practice, Health Care Law, Insurance Defense Law, Labor and Employment Law, Medical Malpractice Law, Natural Resources Law, Real Estate Law, Tax Law
Roswell, NM........................Bankruptcy Law, Civil Trial Practice, Commercial Law, Insurance Defense Law, Natural Resources Law, Personal Injury Law
Santa Fe, NM........................Civil Trial Practice, Environmental Law, Insurance Defense Law, Natural Resources Law, Personal Injury Law, Real Estate Law
Amarillo, TX........................Appellate Practice, Banking Law, Bankruptcy Law, Civil Trial Practice, Commercial Law, Insurance Defense Law, Natural Resources Law, Probate and Estate Planning Law, Product Liability Law, Public Utilities Law, Tax Law
Midland, TX........................Banking Law, Civil Trial Practice, Commercial Law, Natural Resources Law

HINKLE, EBERHART & ELKOURI, L.L.C.
Wichita, KS........................General Practice, Municipal Bond/Public Authority Financing Law, Tax Law

HINKLE KECK & GUNDLACH
Danville, IN........................General Practice

HINMAN, HOWARD & KATTELL
Binghamton, NY........................Civil Trial Practice, General Practice, Labor and Employment Law, Municipal Bond/Public Authority Financing Law, Natural Resources Law, Tax Law

HINSHAW, WINKLER, DRAA, MARSH & STILL
San Jose, CA........................Civil Trial Practice, Insurance Defense Law

HINTON & COX
Houston, TX........................Civil Trial Practice

HIRN DOHENY REED & HARPER
Louisville, KY........................Banking Law, Civil Trial Practice, General Practice, Tax Law

HIRSCH, PARTIN & GROGAN, P.C.
Columbus, GA........................Family Law

HIRSCHHORN, AUSTIN, P.C.
Birmingham, MI........................Bankruptcy Law, Business Law, Civil Trial Practice, Commercial Law, General Practice

HIRSH, DAVIS, WALKER & PICCARRETA, P.C.
Tucson, AZ........................Criminal Trial Practice

HIRST & APPLEGATE, A PROFESSIONAL CORPORATION
Cheyenne, WY........................General Practice

HISHON & BURBAGE
Atlanta, GA........................Business Law, Civil Trial Practice, General Practice, Tax Law

HITT, SACHNER & COLEMAN
Cheshire, CT........................General Practice, Medical Malpractice Law

HOAGLAND, LONGO, MORAN, DUNST & DOUKAS
New Brunswick, NJ........................Civil Trial Practice, General Practice, Insurance Defense Law, Real Estate Law

HOBBS, LARRY F., P.C.
Denver, CO........................Labor and Employment Law

HOBBS, STRAUS, DEAN & WALKER
Washington, DC........................General Practice

HOBSON, CADY & CADY
Hampton, IA........................Civil Trial Practice, General Practice

HOCHBERG, KRIEGER, DANZIG & GARUBO
Roseland, NJ........................Civil Trial Practice, Family Law

HOCHMAN, SALKIN AND DEROY, A PROFESSIONAL CORPORATION
Beverly Hills, CA........................Business Law, Criminal Trial Practice, Probate and Estate Planning Law, Tax Law

HODES & BRAUN, P.A.
Short Hills, NJ........................Family Law

HODGES & DAVIS, P.C.
Merrillville, IN........................Civil Trial Practice, Commercial Law, General Practice, Health Care Law, Real Estate Law
Portage, IN........................Civil Trial Practice, Commercial Law, General Practice, Health Care Law, Real Estate Law

HODGES, DOUGHTY AND CARSON
Knoxville, TN .... Bankruptcy Law, Civil Trial Practice, General Practice, Insurance Defense Law, Medical Malpractice Law, Product Liability Law

HODGSON, RUSS, ANDREWS, WOODS & GOODYEAR
Buffalo, NY .... Civil Trial Practice, General Practice, Immigration and Naturalization Law, Labor and Employment Law, Patent, Trademark, Copyright and Unfair Competition Law, Tax Law

HODOSH, SPINELLA & ANGELONE
Providence, RI .... Civil Trial Practice, General Practice, Insurance Defense Law, Personal Injury Law

HOEPPNER WAGNER AND EVANS
Merrillville, IN .... General Practice, Insurance Defense Law, Labor and Employment Law, Product Liability Law
Valparaiso, IN .... General Practice, Insurance Defense Law, Labor and Employment Law, Product Liability Law

HOFF, CURTIS, PACHT, CASSIDY & FRAME, P.C.
Burlington, VT .... General Practice

HOFF, SVINGEN, ATHENS & RUSSELL
Fergus Falls, MN .... General Practice

HOFFERT, MYLES B., & ASSOCIATES, P.C.
Southfield, MI .... Tax Law

HOFFMAN, JAMES P. LAW OFFICES OF
Keokuk, IA .... Personal Injury Law

HOFFMAN & HERTZIG, P.A.
Miami, FL .... Civil Trial Practice

HOFFMAN, LUHMAN & BUSCH
Lafayette, IN .... Bankruptcy Law, General Practice, Insurance Defense Law, Personal Injury Law

HOFFMAN, WACHTELL, KOSTER, MAIER & MANDEL
White Plains, NY .... General Practice, Insurance Defense Law, Municipal and Zoning Law, Real Estate Law

HOFFMANN & BARON
Jericho, NY .... Patent, Trademark, Copyright and Unfair Competition Law

HOFHEIMER, NUSBAUM, MCPHAUL & SAMUELS, A PROFESSIONAL CORPORATION
Norfolk, VA .... General Practice

HOGAN, THOMAS R. LAW OFFICES OF
San Jose, CA .... Civil Trial Practice, General Practice

HOGAN & HARTSON L.L.P.
Washington, DC .... Banking Law, Communications Law, General Practice, Tax Law

HOGAN & HOGAN
East Providence, RI .... General Practice

HOGAN & RINI, P.C.
New Haven, CT .... Banking Law, Business Law, Civil Trial Practice, Labor and Employment Law, Municipal and Zoning Law, Securities Law

HOGAN, SMITH, ALSPAUGH, SAMPLES & PRATT, P.C.
Birmingham, AL .... Environmental Law, General Practice, Medical Malpractice Law

HOGUE, HILL, JONES, NASH AND LYNCH
Wilmington, NC .... Civil Trial Practice, General Practice, Insurance Defense Law

HOHLT, HOUSE, DEMOSS & JOHNSON
Du Quoin, IL .... General Practice
Nashville, IL .... General Practice
Pinckneyville, IL .... General Practice, Natural Resources Law

HOHMANN, WERNER & TAUBE, L.L.P.
Austin, TX .... Banking Law, Civil Trial Practice, Insurance Defense Law
Houston, TX .... Civil Trial Practice, Insurance Defense Law

HOLAHAN, MALLOY, MAYBAUGH & MONNICH
Troy, MI .... Civil Trial Practice, Insurance Defense Law, Medical Malpractice Law, Personal Injury Law, Probate and Estate Planning Law

HOLBROOK, HEAVEN & FAY, P.A.
Kansas City, KS .... Civil Trial Practice, General Practice, Insurance Defense Law

HOLBROOK & PITT
Ashland, KY .... Real Estate Law

HOLCOMB, DUNBAR, CONNELL, CHAFFIN & WILLARD, A PROFESSIONAL ASSOCIATION
Aberdeen, MS .... Bankruptcy Law, Civil Trial Practice, Commercial Law, Environmental Law, General Practice, Insurance Defense Law, Labor and Employment Law, Probate and Estate Planning Law
Clarksdale, MS .... Bankruptcy Law, Civil Trial Practice, Commercial Law, Environmental Law, General Practice, Insurance Defense Law, Probate and Estate Planning Law
Jackson, MS .... Bankruptcy Law, Civil Trial Practice, Commercial Law, Environmental Law, General Practice, Insurance Defense Law, Labor and Employment Law, Probate and Estate Planning Law
Oxford, MS .... Bankruptcy Law, Civil Trial Practice, Commercial Law, Environmental Law, General Practice, Insurance Defense Law, Labor and Employment Law, Probate and Estate Planning Law
Southaven, MS .... Bankruptcy Law, Civil Trial Practice, Commercial Law, General Practice, Insurance Defense Law, Labor and Employment Law, Probate and Estate Planning Law

HOLCOMBE, BOMAR, COTHRAN AND GUNN, P.A.
Spartanburg, SC .... Civil Trial Practice, General Practice

HOLDEN, KIDWELL, HAHN & CRAPO
Idaho Falls, ID .... General Practice

HOLLAND & ASSOCIATES
Longmeadow, MA .... Patent, Trademark, Copyright and Unfair Competition Law
Springfield, MA .... Patent, Trademark, Copyright and Unfair Competition Law

HOLLAND, DONOVAN, BECKETT & HERMANS, PROFESSIONAL ASSOCIATION
Exeter, NH .... General Practice, Municipal and Zoning Law, Real Estate Law, Tax Law

HOLLAND & HART
Aspen, CO .... General Practice
Boulder, CO .... General Practice
Colorado Springs, CO .... General Practice
Denver, CO .... Antitrust Law, Banking Law, Bankruptcy Law, Civil Trial Practice, Environmental Law, General Practice, Labor and Employment Law, Municipal Bond/Public Authority Financing Law, Natural Resources Law, Patent, Trademark, Copyright and Unfair Competition Law, Real Estate Law, Tax Law, Trademark, Copyright and Unfair Competition Law
Washington, DC .... General Practice
Boise, ID .... General Practice
Billings, MT .... General Practice
Cheyenne, WY .... General Practice
Jackson, WY .... General Practice

HOLLAND & HOLLAND
Indianapolis, IN .... Civil Trial Practice, Personal Injury Law

HOLLAND & KNIGHT
Washington, DC .... General Practice
Fort Lauderdale, FL .... General Practice
Jacksonville, FL .... General Practice
Lakeland, FL .... General Practice
Miami, FL .... General Practice
Orlando, FL .... General Practice
St. Petersburg, FL .... General Practice
Tallahassee, FL .... General Practice
Tampa, FL .... General Practice
West Palm Beach, FL .... General Practice

HOLLAND, RAY & UPCHURCH, P.A.
Tupelo, MS .... Banking Law, Commercial Law, General Practice, Insurance Defense Law, Labor and Employment Law, Medical Malpractice Law, Probate and Estate Planning Law, Real Estate Law

HOLLAND, STARLING, SEVERS, STADLER & FRIEDLAND, P.A.
Titusville, FL .... General Practice

HOLLEMAN, BOYCE, A PROFESSIONAL ASSOCIATION
Gulfport, MS .... Civil Trial Practice, Criminal Trial Practice, Family Law, General Practice, Personal Injury Law

HOLLEY, WILLIAM
San Jose, CA .... General Practice

HOLLEY, ALBERTSON & POLK, P.C.
Golden, CO .... Civil Trial Practice, Real Estate Law

HOLLEY & GALEN
Los Angeles, CA .... General Practice, Probate and Estate Planning Law, Tax Law

HOLLIDAY, JAMES S. JR.
Baton Rouge, LA .... Business Law, Construction Law

HOLLIMAN, LANGHOLZ, RUNNELS, HOLDEN, FORSMAN & SELLERS, A PROFESSIONAL CORPORATION
Tulsa, OK .... General Practice, Natural Resources Law, Securities Law

HOLLINS, WAGSTER & YARBROUGH, P.C.
Nashville, TN .... Civil Trial Practice, Criminal Trial Practice

HOLLINSHEAD, MENDELSON, BRESNAHAN & NIXON, P.C.
Pittsburgh, PA .... Real Estate Law

HOLLISTER & BRACE, A PROFESSIONAL CORPORATION
Santa Barbara, CA .... Civil Trial Practice, General Practice

HOLLOMAN, CHARLES R., P.A.
Ocala, FL .... Criminal Trial Practice

HOLLOWAY, DOBSON, HUDSON, BACHMAN, ALDEN, JENNINGS, ROBERTSON & HOLLOWAY, A PROFESSIONAL CORPORATION
Oklahoma City, OK .... Civil Trial Practice, Environmental Law, Insurance Defense Law, Personal Injury Law

HOLLOWAY ODEGARD & SWEENEY, P.C.
Phoenix, AZ .... Insurance Defense Law

HOLMAN, MCCOLLUM & HANSEN, P.C.
Prairie Village, KS .... Banking Law, Business Law, Civil Trial Practice, Family Law, General Practice, Labor and Employment Law, Probate and Estate Planning Law, Tax Law

HOLME ROBERTS & OWEN LLC
Boulder, CO .... General Practice
Colorado Springs, CO .... General Practice
Denver, CO .... Banking Law, Bankruptcy Law, Business Law, Civil Trial Practice, Environmental Law, General Practice, Health Care Law, International Business Law, Labor and Employment Law, Municipal Bond/Public Authority Financing Law, Natural Resources Law, Patent, Trademark, Copyright and Unfair Competition Law, Probate and Estate Planning Law, Public Utilities Law, Real Estate Law, Securities Law, Tax Law
Salt Lake City, UT .... General Practice
London, England .... General Practice

HOLMES & THOMSON, L.L.P.
Charleston, SC .... General Practice

HOLPER WELSH & MITCHELL, LTD.
Minneapolis, MN .... Bankruptcy Law

HOLT, LONGEST, WALL & LILES, P.L.L.C.
Burlington, NC .... General Practice

HOLT, NEY, ZATCOFF & WASSERMAN
Atlanta, GA .... Business Law, Civil Trial Practice, Environmental Law, General Practice, Health Care Law, Municipal and Zoning Law, Personal Injury Law, Real Estate Law, Tax Law

HOLT & WATT
Reidsville, NC .... General Practice

HOLTON & HOWARD, A PROFESSIONAL CORPORATION
Nashville, TN .... Probate and Estate Planning Law, Tax Law

HOLTORF, KOVARIK, ELLISON & MATHIS, P.C.
Gering, NE .... General Practice, Insurance Defense Law

HOLTZMAN, ERIC H.
Hauppauge, NY .... Civil Trial Practice, Commercial Law, General Practice, Product Liability Law

HOLTZMANN, WISE & SHEPARD
Palo Alto, CA .... General Practice
New York, NY .... General Practice

HOLZWARTH, WILLIAM C., LAW OFFICES OF
Irvine, CA .... Civil Trial Practice, Real Estate Law

HONAKER, HAMPTON & NEWMAN
Rock Springs, WY .... Personal Injury Law

HONIGMAN MILLER SCHWARTZ AND COHN
Los Angeles, CA .... Bankruptcy Law, Civil Trial Practice, General Practice
Orlando, FL .... General Practice, Municipal Bond/Public Authority Financing Law, Real Estate Law, Tax Law
Tampa, FL .... Civil Trial Practice, Environmental Law, General Practice, Natural Resources Law
West Palm Beach, FL .... Environmental Law, General Practice, Natural Resources Law, Real Estate Law
Detroit, MI .... Antitrust Law, Bankruptcy Law, Civil Trial Practice, Communications Law, Criminal Trial Practice, Environmental Law, General Practice, Health Care Law, Labor and Employment Law, Municipal Bond/Public Authority Financing Law, Natural Resources Law, Real Estate Law, Tax Law
Lansing, MI .... Civil Trial Practice, Environmental Law, General Practice, Insurance Defense Law, Natural Resources Law, Real Estate Law, Tax Law, Transportation Law

HOOD LAW FIRM
Charleston, SC .... Civil Trial Practice, General Practice, Insurance Defense Law, Medical Malpractice Law, Personal Injury Law, Product Liability Law

HOOD, THORNBRUGH & RAYNOLDS, P.C.
Tulsa, OK .... Family Law

HOOGENDOORN, TALBOT, DAVIDS, GODFREY & MILLIGAN
Chicago, IL .... Probate and Estate Planning Law, Real Estate Law, Tax Law

HOOKER, ROBERT THE LAW OFFICE OF
Tucson, AZ .... Criminal Trial Practice

HOOPER, HATHAWAY, PRICE, BEUCHE & WALLACE
Ann Arbor, MI .... Business Law, Civil Trial Practice, Criminal Trial Practice, Environmental Law, General Practice, Labor and Employment Law, Probate and Estate Planning Law, Real Estate Law

HOOPER LAW OFFICES, P.C.
Riverton, WY .... Civil Trial Practice

HOOPER, LUNDY & BOOKMAN, INC.
Los Angeles, CA .... Health Care Law

HOOVER LEGAL ASSOCIATES, A PROFESSIONAL CORPORATION
Dallas, TX .... General Practice

HOOVER & STOREY
Little Rock, AR .... Administrative Law, Banking Law, Bankruptcy Law, Business Law, Civil Trial Practice, Commercial Law, Construction Law, Employment Benefits Law, General Practice, Probate and Estate Planning Law, Real Estate Law, Securities Law, Tax Law

HOPE & CAUSEY, P.C.
Conroe, TX .... Insurance Defense Law

HOPE, MILLS, BOLIN, COLLINS & RAMSEY
Garden City, KS .... General Practice

HOPKINS, THEODORE J. JR.
Columbia, SC .... Tax Law

HOPKINS, DODSON, CRAWLEY, BAGWELL, UPSHAW & PERSONS
Gulfport, MS .... Civil Trial Practice, Environmental Law, Insurance Defense Law, Probate and Estate Planning Law

HOPKINS, RODEN, CROCKETT, HANSEN & HOOPES
Boise, ID .... General Practice
Idaho Falls, ID .... General Practice

HOPKINS & THOMAS
Atlanta, GA .... Patent, Trademark, Copyright and Unfair Competition Law

HOPPE, FREY, HEWITT & MILLIGAN
Warren, OH .... General Practice

HOPPER AND KANOUFF, A PROFESSIONAL CORPORATION
Denver, CO .... Business Law, Securities Law

HOPPER & PLUNK, P.C.
Savannah, TN .... Civil Trial Practice, General Practice, Insurance Defense Law, Real Estate Law

HOPPER, WENZEL & GALLIHER, P.C.
Indianapolis, IN .... Bankruptcy Law, Commercial Law

HOPPING BOYD GREEN & SAMS
Tallahassee, FL .... Administrative Law, Communications Law, Environmental Law, General Practice, Municipal and Zoning Law, Natural Resources Law

HORGER, BARNWELL & REID
Orangeburg, SC .... General Practice

HORGER, HORGER & LANIER
Orangeburg, SC .... General Practice

HORN, JEROLD I.
Peoria, IL .... Probate and Estate Planning Law

HORN, GOLDBERG, GORNY, DANIELS, PLACKTER & WEISS, A PROFESSIONAL CORPORATION
Atlantic City, NJ .... General Practice

HORNBERGER & CRISWELL
Los Angeles, CA .... Appellate Practice, Civil Trial Practice, Environmental Law, Insurance Defense Law

HORNBUCKLE & CLARK, P.C.
San Antonio, TX .... Personal Injury Law

HORNE, KAPLAN AND BISTROW, P.C.
Phoenix, AZ .... Civil Trial Practice, Commercial Law, Construction Law, Trademark, Copyright and Unfair Competition Law

HORNING JANIN & HARVEY
San Francisco, CA ....Civil Trial Practice

HORNSBY, WATSON & MEGINNISS
Huntsville, AL..........................Civil Trial Practice, Personal Injury Law, Product Liability Law

HORNTHAL, RILEY, ELLIS & MALAND, L.L.P.
Elizabeth City, NC..................Civil Trial Practice, Criminal Trial Practice, General Practice

HOROWITZ, DONALD LAW OFFICES OF
Hackensack, NJ.......................Civil Trial Practice, Criminal Trial Practice

HOROWITZ, EDWARD J., A PROFESSIONAL CORPORATION
Los Angeles, CA.....................Appellate Practice

HOROWITZ & GUDEMAN, P.C.
Farmington Hills, MI..............Probate and Estate Planning Law, Real Estate Law

HOROWITZ, ILANA
Cleveland, OH.........................Family Law

HORTON, KNOX, CARTER & FOOTE
El Centro, CA..........................General Practice

HORTY, SPRINGER & MATTERN, P.C.
Pittsburgh, PA.........................Health Care Law

HORVITZ & LEVY
Los Angeles, CA.....................Appellate Practice, Health Care Law, Insurance Defense Law

HORWATT, MICHAEL, & ASSOCIATES, P.C.
McLean, VA..............................Business Law, Commercial Law, Real Estate Law

HOSKIN, FARINA, ALDRICH & KAMPF, PROFESSIONAL CORPORATION
Grand Junction, CO.................General Practice

HOSTAK, HENZL & BICHLER, S.C.
Racine, WI...............................General Practice

HOSTETLER & KOWALIK, P.C.
Indianapolis, IN.......................Bankruptcy Law, Commercial Law

HOSTETLER & MCNEILL
Raeford, NC.............................General Practice

HOTTELL, DENNIS M. & ASSOCIATES
Fairfax, VA..............................Family Law

HOUGHTON, POTTER, SWEENEY & BRENNER, A PROFESSIONAL CORPORATION
Detroit, MI...............................Civil Trial Practice, Insurance Defense Law, Labor and Employment Law, Municipal and Zoning Law, Personal Injury Law, Probate and Estate Planning Law, Real Estate Law, Tax Law

HOURIGAN, KLUGER, SPOHRER & QUINN, A PROFESSIONAL CORPORATION
Wilkes-Barre, PA.....................General Practice, Labor and Employment Law, Medical Malpractice Law, Personal Injury Law, Probate and Estate Planning Law, Real Estate Law

HOUSE, GOLDEN, KINGSMILL & RIESS, L.L.P.
New Orleans, LA.....................Civil Trial Practice

HOUSEMAN, FEIND, GALLO & MALLOY
Grafton, WI.............................General Practice

HOUSLEY GOLDBERG KANTARIAN & BRONSTEIN, P.C.
Washington, DC.......................Banking Law

HOUSTON, HOUSTON & DONNELLY
Pittsburgh, PA.........................General Practice, Probate and Estate Planning Law

HOUSTON AND OSBORN, P.C.
Stillwater, OK..........................General Practice

HOUSTON AND THOMPSON, P.C.
Scottsburg, IN..........................General Practice

HOUTCHENS, DANIEL & GREENFIELD
Greeley, CO..............................General Practice

HOVER, JOHN C., P.C.
Phoenix, AZ.............................Bankruptcy Law, Civil Trial Practice, Commercial Law, Real Estate Law

HOVERSTEN, STROM, JOHNSON & RYSAVY
Austin, MN...............................Civil Trial Practice, Criminal Trial Practice, General Practice, Insurance Defense Law, Real Estate Law

HOVEY, KIRBY, THORNTON & HAHN, A PROFESSIONAL CORPORATION
San Diego, CA..........................Bankruptcy Law, Civil Trial Practice, Commercial Law, Construction Law, Environmental Law, Municipal and Zoning Law, Real Estate Law

HOVEY, WILLIAMS, TIMMONS & COLLINS
Kansas City, MO......................Patent, Trademark, Copyright and Unfair Competition Law

HOWARD, BRAWNER & STONE
Miami, FL..................................General Practice

HOWARD, CARSWELL & BENNETT, P.C.
Jesup, GA.................................General Practice

HOWARD, FROM, STALLINGS & HUTSON, P.A.
Raleigh, NC..............................Family Law, Personal Injury Law, Real Estate Law

HOWARD & GREEN, L.L.P.
Raleigh, NC..............................Family Law, General Practice

HOWARD & HOWARD
Mount Vernon, IL......................General Practice
Bloomfield Hills, MI.................Antitrust Law, Banking Law, Bankruptcy Law, Business Law, Civil Trial Practice, Environmental Law, General Practice, Health Care Law, Immigration and Naturalization Law, Insurance Defense Law, Labor and Employment Law, Municipal Bond/Public Authority Financing Law, Patent, Trademark, Copyright and Unfair Competition Law, Real Estate Law, Tax Law
Kalamazoo, MI.........................Banking Law, Bankruptcy Law, Business Law, Civil Trial Practice, Commercial Law, Environmental Law, General Practice, Health Care Law, Insurance Defense Law, Labor and Employment Law, Tax Law
Lansing, MI...............................Antitrust Law, Banking Law, Business Law, Civil Trial Practice, Commercial Law, Environmental Law, General Practice, Insurance Defense Law, Labor and Employment Law, Real Estate Law, Tax Law

HOWARD, LEINO & HOWARD, P.C.
Alexandria, VA.........................General Practice

HOWARD, LEWIS & PETERSEN, P.C.
Provo, UT..................................Banking Law, Civil Trial Practice, Commercial Law, Family Law, General Practice, Personal Injury Law

HOWARD, MACKIE
Calgary, AB, Canada...............General Practice

HOWARD, MOSS, LOVEDER, STRICKROTH & WALKER
Santa Ana, CA..........................Insurance Defense Law

HOWARTH, ROBERT F. JR.
Columbus, OH..........................General Practice

HOWD, LAVIERI & FINCH
Winsted, CT..............................General Practice

HOWD & LUDORF
Hartford, CT.............................Insurance Defense Law

HOWE, GEDNEY M., III, P.A.
Charleston, SC..........................Civil Trial Practice, Criminal Trial Practice

HOWE, WATERS & CARPENTER, P.A.
Hendersonville, NC..................General Practice

HOWELL, JOEL W. III
Jackson, MS.............................Civil Trial Practice

HOWELL, GATELY, WHITNEY & CARTER
Towson, MD.............................Appellate Practice, Civil Trial Practice, General Practice, Insurance Defense Law, Product Liability Law

HOWELL, LEMBHARD G., P.S., LAW OFFICES OF
Seattle, WA..............................Personal Injury Law

HOWELL O'NEAL & JOHNSON
Jacksonville, FL.......................Personal Injury Law

HOWREY & SIMON
Washington, DC.......................General Practice

HOY & HOY
Sioux Falls, SD........................Civil Trial Practice

HOYLE, WILLIAM V. JR.
Newport News, VA..................Civil Trial Practice, General Practice

HOYLE, MORRIS & KERR
Philadelphia, PA......................Civil Trial Practice, General Practice

HOYT, COLGAN & ANDREU, P.A.
Tampa, FL.................................Civil Trial Practice

HUBBARD, CATES & LONG
Roxboro, NC.............................General Practice

HUBBARD, FOX, THOMAS, WHITE & BENGTSON, P.C.
Lansing, MI..............................Business Law, Civil Trial Practice

HUBER & GOODWIN
Eureka, CA...............................General Practice

HUBER, KELLEY, BOOK, CORTESE & HAPPE
Des Moines, IA........................Insurance Defense Law

HUCKABAY, MUNSON, ROWLETT & TILLEY, P.A.
Little Rock, AR .... Civil Trial Practice, Insurance Defense Law, Medical Malpractice Law, Personal Injury Law

HUCKABY, FLEMING, FRAILEY, CHAFFIN, CORDELL, GREENWOOD & PERRYMAN
Oklahoma City, OK .... Civil Trial Practice

HUDDLE AND ROSE CO., L.P.A.
Lancaster, OH .... General Practice

HUDDLESTON, BOLEN, BEATTY, PORTER & COPEN
Charleston, WV .... General Practice
Huntington, WV .... General Practice

HUDDLESTON & HUDDLESTON
Bowling Green, KY .... Bankruptcy Law, Civil Trial Practice

HUDSON, MARTIN, FERRANTE & STREET
Monterey, CA .... General Practice

HUDSON, POTTS & BERNSTEIN
Monroe, LA .... General Practice

HUFF, GAYLE G.
Harlan, KY .... Insurance Defense Law, Labor and Employment Law

HUFF & HUFF
Marshall, NC .... General Practice

HUFFAKER & BARNES, A PROFESSIONAL CORPORATION
Santa Fe, NM .... Administrative Law, Commercial Law, Environmental Law, Health Care Law, Natural Resources Law

HUFFAKER, GREEN & HUFFAKER
Tahoka, TX .... General Practice

HUFFER AND HUFFER CO., L.P.A.
Circleville, OH .... General Practice, Probate and Estate Planning Law

HUFFMAN ARRINGTON KIHLE GABERINO & DUNN, A PROFESSIONAL CORPORATION
Tulsa, OK .... Banking Law, Bankruptcy Law, General Practice, Securities Law

HUFSTEDLER & KAUS
Los Angeles, CA .... Antitrust Law, Appellate Practice, Bankruptcy Law, Civil Trial Practice, Environmental Law, Family Law, General Practice, Tax Law

HUGHES, AMYS
Toronto, ON, Canada .... Insurance Defense Law

HUGHES HUBBARD & REED
Los Angeles, CA .... General Practice
Washington, DC .... General Practice
Miami, FL .... General Practice
New York, NY .... General Practice
Paris, France .... General Practice

HUGHES AND HUGHES
Indianapolis, IN .... Appellate Practice, Civil Trial Practice, Real Estate Law

HUGHES & LUCE, L.L.P.
Austin, TX .... Administrative Law, General Practice
Dallas, TX .... Banking Law, Bankruptcy Law, Business Law, Civil Trial Practice, Commercial Law, General Practice, Probate and Estate Planning Law, Real Estate Law, Tax Law
Houston, TX .... General Practice

HUGHES, MATHEWS & DIDIER, P.A.
St. Cloud, MN .... Civil Trial Practice, Commercial Law, General Practice

HUGHES & NUNN
San Diego, CA .... Admiralty/Maritime Law, Antitrust Law, Product Liability Law

HUGHES, PETER J., A PROFESSIONAL CORPORATION
San Diego, CA .... Criminal Trial Practice

HUGHES, THOREEN & KNAPP, P.A.
St. Cloud, MN .... Civil Trial Practice, Commercial Law, General Practice

HUGHES, WHITE, ADAMS & GRANT
Oklahoma City, OK .... Civil Trial Practice, Criminal Trial Practice, General Practice, Personal Injury Law

HUGIE, ELDON R., A PROFESSIONAL CORPORATION
Bakersfield, CA .... Business Law, General Practice, Probate and Estate Planning Law, Real Estate Law, Tax Law

HUIE, FERNAMBUCQ AND STEWART
Birmingham, AL .... Medical Malpractice Law

HULBERT, DANIEL & LAWSON
Perry, GA .... General Practice

HULL, TOWILL, NORMAN & BARRETT, A PROFESSIONAL CORPORATION
Augusta, GA .... Business Law, Civil Trial Practice, General Practice, Real Estate Law

HULLVERSON LAW FIRM, THE
St. Louis, MO .... Personal Injury Law

HULL, WEBBER & REIS
Rutland, VT .... Banking Law, Environmental Law, General Practice, Insurance Defense Law, Medical Malpractice Law, Product Liability Law

HULSEY, OLIVER & MAHAR
Gainesville, GA .... Civil Trial Practice, General Practice

HULSTRAND ANDERSON LARSON & HANSON
Willmar, MN .... General Practice

HUMMEL & COAN
Louisville, KY .... General Practice, Insurance Defense Law

HUMPHREYS DUNLAP WELLFORD ACUFF & STANTON, A PROFESSIONAL CORPORATION
Memphis, TN .... General Practice

HUNEGS, STONE, KOENIG & DOLAN, P.A.
Minneapolis, MN .... Admiralty/Maritime Law, Civil Trial Practice, Personal Injury Law

HUNT, ERNEST L. JR.
Vista, CA .... Probate and Estate Planning Law, Real Estate Law

HUNT, COLAW & ADAMS, INC.
Santa Ana, CA .... Personal Injury Law

HUNT, HERMANSEN, MCKIBBEN & ENGLISH, L.L.P.
Corpus Christi, TX .... Civil Trial Practice, Insurance Defense Law

HUNT, LEES, FARRELL & KESSLER
Charleston, WV .... Civil Trial Practice, Criminal Trial Practice, General Practice, Medical Malpractice Law, Personal Injury Law

HUNT, SUEDHOFF, BORROR & EILBACHER
Fort Wayne, IN .... Civil Trial Practice, Commercial Law

HUNTER, MACLEAN, EXLEY & DUNN, P.C.
Savannah, GA .... General Practice

HUNTER, SMITH & DAVIS
Johnson City, TN .... General Practice
Kingsport, TN .... Banking Law, Civil Trial Practice, Environmental Law, General Practice, Labor and Employment Law, Municipal Bond/Public Authority Financing Law, Natural Resources Law, Tax Law

HUNTER & SOMMERS
Waukesha, WI .... General Practice

HUNTER, WHARTON & STROUPE
Raleigh, NC .... General Practice

HUNTINGTON & HAVILAND, A PROFESSIONAL CORPORATION
San Diego, CA .... Family Law

HUPP, LANUTI, IRION & MARTIN, P.C.
Ottawa, IL .... General Practice, Insurance Defense Law

HUPPERT & SWINDLEHURST, P.C.
Livingston, MT .... General Practice

HURBIS, CMEJREK & CLINTON
Ann Arbor, MI .... Civil Trial Practice, Construction Law, Insurance Defense Law, Personal Injury Law, Product Liability Law

HURLEY, BRYANT, LOVLIEN, LYNCH, JARVIS AND RE
Bend, OR .... General Practice

HURLEY, FOX, SELIG & KELLEHER
New City, NY .... General Practice
Stony Point, NY .... Civil Trial Practice, General Practice

HURLEY, JOSEPH A., P.A.
Wilmington, DE .... Criminal Trial Practice

HURTH, YEAGER & SISK
Boulder, CO .... General Practice

HURWITZ & FINE, P.C.
Buffalo, NY .... Bankruptcy Law, General Practice, Health Care Law, Insurance Defense Law, Probate and Estate Planning Law, Tax Law

HURWITZ & SAGARIN, P.C.
Milford, CT .... General Practice, Personal Injury Law

HUSBAND, B. PAUL
Valencia, CA .... Tax Law

HUTCHESON & GRUNDY, L.L.P.
Houston, TX .... General Practice

HUTCHINS, TYNDALL, DOUGHTON & MOORE
Winston-Salem, NC .... Civil Trial Practice, General Practice

HUTCHINS, WHEELER & DITTMAR, A PROFESSIONAL CORPORATION
Boston, MA .... General Practice

HUTCHISON BOYLE BROOKS & FISHER, A PROFESSIONAL CORPORATION
Dallas, TX .... Municipal Bond/Public Authority Financing Law

HUTSON, SAWYER, CHAPMAN & REILLY
Troy, MI .... Civil Trial Practice, Family Law, Personal Injury Law, Real Estate Law

HUTTON INGRAM YUZEK GAINEN CARROLL & BERTOLOTTI
New York, NY .... Appellate Practice, Banking Law, Business Law, Civil Trial Practice, Commercial Law, Construction Law, General Practice, Insurance Defense Law, International Business Law, Real Estate Law, Securities Law, Tax Law

HUTTON, LAURY, HESSER, LIETZ & WILCOX
Danville, IL .... Civil Trial Practice, General Practice, Insurance Defense Law

HVASS, WEISMAN & KING, CHARTERED
Minneapolis, MN .... Civil Trial Practice, General Practice, Labor and Employment Law, Medical Malpractice Law, Personal Injury Law, Product Liability Law

HYATT & HYATT, P.C.
Decatur, GA .... General Practice, Personal Injury Law

HYDE AND CANOFF
San Diego, CA .... Business Law, Civil Trial Practice, Real Estate Law

HYDE & HOLCOMB
Walnut Creek, CA .... Civil Trial Practice

HYLTON & GONZALES
Baltimore, MD .... Civil Trial Practice, General Practice, Probate and Estate Planning Law

HYMAN AND LIPPITT, P.C.
Birmingham, MI .... Business Law, Civil Trial Practice, Family Law

HYMES AND COONTS
Buckhannon, WV .... Civil Trial Practice, General Practice

HYNES JOHNSON & HEALY
Chicago, IL .... General Practice

ICE MILLER DONADIO & RYAN
Indianapolis, IN .... Antitrust Law, Banking Law, Bankruptcy Law, Civil Trial Practice, Commercial Law, Communications Law, Construction Law, Employment Benefits Law, Environmental Law, General Practice, Health Care Law, Immigration and Naturalization Law, Insurance Defense Law, International Business Law, Labor and Employment Law, Medical Malpractice Law, Municipal Bond/Public Authority Financing Law, Natural Resources Law, Personal Injury Law, Probate and Estate Planning Law, Real Estate Law, Securities Law, Tax Law, Trademark, Copyright and Unfair Competition Law

IFSHIN & FRIEDMAN
Washington, DC .... Civil Trial Practice

IKARD & GOLDEN, P.C.
Austin, TX .... Probate and Estate Planning Law

IMHOFF & LYNCH
Boise, ID .... General Practice, Insurance Defense Law, Labor and Employment Law

INDIANO, WILLIAMS & WEINSTEIN-BACAL
San Juan, PR .... Bankruptcy Law, Civil Trial Practice, Commercial Law, Construction Law, Personal Injury Law

INGERSOLL AND BLOCH, CHARTERED
Washington, DC .... Real Estate Law

INGE, TWITTY & DUFFY
Mobile, AL .... Civil Trial Practice, General Practice

INGHAM, SAMUEL D. III
Beverly Hills, CA .... Probate and Estate Planning Law, Tax Law

INGLESBY, FALLIGANT, HORNE, COURINGTON & NASH, A PROFESSIONAL CORPORATION
Savannah, GA .... Bankruptcy Law, General Practice, Real Estate Law

INGLISH & MONACO, P.C.
Jefferson City, MO .... Insurance Defense Law

INGRAM AND INGRAM
Potsdam, NY .... General Practice

INSLEE, BEST, DOEZIE & RYDER, P.S.
Bellevue, WA .... General Practice

INZER, STIVENDER, HANEY & JOHNSON, P.A.
Gadsden, AL .... Civil Trial Practice, General Practice

IRELAND, CARROLL & KELLEY, P.C.
Tyler, TX .... Civil Trial Practice, Criminal Trial Practice

IRELAND, STAPLETON, PRYOR & PASCOE, P.C.
Denver, CO .... Antitrust Law, Civil Trial Practice, General Practice

IRSFELD, IRSFELD & YOUNGER
Glendale, CA .... Civil Trial Practice, General Practice

ISAACS, ALLEY & HARVEY, L.L.P.
Columbia, SC .... Business Law, Commercial Law, Family Law, Real Estate Law

ISAACSON ISAACSON & GRIMES
Greensboro, NC .... Business Law, Commercial Law, General Practice, Municipal and Zoning Law, Real Estate Law

ISEMAN, CUNNINGHAM, RIESTER & HYDE
Albany, NY .... Civil Trial Practice, Construction Law, Health Care Law, Personal Injury Law, Real Estate Law, Tax Law

ISRAELSON, SALSBURY, CLEMENTS & BEKMAN
Baltimore, MD .... Admiralty/Maritime Law, Civil Trial Practice, Medical Malpractice Law, Personal Injury Law, Product Liability Law

ISRAEL AND WOOD, P.C.
Pittsburgh, PA .... Insurance Defense Law

IVENER, MARK A., A LAW CORPORATION
Los Angeles, CA .... Immigration and Naturalization Law

IVERSEN, JUDD C., A PROFESSIONAL CORPORATION
San Francisco, CA .... Civil Trial Practice, Criminal Trial Practice

IVERSON, YOAKUM, PAPIANO & HATCH
Los Angeles, CA .... Commercial Law

IVES, EMERSON & MANAHAN
Delphi, IN .... General Practice

IVESTER, SKINNER & CAMP, P.A.
Little Rock, AR .... Banking Law, Commercial Law, Communications Law, General Practice, Patent, Trademark, Copyright and Unfair Competition Law, Securities Law, Tax Law

IVEY, BARNUM & O'MARA
Greenwich, CT .... Civil Trial Practice, Commercial Law, General Practice, Probate and Estate Planning Law, Real Estate Law, Tax Law

IVEY, IVEY, MCCLELLAN & GATTON, L.L.P.
Greensboro, NC .... General Practice

IVINS, PHILLIPS & BARKER, CHARTERED
Washington, DC .... Probate and Estate Planning Law, Tax Law

IVONE, DEVINE & JENSEN
Lake Success, NY .... Civil Trial Practice, Construction Law, Insurance Defense Law, Medical Malpractice Law

JACKL & KATZEN
Walnut Creek, CA .... Business Law, Civil Trial Practice, Construction Law, Real Estate Law

JACKS, ADAMS & WESTERFIELD, P.A.
Cleveland, MS .... General Practice, Insurance Defense Law

JACKSON, BROWN & EFTING
Sunnyvale, CA .... Family Law

JACKSON & CAMPBELL, P.C.
Washington, DC .... General Practice

JACKSON EMERICH PEDREIRA & NAHIGIAN, A PROFESSIONAL CORPORATION
Fresno, CA .... Business Law, Civil Trial Practice, Health Care Law, Municipal Bond/Public Authority Financing Law, Tax Law

JACKSON, HARRIS, BURLINGAME & HUBERT
Danielson, CT .... General Practice

JACKSON, HICKS & FITZGERALD
Roxboro, NC .... General Practice

JACKSON & JESSUP, P.C.
Arlington, VA .... Transportation Law

JACKSON & KELLY
Washington, DC — General Practice
Lexington, KY — General Practice
Charleston, WV — Administrative Law, Admiralty/Maritime Law, Antitrust Law, Banking Law, Bankruptcy Law, Civil Trial Practice, Commercial Law, Construction Law, Criminal Trial Practice, Employment Benefits Law, Environmental Law, General Practice, Health Care Law, Insurance Defense Law, Labor and Employment Law, Municipal Bond/Public Authority Financing Law, Natural Resources Law, Probate and Estate Planning Law, Public Utilities Law, Real Estate Law, Securities Law, Tax Law, Transportation Law
Charles Town, WV — General Practice
Clarksburg, WV — General Practice
Martinsburg, WV — General Practice
Morgantown, WV — General Practice
New Martinsville, WV — General Practice

JACKSON, LILLA & MCFERRIN, P.C.
Kansas City, MO — Civil Trial Practice, General Practice

JACKSON, O'KEEFE AND PHELAN
Hartford, CT — Civil Trial Practice, Family Law, General Practice, Insurance Defense Law, Medical Malpractice Law, Personal Injury Law

JACKSON, TUFTS, COLE & BLACK
San Francisco, CA — General Practice
San Jose, CA — General Practice

JACKSON & WALKER, L.L.P.
Dallas, TX — Antitrust Law, Civil Trial Practice, Communications Law, General Practice, Tax Law
Fort Worth, TX — General Practice
Houston, TX — General Practice

JACOB & WEINGARTEN, PROFESSIONAL CORPORATION
Troy, MI — Bankruptcy Law, Real Estate Law

JACOBS, DARLEEN M., A PROFESSIONAL LAW CORPORATION
New Orleans, LA — Admiralty/Maritime Law, Personal Injury Law

JACOBS & JACOBS
New Haven, CT — Medical Malpractice Law, Personal Injury Law

JACOBSON, MIRIAM N.
Philadelphia, PA — Real Estate Law

JACOBSON, BRISTOL, GARRETT & SWARTZ
Waukon, IA — General Practice

JACOBSON, PRICE, HOLMAN & STERN
Washington, DC — Patent, Trademark, Copyright and Unfair Competition Law

JACOBSON & SCHWARTZ
Rockville Centre, NY — Insurance Defense Law

JACOBSON & TRIGGS
New York, NY — Civil Trial Practice

JACOBUS, BOLTZ & MELAMED
Houston, TX — Real Estate Law

JAFFE & CLEMENS
Beverly Hills, CA — Family Law

JAFFE, RAITT, HEUER & WEISS, PROFESSIONAL CORPORATION
Detroit, MI — Bankruptcy Law, Business Law, Civil Trial Practice, Employment Benefits Law, Environmental Law, Family Law, General Practice, Health Care Law, Municipal Bond/Public Authority Financing Law, Municipal and Zoning Law, Probate and Estate Planning Law, Real Estate Law, Securities Law, Tax Law
Monroe, MI — General Practice, Municipal and Zoning Law
Southfield, MI — General Practice

JAFFE, RICHARD S., P.C.
Birmingham, AL — Criminal Trial Practice, Personal Injury Law

JAKEWAY, EDWIN W.
Grand Blanc, MI — Personal Injury Law

JAKLE AND HROMADKA
Santa Monica, CA — Probate and Estate Planning Law

JAMES, DANIEL H.
West Palm Beach, FL — Civil Trial Practice

JAMES, BERNHEIM & HICKS
Santa Rosa, CA — General Practice

JAMES & BIAGIOLI, P.C.
Independence, MO — Family Law, Personal Injury Law

JAMES, GRAY & MCCAFFERTY, P.C.
Great Falls, MT — Civil Trial Practice

JAMES LAW FIRM, THE, P.C.
Des Moines, IA — Medical Malpractice Law, Personal Injury Law

JAMES, LOWE & MOBLEY
Haleyville, AL — Civil Trial Practice, General Practice, Insurance Defense Law

JAMES, POTTS AND WULFERS
Tulsa, OK — Banking Law, Business Law, Commercial Law, Probate and Estate Planning Law, Real Estate Law, Tax Law

JAMIESON, MOORE, PESKIN & SPICER, A PROFESSIONAL CORPORATION
Princeton, NJ — General Practice
Trenton, NJ — General Practice

JAMIN, EBELL, BOLGER & GENTRY, A PROFESSIONAL CORPORATION
Kodiak, AK — General Practice

JANECKY, NEWELL, POTTS, HARE & WELLS, P.C.
Mobile, AL — Insurance Defense Law
Pensacola, FL — Insurance Defense Law

JANET & STRAUSBERG
Baltimore, MD — Medical Malpractice Law, Personal Injury Law, Product Liability Law

JANIK & DUNN
Cleveland, OH — Appellate Practice, Civil Trial Practice, Construction Law, Environmental Law, General Practice, Insurance Defense Law, Labor and Employment Law, Personal Injury Law, Product Liability Law, Securities Law, Trademark, Copyright and Unfair Competition Law

JANSSEN, MALLOY, MARCHI, NEEDHAM & MORRISON
Eureka, CA — General Practice

JANUSZEWSKI, MCQUILLAN AND DENIGRIS
New Britain, CT — General Practice

JAQUA & WHEATLEY, P.C.
Eugene, OR — Civil Trial Practice

JARDINE, LOGAN & O'BRIEN
St. Paul, MN — Civil Trial Practice, General Practice, Insurance Defense Law, Personal Injury Law

JARDINE & PAGANO, A PROFESSIONAL CORPORATION
Springfield, NJ — Labor and Employment Law, Probate and Estate Planning Law

JARDINE, STEPHENSON, BLEWETT AND WEAVER, P.C.
Great Falls, MT — General Practice

JARRELL, HICKS & SASSER
Spotsylvania, VA — General Practice

JASINSKI AND PARANAC, A PROFESSIONAL CORPORATION
Newark, NJ — Labor and Employment Law

JASPAN, GINSBERG, SCHLESINGER, SILVERMAN & HOFFMAN
Garden City, NY — Bankruptcy Law, Commercial Law, Environmental Law, General Practice, Labor and Employment Law, Real Estate Law

JAVERBAUM WURGAFT & HICKS
Springfield, NJ — Civil Trial Practice, Personal Injury Law, Product Liability Law

JAYCOX, JACK S., LAW OFFICES, LTD.
Bloomington, MN — Family Law

JEANES, LYLE H., II, P.C.
Paris, TX — Civil Trial Practice, General Practice, Insurance Defense Law

JEFFER, HOPKINSON, VOGEL, COOMBER & PEIFFER
Hawthorne, NJ — Civil Trial Practice, General Practice, Municipal Bond/Public Authority Financing Law, Real Estate Law

JEFFERS, DANIELSON, SONN & AYLWARD, P.S.
Wenatchee, WA — General Practice

JEFFRIES, OLSON, FLOM, OPPEGARD & HOGAN, P.A.
Moorhead, MN — General Practice
Fargo, ND — Civil Trial Practice, General Practice

JEFFS AND JEFFS, P.C.
Provo, UT — Civil Trial Practice, General Practice, Insurance Defense Law

JELLIFFE, FERRELL & MORRIS
Harrisburg, IL — Civil Trial Practice, Criminal Trial Practice, General Practice, Insurance Defense Law

JENKINS, JOHN R. JR.
Aulander, NC..........General Practice

JENKINS, RICHARD E.
Durham, NC..........Patent, Trademark, Copyright and Unfair Competition Law

JENKINS & EELLS
Atlanta, GA..........General Practice

JENKINS, FENSTERMAKER, KRIEGER, KAYES, FARRELL & AGEE
Huntington, WV..........Civil Trial Practice, General Practice, Insurance Defense Law, Medical Malpractice Law, Real Estate Law

JENKINS & JENKINS, P.C.
Waxahachie, TX..........General Practice

JENKS, SURDYK & COWDREY CO., L.P.A.
Dayton, OH..........Civil Trial Practice, Insurance Defense Law

JENNE, SCOTT & BRYANT
Cleveland, TN..........Civil Trial Practice, Criminal Trial Practice, General Practice, Insurance Defense Law

JENNER & AUXIER
Madison, IN..........General Practice

JENNINGS & HAUG
Phoenix, AZ..........Civil Trial Practice, Construction Law

JENNINGS, STROUSS AND SALMON, P.L.C.
Phoenix, AZ..........Antitrust Law, Banking Law, Bankruptcy Law, Civil Trial Practice, Environmental Law, General Practice, Health Care Law, Insurance Defense Law, Labor and Employment Law, Medical Malpractice Law, Municipal Bond/Public Authority Financing Law, Natural Resources Law, Personal Injury Law, Probate and Estate Planning Law, Real Estate Law, Securities Law, Tax Law, Trademark, Copyright and Unfair Competition Law

JENSEN BAIRD GARDNER & HENRY
Biddeford, ME..........General Practice
Portland, ME..........Banking Law, Civil Trial Practice, General Practice, Real Estate Law

JENSEN & KELLEY, P.A.
Phoenix, AZ..........Family Law

JEPPSON & LEE, A PROFESSIONAL CORPORATION
Reno, NV..........General Practice

JEWELL, GATZ, COLLINS, FITZGERALD & DELAY
Norfolk, NE..........General Practice

JIMENEZ, JORGE R.
San Juan, PR..........Antitrust Law, Banking Law, Civil Trial Practice, Commercial Law, Real Estate Law

JIMÉNEZ, GRAFFAM & LAUSELL
San Juan, PR..........Admiralty/Maritime Law, Civil Trial Practice, Environmental Law, General Practice, Insurance Defense Law, Labor and Employment Law, Personal Injury Law, Transportation Law

JINKERSON, GUYTON N.
San Jose, CA..........Criminal Trial Practice

JOHN, HENGERER & ESPOSITO
Washington, DC..........Natural Resources Law

JOHNS & FLAHERTY, S.C.
La Crosse, WI..........General Practice

JOHNSEN, ROGER A.
Philadelphia, PA..........General Practice, International Business Law

JOHNSON, JOSEPH R. JR. & ASSOCIATES
Lynchburg, VA..........Civil Trial Practice, Criminal Trial Practice, Family Law, Personal Injury Law

JOHNSON, PHILLIP E. LAW OFFICES OF
Augusta, ME..........Civil Trial Practice, Insurance Defense Law, Labor and Employment Law

JOHNSON, R. TENNEY
Washington, DC..........Administrative Law

JOHNSON, RONALD W.
La Jolla, CA..........Family Law

JOHNSON, WILLIAM M.
Frankfort, KY..........Real Estate Law

JOHNSON, ALLEN, JONES & DORNBLASER
Tulsa, OK..........Business Law, Commercial Law, Health Care Law, Probate and Estate Planning Law, Securities Law, Tax Law

JOHNSON, ANDERSON & ZELLMER
Mankato, MN..........Family Law, General Practice, Probate and Estate Planning Law

JOHNSON, AYERS & MATTHEWS
Roanoke, VA..........Civil Trial Practice, General Practice, Insurance Defense Law

JOHNSON & BELL, LTD.
Chicago, IL..........Civil Trial Practice, Environmental Law, Insurance Defense Law, Medical Malpractice Law

JOHNSON, BLAKELY, POPE, BOKOR, RUPPEL & BURNS, P.A.
Clearwater, FL..........General Practice
Tampa, FL..........General Practice

JOHNSON, BOOZE & BURGESS
Johnson City, TN..........General Practice

JOHNSON & BOWEN
El Paso, TX..........General Practice

JOHNSON, C. CLAYTON, CO., A LEGAL PROFESSIONAL ASSOCIATION
Portsmouth, OH..........General Practice, Probate and Estate Planning Law

JOHNSON & DAVIS
Harlingen, TX..........General Practice

JOHNSON, DON, P.S.C.
Fort Thomas, KY..........Civil Trial Practice, General Practice

JOHNSON, ERB, GIBB, BICE & CARLSON, P.C.
Fort Dodge, IA..........General Practice

JOHNSON, GALLAGHER, BURGIO & MARTIN
Caldwell, NJ..........Personal Injury Law, Product Liability Law

JOHNSON, GREEN & LOCKLIN, P.A.
Milton, FL..........General Practice

JOHNSON, GRUSIN, KEE & SURPRISE, P.C.
Memphis, TN..........General Practice, Real Estate Law

JOHNSON, HALL AND LAWHEAD, PROFESSIONAL CORPORATION
Indianapolis, IN..........Business Law, Probate and Estate Planning Law

JOHNSON, HANSEN, SHAMBEAU, MARONEY & ANDERSON, S.C.
Waupaca, WI..........General Practice

JOHNSON, HEIDEPRIEM, MINER & MARLOW
Yankton, SD..........General Practice

JOHNSON, HESTER & WALTER
Ottumwa, IA..........General Practice

JOHNSON, HOULIHAN, PAULSON & PRIEBE, S.C.
Rhinelander, WI..........General Practice

JOHNSON HUFFMAN, A PROF. CORP. OF LAWYERS
Rapid City, SD..........Environmental Law, General Practice, Medical Malpractice Law, Natural Resources Law

JOHNSON AND JOHNSON, P.A.
Lillington, NC..........General Practice

JOHNSON, JOHNSON, WHITTLE, SNELGROVE & WEEKS, P.A.
Aiken, SC..........Civil Trial Practice, Criminal Trial Practice, Family Law, General Practice, Personal Injury Law, Real Estate Law

JOHNSON & LAMBETH
Wilmington, NC..........Criminal Trial Practice, Insurance Defense Law

JOHNSON, MARTIN, RUSSELL, ENGLISH, SCOMA & BENEKE, P.C.
Princeton, IL..........General Practice, Insurance Defense Law

JOHNSON AND MONTGOMERY
Atlanta, GA..........Business Law

JOHNSON & ROCHE
McLean, VA..........Personal Injury Law

JOHNSON, ROSATI, GALICA, SHIFMAN, LABARGE, ASELTYNE, SUGAMELI & FIELD, P.C.
Farmington Hills, MI..........Labor and Employment Law, Municipal and Zoning Law

JOHNSON, RUDDY, NORMAN & MCCONATY, A PROFESSIONAL CORPORATION
Denver, CO..........Civil Trial Practice, Medical Malpractice Law

JOHNSON, SCHACHTER, LEWIS & COLLINS, A PROFESSIONAL CORPORATION
Sacramento, CA..........Civil Trial Practice, Insurance Defense Law, Product Liability Law

JOHNSON, SIMMERMAN & BROUGHTON, L.C.
Clarksburg, WV..........Civil Trial Practice, Construction Law, Environmental Law, General Practice, Medical Malpractice Law, Personal Injury Law, Probate and Estate Planning Law, Tax Law

JOHNSON, SMITH, DENSBORN, WRIGHT & HEATH
Indianapolis, IN .... Administrative Law, Banking Law, Bankruptcy Law, Civil Trial Practice, Commercial Law, Environmental Law, General Practice, Health Care Law, Insurance Defense Law, Real Estate Law, Securities Law

JOHNSON, SUDENGA, LATHAM & PEGLOW
Marshalltown, IA .... General Practice

JOHNSON & TAYLOR
Pontiac, IL .... Probate and Estate Planning Law

JOHNSON & TOWER
Corpus Christi, TX .... Personal Injury Law

JOHNSON & VALENTINE
Detroit, MI .... Business Law, Civil Trial Practice

JOHNSON & WARD
Atlanta, GA .... Business Law, Personal Injury Law, Product Liability Law

JOHNSTON, BARTON, PROCTOR, SWEDLAW & NAFF
Birmingham, AL .... Antitrust Law, Communications Law, General Practice, Labor and Employment Law, Securities Law, Tax Law

JOHNSTON & BUDNER, A PROFESSIONAL CORPORATION
Dallas, TX .... Civil Trial Practice, Commercial Law

JOHNSTON, HINESLEY, FLOWERS & CLENNEY, P.C., A PROFESSIONAL CORPORATION
Dothan, AL .... Tax Law

JOHNSTON, HOLROYD & ASSOCIATES
Princeton, WV .... General Practice

JOHNSTON & MCSHANE, P.C.
New York, NY .... Civil Trial Practice, Environmental Law, Insurance Defense Law, Product Liability Law

JOHNSTONE, ADAMS, BAILEY, GORDON AND HARRIS
Mobile, AL .... Admiralty/Maritime Law, Antitrust Law, Banking Law, Bankruptcy Law, Business Law, Civil Trial Practice, Construction Law, Employment Benefits Law, Environmental Law, General Practice, Health Care Law, Insurance Defense Law, Labor and Employment Law, Natural Resources Law, Probate and Estate Planning Law, Real Estate Law, Tax Law

JOLLEY, URGA, WIRTH & WOODBURY
Las Vegas, NV .... Banking Law, Bankruptcy Law, Civil Trial Practice, Commercial Law, Construction Law, Environmental Law, Family Law, General Practice, Labor and Employment Law, Natural Resources Law, Personal Injury Law, Probate and Estate Planning Law, Real Estate Law

JOLLY & BLAU
Newport, KY .... General Practice, Insurance Defense Law

JONES, O. F. III, LAW OFFICE OF
Victoria, TX .... Civil Trial Practice

JONES, RANDOLPH B.
Nashville, TN .... Business Law

JONES & BAHRET CO., L.P.A.
Toledo, OH .... Civil Trial Practice, Insurance Defense Law

JONES, BLECHMAN, WOLTZ & KELLY, P.C.
Newport News, VA .... General Practice

JONES, BOYKIN & ASSOCIATES, PROFESSIONAL CORPORATION
Savannah, GA .... Personal Injury Law

JONES, CHARTERED
Pocatello, ID .... General Practice

JONES, CORK & MILLER
Macon, GA .... Civil Trial Practice, General Practice

JONES, DAY, REAVIS & POGUE
Irvine, CA .... General Practice, Municipal Bond/Public Authority Financing Law
Los Angeles, CA .... Antitrust Law, Bankruptcy Law, General Practice, Immigration and Naturalization Law, Municipal Bond/Public Authority Financing Law, Patent, Trademark, Copyright and Unfair Competition Law, Tax Law
Washington, DC .... Antitrust Law, General Practice, Immigration and Naturalization Law, Municipal Bond/Public Authority Financing Law, Tax Law
Atlanta, GA .... Antitrust Law, Civil Trial Practice, General Practice, Labor and Employment Law, Municipal Bond/Public Authority Financing Law, Tax Law
Chicago, IL .... Antitrust Law, General Practice, Municipal Bond/Public Authority Financing Law, Tax Law
New York, NY .... General Practice, Municipal Bond/Public Authority Financing Law
Cleveland, OH .... Antitrust Law, Civil Trial Practice, General Practice, Labor and Employment Law, Municipal Bond/Public Authority Financing Law, Patent, Trademark, Copyright and Unfair Competition Law, Real Estate Law, Tax Law, Trademark, Copyright and Unfair Competition Law
Columbus, OH .... General Practice, Municipal Bond/Public Authority Financing Law
Pittsburgh, PA .... General Practice, Municipal Bond/Public Authority Financing Law
Dallas, TX .... Antitrust Law, General Practice, Municipal Bond/Public Authority Financing Law
Brussels, Belgium .... General Practice
London, England .... General Practice
Paris, France .... General Practice
Frankfurt/Main, Germany .... General Practice
Hong Kong, Hong Kong (British Crown Colony) .... General Practice
Tokyo, Japan .... General Practice
Geneva, Switzerland .... General Practice
Taipei, Taiwan .... General Practice

JONES, E. STEWART
Troy, NY .... Civil Trial Practice, Criminal Trial Practice, General Practice

JONES, FLYGARE, GALEY, BROWN & WHARTON
Lubbock, TX .... General Practice, Health Care Law, Insurance Defense Law

JONES, FOSTER, JOHNSTON & STUBBS, P.A.
West Palm Beach, FL .... Civil Trial Practice, General Practice, Natural Resources Law, Tax Law

JONES, GALLIGAN & KEY, L.L.P.
Weslaco, TX .... General Practice

JONES, GARY L., CO., L.P.A.
Columbus, OH .... Administrative Law

JONES, GILBREATH, JACKSON & MOLL
Fort Smith, AR .... Civil Trial Practice, General Practice, Insurance Defense Law

JONES, GIVENS, GOTCHER & BOGAN, A PROFESSIONAL CORPORATION
Tulsa, OK .... Business Law, General Practice

JONES HALL HILL & WHITE,, A PROFESSIONAL LAW CORPORATION
San Francisco, CA .... Municipal Bond/Public Authority Financing Law

JONES, HEWSON & WOOLARD
Charlotte, NC .... General Practice

JONES & JONES
Fayetteville, AR .... Insurance Defense Law
Mineola, NY .... Civil Trial Practice

JONES, JONES, CLOSE & BROWN, CHARTERED
Las Vegas, NV .... Bankruptcy Law, Civil Trial Practice, General Practice, Real Estate Law
Reno, NV .... Bankruptcy Law

JONES, JONES & CURRY, INC., A PROFESSIONAL CORPORATION
Marshall, TX .... General Practice

JONES, JONES, VINES & HUNKINS
Wheatland, WY .... General Practice

JONES, KEY, MELVIN & PATTON, P.A.
Franklin, NC .... General Practice

JONES KURTH & TREAT, P.C.
San Antonio, TX .... Civil Trial Practice, Insurance Defense Law

JONES, NORPELL, LIST, MILLER & HOWARTH
Newark, OH .... General Practice

JONES, OBENCHAIN, FORD, PANKOW, LEWIS & WOODS
South Bend, IN .... Bankruptcy Law, Civil Trial Practice, Health Care Law, Insurance Defense Law, Labor and Employment Law, Real Estate Law

JONES, OSTEEN, JONES & ARNOLD
Hinesville, GA .... General Practice

JONES PATTERSON BOLL & TUCKER, PROFESSIONAL CORPORATION
Columbus, IN .... Civil Trial Practice, General Practice, Health Care Law

JONES, SKELTON & HOCHULI
Phoenix, AZ .... Civil Trial Practice, Commercial Law, Insurance Defense Law, Medical Malpractice Law

JONES, SNEAD, WERTHEIM, RODRIGUEZ & WENTWORTH, P.A.
Santa Fe, NM .... Civil Trial Practice, General Practice, Patent, Trademark, Copyright and Unfair Competition Law, Transportation Law

JONES, TÊTE, NOLEN, HANCHEY, SWIFT & SPEARS, L.L.P.
Lake Charles, LA....................Admiralty/Maritime Law, Bankruptcy Law, Civil Trial Practice, General Practice, Insurance Defense Law, Labor and Employment Law, Probate and Estate Planning Law

JONES, TROUSDALE & THOMPSON
Florence, AL..........................Insurance Defense Law, Product Liability Law

JONES, WALDO, HOLBROOK & MCDONOUGH, A PROFESSIONAL CORPORATION
Washington, DC......................General Practice
St. George, UT.......................General Practice
Salt Lake City, UT..................Antitrust Law, Civil Trial Practice, General Practice, Labor and Employment Law, Natural Resources Law, Real Estate Law

JONES, WALKER, WAECHTER, POITEVENT, CARRÈRE & DENÈGRE
New Orleans, LA.....................General Practice

JONES & WYATT
Enid, OK.................................Civil Trial Practice, Criminal Trial Practice

JORDAN COYNE & SAVITS
Washington, DC......................Insurance Defense Law
Baltimore, MD........................Insurance Defense Law
Rockville, MD.........................Insurance Defense Law
Fairfax, VA.............................Insurance Defense Law
Leesburg, VA..........................Insurance Defense Law

JORDAN AND HAMBURG
New York, NY.........................Patent, Trademark, Copyright and Unfair Competition Law

JORDAN & O'DONNELL
Brunswick, GA........................Civil Trial Practice

JORDAN, OLIVER & WALTERS
Winterset, IA...........................General Practice

JORDON, WAYNE A.
Alamogordo, NM......................General Practice

JORGENSON, SIEGEL, MCCLURE & FLEGEL
Menlo Park, CA.......................General Practice

JORY, PETERSON, WATKINS & SMITH
Fresno, CA..............................Business Law, Civil Trial Practice, Commercial Law, Labor and Employment Law

JOSEPH, RAYMOND
Lansing, MI.............................Civil Trial Practice, Insurance Defense Law, Product Liability Law

JOSEPH, GREENWALD AND LAAKE, P.A.
Greenbelt, MD.........................General Practice

JOSEPHS, BONNIE P.
New York, NY.........................Civil Trial Practice

JOSLYN KEYDEL & WALLACE
Detroit, MI..............................Probate and Estate Planning Law

JOSSELSON, POTTER & ROBERTS
Portland, OR...........................Environmental Law, Municipal and Zoning Law, Real Estate Law

JOYCE, MEREDITH, FLITCROFT & NORMAND
Oak Ridge, TN.........................General Practice

JOYCE AND POLLARD
Tulsa, OK................................Banking Law, Business Law, Civil Trial Practice, General Practice, Probate and Estate Planning Law

JUBANYIK, VARBALOW, TEDESCO, SHAW & SHAFFER
Cherry Hill, NJ........................Banking Law, General Practice

JUERGENSMEYER, STRAIN, AND ASSOCIATES
Elgin, IL..................................Personal Injury Law

JUGE, NAPOLITANO, LEYVA & GUILBEAU
Metairie, LA............................Insurance Defense Law, Labor and Employment Law

JULIAN & PERTZ, P.C.
Utica, NY.................................Personal Injury Law

JULIEN & SCHLESINGER, P.C.
New York, NY.........................Civil Trial Practice, Medical Malpractice Law, Personal Injury Law, Product Liability Law

JUNKER & THOMPSON, A PROFESSIONAL CORPORATION
Seattle, WA.............................International Business Law

KABALA & GEESEMAN, A PROFESSIONAL CORPORATION
Pittsburgh, PA.........................General Practice

KADISH & BENDER, A LEGAL PROFESSIONAL ASSOCIATION
Cleveland, OH.........................Business Law, Employment Benefits Law, General Practice, Probate and Estate Planning Law, Real Estate Law, Tax Law

KAHN, DEES, DONOVAN & KAHN
Evansville, IN..........................Admiralty/Maritime Law, Banking Law, Civil Trial Practice, Environmental Law, General Practice, Health Care Law, Insurance Defense Law, Labor and Employment Law, Real Estate Law, Tax Law

KAHN, KLEINMAN, YANOWITZ & ARNSON CO., L.P.A.
Cleveland, OH.........................General Practice

KAHN, SMITH & COLLINS, P.A.
Baltimore, MD.........................Administrative Law, Labor and Employment Law, Medical Malpractice Law

KAHRS, NELSON, FANNING, HITE & KELLOGG
Wichita, KS.............................Civil Trial Practice, General Practice, Insurance Defense Law

KAISER, JACK I. LAW OFFICES
San Francisco, CA...................Immigration and Naturalization Law

KAJAN AND MATHER, A PROFESSIONAL CORPORATION
Beverly Hills, CA.....................Tax Law

KALAMAROS, EDWARD N., & ASSOCIATES, PROFESSIONAL CORPORATION
South Bend, IN.........................Civil Trial Practice, General Practice, Insurance Defense Law, Personal Injury Law, Product Liability Law

KALCHEIM, SCHATZ & BERGER
Chicago, IL..............................Family Law

KALEEL & KALEEL, P.A.
St. Petersburg, FL....................Civil Trial Practice

KALISH & WARD, PROFESSIONAL ASSOCIATION
Tampa, FL................................Business Law, Employment Benefits Law, Probate and Estate Planning Law, Real Estate Law, Securities Law, Tax Law

KAMBERG, BERMAN, P.C.
Springfield, MA........................Bankruptcy Law, Commercial Law, Environmental Law

KAMER & RICCIARDI
Las Vegas, NV.........................Labor and Employment Law

KANAGA, LAWRENCE W.
Westport, CT............................Civil Trial Practice, Medical Malpractice Law, Personal Injury Law

KANANACK, MURGATROYD, BAUM & HEDLUND, A PROFESSIONAL CORPORATION
Los Angeles, CA......................Civil Trial Practice, Personal Injury Law
Washington, DC........................Civil Trial Practice, Personal Injury Law

KANE, DALSIMER, SULLIVAN, KURUCZ, LEVY, EISELE AND RICHARD
New York, NY...........................Patent, Trademark, Copyright and Unfair Competition Law

KANE, DONLEY & SHAFFER
Colorado Springs, CO...............Civil Trial Practice, General Practice, Insurance Defense Law

KANE, KANE & KANE
Pawhuska, OK..........................General Practice

KANE, SICURO & SIMON
Ravenna, OH............................General Practice

KANE & WHELAN
Glendale, CA............................Insurance Defense Law

KANIA, LINDNER, LASAK AND FEENEY
Bala Cynwyd, PA......................Business Law, Civil Trial Practice, Commercial Law, Real Estate Law

KANTROW, SPAHT, WEAVER & BLITZER, A PROFESSIONAL LAW CORPORATION
Baton Rouge, LA.......................Civil Trial Practice, Commercial Law, General Practice, Probate and Estate Planning Law, Real Estate Law

KAPLAN, HOWARD GORDON, LTD.
Chicago, IL................................Business Law

KAPLAN, STRANGIS AND KAPLAN, P.A.
Minneapolis, MN.......................General Practice

KAPLOWITZ AND WISE, A PROFESSIONAL CORPORATION
Linden, NJ.................................Civil Trial Practice

KAPNER, LEWIS, P.A.
West Palm Beach, FL...............Civil Trial Practice, Family Law

KAPS & BARTO
Hackensack, NJ........................Business Law, Civil Trial Practice, Commercial Law, Environmental Law

KARASZKIEWICZ, KIRK T., & ASSOCIATES, P.C.
Philadelphia, PA.......................Criminal Trial Practice

KAROWSKY, WITWER, MILLER & OLDENBURG
Greeley, CO....................General Practice

KARP & WEISS, P.C.
Tucson, AZ....................Family Law

KARSH AND FULTON, PROFESSIONAL CORPORATION
Denver, CO....................Commercial Law, Real Estate Law

KASDIN, PETER D., LTD.
Chicago, IL....................Medical Malpractice Law, Personal Injury Law

KASDORF, LEWIS & SWIETLIK, S.C.
Milwaukee, WI....................Civil Trial Practice, Insurance Defense Law

KASE & DRUKER
Garden City, NY....................Appellate Practice, Criminal Trial Practice, General Practice

KASIBORSKI, RONAYNE & FLASKA, A PROFESSIONAL CORPORATION
Detroit, MI....................General Practice

KASSAB ARCHBOLD JACKSON & O'BRIEN
Media, PA....................Bankruptcy Law, Commercial Law, Environmental Law, Family Law, General Practice, Labor and Employment Law, Medical Malpractice Law, Municipal Bond/Public Authority Financing Law, Personal Injury Law, Probate and Estate Planning Law, Product Liability Law, Real Estate Law

KASSEBAUM & JOHNSON
Wichita, KS....................Insurance Defense Law

KASSEL & KASSEL
San Bernardino, CA....................Criminal Trial Practice, General Practice, Health Care Law, Personal Injury Law

KATARINCIC & SALMON
Pittsburgh, PA....................Civil Trial Practice, Securities Law

KATSKEE, HENATSCH & SUING
Omaha, NE....................Civil Trial Practice, General Practice, Insurance Defense Law

KATZ, BIERER & BRADY, INC.
Larkspur, CA....................Civil Trial Practice, Personal Injury Law

KATZ, FROME AND BLEECKER, P.A.
Rockville, MD....................Bankruptcy Law, Business Law, Civil Trial Practice, Family Law, Probate and Estate Planning Law

KATZ, GREENBERGER & NORTON
Cincinnati, OH....................Bankruptcy Law, Business Law, Civil Trial Practice, Immigration and Naturalization Law, International Business Law

KATZ, KANTOR & PERKINS
Bluefield, WV....................General Practice

KATZ, KUTTER, HAIGLER, ALDERMAN, MARKS & BRYANT, PROFESSIONAL ASSOCIATION
Tallahassee, FL....................Administrative Law

KATZ, MCANDREWS, BALCH, LEFSTEIN & FIEWEGER, P.C.
Rock Island, IL....................Civil Trial Practice, General Practice

KATZ, TELLER, BRANT & HILD, A LEGAL PROFESSIONAL ASSOCIATION
Cincinnati, OH....................Business Law, Civil Trial Practice, Employment Benefits Law, Family Law, General Practice, Health Care Law, Probate and Estate Planning Law

KATZMAN KATZMAN & PYLITT, A PROFESSIONAL CORPORATION
Indianapolis, IN....................Business Law, Civil Trial Practice, General Practice

KAUFFMAN & SCHWARTZ, P.A.
Boca Raton, FL....................Family Law, Personal Injury Law, Probate and Estate Planning Law, Real Estate Law

KAUFMAN & CANOLES, A PROFESSIONAL CORPORATION
Newport News, VA....................General Practice
Norfolk, VA....................General Practice
Virginia Beach, VA....................General Practice

KAUFMAN, COREN, RESS & WEIDMAN
Philadelphia, PA....................Civil Trial Practice

KAUFMAN & CUMBERLAND CO., L.P.A.
Cleveland, OH....................Business Law, Civil Trial Practice, Environmental Law, General Practice
Columbus, OH....................Environmental Law

KAUFMAN & FLORENCE
Lebanon, OH....................General Practice

KAUFMAN & GREEN, L.L.P.
Wilmington, NC....................Banking Law, Real Estate Law

KAUFMAN MILLER DICKSTEIN & GRUNSPAN, P.A.
Miami, FL....................Commercial Law

KAUFMAN, NANESS, SCHNEIDER & ROSENSWEIG, P.C.
Melville, NY....................Labor and Employment Law

KAUFMAN AND PAYTON
Farmington Hills, MI....................Admiralty/Maritime Law, Appellate Practice, Business Law, Civil Trial Practice, Commercial Law, Environmental Law, Immigration and Naturalization Law, Insurance Defense Law, International Business Law, Medical Malpractice Law, Personal Injury Law, Probate and Estate Planning Law, Product Liability Law, Real Estate Law

KAUFMAN, REIBACH & RICHIE, INC.
Austin, TX....................Civil Trial Practice, Municipal and Zoning Law
San Antonio, TX....................Civil Trial Practice, Municipal and Zoning Law

KAUFMAN & ROTHFEDER, P.C.
Montgomery, AL....................Real Estate Law, Tax Law

KAUFMAN & YOUNG, A PROFESSIONAL CORPORATION
Beverly Hills, CA....................Family Law

KAVALLER, MILES L., A PROFESSIONAL LAW CORPORATION
Beverly Hills, CA....................Transportation Law

KAVANAGH, SCULLY, SUDOW, WHITE & FREDERICK, P.C.
Peoria, IL....................Civil Trial Practice, General Practice

KAY, J. BENJAMIN III
Augusta, GA....................Bankruptcy Law

KAY & ANDERSEN, S.C.
Madison, WI....................Civil Trial Practice, Construction Law, General Practice

KAY, CASTO, CHANEY, LOVE & WISE
Charleston, WV....................Civil Trial Practice, General Practice

KAY, EDWARD M., P.A.
Fort Lauderdale, FL....................Criminal Trial Practice

KAYE, ALLEN E., P.C.
New York, NY....................Immigration and Naturalization Law

KAYE, SCHOLER, FIERMAN, HAYS & HANDLER
Los Angeles, CA....................General Practice
Washington, DC....................General Practice
New York, NY....................General Practice
Beijing (Peking), People's Republic of China....................General Practice
Hong Kong, Hong Kong (British Crown Colony)....................General Practice

KAYSER & REDFERN
New York, NY....................General Practice

KAZAN, MCCLAIN, EDISES, SIMON & ABRAMS, A PROFESSIONAL LAW CORPORATION
Oakland, CA....................Civil Trial Practice, Personal Injury Law

KEAN, MILLER, HAWTHORNE, D'ARMOND, MCCOWAN & JARMAN, L.L.P.
Baton Rouge, LA....................Civil Trial Practice, Commercial Law, Environmental Law, General Practice, Labor and Employment Law, Natural Resources Law, Probate and Estate Planning Law, Public Utilities Law, Tax Law

KEANE & BEANE, P.C.
White Plains, NY....................Commercial Law, Environmental Law, General Practice, Labor and Employment Law, Municipal and Zoning Law, Real Estate Law

KEARNEY, JEFF, & ASSOCIATES
Fort Worth, TX....................Criminal Trial Practice

KEATING, MUETHING & KLEKAMP
Cincinnati, OH....................Banking Law, Civil Trial Practice, General Practice, Insurance Defense Law, Medical Malpractice Law, Real Estate Law, Tax Law

KECK, MAHIN & CATE
Washington, DC....................General Practice
Chicago, IL....................Antitrust Law, General Practice

KEEFE, BRENNAN & BRENNAN
Quincy, IL....................General Practice

KEEFE & DEPAULI, P.C.
Fairview Heights, IL....................Civil Trial Practice

KEEFER, O'REILLY & FERRARIO
Las Vegas, NV....................Business Law, Civil Trial Practice

KEEFER, WOOD, ALLEN & RAHAL
Harrisburg, PA....................Civil Trial Practice, General Practice, Health Care Law, Tax Law

KEEGAN, KEEGAN & ASSOCIATES, P.C.
White Plains, NY....................Personal Injury Law

KEENER & KEENER
Centre, AL ....General Practice

KEGAN & KEGAN, LTD.
Chicago, IL....................Patent, Trademark, Copyright and Unfair Competition Law

KEGEL, CHESTERS, LAPP & MILLER
Lancaster, PA....................General Practice

KEHART, SHAFTER, HUGHES & WEBBER, P.C.
Decatur, IL....................General Practice

KEHOE, DENNIS J., A LAW CORPORATION
Aptos, CA ....Civil Trial Practice, Environmental Law, Personal Injury Law

KEITH, DARRELL, P.C., LAW FIRM OF
Fort Worth, TX ....Medical Malpractice Law

KEITH, MACK, LEWIS, COHEN & LUMPKIN
Miami, FL....................General Practice

KEKER & VAN NEST
San Francisco, CA ....Civil Trial Practice

KELLAHIN AND KELLAHIN
Santa Fe, NM....................Natural Resources Law

KELLER AND CURTIN CO., L.P.A.
Cleveland, OH....................Civil Trial Practice, Environmental Law, General Practice, Insurance Defense Law, Product Liability Law

KELLER & PITTS
Florence, AL ....Insurance Defense Law, Probate and Estate Planning Law, Tax Law

KELLER, REYNOLDS, DRAKE, JOHNSON & GILLESPIE, P.C.
Helena, MT ....Civil Trial Practice, Insurance Defense Law

KELLER ROHRBACK
Seattle, WA ....Antitrust Law, Civil Trial Practice, General Practice, Insurance Defense Law

KELLER, THOMA, SCHWARZE, SCHWARZE, DUBAY & KATZ, P.C.
Detroit, MI....................Civil Trial Practice, Employment Benefits Law, General Practice, Labor and Employment Law, Probate and Estate Planning Law

KELLETT, GILLIS & KELLETT, P.A.
Fort Payne, AL....................General Practice, Insurance Defense Law

KELLEY, BELCHER & BROWN, A PROFESSIONAL CORPORATION
Bloomington, IN ....Civil Trial Practice, Insurance Defense Law, Personal Injury Law, Product Liability Law

KELLEY, JASONS, MCGUIRE & SPINELLI
Philadelphia, PA ....Civil Trial Practice, Commercial Law, Insurance Defense Law, Medical Malpractice Law, Personal Injury Law, Product Liability Law

KELLEY & KELLEY
Bardstown, KY ....General Practice

KELLEY & LOVETT, P.C.
Albany, GA....................Bankruptcy Law

KELLEY, MCCANN & LIVINGSTONE
Cleveland, OH....................Appellate Practice, Bankruptcy Law, Business Law, Civil Trial Practice, Environmental Law, Family Law, General Practice, Municipal and Zoning Law, Real Estate Law, Securities Law

KELLEY & MURPHY
Blue Bell, PA....................General Practice

KELLEY, SCRITSMIER & BYRNE, P.C.
North Platte, NE ....General Practice

KELLEY, WEBER, PIETZ & SLATER, S.C.
Wausau, WI....................Civil Trial Practice

KELL & LYNCH, P.C.
Birmingham, MI....................Civil Trial Practice, Commercial Law, Insurance Defense Law

KELL, NUELLE & LOIZZO
Woodstock, IL ....General Practice

KELLOGG, WHITE, EVANS AND GRAY
Manteo, NC ....General Practice

KELLY AFFLECK GREENE
Toronto, ON, Canada....................Bankruptcy Law, Civil Trial Practice

KELLY, BAUERSFELD & LOWRY
Woodland Hills, CA ....Patent, Trademark, Copyright and Unfair Competition Law

KELLY & BERENS, P.A.
Minneapolis, MN ....Appellate Practice, Civil Trial Practice

KELLY, BLACK, BLACK, BYRNE & BEASLEY, PROFESSIONAL ASSOCIATION
Miami, FL ....Civil Trial Practice, General Practice

KELLY, HART & HALLMAN, A PROFESSIONAL CORPORATION
Fort Worth, TX ....General Practice

KELLY, J. MICHAEL, & ASSOCIATES, A PROF. CORP.
Santa Monica, CA....................Family Law, Personal Injury Law

KELLY, JAMES P., & ASSOCIATES, P.C.
Atlanta, GA ....Business Law, Health Care Law

KELLY, RAMMELKAMP, MUEHLENWEG, LUCERO & LEÓN, A PROFESSIONAL ASSOCIATION
Albuquerque, NM....................Banking Law, Civil Trial Practice, General Practice, Health Care Law, Labor and Employment Law, Real Estate Law, Tax Law

KELLY, RODE & KELLY, LLP
Mineola, NY....................General Practice

KELLY & RYBERG, S.C.
Eau Claire, WI....................Civil Trial Practice, Insurance Defense Law

KELLY, TIMOTHY F., LAW OFFICES OF
Munster, IN ....Civil Trial Practice, General Practice, Insurance Defense Law, Labor and Employment Law, Medical Malpractice Law, Personal Injury Law, Product Liability Law

KELSCH, KELSCH, RUFF & AUSTIN
Mandan, ND....................General Practice

KEMP AND KEMP
Hopkinsville, KY ....General Practice

KEMP, SMITH, DUNCAN & HAMMOND, A PROFESSIONAL CORPORATION
Albuquerque, NM....................General Practice
El Paso, TX....................Antitrust Law, General Practice, Labor and Employment Law, Tax Law

KEMPE, JOSEPH C., PROFESSIONAL ASSOCIATION
Jupiter, FL....................Probate and Estate Planning Law, Tax Law
Stuart, FL....................Probate and Estate Planning Law, Tax Law
Vero Beach, FL....................Probate and Estate Planning Law, Tax Law

KENDALL, HUGH F., ATTORNEY, P.C.
Chattanooga, TN ....Probate and Estate Planning Law, Real Estate Law, Tax Law

KENDRICK, JOHN A.
Washington, DC....................Probate and Estate Planning Law

KENDRICKS, BORDEAU, ADAMINI, KEEFE, SMITH, GIRARD AND SEAVOY, P.C.
Marquette, MI....................General Practice

KENEFICK, THOMAS A. III
Springfield, MA....................Medical Malpractice Law

KENNEDY, JAMES L. JR.
Ketchum, ID ....Environmental Law, Natural Resources Law, Real Estate Law

KENNEDY & CHRISTOPHER, P.C.
Denver, CO ....Civil Trial Practice, Medical Malpractice Law

KENNEDY, CICCONETTI & RICKETT, A L.P.A.
Wooster, OH ....Civil Trial Practice

KENNEDY & COMERFORD
Mineola, NY....................Commercial Law, General Practice, Insurance Defense Law, Real Estate Law

KENNEDY COVINGTON LOBDELL & HICKMAN, L.L.P.
Charlotte, NC....................General Practice
Rock Hill, SC....................General Practice

KENNEDY, FULTON & KOONTZ
Chattanooga, TN ....Bankruptcy Law, Commercial Law

KENNEDY, HOLLAND, DELACY & SVOBODA
Omaha, NE ....General Practice

KENNEDY & KENNEDY
Bloomfield, NJ ....Civil Trial Practice, Insurance Defense Law

KENNEDY & NERVIG
Wadena, MN....................General Practice

KENNEDY, RICHARD R., A PROFESSIONAL LAW CORPORATION
Lafayette, LA ....Admiralty/Maritime Law, Civil Trial Practice, General Practice, Personal Injury Law

KENNERLY, MONTGOMERY & FINLEY, P.C.
Knoxville, TN ....Civil Trial Practice, Commercial Law, General Practice, Insurance Defense Law

KENNEY & KEARNEY
Cherry Hill, NJ .... Civil Trial Practice

KENNY, BRIMMER, MELLEY & MAHONEY
Hartford, CT .... Environmental Law, General Practice, Insurance Defense Law, Medical Malpractice Law, Personal Injury Law

KENNY NACHWALTER SEYMOUR ARNOLD CRITCHLOW & SPECTOR, PROFESSIONAL ASSOCIATION
Miami, FL .... Antitrust Law, Civil Trial Practice, General Practice, Trademark, Copyright and Unfair Competition Law

KENNY & STEARNS
Newark, NJ .... Admiralty/Maritime Law, Civil Trial Practice
New York, NY .... Admiralty/Maritime Law, Civil Trial Practice

KENT, HAZZARD, JAEGER, GREER, WILSON & FAY
White Plains, NY .... Civil Trial Practice, General Practice, Probate and Estate Planning Law, Real Estate Law

KENT & MCBRIDE, P.C.
Philadelphia, PA .... Environmental Law, Insurance Defense Law

KENT, WORSHAM, WILLIAMSON & BRANNON
Savannah, GA .... Insurance Defense Law

KENYON & KENYON
Washington, DC .... Patent, Trademark, Copyright and Unfair Competition Law
New York, NY .... Patent, Trademark, Copyright and Unfair Competition Law

KEOGH, BURKHART & VETTER
Norwalk, CT .... General Practice

KEPLEY, MACCONNELL & EYRICH, A LEGAL PROFESSIONAL ASSOCIATION
Cincinnati, OH .... Business Law, Civil Trial Practice, Personal Injury Law, Public Utilities Law, Real Estate Law

KERNAN AND KERNAN, P.C.
Utica, NY .... General Practice

KERR, ANN LOUGHRIDGE
Clearwater, FL .... Family Law

KERR, FITZ-GERALD & KERR, L.L.P.
Midland, TX .... Banking Law, General Practice

KERR, IRVINE, RHODES & ABLES, A PROFESSIONAL CORPORATION
Oklahoma City, OK .... Administrative Law, Civil Trial Practice, Environmental Law, General Practice, Insurance Defense Law

KERR, RUSSELL AND WEBER
Detroit, MI .... Antitrust Law, Appellate Practice, Civil Trial Practice, Commercial Law, Construction Law, Employment Benefits Law, Environmental Law, General Practice, Health Care Law, Insurance Defense Law, Labor and Employment Law, Medical Malpractice Law, Probate and Estate Planning Law, Real Estate Law, Tax Law

KERSTEN & CARLSON
Fort Dodge, IA .... General Practice

KERSTEN & MCKINNON, S.C.
Milwaukee, WI .... Antitrust Law, Civil Trial Practice, Medical Malpractice Law, Personal Injury Law

KESLER & RUST, A PROFESSIONAL CORPORATION
Salt Lake City, UT .... Business Law

KESSLER & KESSLER
Uvalde, TX .... General Practice

KETCHAM & KETCHAM
Columbus, OH .... Criminal Trial Practice

KEULING-STOUT, P.C.
Big Stone Gap, VA .... Civil Trial Practice, General Practice

KEYES AND DONNELLAN, P.C.
Springfield, MA .... Personal Injury Law

KEYSER MASON BALL
Mississauga, ON, Canada .... General Practice
Toronto, ON, Canada .... General Practice

KEYWELL AND ROSENFELD
Troy, MI .... Business Law, Civil Trial Practice, Labor and Employment Law, Probate and Estate Planning Law

KEZIAH, GATES & SAMET, L.L.P.
High Point, NC .... General Practice

KIEFER & RUDMAN, A PROFESSIONAL LAW CORPORATION
Metairie, LA .... Civil Trial Practice, Probate and Estate Planning Law, Real Estate Law

KIERNAN, PLUNKETT & REDIHAN
Providence, RI .... Civil Trial Practice, Environmental Law, Insurance Defense Law

KIERNAN & STRENK
Morristown, NJ .... Commercial Law

KIESLER & BERMAN
Chicago, IL .... Insurance Defense Law

KIGER MESSER & ALPERN
Pittsburgh, PA .... Civil Trial Practice, General Practice, Insurance Defense Law, Personal Injury Law, Product Liability Law

KIGHTLINGER & GRAY
Evansville, IN .... General Practice
Indianapolis, IN .... Civil Trial Practice, General Practice

KILGORE, DONALD C.
Portsmouth, VA .... General Practice

KILGORE & KILGORE, A PROFESSIONAL CORPORATION
Dallas, TX .... Civil Trial Practice, General Practice, Natural Resources Law

KILLIAN & GEPHART
Harrisburg, PA .... Administrative Law, Civil Trial Practice, Criminal Trial Practice, Environmental Law, Labor and Employment Law

KILLIAN, NICHOLAS, FISCHER, WIRKEN, COOK & PEW, P.L.C.
Mesa, AZ .... General Practice

KILLWORTH, GOTTMAN, HAGAN & SCHAEFF
Dayton, OH .... Patent, Trademark, Copyright and Unfair Competition Law

KILPATRICK & CODY
Washington, DC .... General Practice
Atlanta, GA .... Antitrust Law, Communications Law, General Practice, Immigration and Naturalization Law, Labor and Employment Law, Municipal Bond/Public Authority Financing Law, Patent, Trademark, Copyright and Unfair Competition Law
Augusta, GA .... Civil Trial Practice, General Practice

KIMBALL & CURRY, P.C.
Phoenix, AZ .... Environmental Law, Natural Resources Law

KIMBALL, PARR, WADDOUPS, BROWN & GEE, A PROFESSIONAL CORPORATION
Salt Lake City, UT .... Civil Trial Practice, Environmental Law, General Practice, Insurance Defense Law, Natural Resources Law, Real Estate Law

KIMBLE, GOTHREAU & NELSON, P.C.
Tucson, AZ .... Civil Trial Practice, General Practice, Insurance Defense Law

KIMBLE, MACMICHAEL & UPTON, A PROFESSIONAL CORPORATION
Fresno, CA .... Bankruptcy Law, Civil Trial Practice, Environmental Law, Health Care Law, Patent, Trademark, Copyright and Unfair Competition Law, Real Estate Law

KIMBRELL & HAMANN, PROFESSIONAL ASSOCIATION
Miami, FL .... General Practice

KIMBROUGH, ROBERT A.
Sarasota, FL .... Probate and Estate Planning Law

KIMERER, LAVELLE, HAY & HOOD, P.L.C.
Phoenix, AZ .... Civil Trial Practice, Criminal Trial Practice, General Practice, Securities Law

KIMMEL, JAMES S.
Littleton, CO .... General Practice

KIMMEL, WEISS & CARTER, P.A.
Wilmington, DE .... Civil Trial Practice, Personal Injury Law

KINCAID, CULTICE & GEYER
Zanesville, OH .... General Practice

KINCAID, GIANUNZIO, CAUDLE & HUBERT, A PROFESSIONAL CORPORATION
Oakland, CA .... Insurance Defense Law
San Francisco, CA .... Insurance Defense Law
Walnut Creek, CA .... Insurance Defense Law

KINDEL & ANDERSON
Irvine, CA .... General Practice
Los Angeles, CA .... Civil Trial Practice, General Practice, Labor and Employment Law, Probate and Estate Planning Law, Tax Law
San Francisco, CA .... General Practice
Woodland Hills, CA .... General Practice

KING, JOHN ROBERT LAW OFFICE OF
McAllen, TX..........Civil Trial Practice, Family Law, Real Estate Law

KING, ALLEN & ARNOLD
Charleston, WV..........Administrative Law, Civil Trial Practice, Criminal Trial Practice

KING & BALLOW
San Diego, CA..........General Practice, Immigration and Naturalization Law
Nashville, TN..........Antitrust Law, Civil Trial Practice, Communications Law, General Practice, Labor and Employment Law, Tax Law, Trademark, Copyright and Unfair Competition Law

KING & CROFT
Atlanta, GA..........Civil Trial Practice

KING, DEEP AND BRANAMAN
Henderson, KY..........Civil Trial Practice, General Practice, Insurance Defense Law, Natural Resources Law, Real Estate Law

KING & KING
Pittsburgh, PA..........Family Law, Personal Injury Law
Greeneville, TN..........Family Law, General Practice, Personal Injury Law

KING AND KING
Jackson, WY..........Civil Trial Practice, Personal Injury Law

KING, MCCARDLE, HERMAN, FREUND & OLEXA
Allentown, PA..........General Practice

KING, PAGANO & HARRISON
New York, NY..........Civil Trial Practice

KING, ROBERTS & BEELER
Oklahoma City, OK..........Antitrust Law, Civil Trial Practice, Insurance Defense Law

KING AND SCHICKLI
Lexington, KY..........Patent, Trademark, Copyright and Unfair Competition Law

KING & SPALDING
Washington, DC..........General Practice
Atlanta, GA..........General Practice
New York, NY..........General Practice

KING & VERNON, P.A.
Columbia, SC..........Civil Trial Practice, Criminal Trial Practice, Family Law, General Practice

KINGCADE, THOMAS E., PROFESSIONAL ASSOCIATION
West Palm Beach, FL..........Civil Trial Practice, Personal Injury Law

KINGERY DURREE WAKEMAN & RYAN, ASSOC.
Peoria, IL..........Civil Trial Practice, General Practice

KINNEY & LANGE, P.A.
Minneapolis, MN..........Patent, Trademark, Copyright and Unfair Competition Law

KINSELLA, BOESCH, FUJIKAWA & TOWLE
Los Angeles, CA..........Civil Trial Practice

KINSEY, ALLEBAUGH & KING
Steubenville, OH..........Banking Law, General Practice, Insurance Defense Law, Real Estate Law

KIPLE, KIPLE, DENEFE, BEAVER & GARDNER
Ottumwa, IA..........General Practice

KIPP AND CHRISTIAN, P.C.
Salt Lake City, UT..........Banking Law, Civil Trial Practice, General Practice, Insurance Defense Law, Personal Injury Law

KIRBO & KENDRICK
Bainbridge, GA..........General Practice

KIRBY, JACK ARTHUR
Rosemont, PA..........Probate and Estate Planning Law

KIRBY, PATRICK M., A PROF. CORP., LAW OFFICES OF
Flint, MI..........Civil Trial Practice, Insurance Defense Law, Labor and Employment Law

KIRCH, DAVID W.
Aurora, CO..........Probate and Estate Planning Law

KIRSCHNER, MAIN, PETRIE, GRAHAM, TANNER & DEMONT, PROFESSIONAL ASSOCIATION
Jacksonville, FL..........Bankruptcy Law, Commercial Law

KIRSHENBAUM LAW ASSOCIATES
Warwick, RI..........Civil Trial Practice, Family Law, Personal Injury Law

KIRSHMAN, HARRIS & COOPER, A PROFESSIONAL CORPORATION
Las Vegas, NV..........Labor and Employment Law

KIRTON & MCCONKIE, A PROFESSIONAL CORPORATION
Salt Lake City, UT..........Civil Trial Practice, Commercial Law, General Practice, Insurance Defense Law, Personal Injury Law, Probate and Estate Planning Law, Real Estate Law

KIRVEN & KIRVEN, P.C.
Buffalo, WY..........General Practice, Real Estate Law

KIRWAN & BARRETT, P.C.
Bozeman, MT..........Appellate Practice, Banking Law, Business Law, Civil Trial Practice, Commercial Law, Construction Law, Labor and Employment Law, Municipal and Zoning Law, Personal Injury Law, Probate and Estate Planning Law, Real Estate Law

KIRWAN, GOGER, CHESIN & PARKS, P.C.
Atlanta, GA..........Administrative Law, Bankruptcy Law, Criminal Trial Practice

KISSOON AND CLUGG
Edina, MN..........Family Law

KITCH, DRUTCHAS, WAGNER & KENNEY, P.C.
Ann Arbor, MI..........General Practice
Detroit, MI..........Civil Trial Practice, Environmental Law, General Practice, Health Care Law, Insurance Defense Law, Labor and Employment Law, Medical Malpractice Law, Personal Injury Law
Lansing, MI..........General Practice
Mount Clemens, MI..........General Practice
Troy, MI..........General Practice

KITCHEN, DEERY & BARNHOUSE
Cleveland, OH..........Civil Trial Practice, Criminal Trial Practice, Insurance Defense Law

KITCHENS, BENTON, KITCHENS & WARREN, A PROFESSIONAL LAW CORPORATION
Minden, LA..........General Practice

KITTELSEN, BARRY, ROSS, WELLINGTON AND THOMPSON
Monroe, WI..........General Practice

KITTREDGE, DONLEY, ELSON, FULLEM & EMBICK
Philadelphia, PA..........Civil Trial Practice, Environmental Law, Insurance Defense Law, Labor and Employment Law

KIZER AND BLACK
Maryville, TN..........General Practice

KIZER, BONDS, CROCKER & HUGHES
Milan, TN..........General Practice

KIZER, HOOD & MORGAN, L.L.P.
Baton Rouge, LA..........Bankruptcy Law, Real Estate Law

KIZER & NEU
Bremen, IN..........General Practice
Plymouth, IN..........General Practice

KLAINE, WILEY, HOFFMANN & MEURER, A LEGAL PROFESSIONAL ASSOCIATION
Cincinnati, OH..........Business Law, Employment Benefits Law, General Practice, Labor and Employment Law, Probate and Estate Planning Law, Real Estate Law, Securities Law, Tax Law

KLARQUIST, SPARKMAN, CAMPBELL, LEIGH & WHINSTON
Portland, OR..........Patent, Trademark, Copyright and Unfair Competition Law

KLAUBER & JACKSON
Hackensack, NJ..........Patent, Trademark, Copyright and Unfair Competition Law, Trademark, Copyright and Unfair Competition Law

KLAUSNER HUNTER & SEID
Somerville, NJ..........General Practice

KLEHR, HARRISON, HARVEY, BRANZBURG & ELLERS
Philadelphia, PA..........Banking Law, Bankruptcy Law, Business Law, Commercial Law, General Practice, Real Estate Law, Securities Law, Tax Law

KLEIN AND ASSOCIATES, P.A.
North Miami, FL..........Business Law, Civil Trial Practice, Real Estate Law

KLEIN, JOSEPH A., A PROFESSIONAL CORPORATION
Harrisburg, PA..........Civil Trial Practice, Medical Malpractice Law, Municipal and Zoning Law, Personal Injury Law, Real Estate Law

KLEIN, STODDARD & BUCK
De Kalb, IL..........General Practice
Sycamore, IL..........General Practice

KLEIN, WEGIS, DENATALE, GOLDNER & MUIR
Bakersfield, CA..........Bankruptcy Law, Civil Trial Practice, Commercial Law, Construction Law, Environmental Law, General Practice, Labor and Employment Law, Personal Injury Law, Probate and Estate Planning Law, Real Estate Law, Tax Law

Santa Ana, CA .... Civil Trial Practice, General Practice

KLEINBARD, BELL & BRECKER
Philadelphia, PA .... General Practice, Labor and Employment Law

KLEINPETER & KLEINPETER
Baton Rouge, LA .... Civil Trial Practice, Insurance Defense Law

KLENDA, MITCHELL, AUSTERMAN & ZUERCHER
Wichita, KS .... General Practice

KLETT LIEBER ROONEY & SCHORLING, A PROFESSIONAL CORPORATION
Philadelphia, PA .... General Practice
Pittsburgh, PA .... General Practice, Labor and Employment Law, Municipal Bond/Public Authority Financing Law, Natural Resources Law, Tax Law

KLETTE AND KLETTE
Covington, KY .... Banking Law, General Practice, Probate and Estate Planning Law, Real Estate Law

KLIEBENSTEIN, HERONIMUS, SCHMIDT & GEER
Grundy Center, IA .... General Practice

KLING, FRED
Albany, MO .... General Practice

KLOS, FLYNN & PAPENFUSS, CHARTERED
La Crosse, WI .... General Practice

KLOSTER, RUDDELL, HORNBURG, COCHRAN, STANTON & SMITH
Visalia, CA .... General Practice

KLOVSKY, KUBY AND HARRIS
Philadelphia, PA .... Civil Trial Practice

KLUGER, PERETZ, KAPLAN & BERLIN, P.A.
Miami, FL .... Civil Trial Practice

KLUTTZ, REAMER, BLANKENSHIP & HAYES, L.L.P.
Salisbury, NC .... General Practice, Insurance Defense Law

KNEE & MASON
Los Angeles, CA .... Labor and Employment Law

KNIGHT, DAHOOD, MCLEAN, EVERETT & DAYTON
Anaconda, MT .... General Practice

KNIGHT, DUDLEY, DEZERN & CLARKE, P.L.L.C.
Norfolk, VA .... General Practice

KNIGHT, FORD, WRIGHT, ATWILL, PARSHALL & BAKER
Columbia, MO .... General Practice

KNIGHT, MACLAY & MASAR
Missoula, MT .... General Practice, Real Estate Law

KNIGHT, MANZI, BRENNAN, OSTROM AND HAM, A PROFESSIONAL ASSOCIATION
Upper Marlboro, MD .... General Practice

KNOBBE, MARTENS, OLSON & BEAR
Newport Beach, CA .... Patent, Trademark, Copyright and Unfair Competition Law

KNOTT, JOHN K. JR.
Cheshire, CT .... Municipal and Zoning Law

KNOWLES & ASSOCIATES
Carmel, IN .... Bankruptcy Law, Business Law, Civil Trial Practice, Criminal Trial Practice, Probate and Estate Planning Law

KNOX, RICHARD H.
Philadelphia, PA .... Probate and Estate Planning Law

KNOX MCLAUGHLIN GORNALL & SENNETT, P.C.
Erie, PA .... General Practice

KNOX RICKSEN
Fairfield, CA .... General Practice
Oakland, CA .... General Practice

KNOX AND SWAN
Thomson, GA .... General Practice

KNOX & TOLLEFSON, P.C.
Irving, TX .... Insurance Defense Law

KNUDSEN, BERKHEIMER, RICHARDSON & ENDACOTT
Lincoln, NE .... General Practice, Securities Law

KOBAYASHI, SUGITA & GODA
Honolulu, HI .... Business Law, General Practice, Real Estate Law

KOCH, JOHNSON, WEBER & GOHEEN
Hamilton, MT .... General Practice

KOCHA, STUART E., P.A.
West Palm Beach, FL .... Civil Trial Practice, General Practice, Medical Malpractice Law

KOEPPEL MARTONE LEISTMAN & HERMAN
Mineola, NY .... Real Estate Law

KOHN, MICHAEL G.
Cincinnati, OH .... Civil Trial Practice

KOHN, BOOKSTEIN & KARP, P.C.
Albany, NY .... General Practice, Labor and Employment Law, Probate and Estate Planning Law, Tax Law

KOHN, SHANDS, ELBERT, GIANOULAKIS & GILJUM
St. Louis, MO .... Antitrust Law, Labor and Employment Law, Tax Law

KOHNER, MANN & KAILAS, S.C.
Milwaukee, WI .... Banking Law, Bankruptcy Law, Business Law, Civil Trial Practice, Commercial Law, Construction Law

KOHORST LAW FIRM
Harlan, IA .... General Practice, Insurance Defense Law

KOHRS & FISKE
Santa Monica, CA .... Insurance Defense Law

KOKJER, KIRCHER, BOWMAN & JOHNSON, A PROFESSIONAL CORPORATION
Kansas City, MO .... Patent, Trademark, Copyright and Unfair Competition Law

KOLEY, JESSEN, DAUBMAN & RUPIPER, PROFESSIONAL CORPORATION
Omaha, NE .... General Practice

KOLISCH HARTWELL DICKINSON MCCORMACK & HEUSER, A PROFESSIONAL CORPORATION
Portland, OR .... Patent, Trademark, Copyright and Unfair Competition Law

KOLLMAN & SHEEHAN, P.A.
Baltimore, MD .... Business Law, Labor and Employment Law

KOLSBY, GORDON, ROBIN, SHORE & ROTHWEILER, A PROFESSIONAL CORPORATION
Philadelphia, PA .... Civil Trial Practice, Medical Malpractice Law

KOLVOORD, OVERTON AND WILSON
Essex Junction, VT .... General Practice, Probate and Estate Planning Law

KOMIE AND ASSOCIATES, LAW OFFICES
Chicago, IL .... Civil Trial Practice, Criminal Trial Practice, Family Law

KOMMERS, KASTING & ROTH
Bozeman, MT .... General Practice

KONIG, RICHARD W.
Stockton, CA .... Probate and Estate Planning Law

KOOMAN, RICHARD W. II, LAW OFFICES OF
Clarion, PA .... Commercial Law, General Practice, Insurance Defense Law

KOONS, JOHN P.
Dallas, TX .... Banking Law

KOONS, FULLER & VANDEN EYKEL, A PROFESSIONAL CORPORATION
Dallas, TX .... Family Law

KOONZ, MCKENNEY, JOHNSON & REGAN, P.C.
Washington, DC .... Personal Injury Law

KOPELMAN AND PAIGE, P.C.
Boston, MA .... Civil Trial Practice, Environmental Law, General Practice, Insurance Defense Law, Municipal and Zoning Law

KOPFF, NARDELLI & DOPF
New York, NY .... Civil Trial Practice, Insurance Defense Law, Medical Malpractice Law, Personal Injury Law

KOPPLE & KLINGER
Los Angeles, CA .... Tax Law

KOPS AND FENNER, P.C.
Philadelphia, PA .... Personal Injury Law

KORDES, CLAYTON & AMBROSE, P.A.
Brielle, NJ .... General Practice

KOREN, BERTELL & HOEY
Buffalo, NY .... General Practice, Insurance Defense Law, Personal Injury Law

KORNEY & HELDT
Birmingham, MI .... Labor and Employment Law, Personal Injury Law

KORNFIELD, PAUL & BUPP, A PROFESSIONAL CORPORATION
Oakland, CA .... Bankruptcy Law

KORNIEVSKY, GEORGE M., A PROFESSIONAL CORPORATION
Newport Beach, CA................Family Law

KORTHALS, JOHN L.
Pompano Beach, FL ....General Practice

KOSLOV & CADY
Los Angeles, CA......................Civil Trial Practice, Construction Law, Insurance Defense Law, Product Liability Law

KOSTELANETZ & FINK
New York, NY........................Criminal Trial Practice, Tax Law

KOTTKAMP & O'ROURKE
Pendleton, OR..........................General Practice

KRAEMER, BURNS, MYTELKA & LOVELL, P.A.
Springfield, NJ ....Civil Trial Practice

KRAFT, WALSER, NELSON, HETTIG & HONSEY
Hutchinson, MN......................General Practice
Olivia, MN ....General Practice
Renville, MN..........................General Practice

KRALOVEC, MARQUARD, DOYLE & GIBBONS, CHARTERED
Chicago, IL...............................Civil Trial Practice, Insurance Defense Law

KRAMER, LYNNE ADAIR LAW OFFICES OF
Commack, NY ....Family Law

KRAMER, LEVIN, NAFTALIS, NESSEN, KAMIN & FRANKEL
New York, NY.........................Civil Trial Practice, General Practice

KRAMER, PAUL R., P.A.
Baltimore, MD........................Criminal Trial Practice

KRAMON & GRAHAM, P.A.
Baltimore, MD........................General Practice

KRASNER & CHEN
New York, NY.........................Banking Law, Commercial Law, Real Estate Law

KRASNY AND DETTMER
Melbourne, FL.........................Civil Trial Practice, General Practice, Probate and Estate Planning Law, Real Estate Law

KRAUS, SHERRY S.
Rochester, NY..........................Tax Law

KREDER, BROOKS, HAILSTONE & LUDWIG
Scranton, PA ....Civil Trial Practice, General Practice, Personal Injury Law, Product Liability Law

KREIS, ENDERLE, CALLANDER & HUDGINS, A PROFESSIONAL CORPORATION
Kalamazoo, MI ....Banking Law, Bankruptcy Law, Civil Trial Practice, Commercial Law, Construction Law, Environmental Law, Family Law, General Practice, Health Care Law, Labor and Employment Law, Municipal and Zoning Law, Probate and Estate Planning Law, Real Estate Law, Tax Law

KREITZMAN, MORTENSEN & SIMON
New York, NY.........................Labor and Employment Law

KRENTZMAN, PAUL L.
Beverly Hills, CA....................Personal Injury Law

KREUSLER-WALSH, JANE
West Palm Beach, FL.............Civil Trial Practice

KRIEGER, ALBERT J., P.A.
Miami, FL ....Criminal Trial Practice

KRIEGER & KRIEGER
Omaha, NE ....Immigration and Naturalization Law

KRIST, GUNN, WELLER, NEUMANN & MORRISON, L.L.P.
Houston, TX ....Civil Trial Practice, Personal Injury Law

KRISTENSEN, CUMMINGS & MURTHA, P.C.
Brattleboro, VT........................General Practice, Probate and Estate Planning Law

KRIVCHER, MAGIDS, NEAL, COTTAM & CAMPBELL, P.C.
Memphis, TN...........................General Practice, Insurance Defense Law

KRIVIS, PASSOVOY & SPILE
Encino, CA...............................Insurance Defense Law

KROGER, GARDIS & REGAS
Indianapolis, IN.......................Appellate Practice, Bankruptcy Law, Business Law, Commercial Law, Environmental Law, Probate and Estate Planning Law, Real Estate Law

KROLL & TRACT
New York, NY..........................General Practice

KROLOFF, BELCHER, SMART, PERRY & CHRISTOPHERSON
Stockton, CA............................General Practice

KRONICK, MOSKOVITZ, TIEDEMANN & GIRARD, A PROFESSIONAL CORPORATION
Sacramento, CA ....Environmental Law, General Practice

KRONISCH, SCHKEEPER AND LESSER, A PROFESSIONAL CORPORATION
Livingston, NJ.........................Civil Trial Practice

KRONISH, LIEB, WEINER & HELLMAN
New York, NY.........................General Practice

KROOTH & ALTMAN
Washington, DC......................General Practice

KRUEGER & CAHILL
Wailuku, HI ....General Practice

KRUGLIAK, WILKINS, GRIFFITHS & DOUGHERTY CO., L.P.A.
Canton, OH.............................General Practice

KRUKOWSKI & COSTELLO, S.C.
Milwaukee, WI........................Labor and Employment Law

KRUPNICK CAMPBELL MALONE ROSELLI BUSER & SLAMA, P.A.
Fort Lauderdale, FL...............Admiralty/Maritime Law, Civil Trial Practice, General Practice, Personal Injury Law

KRUSE, LANDA & MAYCOCK, L.L.C.
Salt Lake City, UT..................Bankruptcy Law

KRUSE & LYNCH, P.C.
Colorado Springs, CO.............Probate and Estate Planning Law

KRUSEN EVANS & BYRNE
Philadelphia, PA ....Admiralty/Maritime Law, General Practice

KRYS BOYLE GOLZ REICH FREEDMAN BEAN & SCOTT, P.C.
Denver, CO ....Securities Law

KUBICKI DRAPER
Fort Lauderdale, FL...............General Practice
Miami, FL ....Civil Trial Practice, General Practice
West Palm Beach, FL..............General Practice

KUEHN, TRENTMAN & O'GARA
Belleville, IL ....Criminal Trial Practice, Personal Injury Law

KUHS, PARKER & STANTON
Bakersfield, CA ....Civil Trial Practice, Construction Law, General Practice, Municipal Bond/Public Authority Financing Law, Real Estate Law

KULZER & DIPADOVA, A PROFESSIONAL CORPORATION
Haddonfield, NJ......................Tax Law

KUMMER KAEMPFER BONNER & RENSHAW
Las Vegas, NV ....Commercial Law, Insurance Defense Law, Securities Law

KUMMER, KNOX, NAUGHTON & HANSBURY
Parsippany, NJ ....Civil Trial Practice, Commercial Law, Environmental Law, Securities Law

KUNIHOLM, ELIZABETH F.
Raleigh, NC............................Medical Malpractice Law

KUNKEL MILLER & HAMENT
Fort Myers, FL ....Labor and Employment Law
Sarasota, FL...........................Labor and Employment Law
Tampa, FL ....Labor and Employment Law

KUPFER, RICHARD A., P.A.
West Palm Beach, FL.............Appellate Practice

KURZMAN & EISENBERG
White Plains, NY ....General Practice, Probate and Estate Planning Law, Real Estate Law, Tax Law

KUSSMAN & WHITEHILL
Los Angeles, CA.....................Medical Malpractice Law, Personal Injury Law

KUTAK ROCK
Denver, CO ....General Practice
Washington, DC......................General Practice
Atlanta, GA ....General Practice
Omaha, NE ....General Practice

KUTNER, RUBINOFF & BUSH
Miami, FL ....Civil Trial Practice, General Practice

KUTTNER LAW OFFICES
Millburn, NJ............................Civil Trial Practice, Criminal Trial Practice, Insurance Defense Law, Personal Injury Law, Probate and Estate Planning Law

KUYKENDALL, JOHNSTON & KUYKENDALL, P.C.
Winchester, VA ....General Practice

LABARRE & ASSOCIATES, P.C.
Portland, OR ....Civil Trial Practice, Commercial Law, Personal Injury Law, Securities Law

L'ABBATE, BALKAN, COLAVITA & CONTINI, L.L.P.
Garden City, NY....................Civil Trial Practice, General Practice, Insurance Defense Law, Product Liability Law

LABE, ROBERT B., P.C.
Southfield, MI..........................Business Law, Probate and Estate Planning Law, Tax Law

LABORDE & LAFARGUE
Marksville, LA..........................General Practice

LABRUM AND DOAK
Woodbury, NJ............................General Practice
Bethlehem, PA...........................General Practice
Norristown, PA..........................General Practice
Philadelphia, PA........................General Practice

LACEY & JONES
Birmingham, MI..........................Civil Trial Practice, Insurance Defense Law

LACEY, O'MAHONEY, MAHONEY, SAGER & KING
Kokomo, IN..............................General Practice

LACKEY & LACKEY
Shelby, NC..............................General Practice

LACKEY, NUSBAUM, HARRIS, RENY & TORZEWSKI, A LEGAL PROFESSIONAL ASSOCIATION
Toledo, OH..............................Admiralty/Maritime Law, Family Law, Labor and Employment Law, Personal Injury Law

LACY, KATZEN, RYEN & MITTLEMAN
Rochester, NY...........................General Practice

LADAR & KNAPP
San Francisco, CA.......................Criminal Trial Practice

LADNER DOWNS
Vancouver, BC, Canada...................General Practice, Real Estate Law

LAFF, WHITESEL, CONTE & SARET, LTD., A PROFESSIONAL CORPORATION
Chicago, IL.............................Patent, Trademark, Copyright and Unfair Competition Law

LAFLEUR BROWN
Toronto, ON, Canada.....................General Practice
Montreal, QU, Canada....................General Practice
Quebec, QU, Canada......................General Practice
Brussels, Belgium.......................General Practice

LA FLEUR, LA FLEUR & LA FLEUR, P.C.
Rapid City, SD..........................General Practice

LAFLIN, LIEUWEN, TUCKER, PICK & HEER, P.A.
Albuquerque, NM.........................Tax Law

LA FOLLETTE, JOHNSON, DE HAAS, FESLER & AMES, A PROFESSIONAL CORPORATION
Los Angeles, CA.........................Civil Trial Practice, Insurance Defense Law, Medical Malpractice Law, Personal Injury Law, Product Liability Law

LAFOLLETTE & SINYKIN
Madison, WI.............................Banking Law, Civil Trial Practice, General Practice, Personal Injury Law

LAGERLOF, SENECAL, BRADLEY & SWIFT
Los Angeles, CA.........................Civil Trial Practice, General Practice
Pasadena, CA............................Administrative Law, Bankruptcy Law, Civil Trial Practice, Environmental Law, Municipal and Zoning Law, Natural Resources Law, Probate and Estate Planning Law, Real Estate Law

LA GRANGE, FREDBECK & DEPPE
Franklin, IN............................General Practice

LAGUE, NEWMAN & IRISH, A PROFESSIONAL CORPORATION
Muskegon, MI............................General Practice

LAIDLAW, SALLY J.
Oakland, CA.............................Family Law

LAKE, TINDALL & THACKSTON
Paducah, KY.............................Admiralty/Maritime Law
Greenville, MS..........................Admiralty/Maritime Law, General Practice

LAMB, WINDLE & MCERLANE, P.C.
West Chester, PA........................Administrative Law, Civil Trial Practice, Environmental Law, General Practice, Municipal Bond/Public Authority Financing Law, Municipal and Zoning Law, Personal Injury Law, Probate and Estate Planning Law, Real Estate Law

LAMBERT, PAUL WATSON
Tallahassee, FL.........................Administrative Law

LAMBERT & ROFFMAN
Madison, GA.............................General Practice

LAMBERTH, BONAPFEL, CIFELLI, WILLSON & STOKES, P.A.
Atlanta, GA.............................Bankruptcy Law, Business Law

LAMKIN, VAN EMAN, TRIMBLE, BEALS & ROURKE
Columbus, OH............................Civil Trial Practice, Medical Malpractice Law, Personal Injury Law, Product Liability Law

LAMMERS, LAMMERS, KLEIBACKER & PARENT
Madison, SD.............................General Practice

LANCASTER & ASSOCIATES
Santa Ana, CA...........................Business Law, Insurance Defense Law, Real Estate Law

LANCY, JOHN S., & ASSOCIATES, A PROFESSIONAL CORPORATION
Phoenix, AZ.............................Business Law, Real Estate Law, Securities Law

LANDELS, RIPLEY & DIAMOND
Sacramento, CA..........................General Practice
San Francisco, CA.......................General Practice

LANDIS, DAVID M., P.A.
Orlando, FL.............................General Practice

LANDIS, GRAHAM, FRENCH, HUSFELD, SHERMAN & FORD, P.A.
Daytona Beach, FL.......................General Practice
De Land, FL.............................General Practice
Deltona, FL.............................General Practice

LANDOE, BROWN, PLANALP & BRAAKSMA, P.C.
Bozeman, MT.............................General Practice

LANDRUM & SHOUSE
Lexington, KY...........................Business Law, Civil Trial Practice, Commercial Law, Environmental Law, Family Law, General Practice, Insurance Defense Law, Labor and Employment Law, Personal Injury Law, Probate and Estate Planning Law, Real Estate Law
Louisville, KY..........................Business Law, Family Law, General Practice, Insurance Defense Law, Personal Injury Law

LANDWEHR & HOF
New Orleans, LA.........................Bankruptcy Law

LANE, AITKEN & MCCANN
Washington, DC..........................Patent, Trademark, Copyright and Unfair Competition Law, Trademark, Copyright and Unfair Competition Law

LANE, FERTITTA, LANE, JANNEY & THOMAS
Baton Rouge, LA.........................Insurance Defense Law

LANE, LANE AND KELLY
Braintree, MA...........................General Practice

LANE, MARC J., THE LAW OFFICES OF, A PROFESSIONAL CORPORATION
Chicago, IL.............................Business Law, Tax Law

LANE POWELL SPEARS LUBERSKY
Los Angeles, CA.........................Product Liability Law
Portland, OR............................Antitrust Law, General Practice, Labor and Employment Law
Seattle, WA.............................Antitrust Law, Bankruptcy Law, Civil Trial Practice, Environmental Law, General Practice, Labor and Employment Law, Real Estate Law, Tax Law

LANE, ROSEN AND STARKEY, P.C.
Willimantic, CT.........................General Practice

LANE, TROHN, CLARKE, BERTRAND, VREELAND & JACOBSEN, P.A.
Bradenton, FL...........................Civil Trial Practice, General Practice
Lakeland, FL............................Civil Trial Practice, General Practice

LANE & WATERMAN
Rock Island, IL.........................General Practice
Davenport, IA...........................General Practice

LANER, MUCHIN, DOMBROW, BECKER, LEVIN AND TOMINBERG, LTD.
Chicago, IL.............................Employment Benefits Law, Labor and Employment Law

LANG, HENRY M. Q.C.
Sault Ste. Marie, ON, Canada............Civil Trial Practice

LANG MICHENER
Ottawa, ON, Canada......................General Practice
Toronto, ON, Canada.....................General Practice

LANG, RICHERT & PATCH, A PROFESSIONAL CORPORATION
Fresno, CA..............................Bankruptcy Law, Civil Trial Practice, Construction Law, Environmental Law, General Practice, Labor and Employment Law, Medical Malpractice Law, Personal Injury Law, Real Estate Law

LANGBERG, LESLIE & GABRIEL
Los Angeles, CA.........................Appellate Practice, Civil Trial Practice, Labor and Employment Law, Trademark, Copyright and Unfair Competition Law

LANGDON, JACK A., P.A.
St. Augustine, FL....................Insurance Defense Law

LANGFORD, HILL & TRYBUS, P.A.
Tampa, FL....................Administrative Law, Banking Law, Bankruptcy Law, Civil Trial Practice, Commercial Law, Environmental Law, Family Law, Insurance Defense Law, Probate and Estate Planning Law, Real Estate Law, Tax Law

LANGLOIS ROBERT
Montreal, QU, Canada....................General Practice

LANIER FORD SHAVER & PAYNE, P.C.
Huntsville, AL....................General Practice

LANO, NELSON, O'TOOLE & BENGTSON, LTD.
Grand Rapids, MN....................General Practice, Insurance Defense Law

LAPORTE, DANIEL G. AND ASSOCIATES
Akron, OH....................Probate and Estate Planning Law, Real Estate Law, Tax Law

LARGE, SCAMMELL & DANZIGER, A PROFESSIONAL CORPORATION
Flemington, NJ....................Commercial Law, General Practice, Real Estate Law

LARK, MAKOWSKI, MARATECK & KONOPKA
Shamokin, PA....................General Practice

LARKY, SHELDON G.
Birmingham, MI....................Family Law

LA ROSSA, MITCHELL & ROSS
New York, NY....................Criminal Trial Practice, General Practice

LARSEN, LYNN B.
Salt Lake City, UT....................Construction Law

LARSON & BOBENHAUSEN, PROFESSIONAL ASSOCIATION
Clearwater, FL....................Banking Law, Commercial Law, Real Estate Law

LARSON & BURNHAM, A PROFESSIONAL CORPORATION
Oakland, CA....................General Practice

LARSON AND TAYLOR
Arlington, VA....................Patent, Trademark, Copyright and Unfair Competition Law

LASATER & KNIGHT
Tyler, TX....................General Practice

LASCHER & LASCHER, A PROFESSIONAL CORPORATION
Ventura, CA....................Appellate Practice, General Practice

LASER, POKORNY, SCHWARTZ, FRIEDMAN & ECONOMOS, P.C.
Chicago, IL....................Banking Law, General Practice

LASER, SHARP, WILSON, BUFFORD & WATTS, P.A.
Little Rock, AR....................Civil Trial Practice, Commercial Law, General Practice, Insurance Defense Law, Medical Malpractice Law

LASKIN & GRAHAM
Glendale, CA....................Commercial Law, Municipal and Zoning Law, Real Estate Law

LASKY, HAAS & COHLER, PROFESSIONAL CORPORATION
San Francisco, CA....................Civil Trial Practice

LASORTE, ALFRED A. JR.
West Palm Beach, FL....................Civil Trial Practice

LASPADA, ANTHONY J., P.A.
Tampa, FL....................Criminal Trial Practice

LASTER, G. A.
San Mateo, CA....................Municipal Bond/Public Authority Financing Law

LATHROP & CLARK
Madison, WI....................General Practice, Patent, Trademark, Copyright and Unfair Competition Law, Trademark, Copyright and Unfair Competition Law

LATHROP & NORQUIST, L.C.
Overland Park, KS....................General Practice
Kansas City, MO....................General Practice

LATHROP & RUTLEDGE, A PROFESSIONAL CORPORATION
Cheyenne, WY....................Civil Trial Practice, General Practice, Insurance Defense Law

LAUCHENGCO, JOSÉ Y. JR.
Los Angeles, CA....................Criminal Trial Practice, Personal Injury Law

LAUER, E. STEVEN, P.A.
Vero Beach, FL....................Probate and Estate Planning Law, Tax Law

LAUER AND MONAHAN, P.C.
Easton, PA....................General Practice

LAUFMAN, ALAN K., J.D., M.D., A PROF. CORP., LAW OFFICES OF
Dallas, TX....................Medical Malpractice Law, Personal Injury Law, Product Liability Law

LAUGHLIN, PETERSON & LANG
Omaha, NE....................Civil Trial Practice, General Practice, Probate and Estate Planning Law, Real Estate Law, Tax Law

LAU, LANE, PIEPER, CONLEY & MCCREADIE, P.A.
Tampa, FL....................Admiralty/Maritime Law, General Practice

LAUTSCH, JOHN C., A PROFESSIONAL CORPORATION
Newport Beach, CA....................Appellate Practice, Business Law, Civil Trial Practice, Probate and Estate Planning Law

LAVENDER, ROCHELLE, BARNETTE & PICKETT
Texarkana, AR....................Civil Trial Practice, General Practice

LAVERY, DE BILLY
Montreal, QU, Canada....................General Practice

LAVIN, COLEMAN, FINARELLI & GRAY
New York, NY....................Civil Trial Practice, Insurance Defense Law, Product Liability Law
Philadelphia, PA....................Civil Trial Practice, Insurance Defense Law, Product Liability Law

LAWLER, ANDREW M., P.C.
New York, NY....................Criminal Trial Practice

LAWRENCE, WILLIAM V.
Craig, CO....................Probate and Estate Planning Law

LAWRENCE, KAMIN, SAUNDERS & UHLENHOP
Chicago, IL....................Civil Trial Practice, Construction Law, Securities Law

LAWRENCE AND LAWRENCE
Louisville, KY....................Probate and Estate Planning Law

LAWRENCE, RICHARD D., AND ASSOCIATES CO., L.P.A.
Cincinnati, OH....................Medical Malpractice Law, Personal Injury Law

LAWS & MURDOCH, P.A.
Russellville, AR....................General Practice

LAWSON LUNDELL LAWSON & MCINTOSH
Vancouver, BC, Canada....................Business Law

LAWTON & CATES, S.C.
Madison, WI....................Civil Trial Practice, Construction Law, Criminal Trial Practice, Labor and Employment Law, Personal Injury Law

LAWWELL, DALE & GRAHAM
Columbia, TN....................General Practice

LAYFIELD, ROTHSCHILD & MORGAN
Columbus, GA....................General Practice, Insurance Defense Law, Tax Law

LEACH & ENGLISH
San Francisco, CA....................Civil Trial Practice

LEACH, MCGREEVY, BAUTISTA & BRASS
San Francisco, CA....................Construction Law, Environmental Law, Insurance Defense Law

LEACH, SULLIVAN, SULLIVAN & WATKINS
Duncan, OK....................General Practice, Probate and Estate Planning Law

LEAHY & DENAULT
Claremont, NH....................General Practice

LEAKE & ANDERSSON
New Orleans, LA....................Civil Trial Practice, Commercial Law, Construction Law, General Practice, Insurance Defense Law

LEARMAN & MCCULLOCH AND REISING, ETHINGTON, BARNARD, PERRY & MILTON
Saginaw, MI....................Patent, Trademark, Copyright and Unfair Competition Law

LEATH, BYNUM, KITCHIN & NEAL, P.A.
Rockingham, NC....................General Practice

LEATHERMAN, WITZLER, DOMBEY & HART
Perrysburg, OH....................General Practice, Probate and Estate Planning Law

LEATHERWOOD WALKER TODD & MANN, P.C.
Greenville, SC....................Antitrust Law, Civil Trial Practice, Environmental Law, General Practice, Insurance Defense Law, Tax Law
Spartanburg, SC....................Civil Trial Practice, General Practice, Insurance Defense Law

LEAVITT, SULLY & RIVERS
Las Vegas, NV....................Business Law, Civil Trial Practice, Construction Law, Municipal and Zoning Law, Real Estate Law, Securities Law

LEAVY, SCHULTZ, DAVIS & FEARING, P.S.
Kennewick, WA....................General Practice

LEBENSFELD & ASSOCIATES, P.C.
Red Bank, NJ....................General Practice

LEBOVITS & DAVID, A PROFESSIONAL CORPORATION
Los Angeles, CA....................Civil Trial Practice, Personal Injury Law

LEE, RAYMOND JR.
Tuscola, IL....................General Practice

LEE, RON L.
Cottonwood, AZ....................Personal Injury Law

LEE, JOHN PETER, LTD.
Las Vegas, NV....................Bankruptcy Law, Civil Trial Practice, General Practice

LEE, KIM, WONG, YEE & LAU, ATTORNEYS AT LAW, A LAW CORPORATION
Honolulu, HI....................Civil Trial Practice, Medical Malpractice Law

LEE AND LEE
Lumberton, NC....................General Practice

LEE, MARTIN, GREEN & REITER, INC.
Bellefonte, PA....................General Practice
State College, PA....................General Practice

LEE & MCINISH
Dothan, AL....................Civil Trial Practice, General Practice

LEE, SCHULTE, EATON & BARRON
Jupiter, FL....................General Practice
Miami, FL....................General Practice

LEE, WILSON & ERTER
Sumter, SC....................Civil Trial Practice, General Practice, Insurance Defense Law

LEEMON, WEINSTINE, SHIRK & MELLOTT
Mount Carroll, IL....................Civil Trial Practice, General Practice

LEESFIELD, LEIGHTON, RUBIO & HILLENCAMP, P.A.
Miami, FL....................Civil Trial Practice, General Practice

LEFEBVRE, FRANCIS, BUREAU
New York, NY....................Business Law, Tax Law

LEFTWICH & DOUGLAS
Washington, DC....................General Practice

LEHNARDT, DETLEF G.
Kansas City, MO....................Business Law, International Business Law, Real Estate Law

LEHR, MIDDLEBROOKS & PROCTOR, P.C.
Birmingham, AL....................Labor and Employment Law

LEIB, ALTON
Los Angeles, CA....................Civil Trial Practice

LEIBOVIT, LOUIS
Palm Beach, FL....................Probate and Estate Planning Law, Real Estate Law

LEICK, HAMMONS AND BRITTAIN
Corbin, KY....................General Practice

LEITMAN, SIEGAL, PAYNE & CAMPBELL, P.C.
Birmingham, AL....................General Practice

LELAND, PARACHINI, STEINBERG, FLINN, MATZGER & MELNICK
San Francisco, CA....................General Practice

LEMLE & KELLEHER, L.L.P.
New Orleans, LA....................Admiralty/Maritime Law, General Practice, Natural Resources Law

LEMON, REED, ARMEY, HEARN & LEININGER
Warsaw, IN....................Civil Trial Practice, General Practice, Probate and Estate Planning Law

LEMON, SHEARER, EHRLICH, PHILLIPS & GOOD, A PROFESSIONAL CORPORATION
Perryton, TX....................Civil Trial Practice, General Practice, Natural Resources Law

LENAHAN & DEMPSEY, A PROFESSIONAL CORPORATION
Scranton, PA....................Civil Trial Practice, General Practice, Insurance Defense Law, Personal Injury Law, Securities Law

LENGVARI BRAMAN BARBACKI MOREAU, S.E.N.C.
Montreal, QU, Canada....................Business Law, Commercial Law

LENOX, SOCEY, WILGUS, FORMIDONI & CASEY
Trenton, NJ....................Civil Trial Practice, Insurance Defense Law, Medical Malpractice Law

LENTZ, CANTOR, KILGORE & MASSEY, LTD.
Frazer, PA....................General Practice

LEON, JACK PAUL
San Antonio, TX....................Civil Trial Practice, Criminal Trial Practice

LEONARD FELKER ALTFELD & BATTAILE, P.C.
Tucson, AZ....................Banking Law, Bankruptcy Law, Civil Trial Practice, Real Estate Law

LEONARD & LYDE
Chico, CA....................General Practice
Oroville, CA....................General Practice

LEONARD & MORRISON
Fort Lauderdale, FL....................General Practice

LEONARD, RALSTON, STANTON & DANKS
Washington, DC....................Bankruptcy Law, Civil Trial Practice

LEONARD, STREET AND DEINARD, PROFESSIONAL ASSOCIATION
Minneapolis, MN....................General Practice, Labor and Employment Law, Municipal Bond/Public Authority Financing Law, Natural Resources Law, Tax Law

LEOPOLD, PETRICH & SMITH, A PROFESSIONAL CORPORATION
Los Angeles, CA....................Civil Trial Practice, Patent, Trademark, Copyright and Unfair Competition Law

LEPLEY, PATRICK H.
Bellevue, WA....................Personal Injury Law

LERNER, DAVID, LITTENBERG, KRUMHOLZ & MENTLIK
Westfield, NJ....................Patent, Trademark, Copyright and Unfair Competition Law

LERNER, SAMPSON & ROTHFUSS, A LEGAL PROFESSIONAL ASSOCIATION
Cincinnati, OH....................Bankruptcy Law, Commercial Law, Real Estate Law

LESESNE & CONNETTE
Charlotte, NC....................Labor and Employment Law

LESH, CASNER & MILLER, A LEGAL PROFESSIONAL ASSOCIATION
Canton, OH....................Civil Trial Practice, General Practice, Insurance Defense Law, Real Estate Law

LESHER & WILLIAMS, A PROFESSIONAL CORPORATION
Tucson, AZ....................General Practice

LESLIE & SMITH, P.C.
El Paso, TX....................Bankruptcy Law

LESS, GETZ & LIPMAN
Memphis, TN....................Construction Law

LESSER & KAPLIN, PROFESSIONAL CORPORATION
Blue Bell, PA....................Banking Law, Bankruptcy Law, Civil Trial Practice, Commercial Law, Real Estate Law

LEV, SPALTER & BERLIN, P.C.
Norwalk, CT....................Real Estate Law, Securities Law

LEVANDER, GILLEN & MILLER, P.A.
South St. Paul, MN....................General Practice

LEVEEN, BARRY G.
Westwood, NJ....................Business Law, International Business Law

LEVENE & EISENBERG, A PROFESSIONAL CORPORATION
Los Angeles, CA....................Bankruptcy Law

LEVENFELD, EISENBERG, JANGER, GLASSBERG, SAMOTNY & HALPER
Chicago, IL....................Banking Law, Real Estate Law

LEVENS, WILLIAM P.
Tampa, FL....................Personal Injury Law

LEVENTHAL AND BOGUE, P.C.
Denver, CO....................Civil Trial Practice, General Practice

LEVENTHAL SLADE & KRANTZ
New York, NY....................Civil Trial Practice, Criminal Trial Practice

LEVETT, ROCKWOOD & SANDERS, PROFESSIONAL CORPORATION
Westport, CT....................Appellate Practice, Business Law, General Practice

LEVIN, MARK
Roseland, NJ....................Probate and Estate Planning Law, Tax Law

LEVIN & D'AGOSTINO
Hartford, CT....................General Practice, Real Estate Law

LEVIN, FISHBEIN, SEDRAN & BERMAN
Philadelphia, PA....................Admiralty/Maritime Law, Antitrust Law, Civil Trial Practice, Environmental Law, Medical Malpractice Law, Product Liability Law, Securities Law

LEVIN & FULP
Beaufort, SC .... General Practice

LEVINE & ASSOCIATES
Los Angeles, CA .... Business Law

LEVINE, HIRSCH, SEGALL & NORTHCUTT, P.A.
Tampa, FL .... Civil Trial Practice, Personal Injury Law

LEVINE, SAMUEL JAY, P.C.
Arlington, VA .... Immigration and Naturalization Law

LEVINE, STALLER, SKLAR, CHAN & BRODSKY, P.A.
Atlantic City, NJ .... Commercial Law, Probate and Estate Planning Law, Real Estate Law, Tax Law

LEVINGSTON & LEVINGSTON
Cleveland, MS .... General Practice

LEVIT & MANN
Richmond, VA .... Civil Trial Practice, Criminal Trial Practice, Labor and Employment Law, Personal Injury Law

LEVITAN & FRIELAND, P.C.
Newark, NJ .... General Practice

LEVY, HERBERT MONTE
New York, NY .... Appellate Practice

LEVY, EHRLICH & KRONENBERG, A PROFESSIONAL CORPORATION
Newark, NJ .... General Practice, Probate and Estate Planning Law, Tax Law

LEVY, JAMES L., A PROFESSIONAL CORPORATION
St. Albans, VT .... General Practice

LEVY & PREATE
Scranton, PA .... Commercial Law, General Practice, Real Estate Law

LEVY, ROBERT S., P.A.
West Palm Beach, FL .... General Practice

LEWALLEN, JO BETSY LAW OFFICES OF
Austin, TX .... Family Law

LEWIS, JOHN B.
Sacramento, CA .... Civil Trial Practice

LEWIS & BACON, A PROFESSIONAL CORPORATION
Sacramento, CA .... Insurance Defense Law

LEWIS, BERGER & FERRARO
Stuart, FL .... Criminal Trial Practice, Family Law, Personal Injury Law

LEWIS & KAPPES, PROFESSIONAL CORPORATION
Indianapolis, IN .... General Practice

LEWIS, KING, KRIEG & WALDROP, P.C.
Knoxville, TN .... Civil Trial Practice, General Practice
Nashville, TN .... Civil Trial Practice, General Practice

LEWIS AND LEWIS
Terre Haute, IN .... Civil Trial Practice, General Practice

LEWIS & MCKENNA
Saddle River, NJ .... Civil Trial Practice, Commercial Law, Insurance Defense Law

LEWIS, PRESTON & EASTON
Elizabethtown, KY .... General Practice

LEWIS, RICE & FINGERSH
St. Louis, MO .... Admiralty/Maritime Law, Antitrust Law, Civil Trial Practice, General Practice, Labor and Employment Law, Municipal Bond/Public Authority Financing Law, Tax Law

LEWIS AND ROCA
Phoenix, AZ .... Antitrust Law, Banking Law, Bankruptcy Law, Business Law, Civil Trial Practice, Commercial Law, Criminal Trial Practice, Environmental Law, General Practice, Health Care Law, Labor and Employment Law, Real Estate Law, Securities Law, Tax Law, Trademark, Copyright and Unfair Competition Law
Tucson, AZ .... Real Estate Law

LEWIS & ROGERS
Plattsburgh, NY .... General Practice

LEWIS, SKAGGS & REYNA, L.L.P.
McAllen, TX .... Civil Trial Practice, General Practice, Insurance Defense Law

LEWIS, TAYLOR & TODD, P.C.
La Grange, GA .... General Practice

LEWIS & TRATTNER
Washington, DC .... Trademark, Copyright and Unfair Competition Law

LEWIS, TRICHILO, BANCROFT, MCGAVIN & HORVATH, P.C.
Fairfax, VA .... Civil Trial Practice, Insurance Defense Law

LEWIS & WAGNER
Indianapolis, IN .... Civil Trial Practice, Insurance Defense Law, Product Liability Law

LEWIS, WHITE & CLAY, A PROFESSIONAL CORPORATION
Washington, DC .... Environmental Law, Municipal Bond/Public Authority Financing Law, Securities Law
Detroit, MI .... Civil Trial Practice, Environmental Law, Health Care Law, Municipal Bond/Public Authority Financing Law, Real Estate Law, Securities Law

LEYDIG, VOIT & MAYER, LTD.
Chicago, IL .... Patent, Trademark, Copyright and Unfair Competition Law
Rockford, IL .... Patent, Trademark, Copyright and Unfair Competition Law

LIBERT, VICTOR E. LAW OFFICE OF
Simsbury, CT .... Patent, Trademark, Copyright and Unfair Competition Law

LICATA, ARTHUR F., P.C.
Boston, MA .... General Practice

LICCARDO, ROSSI, STURGES & MCNEIL, A PROFESSIONAL LAW CORPORATION
San Jose, CA .... Personal Injury Law, Probate and Estate Planning Law, Real Estate Law

LICHT & SEMONOFF
Providence, RI .... Civil Trial Practice, General Practice, Tax Law

LICHTENAUER, ROBERT A.
Indianapolis, IN .... Probate and Estate Planning Law, Tax Law

LIDDLE, ROBINSON & SHOEMAKER
New York, NY .... Civil Trial Practice, Family Law, Labor and Employment Law

LIDDY SULLIVAN GALWAY & BEGLER, P.C.
New York, NY .... Patent, Trademark, Copyright and Unfair Competition Law

LIEBERMAN, DODGE, SENDROW & GERDING, LTD.
Phoenix, AZ .... Civil Trial Practice, General Practice

LIEBERTHAL, DAVID H.
Tucson, AZ .... Family Law

LIEBMAN, EMMANUEL, CHARTERED, A PROF. CORP.
Cherry Hill, NJ .... Tax Law

LIEFF, CABRASER & HEIMANN
San Francisco, CA .... Antitrust Law, Environmental Law, Labor and Employment Law, Product Liability Law, Securities Law

LIGGIO & LUCKMAN
West Palm Beach, FL .... Admiralty/Maritime Law, Personal Injury Law

LIGHTCAP, ROBERT P.
Latrobe, PA .... Construction Law

LIGHTFOOT, FRANKLIN, WHITE & LUCAS
Birmingham, AL .... Antitrust Law, Civil Trial Practice, Environmental Law, Personal Injury Law, Securities Law

LILES, GAVIN & COSTANTINO
Jacksonville, FL .... Civil Trial Practice, Commercial Law, Medical Malpractice Law, Personal Injury Law

LILLEY, DANIEL G., P.A.
Portland, ME .... Criminal Trial Practice

LILLY & LILLY, P.C.
Kalamazoo, MI .... Civil Trial Practice, Employment Benefits Law, General Practice, Insurance Defense Law, Labor and Employment Law

LILLY & WISE
Jackson, MS .... Appellate Practice, Civil Trial Practice, International Business Law

LIMANDRI, CHARLES S.
San Diego, CA .... Civil Trial Practice

LIMBACH & LIMBACH
San Francisco, CA .... Patent, Trademark, Copyright and Unfair Competition Law

LINDABURY, MCCORMICK & ESTABROOK, A PROFESSIONAL CORPORATION
Westfield, NJ .... Civil Trial Practice, Commercial Law, Construction Law, General Practice, Health Care Law, Labor and Employment Law, Municipal Bond/Public Authority Financing Law, Real Estate Law, Tax Law

LINDHORST & DREIDAME CO., L.P.A.
Cincinnati, OH....................Civil Trial Practice, General Practice, Insurance Defense Law, Medical Malpractice Law

LINDLEY, LAZAR & SCALES, A PROFESSIONAL CORPORATION
San Diego, CA....................Banking Law, Bankruptcy Law, Business Law, Civil Trial Practice, Commercial Law, Construction Law, General Practice, Health Care Law, Probate and Estate Planning Law, Real Estate Law, Tax Law

LINDNER & MARSACK, S.C.
Milwaukee, WI....................Labor and Employment Law

LINDSAY, HART, NEIL & WEIGLER
Portland, OR....................Admiralty/Maritime Law, General Practice

LINDSEY AND SCHRIMSHER, P.A.
Charlotte, NC....................Bankruptcy Law, General Practice, Probate and Estate Planning Law

LINES, HINSON AND LINES
Quincy, FL....................General Practice

LING, JOE
Long Beach, CA....................Civil Trial Practice

LINOWES AND BLOCHER
Washington, DC....................General Practice
Silver Spring, MD....................General Practice

LINSEY, STRAIN & WORSFOLD, P.C.
Grand Rapids, MI....................Civil Trial Practice, Insurance Defense Law, Personal Injury Law

LINZER, LANG & DITSCH, P.C.
Phoenix, AZ....................Business Law, Civil Trial Practice, Real Estate Law

LIONEL SAWYER & COLLINS
Las Vegas, NV....................Bankruptcy Law, Civil Trial Practice, General Practice, Labor and Employment Law, Real Estate Law
Reno, NV....................General Practice

LIPE, GREEN, PASCHAL, TRUMP & BRAGG, A PROFESSIONAL CORPORATION
Tulsa, OK....................Bankruptcy Law, Civil Trial Practice, Commercial Law, General Practice, Personal Injury Law

LIPKIN, STANLEY G.
Denver, CO....................Family Law

LIPKIN, MARSHALL, BOHORAD & THORNBURG, A PROFESSIONAL CORPORATION
Pottsville, PA....................General Practice

LIPMAN, ANTONELLI, BATT, DUNLAP, WODLINGER & GILSON, A PROFESSIONAL CORPORATION
Vineland, NJ....................General Practice

LIPMAN & KATZ, P.A.
Augusta, ME....................Civil Trial Practice

LIPPMAN, MAHFOUZ & MARTIN
Morgan City, LA....................General Practice

LIPSCOMB, J. RANDOLPH
Columbus, MS....................Civil Trial Practice

LIPSHULTZ AND HONE, CHARTERED
Silver Spring, MD....................Environmental Law, General Practice, Insurance Defense Law

LIPSHUTZ, GREENBLATT & KING
Atlanta, GA....................Civil Trial Practice, General Practice

LIPSITZ, GREEN, FAHRINGER, ROLL, SALISBURY & CAMBRIA
Buffalo, NY....................Civil Trial Practice, General Practice, Labor and Employment Law

LISA & SOUSA, LTD.
Providence, RI....................Commercial Law, Probate and Estate Planning Law, Real Estate Law

LISLE LAW FIRM, P.C.
Springdale, AR....................Civil Trial Practice, Commercial Law

LISMAN & LISMAN, A PROFESSIONAL CORPORATION
Burlington, VT....................Administrative Law, Bankruptcy Law, General Practice, Medical Malpractice Law, Personal Injury Law, Probate and Estate Planning Law, Real Estate Law, Tax Law

LISSNER, KILLIAN, CUNNINGHAM AND BOYD
Brunswick, GA....................Personal Injury Law

LISTON/LANCASTER
Grenada, MS....................Civil Trial Practice, General Practice
Winona, MS....................Civil Trial Practice, General Practice

LITMAN, ASCHE, LUPKIN, GIOIELLA & BASSIN
New York, NY....................Civil Trial Practice, Criminal Trial Practice, Medical Malpractice Law, Personal Injury Law

LITMAN LAW OFFICES, LTD.
Arlington, VA....................Patent, Trademark, Copyright and Unfair Competition Law

LITMAN LITMAN HARRIS & BROWN, P.C.
Pittsburgh, PA....................Civil Trial Practice, Commercial Law, General Practice, Personal Injury Law

LITMAN, MCMAHON AND BROWN
Kansas City, MO....................Patent, Trademark, Copyright and Unfair Competition Law

LITTEN & SIPE
Harrisonburg, VA....................General Practice

LITTLEJOHN, TALMADGE D.
New Albany, MS....................Civil Trial Practice, Personal Injury Law, Real Estate Law

LITTLE, LITTLE, LITTLE, WINDEL & COPPEDGE
Madill, OK....................General Practice

LITWIN & HOLSINGER
Hackensack, NJ....................Civil Trial Practice, Probate and Estate Planning Law, Tax Law

LITZ, RONALD A. & ASSOCIATES
Los Angeles, CA....................Business Law, Civil Trial Practice, Family Law

LIVINGSTON & KALETA
Miami, FL....................General Practice, International Business Law

LIVINGSTON, PORTER & PAULK, P.C.
Scottsboro, AL....................Civil Trial Practice, General Practice, Insurance Defense Law

LIZZA, MULCAHY & CASEY, P.C.
Detroit, MI....................Civil Trial Practice

LLOYD, GOSSELINK, FOWLER, BLEVINS & MATHEWS, P.C.
Austin, TX....................Environmental Law

LLOYD & MCDANIEL
Louisville, KY....................Bankruptcy Law, Commercial Law

LLOYD, SCHREIBER & GRAY, P.C.
Birmingham, AL....................Insurance Defense Law

LLOYD & WEISSENBERGER
Cincinnati, OH....................Civil Trial Practice

LOBEL, WINTHROP & BROKER
Irvine, CA....................Bankruptcy Law, Commercial Law, General Practice

LOCKE PURNELL RAIN HARRELL, A PROFESSIONAL CORPORATION
Dallas, TX....................General Practice

LOCKE REYNOLDS BOYD & WEISELL
Indianapolis, IN....................Banking Law, Civil Trial Practice, Construction Law, General Practice, Health Care Law, Insurance Defense Law, Labor and Employment Law, Medical Malpractice Law, Patent, Trademark, Copyright and Unfair Competition Law, Personal Injury Law, Product Liability Law, Securities Law, Tax Law

LOCKYEAR & KORNBLUM
Evansville, IN....................Civil Trial Practice, Personal Injury Law

LODEN, ELLIOT H., ATTORNEY AT LAW, A LAW CORPORATION
Honolulu, HI....................Probate and Estate Planning Law

LODGE & HELLER
Carlsbad, CA....................Civil Trial Practice, Probate and Estate Planning Law

LOEB AND LOEB
Los Angeles, CA....................Antitrust Law, Appellate Practice, Banking Law, Bankruptcy Law, Civil Trial Practice, Environmental Law, General Practice, Labor and Employment Law, Probate and Estate Planning Law, Real Estate Law, Tax Law, Trademark, Copyright and Unfair Competition Law
New York, NY....................Antitrust Law, Appellate Practice, Banking Law, Civil Trial Practice, General Practice, Probate and Estate Planning Law, Real Estate Law, Tax Law, Trademark, Copyright and Unfair Competition Law
Rome, Italy....................General Practice

LOFTON, LIONEL S.
Charleston, SC....................Criminal Trial Practice

LOGAN, GARY
Las Vegas, NV....................Medical Malpractice Law, Personal Injury Law

LOGAN, JOHN W. JR. & ASSOCIATES
Willow Grove, PA....................Patent, Trademark, Copyright and Unfair Competition Law

LOGOTHETIS & PENCE
Dayton, OH....................Labor and Employment Law

LOHF, SHAIMAN & JACOBS, P.C.
Denver, CO .... Business Law, Natural Resources Law, Real Estate Law, Tax Law

LOMELL, MUCCIFORI, ADLER, RAVASCHIERE, AMABILE & PEHLIVANIAN, A PROFESSIONAL CORPORATION
Toms River, NJ .... Civil Trial Practice

LOMMEN, NELSON, COLE & STAGEBERG, P.A.
Minneapolis, MN .... Business Law, Civil Trial Practice, Insurance Defense Law, Real Estate Law

LONABAUGH AND RIGGS
Sheridan, WY .... Civil Trial Practice, Insurance Defense Law, Natural Resources Law

LONDON FISCHER
New York, NY .... Admiralty/Maritime Law, Appellate Practice, Civil Trial Practice, Construction Law, Insurance Defense Law, Product Liability Law

LONDON, YANCEY, ELLIOTT & BURGESS
Birmingham, AL .... Insurance Defense Law

LONG ALDRIDGE & NORMAN
Atlanta, GA .... Administrative Law, Banking Law, Bankruptcy Law, Business Law, Civil Trial Practice, Communications Law, Employment Benefits Law, Environmental Law, General Practice, Health Care Law, Immigration and Naturalization Law, Labor and Employment Law, Municipal Bond/Public Authority Financing Law, Probate and Estate Planning Law, Public Utilities Law, Real Estate Law, Securities Law, Tax Law

LONG, BURNER, PARKS & SEALY, A PROFESSIONAL CORPORATION
Austin, TX .... Civil Trial Practice, Insurance Defense Law, Personal Injury Law

LONG & JAUDON, P.C.
Denver, CO .... Civil Trial Practice, General Practice, Insurance Defense Law, Labor and Employment Law, Medical Malpractice Law

LONG & LEVIT
San Francisco, CA .... General Practice

LONG & LONG
Chapel Hill, NC .... Civil Trial Practice, Criminal Trial Practice, Family Law, Personal Injury Law

LONG, PARKER & PAYNE, P.A.
Asheville, NC .... Civil Trial Practice, Criminal Trial Practice

LONG, WEINBERG, ANSLEY AND WHEELER
Atlanta, GA .... Civil Trial Practice, General Practice

LOOMIS, EWERT, EDERER, PARSLEY, DAVIS & GOTTING, P.C.
Lansing, MI .... General Practice

LOONEY & GROSSMAN
Boston, MA .... General Practice

LOONEY, NICHOLS, JOHNSON & HAYES
Oklahoma City, OK .... Civil Trial Practice, General Practice

LOPATIN, MILLER, FREEDMAN, BLUESTONE, HERSKOVIC & HEILMANN, A PROFESSIONAL CORPORATION
Detroit, MI .... Civil Trial Practice, General Practice, Medical Malpractice Law, Personal Injury Law

LOPEZ, DAVID T. & ASSOCIATES
Houston, TX .... Labor and Employment Law

LORAINE, THOMAS E., P.C.
Lake Ozark, MO .... Construction Law, Environmental Law, Personal Injury Law, Product Liability Law, Real Estate Law

LORANCE & THOMPSON, A PROFESSIONAL CORPORATION
Houston, TX .... Civil Trial Practice, Insurance Defense Law, Medical Malpractice Law, Personal Injury Law, Product Liability Law, Real Estate Law

LORD, BISSELL & BROOK
Los Angeles, CA .... General Practice
Atlanta, GA .... General Practice
Chicago, IL .... General Practice
Rockford, IL .... General Practice

LORENZO & KULAKOWSKI, P.C.
Punxsutawney, PA .... Civil Trial Practice, Personal Injury Law

LORUSSO & LOUD
Portsmouth, NH .... Patent, Trademark, Copyright and Unfair Competition Law

LOSEY & ASSOCIATES
San Francisco, CA .... Tax Law

LOSKAMP, ALVIN N., A LAW CORPORATION
Burbank, CA .... Business Law, Probate and Estate Planning Law

LOTT, FRANKLIN, FONDA & FLANAGAN
Greenwood, MS .... General Practice

LOUIS & FROELICH, A LEGAL PROFESSIONAL ASSOCIATION
Dayton, OH .... Business Law, General Practice, Immigration and Naturalization Law, Probate and Estate Planning Law, Real Estate Law

LOVE, THORNTON, ARNOLD & THOMASON, P.A.
Greenville, SC .... Civil Trial Practice, Criminal Trial Practice, General Practice, Insurance Defense Law, Medical Malpractice Law

LOVELESS, BANKS & LYONS
Mobile, AL .... Civil Trial Practice, General Practice

LOVETT & LAMAR
Owensboro, KY .... Bankruptcy Law, Civil Trial Practice, Commercial Law, General Practice, Labor and Employment Law, Real Estate Law

LOVETT & SMITH, LTD.
Minneapolis, MN .... Bankruptcy Law, General Practice, Probate and Estate Planning Law

LOVITT & HANNAN, INC.
San Francisco, CA .... Civil Trial Practice

LOWE, STEIN, HOFFMAN, ALLWEISS & HAUVER, L.L.P.
New Orleans, LA .... General Practice

LOWEN & ABUT, P.A.
Fort Lee, NJ .... General Practice

LOWENHAUPT & CHASNOFF, L.L.C.
St. Louis, MO .... General Practice, Tax Law

LOWENSTEIN, SANDLER, KOHL, FISHER & BOYLAN, A PROFESSIONAL CORPORATION
Newark, NJ .... General Practice
Roseland, NJ .... Banking Law, Civil Trial Practice, Criminal Trial Practice, Environmental Law, General Practice, Tax Law
Somerville, NJ .... Civil Trial Practice, General Practice

LOWERY AND LOWERY, P.C.
Denver, CO .... Civil Trial Practice, Criminal Trial Practice, General Practice

LOWRY, CLEMENTS & POWELL, P.C.
Scottsdale, AZ .... Probate and Estate Planning Law

LOWRY & JOHNSON
Valley Falls, KS .... General Practice

LOWTHORP, RICHARDS, MCMILLAN, MILLER, CONWAY & TEMPLEMAN, A PROFESSIONAL CORPORATION
Oxnard, CA .... General Practice

LUBIN, STANLEY LAW OFFICE OF
Phoenix, AZ .... Labor and Employment Law

LUBIN AND GANO, P.A.
West Palm Beach, FL .... Criminal Trial Practice

LUCAS, KATHLEEN M.
San Francisco, CA .... Civil Trial Practice, Labor and Employment Law

LUCAS BOWKER & WHITE
Edmonton, AB, Canada .... Banking Law, Civil Trial Practice, Commercial Law, Environmental Law, General Practice, Labor and Employment Law, Medical Malpractice Law, Probate and Estate Planning Law

LUCAS, HOLCOMB & MEDREA
Merrillville, IN .... General Practice

LUCAS & MONAGHAN, P.C.
Miles City, MT .... General Practice

LUCCO BROWN & MUDGE
Edwardsville, IL .... Civil Trial Practice

LUCE, FORWARD, HAMILTON & SCRIPPS
La Jolla, CA .... General Practice
San Diego, CA .... Banking Law, Bankruptcy Law, Business Law, Environmental Law, Family Law, General Practice, Labor and Employment Law, Real Estate Law

LUCERO, LESTER & SIGMOND
Alamosa, CO .... Civil Trial Practice, General Practice

LUCHSINGER, JOHN A.
Media, PA .... Medical Malpractice Law

LUCKETT LAW FIRM, A PROFESSIONAL ASSOCIATION
Clarksdale, MS .... General Practice, Insurance Defense Law

LUDENS, POTTER & BURCH
Morrison, IL .... General Practice

LUDLUM & LUDLUM
Austin, TX ....Civil Trial Practice, Insurance Defense Law, Medical Malpractice Law, Personal Injury Law

LUDWIG GOLDBERG & KRENZEL, A PROFESSIONAL CORPORATION
San Francisco, CA ....Employment Benefits Law

LUDWIGSON, THOMPSON, HAYES & BELL
Bellingham, WA ....General Practice

LUEDEKA, NEELY & GRAHAM, P.C.
Knoxville, TN ....Patent, Trademark, Copyright and Unfair Competition Law

LUEDERS, ROBERTSON & KONZEN
Granite City, IL ....General Practice

LUNDEEN, DAVID F.
Fergus Falls, MN ....General Practice

LUNDIN, JOHN W., P.S.
Seattle, WA ....Civil Trial Practice, Criminal Trial Practice

LUND LAW FIRM, CHARTERED, A PROFESSIONAL CORPORATION
Oberlin, KS ....General Practice

LUNDY, DAVID A.
Fort Wayne, IN ....Patent, Trademark, Copyright and Unfair Competition Law
Indianapolis, IN ....Patent, Trademark, Copyright and Unfair Competition Law

LUNDY & DAVIS, L.L.P.
Lake Charles, LA ....Admiralty/Maritime Law, Commercial Law

LUPER, WOLINETZ, SHERIFF & NEIDENTHAL, A LEGAL PROFESSIONAL ASSOCIATION
Columbus, OH ....Bankruptcy Law, Family Law

LUPO, KOCZKUR & PETRELLA, P.C.
Detroit, MI ....Insurance Defense Law, Product Liability Law

LURVEY & SHAPIRO
Los Angeles, CA ....Family Law

LUSK & LUSK
Guntersville, AL ....General Practice, Insurance Defense Law

LUSTBADER, PHILIP M., & DAVID LUSTBADER, A PROFESSIONAL CORPORATION
Livingston, NJ ....Civil Trial Practice, Insurance Defense Law, Medical Malpractice Law, Personal Injury Law

LUTHER, ANDERSON, CLEARY & RUTH, P.C.
Chattanooga, TN ....Insurance Defense Law

LUTZ, SHAFRANSKI, GORMAN AND MAHONEY, P.A.
New Brunswick, NJ ....Civil Trial Practice, Personal Injury Law

LUVAAS, COBB, RICHARDS & FRASER, P.C.
Eugene, OR ....General Practice, Insurance Defense Law

LUXAN & MURFITT
Helena, MT ....General Practice

LUXENBERG, GARBETT & KELLY, P.C.
New Castle, PA ....Insurance Defense Law

LYLES, HAMMETT, DARR AND CLARK
Spartanburg, SC ....General Practice

LYMAN, RICHARD W. JR.
Manhattan Beach, CA ....General Practice, Real Estate Law

LYNBERG & WATKINS, A PROFESSIONAL CORPORATION
Los Angeles, CA ....Civil Trial Practice

LYNCH, CHAPPELL & ALSUP, A PROFESSIONAL CORPORATION
Midland, TX ....General Practice, Natural Resources Law, Tax Law

LYNCH, DALLAS, SMITH & HARMAN, P.C.
Cedar Rapids, IA ....Civil Trial Practice, General Practice

LYNCH, GALLAGHER, LYNCH & MARTINEAU
Mount Pleasant, MI ....General Practice, Natural Resources Law

LYNCH, LYNCH & LYNCH
Winchester, TN ....General Practice

LYNCH, MANN, SMITH & MANN
Beckley, WV ....Civil Trial Practice, General Practice, Insurance Defense Law

LYNCH, TRAUB, KEEFE AND ERRANTE, A PROFESSIONAL CORPORATION
New Haven, CT ....General Practice, Labor and Employment Law, Medical Malpractice Law, Transportation Law

LYNN, JACKSON, SHULTZ & LEBRUN, P.C.
Rapid City, SD ....Civil Trial Practice, Criminal Trial Practice, Employment Benefits Law, General Practice

LYON, LYMAN R.
Troy, MI ....Patent, Trademark, Copyright and Unfair Competition Law

LYON, SCULLY & FITZPATRICK
Holyoke, MA ....General Practice

LYON, WEIGAND, SUKO & GUSTAFSON, P.S.
Yakima, WA ....General Practice

LYONS & BEAUDRY, P.A.
Sarasota, FL ....Probate and Estate Planning Law, Real Estate Law

LYONS, BRANDT, COOK & HIRAMATSU
Honolulu, HI ....General Practice

LYONS, PIPES & COOK, P.C.
Mobile, AL ....Admiralty/Maritime Law, Appellate Practice, Banking Law, Bankruptcy Law, Civil Trial Practice, Commercial Law, Environmental Law, General Practice, Labor and Employment Law, Municipal Bond/Public Authority Financing Law, Natural Resources Law, Probate and Estate Planning Law, Product Liability Law, Real Estate Law, Tax Law

LYTAL & REITER
West Palm Beach, FL ....Medical Malpractice Law, Personal Injury Law, Product Liability Law

LYTLE, THOMAS F.
Sacramento, CA ....Personal Injury Law

LYTLE SOULÉ & CURLEE
Oklahoma City, OK ....Civil Trial Practice, General Practice

MACARONIS LAW FIRM
Lowell, MA ....Personal Injury Law

MACCARTHY, POJANI & HURLEY
Worcester, MA ....Banking Law, Civil Trial Practice, General Practice, Insurance Defense Law

MACCARTNEY, MACCARTNEY, KERRIGAN & MACCARTNEY
Nyack, NY ....General Practice, Personal Injury Law

MACDONALD, FITZGERALD, MACDONALD & SIMON, P.C.
Flint, MI ....General Practice, Personal Injury Law, Product Liability Law

MACDONALD AND GOREN, P.C.
Birmingham, MI ....Business Law, Civil Trial Practice, Employment Benefits Law, Probate and Estate Planning Law, Real Estate Law, Tax Law

MACDONALD, ILLIG, JONES & BRITTON
Erie, PA ....General Practice

MACELREE, HARVEY, GALLAGHER, FEATHERMAN & SEBASTIAN, LTD.
Kennett Square, PA ....General Practice
West Chester, PA ....Banking Law, Civil Trial Practice, General Practice, Personal Injury Law

MACERA & JARZYNA
Ottawa, ON, Canada ....Patent, Trademark, Copyright and Unfair Competition Law

MACEY, WILENSKY, COHEN, WITTNER & KESSLER
Atlanta, GA ....Bankruptcy Law, Civil Trial Practice, General Practice, Real Estate Law

MACFARLANE AUSLEY FERGUSON & MCMULLEN
Clearwater, FL ....General Practice
Tallahassee, FL ....General Practice
Tampa, FL ....General Practice

MACGOWAN, EUGENIA
San Francisco, CA ....Family Law

MACIE, JAMES J.
Atlanta, GA ....Family Law
Jonesboro, GA ....Family Law

MACKENZIE GERVAIS, S.E.N.C.
Montreal, QU, Canada ....General Practice

MACKENZIE & PEDEN, P.S.C.
Louisville, KY ....General Practice

MACKEY & WILLS, P.A.
Little Rock, AR ....Banking Law

MACKIN, RALPH R.
Purdys, NY ....General Practice

MACKOFF, KELLOGG, KIRBY & KLOSTER, P.C.
Dickinson, ND ....General Practice

MAC LACHLAN, BURFORD & ARIAS, A LAW CORPORATION
San Bernardino, CA ....Civil Trial Practice, Construction Law, General Practice, Insurance Defense Law, Personal Injury Law, Product Liability Law

MACLEAN & JACQUES, LTD.
Phoenix, AZ ....Commercial Law, Family Law, Real Estate Law

MACMILLAN & STANLEY
Delray Beach, FL....................Probate and Estate Planning Law

MACPHERSON LESLIE & TYERMAN
Regina, SK, Canada....................Business Law, Commercial Law, Construction Law, Environmental Law, General Practice, Immigration and Naturalization Law, Natural Resources Law, Securities Law

MACVEAN, LEWIS, SHERWIN & MCDERMOTT, P.C.
Middletown, NY....................Banking Law, Civil Trial Practice, General Practice, Real Estate Law

MADDALONE, JOSEPH R. JR.
Hempstead, NY....................Civil Trial Practice, Criminal Trial Practice

MADDEN, JONES & COLE, A PROFESSIONAL CORPORATION
Long Beach, CA....................Business Law, Civil Trial Practice, Construction Law, General Practice

MADDEN, MADDEN AND DEL DUCA, P.A.
Haddonfield, NJ....................General Practice

MADDIN, HAUSER, WARTELL, ROTH, HELLER & PESSES, P.C.
Southfield, MI....................Business Law, Probate and Estate Planning Law, Real Estate Law, Tax Law

MADDOX LAW FIRM, PROFESSIONAL CORPORATION
Hobbs, NM....................General Practice

MADDOX, STARNES & NIX
Conyers, GA....................General Practice

MADEWELL & JARED
Cookeville, TN....................Civil Trial Practice, General Practice, Insurance Defense Law

MADIGAN & SCOTT, INC.
Springfield, VA....................Business Law, Civil Trial Practice, Real Estate Law

MAEDER, JEROME A., LAW OFFICES, S.C.
Wausau, WI....................Medical Malpractice Law, Personal Injury Law

MAGEE, E. FREMONT, P.A.
Baltimore, MD....................Civil Trial Practice, Employment Benefits Law, Labor and Employment Law

MAGEE, PAGANO & ISHERWOOD
Wall Township, NJ....................General Practice

MAGER LIEBENBERG & WHITE
Philadelphia, PA....................Antitrust Law, Appellate Practice, Commercial Law, Labor and Employment Law, Securities Law

MAGER, MERCER, SCOTT & ALBER, P.C.
Detroit, MI....................Banking Law, Civil Trial Practice, Commercial Law, Construction Law, Insurance Defense Law, Real Estate Law

MAGGIO & KATTAR
Washington, DC....................Immigration and Naturalization Law

MAGRUDER & ASSOCIATES, P.C.
McLean, VA....................General Practice

MAGUIRE, SAMUEL F.
Augusta, GA....................Civil Trial Practice

MAGUIRE, VOORHIS & WELLS, P.A.
Orlando, FL....................Immigration and Naturalization Law, Patent, Trademark, Copyright and Unfair Competition Law

MAHASSNI, HASSAN, LAW OFFICE OF
Jeddah, Saudi Arabia....................General Practice

MAHER, GIBSON AND GUILEY, A PROF. ASSN. OF LAWYERS
Orlando, FL....................Medical Malpractice Law, Personal Injury Law, Product Liability Law

MAHL TULLY, A PROFESSIONAL CORPORATION
San Jose, CA....................Construction Law, Environmental Law

MAHONEY, DOUGHERTY AND MAHONEY, PROFESSIONAL ASSOCIATION
Minneapolis, MN....................Civil Trial Practice, Insurance Defense Law

MAIDER & SMITH
Gloversville, NY....................Administrative Law, General Practice

MAKOUL, RICHARD J.
Allentown, PA....................Civil Trial Practice, Criminal Trial Practice, Personal Injury Law

MALIN, HALEY, DIMAGGIO AND CROSBY, P.A.
Fort Lauderdale, FL....................Patent, Trademark, Copyright and Unfair Competition Law
Miami, FL....................Patent, Trademark, Copyright and Unfair Competition Law
West Palm Beach, FL....................Patent, Trademark, Copyright and Unfair Competition Law

MALLINCKRODT & MALLINCKRODT
Salt Lake City, UT....................Patent, Trademark, Copyright and Unfair Competition Law

MALLOY, JOHN CYRIL
Miami, FL....................General Practice, Patent, Trademark, Copyright and Unfair Competition Law, Trademark, Copyright and Unfair Competition Law

MALNICK, DAVID, A PROFESSIONAL CORPORATION
San Jose, CA....................Personal Injury Law

MALONE, THOMAS WILLIAM
Atlanta, GA....................Personal Injury Law

MALONEY, GALLUP, ROACH, BROWN & MCCARTHY, P.C.
Buffalo, NY....................Civil Trial Practice, General Practice

MALONEY, GERRA, MEHLMAN & KATZ
New York, NY....................Business Law, Securities Law, Tax Law

MALONEY & MALONEY
Aberdeen, SD....................Construction Law, Employment Benefits Law, Labor and Employment Law

MALONEY & MULLEN, A PROFESSIONAL CORPORATION
Santa Monica, CA....................Civil Trial Practice, General Practice

MALOON, MALOON & BARCLAY CO., L.P.A.
Columbus, OH....................Medical Malpractice Law

MALOVOS & KONEVICH
Los Altos, CA....................Business Law, Family Law, Probate and Estate Planning Law, Real Estate Law

MALOY & JENKINS
Atlanta, GA....................Criminal Trial Practice

MANAHAN & BLUTH, LAW OFFICE, CHARTERED
Mankato, MN....................Criminal Trial Practice, Family Law

MANCHESTER, BENNETT, POWERS & ULLMAN, A LEGAL PROFESSIONAL ASSOCIATION
Youngstown, OH....................General Practice

MANCHESTER LAW OFFICES, PROFESSIONAL CORPORATION
Burlington, VT....................Civil Trial Practice, Commercial Law, Environmental Law, General Practice, Medical Malpractice Law, Natural Resources Law, Personal Injury Law

MANCHESTER & PIGNATO, P.C.
Oklahoma City, OK....................Construction Law, Environmental Law, Insurance Defense Law

MANCHESTER & WILLIAMS
San Jose, CA....................Criminal Trial Practice

MANCKE, WAGNER, HERSHEY AND TULLY
Harrisburg, PA....................Civil Trial Practice, Criminal Trial Practice, Family Law, General Practice, Personal Injury Law, Transportation Law

MANDEL, LIPTON AND STEVENSON LIMITED
Chicago, IL....................Civil Trial Practice, Family Law, General Practice, Immigration and Naturalization Law

MANDELL, LEWIS & GOLDBERG, A PROFESSIONAL CORPORATION
McLean, VA....................Communications Law, Labor and Employment Law, Securities Law

MANDELSTAMM, JEROME R.
St. Louis, MO....................Business Law, Probate and Estate Planning Law, Real Estate Law

MANESS, MICHAEL A.
Houston, TX....................General Practice

MANEY, DAMSKER, HARRIS & JONES, P.A.
Tampa, FL....................Appellate Practice, Civil Trial Practice, Criminal Trial Practice, Family Law, Tax Law

MANG, RETT & MINNICK, P.A.
Tallahassee, FL....................Insurance Defense Law, Labor and Employment Law

MANGAN, DALTON, TRENKLE, REBEIN & DOLL, CHARTERED
Dodge City, KS....................General Practice

MANGHAM, DAVIS AND OGLESBEE
Lafayette, LA....................Administrative Law, Admiralty/Maritime Law, Appellate Practice, Civil Trial Practice, Environmental Law, General Practice, Insurance Defense Law, Natural Resources Law, Real Estate Law

MANGUM, WALL, STOOPS & WARDEN, P.L.L.C.
Flagstaff, AZ....................Civil Trial Practice, General Practice, Insurance Defense Law, Personal Injury Law, Probate and Estate Planning Law

MANIER, HEROD, HOLLABAUGH & SMITH, A PROFESSIONAL CORPORATION
Nashville, TN..........Bankruptcy Law, Business Law, Commercial Law, Environmental Law, General Practice, Insurance Defense Law, Medical Malpractice Law, Probate and Estate Planning Law, Product Liability Law, Real Estate Law, Tax Law

MANKO, GOLD & KATCHER
Bala Cynwyd, PA..........Environmental Law

MANN, HENRY B.
Louisville, KY..........Probate and Estate Planning Law, Real Estate Law

MANN & MITCHELL
Providence, RI..........Criminal Trial Practice

MANN, TREVINO, HALE & GALLEGO
Laredo, TX..........General Practice

MANN, UNGAR & SPECTOR, P.A.
Philadelphia, PA..........Commercial Law, Securities Law

MANN, WALTER, BURKART, WEATHERS & WALTER, L.C.
Springfield, MO..........General Practice

MANNING, J. RICHARD
Seattle, WA..........Business Law, Construction Law

MANNING, FULTON & SKINNER, P.A.
Raleigh, NC..........Civil Trial Practice, General Practice

MANNING, KINKEAD, BROOKS & BRADBURY, A PROFESSIONAL CORPORATION
Norristown, PA..........Bankruptcy Law, Business Law, Civil Trial Practice, Family Law, General Practice, Insurance Defense Law, Personal Injury Law, Probate and Estate Planning Law, Real Estate Law

MANNINO GRIFFITH, P.C.
Philadelphia, PA..........Banking Law, Civil Trial Practice

MANOS, MARTIN, PERGRAM & BROWNING
Delaware, OH..........General Practice

MANSFIELD & TANICK, P.A.
Minneapolis, MN..........Bankruptcy Law, Civil Trial Practice, Labor and Employment Law, Probate and Estate Planning Law

MANTA AND WELGE
Philadelphia, PA..........Civil Trial Practice, Environmental Law, Insurance Defense Law, Product Liability Law

MANTOOTH, JOHN
Purcell, OK..........Civil Trial Practice, General Practice

MANWEILER, BEVIS & CAMERON, P.A.
Boise, ID..........General Practice

MANWELL & MILTON
San Francisco, CA..........Business Law, Securities Law

MAPOTHER & MAPOTHER
Louisville, KY..........Banking Law, Bankruptcy Law, Real Estate Law

MAPP, HARRY L. JR.
Halifax, VA..........Civil Trial Practice, General Practice

MARCH, HURWITZ, DEMARCO & MITCHELL
Media, PA..........Civil Trial Practice

MARCH & MYATT, P.C.
Fort Collins, CO..........General Practice

MARCO, MARCO & BAILEY
Medina, OH..........General Practice

MARCUM & TRIPLETT
Lowmansville, KY..........General Practice, Personal Injury Law

MARCUS, LYN H.
Los Angeles, CA..........International Business Law

MARCUS & SHAPIRA
Pittsburgh, PA..........Antitrust Law, Bankruptcy Law, Civil Trial Practice, Commercial Law, Family Law, General Practice, Insurance Defense Law, Labor and Employment Law, Personal Injury Law, Probate and Estate Planning Law, Real Estate Law, Securities Law, Tax Law

MARGER, JOHNSON, MCCOLLOM & STOLOWITZ, P.C.
Portland, OR..........Patent, Trademark, Copyright and Unfair Competition Law

MARGOLIN, EPHRAIM LAW OFFICES OF
San Francisco, CA..........Appellate Practice, Criminal Trial Practice

MARGOLIS & CASSIDY
Milwaukee, WI..........Family Law

MARGOLIS, EDELSTEIN & SCHERLIS
Philadelphia, PA..........Civil Trial Practice, Environmental Law, Insurance Defense Law

MARGOLIS, GEORGE & PORT
Uniontown, PA..........General Practice

MARING LAW OFFICE, P.C.
Fargo, ND..........Personal Injury Law

MARINO & DALLINGER
Encino, CA..........Business Law, Civil Trial Practice, Probate and Estate Planning Law, Real Estate Law

MARISCAL, WEEKS, MCINTYRE & FRIEDLANDER, P.A.
Phoenix, AZ..........Bankruptcy Law, Family Law, General Practice

MARKEL, SCHAFER, P.C.
Pittsburgh, PA..........Civil Trial Practice, Commercial Law, Real Estate Law

MARKOW, WALKER, REEVES & ANDERSON, P.A.
Jackson, MS..........Environmental Law, Insurance Defense Law, Medical Malpractice Law

MARK & PEARLSTEIN, P.A.
Phoenix, AZ..........Family Law, Insurance Defense Law, Medical Malpractice Law, Personal Injury Law

MARKS & BROOKLIER
Beverly Hills, CA..........Criminal Trial Practice

MARKS, GRAY, CONROY & GIBBS, P.A.
Jacksonville, FL..........General Practice

MARKS & MADSEN
Sioux City, IA..........General Practice

MARKS & MURASE
Los Angeles, CA..........General Practice
Washington, DC..........General Practice
New York, NY..........General Practice

MARKS, O'NEILL, REILLY & O'BRIEN, P.C.
Philadelphia, PA..........Environmental Law, Insurance Defense Law

MARKS, SHELL, MANESS & MARKS
Clarksville, TN..........General Practice

MARKSON, ALDAN O.
Kenilworth, NJ..........General Practice, Real Estate Law

MARONEY, CROWLEY & BANKSTON, L.L.P.
Austin, TX..........Civil Trial Practice

MARRINER & CRUMRINE
Washington, PA..........General Practice

MARROLETTI, ALFRED AND ASSOCIATES
Philadelphia, PA..........Civil Trial Practice, Family Law, General Practice, Personal Injury Law

MARS, RICHARD D., P.A.
Bartow, FL..........Criminal Trial Practice

MARSH, DAY & CALHOUN
Bridgeport, CT..........General Practice
Southport, CT..........General Practice

MARSH, SPAEDER, BAUR, SPAEDER & SCHAAF
Erie, PA..........General Practice, Insurance Defense Law, Tax Law

MARSHALL, THOMAS E. LAW OFFICES OF
Detroit, MI..........Labor and Employment Law

MARSHALL, DENNEHEY, WARNER, COLEMAN AND GOGGIN
Philadelphia, PA..........Civil Trial Practice, General Practice

MARSHALL AND GONZALEZ
Houston, TX..........Insurance Defense Law
McAllen, TX..........Insurance Defense Law

MARSHALL, WILLIAMS & GORHAM, L.L.P.
Wilmington, NC..........Admiralty/Maritime Law, Civil Trial Practice, General Practice

MARTIN, ADE, BIRCHFIELD & MICKLER, P.A.
Jacksonville, FL..........General Practice

MARTIN, BACON & MARTIN, P.C.
Mount Clemens, MI..........Medical Malpractice Law, Personal Injury Law, Product Liability Law

MARTIN, BROWN & SULLIVAN, LTD.
Chicago, IL..........Civil Trial Practice, Criminal Trial Practice, Tax Law

MARTIN, BROWNE, HULL & HARPER
Springfield, OH..........General Practice

MARTIN, CHAPMAN, SCHILD & LASSAW, CHARTERED
Boise, ID....General Practice, Probate and Estate Planning Law
Sun Valley, ID....Probate and Estate Planning Law

MARTIN, CHURCHILL, OVERMAN, HILL & COLE, CHARTERED
Wichita, KS....Labor and Employment Law

MARTIN, FIGURSKI & HARRILL
New Port Richey, FL....Administrative Law, Civil Trial Practice, Real Estate Law

MARTIN, GUNN & MARTIN, A PROFESSIONAL CORPORATION
Westmont, NJ....General Practice

MARTIN & HUDSON
Pasadena, CA....Probate and Estate Planning Law, Tax Law

MARTIN, INGLES & INGLES, LTD.
Gloucester, VA....General Practice

MARTIN, JOHN F., A PROF. CORP., LAW OFFICES OF
Walnut Creek, CA....Business Law

MARTIN, JOHN O., P.C.
Denver, CO....Civil Trial Practice

MARTIN LAW OFFICE
Oklahoma City, OK....Criminal Trial Practice

MARTIN, LUTZ & BROWER, P.C.
Las Cruces, NM....General Practice

MARTIN, MAGNUSON, MCCARTHY & KENNEY
Boston, MA....General Practice, Insurance Defense Law

MARTIN & MARTIN, P.A.
Lakeland, FL....General Practice

MARTIN, MATTOON, MATZKE & MATTOON
Sidney, NE....General Practice

MARTIN, OCKERMAN & BRABANT
Lexington, KY....Business Law, General Practice, Real Estate Law

MARTIN, PERGRAM & BROWNING CO., L.P.A.
Columbus, OH....General Practice

MARTIN, PICKLESIMER, JUSTICE & VINCENT
Ashland, KY....Civil Trial Practice, General Practice, Insurance Defense Law

MARTIN, PRINGLE, OLIVER, WALLACE & SWARTZ, L.C.
Wichita, KS....General Practice

MARTIN, RONALD T., P.A.
Boca Raton, FL....Tax Law

MARTIN, RYAN & ANDRADA, A PROFESSIONAL CORPORATION
Oakland, CA....Civil Trial Practice, Construction Law, Insurance Defense Law

MARTIN, SHOWERS, SMITH & MCDONALD
Hillsboro, TX....General Practice

MARTIN, TATE, MORROW & MARSTON, P.C.
Memphis, TN....Admiralty/Maritime Law, Civil Trial Practice, General Practice, Tax Law

MARTIN, VAN DE WALLE, DONOHUE, MANDRACCHIA & MCGAHAN
Great Neck, NY....Civil Trial Practice, Commercial Law, General Practice

MARTINDALE & BRZYTWA
Cleveland, OH....Civil Trial Practice

MARTINDELL, SWEARER & SHAFFER
Hutchinson, KS....General Practice

MARTINEAU WALKER
Montreal, QU, Canada....General Practice
Quebec, QU, Canada....General Practice

MARTINEZ, GEORGE C.
San Francisco, CA....Civil Trial Practice

MARTINEZ & DALTON, PROFESSIONAL ASSOCIATION
Orlando, FL....Civil Trial Practice, Medical Malpractice Law, Personal Injury Law, Product Liability Law

MÁRTINEZ ODELL & CALABRIA
San Juan, PR....Banking Law, Bankruptcy Law, Civil Trial Practice, Commercial Law, Environmental Law, General Practice, Labor and Employment Law, Real Estate Law, Tax Law

MARTSON, DEARDORFF, WILLIAMS & OTTO, A PROFESSIONAL CORPORATION
Carlisle, PA....General Practice

MARZIK, ROBERT K., P.C., LAW OFFICES OF
Stratford, CT....Admiralty/Maritime Law

MASCAGNI, FRANK III
Louisville, KY....Criminal Trial Practice, General Practice

MASERITZ, GUY B. LAW OFFICES OF
Columbia, MD....Business Law, Securities Law

MASINTER & LACY
Charleston, WV....Medical Malpractice Law, Personal Injury Law

MASKALERIS & ASSOCIATES
Morristown, NJ....Civil Trial Practice, Criminal Trial Practice, Medical Malpractice Law, Personal Injury Law, Product Liability Law

MASLON EDELMAN BORMAN & BRAND
Minneapolis, MN....Civil Trial Practice, General Practice

MASON, GRIFFIN & PIERSON, A PROFESSIONAL CORPORATION
Princeton, NJ....General Practice

MASON, J. CHENEY, P.A.
Orlando, FL....Criminal Trial Practice

MASON, KOLEHMAINEN, RATHBURN & WYSS
Chicago, IL....Patent, Trademark, Copyright and Unfair Competition Law

MASON, STEINHARDT, JACOBS & PERLMAN, PROFESSIONAL CORPORATION
Southfield, MI....Commercial Law, Environmental Law, General Practice, Real Estate Law, Tax Law

MASON & THOMAS
Sacramento, CA....Civil Trial Practice, Insurance Defense Law, Personal Injury Law

MASSA, PATRICK C., P.A., LAW OFFICES OF
North Palm Beach, FL....Civil Trial Practice, Personal Injury Law

MASSENGILL, CALDWELL, HYDER & BUNN, P.C.
Bristol, TN....General Practice

MASSEY, M. CRAIG
Lakeland, FL....General Practice

MAST, FRANK & ASSOCIATES
Pittsburgh, PA....Civil Trial Practice, Tax Law

MASTERS & TAYLOR, L.C.
Charleston, WV....Personal Injury Law

MASUD, GILBERT & PATTERSON, P.C.
Saginaw, MI....Labor and Employment Law

MATHENY, POIDMORE & SEARS
Sacramento, CA....Bankruptcy Law, Civil Trial Practice, Employment Benefits Law, Insurance Defense Law, Personal Injury Law, Real Estate Law

MATHESON, PARR, SCHULER, EWALD, ESTER & JOLLY
Troy, MI....General Practice, Labor and Employment Law, Transportation Law

MATHEWS, ATKINSON, GUGLIELMO, MARKS & DAY
Baton Rouge, LA....General Practice, Insurance Defense Law

MATHEWS, DINSDALE & CLARK
Toronto, ON, Canada....Labor and Employment Law

MATHEWS SMITH RAILEY & DECUBELLIS, P.A.
Orlando, FL....Civil Trial Practice, General Practice

MATHEWS, WOODBRIDGE & COLLINS, A PROFESSIONAL CORPORATION
Princeton, NJ....Trademark, Copyright and Unfair Competition Law

MATHISON & MATHISON
Palm Beach Gardens, FL....Personal Injury Law
West Palm Beach, FL....Personal Injury Law

MATSUBARA, LEE & KOTAKE, ATTORNEYS AT LAW, A LAW CORPORATION
Honolulu, HI....Civil Trial Practice

MATTHEWS & BRANSCOMB, A PROFESSIONAL CORPORATION
Austin, TX....General Practice, Labor and Employment Law
Corpus Christi, TX....Civil Trial Practice, General Practice, Labor and Employment Law, Natural Resources Law, Probate and Estate Planning Law, Real Estate Law, Tax Law
San Antonio, TX....Antitrust Law, Civil Trial Practice, Communications Law, Criminal Trial Practice, General Practice, Labor and Employment Law, Municipal Bond/Public Authority Financing Law, Natural Resources Law, Patent, Trademark, Copyright and Unfair Competition Law, Tax Law, Trademark, Copyright and Unfair Competition Law, Transportation Law

MATTHIAS & BERG
Los Angeles, CA....International Business Law, Securities Law, Tax Law

MATTIONI, MATTIONI & MATTIONI, LTD.
Philadelphia, PA....Admiralty/Maritime Law, Civil Trial Practice, General Practice

MATTOCH, IAN L.
Honolulu, HI....Personal Injury Law

MATTOX & MATTOX
New Albany, IN....General Practice

MATTSON, MADDEN & POLITO
Newark, NJ....Civil Trial Practice, General Practice

MATTSON, RICKETTS, DAVIES, STEWART & CALKINS
Lincoln, NE....General Practice

MATZ, JEFFREY A., A PROFESSIONAL CORPORATION
Scottsdale, AZ....Civil Trial Practice, Insurance Defense Law, Labor and Employment Law, Medical Malpractice Law, Personal Injury Law, Product Liability Law

MAUPIN TAYLOR ELLIS & ADAMS, P.A.
Raleigh, NC....General Practice, Labor and Employment Law

MAURER, EUGENE J., JR., P.A.
Wilmington, DE....Civil Trial Practice, Criminal Trial Practice, Family Law, Personal Injury Law

MAURER LAW FIRM
La Jolla, CA....Construction Law, Personal Injury Law

MAUZY LAW FIRM
Minneapolis, MN....Criminal Trial Practice

MAXEY LAW OFFICES, P.S.
Spokane, WA....Criminal Trial Practice, Family Law

MAXWELL, MAXWELL, DICK, WALSH & LISKO
Waynesboro, PA....General Practice

MAY, ADAM, GERDES & THOMPSON
Pierre, SD....General Practice

MAY, JOHNSON, DOYLE & BECKER, P.C.
Sioux Falls, SD....General Practice

MAY AND MAY, PROFESSIONAL CORPORATION
Southfield, MI....Probate and Estate Planning Law

MAY, SIMPSON & STROTE, A PROFESSIONAL CORPORATION
Bloomfield Hills, MI....Business Law, Civil Trial Practice, Commercial Law, Construction Law, General Practice, Real Estate Law
Detroit, MI....General Practice

MAYER, BROWN & PLATT
Los Angeles, CA....General Practice
Washington, DC....General Practice
Chicago, IL....General Practice
New York, NY....General Practice
Houston, TX....General Practice
Brussels, Belgium....General Practice
London, England....General Practice
Berlin, Germany....General Practice
Tokyo, Japan....General Practice

MAYER, FRIEDLICH, SPIESS, TIERNEY, BROWN & PLATT
Chicago, IL....General Practice

MAYER, SMITH & ROBERTS, L.L.P.
Shreveport, LA....Civil Trial Practice, General Practice, Insurance Defense Law

MAYFIELD AND BROOKS
Lafayette, IN....General Practice, Probate and Estate Planning Law

MAYFIELD AND PERRENOT, A PROFESSIONAL CORPORATION
El Paso, TX....Banking Law, General Practice

MAYNE & MAYNE
Sioux City, IA....General Practice, Insurance Defense Law

MAYNES, BRADFORD, SHIPPS & SHEFTEL
Durango, CO....General Practice

MAYOR, DAY, CALDWELL & KEETON, L.L.P.
Houston, TX....General Practice

MAYS, KARBERG & WACHTER
Cleveland, OH....Real Estate Law

MAZANEC, RASKIN & RYDER CO., L.P.A.
Cleveland, OH....Insurance Defense Law
Columbus, OH....Insurance Defense Law

MCAFEE & TAFT, A PROFESSIONAL CORPORATION
Oklahoma City, OK....General Practice, Natural Resources Law, Tax Law

MCALILEY, THOMAS W., P.A.
Miami, FL....Admiralty/Maritime Law, Civil Trial Practice, Criminal Trial Practice, Personal Injury Law

MCALLISTER & GALLAGHER, P.C.
Philadelphia, PA....Personal Injury Law, Public Utilities Law

MCALLISTER, WESTMORELAND, VESPER & SCHWARTZ, A PROFESSIONAL CORPORATION
Atlantic City, NJ....General Practice
West Atlantic City, NJ....General Practice

MCALMON, GEORGE A.
El Paso, TX....Civil Trial Practice

MCALOON & FRIEDMAN, P.C.
New York, NY....Civil Trial Practice, Health Care Law, Medical Malpractice Law

MCANANY, VAN CLEAVE & PHILLIPS, P.A.
Kansas City, KS....Civil Trial Practice, General Practice, Insurance Defense Law, Personal Injury Law
Lenexa, KS....General Practice

MCANDREWS, HELD & MALLOY, LTD.
Chicago, IL....Antitrust Law, Civil Trial Practice, Patent, Trademark, Copyright and Unfair Competition Law

MCANERNEY & MILLAR
Darien, CT....General Practice

MCBRAYER, MCGINNIS, LESLIE & KIRKLAND
Frankfort, KY....General Practice
Greenup, KY....General Practice
Lexington, KY....General Practice

MCBRIDE BAKER & COLES
Chicago, IL....Antitrust Law, Business Law, Employment Benefits Law, General Practice, Labor and Employment Law, Probate and Estate Planning Law, Real Estate Law, Securities Law, Tax Law

MCBRIDE AND MCBRIDE, P.C.
Grove City, PA....General Practice

MCCABE & COZZENS
Mineola, NY....Insurance Defense Law

MCCABE & MACK
Poughkeepsie, NY....General Practice

MCCABE, O'DONNELL & WRIGHT, A PROFESSIONAL ASSOCIATION
Phoenix, AZ....General Practice, Probate and Estate Planning Law, Real Estate Law, Tax Law

MCCAFFREY, THOMAS M.
New York, NY....Admiralty/Maritime Law

MCCAFFREY & TAWWATER
Oklahoma City, OK....Civil Trial Practice, Labor and Employment Law, Medical Malpractice Law, Personal Injury Law

MCCAHILL, JOHN A.
Alexandria, VA....Criminal Trial Practice

MCCAHILL, JOHN A.
Washington, DC....Criminal Trial Practice

MCCALLAR AND ASSOCIATES
Savannah, GA....Civil Trial Practice, Insurance Defense Law

MCCAMPBELL & YOUNG, A PROFESSIONAL CORPORATION
Knoxville, TN....Banking Law, Bankruptcy Law, Civil Trial Practice, Commercial Law, Communications Law, General Practice, Natural Resources Law, Real Estate Law, Tax Law

MCCANDLESS & HUNT
Portland, ME....General Practice, Probate and Estate Planning Law, Tax Law

MCCANN, GARLAND, RIDALL & BURKE
Pittsburgh, PA....Civil Trial Practice, General Practice, Probate and Estate Planning Law, Real Estate Law

MCCANNA, KONZ, DUDAS, & ASSOCIATES, S.C.
Appleton, WI....Civil Trial Practice, Insurance Defense Law

MCCARROLL, NUNLEY & HARTZ
Owensboro, KY....General Practice

MCCARTER & ENGLISH
Wilmington, DE....General Practice
Cherry Hill, NJ....Civil Trial Practice, General Practice
Newark, NJ....Admiralty/Maritime Law, Antitrust Law, Banking Law, Bankruptcy Law, Civil Trial Practice, Commercial Law, Communications Law, Family Law, General Practice, Health Care Law, Insurance Defense Law, Labor and Employment Law, Municipal Bond/Public Authority Financing Law, Natural Resources Law, Personal Injury Law, Probate and Estate Planning Law, Real Estate Law, Tax Law, Trademark, Copyright and Unfair Competition Law, Transportation Law

New York, NY....................General Practice

MCCARTHY, JOHN C.
Claremont, CA....................Civil Trial Practice, Labor and Employment Law

MCCARTHY, BACON & COSTELLO
Lanham, MD....................General Practice

MCCARTHY, BOULEY, FOSTER & ELDRIDGE, P.C.
Cambridge, MA....................Medical Malpractice Law

MCCARTHY, PALMER, VOLKEMA, BOYD & THOMAS, A LEGAL PROFESSIONAL ASSOCIATION
Columbus, OH....................Civil Trial Practice, Medical Malpractice Law, Personal Injury Law, Product Liability Law

MCCARTHY AND SCHATZMAN, P.A.
Princeton, NJ....................Banking Law, Civil Trial Practice, Family Law, General Practice, Probate and Estate Planning Law, Real Estate Law

MCCARTHY, SUMMERS, BOBKO, MCKEY & BONAN, P.A.
Stuart, FL....................Civil Trial Practice, Family Law, Personal Injury Law, Real Estate Law

MCCARTHY TÉTRAULT
Vancouver, BC, Canada....................General Practice
London, ON, Canada....................General Practice
Ottawa, ON, Canada....................General Practice
Toronto, ON, Canada....................General Practice
Montreal, QU, Canada....................General Practice
Quebec, QU, Canada....................General Practice
London, England....................General Practice

MCCARTHY, WILSON & ETHRIDGE
Rockville, MD....................General Practice

MCCARTY, JAMES RICHARD, P.C.
Casper, WY....................Civil Trial Practice, Personal Injury Law

MCCASLIN, IMBUS & MCCASLIN, A LEGAL PROFESSIONAL ASSOCIATION
Cincinnati, OH....................Insurance Defense Law

MCCAUGHEY & METOS
Salt Lake City, UT....................Criminal Trial Practice

MCCAULEY & ASSOCIATES
Costa Mesa, CA....................Civil Trial Practice, General Practice

MCCAY, JAMES K.
Baton Rouge, LA....................Real Estate Law

MCCLAIN & STRAUSS, P.A.
Tampa, FL....................Insurance Defense Law

MCCLELLAN & ASSOCIATES, A PROFESSIONAL CORPORATION
San Diego, CA....................Civil Trial Practice, Personal Injury Law, Product Liability Law

MCCLELLAN, POWERS, EHMLING & DIX, P.C.
Gallatin, TN....................Civil Trial Practice

MCCLESKEY, HARRIGER, BRAZILL & GRAF, L.L.P.
Lubbock, TX....................General Practice

MCCLURE, DAVID R.
El Paso, TX....................Family Law

MCCLURE, MCCLURE & KAMMEN
Indianapolis, IN....................Criminal Trial Practice, Family Law, Health Care Law, Probate and Estate Planning Law

MCCLURE & MILLER
Erie, PA....................General Practice

MCCLURE, RAMSAY & DICKERSON
Toccoa, GA....................Civil Trial Practice, General Practice, Insurance Defense Law

MCCLUSKEY, HUGH B.
Parsippany, NJ....................Probate and Estate Planning Law

MCCONN, FISHER, OLSON AND DALEY, LTD.
Grand Forks, ND....................General Practice

MCCONNAUGHHAY, ROLAND, MAIDA & CHERR, P.A.
Tallahassee, FL....................Civil Trial Practice

MCCONNELL AND FINNERTY
North Vernon, IN....................General Practice

MCCONNELL & MENDELSON
Chicago, IL....................Antitrust Law, Commercial Law

MCCONNELL VALDÉS
San Juan, PR....................General Practice

MCCORMACK, COONEY, HILLMAN & ELDER
Omaha, NE....................General Practice

MCCORMICK, BARSTOW, SHEPPARD, WAYTE & CARRUTH
Fresno, CA....................Business Law, General Practice, Insurance Defense Law

MCCORMICK AND CHRISTOPH
Boulder, CO....................Criminal Trial Practice, Personal Injury Law

MCCORMICK, KIDMAN & BEHRENS
Costa Mesa, CA....................Environmental Law, General Practice, Natural Resources Law

MCCORMICK, REEDER, NICHOLS, BAHL, KNECHT & PERSON
Williamsport, PA....................Banking Law, Civil Trial Practice, General Practice, Medical Malpractice Law, Real Estate Law

MCCORRISTON MIHO MILLER MUKAI
Honolulu, HI....................Business Law, Civil Trial Practice, General Practice, Insurance Defense Law, International Business Law, Real Estate Law, Tax Law

MCCOY, HAWTHORNE, ROBERTS & BEGNAUD, LTD., A LAW CORPORATION
Natchitoches, LA....................General Practice

MCCOY, WEAVER, WIGGINS, CLEVELAND & RAPER
Fayetteville, NC....................General Practice

MCCOY, WILKINS, STEPHENS & TIPTON, P.A.
Jackson, MS....................Insurance Defense Law

MCCRARY, BARRY N.
Talladega, AL....................Civil Trial Practice

MCCREEDY AND COX
Cranford, NJ....................Appellate Practice, Civil Trial Practice, Insurance Defense Law, Medical Malpractice Law, Personal Injury Law, Product Liability Law

MCCUBBIN, DENNIS T.
St. Louis, MO....................Civil Trial Practice

MCCURLEY, WEBB, KINSER, MCCURLEY & NELSON, L.L.P.
Dallas, TX....................Family Law

MCCUTCHEN, BLANTON, RHODES & JOHNSON
Columbia, SC....................Appellate Practice, Civil Trial Practice, General Practice, Insurance Defense Law

MCCUTCHEN, DOYLE, BROWN & ENERSEN
Los Angeles, CA....................General Practice
San Francisco, CA....................General Practice
San Jose, CA....................General Practice
Walnut Creek, CA....................General Practice
Washington, DC....................General Practice
Taipei, Taiwan....................General Practice

MCCUTCHEON, MCCUTCHEON & BAXTER, P.A.
Conway, SC....................General Practice

MCDANIEL, DUKE A.
Petersburg, WV....................General Practice

MCDANIEL, HALL, CONERLY & LUSK, P.C.
Birmingham, AL....................General Practice

MCDAVID, NOBLIN & WEST
Jackson, MS....................Administrative Law, Civil Trial Practice, Natural Resources Law, Probate and Estate Planning Law, Real Estate Law

MCDERMOTT & MCGEE
Millburn, NJ....................Civil Trial Practice, General Practice, Insurance Defense Law, Medical Malpractice Law, Personal Injury Law

MCDERMOTT, WILL & EMERY
Los Angeles, CA....................General Practice, Trademark, Copyright and Unfair Competition Law
Newport Beach, CA....................General Practice, Labor and Employment Law
Washington, DC....................Antitrust Law, General Practice, Tax Law, Trademark, Copyright and Unfair Competition Law
Miami, FL....................General Practice, Labor and Employment Law, Trademark, Copyright and Unfair Competition Law
Chicago, IL....................Admiralty/Maritime Law, Antitrust Law, General Practice, Labor and Employment Law, Tax Law, Trademark, Copyright and Unfair Competition Law
Boston, MA....................General Practice, Labor and Employment Law, Trademark, Copyright and Unfair Competition Law
New York, NY....................General Practice, Labor and Employment Law, Trademark, Copyright and Unfair Competition Law

MCDONALD, BROWN & FAGEN
Dallas Center, IA....................General Practice

MCDONALD, CARANO, WILSON, MCCUNE, BERGIN, FRANKOVICH & HICKS
Las Vegas, NV....................Civil Trial Practice, Commercial Law, General Practice, Probate and Estate Planning Law
Reno, NV....................Civil Trial Practice, Commercial Law, Construction Law, Employment Benefits Law, Environmental Law, General Practice, Labor and Employment Law, Municipal and Zoning Law, Probate and Estate Planning Law, Real Estate Law, Tax Law

MCDONALD GROUP, THE, P.C.
Erie, PA .... General Practice

MCDONALD & HAYDEN
Toronto, ON, Canada .... Real Estate Law, Tax Law

MCDONALD, HOPKINS, BURKE & HABER CO., L.P.A.
Cleveland, OH .... General Practice

MCDONALD KUHN
Memphis, TN .... General Practice, Insurance Defense Law

MCDONALD, SAELTZER, MORRIS, CREEGGAN & WADDOCK
Sacramento, CA .... Civil Trial Practice, Insurance Defense Law

MCDONALD SANDERS, A PROFESSIONAL CORPORATION
Fort Worth, TX .... General Practice

MCDONALD, WILLIAM R., P.C.
Denver, CO .... Tax Law

MCDONNELL LAW OFFICES
Naples, FL .... Civil Trial Practice

MCDONOUGH, HOLLAND & ALLEN, A PROFESSIONAL CORPORATION
Sacramento, CA .... General Practice

MCDONOUGH, KORN & EICHHORN, A PROFESSIONAL CORPORATION
Springfield, NJ .... Civil Trial Practice, Criminal Trial Practice, General Practice, Insurance Defense Law, Medical Malpractice Law, Product Liability Law

MCDONOUGH, O'DELL, WIELAND & WILLIAMS
Orlando, FL .... Insurance Defense Law, Personal Injury Law

MCDOUGAL, EVANS & BENNETT, P.C.
Tulsa, OK .... Probate and Estate Planning Law

MCDOUGALL, READY
Regina, SK, Canada .... Banking Law, Civil Trial Practice, Commercial Law, General Practice, Probate and Estate Planning Law, Product Liability Law
Saskatoon, SK, Canada .... General Practice

MCDOWELL, WICK, DALY, GALLUP, HAUSER AND HARTLE
Bradford, PA .... General Practice

MCDUFF, JOHN, P.C., A PROFESSIONAL CORPORATION
Austin, TX .... Business Law, Probate and Estate Planning Law, Real Estate Law, Tax Law

MCELROY, CAMRUD, MADDOCK & OLSON, LTD.
Grand Forks, ND .... General Practice

MCELROY, DEUTSCH AND MULVANEY
Morristown, NJ .... Civil Trial Practice, Commercial Law, Construction Law, Environmental Law, General Practice, Insurance Defense Law

MCEWEN, SCHMITT & CO.
Vancouver, BC, Canada .... Admiralty/Maritime Law

MCFADDEN, EVANS & SILL
Washington, DC .... Communications Law

MCFALL, SHERWOOD & SHEEHY, A PROFESSIONAL CORPORATION
Houston, TX .... Civil Trial Practice, General Practice, Insurance Defense Law, Medical Malpractice Law, Personal Injury Law

MCFARLAIN, WILEY, CASSEDY & JONES, PROFESSIONAL ASSOCIATION
Tallahassee, FL .... Administrative Law, Appellate Practice, Civil Trial Practice, Health Care Law, Insurance Defense Law, Personal Injury Law, Product Liability Law

MCFARLAND & MCFARLAND
Tryon, NC .... General Practice

MCGAHN & FRISS
Atlantic City, NJ .... General Practice

MCGEE & GELMAN
Buffalo, NY .... Civil Trial Practice, General Practice, Patent, Trademark, Copyright and Unfair Competition Law

MCGEE, HANKLA, BACKES & WHEELER, P.C.
Minot, ND .... Commercial Law, General Practice, Health Care Law, Insurance Defense Law, Probate and Estate Planning Law

MCGILL, GOTSDINER, WORKMAN & LEPP, P.C.
Omaha, NE .... Civil Trial Practice, General Practice, Health Care Law, International Business Law, Tax Law

MCGILLICUDDY, TERRENCE J., P.C.
Phoenix, AZ .... Personal Injury Law

MCGINLEY, LANE, MUELLER, O'DONNELL & REYNOLDS, P.C.
Ogallala, NE .... General Practice

MCGINNIS, LOCHRIDGE & KILGORE, L.L.P.
Austin, TX .... Banking Law, Civil Trial Practice, General Practice, Natural Resources Law, Real Estate Law, Tax Law, Transportation Law
Houston, TX .... General Practice

MCGIVERN, SCOTT, GILLIARD, CURTHOYS & ROBINSON
Tulsa, OK .... Insurance Defense Law, Labor and Employment Law

MCGLONE LAW OFFICE
Terre Haute, IN .... Personal Injury Law, Product Liability Law

MCGOLRICK, J. EDWARD, JR., P.C.
Manassas, VA .... Personal Injury Law

MCGOUGAN, WRIGHT, WORLEY AND HARPER
Tabor City, NC .... General Practice

MCGOVERN, CONNELLY & DAVIDSON
New Rochelle, NY .... General Practice, Tax Law

MCGOWAN, EDWARD M.
Maspeth, NY .... General Practice, Probate and Estate Planning Law, Real Estate Law, Tax Law

MCGRATH, J. NICHOLAS, P.C.
Aspen, CO .... Civil Trial Practice, General Practice, Real Estate Law

MCGRATH, NORTH, MULLIN & KRATZ, P.C.
Omaha, NE .... Antitrust Law, Civil Trial Practice, General Practice, Labor and Employment Law, Tax Law

MCGREGOR, DAHL & KLUG
Fresno, CA .... General Practice

MCGREGOR, MALCOLM, INC., A PROFESSIONAL CORPORATION, LAW OFFICES OF
El Paso, TX .... General Practice

MCGUANE AND MALONE, PROFESSIONAL CORPORATION
Denver, CO .... Family Law

MCGUIRE, KEHL & NEALON
New York, NY .... Appellate Practice, Commercial Law, Labor and Employment Law

MCGUIRE & MCGUIRE, P.C.
Worcester, MA .... Civil Trial Practice, Criminal Trial Practice, General Practice

MCGUIRE, PRATT, MASIO & FARRANCE, P.A.
Bradenton, FL .... Commercial Law, Environmental Law, Municipal and Zoning Law

MCGUIRE, WOOD & BISSETTE, P.A.
Asheville, NC .... Civil Trial Practice, General Practice

MCGUIRE, WOODS, BATTLE & BOOTHE
Washington, DC .... General Practice
Jacksonville, FL .... General Practice
Alexandria, VA .... General Practice
Charlottesville, VA .... General Practice
McLean, VA .... General Practice
Norfolk, VA .... General Practice
Richmond, VA .... Antitrust Law, General Practice, Labor and Employment Law, Municipal Bond/Public Authority Financing Law, Tax Law

MCGUIRL, ROBERT J. LAW OFFICES OF
Westwood, NJ .... Product Liability Law

MCHENRY AND MITCHELL
Little Rock, AR .... Medical Malpractice Law

MCHIE, MYERS, MCHIE & ENSLEN
Hammond, IN .... Civil Trial Practice, General Practice

MCINERNEY, GARY J., P.C.
Grand Rapids, MI .... General Practice

MCINNES COOPER & ROBERTSON
Halifax, NS, Canada .... Administrative Law, Admiralty/Maritime Law, Banking Law, Bankruptcy Law, Business Law, Civil Trial Practice, Commercial Law, Construction Law, Employment Benefits Law, Environmental Law, Family Law, General Practice, Health Care Law, Insurance Defense Law, Labor and Employment Law, Municipal and Zoning Law, Natural Resources Law, Personal Injury Law, Probate and Estate Planning Law, Real Estate Law, Tax Law, Transportation Law

MCINTEE & WHISENAND, P.C.
Williston, ND .... General Practice

MCINTOSH, SHERARD & SULLIVAN
Anderson, SC .... General Practice

MCKAY & GUÉRARD, P.A.
Charleston, SC .... General Practice
Columbia, SC .... General Practice

MCKAY, JOHN J., JR., P.A.
Hilton Head Island, SC .... Civil Trial Practice

MCKAY, MCKAY, HENRY & FOSTER, P.A.
Columbia, SC .... Civil Trial Practice, General Practice, Medical Malpractice Law, Product Liability Law

MCKEE & BARGE
Atlanta, GA .... Labor and Employment Law

MCKEEVER, STUART A.
Westport, CT .... Civil Trial Practice, Criminal Trial Practice, General Practice, Probate and Estate Planning Law, Real Estate Law, Tax Law

MCKELLIGOTT, JOHN P.
Philadelphia, PA .... Personal Injury Law

MCKENDREE, JOHN W., LAW OFFICES OF
Denver, CO .... Labor and Employment Law

MCKENNEY, THOMSEN AND BURKE
Baltimore, MD .... Probate and Estate Planning Law, Tax Law

MCKEOWN, FITZGERALD, ZOLLNER, BUCK, HUTCHISON & RUTTLE
Joliet, IL .... Civil Trial Practice, General Practice, Personal Injury Law, Probate and Estate Planning Law

MCKERCHER, MCKERCHER & WHITMORE
Saskatoon, SK, Canada .... Banking Law, Bankruptcy Law, Civil Trial Practice, Family Law, General Practice, Insurance Defense Law, Probate and Estate Planning Law, Real Estate Law, Tax Law

MCKIBBEN, GRANT & ASSOCIATES, A PROF. ASSN., LAW OFFICES OF
Jackson, MS .... Natural Resources Law

MCKINLEY & SMITH
Sacramento, CA .... Civil Trial Practice, Health Care Law

MCKINNON AND MCKINNON
Holland, MI .... Patent, Trademark, Copyright and Unfair Competition Law

MCKIRDY AND RISKIN, A PROFESSIONAL CORPORATION
Morristown, NJ .... Civil Trial Practice, Real Estate Law

MCKISSOCK & HOFFMAN, P.C.
Philadelphia, PA .... Civil Trial Practice, Commercial Law, Health Care Law, Insurance Defense Law, Medical Malpractice Law, Product Liability Law

MCKNIGHT, HUDSON, LEWIS & HENDERSON
Memphis, TN .... Labor and Employment Law

MCLAIN & MERRITT, P.C.
Atlanta, GA .... Family Law, Probate and Estate Planning Law

MCLANE, GRAF, RAULERSON & MIDDLETON, PROFESSIONAL ASSOCIATION
Manchester, NH .... Civil Trial Practice, General Practice

MCLARTY, ROBINSON & VAN VOORHIES
Decatur, GA .... General Practice

MCLAUGHLIN, LESLIE G.
Midland, TX .... Civil Trial Practice, General Practice, Insurance Defense Law, Personal Injury Law

MCLAUGHLIN & COOPER, A PROFESSIONAL CORPORATION
Trenton, NJ .... General Practice

MCLAUGHLIN AND FLORINI, LTD.
Sullivan, IL .... General Practice

MCLAUGHLIN & FOLAN, P.C.
New Bedford, MA .... Civil Trial Practice, Insurance Defense Law

MCLEAN PETERSON LAW FIRM, CHARTERED
Mankato, MN .... Banking Law, General Practice

MCLENNAN ROSS
Edmonton, AB, Canada .... Civil Trial Practice, General Practice, Labor and Employment Law

MCLEOD, ALEXANDER, POWEL & APFFEL, A PROFESSIONAL CORPORATION
Galveston, TX .... General Practice

MCLEOD, BENTON, BEGNAUD & MARSHALL
Athens, GA .... Civil Trial Practice, General Practice

MCLEOD, IAN C., P.C.
Okemos, MI .... Patent, Trademark, Copyright and Unfair Competition Law

MCLEOD, VERLANDER, EADE & VERLANDER
Monroe, LA .... Bankruptcy Law, Civil Trial Practice, Criminal Trial Practice, Family Law, General Practice, Health Care Law, Personal Injury Law

MCMAHON, GROW & GETTY
Rome, NY .... General Practice

MCMAHON, SUROVIK, SUTTLE, BUHRMANN, COBB & HICKS, A PROFESSIONAL CORPORATION
Abilene, TX .... General Practice

MCMAHON, TIDWELL, HANSEN, ATKINS & PEACOCK, P.C.
Odessa, TX .... General Practice

MCMANIMON & SCOTLAND
Newark, NJ .... Banking Law, Environmental Law, General Practice, Municipal Bond/Public Authority Financing Law, Securities Law

MCMASTER, CLIFFORD F.
Fort Worth, TX .... Bankruptcy Law

MCMASTER MEIGHEN
Montreal, QU, Canada .... Admiralty/Maritime Law, Banking Law, Bankruptcy Law, Civil Trial Practice, Commercial Law, Environmental Law, General Practice, Insurance Defense Law, Labor and Employment Law, Municipal Bond/Public Authority Financing Law, Personal Injury Law, Probate and Estate Planning Law, Real Estate Law, Tax Law, Transportation Law

MCMATH LAW FIRM, THE, P.A.
Little Rock, AR .... Civil Trial Practice, Medical Malpractice Law

MCMILLAN BINCH
Mississauga, ON, Canada .... General Practice
Toronto, ON, Canada .... General Practice

MCMILLAN, CONSTABILE, MAKER & MURPHY
Larchmont, NY .... General Practice

MCMURRY & LIVINGSTON
Paducah, KY .... General Practice

MCNAIRY, CLIFFORD & CLENDENIN
Greensboro, NC .... Criminal Trial Practice, Personal Injury Law

MCNAMAR, FEARNOW & MCSHARAR, P.C.
Indianapolis, IN .... Administrative Law, Health Care Law

MCNAMARA, HOUSTON, DODGE, MCCLURE & NEY
Walnut Creek, CA .... Insurance Defense Law, Real Estate Law

MCNAMARA, KELLY & WELSH
Jackson, MS .... Civil Trial Practice, Commercial Law, Personal Injury Law

MCNEER, HIGHLAND & MCMUNN
Clarksburg, WV .... Administrative Law, Banking Law, Bankruptcy Law, Business Law, Civil Trial Practice, General Practice, Insurance Defense Law, Probate and Estate Planning Law, Tax Law
Martinsburg, WV .... Civil Trial Practice, General Practice, Insurance Defense Law
Morgantown, WV .... Civil Trial Practice, General Practice, Insurance Defense Law

MCNEES, WALLACE & NURICK
Harrisburg, PA .... Bankruptcy Law, Civil Trial Practice, Commercial Law, Construction Law, Employment Benefits Law, Environmental Law, General Practice, Health Care Law, Insurance Defense Law, Labor and Employment Law, Patent, Trademark, Copyright and Unfair Competition Law, Probate and Estate Planning Law, Real Estate Law, Securities Law, Tax Law, Transportation Law

MCNEIL, SILVEIRA & RICE
San Rafael, CA .... Business Law

MCNERNEY, PAGE, VANDERLIN & HALL
Williamsport, PA .... Civil Trial Practice, General Practice, Labor and Employment Law

MCNICHOLAS & MCNICHOLAS
Los Angeles, CA .... Civil Trial Practice

MCPHAIL, IAN D., A PROFESSIONAL CORPORATION
Carmel, CA .... Probate and Estate Planning Law

MCPHARLIN & SPRINKLES
San Jose, CA .... Business Law, Civil Trial Practice, Construction Law, Labor and Employment Law

MCPHEE, DEAN W.
San Francisco, CA .... Civil Trial Practice, Construction Law, Real Estate Law

MCPHERSON, WILLIAM H.
Fairfield, CA .... Family Law

MCPHERSON, WILLIAM V. JR.
Durham, NC .... Probate and Estate Planning Law, Tax Law

MCPHILLIPS, FITZGERALD & MEYER
Glens Falls, NY .... General Practice

MCQUADES, THE, CO., L.P.A.
Swanton, OH .... General Practice, Personal Injury Law

MCQUAIDE, BLASKO, SCHWARTZ, FLEMING & FAULKNER, INC.
State College, PA .... General Practice

MCREYNOLDS, MARY A., P.C.
Washington, DC .... Civil Trial Practice, Commercial Law

MCREYNOLDS & WELCH, P.C.
Atlanta, GA .... Construction Law

MCSHANE & BOWIE
Grand Rapids, MI .... General Practice, Real Estate Law, Securities Law

MCSHANE, BREITFELLER & WITTEN
Columbus, OH .... Antitrust Law, Civil Trial Practice

MCTAGUE LAW FIRM
Windsor, ON, Canada .... Commercial Law, General Practice, Labor and Employment Law

MCTIGHE, WEISS, O'ROURKE & MILNER, P.C.
Norristown, PA .... General Practice

MCTURNAN & TURNER
Indianapolis, IN .... Antitrust Law, Appellate Practice, Civil Trial Practice, Securities Law

MCVAY, WILLIAM W.
Pittsburgh, PA .... Personal Injury Law

MCWHORTER, COBB & JOHNSON, L.L.P.
Lubbock, TX .... General Practice

MCWILLIAMS AND MINTZER, P.C.
Philadelphia, PA .... Civil Trial Practice, Health Care Law, Medical Malpractice Law

MEAD, HECHT, CONKLIN & GALLAGHER
White Plains, NY .... General Practice

MEAD, MEAD & THOMPSON
Salem, IN .... General Practice

MEADOWS, OWENS, COLLIER, REED, COUSINS & BLAU, L.L.P.
Dallas, TX .... General Practice, Tax Law

MEADOWS, RILEY, KOENENN AND TEEL, P.A.
Gulfport, MS .... Civil Trial Practice, Family Law, General Practice, Probate and Estate Planning Law, Real Estate Law

MEAGHER & GEER
Minneapolis, MN .... General Practice

MEAHER, AUGUSTINE, III, P.C.
Mobile, AL .... Civil Trial Practice, General Practice

MEARDON, SUEPPEL, DOWNER & HAYES P.L.C.
Iowa City, IA .... Civil Trial Practice, General Practice, Municipal and Zoning Law

MEDVIN & ELBERG
Newark, NJ .... Civil Trial Practice, General Practice, Personal Injury Law

MEEHAN & MEEHAN
Bridgeport, CT .... Criminal Trial Practice, Personal Injury Law

MEEKS & JERNIGAN, P.A.
Little Rock, AR .... General Practice

MEENAN, KEVIN
Pasadena, CA .... Civil Trial Practice, Construction Law, Personal Injury Law

MEHAFFY & WEBER, A PROFESSIONAL CORPORATION
Beaumont, TX .... Admiralty/Maritime Law, Civil Trial Practice, Environmental Law, General Practice
Houston, TX .... Civil Trial Practice, Environmental Law
Orange, TX .... Civil Trial Practice, Environmental Law, General Practice

MEHRENS, CRAIG, P.A.
Phoenix, AZ .... Criminal Trial Practice

MEIGHEN DEMERS
Toronto, ON, Canada .... General Practice

MEISEL, DAVID S., P.A.
West Palm Beach, FL .... Tax Law

MEISNER AND HODGDON, P.C.
Bingham Farms, MI .... Business Law, Civil Trial Practice, Probate and Estate Planning Law, Real Estate Law

MEISSNER & TIERNEY, S.C.
Milwaukee, WI .... Business Law, Communications Law, Employment Benefits Law, Environmental Law, Probate and Estate Planning Law, Real Estate Law, Securities Law, Tax Law

MELAT, PRESSMAN, EZELL & HIGBIE
Colorado Springs, CO .... Civil Trial Practice, Personal Injury Law

MELENDI, GIBBONS & GARCIA, A PROFESSIONAL ASSOCIATION
Tampa, FL .... General Practice

MELLADO & MELLADO-VILLARREAL
San Juan, PR .... Civil Trial Practice, General Practice, Real Estate Law

MELLEY, STEVEN M.
Rhinebeck, NY .... Personal Injury Law

MELLI, WALKER, PEASE & RUHLY, S.C.
Madison, WI .... General Practice, Labor and Employment Law

MELTON, FLOYD M. JR.
Greenwood, MS .... Probate and Estate Planning Law

MELTON, WILLIAM D.
Evergreen, AL .... General Practice

MELVILLE & FOWLER, P.A.
Fort Pierce, FL .... Civil Trial Practice, Probate and Estate Planning Law

MELVIN & MELVIN
Syracuse, NY .... General Practice

MENDELSOHN ROSENTZVEIG SHACTER
Montreal, QU, Canada .... General Practice, Patent, Trademark, Copyright and Unfair Competition Law, Tax Law

MENDES & MOUNT
Los Angeles, CA .... General Practice
New York, NY .... Admiralty/Maritime Law, Civil Trial Practice, Insurance Defense Law

MENG & UREY
Upper Marlboro, MD .... General Practice

MENKE, FAHRNEY & CARROLL, A PROFESSIONAL CORPORATION
Costa Mesa, CA .... Business Law, Commercial Law

MENN, NELSON, SHARRATT, TEETAERT & BEISENSTEIN, LTD.
Appleton, WI .... Business Law, Commercial Law, Insurance Defense Law, Personal Injury Law, Probate and Estate Planning Law, Real Estate Law

MENTER, RUDIN & TRIVELPIECE, P.C.
Syracuse, NY .... Tax Law

MERANZE AND KATZ
Philadelphia, PA .... Labor and Employment Law

MERCALDO, RONALD D., LTD.
Tucson, AZ .... Personal Injury Law

MERCER & MERCER
Pittsburgh, PA .... Personal Injury Law

MERCHANT, GOULD, SMITH, EDELL, WELTER & SCHMIDT, PROFESSIONAL ASSOCIATION
Minneapolis, MN .... Patent, Trademark, Copyright and Unfair Competition Law
St. Paul, MN .... Patent, Trademark, Copyright and Unfair Competition Law

MERKEL & COCKE, A PROFESSIONAL ASSOCIATION
Clarksdale, MS .... Civil Trial Practice, Medical Malpractice Law, Tax Law

MERLINE & THOMAS, P.A.
Greenville, SC .... Probate and Estate Planning Law, Tax Law

MEROLLA & KANE
Providence, RI .... General Practice

MERRILL & MERRILL, CHARTERED
Pocatello, ID .... Appellate Practice, Banking Law, Business Law, Civil Trial Practice, General Practice, Health Care Law, Insurance Defense Law, Probate and Estate Planning Law, Public Utilities Law, Real Estate Law, Tax Law

MERRILL, PORCH, DILLON & FITE, P.A.
Anniston, AL .... General Practice

MERRITT, JERALYN E.
Denver, CO .... Criminal Trial Practice

MERSHON, SAWYER, JOHNSTON, DUNWODY & COLE
Miami, FL..............Antitrust Law, Banking Law, Bankruptcy Law, Civil Trial Practice, Commercial Law, Environmental Law, General Practice, Labor and Employment Law, Probate and Estate Planning Law, Real Estate Law, Tax Law, Trademark, Copyright and Unfair Competition Law
Naples, FL..............General Practice

MESERVE, MUMPER & HUGHES
Irvine, CA..............General Practice
Los Angeles, CA..............General Practice

MESH, GENE & ASSOCIATES
Cincinnati, OH..............General Practice

MESHBESHER & SPENCE, LTD.
Minneapolis, MN..............Civil Trial Practice, Criminal Trial Practice, General Practice, Medical Malpractice Law, Personal Injury Law

MESIROV GELMAN JAFFE CRAMER & JAMIESON
Philadelphia, PA..............General Practice

MESSINA BUFALINI BULZOMI
Tacoma, WA..............Personal Injury Law

METNICK, WISE, CHERRY & FRAZIER
Springfield, IL..............Civil Trial Practice, Criminal Trial Practice, Family Law

METTE, EVANS & WOODSIDE, A PROFESSIONAL CORPORATION
Harrisburg, PA..............Administrative Law, Banking Law, Civil Trial Practice, Commercial Law, Construction Law, Environmental Law, General Practice, Municipal Bond/Public Authority Financing Law, Real Estate Law, Tax Law

METZGER, WICKERSHAM, KNAUSS & ERB
Harrisburg, PA..............Civil Trial Practice, General Practice, Insurance Defense Law, Medical Malpractice Law, Personal Injury Law, Probate and Estate Planning Law, Product Liability Law

MEYER, CAPEL, HIRSCHFELD, MUNCY, JAHN & ALDEEN, P.C.
Champaign, IL..............General Practice

MEYER, FLUEGGE AND TENNEY, P.S.
Yakima, WA..............General Practice

MEYER, HENDRICKS, VICTOR, OSBORN & MALEDON, A PROFESSIONAL ASSOCIATION
Phoenix, AZ..............Administrative Law, Antitrust Law, Banking Law, Bankruptcy Law, Business Law, Civil Trial Practice, Communications Law, Criminal Trial Practice, Environmental Law, General Practice, Insurance Defense Law, Labor and Employment Law, Municipal and Zoning Law, Natural Resources Law, Personal Injury Law, Real Estate Law, Securities Law, Tax Law, Trademark, Copyright and Unfair Competition Law

MEYER, JIM, & ASSOCIATES, P.C.
Waco, TX..............Civil Trial Practice, Family Law, Personal Injury Law

MEYER, KIRK, SNYDER & SAFFORD
Bloomfield Hills, MI..............Business Law, Civil Trial Practice, General Practice, Probate and Estate Planning Law, Real Estate Law
Detroit, MI..............Family Law, General Practice

MEYER, MEYER & METLI
Smithtown, NY..............Banking Law, General Practice

MEYER AND SWATKOSKI ASSOCIATES, A PROFESSIONAL CORPORATION
Wilkes-Barre, PA..............Civil Trial Practice

MEYER, UNKOVIC & SCOTT
Pittsburgh, PA..............General Practice

MEYERS, BILLINGSLEY, SHIPLEY, RODBELL & ROSENBAUM, P.A.
Riverdale, MD..............Civil Trial Practice, General Practice, Municipal Bond/Public Authority Financing Law

MEYERS, HENTEMANN, SCHNEIDER & REA CO., L.P.A.
Cleveland, OH..............Civil Trial Practice, General Practice, Insurance Defense Law, Product Liability Law

MEYERS, O. CHRISTOPHER, INC.
Lawton, OK..............Tax Law

MEYERSON, JACK A.
Philadelphia, PA..............Criminal Trial Practice

MEYNER AND LANDIS
Newark, NJ..............Banking Law, Civil Trial Practice, Commercial Law, Immigration and Naturalization Law, Probate and Estate Planning Law, Real Estate Law

MEZEY & MEZEY, A PROFESSIONAL CORPORATION
Princeton, NJ..............Insurance Defense Law, Real Estate Law

MEZVINSKY, EDWARD M.
Narberth, PA..............General Practice, International Business Law

MICHAEL, ROBERT J.
Rochester, NY..............Medical Malpractice Law, Personal Injury Law, Product Liability Law

MICHAEL, BEST & FRIEDRICH
Madison, WI..............General Practice
Milwaukee, WI..............Antitrust Law, General Practice, Labor and Employment Law, Municipal Bond/Public Authority Financing Law, Natural Resources Law, Patent, Trademark, Copyright and Unfair Competition Law, Tax Law

MICHAELIS, MONTANARI & JOHNSON, A PROFESSIONAL LAW CORPORATION
Westlake Village, CA..............Insurance Defense Law

MICHAELS & BELL, P.C.
Auburn, NY..............Civil Trial Practice

MICHAELSON, BENJAMIN, JR., P.A.
Annapolis, MD..............Real Estate Law

MICHELI, BALDWIN, BOPELEY & NORTHRUP
Zanesville, OH..............Civil Trial Practice, Insurance Defense Law

MICHENER, LARIMORE, SWINDLE, WHITAKER, FLOWERS, SAWYER, REYNOLDS & CHALK, L.L.P.
Fort Worth, TX..............Business Law, Tax Law

MICHIE, HAMLETT, LOWRY, RASMUSSEN AND TWEEL, P.C.
Charlottesville, VA..............General Practice, Tax Law

MICKEY, WILSON, WEILER & RENZI, P.C.
Aurora, IL..............General Practice

MIDDENDORF, HENRY S. JR.
New York, NY..............General Practice

MIDDLEBERG, RIDDLE & GIANNA
New Orleans, LA..............Commercial Law, Insurance Defense Law, Real Estate Law
Dallas, TX..............Civil Trial Practice, Insurance Defense Law, Real Estate Law

MIDDLETON & REUTLINGER, P.S.C.
Louisville, KY..............Antitrust Law, Banking Law, Bankruptcy Law, Civil Trial Practice, Environmental Law, General Practice, Insurance Defense Law, Patent, Trademark, Copyright and Unfair Competition Law, Personal Injury Law, Probate and Estate Planning Law, Securities Law, Tax Law

MIDLEN & GUILLOT, CHARTERED
Washington, DC..............Business Law, Communications Law, Trademark, Copyright and Unfair Competition Law

MIEL MIEL & PERRY
Stanton, MI..............General Practice

MIKOS, KENNETH R., P.A.
Fort Lauderdale, FL..............Civil Trial Practice, General Practice

MIKUS LAW ASSOCIATES
Lancaster, PA..............Personal Injury Law

MILBANK, TWEED, HADLEY & MCCLOY
Los Angeles, CA..............General Practice
Washington, DC..............General Practice
New York, NY..............Banking Law, Civil Trial Practice, General Practice
London, England..............General Practice
Hong Kong, Hong Kong (British Crown Colony)..............General Practice
Tokyo, Japan..............General Practice
Moscow, Russia..............General Practice
Singapore, Singapore..............General Practice

MILBERG WEISS BERSHAD HYNES & LERACH
New York, NY..............Antitrust Law, Civil Trial Practice

MILES AND MILES, A PROFESSIONAL ASSOCIATION
Plymouth, MA..............Family Law

MILES, SEARS & EANNI, A PROFESSIONAL CORPORATION
Fresno, CA..............Civil Trial Practice, Medical Malpractice Law, Personal Injury Law

MILES & STOCKBRIDGE, A PROFESSIONAL CORPORATION
Washington, DC..............General Practice
Baltimore, MD..............General Practice, Municipal Bond/Public Authority Financing Law, Tax Law
Towson, MD..............General Practice
Fairfax, VA..............General Practice

MILES & TIERNEY
Las Vegas, NV..............Banking Law, Environmental Law, Real Estate Law

MILIDES, GUS
Easton, PA .... General Practice, Medical Malpractice Law, Personal Injury Law, Product Liability Law

MILITELLO, ZANCK & COEN, P.C.
Crystal Lake, IL .... General Practice

MILLAR, HODGES & BEMIS
Newport Beach, CA .... Probate and Estate Planning Law

MILLBERG & GORDON
Raleigh, NC .... Civil Trial Practice

MILLER, J. JEROME
Destin, FL .... General Practice, Municipal and Zoning Law, Probate and Estate Planning Law

MILLER, JOHN E.
Palo Alto, CA .... Family Law, Probate and Estate Planning Law

MILLER, THOMAS W.
Cincinnati, OH .... Criminal Trial Practice

MILLER, BARNES AND CHRISTIAN
Lancaster, OH .... General Practice

MILLER, CANFIELD, PADDOCK AND STONE, P.L.C.
Ann Arbor, MI .... Antitrust Law, Banking Law, Bankruptcy Law, Civil Trial Practice, Environmental Law, Family Law, General Practice, Insurance Defense Law, International Business Law, Labor and Employment Law, Natural Resources Law, Probate and Estate Planning Law, Real Estate Law, Securities Law, Tax Law, Transportation Law
Birmingham, MI .... General Practice
Bloomfield Hills, MI .... General Practice, International Business Law, Securities Law
Detroit, MI .... Admiralty/Maritime Law, Antitrust Law, Banking Law, Bankruptcy Law, Civil Trial Practice, Communications Law, Environmental Law, Family Law, General Practice, Insurance Defense Law, International Business Law, Labor and Employment Law, Medical Malpractice Law, Municipal Bond/Public Authority Financing Law, Natural Resources Law, Patent, Trademark, Copyright and Unfair Competition Law, Personal Injury Law, Probate and Estate Planning Law, Real Estate Law, Securities Law, Tax Law, Transportation Law
Grand Rapids, MI .... Antitrust Law, Banking Law, Bankruptcy Law, General Practice, International Business Law, Personal Injury Law, Securities Law
Kalamazoo, MI .... Antitrust Law, Banking Law, Bankruptcy Law, Civil Trial Practice, Commercial Law, Environmental Law, Family Law, General Practice, Insurance Defense Law, International Business Law, Labor and Employment Law, Medical Malpractice Law, Patent, Trademark, Copyright and Unfair Competition Law, Personal Injury Law, Probate and Estate Planning Law, Real Estate Law, Securities Law, Tax Law, Transportation Law
Lansing, MI .... Antitrust Law, Banking Law, Bankruptcy Law, General Practice, Labor and Employment Law, Probate and Estate Planning Law, Real Estate Law
Monroe, MI .... General Practice, International Business Law, Securities Law

MILLER CARSON BOXBERGER & MURPHY
Bloomington, IN .... General Practice
Fort Wayne, IN .... General Practice

MILLER, CASSIDY, LARROCA & LEWIN
Washington, DC .... Civil Trial Practice, Criminal Trial Practice

MILLER & CHEVALIER, CHARTERED
Washington, DC .... General Practice, Tax Law

MILLER & CHRISTENBURY, P.C.
Philadelphia, PA .... Patent, Trademark, Copyright and Unfair Competition Law

MILLER & COMPANY, P.C.
Kansas City, MO .... International Business Law

MILLER, EGGLESTON & ROSENBERG, LTD.
Burlington, VT .... Antitrust Law, Civil Trial Practice, General Practice, Health Care Law, Tax Law

MILLER & ENTWISLE
Pittsburgh, PA .... General Practice

MILLER & FAIGNANT, A PROFESSIONAL CORPORATION
Rutland, VT .... Appellate Practice, Civil Trial Practice, General Practice, Insurance Defense Law, Medical Malpractice Law, Personal Injury Law, Product Liability Law

MILLER & GALDIERI
Jersey City, NJ .... Civil Trial Practice

MILLER, HALE AND HARRISON
Boulder, CO .... Criminal Trial Practice, Personal Injury Law

MILLER, HAMILTON, SNIDER & ODOM, L.L.C.
Mobile, AL .... Antitrust Law, Banking Law, Civil Trial Practice, General Practice, Securities Law, Transportation Law

MILLER, J. BRUCE, LAW GROUP
Louisville, KY .... Civil Trial Practice, General Practice

MILLER, KENNETH C., LTD.
Chicago, IL .... Medical Malpractice Law, Personal Injury Law, Product Liability Law

MILLER, KISTLER & CAMPBELL, INC.
Bellefonte, PA .... Civil Trial Practice
State College, PA .... Civil Trial Practice

MILLER LAW OFFICES, THE
Studio City, CA .... Immigration and Naturalization Law

MILLER, MANNIX & PRATT, P.C.
Glens Falls, NY .... General Practice

MILLER & MARTIN
Chattanooga, TN .... General Practice

MILLER, MELVIN B., LTD.
Philadelphia, PA .... Business Law, Real Estate Law

MILLER AND MILLER
Louisville, KY .... Admiralty/Maritime Law

MILLER & MILLER, LTD.
Phoenix, AZ .... Civil Trial Practice, Criminal Trial Practice, Medical Malpractice Law, Personal Injury Law

MILLER & MILLER, P.C.
Haverstraw, NY .... General Practice, Personal Injury Law

MILLER, MILLER & CANBY, CHARTERED
Frederick, MD .... General Practice
Rockville, MD .... General Practice

MILLER, MONSON & PESHEL
San Diego, CA .... Probate and Estate Planning Law

MILLER, MORTON, CAILLAT & NEVIS
San Jose, CA .... General Practice

MILLER MULLER MENDELSON & KENNEDY
Indianapolis, IN .... Business Law, Civil Trial Practice, Medical Malpractice Law, Personal Injury Law, Product Liability Law

MILLER, NANCY D., P.C., LAW OFFICES OF
Denver, CO .... Bankruptcy Law, Real Estate Law

MILLER, NASH, WIENER, HAGER & CARLSEN
Portland, OR .... Admiralty/Maritime Law, Antitrust Law, General Practice, Labor and Employment Law, Patent, Trademark, Copyright and Unfair Competition Law

MILLER, PEARSON, GLOE, BURNS, BEATTY & COWIE, P.C.
Decorah, IA .... General Practice, Insurance Defense Law

MILLER, PITT & MCANALLY, P.C.
Tucson, AZ .... Civil Trial Practice, General Practice, Personal Injury Law

MILLER, PORTER & MULLER
Princeton, NJ .... General Practice

MILLER, RICHARD F., A PROFESSIONAL CORPORATION
Pasadena, CA .... Probate and Estate Planning Law

MILLER, ROBERT E., INC., A PROFESSIONAL CORPORATION
Menlo Park, CA .... Business Law

MILLER & SANFORD, A PROFESSIONAL CORPORATION
Springfield, MO .... Civil Trial Practice, General Practice

MILLER, SCHWARTZ AND MILLER, P.A.
Hollywood, FL .... General Practice

MILLER, SHAKMAN, HAMILTON, KURTZON & SCHLIFKE
Chicago, IL .... General Practice

MILLER, SIMPSON & TATUM
Savannah, GA .... General Practice

MILLER, STARR & REGALIA, A PROFESSIONAL LAW CORPORATION
Oakland, CA .... General Practice
Walnut Creek, CA .... General Practice

MILLER & STEINBERG
Rockville, MD .... Family Law, General Practice

MILLER, STRATVERT, TORGERSON & SCHLENKER, P.A.
Albuquerque, NM .... Banking Law, Business Law, Civil Trial Practice, General Practice, Insurance Defense Law, Natural Resources Law, Probate and Estate Planning Law, Real Estate Law, Tax Law

Farmington, NM....................Banking Law, Business Law, General Practice, Insurance Defense Law, Natural Resources Law, Real Estate Law
Las Cruces, NM....................Banking Law, Commercial Law, Insurance Defense Law, Natural Resources Law, Real Estate Law

MILLER THOMSON
Markham, ON, Canada...........General Practice
Toronto, ON, Canada............General Practice

MILLER, TOLBERT, MUEHLHAUSEN, MUEHLHAUSEN & GROFF, P.C.
Logansport, IN.......................General Practice

MILLIKEN LAW FIRM
Bowling Green, KY.................Civil Trial Practice, Criminal Trial Practice, General Practice, Medical Malpractice Law

MILLING, BENSON, WOODWARD, HILLYER, PIERSON & MILLER
Baton Rouge, LA....................Environmental Law
New Orleans, LA....................Admiralty/Maritime Law, Antitrust Law, General Practice, Labor and Employment Law, Natural Resources Law, Tax Law

MILLISOR & NOBIL, A LEGAL PROFESSIONAL ASSOCIATION
Cleveland, OH.........................Employment Benefits Law, Labor and Employment Law
Columbus, OH.........................Employment Benefits Law, Labor and Employment Law

MILLS & CHASTEEN, P.C. ATTORNEYS AT LAW
Fitzgerald, GA.........................General Practice

MILLS & MORAITAKIS
Atlanta, GA.............................Civil Trial Practice, Product Liability Law

MILLS, RICHARD J., & ASSOCIATES
Pittsburgh, PA........................Civil Trial Practice, Insurance Defense Law, Product Liability Law, Transportation Law

MILLS, SHIRLEY, ECKEL & BASSETT, L.L.P.
Galveston, TX..........................General Practice
Houston, TX............................General Practice

MILLS & WHITTEN, A PROFESSIONAL CORPORATION
Oklahoma City, OK..................Civil Trial Practice, Insurance Defense Law, Medical Malpractice Law, Personal Injury Law

MILLSTEIN, DAVID J.
Greensburg, PA.......................Appellate Practice, Business Law, Civil Trial Practice, General Practice, Real Estate Law

MILNER, C. GEORGE, ESQ., A PROF. CORP.
Philadelphia, PA.....................Civil Trial Practice

MILNER, LOBEL, GORANSON, SORRELS, UDASHEN & WELLS
Dallas, TX...............................Criminal Trial Practice

MILTON, LAURENCE & DIXON
Worcester, MA.........................Insurance Defense Law

MINOR, BELL & NEAL, P.C.
Dalton, GA...............................General Practice

MINOR AND GUICE
Biloxi, MS................................Admiralty/Maritime Law, Civil Trial Practice, Personal Injury Law, Product Liability Law

MINSKY, MCCORMICK & HALLAGAN, P.C.
Chicago, IL..............................Immigration and Naturalization Law

MINTMIRE & ASSOCIATES
Palm Beach, FL........................Civil Trial Practice, Probate and Estate Planning Law

MINTON, BURTON, FOSTER & COLLINS, A PROFESSIONAL CORPORATION
Austin, TX...............................Civil Trial Practice, Criminal Trial Practice

MINTON, MICHAEL HARRY, A PROFESSIONAL CORPORATION
Chicago, IL..............................Family Law

MINTON, MINTON AND RAND
Los Angeles, CA......................Business Law, Probate and Estate Planning Law, Real Estate Law

MINTZ, LEVIN, COHN, FERRIS, GLOVSKY AND POPEO, P.C.
Washington, DC.......................General Practice
Boston, MA..............................Antitrust Law, Civil Trial Practice, Communications Law, Criminal Trial Practice, General Practice, Municipal Bond/Public Authority Financing Law

MIRICK, O'CONNELL, DEMALLIE & LOUGEE
Worcester, MA.........................General Practice

MIROFF, CROSS, RUPPERT & KLINEMAN
Indianapolis, IN......................Family Law

MISKO, HOWIE & SWEENEY
Dallas, TX...............................Civil Trial Practice, Medical Malpractice Law, Personal Injury Law, Product Liability Law

MITCHELL, LINCOLN A.
Palo Alto, CA..........................Family Law

MITCHELL & ARMSTRONG, LTD.
Marion, IL...............................General Practice, Insurance Defense Law

MITCHELL, BRISSO, DELANEY, REINHOLTSEN & VRIEZE
Eureka, CA..............................General Practice, Insurance Defense Law

MITCHELL & DECLERCK, P.C.
Enid, OK.................................General Practice

MITCHELL, EDDIE C., P.A.
Winston-Salem, NC..................Criminal Trial Practice

MITCHELL HURST JACOBS & DICK
Indianapolis, IN......................Business Law, Civil Trial Practice, Medical Malpractice Law, Personal Injury Law, Product Liability Law, Real Estate Law

MITCHELL, JOINER, HARDESTY & LOWTHER
Madisonville, KY.....................General Practice, Labor and Employment Law

MITCHELL, MCNUTT, THREADGILL, SMITH & SAMS, P.A.
Columbus, MS..........................General Practice
Tupelo, MS...............................General Practice

MITCHELL & MITCHELL, P.C.
Dalton, GA...............................Civil Trial Practice, General Practice

MITCHELL, MITCHELL, GRAY & GALLAGHER, A PROFESSIONAL CORPORATION
Williamsport, PA......................Civil Trial Practice, Insurance Defense Law, Medical Malpractice Law, Personal Injury Law, Product Liability Law

MITCHELL, NEUBAUER, SHAW & HANSON, P.C.
Mount Vernon, IL.....................General Practice

MITCHELL & RALLINGS
Charlotte, NC..........................Bankruptcy Law, Civil Trial Practice, Commercial Law

MITCHELL, SAM C., & ASSOCIATES
West Frankfort, IL...................Personal Injury Law

MITCHELL, SILBERBERG & KNUPP
Los Angeles, CA......................Antitrust Law, Commercial Law, Environmental Law, General Practice, Labor and Employment Law, Probate and Estate Planning Law, Tax Law

MITCHELL, VOGE, BEASLEY AND CORBAN
Tupelo, MS...............................General Practice

MITHOFF & JACKS, L.L.P.
Austin, TX...............................Civil Trial Practice, Personal Injury Law

MIZE, JAMES M.
Sacramento, CA.......................Family Law

MOBBS, DENNY E.
Cleveland, TN..........................Civil Trial Practice, General Practice, Insurance Defense Law

MOCK, SCHWABE, WALDO, ELDER, REEVES & BRYANT, A PROFESSIONAL CORPORATION
Oklahoma City, OK..................Banking Law, Bankruptcy Law, Civil Trial Practice, General Practice, Natural Resources Law, Real Estate Law, Securities Law, Tax Law

MODRALL, SPERLING, ROEHL, HARRIS & SISK, P.A.
Albuquerque, NM.....................General Practice
Las Cruces, NM.......................General Practice
Santa Fe, NM...........................General Practice

MOEN, BRUCE R.
Seattle, WA.............................Probate and Estate Planning Law

MOEN, SHEEHAN, MEYER, LTD.
La Crosse, WI..........................General Practice

MOFFATT, THOMAS, BARRETT, ROCK & FIELDS, CHARTERED
Boise, ID.................................Antitrust Law, Civil Trial Practice, Environmental Law, General Practice, Labor and Employment Law, Natural Resources Law, Patent, Trademark, Copyright and Unfair Competition Law, Trademark, Copyright and Unfair Competition Law, Transportation Law

MOGEL, SPEIDEL, BOBB & KERSHNER, A PROFESSIONAL CORPORATION
Reading, PA.............................Banking Law, Business Law, Family Law, General Practice, Probate and Estate Planning Law

MOGILL, KENNETH M.
Detroit, MI...............................Appellate Practice, Criminal Trial Practice

MOHAN, ALEWELT, PRILLAMAN & ADAMI
Springfield, IL.........................Environmental Law, General Practice, Real Estate Law, Tax Law

MOHER & CANNELLO, P.C.
Sault Ste. Marie, MI .... Civil Trial Practice, General Practice, Personal Injury Law

MOHR, HACKETT, PEDERSON, BLAKLEY, RANDOLPH & HAGA, P.C.
Phoenix, AZ .... General Practice

MOHR, LEE R., A PROFESSIONAL LAW CORPORATION
Palm Springs, CA .... Family Law

MOLINE & SHOSTAK
St. Louis, MO .... Business Law, Civil Trial Practice, Criminal Trial Practice, Securities Law

MOLLER, HORTON & SHIELDS, P.C.
Hartford, CT .... General Practice, Insurance Defense Law

MOLLICA, MURRAY & HOGUE
Pittsburgh, PA .... Business Law, Construction Law, Insurance Defense Law, Municipal and Zoning Law, Real Estate Law

MOLLIGAN, COX & MOYER, A PROFESSIONAL CORPORATION
San Francisco, CA .... Antitrust Law, Civil Trial Practice, Medical Malpractice Law, Personal Injury Law, Product Liability Law

MOLLOY, JONES & DONAHUE, P.C.
Tucson, AZ .... General Practice

MOMBACH, BOYLE & HARDIN, P.A.
Fort Lauderdale, FL .... Commercial Law

MONAGHAN & GOLD, P.C.
Elkins Park, PA .... Appellate Practice, Civil Trial Practice, Commercial Law, Insurance Defense Law, Labor and Employment Law, Medical Malpractice Law, Product Liability Law

MONDSCHEIN, JOHN R.
Allentown, PA .... Family Law

MONE, D'AMBROSE & HANYEN, P.C.
Brockton, MA .... Insurance Defense Law

MONK, GOODWIN
Winnipeg, MB, Canada .... General Practice

MONNET, HAYES, BULLIS, THOMPSON & EDWARDS
Oklahoma City, OK .... Civil Trial Practice, General Practice, Natural Resources Law

MONSEY & ANDREWS
Las Vegas, NV .... Commercial Law, Probate and Estate Planning Law, Real Estate Law

MONTAGUE, PITTMAN & VARNADO, A PROFESSIONAL ASSOCIATION
Hattiesburg, MS .... Environmental Law, General Practice

MONTANO, SUMMERS, MULLEN, MANUEL, OWENS AND GREGORIO, A PROFESSIONAL CORPORATION
Cherry Hill, NJ .... Civil Trial Practice, General Practice, Insurance Defense Law, Personal Injury Law

MONTEDONICO, HAMILTON & ALTMAN, P.C.
Washington, DC .... General Practice
Fairfax, VA .... General Practice
Richmond, VA .... General Practice

MONTELEONE & MCCRORY
Los Angeles, CA .... General Practice

MONTFORT, HEALY, MCGUIRE & SALLEY
Garden City, NY .... Civil Trial Practice, Environmental Law, General Practice

MONTGOMERY & ANDREWS, PROFESSIONAL ASSOCIATION
Albuquerque, NM .... Patent, Trademark, Copyright and Unfair Competition Law
Santa Fe, NM .... Administrative Law, Civil Trial Practice, Environmental Law, General Practice, Labor and Employment Law, Natural Resources Law, Tax Law

MONTGOMERY, BARNETT, BROWN, READ, HAMMOND & MINTZ
New Orleans, LA .... Admiralty/Maritime Law

MONTGOMERY, GREEN, JARVIS, KOLODNY AND MARKUSSON, A PROFESSIONAL CORPORATION
Denver, CO .... Civil Trial Practice, Insurance Defense Law

MONTGOMERY & LARMOYEUX
West Palm Beach, FL .... Civil Trial Practice, General Practice

MONTGOMERY LITTLE & MCGREW, P.C.
Denver, CO .... Civil Trial Practice, Commercial Law, General Practice

MONTGOMERY, MCCRACKEN, WALKER & RHOADS
Philadelphia, PA .... General Practice

MONTGOMERY, MICHAEL B., A LAW CORPORATION
El Monte, CA .... Municipal Bond/Public Authority Financing Law, Municipal and Zoning Law, Real Estate Law

MONTGOMERY & PEAVY, L.L.P.
Graham, TX .... Probate and Estate Planning Law

MOODIE & MOODIE
West Point, NE .... General Practice

MOODY, STROPLE & KLOEPPEL, LTD.
Portsmouth, VA .... Civil Trial Practice, Personal Injury Law

MOONEY, F. BENTLEY, JR., A LAW CORPORATION
North Hollywood, CA .... Business Law, Probate and Estate Planning Law

MOONEY LAW FIRM
Jonesboro, AR .... General Practice

MOORE, DONALD HUGH
Marina Del Rey, CA .... Insurance Defense Law

MOORE, REID JR.
West Palm Beach, FL .... Probate and Estate Planning Law

MOORE & BERKOWITZ
Southampton, PA .... Civil Trial Practice

MOORE, CHAMBLISS, ALLEN AND TYNDALL
Moultrie, GA .... General Practice

MOORE, CHRISTOPHER M., & ASSOCIATES, A LAW CORPORATION
Torrance, CA .... Family Law, Probate and Estate Planning Law

MOORE, COSTELLO & HART
Minneapolis, MN .... Commercial Law, Construction Law, Insurance Defense Law
St. Paul, MN .... Commercial Law, Construction Law, Insurance Defense Law

MOORE & CRAVITZ
Selinsgrove, PA .... General Practice, Probate and Estate Planning Law

MOORE, GEORGE E., A PROFESSIONAL LAW CORPORATION
Pasadena, CA .... Medical Malpractice Law, Personal Injury Law

MOORE & HANSEN
Minneapolis, MN .... Patent, Trademark, Copyright and Unfair Competition Law

MOORE, MEEGAN, HANSCHU & KASSENBROCK
Sacramento, CA .... Civil Trial Practice, General Practice

MOORE, MORROW & FRYMIRE
Madisonville, KY .... General Practice

MOORE, RADER, CLIFT AND FITZPATRICK, P.C.
Cookeville, TN .... Civil Trial Practice, General Practice, Insurance Defense Law

MOORE & ROGERS
Marietta, GA .... Civil Trial Practice, Insurance Defense Law, Real Estate Law

MOORE & SERIO
Clarendon, AR .... General Practice

MOORE, STOUT, WADDELL & LEDFORD
Kingsport, TN .... Civil Trial Practice, General Practice, Labor and Employment Law, Probate and Estate Planning Law

MOORE & VAN ALLEN, PLLC
Charlotte, NC .... General Practice, Tax Law
Durham, NC .... Civil Trial Practice, General Practice
Raleigh, NC .... General Practice

MOORE, VIRGADAMO & LYNCH, LTD.
Newport, RI .... General Practice

MOOTS, COPE & STANTON, A LEGAL PROFESSIONAL ASSOCIATION
Columbus, OH .... Family Law, Labor and Employment Law

MORAN & MORAN
Toledo, OH .... Family Law, General Practice

MORCHOWER, MICHAEL
Richmond, VA .... Criminal Trial Practice

MOREHOUSE, HARLOW & WELDY
Fairfield, CT .... General Practice

MORGAN, JOSEPH A.
El Paso, TX .... Personal Injury Law

MORGAN, BROWN & JOY
Boston, MA .... Labor and Employment Law

MORGAN, CARRATT AND O'CONNOR, P.A.
Fort Lauderdale, FL .... General Practice

MORGAN & FINNEGAN, L.L.P.
Washington, DC......Patent, Trademark, Copyright and Unfair Competition Law
New York, NY......Patent, Trademark, Copyright and Unfair Competition Law

MORGAN AND GOTCHER
Greenville, TX......General Practice, Probate and Estate Planning Law

MORGAN & HANSEN
Salt Lake City, UT......Civil Trial Practice, General Practice, Insurance Defense Law, Personal Injury Law

MORGAN, MELHUISH, MONAGHAN, ARVIDSON, ABRUTYN & LISOWSKI
Livingston, NJ......Civil Trial Practice, General Practice, Insurance Defense Law, Personal Injury Law

MORGAN & POTTINGER, P.S.C.
Louisville, KY......Bankruptcy Law, General Practice

MORGAN, RUBY, SCHOFIELD, FRANICH & FREDKIN
San Jose, CA......Civil Trial Practice, General Practice

MORGENSTEIN & JUBELIRER
San Francisco, CA......Civil Trial Practice, General Practice

MORGERA, VINCENT D.
Providence, RI......Admiralty/Maritime Law, Civil Trial Practice, Medical Malpractice Law, Personal Injury Law, Product Liability Law

MORIARTY, DONOGHUE & LEJA, P.C.
Springfield, MA......Civil Trial Practice, Personal Injury Law

MORITT, HOCK & HAMROFF
Hempstead, NY......Bankruptcy Law, Civil Trial Practice, Commercial Law

MORLEY CASKIN
Washington, DC......Administrative Law, Natural Resources Law

MORMAN, SMIT, HUGHES, STRAIN, MOLSTAD & HAIVALA
Sturgis, SD......General Practice

MORNEAU & MURPHY
Jamestown, RI......Bankruptcy Law, Civil Trial Practice, General Practice

MOROSCO, B. ANTHONY
White Plains, NY......Criminal Trial Practice

MORRILL BROWN & THOMAS
Rapid City, SD......General Practice

MORRIS, JOHN W.
Philadelphia, PA......Appellate Practice, Commercial Law, Criminal Trial Practice

MORRIS BRIGNONE & PICKERING
Las Vegas, NV......Commercial Law, Labor and Employment Law, Product Liability Law

MORRIS, CLOUD AND CONCHIN, P.C.
Huntsville, AL......Civil Trial Practice

MORRIS & FLOREY, L.L.P.
Austin, TX......Criminal Trial Practice

MORRIS, GARLOVE, WATERMAN & JOHNSON
Louisville, KY......General Practice, Insurance Defense Law, Real Estate Law, Tax Law

MORRIS, HAYNES, INGRAM & HORNSBY
Alexander City, AL......Personal Injury Law, Product Liability Law

MORRIS, J. SCOTT, P.C.
Austin, TX......Probate and Estate Planning Law, Tax Law

MORRIS, JAMES, HITCHENS & WILLIAMS
Dover, DE......General Practice
Wilmington, DE......Civil Trial Practice, General Practice

MORRIS, LAING, EVANS, BROCK & KENNEDY, CHARTERED
Wichita, KS......Bankruptcy Law, Civil Trial Practice, General Practice, Natural Resources Law

MORRIS AND MORRIS
Wilmington, DE......General Practice, Securities Law
Richmond, VA......Banking Law, Civil Trial Practice, General Practice

MORRIS, NEIL A., ASSOCIATES, P.C.
Philadelphia, PA......Labor and Employment Law

MORRIS, NICHOLS, ARSHT & TUNNELL
Wilmington, DE......General Practice, Tax Law

MORRIS, PAUL, PROFESSIONAL ASSOCIATION
Miami, FL......Appellate Practice

MORRIS, ROBERT L., & ASSOCIATES, P.C.
Denver, CO......Labor and Employment Law

MORRISON AND MORRISON
Whitefish, MT......Civil Trial Practice

MORRISON, MORRISON & MILLS, P.A.
Tampa, FL......Banking Law, Municipal Bond/Public Authority Financing Law, Municipal and Zoning Law

MORRISON & SHELTON, A PROFESSIONAL CORPORATION
Wichita Falls, TX......Civil Trial Practice, General Practice, Personal Injury Law

MORROW, GORDON & BYRD
Newark, OH......General Practice

MORROW & OTOROWSKI
Bainbridge Island, WA......Personal Injury Law

MORROW, SEDIVY & BENNETT, PROFESSIONAL CORPORATION
Bozeman, MT......General Practice

MORSE & BRATT
Vancouver, WA......General Practice

MORSE & MOWBRAY, A PROFESSIONAL CORPORATION
Las Vegas, NV......Civil Trial Practice

MORTIMER SOURWINE MOUSEL & SLOANE, LTD.
Reno, NV......Civil Trial Practice, General Practice

MORTON, C. RICHARD
West Chester, PA......General Practice

MORTON & LACY
San Francisco, CA......Civil Trial Practice, Insurance Defense Law

MORTON, REED & COUNTS
St. Joseph, MO......General Practice

MORVILLO, ABRAMOWITZ, GRAND, IASON & SILBERBERG, P.C.
New York, NY......Criminal Trial Practice, General Practice

MOSCATO, BYERLY & SKOPIL
Portland, OR......Insurance Defense Law

MOSER AND MARSALEK, P.C.
St. Louis, MO......Civil Trial Practice, General Practice

MOSER & MOSER
Washington, DC......Commercial Law
Albany, NY......Commercial Law, Real Estate Law
New York, NY......Commercial Law, Real Estate Law
Philadelphia, PA......Commercial Law

MOSES, MARGARET L.
Roseland, NJ......Commercial Law, International Business Law

MOSHOS, HADEN & DE DEO, P.C.
Fairfax, VA......General Practice

MOSLEY, CLARE & TOWNES
Louisville, KY......Civil Trial Practice, Family Law, Immigration and Naturalization Law

MOSS & BARNETT, A PROFESSIONAL ASSOCIATION
Minneapolis, MN......General Practice

MOSS, BENTON, WALLIS & PETTIGREW
Jackson, TN......Civil Trial Practice, General Practice, Insurance Defense Law

MOSS & ENOCHIAN, A LAW CORPORATION
Redding, CA......General Practice

MOSS, HENDERSON, VAN GAASBECK, BLANTON & KOVAL, P.A.
Vero Beach, FL......Civil Trial Practice, General Practice, Medical Malpractice Law

MOSS & STRICKLER, P.A.
Bethesda, MD......Family Law

MOULTON, BELLINGHAM, LONGO & MATHER, P.C.
Billings, MT......General Practice

MOUNCE & GALATZAN, A PROFESSIONAL CORPORATION
El Paso, TX......Antitrust Law, Banking Law, General Practice, Labor and Employment Law, Probate and Estate Planning Law

MOUND, COTTON & WOLLAN
New York, NY......Civil Trial Practice, Insurance Defense Law, International Business Law

MOUNTAIN, DEARBORN & WHITING
Worcester, MA......General Practice

MOYE, GILES, O'KEEFE, VERMEIRE & GORRELL
Denver, CO......General Practice

MOYERS, MARTIN, SANTEE, IMEL & TETRICK
Tulsa, OK .... General Practice

MOYLER, MOYLER, RAINEY & COBB
Franklin, VA .... General Practice

MOYNAHAN, BULLEIT, KINKEAD & IRVIN
Lexington, KY .... General Practice

MOZLEY, FINLAYSON & LOGGINS
Atlanta, GA .... Business Law, Civil Trial Practice, Insurance Defense Law

MUDD, MUDD & FITZGERALD, P.A.
La Plata, MD .... General Practice

MUDGE ROSE GUTHRIE ALEXANDER & FERDON
New York, NY .... Civil Trial Practice, Criminal Trial Practice, General Practice, Labor and Employment Law, Municipal Bond/Public Authority Financing Law, Tax Law
Paris, France .... General Practice

MUEGENBURG, NORMAN & DOWLER, A PROFESSIONAL LAW CORPORATION
Ventura, CA .... General Practice

MUELLER AND SMITH, A LEGAL PROFESSIONAL ASSOCIATION
Columbus, OH .... Patent, Trademark, Copyright and Unfair Competition Law

MUELLER, THOMAS F., A PROFESSIONAL CORPORATION
San Jose, CA .... Criminal Trial Practice

MUIR, COSTELLO & CARLSON
Jackson, MN .... General Practice

MULDOON, MURPHY & FAUCETTE
Washington, DC .... Banking Law, Securities Law

MULHEARN & MULHEARN
Natchez, MS .... Civil Trial Practice, Criminal Trial Practice

MULLEN & HENZELL
Santa Barbara, CA .... Civil Trial Practice, General Practice

MULLEN, MACINNES & REDDING
Austin, TX .... Civil Trial Practice, Insurance Defense Law, Personal Injury Law

MULLER, MINTZ, KORNREICH, CALDWELL, CASEY, CROSLAND & BRAMNICK, P.A.
Miami, FL .... Labor and Employment Law
Orlando, FL .... Labor and Employment Law

MULLIGAN & MULLIGAN
Hackettstown, NJ .... Family Law, Personal Injury Law

MULLINS, THOMASON & HARRIS, A PROFESSIONAL CORPORATION
Norton, VA .... General Practice

MULLOY, WALZ, WETTERER, FORE & SCHWARTZ
Louisville, KY .... Business Law, Commercial Law, General Practice, Real Estate Law, Securities Law

MULOCK, COLEMAN & THOMPSON, P.A.
Bradenton, FL .... Medical Malpractice Law, Personal Injury Law

MULVANEY, KAHAN & BARRY, A PROFESSIONAL CORPORATION
San Diego, CA .... Banking Law, Bankruptcy Law, Civil Trial Practice, General Practice

MUNDY & GAMMAGE, P.C.
Cedartown, GA .... Civil Trial Practice, General Practice, Personal Injury Law

MUNDY, ROGERS & FRITH
Roanoke, VA .... Family Law, Medical Malpractice Law, Personal Injury Law

MUNGER AND MUNGER, P.L.C.
Tucson, AZ .... Commercial Law, Probate and Estate Planning Law, Real Estate Law

MUNGER, TOLLES & OLSON
Los Angeles, CA .... General Practice

MUNLEY, MATTISE, KELLY & CARTWRIGHT
Scranton, PA .... Appellate Practice, Civil Trial Practice, Personal Injury Law

MUNZER, STEPHEN I., & ASSOCIATES, P.C.
New York, NY .... Real Estate Law

MURAI, WALD, BIONDO & MORENO, P.A.
Miami, FL .... Civil Trial Practice, General Practice, International Business Law

MURCHIE, CALCUTT & BOYNTON
Beulah, MI .... General Practice
Cadillac, MI .... General Practice
Charlevoix, MI .... General Practice
Leland, MI .... General Practice
Traverse City, MI .... Banking Law, Bankruptcy Law, Civil Trial Practice, Commercial Law, General Practice, Labor and Employment Law, Personal Injury Law, Real Estate Law

MURCHISON & PAULSON
Charlotte, NC .... Real Estate Law

MURCHISON, TAYLOR, KENDRICK, GIBSON & DAVENPORT, L.L.P.
Wilmington, NC .... Civil Trial Practice, General Practice

MURNANE, CONLIN, WHITE & BRANDT, P.A.
St. Paul, MN .... General Practice

MUROV & WARD, A PROFESSIONAL LAW CORPORATION
New Orleans, LA .... Immigration and Naturalization Law

MURPHY, WILLIAM T.
Providence, RI .... Banking Law, Civil Trial Practice, Commercial Law, Criminal Trial Practice, Insurance Defense Law, Labor and Employment Law

MURPHY & ASSOCIATES
Washington, DC .... International Business Law

MURPHY, BARTOL & O'BRIEN
Mineola, NY .... Civil Trial Practice

MURPHY, BUTTERFIELD, HOLLAND & PRICE, P.C.
Williamsport, PA .... Banking Law, Probate and Estate Planning Law

MURPHY & DESMOND, S.C.
Madison, WI .... General Practice

MURPHY, GILLICK, WICHT & PRACHTHAUSER
Appleton, WI .... Personal Injury Law
Milwaukee, WI .... Civil Trial Practice, Personal Injury Law

MURPHY, GOERING, ROBERTS & BERKMAN, P.C.
Tucson, AZ .... Civil Trial Practice, General Practice, Insurance Defense Law, Personal Injury Law

MURPHY, HUPP, FOOTE, MIELKE AND KINNALLY
Aurora, IL .... Environmental Law, General Practice, Insurance Defense Law, Personal Injury Law

MURPHY, LUTEY, SCHMITT & BECK
Prescott, AZ .... Civil Trial Practice, General Practice, Personal Injury Law

MURPHY AND MURPHY
Bryn Mawr, PA .... General Practice, Probate and Estate Planning Law, Real Estate Law

MURPHY & OLIVER, P.C.
Norristown, PA .... Civil Trial Practice, Insurance Defense Law, Personal Injury Law

MURPHY, PEARSON, BRADLEY & FEENEY, A PROFESSIONAL CORPORATION
San Francisco, CA .... Civil Trial Practice, Commercial Law, Medical Malpractice Law, Real Estate Law

MURPHY, PEDERSON, WAITE & WILLIAMS
North Platte, NE .... General Practice

MURPHY, REID & PILOTTE, P.A.
Palm Beach, FL .... General Practice, Probate and Estate Planning Law, Real Estate Law, Tax Law

MURPHY, ROBINSON, HECKATHORN & PHILLIPS, P.C.
Kalispell, MT .... General Practice, Insurance Defense Law

MURPHY & SHEPARD
Lucedale, MS .... General Practice

MURPHY, SMITH & POLK, A PROFESSIONAL CORPORATION
Chicago, IL .... Employment Benefits Law, Labor and Employment Law

MURPHY, THOMPSON & GUNTER, A PROFESSIONAL LAW PARTNERSHIP
Monterey, CA .... Civil Trial Practice, Real Estate Law

MURRAY, JACOBS & ABEL
Alexandria, VA .... Civil Trial Practice

MURRAY LAW FIRM
New Orleans, LA .... Personal Injury Law

MURTAUGH, MILLER, MEYER & NELSON
Costa Mesa, CA .... Civil Trial Practice, Construction Law, General Practice, Insurance Defense Law

MUSCARELLA, BOCHET, LAHIFF, PECK & EDWARDS, P.C.
Fair Lawn, NJ .... Civil Trial Practice, Insurance Defense Law

MUSGRAVE & THEIS, P.C.
Denver, CO .... Administrative Law, Antitrust Law, Civil Trial Practice

MUSHKIN, MARTIN
New York, NY....General Practice

MUSICK, PEELER & GARRETT
Los Angeles, CA....Antitrust Law, General Practice, Labor and Employment Law, Tax Law

MUSSELMAN, ROBERT M. & ASSOCIATES
Charlottesville, VA....Bankruptcy Law, Probate and Estate Planning Law, Tax Law

MYER, SWANSON & ADAMS, P.C.
Denver, CO....Business Law, Civil Trial Practice, Commercial Law, General Practice, Probate and Estate Planning Law

MYERS, FRANK B.
Newport Beach, CA....Construction Law, International Business Law

MYERS, DAUGHERITY, BERRY & O'CONOR, LTD.
Ottawa, IL....General Practice, Personal Injury Law
Streator, IL....General Practice

MYERS, HOPPIN, BRADLEY AND DEVITT, P.C.
Denver, CO....Environmental Law, Family Law, Medical Malpractice Law, Municipal and Zoning Law, Personal Injury Law, Probate and Estate Planning Law, Tax Law

MYERS & JENKINS, A PROFESSIONAL CORPORATION
Phoenix, AZ....Bankruptcy Law, Civil Trial Practice, Commercial Law

MYERS KRAUSE & STEVENS, CHARTERED
Naples, FL....Probate and Estate Planning Law, Real Estate Law

MYLOTTE, DAVID & FITZPATRICK
Philadelphia, PA....Civil Trial Practice

MYRICK, SEAGRAVES, ADAMS & DAVIS
Grants Pass, OR....Family Law, General Practice, Personal Injury Law

NACHMAN, ERWIN B.
Newport News, VA....Bankruptcy Law

NACHSHIN & WESTON
Los Angeles, CA....Family Law

NACK, RICHARDSON & KELLY
Galena, IL....General Practice

NADELHOFFER, KUHN, MITCHELL, MOSS, SALOGA & LECHOWICZ, P.C.
Naperville, IL....General Practice

NAEGELE, TIMOTHY D. & ASSOCIATES
Washington, DC....Banking Law, General Practice

NAGEL, A. PATRICK
Irvine, CA....Labor and Employment Law

NAGLE, KRUG & WINTERS
Burlingame, CA....Insurance Defense Law

NAJJAR DENABURG, P.C.
Birmingham, AL....Family Law, General Practice

NAMACK, CLARK & KEENEY
Sarasota, FL....Probate and Estate Planning Law

NAMAN, HOWELL, SMITH & LEE, A PROFESSIONAL CORPORATION
Austin, TX....General Practice
Waco, TX....General Practice

NANCE, CACCIATORE, SISSERSON, DURYEA AND HAMILTON
Melbourne, FL....Civil Trial Practice, General Practice

NAREY, CHOZEN AND SAUNDERS
Spirit Lake, IA....General Practice

NARRON, O'HALE & WHITTINGTON, P.A.
Smithfield, NC....General Practice

NASATIR, HIRSCH & PODBERESKY
Santa Monica, CA....Criminal Trial Practice

NASH & COMPANY, A PROFESSIONAL CORPORATION
Pittsburgh, PA....General Practice, Health Care Law

NASH & JONES, P.C., LAW OFFICES OF
Tucson, AZ....Criminal Trial Practice

NASH, NASH, STOESS & BROWN
Louisville, KY....General Practice

NASH, SPINDLER, DEAN & GRIMSTAD
Manitowoc, WI....General Practice

NASON, GILDAN, YEAGER, GERSON & WHITE, P.A.
West Palm Beach, FL....Civil Trial Practice, General Practice

NASSER LAW OFFICES, P.C.
Sioux Falls, SD....Insurance Defense Law, Personal Injury Law

NATISS & FERENZO, P.C.
Roslyn Heights, NY....General Practice

NAUFUL, ERNEST J., JR., P.C.
Columbia, SC....Civil Trial Practice, General Practice, Medical Malpractice Law, Product Liability Law

NAUGHTIN, MULVAHILL AND MURRAY
Hibbing, MN....General Practice

NAUMAN, SMITH, SHISSLER & HALL
Harrisburg, PA....Banking Law, Bankruptcy Law, Civil Trial Practice, Environmental Law, General Practice, Insurance Defense Law, Probate and Estate Planning Law, Real Estate Law, Tax Law

NAVRATIL, HARDY & BOURGEOIS
Baton Rouge, LA....Insurance Defense Law

NEAL & ASSOCIATES
Oakland, CA....Bankruptcy Law, Probate and Estate Planning Law

NEAL, CRAVEN & ROMER
Jamestown, TN....General Practice

NEAL, EARL L., & ASSOCIATES
Chicago, IL....Municipal and Zoning Law, Real Estate Law

NEAL & HARWELL
Nashville, TN....Civil Trial Practice, Criminal Trial Practice, General Practice

NEAL, J. W., P.C.
Hobbs, NM....General Practice

NEAL, NEAL & STEWART, P.C.
Flint, MI....Civil Trial Practice

NEARY, BRIAN J.
Hackensack, NJ....Appellate Practice, Criminal Trial Practice

NEBLETT, BEARD & ARSENAULT
Alexandria, LA....Civil Trial Practice

NEEDELL & MCGLONE, A PROFESSIONAL CORPORATION
Trenton, NJ....Civil Trial Practice, Commercial Law, Construction Law, Environmental Law, Insurance Defense Law, Product Liability Law

NEEL, HOOPER & KALMANS, P.C.
Houston, TX....Labor and Employment Law

NEELY & BRIEN
Mayfield, KY....General Practice

NEIDER & BOUCHER, S.C.
Madison, WI....Business Law

NEIGHER, ALAN
Westport, CT....Civil Trial Practice, Communications Law

NEIL, DYMOTT, PERKINS, BROWN & FRANK, A PROFESSIONAL CORPORATION
San Diego, CA....Insurance Defense Law, Medical Malpractice Law, Product Liability Law

NEILL GRIFFIN JEFFRIES & LLOYD, CHARTERED
Fort Pierce, FL....Civil Trial Practice, Personal Injury Law, Real Estate Law

NELSON, ERNEST J. JR.
Decatur, GA....General Practice

NELSON, BOYD, MACDONALD, MITCHELL, MASON & HEDIN
San Rafael, CA....General Practice

NELSON, CASEY, TRIPP & DOW, P.A.
Owatonna, MN....General Practice

NELSON, DRIES & ZIMMERMAN, S.C.
Brookfield, WI....Civil Trial Practice, Insurance Defense Law

NELSON, GORDON & BURSTEIN
New York, NY....General Practice

NELSON HESSE CYRIL SMITH WIDMAN HERB CAUSEY & DOOLEY
Sarasota, FL....Civil Trial Practice, General Practice

NELSON, J. BARLOW, INC.
Tulsa, OK....Probate and Estate Planning Law

NELSON, MCMAHAN, PARKER & NOBLETT
Chattanooga, TN....Insurance Defense Law, Municipal and Zoning Law, Personal Injury Law

NELSON MULLINS RILEY & SCARBOROUGH, L.L.P.
Columbia, SC....Civil Trial Practice, General Practice, Tax Law

Greenville, SC..........Civil Trial Practice, General Practice, Tax Law
Lexington, SC..........General Practice
Myrtle Beach, SC..........Civil Trial Practice, General Practice

NELSON & NELSON
Washington, DC..........Civil Trial Practice
Bethesda, MD..........Civil Trial Practice

NELSON OYEN TORVIK
Montevideo, MN..........General Practice

NELSON, PERLOV & LEE, A PROFESSIONAL CORPORATION
Los Altos, CA..........Personal Injury Law

NEMEROFF, ROBERTS & SAFFREN, A PROFESSIONAL CORPORATION
Philadelphia, PA..........Civil Trial Practice, Criminal Trial Practice, Personal Injury Law, Real Estate Law

NEMETH, JOHN C. & ASSOCIATES
Columbus, OH..........Civil Trial Practice, Insurance Defense Law

NEPPLE, VAN DER KAMP & FLYNN, P.C.
Rock Island, IL..........Probate and Estate Planning Law, Tax Law

NESSER, KING & LEBLANC
New Orleans, LA..........Admiralty/Maritime Law, Banking Law, Bankruptcy Law, Civil Trial Practice, Construction Law, Environmental Law, General Practice, Insurance Defense Law, Tax Law

NETZORG & MCKEEVER, PROFESSIONAL CORPORATION
Denver, CO..........Business Law, Civil Trial Practice, Commercial Law, Natural Resources Law, Securities Law

NEU, MINNICH, COMITO & HALL, P.C.
Carroll, IA..........General Practice

NEUMEYER & BOYD
Los Angeles, CA..........Appellate Practice, Insurance Defense Law

NEUMILLER & BEARDSLEE, A PROFESSIONAL CORPORATION
Stockton, CA..........General Practice

NEVILLE, WILLIAM V. JR.
Eufaula, AL..........General Practice, Real Estate Law

NEVORAL, BERNARD R., AND ASSOCIATES, LTD.
Chicago, IL..........Civil Trial Practice, Personal Injury Law, Product Liability Law

NEWBERRY, HARGROVE & RAMBICURE, P.S.C.
Lexington, KY..........General Practice

NEWBROUGH, JOHNSTON, BREWER, MADDUX AND NADLER
Ames, IA..........General Practice

NEWBY, LEWIS, KAMINSKI & JONES
La Porte, IN..........Civil Trial Practice, General Practice, Insurance Defense Law, Labor and Employment Law, Product Liability Law

NEWCOMER, SHAFFER, BIRD & SPANGLER
Bryan, OH..........General Practice

NEWITT & BRUNY
Charlotte, NC..........Business Law

NEWLAN, DOUGLAS H.
Redding, CA..........Insurance Defense Law

NEWMAN, CRAIG
Casper, WY..........Natural Resources Law

NEWMAN, DAVID, & ASSOCIATES, P.C.
La Plata, MD..........Criminal Trial Practice, Medical Malpractice Law, Patent, Trademark, Copyright and Unfair Competition Law, Product Liability Law

NEWMAN SCHLAU FITCH & LANE, P.C.
New York, NY..........Civil Trial Practice, Insurance Defense Law

NEWMAN & SCHWARTZ
New York, NY..........Criminal Trial Practice

NEWMARK IRVINE, P.A.
Phoenix, AZ..........Tax Law

NEWSOM, GRAHAM, HEDRICK & KENNON, P.A.
Durham, NC..........Civil Trial Practice, General Practice

NEWTON - KIGHT
Everett, WA..........General Practice

NEXSEN PRUET JACOBS & POLLARD, LLP
Columbia, SC..........General Practice

NIBLOCK LAW FIRM
Fayetteville, AR..........Civil Trial Practice

NICHOLS, CAFFREY, HILL & EVANS, L.L.P.
Greensboro, NC..........Civil Trial Practice, General Practice

NICHOLS, JONES & MCCOWN
Tuscola, IL..........General Practice

NICHOLSON, FLETCHER & DEGROW
Port Huron, MI..........Civil Trial Practice, Environmental Law, General Practice, Insurance Defense Law, Labor and Employment Law, Municipal and Zoning Law

NICHOLSON, TURNER, WALKER & WHITE
St. Stephen, NB, Canada..........General Practice

NICKLAUS, VALLE, CRAIG & WICKS
Miami, FL..........Admiralty/Maritime Law, Civil Trial Practice, Commercial Law, Insurance Defense Law, Personal Injury Law, Product Liability Law

NICOLAS, MORRIS & BARROW
Corpus Christi, TX..........Family Law, General Practice

NICOLETTE & PERKINS, P.A.
Oradell, NJ..........Administrative Law, Bankruptcy Law, Commercial Law, General Practice

NICOLINI & PARADISE
Mineola, NY..........Civil Trial Practice, Insurance Defense Law

NIEBLER, PYZYK & WAGNER
Menomonee Falls, WI..........General Practice, Real Estate Law

NIEWALD, WALDECK & BROWN, A PROFESSIONAL CORPORATION
Kansas City, MO..........Civil Trial Practice, General Practice

NIGHTINGALE, LILES, DENNARD & CARMICAL
Brunswick, GA..........General Practice

NILES, BARTON & WILMER
Baltimore, MD..........Admiralty/Maritime Law, General Practice

NILLES, HANSEN & DAVIES, LTD.
Fargo, ND..........Banking Law, Civil Trial Practice, Commercial Law, General Practice, Insurance Defense Law, Labor and Employment Law, Personal Injury Law, Probate and Estate Planning Law, Real Estate Law, Tax Law

NILSSON, WURST & GREEN
Los Angeles, CA..........Patent, Trademark, Copyright and Unfair Competition Law

NIMS, HOWES, COLLISON, HANSEN & LACKERT
New York, NY..........Trademark, Copyright and Unfair Competition Law

NIRO, SCAVONE, HALLER & NIRO
Chicago, IL..........Patent, Trademark, Copyright and Unfair Competition Law

NIX, HOLTSFORD & VERCELLI, P.C.
Montgomery, AL..........Environmental Law, Insurance Defense Law

NIXON & VANDERHYE, P.C.
Arlington, VA..........Patent, Trademark, Copyright and Unfair Competition Law

NOBILE, MAGARIAN & DISALVO
Bronxville, NY..........General Practice

NOBLE & SULLIVAN
Cleveland, OH..........Natural Resources Law

NOLAN & ARMSTRONG
Palo Alto, CA..........Criminal Trial Practice

NOLAN, PLUMHOFF & WILLIAMS, CHARTERED
Towson, MD..........Civil Trial Practice, Criminal Trial Practice, General Practice, Personal Injury Law

NOLAND, HAMERLY, ETIENNE & HOSS, A PROFESSIONAL CORPORATION
Salinas, CA..........General Practice

NOONAN & PROKUP
Allentown, PA..........Probate and Estate Planning Law

NOONAN, THOMAS J., P.C., LAW OFFICES OF
St. Louis, MO..........Commercial Law, Insurance Defense Law

NORDMAN, CORMANY, HAIR & COMPTON
Oxnard, CA..........Bankruptcy Law, General Practice

NORMAN, THRALL, ANGLE & GUY
Jacksonville, TX..........Civil Trial Practice, General Practice, Insurance Defense Law
Rusk, TX..........Civil Trial Practice, General Practice, Insurance Defense Law

NORMANDIN, CHENEY & O'NEIL
Laconia, NH..........Banking Law, Civil Trial Practice, Commercial Law, General Practice, Personal Injury Law, Probate and Estate Planning Law, Product Liability Law, Real Estate Law

NORMINTON & WIITA
Beverly Hills, CA....................Civil Trial Practice

NORRIS, FLOYD H.
Los Angeles, CA....................Probate and Estate Planning Law

NORRIS, CHOPLIN & SCHROEDER
Indianapolis, IN....................Environmental Law, Insurance Defense Law, Personal Injury Law

NORTH, STEVEN E., P.C.
New York, NY....................Medical Malpractice Law, Personal Injury Law

NORTHCUTT, CLARK, GARDNER, HRON & POWELL
Ponca City, OK....................General Practice

NORTHEN, BLUE, ROOKS, THIBAUT, ANDERSON & WOODS, L.L.P.
Chapel Hill, NC....................Bankruptcy Law, Business Law, Civil Trial Practice, Family Law, Personal Injury Law

NORTON & CHRISTENSEN
Goshen, NY....................Construction Law, Environmental Law, General Practice

NORTON, WASSERMAN, JONES & KELLY
Salina, KS....................Civil Trial Practice

NORVELL & ASSOCIATES, A PROFESSIONAL CORPORATION
Abilene, TX....................Civil Trial Practice, Personal Injury Law

NOSEK, FRANCIS J., JR., A PROFESSIONAL CORPORATION
Anchorage, AK....................Real Estate Law

NOTARO & MICHALOS P.C.
New York, NY....................Patent, Trademark, Copyright and Unfair Competition Law, Trademark, Copyright and Unfair Competition Law

NOTTAGE AND WARD
Chicago, IL....................Family Law

NOTTINGHAM, ENGEL, GORDON & KERR
Syracuse, NY....................Civil Trial Practice, General Practice

NOVACK AND MACEY
Chicago, IL....................Civil Trial Practice

NOVAKOV, DAVIDSON & FLYNN, A PROFESSIONAL CORPORATION
Dallas, TX....................Banking Law, Business Law, Civil Trial Practice, General Practice, Probate and Estate Planning Law, Real Estate Law, Tax Law

NOVEY & MENDELSON
Tallahassee, FL....................Family Law, Real Estate Law

NOVINS, YORK & PENTONY, A PROFESSIONAL CORPORATION
Toms River, NJ....................Civil Trial Practice, Criminal Trial Practice, General Practice

NOVOSELSKY, DAVID A. & ASSOCIATES
Chicago, IL....................Appellate Practice

NUKES, PERANTINIDES & NOLAN CO., L.P.A.
Akron, OH....................Civil Trial Practice, General Practice, Insurance Defense Law

NURENBERG, PLEVIN, HELLER & MCCARTHY CO., L.P.A.
Cleveland, OH....................Civil Trial Practice, General Practice, Medical Malpractice Law, Personal Injury Law

NUTTER, MCCLENNEN & FISH
Boston, MA....................General Practice

OATES, HUGHES & KNEZEVICH, P.C.
Aspen, CO....................Civil Trial Practice, General Practice

OATS & HUDSON
Lafayette, LA....................Admiralty/Maritime Law

O'BANNON & O'BANNON
Florence, AL....................Insurance Defense Law

OBENSHAIN, WILEY S., III, P.C.
Augusta, GA....................Civil Trial Practice, Insurance Defense Law

OBERDANK, LAWRENCE M., CO., L.P.A.
Cleveland, OH....................Labor and Employment Law

OBERMAN & OBERMAN
Charleston, SC....................Civil Trial Practice, Family Law, Real Estate Law

OBERMAYER, REBMANN, MAXWELL & HIPPEL
Philadelphia, PA....................General Practice

O'BRIANT, O'BRIANT, BUNCH, WHATLEY & ROBINS
Asheboro, NC....................General Practice

O'BRIEN, WILLIAM M.
Cambridge, MA....................Banking Law, Commercial Law, General Practice, Real Estate Law

O'BRIEN, EHRICK, WOLF, DEANER & MAUS
Rochester, MN....................General Practice

O'BRIEN, JOHN D., LTD.
Las Vegas, NV....................Civil Trial Practice, Probate and Estate Planning Law

O'BRIEN, LIOTTA & MANDEL
Union, NJ....................Business Law

O'BRIEN AND O'BRIEN
Ann Arbor, MI....................Civil Trial Practice, Criminal Trial Practice, Personal Injury Law

O'BRIEN, O'ROURKE & HOGAN
Chicago, IL....................Civil Trial Practice, Construction Law, Real Estate Law

O'BRIEN, SHAFNER, STUART, KELLY & MORRIS, P.C.
Groton, CT....................General Practice, Personal Injury Law
Norwich, CT....................General Practice

O'BRIEN, TANSKI, TANZER & YOUNG
Hartford, CT....................General Practice, Health Care Law

O'CONNELL AND ARONOWITZ, P.C.
Albany, NY....................Civil Trial Practice, Criminal Trial Practice, General Practice, Health Care Law

O'CONNELL & MAYHUGH, P.C.
Warrenton, VA....................General Practice

O'CONNELL & NEWMAN
Tucson, AZ....................Probate and Estate Planning Law, Tax Law

O'CONNOR, CAVANAGH, ANDERSON, WESTOVER, KILLINGSWORTH & BESHEARS, A PROFESSIONAL ASSOCIATION
Nogales, AZ....................Administrative Law, Civil Trial Practice, Commercial Law, General Practice, International Business Law, Real Estate Law, Tax Law
Phoenix, AZ....................Administrative Law, Antitrust Law, Banking Law, Bankruptcy Law, Civil Trial Practice, Commercial Law, Construction Law, Environmental Law, General Practice, Health Care Law, Insurance Defense Law, International Business Law, Labor and Employment Law, Patent, Trademark, Copyright and Unfair Competition Law, Product Liability Law, Real Estate Law, Securities Law, Tax Law
Sun City, AZ....................General Practice, Probate and Estate Planning Law, Tax Law
Tucson, AZ....................Bankruptcy Law, Civil Trial Practice, Commercial Law, Construction Law, Environmental Law, General Practice, Health Care Law, Insurance Defense Law, Labor and Employment Law, Product Liability Law, Real Estate Law, Securities Law

O'CONNOR, COHN, DILLON & BARR, A LAW CORPORATION
San Francisco, CA....................Civil Trial Practice, Medical Malpractice Law, Product Liability Law

O'CONNOR, GACIOCH & POPE
Binghamton, NY....................Construction Law, Environmental Law, Insurance Defense Law, Labor and Employment Law

O'CONNOR & HANNAN
Washington, DC....................General Practice
Minneapolis, MN....................Antitrust Law, General Practice, Municipal Bond/Public Authority Financing Law, Tax Law

O'CONNOR, MCGUINNESS, CONTE, DOYLE, OLESON & COLLINS
White Plains, NY....................General Practice, Insurance Defense Law, Probate and Estate Planning Law

O'CONNOR & RHATICAN, A PROFESSIONAL CORPORATION
Chatham, NJ....................Civil Trial Practice, Medical Malpractice Law, Personal Injury Law

O'CONNOR AND RYAN, P.C.
Fitchburg, MA....................Civil Trial Practice, Personal Injury Law

O'CONNOR & THOMAS, P.C.
Dubuque, IA....................General Practice

ODELL, JAMES R., P.S.C.
Lexington, KY....................General Practice

ODIN, FELDMAN & PITTLEMAN, P.C.
Fairfax, VA....................Banking Law, Civil Trial Practice, Commercial Law, Family Law, General Practice, Labor and Employment Law, Real Estate Law, Tax Law, Trademark, Copyright and Unfair Competition Law

ODOM, ELLIOTT, WINBURN AND WATSON
Fayetteville, AR....................Civil Trial Practice, Personal Injury Law

O'DONNELL, RAMIS, CREW, CORRIGAN & BACHRACH
Portland, OR....................Antitrust Law, Business Law, Civil Trial Practice, Environmental Law, Labor and Employment Law, Municipal and Zoning Law, Personal Injury Law, Real Estate Law

O'DONNELL, WEISS & MATTEI, P.C.
Pottstown, PA....General Practice

O'DONOGHUE & O'DONOGHUE
Washington, DC....Labor and Employment Law

O'DONOHUE & O'DONOHUE
Toronto, ON, Canada....General Practice

OFFERMANN, CASSANO, PIGOTT & GRECO
Buffalo, NY....General Practice

OFFUTT, HORMAN, BURDETTE & FREY, P.A.
Frederick, MD....General Practice

O'FLARITY, JAMES P., P.A.
West Palm Beach, FL....Family Law

OGBURN, JOHN N. JR.
Asheboro, NC....Business Law, Probate and Estate Planning Law

OGDEN, LEN W. JR.
Paducah, KY....Criminal Trial Practice

OGDEN NEWELL & WELCH
Louisville, KY....Administrative Law, Antitrust Law, Appellate Practice, Business Law, Civil Trial Practice, Commercial Law, Communications Law, Criminal Trial Practice, Employment Benefits Law, Environmental Law, General Practice, Health Care Law, Insurance Defense Law, Labor and Employment Law, Medical Malpractice Law, Municipal Bond/Public Authority Financing Law, Probate and Estate Planning Law, Product Liability Law, Public Utilities Law, Real Estate Law, Securities Law, Tax Law

OGILVIE, GEORGE F.
Las Vegas, NV....General Practice

OGILVIE, DAVID A., P.C.
Denver, CO....Criminal Trial Practice

OGILVY RENAULT
Ottawa, ON, Canada....General Practice
Montreal, QU, Canada....General Practice
Quebec, QU, Canada....General Practice

OGLETREE, DEAKINS, NASH, SMOAK & STEWART
Washington, DC....Labor and Employment Law
Atlanta, GA....Labor and Employment Law
Raleigh, NC....Labor and Employment Law
Charleston, SC....Labor and Employment Law
Columbia, SC....Labor and Employment Law
Greenville, SC....Environmental Law, Labor and Employment Law

O'HAIRE, QUINN, CANDLER & O'HAIRE
Vero Beach, FL....Civil Trial Practice, General Practice

O'HARA & HANLON
Syracuse, NY....General Practice

O'HARA, RUBERG, TAYLOR, SLOAN AND SERGENT
Covington, KY....Civil Trial Practice, Family Law, General Practice

O'HARE & HEITCZMAN
Bethlehem, PA....Civil Trial Practice, Criminal Trial Practice, General Practice

OHNEGIAN, DONALD C.
Ramsey, NJ....Civil Trial Practice, General Practice, Probate and Estate Planning Law

OHNSTAD TWICHELL, P.C.
West Fargo, ND....Criminal Trial Practice, General Practice, Municipal Bond/Public Authority Financing Law, Probate and Estate Planning Law

OHRENSTEIN, BENJAMIN S.
Haverford, PA....Business Law, General Practice, Probate and Estate Planning Law

OHRENSTEIN & BROWN
New York, NY....Civil Trial Practice, Insurance Defense Law

OLDFATHER & MORRIS
Louisville, KY....Civil Trial Practice, Family Law, General Practice, Medical Malpractice Law, Personal Injury Law, Product Liability Law

OLDFIELD & COKER
Oklahoma City, OK....Insurance Defense Law, Labor and Employment Law, Personal Injury Law

O'LEARY, O'LEARY, JACOBS, MATTSON, PERRY & MASON, P.C.
Southfield, MI....Appellate Practice, Civil Trial Practice, Insurance Defense Law, Medical Malpractice Law, Transportation Law

OLENDER, JACK H., AND ASSOCIATES, P.C.
Washington, DC....Medical Malpractice Law

OLES, MORRISON & RINKER
Seattle, WA....Construction Law, General Practice, Insurance Defense Law

OLINS, FOERSTER & HAYES
San Diego, CA....Family Law, Labor and Employment Law, Personal Injury Law

OLIVE AND OLIVE, P.A.
Durham, NC....Patent, Trademark, Copyright and Unfair Competition Law

OLIVEIRA, RONALD E.
Pittsfield, MA....General Practice

OLIVER, DUCKWORTH, SPARGER & WINKLE, P.C.
Jonesboro, GA....Civil Trial Practice, General Practice

OLIVER, OLIVER & WALTZ, P.C.
Cape Girardeau, MO....Civil Trial Practice, General Practice, Insurance Defense Law

OLIVER, WALKER, CARLTON AND WILSON
Columbia, MO....General Practice

OLSON, GIBBONS, SARTAIN, NICOUD, BIRNE & SUSSMAN, L.L.P.
Dallas, TX....Bankruptcy Law, Civil Trial Practice, Commercial Law

OLTMAN AND FLYNN
Fort Lauderdale, FL....Patent, Trademark, Copyright and Unfair Competition Law

OLUP & ASSOCIATES
Minneapolis, MN....Family Law

O'MALLEY & HARRIS, P.C.
Scranton, PA....Civil Trial Practice, General Practice, Insurance Defense Law, Medical Malpractice Law

O'MEARA, ECKERT, POUROS & GONRING
West Bend, WI....General Practice

O'MELIA, SCHIEK & MCELDOWNEY, S.C.
Rhinelander, WI....General Practice

O'MELVENY & MYERS
Los Angeles, CA....Banking Law, Civil Trial Practice, General Practice, Insurance Defense Law, Labor and Employment Law, Municipal Bond/Public Authority Financing Law, Real Estate Law, Tax Law
Newport Beach, CA....General Practice
San Francisco, CA....General Practice
Washington, DC....Communications Law, General Practice
New York, NY....General Practice
London, England....General Practice
Hong Kong, Hong Kong (British Crown Colony)....General Practice
Tokyo, Japan....General Practice

OMINSKY, WELSH & STEINBERG, P.C.
Philadelphia, PA....Civil Trial Practice, General Practice, Personal Injury Law, Real Estate Law

OMOHUNDRO, PALMERLEE AND DURRANT
Buffalo, WY....Commercial Law, Environmental Law, General Practice, Natural Resources Law, Probate and Estate Planning Law, Real Estate Law
Gillette, WY....General Practice

O'NEAL, BROWN & SIZEMORE, A PROFESSIONAL CORPORATION
Macon, GA....General Practice, Personal Injury Law

O'NEAL, WALKER & BOEHM
Chattanooga, TN....Personal Injury Law

ONEBANE, DONOHOE, BERNARD, TORIAN, DIAZ, MCNAMARA & ABELL
Lafayette, LA....Civil Trial Practice, General Practice, Insurance Defense Law

O'NEIL, EICHIN, MILLER, BRECKINRIDGE & SAPORITO, A LAW CORPORATION
New Orleans, LA....Admiralty/Maritime Law, Insurance Defense Law

O'NEILL & BORGES
San Juan, PR....Bankruptcy Law, Civil Trial Practice, Environmental Law, General Practice, Immigration and Naturalization Law, Labor and Employment Law, Real Estate Law, Tax Law, Trademark, Copyright and Unfair Competition Law

O'NEILL, CHAPIN, MARKS, LIEBMAN, COOPER & CARR
Orlando, FL....Civil Trial Practice, Commercial Law, Insurance Defense Law

O'NEILL, JOSEPH D., A PROFESSIONAL CORPORATION
Vineland, NJ....Criminal Trial Practice, Personal Injury Law

O'NEILL, LYSAGHT & SUN
Santa Monica, CA....................Appellate Practice, Civil Trial Practice, Commercial Law, Criminal Trial Practice

O'NEILL, WALLACE & DOYLE, P.C.
Saginaw, MI....................General Practice, Insurance Defense Law

OOT LAW OFFICES
East Syracuse, NY....................General Practice

OPPENHEIMER, BLEND, HARRISON & TATE, INC.
San Antonio, TX....................General Practice

OPPERMAN & ASSOCIATES, P.C.
Denver, CO....................Civil Trial Practice, Real Estate Law

ORANS, ELSEN & LUPERT
New York, NY....................Appellate Practice, Civil Trial Practice, Criminal Trial Practice, Family Law, International Business Law, Securities Law

O'REAR & O'REAR
Jasper, AL....................Business Law, Civil Trial Practice, Probate and Estate Planning Law, Real Estate Law

O'REILLY & COLLINS, A PROFESSIONAL CORPORATION
Menlo Park, CA....................Civil Trial Practice, Personal Injury Law, Product Liability Law

O'REILLY, CUNNINGHAM, NORTON & MANCINI, PROFESSIONAL CORPORATION
Wheaton, IL....................Civil Trial Practice

O'REILLY, NOSEWORTHY
St. John's, NF, Canada....................General Practice

O'REILLY, RANCILIO, NITZ, ANDREWS & TURNBULL, P.C.
Sterling Heights, MI....................General Practice

ORGAIN, BELL & TUCKER, L.L.P.
Beaumont, TX....................General Practice

O'RIORDEN, MANN, HOOTMAN, INGRAM & DUNKLE, P.A.
Sarasota, FL....................Insurance Defense Law

ORLOFF, LOWENBACH, STIFELMAN & SIEGEL, A PROFESSIONAL CORPORATION
Roseland, NJ....................Civil Trial Practice, Commercial Law, General Practice, Probate and Estate Planning Law, Tax Law

ORLOW AND ORLOW, P.C.
Philadelphia, PA....................Immigration and Naturalization Law

ORMAN, JAMES M.
Philadelphia, PA....................Probate and Estate Planning Law

O'ROURKE, ALLAN & FONG
Glendale, CA....................Civil Trial Practice, Construction Law, Real Estate Law

O'ROURKE & JOSEPH, P.C.
Flint, MI....................Civil Trial Practice, Criminal Trial Practice

ORR & RENO, PROFESSIONAL ASSOCIATION
Concord, NH....................Civil Trial Practice, Commercial Law, Environmental Law, General Practice, Health Care Law, Labor and Employment Law, Personal Injury Law, Probate and Estate Planning Law, Real Estate Law, Tax Law

ORTON, TOOMAN, HALE AND MCKOWN, P.C.
Allegan, MI....................General Practice

OSBORN HINER & LISHER, P.C.
Indianapolis, IN....................Civil Trial Practice, Insurance Defense Law, Product Liability Law

OSBORN, MALCOLM E., P.A.
Winston-Salem, NC....................Tax Law

OSBORN, REED, BURKE & TOBIN
Rochester, NY....................General Practice

OSBORNE AND AIKIN, P.A.
Orlando, FL....................Civil Trial Practice

OSBORNE, LOWE, HELMAN & SMITH, L.L.P.
Austin, TX....................Probate and Estate Planning Law

OSBORNE, OSBORNE & DECLAIRE, P.A.
Boca Raton, FL....................General Practice, Probate and Estate Planning Law

O'SHAUGHNESSY, PHILLIPS P., P.A.
Baltimore, MD....................Civil Trial Practice, General Practice

OSHINS & GIBBONS
[illegible]gas, NV....................General Practice, Probate and Estate Planning Law

[illegible]SKIN & HARCOURT
[illegible] ON, Canada....................General Practice, Patent, Trademark, Copyright and Unfair Competition Law

Toronto, ON, Canada....................General Practice, Patent, Trademark, Copyright and Unfair Competition Law

OSLER RENAULT
London, England....................General Practice
Paris, France....................General Practice
Hong Kong, Hong Kong (British Crown Colony)....................General Practice

OSTROVE, KRANTZ & OSTROVE, A PROFESSIONAL CORPORATION
Los Angeles, CA....................General Practice

O'SULLIVAN, BEAUCHAMP, KELLY & WHIPPLE
Port Huron, MI....................General Practice

OSWALD & COTTEY, A PROFESSIONAL CORPORATION
Kirksville, MO....................Civil Trial Practice, General Practice

OTERI, WEINBERG & LAWSON
Boston, MA....................Criminal Trial Practice

OTHS & HEISER
Wellston, OH....................Probate and Estate Planning Law

OTSTOTT, GEORGE A., & ASSOCIATES, A PROF. CORP.
Dallas, TX....................Medical Malpractice Law, Personal Injury Law, Product Liability Law

OTTEN, JOHNSON, ROBINSON, NEFF & RAGONETTI, P.C.
Denver, CO....................General Practice

OTTERBOURG, STEINDLER, HOUSTON & ROSEN, P.C.
New York, NY....................Antitrust Law, Appellate Practice, Banking Law, Bankruptcy Law, Business Law, Civil Trial Practice, Commercial Law, Construction Law, Employment Benefits Law, General Practice, International Business Law, Probate and Estate Planning Law, Real Estate Law, Securities Law, Trademark, Copyright and Unfair Competition Law

OTTERMAN & ALLEN, P.C.
Barre, VT....................Probate and Estate Planning Law

OTTO, PORTERFIELD & POST
Vail, CO....................Banking Law, General Practice, Real Estate Law

OTTS, MOORE & JORDAN
Brewton, AL....................General Practice

OUGHTERSON, OUGHTERSON, PREWITT & SUNDHEIM, P.A.
Stuart, FL....................General Practice, Probate and Estate Planning Law

OUTERBRIDGE AND MILLER
Toronto, ON, Canada....................Civil Trial Practice

OUTTEN, BARRETT, BURR & SHARRETT, P.C.
Emporia, VA....................General Practice
Lawrenceville, VA....................General Practice

OVERBEY, HAWKINS & SELZ
Rustburg, VA....................Civil Trial Practice, General Practice

OVERSTREET RITCH & THACKER
Kissimmee, FL....................General Practice

OWEN, WILLIAM L.
Little Rock, AR....................Civil Trial Practice, Real Estate Law

OWEN, LYLE, VOSS & OWEN, P.C.
Plainview, TX....................General Practice

OWEN & MELBYE, A PROFESSIONAL CORPORATION
Redwood City, CA....................General Practice, Insurance Defense Law

OWEN SHOUP & KINZIE
Indianapolis, IN....................Employment Benefits Law, Labor and Employment Law

OWENS DAVIES MACKIE, A PROFESSIONAL SERVICES CORPORATION
Olympia, WA....................General Practice

OWLETT, LEWIS & GINN, P.C.
Wellsboro, PA....................General Practice, Probate and Estate Planning Law, Real Estate Law, Tax Law

OXFORD, MCKELVEY & JONES, P.C.
Americus, GA....................Commercial Law, Personal Injury Law, Real Estate Law

OXLEY, MALONE, FITZGERALD & HOLLISTER
Findlay, OH....................General Practice, Insurance Defense Law

OZZARD WHARTON, A PROFESSIONAL PARTNERSHIP
Somerville, NJ....................Banking Law, Civil Trial Practice, Commercial Law, Environmental Law, Family Law, General Practice, Insurance Defense Law, Municipal Bond/Public Authority Financing Law, Municipal and Zoning Law, Personal Injury Law, Probate and Estate Planning Law, Real Estate Law

PACIFICO, PAUL J. LAW OFFICES OF
Westport, CT............................Appellate Practice, Civil Trial Practice, Family Law, Personal Injury Law

PADBERG, MCSWEENEY, SLATER & MERZ, A PROFESSIONAL CORPORATION
St. Louis, MO............................Civil Trial Practice, Medical Malpractice Law, Personal Injury Law, Product Liability Law, Real Estate Law

PADGETT & SHAW, P.A.
Coral Gables, FL ....General Practice

PAGE & BACEK
Atlanta, GA ....General Practice

PAGE, MANNINO & PERESICH
Biloxi, MS................................General Practice, Insurance Defense Law, Medical Malpractice Law, Personal Injury Law, Product Liability Law
Gulfport, MS............................General Practice, Insurance Defense Law, Medical Malpractice Law, Personal Injury Law, Product Liability Law
Jackson, MS ....General Practice, Insurance Defense Law, Medical Malpractice Law, Personal Injury Law, Product Liability Law

PAGE, POLIN, BUSCH & BOATWRIGHT, A PROFESSIONAL CORPORATION
San Diego, CA ....Bankruptcy Law, Business Law, Civil Trial Practice, General Practice, International Business Law, Tax Law

PAGLIUSO, JAMES J.
Glendale, CA...........................Medical Malpractice Law

PAIN AND GARLAND
Anadarko, OK ....General Practice

PAINE EDMONDS
Vancouver, BC, Canada...........General Practice, Insurance Defense Law

PAINE, MCELREATH & HYDER, P.C.
Augusta, GA ....Commercial Law

PAINTER, RATTERREE & BART
Savannah, GA ....General Practice, Product Liability Law

PAJCIC & PAJCIC, P.A.
Jacksonville, FL ....Personal Injury Law

PALAZZO, ROBERT P.
Los Angeles, CA ....International Business Law

PALEY, ROTHMAN, GOLDSTEIN, ROSENBERG & COOPER, CHARTERED
Bethesda, MD ....General Practice, Tax Law

PALKOVITZ, HERBERT
Cleveland, OH.........................Family Law

PALMATIER, SJOQUIST & HELGET, P.A.
Minneapolis, MN ....Patent, Trademark, Copyright and Unfair Competition Law

PALMER, ALLEN & MCTAGGART, L.L.P.
Dallas, TX...............................Appellate Practice, Banking Law, Business Law, Commercial Law, Probate and Estate Planning Law, Real Estate Law

PALMER BIEZUP & HENDERSON
Philadelphia, PA ....Admiralty/Maritime Law, Civil Trial Practice, Insurance Defense Law

PALMER & DODGE
Boston, MA.............................Antitrust Law, Banking Law, Bankruptcy Law, Business Law, Civil Trial Practice, Construction Law, Employment Benefits Law, Environmental Law, General Practice, Immigration and Naturalization Law, Insurance Defense Law, International Business Law, Labor and Employment Law, Municipal Bond/Public Authority Financing Law, Personal Injury Law, Probate and Estate Planning Law, Real Estate Law, Securities Law, Tax Law, Trademark, Copyright and Unfair Competition Law

PALMER LAW FIRM
Dyersburg, TN........................Personal Injury Law

PALMER & LOWRY
Topeka, KS.............................Medical Malpractice Law, Personal Injury Law

PALMER, O'CONNELL, LEGER, RODERICK, GLENNIE
Saint John, NB, Canada ....General Practice

PALMIERI, TYLER, WIENER, WILHELM & WALDRON
Irvine, CA...............................General Practice

PALUMBO, JOSEPH R. JR.
Middletown, RI.......................Civil Trial Practice, Personal Injury Law

PANIELLO, JOSEPH M.
Tampa, FL ....Real Estate Law

PANITCH SCHWARZE JACOBS & NADEL, P.C.
Philadelphia, PA ....Patent, Trademark, Copyright and Unfair Competition Law

PAPA, HERMAN D.
San Francisco, CA ....Civil Trial Practice

PAPERNICK AND GEFSKY, A PROFESSIONAL CORPORATION
Pittsburgh, PA ....Real Estate Law

PARDIECK, GILL & VARGO, A PROFESSIONAL CORPORATION
Indianapolis, IN......................Medical Malpractice Law, Personal Injury Law, Product Liability Law
Seymour, IN............................Medical Malpractice Law, Personal Injury Law, Product Liability Law

PARHAM, HELMS & HARRIS
Charlotte, NC..........................Real Estate Law

PARHAM & SMITH
Greenville, SC.........................Civil Trial Practice, Medical Malpractice Law, Personal Injury Law

PARICHAN, RENBERG, CROSSMAN & HARVEY, LAW CORPORATION
Fresno, CA..............................Business Law, Civil Trial Practice, Insurance Defense Law, Probate and Estate Planning Law

PARILLA, MILITZOK & SHEDDEN
Irvine, CA...............................Business Law, Real Estate Law

PARKER, BRANTLEY & WILKERSON, P.C.
Montgomery, AL ....Bankruptcy Law, Civil Trial Practice, Communications Law, Health Care Law, Insurance Defense Law, Public Utilities Law

PARKER CHAPIN FLATTAU & KLIMPL, L.L.P.
New York, NY.........................Antitrust Law, Banking Law, Bankruptcy Law, Civil Trial Practice, Commercial Law, General Practice, Health Care Law, Insurance Defense Law, Labor and Employment Law, Medical Malpractice Law, Probate and Estate Planning Law, Product Liability Law, Real Estate Law, Securities Law, Tax Law

PARKER, HAYES & LOVINGER, P.C.
Hillsdale, MI ....General Practice

PARKER, HUDSON, RAINER & DOBBS
Atlanta, GA ....Antitrust Law, Bankruptcy Law, Business Law, Commercial Law, Health Care Law, Securities Law

PARKER, JOHNSON & PARKER, P.S.
Hoquiam, WA..........................General Practice

PARKER, LAWRENCE, CANTRELL & DEAN
Nashville, TN..........................Civil Trial Practice, General Practice

PARKER, MCCAY & CRISCUOLO, P.A.
Cherry Hill, NJ ....Civil Trial Practice, General Practice
Marlton, NJ.............................Civil Trial Practice, General Practice

PARKERSON & SHELFER
Decatur, GA............................Insurance Defense Law, Personal Injury Law

PARKOWSKI, NOBLE & GUERKE, PROFESSIONAL ASSOCIATION
Dover, DE ....Civil Trial Practice, Environmental Law, General Practice, Real Estate Law

PARKS, BENNETT & STEWART
Naples, FL...............................Probate and Estate Planning Law, Real Estate Law

PARLEE MCLAWS
Edmonton, AB, Canada ....Administrative Law, Appellate Practice, Banking Law, Bankruptcy Law, Business Law, Civil Trial Practice, Commercial Law, Construction Law, Employment Benefits Law, Environmental Law, General Practice, Immigration and Naturalization Law, Insurance Defense Law, International Business Law, Municipal and Zoning Law, Natural Resources Law, Personal Injury Law, Probate and Estate Planning Law, Public Utilities Law, Real Estate Law, Securities Law, Tax Law

PARMENTER O'TOOLE
Muskegon, MI.........................Banking Law, Civil Trial Practice, Criminal Trial Practice, Family Law, General Practice, Real Estate Law

PARR RICHEY OBREMSKEY & MORTON
Indianapolis, IN ....General Practice
Lebanon, IN............................General Practice

PARRA, DEL VALLE, FRAU & LIMERES
Ponce, PR................................General Practice

PARRISH, BAILEY & MORSCH, P.A.
Orlando, FL ....Medical Malpractice Law, Personal Injury Law, Product Liability Law

PARRY MURRAY WARD & MOXLEY, A PROFESSIONAL CORPORATION
Salt Lake City, UT..................Civil Trial Practice, Commercial Law, Environmental Law, General Practice

PARSINEN BOWMAN & LEVY, A PROFESSIONAL ASSOCIATION
Minneapolis, MN.................Civil Trial Practice, General Practice, Securities Law, Tax Law

PARSONS BEHLE & LATIMER, A PROFESSIONAL CORPORATION
Salt Lake City, UT..................Administrative Law, Antitrust Law, Banking Law, Bankruptcy Law, Business Law, Civil Trial Practice, Communications Law, Construction Law, Employment Benefits Law, Environmental Law, Health Care Law, Immigration and Naturalization Law, International Business Law, Labor and Employment Law, Medical Malpractice Law, Natural Resources Law, Personal Injury Law, Real Estate Law, Securities Law, Tax Law

PARSONS, LEE & JULIANO, P.C.
Birmingham, AL.....................General Practice

PASSEN, STEPHEN M., LTD.
Chicago, IL.........................Medical Malpractice Law, Personal Injury Law

PASTOR, MARK D., LAW CORPORATION
Los Angeles, CA....................Tax Law

PATE & DODSON
Beaumont, TX.......................Insurance Defense Law

PATERSON, MACDOUGALL
Toronto, ON, Canada..............Insurance Defense Law

PATLA, STRAUS, ROBINSON & MOORE, P.A.
Asheville, NC.......................General Practice

PATRICK, HARPER AND DIXON
Hickory, NC..........................General Practice

PATRICK, KEVIN L., P.C.
Aspen, CO.............................Environmental Law, Natural Resources Law

PATRICK & LACY, P.C.
Birmingham, AL.....................Antitrust Law, Appellate Practice, Civil Trial Practice, Securities Law

PATTEN, WORNOM & WATKINS, L.C.
Newport News, VA.................Bankruptcy Law, General Practice

PATTERSON, W. R. (PAT) JR.
Louisville, KY........................Civil Trial Practice, Personal Injury Law

PATTERSON, BELKNAP, WEBB & TYLER, LLP
New York, NY........................Civil Trial Practice, General Practice

PATTERSON, CLAUSSEN, SANTOS & HUME
Miami, FL..............................Civil Trial Practice, General Practice, International Business Law, Real Estate Law

PATTERSON, DILTHEY, CLAY & BRYSON, L.L.P.
Raleigh, NC...........................Insurance Defense Law, Personal Injury Law

PATTERSON & HARMON, P.A.
Deerfield Beach, FL................General Practice

PATTERSON, LORENTZEN, DUFFIELD, TIMMONS, IRISH, BECKER & ORDWAY
Des Moines, IA......................Civil Trial Practice, General Practice, Insurance Defense Law, Personal Injury Law

PATTERSON & PATTERSON
Aberdeen, MS.........................Bankruptcy Law, Civil Trial Practice, General Practice, Labor and Employment Law, Natural Resources Law

PATTERSON, PHIFER & PHILLIPS, P.C.
Detroit, MI.............................Civil Trial Practice

PATTERSON, RICHARD A., P.C.
Bloomfield Hills, MI...............Insurance Defense Law

PATTERSON, RICHARDS, HESSERT, WENDORFF & ELLISON
Wausau, WI............................Environmental Law, General Practice

PATTERSON & WEIR
Philadelphia, PA....................Banking Law, Bankruptcy Law, Business Law, Commercial Law

PATTIE & DALEY
Christiansted, St. Croix, VI.....General Practice

PATTISHALL, MCAULIFFE, NEWBURY, HILLIARD & GERALDSON
Chicago, IL............................International Business Law, Trademark, Copyright and Unfair Competition Law

PATTON, DAVID D., & ASSOCIATES, P.C.
Bloomfield Hills, MI...............Administrative Law, Business Law, Civil Trial Practice, Insurance Defense Law, Labor and Employment Law, Medical Malpractice Law, Personal Injury Law

PATTON, HALTOM, ROBERTS, MCWILLIAMS & GREER, L.L.P.
Texarkana, TX.......................Bankruptcy Law, Civil Trial Practice, General Practice, Insurance Defense Law, Personal Injury Law, Probate and Estate Planning Law, Real Estate Law, Tax Law

PATTON, LATHAM, LEGGE & COLE
Athens, AL.............................General Practice, Insurance Defense Law

PATTON, STARNES, THOMPSON, AYCOCK & TEELE, P.A.
Morganton, NC.......................General Practice

PATULA & ASSOCIATES
Chicago, IL............................Patent, Trademark, Copyright and Unfair Competition Law

PATURIS, E. MICHAEL
Alexandria, VA.......................Business Law, Probate and Estate Planning Law, Tax Law

PAUL, HASTINGS, JANOFSKY & WALKER
Costa Mesa, CA......................General Practice
Los Angeles, CA.....................General Practice
Santa Monica, CA...................General Practice
Stamford, CT..........................General Practice
Washington, DC......................General Practice
Atlanta, GA............................General Practice
New York, NY........................General Practice
Tokyo, Japan..........................General Practice

PAULIG AND SINGER
Urbana, OH............................General Practice

PAUL, JOHNSON, PARK & NILES, ATTORNEYS AT LAW, A LAW CORPORATION
Honolulu, HI..........................General Practice
Wailuku, HI...........................General Practice

PAULLING & JAMES
Darlington, SC........................General Practice

PAUL & PAUL
Philadelphia, PA....................Patent, Trademark, Copyright and Unfair Competition Law, Trademark, Copyright and Unfair Competition Law

PAULSON, HANKEL, BRUNER & NICHOLS, S.C.
Racine, WI.............................General Practice, Insurance Defense Law

PAULSON, NACE & NORWIND
Washington, DC......................Civil Trial Practice, Medical Malpractice Law, Personal Injury Law

PAULSON, NACE, NORWIND & SELLINGER
Rockville, MD........................Civil Trial Practice, Medical Malpractice Law, Personal Injury Law

PAUL, WEISS, RIFKIND, WHARTON & GARRISON
Washington, DC......................General Practice
New York, NY........................General Practice
Paris, France..........................General Practice

PAVALON & GIFFORD
Chicago, IL............................Civil Trial Practice, Medical Malpractice Law, Personal Injury Law

PAVETTI & FREEMAN
New London, CT.....................General Practice, Real Estate Law

PAXTON, CROW, BRAGG, SMITH & KEYSER, P.A.
Vero Beach, FL.......................Civil Trial Practice
West Palm Beach, FL..............Civil Trial Practice

PAYNE & BLANCHARD, L.L.P.
Dallas, TX..............................Civil Trial Practice, General Practice

PAYNE, GATES, FARTHING & RADD, P.C.
Norfolk, VA............................Civil Trial Practice, Personal Injury Law

PAYNE & JONES, CHARTERED
Overland Park, KS..................General Practice

PAYNE, LOEB & RAY
Charleston, WV......................Civil Trial Practice, General Practice, Probate and Estate Planning Law, Tax Law

PAYNE, WOOD & LITTLEJOHN
Glen Cove, NY.......................General Practice
Melville, NY..........................General Practice

PAYNTER, W.B., P.C.
Akron, CO..............................General Practice

PEABODY & ARNOLD
Boston, MA............................General Practice

PEACOCK, KELLER, YOHE, DAY & ECKER
Washington, PA......................Business Law, Civil Trial Practice, General Practice, Probate and Estate Planning Law

PEAR SPERLING EGGAN & MUSKOVITZ, P.C.
Ann Arbor, MI........................Banking Law, Civil Trial Practice, Family Law, General Practice, Labor and Employment Law, Probate and Estate Planning Law, Real Estate Law

Ypsilanti, MI .... Civil Trial Practice, General Practice, Probate and Estate Planning Law

PEARCE AND DURICK
Bismarck, ND .... Civil Trial Practice, Commercial Law, Communications Law, General Practice, Insurance Defense Law, Labor and Employment Law, Natural Resources Law, Product Liability Law, Real Estate Law, Tax Law

PEARCE & MASSLER
Hackensack, NJ........................... General Practice

PEARLMAN & PEARLMAN, PROFESSIONAL CORPORATION
Charleston, SC .... Tax Law

PEARLMAN, PIANIN & SCHAEFER
Southfield, MI .... Personal Injury Law

PEARLSTINE/SALKIN ASSOCIATES
Lansdale, PA........................... Banking Law, Business Law, Civil Trial Practice, Environmental Law, Labor and Employment Law, Personal Injury Law, Probate and Estate Planning Law, Product Liability Law, Real Estate Law, Tax Law

PEARNE, GORDON, MCCOY & GRANGER
Cleveland, OH........................... Patent, Trademark, Copyright and Unfair Competition Law

PECTOL, RICHARD W., P.C. & ASSOCIATES
Johnson City, TN........................... Civil Trial Practice, Criminal Trial Practice, General Practice

PEDLEY, ROSS, ZIELKE & GORDINIER
Louisville, KY........................... Civil Trial Practice, Insurance Defense Law, Securities Law

PEEL, RICHARD L., P.A.
Russellville, AR .... Civil Trial Practice

PEGALIS & WACHSMAN, P.C.
Great Neck, NY........................... Civil Trial Practice, General Practice, Medical Malpractice Law

PEIRSOL, FREDERICK W.
Winter Park, FL........................... General Practice, Probate and Estate Planning Law

PELINO & LENTZ, A PROFESSIONAL CORPORATION
Philadelphia, PA .... General Practice

PELLEGRINI & SEELEY, P.C.
Springfield, MA........................... Civil Trial Practice, General Practice

PELLETTIERI, RABSTEIN AND ALTMAN
Princeton, NJ .... Civil Trial Practice, Commercial Law, Personal Injury Law

PENCE, LINDA L. LAW OFFICES OF
Indianapolis, IN........................... Civil Trial Practice, Criminal Trial Practice, Tax Law

PENCE & HOUSLEY
Norman, OK........................... General Practice

PENCE AND MACMILLAN
Laramie, WY........................... Civil Trial Practice

PENDLETON & PENDLETON, P.A.
Lincolnton, NC........................... General Practice

PENIX, PENIX & LUSBY
Jonesboro, AR .... General Practice

PENLAND & BLOCK, P.A.
Jacksonville, FL .... Civil Trial Practice

PENNIE & EDMONDS
Washington, DC........................... Patent, Trademark, Copyright and Unfair Competition Law
New York, NY........................... Patent, Trademark, Copyright and Unfair Competition Law, Trademark, Copyright and Unfair Competition Law

PENNINGTON & HABEN, P.A.
Tallahassee, FL .... General Practice

PEPER, MARTIN, JENSEN, MAICHEL AND HETLAGE
St. Louis, MO........................... Business Law, Civil Trial Practice, Environmental Law, General Practice, Health Care Law, Labor and Employment Law, Real Estate Law, Tax Law

PEPPER, JOHN J. Q.C. AND ASSOCIATES
Montreal, QU, Canada .... Civil Trial Practice

PEPPER, HAMILTON & SCHEETZ
Wilmington, DE........................... General Practice
Washington, DC........................... General Practice
Detroit, MI........................... General Practice
Harrisburg, PA........................... General Practice
Philadelphia, PA .... General Practice

PEPPER, W. ALLEN, JR., P.A.
Cleveland, MS........................... Civil Trial Practice

PERDUE & CLORE, L.L.P.
Houston, TX........................... Medical Malpractice Law, Personal Injury Law

PERINI, VINCENT WALKER, P.C.
Dallas, TX........................... Criminal Trial Practice

PERKIN & HOSODA
Honolulu, HI........................... Civil Trial Practice

PERKINS COIE
Washington, DC........................... General Practice
Bellevue, WA........................... General Practice
Seattle, WA .... Antitrust Law, General Practice, Labor and Employment Law, Municipal Bond/Public Authority Financing Law, Tax Law

PERKINS, SACKS, HANNAN, REILLY AND PETERSEN
Council Bluffs, IA........................... Bankruptcy Law, General Practice, Personal Injury Law

PERKINS, THOMPSON, HINCKLEY & KEDDY, P.A.
Portland, ME .... Civil Trial Practice, General Practice

PERLMAN, PETER, LAW OFFICES, P.S.C.
Lexington, KY .... Civil Trial Practice, Personal Injury Law

PERMAN & GREEN
Fairfield, CT........................... Patent, Trademark, Copyright and Unfair Competition Law, Trademark, Copyright and Unfair Competition Law

PERRIN, PERRIN, MANN & PATTERSON
Spartanburg, SC........................... Commercial Law, General Practice

PERRONI LAW FIRM, THE, P.A.
Little Rock, AR........................... Civil Trial Practice, Criminal Trial Practice

PERRY, GARY G.
Sacramento, CA........................... Tax Law

PERRY, FIALKOWSKI & PERRY
Philadelphia, PA .... Medical Malpractice Law, Product Liability Law

PERRY, GENTRY, PERRY & MARSH
Hobart, OK........................... General Practice

PERRY, PATRICK, FARMER & MICHAUX, P.A.
Charlotte, NC........................... General Practice, Real Estate Law
Raleigh, NC........................... General Practice, Real Estate Law

PERSON, DONALD R. THE LAW OFFICE OF
Sacramento, CA .... Real Estate Law

PERSON, WHITWORTH, RAMOS, BORCHERS & MORALES
Laredo, TX........................... General Practice

PESKIND HYMSON & GOLDSTEIN, P.C.
Scottsdale, AZ........................... Bankruptcy Law, Business Law, Civil Trial Practice, Commercial Law, Construction Law, Real Estate Law

PETEFISH, CURRAN, IMMEL & HEEB
Lawrence, KS........................... General Practice

PETERS, DONALD, A LAW CORPORATION
Newport Beach, CA........................... Medical Malpractice Law, Personal Injury Law

PETERS, FULLER, RUSH, FARNSWORTH & HABIB
Chico, CA........................... General Practice

PETERS LAW FIRM, P.C.
Council Bluffs, IA........................... Civil Trial Practice, General Practice

PETERS, R. TIMOTHY, P.A.
Clearwater, FL........................... Civil Trial Practice

PETERS, ROBERTSON, LAX, PARSONS & WELCHER
Fort Lauderdale, FL........................... General Practice
Fort Myers, FL........................... General Practice
Miami, FL........................... General Practice
West Palm Beach, FL........................... General Practice

PETERSEN, MOSS, OLSEN, CARR, ESKELSON & HALL
Idaho Falls, ID........................... General Practice

PETERSON & BASHA, P.C.
Vienna, VA........................... Business Law, Civil Trial Practice, Probate and Estate Planning Law, Real Estate Law, Tax Law

PETERSON, BERNARD, VANDENBERG, ZEI, GEISLER & MARTIN
Fort Lauderdale, FL........................... Civil Trial Practice, Insurance Defense Law

PETERSON & KOCOUREK
Council Bluffs, IA........................... General Practice

PETERSON, MYERS, CRAIG, CREWS, BRANDON & PUTERBAUGH, P.A.
Lakeland, FL..........Banking Law, Civil Trial Practice, Environmental Law, General Practice, Real Estate Law, Tax Law
Lake Wales, FL..........Banking Law, Civil Trial Practice, Environmental Law, General Practice, Real Estate Law, Tax Law
Winter Haven, FL..........Banking Law, Civil Trial Practice, Environmental Law, Family Law, General Practice, Real Estate Law

PETERSON & ROSS
Chicago, IL..........General Practice

PETERSON, SCHMITZ, MOENCH & SCHMIDT, A PROFESSIONAL CORPORATION
Bismarck, ND..........Banking Law, Civil Trial Practice, Commercial Law, Criminal Trial Practice, Family Law, General Practice, Medical Malpractice Law, Personal Injury Law, Product Liability Law

PETILLON & HANSEN
Torrance, CA..........Securities Law

PETOCK, MICHAEL F.
Valley Forge, PA..........Patent, Trademark, Copyright and Unfair Competition Law, Trademark, Copyright and Unfair Competition Law

PETREE STOCKTON, L.L.P.
Charlotte, NC..........General Practice
Raleigh, NC..........General Practice
Winston-Salem, NC..........General Practice

PETRIKIN, WELLMAN, DAMICO, CARNEY & BROWN, A PROFESSIONAL CORPORATION
Media, PA..........General Practice

PETRONE & PETRONE, P.C.
Utica, NY..........Environmental Law

PETRUCCELLI & MARTIN
Portland, ME..........Appellate Practice, Civil Trial Practice, General Practice

PETRY & PETRY, P.C.
Carrizo Springs, TX..........General Practice

PETTIS & MCDONALD, P.A.
Tampa, FL..........Patent, Trademark, Copyright and Unfair Competition Law

PETTIT & MARTIN
San Francisco, CA..........General Practice

PETTY, DAVID K., A PROFESSIONAL CORPORATION
Guymon, OK..........General Practice

PEZZOLA & REINKE, A PROFESSIONAL CORPORATION
Oakland, CA..........Business Law, Health Care Law, Patent, Trademark, Copyright and Unfair Competition Law, Securities Law, Tax Law

PFAU, PFAU & MARANDO
Youngstown, OH..........Insurance Defense Law

PFEIFER, MAXWELL S.
Bronx, NY..........Civil Trial Practice, General Practice, Personal Injury Law, Product Liability Law

PHEBUS, WINKELMANN, WONG & BRAMFELD
Urbana, IL..........General Practice

PHELPS, J. MICHAEL
San Francisco, CA..........Civil Trial Practice

PHELPS DUNBAR, L.L.P.
Baton Rouge, LA..........Civil Trial Practice, General Practice
New Orleans, LA..........Admiralty/Maritime Law, Banking Law, Civil Trial Practice, Environmental Law, General Practice, Labor and Employment Law, Natural Resources Law, Tax Law
Jackson, MS..........Civil Trial Practice, General Practice, Labor and Employment Law
Tupelo, MS..........Civil Trial Practice, General Practice
Houston, TX..........Admiralty/Maritime Law

PHELPS & FARA
Indianapolis, IN..........Family Law

PHELPS, JENKINS, GIBSON & FOWLER
Tuscaloosa, AL..........Business Law, Civil Trial Practice, General Practice, Insurance Defense Law, Tax Law

PHELPS, KASTEN, RUYLE & BURNS
Carlinville, IL..........Civil Trial Practice, General Practice

PHILIPS AND HOPKINS, P.C.
Denton, TX..........Criminal Trial Practice, Family Law, General Practice, Probate and Estate Planning Law, Real Estate Law

PHILLIPS, GARDILL, KAISER & ALTMEYER
Wheeling, WV..........General Practice

PHILLIPS, JAMES J., A PROFESSIONAL CORPORATION
Pleasanton, CA..........Probate and Estate Planning Law

PHILLIPS, LYTLE, HITCHCOCK, BLAINE & HUBER
Buffalo, NY..........General Practice, Labor and Employment Law, Tax Law
Jamestown, NY..........General Practice
New York, NY..........General Practice
Rochester, NY..........General Practice

PHILLIPS MCFALL MCCAFFREY MCVAY & MURRAH, P.C.
Oklahoma City, OK..........General Practice

PHILLIPS, MOORE, LEMPIO & FINLEY
San Francisco, CA..........Patent, Trademark, Copyright and Unfair Competition Law

PHILLIPS, OLORE & DUNLAVEY, P.A.
Presque Isle, ME..........General Practice

PHIPPS, BENJAMIN K.
Tallahassee, FL..........General Practice

PIAZZA, MELMED & BERKOWITZ
Stamford, CT..........Personal Injury Law

PICCO MACK HERBERT, A PROFESSIONAL CORPORATION
Trenton, NJ..........Environmental Law

PICHA & SALISBURY
Rockford, IL..........Insurance Defense Law

PICKARD, STEPHEN R., P.C.
Alexandria, VA..........Personal Injury Law

PICKENS, BARNES & ABERNATHY
Cedar Rapids, IA..........Civil Trial Practice, Insurance Defense Law

PICKETT, STANLEY S.
Greenbelt, MD..........General Practice, Probate and Estate Planning Law, Real Estate Law

PICKREL, SCHAEFFER & EBELING CO., L.P.A.
Dayton, OH..........General Practice, Insurance Defense Law, Labor and Employment Law

PICO & MITCHELL
Las Vegas, NV..........Civil Trial Practice, General Practice, Insurance Defense Law, Real Estate Law

PIERCE, ATWOOD, SCRIBNER, ALLEN, SMITH & LANCASTER
Augusta, ME..........Administrative Law, Bankruptcy Law, Civil Trial Practice, Criminal Trial Practice, General Practice, Health Care Law, Medical Malpractice Law, Personal Injury Law, Product Liability Law
Camden, ME..........General Practice, Probate and Estate Planning Law, Real Estate Law
Portland, ME..........Administrative Law, Banking Law, Bankruptcy Law, Business Law, Civil Trial Practice, Commercial Law, Criminal Trial Practice, Employment Benefits Law, Environmental Law, General Practice, Health Care Law, Immigration and Naturalization Law, Insurance Defense Law, Labor and Employment Law, Municipal Bond/Public Authority Financing Law, Municipal and Zoning Law, Natural Resources Law, Personal Injury Law, Probate and Estate Planning Law, Public Utilities Law, Real Estate Law, Tax Law

PIERCE, CARR & ALFORD, P.C.
Mobile, AL..........Appellate Practice, Civil Trial Practice, Real Estate Law

PIERCE COUCH HENDRICKSON BAYSINGER & GREEN
Oklahoma City, OK..........General Practice, Insurance Defense Law, Medical Malpractice Law, Product Liability Law

PIERCE, J. WAYNE, P.A., LAW OFFICES OF
Atlanta, GA..........Civil Trial Practice, Health Care Law, Insurance Defense Law, Medical Malpractice Law, Personal Injury Law

PIERCE & PIERCE, P.C.
Birmingham, MI..........Business Law, Tax Law

PIERCE, SAMUEL P., JR., P.C.
Atlanta, GA..........Medical Malpractice Law, Product Liability Law

PIERSON, PIERSON & NOLAN
Baltimore, MD..........Civil Trial Practice, General Practice

PIETRAGALLO, BOSICK & GORDON
Pittsburgh, PA..........Civil Trial Practice, General Practice, Insurance Defense Law, Personal Injury Law

PIETTE & JACOBSON, S.C.
Milwaukee, WI..........Insurance Defense Law

PIGG, GAIL P.
Nashville, TN .... Civil Trial Practice, Real Estate Law

PIKE, GARY, A PROF. CORP., LAW OFFICES OF
San Diego, CA .... Family Law

PILECKAS, PAUL L.
Rome, NY .... General Practice, Personal Injury Law

PILIERO GOLDSTEIN JENKINS & HALL
New York, NY .... Antitrust Law, Appellate Practice, Business Law, Civil Trial Practice, Commercial Law, Securities Law

PILKINGTON, JOSEPH H., & CO., L.P.A.
Toledo, OH .... Commercial Law, Real Estate Law

PILKINTON, PILKINTON & YOCOM
Hope, AR .... General Practice

PILLAR AND MULROY, P.C.
Pittsburgh, PA .... Family Law, Transportation Law

PILLSBURY MADISON & SUTRO
Los Angeles, CA .... Admiralty/Maritime Law, Antitrust Law, Civil Trial Practice, General Practice, Tax Law
San Diego, CA .... Admiralty/Maritime Law, General Practice
San Francisco, CA .... General Practice
San Jose, CA .... General Practice
Washington, DC .... General Practice

PINKERTON & ASSOCIATES
Tulsa, OK .... Civil Trial Practice

PINKERTON AND FRIEDMAN, PROFESSIONAL CORPORATION
Munster, IN .... Business Law, Employment Benefits Law, Probate and Estate Planning Law, Tax Law

PIPER & MARBURY
Washington, DC .... General Practice
Baltimore, MD .... Antitrust Law, General Practice, Labor and Employment Law, Municipal Bond/Public Authority Financing Law, Tax Law

PIPER, WELLMAN & BOWERS
Lexington, KY .... Civil Trial Practice, General Practice, Health Care Law, Insurance Defense Law, Personal Injury Law

PIPKIN & KNOTT, L.L.P.
Raleigh, NC .... General Practice, Personal Injury Law

PIPPINGER, TROPP & MATASSINI, P.A.
Tampa, FL .... Civil Trial Practice, Criminal Trial Practice, Family Law, Personal Injury Law

PITBLADO & HOSKIN
Winnipeg, MB, Canada .... General Practice

PITLUCK & KIDO
Honolulu, HI .... Antitrust Law, Business Law, Real Estate Law

PITNEY, HARDIN, KIPP & SZUCH
Morristown, NJ .... Antitrust Law, Civil Trial Practice, Environmental Law, General Practice, Labor and Employment Law, Probate and Estate Planning Law, Real Estate Law, Tax Law

PITROF & STARKEY
Prince Frederick, MD .... General Practice
Upper Marlboro, MD .... General Practice

PITTMAN, HOOKS, MARSH, DUTTON & HOLLIS, P.C.
Birmingham, AL .... Admiralty/Maritime Law, Medical Malpractice Law, Personal Injury Law, Product Liability Law

PITTS, PITTS & THOMPSON
Selma, AL .... General Practice

PIVO & HALBREICH
Irvine, CA .... Civil Trial Practice, Insurance Defense Law, Probate and Estate Planning Law

PIZER & MICHAELSON INC.
Los Angeles, CA .... Bankruptcy Law, Commercial Law
Santa Ana, CA .... Commercial Law

PLASSMAN, RUPP, HENSAL & SHORT
Archbold, OH .... General Practice

PLATZ & THOMPSON, P.A.
Lewiston, ME .... Civil Trial Practice, Commercial Law, General Practice, Insurance Defense Law

PLAUCHÉ SMITH & NIESET, A PROFESSIONAL LAW CORPORATION
Lake Charles, LA .... Admiralty/Maritime Law, Civil Trial Practice, General Practice, Insurance Defense Law, Personal Injury Law

PLAUT LIPSTEIN MORTIMER, PC
Lakewood, CO .... Civil Trial Practice, Labor and Employment Law, Personal Injury Law

PLEDGER & SANTONI
McLean, VA .... Civil Trial Practice, Insurance Defense Law, Medical Malpractice Law

PLEUS, ADAMS, DAVIS & SPEARS, P.A.
Orlando, FL .... Civil Trial Practice, General Practice

PLEWS SHADLEY RACHER & BRAUN
Indianapolis, IN .... Administrative Law, Appellate Practice, Environmental Law, Natural Resources Law

PLOTTEL, ROLAND
New York, NY .... Patent, Trademark, Copyright and Unfair Competition Law

PLOURDE & LEONARD, LTD.
Providence, RI .... Tax Law

PLOWMAN, SPIEGEL & LEWIS, P.C.
Pittsburgh, PA .... Bankruptcy Law, Civil Trial Practice, Construction Law, Environmental Law, General Practice, Insurance Defense Law, Real Estate Law

PLUMMER & FARMER
Houston, TX .... Civil Trial Practice, Family Law

PLUNKETT, GIBSON & ALLEN, INC.
San Antonio, TX .... Civil Trial Practice, General Practice, Insurance Defense Law

PLUNKETT & JAFFE, P.C.
New York, NY .... Civil Trial Practice

PLUNKETT & PLUNKETT, P.C.
Salem, MA .... General Practice

POAGUE, WALL, ESHELMAN & COX
Clinton, MO .... General Practice

PODELL & PODELL
Milwaukee, WI .... Family Law

PODELL, RICHARD J., & ASSOCIATES, S.C.
Milwaukee, WI .... Family Law

PODHURST, ORSECK, JOSEFSBERG, EATON, MEADOW, OLIN & PERWIN, P.A.
Miami, FL .... Appellate Practice, Civil Trial Practice, Criminal Trial Practice, General Practice, Personal Injury Law

POEHLMANN, THEODORE A. E.
Woodstock, IL .... Civil Trial Practice

POHL & BROWN, P.A.
Kissimmee, FL .... Administrative Law, Antitrust Law, Appellate Practice, Banking Law, Business Law, Civil Trial Practice, Commercial Law, Construction Law, Environmental Law, International Business Law, Labor and Employment Law, Municipal and Zoning Law, Probate and Estate Planning Law, Real Estate Law, Tax Law
Orlando, FL .... Administrative Law, Antitrust Law, Appellate Practice, Banking Law, Business Law, Civil Trial Practice, Commercial Law, Construction Law, Environmental Law, International Business Law, Labor and Employment Law, Municipal and Zoning Law, Probate and Estate Planning Law, Real Estate Law, Tax Law
Winter Park, FL .... Administrative Law, Antitrust Law, Appellate Practice, Banking Law, Business Law, Civil Trial Practice, Commercial Law, Construction Law, Environmental Law, International Business Law, Labor and Employment Law, Municipal and Zoning Law, Probate and Estate Planning Law, Real Estate Law, Tax Law

POLIDORI, GEROME, FRANKLIN AND JACOBSON
Lakewood, CO .... Civil Trial Practice, Family Law, General Practice, Personal Injury Law, Probate and Estate Planning Law

POLING, MCGAW & POLING, P.C.
Troy, MI .... Business Law, Civil Trial Practice, Construction Law, Employment Benefits Law, Insurance Defense Law, Personal Injury Law, Probate and Estate Planning Law, Real Estate Law

POLITO & SMOCK, P.C.
Pittsburgh, PA .... Admiralty/Maritime Law, Labor and Employment Law

POLLI, ROBERT P.
Tampa, FL .... Appellate Practice, Criminal Trial Practice

POLLOCK, MEYERS, EICKSTEADT & WEECH, LTD.
Marengo, IL .... General Practice

POLSTER, LIEDER, WOODRUFF & LUCCHESI, L.C.
St. Louis, MO .... Patent, Trademark, Copyright and Unfair Competition Law

POMS, SMITH, LANDE & ROSE, PROFESSIONAL CORPORATION
Irvine, CA.......Patent, Trademark, Copyright and Unfair Competition Law
Los Angeles, CA.......Patent, Trademark, Copyright and Unfair Competition Law

PONZOLI, WASSENBERG & SPERKACZ, P.A.
Miami, FL.......Insurance Defense Law

POOLE & POOLE
Greenville, AL.......General Practice

POPE AND HUDGENS, P.A.
Newberry, SC.......General Practice

POPE, MCGLAMRY, KILPATRICK & MORRISON
Atlanta, GA.......Civil Trial Practice, General Practice, Medical Malpractice Law, Personal Injury Law
Columbus, GA.......Civil Trial Practice, General Practice, Medical Malpractice Law, Personal Injury Law

POPE, MCMILLAN, GOURLEY, KUTTEH & SIMON
Statesville, NC.......General Practice

POPE, POPE AND DRAYER
Clarion, PA.......General Practice

POPE & RODGERS
Columbia, SC.......Civil Trial Practice

POPHAM, HAIK, SCHNOBRICH & KAUFMAN, LTD.
Washington, DC.......General Practice
Minneapolis, MN.......General Practice

POPKOFF & STERN
Los Angeles, CA.......Probate and Estate Planning Law

PORTER, FAIRCHILD, WACHTER & HANEY, P.A.
Topeka, KS.......Civil Trial Practice, Criminal Trial Practice, General Practice

PORTERFIELD, HARPER & MILLS, P.A.
Birmingham, AL.......Civil Trial Practice, General Practice, Medical Malpractice Law

PORTER, J. CHESTER, & ASSOCIATES
Shepherdsville, KY.......Banking Law

PORTER, JOHN T., P.A., LAW OFFICES OF
Albuquerque, NM.......Banking Law, Commercial Law

PORTER & PORTER
Cincinnati, OH.......Probate and Estate Planning Law

PORTER, SCOTT, WEIBERG & DELEHANT, A PROFESSIONAL CORPORATION
Sacramento, CA.......Civil Trial Practice, Medical Malpractice Law

PORTER & STEEL, PLLC
Research Triangle Park, NC.......Real Estate Law

PORTER, WRIGHT, MORRIS & ARTHUR
Washington, DC.......General Practice
Naples, FL.......General Practice
Cincinnati, OH.......General Practice
Cleveland, OH.......General Practice
Columbus, OH.......Antitrust Law, Banking Law, Bankruptcy Law, Civil Trial Practice, Environmental Law, General Practice, Labor and Employment Law, Municipal Bond/Public Authority Financing Law, Patent, Trademark, Copyright and Unfair Competition Law, Tax Law
Dayton, OH.......General Practice

PORTIGAL, HAMMERTON & ALLEN
Santa Ana, CA.......Probate and Estate Planning Law

PORTNOY, PIDGEON & ROTH, P.C.
Bloomfield Hills, MI.......Civil Trial Practice, Health Care Law, Medical Malpractice Law, Personal Injury Law, Product Liability Law

PORZIO, BROMBERG & NEWMAN, A PROFESSIONAL CORPORATION
Morristown, NJ.......Civil Trial Practice, Commercial Law, Environmental Law, General Practice, Personal Injury Law

POST, POLAK, GOODSELL & MACNEILL, P.A.
Roseland, NJ.......Civil Trial Practice, Commercial Law, Environmental Law, Family Law, Labor and Employment Law, Medical Malpractice Law, Natural Resources Law, Real Estate Law

POST & POST
High Point, NC.......General Practice

LL, P.C.
, PA.......Civil Trial Practice

LOMGREN & STRAVERS
A.......Insurance Defense Law, Medical Malpractice Law

POTTER ANDERSON & CORROON
Wilmington, DE.......Banking Law, Bankruptcy Law, Civil Trial Practice, Employment Benefits Law, Environmental Law, General Practice, Municipal Bond/Public Authority Financing Law, Personal Injury Law, Probate and Estate Planning Law, Tax Law

POTTER & HAMILTON
Jackson, MI.......Family Law, General Practice

POTTS, DENNIS W., ATTORNEY AT LAW, A LAW CORPORATION
Honolulu, HI.......Personal Injury Law

POTTS & YOUNG
Florence, AL.......General Practice, Personal Injury Law, Product Liability Law

POULIOT, MERCURE
Montreal, QU, Canada.......General Practice

POULSON, JON C.
Accomac, VA.......Civil Trial Practice, Real Estate Law

POULSON, ODELL & PETERSON
Denver, CO.......Natural Resources Law

POWELL & FREDERICK
Birmingham, AL.......Employment Benefits Law, Labor and Employment Law

POWELL, GOLDSTEIN, FRAZER & MURPHY
Washington, DC.......General Practice
Atlanta, GA.......General Practice, Immigration and Naturalization Law, Municipal Bond/Public Authority Financing Law

POWELL, JONES & REID
Destin, FL.......General Practice
Niceville, FL.......General Practice

POWELL, PEEK & WEAVER
Andalusia, AL.......General Practice

POWELL, POWELL & AAMODT
Bemidji, MN.......Civil Trial Practice, Insurance Defense Law

POWELL, TRACHTMAN, LOGAN, CARRLE & BOWMAN, A PROFESSIONAL CORPORATION
King Of Prussia, PA.......Civil Trial Practice, Commercial Law, Construction Law, Insurance Defense Law

POWER, BOWEN & VALIMONT
Doylestown, PA.......Civil Trial Practice, General Practice
Sellersville, PA.......Civil Trial Practice

POWER ROGERS & SMITH, P.C.
Chicago, IL.......Civil Trial Practice, Medical Malpractice Law, Personal Injury Law

POWERS, CLEGG & WILLARD
Baton Rouge, LA.......Banking Law, Business Law, Civil Trial Practice, General Practice

POWERS & HALL, PROFESSIONAL CORPORATION
Boston, MA.......Business Law, General Practice

POWERS, PYLES, SUTTER & VERVILLE, P.C.
Washington, DC.......Health Care Law

POYNTER & GEARHART, P.A.
Mountain Home, AR.......General Practice

POZNER HUTT KAPLAN, P.C.
Denver, CO.......Criminal Trial Practice

PRATHER & ASSOCIATES, P.C.
Detroit, MI.......Civil Trial Practice, Family Law, General Practice, Labor and Employment Law, Personal Injury Law

PRATHER, JOHN G., THE FIRM OF
Somerset, KY.......General Practice

PRAVEL, HEWITT, KIMBALL & KRIEGER, A PROFESSIONAL CORPORATION
Houston, TX.......Patent, Trademark, Copyright and Unfair Competition Law

PRAY, WALKER, JACKMAN, WILLIAMSON & MARLAR, A PROFESSIONAL CORPORATION
Tulsa, OK.......Civil Trial Practice, General Practice

PREAUS, RODDY & KREBS
New Orleans, LA.......Bankruptcy Law, Civil Trial Practice, Construction Law, Insurance Defense Law

PREMINGER, DANIEL M., P.C.
Philadelphia, PA.......Appellate Practice, Criminal Trial Practice

PRENOVOST, NORMANDIN, BERGH & DAWE, A PROFESSIONAL CORPORATION
Santa Ana, CA.......Banking Law, Bankruptcy Law, Commercial Law

PRERAU & TEITELL
New York, NY........................Probate and Estate Planning Law, Tax Law
White Plains, NY....................Probate and Estate Planning Law, Tax Law

PRESCOTT, BULLARD & MCLEOD
New Bedford, MA..................General Practice

PRESCOTT & PRESCOTT
Dallas, TX............................General Practice

PRESSLY & PRESSLY, P.A.
West Palm Beach, FL.............Probate and Estate Planning Law, Real Estate Law

PRESTON GATES & ELLIS
Seattle, WA............................Environmental Law, Municipal and Zoning Law

PRESTON & PRESTON, P.C.
Douglas, GA..........................General Practice

PRETI, FLAHERTY, BELIVEAU & PACHIOS
Augusta, ME..........................General Practice
Portland, ME.........................Administrative Law, Bankruptcy Law, Business Law, Civil Trial Practice, Commercial Law, Communications Law, Environmental Law, General Practice, Health Care Law, Insurance Defense Law, Labor and Employment Law, Medical Malpractice Law, Municipal Bond/Public Authority Financing Law, Probate and Estate Planning Law, Real Estate Law, Tax Law
Rumford, ME..........................General Practice

PRETTY, SCHROEDER, BRUEGGEMANN & CLARK, A PROFESSIONAL CORPORATION
Los Angeles, CA.....................Patent, Trademark, Copyright and Unfair Competition Law

PRETZEL & STOUFFER, CHARTERED
Chicago, IL............................Business Law, Civil Trial Practice, General Practice, Health Care Law, Insurance Defense Law, Real Estate Law, Tax Law

PREVIANT, GOLDBERG, UELMEN, GRATZ, MILLER & BRUEGGEMAN, S.C.
Milwaukee, WI........................Labor and Employment Law

PRICE & BARKER
Indianapolis, IN......................Civil Trial Practice, Commercial Law, Medical Malpractice Law, Personal Injury Law, Product Liability Law

PRICE, HENEVELD, COOPER, DEWITT & LITTON
Grand Rapids, MI...................International Business Law, Patent, Trademark, Copyright and Unfair Competition Law, Trademark, Copyright and Unfair Competition Law

PRICE, JACK N., P.C.
Austin, TX.............................Civil Trial Practice

PRICE OKAMOTO HIMENO & LUM, ATTORNEYS AT LAW, A LAW CORPORATION
Honolulu, HI..........................Medical Malpractice Law, Personal Injury Law, Real Estate Law

PRICE & ZIRULNIK
Jackson, MS...........................Business Law, Civil Trial Practice, Family Law, General Practice, Personal Injury Law

PRICKETT, JONES, ELLIOTT, KRISTOL & SCHNEE
Dover, DE..............................General Practice
Wilmington, DE......................General Practice, Insurance Defense Law
Kennett Square, PA.................General Practice

PRIFTI, WILLIAM M.
Lynnfield, MA.......................Securities Law

PRIMMER & PIPER, PROFESSIONAL CORPORATION
St. Johnsbury, VT..................Administrative Law, Banking Law, Environmental Law, Securities Law

PRINCE, GLICK & MCFARLANE, P.A., LAW OFFICES
Fort Lauderdale, FL...............Civil Trial Practice, General Practice, Personal Injury Law

PRINCE, YEATES & GELDZAHLER
Park City, UT.........................General Practice
Salt Lake City, UT..................General Practice, Labor and Employment Law, Real Estate Law, Tax Law

PRINCE, YOUNGBLOOD & MASSAGEE
Hendersonville, NC................General Practice

PRINDLE, MALAND, SELLNER, STENNES AND KNUTSEN, CHARTERED
Montevideo, MN.....................General Practice

PRINGLE & PRINGLE, A PROFESSIONAL CORPORATION
Oklahoma City, OK.................Banking Law, Bankruptcy Law, General Practice, Securities Law

PRITCHARD, MCCALL & JONES
Birmingham, AL.....................Bankruptcy Law, Business Law, Civil Trial Practice, Commercial Law, General Practice, Medical Malpractice Law, Personal Injury Law, Probate and Estate Planning Law, Product Liability Law, Real Estate Law, Tax Law

PRITCHARD & THOMAS, PROFESSIONAL CORPORATION
Detroit, MI............................Criminal Trial Practice

PROCOPIO, CORY, HARGREAVES AND SAVITCH
San Diego, CA.......................Banking Law, Bankruptcy Law, Civil Trial Practice, General Practice, Real Estate Law, Tax Law

PROENZA, WHITE & ROBERTS, P.A.
Miami, FL...............................Civil Trial Practice, General Practice

PROKSCH, DDR. & PARTNER
Vaduz, Liechtenstein..............International Business Law

PROSKAUER ROSE GOETZ & MENDELSOHN, LLP
Los Angeles, CA.....................General Practice
Washington, DC.....................General Practice
New York, NY........................General Practice, Labor and Employment Law
Paris, France..........................General Practice

PROVIZER, LICHTENSTEIN & PHILLIPS, P.C.
Southfield, MI........................Insurance Defense Law, Personal Injury Law

PROVOSTY, SADLER & DELAUNAY
Alexandria, LA.......................General Practice

PRUITT, GUSHEE & BACHTELL
Salt Lake City, UT..................Natural Resources Law

PRUITT & PRUITT, P.A.
West Palm Beach, FL.............Civil Trial Practice, General Practice, Medical Malpractice Law

PRYOR, CARNEY AND JOHNSON, A PROFESSIONAL CORPORATION
Denver, CO............................Civil Trial Practice, General Practice, Insurance Defense Law, Medical Malpractice Law

PRYOR, FLYNN, PRIEST & HARBER
Knoxville, TN.........................Civil Trial Practice, Criminal Trial Practice, General Practice, Medical Malpractice Law, Personal Injury Law, Product Liability Law

PRYOR & MANDELUP, P.C.
Westbury, NY.........................Bankruptcy Law, Civil Trial Practice

PUCCI & GOLDIN, INC.
Providence, RI.......................General Practice

PUCCINELLI & PUCCINELLI
Elko, NV................................General Practice

PUCILLO, ANTHONY E., P.A.
West Palm Beach, FL.............Civil Trial Practice

PUCKETT, CHARLES H. III
Houston, TX...........................Business Law, Natural Resources Law

PUGH, IRBY G.
Orlando, FL............................Environmental Law, Personal Injury Law

PULASKI, GIEGER & LABORDE, A PROFESSIONAL LAW CORPORATION
New Orleans, LA....................Environmental Law, Insurance Defense Law, Product Liability Law, Transportation Law

PURDY AND FLYNN
Fort Lauderdale, FL...............Personal Injury Law

PURVIS, GRAY, SCHUETZE & GORDON
Boulder, CO...........................Civil Trial Practice, General Practice, Personal Injury Law
Denver, CO............................Civil Trial Practice, Personal Injury Law

PUTBRESE & HUNSAKER
McLean, VA............................Communications Law

PUTNEY, TWOMBLY, HALL & HIRSON
New York, NY........................General Practice

PYSZKA, KESSLER, MASSEY, WELDON, CATRI, HOLTON & DOUBERLEY, P.A.
Fort Lauderdale, FL...............Civil Trial Practice, General Practice
Miami, FL...............................Civil Trial Practice, General Practice

PYTELL, R.H., & ASSOCIATES, P.C.
Detroit, MI............................Business Law, Probate and Estate Planning Law

QUADROS & JOHNSON
San Mateo, CA.......................General Practice

QUALE, HARTMANN, BOHL, REYNOLDS & PULSFUS
Baraboo, WI...........................General Practice

QUANDT, GIFFELS & BUCK CO., L.P.A.
Cleveland, OH........................Civil Trial Practice, General Practice, Insurance Defense Law

QUARLES & BRADY
Milwaukee, WI........................Administrative Law, Antitrust Law, Banking Law, Bankruptcy Law, Business Law, Civil Trial Practice, Commercial Law, Construction Law, Employment Benefits Law, Environmental Law, Family Law, General Practice, Health Care Law, Immigration and Naturalization Law, International Business Law, Labor and Employment Law, Municipal Bond/Public Authority Financing Law, Municipal and Zoning Law, Patent, Trademark, Copyright and Unfair Competition Law, Probate and Estate Planning Law, Product Liability Law, Public Utilities Law, Real Estate Law, Securities Law, Tax Law

QUELLER & FISHER
New York, NY........................Civil Trial Practice, Construction Law, Medical Malpractice Law, Personal Injury Law

QUIGLEY, DILL & QUIGLEY
Valentine, NE........................General Practice

QUINLIVAN, SHERWOOD, SPELLACY & TARVESTAD, P.A.
St. Cloud, MN........................Insurance Defense Law

QUINN, WILLIAM G. III
Decatur, GA........................Civil Trial Practice, Criminal Trial Practice

QUINN, BUSECK, LEEMHUIS, TOOHEY & KROTO, INC.
Erie, PA........................General Practice

QUINN, EIESLAND, DAY & BARKER
Belle Fourche, SD........................Civil Trial Practice
Rapid City, SD........................Civil Trial Practice

QUINN, JOHNSTON, HENDERSON & PRETORIUS, CHARTERED
Peoria, IL........................Civil Trial Practice, General Practice

QUINN, KULLY AND MORROW, A PROFESSIONAL LAW CORPORATION
Los Angeles, CA........................Antitrust Law, Appellate Practice, Civil Trial Practice, General Practice

QUINN, PATTERSON & WILLARD
Columbia, SC........................Civil Trial Practice, General Practice, Real Estate Law

QUINN & SUHR
White Plains, NY........................General Practice

QUISUMBING TORRES & EVANGELISTA
Metro Manila, Republic of The Philippines........................General Practice

RABBITT, PITZER & SNODGRASS, P.C.
St. Louis, MO........................General Practice

RABE, GEORGE F.
Lexington, KY........................Civil Trial Practice

RABIL, LOUIS
Washington, DC........................General Practice

RABINOWITZ, RAFAL, SWARTZ, TALIAFERRO & GILBERT, P.C.
Norfolk, VA........................Admiralty/Maritime Law, Civil Trial Practice, Criminal Trial Practice, Personal Injury Law

RABON, WOLF & RABON
Hugo, OK........................General Practice

RACCUGLIA, ANTHONY C. & ASSOCIATES
Peru, IL........................Civil Trial Practice, Medical Malpractice Law, Personal Injury Law, Product Liability Law

RACINE, OLSON, NYE, COOPER & BUDGE, CHARTERED
Pocatello, ID........................General Practice

RACKEMANN, SAWYER & BREWSTER, PROFESSIONAL CORPORATION
Boston, MA........................Business Law, Civil Trial Practice, Environmental Law, General Practice, Probate and Estate Planning Law, Real Estate Law, Tax Law

RADEY HINKLE THOMAS & MCARTHUR
Tallahassee, FL........................Administrative Law, Antitrust Law, Appellate Practice, Civil Trial Practice, Commercial Law, Environmental Law, General Practice, Health Care Law

RAEKES, RETTIG, OSBORNE, FORGETTE & O'DONNELL
Kennewick, WA........................General Practice

RAGGIO, CAPPEL, CHOZEN & BERNIARD
Lake Charles, LA........................Civil Trial Practice, General Practice

RAGSDALE, LIGGETT & FOLEY
Raleigh, NC........................Civil Trial Practice

RAICHLE, BANNING, WEISS & STEPHENS
Buffalo, NY........................General Practice

RAINEY & BARKSDALE
Okmulgee, OK........................General Practice

RAINEY, KIZER, BUTLER, REVIERE & BELL
Jackson, TN........................Banking Law, Bankruptcy Law, Civil Trial Practice, General Practice, Insurance Defense Law, Personal Injury Law

RAINEY, ROSS, RICE & BINNS
Oklahoma City, OK........................Bankruptcy Law, General Practice, Public Utilities Law

RAINS & POGREBIN, P.C.
Mineola, NY........................Labor and Employment Law

RAINWATER, HUMBLE & VOWELL
Knoxville, TN........................Appellate Practice, Medical Malpractice Law, Personal Injury Law, Probate and Estate Planning Law, Product Liability Law

RAISBECK, LARA, RODRIGUEZ & RUEDA
Bogotá, Colombia........................General Practice

RAJKOWSKI HANSMEIER LTD.
St. Cloud, MN........................Environmental Law, Insurance Defense Law

RAKESTRAW & RAKESTRAW
Findlay, OH........................General Practice

RAMBOW & AWSUMB, P.A.
Minneapolis, MN........................Personal Injury Law

RAMEY, GEORGE H.
Yukon, OK........................Civil Trial Practice

RAMIREZ, ANTHONY B., P.C.
St. Louis, MO........................General Practice

RAMMELKAMP, BRADNEY, DAHMAN, KUSTER, KEATON, FRITSCHE & LINDSAY, P.C.
Jacksonville, IL........................General Practice

RAMSAY, BRIDGFORTH, HARRELSON & STARLING
Pine Bluff, AR........................General Practice

RAMSAY & CALLOWAY
Atlanta, GA........................Real Estate Law

RAND, ALGEIER, TOSTI & WOODRUFF, A PROFESSIONAL CORPORATION
Morristown, NJ........................Commercial Law

RANGEL & CHRISS
Corpus Christi, TX........................Civil Trial Practice, Personal Injury Law

RANKIN, SPROAT & POLLACK
Oakland, CA........................Insurance Defense Law, Medical Malpractice Law

RANSMEIER & SPELLMAN, PROFESSIONAL CORPORATION
Concord, NH........................Business Law, Commercial Law, General Practice, Probate and Estate Planning Law, Product Liability Law

RAPPAPORT & FURMAN
Philadelphia, PA........................Real Estate Law

RAPPORT, MEYERS, GRIFFEN & WHITBECK
Hudson, NY........................General Practice

RATH, YOUNG, PIGNATELLI AND OYER, P.A.
Concord, NH........................Medical Malpractice Law, Public Utilities Law

RATHJE, WOODWARD, DYER & BURT
Wheaton, IL........................General Practice

RATHMAN, COMBS, SCHAEFER & KAUP
Middletown, OH........................General Practice

RATNER & PRESTIA, A PROFESSIONAL CORPORATION
Valley Forge, PA........................Patent, Trademark, Copyright and Unfair Competition Law, Trademark, Copyright and Unfair Competition Law

RAUSCHER, DAVID J., P.C.
St. Louis, MO........................Personal Injury Law

RAVEN, KIRSCHNER & NORELL, P.C.
Tucson, AZ........................Administrative Law, Banking Law, Bankruptcy Law, Business Law, Civil Trial Practice, General Practice, Health Care Law, Labor and Employment Law, Municipal Bond/Public Authority Financing Law, Real Estate Law

RAVIN, GREENBERG & MARKS, A PROFESSIONAL CORPORATION
Roseland, NJ........................Bankruptcy Law

RAWLE & HENDERSON
Philadelphia, PA........................Admiralty/Maritime Law, General Practice

RAWLINGS, NIELAND, PROBASCO, KILLINGER, ELLWANGER, JACOBS & MOHRHAUSER
Sioux City, IA........................General Practice

RAWLINGS, OLSON & CANNON, A PROFESSIONAL CORPORATION
Las Vegas, NV........................Civil Trial Practice, Insurance Defense Law

RAWLS, DICKINSON AND LEDFORD, P.A.
Charlotte, NC........................Criminal Trial Practice

RAY, RONALD D.
Louisville, KY........................Civil Trial Practice

RAY, QUINNEY & NEBEKER, A PROFESSIONAL CORPORATION
Provo, UT........................General Practice
Salt Lake City, UT........................Antitrust Law, Banking Law, Bankruptcy Law, Civil Trial Practice, Commercial Law, General Practice, Insurance Defense Law, Labor and Employment Law, Municipal Bond/Public Authority Financing Law, Natural Resources Law, Real Estate Law, Tax Law

REISING, ETHINGTON, BARNARD, PERRY & MILTON AND LEARMAN & MCCULLOCH
Troy, MI....Patent, Trademark, Copyright and Unfair Competition Law

REITER, ARNOLD E.
Mahwah, NJ....Probate and Estate Planning Law

RENALDO, MYERS, REGAN & PALUMBO, P.C.
Buffalo, NY....Personal Injury Law

RENDIGS, FRY, KIELY & DENNIS
Cincinnati, OH....Admiralty/Maritime Law, Civil Trial Practice, General Practice, Insurance Defense Law

RENDLEN, RENDLEN, REDINGTON AND BASTIAN, P.C.
Hannibal, MO....General Practice

RENICK, SINGER, KAMBER & FISCHER
Lake Worth, FL....Civil Trial Practice, Family Law

RENNER, KENNER, GREIVE, BOBAK, TAYLOR & WEBER, A LEGAL PROFESSIONAL ASSOCIATION
Akron, OH....Patent, Trademark, Copyright and Unfair Competition Law

RENNER, OTTO, BOISSELLE & SKLAR
Cleveland, OH....Patent, Trademark, Copyright and Unfair Competition Law

RENO, O'BYRNE & KEPLEY, P.C.
Champaign, IL....General Practice

RENO, ZAHM, FOLGATE, LINDBERG & POWELL
Rockford, IL....Civil Trial Practice, General Practice

RETHERFORD, MULLEN, JOHNSON & BRUCE
Colorado Springs, CO....Civil Trial Practice, General Practice, Insurance Defense Law, Personal Injury Law

REUSSILLE, MAUSNER, CAROTENUTO, BRUNO & BARGER
Red Bank, NJ....General Practice

REVELLE, BURLESON, LEE & REVELLE
Murfreesboro, NC....General Practice

REYNOLDS, BEEBY & MAGNUSON, P.C.
Troy, MI....Civil Trial Practice, Insurance Defense Law

REYNOLDS, CARONIA & GIANELLI
Hauppauge, NY....General Practice

REYNOLDS & CONWAY, P.C.
Springfield, MO....General Practice

REYNOLDS, FORKER, BERKLEY, SUTER, ROSE & DOWER
Hutchinson, KS....General Practice

REYNOLDS & MCARTHUR
Atlanta, GA....Civil Trial Practice, Medical Malpractice Law, Personal Injury Law, Product Liability Law
Macon, GA....Civil Trial Practice, Medical Malpractice Law, Personal Injury Law, Product Liability Law
Asheville, NC....Civil Trial Practice, Medical Malpractice Law, Personal Injury Law, Product Liability Law

REYNOLDS & SYDOW, L.L.P.
Houston, TX....Business Law, Civil Trial Practice, Personal Injury Law

REZNIK & REZNIK, A LAW CORPORATION
Los Angeles, CA....Environmental Law

RHOADES, RUFUS VON THULEN
Los Angeles, CA....Tax Law

RHOADES, MCKEE, BOER, GOODRICH & TITTA
Grand Rapids, MI....Business Law, Insurance Defense Law

RHOADS & SINON
Harrisburg, PA....Banking Law, Civil Trial Practice, Environmental Law, General Practice, Municipal Bond/Public Authority Financing Law, Tax Law

RHODA, STOUDT & BRADLEY
Reading, PA....General Practice

RHODES COATS AND BENNETT, L.L.P.
Greensboro, NC....Patent, Trademark, Copyright and Unfair Competition Law
Raleigh, NC....Patent, Trademark, Copyright and Unfair Competition Law

RHODES, HIERONYMUS, JONES, TUCKER & GABLE
Tulsa, OK....Civil Trial Practice, Insurance Defense Law

[illegible] HUBBARD & LEOPOLD, ATTORNEYS AT LAW, P.A.
[illegible] Palm Beach, FL....Civil Trial Practice, Personal Injury Law

RICE, DOLAN & KERSHAW
Providence, RI....General Practice, Insurance Defense Law, Medical Malpractice Law

RICE FOWLER
New Orleans, LA....Admiralty/Maritime Law, Commercial Law, Insurance Defense Law, International Business Law, Transportation Law
San Diego, CA....Admiralty/Maritime Law, Commercial Law, Insurance Defense Law, International Business Law, Transportation Law
San Francisco, CA....Admiralty/Maritime Law, Commercial Law, Insurance Defense Law, International Business Law, Transportation Law

RICE & HENDRICKSON
Harlan, KY....General Practice, Insurance Defense Law, Labor and Employment Law

RICE, MARTIN ERROL, P.A.
St. Petersburg, FL....Civil Trial Practice, General Practice

RICH & D'AMBROSIO, P.S.C.
Louisville, KY....Labor and Employment Law

RICH, FUIDGE, MORRIS & SANBROOK, INC.
Marysville, CA....General Practice

RICH, MAY, BILODEAU & FLAHERTY, P.C.
Boston, MA....Business Law, Civil Trial Practice, Environmental Law, General Practice, Labor and Employment Law, Public Utilities Law, Real Estate Law, Securities Law

RICHARD, DISANTI, HAMILTON & GALLAGHER, A PROFESSIONAL CORPORATION
Media, PA....General Practice, Personal Injury Law

RICHARDS, GATES T.
Cincinnati, OH....Civil Trial Practice, Medical Malpractice Law, Personal Injury Law

RICHARDS, BRANDT, MILLER & NELSON, A PROFESSIONAL CORPORATION
Salt Lake City, UT....Business Law, Insurance Defense Law, Tax Law

RICHARDS, DOUGLAS, P.C.
Springfield, VT....General Practice

RICHARDS, GILKEY, FITE, SLAUGHTER, PRATESI & WARD, P.A.
Clearwater, FL....General Practice, Probate and Estate Planning Law, Real Estate Law

RICHARDS, LAYTON & FINGER, P.A.
Wilmington, DE....General Practice, Tax Law

RICHARDS AND MEOLA
Warren, OH....Insurance Defense Law

RICHARDS, PAUL, RICHARDS & SIEGEL
Tulsa, OK....Civil Trial Practice, Insurance Defense Law, Medical Malpractice Law

RICHARDSON, BARRICKMAN, DICKINSON & TRAVIS
Glasgow, KY....General Practice

RICHARDSON, DANIELL, SPEAR & UPTON, P.C.
Mobile, AL....Personal Injury Law

RICHARDSON, PLOWDEN, GRIER AND HOWSER, P.A.
Columbia, SC....Appellate Practice, Business Law, Civil Trial Practice, Construction Law, Environmental Law, General Practice, Health Care Law, Insurance Defense Law, Medical Malpractice Law, Personal Injury Law, Product Liability Law, Real Estate Law

RICHARDSON AND RICHARDSON
Red Wing, MN....General Practice

RICHARDSON & TROUBH, A PROFESSIONAL CORPORATION
Portland, ME....Banking Law, Civil Trial Practice, General Practice, Insurance Defense Law, Product Liability Law

RICHARDSON, TROUBH & BADGER, A PROFESSIONAL CORPORATION
Bangor, ME....Civil Trial Practice, Criminal Trial Practice, General Practice, Insurance Defense Law

RICHESON AND BROWN, P.A.
Fort Pierce, FL....Labor and Employment Law
Orlando, FL....Labor and Employment Law
West Palm Beach, FL....Labor and Employment Law

RICHEY, MUNROE, RODRIGUEZ & DIAZ, P.A.
Miami, FL....Appellate Practice, Civil Trial Practice, Criminal Trial Practice

RICHILANO, JOHN M., P.C.
Denver, CO....Civil Trial Practice, Criminal Trial Practice

RICHMOND AND FISHBURNE
Charlottesville, VA....Civil Trial Practice, General Practice, Insurance Defense Law, Probate and Estate Planning Law, Real Estate Law

RICKEL & BAUN, A PROFESSIONAL CORPORATION
Detroit, MI....................Business Law
Grosse Pointe Farms, MI........Business Law

RICKS & ANDERSON, A LAW CORPORATION
Santa Ana, CA....................Civil Trial Practice, Labor and Employment Law

RIDDLE, DON R., P.C.
Houston, TX....................Personal Injury Law

RIDEN, EARLE & KIEFNER, P.A.
St. Petersburg, FL....................General Practice

RIDENOUR, RIDENOUR & FOX
Clinton, TN....................Personal Injury Law

RIDENOUR, SWENSON, CLEERE & EVANS, P.C.
Phoenix, AZ....................Banking Law, Civil Trial Practice, Commercial Law, Insurance Defense Law, Real Estate Law

RIDGE, HOLLEY & MORRIS
Graham, NC....................General Practice

RIEBESELL, H. F., JR., P.C.
Denver, CO....................Business Law

RIECKER, VAN DAM, GANNON, LOOBY & BARKER, P.C.
Midland, MI....................General Practice

RIEDERS, TRAVIS, MUSSINA, HUMPHREY & HARRIS
Williamsport, PA....................Appellate Practice, Civil Trial Practice, Medical Malpractice Law, Personal Injury Law, Product Liability Law

RIESENBURGER & KIZNER, P.C.
Vineland, NJ....................Civil Trial Practice, General Practice

RIEVES & MAYTON
West Memphis, AR....................Civil Trial Practice, General Practice, Insurance Defense Law, Product Liability Law

RIFE & DAUGHERTY
Huntington, WV....................Real Estate Law, Tax Law

RIGBY, THATCHER, ANDRUS, RIGBY, KAM & MOELLER, CHARTERED
Rexburg, ID....................General Practice

RIKER, DANZIG, SCHERER, HYLAND & PERRETTI
Morristown, NJ....................General Practice
Trenton, NJ....................General Practice

RIKLI, DONALD C.
Highland, IL....................General Practice

RILEY, JESSE L. JR.
Russellville, KY....................General Practice

RILEY & HOGGATT, P.C.
Sierra Vista, AZ....................General Practice

RILEY, MCNULTY & HEWITT, P.C.
Pittsburgh, PA....................Civil Trial Practice, Commercial Law, General Practice

RILEY, ROBERT F., P.C.
Dearborn, MI....................Civil Trial Practice

RILEY AND ROUMELL, P.C.
Detroit, MI....................General Practice, Labor and Employment Law

RILEY, TOM, LAW FIRM, P.C.
Cedar Rapids, IA....................Personal Injury Law

RINELLA AND RINELLA, LTD.
Chicago, IL....................Family Law

RINGO & STUBER, P.C.
Corvallis, OR....................General Practice

RINOS & PACKER
Santa Ana, CA....................General Practice, Medical Malpractice Law

RIPPLINGER, GEORGE, & ASSOCIATES
Belleville, IL....................Civil Trial Practice, Personal Injury Law

RISCASSI AND DAVIS, P.C.
Hartford, CT....................Civil Trial Practice, Personal Injury Law

RISELING & ASSOCIATES, A PROFESSIONAL CORPORATION
Tulsa, OK....................Probate and Estate Planning Law

RISJORD & JAMES
Overland Park, KS....................Product Liability Law

RITCHIE, JAMES B., A PROFESSIONAL CORPORATION
Atlanta, GA....................Construction Law

RITCHIE & REDIKER, P.C.
Birmingham, AL....................Securities Law

RITER, MAYER, HOFER, WATTIER & BROWN
Pierre, SD....................General Practice

RITTER, HANFORD AND PRYOR
Bridgeton, NJ....................General Practice

RITTER, ROBINSON, MCCREADY & JAMES
Toledo, OH....................Civil Trial Practice, General Practice, Insurance Defense Law, Municipal and Zoning Law, Personal Injury Law, Probate and Estate Planning Law, Real Estate Law

RIVKIN, RADLER & KREMER
Uniondale, NY....................Civil Trial Practice, General Practice

RIVLIN, LEWIS A.
Washington, DC....................General Practice

RIXEY AND RIXEY
Virginia Beach, VA....................Family Law

ROACH AND WHEAT
Louisville, KY....................Trademark, Copyright and Unfair Competition Law

ROAN & AUTREY, A PROFESSIONAL CORPORATION
Austin, TX....................Administrative Law, Insurance Defense Law

ROBBINS, BERLINER & CARSON
Los Angeles, CA....................Patent, Trademark, Copyright and Unfair Competition Law

ROBBINS & GREEN, A PROFESSIONAL ASSOCIATION
Phoenix, AZ....................Bankruptcy Law, Civil Trial Practice, Commercial Law, General Practice, Insurance Defense Law, Personal Injury Law, Real Estate Law

ROBBINS, KENNETH S., ATTORNEY AT LAW, A LAW CORPORATION, LAW OFFICE OF
Honolulu, HI....................Appellate Practice, Civil Trial Practice, Construction Law, Health Care Law, Insurance Defense Law, Medical Malpractice Law, Personal Injury Law, Product Liability Law

ROBBINS, TUNKEY, ROSS, AMSEL, RABEN & WAXMAN, P.A.
Miami, FL....................Appellate Practice, Criminal Trial Practice

ROBE AND ROBE
Athens, OH....................General Practice

ROBENALT & ROBENALT
Lima, OH....................General Practice

ROBERT & MILLER
Louisville, KY....................Patent, Trademark, Copyright and Unfair Competition Law

ROBERTS, WILLIAM B.
Naples, FL....................Business Law

ROBERTS, ALLEN P., P.A.
Camden, AR....................General Practice

ROBERTS, BETZ & BLOSS, P.C.
Grand Rapids, MI....................Civil Trial Practice, Commercial Law, Construction Law, Environmental Law, Insurance Defense Law, Personal Injury Law

ROBERTS, GARY, & ASSOCIATES, P.A.
West Palm Beach, FL....................Medical Malpractice Law

ROBERTS, GARY W., P.A., LAWYERS
West Palm Beach, FL....................Personal Injury Law

ROBERTS, MARK SCOTT, AND ASSOCIATES, A PROF. LAW CORP.
Fullerton, CA....................Probate and Estate Planning Law

ROBERTS & MORGAN
Riverside, CA....................General Practice

ROBERTS, ROBERTS & INGRAM
Cordele, GA....................General Practice

ROBERTS & SMITH
Lexington, KY....................Criminal Trial Practice, General Practice, Insurance Defense Law, Personal Injury Law

ROBERTS, SOJKA & DORAN, P.A.
New Port Richey, FL....................Personal Injury Law

ROBERTS, SOKOL, ASHBY & JONES
Fredericksburg, VA....................Civil Trial Practice, Commercial Law, General Practice

ROBERTSON, W. R. III
Marietta, GA....................Business Law, Family Law, Probate and Estate Planning Law

ROBERTSON, MONAGLE & EASTAUGH, A PROFESSIONAL CORPORATION
Anchorage, AK....................General Practice

ROBERTSON & SEEKINGS
Charleston, SC ....Business Law, Construction Law

ROBERTSON & WILLIAMS, INC.
Oklahoma City, OK................General Practice

ROBERTSON, WILLIAMS & MCDONALD, P.A.
Orlando, FL ....Civil Trial Practice, Commercial Law, Environmental Law

ROBINETTE, DUGAN & JAKUBOWSKI, P.A.
Baltimore, MD ....Civil Trial Practice, Medical Malpractice Law, Personal Injury Law

ROBINSON, BERT K.
Baton Rouge, LA.....................Business Law, Civil Trial Practice, Construction Law, Personal Injury Law, Probate and Estate Planning Law, Product Liability Law

ROBINSON, CHARLES F.
Clearwater, FL ....Probate and Estate Planning Law

ROBINSON, MARIETTA S.
Detroit, MI...............................Medical Malpractice Law

ROBINSON, PETER B.
Lowell, MA ....Business Law

ROBINSON, BARNETT, JR., P.A.
Boca Raton, FL ....General Practice
Coral Gables, FL ....General Practice

ROBINSON, BRADSHAW & HINSON, P.A.
Charlotte, NC...........................General Practice
Rock Hill, SC...........................General Practice

ROBINSON, DIAMANT, BRILL & KLAUSNER, A PROFESSIONAL CORPORATION
Los Angeles, CA ....Bankruptcy Law

ROBINSON DONOVAN MADDEN & BARRY, P.C.
Springfield, MA........................Civil Trial Practice, Environmental Law, General Practice

ROBINSON LAW FIRM, THE
Washington, DC.......................Civil Trial Practice, Criminal Trial Practice

ROBINSON, LOCKE, GAGE, FITE & WILLIAMS
Muskogee, OK ....Civil Trial Practice, General Practice

ROBINSON MAREADY LAWING & COMERFORD
Winston-Salem, NC ....General Practice

ROBINSON, MCFADDEN & MOORE, P.C.
Columbia, SC...........................Civil Trial Practice, General Practice, Insurance Defense Law, Personal Injury Law

ROBINSON, PALMER & LOGAN
Bakersfield, CA ....Civil Trial Practice, General Practice, Insurance Defense Law

ROBINSON, PHILLIPS & CALCAGNIE, A PROFESSIONAL CORPORATION
Mission Viejo, CA....................Civil Trial Practice, Personal Injury Law

ROBINSON, ST. JOHN & WAYNE
Newark, NJ ....Antitrust Law, Banking Law, Civil Trial Practice, Criminal Trial Practice, General Practice, Insurance Defense Law, Municipal Bond/Public Authority Financing Law, Tax Law

ROBINSON SHEPPARD SHAPIRO, G.P.
Montreal, QU, Canada ....General Practice

ROBINSON & WOOD, INC.
San Jose, CA ....Insurance Defense Law

ROBISON, BELAUSTEGUI, ROBB AND SHARP, A PROFESSIONAL CORPORATION
Reno, NV ....General Practice

ROBISON, CURPHEY & O'CONNELL
Toledo, OH ....General Practice, Insurance Defense Law, Medical Malpractice Law

ROBMAN & SEELEY
Pasadena, CA..........................Civil Trial Practice

ROBY & HOOD
Fort Wayne, IN........................Civil Trial Practice, Personal Injury Law

ROCAP, WITCHGER & THRELKELD
Indianapolis, IN ....Commercial Law, General Practice, Insurance Defense Law

ROCHE, JOHN J. & ASSOCIATES
Cambridge, MA ....Probate and Estate Planning Law

ROCHE, CARENS & DEGIACOMO
Boston, MA..............................Bankruptcy Law, Business Law, General Practice

ROCHE CORRIGAN MCCOY & BUSH
Albany, NY..............................Construction Law, General Practice, Insurance Defense Law, Personal Injury Law

ROCHE AND MURPHY
Franklin, MA ....Civil Trial Practice, Municipal and Zoning Law, Real Estate Law

ROCKEY, RIFKIN AND RYTHER
Chicago, IL..............................Patent, Trademark, Copyright and Unfair Competition Law

ROCKHILL, PINNICK, PEQUIGNOT, HELM & LANDIS
Warsaw, IN ....Business Law, Civil Trial Practice, Insurance Defense Law

ROCKS, JOANNE S.
Anaheim, CA ....Tax Law

RODA, JOSEPH F., P.C.
Lancaster, PA..........................Civil Trial Practice, Commercial Law, Personal Injury Law

RODERICK, MYERS & LINTON
Akron, OH ....Civil Trial Practice, General Practice, Insurance Defense Law

RODEY, DICKASON, SLOAN, AKIN & ROBB, P.A.
Albuquerque, NM....................Administrative Law, Antitrust Law, Banking Law, Bankruptcy Law, Business Law, Commercial Law, Construction Law, Criminal Trial Practice, General Practice, Health Care Law, Insurance Defense Law, International Business Law, Labor and Employment Law, Medical Malpractice Law, Natural Resources Law, Personal Injury Law, Probate and Estate Planning Law, Product Liability Law, Public Utilities Law, Real Estate Law, Securities Law, Tax Law
Santa Fe, NM..........................General Practice

RODGERS, JAMES R.
Blackwell, OK ....General Practice, Probate and Estate Planning Law

RODGERS, MENARD & COPPOLA
Buffalo, NY ....Civil Trial Practice, General Practice, Insurance Defense Law

RODMAN, HOLSCHER, FRANCISCO & PECK, P.A.
Washington, NC.......................General Practice

RODRIGUEZ, COLVIN & CHANEY
Brownsville, TX ....Banking Law, General Practice

ROEMER & HARNIK
Indian Wells, CA ....Probate and Estate Planning Law, Real Estate Law

ROGAN & WELCH
Rogersville, TN.......................General Practice

ROGERS, BOWERS, DEMPSEY AND PALADINO
West Palm Beach, FL ....Tax Law

ROGERS & GREENBERG
Dayton, OH..............................Business Law, Family Law, General Practice

ROGERS & HARDIN
Atlanta, GA ....General Practice

ROGERS, HOWELL & HAFERKAMP
St. Louis, MO..........................Patent, Trademark, Copyright and Unfair Competition Law

ROGERS, JOSEPH, O'DONNELL & QUINN, A PROFESSIONAL CORPORATION
San Francisco, CA ....Civil Trial Practice, General Practice

ROGERS, LAUGHLIN, NUNNALLY, HOOD & CRUM
Greeneville, TN ....Civil Trial Practice, General Practice

ROGERS, MAGRUDER, SUMNER & BRINSON
Rome, GA................................General Practice

ROGERS & MILNE
Toronto, ON, Canada..............Patent, Trademark, Copyright and Unfair Competition Law

ROGERS & ROGERS
Las Vegas, NV ....Communications Law

ROGERS, TOWERS, BAILEY, JONES & GAY, P.A.
Jacksonville, FL ....General Practice
Tallahassee, FL ....General Practice

ROGERS & WELLS
Los Angeles, CA ....General Practice
Washington, DC......................General Practice
New York, NY.........................Civil Trial Practice, General Practice
London, England ....General Practice
Paris, France...........................General Practice

ROHDE, DALES, MELZER, TE WINKLE & GASS
Sheboygan, WI ....General Practice

ROHLFF, HOWIE & FRISCHHOLZ
San Jose, CA ....Insurance Defense Law, Product Liability Law

ROHRBACHER, NICHOLSON & LIGHT, CO., L.P.A.
Adrian, MI ....Environmental Law
Monroe, MI.............................Environmental Law

ROLAND & SCHLEGEL, P.C.
Reading, PA ....General Practice

ROLFES, GARVEY, WALKER & ROBBINS
Greensburg, IN ....General Practice

ROLLESTON, MORETON JR.
Atlanta, GA ....Business Law

ROLLINS, SMALKIN, RICHARDS & MACKIE
Baltimore, MD ....Civil Trial Practice, Insurance Defense Law, Personal Injury Law

ROOKS, PITTS AND POUST
Chicago, IL.............................General Practice

ROPERS, MAJESKI, KOHN & BENTLEY, A PROFESSIONAL CORPORATION
Los Angeles, CA......................General Practice
Redwood City, CA ....General Practice
Sacramento, CA ....General Practice
San Francisco, CA ....General Practice
San Jose, CA ....General Practice
Santa Rosa, CA.......................General Practice

ROPES & GRAY
Washington, DC......................General Practice
Boston, MA.............................Civil Trial Practice, General Practice, Tax Law

ROSE & BRUTOCAO
Pasadena, CA ....Antitrust Law, Trademark, Copyright and Unfair Competition Law

ROSE, KOHL & DAVENPORT, LTD.
Santa Fe, NM..........................Civil Trial Practice, Probate and Estate Planning Law, Securities Law, Tax Law

ROSE LAW FIRM, A PROFESSIONAL ASSOCIATION
Little Rock, AR ....Banking Law, Bankruptcy Law, Civil Trial Practice, Commercial Law, Communications Law, General Practice, Insurance Defense Law, Labor and Employment Law, Municipal Bond/Public Authority Financing Law, Personal Injury Law, Probate and Estate Planning Law, Real Estate Law, Tax Law

ROSE PADDEN & PETTY, L.C.
Fairmont, WV ....General Practice, Insurance Defense Law
Morgantown, WV ....General Practice, Insurance Defense Law

ROSE, RAND, ORCUTT, CAULEY & BLAKE, P.A.
Wilson, NC..............................General Practice

ROSE, RAY, WINFREY, O'CONNOR & LESLIE, P.A.
Fayetteville, NC ....General Practice, Immigration and Naturalization Law

ROSE & ROSE
Kenosha, WI ....Criminal Trial Practice, General Practice

ROSE, SCHMIDT, HASLEY & DISALLE, P.C.
Pittsburgh, PA ....Antitrust Law, Civil Trial Practice, General Practice, Labor and Employment Law

ROSE, SUNDSTROM & BENTLEY
Tallahassee, FL ....Administrative Law, Environmental Law, Health Care Law, Public Utilities Law, Real Estate Law

ROSEN, CHARLES A.
Roseland, NJ...........................Commercial Law, General Practice

ROSEN, BIEN & ASARO
San Francisco, CA ....Antitrust Law, Appellate Practice, Civil Trial Practice, Commercial Law, Labor and Employment Law, Securities Law, Trademark, Copyright and Unfair Competition Law

ROSEN, DAINOW & JACOBS
New York, NY.........................Patent, Trademark, Copyright and Unfair Competition Law

ROSEN & LOVELL, P.C.
Detroit, MI ....Construction Law, Personal Injury Law, Product Liability Law

ROSEN, ROSEN & HAGOOD, P.A.
Charleston, SC ....Administrative Law, Bankruptcy Law, Civil Trial Practice, Construction Law, Family Law, General Practice, Labor and Employment Law, Medical Malpractice Law, Personal Injury Law, Probate and Estate Planning Law

ROSENBAUM & ROSENBAUM, P.S.C.
Lexington, KY ....General Practice

ROSENBERG, KIRSHNER, P.A.
Pittsburgh, PA ....Family Law, General Practice, Insurance Defense Law

ROSENBERG LAW FIRM, THE
Des Moines, IA ....Business Law, Criminal Trial Practice, General Practice, Personal Injury Law

ROSENBERG, ROBERT MERRILL, P.A.
Minneapolis, MN....................General Practice, Real Estate Law

ROSENBLATT, STANLEY M., PROFESSIONAL ASSOCIATION
Miami, FL ....Civil Trial Practice

ROSENBLUM & FILAN
Stamford, CT..........................Civil Trial Practice, Health Care Law, Medical Malpractice Law
New York, NY.........................Medical Malpractice Law
White Plains, NY ....Medical Malpractice Law

ROSENBLUM, WOLF & LLOYD, A PROFESSIONAL CORPORATION
Secaucus, NJ...........................Real Estate Law, Tax Law

ROSENFELD & WOLFF, A PROFESSIONAL CORPORATION
Los Angeles, CA ....Business Law, Real Estate Law

ROSENMAN & COLIN
Washington, DC......................General Practice
New York, NY.........................General Practice

ROSENN, JENKINS & GREENWALD
Wilkes-Barre, PA ....Bankruptcy Law, General Practice, Labor and Employment Law, Probate and Estate Planning Law, Real Estate Law, Tax Law

ROSENOW, JOHNSON, GRAFFE, KEAY, POMEROY & MONIZ
Tacoma, WA ....Health Care Law, Medical Malpractice Law

ROSENSTEIN, FIST & RINGOLD, A PROFESSIONAL CORPORATION
Tulsa, OK ....General Practice

ROSENTHAL, MONHAIT, GROSS & GODDESS, P.A.
Wilmington, DE......................Civil Trial Practice, General Practice

ROSENTHAL AND SCHANFIELD, PROFESSIONAL CORPORATION
Chicago, IL.............................Civil Trial Practice, General Practice

ROSENTHAL, SIEGEL, MUENKEL & WOLF
Buffalo, NY ....Personal Injury Law

ROSENTHAL AND WEISBERG, P.C.
Philadelphia, PA ....Personal Injury Law

ROSENWALD, LAWRENCE S., P.C.
Philadelphia, PA ....Civil Trial Practice, Commercial Law, Real Estate Law

ROSENZWEIG, JONES & MACNABB, P.C.
Newnan, GA ....Civil Trial Practice, General Practice, Real Estate Law

ROSENZWEIG, SCHULZ & GILLOMBARDO CO., L.P.A.
Cleveland, OH.........................General Practice

ROSEPINK & ESTES
Scottsdale, AZ.........................Probate and Estate Planning Law, Tax Law

ROSHOLT, ROBERTSON & TUCKER, CHARTERED
Boise, ID.................................Bankruptcy Law, Business Law, Commercial Law, Natural Resources Law
Twin Falls, ID.........................Business Law, Commercial Law, Municipal and Zoning Law, Natural Resources Law, Real Estate Law

ROSS, HARRIET
San Francisco, CA ....Criminal Trial Practice

ROSS, JAMES E. & ASSOCIATES
Houston, TX ....Admiralty/Maritime Law, General Practice, Insurance Defense Law

ROSS, BRITTAIN & SCHONBERG CO., L.P.A.
Cleveland, OH.........................Labor and Employment Law

ROSS, DIXON & MASBACK
Washington, DC......................Civil Trial Practice

ROSS & HARDIES
Chicago, IL.............................General Practice

ROSS, HUNT, SPELL & ROSS, A PROFESSIONAL ASSOCIATION
Clarksdale, MS.......................Administrative Law, General Practice, Natural Resources Law, Real Estate Law

ROSS & ROSS
Monticello, AR ....General Practice

ROSS, SACKS & GLAZIER
Los Angeles, CA .... Probate and Estate Planning Law

ROSSI, MURNANE, BALZANO & HUGHES
Utica, NY .... General Practice

ROSSIE, BETHEA, LUCKETT, PARKER & LAUGHLIN, P.C.
Memphis, TN .... General Practice

ROSSMAN, BAUMBERGER & REBOSO, A PROFESSIONAL ASSOCIATION
Miami, FL .... Civil Trial Practice

ROST & GEIGER
Wailuku, HI .... Personal Injury Law

ROTH, MICHAEL DUNDON LAW OFFICES OF
Los Angeles, CA .... Health Care Law

ROTH, STEPHEN H.
Hackensack, NJ .... Commercial Law, Family Law, Real Estate Law

ROTH, DUNCAN & LABARGA, P.A.
West Palm Beach, FL .... Criminal Trial Practice, Personal Injury Law

ROTH, VAN AMBERG, GROSS, ROGERS & ORTIZ
Santa Fe, NM .... Civil Trial Practice, Personal Injury Law, Real Estate Law

ROTHBERG, GALLMEYER, FRUECHTENICHT & LOGAN
Fort Wayne, IN .... Banking Law, General Practice

ROTHMAN GORDON FOREMAN & GROUDINE, P.C.
Pittsburgh, PA .... Civil Trial Practice, Communications Law, General Practice, Labor and Employment Law

ROTHSCHILD, BARRY & MYERS
Chicago, IL .... Antitrust Law

ROTHSCHILD & WISHEK
Sacramento, CA .... Criminal Trial Practice

ROTHSTEIN, DONATELLI, HUGHES, DAHLSTROM, CRON & SCHOENBURG
Santa Fe, NM .... Civil Trial Practice, Criminal Trial Practice

ROUNTREE & SEAGLE, L.L.P.
Wilmington, NC .... Admiralty/Maritime Law, Civil Trial Practice, General Practice

ROUTMAN, MOORE, GOLDSTONE & VALENTINO
New Castle, PA .... General Practice
Sharon, PA .... General Practice

ROWAN & QUIRK
Rockville, MD .... Civil Trial Practice, General Practice

ROWE, FOLEY & GARDNER
South Bend, IN .... Civil Trial Practice, General Practice, Insurance Defense Law, Personal Injury Law, Product Liability Law

ROWLEY, FORREST, O'DONNELL & HITE, P.C.
Albany, NY .... Administrative Law, Business Law, Civil Trial Practice, Commercial Law, Employment Benefits Law, Environmental Law, General Practice, Insurance Defense Law, Labor and Employment Law, Personal Injury Law

ROWLEY LAW FIRM, P.C.
Clovis, NM .... General Practice

ROY, BIVINS, JUDICE & HENKE, A PROFESSIONAL LAW CORPORATION
Lafayette, LA .... Admiralty/Maritime Law, General Practice, Medical Malpractice Law, Product Liability Law, Public Utilities Law

ROY & LAMBERT
Springdale, AR .... General Practice

ROY, LANSING J., P.A., LAW OFFICE OF
Jacksonville, FL .... Bankruptcy Law

ROYALL, KOEGEL & WELLS
Washington, DC .... General Practice

ROYALL KOEGEL & WELLS
New York, NY .... General Practice

ROYALS & HARTUNG
Jackson, MS .... Criminal Trial Practice

ROYCE, GRIMM, VRANJES, MCCORMICK & GRAHAM
San Diego, CA .... Insurance Defense Law, Patent, Trademark, Copyright and Unfair Competition Law

ROYLANCE, ABRAMS, BERDO & GOODMAN
Washington, DC .... Patent, Trademark, Copyright and Unfair Competition Law

ROYSTON, MUELLER, MCLEAN & REID
Towson, MD .... General Practice

ROYSTON, RAYZOR, VICKERY & WILLIAMS, L.L.P.
Brownsville, TX .... General Practice
Corpus Christi, TX .... General Practice
Galveston, TX .... General Practice
Houston, TX .... Admiralty/Maritime Law, General Practice

ROZELLE, SULLIVAN AND CALL
Palm Beach, FL .... Civil Trial Practice, General Practice

RUBENSTEIN, NOVAK, EINBUND, PAVLIK & CELEBREZZE
Cleveland, OH .... Bankruptcy Law, Civil Trial Practice, Medical Malpractice Law, Personal Injury Law, Product Liability Law

RUBENSTEIN PLOTKIN, PROFESSIONAL CORPORATION
Southfield, MI .... Probate and Estate Planning Law, Tax Law

RUBIN & ASSOCIATES
Paoli, PA .... Civil Trial Practice

RUBIN BAUM LEVIN CONSTANT & FRIEDMAN
New York, NY .... General Practice

RUBIN & DORNBAUM
Newark, NJ .... Immigration and Naturalization Law

RUBIN, GLICKMAN AND STEINBERG, A PROFESSIONAL CORPORATION
Lansdale, PA .... Criminal Trial Practice, Family Law, Personal Injury Law, Probate and Estate Planning Law

RUBIN HAYS & FOLEY
Louisville, KY .... Banking Law, Bankruptcy Law, Civil Trial Practice, Family Law, General Practice, Municipal Bond/Public Authority Financing Law, Personal Injury Law, Probate and Estate Planning Law, Real Estate Law, Securities Law, Tax Law

RUBIN & LEVIN, P.C.
Indianapolis, IN .... Bankruptcy Law, Commercial Law

RUBIN AND RUDMAN
Boston, MA .... Business Law, Civil Trial Practice, General Practice, Real Estate Law

RUCCI, GLEASON & BURNHAM
Darien, CT .... General Practice

RUCKELSHAUS, ROLAND, HASBROOK & O'CONNOR
Indianapolis, IN .... General Practice, Labor and Employment Law

RUDASILL & RUDASILL
Clinton, IL .... General Practice

RUDDY, BRADLEY & KOLKHORST, A PROFESSIONAL CORPORATION
Juneau, AK .... Civil Trial Practice

RUDERMAN, ALAN
Chattanooga, TN .... Patent, Trademark, Copyright and Unfair Competition Law

RUDER, WARE & MICHLER, S.C.
Wausau, WI .... General Practice

RUDLOFF, GOLDEN & EVANS
Bowling Green, KY .... Civil Trial Practice, Insurance Defense Law, Personal Injury Law

RUDNICK & WOLFE
Chicago, IL .... General Practice

RUDOLF & MAHER, P.A.
Chapel Hill, NC .... Criminal Trial Practice

RUFF, BOND, COBB, WADE & MCNAIR, L.L.P.
Charlotte, NC .... Civil Trial Practice, General Practice, Real Estate Law

RUFF, REX R., P.C.
Marietta, GA .... Family Law

RUHNKE & BARRETT
West Orange, NJ .... Appellate Practice, Criminal Trial Practice

RULEY & EVERETT
Parkersburg, WV .... General Practice, Insurance Defense Law

RUMAN, CLEMENTS, TOBIN & HOLUB, P.C.
Hammond, IN .... Personal Injury Law

RUMMAGE, KAMUF, YEWELL, PACE & CONDON
Owensboro, KY .... Business Law, Civil Trial Practice, Criminal Trial Practice, Family Law, General Practice, Personal Injury Law, Real Estate Law

RUMMONDS, WILLIAMS & MAIR
Aptos, CA .... Civil Trial Practice, Personal Injury Law

RUMRELL & JOHNSON, P.A.
Jacksonville, FL .... Admiralty/Maritime Law, Insurance Defense Law

RUMSEY, RALPH S.
Ann Arbor, MI ....Tax Law

RUMSEY & BUGG, A PROFESSIONAL CORPORATION
Irvington, VA....................General Practice

RUNFOLA, JOHN M.
San Francisco, CA ....Criminal Trial Practice

RUNYON AND RUNYON
Clarksville, TN....................Family Law, Personal Injury Law, Probate and Estate Planning Law

RUOCCO, SAUCEDO & CORSIGLIA, A LAW CORPORATION
San Jose, CA ....Medical Malpractice Law, Personal Injury Law

RUPE & GIRARD, LAW OFFICES, P.A.
Wichita, KS ....Labor and Employment Law

RUPPERT, BRONSON, CHICARELLI & SMITH CO., L.P.A.
Franklin, OH....................Insurance Defense Law, Medical Malpractice Law, Personal Injury Law

RUS, MILIBAND, WILLIAMS & SMITH
Irvine, CA....................General Practice

RUSH MOORE CRAVEN SUTTON MORRY & BEH
Honolulu, HI....................General Practice

RUSH & RUSH
Salida, CO ....General Practice

RUSH & SEIKEN, P.C.
Philadelphia, PA ....Personal Injury Law

RUSHING & GUICE
Biloxi, MS....................Civil Trial Practice, Commercial Law, General Practice, Probate and Estate Planning Law, Real Estate Law

RUSHTON, STAKELY, JOHNSTON & GARRETT, P.A.
Montgomery, AL ....Civil Trial Practice, General Practice

RUSS, JAMES M., P.A., LAW OFFICES OF
Orlando, FL ....Civil Trial Practice, Criminal Trial Practice

RUSSELL & BATCHELOR
Grand Rapids, MI ....Real Estate Law, Tax Law

RUSSELL, BROWN, BICKEL & BRECKENRIDGE
Nevada, MO....................General Practice

RUSSELL & DUMOULIN
Vancouver, BC, Canada..........Admiralty/Maritime Law, Antitrust Law, Banking Law, Bankruptcy Law, Business Law, Civil Trial Practice, Communications Law, Construction Law, Environmental Law, Family Law, General Practice, Immigration and Naturalization Law, Insurance Defense Law, Labor and Employment Law, Natural Resources Law, Personal Injury Law, Probate and Estate Planning Law, Real Estate Law, Tax Law, Trademark, Copyright and Unfair Competition Law

RUSSELL & HULL, P.A.
Orlando, FL ....Civil Trial Practice, Construction Law, Real Estate Law

RUSSELL & MIRKOVICH
Long Beach, CA....................Admiralty/Maritime Law, Civil Trial Practice, General Practice, International Business Law

RUSSELL, TURNER, LAIRD & JONES, L.L.P.
Fort Worth, TX ....Civil Trial Practice, Commercial Law, Medical Malpractice Law, Personal Injury Law, Product Liability Law

RUSSO & TALISMAN, P.A.
Miami, FL ....Appellate Practice

RUST, RUST & SILVER, A PROFESSIONAL CORPORATION
Fairfax, VA ....Banking Law, Business Law, Civil Trial Practice, Commercial Law, Municipal and Zoning Law, Personal Injury Law, Real Estate Law

RUTAN & TUCKER
Costa Mesa, CA....................Bankruptcy Law, Business Law, Civil Trial Practice, Commercial Law, Construction Law, Environmental Law, General Practice, Labor and Employment Law, Municipal Bond/Public Authority Financing Law, Municipal and Zoning Law, Probate and Estate Planning Law, Real Estate Law, Tax Law

RUTH & MACNEILLE, PROFESSIONAL ASSOCIATION
Hilton Head Island, SC..........Civil Trial Practice, Probate and Estate Planning Law, Tax Law

RUTKIN AND EFFRON, P.C.
Westport, CT....................Family Law, Personal Injury Law

RUTLEDGE, MANION, RABAUT, TERRY & THOMAS, P.C.
Detroit, MI....................Insurance Defense Law

RUTTER, THOMAS B., LTD.
Philadelphia, PA ....Appellate Practice, Civil Trial Practice, Criminal Trial Practice

RYALS, ROBINSON & SAFFO, P.C.
Wilmington, NC....................General Practice

RYAN, BENNETT & RADLOFF
Charleston, IL....................General Practice
Mattoon, IL....................Civil Trial Practice, Criminal Trial Practice, General Practice

RYAN, GEISTER & WHALEY, A PROFESSIONAL CORPORATION
Oklahoma City, OK....................General Practice

RYAN, MARTIN, COSTELLO, ALLISON & LEITER, P.C.
Springfield, MA....................Civil Trial Practice, General Practice

RYAN, RUSSELL, OGDEN & SELTZER
Reading, PA....................Administrative Law, Civil Trial Practice, Public Utilities Law

RYAN, RYAN, JOHNSON, CLEAR & DELUCA
Stamford, CT....................Civil Trial Practice, General Practice

RYAN, RYAN & ZIMMERMAN
Aitkin, MN....................General Practice

RYAN SMITH & CARBINE, LTD.
Rutland, VT ....General Practice

RYDBERG, GOLDSTEIN & BOLVES, P.A.
Tampa, FL ....Bankruptcy Law, Commercial Law, Environmental Law, Municipal and Zoning Law, Real Estate Law

RYLAND AND DAVIS, A PROFESSIONAL CORPORATION
Warsaw, VA ....General Practice

RYMER, WM. W.
Providence, RI....................Patent, Trademark, Copyright and Unfair Competition Law

RYWANT, ALVAREZ, JONES & RUSSO, PROFESSIONAL ASSOCIATION
Tampa, FL ....Civil Trial Practice, Insurance Defense Law, Product Liability Law

SABBATH & MEHESAN, CHARTERED, THE LAW FIRM OF
Las Vegas, NV ....Labor and Employment Law

SABLE, MAKOROFF & GUSKY, P.C.
Pittsburgh, PA ....Bankruptcy Law, Civil Trial Practice

SACCA AND SACCA
Lockport, NY....................General Practice

SACHNOFF & WEAVER, LTD.
Chicago, IL....................General Practice

SACHS, BERMAN & SHURE, SKLARZ & GALLANT, P.C.
New Haven, CT ....General Practice, Real Estate Law, Tax Law

SACKS, MASON J., INC., A PROF. LAW CORP.
Los Gatos, CA ....Probate and Estate Planning Law

SACKS MONTGOMERY, P.C.
New York, NY....................Civil Trial Practice, Construction Law

SACKS, SACKS & IMPREVENTO
Norfolk, VA ....Civil Trial Practice, Criminal Trial Practice, General Practice, Personal Injury Law

SACKS TIERNEY, P.A.
Phoenix, AZ ....Bankruptcy Law, Civil Trial Practice, General Practice

SACKS & ZWEIG
Santa Monica, CA....................Business Law, Civil Trial Practice, General Practice, Real Estate Law

SACOPULOS, JOHNSON, CARTER & SACOPULOS
Terre Haute, IN ....Insurance Defense Law

SAEGERT, ANGENEND & AUGUSTINE, P.C.
Austin, TX ....Administrative Law, Civil Trial Practice, Environmental Law, Probate and Estate Planning Law

SAGER, PAVLICK & WIRTZ, S.C.
Fond du Lac, WI ....General Practice

SAIBER SCHLESINGER SATZ & GOLDSTEIN
Newark, NJ ....Appellate Practice, Banking Law, Bankruptcy Law, Civil Trial Practice, Criminal Trial Practice, General Practice, Insurance Defense Law, Securities Law, Tax Law

SAIKLEY, GARRISON & COLOMBO, LTD.
Danville, IL ....Commercial Law

ST. CLAIR, DALLING & MEACHAM
Idaho Falls, ID....................General Practice

ST. CLAIR, MCFETRIDGE, GRIFFIN & LEGERNES, A PROFESSIONAL CORPORATION
San Francisco, CA ....Insurance Defense Law

ST. JOHN, HOWARD C. AND ASSOCIATES
Kingston, NY..........................General Practice

ST. JOHN & ST. JOHN
Cullman, AL...........................Civil Trial Practice, General Practice

ST. ONGE STEWARD JOHNSTON & REENS
Stamford, CT...........................Patent, Trademark, Copyright and Unfair Competition Law

SAITLIN, PATZIK & FRANK, LTD.
Chicago, IL..............................Securities Law, Tax Law

SALEH, JOHN
Lamesa, TX..............................Civil Trial Practice

SALERNO, COZZARELLI, MAUTONE, DE SALVO & NUSSBAUM, A PROFESSIONAL CORPORATION
Verona, NJ...............................General Practice, Municipal and Zoning Law

SALES, RONALD, LAWYER, P.A.
West Palm Beach, FL.............Civil Trial Practice, Family Law

SALITERMAN & SIEFFERMAN LAW FIRM
Minneapolis, MN.....................General Practice, Securities Law

SALLY & FITCH
Boston, MA..............................Civil Trial Practice

SALMON, GODSMAN & NICHOLSON, PROFESSIONAL CORPORATION
Englewood, CO........................Personal Injury Law

SALVI, PATRICK A., P.C., LAW OFFICES OF
Waukegan, IL..........................Medical Malpractice Law, Personal Injury Law

SAMEL, JEFFREY & ASSOCIATES
New York, NY..........................Insurance Defense Law, Personal Injury Law, Product Liability Law

SAMET & GAGE, P.C.
Tucson, AZ ....Personal Injury Law

SAMFORD, DENSON, HORSLEY, PETTEY & MARTIN
Opelika, AL.............................General Practice

SAMS, MARTIN & LISTER, P.A.
Miami, FL................................Civil Trial Practice, General Practice, Personal Injury Law

SAMS AND SAMS
Beaufort, SC ....Civil Trial Practice, General Practice

SAMUEL AND BALLARD, A PROFESSIONAL CORPORATION
Philadelphia, PA ....Civil Trial Practice, Commercial Law, Labor and Employment Law, Personal Injury Law

SAMUELS, MILLER, SCHROEDER, JACKSON & SLY
Decatur, IL..............................General Practice

SAMUELSON & JACOB
Hackensack, NJ.......................Patent, Trademark, Copyright and Unfair Competition Law

SAMUELSON RIEGER & YOVINO
Garden City, NY ....Family Law

SANDENAW, T. A., LAW OFFICE OF
Las Cruces, NM.......................Civil Trial Practice, Insurance Defense Law, Medical Malpractice Law

SANDERS, AUSTIN, SWOPE & FLANIGAN
Princeton, WV.........................Civil Trial Practice, Personal Injury Law, Product Liability Law

SANDERS, HAUGEN & SEARS
Newnan, GA ....General Practice

SANDERS, ROBERT E., AND ASSOCIATES, P.S.C.
Covington, KY ....Civil Trial Practice, Criminal Trial Practice, Medical Malpractice Law, Personal Injury Law, Product Liability Law

SANFORD, SPELLINGS, KUHL & PERKINS, L.L.P.
Austin, TX ....Administrative Law, Municipal Bond/Public Authority Financing Law, Municipal and Zoning Law

SANSONE, CHARLES F.
Tampa, FL ....Civil Trial Practice, Personal Injury Law, Product Liability Law

SANTEN & HUGHES, A LEGAL PROFESSIONAL ASSOCIATION
Cincinnati, OH.........................Bankruptcy Law, Civil Trial Practice, Commercial Law, General Practice, Medical Malpractice Law, Personal Injury Law, Probate and Estate Planning Law, Tax Law

SAPERSTEIN, GOLDSTEIN, DEMCHAK & BALLER, A PROFESSIONAL CORPORATION
Oakland, CA ....Labor and Employment Law

SARNOFF & BACCASH
Chicago, IL..............................Tax Law

SARRAIL, LYNCH & HALL
San Francisco, CA ....Insurance Defense Law, Product Liability Law

SASSCER, CLAGETT & BUCHER
Upper Marlboro, MD ....General Practice

SASSER, DONALD J., P.A.
Boca Raton, FL........................Family Law, General Practice
West Palm Beach, FL..............Family Law, General Practice

SATTERLEE STEPHENS BURKE & BURKE
New York, NY..........................General Practice, Immigration and Naturalization Law, Municipal Bond/Public Authority Financing Law, Natural Resources Law

SAUL, EWING, REMICK & SAUL
New York, NY..........................General Practice
Malvern, PA.............................General Practice
Philadelphia, PA ....Antitrust Law, General Practice, Municipal Bond/Public Authority Financing Law

SAUNDERS & MONROE
Chicago, IL..............................Antitrust Law, Civil Trial Practice, Communications Law, Public Utilities Law, Securities Law

SAVAGE, GARMER & ELLIOTT, P.S.C.
Lexington, KY ....Civil Trial Practice, Medical Malpractice Law, Personal Injury Law

SAVAGE, KRIM & SIMONS, P.A.
Ocala, FL.................................General Practice

SAVAGE, ROYALL AND SHEHEEN
Camden, SC.............................Civil Trial Practice, General Practice

SAVERI AND SAVERI, A PROFESSIONAL CORPORATION
San Francisco, CA ....Antitrust Law, Securities Law

SAVETT FRUTKIN PODELL & RYAN, P.C.
Philadelphia, PA ....Civil Trial Practice, Securities Law

SAWYER, J. E. JR.
Enterprise, AL..........................Civil Trial Practice, General Practice

SAWYER, DAVIS & HALPERN
Garden City, NY ....Civil Trial Practice, Family Law, General Practice, Medical Malpractice Law, Personal Injury Law, Probate and Estate Planning Law

SAYRE LAW OFFICES
Seattle, WA ....General Practice

SAYRE & WITTGRAF
Cherokee, IA ....General Practice

SCADDEN, HAMILTON & RYAN
San Francisco, CA ....Civil Trial Practice, Insurance Defense Law, Product Liability Law

SCALLEY & READING, A PROFESSIONAL CORPORATION
Salt Lake City, UT...................Environmental Law, Insurance Defense Law

SCANLAN AND SCANLAN, A PROFESSIONAL CORPORATION
Philadelphia, PA ....Admiralty/Maritime Law, Labor and Employment Law

SCANLON & GEARINGER CO., L.P.A.
Akron, OH ....Civil Trial Practice, General Practice

SCANLON, HOWLEY, SCANLON & DOHERTY
Scranton, PA...........................Civil Trial Practice, General Practice, Medical Malpractice Law

SCARIANO, KULA, ELLCH AND HIMES, CHARTERED
Chicago, IL..............................Civil Trial Practice, Employment Benefits Law, Insurance Defense Law, Labor and Employment Law, Municipal Bond/Public Authority Financing Law, Municipal and Zoning Law

SCARPELLO & ALLING, LTD. A PROFESSIONAL CORPORATION
Carson City, NV ....General Practice
Stateline, NV ....General Practice

SCARZAFAVA, JOHN, LAW OFFICE OF
Oneonta, NY ....Personal Injury Law, Product Liability Law

SCHAAF & HODGES
Marietta, GA............................Real Estate Law

SCHACHTER, KRISTOFF, ORENSTEIN & BERKOWITZ
San Francisco, CA ....Labor and Employment Law

SCHACHTER, TROMBADORE, OFFEN, STANTON & PAVICS, A PROFESSIONAL CORPORATION
Somerville, NJ ....Bankruptcy Law, Civil Trial Practice, Commercial Law, Criminal Trial Practice, Family Law, Personal Injury Law

SCHADEN, LAMPERT & LAMPERT
Denver, CO ....Medical Malpractice Law, Personal Injury Law, Product Liability Law

SCHAFER, GERALD S.
Greensboro, NC ....Bankruptcy Law

SCHAFFENEGGER, WATSON & PETERSON, LTD.
Chicago, IL ....Appellate Practice, Civil Trial Practice, Insurance Defense Law, Personal Injury Law, Product Liability Law

SCHAFFER, LAMBRIGHT, ODOM & SPARKS
Houston, TX ....Criminal Trial Practice

SCHAFFNER & VAN DER SNICK, P.C.
Geneva, IL ....Family Law

SCHANTZ, SCHATZMAN, AARONSON & CAHAN, P.A.
Miami, FL ....General Practice

SCHAPER & STEFFENS
Broken Bow, NE ....General Practice, Probate and Estate Planning Law, Real Estate Law

SCHATZ & SCHATZ, RIBICOFF & KOTKIN
Hartford, CT ....General Practice
Stamford, CT ....General Practice

SCHEDLER, MARTIN, P.C.
Portland, OR ....Transportation Law

SCHEFFLER, WILLIAM L.
Westport, CT ....Business Law, Immigration and Naturalization Law, Municipal and Zoning Law, Probate and Estate Planning Law, Real Estate Law

SCHEINBERG, SCHNEPS, DE PETRIS & DE PETRIS
Riverhead, NY ....General Practice

SCHEKTER RISHTY GOLDSTEIN & BLUMENTHAL, P.C.
New York, NY ....General Practice

SCHELL BRAY AYCOCK ABEL & LIVINGSTON, L.L.P.
Greensboro, NC ....General Practice, Tax Law

SCHELLINGER & DOYLE, S.C.
Milwaukee, WI ....Insurance Defense Law

SCHENCK, PRICE, SMITH & KING
Morristown, NJ ....General Practice

SCHERFFIUS, ANDREW M., P.C.
Atlanta, GA ....Civil Trial Practice, Medical Malpractice Law, Personal Injury Law

SCHERNER & HANSON
Columbus, OH ....Civil Trial Practice, Medical Malpractice Law, Personal Injury Law

SCHESSLER, JOHN
Ontario, CA ....Probate and Estate Planning Law

SCHEUER, YOST & PATTERSON, A PROFESSIONAL CORPORATION
Santa Fe, NM ....Banking Law, Civil Trial Practice, Environmental Law, General Practice, Labor and Employment Law, Probate and Estate Planning Law, Real Estate Law

SCHIFF HARDIN & WAITE
Washington, DC ....General Practice
Chicago, IL ....General Practice
Peoria, IL ....General Practice
New York, NY ....General Practice

SCHIFFMACHER, WEINSTEIN, BOLDT & RACINE, PROFESSIONAL CORPORATION
Los Angeles, CA ....Tax Law

SCHILLER & ASSOCIATES, P.C.
New York, NY ....Health Care Law

SCHILLER, DU CANTO AND FLECK
Chicago, IL ....Family Law
Lake Forest, IL ....Family Law

SCHILLING, JOHN R., A PROFESSIONAL CORPORATION
Newport Beach, CA ....Family Law

SCHINDLER & MEYER, PROFESSIONAL CORPORATION
San Francisco, CA ....Probate and Estate Planning Law

SCHINDLER AND OLSON
Mishawaka, IN ....General Practice, Personal Injury Law, Probate and Estate Planning Law, Real Estate Law

SCHINE & JULIANELLE, P.C.
Orange, CT ....Business Law, Civil Trial Practice, Probate and Estate Planning Law

SCHLANGER, MILLS, MAYER & GROSSBERG, L.L.P.
Houston, TX ....General Practice

SCHLECHT, SHEVLIN & SHOENBERGER, A LAW CORPORATION
Palm Springs, CA ....Business Law, General Practice, Probate and Estate Planning Law, Real Estate Law

SCHLICHTER, BOGARD & DENTON
St. Louis, MO ....Personal Injury Law

SCHLUSSER, REIVER, HUGHES & SISK
Wilmington, DE ....Business Law, Probate and Estate Planning Law, Tax Law

SCHMELZLE AND KROEGER
Freeport, IL ....General Practice

SCHMIDT, C.L. MIKE, P.C., THE LAW FIRM OF
Dallas, TX ....Civil Trial Practice, Medical Malpractice Law, Personal Injury Law

SCHMIDT & KUEHNE, A PROFESSIONAL LAW CORPORATION
Baton Rouge, LA ....Employment Benefits Law, Tax Law

SCHMIDT & RONCA, P.C.
Harrisburg, PA ....Personal Injury Law

SCHMIDT, SCHROYER, COLWILL & MORENO, P.C.
Pierre, SD ....General Practice

SCHMIDT, THOMPSON, JOHNSON & MOODY, P.A.
Willmar, MN ....Civil Trial Practice, General Practice, Insurance Defense Law

SCHMIEDESKAMP, ROBERTSON, NEU & MITCHELL
Quincy, IL ....Civil Trial Practice, General Practice

SCHMITTINGER & RODRIGUEZ, PROFESSIONAL ASSOCIATION
Dover, DE ....General Practice

SCHMITZ & OPHAUG
Northfield, MN ....General Practice

SCHNADER, HARRISON, SEGAL & LEWIS
Washington, DC ....General Practice
New York, NY ....General Practice
Philadelphia, PA ....Communications Law, General Practice, Labor and Employment Law

SCHNAPP, GRAHAM, REID & FULTON
Fredericktown, MO ....General Practice

SCHNEIDER, GELB, GOFFER & HICKEY, P.C.
Scranton, PA ....Civil Trial Practice

SCHNEIDER, KLEINICK, WEITZ, DAMASHEK, GODOSKY & GENTILE
New York, NY ....Civil Trial Practice, Medical Malpractice Law, Personal Injury Law

SCHNEIDER LAW FIRM, A PROFESSIONAL ASSOCIATION
Willmar, MN ....Civil Trial Practice, Personal Injury Law, Product Liability Law

SCHNEIDER, LUCE, QUILLINAN & MORGAN
Mountain View, CA ....Civil Trial Practice, Probate and Estate Planning Law, Real Estate Law, Tax Law

SCHNEIDER & MCWILLIAMS, P.C.
George West, TX ....General Practice

SCHNEIDER, REILLY, ZABIN & COSTELLO, P.C.
Boston, MA ....Civil Trial Practice

SCHNEIDER & SIEGEL, P.C.
Memphis, TN ....Probate and Estate Planning Law

SCHNEIDLER, JON G.
Seattle, WA ....Municipal and Zoning Law, Real Estate Law

SCHNORF & SCHNORF CO., L.P.A., A PROFESSIONAL CORPORATION
Toledo, OH ....Civil Trial Practice, General Practice, Insurance Defense Law, Labor and Employment Law; Personal Injury Law

SCHOBER & ULATOWSKI, S.C.
Green Bay, WI ....Business Law, Civil Trial Practice, Insurance Defense Law, Transportation Law

SCHOCH & WOODRUFF, L.L.P.
High Point, NC ....General Practice

SCHOCHOR, FEDERICO AND STATON, P.A.
Baltimore, MD ....Civil Trial Practice, Medical Malpractice Law, Personal Injury Law

SCHOELLERMAN, JACK L.
Irvine, CA....Business Law

SCHOEL, OGLE, BENTON AND CENTENO
Birmingham, AL....Antitrust Law, Bankruptcy Law, Civil Trial Practice, Construction Law

SCHOEN, DENNIS T., P.C., LAW OFFICES
Chicago, IL....Personal Injury Law

SCHOEN & SMITH, LTD.
Chicago, IL....Insurance Defense Law, Product Liability Law

SCHOENBAUM, CURPHY & SCANLAN, P.C.
San Antonio, TX....Business Law, Employment Benefits Law, Probate and Estate Planning Law, Real Estate Law, Tax Law

SCHOIFET, EDWARD, A PROFESSIONAL CORPORATION
New Brunswick, NJ....Family Law

SCHOLDER, PAUL A., ATTORNEY AT LAW, P.C.
New Haven, CT....Civil Trial Practice, Insurance Defense Law, Personal Injury Law

SCHOLZ, LOOS, PALMER, SIEBERS & DUESTERHAUS
Quincy, IL....General Practice

SCHOTTENSTEIN, ZOX & DUNN, A LEGAL PROFESSIONAL ASSOCIATION
Columbus, OH....General Practice, Health Care Law, Labor and Employment Law

SCHRADER, RECHT, BYRD, COMPANION & GURLEY
Wheeling, WV....Banking Law, Bankruptcy Law, Civil Trial Practice, Criminal Trial Practice, Employment Benefits Law, Family Law, General Practice, Insurance Defense Law, Labor and Employment Law, Medical Malpractice Law, Personal Injury Law, Real Estate Law, Tax Law

SCHRAGGER, LAVINE & NAGY, A PROFESSIONAL CORPORATION
Trenton, NJ....General Practice, Labor and Employment Law, Probate and Estate Planning Law, Real Estate Law

SCHRAMM & PINES, L.L.C.
St. Louis, MO....Business Law, Civil Trial Practice, International Business Law

SCHRAMM & RADDUE
Santa Barbara, CA....Business Law, General Practice, Tax Law

SCHRECK, JONES, BERNHARD, WOLOSON & GODFREY, CHARTERED
Las Vegas, NV....Bankruptcy Law, Commercial Law, Labor and Employment Law, Real Estate Law

SCHREEDER, WHEELER & FLINT
Atlanta, GA....Bankruptcy Law, Civil Trial Practice, Construction Law, Real Estate Law

SCHROEDER & HRUBY, LTD.
Wheaton, IL....Personal Injury Law

SCHROEDER & LARCHE, P.A.
Boca Raton, FL....Probate and Estate Planning Law, Real Estate Law

SCHROPP, BUELL & ELLIGETT, PROFESSIONAL ASSOCIATION
Tampa, FL....Civil Trial Practice

SCHUCHARDT, ROBERT G.
San Francisco, CA....General Practice

SCHUERING ZIMMERMAN SCULLY & NOLEN
Sacramento, CA....Insurance Defense Law, Medical Malpractice Law, Product Liability Law

SCHULLER, STEPHEN A., INCORPORATED
Tulsa, OK....General Practice, Real Estate Law

SCHULMAN, LEROY AND BENNETT, P.C.
Nashville, TN....General Practice

SCHULMAN & MCMILLAN, INCORPORATED
Costa Mesa, CA....Criminal Trial Practice

SCHULTEN & WARD
Atlanta, GA....Business Law, Civil Trial Practice, Labor and Employment Law

SCHULTE ROTH & ZABEL
New York, NY....Civil Trial Practice, Criminal Trial Practice, General Practice

SCHULTZ, JACK M., P.C.
Southfield, MI....Tax Law

SCHULTZ, SALISBURY, CAUBLE, VERSTEEG & DOLE
Grants Pass, OR....General Practice

SCHUMACHER, STEPHEN J.
Newport Beach, CA....Tax Law

SCHUMAN & BUTZ
Toms River, NJ....General Practice

SCHUREMAN, FRAKES, GLASS & WULFMEIER
Detroit, MI....Civil Trial Practice, Family Law, General Practice, Insurance Defense Law, Personal Injury Law

SCHUTTER, DAVID C. & ASSOCIATES
Honolulu, HI....Civil Trial Practice, Personal Injury Law

SCHWALB, DONNENFELD, BRAY & SILBERT, A PROFESSIONAL CORPORATION
Washington, DC....Civil Trial Practice

SCHWARTZ, JOHN B. & ASSOCIATES
Chicago, IL....Medical Malpractice Law, Personal Injury Law

SCHWARTZ, THEODORE F.
Clayton, MO....Commercial Law

SCHWARTZ, ARTHUR M., P.C.
Denver, CO....Criminal Trial Practice

SCHWARTZ & BLACKMAN
Philadelphia, PA....Civil Trial Practice

SCHWARTZ, BON, WALKER & STUDER
Casper, WY....Business Law, Civil Trial Practice, Personal Injury Law

SCHWARTZ & CAMPBELL, L.L.P.
Houston, TX....Admiralty/Maritime Law, Appellate Practice, Business Law, Civil Trial Practice, Commercial Law, Construction Law, Insurance Defense Law, Labor and Employment Law

SCHWARTZ AND ELLIS, LTD.
Arlington, VA....Civil Trial Practice, Family Law, International Business Law, Medical Malpractice Law, Personal Injury Law

SCHWARTZ & JALKANEN, P.C.
Southfield, MI....Civil Trial Practice, Insurance Defense Law, Medical Malpractice Law, Personal Injury Law, Product Liability Law

SCHWARTZ, KOBB & SCHEINERT
Nanuet, NY....General Practice

SCHWARTZ, MANES & RUBY, A LEGAL PROFESSIONAL ASSOCIATION
Cincinnati, OH....Business Law, General Practice, Probate and Estate Planning Law, Tax Law

SCHWARTZ & SCHWARTZ
Media, PA....Personal Injury Law
Hallettsville, TX....Personal Injury Law

SCHWARTZ, SIMON, EDELSTEIN, CELSO & KESSLER
Livingston, NJ....Civil Trial Practice, Labor and Employment Law

SCHWARTZ, STEINSAPIR, DOHRMANN & SOMMERS
Los Angeles, CA....Civil Trial Practice, Employment Benefits Law, Labor and Employment Law, Real Estate Law

SCHWARTZ, WISOT & RODOV, A PROFESSIONAL LAW CORPORATION
Beverly Hills, CA....Bankruptcy Law, Civil Trial Practice, Real Estate Law

SCHWARTZBACH, M. GERALD
San Francisco, CA....Criminal Trial Practice, Labor and Employment Law, Personal Injury Law

SCHWARTZMAN, JAMES C. & ASSOCIATES
Philadelphia, PA....Civil Trial Practice, Criminal Trial Practice

SCOBLIONKO, SCOBLIONKO, MUIR & BARTHOLOMEW, A PROFESSIONAL CORPORATION
Allentown, PA....General Practice

SCOFIELD, MICHAEL S. LAW OFFICES OF
Charlotte, NC....Criminal Trial Practice

SCOFIELD, GERARD, VERON, SINGLETARY & POHORELSKY, A PROFESSIONAL LAW CORPORATION
Lake Charles, LA....Civil Trial Practice, General Practice

SCOTT, DAVID V.
New Albany, IN....Civil Trial Practice, Personal Injury Law, Product Liability Law

SCOTT, DOUGLASS, LUTON & MCCONNICO, L.L.P.
Austin, TX....Administrative Law, Civil Trial Practice, Insurance Defense Law, Natural Resources Law

SCOTT, HULSE, MARSHALL, FEUILLE, FINGER & THURMOND, P.C.
El Paso, TX....General Practice

SCOTT, ROYCE, HARRIS, BRYAN, BARRA & JORGENSEN, PROFESSIONAL ASSOCIATION
Palm Beach Gardens, FL....Civil Trial Practice, Environmental Law, General Practice, Natural Resources Law

SCOTT, VOGRIN, RIESTER & JAMIOLKOWSKI, A PROFESSIONAL CORPORATION
Pittsburgh, PA .... Criminal Trial Practice, Personal Injury Law, Probate and Estate Planning Law

SCOTTEN & HINSHAW
New Castle, IN .... General Practice

SCROGGINS & WILLIAMSON
Atlanta, GA .... Bankruptcy Law

SCRUGGS, JORDAN & DODD, P.A.
Fort Payne, AL .... Banking Law, Civil Trial Practice, General Practice, Insurance Defense Law, Personal Injury Law

SCUDDER LAW FIRM, P.C.
Lincoln, NE .... Labor and Employment Law, Probate and Estate Planning Law, Real Estate Law, Securities Law

SCUDERI, PETER J.
Philadelphia, PA .... Criminal Trial Practice

SCUTTI, JIM, P.A.
Boca Raton, FL .... Securities Law

SEALE, SMITH, ZUBER & BARNETTE
Baton Rouge, LA .... Civil Trial Practice, Commercial Law, Insurance Defense Law, Personal Injury Law

SEARCY DENNEY SCAROLA BARNHART & SHIPLEY, PROFESSIONAL ASSOCIATION
West Palm Beach, FL .... Civil Trial Practice, Commercial Law, General Practice, Medical Malpractice Law, Personal Injury Law, Product Liability Law

SEARS, ANDERSON & SWANSON, P.C.
Colorado Springs, CO .... Civil Trial Practice, Personal Injury Law

SEBALY, SHILLITO & DYER
Dayton, OH .... Business Law, Civil Trial Practice, Environmental Law, Health Care Law, Labor and Employment Law, Securities Law

SEBAT, SWANSON, BANKS, GARMAN & TOWNSLEY
Danville, IL .... Civil Trial Practice, General Practice

SECOR, CASSIDY & MCPARTLAND, P.C.
Danbury, CT .... Appellate Practice, General Practice
Southbury, CT .... Appellate Practice, General Practice
Waterbury, CT .... Appellate Practice, General Practice

SECREST, HILL & FOLLUO
Tulsa, OK .... Insurance Defense Law, Medical Malpractice Law, Product Liability Law

SEDER & CHANDLER
Worcester, MA .... Bankruptcy Law, Business Law, Civil Trial Practice

SEDGWICK, DETERT, MORAN & ARNOLD
San Francisco, CA .... General Practice

SEDKY, WITTIE & LETSCHE
Washington, DC .... General Practice

SEELEY & BERGLASS
Southport, CT .... Business Law, Tax Law

SEELEY, SAVIDGE AND AUSSEM, A LEGAL PROFESSIONAL ASSOCIATION
Cleveland, OH .... Civil Trial Practice, Commercial Law, Environmental Law, Family Law, General Practice, Insurance Defense Law, Labor and Employment Law, Municipal and Zoning Law, Probate and Estate Planning Law, Real Estate Law, Securities Law

SEGAL, WILLIAM J., P.A.
North Miami Beach, FL .... Probate and Estate Planning Law, Real Estate Law

SEGRÉ & SENSER, P.C.
Philadelphia, PA .... Real Estate Law

SEHAM SEHAM MELTZ & PETERSEN
New York, NY .... Labor and Employment Law, Public Utilities Law

SEIBERT, KASSERMAN, FARNSWORTH, GILLENWATER, GLAUSER, RICHARDSON & CURTIS, L.C.
Wheeling, WV .... Civil Trial Practice, General Practice, Insurance Defense Law, Probate and Estate Planning Law

SEIDEL, GONDA, LAVORGNA & MONACO, P.C.
Philadelphia, PA .... Patent, Trademark, Copyright and Unfair Competition Law

SEIGFREID, RUNGE, LEONATTI, POHLMEYER & SEIGFREID, P.C.
Mexico, MO .... Civil Trial Practice, General Practice, Probate and Estate Planning Law

SEILLER & HANDMAKER
Louisville, KY .... Bankruptcy Law, Business Law, Civil Trial Practice, Criminal Trial Practice, Family Law, General Practice, Personal Injury Law, Trademark, Copyright and Unfair Competition Law

SELF, GIDDENS & LEES, INC.
Oklahoma City, OK .... Banking Law, Bankruptcy Law, Civil Trial Practice, Commercial Law, Natural Resources Law, Real Estate Law

SELF & SELF
Florence, AL .... Civil Trial Practice, Personal Injury Law
Tuscumbia, AL .... Civil Trial Practice

SELKER & FURBER
Cleveland, OH .... Business Law, Civil Trial Practice, Real Estate Law

SELLAR, RICHARDSON, STUART & CHISHOLM, P.C.
Roseland, NJ .... Civil Trial Practice, Insurance Defense Law

SELL & MELTON
Macon, GA .... Banking Law, Bankruptcy Law, Business Law, Civil Trial Practice, General Practice, Health Care Law, Personal Injury Law

SELNER, GLASER, KOMEN, BERGER & GALGANSKI, P.C.
St. Louis, MO .... General Practice

SELTZER CAPLAN WILKINS & MCMAHON, A PROFESSIONAL CORPORATION
San Diego, CA .... Antitrust Law, Civil Trial Practice, General Practice, Tax Law

SELTZER AND ROSEN, P.C.
Washington, DC .... Construction Law, Environmental Law

SEMMES, BOWEN & SEMMES
Baltimore, MD .... General Practice

SEMPLE & JACKSON, P.C.
Denver, CO .... Labor and Employment Law

SEMPLINER, THOMAS AND BOAK
Plymouth, MI .... Civil Trial Practice, Real Estate Law

SERKLAND, LUNDBERG, ERICKSON, MARCIL & MCLEAN, LTD.
Fargo, ND .... General Practice

SERKO & SIMON
New York, NY .... International Business Law

SERLING, MICHAEL B., P.C.
Birmingham, MI .... Personal Injury Law

SERVICE, GASSER & KERL
Pocatello, ID .... General Practice

SESSIONS & FISHMAN, L.L.P.
New Orleans, LA .... General Practice

SESSUMS & MASON, P.A.
Tampa, FL .... Family Law

SEVERSON & WERSON, A PROFESSIONAL CORPORATION
San Francisco, CA .... General Practice

SEWARD & KISSEL
Washington, DC .... General Practice
New York, NY .... General Practice

SEWARD, TALLY & PIGGOTT, P.C.
Bay City, MI .... General Practice

SHACK, RICHARD M.
Orange, CA .... Family Law

SHACKELFORD, HONENBERGER, THOMAS & WILLIS, P.L.C.
Orange, VA .... Civil Trial Practice, Criminal Trial Practice, General Practice

SHACKLEFORD, FARRIOR, STALLINGS & EVANS, PROFESSIONAL ASSOCIATION
Tampa, FL .... General Practice

SHACKLEFORD, SHACKLEFORD & PHILLIPS, P.A.
El Dorado, AR .... General Practice

SHACKLETON, HAZELTINE AND BISHOP
Ship Bottom, NJ .... General Practice

SHACK & SIEGEL, P.C.
New York, NY .... Business Law, Commercial Law, Labor and Employment Law, Probate and Estate Planning Law, Real Estate Law, Securities Law, Trademark, Copyright and Unfair Competition Law

SHADOAN AND MICHAEL
Rockville, MD .... Medical Malpractice Law, Personal Injury Law, Product Liability Law

SHAFER, DAVIS, ASHLEY, O'LEARY & STOKER, A PROFESSIONAL CORPORATION
Odessa, TX .... General Practice

SHAFER, SWICK, BAILEY, IRWIN & STACK
Meadville, PA....................General Practice

SHAFFER, JOHN C., JR., A PROF. LAW CORP., LAW OFFICES OF
Menlo Park, CA....................Civil Trial Practice, Labor and Employment Law, Personal Injury Law

SHAFFER AND SHAFFER
Madison, WV....................Civil Trial Practice, General Practice, Insurance Defense Law, Personal Injury Law, Real Estate Law

SHAFT, REIS, SHAFT & SOGARD, LTD.
Grand Forks, ND....................General Practice

SHAHEEN, JACOBS & ROSS, P.C.
Detroit, MI....................Banking Law, Commercial Law, Real Estate Law

SHAIN, SCHAFFER & RAFANELLO, A PROFESSIONAL CORPORATION
Bernardsville, NJ....................Banking Law, General Practice, Real Estate Law

SHAINES & MCEACHERN, PROFESSIONAL ASSOCIATION
Portsmouth, NH....................General Practice

SHAMBAUGH, KAST, BECK & WILLIAMS
Fort Wayne, IN....................Civil Trial Practice, General Practice, Probate and Estate Planning Law, Tax Law

SHAMBERG, JOHNSON, BERGMAN & MORRIS, CHARTERED
Overland Park, KS....................Civil Trial Practice, Environmental Law, Medical Malpractice Law, Personal Injury Law, Product Liability Law

SHAMBERG MARWELL CHERNEFF HOCHERMAN DAVIS & HOLLIS, P.C.
Mount Kisco, NY....................General Practice

SHAMBERG, WOLF, MCDERMOTT & DEPUÉ
Grand Island, NE....................General Practice

SHAND, MCLACHLAN & NEWBOLD, P.C.
Durango, CO....................Banking Law, Civil Trial Practice, Insurance Defense Law, Probate and Estate Planning Law, Real Estate Law

SHANLEY & FISHER, A PROFESSIONAL CORPORATION
Morristown, NJ....................Banking Law, Bankruptcy Law, Civil Trial Practice, Environmental Law, General Practice, Labor and Employment Law, Real Estate Law, Tax Law

SHANLEY, SWEENEY & REILLY, P.C.
Albany, NY....................Environmental Law, General Practice, Real Estate Law

SHANTZ AND BOOKER, PROFESSIONAL CORPORATION
Bloomfield Hills, MI....................General Practice
Detroit, MI....................General Practice

SHAPIRO, WILLIAM D.
San Bernardino, CA....................Personal Injury Law

SHAPIRO & ASSOCIATES
Boston, MA....................Insurance Defense Law, Personal Injury Law

SHAPIRO, COHEN, ANDREWS, FINLAYSON
Ottawa, ON, Canada....................Patent, Trademark, Copyright and Unfair Competition Law

SHAPIRO, FUSSELL, WEDGE, SMOTHERMAN & MARTIN
Atlanta, GA....................Construction Law, Labor and Employment Law

SHAPIRO & SHAPIRO
Hackensack, NJ....................Bankruptcy Law, Business Law, Commercial Law, Real Estate Law

SHAPIRO AND SHAPIRO
Arlington, VA....................Patent, Trademark, Copyright and Unfair Competition Law
Vineland, NJ....................General Practice

SHAPO, FREEDMAN & FLETCHER, P.A.
Miami, FL....................General Practice, Real Estate Law

SHARLOCK, REPCHECK & MAHLER
Pittsburgh, PA....................General Practice

SHARP, MICHAEL R.
Austin, TX....................Administrative Law, Health Care Law

SHARP, TERRY, P.C., LAW OFFICE OF
Mount Vernon, IL....................Bankruptcy Law, Commercial Law, Real Estate Law

SHARPE & KRUEGER
Kingsville, TX....................General Practice

SHARPNACK, BIGLEY, DAVID & RUMPLE
Columbus, IN....................Civil Trial Practice, Family Law, General Practice, Insurance Defense Law, Probate and Estate Planning Law

SHARTSIS, FRIESE & GINSBURG
San Francisco, CA....................General Practice

SHAW & ASSOCIATES, A PROFESSIONAL CORPORATION
Houston, TX....................Real Estate Law

SHAW, ELLIOT S., P.A.
West Palm Beach, FL....................Probate and Estate Planning Law

SHAW, GERALD M., A PROFESSIONAL CORPORATION
Corona Del Mar, CA....................Civil Trial Practice

SHAW, LEDBETTER, HORNBERGER, COGBILL & ARNOLD
Fort Smith, AR....................General Practice, Insurance Defense Law

SHAW, LICITRA, PARENTE, ESERNIO & SCHWARTZ, P.C.
Garden City, NY....................Bankruptcy Law, General Practice

SHAW, MADDOX, GRAHAM, MONK & BOLING
Rome, GA....................Civil Trial Practice, General Practice

SHAW, PITTMAN, POTTS & TROWBRIDGE
Washington, DC....................General Practice
Alexandria, VA....................General Practice
McLean, VA....................General Practice

SHAW AND SHAW, A PROFESSIONAL LAW CORPORATION
Homer, LA....................Civil Trial Practice, Natural Resources Law, Probate and Estate Planning Law

SHAWE & ROSENTHAL
Baltimore, MD....................Labor and Employment Law

SHAWN, MANN & NIEDERMAYER, L.L.P.
Washington, DC....................Bankruptcy Law, Civil Trial Practice, Commercial Law, International Business Law, Real Estate Law, Trademark, Copyright and Unfair Competition Law, Transportation Law

SHAWWAF, SAUD M.A., LAW OFFICE OF
Riyadh, Saudi Arabia....................General Practice

SHAY, SLOCUM & DEWEY
New Haven, CT....................Civil Trial Practice, Insurance Defense Law, Personal Injury Law

SHAYNE, DACHS, STANISCI, CORKER & SAUER
Mineola, NY....................Insurance Defense Law, Medical Malpractice Law, Personal Injury Law

SHEA, JOSEPH W. III, LAW OFFICES OF
Cincinnati, OH....................Civil Trial Practice, Medical Malpractice Law, Personal Injury Law, Product Liability Law

SHEA & GARDNER
Washington, DC....................General Practice

SHEA AND SHEA
Bryn Mawr, PA....................Probate and Estate Planning Law, Real Estate Law

SHEA & SHEA, A PROFESSIONAL LAW CORPORATION
San Jose, CA....................Personal Injury Law

SHEA & WILKS, P.C.
Phoenix, AZ....................Commercial Law

SHEAHAN, ROBERT E. & ASSOCIATES
High Point, NC....................Labor and Employment Law

SHEARER, TEMPLER, PINGEL & KAPLAN, A PROFESSIONAL CORPORATION
Des Moines, IA....................Commercial Law, Construction Law, General Practice, Labor and Employment Law, Probate and Estate Planning Law

SHEARMAN & STERLING
Los Angeles, CA....................General Practice
San Francisco, CA....................General Practice
Washington, DC....................General Practice
New York, NY....................General Practice
Beijing (Peking), People's Republic of China....................General Practice
London, England....................General Practice
Paris, France....................General Practice
Düsseldorf, Germany....................General Practice
Frankfurt/Main, Germany....................General Practice
Hong Kong, Hong Kong (British Crown Colony)....................General Practice
Budapest, Hungary....................General Practice
Tokyo, Japan....................General Practice
Taipei, Taiwan....................General Practice
Abu Dhabi, United Arab Emirates....................General Practice

SHEEHAN, BARNETT & HAYS, P.S.C.
Danville, KY....................Commercial Law, General Practice, Insurance Defense Law

SHEEHAN PHINNEY BASS + GREEN, PROFESSIONAL ASSOCIATION
Manchester, NH....................General Practice

SHEEHAN, SHEEHAN & STELZNER, P.A.
Albuquerque, NM....................Civil Trial Practice, Commercial Law, Construction Law, Employment Benefits Law, Insurance Defense Law, Personal Injury Law, Real Estate Law

SHEEHE & VENDITTELLI, P.A.
Miami, FL....................General Practice, International Business Law

SHEEHEY BRUE GRAY & FURLONG, PROFESSIONAL CORPORATION
Burlington, VT....................Banking Law, Civil Trial Practice, Environmental Law, General Practice, Health Care Law, Real Estate Law, Securities Law, Tax Law

SHEEHY, LOVELACE & MAYFIELD, P.C. A PROFESSIONAL CORPORATION
Waco, TX....................General Practice

SHEEHY & SHEEHY
Jersey City, NJ....................General Practice, Tax Law

SHEFFER, HOFFMAN, THOMASON & MORTON
Henderson, KY....................General Practice
Owensboro, KY....................General Practice
Paducah, KY....................General Practice

SHEFT & SHEFT
New York, NY....................Environmental Law, Insurance Defense Law, Medical Malpractice Law, Product Liability Law

SHEFTE, PINCKNEY & SAWYER
Charlotte, NC....................Patent, Trademark, Copyright and Unfair Competition Law

SHEIMAN, RONALD L.
Westport, CT....................Business Law, Probate and Estate Planning Law, Tax Law

SHELL, BUFORD, BUFKIN, CALLICUTT & PERRY
Jackson, MS....................Civil Trial Practice, Insurance Defense Law

SHELL, FLEMING, DAVIS & MENGE, P.A.
Pensacola, FL....................General Practice

SHELLOW, SHELLOW & GLYNN, S.C.
Milwaukee, WI....................Criminal Trial Practice

SHEPHERD, GARY & MCWHORTER
Swainsboro, GA....................General Practice

SHEPHERD & MONK
Carrollton, KY....................Probate and Estate Planning Law

SHEPPARD, BRETT & STEWART, P.A.
Fort Myers, FL....................General Practice

SHEPPARD, MULLIN, RICHTER & HAMPTON
Los Angeles, CA....................Antitrust Law, Banking Law, General Practice, Labor and Employment Law, Natural Resources Law, Real Estate Law, Tax Law
Newport Beach, CA....................General Practice
San Diego, CA....................General Practice
San Francisco, CA....................General Practice

SHEPPARD & WHITE, P.A.
Jacksonville, FL....................Criminal Trial Practice

SHERARD, SHERARD AND JOHNSON
Wheatland, WY....................General Practice

SHERBURNE, POWERS & NEEDHAM, P.C.
Boston, MA....................Banking Law, Bankruptcy Law, Business Law, Commercial Law, Construction Law, Criminal Trial Practice, Family Law, General Practice, Labor and Employment Law, Municipal and Zoning Law, Patent, Trademark, Copyright and Unfair Competition Law, Personal Injury Law, Probate and Estate Planning Law, Real Estate Law, Tax Law

SHERIDAN ROSS & MCINTOSH, A PROFESSIONAL CORPORATION
Denver, CO....................Patent, Trademark, Copyright and Unfair Competition Law, Trademark, Copyright and Unfair Competition Law

SHERIN AND LODGEN
Boston, MA....................Business Law, Civil Trial Practice, General Practice, Real Estate Law

SHERMAN, STEPHEN A. & ASSOCIATES
Oklahoma City, OK....................Commercial Law, Real Estate Law

SHERMAN, WILLIAM F.
Little Rock, AR....................General Practice

SHERMAN AND CREGG
Andover, MA....................General Practice

SHERMAN & HOWARD, L.L.C.
Colorado Springs, CO....................General Practice
Denver, CO....................Antitrust Law, Banking Law, Civil Trial Practice, General Practice, Labor and Employment Law, Municipal Bond/Public Authority Financing Law, Natural Resources Law, Probate and Estate Planning Law, Tax Law

SHERMAN, MEEHAN & CURTIN, P.C.
Washington, DC....................General Practice

SHERMAN, OLSHER & SHERMAN
Black River Falls, WI....................General Practice

SHERMAN, RICHARD A., P.A., LAW OFFICES OF
Fort Lauderdale, FL....................Appellate Practice

SHERMAN, SILVERSTEIN, KOHL, ROSE & PODOLSKY, A PROFESSIONAL CORPORATION
Pennsauken, NJ....................General Practice

SHERMETA, CHIMKO AND KILPATRICK, P.C.
Rochester, MI....................Bankruptcy Law, Commercial Law

SHERRILL, CROSNOE & GOFF, A PROFESSIONAL CORPORATION
Wichita Falls, TX....................General Practice

SHERRILL AND ROGERS, PC
Columbia, SC....................Family Law, General Practice, Probate and Estate Planning Law, Real Estate Law

SHERWOOD AND HARDGROVE
Los Angeles, CA....................Real Estate Law

SHIBLEY RIGHTON
Toronto, ON, Canada....................General Practice

SHIELDS LAW OFFICE, P.A.
St. John, KS....................General Practice

SHIGLEY, KENNETH L.
Atlanta, GA....................Personal Injury Law, Product Liability Law

SHIMKO, TIMOTHY A., & ASSOCIATES, A LEGAL PROF. ASSN.
Cleveland, OH....................Antitrust Law, Civil Trial Practice, Labor and Employment Law, Medical Malpractice Law, Personal Injury Law, Product Liability Law

SHIMMEL, HILL, BISHOP & GRUENDER, P.C.
Phoenix, AZ....................Civil Trial Practice, General Practice, Insurance Defense Law, Labor and Employment Law

SHINE & MASON LAW OFFICE
Kingsport, TN....................General Practice, Labor and Employment Law

SHINGLES & CAPPELLI
Philadelphia, PA....................Civil Trial Practice, Criminal Trial Practice

SHINN LAWYERS
Lamar, CO....................General Practice

SHIPLEY, INHOFE & STRECKER
Tulsa, OK....................Civil Trial Practice, Environmental Law, Labor and Employment Law

SHIPLEY & KOS
Fort Wayne, IN....................Bankruptcy Law, Commercial Law

SHIPMAN & GOODWIN
Hartford, CT....................Environmental Law, General Practice, Labor and Employment Law, Probate and Estate Planning Law
Lakeville, CT....................General Practice
Stamford, CT....................General Practice

SHIPMAN, UTRECHT & DIXON CO., L.P.A.
Troy, OH....................Civil Trial Practice, General Practice, Insurance Defense Law

SHIREY, EDWARDS & GLASS
Muncie, IN....................General Practice, Probate and Estate Planning Law

SHIRK, WORK, ROBINSON & WORK, A PROFESSIONAL CORPORATION
Oklahoma City, OK....................General Practice, Municipal Bond/Public Authority Financing Law

SHLIMBAUM, SHLIMBAUM AND JABLONSKI
Islip, NY....................General Practice

SHOFI, SMITH, HENNEN, JENKINS, STANLEY & GRAMOVOT, P.A.
Tampa, FL....................Insurance Defense Law

SHORT, KEVIN J.
Minneapolis, MN....................Criminal Trial Practice

SHORT CRESSMAN & BURGESS
Seattle, WA....................Construction Law, General Practice, Real Estate Law, Tax Law

SHORT, GENTRY & BISHOP, P.A.
Fort Scott, KS....................General Practice

SHORT & JENKINS, A PROFESSIONAL LEGAL CORPORATION
Houston, TX....................Family Law

SHOUN, SMITH & BACH, P.C.
Fairfax, VA....................Family Law

SHRAGER, MCDAID, LOFTUS, FLUM & SPIVEY
Philadelphia, PA .... Personal Injury Law

SHUFORD & CADDELL
Salisbury, NC .... General Practice

SHUGHART THOMSON & KILROY, A PROFESSIONAL CORPORATION
Overland Park, KS .... General Practice
Kansas City, MO .... Antitrust Law, Civil Trial Practice, General Practice, Labor and Employment Law

SHULL, COSGROVE, HELLIGE, DU BRAY & LUNDBERG
Sioux City, IA .... General Practice, Probate and Estate Planning Law

SHULMAN, ROGERS, GANDAL, PORDY & ECKER, P.A.
Rockville, MD .... Civil Trial Practice, Commercial Law, General Practice

SHULTZ & ROLLINS, LTD.
Tucson, AZ .... Civil Trial Practice, Personal Injury Law

SHUMACKER & THOMPSON
Chattanooga, TN .... Bankruptcy Law, Civil Trial Practice, Environmental Law, General Practice, Probate and Estate Planning Law, Real Estate Law, Tax Law

SHUMAKER, LOOP & KENDRICK
Toledo, OH .... General Practice

SHUMAKER WILLIAMS, A PROFESSIONAL CORPORATION
Harrisburg, PA .... Banking Law

SHUMAN, ANNAND & POE
Charleston, WV .... General Practice, Insurance Defense Law

SHUMARD, THOMAS J.
Phoenix, AZ .... Probate and Estate Planning Law

SHUMATE, FLAHERTY & EUBANKS
Richmond, KY .... General Practice

SHUMWAY & MERLE
Southport, CT .... Environmental Law

SHUTLER AND LOW
Chantilly, VA .... Environmental Law

SHUTTLEWORTH & INGERSOLL, P.C.
Cedar Rapids, IA .... Administrative Law, Banking Law, Civil Trial Practice, General Practice, Insurance Defense Law, Labor and Employment Law, Patent, Trademark, Copyright and Unfair Competition Law, Probate and Estate Planning Law, Real Estate Law, Tax Law

SHUTTLEWORTH RULOFF GIORDANO AND KAHLE, P.C.
Virginia Beach, VA .... Civil Trial Practice, Criminal Trial Practice

SHUTTS & BOWEN
Miami, FL .... Admiralty/Maritime Law, Antitrust Law, General Practice, Tax Law
Orlando, FL .... General Practice
West Palm Beach, FL .... General Practice

SICHOL & HICKS, P.C.
Suffern, NY .... General Practice

SIDLEY & AUSTIN
Los Angeles, CA .... General Practice
Washington, DC .... General Practice
Chicago, IL .... General Practice
New York, NY .... General Practice
London, England .... General Practice
Tokyo, Japan .... General Practice

SIEBEN, GROSE, VON HOLTUM, MCCOY & CAREY, LTD.
Minneapolis, MN .... Medical Malpractice Law, Personal Injury Law

SIEBEN, POLK, LAVERDIERE, JONES & HAWN, A PROFESSIONAL ASSOCIATION
Hastings, MN .... Civil Trial Practice, Personal Injury Law

SIEGEL, LOUIS H. LAW OFFICES OF
Buffalo, NY .... Insurance Defense Law, Personal Injury Law

SIEGEL, BRILL, GREUPNER & DUFFY, P.A.
Minneapolis, MN .... Antitrust Law, Civil Trial Practice, General Practice

SIEGEL, MANDELL & DAVIDSON, P.C.
New York, NY .... Administrative Law, Business Law

SIEGEL, O'CONNOR, SCHIFF & ZANGARI, P.C.
Hartford, CT .... Labor and Employment Law, Tax Law
New Haven, CT .... Labor and Employment Law, Tax Law

SIEGEL, SOMMERS & SCHWARTZ
New York, NY .... Bankruptcy Law

SIEGFRIED, RIVERA, LERNER, DE LA TORRE & PETERSEN, P.A.
Miami, FL .... Commercial Law, Construction Law, Real Estate Law

SIEMION, HUCKABAY, BODARY, PADILLA, MORGANTI & BOWERMAN, P.C.
Detroit, MI .... Civil Trial Practice, Insurance Defense Law

SIFERD & SIFERD
Lima, OH .... Civil Trial Practice

SIGLER & SMITH LAW OFFICE
Torrington, WY .... Civil Trial Practice

SIGMON, MACKIE & HUTTON, P.A.
Hickory, NC .... General Practice

SIKORA AND PRICE, INCORPORATED
Santa Ana, CA .... General Practice

SILBER, LOUIS M., P.A., LAW OFFICES OF
West Palm Beach, FL .... Civil Trial Practice, General Practice

SILBERT, MARC M.
Philadelphia, PA .... Employment Benefits Law

SILK, ADLER & COLVIN, A LAW CORPORATION
San Francisco, CA .... Tax Law

SILLS, NANCY M.
Albany, NY .... Probate and Estate Planning Law

SILLS CUMMIS ZUCKERMAN RADIN TISCHMAN EPSTEIN & GROSS, A PROFESSIONAL CORPORATION
Atlantic City, NJ .... General Practice
Newark, NJ .... Administrative Law, Banking Law, Bankruptcy Law, Business Law, Civil Trial Practice, Commercial Law, Communications Law, Construction Law, Criminal Trial Practice, Environmental Law, General Practice, Health Care Law, Insurance Defense Law, Labor and Employment Law, Municipal Bond/Public Authority Financing Law, Patent, Trademark, Copyright and Unfair Competition Law, Personal Injury Law, Probate and Estate Planning Law, Real Estate Law, Tax Law, Transportation Law
New York, NY .... General Practice

SILLS, LAW, ESSAD, FIEDLER & CHARBONEAU, P.C.
Bloomfield Hills, MI .... Business Law

SILVER, GOLUB & TEITELL
Stamford, CT .... Civil Trial Practice, Criminal Trial Practice, Family Law, General Practice, Labor and Employment Law, Medical Malpractice Law, Personal Injury Law, Product Liability Law

SILVERMAN, MELVIN L.
Los Angeles, CA .... Family Law

SILVERMAN COOPERSMITH HILLMAN & FRIMMER, A PROFESSIONAL CORPORATION
Philadelphia, PA .... Insurance Defense Law

SILVERMAN & KUDISCH, P.C.
Boston, MA .... Bankruptcy Law, Business Law

SILVERMAN, OWEN A., INC., A PROFESSIONAL CORPORATION
Torrance, CA .... Personal Injury Law

SILVERS AND SIMPSON, PROFESSIONAL CORPORATION
Savannah, GA .... Probate and Estate Planning Law, Tax Law

SILVERSTEIN & OSACH, P.C.
New Haven, CT .... Tax Law

SIM, HUGHES, ASHTON & MCKAY
Toronto, ON, Canada .... Patent, Trademark, Copyright and Unfair Competition Law

SIMMONS, BRUNSON, SASSER AND CALLIS, ATTORNEYS, P.A.
Gadsden, AL .... Civil Trial Practice, General Practice, Insurance Defense Law

SIMMONS AND DERR
Winnfield, LA .... General Practice, Probate and Estate Planning Law, Real Estate Law

SIMMONS, OLSEN, EDIGER AND SELZER, P.C.
Scottsbluff, NE .... General Practice

SIMMONS, PERRINE, ALBRIGHT & ELLWOOD, L.L.P.
Cedar Rapids, IA .... Civil Trial Practice, General Practice, Insurance Defense Law, Labor and Employment Law, Probate and Estate Planning Law, Real Estate Law

SIMMONS, WARREN & SZCZECKO, PROFESSIONAL ASSOCIATION
Decatur, GA .... Business Law, Civil Trial Practice, Family Law, General Practice, Real Estate Law

SIMON, FITZGERALD, COOKE, REED & WELCH
Shreveport, LA..........Bankruptcy Law, General Practice

SIMON, MCKINSEY, MILLER, ZOMMICK, SANDOR & DUNDAS, A LAW CORPORATION
Long Beach, CA..........General Practice

SIMON, MOSKOWITZ & MANDELL, P.A.
Fort Lauderdale, FL..........Banking Law, Commercial Law

SIMON & SCHMIDT
Delray Beach, FL..........General Practice

SIMON AND SIMON
Kansas City, MO..........Criminal Trial Practice

SIMONDS, WINSLOW, WILLIS & ABBOTT, A PROFESSIONAL ASSOCIATION
Boston, MA..........General Practice, Real Estate Law

SIMONSON & COHEN, P.C.
Staten Island, NY..........Civil Trial Practice, Family Law, General Practice, Personal Injury Law, Probate and Estate Planning Law, Product Liability Law, Real Estate Law

SIMONSON HESS & LEIBOWITZ, P.C.
New York, NY..........Civil Trial Practice, Medical Malpractice Law, Personal Injury Law

SIMPSON AYCOCK, P.A.
Morganton, NC..........General Practice

SIMPSON & BERRY, P.C.
Birmingham, MI..........Banking Law, Business Law, Civil Trial Practice, Commercial Law, Construction Law, Environmental Law, Real Estate Law

SIMPSON, KABLACK & BELL
Indiana, PA..........General Practice

SIMPSON, KEPLER & EDWARDS
Cody, WY..........General Practice, Probate and Estate Planning Law

SIMPSON THACHER & BARTLETT
New York, NY..........General Practice
Columbus, OH..........General Practice
London, England..........General Practice
Hong Kong, Hong Kong (British Crown Colony)..........General Practice
Tokyo, Japan..........General Practice

SIMPSON, WIGLE
Hamilton, ON, Canada..........General Practice

SIMS & FLEMING, P.C.
Tifton, GA..........General Practice

SIMS MOORE HILL & GANNON, L.L.P.
Hillsboro, TX..........General Practice

SINCLAIR, I.B. LAW OFFICES
Media, PA..........Family Law

SINCLAIR, LOUIS, HEATH, NUSSBAUM & ZAVERTNIK, P.A.
Miami, FL..........Civil Trial Practice

SINDEL & SINDEL, P.C.
St. Louis, MO..........Criminal Trial Practice, Personal Injury Law

SINGER, PASLEY, HOLM, TIMMONS, MATHISON & CURTIS
Ames, IA..........General Practice

SINGLETON, THOMAS J.
Mount Kisco, NY..........General Practice

SINGLETON, MURRAY, CRAVEN & INMAN
Fayetteville, NC..........General Practice

SINGLETON URQUHART MACDONALD
Vancouver, BC, Canada..........Construction Law, General Practice, Insurance Defense Law

SINKLER & BOYD, P.A.
Charleston, SC..........Admiralty/Maritime Law, Civil Trial Practice, General Practice, Municipal Bond/Public Authority Financing Law
Columbia, SC..........Admiralty/Maritime Law, Civil Trial Practice, General Practice, Municipal Bond/Public Authority Financing Law
Greenville, SC..........Municipal Bond/Public Authority Financing Law

SIRIANNI & YOUTZ
Seattle, WA..........Business Law

SIRKIN PINALES MEZIBOV & SCHWARTZ
Cincinnati, OH..........Civil Trial Practice, Criminal Trial Practice, Labor and Employment Law

SIROTA & SIROTA
New York, NY..........Securities Law

SIROTE & PERMUTT, P.C.
Birmingham, AL..........Antitrust Law, Banking Law, Bankruptcy Law, Civil Trial Practice, Commercial Law, Employment Benefits Law, Environmental Law, Family Law, General Practice, Health Care Law, International Business Law, Labor and Employment Law, Municipal Bond/Public Authority Financing Law, Patent, Trademark, Copyright and Unfair Competition Law, Probate and Estate Planning Law, Real Estate Law, Tax Law
Huntsville, AL..........Antitrust Law, Banking Law, Bankruptcy Law, Civil Trial Practice, Commercial Law, Environmental Law, Family Law, General Practice, Health Care Law, Immigration and Naturalization Law, International Business Law, Labor and Employment Law, Municipal Bond/Public Authority Financing Law, Patent, Trademark, Copyright and Unfair Competition Law, Probate and Estate Planning Law, Real Estate Law, Tax Law
Mobile, AL..........Antitrust Law, Banking Law, Bankruptcy Law, Civil Trial Practice, Commercial Law, Environmental Law, Family Law, General Practice, Health Care Law, Labor and Employment Law, Municipal Bond/Public Authority Financing Law, Patent, Trademark, Copyright and Unfair Competition Law, Probate and Estate Planning Law, Real Estate Law, Tax Law
Montgomery, AL..........Civil Trial Practice, General Practice, Municipal Bond/Public Authority Financing Law, Probate and Estate Planning Law, Tax Law

SISKIND, CROMARTY, IVEY & DOWLER
London, ON, Canada..........General Practice

SITLINGER, MCGLINCY, STEINER, THEILER & KAREM
Louisville, KY..........Insurance Defense Law

SIXBEY, FRIEDMAN, LEEDOM & FERGUSON, P.C.
McLean, VA..........Patent, Trademark, Copyright and Unfair Competition Law

SKADDEN, ARPS, SLATE, MEAGHER & FLOM
Wilmington, DE..........General Practice
Washington, DC..........General Practice
New York, NY..........Bankruptcy Law, Criminal Trial Practice, General Practice, Labor and Employment Law, Municipal Bond/Public Authority Financing Law

SKEEN & PEARLMAN, P.C.
Denver, CO..........Bankruptcy Law

SKELLEY ROTTNER, P.C.
Hartford, CT..........General Practice, Insurance Defense Law

SKELTON, TAINTOR & ABBOTT, A PROFESSIONAL CORPORATION
Auburn, ME..........General Practice

SKEMP, WILLIAM, LAW FIRM, S.C.
La Crosse, WI..........Insurance Defense Law, Personal Injury Law

SKIPPER, RONALD G.
San Bernardino, CA..........Personal Injury Law

SKJERVEN, MORRILL, MACPHERSON, FRANKLIN & FRIEL
San Francisco, CA..........General Practice, Patent, Trademark, Copyright and Unfair Competition Law
San Jose, CA..........General Practice, Patent, Trademark, Copyright and Unfair Competition Law
Austin, TX..........Patent, Trademark, Copyright and Unfair Competition Law

SKOLER, ABBOTT & PRESSER, P.C.
Springfield, MA..........Labor and Employment Law
Worcester, MA..........Labor and Employment Law

SKOLOFF & WOLFE
Livingston, NJ..........Civil Trial Practice, Family Law, Real Estate Law, Tax Law

SKOOG, RICHARD O., P.A.
Ottawa, KS..........General Practice

SKORNIA LAW FIRM, THE
San Jose, CA..........Business Law

SKOUSEN, SKOUSEN, GULBRANDSEN & PATIENCE, P.C.
Mesa, AZ..........Personal Injury Law

SKULINA & HILL
Cleveland, OH..........Civil Trial Practice

SLATER LAW FIRM, A PROFESSIONAL CORPORATION
New Orleans, LA..........Antitrust Law, Business Law, Personal Injury Law, Product Liability Law, Transportation Law

SLATES, RONALD P., A PROFESSIONAL CORPORATION
Los Angeles, CA..........Bankruptcy Law, Business Law

SLATTERY, HAUSMAN & HOEFLE, LTD.
Milwaukee, WI..........Civil Trial Practice, Insurance Defense Law, Personal Injury Law

SLAUGHTER & REDINGER, P.C.
Charlottesville, VA....Civil Trial Practice, Probate and Estate Planning Law

SLAWSON & GLICK
Palm Beach Gardens, FL....Civil Trial Practice, Personal Injury Law

SLEPIN & SLEPIN
Tallahassee, FL....Administrative Law, Appellate Practice

SLOAN, TODD M. LAW OFFICES OF
Malibu, CA....Civil Trial Practice

SLOAN, RUBENS & PEEPLES
West Memphis, AR....General Practice

SLOMSKI, RAYMOND J., P.C., LAW OFFICES OF
Phoenix, AZ....Medical Malpractice Law, Personal Injury Law

SLOSSER & HUDGINS, P.L.C., LAW OFFICES OF
Tucson, AZ....Probate and Estate Planning Law

SLOTCHIVER & SLOTCHIVER
Charleston, SC....Civil Trial Practice, Tax Law

SLOVER & LOFTUS
Washington, DC....Transportation Law

SLUTES, SAKRISON, EVEN, GRANT & PELANDER, P.C.
Tucson, AZ....Civil Trial Practice, General Practice, Insurance Defense Law

SLUTSKY & SLUTSKY CO., L.P.A.
Cincinnati, OH....Bankruptcy Law

SMALL, J. MICHAEL LAW OFFICE OF
Alexandria, LA....Criminal Trial Practice

SMALLEY, ROBERT H., JR., PROFESSIONAL CORPORATION
Griffin, GA....Banking Law, Civil Trial Practice, General Practice

SMALL LARKIN & KIDDÉ
Los Angeles, CA....Patent, Trademark, Copyright and Unfair Competition Law

SMALL, TOTH, BALDRIDGE & VAN BELKUM, P.C.
Bingham Farms, MI....Civil Trial Practice, Insurance Defense Law, Medical Malpractice Law

SMALLWOOD-COOK & SCHMIEDER
Warsaw, NY....General Practice

SMART & BIGGAR
Ottawa, ON, Canada....Patent, Trademark, Copyright and Unfair Competition Law
Toronto, ON, Canada....Patent, Trademark, Copyright and Unfair Competition Law
Montreal, QU, Canada....Patent, Trademark, Copyright and Unfair Competition Law

SMITH, DANIEL T.
Denver, CO....Criminal Trial Practice

SMITH, ROBERT B.
Jesup, GA....Civil Trial Practice

SMITH, RUFUS R. JR., & ASSOCIATES
Dothan, AL....Civil Trial Practice

SMITH, A. RUSSELL
Akron, OH....Civil Trial Practice, Medical Malpractice Law

SMITH, BARTLETT, HEEKE & CARPENTER
Jeffersonville, IN....General Practice

SMITH & BRATCHER, INC.
Waco, TX....General Practice

SMITH, BRENDAN P., A PROFESSIONAL CORPORATION
Providence, RI....Tax Law

SMITH & BROOKER, P.C.
Bay City, MI....General Practice
Flint, MI....General Practice
Saginaw, MI....Civil Trial Practice, General Practice, Labor and Employment Law

SMITH, CARTER, ROSE, FINLEY & GRIFFIS, A PROFESSIONAL CORPORATION
San Angelo, TX....General Practice

SMITH, CURRIE & HANCOCK
Atlanta, GA....Construction Law, Labor and Employment Law

SMITH DEBNAM HIBBERT & PAHL
Raleigh, NC....Bankruptcy Law, Civil Trial Practice, General Practice

SMITH & DEBONIS
East Chicago, IN....Civil Trial Practice

SMITH ELLIOTT SMITH & GARMEY, P.A.
Kennebunk, ME....General Practice
Portland, ME....General Practice, Medical Malpractice Law, Personal Injury Law
Saco, ME....Civil Trial Practice, Criminal Trial Practice, General Practice, Medical Malpractice Law, Personal Injury Law

SMITH, FINKELSTEIN, LUNDBERG, ISLER AND YAKABOSKI
Riverhead, NY....General Practice

SMITH, GENDLER, SHIELL, SHEFF & FORD, P.A.
Minneapolis, MN....Real Estate Law

SMITH, GILLIAM AND WILLIAMS
Gainesville, GA....General Practice, Insurance Defense Law, Real Estate Law, Tax Law

SMITH, GOLDSTEIN & MAGRAM, A PROFESSIONAL CORPORATION
Burlington, NJ....Civil Trial Practice, General Practice, Personal Injury Law

SMITH, GRIMSLEY, BAUMAN, PINKERTON, PETERMANN, SAXER & WELLS
Fort Walton Beach, FL....General Practice

SMITH & HALE
Columbus, OH....Real Estate Law

SMITH, HAUGHEY, RICE & ROEGGE, P.C.
East Lansing, MI....General Practice, Medical Malpractice Law
Grand Rapids, MI....Civil Trial Practice, General Practice, Insurance Defense Law, Medical Malpractice Law
Traverse City, MI....General Practice, Medical Malpractice Law

SMITH, HELENIUS & HAYES, A LAW CORPORATION
San Luis Obispo, CA....Civil Trial Practice, Insurance Defense Law

SMITH HELMS MULLISS & MOORE, L.L.P.
Charlotte, NC....Antitrust Law, Bankruptcy Law, Criminal Trial Practice, Environmental Law, General Practice, Health Care Law, Immigration and Naturalization Law, Labor and Employment Law, Municipal Bond/Public Authority Financing Law, Real Estate Law, Tax Law
Greensboro, NC....Bankruptcy Law, Criminal Trial Practice, Environmental Law, General Practice, Health Care Law, Immigration and Naturalization Law, Labor and Employment Law, Real Estate Law, Tax Law
Raleigh, NC....Antitrust Law, Bankruptcy Law, Criminal Trial Practice, Environmental Law, General Practice, Health Care Law, Immigration and Naturalization Law, Real Estate Law, Tax Law

SMITH HULSEY & BUSEY
Jacksonville, FL....General Practice

SMITH, JOHNSON & BRANDT, ATTORNEYS, P.C.
Traverse City, MI....Commercial Law, General Practice

SMITH, JOSEPH C., P.C.
Detroit, MI....Medical Malpractice Law, Product Liability Law

SMITH, KATZENSTEIN & FURLOW
Wilmington, DE....Bankruptcy Law, Business Law, Civil Trial Practice, Commercial Law, General Practice, Insurance Defense Law, Labor and Employment Law, Medical Malpractice Law, Personal Injury Law, Product Liability Law

SMITH, KELLER, MINER & O'SHEA
Buffalo, NY....Civil Trial Practice, Personal Injury Law

SMITH, KEN MCFARLANE, P.C.
Arlington, VA....Probate and Estate Planning Law

SMITH & KOTCHKA, LTD.
Las Vegas, NV....Labor and Employment Law

SMITH, LANDMEIER & SKAAR, P.C.
Geneva, IL....General Practice, Municipal and Zoning Law, Probate and Estate Planning Law, Trademark, Copyright and Unfair Competition Law

SMITH, LEWIS, BECKETT, POWELL & ROARK
Columbia, MO....General Practice

SMITH, LYONS, TORRANCE, STEVENSON & MAYER
Toronto, ON, Canada....General Practice

SMITH, MARSHALL AND WEAVER
Cleveland, OH....Civil Trial Practice, Insurance Defense Law, Product Liability Law

SMITH MAZURE DIRECTOR WILKINS YOUNG YAGERMAN & TARALLO, P.C.
New York, NY....Civil Trial Practice, Insurance Defense Law

SMITH, MCELWAIN & WENGERT
Sioux City, IA....Labor and Employment Law

SMITH, MERRIFIELD & RICHARDS, L.L.P.
Dallas, TX .... Real Estate Law

SMITH, MURPHY & SCHOEPPERLE
Buffalo, NY .... Civil Trial Practice, General Practice, Insurance Defense Law

SMITH PETERSON LAW FIRM
Council Bluffs, IA .... Business Law, Commercial Law, Insurance Defense Law, Labor and Employment Law, Probate and Estate Planning Law, Real Estate Law, Tax Law

SMITH, RANSCHT, CONNORS, MUTINO, NORDELL & SIRIGNANO, P.C.
White Plains, NY .... General Practice, Municipal Bond/Public Authority Financing Law, Probate and Estate Planning Law, Tax Law

SMITH, SAUER, DEMARIA & JOHNSON
Pensacola, FL .... General Practice

SMITH, SCHODER, ROUSE & BOUCK, P.A.
Daytona Beach, FL .... Medical Malpractice Law, Personal Injury Law

SMITH, SHARP, BENSON, JAHN & FEILMEYER
Ames, IA .... General Practice

SMITH, SMART, HANCOCK, TABLER & SCHWENSEN
Seattle, WA .... Banking Law, Civil Trial Practice, Real Estate Law

SMITH & SMITH
Beverly Hills, CA .... Construction Law, Probate and Estate Planning Law
Vero Beach, FL .... Civil Trial Practice, General Practice

SMITH AND SMITH
Louisville, KY .... Labor and Employment Law

SMITH & SMITH
Dallas, TX .... General Practice

SMITH, SMITH & MONTGOMERY
Bellefontaine, OH .... General Practice

SMITH, SOMERVILLE & CASE
Baltimore, MD .... General Practice

SMITH, STRATTON, WISE, HEHER & BRENNAN
Princeton, NJ .... General Practice
Trenton, NJ .... General Practice

SMITH, STROUD, MCCLERKIN, DUNN & NUTTER
Texarkana, AR .... Civil Trial Practice, General Practice, Medical Malpractice Law, Natural Resources Law

SMITH, WELCH & STUDDARD
McDonough, GA .... Civil Trial Practice, Family Law, General Practice, Municipal and Zoning Law, Real Estate Law

SMITH & WELLS
Manchester, KY .... General Practice

SMITH, WILLIAMS & BOWLES, P.A.
Tampa, FL .... Civil Trial Practice, Environmental Law, Insurance Defense Law, Real Estate Law

SMITH, WOLNITZEK, SCHACHTER & ROWEKAMP, P.S.C.
Covington, KY .... Civil Trial Practice, Family Law, General Practice

SMOAK, RICHARD
Panama City, FL .... General Practice

SMOOT ADAMS EDWARDS & GREEN, P.A.
Fort Myers, FL .... Civil Trial Practice, General Practice, Insurance Defense Law, Real Estate Law, Tax Law

SMYTH & LACK
Huntington, NY .... Banking Law, Bankruptcy Law, General Practice, Probate and Estate Planning Law, Real Estate Law

SNEED, LANG, ADAMS & BARNETT, A PROFESSIONAL CORPORATION
Tulsa, OK .... Antitrust Law, Banking Law, Bankruptcy Law, Civil Trial Practice, Commercial Law, Criminal Trial Practice, Insurance Defense Law, Natural Resources Law, Personal Injury Law, Probate and Estate Planning Law, Real Estate Law, Securities Law, Tax Law

SNELBAKER & BRENNEMAN, A PROFESSIONAL CORPORATION
Mechanicsburg, PA .... General Practice

SNELL, RICHARD G.
Dayton, OH .... General Practice

SNELLGROVE, LASER, LANGLEY, LOVETT & CULPEPPER
Jonesboro, AR .... General Practice, Medical Malpractice Law

SNELLINGS, BREARD, SARTOR, INABNETT & TRASCHER
Monroe, LA .... Civil Trial Practice, General Practice

SNELL & WILMER
Phoenix, AZ .... Antitrust Law, Banking Law, Bankruptcy Law, Civil Trial Practice, Commercial Law, Construction Law, Criminal Trial Practice, Employment Benefits Law, Environmental Law, General Practice, Health Care Law, Labor and Employment Law, Municipal Bond/Public Authority Financing Law, Natural Resources Law, Probate and Estate Planning Law, Real Estate Law, Tax Law
Tucson, AZ .... Antitrust Law, Banking Law, Bankruptcy Law, Real Estate Law
Irvine, CA .... General Practice

SNOW, CHRISTENSEN & MARTINEAU
Salt Lake City, UT .... General Practice

SNOW, NUFFER, ENGSTROM, DRAKE, WADE & SMART, A PROFESSIONAL CORPORATION
St. George, UT .... General Practice

SNOWISS, STEINBERG, FAULKNER AND RAE
Lock Haven, PA .... General Practice

SNYDER, WILLIAM A.
Davie, FL .... Probate and Estate Planning Law

SNYDER, GRONER & SCHIEB
Sarasota, FL .... Securities Law
Venice, FL .... Civil Trial Practice, Personal Injury Law

SOCKRIDER, BOLIN & ANGLIN, A PROFESSIONAL LAW CORPORATION
Shreveport, LA .... Business Law, Personal Injury Law

SOKOL, BEHOT AND FIORENZO
Hackensack, NJ .... Commercial Law, Environmental Law, General Practice, Real Estate Law

SOKOLOFF, CHARLES S., INCORPORATED
Woonsocket, RI .... Real Estate Law

SOLOMON, DAVID
Helena, AR .... General Practice

SOLOMON, JAY I.
Atlanta, GA .... Immigration and Naturalization Law

SOLOMON, KAHN, BUDMAN & STRICKER
Charleston, SC .... Civil Trial Practice, Family Law, Personal Injury Law, Real Estate Law

SOMERS & ASSOCIATES
Tampa, FL .... Civil Trial Practice

SOMMER & BARNARD, ATTORNEYS AT LAW, PC
Indianapolis, IN .... Administrative Law, Antitrust Law, Bankruptcy Law, Business Law, Civil Trial Practice, Commercial Law, Environmental Law, General Practice, Labor and Employment Law, Real Estate Law, Securities Law

SOMMERS, SCHWARTZ, SILVER & SCHWARTZ, P.C.
Southfield, MI .... Appellate Practice, Banking Law, Business Law, Civil Trial Practice, Commercial Law, Criminal Trial Practice, Environmental Law, Family Law, General Practice, Health Care Law, Insurance Defense Law, Labor and Employment Law, Medical Malpractice Law, Personal Injury Law, Probate and Estate Planning Law, Product Liability Law, Real Estate Law, Tax Law

SONDERBY, PETER R., P.C.
Chicago, IL .... Civil Trial Practice

SONNENSCHEIN NATH & ROSENTHAL
Los Angeles, CA .... General Practice
San Francisco, CA .... General Practice
Washington, DC .... General Practice
Chicago, IL .... General Practice
St. Louis, MO .... General Practice
New York, NY .... General Practice

SONNETT, NEAL R., P.A.
Miami, FL .... Criminal Trial Practice

SORLING, NORTHRUP, HANNA, CULLEN AND COCHRAN, LTD.
Springfield, IL .... General Practice

SOROKIN SOROKIN GROSS HYDE & WILLIAMS, P.C.
Hartford, CT .... Administrative Law, Antitrust Law, Appellate Practice, Business Law, Civil Trial Practice, Commercial Law, Construction Law, Employment Benefits Law, Family Law, General Practice, Insurance Defense Law, Probate and Estate Planning Law, Real Estate Law, Securities Law, Tax Law

SOTIROFF ABRAMCZYK & RAUSS, P.C.
Bingham Farms, MI .... Business Law, Labor and Employment Law, Real Estate Law

SOULES & WALLACE, ATTORNEYS AT LAW, A PROFESSIONAL CORPORATION
San Antonio, TX .... General Practice

SOUTHWELL & O'ROURKE, P.S.
Spokane, WA .... Bankruptcy Law

SOUTTER, NICHOLAS B.
Wellesley, MA .... Civil Trial Practice, Criminal Trial Practice, General Practice

SPAIN, GILLON, GROOMS, BLAN & NETTLES
Birmingham, AL .... Antitrust Law, Banking Law, Civil Trial Practice, Commercial Law, Environmental Law, General Practice, Insurance Defense Law, Labor and Employment Law, Municipal Bond/Public Authority Financing Law, Personal Injury Law, Probate and Estate Planning Law, Real Estate Law, Tax Law

SPAIN, MERRELL AND MILLER
Poplar Bluff, MO .... Insurance Defense Law

SPANGENBERG, SHIBLEY, TRACI, LANCIONE & LIBER
Cleveland, OH .... General Practice

SPANGLER, JENNINGS & DOUGHERTY, P.C.
Merrillville, IN .... Civil Trial Practice, General Practice, Insurance Defense Law, Personal Injury Law
Valparaiso, IN .... General Practice

SPANTON, PARSOFF & SIEGEL, P.C.
Melville, NY .... Business Law, Probate and Estate Planning Law, Tax Law

SPARBER, KOSNITZKY, TRUXTON, DE LA GUARDIA SPRATT & BROOKS, P.A.
Miami, FL .... Business Law, Civil Trial Practice, Commercial Law, General Practice, Health Care Law, Probate and Estate Planning Law, Real Estate Law, Securities Law, Tax Law

SPARKS, HAROLD S. III
Fort Worth, TX .... Probate and Estate Planning Law, Real Estate Law

SPARKS & COOK, P.C.
Woodward, OK .... General Practice

SPARKS & SILER, P.C.
Scottsdale, AZ .... Environmental Law, Probate and Estate Planning Law, Real Estate Law

SPEARS, MOORE, REBMAN & WILLIAMS
Chattanooga, TN .... Banking Law, Bankruptcy Law, Civil Trial Practice, Commercial Law, Employment Benefits Law, Environmental Law, General Practice, Insurance Defense Law, Labor and Employment Law, Probate and Estate Planning Law, Tax Law

SPEARS & SPEARS
Ironton, OH .... General Practice, Personal Injury Law, Probate and Estate Planning Law, Real Estate Law

SPECK, JAMES F.
Kansas City, MO .... Criminal Trial Practice

SPECTOR GADON & ROSEN, ATTORNEYS AT LAW, P.C.
Philadelphia, PA .... Business Law, Civil Trial Practice, Commercial Law

SPECTOR & ROSEMAN, A PROFESSIONAL CORPORATION
Philadelphia, PA .... Antitrust Law, Securities Law

SPEER, THOMAS A., P.A.
Sanford, FL .... Civil Trial Practice, General Practice

SPEISER, LAURENCE A., LTD.
Las Vegas, NV .... Business Law

SPELMAN, SAUER, BURDICK & METZGER, P.C.
St. Joseph, MI .... General Practice

SPENCE, CUSTER, SAYLOR, WOLFE & ROSE
Johnstown, PA .... General Practice

SPENCE, MORIARITY & SCHUSTER
Jackson, WY .... Civil Trial Practice, Criminal Trial Practice, General Practice, Personal Injury Law

SPENCER FANE BRITT & BROWNE
Kansas City, MO .... Civil Trial Practice, Environmental Law, General Practice, Insurance Defense Law, Labor and Employment Law

SPENCER, FRANK & SCHNEIDER
Washington, DC .... Patent, Trademark, Copyright and Unfair Competition Law

SPENCER, GLEASON, HEBE & RAGUE
Wellsboro, PA .... Civil Trial Practice, Medical Malpractice Law, Personal Injury Law

SPENCER AND KLEIN, PROFESSIONAL ASSOCIATION
Miami, FL .... Civil Trial Practice, General Practice, International Business Law, Tax Law

SPENCER & SPENCER, PROFESSIONAL ASSOCIATION
Rock Hill, SC .... General Practice

SPENGLER NATHANSON
Toledo, OH .... Banking Law, Bankruptcy Law, Civil Trial Practice, General Practice, Insurance Defense Law, Labor and Employment Law, Municipal Bond/Public Authority Financing Law, Real Estate Law, Tax Law

SPERLING & PERGANDE
Santa Ana, CA .... Bankruptcy Law, Commercial Law, General Practice, Real Estate Law

SPESIA, AYERS, ARDAUGH & WUNDERLICH
Joliet, IL .... General Practice, Personal Injury Law

SPIEGEL LIAO & KAGAY
San Francisco, CA .... Antitrust Law, Appellate Practice

SPIERS AND SPIERS
Radford, VA .... Civil Trial Practice, General Practice

SPIETH, BELL, MCCURDY & NEWELL CO., L.P.A.
Cleveland, OH .... Civil Trial Practice, General Practice, Labor and Employment Law, Probate and Estate Planning Law, Real Estate Law, Tax Law

SPIKE & MECKLER
Elyria, OH .... Civil Trial Practice, Family Law, General Practice, Medical Malpractice Law, Personal Injury Law

SPILMAN, THOMAS & BATTLE
Charleston, WV .... General Practice

SPITLER, VOGTSBERGER & HUFFMAN
Bowling Green, OH .... Business Law, General Practice, Personal Injury Law

SPITZ & CARR
Edmonton, AB, Canada .... Civil Trial Practice

SPIVEY, GRIGG, KELLY & KNISELY, P.C.
Austin, TX .... Civil Trial Practice, Personal Injury Law

SPRADLEY & RIESMEYER, A PROFESSIONAL CORPORATION
Kansas City, MO .... Civil Trial Practice, Public Utilities Law

SPRATT, MCKEOWN & BRADFORD
York, SC .... General Practice

SPRIGMAN, CHARLES J. JR.
Thorofare, NJ .... General Practice

SPRINGER, BUSH & PERRY, A PROFESSIONAL CORPORATION
Pittsburgh, PA .... Antitrust Law, General Practice, Labor and Employment Law, Municipal Bond/Public Authority Financing Law

SPRINGER & STEINBERG, A PROFESSIONAL CORPORATION
Denver, CO .... Criminal Trial Practice, Personal Injury Law

SPURRIER, RICE, WOOD & HALL
Huntsville, AL .... Civil Trial Practice, Insurance Defense Law

SQUIRE, SANDERS & DEMPSEY
Phoenix, AZ .... General Practice
Washington, DC .... General Practice
Jacksonville, FL .... General Practice
Miami, FL .... General Practice
Cleveland, OH .... General Practice
Columbus, OH .... General Practice
Brussels, Belgium .... General Practice
Prague, Czech Republic .... General Practice
London, England .... General Practice
Budapest, Hungary .... General Practice
Bratislava, Slovakia .... General Practice

STACK, FILPI & KAKACEK, CHARTERED
Chicago, IL .... Administrative Law, Commercial Law

STACKHOUSE, SMITH & NEXSEN
Norfolk, VA .... Banking Law, Bankruptcy Law, Business Law, Civil Trial Practice, General Practice, Insurance Defense Law

STAFFORD, STEWART & POTTER
Alexandria, LA .... Civil Trial Practice, General Practice, Insurance Defense Law

STAHANCYK, GAZZOLA, GEARING & RACKNER, P.C.
Portland, OR .... Family Law

STAMMER, MCKNIGHT, BARNUM & BAILEY
Fresno, CA .... Civil Trial Practice, Health Care Law, Insurance Defense Law

STAMPER, BURRAGE & HADLEY
Antlers, OK .... General Practice

STAMPS, THOMAS PATY LAW OFFICE OF
Atlanta, GA .... Business Law, Civil Trial Practice

STANLEY AND BERTRAM
Vanceburg, KY .... Insurance Defense Law, Personal Injury Law, Probate and Estate Planning Law

STANSBURY, RICHARD T., A PROFESSIONAL ASSOCIATION
Baltimore, MD .... Tax Law

STANSELL, LELAND E. JR., P.A.
Miami, FL .... Civil Trial Practice, Insurance Defense Law, Personal Injury Law, Product Liability Law

STANTON, THOMAS M.
Bakersfield, CA .... Civil Trial Practice

STANTON, WILLIAM E.
Stanfordville, NY .... Civil Trial Practice, Criminal Trial Practice, General Practice, Medical Malpractice Law, Personal Injury Law, Product Liability Law

STANWYCK, STEVEN J.
Los Angeles, CA .... Civil Trial Practice, Communications Law

STAPLETON & STAPLETON, A PROFESSIONAL ASSOCIATION
Tustin, CA .... Family Law

STARK DONINGER & SMITH
Indianapolis, IN .... Environmental Law, General Practice, Real Estate Law

STARKEY, KELLY, BLANEY & WHITE
Brick, NJ .... Civil Trial Practice, General Practice

STARK & KEENAN, A PROFESSIONAL ASSOCIATION
Bel Air, MD .... Business Law, Civil Trial Practice, General Practice, Municipal and Zoning Law, Personal Injury Law, Probate and Estate Planning Law, Real Estate Law

STARNES & ATCHISON
Birmingham, AL .... Civil Trial Practice, Construction Law, Environmental Law, Insurance Defense Law, Medical Malpractice Law, Personal Injury Law

STATHAM, JOHNSON & MCCRAY
Evansville, IN .... Banking Law, Civil Trial Practice, Commercial Law, General Practice, Health Care Law, Insurance Defense Law, Labor and Employment Law, Medical Malpractice Law, Probate and Estate Planning Law, Product Liability Law, Real Estate Law

STATON, PERKINSON, DOSTER, POST, SILVERMAN & ADCOCK
Sanford, NC .... General Practice

STAUFFER & ABRAHAM
Alexandria, VA .... Business Law
Vienna, VA .... Banking Law, Civil Trial Practice

STEARNS WEAVER MILLER WEISSLER ALHADEFF & SITTERSON, P.A.
Miami, FL .... Bankruptcy Law, Business Law, Civil Trial Practice, Commercial Law, Environmental Law, Municipal and Zoning Law, Natural Resources Law, Real Estate Law

STEBEL & PASELTINER, P.C.
Woodbury, NY .... Banking Law, Business Law, Commercial Law, Probate and Estate Planning Law, Real Estate Law

STEBELTON, ARANDA & SNIDER, A LEGAL PROFESSIONAL ASSOCIATION
Lancaster, OH .... Business Law, Civil Trial Practice, Family Law, Personal Injury Law

STEEFEL, LEVITT & WEISS, A PROFESSIONAL CORPORATION
San Francisco, CA .... Civil Trial Practice, General Practice

STEELE, STEELE, MCSOLEY & MCSOLEY
Bedford, IN .... Banking Law, Civil Trial Practice, General Practice

STEEL, RUDNICK & RUBEN
Philadelphia, PA .... Immigration and Naturalization Law

STEEL & STEEL
Nashville, AR .... General Practice

STEEN REYNOLDS DALEHITE & CURRIE
Jackson, MS .... Civil Trial Practice, General Practice, Insurance Defense Law, Medical Malpractice Law

STEERS & STEERS, P.S.C.
Franklin, KY .... Civil Trial Practice, Personal Injury Law

STEIN, ARTHUR & ASSOCIATES, LAW OFFICES
Forked River, NJ .... General Practice

STEIN, HARVEY W., A PROFESSIONAL CORPORATION
Oakland, CA .... Business Law

STEIN & MOORE, P.A.
St. Paul, MN .... Bankruptcy Law

STEIN, SPERLING, BENNETT, DE JONG, DRISCOLL, GREENFEIG & METRO, P.A.
Rockville, MD .... Business Law, Civil Trial Practice, Commercial Law, Construction Law, Criminal Trial Practice, Family Law, General Practice, Labor and Employment Law, Personal Injury Law, Probate and Estate Planning Law, Real Estate Law, Tax Law

STEIN, STEPHEN, CHARTERED
Las Vegas, NV .... Criminal Trial Practice

STEINBERG, FOSTER & BARNESS
Manhattan Beach, CA .... Bankruptcy Law, Civil Trial Practice, Probate and Estate Planning Law, Real Estate Law

STEINBERG, NUTTER & BRENT, LAW CORPORATION
Santa Monica, CA .... Bankruptcy Law, Real Estate Law

STEINBOCK, MIRIAM
Oakland, CA .... Family Law

STEINER AND STEINER
Kittanning, PA .... General Practice

STEKETEE, PETER W.
Grand Rapids, MI .... Civil Trial Practice, Tax Law

STENNETT, WILKINSON & PEDEN, A PROFESSIONAL ASSOCIATION
Jackson, MS .... General Practice, Municipal Bond/Public Authority Financing Law

STENSTROM, MCINTOSH, JULIAN, COLBERT, WHIGHAM & SIMMONS, P.A.
Sanford, FL .... Civil Trial Practice, General Practice

STEPANIAN & MUSCATELLO
Butler, PA .... Insurance Defense Law

STEPHENS, BARONI, REILLY & LEWIS
White Plains, NY .... General Practice, Municipal and Zoning Law

STEPHENS LAW FIRM
McLean, VA .... General Practice

STEPHENS, MILLIRONS, HARRISON & WILLIAMS, P.C.
Huntsville, AL .... Banking Law, Civil Trial Practice, Family Law, Real Estate Law

STEPHENSON DALY MOROW AND KURNIK, P.C.
Indianapolis, IN .... Insurance Defense Law

STEPONOVICH & ASSOCIATES, A PROFESSIONAL LAW CORPORATION
Irvine, CA .... Civil Trial Practice

STEPTOE & JOHNSON
Phoenix, AZ .... General Practice
Washington, DC .... Antitrust Law, General Practice, Tax Law, Transportation Law
Charleston, WV .... Civil Trial Practice, Environmental Law, General Practice, Health Care Law, Insurance Defense Law, Labor and Employment Law
Charles Town, WV .... General Practice
Clarksburg, WV .... Civil Trial Practice, Environmental Law, General Practice, Health Care Law, Insurance Defense Law, Labor and Employment Law, Municipal Bond/Public Authority Financing Law
Martinsburg, WV .... Civil Trial Practice, General Practice
Morgantown, WV .... Civil Trial Practice, General Practice

STERLING, SCHILLING & THORBURN, P.C.
Pontiac, MI .... Criminal Trial Practice, Family Law, Probate and Estate Planning Law, Real Estate Law

STERN & EDLIN, P.C.
Atlanta, GA .... Family Law

STERN STEIGER CROLAND, A PROFESSIONAL CORPORATION
Paramus, NJ .... Civil Trial Practice, Family Law, Municipal and Zoning Law, Real Estate Law

STERN & TANNENBAUM, P.A.
North Miami Beach, FL .... General Practice

STERNS & WEINROTH
Trenton, NJ .... Administrative Law, Civil Trial Practice, Commercial Law, General Practice, Real Estate Law

STETINA, BRUNDA AND BUYAN, A PROFESSIONAL CORPORATION
Laguna Hills, CA .... Patent, Trademark, Copyright and Unfair Competition Law

STETTNER, MILLER AND COHN, P.C.
Denver, CO .... Labor and Employment Law

STEVENS, BRAND, GOLDEN, WINTER & SKEPNEK
Lawrence, KS .... General Practice

STEVENS, ENGELS, BISHOP & SPRAGUE
Presque Isle, ME .... Criminal Trial Practice, Family Law, General Practice, Insurance Defense Law, Labor and Employment Law

STEVENS & JOHNSON
Allentown, PA .... General Practice

STEVENS & LEE, A PROFESSIONAL CORPORATION
Reading, PA .... General Practice, Municipal Bond/Public Authority Financing Law, Tax Law

STEVENS, STEVENS & THOMAS, P.C.
Myrtle Beach, SC .... Civil Trial Practice, Commercial Law, Construction Law, Labor and Employment Law, Personal Injury Law, Real Estate Law

STEWART DUE MILLER & PUGH
Indianapolis, IN .... Civil Trial Practice, Insurance Defense Law

STEWART, HUMPHERYS, BURCHETT & SANDELMAN
Chico, CA .... General Practice

STEWART MCKELVEY STIRLING SCALES
Moncton, NB, Canada .... General Practice
Saint John, NB, Canada .... General Practice
St. John's, NF, Canada .... General Practice
Halifax, NS, Canada .... General Practice
Sydney, NS, Canada .... General Practice
Charlottetown, PE, Canada .... General Practice

STEWART, MELVIN & FROST
Gainesville, GA .... General Practice

STEWART AND STEWART
Washington, DC .... General Practice

STEWART & STEWART LAW OFFICES, INC., P.S., A PROF. SERVICE CORP.
Montesano, WA .... General Practice

STEWART, STEWART & O'NEIL
Walnut Creek, CA .... Probate and Estate Planning Law

STEWART TILGHMAN FOX & BIANCHI, P.A.
Miami, FL .... Civil Trial Practice

STICHTER, RIEDEL, BLAIN & PROSSER, P.A.
Tampa, FL .... Bankruptcy Law

STIKEMAN, ELLIOTT
Vancouver, BC, Canada .... General Practice
Ottawa, ON, Canada .... General Practice
Toronto, ON, Canada .... General Practice
Montreal, QU, Canada .... General Practice
London, England .... General Practice
Hong Kong, Hong Kong (British Crown Colony) .... General Practice
Taipei, Taiwan .... General Practice

STILL, NEMIER, TOLARI & LANDRY, P.C.
Farmington Hills, MI .... Insurance Defense Law, Medical Malpractice Law, Product Liability Law

STINSON, JOSEPH M.
Tylertown, MS .... General Practice

STIRBA & HATHAWAY, A PROFESSIONAL CORPORATION
Salt Lake City, UT .... Civil Trial Practice

STIRLING & KLEINTOP
Honolulu, HI .... Family Law

STITES & HARBISON
Frankfort, KY .... General Practice
Lexington, KY .... General Practice, Natural Resources Law
Louisville, KY .... General Practice, Municipal Bond/Public Authority Financing Law

STITES, MCELWAIN & FOWLER
Louisville, KY .... General Practice

STIVISON, DAVID V.
Philadelphia, PA .... Public Utilities Law

STOCK AND LEADER
York, PA .... Civil Trial Practice, General Practice, Labor and Employment Law, Municipal Bond/Public Authority Financing Law

STOCKTON & SADLER
Modesto, CA .... General Practice

STOCKWELL & COOPERMAN, A LEGAL PROFESSIONAL ASSOCIATION
Toledo, OH .... Probate and Estate Planning Law, Real Estate Law, Tax Law

STOCKWELL, HARRIS, ANDERSON & WIDOM, A PROFESSIONAL CORPORATION
Los Angeles, CA .... Insurance Defense Law, Labor and Employment Law

STOCKWELL, SIEVERT, VICCELLIO, CLEMENTS & SHADDOCK
Lake Charles, LA .... General Practice

STOCKWOOD, SPIES, CRAIGEN & LE VAY
Toronto, ON, Canada .... Civil Trial Practice

STOECKLEIN, KOVERMAN & SMITH
Dayton, OH .... Business Law, Probate and Estate Planning Law, Real Estate Law

STOKES & BARTHOLOMEW, P.A.
Nashville, TN .... General Practice

STOKES, EITELBACH & LAWRENCE, P.S.
Seattle, WA .... Antitrust Law, Business Law, Labor and Employment Law, Probate and Estate Planning Law

STOKES LAZARUS & CARMICHAEL
Atlanta, GA .... Administrative Law, Commercial Law, Labor and Employment Law

STOKES & MURPHY
Santa Monica, CA .... Construction Law, Labor and Employment Law
Atlanta, GA .... Construction Law, Labor and Employment Law

STOKKE & RIDDET, A PROFESSIONAL CORPORATION
Santa Ana, CA .... Criminal Trial Practice

STOLDT AND HORAN, A PROFESSIONAL CORPORATION
Hackensack, NJ .... Real Estate Law

STOLL, KEENON & PARK
Frankfort, KY .... General Practice
Lexington, KY .... Administrative Law, Antitrust Law, Banking Law, Bankruptcy Law, Business Law, Civil Trial Practice, Commercial Law, Communications Law, Criminal Trial Practice, Employment Benefits Law, Environmental Law, Family Law, General Practice, Health Care Law, Insurance Defense Law, Labor and Employment Law, Municipal Bond/Public Authority Financing Law, Municipal and Zoning Law, Natural Resources Law, Probate and Estate Planning Law, Real Estate Law, Securities Law, Tax Law
Louisville, KY .... Commercial Law, General Practice

STOLPMAN, KRISSMAN, ELBER, MANDEL & KATZMAN
Long Beach, CA .... Civil Trial Practice, Personal Injury Law, Product Liability Law

STOLTZ, MELVIN I.
Milford, CT .... Patent, Trademark, Copyright and Unfair Competition Law

STOMPOLY, STROUD, GIDDINGS & GLICKSMAN, P.C.
Tucson, AZ .... Business Law, Civil Trial Practice, Family Law, General Practice, Medical Malpractice Law, Personal Injury Law, Probate and Estate Planning Law

STONE, JACK A.
Evansville, IN .... Probate and Estate Planning Law, Tax Law

STONE & CHRISTIAN, P.C.
Macon, GA .... Family Law

STONE, EDWARD H., P.C.
Newport Beach, CA .... Probate and Estate Planning Law

STONE, HARRISON, TURK & SHOWALTER, P.C.
Radford, VA .... Civil Trial Practice, Criminal Trial Practice, General Practice, Personal Injury Law

STONE JESSUP, P.C.
Tulsa, OK .... Municipal Bond/Public Authority Financing Law

STONE, LEYTON & GERSHMAN, A PROFESSIONAL CORPORATION
St. Louis, MO .... Bankruptcy Law, Real Estate Law

STONE, PIGMAN, WALTHER, WITTMANN & HUTCHINSON
New Orleans, LA .... General Practice

STONE, WILLIAM S., P.C.
Blakely, GA .... Personal Injury Law

STONECIPHER, CUNNINGHAM, BEARD & SCHMITT
Pittsburgh, PA .... Bankruptcy Law, Civil Trial Practice, General Practice

STOPHEL & STOPHEL, P.C.
Chattanooga, TN .... Banking Law, Bankruptcy Law, Civil Trial Practice, Commercial Law, Construction Law, Environmental Law, General Practice, Health Care Law, Personal Injury Law, Probate and Estate Planning Law, Real Estate Law, Tax Law

STOTT, HOLLOWELL, PALMER & WINDHAM
Gastonia, NC .... General Practice

STOUT & STOUT
Hobbs, NM .... General Practice

STOUT AND WINTERBOTTOM
Roswell, NM .... Criminal Trial Practice

STRADLING, YOCCA, CARLSON & RAUTH, A PROFESSIONAL CORPORATION
Newport Beach, CA .... General Practice

STRANG, FLETCHER, CARRIGER, WALKER, HODGE & SMITH
Chattanooga, TN .... General Practice

STRASBURGER & PRICE, L.L.P.
Austin, TX .... General Practice

Dallas, TX....................General Practice
Houston, TX....................General Practice
Mexico, D.F., Mexico....................General Practice

STRASSER & ASSOCIATES, A PROFESSIONAL CORPORATION
Nutley, NJ....................Civil Trial Practice, General Practice, Real Estate Law
Saddle River, NJ....................Civil Trial Practice, General Practice, Real Estate Law

STRASSMAN, HARVEY
Los Angeles, CA....................Family Law

STRATER & STRATER, P.A.
York, ME....................General Practice

STRATTON, MAY, HAYS & HOGG, P.S.C.
Pikeville, KY....................General Practice, Insurance Defense Law

STRAUSS & TROY, A LEGAL PROFESSIONAL ASSOCIATION
Covington, KY....................General Practice
Cincinnati, OH....................Business Law, Civil Trial Practice, Employment Benefits Law, General Practice, Insurance Defense Law, Medical Malpractice Law, Real Estate Law, Securities Law, Tax Law

STREATER, MURPHY, GERNANDER, FORSYTHE & TELSTAD, P.A.
Winona, MN....................General Practice

STREET & GRUA
Lansing, MI....................Business Law, Civil Trial Practice, General Practice, Personal Injury Law, Real Estate Law

STREET, STREET, STREET, SCOTT & BOWMAN
Grundy, VA....................General Practice

STREIBICH & SEALE
Memphis, TN....................Trademark, Copyright and Unfair Competition Law

STREICH LANG, A PROFESSIONAL ASSOCIATION
Phoenix, AZ....................Banking Law, Bankruptcy Law, Business Law, Civil Trial Practice, Commercial Law, Environmental Law, General Practice, Natural Resources Law, Patent, Trademark, Copyright and Unfair Competition Law, Real Estate Law, Securities Law, Tax Law
Tucson, AZ....................Bankruptcy Law, Civil Trial Practice, General Practice

STRICKLAND, JACK V. JR.
Fort Worth, TX....................Criminal Trial Practice

STRICKLAND & O'HAIR, P.C.
Tucson, AZ....................Medical Malpractice Law, Natural Resources Law, Personal Injury Law

STRINGARI, FRITZ, KREGER, AHEARN & CRANDALL, P.C.
Detroit, MI....................Civil Trial Practice, Criminal Trial Practice, Employment Benefits Law, Labor and Employment Law

STRINGER, BRISBIN, HUMPHREY
Toronto, ON, Canada....................Labor and Employment Law

STRINGER & ROHLEDER, LTD.
St. Paul, MN....................Civil Trial Practice

STRIPLING, MCMICHAEL & STRIPLING, P.A.
Gainesville, FL....................Civil Trial Practice

STROBL AND MANOOGIAN, P.C.
Bloomfield Hills, MI....................Appellate Practice, Banking Law, Bankruptcy Law, Business Law, Civil Trial Practice, Commercial Law, General Practice, Insurance Defense Law, Probate and Estate Planning Law, Real Estate Law, Securities Law, Tax Law

STRODEL, ROBERT C., LTD.
Peoria, IL....................Civil Trial Practice, General Practice

STROHM, RICHARD L., P.C., LAW OFFICES OF
Phoenix, AZ....................Criminal Trial Practice, Personal Injury Law

STRONG & HANNI, A PROFESSIONAL CORPORATION
Salt Lake City, UT....................Business Law, General Practice, Insurance Defense Law, Labor and Employment Law, Medical Malpractice Law, Probate and Estate Planning Law, Product Liability Law

STRONG, PIPKIN, NELSON & BISSELL, L.L.P.
Beaumont, TX....................General Practice

STRONG, STEVENS, BRISCOE & HAMILTON, P.C.
Philadelphia, PA....................Banking Law, Business Law, Probate and Estate Planning Law, Real Estate Law

STRONG, STRONG & PROKES, A PROFESSIONAL CORPORATION
Maryville, MO....................General Practice

STROOCK & STROOCK & LAVAN
Los Angeles, CA....................General Practice
Washington, DC....................General Practice
Miami, FL....................General Practice
New York, NY....................Bankruptcy Law, General Practice, Tax Law

STROP, THOMAS, BURNS & HOLLIDAY
St. Joseph, MO....................General Practice

STROUD, STROUD, WILLINK, THOMPSON & HOWARD
Madison, WI....................General Practice, Patent, Trademark, Copyright and Unfair Competition Law, Probate and Estate Planning Law

STROUP, JOHNSON & TRESIDDER, P.C.
Petoskey, MI....................General Practice

STROUT & PAYSON, P.A.
Rockland, ME....................General Practice

STRYKER, TAMS & DILL
Newark, NJ....................General Practice

STUART, CHARLES M. JR.
Greenville, SC....................Probate and Estate Planning Law

STUART & BRANIGIN
Lafayette, IN....................Civil Trial Practice, General Practice, Insurance Defense Law

STUART & STRICKLAND, P.A.
Tampa, FL....................Civil Trial Practice, Insurance Defense Law

STUART, TINLEY, PETERS, THORN & HUGHES
Council Bluffs, IA....................General Practice

STUBBS, HITTIG & LEONE, A PROFESSIONAL CORPORATION
San Francisco, CA....................Construction Law, Health Care Law, Insurance Defense Law, Real Estate Law

STUBBS & STUBBS
San Mateo, CA....................Civil Trial Practice

STUCKERT AND YATES
Newtown, PA....................General Practice

STUDDARD & MELBY, A PROFESSIONAL CORPORATION
El Paso, TX....................General Practice

STULTS, STULTS, FORSZT & PAWLOWSKI, A PROFESSIONAL ASSOCIATION
Gary, IN....................Civil Trial Practice, General Practice, Insurance Defense Law

STURGILL, TURNER & TRUITT
Lexington, KY....................Banking Law, Bankruptcy Law, Business Law, Civil Trial Practice, Commercial Law, Construction Law, Environmental Law, General Practice, Insurance Defense Law, Natural Resources Law, Personal Injury Law, Probate and Estate Planning Law, Real Estate Law

STUTH, HARRY P.
Dallas, TX....................Civil Trial Practice

STUTMAN, TREISTER & GLATT, PROFESSIONAL CORPORATION
Los Angeles, CA....................Bankruptcy Law, Commercial Law

STUZIN AND CAMNER, PROFESSIONAL ASSOCIATION
Miami, FL....................Banking Law, Bankruptcy Law, Civil Trial Practice, Commercial Law, General Practice, Insurance Defense Law, Real Estate Law, Securities Law

SUCHERMAN & COLLINS
San Francisco, CA....................Family Law, Probate and Estate Planning Law

SUELTHAUS & KAPLAN, P.C.
St. Louis, MO....................General Practice

SUGARMAN AND SUGARMAN, P.C.
Boston, MA....................General Practice, Medical Malpractice Law, Personal Injury Law

SUGARMAN, WALLACE, MANHEIM & SCHOENWALD
Syracuse, NY....................General Practice

SUITTER AXLAND & HANSON, A PROFESSIONAL LAW CORPORATION
Salt Lake City, UT....................General Practice

SULLIVAN & CROMWELL
Los Angeles, CA....................General Practice
Washington, DC....................General Practice
New York, NY....................Civil Trial Practice, General Practice
Melbourne, Victoria, Australia....................General Practice
London, England....................General Practice
Paris, France....................General Practice
Hong Kong, Hong Kong (British Crown Colony)....................General Practice
Tokyo, Japan....................General Practice

SULLIVAN, DONOVAN, BOND & BONNER
New York, NY........................International Business Law, Municipal Bond/Public Authority Financing Law

SULLIVAN, HALL, BOOTH & SMITH, A PROFESSIONAL CORPORATION
Atlanta, GA ....Civil Trial Practice, Health Care Law, Insurance Defense Law, Medical Malpractice Law, Personal Injury Law, Product Liability Law

SULLIVAN, HAMILTON, SCHULZ, LETZRING, SIMONS, KRETER, TOTH & LEBEUF
Battle Creek, MI ....Civil Trial Practice, General Practice

SULLIVAN, MAHONEY
St. Catharines, ON, Canada ....General Practice

SULLIVAN, WALSH & WOOD
Los Angeles, CA......................Business Law, Civil Trial Practice, General Practice

SULLIVAN & WARD, P.C.
Des Moines, IA........................General Practice

SULLIVAN, WARD, BONE, TYLER & ASHER, P.C.
Southfield, MI ....Insurance Defense Law

SULLIVAN & WORCESTER
Boston, MA..............................General Practice

SULLIVAN, WORKMAN & DEE
Los Angeles, CA......................General Practice

SULLOWAY & HOLLIS
Concord, NH ....General Practice

SULMEYER, KUPETZ, BAUMANN & ROTHMAN, A PROFESSIONAL CORPORATION
Los Angeles, CA......................Bankruptcy Law, Commercial Law

SUMMERS, MCCREA & WYATT, P.C.
Chattanooga, TN ....Civil Trial Practice, Criminal Trial Practice, General Practice, Labor and Employment Law, Medical Malpractice Law, Personal Injury Law

SUMNER & HEWES
Atlanta, GA ....Antitrust Law, Appellate Practice, Civil Trial Practice, Construction Law, Health Care Law

SUMNER & WARREN, P.A.
Dade City, FL..........................General Practice

SUMNERS, CARTER & MCMILLIN, P.A.
New Albany, MS ....General Practice, Insurance Defense Law

SUMRALL, H. CASSEDY, JR., PROFESSIONAL ASSOCIATION
Delray Beach, FL.....................Probate and Estate Planning Law, Real Estate Law

SUNDAHL, POWERS, KAPP & MARTIN
Cheyenne, WY.........................Administrative Law, Civil Trial Practice, Insurance Defense Law

SUPNIK, PAUL D.
Beverly Hills, CA.....................Trademark, Copyright and Unfair Competition Law

SUPPLEE, ROBERT S., P.C.
West Chester, PA.....................Probate and Estate Planning Law

SURRATT, JOHN R., P.A.
Winston-Salem, NC ....Civil Trial Practice, Commercial Law

SUSK, ROBERT A., LAW FIRM OF
San Francisco, CA ....Antitrust Law, Civil Trial Practice, Real Estate Law

SUSMAN, DUFFY & SEGALOFF, P.C.
New Haven, CT.......................Business Law, Civil Trial Practice, General Practice, Real Estate Law

SUSMAN, GERALD S., & ASSOCIATES, P.C.
Philadelphia, PA ....Probate and Estate Planning Law, Tax Law

SUSSMAN SHANK WAPNICK CAPLAN & STILES
Portland, OR...........................Bankruptcy Law, Business Law, Commercial Law, Construction Law, Environmental Law, General Practice, Probate and Estate Planning Law, Real Estate Law, Tax Law

SUSSMAN, WILLIAM C., P.A.
Miami, FL ....Real Estate Law

SUTER DOYLE KESSELRING LAWRENCE & WERNER
Rochester, NY.........................Bankruptcy Law, Commercial Law

SUTHERLAND, ASBILL & BRENNAN
Washington, DC......................Administrative Law, Antitrust Law, Banking Law, Business Law, Civil Trial Practice, Communications Law, Employment Benefits Law, Environmental Law, General Practice, Insurance Defense Law, Natural Resources Law, Probate and Estate Planning Law, Real Estate Law, Tax Law
Atlanta, GA ....Antitrust Law, Banking Law, Bankruptcy Law, Business Law, Civil Trial Practice, Construction Law, Employment Benefits Law, Environmental Law, General Practice, Health Care Law, Immigration and Naturalization Law, Municipal Bond/Public Authority Financing Law, Probate and Estate Planning Law, Real Estate Law, Tax Law, Trademark, Copyright and Unfair Competition Law

SUTHERLAND, JOHN H., P.A.
Vero Beach, FL ....Probate and Estate Planning Law, Real Estate Law

SUTIN, THAYER & BROWNE, A PROFESSIONAL CORPORATION
Albuquerque, NM....................Civil Trial Practice, General Practice
Santa Fe, NM..........................General Practice

SUTKOWSKI & WASHKUHN, LTD.
Peoria, IL................................General Practice

SUTTON, BASSECHES, MAGIDOFF & AMARAL
New York, NY.........................Patent, Trademark, Copyright and Unfair Competition Law, Trademark, Copyright and Unfair Competition Law

SUTTON, DELEEUW, CLARK & DARCY
Pittsford, NY...........................General Practice

SWADEN LAW OFFICES
Edina, MN ....Family Law

SWAIN, HARTSHORN & SCOTT
Peoria, IL................................General Practice

SWAIN, JOHNSON & GARD
Peoria, IL................................General Practice

SWAINE AND HARRIS, P.A.
Lake Placid, FL.......................General Practice
Sebring, FL.............................General Practice

SWANSON, MARTIN & BELL
Chicago, IL..............................Civil Trial Practice, Insurance Defense Law, Medical Malpractice Law, Product Liability Law

SWANSON, MIDGLEY, GANGWERE, KITCHIN & MCLARNEY, L.L.C.
Kansas City, MO ....Antitrust Law, Bankruptcy Law, Civil Trial Practice, Commercial Law, Environmental Law, Family Law, General Practice, Immigration and Naturalization Law, Labor and Employment Law, Natural Resources Law, Probate and Estate Planning Law, Real Estate Law, Tax Law, Transportation Law

SWARTZ, CAMPBELL & DETWEILER
Harrisburg, PA........................General Practice
Media, PA ....General Practice
Philadelphia, PA ....General Practice, Insurance Defense Law

SWARTZ & SWARTZ
Boston, MA..............................Admiralty/Maritime Law, Civil Trial Practice, Environmental Law, Medical Malpractice Law, Personal Injury Law, Product Liability Law

SWEARINGEN, JAMES D.
Pensacola, FL.........................Family Law

SWEENEY, DABAGIA, DONOGHUE, THORNE, JANES & PAGOS
Michigan City, IN....................General Practice

SWEENEY, MASON & WILSON, A PROFESSIONAL LAW CORPORATION
Los Gatos, CA.........................Business Law, Construction Law, Labor and Employment Law

SWEENEY, SHEEHAN & SPENCER, A PROFESSIONAL CORPORATION
Philadelphia, PA ....General Practice, Product Liability Law

SWEET & REDDY, S.C.
Elkhorn, WI ....General Practice, Real Estate Law

SWENDSEID & STERN
Las Vegas, NV........................Municipal Bond/Public Authority Financing Law
Reno, NV ....Municipal Bond/Public Authority Financing Law

SWENSEN PERER & JOHNSON
Pittsburgh, PA ....Civil Trial Practice, Personal Injury Law, Product Liability Law

SWERDLOW, FLORENCE & SANCHEZ, A LAW CORPORATION
Beverly Hills, CA.....................Labor and Employment Law

SWERLING, JACK B.
Columbia, SC..........................Appellate Practice, Criminal Trial Practice

SWINFORD & SIMS, P.S.C.
Cynthiana, KY.........................General Practice

SWISHER & COHRT
Waterloo, IA ....Business Law, Civil Trial Practice, Commercial Law, General Practice, Insurance Defense Law, Labor and Employment Law, Real Estate Law

SYLVESTER & MALEY, INC.
Burlington, VT ....Civil Trial Practice, Medical Malpractice Law, Personal Injury Law

SYPRETT, MESHAD, RESNICK & LIEB
Sarasota, FL...........................General Practice

TABNER, LAUDATO AND RYAN
Albany, NY.....General Practice

TAFARO & FLYNN
New Providence, NJ.....Civil Trial Practice

TAFT & MCSALLY
Cranston, RI.....General Practice, Probate and Estate Planning Law

TAFT, STETTINIUS & HOLLISTER
Washington, DC.....General Practice
Crestview Hills, KY.....General Practice
Cincinnati, OH.....General Practice
Columbus, OH.....General Practice

TALCOTT, LIGHTFOOT, VANDEVELDE, WOEHRLE & SADOWSKY
Los Angeles, CA.....Civil Trial Practice, Criminal Trial Practice

TALIAFERRO AND MEHLING
Covington, KY.....Civil Trial Practice, Insurance Defense Law, Probate and Estate Planning Law, Real Estate Law, Tax Law

TALKINGTON AND CHASE
Iola, KS.....General Practice

TALLMAN, HUDDERS & SORRENTINO, P.C.
Allentown, PA.....Civil Trial Practice, General Practice, Probate and Estate Planning Law

TALT, ALAN R.
Pasadena, CA.....Business Law, Probate and Estate Planning Law

TANENBAUM, ROBERT M.
New York, NY.....General Practice

TANENBAUM, MARK C., P.A.
Charleston, SC.....Civil Trial Practice

TANKARD AND GORDON
Eastville, VA.....General Practice

TANNENBAUM, RICHARD N.
New York, NY.....Civil Trial Practice, Family Law

TANSEY, ROSEBROUGH, GERDING & STROTHER, P.C.
Farmington, NM.....Civil Trial Practice, General Practice, Labor and Employment Law

TARASI & JOHNSON, P.C.
Pittsburgh, PA.....Civil Trial Practice, General Practice, Medical Malpractice Law, Personal Injury Law

TARASKA, GROWER, UNGER AND KETCHAM, P.A.
Orlando, FL.....Insurance Defense Law

TARLOW, BARRY, A PROF. CORP., LAW OFFICES OF
Los Angeles, CA.....Criminal Trial Practice

TARNOW, HERMAN H.
Westport, CT.....Family Law
New York, NY.....Family Law

TARUTIS, GERALD R., INC., P.S.
Seattle, WA.....Health Care Law

TASCHNER, DANA B. LAW OFFICES OF
Dallas, TX.....Business Law, International Business Law

TASCHNER, DANA B., P.C.
Beverly Hills, CA.....Business Law, International Business Law, Product Liability Law

TATE & ASSOCIATES
Richmond, TX.....Civil Trial Practice

TATE, LOWE & ROWLETT, P.C.
Abingdon, VA.....Criminal Trial Practice, General Practice, Personal Injury Law, Real Estate Law

TATE, YOUNG, MORPHIS, BACH AND FARTHING
Hickory, NC.....General Practice

TATLOW & GUMP
Moberly, MO.....General Practice

TATUM & MCDOWELL
Clovis, NM.....General Practice, Probate and Estate Planning Law, Tax Law

TAUB, STEPHEN R.
Garden City, NY.....Family Law

TAUBMAN, SIMPSON, YOUNG & SULENTOR
Long Beach, CA.....Civil Trial Practice, Environmental Law, General Practice, Real Estate Law, Tax Law

TAUSTINE, POST, SOTSKY, BERMAN, FINEMAN & KOHN
Louisville, KY.....Business Law, Medical Malpractice Law, Real Estate Law, Tax Law

TAVSS, FLETCHER, EARLEY & KING, P.C.
Norfolk, VA.....Banking Law, General Practice, Personal Injury Law, Real Estate Law

TAYLOR, NELSON W. III
Morehead City, NC.....General Practice

TAYLOR, ANDERSON & TRAVERS
Boston, MA.....Civil Trial Practice, General Practice, Insurance Defense Law

TAYLOR, ATKINS & OSTROW
Garden City, NY.....Family Law

TAYLOR, BRION, BUKER & GREENE
Coral Gables, FL.....General Practice
Fort Lauderdale, FL.....General Practice
Key West, FL.....General Practice
Miami, FL.....Banking Law, Civil Trial Practice, General Practice
Tallahassee, FL.....General Practice

TAYLOR, CARTER, BUTTERFIELD, RISEMAN, CLARK AND HOWELL, P.C.
Lapeer, MI.....General Practice

TAYLOR & CIRE
Houston, TX.....Civil Trial Practice

TAYLOR & FAUST, A PROFESSIONAL CORPORATION
San Francisco, CA.....Tax Law

TAYLOR, HARP & CALLIER
Columbus, GA.....Civil Trial Practice, Personal Injury Law

TAYLOR & HORBALY
Jacksonville, NC.....Criminal Trial Practice

TAYLOR, JONES, ALEXANDER, SORRELL & MCFALL, LTD.
Southaven, MS.....Civil Trial Practice, Criminal Trial Practice, Family Law, Probate and Estate Planning Law, Real Estate Law

TAYLOR, KELLER & DUNAWAY
London, KY.....Civil Trial Practice, General Practice, Insurance Defense Law

TAYLOR KUPFER SUMMERS & RHODES
Los Angeles, CA.....General Practice
Pasadena, CA.....Business Law, Family Law, General Practice, Probate and Estate Planning Law, Real Estate Law

TAYLOR LOHMEYER CORRIGAN, P.C.
Dallas, TX.....General Practice

TAYLOR MCCORD, A LAW CORPORATION
Ventura, CA.....Civil Trial Practice, Environmental Law, Family Law, Probate and Estate Planning Law

TAYLOR, MILLER, SPROWL, HOFFNAGLE & MERLETTI
Chicago, IL.....General Practice, Insurance Defense Law

TAYLOR, MOSELEY & JOYNER, P.A.
Jacksonville, FL.....Admiralty/Maritime Law, General Practice, Transportation Law

TAYLOR, PORTER, BROOKS & PHILLIPS
Baton Rouge, LA.....General Practice

TAYLOR, ZUNKA, MILNOR & CARTER, LTD.
Charlottesville, VA.....Civil Trial Practice, General Practice, Insurance Defense Law

TEAHAN & CONSTANTINO
Poughkeepsie, NY.....Probate and Estate Planning Law, Tax Law

TEGTMEIER CISNEROS, P.C.
Colorado Springs, CO.....Criminal Trial Practice

TEICHBERG, ARTHUR J., A PROFESSIONAL CORPORATION
New York, NY.....Commercial Law

TEITLER, STANLEY A., P.C.
New York, NY.....Criminal Trial Practice

TELLEEN, TELLEEN, BRAENDLE, HORBERG & THURMAN
Cambridge, IL.....General Practice

TELLER, MARTIN, CHANEY & HASSELL
Vicksburg, MS.....General Practice

TELPNER, SMITH & RUESCH
Council Bluffs, IA.....Banking Law, Bankruptcy Law, General Practice

TEMKIN & STONE, LTD.
Providence, RI.....General Practice

TENER, VAN KIRK, WOLF & MOORE
Pittsburgh, PA.....Probate and Estate Planning Law, Tax Law

TENNEY & TENNEY
Decatur, IL............................Business Law, Civil Trial Practice, Probate and Estate Planning Law

TEPE, THOMAS M.
Cincinnati, OH........................Civil Trial Practice

TEPPER, NANCY BOXLEY, A PROFESSIONAL CORPORATION
Laguna Hills, CA....................Probate and Estate Planning Law

TERAOKA & ASSOCIATES, A LAW CORPORATION
San Francisco, CA..................Business Law

TERRIBERRY, CARROLL & YANCEY, L.L.P.
New Orleans, LA....................Admiralty/Maritime Law, General Practice

TERRY & DITTMAR
Tampa, FL..............................Bankruptcy Law, Civil Trial Practice

TERWILLIGER, WAKEEN, PIEHLER & CONWAY, S.C.
Stevens Point, WI...................Civil Trial Practice, General Practice
Wausau, WI............................Civil Trial Practice, General Practice

TESCHER CHAVES HOCHMAN RUBIN & MULLER, P.A.
Miami, FL...............................Probate and Estate Planning Law, Tax Law

TESTA, HURWITZ & THIBEAULT
Boston, MA.............................General Practice

TEW, ALLEN R., P.A.
Clayton, NC............................General Practice

THACHER PROFFITT & WOOD
Washington, DC.......................General Practice
New York, NY.........................Admiralty/Maritime Law, Civil Trial Practice, General Practice

THARP, LIOTTA & JANES
Fairmont, WV.........................General Practice

THARRINGTON, SMITH & HARGROVE
Raleigh, NC............................Administrative Law, Business Law, Civil Trial Practice, Communications Law, Criminal Trial Practice, Family Law

THAXTON, HOUT & HOWARD
Newport, AR...........................General Practice

THAYER, BERNSTEIN, BASS & MONACO, P.C.
Kansas City, MO.....................Family Law

THERIAULT & JOSLIN, P.C.
Montpelier, VT........................General Practice, Insurance Defense Law, Medical Malpractice Law

THERREL BAISDEN & MEYER WEISS
Miami Beach, FL.....................General Practice, Tax Law

THIBODEAU, JOSEPH H., P.C., LAW OFFICES OF
Denver, CO............................Tax Law

THIEBLOT, RYAN, MARTIN & FERGUSON, P.A.
Baltimore, MD........................Admiralty/Maritime Law, Bankruptcy Law, Civil Trial Practice, Commercial Law, Construction Law, Criminal Trial Practice, General Practice, Insurance Defense Law, Transportation Law

THIELEN AND BURKE, A PROFESSIONAL CORPORATION
Long Beach, CA......................Personal Injury Law

THINNES, THOMAS A., P.A.
Phoenix, AZ...........................Criminal Trial Practice

THOMAN SOULE GAGE
Hamilton, ON, Canada...........General Practice

THOMAS, BALLENGER, VOGELMAN AND TURNER, P.C.
Alexandria, VA.......................Bankruptcy Law, Commercial Law, General Practice, Labor and Employment Law, Real Estate Law, Transportation Law

THOMAS, BIRDSONG & CLAYTON, P.C.
Rolla, MO..............................General Practice

THOMAS, FELDMAN & WILSHUSEN, L.L.P.
Dallas, TX..............................Construction Law

THOMAS, KENNEDY, SAMPSON & PATTERSON
Atlanta, GA............................Commercial Law, Insurance Defense Law, Medical Malpractice Law, Municipal Bond/Public Authority Financing Law, Personal Injury Law, Product Liability Law, Real Estate Law

THOMAS & LIBOWITZ, A PROFESSIONAL ASSOCIATION
Baltimore, MD........................Securities Law

THOMAS, MAMER & HAUGHEY
Champaign, IL.......................General Practice

THOMAS & NEESE
Dresden, TN...........................General Practice

THOMAS, SNELL, JAMISON, RUSSELL AND ASPERGER, A PROFESSIONAL CORPORATION
Fresno, CA.............................General Practice

THOMAS & THOMAS
Brazil, IN...............................General Practice

THOMAS, THOMAS & HAFER
Harrisburg, PA........................Civil Trial Practice, Health Care Law, Insurance Defense Law, Labor and Employment Law, Medical Malpractice Law

THOMASON, HENDRIX, HARVEY, JOHNSON & MITCHELL
Memphis, TN..........................Bankruptcy Law, Civil Trial Practice, Environmental Law, General Practice, Insurance Defense Law, Personal Injury Law, Probate and Estate Planning Law

THOMASSON, GILBERT, COOK, REMLEY & MAGUIRE
Cape Girardeau, MO...............Civil Trial Practice, General Practice

THOMPSON, SARAH M.
Philadelphia, PA.....................Civil Trial Practice, Medical Malpractice Law, Personal Injury Law, Product Liability Law

THOMPSON, BETTY A., LTD.
Arlington, VA.........................Family Law

THOMPSON & BOWIE
Portland, ME..........................Civil Trial Practice, Construction Law, Insurance Defense Law, Personal Injury Law, Product Liability Law

THOMPSON CALKINS & SUTTER
Pittsburgh, PA........................General Practice, Insurance Defense Law

THOMPSON, COE, COUSINS & IRONS, L.L.P.
Dallas, TX..............................Administrative Law, Bankruptcy Law, Business Law, Civil Trial Practice, General Practice, Insurance Defense Law, Labor and Employment Law, Real Estate Law

THOMPSON, DANIEL R., P.C.
Washington, DC.....................Administrative Law, Environmental Law

THOMPSON, E.C., III, P.A.
Warsaw, NC............................General Practice

THOMPSON, GARRETT & HINES
Brewton, AL...........................General Practice

THOMPSON, HENRY, GWIN, BRITTAIN & STEVENS, P.A.
Conway, SC............................General Practice

THOMPSON, HINE AND FLORY
Washington, DC.....................Antitrust Law, Banking Law, Business Law, Civil Trial Practice, Commercial Law, Employment Benefits Law, General Practice, Health Care Law, Probate and Estate Planning Law, Real Estate Law, Transportation Law
Akron, OH..............................Civil Trial Practice, Commercial Law, General Practice, Labor and Employment Law
Cincinnati, OH........................Antitrust Law, Bankruptcy Law, Business Law, Civil Trial Practice, Commercial Law, Construction Law, Employment Benefits Law, Environmental Law, Family Law, General Practice, Health Care Law, Immigration and Naturalization Law, Insurance Defense Law, Labor and Employment Law, Municipal Bond/Public Authority Financing Law, Probate and Estate Planning Law, Real Estate Law, Tax Law
Cleveland, OH........................Admiralty/Maritime Law, Antitrust Law, Banking Law, Bankruptcy Law, Business Law, Civil Trial Practice, Commercial Law, Construction Law, Criminal Trial Practice, Employment Benefits Law, Environmental Law, General Practice, Health Care Law, Immigration and Naturalization Law, Insurance Defense Law, Labor and Employment Law, Municipal Bond/Public Authority Financing Law, Municipal and Zoning Law, Probate and Estate Planning Law, Real Estate Law, Tax Law, Trademark, Copyright and Unfair Competition Law
Columbus, OH........................Bankruptcy Law, Business Law, Civil Trial Practice, Commercial Law, Construction Law, Employment Benefits Law, Environmental Law, General Practice, Health Care Law, Labor and Employment Law, Municipal Bond/Public Authority Financing Law, Municipal and Zoning Law, Probate and Estate Planning Law, Real Estate Law, Tax Law
Dayton, OH............................Antitrust Law, Banking Law, Bankruptcy Law, Business Law, Civil Trial Practice, Commercial Law, Construction Law, Employment Benefits Law, Environmental Law, General Practice, Health Care Law, Insurance Defense Law, Labor and Employment Law, Municipal Bond/Public Authority Financing Law, Patent, Trademark, Copyright and Unfair Competition Law, Probate and Estate Planning Law, Real Estate Law, Tax Law, Trademark, Copyright and Unfair Competition Law

Brussels, Belgium ....General Practice

THOMPSON, HUBBARD & OMETER, A LAW CORPORATION
Monterey, CA ....General Practice

THOMPSON AND HUTSON
Washington, DC........................Labor and Employment Law
Greenville, SC..........................Labor and Employment Law

THOMPSON & KNIGHT, A PROFESSIONAL CORPORATION
Austin, TX ....Business Law, Civil Trial Practice, Environmental Law, General Practice, Health Care Law, Insurance Defense Law, International Business Law, Medical Malpractice Law, Municipal and Zoning Law, Securities Law, Trademark, Copyright and Unfair Competition Law
Dallas, TX...............................Antitrust Law, Banking Law, Bankruptcy Law, Business Law, Civil Trial Practice, Construction Law, Employment Benefits Law, Environmental Law, General Practice, Health Care Law, Insurance Defense Law, International Business Law, Labor and Employment Law, Medical Malpractice Law, Municipal and Zoning Law, Natural Resources Law, Patent, Trademark, Copyright and Unfair Competition Law, Probate and Estate Planning Law, Real Estate Law, Securities Law, Tax Law, Trademark, Copyright and Unfair Competition Law
Fort Worth, TX ....Business Law, Civil Trial Practice, General Practice, Health Care Law, Insurance Defense Law, International Business Law, Medical Malpractice Law, Probate and Estate Planning Law, Real Estate Law, Securities Law, Tax Law
Houston, TX ....Business Law, Civil Trial Practice, General Practice, Health Care Law, Insurance Defense Law, Medical Malpractice Law, Natural Resources Law, Securities Law
Monterrey, Nuevo León, Mexico ....Business Law, General Practice, International Business Law, Securities Law

THOMPSON, MARK E., A PROFESSIONAL CORPORATION
Lancaster, CA ....Probate and Estate Planning Law

THOMPSON, MICHAEL, AND ASSOCIATES, L.L.P.
Denison, TX.............................Civil Trial Practice, Family Law

THOMPSON & MITCHELL
Washington, DC........................General Practice
Belleville, IL ....Civil Trial Practice, General Practice, Labor and Employment Law, Tax Law
St. Charles, MO ....General Practice
St. Louis, MO...........................Admiralty/Maritime Law, Antitrust Law, Civil Trial Practice, Environmental Law, General Practice, Labor and Employment Law, Municipal Bond/Public Authority Financing Law, Probate and Estate Planning Law, Tax Law

THOMPSON, PARSONS & O'NEIL
Traverse City, MI.....................Civil Trial Practice, Medical Malpractice Law, Personal Injury Law, Product Liability Law

THOMPSON & SLAGLE, P.C.
Norcross, GA ....Commercial Law, General Practice

THOMPSON, SMITHERS, NEWMAN & WADE
Richmond, VA ....Civil Trial Practice, Insurance Defense Law, Probate and Estate Planning Law, Real Estate Law

THOMPSON & THOMPSON
Centreville, MD........................General Practice

THOMS, DAVID M., & ASSOCIATES, P.C.
Detroit, MI...............................Business Law, Probate and Estate Planning Law, Tax Law

THOMSON, DOUGLAS W., LTD.
St. Paul, MN ....Criminal Trial Practice

THOMSON MURARO RAZOOK & HART, P.A.
Miami, FL ....Communications Law, General Practice, Natural Resources Law, Tax Law

THOMSON & NELSON, A PROFESSIONAL LAW CORPORATION
Whittier, CA.............................General Practice

THOMSON, RHODES & COWIE, P.C.
Pittsburgh, PA ....Civil Trial Practice, General Practice, Real Estate Law

THOMSON, ROGERS
Toronto, ON, Canada...............General Practice

THORBURN, SAKOL & THRONE
Boulder, CO ....Family Law

THORN AND GERSHON
Albany, NY ....Civil Trial Practice, Environmental Law, Insurance Defense Law, Personal Injury Law

THORNDAL, BACKUS, ARMSTRONG & BALKENBUSH, A PROFESSIONAL CORPORATION
Las Vegas, NV ....Civil Trial Practice

THORNE, GRODNIK, RANSEL, DUNCAN, BYRON & HOSTETLER
Elkhart, IN...............................Bankruptcy Law, Civil Trial Practice, Family Law, General Practice, Insurance Defense Law, Personal Injury Law, Probate and Estate Planning Law, Real Estate Law

THORNTON, DAVIS & MURRAY, P.A.
Miami, FL.................................Civil Trial Practice, General Practice

THORNTON, HEGG, REIF, JOHNSTON & DOLAN
Alexandria, MN........................General Practice

THORNTON, PAYNE, WATSON & KLING, P.C.
Bryan, TX.................................General Practice

THORNTON, ROTHMAN & EMAS, P.A.
Miami, FL.................................Criminal Trial Practice

THORNTON, TAYLOR, DOWNS, BECKER, TOLSON & DOHERTY
San Francisco, CA ....Insurance Defense Law

THORNTON, THORNTON & THOMSEN
Westerly, RI ....Probate and Estate Planning Law, Tax Law

THORP, REED & ARMSTRONG
Pittsburgh, PA ....Antitrust Law, Bankruptcy Law, Civil Trial Practice, Commercial Law, Construction Law, Criminal Trial Practice, Employment Benefits Law, Environmental Law, General Practice, Health Care Law, Insurance Defense Law, Labor and Employment Law, Municipal Bond/Public Authority Financing Law, Municipal and Zoning Law, Probate and Estate Planning Law, Product Liability Law, Real Estate Law, Securities Law, Tax Law

THORPE, LAWRENCE W. LAW OFFICES OF
San Francisco, CA ....Family Law

THORSNES, BARTOLOTTA, MCGUIRE & PADILLA
San Diego, CA ....Civil Trial Practice, General Practice

THORSTEINSSONS
Vancouver, BC, Canada...........Tax Law
Toronto, ON, Canada...............Tax Law

THRASHER, DOYLE, PELISH & FRANTI, LTD.
Rice Lake, WI ....Insurance Defense Law

THRASHER, WHITLEY, HAMPTON & MORGAN, A PROFESSIONAL CORPORATION
Atlanta, GA ....Business Law, Securities Law

THRELKELD & THRELKELD, P.S.C.
Williamstown, KY ....Real Estate Law

THROCKMORTON, BECKSTROM, OAKES & TOMASSIAN
Pasadena, CA ....Civil Trial Practice, General Practice

THUILLEZ, FORD, GOLD & CONOLLY
Albany, NY..............................Civil Trial Practice, General Practice

THURMAN, HOWALD, WEBER, BOWLES & SENKEL
Hillsboro, MO..........................Civil Trial Practice, General Practice

TIERNEY, ZULLO, FLAHERTY & MURPHY, P.C.
Norwalk, CT ....General Practice

TILCHIN, HALL & DIEDRICH, P.C.
Farmington Hills, MI ....Real Estate Law

TILFORD, DOBBINS, ALEXANDER & BUCKAWAY
Louisville, KY ....General Practice, Insurance Defense Law

TILLMAN, MCTIER, COLEMAN, TALLEY, NEWBERN & KURRIE
Valdosta, GA ....Civil Trial Practice, General Practice

TIMBERLAKE, SMITH, THOMAS & MOSES, P.C.
Staunton, VA ....General Practice

TIMMIS & INMAN
Detroit, MI...............................Antitrust Law, Appellate Practice, Business Law, Civil Trial Practice, Environmental Law, General Practice, Health Care Law, Insurance Defense Law, Labor and Employment Law, Probate and Estate Planning Law, Real Estate Law, Tax Law

TINDALL & FOSTER, P.C.
Houston, TX.............................Immigration and Naturalization Law

TINGLE, MURVIN, WATSON & BATES, P.C.
Birmingham, AL ....General Practice

TINLEY, NASTRI & RENEHAN
Waterbury, CT ....Civil Trial Practice, Commercial Law, Personal Injury Law

TINSMAN & HOUSER, INC.
San Antonio, TX....................Civil Trial Practice, Commercial Law, Medical Malpractice Law, Personal Injury Law, Product Liability Law

TIPPING, HARRY A., CO., A LEGAL PROF. ASSN.
Akron, OH....................Insurance Defense Law, Labor and Employment Law

TIROLA & HERRING
Westport, CT....................Banking Law, Commercial Law, Family Law, General Practice, Probate and Estate Planning Law, Real Estate Law

TISINGER, TISINGER, VANCE & GREER, A PROFESSIONAL CORPORATION
Carrollton, GA....................Business Law, Commercial Law, General Practice, Health Care Law, Insurance Defense Law, Medical Malpractice Law, Public Utilities Law, Real Estate Law

TOBIN AND DEMPF
Albany, NY....................General Practice, Health Care Law, Labor and Employment Law

TOCHER & BOECKMAN
Redding, CA....................Personal Injury Law

TODD, VANDERBLOEMEN, RESPESS AND BRADY, P.A.
Lenoir, NC....................General Practice

TOGUT, SEGAL & SEGAL
New York, NY....................Bankruptcy Law

TOKYO AOYAMA LAW OFFICE
Tokyo, Japan....................General Practice

TOLES & ASSOCIATES, P.C.
Phoenix, AZ....................Criminal Trial Practice, Personal Injury Law

TOLLEY, VANDENBOSCH & WALTON, P.C.
Grand Rapids, MI....................Civil Trial Practice, Insurance Defense Law, Real Estate Law, Securities Law

TOLMAN • KIRK
Poulsbo, WA....................Civil Trial Practice, Personal Injury Law, Probate and Estate Planning Law

TOMAR, SIMONOFF, ADOURIAN & O'BRIEN, A PROFESSIONAL CORPORATION
Haddonfield, NJ....................Labor and Employment Law, Natural Resources Law
Northfield, NJ....................Environmental Law, Labor and Employment Law

TOMAZIN, THOMAS J., P.C.
Englewood, CO....................Civil Trial Practice, Medical Malpractice Law, Personal Injury Law

TOMB & HERING
Tiffin, OH....................General Practice

TOMICH, LILLIAN LAW OFFICES OF
San Marino, CA....................Civil Trial Practice

TOMPKINS, MCGUIRE & WACHENFELD
Newark, NJ....................Banking Law, Civil Trial Practice, Criminal Trial Practice, General Practice, Insurance Defense Law

TOMPKINS AND MCMASTER
Columbia, SC....................Business Law, Civil Trial Practice, Criminal Trial Practice, General Practice

TOOMS & HOUSE
London, KY....................Civil Trial Practice, General Practice, Insurance Defense Law

TORKILDSON, KATZ, JOSSEM, FONSECA, JAFFE, MOORE & HETHERINGTON, ATTORNEYS AT LAW, A LAW CORPORATION
Honolulu, HI....................General Practice, Labor and Employment Law

TORY TORY DESLAURIERS & BINNINGTON
Toronto, ON, Canada....................General Practice
London, England....................General Practice

TOUSLEY BRAIN
Seattle, WA....................Civil Trial Practice, Construction Law, General Practice, Real Estate Law

TOWNLEY & UPDIKE
New York, NY....................Civil Trial Practice, General Practice

TOWNSEND, COURTLAND K., JR., CHARTERED
Ocean City, MD....................Civil Trial Practice, Criminal Trial Practice

TOWNSEND, HOVDE & MONTROSS
Indianapolis, IN....................Civil Trial Practice, Medical Malpractice Law, Personal Injury Law, Product Liability Law

TOWNSEND & TOWNSEND
Indianapolis, IN....................Medical Malpractice Law, Personal Injury Law

TOWNSEND AND TOWNSEND KHOURIE AND CREW
Palo Alto, CA....................Patent, Trademark, Copyright and Unfair Competition Law
San Francisco, CA....................Patent, Trademark, Copyright and Unfair Competition Law

TRABUE, STURDIVANT & DEWITT
Columbia, TN....................General Practice
Nashville, TN....................General Practice

TRACY & MCQUILLAN, THE LEGAL PROF. CORP. OF
Grand Island, NE....................General Practice, Probate and Estate Planning Law, Tax Law

TRAGER, SUSAN M., A PROFESSIONAL CORPORATION, LAW OFFICES OF
Irvine, CA....................Environmental Law, Natural Resources Law

TRAGOS, GEORGE E.
Clearwater, FL....................Criminal Trial Practice

TRALINS AND ASSOCIATES, P.A.
Miami, FL....................General Practice

TRASK, BRITT & ROSSA, A PROFESSIONAL CORPORATION
Salt Lake City, UT....................Patent, Trademark, Copyright and Unfair Competition Law

TRAUB, BONACQUIST & FOX
New York, NY....................Bankruptcy Law, Business Law

TRAVIS & GOOCH
Washington, DC....................Public Utilities Law

TRAYNOR, RUTTEN & TRAYNOR
Devils Lake, ND....................General Practice

TREECE, ALFREY & MUSAT, P.C.
Denver, CO....................Civil Trial Practice, Environmental Law, Medical Malpractice Law

TREMAYNE, LAY, CARR & BAUER
Clayton, MO....................General Practice

TREMBLAY, MAURILE C., A PROF. CORP., LAW OFFICES OF
La Jolla, CA....................Civil Trial Practice, Insurance Defense Law, Real Estate Law

TREMBLAY & SMITH
Charlottesville, VA....................Civil Trial Practice, General Practice

TRENAM, KEMKER, SCHARF, BARKIN, FRYE, O'NEILL & MULLIS, PROFESSIONAL ASSOCIATION
Tampa, FL....................General Practice

TRENCH, ROSSI E WATANABE
São Paulo, Brazil....................General Practice

TRENTA, THOMAS J., P.C., LAW OFFICES OF
Bloomfield Hills, MI....................Civil Trial Practice, Commercial Law, Family Law, Insurance Defense Law, Medical Malpractice Law

TRENTI LAW FIRM
Virginia, MN....................General Practice

TREPEL & CLARK
San Jose, CA....................Civil Trial Practice

TREXLER, BUSHNELL, GIANGIORGI & BLACKSTONE, LTD.
Chicago, IL....................Patent, Trademark, Copyright and Unfair Competition Law

TRIBLER & ORPETT, A PROFESSIONAL CORPORATION
Chicago, IL....................Civil Trial Practice, Insurance Defense Law

TRINKLE, REDMAN, SWANSON & BYRD, P.A.
Plant City, FL....................General Practice

TRIPLETT, WOOLF & GARRETSON
Wichita, KS....................General Practice

TRIPP, MINOT WELD JR.
San Francisco, CA....................Tax Law

TRIPPET AND KEE
Beaver, OK....................General Practice

TROFF, PETZKE & AMMESON
St. Joseph, MI....................Labor and Employment Law, Probate and Estate Planning Law, Real Estate Law

TROMBADORE, RAYMOND R. AND ANN W., A PROFESSIONAL CORPORATION
Somerville, NJ....................Civil Trial Practice, Commercial Law, Criminal Trial Practice, General Practice, Real Estate Law

TROPE AND TROPE
Los Angeles, CA....................Family Law

TROTH, VAN TILBURG & HALLIGAN
Ashland, OH....................General Practice

TROTTER, JAMES R.
Raleigh, NC....General Practice

TROUTMAN, WILLIAMS, IRVIN, GREEN & HELMS, PROFESSIONAL ASSOCIATION
Kissimmee, FL....Civil Trial Practice, General Practice
Winter Park, FL....Civil Trial Practice, General Practice

TROUTT, NAT G.
Senatobia, MS....Civil Trial Practice

TRUMAN, CRAIG L., P.C.
Denver, CO....Criminal Trial Practice

TRZUSKOWSKI, KIPP, KELLEHER & PEARCE, P.A.
Wilmington, DE....Civil Trial Practice, Family Law, General Practice, Insurance Defense Law, Personal Injury Law

TSCHIDER & SMITH
Bismarck, ND....Civil Trial Practice, Probate and Estate Planning Law, Tax Law

TSOUTSOURIS, JAMES V. LAW OFFICES OF
Valparaiso, IN....Civil Trial Practice, Criminal Trial Practice, General Practice, Personal Injury Law

TUCKER, STEVEN L.
Santa Fe, NM....Appellate Practice

TUCKER ARENSBERG, P.C.
Harrisburg, PA....General Practice
Pittsburgh, PA....Banking Law, Civil Trial Practice, General Practice, Labor and Employment Law, Probate and Estate Planning Law

TUCKER, JETER, JACKSON AND HICKMAN, L.L.P.
Shreveport, LA....Environmental Law, General Practice

TUCKER AND TUCKER
Paoli, IN....General Practice

TUGGLE DUGGINS & MESCHAN, P.A.
Greensboro, NC....General Practice, Tax Law

TULAC, JOHN W.
Diamond Bar, CA....International Business Law

TURK, A. MARCO, LAW CORP.
Santa Monica, CA....Appellate Practice

TURK, PAUL A., JR., P.A.
West Palm Beach, FL....Civil Trial Practice

TURLEY, WINDLE, P.C., LAW OFFICES OF
Dallas, TX....Personal Injury Law

TURNBULL, WASE & LYONS, P.A.
Towson, MD....Family Law

TURNER, BRUCE E.
Dallas, TX....Real Estate Law

TURNER, CHARLES B.
South Orange, NJ....Commercial Law

TURNER, PAUL K. LAW OFFICE OF
Hopkinsville, KY....General Practice

TURNER, RICHARD K.
Sacramento, CA....Administrative Law, Health Care Law

TURNER, GERSTENFELD, WILK, TIGERMAN & YOUNG
Beverly Hills, CA....Civil Trial Practice, General Practice, Probate and Estate Planning Law, Real Estate Law

TURNER, GRANZOW & HOLLENKAMP
Dayton, OH....General Practice

TURNER, JONES & BITTING
Clarinda, IA....General Practice

TURNER & MCDONALD, P.C.
Philadelphia, PA....Civil Trial Practice, Commercial Law, Criminal Trial Practice

TURNER, ONDERDONK, KIMBROUGH & HOWELL, P.A.
Chatom, AL....Civil Trial Practice, Criminal Trial Practice

TURNER, PADGET, GRAHAM & LANEY, P.A.
Columbia, SC....Civil Trial Practice, General Practice, Insurance Defense Law, Personal Injury Law

TURNER, REID, DUNCAN, LOOMER & PATTON, P.C.
Springfield, MO....Civil Trial Practice

TURNER, SEABERRY & WARFORD
Eastland, TX....General Practice

TURNER, STOEVE, GAGLIARDI & GOSS, P.S.
Spokane, WA....General Practice

TURNER, TURNER & TURNER, P.C.
Atlanta, GA....Family Law

TUTTLE, ROGER L.
Midlothian, VA....Medical Malpractice Law

TUTTLE & TAYLOR, A LAW CORPORATION
Los Angeles, CA....General Practice
Sacramento, CA....General Practice

TUTTLE, TAYLOR & HERON
Washington, DC....General Practice

TWITCHELL AND RICE
Santa Maria, CA....General Practice

TWOMEY, LATHAM, SHEA & KELLEY
Riverhead, NY....Environmental Law

TYACK, BLACKMORE & LISTON CO., L.P.A.
Columbus, OH....Criminal Trial Practice, Family Law, Personal Injury Law

TYAN & ASSOCIES
Beirut, Lebanon....General Practice

TYBOUT, REDFEARN & PELL
Wilmington, DE....Appellate Practice, Civil Trial Practice, Insurance Defense Law, Medical Malpractice Law, Personal Injury Law, Product Liability Law

TYDINGS, BRYAN & ADAMS, P.C.
Fairfax, VA....Banking Law, General Practice

TYDINGS & ROSENBERG
Baltimore, MD....General Practice

TYE & TYE
Dayton, OH....General Practice, Probate and Estate Planning Law

TYGART AND SCHULER, P.A.
Jacksonville, FL....Insurance Defense Law, Personal Injury Law

TYLER COOPER & ALCORN
Hartford, CT....General Practice
New Haven, CT....General Practice
Stamford, CT....General Practice

TYNDALL & CAHNERS
San Jose, CA....Criminal Trial Practice, Environmental Law, Medical Malpractice Law

ULMER & BERNE
Cleveland, OH....Business Law, Civil Trial Practice, General Practice, Tax Law

ULRICH, THOMPSON & KESSLER, P.C.
Phoenix, AZ....Antitrust Law, Civil Trial Practice, Health Care Law

ULRICH AND ULRICH, A PROFESSIONAL CORPORATION
Houston, TX....Civil Trial Practice

UNDERBERG & KESSLER
Rochester, NY....Civil Trial Practice, Environmental Law, General Practice, Insurance Defense Law

UNDERWOOD, P. JAMES
Annapolis, MD....General Practice, Real Estate Law

UNDERWOOD, CAMPBELL, BROCK & CERUTTI, P.S.
Spokane, WA....General Practice

UNDERWOOD KINSEY WARREN & TUCKER, P.A.
Charlotte, NC....General Practice

UNDERWOOD, WILSON, BERRY, STEIN & JOHNSON, P.C.
Amarillo, TX....General Practice

UNGERMAN & IOLA
Tulsa, OK....Family Law, Labor and Employment Law, Personal Injury Law

UPCHURCH, BAILEY & UPCHURCH, P.A.
St. Augustine, FL....General Practice

UPSHAW, WILLIAMS, BIGGERS, PAGE & KRUGER
Greenwood, MS....Civil Trial Practice, Environmental Law, General Practice, Insurance Defense Law
Jackson, MS....Civil Trial Practice, General Practice, Insurance Defense Law

URSO, LIGUORI AND URSO
Westerly, RI....General Practice, Labor and Employment Law, Probate and Estate Planning Law, Real Estate Law

USSERY & PARRISH, P.A.
Albuquerque, NM....General Practice

UTZ, LITVAK, SUMMERS, POWERS & MANRING
St. Joseph, MO........................General Practice

VAALER, WARCUP, WOUTAT, ZIMNEY & FOSTER, CHARTERED
Grand Forks, ND...................General Practice

VADEN, EICKENROHT, THOMPSON, BOULWARE & FEATHER, L.L.P.
Houston, TX...........................Patent, Trademark, Copyright and Unfair Competition Law

VAFIADES, BROUNTAS & KOMINSKY
Bangor, ME............................Civil Trial Practice, Criminal Trial Practice, General Practice, Insurance Defense Law, Personal Injury Law, Real Estate Law

VAGLICA & CARLSON
Colorado Springs, CO.............Civil Trial Practice

VAIRO, MECHLIN, TOMASI, JOHNSON & MANCHESTER
Houghton, MI.........................General Practice, Insurance Defense Law

VALENTINE, JOHN C.
Logan, WV..............................General Practice

VALENTINE, ADAMS, LAMAR, ETHERIDGE, SYKES & BRITT, L.L.P.
Nashville, NC.........................General Practice

VALENTINE, STEPHEN K., JR., P.C.
Troy, MI..................................Civil Trial Practice, Labor and Employment Law, Personal Injury Law
West Bloomfield, MI...............Business Law, Civil Trial Practice, Labor and Employment Law, Personal Injury Law, Real Estate Law

VALORE LAW FIRM, P.C.
Atlantic City, NJ.....................General Practice

VANANTWERP, MONGE, JONES & EDWARDS
Ashland, KY...........................Banking Law, Environmental Law, General Practice, Labor and Employment Law, Probate and Estate Planning Law, Real Estate Law

VAN BERKOM, ELLA LAW OFFICE
Minot, ND...............................General Practice

VAN BLOIS & KNOWLES
Oakland, CA............................Civil Trial Practice, Medical Malpractice Law, Personal Injury Law

VAN CAMP, WEST, HAYES & MEACHAM, A PROFESSIONAL ASSOCIATION
Pinehurst, NC..........................General Practice

VAN COTT, BAGLEY, CORNWALL & MCCARTHY, A PROFESSIONAL CORPORATION
Ogden, UT................................General Practice
Park City, UT..........................General Practice
Salt Lake City, UT..................Administrative Law, Antitrust Law, Banking Law, Bankruptcy Law, Business Law, Civil Trial Practice, Commercial Law, Communications Law, Construction Law, Criminal Trial Practice, Employment Benefits Law, Environmental Law, General Practice, Health Care Law, Insurance Defense Law, Labor and Employment Law, Medical Malpractice Law, Natural Resources Law, Patent, Trademark, Copyright and Unfair Competition Law, Personal Injury Law, Probate and Estate Planning Law, Public Utilities Law, Real Estate Law, Securities Law, Tax Law

VANDEBERG JOHNSON & GANDARA
Tacoma, WA............................General Practice

VANDEVEER GARZIA, PROFESSIONAL CORPORATION
Detroit, MI..............................Civil Trial Practice, Environmental Law, General Practice, Insurance Defense Law, Municipal and Zoning Law, Personal Injury Law
Grand Rapids, MI...................General Practice
Mount Clemens, MI.................General Practice

VANDEVENTER, BLACK, MEREDITH & MARTIN
Norfolk, VA............................Admiralty/Maritime Law, Bankruptcy Law, Civil Trial Practice, Environmental Law, General Practice, Immigration and Naturalization Law, Labor and Employment Law, Real Estate Law, Tax Law

VAN HOY, REUTLINGER & TAYLOR
Charlotte, NC..........................Health Care Law, Labor and Employment Law

VAN LANDINGHAM, L. S. JR., LAW OFFICES OF
Arlington, VA.........................Patent, Trademark, Copyright and Unfair Competition Law

VAN LOUCKS & HANLEY
San Jose, CA...........................Civil Trial Practice, General Practice, Insurance Defense Law

VAN MEER & BELANGER, P.A.
South Portland, ME.................Health Care Law, Tax Law

VANN, FRANK C.
Camilla, GA............................General Practice

VANNAH COSTELLO HOWARD & CANEPA
Las Vegas, NV........................Insurance Defense Law, Medical Malpractice Law, Personal Injury Law, Product Liability Law

VANNOY, COLVARD, TRIPLETT & MCLEAN
North Wilkesboro, NC...........General Practice

VANNOY & REEVES
West Jefferson, NC.................General Practice

VAN STEENBERG, CHALOUPKA, MULLIN, HOLYOKE, PAHLKE, SMITH, SNYDER & HOFMEISTER, P.C.
Scottsbluff, NE.......................General Practice

VAN VALER WILLIAMS & HEWITT
Greenwood, IN........................Banking Law, Civil Trial Practice, Commercial Law, General Practice, Health Care Law, Labor and Employment Law, Probate and Estate Planning Law, Real Estate Law

VANVOORHIS, EUGENE
Rochester, NY.........................General Practice

VAN WERT, RONALD K., A PROF. CORP.
Newport Beach, CA.................Civil Trial Practice, Tax Law

VAN WINKLE, PETER B., P.C.
Howell, MI..............................Civil Trial Practice, Family Law, General Practice, Probate and Estate Planning Law, Real Estate Law

VARET & FINK P.C.
Washington, DC......................General Practice
New York, NY.........................Civil Trial Practice, General Practice

VARGAS & BARTLETT
Reno, NV.................................Civil Trial Practice, General Practice, Real Estate Law

VARNUM, RIDDERING, SCHMIDT & HOWLETT
Battle Creek, MI.....................Antitrust Law, Civil Trial Practice, General Practice, Labor and Employment Law, Tax Law, Transportation Law
Grand Rapids, MI..................Antitrust Law, Banking Law, Bankruptcy Law, Business Law, Civil Trial Practice, Environmental Law, Family Law, General Practice, Labor and Employment Law, Municipal Bond/Public Authority Financing Law, Patent, Trademark, Copyright and Unfair Competition Law, Probate and Estate Planning Law, Real Estate Law, Tax Law, Trademark, Copyright and Unfair Competition Law
Kalamazoo, MI.......................General Practice

VAROUTSOS, GEORGE D.
Arlington, VA..........................Criminal Trial Practice, Personal Injury Law

VAUGHAN & HULL, LTD., A PROF. CORP., LAW OFFICES
Elko, NV.................................General Practice

VAUGHAN & SLAYTON
South Boston, VA...................General Practice

VEATCH, CARLSON, GROGAN & NELSON
Los Angeles, CA.....................Civil Trial Practice, Health Care Law, Insurance Defense Law, Medical Malpractice Law

VEDDER, PRICE, KAUFMAN & KAMMHOLZ
Chicago, IL..............................Banking Law, General Practice, Labor and Employment Law, Municipal Bond/Public Authority Financing Law, Tax Law

VEDDER, PRICE, KAUFMAN, KAMMHOLZ & DAY
Washington, DC......................General Practice, Labor and Employment Law

VEGA, BROWN, STANLEY, MARTIN & ZELMAN, P.A.
Naples, FL..............................Civil Trial Practice, Criminal Trial Practice, Family Law, General Practice, Municipal and Zoning Law, Real Estate Law, Tax Law

VEIRANO E ADVOGADOS ASSOCIADOS
Rio de Janeiro, Brazil.............General Practice

VELIKANJE, MOORE & SHORE, INC., P.S.
Yakima, WA............................General Practice

VENABLE, BAETJER AND HOWARD
Baltimore, MD........................Administrative Law, Admiralty/Maritime Law, Antitrust Law, Appellate Practice, Banking Law, Bankruptcy Law, Business Law, Civil Trial Practice, Commercial Law, Communications Law, Construction Law, Criminal Trial Practice, Employment Benefits Law, Environmental Law, Family Law, General Practice, Health Care Law, Immigration and Naturalization Law, Insurance Defense Law, Labor and Employment Law, Municipal Bond/Public Authority Financing Law, Municipal and Zoning Law, Natural Resources Law, Patent, Trademark, Copyright and Unfair Competition Law, Personal Injury Law, Probate and Estate Planning Law, Product Liability Law, Real Estate Law, Securities Law, Tax Law, Trademark, Copyright and Unfair Competition Law, Transportation Law

Rockville, MD.........................Administrative Law, Appellate Practice, Banking Law, Business Law, Civil Trial Practice, General Practice, Labor and Employment Law
Towson, MD...........................Appellate Practice, Banking Law, Business Law, Civil Trial Practice, Commercial Law, Construction Law, General Practice, Insurance Defense Law, Labor and Employment Law, Municipal Bond/Public Authority Financing Law, Personal Injury Law, Probate and Estate Planning Law, Product Liability Law, Real Estate Law
McLean, VA............................Appellate Practice, Banking Law, Civil Trial Practice, Commercial Law, Construction Law, General Practice, Real Estate Law

VENABLE, BAETJER, HOWARD & CIVILETTI
Washington, DC.......................Administrative Law, Admiralty/Maritime Law, Antitrust Law, Appellate Practice, Banking Law, Bankruptcy Law, Business Law, Civil Trial Practice, Commercial Law, Communications Law, Construction Law, Criminal Trial Practice, Employment Benefits Law, Environmental Law, General Practice, Health Care Law, Insurance Defense Law, Labor and Employment Law, Natural Resources Law, Patent, Trademark, Copyright and Unfair Competition Law, Product Liability Law, Real Estate Law, Securities Law, Trademark, Copyright and Unfair Competition Law, Transportation Law

VERDERAIME & DU BOIS, P.A.
Baltimore, MD.........................Civil Trial Practice, Personal Injury Law

VERNER, LIIPFERT, BERNHARD, MCPHERSON AND HAND, CHARTERED
Washington, DC.......................Commercial Law, Communications Law, Environmental Law, General Practice, Labor and Employment Law, Natural Resources Law, Tax Law, Transportation Law

VERRILL & DANA
Portland, ME..........................General Practice

VETTER & WHITE, INCORPORATED
Providence, RI.........................Civil Trial Practice

VIAL, HAMILTON, KOCH & KNOX
Dallas, TX..............................General Practice

VICKERS, RIIS, MURRAY AND CURRAN
Mobile, AL..............................Admiralty/Maritime Law, Business Law, Environmental Law, General Practice, Tax Law

VICTOR, RAYMOND M., P.C.
Norristown, PA........................Medical Malpractice Law, Personal Injury Law, Product Liability Law

VIGIL & HANRATH
Barrington, IL.........................Patent, Trademark, Copyright and Unfair Competition Law

VIMONT & WILLS
Lexington, KY.........................Bankruptcy Law, Commercial Law, Construction Law, General Practice, Labor and Employment Law

VINAR, BENJAMIN
Garden City, NY......................Civil Trial Practice

VINCENT, ORESTE
Catskill, NY............................General Practice

VINCENT, CHOREY, TAYLOR & FEIL, A PROFESSIONAL CORPORATION
Atlanta, GA.............................General Practice, Real Estate Law

VINNEDGE, GAFNEY & GLADSON, INC.
Upland, CA..............................Probate and Estate Planning Law

VINSON & ELKINS
London, England......................General Practice
Washington, DC.......................Civil Trial Practice, General Practice
Austin, TX..............................Civil Trial Practice, General Practice
Dallas, TX..............................Civil Trial Practice, General Practice
Houston, TX............................Admiralty/Maritime Law, Antitrust Law, Civil Trial Practice, General Practice, Labor and Employment Law, Municipal Bond/Public Authority Financing Law, Natural Resources Law, Patent, Trademark, Copyright and Unfair Competition Law, Tax Law

VINYARD AND MOISE, ATTORNEYS AT LAW, P.C.
Abingdon, VA..........................Civil Trial Practice, Criminal Trial Practice, Family Law

VITTAL AND STERNBERG
Los Angeles, CA......................Civil Trial Practice

VLADECK, WALDMAN, ELIAS & ENGELHARD, P.C.
New York, NY..........................Employment Benefits Law, Labor and Employment Law

VLASSIS & VLASSIS
Phoenix, AZ............................Business Law

VLASTOS, BROOKS & HENLEY, P.C.
Casper, WY.............................Civil Trial Practice, General Practice

VOGEL, BRANTNER, KELLY, KNUTSON, WEIR & BYE, LTD.
Fargo, ND...............................Banking Law, Bankruptcy Law, Civil Trial Practice, Commercial Law, Criminal Trial Practice, General Practice, Insurance Defense Law, Labor and Employment Law, Personal Injury Law, Probate and Estate Planning Law, Real Estate Law, Tax Law

VOGEL, SOULS & WOODBINE
Providence, RI.........................Insurance Defense Law, Personal Injury Law

VOGL & MEREDITH
San Francisco, CA...................Civil Trial Practice, Environmental Law, Insurance Defense Law, Probate and Estate Planning Law

VOLK & MONTES, P.C.
El Paso, TX.............................Medical Malpractice Law

VOLK, ROBERTSON & HELLERSTEDT
Pittsburgh, PA........................Labor and Employment Law

VOLLMER, MICHAEL V.
Newport Beach, CA..................Probate and Estate Planning Law

VOLLMER RULONG & ASSOCIATES, P.C.
Pittsburgh, PA........................Bankruptcy Law, Civil Trial Practice

VOLPE, EDWARD L., P.C.
Denver, CO.............................Civil Trial Practice

VOORHEES & ACCIAVATTI
Morris Plains, NJ.....................Civil Trial Practice, Commercial Law

VORYS, SATER, SEYMOUR AND PEASE
Washington, DC.......................General Practice
Cincinnati, OH.........................General Practice
Cleveland, OH.........................General Practice, Labor and Employment Law
Columbus, OH.........................Antitrust Law, Banking Law, Bankruptcy Law, General Practice, Labor and Employment Law, Municipal Bond/Public Authority Financing Law, Natural Resources Law, Real Estate Law, Tax Law

VOUTÉ, LOHRFINK, MAGRO & COLLINS
White Plains, NY.....................General Practice, Insurance Defense Law

VRANESH AND RAISCH, L.L.C.
Boulder, CO............................Environmental Law, Natural Resources Law

VUONO, LAVELLE & GRAY
Pittsburgh, PA........................Civil Trial Practice, Real Estate Law, Tax Law, Transportation Law

WACHLER & KOPSON, PROFESSIONAL CORPORATION
Detroit, MI..............................Health Care Law, Municipal and Zoning Law

WACHTEL, BIEHN & MALM
Lake Havasu City, AZ.............General Practice, Personal Injury Law, Probate and Estate Planning Law

WADE ASH WOODS HILL & FARLEY, P.C.
Denver, CO.............................Probate and Estate Planning Law

WADLEIGH, STARR, PETERS, DUNN & CHIESA
Manchester, NH.......................General Practice

WADSWORTH & DAVIS
Tallahassee, FL.......................Civil Trial Practice, Criminal Trial Practice, Personal Injury Law

WAGNER, BAGOT & GLEASON
New Orleans, LA.....................Admiralty/Maritime Law, Commercial Law, Environmental Law, Insurance Defense Law, International Business Law, Labor and Employment Law

WAGNER, FALCONER & JUDD, LTD.
Minneapolis, MN.....................Commercial Law, Construction Law, General Practice

WAGNER AND GRUNDY
Tulsa, OK................................Family Law

WAGNER & JOHNSTON, P.C.
Atlanta, GA.............................Business Law

WAGNER, MYERS & SANGER, A PROFESSIONAL CORPORATION
Knoxville, TN..........................Civil Trial Practice, General Practice, Health Care Law, Natural Resources Law, Public Utilities Law, Securities Law, Tax Law

WAGNER, NUGENT, JOHNSON & MCAFEE, P.A.
West Palm Beach, FL..............Civil Trial Practice, Personal Injury Law

WAGNER, VAUGHAN & MCLAUGHLIN, P.A.
Tampa, FL...............................Admiralty/Maritime Law, Civil Trial Practice, Commercial Law, Personal Injury Law, Product Liability Law

WAGSTAFF, ALVIS, STUBBEMAN, SEAMSTER & LONGACRE, L.L.P.
Abilene, TX.............................General Practice

WAITE, SCHNEIDER, BAYLESS & CHESLEY CO., L.P.A.
Cincinnati, OH .... Admiralty/Maritime Law, Antitrust Law, Appellate Practice, Civil Trial Practice, Construction Law, International Business Law, Labor and Employment Law, Medical Malpractice Law, Personal Injury Law, Product Liability Law, Public Utilities Law, Securities Law

WAKE, SEE, DIMES & BRYNICZKA
Westport, CT .... Business Law, General Practice, Probate and Estate Planning Law, Tax Law

WALDBAUM, CORN, KOFF AND BERGER, P.C.
Denver, CO .... General Practice

WALDER, SONDAK & BROGAN, A PROFESSIONAL CORPORATION
Roseland, NJ .... Appellate Practice, Civil Trial Practice, Criminal Trial Practice, Environmental Law

WALDRON AND FANN
Murfreesboro, TN .... Personal Injury Law

WALINSKI & TRUNKETT, P.C.
Chicago, IL .... Bankruptcy Law, Commercial Law

WALKER, GEORGE R.
Monterey, CA .... Civil Trial Practice

WALKER & BLACK
Little Rock, AR .... Commercial Law, Probate and Estate Planning Law

WALKER & DURHAM
San Francisco, CA .... Personal Injury Law

WALKER, GEORGE G., INC.
San Francisco, CA .... Criminal Trial Practice

WALKER, HILL, ADAMS, UMBACH, MEADOWS & WALTON
Opelika, AL .... General Practice

WALKER, HULBERT, GRAY & BYRD
Perry, GA .... General Practice

WALKER, JONES, LAWRENCE, PAYNE & DUGGAN, P.C.
Warrenton, VA .... General Practice

WALKER LAW FIRM, THE, A PROFESSIONAL CORPORATION
Newport Beach, CA .... Civil Trial Practice

WALKER, MCKENZIE & WALKER, A PROFESSIONAL CORPORATION
Memphis, TN .... Patent, Trademark, Copyright and Unfair Competition Law

WALKER, ROBERT D., A PROFESSIONAL CORPORATION
Los Angeles, CA .... Civil Trial Practice, Medical Malpractice Law, Personal Injury Law

WALKER & WALKER, P.C.
Knoxville, TN .... Banking Law, Bankruptcy Law, General Practice

WALKER, WATTS, JACKSON & MCFARLAND
Adrian, MI .... Banking Law, General Practice, Real Estate Law

WALKER & WILLIAMS, PROFESSIONAL CORPORATION
Belleville, IL .... General Practice
Edwardsville, IL .... General Practice

WALKUP, MELODIA, KELLY & ECHEVERRIA, A PROFESSIONAL CORPORATION
San Francisco, CA .... Medical Malpractice Law, Personal Injury Law, Product Liability Law

WALLACE, CREECH, SARDA & ZAYTOUN, L.L.P.
Raleigh, NC .... Personal Injury Law

WALLACE & DE MAYO, P.C.
Atlanta, GA .... Bankruptcy Law, Commercial Law

WALLACE, ENGELS, PERTNOY, SOLOWSKY & ALLEN, P.A.
Miami, FL .... Civil Trial Practice

WALLACE, MORRIS, BARWICK & ROCHELLE, P.A.
Kinston, NC .... General Practice

WALLACE, OWENS, LANDERS, GEE, MORROW, WILSON, WATSON & JAMES, A PROFESSIONAL CORPORATION
Miami, OK .... General Practice

WALLACE, SAUNDERS, AUSTIN, BROWN & ENOCHS, CHARTERED
Overland Park, KS .... General Practice

WALLAHAN, BANKS & EICHER, P.C.
Rapid City, SD .... Civil Trial Practice, General Practice

WALLECK, SHANE, STANARD & BLENDER
Woodland Hills, CA .... Business Law, Civil Trial Practice, Communications Law, Probate and Estate Planning Law, Real Estate Law, Tax Law

WALLER LANSDEN DORTCH & DAVIS
Columbia, TN .... General Practice
Nashville, TN .... General Practice

WALLER AND MARK, P.C.
Denver, CO .... Civil Trial Practice

WALLER, SMITH & PALMER, P.C.
New London, CT .... Banking Law, Civil Trial Practice, Commercial Law, General Practice, Municipal and Zoning Law, Probate and Estate Planning Law, Real Estate Law
Old Lyme, CT .... General Practice

WALLERSTEIN, MELVIN J., P.A.
West Orange, NJ .... Probate and Estate Planning Law, Tax Law

WALL, WALL & FRAUENHOFER
Torrington, CT .... General Practice

WALMSLEY AND BLANKENSHIP
Batesville, AR .... General Practice

WALSH, ANDERSON, UNDERWOOD, SCHULZE & ALDRIDGE, P.C.
Austin, TX .... Civil Trial Practice, Insurance Defense Law

WALSH, COLUCCI, STACKHOUSE, EMRICH & LUBELEY, P.C.
Arlington, VA .... Civil Trial Practice, Real Estate Law
Leesburg, VA .... Real Estate Law
Woodbridge, VA .... Real Estate Law

WALSH & FISHER, A PROFESSIONAL ASSOCIATION
Westminster, MD .... General Practice

WALSTON, STABLER, WELLS, ANDERSON & BAINS
Birmingham, AL .... General Practice

WALSWORTH, FRANKLIN & BEVINS
Orange, CA .... Bankruptcy Law, Business Law, Civil Trial Practice, Construction Law, Environmental Law, Insurance Defense Law, Natural Resources Law, Real Estate Law

WALTA, J. GREGORY, P.C.
Colorado Springs, CO .... Civil Trial Practice, Personal Injury Law

WALTER, CONSTON, ALEXANDER & GREEN, P.C.
New York, NY .... General Practice

WALTER & HAVERFIELD
Cleveland, OH .... Communications Law, Employment Benefits Law, Environmental Law, General Practice, Labor and Employment Law, Municipal and Zoning Law

WALTERS, DAVIS, MEEKS & PUJADAS, P.C.
Ocilla, GA .... Civil Trial Practice, Criminal Trial Practice, General Practice

WALTERS, JAMES A., P.C.
Dallas, TX .... General Practice

WALTERS & JOYCE, P.C.
Denver, CO .... Antitrust Law, Civil Trial Practice, General Practice

WALTERS & WARD, A PROFESSIONAL CORPORATION
San Diego, CA .... Probate and Estate Planning Law

WALTHER ASSOCIATES
Santa Fe, NM .... Family Law

WALTHOUR AND GARLAND
Greensburg, PA .... Appellate Practice, Civil Trial Practice, General Practice, Probate and Estate Planning Law

WALTON LANTAFF SCHROEDER & CARSON
Coral Gables, FL .... General Practice
Fort Lauderdale, FL .... General Practice
Miami, FL .... General Practice
West Palm Beach, FL .... General Practice

WALTON, SMITH, PHILLIPS & DIXON, P.C.
Traverse City, MI .... Civil Trial Practice, Personal Injury Law

WALZ & WARBA, P.C.
Big Rapids, MI .... Civil Trial Practice, Personal Injury Law
Traverse City, MI .... Civil Trial Practice, Personal Injury Law

WALZER & WALZER, A LAW CORPORATION
Los Angeles, CA .... Family Law

WANDERER, HANNA & TALARICO
Danbury, CT .... General Practice

WARBURTON, ADAMI, MCNEILL, PAISLEY & MCGUIRE, P.C.
Alice, TX .... General Practice

WARD, CRAIG B., P.A.
Orlando, FL .... General Practice, Probate and Estate Planning Law, Real Estate Law

WARD LAW FIRM, THE, P.A.
Spartanburg, SC .... General Practice

WARD, MAGUIRE & BYBEE
Pocatello, ID .... General Practice

WARD, WARD, WILLEY AND WARD
New Bern, NC .... Civil Trial Practice, General Practice

WARE, DAVID A. M. & ASSOCIATES
Metairie, LA .... Immigration and Naturalization Law

WARE, BRYSON, WEST & KUMMER
Covington, KY .... Civil Trial Practice, General Practice, Insurance Defense Law

WARHOLA, O'TOOLE, LOUGHMAN, ALDERMAN & STUMPHAUZER
Lorain, OH .... General Practice

WARING COX
Memphis, TN .... Civil Trial Practice, General Practice, Insurance Defense Law, Labor and Employment Law, Municipal Bond/Public Authority Financing Law, Real Estate Law, Tax Law

WARLICK MILSTED DOTSON & CARTER
Jacksonville, NC .... General Practice

WARLICK, TRITT & STEBBINS
Augusta, GA .... Banking Law, Civil Trial Practice, Commercial Law, General Practice, Probate and Estate Planning Law, Tax Law

WARNER, CHARLES G. LAW OFFICES OF
Monterey, CA .... Civil Trial Practice

WARNER, MAYOUE & BATES, P.C.
Atlanta, GA .... Family Law

WARNER, NORCROSS & JUDD
Grand Rapids, MI .... Antitrust Law, Banking Law, Bankruptcy Law, Civil Trial Practice, Employment Benefits Law, Environmental Law, General Practice, Health Care Law, Immigration and Naturalization Law, Labor and Employment Law, Natural Resources Law, Patent, Trademark, Copyright and Unfair Competition Law, Real Estate Law, Securities Law, Tax Law, Transportation Law
Holland, MI .... General Practice
Muskegon, MI .... General Practice

WARNER AND SMITH
Fort Smith, AR .... Civil Trial Practice, General Practice

WARNER & STACKPOLE
Boston, MA .... Banking Law, Civil Trial Practice, Environmental Law, General Practice, Insurance Defense Law, Labor and Employment Law, Municipal Bond/Public Authority Financing Law, Probate and Estate Planning Law, Product Liability Law, Real Estate Law, Tax Law

WARNOCK & WARNOCK
Greenup, KY .... General Practice

WARREN & SCHEID, P.C.
Narrows, VA .... General Practice

WARREN & SINKLER
Charleston, SC .... General Practice, Real Estate Law

WARREN AND YOUNG
Ashtabula, OH .... Business Law, General Practice, Insurance Defense Law, Labor and Employment Law

WARSHAFSKY, ROTTER, TARNOFF, REINHARDT & BLOCH, S.C.
Milwaukee, WI .... Personal Injury Law

WASH, MICHAEL A. LAW OFFICES OF
Austin, TX .... Personal Injury Law

WASKER, DORR, WIMMER & MARCOUILLER, P.C.
Des Moines, IA .... Administrative Law, Civil Trial Practice, General Practice, Personal Injury Law, Real Estate Law

WASSERMAN, COMDEN & CASSELMAN
Tarzana, CA .... Civil Trial Practice, General Practice, Insurance Defense Law

WASSERSTROM, DAVID E.
Elkins Park, PA .... Business Law

WATANABE, ING & KAWASHIMA
Honolulu, HI .... Civil Trial Practice, General Practice

WATERFALL, ECONOMIDIS, CALDWELL, HANSHAW & VILLAMANA, P.C.
Tucson, AZ .... Family Law, General Practice, Real Estate Law

WATERS, HOLT & FIELDS
Pampa, TX .... General Practice

WATERS, MCPHERSON, MCNEILL, P.C.
Secaucus, NJ .... Civil Trial Practice, General Practice

WATERS, WARNER & HARRIS
Clarksburg, WV .... Civil Trial Practice, General Practice, Insurance Defense Law, Natural Resources Law, Real Estate Law

WATKINS, JOHN E. JR.
White Plains, NY .... Municipal and Zoning Law

WATKINS, BATES & CAREY
Toledo, OH .... Civil Trial Practice, Commercial Law, General Practice, Health Care Law, Probate and Estate Planning Law, Real Estate Law, Tax Law

WATKINS, BOULWARE, LUCAS, MINER, MURPHY & TAYLOR
St. Joseph, MO .... General Practice

WATKINS & EAGER
Jackson, MS .... Banking Law, Bankruptcy Law, Civil Trial Practice, Commercial Law, Environmental Law, General Practice, Insurance Defense Law, Labor and Employment Law, Natural Resources Law, Personal Injury Law, Tax Law

WATKINS, VANDIVER, KIRVEN, GABLE & GRAY
Anderson, SC .... General Practice

WATKINSON LAIRD RUBENSTEIN LASHWAY & BALDWIN, P.C.
Eugene, OR .... General Practice

WATKISS DUNNING & WATKISS, A PROFESSIONAL CORPORATION
Salt Lake City, UT .... Antitrust Law, Civil Trial Practice, Construction Law, Employment Benefits Law

WATSON, TIMOTHY F. SR.
Newport, AR .... General Practice

WATSON, WILLIAM E. & ASSOCIATES
Wellsburg, WV .... General Practice

WATSON, BLANCHE, WILSON & POSNER
Baton Rouge, LA .... General Practice, Health Care Law, Medical Malpractice Law, Product Liability Law, Tax Law

WATSON & DANA
La Fayette, GA .... General Practice

WATSON, DAVID S., CHARTERED
Sarasota, FL .... Commercial Law, General Practice, Probate and Estate Planning Law

WATSON, FARLEY & WILLIAMS
New York, NY .... Admiralty/Maritime Law, Banking Law, General Practice, Transportation Law

WATSON, GAMMONS & FEES, P.C.
Huntsville, AL .... Appellate Practice, Civil Trial Practice, General Practice, Personal Injury Law, Product Liability Law, Real Estate Law

WATSON, HOLLOW & REEVES
Knoxville, TN .... Civil Trial Practice, Communications Law, Insurance Defense Law, Labor and Employment Law, Medical Malpractice Law, Product Liability Law

WATT & SAWYIER
Chicago, IL .... Banking Law, Civil Trial Practice, Municipal Bond/Public Authority Financing Law, Real Estate Law

WATT, TIEDER & HOFFAR
Irvine, CA .... Civil Trial Practice, Commercial Law, Construction Law, Environmental Law, General Practice, International Business Law, Real Estate Law
Washington, DC .... Civil Trial Practice, Commercial Law, Construction Law, Environmental Law, General Practice, International Business Law, Real Estate Law
McLean, VA .... Civil Trial Practice, Commercial Law, Construction Law, Environmental Law, General Practice, International Business Law, Real Estate Law

WEARY, DAVIS, HENRY, STRUEBING & TROUP
Junction City, KS .... General Practice

WEATHERLY, CHARLES L.
Atlanta, GA .... Administrative Law, Civil Trial Practice

WEAVER, MOSEBACH, PIOSA, HIXSON & MARLES
Allentown, PA .... General Practice, Municipal and Zoning Law

WEAVER & WEAVER, P.A.
Fort Lauderdale, FL .... Admiralty/Maritime Law, Civil Trial Practice, Personal Injury Law

WEBB, BURNETT, JACKSON, CORNBROOKS, WILBER, VORHIS & DOUSE
Salisbury, MD .... General Practice

WEBB, CARLOCK, COPELAND, SEMLER & STAIR
Atlanta, GA .... Civil Trial Practice, Insurance Defense Law

WEBB, SANDERS, DEATON, BALDUCCI & SMITH
Tupelo, MS .... Business Law, Civil Trial Practice, General Practice, Insurance Defense Law

WEBB, STOKES & SPARKS
San Angelo, TX .... Personal Injury Law

WEBB, TANNER & POWELL
Lawrenceville, GA .... Banking Law, Business Law, General Practice

WEBB ZIESENHEIM BRUENING LOGSDON ORKIN & HANSON, P.C.
Pittsburgh, PA .... Patent, Trademark, Copyright and Unfair Competition Law

WEBBER, CHRISTOPHER A. JR.
Rutland, VT .... Probate and Estate Planning Law

WEBBER, JOSEPH P. LAW OFFICES OF
Austin, TX .... Civil Trial Practice

WEBBER & THIES, P.C.
Urbana, IL .... General Practice, Tax Law

WEBER, JAMES E., P.A.
West Palm Beach, FL .... Civil Trial Practice, Probate and Estate Planning Law

WEBER, MUTH & WEBER
Ramsey, NJ .... Banking Law, General Practice, Probate and Estate Planning Law, Real Estate Law

WEBER, PERRA & WILSON, P.C.
Brattleboro, VT .... Civil Trial Practice, Environmental Law, Family Law, General Practice, Probate and Estate Planning Law

WEBER & ROSE, PROFESSIONAL SERVICE CORPORATION
Louisville, KY .... Insurance Defense Law, Medical Malpractice Law, Probate and Estate Planning Law

WEBER & STERLING
Maumee, OH .... Probate and Estate Planning Law

WEBER, SWANSON & DETTMANN
Marquette, MI .... Civil Trial Practice, Insurance Defense Law

WEBSTER, CHAMBERLAIN & BEAN
Washington, DC .... Administrative Law

WEBSTER & WEBSTER, P.C.
Uniontown, PA .... General Practice

WEEKS & HUTCHINS
Waterville, ME .... General Practice

WEEMS, WRIGHT, SCHIMPF, HAYTER & CARMOUCHE, A PROFESSIONAL LAW CORPORATION
Shreveport, LA .... Civil Trial Practice, Construction Law, Real Estate Law

WEGMANN, GASAWAY, STEWART, SCHNEIDER, DIEFFENBACH, TESREAU, STOLL & SHERMAN, P.C.
Hillsboro, MO .... General Practice

WEHNER AND PERLMAN
Los Angeles, CA .... Business Law

WEHR, BERGER, LANE & STEVENS
Davenport, IA .... General Practice

WEHRLE & SMITH, P.C.
Martinsville, IN .... General Practice

WEIER, HOCKENSMITH & SHERBY, P.C.
St. Louis, MO .... General Practice

WEIGHT, MICHAEL A., ATTORNEY AT LAW, A LAW CORPORATION
Honolulu, HI .... Criminal Trial Practice

WEILER, LEONARD D., A PROFESSIONAL CORPORATION
San Ramon, CA .... Family Law

WEILL & WEILL
Chattanooga, TN .... Civil Trial Practice, Personal Injury Law

WEIL & WRIGHT
Carlsbad, CA .... Banking Law, Civil Trial Practice, Commercial Law, Real Estate Law

WEINBERG & BELL, ATTORNEYS AT LAW, A LAW CORPORATION
Honolulu, HI .... Civil Trial Practice, Medical Malpractice Law, Personal Injury Law

WEINBERG, CAMPBELL, SLONE & SLONE, P.S.C.
Hindman, KY .... Environmental Law, General Practice, Natural Resources Law, Personal Injury Law, Product Liability Law

WEINBERG, HOFFMAN & CASEY
Larkspur, CA .... Business Law, Insurance Defense Law, Medical Malpractice Law, Personal Injury Law, Product Liability Law

WEINBERG, MCCORMICK AND CHATZINOFF, A PROFESSIONAL ASSOCIATION
Haddonfield, NJ .... Bankruptcy Law, Family Law

WEINBERG & STEIN, A PROFESSIONAL CORPORATION
Norfolk, VA .... Family Law, Real Estate Law

WEINBRENNER, RICHARDS, PAULOWSKY & RAMIREZ, P.A.
Las Cruces, NM .... Banking Law, Family Law, General Practice, Insurance Defense Law, Probate and Estate Planning Law, Real Estate Law

WEINER, SAM B.
Columbus, OH .... Criminal Trial Practice

WEINER, JEFFREY S., P.A.
Miami, FL .... Criminal Trial Practice

WEINGARDEN & HAUER, P.C.
Birmingham, MI .... Business Law, Family Law, Probate and Estate Planning Law, Tax Law

WEINHAUS AND DOBSON
St. Louis, MO .... Employment Benefits Law, Labor and Employment Law

WEINSTEIN, JEFFREY P., A PROFESSIONAL CORPORATION
Livingston, NJ .... Family Law

WEINSTEIN, STEPHEN S., A PROFESSIONAL CORPORATION
Morristown, NJ .... Civil Trial Practice, Criminal Trial Practice, Medical Malpractice Law, Personal Injury Law, Product Liability Law

WEINTRAUB & ASSOCIATES, A PROFESSIONAL LAW CORPORATION
San Diego, CA .... Probate and Estate Planning Law, Securities Law

WEINTRAUB, ROBINSON, WEINTRAUB, STOCK & BENNETT, P.C.
Memphis, TN .... General Practice, Labor and Employment Law

WEIR, JAMES A.
Colorado Springs, CO .... Probate and Estate Planning Law, Real Estate Law

WEIR & FOULDS
Mississauga, ON, Canada .... General Practice
Toronto, ON, Canada .... General Practice

WEIR AND WALLEY
Metairie, LA .... Commercial Law, Probate and Estate Planning Law

WEISMAN BOWEN & GROSS
Pittsburgh, PA .... Bankruptcy Law, Civil Trial Practice, Commercial Law

WEISMAN & LUBELL
Westport, CT .... Civil Trial Practice, Family Law, General Practice, Municipal Bond/Public Authority Financing Law, Municipal and Zoning Law

WEISS, LOREN E.
Salt Lake City, UT .... Civil Trial Practice, Criminal Trial Practice

WEISS & FREDERICK
Louisville, KY .... Civil Trial Practice, Personal Injury Law

WEISS & HANDLER, P.A.
Boca Raton, FL .... Civil Trial Practice, Family Law, Personal Injury Law, Real Estate Law

WEISSBURG AND ARONSON, INC.
Los Angeles, CA .... Health Care Law

WEIST, WILLIAM B.
Fowler, IN .... General Practice, Probate and Estate Planning Law

WEISZ & ASSOCIATES
Atlanta, GA .... Administrative Law, Business Law, Commercial Law, Construction Law

WELBAUM, ZOOK & JONES
Miami, FL .... Civil Trial Practice, Construction Law, General Practice

WELBORN SULLIVAN MECK & TOOLEY, P.C.
Denver, CO .... Environmental Law, General Practice, Natural Resources Law

WELDON, E. DURWARD
Georgetown, KY .... General Practice, Probate and Estate Planning Law, Real Estate Law

WELDON, HUSTON & KEYSER
Mansfield, OH .... General Practice

WELLER FRIEDRICH, LLC
Denver, CO .... Banking Law, Bankruptcy Law, Civil Trial Practice, Commercial Law, Construction Law, Environmental Law, Insurance Defense Law

WELLER, GREEN, MCGOWN & TOUPS, L.L.P.
Beaumont, TX .... Insurance Defense Law, Personal Injury Law

WELLER, MILLER, CARRIER, MILLER & HICKIE
Johnson City, TN....................Civil Trial Practice, General Practice

WELLER, WICKS & WALLACE, PROFESSIONAL CORPORATION
Pittsburgh, PA ....Natural Resources Law, Probate and Estate Planning Law, Tax Law

WELLES & MCGRATH
Scranton, PA ....Civil Trial Practice, General Practice

WELLS & BLOSSOM
Wallace, NC ....General Practice

WELLS, GALLAGHER, ROEDER & MILLAGE
Bettendorf, IA ....General Practice

WELLS MARBLE & HURST
Jackson, MS ....Civil Trial Practice, General Practice, Insurance Defense Law, Tax Law

WELLS, MOORE, SIMMONS & NEELD
Jackson, MS ....General Practice

WELLS, PEYTON, BEARD, GREENBERG, HUNT & CRAWFORD, L.L.P.
Beaumont, TX..........................Admiralty/Maritime Law, General Practice

WELLS, PORTER & SCHMITT
Paintsville, KY.........................General Practice, Insurance Defense Law

WELLS AND SINGER, P.A.
Bordentown, NJ.......................General Practice
Mount Holly, NJ.......................General Practice
Robbinsville, NJ.......................General Practice

WELMAKER & WELMAKER, P.C.
San Antonio, TX......................General Practice

WELMAN, BEATON, MCVEY, HIVELY & GODLEY
Kennett, MO............................General Practice
Malden, MO.............................General Practice

WELP, HARRISON, BRENNECKE & MOORE
Marshalltown, IA......................General Practice

WELTS & WELTS
Mount Vernon, WA..................Personal Injury Law

WELTY, JEAN L.
New Haven, CT ....Family Law

WEMPLE & DALY
Schenectady, NY......................General Practice

WENDEROTH, LIND & PONACK
Washington, DC.......................Patent, Trademark, Copyright and Unfair Competition Law

WENTWORTH, THEODORE S., LAW OFFICES OF
Newport Beach, CA..................Personal Injury Law

WERNLE, RISTINE & AYERS, L.P.C.
Crawfordsville, IN...................General Practice

WESIERSKI & ZUREK
Irvine, CA................................Civil Trial Practice

WESNER, KEMPTON, RUSSELL AND DOMINIQUE
Jefferson City, MO...................General Practice
Sedalia, MO.............................General Practice

WESSELS, STOJAN & STEPHENS, P.C.
Rock Island, IL........................General Practice

WEST, ROBIN PAGE
Baltimore, MD.........................Civil Trial Practice, Personal Injury Law, Product Liability Law

WEST, DAVID WM., P.C., LAW OFFICES OF
Phoenix, AZ ....General Practice

WEST & JONES
Clarksburg, WV ....Civil Trial Practice, General Practice, Medical Malpractice Law, Personal Injury Law, Real Estate Law

WEST LAW FIRM, THE
Shawnee, OK...........................Personal Injury Law

WEST & ROSE
Kingsport, TN..........................Civil Trial Practice, Insurance Defense Law

WESTERVELT, GEORGE W. JR.
Stroudsburg, PA.......................Personal Injury Law

WESTERVELT, JOHNSON, NICOLL & KELLER
Peoria, IL................................General Practice

WESTMAN & LINTZ
Cocoa, FL................................General Practice

WESTON HURD FALLON PAISLEY & HOWLEY
Cleveland, OH.........................Civil Trial Practice, Environmental Law, General Practice, Insurance Defense Law, Patent, Trademark, Copyright and Unfair Competition Law, Tax Law

WETTEROTH, WARREN C.
Bakersfield, CA ....Civil Trial Practice

WHARTON, ALDHIZER & WEAVER, P.L.C.
Harrisonburg, VA ....General Practice, Insurance Defense Law, Real Estate Law, Tax Law

WHARTON, LEVIN, EHRMANTRAUT, KLEIN & NASH, A PROFESSIONAL ASSOCIATION
Annapolis, MD ....General Practice
Baltimore, MD ....General Practice
Bethesda, MD ....General Practice

WHEATLEY, CAMPAGNOLO & SESSIONS, L.L.P.
San Antonio, TX.....................Banking Law, Business Law, Construction Law, Environmental Law

WHEATLY, WHEATLY, NOBLES & WEEKS, P.A.
Beaufort, NC ....Civil Trial Practice, Criminal Trial Practice, General Practice

WHEELER & KORPECK
Silver Spring, MD ....General Practice

WHEELER & KROMHOLZ
Milwaukee, WI.......................Patent, Trademark, Copyright and Unfair Competition Law

WHEELER, THOMPSON, PARKER & COUNTS
Easton, MD..............................General Practice

WHEELER UPHAM, A PROFESSIONAL CORPORATION
Grand Rapids, MI ....Appellate Practice, Business Law, Civil Trial Practice, Commercial Law, Employment Benefits Law, Environmental Law, General Practice, Insurance Defense Law, Probate and Estate Planning Law, Product Liability Law, Real Estate Law, Transportation Law

WHEELUS, KYLE JR.
Beaumont, TX..........................Insurance Defense Law

WHELCHEL, BROWN, READDICK & BUMGARTNER
Brunswick, GA.........................Civil Trial Practice, General Practice

WHELCHEL, DUNLAP & GIGNILLIAT
Gainesville, GA........................General Practice

WHELCHEL, WHELCHEL & CARLTON
Moultrie, GA............................General Practice

WHIPPS, EDWARD F. & ASSOCIATES
Columbus, OH ....Family Law

WHITAKER & DICKENS
Roanoke Rapids, NC...............General Practice

WHITE, DAN E.
Atlanta, GA ....Immigration and Naturalization Law

WHITE & ALLEN, P.A.
Kinston, NC.............................Civil Trial Practice, General Practice

WHITE & CASE
Washington, DC......................General Practice
New York, NY.........................Civil Trial Practice, Criminal Trial Practice, General Practice
London, England ....General Practice
Paris, France...........................General Practice
Hong Kong, Hong Kong (British Crown Colony)...........General Practice
Tokyo, Japan...........................General Practice
Singapore, Singapore..............General Practice
Ankara, Turkey.......................General Practice
Istanbul, Turkey......................General Practice
Stockholm, Sweden ....General Practice

WHITE, COFFEY, GALT & FITE, P.C.
Oklahoma City, OK................General Practice

WHITE AND CRUMPLER
Winston-Salem, NC ....Criminal Trial Practice, Family Law, Personal Injury Law

WHITE, DENNIS R., P.A.
Naples, FL...............................Probate and Estate Planning Law

WHITE, FLEISCHNER & FINO
New York, NY.........................Environmental Law, Insurance Defense Law, Medical Malpractice Law, Personal Injury Law, Product Liability Law

WHITEFORD, TAYLOR & PRESTON
Washington, DC....................General Practice
Baltimore, MD....................General Practice, Labor and Employment Law, Municipal Bond/Public Authority Financing Law
Towson, MD....................General Practice

WHITE, HALL & DIXON
Elizabeth City, NC....................Civil Trial Practice, General Practice

WHITE, HAMILTON, WYCHE & SHELL, P.C.
Petersburg, VA....................General Practice

WHITE, HUSEMAN, PLETCHER & POWERS
Corpus Christi, TX....................Admiralty/Maritime Law, Civil Trial Practice

WHITE, INKER, ARONSON, P.C.
Boston, MA....................Family Law, General Practice

WHITE, KOCH, KELLY & MCCARTHY, A PROFESSIONAL ASSOCIATION
Santa Fe, NM....................Commercial Law, Criminal Trial Practice, Family Law, General Practice, Insurance Defense Law, Labor and Employment Law, Probate and Estate Planning Law, Real Estate Law

WHITEMAN OSTERMAN & HANNA
Albany, NY....................Civil Trial Practice, Environmental Law, Municipal and Zoning Law

WHITE, PECK, CARRINGTON AND MCDONALD
Mount Sterling, KY....................General Practice

WHITE & REASOR
Nashville, TN....................Banking Law, Civil Trial Practice, Commercial Law, Personal Injury Law, Real Estate Law

WHITE, REGEN & STUART
Dickson, TN....................General Practice

WHITES LAW OFFICES
Princeton, WV....................Civil Trial Practice, Insurance Defense Law

WHITESELL LAW FIRM
Iowa Falls, IA....................General Practice

WHITESIDES, ROBINSON, BLUE, WILSON & SMITH
Gastonia, NC....................Civil Trial Practice, Real Estate Law

WHITE AND STEELE, PROFESSIONAL CORPORATION
Denver, CO....................Civil Trial Practice, General Practice, Insurance Defense Law, Product Liability Law, Public Utilities Law

WHITE, WHITE, ASKEW & CRENSHAW
Hopkinsville, KY....................General Practice

WHITFIELD & EDDY, P.L.C.
Des Moines, IA....................Banking Law, Civil Trial Practice, General Practice, Insurance Defense Law

WHITING, STANLEY E.
Winner, SD....................General Practice

WHITING, HAGG & HAGG
Rapid City, SD....................General Practice

WHITLOW, ROBERTS, HOUSTON & RUSSELL
Paducah, KY....................Admiralty/Maritime Law, Banking Law, Bankruptcy Law, Civil Trial Practice, General Practice, Labor and Employment Law, Tax Law

WHITMAN BREED ABBOTT & MORGAN
Greenwich, CT....................General Practice
Washington, DC....................General Practice
New York, NY....................General Practice
London, England....................General Practice

WHITNEY, NEWMAN, MERSCH & OTTO
Aurora, NE....................General Practice

WIBLE, CHARLES S., P.S.C., LAW OFFICES OF
Owensboro, KY....................Personal Injury Law

WICKENS, HERZER & PANZA, A LEGAL PROFESSIONAL ASSOCIATION
Lorain, OH....................General Practice

WICK, STREIFF, MEYER, METZ & O'BOYLE, P.C.
Pittsburgh, PA....................Business Law, Civil Trial Practice, Tax Law, Transportation Law

WIEDERHOLD, MOSES, BULFIN & RUBIN, P.A.
West Palm Beach, FL....................Civil Trial Practice, Insurance Defense Law

WIENER, WEISS, MADISON & HOWELL, A PROFESSIONAL CORPORATION
Shreveport, LA....................Bankruptcy Law, Civil Trial Practice, General Practice, Insurance Defense Law, Natural Resources Law, Personal Injury Law, Probate and Estate Planning Law, Tax Law

WIER, RICHARD R., JR., A PROF. ASSOC., THE LAW OFFICES OF
Wilmington, DE....................Labor and Employment Law

WIESE LAW FIRM, P.A.
Minneapolis, MN....................Business Law

WIEST, WIEST, SAYLOR & MUOLO
Sunbury, PA....................General Practice

WIGGIN & DANA
Hartford, CT....................General Practice
New Haven, CT....................Antitrust Law, Civil Trial Practice, General Practice, Health Care Law, Labor and Employment Law, Patent, Trademark, Copyright and Unfair Competition Law

WIGGIN & NOURIE, P.A.
Manchester, NH....................General Practice

WIGGINS & MASSON
Ithaca, NY....................General Practice, Personal Injury Law

WILBERT AND TOWNER, P.A.
Pittsburg, KS....................General Practice

WILBRAHAM, LAWLER & BUBA, A PROFESSIONAL CORPORATION
Philadelphia, PA....................Environmental Law, Insurance Defense Law, Product Liability Law

WILBURN, MASTERSON & SMILING
Tulsa, OK....................Insurance Defense Law, Medical Malpractice Law

WILCOX, ARTHUR M. JR.
San Diego, CA....................Real Estate Law

WILCOX, WILCOX, DUPLESSIE, WESTERLUND & ENRIGHT
Eau Claire, WI....................Civil Trial Practice, General Practice, Insurance Defense Law, Real Estate Law

WILCOXEN, WILLIAM M.
Laguna Beach, CA....................Probate and Estate Planning Law

WILDMAN, HARROLD, ALLEN & DIXON
Chicago, IL....................Appellate Practice, Business Law, General Practice, Insurance Defense Law

WILDS, JOHN L.
Sioux Falls, SD....................Probate and Estate Planning Law, Real Estate Law

WILENTZ, GOLDMAN & SPITZER, A PROFESSIONAL CORPORATION
Eatontown, NJ....................General Practice
Perth Amboy, NJ....................General Practice
Woodbridge, NJ....................Banking Law, Civil Trial Practice, Commercial Law, Criminal Trial Practice, Environmental Law, Family Law, General Practice, Labor and Employment Law, Municipal Bond/Public Authority Financing Law, Probate and Estate Planning Law, Real Estate Law, Tax Law

WILEY, REIN & FIELDING
Washington, DC....................General Practice

WILF, MERVIN M., LTD.
Boston, MA....................Employment Benefits Law, Probate and Estate Planning Law, Tax Law
Philadelphia, PA....................Employment Benefits Law, Probate and Estate Planning Law, Tax Law

WILKE, FLEURY, HOFFELT, GOULD & BIRNEY
Sacramento, CA....................Administrative Law, Antitrust Law, Bankruptcy Law, Business Law, Civil Trial Practice, Construction Law, Environmental Law, General Practice, Health Care Law, Labor and Employment Law, Medical Malpractice Law, Probate and Estate Planning Law, Real Estate Law, Tax Law

WILKES, ARTIS, HEDRICK & LANE, CHARTERED
Washington, DC....................General Practice, Real Estate Law

WILKINS, JOHN C. (JACK) III
Bartow, FL....................Criminal Trial Practice

WILKINS, FROHLICH, JONES, HEVIA, RUSSELL & SUTTER, P.A.
Port Charlotte, FL....................General Practice

WILKINS & SLUSHER
McAllen, TX....................General Practice, Probate and Estate Planning Law

WILKINSON, BARKER, KNAUER & QUINN
Washington, DC....................Communications Law, General Practice

WILKINSON, CARMODY & GILLIAM
Shreveport, LA....................Appellate Practice, Civil Trial Practice, Environmental Law, General Practice, Insurance Defense Law, Labor and Employment Law, Public Utilities Law, Transportation Law

WILKINSON, GOELLER, MODESITT, WILKINSON & DRUMMY
Terre Haute, IN....................Bankruptcy Law, Civil Trial Practice, General Practice, Health Care Law, Insurance Defense Law, Probate and Estate Planning Law, Product Liability Law, Tax Law

WILLARDSON, LIPSCOMB & BENDER
Wilkesboro, NC........................General Practice

WILLCOX, PIROZZOLO AND MCCARTHY, PROFESSIONAL CORPORATION
Boston, MA........................Civil Trial Practice, General Practice, Patent, Trademark, Copyright and Unfair Competition Law

WILLCOX & SAVAGE, P.C.
Norfolk, VA........................General Practice

WILLIAMS, JOHN R. LAW OFFICES OF
New Haven, CT........................Appellate Practice, Civil Trial Practice, Criminal Trial Practice, Personal Injury Law

WILLIAMS & ANDERSON
Little Rock, AR........................Antitrust Law, Civil Trial Practice, Commercial Law, General Practice, Municipal Bond/Public Authority Financing Law, Securities Law, Tax Law

WILLIAMS, BOGER, GRADY, DAVIS & TUTTLE, P.A.
Concord, NC........................General Practice

WILLIAMS, BRASFIELD, WERTZ, FULLER, GOLDMAN, FREEMAN & LOVELL, P.A.
St. Petersburg, FL........................Medical Malpractice Law, Personal Injury Law

WILLIAMS, CALIRI, MILLER & OTLEY, A PROFESSIONAL CORPORATION
Wayne, NJ........................Banking Law, General Practice, Insurance Defense Law, Real Estate Law

WILLIAMS, CHARLES J., A PROFESSIONAL CORPORATION
Martinez, CA........................Municipal and Zoning Law

WILLIAMS & CONNOLLY
Washington, DC........................Civil Trial Practice, Criminal Trial Practice, General Practice, Tax Law

WILLIAMS, COONEY & SHEEHY
Bridgeport, CT........................Civil Trial Practice, General Practice, Insurance Defense Law, Medical Malpractice Law, Personal Injury Law, Product Liability Law

WILLIAMS, EBB H., III, P.C.
Martinsville, VA........................Personal Injury Law

WILLIAMS, FRANK J., LTD.
Providence, RI........................General Practice, Labor and Employment Law

WILLIAMS, HERSHMAN & WISLER, P.A.
Wilmington, DE........................General Practice, Probate and Estate Planning Law, Real Estate Law, Tax Law

WILLIAMS, KASTNER & GIBBS
Bellevue, WA........................General Practice
Seattle, WA........................Antitrust Law, General Practice, Labor and Employment Law, Tax Law

WILLIAMS KELLY & GREER, A PROFESSIONAL CORPORATION
Norfolk, VA........................General Practice

WILLIAMS LAW OFFICE
Port Angeles, WA........................Personal Injury Law

WILLIAMS & MCCARTHY, A PROFESSIONAL CORPORATION
Oregon, IL........................Civil Trial Practice, General Practice
Rockford, IL........................Civil Trial Practice, General Practice, Tax Law

WILLIAMS AND MONTGOMERY, LTD.
Chicago, IL........................Civil Trial Practice, General Practice

WILLIAMS, MULLEN, CHRISTIAN & DOBBINS, A PROFESSIONAL CORPORATION
Richmond, VA........................Administrative Law, Antitrust Law, Banking Law, Bankruptcy Law, Business Law, Civil Trial Practice, Commercial Law, Communications Law, Construction Law, Employment Benefits Law, Environmental Law, General Practice, Health Care Law, Immigration and Naturalization Law, Insurance Defense Law, International Business Law, Labor and Employment Law, Municipal Bond/Public Authority Financing Law, Municipal and Zoning Law, Probate and Estate Planning Law, Real Estate Law, Securities Law, Tax Law, Trademark, Copyright and Unfair Competition Law

WILLIAMS & NENNEY
Los Angeles, CA........................Probate and Estate Planning Law

WILLIAMS, PARKER, HARRISON, DIETZ & GETZEN, PROFESSIONAL ASSOCIATION
Sarasota, FL........................Banking Law, Civil Trial Practice, General Practice, International Business Law, Municipal Bond/Public Authority Financing Law, Probate and Estate Planning Law, Real Estate Law, Tax Law

WILLIAMS, PATTILLO & SQUIRES, L.L.P.
Waco, TX........................Civil Trial Practice

WILLIAMS, PORTER, DAY & NEVILLE, P.C.
Casper, WY........................Civil Trial Practice, Environmental Law, General Practice, Insurance Defense Law

WILLIAMS, ROBINSON, TURLEY & WHITE, A PROFESSIONAL CORPORATION
Rolla, MO........................General Practice

WILLIAMS, SCHAEFER, RUBY & WILLIAMS, PROFESSIONAL CORPORATION
Birmingham, MI........................Environmental Law, Family Law, Municipal and Zoning Law, Probate and Estate Planning Law, Real Estate Law

WILLIAMS & SENNETT CO., L.P.A.
Hudson, OH........................Civil Trial Practice

WILLIAMS, STROBEL, MALONE, MASON & RALPH, P.A.
Dodge City, KS........................General Practice

WILLIAMS & TRINE, P.C.
Boulder, CO........................Civil Trial Practice, Personal Injury Law

WILLIAMS & WAGONER
Louisville, KY........................Insurance Defense Law

WILLIAMS, WILLIAMS AND MONTGOMERY, P.A.
Picayune, MS........................General Practice
Poplarville, MS........................Admiralty/Maritime Law, Civil Trial Practice, General Practice, Personal Injury Law

WILLIAMS WOOLLEY COGSWELL NAKAZAWA & RUSSELL
Long Beach, CA........................Admiralty/Maritime Law, Civil Trial Practice, International Business Law, Transportation Law

WILLIAMSON, STEPHEN T.
Louisville, CO........................Natural Resources Law

WILLIAMSON, DEAN, BROWN, WILLIAMSON & PURCELL, L.L.P.
Laurinburg, NC........................General Practice

WILLIAMSON & WALTON
Whiteville, NC........................General Practice

WILLIS & KNIGHT
Nashville, TN........................Civil Trial Practice

WILLIS & SACKETT
Perry, IA........................General Practice

WILLKIE FARR & GALLAGHER
Washington, DC........................General Practice
New York, NY........................Civil Trial Practice, General Practice, Municipal Bond/Public Authority Financing Law
London, England........................General Practice
Paris, France........................General Practice

WILLMAN & ARNOLD
Pittsburgh, PA........................Environmental Law, Insurance Defense Law

WILLONER, CALABRESE & ROSEN, P.A.
College Park, MD........................General Practice

WILLS LAW FIRM, THE
Colorado Springs, CO........................Civil Trial Practice, General Practice, Personal Injury Law

WILMER, CUTLER & PICKERING
Washington, DC........................Antitrust Law, Banking Law, Bankruptcy Law, Business Law, Civil Trial Practice, Communications Law, Criminal Trial Practice, Environmental Law, General Practice, Insurance Defense Law, International Business Law, Securities Law, Tax Law, Transportation Law
Brussels, Belgium........................General Practice
London, England........................General Practice
Berlin, Germany........................General Practice

WILMER & GREATHOUSE
Middletown, OH........................General Practice

WILMETH LAW FIRM
Hartsville, SC........................General Practice

WILSHIRE SCOTT & DYER, A PROFESSIONAL CORPORATION
Houston, TX........................Appellate Practice, Banking Law, Civil Trial Practice, Environmental Law

WILSON, GUY C.
Scottsdale, AZ........................Probate and Estate Planning Law, Real Estate Law, Tax Law

WILSON AND BARROWS, LTD.
Elko, NV........................General Practice, Probate and Estate Planning Law, Real Estate Law

WILSON, BAVE, CONBOY, COZZA & COUZENS, P.C.
White Plains, NY........................General Practice, Insurance Defense Law, Personal Injury Law

WILSON, BORROR, DUNN, SCOTT & DAVIS
San Bernardino, CA........................Civil Trial Practice, General Practice, Insurance Defense Law, Probate and Estate Planning Law

WILSON, CARNAHAN & MCCOLL, CHARTERED
Boise, ID....Civil Trial Practice, Commercial Law, Family Law, Real Estate Law

WILSON, DECAMP & TALBOTT, P.S.C.
Lexington, KY....General Practice

WILSON, ELSER, MOSKOWITZ, EDELMAN & DICKER
New York, NY....Civil Trial Practice, Insurance Defense Law

WILSON, ENGSTROM, CORUM, DUDLEY & COULTER
Little Rock, AR....Civil Trial Practice, Criminal Trial Practice

WILSON, HALL & CRAIG, PROFESSIONAL CORPORATION
Eldora, IA....General Practice

WILSON, JOHNSON & JAFFER, P.A.
Sarasota, FL....Business Law, Probate and Estate Planning Law, Real Estate Law

WILSON, JOHNSON & PRESSER
Owensboro, KY....Probate and Estate Planning Law

WILSON, KEHOE & WININGHAM
Indianapolis, IN....Personal Injury Law, Product Liability Law

WILSON & MCILVAINE
Chicago, IL....Antitrust Law, Banking Law, Civil Trial Practice, Environmental Law, General Practice, Probate and Estate Planning Law, Real Estate Law, Securities Law

WILSON, MCRAE, IVY, SEVIER, MCTYIER AND STRAIN
Memphis, TN....General Practice, Insurance Defense Law

WILSON, SONSINI, GOODRICH & ROSATI, PROFESSIONAL CORPORATION
Palo Alto, CA....General Practice

WILSON, WHITE & COPELAND
Dallas, TX....Tax Law

WILSON, WILSON & PLAIN
Owensboro, KY....Banking Law, General Practice, Insurance Defense Law, Probate and Estate Planning Law

WILSON, WORLEY, GAMBLE & WARD, P.C.
Kingsport, TN....Civil Trial Practice, General Practice, Tax Law

WIMER LAW OFFICES, P.C.
Pittsburgh, PA....Civil Trial Practice, Personal Injury Law

WINDELS, MARX, DAVIES & IVES
New York, NY....General Practice

WINDERWEEDLE, HAINES, WARD & WOODMAN, P.A.
Orlando, FL....General Practice, Probate and Estate Planning Law, Real Estate Law
Winter Park, FL....General Practice, Probate and Estate Planning Law, Real Estate Law

WINEGARDEN, SHEDD, HALEY, LINDHOLM & ROBERTSON
Flint, MI....Banking Law, Bankruptcy Law, Business Law, Civil Trial Practice, Commercial Law, Construction Law, Environmental Law, Family Law, General Practice, Labor and Employment Law, Personal Injury Law, Probate and Estate Planning Law, Real Estate Law, Tax Law

WINETSKY AND WINETSKY
Linden, NJ....General Practice

WINGATE & CULLEN
Brooklyn, NY....Banking Law, General Practice
Melville, NY....Banking Law, General Practice

WINGERT, GREBING, ANELLO & BRUBAKER
San Diego, CA....Civil Trial Practice, Insurance Defense Law, Probate and Estate Planning Law

WINGET & KANE
Peoria, IL....Civil Trial Practice, Family Law

WINIKATES & WINIKATES
Frisco, TX....Banking Law, Civil Trial Practice, Probate and Estate Planning Law

WINKJER MCKENNETT STENEHJEM REIERSON & FORSBERG, P.C.
Williston, ND....General Practice

WINSTEAD SECHREST & MINICK P.C.
Austin, TX....General Practice
Dallas, TX....General Practice
Houston, TX....General Practice

WINSTEIN, KAVENSKY & WALLACE
Rock Island, IL....Civil Trial Practice

WINSTON, BARRY T.
Chapel Hill, NC....Civil Trial Practice, Criminal Trial Practice

WINSTON & CASHATT, LAWYERS, A PROFESSIONAL SERVICE CORPORATION
Spokane, WA....Construction Law, General Practice

WINSTON, REUBER & BYRNE, LAWYERS, A PROFESSIONAL CORPORATION
Mason City, IA....General Practice, Probate and Estate Planning Law, Real Estate Law

WINSTON & STRAWN
Washington, DC....General Practice
Chicago, IL....Antitrust Law, General Practice
New York, NY....General Practice

WINTER & RHODEN
Gaffney, SC....General Practice

WINTERS, DAVID C.
Columbus, OH....Criminal Trial Practice

WINTERS, BREWSTER, CROSBY & PATCHETT
Marion, IL....General Practice

WINTERS & FORTE
Cheshire, CT....Business Law, Probate and Estate Planning Law, Tax Law

WINTHROP, STIMSON, PUTNAM & ROBERTS
Stamford, CT....General Practice
Washington, DC....General Practice
Palm Beach, FL....General Practice
New York, NY....Antitrust Law, Banking Law, Bankruptcy Law, Civil Trial Practice, General Practice, Tax Law
Brussels, Belgium....General Practice
London, England....General Practice
Hong Kong, Hong Kong (British Crown Colony)....General Practice
Tokyo, Japan....General Practice

WINTHROP & WEINSTINE, A PROFESSIONAL ASSOCIATION
St. Paul, MN....General Practice

WISE CARTER CHILD & CARAWAY, PROFESSIONAL ASSOCIATION
Jackson, MS....Civil Trial Practice, General Practice, Health Care Law, Insurance Defense Law, Medical Malpractice Law, Probate and Estate Planning Law

WISE & COLE, P.A.
Charleston, SC....Bankruptcy Law

WISE & MARSAC, PROFESSIONAL CORPORATION
Detroit, MI....Business Law, Civil Trial Practice

WISE, WIEZOREK, TIMMONS & WISE, A PROFESSIONAL CORPORATION
Long Beach, CA....Civil Trial Practice, General Practice

WISEHART & KOCH
New York, NY....Labor and Employment Law

WISHART, NORRIS, HENNINGER & PITTMAN, P.A.
Burlington, NC....General Practice

WISTI & JAASKELAINEN, P.C.
Hancock, MI....Civil Trial Practice, Construction Law, Criminal Trial Practice, Personal Injury Law

WITHERS, BRANT, IGOE & MULLENNIX, P.C.
Liberty, MO....General Practice

WITHERSPOON, JOHN F.
Washington, DC....Patent, Trademark, Copyright and Unfair Competition Law

WITHERSPOON, KELLEY, DAVENPORT & TOOLE, P.S.
Spokane, WA....Communications Law, General Practice

WITMER & THUOTTE
Boston, MA....Commercial Law, Family Law, Personal Injury Law

WITT, GAITHER & WHITAKER, P.C.
Chattanooga, TN....Civil Trial Practice, General Practice, Labor and Employment Law

WITTER AND HARPOLE
Los Angeles, CA....General Practice

WITTLIN GOLDSTON & CAPUTO, P.C.
Pittsburgh, PA....Administrative Law, Business Law, Commercial Law, General Practice, Probate and Estate Planning Law, Real Estate Law

WITTNER, POGER, ROSENBLUM & SPEWAK, P.C.
St. Louis, MO....Business Law, Civil Trial Practice, Criminal Trial Practice, Personal Injury Law

WOBENSMITH, ZACHARY T. III
Valley Forge, PA....Patent, Trademark, Copyright and Unfair Competition Law, Trademark, Copyright and Unfair Competition Law

WOFSEY, ROSEN, KWESKIN & KURIANSKY
Stamford, CT....Banking Law, Civil Trial Practice, Commercial Law, Family Law, Personal Injury Law, Probate and Estate Planning Law, Tax Law

WOHLFORTH, ARGETSINGER, JOHNSON & BRECHT, A PROFESSIONAL CORPORATION
Anchorage, AK....Commercial Law, Real Estate Law

WOLF, ROBERT W.
Forest City, NC....General Practice

WOLF AND AKERS, A LEGAL PROFESSIONAL ASSOCIATION
Cleveland, OH....Family Law

WOLF, BLOCK, SCHORR AND SOLIS-COHEN
Philadelphia, PA....Antitrust Law, General Practice, Labor and Employment Law, Municipal Bond/Public Authority Financing Law, Tax Law

WOLFE, RICHARD B.
Sherman Oaks, CA....Personal Injury Law

WOLFF, DONALD L.
Clayton, MO....Criminal Trial Practice

WOLFF & SAMSON, P.A.
Roseland, NJ....Civil Trial Practice, Environmental Law, General Practice, Insurance Defense Law, Municipal Bond/Public Authority Financing Law, Tax Law

WOLFSDORF, BERNARD P., A PROFESSIONAL CORPORATION
Los Angeles, CA....Immigration and Naturalization Law

WOLSKE & BLUE, A LEGAL PROFESSIONAL ASSOCIATION
Columbus, OH....Appellate Practice, Medical Malpractice Law, Personal Injury Law

WOMACK, LANDIS, PHELPS, MCNEILL & MCDANIEL, A PROFESSIONAL ASSOCIATION
Jonesboro, AR....General Practice, Insurance Defense Law

WOMACK & RHYNE
La Fayette, GA....General Practice

WOMBLE CARLYLE SANDRIDGE & RICE
Charlotte, NC....Appellate Practice, Banking Law, Business Law, Civil Trial Practice, Commercial Law, Construction Law, Employment Benefits Law, Environmental Law, General Practice, Insurance Defense Law, International Business Law, Municipal Bond/Public Authority Financing Law, Natural Resources Law, Real Estate Law, Securities Law, Tax Law
Raleigh, NC....Administrative Law, Antitrust Law, Appellate Practice, Banking Law, Business Law, Civil Trial Practice, Commercial Law, Construction Law, Employment Benefits Law, Environmental Law, Family Law, General Practice, Insurance Defense Law, International Business Law, Labor and Employment Law, Municipal Bond/Public Authority Financing Law, Natural Resources Law, Patent, Trademark, Copyright and Unfair Competition Law, Real Estate Law, Securities Law, Tax Law
Winston-Salem, NC....Administrative Law, Antitrust Law, Appellate Practice, Banking Law, Bankruptcy Law, Business Law, Civil Trial Practice, Commercial Law, Communications Law, Construction Law, Employment Benefits Law, Environmental Law, Family Law, General Practice, Health Care Law, Insurance Defense Law, International Business Law, Labor and Employment Law, Municipal Bond/Public Authority Financing Law, Municipal and Zoning Law, Natural Resources Law, Patent, Trademark, Copyright and Unfair Competition Law, Probate and Estate Planning Law, Product Liability Law, Real Estate Law, Securities Law, Tax Law

WONG, MARGARET W. & ASSOCIATES
Cleveland, OH....Immigration and Naturalization Law

WONG, MICHAEL J. Y.
Honolulu, HI....Family Law, Personal Injury Law

WOO, VERNON Y. T.
Honolulu, HI....General Practice

WOOD, CHARLES J. JR.
Wallingford, CT....General Practice, Insurance Defense Law

WOODALL AND MACKENZIE, P.C.
Savannah, GA....Civil Trial Practice, Insurance Defense Law

WOODARD, EMHARDT, NAUGHTON, MORIARTY & MCNETT
Indianapolis, IN....Patent, Trademark, Copyright and Unfair Competition Law

WOODARD, HALL & PRIMM, A PROFESSIONAL CORPORATION
Houston, TX....General Practice

WOODBRIDGE & REAMY
Fredericksburg, VA....Civil Trial Practice, Criminal Trial Practice

WOODBURN AND WEDGE
Las Vegas, NV....Business Law, Civil Trial Practice, Commercial Law, Natural Resources Law, Probate and Estate Planning Law, Real Estate Law
Reno, NV....Business Law, Civil Trial Practice, Commercial Law, Natural Resources Law, Probate and Estate Planning Law, Real Estate Law

WOODBURY, J. WAYNE
Silver City, NM....General Practice

WOODCOCK WASHBURN KURTZ MACKIEWICZ & NORRIS
Philadelphia, PA....Patent, Trademark, Copyright and Unfair Competition Law

WOOD, CRIST & VALENTI, P.A.
Tampa, FL....Insurance Defense Law

WOODEN MCLAUGHLIN & STERNER
Indianapolis, IN....General Practice

WOOD, HERRON & EVANS
Cincinnati, OH....Patent, Trademark, Copyright and Unfair Competition Law

WOOD & LAMPING
Cincinnati, OH....Civil Trial Practice, General Practice, Insurance Defense Law

WOOD, ODOM AND EDGE, P.A.
Newnan, GA....General Practice

WOOD, PHILLIPS, VAN SANTEN, HOFFMAN & ERTEL
Chicago, IL....Patent, Trademark, Copyright and Unfair Competition Law

WOOD, RIS & HAMES, PROFESSIONAL CORPORATION
Denver, CO....Civil Trial Practice, General Practice, Insurance Defense Law

WOODROOF & WOODROOF
Athens, AL....General Practice

WOODROW, ROUSHAR & CAREY
Montrose, CO....General Practice

WOODRUFF, O'HAIR & POSNER, INC. A LAW CORPORATION
Sacramento, CA....Family Law

WOODS, RONALD G.
Houston, TX....Criminal Trial Practice

WOODS & AITKEN
Lincoln, NE....General Practice

WOODS & BATES
Lincoln, IL....General Practice

WOODS & PARTNERS
Montreal, QU, Canada....General Practice

WOODS AND SNYDER
Olive Branch, MS....Civil Trial Practice

WOODSON, FORD, SAYERS, LAWTHER, SHORT, PARROTT & HUDSON
Salisbury, NC....General Practice

WOOD, SPRINGER & LYLE, A PROFESSIONAL CORPORATION
Denton, TX....Appellate Practice, Civil Trial Practice, Personal Injury Law

WOOD TATUM SANDERS & MURPHY
Portland, OR....Admiralty/Maritime Law, General Practice, Insurance Defense Law

WOODWARD AND ASSOCIATES
Austin, TX....International Business Law

WOODWARD & EPLEY
Magnolia, AR....General Practice

WOODWARD, HOBSON & FULTON
Louisville, KY....Antitrust Law, Civil Trial Practice, Environmental Law, General Practice, Health Care Law, Insurance Defense Law, Labor and Employment Law, Product Liability Law

WOODWARD, LEVENTIS, UNGER, DAVES, HERNDON AND COTHRAN
Columbia, SC....Banking Law, Business Law, Civil Trial Practice, Personal Injury Law, Real Estate Law

WOODWARD, MILES & FLANNAGAN, P.C.
Bristol, VA....Civil Trial Practice, General Practice, Insurance Defense Law, Real Estate Law

WOODWORTH, GLENN, P.A., LAW OFFICE OF
St. Petersburg, FL....Civil Trial Practice

WOOLSEY, FISHER, WHITEAKER & MCDONALD, A PROFESSIONAL CORPORATION
Springfield, MO....Civil Trial Practice, Environmental Law, General Practice

WOOTEN & HART, A PROFESSIONAL CORPORATION
Roanoke, VA....................Insurance Defense Law

WOOTTON & SLAGLE, P.A.
Hot Springs National Park, AR....................General Practice

WORDEN, THANE & HAINES, P.C.
Missoula, MT....................General Practice

WORKMAN, NYDEGGER & SEELEY, A PROFESSIONAL CORPORATION
Salt Lake City, UT....................Patent, Trademark, Copyright and Unfair Competition Law

WORREL & WORREL
Fresno, CA....................Patent, Trademark, Copyright and Unfair Competition Law

WOTITZKY & WOTITZKY
Punta Gorda, FL....................General Practice

WRAY & KRACHT
Baton Rouge, LA....................Construction Law

WRENN, JAMES R., JR., P.C.
Midlothian, VA....................Administrative Law

WRIGHT & BONDS
Little Rock, AR....................Real Estate Law, Securities Law

WRIGHT, CHANEY, BERRY & DANIEL, P.A.
Arkadelphia, AR....................General Practice

WRIGHT, CONSTABLE & SKEEN
Baltimore, MD....................Admiralty/Maritime Law, General Practice
Elkton, MD....................General Practice

WRIGHT, DALE & JETT
Guymon, OK....................General Practice

WRIGHT AND DUNKUM
Buckingham, VA....................General Practice

WRIGHT, EVANS AND DALY
Evansville, IN....................Civil Trial Practice, General Practice, Insurance Defense Law, Real Estate Law

WRIGHT, HENSON, SOMERS, SEBELIUS, CLARK & BAKER
Topeka, KS....................Banking Law, Bankruptcy Law, Civil Trial Practice, General Practice, Insurance Defense Law, Labor and Employment Law, Medical Malpractice Law, Patent, Trademark, Copyright and Unfair Competition Law, Personal Injury Law

WRIGHT, JUDD & WINCKLER
Las Vegas, NV....................Civil Trial Practice, Criminal Trial Practice

WRIGHT, LINDSEY & JENNINGS
Little Rock, AR....................Admiralty/Maritime Law, Antitrust Law, General Practice, Labor and Employment Law, Municipal Bond/Public Authority Financing Law

WRIGHT & MILLS, P.A.
Skowhegan, ME....................Civil Trial Practice, Criminal Trial Practice, General Practice, Personal Injury Law

WRIGHT, POWERS AND MCINTOSH
Florence, SC....................General Practice

WRIGHT, STOUT & FITE
Muskogee, OK....................General Practice

WRIGHT, TOLLIVER AND GUTHALS, A PROFESSIONAL SERVICE CORPORATION
Billings, MT....................Bankruptcy Law, Commercial Law

WRIGHT AND WRIGHT, A PROFESSIONAL CORPORATION
Guntersville, AL....................General Practice, Real Estate Law

WUNSCH, JOHN C., P.C.
Chicago, IL....................Personal Injury Law

WYATT & CUNNINGHAM
Charlotte, NC....................Civil Trial Practice, Criminal Trial Practice

WYATT, EARLY, HARRIS, WHEELER & HAUSER, L.L.P.
High Point, NC....................Civil Trial Practice, General Practice

WYATT, TARRANT & COMBS
New Albany, IN....................General Practice
Frankfort, KY....................General Practice
Lexington, KY....................General Practice
Louisville, KY....................Banking Law, Civil Trial Practice, Communications Law, General Practice
Nashville, TN....................Communications Law, General Practice, Trademark, Copyright and Unfair Competition Law

WYCHE, BURGESS, FREEMAN & PARHAM, PROFESSIONAL ASSOCIATION
Greenville, SC....................Antitrust Law, Banking Law, Bankruptcy Law, Civil Trial Practice, Communications Law, Employment Benefits Law, Environmental Law, General Practice, Health Care Law, Insurance Defense Law, Labor and Employment Law, Municipal Bond/Public Authority Financing Law, Probate and Estate Planning Law, Real Estate Law, Securities Law, Tax Law

WYCHE & STORY
Raleigh, NC....................General Practice

WYLIE, PAUL R., A PROFESSIONAL CORPORATION
Bozeman, MT....................Antitrust Law, Patent, Trademark, Copyright and Unfair Competition Law

WYNN, MARY ELLEN
Stamford, CT....................Family Law

WYRSCH ATWELL MIRAKIAN LEE & HOBBS, P.C.
Kansas City, MO....................Civil Trial Practice, Criminal Trial Practice, General Practice

YANITY, JOSEPH BLAIR JR.
Athens, OH....................General Practice

YARLING, ROBINSON, HAMMEL & LAMB
Indianapolis, IN....................Bankruptcy Law, Civil Trial Practice, Commercial Law, Insurance Defense Law, Personal Injury Law

YAROSKY, DAVIAULT, LA HAYE, STOBER & ISAACS
Montreal, QU, Canada....................Criminal Trial Practice

YATES, MCLAMB & WEYHER, L.L.P.
Raleigh, NC....................Insurance Defense Law

YEARY & ASSOCIATES, P.C.
Abingdon, VA....................Criminal Trial Practice, General Practice, Personal Injury Law, Real Estate Law

YENGICH, RICH & XAIZ
Salt Lake City, UT....................Criminal Trial Practice

YERRID, KNOPIK & VALENZUELA, P.A.
Tampa, FL....................Personal Injury Law, Product Liability Law

YODER, AINLAY, ULMER & BUCKINGHAM
Goshen, IN....................General Practice

YONKEE & TONER
Sheridan, WY....................Civil Trial Practice, General Practice

YORK, MCRAE & YORK
Cedartown, GA....................General Practice

YOSHA, LADENDORF & TODD
Indianapolis, IN....................Civil Trial Practice, Medical Malpractice Law, Personal Injury Law, Product Liability Law

YOST, HARVEY D. II
Perry, OK....................Probate and Estate Planning Law, Real Estate Law

YOUNG, DAMON LAW OFFICES OF
Texarkana, TX....................Criminal Trial Practice, Personal Injury Law

YOUNG & ALEXANDER CO., L.P.A.
Dayton, OH....................Civil Trial Practice, Environmental Law, General Practice, Insurance Defense Law, Medical Malpractice Law, Real Estate Law, Tax Law

YOUNG & ASSOCIATES, P.C.
Southfield, MI....................Antitrust Law, Civil Trial Practice

YOUNG, B. RICHARD, P.A.
Pensacola, FL....................Civil Trial Practice, Insurance Defense Law, Product Liability Law

YOUNG, BERKMAN, BERMAN & KARPF, PROFESSIONAL ASSOCIATION
North Miami Beach, FL....................Family Law

YOUNG, BOGLE, MCCAUSLAND, WELLS & CLARK, P.A.
Wichita, KS....................Civil Trial Practice, Commercial Law, Environmental Law, General Practice, Insurance Defense Law, Natural Resources Law, Personal Injury Law, Probate and Estate Planning Law, Real Estate Law

YOUNG, CLEMENT, RIVERS & TISDALE
Charleston, SC....................Civil Trial Practice, Environmental Law, General Practice, Insurance Defense Law, Labor and Employment Law, Medical Malpractice Law, Tax Law

YOUNG, CONAWAY, STARGATT & TAYLOR
Georgetown, DE....................General Practice
Wilmington, DE....................General Practice

YOUNG, DIMIERO & SAYOVITZ, A PROFESSIONAL CORPORATION
West Orange, NJ....................General Practice

YOUNG, HASKINS, MANN & GREGORY, A PROFESSIONAL CORPORATION
Martinsville, VA....................General Practice

YOUNG AND HUBBELL
Lebanon, OH....................General Practice

YOUNG, MOORE, HENDERSON & ALVIS, P.A.
Raleigh, NC....................Civil Trial Practice, General Practice

YOUNG & PERL, P.C.
Memphis, TN....................Employment Benefits Law, General Practice, Labor and Employment Law

YOUNG, RICHARD W., A PROFESSIONAL CORPORATION
Reno, NV ....Criminal Trial Practice, Family Law

YOUNG & RILEY
Indianapolis, IN ....Personal Injury Law, Product Liability Law

YOUNG, SANDERS & FELDMAN, INC.
Anchorage, AK ....Civil Trial Practice, Criminal Trial Practice, Personal Injury Law, Product Liability Law

YOUNG WOOLDRIDGE, LAW OFFICES OF
Bakersfield, CA ....Civil Trial Practice, General Practice, Personal Injury Law

YOUNKIN, JACK C.
Shamokin, PA ....Civil Trial Practice, General Practice

YOW, CULBRETH & FOX
Wilmington, NC....Criminal Trial Practice, Personal Injury Law

YTURRI, ROSE, BURNHAM, BENTZ & HELFRICH
Ontario, OR ....General Practice

YUDES, JAMES P., A PROFESSIONAL CORPORATION
Springfield, NJ ....Family Law

YUKEVICH, BLUME & ZANGRILLI
Pittsburgh, PA ....Business Law, Civil Trial Practice, Securities Law

ZAGRANS, ERIC H.
Elyria, OH ....Antitrust Law, Appellate Practice, Civil Trial Practice, Product Liability Law, Securities Law

ZAHND, DIETRICH & ROSS
Maryville, MO....General Practice

ZALKIND, RODRIGUEZ, LUNT & DUNCAN
Boston, MA....Criminal Trial Practice

ZALTAS, MEDOFF & RAIDER
Natick, MA ....General Practice

ZALUTSKY & KLARQUIST, P.C.
Portland, OR....Employment Benefits Law, Tax Law

ZAMANSKY PROFESSIONAL ASSOCIATION
Minneapolis, MN ....Business Law, Real Estate Law

ZARIN, IRA J. LAW OFFICES OF
Newark, NJ ....Medical Malpractice Law, Personal Injury Law, Product Liability Law

ZARLEY, MCKEE, THOMTE, VOORHEES & SEASE
Des Moines, IA....Patent, Trademark, Copyright and Unfair Competition Law
Omaha, NE ....Patent, Trademark, Copyright and Unfair Competition Law

ZARWIN, BAUM, DEVITO, KAPLAN & O'DONNELL, P.C.
Philadelphia, PA ....Civil Trial Practice, Insurance Defense Law

ZAVARELLO, A. WILLIAM, CO., L.P.A.
Akron, OH ....Civil Trial Practice, General Practice, Medical Malpractice Law

ZAZZALI, ZAZZALI, FAGELLA & NOWAK, A PROFESSIONAL CORPORATION
Newark, NJ ....Appellate Practice, Civil Trial Practice, General Practice, Labor and Employment Law

ZEANAH, HUST, SUMMERFORD & DAVIS, L.L.C.
Tuscaloosa, AL ....Civil Trial Practice, General Practice, Insurance Defense Law

ZEFF AND ZEFF, P.C.
Detroit, MI....Civil Trial Practice, Personal Injury Law

ZEGAS, ALAN L.
West Orange, NJ....Appellate Practice, Civil Trial Practice, Criminal Trial Practice, General Practice

ZEIGLER CARTER COHEN & KOCH
Indianapolis, IN ....Insurance Defense Law

ZEIHER, WILLIAM A., P.A.
Fort Lauderdale, FL....Probate and Estate Planning Law, Real Estate Law

ZELDES, NEEDLE & COOPER, A PROFESSIONAL CORPORATION
Bridgeport, CT ....General Practice

ZELLE & LARSON
Minneapolis, MN ....Civil Trial Practice, General Practice

ZELLER & STRULOWITZ
West Orange, NJ....Tax Law

ZEMAN, WILLIAM S.
West Hartford, CT....Labor and Employment Law

ZERRENNER & ROANE
Grand Rapids, MI ....Family Law

ZICKERT, LLOYD L.
Chicago, IL....Patent, Trademark, Copyright and Unfair Competition Law

ZIDE & O'BIECUNAS
Los Angeles, CA ....Commercial Law

ZIEGLER, CLOUDY, PETERSON, WOODELL & SEAVER
Ketchikan, AK ....General Practice

ZIEGLER & GINSBURG, P.A.
Miami, FL ....Bankruptcy Law, Real Estate Law

ZIEGLER, METZGER & MILLER
Cleveland, OH....Bankruptcy Law, Civil Trial Practice, Commercial Law, General Practice, Personal Injury Law, Probate and Estate Planning Law, Real Estate Law, Tax Law

ZIEMER, STAYMAN, WEITZEL & SHOULDERS
Evansville, IN....Banking Law, Bankruptcy Law, Business Law, Commercial Law, Construction Law, Health Care Law

ZIERCHER & HOCKER, P.C.
St. Louis, MO....General Practice

ZIMMER AND DUNCAN
Parker, SD ....General Practice

ZIMMER KUNZ, PROFESSIONAL CORPORATION
Pittsburgh, PA ....Civil Trial Practice, General Practice, Insurance Defense Law

ZIMMER AND ZIMMER, L.L.P.
Wilmington, NC....Criminal Trial Practice, Personal Injury Law

ZIMMERMAN, ROY B.
Alexandria, VA ....Bankruptcy Law

ZIMMERMAN, LIEBERMAN & DERENZO
Pottsville, PA ....General Practice

ZIMMERMAN, PFANNEBECKER & NUFFORT
Lancaster, PA....Civil Trial Practice

ZIMMERMAN, SHUFFIELD, KISER & SUTCLIFFE, P.A.
Orlando, FL ....Civil Trial Practice, General Practice

ZIMRING, STUART D.
Los Angeles, CA ....Probate and Estate Planning Law

ZINOBER & MCCREA, P.A.
Tampa, FL ....General Practice, Labor and Employment Law

ZINSER AND DOMINA
Nashville, TN....Labor and Employment Law

ZIPPERER & LORBERBAUM, P.C.
Savannah, GA ....Civil Trial Practice, Criminal Trial Practice

ZISMAN AND INGRAHAM, P.C.
Denver, CO ....Probate and Estate Planning Law, Tax Law

ZOLLA AND MEYER
Los Angeles, CA ....Family Law

ZOLLNER, ROBERT S.
Andover, MA....Municipal and Zoning Law

ZUCKER, FACHER AND ZUCKER, A PROFESSIONAL CORPORATION
West Orange, NJ....Banking Law, Insurance Defense Law, Personal Injury Law

ZUCKERMAN, SPAEDER, GOLDSTEIN, TAYLOR & BETTER
Baltimore, MD ....Civil Trial Practice, Criminal Trial Practice

ZUCKERMAN, SPAEDER, GOLDSTEIN, TAYLOR & KOLKER
Washington, DC....Bankruptcy Law, Business Law, Civil Trial Practice, Criminal Trial Practice, Probate and Estate Planning Law, Tax Law
New York, NY....Civil Trial Practice, Criminal Trial Practice

ZUCKERMAN, SPAEDER, TAYLOR & EVANS
Miami, FL ....Antitrust Law, Civil Trial Practice, Criminal Trial Practice, Real Estate Law
Tampa, FL ....Antitrust Law, Banking Law, Civil Trial Practice, Criminal Trial Practice, Real Estate Law

ZUGER KIRMIS & SMITH
Bismarck, ND ....Civil Trial Practice, General Practice

ZUKOWSKI, ROGERS, FLOOD & MCARDLE
Crystal Lake, IL....General Practice, Municipal and Zoning Law

ZUMBRUNN, LYNN E., A LAW CORPORATION
Victorville, CA ....Civil Trial Practice, Family Law

ZWEIG, DAVID S., LAW FIRM OF
San Diego, CA ....Tax Law

PRACTICE AREAS SECTION

ADMINISTRATIVE LAW

ALABAMA

*BIRMINGHAM,** Jefferson Co.

BALCH & BINGHAM (AV)

1710 Sixth Avenue North, P.O. Box 306, 35201
Telephone: 205-251-8100
Facsimile: 205-226-8798
Other Birmingham, Alabama Office: 1901 Sixth Avenue North, 35203.
Telephone: 205-251-8100.
Facsimile: 205-226-8799.
Montgomery, Alabama Office: The Winter Building, 2 Dexter Avenue, 36101.
Telephone: 205-834-6500.
Facsimile: 205-269-3115.
Huntsville, Alabama Office: Suite 810, 200 West Court Square, 35801.
Telephone: 205-551-0171.
Facsimile: 205-551-0174.
Washington, D.C. Office: Suite 800, 1101 Connecticut Avenue, N.W., 20036.
Telephone: 202-296-0387.
Facsimile: 202-452-8180.

MEMBERS OF FIRM

Rodney O. Mundy
Dan H. McCrary

Counsel for: Alabama Power Co.; Blue Cross and Blue Shield of Alabama; The Boeing Company; Brasfield & Gorrie, Inc.; Compass Bancshares, Inc.; Harbert Corp.; Kimberly-Clark Corp.; Southern Company Services, Inc.; Southern Research Institute; Vesta Insurance Group, Inc.

For Complete List of Firm Personnel, See General Section

For full biographical listings, see the Martindale-Hubbell Law Directory

*MOBILE,** Mobile Co.

ARMBRECHT, JACKSON, DEMOUY, CROWE, HOLMES & REEVES (AV)

1300 AmSouth Center, P.O. Box 290, 36601
Telephone: 334-432-6751
Facsimile: 334-432-6843; 433-3821

MEMBERS OF FIRM

Wm. H. Armbrecht (1908-1991)
Theodore K. Jackson (1910-1981)
Marshall J. DeMouy
Wm. H. Armbrecht, III
Rae M. Crowe
Broox G. Holmes
W. Boyd Reeves
E. B. Peebles III
William B. Harvey
Kirk C. Shaw
Norman E. Waldrop, Jr.
Conrad P. Armbrecht
Edward G. Hawkins
Grover E. Asmus II
David A. Bagwell
Douglas L. Brown
Donald C. Radcliff
Christopher I. Gruenewald
James Donald Hughes
M. Kathleen Miller
Edward A. Dean
David E. Hudgens
Ray Morgan Thompson
James Dale Smith
Duane A. Graham
Robert J. Mullican
Wm. Steele Holman, II
Coleman F. Meador
Broox G. Holmes, Jr.

ASSOCIATES

James E. Robertson, Jr.
Scott G. Brown
Clifford C. Brady
Richard W. Franklin
Stephen Russell Copeland
Tara T. Bostick
Rodney R. Cate
James F. Watkins

Representative Clients: AmSouth Bank N.A. (Regional Counsel); Burlington Northern Railroad Co. (District Counsel); Ryan-Walsh, Inc.; Scott Paper Co.; Travelers Insurance Co.

For Complete List of Firm Personnel, See General Section

For full biographical listings, see the Martindale-Hubbell Law Directory

*MONTGOMERY,** Montgomery Co.

CAPOUANO, WAMPOLD, PRESTWOOD & SANSONE, P.A. (AV)

350 Adams Avenue, P.O. Box 1910, 36102-1910
Telephone: 334-264-6401
Fax: 334-834-4954

Leon M. Capouano
Alvin T. Prestwood
Jerome D. Smith
Ellis D. Hanan
Joseph P. Borg
Joseph W. Warren

OF COUNSEL

Charles H. Wampold, Jr.

(See Next Column)

Thomas B. Klinner
Linda Smith Webb
James M. Sizemore, Jr.

Counsel for: First Alabama Bank of Montgomery, N.A.; Union Bank and Trust Co.; Real Estate Financing, Inc.; SouthTrust Bank; AmSouth Bank; Central Bank; City Federal Savings & Loan Assoc.; Colonial Mortgage Co.; Lomas & Nettleton; First Bank of Linden.

For full biographical listings, see the Martindale-Hubbell Law Directory

ARIZONA

*NOGALES,** Santa Cruz Co.

O'CONNOR, CAVANAGH, ANDERSON, WESTOVER, KILLINGSWORTH & BESHEARS, A PROFESSIONAL ASSOCIATION (AV)

1827 North Mastick Way, 85621
Telephone: 602-761-4215
FAX: 602-761-3505
Phoenix, Arizona Office: One East Camelback Road, Suite 1100, 85012.
Telephone: 602-263-2400.
FAX: 602-263-2900.
Tucson, Arizona Office: Suite 2200, One South Church Avenue, 85701.
Telephone: 602-882-8912.
FAX: 602-624-9564.
Sun City, Arizona Office: 13250 North Del Webb Boulevard, Suite B, 85351.
Telephone: 602-263-2808.
FAX: 602-933-3100.

OF COUNSEL

James D. Robinson

Representative Clients: Omega Produce Co.; Frank's Distributing, Inc.; City of Nogales; Collectron of Ariz., Inc.; James K. Wilson Produce Co.; Agricola Bon, S. de R.L. de C.V.; Angel Demerutis E.; Rene Carrillo C.; Arturo Lomeli; Theojary Crisantes E.

For Complete List of Firm Personnel, See General Section

For full biographical listings, see the Martindale-Hubbell Law Directory

*PHOENIX,** Maricopa Co.

CARMICHAEL & POWELL, PROFESSIONAL CORPORATION (AV)

7301 North 16th Street, 85020-5224
Telephone: 602-861-0777
Facsimile: 602-870-0296

Ronald W. Carmichael
Donald W. Powell
Laurence B. Stevens
Sid A. Horwitz

Stephen Manes
Craig A. Raby
Brian A. Hatch
Richard C. Gramlich

Representative Clients: Home Builders Association of Central Arizona.

For full biographical listings, see the Martindale-Hubbell Law Directory

FENNEMORE CRAIG, A PROFESSIONAL CORPORATION (AV)

Two North Central, Suite 2200, 85004
Telephone: 602-257-8700
Fax: 602-257-8527
Scottsdale, Arizona Office: 6263 North Scottsdale Road, Suite 290, 85250.
Telephone: 602-257-5400.
Fax: 602-945-4932.
Tucson, Arizona Office: One South Church Avenue, Suite 1030, 85701.
Telephone: 602-624-9312.
Fax: 602-882-7383.

C. Webb Crockett
Michael Preston Green
John G. Ryan
Timothy Berg
Andrew M. Federhar
Robert D. Anderson

Representative Clients: ASARCO Incorporated; AT&T Communications; Bridgestone/Firestone, Inc.; Catellus Development Corp.; Citibank (Arizona); First Interstate Bank of Arizona; GIANT Industries; Phelps Dodge Corporation; The Atchison, Topeka & Santa Fe Railway, Co.; US WEST Communications.

For Complete List of Firm Personnel, See General Section

For full biographical listings, see the Martindale-Hubbell Law Directory

MEYER, HENDRICKS, VICTOR, OSBORN & MALEDON, A PROFESSIONAL ASSOCIATION (AV)

2929 North Central Avenue Suite 2100, 85012-2794
Telephone: 602-640-9000
Facsimile: (24 Hrs.) 602-640-9050
Mailing Address: P.O. Box 33449, 85067-3449,

(See Next Column)

MEYER, HENDRICKS, VICTOR, OSBORN & MALEDON A PROFESSIONAL ASSOCIATION, *Phoenix—Continued*

Paul J. Meyer
Andrew D. Hurwitz
Randall C. Nelson
Jay I. Moyes
John A. LaSota, Jr.
James G. Derouin
William M. Hardin
Jeffrey C. Zimmerman
David B. Rosenbaum
W. Scott Bales
Bruce E. Meyerson
Lucia Fakonas Howard
Robert V. Kerrick

Evan Haglund

Reference: Bank One Arizona, NA.

For Complete List of Firm Personnel, See General Section

For full biographical listings, see the Martindale-Hubbell Law Directory

O'CONNOR, CAVANAGH, ANDERSON, WESTOVER, KILLINGSWORTH & BESHEARS, A PROFESSIONAL ASSOCIATION (AV)

One East Camelback Road, Suite 1100, 85012-1656
Telephone: 602-263-2400
FAX: 602-263-2900
Sun City, Arizona Office: 13250 North Del Webb Boulevard, Suite B, 85351.
Telephone: 602-263-2808.
FAX: 602-933-3100.
Tucson, Arizona Office: Suite 2200, One South Church Avenue, 85701.
Telephone: 602-882-8912.
FAX: 602-624-9564.
Nogales, Arizona Office: 1827 North Mastick Way, 85621.
Telephone: 602-761-4215.
FAX: 602-761-3505.

Jeffrey B. Smith
Jolyon Grant
Paul J. Roshka, Jr.
Raymond S. Heyman

Timothy F. Bolden
Jamal F. Allen

Representative Clients: Bashas', Inc.; Arzona Payphone Assn.; Nevada Payphone Assn.; Phoenix Children's Hospital; Happy Trails Golf Resort; American Network Securities, Inc.; Charles Schwab & Co., Inc.; Fidelity Brokerage Services, Inc.; Walgreens Company; Norcross Securities, Inc.

For Complete List of Firm Personnel, See General Section

For full biographical listings, see the Martindale-Hubbell Law Directory

*TUCSON,** Pima Co.

COREY & FARRELL, P.C. (AV)

Suite 830, Norwest Tower, One South Church Avenue, 85701-1620
Telephone: 602-882-4994
Telefax: 602-884-7757

Barry M. Corey
Kristen B. Klotz

Representative Clients: Amphitheater Public School District; Civil Service Commission of the City of Tucson; La Quinta Homes, Inc.; Pima County Merit System Commission; DANKA-Uni-Copy Corp.; Introspect Health Care Corp.

For full biographical listings, see the Martindale-Hubbell Law Directory

RAVEN, KIRSCHNER & NORELL, P.C. (AV)

Suite 1600, One South Church Avenue, 85701-1612
Telephone: 602-628-8700
Telefax: 602-798-5200

Dennis J. Clancy
Susan M. Freund
Mark B. Raven
S. Leonard Scheff

Representative Clients: Pace American Bonding Company; Citibank (Arizona); Continental Medical Systems, Inc.; El Paso Natural Gas Co.; Norwest Bank Arizona; El Rio-Santa Cruz Neighborhood Health Center, Inc.; Resolution Trust Corp.; Sierra Vista Community Hospital; Southern Arizona Rehabilitation Hospital; Ford Motor Credit.

For Complete List of Firm Personnel, See General Section

For full biographical listings, see the Martindale-Hubbell Law Directory

ARKANSAS

*LITTLE ROCK,** Pulaski Co.

HOOVER & STOREY (AV)

111 Center Street, 11th Floor, 72201-4445
Telephone: 501-376-8500
Facsimile: 501-372-3255

(See Next Column)

MEMBERS OF FIRM

Paul W. Hoover, Jr.
O. H. Storey, III
John Kooistra, III
Lawrence Joseph Brady
William P. Dougherty
Max C. Mehlburger
Joyce Bradley Babin
Herbert W. Kell, Jr.
Letty McAdams

For full biographical listings, see the Martindale-Hubbell Law Directory

CALIFORNIA

PASADENA, Los Angeles Co.

LAGERLOF, SENECAL, BRADLEY & SWIFT (AV)

301 North Lake Avenue, 10th Floor, 91101-4107
Telephone: 818-793-9400
FAX: 818-793-5900

MEMBERS OF FIRM

Joseph J. Burris (1913-1980)
Stanley C. Lagerlof
H. Melvin Swift, Jr.
H. Jess Senecal
Jack T. Swafford
John F. Bradley
Timothy J. Gosney
William F. Kruse
Thomas S. Bunn, III
Andrew D. Turner
Rebecca J. Thyne

ASSOCIATES

Paul M. Norman
John F. Machtinger
James D. Ciampa
Ellen M. Burkhart

LEGAL SUPPORT PERSONNEL

Ronald E. Hagler

Representative Clients: Anchor Glass Container Corporation; Bethlehem Steel Corp.; Orthopaedic Hospital; Palmdale Water District; Public Water Agencies Group; Walnut Valley Water District.
Special Counsel: City of Redondo Beach, Calif.; Ventura Port Dist., Calif.

For full biographical listings, see the Martindale-Hubbell Law Directory

*SACRAMENTO,** Sacramento Co.

HARMATA LAW OFFICES (AV)

2201 Q Street, 95816
Telephone: 916-442-2842
Fax: 916-442-2015

Donald D. Harmata

LEGAL SUPPORT PERSONNEL
PARALEGAL

Debra D. Morrow

Representative Clients: Control Data Corporation; Deloitte & Touche; General Electric Company; Myers Electric, Inc.; Syblon-Reid Co.; Systemhouse Inc.; TRW, Inc.

For full biographical listings, see the Martindale-Hubbell Law Directory

RICHARD K. TURNER (AV)

555 Capitol Mall, Suite 1500, 95814
Telephone: 916-557-1111

For full biographical listings, see the Martindale-Hubbell Law Directory

WILKE, FLEURY, HOFFELT, GOULD & BIRNEY (AV)

A Partnership including Professional Corporations
400 Capitol Mall, Suite 2200, 95814-4408
Telephone: 916-441-2430
Telefax: 916-442-6664
Mailing Address: P.O. Box 15559, 95852-0559

MEMBERS OF FIRM

Richard H. Hoffelt (Inc.)
William A. Gould, Jr., (Inc.)
Philip R. Birney (Inc.)
Thomas G. Redmon (Inc.)
Scott L. Gassaway
Donald Rex Heckman II (Inc.)
Alan G. Perkins
Bradley N. Webb
Ernest James Krtil
Robert R. Mirkin
Matthew W. Powell
Mark L. Andrews
Stephen K. Marmaduke
David A. Frenznick
John R. Valencia
Angus M. MacLeod

ASSOCIATES

Paul A. Dorris
Kelli M. Kennaday
Tracy S. Hendrickson
Joseph G. De Angelis
Jennifer L. Kennedy
Anthony J. DeCristoforo
Rachel N. Kook
Alicia F. From
Michael Polis
Matthew J. Smith
Wayne L. Ordos

(See Next Column)

WILKE, FLEURY, HOFFELT, GOULD & BIRNEY—*Continued*

OF COUNSEL

Sherman C. Wilke
Anita Seipp Marmaduke
Benjamin G. Davidian

Representative Clients: NOR-CAL Mutual Insurance Co.; California Optometric Assn.; KPMG Peat Marwick; Glaxo, Inc.

For full biographical listings, see the Martindale-Hubbell Law Directory

COLORADO

*DENVER,** Denver Co.

BROWNSTEIN HYATT FARBER & STRICKLAND, P.C. (AV)

Twenty-Second Floor, 410 Seventeenth Street, 80202-4437
Telephone: 303-534-6335
Telecopier: 303-623-1956

Steven W. Farber
Thomas L. Strickland
Andrew W. Loewi
Charles B. White
Gary M. Reiff
Wayne F. Forman
Bruce A. James
P. Cole Finegan

Carrie A. Mineart
Mark J. Mathews

Representative Clients: The Denver Broncos; Hertz Corp.; La Petite Academy, Inc.; Morrison Knudsen Corporation; Pfizer, Inc.; Rose Medical Center/Rose Health Care Systems; Safeway, Inc.; Schmidt Construction Co.; Siemens Transportation Systems; Trammell Crow Company.

For Complete List of Firm Personnel, See General Section

For full biographical listings, see the Martindale-Hubbell Law Directory

MUSGRAVE & THEIS, P.C. (AV)

Mellon Financial Center, 1775 Sherman Street, Suite 2950, 80203
Telephone: 303-863-8686
Facsimile: 303-863-0423

B. Lawrence Theis
Bobbee J. Musgrave

Jane G. Ebisch

OF COUNSEL

Thomas P. McMahon

Representative Clients: Anheuser-Busch Companies; City and County of Denver; Schuller International; Sashco, Inc.; Tri-County Cablevision, Inc.
Reference: Norwest Bank of Buckingham Square.

For full biographical listings, see the Martindale-Hubbell Law Directory

CONNECTICUT

*HARTFORD,** Hartford Co.

SOROKIN SOROKIN GROSS HYDE & WILLIAMS P.C. (AV)

One Corporate Center, 06103
Telephone: 203-525-6645
Fax: 203-522-1781
Simsbury, Connecticut Office: 730 Hopmeadow Street.
Telephone: 203-651-9348.
Rocky Hill, Connecticut Office: 2360 Main Street.
Telephone: 203-563-9305.
Fax: 203-529-6931.
Glastonbury, Connecticut Office: 124 Hebron Avenue.
Telephone: 203-659-8801.

Richard G. Convicer
Clifford J. Grandjean
Lewis Rabinovitz
Richard D. Tulisano (Resident, Rocky Hill Office)

OF COUNSEL

Ethel Silver Sorokin
Milton Sorokin

For Complete List of Firm Personnel, See General Section

For full biographical listings, see the Martindale-Hubbell Law Directory

DISTRICT OF COLUMBIA

WASHINGTON, D.C. Co.

* indicates certain Bar Register subscribers, in cities of comparable size and importance, who maintain an additional office in Washington, D.C. and who have arranged for representation as a part of the Washington, D.C. listings that follow

* BAKER & BOTTS, L.L.P. (AV)

A Registered Limited Liability Partnership
The Warner, 1299 Pennsylvania Avenue, N.W., 20004-2400
Telephone: 202-639-7700
Fax: 202-639-7832
Houston, Texas Office: One Shell Plaza, 910 Louisiana.
Telephone: 713-229-1234.
Austin, Texas Office: 1600 San Jacinto Center, 98 San Jacinto Boulevard.
Telephone: 512-322-2500.
Dallas, Texas Office: 2001 Ross Avenue.
Telephone: 214-953-6500.
New York, New York Office: 805 Third Avenue, Suite 2000.
Telephone: 212-705-5000.
Moscow, Russian Federation Office: 10 ul. Pushkinskaya, 103031.
Telephone: 7095/921-5300 (Local); 7501/929-7070 (International).

MEMBERS OF FIRM

Bruce F. Kiely
William D. Kramer
Charles M. Darling, IV
Randolph Quaile McManus
Thomas J. Eastment
B. Donovan Picard
Steven R. Hunsicker
John B. Veach, III
John B. McDaniel

ASSOCIATES

Claude A. Allen
Debra Raggio Bolton
Sue Ann Dilts
Andrea Fraser-Reid Farr
Drew J. Fossum
Jennifer S. Leete (Not admitted in DC)
Mark K. Lewis
Paul T. Luther
Martin T. Lutz
Michael X. Marinelli
Jeffrey A. Stonerock
Cheryl J. Walker

For Complete List of Firm Personnel, See General Section

For full biographical listings, see the Martindale-Hubbell Law Directory

BAKER & HOSTETLER (AV)

Washington Square, Suite 1100, 1050 Connecticut Avenue, N.W., 20036-5304
Telephone: 202-861-1500
In Cleveland, Ohio: 3200 National City Center, 1900 East Ninth Street.
Telephone: 216-621-0200.
In Columbus, Ohio: Capitol Square, Suite 2100, 65 East State Street.
Telephone: 614-228-1541.
In Denver, Colorado: 303 East 17th Avenue, Suite 1100.
Telephone: 303-861-0600.
In Houston, Texas: 1000 Louisiana, Suite 2000.
Telephone: 713-751-1600.
In Long Beach, California: 300 Oceangate, Suite 620.
Telephone: 310-432-2827.
In Los Angeles, California: 600 Wilshire Boulevard.
Telephone: 213-624-2400.
In Orlando, Florida: SunBank Center, Suite 2300, 200 South Orange Avenue.
Telephone: 305-841-1111.
In College Park, Maryland: 9658 Baltimore Boulevard, Suite 206.
Telephone: 301-441-2781.
In Alexandria, Virginia: 437 North Lee Street.
Telephone: 703-549-1294.
In San Francisco, California: One Sansome Street, Suite 2000.
Telephone: 415-951-4705.

PARTNERS

Frederick H. Graefe
Richard A. Hauser

OF COUNSEL

E. Mark Braden
Richard H. Jones
Laurence Levitan

For Complete List of Firm Personnel, See General Section

For full biographical listings, see the Martindale-Hubbell Law Directory

BRICKFIELD, BURCHETTE & RITTS, P.C. (AV)

8th Floor, West Tower, 1025 Thomas Jefferson Street, N.W., 20007-0805
Telephone: 202-342-0800
Fax: 202-342-0807
Austin, Texas Office: Suite 1050, 1005 Congress Avenue.
Telephone: 512-472-1081.

(See Next Column)

BRICKFIELD, BURCHETTE & RITTS P.C., *Washington—Continued*

Peter J. P. Brickfield
William H. Burchette
Mark C. Davis (Not admitted in DC; Resident, Austin, Texas Office)
Daniel C. Kaufman
Michael E. Kaufmann
Peter J. Mattheis
Michael N. McCarty
Frederick H. Ritts
Fernando Rodriguez (Not admitted in DC; Resident, Austin, Texas Office)
Christine C. Ryan
Garrett A. Stone

COUNSEL

Philip L. Chabot, Jr.
Foster De Reitzes
Robert L. McCarty
A. Hewitt Rose

Lisa A. Cottle (Not admitted in DC)
Vincent P. Duane
Julie B. Greenisen (Not admitted in DC)
Stephen J. Karina (Not admitted in DC)
Sandra E. Rizzo
Sonnet C. Schmidt (Not admitted in DC)

LEGAL SUPPORT PERSONNEL

Jean Levicki

For full biographical listings, see the Martindale-Hubbell Law Directory

GEORGE M. COBURN (AV)

1661 Crescent Place, N.W., Suite 208, 20009-4047
Telephone: 202-234-2054
Fax: 202-234-2054

For full biographical listings, see the Martindale-Hubbell Law Directory

DAVIS & HARMAN (AV)

Suite 1200, 1455 Pennsylvania Avenue, N.W., 20004
Telephone: 202-347-2230

MEMBERS OF FIRM

Thomas A. Davis
William B. Harman, Jr.
John T. Adney
Joseph F. McKeever, III
Barbara Groves Mattox
Richard S. Belas

ASSOCIATES

Mark E. Griffin
Craig R. Springfield
David L. Wunder

OF COUNSEL

Gail Bramblett Wilkins
William T. Gibb, III

For full biographical listings, see the Martindale-Hubbell Law Directory

DUNAWAY & CROSS, A PROFESSIONAL CORPORATION (AV)

Suite 400, 1146 19th Street, N.W., 20036
Telephone: 202-862-9700

Mac S. Dunaway
Gary E. Cross
George C. Courtot
Stanley J. Green

Matthew F. Hall
Christopher E. Anders
Joan R. Vail (Not admitted in DC)

COUNSEL

Raymond P. Shafer (Not admitted in DC)

For full biographical listings, see the Martindale-Hubbell Law Directory

FRANK W. FRISK, JR., P.C. (AV)

Suite 125, Canal Square, 1054 Thirty-First Street, N.W., 20007
Telephone: 202-333-8433
Fax: 202-333-8431

Frank W. Frisk, Jr.

For full biographical listings, see the Martindale-Hubbell Law Directory

R. TENNEY JOHNSON (AV)

Suite 600, 2300 N Street, N.W., 20037-1122
Telephone: 202-663-9030
Fax: 202-663-9040

For full biographical listings, see the Martindale-Hubbell Law Directory

MORLEY CASKIN (AV)

1225 Eye Street, N.W., Suite 402, 20005
Telephone: 202-789-1100
Facsimile: 202-289-3928

OF COUNSEL

Stanley M. Morley (1912-1991)

MEMBERS OF FIRM

Joel F. Zipp
William A. Mogel
George H. Williams, Jr.
Paul W. Diehl

For full biographical listings, see the Martindale-Hubbell Law Directory

REICHLER, MILTON & MEDEL (AV)

Suite 1200, 1747 Pennsylvania Avenue, N.W., 20006-4604
Telephone: 202-223-1200
Telex: 494-3588
Fax: 202-785-6687

Paul S. Reichler
Kathleen M. Milton
Arthur V. Medel

ASSOCIATES

Janis H. Brennan
Padideh Ala'i
Traci Duvall Humes
Alima Joned (Not admitted in DC)

For full biographical listings, see the Martindale-Hubbell Law Directory

SUTHERLAND, ASBILL & BRENNAN (AV)

1275 Pennsylvania Avenue, N.W., 20004-2404
Telephone: 202-383-0100
Cable Address: "Sutab Wash"
Telex: 89-501
Facsimile: 202-637-3593
Atlanta, Georgia Office: 999 Peachtree Street, N. E., 30309-3996.
Telephone: 404-853-8000.
New York, N.Y. Office: 1270 Avenue of the Americas, 10020-1700.
Telephone: 212-332-3000.
Austin, Texas Office: 111 Congress Avenue, 23rd Floor, 78701-4079.
Telephone: 512-469-3350.

Robert W. Clark
Jacob Dweck
Philip R. Ehrenkranz
N. Beth Emery
Edward J. Grenier, Jr.
Karen L. Grimm
Joel E. Hoffman
Glen S. Howard
Frank J. Martin, Jr.
Randolph J. May
Keith R. McCrea
Michael T. Mishkin
William H. Penniman
Peter H. Rodgers
Beverly J. Rudy
Michael J. Shea
Kenneth G. Starling

COUNSEL

Timothy J. Cooney
Sterling H. Smith

For Complete List of Firm Personnel, See General Section

For full biographical listings, see the Martindale-Hubbell Law Directory

DANIEL R. THOMPSON, P.C. (AV)

Suite 925, 1620 I Street, N.W., 20006
Telephone: 202-293-5800
Facsimile: 202-463-8998

Daniel R. Thompson
Gregory E. Thompson
John B. Hallagan

Reference: NationsBank, Washington, D.C.

For full biographical listings, see the Martindale-Hubbell Law Directory

* VENABLE, BAETJER, HOWARD & CIVILETTI (AV)

A Partnership including Professional Corporations
Suite 1000, 1201 New York Avenue, N.W., 20005
Telephone: 202-962-4800
Fax: 202-962-8300
Baltimore, Maryland Office: Venable, Baetjer and Howard, 1800 Mercantile Bank & Trust Building, 2 Hopkins Plaza.
Telephone: 410-244-7400.
McLean, Virginia Office: Venable, Baetjer and Howard, Suite 400, 2010 Corporate Ridge.
Telephone: 703-760-1600.
Rockville, Maryland Office: Venable, Baetjer and Howard, Suite 500, One Church Street, P. O. Box 1906.
Telephone: 301-217-5600.
Towson, Maryland Office: Venable, Baetjer and Howard, 210 Allegheny Avenue, P. O. Box 5517.
Telephone: 410-494-6200.

MEMBERS OF FIRM

Thomas J. Madden
Ronald R. Glancz
Robert P. Bedell (Not admitted in DC)
Michael Schatzow (Also at Baltimore and Towson, Maryland Offices)
John F. Cooney
N. Frank Wiggins
Jeffrey D. Knowles
John J. Pavlick, Jr.
Gary M. Hnath

ASSOCIATE

James W. Hedlund (Not admitted in DC)

For Complete List of Firm Personnel, See General Section

For full biographical listings, see the Martindale-Hubbell Law Directory

WEBSTER, CHAMBERLAIN & BEAN (AV)

Suite 1000, 1747 Pennsylvania Avenue, N.W., 20006
Telephone: 202-785-9500

(See Next Column)

WEBSTER, CHAMBERLAIN & BEAN—*Continued*

MEMBERS OF FIRM

George D. Webster
J. Coleman Bean
Arthur L. Herold
Alan P. Dye
Edward D. Coleman
Burkett Van Kirk
Frank M. Northam
Gerard P. Panaro
John W. Hazard, Jr.
Hugh K. Webster

OF COUNSEL

Charles E. Chamberlain

ASSOCIATES

Charles M. Watkins
David P. Goch (Not admitted in DC)
Brenley J. Locke (Not admitted in DC)

For full biographical listings, see the Martindale-Hubbell Law Directory

FLORIDA

*KISSIMMEE,** Osceola Co.

POHL & BROWN, P.A.

(See Winter Park)

NEW PORT RICHEY, Pasco Co.

MARTIN, FIGURSKI & HARRILL (AV)

A Partnership of Professional Associations
Suite B-1, 8406 Massachusetts Avenue, P.O. Box 786, 34653
Telephone: 813-842-8439
Clearwater, Florida Office: 28059 U.S. Highway 19, Suite 202.
Telephone: 813-796-3259.
Fax: 813-796-3598.

MEMBERS OF FIRM

Daniel N. Martin (P.A.)
Gerald A. Figurski (P.A.)
James Benjamin Harrill (P.A.)

Representative Clients: Regency Communities, Inc., formerly Minieri Communities of Florida, Inc.; Greene Builders, Inc.; Mobil Oil Corp.; Barnett Bank of Pasco County; Hospital Corporation of America; U.S. Home Corp. *Approved Attorneys For:* Attorneys' Title Insurance Fund; First American Title Insurance Co.; Commonwealth Land Title Insurance Company. *Reference:* Barnett Bank of Pasco County.

For full biographical listings, see the Martindale-Hubbell Law Directory

*ORLANDO,** Orange Co.

POHL & BROWN, P.A.

(See Winter Park)

*TALLAHASSEE,** Leon Co.

GATLIN, WOODS, CARLSON & COWDERY (AV)

A Partnership including a Professional Corporation
The Mahan Station, 1709-D Mahan Drive, 32308
Telephone: 904-877-7191
Telecopier: 904-877-9031

MEMBERS OF FIRM

B. Kenneth Gatlin (P.A.)
Thomas F. Woods
John D. Carlson
Kathryn G. W. Cowdery

ASSOCIATE

Wayne L. Schiefelbein

For full biographical listings, see the Martindale-Hubbell Law Directory

HOPPING BOYD GREEN & SAMS (AV)

123 South Calhoun Street, P.O. Box 6526, 32314
Telephone: 904-222-7500
Fax: 904-224-8551

MEMBERS OF FIRM

Carlos Alvarez
James S. Alves
Brian H. Bibeau
Kathleen L. Blizzard
Elizabeth C. Bowman
William L. Boyd, IV
Richard S. Brightman
Peter C. Cunningham
Ralph A. DeMeo
Thomas M. DeRose
William H. Green
Wade L. Hopping
Frank E. Matthews
Richard D. Melson
David L. Powell
William D. Preston
Carolyn S. Raepple
Gary P. Sams
Robert P. Smith
Cheryl G. Stuart

(See Next Column)

ASSOCIATES

Kristin M. Conroy
Charles A. Culp, Jr.
Connie C. Durrence
Jonathan S. Fox
James Calvin Goodlett
Gary K. Hunter, Jr.
Dalana W. Johnson
Jonathan T. Johnson
Angela R. Morrison
Gary V. Perko
Karen Peterson
Michael P. Petrovich
Douglas S. Roberts
R. Scott Ruth
Julie Rome Steinmeyer

OF COUNSEL

W. Robert Fokes

Representative Clients: Amelia Island Plantation; American Cyanamid Co.; ARC America Corp.; Association of American Publishers; Association of Physical Fitness Centers; Cement Products Corp.; CF Industries; Champion Realty; Chemical Bank; Deseret Properties.

For full biographical listings, see the Martindale-Hubbell Law Directory

KATZ, KUTTER, HAIGLER, ALDERMAN, MARKS & BRYANT, PROFESSIONAL ASSOCIATION (AV)

106 East College Avenue, 12th Floor, P.O. Box 1877, 32301
Telephone: 904-224-9634
Telecopier: 904-224-0781; 222-0103

Silvia Morell Alderman
Daniel C. Brown
Bill L. Bryant, Jr.
J. Riley Davis
Martin R. Dix
Paul R. Ezatoff, Jr.
William M. Furlow
Mitchell B. Haigler
Edward S. Jaffry
Allan J. Katz
Edward L. Kutter
Richard P. Lee
John C. Lovett
John R. Marks, III
Brian M. Nugent
Gary P. Timin
J. Larry Williams
David A. Yon
Paul A. Zeigler

Donna E. Blanton
Alan Harrison Brents
Richard E. Coates
Jose A. Diez-Arguelles
Kenneth W. Donnelly
David P. Healy
Mark E. Kaplan
Christopher B. Lunny
Tavis L. Miller
Bruce D. Platt

OF COUNSEL

Patrick F. Maroney
Arthur L. Stern, III

LEGAL SUPPORT PERSONNEL

Gerald C. Wester (Governmental Consultant)
Monica A. Lasseter (Governmental Consultant)
E. Clinton Smawley (Governmental Consultant)
Pat Griffith O'Connell (Governmental Consultant)
J. Andrew Keller, III (Executive Director)

For full biographical listings, see the Martindale-Hubbell Law Directory

PAUL WATSON LAMBERT (AV)

2851 Remington Green Circle, Suite C, 32308-3749
Telephone: 904-385-9393
Fax: 904-385-8045

Agent for: Agency for Health Care Administration; Department of Business and Professional Regulation; Department of Insurance; Department of Health and Rehabilitation Services.

For full biographical listings, see the Martindale-Hubbell Law Directory

MCFARLAIN, WILEY, CASSEDY & JONES, PROFESSIONAL ASSOCIATION (AV)

215 South Monroe Street, Suite 600, P.O. Box 2174, 32316-2174
Telephone: 904-222-2107
Telecopier: 904-222-8475

Richard C. McFarlain
William B. Wiley
Marshall R. Cassedy
Douglas P. Jones
Charles A. Stampelos
Linda McMullen
H. Darrell White, Jr.
Christopher Barkas

Harold R. Mardenborough, Jr.
Katherine Hairston LaRosa
J. Robert Griffin

OF COUNSEL

Betty J. Steffens

For full biographical listings, see the Martindale-Hubbell Law Directory

RADEY HINKLE THOMAS & MCARTHUR (AV)

Suite 1000 Monroe-Park Tower, 101 North Monroe Street, P.O. Drawer 11307, 32302
Telephone: 904-681-7766
Telecopier: 904-681-0506

(See Next Column)

RADEY HINKLE THOMAS & MCARTHUR, *Tallahassee—Continued*

John Radey
Elizabeth Waas McArthur
Jeffrey L. Frehn

Representative Clients: Ringling Bros. Barnum-Bailey Combined Shows; Tampa General Hospital; Columbia/HCA Healthcare Corp.; Tallahassee Community Hospital; Lawnwood Regional Medical Center; Central Florida Regional Hospital.

For Complete List of Firm Personnel, See General Section

For full biographical listings, see the Martindale-Hubbell Law Directory

ROSE, SUNDSTROM & BENTLEY (AV)

A Partnership including Professional Associations
2548 Blairstone Pines Drive, P.O. Box 1567, 32302-1567
Telephone: 904-877-6555
Telecopier: 904-656-4029

MEMBERS OF FIRM

Chris H. Bentley (P.A.)
F. Marshall Deterding
Martin S. Friedman (P.A.)
John R. Jenkins
Robert M. C. Rose (P.A.)
William E. Sundstrom (P.A.)
Diane D. Tremor (P.A.)
John L. Wharton

ASSOCIATE

Robert A. Antista

Representative Clients: Aloha Utilities, Inc.; Arbor Health Care Co.; Bonita Springs Water System, Inc.; East Central Florida Services, Inc.; Florida Waterworks Assn.; Hydratech Utilities, Inc.; National Premium Budget Plan Corp.; Orange-Osceola Utilities, Inc.; Utility Board of the City of Key West.
Reference: Barnett Bank, Tallahassee.

For full biographical listings, see the Martindale-Hubbell Law Directory

SLEPIN & SLEPIN (AV)

1114 East Park Avenue, 32301
Telephone: 904-224-5200

Stephen Marc Slepin

OF COUNSEL

Matthew M. Slepin

For full biographical listings, see the Martindale-Hubbell Law Directory

*TAMPA,** Hillsborough Co.

LANGFORD, HILL & TRYBUS, P.A. (AV)

Suite 800, Bayshore Place, 601 Bayshore Boulevard, 33606
Telephone: 813-251-5533
Telecopier: 813-251-1900
Wats: 1-800-277-2005

E. C. Langford
Edward A. Hill
Ronald H. Trybus
Ronald G. Hock
Catherine M. Catlin
Debra M. Kubicsek
William B. Smith

Fredrique B. Boire
Muriel Desloovere
Kevin H. O'Neill
Vicki L. Page
Frederick T. Reeves
Barbara A. Sinsley
Stephens B. Woodrough (Not admitted in FL)
Anthony G. Woodward

Representative Clients: Affiliated of Florida, Inc.; American Federation Insurance Co.; Armor Insurance; Bank of Tampa; Central Bank of Tampa; Cintas Corp.; Container Corporation of America; CU Financial Services; Farm Stores, Inc.; First Union Home Equity Bank.

For full biographical listings, see the Martindale-Hubbell Law Directory

WINTER PARK, Orange Co.

POHL & BROWN, P.A. (AV)

280 West Canton Avenue, Suite 410, P.O. Box 3208, 32789
Telephone: 407-647-7645; 407-647-POHL
Telefax: 407-647-2314

Frank L. Pohl
Usher L. Brown
Houston E. Short
Dwight I. Cool
William W. Pouzar
Mary B. Van Leuven

OF COUNSEL

Frederick W. Peirsol

Representative Clients: Orange County Comptroller; Osceola County; School Board of Osceola County, Florida; Osceola Tourist Development Council; NationsBank of Florida, N.A.; SunBank, N.A.; The Bank of Winter Park; Bekins Moving and Storage Co., Inc.; Champion Boats, Inc.; KeyCom Telephone Systems, Inc.

For full biographical listings, see the Martindale-Hubbell Law Directory

GEORGIA

*ATLANTA,** Fulton Co.

CHILIVIS & GRINDLER (AV)

3127 Maple Drive, N.E., 30305
Telephone: 404-233-4171
Facsimile: 404-261-2842

Nickolas P. Chilivis
Gary G. Grindler
Anthony L. Cochran
John K. Larkins, Jr.
Thomas D. Bever
Daniel P. Griffin
Carol M. Kayser
Merrilee Aynes Gober
John D. Dalbey
Pamela B. Adams

For full biographical listings, see the Martindale-Hubbell Law Directory

HARKLEROAD & HERMANCE, A PROFESSIONAL CORPORATION (AV)

2500 Cain Tower-Peachtree Center, 229 Peachtree Street, N.E., 30303
Telephone: 404-588-9211
Telex II: 810-751-3228
Telecopier: 404-659-0860

James P. Hermance

For full biographical listings, see the Martindale-Hubbell Law Directory

KIRWAN, GOGER, CHESIN & PARKS, P.C. (AV)

2600 The Grand, 75 Fourteenth Street, 30309
Telephone: 404-873-8000
Facsimile: 404-873-8050

A. Lee Parks, Jr.
Larry H. Chesin
Robert B. Remar

Harlan S. Miller, III

Representative Client: Anheuser Busch Cos., Inc.
Reference: Trust Company Bank.

For full biographical listings, see the Martindale-Hubbell Law Directory

LONG ALDRIDGE & NORMAN (AV)

A Partnership including Professional Corporations
One Peachtree Center, Suite 5300, 303 Peachtree Street, 30308
Telephone: 404-527-4000
Telecopier: 404-527-4198
Washington, D.C. Office: Suite 950, 1615 L Street, 20036.
Telephone: 202-223-7033.
Telecopier: 202-223-7013.

MEMBERS OF FIRM

Douglas L. Beresford (Resident, Washington, D.C. Office)
Gordon D. Giffin
John E. Holtzinger, Jr. (Resident, Washington, D.C. Office)
Albert G. Norman, Jr.
Russell N. Sewell, Jr.
Jacolyn A. Simmons (Resident, Washington, D.C. Office)
John T. Stough, Jr. (Resident, Washington, D.C. Office)
Robert I. White (Resident, Washington, D.C. Office)

ASSOCIATES

L. Craig Dowdy
Kevin M. Downey (Resident, Washington, D.C. Office)
Jennifer D. Malinovsky
Kyle Michel (Resident, Washington, D.C. Office)
Joel D. Newton (Resident, Washington, D.C. Office)

OF COUNSEL

Nancy A. White (Resident, Washington, D.C. Office)

For Complete List of Firm Personnel, See General Section

For full biographical listings, see the Martindale-Hubbell Law Directory

STOKES LAZARUS & CARMICHAEL (AV)

80 Peachtree Park Drive, N.E., 30309-1320
Telephone: 404-352-1465
Fax: 404-352-8463

MEMBERS OF FIRM

Marion B. Stokes
Wayne H. Lazarus
William K. Carmichael
Michael J. Ernst

ASSOCIATES

Richard J. Joseph
C. W. Tab Billingsley, Jr.
Douglas L. Brooks
Derek W. Johanson

For full biographical listings, see the Martindale-Hubbell Law Directory

Atlanta—Continued

CHARLES L. WEATHERLY (AV)

3151 Maple Drive, N.E., 30305
Telephone: 404-365-5045
Fax: 404-365-5041

For full biographical listings, see the Martindale-Hubbell Law Directory

WEISZ & ASSOCIATES (AV)

Suite 900 Live Oak Center, 3475 Lenox Road, N.E., 30326-1232
Telephone: 404-233-7888
Facsimile: 404-261-1925

Peter R. Weisz

ASSOCIATE

Cathy Rae Nash

LEGAL SUPPORT PERSONNEL

PARALEGALS

Jo Anne Gunn

For full biographical listings, see the Martindale-Hubbell Law Directory

HAWAII

*HONOLULU,** Honolulu Co.

DWYER IMANAKA SCHRAFF KUDO MEYER & FUJIMOTO ATTORNEYS AT LAW, A LAW CORPORATION (AV)

1800 Pioneer Plaza, 900 Fort Street Mall, 96813
Telephone: 808-524-8000
Telecopier: 808-526-1419
Mailing Address: P.O. Box 2727, 96803

John R. Dwyer, Jr.
Mitchell A. Imanaka
Paul A. Schraff
Benjamin A. Kudo (Atty. at Law, A Law Corp.)
William G. Meyer, III
Wesley M. Fujimoto
Ronald Van Grant
Jon M. H. Pang
Blake W. Bushnell
Kenn N. Kojima

Adelbert Green
Richard T. Asato, Jr.
Scott W. Settle
Darcie S. Yoshinaga
Tracy Timothy Woo
Lawrence I. Kawasaki
Douglas H. Inouye
Christine A. Low

OF COUNSEL

Randall Y. Iwase

For full biographical listings, see the Martindale-Hubbell Law Directory

ILLINOIS

*CHICAGO,** Cook Co.

STACK, FILPI & KAKACEK, CHARTERED (AV)

Suite 411, 140 South Dearborn Street, 60603-5298
Telephone: 312-782-0690; 236-5032
Telecopier: 312-782-0936
Telex: 25-3862 Counsel Cgo

Paul F. Stack
Robert A. Filpi
John J. Kakacek

OF COUNSEL

John H. Shurtleff
Michael A. McPartlin

For full biographical listings, see the Martindale-Hubbell Law Directory

INDIANA

*INDIANAPOLIS,** Marion Co.

HACKMAN MCCLARNON HULETT & CRACRAFT (AV)

2400 One Indiana Square, 46204
Telephone: 317-636-5401
Facsimile: 317-686-3288

MEMBERS OF FIRM

James R. McClarnon
Marvin L. Hackman
Robert S. Hulett
Michael B. Cracraft
Timothy K. Ryan
Philip B. McKiernan
Vicki L. Anderson

(See Next Column)

ASSOCIATES

Jane A. Phillips
Jeffrey G. Jackson
Thomas F. Bedsole
Thomas A. Dickey

OF COUNSEL

John D. Cochran, Jr.
Mark S. Alderfer

Representative Clients: Ameritech Indiana; AT&T Technologies, Inc.; Citizens Gas & Coke Utility; Texas Eastern Products Pipeline Co.; Indiana Municipal Power Agency; Indiana Municipal Electric Assn.

For full biographical listings, see the Martindale-Hubbell Law Directory

JOHNSON, SMITH, DENSBORN, WRIGHT & HEATH (AV)

One Indiana Square Suite 1800, 46204
Telephone: 317-634-9777
Telecopier: 317-636-9061

MEMBERS OF FIRM

Robert B. Hebert
James T. Smith
Martha Taylor Starkey

ASSOCIATE

David A. Tucker

For Complete List of Firm Personnel, See General Section

For full biographical listings, see the Martindale-Hubbell Law Directory

MCNAMAR, FEARNOW & MCSHARAR, P.C. (AV)

Bank One Center Tower, 111 Monument Circle, Suite 4500, 46204-5145
Telephone: 317-630-4500
Fax: 317-630-4501

David F. McNamar
Randall R. Fearnow
Janet A. McSharar
Alastair J. Warr

For full biographical listings, see the Martindale-Hubbell Law Directory

PLEWS SHADLEY RACHER & BRAUN (AV)

1346 North Delaware Street, 46202-2415
Telephone: 317-637-0700
Telecopier: 317-637-0710

MEMBERS OF FIRM

George M. Plews
Sue A. Shadley
Peter M. Racher
Christopher J. Braun

ASSOCIATES

Harinder Kaur
Leonardo D. Robinson
Frederick D. Emhardt
S. Curtis DeVoe
Jeffrey D. Claflin
John E. Klarquist
Jeffrey D. Featherstun
Amy K. Luigs
Donna C. Marron

OF COUNSEL

Craig A. Wood
Christine C. H. Plews
M. Scott Barrett

For full biographical listings, see the Martindale-Hubbell Law Directory

SOMMER & BARNARD, ATTORNEYS AT LAW, PC (AV)

4000 Bank One Tower, 111 Monument Circle, P.O. Box 44363, 46244-0363
Telephone: 317-630-4000
FAX: 317-236-9802
North Office: 8900 Keystone Crossing, Suite 1046, Indianapolis, Indiana, 46240-2134.
Telephone: 317-630-4000.
FAX: 317-844-4780.

James K. Sommer
William C. Barnard
James E. Hughes
Edward W. Harris, III
Frederick M. King
Jerald I. Ancel
Eric R. Johnson
Gordon L. Pittenger
Lynn Brundage Jongleux
Frank J. Deveau
John E. Taylor
Michael C. Terrell
Marlene Reich
Richard C. Richmond, III
Julianne S. Lis-Milam
Steven C. Shockley
Stephen B. Cherry
Robert J. Hicks
Lawrence A. Vanore
Donald C. Biggs
Debra McVicker Lynch

Gayle A. Reindl
Ann Carr Mackey
Gregory J. Seketa
Sandra L. Gosling
Edwin J. Broecker
Thomas R. DeVoe
Mary T. Doherty
William K. Boncosky

OF COUNSEL

Jerry Williams
Glenn Scolnik
Philip L. McCool
Charles E. Valliere
Verl L. Myers

Representative Clients: Comerica Bank; Excel Industries; Federal Express; Kimball International; Monsanto; Renault Automation; Repport International; TRW, Inc.

For full biographical listings, see the Martindale-Hubbell Law Directory

IOWA

*CEDAR RAPIDS,** Linn Co.

SHUTTLEWORTH & INGERSOLL, P.C. (AV)

500 Firstar Bank Building, P.O. Box 2107, 52406-2107
Telephone: 319-365-9461
Fax: 319-365-8443

Thomas M. Collins
James C. Nemmers
Michael O. McDermott
Richard S. Fry
Richard C. Garberson
Gary J. Streit
Carroll J. Reasoner
Steven J. Pace
Glenn L. Johnson
Thomas P. Peffer
Kevin H. Collins
William P. Prowell
Diane Kutzko
Mark L. Zaiger
William S. Hochstetler

William H. Courter

OF COUNSEL

Ralph W. Gearhart

COUNSEL

Joan Lipsky
James D. Hodges, Jr.

Representative Clients: Amana Society; Archer-Daniels-Midland Co.; Cargill, Inc.; Firstar Bank Cedar Rapids, N.A.; General Mills, Inc.; Iowa Electric Light and Power Co.; MCI; McLeod Telecommunications Group, Inc.; PMX Industries, Inc.

For Complete List of Firm Personnel, See General Section

For full biographical listings, see the Martindale-Hubbell Law Directory

*DES MOINES,** Polk Co.

WASKER, DORR, WIMMER & MARCOUILLER, P.C. (AV)

801 Grand Avenue, Suite 3100, 50309-8036
Telephone: 515-283-1801
Facsimile: 515-283-1802

Charles F. Wasker
Fred L. Dorr
William J. Wimmer
D. Mark Marcouiller

Robert A. Sims
David A. Bolte
Jennifer Ann Tyler
Matthew D. Kern

For Complete List of Firm Personnel, See General Section

For full biographical listings, see the Martindale-Hubbell Law Directory

KANSAS

*TOPEKA,** Shawnee Co.

FOULSTON & SIEFKIN (AV)

(Formerly Foulston, Siefkin, Powers & Eberhardt)
1515 Bank IV Tower, 534 Kansas Avenue, 66603
Telephone: 913-233-3600
FAX: 913-233-1610
Wichita, Kansas Office: 700 Fourth Financial Center, Broadway at Douglas. 67202.
Telephone: 316-267-6371.
Facsimile: 316-267-6345.
Member: Lex Mundi, A Global Association of Independent Firms

MEMBERS OF FIRM

William H. Dye (Resident, Wichita Office)
Mary Kathleen Babcock (Resident, Wichita Office)
Gloria G. Farha Flentje (Resident, Wichita Office)

SPECIAL COUNSEL

James L. Grimes, Jr.

For full biographical listings, see the Martindale-Hubbell Law Directory

*WICHITA,** Sedgwick Co.

FOULSTON & SIEFKIN (AV)

(Formerly Foulston, Siefkin, Powers & Eberhardt)
700 Fourth Financial Center, Broadway at Douglas, 67202
Telephone: 316-267-6371
Facsimile: 316-267-6345
Topeka, Kansas Office: 1515 Bank IV Tower, 534 Kansas Avenue. 66603.
Telephone: 913-233-3600.
FAX: 913-233-1610.
Member: Lex Mundi, A Global Association of Independent Firms

(See Next Column)

MEMBERS OF FIRM

William H. Dye
Mary Kathleen Babcock
Gloria G. Farha Flentje

SPECIAL COUNSEL

James L. Grimes, Jr. (Resident, Topeka Office)

For Complete List of Firm Personnel, See General Section

For full biographical listings, see the Martindale-Hubbell Law Directory

KENTUCKY

COVINGTON, Kenton Co.

GREENEBAUM DOLL & McDONALD (AV)

A Partnership including Professional Service Corporations
50 East Rivercenter Boulevard, P.O. Box 2050, 41012-2050
Telephone: 606-655-4200
Telecopier: 606-655-4239
Louisville, Kentucky Office: 3300 National City Tower.
Telephone: 502-589-4200.
Fax: 502-587-3695.
Lexington, Kentucky Office: 1400 Vine Center Tower.
Telephone: 606-231-8500.
Fax: 606-255-2742.
Cincinnati, Ohio Office: 832 Main Street.
Telephone: 513-421-8087.
Fax: 513-421-8089.

MEMBERS OF FIRM

Wm. T. Robinson, III
Eric L. Ison
Jeffrey A. McKenzie

Representative Clients: Aetna Life Insurance Co.; ANDALEX Resources, Inc.; Ashland Oil, Inc.; A T & T Communications, Inc.; Bethlehem Steel Corp.; Brown-Forman Corp.; Citizens Fidelity Bank & Trust Co.; Humana, Inc.; KFC National Cooperative Advertising Program, Inc.
*A Professional Service Corporation

For Complete List of Firm Personnel, See General Section

For full biographical listings, see the Martindale-Hubbell Law Directory

*LEXINGTON,** Fayette Co.

GREENEBAUM DOLL & McDONALD (AV)

A Partnership including Professional Service Corporations
1400 Vine Center Tower, 40508
Telephone: 606-231-8500
Telecopier: 606-255-2742
Telex: 213029
Louisville, Kentucky Office: 3300 National City Tower.
Telephone: 502-589-4200.
Fax: 502-587-3695.
Covington, Kentucky Office: 50 East River Center Boulevard, P.O. Box 2050.
Telephone: 606-655-4200.
Fax: 606-655-4239.
Cincinnati, Ohio Office: 832 Main Street.
Telephone: 513-421-8087.
Fax: 513-421-8089.

MEMBERS OF FIRM

Wm. T. Robinson, III
Eric L. Ison
Marcus P. McGraw (Resident)
Bruce E. Cryder
John C. Bender (Resident)
David A. Owen (Resident)

ASSOCIATE

John A. Kolanz (Resident)

Representative Clients: Aetna Life Insurance Co.; ANDALEX Resources, Inc.; Ashland Oil, Inc.; AT&T Communications, Inc.; Bethlehem Steel Corp.; Brown-Forman Corp.; Columbia Gas & Transmission Co.; Commonwealth Aluminum Corp.; Consolidation Coal Co.; Costain Coal, Inc.
*A Professional Service Corporation

For Complete List of Firm Personnel, See General Section

For full biographical listings, see the Martindale-Hubbell Law Directory

STOLL, KEENON & PARK (AV)

201 E. Main Street, Suite 1000, 40507-1380
Telephone: 606-231-3000
Telecopier: 606-253-1093; 606-253-1027
Frankfort, Kentucky Office: 326 West Main Street.
Telephone: 502-875-6000.
Telecopier: 502-875-6008.
Louisville, Kentucky Office: 400 West Market Street, Suite 2650, 40202.
Telephone: 502-568-9100.
Telecopier: 502-568-6340.

(See Next Column)

STOLL, KEENON & PARK—*Continued*

MEMBERS OF FIRM

Bennett Clark — Robert M. Watt, III
Richard M. Guarnieri

Representative Clients: Bank One, Lexington, NA; Farmers Capital Bank Corp.; The Tokai Bank Ltd.; Link Belt Construction Equipment Co.; General Motors Corp.; International Business Machines Corp.; Ohbayashi Corp.; R. J. Reynolds Tobacco Co.; Rockwell International Corp.; Square D Co.

For Complete List of Firm Personnel, See General Section

For full biographical listings, see the Martindale-Hubbell Law Directory

*LOUISVILLE,** Jefferson Co.

GREENEBAUM DOLL & McDONALD (AV)

A Partnership including Professional Service Corporations
3300 National City Tower, 40202
Telephone: 502-589-4200
Fax: 502-587-3695
Lexington, Kentucky Office: 1400 Vine Center Tower.
Telephone: 606-231-8500.
Fax: 606-255-2742.
Covington, Kentucky Office: 50 East River Center Boulevard, P.O. Box 2050.
Telephone: 606-655-4200.
Fax: 606-655-4239.
Cincinnati, Ohio Office: 832 Main Street.
Telephone: 513-421-8087.
Fax: 513-421-8089.

Wm. T. Robinson, III — Holland N. McTyeire, V
Eric L. Ison — Jeffrey A. McKenzie
Marcus P. McGraw (Resident at Lexington, Kentucky) — John C. Bender (Resident at Lexington, Kentucky)
Bruce E. Cryder (Lexington, Kentucky and Cincinnati, Ohio) — David A. Owen (Resident at Lexington, Kentucky)

ASSOCIATE

John A. Kolanz (Resident at Lexington, Kentucky)

Representative Clients: Aetna Life Insurance Co.; ANDALEX Resources, Inc.; Ashland Oil, Inc.; A T & T Communications, Inc.; Bethlehem Steel Corp.; Brown-Forman Corp.; Humana, Inc.; Kentucky Kingdom, Inc.; KFC National Cooperative Advertising Program, Inc.
*A Professional Service Corporation

For Complete List of Firm Personnel, See General Section

For full biographical listings, see the Martindale-Hubbell Law Directory

OGDEN NEWELL & WELCH (AV)

1200 One Riverfront Plaza, 40202-2973
Telephone: 502-582-1601
Fax: 502-581-9564

MEMBERS OF FIRM

Richard F. Newell — Walter Lapp Sales
Kendrick R. Riggs

ASSOCIATES

John Wade Hendricks — James G. Campbell
Allyson K. Sturgeon

Counsel for: KU Energy Corp.; Kentucky Utilities Co.; Brown-Forman Corp.; B. F. Goodrich Co.; Brown & Williamson Tobacco Corp.; J.J.B. Hilliard, W.L. Lyons, Inc.; Interlock Industries, Inc.; Akzo Coatings, Inc.; United Medical Corp.; Bank of Louisville.

For Complete List of Firm Personnel, See General Section

For full biographical listings, see the Martindale-Hubbell Law Directory

LOUISIANA

*LAFAYETTE,** Lafayette Parish

MANGHAM, DAVIS AND OGLESBEE (AV)

Suite 1400 First National Bank Towers, 600 Jefferson Street, P.O. Box 93110, 70509-3110
Telephone: 318-233-6200
Fax: 318-233-6521

Michael R. Mangham — Michael G. Oglesbee
Louis R. Davis — Herman E. Garner, Jr.

ASSOCIATES

Dawn Mayeux Fuqua — Lisa Hanchey Sevier

SPECIAL COUNSEL

Michael J. O'Shee

(See Next Column)

OF COUNSEL

George W. Hardy, III — Robert E. Rowe

Reference: The First National Bank of Lafayette, Lafayette, Louisiana.

For full biographical listings, see the Martindale-Hubbell Law Directory

*SHREVEPORT,** Caddo Parish

BARLOW AND HARDTNER L.C. (AV)

Tenth Floor, Louisiana Tower, 401 Edwards Street, 71101-3289
Telephone: 318-227-1131
Telecopier: 318-227-1141
Mailing Address: P.O. Box 8, Shreveport, Louisiana, 71161-0008

Ray A. Barlow — Clair F. White
Malcolm S. Murchison — Philip E. Downer, III
David R. Taggart — Michael B. Donald

Representative Clients: Anderson Oil & Gas, Inc.; Brammer Engineering, Inc.; Central Louisiana Electric Co., Inc.; Central and South West; Franks Petroleum Inc.; Kelly Oil Corporation; Louisiana Intrastate Gas Corp.; NorAm Energy Corp. (formerly Arkla, Inc.); Panhandle Eastern Corp.; Southwestern Electric Power Company.

For Complete List of Firm Personnel, See General Section

For full biographical listings, see the Martindale-Hubbell Law Directory

MAINE

*AUGUSTA,** Kennebec Co.

* indicates certain Bar Register subscribers whose principal office is located elsewhere in the state and who have arranged for representation as a part of the state capital listings that follow

*** PIERCE, ATWOOD, SCRIBNER, ALLEN, SMITH & LANCASTER (AV)**

77 Winthrop Street, 04330
Telephone: 207-622-6311
Fax: 207-623-9367
Portland, Maine Office: One Monument Square.
Telephone: 207-773-6411.
Camden, Maine Office: 36 Chestnut Street, P.O. Box 780.
Telephone: 207-236-4333.

MEMBERS OF FIRM

Warren E. Winslow, Jr. — Joseph M. Kozak
Malcolm L. Lyons — Michael D. Seitzinger
John C. Nivison

ASSOCIATES

Daniel J. Stevens — Benjamin P. Townsend
Christine F. Burke

For full biographical listings, see the Martindale-Hubbell Law Directory

*PORTLAND,** Cumberland Co.

PIERCE, ATWOOD, SCRIBNER, ALLEN, SMITH & LANCASTER (AV)

One Monument Square, 04101
Telephone: 207-773-6411
Fax: 207-773-3419
Augusta, Maine Office: 77 Winthrop Street.
Telephone: 207-622-6311.
Camden, Maine Office: 36 Chestnut Street, P.O. Box 780.
Telephone: 207-236-4333.

MEMBERS OF FIRM

Daniel E. Boxer — Philip F. W. Ahrens, III
John D. Delahanty — Kenneth Fairbanks Gray
Robert A. Moore — Elizabeth R. Butler
Thomas R. Doyle — William E. Taylor

ASSOCIATES

Dixon P. Pike — Matthew D. Manahan
Kate L. Geoffroy — Adam H. Steinman
David P. Littell

For Complete List of Firm Personnel, See General Section

For full biographical listings, see the Martindale-Hubbell Law Directory

PRETI, FLAHERTY, BELIVEAU & PACHIOS (AV)

443 Congress Street, P.O. Box 11410, 04104-7410
Telephone: 207-791-3000
Telecopier: 207-791-3111
Augusta, Maine Office: 45 Memorial Circle, P.O. Box 1058, 04332-1058.
Telephone: 207-623-5300.
Telecopier: 207-623-2914.

(See Next Column)

PRETI, FLAHERTY, BELIVEAU & PACHIOS, *Portland—Continued*

Rumford, Maine Office: 150 Congress Street, P.O. Drawer L, 04276-2035.
Telephone: 207-364-4593.
Telecopier: 207-369-9421.

MEMBERS OF FIRM

Severin M. Beliveau (Augusta Office)
Harold C. Pachios
Bruce C. Gerrity (Augusta Office)
Anthony W. Buxton (Augusta Office)
Virginia E. Davis (Augusta Office)
Estelle A. Lavoie
Joseph G. Donahue (Augusta Office)
David B. Van Slyke

ASSOCIATES

Mark B. LeDuc (Augusta Office)
Jeanne T. Cohn-Connor
Ann R. Robinson (Augusta Office)
Deirdre M. O'Callaghan (Augusta Office)
Charles F. Dingman (Augusta Office)

Representative Clients: American Insurance Assn.; New England Cable Television Assn.; Industrial Energy Consumer Group; Canadian Pacific Railroad; Bangor Hydroelectric Co.; Maine Oil Dealers Assn.; American Express; The Hampton Group; Maine Auto Dealers Assn.; Medco Containment Services.

For Complete List of Firm Personnel, See General Section

For full biographical listings, see the Martindale-Hubbell Law Directory

MARYLAND

*BALTIMORE,** (Independent City)

KAHN, SMITH & COLLINS, P.A. (AV)

110 Saint Paul Street, 6th Floor, 21202
Telephone: 410-244-1010
Telecopier: 410-244-8001

Andrew H. Kahn
Joel A. Smith
Francis J. Collins

David Vernon Diggs
Christyne L. Neff

For full biographical listings, see the Martindale-Hubbell Law Directory

VENABLE, BAETJER AND HOWARD (AV)

A Partnership including Professional Corporations
1800 Mercantile Bank & Trust Building, 2 Hopkins Plaza, 21201
Telephone: 410-244-7400
Washington, D.C. Office: Venable, Baetjer, Howard & Civiletti. Suite 1000, 1201 New York Avenue, N.W.
Telephone: 202-962-4800.
McLean, Virginia Office: Suite 400, 2010 Corporate Ridge.
Telephone: 703-760-1600.
Rockville, Maryland Office: Suite 500, One Church Street, P. O. Box 1906.
Telephone: 301-217-5600.
Towson, Maryland Office: 210 Allegheny Avenue, P. O. Box 5517.
Telephone: 410-494-6200.

MEMBERS OF FIRM

Thomas P. Perkins, III (P.C.)
Roger W. Titus (Resident, Rockville, Maryland Office)
Thomas J. Madden (Not admitted in MD; Resident, Washington, D.C. Office)
William L. Walsh, Jr. (P.C.) (Not admitted in MD; Resident, McLean, Virginia Office)
Ronald R. Glancz (Not admitted in MD; Resident, Washington, D.C. Office)
Robert P. Bedell (Not admitted in MD; Resident, Washington, D.C. Office)
Kenneth C. Bass, III (Not admitted in MD; Also at Washington, D.C. and McLean, Virginia Offices)
Paul F. Strain (P.C.)
Paul T. Glasgow (Resident, Rockville, Maryland Office)
Sondra Harans Block (Resident, Rockville, Maryland Office)
Michael Schatzow (Also at Washington, D.C. and Towson, Maryland Offices)
John F. Cooney (Not admitted in MD; Resident, Washington, D.C. Office)
N. Frank Wiggins (Resident, Washington, D.C. Office)
L. Paige Marvel
Susan K. Gauvey (Also at Towson, Maryland Office)
H. Russell Frisby, Jr.
Jeffrey D. Knowles (Not admitted in MD; Resident, Washington, D.C. Office)
John J. Pavlick, Jr. (Not admitted in MD; Resident, Washington, D. C. Office)
M. King Hill, III (Resident, Towson, Maryland Office)
Gary M. Hnath (Resident, Washington, D.C. Office)

OF COUNSEL

Emried D. Cole, Jr.
Judith A. Armold

(See Next Column)

ASSOCIATES

Paul D. Barker, Jr.
Matthew L. Iwicki
G. Page Wingert (Resident, Towson, Maryland Office)

For Complete List of Firm Personnel, See General Section

For full biographical listings, see the Martindale-Hubbell Law Directory

*ROCKVILLE,** Montgomery Co.

VENABLE, BAETJER AND HOWARD (AV)

A Partnership including Professional Corporations
Suite 500, One Church Street, P.O. Box 1906, 20850-4129
Telephone: 301-217-5600
FAX: 301-217-5617
Baltimore, Maryland Office: 1800 Mercantile Bank & Trust Building, 2 Hopkins Plaza.
Telephone: 410-244-7400.
Washington, D.C. Office: Venable, Baetjer, Howard & Civiletti. Suite 1000, 1201 New York Avenue, N.W.
Telephone: 202-962-4800.
McLean, Virginia Office: Suite 400, 2010 Corporate Ridge.
Telephone: 703-760-1600.
Towson, Maryland, Office: 210 Allegheny Avenue, P. O. Box 5517.
Telephone: 410-494-6200.

MEMBERS OF FIRM

Roger W. Titus
Paul T. Glasgow
Sondra Harans Block

For Complete List of Firm Personnel, See General Section

For full biographical listings, see the Martindale-Hubbell Law Directory

SILVER SPRING, Montgomery Co.

ALEXANDER, GEBHARDT, APONTE & MARKS, L.L.C. (AV)

Lee Plaza-Suite 805, 8601 Georgia Avenue, 20910
Telephone: 301-589-2222
Facsimile: 301-589-2523
Washington, D.C. Office: 1314 Nineteenth Street, N.W., 20036.
Telephone: 202-835-1555.
New York, New York Office: 330 Madison Avenue, 36th Floor.
Telephone: 212-808-0008.
Fax: 212-599-1028.

Koteles Alexander (Not admitted in MD)
Mari Carmen Aponte (Not admitted in MD; Resident Washington, D.C. Office)

OF COUNSEL

Eduardo Peña, Jr. (Not admitted in MD)
Michelle C. Clay (Not admitted in MD)

Susan C. Lee (Not admitted in MD)
Eleanor Pelta (Not admitted in MD)

Reference: Riggs National Bank of Washington, D.C.

For full biographical listings, see the Martindale-Hubbell Law Directory

MICHIGAN

*ANN ARBOR,** Washtenaw Co.

BUTZEL LONG, A PROFESSIONAL CORPORATION (AV)

Suite 400, 121 West Washington, 48104-1345
Telephone: 313-995-3110
Telecopier: 313-995-1777
Detroit, Michigan Office: Suite 900, 150 West Jefferson.
Telephone: 313-225-7000.
Telecopier: 313-225-7080.
Birmingham, Michigan Office: Suite 200, 32270 Telegraph Road.
Telephone: 810-258-1616.
Telecopier: 810-258-1439.
Lansing, Michigan Office: 118 West Ottawa Street.
Telephone: 517-372-6622.
Telecopier: 372-6672.
Grosse Pointe Farms, Michigan Office: Suite 260, 21 Kercheval.
Telephone: 313-886-5446.
Telecopier: 313-886-2114.

Robert M. Vercruysse
Robert A. Boonin

For Complete List of Firm Personnel, See General Section

For full biographical listings, see the Martindale-Hubbell Law Directory

BIRMINGHAM, Oakland Co.

Butzel Long, A Professional Corporation (AV)

Suite 200, 32270 Telegraph Road, 48025
Telephone: 810-258-1616
Telecopier: 810-258-1439
Detroit, Michigan Office: Suite 900, 150 West Jefferson.
Telephone: 313-225-7000.
Telecopier: 313-225-7080.
Lansing, Michigan Office: 118 West Ottawa Street.
Telephone: 517-372-6622.
Telecopier: 517-372-6672.
Ann Arbor, Michigan Office: Suite 400, 121 West Washington.
Telephone: 313-995-3110.
Telecopier: 313-995-1777.
Grosse Pointe Farms, Michigan Office: Suite 260, 21 Kercheval.
Telephone: 313-886-5446.
Telecopier: 313-886-2114.

Gordon W. Didier
Brian P. Henry

For Complete List of Firm Personnel, See General Section

For full biographical listings, see the Martindale-Hubbell Law Directory

BLOOMFIELD HILLS, Oakland Co.

David D. Patton & Associates, P.C. (AV)

100 Bloomfield Hills Parkway, Suite 110, 48304
Telephone: 810-258-6020
Fax: 810-258-6052

David D. Patton

Ellen Bartman Jannette
James A. Reynolds, Jr.
Patricia C. White
David H. Patton (1912-1993)

For full biographical listings, see the Martindale-Hubbell Law Directory

*DETROIT,** Wayne Co.

Bodman, Longley & Dahling (AV)

34th Floor 100 Renaissance Center, 48243
Telephone: 313-259-7777
Fax: 313-393-7579
Troy, Michigan Office: Suite 2020, 755 West Big Beaver Road.
Telephone: 810-362-2110.
Ann Arbor, Michigan Office: 110 Miller, Suite 300.
Telephone: 313-761-3780.
Northern Michigan Office: 229 Court Street, P.O. Box 405, Cheboygan.
Telephone: 616-627-4351.

MEMBERS OF FIRM

Richard D. Rohr
James A. Smith
Randolph S. Perry (Ann Arbor Office)
F. Thomas Lewand

Representative Clients: Abitibi Price Group; Archdiocese of Detroit; Comerica Bank; The Detroit Lions, Inc.; Ford Estates; General Motors Corporation; Charles Steward Mott Foundation; Norfolk Southern Corporation; Panhandle Eastern Corporation; State Farm Mutual Automobile Insurance Company.

For Complete List of Firm Personnel, See General Section

For full biographical listings, see the Martindale-Hubbell Law Directory

Brady Hathaway, Professional Corporation (AV)

1330 Buhl Building, 48226-3602
Telephone: 313-965-3700
Telecopier: 313-965-2830

Thomas M. J. Hathaway

Representative Clients: Beam Stream, Inc.; Bundy Tubing Company; Century 21 Real Estate Corp.; Datamedia Corporation; Energy Conversion Devices, Inc.; Michigan Gas Utilities; Pony Express Courier Corp.; Schering Corporation; Warner-Lambert; Wolverine Technologies.

For Complete List of Firm Personnel, See General Section

For full biographical listings, see the Martindale-Hubbell Law Directory

Butzel Long, A Professional Corporation (AV)

Suite 900, 150 West Jefferson, 48226
Telephone: 313-225-7000
Telecopier: 313-225-7080
Birmingham, Michigan Office: Suite 200, 32270 Telegraph Road.
Telephone: 810-258-1616.
Telecopier: 810-258-1439.
Lansing, Michigan Office: 118 West Ottawa Street.
Telephone: 517-372-6622.
Telecopier: 517-372-6672.
Ann Arbor, Michigan Office: Suite 400, 121 West Washington.
Telephone: 313-995-3110.
Telecopier: 313-995-1777.

(See Next Column)

Grosse Pointe Farms, Michigan Office: Suite 260, 21 Kercheval.
Telephone: 313-886-5446.
Telecopier: 313-886-2114.

Robert J. Battista
William R. Ralls (Lansing)
Robert M. Vercruysse
John P. Hancock, Jr.
Leonard F. Charla
James C. Bruno
Gordon W. Didier
Lynne E. Deitch
Brian P. Henry (Birmingham and Lansing)
Robert A. Boonin

Leland R. Rosier (Lansing)
Wendel Vincent Hall (Lansing)

Representative Clients: Bridgestone/Firestone, Inc.; The Detroit News, Inc.; Detroit Diesel Corp.; Kelly Services; Kelsey Hayes Co.; Merrill Lynch & Co., Inc.; Stroh Brewery Co.; Takata Corp.; United Parcel Services of America, Inc.; The University of Michigan.

For Complete List of Firm Personnel, See General Section

For full biographical listings, see the Martindale-Hubbell Law Directory

Clark, Klein & Beaumont (AV)

1600 First Federal Building, 1001 Woodward Avenue, 48226
Telephone: 313-965-8300
Facsimile: 313-962-4348
Bloomfield Hills Office: 1533 North Woodward Avenue, Suite 220, 48304.
Telephone: 810-258-2900.
Facsimile: 810-258-2949.

MEMBERS OF FIRM

Richard C. Marsh
James E. Baiers

Representative Clients: Booth Communications, Inc.; LCI International Telecom Corp.

For Complete List of Firm Personnel, See General Section

For full biographical listings, see the Martindale-Hubbell Law Directory

Eames, Wilcox, Mastej, Bryant, Swift & Riddell (AV)

1400 Buhl Building, 48226-3602
Telephone: 313-963-3750
Facsimile: 313-963-8485

MEMBERS OF FIRM

Leonard A. Wilcox, Jr.
Ronald J. Mastej
John W. Bryant
Jerry R. Swift
Neill T. Riddell
Elizabeth Roberto
Kevin N. Summers

ASSOCIATE

Keith M. Aretha

OF COUNSEL

Rex Eames
Robert E. Gesell
William B. McIntyre, Jr.

Representative Clients: ABF Freight System, Inc.; Chrysler Credit Corp.; City Transfer Co.; Engineered Heat Treat, Inc.; Fetz Engineering Co.; I E & E Industries, Inc.; Schneider Transport; Tank Carrier Employers Association of Michigan; TNT Transport Group, Inc.; Waste Management of Michigan.

For full biographical listings, see the Martindale-Hubbell Law Directory

LANSING, Ingham Co.

Butzel Long, A Professional Corporation (AV)

118 West Ottawa Street, 48933
Telephone: 517-372-6622
Telecopier: 517-372-6672
Detroit, Michigan Office: Suite 900, 150 West Jefferson.
Telephone: 313-225-7000.
Telecopier: 313-225-7080.
Birmingham, Michigan Office: Suite 200, 32270 Telegraph Road.
Telephone: 810-258-1616.
Telecopier: 810-258-1439.
Ann Arbor, Michigan Office: Suite 400, 121 West Washington.
Telephone: 313-995-3110.
Telecopier: 313-995-1777.
Grosse Pointe Farms, Michigan Office: Suite 260, 21 Kercheval.
Telephone: 313-886-5446.
Telecopier: 313-886-2114.

William R. Ralls (Resident)
Brian P. Henry

James J. Urban (Resident)
Leland R. Rosier (Resident)
Wendel Vincent Hall (Resident)

For full biographical listings, see the Martindale-Hubbell Law Directory

Dunnings & Frawley, P.C. (AV)

Duncan Building, 530 South Pine Street, 48933-2299
Telephone: 517-487-8222
Fax: 517-487-2026

Stuart J. Dunnings, Jr.
John J. Frawley

(See Next Column)

DUNNINGS & FRAWLEY P.C., *Lansing—Continued*

Stuart J. Dunnings, III
Steven D. Dunnings

Representative Clients: Lansing Board of Education; Lansing Housing Commission; Ford Motor Co.
References: First of America; Michigan National Bank.

For full biographical listings, see the Martindale-Hubbell Law Directory

MISSISSIPPI

*CLARKSDALE,** Coahoma Co.

ROSS, HUNT, SPELL & ROSS, A PROFESSIONAL ASSOCIATION (AV)

123 Court Street, P.O. Box 1196, 38614
Telephone: 601-627-5251
Telecopier No.: 601-627-5254
Clinton, Mississippi Office: 203 Monroe Street.
Telephone: 601-924-2655.

Tom T. Ross (1903-1993)
David R. Hunt
Tom T. Ross, Jr.

Representative Client: Beech Aircraft Corp., Wichita, Kansas.

For Complete List of Firm Personnel, See General Section

For full biographical listings, see the Martindale-Hubbell Law Directory

*GULFPORT,** Harrison Co.

DUKES, DUKES, KEATING AND FANECA, P.A. (AV)

2308 East Beach Boulevard, P.O. Drawer W, 39501
Telephone: 601-868-1111
FAX: 601-863-2886

Hugh D. Keating
Cy Faneca

For full biographical listings, see the Martindale-Hubbell Law Directory

*JACKSON,** Hinds Co.

McDAVID, NOBLIN & WEST (AV)

Suite 1000, Security Centre North, 200 South Lamar Street, 39201
Telephone: 601-948-3305
Telecopier: 601-354-4789

MEMBERS OF FIRM

John Land McDavid
William C. Noblin, Jr.
W. Eric West
John Sanford McDavid
John C. Robertson

OF COUNSEL

Lowell F. Stephens

For full biographical listings, see the Martindale-Hubbell Law Directory

MONTANA

*BILLINGS,** Yellowstone Co.

CROWLEY, HAUGHEY, HANSON, TOOLE & DIETRICH (AV)

500 Transwestern II, 490 North 31st Street, P.O. Box 2529, 59103
Telephone: 406-252-3441
Fax: 406-259-4159
Helena, Montana Office: IBM Building, 100 North Park Avenue, Suite 300, 59601.
Telephone: 406-449-4165.
Fax: 406-449-5149.

MEMBERS OF FIRM

Terry B. Cosgrove
Janice L. Rehberg

ASSOCIATE

Michael S. Lahr

Representative Clients: Montana Power Co.; First Interstate Bank of Commerce; MDU Resources Group, Inc.; Chevron U.S.A., Inc.; Noranda Minerals Corp.; United Parcel Service.
Insurance Clients: Farmers Insurance Group; New York Life Insurance Co.

For Complete List of Firm Personnel, See General Section

For full biographical listings, see the Martindale-Hubbell Law Directory

NEVADA

*LAS VEGAS,** Clark Co.

ALVERSON, TAYLOR, MORTENSEN & NELSON (AV)

3821 W. Charleston Boulevard, 89102
Telephone: 702-384-7000
FAX: 702-385-7000

MEMBERS OF FIRM

J. Bruce Alverson
Eric K. Taylor
David J. Mortensen
Erven T. Nelson
LeAnn Sanders
David R. Clayson

ASSOCIATES

Milton J. Eichacker
Douglas D. Gerrard
Marie Ellerton
James H. Randall
Peter Dubowsky
Hayley B. Chambers
Michael D. Stevenson
Cookie Lea Olshein
Kenneth M. Marias
Jeffrey H. Ballin
Jeffrey W. Daly
Kenneth R. Ivory
Edward D. Boyack
Sandra Smagac
Jill M. Chase
Francis F. Lin

Representative Clients: Checker Cab Company; Nevada Fleet Management, Inc.; Star Cab Co.; Yellow Cab Company; National Moving & Storage, Inc.; Southwest Pools & Landscaping; White Gove Delivery, Inc.; Fleet Deliver Service Northwest.

For full biographical listings, see the Martindale-Hubbell Law Directory

HILBRECHT & ASSOCIATES, CHARTERED (AV)

723 South Casino Center Boulevard, 89101-6716
Telephone: 702-384-1036
Telefax: 702-384-2LAW

Norman Ty Hilbrecht

Morgan Drew Davis
Eric A. Daly (Not admitted in NV)

Representative Clients: Bell Trans; Bell United Insurance; Bristol-Myers Squibb; Calzona Tankways; Coldwell Banker; Desert Chrysler-Plymouth; Enstrom Helicopter Co.; Paul Revere Insurance; United Companies.
Reference: American Bank of Commerce.

For full biographical listings, see the Martindale-Hubbell Law Directory

NEW JERSEY

*HACKENSACK,** Bergen Co.

DEENER, FEINGOLD & STERN, A PROFESSIONAL CORPORATION (AV)

2 University Plaza, Suite 602, 07601
Telephone: 201-343-8788
Fax: 201-343-4640

Jerome A. Deener
Cal R. Feingold
Robert A. Stern

Debra T. Hirsch
David M. Edelblum
Anthony M. Vizzoni
James J. Costello, Jr. (Not admitted in NJ)

References: United Jersey Bank; Midlantic Bank; Midland Bank and Trust Co. (Trust Department); Fidelity Bank; Hudson United Bank.

For full biographical listings, see the Martindale-Hubbell Law Directory

LIVINGSTON, Essex Co.

GENOVA, BURNS, TRIMBOLI & VERNOIA (AV)

Eisenhower Plaza II, 354 Eisenhower Parkway, 07039
Telephone: 201-533-0777
Facsimile: 201-533-1112
Trenton, New Jersey Office: Suite One, 160 West State Street.
Telephone: 609-393-1131.

MEMBERS OF FIRM

Angelo J. Genova
James M. Burns
Stephen E. Trimboli
Francis J. Vernoia

ASSOCIATES

Meryl G. Nadler
John C. Petrella
James J. McGovern, III
Kathleen M. Connelly
Joseph Licata
Elaine M. Reyes
Lynn S. Degen
James J. Gillespie
T. Sean Jackson

For full biographical listings, see the Martindale-Hubbell Law Directory

*NEWARK,** Essex Co.

FOX AND FOX (AV)

570 Broad Street, 07102
Telephone: 201-622-3624
Telecopier: 201-622-6220

MEMBERS OF FIRM

David I. Fox
Arthur D. Grossman
Paul I. Rosenberg
Kenneth H. Fast
Martin Kesselhaut
Dennis J. Alessi
Gabriel H. Halpern
Steven A. Holt
Nancy C. McDonald

OF COUNSEL

Jacob Fox (1898-1992)
Martin S. Fox
Robert J. Rohrberger
Robert S. Catapano-Friedman

ASSOCIATES

Robert P. Donovan
Stacey B. Rosenberg
Susan R. Fox
Virginia S. Ryan
Ronnie Ann Powell
Katherine J. Welsh
Craig S. Gumpel
Brett Alison Rosenberg
Alfred V. Acquaviva
Anthony F. Vitiello

For full biographical listings, see the Martindale-Hubbell Law Directory

SILLS CUMMIS ZUCKERMAN RADIN TISCHMAN EPSTEIN & GROSS, A PROFESSIONAL CORPORATION (AV)

One Riverfront Plaza, 07102-5400
Telephone: 201-643-7000
Fax: 201-643-6500
Telex: 820630 Sillsbeck Nwk
Atlantic City, New Jersey Office: 17 Gordon's Alley.
Telephone: 609-344-2800.
New York, N.Y. Office: 250 Park Avenue.
Telephone: 212-643-7000.

Clive S. Cummis
Stephen J. Moses
Noah Bronkesh (Resident at Atlantic City, N.J. Office)
Lester Aron
Kenneth F. Oettle
Philip R. Sellinger
Robert M. Axelrod
Richard J. Schulman (Not admitted in NJ)
James M. Hirschhorn
Mark J. Blunda

Patricia M. Kerins
Cherie L. Maxwell
Glenn E. Davis
Eileen O'Donnell
Richard S. Schkolnick
Paul P. Josephson
Bryan S. Greenberg

Representative Clients: GAF Corporation; Rockland Electric; Orange & Rockland Electric Co.; Public Service Enterprise Group; Bally Manufacturing Corp.; GTE Sprint; GAF Corporation; U.S. Generating Co.; Bertex Laboratories, Inc.; Jersey City Medical Center.;

For Complete List of Firm Personnel, See General Section

For full biographical listings, see the Martindale-Hubbell Law Directory

ORADELL, Bergen Co.

NICOLETTE & PERKINS, P.A. (AV)

555 Kinderkamack Road, P.O. Box 549, 07649
Telephone: 201-261-9300
Telecopier: 201-261-8855

David A. Nicolette, Jr.
Eric R. Perkins

Evelyn J. Marose
Jeanette A. Odynski

For full biographical listings, see the Martindale-Hubbell Law Directory

*TRENTON,** Mercer Co.

STERNS & WEINROTH (AV)

50 West State Street, Suite 1400, P.O. Box 1298, 08607-1298
Telephone: 609-392-2100
Fax: 609-392-7956
Atlantic City, New Jersey Office: 2901 Atlantic Avenue, Suite 201, 08401.
Telephone: 609-340-8300.
Fax: 609-340-8722.
Washington, D.C. Office: 1150 Seventeenth Street, N.W., Suite 600, 20036.
Telephone: 202-296-3432.

Joseph A. Fusco (Resident, Atlantic City)
Elmer M. Matthews
Paul M. O'Gara
Mark D. Schorr
Joel H. Sterns
Susan Stryker
Richard K. Weinroth

Karen A. Confoy
Richard J. Van Wagner

For Complete List of Firm Personnel, See General Section

For full biographical listings, see the Martindale-Hubbell Law Directory

NEW MEXICO

*ALBUQUERQUE,** Bernalillo Co.

CAMPBELL, PICA, OLSON & SEEGMILLER (AV)

6565 Americas Parkway, N.E., Suite 800, P.O. Box 35459, 87176
Telephone: 505-883-9110
Fax: 505-884-3882

MEMBERS OF FIRM

Lewis O. Campbell
Nicholas R. Pica
David C. Olson
Douglas Seegmiller

ASSOCIATES

Brad Vaughn
Roger A. Stansbury
Philip Craig Snyder
Arthur J. G. Lacerte, Jr.
Jeffrey C. Gilmore

Representative Clients: Phelps Dodge Corporation; Chino Mines Company; Large Power Users Coalition; Sara Lee Corporation; General Electric Capital Corporation; New Mexico Retail Association; Compania Minera Ojos Del Salado S.A.

For full biographical listings, see the Martindale-Hubbell Law Directory

RODEY, DICKASON, SLOAN, AKIN & ROBB, P.A. (AV)

Albuquerque Plaza, Suite 2200, 201 Third Street, N.W., P.O. Box 1888, 87103-1888
Telephone: 505-765-5900
Fax: 505-768-7395
Santa Fe, New Mexico Office: Suite 101 Marcy Plaza, 123 East Marcy Street, P.O. Box 1357, 87504-1357.
Telephone: 505-984-0100.
Fax: 505-989-9542.

John P. Salazar
James P. Fitzgerald
Joseph B. Rochelle
Angela M. Martinez
Patricia M. Taylor

David W. Bunting

For Complete List of Firm Personnel, See General Section

For full biographical listings, see the Martindale-Hubbell Law Directory

*SANTA FE,** Santa Fe Co.

HUFFAKER & BARNES, A PROFESSIONAL CORPORATION (AV)

155 Grant Avenue, P.O. Box 1868, 87504-1868
Telephone: 505-988-8921
Fax: 505-983-3927

Gregory D. Huffaker, Jr.
Julia Hosford Barnes
Bradley C. Barron
Sharon A. Higgins (Not admitted in NM)

Representative Clients: Chevron U.S.A. Products Inc.; Federal Deposit Insurance Corp.; Resolution Trust Corporation; Alphagraphics of Santa Fe and Los Alamos; Basis International, Ltd.; San Juan Concrete Co.; S.I. Baker; Sasco Electric; Hy Power, Inc.; University of Pennsylvania.

For full biographical listings, see the Martindale-Hubbell Law Directory

MONTGOMERY & ANDREWS, PROFESSIONAL ASSOCIATION (AV)

325 Paseo de Peralta, P.O. Box 2307, 87504-2307
Telephone: 505-982-3873
Albuquerque, New Mexico Office: Suite 1300 Albuquerque Plaza, 201 Third Street, N.W., P.O. Box 26927.
Telephone: 505-242-9677.
FAX: 505-243-2542.

Gary Kilpatric
Thomas W. Olson
John B. Draper
Nancy M. Anderson King
Galen M. Buller
Edmund H. Kendrick
Louis W. Rose

Representative Clients: US WEST Communications; Aetna Life & Casualty Insurance Co.; Travelers Insurance Co.; American International Group; New Mexico-American Water Company; Zia Natural Gas Company; Mobil Exploration and Producing U.S., Inc.; Sangre de Cristo Water Company; Intel Corporation; LAC Minerals (USA), Inc.

For Complete List of Firm Personnel, See General Section

For full biographical listings, see the Martindale-Hubbell Law Directory

NEW YORK

*ALBANY,** Albany Co.

ROWLEY, FORREST, O'DONNELL & HITE, P.C. (AV)

90 State Street Suite 729, 12207-1715
Telephone: 518-434-6187
Fax: 518-434-1287

Richard R. Rowley
Thomas J. Forrest
Brian J. O'Donnell
Robert S. Hite
John H. Beaumont
Mark S. Pelersi
David C. Rowley

James J. Seaman
David P. Miranda
Kevin S. Casey
Richard W. Bader
Daniel W. Coffey
Thomas D. Spain

OF COUNSEL

Rush W. Stehlin

Reference: Norstar Bank.

For full biographical listings, see the Martindale-Hubbell Law Directory

GLOVERSVILLE, Fulton Co.

MAIDER & SMITH (AV)

37 East Fulton Street, 12078
Telephone: 518-725-7195
Fax: 518-773-3343

MEMBERS OF FIRM

Wesley H. Maider (1879-1955)
Lydon F. Maider
Robert L. Maider
Peter K. Smith

General Counsel for: City National Bank & Trust Co.; St. Thomas, Inc.
Local Counsel for: Sentry Insurance Co.
Reference: City National Bank & Trust Co.

For full biographical listings, see the Martindale-Hubbell Law Directory

*NEW YORK,** New York Co.

ABRAMS & MARTIN, P.C. (AV)

120 Wall Street, 10005
Telephone: 212-422-1200
Fax: 212-968-7573

Henry H. Abrams (1910-1977)
Alan J. Martin
Mark E. Abrams
Michael E. Gorelick
Daniel J. Friedman
Glenn A. Jacobson

Melvin P. Meyer
Norman Landres
Kevin J. Spencer
Pamela R. Wolff
Martin I. Nagel
Allen A. Kolber

OF COUNSEL

Harold A. Craig, Jr.

Representative Clients: Underwriters at Lloyds; New York Property Insurance Underwriting Assn.; American International Group; Jefferson Insurance Co.; Homestead Insurance Co.

For full biographical listings, see the Martindale-Hubbell Law Directory

SIEGEL, MANDELL & DAVIDSON, P.C. (AV)

1515 Broadway One Astor Plaza, 10036
Telephone: 212-944-7900
Telecopier: 212-944-8497
Washington, D.C. Office: 1990 M Street, N.W., Suite 340, 20036.
Telephone: 202-223-8304.
Telecopier: 202-223-8305.

Samuel T. Siegel (1882-1948)
Sidney Mandell (1889-1969)
Joshua M. Davidson (1911-1981)
Harvey A. Isaacs
Brian S. Goldstein
Steven S. Weiser
Louis S. Shoichet
Ellen E. Rosenberg
Edward B. Ackerman
Robert T. Stack

Paul A. Horowitz
Arthur W. Bodek
Laurence M. Friedman
David A. Eisen
Amy J. Johannesen
Maytee Pereira
Brett Harris

For full biographical listings, see the Martindale-Hubbell Law Directory

NORTH CAROLINA

*RALEIGH,** Wake Co.

* indicates certain Bar Register subscribers whose principal office is located elsewhere in the state and who have arranged for representation as a part of the state capital listings that follow

EVERETT, GASKINS, HANCOCK & STEVENS (AV)

The Professional Building, Suite 600, 127 West Hargett Street, P.O. Box 911, 27602
Telephone: 919-755-0025
Fax: 919-755-0009
Durham, North Carolina Office: Suite 300, 301 West Main Street, P.O. Box 586.
Telephone: 919-682-5691.
Fax: 919-682-5469.

LEGAL SUPPORT PERSONNEL

Alison R. Weigold

For Complete List of Firm Personnel, See General Section

For full biographical listings, see the Martindale-Hubbell Law Directory

THARRINGTON, SMITH & HARGROVE (AV)

209 Fayetteville Street Mall, P.O. Box 1151, 27602
Telephone: 919-821-4711
Telecopier: 919-829-1583

MEMBERS OF FIRM

Carlisle W. Higgins (1887-1980)
J. Harold Tharrington
Roger W. Smith
Wade M. Smith
George T. Rogister, Jr.
Carlyn G. Poole
Douglas E. Kingsbery
Randall M. Roden
Michael Crowell
Ann L. Majestic
C. Allison Brown Schafer

ASSOCIATES

Melissa Hill
Daniel W. Clark
Jonathan A. Blumberg
Debra R. Nickels
Rod Malone
E. Hardy Lewis
Jaye Powell Meyer

LEGAL SUPPORT PERSONNEL

Michael M. Cogswell

Representative Clients: North Carolina Association of Broadcasters; AT&T Communications; ABC-TV Network Affiliates Assn.; North Carolina Cable Television Assn.; Time-Warner Communications; Virginia Association of Broadcasters; Pulitzer Broadcasting; The Hearst Corporation.

For full biographical listings, see the Martindale-Hubbell Law Directory

* **WOMBLE CARLYLE SANDRIDGE & RICE** (AV)

A Professional Limited Liability Company
2100 First Union Capitol Center, 150 Fayetteville Street Mall, P.O. Box 831, 27602
Telephone: 919-755-2100
Telecopy: 919-755-2150
Telex: 806498
Charlotte, North Carolina Office: 3300 One First Union Center, 301 South College Street.
Telephone: 704-331-4900.
Telecopy: 704-331-4955.
Telex: 853609.
Winston-Salem, North Carolina Office: 1600 Southern National Financial Center.
Telephone: 919-721-3600.
Telecopy: 919-721-3660.
Telex: 806498.
Atlanta, Georgia Office: One Ninety One Peachtree Tower, 191 Peachtree Street N.E., Suite 3250.
Telephone: 404-614-2580.
Fax: 404-614-2595.

RESIDENT PARTNERS

E. Lawrence Davis, III
Johnny M. Loper

RESIDENT ASSOCIATES

Yvonne C. Bailey
Samuel M. Taylor

Representative Clients: Aetna Casualty and Surety Co., Inc.; ALSCO/AmeriMark Building Products, Inc.; Aoki Corporation America, Inc.; Empire of Carolina, Inc.; Hackney Brothers, Inc.; Lawyers Mutual Liability Insurance Company of North Carolina; Meredith College; Monk-Austin, Inc.; Regency Park Corporation; Wachovia Bank of North Carolina, N.A.

For Complete List of Firm Personnel, See General Section

For full biographical listings, see the Martindale-Hubbell Law Directory

*WINSTON-SALEM,** Forsyth Co.

WOMBLE CARLYLE SANDRIDGE & RICE (AV)

A Professional Limited Liability Company
1600 Southern National Financial Center, P.O. Drawer 84, 27102
Telephone: 910-721-3600
Telecopy: 910-721-3660
Telex: 806498
Charlotte, North Carolina Office: 3300 One First Union Center, 301 South College Street.
Telephone: 704-331-4900.
Telecopy: 704-331-4955.
Telex: 853609.
Raleigh, North Carolina Office: 2100 First Union Capitol Center, 150 Fayetteville Street Mall, P.O. Box 831.
Telephone: 919-755-2100.
Telecopy: 919-755-2150.
Telex: 806498.
Atlanta, Georgia Office: One Ninety One Peachtree Tower, 191 Peachtree Street, N.E., Suite 3250.
Telephone: 404-614-2580.
Fax: 404-614-2595.

OF COUNSEL

Ashley O. Thrift

Representative Clients: Brad Ragan, Inc.; Brenner Companies; Food Lion, Inc.; Hanes Companies, Inc.; North Carolina Baptist Hospitals, Inc.; R.J. Reynolds Tobacco Company; Summit Communications Group, Inc.; Thomasville Furniture Industries, Inc.; Wachovia Corporation; Wake Forest University.

For Complete List of Firm Personnel, See General Section

For full biographical listings, see the Martindale-Hubbell Law Directory

OHIO

*CINCINNATI,** Hamilton Co.

BARRETT & WEBER A LEGAL PROFESSIONAL ASSOCIATION (AV)

400 Atlas Building, 524 Walnut Street, 45202-3114
Telephone: 513-721-2120
Facsimile: 513-721-2139

C. Francis Barrett

For full biographical listings, see the Martindale-Hubbell Law Directory

DINSMORE & SHOHL (AV)

1900 Chemed Center, 255 East Fifth Street, 45202-3172
Telephone: 513-977-8200
FAX: 513-977-8141
Florence, Kentucky Office: Turfway Ridge Office Park, 7300 Turfway Road, Suite 430 41042-1355.
Telephone: 606-283-0515.
FAX: 606-283-6017.
Dayton, Ohio Office: 500 Courthouse Plaza, S.W., 10 N. Ludlow Street, 45402-1834.
Telephone: 513-228-8012.
FAX: 513-461-2543.
Columbus, Ohio Office: NBD Bank Building, Suite 330, 175 South Third Street, 43215-5134.
Telephone: 614-224-7887.
FAX: 614-224-7882.

MEMBERS OF FIRM

John M. Kunst, Jr.
Vincent B. Stamp
Mark A. Vander Laan
David H. Beaver
Joel S. Taylor (Resident, Columbus, Ohio Office)

ASSOCIATES

Joan M. Verchot
Michael L. Squillace (Resident, Columbus, Ohio Office)
William M. Mattes (Resident, Columbus, Ohio Office)
Dianne Goss Paynter (Resident, Columbus, Ohio Office)

For Complete List of Firm Personnel, See General Section

For full biographical listings, see the Martindale-Hubbell Law Directory

GOODMAN & GOODMAN A LEGAL PROFESSIONAL ASSOCIATION (AV)

123 East Fourth Street, 45202
Telephone: 513-621-1505; 1-800-494-4529
FAX: 513-621-6900

Stanley Goodman
Ronald J. Goodman

For full biographical listings, see the Martindale-Hubbell Law Directory

*COLUMBUS,** Franklin Co.

EMENS, KEGLER, BROWN, HILL & RITTER (AV)

Capitol Square Suite 1800, 65 East State Street, 43215-4294
Telephone: 614-462-5400
Telecopier: 614-464-2634
Cable Address: "Law EKBHR"
Telex: 246671

William J. Brown
Lawrence F. Feheley
Gene W. Holliker
Charles J. Kegler
Roger P. Sugarman
Frank A. Titus
R. Douglas Wrightsel

COUNSEL

Chalmers P. Wylie

Denise Cleary Clayton
Daniel G. Hilson
Todd F. Palmer
Richard W. Schuermann, Jr.
Robert C. Schuler

Representative Clients: Chambers Development Company, Inc.; Medco Containment Services, Inc.; Mid-American Waste Systems, Inc.; Ohio Manufactured Housing Association.

For Complete List of Firm Personnel, See General Section

For full biographical listings, see the Martindale-Hubbell Law Directory

GARY L. JONES CO., L.P.A. (AV)

42 East Gay Street, Suite 1500, 43215
Telephone: 614-221-2300

Gary L. Jones

For full biographical listings, see the Martindale-Hubbell Law Directory

OKLAHOMA

*OKLAHOMA CITY,** Oklahoma Co.

KERR, IRVINE, RHODES & ABLES, A PROFESSIONAL CORPORATION (AV)

600 Bank of Oklahoma Plaza, 73102-4267
Telephone: 405-272-9221
Fax: 405-236-3121

Horace G. Rhodes
Jo Angela Ables
James W. Rhodes
F. Andrew Fugitt

Michael D. Coleman
James R. Barnett
R. Thomas Lay

For Complete List of Firm Personnel, See General Section

For full biographical listings, see the Martindale-Hubbell Law Directory

PENNSYLVANIA

*HARRISBURG,** Dauphin Co.

BUCHANAN INGERSOLL, PROFESSIONAL CORPORATION (AV)

Vartan Parc, 30 North Third Street, 17101
Telephone: 717-237-4800
Telecopier: 717-233-0852
Pittsburgh, Pennsylvania Office: 5800 USX Tower, 600 Grant Street.
Telephone: 412-562-8800.
Philadelphia, Pennsylvania Office: Two Logan Square, Twelfth Floor, 18th & Arch Streets.
Telephone: 215-665-8700.
Tampa, Florida Office: 101 East Kennedy Boulevard, Suite 1030.
Telephone: 813-222-8180.
North Miami Beach, Florida Office: 19495 Biscayne Boulevard.
Telephone: 305-933-5600.
Lexington, Kentucky Office: 1210 Vine Center Office Tower, 333 West Vine Street.
Telephone: 606-225-5333.
Princeton, New Jersey Office: Buchanan Ingersoll, A Partnership, College Centre, 500 College Road East.
Telephone: 609-452-2666.

Daniel E. Beren
Andrew S. Gordon
Mary Hannah Leavitt

(See Next Column)

BUCHANAN INGERSOLL PROFESSIONAL CORPORATION, *Harrisburg—Continued*

SENIOR ATTORNEYS

Richard H. Friedman | Kathryn Speaker MacNett
Michael L. Solomon

For Complete List of Firm Personnel, See General Section

For full biographical listings, see the Martindale-Hubbell Law Directory

HEPFORD, SWARTZ & MORGAN (AV)

111 North Front Street, P.O. Box 889, 17108-0889
Telephone: 717-234-4121
Fax: 717-232-6802
Lewistown, Pennsylvania Office: 12 South Main Street, P.O. Box 867.
Telephone: 717-248-3913.

MEMBERS OF FIRM

H. Joseph Hepford
Lee C. Swartz
James G. Morgan, Jr.
Sandra L. Meilton
Stephen M. Greecher, Jr.
Dennis R. Sheaffer

COUNSEL

Stanley H. Siegel (Resident, Lewistown Office)

ASSOCIATES

Richard A. Estacio
Michael H. Park
Andrew K. Stutzman

For full biographical listings, see the Martindale-Hubbell Law Directory

KILLIAN & GEPHART (AV)

218 Pine Street, P.O. Box 886, 17108
Telephone: 717-232-1851
Telecopier: 717-238-0592

MEMBERS OF FIRM

John D. Killian
Smith B. Gephart
Thomas W. Scott
Jane Penny Malatesta
Terrence J. McGowan
Ronda K. Kiser
Paula J. McDermott

ASSOCIATES

Shaun E. O'Toole
J. Paul Helvy

Reference: Dauphin Deposit Bank & Trust Co.

For full biographical listings, see the Martindale-Hubbell Law Directory

METTE, EVANS & WOODSIDE, A PROFESSIONAL CORPORATION (AV)

3401 North Front Street, P.O. Box 5950, 17110-0950
Telephone: 717-232-5000
Telecopier: 717-236-1816

Howell C. Mette
James W. Evans
Charles B. Zwally
Christopher C. Conner
Michael D. Reed
Robert P. Haynes III

David A. Fitzsimons
Robyn J. Katzman

Counsel for: The B. F. Goodrich Co.; Juniata Valley Financial Corp.; MCI Telecommunications Corp.; Monongahela Power Co.; The Procter and Gamble Paper Products Co.; United States Fidelity and Guaranty Co.; Community Banks; GTE Products Corp.; Commerce Bank.

For Complete List of Firm Personnel, See General Section

For full biographical listings, see the Martindale-Hubbell Law Directory

*PHILADELPHIA,** Philadelphia Co.

ABRAMSON, FREEDMAN & THALL (AV)

2128 Locust Street, 19103
Telephone: 215-545-2400
Telecopier: 215-545-8537
Haddonfield, New Jersey Office: 20 Kings Highway West.
Telephone: 609-795-5363.
Fax: 609-354-0020.

MEMBERS OF FIRM

Gilbert B. Abramson
Jeffrey M. Freedman
Bruce L. Thall

ASSOCIATES

Michael J. Troiani
Michael B. Tolcott
Stanley B. Cheiken (Resident, Haddonfield, New Jersey Office)

For full biographical listings, see the Martindale-Hubbell Law Directory

BUCHANAN INGERSOLL, PROFESSIONAL CORPORATION (AV)

Two Logan Square Twelfth Floor, 18th & Arch Streets, 19103
Telephone: 215-665-8700
Telecopier: 215-569-2066
Pittsburgh, Pennsylvania Office: 5800 USX Tower, 600 Grant Street.
Telephone: 412-562-8800.

(See Next Column)

Harrisburg, Pennsylvania Office: Vartan Parc, 30 North Third Street.
Telephone: 717-237-4800.
Tampa, Florida Office: 101 East Kennedy Boulevard, Suite 1030.
Telephone: 813-222-8180.
North Miami Beach, Florida Office: 19495 Biscayne Boulevard.
Telephone: 305-933-5600.
Lexington, Kentucky Office: 1210 Vine Center Office Tower, 333 West Vine Street.
Telephone: 606-225-5333.
Princeton, New Jersey Office: Buchanan Ingersoll, A Partnership, College Centre, 500 College Road East.
Telephone: 609-452-2666.

SENIOR ATTORNEY

Mary Ellen Krober

For Complete List of Firm Personnel, See General Section

For full biographical listings, see the Martindale-Hubbell Law Directory

DUANE, MORRIS & HECKSCHER (AV)

Suite 4200 One Liberty Place, 19103-7396
Telephone: 215-979-1000
FAX: 215-979-1020
Harrisburg, Pennsylvania Office: 305 North Front Street, 5th Floor, P.O. Box 1003.
Telephone: 717-237-5500.
Fax: 717-232-4015.
Wilmington, Delaware Office: Suite 1500, 1201 Market Street.
Telephone: 302-571-5550.
Fax: 302-571-5560.
New York, N.Y. Office: 112 E. 42nd Street, Suite 2125.
Telephone: 212-499-0410.
Fax: 212-499-0420.
Wayne, Pennsylvania Office 735 Chesterbrook Boulevard, Suite 300.
Telephone: 610-647-3555.
Allentown, Pennsylvania Office: 968 Postal Road, Suite 200.
Telephone: 610-266-3650.
Fax: 610-640-2619.
Cherry Hill, New Jersey Office: 51 Haddonfield Road, Suite 340.
Telephone: 609-488-7300.
Fax: 609-488-7021.

MEMBERS OF FIRM

Roland Morris
Robert L. Pratter
Bruce J. Kasten
Amy E. Wilkinson
David C. Toomey
Jane Leslie Dalton
David E. Loder
Seth v.d.H. Cooley

ASSOCIATES

Thomas G. Servodidio
David L. Frank
Nancy Conrad
E. Lynne Hirsch
Sheila McVey Mangan
Linda Marie Doyle
Bruce A. Gelting (Resident, Harrisburg, Pennsylvania Office)
Larry D. Silver
Lisa W. Clark
Deborah Tate Pecci
Martin A. Fritz (Resident, Harrisburg, Pennsylvania Office)
Paula Terese Ryan

For Complete List of Firm Personnel, See General Section

For full biographical listings, see the Martindale-Hubbell Law Directory

*PITTSBURGH,** Allegheny Co.

ADERSON, FRANK & STEINER, A PROFESSIONAL CORPORATION (AV)

2320 Grant Building, 15219
Telephone: 412-263-0500
Fax: 412-263-0565

Sanford M. Aderson
Edward A. Witt
Nancy L. Rackoff

For full biographical listings, see the Martindale-Hubbell Law Directory

BUCHANAN INGERSOLL, PROFESSIONAL CORPORATION (AV)

5800 USX Tower, 600 Grant Street, 15219
Telephone: 412-562-8800
Telecopier: 412-562-1041
Philadelphia, Pennsylvania Office: Two Logan Square, Twelfth Floor, 18th & Arch Streets.
Telephone: 215-665-8700.
Harrisburg, Pennsylvania Office: Vartan Parc, 30 North Third Street.
Telephone: 717-237-4800.
Tampa, Florida Office: 101 East Kennedy Boulevard, Suite 1030.
Telephone: 813-222-8180.
North Miami Beach, Florida Office: 19495 Biscayne Boulevard.
Telephone: 305-933-5600.
Lexington, Kentucky Office: 1210 Vine Center Office Tower, 333 West Vine Street.
Telephone: 606-225-5333.

(See Next Column)

BUCHANAN INGERSOLL PROFESSIONAL CORPORATION—*Continued*

Princeton, New Jersey Office: Buchanan Ingersoll, A Partnership, College Centre, 500 College Road East.
Telephone: 609-452-2666.

Donald T. O'Connor — P. Jerome Richey

SENIOR ATTORNEY

Cristopher Charles Hoel

John M. Cerilli — Paul J. Corrado

For Complete List of Firm Personnel, See General Section

For full biographical listings, see the Martindale-Hubbell Law Directory

WITTLIN GOLDSTON & CAPUTO, P.C. (AV)

213 Smithfield Street, Suite 200, 15222
Telephone: 412-261-4200
Telecopier: 412-261-9137

Linda Leebov Goldston — Louis E. Caputo
William L. Stang

For Complete List of Firm Personnel, See General Section

For full biographical listings, see the Martindale-Hubbell Law Directory

*READING,** Berks Co.

RYAN, RUSSELL, OGDEN & SELTZER (AV)

1100 Berkshire Boulevard, P.O. Box 6219, 19610-0219
Telephone: 610-372-4761
Fax: 610-372-4177

Samuel B. Russell — Alan Michael Seltzer
W. Edwin Ogden — Harold J. Ryan (1896-1972)
John S. McConaghy (1907-1981)

ASSOCIATES

Jeffrey A. Franklin — Janet E. Arnold

For full biographical listings, see the Martindale-Hubbell Law Directory

*WEST CHESTER,** Chester Co.

LAMB, WINDLE & MCERLANE, P.C. (AV)

24 East Market Street, P.O. Box 565, 19381-0565
Telephone: 610-430-8000
Telecopier: 610-692-0877

COUNSEL

Theodore O. Rogers

William H. Lamb — John D. Snyder
Susan Windle Rogers — William P. Mahon
James E. McErlane — Guy A. Donatelli
E. Craig Kalemjian — Vincent M. Pompo
James C. Sargent, Jr. — James J. McEntee III

Tracy Blake DeVlieger — Daniel A. Loewenstern
P. Andrew Schaum — Thomas F. Oeste
Lawrence J. Persick — John W. Pauciulo
Thomas K. Schindler — Andrea B. Pettine
John J. Cunningham

Representative Clients: Chester County; First Financial Savings Bank, PaSA; Bank of Chester County; Jefferson Bank; Downingtown Area and Great Valley School Districts; Philadelphia Electric Company; Central and Western Chester County Industrial Development Authority; Valley Forge Sewer Authority; Manito Title Insurance Company.

For full biographical listings, see the Martindale-Hubbell Law Directory

SOUTH CAROLINA

*CHARLESTON,** Charleston Co.

HAYNSWORTH, MARION, MCKAY & GUÉRARD, L.L.P (AV)

#2 Prioleau Street, P.O. Box 1119, 29402
Telephone: 803-722-7606
Telecopier: 803-723-5263
Columbia, South Carolina Office: Suite 2400 AT&T Building, 1201 Main Street, P.O. Drawer 7157, 29202.
Telephone: 803-765-1818.
Telecopier: 803-765-2399.
Greenville, South Carolina Office: Two Insignia Financial Plaza, 75 Beattie Place, P.O. Box 2048, 29602.
Telephone: 803-240-3200.
Telecopier: 803-240-3300.

(See Next Column)

MEMBERS OF FIRM

W. E. Applegate, III — James J. Hinchey, Jr. (Resident)
William C. Cleveland — Donald Bancroft Meyer

ASSOCIATES

James E. Lady — Coleman Miller Legerton
Paul M. Lynch — J. Walker Coleman, IV
Meredith Grier Buyck

Counsel for: Bank of South Carolina; Baker Hospital; Healthsource of South Carolina; Allstate Insurance Co.; CSX Corporation; Lloyd's Underwriters; Coward-Hund Construction Co.; City of Hanahan; Duke Power Company; Anheuser Busch Company; Roper Hospital.

For Complete List of Firm Personnel, See General Section

For full biographical listings, see the Martindale-Hubbell Law Directory

ROSEN, ROSEN & HAGOOD, P.A. (AV)

134 Meeting Street, Suite 200, P.O. Box 893, 29402
Telephone: 803-577-6726

Morris D. Rosen — H. Brewton Hagood
Robert N. Rosen — Alice F. Paylor
Richard S. Rosen — Donald B. Clark

Randy Horner

Reference: NationsBank of South Carolina, N.A.

For Complete List of Firm Personnel, See General Section

For full biographical listings, see the Martindale-Hubbell Law Directory

*COLUMBIA,** Richland Co.

* indicates certain Bar Register subscribers whose principal office is located elsewhere in the state and who have arranged for representation as a part of the state capital listings that follow

*** HAYNSWORTH, MARION, MCKAY & GUÉRARD, L.L.P. (AV)**

Suite 2400 A T & T Building, 1201 Main Street, P.O. Drawer 7157, 29202
Telephone: 803-765-1818
Telecopier: 803-765-2399
Greenville, South Carolina Office: Two Insignia Financial Plaza, 75 Beattie Place, P.O. Box 2048, 29602.
Telephone: 803-240-3200.
Telecopier: 803-240-3300.
Charleston, South Carolina Office: #2 Prioleau Street, P.O. Box 1119, 29402.
Telephone: 803-722-7606.
Telecopier: 803-723-5263.

OF COUNSEL

Julius W. McKay

SPECIAL COUNSEL

Julian W. Walker, Jr.

MEMBERS OF FIRM

William P. Simpson — Gary W. Morris
Henry P. Wall

ASSOCIATES

Stephen F. McKinney — Boyd B. Nicholson, Jr.
Edward G. Kluiters — Jill R. Quattlebaum

Counsel for: St. Paul Insurance Group; Allstate Insurance Co.; Fluor-Daniel Corp.; South Carolina Jobs - Economic Development Authority; Anheuser Busch Company; CSX Transportation; Ernst & Young, LLP; Willis Corroon of South Carolina, Inc.; Westinghouse Savannah River Co.; Wachovia Bank of South Carolina, N.A.

For Complete List of Firm Personnel, See General Section

For full biographical listings, see the Martindale-Hubbell Law Directory

*GREENVILLE,** Greenville Co.

HAYNSWORTH, MARION, MCKAY & GUÉRARD, L.L.P. (AV)

Two Insignia Financial Plaza, 75 Beattie Place, P.O. Box 2048, 29602
Telephone: 803-240-3200
Telecopier: 803-240-3300
Columbia, South Carolina Office: Suite 2400 A T & T Building, 1201 Main Street, P.O. Drawer 7157, 29202
Telephone: 803-765-1818.
Telecopier: 803-765-2399.
Charleston, South Carolina Office: #2 Prioleau Street, P.O. Box 1119, 29402.
Telephone: 803-722-7606.
Telecopier: 803-723-5263.

MEMBER OF FIRM

Donald L. Ferguson

(See Next Column)

HAYNSWORTH, MARION, MCKAY & GUÉRARD L.L.P., *Greenville—Continued*

ASSOCIATE
Melissa Miller Anderson

Counsel for: Duke Power Co.; Liberty Mutual Insurance Co.; Equitable Life Assurance Society of the United States; St. Paul Insurance Group; Allstate Insurance Co.; Fluor-Daniel Corp.; Snyalloy Corporation; Greenville Hospital System.

For Complete List of Firm Personnel, See General Section

For full biographical listings, see the Martindale-Hubbell Law Directory

TEXAS

*AUSTIN,** Travis Co.

* indicates certain Bar Register subscribers whose principal office is located elsewhere in the state and who have arranged for representation as a part of the state capital listings that follow

BAKER & BOTTS, L.L.P. (AV)

1600 San Jacinto Center, 98 San Jacinto Boulevard, 78701
Telephone: 512-322-2500
Fax: 512-322-2501
Houston, Texas Office: One Shell Plaza, 910 Louisiana.
Telephone: 713-229-1234.
Dallas, Texas Office: 2001 Ross Avenue.
Telephone: 214-953-6500.
Washington, D.C. Office: The Warner, 1299 Pennsylvania Avenue, N.W.
Telephone: 202-639-7700.
New York, New York Office: 885 Third Avenue, Suite 2000.
Telephone: 212-705-5000.
Moscow, Russian Federation Office: 10 ul. Pushkinskaya, 103031.
Telephone: 7095/921-5300 (Local); 7501/929-7070 (International).

MEMBER OF FIRM
Robert T. Stewart

OF COUNSEL
Joe R. Greenhill
Bob E. Shannon
Robert D. Simpson

ASSOCIATES
Derek R. McDonald
Mark R. Robeck

For Complete List of Firm Personnel, See General Section

For full biographical listings, see the Martindale-Hubbell Law Directory

DAVIS & DAVIS, P.C. (AV)

Arboretum Plaza One, 9th Floor, 9442 Capitol of Texas Highway, P.O. Box 1588, 78767
Telephone: 512-343-6248
Fax: 512-343-0121

C. Dean Davis
Alexis J. Fuller, Jr.
Fred E. Davis
Francis A. (Tony) Bradley
Ruth Russell-Schafer

Bill Cline, Jr.
A. A. Jack Ross, IV
Robert L. Hargett
Kevin Wayde Morse
Michael L. Neely
Mark Alan Keene
Brian Gregory Jackson
Kenda B. Dalrymple

For Complete List of Firm Personnel, See General Section

For full biographical listings, see the Martindale-Hubbell Law Directory

THOMAS A. FORBES (AV)

Suite 2300 515 Congress Avenue, 78701
Telephone: 512-480-5655
Fax: 512-478-1976

For full biographical listings, see the Martindale-Hubbell Law Directory

GRAVES, DOUGHERTY, HEARON & MOODY, A PROFESSIONAL CORPORATION (AV)

Suite 2300, 515 Congress Avenue, P.O. Box 98, 78767
Telephone: 512-480-5600
Kerrville, Texas Office: 222 Sidney Baker South.
Telephone: 210-257-7311.
Fax: 210-896-7273.

SHAREHOLDERS
Michael Diehl
Glenn E. Johnson
Robert J. Hearon, Jr.
Robin A. Melvin
Thomas B. Hudson, Jr.
Dan Moody, Jr.
Selden Anne Wallace

(See Next Column)

Michelle Bourianoff Bray

For Complete List of Firm Personnel, See General Section

For full biographical listings, see the Martindale-Hubbell Law Directory

* **HUGHES & LUCE, L.L.P.** (AV)

A Registered Limited Liability Partnership including Professional Corporations
111 Congress, Suite 900, 78701
Telephone: 512-482-6800
Fax: 512-482-6859
Dallas, Texas Office: 1717 Main Street, Suite 2800.
Telephone: 214-939-5500.
Fax: 214-939-6100.
Houston, Texas Office: Three Allen Center, 333 Clay Street, Suite 3800.
Telephone: 713-754-5200.
Fax: 713-754-5206.
Fort Worth, Texas Office: 2421 Westport Parkway, Suite 500A.
Telephone: 817-439-3000.
Fax: 817-439-4222.

MEMBER OF FIRM
Alexander J. Gonzales

SENIOR COUNSEL
Mack Wallace

For Complete List of Firm Personnel, See General Section

For full biographical listings, see the Martindale-Hubbell Law Directory

ROAN & AUTREY, A PROFESSIONAL CORPORATION (AV)

710 First State Bank Tower, 400 West Fifteenth Street, 78701-4200
Telephone: 512-474-4200
FAX: 512-469-0470; 512-469-0474

Forrest C. Roan
Jeff W. Autrey
Stephen L. Phillips

OF COUNSEL
Robert McFarland

LEGAL SUPPORT PERSONNEL
DIRECTOR OF GOVERNMENT RELATIONS
Dana Chiodo

DIRECTOR OF WORKERS' COMPENSATION
N.J. "Nick" Huestis

For full biographical listings, see the Martindale-Hubbell Law Directory

SAEGERT, ANGENEND & AUGUSTINE, P.C. (AV)

1145 West Fifth Street, Suite 300, 78703
Telephone: 512-474-6521
Fax: 512-477-4512

Jerry C. Saegert
Harrell Glenn Hall, Jr.
Paul D. Angenend
Wendall Corrigan
John C. Augustine
Rebecca K. Knapik
Mark D. Swanson
Walter C. Guebert
John R. Whisenhunt (1949-1994)
Paul Vincent Mouer

For full biographical listings, see the Martindale-Hubbell Law Directory

SANFORD, SPELLINGS, KUHL & PERKINS, L.L.P. (AV)

400 West 15th Street, Suite 1630, 78701
Telephone: 512-472-9090
FAX: 512-472-9182
Houston, Texas Office: 1180 Galleria Financial Center, 5075 Westheime.
Telephone: 713-850-9000.
Fax: 713-850-1330.

RESIDENT MEMBERS
Marion Sanford, Jr.
Robert D. Spellings

For full biographical listings, see the Martindale-Hubbell Law Directory

SCOTT, DOUGLASS, LUTON & MCCONNICO, L.L.P. (AV)

A Limited Liability Partnership including a Professional Corporation
One American Center, 600 Congress Avenue, 15th Floor, 78701-3234
Telephone: 512-495-6300
Fax: 512-474-0731
Houston, Texas Office: 40th Floor, NationsBank Center, 700 Louisiana Street.
Telephone: 713-225-8400.
Dallas, Texas Office: NationsBank Plaza, 901 Main Street, Suite 2800.
Telephone: 214-651-5300.

MEMBERS OF FIRM
Wallace H. Scott, Jr.
James N. Cowden
Frank P. Youngblood
Richard P. Marshall, Jr.
H. Philip Whitworth, Jr.
Carroll Greer Martin
John G. Soule
Steve Selby
Stephen E. McConnico
Elizabeth N. Miller

(See Next Column)

SCOTT, DOUGLASS, LUTON & MCCONNICO L.L.P.—*Continued*

MEMBERS OF FIRM (Continued)

John W. Camp
Daniel W. Bishop, II
Ray H. Langenberg
Thomas A. Albright
Douglas J. Dashiell
Ray N. Donley
Phyllis M. Pollard
Christopher Fuller
Casey L. Dobson
Jennifer Knauth Lipinski
Daniel C. Bitting
Sam Johnson
Robert A. Summers
Mark W. Eidman
Julie Ann Springer

OF COUNSEL

Bob Bullock
Martin L. Allday

ASSOCIATES

Jeffrey G. Henry
James P. Ray
Jane M. N. Webre
Steven J. Wingard
Elizabeth B. Pearsall
Anna M. Norris
James D. Clayton
Rebecca M. Hudson

For full biographical listings, see the Martindale-Hubbell Law Directory

MICHAEL R. SHARP (AV)

1820 One American Center, 600 Congress Avenue, 78701
Telephone: 512-473-2265

LEGAL SUPPORT PERSONNEL

Kimberly Stamper (Legal Assistant)

For full biographical listings, see the Martindale-Hubbell Law Directory

*DALLAS,** Dallas Co.

BAKER & BOTTS, L.L.P. (AV)

2001 Ross Avenue, 75201
Telephone: 214-953-6500
Fax: 214-953-6503
Houston, Texas Office: One Shell Plaza, 910 Louisiana.
Telephone: 713-229-1234.
Washington, D.C. Office: The Warner, 1299 Pennsylvania Avenue, N.W.
Telephone: 202-639-7700.
Austin, Texas Office: 1600 San Jacinto Center, 98 San Jacinto Boulevard.
Telephone: 512-322-2500.
New York, New York Office: 885 Third Avenue, Suite 2000.
Telephone: 212-705-5000.
Moscow, Russian Federation Office: 10 ul. Pushkinskaya, 103031.
Telephone: 7095/921-5300 (Local); 7095/929-7070.

MEMBERS OF FIRM

Stan Hinton
Edwin J. Tomko

ASSOCIATES

B. Borden Johnson
Paul W. Searles

For Complete List of Firm Personnel, See General Section
For full biographical listings, see the Martindale-Hubbell Law Directory

THOMPSON, COE, COUSINS & IRONS, L.L.P. (AV)

200 Crescent Court, Eleventh Floor, 75201-1840
Telephone: 214-871-8200 (Dallas)
512-480-8770 (Austin)
FAX: 214-871-8209

MEMBERS OF FIRM

Emory L. White, Jr.
Richard S. Geiger
Jack M. Cleaveland, Jr.
Rodney D. Bucker

ASSOCIATE

Michael W. Jones

Representative Clients: Alexander & Alexander, Inc.; Association of Fire and Casualty Companies of Texas; Great American Insurance Companies; Universal Surety of America; National Council on Compensation Insurance; Skandia Insurance Group; Texas Automobile Insurance Service Office; Texas Automobile Insurance Plan; Transamerica Insurance Group; Maclean Oddy & Associates, Inc.

For Complete List of Firm Personnel, See General Section
For full biographical listings, see the Martindale-Hubbell Law Directory

*HOUSTON,** Harris Co.

BAKER & BOTTS, L.L.P. (AV)

One Shell Plaza, 910 Louisiana, 77002
Telephone: 713-229-1234
Cable Address: "Boterlove"
Fax: 713-229-1522
Washington, D.C. Office: The Warner, 1299 Pennsylvania Avenue, N.W.
Telephone: 202-639-7700.
New York, New York Office: 885 Third Avenue, Suite 2000.
Telephone: 212-705-5000.
Austin, Texas Office: 1600 San Jacinto Center, 98 San Jacinto Boulevard.
Telephone: 512-322-2500.
Dallas, Texas Office: 2001 Ross Avenue.
Telephone: 214-953-6500.

(See Next Column)

Moscow, Russian Federation Office: 10 ul. Pushkinskaya, 103031.
Telephone: 7095/921-5300 (Local); 7095/929-7070 (International).

MEMBERS OF FIRM

Finis E. Cowan
I. Jay Golub
Jefferson Gregory Copeland
Scott E. Rozzell
George F. Goolsby

ASSOCIATES

James H. Barkley
Sarah Sharlot Dietrich
Clayton L. Smith
Mark S. Snell
Michael T. Swaim

For Complete List of Firm Personnel, See General Section
For full biographical listings, see the Martindale-Hubbell Law Directory

*SAN ANTONIO,** Bexar Co.

GARDNER & FERGUSON, INC., A PROFESSIONAL CORPORATION (AV)

745 East Mulberry, Suite 100, 78212
Telephone: 210-733-8191
Fax: 210-733-5538

Holmes T. Bennett
Wm. Richard Davis
Donald O. Ferguson
William W. Sommers
Carl Payne 'Chip' Tobey, Jr.
Thomas J. Walthall, Jr.

Mark M. Ferguson

Representative Clients: Litho-Press, Inc.; Morrisen Knudsen.

For full biographical listings, see the Martindale-Hubbell Law Directory

UTAH

*SALT LAKE CITY,** Salt Lake Co.

PARSONS BEHLE & LATIMER, A PROFESSIONAL CORPORATION (AV)

One Utah Center, 201 South Main Street, Suite 1800, P.O. Box 45898, 84145-0898
Telephone: 801-532-1234
Telecopy: 801-536-6111

F. Robert Reeder
Dallin W. Jensen
Val R. Antczak

Representative Clients: Amoco Oil Company; Hercules, Inc.; Kennecott Corporation; Kimberly Clark Corporation; National Semiconductor Corporation; Western Zirconium.

For full biographical listings, see the Martindale-Hubbell Law Directory

VAN COTT, BAGLEY, CORNWALL & MCCARTHY, A PROFESSIONAL CORPORATION (AV)

Suite 1600, 50 South Main Street, P.O. Box 45340, 84145
Telephone: 801-532-3333
Telex: 453149
Telecopier: 801-534-0058
Ogden, Utah Office: Suite 900, 2404 Washington Boulevard.
Telephone: 801-394-5783.
Park City, Utah Office: 314 Main Street, Suite 205.
Telephone: 801-649-3889.
Reno, Nevada Office: Jeppson & Lee, 100 West Liberty, Suite 990.
Telephone: 702-333-6800.

Gregory P. Williams
Alan L. Sullivan
John T. Nielsen
H. Michael Keller
Patricia M. Leith
R. Stephen Marshall

OF COUNSEL

Leonard J. Lewis

For Complete List of Firm Personnel, See General Section
For full biographical listings, see the Martindale-Hubbell Law Directory

VERMONT

*BURLINGTON,** Chittenden Co.

BURAK & ANDERSON (AV)

Executive Square, 346 Shelburne Street, P.O. Box 64700, 05406-4700
Telephone: 802-862-0500
Telecopier: 802-862-8176

(See Next Column)

BURAK & ANDERSON, *Burlington—Continued*

MEMBERS OF FIRM

Michael L. Burak
Thomas R. Melloni
Jon Anderson
David M. Hyman

ASSOCIATES

Robert I. Goetz
Andrew H. Montroll

For Complete List of Firm Personnel, See General Section

For full biographical listings, see the Martindale-Hubbell Law Directory

LISMAN & LISMAN, A PROFESSIONAL CORPORATION (AV)

84 Pine Street, P.O. Box 728, 05402-0728
Telephone: 802-864-5756
Fax: 802-864-3629

Carl H. Lisman
Mary G. Kirkpatrick
Allen D. Webster
E. William Leckerling, III
Douglas K. Riley

Judith Lillian Dillon
Richard W. Kozlowski

OF COUNSEL

Bernard Lisman
Louis Lisman

For full biographical listings, see the Martindale-Hubbell Law Directory

*MIDDLEBURY,** Addison Co.

CONLEY & FOOTE (AV)

11 South Pleasant Street, P.O. Drawer 391, 05753
Telephone: 802-388-4061
Fax: 802-388-0210

MEMBERS OF FIRM

John T. Conley (1900-1971)
D. Michael Mathes
Ralph A. Foote
Richard P. Foote
Charity A. Downs
Janet P. Shaw

For full biographical listings, see the Martindale-Hubbell Law Directory

*ST. JOHNSBURY,** Caledonia Co.

PRIMMER & PIPER, PROFESSIONAL CORPORATION (AV)

52 Summer Street, P.O. Box 159, 05819
Telephone: 802-748-5061
Facsimile: 802-748-3976
Montpelier, Vermont Office: 44 East State Street, 05602. Box 1309.
Telephone: 802-223-2102.
Fax: 802-223-2628.

John L. Primmer
Jeffrey P. Johnson
William B. Piper
Robert W. Martin, Jr.
Denise J. Deschenes
James E. Clemons

Trevor R. Lewis
James D. Huber

For full biographical listings, see the Martindale-Hubbell Law Directory

VIRGINIA

MIDLOTHIAN, Chesterfield Co.

JAMES R. WRENN, JR., P.C. (AV)

Suite C, 14031 Steeplestone Drive, 23113-6416
Telephone: 804-378-2037
Fax: 804-378-2039

James R. Wrenn, Jr.

Reference: First Virginia Bank-Colonial, Richmond, Virginia.

For full biographical listings, see the Martindale-Hubbell Law Directory

*RICHMOND,** (Ind. City; Seat of Henrico Co.)

WILLIAMS, MULLEN, CHRISTIAN & DOBBINS, A PROFESSIONAL CORPORATION (AV)

Two James Center, 1021 East Cary Street, P.O. Box 1320, 23210-1320
Telephone: 804-643-1991
Fax: 804-783-6456
Glen Allen, Virginia Office: 4401 Waterfront Drive, Suite 140.
Telephone: 804-965-9168.
Fax: 804-965-0955.
Washington, D.C. Office: 1575 Eye Street, N.W.
Telephone: 202-289-6200.
Fax: 202-289-4126.

(See Next Column)

Ralph L. Axselle, Jr.
Walter H. Ryland
Sarah Hopkins Finley
C. William Waechter, Jr.
Timothy G. Hayes
Clayton L. Walton
Reginald N. Jones
Thomas B. McVey (Not admitted in VA; Resident, Washington, D.C. Office)

Heidi Wilson Abbott

For Complete List of Firm Personnel, See General Section

For full biographical listings, see the Martindale-Hubbell Law Directory

WASHINGTON

*SEATTLE,** King Co.

GAITÁN & CUSACK (AV)

30th Floor Two Union Square, 601 Union Street, 98101-2324
Telephone: 206-521-3000
Facsimile: 206-386-5259
Anchorage, Alaska Office: 425 G Street, Suite 760.
Telephone: 907-278-3001.
Facsimile: 907-278-6068.
San Francisco, California Office: 275 Battery Street, 20th Floor.
Telephone: 415-398-5562.
Fax: 415-398-4033.
Washington, D.C. Office: 2000 L Street, Suite 200.
Telephone: 202-296-4637.
Fax: 202-296-4650.

MEMBERS OF FIRM

José E. Gaitán
William F. Knowles
Kenneth J. Cusack (Resident, Anchorage, Alaska Office)
Ronald L. Bozarth

OF COUNSEL

Howard K. Todd
Christopher A. Byrne
Gary D. Gayton
Patricia D. Ryan
Michel P. Stern (Also practicing alone, Bellevue, Washington)

ASSOCIATES

Mary F. O'Boyle
Robert T. Mimbu
Bruce H. Williams
Cristina C. Kapela
David J. Onsager
Camilla M. Hedberg
Diana T. Jimenez
John E. Lenker
Kathleen C. Healy

Representative Clients: North Shore Utility District; State of Washington.

For full biographical listings, see the Martindale-Hubbell Law Directory

WEST VIRGINIA

*CHARLESTON,** Kanawha Co.

JACKSON & KELLY (AV)

1600 Laidley Tower, P.O. Box 553, 25322
Telephone: 304-340-1000
Fax: 304-340-1130
Martinsburg, West Virginia Office: 300 Foxcroft Avenue, P.O. Box 1068.
Telephone: 304-263-8800.
Morgantown, West Virginia Office: 6000 Hampton Center, P.O. Box 619.
Telephone: 304-599-3000.
New Martinsville, West Virginia Office: 256 Russell Avenue, P.O. Box 68.
Telephone: 304-455-1751.
Charles Town, West Virginia Office: 700 East Washington Street, P.O. Box 983.
Telephone: 304-728-6088.
Clarksburg, West Virginia Office: 203 Main Street, P.O. Box 1587.
Telephone: 304-623-3002.
Lexington, Kentucky Office: 175 East Main Street, Suite 500, P.O. Box 2150.
Telephone: 606-255-9500.
Washington, D. C. Office: 2401 Pennsylvania Avenue, N.W., Suite 400.
Telephone: 202-973-0200.
Denver, Colorado Office: Suite 2710, 1660 Lincoln Street.
Telephone: 303-837-0003.

MEMBERS OF FIRM

John L. McClaugherty
John Philip Melick
Thomas E. Potter
William E. Doll, Jr. (Resident, Lexington, Kentucky Office)
W. Warren Upton
Michael A. Albert
Thad S. Huffman (Resident, Washington, D.C. Office)
Allen R. Prunty
James W. Thomas
L. Poe Leggette (Resident, Washington, D.C. Office)
Samme L. Gee

(See Next Column)

JACKSON & KELLY—*Continued*

ASSOCIATES

Brooks K. Barkwill (New Martinsville, West Virginia Office)

Representative Clients: Central West Virginia Regional Airport Authority; Kanawha Valley Regional Transportation Authority; Kanawha County Parks and Recreation Commission; Consol Inc.; Pittston Coal Co.; Union Carbide Corp.; Rhone-Poulenc Ag Co.

For Complete List of Firm Personnel, See General Section

For full biographical listings, see the Martindale-Hubbell Law Directory

KING, ALLEN & ARNOLD (AV)

1300 Bank One Center, P.O. Box 3394, 25333
Telephone: 304-345-7250
Telecopier: 304-345-9941

Robert B. King	S. Benjamin Bryant
George G. Guthrie	Raymond Keener, III
Robert B. Allen	Wm. Scott Wickline
James S. Arnold	Robert A. Campbell
R. Terrance Rodgers	W. Mark Burnette
Robert A. Goldberg	J. Miles Morgan
Stephen B. Farmer	Pamela Lynn Kandzari
John J. Polak	Michelle M. Price
Robert D. Cline, Jr.	Kimberly S. Fenwick

For full biographical listings, see the Martindale-Hubbell Law Directory

*CLARKSBURG,** Harrison Co.

MCNEER, HIGHLAND & MCMUNN (AV)

Empire Building, P.O. Drawer 2040, 26301
Telephone: 304-623-6636
Facsimile: 304-623-3035
Morgantown Office: McNeer, Highland & McMunn, Baker & Armistead, 168 Chancery Row. P.O. Box 1615.
Telephone: 304-292-8473.
Fax: 304-292-1528.
Martinsburg, Office: 1446-1 Edwin Miller Boulevard. P.O. Box 2509.
Telephone: 304-264-4621.
Fax: 304-264-8623.

MEMBERS OF FIRM

C. David McMunn	Dennis M. Shreve
J. Cecil Jarvis	Geraldine S. Roberts
James A. Varner	Harold M. Sklar
George B. Armistead (Resident, Morgantown Office)	Jeffrey S. Bolyard
Catherine D. Munster	Steven R. Bratke
Robert W. Trumble (Resident, Martinsburg Office)	Michael J. Novotny (Resident, Martinsburg Office)

OF COUNSEL

James E. McNeer	Cecil B. Highland, Jr.

William L. Fury

Representative Clients: One Valley Bank of Clarksburg, National Association; Bruceton Bank; Harrison County Bank; Nationwide Mutual Insurance Cos.; Clarksburg Publishing Co.; C.I.T. Financial Services; State Automobile Mutual Insurance Co.; United Hospital Center, Inc.; West Virginia Coals, Inc.; Swanson Plating Company.

For Complete List of Firm Personnel, See General Section

For full biographical listings, see the Martindale-Hubbell Law Directory

WISCONSIN

*MILWAUKEE,** Milwaukee Co.

QUARLES & BRADY (AV)

411 East Wisconsin Avenue, 53202-4497
Telephone: 414-277-5000
Cable Address: "Lawdock"
Fax: 414-271-3552.
TWX: 910-262-3426
Madison, Wisconsin Office: Firstar Plaza, One South Pinckney Street, P.O. Box 2113.
Telephone: 608-251-5000.
Fax: 608-251-9166.
West Palm Beach, Florida Office: 222 Lakeview Avenue, 4th Floor.
Telephone: 407-653-5000.
Fax: 407-653-5333.
Naples, Florida Office: Barnett Center, 4501 Tamiami Trail North.
Telephone: 813-262-5959.
Fax: 813-434-4999.
Phoenix, Arizona Office: One Camelback Building, One East Camelback Road, Suite 400.
Telephone: 602-230-5500.
Fax: 602-230-5598.

(See Next Column)

MEMBERS OF FIRM
(ALPHABETICALLY BY YEAR OF ADMISSION TO BAR)

Charles Q. Kamps	Larry J. Martin
P. Robert Fannin (Resident, Phoenix, Arizona Office)	Anthony H. Driessen
	Thomas P. McElligott

Nancy K. Peterson

ASSOCIATES

Erica M. Eisinger (Resident, Madison Office)	Patricia M. Anania (Resident, Phoenix, Arizona Office)

For Complete List of Firm Personnel, See General Section

For full biographical listings, see the Martindale-Hubbell Law Directory

WYOMING

*CASPER,** Natrona Co.

BROWN & DREW (AV)

Casper Business Center, Suite 800, 123 West First Street, 82601-2486
Telephone: 307-234-1000
800-877-6755
Telefax: 307-265-8025

MEMBERS OF FIRM

Morris R. Massey	Donn J. McCall
Harry B. Durham, III	John A. Warnick
W. Thomas Sullins, II	Thomas F. Reese

Jeffrey C. Brinkerhoff

ASSOCIATES

Jon B. Huss	Courtney Robert Kepler
Carol Warnick	Drew A. Perkins

Attorneys for: First Interstate Bank of Wyoming, N.A.; Norwest Bank Wyoming, N.A.; The CIT Group/Industrial Financing; The Doctor's Co.; MED-MARC; WOTCO, Inc.; Chevron USA; Kerr-McGee Corp.; Chicago and NorthWestern Transportation Company.

For Complete List of Firm Personnel, See General Section

For full biographical listings, see the Martindale-Hubbell Law Directory

*CHEYENNE,** Laramie Co.

SUNDAHL, POWERS, KAPP & MARTIN (AV)

American National Bank Building, 1912 Capitol Avenue, Suite 300, P.O. Box 328, 82001
Telephone: 307-632-6421
FAX: 307-632-7216

MEMBERS OF FIRM

John Alan Sundahl	Paul Kapp
George E. Powers, Jr.	Raymond W. Martin

ASSOCIATES

John A. Coppede	Kay Lynn Bestol

A list of Representative Clients will be furnished upon request.

For full biographical listings, see the Martindale-Hubbell Law Directory

CANADA
ALBERTA

*EDMONTON,** Edmonton Jud. Dist.

PARLEE MCLAWS (AV)

15th Floor Manulife Place, 10180 101st Street, T5J 4K1
Telephone: 403-423-8500
Telecopier: 403-423-2870
Calgary, Alberta Office: 3400, Western Canadian Place, 707 - 8th Avenue, S.W.
Telephone: 403-294-7000.
Telecopier: 403-265-8263.

MEMBERS OF FIRM

C. H. Kerr, Q.C.	R. A. Newton, Q.C.
M. D. MacDonald	T. A. Cockrall, Q.C.
K. F. Bailey, Q.C.	H. D. Montemurro
R. B. Davison, Q.C.	F. J. Niziol
F. R. Haldane	R. W. Wilson
P. E. J. Curran	I. L. MacLachlan
D. G. Finlay	R. O. Langley
J. K. McFadyen	R. G. McBean
R. C. Secord	J. T. Neilson
D. L. Kennedy	E. G. Rice
D. C. Rolf	J. F. McGinnis
D. F. Pawlowski	J. H. H. Hockin
A. A. Garber	G. W. Jaycock

(See Next Column)

PARLEE MCLAWS, *Edmonton—Continued*

MEMBERS OF FIRM (Continued)

R. P. James
M. J. K. Nikel
D. C. Wintermute
B. J. Curial
J. L. Cairns
S. L. May
M. S. Poretti

ASSOCIATES

C. R. Head
P. E. S. J. Kennedy
A.W. Slemko
R. Feraco
L. H. Hamdon
R.J. Billingsley
K.A. Smith
N.B.R. Thompson
K. D. Fallis-Howell
P. A. Shenher
D. S. Tam
I. C. Johnson
J.W. McClure
K.G. Koshman
F.H. Belzil
D.D. Dubrule
R.A. Renz
G. T. Lund
J.G. Paulson
W.D. Johnston
K. E. Buss
G. E. Flemming
B. L. Andriachuk
K. P. Nayyer

For full biographical listings, see the Martindale-Hubbell Law Directory

CANADA NEW BRUNSWICK

*SAINT JOHN,** Saint John Co.

CLARK, DRUMMIE & COMPANY (AV)

40 Wellington Row, P.O. Box 6850 Station "A", E2L 4S3
Telephone: 506-633-3800
Telecopier (Automatic): 506-633-3811

MEMBERS OF FIRM

Deno P. Pappas, Q.C.
M. Robert Jette
Karen M. Colpitts

Reference: Royal Bank of Canada.

For Complete List of Firm Personnel, See General Section

For full biographical listings, see the Martindale-Hubbell Law Directory

CANADA NOVA SCOTIA

*HALIFAX,** Halifax Co.

MCINNES COOPER & ROBERTSON (AV)

1601 Lower Water Street, P.O. Box 730, B3J 2V1
Telephone: 902-425-6500
Fax: 902-425-6350
St. John's, Newfoundland Office: Suite 602, Scotia Centre, 235 Water Street, P.O. Box 547. A1C, 5K8.
Telephone: 709-726-9500.
Fax: 709-726-9550.

Peter McLellan, Q.C.
John D. Stringer
Harvey L. Morrison

Attorneys for: Bank of Nova Scotia; Imperial Oil, Limited; Frank B. Hall & Co., Inc. (New York); American Steamship Owners Protection & Indemnity Association, Inc.; Coca-Cola, Ltd.; Scott Worldwide Inc.; Hong Kong Bank of Canada.

For Complete List of Firm Personnel, See General Section

For full biographical listings, see the Martindale-Hubbell Law Directory

CANADA ONTARIO

*TORONTO,** Regional Munic. of York

BORDEN & ELLIOT (AV)

Barristers & Solicitors
Scotia Plaza, 40 King Street West, M5H 3Y4
Telephone: 416-367-6000
Telecopier: 416-367-6749
Internet: @ borden.com
A Member of the national association of Borden DuMoulin Howard Gervais, comprising Borden & Elliot in Toronto, Ontario, Russell & DuMoulin in Vancouver, British Columbia, Howard, Mackie in Calgary, Alberta and Mackenzie Gervais in Montréal, Québec. Borden DuMoulin Howard Gervais also operates an office in London, England.

MEMBER AND ASSOCIATES

Dennis R. O'Connor, Q.C.

For Complete List of Firm Personnel, See General Section

For full biographical listings, see the Martindale-Hubbell Law Directory

CANADA PRINCE EDWARD ISLAND

*CHARLOTTETOWN,** Queen's Co.

CAMPBELL, LEA, MICHAEL, MCCONNELL & PIGOT (AV)

15 Queen Street, P.O. Box 429, C1A 7K7
Telephone: 902-566-3400
Telecopier: 902-566-9266

MEMBERS OF FIRM

William G. Lea, Q.C.
Paul D. Michael, Q.C.
Kenneth L. Godfrey

General Counsel in Prince Edward Island for: Canadian Imperial Bank of Commerce; Maritime Electric Co., Ltd.; Michelin Tires (Canada) Ltd.; Newsco Investments Ltd. (Dundas Farms); Queen Elizabeth Hospital Inc.; Imperial Oil Limited; General Motors of Canada; Co-op Atlantic; Liberty Mutual; Employers Reinsurance Group.

For Complete List of Firm Personnel, See General Section

For full biographical listings, see the Martindale-Hubbell Law Directory

ADMIRALTY/MARITIME LAW

ALABAMA

*BIRMINGHAM,** Jefferson Co.

CABANISS, JOHNSTON, GARDNER, DUMAS & O'NEAL (AV)

Park Place Tower, 2001 Park Place North, Suite 700, P.O. Box 830612, 35283-0612
Telephone: 205-252-8800
Telecopier: 205-716-5389
Mobile, Alabama Office: 700 AmSouth Center, P.O. Box 2906.
Telephone: 205-433-6961.
Telecopier: 205-433-1060.

MEMBERS OF FIRM

Crawford S. McGivaren, Jr.
Patrick H. Sims (Resident at Mobile Office)
R. Boyd Miller (Mobile Office)

Counsel for: Alabaster Industries, Inc.; Schuler Industries, Inc.; Carraway Methodist Hospitals of Alabama; Doster Construction Co., Inc.; Liberty Mutual Insurance Co.; John Alden Life Insurance Co.; MacMillan Bloedel Inc.; Norfolk Southern Corp.; O'Neal Steel, Inc.

For Complete List of Firm Personnel, See General Section

For full biographical listings, see the Martindale-Hubbell Law Directory

PITTMAN, HOOKS, MARSH, DUTTON & HOLLIS, P.C. (AV)

1100 Park Place Tower, 35203
Telephone: 205-322-8880
Telecopier: 205-328-2711

W. Lee Pittman
Kenneth W. Hooks
David H. Marsh
Tom Dutton
L. Andrew Hollis, Jr.
Jeffrey C. Kirby
Ralph Bohanan, Jr.
Nat Bryan

Jeffrey C. Rickard
Susan J. Silvernail
Nici F. Williams
Chris T. Hellums
Adam P. Morel

OF COUNSEL

James H. Davis (Not admitted in AL)
Myra B. Staggs

For full biographical listings, see the Martindale-Hubbell Law Directory

*MOBILE,** Mobile Co.

ARMBRECHT, JACKSON, DEMOUY, CROWE, HOLMES & REEVES (AV)

1300 AmSouth Center, P.O. Box 290, 36601
Telephone: 334-432-6751
Facsimile: 334-432-6843; 433-3821

MEMBERS OF FIRM

Wm. H. Armbrecht (1908-1991)
Theodore K. Jackson (1910-1981)
F.M. Keeling (1943-1993)
Marshall J. DeMouy
Wm. H. Armbrecht, III
Rae M. Crowe
Broox G. Holmes
W. Boyd Reeves
E. B. Peebles III
William B. Harvey
Kirk C. Shaw
Norman E. Waldrop, Jr.
Conrad P. Armbrecht
Edward G. Hawkins
Grover E. Asmus II
David A. Bagwell
Douglas L. Brown
Donald C. Radcliff
Christopher I. Gruenewald
James Donald Hughes
M. Kathleen Miller
Dabney Bragg Foshee
Edward A. Dean
David E. Hudgens
Ray Morgan Thompson
James Dale Smith
Duane A. Graham
Robert J. Mullican
Wm. Steele Holman, II
Coleman F. Meador
Broox G. Holmes, Jr.

ASSOCIATES

James E. Robertson, Jr.
Scott G. Brown
Clifford C. Brady
Richard W. Franklin
Stephen Russell Copeland
Tara T. Bostick
Rodney R. Cate
James F. Watkins
P. Vincent Gaddy
Richard G. Brock

Representative Clients: Ryan-Walsh Stevedoring Co.; Cove Shipping Co.; Warrior & Gulf Navigation Co.; Cooper Stavedoring Co.; Strachan Shipping Co.; Mobile River Terminal; National Marine, Inc.; ProMar Insurance Co.

For full biographical listings, see the Martindale-Hubbell Law Directory

CUNNINGHAM, BOUNDS, YANCE, CROWDER & BROWN (AV)

1601 Dauphin Street, P.O. Box 66705, 36660
Telephone: 334-471-6191
Fax: 334-479-1031

Richard Bounds
James A. Yance
John T. Crowder, Jr.
Robert T. Cunningham, Jr.
Joseph M. Brown, Jr.
Gregory B. Breedlove
Andrew T. Citrin
Michael A. Worel

David G. Wirtes, Jr.
Randolph B. Walton
Toby D. Brown
Mitchell K. Shelly

OF COUNSEL

Robert T. Cunningham
Valentino D. B. Mazzia

References: First Alabama Bank; AmSouth Bank, N.A.

For full biographical listings, see the Martindale-Hubbell Law Directory

DIAMOND, HASSER & FROST (AV)

1325 Dauphin Street, P.O. Drawer 40600, 36640
Telephone: 334-432-3362
Fax: 334-432-3367

MEMBERS OF FIRM

Ross Diamond, Jr. (1919-1978)
Ross M. Diamond, III
James E. Hasser, Jr.
James H. Frost

References: First Alabama Bank, Mobile; AM South Bank, Mobile.

For full biographical listings, see the Martindale-Hubbell Law Directory

HAND, ARENDALL, BEDSOLE, GREAVES & JOHNSTON (AV)

3000 First National Bank Building, P.O. Box 123, Drawer C, 36601
Telephone: 334-432-5511
Fax: 334-694-6375
Washington, D.C. Office: 410 First Street, S.E., Suite 300. 20003.
Telephone: 202-863-0053.
Fax: 202-863-0096.

MEMBERS OF FIRM

Alexander F. Lankford, III
G. Hamp Uzzelle, III
Joseph Hodge Alves, III
Joe E. Basenberg
Douglas L. McCoy
Blane H. Crutchfield
Brian P. McCarthy

For Complete List of Firm Personnel, See General Section

For full biographical listings, see the Martindale-Hubbell Law Directory

JOHNSTONE, ADAMS, BAILEY, GORDON AND HARRIS (AV)

Royal St. Francis Building, 104 St. Francis Street, P.O. Box 1988, 36633
Telephone: 334-432-7682
Facsimile: 334-432-2800
Telex: 782040

MEMBERS OF FIRM

Joseph M. Allen, Jr.
Thomas S. Rue
Alan C. Christian
Gregory C. Buffalow

Representative Clients: The West of England Ship Owners Mutual Protection and Indemnity Assn. (Luxembourg); The Standard Steamship Owners Protection and Indemnity Assn. (Bermuda) Ltd.; Waterman Steamship Corp.; Lykes Bros. Steamship Co., Inc.; Ocean Marine Division of The Travelers; Dravo Natural Resources Co.; The Shipowners' Mutual Protection and Indemnity Assn. (Luxemburg); Sea-Land Service, Inc.

For Complete List of Firm Personnel, See General Section

For full biographical listings, see the Martindale-Hubbell Law Directory

LYONS, PIPES & COOK, P.C. (AV)

2 North Royal Street, P.O. Box 2727, 36652-2727
Telephone: 334-432-4481
Cable Address: "Lysea"
Telecopier: 334-433-1820

G. Sage Lyons
Wesley Pipes
Marion A. Quina, Jr.
Walter M. Cook, Jr.
Allen E. Graham

General Counsel: Alabama State Docks Department (an agency of the State of Alabama); Southern Steamship Agency, Inc.
Counsel: McKenzie Tank Lines, Inc.; SCNO Barge Lines, Inc.; Scott Paper Co.; Shell Oil Corp.
Trial Counsel: Aetna Life and Casualty Co.; Chubb Group of Insurance Companies.

For Complete List of Firm Personnel, See General Section

For full biographical listings, see the Martindale-Hubbell Law Directory

VICKERS, RIIS, MURRAY AND CURRAN (AV)

8th Floor, First Alabama Bank Building, P.O. Box 2568, 36652
Telephone: 334-432-9772
Fax: 334-432-9781

(See Next Column)

VICKERS, RIIS, MURRAY AND CURRAN, *Mobile—Continued*

MEMBERS OF FIRM

J. Manson Murray
Thomas E. Sharp, III
J. W. Goodloe, Jr.
J. Marshall Gardner

Representative Clients: Dravo Natural Resources Co.; Midstream Fuel Services; John E. Graham & Sons; McPhillips Manufacturing Co.; Spring Hill College; Steiner Shipyard, Inc.; Homeowners Marketing Services, Inc.; Marine Office of America Corp.; Cummins Alabama, Inc.; Ben M. Radcliff Contractor, Inc.

For Complete List of Firm Personnel, See General Section

For full biographical listings, see the Martindale-Hubbell Law Directory

ARKANSAS

*LITTLE ROCK,** Pulaski Co.

WRIGHT, LINDSEY & JENNINGS (AV)

2200 Worthen Bank Building, 200 West Capitol Avenue, 72201
Telephone: 501-371-0808
Fax: 501-376-9442
Fayetteville, Arkansas Office: 101 West Mountain Street, Suite 206, 72701.
Telephone: 501-575-0808.
Fax: 501-575-0999.
Russellville, Arkansas Office: Suite E, 1110 West B Street.
Telephone: 501-968-7995.

Gordon S. Rather, Jr.
Bettina E. Brownstein

Representative Clients: Chotin Transportation, Inc.; Exxon; General Electric Capital Corp.; The Home Insurance Co.; Liberty Mutual Insurance Co.; Lloyd's of London; Mid-South Dredging Co.; Reliance Insurance Co.; The Travelers Insurance Co.; Turnaboat Services, Ltd.; Union Carbide Corp.

For Complete List of Firm Personnel, See General Section

For full biographical listings, see the Martindale-Hubbell Law Directory

CALIFORNIA

IRVINE, Orange Co.

ANDRADE & ASSOCIATES (AV)

Marine National Bank Building, 18401 Von Karman, Suite 350, 92715
Telephone: 714-553-1951
Telecopier: 714-553-0655

Richard B. Andrade

ASSOCIATES

Jack W. Fleming
Andrew C. Muzi
Steven S. Hanagami

OF COUNSEL

Kurt Kupferman

Representative Clients: American International Cos.; American Home Assurance; Insurance Company of North America (INA); National Union Fire Insurance of Pittsburgh, PA; Aetna Insurance Co.; Fremont Insurance Co.; Maryland Casualty; Commercial Union Insurance Co.; Superior National Insurance Co.

For full biographical listings, see the Martindale-Hubbell Law Directory

LONG BEACH, Los Angeles Co.

LAW OFFICES OF JAMES H. ACKERMAN (AV)

Suite 1440, One World Trade Center, 90831-1440
Telephone: 310-436-9911
Cable Address: "Jimack"
Telecopier: 310-436-1897

References: Farmers and Merchants Bank (Long Beach Main Office); Sumitomo Bank of California (Long Beach Main Office).

For full biographical listings, see the Martindale-Hubbell Law Directory

BAKER & HOSTETLER (AV)

300 Oceangate, Suite 620, 90802-6807
Telephone: 310-432-2827
FAX: 310-432-6698
In Cleveland, Ohio: 3200 National City Center, 1900 East Ninth Street.
Telephone: 216-621-0200.
In Columbus, Ohio: Capitol Square, Suite 2100, 65 East State Street.
Telephone: 614-228-1541.
In Denver, Colorado: 303 East 17th Avenue, Suite 1100.
Telephone: 303-861-0600.

(See Next Column)

In Houston, Texas: 1000 Louisiana, Suite 2000.
Telephone: 713-236-0020.
In Los Angeles, California: 600 Wilshire Boulevard.
Telephone: 213-624-2400.
In Orlando, Florida: SunBank Center, Suite 2300, 200 South Orange Avenue.
Telephone: 407-649-4000.
In Washington, D. C.: Washington Square, Suite 1100, 1050 Connecticut Avenue, N. W.
Telephone: 202-861-1500.
In College Park, Maryland: 9658 Baltimore Boulevard, Suite 206.
Telephone: 301-441-2781.
In Alexandria, Virginia: 437 North Lee Street.
Telephone: 703-549-1294.
In San Francisco, California: One Sansome Street, Suite 2000.
Telephone: 415-951-4705.

PARTNERS

Robert E. Coppola (Partner in Charge)
Kenneth E. Johnson
David A. Kettel
Christina L. Owen

ASSOCIATES

Paul W. Chandler
Andrew H. Do

For Complete List of Firm Personnel, See General Section

For full biographical listings, see the Martindale-Hubbell Law Directory

FISHER & PORTER, A LAW CORPORATION (AV)

110 Pine Avenue, 11th Floor, P.O. Box 22686, 90801-5686
Telephone: 310-435-5626
Telex: 284549 FPKLAW UR
Fax: 310-432-5399

Gerald M. Fisher
Therese G. Groff
David S. Porter
Michael W. Lodwick
Frank C. Brucculeri

George P. Hassapis
Steven Y. Otera
Stephen Chace Bass
Jay Russell Sever
Robert M. White, Jr.
Vicki L. Hassman
Paul J. Rubino
Linda A. Mancini

OF COUNSEL

Stephen C. Klausen

For full biographical listings, see the Martindale-Hubbell Law Directory

FLYNN, DELICH & WISE (AV)

One World Trade Center, Suite 1800, 90831-1800
Telephone: 310-435-2626
Fax: 310-437-7555
San Francisco, California Office: Suite 1750, 580 California Street.
Telephone: 415-693-5566.
Fax: 415-693-0410.

Erich P. Wise
Nicholas S. Politis

Thomas C. Jorgensen

Representative Clients: American Hawaii Cruises; Holland America Line; Through Transport Mutual Insurance Association, Ltd.; The Britannia Steam Ship Insurance Association Limited; The Steamship Mutual Underwriting Association (Bermuda) Ltd.; General Steamship Corp., Ltd.; Commodore Cruise Line, Ltd.; Interocean Steamship Corporation; Sea-Land Service, Inc.; Hatteras Yachts.

For full biographical listings, see the Martindale-Hubbell Law Directory

RUSSELL & MIRKOVICH (AV)

One World Trade Center, Suite 1450, 90831-1450
Telephone: 310-436-9911
FAX: 310-436-1897

Carlton E. Russell
Joseph N. Mirkovich

Representative Clients: Stevedore Services of America; Rados International; Crosby & Overton, Inc.

For Complete List of Firm Personnel, See General Section

For full biographical listings, see the Martindale-Hubbell Law Directory

WILLIAMS WOOLLEY COGSWELL NAKAZAWA & RUSSELL (AV)

111 West Ocean Boulevard, Suite 2000, 90802-4614
Telephone: 310-495-6000
Telecopier: 310-435-1359
Telex: ITT: 4933872; WU: 984929

MEMBERS OF FIRM

Reed M. Williams
Alan Nakazawa
David E. R. Woolley
Blake W. Larkin
Forrest R. Cogswell
Thomas A. Russell

(See Next Column)

WILLIAMS WOOLLEY COGSWELL NAKAZAWA & RUSSELL—*Continued*

ASSOCIATES

B. Alexander Moghaddam   Dennis R. Acker

For full biographical listings, see the Martindale-Hubbell Law Directory

*LOS ANGELES,** Los Angeles Co.

BAKER & HOSTETLER (AV)

600 Wilshire Boulevard, 90017-3212
Telephone: 213-624-2400
FAX: 213-975-1740
In Cleveland, Ohio, 3200 National City Center, 1900 East Ninth Street. Telephone: 216-621-0200.
In Columbus, Ohio, Capitol Square, Suite 2100, 65 East State Street. Telephone: 614-228-1541.
In Denver, Colorado, 303 East 17th Avenue, Suite 1100. Telephone: 303-861-0600.
In Houston, Texas, 1000 Louisiana, Suite 2000. Telephone: 713-236-0020.
In Long Beach, California: 300 Oceangate, Suite 620.
Telephone: 310-432-2827.
In Orlando, Florida, SunBank Center, Suite 2300, 200 South Orange Avenue. Telephone: 407-649-4000.
In Washington, D. C., Washington Square, Suite 1100, 1050 Connecticut Avenue, N. W. Telephone: 202-861-1500.
In College Park, Maryland, 9658 Baltimore Boulevard, Suite 206. Telephone: 301-441-2781.
In Alexandria, Virginia, 437 North Lee Street. Telephone: 703-549-1294.
In San Francisco, California: One Sansome Street, Suite 2000.
Telephone: 415-951-4705.

MEMBERS OF FIRM IN LOS ANGELES, CALIFORNIA

Sheldon A. Gebb (Managing Partner-Los Angeles and Long Beach, California and Houston, Texas Offices)

PARTNERS

William P. Barry   Richard C. Giller

ASSOCIATE

Kathleen E. Bailey

For Complete List of Firm Personnel, See General Section

For full biographical listings, see the Martindale-Hubbell Law Directory

HAWKINS, SCHNABEL, LINDAHL & BECK (AV)

660 South Figueroa Street, Suite 1500, 90017
Telephone: 213-488-3900
Telecopier: 213-486-9883
Cable Address: "Haslin"

MEMBERS OF FIRM

Roger E. Hawkins   Laurence H. Schnabel
George M. Lindahl

For full biographical listings, see the Martindale-Hubbell Law Directory

PILLSBURY MADISON & SUTRO (AV)

Citicorp Plaza, 725 South Figueroa Street, Suite 1200, 90017-2513
Telephone: 213-488-7100
Fax: 213-629-1033
Costa Mesa, California Office: Plaza Tower, 600 Anton Boulevard, Suite 1100, 92626.
Telephone: 714-436-6800.
Fax: 714-662-6999.
Menlo Park, California Office: 2700 Sand Hill Road, 94025.
Telephone: 415-233-4500.
Fax: 415-233-4545.
Sacramento, California Office: 400 Capitol Mall, Suite 1700, 95814.
Telephone: 916-329-4700.
Fax: 916-441-3583.
San Diego, California Office: 101 West Broadway, Suite 1800, 92101.
Telephone: 619-234-5000.
Fax: 619-236-1995.
San Francisco, California Office: 225 Bush Street, 94104.
Telephone: 415-983-1000.
Fax: 415-398-2096.
San Jose, California Office: Ten Almaden Boulevard, 95113.
Telephone: 408-947-4000.
Fax: 408-287-8341.
Washington, D. C. Office: 1667 K Street, N.W., Suite 1100, Suite 20006.
Telephone: 202-887-0300.
Fax: 202-296-7605.
New York, New York Office: One Liberty Plaza, 165 Broadway, 51st Floor.
Telephone: 212-374-1890.
Fax: 212-374-1852.
Hong Kong Office: 6/F Asia Pacific Finance Tower, Citibank Plaza, 3 Garden Road, Central.
Telephone: 011-852-509-7100.
Fax: 011-852-509-7188.

(See Next Column)

Tokyo, Japan Office: Churchill and Shimazaki, Gaiko-Jimo-Bengoshi Jimusho, 11-12, Toranomon, 5-chome Minato-ku, Tokyo 105, Japan.
Telephone: 800-729-9830; 011-81-3-5472-6561.
Fax: 011-81-3-5472-5761.

MEMBER OF FIRM

Lawrence D. Bradley, Jr.

For Complete List of Firm Personnel, See General Section

For full biographical listings, see the Martindale-Hubbell Law Directory

*SAN DIEGO,** San Diego Co.

DOUGHERTY & HILDRE (AV)

2550 Fifth Avenue, Suite 600, 92103-5624
Telephone: 619-232-9131
Telefax: 619-232-7317

William O. Dougherty   Daniel H. Cargnelutti
Donald F. Hildre   Fred M. Dudek
Mona H. Freedman

For full biographical listings, see the Martindale-Hubbell Law Directory

GRAY CARY WARE & FREIDENRICH, A PROFESSIONAL CORPORATION (AV)

Gray Cary Established in 1927
Ware & Freidenrich Established in 1969
401 "B" Street, Suite 1700, 92101
Telephone: 619-699-2700
Telecopier: 619-236-1048
Palo Alto, California Office: 400 Hamilton Avenue.
Telephone: 415-328-6561.
La Jolla, California Office: Suite 575, 1200 Prospect Street.
Telephone: 619-454-9101.
El Centro, California Office: 1224 State Street, P.O. Box 2890.
Telephone: 619-353-6140.

Robert W. Ayling   Jan Shirley Driscoll
William N. Kammer

Representative Clients: American Tunaboat Assn.; Bank of America; C.A. Parr (Agencies), Ltd.; Underwriters at Lloyds; Wells Fargo Bank; Kettenburg Marine; San Diego Yacht Club; America Foundation.

For Complete List of Firm Personnel, See General Section

For full biographical listings, see the Martindale-Hubbell Law Directory

HUGHES & NUNN (AV)

A Partnership including a Professional Corporation
450 "B" Street, Suite 2000, 92101
Telephone: 619-231-1661
Telecopier: 619-236-9271

MEMBERS OF FIRM

William D. Hughes (A Professional Corporation)   Randall M. Nunn
Scott D. Schabacker

ASSOCIATES

Lucia Rivas   E. Kenneth Purviance
Regan Furcolo

For full biographical listings, see the Martindale-Hubbell Law Directory

PILLSBURY MADISON & SUTRO (AV)

101 West Broadway, Suite 1800, 92101
Telephone: 619-234-5000
Telex: 559755
FAX: 619-236-1995
Costa Mesa, California Office: Plaza Tower, 600 Anton Boulevard, Suite 1100,92626.
Telephone: 714-436-6800.
Fax: 714-662-6999.
Los Angeles, California Office: Citicorp Plaza, 725 South Figueroa, Suite 1200, 90017.
Telephone: 213-488-7100.
Fax: 213-629-1033.
New York, New York Office: One Liberty Plaza, 165 Broadway, 51st Floor.
Telephone: 212-374-1890.
Fax: 212-374-1852.
Menlo Park, California Office: 2700 Sand Hill Road, 94025.
Telephone: 415-233-4500.
Fax: 415-233-4545.
Sacramento, California Office: 400 Capitol Mall, Suite 1700, 95814.
Telephone: 916-329-4700.
Fax: 916-441-3583.
San Francisco, California Office: 225 Bush Street, 94104.
Telephone: 415-983-1000.
Fax: 415-398-2096.
San Jose, California Office: Ten Almaden Boulevard, 95113.
Telephone: 408-947-4000.
Fax: 408-287-8341.

(See Next Column)

PILLSBURY MADISON & SUTRO, *San Diego—Continued*

Washington, D.C. Office: Suite 1100, 1667 K Street, N.W., 20006.
Telephone: 202-887-0300.
Fax: 202-296-7605.
Hong Kong Office: 6/F Asia Pacific Finance Tower, Citibank Plaza, 3 Garden Road, Central.
Telephone: 011-852-509-7100.
Fax: 011-852-509-7188.
Tokyo, Japan Office: Churchill and Shimazaki, Gaikokuho-Jimu-Bengoshi-Jimusho, 11-12, Toranomon 5-Chome, Minato-Ku, Tokyo, 105, Japan.
Telephone: 800-729-9830; 011-81-3-5472-6561.
Fax: 011-81-3-5472-5761.

MEMBER OF FIRM

Daniel C. Minteer

For Complete List of Firm Personnel, See General Section

For full biographical listings, see the Martindale-Hubbell Law Directory

RICE FOWLER BOOTH & BANNING (AV)

Emerald - Shapery Center, 402 W. Broadway, Suite 850, 92101
Telephone: 619-230-0030
Telecopier: 619-230-1350
New Orleans, Louisiana Office: 36th Floor, Place St. Charles, 201 St. Charles Avenue, 70130
Telephone: 504-523-2600.
Telecopier: 504-523-2705.
Telex: 9102507910. ELN: 62548910.
London, England Office: Suite 692, Level 6 Lloyd's, 1 Lime Street, London EC3M 7DQ England.
Telephone: 071-327-4222.
Telecopier: 071-929-0043.
San Francisco, California Office: Embarcadero Center West, 275 Battery Street, 27th Floor, 94111.
Telephone: 415-399-9191.
Telecopier: 415-399-9192.
Telex: 451981.
Beijing, China Office: Beijing International Convention Centre, Suite 7024, No. 8 Beichendong Road, Chaoyang District, 100101, P.R.C.
Telephone: (861) 493-4250.
Telecopier: (861) 493-4251.
Bogota, Colombia Office: Avenida Jimenez #4-03 Officina 10-05.
Telephone: (571) 342-1062.
Telecopier: (571) 342-1062.

PARTNERS

William L. Banning
Keith Zakarin
Robert B. Krueger, Jr.

ASSOCIATE

Juan Carlos Dominguez

For full biographical listings, see the Martindale-Hubbell Law Directory

*SAN FRANCISCO,** San Francisco Co.

BOSTWICK & TEHIN (AV)

A Partnership including Professional Corporations
Bank of America Center, 555 California Street, 33rd Floor, 94104-1609
Telephone: 415-421-5500
Fax: 415-421-8144
Honolulu, Hawaii Office: Suite 900, 333 Queen Street.
Telephone: 808-536-7771.

MEMBERS OF FIRM

James S. Bostwick (Professional Corporation)
Nikolai Tehin (Professional Corporation)
Pamela J. Stevens

ASSOCIATES

James J. O'Donnell
Sara A. Smith
Baron J. Drexel

For full biographical listings, see the Martindale-Hubbell Law Directory

BOUGHEY, GARVIE & BUSHNER (AV)

One Post Street, 24th Floor, 94104-5228
Telephone: 415-398-4500
Telex: WU 408661
FAX: 415-398-2455

MEMBERS OF FIRM

James D. Boughey
Robert C. Garvie
Ronald S. Bushner

Donald A. Velez, Jr.
Eileen R. Ridley
Christine M. Renne
Nicholas R. Mack
Lawrence D. Goldberg
Todd Holcomb
Jeffrey George Benz
Ginger M. English

For full biographical listings, see the Martindale-Hubbell Law Directory

PHILIP A. FANT (AV⊤)

88 Kearny Street, Suite 1100, 94108-5530
Telephone: 415-982-2006
FAX: 415-393-8087

For full biographical listings, see the Martindale-Hubbell Law Directory

FLYNN, DELICH & WISE (AV)

Suite 1750, 580 California Street, 94104
Telephone: 415-693-5566
Fax: 415-693-0410
Long Beach, California Office: 1 World Trade Center, Suite 1800.
Telephone: 310-435-2626.
Fax: 310-437-7555.

John Allen Flynn
Sam D. Delich
James B. Nebel

Faye Lee

Representative Clients: American Hawaii Cruises; Holland America Line; Through Transport Mutual Insurance Association, Ltd.; The Britannia Steam Ship Insurance Association Limited; The Steamship Mutual Underwriting Association (Bermuda) Ltd.; General Steamship Corp., Ltd.; Commodore Cruise Line, Ltd.; Interocean Steamship Corporation; Sea-Land Service, Inc.; Hatteras Yachts.

For full biographical listings, see the Martindale-Hubbell Law Directory

GRAHAM & JAMES (AV)

Suite 300 Alcoa Building, One Maritime Plaza, 94111
Telephone: 415-954-0200
Cable Address: "Chalgray"
Telex: WU 340143; WUI 67565
Telecopier: 415-391-2493
Other offices located in: Los Angeles, Newport Beach, Palo Alto, Sacramento and Fresno, California; Washington, D.C.; New York, New York; Milan, Italy; Beijing, China; Tokyo, Japan; London, England; Dusseldorf, Germany; Taipei, Taiwan.
Associated Offices: Deacons in Association with Graham & James, Hong Kong; Sly and Weigall, Sydney, Melbourne, Brisbane, Perth and Canberra, Australia.
Affiliated Offices: Graham & James in Affiliation with Taylor Joynson Garrett, London, England, Bucharest, Romania and Brussels, Belgium; Hanafiah Soeharto Ponggawa, Jakarta, Indonesia; Deacons and Graham & James, Bangkok, Thailand; Haarmann, Hemmelrath & Partner, Berlin, Munich, Leipzig, Frankfurt and Dusseldorf, Germany; Mishare M. Al-Ghazali & Partners, Kuwait; Sly & Weigall Deacons in Association with Graham & James, Hanoi, Vietnam and Guangzhou, China; Gallastegui y Lozano, S.C., Mexico City, Mexico; Law Firm of Salah Al-Hejailan, Jeddah and Riyadh, Saudi Arabia.

Eric M. Danoff
Rupert P. Hansen, Jr.
Andrew I. Port

For Complete List of Firm Personnel, See General Section

For full biographical listings, see the Martindale-Hubbell Law Directory

RICE FOWLER BOOTH & BANNING (AV)

Embarcadero Center West, 275 Battery Street, 27th Floor, 94111
Telephone: 415-399-9191
Telecopier: 415-399-9192
Telex: 451981
New Orleans, Louisiana Office: Place St. Charles, 36th Floor, 201 St. Charles Avenue, 70130.
Telephone: 504-523-2600.
Telecopier: 504-523-2705.
Telex: 9102507910. ELN 62548910.
San Diego, California Office: Emerald-Shapery Center, 402 W. Broadway, Suite 850, 92101.
Telephone: 619-230-0030.
Telecopier: 619-230-1350.
London, England Office: Suite 692, Level 6 Lloyd's, 1 Lime Street, London EC3M 7DQ England.
Telephone: 071-327-4222.
Telecopier: 071-929-0043.
Beijing, China Office: Beijing International Convention Centre, Suite 7024, No. 8 Beichendong Road, Chaoyang District, 100101, P.R.C.
Telephone: (861) 493-4250.
Telecopier: (861) 493-4251.
Bogota, Colombia Office: Avenida Jimenez #4-03 Oficina 10-05, Bogota, Colombia.
Telephone: (571) 342-1062.
Telecopier: (571) 342-1062.

MEMBERS OF FIRM

Forrest Booth
Kurt L. Micklow
Norman J. Ronneberg, Jr.

(See Next Column)

RICE FOWLER BOOTH & BANNING—*Continued*

ASSOCIATES

Cynthia L. Mitchell
Lynn Haggerty King
Edward M. Bull, III
Kim O. Dincel
Amy Jo Poor
Janice Amenta-Jones
Heidi Loken Benas

For full biographical listings, see the Martindale-Hubbell Law Directory

CONNECTICUT

STRATFORD, Fairfield Co.

LAW OFFICES OF ROBERT K. MARZIK, P.C. (AV)

1512 Main Street, 06497
Telephone: 203-375-4803
Telecopier: 203-386-0136
New York, New York Office: 120 East 41st Street.
Telephone: 212-683-2805.

Robert K. Marzik

For full biographical listings, see the Martindale-Hubbell Law Directory

DISTRICT OF COLUMBIA

WASHINGTON, D.C. Co.

***** indicates certain Bar Register subscribers, in cities of comparable size and importance, who maintain an additional office in Washington, D.C. and who have arranged for representation as a part of the Washington, D.C. listings that follow

H. CLAYTON COOK, JR. (AV)

2828 Pennsylvania Avenue, N.W., 20007
Telephone: 202-338-8088
Rapifax: 202-338-1843
McLean, Virginia Office: 1011 Langley Hill Drive. 22101.
Telephone: 703-821-2468.
Rapifax: 703-821-2469.

For full biographical listings, see the Martindale-Hubbell Law Directory

*** VENABLE, BAETJER, HOWARD & CIVILETTI (AV)**

A Partnership including Professional Corporations
Suite 1000, 1201 New York Avenue, N.W., 20005
Telephone: 202-962-4800
Fax: 202-962-8300
Baltimore, Maryland Office: Venable, Baetjer and Howard, 1800 Mercantile Bank & Trust Building, 2 Hopkins Plaza.
Telephone: 410-244-7400.
McLean, Virginia Office: Venable, Baetjer and Howard, Suite 400, 2010 Corporate Ridge.
Telephone: 703-760-1600.
Rockville, Maryland Office: Venable, Baetjer and Howard, Suite 500, One Church Street, P. O. Box 1906.
Telephone: 301-217-5600.
Towson, Maryland Office: Venable, Baetjer and Howard, 210 Allegheny Avenue, P. O. Box 5517.
Telephone: 410-494-6200.

MEMBER OF FIRM

Douglas D. Connah, Jr. (P.C.) (Also at Baltimore, Maryland Office)

ASSOCIATE

Fred Joseph Federici, III

For Complete List of Firm Personnel, See General Section

For full biographical listings, see the Martindale-Hubbell Law Directory

FLORIDA

*FORT LAUDERDALE,** Broward Co.

KRUPNICK CAMPBELL MALONE ROSELLI BUSER & SLAMA, P.A. (AV)

700 Southeast 3rd Avenue, 33316
Telephone: 305-763-8181
FAX: 305-763-8292

(See Next Column)

Jon E. Krupnick
Walter G. Campbell, Jr.
Kevin A. Malone
Richard J. Roselli
Thomas E. Buser
Joseph J. Slama
Kelly D. Hancock
Lisa A. McNelis

Kelley Badger Gelb
Elaine P. Krupnick
Scott S. Liberman
Robert J. McKee
Adria E. Quintela

Reference: Citizens and Southern Bank.

For full biographical listings, see the Martindale-Hubbell Law Directory

WEAVER & WEAVER, P.A. (AV)

500 Southeast Sixth Street, P.O. Box 14663, 33302-4663
Telephone: 305-763-2511
Miami: 305-944-4452
West Palm Beach: 407-655-6012
FAX: 305-764-3590

Ben J. Weaver
Dianne Jay Weaver

For full biographical listings, see the Martindale-Hubbell Law Directory

*JACKSONVILLE,** Duval Co.

GABEL & HAIR (AV)

76 South Laura Street, Suite 1600, 32202-3421
Telephone: 904-353-7329
Cable Address: "Wahlgabel"
Fax: 904-358-1637

MEMBERS OF FIRM

George D. Gabel, Jr.
Mattox S. Hair
Joel B. Toomey
Robert M. Dees
Sheldon Boney Forte
Timothy J. Conner
Suzanne Meyer Schnabel

ASSOCIATES

Christine S. Mayo
Michael L. Berry, Jr.
Karen Harris Hildebrand

Scott M. Loftin (1878-1953)
Harold B. Wahl (1907-1993)

Representative Clients: The Japan Ship Owners Mutual Protection & Indemnity Association; Liverpool & London Steamship Protection & Indemnity Association; The Standard Steamship Owners Protection & Indemnity Association, Ltd.; The Steamship Mutual Underwriting Association, Ltd.; A. B. Indemnitas; Trampfahrt P&I, Hamburg; Scandinavian Marine Claims Office, Inc.; Exxon Corp.; Marine Office of America Corp.; Water Quality Insurance Syndicate.

For full biographical listings, see the Martindale-Hubbell Law Directory

RUMRELL & JOHNSON, P.A. (AV)

One Harbert Center, 7077 Bonneval Road, Suite 200, 32216
Telephone: 904-296-3200
Telecopier: 904-296-3204

Richard G. Rumrell
Gregory W. Johnson
Lindsey C. Brock III
Joanne Reed Day
Ross Logan Bilbrey
W. David Vaughn

For full biographical listings, see the Martindale-Hubbell Law Directory

TAYLOR, MOSELEY & JOYNER, P.A. (AV)

501 West Bay Street, 32202
Telephone: 904-356-1306
Cable Address: "Ragland"
Telex: 5-6374
Telecopier: 904-354-0194

Reuben Ragland (1882-1954)
Louis Kurz (1891-1965)
E. Dale Joyner (1943-1993)
Neil C. Taylor
James F. Moseley
Robert E. Warren
Joseph W. Prichard, Jr.
Robert B. Parrish
Andrew J. Knight II
Richard K. Jones
James F. Moseley, Jr.
Phillip A. Buhler
Melanie E. Shepherd
Victor J. Zambetti
Mathew G. Nasrallah

Stanley M. Weston

OF COUNSEL

James E. Williams

Counsel for: CSX Transportation; Britannia Steam Ship Insurance Assn., Ltd.; The West of England Protection & Indemnity Assn. (Luxembourg); Crowley American Transport Services, Inc.; Howard Johnson Co.; United Kingdom Mutal Steamship Assurance Assn., Ltd. (Bermuda); General Food Corp.; The London Steam-Ship Owners' Mutual Insurance Assn., Ltd.

For full biographical listings, see the Martindale-Hubbell Law Directory

*MIAMI,** Dade Co.

CLARKE & SILVERGLATE, PROFESSIONAL ASSOCIATION (AV)

100 North Biscayne Boulevard, Suite 2401, 33132
Telephone: 305-377-0700
Fax: 305-377-3001

Mercer K. Clarke
Spencer H. Silverglate
Kelly Anne Luther

For full biographical listings, see the Martindale-Hubbell Law Directory

FOWLER, WHITE, BURNETT, HURLEY, BANICK & STRICKROOT, A PROFESSIONAL ASSOCIATION (AV)

International Place, Seventeenth Floor, 100 S.E. Second Street, 33131
Telephone: 305-358-6550
Cable Address: "Fowhite"
Telex: 6811696

Allan R. Kelley
Charles G. DeLeo
Cromwell A. Anderson
Curtis J. Mase

Beverly D. Eisenstadt
Darren R. Latham
James D. Gassenheimer
Heather B. Brock

Representative Clients: Royal Caribbean Cruise Line; United Kingdom Mutual Steamship Assurance Assn.; Steamship Mutual Underwriting Association, Ltd.; Japan Shipowners Mutual P & I Assn.; Assuranceforeningen GARD (Gjensidig); Assuranceforeningen SKULD; London Steamship Owners' Mutual Insurance Assn., Ltd.; Transnave Steamship Co.; Sealand Services, Inc.; Sun Bank, N.A.

For Complete List of Firm Personnel, See General Section

For full biographical listings, see the Martindale-Hubbell Law Directory

HAYDEN AND MILLIKEN, P.A. (AV)

Suite 63, 5915 Ponce de Leon Boulevard, 33146-2477
Telephone: 305-662-1523
Fax: 305-663-1358
Tampa, Florida Office: 615 De Leon Street 33606-2719.
Telephone: 813-251-1770.
Fax: 813-254-5436.

Reginald M. Hayden, Jr.
William Barry Milliken
William R. Boeringer
Timothy P. Shusta (Resident, Tampa, Florida Office)
Jan M. Kuylenstierna
James N. Hurley
Michael J. Cappucio
Joseph K. Birch (Resident, Tampa, Florida Office)

Representative Clients: Regency Cruise Lines; Seaboard Marine, Ltd.; Tropical Shipping and Construction Co., Ltd.; Great American Insurance Co.; Marine Office of America Corp.; St. Paul Fire and Marine Insurance Co.; Britannia P & I; New Castle P & I; Steamship Mutual; The Swedish Club; Through Transport Mutual.
Reference: Dadeland Bank.

For full biographical listings, see the Martindale-Hubbell Law Directory

THOMAS W. MCALILEY, P.A. (AV)

3260 Miami Center, 201 South Biscayne Boulevard, 33131
Telephone: 305-373-6551
Telecopier: 305-358-3404

Thomas W. McAliley

For full biographical listings, see the Martindale-Hubbell Law Directory

NICKLAUS, VALLE, CRAIG & WICKS (AV)

15th Floor New World Tower, 100 North Biscayne Boulevard, 33132
Telephone: 305-358-2888
Facsimile: 305-358-5501
Fort Lauderdale, Florida Office: Suite 101N, Justice Building, 524 South Andrews Avenue, 33301.
Telephone: 305-523-1858.
Facsimile: 305-523-8068.

MEMBERS OF FIRM

Edward R. Nicklaus
Laurence F. Valle
Lawrance B. Craig, III
William R. Wicks, III
James W. McCready, III
Michael W. Whitaker

ASSOCIATES

Richard D. Settler
Kevin M. Fitzmaurice
Timothy Maze Hartley
Keith S. Grybowski
Patricia Blanco
Michael J. Lynott

For full biographical listings, see the Martindale-Hubbell Law Directory

SHUTTS & BOWEN (AV)

A Partnership including Professional Associations
1500 Miami Center, 201 South Biscayne Boulevard, 33131
Telephone: 305-358-6300
Cable Address: "Shuttsbo"
Telefax: 305-381-9982
Key Largo, Florida Office: Suite A206, 31 Ocean Reef Drive.
Telephone: 305-367-2881.
Orlando, Florida Office: 20 North Orange Avenue, Suite 1000.
Telephone: 407-423-3200.
Fax: 407-425-8316.
West Palm Beach, Florida Office: One Clearlake Centre, 250 Australian Avenue South, Suite 500.
Telephone: 407-835-8500.
Fax: 407-650-8530.
Amsterdam, The Netherlands Office: Shutts & Bowen, B.V., Europa Boulevard 59, 1083 AD, Amsterdam.
Telephone: (31 20) 661-0969.
Fax: (31 20) 642-1475.
London, England Office: 48 Mount Street, London W1Y 5RE.
Telephone: 4471493-4840.
Telefax: 4471493-4299.

MEMBER OF FIRM

Richard M. Leslie (P.A.)

Representative Clients: Paquet Cruises, Inc.; Ulysses Cruises Inc.; Dolphin Cruises Inc.; Holland America Cruises; West of England P and I Club; Lykes Bros. Steamship; United Kingdom P and I Club.

For Complete List of Firm Personnel, See General Section

For full biographical listings, see the Martindale-Hubbell Law Directory

*TAMPA,** Hillsborough Co.

HAYDEN AND MILLIKEN, P.A. (AV)

615 De Leon Street, 33606-2719
Telephone: 813-251-1770
Fax: 813-254-5436
Miami, Florida Office: Suite 63, 5915 Ponce de Leon Boulevard.
Telephone: 305-662-1523.
Fax: 305-663-1358.

Reginald M. Hayden, Jr.
William Barry Milliken
Timothy P. Shusta (Resident)
Joseph K. Birch (Resident)

Representative Clients: Regency Cruise Lines; Seaboard Marine, Ltd.; Tropical Shipping and Construction Co., Ltd.; Great American Insurance Co.; Marine Office of America Corp.; St. Paul Fire and Marine Insurance Co.; Britannia P & I; New Castle P & I; Steamship Mutual; Through Transport.
Reference: Dadeland Bank.

For full biographical listings, see the Martindale-Hubbell Law Directory

LAU, LANE, PIEPER, CONLEY & MCCREADIE, P.A. (AV)

Suite 1700, 100 South Ashley, P.O. Box 838, 33601
Telephone: 813-229-2121
Telecopier: 813-228-7710
Port Canaveral, Florida Office: 405 Atlantis Road, Suite B.
Telephone: 407-799-3400.
Telecopier: 813-228-7710.

James V. Lau
Charles C. Lane
Nathaniel G. W. Pieper
Mary A. Lau
Timothy C. Conley
David W. McCreadie
Annette Horan
Earl R. McMillin (Resident, Port Canaveral Office)
David F. Pope
Daintry E. Cleary

For full biographical listings, see the Martindale-Hubbell Law Directory

WAGNER, VAUGHAN & MCLAUGHLIN, P.A. (AV)

708 Jackson Street (Corner of Jefferson), and 601 Bayshore Boulevard, Suite 910, 33602
Telephone: 813-223-7421; 813-225-4000
FAX: 813-221-0254; 813-225-4010

Bill Wagner (Resident, Bayshore Boulevard Office)
Roger A. Vaughan, Jr.
John J. McLaughlin

Alan F. Wagner (Resident, Bayshore Boulevard Office)
Ruth Whetstone Wagner (Resident, Bayshore Boulevard Office)
Denise E. Vaughan
Weldon "Web" Earl Brennan (Resident, Bayshore Boulevard Office)
Bob Vaughan

For full biographical listings, see the Martindale-Hubbell Law Directory

*WEST PALM BEACH,** Palm Beach Co.

LIGGIO & LUCKMAN (AV)

213 Southern Boulevard, 33405
Telephone: 407-833-6604
Fax: 407-833-0870

(See Next Column)

LIGGIO & LUCKMAN—*Continued*

MEMBERS OF FIRM

Jeffrey M. Liggio
Eric H. Luckman

LEGAL SUPPORT PERSONNEL

Yara B. Vega (Paralegal)

For full biographical listings, see the Martindale-Hubbell Law Directory

GEORGIA

*SAVANNAH,** Chatham Co.

CHAMLEE, DUBUS & SIPPLE (AV)

Suite 301 Cluskey Building, 127 Abercorn Street, P.O. Box 9523, 31412
Telephone: 912-232-3311
Cable Address: "Floodtide"
Telex: 804733
Telecopier: 912-232-3253

MEMBERS OF FIRM

George H. Chamlee
Gustave R. Dubus, III
David F. Sipple

For full biographical listings, see the Martindale-Hubbell Law Directory

HAWAII

*HONOLULU,** Honolulu Co.

ALCANTARA & FRAME ATTORNEYS AT LAW, A LAW CORPORATION (AV)

Suite 1100 Pioneer Plaza, 900 Fort Street Mall, 96813
Telephone: 808-536-6922
Fax: 808-521-8898
Telex: 650-225-8816
WUI: 101-650 225-8816
MCI ID: 225-8816

Leonard F. Alcantara
Robert G. Frame
Bryan Y. Y. Ho

Joy Lee Cauble
John O'Kane, Jr.
Evelyn J. Black
Mary A. Cox
Michael D. Formby
Eldon M. Ching

Reference: City Bank, Honolulu.

For full biographical listings, see the Martindale-Hubbell Law Directory

ASHFORD & NAKAMURA (AV)

2910 Pacific Tower, 1001 Bishop Street, 96813
Telephone: 808-528-0444
Telex: 723-8158
Telecopier: (808) 533-0761
Cable Address: Justlaw

George W. Ashford, Jr.
Lee T. Nakamura

Ann C. Kemp
Francis T. O'Brien

Representative Clients: Baker Industries, Inc.; Burns International Security Services; Clark Equipment Co.; Great Lakes Chemical Corporation; California Union Insurance Co.; Fireman's Fund Insurance Companies; Great American Insurance Companies; Guaranty National Companies; Horace Mann Insurance Company; Marine Office of America Corp.

For full biographical listings, see the Martindale-Hubbell Law Directory

CRONIN, FRIED, SEKIYA, KEKINA & FAIRBANKS ATTORNEYS AT LAW, A LAW CORPORATION (AV)

1900 Davies Pacific Center, 841 Bishop Street, 96813
Telephone: 808-524-1433
FAX: 808-536-2073

Paul F. Cronin
L. Richard Fried, Jr.
Gerald Y. Sekiya
Wayne K. Kekina
David L. Fairbanks
John D. Thomas, Jr.
Stuart A. Kaneko
Bert S. Sakuda
Allen K. Williams
Keith K. H. Young

Patrick W. Border
Gregory L. Lui-Kwan
Patrick F. McTernan
Irene M. Nakano

For full biographical listings, see the Martindale-Hubbell Law Directory

ILLINOIS

*CHICAGO,** Cook Co.

BELGRADE AND O'DONNELL, A PROFESSIONAL CORPORATION (AV)

311 South Wacker Drive, Suite 2770, 60606
Telephone: 312-360-9500
Facsimile: 312-360-9550

Steven B. Belgrade
John A. O'Donnell
George M. Velcich
Kim Richard Kardas
Andrea J. McIntyre
Joseph G. Howard

For full biographical listings, see the Martindale-Hubbell Law Directory

McDERMOTT, WILL & EMERY (AV)

A Partnership including Professional Corporations
227 West Monroe Street, 60606-5096
Telephone: 312-372-2000
Telex: 253565 Milam CGO
Facsimile: 312-984-7700
Boston, Massachusetts Office: 75 State Street, Suite 1700.
Telephone: 617-345-5000.
Telex: 951324 MILAM BSN.
Facsimile: 617-345-5077.
Miami, Florida Office: 201 South Biscayne Boulevard.
Telephone: 305-358-3500.
Telex: 441777 LEYES.
Facsimile: 305-347-6500.
Washington, D.C. Office: 1850 K Street, N.W.
Telephone: 202-887-8000.
Telex: 253565 MILAM CGO.
Facsimile: 202-778-8087.
Los Angeles, California Office: 2049 Century Park East.
Telephone: 310-277-4110.
Facsimile: 310-277-4730.
Newport Beach, California Office: 1301 Dove Street, Suite 500.
Telephone: 714-851-0633.
Facsimile: 714-851-9348.
New York, N.Y. Office: 1211 Avenue of the Americas.
Telephone: 212-768-5400.
Facsimile: 212-768-5444.
St. Petersburg, Russia Office: 2/2 Tchaikovsky Street, #517, 191187 St. Petersburg, Russia.
Telephone: (7) (812) 273-9831.
Facsimile: (7) (812) 273-9831.
Tallinn, Estonia Office: Tallinn Business Center, 6 Harju Street, EE0001 Tallinn, Estonia.
Telephone: 372 6 31-05-53.
Facsimile: 372 6 31-05-54.
Vilnius, Lithuania Office: Smetonos 6, 2600 Vilnius, Lithuania.
Telephone: 370 2 61-43-08.
Facsimile: 370 2 22-79-55.
Associated (Independent) Offices:
Brussels, Belgium: Uettwiller Grelon Lippens Dekeyser, 73 avenue Vandendriessche, 1150 Brussels, Belgium.
Telephone: (32) (2) 772-87-50.
Facsimile: (32) (2) 772-87-52.
London, England: Paisner & Co, Bouverie House, 154 Fleet Street, London EC4A 2DQ, England.
Telephone: (44) (71) 353-0299.
Facsimile: (44) (71) 583-8621.
Paris, France: Uettwiller Grelon Gout Canat & Associes, 68, boulevard de Courcelles, 75017 Paris, France.
Telephone: (33) (1) 48 88 89 00.
Facsimile: (33) (1) 48 88 05 50.

MEMBER OF FIRM

Paul J. Kozacky

For Complete List of Firm Personnel, See General Section

For full biographical listings, see the Martindale-Hubbell Law Directory

RAY, ROBINSON, CARLE, DAVIES & SNYDER (AV)

A Partnership including a Professional Corporation
850 West Jackson Boulevard, Suite 310, 60607-3011
Telephone: 312-421-3110
Telex: 25200 BRADMIR CGO
Cable Address: Lakelaw-Chicago
Facsimile: 312-421-2808
Cleveland, Ohio Office: 1650 The East Ohio Building, 1717 East 9th Street.
Telephone: 216-861-4533.
Telex: 810-421-8402.
Cable Address: Lakelaw-Cleveland.
Facsimile: 216-861-4568.

(See Next Column)

RAY, ROBINSON, CARLE, DAVIES & SNYDER, *Chicago—Continued*

Michael A. Snyder, Ltd.

Richard A. Forster
William P. Ryan
Charles A. Rozhon
Shanshan Zhou

OF COUNSEL

Theodore C. Robinson

For full biographical listings, see the Martindale-Hubbell Law Directory

EAST ST. LOUIS, St. Clair Co.

CARR, KOREIN, TILLERY, KUNIN, MONTROY & GLASS (AV)

412 Missouri Avenue, 62201
Telephone: 618-274-0434
Telecopier: 618-274-8369
St. Louis, Missouri Office: 701 Market Street, Suite 300.
Telephone: 314-241-4844.
Telecopier: 314-241-3525.
Belleville, Illinois Office: 5520 West Main.
Telephone: 618-277-1180.

MEMBER OF FIRM

Sandor Korein

Rivers Counsel for: National Maritime Union of America.

For Complete List of Firm Personnel, See General Section

For full biographical listings, see the Martindale-Hubbell Law Directory

INDIANA

*EVANSVILLE,** Vanderburgh Co.

KAHN, DEES, DONOVAN & KAHN (AV)

P.O. Box 3646, 47735-3646
Telephone: 812-423-3183
Fax: 812-423-3841

MEMBERS OF FIRM

Jeffrey A. Wilhite
Jeffrey W. Ahlers

ASSOCIATE

Richard O. Hawley, Jr.

Representative Clients: Neare Gibbs Maritime Insurance; United States Fidelity & Guarantee; Ohio Valley Marine Service; Mulzer Crushed Stone; Mt. Veron Barge Service.

For Complete List of Firm Personnel, See General Section

For full biographical listings, see the Martindale-Hubbell Law Directory

KENTUCKY

*LOUISVILLE,** Jefferson Co.

MILLER AND MILLER (AV)

Suite 602, One Riverfront Plaza, 40202
Telephone: 502-581-1224
Fax: 502-581-1227

MEMBERS OF FIRM

W. Scott Miller (1904-1988)
W. Scott Miller, Jr.
Stephanie R. Miller

References: National City Bank; Liberty National Bank.

For full biographical listings, see the Martindale-Hubbell Law Directory

*PADUCAH,** McCracken Co.

LAKE, TINDALL & THACKSTON (AV⊤)

Formerly Firm of Wynn, Hafter, Lake & Tindall
One Executive Boulevard Suite 318, P.O. Box 30, 42002
Telephone: 502-442-1900
Facsimile: 502-442-8247
Greenville, Mississippi Office: 127 South Poplar Street, P.O. Box 918.
Telephone: 601-378-2121.
Facsimile: 601-378-2183.
Jackson, Mississippi Office: 350 Security Centre North, 200 South Lamar Street, P.O. Box 1787.
Telephone: 601-948-2121.
Facsimile: 601-948-0603.

(See Next Column)

Edwin Spivey Gault (Resident)
Carl J. Marshall (Resident)

For full biographical listings, see the Martindale-Hubbell Law Directory

WHITLOW, ROBERTS, HOUSTON & RUSSELL (AV)

Old National Bank Building, 300 Broadway, P.O. Box 995, 42001
Telephone: 502-443-4516
FAX: 502-443-4571

MEMBERS OF FIRM

Richard C. Roberts
E. Frederick Straub, Jr.
Mark S. Medlin

ASSOCIATE

Ronald F. Kupper

Counsel for: Crounse Corporation; American Electric Power.

For Complete List of Firm Personnel, See General Section

For full biographical listings, see the Martindale-Hubbell Law Directory

LOUISIANA

*BATON ROUGE,** East Baton Rouge Parish

GEORGE AND GEORGE, LTD., A PROFESSIONAL LAW CORPORATION (AV)

8110 Summa Avenue, 70809
Telephone: 504-769-3064
Fax: 504-766-9974
Toll Free Numbers: 1-800-654-2335
Nationwide: 1-800-843-5702

James A. George

Reference: Hibernia National Bank of Baton Rouge.

For full biographical listings, see the Martindale-Hubbell Law Directory

*LAFAYETTE,** Lafayette Parish

DOMENGEAUX, WRIGHT, MOROUX & ROY, A PROFESSIONAL LAW CORPORATION (AV)

556 Jefferson Street, Suite 500, P.O. Box 3668, 70502-3668
Telephone: 318-233-3033; 1-800-375-3106
Fax: 318-232-8213
Hammond, Louisiana Office: Magnolia Plaza, Suite K, 1007 West Thomas Street, P. O. Box 1558.
Telephone: 504-542-4963; 1-800-423-1160.

James Domengeaux (1907-1988)
Anthony D. Moroux (1948-1993)
Bob F. Wright (A Professional Law Corporation)
James Parkerson Roy (A Professional Law Corporation)
Robert K. Tracy (A Professional Law Corporation)
Thomas R. Edwards (A Professional Law Corporation)
Frank Edwards (Resident, Hammond Office)
James Wattigny
James H. Domengeaux
R. Hamilton Davis
Gilbert Hennigan Dozier
Carla Marie Perron
Tyron D. Picard

OF COUNSEL

Jerome E. Domengeaux

Reference: Mid-South National Bank; Advocate Financial, L.L.C.

For full biographical listings, see the Martindale-Hubbell Law Directory

HILL & BEYER, A PROFESSIONAL LAW CORPORATION (AV)

101 LaRue France, Suite 502, P.O. Box 53006, 70505-3006
Telephone: 318-232-9733
Fax: 1-318-237-2566

John K. Hill, Jr.
Bret C. Beyer
David R. Rabalais
Lisa C. McCowen
Eugene P. Matherne
Robert B. Purser
Erin J. Sherburne
Harold Adam Lawrence

For full biographical listings, see the Martindale-Hubbell Law Directory

RICHARD R. KENNEDY A PROFESSIONAL LAW CORPORATION (AV)

309 Polk Street, P.O. Box 3243, 70502-3243
Telephone: 318-232-1934
Fax: 318-232-9720

Richard R. Kennedy

For full biographical listings, see the Martindale-Hubbell Law Directory

Lafayette—Continued

MANGHAM, DAVIS AND OGLESBEE (AV)

Suite 1400 First National Bank Towers, 600 Jefferson Street, P.O. Box 93110, 70509-3110
Telephone: 318-233-6200
Fax: 318-233-6521

Michael R. Mangham
Louis R. Davis
Michael G. Oglesbee
Herman E. Garner, Jr.

ASSOCIATES

Dawn Mayeux Fuqua
Lisa Hanchey Sevier

SPECIAL COUNSEL

Michael J. O'Shee

OF COUNSEL

George W. Hardy, III
Robert E. Rowe

Reference: The First National Bank of Lafayette, Lafayette, Louisiana.

For full biographical listings, see the Martindale-Hubbell Law Directory

OATS & HUDSON (AV)

Suite 400 Gordon Square, 100 East Vermilion Street, 70501
Telephone: 318-233-1100
Facsimile: 318-233-1178

Stephen J. Oats
William M. Hudson, III
Patrick B. McIntire
Edgar D. Gankendorff
J. Marshall Montgomery
Robert A. Mahtook, Jr.

OF COUNSEL

Oscar E. Reed, Jr.

For full biographical listings, see the Martindale-Hubbell Law Directory

ROY, BIVINS, JUDICE & HENKE, A PROFESSIONAL LAW CORPORATION (AV)

600 Jefferson Street, Suite 800, P.O. Drawer Z, 70502
Telephone: 318-233-7430
Telecopier: 318-233-8403
Telex: 9102505130

Harmon F. Roy
John A. Bivins
Ronald J. Judice
Kenneth M. Henke
W. Alan Lilley
Philip E. Roberts
Patrick M. Wartelle

Representative Clients: Employers Insurance of Wausau; Louisiana Medical Mutual Ins. Co.; C.N.A.; Aetna Casualty & Surety; Zurich Ins. Co.; Our Lady of Lourdes Regional Medical Center, Inc.; St Paul Fire & Marine Ins. Co.; First Financial Insurance Company.

For full biographical listings, see the Martindale-Hubbell Law Directory

*LAKE CHARLES,** Calcasieu Parish

BAGGETT, MCCALL & BURGESS, A PROFESSIONAL LAW CORPORATION (AV)

3006 Country Club Road, P.O. Drawer 7820, 70606-7820
Telephone: 318-478-8888
Fax: 318-478-8946

William B. Baggett
Robert C. McCall
Roger G. Burgess
William B. Baggett, Jr.

For Complete List of Firm Personnel, See General Section

For full biographical listings, see the Martindale-Hubbell Law Directory

BERGSTEDT & MOUNT (AV)

Second Floor, Magnolia Life Building, P.O. Drawer 3004, 70602-3004
Telephone: 318-433-3004
Facsimile: 318-433-8080

MEMBERS OF FIRM

Thomas M. Bergstedt
Benjamin W. Mount

ASSOCIATES

Van C. Seneca
Thomas J. Gayle
Gregory P. Marceaux

OF COUNSEL

Charles S. Ware

Representative Clients: Armstrong World Industries; Ashland Oil Co.; CIGNA Property & Casualty Companies; Homequity; Lake Area Medical Center; Leach Company; Olin Corporation; Terra Corporation; Town of Iowa; R. D. Werner Company.

For Complete List of Firm Personnel, See General Section

For full biographical listings, see the Martindale-Hubbell Law Directory

JONES, TÊTE, NOLEN, HANCHEY, SWIFT & SPEARS, L.L.P. (AV)

First Federal Building, P.O. Box 910, 70602
Telephone: 318-439-8315
Telefax: 436-5606; 433-5536

MEMBERS OF FIRM

Sam H. Jones (1897-1978)
William R. Tête
William M. Nolen
James C. Hanchey
Carl H. Hanchey
William B. Swift
Kenneth R. Spears
Edward J. Fonti
Charles N. Harper
Gregory W. Belfour
Robert J. Tête
Yul D. Lorio

OF COUNSEL

John A. Patin
Edward D. Myrick

ASSOCIATES

Lilynn A. Cutrer
Lydia Ann Guillory-Lee
Clint David Bischoff

General Counsel for: First Federal Savings & Loan Association of Lake Charles; Beauregard Electric Cooperative, Inc.

Representative Clients: Atlantic Richfield Company; CITGO Petroleum Corp.; Conoco Inc.; HIMONT U.S.A., Inc.; ITT Hartford; Olin Corporation; OXY USA Inc.; Premier Bank, National Association; W.R. Grace & Co.

For full biographical listings, see the Martindale-Hubbell Law Directory

LUNDY & DAVIS, L.L.P. (AV)

A Partnership including a Professional Corporation
Calcasieu Marine Tower, One Lakeshore Drive, Suite 1600, P.O. Box 3009, 70602
Telephone: 318-439-0707
FAX: 318-439-1029
Jackson, Mississippi Office: 111 East Capitol Street, Suite 250.
Telephone: 601-948-3010.
Facsimile: 601-948-2143.
Houston, Texas Office: 13101 Northwest Freeway.
Telephone: 713-690-8949.
Facsimile: 713-690-8919.
Biloxi, Mississippi Office: 999 Howard Avenue.
Telephone: 601-435-7733.
Facsimile: 601-435-7737.

MEMBERS OF FIRM

Hunter W. Lundy
Clayton A. L. Davis
Matthew E. Lundy
Jerry A. Johnson
Winfield E. Little, Jr., (A Professional Corporation)
David A. Bowers (Resident, Jackson, Mississippi Office)

ASSOCIATES

Jackey W. South
DeAnn Gibson
Samuel B. Gabb

OF COUNSEL

Edgar F. Barnett (Resident, Houston, Texas Office)
Walter L. Nixon, Jr.

For full biographical listings, see the Martindale-Hubbell Law Directory

PLAUCHÉ SMITH & NIESET, A PROFESSIONAL LAW CORPORATION (AV)

1123 Pithon Street, P.O. Drawer 1705, 70602
Telephone: 318-436-0522
Facsimile: 318-436-9637

S. W. Plauché (1889-1952)
S. W. Plauché, Jr. (1915-1966)
A. Lane Plauché
Allen L. Smith, Jr.
James R. Nieset
Frank M. Walker, Jr.
Michael J. McNulty, III
Jeffrey M. Cole
Andrew R. Johnson, IV
Charles V. Musso, Jr.
Christopher P. Ieyoub
H. David Vaughan, II
Rebecca S. Young
Stephanie A. Landry

Representative Clients: CIGNA; CNA Insurance Cos.; Commercial Union Insurance Cos.; Crum & Forster; General Motors Corp.; Reliance Insurance Cos.; Royal Insurance Group; State Farm; U.S. Insurance Group.

For full biographical listings, see the Martindale-Hubbell Law Directory

METAIRIE, Jefferson Parish

HAILEY, MCNAMARA, HALL, LARMANN & PAPALE (AV)

A Partnership including Law Corporations
Suite 1400, One Galleria Boulevard, P.O. Box 8288, 70011
Telephone: 504-836-6500
Fax: 504-836-6565

MEMBERS OF FIRM

James W. Hailey, Jr., (P.L.C.)
Henry D. McNamara, Jr., (P.L.C.)
W. Marvin Hall (P.L.C.)
Antonio E. Papale, Jr., (P.L.C.)
Laurence E. Larmann (P.L.C.)
Richard A. Chopin (P.L.C.)
Kevin L. Cole
Michael P. Mentz
Richard T. Simmons, Jr.,(P.L.C.)
Nelson W. Wagar, III, (P.L.C.)
Michael J. Vondenstein

(See Next Column)

HAILEY, MCNAMARA, HALL, LARMANN & PAPALE, *Metairie—Continued*

MEMBERS OF FIRM (Continued)

Brian ReBoul
David K. Persons
Thomas M. Richard
Dominic J. Ovella
Elizabeth Smyth Sirgo
C. Kelly Lightfoot
John T. Culotta (P.L.C.)
John E. Unsworth, Jr.
Julie DiFulco Robles

ASSOCIATES

William R. Seay, Jr.
Cyril B. Burck, Jr.
Claude A. Greco
Valerie T. Schexnayder
John Price McNamara
W. Evan Plauche
Brian T. Carr
Kurt D. Engelhardt
W. Glenn Burns

OF COUNSEL

John P. Volz

Representative Clients: Certain Underwriters at Lloyds of London; Diamond Offshore Drilling Inc.; First American Title Insurance Company; The Flintkote Co.; Litton Industries; Martin Marietta Manned Space Systems; Rheem Manufacturing Co.; Rowan Companies, Inc; State Farm Fire & Casualty Co.; Textron, Inc; Travelers Companies.

For full biographical listings, see the Martindale-Hubbell Law Directory

*NEW ORLEANS,** Orleans Parish

CAPITELLI & WICKER (AV)

2950 Energy Centre, 1100 Poydras Street, 70163-2950
Telephone: 504-582-2425
FAX: 504-582-2422

Ralph Capitelli
T. Carey Wicker, III
Paul Michael Elvir, Jr.

OF COUNSEL

Terry Q. Alarcon

For full biographical listings, see the Martindale-Hubbell Law Directory

CHAFFE, MCCALL, PHILLIPS, TOLER & SARPY (AV)

A Partnership including a Professional Law Corporation
2300 Energy Centre, 1100 Poydras Street, 70163-2300
Telephone: 504-585-7000
Telecopier: 504-585-7075
Cable Address: "Denegre"
Telex: (AT&T) 460122 CMPTS
Baton Rouge, Louisiana Office: 202 Two United Plaza, 8550 United Plaza Boulevard.
Telephone: 504-922-4300.
Fax: 504-922-4304.

MEMBERS OF FIRM

Leon Sarpy
Donald A. Lindquist
Robert B. Deane
J. Dwight LeBlanc, Jr.
Robert B. Fisher, Jr.
Derek Anthony Walker
Kenneth J. Servay
Daniel L. Daboval
Thomas D. Forbes
John H. Clegg

ASSOCIATES

Daphne P. McNutt
Eric J. Simonson
Scott A. Soule

Representative Clients: Liverpool and London Steamship Protection and Indemnity Association, Ltd.; The West of England Ship Owners Mutual Insurance Association (Luxembourg); The United Kingdom Mutual Steamship Assurance Association (Bermuda) Ltd.; The Sunderland Steamship Protecting & Indemnity Association; The Standard Steamship Owners' Protection and Indemnity Association (Bermuda) Ltd.; The Britannia Steam Ship Insurance Association Ltd.; The Japan Ship Owners' Mutual Protection and Indemnity Association; The North of England Protecting and Indemnity Association Ltd.; Newcastle Protection and Indemnity Association; Nedlloyd Bulk B.V.

For Complete List of Firm Personnel, See General Section

For full biographical listings, see the Martindale-Hubbell Law Directory

CHRISTOVICH AND KEARNEY, L.L.P. (AV)

Suite 2300 Pan American Life Center, 601 Poydras Street, 70130-6078
Telephone: 504-561-5700
FAX: 504-561-5743
Houston, Texas Office: 700 Louisiana, Suite 4550, 77002.
Telephone: 713-225-2255.
Fax: 713-225-1112.

MEMBERS OF FIRM

Alvin R. Christovich, Jr.
William K. Christovich
J. Walter Ward, Jr.
Lawrence J. Ernst
James F. Holmes
Robert E. Peyton
C. Edgar Cloutier
Charles W. Schmidt, III
Richard K. Christovich
Terry Christovich Gay
Paul G. Preston
Michael M. Christovich
E. Phelps Gay
Thomas C. Cowan
Geoffrey P. Snodgrass
J. Warren Gardner, Jr.
Kevin R. Tully
Lance R. Rydberg

(See Next Column)

MEMBERS OF FIRM (Continued)

Elizabeth S. Cordes
John K. Leach
Fred T. Hinrichs
Daniel A. Rees
Charles M. Lanier, Jr.

ASSOCIATES

Lyon H. Garrison
Philip J. Borne
Anthony Reginelli, Jr.
Paige F. Rosato
J. Roslyn Lemmon
James Aristide Holmes
Richard J. Garvey, Jr.
Scott P. Yount
Patricia Broussard
Patrick W. Drouilhet (Not admitted in LA)
Cheryl A. Smith (Not admitted in LA)

OF COUNSEL

Nannette Jolivette-Brown

Representative Clients: AMOCO; Atlantic Richfield Co.; Brown & Root, Inc.; Dual Drilling Co.; Freeport-McMoran; Grace Offshore Co.; Oceaneering International; Texas Eastern; Union Oil of California; Western Oceanic, Inc.

For full biographical listings, see the Martindale-Hubbell Law Directory

DEUTSCH, KERRIGAN & STILES (AV)

A Partnership including Professional Law Corporations
755 Magazine Street, 70130-3672
Telephone: 504-581-5141
Cable Address: "Dekest"
Telex: 584358
Telecopier: 504-566-1201

MEMBERS OF FIRM

Bertrand M. Cass, Jr.
Francis J. Barry, Jr.
Allen F. Campbell
G. Alex Weller
A. Wendel Stout, III

OF COUNSEL

Brunswick G. Deutsch (P.L.C.)

ASSOCIATE

Gene Ray Smith

For Complete List of Firm Personnel, See General Section

For full biographical listings, see the Martindale-Hubbell Law Directory

GAINSBURGH, BENJAMIN, FALLON, DAVID & ATES (AV)

A Partnership including Professional Law Corporations
2800 Energy Centre, 1100 Poydras, 70163-2800
Telephone: 504-522-2304
Telecopier: 504-528-9973

OF COUNSEL

Samuel C. Gainsburgh (P.L.C.)

MEMBERS OF FIRM

Jack C. Benjamin (P.L.C.)
Eldon E. Fallon (P.L.C.)
Robert J. David
George S. Meyer (1939-1977)
J. Robert Ates (P.L.C.)
Gerald E. Meunier
Nick F. Noriea, Jr.
Irving J. Warshauer
Stevan C. Dittman
Madeleine M. Landrieu

ASSOCIATES

Darryl M. Phillips
Andrew A. Lemmon
Michael G. Calogero

For full biographical listings, see the Martindale-Hubbell Law Directory

HEBERT, MOULEDOUX & BLAND, A PROFESSIONAL LAW CORPORATION (AV)

Pan-American Life Center, Suite 1650, 601 Poydras Street, 70130
Telephone: 504-525-3333
Cable Address: "HMBL"
Telex: 588-092;
Fax: 504-523-4224

Maurice C. Hebert, Jr.
André J. Mouledoux
Wilton E. Bland, III
Georges M. Legrand
Roch P. Poelman
Alan Guy Brackett
David M. Flotte
C. William Emory
Franck F. LaBiche, Jr.
C. Michael Parks
Daniel J. Hoerner
John H. Musser, V

Representative Clients: Archer-Daniels Midland Company; Bisso Marine Company, Inc.; Carline Geismar Fleet, Inc.; Cooper/T. Smith Stevedoring Company, Inc.; Delta Queen Steamboat Co.; Diamond Offshore Drilling, Inc.; LOOP INC.; Marine Equipment Management Corporation; McDermott Incorporated; Olympic Marine Company.

For full biographical listings, see the Martindale-Hubbell Law Directory

DARLEEN M. JACOBS A PROFESSIONAL LAW CORPORATION (AV)

823 St. Louis Street, 70112
Telephone: 504-522-3287; 522-0155
Cable Address: "Darjac."

(See Next Column)

DARLEEN M. JACOBS A PROFESSIONAL LAW CORPORATION—*Continued*

Darleen M. Jacobs
Honorable S. Sanford Levy (1902-1989)

For full biographical listings, see the Martindale-Hubbell Law Directory

LEMLE & KELLEHER, L.L.P. (AV)

A Partnership including Professional Law Corporations
21st Floor, Pan-American Life Center, 601 Poydras Street, 70130-6097
Telephone: 504-586-1241
FAX: 504-584-9142
Cable Address: "Lemmor"
Telex: WU 584272
Baton Rouge, Louisiana Office: One American Place, 301 Main Street, Suite 1800, 70825.
Telephone: 504-387-5068.
FAX: 504-387-4995.
London, England Office: 1 Seething Lane, EC3N 4AX.
Telephone: 071-702-1446.
FAX: 071-702-1447.

MEMBERS OF FIRM

George A. Frilot, III (A Professional Law Corp.)
Thomas W. Thorne, Jr.
James H. Daigle (A Professional Law Corporation)
Ashton R. O'Dwyer, Jr. (A Professional Law Corp.)
Edward F. Kohnke, IV
Richard B. Foster
Michael A. McGlone
Hal C. Welch
Douglas P. Matthews
James H. Brown, Jr.
David A. Olson
Miles P. Clements
Scott S. Partridge
James F. Shuey
Charles R. Talley
James R. Silverstein
Andrew S. de Klerk
Allen J. Krouse, III
J. Dwight LeBlanc, III

ASSOCIATES

E. John Heiser
Kent B. Ryan
Patrick J. McShane
Glenn P. Orgeron

Counsel for: Continental Grain Co.; Dow Chemical Co.; Ohio River Co./-Midland Enterprises; Tidewater, Inc.; United Kingdom Mutual Steam Ship Assn.

For Complete List of Firm Personnel, See General Section

For full biographical listings, see the Martindale-Hubbell Law Directory

MILLING, BENSON, WOODWARD, HILLYER, PIERSON & MILLER (AV)

A Partnership including Professional Law Corporations
Suite Twenty-Three Hundred, 909 Poydras Street, 70112-1017
Telephone: 504-569-7000
Cable Address: "Milling"
Telex: 58-4211
Telecopier: 504-569-7001
ABA net: 15656
MCI Mail: "Milling"
Lafayette, Louisiana Office: 101 LaRue France, Suite 200.
Telephone: 318-232-3929.
Telecopier: 318-233-4957.
Baton Rouge, Louisiana Office: Suite 402, 8555 United Plaza Blvd.
Telephone: 504-928-688.
Fax: 504-928-6881.

MEMBERS OF FIRM

Neal D. Hobson (P.C.)
Bruce R. Hoefer, Jr. (P.C.)
Patrick A. Talley (P.C.)

ASSOCIATE

Benjamin O. Schupp

See General Section for list of Representative Clients.

For Complete List of Firm Personnel, See General Section

For full biographical listings, see the Martindale-Hubbell Law Directory

MONTGOMERY, BARNETT, BROWN, READ, HAMMOND & MINTZ (AV)

A Registered Limited Liability Partnership
3200 Energy Centre, 1100 Poydras Street, 70163-3200
Telephone: 504-585-3200
Cable Address: "MONBAR"
Telex: 58-7389
FAX: 504-585-7688

MEMBERS OF FIRM

John B. Gooch, Jr.
A. Gordon Grant, Jr.
Frederick T. Haas, III
John C. Person
Christopher E. Carey
Patrick E. O'Keefe
Robert E. Durgin

(See Next Column)

A. Carter Mills, IV

Representative Clients: Atlantic Companies; The Delta Queen Steamboat Company; The CIGNA Cos.; International Marine Underwriters; MOAC (Marine Office of America Corp.); Underwriters at Lloyds; Fireman's Fund Insurance Companies; Crum & Forster Insurance Group; Water Quality Insurance Syndicate; Hatteras Yachts.

For full biographical listings, see the Martindale-Hubbell Law Directory

NESSER, KING & LEBLANC (AV)

Suite 3800 Place St. Charles, 201 St. Charles Avenue, 70170
Telephone: 504-582-3800
Telecopier: 504-582-1233

John T. Nesser, III
Henry A. King
Joseph E. LeBlanc, Jr.
David S. Bland
Patricia Ann Krebs
Robert J. Burvant
Eric Earl Jarrell
Liane K. Hinrichs

Jeffrey M. Burmaster
Jeffrey A. Mitchell
Margaret M. Sledge
Josh M. Kantrow
Elton A. Foster
Elizabeth S. Wheeler
Robert J. Bergeron
Timothy S. Madden
Elizabeth A. Meek

OF COUNSEL

Clare P. Hunter
George B. Jurgens, III
J. Grant Coleman
Len R. Brignac
George Farber, Jr.

For full biographical listings, see the Martindale-Hubbell Law Directory

O'NEIL, EICHIN, MILLER, BRECKINRIDGE & SAPORITO, A LAW CORPORATION (AV)

One Poydras Plaza, 22nd Floor, 70113
Telephone: 504-525-3200
Cable Address: ONEMILL NLN
Telex: ITT 460125
Answer Back: ONEMILL NLN
Facsimile: 504-529-7389 (Groups 1, 2 & 3)

William E. O'Neil
Earl S. Eichin, Jr.
Machale A. Miller
Alexander N. Breckinridge, IV
Jerry L. Saporito
I. Matthew Williamson
Randell E. Treadaway
Lindsay A. Larson, III
John F. Fay, Jr.
Alfred J. Rufty
Marva Jo Wyatt
Michael D. Sledge
Maria M. Bartush
Anne Flower Redd

For full biographical listings, see the Martindale-Hubbell Law Directory

PHELPS DUNBAR, L.L.P. (AV)

Texaco Center, 400 Poydras Street, 70130-3245
Telephone: 504-566-1311
Telecopier: 504-568-9130, 504-568-9007
Cable Address: "Howspencer"
Telex: 584125 WU
Telex: 6821155 WUI
Baton Rouge, Louisiana Office: Suite 701, City National Bank Building, P.O. Box 4412.
Telephone: 504-346-0285.
Telecopier: 504-381-9197.
Jackson, Mississippi Office: Suite 500, Security Centre North, 200 South Lamar Street, P.O. Box 23066.
Telephone: 601-352-2300.
Telecopier: 601-360-9777.
Tupelo, Mississippi Office: Seventh Floor, One Mississippi Plaza, P.O. Box 1220.
Telephone: 601-842-7907.
Telecopier: 601-842-3873.
Houston, Texas Office: Suite 501, 4 Houston Center, 1331 Lamar Street.
Telephone: 713-659-1386.
Telecopier: 713-659-1388.
London, England Office: Suite 976, Level 9, Lloyd's, 1 Lime Street, London EC3M 7DQ England.
Telephone: 011-44-71-929-4765.
Telecopier: 011-44-71-929-0046.
Telex: 987321.

OF COUNSEL

John W. Sims
Charles Edward Dunbar, III
J. Barbee Winston

MEMBERS OF FIRM

George W. Healy, III
James Bradley Kemp, Jr.
James H. Roussel
Charles M. Steen
Walker W. (Bill) Jones, III (Not admitted in LA; Jackson and Tupelo, Mississippi Offices)
Kent E. Westmoreland (Not admitted in LA; Resident, Houston, Texas Office)
Claude LeRoy Stuart, III (Not admitted in LA; Resident, Houston, Texas Office)
Robert C. Clotworthy

(See Next Column)

PHELPS DUNBAR L.L.P., *New Orleans—Continued*

MEMBERS OF FIRM (Continued)

George M. Gilly
Christopher O. Davis
Robert P. McCleskey, Jr.
Julia Marie Adams (Not admitted in LA; Resident, Houston, Texas Office)
Brian D. Wallace
Mark C. Dodart

COUNSEL

Edwin K. Legnon

ASSOCIATES

David A. Abramson
Sheryl Bey (Resident, Jackson, Mississippi Office)
Evan T. Caffrey (Not admitted in LA; Resident, Houston, Texas Office)
Laurie Dearman Clark
Laura E. Cormier (Not admitted in LA; Resident, Houston, Texas Office)
Malinda York Crouch (Not admitted in LA; Resident, Houston, Texas Office)
John C. Cunningham (Not admitted in LA; Resident, Houston, Texas Office)
Warren A. Cuntz, Jr.
Eric P. Halber
Richard Leo Harrell (Resident, Houston, Texas Office)
William B. Hidalgo
Stephanie G. McShane
William J. Riviere
Daniel C. Rodgers
David B. Sharpe
Michael F. Walther (Resident, Houston, Texas Office)
Dawei Zhang

Representative Clients: American Steamship Owners Mutual P & I Association; The Britannia Steamship Insurance Assn., Ltd.; Edison Chouest Offshore, Inc.; Halliburton Company; John E. Chance & Associates, Inc.; McDonough Marine Service, A Division of MARMAC Corp.; Southern Marine & Aviation Underwriters, Inc.; Standard Steamship Owners P&I Association; The Steamship Mutual Underwriting Association, Ltd.; Underwriters at Lloyd's, London.

For Complete List of Firm Personnel, See General Section

For full biographical listings, see the Martindale-Hubbell Law Directory

RICE FOWLER (AV)

Place St. Charles, 36th Floor, 201 St. Charles Avenue, 70130
Telephone: 504-523-2600
Telecopier: 504-523-2705
Telex: 9102507910
ELN 62548910
London, England Office: Suite 692, Level 6 Lloyd's, 1 Lime Street, London EC3M 7DQ England.
Telephone: 071-327-4222.
Telecopier: 071-929-0043.
San Francisco, California Office: Embarcadero Center West, 275 Battery Street, 27th Floor, 94111.
Telephone: 415-399-9191.
Telecopier: 415-399-9192.
Telex: 451981.
San Diego, California Office: Emerald-Shapery Center, 402 W. Broadway, Suite 850, 92101.
Telephone: 619-230-0030.
Telecopier: 619-230-1350.
Beijing, China Office: Beijing International Convention Centre, Suite 7024, No. 8 Beichendong Road, Chaoyang District, 100101, P.R.C.
Telephone: (861) 493-4250.
Telecopier: (861) 493-4251.
Bogota, Colombia Office: Avenida Jimenez #4-03 Oficina 10-05.
Telephone: (571) 342-1062.
Telecopier: (571) 342-1062.

MEMBERS OF FIRM

Winston Edward Rice
George J. Fowler, III
Antonio J. Rodriguez
Thomas H. Kingsmill, III
Paul N. Vance
Delos E. Flint, Jr.
Edward F. LeBreton, III
Docia L. Dalby
Mary Campbell Hubbard
Jon W. Wise
Mat M. Gray, III

OF COUNSEL

T. C. W. Ellis

ASSOCIATES

Mary E. Kerrigan
Susan Molero Vance
Samuel A. Giberga
John F. Billera
D. Roxanne Perkins
Jeffry L. Sanford
Alanson T. Chenault, IV
Cindy T. Matherne
Barry A. Brock
Walter F. Wolf, III
Robert R. Johnston
Virginia R. Quijada
William J. Sommers, Jr.

For full biographical listings, see the Martindale-Hubbell Law Directory

TERRIBERRY, CARROLL & YANCEY, L.L.P. (AV)

3100 Energy Centre, 1100 Poydras Street, 70163-3100
Telephone: 504-523-6451
Cable Address: "Terrib"
Telex: 6821224 (WUI)
Fax: 504-524-3257

MEMBERS OF FIRM

Benjamin W. Yancey (1906-1991)
Walter Carroll, Jr. (Retired)
Maurie D. Yager
G. Edward Merritt
James L. Schupp, Jr.
John A. Bolles
Charles F. Lozes
Robert J. Barbier
Rufus C. Harris, III
Hugh Ramsay Straub
Robert S. Reich
David B. Lawton
Roger D. Allen
Janet Wessler Marshall
D. Kirk Boswell
Gary A. Hemphill
Laurence R. De Buys, IV
Kevin J. LaVie
Stephen E. Mattesky

COUNSEL

Andrew T. Martinez
Cynthia Anne Wegmann

ASSOCIATES

Robert B. Acomb, III
Gerald M. Baca
Michael M. Butterworth
John A. Scialdone

Representative Clients: Assuranceforeningen Gard; Assuranceforeningen Skuld; Certain Underwriters at Lloyd's; The London Steam-Ship Owners' Mutual Insurance Assn. Ltd.; Lykes Bros. Steamship Co., Inc.; New Orleans Steamship Assn.; Nordisk Skibsrederforening (Northern Shipowners Defence Club); Scandinavian Marine Claims Office, Inc.; Steamship Mutual Underwriting Assn. Ltd.; United Kingdom Mutual Steam Ship Assurance Assn. Ltd.

For full biographical listings, see the Martindale-Hubbell Law Directory

WAGNER, BAGOT & GLEASON (AV)

Suite 2660, Poydras Center, 650 Poydras Street, 70130-6102
Telephone: 504-525-2141
Telecopier: 504-523-1587
TWX: 5106017673
ELN: 62928850
"INCISIVE"

Thomas J. Wagner
Michael H. Bagot, Jr.
Harvey G. Gleason
Whitney L. Cole
Eric D. Suben

For full biographical listings, see the Martindale-Hubbell Law Directory

MARYLAND

*BALTIMORE,** (Independent City)

ISRAELSON, SALSBURY, CLEMENTS & BEKMAN (AV)

300 West Pratt Street, Suite 450, 21201
Telephone: 410-539-6633
FAX: 410-625-9554

MEMBERS OF FIRM

Stuart Marshall Salsbury
Paul D. Bekman
Daniel M. Clements
Matthew Zimmerman
Laurence A. Marder

Suzanne K. Farace
Scott R. Scherr
Carol J. Glover

COUNSEL TO THE FIRM

Max R. Israelson

OF COUNSEL

Samuel Omar Jackson, Jr. (Semi-Retired)

For full biographical listings, see the Martindale-Hubbell Law Directory

NILES, BARTON & WILMER (AV)

1400 Legg Mason Tower, 111 South Calvert Street, 21202-6185
Telephone: 410-783-6300
Cable Address: "Nilwo"
Telecopier: 410-783-6363

MEMBERS OF FIRM

Paul B. Lang
Robert P. O'Brien
Steven E. Leder

For Complete List of Firm Personnel, See General Section

For full biographical listings, see the Martindale-Hubbell Law Directory

THIEBLOT, RYAN, MARTIN & FERGUSON, P.A. (AV)

4th Floor, The World Trade Center, 21202-3091
Telephone: 410-837-1140
Washington, D.C. Line: 202-628-8223
Fax: 410-837-3282

(See Next Column)

THIEBLOT, RYAN, MARTIN & FERGUSON P.A.—*Continued*

Robert J. Thieblot
Anthony W. Ryan
J. Edward Martin, Jr.
Robert L. Ferguson, Jr.
Bruce R. Miller
Robert D. Harwick, Jr.
Thomas J. Schetelich
Christopher J. Heffernan

M. Brooke Murdock
Anne M. Hrehorovich
Donna Marie Raffaele
Michael N. Russo, Jr.
Jodi K. Ebersole
Hamilton Fisk Tyler
Peter Joseph Basile

Representative Clients: Ford Motor Credit Co.; USF & G Co.; The American Road Insurance Co.; Fidelity Engineering Corp.; The North Charles Street Design Organization; Record Collections, Inc.; Toyota Motor Credit Co.

For full biographical listings, see the Martindale-Hubbell Law Directory

VENABLE, BAETJER AND HOWARD (AV)

A Partnership including Professional Corporations
1800 Mercantile Bank & Trust Building, 2 Hopkins Plaza, 21201
Telephone: 410-244-7400
Washington, D.C. Office: Venable, Baetjer, Howard & Civiletti. Suite 1000, 1201 New York Avenue, N.W.
Telephone: 202-962-4800.
McLean, Virginia Office: Suite 400, 2010 Corporate Ridge.
Telephone: 703-760-1600.
Rockville, Maryland Office: Suite 500, One Church Street, P. O. Box 1906.
Telephone: 301-217-5600.
Towson, Maryland Office: 210 Allegheny Avenue, P. O. Box 5517.
Telephone: 410-494-6200.

MEMBERS OF FIRM

Douglas D. Connah, Jr. (P.C.) (Also at Washington, D.C. Office)
Lars E. Anderson (Not admitted in MD; Resident, McLean, Virginia Office)

ASSOCIATE

Fred Joseph Federici, III (Resident, Washington, D.C. Office)

For Complete List of Firm Personnel, See General Section

For full biographical listings, see the Martindale-Hubbell Law Directory

WRIGHT, CONSTABLE & SKEEN (AV)

250 West Pratt Street, 13th Floor, 21201-2423
Telephone: 410-539-5541
Telex: 710 234-2383 CALDAS
Fax: 301-659-1350
Elkton, Maryland Office: 138 East Main Street.
Telephone: 301-398-1844.

MEMBERS OF FIRM

James W. Constable
James D. Skeen
Stephen F. White

Representative Clients: General Ship Repair Corp.; Egan Marine Contracting Co., Inc.; Atlantic Mutual Insurance Co.; Marine Office of America Corp.; Recovery Services International; Toplis & Harding, Inc.; Firemen's Fund; Royal Insurance Co.; Gradman & Holler, Gmbh; Arkwright-Boston Insurance.

For Complete List of Firm Personnel, See General Section

For full biographical listings, see the Martindale-Hubbell Law Directory

MASSACHUSETTS

*BOSTON,** Suffolk Co.

BINGHAM, DANA & GOULD (AV)

150 Federal Street, 02110
Telephone: 617-951-8000
Cable Address: "Blodgham Bsn"
Telex: 275147 BDGBSN UR
Telecopy: 617-951-8736
Hartford, Connecticut Office: 100 Pearl Street.
Telephone: 203-244-3770.
Telecopy: 203-527-5188.
London, England Office: 39 Victoria Street, SWIH 0EE.
Telephone: 011-44-71-799-2646.
Telecopy: 011-44-71-799-2654.
Telex: 888179 BDGLDN G.
Cable Address: "Blodgham Ldn".
Washington, D.C. Office: 1550 M Street, N.W.
Telephone: 202-822-9320.
Telecopy: 202-833-1506.

MEMBERS OF FIRM

Charles L. Janes
Robert E. McDonnell
Neal A. Rosen
Thomas H. Walsh, Jr.

(See Next Column)

ASSOCIATES

John J. Finn
Jeffrey S. King

For Complete List of Firm Personnel, See General Section

For full biographical listings, see the Martindale-Hubbell Law Directory

SWARTZ & SWARTZ (AV)

10 Marshall Street, 02108
Telephone: 617-742-1900
Fax: 617-367-7193

Edward M. Swartz
Alan L. Cantor
Joseph A. Swartz
Victor A. Denaro
Joan E. Swartz
James A. Swartz
Robert S. Berger
Harold David Levine

OF COUNSEL

Fredric A. Swartz

For full biographical listings, see the Martindale-Hubbell Law Directory

MICHIGAN

*DETROIT,** Wayne Co.

BRADY HATHAWAY, PROFESSIONAL CORPORATION (AV)

1330 Buhl Building, 48226-3602
Telephone: 313-965-3700
Telecopier: 313-965-2830

Thomas M. J. Hathaway

Representative Clients: Beam Stream, Inc.; Bundy Tubing Company; Century 21 Real Estate Corp.; Datamedia Corporation; Energy Conversion Devices, Inc.; Michigan Gas Utilities; Pony Express Courier Corp.; Schering Corporation; Warner-Lambert; Wolverine Technologies.

For Complete List of Firm Personnel, See General Section

For full biographical listings, see the Martindale-Hubbell Law Directory

BUTZEL LONG, A PROFESSIONAL CORPORATION (AV)

Suite 900, 150 West Jefferson, 48226
Telephone: 313-225-7000
Telecopier: 313-225-7080
Birmingham, Michigan Office: Suite 200, 32270 Telegraph Road.
Telephone: 810-258-1616.
Telecopier: 810-258-1439.
Lansing, Michigan Office: 118 West Ottawa Street.
Telephone: 517-372-6622.
Telecopier: 517-372-6672.
Ann Arbor, Michigan Office: Suite 400, 121 West Washington.
Telephone: 313-995-3110.
Telecopier: 313-995-1777.
Grosse Pointe Farms, Michigan Office: Suite 260, 21 Kercheval.
Telephone: 313-886-5446.
Telecopier: 313-886-2114.

C. Peter Theut
James Y. Stewart

Brian J. Miles
Daniel R. W. Rustmann

Representative Clients: Michigan Boating Industries Association; National Marine Bankers Association; Excel Marine, Inc.; Markley Marine, Inc.; First National Bank-Mt. Clemens; Michigan Marine Salvage, Inc.; Great Lakes Prepaid Towing, Inc.; Toledo Overseas Terminal, Inc.; Through Transit Mutual Assurance, Ltd.; Comerica Bank.

For Complete List of Firm Personnel, See General Section

For full biographical listings, see the Martindale-Hubbell Law Directory

FOSTER, MEADOWS & BALLARD, P.C. (AV)

3200 Penobscot Building, 48226
Telephone: 313-961-3234
Cable Address: "Foster"
Telex: 23-5823
Facsimile: 313-961-6184

Sparkman D. Foster (1897-1967)
John L. Foster
Charles R. Hrdlicka
Paul D. Galea
Richard A. Dietz
Robert H. Fortunate
Robert G. Lahiff
Camille A. Raffa-Dietz

Michael J. Liddane
Paul A. Kettunen

OF COUNSEL

John F. Langs
John A. Mundell, Jr.

Counsel for: Air Canada; Canadian National Railways; Grand Trunk Western Railroad; Alexander and Alexander; Shand Morahan; Utica Mutual.

(See Next Column)

FOSTER, MEADOWS & BALLARD P.C., *Detroit—Continued*

Admiralty Counsel for: Ford Motor; Bob Lo Co.

For full biographical listings, see the Martindale-Hubbell Law Directory

MILLER, CANFIELD, PADDOCK AND STONE, P.L.C. (AV)

A Professional Limited Liability Company
Founded in 1852 by Sidney Davy Miller
150 West Jefferson, Suite 2500, 48226-4415
Telephone: 313-963-6420
Fax: 313-496-7500
Cable Address: "Stem Detroit"
Detroit, Michigan Office: 150 West Jefferson, Suite 2500, 48226-4415.
Telephone: 313-963-6420.
Fax: 313-496-7500.
Cable Address: "Stem Detroit."
Ann Arbor, Michigan Office: 101 North Main Street, 7th Floor, 48104-1400.
Telephone: 313-663-2445.
Fax: 313-747-7147.
Bloomfield Hills, Michigan Office: Suite 100, Pinehurst Office Center, 1400 North Woodward, 48303-2014.
Telephone: 313-645-5000.
Fax: 313-645-1917.
Grand Rapids, Michigan Office: 1200 Campau Square Plaza, 99 Monroe, N.W., 49503-2639.
Telephone: 616-454-8656.
Fax: 616-776-6322.
Howell, Michigan Office: 121 South Barnard Street, Suite 4, 48843-2305.
Telephone: 517-546-7600.
Telecopier: 517-546-6974.
Kalamazoo, Michigan Office: 444 West Michigan Avenue, 49007-3752.
Telephone: 616-381-7030.
Fax: 616-382-0244.
Lansing, Michigan Office: One Michigan Avenue, Suite 900, 48933-1609.
Telephone: 517-487-2070.
Fax: 517-374-6304.
Monroe, Michigan Office: The Executive Centre, 214 East Elm Avenue, 48161-2682.
Telephone: 313-243-2000.
Fax: 313-243-0901.
Washington, D.C. Office: 1225 Nineteenth Street, N.W., Suite 400. 20036.
Telephone: 202-429-5575; 785-0600.
Fax: 202-331-1118; 785-1234.
Pensacola, Florida Office: 25 West Cedar, 32501.
Telephone: 904-469-1088.
Fax: 904-432-0677.
St. Petersburg, Florida Office: 100 Second Avenue S., Suite 7045, 33701.
Telephone: 813-982-6000.
Fax: 813-892-6002.
Gdansk, Poland Office: Suite 322, Dom Technika Building, Ul. Rajska 6, 80-850.
Telephone: 011-485-831-2808.
Fax: 011-485-831-4719.
Warsaw, Poland Office: Ul. Marszalkowska 82, Suite 561, 00-517.
Telephone: 011-482-623-6457 and 6458.
Fax: 011-482-623-6459.

MEMBERS OF FIRM

Lawrence A. King (P.C.) (Bloomfield Hills Office)
John B. DeVine (Ann Arbor Office)
Robert E. Hammell
Joseph F. Maycock, Jr.
Allen Schwartz
John W. Gelder
George E. Parker, III
Richard A. Jones (P.C.) (Bloomfield Hills Office)
Stevan Uzelac (P.C.)
Gilbert E. Gove
Robert S. Ketchum
Samuel J. McKim, III, (P.C.)
Rocque E. Lipford (P.C.) (Monroe Office)
Joel L. Piell
Robert E. Gilbert (Ann Arbor Office)
Eric V. Brown, Jr. (Kalamazoo Office)
Bruce D. Birgbauer
George T. Stevenson
John A. Thurber (P.C.) (Bloomfield Hills Office)
Orin D. Brustad
Carl H. von Ende
Erik H. Serr (Ann Arbor Office)
Allyn D. Kantor (Ann Arbor Office)
Mark E. Schlussel
Charles E. Ritter (Kalamazoo Office)
Thomas G. Parachini
John A. Campbell (Kalamazoo Office)
David D. Joswick (P.C.)
Charles L. Burleigh, Jr.
John A. Marxer (P.C.) (Bloomfield Hills Office)
Gregory L. Curtner
Dennis R. Neiman
Kenneth E. Konop (Bloomfield Hills Office)
Leonard D. Givens
W. Mack Faison
Joseph F. Galvin
Thomas J. Heiden (Grand Rapids Office)
Ronald H. Riback (Bloomfield Hills Office)
James W. Williams (Bloomfield Hills Office)
Thomas P. Hustoles (Kalamazoo Office)
William J. Danhof (Lansing Office)
Clarence L. Pozza, Jr.
Jerry T. Rupley
Michael W. Hartmann
Kent E. Shafer
James C. Foresman
John J. Collins, Jr.
John R. Cook (Kalamazoo Office)
Lawrence D. Owen (Lansing Office)

(See Next Column)

MEMBERS OF FIRM (Continued)

Thomas W. Linn
Stephen G. Palms
Jerome R. Watson
Frank L. Andrews (Detroit and Bloomfield Hills Offices)
Donna J. Donati
Donald W. Keim
Larry J. Saylor
Mark E. Putney (Grand Rapids Office)
James G. Vantine, Jr. (Kalamazoo and Grand Rapids Offices)
Richard J. Seryak
Michael R. Atkins (Lansing Office)
Leland D. Barringer
Timothy D. Sochocki (Ann Arbor Office)
Thomas C. Phillips (Grand Rapids and Lansing Offices)
Christopher J. Dembowski (Lansing Office)
Marjory G. Basile
Terrence M. Crawford
Ryan H. Haywood
Michael J. Hodge (Lansing Office)
J. Kevin Trimmer (Bloomfield Hills Office)
Steven D. Weyhing (Lansing Office)
Richard A. Gaffin (Grand Rapids Office)
Kevin M. McCarthy (Kalamazoo Office)
Ronald E. Baylor (Kalamazoo Office)
Gary A. Bruder (Ann Arbor Office)
Beverly Hall Burns
Charles S. Mishkind (Grand Rapids, Lansing and Kalamazoo Offices)
Stephen J. Ott
Amanda Van Dusen
Peter W. Waldmeir
Thomas G. Appleman
Thomas H. Van Dis (Kalamazoo Office)
Walter Briggs Connolly, Jr.
Michael P. Coakley
Cynthia B. Faulhaber
Jeffrey M. McHugh
Susan Hedges Patton (Ann Arbor Office)
Robert F. Rhoades
James E. Spurr (Kalamazoo Office)
Gregory V. Di Censo (Bloomfield Hills Office)
Michael L. Lencione
Stephen M. Tuuk (Grand Rapids Office)
Robert D. VanderLaan (Grand Rapids Office)
Brad B. Arbuckle (Bloomfield Hills Office)
Mark T. Boonstra
Harold W. Bulger, Jr.
Michael G. Campbell (Grand Rapids Office)
David A. French (Ann Arbor Office)
Michael A. Limauro
Karen Ann McCoy
Kevin J. Moody (Lansing Office)
Steven M. Stankewicz (Kalamazoo Office)
Robert E. Lee Wright
Andrea L. Fischer
Michael A. Indenbaum
Alison B. Marshall (Washington, D.C. Office)
J. David Reck (Ann Arbor and Howell Offices)
Michael H. Traison
Jonathan S. Green
Le Roy L. Asher, Jr.
Vernon Bennett III (Grand Rapids and Kalamazoo Offices)
Douglas W. Crim (Grand Rapids Office)
Pamela Chapman Enslen (Kalamazoo Office)
Michael P. McGee
David N. Parsigian (Ann Arbor Office)
Jay B. Rising (Lansing Office)
Deborah W. Thompson
Richard T. Urbis
Richard F. X. Urisko
Steven A. Roach

Richard A. Walawender

OF COUNSEL

William G. Butler
John A. Gilray, Jr., (P.C.) (Bloomfield Hills Office)
Eric V. Brown, Sr. (Kalamazoo Office)
Edmond F. DeVine (Ann Arbor Office)
James E. Tobin
Stratton S. Brown
Richard B. Gushée
Peter P. Thurber
George J. Slykhouse (Grand Rapids Office)
Gerard Thomas (Kalamazoo Office)
George E. Bushnell, Jr.
Henry R. Nolte, Jr. (Bloomfield Hills Office)
Donald B. Lifton
Anne H. Hiemstra
Richard I. Lott (Pensacola, Florida Office)
Nicholas P. Miller (Washington, D.C. Office)
Joseph Van Eaton (Washington, D.C. Office)
Tillman L. Lay (Washington, D.C. Office)
William R. Malone (Washington, D.C. Office)
Steven C. Kahn (Washington, D.C. Office)
Stephen J. Markman
David K. McLeod

SENIOR ATTORNEYS

Charles E. Scholl (Grand Rapids Office)
David E. Hathaway (Grand Rapids Office)
Julianna B. Miller
Leo P. Goddeyne (Kalamazoo Office)
Charles A. Duerr, Jr. (Ann Arbor Office)
Michael J. Taylor (Grand Rapids Office)
Don M. Schmidt (Kalamazoo Office)
Ronald D. Gardner (Ann Arbor Office)
Elise Levasseur Rohn
William B. Beach
Abigail Elias
David F. Dixon
Robert J. Sandler
Lawrence M. Dudek
Irene Bruce Hathaway
Sherry Katz-Crank (Lansing Office)
Marta A. Manildi (Ann Arbor Office)
Gary W. Faria
David J. Hasper (Grand Rapids Office)
Susan E. Juroe (Washington, D.C. Office)
Michael A. Alaimo
David A. Gatchell (St. Petersburg Office)
John G. VanSlambrouck
Celeste M. Moy (Washington, D.C. Office)

(See Next Column)

MILLER, CANFIELD, PADDOCK AND STONE P.L.C.—*Continued*

ASSOCIATES

Brian J. Doren
Ilana A. Stein Ben-Ze'ev
Walter A. Payne, III
Ronald E. Hodess (Bloomfield Hills Office)
Ellen M. Tickner
George D. Mesritz
John C. Shea (Lansing Office)
Kathryn L. Ossian
Donald J. Hutchinson
Megan P. Norris
Kurt N. Sherwood (Kalamazoo Office)
Patricia D. Lott (Pensacola Office)
Frederick E. Ellrod III (Washington, D.C. Office)
Jereen G. Trudell (Bloomfield Hills Office)
Richard I. Loebl
Gary E. Mitchell (Grand Rapids Office)
Matthew C. Ames (Washington, D.C. Office)
Ballard Jay Yelton III (Kalamazoo Office)
Michael A. Luberto, Jr.
Clifford T. Flood (Lansing Office)
Linda M. Bruton
William L. Rosin (Bloomfield Hills Office)
Thomas R. Cox
Lori L. Purkey (Kalamazoo Office)
L. Jeffrey Zauberman
Joanne B. Faycurry
Janet R. Chrzanowski
Dawn M. Schluter (Bloomfield Hills Office)
A. Paul Thowsen (Ann Arbor Office)
Robert J. Haddad
John H. Willems
Erich H. Hintzen
James R. Lancaster, Jr. (Lansing Office)
Carol A. Jizmejian
Joan L. Kramlich (Lansing Office)
John O. Renken (Ann Arbor and District of Columbia Offices)
Terry Xiaotian Gao (Washington, D.C. Office)
Frederick A. Acomb
Joseph G. Sullivan
Lisa D. Pick
Elizabeth J. Partington (Pensacola Office)
Louise B. Wright (Kalamazoo Office)
John C. Arndts
Brian S. Westenberg
Amy S. Davis
A. Michael Palizzi
Sally A. Hamby
Patrick F. McGow
Brian K. Telfair
Paul G. Machesky
Mark A. Randon
Michael C. Fayz
Jeffrey S. Starman
Anna M. Maiuri (Bloomfield Hills Office)
Thomas D. Colis
Dean M. Altobelli (Lansing Office)
Derek T. Montgomery
Amy J. Broman (Ann Arbor Office)
Diane B. Cabbell (Ann Arbor Office)
Steven G. Cohen
Kristin M. Neun (Washington, D.C. Office)
David A. Nacht
Bradley C. White (Grand Rapids Office)
Sean P. Culliton (Pensacola Office)
Jeffrey D. Adelman
Meg Hackett Carrier (Grand Rapids Office)
Linda M. Ledbetter (Ann Arbor Office)
Catherine M. Patterson
Suzanne L. DeVine (Ann Arbor Office)
Karen M. Hassevoort (Kalamazoo Office)

Representative Firm Clients: Chrysler Corp.; Comerica, Inc.; City of Detroit, Mich.; Detroit Tigers, Inc.; First of Michigan; Fretter, Inc.; Ford Motor Co.; Ford Motor Credit Co.; Great Lakes Bancorp; Henry Ford Hospital.

For full biographical listings, see the Martindale-Hubbell Law Directory

FARMINGTON HILLS, Oakland Co.

KAUFMAN AND PAYTON (AV)

200 Northwestern Financial Center, 30833 Northwestern Highway, 48334
Telephone: 810-626-5000
Telefacsimile: 810-626-2843
Grand Rapids, Michigan Office: 420 Trust Building.
Telephone: 616-459-4200.
Fax: 616-459-4929.
Traverse City, Michigan Office: 122 West State Street.
Telephone: 616-947-4050.
Fax: 616-947-7321.

Alan Jay Kaufman
Donald L. Payton
Kenneth C. Letherwood
Stephen R. Levine
Thomas L. Vitu
Ralph C. Chapa, Jr.
Raymond I. Foley, II
Jeffrey K. Van Hattum
Leo D. Neville

For full biographical listings, see the Martindale-Hubbell Law Directory

MINNESOTA

*MINNEAPOLIS,** Hennepin Co.

HUNEGS, STONE, KOENIG & DOLAN, P.A. (AV)

565 Northstar East, 608 Second Avenue South, 55402
Telephone: 612-339-4511; 800-328-4340
Fax: 612-339-5150

(See Next Column)

William H. DeParcq (1905-1988)
Richard Gene Hunegs
Robert N. Stone
Ralph E. Koenig
Robert T. Dolan

Frances S. P. Li
Lawrence Alan Thomas

Reference: First Bank of Minneapolis.

For full biographical listings, see the Martindale-Hubbell Law Directory

MISSISSIPPI

BILOXI, Harrison Co.

MINOR AND GUICE (AV)

A Partnership including a Professional Association
160 Main Street, Drawer 1388, 39533
Telephone: 601-374-5151
FAX: 601-374-6630

Paul S. Minor (P.A.)
Judy M. Guice

Mark D. Lumpkin
Michael Bruffey

For full biographical listings, see the Martindale-Hubbell Law Directory

*COLUMBIA,** Marion Co.

AULTMAN, TYNER, MCNEESE & RUFFIN, LTD., A PROFESSIONAL LAW CORPORATION (AV)

329 Church Street, P.O. Drawer 707, 39429
Telephone: 601-736-2222
Hattiesburg, Mississippi Office: 315 Hemphill Street, P.O. Drawer 750.
Telephone: 601-583-2671.
Gulfport, Mississippi Office: 1201 25th Avenue, Suite 300, P.O. Box 607.
Telephone: 601-863-6913.

Thomas D. McNeese
Richard F. Yarborough, Jr.

Lawrence E. Hahn

OF COUNSEL

Ernest Ray Duff

Representative Clients: Hercules, Inc.; United States Steel Corp.; Ford Motor Co.; International Paper Co.; Phillips Petroleum Co.; Aetna Casualty & Surety Co.; CNA Group; Liberty Mutual Insurance Co.; St. Paul Fire & Marine Insurance Co.; Fireman's Fund.

For full biographical listings, see the Martindale-Hubbell Law Directory

*GREENVILLE,** Washington Co.

LAKE, TINDALL & THACKSTON (AV)

Formerly Firm of Wynn, Hafter, Lake & Tindall
127 South Poplar Street, P.O. Box 918, 38701
Telephone: 601-378-2121
Facsimile: 601-378-2183
Paducah, Kentucky Office: One Executive Boulevard, Suite 318, P.O. Box 30.
Telephone: 502-442-1900.
Facsimile: 502-442-8247.
Jackson, Mississippi Office: 350 Security Centre North, 200 South Lamar Street, P.O. Box 1787.
Telephone: 601-948-2121.
Facsimile: 601-948-0603.

Franklin S. Thackston, Jr.
Edwin Spivey Gault (Resident Paducah Office)
Clinton W. Walker, III
Carl J. Marshall (Resident Paducah Office)

General Counsel for: Greenville Bank (Branch of Deposit Guaranty National Bank of Jackson); Bunge Towing, Inc.; SUPERVALU INC., Lewis Grocer Division; Greenville Port Commission; Stein Mart Inc.; Delta and Pine Land Co.
Local Counsel For: Insurance: Aetna Casualty & Surety Co.; Cigna-Aetna Insurance Co.; Allstate Insurance Co.; Shelter Insurance Co.

For Complete List of Firm Personnel, See General Section

For full biographical listings, see the Martindale-Hubbell Law Directory

*GULFPORT,** Harrison Co.

AULTMAN, TYNER, MCNEESE & RUFFIN, LTD., A PROFESSIONAL LAW CORPORATION (AV)

1201 25th Avenue, Suite 300, P.O. Box 607, 39502
Telephone: 601-863-6913
Hattiesburg, Mississippi Office: 315 Hemphill Street, P.O. Drawer 750.
Telephone: 601-583-2671.

(See Next Column)

AULTMAN, TYNER, MCNEESE & RUFFIN, LTD. A PROFESSIONAL LAW CORPORATION, *Gulfport—Continued*

Columbia, Mississippi Office: 329 Church Street, P.O. Drawer 707.
Telephone: 601-736-2222.

Ben E. Sheely
Paul J. Delcambre, Jr.
Dorrance (Dee) Aultman, Jr.

For full biographical listings, see the Martindale-Hubbell Law Directory

DUKES, DUKES, KEATING AND FANECA, P.A. (AV)

2308 East Beach Boulevard, P.O. Drawer W, 39501
Telephone: 601-868-1111
FAX: 601-863-2886

Walter W. Dukes
Hugh D. Keating
Cy Faneca

David Charles Goff

For full biographical listings, see the Martindale-Hubbell Law Directory

FRANKE, RAINEY & SALLOUM (AV)

2605 14th Street, P.O. Drawer 460, 39502
Telephone: 601-868-7070
Telecopier: 601-868-7090

MEMBERS OF FIRM

Paul M. Franke, Jr.
William M. Rainey
Richard P. Salloum
Paul B. Howell
Ronald T. Russell
Fredrick B. Feeney, II
Traci M. Castille

ASSOCIATES

Kaleel G. Salloum, Jr.
Ruth E. Bennett
Donald P. Moore
Roland F. Samson, III
Jeffrey S. Bruni
Stefan G. Bourn

For full biographical listings, see the Martindale-Hubbell Law Directory

*HATTIESBURG,** Forrest Co.

AULTMAN, TYNER, MCNEESE & RUFFIN, LTD., A PROFESSIONAL LAW CORPORATION (AV)

315 Hemphill Street, P.O. Drawer 750, 39403-0750
Telephone: 601-583-2671
Columbia, Mississippi Office: 329 Church Street, P.O. Drawer 707.
Telephone: 601-736-2222.
Gulfport, Mississippi Office: 1201 25th Avenue, Suite 300, P.O. Box 607.
Telephone: 601-863-6913.

Dorrance Aultman
Thomas W. Tyner
Thomas D. McNeese (Resident, Columbia Office)
Louie F. Ruffin
Richard F. Yarborough, Jr. (Resident, Columbia Office)
Ben E. Sheely (Resident, Gulfport Office)
Patrick H. Zachary
Paul J. Delcambre, Jr. (Resident, Gulfport Office)
Robert J. Dambrino, III
Vicki R. Leggett
R. Curtis Smith, II
Dorrance (Dee) Aultman, Jr. (Resident, Gulfport Office)
William Nelson Graham

James L. Quinn
Walter J. Eades
Lawrence E. Hahn (Resident, Columbia Office)
Carol Ann Estes
Victor A. DuBose

OF COUNSEL

Ernest Ray Duff (Resident, Columbia Office)

Representative Clients: Hercules, Inc.; U.S. Steel Corp.; Ford Motor Co.; Phillips Petroleum Co.; Aetna Casualty & Surety Co.; CNA Group; Liberty Mutual Insurance Co.; St. Paul Fire & Marine Insurance Co.; Fireman's Fund.

For full biographical listings, see the Martindale-Hubbell Law Directory

*POPLARVILLE,** Pearl River Co.

WILLIAMS, WILLIAMS AND MONTGOMERY, P.A. (AV)

109 Erlanger Street, P.O. Box 113, 39470
Telephone: 601-795-4572
FAX: 601-795-8382
Picayune, Mississippi Office: 900 Highway 11 South, P.O. Box 1058.
Telephone: 601-798-0480.
FAX: 601-798-5481.

E. B. Williams (1890-1976)
E. B. Williams, Jr. (1917-1990)
Lampton O'Neal Williams
Joseph H. Montgomery
E. Bragg Williams, III
L. O'Neal Williams, Jr.

Michael E. Patten
Anne M. Parker

Representative Clients: Hancock Bank, Bank of Commerce Branch; Wesley's Fertilizer Plant, Inc.; Wesley Oil and Gas Co., Inc.; Garrett Industries, Inc.; Bass Pecan Co., Lumberton, Miss.; Joe N. Miles & Sons Lumber Co., Inc., Lumberton and Silver Creek, Miss. and Bogalusa, La.

(See Next Column)

Reference: Hancock Bank, Bank of Commerce Branch, Poplarville, Mississippi.

For full biographical listings, see the Martindale-Hubbell Law Directory

MISSOURI

ST. LOUIS, (Independent City)

EVANS & DIXON (AV)

1200 Saint Louis Place, 200 North Broadway, 63102-2749
Telephone: 314-621-7755
Kansas City, Missouri Office: City Center Square, 1100 Main Street, Suite 2000, 64105-2119.
Telephone: 816-472-4600.
Edwardsville, Illinois Office: 17 Ginger Creek Meadows, P.O. Box 405. 62025-3508.
Telephone: 618-656-8505.
Leawood, Kansas Office: 8016 State Line Road, Suite 207. 66208-3713.
Telephone: 913-649-5386.

MEMBERS OF FIRM

Edward W. Warner
Eugene K. Buckley
Robert W. Wilson (Resident, Edwardsville, Illinois Office)
Edward M. Vokoun
Raymond J. Flunker
Robert J. Krehbiel

Attorneys for: Travelers Insurance Co.; Commercial Union; Firemen's Fund Insurance; Hartford Insurance; Liberty Mutual Insurance.

For Complete List of Firm Personnel, See General Section

For full biographical listings, see the Martindale-Hubbell Law Directory

GOLDSTEIN AND PRICE, L.C. (AV)

The Boatmen's Tower, Suite 1000, 100 North Broadway, 63102
Telephone: 314-421-0710
Telecopier: 314-421-2832

Hubert I. Binowitz (1933-1990)
Gary T. Sacks
Daryl F. Sohn
Robert Dale Nienhuis
John R. Halpern
Simon Tonkin
Alan K. Goldstein
Jeanne Knowles Townsend

OF COUNSEL

Elmer Price
Milton I. Goldstein

James K. Mondl
Douglas E. Gossow
Timothy I. Nicholson

Representative Clients: American River Transportation Co.; Apex Oil Co.; Commercial Union Insurance Cos.; Marine Office of America Corp.; Midland Enterprises Inc.; Peavey Barge Line, division of ConAgra, Inc.; Riverway Harbor Services, St. Louis, Inc.; Southern Towing Co.; GRE America.

For full biographical listings, see the Martindale-Hubbell Law Directory

LEWIS, RICE & FINGERSH (AV)

A Partnership including Partnerships and Individuals
500 North Broadway, Suite 2000, 63102-2147
Telephone: 314-444-7600
Telecopier: 314-241-6056
Clayton, Missouri Office: Suite 400, 8182 Maryland Avenue.
Telephone: 314-444-7600.
Belleville, Illinois Office: 325 South High Street.
Telephone: 618-234-8636.
Hays, Kansas Office: 201 W. 11th St.
Telephone: 913-625-3997.
Leawood, Kansas Office: Suite 375, 8900 State Line.
Telephone: 913-381-8898.
Kansas City, Missouri Office: 1010 Walnut, Suite 500.
Telephone: 816-421-2500.

RESIDENT PARTNERS

James W. Herron
Andrew Rothschild
James V. O'Brien

For Complete List of Firm Personnel, See General Section

For full biographical listings, see the Martindale-Hubbell Law Directory

THOMPSON & MITCHELL (AV)

One Mercantile Center, Suite 3300, 63101
Telephone: 314-231-7676
Telecopier: 314-342-1717
Belleville, Illinois Office: 525 West Main Street.
Telephone: 618-277-4700; 314-271-1800.
Telecopier: 618-236-3434.
St. Charles, Missouri Office: 200 North Third Street.
Telephone: 314-946-7717.
Telecopier: 314-946-4938.

(See Next Column)

THOMPSON & MITCHELL—*Continued*

Washington, D.C. Office: 700 14th Street, N.W., Suite 900.
Telephone: 202-508-1000.
Telecopier: 202-508-1010.

MEMBERS OF FIRM

Michael D. O'Keefe
Donald B. Dorwart
Raymond L. Massey
Gary Mayes
Allen D. Allred
William R. Bay
Jan Robey Alonzo
Nicholas J. Lamb

ASSOCIATES

David S. Corwin
Roger A. Keller, Jr.
T. Evan Schaeffer
Anthony G. Simon

WASHINGTON, D.C. OFFICE

MEMBERS OF FIRM

Barbara B. Powell
Gerald D. Stoltz
Marjorie F. Krumholz

Representative Clients: American Commercial Lines, Inc.; Ashland Oil & affiliated Companies; Clipper Cruise Line, Inc.; Continental Grain; Diamond M Company; Dixie Carriers, Inc.; Garvey International & Subsidiaries; Marine Equipment Management Corporation; Riverway Co.

For Complete List of Firm Personnel, See General Section

For full biographical listings, see the Martindale-Hubbell Law Directory

NEW JERSEY

*CAMDEN,** Camden Co.

BROWN & CONNERY (AV)

518 Market Street, P.O. Box 1449, 08101
Telephone: 609-365-5100
Facsimile: 609-858-4967
Westmont, New Jersey Office: 360 Haddon Avenue. P.O. Box 539.
Telephone: 609-854-8900.

MEMBERS OF FIRM

Thomas F. Connery, Jr.
William J. Cook
Warren W. Faulk
Dennis P. Blake
William M. Tambussi

Representative Clients: Delaware River Port Authority; Underwood-Memorial Hospital; Garden State Water Company; Honeywell, Inc.; Philadelphia Newspapers, Inc.; Port Authority Transit Co.; Resolution Trust Corp.; General Electric; Mercedes-Benz Credit Corp.; American Red Cross.

For Complete List of Firm Personnel, See General Section

For full biographical listings, see the Martindale-Hubbell Law Directory

*NEWARK,** Essex Co.

CARPENTER, BENNETT & MORRISSEY (AV)

(Formerly Carpenter, Gilmour & Dwyer)
Three Gateway Center, 17th Floor, 100 Mulberry Street, 07102-4079
Telephone: 201-622-7711
New York City: 212-943-6530
Telex: 139405
Telecopier: 201-622-5314
EasyLink: 62827845
ABA/net: CARPENTERB

MEMBER OF FIRM

John P. Dwyer

Reference: United Jersey Bank.

For Complete List of Firm Personnel, See General Section

For full biographical listings, see the Martindale-Hubbell Law Directory

GOLDSTEIN TILL & LITE (AV)

Suite 800, 744 Broad Street, 07102-3803
Telephone: 201-623-3000
FAX: 201-623-0858
Telex: 262320 USA UR

MEMBERS OF FIRM

Andrew J. Goldstein
Joseph J. DePalma

For full biographical listings, see the Martindale-Hubbell Law Directory

KENNY & STEARNS (AV)

56 Park Place, 07102
Telephone: 201-624-7779
New York, N.Y. Office: 26 Broadway.
Telephone: 212-422-6111.
FAX: 212-422-6544.

(See Next Column)

PARTNERS IN CHARGE

James M. Kenny
Joseph T. Stearns

For full biographical listings, see the Martindale-Hubbell Law Directory

MCCARTER & ENGLISH (AV)

Four Gateway Center, 100 Mulberry Street, P.O. Box 652, 07101-0652
Telephone: 201-622-4444
Telecopier: 201-624-7070
Cable Address: "McCarter" Newark
Cherry Hill, New Jersey Office: 1810 Chapel Avenue West.
Telephone: 609-662-8444.
Telecopier: 609-662-6203.
New York, New York Office: Suite 1519, One World Trade Center.
Telephone: 212-466-9018.
Telecopier: 212-432-6568.
Boca Raton, Florida Office: 2255 Glades Road, Suite 319-A.
Telephone: 407-994-6262.
Telecopier: 407-241-0798.
Wilmington, Delaware Office: Mellon Bank Center, 919 Market Street.
Telephone: 302-654-8010.
Telecopier: 302-654-0795.

MEMBERS OF FIRM

Thomas F. Daly
James F. Hammill (Resident Partner, Cherry Hill, New Jersey Office)

For Complete List of Firm Personnel, See General Section

For full biographical listings, see the Martindale-Hubbell Law Directory

WESTMONT, Camden Co.

BROWN & CONNERY (AV)

360 Haddon Avenue, P.O. Box 539, 08108
Telephone: 609-854-8900
Facsimile: 609-858-4967
Camden, New Jersey Office: 518 Market Street, P.O. Box 1449.
Telephone: 609-365-5100.
Telecopier: 609-858-4967.

MEMBERS OF FIRM

Thomas F. Connery, Jr.
William J. Cook
Warren W. Faulk
Dennis P. Blake
William M. Tambussi

Representative Clients: Delaware River Port Authority; Underwood-Memorial Hospital; Garden State Water Company; Honeywell, Inc. Philadelphia Newspapers, Inc.; Port Authority Transit Co.; Resolution Trust Corp.; General Electric; Mercedez-Benz Credit Corp.; American Red Cross.

For Complete List of Firm Personnel, See General Section

For full biographical listings, see the Martindale-Hubbell Law Directory

NEW YORK

*NEW YORK,** New York Co.

BADIAK WILL & MALOOF (AV)

Suite 1040 120 Broadway, 10271
Telephone: 212-376-6767
Telecopier: 212-376-6770
Telex: 6716686 BANDW
North Miami Beach, Florida Office: Badiak, Will & Kallen, 17071 West Dixie Highway, P.O. Box 600550.
Telephone: 305-945-1851.

MEMBERS OF FIRM

Roman Badiak
Alfred J. Will
Charles C. Goodenough
James J. Ruddy
John D. Kallen (Not admitted in NY; Resident, North Miami, Florida Office)
David L. Maloof (1924-1992)

ASSOCIATES

Paul A. Walsh
Stephen A. Frank
Lynn S. Waterman (Not admitted in NY; Resident, North Miami, Florida Office)

OF COUNSEL

Joseph B. McDonald

For full biographical listings, see the Martindale-Hubbell Law Directory

BECK & HALBERG (AV)

40 Exchange Place, 10005
Telephone: 212-344-7320
Cable Address: "Romherblaw New York"
Telex: 127345

(See Next Column)

BECK & HALBERG, *New York—Continued*

MEMBERS OF FIRM

Herbert B. Halberg
Elissa Panster (Not admitted in NY)

OF COUNSEL

Roman Beck (1904-1992)

For full biographical listings, see the Martindale-Hubbell Law Directory

BIGHAM ENGLAR JONES & HOUSTON (AV)

14 Wall Street, 10005-2140
Telephone: 212-732-4646
Cable: "Kedge"
RCA Telex: 235332 BEJHUR
Telefax: 2126190781 GR I II III; 2122279491 GR I II III
London, England Office: Lloyd's Suite 699, 1 Lime Street.
Telephone: 71-283-9541.
Telex: 893323 BEJH G.
Telefax: 016262382 GR I II III.
Newark, New Jersey Office: One Gateway Center.
Telephone: 201-643-1303.
Telecopier: 201-643-1124.
Washington, D.C. Office: 1919 Pennsylvania Avenue, N.W., Suite 300.
Telephone: 202-736-2150.
Telefax: 202-223-6739.
Long Beach, California Office: 301 Ocean Boulevard, Suite 800.
Telephone: 310-437-5155.
Telefax: 310-495-3273.

MEMBERS OF FIRM

Douglas A. Jacobsen
James S. McMahon, Jr.
John T. Kochendorfer
Louis G. Juliano
George R. Daly
John E. Cone, Jr.
Francis A. Montbach
Robert J. Phillips, Jr.
William R. Connor, III
Marilyn L. Lytle
Donald T. Rave, Jr.
Stephen V. Rible
Helen M. Benzie
Lawrence B. Brennan

ASSOCIATE

Frederick A. Lovejoy

For Complete List of Firm Personnel, See General Section

For full biographical listings, see the Martindale-Hubbell Law Directory

CHALOS & BROWN, P.C. (AV)

300 East 42nd Street, 10017-5982
Telephone: 212-661-5440
Telecopier: 212-697-8999
Telex: 238470 (RCA)
Clifton, New Jersey Office: 1118 Clifton Avenue.
Telephone: 201-779-1116.

Michael G. Chalos
Robert J. Brown
Harry A. Gavalas
Stephan Skoufalos
Thomas M. Russo
Martin F. Casey
Robert J. Seminara

Edward P. Flood
Timothy G. Hourican
Fred G. Wexler
Steven G. Friedberg
George J. Tsimis
Martin F. Marvet
Laurence Curran

References: Citibank, N.A.; Chase Manhattan Bank.

For full biographical listings, see the Martindale-Hubbell Law Directory

DE ORCHIS & PARTNERS (AV)

One Battery Park Plaza, Second Floor, 10004-1480
Telephone: 212-425-9797
Cable Address: "Deopartner"
Telex: 960-384
Telecopier: 212-509-7886
Union, New Jersey Office: 1495 Morris Avenue, P.O. Box 1718.
Telephone: 908-467-4740.
Telefax: 908-687-0255.

MEMBERS OF FIRM

M. E. De Orchis
Vincent M. De Orchis
John A. Orzel

OF COUNSEL
NEW JERSEY OFFICE

James J. Byrnes (Not admitted in NY)
John J. Guidera (Not admitted in NY)

ASSOCIATES

Arthur P. Zapolski
Kevin L. Gould

For full biographical listings, see the Martindale-Hubbell Law Directory

GILMARTIN, POSTER & SHAFTO (AV)

One William Street, 10004
Telephone: 212-425-3220
Telex: 235073
Cable Address: "Lawpost"
Telecopier: (212) 425-3130

MEMBERS OF FIRM

Richard A. Bertocci
Patrick J. Gilmartin
Michael C. Lambert
Joseph A. Lenczycki, Jr.
Harold S. Poster
Robert L. Poster
Donald B. Shafto

ASSOCIATE

William K. Sheehy

For full biographical listings, see the Martindale-Hubbell Law Directory

HEALY & BAILLIE (AV)

29 Broadway, 10006-3293
Telephone: 212-943-3980
Cable Address: "Mainbrace New York"
Telex: 422089
Telecopier: (212) 425-0131
MCI E-MAIL: 566-4694
Hong Kong Office: Luk Hoi Tong Building, Suite 1301, 31 Queen's Road Central.
Telephone: 852-2537-8628.
Telecopier: 852-2521-9072. MCI E-MAIL: 641-2689.

MEMBERS OF FIRM

Allan A. Baillie (1911-1983)
W. Cameron Beard
Andrew V. Buchsbaum
William N. France, II
Jack A. Greenbaum
Simon Harter
Jeremy J. Harwood
Nicholas J. Healy
John D. Kimball
John C. Koster
Andrew N. Krinsky
LeRoy Lambert
Philip S. LaPenta
Howard M. McCormack
Glen T. Oxton
Gordon W. Paulsen
Robert G. Shaw
Richard V. Singleton, II
Genrong Yu (Resident Partner, Hong Kong Office)

ASSOCIATES

Ronald Betancourt
Evanthia Coffee
Todd P. Kenyon
Matthew A. Marion
Cornelius J. O'Reilly
Susan Emma Olick
Shari M. Rubin

For full biographical listings, see the Martindale-Hubbell Law Directory

KENNY & STEARNS (AV)

26 Broadway, 10004
Telephone: 212-422-6111
FAX: 212-422-6544
Newark, New Jersey Office: 56 Park Place.
Telephone: 201-624-7779.

MEMBERS OF FIRM

James M. Kenny
Joseph T. Stearns
Stephen J. Buckley

William J. Manning, Jr.
Gino A. Zonghetti
Matthew Patrick McCloskey

For full biographical listings, see the Martindale-Hubbell Law Directory

LONDON FISCHER (AV)

375 Park Avenue, 10152
Telephone: 212-888-3636
Facsimile: 212-888-3974

MEMBERS OF FIRM

Bernard London
James L. Fischer
John W. Manning
Daniel Zemann, Jr.
John E. Sparling

ASSOCIATES

Richard S. Endres
Nicholas Kalfa
Evan D. Lieberman
Amy M. Kramer
Robert S. Sunshine
Robert M. Vecchione
John P. Bruen
Christina M. Ambrosio
William C. Nanis
Michael P. Mezzacappa
Douglas W. Hammond
Michael S. Leavy
Robert L. Honig

For full biographical listings, see the Martindale-Hubbell Law Directory

THOMAS M. MCCAFFREY (AV)

80 Wall Street, 10005
Telephone: 212-344-1953

For full biographical listings, see the Martindale-Hubbell Law Directory

New York—Continued

MENDES & MOUNT (AV)

750 Seventh Avenue, 10019
Telephone: 212-261-8000
Telecopier: 212-261-8750
Cable Address: "Menmount"
Telex: WUI 620392; 620332
Los Angeles, California Office: Citicorp Plaza, 725 South Figueroa Street, Nineteenth Floor.
Telephone: 213-955-7700.
Telecopy: 213-955-7725.
Telex: 6831520.
Cable Address: "MNDMT."
Newark, New Jersey Office: 1 Newark Center.
Telephone: 201-639-7300.
Fax: 201-639-7350.

MEMBER OF FIRM

William J. McAndrews

For full biographical listings, see the Martindale-Hubbell Law Directory

THACHER PROFFITT & WOOD (AV)

Two World Trade Center, 10048
Telephone: 212-912-7400
Cable Address: "Wallaces, New York"
Telex: 226733TPCW; 669578TPW
Facsimile: 212-912-7751; 912-7752
Washington, D.C. Office: 1500 K Street, N.W.
Telephone: 202-347-8400.
Facsimile: 202-347-6238.
White Plains, New York Office: 50 Main Street.
Telephone: 914-421-4100.
Facsimile: 914-421-4150/4151.

MEMBERS OF FIRM

Charles D. Brown
Joel B. Harris
Charles A. Dietzgen
Lauris G. L. Rall
John M. Woods

COUNSEL

Dwight B. Demeritt, Jr.
Edward C. Kalaidjian
Raymond S. Jackson, Jr.
Cornelius S. Van Rees

ASSOCIATES

A. James Cotins
Joseph G. Grasso
Gerald J. Ferguson
Maria M. Livanos
Usher T. Winslett

For Complete List of Firm Personnel, See General Section

For full biographical listings, see the Martindale-Hubbell Law Directory

WATSON, FARLEY & WILLIAMS (AV)

380 Madison Avenue, 10017
Telephone: 212-922-2200
Telex: 6790626 WFW NY
Fax: 212-922-1512
London, England Office: 15 Appold Street, London EC2A 2HB.
Telephone: (44 71) 814 8000.
Telex: 8955707 WFW LON G.
Fax: (44 71) 814 8141.
Paris, France Office: 19 rue de Marignan, 75008 Paris.
Telephone: (33 1) 45 63 15 15.
Telex: WFW PAR 651096 F.
Fax: (33 1) 45 61 09 01.
Oslo, Norway Office: Beddingen 8, Aker Brygge, 0250 Oslo.
Telephone: (47 22) 83 83 08.
Telex: 79209 WFW N.
Fax: (47 22) 83 83 13.
Athens, Greece Office: Alassia Building, Defteras Merarchias 13, 185-35 Piraeus.
Telephone: (30 1) 422 3660.
Telex: 24 1311 WFW GR.
Fax: (30 1) 422 3664.
Moscow, Russia Office: 36 Myaskovskovo Street, Moscow 121019.
Telephone: (7 502) 224 1700 (international only); (7 095) 291 8046/5968.
Fax: (7 502) 224 1701 (international only); (7 095) 202 9027.
Copenhagen, Denmark Office: Lille Kongensgade 20 DK-1074 Copenhagen K.
Telephone: (45 33) 91 33 03.
Fax: (45 33) 91 49 12.

MEMBERS OF FIRM

Derick W. Betts, Jr.
Alfred E. Yudes, Jr.
Leo Chang
Thatcher A. Stone
John E. Nelson II
Joseph G. Braunreuther
David N. Osborne
Peter S. Smedresman
John S. Osborne, Jr.
Philip H. Spector
R. Jay Fortin

For Complete List of Firm Personnel, See General Section

For full biographical listings, see the Martindale-Hubbell Law Directory

NORTH CAROLINA

*BEAUFORT,** Carteret Co.

DAVIS, MURRELLE & LUMSDEN, P.A. (AV)

Beaufort Professional Center, 412 Front Street, P.O. Box 819, 28516
Telephone: 919-728-4080
FAX: 919-728-3235

Edward L. Murrelle
Treve B. Lumsden

Janet M. Lyles

OF COUNSEL

Warren J. Davis

Representative Clients: NationsBank; Cooperative Bank for Savings; Zapata Haynie Corp.; Roman Catholic Diocese of Raleigh for Carteret County; International Longshoreman's Association Local 1807; Town of Cedar Point; John Yancey Corp.; Morehead City Export Terminal, Inc.; Morehead City Docking Masters Assoc., Inc.; Crow Hill Farms, Inc.

For full biographical listings, see the Martindale-Hubbell Law Directory

*WILMINGTON,** New Hanover Co.

CLARK, NEWTON, HINSON & MCLEAN, L.L.P. (AV)

509 Princess Street, 28401
Telephone: 910-762-8743
Facsimile: 910-762-6206

George T. Clark, Jr.
Reid G. Hinson
John Richard Newton
J. Dickson McLean

Representative Clients: North Carolina Natural Gas; North Carolina Shipping Assn. P&I CLUBS: The Britannia Club; Liverpool & London P&I Club; London Steamship Mutual P&I; Standard Steamship P&I; Steamship Mutual P&I Club; The Swedish Club; The Gard; United Kingdom Club; West of England Shipowners Mutual Insurance Assn.

For full biographical listings, see the Martindale-Hubbell Law Directory

MARSHALL, WILLIAMS & GORHAM, L.L.P. (AV)

14 South Fifth Street, P.O. Drawer 2088, 28402-2088
Telephone: 910-763-9891
Telecopier: 910-343-8604

MEMBERS OF FIRM

Lonnie B. Williams
John Dearman Martin
John L. Coble

Representative Clients: Almont Shipping Company; Skuld; Danish Shipowner's Defense Assoc.; McAllister Towing; Akzo Salt and Basic Chemical.

For Complete List of Firm Personnel, See General Section

For full biographical listings, see the Martindale-Hubbell Law Directory

ROUNTREE & SEAGLE, L.L.P. (AV)

2419 Market Street, P.O. Box 1409, 28402-1409
Telephone: 910-763-3404
Telecopier: 910-763-0320

MEMBERS OF FIRM

George Rountree, III
J. Harold Seagle
Charles M. Lineberry, Jr.

Representative Clients: American International Marine Agency; Fireman's Fund Insurance Cos.; The Japan Shipowners' Mutual Protection & Indemnity Assn., Ltd.
Approved Attorneys for: Chicago Title Insurance Co.; Commonwealth Land Insurance Co.; Investors Title Insurance Co.; Lawyers Title Insurance Corp.
References: Centura Bank; First Union National Bank of North Carolina; NationsBank of North Carolina, N.A.

For Complete List of Firm Personnel, See General Section

For full biographical listings, see the Martindale-Hubbell Law Directory

OHIO

*CINCINNATI,** Hamilton Co.

DINSMORE & SHOHL (AV)

1900 Chemed Center, 255 East Fifth Street, 45202-3172
Telephone: 513-977-8200
FAX: 513-977-8141
Florence, Kentucky Office: Turfway Ridge Office Park, 7300 Turfway Road, Suite 430 41042-1355.
Telephone: 606-283-0515.
FAX: 606-283-6017.

(See Next Column)

DINSMORE & SHOHL, *Cincinnati—Continued*

Dayton, Ohio Office: 500 Courthouse Plaza, S.W., 10 N. Ludlow Street, 45402-1834.
Telephone: 513-228-8012.
FAX: 513-461-2543.
Columbus, Ohio Office: NBD Bank Building, Suite 330, 175 South Third Street, 43215-5134.
Telephone: 614-224-7887.
FAX: 614-224-7882.

MEMBERS OF FIRM

Gordon C. Greene | Michael D. Eagen

For Complete List of Firm Personnel, See General Section

For full biographical listings, see the Martindale-Hubbell Law Directory

RENDIGS, FRY, KIELY & DENNIS (AV)

900 Central Trust Tower, 45202
Telephone: 513-381-9200
FAX: 513-381-9206
Courtesy Office: Kentucky National Bank Tower, Suite 1610, 50 East Rivercenter Boulevard, Covington, Kentucky.

MEMBER OF FIRM

Donald C. Adams, Jr.

Local Counsel for: Associated Aviation Underwriters; Commercial Union Assurance Co.; Continental National American Group; The Medical Protective Co.; St. Paul Insurance Co.; Sherwin-Williams; State Automobile Mutual Insurance Co.; U.S. Aviation Underwriters; Zurich Insurance Co.

For Complete List of Firm Personnel, See General Section

For full biographical listings, see the Martindale-Hubbell Law Directory

WAITE, SCHNEIDER, BAYLESS & CHESLEY CO., L.P.A. (AV)

1513 Central Trust Tower, Fourth and Vine Streets, 45202
Telephone: 513-621-0267
Fax: 513-381-2375; 621-0262

Stanley M. Chesley

Thomas F. Rehme
Fay E. Stilz
Louise M. Roselle
Dwight Tillery
D. Arthur Rabourn
Jerome L. Skinner
Janet G. Abaray
Paul M. De Marco
Terrence L. Goodman
Sherrill P. Hondorf
Colleen M. Hegge
Dianna Pendleton
Randy F. Fox
Glenn D. Feagan
Theresa L. Groh
Theodore N. Berry
Jane H. Walker
Renée Infante
Allen P. Grunes

OF COUNSEL

Jos. E. Rosen | James F. Keller

For full biographical listings, see the Martindale-Hubbell Law Directory

*CLEVELAND,** Cuyahoga Co.

RAY, ROBINSON, CARLE, DAVIES & SNYDER (AV)

1650 The East Ohio Building, 1717 East 9th Street, 44114-2898
Telephone: 216-861-4533
Telex: 810-421-8402
Cable Address: Lakelaw-Cleveland
Facsimile: 216-861-4568
Chicago, Illinois Office: 850 West Jackson Blvd, Suite 310.
Telephone: 312-421-3110.
Cable Address: Lakelaw-Chicago.
Facsimile: 312-421-2808.

MEMBERS OF FIRM

William D. Carle, III
David G. Davies
Michael A. Snyder, Ltd. (Resident at Chicago, Illinois Office)
Douglas R. Denny
Gene B. George
Julia R. Brouhard

ASSOCIATES

Robert T. Coniam
Sandra Maurer Kelly
Richard F. Schultz
Richard A. Forster (Resident at Chicago, Illinois Office)
William P. Ryan (Resident at Chicago, Illinois Office)
Charles A. Rozhon (Resident at Chicago, Illinois Office)
Shanshan Zhou (Resident at Chicago, Illinois Office)
Thomas More Wynne

OF COUNSEL

Lucian Y. Ray (1903-1987)
Theodore C. Robinson (Resident at Chicago, Illinois Office)

Representative Clients: Bethlehem Steel Corp., Great Lakes Steamship Division; U.S. Steel Corp., Great Lakes Fleet; Canada Steamship Lines; The M.A. Hanna Co.; Inland Steel Corp.; Assuranceforeningen Gard; Assuranceforeningen Skuld; West of England Shipowners P & I Assn., Ltd.; The London Steam-Ship Owners Insurance Assn.; Inland Lakes Management.

(See Next Column)

For full biographical listings, see the Martindale-Hubbell Law Directory

THOMPSON, HINE AND FLORY (AV)

1100 National City Bank Building, 629 Euclid Avenue, 44114-3070
Telephone: 216-566-5500
Fax: 216-566-5583
Telex: 980217
Cable Address: "Thomflor"
Akron, Ohio Office: 50 S. Main Street, Suite 502, 44308-1828.
Telephone: 216-376-8090.
Fax: 216-376-8386.
Cincinnati, Ohio Office: 312 Walnut Street, 14th Floor, 45202-4029.
Telephone: 513-352-6700.
Fax: 513-241-4771.
Telex: 938003.
Columbus, Ohio Office: One Columbus, 10 West Broad Street, 43215-3435.
Telephone: 614-469-3200.
Fax: 614-469-3361.
Dayton, Ohio Office: 2000 Courthouse Plaza, N.E., 45402-1706.
Telephone: 513-443-6600.
Fax: 513-443-6637; 443-6635.
Palm Beach, Florida Office: 125 Worth Avenue, Suite 117, 33480-4466.
Telephone: 407-833-5900.
Fax: 407-833-5951.
Washington, D.C. Office: 1920 N Street, N.W., 20036-1601.
Telephone: 202-331-8800.
Fax: 202-331-8330.
Telex: 904173.
Cable Address: "Caglaw".
Brussels, Belgium Office: Rue des Chevaliers, Ridderstraat 14 - B.10, B - 1050.
Telephone: 011(32-2) 511-9326.
Fax: 011(32-2) 513-9206.

MEMBERS OF FIRM

Douglas N. Barr
Richard C. Binzley
Thomas A. Heffernan
Harold W. Henderson

For Complete List of Firm Personnel, See General Section

For full biographical listings, see the Martindale-Hubbell Law Directory

*TOLEDO,** Lucas Co.

LACKEY, NUSBAUM, HARRIS, RENY & TORZEWSKI A LEGAL PROFESSIONAL ASSOCIATION (AV)

Two Maritime Plaza Third Floor, 43604
Telephone: 419-243-1105
Fax: 419-243-8953

Jay Harris | D. Michael Reny

References: Fifth Third Bank; Society Bank.

For full biographical listings, see the Martindale-Hubbell Law Directory

OREGON

*PORTLAND,** Multnomah Co.

LINDSAY, HART, NEIL & WEIGLER (AV)

Suite 3400, 1300 S.W. Fifth Avenue, 97201-5696
Telephone: 503-226-7677
Telecopier: 503-226-7697
Washington, D.C. Office: 1201 Pennsylvania Avenue, N.W., Suite 821, 20004.
Telephone: 202-467-8383.
Fax: 202-467-8581.

MEMBERS OF FIRM

Dennis J. Lindsay
Carl R. Neil
Jerard S. Weigler
Thomas E. McDermott

For Complete List of Firm Personnel, See General Section

For full biographical listings, see the Martindale-Hubbell Law Directory

MILLER, NASH, WIENER, HAGER & CARLSEN (AV)

111 S.W. Fifth Avenue, 97204-3699
Telephone: 503-224-5858
Telex: 364462, Kingmar PTL
Facsimile: 503-224-0155, 503-224-2450
Seattle, Washington Office: 4400 Two Union Square, 601 Union Street, 98101-2322.
Telephone: 206-622-8484.
Facsimile: 206-622-7485.

PORTLAND, OREGON PARTNERS

Dean D. DeChaine
Jeffrey J. Druckman
James F. Dulcich
M. Christie Helmer
Louis G. Henry

(See Next Column)

MILLER, NASH, WIENER, HAGER & CARLSEN—*Continued*

Representative Clients: The London Steam-Ship Owners' Mutual Insurance Assn., Ltd.; Mitsui Marine & Fire Insurance Co., Ltd.; The Charterers Mutual Assurance Association Limited; International Marine Underwriters; Ocean Marine Mutual Protection & Indemnity Assn.; Transmarine Mutual Assurance Assn.

For Complete List of Firm Personnel, See General Section

For full biographical listings, see the Martindale-Hubbell Law Directory

WOOD TATUM SANDERS & MURPHY (AV)

1001 S.W. Fifth Avenue, Suite 1300, 97204
Telephone: 503-224-5430
Cable Address: "Linwood"
Telex: 296522
Facsimile: 503-241-7235

MEMBERS OF FIRM

Robert I. Sanders
Craig C. Murphy
Kim Jefferies
Todd A. Zilbert

ASSOCIATE

John H. Chambers

Representative Clients: American President Lines, Ltd.; Assuranceforeningen Gard; Assuranceforeningen Skuld; Britannia Steam Ship Ins. Association, Ltd.; British Marine Mutual; Japan Ship Owners' Mutual P & I Assn.; Keystone Shipping Co.; Liverpool & London Steamship P & I; Mobil Oil Corp.; Newcastle P & I Assn.; North of England P & I Assoc.; Shipowners Claims Bureau; Shipowners Mutual P & I Assn.; Standard Steamship Owners P & I Assn.; Steamship Mutual Underwriting Assn.; Sveriges Angfartygs Assurans Forening; United Kingdom Mutual S.S.; West of England P & I Assn.

For Complete List of Firm Personnel, See General Section

For full biographical listings, see the Martindale-Hubbell Law Directory

PENNSYLVANIA

*PHILADELPHIA,** Philadelphia Co.

MARVIN I. BARISH LAW OFFICES A PROFESSIONAL CORPORATION (AV)

625 Walnut Street, Suite 801, 19106-3308
Telephone: 215-923-8900; 800-233-7101
Cable Address: "Marsbar-Philadelphia"
Fax: 215-351-0593

Marvin I. Barish

Robert J. Meyers
Stacey E. Barish
Timothy Garvey

For full biographical listings, see the Martindale-Hubbell Law Directory

CLARK, LADNER, FORTENBAUGH & YOUNG (AV)

One Commerce Square, 2005 Market Street, 19103
Telephone: 215-241-1800
Telex: 831462
Cable Address: "Clarklad"
Telecopier: 215-241-1857
Cherry Hill, New Jersey Office: Woodland Falls Corporate Park, 200 Lake Drive East, Suite 300.
Telephone: 609-779-0900.
Telecopier: 609-779-8720.
Conshohocken, Pennsylvania Office: Plymouth Corporate Center, 625 West Ridge Pike-Building E, Suite 300.
Telephone: 215-825-7000.
Fax: 215-825-1480.

MEMBERS OF FIRM

Edward V. Cattell, Jr. (Resident, Cherry Hill, New Jersey Office)
William G. Downey
Stuart M. Goldstein (Resident, Cherry Hill, New Jersey Office)
James W. Johnson
E. Michael Keating, III
Jeffrey S. Moller

CHERRY HILL, NEW JERSEY
RESIDENT ASSOCIATE

W. Steven Berman

Representative Clients: BP America Inc.; Express Marine Inc.; International Marine Underwriters; Maritrans Operating Partners L.P.; N.J. Commercial Fishermen's Association, Inc.; Pilots Association for the River & Bay Delaware; S.C. Loveland Company; Sunderland Marine Mutual Insurance Association, Ltd.; Viking Yacht Co.; Waterfront Corporation.

For Complete List of Firm Personnel, See General Section

For full biographical listings, see the Martindale-Hubbell Law Directory

KRUSEN EVANS & BYRNE (AV)

Suite 1100, The Curtis Center, 601 Walnut Street, 19106-3393
Telephone: 215-923-4400
Cable Address: "Kesel"
Telex: 83-4201
Telecopier: 215-925-0218
Westmont, New Jersey Office: Sentry Office Plaza, 216 Haddon Avenue, Suite 500, 08108-2813.
Telephone: 609-858-3444.
Telecopier: 609-858-6707.

MEMBERS OF FIRM

James F. Young
Joseph A. Barone
E. Alfred Smith
Thomas A. Bell
A. Robert Degen
James A. Yulman
Peter Hansen Bach (Resident, Westmont, New Jersey Office)
Robert S. Forster, Jr.
William C. Miller
Mary Elisa Reeves
Sandra L. Knapp

OF COUNSEL

Eugene R. Lippman

ASSOCIATES

Donna L. Adelsberger
Gabriel Dino Cieri
Yolanda A. Konopacka
Diana L. Moro-Bishop
Robert M. Kline
Susan J. Wiener
June A. Taima (Not admitted in PA)

For Complete List of Firm Personnel, See General Section

For full biographical listings, see the Martindale-Hubbell Law Directory

LEVIN, FISHBEIN, SEDRAN & BERMAN (AV)

Suite 600, 320 Walnut Street, 19106
Telephone: 215-592-1500
Fax: 215-592-4663

MEMBERS OF FIRM

Arnold Levin
Michael D. Fishbein
Howard J. Sedran
Laurence S. Berman
Frederick S. Longer

Robert M. Unterberger
Craig D. Ginsburg
Jonathan Shub
Cheryl R. Brown Hill
Roberta Shaner

For full biographical listings, see the Martindale-Hubbell Law Directory

MATTIONI, MATTIONI & MATTIONI, LTD. (AV)

399 Market Street, 2nd Floor, 19106
Telephone: 215-629-1600
Cable Address: "Mattioni"
TWX: 710-670-1373
Fax: 215-923-2 227
Westmont, New Jersey Office: Suite 502 Sentry Office Plaza, 216 Haddon Avenue, 08108.
Telephone: 609-772-0098.

Dante Mattioni
Faustino Mattioni
John Mattioni
Blasco Mattioni *
Eugene Mattioni
Kenneth M. Giannantonio
Francis X. Kelly
George R. Zacharkow
Andrew H. Quinn
Eva Helena Bleich
Robert W. Weidner, Jr.
Scott J. Schwarz
Stephen M. Martin
Robert R. Hyde
Bruce A. O'Neill
John J. Sellinger
Stephen J. Galati
Anthony Granato
Kristi L. Treadway
Philip J. Ford
Joseph F. Bouvier
Michael Mattioni
John E. Minihan
Alan Mattioni
Louis J. Apoldo
Joseph P. Corcoran III
Scott William Barton
Heather A. Cicalese
Frank Carano *

LEGAL SUPPORT PERSONNEL

PARALEGALS

Rosaria Tesauro
Carmela Valeno
Tracey L. Smith
Andrea L. D'Alessandro
Linda A. Morris
Karen L. Knauss

*Counsel to the Firm

For full biographical listings, see the Martindale-Hubbell Law Directory

PALMER BIEZUP & HENDERSON (AV)

Suite 956 Public Ledger Building, 620 Chestnut Street Independence Mall West, 19106-3409
Telephone: 215-625-9900
Cable Address: "Palmbee" Phila
Telex: ITT: 476-1102
FAX: 215-625-0185
New York, New York Office: 53 Wall Street, 10005.
Telephone: 212-406-1855.
Fax: 215-625-0185.
Telex: ITT 476-1102.

(See Next Column)

PALMER BIEZUP & HENDERSON, *Philadelphia—Continued*

Wilmington, Delaware Office: 1223 Foulk Road, 19803.
Telephone: 302-594-0895.
Fax: 215-625-0185.
Telex: ITT 476-1102.
Camden, New Jersey Office: 211 North 5th Street. 08102-1203.
Telephone: 609-428-7717.
Fax: 215-625-0185.
Telex: ITT 476-1102.

MEMBERS OF FIRM

Richard W. Palmer
J. Welles Henderson
Raul Betancourt
Alfred J. Kuffler
Michael B. McCauley
Stephen M. Calder
Richard Q. Whelan
Timothy J. Abeel
Frank P. De Giulio
Kevin G. O'Donovan

David P. Thompson
Gary Francis Seitz
Richard C. Mason
Richard S. Tweedie
Peter J. Williams
Betsy A. Stone
Jon Michael Dumont
Lawrence D. Jackson
James J. Musial
Kevin Haney
Thomas P. Mundy
Paul D. Rowe, Jr.

COUNSEL

Raymond T. Letulle
H. Coleman Switkay

For full biographical listings, see the Martindale-Hubbell Law Directory

RAWLE & HENDERSON (AV)

(Rawle Law Offices Founded 1783)
The Widener Building, One South Penn Square, 19107
Telephone: 215-575-4200
Cable Address: "Rawle" Philadelphia
Telex: 83-4286
Telecopier: 215-563-2583
Marlton, New Jersey Office: Suite 104, Ten Lake Center Executive Park, 401 Route 73 North.
Telephone: 609-596-4800.
Telecopier: 609-596-6164.

Henry C. Lucas, III
Carl D. Buchholz, III

David A. O'Brien
Lawrence D. Wright
Michael P. Zipfel

For Complete List of Firm Personnel, See General Section

For full biographical listings, see the Martindale-Hubbell Law Directory

SCANLAN AND SCANLAN, A PROFESSIONAL CORPORATION (AV)

Suite 701, One Penn Square West, 30 South 15th Street, 19102
Telephone: 215-564-6399
Cable Address: "Scanlan"
Telecopier: 215-564-2242

Francis A. Scanlan
Francis X. Scanlan
Ricardo A. Byron

For full biographical listings, see the Martindale-Hubbell Law Directory

*PITTSBURGH,** Allegheny Co.

BUCHANAN INGERSOLL, PROFESSIONAL CORPORATION (AV)

5800 USX Tower, 600 Grant Street, 15219
Telephone: 412-562-8800
Telecopier: 412-562-1041
Philadelphia, Pennsylvania Office: Two Logan Square, Twelfth Floor, 18th & Arch Streets.
Telephone: 215-665-8700.
Harrisburg, Pennsylvania Office: Vartan Parc, 30 North Third Street.
Telephone: 717-237-4800.
Tampa, Florida Office: 101 East Kennedy Boulevard, Suite 1030.
Telephone: 813-222-8180.
North Miami Beach, Florida Office: 19495 Biscayne Boulevard.
Telephone: 305-933-5600.
Lexington, Kentucky Office: 1210 Vine Center Office Tower, 333 West Vine Street.
Telephone: 606-225-5333.
Princeton, New Jersey Office: Buchanan Ingersoll, A Partnership, College Centre, 500 College Road East.
Telephone: 609-452-2666.

Michael J. Flinn

For Complete List of Firm Personnel, See General Section

For full biographical listings, see the Martindale-Hubbell Law Directory

GACA, MATIS & HAMILTON, A PROFESSIONAL CORPORATION (AV)

300 Four PPG Place, 15222-5404
Telephone: 412-338-4750
Fax: 412-338-4742

(See Next Column)

Giles J. Gaca
Thomas A. Matis
Mark R. Hamilton
John W. Jordan, IV
Alan S. Baum
Thomas P. McGinnis
Bernard R. Rizza
Jeffrey A. Ramaley
Stephen J. Dalesio
John Timothy Hinton, Jr.
Shawn Lynne Reed

LEGAL SUPPORT PERSONNEL

PARALEGALS

Tina M. Shanafelt
Jill M. Peterson

For full biographical listings, see the Martindale-Hubbell Law Directory

POLITO & SMOCK, P.C. (AV)

Suite 400, Four Gateway Center, 15222
Telephone: 412-394-3333
Fax: 412-232-1799

Anthony J. Polito
Leonard Fornella

Robert J. Henderson

For full biographical listings, see the Martindale-Hubbell Law Directory

RHODE ISLAND

*PROVIDENCE,** Providence Co.

HANSON, CURRAN, PARKS & WHITMAN (AV)

146 Westminster Street, 02903-2218
Telephone: 401-421-2154
Telecopier: 401-521-7040

Kirk Hanson (1948-1991)

MEMBERS OF FIRM

A. Lauriston Parks
David P. Whitman
Michael T. F. Wallor
Robert D. Parrillo
Dennis J. McCarten
James T. Murphy
Seth E. Bowerman
Thomas R. Bender

ASSOCIATES

Amy Beretta
Mark W. Dana
Richard H. Burrows
Daniel P. McKiernan

OF COUNSEL

William A. Curran

General Counsel for: Medical Malpractice Joint Underwriting Association of Rhode Island.
Rhode Island Counsel for: Amica Mutual Insurance Co.; CIGNA; St. Paul Insurance Cos.; Occidental Life Insurance Co.; Exchange Mutual Insurance Co.; Aetna Casualty & Surety Co.

For full biographical listings, see the Martindale-Hubbell Law Directory

VINCENT D. MORGERA (AV)

One Old Stone Square, 02903-7104
Telephone: 401-456-0300
Telecopier: 401-456-0303

For full biographical listings, see the Martindale-Hubbell Law Directory

SOUTH CAROLINA

*CHARLESTON,** Charleston Co.

BUIST, MOORE, SMYTHE & MCGEE, P.A. (AV)

Successors to Buist, Buist, Smythe and Smythe and Moore, Mouzon and McGee.
Five Exchange Street, P.O. Box 999, 29402
Telephone: 803-722-3400
Cable Address: "Conferees"
Telex: 57-6488
Telecopier: 803-723-7398
North Charleston, South Carolina Office: Atrium Northwood Office Building, 7301 Rivers Avenue, Suite 288. Zip: 29406-2859.
Telephone: 803-797-3000.
Telecopier: 803-863-5500.

Benj. Allston Moore, Jr.
Gordon D. Schreck

David M. Collins
Douglas M. Muller

Representative Clients: Transport Mutual Services, Inc.; Turnabout Services, Inc.; Lamorte Burns & Co., Inc.; Shipowners Claims Bureau, Inc.; MOAC; Home Insurance Co. (Hull and Marin Risks); Frank B. Hall & Co., Inc.;

(See Next Column)

BUIST, MOORE, SMYTHE & MCGEE P.A.—*Continued*

Japan Shipowners Mutual P & I Co.; All English and Scandinavian P & I Clubs; White Stack Towing; Lykes Bros. Steamship Co. Inc.

For Complete List of Firm Personnel, See General Section

For full biographical listings, see the Martindale-Hubbell Law Directory

SINKLER & BOYD, P.A. (AV)

160 East Bay Street, P.O. Box 340, 29402-0340
Telephone: 803-722-3366
FAX: 803-722-2266
Columbia, South Carolina Office: Suite 1200 The Palmetto Center, 1426 Main Street, P.O. Box 11889.
Telephone: 803-779-3080.
FAX: 803-765-1243.
Greenville, South Carolina Office: 15 South Main Street, Suite 500, Wachovia Building, P.O. Box 275.
Telephone: 803-467-1100.
FAX: 803-467-1521.

Stephen E. Darling
Marvin D. Infinger
Bert Glenn Utsey III

Edward K. Pritchard III

Representative Clients: Allsouth Stevedoring Co.; Metal Trades, Inc.; Palmetto Shipping & Stevedoring Co.; Carolina Maritime Co.; Strachan Shipping Co.; Charleston Line Handling, Inc.; Swygert Shipyards, Inc.; Stevens Shipping Co.

For Complete List of Firm Personnel, See General Section

For full biographical listings, see the Martindale-Hubbell Law Directory

*COLUMBIA,** Richland Co.

SINKLER & BOYD, P.A. (AV)

Suite 1200 The Palmetto Center, 1426 Main Street, P.O. Box 11889, 29211-1889
Telephone: 803-779-3080
FAX: 803-765-1243
Charleston, South Carolina Office: 160 East Bay Street, P.O. Box 340.
Telephone: 803-722-3366.
FAX: 803-722-2266.
Greenville, South Carolina Office: 15 South Main Street, Suite 500, Wachovia Building, P.O. Box 275.
Telephone: 803-467-1100.
FAX: 803-467-1521.

Charles H. Gibbs (1915-1993)
Stephen E. Darling (Resident, Charleston Office)
Marvin D. Infinger (Resident, Charleston Office)
Bert Glenn Utsey III (Resident, Charleston Office)

Edward K. Pritchard, III (Resident, Charleston Office)

Representative Clients: Allsouth Stevedoring Co.; Metal Trades, Inc.; Palmetto Shipping & Stevedoring Co.; Carolina Maritime Co.; Strachan Shipping Co.; Charleston Line Handling, Inc.; Swygert Shipyards, Inc.; Stevens Shipping Co.

For Complete List of Firm Personnel, See General Section

For full biographical listings, see the Martindale-Hubbell Law Directory

TENNESSEE

*MEMPHIS,** Shelby Co.

BATEMAN & CHILDERS (AV)

Suite 1010 Cotton Exchange Building, 65 Union Avenue, P.O. Box 3351, 38173-0351
Telephone: 901-526-0412
Telecopier: (901) 525-8466

MEMBERS OF FIRM

William C. Bateman, Jr.
Jack Alford Childers, Jr.

For Complete List of Firm Personnel, See General Section

For full biographical listings, see the Martindale-Hubbell Law Directory

FARRIS, HANCOCK, GILMAN, BRANAN & HELLEN (AV)

50 North Front Street, Suite 1400, 38103
Telephone: 901-576-8200
Fax: 901-576-8250
East Memphis, Tennessee Office: Suite 400 United American Bank Building, 5384 Poplar Avenue.
Telephone: 901-763-4000.
Fax: 901-763-4095.

(See Next Column)

MEMBERS OF FIRM

G. Ray Bratton
Eugene Stone Forrester, Jr.

ASSOCIATE

Gregory W. O'Neal

For Complete List of Firm Personnel, See General Section

For full biographical listings, see the Martindale-Hubbell Law Directory

MARTIN, TATE, MORROW & MARSTON, P.C. (AV)

The Falls Building, Suite 1100, 22 North Front Street, 38103-1182
Telephone: 901-522-9000
Telecopier: 901-527-3746

W. Emmett Marston
Lee L. Piovarcy
William Joseph Landers, II

For Complete List of Firm Personnel, See General Section

For full biographical listings, see the Martindale-Hubbell Law Directory

TEXAS

*BEAUMONT,** Jefferson Co.

BENCKENSTEIN & OXFORD, L.L.P. (AV)

First Interstate Bank Building, P.O. Box 150, 77704
Telephone: 409-833-9182
Cable Address: "Bmor"
Telex: 779485
Telefax: 409-833-8819
Austin, Texas Office: Suite 810, 400 West 15th Street, 78701.
Telephone: 512-474-8586.
Telefax: 512-478-3064.

MEMBERS OF FIRM

L. J. Benckenstein (1894-1966)
F. L. Benckenstein (1918-1987)
Hubert Oxford, III
Alan G. Sampson
Frank D. Calvert
Dana Timaeus
Mary Ellen Blade
William H. Yoes
William M. Tolin, III
Kip Kevin Lamb
Frances Blair Bethea
Robert J. Rose, Sr.

ASSOCIATES

Susan J. Oliver
F. Blair Clarke
Keith A. Pardue (Resident, Austin, Texas Office)
Josiah Wheat, Jr.
Steve Johnson
Michael Keith Eaves
Nikki L. Redden

Representative Clients: Marine Office of American Corporation (MOAC); Moran Towing and Transportation Co., Inc.

For Complete List of Firm Personnel, See General Section

For full biographical listings, see the Martindale-Hubbell Law Directory

MEHAFFY & WEBER, A PROFESSIONAL CORPORATION (AV)

2615 Calder Avenue, P.O. Box 16, 77704
Telephone: 409-835-5011
Fax: 409-835-5729; 835-5177
Orange, Texas Office: 1006 Green Avenue, P.O. Drawer 189.
Telephone: 409-886-7766.
Houston, Texas Office: One Allen Center, 500 Dallas, Suite 1200.
Telephone: 713-655-1200.

James W. Mehaffy (1914-1985)
Dewey J. Gonsoulin
Daniel V. Flatten
M. C. Carrington

OF COUNSEL

Otto J. Weber, Jr.

Representative Clients: Southern Pacific Lines; E.I. du Pont de Nemours and Company; Bethlehem Steel Corp.; The Kansas City Southern Railway Co.; FMC Corp.; Eli Lilly & Company; Merrell Dow; Jefferson County Tax Appraisal District.
Approved Attorneys for: Stewart Title Guaranty Co.

For Complete List of Firm Personnel, See General Section

For full biographical listings, see the Martindale-Hubbell Law Directory

WELLS, PEYTON, BEARD, GREENBERG, HUNT & CRAWFORD, L.L.P. (AV)

6th Floor, Petroleum Building, P.O. Box 3708, 77704-3708
Telephone: 409-838-2644
FAX: 409-838-4713

MEMBERS OF FIRM

Walter J. Crawford, Jr.
Joseph Martin Green
Mark Freeman

ASSOCIATE

Randall D. Collins

(See Next Column)

WELLS, PEYTON, BEARD, GREENBERG, HUNT & CRAWFORD L.L.P., *Beaumont—Continued*

OF COUNSEL

Louis H. Beard

For Complete List of Firm Personnel, See General Section

For full biographical listings, see the Martindale-Hubbell Law Directory

*CORPUS CHRISTI,** Nueces Co.

WHITE, HUSEMAN, PLETCHER & POWERS (AV)

600 Leopard Street, Suite 2100, P.O. Box 2707, 78403-2707
Telephone: 512-883-3563
Fax: 512-883-0210

David Yancey White

Reference: First City Bank, Corpus Christi, Texas.

For full biographical listings, see the Martindale-Hubbell Law Directory

*HOUSTON,** Harris Co.

BAKER & BOTTS, L.L.P. (AV)

One Shell Plaza, 910 Louisiana, 77002
Telephone: 713-229-1234
Cable Address: "Boterlove"
Fax: 713-229-1522
Washington, D.C. Office: The Warner, 1299 Pennsylvania Avenue, N.W.
Telephone: 202-639-7700.
New York, New York Office: 885 Third Avenue, Suite 2000.
Telephone: 212-705-5000.
Austin, Texas Office: 1600 San Jacinto Center, 98 San Jacinto Boulevard.
Telephone: 512-322-2500.
Dallas, Texas Office: 2001 Ross Avenue.
Telephone: 214-953-6500.
Moscow, Russian Federation Office: 10 ul. Pushkinskaya, 103031.
Telephone: 7095/921-5300 (Local); 7095/929-7070 (International).

MEMBER OF FIRM

Joseph D. Cheavens

ASSOCIATES

Nancy K. Archer-Yanochik
William C. Bullard
James M. Grace, Jr.
M. Lamont Jones

For Complete List of Firm Personnel, See General Section

For full biographical listings, see the Martindale-Hubbell Law Directory

BILLINGS & SOLOMON, P.C. (AV)

460 Riviana Building, 2777 Allen Parkway, 77019-2174
Telephone: 713-528-2111
Telex: 775-533.
Fax: 713-528-0980

Frank E. Billings
Cecil L. Solomon

Richard P. Martini
Ford C. Thanheiser
James C. Bollom

For full biographical listings, see the Martindale-Hubbell Law Directory

BROWN, SIMS, WISE & WHITE, A PROFESSIONAL CORPORATION (AV)

One Post Oak Central, 21st Floor, 2000 Post Oak Boulevard, 77056-4496
Telephone: 713-629-1580
Fax: 713-629-5027
Telex: 775557

G. Byron Sims
James D. Wise, Jr.
Ronald L. White
Kenneth G. Engerrand
Lyn Van Dusen
Thomas O. Deen
Innes Alexander Henderson Mackillop
James N. Isbell
Gregory M. Sullivan

OF COUNSEL

Thomas A. Brown

Polly A. Kinnibrugh
Charles M. Brackett
Deanna H. Brewer
Thomas W. Burch, III
Michael D. Williams
Richard E. Hanson
Mark C. Clemer
James R. Koecher
Randa L. Duncan
Ronnie W. Baham, Jr.
John R. Walker
William A. Galerston
Robert J. Hamm
Cynthia A. Galvan
Michael A. Varner
Stephen T. Smith
Walter Joseph Gallant
Philip Robert Brinson
Marc C. Mayfield
Gus David Oppermann, V
Douglas J. Shoemaker
Christopher A. Kesler
Monica A. Fekete
Leslie Downs Geer

For full biographical listings, see the Martindale-Hubbell Law Directory

PHELPS DUNBAR, L.L.P. (AV)

Suite 501, 4 Houston Center, 1331 Lamar Street, 77010
Telephone: 713-659-1386
Telecopier: 713-659-1388
New Orleans, Louisiana Office: Texaco Center, 400 Poydras Street.
Telephone 504-566-1311.
Telecopier: 504-568-9130, 504-568-9007.
Cable Address: "Howspencer."
Telex: 584125 WU.
Telex: 6821155 WUI.
Baton Rouge, Louisiana Office: Suite 701, City National Bank Building, P.O. Box 4412.
Telephone: 504-346-0285.
Telecopier: 504-381-9197.
Jackson, Mississippi Office: Suite 500, Security Centré North, 200 South Lamar Street, P.O. Box 23066.
Telephone: 601-352-2300.
Telecopier: 601-360-9777.
Tupelo, Mississippi Office: Seventh Floor, One Mississippi Plaza, P.O. Box 1220.
Telephone: 601-842-7907.
Telecopier: 601-842-3873.
London, England Office: Suite 976, Level 9, Lloyd's, 1 Lime Street London EC3M 7DQ England.
Telephone: 011-44-171-929-4765.
Telecopier: 011-44-171-929-0046.
Telex: 987321.

RESIDENT PARTNERS

Kent E. Westmoreland
Julia Marie Adams

RESIDENT ASSOCIATES

Evan T. Caffrey
Laura E. Cormier
Malinda York Crouch
John C. Cunningham
Richard Leo Harrell
Karen Klaas Milhollin
John L. Schouest

Representative Clients: Americas Insurance Company; Edison Chouest Offshore, Inc.; ENTEX, A Division of NORAM; GATX Terminals Corp.; Global Industries; John E. Chance & Associates, Inc.; McDonough Marine Service, A Division of MARMAC Corp.; Southern Marine & Aviation Underwriters, Inc.; Underwriters at Lloyd's, London; Various I.L.U. Companies.

For full biographical listings, see the Martindale-Hubbell Law Directory

JAMES E. ROSS & ASSOCIATES (AV)

3209 Montrose Boulevard, 77006
Telephone: 713-523-8087
Telecopier: 713-523-8224

Edwin K. Nelson, IV

For full biographical listings, see the Martindale-Hubbell Law Directory

ROYSTON, RAYZOR, VICKERY & WILLIAMS, L.L.P. (AV)

2200 Texas Commerce Tower, 77002-2913
Telephone: 713-224-8380
Cable Address: "Houport"
Telex: 6869017
Telecopier: 713-225-9945
Galveston, Texas Office: 205 Cotton Exchange Building, 2102 Mechanic Street.
Telephone: 409-763-1623.
Cable Address: "Royston"
Telex: 765-449.
Telecopier: 409-763-3853.
Brownsville, Texas Office: 55 Cove Circle, P.O. Box 3509.
Telephone: 210-542-4377.
Cable Address: "Padre"
Telex: 767-817.
Telecopier: 210-542-4370.
Corpus Christi, Texas Office: 1700 Wilson Plaza West, 606 North Carancahua.
Telephone: 512-884-8808.
Cable Address: "CC PORT"
Telex: 6866625.
Telecopier: 512-884-7261.

OF COUNSEL

Decatur J. Holcombe

PARTNERS

Edward D. Vickery
Gus A. Schill, Jr.
Ben L. Reynolds
Kenneth D. Kuykendall
Ted C. Litton
William M. Jensen
W. Robins Brice
James P. Cooney
Bradley A. Jackson
Robert H. Etnyre, Jr.
James G. Blain, II
John M. Elsley
David R. Walker
Tobi A. Tabor
John F. Unger
Mark Cohen
William R. Towns
Marilyn Tanner Hebinck
Kim J. Fletcher

(See Next Column)

ROYSTON, RAYZOR, VICKERY & WILLIAMS L.L.P.—*Continued*

Representative Clients: G & H Towing Co.; Lykes Bros. Steamship Co., Inc.; American International Underwriters Corp.; West of England Steam Ship Owners' Protection and Indemnity Assn., Ltd.; The United Kingdom Mutual Steam Ship Assurance Assn. Ltd.; Underwriter at Lloyds; Institute of London Underwriters.

For Complete List of Firm Personnel, See General Section

For full biographical listings, see the Martindale-Hubbell Law Directory

SCHWARTZ & CAMPBELL, L.L.P. (AV)

1221 McKinney, Suite 1000, 77010
Telephone: 713-752-0017
Telecopier: 713-752-0327

Richard A. Schwartz
Marshall S. Campbell

Monica F. Oathout
Stephen A. Mendel
Samuel E. Dunn
Harold W. Hargis
Phillip W. Bechter
Laura M. Taylor
Michael D. Hudgins

LEGAL SUPPORT PERSONNEL

PARALEGALS

Nannette Koger
Bettye Vaughan Johnson
Lenore Chomout
Maria Pinillos

For full biographical listings, see the Martindale-Hubbell Law Directory

VINSON & ELKINS L.L.P. (AV)

2300 First City Tower, 1001 Fannin, 77002-6760
Telephone: 713-758-2222
Fax: 713-758-2346
International Telex: 6868314
Cable Address: Vinelkins
Austin, Texas Office: One American Center, 600 Congress Avenue.
Telephone: 512-495-8400.
Fax: 512-495-8612.
Dallas, Texas Office: 3700 Trammell Crow Center, 2001 Ross Avenue.
Telephone: 214-220-7700.
Fax: 214-220-7716.
Washington, D.C. Office: The Willard Office Building, 1455 Pennsylvania Avenue, N.W.
Telephone: 202-639-6500.
Fax: 202-639-6604.
Cable Address: Vinelkins.
London, England Office: 47 Charles Street, Berkeley Square, London, W1X 7PB, England.
Telephone: 011 (44-171) 491-7236.
Fax: 011 (44-71) 499-5320.
Cable Address: Vinelkins London W.1.
Moscow, Russian Federation Office: 16 Alexey Tolstoy Street, Second Floor, Moscow, 103001 Russian Federation.
Telephone: 011 (70-95) 956-1995.
Telecopy: 011 (70-95) 956-1996.
Mexico City, Mexico Office: Aristóteles 77, 5°Piso, Colonia Chapultepec Polanco, 11560 Mexico, D.F.
Telephone: (52-5) 280-7828.
Fax: (52-5) 280-9223.
Singapore Office: 50 Raffles Place, #19-05 Shell Tower, 0104. U.S. Voice Mailbox: 713-758-3500.
Telephone: (65) 536-8300.
Fax: (65) 536-8311.

Theodore G. Dimitry
Eugene J. Silva

ASSOCIATES

Joël Elaine Baird
Timothy K. Borchers
Daniel S. Cahill
Matthew D. Eisele
Joshua S. Force
Dana C. Livingston
Thomas Nork
Kevin Michael O'Gorman
Frank A. Parigi
Jeffrey L. Raizner

For Complete List of Firm Personnel, See General Section

For full biographical listings, see the Martindale-Hubbell Law Directory

VIRGINIA

MCLEAN, Fairfax Co.

H. CLAYTON COOK, JR. (AV)

1011 Langley Hill Drive, 22101
Telephone: 703-821-2468
Rapifax: 703-821-2469
Washington, D.C. Office: 2828 Pennsylvania Avenue, N.W. 20007.
Telephone: 202-338-8088.
Rapifax: 202-338-1843.

For full biographical listings, see the Martindale-Hubbell Law Directory

NORFOLK, (Independent City)

CRENSHAW, WARE AND MARTIN, P.L.C. (AV)

Suite 1200 NationsBank Center, One Commercial Place, 23510-2111
Telephone: 804-623-3000
FAX: 804-623-5735

Francis N. Crenshaw
Guilford D. Ware
Howard W. Martin, Jr.
Timothy A. Coyle
Ann K. Sullivan
James L. Chapman, IV
John T. Midgett
Martha M. Poindexter

Melanie Fix
David H. Sump
Donald C. Schultz
Kristen L. Hodeen

Representative Clients: American International Group; Cargill, Inc.; Exxon Co., U.S.A.; Norfolk Dredging Co.; Ramsey Scarlett & Co., Inc.

For full biographical listings, see the Martindale-Hubbell Law Directory

RABINOWITZ, RAFAL, SWARTZ, TALIAFERRO & GILBERT, P.C. (AV)

Wainwright Building, Suite 700, 229 West Bute Street, P.O. Box 3332, 23514
Telephone: 804-622-3931; 623-6674
FAX: 804-626-1003

Ralph Rabinowitz

For full biographical listings, see the Martindale-Hubbell Law Directory

VANDEVENTER, BLACK, MEREDITH & MARTIN (AV)

500 World Trade Center, 23510
Telephone: 804-446-8600
Cable Address: "Hughsvan"
Telex: 823-671
Telecopier: 446-8670
North Carolina, Kitty Hawk Office: 6 Juniper Trail.
Telephone: 919-261-5055.
Fax: 919-261-8444.
London, England Office: Suite 692, Level 6, Lloyd's, 1 Lime Street.
Telephone: (071) 623-2081.
Facsimile: (071) 929-0043.
Telex: 987321.

MEMBERS OF FIRM

Walter B. Martin, Jr.
Charles F. Tucker
Morton H. Clark
John M. Ryan
George William Birkhead
Carter T. Gunn
Henry P. Bouffard

For Complete List of Firm Personnel, See General Section

For full biographical listings, see the Martindale-Hubbell Law Directory

WASHINGTON

*SEATTLE,** King Co.

JOHN S. CONGALTON (AV)

5700 Columbia Center, 701 Fifth Avenue, 98104-7094
Telephone: 206-623-8300
Fax: 206-292-9736

For full biographical listings, see the Martindale-Hubbell Law Directory

GARVEY, SCHUBERT & BARER (AV)

1191 Second Avenue, 18th Floor, 98101
Telephone: 206-464-3939
Cable Address: "Lex, Seattle"
Telex: 32-1037
Telecopier: 206-464-0125
Washington, D.C. Office: 5th Floor, 1000 Potomac Street, N.W., 20007.
Telephone: 202-965-7880.
Telecopier: 202-965-1729.
Portland, Oregon Office: Eleventh Floor, 121 S.W. Morrison Street, 97204.
Telephone: 503-228-3939.
Telecopier: 503-226-0259.

MEMBERS OF FIRM

Barbara L. Holland
Stephen B. Johnson
James G. Kibble
E. Charles Routh
Alan P. Sherbrooke
Gary J. Strauss
Donald P. Swisher
David R. West

RESIDENT ASSOCIATES

Pegeen Mulhern
Carol L. Saboda
Donald B. Scaramastra
Susan Richardson Willert

(See Next Column)

GARVEY, SCHUBERT & BARER, *Seattle—Continued*

OF COUNSEL

Stanley H. Barer | M. John Bundy

Representative Clients: B.P. America, Inc.; China Ocean Shipping (Group) Company; Foss Maritime Co.; Totem Ocean Trailer Express, Inc.; United Kingdom Mutual Steamship Assurance Assn.

For Complete List of Firm Personnel, See General Section

For full biographical listings, see the Martindale-Hubbell Law Directory

WEST VIRGINIA

*CHARLESTON,** Kanawha Co.

JACKSON & KELLY (AV)

1600 Laidley Tower, P.O. Box 553, 25322
Telephone: 304-340-1000
Fax: 304-340-1130
Martinsburg, West Virginia Office: 300 Foxcroft Avenue, P.O. Box 1068.
Telephone: 304-263-8800.
Morgantown, West Virginia Office: 6000 Hampton Center, P.O. Box 619.
Telephone: 304-599-3000.
New Martinsville, West Virginia Office: 256 Russell Avenue, P.O. Box 68.
Telephone: 304-455-1751.
Charles Town, West Virginia Office: 700 East Washington Street, P.O. Box 983.
Telephone: 304-728-6088.
Clarksburg, West Virginia Office: 203 Main Street, P.O. Box 1587.
Telephone: 304-623-3002.
Lexington, Kentucky Office: 175 East Main Street, Suite 500, P.O. Box 2150.
Telephone: 606-255-9500.
Washington, D. C. Office: 2401 Pennsylvania Avenue, N.W., Suite 400.
Telephone: 202-973-0200.
Denver, Colorado Office: Suite 2710, 1660 Lincoln Street.
Telephone: 303-837-0003.

MEMBERS OF FIRM

Alvin L. Emch
Larry W. Blalock (Administrative Manager, New Martinsville, West Virginia Office)
Thomas J. Hurney, Jr.
William J. Powell

For Complete List of Firm Personnel, See General Section

For full biographical listings, see the Martindale-Hubbell Law Directory

WISCONSIN

*MILWAUKEE,** Milwaukee Co.

COOK & FRANKE S.C. (AV)

660 East Mason Street, 53202
Telephone: 414-271-5900
Facsimile: 414-271-2002

William A. Jennaro | Kathy L. Nusslock

Representative Clients: The United Kingdom Mutual Steam Ship Assurance Association; The Liverpool and London Steamship P&I Association, Ltd.; The Standard Steamship Owners' P&I Association, Ltd.; GARD; Newcastle P&I Association; The Steamship Mutual Underwriting Association, Ltd.; The North of England P&I Association, Ltd.; The Britannia Steamship Insurance Association, Ltd.; The London Steamship Owners' Mutual Insurance Association, Ltd.

For Complete List of Firm Personnel, See General Section

For full biographical listings, see the Martindale-Hubbell Law Directory

DAVIS & KUELTHAU, S.C. (AV)

111 East Kilbourn Avenue, Suite 1400, 53202-6613
Telephone: 414-276-0200
Facsimile: 414-276-9369
Cable Address: "Shiplaw"

James E. Braza
William E. Callahan, Jr.
Maria K. Myers
David W. Neeb
Harney B. Stover, Jr.

Louis F. Raymond

Admiralty Counsel For: American Steamship Owners Mutual Protection and Indemnity Assn., Inc.; Great Lakes Towing Co.; Marine Defense Group, Ltd.; Marine Office of America Corp.; Meehan Seaway Service, Ltd.; The

(See Next Column)

Mutual Assurance Association SKULD; Scandinavian Marine Claims Office, Inc.; Shipowners Claims Bureau, Inc.; Swedish Shipowners Insurance Assn.

For full biographical listings, see the Martindale-Hubbell Law Directory

PUERTO RICO

SAN JUAN, San Juan Dist.

JIMÉNEZ, GRAFFAM & LAUSELL

Formerly Jiménez & Fusté
Suite 505, Midtown Building, 421 Muñoz Rivera Avenue, Hato Rey, P.O. Box 366104, 00936-6104
Telephone: 809-767-1030; 767-1000; 767-1061; 767-1064
Telefax: 809-751-4068;
Cable: "Nezte"; RCA
Telex: 325-2730

MEMBERS OF FIRM

Nicolás Jiménez
William A. Graffam
Steven C. Lausell
J. Ramón Rivera-Morales
José Juan Torres-Escalera
Raquel M. Dulzaides
Manuel San Juan

ASSOCIATES

Manolo T. Rodríguez-Bird
Patricia Garrity
Carlos E. Bayrón
Isabel J. Vélez-Serrano
Edgardo A. Vega-López

Representative Clients: Crowley Maritime Corp.; Sea-Land Services, Inc.; The United Kingdom Steamship P & I Association; The Japan Ship Owners' Mutual Protection & Indemnity Association.

For Complete List of Firm Personnel, See General Section

For full biographical listings, see the Martindale-Hubbell Law Directory

CANADA
BRITISH COLUMBIA

*VANCOUVER,** Vancouver Co.

MCEWEN, SCHMITT & CO. (AV)

1615 - 1055 West Georgia Street, P.O. Box 11174 - Royal Centre, V6E 3R5
Telephone: 604-683-1223
Telecopier: 604-683-2359
Telex: 04-51388

MEMBERS OF FIRM

David F. McEwen
Douglas G. Schmitt
Elyn M. R. Underhill
Christopher J. Giaschi
John M. McEwen (1911-1988)

For full biographical listings, see the Martindale-Hubbell Law Directory

RUSSELL & DUMOULIN (AV)

2100-1075 West Georgia Street, V6E 3G2
Telephone: 604-631-3131
Fax: 604-631-3232
A Member of the national association of Borden DuMoulin Howard Gervais, comprising Russell & DuMoulin, Vancouver, British Columbia; Howard Mackie, Calgary, Alberta; Borden & Elliot, Toronto, Ontario; Mackenzie Gervais, Montreal, Quebec and Borden DuMoulin Howard Gervais, London, England.
Strategic Alliance with Perkins Coie with offices in Seattle, Spokane and Bellevue, Washington; Portland, Oregon; Anchorage, Alaska; Los Angeles, California; Washington, D.C.; Hong Kong and Taipei, Taiwan.
Represented in Hong Kong by Vincent T.K. Cheung, Yap & Co.

MEMBERS OF FIRM

Murray B. Blok | Christopher Harvey, Q.C.

Representative Clients: Alcan Smelters & Chemicals Ltd.; The Bank of Nova Scotia; Canada Trust Co.; The Canada Life Assurance Co.; Forest Industrial Relations Ltd.; Honda Canada Inc.; IBM Canada Ltd.; Macmillan Bloedel Ltd.; Nissho Iwai Canada Ltd.; The Toronto-Dominion Bank.

For Complete List of Firm Personnel, See General Section

For full biographical listings, see the Martindale-Hubbell Law Directory

CANADA NEW BRUNSWICK

*SAINT JOHN,** Saint John Co.

Clark, Drummie & Company (AV)

40 Wellington Row, P.O. Box 6850 Station "A", E2L 4S3
Telephone: 506-633-3800
Telecopier (Automatic): 506-633-3811

MEMBERS OF FIRM

M. Robert Jette
Patrick J. P. Ervin

Reference: Royal Bank of Canada.

For Complete List of Firm Personnel, See General Section

For full biographical listings, see the Martindale-Hubbell Law Directory

CANADA NOVA SCOTIA

*HALIFAX,** Halifax Co.

McInnes Cooper & Robertson (AV)

1601 Lower Water Street, P.O. Box 730, B3J 2V1
Telephone: 902-425-6500
Fax: 902-425-6350
St. John's, Newfoundland Office: Suite 602, Scotia Centre, 235 Water Street, P.O. Box 547. A1C, 5K8.
Telephone: 709-726-9500.
Fax: 709-726-9550.

James E. Gould, Q.C.
Wylie Spicer
Thomas E. Hart

ASSOCIATE

Hugh Wright

Attorneys for: Bank of Nova Scotia; Imperial Oil, Limited; Frank B. Hall & Co., Inc. (New York); American Steamship Owners Protection & Indemnity Association, Inc.; Coca-Cola, Ltd.; Scott Worldwide Inc.; Hong Kong Bank of Canada.

For Complete List of Firm Personnel, See General Section

For full biographical listings, see the Martindale-Hubbell Law Directory

CANADA ONTARIO

*TORONTO,** Regional Munic. of York

Borden & Elliot (AV)

Barristers & Solicitors
Scotia Plaza, 40 King Street West, M5H 3Y4
Telephone: 416-367-6000
Telecopier: 416-367-6749
Internet: @ borden.com
A Member of the national association of Borden DuMoulin Howard Gervais, comprising Borden & Elliot in Toronto, Ontario, Russell & DuMoulin in Vancouver, British Columbia, Howard, Mackie in Calgary, Alberta and Mackenzie Gervais in Montréal, Québec. Borden DuMoulin Howard Gervais also operates an office in London, England.

MEMBER AND ASSOCIATES

Norman G. Letalik

For Complete List of Firm Personnel, See General Section

For full biographical listings, see the Martindale-Hubbell Law Directory

CANADA QUEBEC

*MONTREAL,** Montreal Dist.

McMaster Meighen (AV)

A General Partnership
7th Floor, 630 René-Lévesque Boulevard West, H3B 4H7
Telephone: 514-879-1212
Telecopier: 514-878-0605
Cable Address: "Cammerall"
Telex: "Cammerall MTL" 05-268637
Affiliated with Fraser & Beatty in Toronto, North York, Ottawa and Vancouver.

MEMBERS OF FIRM

Sean J. Harrington
P. Jeremy Bolger
Nancy G. Cleman
Jon H. Scott
Nicholas J. Spillane
Peter G. Pamel

COUNSEL

A. Stuart Hyndman, Q.C.

For Complete List of Firm Personnel, See General Section

For full biographical listings, see the Martindale-Hubbell Law Directory

ANTITRUST LAW

ALABAMA

*BIRMINGHAM,** Jefferson Co.

BALCH & BINGHAM (AV)

1710 Sixth Avenue North, P.O. Box 306, 35201
Telephone: 205-251-8100
Facsimile: 205-226-8798
Other Birmingham, Alabama Office: 1901 Sixth Avenue North, 35203.
Telephone: 205-251-8100.
Facsimile: 205-226-8799.
Montgomery, Alabama Office: The Winter Building, 2 Dexter Avenue, 36101.
Telephone: 205-834-6500.
Facsimile: 205-269-3115.
Huntsville, Alabama Office: Suite 810, 200 West Court Square, 35801.
Telephone: 205-551-0171.
Facsimile: 205-551-0174.
Washington, D.C. Office: Suite 800, 1101 Connecticut Avenue, N.W., 20036.
Telephone: 202-296-0387.
Facsimile: 202-452-8180.

COUNSEL

S. Eason Balch

MEMBERS OF FIRM

Michael L. Edwards
John F. Mandt

Counsel for: Alabama Power Co.; Blue Cross and Blue Shield of Alabama; The Boeing Company; Brasfield & Gorrie, Inc.; Compass Bancshares, Inc.; Harbert Corp.; Kimberly-Clark Corp.; Southern Company Services, Inc.; Southern Research Institute; Vesta Insurance Group, Inc.

For Complete List of Firm Personnel, See General Section

For full biographical listings, see the Martindale-Hubbell Law Directory

BERKOWITZ, LEFKOVITS, ISOM & KUSHNER, A PROFESSIONAL CORPORATION (AV)

1600 SouthTrust Tower, 420 North Twentieth Street, 35203
Telephone: 205-328-0480
Telecopier: 205-322-8007

Lee H. Zell
B. G. Minisman, Jr.
Susan S. Wagner
Marvin T. Griff

Representative Clients: AlaTenn Resources, Inc.; B.A.S.S., Inc.; Hanna Steel Co., Inc.; Liberty Trouser Co., Inc.; McDonald's Corp.; Parisian, Inc.; Southern Pipe & Supply Co., Inc.

For Complete List of Firm Personnel, See General Section

For full biographical listings, see the Martindale-Hubbell Law Directory

BRADLEY, ARANT, ROSE & WHITE (AV)

1400 Park Place Tower, 2001 Park Place, 35203
Telephone: 205-521-8000
Telex: 494-1324
Facsimile: 205-251-8611, 251-8665, 252-0264
Facsimile (Southtrust Office): 205-251-9915
Huntsville, Alabama Office: 200 Clinton Avenue West, Suite 900.
Telephone: 205-517-5100.
Facsimile: 205-533-5069.

MEMBERS OF FIRM

John James Coleman, Jr.
John H. Morrow
Thad Gladden Long
James Patrick Alexander
Linda A. Friedman
Joseph B. Mays, Jr.
Patricia Trott Mandt

ASSOCIATES

James S. Christie, Jr.
John E. Goodman
Susan Donovan Josey

Counsel for: SouthTrust Bank of Alabama, National Association; Stockham Valves & Fittings, Inc.; Wolverine Tube, Inc.; Blount, Inc.; Coca-Cola Bottling Company United, Inc.; Russell Corp.; Walter Industries, Inc.

For Complete List of Firm Personnel, See General Section

For full biographical listings, see the Martindale-Hubbell Law Directory

BURR & FORMAN (AV)

3000 SouthTrust Tower, 420 North 20th Street, 35203
Telephone: 205-251-3000
Telecopier: 205-458-5100
Huntsville, Alabama Office: Suite 204, Regency Center, 400 Meridian Street.
Telephone: 205-551-0010.

MEMBERS OF FIRM

John D. Clements
James Ross Forman, III
J. Patrick Logan
Gary M. London
J. Hunter Phillips, III

OF COUNSEL

A. Jackson Noble, Jr.

ASSOCIATE

Darin W. Collier

For Complete List of Firm Personnel, See General Section

For full biographical listings, see the Martindale-Hubbell Law Directory

JOHNSTON, BARTON, PROCTOR, SWEDLAW & NAFF (AV)

2900 AmSouth/Harbert Plaza, 1901 Sixth Avenue North, 35203-2618
Telephone: 205-458-9400
Telecopier: 205-458-9500

MEMBERS OF FIRM

Harvey Deramus (1904-1970)
Alfred M. Naff (1923-1993)
James C. Barton
G. Burns Proctor, Jr.
Sydney L. Lavender
Jerome K. Lanning
Don B. Long, Jr.
Charles L. Robinson
J. William Rose, Jr.
Gilbert E. Johnston, Jr.
David P. Whiteside, Jr.
Ralph H. Smith II
James C. Barton, Jr.
Thomas E. Walker
Anne P. Wheeler
Raymond P. Fitzpatrick, Jr.
Hollinger F. Barnard
William D. Jones III
David W. Proctor
Oscar M. Price III
W. Hill Sewell
Robert S. Vance, Jr.
Richard J. Brockman
Anthony A. Joseph

OF COUNSEL

Gilbert E. Johnston
Alfred Swedlaw
Alan W. Heldman

ASSOCIATES

William K. Hancock
James P. Pewitt
Scott Wells Ford
David M. Hunt
Lee M. Pope
Haskins W. Jones
James M. Parker, Jr.
Michael H. Johnson
Russell L. Irby, III
R. Scott Clark
Helen Kathryn Downs

General Counsel for: Allied Products Co.; Anderson News Co.; The Birmingham News Co. (Publishers of The Birmingham News and owner of The Huntsville Times Co.).
Counsel for: General Motors Corp.; General Electric Credit Corp.

For full biographical listings, see the Martindale-Hubbell Law Directory

LIGHTFOOT, FRANKLIN, WHITE & LUCAS (AV)

300 Financial Center, 505 20th Street North, 35203-2706
Telephone: 205-581-0700
Facsimile: 205-581-0799

MEMBERS OF FIRM

Warren B. Lightfoot
Samuel H. Franklin
John M. Johnson
E. Glenn Waldrop, Jr.

ASSOCIATES

Sarah Bruce Jackson
Wynn M. Shuford

Counsel for: AT&T; Ford Motor Co.; Emerson Electric Co.; Monsanto Co.; Chrysler Corp.; Unocal Corp.; The Upjohn Co.; Bristol-Myers Squibb Co.; The Goodyear Tire & Rubber Co.; Mitsubishi Motor Sales of America, Inc.

For full biographical listings, see the Martindale-Hubbell Law Directory

PATRICK & LACY, P.C. (AV)

1201 Financial Center, 35203
Telephone: 205-323-5665
Telecopier: 205-324-6221

J. Vernon Patrick, Jr.
Alex S. Lacy
William M. Acker, III
Elizabeth N. Pitman
Joseph A. Cartee

For full biographical listings, see the Martindale-Hubbell Law Directory

SCHOEL, OGLE, BENTON AND CENTENO (AV)

600 Financial Center, 505 North 20th Street, P.O. Box 1865, 35201-1865
Telephone: 205-521-7000
Telecopier: 205-521-7007

(See Next Column)

SCHOEL, OGLE, BENTON AND CENTENO, *Birmingham—Continued*

MEMBERS OF FIRM

Jerry W. Schoel
Richard F. Ogle
Lee R. Benton
Paul A. Liles
Douglas J. Centeno
Melinda Murphy Dionne
Gilbert M. Sullivan, Jr.
David O. Upshaw
Paul Avron
Lynn McCreery Shaw

Reference: National Bank of Commerce; First Alabama Bank.

For full biographical listings, see the Martindale-Hubbell Law Directory

SIROTE & PERMUTT, P.C. (AV)

2222 Arlington Avenue, South, P.O. Box 55727, 35255
Telephone: 205-933-7111
Facsimile: 205-930-5301
Huntsville, Alabama Office: 200 Clinton Avenue, N.W., Suite 1000.
Telephone: 205-536-1711.
Facsimile: 205-534-9650.
Mobile, Alabama Office: One St. Louis Centre, Suite 1000.
Telephone: 205-432-1671.
Facsimile: 205-434-0196.
Montgomery, Alabama Office: Colonial Commerce Center, Suite 305 One Commerce Street.
Telephone: 205-261-3400.
Facsimile: 205-261-3434.
Tuscaloosa, Alabama Office: 2216 14th Street.
Telephone: 205-752-2089.

C. Lee Reeves
J. Rushton McClees
James Sarven Williams

Representative Clients: International Business Machines (IBM); General Motors Corp.; Colonial Bank; Bruno's, Inc.; University of Alabama Hospitals; Westinghouse Electric Corp.; First Alabama Bank; Monsanto Chemical Company; South Central Bell; Prudential Insurance Company; American Home Products, Inc.; Minnesota Mining and Manufacturing, Inc. (3M).

For Complete List of Firm Personnel, See General Section

For full biographical listings, see the Martindale-Hubbell Law Directory

SPAIN, GILLON, GROOMS, BLAN & NETTLES (AV)

The Zinszer Building, 2117 2nd Avenue North, 35203
Telephone: 205-328-4100
Telecopier: 205-324-8866

MEMBERS OF FIRM

Ollie L. Blan, Jr.
Alton B. Parker, Jr.

General Counsel for: Liberty National Life Insurance Co.; United States Fidelity & Guaranty Co.; Piggly Wiggly Alabama Distributing Co.; AmSouth Mortgage Co., Inc.; Alabama Insurance Guaranty Association; Alabama Life and Disability Insurance Guaranty Association; Alabama Insurance Underwriters Association.
Counsel for: The Prudential Insurance Company of America; Government Employees Insurance Co.; Massachusetts Mutual Life Insurance Co.

For Complete List of Firm Personnel, See General Section

For full biographical listings, see the Martindale-Hubbell Law Directory

*HUNTSVILLE,** Madison Co.

SIROTE & PERMUTT, P.C. (AV)

Suite 1000, 200 Clinton Avenue, N.W., 35801
Telephone: 205-536-1711
Facsimile: 205-534-9650
Birmingham, Alabama Office: 2222 Arlington Avenue, South, P.O. Box 55727.
Telephone: 205-933-7111.
Facsimile: 205-930-5301.
Mobile, Alabama Office: One St. Louis Centre, Suite 1000.
Telephone: 205-432-1671.
Facsimile: 205-434-0196.
Montgomery, Alabama Office: Colonial Commerce Center, Suite 305, One Commerce Street.
Telephone: 205-261-3400.
Facsimile: 205-261-3434.
Tuscaloosa, Alabama Office: 2216 14th Street.
Telephone: 205-752-2089.

Julian D. Butler
George W. Royer, Jr.
Roderic G. Steakley

For Complete List of Firm Personnel, See General Section

For full biographical listings, see the Martindale-Hubbell Law Directory

*MOBILE,** Mobile Co.

JOHNSTONE, ADAMS, BAILEY, GORDON AND HARRIS (AV)

Royal St. Francis Building, 104 St. Francis Street, P.O. Box 1988, 36633
Telephone: 334-432-7682
Facsimile: 334-432-2800
Telex: 782040

(See Next Column)

MEMBERS OF FIRM

William H. Hardie, Jr.
Celia J. Collins

For a list of Representative Clients, see General Section.

For Complete List of Firm Personnel, See General Section

For full biographical listings, see the Martindale-Hubbell Law Directory

MILLER, HAMILTON, SNIDER & ODOM, L.L.C. (AV)

254-256 State Street, P.O. Box 46, 36601
Telephone: 334-432-1414
Telecopier: 334-433-4106
Montgomery, Alabama Office: Suite 802, One Commerce Street.
Telephone: 205-834-5550.
Telecopier: 205-265-4533.
Washington, D.C. Office: Miller, Hamilton, Snider, Odom & Bridgeman, L.L.C., Suite 1150, 1747 Pennsylvania Avenue, N.W.
Telephone: 202-429-9223.
Telecopier: 202-293-2068.

MEMBERS OF FIRM

Thomas Troy Zieman, Jr.
Lester M. Bridgeman

Representative Clients: The Colonial BancGroup, Inc.; Colonial Mortgage Co.; Chase Manhattan Bank, N.A.; The Mitchell Co.; Poole Truck Line, Inc.; Brittania Airways, Ltd. (U.K.); Air Europe (Italy); K-Mart Corporation; K & B Alabama Corp.; Ford Consumer Finance Company, Inc.

For Complete List of Firm Personnel, See General Section

For full biographical listings, see the Martindale-Hubbell Law Directory

SIROTE & PERMUTT, P.C. (AV)

One St. Louis Centre, Suite 1000, P.O. Drawer 2025, 36652-2025
Telephone: 334-432-1671
Facsimile: 334-434-0196
Birmingham, Alabama Office: 2222 Arlington Avenue, South, P.O. Box 55727.
Telephone: 205-933-7111.
Facsimile: 205-930-5301.
Huntsville, Alabama Office: 200 Clinton Avenue, N.W., Suite 1000.
Telephone: 205-536-1711.
Facsimile: 205-534-9650.
Montgomery, Alabama Office: Colonial Commerce Center, Suite 305, One Commerce Street.
Telephone: 205-261-3400.
Facsimile: 205-261-3434.
Tuscaloosa, Alabama Office: 2216 14th Street.
Telephone: 205-752-2089.

Richard H. Sforzini, Jr.
Steven L. Nicholas

For Complete List of Firm Personnel, See General Section

For full biographical listings, see the Martindale-Hubbell Law Directory

ARIZONA

*PHOENIX,** Maricopa Co.

BROWN & BAIN, A PROFESSIONAL ASSOCIATION (AV)

2901 North Central Avenue, P.O. Box 400, 85001-0400
Telephone: 602-351-8000
Cable: TWX 910-951-0646
Telecopier: 602-351-8516
Palo Alto, California Affiliated Office: Brown & Bain, 600 Hansen Way.
Telephone: 415-856-9411.
Telecopier: 415-856-6061.
Tucson, Arizona Affiliated Office: Brown & Bain, A Professional Association. One South Church Avenue, Nineteenth Floor, P.O. Box 2265.
Telephone: 602-798-7900
Telecopier: 602-798-7945.

Lois W. Abraham (Resident at Palo Alto Office)
Robert E. B. Allen
Michael F. Bailey
C. Randall Bain
Philip P. Berelson (Resident at Palo Alto Office)
Alan H. Blankenheimer
Jack E. Brown
John A. Buttrick
Howard Ross Cabot
H. Michael Clyde
Paul F. Eckstein
Terry E. Fenzl
Douglas Gerlach (On leave)
Philip R. Higdon (Resident at Tucson Office)
Karl J. Kramer (Resident at Palo Alto Office)
Don F. Kumamoto (Resident at Palo Alto Office)
Martin L. Lagod (Resident at Palo Alto Office)
Joseph E. Mais
Joseph W. Mott
Joel W. Nomkin
Christopher R. Ottenweller (Resident at Palo Alto Office)
Michael W. Patten
Charles S. Price

(See Next Column)

BROWN & BAIN A PROFESSIONAL ASSOCIATION—*Continued*

Daniel P. Quigley
John W. Rogers
Lawrence G. D. Scarborough
D. Bruce Sewell
(Resident at Palo Alto Office)
Craig W. Soland
Antonio T. Viera
Kim E. Williamson

Susan D. Berney-Key
(Resident at Palo Alto Office)
Charles A. Blanchard
Chad S. Campbell
Jonathan M. James
Anthony L. Marks
Kelly A. O'Connor
Christopher J. Raboin

For Complete List of Firm Personnel, See General Section

For full biographical listings, see the Martindale-Hubbell Law Directory

FENNEMORE CRAIG, A PROFESSIONAL CORPORATION (AV)

Two North Central, Suite 2200, 85004
Telephone: 602-257-8700
Fax: 602-257-8527
Scottsdale, Arizona Office: 6263 North Scottsdale Road, Suite 290, 85250.
Telephone: 602-257-5400.
Fax: 602-945-4932.
Tucson, Arizona Office: One South Church Avenue, Suite 1030, 85701.
Telephone: 602-624-9312.
Fax: 602-882-7383.

Timothy J. Burke
C. Owen Paepke
Janet W. Lord

Representative Clients: ASARCO Incorporated; AT&T Communications; Bridgestone/Firestone, Inc.; Catellus Development Corp.; Citibank (Arizona); First Interstate Bank of Arizona; GIANT Industries; Phelps Dodge Corporation; The Atchison, Topeka & Santa Fe Railway, Co.; US WEST Communications.

For Complete List of Firm Personnel, See General Section

For full biographical listings, see the Martindale-Hubbell Law Directory

JENNINGS, STROUSS AND SALMON, P.L.C. (AV)

A Professional Limited Liability Company
One Renaissance Square, Two North Central, 85004-2393
Telephone: 602-262-5911
Fax: 602-253-3255

David L. White

For Complete List of Firm Personnel, See General Section

For full biographical listings, see the Martindale-Hubbell Law Directory

LEWIS AND ROCA (AV)

A Partnership including Professional Corporations
40 North Central Avenue, 85004-4429
Telephone: 602-262-5311
Fax: 602-262-5747
Tucson, Arizona Office: One South Church Avenue, Suite 700.
Telephone: 602-622-2090.
Fax: 602-622-3088.

MEMBERS OF FIRM

John P. Frank
Edward M. Mansfield
George L. Paul
Karen Carter Owens

Representative Clients: The Heil Company; Rockford Corporation; St. Peters Community Hospital; Samaritan Health System; Arizona Hospital Association.

For Complete List of Firm Personnel, See General Section

For full biographical listings, see the Martindale-Hubbell Law Directory

MEYER, HENDRICKS, VICTOR, OSBORN & MALEDON, A PROFESSIONAL ASSOCIATION (AV)

2929 North Central Avenue Suite 2100, 85012-2794
Telephone: 602-640-9000
Facsimile: (24 Hrs.) 602-640-9050
Mailing Address: P.O. Box 33449, 85067-3449,

Ed Hendricks
William J. Maledon
Larry A. Hammond
Robert L. Palmer
R. Douglas Dalton
Don Bivens
Brett L. Dunkelman

Reference: Bank One Arizona, NA.

For Complete List of Firm Personnel, See General Section

For full biographical listings, see the Martindale-Hubbell Law Directory

O'CONNOR, CAVANAGH, ANDERSON, WESTOVER, KILLINGSWORTH & BESHEARS, A PROFESSIONAL ASSOCIATION (AV)

One East Camelback Road, Suite 1100, 85012-1656
Telephone: 602-263-2400
FAX: 602-263-2900
Sun City, Arizona Office: 13250 North Del Webb Boulevard, Suite B, 85351.
Telephone: 602-263-2808.
FAX: 602-933-3100.
Tucson, Arizona Office: Suite 2200, One South Church Avenue, 85701.
Telephone: 602-882-8912.
FAX: 602-624-9564.
Nogales, Arizona Office: 1827 North Mastick Way, 85621.
Telephone: 602-761-4215.
FAX: 602-761-3505.

Harry J. Cavanagh
Stephen E. Richman
David A. Van Engelhoven

Representative Clients: Karsten Manufacturing Corp.; Arizona Physicians, IPA; Good Samaritan Health Systems; Samsung Electronics Corp.

For Complete List of Firm Personnel, See General Section

For full biographical listings, see the Martindale-Hubbell Law Directory

SNELL & WILMER (AV)

One Arizona Center, 85004-0001
Telephone: 602-382-6000
Fax: 602-382-6070
Tucson, Arizona Office: 1500 Norwest Tower, One South Church Avenue 85701-1612.
Telephone: 602-882-1200.
Fax: 602-884-1294.
Orange County Office: 1920 Main Street, Suite 1200, P.O. Box 19601, Irvine, California, 92714.
Telephone: 714-253-2700.
Fax: 714-955-2507.
Salt Lake City, Utah Office: Broadway Centre, 111 East Broadway, Suite 900, 84111.
Telephone: 801-237-1900.
Fax: 801-237-1950.

MEMBERS OF FIRM

John J. Bouma
Arthur P. Greenfield
Daniel J. McAuliffe
E. Jeffrey Walsh

SENIOR ATTORNEY

Bruce P. White

Representative Clients: Arizona Public Service; Arvin Industries; Baptist Hospitals and Health Systems; Coca-Cola Bottling Co. of Phoenix; Good Samaritan Hospital Medical Staff; Holsum Bakery; Lincoln Health Systems; Maricopa Foundation for Medical Care; Phoenix Board of Realtors; The Tanner Companies.

For Complete List of Firm Personnel, See General Section

For full biographical listings, see the Martindale-Hubbell Law Directory

ULRICH, THOMPSON & KESSLER, P.C. (AV)

Suite 1000, 3030 North Central Avenue, 85012-2717
Telephone: 602-248-9465
Fax: 602-248-0165

Paul G. Ulrich
Donn G. Kessler

For full biographical listings, see the Martindale-Hubbell Law Directory

*TUCSON,** Pima Co.

SNELL & WILMER (AV)

1500 Norwest Tower, One South Church Avenue, 85701-1612
Telephone: 602-882-1200
Fax: 602-884-1294
Phoenix, Arizona Office: One Arizona Center, 85004-0001.
Telephone: 602-382-6000.
Fax: 602-382-6070.
Orange County Office: 1920 Main Street, Suite 1200, P.O. Box 19601, Irvine, California, 92714.
Telephone: 714-253-2700
Fax: 714-955-2507.
Salt Lake City, Utah Office: Broadway Centre, 111 East Broadway, Suite 900, 84111.
Telephone: 801-237-1900.
Fax: 801-237-1950.

MEMBERS OF FIRM

David A. Paige
Sandra S. Froman

Representative Clients: Arizona Public Service Company; Arvin Industries; Baptist Hospitals and Health Systems; Coca Cola Bottling Co. of Phoenix; Good Samaritan Hospital Medical Staff; Holsum Bakery; Lincoln Health Systems; Maricopa Foundation for Medical Care; Phoenix Board of Realtors; The Tanner Companies.

For full biographical listings, see the Martindale-Hubbell Law Directory

ARKANSAS

LITTLE ROCK,* Pulaski Co.

FRIDAY, ELDREDGE & CLARK (AV)

A Partnership including Professional Associations
Formerly, Smith, Williams, Friday, Eldredge & Clark
2000 First Commercial Building, 400 West Capitol, 72201-3493
Telephone: 501-376-2011
Telecopier: 501-376-2147; 376-6369

MEMBER OF FIRM

James M. Simpson, Jr., (P.A.)

Counsel for: Union Pacific System; St. Paul Insurance Co.; Liberty Mutual Insurance Co.; Cigna Property & Casualty Co.; Arkansas Power & Light Co.; Dillard Department Stores, Inc.; First Commercial Corp.; Browning Arms Co.; Phillips Petroleum Co.; Aetna Casualty & Surety Co.

For Complete List of Firm Personnel, See General Section

For full biographical listings, see the Martindale-Hubbell Law Directory

WILLIAMS & ANDERSON (AV)

Twenty-Second Floor, 111 Center Street, 72201
Telephone: 501-372-0800
FAX: 501-372-6453

MEMBERS OF FIRM

Philip S. Anderson
Peter G. Kumpe
J. Leon Holmes

Representative Clients: Arkansas Development Finance Authority; Coregis; Dean Witter Reynolds Inc.; Entergy Power, Inc.; Little Rock Newspapers, Inc. d/b/a/ Arkansas Democrat-Gazette; Texaco, Inc.; Transport Indemnity Insurance Co.; Wal-Mart Stores, Inc.

For Complete List of Firm Personnel, See General Section

For full biographical listings, see the Martindale-Hubbell Law Directory

WRIGHT, LINDSEY & JENNINGS (AV)

2200 Worthen Bank Building, 200 West Capitol Avenue, 72201
Telephone: 501-371-0808
Fax: 501-376-9442
Fayetteville, Arkansas Office: 101 West Mountain Street, Suite 206, 72701.
Telephone: 501-575-0808.
Fax: 501-575-0999.
Russellville, Arkansas Office: Suite E, 1110 West B Street.
Telephone: 501-968-7995.

Ronald A. May
M. Samuel Jones, III
N. M. Norton, Jr.
Charles L. Schlumberger
Nancy Bellhouse May

Representative Clients: American Telephone & Telegraph Company; Central Arkansas Radiation Therapy Institute; Coleman Dairy, Inc.; Federal Compress & Warehouse Co.; Hudson Foods, Inc.; J.B. Hunt Transport Services, Inc.; Riceland Foods, Inc.; St. Louis Southwestern Railway Co. (Cotton Belt); Timex Corporation; United Parcel Service, Inc.; Worthen National Bank of Arkansas.

For Complete List of Firm Personnel, See General Section

For full biographical listings, see the Martindale-Hubbell Law Directory

CALIFORNIA

LOS ANGELES,* Los Angeles Co.

ADAMS, DUQUE & HAZELTINE (AV)

A Partnership including Professional Corporations
777 South Figueroa Street, Tenth Floor, 90017
Telephone: 213-620-1240
FAX: 213-896-5500
San Francisco, California Office: 500 Washington Street.
Telephone: 415-982-1240.
FAX: 415-982-0130.

MEMBER OF FIRM

C. Forrest Bannan

For Complete List of Firm Personnel, See General Section

For full biographical listings, see the Martindale-Hubbell Law Directory

BLECHER & COLLINS, A PROFESSIONAL CORPORATION (AV)

611 West Sixth Street, 20th Floor, 90017
Telephone: 213-622-4222
Telecopier: 213-622-1656

Maxwell M. Blecher
Harold R. Collins, Jr.
Douglas H. Altschuler
Mark D. Baute
Florence F. Cameron
Ralph C. Hofer
William C. Hsu
Jinna Kim
Benjamin D. Nieberg
James Robert Noblin
Donald R. Pepperman
Alicia G. Rosenberg

OF COUNSEL

John J. McCauley

For full biographical listings, see the Martindale-Hubbell Law Directory

CORINBLIT & SELTZER, A PROFESSIONAL CORPORATION (AV)

Suite 820 Wilshire Park Place, 3700 Wilshire Boulevard, 90010-3085
Telephone: 213-380-4200
Telecopier: 213-385-7503; 385-4560

Marc M. Seltzer

OF COUNSEL

Jack Corinblit
Earl P. Willens

Gretchen M. Nelson
Christina A. Snyder
George A. Shohet

Reference: Bank of America (Wilshire & Harvard Office).

For full biographical listings, see the Martindale-Hubbell Law Directory

LAW OFFICES OF RICHARD I. FINE & ASSOCIATES A PROFESSIONAL CORPORATION (AV)

Suite 1000, 10100 Santa Monica Boulevard (Century City), 90067-4090
Telephone: 310-277-5833
Rapifax: 310-277-1543

Richard I. Fine

OF COUNSEL

Brian D. Krantz

LEGAL SUPPORT PERSONNEL

Mary Benson (Senior Paralegal)

For full biographical listings, see the Martindale-Hubbell Law Directory

HUFSTEDLER & KAUS (AV)

A Partnership including Professional Corporations
Thirty-Ninth Floor, 355 South Grand Avenue, 90071-3101
Telephone: 213-617-7070
Fax: 213-617-6170

MEMBERS OF FIRM

Seth M. Hufstedler (Professional Corporation)
Shirley M. Hufstedler (Professional Corporation)
Otto M. Kaus
Joseph L. Wyatt, Jr.
John Sobieski
Burton J. Gindler
Fred L. Leydorf
Jerome H. Craig (Professional Corporation)
Thomas J. Ready (Professional Corporation)
Patricia Dominis Phillips
Dudley M. Lang
John P. Olson
Dennis M. Perluss
Margot A. Metzner
Leonard L. Gumport
Dan Marmalefsky
Gary Plessman
Michael V. Toumanoff
Susan I. Schutzbank Montgomery
Mark R. McDonald

ASSOCIATES

John W. (Jack) Alden Jr.
David K. Barrett
Eliot F. Krieger

Reference: First Interstate Bank, 707 Wilshire.

For Complete List of Firm Personnel, See General Section

For full biographical listings, see the Martindale-Hubbell Law Directory

JONES, DAY, REAVIS & POGUE (AV)

555 West Fifth Street Suite 4600, 90013-1025
Telephone: 213-489-3939
Telex: 181439 UD
Telecopier: 213-243-2539
In Irvine, California: 2603 Main Street, Suite 900.
Telephone: 714-851-3939.
Telex: 194911 Lawyers LSA.
Telecopier: 714-553-7539.
In Atlanta, Georgia: 3500 One Peachtree Center, 303 Peachtree Street, N.E.
Telephone: 404-521-3939.
Cable Address: "Attorneys Atlanta".
Telex: 54-2711.
Telecopier: 404-581-8330.

(See Next Column)

JONES, DAY, REAVIS & POGUE—*Continued*

In Brussels, Belgium: Avenue Louise 480, 7th Floor, B-1050 Brussels.
Telephone: 011-32-2-645-14-11.
Telecopier: 011-32-2-645-14-45.
In Chicago, Illinois: 77 West Wacker.
Telephone: 312-782-3939.
Telecopier: 312-782-8585.
In Cleveland, Ohio: North Point, 901 Lakeside Avenue.
Telephone: 216-586-3939.
Cable Address: "Attorneys Cleveland."
Telex: 980389.
Telecopier: 216-579-0212.
In Columbus, Ohio: 1900 Huntington Center.
Telephone: 614-469-3939.
Cable Address: "Attorneys Columbus."
Telecopier: 614-461-4198.
In Dallas, Texas: 2300 Trammell Crow Center, 2001 Ross Avenue.
Telephone: 214-220-3939.
Cable Address: "Attorneys Dallas."
Telex: 730852.
Telecopier: 214-969-5100.
In Frankfurt, Germany: Triton Haus, Bockenheimer Landstrasse 42, 60323 Frankfurt am Main.
Telephone: 49-69-9726-3939.
Telecopier: 49-69-9726-3993.
In Geneva, Switzerland: 20, rue de Candolle.
Telephone: 011-41-22-320-2339.
Telecopier: 011-41-22-320-1232.
In Hong Kong: 1501 One Exchange Square, 8 Connaught Place.
Telephone: 011-852-2526-6895.
Telecopier: 011-852-2810-5787.
In London England: One Mount Street.
Telephone: 011-44-71-493-9361.
Cable Address: "Surgoe London WI."
Telecopier: 011-44-71-493-9666.
In New York, New York: 599 Lexington Avenue.
Telephone: 212-326-3939.
Cable Address: "JONESDAY NEWYORK."
Telex: 237013 JDRP UR.
Telecopier: 212-755-7306.
In Paris, France: 62, rue du Faubourg Saint-Honore.
Telephone: 011-33-1-44-71-3939.
Cable Address: "Surgoe Paris."
Telex: 290156 Surgoe.
Telecopier: 011-33-1-49-24-0471.
In Pittsburgh, Pennsylvania: 500 Grant Street, 31st Floor.
Telephone: 412-391-3939.
Cable Address: "Attorneys Pittsburgh".
Telecopier: 412-394-7959.
In Riyadh, Saudi Arabia: Law Offices of Saud M.A. Shawwaf, P.O. Box 2700.
Telephones: 011 (966-1) 465-6543, 011 (966-1) 464-8534 or 011 (966-1) 464-8540.
Telex: 401831 SAUCON SJ.
Telecopier: (966-1) 464-8480.
In Taipei, Taiwan: 8th Floor, 2 Tun Hwa South Road, Section 2.
Telephone: 011 (886-2) 704-6808.
Telecopier: 011 (886-2) 704-6791.
In Tokyo, Japan: Toranomon MT Building, 4th Floor, 10-3, Toranomon 3-Chome, Minato-Ku, Tokyo 105, Japan.
Telephone: 011-81-3-3433-3939.
Telecopier: 011-81-3-5401-2725.
In Washington, D.C.: Metropolitan Square, 1450 G Street, N.W.
Telephone: 202-879-3939.
Cable Address: "Attorneys Washington."
Telex: 89-2410 ATTORNEYS WASH.
Telecopier: 202-737-2832.

MEMBERS OF FIRM IN LOS ANGELES

Gerald W. Palmer
Frederick L. McKnight
Louis L. Touton
Jeffrey A. LeVee

For Complete List of Firm Personnel, See General Section

For full biographical listings, see the Martindale-Hubbell Law Directory

LOEB AND LOEB (AV)

A Partnership including Professional Corporations
Suite 1800, 1000 Wilshire Boulevard, 90017-2475
Telephone: 213-688-3400
Telecopier: 213-688-3460; 688-3461; 688-3462
Century City, California Office: Suite 2200, 10100 Santa Monica Boulevard, Los Angeles, 90067-4164.
Telephone: 310-282-2000.
Telecopier: 310-282-2191; 282-2192.
New York, N.Y. Office: 345 Park Avenue, 10154-0037.
Telephone: 212-407-4000.
Facsimile: 212-407-4990.
Nashville, Tennessee Office: 45 Music Square West, 37203-3205.
Telephone: 615-749-8300;
Facsimile: 615-749-8308.
Rome, Italy Office: Piazza Digione 1, 00197.
Telephone: 011-396-808-8456.
Telecopier: 011-396-674-8223.

(See Next Column)

MEMBERS OF FIRM

Phillip E. Adler (A P.C.)
Howard I. Friedman (A P.C.)
Robert A. Holtzman (A P.C.)
Robert A. Meyer
Charles H. Miller (New York City Office)
David B. Shontz (New York City Office)

OF COUNSEL

Harry First (New York City Office)
Alfred I. Rothman (A P.C.)
Albert F. Smith (A P.C.)

For Complete List of Firm Personnel, See General Section

For full biographical listings, see the Martindale-Hubbell Law Directory

MITCHELL, SILBERBERG & KNUPP (AV)

A Partnership of Professional Corporations
11377 West Olympic Boulevard, 90064
Telephone: 310-312-2000
Cable Address: "Silmitch"
Telex: 69-1347
Telecopier: 310-312-3200

MEMBERS OF FIRM

Edward M. Medvene (A Professional Corporation)
Thomas P. Lambert (A Professional Corporation)
Roy L. Shults (A Professional Corporation)
Richard R. Mainland (A Professional Corporation)

Reference: First Interstate Bank of California (Headquarters, Los Angeles, California).

For Complete List of Firm Personnel, See General Section

For full biographical listings, see the Martindale-Hubbell Law Directory

MUSICK, PEELER & GARRETT (AV)

Suite 2000, One Wilshire Boulevard, 90017-3321
Telephone: 213-629-7600
Cable Address: "Peelgar"
Facsimile: 213-624-1376
San Diego, California Office: 1900 Home Savings Tower, 225 Broadway.
Telephone: 619-231-2500.
Facsimile: 619-231-1234.
San Francisco, California Office: Suite 1300, Steuart Street Tower, One Market Plaza.
Telephone: 415-281-2000.
Facsimile: 415-281-2010.
Sacramento, California Office: Suite 100, 1121 L Street.
Telephone: 916-442-1200.
Facsimile: 916-442-8644.
Fresno, California Office: 6041 North First Street.
Telephone: 209-228-1000.
Facsimile: 209-447-4670.

MEMBER OF FIRM

William McD. Miller, III

For Complete List of Firm Personnel, See General Section

For full biographical listings, see the Martindale-Hubbell Law Directory

PILLSBURY MADISON & SUTRO (AV)

Citicorp Plaza, 725 South Figueroa Street, Suite 1200, 90017-2513
Telephone: 213-488-7100
Fax: 213-629-1033
Costa Mesa, California Office: Plaza Tower, 600 Anton Boulevard, Suite 1100, 92626.
Telephone: 714-436-6800.
Fax: 714-662-6999.
Menlo Park, California Office: 2700 Sand Hill Road, 94025.
Telephone: 415-233-4500.
Fax: 415-233-4545.
Sacramento, California Office: 400 Capitol Mall, Suite 1700, 95814.
Telephone: 916-329-4700.
Fax: 916-441-3583.
San Diego, California Office: 101 West Broadway, Suite 1800, 92101.
Telephone: 619-234-5000.
Fax: 619-236-1995.
San Francisco, California Office: 225 Bush Street, 94104.
Telephone: 415-983-1000.
Fax: 415-398-2096.
San Jose, California Office: Ten Almaden Boulevard, 95113.
Telephone: 408-947-4000.
Fax: 408-287-8341.
Washington, D. C. Office: 1667 K Street, N.W., Suite 1100, Suite 20006.
Telephone: 202-887-0300.
Fax: 202-296-7605.
New York, New York Office: One Liberty Plaza, 165 Broadway, 51st Floor.
Telephone: 212-374-1890.
Fax: 212-374-1852.
Hong Kong Office: 6/F Asia Pacific Finance Tower, Citibank Plaza, 3 Garden Road, Central.
Telephone: 011-852-509-7100.
Fax: 011-852-509-7188.

(See Next Column)

PILLSBURY MADISON & SUTRO, *Los Angeles—Continued*

Tokyo, Japan Office: Churchill and Shimazaki, Gaiko-Jimo-Bengoshi Jimusho, 11-12, Toranomon, 5-chome Minato-ku, Tokyo 105, Japan.
Telephone: 800-729-9830; 011-81-3-5472-6561.
Fax: 011-81-3-5472-5761.

MEMBERS OF FIRM

Kenneth R. Chiate
Karen L. Heilman
Sidney K. Kanazawa
James A. Magee
Patrick G. Rogan
William E. Stoner
John Randolph Haag
Amy D. Hogue
Jennie L. La Prade
Charles E. Patterson
Matthew R. Rogers
Mark K. Suzumoto
David B. Van Etten

ASSOCIATES

Michael J. Finnegan
William T. Gillespie

For Complete List of Firm Personnel, See General Section

For full biographical listings, see the Martindale-Hubbell Law Directory

QUINN, KULLY AND MORROW, A PROFESSIONAL LAW CORPORATION (AV)

Eighth Floor 520 South Grand Avenue, 90071
Telephone: 213-622-0300
Telecopier: 213-622-3799

John J. Quinn
Margaret M. Morrow
Laurence J. Hutt
Lawrence A. Cox

For Complete List of Firm Personnel, See General Section

For full biographical listings, see the Martindale-Hubbell Law Directory

SHEPPARD, MULLIN, RICHTER & HAMPTON (AV)

A Partnership including Professional Corporations
Forty-Eighth Floor, 333 South Hope Street, 90071-1406
Telephone: 213-620-1780
Telecopier: 213-620-1398
Cable Address: "Sheplaw"
Telex: 19-4424
Orange County, California Office: Seventh Floor, 4695 MacArthur Court, Newport Beach.
Telephone: 714-752-6400.
Telecopier: 714-851-0739.
Telex: 19-4424.
San Francisco, California Office: Seventeenth Floor, Four Embarcadero Center.
Telephone: 415-434-9100.
Telecopier: 415-434-3947.
Telex: 19-4424.
San Diego, California Office: Nineteenth Floor, 501 West Broadway.
Telephone: 619-338-6500.
Telecopier: 619-234-3815.
Telex: 19-4424.

MEMBERS OF FIRM

James J. Carroll, III *
Joseph F. Coyne, Jr.
André J. Cronthall
Joseph A. Darrell (San Francisco Office)
Phillip A. Davis
Polly Towill Dennis
Frank Falzetta
Robert B. Flaig
Dale E. Fredericks (San Francisco Office)
Randolph B. Godshall (Orange County Office)
Gerald N. Gordon
Gordon A. Greenberg
Andrew J. Guilford (Orange County Office)
Harold E. Hamersmith
Don T. Hibner, Jr.
Gregory A. Long *
Charles H. MacNab, Jr. (San Francisco Office)
Paul S. Malingagio
James F. McShane
James J. Mittermiller (San Diego Office)
Gary J. Nevolo (San Francisco Office)
Kathyleen A. O'Brien
Stephen J. O'Neil
John R. Pennington
Fred R. Puglisi
Kent R. Raygor
Paul M. Reitler *
Mark Riera
John F. Runkel, Jr. (San Francisco Office)
D. Ronald Ryland (San Francisco Office)
James L. Sanders
Pierce T. Selwood *
Richard L. Stone
Finley L. Taylor * (Orange County Office)
Stephen C. Taylor *
Timothy B. Taylor (San Diego Office)
Jane L. Thomas (San Francisco Office)
Carlton A. Varner *
Edward D. Vogel (San Diego Office)
Michael J. Weaver * (San Diego Office)
Darryl M. Woo (San Francisco Office)
Roy G. Wuchitech (Director, The Sheppard, Mullin Environmental Practice Group)

SPECIAL COUNSEL

M. Elizabeth McDaniel (San Francisco Office)

(See Next Column)

ASSOCIATES

Fredric I. Albert (Orange County Office)
Cindy Thomas Archer (Orange County Office)
Vincent J. Axelson (San Diego Office)
Carrie Battilega (San Diego Office)
Robert S. Beall (Orange County Office)
David M. Beckwith (San Diego Office)
Barbara A. Benner (Orange County Office)
Jason Brauser
Ann A. Byun
Justine Mary Casey (Orange County Office)
Thomas A. Counts (San Francisco Office)
Angela A. Dahl (San Diego Office)
Kristina M. Diaz
Karin A. Dougan (San Diego Office)
Phillip J. Eskenazi
Ann H. Fromholz
Robert S. Gerber (San Diego Office)
Kristen A. Jensen (San Francisco Office)
Beverly Johnson
Mark D. Johnson
Rebecca C. Klipfel (Orange County Office)
Laura A. Larks
H. Anthony Lewis (San Diego Office)
Philip A. Magen (San Diego Office)
Alan H. Martin (Orange County Office)
Candace L. Matson
Maureen C. McLaughlin (San Francisco Office)
Dani Jo Young Merryman
Paul M. Miloknay
Elena Muravina
Cindy M. Oakes (San Francisco Office)
Jeffrey J. Parker
David A. Pursley (San Francisco Office)
Lynne M. Rasmussen
Scott F. Roybal
Betty J. Santohigashi (San Diego Office)
Lara A. Saunders (Orange County Office)
Richard C. Seavey
Kay S. Solomon
Michael St. Denis
Michael D. Stewart (Orange County Office)
Barry Sullivan
Lei K. Udell (San Diego Office)
Perry Joseph Viscounty (Orange County Office)
Holly O. Whatley
John A. Yacovelle (San Diego Office)

*Professional Corporation

For Complete List of Firm Personnel, See General Section

For full biographical listings, see the Martindale-Hubbell Law Directory

PALO ALTO, Santa Clara Co.

FTHENAKIS & VOLK (AV)

540 University Avenue, Suite 300, 94301
Telephone: 415-326-1397
Telecopier: 415-326-3203

MEMBERS OF FIRM

Basil P. Fthenakis
John D. Volk

ASSOCIATE

Oliver P. Colvin

For full biographical listings, see the Martindale-Hubbell Law Directory

GRAY CARY WARE & FREIDENRICH, A PROFESSIONAL CORPORATION (AV)

Gray Cary Established in 1927
Ware & Freidenrich Established in 1969
400 Hamilton Avenue, 94301-1825
Telephone: 415-328-6561
Telex: 348-372
Telecopier: 415-327-3699
San Diego, California Office: 401 B Street, Suite 1700.
Telephone: 619-699-2700.
La Jolla, California Office: 1200 Prospect Street, Suite 575.
Telephone: 619-454-9101.
El Centro, California Office: 1224 State Street, P.O. Box 2890.
Telephone: 619-353-6140.

Douglas B. Aikins
Cynthia B. Carlson
John Howard Clowes
Lawrence A. Cogan
Steven G. Cohen
Ian N. Feinberg
Mark Fowler
Diane Holt Frankle
Thomas M. French
Thomas W. Furlong
Gregory M. Gallo
Penny Howe Gallo
Hugh Goodwin, Jr.
Judith V. Gordon
Robert N. Grant
Louis B. Green
John B. Hale
George H. Hohnsbeen, II
Aimée E. Jorgensen
James M. Koshland
Eric J. Lapp
Mary LaVigne-Butler
Jeffrey J. Lederman
Patrick J. McGaraghan
Marvin Meisel
Robert H. Miller
Timothy J. Moore
Carla S. Newell
Mark F. Radcliffe
Jonathan E. Rattner
Arthur C. Rinsky
Bradley J. Rock
Robert T. Russell
Bruce E. Schaeffer
John R. Shuman, Jr.
Stacy Snowman
Jay M. Spitzen
Jeffrey A. Trant
Richard I. Yankwich

(See Next Column)

GRAY CARY WARE & FREIDENRICH A PROFESSIONAL CORPORATION—*Continued*

James E. Anderson
Beth Detweiler Castleberry
Susan Goodhue
William H. Hoffman
Daniel K. Seubert

RETIRED PARTNERS

John Freidenrich
Leonard Ware

OF COUNSEL

Marta L. Morando

Representative Clients: Automobile Club of South California; Bank of America; Brooktree Corp.; C. A. Parr (Agencies), Ltd.; IMED; Pacific Bell; McMillin Development Co.; Scripps Clinic and Research Fdtn.; SeaWorld, Inc.; Underwriters at Lloyds; Wells Fargo Bank.

For Complete List of Firm Personnel, See General Section

For full biographical listings, see the Martindale-Hubbell Law Directory

PASADENA, Los Angeles Co.

ROSE & BRUTOCAO (AV)

225 South Lake Avenue, 9th Floor, 91101
Telephone: 818-683-8787; 818-788-8494
Fax: 818-683-0755;
Internet: RobertRose@rbpas.cc mail.compuserve.com
cc: Mail: RBPAS (818) 683-3890

MEMBER OF FIRM

Robert J. Rose

Reference: California State Bank (Covina Branch).

For full biographical listings, see the Martindale-Hubbell Law Directory

*SACRAMENTO,** Sacramento Co.

WILKE, FLEURY, HOFFELT, GOULD & BIRNEY (AV)

A Partnership including Professional Corporations
400 Capitol Mall, Suite 2200, 95814-4408
Telephone: 916-441-2430
Telefax: 916-442-6664
Mailing Address: P.O. Box 15559, 95852-0559

MEMBERS OF FIRM

Richard H. Hoffelt (Inc.)
William A. Gould, Jr., (Inc.)
Philip R. Birney (Inc.)
Thomas G. Redmon (Inc.)
Scott L. Gassaway
Donald Rex Heckman II (Inc.)
Alan G. Perkins
Bradley N. Webb
Ernest James Krtil
Robert R. Mirkin
Matthew W. Powell
Mark L. Andrews
Stephen K. Marmaduke
David A. Frenznick
John R. Valencia
Angus M. MacLeod

ASSOCIATES

Paul A. Dorris
Kelli M. Kennaday
Tracy S. Hendrickson
Joseph G. De Angelis
Jennifer L. Kennedy
Anthony J. DeCristoforo
Rachel N. Kook
Alicia F. From
Michael Polis
Matthew J. Smith
Wayne L. Ordos

OF COUNSEL

Sherman C. Wilke
Anita Seipp Marmaduke
Benjamin G. Davidian

Representative Clients: NOR-CAL Mutual Insurance Co.; California Optometric Assn.; KPMG Peat Marwick; Glaxo, Inc.

For full biographical listings, see the Martindale-Hubbell Law Directory

*SAN DIEGO,** San Diego Co.

FERRIS & BRITTON, A PROFESSIONAL CORPORATION (AV)

1600 First National Bank Center, 401 West A Street, 92101
Telephone: 619-233-3131
Fax: 619-232-9316

Christopher Q. Britton
Michael R. Weinstein

OF COUNSEL

Allan J. Reniche

Representative Clients: Allstate Insurance Co.; Cox Communications, Inc.; Enterprise Rent-a-Car; Exxon; Immuno Pharmaceutics, Inc.; Invitrogen Corporation; Teleport Communications Group; Southwest Airlines; Times-Mirror Cable Television.

For Complete List of Firm Personnel, See General Section

For full biographical listings, see the Martindale-Hubbell Law Directory

GRAY CARY WARE & FREIDENRICH, A PROFESSIONAL CORPORATION (AV)

Gray Cary Established in 1927
Ware & Freidenrich Established in 1969
401 "B" Street, Suite 1700, 92101
Telephone: 619-699-2700
Telecopier: 619-236-1048
Palo Alto, California Office: 400 Hamilton Avenue.
Telephone: 415-328-6561.
La Jolla, California Office: Suite 575, 1200 Prospect Street.
Telephone: 619-454-9101.
El Centro, California Office: 1224 State Street, P.O. Box 2890.
Telephone: 619-353-6140.

R. Reaves Elledge, Jr.
Browning E. Marean, III
Edward J. McIntyre
Jeffrey M. Shohet
James F. Stiven

Representative Clients: The Copley Press, Inc.; G. A. Technologies, Inc.; General Dynamics Corp.; Science Applications International Corp.; Westinghouse Electric Corp.

For Complete List of Firm Personnel, See General Section

For full biographical listings, see the Martindale-Hubbell Law Directory

HUGHES & NUNN (AV)

A Partnership including a Professional Corporation
450 "B" Street, Suite 2000, 92101
Telephone: 619-231-1661
Telecopier: 619-236-9271

MEMBERS OF FIRM

William D. Hughes (A Professional Corporation)
Randall M. Nunn
Scott D. Schabacker

ASSOCIATES

Lucia Rivas
E. Kenneth Purviance
Regan Furcolo

For full biographical listings, see the Martindale-Hubbell Law Directory

SELTZER CAPLAN WILKINS & MCMAHON, A PROFESSIONAL CORPORATION (AV)

2100 Symphony Towers, 750 B Street, 92101
Telephone: 619-685-3003
Fax: 619-685-3100

Gerald L. McMahon
Reginald A. Vitek
Dennis J. Wickham

Representative Clients: Girard Savings Bank; W.R. Grace & Co--Conn.; McDonnell-Douglas Corp.; McMillin Communities; Philip Morris Incorporated; Taco Bell Corp.; Western Financial Savings Bank.

For Complete List of Firm Personnel, See General Section

For full biographical listings, see the Martindale-Hubbell Law Directory

*SAN FRANCISCO,** San Francisco Co.

CARR & MUSSMAN, A PROFESSIONAL CORPORATION (AV)

3 Embarcadero Center, Suite 1060, 94111
Telephone: 415-391-7112
Telecopier: 415-391-7124

Timothy E. Carr
William E. Mussman
William E. Mussman, III

Michael T. Healy

For full biographical listings, see the Martindale-Hubbell Law Directory

FURTH, FAHRNER & MASON (AV)

Furth Building, Suite 1000, 201 Sansome Street, 94104
Telephone: 415-433-2070
Telecopier: 415-982-2076
Healdsburg, California Office: 10300 Chalk Hill Road.
Telephone: 707-838-4379.
FAX: 707-838-9685.

MEMBERS OF FIRM

Frederick P. Furth
Daniel S. Mason
Thomas R. Fahrner
Bruce J. Wecker
Michael P. Lehmann
Craig C. Corbitt
Michele C. Jackson
George F. Bishop
Scott R. Campbell
Joseph W. Bell

Brett L. Raven
Christopher T. Micheletti
Wesley E. Overson, Jr.
Steven S. Lubliner
Emily Platt
David A. Hoskins
Valerie M. Wagner

For full biographical listings, see the Martindale-Hubbell Law Directory

San Francisco—Continued

GOLD & BENNETT, A PROFESSIONAL LAW CORPORATION (AV)

595 Market Street, Suite 2300, 94105
Telephone: 415-777-2230
Fax: 415-777-5189

Paul F. Bennett
Solomon B. Cera

George S. Trevor
Glenn MacRae Goffin
Gregory C. Moore
Marc Rosner
Robert A. Jigarjian
B. F. Pierce Gore

For full biographical listings, see the Martindale-Hubbell Law Directory

LIEFF, CABRASER & HEIMANN (AV)

Embarcadero Center West, 30th Floor, 275 Battery Street, 94111
Telephone: 415-956-1000
Telecopier: 415-956-1008

Robert L. Lieff
Elizabeth J. Cabraser
Richard M. Heimann
William Bernstein
William B. Hirsch
James M. Finberg
Karen E. Karpen
Michael F. Ram
William M. Audet
Joseph R. Saveri
Steven E. Fineman
Donald C. Arbitblit
Robert J. Nelson

Kristine E. Bailey
Suzanne A. Barr
Kelly M. Dermody
Deborah A. Kemp
Anthony K. Lee
Jacqueline E. Mottek
Kimberly W. Pate
Melanie M. Piech
Morris A. Ratner
Rhonda L. Woo

For full biographical listings, see the Martindale-Hubbell Law Directory

MOLLIGAN, COX & MOYER, A PROFESSIONAL CORPORATION (AV)

703 Market Street, Suite 1800, 94103
Telephone: 415-543-9464
Fax: 415-777-1828

Ingemar E. Hoberg (1903-1971)
John H. Finger (1913-1991)
Phillip E. Brown (Retired)
Peter N. Molligan
Stephen T. Cox
David W. Moyer

John C. Hentschel
Guy D. Loranger
Nicholas J. Piediscazzi

OF COUNSEL

Kenneth W. Rosenthal
Barbara A. Zuras

For full biographical listings, see the Martindale-Hubbell Law Directory

ROSEN, BIEN & ASARO (AV)

Eighth Floor, 155 Montgomery Street, 94104
Telephone: 415-433-6830
Fax: 415-433-7104

Sanford Jay Rosen
Michael W. Bien
Andrea G. Asaro

Stephen M. Liacouras
Hilary A. Fox
Thomas Nolan
Mary Ann Cryan (Not admitted in CA)
Donna Petrine

For full biographical listings, see the Martindale-Hubbell Law Directory

SAVERI AND SAVERI, A PROFESSIONAL CORPORATION (AV)

41st Floor, Spear Street Tower, One Market Plaza, 94105-1001
Telephone: 415-243-4005
Fax: 415-243-4009

Richard Saveri
Guido Saveri

OF COUNSEL

John A. Kithas

For full biographical listings, see the Martindale-Hubbell Law Directory

SPIEGEL LIAO & KAGAY (AV)

88 Kearny Street, Suite 1310, 94108-5530
Telephone: 415-956-5959
Telecopier: 415-362-1431

Michael I. Spiegel
Charles M. Kagay

OF COUNSEL

Bartholomew Lee
Wayne M. Liao

For full biographical listings, see the Martindale-Hubbell Law Directory

LAW FIRM OF ROBERT A. SUSK (AV)

101 California Street, Suite 3550, 94111-5847
Telephone: 415-982-3950
Fax: 415-982-6143

Robert A. Susk
Leslie J. Mann
Phillip H. Kalsched

For full biographical listings, see the Martindale-Hubbell Law Directory

COLORADO

*DENVER,** Denver Co.

DUFFORD & BROWN, P.C. (AV)

1700 Broadway, Suite 1700, 80290-1701
Telephone: 303-861-8013
Facsimile: 303-832-3804

Thomas G. Brown
David W. Furgason
Gregory A. Ruegsegger
Edward D. White

Representative Clients: CF&I Steel, L.P.; The Colorado and Wyoming Railway Co.

For Complete List of Firm Personnel, See General Section

For full biographical listings, see the Martindale-Hubbell Law Directory

HOLLAND & HART (AV)

Suite 2900, 555 Seventeenth Street, P.O. Box 8749, 80201
Telephone: 303-295-8000
Cable Address: "Holhart Denver"
Telecopier: 303-295-8261
TWX: 910-931-0568
Denver Tech Center, Colorado Office: Suite 1050, 4601 DTC Boulevard.
Telephone: 303-290-1600.
Telecopier: 303-290-1606.
Aspen, Colorado Office: 600 East Main Street.
Telephone: 303-925-3476.
Telecopier: 303-925-9367.
Boulder, Colorado Office: Suite 500, 1050 Walnut.
Telephone: 303-473-2700.
Telecopier: 303-473-2720.
Colorado Springs, Colorado Office: Suite 1000, 90 S. Cascade Avenue.
Telephone: 719-475-7730.
Telex: 82077 SHHTLX.
Telecopier: 719-634-2461.
Washington, D.C. Office: Suite 310, 1001 Pennsylvania Avenue, N.W.
Telephone: 202-638-5500.
Telecopier: 202-737-8998.
Boise, Idaho Office: Suite 1400, West One Plaza, 101 South Capitol Boulevard, P.O. Box 2527.
Telephone: 208-342-5000.
Telecopier: 208-343-8869.
Billings, Montana Office: Suite 1500, First Interstate Center, 401 North 31st Street, P.O. Box 639.
Telephone: 406-252-2166.
Telecopier: 406-252-1669.
Salt Lake City, Utah Office: Suite 880, 111 East Broadway.
Telephone: 801-578-6000.
FAX: 801-578-6010.
Cheyenne, Wyoming Office: Holland & Hart, A Partnership including Professional Corporations, Suite 500, 2020 Carey Avenue, P.O. Box 1347.
Telephone: 307-778-4200.
Telecopier: 307-778-8175.
Jackson, Wyoming Office: Holland & Hart, A Partnership including Professional Corporations, Suite 2, 175 South King Street, P.O. Box 68.
Telephone: 307-739-9741.
Telecopier: 307-739-9744.

MEMBERS OF FIRM

William C. McClearn
Harry L. Hobson
Gordon G. Greiner
Jane Michaels
James E. Hartley

DENVER TECH CENTER, COLORADO RESIDENT PARTNER

William W. Maywhort

BOULDER, COLORADO PARTNER

William E. Mooz, Jr.

COLORADO SPRINGS, COLORADO PARTNER

Gary R. Burghart (Resident)

BOISE, IDAHO RESIDENT PARTNER

B. Newal Squyres, Jr.

BILLINGS, MONTANA PARTNER

Paul D. Miller

(See Next Column)

HOLLAND & HART—*Continued*

CHEYENNE, WYOMING PARTNER

Donald I. Schultz (P.C.)

For Complete List of Firm Personnel, See General Section

For full biographical listings, see the Martindale-Hubbell Law Directory

IRELAND, STAPLETON, PRYOR & PASCOE, P.C. (AV)

Suite 2600, 1675 Broadway, 80202
Telephone: 303-623-2700
Telecopier: 303-623-2062

Tucker K. Trautman

Representative Clients: Aspen Highlands Skiing Corp.; NBI, Inc.; Dillon Companies, Inc.; Harcourt, Brace, Jovanovich Legal, Inc.

For Complete List of Firm Personnel, See General Section

For full biographical listings, see the Martindale-Hubbell Law Directory

MUSGRAVE & THEIS, P.C. (AV)

Mellon Financial Center, 1775 Sherman Street, Suite 2950, 80203
Telephone: 303-863-8686
Facsimile: 303-863-0423

B. Lawrence Theis — Bobbee J. Musgrave

OF COUNSEL

Thomas P. McMahon

Representative Clients: Anheuser-Busch Companies; City and County of Denver; Schuller International; Sashco, Inc.; Tri-County Cablevision, Inc.
Reference: Norwest Bank of Buckingham Square.

For full biographical listings, see the Martindale-Hubbell Law Directory

REIMAN & ASSOCIATES, P.C. (AV)

1600 Broadway, Suite 1640, 80202
Telephone: 303-860-1500
Fax: 303-839-4380

Jeffrey Reiman

Marcie K. Bayaz — James Birch

For full biographical listings, see the Martindale-Hubbell Law Directory

SHERMAN & HOWARD L.L.C. (AV)

Attorneys at Law
633 Seventeenth Street, Suite 3000, 80202
Telephone: 303-297-2900
Telecopier: 303-298-0940
Colorado Springs, Colorado Office: Suite 1500, 90 South Cascade Avenue, 80903.
Telephone: 719-475-2440.
Las Vegas, Nevada Office: Swendseid & Stern a member in Sherman & Howard L.L.C., 317 Sixth Street, 89101.
Telephone: 702-387-6073.
Reno, Nevada Office: Swendseid & Stern, a member in Sherman & Howard L.L.C., 50 West Liberty Street, Suite 660, 89501.
Telephone: 702-323-1980.

James E. Hautzinger — Paul Curtis Daw

Representative Clients: AT&T Corp.; Eastman Kodak Co.; Newmont Gold Corp.; Keystone Resort; Tele-Communications, Inc.; VICORP Restaurants, Inc.

For Complete List of Firm Personnel, See General Section

For full biographical listings, see the Martindale-Hubbell Law Directory

WALTERS & JOYCE, P.C. (AV)

2015 York Street, 80205
Telephone: 303-322-1404
FAX: 303-377-5668

William E. Walters, III

Reference: Norwest Bank of Buckingham Square.

For Complete List of Firm Personnel, See General Section

For full biographical listings, see the Martindale-Hubbell Law Directory

CONNECTICUT

*HARTFORD,** Hartford Co.

DAY, BERRY & HOWARD (AV)

Cityplace, 06103-3499
Telephone: 203-275-0100
Telecopier: 203-275-0343
Stamford, Connecticut Office: One Canterbury Green.
Telephone: 203-977-7300.
Telecopier: 203-977-7301.
Boston, Massachusetts Office: 260 Franklin Street.
Telephone: 617-345-4600.
Telex: 990686.
Telecopier: 617-345-4745.

Scott P. Moser — Richard M. Reynolds
James Sicilian

For Complete List of Firm Personnel, See General Section

For full biographical listings, see the Martindale-Hubbell Law Directory

SOROKIN SOROKIN GROSS HYDE & WILLIAMS P.C. (AV)

One Corporate Center, 06103
Telephone: 203-525-6645
Fax: 203-522-1781
Simsbury, Connecticut Office: 730 Hopmeadow Street.
Telephone: 203-651-9348.
Rocky Hill, Connecticut Office: 2360 Main Street.
Telephone: 203-563-9305.
Fax: 203-529-6931.
Glastonbury, Connecticut Office: 124 Hebron Avenue.
Telephone: 203-659-8801.

Clifford J. Grandjean — Richard C. Robinson

For Complete List of Firm Personnel, See General Section

For full biographical listings, see the Martindale-Hubbell Law Directory

*NEW HAVEN,** New Haven Co.

WIGGIN & DANA (AV)

One Century Tower, 06508-1832
Telephone: 203-498-4400
Telefax: 203-782-2889
Hartford, Connecticut Office: One CityPlace.
Telephone: 203-297-3700.
FAX: 203-525-9380.
Stamford, Connecticut Office: Three Stamford Plaza, 301 Tresser Boulevard.
Telephone: 203-363-7600.
Telefax: 203-363-7676.

MEMBERS OF FIRM

Shaun S. Sullivan — Patrick J. Monahan, II (Resident at Hartford)
Mark R. Kravitz — Robert M. Langer (Resident at Hartford)
Edward Wood Dunham
William G. Millman, Jr.

ASSOCIATES

Michelle Wilcox DeBarge — Thomas J. Witt (Resident at Hartford)
Merton G. Gollaher

For Complete List of Firm Personnel, See General Section

For full biographical listings, see the Martindale-Hubbell Law Directory

DISTRICT OF COLUMBIA

WASHINGTON, D.C. Co.

***** **indicates certain Bar Register subscribers, in cities of comparable size and importance, who maintain an additional office in Washington, D.C. and who have arranged for representation as a part of the Washington, D.C. listings that follow**

BAKER & HOSTETLER (AV)

Washington Square, Suite 1100, 1050 Connecticut Avenue, N.W., 20036-5304
Telephone: 202-861-1500
In Cleveland, Ohio: 3200 National City Center, 1900 East Ninth Street.
Telephone: 216-621-0200.
In Columbus, Ohio: Capitol Square, Suite 2100, 65 East State Street.
Telephone: 614-228-1541.
In Denver, Colorado: 303 East 17th Avenue, Suite 1100.
Telephone: 303-861-0600.
In Houston, Texas: 1000 Louisiana, Suite 2000.
Telephone: 713-751-1600.

(See Next Column)

BAKER & HOSTETLER, *Washington—Continued*

In Long Beach, California: 300 Oceangate, Suite 620.
Telephone: 310-432-2827.
In Los Angeles, California: 600 Wilshire Boulevard.
Telephone: 213-624-2400.
In Orlando, Florida: SunBank Center, Suite 2300, 200 South Orange Avenue.
Telephone: 305-841-1111.
In College Park, Maryland: 9658 Baltimore Boulevard, Suite 206.
Telephone: 301-441-2781.
In Alexandria, Virginia: 437 North Lee Street.
Telephone: 703-549-1294.
In San Francisco, California: One Sansome Street, Suite 2000.
Telephone: 415-951-4705.

PARTNERS

Gerald A. Connell — Louis R. Sernoff
John Daniel Reaves — Lee H. Simowitz
Alan S. Ward

ASSOCIATES

Jenifer M. Brown — John M. Taladay

For Complete List of Firm Personnel, See General Section

For full biographical listings, see the Martindale-Hubbell Law Directory

*** BELL, BOYD & LLOYD (AV)**

1615 L Street, N.W., 20036
Telephone: 202-466-6300
FAX: 202-463-0678
Chicago, Illinois Office: Three First National Plaza, Suite 3300, 70 West Madison Street.
Telephone: 312-372-1121.
FAX: 312-372-2098.

RESIDENT PARTNERS

John C. Christie, Jr. — Patrick J. Roach

For Complete List of Firm Personnel, See General Section

For full biographical listings, see the Martindale-Hubbell Law Directory

DOW, LOHNES & ALBERTSON (AV)

Suite 500, 1255 Twenty-Third Street, N.W., 20037-1194
Telephone: 202-857-2500
Telecopier: (202) 857-2900
Atlanta, Georgia Office: One Ravinia Drive, Suite 1600.
Telephone: 404-901-8800.
Telecopier: (404) 901-8874.

MEMBERS OF THE FIRM

Jonathan D. Hart — James A. Treanor, III

For Complete List of Firm Personnel, See General Section

For full biographical listings, see the Martindale-Hubbell Law Directory

DUNAWAY & CROSS, A PROFESSIONAL CORPORATION (AV)

Suite 400, 1146 19th Street, N.W., 20036
Telephone: 202-862-9700

Mac S. Dunaway — George C. Courtot
Gary E. Cross — Stanley J. Green

Matthew F. Hall — Joan R. Vail
Christopher E. Anders — (Not admitted in DC)

COUNSEL

Raymond P. Shafer (Not admitted in DC)

For full biographical listings, see the Martindale-Hubbell Law Directory

GROVE, JASKIEWICZ AND COBERT (AV)

Suite 400, 1730 M Street, N.W., 20036
Telephone: 202-296-2900
Telecopier: 202-296-1370
Baltimore, Maryland Office: The Park Plaza, 800 North Charles Street, Suite 400.
Telephone: 301-727-7010.

MEMBERS OF FIRM

William J. Grove (1914-1988) — Robert L. Cope
Ronald N. Cobert — Joseph Michael Roberts
Paul H. Lamboley (Not admitted in DC) — Andrew M. Danas
Edward J. Kiley — Andrew M. Whitman (Not admitted in DC)

OF COUNSEL

Leonard A. Jaskiewicz — Lawrence E. Dubé, Jr.
James F. Flint — James K. Jeanblanc
Edmund M. Jaskiewicz

For full biographical listings, see the Martindale-Hubbell Law Directory

*** JONES, DAY, REAVIS & POGUE (AV)**

Metropolitan Square, 1450 G Street, N.W., 20005-2088
Telephone: 202-879-3939
Cable Address: "Attorneys Washington"
Telex: W.U. (Domestic) 89-2410 ATTORNEYS WASH (International) 64363 ATTORNEYS WASH
Telecopier: 202-737-2832
In Atlanta, Georgia: 3500 One Peachtree Center, 303 Peachtree Street, N.E .
Telephone: 404-521-3939.
Cable Address: "Attorneys Atlanta".
Telex: 54-2711.
Telecopier: 404-581-8330.
In Brussels, Belgium: Avenue Louise 480, 7th Floor, B-1050 Brussels.
Telephone: 011-32-2-645-14-11.
Telecopier: 011-32-2-645-14-45.
In Chicago, Illinois: 77 West Wacker.
Telephone: 312-782-3939.
Telecopier: 312-782-8585.
In Cleveland, Ohio: North Point, 901 Lakeside Avenue.
Telephone: 216-586-3939.
Cable Address: "Attorneys Cleveland."
Telex: 980389.
Telecopier: 216-579-0212.
In Columbus, Ohio: 1900 Huntington Center.
Telephone: 614-469-3939.
Cable Address: "Attorneys Columbus."
Telecopier: 614-461-4198.
In Dallas, Texas: 2300 Trammell Crow Center, 2001 Ross Avenue.
Telephone: 214-220-3939.
Cable Address: "Attorneys Dallas."
Telex: 730852.
Telecopier: 214-969-5100.
In Frankfurt, Germany: Triton Haus, Bockenheimer Landstrasse 42, 60323 Frankfurt am Main.
Telephone: 49-69-9726-3939.
Telecopier: 49-69-9726-3993.
In Geneva, Switzerland: 20, rue de Candolle.
Telephone: 011-41-22-320-2339.
Telecopier: 011-41-22-320-1232.
In Hong Kong: 1501 One Exchange Square, 8 Connaught Place.
Telephone: 011-852-2526-6895.
Telecopier: 011-852-2810-5787.
In Irvine, California: 2603 Main Street, Suite 900 .
Telephone: 714-851-3939.
Telex: 194911 Lawyers LSA.
Telecopier: 714-553-7539.
In London, England: One Mount Street.
Telephone: 011-44-71-493-9361.
Cable Address: "Surgoe London WI."
Telecopier: 011-44-71-493-9666.
In Los Angeles, California: 555 West Fifth Street, Suite 4600.
Telephone: 213-489-3939.
Telex: 181439 UD.
Telecopier: 213-243-2539.
In New York, New York: 599 Lexington Avenue.
Telephone: 212-326-3939.
Cable Address: "JONESDAY NEWYORK."
Telex: 237013 JDRP UR.
Telecopier: 212-755-7306.
In Paris, France: 62, rue du Faubourg Saint-Honore.
Telephone: 011-33-1-44-71-3939.
Cable Address: "Surgoe Paris."
Telex: 290156 Surgoe.
Telecopier: 011-33-1-49-24-0471.
In Pittsburgh, Pennsylvania: 500 Grant Street, 31st Floor.
Telephone: 412-391-3939.
Cable Address: "Attorneys Pittsburgh".
Telecopier: 412-394-7959.
In Riyadh, Saudi Arabia: Law Offices of Saud M.A. Shawwaf, P.O. Box 2700.
Telephones: 011 (966-1) 465-6543, 011 (966-1) 464-8534 or 011 (966-1) 464-8540.
Telex: 401831 SAUCON SJ.
Telecopier: (966-1) 464-8480.
In Taipai, Taiwan: 8th Floor, 2 Tun Hwa South Road, Section 2.
Telephone: 011 (886-2) 704-6808.
Telecopier: 011 (886-2) 704-6791.
In Tokyo, Japan: Toranomon MT Building, 4th Floor, 10-3, Toranomon 3-Chome, Minato-Ku, Tokyo 105, Japan.
Telephone: 011-81-3-3433-3939.
Telecopier: 011-81-3-5401-2725.

MEMBERS OF FIRM IN WASHINGTON, D.C.

Joe Sims — Timothy J. Finn
Tom D. Smith — Toby G. Singer
Phillip A. Proger — Kathryn M. Fenton
Thomas F. Cullen, Jr. — Kevin D. McDonald
Charles A. James

OF COUNSEL

William E. Swope

SENIOR ATTORNEY

Robert C. Jones

(See Next Column)

JONES, DAY, REAVIS & POGUE—*Continued*

ASSOCIATES

Karen E. Silverman	Hendrik A. Bourgeois
Stephen D. Kiess	(Not admitted in DC)

For Complete List of Firm Personnel, See General Section

For full biographical listings, see the Martindale-Hubbell Law Directory

* McDERMOTT, WILL & EMERY (AV)

A Partnership including Professional Corporations
1850 K Street, N.W., 20006-2296
Telephone: 202-887-8000
Telex: 253565 MILAM CGO
Facsimile: 202-778-8087
Chicago, Illinois Office: 227 West Monroe Street.
Telephone: 312-372-2000.
Telex: 253565 MILAM CGO.
Facsimile: 312-984-7700.
Boston, Massachusetts Office: 75 State Street, Suite 1700.
Telephone: 617-345-5000.
Telex: 951324 MILAM BSN.
Facsimile: 617-345-5077.
Miami, Florida Office: 201 South Biscayne Boulevard.
Telephone: 305-358-3500.
Telex: 441777 LEYES.
Facsimile: 305-347-6500.
Los Angeles, California Office: 2049 Century Park East.
Telephone: 310-277-4110.
Facsimile: 310-277-4730.
Newport Beach, California Office: 1301 Dove Street, Suite 500.
Telephone: 714-851-0633.
Facsimile: 714-851-9348.
New York, N.Y. Office: 1211 Avenue of the Americas.
Telephone: 212-768-5400.
Facsimile: 212-768-5444.
St. Petersburg, Russia Office: 2/2 Tchaikovsky Street, #517, 191187 St. Petersburg, Russia.
Telephone: (7) (812) 273-9831.
Facsimile: (7) (812) 273-9831.
Tallinn, Estonia Office: Tallinn Business Center, 6 Harju Street, EE0001 Tallinn, Estonia.
Telephone: 372 6 31-05-53.
Facsimile: 372 6 31-05-54.
Vilnius, Lithuania Office: Smetonos 6, 2600 Vilnius, Lithuania.
Telephone: 370 2 61-43-08.
Facsimile: 370 2 22-79-55.
Associated (Independent) Offices:
Brussels, Belgium: Uettwiller Grelon Lippens Dekeyser, 73 avenue Vandendriessche, 1150 Brussels, Belgium.
Telephone: (32) (2) 772-87-50.
Facsimile: (32) (2) 772-87-52.
London, England: Paisner & Co, Bouverie House, 154 Fleet Street, London EC4A 2DQ, England.
Telephone: (44) (71) 353-0299.
Facsimile: (44) (71) 583-8621.
Paris, France: Uettwiller Grelon Gout Canat & Associes, 68, boulevard de Courcelles, 75017 Paris, France.
Telephone: (33) (1) 48 88 89 00.
Facsimile: (33) (1) 48 88 05 50.

MEMBERS OF FIRM

William H. Barrett	Amy E. Hancock
Jeanne A. Carpenter	Robert S. Schwartz
Michael E. Friedlander	Carl W. Schwarz
Nathalie F. P. Gilfoyle	James H. Sneed
Seth D. Greenstein	Timothy J. Waters

COUNSEL

Ronald A. Bloch

For Complete List of Firm Personnel, See General Section

For full biographical listings, see the Martindale-Hubbell Law Directory

STEPTOE & JOHNSON (AV)

1330 Connecticut Avenue, N.W., 20036
Telephone: 202-429-3000
Cable Address: "Stepjohn"
Telex: 89-2503
Telecopier: 202-429-3902
Phoenix, Arizona Office: Two Renaissance Square, 40 N. Central Avenue, Suite 2400, 85004.
Telephone: 602-257-5200.
Moscow, Russia Office: Steptoe & Johnson International Affiliate in Moscow. 25 Tsvetnoy Boulevard, Building 3 Moscow, Russia 103051.
Telephone: 011-7-501-929-9700.
Fax: 501-929-9701.

(See Next Column)

MEMBERS

Betty Jo Christian	Robert W. Fleishman
Robert E. Jordan, III	Mark F. Horning
Richard O. Cunningham	Ellen M. McNamara
David L. Roll	Timothy M. Walsh
Richard H. Porter	Stephen A. Fennell
Daniel J. Plaine	Samuel M. Sipe, Jr.
John R. Labovitz	Philip L. Malet
F. Michael Kail	Edward J. Krauland

John D. Graubert

OF COUNSEL

Richard A. Whiting	Richard Diamond

For Complete List of Firm Personnel, See General Section

For full biographical listings, see the Martindale-Hubbell Law Directory

SUTHERLAND, ASBILL & BRENNAN (AV)

1275 Pennsylvania Avenue, N.W., 20004-2404
Telephone: 202-383-0100
Cable Address: "Sutab Wash"
Telex: 89-501
Facsimile: 202-637-3593
Atlanta, Georgia Office: 999 Peachtree Street, N. E., 30309-3996.
Telephone: 404-853-8000.
New York, N.Y. Office: 1270 Avenue of the Americas, 10020-1700.
Telephone: 212-332-3000.
Austin, Texas Office: 111 Congress Avenue, 23rd Floor, 78701-4079.
Telephone: 512-469-3350.

Karen L. Grimm	Kenneth G. Starling
Robert G. Levy (Not admitted in DC)	

For Complete List of Firm Personnel, See General Section

For full biographical listings, see the Martindale-Hubbell Law Directory

* THOMPSON, HINE AND FLORY (AV)

1920 N Street, N.W., 20036-1601
Telephone: 202-331-8800
Fax: 202-331-8330
Telex: 904173
Cable Address: "Caglaw"
Akron, Ohio Office: 50 S. Main Street, Suite 502, 44308-1828.
Telephone: 216-376-8090.
Fax: 216-376-8386.
Cincinnati, Ohio Office: 312 Walnut Street, 14th Floor, 45202-4029.
Telephone: 513-352-6700.
Fax: 513-241-4771.
Telex: 938003.
Cleveland, Ohio Office: 1100 National City Bank Building, 629 Euclid Avenue, 44114.
Telephone: 216-566-5500.
Fax: 216-566-5583.
Telex: 980217. Cable Address "Thomflor".
Columbus, Ohio Office: One Columbus, 10 West Broad Street, 43215-34353.
Telephone: 614-469-3200.
Fax: 614-469-3361.
Dayton, Ohio Office: 2000 Courthouse Plaza, N.E., 45402-1706.
Telephone: 513-443-6600.
Fax: 513-443-6637, 513-443-6635.
Palm Beach, Florida Office: 125 Worth Avenue, 33480-4466.
Telephone: 407-833-5900.
Fax: 407-833-5951.
Brussels, Belgium Office: Rue Des Chevaliers, Ridderstraat 14 - B.10, B-1050.
Telephone: 011-32-2-511-9326.
Fax: 011-32-2-513-9206.

MEMBER OF FIRM

Charles L. Freed

For Complete List of Firm Personnel, See General Section

For full biographical listings, see the Martindale-Hubbell Law Directory

* VENABLE, BAETJER, HOWARD & CIVILETTI (AV)

A Partnership including Professional Corporations
Suite 1000, 1201 New York Avenue, N.W., 20005
Telephone: 202-962-4800
Fax: 202-962-8300
Baltimore, Maryland Office: Venable, Baetjer and Howard, 1800 Mercantile Bank & Trust Building, 2 Hopkins Plaza.
Telephone: 410-244-7400.
McLean, Virginia Office: Venable, Baetjer and Howard, Suite 400, 2010 Corporate Ridge.
Telephone: 703-760-1600.
Rockville, Maryland Office: Venable, Baetjer and Howard, Suite 500, One Church Street, P.O. Box 1906.
Telephone: 301-217-5600.

(See Next Column)

VENABLE, BAETJER, HOWARD & CIVILETTI, *Washington—Continued*

Towson, Maryland Office: Venable, Baetjer and Howard, 210 Allegheny Avenue, P. O. Box 5517.
Telephone: 410-494-6200.

MEMBERS OF FIRM

Benjamin R. Civiletti (P.C.) (Also at Baltimore and Towson, Maryland Offices)
Douglas D. Connah, Jr. (P.C.) (Also at Baltimore, Maryland Office)
Kenneth C. Bass, III (Also at McLean, Virginia Office)
Edward F. Glynn, Jr.
Michael Schatzow (Also at Baltimore and Towson, Maryland Offices)
James K. Archibald (Also at Baltimore and Towson, Maryland Offices)
James R. Myers
Jeffrey D. Knowles
William D. Coston
Maurice Baskin
Amy Berman Jackson
William D. Quarles (Also at Towson, Maryland Office)

ASSOCIATE

David W. Goewey

For Complete List of Firm Personnel, See General Section

For full biographical listings, see the Martindale-Hubbell Law Directory

WILMER, CUTLER & PICKERING (AV)

2445 M Street, N.W., 20037-1420
Telephone: 202-663-6000
Facsimile: 202-663-6363
Internet: Law@Wilmer.Com
European Offices:
4 Carlton Gardens, London, SW1Y 5AA, England. Telephone: 011 (4471) 839-4466.
Facsimile: 011 (4471) 839-3537.
Rue de la Loi 15 Wetstraat, B-1040 Brussels, Belgium. Telephone: 011 (322) 231-0903.
Facsimile: 011 (322) 230-4322.
Friedrichstrasse 95, D-10117 Berlin, Germany. Telephone: 011 (4930) 2643-3601.
Facsimile: 011 (4930) 2643-3630.

MEMBERS OF FIRM

Robert A. Hammond, III
Daniel K. Mayers
James S. Campbell
Ronald J. Greene
Gary D. Wilson
C. Loring Jetton, Jr.
A. Douglas Melamed
William J. Kolasky, Jr.
John Rounsaville, Jr.
James S. Venit (Not admitted in DC; Resident, European Office, Brussels, Belgium)

COUNSEL

Dr. Andreas Weitbrecht (Not admitted in DC; Resident, European Office, Brussels, Belgium)

SPECIAL COUNSEL

John J. Kallaugher (Not admitted in DC; Resident, European Office, London, England)

For Complete List of Firm Personnel, See General Section

For full biographical listings, see the Martindale-Hubbell Law Directory

FLORIDA

*KISSIMMEE,** Osceola Co.

POHL & BROWN, P.A.

(See Winter Park)

*MIAMI,** Dade Co.

KENNY NACHWALTER SEYMOUR ARNOLD CRITCHLOW & SPECTOR, PROFESSIONAL ASSOCIATION (AV)

1100 Miami Center, 201 South Biscayne Boulevard, 33131-4327
Telephone: 305-373-1000
Facsimile: 305-372-1861
ABA/net: 18338
Rogersville, Tennessee Office: 107 East Main Street, Suite 301, 37857-3347.
Telephone: 615-272-5300.
Facsimile: 615-272-4961.

James J. Kenny
Michael Nachwalter
Richard Alan Arnold
Brian F. Spector
Kevin J. Murray
William J. Blechman
Harry R. Schafer
David H. Lichter
Scott E. Perwin

Representative Clients: Albertson's, Inc.; American Cyanamid Co.; American Stores; A&P, Inc.; Cartier, Inc.; Charterhouse Group International, Inc.; City Gas Company of Florida; Ethan Allen; GTE Directories; The Kroger Co.; Nestle Food Co.; Safeway, Inc.

(See Next Column)

For Complete List of Firm Personnel, See General Section

For full biographical listings, see the Martindale-Hubbell Law Directory

MERSHON, SAWYER, JOHNSTON, DUNWODY & COLE (AV)

A Partnership including Professional Associations
Suite 4500 First Union Financial Center, 200 South Biscayne Boulevard, 33131-2387
Telephone: 305-358-5100
Cable Address: "Mercole"
Telex: 515705
Fax: 305-376-8654
Naples, Florida Office: Pelican Bay Corporate Centre, Suite 501, 5551 Ridgewood Drive.
Telephone: 813-598-1055.
Fax: 813-598-1868.
West Palm Beach, Florida Office: 777 South Flagler Drive, Suite 900.
Telephone: 407-659-5990.
Fax: 407-659-6313.
Key West, Florida Office: 3132 North Side Drive, Suite 102.
Telephone: 305-296-1774.
Fax: 305-296-1715
London, England Office: Blake Lodge, Bridge Lane, London SW11 3AD, England.
Telephone: 44-71-978-7748.
Fax: 44-71-350-0156.

MEMBER OF FIRM

William J. Dunaj (P.A.)

ASSOCIATE

Rona F. Morrow

Representative Clients: Arvida/JMB Partners; Bankers Trust Co.; Biscayne Kennel Club, Inc.; The Chase Manhattan Bank, N.A.; Lennar Corp.; Reynolds Metals Co.; United States Sugar Corp.; University of Miami.

For Complete List of Firm Personnel, See General Section

For full biographical listings, see the Martindale-Hubbell Law Directory

SHUTTS & BOWEN (AV)

A Partnership including Professional Associations
1500 Miami Center, 201 South Biscayne Boulevard, 33131
Telephone: 305-358-6300
Cable Address: "Shuttsbo"
Telefax: 305-381-9982
Key Largo, Florida Office: Suite A206, 31 Ocean Reef Drive.
Telephone: 305-367-2881.
Orlando, Florida Office: 20 North Orange Avenue, Suite 1000.
Telephone: 407-423-3200.
Fax: 407-425-8316.
West Palm Beach, Florida Office: One Clearlake Centre, 250 Australian Avenue South, Suite 500.
Telephone: 407-835-8500.
Fax: 407-650-8530.
Amsterdam, The Netherlands Office: Shutts & Bowen, B.V., Europa Boulevard 59, 1083 AD, Amsterdam.
Telephone: (31 20) 661-0969.
Fax: (31 20) 642-1475.
London, England Office: 48 Mount Street, London W1Y 5RE.
Telephone: 4471493-4840.
Telefax: 4471493-4299.

MEMBERS OF FIRM

Frank B. Shutts (1870-1947)
Crate D. Bowen (1871-1959)
Gary M. Bagliebter
Arnold L. Berman (Resident at West Palm Beach Office)
Joseph D. Bolton
Bowman Brown (P.A.)
Andrew M. Brumby (Resident at Orlando Office)
Judith A. Burke
Sheila M. Cesarano
Jonathan Cohen
Kevin D. Cowan
Luis A. de Armas
Jean-Charles Dibbs
James F. Durham, II
Charles Robinson Fawsett (P.A.)
Esteban A. Ferrer
Robert G. Fracasso, Jr.
Robert A. Freyer (Resident at Orlando Office)
Roger Friedbauer
Andrew L. Gordon
Michael L. Gore (Resident at Orlando Office)
Robert E. Gunn (P.A.) (Resident at West Palm Beach Office)
John K. Harris, Jr.
Edmund T. Henry, III
William N. Jacobs
Marvin A. Kirsner (Resident at West Palm Beach Office)
John Thomas Kolinski
Richard M. Leslie (P.A.)
Maxine Master Long
Don A. Lynn (P.A.)
Lee D. Mackson
Antonio Martinez, Jr., (P.A.)
Joseph F. McSorley (Resident at West Palm Beach Office)
John E. Meagher
Arthur J. Menor (Resident at West Palm Beach Office)
Robert D. Miller (Resident at West Palm Beach Office)
Alan I. Mishael
C. Richard Morgan
Timothy J. Murphy
Phillip G. Newcomm (P.A.)
Louis Nostro
Harold E. Patricoff Jr.
Stephen L. Perrone (P.A.)
Geoffrey Randall
Sally M. Richardson
Margaret A. Rolando
Allan M. Rubin
Raul J. Salas
Robert A. Savill (Resident at Orlando Office)

(See Next Column)

SHUTTS & BOWEN—*Continued*

MEMBERS OF FIRM (Continued)

Rosemarie N. Sanderson Schade (P.A.) (Resident at Amsterdam, The Netherlands)
Alfred G. Smith, II
William F. Smith
Robert C. Sommerville (P.A.) (Resident; West Palm Beach Office)
Kimarie R. Stratos
Xavier L. Suarez
Robert E. Venney
Barbara E. Vicevich (P.A.)
Robert A. Wainger
Joseph Donald Wasil
John B. White (P.A.)
James G. Willard (Resident at Orlando Office)
Scott G. Williams (Resident at West Palm Beach Office)
Kenneth W. Wright (Resident at Orlando Office)

ASSOCIATES

Katrina D. Baker
Mark J. Boulris
Christopher W. Boyett
Thomas P. Callan (Resident at Orlando Office)
Steven L. Chudnow
Gregory L. Denes
Kathleen L. Deutsch
Terry B. Fein
Robert B. Goldman (Resident at West Palm Beach Office)
Joseph M. Goldstein
Mary Ruth Houston (Resident at Orlando Office)
Jeffrey M. Landau
Lourdes B. Martinez-Esquivel
William G. Mc Cullough
Patrick M. Muldowney (Resident at Orlando Office)
Lisa R. Pearson (Resident, Orlando Office)
Andrew P. Tetzeli
Geoffrey L. Travis
Daniel J. Weidmann (Resident in Orlando)
Robert Wexler (Resident at West Palm Beach Office)

OF COUNSEL

Jordan Bittel (P.A.)
John S. Chowning (P.A.)
John R. Day (P.A.)
Stephen J. Gray (Resident, London, England Office)
Rod Jones (Resident at Orlando Office)
Marshall J. Langer (P.A.) (Resident, London, England Office)
Preston L. Prevatt

CONSULTING ATTORNEY

Patrick L. Murray (Not admitted in the United States)

Representative Clients: Southern Bell Telephone Co.; BellSouth Advertising & Publishing Co.; General Electric Co.; Equitable Life Assurance Society of the U.S.; New England Mutual Life Insurance Co.; New York Life Insurance Co.; Dadeland Bank.

For full biographical listings, see the Martindale-Hubbell Law Directory

ZUCKERMAN, SPAEDER, TAYLOR & EVANS (AV)

Miami Center, 201 South Biscayne Boulevard, Suite 900, 33131
Telephone: 305-358-5000; 305-579-0110
Broward County: 305-523-0277
Fax: 305-579-9749
Tampa, Florida Office: 101 East Kennedy Boulevard, Suite 3140.
Telephone: 813-221-1010.
Fax: 813-223-7961.
Ft. Lauderdale, Florida Office: One East Broward Boulevard, Suite 700.
Telephone: 305-356-0463.
Fax: 305-356-0406.
Washington, D.C. Office: Zuckerman, Spaeder, Goldstein, Taylor & Kolker, 1201 Connecticut Avenue, N.W.
Telephone: 202-778-1800.
Fax: 202-822-8106.
Baltimore, Maryland Office: Zuckerman, Spaeder, Goldstein, Taylor & Better, Suite 2440, 100 East Pratt Street.
Telephone: 410-332-0444.
Fax: 410-659-0436.
New York, N.Y. Office: Zuckerman, Spaeder, Goldstein, Taylor & Kolker, 1114 Avenue of the Americas, 45th Floor, Grace Building.
Telephone: 212-479-6500.
Fax: 212-479-6512.

MEMBERS OF FIRM

Ronald B. Ravikoff (Resident)
Roger C. Spaeder (Resident, Washington, D.C. Office)

For full biographical listings, see the Martindale-Hubbell Law Directory

*ORLANDO,** Orange Co.

DEMPSEY & ASSOCIATES, P.A. (AV)

605 East Robinson Street, P.O. Box 1980, 32802-1980
Telephone: 407-422-5166
Mailing Address: 1031 West Morse Boulevard, Suite 200, Winter Park, Florida, 32789
Winter Park, Florida Office: 1031 West Morse Boulevard, Suite 200, 32789.
Telephone: 407-740-7778.
Telecopier: 407-740-0911.

Bernard H. Dempsey, Jr.
Michael C. Sasso

M. Susan Sacco
William P. Weatherford, Jr.
Daniel N. Brodersen
Lori R. Benton
Barbara B. Smithers

(See Next Column)

OF COUNSEL

Gary S. Salzman

Reference: First Union National Bank of Florida.

For full biographical listings, see the Martindale-Hubbell Law Directory

POHL & BROWN, P.A.

(See Winter Park)

*TALLAHASSEE,** Leon Co.

RADEY HINKLE THOMAS & MCARTHUR (AV)

Suite 1000 Monroe-Park Tower, 101 North Monroe Street, P.O. Drawer 11307, 32302
Telephone: 904-681-7766
Telecopier: 904-681-0506

Robert L. Hinkle
Harry O. Thomas

Representative Clients: Johnson & Johnson; Vision Products, Inc.; Micro Flo Corp.; Johnson & Johnson Orthopedic Inc.; Anesthesiology Associates of Tallahassee.

For Complete List of Firm Personnel, See General Section

For full biographical listings, see the Martindale-Hubbell Law Directory

*TAMPA,** Hillsborough Co.

MICHAEL C. ADDISON (AV)

Suite 2175, 100 North Tampa Street, 33602-5145
Telephone: 813-223-2000
Facsimile: 813-228-6000
Mailing Address: P.O. Box 2175, Tampa, Florida, 33601-2175

For full biographical listings, see the Martindale-Hubbell Law Directory

ZUCKERMAN, SPAEDER, TAYLOR & EVANS (AV)

101 East Kennedy Boulevard, Suite 3140, 33602
Telephone: 813-221-1010
Fax: 813-223-7961
Miami, Florida Office: Suite 900, Miami Center, 201 South Biscayne Boulevard.
Telephones: 305-358-5000; 305-579-0110; Broward County: 305-523-0277.
Fax: 305-579-9749.
Ft. Lauderdale, Florida Office: One East Broward Boulevard, Suite 700.
Telephone: 305-356-0463.
Fax: 305-356-0406.
Washington, D.C. Office: Zuckerman, Spaeder, Goldstein, Taylor & Kolker, 1201 Connecticut Avenue, N.W.
Telephone: 202-778-1800.
Fax: 202-822-8106.
Baltimore, Maryland Office: Zuckerman, Spaeder, Goldstein, Taylor & Better, Suite 2440, 100 East Pratt Street.
Telephone: 410-332-0444.
Fax: 410-659-0436.
New York, N.Y. Office: Zuckerman, Spaeder, Goldstein, Taylor & Kolker, 1114 Avenue of the Americas, 45th Floor, Grace Building.
Telephone: 212-479-6500.
Fax: 212-479-6512.

MEMBER OF FIRM

Ronald B. Ravikoff (Resident, Miami, Florida Office)

For full biographical listings, see the Martindale-Hubbell Law Directory

WINTER PARK, Orange Co.

POHL & BROWN, P.A. (AV)

280 West Canton Avenue, Suite 410, P.O. Box 3208, 32789
Telephone: 407-647-7645; 407-647-POHL
Telefax: 407-647-2314

Frank L. Pohl
Usher L. Brown
Houston E. Short
Dwight I. Cool
William W. Pouzar
Mary B. Van Leuven

OF COUNSEL

Frederick W. Peirsol

Representative Clients: Orange County Comptroller; Osceola County; School Board of Osceola County, Florida; Osceola Tourist Development Council; NationsBank of Florida, N.A.; SunBank, N.A.; The Bank of Winter Park; Bekins Moving and Storage Co., Inc.; Champion Boats, Inc.; KeyCom Telephone Systems, Inc.

For full biographical listings, see the Martindale-Hubbell Law Directory

GEORGIA

*ATLANTA,** Fulton Co.

ALSTON & BIRD (AV)

A Partnership including Professional Corporations
One Atlantic Center, 1201 West Peachtree Street, 30309-3424
Telephone: 404-881-7000
Telecopier: 404-881-7777
Cable Address: AMGRAM GA
Telex: 54-2996
Easylink: 62985848
Washington, D.C. Office: 700 Thirteenth Street, Suite 350 20005-3960.
Telephone: 202-508-3300.
Telecopier: 202-508-3333.

MEMBERS OF FIRM

John K. Train III
Kevin E. Grady
Frank G. Smith III
Martin J. Elgison
H. Stephen Harris, Jr.
Michael P. Kenny
Randall L. Allen

COUNSEL

J. Kennard Neal

ASSOCIATES

Karen B. Baynes
Laura J. Coleman
Scott C. Commander
John P. Fry
Beth E. Kirby
H. Suzanne Smith
David J. Stewart
Teresa D. Thebaut
James J. Wolfson
Susan L. Wright

Representative Clients: Borden, Inc.; Chrysler Corp.; Genuine Parts Company; Gold Kist Inc.; NationsBank Corporation; Technical Association of the Pulp and Paper Industry, Inc.

For Complete List of Firm Personnel, See General Section

For full biographical listings, see the Martindale-Hubbell Law Directory

BONDURANT, MIXSON & ELMORE (AV)

1201 W. Peachtree Street Suite 3900, 30309
Telephone: 404-881-4100
FAX: 404-881-4111

MEMBERS OF FIRM

Emmet J. Bondurant II
H. Lamar Mixson
M. Jerome Elmore
Edward B. Krugman
James C. Morton
Jeffrey O. Bramlett
Dirk G. Christensen
Jane E. Fahey
Jeffrey D. Horst
John E. Floyd
Carolyn R. Gorwitz
Michael A. Sullivan

ASSOCIATES

Mary Jo Bradbury
P. Richard Game
Robin M. Hutchinson
J. Scott McClain
Keenan Rance Sephus Nix
Jill A. Pryor
Michael B. Terry
Joshua F. Thorpe

Representative Clients: The Aetna Casualty and Surety Company; Bottlers of Coca-Cola, U.S.A.; Brinks Home Security Systems, Inc.; Delta Air Lines, Inc.; Fina Oil and Chemical Company; JMB Realty Corp.; The Paradies Shops, Inc.; Sanifill, Inc.; Trammell Crow Co.

For Complete List of Firm Personnel, See General Section

For full biographical listings, see the Martindale-Hubbell Law Directory

JONES, DAY, REAVIS & POGUE (AV)

3500 One Peachtree Center, 303 Peachtree Street, N.E., 30308-3242
Telephone: 404-521-3939
Cable Address: "Attorneys Atlanta"
Telex: 54-2711
Telecopier: 404-581-8330
In Brussels, Belgium: Avenue Louise 480, 7th Floor, B-1050 Brussels.
Telephone: 011-32-2-645-14-11.
Telecopier: 011-32-2-645-14-45.
In Chicago, Illinois: 77 West Wacker.
Telephone: 312-782-3939.
Telecopier: 312-782-8585.
In Cleveland, Ohio: North Point. 901 Lakeside Avenue.
Telephone: 216-586-3939.
Cable Address: "Attorneys Cleveland".
Telex: 980389.
Telecopier: 216-579-0212.
In Columbus, Ohio: 1900 Huntington Center.
Telephone: 614-469-3939.
Cable Address: "Attorneys Columbus".
Telecopier: 614-461-4198.
In Dallas, Texas: 2300 Trammell Crow Center, 2001 Ross Avenue.
Telephone: 214-220-3939.
Cable Address: "Attorneys Dallas."
Telex: 730852.
Telecopier: 214-969-5100.

(See Next Column)

In Frankfurt, Germany: Westendstrasse 41, 60325 Frankfurt am Main.
Telephone: 011-49-69-7438-3939.
Telecopier: 011-49-69-741-1686.
In Geneva, Switzerland: 20, rue de Candolle.
Telephone: 011-41-22-320-2339.
Telecopier: 011-41-22-320-1232.
In Hong Kong: 1501 One Exchange Square, 8 Connaught Place.
Telephone: 011-852-526-6895.
Telecopier: 011-852-810-5787.
In Irvine, California: 2603 Main Street, Suite 900.
Telephone: 714-851-3939.
Telex: 194911 Lawyers LSA.
Telecopier: 714-553-7539.
In London, England: One Mount Street.
Telephone: 011-44-71-493-9361.
Cable Address: "Surgoe London WI."
Telecopier: 011-44-71-493-9666.
In Los Angeles, California: 555 West Fifth Street, Suite 4600.
Telephone: 213-489-3939.
Telex: 181439 UD.
Telecopier: 213-243-2539.
In New York, New York: 599 Lexington Avenue.
Telephone: 212-326-3939.
Cable Address: "JONESDAY NEWYORK."
Telex: 237013 JDRP UR.
Telecopier: 212-755-7306.
In Paris, France: 62, rue du Faubourg Saint-Honore.
Telephone: 011-33-1-44-71-3939.
Cable Address: "Surgoe Paris."
Telex: 290156 Surgoe.
Telecopier: 011-33-1-49-24-0471.
In Pittsburgh, Pennsylvania: 500 Grant Street, 31st Floor.
Telephone: 412-391-3939.
Cable Address: "Attorneys Pittsburgh".
Telecopier: 412-394-7959.
In Riyadh, Saudi Arabia: Law Offices of Saud M.A. Shawwaf, P.O. Box 2700.
Telephones: 011 (966-1) 465-6543, 011 (966-1) 464-8534 or 011 (966-1) 464-8540.
Telex: 401831 SAUCON SJ.
Telecopier: (966-1) 464-8480.
In Taipei, Taiwan: 7th Floor, 2 Tun Hwa South Road, Section 2.
Telephone: 011 (886-2) 704-6808 and 704-6809.
Telecopier: 011 (886-2) 704-6791.
In Tokyo, Japan: Shiroyama JT Mori Bldg., 15th Floor, 3-1, Toranomon 4-chome Minato-ku.
Telephone: 011-81-3-3433-3939.
Telecopier: 011-81-3-5401-2725.
In Washington, D.C.: Metropolitan Square, 1450 G Street, N.W.
Telephone: 202-879-3939.
Cable Address: "Attorneys Washington."
Telex: 89-2410 ATTORNEYS WASH.
Telecopier: 202-737-2832. 2-737-2832.

MEMBERS OF FIRM IN ATLANTA

Girard E. Boudreau, Jr.
William B. B. Smith

SENIOR ATTORNEY

L. Trammell Newton, Jr.

For Complete List of Firm Personnel, See General Section

For full biographical listings, see the Martindale-Hubbell Law Directory

KILPATRICK & CODY (AV)

Suite 2800, 1100 Peachtree Street, 30309-4530
Telephone: 404-815-6500
Telephone Copier: 404-815-6555
Telex: 54-2307
Washington, D.C. Office: Suite 800, 700 13th Street, N.W., 20005.
Telephone: 202-508-5800. Telephone Copier: 202-508-5858.
Brussels, Belgium Office: Avenue Louise 65, BTE 3, 1050 Brussels.
Telephone: (32) (2) 533-03-00.
Telecopier: (32) (2) 534-86-38.
London, England Office: 68 Pall Mall, London, SW1Y 5ES, England.
Telephone: (44) (71) 321 0477.
Telecopier: (44) (71) 930 9733.
Augusta, Georgia Office: Suite 1400 First Union Bank Building, P.O. Box 2043, 30903. Telephone (706) 724-2622. Telecopier (706) 722-0219.

MEMBERS OF FIRM

Miles J. Alexander
Elliott H. Levitas
Jerre B. Swann
A. Stephens Clay
Susan A. Cahoon
Virginia S. Taylor
Frederick H. von Unwerth

Representative Clients: Southern Bell Telephone and Telegraph Co.; Lockheed Aeronautical Systems Co.; Frito-Lay, Inc.; Scientific-Atlanta, Inc.; Scripto-Tokai, Inc.; Bank South Corporation; PepsiCo.

For Complete List of Firm Personnel, See General Section

For full biographical listings, see the Martindale-Hubbell Law Directory

Atlanta—Continued

PARKER, HUDSON, RAINER & DOBBS (AV)

1500 Marquis Two Tower, 285 Peachtree Center Avenue, N.E., 30303
Telephone: 404-523-5300
FAX: 404-522-8409
Tallahassee, Florida Office: The Perkins House, 118 North Gadsden Street, 32301.
Telephone: 904-681-0191.
FAX: 904-681-9493.

MEMBER OF FIRM

J. Marbury Rainer

For full biographical listings, see the Martindale-Hubbell Law Directory

SUMNER & HEWES (AV)

Suite 700, The Hurt Building, 50 Hurt Plaza, 30303
Telephone: 404-588-9000

PARTNERS

William E. Sumner
Nancy Becker Hewes
Stephen J. Anderson
David A. Webster

ASSOCIATES

Rosemary Smith
Andrew A. Davenport
Marguerite Patrick Bryan
Michelle Harris Jordan
Edith M. Shine

For full biographical listings, see the Martindale-Hubbell Law Directory

SUTHERLAND, ASBILL & BRENNAN (AV)

999 Peachtree Street, N.E., 30309-3996
Telephone: 404-853-8000
Facsimile: 404-853-8806
Washington, D.C. Office: 1275 Pennsylvania Avenue, N.W., 20004-2404.
Telephone: 202-383-0100.
New York, N.Y. Office: 1270 Avenue of the Americas, 10020-1700.
Telephone: 212-332-3000.
Austin, Texas Office: 111 Congress Avenue, 23rd Floor, 78701-4079.
Telephone: 512-469-3350.

David Robert Cumming, Jr.
Carey P. DeDeyn
William M. Hames
Charles T. Lester, Jr.
James R. McGibbon

For Complete List of Firm Personnel, See General Section

For full biographical listings, see the Martindale-Hubbell Law Directory

HAWAII

*HONOLULU,** Honolulu Co.

PITLUCK & KIDO (AV)

701 Bishop Street, 96813
Telephone: 808-523-5030
Telecopier: 808-545-4015

MEMBERS OF FIRM

Wayne Marshall Pitluck
Alan Takashi Kido
Dana Kiyomi Nalani Sato

James Mauliola Keaka Stone, Jr.
Margaret Ann Leong

Reference: Bank of Hawaii.

For full biographical listings, see the Martindale-Hubbell Law Directory

IDAHO

*BOISE,** Ada Co.

EBERLE, BERLIN, KADING, TURNBOW & MCKLVEEN, CHARTERED (AV)

Capitol Park Plaza, 300 North Sixth Street, P.O. Box 1368, 83701
Telephone: 208-344-8535
Facsimile: 208-344-8542

R.M. Turnbow
William A. Fuhrman

Representative Clients: TJ International; Key Bank of Idaho; Agri Beef Co.

For Complete List of Firm Personnel, See General Section

For full biographical listings, see the Martindale-Hubbell Law Directory

ELAM & BURKE, A PROFESSIONAL ASSOCIATION (AV)

Key Financial Center, 702 West Idaho Street, P.O. Box 1539, 83701
Telephone: 208-343-5454
Telecopier: 208-384-5844

William G. Dryden
William J. Batt

Representative Clients: Morrison-Knudsen, Inc.; Texas Instruments, Inc.; Prudential Securities, Inc.; Pechiney Corp.; Dow Corning Corporation; U.S. West Communications; State Farm Insurance Cos.; Sinclair Oil Company d/b/a Sun Valley Company; Farmers Insurance Group; Hecla Mining Company.

For Complete List of Firm Personnel, See General Section

For full biographical listings, see the Martindale-Hubbell Law Directory

MOFFATT, THOMAS, BARRETT, ROCK & FIELDS, CHARTERED (AV)

First Security Building, 911 West Idaho Street, Suite 300, P.O. Box 829, 83701
Telephone: 208-345-2000
FAX: 208-385-5384
Idaho Falls Office: 525 Park Avenue, Suite 2D, P.O. Box 1367, 83403.
Telephone: 208-522-6700.
FAX: 208-522-5111.
Pocatello, Idaho Office: 1110 Call Creek Drive, P.O. Box 4941, 83201.
Telephone: 208-233-2001.

R. B. Rock
Michael E. Thomas

Representative Clients: BMC West Corporation; Chevron, U.S.A.; First Security Bank of Idaho, N.A.; General Motors Corp.; Idaho Potato Commission; Intermountain Gas Co.; John Alden Life Insurance Co.; Micron, Inc.; Royal Insurance Cos.; St. Luke's Regional Medical Center & Mountain States Tumor Institute.

For Complete List of Firm Personnel, See General Section

For full biographical listings, see the Martindale-Hubbell Law Directory

ILLINOIS

*CHICAGO,** Cook Co.

BELL, BOYD & LLOYD (AV)

Three First National Plaza Suite 3300, 70 West Madison Street, 60602
Telephone: 312-372-1121
FAX: 312-372-2098
Washington, D.C. Office: 1615 L Street, N.W.
Telephone: 202-466-6300.
FAX: 202-463-0678.

MEMBERS OF FIRM

Michael J. Abernathy
William F. Dolan
Joseph V. Giffin
Victor E. Grimm
Robert T. Johnson, Jr.
Scott M. Mendel
Rebecca C. Meriwether
John R. Myers
Michael Sennett

OF COUNSEL

John T. Loughlin

ASSOCIATES

Michael Chimitris
Julie M. Rubins
Stephen H. Wenc

For Complete List of Firm Personnel, See General Section

For full biographical listings, see the Martindale-Hubbell Law Directory

FREEMAN, FREEMAN & SALZMAN, P.C. (AV)

Suite 3200, 401 North Michigan Avenue, 60611
Telephone: 312-222-5100
Facsimile: 312-822-0870

Lee A. Freeman
Lee A. Freeman, Jr.
Jerrold E. Salzman
John F. Kinney
James T. Malysiak
Glynna W. Freeman
Phillip L. Stern
Albert F. Ettinger
Derek J. Meyer
Scott A. Browdy
Chris S. Gair
Christopher M. Kelly (Not admitted in IL)

For full biographical listings, see the Martindale-Hubbell Law Directory

HALFPENNY, HAHN, ROCHE & MARCHESE (AV)

Suite 3330, 20 North Wacker Drive, 60606-2806
Telephone: 312-782-1829
FAX: 312-782-4868

(See Next Column)

HALFPENNY, HAHN, ROCHE & MARCHESE, *Chicago—Continued*

MEMBERS OF FIRM

Thomas F. Roche
Louis R. Marchese
Neil J. Kuenn
George W. Keeley
Michael T. Reid

ASSOCIATES

Thomas E. Roche
Robert W. Baker

Counsel For: National Association of Electrical Distributors, Construction Industry Manufacturers Assn; National Association of Wholesale-Distributors; National Association of Chain Manufacturers; Spring Research Institute; Chicago-Midwest Credit Management Assn.; Automotive Wholesalers of Illinois; Industrial Distribution Assn.; Wholesale Stationers Assn.; Woodworking Machinery Importers Assn.

For full biographical listings, see the Martindale-Hubbell Law Directory

ARAM A. HARTUNIAN AND ASSOCIATES (AV)

122 South Michigan Avenue, Suite 1850, 60603
Telephone: 312: 427-3600
FAX: 312-427-1850

Aram A. Hartunian

ASSOCIATE

Steven Paul Schneck

For full biographical listings, see the Martindale-Hubbell Law Directory

JONES, DAY, REAVIS & POGUE (AV)

77 West Wacker, 60601-1692
Telephone: 312-782-3939
Telecopier: 312-782-8585
In Atlanta, Georgia: 3500 One Peachtree Center, 303 Peachtree Street, N.E.
Telephone: 404-521-3939.
Cable Address: "Attorneys Atlanta".
Telex: 54-2711.
Telecopier: 404-581-8330.
In Brussels, Belgium: Avenue Louise 480, 7th Floor, B-1050 Brussels.
Telephone: 011-32-2-645-14-11.
Telecopier: 011-32-2-645-14-45.
In Cleveland, Ohio: North Point, 901 Lakeside Avenue.
Telephone: 216-586-3939.
Cable Address: "Attorneys Cleveland."
Telex: 980389.
Telecopier: 216-579-0212.
In Columbus, Ohio: 1900 Huntington Center.
Telephone: 614-469-3939.
Cable Address: "Attorneys Columbus."
Telecopier: 614-461-4198.
In Dallas, Texas: 2300 Trammell Crow Center, 2001 Ross Avenue.
Telephone: 214-220-3939.
Cable Address: "Attorneys Dallas."
Telex: 730852.
Telecopier: 214-969-5100.
In Frankfurt, Germany: Westendstrasse 41, 60325 Frankfurt am Main.
Telephone: 011-49-69-7438-3939.
Telecopier: 011-49-69-741-1686.
In Geneva, Switzerland: 20, rue de Candolle.
Telephone: 011-41-22-320-2339.
Telecopier: 011-41-22-320-1232.
In Hong Kong: 1501 One Exchange Square, 8 Connaught Place.
Telephone: 011-852-526-6895.
Telecopier: 011-852-810-5787.
In Irvine, California: 2603 Main Street, Suite 900.
Telephone: 714-851-3939.
Telex: 194911 Lawyers LSA.
Telecopier: 714-553-7539.
In London, England: One Mount Street.
Telephone: 011-44-71-493-9361.
Cable Address: "Surgoe London WI."
Telecopier: 011-44-71-493-9666.
In Los Angeles, California: 555 West Fifth Street, Suite 4600.
Telephone: 213-489-3939.
Telex: 181439 UD.
Telecopier: 213-243-2539.
In New York, New York: 599 Lexington Avenue.
Telephone: 212-326-3939.
Cable Address: "JONESDAY NEWYORK."
Telex: 237013 JDRP UR.
Telecopier: 212-755-7306.
In Paris, France: 62, rue du Faubourg Saint-Honore.
Telephone: 011-33-1-44-71-3939.
Cable Address: "Surgoe Paris."
Telex: 290156 Surgoe.
Telecopier: 011-33-1-49-24-0471.
In Pittsburgh, Pennsylvania: 500 Grant Street, 31st Floor.
Telephone: 412-391-3939.
Cable Address: "Attorneys Pittsburgh."
Telecopier: 412-394-7959.

(See Next Column)

In Riyadh, Saudi Arabia: Law Offices of Saud M.A. Shawwaf, P.O. Box 2700.
Telephones: 011 (966-1) 465-6543, 011 (966-1) 464-8534 or 011 (966-1) 464-8540.
Telex: 401831 SAUCON SJ.
Telecopier: (966-1) 464-8480.
In Taipei, Taiwan: 7th Floor, 2 Tun Hwa South Road, Section 2.
Telephone: 011 (886-2) 704-6808 and 704-6809.
Telecopier: 011 (886-2) 704-6791.
In Tokyo, Japan: Shiroyama JT Mori Bldg., 15th Floor, 3-1, Toranomon 4-chome, Minato-Ku.
Telephone: 011-81-3-3433-3939.
Telecopier: 011-81-3-5401-2725.
In Washington, D.C.: Metropolitan Square, 1450 G Street, N.W.
Telephone: 202-879-3939.
Cable Address: "Attorneys Washington."
Telex: 89-2410 ATTORNEYS WASH.
Telecopier: 202-737-2832.

MEMBER OF FIRM IN CHICAGO

Thomas F. Gardner

For Complete List of Firm Personnel, See General Section

For full biographical listings, see the Martindale-Hubbell Law Directory

KECK, MAHIN & CATE (AV)

A Partnership including Professional Corporations
77 West Wacker Drive Suite 4900, 60601-1693
Telephone: 312-634-7700
Cable Address: "Hamscott"
Telex: 25-3411
Fax: 312-634-5000
Washington, D.C. Office: Penthouse, 1201 New York Avenue, N.W.
Telephone: 202-789-3400.
Telecopier: 202-789-1158.
Peoria, Illinois Office: Suite 640, 331 Fulton Street.
Telephone: 309-673-1681.
Oakbrook Terrace, Illinois Office: Suite 1000, One Mid America Plaza.
Telephone: 708-954-2100.
Telecopier: 708-954-2112.
Schaumburg, Illinois Office: Suite 250 Schaumburg Corporate Center, 1515 East Woodfield Road.
Telephone: 708-330-1200.
Telecopier: 708-330-1220.
Houston, Texas Office: 2800 First City Main Building, 1021 Main Street.
Telephone: 713-951-0990.
Telecopier: 713-951-0987.
Los Angeles, California Office: 2029 Century Park East.
Telephone: 310-284-8771.
Fax: 310-284-8359.
New York, N.Y. Office: 220 E. 42nd Street.
Telephone: 212-682-3060.
Fax: 212-490-3918.
San Francisco, California Office: One Maritime Plaza, Golden Gateway Center, 23rd Floor.
Telephone: 415-392-7077.
Fax: 415-392-3969.

MEMBERS OF FIRM

Jonathan G. Bunge (P.C.)
William C. Ives
Thomas W. Johnston
Sheldon Karon
Robin R. Lunn
Philip L. O'Neill (Resident, Washington, D.C. Office)
Robert W. Pratt
Richard L. Reinish

OF COUNSEL

Robert C. Keck

For Complete List of Firm Personnel, See General Section

For full biographical listings, see the Martindale-Hubbell Law Directory

MCANDREWS, HELD & MALLOY, LTD. (AV)

Northwestern Atrium Center Suite 3400, 500 West Madison Street, 60661
Telephone: 312-707-8889
Telecopier: 312-707-9155
Telex: 650-388-1248

George P. McAndrews
John J. Held
Timothy J. Malloy
William M. Wesley
Lawrence M. Jarvis
Robert C. Ryan
Gregory J. Vogler
Jean Dudek Kuelper
Herbert D. Hart III
Robert W. Fieseler
D. David Hill
Thomas J. Wimbiscus
Steven J. Hampton
Alejandro Menchaca
Priscilla F. Gallagher
Stephen F. Sherry
Patrick J. Arnold, Jr.
Robert B. Polit
George Wheeler
Christopher C. Winslade
Edward A. Mas, II
Gregory C. Schodde
John S. Artz
David D. Headrick
Sharon A. Hwang
Phyllis T. Turner Brim
Jeff D. Wheeler

(See Next Column)

McANDREWS, HELD & MALLOY LTD.—*Continued*

OF COUNSEL

S. Jack Sauer Donald P. Reynolds

For full biographical listings, see the Martindale-Hubbell Law Directory

McBRIDE BAKER & COLES (AV)

500 West Madison Street 40th Floor, 60661
Telephone: 312-715-5700
Cable Address: "Chilaw"
Telex: 270258
Telecopier: 312-993-9350

MEMBERS OF FIRM

Henry S. Allen, Jr.
Malcolm H. Brooks
John P. Ryan, Jr.
Robert C. Schnitz
Steven B. Varick

For Complete List of Firm Personnel, See General Section

For full biographical listings, see the Martindale-Hubbell Law Directory

McCONNELL & MENDELSON (AV)

140 South Dearborn Street, Suite 815, 60603
Telephone: 312-263-1212
Telecopier: 312-263-0402

Francis J. McConnell
Richard A. Sloan
Peter S. Lubin

Reference: The Northern Trust Co., Chicago, Illinois.

For full biographical listings, see the Martindale-Hubbell Law Directory

McDERMOTT, WILL & EMERY (AV)

A Partnership including Professional Corporations
227 West Monroe Street, 60606-5096
Telephone: 312-372-2000
Telex: 253565 Milam CGO
Facsimile: 312-984-7700
Boston, Massachusetts Office: 75 State Street, Suite 1700.
Telephone: 617-345-5000.
Telex: 951324 MILAM BSN.
Facsimile: 617-345-5077.
Miami, Florida Office: 201 South Biscayne Boulevard.
Telephone: 305-358-3500.
Telex: 441777 LEYES.
Facsimile: 305-347-6500.
Washington, D.C. Office: 1850 K Street, N.W.
Telephone: 202-887-8000.
Telex: 253565 MILAM CGO.
Facsimile: 202-778-8087.
Los Angeles, California Office: 2049 Century Park East.
Telephone: 310-277-4110.
Facsimile: 310-277-4730.
Newport Beach, California Office: 1301 Dove Street, Suite 500.
Telephone: 714-851-0633.
Facsimile: 714-851-9348.
New York, N.Y. Office: 1211 Avenue of the Americas.
Telephone: 212-768-5400.
Facsimile: 212-768-5444.
St. Petersburg, Russia Office: 2/2 Tchaikovsky Street, #517, 191187 St. Petersburg, Russia.
Telephone: (7) (812) 273-9831.
Facsimile: (7) (812) 273-9831.
Tallinn, Estonia Office: Tallinn Business Center, 6 Harju Street, EE0001 Tallinn, Estonia.
Telephone: 372 6 31-05-53.
Facsimile: 372 6 31-05-54.
Vilnius, Lithuania Office: Smetonos 6, 2600 Vilnius, Lithuania.
Telephone: 370 2 61-43-08.
Facsimile: 370 2 22-79-55.
Associated (Independent) Offices:
Brussels, Belgium: Uettwiller Grelon Lippens Dekeyser, 73 avenue Vandendriessche, 1150 Brussels, Belgium.
Telephone: (32) (2) 772-87-50.
Facsimile: (32) (2) 772-87-52.
London, England: Paisner & Co, Bouverie House, 154 Fleet Street, London EC4A 2DQ, England.
Telephone: (44) (71) 353-0299.
Facsimile: (44) (71) 583-8621.
Paris, France: Uettwiller Grelon Gout Canat & Associes, 68, boulevard de Courcelles, 75017 Paris, France.
Telephone: (33) (1) 48 88 89 00.
Facsimile: (33) (1) 48 88 05 50.

MEMBERS OF FIRM

Robert E. Bouma
Byron L. Gregory
Steven P. Handler *
Janet M. Koran
David Marx, Jr.
William P. Schuman
Mark L. Yeager

*Denotes a lawyer employed by a Professional Corporation which is a member of the Firm.

(See Next Column)

For Complete List of Firm Personnel, See General Section

For full biographical listings, see the Martindale-Hubbell Law Directory

ROTHSCHILD, BARRY & MYERS (AV)

A Partnership including Professional Corporations
Suite 3900 Xerox Centre, 55 West Monroe Street, 60603-5012
Telephone: 312-372-2345
FAX: 312-372-2350

MEMBERS OF FIRM

Edward I. Rothschild (P.C.)
Norman J. Barry (P.C.)
William G. Myers (P.C.)
Melvin I. Mishkin
John J. Coffey, III
Joseph P. Della Maria, Jr.
Roger J. Guerin
Michael J. Wall
Daniel Cummings
Christopher G. Walsh, Jr.
Kenneth P. Taube
Jonathan E. Rothschild
Alan S. Madans

COUNSEL

Philip B. Kurland

ASSOCIATES

Mary T. Meegan
John G. Dalton
John A. Knight
Kevin J. Moore
Elizabeth Staggs

For full biographical listings, see the Martindale-Hubbell Law Directory

SAUNDERS & MONROE (AV)

Suite 4201, 205 North Michigan Avenue, 60601
Telephone: 312-946-9000
Facsimile: 312-946-0528

MEMBERS OF FIRM

George L. Saunders, Jr.
Lee A. Monroe
Thomas F. Bush, Jr.
Matthew E. Van Tine

Thomas A. Doyle
Christina J. Norton
Gwen A. Niedbalski

For full biographical listings, see the Martindale-Hubbell Law Directory

WILSON & McILVAINE (AV)

500 West Madison, Suite 3700, 60661-2511
Telephone: 312-715-5000
Telecopier: 312-715-5155

PARTNER

Kendall R. Meyer

For Complete List of Firm Personnel, See General Section

For full biographical listings, see the Martindale-Hubbell Law Directory

WINSTON & STRAWN (AV)

35 West Wacker Drive, 60601
Telephone: 312-558-5600
Cable Address: "Winston Chicago"
Facsimile: 312-558-5700
Washington, D.C. Office: 1400 L Street, N.W.
Telephone: 202-371-5700.
Telecopier: 202-371-5950.
Telex: 440574 INTLAW UI.
New York, N.Y. Office: 175 Water Street.
Telephone: 212-269-2500.
Telecopier: 212-952-1474/5.
Cable Address: "Coledeitz, NYK".
Telex: (RCA) 232459.
Geneva, Switzerland Office: 43 Rue du Rhone, 1204.
Telephone: (4122) 7810506.
Fax: (4122) 7810361.

MEMBERS OF FIRM

Edward L. Foote
John W. Stack
Duane M. Kelley
R. Mark McCareins

Representative Clients: Windmere Corp.; Tropicana Products; Illinois Bell Telephone Co.; Amertech; Marmon Group.

For Complete List of Firm Personnel, See General Section

For full biographical listings, see the Martindale-Hubbell Law Directory

INDIANA

*INDIANAPOLIS,** Marion Co.

BOSE MCKINNEY & EVANS (AV)

2700 First Indiana Plaza, 135 North Pennsylvania Street, 46204
Telephone: 317-684-5000
Facsimile: 317-684-5173
Indianapolis North Office: Suite 1201, 8888 Keystone Crossing, 46240.
Telephone: 317-574-3700.
Facsimile: 317-574-3716.

MEMBERS OF FIRM

Kendall C. Crook
Ronald E. Elberger
Stephen E. Arthur

ASSOCIATES

Gary L. Chapman
J. Scott Enright

Representative Clients: Agmax, Inc.; Ameritech Publishing; Erbrich Products Co., Inc.; First Indiana Bank; Indiana Supply Corp.; Kenra Laboratories Inc.; Lawyers Title Insurance Corp.; Muncie Power Products, Inc.; Indianapolis Life Insurance Co.; BMW Constructors, Inc.; Indiana Academy of Ophthalmology, Inc.

For Complete List of Firm Personnel, See General Section

For full biographical listings, see the Martindale-Hubbell Law Directory

ICE MILLER DONADIO & RYAN (AV)

One American Square Box 82001, 46282-0002
Telephone: 317-236-2100
Fax: 317-236-2219

MEMBERS OF FIRM

Philip A. Whistler
Fred R. Biesecker
Gregory L. Pemberton

ASSOCIATE

Timothy A. Brooks

Counsel for: American United Life Insurance Co.; Chrysler Corp.; Ford Motor Company; General Electric Company; Indiana Bankers Assn.; Biomet; Union City Body Company; Coca Cola Company; RJR Nabisco; Indiana Association of Cities and Towns.

For Complete List of Firm Personnel, See General Section

For full biographical listings, see the Martindale-Hubbell Law Directory

MCTURNAN & TURNER (AV)

2070 Market Tower, 10 West Market Street, 46204
Telephone: 317-464-8181
Telecopier: 317-464-8131

Lee B. McTurnan
Wayne C. Turner
Judy L. Woods
Jacqueline Bowman Ponder
Steven M. Badger
Matthew W. Foster

For full biographical listings, see the Martindale-Hubbell Law Directory

SOMMER & BARNARD, ATTORNEYS AT LAW, PC (AV)

4000 Bank One Tower, 111 Monument Circle, P.O. Box 44363, 46244-0363
Telephone: 317-630-4000
FAX: 317-236-9802
North Office: 8900 Keystone Crossing, Suite 1046, Indianapolis, Indiana, 46240-2134.
Telephone: 317-630-4000.
FAX: 317-844-4780.

William C. Barnard
James E. Hughes
Edward W. Harris, III
Gordon L. Pittenger

Gayle A. Reindl

Representative Clients: Excel Industries, Inc.; Monsanto Co.; Comerica Bank; Federal Express; Renault Automation; Reppert International; Kimball International; TRW, Inc.

For Complete List of Firm Personnel, See General Section

For full biographical listings, see the Martindale-Hubbell Law Directory

IOWA

*DES MOINES,** Polk Co.

DICKINSON, MACKAMAN, TYLER & HAGEN, P.C. (AV)

Suite 1600 Hub Tower, 699 Walnut Street, 50309-3986
Telephone: 515-244-2600
Telecopier: 515-246-4550

(See Next Column)

L. J. Dickinson (1873-1968)
L. Call Dickinson (1905-1974)
Addison M. Parker (Retired)
John H. Raife (Retired)
Robert B. Throckmorton (Retired)
Helen C. Adams
Brent R. Appel
Barbara G. Barrett
John W. Blyth
L. Call Dickinson, Jr.
Jeanine M. Freeman
David J. Grace
Craig F. Graziano
Howard O. Hagen
J. Russell Hixson
Paul E. Horvath
F. Richard Lyford
John R. Mackaman
Richard A. Malm
James W. O'Brien
Arthur F. Owens
Rebecca Boyd Parrott
David M. Repp
Robert C. Rouwenhorst
Russell L. Samson
David S. Steward
Philip E. Stoffregen
Francis (Frank) J. Stork
Jon P. Sullivan
Celeste L. Tito (Not admitted in IA)
Paul R. Tyler
John K. Vernon
J. Marc Ward
Linda S. Weindruch

OF COUNSEL

Robert E. Mannheimer

Representative Clients: Archer-Daniels-Midland Co.; Board of Water Works Trustees, Des Moines, Iowa; Merchants Bonding Co. (Mutual); Norwest Bank, N.A.

For full biographical listings, see the Martindale-Hubbell Law Directory

KANSAS

*WICHITA,** Sedgwick Co.

FLEESON, GOOING, COULSON & KITCH, L.L.C. (AV)

125 North Market Street, Suite 1600, P.O. Box 997, 67201-0997
Telephone: 316-267-7361
Telecopier: 316-267-1754

Gerrit H. Wormhoudt
Thomas D. Kitch
Gregory J. Stucky

Attorneys for: Bank IV, Wichita, N.A; Intrust Bank, N.A.; Wichita Eagle and Beacon Publishing Co., Inc.; Southwest Kansas Royalty Owners Assn.; Liberty Mutual Insurance Co.; Grant Thornton; The Law Company; Vulcan Materials Co.; The Wichita State University Board of Trustees.

For Complete List of Firm Personnel, See General Section

For full biographical listings, see the Martindale-Hubbell Law Directory

FOULSTON & SIEFKIN (AV)

(Formerly Foulston, Siefkin, Powers & Eberhardt)
700 Fourth Financial Center, Broadway at Douglas, 67202
Telephone: 316-267-6371
Facsimile: 316-267-6345
Topeka, Kansas Office: 1515 Bank IV Tower, 534 Kansas Avenue. 66603.
Telephone: 913-233-3600.
FAX: 913-233-1610.
Member: Lex Mundi, A Global Association of Independent Firms

MEMBERS OF FIRM

Robert L. Howard
James D. Oliver
Jim H. Goering

For Complete List of Firm Personnel, See General Section

For full biographical listings, see the Martindale-Hubbell Law Directory

KENTUCKY

*LEXINGTON,** Fayette Co.

STOLL, KEENON & PARK (AV)

201 E. Main Street, Suite 1000, 40507-1380
Telephone: 606-231-3000
Telecopier: 606-253-1093; 606-253-1027
Frankfort, Kentucky Office: 326 West Main Street.
Telephone: 502-875-6000.
Telecopier: 502-875-6008.
Louisville, Kentucky Office: 400 West Market Street, Suite 2650, 40202.
Telephone: 502-568-9100.
Telecopier: 502-568-6340.

MEMBERS OF FIRM

William E. Johnson
Samuel D. Hinkle, IV
Donald P. Wagner

Representative Clients: Bank One, Lexington, NA; Farmers Capital Bank Corp.; The Tokai Bank Ltd.; Link Belt Construction Equipment Co.; General Motors Corp.; International Business Machines Corp.; Ohbayashi Corp.; R. J. Reynolds Tobacco Co.; Rockwell International Corp.; Square D Co.

(See Next Column)

STOLL, KEENON & PARK—*Continued*

For Complete List of Firm Personnel, See General Section

For full biographical listings, see the Martindale-Hubbell Law Directory

*LOUISVILLE,** Jefferson Co.

GREENEBAUM DOLL & MCDONALD (AV)

A Partnership including Professional Service Corporations
3300 National City Tower, 40202
Telephone: 502-589-4200
Fax: 502-587-3695
Lexington, Kentucky Office: 1400 Vine Center Tower.
Telephone: 606-231-8500.
Fax: 606-255-2742.
Covington, Kentucky Office: 50 East River Center Boulevard, P.O. Box 2050.
Telephone: 606-655-4200.
Fax: 606-655-4239.
Cincinnati, Ohio Office: 832 Main Street.
Telephone: 513-421-8087.
Fax: 513-421-8089.

Peggy B. Lyndrup
Holland N. McTyeire, V

Representative Clients: A T & T Communications, Inc.; Ashland Oil, Inc.; Carrier Vibrating, Inc.; Courtaulds Coatings Inc. (Porter Paint Co.); Hillerich & Bradsby; Humana Inc.; Louisville Gas and Electric; Toyota Motor Manufacturing, U.S.A., Inc.; Transco Energy Corp.; University of Louisville.

For Complete List of Firm Personnel, See General Section

For full biographical listings, see the Martindale-Hubbell Law Directory

MIDDLETON & REUTLINGER, P.S.C. (AV)

2500 Brown and Williamson Tower, 40202-3410
Telephone: 502-584-1135
Fax: 502-561-0442
Jeffersonville, Indiana Office: 605 Watt Street, 47130.
Telephone: 812-282-4886.

Charles G. Middleton, III
C. Kent Hatfield
William Jay Hunter, Jr.
John M. Franck II

Counsel For: Louisville Gas & Electric Co.; Logan Aluminum, Inc.; The Kroger Co.; MCI Telecommunications Corp.; EnTrade Corp.; Stevens Contractors, Inc.; Associated General Contractors of Kentucky; Builders Exchange of Louisville, Inc.

For Complete List of Firm Personnel, See General Section

For full biographical listings, see the Martindale-Hubbell Law Directory

OGDEN NEWELL & WELCH (AV)

1200 One Riverfront Plaza, 40202-2973
Telephone: 502-582-1601
Fax: 502-581-9564

MEMBERS OF FIRM

James S. Welch
Ernest W. Williams
David A. Harris

Counsel for: KU Energy Corp.; Kentucky Utilities Co.; Brown-Forman Corp.; B.F. Goodrich Co.; Brown & Williamson Tobacco Corp.; J.J.B. Hilliard, W.L. Lyons, Inc.; Akzo Coatings, Inc.; United Medical Corp.; Bramco, Inc.; Bank of Louisville.

For Complete List of Firm Personnel, See General Section

For full biographical listings, see the Martindale-Hubbell Law Directory

WOODWARD, HOBSON & FULTON (AV)

2500 National City Tower, 101 South Fifth Street, 40202
Telephone: 502-581-8000
Fax: 502-581-8111
Lexington, Kentucky Office: National City Plaza, 301 East Main Street, Suite 650.
Telephone: 606-244-7100.
Telecopier: 606-244-7111.

MEMBER OF FIRM

Kenneth L. Anderson

Representative Clients: International Minerals & Chemical Corp.; Ralston Purina Co.; Sears, Roebuck & Co.

For Complete List of Firm Personnel, See General Section

For full biographical listings, see the Martindale-Hubbell Law Directory

LOUISIANA

*BATON ROUGE,** East Baton Rouge Parish

BREAZEALE, SACHSE & WILSON, L.L.P. (AV)

Twenty-Third Floor, One American Place, P.O. Box 3197, 70821-3197
Telephone: 504-387-4000
Fax: 504-387-5397
New Orleans, Louisiana Office: Place St. Charles, Suite 4214, 201 St. Charles Avenue.
Telephone: 504-582-1170.
Fax: 504-582-1164.

MEMBERS OF FIRM

Gordon A. Pugh
Claude F. Reynaud, Jr.
Emile C. Rolfs, III
John F. Whitney (Resident, New Orleans Office)
Joseph E. Friend (Resident, New Orleans Office)
Jude C. Bursavich

ASSOCIATES

James R. Chastain, Jr.
Linda Perez Clark
Luis A. Leitzelar

Counsel for: Hibernia National Bank; South Central Bell Telephone Co.; Allied-Signal Corp.; Reynolds Metal Co.; Illinois Central Railroad Co.; The Continental Insurance Cos.; Fireman's Fund American Group; Chicago Bridge & Iron Co.; Montgomery Ward & Co.

For Complete List of Firm Personnel, See General Section

For full biographical listings, see the Martindale-Hubbell Law Directory

*LAFAYETTE,** Lafayette Parish

DOMENGEAUX, WRIGHT, MOROUX & ROY, A PROFESSIONAL LAW CORPORATION (AV)

556 Jefferson Street, Suite 500, P.O. Box 3668, 70502-3668
Telephone: 318-233-3033; 1-800-375-3106
Fax: 318-232-8213
Hammond, Louisiana Office: Magnolia Plaza, Suite K, 1007 West Thomas Street, P. O. Box 1558.
Telephone: 504-542-4963; 1-800-423-1160.

James Domengeaux (1907-1988)
Anthony D. Moroux (1948-1993)
Bob F. Wright (A Professional Law Corporation)
James Parkerson Roy (A Professional Law Corporation)
Robert K. Tracy (A Professional Law Corporation)
Thomas R. Edwards (A Professional Law Corporation)
Frank Edwards (Resident, Hammond Office)
James Wattigny
James H. Domengeaux
R. Hamilton Davis
Gilbert Hennigan Dozier
Carla Marie Perron
Tyron D. Picard

OF COUNSEL

Jerome E. Domengeaux

Reference: Mid-South National Bank; Advocate Financial, L.L.C.

For full biographical listings, see the Martindale-Hubbell Law Directory

*NEW ORLEANS,** Orleans Parish

DEUTSCH, KERRIGAN & STILES (AV)

A Partnership including Professional Law Corporations
755 Magazine Street, 70130-3672
Telephone: 504-581-5141
Cable Address: "Dekest"
Telex: 584358
Telecopier: 504-566-1201

MEMBER OF FIRM

Charles K. Reasonover (P.L.C.)

OF COUNSEL

Ralph L. Kaskell, Jr.

For Complete List of Firm Personnel, See General Section

For full biographical listings, see the Martindale-Hubbell Law Directory

MILLING, BENSON, WOODWARD, HILLYER, PIERSON & MILLER (AV)

A Partnership including Professional Law Corporations
Suite Twenty-Three Hundred, 909 Poydras Street, 70112-1017
Telephone: 504-569-7000
Cable Address: "Milling"
Telex: 58-4211
Telecopier: 504-569-7001
ABA net: 15656
MCI Mail: "Milling"
Lafayette, Louisiana Office: 101 LaRue France, Suite 200.
Telephone: 318-232-3929.
Telecopier: 318-233-4957.

(See Next Column)

MILLING, BENSON, WOODWARD, HILLYER, PIERSON & MILLER, *New Orleans—Continued*

Baton Rouge, Louisiana Office: Suite 402, 8555 United Plaza Blvd.
Telephone: 504-928-688.
Fax: 504-928-6881.

MEMBERS OF FIRM

James K. Irvin (P.C.) Katherine Goldman (P.C.)

See General Section for list of Representative Clients.

For Complete List of Firm Personnel, See General Section

For full biographical listings, see the Martindale-Hubbell Law Directory

SLATER LAW FIRM, A PROFESSIONAL CORPORATION (AV)

650 Poydras Street Suite 2400, 70130-6101
Telephone: 504-523-7333
Fax: 504-528-1080

Benjamin R. Slater, Jr. Mark E. Van Horn
Benjamin R. Slater, III Kevin M. Wheeler

Anne Elise Brown Donald J. Miester, Jr.

OF COUNSEL

Michael O. Waguespack

Representative Clients: Norfolk Southern Corporation; New Orleans Steamship Association; Anheuser-Busch, Inc.; The Quaker Oats Company; Primerica Financial Services; Electric Mutual Liability Insurance Company; Diversified Foods and Seasonings; American International Gaming Association, Inc.

For full biographical listings, see the Martindale-Hubbell Law Directory

*SHREVEPORT,** Caddo Parish

BARLOW AND HARDTNER L.C. (AV)

Tenth Floor, Louisiana Tower, 401 Edwards Street, 71101-3289
Telephone: 318-227-1131
Telecopier: 318-227-1141
Mailing Address: P.O. Box 8, Shreveport, Louisiana, 71161-0008

David R. Taggart Michael B. Donald

Representative Clients: Kelley Oil Corporation; NorAm Energy Corp. (formerly Arkla, Inc.); Central and South West; Panhandle Eastern Corp.; Pennzoil Producing Co.; Johnson Controls, Inc.; Ashland Oil, Inc.; Southwestern Electric Power Company; Brammer Engineering, Inc.; General Electric Co.

For Complete List of Firm Personnel, See General Section

For full biographical listings, see the Martindale-Hubbell Law Directory

MAINE

*BANGOR,** Penobscot Co.

EATON, PEABODY, BRADFORD & VEAGUE, P.A. (AV)

Fleet Center-Exchange Street, P.O. Box 1210, 04402-1210
Telephone: 207-947-0111
Telecopier: 207-942-3040
Augusta, Maine Office: 2 Central Plaza.
Telephone: 207-622-3747.
Telecopier: 207-622-9732.
Brunswick, Maine Office: 167 Park Row.
Telephone: 207-729-1144.
Telecopier: 207-729-1140.
Camden, Maine Office: 7-9 Washington Street.
Telephone: 207-236-3325.
Telecopier: 207-236-8611.
Dover-Foxcroft, Maine Office: 30 East Main Street.
Telephone: 207-564-8378.
Telecopier: 207-564-7059.

Daniel G. McKay Gordon H. S. Scott (Resident, Augusta Office)

Thad B. Zmistowski

A List of Representative Clients available upon request.

For Complete List of Firm Personnel, See General Section

For full biographical listings, see the Martindale-Hubbell Law Directory

MARYLAND

*BALTIMORE,** (Independent City)

PIPER & MARBURY (AV)

Charles Center South, 36 South Charles Street, 21201-3010
Telephone: 410-539-2530
FAX: 410-539-0489
Washington, D.C. Office: 1200 Nineteenth Street, N.W., 20036-2430.
Telephone: 202-861-3900.
FAX: 202-223-2085.
Easton, Maryland Office: 117 Bay Street, 21601-2703.
Telephone: 410-820-4460.
FAX: 410-820-4463.
Garrison, New York Office: Garrison Landing.
Telephone: 914-424-3711.
Fax: 914-424-3045.
New York, N.Y. Office: 31 West 52nd Street, 10019-6118.
Telephone: 212-261-2000.
FAX: 212-261-2001.
Philadelphia, Pennsylvania Office: Suite 1500, 2 Penn Center Plaza, 19102-1715.
Telephone: 215-656-3300.
FAX: 215-656-3301.
London, England Office: 14 Austin Friars, EC2N 2HE.
Telephone: 071-638-3833.
FAX: 071-638-1208.

MEMBERS OF FIRM

Lewis A. Noonberg (Resident, Washington, D.C. Office)
Jeffrey F. Liss (Resident, Washington, D.C. Office)
Jeffrey D. Herschman
Michael F. Brockmeyer

ASSOCIATES

H. Mark Stichel
Leonard L. Gordon (Resident, Washington, D.C. Office)

For Complete List of Firm Personnel, See General Section

For full biographical listings, see the Martindale-Hubbell Law Directory

VENABLE, BAETJER AND HOWARD (AV)

A Partnership including Professional Corporations
1800 Mercantile Bank & Trust Building, 2 Hopkins Plaza, 21201
Telephone: 410-244-7400
Washington, D.C. Office: Venable, Baetjer, Howard & Civiletti. Suite 1000, 1201 New York Avenue, N.W.
Telephone: 202-962-4800.
McLean, Virginia Office: Suite 400, 2010 Corporate Ridge.
Telephone: 703-760-1600.
Rockville, Maryland Office: Suite 500, One Church Street, P. O. Box 1906.
Telephone: 301-217-5600.
Towson, Maryland Office: 210 Allegheny Avenue, P. O. Box 5517.
Telephone: 410-494-6200.

MEMBERS OF FIRM

Benjamin R. Civiletti (P.C.) (Also at Washington, D.C. and Towson, Maryland Offices)
John Henry Lewin, Jr. (P.C.)
Douglas D. Connah, Jr. (P.C.) (Also at Washington, D.C. Office)
Kenneth C. Bass, III (Not admitted in MD; Also at Washington, D.C. and McLean, Virginia Offices)
Edward F. Glynn, Jr. (Not admitted in MD; Resident, Washington, D.C. Office)
Michael Schatzow (Also at Washington, D.C. and Towson, Maryland Offices)
James K. Archibald (Also at Washington, D.C. and Towson, Maryland Offices)
G. Stewart Webb, Jr.
James R. Myers (Not admitted in MD; Resident, Washington, D.C. Office)
Jeffrey D. Knowles (Not admitted in MD; Resident, Washington, D.C. Office)
William D. Coston (Not admitted in MD; Resident, Washington, D.C. Office)
Maurice Baskin (Resident, Washington, D.C. Office)
Amy Berman Jackson (Not admitted in MD; Resident, Washington, D.C. Office)
William D. Quarles (Also at Washington, D.C. and Towson, Maryland Offices)
Christopher R. Mellott
James A. Dunbar (Also at Washington, D.C. Office)

OF COUNSEL

Emried D. Cole, Jr.

ASSOCIATES

David W. Goewey (Not admitted in MD; Resident, Washington, D.C. Office)
James W. Hedlund (Not admitted in MD; Resident, Washington, D.C. Office)
Vicki Margolis

For Complete List of Firm Personnel, See General Section

For full biographical listings, see the Martindale-Hubbell Law Directory

MASSACHUSETTS

*BOSTON,** Suffolk Co.

BROWN & STADFELD (AV)

66 Long Wharf, 02110
Telephone: 617-720-4200
Fax: 617-720-0240

Harold Brown
L. Seth Stadfeld

L. Michael Hankes
Linda J. Keogh
Catherine M. Keenan

For Complete List of Firm Personnel, See General Section

For full biographical listings, see the Martindale-Hubbell Law Directory

GOODWIN, PROCTER & HOAR (AV)

A Partnership including Professional Corporations
Exchange Place, 02109-2881
Telephone: 617-570-1000
Cable Address: "Goodproct, Boston"
Telex: 94-0640
Telecopier: 617-523-1231
Washington, D.C. Office: 901 Fifteenth Street, N.W., Suite 410.
Telephone: 202-414-6160.
Telecopier: 202-789-1720.
Albany, New York Office: One Steuben Place.
Telephone: 518-472-9460.
Telecopier: 518-472-9472.

OF COUNSEL
Donald B. Gould

For Complete List of Firm Personnel, See General Section

For full biographical listings, see the Martindale-Hubbell Law Directory

HANIFY & KING, PROFESSIONAL CORPORATION (AV)

One Federal Street, 02110-2007
Telephone: 617-423-0400
Telefax: 617-423-0498

James Coyne King
John D. Hanify
Harold B. Murphy
David Lee Evans
Daniel J. Lyne
Donald F. Farrell, Jr.
Barbara Wegener Pfirrman
Gerard P. Richer
Timothy P. O'Neill

Gordon M. Jones, III
Kara L. Thornton
Jean A. Musiker
Ann M. Chiacchieri
Melissa J. Cassedy
Kara M. Lucciola
Philip C. Silverman
Michael R. Perry
Jeffrey S. Cedrone
Charles A. Dale, III
Joseph F. Cortellini
Hiram N. Pan
Amy Conroy
Michael S. Bloom
Andrew G. Lizotte
Peter D. Lee
Martin F. Gaynor, III

For full biographical listings, see the Martindale-Hubbell Law Directory

MINTZ, LEVIN, COHN, FERRIS, GLOVSKY AND POPEO, P.C. (AV)

One Financial Center, 02111
Telephone: 617-542-6000
FAX: 617-542-2241
Washington, D.C. Office: 701 Pennsylvania Avenue, N.W. Suite 900.
Telephone: 202-434-7300.
Fax: 202-434-7400.

Jerome Gotkin
R. Robert Popeo
Bruce D. Sokler (Resident, Washington, D.C. Office)
Charles Alan Samuels (Resident, Washington, D.C. Office)
Bruce F. Metge

Christopher J. Harvie (Not admitted in MA)

For Complete List of Firm Personnel, See General Section

For full biographical listings, see the Martindale-Hubbell Law Directory

PALMER & DODGE (AV)

(Storey Thorndike Palmer & Dodge)
One Beacon Street, 02108
Telephone: 617-573-0100
Telecopier: 617-227-4420
Telex: 951104
Cable Address: "Storeydike," Boston

(See Next Column)

MEMBERS OF FIRM
Michael T. Gass
Thane D. Scott

For Complete List of Firm Personnel, See General Section

For full biographical listings, see the Martindale-Hubbell Law Directory

MICHIGAN

*ANN ARBOR,** Washtenaw Co.

MILLER, CANFIELD, PADDOCK AND STONE, P.L.C. (AV)

A Professional Limited Liability Company
Founded in 1852 by Sidney Davy Miller
101 North Main Street, Seventh Floor, 48104-1400
Telephone: 313-663-2445
Fax: 313-747-7147
Detroit, Michigan Office: 150 West Jefferson, Suite 2500, 48226-4415.
Telephone: 313-963-6420.
Fax: 313-496-7500.
Cable Address: "Stem Detroit."
Bloomfield Hills, Michigan Office: Suite 100, Pinehurst Office Center, 1400 North Woodward, 48303-2014.
Telephone: 313-645-5000.
Fax: 313-645-1917.
Grand Rapids, Michigan Office: 1200 Campau Square Plaza, 99 Monroe, N.W., 49503-2639.
Telephone: 616-454-8656.
Fax: 616-776-6322.
Howell, Michigan Office: 121 South Barnard Street, Suite 4, 48843-2305.
Telephone: 517-546-7600.
Telecopier: 517-546-6974.
Kalamazoo, Michigan Office: 444 West Michigan Avenue, 49007-3752.
Telephone: 616-381-7030.
Fax: 616-382-0244.
Lansing, Michigan Office: One Michigan Avenue, Suite 900, 48933-1609.
Telephone: 517-487-2070.
Fax: 517-374-6304.
Monroe, Michigan Office: The Executive Centre, 214 East Elm Avenue, 48161-2682.
Telephone: 313-243-2000.
Fax: 313-243-0901.
Washington, D.C. Office: 1225 Nineteenth Street, N.W., Suite 400. 20036.
Telephone: 202-429-5575; 785-0600.
Fax: 202-331-1118; 785-1234.
Pensacola, Florida Office: 25 West Cedar, 32501.
Telephone: 904-469-1088.
Fax: 904-432-0677.
St. Petersburg, Florida Office: 100 Second Avenue S., Suite 7045, 33701.
Telephone: 813-982-6000.
Fax: 813-892-6002.
Gdansk, Poland Office: Suite 322, Dom Technika Building, Ul. Rajska 6, 80-850.
Telephone: 011-485-831-2808.
Fax: 011-485-831-4719.
Warsaw, Poland Office: Ul. Marszalkowska 82, Suite 561, 00-517.
Telephone: 011-482-623-6457 and 6458.
Fax: 011-482-623-6459.

RESIDENT PARTNER
Robert E. Gilbert

OF COUNSEL
Edmond F. DeVine

Representative Firm Clients: Chrysler Corp.; Comerica, Inc.; City of Detroit, Mich.; Detroit Tigers, Inc.; First of Michigan; Fretter, Inc.; Ford Motor Co.; Ford Motor Credit Co.; Great Lakes Bancorp; Henry Ford Hospital.

For Complete List of Firm Personnel, See General Section

For full biographical listings, see the Martindale-Hubbell Law Directory

BATTLE CREEK, Calhoun Co.

VARNUM, RIDDERING, SCHMIDT & HOWLETT (AV)

4950 West Dickman Road, Suite B-1, 49015
Telephone: 616-962-7144
Grand Rapids, Michigan Office: Bridgewater Place, P.O. Box 352, 49501-0352.
Telephone: 616-336-6000; 800-262-0011.
Facsimile: 616-336-7000.
Telex: 1561593 VARN.
Lansing, Michigan Office: The Victor Center, Suite 810, 201 North Washington Square, 48933.
Telephone: 517-482-6237.
Facsimile: 517-482-6937.
Kalamazoo, Michigan Office: 350 East Michigan Avenue, 49007.
Telephone: 616-382-2300.
Facsimile: 616-382-2382.

(See Next Column)

VARNUM, RIDDERING, SCHMIDT & HOWLETT, *Battle Creek—Continued*

Grand Haven, Michigan Office: 321 Washington Street, P.O. Box 288, 49417.
Telephone: 616-846-7100.
Facsimile: 616-846-7101.
Detroit, Michigan Office: 440 East Congress, Fourth Floor, 48226.
Telephone: 313-961-1600.
Facsimile: 313-961-1636.

MEMBER OF FIRM

Carl E. Ver Beek

For full biographical listings, see the Martindale-Hubbell Law Directory

BLOOMFIELD HILLS, Oakland Co.

HOWARD & HOWARD ATTORNEYS, P.C. (AV)

The Pinehurst Office Center, Suite 101, 1400 North Woodward Avenue, 48304-2856
Telephone: 810-645-1483
Telecopier: 810-645-1568
Kalamazoo, Michigan Office: The Kalamazoo Building, Suite 400, 107 West Michigan Avenue.
Telephone: 616-382-1483.
Telecopier: 616-382-1568.
Lansing, Michigan Office: The Phoenix Building, Suite 500, 222 Washington Square, North.
Telephone: 517-485-1483.
Telecopier: 517-485-1568.
Peoria, Illinois Office: Howard & Howard, P.C., The Creve Coeur Building, Suite 200, 321 Liberty Street.
Telephone: 309-672-1483.
Telecopier: 309-672-1568.

Thomas R. Curran, Jr.
Paul Green
Thomas J. Tallerico
John E. Young

Representative Clients: For Representative Client list, see General Practice, Bloomfield Hills, MI.

For Complete List of Firm Personnel, See General Section

For full biographical listings, see the Martindale-Hubbell Law Directory

*DETROIT,** Wayne Co.

BODMAN, LONGLEY & DAHLING (AV)

34th Floor 100 Renaissance Center, 48243
Telephone: 313-259-7777
Fax: 313-393-7579
Troy, Michigan Office: Suite 2020, 755 West Big Beaver Road.
Telephone: 810-362-2110.
Ann Arbor, Michigan Office: 110 Miller, Suite 300.
Telephone: 313-761-3780.
Northern Michigan Office: 229 Court Street, P.O. Box 405, Cheboygan.
Telephone: 616-627-4351.

MEMBERS OF FIRM

Richard D. Rohr
Theodore Souris
Michael B. Lewiston
Herold McC. Deason
David G. Chardavoyne

COUNSEL

Robert A. Nitschke

Representative Clients: Abitibi Price Group; Archdiocese of Detroit; Comerica Bank; The Detroit Lions, Inc.; Ford Estates; General Motors Corporation; Charles Stewart Mott Foundation; Norfolk Southern Corporation; Panhandle Eastern Corporation; State Farm Mutual Automobile Insurance Company.

For Complete List of Firm Personnel, See General Section

For full biographical listings, see the Martindale-Hubbell Law Directory

BUTZEL LONG, A PROFESSIONAL CORPORATION (AV)

Suite 900, 150 West Jefferson, 48226
Telephone: 313-225-7000
Telecopier: 313-225-7080
Birmingham, Michigan Office: Suite 200, 32270 Telegraph Road.
Telephone: 810-258-1616.
Telecopier: 810-258-1439.
Lansing, Michigan Office: 118 West Ottawa Street.
Telephone: 517-372-6622.
Telecopier: 517-372-6672.
Ann Arbor, Michigan Office: Suite 400, 121 West Washington.
Telephone: 313-995-3110.
Telecopier: 313-995-1777.
Grosse Pointe Farms, Michigan Office: Suite 260, 21 Kercheval.
Telephone: 313-886-5446.
Telecopier: 313-886-2114.

(See Next Column)

Richard E. Rassel
Philip J. Kessler
Leonard M. Niehoff
Sheldon H. Klein

Representative Clients: Bridgestone/Firestone, Inc.; The Detroit News, Inc.; Detroit Diesel Corp.; Kelly Services; Kelsey Hayes Co.; Merrill Lynch & Co., Inc.; Stroh Brewery Co.; Takata Corp.; United Parcel Services of America, Inc.; The University of Michigan.

For Complete List of Firm Personnel, See General Section

For full biographical listings, see the Martindale-Hubbell Law Directory

CLARK, KLEIN & BEAUMONT (AV)

1600 First Federal Building, 1001 Woodward Avenue, 48226
Telephone: 313-965-8300
Facsimile: 313-962-4348
Bloomfield Hills Office: 1533 North Woodward Avenue, Suite 220, 48304.
Telephone: 810-258-2900.
Facsimile: 810-258-2949.

MEMBERS OF FIRM

D. Kerry Crenshaw
David M. Hayes
Robert L. Weyhing, III
David E. Nims, III
David H. Paruch
Jonathan T. Walton, Jr.
John J. Hern, Jr.
John E. Berg

ASSOCIATES

Patrice A. Villani
Georgette Borrego Dulworth

For Complete List of Firm Personnel, See General Section

For full biographical listings, see the Martindale-Hubbell Law Directory

DICKINSON, WRIGHT, MOON, VAN DUSEN & FREEMAN (AV)

500 Woodward Avenue, Suite 4000, 48226-3425
Telephone: 313-223-3500
Facsimile: 313-223-3598
Bloomfield Hills, Michigan Office: 525 North Woodward Avenue, Suite 2000.
Telephone: 810-433-7200.
Facsimile: 810-433-7274.
Grand Rapids, Michigan Office: 200 Ottawa Avenue, N.W., Suite 900.
Telephone: 616-458-1300.
Facsimile: 616-458-6753.
Lansing, Michigan Office: Suite 200, 215 South Washington Square.
Telephone: 517-371-1730.
Facsimile: 517-487-4700.
Washington, D.C. Office: Suite 800, 1901 L Street, N.W.
Telephone: 202-457-0160.
Facsimile: 202-659-1559.
Chicago, Illinois Office: 225 West Washington, Suite 400.
Telephone: 312-220-0300.
Facsimile: 312-220-0021.
Warsaw, Poland Office: 46 Wilcza Street, 4th Floor, 00-679.
Telephone: (48-22) 299-241.
Facsimile: (48-2) 628-4107. Komertel Satellite Phone: (48-39) 121-510.

MEMBERS OF FIRM

Fred W. Freeman
John A. Krsul, Jr.
Kenneth J. McIntyre
Philip M. Frost

CONSULTING PARTNER

Grady Avant, Jr.

Representative Clients: Federal-Mogul Corp.; Florists' Transworld Delivery Assn.; GMF Robotics Corp.; Kmart Corp.; Kuhlman Corp.; Michigan Consolidated Gas Co.; NBD Bank, N.A.

For Complete List of Firm Personnel, See General Section

For full biographical listings, see the Martindale-Hubbell Law Directory

DYKEMA GOSSETT (AV)

400 Renaissance Center, 48243-1668
Telephone: 313-568-6800
Cable Address: "Dyke-Detroit"
Telex: 23-0121
Fax: 313-568-6594
Ann Arbor, Michigan Office: 315 East Eisenhower Parkway, Suite 100, 48108-3306.
Telephone: 313-747-7660.
Fax: 313-747-7696.
Bloomfield Hills, Michigan Office: 1577 North Woodward Avenue, Suite 300, 48304-2820.
Telephone: 810-540-0700.
Fax: 810-540-0763.
Grand Rapids, Michigan Office: 200 Oldtown Riverfront Building, 248 Louis Campau Promenade, N.W., 49503-2668.
Telephone: 616-776-7500.
Fax: 616-776-7573.
Lansing, Michigan Office: 800 Michigan National Tower, 48933-1707.
Telephone: 517-374-9100.
Fax: 517-374-9191.
Washington, D.C. Office: Franklin Square, Suite 300 West Tower, 1300 I Street, N.W., 20005-3306.
Telephone: 202-522-8600.
Fax: 202-522-8669.

(See Next Column)

DYKEMA GOSSETT—*Continued*

Chicago, Illinois Office: Three First National Plaza, Suite 1400, 70 W. Madison, 60602-4270.
Telephone: 312-214-3380.
Fax: 312-214-3441.

MEMBERS OF FIRM

Ted T. Amsden
Barbara L. Goldman
Dennis M. Haffey (Resident at Bloomfield Hills Office)
Debra M. McCulloch
Howard E. O'Leary, Jr. (Resident at Washington, D.C. Office)
Thomas W. B. Porter
Lori M. Silsbury (Resident at Lansing Office)
Daniel J. Stephenson (Resident at Ann Arbor Office)
Roger K. Timm
Fred L. Woodworth (Resident at Washington, D.C. Office)

ASSOCIATES

Martin R. Fischer (Not admitted in MI; Resident at Washington, D.C. Office)
Judy Parker Jenkins (Not admitted in MI; Resident at Washington, D.C. Office)
Ava K. Ortner
Mark W. Osler
Thomas M. Pastore

For Complete List of Firm Personnel, See General Section

For full biographical listings, see the Martindale-Hubbell Law Directory

---

HONIGMAN MILLER SCHWARTZ AND COHN (AV)

A Partnership including Professional Corporations
2290 First National Building, 48226
Telephone: 313-256-7800
Telecopier: 313-962-0176
Telex: 235705
Lansing, Michigan Office: Phoenix Building, 222 North Washington Square, Suite 400.
Telephone: 517-484-8282.
West Palm Beach, Florida Office: Suite 800 Esperante Building, 222 Lakeview Avenue.
Telephone: 407-838-4500.
Tampa, Florida Office: 2700 Landmark Centre, 401 E. Jackson Street.
Telephone: 813-221-6600.
Orlando, Florida Office: 390 North Orange Avenue, Suite 1300.
Telephone: 407-648-0300.
Houston, Texas Office: 3100 First Interstate Bank Plaza, 1000 Louisiana.
Telephone: 713-650-2600.
Los Angeles, California Office: McNeill Plaza, Suite 820, 15260 Ventura Boulevard, 91403.
Telephone: 818-784-2900.

MEMBERS OF FIRM

Maurice S. Binkow
Gerald S. Cook
David A. Ettinger
Howard B. Iwrey
Stephen Wasinger

ASSOCIATES

Stanford P. Berenbaum
William L. Fealko, III (Not admitted in MI)

RESIDENT IN TAMPA, FLORIDA OFFICE

MEMBER

Harry Christopher Goplerud (P.A.)

Representative Clients: American Speedy Printing Company, Inc.; Bronson Healthcare Group, Inc; Citicorp; Compuware; Handleman Co.; J.P. Industries, Inc.; Intergraph Corporation; Mercy Health Services; Prime Computer, Inc.; T & N, Inc.

For Complete List of Firm Personnel, See General Section

For full biographical listings, see the Martindale-Hubbell Law Directory

---

KERR, RUSSELL AND WEBER (AV)

One Detroit Center, 500 Woodward Avenue, Suite 2500, 48226-3406
Telephone: 313-961-0200
Telecopier: 313-961-0388
Bloomfield Hills, Michigan Office: 3883 Telegraph Road.
Telephone: 810-649-5990.
East Lansing, Michigan Office: 1301 North Hagadorn Road.
Telephone: 517-336-6767.

William A. Sankbeil
Monte D. Jahnke
Joanne Geha Swanson

For Complete List of Firm Personnel, See General Section

For full biographical listings, see the Martindale-Hubbell Law Directory

---

MILLER, CANFIELD, PADDOCK AND STONE, P.L.C. (AV)

A Professional Limited Liability Company
Founded in 1852 by Sidney Davy Miller
150 West Jefferson, Suite 2500, 48226-4415
Telephone: 313-963-6420
Fax: 313-496-7500
Cable Address: "Stem Detroit"
Detroit, Michigan Office: 150 West Jefferson, Suite 2500, 48226-4415.
Telephone: 313-963-6420.
Fax: 313-496-7500.
Cable Address: "Stem Detroit."
Ann Arbor, Michigan Office: 101 North Main Street, 7th Floor, 48104-1400.
Telephone: 313-663-2445.
Fax: 313-747-7147.
Bloomfield Hills, Michigan Office: Suite 100, Pinehurst Office Center, 1400 North Woodward, 48303-2014.
Telephone: 313-645-5000.
Fax: 313-645-1917.
Grand Rapids, Michigan Office: 1200 Campau Square Plaza, 99 Monroe, N.W., 49503-2639.
Telephone: 616-454-8656.
Fax: 616-776-6322.
Howell, Michigan Office: 121 South Barnard Street, Suite 4, 48843-2305.
Telephone: 517-546-7600.
Telecopier: 517-546-6974.
Kalamazoo, Michigan Office: 444 West Michigan Avenue, 49007-3752.
Telephone: 616-381-7030.
Fax: 616-382-0244.
Lansing, Michigan Office: One Michigan Avenue, Suite 900, 48933-1609.
Telephone: 517-487-2070.
Fax: 517-374-6304.
Monroe, Michigan Office: The Executive Centre, 214 East Elm Avenue, 48161-2682.
Telephone: 313-243-2000.
Fax: 313-243-0901.
Washington, D.C. Office: 1225 Nineteenth Street, N.W., Suite 400. 20036.
Telephone: 202-429-5575; 785-0600.
Fax: 202-331-1118; 785-1234.
Pensacola, Florida Office: 25 West Cedar, 32501.
Telephone: 904-469-1088.
Fax: 904-432-0677.
St. Petersburg, Florida Office: 100 Second Avenue S., Suite 7045, 33701.
Telephone: 813-982-6000.
Fax: 813-892-6002.
Gdansk, Poland Office: Suite 322, Dom Technika Building, Ul. Rajska 6, 80-850.
Telephone: 011-485-831-2808.
Fax: 011-485-831-4719.
Warsaw, Poland Office: Ul. Marszalkowska 82, Suite 561, 00-517.
Telephone: 011-482-623-6457 and 6458.
Fax: 011-482-623-6459.

MEMBERS OF FIRM

George E. Parker, III
Rocque E. Lipford (P.C.) (Monroe Office)
David D. Joswick (P.C.)
Gregory L. Curtner
Larry J. Saylor
Mark T. Boonstra

OF COUNSEL

Edmond F. DeVine (Ann Arbor Office)
Richard B. Gushée

Representative Firm Clients: Chrysler Corp.; Comerica, Inc.; City of Detroit, Mich.; Detroit Tigers, Inc.; First of Michigan; Fretter, Inc.; Ford Motor Co.; Ford Motor Credit Co.; Great Lakes Bancorp; Henry Ford Hospital.

For Complete List of Firm Personnel, See General Section

For full biographical listings, see the Martindale-Hubbell Law Directory

---

TIMMIS & INMAN (AV)

300 Talon Centre, 48207
Telephone: 313-396-4200
Telecopier: 313-396-4228

MEMBERS OF FIRM

Wayne C. Inman
Charles W. Royer
Henry J. Brennan, III
Lisa R. Gorman

ASSOCIATES

Bradley J. Knickerbocker
Mark Robert Adams

Representative Client: F & M Distributors.

For Complete List of Firm Personnel, See General Section

For full biographical listings, see the Martindale-Hubbell Law Directory

*GRAND RAPIDS,** Kent Co.

Miller, Canfield, Paddock and Stone, P.L.C. (AV)

A Professional Limited Liability Company
Founded in 1852 by Sidney Davy Miller
1200 Campau Square Plaza, 99 Monroe, N.W., P.O. Box 329, 49503-2639
Telephone: 616-454-8656
Fax: 616-776-6322
Detroit, Michigan Office: 150 West Jefferson, Suite 2500, 48226-4415.
Telephone: 313-963-6420.
Fax: 313-496-7500.
Cable Address: "Stem Detroit."
Ann Arbor, Michigan Office: 101 North Main Street, 7th Floor, 48104-1400.
Telephone: 313-663-2445.
Fax: 313-747-7147.
Bloomfield Hills, Michigan Office: Suite 100, Pinehurst Office Center, 1400 North Woodward, 48303-2014.
Telephone: 313-645-5000.
Fax: 313-645-1917.
Howell, Michigan Office: 121 South Barnard Street, Suite 4, 48843-2305.
Telephone: 517-546-7600.
Telecopier: 517-546-6974.
Kalamazoo, Michigan Office: 444 West Michigan Avenue, 49007-3752.
Telephone: 616-381-7030.
Fax: 616-382-0244.
Lansing, Michigan Office: One Michigan Avenue, Suite 900, 48933-1609.
Telephone: 517-487-2070.
Fax: 517-374-6304.
Monroe, Michigan Office: The Executive Centre, 214 East Elm Avenue, 48161-2682.
Telephone: 313-243-2000.
Fax: 313-243-0901.
Washington, D.C. Office: 1225 Nineteenth Street, N.W., Suite 400. 20036.
Telephone: 202-429-5575; 785-0600;
Fax: 202-331-1118; 785-1234.
Pensacola, Florida Office: 25 West Cedar 32501.
Telephone: 904-469-1088.
Fax: 904-432-0677.
St. Petersburg Florida Office: 100 Second Avenue S., Suite 7045, 33701.
Telephone: 813-982-6000.
Fax: 813-892-6002.
Gdansk, Poland Office: Suite 322, Dom Technika Building, Ul. Rajska 6, 80-850.
Telephone: 011-485-831-2808.
Fax: 011-485-831-4719.
Warsaw, Poland Office: Ul. Marszalkowska 82, Suite 561, 00-517.
Telephone: 011-482-623-6457 and 6458.
Fax: 011-482-623-6459.

MEMBERS OF FIRM

Thomas J. Heiden (Resident)
Mark E. Putney (Resident)
Thomas C. Phillips
Richard A. Gaffin
Charles S. Mishkind (Detroit, Lansing and Kalamazoo Offices)
Stephen M. Tuuk (Resident)
Robert D. VanderLaan (Resident)
Michael G. Campbell (Resident)
Robert E. Lee Wright
Vernon Bennett III
Douglas W. Crim (Resident)

OF COUNSEL

George J. Slykhouse (Resident)

SENIOR ATTORNEYS

Charles E. Scholl (Resident)
David E. Hathaway (Resident)
Michael J. Taylor (Resident)
David J. Hasper (Resident)

ASSOCIATES

Gary E. Mitchell (Resident)
John C. Arndts (Resident)
Bradley C. White
Meg Hackett Carrier (Resident)

Representative Firm Clients: Chrysler Corp.; Comerica, Inc.; City of Detroit, Mich.; Detroit Tigers, Inc.; First of Michigan; Fretter, Inc.; Ford Motor Co.; Ford Motor Credit Co.; Great Lakes Bancorp; Henry Ford Hospital.

For full biographical listings, see the Martindale-Hubbell Law Directory

Varnum, Riddering, Schmidt & Howlett (AV)

Bridgewater Place, P.O. Box 352, 49501-0352
Telephone: 616-336-6000
800-262-0011
Facsimile: 616-336-7000
Telex: 1561593 VARN
Lansing, Michigan Office: The Victor Center, Suite 810, 210 North Washington Square, 48933.
Telephone: 517-482-6237.
Facsimile: 517-482-6937.
Kalamazoo, Michigan Office: 350 East Michigan Avenue, 49007.
Telephone: 616-382-2300.
Facsimile: 616-382-2382.
Grand Haven, Michigan Office: 321 Washington Street, P.O. Box 288, 49417.
Telephone: 616-846-7100.
Facsimile: 616-846-7101.

(See Next Column)

Battle Creek, Michigan Office: 4950 West Dickman Road, Suite B-1, 49015.
Telephone: 616-962-7144.
Detroit, Michigan Office: 440 East Congress, Fourth Floor, 48226.
Telephone: 313-961-1600.
Facsimile: 313-961-1636.

MEMBERS OF FIRM

J. Terry Moran
Robert L. Diamond
William J. Lawrence III
Jeffrey W. Beswick (Resident at Grand Haven Office)

ASSOCIATES

Kathleen P. Fochtman
Steven J. Morren
Jon M. Bylsma

Counsel for: Donnelly Corporation ; First Michigan Bank Corporation; Gainey Corporation; Gentex Corporation; Grand Rapids Association of Realtors; Harrow Products, Inc.; Herman Miller, Inc.; Holland Hitch Co.; X-Rite Incorporated; S-2 Yachts, Inc.

For Complete List of Firm Personnel, See General Section

For full biographical listings, see the Martindale-Hubbell Law Directory

Warner, Norcross & Judd (AV)

900 Old Kent Building, 111 Lyon Street, N.W., 49503-2489
Telephone: 616-752-2000
Fax: 616-752-2500
Muskegon, Michigan Office: 400 Terrace Plaza, P.O. Box 900.
Telephone: 616-727-2600.
Fax: 616-727-2699.
Holland, Michigan Office: Curtis Center, Suite 300, 170 College Avenue.
Telephone: 616-396-9800.
Fax: 616-396-3656.

MEMBERS OF FIRM

R. Malcolm Cumming
William K. Holmes
J. A. Cragwall, Jr.
Stephen C. Waterbury
Tracy T. Larsen
Richard L. Bouma

General Counsel for: Bissell Inc.; Blodgett Memorial Medical Center; Guardsman Products, Inc.; Haworth, Inc.; Kysor Industrial Corp.; Michigan Bankers Assn.; Old Kent Financial Corp.; Steelcase Inc.; Wolverine World Wide Inc.

For Complete List of Firm Personnel, See General Section

For full biographical listings, see the Martindale-Hubbell Law Directory

*KALAMAZOO,** Kalamazoo Co.

Miller, Canfield, Paddock and Stone, P.L.C. (AV)

A Professional Limited Liability Company
Founded in 1852 by Sidney Davy Miller
444 West Michigan Avenue, 49007-3752
Telephone: 616-381-7030
Fax: 616-382-0244
Detroit, Michigan Office: 150 West Jefferson, Suite 2500, 48226-4415.
Telephone: 313-963-6420.
Fax: 313-496-7500.
Cable Address: "Stem Detroit."
Ann Arbor, Michigan Office: 101 North Main Street, 7th Floor, 48104-1400.
Telephone: 313-663-2445.
Fax: 313-747-7147.
Bloomfield Hills, Michigan Office: Suite 100, Pinehurst Office Center, 1400 North Woodward, 48303-2014.
Telephone: 313-645-5000.
Fax: 313-645-1917.
Grand Rapids, Michigan Office: 1200 Campau Square Plaza, 99 Monroe, N.W., 49503-2639.
Telephone: 616-454-8656.
Fax: 616-776-6322.
Howell, Michigan Office: 121 South Barnard Street, Suite 4, 48843-2305.
Telephone: 517-546-7600.
Telecopier: 517-546-6974.
Lansing, Michigan Office: One Michigan Avenue, Suite 900, 48933-1609.
Telephone: 517-487-2070.
Fax: 517-374-6304.
Monroe, Michigan Office: The Executive Centre, 214 East Elm Avenue, 48161-2682.
Telephone: 313-243-2000.
Fax: 313-243-0901.
Washington, D.C. Office: 1225 Nineteenth Street, N.W., Suite 400. 20036.
Telephone: 202-429-5575; 785-0600.
Fax: 202-331-1118; 785-1234.
Pensacola, Florida Office: 25 West Cedar, 32501.
Telephone: 904-469-1088.
Fax: 904-432-0677.
St. Petersburg, Florida Office: 100 Second Avenue S., Suite 7045,33701.
Telephone: 813-982-6000.
Fax: 813-892-6002.
Gdansk, Poland Office: Suite 322, Dom Technika Building, Ul. Rajska 6, 80-850.
Telephone: 011-485-831-2808.
Fax: 011-485-831-4719.

(See Next Column)

MILLER, CANFIELD, PADDOCK AND STONE P.L.C.—*Continued*

Warsaw, Poland Office: Ul. Marszalkowska 82, Suite 561, 00-517.
Telephone: 011-482-623-6457 and 6458.
Fax: 011-482-623-6459.

MEMBER OF FIRM

Eric V. Brown, Jr. (Resident)

Representative Firm Clients: Chrysler Corp.; Comerica, Inc.; City of Detroit, Mich.; Detroit Tigers, Inc.; First of Michigan; Fretter, Inc.; Ford Motor Co.; Ford Motor Credit Co.; Great Lakes Bancorp; Henry Ford Hospital.

For Complete List of Firm Personnel, See General Section

For full biographical listings, see the Martindale-Hubbell Law Directory

LANSING, Ingham Co.

HOWARD & HOWARD ATTORNEYS, P.C. (AV)

The Phoenix Building, Suite 500, 222 Washington Square, North, 48933-1817
Telephone: 517-485-1483
Telecopier: 517-485-1568
Kalamazoo, Michigan Office: The Kalamazoo Building, Suite 400, 107 West Michigan Avenue.
Telephone: 616-382-1483.
Telecopier: 616-382-1568.
Bloomfield Hills, Michigan Office: The Pinehurst Office Center, Suite 101, 1400 North Woodward Avenue.
Telephone: 810-645-1483.
Telecopier: 810-645-1568.
Peoria, Illinois Office: Howard & Howard, P.C., The Creve Coeur Building, Suite 200, 321 Liberty Street.
Telephone: 309-672-1483.
Telecopier: 309-672-1568.

Todd D. Chamberlain

Representative Clients: For Representative Client list, see General Practice, Lansing, MI.

For Complete List of Firm Personnel, See General Section

For full biographical listings, see the Martindale-Hubbell Law Directory

MILLER, CANFIELD, PADDOCK AND STONE, P.L.C. (AV)

A Professional Limited Liability Company
Founded in 1852 by Sidney Davy Miller
Suite 900, One Michigan Avenue, 48933-1609
Telephone: 517-487-2070
Fax: 517-374-6304
Detroit, Michigan Office: 150 West Jefferson, Suite 2500, 48226-4415.
Telephone: 313-963-6420.
Fax: 313-496-7500.
Cable Address: "Stem Detroit."
Ann Arbor, Michigan Office: 101 North Main Street, 7th Floor, 48104-1400.
Telephone: 313-663-2445.
Fax: 313-747-7147.
Bloomfield Hills, Michigan Office: Suite 100, Pinehurst Office Center, 1400 North Woodward, 48303-2014.
Telephone: 313-645-5000.
Fax: 313-645-1917.
Grand Rapids, Michigan Office: 1200 Campau Square Plaza, 99 Monroe, N.W., 49503-2639.
Telephone: 616-454-8656.
Fax: 616-776-6322.
Howell, Michigan Office: 121 South Barnard Street, Suite 4, 48843-2305.
Telephone: 517-546-7600.
Telecopier: 517-546-6974.
Kalamazoo, Michigan Office: 444 West Michigan Avenue, 49007-3752.
Telephone: 616-381-7030.
Fax: 616-382-0244.
Monroe, Michigan Office: The Executive Centre, 214 East Elm Avenue, 48161-2682.
Telephone: 313-243-2000.
Fax: 313-243-0901.
Washington, D.C. Office: 1225 Nineteenth Street, N.W., Suite 400. 20036.
Telephone: 202-429-5575; 785-0600.
Fax: 202-331-1118; 785-1234.
Pensacola, Florida Office: 25 West Cedar, 32501.
Telephone: 904-469-1088.
Fax: 904-432-0677.
St. Petersburg Office: 100 Second Avenue S., Suite 7045, 33701.
Telephone: 813-982-6000.
Fax: 813-892-6002.
Gdansk, Poland Office: Suite 322, Dom Technika Building, Ul. Rajska 6, 80-850.
Telephone: 011-485-831-2808.
Fax: 011-485-831-4719.
Warsaw, Poland Office: Ul. Marszalkowska 82, Suite 561, 00-517.
Telephone: 011-482-623-6457 and 6458.
Fax: 011-482-623-6459.

(See Next Column)

MEMBER OF FIRM

William J. Danhof (Resident)

Representative Firm Clients: Chrysler Corp.; Comerica, Inc.; City of Detroit, Mich.; Detroit Tigers, Inc.; First of Michigan; Fretter, Inc.; Ford Motor Co.; Ford Motor Credit Co.; Great Lakes Bancorp; Henry Ford Hospital.

For Complete List of Firm Personnel, See General Section

For full biographical listings, see the Martindale-Hubbell Law Directory

SOUTHFIELD, Oakland Co.

YOUNG & ASSOCIATES, P.C. (AV)

Suite 305 Westview Office Center, 26200 American Drive, 48034
Telephone: 810-353-8620
Telecopier: 810-353-6559

Rodger D. Young

Anthony Cho — Michael J. Fergestrom

Representative Clients: ADT; Commtract Corp.; GTE; Phillips Service Industries, NC. (PSI); Regal Plastics; Siemens; The Virtual Group

For full biographical listings, see the Martindale-Hubbell Law Directory

MINNESOTA

*MINNEAPOLIS,** Hennepin Co.

FREDRIKSON & BYRON, P.A. (AV)

1100 International Centre, 900 Second Avenue South, 55402-3397
Telephone: 612-347-7000
Telex: 290569 FREDRIKSON MPS
Telecopier: 612-347-7077
European Office: 79 Knightsbridge, London SW1X 7RB England.
Telephone: 44-71-823-2338.
Telecopier: 44-71-235-2683.

Quentin T. Johnson — John A. Satorius
Sharon K. Freier

For Complete List of Firm Personnel, See General Section

For full biographical listings, see the Martindale-Hubbell Law Directory

O'CONNOR & HANNAN (AV)

3800 IDS Center, 80 South Eighth Street, 55402-2254
Telephone: 612-343-1200
Telecopy: 612-343-1256
Washington, D.C. Office: 1919 Pennsylvania Avenue, N.W., Suite 800.
Telephone: 202-887-1400.
Telecopy: 202-466-2198.

MEMBER OF FIRM

Joe A. Walters

WASHINGTON, D.C. OFFICE

David R. Melincoff *

A List of Representative Clients will be furnished upon request.
*Not admitted in Minn.

For Complete List of Firm Personnel, See General Section

For full biographical listings, see the Martindale-Hubbell Law Directory

SIEGEL, BRILL, GREUPNER & DUFFY, P.A. (AV)

1300 Washington Square, 100 Washington Avenue South, 55401
Telephone: 612-339-7131
Telecopier: 612-339-6591

Richard Siegel — Thomas H. Goodman
Josiah E. Brill, Jr. — John S. Watson
James R. Greupner — Wm. Christopher Penwell
Gerald S. Duffy — Susan M. Voigt
Wood R. Foster, Jr. — Anthony James Gleekel
Joel H. Jensen

Sherri L. Rohlf — Rosemary Tuohy
Brian E. Weisberg — Jordan M. Lewis
James A. Yarosh

RETIRED

Maurice L. Grossman (P.A.) — Sheldon D. Karlins (P.A.)

Representative Clients: Champion Auto Stores, Inc.; Holiday Inns; Ron-Vik, Inc.; Super America Stations, Inc.; Ashland Oil, Inc.; Aveda Corporation; Applied Spectrum Technology, Inc.; Richard Manufacturing Co.; Mann Theaters; Homecraft Builders, Inc.

For full biographical listings, see the Martindale-Hubbell Law Directory

MISSISSIPPI

*JACKSON,** Hinds Co.

ALSTON, RUTHERFORD, TARDY & VAN SLYKE (AV)

121 North State Street, P.O. Drawer 1532, 39215-1532
Telephone: 601-948-6882
Fax: 601-948-6902

MEMBERS OF FIRM

Alex A. Alston, Jr. Kenneth A. Rutherford

Counsel for: Ford Motor Co.; E.I. DuPont de Nemours Co.; Gannett Co., Inc.; Conoco, Inc.; Jostens, Inc.; General Electric Company; Georgia-Pacific Corp.; Dean Witter Reynolds, Inc.; Prudential Securities, Inc.; Transcontinental Gas Pipeline Inc.

For Complete List of Firm Personnel, See General Section

For full biographical listings, see the Martindale-Hubbell Law Directory

MISSOURI

KANSAS CITY, Jackson, Clay & Platte Cos.

BLACKWELL SANDERS MATHENY WEARY & LOMBARDI L.C. (AV)

Suite 1100, Two Pershing Square, 2300 Main Street, 64108
Telephone: 816-274-6800
Telecopier: 816-274-6914
Overland Park, Kansas Office: 40 Corporate Woods, Suite 1200, 9401 Indian Creek Parkway.
Telephone: 913-345-8400.
Telecopier: 913-344-6375.

MEMBERS OF FIRM

John Keith Brungardt Floyd R. Finch, Jr.
John R. Phillips

Representative Clients: Cook Paint & Varnish Co.; Puritan-Bennett Corp.; Universal Underwriters; UtiliCorp United Inc.

For Complete List of Firm Personnel, See General Section

For full biographical listings, see the Martindale-Hubbell Law Directory

SHUGHART THOMSON & KILROY, A PROFESSIONAL CORPORATION (AV)

Twelve Wyandotte Plaza, 120 West 12th Street, 64105
Telephone: 816-421-3355
Overland Park, Kansas Office: Suite 1100, 32 Corporate Woods, 9225 Indian Creek Parkway 66210.
Telephone: 913-451-3355.

R. Lawrence Ward John M. Kilroy, Jr.
Robert R. Raymond Dennis D. Palmer
George E. Leonard William E. Quirk
Philip W. Bledsoe

For Complete List of Firm Personnel, See General Section

For full biographical listings, see the Martindale-Hubbell Law Directory

SWANSON, MIDGLEY, GANGWERE, KITCHIN & MCLARNEY, L.L.C. (AV)

1500 Commerce Trust Building, 922 Walnut, 64106-1848
Telephone: 816-842-6100
Overland Park, Kansas Office: The NCAA Building, Suite 350, 6201 College Boulevard.
Telephone: 816-842-6100.

John J. Kitchin Lawrence M. Maher

Counsel for: General Electric Co.; Chrysler Corp.; Yellow Freight System, Inc.; The Prudential Insurance Co. of America; Metropolitan Life Insurance Co.; National Collegiate Athletic Assn.; Land Title Insurance Co.; Safeway Stores, Inc.; The Lee Apparel Co.; Mayflower Contract Services.

For Complete List of Firm Personnel, See General Section

For full biographical listings, see the Martindale-Hubbell Law Directory

ST. LOUIS, (Independent City)

ARMSTRONG, TEASDALE, SCHLAFLY & DAVIS (AV)

A Partnership including Professional Corporations
One Metropolitan Square, 63102-2740
Telephone: 314-621-5070
Facsimile: 314-621-5065
Twx: 910 761-2246
Cable: ATKV LAW
Kansas City, Missouri Office: 1700 City Center Square. 1100 Main Street, 64105.
Telephone: 816-221-3420.
Facsimile: 816-221-0786.
Belleville, Illinois Office: 23 South First Street, 62220.
Telephone: 618-397-4411.
Olathe, Kansas Office: 100 East Park, 66061.
Telephone: 913-345-0706.

MEMBERS OF FIRM

Thomas Cummings (P.C.) Jay A. Summerville
Glenn E. Davis

OF COUNSEL

John J. Cole (P.C.) Charles E. Dapron

Representative Clients: Anheuser-Busch, Inc.; Big River Minerals; Blue Cross Health Services, Inc. of Missouri; Christian Hospitals; Southwestern Bell Telephone; Toyota Motor Company; Union Electric Co.; Continental Baking; Jefferson Smurfit; Maytag Corporation.

For Complete List of Firm Personnel, See General Section

For full biographical listings, see the Martindale-Hubbell Law Directory

KOHN, SHANDS, ELBERT, GIANOULAKIS & GILJUM (AV)

24th Floor, One Mercantile Center, 63101
Telephone: 314-241-3963
Telecopier: 314-241-2509

Alan C. Kohn John Gianoulakis
Mark J. Bremer

For full biographical listings, see the Martindale-Hubbell Law Directory

LEWIS, RICE & FINGERSH (AV)

A Partnership including Partnerships and Individuals
500 North Broadway, Suite 2000, 63102-2147
Telephone: 314-444-7600
Telecopier: 314-241-6056
Clayton, Missouri Office: Suite 400, 8182 Maryland Avenue.
Telephone: 314-444-7600.
Belleville, Illinois Office: 325 South High Street.
Telephone: 618-234-8636.
Hays, Kansas Office: 201 W. 11th St.
Telephone: 913-625-3997.
Leawood, Kansas Office: Suite 375, 8900 State Line.
Telephone: 913-381-8898.
Kansas City, Missouri Office: 1010 Walnut, Suite 500.
Telephone: 816-421-2500.

RESIDENT PARTNERS

Robert Smith Allen Barry A. Short
Allen S. Boston Richard B. Walsh, Jr.

For Complete List of Firm Personnel, See General Section

For full biographical listings, see the Martindale-Hubbell Law Directory

THOMPSON & MITCHELL (AV)

One Mercantile Center, Suite 3300, 63101
Telephone: 314-231-7676
Telecopier: 314-342-1717
Belleville, Illinois Office: 525 West Main Street.
Telephone: 618-277-4700; 314-271-1800.
Telecopier: 618-236-3434.
St. Charles, Missouri Office: 200 North Third Street.
Telephone: 314-946-7717.
Telecopier: 314-946-4938.
Washington, D.C. Office: 700 14th Street, N.W., Suite 900.
Telephone: 202-508-1000.
Telecopier: 202-508-1010.

MEMBERS OF FIRM

William G. Guerri James J. Raymond
David F. Ulmer Mary M. Bonacorsi
W. Stanley Walch Kenton E. Knickmeyer
Michael J. Morris

WASHINGTON, D.C. OFFICE
MEMBERS OF FIRM

Michael A. Greenspan John V. Austin

Representative Clients: Chrysler Corp.; Manildra Milling Company; Mercantile Bancorporation Inc.; Midland Development Group; Peabody Coal Co.; Shell Oil Co.; Union Pacific Railroad Company.

(See Next Column)

THOMPSON & MITCHELL—*Continued*

For Complete List of Firm Personnel, See General Section

For full biographical listings, see the Martindale-Hubbell Law Directory

MONTANA

*BOZEMAN,** Gallatin Co.

PAUL R. WYLIE A PROFESSIONAL CORPORATION (AV Ⓣ)

1805 West Dickerson #2, Suite 3, 59715
Telephone: 406-585-7344
Telecopier: 406-585-7358

Paul R. Wylie

Reference: First Security Bank, Bozeman, Montana.

For full biographical listings, see the Martindale-Hubbell Law Directory

NEBRASKA

*OMAHA,** Douglas Co.

MCGRATH, NORTH, MULLIN & KRATZ, P.C. (AV)

Suite 1400, One Central Park Plaza, 68102
Telephone: 402-341-3070
Telecopy: 402-341-0216
Telex: 797122 MNMKOM

Bruce C. Rohde
David H. Roe
John P. Passarelli
Sandra D. Morar

Representative Clients: ConAgra, Inc.; Valmont Industries, Inc.; Physicians Mutual Insurance Company; Omaha Airport Authority; American Family Insurance Group; Dow Chemical; Lloyds of London; Mutual of Omaha; The Pacesetter Corporation.

For Complete List of Firm Personnel, See General Section

For full biographical listings, see the Martindale-Hubbell Law Directory

NEW JERSEY

*HACKENSACK,** Bergen Co.

BRESLIN & TROVINI (AV)

14 Washington Place, 07601
Telephone: 201-343-5678
Telefax: 201-343-0369

MEMBERS OF FIRM

Michael J. Breslin, Jr.
Vincent P. Trovini

ASSOCIATES

Daniel P. McNerney
Victoria L. Tomasella
David S. Lafferty

OF COUNSEL

J. Emmet Cassidy (1919-1989)

Reference: Bridge View Bank.

For full biographical listings, see the Martindale-Hubbell Law Directory

*MORRISTOWN,** Morris Co.

PITNEY, HARDIN, KIPP & SZUCH (AV)

Park Avenue at Morris County, P.O. Box 1945, 07962-1945
Telephone: 201-966-6300
New York City: 212-926-0331
Telex: 642014
Telecopier: 201-966-1550

MEMBERS OF FIRM

Clyde A. Szuch
Frederick L. Whitmer
Murray J. Laulicht
James E. Tyrrell, Jr.

Representative Clients: AlliedSignal Inc.; AT&T; Base Ten Systems, Inc.; Exxon Corp.; Ford Motor Co.; Midlantic National Bank; Sony Electronics, Inc.; Union Carbide Corp.; United Parcel Services, Inc.; Warner-Lambert Co.

For Complete List of Firm Personnel, See General Section

For full biographical listings, see the Martindale-Hubbell Law Directory

*NEWARK,** Essex Co.

CARPENTER, BENNETT & MORRISSEY (AV)

(Formerly Carpenter, Gilmour & Dwyer)
Three Gateway Center, 17th Floor, 100 Mulberry Street, 07102-4079
Telephone: 201-622-7711
New York City: 212-943-6530
Telex: 139405
Telecopier: 201-622-5314
EasyLink: 62827845
ABA/net: CARPENTERB

MEMBERS OF FIRM

Michael S. Waters
Robert J. Stickles
John F. Lynch, Jr.
Scott J. Sheldon

ASSOCIATE

Lois H. Goodman

Representative Clients: General Motors Corp.; E. I. du Pont de Nemours and Company; Texaco Inc.; AT&T; Litton Industries; ITT Corp.; International Flavors & Fragrances Inc.; New Jersey Hospital Association; Prudential Insurance Company of America; United Jersey Bank.

For Complete List of Firm Personnel, See General Section

For full biographical listings, see the Martindale-Hubbell Law Directory

CRUMMY, DEL DEO, DOLAN, GRIFFINGER & VECCHIONE, A PROFESSIONAL CORPORATION (AV)

One Riverfront Plaza, 07102
Telephone: 201-596-4500
Telecopier: 201-596-0545
Cable-Telex: 138154
Brussels, Belgium Office: Crummy, Del Deo, Dolan, Griffinger & Vecchione. Avenue Louise 475, BTE. 8, B-1050.
Telephone: 011-322-646-0019.
Telecopier: 011-322-646-0152.

Ralph N. Del Deo
Richard S. Zackin
John T. Dolan
David M. Hyman
Michael R. Griffinger
Arnold B. Calmann
Michael D. Loprete
Terry R. Broderick (Not admitted in NJ; Resident, Brussels, Belgium Office)
John A. Ridley

Representative Clients: Hoffmann-La Roche Inc.; McGraw-Hill, Inc.; Mitsubishi Electric Corp.; United Parcel Service, Inc.; Pratt Hotel Corp.

For Complete List of Firm Personnel, See General Section

For full biographical listings, see the Martindale-Hubbell Law Directory

HELLRING LINDEMAN GOLDSTEIN & SIEGAL (AV)

One Gateway Center, 07102-5386
Telephone: 201-621-9020
Telecopier: 201-621-7406

Jonathan L. Goldstein
Robert S. Raymar
Richard D. Shapiro
Stephen L. Dreyfuss
Matthew E. Moloshok

For Complete List of Firm Personnel, See General Section

For full biographical listings, see the Martindale-Hubbell Law Directory

MCCARTER & ENGLISH (AV)

Four Gateway Center, 100 Mulberry Street, P.O. Box 652, 07101-0652
Telephone: 201-622-4444
Telecopier: 201-624-7070
Cable Address: "McCarter" Newark
Cherry Hill, New Jersey Office: 1810 Chapel Avenue West.
Telephone: 609-662-8444.
Telecopier: 609-662-6203.
New York, New York Office: Suite 1519, One World Trade Center.
Telephone: 212-466-9018.
Telecopier: 212-432-6568.
Boca Raton, Florida Office: 2255 Glades Road, Suite 319-A.
Telephone: 407-994-6262.
Telecopier: 407-241-0798.
Wilmington, Delaware Office: Mellon Bank Center, 919 Market Street.
Telephone: 302-654-8010.
Telecopier: 302-654-0795.

MEMBERS OF FIRM

Eugene M. Haring
Richard M. Eittreim

For Complete List of Firm Personnel, See General Section

For full biographical listings, see the Martindale-Hubbell Law Directory

Newark—Continued

ROBINSON, ST. JOHN & WAYNE (AV)

Two Penn Plaza East, 07105-2249
Telephone: 201-491-3300
Fax: 201-491-3333
Rochester, New York Office: Robinson, St. John & Curtin. First Federal Plaza.
Telephone: 716-262-6780.
Fax: 716-262-6755.
New York, New York Office: 245 Park Avenue.
Telephone: 212-953-0700.
Fax: 212-880-6555.

MEMBER OF FIRM

Paul J. Linker

For Complete List of Firm Personnel, See General Section

For full biographical listings, see the Martindale-Hubbell Law Directory

NEW MEXICO

*ALBUQUERQUE,** Bernalillo Co.

EAVES, BARDACKE & BAUGH, P.A. (AV)

6400 Uptown Boulevard N.E., Suite 110-W, P.O. Box 35670, 87176
Telephone: 505-888-4300
Facsimile: 505-883-4406

John M. Eaves
Paul Bardacke
John G. Baugh
Kerry Kiernan
Peter S. Kierst
David V. Halliburton
David A. Garcia
Lisabeth L. Occhialino

OF COUNSEL

Marianne Woodard
Jennifer J. Pruett
Susan C. Kery

For full biographical listings, see the Martindale-Hubbell Law Directory

HINKLE, COX, EATON, COFFIELD & HENSLEY (AV)

Suite 800, 500 Marquette, N.W., P.O. Box 2043, 87103
Telephone: 505-768-1500
FAX: 505-768-1529
Roswell, New Mexico Office: Suite 700, United Bank Plaza, P.O. Box 10, 88202.
Telephone: 505-622-6510.
FAX: 505-623-9332.
Midland, Texas Office: 6 Desta Drive, Suite 2800, P.O. Box 3580, 79705.
Telephone: 915-683-4691.
FAX: 915-683-6518.
Amarillo, Texas Office: 1700 Bank One Center. P.O. Box 9238, 79105-9238.
Telephone: 806-372-5569.
FAX: 806-372-9761.
Santa Fe, New Mexico Office: 218 Montezuma, P.O. Box 2068, 87504.
Telephone: 505-982-4554.
FAX: 505-982-8623.
Austin, Texas Office: 401 West 15th Street, Suite 800, 78701.
Telephone: 512-476-7137.
FAX: 512-476-5431.
Associated Office: Hoffman & Stephens, P.C., 401 West 15th Street, Suite 800, 78701.
Telephone: 512-476-5434.
Fax: 512-476-5431.

Eric D. Lanphere
Marshall G. Martin
James J. Wechsler
(Santa Fe Office)

Representative Clients: Anadarko Petroleum Corp.; Atlantic Richfield Co.; Bass Enterprises Production Co.; BHP Petroleum; Caroon & Black Management, Inc.; Chevron, USA, Inc.; CIGNA; City of Albuquerque; Coastal Oil & Gas Corp. Co.; Ethicon Inc., A Johnson & Johnson, Co.; Diagnostik; Conoco; Texaco; Presbyterian Healthcare Services.

For Complete List of Firm Personnel, See General Section

For full biographical listings, see the Martindale-Hubbell Law Directory

RODEY, DICKASON, SLOAN, AKIN & ROBB, P.A. (AV)

Albuquerque Plaza, Suite 2200, 201 Third Street, N.W., P.O. Box 1888, 87103-1888
Telephone: 505-765-5900
Fax: 505-768-7395
Santa Fe, New Mexico Office: Suite 101 Marcy Plaza, 123 East Marcy Street, P.O. Box 1357, 87504-1357.
Telephone: 505-984-0100.
Fax: 505-989-9542.

(See Next Column)

William S. Dixon
John P. Burton
(Resident, Santa Fe Office)
Rex D. Throckmorton
Edward Ricco
David C. Davenport, Jr.
(Resident, Santa Fe Office)
Charles Kipps Purcell

For Complete List of Firm Personnel, See General Section

For full biographical listings, see the Martindale-Hubbell Law Directory

*SANTA FE,** Santa Fe Co.

CAMPBELL, CARR, BERGE & SHERIDAN, P.A. (AV)

110 North Guadalupe, P.O. Box 2208, 87504-2208
Telephone: 505-988-4421
Telecopier: 505-983-6043

Michael B. Campbell
William F. Carr
Bradford C. Berge
Mark F. Sheridan

Michael H. Feldewert
Tanya M. Trujillo
Nancy A. Rath

For Complete List of Firm Personnel, See General Section

For full biographical listings, see the Martindale-Hubbell Law Directory

GALLEGOS LAW FIRM, P.C. (AV)

141 East Palace Avenue, 87501
Telephone: 505-983-6686
Telefax: 505-986-0741

J. E. Gallegos
Mary E. Walta
Michael J. Condon
David Sandoval
Glenn Theriot

For full biographical listings, see the Martindale-Hubbell Law Directory

NEW YORK

*NEW YORK,** New York Co.

ANDERSON KILL OLICK & OSHINSKY, P.C. (AV)

1251 Avenue of the Americas, 10020-1182
Telephone: 212-278-1000
Cable Address: "Neweralaw New York"
Telex: WU 12-7022; WUI 66513.
Fax: 212-278-1733
Washington, D.C. Office: Anderson Kill Olick & Oshinsky, 2000 Pennsylvania Avenue, N.W., Suite 7500.
Telephone: 202-728-3100.
Fax: 202-728-3199.
Philadelphia, Pennsylvania Office: 1600 Market Street.
Telephone: 215-568-4202.
Fax: 215-568-4573.
Newark, New Jersey Office: One Gateway Center, Suite 0901.
Telephone: 201-642-5858.
Fax: 201-621-6361.
San Francisco, California Office: Citicorp Center, One Samsone Street, Suite 1610.
Telephone: 415-677-1450.
Fax: 415-677-1475.
New Haven, Connecticut Office: 59 Elm Street.
Telephone: 203-777-2230.
Fax: 203-777-9717.
Phoenix, Arizona Office: One Renaissance Square, Two North Central, Suite 1250.
Telephone: 602-252-0002.
Fax: 601-252-0003.

Edward P. Abbot
Lisa M. Anastos
(Not admitted in NY)
Eugene R. Anderson
Peter J. Andrews
John B. Berringer
Chaim B. Book
Amy G. Borress-Glass
Stefan R. Boshkov
Martin F. Brecker
Ronald S. Brody
Mark M. Brown
(Not admitted in NY)
Anna S. Chacko
Jordan M. Cohen
Leonard A. Cohen
Robin L. Cohen
Steven Cooper
Howard E. Cotton
Samantha S. Daniels
Jennifer W. Darger
Duncan N. Darrow
Risa F. Davis
Steven J. Dolmanisth
John H. Doyle, III
Stephen A. Dvorkin
David J. Egidi
David A. Einhorn
Bennett Ellenbogen
Jean M. Farrell
Wendy Ferber
Gloria J. Frank
John W. Fried
Karen L. Illuzzi Gallinari
John P. Gasior
Linda Gerstel
Ann S. Ginsberg
Jeffrey L. Glatzer
Michael S. Gordon
M. Beth Gorrie
Telma M. Grayson
Tara A. Griffin

(See Next Column)

ANDERSON KILL OLICK & OSHINSKY P.C.—*Continued*

John H. Gross
Michael Gurland
Philippa M. Haggar
Finley T. R. Harckham
Richard L. Hartz
Mary Angela Hawke
Sarah B. Hechtman
Robert M. Horkovich
Leslie Sue Howard
Shahan Islam
Raymond A. Joao
T. Michael Johnson
Laura V. Jones
Gabriella Jordan
Edward M. Joyce
Robert A. Karin
John H. Kazanjian
Michael J. Keane
R. Mark Keenan
Thomas L. Kent
Lawrence Kill
Mark E. Klein
Ann V. Kramer
Joan L. Lewis
Diane E. Lifton
Henry A. Lowet
Nestor P. Maddatu
Tracy Ellen Makow
Steven M. Manket
Susan M. Marotta
Raj Mehra
Jeffrey A. Moross
Avraham C. Moskowitz
Frank S. Occhipinti
Arthur S. Olick
Randy Paar
Susan G. Papano
William G. Passannante
Amalia Gisela Pena
Michelle Perez
Bennett Pine
Mayda Prego
Anthony Princi
J. Andrew Rahl, Jr.
Jane Revellino
David Garfield Roland
Harry Rothenberg
Lia B. Royle
Melvin Salberg
Seth B. Schafler
David M. Schlecker
David J. Schwartz
Lori C. Seegers
Edan Dawn Segal
Irving Shafran
Jordan W. Siev
Mark D. Silverschotz
James Walker Smith
Neal S. Smolar
Erik T. Sorensen
A. Thomas Southwick
Jay B. Spievack
Michael W. Stamm
Kevin N. Starkey
Eric D. Statman
Robert J. Stevens
Charles Addison Stewart, III
Catherine M. (Kay) Stockwell
Irene C. Warshauer
Margaret Armstrong Weiner
Mark L. Weyman
John P. Winsbro
Judith A. Yavitz
Nazim Zilkha
Jean E. Zimmerman
Nicholas J. Zoogman

OF COUNSEL

Roy Babitt
Richard W. Collins
Dona Seeman Kahn
Melvin S. Slade
David Toren

For full biographical listings, see the Martindale-Hubbell Law Directory

---

BRAUNSCHWEIG RACHLIS FISHMAN & RAYMOND, P.C. (AV)

1114 Avenue of the Americas, 10036
Telephone: 212-944-5200
Telecopier: 212-944-5210

Robert Braunschweig
Stephen P. H. Rachlis
Bernard H. Fishman
Richard C. Raymond

OF COUNSEL

Jeffrey M. Herrmann
Jeffrey H. Teitel (Not admitted in NY)
William G. Halby
Gerard C. Smetana (P.C.)
Martin W. McCormack
Jacob Dolinger (Not admitted in NY)

Bruce D. Osborne

LEGAL SUPPORT PERSONNEL

William Hershkowitz

For full biographical listings, see the Martindale-Hubbell Law Directory

---

LOEB AND LOEB (AV)

A Partnership including Professional Corporations
345 Park Avenue, 10154-0037
Telephone: 212-407-4000
Facsimile: 212-407-4990
Los Angeles, California Office: Suite 1800, 1000 Wilshire Boulevard, 90017-2475.
Telephone: 213-688-3400.
Cable Address: "Loband LSA".
Telecopier: 213-688-3460; 688-3461; 688-3462.
Century City (Los Angeles), California Office: Suite 2200, 10100 Santa Monica Boulevard, Los Angeles, 90067-4164.
Telephone: 310-282-2000.
Telecopier: 310-282-2191; 282-2192.
Nashville, Tennessee Office: 45 Music Square West, 37203-3205.
Telephone: 615-749-8300.
Facsimile: 615-749-8308.
Rome, Italy Office: Piazza Digione 1, 00197.
Telephone: 011-396-808-8456.
Telecopier: 011-396-674-8223.

MEMBERS OF FIRM

Charles H. Miller
David B. Shontz

(See Next Column)

OF COUNSEL

Harry First

For Complete List of Firm Personnel, See General Section
For full biographical listings, see the Martindale-Hubbell Law Directory

---

MILBERG WEISS BERSHAD HYNES & LERACH (AV)

One Pennsylvania Plaza, 10119
Telephone: 212-594-5300
San Diego, California Office: 600 West Broadway, 1800 One America Plaza.
Telephone: 619-231-1058.
San Francisco, California Office: 222 Kearny Street, 10th Floor.
Telephone: 415-288-4545.
Fax: 415-288-4534.

MEMBERS OF FIRM

Melvyn I. Weiss
Lawrence Milberg (1913-1989)
David J. Bershad
Jared Specthrie
William S. Lerach (Resident at San Diego Office)
Sol Schreiber
Jerome M. Congress
Richard M. Meyer
Patricia M. Hynes
Keith F. Park (Resident at San Diego Office)
Sharon Levine Mirsky
Robert P. Sugarman
John E. Grasberger (Resident at San Francisco Office)
Leonard B. Simon (Resident at San Diego Office)
Arnold N. Bressler
Alan Schulman (Resident at San Diego Office)
Jan Mark Adler (Resident at San Diego Office)
Michael C. Spencer
Anita Meley Laing (Resident at San Diego Office)
Blake M. Harper (Resident at San Diego Office)
Steven G. Schulman
Robert A. Wallner
Sanford P. Dumain
Patrick Coughlin (Resident at San Diego Office)
George A. Bauer III
Kevin P. Roddy (Resident at San Diego Office)
Dennis Stewart (Resident at San Diego Office)
Barry A. Weprin
Richard H. Weiss
Helen J. Hodges (Resident at San Diego Office)
Eric A. Isaacson (Resident at San Diego Office)
Alan M. Mansfield (Resident at San Diego Office)
Lee S. Shalov
John J. Stoia, Jr. (Resident at San Francisco Office)

ASSOCIATES

Jeffrey S. Abraham
Helen B. Alley (Not admitted in NY)
Joy A. Bull (Resident at San Diego Office)
James A. Caputo (Resident at San Diego Office)
Deborah Clark-Weintraub
George H. Cohen
Lori G. Feldman
Keith M. Fleischman
Susan Gonick (Resident at San Diego Office)
Mary M. Hurley (Resident at San Diego Office)
John W. Jeffrey (Resident at San Diego Office)
Edith M. Kallas
Jay Kenneth Kupietzky
Pamela M. Parker (Resident at San Diego Office)
Steven W. Pepich (Resident at San Diego Office)
Theodore J. Pintar (Resident at San Diego Office)
Janine L. Pollack
Henry Rosen (Resident at San Diego Office)
Ralph M. Stone
Alison M. Tattersall (Resident at San Francisco Office)
Joshua H. Vinik
Erin C. Ward (Resident at San Diego Office)
Jeff S. Westerman (Resident at San Diego Office)

OF COUNSEL

Charles S. Crandall (Resident at San Diego Office)

For full biographical listings, see the Martindale-Hubbell Law Directory

---

OTTERBOURG, STEINDLER, HOUSTON & ROSEN, P.C. (AV)

230 Park Avenue, 10169
Telephone: 212-661-9100
Cable Address: "Otlerton";
Telecopier: 212-682-6104
Telex: 960916

Bernard Beitel
Peter L. Feldman

Lloyd M. Green

For Complete List of Firm Personnel, See General Section
For full biographical listings, see the Martindale-Hubbell Law Directory

---

PARKER CHAPIN FLATTAU & KLIMPL, L.L.P. (AV)

1211 Avenue of the Americas, 10036
Telephone: 212-704-6000
Telecopier: 212-704-6288
Cable Address: "Lawpark"
Telex: 640347
Great Neck, New York Office: 175 Great Neck Road.
Telephone: 516-482-4422.
Telecopier: 516-482-4469.

(See Next Column)

PARKER CHAPIN FLATTAU & KLIMPL L.L.P., *New York—Continued*

MEMBERS OF FIRM

Barry J. Brett
Aurora Cassirer
Charles P. Greenman
Stephen G. Rinehart
Alvin M. Stein
Patricia Lynne Truscelli

OF COUNSEL

Mark I. Schlesinger

ASSOCIATE

Katherine Cooney Ash

For Complete List of Firm Personnel, See General Section

For full biographical listings, see the Martindale-Hubbell Law Directory

PILIERO GOLDSTEIN JENKINS & HALL (AV)

292 Madison Avenue, 10017
Telephone: 212-213-8200
Fax: 212-685-2028
Carlstadt, New Jersey Office: One Palmer Terrace.
Telephone: 201-507-5157.
FAX: 201-507-5221.
Washington, D.C. Office: 888 17th Street, N.W., Suite 1100.
Telephone: 202-467-6991.
FAX: 202-467-6703.

MEMBERS OF FIRM

Edward J. Goldstein
Christopher P. Hall
Jon Mark Jenkins
Robert D. Piliero

ASSOCIATES

John William LaRocca
Juliana M. Moday
Elaine B. Michetti
(Not admitted in NY)

OF COUNSEL

Ricardo J. Davila

For full biographical listings, see the Martindale-Hubbell Law Directory

WINTHROP, STIMSON, PUTNAM & ROBERTS (AV)

One Battery Park Plaza, 10004-1490
Telephone: 212-858-1000
Telex: 62854 WINSTIM
Telefax: 212-858-1500
Stamford, Connecticut Office: Financial Centre, 695 East Main Street, P.O. Box 6760, 06904-6760.
Telephone: 203-348-2300.
Washington, D.C. Office: 1133 Connecticut Avenue, N.W., 20036.
Telephone: 202-775-9800.
Palm Beach, Florida Office: 125 Worth Avenue, 33480.
Telephone: 407-655-7297.
London Office: 2 Throgmorton Avenue, London EC2N 2AP, England.
Telephone: 011-4471-628-4931.
Brussels Office: Rue Du Taciturne 42, B-1040 Brussels, Belgium.
Telephone: 011-322-230-1392.
Tokyo, Japan Office: 608 Atagoyama Bengoshi Building 6-7, Atago 1-chome, Minato-ku, Tokyo 105 Japan.
Telephone: 011-813-3437-9740.
Hong Kong Office: 2505 Asia Pacific Finance Tower, Citibank Plaza, 3 Garden Road, Central.
Telephone: 011-852-530-3400.

MEMBERS OF FIRM

Leo T. Crowley
Sutton Keany
David G. Keyko
David M. Lindley
Edwin J. Wesely

SENIOR COUNSEL

Merrell E. Clark, Jr.

CONNECTICUT OFFICE
MEMBER OF FIRM

Thomas F. Clauss, Jr.

COUNSEL

Thomas R. Trowbridge, III

WASHINGTON, D.C. OFFICE
MEMBERS OF FIRM

Donald A. Carr

WASHINGTON, D.C.
COUNSEL

Aileen Meyer

For Complete List of Firm Personnel, See General Section

For full biographical listings, see the Martindale-Hubbell Law Directory

*SYRACUSE,** Onondaga Co.

BOND, SCHOENECK & KING (AV)

18th Floor One Lincoln Center, 13202-1355
Telephone: 315-422-0121
Fax: 315-422-3598
Albany, New York Office: 111 Washington Avenue.
Telephone: 518-462-7421.
Fax: 518-462-7441.

(See Next Column)

Boca Raton, Florida Office: 5355 Town Center Road, Suite 1002.
Telephone: 407-368-1212.
Fax: 407-338-9955.
Naples, Florida Office: 1167 Third Street South.
Telephone: 813-262-6812.
Fax: 813-262-6908.
Oswego, New York Office: 130 East Second Street.
Telephone: 315-343-9116.
Fax: 315-343-1231.
Overland Park, Kansas Office: 7500 College Boulevard, Suite 910.
Telephone: 913-345-8001.
Fax: 913-345-9017.

MEMBERS OF FIRM

Charles T. Beeching, Jr.
Margaret M. Cassady

General Counsel for: Syracuse University; Unity Mutual Life Insurance Co.; Manufacturers Association of Central New York.
Regional or Special Counsel for: Newhouse Broadcasting Corp. (WSYR, AM-FM); Syracuse Herald-Post Standard Newspapers.; Miller Brewing Co.; Allied Corp.; General Electric Co.; National Grange.

For Complete List of Firm Personnel, See General Section

For full biographical listings, see the Martindale-Hubbell Law Directory

NORTH CAROLINA

*CHARLOTTE,** Mecklenburg Co.

SMITH HELMS MULLISS & MOORE, L.L.P. (AV)

227 North Tryon Street, P.O. Box 31247, 28231
Telephone: 704-343-2000
Telecopier: 704-334-8467
Telex: 572460
Greensboro, North Carolina Office: Smith Helms Mulliss & Moore, Suite 1400 First Union Tower, 300 North Greene Street, P.O. Box 21927.
Telephone: 910-378-5200.
Telecopier: 910-379-9558.
Raleigh, North Carolina Office: 316 West Edenton Street, P.O. Box 27525.
Telephone: 919-755-8700.
Telecopier: 919-828-7938.

COUNSEL

James H. Guterman

MEMBER OF FIRM

E. Osborne Ayscue, Jr.

For Complete List of Firm Personnel, See General Section

For full biographical listings, see the Martindale-Hubbell Law Directory

*RALEIGH,** Wake Co.

* indicates certain Bar Register subscribers whose principal office is located elsewhere in the state and who have arranged for representation as a part of the state capital listings that follow

ALLEN AND PINNIX (AV)

20 Market Plaza, Suite 200, P.O. Drawer 1270, 27602
Telephone: 919-755-0505
Telecopier: 919-829-8098
Woodlawn Green, Charlotte, North Carolina Telephone: 704-522-8069

MEMBERS OF FIRM

Noel L. Allen
Paul Christian Ridgeway

General Counsel for: North Carolina State Board of CPA Examiners; North Carolina Board of Architecture.

For full biographical listings, see the Martindale-Hubbell Law Directory

*** SMITH HELMS MULLISS & MOORE, L.L.P. (AV)**

316 West Edenton Street, P.O. Box 27525, 27611-7525
Telephone: 919-755-8700
Telecopier: 919-828-7938
Charlotte, North Carolina Office: 227 North Tryon Street, P.O. Box 31247.
Telephone: 704-343-2000.
Telecopier: 704-334-8467.
Telex: 572460.
Greensboro, North Carolina Office: Smith Helms Mulliss & Moore, Suite 1400 First Union Tower, 300 North Greene Street, P.O. Box 21927.
Telephone: 910-378-5200.
Telecopier: 910-379-9558.

MEMBER OF FIRM

Richard W. Ellis

ASSOCIATE

Matthew W. Sawchak

For Complete List of Firm Personnel, See General Section

For full biographical listings, see the Martindale-Hubbell Law Directory

Raleigh—Continued

*** WOMBLE CARLYLE SANDRIDGE & RICE (AV)**

A Professional Limited Liability Company

2100 First Union Capitol Center, 150 Fayetteville Street Mall, P.O. Box 831, 27602
Telephone: 919-755-2100
Telecopy: 919-755-2150
Telex: 806498
Charlotte, North Carolina Office: 3300 One First Union Center, 301 South College Street.
Telephone: 704-331-4900.
Telecopy: 704-331-4955.
Telex: 853609.
Winston-Salem, North Carolina Office: 1600 Southern National Financial Center.
Telephone: 919-721-3600.
Telecopy: 919-721-3660.
Telex: 806498.
Atlanta, Georgia Office: One Ninety One Peachtree Tower, 191 Peachtree Street N.E., Suite 3250.
Telephone: 404-614-2580.
Fax: 404-614-2595.

RESIDENT PARTNERS

E. Lawrence Davis, III | Pressly M. Millen

RESIDENT ASSOCIATE

Samuel M. Taylor

Representative Clients: Aetna Casualty and Surety Co., Inc.; ALSCO/AmeriMark Building Products, Inc.; Aoki Corporation America, Inc.; Empire of Carolina, Inc.; Hackney Brothers, Inc.; Lawyers Mutual Liability Insurance Company of North Carolina; Meredith College; Monk-Austin, Inc.; Regency Park Corporation; Wachovia Bank of North Carolina, N.A.

For Complete List of Firm Personnel, See General Section

For full biographical listings, see the Martindale-Hubbell Law Directory

*WINSTON-SALEM,** Forsyth Co.

WOMBLE CARLYLE SANDRIDGE & RICE (AV)

A Professional Limited Liability Company

1600 Southern National Financial Center, P.O. Drawer 84, 27102
Telephone: 910-721-3600
Telecopy: 910-721-3660
Telex: 806498
Charlotte, North Carolina Office: 3300 One First Union Center, 301 South College Street.
Telephone: 704-331-4900.
Telecopy: 704-331-4955.
Telex: 853609.
Raleigh, North Carolina Office: 2100 First Union Capitol Center, 150 Fayetteville Street Mall, P.O. Box 831.
Telephone: 919-755-2100.
Telecopy: 919-755-2150.
Telex: 806498.
Atlanta, Georgia Office: One Ninety One Peachtree Tower, 191 Peachtree Street, N.E., Suite 3250.
Telephone: 404-614-2580.
Fax: 404-614-2595.

MEMBERS OF FIRM

James K. Phillips | Mark N. Poovey

ASSOCIATES

David A. Shirlen | Timothy A. Thelen

OF COUNSEL

Ashley O. Thrift

Representative Clients: Brad Ragan, Inc.; Brenner Companies; Food Lion, Inc.; Hanes Companies, Inc.; North Carolina Baptist Hospitals, Inc.; R.J. Reynolds Tobacco Company; Summit Communications Group, Inc.; Thomasville Furniture Industries, Inc.; Wachovia Corporation; Wake Forest University.

For Complete List of Firm Personnel, See General Section

For full biographical listings, see the Martindale-Hubbell Law Directory

OHIO

*CINCINNATI,** Hamilton Co.

DINSMORE & SHOHL (AV)

1900 Chemed Center, 255 East Fifth Street, 45202-3172
Telephone: 513-977-8200
FAX: 513-977-8141
Florence, Kentucky Office: Turfway Ridge Office Park, 7300 Turfway Road, Suite 430 41042-1355.
Telephone: 606-283-0515.
FAX: 606-283-6017.
Dayton, Ohio Office: 500 Courthouse Plaza, S.W., 10 N. Ludlow Street, 45402-1834.
Telephone: 513-228-8012.
FAX: 513-461-2543.
Columbus, Ohio Office: NBD Bank Building, Suite 330, 175 South Third Street, 43215-5134.
Telephone: 614-224-7887.
FAX: 614-224-7882.

MEMBERS OF FIRM

Thomas S. Calder | Mark L. Silbersack
John W. Beatty | Richard J. Beckmann (Resident, Dayton, Ohio Office)

For Complete List of Firm Personnel, See General Section

For full biographical listings, see the Martindale-Hubbell Law Directory

FROST & JACOBS (AV)

2500 PNC Center, 201 East Fifth Street, P.O. Box 5715, 45201-5715
Telephone: 513-651-6800
Cable Address: "Frostjac"
Telex: 21-4396 F & J CIN
Telecopier: 513-651-6981
Columbus, Ohio Office: One Columbus, 10 West Broad Street.
Telephone: 614-464-1211.
Telecopier: 614-464-1737.
Lexington, Kentucky Office: 1100 Vine Center Tower, 333 West Vine Street.
Telephone: 606-254-1100.
Telecopier: 606-253-2990.
Middletown, Ohio Office: 400 First National Bank Building, 2 North Main Street.
Telephone: 513-422-2001.
Telecopier: 513-422-3010.
Naples, Florida Office: 4001 Tamiami Trail North, Suite 220.
Telephone: 813-261-0582.
Telecopier: 813-261-2083.

MEMBERS OF FIRM

James R. Adams | Myron L. Dale

SENIOR PARTNER

John K. Rose

Representative Clients: Armco Inc.; Arthur Andersen & Co.; Cincinnati Bell Inc.; Cincinnati Milacron Inc.; Federated Department Stores Inc.; Mercy Health Systems; PNC Bank, Ohio, National Association; U.S. Shoe Corporation; Sencorp.; totes incorporated.

For Complete List of Firm Personnel, See General Section

For full biographical listings, see the Martindale-Hubbell Law Directory

THOMPSON, HINE AND FLORY (AV)

312 Walnut Street, 14th Floor, 45202-4029
Telephone: 513-352-6700
Fax: 513-241-4771;
Telex: 938003
Akron, Ohio Office: 50 S. Main Street, Suite 502, 44308-1828.
Telephone: 216-376-8090.
Fax: 216-376-8386.
Cleveland, Ohio Office: 1100 National City Bank Building, 629 Euclid Avenue, 44114-3070.
Telephone: 216-566-5500.
Fax: 216-556-5583.
Telex: 980217.
Cable Address: "Thomflor".
Columbus, Ohio Office: One Columbus, 10 West Broad Street, 43215-3435.
Telephone: 614-469-3200.
Fax: 614-469-3361.
Dayton, Ohio Office: 2000 Courthouse Plaza, N.E., 45402-1706.
Telephone: 513-443-6600.
Fax: 513-443-6637; 443-6635.
Palm Beach, Florida Office: 125 Worth Avenue, 33480-4466.
Telephone: 407-833-5900.
Fax: 407-833-5951.
Washington, D.C. Office: 1920 N Street, N.W., 20036-1601.
Telephone: 202-331-8800.
Fax: 202-331-8330.
Telex: 904173.
Cable Address: "Caglaw".

(See Next Column)

THOMPSON, HINE AND FLORY, *Cincinnati—Continued*

Brussels, Belgium Office: Rue des Chevaliers / Ridderstraat 14 - B.10, B - 1050.
Telephone: 011(32-2) 511-9326.
Fax: 011(-32-2) 513-9206.

MEMBER OF FIRM
Stephen J. Butler
ASSOCIATE
Howard B. Gee

For Complete List of Firm Personnel, See General Section

For full biographical listings, see the Martindale-Hubbell Law Directory

WAITE, SCHNEIDER, BAYLESS & CHESLEY CO., L.P.A. (AV)

1513 Central Trust Tower, Fourth and Vine Streets, 45202
Telephone: 513-621-0267
Fax: 513-381-2375; 621-0262

Stanley M. Chesley

Thomas F. Rehme	Sherrill P. Hondorf
Fay E. Stilz	Colleen M. Hegge
Louise M. Roselle	Dianna Pendleton
Dwight Tillery	Randy F. Fox
D. Arthur Rabourn	Glenn D. Feagan
Jerome L. Skinner	Theresa L. Groh
Janet G. Abaray	Theodore N. Berry
Paul M. De Marco	Jane H. Walker
Terrence L. Goodman	Renée Infante

Allen P. Grunes

OF COUNSEL

Jos. E. Rosen	James F. Keller

For full biographical listings, see the Martindale-Hubbell Law Directory

*CLEVELAND,** Cuyahoga Co.

ARTER & HADDEN (AV)

1100 Huntington Building, 925 Euclid Avenue, 44115-1475
Telephone: 216-696-1100
Telex: 98-5384
In Columbus, Ohio: 21st Floor, One Columbus, 10 West Broad Street. 43215-3422.
Telephone: 614-221-3155.
In Washington, D.C.: 1801 K Street, N.W., Suite 400K. 20006-3480.
Telephone: 202-775-7100.
In Dallas, Texas: 1717 Main Street, Suite 4100. 75201-4605.
Telephone: 214-761-2100.
In Los Angeles, California: 700 South Flower Street. 90017-4101.
Telephone: 213-629-9300.
In Irvine, California: Two Park Plaza, Suite 700, Jamboree Center.
Telephone: 714-252-7500.
In Austin, Texas: 100 Congress Avenue, Suite 1800.
Telephone: 512-479-6403.
In San Antonio, Texas: Suite 540, Harte-Hanks Tower, 7710 Jones Maltsberger Road.
Telephone: 210-805-8497.

MEMBERS OF FIRM

Walter A. Bates	Frank R. Osborne
M. Neal Rains	Anthony C. LaPlaca

OF COUNSEL
Stanley M. Fisher
ASSOCIATES

Carter E. Strang	Cynthia C. Schafer

For Complete List of Firm Personnel, See General Section

For full biographical listings, see the Martindale-Hubbell Law Directory

BAKER & HOSTETLER (AV)

3200 National City Center, 1900 East Ninth Street, 44114-3485
Telephone: 216-621-0200
Telecopier: 216-696-0740
TWX: 810 421 8375
RCA Telex: 215032
In Columbus, Ohio: Capitol Square, Suite 2100, 65 East State Street.
Telephone: 614-228-1541.
In Denver, Colorado: 303 East 17th Avenue, Suite 1100.
Telephone: 303-861-0600.
In Houston, Texas: 1000 Louisiana, Suite 2000.
Telephone: 713-751-1600.
In Long Beach, California: 300 Oceangate, Suite 620.
Telephone: 310-432-2827.
In Los Angeles, California: 600 Wilshire Boulevard.
Telephone: 213-624-2400.
In Orlando, Florida: SunBank Center, Suite 2300, 200 South Orange Avenue.
Telephone: 407-649-4000.

(See Next Column)

In Washington, D. C.: Washington Square, Suite 1100, 1050 Connecticut Avenue, N.W.
Telephone: 202-861-1500.
In College Park, Maryland: 9658 Baltimore Boulevard, Suite 206.
Telephone: 301-441-2781.
In Alexandria, Virginia: 437 North Lee Street.
Telephone: 703-549-1294.
In San Francisco, California: One Sansome Street, Suite 2000.
Telephone: 415-951-4705.

PARTNERS

Paul P. Eyre	John D. Parker
	Ernest E. Vargo, Jr.

For Complete List of Firm Personnel, See General Section

For full biographical listings, see the Martindale-Hubbell Law Directory

JONES, DAY, REAVIS & POGUE (AV)

North Point, 901 Lakeside Avenue, 44114
Telephone: 216-586-3939
Cable Address: "Attorneys Cleveland"
Telex: 980389
Telecopier: 216-579-0212
In Columbus, Ohio: 1900 Huntington Center.
Telephone: 614-469-3939.
Cable Address: "Attorneys Columbus."
Telecopier: 614-461-4198.
In Atlanta, Georgia: 3500 One Peachtree Center, 303 Peachtree Street, N.E.
Telephone: 404-521-3939.
Cable Address: "Attorneys Atlanta".
Telex: 54-2711.
Telecopier: 404-581-8330.
In Brussels, Belgium: Avenue Louise 480, 7th Floor. B-1050 Brussels.
Telephone: 011-32-2-645-14-11.
Telecopier: 011-32-2-645-14-45.
In Chicago, Illinois: 77 West Wacker.
Telephone: 312-782-3939.
Telecopier: 312-782-8585.
In Dallas, Texas: 2300 Trammell Crow Center, 2001 Ross Avenue.
Telephone: 214-220-3939.
Cable Address: "Attorneys Dallas."
Telex: 730852.
Telecopier: 214-969-5100.
In Frankfurt, Germany: Triton Haus, Bockenheimer Landstrasse 42, 60323 Frankfurt am Main.
Telephone: 49-69-9726-3939.
Telecopier: 49-69-9726-3993.
In Geneva, Switzerland: 20, rue de Candolle.
Telephone: 011-41-22-320-2339.
Telecopier: 011-41-22-320-1232.
In Hong Kong: 1501 One Exchange Square, 8 Connaught Place.
Telephone: 011-852-2526-6895.
Telecopier: 011-852-2810-5787.
In Irvine, California: 2603 Main Street, Suite 900.
Telephone: 714-851-3939.
Telex: 194911 Lawyers LSA.
Telecopier: 714-553-7539.
In London, England: One Mount Street.
Telephone: 011-44-71-493-9361.
Cable Address: "Surgoe London WI."
Telecopier: 011-44-71-493-9666.
In Los Angeles, California: 555 West Fifth Street, Suite 4600.
Telephone: 213-489-3939.
Telex: 181439 UD.
Telecopier: 213-243-2539.
In New York, New York: 599 Lexington Avenue.
Telephone: 212-326-3939.
Cable Address: "JONESDAY NEWYORK."
Telex: 237013 JDRP UR.
Telecopier: 212-755-7306.
In Paris, France: 62, rue du Faubourg Saint-Honore.
Telephone: 011-33-1-44-71-3939.
Cable Address: "Surgoe Paris."
Telex: 290156 Surgoe.
Telecopier: 011-33-1-49-24-0471.
In Pittsburgh, Pennsylvania: 500 Grant Street, 31st Floor.
Telephone: 412-391-3939.
Cable Address: "Attorneys Pittsburgh".
Telecopier: 412-394-7959.
In Riyadh, Saudi Arabia: Law Offices of Saud M.A. Shawwaf, P.O. Box 2700.
Telephones: 011 (966-1) 465-6543, 011 (966-1) 464-8534 or 011 (966-1) 464-8540.
Telex: 401831 SAUCON SJ.
Telecopier: (966-1) 464-8480.
In Taipei, Taiwan: 8th Floor, Tun Hwa South Road, Section 2.
Telephone: 011 (886-2) 704-6808.
Telecopier: 011 (886-2) 704-6791.
In Tokyo, Japan: Toranomon MT Building, 4th Floor, 10-3, Toranomon 3-Chome, Minato-Ku, Tokyo 105, Japan.
Telephone: 011-81-3-3433-3939.
Telecopier: 011-81-3-5401-2725.

(See Next Column)

JONES, DAY, REAVIS & POGUE—*Continued*

In Washington, D.C.: Metropolitan Square, 1450 G Street, N.W.
Telephone: 202-879-3939.
Cable Address: "Attorneys Washington."
Telex: 89-2410 ATTORNEYS WASH.
Telecopier: 202-737-2832.

MEMBERS OF FIRM

William Thomas Plesec | Joseph F. Winterscheid
Robert H. Rawson, Jr. | Thomas Demitrack
Hugh R. Whiting | Stephen J. Squeri

ASSOCIATES

Michelle K. Fischer | Deborah Platt Herman

For Complete List of Firm Personnel, See General Section

For full biographical listings, see the Martindale-Hubbell Law Directory

TIMOTHY A. SHIMKO & ASSOCIATES A LEGAL PROFESSIONAL ASSOCIATION (AV)

2010 Huntington Building, 925 Euclid Avenue, 44115
Telephone: 216-241-8300
Fax: 216-241-2702

Timothy A. Shimko

Janet I. Stich | Ronald K. Starkey
Theresa A. Tarchinski | Frank E. Piscitelli, Jr.

OF COUNSEL

Frank B. Mazzone

Reference: National City Bank, Cleveland.

For full biographical listings, see the Martindale-Hubbell Law Directory

THOMPSON, HINE AND FLORY (AV)

1100 National City Bank Building, 629 Euclid Avenue, 44114-3070
Telephone: 216-566-5500
Fax: 216-566-5583
Telex: 980217
Cable Address: "Thomflor"
Akron, Ohio Office: 50 S. Main Street, Suite 502, 44308-1828.
Telephone: 216-376-8090.
Fax: 216-376-8386.
Cincinnati, Ohio Office: 312 Walnut Street, 14th Floor, 45202-4029.
Telephone: 513-352-6700.
Fax: 513-241-4771.
Telex: 938003.
Columbus, Ohio Office: One Columbus, 10 West Broad Street, 43215-3435.
Telephone: 614-469-3200.
Fax: 614-469-3361.
Dayton, Ohio Office: 2000 Courthouse Plaza, N.E., 45402-1706.
Telephone: 513-443-6600.
Fax: 513-443-6637; 443-6635.
Palm Beach, Florida Office: 125 Worth Avenue, Suite 117, 33480-4466.
Telephone: 407-833-5900.
Fax: 407-833-5951.
Washington, D.C. Office: 1920 N Street, N.W., 20036-1601.
Telephone: 202-331-8800.
Fax: 202-331-8330.
Telex: 904173.
Cable Address: "Caglaw".
Brussels, Belgium Office: Rue des Chevaliers, Ridderstraat 14 - B.10, B - 1050.
Telephone: 011(32-2) 511-9326.
Fax: 011(32-2) 513-9206.

MEMBERS OF FIRM

Thomas J. Collin | John F. McClatchey (Retired)
Leslie W. Jacobs | James B. Niehaus
George F. Karch, Jr. | Thomas F. Zych

ASSOCIATES

Suzanne E. Bretz | Donald P. Screen

SENIOR ATTORNEY

Annette Tucker Sutherland

For Complete List of Firm Personnel, See General Section

For full biographical listings, see the Martindale-Hubbell Law Directory

*COLUMBUS,** Franklin Co.

MCSHANE, BREITFELLER & WITTEN (AV)

600 South High Street, 43215
Telephone: 614-221-1919
Telecopier: 614-221-2881

MEMBERS OF FIRM

Eugene F. McShane | Ralph E. Breitfeller
Alan C. Witten

Reference: Bank One of Columbus, N.A.

For full biographical listings, see the Martindale-Hubbell Law Directory

PORTER, WRIGHT, MORRIS & ARTHUR (AV)

41 South High Street, 43215-6194
Telephone: 614-227-2000; (800-533-2794)
Telex: 6503213584 MCI
Fax: 614-227-2100
Dayton, Ohio Office: One Dayton Centre, One South Main Street, 45402.
Telephones: 513-228-2411; (800-533-4434).
Fax: 513-449-6820.
Cincinnati, Ohio Office: 250 E. Fifth Street, 45202-4166.
Telephones: 513-381-4700; (800-582-5813).
Fax: 513-421-0991.
Cleveland, Ohio Office: 925 Euclid Avenue, 44115-1483.
Telephones: 216-443-9000; (800-824-1980).
Fax: 216-443-9011.
Washington, D.C. Office: 1233 20th Street, N.W., 20036-2395.
Telephones: 202-778-3000; (800-456-7962).
Fax: 202-778-3063.
Naples, Florida Office: 4501 Tamiami Trail North, 33940-3060.
Telephones: 813-263-8898;(800-876-7962).
Fax: 813-436-2990.

MEMBERS OF FIRM
COLUMBUS, OHIO OFFICE

Edwin M. Baranowski | Robert J. Nordstrom
Dixon F. Miller | Jean Yingling Teteris

CINCINNATI, OHIO OFFICE
RESIDENT MEMBER

Jerome J. Metz, Jr.

Representative Clients: Alco-Standard Corporation; American Electric Power Service Corporation; Battelle Memorial Institute; Columbus/Southern Power Co.; Ford Motor Co.; Huntington Bancshares Incorporated; Ohio State Medical Association; Rockwell International Corp.; Technical Rubber Co.

For Complete List of Firm Personnel, See General Section

For full biographical listings, see the Martindale-Hubbell Law Directory

VORYS, SATER, SEYMOUR AND PEASE (AV)

52 East Gay Street, P.O. Box 1008, 43216-1008
Telephone: 614-464-6400
Telex: 241348
Telecopier: 614-464-6350
Cable Address: "Vorysater"
Washington, D.C. Office: Suite 1111, 1828 L Street, N.W., 20036-5104.
Telephone: 202-467-8800.
Telex: 440693.
Telecopier: 202-467-8900.
Cleveland, Ohio Office: 2100 One Cleveland Center, 1375 East Ninth Street, 44114-1724.
Telephone: 216-479-6100.
Telecopier: 216-479-6060.
Cincinnati, Ohio Office: Suite 2100, 221 East Fourth Street, P.O. Box 0236, 45201-0236.
Telephone: 513-723-4000.
Telecopier: 513-723-4056.

MEMBERS OF FIRM

John C. Elam | Ivery D. Foreman
James P. Kennedy | Laura G. Kuykendall
Jacob E. Davis, II | Carl D. Smallwood
David S. Cupps | Ellen A. Efros (Resident, Washington, D.C. Office)
Michael J. Canter
James A. Wilson

David A. Westrup

OF COUNSEL

Russell P. Herrold, Jr.

Local Counsel: Abbott Laboratories; Anheuser-Busch, Inc.; Connecticut General Life Insurance Co.; Exxon Company U.S.A.; General Motors Corp.; The Kroger Co.; Lennox Industries, Inc.; Navistar International Corporation; Ohio Manufacturers Assn.; Wendy's International, Inc.

For Complete List of Firm Personnel, See General Section

For full biographical listings, see the Martindale-Hubbell Law Directory

*DAYTON,** Montgomery Co.

THOMPSON, HINE AND FLORY (AV)

2000 Courthouse Plaza, N.E., 45402-1706
Telephone: 513-443-6600
Fax: 513-443-6637; 443-6635
Akron, Ohio Office: 50 S. Main Street, Suite 502, 44308-1828.
Telephone: 216-376-8090.
Fax: 216-376-8386.
Cincinnati, Ohio Office: 312 Walnut Street, 14th Floor, 45202-4029.
Telephone: 513-352-6700.
Fax: 513-241-4771.
Telex: 938003.

(See Next Column)

THOMPSON, HINE AND FLORY, *Dayton—Continued*

Cleveland, Ohio Office: 1100 National City Bank Building, 629 Euclid Avenue, 44114-3070.
Telephone: 216-566-5500.
Fax: 216-556-5583.
Telex: 980217.
Cable Address: "Thomflor".
Columbus, Ohio Office: One Columbus, 10 West Broad Street, 43215-3435.
Telephone: 614-469-3200.
Fax: 614-469-3361.
Palm Beach, Florida Office: 125 Worth Avenue, 33480-4466.
Telephone: 407-833-5900.
Fax: 407-833-5951.
Washington, D.C. Office: 1920 N Street, N.W., 20036-1601.
Telephone: 202-331-8800.
Fax: 202-331-8330.
Telex: 904173.
Cable Address: "Caglaw".
Brussels, Belgium Office: Rue des Chevaliers / Ridderstraat 14 - B.10, B - 1050.
Telephone: 011(32-2) 511-9326.
Fax: 011(32-2) 513-9206.

MEMBERS OF FIRM

Barry M. Block
Stanley A. Freedman
Sue K. McDonnell

SENIOR ATTORNEY

Richard A. Ciambrone

For Complete List of Firm Personnel, See General Section

For full biographical listings, see the Martindale-Hubbell Law Directory

*ELYRIA,** Lorain Co.

ERIC H. ZAGRANS (AV)

474 Overbrook Road, 44035-3623
Telephone: 216-365-5400
Facsimile: 216-365-5100

For full biographical listings, see the Martindale-Hubbell Law Directory

OKLAHOMA

*OKLAHOMA CITY,** Oklahoma Co.

ANDREWS DAVIS LEGG BIXLER MILSTEN & PRICE, A PROFESSIONAL CORPORATION (AV)

500 West Main, 73102
Telephone: 405-272-9241
FAX: 405-235-8786

John F. Fischer, II
Don G. Holladay
Robert D. Nelon
R. Brown Wallace

Representative Clients: Maryland Casualty Co.; Oklahoma City Media Credit Executives; Oklahoma State Medical Assn.; United Bank Services.

For Complete List of Firm Personnel, See General Section

For full biographical listings, see the Martindale-Hubbell Law Directory

CONNER & WINTERS, A PROFESSIONAL CORPORATION (AV)

204 North Robinson, Suite 950, 73102
Telephone: 405-232-7711
Facsimile: 405-232-2695
Tulsa, Oklahoma Office: 15 East 5th Street, Suite 2400, 74103.
Telephone: 918-586-5711.
Facsimile: 918-586-8982.

Peter B. Bradford
Raymond E. Tompkins
Timothy J. Bomhoff

For full biographical listings, see the Martindale-Hubbell Law Directory

CROWE & DUNLEVY, A PROFESSIONAL CORPORATION (AV)

1800 Mid-America Tower, 20 North Broadway, 73102-8273
Telephone: 405-235-7700
Fax: 405-239-6651
Tulsa, Oklahoma Office: Crowe & Dunlevy, 500 Kennedy Building, 321 South Boston.
Telephone: 918-592-9800.
Fax: 918-592-9801.
Norman, Oklahoma Office: Crowe & Dunlevy, Luttrell, Pendarvis & Rawlinson, 104 East Eufaula Street.
Telephone: 405-321-7317.
Fax: 405-360-4002.

(See Next Column)

D. Kent Meyers
Clyde A. Muchmore
Mack J. Morgan III
Harvey D. Ellis, Jr.
Robert E. Bacharach

Joel S. Allen

OF COUNSEL

John W. Swinford

For Complete List of Firm Personnel, See General Section

For full biographical listings, see the Martindale-Hubbell Law Directory

KING, ROBERTS & BEELER (AV)

Suite 600, 15 N. Robinson, 73102
Telephone: 405-239-6143
Fax: 405-236-3934

MEMBERS OF FIRM

Tom L. King
K. David Roberts
Jeff R. Beeler

ASSOCIATES

Teresa Thomas Cauthorn
Tracy L. Pierce
Richard M. Glasgow
Linda Prine Brown
Phillip P. Owens II

References: Liberty Bank & Trust; City Bank & Trust.

For full biographical listings, see the Martindale-Hubbell Law Directory

*TULSA,** Tulsa Co.

CRAWFORD, CROWE & BAINBRIDGE, P.A. (AV)

1714 First National Building, 74103
Telephone: 918-587-1128
Fax: 918-587-3975

B. Hayden Crawford
Harry M. Crowe, Jr.
Robert L. Bainbridge
Kyle B. Haskins
Eric B. Bolusky

For full biographical listings, see the Martindale-Hubbell Law Directory

DOYLE & HARRIS, A PROFESSIONAL CORPORATION (AV)

Southern Hills Tower, 2431 East 61st Street, Suite 260, P.O. Box 1679, 74101-1679
Telephone: 918-743-1276
Fax: 918-748-8215

Stan P. Doyle
Steven M. Harris

Michael D. Davis
Douglas R. Haughey
Randall T. Duncan

Reference: Peoples State Bank.

For full biographical listings, see the Martindale-Hubbell Law Directory

GABLE & GOTWALS (AV)

2000 Bank IV Center, 15 West Sixth Street, 74119-5447
Telephone: 918-582-9201
Facsimile: 918-586-8383

Teresa B. Adwan
Pamela S. Anderson
John R. Barker
David L. Bryant
Gene C. Buzzard
Dennis Clarke Cameron
Timothy A. Carney
Renee DeMoss
Elsie C. Draper
Sidney G. Dunagan
Theodore Q. Eliot
Richard W. Gable
Jeffrey Don Hassell
Patricia Ledvina Himes
Oliver S. Howard
Richard D. Koljack, Jr.
J. Daniel Morgan
Joseph W. Morris
Elizabeth R. Muratet
Richard B. Noulles
Ronald N. Ricketts
John Henry Rule
M. Benjamin Singletary
James M. Sturdivant
Patrick O. Waddel
Michael D. Hall
David Edward Keglovits
Stephen W. Lake
Kari S. McKee
Terry D. Ragsdale
Jeffrey C. Rambach

OF COUNSEL

G. Ellis Gable
Charles P. Gotwals, Jr.

For full biographical listings, see the Martindale-Hubbell Law Directory

SNEED, LANG, ADAMS & BARNETT, A PROFESSIONAL CORPORATION (AV)

2300 Williams Center Tower II, Two West Second Street, 74103
Telephone: 918-583-3145
Telecopier: 918-582-0410

(See Next Column)

SNEED, LANG, ADAMS & BARNETT A PROFESSIONAL CORPORATION—*Continued*

James C. Lang
D. Faith Orlowski
Brian S. Gaskill
G. Steven Stidham
Stephen R. McNamara
Thomas E. Black, Jr.
Robbie Emery Burke
C. Raymond Patton, Jr.
Frederick K. Slicker
Richard D. Black
John D. Russell
Jeffrey S. Swyers

OF COUNSEL

James L. Sneed
O. Edwin Adams
Howard G. Barnett, Jr.

Representative Clients: Amoco Production Company; Continental Bank; Deloitte & Touche; Enron Corporation; Halliburton Energy Services; Helmerich & Payne, Inc.; Lehman Brothers, Inc.; Shell Oil Company; Smith Barney, Inc.; State Farm Mutual Automobile Insurance Company.

For full biographical listings, see the Martindale-Hubbell Law Directory

OREGON

*PORTLAND,** Multnomah Co.

LANE POWELL SPEARS LUBERSKY (AV)

520 S.W. Yamhill Street, Suite 800, 97204-1383
Telephone: 503-226-6151
Telecopier: 224-0388
Other Offices at: Seattle, Mount Vernon and Olympia, Washington; Los Angeles and San Francisco, California; Anchorage, Alaska; London, England.

MEMBERS OF FIRM

Craig D. Bachman
James E. Bartels
Jeffrey M. Batchelor
James H. Clarke
Wayne Hilliard
Milo Petranovich
Donald H. Pyle

ASSOCIATES

Robert W. Roley
Darsee R. Staley

For Complete List of Firm Personnel, See General Section

For full biographical listings, see the Martindale-Hubbell Law Directory

MILLER, NASH, WIENER, HAGER & CARLSEN (AV)

111 S.W. Fifth Avenue, 97204-3699
Telephone: 503-224-5858
Telex: 364462, Kingmar PTL
Facsimile: 503-224-0155, 503-224-2450
Seattle, Washington Office: 4400 Two Union Square, 601 Union Street, 98101-2322.
Telephone: 206-622-8484.
Facsimile: 206-622-7485.

PORTLAND, OREGON PARTNERS

Jeffrey D. Austin
John D. Burns
Clifford N. Carlsen, Jr.
William B. Crow
Dean D. DeChaine
Jeffrey J. Druckman
Thomas C. Sand
Norman J. Wiener
R. Alan Wight

SEATTLE, WASHINGTON PARTNER

James R. Hermsen

Representative Clients: U.S. Bancorp; United States National Bank of Oregon; Louisiana-Pacific Corp.; Willamette Industries, Inc.; Portland Public Schools; St. Vincent Hospital and Medical Center; Merrill Lynch, Pierce, Fenner & Smith, Inc.

For Complete List of Firm Personnel, See General Section

For full biographical listings, see the Martindale-Hubbell Law Directory

O'DONNELL, RAMIS, CREW, CORRIGAN & BACHRACH (AV)

Ballow & Wright Building, 1727 N.W. Hoyt Street, 97209
Telephone: 503-222-4402
FAX: 503-243-2944
Clackamas County Office: Suite 202, 181 N. Grant, Canby.
Telephone: 503-266-1149.

MEMBERS OF FIRM

Mark P. O'Donnell
Timothy V. Ramis
Stephen F. Crew
Charles E. Corrigan
Jeff H. Bachrach

SPECIAL COUNSEL

James M. Coleman

ASSOCIATES

Pamela J. Beery
Mark L. Busch
Gary Firestone
G. Frank Hammond
William A. Monahan
William J. Stalnaker
Ty K. Wyman

(See Next Column)

LEGAL SUPPORT PERSONNEL

Margaret M. Daly
Mary C. Meyers
Laurel L. Ramsey
G. William Selzer
Dawna S. Shattuck (Legal Assistant)

For full biographical listings, see the Martindale-Hubbell Law Directory

PENNSYLVANIA

*HARRISBURG,** Dauphin Co.

GOLDBERG, KATZMAN & SHIPMAN, P.C. (AV)

320 Market Street - Strawberry Square, P.O. Box 1268, 17108-1268
Telephone: 717-234-4161
Telecopier: 717-234-6808; 717-234-6810

Ronald M. Katzman
Michael A. Finio

Reference: Fulton Bank.

For Complete List of Firm Personnel, See General Section

For full biographical listings, see the Martindale-Hubbell Law Directory

*PHILADELPHIA,** Philadelphia Co.

BALLARD SPAHR ANDREWS & INGERSOLL (AV)

1735 Market Street, 51st Floor, 19103-7599
Telephone: 215-665-8500
Fax: 215-864-8999
Denver, Colorado Office: Seventeenth Street Plaza Building, Suite 2300, 1225 17th Street.
Telephone: 303-292-2400.
Fax: 303-296-3956.
Kaunas, Lithuania Office: Donelaicio g., 71-2, Kaunas 3000.
Telephone: (370-7) 20 56 66.
Fax: (370-7) 20 56 91.
Salt Lake City, Utah Office: One Utah Center, Suite 1200, 201 South Main Street.
Telephone: 801-531-3000.
Fax: 801-531-3001.
Washington, D.C. Office: Suite 900 East, 555 13th Street, N.W.
Telephone: 202-383-8800.
Fax: 202-383-8877; 383-8893.
Baltimore, Maryland Office: 300 East Lombard Street. 19th Floor.
Telephone: 410-528-5600.
Fax: 410-528-5650.
Camden, New Jersey Office: 800 Hudson Square, 5th Floor.
Telephone: 609-541-5577.
Fax: 609-541-8272.

Carl W. Hittinger
Geoffrey A. Kahn
Matthew M. Strickler

For Complete List of Firm Personnel, See General Section

For full biographical listings, see the Martindale-Hubbell Law Directory

BARRACK, RODOS & BACINE (AV)

A Partnership including Professional Corporations
3300 Two Commerce Square, 2001 Market Street, 19103
Telephone: 215-963-0600
Telecopier: 215-963-0838
San Diego, California Office: Suite 1700, 600 West Broadway.
Telephone: 619-230-0800.
Telecopier: 619-230-1874.

Leonard Barrack (P.C.)
Gerald J. Rodos (P.C.)
Daniel E. Bacine (P.C.)
Sheldon L. Albert
Samuel R. Simon
M. Richard Komins
Edward M. Gergosian (Resident, San Diego, California Office)
Kirk B. Hulett (Resident, San Diego, California Office)
Robert Lipman
Jeffrey W. Golan
Anthony J. Bolognese
James J. Greenfield
Douglas J. Campion (Resident, San Diego, California Office)
Stephen R. Basser (Resident, San Diego, California Office)
Leslie Bornstein Molder
Robert A. Hoffman
Randal J. Rein (Resident, San Diego, California Office)
Lisa Clare Atkinson (Resident, San Diego, California Office)

For full biographical listings, see the Martindale-Hubbell Law Directory

BERGER & MONTAGUE, P.C. (AV)

1622 Locust Street, 19103
Telephone: 215-875-3000
Telecopier: 215-875-4604; 875-4608

David Berger
Harold Berger
H. Laddie Montague, Jr.
Stanley R. Wolfe
Merrill G. Davidoff
Sherrie Raiken Savett
Daniel Berger
Jay Robert Stiefel

(See Next Column)

BERGER & MONTAGUE P.C., *Philadelphia—Continued*

Gary E. Cantor
Howard I. Langer
Stephen A. Whinston
Martin I. Twersky
Todd S. Collins
Carole A. Broderick
Janice Siegel
Peter R. Kahana
Ruthanne Gordon
Alan M. Sandals
Stephen D. Ramos
Karen S. Orman
Jeanne A. Markey
Lawrence Deutsch
Jonathan D. Berger

Kenneth L. Fox
Lawrence J. Lederer
Peter B. Nordberg
Sheryl S. Levy
Patricia D. Gugin
Andrew J. Lapat
John R. Taylor
Thomas F. Hughes
Catherine Ann Sullivan
Andrew Brenner
Stuart J. Guber
Michael L. Block
Barbara Lowe
Jerome M. Marcus
Susan Jaffe Sarner
Bart D. Cohen
Michael T. Fantini
Jeffrey M. Krulik
David F. Sorensen
Arthur Stock
Jonathan Auerbach
Ivonia K. Slade
Patrick E. Bradley
Genna C. Driscoll
Bret P. Flaherty
Charles Pearsall Goodwin
Joel M. Sweet
Nina Amster
Audrey A. Kraus
Leah R. Stolker

Reference: Corestates Bank N.A.

For full biographical listings, see the Martindale-Hubbell Law Directory

BUCHANAN INGERSOLL, PROFESSIONAL CORPORATION (AV)

Two Logan Square Twelfth Floor, 18th & Arch Streets, 19103
Telephone: 215-665-8700
Telecopier: 215-569-2066
Pittsburgh, Pennsylvania Office: 5800 USX Tower, 600 Grant Street.
Telephone: 412-562-8800.
Harrisburg, Pennsylvania Office: Vartan Parc, 30 North Third Street.
Telephone: 717-237-4800.
Tampa, Florida Office: 101 East Kennedy Boulevard, Suite 1030.
Telephone: 813-222-8180.
North Miami Beach, Florida Office: 19495 Biscayne Boulevard.
Telephone: 305-933-5600.
Lexington, Kentucky Office: 1210 Vine Center Office Tower, 333 West Vine Street.
Telephone: 606-225-5333.
Princeton, New Jersey Office: Buchanan Ingersoll, A Partnership, College Centre, 500 College Road East.
Telephone: 609-452-2666.

Alan C. Kessler

For Complete List of Firm Personnel, See General Section

For full biographical listings, see the Martindale-Hubbell Law Directory

GERMAN, GALLAGHER & MURTAGH, A PROFESSIONAL CORPORATION (AV)

Fifth Floor, The Bellevue, 200 South Broad Street, 19102
Telephone: 215-545-7700
Telecopier: 215-732-4182
Cherry Hill, New Jersey Office: Suite 643, 1040 North Kings Highway.
Telephone: 609-667-7676.
Lancaster, Pennsylvania Office: 40 East Grant Street.
Telephone: 717-293-8070.

Edward C. German
Michael D. Gallagher
Dean F. Murtagh
Philip A. Ryan
Robert P. Corbin
David P. Rovner
Kathryn A. Dux
Gary R. Gremminger
Kim Plouffe
Jeffrey N. German
John P. Shusted

Kathleen M. Carson
Kevin R. McNulty
Linda Porr Sweeney
Gary H. Hunter
Frank A. Gerolamo, III
Milan K. Mrkobrad
Thomas M. Going
Vincent J. Di Stefano, Jr.
Jack T. Ribble, Jr.
Kimberly J. Keiser
Bernard E. Jude Quinn
Gerald C. Montella
Lisa Beth Zucker
Shelby L. Mattioli
Daniel J. Divis
D. Selaine Belver
Christine L. Davis
Daniel L. Grill
Marta I. Sierra-Epperson
Paul G. Kirk
Aileen R. Thompson
Otis V. Maynard
Gregory S. Capps

For full biographical listings, see the Martindale-Hubbell Law Directory

LEVIN, FISHBEIN, SEDRAN & BERMAN (AV)

Suite 600, 320 Walnut Street, 19106
Telephone: 215-592-1500
Fax: 215-592-4663

(See Next Column)

MEMBERS OF FIRM

Arnold Levin
Michael D. Fishbein
Howard J. Sedran
Laurence S. Berman
Frederick S. Longer

Robert M. Unterberger
Craig D. Ginsburg
Jonathan Shub
Cheryl R. Brown Hill
Roberta Shaner

For full biographical listings, see the Martindale-Hubbell Law Directory

MAGER LIEBENBERG & WHITE (AV)

Two Penn Center, Suite 415, 19102
Telephone: 215-569-6921
Telecopier: 215-569-6931

MEMBERS OF FIRM

Carol A. Mager
Roberta D. Liebenberg
Ann D. White

ASSOCIATES

Matthew D. Baxter
Brett M. L. Blyshak
Michael J. Salmanson
W. Scott Magargee
Nancy F. DuBoise

OF COUNSEL

Anna M. Durbin

For full biographical listings, see the Martindale-Hubbell Law Directory

SAUL, EWING, REMICK & SAUL (AV)

3800 Centre Square West, 19102
Telephone: 215-972-7777
Cable Address: "Bidsal"
TWX: 83-4798
Telecopier: XEROX 7020 215-972-7725
Wilmington, Delaware Office: 222 Delaware Avenue, P.O. Box 1266, 19899-1266. For Courier Delivery: 222 Delaware Avenue, Suite 1200, 19801.
Telephone: 302-421-6800.
Cable Address: "Bidsal."
TWX: 83-4798.
Telecopier: XEROX 7020 302-421-6813.
New York, N.Y. Office: Twenty-first Floor, 237 Park Avenue.
Telephone: 212-551-3502.
TWX: 425170.
Telecopier: 212-697-8486.
Malvern, Pennsylvania Office: Suite 200, Great Valley Corporate Center, 300 Chester Field Parkway.
Telephone: 215-251-5050.
Cable Address: "BIDSAL".
TWX: 83-4798.
Telecopier: 215-651-5930.
Voorhees, New Jersey Office: Plaza 1000, Main Street, Suite 206 Evesham & Kresson Roads.
Telephone: 609-424-0098.
Telecopier: XEROX 7020 609-424-2204.
Harrisburg, Pennsylvania Office: 240 North 3rd Street, P.O. Box 1291, 17108-1291. For Courier Delivery: 240 N. 3rd Street, Suite 700, 17101.
Telephone: 717-238-8300.
Telecopier: 717-238-4622.
Trenton, New Jersey Office: Capital Center, 50 East State Street, 08608.
Telephone: 609-393-0057.
Fax: 609-393-5962.

MEMBERS OF FIRM

Robert N. de Luca
Paul M. Hummer
Paul C. Madden
Walter R. Milbourne
Scott D. Patterson (Resident, Malvern Office)
Linda Richenderfer
James G. Rosenberg
John F. Stoviak
J. Clayton Undercofler

OF COUNSEL

Robert W. Sayre

ASSOCIATES

William Michael Janssen
James O'Toole, Jr.

For Complete List of Firm Personnel, See General Section

For full biographical listings, see the Martindale-Hubbell Law Directory

SPECTOR & ROSEMAN, A PROFESSIONAL CORPORATION (AV)

2000 Market Street, 12th Floor, 19103
Telephone: 215-864-2400
Telecopier: 215-864-2424
San Diego, California Office: 600 West Broadway, 1800 One American Plaza, 92101.
Telephone: 619-338-4514.
Telecopier: 619-231-7423.

Eugene A. Spector
Robert M. Roseman
Mark S. Goldman
Paul J. Scarlato

Jeffrey L. Kodroff
Ellen A. Gusikoff (Not admitted in PA)
Jacob A. Goldberg
Debra M. Kahn

For full biographical listings, see the Martindale-Hubbell Law Directory

Philadelphia—Continued

WOLF, BLOCK, SCHORR AND SOLIS-COHEN (AV)

Twelfth Floor, Packard Building, S.E. Corner 15th and Chestnut Streets, 19102-2678
Telephone: 215-977-2000
Cable Address: "WOLBLORR PHA"
TWX: 710-670-1927
Telecopiers: 977-2334; 977-2346
Malvern, Pennsylvania Office: 20 Valley Stream Parkway.
Telephone: 215-889-4900.
Fax: 215-889-4916.
Harrisburg, Pennsylvania Office: 305 North Front Street, Suite 401.
Telephone: 717-237-7160.
Fax: 717-237-7161.

MEMBERS OF FIRM

Ian A. L. Strogatz | Burt M. Rublin

OF COUNSEL

Franklin Poul

For Complete List of Firm Personnel, See General Section

For full biographical listings, see the Martindale-Hubbell Law Directory

*PITTSBURGH,** Allegheny Co.

BUCHANAN INGERSOLL, PROFESSIONAL CORPORATION (AV)

5800 USX Tower, 600 Grant Street, 15219
Telephone: 412-562-8800
Telecopier: 412-562-1041
Philadelphia, Pennsylvania Office: Two Logan Square, Twelfth Floor, 18th & Arch Streets.
Telephone: 215-665-8700.
Harrisburg, Pennsylvania Office: Vartan Parc, 30 North Third Street.
Telephone: 717-237-4800.
Tampa, Florida Office: 101 East Kennedy Boulevard, Suite 1030.
Telephone: 813-222-8180.
North Miami Beach, Florida Office: 19495 Biscayne Boulevard.
Telephone: 305-933-5600.
Lexington, Kentucky Office: 1210 Vine Center Office Tower, 333 West Vine Street.
Telephone: 606-225-5333.
Princeton, New Jersey Office: Buchanan Ingersoll, A Partnership, College Centre, 500 College Road East.
Telephone: 609-452-2666.

Bruce A. Americus | Gregory A. Pearson
Wendelynne J. Newton | Thomas L. VanKirk

Thomas G. Buchanan

For Complete List of Firm Personnel, See General Section

For full biographical listings, see the Martindale-Hubbell Law Directory

DICKIE, MCCAMEY & CHILCOTE, A PROFESSIONAL CORPORATION (AV)

Suite 400, Two PPG Place, 15222-5402
Telephone: 412-281-7272
Fax: 412-392-5367
Wheeling, West Virginia Office: Suite 2002, 1233 Main Street, 26003-2839.
Telephone: 304-233-1022.
Facsimile: 304-233-1026.

David B. Fawcett | Charles W. Kenrick
David J. Armstrong | George Edward McGrann
Wilbur McCoy Otto | Larry A. Silverman
Clayton A. Sweeney | Steven B. Larchuk
Daniel P. Stefko | Judith Ference Olson
M. Richard Dunlap | Dorothy A. Davis

For Complete List of Firm Personnel, See General Section

For full biographical listings, see the Martindale-Hubbell Law Directory

MARCUS & SHAPIRA (AV)

35th Floor, One Oxford Centre, 301 Grant Street, 15219-6401
Telephone: 412-471-3490
Telecopier: 412-391-8758

MEMBERS OF FIRM

Bernard D. Marcus | Susan Gromis Flynn
Daniel H. Shapira | Darlene M. Nowak
George P. Slesinger | Glenn M. Olcerst
Robert L. Allman, II | Elly Heller-Toig
Estelle F. Comay | Sylvester A. Beozzo

OF COUNSEL

John M. Burkoff

SPECIAL COUNSEL

Jane Campbell Moriarty

(See Next Column)

ASSOCIATES

Scott D. Livingston | Lori E. McMaster
Robert M. Barnes | Melody A. Pollock
Stephen S. Zubrow | James F. Rosenberg
David B. Rodes | Amy M. Gottlieb

For full biographical listings, see the Martindale-Hubbell Law Directory

ROSE, SCHMIDT, HASLEY & DISALLE, P.C. (AV)

900 Oliver Building, 15222-2310
Telephone: 412-434-8600
Fax: 412-263-2829
Washington, Pennsylvania Office: 7th Floor, Millcraft Center.
Telephone: 412-228-8883.

Steven M. Petrikis

For Complete List of Firm Personnel, See General Section

For full biographical listings, see the Martindale-Hubbell Law Directory

SPRINGER, BUSH & PERRY, A PROFESSIONAL CORPORATION (AV)

Two Gateway Center, Fifteenth Floor, 15222
Telephone: 412-281-4900
Fax: 412-261-1645
Moon Township, Pennsylvania Office: 500 Cherrington Parkway, Suite 420, Coraopolis, Pennsylvania, 15108.
Telephone: 412-269-4200.
Fax: 412-269-9638.

Joseph Friedman | Stephen F. Ban

COUNSEL

Malcolm Anderson

For Complete List of Firm Personnel, See General Section

For full biographical listings, see the Martindale-Hubbell Law Directory

THORP, REED & ARMSTRONG (AV)

One Riverfront Center, 15222
Telephone: 412-394-7711
Fax: 412-394-2555

MEMBERS OF FIRM

Kevin C. Abbott | Edward B. Harmon
James D. Chiafullo | Deborah P. Powell
George P. Faines | William M. Wycoff

OF COUNSEL

Stuart C. Gaul | Charles Weiss

For Complete List of Firm Personnel, See General Section

For full biographical listings, see the Martindale-Hubbell Law Directory

RHODE ISLAND

*PROVIDENCE,** Providence Co.

BLISH & CAVANAGH (AV)

Commerce Center, 30 Exchange Terrace, 02903
Telephone: 401-831-8900
Telecopier: 401-751-7542

MEMBERS OF FIRM

John H. Blish | William R. Landry
Joseph V. Cavanagh, Jr. | Michael DiBiase

Stephen J. Reid, Jr.

Karen A. Pelczarski | Raymond A. Marcaccio

Scott P. Tierney

Representative Clients: Providence Journal Co.; Fleet Financial Group; Rhode Island Hospital Trust National Bank; Allstate Insurance Co.; U-Haul International, Inc.; Delta Dental of Rhode Island; Gilbane Building Co.; Colony Communications; Providence Housing Authority.

For full biographical listings, see the Martindale-Hubbell Law Directory

EDWARDS & ANGELL (AV)

2700 Hospital Trust Tower, 02903
Telephone: 401-274-9200
Telecopier: 401-276-6611
Cable Address: "Edwangle Providence"
Telex: 952001 "E A PVD"
Boston, Massachusetts Office: 101 Federal Street, 02110.
Telephone: 617-439-444.
Telecopier: 617-439-4170.

(See Next Column)

EDWARDS & ANGELL, *Providence—Continued*

New York, New York Office: 750 Lexington Avenue, 10022.
Telephone: 212-308-4411.
Telecopier: 212-308-4844.
Palm Beach, Florida Office: 250 Royal Palm Way, 33480.
Telephone: 407-833-7700.
Telecopier: 407-655-8719.
Newark, New Jersey Office: Gateway three, 07120.
Telephone: 201-623-7717.
Telecopier: 201-623-7717.
Hartford, Connecticut Office: 750 Main Street, 14th Floor, 06103.
Telephone: 203-525-5065.
Telecopier: 203-527-4198.
Newport, Rhode Island Office: 130 Bellevue Avenue, 02840.
Telephone: 401-849-7800.
Telecopier: 401-849-7887.

MEMBERS OF FIRM

S. Michael Levin
Patricia A. Sullivan Zesk

ASSOCIATE

Jon M. Anderson

For Complete List of Firm Personnel, See General Section

For full biographical listings, see the Martindale-Hubbell Law Directory

FLANDERS + MEDEIROS INC. (AV)

One Turks Head Place, Suite 700, 02903
Telephone: 401-831-0700
Telecopier: 401-274-2752

Matthew F. Medeiros
Robert G. Flanders, Jr.
Robert Karmen

Neal J. McNamara
Fausto C. Anguilla
Amelia E. Edwards
Stacey P. Nakasian

For full biographical listings, see the Martindale-Hubbell Law Directory

SOUTH CAROLINA

*GREENVILLE,** Greenville Co.

LEATHERWOOD WALKER TODD & MANN, P.C. (AV)

100 East Coffee Street, P.O. Box 87, 29602
Telephone: 803-242-6440
FAX: 803-233-8461
Spartanburg, South Carolina Office: 1451 East Main Street, P.O. Box 3188.
Telephone: 803-582-4365.
Telefax: 803-583-8961.

James H. Watson
J. Brantley Phillips, Jr.
John E. Johnston
Harvey G. Sanders, Jr.
O. Jack Taylor, Jr.
Natalma M. McKnew
Steven E. Farrar
Nancy Hyder Robinson

COUNSEL

J. D. Todd, Jr.
Fletcher C. Mann

Counsel for: John D. Hollingsworth on Wheels, Inc.; Bi-Lo, Inc.; Suitt Construction, Co., Inc.; Platt Saco Lowell Corporation; The Litchfield Company of South Carolina.
Representative Clients: NationsBank; Springs Industries, Inc.; American Federal Bank, F.S.B.; General Motor Acceptance Corp.

For Complete List of Firm Personnel, See General Section

For full biographical listings, see the Martindale-Hubbell Law Directory

WYCHE, BURGESS, FREEMAN & PARHAM, PROFESSIONAL ASSOCIATION (AV)

44 East Camperdown Way, P.O. Box 728, 29602-0728
Telephone: 803-242-8200
Telecopier: 803-235-8900

David L. Freeman
James C. Parham, Jr.
William W. Kehl
Henry L. Parr, Jr.

Counsel for: Multimedia, Inc.; Delta Woodside Industries, Inc.; Milliken & Company; Ryan's Family Steak Houses, Inc.; St. Francis Hospital; Span-America Medical Systems, Inc.; Carolina First Bank; KEMET Electronics Corp.; Builder Marts of America, Inc.; One Price Clothing, Inc.

For Complete List of Firm Personnel, See General Section

For full biographical listings, see the Martindale-Hubbell Law Directory

TENNESSEE

*MEMPHIS,** Shelby Co.

ARMSTRONG ALLEN PREWITT GENTRY JOHNSTON & HOLMES (AV)

80 Monroe Avenue Suite 700, 38103
Telephone: 901-523-8211
Telecopier: 901-524-4936
Jackson, Missippi Office: 1350 One Jackson Place, 188 East Capitol Street.
Telephone: 601-948-8020.
Telecopier: 601-948-8389.

MEMBERS OF FIRM

Gavin M. Gentry
Thomas F. Johnston
S. Russell Headrick
Mark S. Norris

For Complete List of Firm Personnel, See General Section

For full biographical listings, see the Martindale-Hubbell Law Directory

*NASHVILLE,** Davidson Co.

BASS, BERRY & SIMS (AV)

2700 First American Center, 37238-2700
Telephone: 615-742-6200
Telecopy: 615-742-6293
Knoxville, Tennessee Office: 1700 Riverview Tower, 900 S. Gay Street, P.O. Box 1509, 37901-1509.
Telephone: 615-521-6200.
Telecopy: 615-521-6234.

MEMBERS OF FIRM

James O. Bass, Jr.
Robert J. Walker
Steven A. Riley
R. Dale Grimes
Bennett L. Ross

Representative Clients: BellSouth Telecommunications, Inc.; The Vanderbilt University; Ingram Industries, Inc.; Amana Refrigeration, Inc.; Blue Cross and Blue Shield of Tennessee, Inc.; Opryland USA, Inc.; Service Merchandise Company, Inc.; Voluntary Hospitals of America, Inc.; Levi Strauss & Co., Inc.; Rogers Group, Inc.

For full biographical listings, see the Martindale-Hubbell Law Directory

KING & BALLOW (AV)

1200 Noel Place, 200 Fourth Avenue, North, 37219
Telephone: 615-259-3456
Fax: 615-254-7907
San Diego, California Office: 2700 Symphony Towers, 750 B Street, 92101.
Telephone: 619-236-9401.
Fax: 619-236-9437.
San Francisco, California Office: 100 First Street, Suite 2700, 94105.
Telephone: 415-541-7803.
Fax: 415-541-7805.

MEMBERS OF FIRM

Frank S. King, Jr.
Robert L. Ballow
Alan L. Marx
Paul H. Duvall (Resident, San Diego, California Office)
Steven C. Douse
Mark E. Hunt

ASSOCIATE

Patrick M. Thomas

Representative Clients: Alameda Newspapers, Hayward, California; Denver Post, Denver, Colorado; Garden State Newspapers, Woodbury, New Jersey; Houston Post, Houston, Texas; Ingram Industries, Inc., Nashville, Tennessee; Media News Group, Houston, Texas; Union Tribune, San Diego, California; Media General, Richmond, Virginia; York Newspaper Co., York, Pennsylvania; Nashville Banner, Nashville, Tennessee; National Newspaper Association, Washington, D.C.

For Complete List of Firm Personnel, See General Section

For full biographical listings, see the Martindale-Hubbell Law Directory

TEXAS

*DALLAS,** Dallas Co.

BAKER & BOTTS, L.L.P. (AV)

2001 Ross Avenue, 75201
Telephone: 214-953-6500
Fax: 214-953-6503
Houston, Texas Office: One Shell Plaza, 910 Louisiana.
Telephone: 713-229-1234.
Washington, D.C. Office: The Warner, 1299 Pennsylvania Avenue, N.W.
Telephone: 202-639-7700.
Austin, Texas Office: 1600 San Jacinto Center, 98 San Jacinto Boulevard.
Telephone: 512-322-2500.

(See Next Column)

BAKER & BOTTS L.L.P.—*Continued*

New York, New York Office: 885 Third Avenue, Suite 2000.
Telephone: 212-705-5000.
Moscow, Russian Federation Office: 10 ul. Pushkinskaya, 103031.
Telephone: 7095/921-5300 (Local); 7095/929-7070.

MEMBERS OF FIRM

Ronald L. Palmer — Robert W. Kantner
Robert W. Jordan — Catharina J. H. D. Haynes

ASSOCIATE

Samara Lackman Kline

For Complete List of Firm Personnel, See General Section

For full biographical listings, see the Martindale-Hubbell Law Directory

CARRINGTON, COLEMAN, SLOMAN & BLUMENTHAL, L.L.P. (AV)

200 Crescent Court, Suite 1500, 75201
Telephone: 214-855-3000
Telecopy: 214-855-1333

MEMBERS OF FIRM

James E. Coleman, Jr. — Lyman G. Hughes
Marvin S. Sloman — Tyler A. Baker, III
Fletcher L. Yarbrough — Tim Gavin
Diane M. Sumoski

For Complete List of Firm Personnel, See General Section

For full biographical listings, see the Martindale-Hubbell Law Directory

JACKSON & WALKER, L.L.P. (AV)

901 Main Street, Suite 6000, 75202-3797
Telephone: 214-953-6000
Fax: 214-953-5822
Fort Worth, Texas Office: 777 Main Street, Suite 1800.
Telephone: 817-334-7200.
Fax: 817-334-7290.
Houston, Texas Office: 1100 Louisiana, Suite 4200.
Telephone: 713-752-4200.
Fax: 713-752-4221.
San Antonio, Texas Office: 112 E. Pecan Street, Suite 2100.
Telephone: 210-978-7700.
Fax: 210-978-7790.

MEMBERS OF FIRM

H. Dudley Chambers — Robert F. Henderson

OF COUNSEL

Ralph E. Hartman — Mary Emma Ackels Karam

Representative Clients Furnished Upon Request.

For Complete List of Firm Personnel, See General Section

For full biographical listings, see the Martindale-Hubbell Law Directory

JONES, DAY, REAVIS & POGUE (AV)

2300 Trammell Crow Center, 2001 Ross Avenue, 75201
Telephone: 214-220-3939
Cable Address: "Attorneys Dallas"
Telex: 730852
Telecopier: 214-969-5100
In Atlanta, Georgia: 3500 One Peachtree Center, 303 Peachtree Street, N.E.
Telephone: 404-521-3939.
Cable Address: "Attorneys Atlanta".
Telex: 54-2711.
Telecopier: 404-581-8330.
In Brussels, Belgium: Avenue Louise 480, 7th Floor, B-1050 Brussels.
Telephone: 011-32-2-645-14-11.
Telecopier: 011-32-2-645-14-45.
In Chicago, Illinois: 77 West Wacker.
Telephone: 312-782-3939.
Telecopier: 312-782-8585.
In Cleveland, Ohio: North Point, 901 Lakeside Avenue.
Telephone: 216-586-3939.
Cable Address: "Attorneys Cleveland."
Telex: 980389.
Telecopier: 216-579-0212.
In Columbus, Ohio: 1900 Huntington Center.
Telephone: 614-469-3939.
Cable Address: "Attorneys Columbus."
Telecopier: 614-461-4198.
In Frankfurt, Germany: Triton Haus, Bockenheimer Landstrasse 42, 60323 Frankfurt am Main.
Telephone: 49-69-9726-3939.
Telecopier: 49-69-9726-3993.
In Geneva, Switzerland: 20, rue de Candolle.
Telephone: 011-41-22-320-2339.
Telecopier: 011-41-22-320-1232.
In Hong Kong: 1501 One Exchange Square, 8 Connaught Place.
Telephone: 011-852-2526-6895.
Telecopier: 011-852-2810-5787.

(See Next Column)

In Irvine, California: 2603 Main Street, Suite 900.
Telephone: 714-851-3939.
Telex: 194911 Lawyers LSA.
Telecopier: 714-553-7539.
In London, England: One Mount Street.
Telephone: 011-44-71-493-9361.
Cable Address: "Surgoe London WI."
Telecopier: 011-44-71-493-9666.
In Los Angeles, California: 555 West Fifth Street, Suite 4600.
Telephone: 213-489-3939.
Telex: 181439 UD.
Telecopier: 213-243-2539.
In New York, New York: 599 Lexington Avenue.
Telephone: 212-326-3939.
Cable Address: "JONESDAY NEWYORK."
Telex: 237013 JDRP UR.
Telecopier: 212-755-7306.
In Paris, France: 62, rue du Faubourg Saint-Honore.
Telephone: 011-33-1-44-71-3939.
Cable Address: "Surgoe Paris."
Telex: 290156 Surgoe.
Telecopier: 011-33-1-49-24-0471.
In Pittsburgh, Pennsylvania: 500 Grant Street, 31st Floor.
Telephone: 412-391-3939.
Cable Address: "Attorneys Pittsburgh".
Telecopier: 412-394-7959.
In Riyadh, Saudi Arabia: Law Offices of Saud M.A. Shawwaf, P.O. Box 2700.
Telephones: 011 (966-1) 465-6543, 011 (966-1) 464-8534 or 011 (966-1) 464-8540.
Telex: 401831 SAUCON SJ.
Telecopier: (966-1) 464-8480.
In Taipei, Taiwan: 8th Floor, 2 Tun Hwa South Road, Section 2.
Telephone: 011 (886-2) 704-6808.
Telecopier: 011 (886-2) 704-6791.
In Tokyo, Japan: Toranomon MT Building, 4th Floor, 10-3, Toranomon, 3-Chome, Minato-Ku, Tokyo 105, Japan.
Telephone: 011-81-3-3433-3939.
Telecopier: 011-81-3-5401-2725.
In Washington, D.C.: Metropolitan Square, 1450 G Street, N.W.
Telephone: 202-879-3939.
Cable Address: "Attorneys Washington."
Telex: 89-2410 ATTORNEYS WASH.
Telecopier: 202-737-2832.

MEMBERS OF FIRM IN DALLAS

Chester J. Hinshaw — Keith C. McDole
Joseph L. McEntee — Thomas R. Jackson
Patricia Villareal

For Complete List of Firm Personnel, See General Section

For full biographical listings, see the Martindale-Hubbell Law Directory

THOMPSON & KNIGHT, A PROFESSIONAL CORPORATION (AV)

(Attorneys and Counselors)
1700 Pacific Avenue Suite 3300, 75201
Telephone: 214-969-1700
Telecopy: 214-969-1751
Cable Address: "Tomtex"
Telex: 732298
Austin, Texas Office: 1200 San Jacinto Center, 98 San Jacinto Boulevard, 78701.
Telephone: 512-469-6100.
Telecopy: 512-469-6180.
Fort Worth, Texas Office: 801 Cherry Street, Suite 1600, 76102.
Telephone: 817-347-1700.
Telecopy: 817-347-1799.
Houston, Texas Office: 1700 Texas Commerce Tower, 600 Travis, 77002.
Telephone: 713-217-2800.
Telecopy: 713-217-2828.
Monterrey, Mexico Office: Edificio Losoles PD-4, Av. Lázaro Cárdenas No. 2400 Pte., San Pedro Garza Garcia, Nuevo Léon C.P. 66220.
Telephone: (52-8) 363-0096.
Telecopy: (52-8) 363-3067.

SHAREHOLDERS

Gregory S. C. Huffman — Judy C. Norris
Timothy R. McCormick — Molly Steele

ASSOCIATES

Michael E. Schonberg — David S. White

For Complete List of Firm Personnel, See General Section

For full biographical listings, see the Martindale-Hubbell Law Directory

*EL PASO,** El Paso Co.

KEMP, SMITH, DUNCAN & HAMMOND, A PROFESSIONAL CORPORATION (AV)

2000 State National Bank Plaza, 79901, P.O. Drawer 2800, 79999
Telephone: 915-533-4424
Fax: 915-546-5360
Albuquerque, New Mexico Office: 500 Marquette, N.W., Suite 1200, P.O. Box 1276.
Telephone: 505-247-2315.
Fax: 505-764-5480.

SENIOR ATTORNEY

Mark N. Osborn

Attorneys for: State National Bank; Circle K Corporation; A. C. Nielsen; Magnolia Coca Cola.

For Complete List of Firm Personnel, See General Section

For full biographical listings, see the Martindale-Hubbell Law Directory

MOUNCE & GALATZAN, A PROFESSIONAL CORPORATION (AV)

7th Floor, Texas Commerce Bank Building, 79901-1334
Telephone: 915-532-3911
Fax: 915-541-1597

Sabre Anthony Safi

Attorneys for: El Paso Natural Gas Co.; Texas Commerce Bank National Association; El Paso Independent School District; Commercial Union Assurance Cos.; State Farm Mutual Automobile Insurance Co.; Employers Insurance of Texas; Greater El Paso Association of Realtors.

For Complete List of Firm Personnel, See General Section

For full biographical listings, see the Martindale-Hubbell Law Directory

*HOUSTON,** Harris Co.

BAKER & BOTTS, L.L.P. (AV)

One Shell Plaza, 910 Louisiana, 77002
Telephone: 713-229-1234
Cable Address: "Boterlove"
Fax: 713-229-1522
Washington, D.C. Office: The Warner, 1299 Pennsylvania Avenue, N.W.
Telephone: 202-639-7700.
New York, New York Office: 885 Third Avenue, Suite 2000.
Telephone: 212-705-5000.
Austin, Texas Office: 1600 San Jacinto Center, 98 San Jacinto Boulevard.
Telephone: 512-322-2500.
Dallas, Texas Office: 2001 Ross Avenue.
Telephone: 214-953-6500.
Moscow, Russian Federation Office: 10 ul. Pushkinskaya, 103031.
Telephone: 7095/921-5300 (Local); 7095/929-7070 (International).

MEMBERS OF FIRM

E. William Barnett
Robert J. Malinak
Rufus W. Oliver, III
J. Michael Baldwin

ASSOCIATES

Thomas R. Ajamie
Parker Bond Binion
David Charles Hricik
William Karl Kroger
J. Bruce McDonald
Cynthia D. Vreeland

For Complete List of Firm Personnel, See General Section

For full biographical listings, see the Martindale-Hubbell Law Directory

VINSON & ELKINS L.L.P. (AV)

2300 First City Tower, 1001 Fannin, 77002-6760
Telephone: 713-758-2222
Fax: 713-758-2346
International Telex: 6868314
Cable Address: Vinelkins
Austin, Texas Office: One American Center, 600 Congress Avenue.
Telephone: 512-495-8400.
Fax: 512-495-8612.
Dallas, Texas Office: 3700 Trammell Crow Center, 2001 Ross Avenue.
Telephone: 214-220-7700.
Fax: 214-220-7716.
Washington, D.C. Office: The Willard Office Building, 1455 Pennsylvania Avenue, N.W.
Telephone: 202-639-6500.
Fax: 202-639-6604.
Cable Address: Vinelkins.
London, England Office: 47 Charles Street, Berkeley Square, London, W1X 7PB, England.
Telephone: 011 (44-171) 491-7236.
Fax: 011 (44-71) 499-5320.
Cable Address: Vinelkins London W.1.
Moscow, Russian Federation Office: 16 Alexey Tolstoy Street, Second Floor, Moscow, 103001 Russian Federation.
Telephone: 011 (70-95) 956-1995.
Telecopy: 011 (70-95) 956-1996.

(See Next Column)

Mexico City, Mexico Office: Aristóteles 77, 5ºPiso, Colonia Chapultepec Polanco, 11560 Mexico, D.F.
Telephone: (52-5) 280-7828.
Fax: (52-5) 280-9223.
Singapore Office: 50 Raffles Place, #19-05 Shell Tower, 0104. U.S. Voice Mailbox: 713-758-3500.
Telephone: (65) 536-8300.
Fax: (65) 536-8311.

MEMBER OF FIRM

Harry M. Reasoner (Managing Partner)

Scott J. Atlas
Page I. Austin
David M. Bond
Travis C. Broesche
Christopher W. Byrd
John L. Carter
Lawrence J. Fossi
Celso M. Gonzalez-Falla
David T. Harvin
David T. Hedges, Jr.
Max Hendrick, III
Karen Jewell
Clara L. Meek
John L. Murchison, Jr.
Charles T. Newton, Jr.
Charles W. Schwartz
Alison L. Smith
Karl S. Stern
Walter B. Stuart IV
W. Dalton Tomlin

Allan Van Fleet

ASSOCIATES

Ernest J. Blansfield, Jr.
Bruce A. Blefeld
Kathleen M. Bone
Jack F. Burleigh
Dale Carpenter
Edward A. Carr
N. Scott Fletcher
Carlos Garcia
Wallis M. Hampton
Erica L. Krennerich
Margaret Christina Ling
James Lloyd Loftis
Andrew James Logan
Manuel Lopez
D'Waine M. Massey
Christopher H. Meakin
Betty R. Owens
James Arthur Reeder, Jr.
Bryant Siddoway
Karen A. Wardell

Richard C. Williams

For Complete List of Firm Personnel, See General Section

For full biographical listings, see the Martindale-Hubbell Law Directory

*SAN ANTONIO,** Bexar Co.

COX & SMITH INCORPORATED (AV)

112 East Pecan Street, Suite 1800, 78205
Telephone: 210-554-5500
Telecopier: 210-226-8395

J. Burleson Smith
Keith E. Kaiser
James B. Smith, Jr.
A. Michael Ferrill

Representative Clients: Boral Industries, Inc.; Incornate Ward Health Services; James Avery Craftsman, Inc.; Nashua Corporation; National Bancshares Corporation of Texas; Owens Corning Fiberglass Corp.; Southwest Venture Partnerships; Tesoro Petroleum Corp.; Winn's Stores, Inc.

For Complete List of Firm Personnel, See General Section

For full biographical listings, see the Martindale-Hubbell Law Directory

MATTHEWS & BRANSCOMB, A PROFESSIONAL CORPORATION (AV)

One Alamo Center, 106 S. St. Mary's Street, Suite 800, 78205
Telephone: 210-226-4211
Facsimile: 210-226-0521
Telex: 5106009283
Cable Code: MBLAW
Austin, Texas Office: 301 Congress Avenue, Suite 2050.
Telephone: 512-305-4400.
Facsimile: 512-305-4413.
Corpus Christi, Texas Office: 802 N. Carancahua, Suite 1900.
Telephone: 512-888-9261.
Facsimile: 512-888-8504.
Eagle Pass, Texas Office: 675 Main Street.
Telephone: 210-773-6700.
Facsimile: 210-757-4045.
Uvalde, Texas Office: 200 E. Nopal #208.
Telephone: 210-278-4597.
Facsimile: 210-278-4806.
(Associated with Hall, Quintanilla & Alarcon, L.C., Laredo, Texas, under the name of Hall, Quintanilla, Alarcon, Matthews & Branscomb, P.L.L.C.)

Howard P. Newton
Charles J. Fitzpatrick
Judith R. Blakeway
Mark A. Phariss

Representative Clients: Coca Cola Bottling Company of the Southwest; Concord Oil Co.; Ellison Enterprises, Inc.; H. E. Butt Grocery Co.; Frank B. Hall & Co., Inc.; The Hearst Corp., San Antonio Light Division; San Antonio Gas & Electric Utilities (City Board); Southern Pacific Transportation Co.; Southwest Texas Methodist Hospital.

For Complete List of Firm Personnel, See General Section

For full biographical listings, see the Martindale-Hubbell Law Directory

UTAH

*SALT LAKE CITY,** Salt Lake Co.

BURBIDGE AND MITCHELL (AV)

Suite 2001, 139 East South Temple, 84111
Telephone: 801-355-6677
Fax: 801-355-2341

Richard D. Burbidge
Stephen B. Mitchell

ASSOCIATES

Douglas H. Holbrook
Gary R. Johnson

Representative Clients: ARCO; Revere National Corp.; SmithKline/Beecham Corp.; Hydro Flame Corp.; Guardian State Bank; Guardian Title Company.

For full biographical listings, see the Martindale-Hubbell Law Directory

CALLISTER, NEBEKER & MCCULLOUGH, A PROFESSIONAL CORPORATION (AV)

800 Kennecott Building, 84133
Telephone: 801-530-7300
Telecopier: 801-364-9127

James R. Holbrook
Mark L. Callister

Representative Clients: GTE Directories Corp.; University of Utah; Zions First National Bank.

For Complete List of Firm Personnel, See General Section

For full biographical listings, see the Martindale-Hubbell Law Directory

JONES, WALDO, HOLBROOK & MCDONOUGH, A PROFESSIONAL CORPORATION (AV)

1500 First Interstate Plaza, 170 South Main Street, 84101
Telephone: 801-521-3200
Telecopier: 801-328-0537
Mailing Address: P.O. Box 45444, 84145-0444
St. George, Utah Office: The Tabernacle Tower Building, 249 East Tabernacle.
Telephone: 801-628-1627.
Telecopier: 801-628-5225.
Washington, D.C. Office: Suite 900, 2300 M Street, N.W.
Telephone: 202-296-5950.
Telecopier: 202-293-2509.

Donald B. Holbrook
Andrew H. Stone

Michael J. Kelley
Jeffrey N. Walker

Representative Clients: Blue Cross and Blue Shield of Utah; American Stores Cos.; Utah Power & Light Co.; Newspaper Agency Corp.; Kearns Tribune Corp.

For Complete List of Firm Personnel, See General Section

For full biographical listings, see the Martindale-Hubbell Law Directory

PARSONS BEHLE & LATIMER, A PROFESSIONAL CORPORATION (AV)

One Utah Center, 201 South Main Street, Suite 1800, P.O. Box 45898, 84145-0898
Telephone: 801-532-1234
Telecopy: 801-536-6111

Keith E. Taylor
Raymond J. Etcheverry
Francis M. Wikstrom
David G. Mangum
C. Kevin Speirs
David M. Bennion

OF COUNSEL

Mark A. Glick

Representative Clients: Baker Hughes Inc.; DYNO NOBEL INC.

For full biographical listings, see the Martindale-Hubbell Law Directory

RAY, QUINNEY & NEBEKER, A PROFESSIONAL CORPORATION (AV)

Suite 400 Deseret Building, 79 South Main Street, P.O. Box 45385, 84145-0385
Telephone: 801-532-1500
Telecopier: 801-532-7543
Provo, Utah Office: 210 First Security Bank Building, 92 North University Avenue.
Telephone: 801-226-7210.
Telecopier: 801-375-8379.

Jonathan A. Dibble
James S. Jardine
Allan T. Brinkerhoff
Keith A. Kelly

Representative Clients: First Security Bank of Utah, N.A.; Borden, Inc.; Southern Pacific Transportation; Utah Power & Light Co.; Travelers Insurance Co.; Greyhound Leasing & Financial; Holy Cross Hospital and Health System; Amoco Production Co.

(See Next Column)

For Complete List of Firm Personnel, See General Section

For full biographical listings, see the Martindale-Hubbell Law Directory

VAN COTT, BAGLEY, CORNWALL & MCCARTHY, A PROFESSIONAL CORPORATION (AV)

Suite 1600, 50 South Main Street, P.O. Box 45340, 84145
Telephone: 801-532-3333
Telex: 453149
Telecopier: 801-534-0058
Ogden, Utah Office: Suite 900, 2404 Washington Boulevard.
Telephone: 801-394-5783.
Park City, Utah Office: 314 Main Street, Suite 205.
Telephone: 801-649-3889.
Reno, Nevada Office: Jeppson & Lee, 100 West Liberty, Suite 990.
Telephone: 702-333-6800.

E. Scott Savage
Kenneth W. Yeates
John A. Snow
David A. Greenwood
Alan L. Sullivan
John T. Nielsen
Michael F. Richman
Jeffrey E. Nelson
Patricia M. Leith
R. Stephen Marshall
Eric C. Olson
Patrick J. O'Hara
John A. Anderson
Scott M. Hadley (Resident, Ogden, Utah Office)
Donald L. Dalton
David L. Arrington
Casey K. McGarvey
Kathryn Holmes Snedaker
Phyllis J. Vetter
Jeremy M. Hoffman
Bryon J. Benevento

OF COUNSEL

Clifford L. Ashton
James P. Cowley

Robert W. Payne
James D. Gilson
Elizabeth D. Winter
Jon E. Waddoups
Melyssa D. Davidson
Craig W. Dallon
Michele Ballantyne
Michael T. Roberts (Resident, Ogden, Utah Office)

Representative Clients: Burlington Northern Railroad; Denver & Rio Grande Western Railroad Co.; Eli Lilly & Co.; Intermountain Health Care, Inc.; Key Bank of Utah; Kimberly-Clark; Martin Marrietta, Inc.; Newmont Gold, Inc.; N.V. Swire Bottlers, Inc.; UNISYS.

For Complete List of Firm Personnel, See General Section

For full biographical listings, see the Martindale-Hubbell Law Directory

WATKISS DUNNING & WATKISS, A PROFESSIONAL CORPORATION (AV)

Broadway Centre, Suite 800, 111 East Broadway, 84111-2304
Telephone: 801-530-1500
Telecopier: 801-530-1520

David K. Watkiss
Elizabeth T. Dunning
David B. Watkiss

Carolyn Cox
Mary J. Woodhead

OF COUNSEL

Karen Campbell Jenson

For full biographical listings, see the Martindale-Hubbell Law Directory

VERMONT

*BURLINGTON,** Chittenden Co.

MILLER, EGGLESTON & ROSENBERG, LTD. (AV)

150 South Champlain Street, P.O. Box 1489, 05402-1489
Telephone: 802-864-0880
Telecopier: 802-864-0328

Michael B. Rosenberg
Anne E. Cramer

Peter F. Young

For Complete List of Firm Personnel, See General Section

For full biographical listings, see the Martindale-Hubbell Law Directory

VIRGINIA

NORFOLK, (Independent City)

Thomas J. Harlan, Jr., P.C. (AV)

1200 Dominion Tower, 999 Waterside Drive, 23510
Telephone: 804-625-8300
FAX: 804-625-3714

Thomas J. Harlan, Jr.

John M. Flora
Kevin M. Thompson (Not admitted in VA)

LEGAL SUPPORT PERSONNEL

Mary Hayse Grant Wareing (Paralegal)
Barry Wade Vanderhoof (Paralegal)

Reference: Commerce Bank.

For full biographical listings, see the Martindale-Hubbell Law Directory

*RICHMOND,** (Ind. City; Seat of Henrico Co.)

McGuire, Woods, Battle & Boothe (AV)

One James Center, 901 East Cary Street, 23219-4030
Telephone: 804-775-1000
Fax: 804-775-1061
Alexandria, Virginia Office: Transpotomac Plaza, Suite 1000, 1199 North Fairfax Street, 22314-1437.
Telephone: 703-739-6200.
Fax: 703-739-6270.
Baltimore, Maryland Office: The Blaustein Building, One North Charles Street, 21201-3793.
Telephone: 410-659-4400.
Fax: 410-659-4599.
Charlottesville, Virginia Office: Court Square Building, P.O. Box 1288, 22902-1288.
Telephone: 804-977-2500.
Fax: 804-980-2222.
Jacksonville, Florida Office: Barnett Center, Suite 2750, 50 North Laura Street, 32202-3635.
Telephone: 904-798-3200.
Fax: 904-798-3207.
McLean, (Tysons Corner) Virginia Office: 8280 Greensboro Drive, Suite 900, Tysons Corner, 22102-3892.
Telephone: 703-712-5000.
Fax: 703-712-5050.
Norfolk, Virginia Office: World Trade Center, Suite 9000, 101 West Main Street, 23510-1655.
Telephone: 804-640-3700.
Fax: 804-640-3701.
Washington, D.C. Office: The Army and Navy Club Building, 1627 Eye Street, N.W., 20006-4007.
Telephone: 202-857-1700.
Fax: 202-857-1737.
Brussels, Belgium Office: 250 Avenue Louise, Ste. 64, 1050.
Telephone: (32 2) 629 42 11.
Fax: (32 2) 629 42 22.
Zürich, Switzerland Office: P.O. Box 4930, Bahnhofstrasse 3, 8022.
Telephone: (41 1) 225 20 00.
Fax: (41 1) 225 20 20.

MEMBERS OF FIRM

C. Torrence Armstrong (Resident, Alexandria Office)
J. Robert Brame III
Howard Feller
Larry D. Sharp (Resident, Washington, D.C. Office)
James H. Walsh
Anne Marie Whittemore

For Complete List of Firm Personnel, See General Section

For full biographical listings, see the Martindale-Hubbell Law Directory

Williams, Mullen, Christian & Dobbins, A Professional Corporation (AV)

Two James Center, 1021 East Cary Street, P.O. Box 1320, 23210-1320
Telephone: 804-643-1991
Fax: 804-783-6456
Glen Allen, Virginia Office: 4401 Waterfront Drive, Suite 140.
Telephone: 804-965-9168.
Fax: 804-965-0955.
Washington, D.C. Office: 1575 Eye Street, N.W.
Telephone: 202-289-6200.
Fax: 202-289-4126.

Stephen E. Baril
David R. Johnson
Robin Robertson Starr

For Complete List of Firm Personnel, See General Section

For full biographical listings, see the Martindale-Hubbell Law Directory

WASHINGTON

*SEATTLE,** King Co.

Keller Rohrback (AV)

1201 Third Avenue, Suite 3200, 98101-3052
Telephone: 206-623-1900
FAX: 206-623-3384
Bremerton, Washington Office: 400 Warren Avenue.
Telephone: 360-479-5151.
Fax: 360-479-7403.

MEMBERS OF FIRM

Robert K. Keller (1916-1992)
Pinckney M. Rohrback (1923-1994)
Lynn Lincoln Sarko (Mr.)
John H. Bright
Michael Woerner

ASSOCIATES

T. David Copley
Rob J. Crichton
Juli E. Farris
Mark A. Griffin

Attorneys For: Wisconsin Electric Power Company; Wisconsin Public Service Corporation; PMC, Inc.; Klauser Corporation; Robert Orr - Sysco Food Distribution Company; Hinds - Bock Corporation; Wisconsin Power & Light Company; American Suzuki Motor Corp.; KAYU - TV.

For Complete List of Firm Personnel, See General Section

For full biographical listings, see the Martindale-Hubbell Law Directory

Lane Powell Spears Lubersky (AV)

A Partnership including Professional Corporations
1420 Fifth Avenue, Suite 4100, 98101-2338
Telephone: 206-223-7000
Cable Address: "Embe"
Telex: 32-8808
Telecopier: 206-223-7107
Other Offices at: Mount Vernon and Olympia, Washington; Los Angeles and San Francisco, California; Anchorage, Alaska; Portland, Oregon; London, England.

MEMBERS OF FIRM

D. Wayne Gittinger
Richard C. Siefert
James L. Robart
Larry S. Gangnes (P.S.)

OF COUNSEL

John R. Tomlinson

Representative Clients: Cavenham Forest Industries Division of Hanson, PLC; Cedar Shake & Shingle Bureau; Coca-Cola Bottling Co. of Yakima & Tri-Cities; Fred Hutchinson Cancer Research Center; Mitsui & Co., Ltd.; Nordstrom, Inc.; Simpson Investment Co. and Affiliates; Texaco, Inc.

For Complete List of Firm Personnel, See General Section

For full biographical listings, see the Martindale-Hubbell Law Directory

Perkins Coie (AV)

A Law Partnership including Professional Corporations
Strategic Alliance with Russell & DuMoulin
1201 Third Avenue, 40th Floor, 98101-3099
Telephone: 206-583-8888
Facsimile: 206-583-8500
Cable Address: "Perki ns Seattle."
Telex: 32-0319 PERKINS SEA
Anchorage, Alaska Office: 1029 West Third Avenue, Suite 300.
Telephone: 907-279-8561.
Facsimile: 907-276-3108.
Telex: 32-0319 PERKINS SEA.
Los Angeles, California Office: 1999 Avenue of the Stars, Ninth Floor.
Telephone: 310-788-9900.
Telex: 32-0319 PERKINS SEA.
Facsimile: 310-788-3399.
Washington, D.C. Office: 607 Fourteenth Street, N.W.
Telephone: 202-628-6600.
Facsimile: 202-434-1690.
Telex: 44-0277 PCSO.
Portland, Oregon Office: U.S. Bancorp Tower, Suite 2500, 111 S.W. Fifth Avenue.
Telephone: 503-295-4400.
Facsimile: 503-295-6793.
Telex: 32-0319 PERKINS SEA.
Bellevue, Washington Office: Suite 1800, One Bellevue Center, 411 - 108th Avenue N.E.
Telephone: 206-453-6980.
Facsimile: 206-453-7350.
Telex: 32-0319 PERKINS SEA.
Spokane, Washington Office: North 221 Wall Street, Suite 600.
Telephone: 509-624-2212.
Facsimile: 509-458-3399.
Telex: 32-0319 PERKINS SEA.
Olympia, Washington Office: 1110 Capitol Way South, Suite 405.
Telephone: 206-956-3300.

(See Next Column)

PERKINS COIE—*Continued*

Strategic Alliance with Russell & DuMoulin, 1700-1075 West Georgia Street, Vancouver, B.C. V6E 3G2. Telephone: 604-631-3131.
Hong Kong Office: 23rd Floor Asia Pacific Finance Tower, Citibank Plaza, 3 Garden Road.
Telephone: 852-2878-1177.
Facsimile: 852-2524-9988. DX-9230-IC.
London, England Office: 36/38 Cornhill, ECV3 3ND.
Telephone: 071-369-9966.
Facsimile: 071-369-9968.
Taipei, Taiwan Office: 8/F TFIT Tower, 85 Jen AiRoad, Sec. 4,Taipei 106, Taiwan, R.O.C.
Telephone: 886-2-778-1177.
Facsimile: 086-2-777-9898.

PARTNERS/SHAREHOLDERS

Richard L. Baum
Thomas L. Boeder
David J. Burman
Ronald M. Gould
Ramer B. Holtan, Jr.

Counsel for: The Boeing Company; Puget Sound Power & Light Company; Alaska Air Group, Inc.; Bristol-Myers Company (Genetic Systems Corporation); Seven Gables Corporation; SmithKline Beckman; Westmark International, Inc.; Weyerhaeuser Company; Advanced Technologies Laboratories; Landmark Theatre Corporation.

For Complete List of Firm Personnel, See General Section

For full biographical listings, see the Martindale-Hubbell Law Directory

STOKES, EITELBACH & LAWRENCE, P.S. (AV)

800 Fifth Avenue, Suite 4000, 98104-3199
Telephone: 206-626-6000
Fax: 206-464-1496

Byron E. Springer, Jr.
Robert Stokes, Jr.

For full biographical listings, see the Martindale-Hubbell Law Directory

WILLIAMS, KASTNER & GIBBS (AV)

4100 Two Union Square, 601 Union Street, P.O. Box 21926, 98111-3926
Telephone: 206-628-6600
Fax: 206-628-6611
Bellevue, Washington Office: 2000 Skyline Tower, 10900 N.E. Fourth Street, P.O. Box 1800, 98004-5841.
Telephone: 206-462-4700.
Fax: 206-451-0714.
Tacoma, Washington Office: 1000 Financial Center, 1145 Broadway, 98402-3502.
Telephone: 206-593-5620; Seattle: 628-2420.
Fax: 206-593-5625.
Vancouver, Washington Office: First Independent Place, 1220 Main Street, Suite 510.
Telephone: 206-696-0248.
Fax: 206-696-2051.

MEMBERS OF FIRM

Peter E. Peterson (Resident Partner, Bellevue Office)
P. Arley Harrel
Jerry B. Edmonds

OF COUNSEL

DeWitt Williams

Representative Clients: Aetna Casulaty & Surety Co.; Atlantic-Richfield Co.; CIGNA; CNA Insurance; Continental Can Company, Inc.; Cushman & Wakefield of Washington, Inc.; General Motors Acceptance Corp.; Loomis Armored, Inc.; Mayne Nickless Incorporated; UNICO Properties, Inc.

For Complete List of Firm Personnel, See General Section

For full biographical listings, see the Martindale-Hubbell Law Directory

WEST VIRGINIA

*CHARLESTON,** Kanawha Co.

JACKSON & KELLY (AV)

1600 Laidley Tower, P.O. Box 553, 25322
Telephone: 304-340-1000
Fax: 304-340-1130
Martinsburg, West Virginia Office: 300 Foxcroft Avenue, P.O. Box 1068.
Telephone: 304-263-8800.
Morgantown, West Virginia Office: 6000 Hampton Center, P.O. Box 619.
Telephone: 304-599-3000.
New Martinsville, West Virginia Office: 256 Russell Avenue, P.O. Box 68.
Telephone: 304-455-1751.
Charles Town, West Virginia Office: 700 East Washington Street, P.O. Box 983.
Telephone: 304-728-6088.
Clarksburg, West Virginia Office: 203 Main Street, P.O. Box 1587.
Telephone: 304-623-3002.

(See Next Column)

Lexington, Kentucky Office: 175 East Main Street, Suite 500, P.O. Box 2150.
Telephone: 606-255-9500.
Washington, D. C. Office: 2401 Pennsylvania Avenue, N.W., Suite 400.
Telephone: 202-973-0200.
Denver, Colorado Office: Suite 2710, 1660 Lincoln Street.
Telephone: 303-837-0003.

MEMBERS OF FIRM

James Knight Brown
James R. Snyder
David Allen Barnette

For Complete List of Firm Personnel, See General Section

For full biographical listings, see the Martindale-Hubbell Law Directory

*MORGANTOWN,** Monongalia Co.

FUSCO & NEWBRAUGH (AV)

2400 Cranberry Square, 26505-9209
Telephone: 304-594-1000
Telecopier: 304-594-1181

Andrew G. Fusco
Thomas H. Newbraugh

Representative Clients: Mylan Pharmaceuticals, Inc.
Reference: One Valley Bank.

For Complete List of Firm Personnel, See General Section

For full biographical listings, see the Martindale-Hubbell Law Directory

WISCONSIN

*MILWAUKEE,** Milwaukee Co.

FOLEY & LARDNER (AV)

Firstar Center, 777 East Wisconsin Avenue, 53202-5367
Telephone: 414-271-2400
Telex: 26-819 (Foley Lard Mil)
Facsimile: 414-297-4900
Madison, Wisconsin Office: 150 E. Gilman Street, P.O. Box 1497.
Telephone: 608-257-5035.
Facsimile: 608-258-4258.
Chicago, Illinois Office: Suite 3300, One IBM Plaza, 330 N. Wabash Avenue.
Telephone: 312-755-1900.
Facsimile: 312-755-1925.
Washington, D.C. Office: Washington Harbour, Suite 500, 3000 K Street, N.W.
Telephone: 202-672-5300.
Telex: 904136 (Foley Lard Wash).
Facsimile: 202-672-5399.
Annapolis, Maryland Office: Suite 102, 175 Admiral Cochrane Drive.
Telephone: 301-266-8077.
Telex: 899149 (Oldtownpat).
Facsimile: 301-266-8664.
Jacksonville, Florida Office: The Greenleaf Building, 200 Laura Street. P.O. Box 240.
Telephone: 904-359-2000.
Facsimile: 904-359-8700.
Orlando, Florida Office: Suite 1800, 111 North Orange Avenue, P.O. Box 2193.
Telephone: 407-423-7656.
Telex: 441781 (HQ ORL).
Facsimile: 407-648-1743.
Tallahassee, Florida Office: Suite 450, 215 South Monroe Street, P.O. Box 508.
Telephone: 904-222-6100.
Facsimile: 904-224-0496.
Tampa, Florida Offices: Suite 2700, One Hundred Tampa Street, P.O. Box 3391.
Telephones: 813-229-2300; Pinellas County: 813-442-3296.
Facsimile: 813-221-4210.
West Palm Beach, Florida Office: Suite 200, Phillips Point East Tower, 777 South Flagler Drive.
Telephone: 407-655-5050.
Facsimile: 407-655-6925.

PARTNERS

Russell J. Barron
David E. Beckwith
Ralf-Reinhard Böer
Richard H. Casper
Robert A. DuPuy
Richard S. Florsheim
Howard W. Fogt, Jr. (Washington, D.C. Office)
Maurice J. McSweeney
John S. Skilton (Madison, Wisconsin Office)
Christian G. Steinmetz
Egerton K. van den Berg (Orlando, Florida Office)
Jay N. Varon (Washington, D.C. Office)
Ronald M. Wawrzyn
Edwin P. Wiley

(See Next Column)

FOLEY & LARDNER, *Milwaukee—Continued*

RETIRED PARTNER

James P. Brody

For Complete List of Firm Personnel, See General Section

For full biographical listings, see the Martindale-Hubbell Law Directory

GIBBS, ROPER, LOOTS & WILLIAMS, S.C. (AV)

735 North Water Street, 53202
Telephone: 414-273-7000
Fax: 414-273-7897

William J. French
Robert L. Gegios

For Complete List of Firm Personnel, See General Section

For full biographical listings, see the Martindale-Hubbell Law Directory

KERSTEN & MCKINNON, S.C. (AV)

231 West Wisconsin Avenue, Suite 1200, 53203
Telephone: 414-271-0054
Fax: 414-271-7131

Charles J. Kersten (1925-1972)
J. P. McKinnon (1943-1973)
Arlo McKinnon
E. Campion Kersten
George P. Kersten
Kenan J. Kersten
Dyan Evans Barbeau
Leslie Van Buskirk
Sheila M. Hanrahan

For full biographical listings, see the Martindale-Hubbell Law Directory

MICHAEL, BEST & FRIEDRICH (AV)

100 East Wisconsin Avenue, 53202-4108
Telephone: 414-271-6560
Telecopier: 414-277-0656
Cable Address: "Mibef"
Madison, Wisconsin Office: One South Pinckney Street, Firstar Plaza, P.O. Box 1806, 53701-1806.
Telephone: 608-257-3501.
Telecopier: 283-2275.
Chicago, Illinois Office: 135 South LaSalle Street, Suite 1610, 60603-4391.
Telephone: 312-845-5800.
Telecopier: 312-845-5828.
Affiliated Law Firm: Edward D. Heffernan, Penthouse One, 1019 19th Street, N.W., Washington, D.C. 20036.
Telephone: 202-331-7444.

PARTNERS

John K. MacIver
John J. McHugh (Resident Partner, Chicago, Illinois Office)
Rickard T. O'Neil
David J. Hanson (Resident Partner, Madison, Wisconsin Office)
David V. Meany
John E. Noel (Resident Partner, Chicago, Illinois Office)

For Complete List of Firm Personnel, See General Section

For full biographical listings, see the Martindale-Hubbell Law Directory

QUARLES & BRADY (AV)

411 East Wisconsin Avenue, 53202-4497
Telephone: 414-277-5000
Cable Address: "Lawdock"
Fax: 414-271-3552.
TWX: 910-262-3426
Madison, Wisconsin Office: Firstar Plaza, One South Pinckney Street, P.O. Box 2113.
Telephone: 608-251-5000.
Fax: 608-251-9166.
West Palm Beach, Florida Office: 222 Lakeview Avenue, 4th Floor.
Telephone: 407-653-5000.
Fax: 407-653-5333.
Naples, Florida Office: Barnett Center, 4501 Tamiami Trail North.
Telephone: 813-262-5959.
Fax: 813-434-4999.
Phoenix, Arizona Office: One Camelback Building, One East Camelback Road, Suite 400.
Telephone: 602-230-5500.
Fax: 602-230-5598.

MEMBERS OF FIRM
(ALPHABETICALLY BY YEAR OF ADMISSION TO BAR)

Harry G. Holz
Thomas W. Ehrmann
Samuel J. Recht
Michael L. Zaleski (Resident, Madison Office)
Wayne E. Babler, Jr.
Peter C. Karegeannes
Quinn W. Martin
Darryl S. Bell
Michael H. Schaalman

OF COUNSEL

Elwin J. Zarwell
William A. Stearns

ASSOCIATE

Deborah L. Skurulsky

For Complete List of Firm Personnel, See General Section

For full biographical listings, see the Martindale-Hubbell Law Directory

PUERTO RICO

SAN JUAN, San Juan Dist.

FIDDLER, GONZÁLEZ & RODRÍGUEZ

Chase Manhattan Bank Building (Hato Rey), P.O. Box 363507, 00936-3507
Telephone: 809-753-3113
Telecopier: 809-759-3123

MEMBERS OF FIRM

Salvador Antonetti-Zequeira
Diego A. Ramos

Representative Clients: The Chase Manhattan Bank, N.A.; Kodak Caribbean Ltd.; Westinghouse Electric Corp.; Pfizer, Inc.; Merck & Co., Inc.; American Cyanamid Co.; Metropolitan Life Insurance Co.; Bacardi Corp.

For Complete List of Firm Personnel, See General Section

For full biographical listings, see the Martindale-Hubbell Law Directory

JORGE R. JIMENEZ

Suite 807 Bankers Finance Tower, 654 Muñoz Rivera Avenue (Hato Rey), 00918
Telephone: 809-763-0106
Fax: 809-763-0574

For full biographical listings, see the Martindale-Hubbell Law Directory

CANADA BRITISH COLUMBIA

*VANCOUVER,** Vancouver Co.

RUSSELL & DUMOULIN (AV)

2100-1075 West Georgia Street, V6E 3G2
Telephone: 604-631-3131
Fax: 604-631-3232
A Member of the national association of Borden DuMoulin Howard Gervais, comprising Russell & DuMoulin, Vancouver, British Columbia; Howard Mackie, Calgary, Alberta; Borden & Elliot, Toronto, Ontario; Mackenzie Gervais, Montreal, Quebec and Borden DuMoulin Howard Gervais, London, England.
Strategic Alliance with Perkins Coie with offices in Seattle, Spokane and Bellevue, Washington; Portland, Oregon; Anchorage, Alaska; Los Angeles, California; Washington, D.C.; Hong Kong and Taipei, Taiwan.
Represented in Hong Kong by Vincent T.K. Cheung, Yap & Co.

MEMBER OF FIRM

Charles F. Willms

Representative Clients: Alcan Smelters & Chemicals Ltd.; The Bank of Nova Scotia; Canada Trust Co.; The Canada Life Assurance Co.; Forest Industrial Relations Ltd.; Honda Canada Inc.; IBM Canada Ltd.; Macmillan Bloedel Ltd.; Nissho Iwai Canada Ltd.; The Toronto-Dominion Bank.

For Complete List of Firm Personnel, See General Section

For full biographical listings, see the Martindale-Hubbell Law Directory

CANADA ONTARIO

*TORONTO,** Regional Munic. of York

BORDEN & ELLIOT (AV)

Barristers & Solicitors
Scotia Plaza, 40 King Street West, M5H 3Y4
Telephone: 416-367-6000
Telecopier: 416-367-6749
Internet: @ borden.com
A Member of the national association of Borden DuMoulin Howard Gervais, comprising Borden & Elliot in Toronto, Ontario, Russell & DuMoulin in Vancouver, British Columbia, Howard, Mackie in Calgary, Alberta and Mackenzie Gervais in Montréal, Québec. Borden DuMoulin Howard Gervais also operates an office in London, England.

BORDEN & ELLIOT—*Continued*

MEMBER AND ASSOCIATES

Simon B. Scott, Q.C.

For Complete List of Firm Personnel, See General Section

For full biographical listings, see the Martindale-Hubbell Law Directory

APPELLATE PRACTICE

ALABAMA

*BIRMINGHAM,** Jefferson Co.

PATRICK & LACY, P.C. (AV)

1201 Financial Center, 35203
Telephone: 205-323-5665
Telecopier: 205-324-6221

J. Vernon Patrick, Jr.
Alex S. Lacy
William M. Acker, III
Elizabeth N. Pitman
Joseph A. Cartee

For full biographical listings, see the Martindale-Hubbell Law Directory

*HUNTSVILLE,** Madison Co.

WATSON, GAMMONS & FEES, P.C. (AV)

200 Clinton Avenue, N.W., Suite 800, P.O. Box 46, 35804
Telephone: 205-536-7423
Telecopier: 205-536-2689

Herman Watson, Jr.
Robert C. Gammons
Michael L. Fees
Joseph A. Jimmerson
J. Barton Warren
Charles H. Pullen
Billie B. Line, Jr.

OF COUNSEL

George K. Williams

LEGAL SUPPORT PERSONNEL

James W. Lowery, Jr. (Administrator)

For full biographical listings, see the Martindale-Hubbell Law Directory

*MOBILE,** Mobile Co.

LYONS, PIPES & COOK, P.C. (AV)

2 North Royal Street, P.O. Box 2727, 36652-2727
Telephone: 334-432-4481
Cable Address: "Lysea"
Telecopier: 334-433-1820

Joseph H. Lyons (1874-1957)
Sam W. Pipes, III (1916-1982)
Walter M. Cook (1915-1988)
G. Sage Lyons
Wesley Pipes
Norton W. Brooker, Jr.
Cooper C. Thurber
Marion A. Quina, Jr.
Thomas F. Garth
Claude D. Boone
Walter M. Cook, Jr.
John Patrick Courtney, III
Reggie Copeland, Jr.
Charles L. Miller, Jr.
W. David Johnson, Jr.
Joseph J. Minus, Jr.
Caroline C. McCarthy
William E. Shreve, Jr.
R. Mark Kirkpatrick
Kenneth A. Nixon
Dan S. Cushing
Allen E. Graham
Michael C. Niemeyer
John C. Bell
Richard D. Morrison
M. Warren Butler
Christopher Lee George

General Counsel: Inchcape Shipping Services.
Counsel: The Hertz Corp.; McKenzie Tank Lines, Inc.; SCNO Barge Lines, Inc.; Scott Paper Co.; Shell Oil Corp.
Trial Counsel: Aetna Life & Casualty Co.; Chubb Group of Insurance Companies.

For full biographical listings, see the Martindale-Hubbell Law Directory

PIERCE, CARR & ALFORD, P.C. (AV)

Suite 900 Montlimar Place Office Building, 1110 Montlimar Drive, P.O. Box 16046, 36616
Telephone: 334-344-5151
FAX: 334-344-9696

Donald F. Pierce
Davis Carr
Helen Johnson Alford
Goodman G. Ledyard
Forrest S. Latta
H. William Wasden
Andrew C. Clausen

James W. Lampkin II
John Chas. S. Pierce
Pamela Kirkwood Millsaps
Mignon Mestayer DeLashmet
Rachel D. Sanders
C. William Daniels, Jr.

Representative Clients: Grove Worldwide; Beloit Corp.; Koehring Cranes & Excavators; Winnebago; Toyota Motor Sales Corp.; Blue Cross and Blue Shield; Charter Medical Corp.; Connecticut Mutual Life Ins. Co.; Nationwide Insurance Cos.

(See Next Column)

For full biographical listings, see the Martindale-Hubbell Law Directory

*MONTGOMERY,** Montgomery Co.

CAPOUANO, WAMPOLD, PRESTWOOD & SANSONE, P.A. (AV)

350 Adams Avenue, P.O. Box 1910, 36102-1910
Telephone: 334-264-6401
Fax: 334-834-4954

Leon M. Capouano
Alvin T. Prestwood
Jerome D. Smith
Ellis D. Hanan
Joseph P. Borg
Joseph W. Warren

OF COUNSEL

Charles H. Wampold, Jr.

Thomas B. Klinner
Linda Smith Webb
James M. Sizemore, Jr.

Counsel for: First Alabama Bank of Montgomery, N.A.; Union Bank and Trust Co.; Real Estate Financing, Inc.; SouthTrust Bank; AmSouth Bank; Central Bank; City Federal Savings & Loan Assoc.; Colonial Mortgage Co.; Lomas & Nettleton; First Bank of Linden.

For full biographical listings, see the Martindale-Hubbell Law Directory

ARIZONA

*PHOENIX,** Maricopa Co.

BROWN & BAIN, A PROFESSIONAL ASSOCIATION (AV)

2901 North Central Avenue, P.O. Box 400, 85001-0400
Telephone: 602-351-8000
Cable: TWX 910-951-0646
Telecopier: 602-351-8516
Palo Alto, California Affiliated Office: Brown & Bain, 600 Hansen Way.
Telephone: 415-856-9411.
Telecopier: 415-856-6061.
Tucson, Arizona Affiliated Office: Brown & Bain, A Professional Association. One South Church Avenue, Nineteenth Floor, P.O. Box 2265.
Telephone: 602-798-7900
Telecopier: 602-798-7945.

C. Randall Bain
Alan H. Blankenheimer
Paul F. Eckstein
Jodi Knobel Feuerhelm
Joel W. Nomkin
Lawrence G. D. Scarborough

For Complete List of Firm Personnel, See General Section

For full biographical listings, see the Martindale-Hubbell Law Directory

BURCH & CRACCHIOLO, P.A. (AV)

702 East Osborn Road, Suite 200, 85014
Telephone: 602-274-7611
Fax: 602-234-0341
Mailing Address: P.O. Box 16882, Phoenix, AZ, 85011

Daniel Cracchiolo
Jack D. Klausner
Daryl Manhart
Daniel R. Malinski

Marigene Abbott-Dessaint
J. Brent Welker

Representative Clients: Bashas' Inc.; Farmers Insurance Group; U-Haul International, Inc.

For Complete List of Firm Personnel, See General Section

For full biographical listings, see the Martindale-Hubbell Law Directory

CALIFORNIA

COSTA MESA, Orange Co.

COULOMBE KOTTKE & KING, A PROFESSIONAL CORPORATION (AV)

Comerica Bank Tower, 611 Anton Boulevard, Suite 1260, P.O. Box 2410, 92628-2410
Telephone: 714-540-1234
Fax: 714-754-0808; 714-754-0707

Ronald B. Coulombe
Jon S. Kottke
Raymond King

COUNSEL

Mary J. Swanson
Roy B. Woolsey

(See Next Column)

COULOMBE KOTTKE & KING A PROFESSIONAL CORPORATION, *Costa Mesa—Continued*

LEGAL SUPPORT PERSONNEL

PARALEGALS

Karen M. Carrillo
Laura A. Bieser
Vicky M. Pearson

LEGAL ADMINISTRATOR

Sheila O. Elpern

For full biographical listings, see the Martindale-Hubbell Law Directory

ENCINO, Los Angeles Co.

ALLAN F. GROSSMAN (AV)

Suite 304 Encino Law Center, 15915 Ventura Boulevard, 91436
Telephone: 818-990-8200
FAX: 818-990-4616

Reference: First Los Angeles Bank, Woodland Hills.

For full biographical listings, see the Martindale-Hubbell Law Directory

*LOS ANGELES,** Los Angeles Co.

DANIELS, BARATTA & FINE (AV)

A Partnership including a Professional Corporation
1801 Century Park East, 9th Floor, 90067
Telephone: 310-556-7900
Telecopier: 310-556-2807

MEMBERS OF FIRM

John P. Daniels (Inc.)
James M. Baratta
Paul R. Fine
Nathan B. Hoffman
Mary Hulett
Michael B. Geibel
James I. Montgomery, Jr.
Lance D. Orloff
Mark R. Israel

ASSOCIATES

Deborah Kaplan Galer
Ilene Wendy Nebenzahl
Heidi Susan Hart
Janet Sacks
Michael N. Schonbuch
Linda A. Schweitz
Christine S. Chu
Glenn T. Rosenblatt
Scott M. Leavitt
Karen Ann Holloway
Mark A. Vega
Patricio Esquivel
Robert B. Gibson
Brett S. Markson
Michelle R. Press
Scott Ashford Brooks
Craig A. Laidig
Paul E. Blevins
Joan T. Lind
Rodi F. Rispone
Stephanie J. Berman
Michelle C. Hopkins
Robin A. Webb
Ronda Lynn Crowley
Scott A. Spungin
Theodore L. Wilson
Daniel Joseph Kolodziej
Craig Momita
Spencer A. Schneider
Angelo A. DuPlantier, III

OF COUNSEL

Timothy J. Hughes
Drew T. Hanker

For full biographical listings, see the Martindale-Hubbell Law Directory

HORNBERGER & CRISWELL (AV)

444 South Flower, 31st Floor, 90071
Telephone: 213-488-1655
Facsimile: 213-488-1255

MEMBERS OF FIRM

Nicholas W. Hornberger
Leslie E. Criswell
Carla J. Feldman
Ann M. Ghazarians
Michael A. Brewer

ASSOCIATES

Scott Alan Freedman
Marlin E. Howes
Christopher T. Olsen
Scott B. Cloud
Celeste S. Makuta
John Shaffery
Charles I. Karlin
K. Christopher Branch
David F. Berry
James M. Slominski
Gina T. Sponzilli

For full biographical listings, see the Martindale-Hubbell Law Directory

EDWARD J. HOROWITZ A PROFESSIONAL CORPORATION (AV)

Suite 1015, 11661 San Vicente Boulevard, 90049
Telephone: 310-826-6619
FAX: 310-826-8242

Edward J. Horowitz

Reference: Union Bank (Brentwood Branch).

For full biographical listings, see the Martindale-Hubbell Law Directory

HORVITZ & LEVY (AV)

A Partnership including Professional Corporations
18th Floor, 15760 Ventura Boulevard (Encino), 91436
Telephone: 818-995-0800; 213-872-0802
FAX: 818-995-3157

(See Next Column)

Ellis J. Horvitz (A P.C.)
Barry R. Levy (A P.C.)
Peter Abrahams
David M. Axelrad
Frederic D. Cohen
S. Thomas Todd
David S. Ettinger
Daniel J. Gonzalez
Mitchell C. Tilner
Christina J. Imre
Lisa Perrochet
Stephen E. Norris
Sandra J. Smith

Mary F. Dant
Ari R. Kleiman
Lisa R. Jaskol
Julie L. Woods
Holly R. Paul
H. Thomas Watson
John A. Taylor, Jr.
Annette E. Davis
Andrea M. Gauthier
Elizabeth Skorcz Anthony
Christine A. Pagac (Not admitted in CA)
Gary T. Gleb
Bruce Adelstein

Reference: Bank of California (Pasadena, California Office).

For full biographical listings, see the Martindale-Hubbell Law Directory

HUFSTEDLER & KAUS (AV)

A Partnership including Professional Corporations
Thirty-Ninth Floor, 355 South Grand Avenue, 90071-3101
Telephone: 213-617-7070
Fax: 213-617-6170

MEMBERS OF FIRM

Seth M. Hufstedler (Professional Corporation)
Shirley M. Hufstedler (Professional Corporation)
Otto M. Kaus
John Sobieski

For Complete List of Firm Personnel, See General Section

For full biographical listings, see the Martindale-Hubbell Law Directory

LANGBERG, LESLIE & GABRIEL (AV)

An Association including a Professional Corporation
2049 Century Park East Suite 3030, 90067
Telephone: 310-286-7700
Telecopier: 310-284-8355

Barry B. Langberg (A Professional Corporation)
Jody R. Leslie
Joseph M. Gabriel

Eileen M. Cohn
Deborah Drooz
Richard J. Wynne
Beatrice L. Hoffman
Michael M. Baranov
Beth F. Dumas
Dwayne A. Watts
Mitchell J. Langberg

LEGAL SUPPORT PERSONNEL

PARALEGALS

Patricia Urban
Patricia Ann Essig
Jeanne A. Logé

For full biographical listings, see the Martindale-Hubbell Law Directory

LOEB AND LOEB (AV)

A Partnership including Professional Corporations
Suite 1800, 1000 Wilshire Boulevard, 90017-2475
Telephone: 213-688-3400
Telecopier: 213-688-3460; 688-3461; 688-3462
Century City, California Office: Suite 2200, 10100 Santa Monica Boulevard, Los Angeles, 90067-4164.
Telephone: 310-282-2000.
Telecopier: 310-282-2191; 282-2192.
New York, N.Y. Office: 345 Park Avenue, 10154-0037.
Telephone: 212-407-4000.
Facsimile: 212-407-4990.
Nashville, Tennessee Office: 45 Music Square West, 37203-3205.
Telephone: 615-749-8300;
Facsimile: 615-749-8308.
Rome, Italy Office: Piazza Digione 1, 00197.
Telephone: 011-396-808-8456.
Telecopier: 011-396-674-8223.

MEMBERS OF FIRM

Howard I. Friedman (A P.C.)
Andrew S. Garb (A P.C.)
Jeffrey M. Loeb

For Complete List of Firm Personnel, See General Section

For full biographical listings, see the Martindale-Hubbell Law Directory

NEUMEYER & BOYD (AV)

2029 Century Park East, Suite 1100, 90067
Telephone: 310-553-9393
Fax: 310-553-8437

MEMBERS OF FIRM

Richard A. Neumeyer
Carol Boyd

(See Next Column)

NEUMEYER & BOYD—*Continued*

ASSOCIATES

Lydia E. Hachmeister
Jeffrey B. Lehrman
Katherine Tatikian
Susie J. Kater
Daniel F. Sanchez

OF COUNSEL

Steven A. Freeman

For full biographical listings, see the Martindale-Hubbell Law Directory

QUINN, KULLY AND MORROW, A PROFESSIONAL LAW CORPORATION (AV)

Eighth Floor 520 South Grand Avenue, 90071
Telephone: 213-622-0300
Telecopier: 213-622-3799

John J. Quinn
J. David Oswalt
Russel I. Kully
Lawrence A. Cox
Margaret M. Morrow
Polly Horn
Richard C. Smith
Eric L. Dobberteen
Laurence J. Hutt
David S. Eisen
Gregory C. Fant
James I. Ham
Julie M. Ward

Martha Jeannette Clark
Brian K. Condon
Patricia A. Libby
Claire M. Corcoran
Michael H. Walizer
Sharon L. Douglass
D. Jay Ritt
Janine M. Watkins
Kerry R. Bensinger
Tracy E. Loomis
James D. Layden
Kelley P. Potter

OF COUNSEL

Craig N. Hentschel
Lisa S. Kantor

For full biographical listings, see the Martindale-Hubbell Law Directory

NEWPORT BEACH, Orange Co.

JOHN C. LAUTSCH A PROFESSIONAL CORPORATION (AV)

4220 Von Karman, Suite 120, 92660
Telephone: 714-955-9095
Telefax: 714-955-2978

John C. Lautsch

Kurt E. English

For full biographical listings, see the Martindale-Hubbell Law Directory

*SACRAMENTO,** Sacramento Co.

EISEN & JOHNSTON (AV)

980 Ninth Street, Suite 1400, P.O. Box 111, 95812-0111
Telephone: 916-444-6171
Fax: 916-441-5810

MEMBERS OF FIRM

Jay-Allen Eisen
Marian M. Johnston
Ann Perrin Farina

For full biographical listings, see the Martindale-Hubbell Law Directory

HANSEN, BOYD, CULHANE & WATSON (AV)

A Partnership including Professional Corporations
Central City Centre, 1331 Twenty-First Street, 95814
Telephone: 916-444-2550
Telecopier: 916-444-2358

Hartley T. Hansen (Inc.)
Lawrence R. Watson
Kevin R. Culhane (Inc.)
John J. Rueda
David E. Boyd
James J. Banks

OF COUNSEL

Betsy S. Kimball

Lorraine M. Pavlovich
D. Jeffery Grimes
Thomas L. Riordan
Joseph Zuber
James O. Moses

For full biographical listings, see the Martindale-Hubbell Law Directory

*SAN FRANCISCO,** San Francisco Co.

LAW OFFICES OF ELLIOT L. BIEN (AV)

Mills Building, 220 Montgomery Street Tower Suite 1210, 94104
Telephone: 415-291-0300
Fax: 415-291-0409

For full biographical listings, see the Martindale-Hubbell Law Directory

LAW OFFICES OF EPHRAIM MARGOLIN (AV)

Suite 300, 240 Stockton Street, 94108
Telephone: 415-421-4347
Fax: 415-397-9801

ASSOCIATES

Bradford L. Battson
Barry Helft

For full biographical listings, see the Martindale-Hubbell Law Directory

ROSEN, BIEN & ASARO (AV)

Eighth Floor, 155 Montgomery Street, 94104
Telephone: 415-433-6830
Fax: 415-433-7104

Sanford Jay Rosen
Michael W. Bien
Andrea G. Asaro

Stephen M. Liacouras
Mary Ann Cryan (Not admitted in CA)
Hilary A. Fox
Thomas Nolan
Donna Petrine

For full biographical listings, see the Martindale-Hubbell Law Directory

SPIEGEL LIAO & KAGAY (AV)

88 Kearny Street, Suite 1310, 94108-5530
Telephone: 415-956-5959
Telecopier: 415-362-1431

Michael I. Spiegel
Charles M. Kagay

OF COUNSEL

Bartholomew Lee
Wayne M. Liao

For full biographical listings, see the Martindale-Hubbell Law Directory

SANTA MONICA, Los Angeles Co.

O'NEILL, LYSAGHT & SUN (AV)

A Partnership including Professional Corporations
100 Wilshire Boulevard, Suite 700, 90401
Telephone: 310-451-5700
Telecopier: 310-399-7201

Brian O'Neill (A Professional Corporation)
Frederick D. Friedman
Brian A. Sun
Brian C. Lysaght (A Professional Corporation)
Yolanda Orozco
John M. Moscarino

Harriet Beegun Leva
J. Andrew Coombs
David E. Rosen
Ellyn S. Garofalo
Lisa Newman Tucker
Edward A. Klein
Robert L. Meylan

OF COUNSEL

J. Joseph Connolly
Arn H. Tellem (P.C.)

Reference: Santa Monica Bank, Santa Monica.

For full biographical listings, see the Martindale-Hubbell Law Directory

A. MARCO TURK LAW CORPORATION (AV)

2118 Wilshire Boulevard Suite 750, 90403
Telephone: 310-829-6910
Fax: 310-829-7910

A. Marco Turk

For full biographical listings, see the Martindale-Hubbell Law Directory

*VENTURA,** Ventura Co.

LASCHER & LASCHER, A PROFESSIONAL CORPORATION (AV)

605 Poli Street, P.O. Box 25540, 93002
Telephone: 805-648-3228
Fax: 805-643-7692

Edward L. Lascher (1928-1991)
Wendy Cole Lascher

Gabriele Mezger-Lashly

Reference: First National Bank of Ventura.

For full biographical listings, see the Martindale-Hubbell Law Directory

COLORADO

*ASPEN,** Pitkin Co.

AUSTIN, PEIRCE & SMITH, P.C. (AV)

Suite 205, 600 East Hopkins Avenue, 81611
Telephone: 303-925-2600
FAX: 303-925-4720

Ronald D. Austin
Frederick F. Peirce
Thomas Fenton Smith

Rhonda J. Bazil

Counsel for: Clark's Market; Coates, Reid & Waldron Realtors; Crystal Palace Corp.; Snowmass Shopping Center; Coldwell Banker; William Poss & Assoc., Architects; Snowmass Resort Association; Real Estate Affiliates, Inc.; Raleigh Enterprises.

For full biographical listings, see the Martindale-Hubbell Law Directory

*DENVER,** Denver Co.

REES & ASSOCIATES, P.C. (AV)

1675 Broadway, Suite 1400, 80202
Telephone: 303-592-5392
Fax: 303-892-3882

David K. Rees

For full biographical listings, see the Martindale-Hubbell Law Directory

REIMAN & ASSOCIATES, P.C. (AV)

1600 Broadway, Suite 1640, 80202
Telephone: 303-860-1500
Fax: 303-839-4380

Jeffrey Reiman

Marcie K. Bayaz
James Birch

For full biographical listings, see the Martindale-Hubbell Law Directory

CONNECTICUT

DANBURY, Fairfield Co.

SECOR, CASSIDY & MCPARTLAND, P.C. (AV)

301 Main Street, 06810
Telephone: 203-743-9145
Fax: 203-798-9844
Waterbury, Connecticut Office: 41 Church Street, P.O. Box 2818.
Telephone: 203-757-9261.
Fax: 203-756-5762.
Southbury, Connecticut Office: 370 Main Street South.
Telephone: 203-264-8223.
Fax: 203-264-6730.

Martin A. Rader, Jr.
Daniel E. Casagrande
Richard D. Arconti
Robin Edwards Otto
Kim E. Nolan (Resident)

For full biographical listings, see the Martindale-Hubbell Law Directory

*HARTFORD,** Hartford Co.

SOROKIN SOROKIN GROSS HYDE & WILLIAMS P.C. (AV)

One Corporate Center, 06103
Telephone: 203-525-6645
Fax: 203-522-1781
Simsbury, Connecticut Office: 730 Hopmeadow Street.
Telephone: 203-651-9348.
Rocky Hill, Connecticut Office: 2360 Main Street.
Telephone: 203-563-9305.
Fax: 203-529-6931.
Glastonbury, Connecticut Office: 124 Hebron Avenue.
Telephone: 203-659-8801.

Clifford J. Grandjean
Lewis Rabinovitz
Richard C. Robinson

Lisa A. Magliochetti

For Complete List of Firm Personnel, See General Section

For full biographical listings, see the Martindale-Hubbell Law Directory

*NEW HAVEN,** New Haven Co.

LAW OFFICES OF JOHN R. WILLIAMS (AV)

51 Elm Street, 06510
Telephone: 203-562-9931
Fax: 203-776-9494

ASSOCIATES

Diane Polan
Norman A. Pattis
Katrena Engstrom
Denise A. Bailey-Garris

Reference: Founders Bank.

For full biographical listings, see the Martindale-Hubbell Law Directory

SOUTHBURY, New Haven Co.

SECOR, CASSIDY & MCPARTLAND, P.C. (AV)

Successors to Bronson, Lewis, Upson & Secor; Lewis, Hart, Upson & Secor; Upson, Secor, Greene & Cassidy and Upson, Secor, Cassidy & McPartland, P.C.
370 Main Street South, 06488
Telephone: 203-264-8223
Fax: 203-264-6730
Waterbury, Connecticut Office: 41 Church Street, P.O. Box 2818.
Telephone: 203-757-9261.
Fax: 203-756-5762.
Danbury, Connecticut Office: 301 Main Street.
Telephone: 203-743-9145.
Fax: 203-798-9844.

James R. Healey

Attorneys for: The Mattatuck Museum; American Republican, Inc.; The Meriden Record Co.; Hubbard-Hall, Inc.; The Siemon Co.; The Romantic Manufacturing Co.; Engineered Sinterings and Plastics, Inc.; Heminway Corp.; Boutin Industries; County Line Buick-Nissan, Inc.

For full biographical listings, see the Martindale-Hubbell Law Directory

WATERBURY, New Haven Co.

SECOR, CASSIDY & MCPARTLAND, P.C. (AV)

Successors to Bronson, Lewis, Upson & Secor; Lewis, Hart, Upson & Secor; Upson, Secor, Greene & Cassidy and Upson, Secor, Cassidy & McPartland, P.C.
41 Church Street, P.O. Box 2818, 06723-2818
Telephone: 203-757-9261
Fax: 203-756-5762
Danbury, Connecticut Office: 301 Main Street.
Telephone: 203-743-9145.
Fax: 203-798-9844.
Southbury, Connecticut Office: 370 Main Street South. Telephon e: 203-264-8223.
Fax: 203-264-6730.

Nath'l R. Bronson (1860-1949)
Lawrence L. Lewis (1881-1965)
Charles E. Hart (1884-1972)
J. Warren Upson (1903-1992)
John H. Cassidy, Jr.
Donald McPartland
W. Fielding Secor
Martin A. Rader, Jr. (Resident at Danbury Office)
James R. Healey
Thomas P. Rush
Gail E. McTaggart
Richard D. Arconti
Thomas G. Parisot
Daniel E. Casagrande
Elizabeth A. Bozzuto
Patrick W. Finn
Robin Edwards Otto
Pamela D. Siemon
Kim E. Nolan (Resident at Danbury Office)
Eric R. Brown

COUNSEL

William J. Secor, Jr.
Charles E. Hart, 3rd (Not admitted in CT)
Milton A. Seymour

Attorneys For: The Mattatuck Museum; American Republican, Inc.; The Meriden Record Co.; Hubbard-Hall, Inc.; The Siemon Co.; The Romantic Manufacturing Company; Engineered Sinterings and Plastics, Inc.; Heminway Corporation; Boutin Industries; County Line Buick-Nissan, Inc.

For full biographical listings, see the Martindale-Hubbell Law Directory

WESTPORT, Fairfield Co.

ANDREW B. BOWMAN (AV)

1804 Post Road East, 06880
Telephone: 203-259-0599
Fax: 203-255-2570
Reference: Peoples Bank.

For full biographical listings, see the Martindale-Hubbell Law Directory

LEVETT, ROCKWOOD & SANDERS, PROFESSIONAL CORPORATION (AV)

33 Riverside Avenue, P.O. Box 5116, 06881
Telephone: 203-222-0885
Telecopier: 203-226-8025

(See Next Column)

LEVETT, ROCKWOOD & SANDERS PROFESSIONAL CORPORATION—*Continued*

David R. Levett
William O. Rockwood, Jr.
John Sanders
Gregory Griffin
Madeleine F. Grossman
Judy A. Rabkin
Dorit Schutzengel Heimer
Sharon M. Schweitzer
Barbara A. Young
Steven M. Siegelaub
Marc J. Kurzman
Suzanne B. Albani
Alfred U. Pavlis
Peter H. Struzzi

OF COUNSEL

John W. Auchincloss, II

Ellen S. Aho
Edward B. Chansky
Margaret H DeSaussure
Cheryl L. Johnson
Ernest C. Mysogland
Robert W. Riordan
Patricia D. Weitzman

Representative Clients: Advantage Health Corporation; Business Express, Inc.; Cannondale Corporation; Caradon, Inc.; Fabrique de Fer de Charleroi (USA), Inc.; Heyman Properties; Hospital of Saint Raphael; Marketing Corporation of America; St. Vincent's Medical Center; Shawmut Bank, N.A.

For full biographical listings, see the Martindale-Hubbell Law Directory

LAW OFFICES OF PAUL J. PACIFICO (AV)

12 Avery Place, Second Floor, 06880
Telephone: 203-221-8066
Fax: 203-221-8076

LEGAL SUPPORT PERSONNEL

Karen L. Kosinski

For full biographical listings, see the Martindale-Hubbell Law Directory

DELAWARE

*WILMINGTON,** New Castle Co.

TYBOUT, REDFEARN & PELL (AV)

Suite 1100, PNC Bank Building, 300 Delaware Avenue, P.O. Box 2092, 19899
Telephone: 302-658-6901
FAX: 658-4018

F. Alton Tybout
B. Wilson Redfearn
Richard W. Pell
Anne L. Naczi
Nancy E. Chrissinger
David G. Culley

ASSOCIATES

Sherry Ruggiero Fallon
Sean A. Dolan
Elizabeth Daniello Maron
Francis X. Nardo
Michael I. Silverman
Bernadette M. Plaza
Joel R. Brown
John J. Klusman, Jr.
Todd M. Finchler

Representative Clients: CIGNA Ins., Co.; Liberty Mutual Ins., Co.; Hartford Ins., Co.; Universal Underwriters; PHICO; State of Delaware; GAB Business Services Inc.; State Farm Ins., Co.; Alliance of American Insurers; Insurance Guarantee Assn.

For full biographical listings, see the Martindale-Hubbell Law Directory

DISTRICT OF COLUMBIA

WASHINGTON, D.C. Co.

*** indicates certain Bar Register subscribers, in cities of comparable size and importance, who maintain an additional office in Washington, D.C. and who have arranged for representation as a part of the Washington, D.C. listings that follow**

*** VENABLE, BAETJER, HOWARD & CIVILETTI (AV)**

A Partnership including Professional Corporations
Suite 1000, 1201 New York Avenue, N.W., 20005
Telephone: 202-962-4800
Fax: 202-962-8300
Baltimore, Maryland Office: Venable, Baetjer and Howard, 1800 Mercantile Bank & Trust Building, 2 Hopkins Plaza.
Telephone: 410-244-7400.
McLean, Virginia Office: Venable, Baetjer and Howard, Suite 400, 2010 Corporate Ridge.
Telephone: 703-760-1600.
Rockville, Maryland Office: Venable, Baetjer and Howard, Suite 500, One Church Street, P. O. Box 1906.
Telephone: 301-217-5600.

(See Next Column)

Towson, Maryland Office: Venable, Baetjer and Howard, 210 Allegheny Avenue, P. O. Box 5517.
Telephone: 410-494-6200.

MEMBERS OF FIRM

Benjamin R. Civiletti (P.C.) (Also at Baltimore and Towson, Maryland Offices)
Thomas J. Madden
Ronald R. Glancz
David J. Levenson
Douglas D. Connah, Jr. (P.C.) (Also at Baltimore, Maryland Office)
Kenneth C. Bass, III (Also at McLean, Virginia Office)
Max Stul Oppenheimer (P.C.) (Also at Baltimore and Towson, Maryland Offices)
Edward F. Glynn, Jr.
Robert G. Ames (Also at Baltimore, Maryland Office)
Michael Schatzow (Also at Baltimore and Towson, Maryland Offices)
N. Frank Wiggins
James K. Archibald (Also at Baltimore and Towson, Maryland Offices)
Judson W. Starr (Also at Baltimore and Towson, Maryland Offices)
James R. Myers
Jeffrey A. Dunn (Also at Baltimore, Maryland Office)
George F. Pappas (Also at Baltimore, Maryland Office)
James L. Shea (Not admitted in DC; also at Baltimore, Maryland Office)
William D. Coston
Maurice Baskin
Amy Berman Jackson
William D. Quarles (Also at Towson, Maryland Office)
James A. Dunbar (Also at Baltimore, Maryland Office)
Mary E. Pivec (Not admitted in DC; Also at Baltimore, Maryland Office)
Thomas J. Kelly, Jr.
Patrick J. Stewart (Also at Baltimore, Maryland Office)
Gary M. Hnath

OF COUNSEL

Geoffrey R. Garinther (Not admitted in DC; Also at Baltimore, Maryland Office)
Fred W. Hathaway

ASSOCIATES

Carla Draluck Craft
Fred Joseph Federici, III
David W. Goewey
Edward Brendan Magrab (Not admitted in DC)
Samuel T. Morison
Traci H. Mundy (Not admitted in DC)
Melissa Landau Steinman (Not admitted in DC)
Paul N. Wengert

For Complete List of Firm Personnel, See General Section

For full biographical listings, see the Martindale-Hubbell Law Directory

FLORIDA

*FORT LAUDERDALE,** Broward Co.

LAW OFFICES OF RICHARD A. SHERMAN, P.A. (AV)

Suite 302, 1777 South Andrews Avenue, 33316
Telephone: 305-525-5885
Miami: 305-940-7557
Miami, Florida Office: Suite 206 Biscayne Building, 19 West Flagler Street.
Telephone: 305-940-7557

Richard A. Sherman

Rosemary B. Wilder

For full biographical listings, see the Martindale-Hubbell Law Directory

*KISSIMMEE,** Osceola Co.

POHL & BROWN, P.A.

(See Winter Park)

*MIAMI,** Dade Co.

BIERMAN, SHOHAT, LOEWY & PERRY, PROFESSIONAL ASSOCIATION (AV)

Penthouse Two, 800 Brickell Avenue, 33131-2944
Telephone: 305-358-7000
Facsimile: 305-358-4010

Donald I. Bierman
Edward R. Shohat
Ira N. Loewy
Pamela I. Perry
Maria C. Beguiristain

Reference: United National Bank of Miami.

For full biographical listings, see the Martindale-Hubbell Law Directory

HICKS, ANDERSON & BLUM, P.A. (AV)

Twenty Fourth Floor, 100 North Biscayne Boulevard, 33132
Telephone: 305-374-8171
Fax: 305-372-8038

(See Next Column)

HICKS, ANDERSON & BLUM P.A., *Miami—Continued*

Mark Hicks
Ralph O. Anderson
Bambi G. Blum

Jean Anne Kneale
Elizabeth M. Moya-Fernandez
Gary A. Magnarini
Gina E. Caruso
Alyssa M. Campbell
Cindy L. Ebenfeld
Matthew S. Nelles

For full biographical listings, see the Martindale-Hubbell Law Directory

PAUL MORRIS PROFESSIONAL ASSOCIATION (AV)

Penthouse II, 2600 Douglas Road (Coral Gables), 33134
Telephone: 305-446-2020
Fax: 305-442-4371

Paul Morris

For full biographical listings, see the Martindale-Hubbell Law Directory

PODHURST, ORSECK, JOSEFSBERG, EATON, MEADOW, OLIN & PERWIN, P.A. (AV)

Suite 800 City National Bank Building, 25 West Flagler Street, 33130-1780
Telephone: 305-358-2800; Fort Lauderdale: 305-463-4346
Fax: 305-358-2382

Joel D. Eaton
Joel S. Perwin

Reference: City National Bank of Miami; United National Bank of Miami.

For Complete List of Firm Personnel, See General Section

For full biographical listings, see the Martindale-Hubbell Law Directory

RICHEY, MUNROE, RODRIGUEZ & DIAZ, P.A. (AV)

3100 First Union Financial Center, 200 South Biscayne Boulevard, 33131-2327
Telephone: 305-372-8808
Telefax: 305-372-3669; 374-4652
Telex: 4932891 RAMPA

Kirk W. Munroe
Juan J. Rodriguez
William L. Richey
Michael Diaz, Jr.

Tamara R. Piety

For full biographical listings, see the Martindale-Hubbell Law Directory

ROBBINS, TUNKEY, ROSS, AMSEL, RABEN & WAXMAN, P.A. (AV)

2250 Southwest Third Avenue, 33129
Telephone: Dade County 305-858-9550; Broward County 305-522-6244
(All Telephones Open 24 Hours)

Frederick S. Robbins
Alan S. Ross
William R. Tunkey
Robert G. Amsel
David Raben

Benjamin S. Waxman
Sylvia A. Thompson
Marco A. Vazquez

Reference: United National Bank, Miami, Florida.

For full biographical listings, see the Martindale-Hubbell Law Directory

RUSSO & TALISMAN, P.A. (AV)

Suite 2001, Terremark Centre, 2601 South Bayshore Drive (Coconut Grove), 33133
Telephone: 305-859-8100
Fax: 305-856-8823

Elizabeth Koebel Russo
Patrice A. Talisman

Edward A. Licitra
Kimberly L. Boldt

For full biographical listings, see the Martindale-Hubbell Law Directory

NORTH MIAMI BEACH, Dade Co.

BECKHAM & BECKHAM, P.A. (AV)

17071 West Dixie Highway, Suite B, 33160
Telephone: DADE: 305-945-1851; BROWARD: 305-920-9793
Fax: 305-940-8706

Pamela Beckham
Eugene G. Beckham
Robert J. Beckham, Jr.

For full biographical listings, see the Martindale-Hubbell Law Directory

*ORLANDO,** Orange Co.

POHL & BROWN, P.A.

(See Winter Park)

ST. PETERSBURG, Pinellas Co.

CARTER, STEIN, SCHAAF & TOWZEY (AV)

270 First Avenue South, Suite 300, 33701-4306
Telephone: 813-894-4333
Fax: 813-894-0175

Victoria Hunt Carter
Gary M. Schaaf
Henry A. Stein
Phyllis J. Towzey

For full biographical listings, see the Martindale-Hubbell Law Directory

*TALLAHASSEE,** Leon Co.

COLLINS & TRUETT, P.A. (AV)

2804 Remington Green Circle, Suite 4, Post Office Drawer 12429, 32317-2429
Telephone: 904-386-6060
Telecopier: 904-385-8220

Richard B. Collins
Gary A. Shipman

Brett Q. Lucas (Resident)
C. Timothy Gray
Dawn D. Caloca
Rogelio Fontela
Joseph E. Brooks
Charles N. Cleland, Jr.
Clifford W. Rainey

OF COUNSEL

Edgar C. Booth
James A. Dixon, Jr.

Representative Clients: Agency Rent-A-Car; Agricultural Excess and Surplus Insurance Co.; AIG Life Insurance Co.; Alliance Insurance Group; Allstate Insurance Co.; American Empire Surplus Lines Insurance Co.; American International Underwriters Inc.; Atlanta Casualty Insurance Co.; Avis Rent-A-Car; Bankers and Shippers Insurance Co.

For full biographical listings, see the Martindale-Hubbell Law Directory

MCFARLAIN, WILEY, CASSEDY & JONES, PROFESSIONAL ASSOCIATION (AV)

215 South Monroe Street, Suite 600, P.O. Box 2174, 32316-2174
Telephone: 904-222-2107
Telecopier: 904-222-8475

Richard C. McFarlain
Charles A. Stampelos
William B. Wiley
Linda McMullen
Marshall R. Cassedy
H. Darrell White, Jr.
Douglas P. Jones
Christopher Barkas

Harold R. Mardenborough, Jr.
Katherine Hairston LaRosa
J. Robert Griffin

OF COUNSEL

Betty J. Steffens

For full biographical listings, see the Martindale-Hubbell Law Directory

RADEY HINKLE THOMAS & MCARTHUR (AV)

Suite 1000 Monroe-Park Tower, 101 North Monroe Street, P.O. Drawer 11307, 32302
Telephone: 904-681-7766
Telecopier: 904-681-0506

John Radey
Robert L. Hinkle
Elizabeth Waas McArthur

Representative Clients: Electronic Data Systems Corp.; Commonwealth Land Title Insurance Co.; State Mutual Life Insurance Company of America; Tampa General Hospital; Columbia/HCA Healthcare Corp.

For Complete List of Firm Personnel, See General Section

For full biographical listings, see the Martindale-Hubbell Law Directory

SLEPIN & SLEPIN (AV)

1114 East Park Avenue, 32301
Telephone: 904-224-5200

Stephen Marc Slepin

OF COUNSEL

Matthew M. Slepin

For full biographical listings, see the Martindale-Hubbell Law Directory

*TAMPA,** Hillsborough Co.

MANEY, DAMSKER, HARRIS & JONES, P.A. (AV)

606 Madison Street, P.O. Box 172009, 33672-0009
Telephone: 813-228-7371
Fax: 813-223-4846

(See Next Column)

MANEY, DAMSKER, HARRIS & JONES P.A.—*Continued*

Lee S. Damsker   David A. Maney

Patricia F. Kuhlman

For full biographical listings, see the Martindale-Hubbell Law Directory

ROBERT P. POLLI (AV)

Barnett Bank Plaza, 101 East Kennedy Boulevard, Suite 3130, 33602
Telephone: 813-222-8350
Fax: Available Upon Request

For full biographical listings, see the Martindale-Hubbell Law Directory

*WEST PALM BEACH,** Palm Beach Co.

RICHARD A. KUPFER, P.A. (AV)

The Forum, Tower C, Suite 810, 1655 Palm Beach Lakes Boulevard, 33401
Telephone: 407-684-8600
FAX: 407-684-8711

Richard A. Kupfer

LEGAL SUPPORT PERSONNEL

Jan M. Setchell

For full biographical listings, see the Martindale-Hubbell Law Directory

WINTER PARK, Orange Co.

POHL & BROWN, P.A. (AV)

280 West Canton Avenue, Suite 410, P.O. Box 3208, 32789
Telephone: 407-647-7645; 407-647-POHL
Telefax: 407-647-2314

Frank L. Pohl   Dwight I. Cool
Usher L. Brown   William W. Pouzar
Houston E. Short   Mary B. Van Leuven

OF COUNSEL

Frederick W. Peirsol

Representative Clients: Orange County Comptroller; Osceola County; School Board of Osceola County, Florida; Osceola Tourist Development Council; NationsBank of Florida, N.A.; SunBank, N.A.; The Bank of Winter Park; Bekins Moving and Storage Co., Inc.; Champion Boats, Inc.; KeyCom Telephone Systems, Inc.

For full biographical listings, see the Martindale-Hubbell Law Directory

GEORGIA

*ATLANTA,** Fulton Co.

SUMNER & HEWES (AV)

Suite 700, The Hurt Building, 50 Hurt Plaza, 30303
Telephone: 404-588-9000

PARTNERS

William E. Sumner   Stephen J. Anderson
Nancy Becker Hewes   David A. Webster

ASSOCIATES

Rosemary Smith   Marguerite Patrick Bryan
Andrew A. Davenport   Michelle Harris Jordan
Edith M. Shine

For full biographical listings, see the Martindale-Hubbell Law Directory

HAWAII

*HONOLULU,** Honolulu Co.

LAW OFFICE OF KENNETH S. ROBBINS ATTORNEY AT LAW, A LAW CORPORATION (AV)

Suite 2220 Davies Pacific Center, 841 Bishop Street, 96813
Telephone: 808-524-2355
Fax: 808-526-0290

Kenneth S. Robbins

Vincent A. Rhodes   Shinken Naitoh

For full biographical listings, see the Martindale-Hubbell Law Directory

IDAHO

*POCATELLO,** Bannock Co.

MERRILL & MERRILL, CHARTERED (AV)

Key Bank Building, P.O. Box 991, 83204
Telephone: 208-232-2286
Fax: 208-232-2499

Wesley F. Merrill   D. Russell Wight
Stephen S. Dunn   N. Randy Smith
David C. Nye

Representative Clients: Farm Bureau Mutual Insurance Co. of Idaho; J.R. Simplot Co.; Fibreboard Corporation; Owens-Illinois, Inc.; Pittsburgh Corning Corporation; Travelers Insurance Co.; E.I. DuPont.

For Complete List of Firm Personnel, See General Section

For full biographical listings, see the Martindale-Hubbell Law Directory

ILLINOIS

*CHICAGO,** Cook Co.

DOWD & DOWD, LTD. (AV)

Suite 1000, 55 West Wacker Drive, 60601
Telephone: 312-704-4400
Telecopier: 312-704-4500

Joseph V. Dowd   Kenneth Gurber
Michael E. Dowd   Robert C. Yelton III
Patrick C. Dowd

S. Robert Depke   Donald G. Machalinski
Robert J. Golden   John M. McAndrews
Kevin J. Kane   Martha A. Niles
Jeffrey Edward Kehl   Michael G. Patrizio
Joseph J. Leonard   Patrick J. Ruberry
Ronald J. Lukes   Anthony R. Rutkowski
Karen W. Worsek

LEGAL SUPPORT PERSONNEL

Carrie J. Julian   Jill A. Weiseman

OF COUNSEL

Guenther Ahlf   Joel S. Ostrow

Reference: Central National Bank in Chicago.

For full biographical listings, see the Martindale-Hubbell Law Directory

DAVID A. NOVOSELSKY & ASSOCIATES (AV)

120 North La Salle Street, Suite 1400, 60602-2401
Telephone: 312-346-8930

Linda A Bryceland   Margarita T. Kulys
Kevin S. Besetzny   Edward Adam Glavinskas

For full biographical listings, see the Martindale-Hubbell Law Directory

SCHAFFENEGGER, WATSON & PETERSON, LTD. (AV)

Suite 3504, One East Wacker Drive, 60601-1802
Telephone: 312-527-5566
Fax: 312-527-5540

J. V. Schaffenegger (1914-1986)   Donald G. Peterson
Jack L. Watson   Jay Scott Nelson
Michael A. Strom

James L. McKnight

Reference: American National Bank & Trust Co.

For full biographical listings, see the Martindale-Hubbell Law Directory

WILDMAN, HARROLD, ALLEN & DIXON (AV)

225 West Wacker Drive, 30th Floor, 60606-1229
Telephone: 312-201-2000
Cable Address: "Whad"
Fax: 312-201-2555
Aurora, Illinois Office: 1851 W. Galena Boulevard, Suite 210.
Telephone: 708-892-7021.
Fax: 708-892-7158.
Waukegan, Illinois Office: 404 West Water, P. O. Box 890.
Telephone: 708-623-0700.
Fax: 708-244-5273.
Lisle, Illinois Office: 4300 Commerce Court.
Telephone: 708-955-0555.
Libertyville, Illinois Office: 611 South Milwaukee Avenue.
Telephone: 708-680-3030.

(See Next Column)

WILDMAN, HARROLD, ALLEN & DIXON, *Chicago—Continued*

New York, New York Office: Wildman, Harrold, Allen, Dixon & Smith. The International Building, 45 Rockefeller Plaza, Suite 353.
Telephone: 212-632-3850.
Fax: 212-632-3858.
Toronto, Ontario affiliated Office: Keel Cottrelle. 36 Toronto Street, Ninth Floor, Suite 920.
Telephone: 416-367-2900.
Telefax: 416-367-2791.
Telex: 062-18660.
Mississauga, Ontario affiliated Office: Keel Cottrelle. 100 Matatson Avenue East, Suite 104.
Telephone: 416-890-7700.
Fax: 416-890-8006.

MEMBERS OF FIRM

Thomas D. Allen
Ira C. Feldman
Mark P. Miller
James T. Nyeste
Richard C. Palmer
Thomas E. Patterson
Linda E. Spring (Waukegan and Libertyville Offices)
John A. Ybarra

Kathryn S. Bedward
Eric A. Berlin
Julie A. Correll
Elizabeth Keiley
Cynthia A. King
Lauren L. McFarlane
Richard D. Murphy Jr.
Gregory S. Norrod
E. Regan Shepley
Lisa S. Simmons
Vernon P. Squires
Bradley Alan Warrick
Susan M. Weis (Not admitted in IL)

For Complete List of Firm Personnel, See General Section

For full biographical listings, see the Martindale-Hubbell Law Directory

INDIANA

*EVANSVILLE,** Vanderburgh Co.

BOWERS, HARRISON, KENT & MILLER (AV)

25 N.W. Riverside Drive, P.O. Box 1287, 47706-1287
Telephone: 812-426-1231
Fax: 812-464-3676

MEMBERS OF FIRM

F. Wesley Bowers
David V. Miller
George C. Barnett, Jr.
David E. Gray
James P. Casey
Joseph H. Harrison, Jr.

Division Counsel in Indiana for: Southern Railway Co.
District Attorneys for the Southern District of Indiana: CSX Transportation, Inc.
Representative Clients: Permanent Federal Savings Bank; Citizens Realty & Insurance, Inc.

For Complete List of Firm Personnel, See General Section

For full biographical listings, see the Martindale-Hubbell Law Directory

FINE & HATFIELD (AV)

520 N.W. Second Street, P.O. Box 779, 47705-0779
Telephone: 812-425-3592
Telecopier: 812-421-4269

MEMBERS OF FIRM

Thomas H. Bryan
Danny E. Glass
D. Timothy Born
Patricia Kay Woodring

For Complete List of Firm Personnel, See General Section

For full biographical listings, see the Martindale-Hubbell Law Directory

*INDIANAPOLIS,** Marion Co.

HUGHES AND HUGHES (AV)

(Not a Partnership)
Two Meridian Plaza, Suite 202, 10401 North Meridian Street, 46290
Telephone: 317-573-2255
Telecopier: 317-573-2266

David B. Hughes
Gary D. Sallee

For full biographical listings, see the Martindale-Hubbell Law Directory

KROGER, GARDIS & REGAS (AV)

111 Monument Circle, Suite 900, 46204-3059
Telephone: 317-692-9000
Telecopier: 317-264-6832

MEMBERS OF FIRM

James A. Knauer
Brian C. Bosma
William C. Potter, II

(See Next Column)

ASSOCIATES

Marcia E. Roan
William Bock, III

LEGAL SUPPORT PERSONNEL

PARALEGALS

Rhonda K. Peterson

Representative Clients: Beneficial Finance Company of America; National City Bank.

For full biographical listings, see the Martindale-Hubbell Law Directory

MCTURNAN & TURNER (AV)

2070 Market Tower, 10 West Market Street, 46204
Telephone: 317-464-8181
Telecopier: 317-464-8131

Lee B. McTurnan
Wayne C. Turner
Judy L. Woods
Jacqueline Bowman Ponder
Steven M. Badger
Matthew W. Foster

For full biographical listings, see the Martindale-Hubbell Law Directory

PLEWS SHADLEY RACHER & BRAUN (AV)

1346 North Delaware Street, 46202-2415
Telephone: 317-637-0700
Telecopier: 317-637-0710

MEMBERS OF FIRM

George M. Plews
Sue A. Shadley
Peter M. Racher
Christopher J. Braun

ASSOCIATES

Harinder Kaur
Leonardo D. Robinson
Frederick D. Emhardt
S. Curtis DeVoe
Jeffrey D. Claflin
John E. Klarquist
Jeffrey D. Featherstun
Amy K. Luigs
Donna C. Marron

OF COUNSEL

Craig A. Wood
Christine C. H. Plews
M. Scott Barrett

For full biographical listings, see the Martindale-Hubbell Law Directory

KENTUCKY

*BOWLING GREEN,** Warren Co.

CAMPBELL, KERRICK & GRISE (AV)

1025 State Street, P.O. Box 9547, 42102-9547
Telephone: 502-782-8160
FAX: 502-782-5856

MEMBERS OF FIRM

Joe Bill Campbell
Thomas N. Kerrick
John R. Grise
Gregory N. Stivers
H. Brent Brennenstuhl
Deborah Tomes Wilkins

ASSOCIATES

H. Harris Pepper, Jr.
Lanna Martin Kilgore
Laura Hagan

Representative Clients: Dollar General Corp.; Greenview Hospital; Hospital Corporation of America; Hardin Memorial Hospital; Monarch Environmental, Inc.; Mid-South Management Group, Inc.; Western Kentucky University; Service One Credit Union; Trans Financial Bank; TKR Cable.

For full biographical listings, see the Martindale-Hubbell Law Directory

HARLIN & PARKER, P.S.C. (AV)

519 East Tenth Street, P.O. Box 390, 42102-0390
Telephone: 502-842-5611
Telefax: 502-842-2607
Smiths Grove, Kentucky Office: Old Farmers Bank Building.
Telephone: 502-563-4701.

William Jerry Parker
Max B. Harlin, III
James David Bryant
James D. Harris, Jr.

Insurance Clients: Allstate Insurance Co.; CNA Insurance Company; Maryland Casualty Co.
Railroad and Utilities Clients: District Attorneys for South Central Bell Telephone Co.; CSX Transportation, Inc.
Local Counsel for: General Motors Corp.; News Publishing Co.

For Complete List of Firm Personnel, See General Section

For full biographical listings, see the Martindale-Hubbell Law Directory

*LOUISVILLE,** Jefferson Co.

Ogden Newell & Welch (AV)

1200 One Riverfront Plaza, 40202-2973
Telephone: 502-582-1601
Fax: 502-581-9564

MEMBERS OF FIRM

John T. Ballantine
Scott T. Wendelsdorf
Stephen F. Schuster
Gregory J. Bubalo
D. Brian Rattliff

ASSOCIATES

Douglas C. Ballantine
Thomas E. Rutledge

Counsel for: Kentucky Utilities Co.; Brown & Williamson Tobacco Corp.; Brown-Forman Corp.; B. F. Goodrich Co.; J.J.B. Hilliard, W.L. Lyons, Inc.; Interlock Industries, Inc.; Akzo Coatings, Inc.; Kentucky Medical Insurance Company; Medical Protective Company.

For Complete List of Firm Personnel, See General Section

For full biographical listings, see the Martindale-Hubbell Law Directory

LOUISIANA

*LAFAYETTE,** Lafayette Parish

Mangham, Davis and Oglesbee (AV)

Suite 1400 First National Bank Towers, 600 Jefferson Street, P.O. Box 93110, 70509-3110
Telephone: 318-233-6200
Fax: 318-233-6521

Michael R. Mangham
Michael G. Oglesbee
Louis R. Davis
Herman E. Garner, Jr.

ASSOCIATES

Dawn Mayeux Fuqua
Lisa Hanchey Sevier

SPECIAL COUNSEL

Michael J. O'Shee

OF COUNSEL

George W. Hardy, III
Robert E. Rowe

Reference: The First National Bank of Lafayette, Lafayette, Louisiana.

For full biographical listings, see the Martindale-Hubbell Law Directory

*SHREVEPORT,** Caddo Parish

Barlow and Hardtner L.C. (AV)

Tenth Floor, Louisiana Tower, 401 Edwards Street, 71101-3289
Telephone: 318-227-1131
Telecopier: 318-227-1141
Mailing Address: P.O. Box 8, Shreveport, Louisiana, 71161-0008

Ray A. Barlow
David R. Taggart
Malcolm S. Murchison
Philip E. Downer, III
Joseph L. Shea, Jr.
Michael B. Donald
Jay A. Greenleaf

Representative Clients: Brammer Engineering, Inc.; Central and South West; Kelley Oil Corporation; Louisiana Intrastate Gas Corp.; NorAm Energy Corp (formerly Arkla, Inc.); Southwestern Electric Power Company; Wagner & Brown; Central and South West; Panhandle Eastern Corp.; Pennzoil Producing Co.

For Complete List of Firm Personnel, See General Section

For full biographical listings, see the Martindale-Hubbell Law Directory

Wilkinson, Carmody & Gilliam (AV)

1700 Beck Building, 400 Travis Street, P.O. Box 1707, 71166
Telephone: 318-221-4196
Telecopier: 318-221-3705

MEMBERS OF FIRM

John D. Wilkinson (1867-1929)
Bobby S. Gilliam
William Scott Wilkinson (1895-1985)
Mark E. Gilliam
Penny D. Sellers
Arthur R. Carmody, Jr.
Brian D. Landry

Representative Clients: Farmers Insurance Group; Home Federal Savings & Loan Association of Shreveport; The Kansas City Southern Railway Co.; KTAL-TV; Lincoln National Life Insurance Co.; Mobil Oil Co.; Schumpert Medical Center; Sears, Roebuck & Co.; Southern Pacific Transportation Co.; Southwestern Electric Power Co.

For full biographical listings, see the Martindale-Hubbell Law Directory

MAINE

LEWISTON, Androscoggin Co.

Berman & Simmons, P.A. (AV)

129 Lisbon Street, P.O. Box 961, 04243-0961
Telephone: 207-784-3576
Fax: 207-784-7699
Portland, Maine Office: 178 Middle Street.
Telephone: 207-774-5277.
Fax: 207-774-0166.
South Paris, Maine Office: 4 Western Avenue.
Telephone: 207-743- 8775.
Fax: 207-743-8559.
Bridgton, Maine Office: Route 302, Portland Street.
Telephone: 207-647-3125.
Fax: 207-647-3134.

C. Martin Berman
Steven D. Silin
Jack H. Simmons
Valerie Stanfill
John E. Sedgewick
Tyler N. Kolle
William D. Robitzek
Glenn S. Eddy
Julian L. Sweet
David J. Van Dyke
Jeffrey Rosenblatt
David W. Grund
Paul F. Macri
Daniel G. Kagan
Jeffrey A. Thaler
Joy C. Cantrell
Ivy L. Frignoca

For full biographical listings, see the Martindale-Hubbell Law Directory

*PORTLAND,** Cumberland Co.

Petruccelli & Martin (AV)

50 Monument Square, P.O. Box 9733, 04104-5033
Telephone: 207-775-0200
Telecopier: 207-775-2360

MEMBERS OF FIRM

Gerald F. Petruccelli
Joel C. Martin
Daniel W. Bates

ASSOCIATES

Michael K. Martin
Linda C. Russell
James B. Haddow
Kenneth D. Keating
Thomas C. Bradley

Representative Clients: Bangor Hydro-Electric Co.; Chubb Insurance Co.; Coopers & Lybrand; Cumberland Farms; General Electric Capital Corp.; Maine Medical Center; Pine Tree Telephone & Telegraph Co.; KPMG Peat Marwick; Union Mutual Fire Insurance Co.; Vermont Mutual Insurance Co.

For full biographical listings, see the Martindale-Hubbell Law Directory

MARYLAND

*BALTIMORE,** (Independent City)

Venable, Baetjer and Howard (AV)

A Partnership including Professional Corporations
1800 Mercantile Bank & Trust Building, 2 Hopkins Plaza, 21201
Telephone: 410-244-7400
Washington, D.C. Office: Venable, Baetjer, Howard & Civiletti. Suite 1000, 1201 New York Avenue, N.W.
Telephone: 202-962-4800.
McLean, Virginia Office: Suite 400, 2010 Corporate Ridge.
Telephone: 703-760-1600.
Rockville, Maryland Office: Suite 500, One Church Street, P. O. Box 1906.
Telephone: 301-217-5600.
Towson, Maryland Office: 210 Allegheny Avenue, P. O. Box 5517.
Telephone: 410-494-6200.

MEMBERS OF FIRM

Benjamin R. Civiletti (P.C.) (Also at Washington, D.C. and Towson, Maryland Offices)
George Cochran Doub (P.C.)
John Henry Lewin, Jr. (P.C.)
Stanley Mazaroff (P.C.)
Roger W. Titus (Resident, Rockville, Maryland Office)
N. Peter Lareau (P.C.)
Thomas J. Madden (Not admitted in MD; Resident, Washington, D.C. Office)
Ronald R. Glancz (Not admitted in MD; Resident, Washington, D.C. Office)
David J. Levenson (Not admitted in MD; Resident, Washington, D.C. Office)
Douglas D. Connah, Jr. (P.C.) (Also at Washington, D.C. Office)
David T. Stitt (Not admitted in MD; Resident, McLean, Virginia Office)
Kenneth C. Bass, III (Not admitted in MD; Also at Washington, D.C. and McLean, Virginia Offices)
John H. Zink, III (Resident, Towson, Maryland Office)
Bruce E. Titus (Resident, McLean, Virginia Office)
Paul F. Strain (P.C.)
Max Stul Oppenheimer (P.C.) (Also at Washington, D.C. and Towson, Maryland Offices)

(See Next Column)

VENABLE, BAETJER AND HOWARD, *Baltimore—Continued*

MEMBERS OF FIRM (Continued)

William D. Dolan, III (P.C.) (Not admitted in MD; Resident, McLean, Virginia Office)
Paul T. Glasgow (Resident, Rockville, Maryland Office)
Joseph C. Wich, Jr. (Resident, Towson, Maryland Office)
Sondra Harans Block (Resident, Rockville, Maryland Office)
Edward F. Glynn, Jr. (Not admitted in MD; Resident, Washington, D.C. Office)
Craig E. Smith
Robert G. Ames (Also at Washington, D.C. Office)
Michael Schatzow (Also at Washington, D.C. and Towson, Maryland Offices)
Nell B. Strachan
David G. Lane (Resident, McLean, Virginia Office)
N. Frank Wiggins (Resident, Washington, D.C. Office)
L. Paige Marvel
Susan K. Gauvey (Also at Towson, Maryland Office)
James K. Archibald (Also at Washington, D.C. and Towson, Maryland Offices)
G. Stewart Webb, Jr.
George W. Johnston (P.C.)
Judson W. Starr (Not admitted in MD; Also at Washington, D.C. and Towson, Maryland Offices)
James R. Myers (Not admitted in MD; Resident, Washington, D.C. Office)
Jana Howard Carey (P.C.)
Jeffrey A. Dunn (also at Washington, D.C. Office)
George F. Pappas (Also at Washington, D.C. Office)
William D. Coston (Not admitted in MD; Resident, Washington, D.C. Office)
James L. Shea (Also at Washington, D.C. Office)
Jeffrey P. Ayres (P.C.)
Elizabeth C. Honeywell
Maurice Baskin (Resident, Washington, D.C. Office)
Amy Berman Jackson (Not admitted in MD; Resident, Washington, D.C. Office)
William D. Quarles (Also at Washington, D.C. and Towson, Maryland Offices)
C. Carey Deeley, Jr. (Also at Towson, Maryland Office)
Kathleen Gallogly Cox (Resident, Towson, Maryland Office)
Christopher R. Mellott
Cynthia M. Hahn (Resident, Towson, Maryland Office)
M. King Hill, III (Resident, Towson, Maryland Office)
James A. Dunbar (Also at Washington, D.C. Office)
Ronald W. Taylor
Mary E. Pivec (Also at Washington, D.C. Office)
Thomas J. Kelly, Jr. (Not admitted in MD; Resident, Washington, D. C. Office)
David J. Heubeck
Herbert G. Smith, II (Not admitted in MD; Resident, McLean, Virginia Office)
Patrick J. Stewart (Also at Washington, D.C. Office)
Gary M. Hnath (Resident, Washington, D.C. Office)
Michael H. Davis (Resident, Towson, Maryland Office)
Darrell R. VanDeusen

OF COUNSEL

A. Samuel Cook (P.C.) (Resident, Towson, Maryland Office)
Joyce K. Becker
Geoffrey R. Garinther (Also at Washington, D.C. Office)
Mary T. Flynn (Not admitted in MD; Resident, McLean, Virginia Office)
Fred W. Hathaway (Not admitted in MD; Resident, Washington, D.C. Office)

ASSOCIATES

Paul D. Barker, Jr.
Elizabeth Marzo Borinsky
Julian Sylvester Brown (Not admitted in MD; Resident, McLean, Virginia Office)
Daniel William China
Patricia Gillis Cousins (Resident, Rockville, Maryland Office)
Carla Draluck Craft (Resident, Washington, D.C. Office)
Royal W. Craig (Resident, Washington, D.C. Office)
Gregory A. Cross
Marina Lolley Dame (Resident, Towson, Maryland Office)
J. Van L. Dorsey (Resident, Towson, Maryland Office)
Fred Joseph Federici, III (Resident, Washington, D.C. Office)
David W. Goewey (Not admitted in MD; Resident, Washington, D.C. Office)
E. Anne Hamel
David R. Hodnett (Not admitted in MD; Resident, McLean, Virginia Office)
J. Scott Hommer, III (Not admitted in MD; Resident, McLean, Virginia Office)
Todd J. Horn
Maria F. Howell
Mary-Dulany James (Resident, Towson, Maryland Office)
Paula Titus Laboy (Resident, Rockville, Maryland Office)
Gregory L. Laubach (Resident, Rockville, Maryland Office)
Jon M. Lippard (Not admitted in MD; Resident, McLean, Virginia Office)
Edward Brendan Magrab (Resident, Washington, D.C. Office)
Patricia A. Malone (Resident, Towson, Maryland Office)
Vicki Margolis
Christine M. McAnney (Not admitted in MD; Resident, McLean, Virginia Office)
John A. McCauley
Timothy J. McEvoy
Mitchell Y. Mirviss
Samuel T. Morison (Not admitted in MD; Resident, Washington, D.C. Office)
Traci H. Mundy (Not admitted in MD; Resident, Washington, D.C. Office)
Valerie Floyd Portner
John T. Prisbe
Lawrence C. Renbaum
Michael W. Robinson (Not admitted in MD; Resident, McLean, Virginia Office)
John Peter Sarbanes
Catherine L. Schuster
Robert A. Schwinger
Nathan E. Siegel
Todd K. Snyder

(See Next Column)

ASSOCIATES (Continued)

Melissa Landau Steinman (Resident, Washington, D.C. Office)
J. Preston Turner
Terri L. Turner
Paul N. Wengert (Not admitted in MD; Resident, Washington, D.C. Office)

For Complete List of Firm Personnel, See General Section

For full biographical listings, see the Martindale-Hubbell Law Directory

*ROCKVILLE,** Montgomery Co.

VENABLE, BAETJER AND HOWARD (AV)

A Partnership including Professional Corporations
Suite 500, One Church Street, P.O. Box 1906, 20850-4129
Telephone: 301-217-5600
FAX: 301-217-5617
Baltimore, Maryland Office: 1800 Mercantile Bank & Trust Building, 2 Hopkins Plaza.
Telephone: 410-244-7400.
Washington, D.C. Office: Venable, Baetjer, Howard & Civiletti. Suite 1000, 1201 New York Avenue, N.W.
Telephone: 202-962-4800.
McLean, Virginia Office: Suite 400, 2010 Corporate Ridge.
Telephone: 703-760-1600.
Towson, Maryland, Office: 210 Allegheny Avenue, P. O. Box 5517.
Telephone: 410-494-6200.

MEMBERS OF FIRM

Roger W. Titus
Paul T. Glasgow
Sondra Harans Block

ASSOCIATES

Patricia Gillis Cousins
Paula Titus Laboy
Gregory L. Laubach

For Complete List of Firm Personnel, See General Section

For full biographical listings, see the Martindale-Hubbell Law Directory

*TOWSON,** Baltimore Co.

HOWELL, GATELY, WHITNEY & CARTER (AV)

401 Washington Avenue, Twelfth Floor, 21204
Telephone: 410-583-8000
FAX: 410-583-8031

MEMBERS OF FIRM

H. Thomas Howell
William F. Gately
Benjamin R. Goertemiller
Daniel W. Whitney
David A. Carter
William R. Levasseur

ASSOCIATES

Una M. Perez
John S. Bainbridge, Jr.
George D. Bogris
Wendy A. Lassen
Kathleen D. Leslie

For full biographical listings, see the Martindale-Hubbell Law Directory

VENABLE, BAETJER AND HOWARD (AV)

A Partnership including Professional Corporations
210 Allegheny Avenue, P.O. Box 5517, 21204
Telephone: 410-494-6200
FAX: 410-821-0147
Baltimore, Maryland Office: 1800 Mercantile Bank & Trust Building, 2 Hopkins Plaza.
Telephone: 410-244-7400.
Washington, D.C. Office: Venable, Baetjer, Howard & Civiletti. Suite 1000, 1201 New York Avenue, N.W.
Telephone: 202-962-4800.
McLean, Virginia Office: Suite 400, 2010 Corporate Ridge.
Telephone: 703-760-1600.
Rockville, Maryland Office: Suite 500, One Church Street, P. O. Box 1906.
Telephone: 301-217-5600.

PARTNERS

Benjamin R. Civiletti (P.C.) (Also at Washington, D.C. and Baltimore, Maryland Offices)
John H. Zink, III
Max Stul Oppenheimer (P.C.) (Also at Baltimore, Maryland and Washington, D.C. offices)
Joseph C. Wich, Jr.
Michael Schatzow (Also at Baltimore, Maryland and Washington, D.C. Offices)
Susan K. Gauvey (Also at Baltimore, Maryland Office)
James K. Archibald (Also at Baltimore, Maryland and Washington, D.C. Offices)
William D. Quarles (Also at Washington, D.C. Office)
C. Carey Deeley, Jr. (Also at Baltimore, Maryland Office)
Kathleen Gallogly Cox
Cynthia M. Hahn
M. King Hill, III
Michael H. Davis

ASSOCIATES

Marina Lolley Dame
J. Van L. Dorsey
Mary-Dulany James
Patricia A. Malone

For Complete List of Firm Personnel, See General Section

For full biographical listings, see the Martindale-Hubbell Law Directory

MASSACHUSETTS

*SPRINGFIELD,** Hampden Co.

ELY & KING (AV)

One Financial Plaza, 1350 Main Street, 01103
Telephone: 413-781-1920
Telecopier: 413-733-3360

MEMBERS OF FIRM

Joseph Buell Ely (1905-1956)
Raymond T. King (1919-1971)
Frederick M. Kingsbury (1924-1968)
Hugh J. Corcoran (1938-1992)
Richard S. Milstein
Donald A. Beaudry
Richard F. Faille
Leland B. Seabury
Gregory A. Schmidt
Pamela Manson
Anthony T. Rice
Russell J. Mawdsley

ASSOCIATE

Donna M. Brown

Representative Clients: Hartford Accident & Indemnity Co.; Albert Steiger Cos.; Shawmut Bank N.A.; Springfield Institution for Savings; St. Paul Fire & Marine Insurance Co.; The Rouse Co.; Tighe & Bond, Inc.; Northeast Utilities.

For full biographical listings, see the Martindale-Hubbell Law Directory

MICHIGAN

BLOOMFIELD HILLS, Oakland Co.

STROBL AND MANOOGIAN, P.C. (AV)

300 East Long Lake Road, Suite 200, 48304-2376
Telephone: 810-645-0306
Facsimile: 810-645-2690

Thomas J. Strobl
Brian C. Manoogian
John Sharp
James A. Rocchio
Kieran F. Cunningham
Michael E. Thoits
James D. Wilson

James T. Dunn
Sara S. Lisznyai
Brian M. Gottry
Thomas H. Kosik
Keith S. King
Pamela S. Ritter
Robert F. Boesiger
Douglas Young

OF COUNSEL

Glenn S. Arendsen

Representative Clients: American Speedy Printing Centers; Bohn Aluminum Corporations; Flat Rock Metal, Inc.; Sherwood Metal Products, Inc.; Resolution Trust Corporation.

For full biographical listings, see the Martindale-Hubbell Law Directory

*DETROIT,** Wayne Co.

BENDURE & THOMAS (AV)

577 East Larned, Suite 210, 48226-4392
Telephone: 313-961-1525
Fax: 313-961-1553

MEMBERS OF FIRM

Mark R. Bendure
Marc E. Thomas

ASSOCIATES

J. Christopher Caldwell
Victor S. Valenti
Sidney A. Klingler

OF COUNSEL

Nancy L. Bosh
John A. Lydick

For full biographical listings, see the Martindale-Hubbell Law Directory

BODMAN, LONGLEY & DAHLING (AV)

34th Floor 100 Renaissance Center, 48243
Telephone: 313-259-7777
Fax: 313-393-7579
Troy, Michigan Office: Suite 2020, 755 West Big Beaver Road.
Telephone: 810-362-2110.
Ann Arbor, Michigan Office: 110 Miller, Suite 300.
Telephone: 313-761-3780.
Northern Michigan Office: 229 Court Street, P.O. Box 405, Cheboygan.
Telephone: 616-627-4351.

MEMBERS OF FIRM

Henry E. Bodman (1874-1963)
Clifford B. Longley (1888-1954)
Louis F. Dahling (1892-1992)
Pierre V. Heftler
Richard D. Rohr
Theodore Souris
Joseph A. Sullivan
Carson C. Grunewald

(See Next Column)

MEMBERS OF FIRM (Continued)

Walter O. Koch (Troy Office)
Alfred C. Wortley, Jr.
Michael B. Lewiston
George D. Miller, Jr.
Mark W. Griffin (Ann Arbor Office)
Thomas A. Roach (Ann Arbor Office)
Kenneth R. Lango (Troy Office)
James T. Heimbuch
Herold McC. Deason
James A. Smith
James R. Buschmann
George G. Kemsley
Joseph N. Brown
David M. Hempstead
Joseph J. Kochanek
Randolph S. Perry (Ann Arbor Office)
James J. Walsh
David G. Chardavoyne
David W. Hipp
Robert G. Brower
Larry R. Shulman
Charles N. Raimi
Terrence B. Larkin (Troy Office)
Thomas Van Dusen (Troy Office)
Fredrick J. Dindoffer
Robert J. Diehl, Jr.
John C. Cashen (Troy Office)
James C. Conboy, Jr. (Northern Michigan Office)
Lloyd C. Fell (Northern Michigan Office)
F. Thomas Lewand
Michael A. Stack (Northern Michigan Office)
Kathleen A. Lieder (Northern Michigan Office)
Karen L. Piper
Martha Bedsole Goodloe (Troy Office)
Harvey W. Berman (Ann Arbor Office)
Barbara Bowman Bluford
R. Craig Hupp
Lawrence P. Hanson (Northern Michigan Office)
Christopher J. Dine (Troy Office)
Henry N. Carnaby (Troy Office)
Jerold Lax (Ann Arbor Office)
Linda J. Throne (Northern Michigan Office)
Diane L. Akers
Ralph E. McDowell
Susan M. Kornfield (Ann Arbor Office)
Stephen I. Greenhalgh
Kathleen O'Callaghan Hickey
Patrick C. Cauley
Dennis J. Levasseur
David P. Larsen
Gail Pabarue Bennett (Troy Office)
Kay E. Malaney (Troy Office)

COUNSEL

Robert A. Nitschke
John S. Dobson (Ann Arbor Office)
Lewis A. Rockwell
Patricia D. White (Ann Arbor Office)

ASSOCIATES

Gary D. Reeves (Troy Office)
Joseph W. Girardot
Barnett Jay Colvin
David W. Barton (Northern Michigan Office)
Susan E. Conboy (Northern Michigan Office)
Sandra L. Sorini (Ann Arbor Office)
Stephen K. Postema (Ann Arbor Office)
Bonnie S. Sherr
Lisa M. Panourgias
R. Carl Lanfear
Louise-Annette Marcotty
William L. Hoey
Laurie A. Allen (Troy Office)
Marc M. Bakst
A. Craig Klomparens (Northern Michigan Office)
Kim M. Williams
David P. Rea
Jodee Fishman Raines
Nicholas P. Scavone, Jr.
Lydia Pallas Loren (Ann Arbor Office)
Robert C. Skramstad
Deanna L. Dixon
Arthur F. deVaux (Troy Office)

Representative Clients: Abitibi Price Group; Archdiocese of Detroit; Comerica Bank; The Detroit Lions, Inc.; Ford Estates; General Motors Corporation; Charles Stewart Mott Foundation; Norfolk Southern Corporation; Panhandle Eastern Corporation; State Farm Mutual Automobile Insurance Company.

For full biographical listings, see the Martindale-Hubbell Law Directory

DISE & GUREWITZ, P.C. (AV)

3600 Cadillac Tower, 48226
Telephone: 313-963-8155
Telefax: 313-963-8438

John H. Dise, Jr.
Harold Gurewitz

Gina Ursula Puzzuoli
Margaret Sind Raben
G. Gus Morris
Elizabeth M. Malone

OF COUNSEL

Timothy Downs
Gene A. Farber

For full biographical listings, see the Martindale-Hubbell Law Directory

GROSS, NEMETH & SILVERMAN, P.L.C. (AV)

444 Penobscot Building, 48226
Telephone: 313-963-8200
Fax: 313-964-6577

James G. Gross
Mary T. Nemeth
Steven G. Silverman

For full biographical listings, see the Martindale-Hubbell Law Directory

Detroit—Continued

KERR, RUSSELL AND WEBER (AV)

One Detroit Center, 500 Woodward Avenue, Suite 2500, 48226-3406
Telephone: 313-961-0200
Telecopier: 313-961-0388
Bloomfield Hills, Michigan Office: 3883 Telegraph Road.
Telephone: 810-649-5990.
East Lansing, Michigan Office: 1301 North Hagadorn Road.
Telephone: 517-336-6767.

Richard D. Weber
Roy H. Christiansen
William A. Sankbeil
Patrick McLain
Curtis J. DeRoo
Daniel G. Beyer
James R. Case
Thomas R. Williams
Edward C. Cutlip, Jr.
Mark M. Cunningham
Joanne Geha Swanson
Robert J. Pineau
Catherine Bonczak Edwards
David E. Sims
Christopher A. Cornwall
Dennis A. Martin
Patrick J. Haddad
Eric I. Lark
James E. DeLine

OF COUNSEL

Robert G. Russell

For Complete List of Firm Personnel, See General Section

For full biographical listings, see the Martindale-Hubbell Law Directory

KENNETH M. MOGILL (AV)

Suite 1930, One Kennedy Square, 48226
Telephone: 313-962-7210
(Also Member Mogill, Posner & Cohen)

For full biographical listings, see the Martindale-Hubbell Law Directory

TIMMIS & INMAN (AV)

300 Talon Centre, 48207
Telephone: 313-396-4200
Telecopier: 313-396-4228

MEMBERS OF FIRM

Michael T. Timmis
Wayne C. Inman
Robert E. Graziani
George A. Peck
Charles W. Royer
Richard L. Levin
Henry J. Brennan, III
Mark W. Peyser
Richard M. Miettinen

ASSOCIATES

Bradley J. Knickerbocker
George M. Malis
Amy Lynn Ryntz
Mark Robert Adams
Daniel G. Kielczewski
Michael F. Wais
David J. Galbenski

Representative Clients: Stylecraft Printing Company; Stylerite Label Corporation; Retail Resources, Inc.; Deneb Robotics, Inc.; Peabody Management, Inc.; Ferndale Honda, Inc,; Applied Process, Inc.; Insilco Corporation; Variety Foods, Inc.; Certain Underwriters at Lloyds of London.

For Complete List of Firm Personnel, See General Section

For full biographical listings, see the Martindale-Hubbell Law Directory

EAST LANSING, Ingham Co.

FARHAT, STORY & KRAUS, P.C. (AV)

Beacon Place, 4572 South Hagadorn Road, Suite 3, 48823
Telephone: 517-351-3700
Fax: 517-332-4122

Leo A. Farhat
James E. Burns (1925-1979)
Monte R. Story
Richard C. Kraus
Max R. Hoffman Jr.
Chris A. Bergstrom
Kitty L. Groh
Charles R. Toy
David M. Platt

Lawrence P. Schweitzer
Jeffrey J. Short
Kathy A. Breedlove
Thomas L. Sparks

Representative Clients: Big L. Corp.; Michigan Automotive Wholesalers Association.; Hartman-Fabco, Inc.; Lansing Electric Motors, Inc.; Mike Miller Lincoln Mercury; Edward Rose Realty, Inc.; GTE Directory Services Corp.
Reference: Capitol National Bank, City Bank, Old Kent Bank & Trust.

For full biographical listings, see the Martindale-Hubbell Law Directory

FARMINGTON HILLS, Oakland Co.

KAUFMAN AND PAYTON (AV)

200 Northwestern Financial Center, 30833 Northwestern Highway, 48334
Telephone: 810-626-5000
Telefacsimile: 810-626-2843
Grand Rapids, Michigan Office: 420 Trust Building.
Telephone: 616-459-4200.
Fax: 616-459-4929.

(See Next Column)

Traverse City, Michigan Office: 122 West State Street.
Telephone: 616-947-4050.
Fax: 616-947-7321.

Alan Jay Kaufman
Donald L. Payton
Kenneth C. Letherwood
Stephen R. Levine
Thomas L. Vitu
Ralph C. Chapa, Jr.
Raymond I. Foley, II
Jeffrey K. Van Hattum
Leo D. Neville

For full biographical listings, see the Martindale-Hubbell Law Directory

*GRAND RAPIDS,** Kent Co.

WHEELER UPHAM, A PROFESSIONAL CORPORATION (AV)

Second Floor, Trust Building, 40 Pearl Street, N.W., 49503
Telephone: 616-459-7100
Fax: 616-459-6366

Gordon B. Wheeler (1904-1986)
Buford A. Upham (Retired)
Robert H. Gillette
Geoffrey L. Gillis
John M. Roels
Gary A. Maximiuk
Timothy J. Orlebeke
Kenneth E. Tiews
Jack L. Hoffman
Janet C. Baxter
Peter Kladder, III
James M. Shade
Thomas A. Kuiper

Counsel for: Travelers Insurance Co.; Prudential Insurance Co. of America; Farmers Insurance Group; Metropolitan Life Insurance Co.; Conrail Trans.; Monsanto Co.; Firestone Tire & Rubber Co.; Navistar, Inc.; Medtronic, Inc.; Westdale Better Homes and Gardens.

For full biographical listings, see the Martindale-Hubbell Law Directory

SOUTHFIELD, Oakland Co.

O'LEARY, O'LEARY, JACOBS, MATTSON, PERRY & MASON, P.C. (AV)

26777 Central Park Boulevard, Suite 275, 48076
Telephone: 810-799-8260

John P. Jacobs
Kevin P. Hanbury

For full biographical listings, see the Martindale-Hubbell Law Directory

SOMMERS, SCHWARTZ, SILVER & SCHWARTZ, P.C. (AV)

2000 Town Center, Suite 900, 48075
Telephone: 810-355-0300
Telecopier: 810-746-4001
Plymouth, Michigan Office: 747 South Main Street.
Telephone: 313-455-4250.

Richard D. Toth
Patrick Burkett
Carl B. Downing

General Counsel for: City of Taylor; Foodland Distributors; C.A. Muer Corporation; Vlasic & Company; Nederlander Corporation; Woodland Physicians; Midwest Health Centers, P.C.
Representative Clients: Crum & Forster Insurance Company; City of Pontiac; Michigan National Bank; Perry Drugs.

For Complete List of Firm Personnel, See General Section

For full biographical listings, see the Martindale-Hubbell Law Directory

MINNESOTA

*MINNEAPOLIS,** Hennepin Co.

FOSTER, WALDECK, LIND & GRIES, LTD. (AV)

Suite 2300 Metropolitan Centre, 333 South Seventh Street, 55402
Telephone: 612-375-1550
Facsimilie: 612-375-0647
St. Michael, Minnesota Office: 100 East Central, P.O. Box 35, 55376.
Telephone: 612-497-3099. Facsimilie: 612-497-3639.

Thomas A. Foster
Timothy W. Waldeck
Peter E. Lind
John R. Gries
Rolf E. Sonnesyn
David J. Lenhardt
Byron M. Peterson
Steven E. Tomsche

Gregory J. Van Heest
Jennifer L. Kjos
Philip J. Danen

Reference: Firstar Bank of Minnesota, N.A.

For full biographical listings, see the Martindale-Hubbell Law Directory

KELLY & BERENS, P.A. (AV)

Suite 3720 IDS Center, 80 South Eighth Street, 55402
Telephone: 612-349-6171
Telecopier: 612-349-6416

(See Next Column)

KELLY & BERENS P.A.—*Continued*

Timothy D. Kelly
Michael Berens
Wendy A. Snyder
Jeffrey L. Levy
Thomas H. Gunther
Celeste E. Culberth
Erin K. Fogarty

For full biographical listings, see the Martindale-Hubbell Law Directory

MISSISSIPPI

*JACKSON,** Hinds Co.

LILLY & WISE (AV)

Suite 2180 Deposit Guaranty Plaza, 210 East Capitol Street, 39201-2305
Telephone: 601-354-4040; 601-354-0078
Fax: DATA 601-354-2244

Thomas G. Lilly
Joseph P. Wise

For full biographical listings, see the Martindale-Hubbell Law Directory

MISSOURI

KANSAS CITY, Jackson, Clay & Platte Cos.

SHERWIN L. EPSTEIN & ASSOCIATES (AV)

Suite 1700, 1006 Grand Avenue, 64106
Telephone: 816-421-6200
FAX: 816-421-6201

John W. Roe

ASSOCIATE

Mark H. Epstein

LEGAL SUPPORT PERSONNEL

Amy L. Edwards
Christine Marie Leete

For full biographical listings, see the Martindale-Hubbell Law Directory

MONTANA

*BOZEMAN,** Gallatin Co.

KIRWAN & BARRETT, P.C. (AV)

215 West Mendenhall, P.O. Box 1348, 59771-1348
Telephone: 406-586-1553
Fax: 406-586-8971

Peter M. Kirwan
Stephen M. Barrett

Tom W. Stonecipher

For full biographical listings, see the Martindale-Hubbell Law Directory

NEBRASKA

*LINCOLN,** Lancaster Co.

JOHN STEVENS BERRY, P.C. (AV)

2650 North 48th Street, P.O. Box 4554, 68504
Telephone: 402-466-8444
Fax: 402-466-1793

John Stevens Berry

For full biographical listings, see the Martindale-Hubbell Law Directory

NEW JERSEY

CHATHAM, Morris Co.

ARSENEAULT, DONOHUE, SORRENTINO & FASSETT (AV)

560 Main Street, 07928-2119
Telephone: 201-635-3366
FAX: 201-635-0855

(See Next Column)

MEMBERS OF FIRM

Jack Arseneault
Timothy M. Donohue
Joan Sorrentino
David W. Fassett
Frank P. Arleo

ASSOCIATES

David G. Tomeo
William Strazza

OF COUNSEL

Edward J. Plaza

For full biographical listings, see the Martindale-Hubbell Law Directory

CRANFORD, Union Co.

MCCREEDY AND COX (AV)

Second Floor, Six Commerce Drive, 07016-3509
Telephone: 908-709-0400
Fax: 908-709-0405

MEMBERS OF FIRM

Edwin J. McCreedy
Robert F. Cox

ASSOCIATE

Patrick J. Hermesmann

Reference: United Counties Trust Co.

For full biographical listings, see the Martindale-Hubbell Law Directory

*HACKENSACK,** Bergen Co.

BRIAN J. NEARY (AV)

190 Moore Street, 07601
Telephone: 201-488-0544
Fax: 201-488-0240
New York, N.Y. Office: 475 Park Avenue, South, Suite 3300.
Telephone: 212-683-8000.

Yung-Mi Lee

For full biographical listings, see the Martindale-Hubbell Law Directory

MONTVALE, Bergen Co.

BEATTIE PADOVANO (AV)

50 Chestnut Ridge Road, P.O. Box 244, 07645-0244
Telephone: 201-573-1810
Fax: (DEX) 201-573-9736

MEMBERS OF FIRM

James R. Beattie
Ralph J. Padovano
Roger W. Breslin, Jr.
Thomas W. Dunn
Martin W. Kafafian
Adolph A. Romei
Brian R. Martinotti

ASSOCIATES

Emery C. Duell
Brenda J. McAdoo
Kathleen Smyth Cook
Francis B. Sheehan
Susan Calabrese
Antimo A. Del Vecchio
Dean J. Obeidallah
Jeffrey L. Love
Steven A. Weisfeld
S. Joseph Oey
Edward S. Kiel
Christopher Heyer
JoAnne C. Gerber
Robert A. Blass

OF COUNSEL

John J. Lamb

Reference: United Jersey Bank.

For full biographical listings, see the Martindale-Hubbell Law Directory

MOORESTOWN, Burlington Co.

CHIERICI & WRIGHT, A PROFESSIONAL CORPORATION (AV)

Blason Campus - III, 509 South Lenola Road Building Six, 08057-1561
Telephone: 609-234-6300
Fax: 609-234-9490

Donald R. Chierici, Jr.
David B. Wright
Elizabeth Coleman Chierici
Julie C. Smith
Sheri Nelson Oliano
Jaunice M. Canning
Rhonda J. Eiger
Michael A. Foresta
Linda M. Novosel

For full biographical listings, see the Martindale-Hubbell Law Directory

*NEWARK,** Essex Co.

BARRY & MCMORAN, A PROFESSIONAL CORPORATION (AV)

One Newark Center, 07102
Telephone: 201-624-6500
Telecopier: 201-624-4052

John J. Barry
Bruce P. McMoran
Salvatore T. Alfano
Mark Falk
John A. Avery
John P. Flanagan

(See Next Column)

BARRY & MCMORAN A PROFESSIONAL CORPORATION, *Newark—Continued*

Mark F. Kluger
Madeline E. Cox
Joann K. Dobransky
Adam N. Saravay
Thomas F. Doherty
Judson L. Hand
Carmen J. Di Maria

For full biographical listings, see the Martindale-Hubbell Law Directory

SAIBER SCHLESINGER SATZ & GOLDSTEIN (AV)

One Gateway Center, 13th Floor, 07102-5311
Telephone: 201-622-3333
Telecopier: 201-622-3349

MEMBERS OF FIRM

David M. Satz, Jr.
Bruce I. Goldstein
William F. Maderer
David J. D'Aloia
James H. Aibel
Sean R. Kelly
John L. Conover
Lawrence B. Mink
Michael L. Allen
Michael L. Messer
Jeffrey W. Lorell
Jeffrey M. Schwartz
David J. Satz
Joan M. Schwab
Jennine DiSomma
James H. Forte
Vincent F. Papalia

OF COUNSEL

Samuel S. Saiber
Norman E. Schlesinger

COUNSEL

Andrew Alcorn
Robin B. Horn
Randi Schillinger

ASSOCIATES

Audrey M. Weinstein
Robert B. Nussbaum
Michael J. Geraghty
Jonathan S. Davis
Paul S. DeGiulio
Diana L. Sussman
Deanna M. Beacham
Robert W. Geiger
William S. Gyves
Barry P. Kramer
Susan Rozman
Michelle Viola

LEGAL SUPPORT PERSONNEL

DIRECTOR OF FINANCE AND ADMINISTRATION

Ronald Henry

For full biographical listings, see the Martindale-Hubbell Law Directory

ZAZZALI, ZAZZALI, FAGELLA & NOWAK, A PROFESSIONAL CORPORATION (AV)

One Riverfront Plaza, 07102-5410
Telephone: 201-623-1822
Telecopier: 201-623-2209
Trenton, New Jersey Office: 150 West State Street.
Telephone: 609-392-8172.
Telecopier: 609-392-8933.

Andrew F. Zazzali (1925-1969)
Andrew F. Zazzali, Jr.
James R. Zazzali
Robert A. Fagella
Kenneth I. Nowak

Paul L. Kleinbaum
Richard A. Friedman
Kathleen Anne Naprstek
Michael J. Buonoaguro
Aileen M. O'Driscoll
Charles J. Farley, Jr.
Edward H. O'Hare

For full biographical listings, see the Martindale-Hubbell Law Directory

PARSIPPANY, Morris Co.

GENNET, KALLMANN, ANTIN & ROBINSON, A PROFESSIONAL CORPORATION (AV)

6 Campus Drive, 07054-4406
Telephone: 201-285-1919
Fax: 201-285-1177

Stanley W. Kallmann
Mark L. Antin
Harry Robinson, III
Richard S. Nichols

OF COUNSEL

Samuel A. Gennet

Michael Margello
William Gary Hanft
Alan E. Burkholz
Thomas J. Olsen

Representative Clients: Aetna Insurance Co.; Hartford Fire; Lloyds of London; New England Mutuals.
Reference: United Jersey Bank.

For full biographical listings, see the Martindale-Hubbell Law Directory

ROSELAND, Essex Co.

GOLDMAN, JACOBSON, KRAMER, FRADKIN & STARR, A PROFESSIONAL CORPORATION (AV)

(Formerly Starr, Weinberg and Fradkin A Professional Corporation)
101 Eisenhower Parkway, P.O. Box 610, 07068
Telephone: 201-228-5888
Telecopier: 201-228-4606

Edwin Fradkin
Bruce E. Goldman
Scott D. Jacobson
Elliot I. Kramer
Andrew P. Fradkin

For full biographical listings, see the Martindale-Hubbell Law Directory

WALDER, SONDAK & BROGAN, A PROFESSIONAL CORPORATION (AV)

5 Becker Farm Road, 07068
Telephone: 201-992-5300
Telecopier: 201-992-1505; 992-1006

Justin P. Walder
John A. Brogan
Barry A. Kozyra
James A. Plaisted

For full biographical listings, see the Martindale-Hubbell Law Directory

SPRINGFIELD, Union Co.

ELLIOT H. GOURVITZ, P.A. (AV)

150 Morris Avenue, P.O. Box 476, 07081
Telephone: 201-467-3200
Fax: 201-912-0432
New Brunswick, New Jersey Office: 75 Paterson Street.
Fax: 908-545-2840.
New York, New York Office: Elliot H. Gourvitz, 295 Madison Avenue.
Telephone: 212-679-3999.
Fax: 212-370-5822.

Elliot H. Gourvitz

Richard A. Outhwaite
Stacey Z. Rodkin

For full biographical listings, see the Martindale-Hubbell Law Directory

WEST ORANGE, Essex Co.

RUHNKE & BARRETT (AV)

20 Northfield Avenue, 07052
Telephone: 201-325-7970
Fax: 201-325-2248

David A. Ruhnke
Jean deSales Barrett

ALAN L. ZEGAS (AV)

20 Northfield Avenue, 07052
Telephone: 201-736-1011
Fax: 201-325-2248

For full biographical listings, see the Martindale-Hubbell Law Directory

NEW MEXICO

*SANTA FE,** Santa Fe Co.

CATRON, CATRON & SAWTELL, A PROFESSIONAL ASSOCIATION (AV)

2006 Botulph Road, P.O. Box 788, 87504-0788
Telephone: 505-982-1947
Telecopier: 505-986-1013

John S. Catron
Fletcher R. Catron
W. Anthony Sawtell
Michael T. Pottow
Kathrin M. Kinzer-Ellington

Attorneys for: Santa Fe Board of Education; American Express Co.; The Santa Fe Opera; Sunwest Bank of Santa Fe; VNS Health Services, Inc.

For Complete List of Firm Personnel, See General Section

For full biographical listings, see the Martindale-Hubbell Law Directory

STEVEN L. TUCKER (AV)

125 Lincoln Avenue, Suite 400, 87501
Telephone: 505-982-3467
Fax: 505-982-3270

For full biographical listings, see the Martindale-Hubbell Law Directory

NEW YORK

GARDEN CITY, Nassau Co.

KASE & DRUKER (AV)

Suite 225, 1325 Franklin Avenue, 11530
Telephone: 516-746-4300
Telecopier: 516-742-9416
Mamaroneck, New York Office: 136 Palmer Avenue.
Telephone: 914-834-4600.
Telecopier: 914-698-3807.

MEMBERS OF FIRM

John L. Kase
James O. Druker

OF COUNSEL

Philip J. Luongo

LEGAL SUPPORT PERSONNEL

Marie T. DeBonis

For full biographical listings, see the Martindale-Hubbell Law Directory

*NEW YORK,** New York Co.

ARKIN SCHAFFER & SUPINO (AV)

1370 Avenue of the Americas, 10019
Telephone: 212-333-0200
Fax: 212-333-2350
Los Angeles, California Office: 10940 Wilshire Blvd., Suite 700. 90024-3902.
Telephone: 310-443-7689.
Fax: 310-443-7599.

Stanley S. Arkin
Hyman L. Schaffer
Anthony M. Supino

OF COUNSEL

Jeffrey M. Kaplan

ASSOCIATES

Katherine E. Hargrove
Joseph Lee Matalon
Barry S. Pollack (Resident, Los Angeles, California Office)
Harry B. Feder
Marc S. Ullman

For full biographical listings, see the Martindale-Hubbell Law Directory

DUKER & BARRETT (AV)

1585 Broadway, 10036
Telephone: 212-969-5600
Telecopy: 212-969-5650
Albany, New York Office: 100 State Street.
Telephone: 518-434-0600.
Telecopy: 518-434-0665.

David A. Barrett
William F. Duker
Richard L. Crisona
Rodney L. Stenlake
George F. Carpinello
Nicholas A. Gravante, Jr.

OF COUNSEL

Gary K. Harris (Not admitted in NY)
Robert B. Silver
Michael Straus
Jack G. Stern
Karen Caudill Dyer (Not admitted in NY)
Tracey Lynn Altman

Christopher Allegaert
Cynthia Goldman
Kenneth G. Alberstadt
Richard S. Laudor
David A. Berger
Laura A. Hastings
Richard A. Schwartz
Janine Marie Gargiulo
Michael S. Vogel
Scott W. Dales
Rebecca L. Fine

For full biographical listings, see the Martindale-Hubbell Law Directory

HUTTON INGRAM YUZEK GAINEN CARROLL & BERTOLOTTI (AV)

250 Park Avenue, 10177
Telephone: 212-907-9600
Facsimile: 212-907-9681

MEMBERS OF FIRM

Ernest J. Bertolotti
Daniel L. Carroll
Roger Cukras
Larry F. Gainen
G. Thompson Hutton
Samuel W. Ingram, Jr.
Paulette Kendler
Steven Mastbaum
Dean G. Yuzek
David G. Ebert
Shane O'Neill

(See Next Column)

ASSOCIATES

Warren E. Friss
Patricia Hewitt
Gail A. Buchman
Stuart A. Christie
Beth N. Green
Timish K. Hnateyko
Jeanne F. Pucci
Jane Drummey
Adam L. Sifre
Susan Ann Fennelly
Marc J. Schneider

For full biographical listings, see the Martindale-Hubbell Law Directory

HERBERT MONTE LEVY (AV)

60 East 42nd Street, 10165
Telephone: 212-370-4950

For full biographical listings, see the Martindale-Hubbell Law Directory

LOEB AND LOEB (AV)

A Partnership including Professional Corporations
345 Park Avenue, 10154-0037
Telephone: 212-407-4000
Facsimile: 212-407-4990
Los Angeles, California Office: Suite 1800, 1000 Wilshire Boulevard, 90017-2475.
Telephone: 213-688-3400.
Cable Address: "Loband LSA".
Telecopier: 213-688-3460; 688-3461; 688-3462.
Century City (Los Angeles), California Office: Suite 2200, 10100 Santa Monica Boulevard, Los Angeles, 90067-4164.
Telephone: 310-282-2000.
Telecopier: 310-282-2191; 282-2192.
Nashville, Tennessee Office: 45 Music Square West, 37203-3205.
Telephone: 615-749-8300.
Facsimile: 615-749-8308.
Rome, Italy Office: Piazza Digione 1, 00197.
Telephone: 011-396-808-8456.
Telecopier: 011-396-674-8223.

MEMBERS OF FIRM

Charles H. Miller
Michael P. Zweig

For Complete List of Firm Personnel, See General Section

For full biographical listings, see the Martindale-Hubbell Law Directory

LONDON FISCHER (AV)

375 Park Avenue, 10152
Telephone: 212-888-3636
Facsimile: 212-888-3974

MEMBERS OF FIRM

Bernard London
James L. Fischer
John W. Manning
Daniel Zemann, Jr.
John E. Sparling

ASSOCIATES

Richard S. Endres
Nicholas Kalfa
Evan D. Lieberman
Amy M. Kramer
Robert S. Sunshine
Robert M. Vecchione
John P. Bruen
Christina M. Ambrosio
William C. Nanis
Michael P. Mezzacappa
Douglas W. Hammond
Michael S. Leavy
Robert L. Honig

For full biographical listings, see the Martindale-Hubbell Law Directory

MCGUIRE, KEHL & NEALON (AV)

230 Park Avenue, Suite 2830, 10169
Telephone: 212-557-0040
Telecopier: 212-953-0768

MEMBERS OF FIRM

Harold F. McGuire, Jr.
Jeffrey A. Kehl
Arthur V. Nealon
Terri E. Simon

COUNSEL

Marion C. Katzive
Shelley Sanders Kehl

For full biographical listings, see the Martindale-Hubbell Law Directory

ORANS, ELSEN & LUPERT (AV)

33rd Floor, One Rockefeller Plaza, 10020
Telephone: 212-586-2211
Cable Address: "ORELSLU"
Telecopier: 212-765-3662

MEMBERS OF FIRM

Sheldon H. Elsen
Leslie A. Lupert
Gary H. Greenberg
Lawrence Solan
Robert L. Plotz

ASSOCIATES

Melissa A. Cohen
Amelia Anne Nickles
Jonathan J. Englander

For full biographical listings, see the Martindale-Hubbell Law Directory

New York—Continued

Otterbourg, Steindler, Houston & Rosen, P.C. (AV)

230 Park Avenue, 10169
Telephone: 212-661-9100
Cable Address: "Otlerton";
Telecopier: 212-682-6104
Telex: 960916

Kurt J. Wolff
William M. Silverman
Morton L. Gitter
Peter H. Stolzar
Bernard Beitel
Daniel Wallen
Richard J. Rubin
Anthony M. Piccione
Stanley L. Lane, Jr.
Peter L. Feldman

Diane B. Kaplan
Lloyd M. Green
Richard G. Haddad
Enid Nagler Stuart
Howard M. Sendrovitz

For Complete List of Firm Personnel, See General Section

For full biographical listings, see the Martindale-Hubbell Law Directory

Piliero Goldstein Jenkins & Hall (AV)

292 Madison Avenue, 10017
Telephone: 212-213-8200
Fax: 212-685-2028
Carlstadt, New Jersey Office: One Palmer Terrace.
Telephone: 201-507-5157.
FAX: 201-507-5221.
Washington, D.C. Office: 888 17th Street, N.W., Suite 1100.
Telephone: 202-467-6991.
FAX: 202-467-6703.

MEMBERS OF FIRM

Edward J. Goldstein
Christopher P. Hall
Jon Mark Jenkins
Robert D. Piliero

ASSOCIATES

John William LaRocca
Juliana M. Moday
Elaine B. Michetti (Not admitted in NY)

OF COUNSEL

Ricardo J. Davila

For full biographical listings, see the Martindale-Hubbell Law Directory

NORTH CAROLINA

*CHARLOTTE,** Mecklenburg Co.

Womble Carlyle Sandridge & Rice (AV)

A Professional Limited Liability Company
3300 One First Union Center, 301 S. College Street, 28202-6025
Telephone: 704-331-4900
Telecopy: 704-331-4955
Telex: 853609
Winston-Salem, North Carolina Office: 1600 Southern National Financial Center.
Telephone: 919-721-3600.
Telecopy: 919-721-3660.
Telex: 806498.
Raleigh, North Carolina Office: 2100 First Union Capitol Center, 150 Fayetteville Street Mall, P.O. Box 831.
Telephone: 919-755-2100.
Telecopy: 919-755-2150.
Telex: 806498.
Atlanta, Georgia Office: One Ninety One Peachtree Tower, 191 Peachtree Street N.E., Suite 3250.
Telephone: 404-614-2580.
Fax: 404-614-2595.

MEMBERS OF FIRM

Timothy G. Barber
Jim D. Cooley
William C. Raper
F. Lane Williamson

RESIDENT ASSOCIATE

Steven D. Gardner

OF COUNSEL

Bradford A. DeVore

Representative Clients: Childress Klein Properties, Inc.; Food Lion, Inc.; Fieldcrest Cannon, Inc.; J.A. Jones Construction Company; Parkdale Mills, Inc.; Duke Power Company; Bowles Hollowell Conner & Company; ALLTEL Carolina, Inc.; Belk Store Services, Inc.; Philip Holzmann A.G.

For Complete List of Firm Personnel, See General Section

For full biographical listings, see the Martindale-Hubbell Law Directory

*RALEIGH,** Wake Co.

* indicates certain Bar Register subscribers whose principal office is located elsewhere in the state and who have arranged for representation as a part of the state capital listings that follow

* **Womble Carlyle Sandridge & Rice** (AV)

A Professional Limited Liability Company
2100 First Union Capitol Center, 150 Fayetteville Street Mall, P.O. Box 831, 27602
Telephone: 919-755-2100
Telecopy: 919-755-2150
Telex: 806498
Charlotte, North Carolina Office: 3300 One First Union Center, 301 South College Street.
Telephone: 704-331-4900.
Telecopy: 704-331-4955.
Telex: 853609.
Winston-Salem, North Carolina Office: 1600 Southern National Financial Center.
Telephone: 919-721-3600.
Telecopy: 919-721-3660.
Telex: 806498.
Atlanta, Georgia Office: One Ninety One Peachtree Tower, 191 Peachtree Street N.E., Suite 3250.
Telephone: 404-614-2580.
Fax: 404-614-2595.

RESIDENT PARTNERS

Charles A. Edwards
Robert E. Fields, III
Marilyn R. Forbes
Johnny M. Loper
Pressly M. Millen
Robert Harrison Sasser, III

RESIDENT ASSOCIATES

Susan Sawin McFarlane
Elizabeth LeVan Riley

Representative Clients: Aetna Casualty and Surety Co., Inc.; ALSCO/AmeriMark Building Products, Inc.; Aoki Corporation America, Inc.; Empire of Carolina, Inc.; Hackney Brothers, Inc.; Lawyers Mutual Liability Insurance Company of North Carolina; Meredith College; Monk-Austin, Inc.; Regency Park Corporation; Wachovia Bank of North Carolina, N.A.

For Complete List of Firm Personnel, See General Section

For full biographical listings, see the Martindale-Hubbell Law Directory

*WINSTON-SALEM,** Forsyth Co.

Womble Carlyle Sandridge & Rice (AV)

A Professional Limited Liability Company
1600 Southern National Financial Center, P.O. Drawer 84, 27102
Telephone: 910-721-3600
Telecopy: 910-721-3660
Telex: 806498
Charlotte, North Carolina Office: 3300 One First Union Center, 301 South College Street.
Telephone: 704-331-4900.
Telecopy: 704-331-4955.
Telex: 853609.
Raleigh, North Carolina Office: 2100 First Union Capitol Center, 150 Fayetteville Street Mall, P.O. Box 831.
Telephone: 919-755-2100.
Telecopy: 919-755-2150.
Telex: 806498.
Atlanta, Georgia Office: One Ninety One Peachtree Tower, 191 Peachtree Street, N.E., Suite 3250.
Telephone: 404-614-2580.
Fax: 404-614-2595.

MEMBERS OF FIRM

Henry Grady Barnhill, Jr.
Jimmy Hamilton Barnhill
Samuel Fraley Bost
Karen Estelle Carey
Clayton M. Custer
Tyrus V. Dahl, Jr.
Allan R. Gitter
R. Howard Grubbs
Robert S. Pierce
Michael E. Ray
Richard T. Rice
Thomas D. Schroeder
Keith W. Vaughan
William F. Womble, Jr.

ASSOCIATES

Ellen M. Gregg
James R. Morgan, Jr.

Representative Clients: Brad Ragan, Inc.; Brenner Companies; Food Lion, Inc.; Hanes Companies, Inc.; North Carolina Baptist Hospitals, Inc.; R.J. Reynolds Tobacco Company; Summit Communications Group, Inc.; Thomasville Furniture Industries, Inc.; Wachovia Corporation; Wake Forest University.

For Complete List of Firm Personnel, See General Section

For full biographical listings, see the Martindale-Hubbell Law Directory

OHIO

*CINCINNATI,** Hamilton Co.

WAITE, SCHNEIDER, BAYLESS & CHESLEY CO., L.P.A. (AV)
1513 Central Trust Tower, Fourth and Vine Streets, 45202
Telephone: 513-621-0267
Fax: 513-381-2375; 621-0262

Stanley M. Chesley

Thomas F. Rehme
Fay E. Stilz
Louise M. Roselle
Dwight Tillery
D. Arthur Rabourn
Jerome L. Skinner
Janet G. Abaray
Paul M. De Marco
Terrence L. Goodman
Sherrill P. Hondorf
Colleen M. Hegge
Dianna Pendleton
Randy F. Fox
Glenn D. Feagan
Theresa L. Groh
Theodore N. Berry
Jane H. Walker
Renée Infante

Allen P. Grunes

OF COUNSEL

Jos. E. Rosen
James F. Keller

For full biographical listings, see the Martindale-Hubbell Law Directory

*CLEVELAND,** Cuyahoga Co.

JANIK & DUNN (AV)
400 Park Plaza Building, 1111 Chester Avenue, 44114
Telephone: 216-781-9700
Fax: 216-781-1250
Brea, California Office: 2601 Saturn Street, Suite 300.
Telephone: 714-572-1101.
Fax: 714-572-1103.

MEMBERS OF FIRM

Steven G. Janik
Theodore M. Dunn, Jr.

ASSOCIATES

Myra Staresina
David L. Mast

For full biographical listings, see the Martindale-Hubbell Law Directory

KELLEY, MCCANN & LIVINGSTONE (AV)
35th Floor, BP America Building, 200 Public Square, 44114-2302
Telephone: 216-241-3141
FAX: 216-241-3707

MEMBERS OF FIRM

Stephen M. O'Bryan
John D. Brown
Mark J. Valponi
Thomas J. Lee
Carl A. Murway
Steven A. Goldfarb

David H. Wallace

ASSOCIATES

Kurt D. Weaver
Robert A. Brindza, II
Sylvester Summers, Jr.
Peter M. Poulos

For Complete List of Firm Personnel, See General Section

For full biographical listings, see the Martindale-Hubbell Law Directory

*COLUMBUS,** Franklin Co.

WOLSKE & BLUE A LEGAL PROFESSIONAL ASSOCIATION (AV)
580 South High Street, 43215-5672
Telephone: 614-228-6969
Cincinnati, Ohio Office: The Society Bank Center, 36 East Seventh Street, Suite 2120.
Telephone: 513-579-1181.

Walter J. Wolske, Jr.
Jason A. Blue
Gerald S. Leeseberg
Michael S. Miller

Anne M. Valentine
William Mann
David B. Shaver
Douglas J. Blue
Maryellen C. Spirito
Sarah Meirson

Reference: Bank One of Columbus, N.A.

For full biographical listings, see the Martindale-Hubbell Law Directory

*DAYTON,** Montgomery Co.

FREUND, FREEZE & ARNOLD A LEGAL PROFESSIONAL ASSOCIATION (AV)
Suite 1800 One Dayton Centre, One South Main Street, 45402-2017
Telephone: 513-222-2424
Telecopier: 513-222-5369
Cincinnati, Ohio Office: Suite 2110 Carew Tower, 441 Vine Street, 45202-4157.
Telephone: 513-287-8400.
FAX: 513-287-8403.

(See Next Column)

Neil F. Freund
Stephen V. Freeze
Gordon D. Arnold
Patrick J. Janis
Jane M. Lynch
Francis S. McDaniel
Stephen C. Findley
Robert N. Snyder
Christopher W. Carrigg
Scott F. McDaniel
Lisa A. Hesse
Gregory J. Berberich
Mary E. Lentz
Thomas B. Bruns
Shawn M. Blatt
Matthew K. Fox
Fredric L. Young
Philip D. Mervis
Thomas P. Glass
Lori S. Kibby

August T. Janszen

Local Counsel for: Auto-Owners Insurance Co.; CNA Insurance Co.; Crum and Foster Underwriters; Employers Reinsurance Corp.; Farmers Insurance Group; Lloyds of London; Medical Protective; Midwestern Group; State Farm Mutual Automobile Insurance Co.; The Travelers Insurance Co.
Special Trial Counsel for: City of Dayton.

For full biographical listings, see the Martindale-Hubbell Law Directory

*ELYRIA,** Lorain Co.

ERIC H. ZAGRANS (AV)
474 Overbrook Road, 44035-3623
Telephone: 216-365-5400
Facsimile: 216-365-5100

For full biographical listings, see the Martindale-Hubbell Law Directory

PENNSYLVANIA

ELKINS PARK, Montgomery Co.

MONAGHAN & GOLD, P.C. (AV)
7837 Old York Road, 19027
Telephone: 215-782-1800
Fax: 215-782-1010

John F. X. Monaghan, Jr.
Alan Steven Gold

Brian E. Appel
Murray R. Glickman
Barbara Malett Weitz
Tanya M. Sweet

*GREENSBURG,** Westmoreland Co.

DAVID J. MILLSTEIN (AV)
218 South Maple Avenue, 15601
Telephone: 412-837-3333
Fax: 412-837-8344

For full biographical listings, see the Martindale-Hubbell Law Directory

WALTHOUR AND GARLAND (AV)
Park Building, 121 North Main Street, 15601
Telephone: 412-834-4900

MEMBERS OF FIRM

Christ. C. Walthour, Jr.
Robert Wm. Garland

Holly G. Garland

Representative Clients: Peoples National Gas Co.; Baltimore & Ohio Railroad; Old Guard Insurance Company; Manor National Bank.
References: Manor National Bank; Southwest National Bank of Pennsylvania.

For full biographical listings, see the Martindale-Hubbell Law Directory

*HARRISBURG,** Dauphin Co.

ANGINO & ROVNER, P.C. (AV)
4503 North Front Street, 17110-1799
Telephone: 717-238-6791
Fax: 717-238-5610

Richard C. Angino
Neil J. Rovner

Joseph M. Melillo
Terry S. Hyman
David L. Lutz
Michael E. Kosik
Pamela G. Shuman
Catherine M. Mahady-Smith
Richard A. Sadlock
David S. Wisneski
Nijole C. Olson
Michael J. Navitsky
Robin J. Marzella
Lawrence F. Barone
Dawn L. Jennings
Stephen R. Pedersen

References: Harrisburg Credit Exchange; Hamilton Bank.

For full biographical listings, see the Martindale-Hubbell Law Directory

Harrisburg—Continued

HEPFORD, SWARTZ & MORGAN (AV)
111 North Front Street, P.O. Box 889, 17108-0889
Telephone: 717-234-4121
Fax: 717-232-6802
Lewistown, Pennsylvania Office: 12 South Main Street, P.O. Box 867.
Telephone: 717-248-3913.

MEMBERS OF FIRM

H. Joseph Hepford
Lee C. Swartz
James G. Morgan, Jr.
Sandra L. Meilton
Stephen M. Greecher, Jr.
Dennis R. Sheaffer

COUNSEL

Stanley H. Siegel (Resident, Lewistown Office)

ASSOCIATES

Richard A. Estacio
Michael H. Park
Andrew K. Stutzman

For full biographical listings, see the Martindale-Hubbell Law Directory

*PHILADELPHIA,** Philadelphia Co.

F. EMMETT FITZPATRICK, P.C. (AV)
926 Public Ledger Building, 19106
Telephone: 215-925-5200
Fax: 215-925-5991

F. Emmett Fitzpatrick
F. Emmett Fitzpatrick, III

For full biographical listings, see the Martindale-Hubbell Law Directory

NORRIS E. GELMAN (AV)
Suite 750 Curtis Center, Sixth and Walnut Streets, 19106
Telephone: 215-574-0513; 574-0514
Fax: 215-928-1669

ASSOCIATE

Marie-Marcelle Benjamin

For full biographical listings, see the Martindale-Hubbell Law Directory

MAGER LIEBENBERG & WHITE (AV)
Two Penn Center, Suite 415, 19102
Telephone: 215-569-6921
Telecopier: 215-569-6931

MEMBERS OF FIRM

Carol A. Mager
Roberta D. Liebenberg
Ann D. White

ASSOCIATES

Matthew D. Baxter
Brett M. L. Blyshak
Michael J. Salmanson
W. Scott Magargee
Nancy F. DuBoise

OF COUNSEL

Anna M. Durbin

For full biographical listings, see the Martindale-Hubbell Law Directory

JOHN W. MORRIS (AV)
One Penn Square West, Suite 1300, 19102
Telephone: 215-569-5154
Fax: 215-569-2862

For full biographical listings, see the Martindale-Hubbell Law Directory

DANIEL M. PREMINGER, P.C. (AV)
Suite 1050, Robinson Building, 42 South 15th Street, 19102
Telephone: 215-564-1227; 923-7963

Daniel M. Preminger

For full biographical listings, see the Martindale-Hubbell Law Directory

THOMAS B. RUTTER, LTD. (AV)
Suite 750 The Curtis Center, Independence Square West, 19106
Telephone: 215-925-9200
Fax: 215-928-1669

Thomas B. Rutter

Joseph D. Cronin
Lori E. Zeid

For full biographical listings, see the Martindale-Hubbell Law Directory

*SCRANTON,** Lackawanna Co.

MUNLEY, MATTISE, KELLY & CARTWRIGHT (AV)
205 Madison Avenue, P.O. Box 1066, 18503
Telephone: 717-346-7401
Fax: 717-346-3452

MEMBERS OF FIRM

Robert W. Munley
Nicholas S. Mattise
P. Timothy Kelly
Marion Munley
Matthew A. Cartwright
J. Christopher Munley

Reference: First National Bank of Jermyn.

For full biographical listings, see the Martindale-Hubbell Law Directory

*WILLIAMSPORT,** Lycoming Co.

RIEDERS, TRAVIS, MUSSINA, HUMPHREY & HARRIS (AV)
161 West Third Street, P.O. Box 215, 17703-0215
Telephone: 717-323-8711
1-800-326-9259
Fax: 717-323-4192

MEMBERS OF FIRM

Gary T. Harris
John M. Humphrey
Malcolm S. Mussina
Clifford A. Rieders
Ronald C. Travis
Thomas Waffenschmidt
C. Scott Waters

ASSOCIATES

Robert H. Vesely
Jeffrey C. Dohrmann
James Michael Wiley

LEGAL SUPPORT PERSONNEL

Kimberly A. Paulhamus

Representative Clients: Jersey Shore State Bank; Gamble Twp.; Crown American Corp.; Fowler Motors, Inc.; Twin Hills oldsmobile, Inc.; Brady Twp.; Cascade Twp.; Cogan House Twp.; Susquehana Twp.; Upper Fairfield Twp.; Borough of Picture Rocks.

For full biographical listings, see the Martindale-Hubbell Law Directory

RHODE ISLAND

*PROVIDENCE,** Providence Co.

HANSON, CURRAN, PARKS & WHITMAN (AV)
146 Westminster Street, 02903-2218
Telephone: 401-421-2154
Telecopier: 401-521-7040

Kirk Hanson (1948-1991)

MEMBERS OF FIRM

A. Lauriston Parks
David P. Whitman
Michael T. F. Wallor
Robert D. Parrillo
Dennis J. McCarten
James T. Murphy
Seth E. Bowerman
Thomas R. Bender

ASSOCIATES

Amy Beretta
Mark W. Dana
Richard H. Burrows
Daniel P. McKiernan

OF COUNSEL

William A. Curran

General Counsel for: Medical Malpractice Joint Underwriting Association of Rhode Island.
Rhode Island Counsel for: Amica Mutual Insurance Co.; CIGNA; St. Paul Insurance Cos.; Occidental Life Insurance Co.; Exchange Mutual Insurance Co.; Aetna Casualty & Surety Co.

For full biographical listings, see the Martindale-Hubbell Law Directory

SOUTH CAROLINA

*COLUMBIA,** Richland Co.

McCUTCHEN, BLANTON, RHODES & JOHNSON (AV)
1414 Lady Street, P.O. Drawer 11209, 29211
Telephone: 803-799-9791
Telecopier: 803-253-6084
Winnsboro, South Carolina Office: Courthouse Square, 29180.
Telephone: 803-635-6884.

MEMBERS OF FIRM

Thomas E. McCutchen
Hoover C. Blanton
Jeter E. Rhodes, Jr.
T. English McCutchen, III
Pope D. Johnson, III
Evans Taylor Barnette
G. D. Morgan, Jr.
John C. Bradley, Jr.

Representative Clients: Allstate Insurance Co.; Sears, Roebuck and Co.; J.B. White Co.; Anchor Continental Inc.; Western Fire Insurance Co.; Liberty Mutual Insurance Co.; Southeastern Freight Lines; American Mutual Fire Insurance Co.; Continental Life Insurance Co.; State Farm Fire & Casualty Co.

For Complete List of Firm Personnel, See General Section

For full biographical listings, see the Martindale-Hubbell Law Directory

Columbia—Continued

Richardson, Plowden, Grier and Howser, P.A. (AV)
1600 Marion Street, P.O. Drawer 7788, 29202
Telephone: 803-771-4400
Telecopy: 803-779-0016
Myrtle Beach, South Carolina Office: Southern National Bank Building, Suite 202, 601 21st Avenue North, P.O. Box 3646, 29578.
Telephone: 803-448-1008.
FAX: 803-448-1533.

Charles E. Carpenter, Jr. Steven W. Hamm

Deborah Harrison Sheffield

Representative Clients: Insurance: CNA Insurance Co.; The Hartford; Kemper Insurance Co.; Pennsylvania National Mutual Casualty Insurance Co.; Wausau Insurance Cos.; The Reudlinger Cos. Real Estate, Corporate and Banking: Richland Memorial Hospital; First Union Bank; National Bank of South Carolina. Construction: S.C. Department of Transportation.

For Complete List of Firm Personnel, See General Section

For full biographical listings, see the Martindale-Hubbell Law Directory

Jack B. Swerling (AV)
1720 Main Street, Suite 301, 29201
Telephone: 803-765-2626
Fax: 803-799-4059

For full biographical listings, see the Martindale-Hubbell Law Directory

*WALHALLA,** Oconee Co.

Larry C. Brandt, P.A. (AV)
205 West Main Street, P.O. Drawer 738, 29691
Telephone: 803-638-5406
803-638-7873

Larry C. Brandt

D. Bradley Jordan J. Bruce Schumpert

LEGAL SUPPORT PERSONNEL

Debra C. Miller

For full biographical listings, see the Martindale-Hubbell Law Directory

TENNESSEE

*KNOXVILLE,** Knox Co.

Rainwater, Humble & Vowell (AV)
2037 Plaza Tower, P.O. Box 2775, 37901
Telephone: 615-525-0321
Fax: 615-525-2431

MEMBERS OF FIRM

J. Earl Rainwater J. Randolph Humble
Donald K. Vowell

Representative Clients: Acme Construction, Inc.; Curtis Construction Co., Inc.; Knoxville Pediatric Associates, P.C.; National Gas Distributors, Inc.; Neel's Wholesale Produce Co., Inc.; Oldham Insurance Inc.; Sherrod Electric Co., Inc.; Towe Iron Works, Inc.; Wm. S. Trimble Co., Inc.

For full biographical listings, see the Martindale-Hubbell Law Directory

TEXAS

*AMARILLO,** Potter Co.

Hinkle, Cox, Eaton, Coffield & Hensley (AV)
1700 Bank One Center, P.O. Box 9238, 79105-9238
Telephone: 806-372-5569
FAX: 806-372-9761
Roswell, New Mexico Office: 700 United Bank Plaza, P. O. Box 10, 88202.
Telephone: 505-622-6510.
FAX: 505-623-9332.
Midland, Texas Office: 6 Desta Drive, Suite 2800, P.O. Box 3580, 79702.
Telephone: 915-683-4691.
FAX: 915-683-6518.
Santa Fe, New Mexico Office: 218 Montezuma, P.O. Box 2068, 87504.
Telephone: 505-982-4554.
FAX: 505-982-8623.
Albuquerque, New Mexico Office: Suite 800, 500 Marquette, N.W., P.O. Box 2043, 87102.
Telephone: 505-768-1500.
FAX: 505-768-1529.

(See Next Column)

Austin, Texas Office: 401 West 15th Street, Suite 800, 78701.
Telephone: 512-476-7137.
FAX: 512-476-5431.
Associated Office: Hoffman & Stephens, P.C., 401 West 15th Street, Suite 800, 78701.
Telephone: 512-476-5434. Fax; 512-476-5431.

RESIDENT PARTNER

Charles R. Watson, Jr.

Representative Clients: Aerion Industries, Inc.; Amarillo Diagnostic Clinic; Amarillo Federal Credit Union; Amarillo Health Facilities Corp.; Amarillo National Bank; Chrysler Management Corp.; Conoco, Inc.; Federated Insurance; First Interstate Management Co.; Flowers Cattle Co.

For full biographical listings, see the Martindale-Hubbell Law Directory

*DALLAS,** Dallas Co.

Joe B. Abbey (AV)
1717 Main Street, Suite 2220, 75201
Telephone: 214-748-0423
Fax: 214-748-0426

For full biographical listings, see the Martindale-Hubbell Law Directory

Palmer, Allen & McTaggart, L.L.P. (AV)
A Partnership including Professional Corporations
1900 St. Paul Place, 750 North St. Paul Street, 75201
Telephone: 214-969-0069
Telecopy: 214-720-0104
Austin, Texas Office: 6505 Lohmann's Crossing (Lago Vista).
Telephone: 512-267-1993. Mailing Address: P.O. Box 4345, Lago Vista, Texas, 78645.

Steven G. Palmer (P.C.) Robert D. McTaggart (P.C.)
Joe B. Allen III Guy Myrph Foote, Jr., (P.C.)
Brian G. Dicus (P.C.)

OF COUNSEL

Robert S. Leithiser (P.C.) Dick P. Wood, Jr., (P.C.)

For full biographical listings, see the Martindale-Hubbell Law Directory

*DENTON,** Denton Co.

Wood, Springer & Lyle, A Professional Corporation (AV)
513 West Oak, 76201
Telephone: 817-387-0404
Fax: 817-566-6673

R. William Wood Frank G. Lyle
J. Jeffrey Springer C. Jane La Rue
Grace A. Weatherly

For full biographical listings, see the Martindale-Hubbell Law Directory

*HOUSTON,** Harris Co.

C. Charles Dippel (AV)
55 Waugh Drive, Suite 603, 77007-5836
Telephone: 713-862-4445
Fax: 713-862-4665

For full biographical listings, see the Martindale-Hubbell Law Directory

Schwartz & Campbell, L.L.P. (AV)
1221 McKinney, Suite 1000, 77010
Telephone: 713-752-0017
Telecopier: 713-752-0327

Richard A. Schwartz Marshall S. Campbell

Monica F. Oathout Harold W. Hargis
Stephen A. Mendel Phillip W. Bechter
Samuel E. Dunn Laura M. Taylor
Michael D. Hudgins

LEGAL SUPPORT PERSONNEL

PARALEGALS

Nannette Koger Lenore Chomout
Bettye Vaughan Johnson Maria Pinillos

For full biographical listings, see the Martindale-Hubbell Law Directory

Wilshire Scott & Dyer, A Professional Corporation (AV)
4450 First City Tower, 1001 Fannin, 77002
Telephone: 713-651-1221
Telefax: 713-651-0020

(See Next Column)

WILSHIRE SCOTT & DYER A PROFESSIONAL CORPORATION, *Houston*—*Continued*

Eugene B. Wilshire, Jr. Patrick J. Dyer
Jacalyn D. Scott Thomas E. Bilek
Kelly Cox Thornton

For full biographical listings, see the Martindale-Hubbell Law Directory

VERMONT

*BURLINGTON,** Chittenden Co.

BURAK & ANDERSON (AV)

Executive Square, 346 Shelburne Street, P.O. Box 64700, 05406-4700
Telephone: 802-862-0500
Telecopier: 802-862-8176

MEMBER OF FIRM
Michael L. Burak
ASSOCIATE
Brian J. Sullivan

For Complete List of Firm Personnel, See General Section

For full biographical listings, see the Martindale-Hubbell Law Directory

GRAVEL AND SHEA, A PROFESSIONAL CORPORATION (AV)

Corporate Plaza, 76 St. Paul Street, P.O. Box 369, 05402-0369
Telephone: 802-658-0220
Fax: 802-658-1456

Robert B. Hemley Dennis R. Pearson
SPECIAL COUNSEL
Norman Williams

For Complete List of Firm Personnel, See General Section

For full biographical listings, see the Martindale-Hubbell Law Directory

*RUTLAND,** Rutland Co.

MILLER & FAIGNANT, A PROFESSIONAL CORPORATION (AV)

36 Merchants Row, P.O. Box 6688, 05702-6688
Telephone: 802-775-2521
Fax: 802-775-8274

Lawrence Miller John Paul Faignant

Barbara R. Blackman Christopher J. Whelton

LEGAL SUPPORT PERSONNEL
Cynthia L. Bonvouloir Marie T. Fabian

Representative Clients: Travelers Insurance Co.; Government Employees Insurance Co.; Utica Mutual Insurance Co.; Universal Underwriters Insurance Co.
Reference: Travelers Insurance Co.

For full biographical listings, see the Martindale-Hubbell Law Directory

VIRGINIA

MCLEAN, Fairfax Co.

VENABLE, BAETJER AND HOWARD (AV)

A Partnership including Professional Corporations
Suite 400, 2010 Corporate Ridge, 22102
Telephone: 703-760-1600
FAX: 703-821-8949
Baltimore, Maryland Office: 1800 Mercantile Bank & Trust Building, 2 Hopkins Plaza.
Telephone: 410-244-7400.
Washington, D.C. Office: Venable, Baetjer, Howard & Civiletti, Suite 1000, 1201 New York Avenue, N.W.
Telephone: 202-962-4800.
Rockville, Maryland Office: Suite 500, One Church Street, P.O. Box 1906.
Telephone: 301-217-5600.
Towson, Maryland Office: 210 Allegheny Avenue, P. O. Box 5517.
Telephone: 410-494-6200.

MEMBERS OF FIRM
David T. Stitt William D. Dolan, III (P.C.)
Kenneth C. Bass, III (Also at Washington, D.C. Office) David G. Lane
Herbert G. Smith, II
OF COUNSEL
Mary T. Flynn

(See Next Column)

ASSOCIATES
Julian Sylvester Brown Jon M. Lippard
David R. Hodnett Christine M. McAnney
J. Scott Hommer, III Michael W. Robinson

For Complete List of Firm Personnel, See General Section

For full biographical listings, see the Martindale-Hubbell Law Directory

WISCONSIN

*MADISON,** Dane Co.

BALISLE & ROBERSON, S.C. (AV)

217 South Hamilton, Suite 302, P.O. Box 870, 53701-0870
Telephone: 608-259-8702
Fax: 608-259-0807

Linda S. Balisle Linda Roberson
Rachel L. L. Caplan
LEGAL SUPPORT PERSONNEL
Diana K. Fleming

For full biographical listings, see the Martindale-Hubbell Law Directory

*RHINELANDER,** Oneida Co.

ECKERT & STINGL (AV)

158 South Anderson Street, P.O. Box 1247, 54501-1247
Telephone: 715-369-1624
FAX: 715-369-1273

MEMBERS OF FIRM
Michael L. Eckert James O. Moermond, III
Michael J. Stingl Timothy B. Melms
OF COUNSEL
John R. Lund

Reference: M & I Merchants Bank.

For full biographical listings, see the Martindale-Hubbell Law Directory

WYOMING

*CASPER,** Natrona Co.

BROWN & DREW (AV)

Casper Business Center, Suite 800, 123 West First Street, 82601-2486
Telephone: 307-234-1000
800-877-6755
Telefax: 307-265-8025

MEMBERS OF FIRM
Morris R. Massey John A. Warnick
Harry B. Durham, III Thomas F. Reese
W. Thomas Sullins, II Russell M. Blood
Donn J. McCall J. Kenneth Barbe
Jeffrey C. Brinkerhoff
ASSOCIATES
Jon B. Huss P. Jaye Rippley
Carol Warnick Courtney Robert Kepler
Drew A. Perkins
OF COUNSEL
B. J. Baker

Attorneys for: First Interstate Bank of Wyoming, N.A.; Norwest Bank Wyoming, N.A.; The CIT Group/Industrial Financing; Aetna Casualty & Surety Co.; The Doctor's Co.; MEDMARC; WOTCO, Inc.; Chevron USA; Kerr-McGee Corp.; Chicago and NorthWestern Transportation Company.

For Complete List of Firm Personnel, See General Section

For full biographical listings, see the Martindale-Hubbell Law Directory

CANADA
ALBERTA

*CALGARY,** Calgary Jud. Dist.

BENNETT JONES VERCHERE (AV)

4500 Bankers Hall East, 855-2nd Street S.W., T2P 4K7
Telephone: (403) 298-3100
Facsimile: (403) 265-7219
Edmonton, Alberta Office: 1000, 10035-105 Street.
Telephone: (403) 421-8133.
Facsimile: (403) 421-7951.
Toronto, Ontario Office: 3400 1 First Canadian Place. P.O. Box 130.
Telephone: (416) 863-1200.
Facsimile: (416) 863-1716.
Ottawa, Ontario Office: Suite 1800. 350 Alberta Street, Box 25, K1R 1A4.
Telephone: (613) 230-4935.
Facsimile: (613) 230-3836.
Montreal, Quebec Office: Suite 1600, 1 Place Ville Marie.
Telephone: (514) 871-1200.
Facsimile: (514) 871-8115.

MEMBER OF FIRM

Donnel O. Sabey, Q.C.

For Complete List of Firm Personnel, See General Section

For full biographical listings, see the Martindale-Hubbell Law Directory

*EDMONTON,** Edmonton Jud. Dist.

PARLEE McLAWS (AV)

15th Floor Manulife Place, 10180 101st Street, T5J 4K1
Telephone: 403-423-8500
Telecopier: 403-423-2870
Calgary, Alberta Office: 3400, Western Canadian Place, 707 - 8th Avenue, S.W.
Telephone: 403-294-7000.
Telecopier: 403-265-8263.

MEMBERS OF FIRM

C. H. Kerr, Q.C.
M. D. MacDonald
K. F. Bailey, Q.C.
R. B. Davison, Q.C.
F. R. Haldane
P. E. J. Curran
D. G. Finlay
J. K. McFadyen
R. C. Secord
D. L. Kennedy
D. C. Rolf
D. F. Pawlowski
A. A. Garber
R. P. James
D. C. Wintermute
J. L. Cairns
R. A. Newton, Q.C.
T. A. Cockrall, Q.C.
H. D. Montemurro
F. J. Niziol
R. W. Wilson
I. L. MacLachlan
R. O. Langley
R. G. McBean
J. T. Neilson
E. G. Rice
J. F. McGinnis
J. H. H. Hockin
G. W. Jaycock
M. J. K. Nikel
B. J. Curial
S. L. May
M. S. Poretti

ASSOCIATES

C. R. Head
A.W. Slemko
L. H. Hamdon
K.A. Smith
K. D. Fallis-Howell
D. S. Tam
J.W. McClure
F.H. Belzil
R.A. Renz
J.G. Paulson
K. E. Buss
B. L. Andriachuk
P. E. S. J. Kennedy
R. Feraco
R.J. Billingsley
N.B.R. Thompson
P. A. Shenher
I. C. Johnson
K.G. Koshman
D.D. Dubrule
G. T. Lund
W.D. Johnston
G. E. Flemming
K. P. Nayyer

For full biographical listings, see the Martindale-Hubbell Law Directory

CANADA
BRITISH COLUMBIA

*VANCOUVER,** Vancouver Co.

CAMP CHURCH & ASSOCIATES (AV)

4th Floor, The Randall Building, 555 West Georgia Street, V6B 1Z5
Telephone: 604-689-7555
Fax: 604-689-7554

MEMBERS OF FIRM

J.J. Camp, Q.C.
David P. Church
Giuseppe (Joe) Fiorante
Andrew J. Pearson
Sharon D. Matthews

For full biographical listings, see the Martindale-Hubbell Law Directory

CANADA
ONTARIO

KITCHENER, Regional Munic. of Waterloo

GIFFEN, LEE, WAGNER, MORLEY & GARBUTT (AV)

50 Queen Street North, P.O. Box 2396, N2H 6M3
Telephone: 519-578-4150
Fax: 519-578-8740

MEMBERS OF FIRM

Jeffrey J. Mansfield (1955-1991)
J. Peter Giffen, Q.C.
Bruce L. Lee
J. Scott Morley
Brian R. Wagner
Philip A. Garbutt

ASSOCIATES

Edward J. Vanderkloet
Keith C. Masterman
Daniel J. Fife
Jeffrey W. Boich

For full biographical listings, see the Martindale-Hubbell Law Directory

BANKING LAW

ALABAMA

ALBERTVILLE, Marshall Co.

GULLAHORN & HARE, P.C. (AV)

310 West Main Street, P.O. Box 1669, 35950
Telephone: 205-878-1891
FAX: 205-878-1965

Charles R. Hare, Jr. John C. Gullahorn

Representative Clients: First Bank of Boaz; The Home Bank; Bank of Albertville; Peoples Independent Bank of Boaz; AmSouth Bank; Compass Bank of the South; Albertville Industrial Development Board; Boaz Industrial Development Board; Marshall-Dekalb Electric Cooperative; Olympia Construction, Inc.

For full biographical listings, see the Martindale-Hubbell Law Directory

*BIRMINGHAM,** Jefferson Co.

BALCH & BINGHAM (AV)

1710 Sixth Avenue North, P.O. Box 306, 35201
Telephone: 205-251-8100
Facsimile: 205-226-8798
Other Birmingham, Alabama Office: 1901 Sixth Avenue North, 35203.
Telephone: 205-251-8100.
Facsimile: 205-226-8799.
Montgomery, Alabama Office: The Winter Building, 2 Dexter Avenue, 36101.
Telephone: 205-834-6500.
Facsimile: 205-269-3115.
Huntsville, Alabama Office: Suite 810, 200 West Court Square, 35801.
Telephone: 205-551-0171.
Facsimile: 205-551-0174.
Washington, D.C. Office: Suite 800, 1101 Connecticut Avenue, N.W., 20036.
Telephone: 202-296-0387.
Facsimile: 202-452-8180.

MEMBERS OF FIRM

H. Hampton Boles
Stanley M. Brock
Richard L. Pearson
William S. Wright
T. Kurt Miller
Suzanne Ashe
Leonard Charles Tillman

SENIOR ATTORNEY

Virginia S. Boliek

ASSOCIATES

Felton W. Smith
Terri E. Wilson

Counsel For: Alabama Bankers Assn.; Alabama Power Co.; American Express Co.; Blue Cross and Blue Shield of Alabama; Brasfield & Gorrie, Inc.; Compass Bancshares, Inc.; Harbert Corp.; Kimberly-Clark Corp.; Southern Research Institute; The Equitable Life Assurance Society of the United States.

For Complete List of Firm Personnel, See General Section

For full biographical listings, see the Martindale-Hubbell Law Directory

BRADLEY, ARANT, ROSE & WHITE (AV)

1400 Park Place Tower, 2001 Park Place, 35203
Telephone: 205-521-8000
Telex: 494-1324
Facsimile: 205-251-8611, 251-8665, 252-0264
Facsimile (Southtrust Office): 205-251-9915
Huntsville, Alabama Office: 200 Clinton Avenue West, Suite 900.
Telephone: 205-517-5100.
Facsimile: 205-533-5069.

MEMBERS OF FIRM

Edward M. Selfe
John P. Adams
P. Nicholas Greenwood
Laurence Duncan Vinson, Jr.
Carleta Roberts Hawley
J. David Dresher
John E. Hagefstration, Jr.

ASSOCIATES

Kenneth T. Wyatt
J. Paul Compton, Jr.
L. Susan Doss
Amy McNeer Tucker
Paige Maddox Davis

For Complete List of Firm Personnel, See General Section

For full biographical listings, see the Martindale-Hubbell Law Directory

BURR & FORMAN (AV)

3000 SouthTrust Tower, 420 North 20th Street, 35203
Telephone: 205-251-3000
Telecopier: 205-458-5100
Huntsville, Alabama Office: Suite 204, Regency Center, 400 Meridian Street.
Telephone: 205-551-0010.

MEMBERS OF FIRM

J. Fred Powell
Joseph G. Stewart
A. Brand Walton
Eric L. Carlton
George M. Taylor, III
Bruce A. Rawls
Dwight L. Mixson, Jr.
Gene T. Price
Deborah P. Fisher
Gail Livingston Mills

ASSOCIATE

Jeffrey T. Baker

For Complete List of Firm Personnel, See General Section

For full biographical listings, see the Martindale-Hubbell Law Directory

GORDON, SILBERMAN, WIGGINS & CHILDS, A PROFESSIONAL CORPORATION (AV)

1400 SouthTrust Tower, 420 North 20th Street, 35203
Telephone: 205-328-0640
Telecopier: 205-254-1500

Bruce L. Gordon
Ray D. Gibbons

Timothy D. Davis

For Complete List of Firm Personnel, See General Section

For full biographical listings, see the Martindale-Hubbell Law Directory

SIROTE & PERMUTT, P.C. (AV)

2222 Arlington Avenue, South, P.O. Box 55727, 35255
Telephone: 205-933-7111
Facsimile: 205-930-5301
Huntsville, Alabama Office: 200 Clinton Avenue, N.W., Suite 1000.
Telephone: 205-536-1711.
Facsimile: 205-534-9650.
Mobile, Alabama Office: One St. Louis Centre, Suite 1000.
Telephone: 205-432-1671.
Facsimile: 205-434-0196.
Montgomery, Alabama Office: Colonial Commerce Center, Suite 305 One Commerce Street.
Telephone: 205-261-3400.
Facsimile: 205-261-3434.
Tuscaloosa, Alabama Office: 2216 14th Street.
Telephone: 205-752-2089.

Karl B. Friedman
Jerry E. Held
Edward M. Friend, III
James C. Wilson, Jr.
Maurice L. Shevin
J. Scott Sims

Representative Clients: Colonial Bank; First Alabama Bank; International Business Machines (IBM); General Motors Corp.; Bruno's, Inc.; University of Alabama Hospitals; Westinghouse Electric Corp.; Monsanto Chemical Company; South Central Bell; Prudential Insurance Company.

For Complete List of Firm Personnel, See General Section

For full biographical listings, see the Martindale-Hubbell Law Directory

SPAIN, GILLON, GROOMS, BLAN & NETTLES (AV)

The Zinszer Building, 2117 2nd Avenue North, 35203
Telephone: 205-328-4100
Telecopier: 205-324-8866

MEMBERS OF FIRM

Samuel H. Frazier
Alton B. Parker, Jr.
Glenn E. Estess, Jr.
Harold H. Goings

General Counsel for: Liberty National Life Insurance Co.; United States Fidelity & Guaranty Co.; Piggly Wiggly Alabama Distributing Co.; AmSouth Mortgage Co., Inc.; Alabama Insurance Guaranty Association; Alabama Life and Disability Insurance Guaranty Association; Alabama Insurance Underwriters Association.
Counsel for: The Prudential Insurance Company of America; Government Employees Insurance Co.; Massachusetts Mutual Life Insurance Co.

For Complete List of Firm Personnel, See General Section

For full biographical listings, see the Martindale-Hubbell Law Directory

*FORT PAYNE,** De Kalb Co.

SCRUGGS, JORDAN & DODD, P.A. (AV)

207 Alabama Avenue, South, P.O. Box 1109, 35967
Telephone: 205-845-5932
Fax: 205-845-4325

(See Next Column)

SCRUGGS, JORDAN & DODD P.A., *Fort Payne—Continued*

William D. Scruggs, Jr. David Dodd
Robert K. Jordan E. Allen Dodd, Jr.

Representative Clients: Compass Bank of the South; Bank of Powell; First Federal Savings and Loan Association of De Kalb County; The Farmers Home Administration; Federal Land Bank; Nucor, Inc.; "ALABAMA" Bank; State Farm Insurance Company; Allstate Insurance Co., Inc.; USF&G Insurance Co.

For full biographical listings, see the Martindale-Hubbell Law Directory

*GADSDEN,** Etowah Co.

FORD & HUNTER, P.C. (AV)

The Lancaster Building, 645 Walnut Street, Suite 5, P.O. Box 388, 35902
Telephone: 205-546-5432
Fax: 205-546-5435

George P. Ford J. Gullatte Hunter, III
Richard M. Blythe

References: General Motors Acceptance Corp.; AmSouth Bank, N.A.

For Complete List of Firm Personnel, See General Section

For full biographical listings, see the Martindale-Hubbell Law Directory

*HUNTSVILLE,** Madison Co.

BALCH & BINGHAM (AV)

Suite 810, 200 West Court Square, P.O. Box 18668, 35804-8668
Telephone: 205-551-0171
Facsimile: 205-551-0174
Birmingham, Alabama Offices: 1710 Sixth Avenue North, 35203.
Telephone: 205-251-8100.
Facsimile: 205-226-8798. 1901 Sixth Avenue North, 35203.
Telephone: 205-251-8100.
Facsimile: 205-226-8799.
Montgomery, Alabama Office: The Winter Building, 2 Dexter Avenue, 36101.
Telephone: 205-834-6500.
Facsimile: 205-269-3115.
Washington, D.C. Office: Suite 800, 1101 Connecticut Avenue, N.W., 20036.
Telephone: 202-296-0387.
Facsimile: 202-452-8180.

RESIDENT MEMBER OF FIRM

S. Revelle Gwyn

RESIDENT ASSOCIATE

Daniel M. Wilson

Counsel For: Alabama Bankers Assn.; Alabama Power Co.; American Express Co.; Blue Cross and Blue Shield of Alabama; Brasfield & Gorrie, Inc.; Compass Bancshares, Inc.; Harbert Corp.; Kimberly-Clark Corp.; Southern Research Institute; The Equitable Life Assurance Society of the United States.

For Complete List of Firm Personnel, See General Section

For full biographical listings, see the Martindale-Hubbell Law Directory

BURR & FORMAN (AV)

Suite 204, Regency Center, 400 Meridian Street, 35801
Telephone: 205-551-0010
Birmingham, Alabama Office: 3000 SouthTrust Tower, 420 North 20th Street.
Telephone: 205-251-3000.
Telecopier: 205-458-5100.

RESIDENT PARTNER

S. Dagnal Rowe

For full biographical listings, see the Martindale-Hubbell Law Directory

SIROTE & PERMUTT, P.C. (AV)

Suite 1000, 200 Clinton Avenue, N.W., 35801
Telephone: 205-536-1711
Facsimile: 205-534-9650
Birmingham, Alabama Office: 2222 Arlington Avenue, South, P.O. Box 55727.
Telephone: 205-933-7111.
Facsimile: 205-930-5301.
Mobile, Alabama Office: One St. Louis Centre, Suite 1000.
Telephone: 205-432-1671.
Facsimile: 205-434-0196.
Montgomery, Alabama Office: Colonial Commerce Center, Suite 305, One Commerce Street.
Telephone: 205-261-3400.
Facsimile: 205-261-3434.
Tuscaloosa, Alabama Office: 2216 14th Street.
Telephone: 205-752-2089.

(See Next Column)

Joe H. Ritch George W. Royer, Jr.
Roderic G. Steakley

For Complete List of Firm Personnel, See General Section

For full biographical listings, see the Martindale-Hubbell Law Directory

STEPHENS, MILLIRONS, HARRISON & WILLIAMS, P.C. (AV)

333 Franklin Street, P.O. Box 307, 35801
Telephone: 205-533-7711
Telecopier: 205-536-9388

Arthur M. Stephens James G. Harrison
Paul L. Millirons Bruce E. Williams
Vicki Ann Bell

Attorneys for: Lomas Mortgage USA, Inc.; AmSouth Mortgage Co., Inc.

For full biographical listings, see the Martindale-Hubbell Law Directory

*MOBILE,** Mobile Co.

JOHNSTONE, ADAMS, BAILEY, GORDON AND HARRIS (AV)

Royal St. Francis Building, 104 St. Francis Street, P.O. Box 1988, 36633
Telephone: 334-432-7682
Facsimile: 334-432-2800
Telex: 782040

MEMBERS OF FIRM

Charles B. Bailey, Jr. I. David Cherniak
Brock B. Gordon R. Gregory Watts
William H. Hardie, Jr. William Alexander Gray, Jr.

General Counsel for: First Alabama Bank, Mobile; Infirmary Health System/Mobile Infirmary Medical Center/Rotary Rehabilitation Hospital (Multi-Hospital System).
Counsel for: Oil and Gas: Exxon Corp. Business and Corporate: Bell South Telecommunications, Inc.; Aluminum Co. of America; Michelin Tire Corp.; Metropolitan Life Insurance Co.; The Travelers Insurance Cos. Marine: The West of England Ship Owners Mutual Protection and Indemnity Association (Luxembourg); The Standard Steamship Owners' Protection and Indemnity Association (Bermuda) Ltd.

For Complete List of Firm Personnel, See General Section

For full biographical listings, see the Martindale-Hubbell Law Directory

LYONS, PIPES & COOK, P.C. (AV)

2 North Royal Street, P.O. Box 2727, 36652-2727
Telephone: 334-432-4481
Cable Address: "Lysea"
Telecopier: 334-433-1820

G. Sage Lyons Wesley Pipes
W. David Johnson, Jr.

Representative Clients: Chemical Bank; First National Bank of Atmore; SouthTrust Bank of Mobile.

For Complete List of Firm Personnel, See General Section

For full biographical listings, see the Martindale-Hubbell Law Directory

MILLER, HAMILTON, SNIDER & ODOM, L.L.C. (AV)

254-256 State Street, P.O. Box 46, 36601
Telephone: 334-432-1414
Telecopier: 334-433-4106
Montgomery, Alabama Office: Suite 802, One Commerce Street.
Telephone: 205-834-5550.
Telecopier: 205-265-4533.
Washington, D.C. Office: Miller, Hamilton, Snider, Odom & Bridgeman, L.L.C., Suite 1150, 1747 Pennsylvania Avenue, N.W.
Telephone: 202-429-9223.
Telecopier: 202-293-2068.

MEMBERS OF FIRM

John C. H. Miller, Jr. Bradley R. Byrne
Ronald A. Snider George A. LeMaistre, Jr.
Palmer C. Hamilton Mark J. Tenhundfeld
Thomas P. Oldweiler

OF COUNSEL

Lewis G. Odom, Jr.

ASSOCIATE

Eric J. Dyas

Representative Clients: The Colonial BancGroup, Inc.; Colonial Mortgage Co.; Chase Manhattan Bank, N.A.; The Mitchell Co.; Poole Truck Line, Inc.; Brittania Airways, Ltd. (U.K.); Air Europe (Italy); K-Mart Corporation; K & B Alabama Corp.; Ford Consumer Finance Company, Inc.

For Complete List of Firm Personnel, See General Section

For full biographical listings, see the Martindale-Hubbell Law Directory

Mobile—Continued

SIROTE & PERMUTT, P.C. (AV)

One St. Louis Centre, Suite 1000, P.O. Drawer 2025, 36652-2025
Telephone: 334-432-1671
Facsimile: 334-434-0196
Birmingham, Alabama Office: 2222 Arlington Avenue, South, P.O. Box 55727.
Telephone: 205-933-7111.
Facsimile: 205-930-5301.
Huntsville, Alabama Office: 200 Clinton Avenue, N.W., Suite 1000.
Telephone: 205-536-1711.
Facsimile: 205-534-9650.
Montgomery, Alabama Office: Colonial Commerce Center, Suite 305, One Commerce Street.
Telephone: 205-261-3400.
Facsimile: 205-261-3434.
Tuscaloosa, Alabama Office: 2216 14th Street.
Telephone: 205-752-2089.

Stephen R. Windom
Gordon O. Tanner
M. Donald Davis, Jr.
T. Julian Motes

For Complete List of Firm Personnel, See General Section

For full biographical listings, see the Martindale-Hubbell Law Directory

*MONTGOMERY,** Montgomery Co.

* indicates certain Bar Register subscribers whose principal office is located elsewhere in the state and who have arranged for representation as a part of the state capital listings that follow

*** BALCH & BINGHAM (AV)**

The Winter Building, 2 Dexter Avenue, P.O. Box 78, 36101
Telephone: 334-834-6500
Facsimile: 334-269-3115
Birmingham, Alabama Offices: 1710 Sixth Avenue North, 35203.
Telephone: 205-251-8100.
Facsimile: 205-226-8798. 1901 Sixth Avenue North, 35203.
Telephone: 205-251-8100.
Facsimile: 205-226-8799.
Huntsville, Alabama Office: Suite 810, 200 West Court Square, 35801.
Telephone: 205-551-0171.
Facsimile: 205-551-0174.
Washington, D.C. Office: Suite 800, 1101 Connecticut Avenue, N.W., 20036.
Telephone: 202-296-0387.
Facsimile: 202-452-8180.

RESIDENT MEMBER OF FIRM

James A. Byram, Jr.

Counsel For: Alabama Bankers Assn.; Alabama Power Co.; American Express Co.; Blue Cross and Blue Shield of Alabama; Brasfield & Gorrie, Inc.; Compass Bancshares, Inc.; Harbert Corp.; Kimberly-Clark Corp.; Southern Research Institute; The Equitable Life Assurance Society of the United States.

For Complete List of Firm Personnel, See General Section

For full biographical listings, see the Martindale-Hubbell Law Directory

CAPOUANO, WAMPOLD, PRESTWOOD & SANSONE, P.A. (AV)

350 Adams Avenue, P.O. Box 1910, 36102-1910
Telephone: 334-264-6401
Fax: 334-834-4954

Leon M. Capouano
Alvin T. Prestwood
Jerome D. Smith
Ellis D. Hanan
Joseph P. Borg
Joseph W. Warren

OF COUNSEL

Charles H. Wampold, Jr.

Thomas B. Klinner
Linda Smith Webb
James M. Sizemore, Jr.

Counsel for: First Alabama Bank of Montgomery, N.A.; Union Bank and Trust Co.; Real Estate Financing, Inc.; SouthTrust Bank; AmSouth Bank; Central Bank; City Federal Savings & Loan Assoc.; Colonial Mortgage Co.; Lomas & Nettleton; First Bank of Linden.

For full biographical listings, see the Martindale-Hubbell Law Directory

ARIZONA

*PHOENIX,** Maricopa Co.

BROWN & BAIN, A PROFESSIONAL ASSOCIATION (AV)

2901 North Central Avenue, P.O. Box 400, 85001-0400
Telephone: 602-351-8000
Cable: TWX 910-951-0646
Telecopier: 602-351-8516
Palo Alto, California Affiliated Office: Brown & Bain, 600 Hansen Way.
Telephone: 415-856-9411.
Telecopier: 415-856-6061.
Tucson, Arizona Affiliated Office: Brown & Bain, A Professional Association. One South Church Avenue, Nineteenth Floor, P.O. Box 2265.
Telephone: 602-798-7900
Telecopier: 602-798-7945.

Richard Calvin Cooledge
Kyle B. Hettinger
Cynthia Y. McCoy
Joseph W. Mott
Charles Van Cott

Jane L. Rodda (Resident at Tucson Office)

COUNSEL

Michael C. Jones

For Complete List of Firm Personnel, See General Section

For full biographical listings, see the Martindale-Hubbell Law Directory

FENNEMORE CRAIG, A PROFESSIONAL CORPORATION (AV)

Two North Central, Suite 2200, 85004
Telephone: 602-257-8700
Fax: 602-257-8527
Scottsdale, Arizona Office: 6263 North Scottsdale Road, Suite 290, 85250.
Telephone: 602-257-5400.
Fax: 602-945-4932.
Tucson, Arizona Office: One South Church Avenue, Suite 1030, 85701.
Telephone: 602-624-9312.
Fax: 602-882-7383.

Robert P. Robinson
Robert J. Hackett
Cathy L. Reece

Representative Clients: ASARCO Incorporated; AT&T Communications; Bridgestone/Firestone, Inc.; Catellus Development Corp.; Citibank (Arizona); First Interstate Bank of Arizona; GIANT Industries; Phelps Dodge Corporation; The Atchison, Topeka & Santa Fe Railway, Co.; US WEST Communications.

For Complete List of Firm Personnel, See General Section

For full biographical listings, see the Martindale-Hubbell Law Directory

JENNINGS, STROUSS AND SALMON, P.L.C. (AV)

A Professional Limited Liability Company
One Renaissance Square, Two North Central, 85004-2393
Telephone: 602-262-5911
Fax: 602-253-3255

Lee E. Esch
I. Douglas Dunipace
Donald J. Oppenheim
Diane K. Geimer
Anne L. Kleindienst
Carol A. Cluff

For Complete List of Firm Personnel, See General Section

For full biographical listings, see the Martindale-Hubbell Law Directory

LEWIS AND ROCA (AV)

A Partnership including Professional Corporations
40 North Central Avenue, 85004-4429
Telephone: 602-262-5311
Fax: 602-262-5747
Tucson, Arizona Office: One South Church Avenue, Suite 700.
Telephone: 602-622-2090.
Fax: 602-622-3088.

MEMBERS OF FIRM

Gerald K. Smith
Richard N. Goldsmith
Patricia K. Norris
David M. Bixby
Brent C. Gardner
Peter D. Baird
David E. Manch
Thomas H. Campbell
Newman R. Porter
Kenneth Van Winkle, Jr.
Robert H. Mc Kirgan

Representative Clients: Arizona Bank; Bank One, Arizona, NA; Citibank; Northern Trust Bank of Arizona, N.A.

For Complete List of Firm Personnel, See General Section

For full biographical listings, see the Martindale-Hubbell Law Directory

Phoenix—Continued

MEYER, HENDRICKS, VICTOR, OSBORN & MALEDON, A PROFESSIONAL ASSOCIATION (AV)

2929 North Central Avenue Suite 2100, 85012-2794
Telephone: 602-640-9000
Facsimile: (24 Hrs.) 602-640-9050
Mailing Address: P.O. Box 33449, 85067-3449,

Paul J. Meyer
C. Taylor Ashworth
Jones Osborn II
Gary A. Gotto
Jeffrey L. Sellers
William M. Hardin
Thomas H. Curzon
Michelle M. Matiski
David B. Rosenbaum

Reference: Bank One Arizona, NA.

For Complete List of Firm Personnel, See General Section

For full biographical listings, see the Martindale-Hubbell Law Directory

O'CONNOR, CAVANAGH, ANDERSON, WESTOVER, KILLINGSWORTH & BESHEARS, A PROFESSIONAL ASSOCIATION (AV)

One East Camelback Road, Suite 1100, 85012-1656
Telephone: 602-263-2400
FAX: 602-263-2900
Sun City, Arizona Office: 13250 North Del Webb Boulevard, Suite B, 85351.
Telephone: 602-263-2808.
FAX: 602-933-3100.
Tucson, Arizona Office: Suite 2200, One South Church Avenue, 85701.
Telephone: 602-882-8912.
FAX: 602-624-9564.
Nogales, Arizona Office: 1827 North Mastick Way, 85621.
Telephone: 602-761-4215.
FAX: 602-761-3505.

Jeffrey H. Verbin
Gilbert L. Rudolph
Stanley D. Mabbitt

Karl A. Freeburg
Mark W. Daliere

Representative Clients: Bank of America; Chase Manhattan Bank; First Interstate Bank of Arizona, N.A.; M & I Thunderbird Bank; Northern Trust Bank; Sears National Bank; Countrywide Credit Industries; GE Capital Mortgage Services, Inc.; Merrill Lynch Credit Corp.; Norwest Mortgage, Inc.

For Complete List of Firm Personnel, See General Section

For full biographical listings, see the Martindale-Hubbell Law Directory

RIDENOUR, SWENSON, CLEERE & EVANS, P.C. (AV)

302 North First Avenue, Suite 900, 85003
Telephone: 602-254-2143
Fax: 602-254-8670

William G. Ridenour
William D. Fearnow
Gerard R. Cleere
Natalie P. Garth

Kurt A. Peterson

For full biographical listings, see the Martindale-Hubbell Law Directory

SNELL & WILMER (AV)

One Arizona Center, 85004-0001
Telephone: 602-382-6000
Fax: 602-382-6070
Tucson, Arizona Office: 1500 Norwest Tower, One South Church Avenue 85701-1612.
Telephone: 602-882-1200.
Fax: 602-884-1294.
Orange County Office: 1920 Main Street, Suite 1200, P.O. Box 19601, Irvine, California, 92714.
Telephone: 714-253-2700.
Fax: 714-955-2507.
Salt Lake City, Utah Office: Broadway Centre, 111 East Broadway, Suite 900, 84111.
Telephone: 801-237-1900.
Fax: 801-237-1950.

MEMBERS OF FIRM

Jon S. Cohen
David A. Sprentall
Craig K. Williams
Timothy W. Moser

Representative Clients: Bank One, Arizona N.A.; First Securities Bank of Utah; Wells Fargo Bank, N.A.

For Complete List of Firm Personnel, See General Section

For full biographical listings, see the Martindale-Hubbell Law Directory

STREICH LANG, A PROFESSIONAL ASSOCIATION (AV)

Renaissance One, Two N. Central Avenue, 85004-2391
Telephone: 602-229-5200
Fax: 602-229-5690
Tucson, Arizona Office: One S. Church Avenue, Suite 1700.
Telephone: 602-770-8700.
Fax: 602-623-2518.
Las Vegas, Nevada Affiliated Office: Dawson & Associates, 3800 Howard Hughes Parkway, Suite 1500.
Telephone: 702-792-2727.
Fax: 702-792-2676.
Los Angeles, California Office: 444 S. Flower Street, Suite 1530.
Telephone: 213-896-0484.

Douglas O. Guffey
Thomas J. Lang
Nancy L. White

OF COUNSEL

Randall S. Theisen

Natalie A. Spencer
Michael B. Wixom (Resident, Las Vegas Office)

Representative Clients: Allied-Signal Aerospace Company; America West Airlines, Inc.; Atlantic Richfield Co.; Chicago Title; First Interstate Bank of Arizona, N.A.; Magma Copper Co.; Motorola, Inc.; Phelps Dodge Development Corp.; TRW Inc.; The Travelers Companies.

For Complete List of Firm Personnel, See General Section

For full biographical listings, see the Martindale-Hubbell Law Directory

*TUCSON,** Pima Co.

LEONARD FELKER ALTFELD & BATTAILE, P.C. (AV)

250 North Meyer Avenue, P.O. Box 191, 85702-0191
Telephone: 602-622-7733
Fax: 602-622-7967

David J. Leonard
Judith B. Leonard
Sidney L. Felker
Denise Ann Faulk
Clifford B. Altfeld
Donna M. Aversa
John F. Battaile III
Lynne M. Schwartz
Edward O. Comitz

For full biographical listings, see the Martindale-Hubbell Law Directory

RAVEN, KIRSCHNER & NORELL, P.C. (AV)

Suite 1600, One South Church Avenue, 85701-1612
Telephone: 602-628-8700
Telefax: 602-798-5200

Benis E. Bernstein
Barry Kirschner
Dennis J. Clancy
Andrew Oldland Norell
Bradley G.A. Cloud
Mark B. Raven
Sally M. Darcy
S. Leonard Scheff
L. Anthony Fines
Stephen A. Thomas

Representative Clients: Pace American Bonding Company; Citibank (Arizona); Continental Medical Systems, Inc.; El Paso Natural Gas Co.; Norwest Bank Arizona; El Rio-Santa Cruz Neighborhood Health Center, Inc.; Resolution Trust Corp.; Sierra Vista Community Hospital; Southern Arizona Rehabilitation Hospital; Ford Motor Credit.

For Complete List of Firm Personnel, See General Section

For full biographical listings, see the Martindale-Hubbell Law Directory

SNELL & WILMER (AV)

1500 Norwest Tower, One South Church Avenue, 85701-1612
Telephone: 602-882-1200
Fax: 602-884-1294
Phoenix, Arizona Office: One Arizona Center, 85004-0001.
Telephone: 602-382-6000.
Fax: 602-382-6070.
Orange County Office: 1920 Main Street, Suite 1200, P.O. Box 19601, Irvine, California, 92714.
Telephone: 714-253-2700
Fax: 714-955-2507.
Salt Lake City, Utah Office: Broadway Centre, 111 East Broadway, Suite 900, 84111.
Telephone: 801-237-1900.
Fax: 801-237-1950.

MEMBERS OF FIRM

Michael S. Milroy
Curt D. Reimann

Representative Clients: Transit Management, Inc.; Tucson Airport Authority; Allstate Insurance Co.; Bank One, Arizona, NA; Southern Pacific Railroad Co.; Ford Motor Co.; Chrysler Motors Corp.; Toyota Motor Sales, U.S.A., Inc.; Magma Copper Co.; Pinnacle West Capital Corp.; Safeway Inc.; Honeywell, Inc.; Wells Fargo Bank, N.A.

For full biographical listings, see the Martindale-Hubbell Law Directory

ARKANSAS

*LITTLE ROCK,** Pulaski Co.

ALLEN LAW FIRM, A PROFESSIONAL CORPORATION (AV)
950 Centre Place, 212 Center Street, 72201
Telephone: 501-374-7100
Telecopier: 501-374-1611

H. William Allen

Sandra E. Jackson

Representative Clients: Worthen National Bank of Arkansas; National Bank of Commerce.

For full biographical listings, see the Martindale-Hubbell Law Directory

ARNOLD, GROBMYER & HALEY, A PROFESSIONAL ASSOCIATION (AV)
875 Union National Plaza, 124 West Capitol Avenue, P.O. Box 70, 72203
Telephone: 501-376-1171
Fax: 501-375-3548

Benjamin F. Arnold
Mark W. Grobmyer
Charles D. McDaniel
Joe A. Polk
Richard L. Ramsay

For Complete List of Firm Personnel, See General Section

For full biographical listings, see the Martindale-Hubbell Law Directory

FRIDAY, ELDREDGE & CLARK (AV)
A Partnership including Professional Associations
Formerly, Smith, Williams, Friday, Eldredge & Clark
2000 First Commercial Building, 400 West Capitol, 72201-3493
Telephone: 501-376-2011
Telecopier: 501-376-2147; 376-6369

MEMBERS OF FIRM

Paul B. Benham, III, (P.A.)
Richard D. Taylor (P.A.)
Thomas N. Rose (P.A.)
Harry A. Light (P.A.)
John Clayton Randolph (P.A.)

ASSOCIATE

Allison Graves Bazzel

Representative Clients: Arkansas Power & Light Co.; First Commercial Bank; First National Bank of Fort Smith; First National Bank of Marianna; First National Bank of Barryville; Arvest Trust Co., N.A.; Farmers Bank & Trust Co. of Magnolia; Dillard Department Stores, Inc.; Union Pacific Railroad; FDH Bancshares, Inc.

For Complete List of Firm Personnel, See General Section

For full biographical listings, see the Martindale-Hubbell Law Directory

HOOVER & STOREY (AV)
111 Center Street, 11th Floor, 72201-4445
Telephone: 501-376-8500
Facsimile: 501-372-3255

MEMBERS OF FIRM

Paul W. Hoover, Jr.
O. H. Storey, III
John Kooistra, III
Lawrence Joseph Brady
William P. Dougherty
Max C. Mehlburger
Joyce Bradley Babin
Herbert W. Kell, Jr.
Letty McAdams

For full biographical listings, see the Martindale-Hubbell Law Directory

IVESTER, SKINNER & CAMP, P.A. (AV)
Suite 1200, 111 Center Street, 72201
Telephone: 501-376-7788
FAX: 501-376-8536

Hermann Ivester
H. Edward Skinner
Charles R. Camp
Randal B. Frazier
Laura G. Wiltshire
Mildred H. Hansen
S. Scott Luton

For Complete List of Firm Personnel, See General Section

For full biographical listings, see the Martindale-Hubbell Law Directory

MACKEY & WILLS, P.A. (AV)
Suite 555, 401 West Capitol Avenue, 72201
Telephone: 501-376-1555
Fax: 501-376-0823

(See Next Column)

B. Frank Mackey, Jr.
Frank J. Wills, III
Bradley Sean Chafin

For full biographical listings, see the Martindale-Hubbell Law Directory

ROSE LAW FIRM, A PROFESSIONAL ASSOCIATION (AV)
120 East Fourth Street, 72201
Telephone: 501-375-9131
Telecopy: 501-375-1309

George E. Campbell
Herbert C. Rule, III
Allen W. Bird, II
Garland J. Garrett
Thomas P. Thrash
Charles W. Baker
Kevin R. Burns
Richard N. Massey
John T. Hardin
Stephen N. Joiner
Brian Rosenthal
J. Scott Schallhorn

Jeffrey J. Gearhart

Representative Clients: Arkansas Association of Bank Holding Cos.; Federal Deposit Insurance Corp.; Stephens Inc.; Tyson Foods, Inc.; Wal-Mart Stores, Inc.; Worthen Banking Corp.

For Complete List of Firm Personnel, See General Section

For full biographical listings, see the Martindale-Hubbell Law Directory

CALIFORNIA

CARLSBAD, San Diego Co.

WEIL & WRIGHT (AV)
1921 Palomar Oaks Way, Suite 301, 92008
Telephone: 619-438-1214
Telefax: 619-438-2666

Paul M. Weil
Archie T. Wright III
James T. Reed, Jr.
David A. Ebersole

For full biographical listings, see the Martindale-Hubbell Law Directory

COSTA MESA, Orange Co.

COULOMBE KOTTKE & KING, A PROFESSIONAL CORPORATION (AV)
Comerica Bank Tower, 611 Anton Boulevard, Suite 1260, P.O. Box 2410, 92628-2410
Telephone: 714-540-1234
Fax: 714-754-0808; 714-754-0707

Ronald B. Coulombe
Jon S. Kottke
Raymond King

COUNSEL

Mary J. Swanson
Roy B. Woolsey

LEGAL SUPPORT PERSONNEL

PARALEGALS

Karen M. Carrillo
Laura A. Bieser
Vicky M. Pearson

LEGAL ADMINISTRATOR

Sheila O. Elpern

For full biographical listings, see the Martindale-Hubbell Law Directory

IRVINE, Orange Co.

STEVEN CASSELBERRY (AV)
5 Park Plaza, Suite 1440, 92714
Telephone: 714-476-9999
Fax: 714-476-0175

OF COUNSEL

Richard A. Harvey

Representative Clients: Chicago Title Insurance Company; Continental Lawyers Title Insurance Company; El Camino National Bank; First National Bank of Portsmouth; Huntington National Bank; Inland Empire National Bank; Landmark Bank; Omni Bank; Pioneer Savings and Loan Association; Queen City Bank.

For full biographical listings, see the Martindale-Hubbell Law Directory

LONG BEACH, Los Angeles Co.

CAYER, KILSTOFTE & CRATON, A PROFESSIONAL LAW CORPORATION (AV)
Suite 700, 444 West Ocean Boulevard, 90802
Telephone: 310-435-6008
Fax: 310-435-3704

(See Next Column)

CAYER, KILSTOFTE & CRATON A PROFESSIONAL LAW CORPORATION, *Long Beach—Continued*

John J. Cayer
Stephen R. Kilstofte
Curt R. Craton

Stephen B. Clemmer

For full biographical listings, see the Martindale-Hubbell Law Directory

*LOS ANGELES,** Los Angeles Co.

LAW OFFICES OF DAVID B. BLOOM A PROFESSIONAL CORPORATION (AV)

3325 Wilshire Boulevard, Ninth Floor, 90010
Telephone: 213-938-5248; 384-4088
Telecopier: 213-385-2009

David B. Bloom

Stephen S. Monroe (A Professional Corporation)
Raphael A. Rosemblat
James E. Adler
Bonni S. Mantovani
Martin A. Cooper
Roy A. Levun
Cherie S. Raidy
Jonathan Udell
Susan Carole Jay
Edward Idell
Sandra Kamenir
Steven Wayne Lazarus
Andrew Edward Briseno
Harold C. Klaskin
Shelley M. Gould
B. Eric Nelson
John C. Notti
Peter O. Israel
Anthony V. Seferian

For full biographical listings, see the Martindale-Hubbell Law Directory

CLARK & TREVITHICK, A PROFESSIONAL CORPORATION (AV)

800 Wilshire Boulevard, 12th Floor, 90017
Telephone: 213-629-5700
Telecopier: 213-624-9441

Philip W. Bartenetti
John A. Lapinski
Leslie R. Horowitz

OF COUNSEL

Judith Ilene Bloom

References: Wells Fargo Bank (Los Angeles Main Office); National Bank of California.

For Complete List of Firm Personnel, See General Section

For full biographical listings, see the Martindale-Hubbell Law Directory

FRIED, BIRD & CRUMPACKER, A PROFESSIONAL CORPORATION (AV)

10100 Santa Monica Boulevard, Suite 300, 90067-6031
Telephone: 310-551-7400
Facsimile: 310-556-4487

Jack Fried
Brian James Bird
David W. Crumpacker, Jr.
Nikki Wolontis
David M. Schachter

David K. Johnson

For full biographical listings, see the Martindale-Hubbell Law Directory

LOEB AND LOEB (AV)

A Partnership including Professional Corporations
Suite 1800, 1000 Wilshire Boulevard, 90017-2475
Telephone: 213-688-3400
Telecopier: 213-688-3460; 688-3461; 688-3462
Century City, California Office: Suite 2200, 10100 Santa Monica Boulevard, Los Angeles, 90067-4164.
Telephone: 310-282-2000.
Telecopier: 310-282-2191; 282-2192.
New York, N.Y. Office: 345 Park Avenue, 10154-0037.
Telephone: 212-407-4000.
Facsimile: 212-407-4990.
Nashville, Tennessee Office: 45 Music Square West, 37203-3205.
Telephone: 615-749-8300;
Facsimile: 615-749-8308.
Rome, Italy Office: Piazza Digione 1, 00197.
Telephone: 011-396-808-8456.
Telecopier: 011-396-674-8223.

MEMBERS OF FIRM

Phillip E. Adler (A P.C.)
Christopher K. Aidun (New York City Office)
Harold A. Barza
Stephen D. Bomes
Maribeth A. Borthwick (Century City Office)
David B. Eizenman (New York City Office)
Frank E. Feder (A P.C.) (Century City and New York Offices)
Joseph P. Heffernan (A P.C.)
Robert A. Meyer

(See Next Column)

MEMBERS OF FIRM (Continued)

Charles H. Miller (New York City Office)
Susan V. Noonoo
David S. Schaefer (New York City Office)
Richard P. Streicher (New York City Office)

For Complete List of Firm Personnel, See General Section

For full biographical listings, see the Martindale-Hubbell Law Directory

O'MELVENY & MYERS (AV)

400 South Hope Street, 90071-2899
Telephone: 213-669-6000
Cable Address: "Moms"
Facsimile: 213-669-6407
Century City, California Office: 1999 Avenue of the Stars, 7th Floor, 90067-6035.
Telephone: 310-553-6700.
Facsimile: 310-246-6779.
Newport Beach, California Office: 610 Newport Center Drive, Suite 1700, 92660.
Telephone: 714-760-9600.
Cable Address: "Moms".
Facsimile: 714-669-6994.
San Francisco, California Office: Embarcadero Center West Tower, 275 Battery Street, Suite 2600, 94111.
Telephone: 415-984-8700.
Facsimile: 415-984-8701.
New York, N.Y. Office: Citicorp Center, 153 East 53rd Street, 54th Floor, 10022-4611.
Telephone: 212-326-2000.
Facsimile: 212-326-2061.
Washington, D.C. Office: 555 13th Street, N.W., Suite 500 West, 20004-1109.
Telephone: 202-383-5300.
Cable Address: "Moms".
Facsimile: 202-383-5414.
Newark, New Jersey Office: One Gateway Center, 7th Floor, 07102.
Telephone: 201-639-8600.
Facsimile: 201-639-8630.
London, England Office: 10 Finsbury Square, London, EC2A 1LA.
Telephone: 011-44-171-256 8451.
Facsimile: 011-44-171-638-8205.
Tokyo, Japan Office: Sanbancho KB-6 Building, 6 Sanbancho, Chiyoda-ku, Tokyo 102, Japan.
Telephone: 011-81-3-3239-2800.
Facsimile: 011-81-3-3239-2432.
Hong Kong Office: 1104 Lippo Tower, Lippo Centre, 89 Queensway, Central Hong Kong.
Telephone: 011-852-523-8266.
Facsimile: 011-852-522-1760.

MEMBERS OF FIRM

Jean M. Arnwine
Stephen A. Cowan (San Francisco Office)
James H. De Meules
Christopher D. Hall (Not admitted in CA; London, England Office)
L. Jane Hamblen (Not admitted in CA; New York, N.Y. Office)
Marc Hanrahan (New York, N.Y. Office)
Peter T. Healy (San Francisco Office)
Linda Shannon Heumann (Newport Beach Office)
Joseph K. Kim
Matthew T. Kirby
C. James Levin
Warren R. Loui (Century City Office)
Jill H. Matichak (San Francisco Office)
Edward J. McAniff (San Francisco Office)
Kathleen G. McGuinness
Frederick B. McLane
Michael Newman
Christine M. Olsen
John B. Power
William H. Satchell (Washington, D.C. Office)
Jonathan P. Williams

SPECIAL COUNSEL

Christopher M. Crain
Lawrence M. Goldman
Frances Elizabeth Lossing
Dean E. Miller

ASSOCIATES

Avery R. Brown
Marian J. Dillon
Daniel M. Hartman
Robert C. Murray

For Complete List of Firm Personnel, See General Section

For full biographical listings, see the Martindale-Hubbell Law Directory

SHEPPARD, MULLIN, RICHTER & HAMPTON (AV)

A Partnership including Professional Corporations
Forty-Eighth Floor, 333 South Hope Street, 90071-1406
Telephone: 213-620-1780
Telecopier: 213-620-1398
Cable Address: "Sheplaw"
Telex: 19-4424
Orange County, California Office: Seventh Floor, 4695 MacArthur Court, Newport Beach.
Telephone: 714-752-6400.
Telecopier: 714-851-0739.
Telex: 19-4424.

(See Next Column)

SHEPPARD, MULLIN, RICHTER & HAMPTON—*Continued*

San Francisco, California Office: Seventeenth Floor, Four Embarcadero Center.
Telephone: 415-434-9100.
Telecopier: 415-434-3947.
Telex: 19-4424.
San Diego, California Office: Nineteenth Floor, 501 West Broadway.
Telephone: 619-338-6500.
Telecopier: 619-234-3815.
Telex: 19-4424.

MEMBERS OF FIRM

John D. Berchild, Jr.
Kathleen Borrero Bloch (San Francisco Office)
Barbara L. Borden (San Diego Office)
Richard W. Brunette, Jr.
Dean A. Demetre (Orange County Office)
Juliette M. Ebert (San Francisco Office)
Merrill R. Francis *
Geraldine A. Freeman (San Francisco Office)
Marsha D. Galinsky
James Blythe Hodge * (San Francisco Office)
Gregory A. Long *
Charles H. MacNab, Jr. (San Francisco Office)
David J. McCarty
Charles E. McCormick
Prentice L. O'Leary *
Joel R. Ohlgren
Sara Pfrommer
Nancy Baldwin Reimann
D. Ronald Ryland (San Francisco Office)
William M. Scott IV
Richard L. Sommers
Laura S. Taylor (San Diego Office)
Victor A. Vilaplana (San Diego Office)
William R. Wyatt (San Francisco Office)

SPECIAL COUNSEL

Jack Chi-Husan Liu

ASSOCIATES

Rebecca Berg (Orange County Office)
Steven W. Cardoza (Orange County Office)
Linda Fox (San Diego Office)
David T. Han
Donna L. Hueckel
David E. Isenberg
Brian W. Jones (San Francisco Office)
Harold S. Marenus
Alan H. Martin (Orange County Office)
Ryan D. McCortney
Leslie J. McShane
Timothy W. J. O'Brien (San Diego Office)
Michael Reisz
Erlinda G. Shrenger
Mark K. Slater (San Francisco Office)
Mark A. Spitzer
Michael D. Stewart (Orange County Office)
Alan Van Derhoff (San Diego Office)
Nellwyn Voorhies
Margaret W. Wolfe
Timothy J. Yoo

*Professional Corporation

For Complete List of Firm Personnel, See General Section

For full biographical listings, see the Martindale-Hubbell Law Directory

NEWPORT BEACH, Orange Co.

GORDON & WOLF, A PROFESSIONAL CORPORATION (AV)

500 Newport Center Drive Suite 800, 92660
Telephone: 714-720-9200
Fax: 714-720-9250

Alan S. Wolf

Michael R. Pfeifer
Donald R. Davidson, III
Roland P. Reynolds
David Brian Lally
Steven M. Lawrence

OF COUNSEL

Stanley M. Gordon
Peter J. Marshall

For full biographical listings, see the Martindale-Hubbell Law Directory

PASADENA, Los Angeles Co.

CAIRNS, DOYLE, LANS, NICHOLAS & SONI, A LAW CORPORATION (AV)

Ninth Floor, 225 South Lake Avenue, 91101
Telephone: 818-683-3111
Telecopier: 818-683-4999

Rohini Soni (1956-1994)
John D. Cairns
John C. Doyle
Stephen M. Lans
Francisco J. Nicholas

David M. Phillips

Representative Clients: Allstate Insurance Companies; Burger King Corporation; California Insurance Guarantee Association; California United Bank; CIGNA Insurance Companies; City of Pasadena; Cumis Insurance Society, Inc.; Employer's Mutual Insurance Companies; State Farm Insurance Companies; Tokio Marine Insurance.

For full biographical listings, see the Martindale-Hubbell Law Directory

*SAN DIEGO,** San Diego Co.

FERRIS & BRITTON, A PROFESSIONAL CORPORATION (AV)

1600 First National Bank Center, 401 West A Street, 92101
Telephone: 619-233-3131
Fax: 619-232-9316

Michael R. Weinstein

OF COUNSEL

James J. Granby

Representative Clients: Allstate Insurance Co.; Cox Communications, Inc.; Enterprise Rent-a-Car; Exxon; Immuno Pharmaceutics, Inc.; Invitrogen Corporation; Teleport Communications Group; Southwest Airlines; Times-Mirror Cable Television.

For Complete List of Firm Personnel, See General Section

For full biographical listings, see the Martindale-Hubbell Law Directory

GRAY CARY WARE & FREIDENRICH, A PROFESSIONAL CORPORATION (AV)

Gray Cary Established in 1927
Ware & Freidenrich Established in 1969
401 "B" Street, Suite 1700, 92101
Telephone: 619-699-2700
Telecopier: 619-236-1048
Palo Alto, California Office: 400 Hamilton Avenue.
Telephone: 415-328-6561.
La Jolla, California Office: Suite 575, 1200 Prospect Street.
Telephone: 619-454-9101.
El Centro, California Office: 1224 State Street, P.O. Box 2890.
Telephone: 619-353-6140.

G. Eric Georgatos
W. Terrance Guiney
Richard F. Luther
Paul R. Syrowik

Representative Clients: Security Pacific National Bank; Coast Federal Bank, Bank of California; First Interstate Bank; Wells Fargo Bank; Bank of America; Scripps Bank; La Jolla Bank & Trust; San Diego Trust & Savings Bank; Citicorp North America, Inc.

For Complete List of Firm Personnel, See General Section

For full biographical listings, see the Martindale-Hubbell Law Directory

HIGGS, FLETCHER & MACK (AV)

2000 First National Bank Building, 401 West "A" Street, 92101
Telephone: 619-236-1551
ABA Net: 9011
Telex: 382028 HFM UD
Telecopier: 619-696-1410
North County Office: 613 West Valley Parkway, Suite 345. Escondido, California, 92025-2552.
Telephone: 619-743-1201.
Telecopier: 619-743-9926.

MEMBERS OF FIRM

Franklin T. Lloyd
Kurt L. Kicklighter

Representative Clients: Frazee Industries; Kawasaki Motors Corp.; Rohr Industries; Allstate Insurance Co.; Associated Aviation Underwriters; Physicians & Surgeons Insurance Exchange.

For Complete List of Firm Personnel, See General Section

For full biographical listings, see the Martindale-Hubbell Law Directory

LINDLEY, LAZAR & SCALES, A PROFESSIONAL CORPORATION (AV)

One America Plaza, 600 West Broadway, Suite 1400, 92101-3302
Telephone: 619-234-9181
Fax: 619-234-8475

Luke R. Corbett
John M. Seitman
Michael H. Wexler
George C. Lazar

Representative Clients: Bank of Commerce; Palomar Savings & Loan; Bank of New York.

For Complete List of Firm Personnel, See General Section

For full biographical listings, see the Martindale-Hubbell Law Directory

LUCE, FORWARD, HAMILTON & SCRIPPS (AV)

A Partnership including Professional Corporations
600 West Broadway, Suite 2600, 92101
Telephone: 619-236-1414
Fax: 619-232-8311
La Jolla, California Office: 4275 Executive Square, Suite 800, 92037.
Telephone: 619-535-2639.
Fax: 619-453-2812.
Los Angeles, California Office: 777 South Figueroa, 36th Floor, 90017.
Telephone: 213-892-4992.
Fax: 213-892-7731.

(See Next Column)

LUCE, FORWARD, HAMILTON & SCRIPPS, *San Diego—Continued*

San Francisco, California Office: 100 Bush Street, 20th Floor, 94104.
Telephone: 415-395-7900.
Fax: 415-395-7949.
New York, N.Y. Office: Citicorp Center, 153 East 53rd Street, 26th Floor, 10022.
Telephone: 212-754-1414.
Fax: 212-644-9727.

MEMBERS OF FIRM

Edgar A. Luce, Jr. | Mikel R. Bistrow
John B. McNeece III | Margaret M. Mann
Christopher Celentino

OF COUNSEL

Michael T. Andrew | Stephen R. Brown

ASSOCIATES

Teryl S. Murabayashi | Kathryn M. S. Catherwood

For Complete List of Firm Personnel, See General Section

For full biographical listings, see the Martindale-Hubbell Law Directory

MULVANEY, KAHAN & BARRY, A PROFESSIONAL CORPORATION (AV)

Seventeenth Floor, First National Bank Center, 401 West "A" Street, 92101-7994
Telephone: 619-238-1010
Fax: 619-238-1981
Los Angeles, California Office: Union Bank Plaza, 445 South Figueroa Street, Suite 2600.
Telephone: 213-612-7765.
La Jolla, California Office: Glendale Federal Building, 7911 Herschel, Suite 300, P.O Box 1885.
Telephone: 619-454-0142.
Fax: 619-454-7858.
Orange, California Office: The Koll Center, 500 North State College Boulevard, Suite 440.
Telephone: 714-634-7069.
Fax: 714-939-8000.

James F. Mulvaney | Greta C. Botka
Lawrence Kahan | Mark R. Raftery
Everett G. Barry, Jr. | Charles F. Bethel
Donald G. Johnson, Jr. | Carrie L. Gleeson
Robert A. Linn | Diane M. Racicot
Maureen E. Markey | John A. Mayers
Paula Rotenberg | Linda P. Lucal
Melissa A. Blackburn | Steven W. Pite
Rex B. Beatty | Patricia A. Sieveke (Resident, Los Angeles and Orange Offices)
Julie A. Jones
Maureen H. Edwards
Michael S. Umansky

OF COUNSEL

James P. McGowan, Jr. (Resident, La Jolla Office) | Derrick W. Samuelson (Not admitted in CA)

Representative Clients: Union Bank; Wells Fargo Bank; California Commerce Bank; Colonial National Bank; NationsBank; FCC National Bank; Rancho Santa Fe National Bank; San Diego National Bank; VISA USA, Inc.

For full biographical listings, see the Martindale-Hubbell Law Directory

PROCOPIO, CORY, HARGREAVES AND SAVITCH (AV)

2100 Union Bank Building, 530 B Street, 92101
Telephone: 619-238-1900
Telecopier: 619-235-0398

A. T. Procopio (1900-1974) | John H. Barrett (Retired)
Harry Hargreaves (Retired) | Dennis H. McKee (Retired)
Gerald E. Olson (Retired)

MEMBERS OF FIRM

Alec L. Cory | James G. Sandler
Emmanuel Savitch | Philip J. Giacinti, Jr.
Todd E. Leigh | Steven J. Untiedt
Jeffrey Isaacs | Robert K. Butterfield, Jr.
Robert G. Russell, Jr. | Kenneth J. Rose
Kelly M. Edwards | Gerald P. Kennedy
Raymond G. Wright | Thomas W. Turner, Jr.

ASSOCIATE

Matthew W. Argue

Representative Clients: Union Bank; Daley Corp. (highway construction); Associated General Contractors; The Bank of Tokyo, Ltd.; First National Bank; Bank of California; San Diego Trust and Savings Bank.

For Complete List of Firm Personnel, See General Section

For full biographical listings, see the Martindale-Hubbell Law Directory

*SANTA ANA,** Orange Co.

PRENOVOST, NORMANDIN, BERGH & DAWE A PROFESSIONAL CORPORATION (AV)

2020 East First Street, Suite 500, 92705
Telephone: 714-547-2444
Fax: 714-835-2889

Thomas J. Prenovost, Jr. | Steven L. Bergh
Tom Roddy Normandin | Michael G. Dawe

Bruce T. Bauer | Kimberly D. Taylor
Kristen L. Welles Lanham | Nancy R. Tragarz

Reference: Marine National Bank.

For full biographical listings, see the Martindale-Hubbell Law Directory

SANTA MONICA, Los Angeles Co.

HAIGHT, BROWN & BONESTEEL (AV)

A Partnership including Professional Corporations
1620 26th Street, Suite 4000 North, P.O. Box 680, 90404
Telephone: 310-449-6000
Telecopier: 310-829-5117
Telex: 705837
Santa Ana, California Office: Suite 900, 5 Hutton Centre Drive.
Telephone: 714-754-1100.
Telecopier: 714-754-0826.
Riverside, California Office: 3750 University Avenue, Suite 650.
Telephone: 909-341-8300.
Fax: 909-341-8309.
San Francisco, California Office: Suite 300, 201 Sansome Street.
Telephone: 415-986-7700.
Fax: 415-986-6945.

MEMBERS OF FIRM

Morton Rosen | William E. Ireland

OF COUNSEL

R. Roy Finkle

For Complete List of Firm Personnel, See General Section

For full biographical listings, see the Martindale-Hubbell Law Directory

*SANTA ROSA,** Sonoma Co.

BELDEN, ABBEY, WEITZENBERG & KELLY, A PROFESSIONAL CORPORATION (AV)

1105 North Dutton Avenue, P.O. Box 1566, 95402
Telephone: 707-542-5050
Telecopier: 707-542-2589

Richard W. Abbey

Representative Clients: Exchange Bank of Santa Rosa; Westamerica Bank; North Bay Title Co.; Northwestern Title Security Co.; Santa Rosa City School District.

For Complete List of Firm Personnel, See General Section

For full biographical listings, see the Martindale-Hubbell Law Directory

COLORADO

*COLORADO SPRINGS,** El Paso Co.

FLYNN MCKENNA & WRIGHT, LIMITED LIABILITY COMPANY (AV)

20 Boulder Crescent, 80903
Telephone: 719-578-8444
Fax: 719-578-8836

James T. Flynn | R. Tim McKenna
Bruce M. Wright

Michael C. Potarf

Representative Clients: Western National Bank of Colorado; Colorado Springs Savings and Loan Association; Chase Manhattan of Colorado, Inc.; Bank One Colorado Springs N.A.; First National Bank of Canon City; Colorado Bank and Trust Company of La Junta; Merrill Lynch Credit Corporation.

For full biographical listings, see the Martindale-Hubbell Law Directory

*DENVER,** Denver Co.

GLEN B. CLARK, JR., P.C. (AV)

Mile High Center, 1700 Broadway, Suite 1217, 80290
Telephone: 303-832-3000
Fax: 303-832-3044

Glen B. Clark, Jr.

Representative Clients: Citadel Bank, Colorado Springs; Cyclo Manufacturing Co.; Camp Coast to Coast, Inc.; Charter Bank & Trust, Inc.; Corporate Air, Inc.; Vacation Matrix, Inc.

For full biographical listings, see the Martindale-Hubbell Law Directory

IVAN D. FUGATE (AV)

North Valley Bank Building, 9001 North Washington Street, P.O. Box 29429, 80229
Telephone: 303-741-2484

For full biographical listings, see the Martindale-Hubbell Law Directory

HOLLAND & HART (AV)

Suite 2900, 555 Seventeenth Street, P.O. Box 8749, 80201
Telephone: 303-295-8000
Cable Address: "Holhart Denver"
Telecopier: 303-295-8261
TWX: 910-931-0568
Denver Tech Center, Colorado Office: Suite 1050, 4601 DTC Boulevard.
Telephone: 303-290-1600.
Telecopier: 303-290-1606.
Aspen, Colorado Office: 600 East Main Street.
Telephone: 303-925-3476.
Telecopier: 303-925-9367.
Boulder, Colorado Office: Suite 500, 1050 Walnut.
Telephone: 303-473-2700.
Telecopier: 303-473-2720.
Colorado Springs, Colorado Office: Suite 1000, 90 S. Cascade Avenue.
Telephone: 719-475-7730.
Telex: 82077 SHHTLX.
Telecopier: 719-634-2461.
Washington, D.C. Office: Suite 310, 1001 Pennsylvania Avenue, N.W.
Telephone: 202-638-5500.
Telecopier: 202-737-8998.
Boise, Idaho Office: Suite 1400, West One Plaza, 101 South Capitol Boulevard, P.O. Box 2527.
Telephone: 208-342-5000.
Telecopier: 208-343-8869.
Billings, Montana Office: Suite 1500, First Interstate Center, 401 North 31st Street, P.O. Box 639.
Telephone: 406-252-2166.
Telecopier: 406-252-1669.
Salt Lake City, Utah Office: Suite 880, 111 East Broadway.
Telephone: 801-578-6000.
FAX: 801-578-6010.
Cheyenne, Wyoming Office: Holland & Hart, A Partnership including Professional Corporations, Suite 500, 2020 Carey Avenue, P.O. Box 1347.
Telephone: 307-778-4200.
Telecopier: 307-778-8175.
Jackson, Wyoming Office: Holland & Hart, A Partnership including Professional Corporations, Suite 2, 175 South King Street, P.O. Box 68.
Telephone: 307-739-9741.
Telecopier: 307-739-9744.

MEMBERS OF FIRM

David Butler
William E. Murane
James P. Lindsay
Richard M. Koon
Mark R. Levy
Ronald M. Martin
Peter C. Houtsma
Mark D. Safty
Elizabeth A. Sharrer
Mary Ellen Scanlan
Debra S. Fagan

OF COUNSEL

Howard R. Tallman

ASSOCIATES

Elizabeth Carney
Robert P. Detrick
Shari R. Lefkoff
Veronica J. May

DENVER TECH CENTER, COLORADO RESIDENT PARTNERS

William W. Maywhort
Todd W. Miller

ASPEN, COLORADO RESIDENT PARTNER

Charles T. Brandt

COLORADO SPRINGS, COLORADO PARTNERS

Bruce T. Buell
Ronald M. Martin
Ronald A. Lehmann (Resident)

COLORADO SPRINGS, COLORADO RESIDENT ASSOCIATE

Brian T. Murphy

BOISE, IDAHO RESIDENT PARTNER

Larry E. Prince

BOISE, IDAHO RESIDENT OF COUNSEL

Debra K. Ellers

(See Next Column)

BOISE, IDAHO RESIDENT ASSOCIATES

Robert A. Faucher
Linda B. Jones

BILLINGS, MONTANA PARTNERS

Donald W. Quander
David R. Chisholm

BILLINGS, MONTANA RESIDENT ASSOCIATE

Bruce F. Fain

CHEYENNE, WYOMING PARTNER

Patrick R. Day (P.C.)

CHEYENNE, WYOMING OF COUNSEL

Teresa Burkett Buffington

CHEYENNE, WYOMING RESIDENT ASSOCIATE

James R. Belcher

For Complete List of Firm Personnel, See General Section

For full biographical listings, see the Martindale-Hubbell Law Directory

HOLME ROBERTS & OWEN LLC (AV)

Suite 4100, 1700 Lincoln, 80203
Telephone: 303-861-7000
Telex: 45-4460
Telecopier: 303-866-0200
Boulder, Colorado Office: Suite 400, 1401 Pearl Street.
Telephone: 303-444-5955.
Telecopier: 303-444-1063.
Colorado Springs, Colorado Office: Suite 1300, 90 South Cascade Avenue.
Telephone: 719-473-3800.
Telecopier: 719-633-1518.
Salt Lake City, Utah Office: Suite 1100, 111 East Broadway.
Telephone: 801-521-5800.
Telecopier: 801-521-9639.
London, England Office: 4th Floor, Mellier House, 26a Albemarle Street.
Telephone: 44-171-499-8776.
Telecopier: 44-171-499-7769.
Moscow, Russia Office: 14 Krivokolenny Pr., Suite 30, 101000.
Telephone: 095-925-7816.
Telecopier: 095-923-2726.

MEMBERS OF FIRM

James C. Owen Jr.
Martha Traudt Collins
Robert H. Bach

SPECIAL COUNSEL

Stephen P. Ward

For Complete List of Firm Personnel, See General Section

For full biographical listings, see the Martindale-Hubbell Law Directory

SHERMAN & HOWARD L.L.C. (AV)

Attorneys at Law
633 Seventeenth Street, Suite 3000, 80202
Telephone: 303-297-2900
Telecopier: 303-298-0940
Colorado Springs, Colorado Office: Suite 1500, 90 South Cascade Avenue, 80903.
Telephone: 719-475-2440.
Las Vegas, Nevada Office: Swendseid & Stern a member in Sherman & Howard L.L.C., 317 Sixth Street, 89101.
Telephone: 702-387-6073.
Reno, Nevada Office: Swendseid & Stern, a member in Sherman & Howard L.L.C., 50 West Liberty Street, Suite 660, 89501.
Telephone: 702-323-1980.

Garth C. Grissom
James L. Cunningham
Andrew L. Blair, Jr.
Mark L. Fulford
James F. Wood
Kenneth B. Siegel
Cynthia C. Benson
Joseph J. Bronesky
Robert L. Brown
Ronald M. Eddy
Susan Hicks Walker
Stephen S. Halasz

COUNSEL

John W. Low

Representative Clients: The Colorado State Bank of Denver; Rocky Mountain Automated Clearing House Assoc., Denver; Denver Clearing House Association; The Bank N.A.(Breckenridge); Community Bank of Parker; Mountain Parks Bank; Platte Valley Bank (Brighton); Frontier Bank of Denver.

For Complete List of Firm Personnel, See General Section

For full biographical listings, see the Martindale-Hubbell Law Directory

WELLER FRIEDRICH, LLC (AV)

One Civic Center, Suite 2000, 1560 Broadway, P.O. Box 989, 80201-0989
Telephone: 303-812-1200
FAX: 303-812-1212

David K. Kerr
Andrew J. Friedrich
Jerome M. Joseph
Dennis J. Bartlett

(See Next Column)

WELLER FRIEDRICH LLC, *Denver—Continued*

OF COUNSEL

Martin J. Andrew

Representative Clients: Abbott Laboratories; Associated Aviation Underwriters; Commercial Union Insurance Companies.
Reference: Colorado State Bank of Denver.

For full biographical listings, see the Martindale-Hubbell Law Directory

*DURANGO,** La Plata Co.

SHAND, MCLACHLAN & NEWBOLD, P.C. (AV)

124 East Ninth Street, P.O. Drawer I, 81302-2790
Telephone: 303-247-3091
Fax: 303-247-3100

E. Bentley Hamilton (1918-1981)
J. Douglas Shand
Michael E. McLachlan
Keith Newbold

David A. Bode
A. Michael Chapman (Resident)
Sheryl Rogers

For full biographical listings, see the Martindale-Hubbell Law Directory

VAIL, Eagle Co.

OTTO, PORTERFIELD & POST (AV)

0020 Eagle Road, P.O. Box 3149, 81658-3149
Telephone: 303-949-5380
Denver Direct Line: 303-623-5926
Fax: 303-845-9135

Frederick S. Otto
Wendell B. Porterfield, Jr.
William J. Post

Reference: 1st Bank of Vail; Vail Bank.

For full biographical listings, see the Martindale-Hubbell Law Directory

CONNECTICUT

*HARTFORD,** Hartford Co.

GORDON, MUIR AND FOLEY (AV)

Hartford Square North, Ten Columbus Boulevard, 06106-1944
Telephone: 203-525-5361
Telecopier: 203-525-4849

MEMBERS OF FIRM

William S. Gordon, Jr. (1946-1956)
George Muir (1939-1976)
Edward J. Foley (1955-1983)
Peter C. Schwartz
John J. Reid
John H. Goodrich, Jr.
R. Bradley Wolfe
Jon Stephen Berk
William J. Gallitto
Gerald R. Swirsky
Robert J. O'Brien
Philip J. O'Connor
Kenneth G. Williams
Chester J. Bukowski
Mary Ann Santacroce

ASSOCIATES

J. Lawrence Price
Mary Anne Alicia Charron
James G. Kelly
Kevin F. Morin
Claudia A. Baio
Patrick T. Treacy
Andrew J. Hern
Eileen Geel
Christopher L. Slack
Renee W. Dwyer
David B. Heintz

OF COUNSEL

Stephen M. Riley

Reference: Fleet Bank.

For full biographical listings, see the Martindale-Hubbell Law Directory

*NEW HAVEN,** New Haven Co.

HOGAN & RINI, P.C. (AV)

Gold Building, 8th Floor 234 Church Street, 06510
Telephone: 203-787-4191
Telecopier: 203-777-4032

John W. Hogan, Jr.
Joseph L. Rini
Sue A. Cousineau

OF COUNSEL

Mark S. Cousineau

For full biographical listings, see the Martindale-Hubbell Law Directory

NEW LONDON, New London Co.

WALLER, SMITH & PALMER, P.C. (AV)

52 Eugene O'Neill Drive, P.O. Box 88, 06320
Telephone: 203-442-0367
Telecopier: 203-447-9915
Old Lyme, Connecticut Office: 103-A Halls Road.
Telephone: 203-434-8063.

William W. Miner
Robert P. Anderson, Jr.
Robert W. Marrion
Hughes Griffis
Edward B. O'Connell
Frederick B. Gahagan
Linda D. Loucony
Mary E. Driscoll
William E. Wellette

Tracy M. Collins
Donna Richer Skaats

OF COUNSEL

Suzanne Donnelly Kitchings

General Counsel for: Colotone Group.
Counsel for: Union Trust Co.; Coastal Savings Bank; Cash Home Center, Inc.
Local Counsel for: Metropolitan Insurance Co.; Connecticut General Life Insurance Co.

For Complete List of Firm Personnel, See General Section

For full biographical listings, see the Martindale-Hubbell Law Directory

STAMFORD, Fairfield Co.

CHAPMAN & FENNELL (AV)

Three Landmark Square, 06901
Telephone: 203-353-8000
Telecopier: 203-353-8799
New York, New York Office: 330 Madison Avenue.
Telephone: 212-687-3600.
Washington, D.C. Office: 2000 L Street, N.W., Suite 200.
Telephone: 202-822-9351.

MEMBERS OF FIRM

John Haven Chapman
Philip M. Chiappone (Resident, New York, N.Y. Office)
Darrell K. Fennell (Resident, New York, N.Y. Office)
Peter S. Gummo
D. Seeley Hubbard
Eric S. Kamisher (Resident, New York, N.Y. Office)
Brian E. Moran
Victor L. Zimmermann, Jr.

ASSOCIATE

Barton Meyerhoff (Not admitted in CT)

OF COUNSEL

Kevin T. Hoffman
Carol E. Meltzer (Resident, New York, N.Y. Office)
Brainard S. Patton
E. Gabriel Perle (Not admitted in CT)
Victor J. Toth (Resident, Washington, D.C. Office)
Michael Winger (Resident, New York, N.Y. Office)

For full biographical listings, see the Martindale-Hubbell Law Directory

WOFSEY, ROSEN, KWESKIN & KURIANSKY (AV)

600 Summer Street, 06901
Telephone: 203-327-2300
FAX: 203-967-9273

MEMBERS OF FIRM

Abraham Wofsey (1915-1944)
Michael Wofsey (1927-1951)
David M. Rosen (1926-1967)
Julius B. Kuriansky (1910-1992)
Monroe Silverman
Emanuel Margolis
Howard C. Kaplan
Anthony R. Lorenzo
Edward M. Kweskin
David M. Cohen
Marshall Goldberg
Stephen A. Finn
Judith Rosenberg
Robert L. Teicher
Mark H. Henderson

Steven D. Grushkin

OF COUNSEL

Saul Kwartin
Sydney C. Kweskin (Retired)

ASSOCIATES

Brian Bandler
John J.L. Chober
Steven M. Frederick
Eric M. Higgins
James A. Lenes
Valerie E. Maze
Maurice K. Segall
Randall M. Skigen
Gregory J. Williams

Representative Clients: Benenson Realty; Cellular Information Systems, Inc.; Gateway Bank; Hartford Provision Company; Louis Dreyfus Corp.; Norwalk Federation of Teachers; Patient Care, Inc.; People's Bank; Ridgeway Shopping Center and Stamford Housing Authority.

For full biographical listings, see the Martindale-Hubbell Law Directory

WESTPORT, Fairfield Co.

TIROLA & HERRING (AV)

1221 Post Road East, P.O. Box 631, 06881
Telephone: 203-226-8926
Fax: 203-226-9500
New York, New York Office: Suite 4E, 10 Sheridan Square.
Telephone: 212-463-9642.

MEMBERS OF FIRM

Vincent S. Tirola
Elizabeth C. Seeley
Charles Fredericks, Jr.
Buddy O. H. Herring

Dan Shaban
Marc J. Grenier

OF COUNSEL

Edward Kanowitz
C. Michael Carter
Alan D. Lieberson

Reference: The Westport Bank and Trust Co.

For full biographical listings, see the Martindale-Hubbell Law Directory

DELAWARE

*WILMINGTON,** New Castle Co.

POTTER ANDERSON & CORROON (AV)

350 Delaware Trust Building, P.O. Box 951, 19899-0951
Telephone: 302-658-6771
FAX: 658-1192; 655-1190; 655-1199

MEMBERS OF FIRM

Richard L. McMahon
Charles S. McDowell
Leonard S. Togman
David B. Brown
David A. Anderson
Michael M. Ledyard

COUNSEL

W. Laird Stabler, Jr.

OF COUNSEL

Blaine T. Phillips

ASSOCIATES

Harold I. Salmons, III
Lewis C. Ledyard, III

Representative Clients: Chase Manhattan Bank (U.S.A.) N.A.; Delaware Trust Company; First National Bank of Maryland; Mellon Bank (East); Mercantile Bankshares; Midatlantic Bank; Second National Federal Savings Bank; Signet Bank; Wilmington Trust Company.

For Complete List of Firm Personnel, See General Section

For full biographical listings, see the Martindale-Hubbell Law Directory

DISTRICT OF COLUMBIA

WASHINGTON, D.C. Co.

***** indicates certain Bar Register subscribers, in cities of comparable size and importance, who maintain an additional office in Washington, D.C. and who have arranged for representation as a part of the Washington, D.C. listings that follow

BAKER & HOSTETLER (AV)

Washington Square, Suite 1100, 1050 Connecticut Avenue, N.W., 20036-5304
Telephone: 202-861-1500
In Cleveland, Ohio: 3200 National City Center, 1900 East Ninth Street.
Telephone: 216-621-0200.
In Columbus, Ohio: Capitol Square, Suite 2100, 65 East State Street.
Telephone: 614-228-1541.
In Denver, Colorado: 303 East 17th Avenue, Suite 1100.
Telephone: 303-861-0600.
In Houston, Texas: 1000 Louisiana, Suite 2000.
Telephone: 713-751-1600.
In Long Beach, California: 300 Oceangate, Suite 620.
Telephone: 310-432-2827.
In Los Angeles, California: 600 Wilshire Boulevard.
Telephone: 213-624-2400.
In Orlando, Florida: SunBank Center, Suite 2300, 200 South Orange Avenue.
Telephone: 305-841-1111.
In College Park, Maryland: 9658 Baltimore Boulevard, Suite 206.
Telephone: 301-441-2781.
In Alexandria, Virginia: 437 North Lee Street.
Telephone: 703-549-1294.
In San Francisco, California: One Sansome Street, Suite 2000.
Telephone: 415-951-4705.

(See Next Column)

PARTNERS

William J. Conti
Mario V. Mirabelli

For Complete List of Firm Personnel, See General Section

For full biographical listings, see the Martindale-Hubbell Law Directory

*** BELL, BOYD & LLOYD (AV)**

1615 L Street, N.W., 20036
Telephone: 202-466-6300
FAX: 202-463-0678
Chicago, Illinois Office: Three First National Plaza, Suite 3300, 70 West Madison Street.
Telephone: 312-372-1121.
FAX: 312-372-2098.

RESIDENT PARTNER

Henry M. Polmer

For Complete List of Firm Personnel, See General Section

For full biographical listings, see the Martindale-Hubbell Law Directory

CAMERON & HORNBOSTEL (AV)

Suite 700, 818 Connecticut Avenue, N.W., 20006
Telephone: 202-293-4690
Cable Address: "Continent"
Telecopier: 202-293-1877
New York, N.Y. Office: 230 Park Avenue.
Telephone: 212-682-4902.
Cable Address: "Continents, New York".
Telecopier: 212-697-0946.

MEMBERS OF FIRM

Duncan H. Cameron
Alexander W. Sierck
Bertrand J. Delanney (Resident, New York, N.Y. Office)
Frederick Simpich
Larry W. Thomas
Peter A. Hornbostel
Howard L. Vickery (Resident, New York, N.Y. Office)
William K. Ince
Dennis James, Jr.
Bruce Zagaris

ASSOCIATES

Gregory J. Bendlin
Michele C. Sherman
Rachel F. Herold (Resident at the New York Office)

OF COUNSEL

Carolyn W. Davenport (Resident at New York, N.Y. Office)
Richard Pu (Resident, New York, N.Y. Office)

For full biographical listings, see the Martindale-Hubbell Law Directory

FRIEDLANDER, MISLER, FRIEDLANDER, SLOAN & HERZ (AV)

Suite 700, 1101 Seventeenth Street, N.W., 20036
Telephone: 202-872-0800
Cable Address: "FMSHLAW"
Telex: 64273

OF COUNSEL

Jack L. Friedlander

MEMBERS OF FIRM

Stephen H. Friedlander
Morris Kletzkin
Leonard A. Sloan
Jeffrey W. Ochsman
Gerald Herz
Jerome Ostrov
Arnold S. Albert

ASSOCIATES

Jana Kay Guggenheim
Alan Dean Sundburg
Philippa T. Gasnier
Andrew B. Schulwolf (Not admitted in DC)
James J. Gallinaro
Seth B. Shapiro
Mark D. Crawford (Not admitted in DC)
Robert J. Strayhorne

For full biographical listings, see the Martindale-Hubbell Law Directory

HOGAN & HARTSON L.L.P. (AV)

Columbia Square, 555 13th Street, N.W., 20004-1109
Telephone: 202-637-5600
Telex: 89-2757
Cable Address: "Hogander Washington"
Fax: 202-637-5910
Brussels, Belgium Office: Avenue des Arts 41, 1040.
Telephone: (32.2) 505.09.11.
Fax: (32.2) 502.28.60.
London, England Office: Veritas House, 125 Finsbury Pavement, EC2A 1NQ.
Telephone: (44 171) 638.9595.
Fax: (44 171) 638.0884.
Moscow, Russia Office: 33/2 Usacheva Street, Building 3, 119048.
Telephone: (7095) 245-5190.
Fax: (7095) 245-5192.
Paris, France Office: Cabinet Wolfram: 14, rue Chauveau-Lagarde, 75008.
Telephone: (33-1) 44.71.97.00.
Fax: (33-1) 47.42.13.56.

(See Next Column)

HOGAN & HARTSON L.L.P., *Washington—Continued*

Prague, Czech Republic Office: Opletalova 37, 110 00.
Telephone: (42-2) 2422-9009.
Fax: (42-2) 2421-5105.
Warsaw, Poland Office: Marszalkowska 6/6, 00-590.
Telephone: (48 2) 628 0201; Int'l (48) 3912 1413.
Fax: (48 2) 628 7787; Int'l (48) 3912 1511.
Baltimore, Maryland Office: 111 South Calvert Street, 16th Floor.
Telephone: 410-659-2700.
Fax: 410-539-6981.
Bethesda, Maryland Office: Two Democracy Center, Suite 720, 6903 Rockledge Drive.
Telephone: 301-493-0030.
Fax: 301-493-5169.
Colorado Springs, Colorado Office: 518 North Nevada Avenue, Suite 200.
Telephone: 719-635-5900.
Fax: 719-635-2847.
Denver, Colorado Office: One Tabor Center, Suite 1500, 1200 Seventeenth Street.
Telephone: 303-899-7300.
Fax: 303-899-7333.
McLean, Virginia Office: 8300 Greensboro Drive.
Telephone: 703-848-2600.
Fax: 703-448-7650.

MEMBERS OF FIRM

Michael D. Colglazier (Resident, Baltimore, Maryland Office)
Edward C. Dolan
Robert J. Elliott
Kevin G. Gralley (Resident, Baltimore, Maryland Office)
Benton R. Hammond
J. Clinton Kelly (Resident, Baltimore, Maryland Office)
David P. King (Resident, Baltimore, Maryland Office)
Duncan S. Klinedinst (Resident, McLean, Virginia Office)
Kathleen M. Miko
Craig H. Ulman
Pamela G. Winthrop

COUNSEL

Susan E. Joseph

ASSOCIATES

James H. Lystad
Barbara G. Martin (Resident, Baltimore, Maryland Office)
Helen P. McClure
Pamela McKenzie Williams (Resident, Baltimore, Maryland Office)
Philip H. Wright (Resident, Baltimore, Maryland Office)

For Complete List of Firm Personnel, See General Section

For full biographical listings, see the Martindale-Hubbell Law Directory

HOUSLEY GOLDBERG KANTARIAN & BRONSTEIN, P.C. (AV)

Suite 700, 1220 19th Street, N.W., 20036
Telephone: 202-822-9611
Facsimile: 202-822-0140

Allan D. Housley (Not admitted in DC)
Daniel J. Goldberg
Harry K. Kantarian
Leonard S. Volin
Matthew G. Ash
Gary R. Bronstein
Edward B. Crosland, Jr.
James I Lundy, III
Howard S. Parris
Daniel H. Burd
James C. Stewart
Joseph Mark Poerio (Not admitted in DC)
K. Scott Fife (Not admitted in DC)
Cynthia Rebecca Cross

Paul D. Borja (Not admitted in DC)
Joel E. Rappoport
Neil H. Seidman (Not admitted in DC)
Joan S. Guilfoyle (Not admitted in DC)
Daniel Lee Hogans (Not admitted in DC)

References: Savings & Community Bankers of America; North Carolina Alliance of Community Financial Institutions; Kansas Savings and Loan League; American College of Mortgage Attorneys; 1st American Bank, Washington, D.C.

For full biographical listings, see the Martindale-Hubbell Law Directory

MULDOON, MURPHY & FAUCETTE (AV)

5101 Wisconsin Avenue, N.W., 20016
Telephone: 202-362-0840
Telecopier: 202-966-9409; 202-363-5068

MEMBERS OF FIRM

Joseph A. Muldoon, Jr.
George W. Murphy, Jr.
Douglas P. Faucette
John R. Hall
Thomas J. Haggerty (Not admitted in DC)
Richard V. Fitzgerald
Joseph G. Passaic, Jr.
Joseph P. Daly
John Bruno
Mary M. Jackley Sjoquist

(See Next Column)

ASSOCIATES

Leslie Murphy
Althea R. Day
Lori M. Beresford
Christina M. Gattuso (Not admitted in DC)
Ann E. Cox
Cynthia M. Krus (Not admitted in DC)
William E. Donnelly
Anne O'Connell Devereaux
Lawrence M. F. Spaccasi (Not admitted in DC)
Wendy L. Morris (Not admitted in DC)
Patricia A. Murphy (Not admitted in DC)
Kent M. Krudys
Philip G. Feigen (Not admitted in DC)
Andrew F. Campbell
Marc Paul Levy
William J.T. Strahan (Not admitted in DC)
Jeffrey Scibetta
Gwen M. Mulberry (Not admitted in DC)
Madra Michelle Alvis (Not admitted in DC)

OF COUNSEL

Mary V. Harcar
Lewis F. Morse
Ralph E. Frable

For full biographical listings, see the Martindale-Hubbell Law Directory

TIMOTHY D. NAEGELE & ASSOCIATES (AV)

Suite 300, 1250 24th Street, N.W., 20037
Telephone: 202-466-7500
Facsimile: 202-466-3079 or 466-2888
Los Angeles, California Office: Suite 2430, 1900 Avenue of the Stars, 90067
Telephone: 310-557-2300.
Facsimile: 310-457-4014.

ASSOCIATE

Ashley Gauthier (Not admitted in DC)

LEGAL SUPPORT PERSONNEL

LAW CLERKS

Robert C. Kersey
Craig Boyd Garner

For full biographical listings, see the Martindale-Hubbell Law Directory

SUTHERLAND, ASBILL & BRENNAN (AV)

1275 Pennsylvania Avenue, N.W., 20004-2404
Telephone: 202-383-0100
Cable Address: "Sutab Wash"
Telex: 89-501
Facsimile: 202-637-3593
Atlanta, Georgia Office: 999 Peachtree Street, N. E., 30309-3996.
Telephone: 404-853-8000.
New York, N.Y. Office: 1270 Avenue of the Americas, 10020-1700.
Telephone: 212-332-3000.
Austin, Texas Office: 111 Congress Avenue, 23rd Floor, 78701-4079.
Telephone: 512-469-3350.

James M. Cain
James D. Darrow
David A. Massey

For Complete List of Firm Personnel, See General Section

For full biographical listings, see the Martindale-Hubbell Law Directory

* THOMPSON, HINE AND FLORY (AV)

1920 N Street, N.W., 20036-1601
Telephone: 202-331-8800
Fax: 202-331-8330
Telex: 904173
Cable Address: "Caglaw"
Akron, Ohio Office: 50 S. Main Street, Suite 502, 44308-1828.
Telephone: 216-376-8090.
Fax: 216-376-8386.
Cincinnati, Ohio Office: 312 Walnut Street, 14th Floor, 45202-4029.
Telephone: 513-352-6700.
Fax: 513-241-4771.
Telex: 938003.
Cleveland, Ohio Office: 1100 National City Bank Building, 629 Euclid Avenue, 44114.
Telephone: 216-566-5500.
Fax: 216-566-5583.
Telex: 980217. Cable Address "Thomflor".
Columbus, Ohio Office: One Columbus, 10 West Broad Street, 43215-34353.
Telephone: 614-469-3200.
Fax: 614-469-3361.
Dayton, Ohio Office: 2000 Courthouse Plaza, N.E., 45402-1706.
Telephone: 513-443-6600.
Fax: 513-443-6637, 513-443-6635.
Palm Beach, Florida Office: 125 Worth Avenue, 33480-4466.
Telephone: 407-833-5900.
Fax: 407-833-5951.
Brussels, Belgium Office: Rue Des Chevaliers, Ridderstraat 14 - B.10, B-1050.
Telephone: 011-32-2-511-9326.
Fax: 011-32-2-513-9206.

(See Next Column)

THOMPSON, HINE AND FLORY—*Continued*

MEMBERS OF FIRM

Roberta B. Aronson
Louis Pohoryles

ASSOCIATE

Lisa Sullivan Franzen

For Complete List of Firm Personnel, See General Section

For full biographical listings, see the Martindale-Hubbell Law Directory

*** VENABLE, BAETJER, HOWARD & CIVILETTI (AV)**

A Partnership including Professional Corporations
Suite 1000, 1201 New York Avenue, N.W., 20005
Telephone: 202-962-4800
Fax: 202-962-8300
Baltimore, Maryland Office: Venable, Baetjer and Howard, 1800 Mercantile Bank & Trust Building, 2 Hopkins Plaza.
Telephone: 410-244-7400.
McLean, Virginia Office: Venable, Baetjer and Howard, Suite 400, 2010 Corporate Ridge.
Telephone: 703-760-1600.
Rockville, Maryland Office: Venable, Baetjer and Howard, Suite 500, One Church Street, P. O. Box 1906.
Telephone: 301-217-5600.
Towson, Maryland Office: Venable, Baetjer and Howard, 210 Allegheny Avenue, P. O. Box 5517.
Telephone: 410-494-6200.

MEMBERS OF FIRM

Benjamin R. Civiletti (P.C.) (Also at Baltimore and Towson, Maryland Offices)
Ronald R. Glancz
David J. Levenson
Joe A. Shull
Kenneth C. Bass, III (Also at McLean, Virginia Office)
Joel Z. Silver
Edward F. Glynn, Jr.
Thomas B. Hudson (Also at Baltimore, Maryland Office)
James R. Myers
Jeffrey A. Dunn (Also at Baltimore, Maryland Office)
George F. Pappas (Also at Baltimore, Maryland Office)
James L. Shea (Not admitted in DC; also at Baltimore, Maryland Office)
William D. Quarles (Also at Towson, Maryland Office)
James A. Dunbar (Also at Baltimore, Maryland Office)
Bruce H. Jurist (Also at Baltimore, Maryland Office)
Linda L. Lord
Paul A. Serini (Not admitted in DC; Also at Baltimore, Maryland Office)

ASSOCIATES

David S. Darland
D. Brent Gunsalus
Andrew R. Herrup

For Complete List of Firm Personnel, See General Section

For full biographical listings, see the Martindale-Hubbell Law Directory

WILMER, CUTLER & PICKERING (AV)

2445 M Street, N.W., 20037-1420
Telephone: 202-663-6000
Facsimile: 202-663-6363
Internet: Law@Wilmer.Com
European Offices:
4 Carlton Gardens, London, SW1Y 5AA, England. Telephone: 011 (4471) 839-4466.
Facsimile: 011 (4471) 839-3537.
Rue de la Loi 15 Wetstraat, B-1040 Brussels, Belgium. Telephone: 011 (322) 231-0903.
Facsimile: 011 (322) 230-4322.
Friedrichstrasse 95, D-10117 Berlin, Germany. Telephone: 011 (4930) 2643-3601.
Facsimile: 011 (4930) 2643-3630.

MEMBERS OF FIRM

Ronald J. Greene
Michael S. Helfer
Christopher R. Lipsett
Russell J. Bruemmer
Anastasia D. Kelly

COUNSEL

Murray A. Indick

SPECIAL COUNSEL

Thomas J. Delaney (Not admitted in DC)

For Complete List of Firm Personnel, See General Section

For full biographical listings, see the Martindale-Hubbell Law Directory

FLORIDA

*CLEARWATER,** Pinellas Co.

LARSON & BOBENHAUSEN, PROFESSIONAL ASSOCIATION (AV)

16120 U.S. Highway 19 North, Suite 210, P.O. Box 17620, 34622-0620
Telephone: 813-535-5594
Telecopier: 813-535-4266

Roger A. Larson
Gale M. Bobenhausen
Scott Torrie
Camille J. Iurillo

Representative Clients: First Union National Bank of Florida; AmSouth Bank of Florida; Barnett Bank of Pasco County; Barnett Banks, Inc.; SunBank of Tampa Bay, N.A.; Rutenberg Housing Corp.

For full biographical listings, see the Martindale-Hubbell Law Directory

*FORT LAUDERDALE,** Broward Co.

SIMON, MOSKOWITZ & MANDELL, P.A. (AV)

Suite 510, 800 Corporate Drive, 33334
Telephone: 305-491-2000; Boca Raton Line: 407-750-7700
FAX: 305-491-2051

Eric A. Simon
Michael W. Moskowitz
Craig J. Mandell
Kenneth A. Rubin
William G. Salim, Jr.

Greg H. Rosenthal

For full biographical listings, see the Martindale-Hubbell Law Directory

*KISSIMMEE,** Osceola Co.

POHL & BROWN, P.A.

(See Winter Park)

LAKELAND, Polk Co.

PETERSON, MYERS, CRAIG, CREWS, BRANDON & PUTERBAUGH, P.A. (AV)

100 East Main Street, P.O. Box 24628, 33802-4628
Telephone: 813-683-6511; 676-6934
Telecopier: 813-682-8031
Lake Wales, Florida Office: 130 East Central Avenue, P.O. Box 1079.
Telephones: 813-676-7611; 683-8942.
Winter Haven, Florida Office: Suite 300, 141 5th Street, N.W., P.O. Drawer 7608.
Telephone: 813-294-3360

Jack P. Brandon
Beach A Brooks, Jr.
J. Davis Connor
Roy A. Craig, Jr.
Jacob C. Dykxhoorn
Dennis P. Johnson
Kevin C. Knowlton
Douglas A. Lockwood, III
Corneal B. Myers
Cornelius B. Myers, III
Robert E. Puterbaugh
Abel A. Putnam
Thomas B. Putnam, Jr.
Deborah A. Ruster
Stephen R. Senn
Andrea Teves Smith
Kerry M. Wilson

General Counsel For: Barnett Bank of Polk County.
Representative Clients: Mutual Wholesale Co.; Sun Bank/Mid-Florida, N.A.; Chase Commercial Corp.; Barnett Banks, Inc.; Ben Hill Griffin, Inc.; Alcoma Association, Inc.
Approved Attorneys For: Equitable Life Assurance Society of the United States; Federal Land Bank of Columbia, S.C.; Attorneys' Title Insurance Fund.

For full biographical listings, see the Martindale-Hubbell Law Directory

LAKE WALES, Polk Co.

PETERSON, MYERS, CRAIG, CREWS, BRANDON & PUTERBAUGH, P.A. (AV)

130 East Central Avenue, P.O. Box 1079, 33853
Telephone: 813-676-7611; 683-8942
Telecopier: 813-676-0643
Lakeland, Florida Office: 100 East Main Street, P.O. Box 24628.
Telephones: 813-683-6511; 676-6934.
Winter Haven, Florida Office: Suite 300, 141 5th Street, N.W., P.O. Drawer 7608.
Telephone: 813-294-3360.

Jack P. Brandon
Beach A Brooks, Jr.
Beach A Brooks, Jr.
J. Davis Connor
Roy A. Craig, Jr.
Jacob C. Dykxhoorn
Dennis P. Johnson
Kevin C. Knowlton
Douglas A. Lockwood, III
Corneal B. Myers
Cornelius B. Myers, III
Robert E. Puterbaugh
Robert E. Puterbaugh
Abel A. Putnam

(See Next Column)

PETERSON, MYERS, CRAIG, CREWS, BRANDON & PUTERBAUGH P.A., *Lake Wales—Continued*

Thomas B. Putnam, Jr.
Deborah A. Ruster
Stephen R. Senn
Andrea Teves Smith
Kerry M. Wilson

General Counsel for: Barnett Bank of Polk County.
Representative Clients: Mutual Wholesale Co.; Sun Bank/Mid-Florida, N.A.; Chase Commercial Corp.; Barnett Banks, Inc.; Ben Hill Griffin, Inc.; Alcoma Association, Inc.
Approved Attorneys for: Equitable Life Assurance Society of the United States; Federal Land Bank of Columbia, S.C.; Attorneys' Title Insurance Fund.

For full biographical listings, see the Martindale-Hubbell Law Directory

*MIAMI,** Dade Co.

MERSHON, SAWYER, JOHNSTON, DUNWODY & COLE (AV)

A Partnership including Professional Associations
Suite 4500 First Union Financial Center, 200 South Biscayne Boulevard, 33131-2387
Telephone: 305-358-5100
Cable Address: "Mercole"
Telex: 515705
Fax: 305-376-8654
Naples, Florida Office: Pelican Bay Corporate Centre, Suite 501, 5551 Ridgewood Drive.
Telephone: 813-598-1055.
Fax: 813-598-1868.
West Palm Beach, Florida Office: 777 South Flagler Drive, Suite 900.
Telephone: 407-659-5990.
Fax: 407-659-6313.
Key West, Florida Office: 3132 North Side Drive, Suite 102.
Telephone: 305-296-1774.
Fax: 305-296-1715
London, England Office: Blake Lodge, Bridge Lane, London SW11 3AD, England.
Telephone: 44-71-978-7748.
Fax: 44-71-350-0156.

MEMBERS OF FIRM

Barry G. Craig (P.A.)
Douglas F. Darbut
David B. McCrea (P.A.)

ASSOCIATE

Doreen S. Moloney

Representative Clients: Arvida/JMB Partners; Bankers Trust Co.; Biscayne Kennel Club, Inc.; The Chase Manhattan Bank, N.A.; Lennar Corp.; Reynolds Metals Co.; United States Sugar Corp.; University of Miami.

For Complete List of Firm Personnel, See General Section

For full biographical listings, see the Martindale-Hubbell Law Directory

STUZIN AND CAMNER, PROFESSIONAL ASSOCIATION (AV)

25th Floor, 1221 Brickell Avenue, 33131-3260
Telephone: 305-577-0600

Charles B. Stuzin
Alfred R. Camner
Stanley A. Beiley
Marsha D. Bilzin
David S. Garbett
Nina S. Gordon
Barry D. Hunter
Nikki J. Nedbor
Neale J. Poller

Lisa R. Carstarphen
Maria E. Chang
Barry P. Gruher
Gustavo D. Llerena
Sherry D. McMillan
Roger A. Preziosi

OF COUNSEL

Anne Shari Camner

References: Citizens Federal Bank; City National Bank of Miami; Barnett Bank of South Florida, N.A.

For full biographical listings, see the Martindale-Hubbell Law Directory

TAYLOR, BRION, BUKER & GREENE (AV)

Fourteenth Floor, 801 Brickell Avenue, 33131-2900
Telephone: 305-377-6700
Telex: 153653 Taybri
Telecopier: 305-371-4578; 371-4579
Tallahassee, Florida Office: Suite 250, 225 South Adams Street.
Telephone: 904-222-7717.
Telecopier: 904-222-3494.
Key West, Florida Office: 500 Fleming Street.
Telephone: 305-292-1776.
Telecopier: 305-292-1982.
Fort Lauderdale, Florida Office: Barnett Bank Plaza, 12th Floor, One East Broward Boulevard.
Telephone: 305-522-6700.
Telecopier: 305-522-6711.
Coral Gables, Florida Office: 2801 Ponce De Leon Boulevard, Suite 707.
Telephone: 305-445-7577.
Telecopier: 305-446-9944.

(See Next Column)

George F. Allen, Jr.
Leila D. Anderson (Fort Lauderdale)
John S. Andrews (Fort Lauderdale)
Peter C. Bianchi, Jr.
David S. Bowman (Fort Lauderdale)
Wilbur E. Brewton (Tallahassee)
Harold L. Greene
Michael E. Hill
W. Douglas Moody, Jr. (Tallahassee)
Gerald W. Moore
James W. Moore
Thomas J. Palmieri
Robert J. Paterno
Anthony F. Sanchez
Robert S. Singer
Thomas J. Skola
Henry H. Taylor, Jr.
Arnaldo Velez
R. Bruce Wallace

OF COUNSEL

Frank D. Hall (Coral Gables)
Burton Harrison
Robert A. Spottswood

For list of Representative Clients, see General Section.

For Complete List of Firm Personnel, See General Section

For full biographical listings, see the Martindale-Hubbell Law Directory

*ORLANDO,** Orange Co.

POHL & BROWN, P.A.

(See Winter Park)

*SARASOTA,** Sarasota Co.

ABEL, BAND, RUSSELL, COLLIER, PITCHFORD & GORDON, CHARTERED (AV)

Barnett Bank Center, 240 South Pineapple Avenue, P.O. Box 49948, 34230-6948
Telephone: 813-366-6660
FAX: 813-366-3999
Fort Myers, Florida Office: The Tidewater Building, 1375 Jackson Street, Suite 201, 33901.
Telephone: 813-337-0062.
FAX: 813-337-0406.
Venice, Florida Office: Suite 199, 333 South Tamiami Trail, 34285.
Telephone: 813-485-8200.
Fax: 813-488-9436.

David S. Band
Jeffrey S. Russell
Ronald L. Collier
Malcolm J. Pitchford
Cheryl Lasris Gordon
Anthony J. Abate
Steven J. Chase
Kathryn Angell Carr
Michael S. Taaffe
Mark W. McFall
Jan Walters Pitchford

OF COUNSEL

Harvey J. Abel
Johnson S. Savary

Saralyn Abel
Douglas M. Bales
Gregory S. Band
John A. Garner
Mark D. Hildreth
Jane M. Kennedy
Christine Edwards Lamia
Bradley D. Magee
George H. Mazzarantani
Philip C. Zimmerman

References: Barnett Bank of Southwest Florida; Sun Bank/Gulf Coast.

For full biographical listings, see the Martindale-Hubbell Law Directory

WILLIAMS, PARKER, HARRISON, DIETZ & GETZEN, PROFESSIONAL ASSOCIATION (AV)

1550 Ringling Boulevard, 34230-3258
Telephone: 813-366-4800
Telecopier: 813-366-5109
Mailing Address: P.O. Box 3258, Sarasota, Florida, 34230-3258

William T. Harrison, Jr.
George A. Dietz
Monte K. Marshall
James L. Ritchey
Hugh McPheeters, Jr.
William G. Lambrecht
John T. Berteau
John V. Cannon, III
Charles D. Bailey, Jr.
J. Michael Hartenstine
Michele Boardman Grimes
James L. Turner
William M. Seider
Elizabeth C. Marshall
Robert W. Benjamin
Frank Strelec
David A. Wallace
Terri Jayne Salt
Jeffrey A. Grebe
John Leslie Moore
Mark A. Schwartz
Susan Barrett Jewell
Phillip D. Eck

OF COUNSEL

Frazer F. Hilder
William E. Getzen
Elvin W. Phillips

Counsel for: Sarasota-Manatee Airport Authority; Sarasota County Public Hospital Board; William G. & Marie Selby Foundation; Taylor Woodrow Homes Ltd.; The School Board of Sarasota County.
Local Counsel for: NationsBank of Florida; Arvida/JMB Partners.

For Complete List of Firm Personnel, See General Section

For full biographical listings, see the Martindale-Hubbell Law Directory

*TALLAHASSEE,** Leon Co.

DAVIS & TAFF (AV)

210 East College Avenue, Suite 200, P.O. Box 37190, 32315-7190
Telephone: 904-222-6026
Telecopier: 904-224-1039

MEMBERS OF FIRM

Ken Davis
Angus Broward Taff, Jr.

For full biographical listings, see the Martindale-Hubbell Law Directory

*TAMPA,** Hillsborough Co.

GLENN RASMUSSEN & FOGARTY (AV)

1300 First Union Center, 100 South Ashley Drive, P.O. Box 3333, 33601-3333
Telephone: 813-229-3333
Fax: 813-229-5946

Rod Anderson
David E. Arroyo
Robert W. Bivins
Sharon Docherty Danco
Richard E. Fee
David S. Felman
Michael A. Fogarty
Robert B. Glenn
Donald S. Hart, Jr.
Michael S. Hooker
Erin C. Keleher
Bradford D. Kimbro
Guy P. McConnell
Robert C. Rasmussen
Edwin G. Rice
Steven W. Vazquez

Reference: First Union National Bank of Florida.

For full biographical listings, see the Martindale-Hubbell Law Directory

LANGFORD, HILL & TRYBUS, P.A. (AV)

Suite 800, Bayshore Place, 601 Bayshore Boulevard, 33606
Telephone: 813-251-5533
Telecopier: 813-251-1900
Wats: 1-800-277-2005

E. C. Langford
Edward A. Hill
Ronald H. Trybus
Ronald G. Hock
Catherine M. Catlin
Debra M. Kubicsek
William B. Smith

Fredrique B. Boire
Muriel Desloovere
Kevin H. O'Neill
Vicki L. Page
Frederick T. Reeves
Barbara A. Sinsley
Stephens B. Woodrough (Not admitted in FL)
Anthony G. Woodward

Representative Clients: Affiliated of Florida, Inc.; American Federation Insurance Co.; Armor Insurance; Bank of Tampa; Central Bank of Tampa; Cintas Corp.; Container Corporation of America; CU Financial Services; Farm Stores, Inc.; First Union Home Equity Bank.

For full biographical listings, see the Martindale-Hubbell Law Directory

MORRISON, MORRISON & MILLS, P.A. (AV)

1200 West Platt Street Suite 100, 33606
Telephone: 813-258-3311
Telecopier: 813-258-3209

Thomas K. Morrison
Susan B. Morrison
Frederick J. Mills
Tracey Karen Jaensch
James E. Holmes, Jr.

Representative Clients: SouthTrust Bank of West Florida; SouthTrust Bank of Alabama, National Association; NationsBank of Florida, N.A.; Mercantile Bank; Barnett Banks, Inc.; Southern Commerce Bank; Sun Bank of Pasco County; Hillsborough County Industrial Development Authority; Automation Packaging, Inc.; Medical Data Management, Inc.

For full biographical listings, see the Martindale-Hubbell Law Directory

ZUCKERMAN, SPAEDER, TAYLOR & EVANS (AV)

101 East Kennedy Boulevard, Suite 3140, 33602
Telephone: 813-221-1010
Fax: 813-223-7961
Miami, Florida Office: Suite 900, Miami Center, 201 South Biscayne Boulevard.
Telephones: 305-358-5000; 305-579-0110; Broward County: 305-523-0277.
Fax: 305-579-9749.
Ft. Lauderdale, Florida Office: One East Broward Boulevard, Suite 700.
Telephone: 305-356-0463.
Fax: 305-356-0406.
Washington, D.C. Office: Zuckerman, Spaeder, Goldstein, Taylor & Kolker, 1201 Connecticut Avenue, N.W.
Telephone: 202-778-1800.
Fax: 202-822-8106.
Baltimore, Maryland Office: Zuckerman, Spaeder, Goldstein, Taylor & Better, Suite 2440, 100 East Pratt Street.
Telephone: 410-332-0444.
Fax: 410-659-0436.

(See Next Column)

New York, N.Y. Office: Zuckerman, Spaeder, Goldstein, Taylor & Kolker, 1114 Avenue of the Americas, 45th Floor, Grace Building.
Telephone: 212-479-6500.
Fax: 212-479-6512.

MEMBERS OF FIRM

Ronald B. Ravikoff (Resident, Miami, Florida Office)
Michael Steven Greene (Resident, Miami, Florida Office)

ASSOCIATES

Jeffrey P. Agron (Resident, Miami, Florida Office)
Jill M. Granat (Resident, Miami, Florida Office)
Rebeca Sanchez-Roig (Resident, Miami, Florida Office)

For full biographical listings, see the Martindale-Hubbell Law Directory

WINTER HAVEN, Polk Co.

PETERSON, MYERS, CRAIG, CREWS, BRANDON & PUTERBAUGH, P.A. (AV)

Suite 300, 141 5th Street N.W., P.O. Drawer 7608, 33883-7608
Telephone: 813-294-3360
Lake Wales, Florida Office: 130 East Central Avenue, P.O. Box 1079.
Telephones: 813-676-7611; 683-8942.
Lakeland, Florida Office: 100 East Main Street, P.O. Box 24628.
Telephones: 813-683-6511; 676-6934.

Jack P. Brandon
Beach A Brooks, Jr.
J. Davis Connor
Michael S. Craig
Roy A. Craig, Jr.
Jacob C. Dykxhoorn
Dennis P. Johnson
Kevin C. Knowlton
Douglas A. Lockwood, III
Corneal B. Myers
Cornelius B. Myers, III
Robert E. Puterbaugh
Abel A. Putnam
Thomas B. Putnam, Jr.
Deborah A. Ruster
Stephen R. Senn
Andrea Teves Smith
Kerry M. Wilson

General Counsel for: Barnett Bank of Polk County.
Representative Clients: Mutual Wholesale Co.; Sun Bank/Mid-Florida, N.A.; Chase Commercial Corp.; Barnett Banks, Inc.; Ben Hill Griffin, Inc.; Alcoma Association, Inc.
Approved Attorneys for: Attorneys' Title Insurance Fund; Federal Land Bank, Columbia, South Carolina; Equitable Life Assurance Society of the United States.

For full biographical listings, see the Martindale-Hubbell Law Directory

WINTER PARK, Orange Co.

POHL & BROWN, P.A. (AV)

280 West Canton Avenue, Suite 410, P.O. Box 3208, 32789
Telephone: 407-647-7645; 407-647-POHL
Telefax: 407-647-2314

Frank L. Pohl
Usher L. Brown
Houston E. Short
Dwight I. Cool
William W. Pouzar
Mary B. Van Leuven

OF COUNSEL

Frederick W. Peirsol

Representative Clients: Orange County Comptroller; Osceola County; School Board of Osceola County, Florida; Osceola Tourist Development Council; NationsBank of Florida, N.A.; SunBank, N.A.; The Bank of Winter Park; Bekins Moving and Storage Co., Inc.; Champion Boats, Inc.; KeyCom Telephone Systems, Inc.

For full biographical listings, see the Martindale-Hubbell Law Directory

GEORGIA

*ATLANTA,** Fulton Co.

ALSTON & BIRD (AV)

A Partnership including Professional Corporations
One Atlantic Center, 1201 West Peachtree Street, 30309-3424
Telephone: 404-881-7000
Telecopier: 404-881-7777
Cable Address: AMGRAM GA
Telex: 54-2996
Easylink: 62985848
Washington, D.C. Office: 700 Thirteenth Street, Suite 350 20005-3960.
Telephone: 202-508-3300.
Telecopier: 202-508-3333.

MEMBERS OF FIRM

F. Dean Copeland
John L. Douglas
Ralph F. MacDonald III
John A. Buchman (Not admitted in GA)
Laura Glover Thatcher
Frank M. Conner III
Ira H. Parker
David E. Brown, Jr.

(See Next Column)

ALSTON & BIRD, *Atlanta—Continued*

ASSOCIATES

W. Thomas Carter III
John N. Fleming
Daniel M. LeBey
Kimberly Dyslin Rountree
Michael L. Stevens
Thomas L. West III

For Complete List of Firm Personnel, See General Section

For full biographical listings, see the Martindale-Hubbell Law Directory

LONG ALDRIDGE & NORMAN (AV)

A Partnership including Professional Corporations
One Peachtree Center, Suite 5300, 303 Peachtree Street, 30308
Telephone: 404-527-4000
Telecopier: 404-527-4198
Washington, D.C. Office: Suite 950, 1615 L Street, 20036.
Telephone: 202-223-7033.
Telecopier: 202-223-7013.

MEMBERS OF FIRM

John G. Aldridge
David R. Bucey
Thomas D. Hall
Patrick M. McGeehan

ASSOCIATES

James L. Barkin
Mindy S. Planer

OF COUNSEL

James W. Culbreth
C. Edward Kuntz
Gerald D. Walling

For Complete List of Firm Personnel, See General Section

For full biographical listings, see the Martindale-Hubbell Law Directory

SUTHERLAND, ASBILL & BRENNAN (AV)

999 Peachtree Street, N.E., 30309-3996
Telephone: 404-853-8000
Facsimile: 404-853-8806
Washington, D.C. Office: 1275 Pennsylvania Avenue, N.W., 20004-2404.
Telephone: 202-383-0100.
New York, N.Y. Office: 1270 Avenue of the Americas, 10020-1700.
Telephone: 212-332-3000.
Austin, Texas Office: 111 Congress Avenue, 23rd Floor, 78701-4079.
Telephone: 512-469-3350.

Peter H. Dean
B. Knox Dobbins
Thomas B. Hyman, Jr.
Edward W. Kallal, Jr.
Mark D. Kaufman
Richard G. Murphy, Jr.
Haynes R. Roberts

For Complete List of Firm Personnel, See General Section

For full biographical listings, see the Martindale-Hubbell Law Directory

*AUGUSTA,** Richmond Co.

WARLICK, TRITT & STEBBINS (AV)

15th Floor, First Union Bank Building, 30901
Telephone: 706-722-7543
Fax: 706-722-1822
Columbia County Office: 119 Davis Road, Martinez, Georgia 30907.
Telephone: 706-860-7595.
Fax: 705-860-7597.

MEMBERS OF FIRM

William Byrd Warlick
Roy D. Tritt (Resident, Martinez Office)
Charles C. Stebbins, III
E. L. Clark Speese
Michael W. Terry
D. Scott Broyles
Ross S. Snellings
C. Gregory Bryan

OF COUNSEL

Richard E. Miley

For full biographical listings, see the Martindale-Hubbell Law Directory

*COLUMBUS,** Muscogee Co.

DAVIDSON, CALHOUN & MILLER, P.C. (AV)

The Joseph House, 828 Broadway, P.O. Box 2828, 31902-2828
Telephone: 706-327-2552
Telecopier: 706-323-5838

J. Quentin Davidson, Jr.
Charles W. Miller
H. Owen Lee

For Complete List of Firm Personnel, See General Section

For full biographical listings, see the Martindale-Hubbell Law Directory

HATCHER, STUBBS, LAND, HOLLIS & ROTHSCHILD (AV)

Suite 500 The Corporate Center, 233 12th Street, P.O. Box 2707, 31902-2707
Telephone: 706-324-0201
Telecopier: 706-322-7747

(See Next Column)

MEMBERS OF FIRM

Albert W. Stubbs
Alan F. Rothschild
William B. Hardegree
Morton A. Harris
J. Barrington Vaught
Charles T. Staples
James E. Humes, II
Joseph L. Waldrep
Robert C. Martin, Jr.
George W. Mize, Jr.
John M. Tanzine, III
Alan F. Rothschild, Jr.
William C. Pound

ASSOCIATES

Mote W. Andrews III
C. Morris Mullin
Theodore Darryl (Ted) Morgan

General Counsel for: Trust Company Bank of Columbus, N.A.; TOM'S Foods Inc.; Muscogee County Board of Education; Burnham Service Corp.; Kinnett Dairies, Inc.; St. Francis Hospital, Inc.
Local Counsel for: First Union National Bank of Georgia.

For Complete List of Firm Personnel, See General Section

For full biographical listings, see the Martindale-Hubbell Law Directory

*GRIFFIN,** Spalding Co.

ROBERT H. SMALLEY, JR. PROFESSIONAL CORPORATION (AV)

115 North Sixth Street, P.O. Box 907, 30224
Telephone: 404-228-2125
Telecopier: 404-228-5018

Robert H. Smalley, Jr.
Thomas E. Baynham, III

Representative Clients: The Bank of Spalding County; Griffin Spalding County Development Authority; Masada Communications, Ltd. (CATV); Union Camp Corp. (Local Counsel).

For full biographical listings, see the Martindale-Hubbell Law Directory

*LAWRENCEVILLE,** Gwinnett Co.

ANDERSEN, DAVIDSON & TATE, P.C. (AV)

324 West Pike Street, Suite 200, P.O. Box 265, 30246-0265
Telephone: 404-822-0900
Telecopier: 404-822-9680

Thomas J. Andersen
Jeffrey R. Mahaffey

References: Trust Company Bank; The Bank of Gwinnett County; Chicago Title Insurance Co.; Title Insurance Company of Minnesota; Lawyers Title Insurance Co.

For Complete List of Firm Personnel, See General Section

For full biographical listings, see the Martindale-Hubbell Law Directory

WEBB, TANNER & POWELL (AV)

Suite 300 Gwinnett Federal Building, 750 South Perry Street, P.O. Box 27, 30246
Telephone: 404-962-8545; 963-3423
Fax: 404-963-3424

MEMBERS OF FIRM

Jones Webb
William G. Tanner
Anthony O. L. Powell

Attorneys for: Gwinnett Federal Savings & Loan Assn.; City of Lawrenceville, Ga.; Water and Sewer Authority of Gwinnett County; Federal Land Bank of Columbia; Georgia Power Co.; Lawyers Title Insurance Corp.; Young Harris College, Young Harris, Georgia; Chicago Title Insurance Co.

For Complete List of Firm Personnel, See General Section

For full biographical listings, see the Martindale-Hubbell Law Directory

*MACON,** Bibb Co.

HALL, BLOCH, GARLAND & MEYER (AV)

1500 Charter Medical Building, P.O. Box 5088, 31213-3199
Telephone: 912-745-1625
Telecopier: 912-741-8822

MEMBERS OF FIRM

J. E. Hall (1876-1945)
Charles J. Bloch (1893-1974)
Ellsworth Hall, Jr. (1908-1984)
J. René Hawkins (1924-1971)
Ellsworth Hall, III
F. Kennedy Hall
Benjamin M. Garland
J. Patrick Meyer, Jr.
J. Steven Stewart
J. Burton Wilkerson, Jr.
Duncan D. Walker, III
Mark E. Toth

ASSOCIATES

Ramsey T. Way, Jr.
Todd C. Brooks

F. Kennedy Hall, Division Counsel (Georgia): Norfolk Southern Corporation; Norfolk Southern Railway Company.
Counsel for: Wachovia Bank of Georgia, N.A.; Charter Medical Corporation; South Georgia Natural Gas Co.; Helena Chemical Corp.; American Druggist Insurance Cop.; Fickling & Walker Asset and Property Management, Inc.; Navistar International Corporation.

For full biographical listings, see the Martindale-Hubbell Law Directory

Macon—Continued

SELL & MELTON (AV)

A Partnership including a Professional Corporation
14th Floor, Charter Medical Building, P.O. Box 229, 31297-2899
Telephone: 912-746-8521
Telecopier: 912-745-6426

Andrew W. McKenna (1918-1981)
E. S. Sell, Jr.
John D. Comer
Buckner F. Melton
Mitchel P. House, Jr.
Joseph W. Popper, Jr.
Doye E. Green
Edward S. Sell, III
John A. Draughon
R. (Chix) Miller
Russell M. Boston (P.C.)
Brian J. Passante

ASSOCIATES

Doye E. Green, Jr.
Jeffrey B. Hanson

General Counsel for: Macon Telegraph Publishing Co. (The Macon Telegraph); Macon-Bibb County Hospital Authority; County of Bibb; County of Twiggs; Smith & Sons Foods, Inc. (S & S Cafeterias); Macon Bibb County Industrial Authority; Burgess Pigment Co.

For Complete List of Firm Personnel, See General Section

For full biographical listings, see the Martindale-Hubbell Law Directory

*MARIETTA,** Cobb Co.

BARNES, BROWNING, TANKSLEY & CASURELLA (AV)

Suite 225, 166 Anderson Street, 30060
Telephone: 404-424-1500
Fax: 404-424-1740

MEMBERS OF FIRM

Roy E. Barnes
Thomas J. Browning
Charles B. Tanksley
Thomas J. Casurella (1956-1989)
Jerry A. Landers, Jr.
Jeffrey G. Casurella
Benny C. Priest

OF COUNSEL

George T. Smith
Howard D. Rothbloom

For full biographical listings, see the Martindale-Hubbell Law Directory

HAWAII

*HONOLULU,** Honolulu Co.

CADES SCHUTTE FLEMING & WRIGHT (AV)

Formerly Smith, Wild, Beebe & Cades
1000 Bishop Street, P.O. Box 939, 96808
Telephone: 808-521-9200
Telex: 7238589
Telecopier: 808-531-8738
Affiliated Law Firm: Udom-Prok Associates Law Offices, 105/36 Tharinee Mansion, Borom Raj Chananee Road Bangkoknoi, Bangkok, Thailand, 10700.
Telephone: 011 660 435-4146.
Kailua-Kona, Hawaii Office: Hualalai Center, Suite B-303, 75-170 Hualalai Road.
Telephone: 808-329-5811.
Telecopier: 808-326-1175.

MEMBERS OF FIRM

Robert B. Bunn
Douglas E. Prior
E. Gunner Schull
Michael P. Porter
Donald E. Scearce
Richard A. Hicks
Bernice Littman
Nicholas C. Dreher
Mark A. Hazlett
Philip J. Leas
Larry T. Takumi
Nelson N. S. Chun
Darryl H. W. Johnston
Cary S. Matsushige
Gino L. Gabrio
Martin E. Hsia
Gail M. Tamashiro
Grace Nihei Kido
Donna Y. L. Leong
David F.E. Banks

ASSOCIATES

Jeffrey D. Watts
Marjorie A. Lau
Laurie A. Kuribayashi
James H. Ashford
Michele M. Sunahara
Nani Lee (Resident, Kona Office)
Carlito P. Caliboso
Daniel H. Devaney IV
Karen Wong
Jeffrey K. Natori
Dean T. Yamamoto

OF COUNSEL

Harold S. Wright

Counsel for: Amfac, Inc.; First Hawaiian Bank; Bishop Trust Co., Ltd.; The Bank of Tokyo, Ltd.; American Savings Bank, F.S.B.; The Industrial Bank of Japan, Ltd.

(See Next Column)

For Complete List of Firm Personnel, See General Section

For full biographical listings, see the Martindale-Hubbell Law Directory

DWYER IMANAKA SCHRAFF KUDO MEYER & FUJIMOTO ATTORNEYS AT LAW, A LAW CORPORATION (AV)

1800 Pioneer Plaza, 900 Fort Street Mall, 96813
Telephone: 808-524-8000
Telecopier: 808-526-1419
Mailing Address: P.O. Box 2727, 96803

John R. Dwyer, Jr.
Mitchell A. Imanaka
Paul A. Schraff
Benjamin A. Kudo (Atty. at Law, A Law Corp.)
William G. Meyer, III
Wesley M. Fujimoto
Ronald Van Grant
Jon M. H. Pang
Blake W. Bushnell
Kenn N. Kojima

Adelbert Green
Richard T. Asato, Jr.
Scott W. Settle
Darcie S. Yoshinaga
Tracy Timothy Woo
Lawrence I. Kawasaki
Douglas H. Inouye
Christine A. Low

OF COUNSEL

Randall Y. Iwase

For full biographical listings, see the Martindale-Hubbell Law Directory

IDAHO

*BOISE,** Ada Co.

HALL, FARLEY, OBERRECHT & BLANTON (AV)

Key Financial Center, 702 West Idaho Street, Suite 700, P.O. Box 1271, 83701-1271
Telephone: 208-336-0404
Facsimile: 208-336-5193

Richard E. Hall
Donald J. Farley
Phillip S. Oberrecht
Raymond D. Powers
Candy Wagahoff Dale
Robert B. Luce
J. Kevin West
Bart W. Harwood

J. Charles Blanton
John J. Burke
Steven J. Hippler
Thorpe P. Orton
Ronald S. Best (Not admitted in ID)

References: Boise State University; Farm Bureau Mutual Insurance Company of Idaho; Medical Insurance Exchange of California; The St. Paul Cos.

For full biographical listings, see the Martindale-Hubbell Law Directory

*POCATELLO,** Bannock Co.

MERRILL & MERRILL, CHARTERED (AV)

Key Bank Building, P.O. Box 991, 83204
Telephone: 208-232-2286
Fax: 208-232-2499

Dave R. Gallafent

Representative Clients: Key Bank of Idaho; First Nationwide Bank; Jackson State Bank; West One Bank of Idaho; First Interstate Bank of Idaho.

For Complete List of Firm Personnel, See General Section

For full biographical listings, see the Martindale-Hubbell Law Directory

ILLINOIS

*CHICAGO,** Cook Co.

ARONBERG GOLDGEHN DAVIS & GARMISA (AV)

Suite 3000 One IBM Plaza, 60611-3633
Telephone: 312-828-9600
Telecopier: 312-828-9635

MEMBERS OF FIRM

Ronald J. Aronberg
Melvin A. Blum
Robert N. Sodikoff
Andrew S. Williams
Ned S. Robertson
Nathan H. Lichtenstein
William W. Yotis III

ASSOCIATES

Eric D. Kaplan
David H. Sachs

For Complete List of Firm Personnel, See General Section

For full biographical listings, see the Martindale-Hubbell Law Directory

Chicago—Continued

BELL, BOYD & LLOYD (AV)

Three First National Plaza Suite 3300, 70 West Madison Street, 60602
Telephone: 312-372-1121
FAX: 312-372-2098
Washington, D.C. Office: 1615 L Street, N.W.
Telephone: 202-466-6300.
FAX: 202-463-0678.

MEMBERS OF FIRM

Steven E. Ducommun
James P. Hemmer
John P. Morrison
Richard L. Sevcik

ASSOCIATE

Amy S. Powers

For Complete List of Firm Personnel, See General Section

For full biographical listings, see the Martindale-Hubbell Law Directory

LASER, POKORNY, SCHWARTZ, FRIEDMAN & ECONOMOS, P.C. (AV)

205 North Michigan Avenue, 38th Floor, 60601-5914
Telephone: 312-540-0600
Telecopier: 312-540-0610

Jules M. Laser
Stephen J. Pokorny
Marc H. Schwartz
Bruce M. Friedman
Joel A. Stein
Alvin J. Helfgot

Joshua S. Hyman
David A. Shapiro

For Complete List of Firm Personnel, See General Section

For full biographical listings, see the Martindale-Hubbell Law Directory

LEVENFELD, EISENBERG, JANGER, GLASSBERG, SAMOTNY & HALPER (AV)

21st Floor, 33 West Monroe Street, 60603
Telephone: 312-346-8380
Facsimile: 346-8434
Cable Address: "Taxlaw"

MEMBER OF FIRM

Edward J. Halper

For full biographical listings, see the Martindale-Hubbell Law Directory

VEDDER, PRICE, KAUFMAN & KAMMHOLZ (AV)

A Partnership including Vedder, Price, Kaufman & Kammholz, P.C.
222 North La Salle Street, 60601-1003
Telephone: 312-609-7500
Fax: 312-609-5005
Rockford, Illinois Office: Vedder, Price, Kaufman & Kammholz, 4615 East State Street, Suite 201.
Telephone: 815-226-7700.
Washington, D.C. Office: Vedder, Price, Kaufman, Kammholz & Day, 1600 M. Street, N.W.
Telephone: 202-296-0500.
New York, New York Office: Vedder, Price, Kaufman, Kammholz & Day, 805 Third Avenue.
Telephone: 212-407-7700.

MEMBERS OF FIRM

Robert J. Stucker
Daniel O'Rourke
John T. McEnroe
Dalius F. Vasys
William L. Conaghan
Thomas P. Desmond
Douglas M. Hambleton
Daniel C. McKay, II
Dean N. Gerber

ASSOCIATES

Lynne A. Gochanour
Michael A. Nemeroff
Mark J. Handfelt
Catherine A. Lemmer

PARTNER AT NEW YORK CITY

Ronald Scheinberg

PARTNER AT DISTRICT OF COLUMBIA

Thomas A. Brooks

For Complete List of Firm Personnel, See General Section

For full biographical listings, see the Martindale-Hubbell Law Directory

WATT & SAWYIER (AV)

Amalgamated Bank Annex Building, 55 West Van Buren Street, Suite 500, 60605
Telephone: 312-663-1440
Telecopier: 312-663-1410

MEMBERS OF FIRM

Garland W. Watt
Michael T. Sawyier

Representative Clients: First National Bank of Chicago; Chicago Title & Trust Company; North Carolina Mutual Life Insurance Company (Durham, North Carolina); Supreme Life Insurance Company of America; Illinois/Service Federal Savings and Loan Association of Chicago; Sonicraft, Inc.; Universal Casket Company (Cassopolis, Michigan).

For full biographical listings, see the Martindale-Hubbell Law Directory

WILSON & MCILVAINE (AV)

500 West Madison, Suite 3700, 60661-2511
Telephone: 312-715-5000
Telecopier: 312-715-5155

PARTNER

Alexander Terras

ASSOCIATE

William T. McCormick

OF COUNSEL

Kent Chandler, Jr.

For Complete List of Firm Personnel, See General Section

For full biographical listings, see the Martindale-Hubbell Law Directory

INDIANA

*BEDFORD,** Lawrence Co.

STEELE, STEELE, MCSOLEY & MCSOLEY (AV)

Bank One Building, Suite One, 1602 I Street, 47421
Telephone: 812-279-3513
Fax: 812-275-3504

MEMBERS OF FIRM

Byron W. Steele
Brent E. Steele

Representative Clients: Bank One; The First National Bank of Mitchell; The Times Mail (newspaper); Ralph Rogers & Co., Inc.; Indiana Bell Telephone Co.; Texas Gas Transmission Corporation; Edgewood Clinic, Inc. (Medical Professional Corporation); U.S. Gypsum Company and Druthers Restaurant of Mitchell, Inc.

For Complete List of Firm Personnel, See General Section

For full biographical listings, see the Martindale-Hubbell Law Directory

*BLOOMINGTON,** Monroe Co.

BUNGER & ROBERTSON (AV)

226 South College Square, P.O. Box 910, 47402-0910
Telephone: 812-332-9295
Fax: 812-331-8808

MEMBER OF FIRM

Don M. Robertson

OF COUNSEL

Philip C. Hill

Representative Clients: Aetna Insurance Companies; Bloomington Hospital; Commercial Union Group; Indiana Insurance Co.; Liberty Mutual Insurance; Medical Protective Co.; Monroe County Community School Corp.; Professional Golf Car, Inc.; Prudential Insurance Company of America; State Farm Automobile Insurance Co.

For Complete List of Firm Personnel, See General Section

For full biographical listings, see the Martindale-Hubbell Law Directory

*EVANSVILLE,** Vanderburgh Co.

BAMBERGER, FOREMAN, OSWALD AND HAHN (AV)

7th Floor Hulman Building, P.O. Box 657, 47704-0657
Telephone: 812-425-1591
Fax: 812-421-4936

MEMBERS OF FIRM

William P. Foreman
Terry G. Farmer

ASSOCIATES

Douglas W. Patterson
Marjorie A. Meeks

Representative Clients: Citizens Bank of Central Indiana; Citizens Bank of Henderson County; CNB Bancshares, Inc.; CNB Bank of Kentucky; Dubois County Bank; Jasper State Bank; Peoples Bank & Trust Co.; The Citizens National Bank of Evansville; Valley Bank F.S.B.

For Complete List of Firm Personnel, See General Section

For full biographical listings, see the Martindale-Hubbell Law Directory

BOWERS, HARRISON, KENT & MILLER (AV)

25 N.W. Riverside Drive, P.O. Box 1287, 47706-1287
Telephone: 812-426-1231
Fax: 812-464-3676

MEMBERS OF FIRM

Joseph H. Harrison
Paul E. Black
Gary R. Case

(See Next Column)

BOWERS, HARRISON, KENT & MILLER—*Continued*

OF COUNSEL

K. Wayne Kent

Representative Clients: Permanent Federal Savings Bank; The Citizens National Bank of Evansville; First Indiana Bank; Citizens National Bank of Tell City.

For Complete List of Firm Personnel, See General Section

For full biographical listings, see the Martindale-Hubbell Law Directory

KAHN, DEES, DONOVAN & KAHN (AV)

P.O. Box 3646, 47735-3646
Telephone: 812-423-3183
Fax: 812-423-3841

MEMBERS OF FIRM

Alan N. Shovers
Brian P. Williams
Marilyn R. Ratliff
G. Michael Schopmeyer
Jeffrey K. Helfrich

Representative Clients: Union Federal Savings Bank; The National City Bank of Evansville; Citizens National Bank of Evansville; Old National Bancorp; Waterfield Mortgage Co.; American General Finance; German American Bank; Jasper State Bank; Tree Haute First National Bank; American National Bank.

For Complete List of Firm Personnel, See General Section

For full biographical listings, see the Martindale-Hubbell Law Directory

STATHAM, JOHNSON & MCCRAY (AV)

215 North West Martin Luther King Jr. Boulevard, P.O. Box 3567, 47734-3567
Telephone: 812-425-5223
Facsimile: 812-421-4238

MEMBERS OF FIRM

R. Eugene Johnson
Donald J. Fuchs

Representative Clients: Elberfeld State Bank; Evansville Federal Savings Bank; Fidelity Federal Bancorp.; INB Banking Company Southwest; National City Bank of Evansville.

For Complete List of Firm Personnel, See General Section

For full biographical listings, see the Martindale-Hubbell Law Directory

ZIEMER, STAYMAN, WEITZEL & SHOULDERS (AV)

(Formerly Early, Arnold & Ziemer)
1507 Old National Bank Building, P.O. Box 916, 47706
Telephone: 812-424-7575
Telecopier: 812-421-5089

MEMBERS OF FIRM

Robert F. Stayman
Marco L. DeLucio
Stephan E. Weitzel
Gregory G. Meyer

Reference: Old National Bank in Evansville.

For full biographical listings, see the Martindale-Hubbell Law Directory

*FORT WAYNE,** Allen Co.

BARRETT & MCNAGNY (AV)

215 East Berry Street, P.O. Box 2263, 46801-2263
Telephone: 219-423-9551
Telecopier: 219-423-8924
Huntington, Indiana Office: 429 Jefferson Park Mall, P.O. Box 5156.
Telephone: 219-356-7766.
Telecopier: 219-356-7782.

MEMBERS OF FIRM

Howard L. Chapman
Michael P. O'Hara
Richard D. Robinson
Joseph G. Bonahoom
Patrick G. Michaels
Thomas M. Niezer

Counsel For: Fort Wayne National Corp.; Fort Wayne National Bank; Lincoln National Corp.; N.B.D.; Union Federal Savings Bank of Indianapolis; Waterfield Mortgage Company, Incorporated.

For Complete List of Firm Personnel, See General Section

For full biographical listings, see the Martindale-Hubbell Law Directory

ROTHBERG, GALLMEYER, FRUECHTENICHT & LOGAN (AV)

2100 Fort Wayne National Bank Building, 110 West Berry Street, P.O. Box 11647, 46859-1647
Telephone: 219-422-9454
Telefax: 219-422-1622

MEMBERS OF FIRM

Thomas D. Logan
Scott T. Niemann
F. L. Dennis Logan
David R. Smelko
Dennis F. Dykhuizen

(See Next Column)

ASSOCIATES

Gregory Martin Cole
Michael T. Deam
James A. Butz
J. Rickard Donovan

Counsel for: Parkview Memorial Hospital; Cameron Memorial Community Hospital; Norwest Bank Indiana, N.A.; NBD Bank, N.A.; Citizens Banking Company of Anderson; Azar's, Incorporated; Fort Wayne-Allen County Airport Authority; Fort Wayne Public Transportation Corporation; Avis Industrial Corp.; Farm Credit Services of Mid-America, ASA; Slater Fort Wayne Federal Credit Union.

For Complete List of Firm Personnel, See General Section

For full biographical listings, see the Martindale-Hubbell Law Directory

GREENWOOD, Johnson Co.

VAN VALER WILLIAMS & HEWITT (AV)

Suite 400 National City Bank Building, 300 South Madison Avenue, P.O. Box 405, 46142
Telephone: 317-888-1121
Fax: 317-887-4069

MEMBERS OF FIRM

Joe N. Van Valer
Jon E. Williams
Brian C. Hewitt

ASSOCIATES

J. Lee Robbins
John M. White
William M. Waltz
Kim Van Valer Shilts
Mark E. Need

For full biographical listings, see the Martindale-Hubbell Law Directory

HAMMOND, Lake Co.

GALVIN, GALVIN & LEENEY (AV)

5231 Hohman Avenue, 46320
Telephone: 219-933-0380
Fax: 219-933-0471

MEMBERS OF FIRM

Edmond J. Leeney (1897-1978)
Carl N. Carpenter
Timothy P. Galvin, Sr. (1894-1993)
John E. Chevigny
Timothy P. Galvin, Jr.
Francis J. Galvin, Sr. (Retired)
Patrick J. Galvin
W. Patrick Downes

Brian L. Goins
William G. Crabtree II
John H. Lloyd, IV

Representative Clients: Mercantile National Bank of Indiana, N.A.; Citizens Federal Savings and Loan Association; First Federal Savings and Loan of Hammond; Security Federal Bank.

For full biographical listings, see the Martindale-Hubbell Law Directory

*INDIANAPOLIS,** Marion Co.

BOSE MCKINNEY & EVANS (AV)

2700 First Indiana Plaza, 135 North Pennsylvania Street, 46204
Telephone: 317-684-5000
Facsimile: 317-684-5173
Indianapolis North Office: Suite 1201, 8888 Keystone Crossing, 46240.
Telephone: 317-574-3700.
Facsimile: 317-574-3716.

MEMBERS OF FIRM

David A. Butcher
R. J. McConnell
Theodore J. Nowacki
Michael A. Trentadue
Alan W. Becker
Dwight L. Miller

ASSOCIATE

J. Scott Enright

Representative Clients: First Indiana Bank; Francisco State Bank; National City Bank; Old National Bancorp; Citizens Banking Co.; Eli Lilly Federal Credit Union; Monroe County Bank; State Bank of Oxford; Star Financial Bank; Huntington National Bank of Indiana.

For Complete List of Firm Personnel, See General Section

For full biographical listings, see the Martindale-Hubbell Law Directory

ICE MILLER DONADIO & RYAN (AV)

One American Square Box 82001, 46282-0002
Telephone: 317-236-2100
Fax: 317-236-2219

MEMBERS OF FIRM

John A. Grayson
Philip A. Whistler
Evan E. Steger
John T. Murphy
Berkley W. Duck, III
Stephen J. Hackman
Harry L. Gonso
Michael A. Wukmer
Thomas H. Ristine
Michael J. Lewinski
Elizabeth A. Smith

(See Next Column)

ICE MILLER DONADIO & RYAN, *Indianapolis—Continued*

ASSOCIATES

Matthew C. Hook | Michael E. Schrader

Counsel for: Citizens Banking Co.; Federal Deposit Insurance Corp.; Gainer Bank, N.A.; Indiana Bankers Assn.; Irwin Union Bank & Trust Co.; NBD, Indiana, Inc.; Resolution Trust Corp.; Society National Bank, Indiana; Bank; Union County National Bank of Liberty.

For Complete List of Firm Personnel, See General Section

For full biographical listings, see the Martindale-Hubbell Law Directory

JOHNSON, SMITH, DENSBORN, WRIGHT & HEATH (AV)

One Indiana Square Suite 1800, 46204
Telephone: 317-634-9777
Telecopier: 317-636-9061

MEMBERS OF FIRM

John F. Joyce (1948-1994)
Wayne O. Adams, III
Thomas A. Barnard
David J. Carr
Peter D. Cleveland
David R. Day
Donald K. Densborn
Thomas N. Eckerle
Mark W. Ford
G. Ronald Heath
Robert B. Hebert
John David Hoover
Andrew W. Hull
Dennis A. Johnson
Richard L. Johnson
Michael J. Kaye
John R. Kirkwood
David Williams Russell
James T. Smith
David E. Wright

ASSOCIATES

Robert C. Wolf (1949-1993)
Carolyn H. Andretti
David G. Blachly
Robert T. Buday
Jeffrey S. Cohen
Patricia L. Marshall
David D. Robinson
Ronald G. Sentman
Sally Franklin Zweig

OF COUNSEL

Earl Auberry (1923-1989)
Bruce W. Claycombe
Paul D. Gresk
William T. Lawrence
Mark A. Palmer
Catherine A. Singleton

For Complete List of Firm Personnel, See General Section

For full biographical listings, see the Martindale-Hubbell Law Directory

LOCKE REYNOLDS BOYD & WEISELL (AV)

1000 Capital Center South, 201 North Illinois Street, 46204
Telephone: 317-237-3800
Telecopier: 317-237-3900

Stephen J. Dutton
Michael D. Moriarty
Michael J. Schneider
David E. Jose
Jeffrey B. Bailey
Paul G. Reis
Howard R. Cohen

James O. Waanders

Representative Clients: The Huntington National Bank of Indiana; IDS Financial Services; Indiana Corporate Federal Credit Union; NBD Bank, N.A.

For Complete List of Firm Personnel, See General Section

For full biographical listings, see the Martindale-Hubbell Law Directory

*TERRE HAUTE,** Vigo Co.

COX, ZWERNER, GAMBILL & SULLIVAN (AV)

511 Wabash Avenue, P.O. Box 1625, 47808-1625
Telephone: 812-232-6003
Fax: 812-232-6567

MEMBERS OF FIRM

Ernest J. Zwerner (1918-1980)
Benjamin G. Cox (1915-1988)
Gilbert W. Gambill, Jr.
James E. Sullivan
Benjamin G. Cox, Jr.
David W. Sullivan
Robert L. Gowdy
Louis F. Britton
Robert D. Hepburn
Carroll D. Smeltzer
Jeffry A. Lind

ASSOCIATE

Ronald E. Jumps

Counsel for: Terre Haute First National Bank; Farmers Insurance Group; Indiana-American Water Co.; Indiana State University; Merchants National Bank of Terre Haute; Rose-Hulman Institute of Technology; Tribune-Star Publishing Co., Inc.; Weston Paper & Manufacturing Co.

For full biographical listings, see the Martindale-Hubbell Law Directory

IOWA

*CEDAR RAPIDS,** Linn Co.

SHUTTLEWORTH & INGERSOLL, P.C. (AV)

500 Firstar Bank Building, P.O. Box 2107, 52406-2107
Telephone: 319-365-9461
Fax: 319-365-8443

Thomas M. Collins
Richard S. Fry
Gary J. Streit
Carroll J. Reasoner
Steven J. Pace
Thomas P. Peffer
Kevin H. Collins
William P. Prowell
William S. Hochstetler

LeeAnn M. Ferry
Dean D. Carrington

COUNSEL

Joan Lipsky
Theodore J. Collins

Representative Clients: Firstar Bank Cedar Rapids, N.A.; First National Bank of Cedar Rapids; Norwest Bank, Iowa, N.A.

For Complete List of Firm Personnel, See General Section

For full biographical listings, see the Martindale-Hubbell Law Directory

*COUNCIL BLUFFS,** Pottawattamie Co.

TELPNER, SMITH & RUESCH (AV)

25 Main Place, Suite 200, P.O. Box 248, 51502-0248
Telephone: 712-325-9000
Fax: 712-328-1946

MEMBERS OF FIRM

Charles L. Smith
Jack E. Ruesch

Representative Clients: Firstar Bank; Houghton State Bank; City National Bank of Shenandoah; Oakland State Bank; Community National Bank; Resolution Trust Corporation; Federal Deposit Insurance Corporation; Bell Federal Union; Mutual of Omaha Employees Credit Union.

For Complete List of Firm Personnel, See General Section

For full biographical listings, see the Martindale-Hubbell Law Directory

*DES MOINES,** Polk Co.

AHLERS, COONEY, DORWEILER, HAYNIE, SMITH & ALLBEE, P.C. (AV)

100 Court Avenue, Suite 600, 50309-2231
Telephone: 515-243-7611
Fax: 515-243-2149

Robert G. Allbee
Wade R. Hauser III

Representative Clients: Drake University; Insurance Company of North America; West Des Moines State Bank; Koss Construction Co.; Pittsburgh-Des Moines Steel Co.; Sears, Roebuck & Co.; Iowa Association of Municipal Utilities; Iowa State Board of Regents; Kirke Van Orsdel, Inc.; Travelers Insurance Group; WestBank.

For Complete List of Firm Personnel, See General Section

For full biographical listings, see the Martindale-Hubbell Law Directory

DICKINSON, MACKAMAN, TYLER & HAGEN, P.C. (AV)

Suite 1600 Hub Tower, 699 Walnut Street, 50309-3986
Telephone: 515-244-2600
Telecopier: 515-246-4550

L. J. Dickinson (1873-1968)
L. Call Dickinson (1905-1974)
Addison M. Parker (Retired)
John H. Raife (Retired)
Robert B. Throckmorton (Retired)
Helen C. Adams
Brent R. Appel
Barbara G. Barrett
John W. Blyth
L. Call Dickinson, Jr.
Jeanine M. Freeman
David J. Grace
Craig F. Graziano
Howard O. Hagen
J. Russell Hixson
Paul E. Horvath
F. Richard Lyford
John R. Mackaman
Richard A. Malm
James W. O'Brien
Arthur F. Owens
Rebecca Boyd Parrott
David M. Repp
Robert C. Rouwenhorst
Russell L. Samson
David S. Steward
Philip E. Stoffregen
Francis (Frank) J. Stork
Jon P. Sullivan
Celeste L. Tito (Not admitted in IA)
Paul R. Tyler
John K. Vernon
J. Marc Ward
Linda S. Weindruch

OF COUNSEL

Robert E. Mannheimer

Representative Clients: Archer-Daniels-Midland Co.; Board of Water Works Trustees, Des Moines, Iowa; Merchants Bonding Co. (Mutual); Norwest Bank, N.A.

For full biographical listings, see the Martindale-Hubbell Law Directory

Des Moines—Continued

Whitfield & Eddy, P.L.C. (AV)

317 6th Avenue, Suite 1200 Locust at 6th, 50309-4110
Telephone: 515-288-6041
Fax: 515-246-1474

John C. Eddy
Harley A. Whitfield
Rodney P. Kubat
William L. Fairbank
Robert G. Bridges
Thomas H. Burke
George H. Frampton
Wendy L. Carlson
Gary A. Norton
Mark V. Hanson

Jeffrey William Courter
August B. Landis

Representative Clients: Brenton National Bank of Perry; Brenton State Bank of Jefferson; Brenton National Bank, N.A.; Farm Credit Banks of Omaha; Production Credit Association of the Midlands; Citizen States Bank; Decatur County State Bank; Iowa Trust & Savings Bank.

For Complete List of Firm Personnel, See General Section

For full biographical listings, see the Martindale-Hubbell Law Directory

KANSAS

PRAIRIE VILLAGE, Johnson Co.

Holman, McCollum & Hansen, P.C. (AV Ⓣ)

9400 Mission Road Suite 205, 66206
Telephone: 913-648-7272
Fax: 913-383-9596
Kansas City, Missouri Office: 644 West 57th Terrace.
Telephone: 816-333-8522.
Fax: 913-383-9596.

Joseph Y. Holman
Frank B. W. McCollum
Eric L. Hansen
Dana L. Parks
Nancy Merrill Wilson
Amy L. Brown
E. John Edwards III (Not admitted in KS)
Katherine E. Rich

For full biographical listings, see the Martindale-Hubbell Law Directory

*TOPEKA,** Shawnee Co.

Wright, Henson, Somers, Sebelius, Clark & Baker (AV)

Commerce Bank Building, 100 Southeast Ninth Street, 2nd Floor, P.O. Box 3555, 66601-3555
Telephone: 913-232-2200
FAX: 913-232-3344

MEMBERS OF FIRM

Charles N. Henson
Dale L. Somers
Anne Lamborn Baker

Representative Clients: Kaw Valley State Bank & Trust Co.; Kansas Bankers Association; Peoples State Bank of Topeka.

For Complete List of Firm Personnel, See General Section

For full biographical listings, see the Martindale-Hubbell Law Directory

*WICHITA,** Sedgwick Co.

Foulston & Siefkin (AV)

(Formerly Foulston, Siefkin, Powers & Eberhardt)
700 Fourth Financial Center, Broadway at Douglas, 67202
Telephone: 316-267-6371
Facsimile: 316-267-6345
Topeka, Kansas Office: 1515 Bank IV Tower, 534 Kansas Avenue. 66603.
Telephone: 913-233-3600.
FAX: 913-233-1610.
Member: Lex Mundi, A Global Association of Independent Firms

MEMBERS OF FIRM

Benjamin C. Langel
William R. Wood, II

For Complete List of Firm Personnel, See General Section

For full biographical listings, see the Martindale-Hubbell Law Directory

KENTUCKY

ASHLAND, Boyd Co.

VanAntwerp, Monge, Jones & Edwards (AV)

1544 Winchester Avenue Fifth Floor, P.O. Box 1111, 41105-1111
Telephone: 606-329-2929
Fax: 606-329-0490
Ironton, Ohio Office: Cooper & VanAntwerp, A Legal Professional Association, 407 Center Street.
Telephone: 614-532-4366.

MEMBERS OF FIRM

Howard VanAntwerp, III
Gregory Lee Monge
William H. Jones, Jr.
Carl D. Edwards, Jr.
Kimberly Scott McCann

ASSOCIATES

Matthew J. Wixsom
William Mitchell Hall
James D. Keffer
Stephen S. Burchett

Representative Clients: Armco; Bank of Ashland; Calgon Carbon Corp.; King's Daughters' Hospital; Allstate Insurance Co.; Kemper Insurance Group; Commercial Union Cos.; The Mayo Coal Cos.; Maryland Casualty Co.; Merck & Co.

For full biographical listings, see the Martindale-Hubbell Law Directory

*BOWLING GREEN,** Warren Co.

Bell, Orr, Ayers & Moore, P.S.C. (AV)

1010 College Street, P.O. Box 738, 42102-0738
Telephone: 502-781-8111
Telecopier: 502-781-9027

Ray B. Buckberry, Jr.
Kevin C. Brooks

James S. Weisz

General Counsel for: First American National Bank of Kentucky; Farm Credit Services of Mid-America, ACA.; Houchens Industries, Inc. (Food Markets and Shopping Centers); Warren County Board of Education; Bowling Green Municipal Utilities.
Representative Clients: Chicago Title Insurance Co.; Commonwealth Land Title Insurance Co.; Kentucky Farm Bureau Mutual Insurance Co.; Martin Automotive Group; Home Insurance Group.

For Complete List of Firm Personnel, See General Section

For full biographical listings, see the Martindale-Hubbell Law Directory

Catron, Kilgore & Begley (AV)

918 State Street, P.O. Box 280, 42102-0280
Telephone: 502-842-1050
Fax: 502-842-4720

Stephen B. Catron
J. Patrick Kilgore
Ernest Edward Begley, II

Representative Clients: Bowling Green Bank & Trust Company, N.A.; Trans Financial Bank, N.A.; Resolution Trust Corporation; International Paper Company; Convention Center Authority; Bowling Green-Warren County Industrial Park Authority, Inc.; Camping World, Inc.; National Corvette Museum; Minit Mart Foods, Inc.; Kentucky Transportation Cabinet.

For full biographical listings, see the Martindale-Hubbell Law Directory

Cole, Moore & McCracken (AV)

921 College Street-Phoenix Place, P.O. Box 10240, 42102-7240
Telephone: 502-782-6666
FAX: 502-782-8666

MEMBERS OF FIRM

John David Cole
Frank Hampton Moore, Jr.
John H. McCracken
Matthew J. Baker

ASSOCIATES

Howard E. Frasier, Jr.
Douglas W. Gott
Dov Moore
C. Terrell Miller
Michael D. Lindsey

OF COUNSEL

Frank R. Goad

Counsel for: Western Kentucky Cola-Cola Bottling Co.; Clark Distributing Co., Inc.; Scotty's Contracting & Stone Co.
Local Counsel for: General Electric Co.; Bucyrus-Erie Company; Wal-Mart Stores, Inc.; Kroger/Country Oven.
Representative Insurance Clients: Liberty Mutual Insurance Co.; Travelers Insurance Co.; Wausau Insurance Co.

For full biographical listings, see the Martindale-Hubbell Law Directory

English, Lucas, Priest & Owsley (AV)

1101 College Street, P.O. Box 770, 42102-0770
Telephone: 502-781-6500
Telecopier: 502-782-7782

(See Next Column)

ENGLISH, LUCAS, PRIEST & OWSLEY, *Bowling Green—Continued*

MEMBERS OF FIRM

Charles E. English
Whayne C. Priest, Jr.
Keith M. Carwell

General Counsel for: Medical Center at Bowling Green; Warren Rural Electric Cooperative Corporation; Trans Financial Bank, N.A.; Southern Sanitation, Inc.
Representative Clients: Commercial Union Insurance Cos.; Kemper Insurance Group; St. Paul Insurance Co.; Desa International; Kentucky Finance Co.; Sumitomo Electric Wiring Systems, Inc.

For Complete List of Firm Personnel, See General Section

For full biographical listings, see the Martindale-Hubbell Law Directory

HARLIN & PARKER, P.S.C. (AV)

519 East Tenth Street, P.O. Box 390, 42102-0390
Telephone: 502-842-5611
Telefax: 502-842-2607
Smiths Grove, Kentucky Office: Old Farmers Bank Building.
Telephone: 502-563-4701.

William Jerry Parker
Max B. Harlin, III
Jerry A. Burns
Scott Charles Marks
Michael K. Bishop
Mark D. Alcott (Resident, Smith Grove Office)

Insurance Clients: Allstate Insurance Co.; American Hardware Mutual Insurance Co.; CNA Insurance Companies; Maryland Casualty Company; Government Employees Insurance Co.; American International Group.
Railroad and Utilities Clients: District Attorneys for South Central Bell Telephone Co.; CSX Transportation, Inc.
Local Counsel for: General Motors Corp.; Ford Motor Co.; Chrysler Corp.

For Complete List of Firm Personnel, See General Section

For full biographical listings, see the Martindale-Hubbell Law Directory

COVINGTON, Kenton Co.

KLETTE AND KLETTE (AV)

250 Grandview Drive, Suite 250, Ft. Mitchell, 41017-5610
Telephone: 606-344-9966
Fax: 606-344-9900
Cincinnati, Ohio Office: 3905 Brigadoon Drive, 45255.
Telephone: 513-421-6699.

MEMBERS OF FIRM

John H. Klette, Jr.
V. Ruth Klette
Debra S. Fox

LEGAL SUPPORT PERSONNEL

Evelyn Richard (Paralegal)

General Counsel for: The Northern Kentucky Motor Club; First Federal Savings & Loan Association of Covington.

For full biographical listings, see the Martindale-Hubbell Law Directory

*LEXINGTON,** Fayette Co.

FOWLER, MEASLE & BELL (AV)

Kincaid Towers, 300 West Vine Street, Suite 650, 40507-1660
Telephone: 606-252-6700
Fax: 606-255-3735

MEMBERS OF FIRM

Taft A. McKinstry
John E. Hinkel, Jr.
Robert S. Ryan
Michael W. Troutman

Representative Clients: Bank One, Lexington, N.A.; PNC Bank, Kentucky, Inc.; National City Bank & Trust Co.; Fifth-Third Bank; Liberty National Bank; RTC; FDIC.

For Complete List of Firm Personnel, See General Section

For full biographical listings, see the Martindale-Hubbell Law Directory

STOLL, KEENON & PARK (AV)

201 E. Main Street, Suite 1000, 40507-1380
Telephone: 606-231-3000
Telecopier: 606-253-1093; 606-253-1027
Frankfort, Kentucky Office: 326 West Main Street.
Telephone: 502-875-6000.
Telecopier: 502-875-6008.
Louisville, Kentucky Office: 400 West Market Street, Suite 2650, 40202.
Telephone: 502-568-9100.
Telecopier: 502-568-6340.

MEMBERS OF FIRM

William L. Montague
Joseph M. Scott, Jr.
R. David Lester
Herbert A. Miller, Jr.
Harvie B. Wilkinson
J. David Smith, Jr.
Dan M. Rose
Gregory D. Pavey

(See Next Column)

ASSOCIATE

Robert E. Wier

Representative Clients: Farmers Capital Bank Corp.; Bank One, Lexington, NA; Whitaker Bancorp, Inc.; The Tokai Bank, Ltd.; Pikeville National Bank; Central Bank and Trust Co.

For Complete List of Firm Personnel, See General Section

For full biographical listings, see the Martindale-Hubbell Law Directory

STURGILL, TURNER & TRUITT (AV)

155 East Main Street, 40507
Telephone: 606-255-8581
Fax: 606-231-0851

MEMBERS OF FIRM

Jerry D. Truitt
Stephen L. Barker
Ann D. Sturgill
Kevin G. Henry

For Complete List of Firm Personnel, See General Section

For full biographical listings, see the Martindale-Hubbell Law Directory

*LOUISVILLE,** Jefferson Co.

GREENEBAUM DOLL & McDONALD (AV)

A Partnership including Professional Service Corporations
3300 National City Tower, 40202
Telephone: 502-589-4200
Fax: 502-587-3695
Lexington, Kentucky Office: 1400 Vine Center Tower.
Telephone: 606-231-8500.
Fax: 606-255-2742.
Covington, Kentucky Office: 50 East River Center Boulevard, P.O. Box 2050.
Telephone: 606-655-4200.
Fax: 606-655-4239.
Cincinnati, Ohio Office: 832 Main Street.
Telephone: 513-421-8087.
Fax: 513-421-8089.

Michael G. Shaikun *
Ivan M. Diamond
Lawrence K. Banks *
Nicholas R. Glancy (Lexington and Covington, Kentucky)
Janet P. Jakubowicz
Stephen W. Switzer (Resident at Lexington, Kentucky)
Daniel E. Fisher

ASSOCIATES

D. Barry Stilz (Resident at Lexington, Kentucky)
Daniel P. Cherry
John P. Fendig
Gregory R. Schaaf (Resident at Lexington, Kentucky)

Representative Clients: Resolution Trust Co.; Federal Deposit Insurance Corp.; PNC Bank; National City Bank; Liberty National Bank and Trust Company of Louisville; Bank of Louisville and Trust Co.; Citibank, N.A.; Texas Commerce Bank; Continental Illinois Bank; Sovran Financial Corp.
*A Professional Service Corporation

For Complete List of Firm Personnel, See General Section

For full biographical listings, see the Martindale-Hubbell Law Directory

JOHN S. GREENBAUM, P.S.C. (AV)

2700 First National Tower, 40202
Telephone: 502-585-1750
Fax: 502-581-1066

John S. Greenebaum

For full biographical listings, see the Martindale-Hubbell Law Directory

HIRN DOHENY REED & HARPER (AV)

A Partnership including a Professional Service Corporation
2000 Meidinger Tower, 40202
Telephone: 502-585-2450
Telecopiers: 502-585-2207; 585-2529

MEMBERS OF FIRM

Marvin J. Hirn
David W. Harper
James R. Cox
Robert B. Vice
William G. Strench

Representative Clients: Bank of Louisville; Indiana United Bancorp; Bourbon Bancshares, Inc.; Hazard Bancorp, Inc.; Marie R. Turner Holding Co.; First Midwest Bancshares; National City Bank Kentucky; PNC Bank.

For Complete List of Firm Personnel, See General Section

For full biographical listings, see the Martindale-Hubbell Law Directory

Louisville—Continued

MAPOTHER & MAPOTHER (AV)

801 West Jefferson Street, 40202
Telephone: 502-587-5400
Fax: 502-587-5444
Lexington, Kentucky Office: 177 North Upper Street.
Telephone: 606-253-0003.
Fax: 606-255-3961.
Stanton, Kentucky Office: 209 Main Street.
Telephone: 606-663-9037.
Jeffersonville, Indiana Office: 505 East Seventh Street.
Telephone: 812-288-5059.
Fax: 502-587-5444.
Cincinnati, Ohio Office: Kroger Building, Suite 2220, 1014 Vine Street.
Telephone: 513-381-4888.
Fax: 513-381-3117.
Huntington, West Virginia Office: Morris Building, Suite 401, 845 Fourth Avenue.
Telephone: 304-525-1185.
Fax: 304-529-3764.
Evansville, Indiana Office: 329 Main Street.
Telephone: 812-421-9108.
Fax: 812-421-9109.

MEMBERS OF FIRM

Thomas C. Mapother (1907-1986)
William R. Mapother
Thomas L. Canary, Jr. (Resident, Lexington Office)
Elizabeth Lee Thompson (Resident, Lexington Office)
Charles M. Friedman

Brian P. Conaty
Andrea Fried Neichter
Kathryn Pry Coryell (Resident, Jeffersonville, Indiana Office)
Roberta S. Dunlap (Resident, Evansville, Indiana Office)
Terry Risner (Resident, Cincinnati, Ohio Office)
Lee W. Grace
Dean A. Langdon
T. Lawson McSwain, II
Charles Brent Robbins (Resident, Lexington Office)

Representative Clients: General Electric Capital Corp.; Ford Motor Credit Co.; General Motors Acceptance Corp.; Associates Commercial Corp.; Cuna Mutual Insurance Society; Bank One; National City Bank; PNC Bank BancOhio National Bank.

For full biographical listings, see the Martindale-Hubbell Law Directory

MIDDLETON & REUTLINGER, P.S.C. (AV)

2500 Brown and Williamson Tower, 40202-3410
Telephone: 502-584-1135
Fax: 502-561-0442
Jeffersonville, Indiana Office: 605 Watt Street, 47130.
Telephone: 812-282-4886.

Charles G. Middleton, III
Charles D. Greenwell
G. Kennedy Hall, Jr.
David J. Kellerman

Margaret E. Thorp

Counsel for: Chevron USA; Liberty National Bank; Logan Aluminum, Inc.; Louisville Gas & Electric Co.; MCI Telecommunications Corp.; Metropolitan Life Insurance Co.; Kosmos Cement Co.; Porcelain Metal Corp.; The Home Insurance Co.; The Kroger Co.; Demars Haka Development, Inc.

For Complete List of Firm Personnel, See General Section

For full biographical listings, see the Martindale-Hubbell Law Directory

RUBIN HAYS & FOLEY (AV)

First Trust Centre 200 South Fifth Street, 40202
Telephone: 502-569-7550
Telecopier: 502-569-7555

MEMBERS OF FIRM

Wm. Carl Fust
Harry Lee Meyer
David W. Gray
Irvin D. Foley
Joseph R. Gathright, Jr.
Lisa Koch Bryant
Sharon C. Hardy
Charles S. Musson
W. Randall Jones
K. Gail Russell

ASSOCIATE

Christian L. Juckett

OF COUNSEL

James E. Fahey
Newman T. Guthrie

Representative Clients: J.C. Bradford & Co., Inc.; J.J.B. Hilliard, W.L. Lyons, Inc.; Huntington National Bank; Liberty National Bank and Trust Company; National City Bank; PNC Bank; Prudential Bache & Co., Inc.; Prudential Securities, Inc.; Society Bank; Stock Yards Bank and Trust Co.

For full biographical listings, see the Martindale-Hubbell Law Directory

WYATT, TARRANT & COMBS (AV)

Citizens Plaza, 40202
Telephone: 502-589-5235
Telecopier: 502-589-0309
Lexington, Kentucky Office: 1700 Lexington Financial Center.
Telephone: 606-233-2012.
Telecopier: 606-259-0649.
Frankfort, Kentucky Office: The Taylor-Scott Building, 311 West Main Street.
Telephone: 502-223-2104.
Telecopier: 502-227-7681.
New Albany, Indiana Office: The Elsby Building, 117 East Spring Street,
Telephone: 812-945-3561.
Telecopier: 812-949-2524.
Nashville, Tennessee Office: 1500 Nashville City Center, 511 Union Street.
Telephone: 615-244-0020.
Telecopier: 615-256-1726.
Music Row, Nashville Office: 29 Music Square East.
Telephone: 615-255-6161.
Telecopier: 615-254-4490.
Hendersonville, Tennessee Office: 313 E. Main Street, Suite 1.
Telephone: 615-822-8822.
Telecopier: 615-824-4684.

MEMBER OF FIRM

Stewart E. Conner

Representative Clients: CBT Corp.; Cardinal Bancshares, Inc.; Citizens Bank & Trust Company and its affiliates; First Kentucky Trust Co.; Liberty National Bank & Trust Co.; PNC Bank, Kentucky, Inc.; Republic Bank and Trust Co.; Trans Financial Bancorp, Inc.; Trans Financial Bank; Vine Street Trust Co.

For Complete List of Firm Personnel, See General Section

For full biographical listings, see the Martindale-Hubbell Law Directory

*MOREHEAD,** Rowan Co.

DEHNER & ELLIS (AV)

206 East Main Street, 40351
Telephone: 606-783-1504
FAX: 606-784-2744

Truman L. Dehner
John J. Ellis

For full biographical listings, see the Martindale-Hubbell Law Directory

*NEW CASTLE,** Henry Co.

BERRY & FLOYD, P.S.C. (AV)

409 North Main Street, P.O. Box 245, 40050
Telephone: 502-845-2880; 845-2881
Fax: 502-845-4223
Carrollton, Kentucky Office: 523 Highland Avenue.
Telephones: 502-732-6689; 732-6680.
Fax: 502-723-6920.

John M. Berry, Sr. (1900-1991)
John M. Berry, Jr.
James M. Crawford
Ruth H. Baxter
G. Edward James
D. Berry Baxter

OF COUNSEL

Donald K. Floyd

Representative Clients: United Citizens Bank & Trust Co., New Castle, Ky.; First National Bank, Carrollton, Ky.; Farmers Bank of Milton, Ky.; Burley Tobacco Growers Cooperative Assn., Lexington, Ky.; U. S. F. & G. Co.; State Automobile Mutual Insurance Co.; Ohio Casualty Co.; Aetna Casualty & Surety Co.

For full biographical listings, see the Martindale-Hubbell Law Directory

*OWENSBORO,** Daviess Co.

WILSON, WILSON & PLAIN (AV)

414 Masonic Building, 42301
Telephone: 502-926-2525
Telecopier: 502-683-3812

MEMBERS OF FIRM

George S. Wilson, Jr. (1902-1966)
William L. Wilson (1912-1993)
George S. Wilson, III
R. Scott Plain
William L. Wilson, Jr.
Thomas S. Poteat
R. Scott Plain, Jr.

Representative Client: Liberty National Bank, Owensboro, Ky.

For full biographical listings, see the Martindale-Hubbell Law Directory

*PADUCAH,** McCracken Co.

WHITLOW, ROBERTS, HOUSTON & RUSSELL (AV)

Old National Bank Building, 300 Broadway, P.O. Box 995, 42001
Telephone: 502-443-4516
FAX: 502-443-4571

(See Next Column)

WHITLOW, ROBERTS, HOUSTON & RUSSELL, *Paducah—Continued*

MEMBERS OF FIRM

Henry O. Whitlow
Mark C. Whitlow
Gary B. Houston
Randy L. Treece

ASSOCIATES

Anne Fowler Gwinn
Ronald F. Kupper

Counsel for: Peoples First National Bank & Trust Co., Paducah; First Liberty Bank, Calvert City/Benton; First National Bank, LaCenter; Salem Bank, Salem/Smithland; Bank of Murray, Murray; Peoples First Corporation.

For Complete List of Firm Personnel, See General Section

For full biographical listings, see the Martindale-Hubbell Law Directory

*RICHMOND,** Madison Co.

COY, GILBERT & GILBERT (AV)

212 North Second Street, 40475
Telephone: 606-623-3877
Fax: 606-624-5435

MEMBER OF FIRM

James T. Gilbert

ASSOCIATE

Mark A. Shepherd

Representative Clients: Richmond Bank and Trust Company.
General Counsel: Peoples Bank and Trust Co. of Madison County.

For Complete List of Firm Personnel, See General Section

For full biographical listings, see the Martindale-Hubbell Law Directory

*SHEPHERDSVILLE,** Bullitt Co.

J. CHESTER PORTER & ASSOCIATES (AV)

318 South Buckman Street, P.O. Box 767, 40165
Telephone: 502-543-2296; 955-6034
FAX: 502-543-2694
Taylorsville, Kentucky Office: 312 Main Street, P.O. Box 509.
Telephone: 502-477-6412.
FAX: 502-477-2169.

J. Chester Porter

Joseph J. Wantland
Phillip K. Wicker
Linda S. Bouvette (Resident, Taylorsville Office)

OF COUNSEL

William C. Boone, Jr.

For full biographical listings, see the Martindale-Hubbell Law Directory

LOUISIANA

*BATON ROUGE,** East Baton Rouge Parish

POWERS, CLEGG & WILLARD (AV)

7967 Office Park Boulevard, P.O. Box 15948, 70895
Telephone: 504-928-1951
Telecopier: 504-929-9834

MEMBERS OF FIRM

John Dale Powers
Michael V. Clegg
William E. Willard

ASSOCIATES

Neil H. Mixon
Troy J. Charpentier
Mary A. Cazes

General Counsel for: Audubon Insurance Co.
Louisiana Counsel for: Hancock Bank & Trust Co.; Hertz Corp.; Ciba-Geigy Corp.; Utica Mutual Insurance Co.

For full biographical listings, see the Martindale-Hubbell Law Directory

*LAKE CHARLES,** Calcasieu Parish

BERGSTEDT & MOUNT (AV)

Second Floor, Magnolia Life Building, P.O. Drawer 3004, 70602-3004
Telephone: 318-433-3004
Facsimile: 318-433-8080

MEMBERS OF FIRM

Thomas M. Bergstedt
Benjamin W. Mount

ASSOCIATES

Van C. Seneca
Thomas J. Gayle
Gregory P. Marceaux

(See Next Column)

OF COUNSEL

Charles S. Ware

Representative Clients: Armstrong World Industries; Ashland Oil Co.; CIGNA Property & Casualty Companies; Homequity; Lake Area Medical Center; Leach Company; Olin Corporation; Terra Corporation; Town of Iowa; R. D. Werner Company.

For Complete List of Firm Personnel, See General Section

For full biographical listings, see the Martindale-Hubbell Law Directory

*NEW ORLEANS,** Orleans Parish

NESSER, KING & LEBLANC (AV)

Suite 3800 Place St. Charles, 201 St. Charles Avenue, 70170
Telephone: 504-582-3800
Telecopier: 504-582-1233

John T. Nesser, III
Patricia Ann Krebs
Henry A. King
Robert J. Burvant
Joseph E. LeBlanc, Jr.
Eric Earl Jarrell
David S. Bland
Liane K. Hinrichs

Jeffrey M. Burmaster
Elton A. Foster
Jeffrey A. Mitchell
Elizabeth S. Wheeler
Margaret M. Sledge
Robert J. Bergeron
Josh M. Kantrow
Timothy S. Madden
Elizabeth A. Meek

OF COUNSEL

Clare P. Hunter
J. Grant Coleman
George B. Jurgens, III
Len R. Brignac
George Farber, Jr.

For full biographical listings, see the Martindale-Hubbell Law Directory

PHELPS DUNBAR, L.L.P. (AV)

Texaco Center, 400 Poydras Street, 70130-3245
Telephone: 504-566-1311
Telecopier: 504-568-9130, 504-568-9007
Cable Address: "Howspencer"
Telex: 584125 WU
Telex: 6821155 WUI
Baton Rouge, Louisiana Office: Suite 701, City National Bank Building, P.O. Box 4412.
Telephone: 504-346-0285.
Telecopier: 504-381-9197.
Jackson, Mississippi Office: Suite 500, Security Centré North, 200 South Lamar Street, P.O. Box 23066.
Telephone: 601-352-2300.
Telecopier: 601-360-9777.
Tupelo, Mississippi Office: Seventh Floor, One Mississippi Plaza, P.O. Box 1220.
Telephone: 601-842-7907.
Telecopier: 601-842-3873.
Houston, Texas Office: Suite 501, 4 Houston Center, 1331 Lamar Street.
Telephone: 713-659-1386.
Telecopier: 713-659-1388.
London, England Office: Suite 976, Level 9, Lloyd's, 1 Lime Street, London EC3M 7DQ England.
Telephone: 011-44-71-929-4765.
Telecopier: 011-44-71-929-0046.
Telex: 987321.

MEMBERS OF FIRM

Philip deV. Claverie
James A. Stuckey
Robert U. Soniat
Stephen H. Leech, Jr. (Not admitted in LA; Resident, Jackson, Mississippi Office)
F. M. Bush, III (Not admitted in LA; Jackson and Tupelo, Mississippi Offices)
Dana E. Kelly (Not admitted in LA; Resident, Jackson, Mississippi Office)
Harvey D. Wagar, III
E. Clifton Hodge, Jr. (Not admitted in LA; Resident, Jackson, Mississippi Office)
Charles D. Porter (Not admitted in LA; Resident, Jackson, Mississippi Office)
Shaun B. Rafferty
Jean Magee Hogan (Not admitted in LA; Jackson and Tupelo, Mississippi Offices)
Jonathan C. Benda (Resident, Baton Rouge, Louisiana Office)

COUNSEL

J. Michael Cutshaw (Resident, Baton Rouge, Louisiana Office)

ASSOCIATES

Lee R. Adler
Jennifer L. Hantel
Gregory D. Guida (Not admitted in LA; Resident, Jackson, Mississippi Office)
Daniel T. Pancamo

Representative Clients: Bank of Mississippi; Citicorp Real Estate, Inc.; First National Bank of Commerce; Hibernia National Bank; Morgan Guaranty Trust Company of New York; NationsBank; Premier Bank, N.A.; Sunburst Bank; Trustmark National Bank; Whitney National Bank.

For Complete List of Firm Personnel, See General Section

For full biographical listings, see the Martindale-Hubbell Law Directory

*SHREVEPORT,** Caddo Parish

Barlow and Hardtner L.C. (AV)

Tenth Floor, Louisiana Tower, 401 Edwards Street, 71101-3289
Telephone: 318-227-1131
Telecopier: 318-227-1141
Mailing Address: P.O. Box 8, Shreveport, Louisiana, 71161-0008

Malcolm S. Murchison
Joseph L. Shea, Jr.
Clair F. White
Philip E. Downer, III
Michael B. Donald

Representative Clients: Kelley Oil Corporation; NorAm Energy Corp. (formerly Arkla, Inc.); Central and South West; Panhandle Eastern Corp.; Pennzoil Producing Co.; Johnson Controls, Inc.; Ashland Oil, Inc.; Southwestern Electric Power Company; Brammer Engineering, Inc.; General Electric Co.

For Complete List of Firm Personnel, See General Section

For full biographical listings, see the Martindale-Hubbell Law Directory

Bodenheimer, Jones, Klotz & Simmons (AV)

509 Milam Street, 71101
Telephone: 318-221-1507
Fax: 318-221-4560

MEMBERS OF FIRM

J. W. Jones
F. John Reeks, Jr.
Norman I. Lafargue
Claude W. Bookter, Jr.

Representative Client: Pioneer Bank & Trust Company.

For full biographical listings, see the Martindale-Hubbell Law Directory

Cook, Yancey, King & Galloway, A Professional Law Corporation (AV)

1700 Commercial National Tower, 333 Texas Street, P.O. Box 22260, 71120-2260
Telephone: 318-221-6277
Telecopier: 318-227-2606

Sidney B. Galloway
James Robert Jeter
Stephen R. Yancey II
J. William Fleming
Frank M. Dodson
Bernard S. Johnson
Curtis R. Shelton
Lance P. Havener
William C. Kalmbach, III
Laura A. Merkler

A list of representative clients will be furnished upon request.

For Complete List of Firm Personnel, See General Section

For full biographical listings, see the Martindale-Hubbell Law Directory

MAINE

*BANGOR,** Penobscot Co.

Eaton, Peabody, Bradford & Veague, P.A. (AV)

Fleet Center-Exchange Street, P.O. Box 1210, 04402-1210
Telephone: 207-947-0111
Telecopier: 207-942-3040
Augusta, Maine Office: 2 Central Plaza.
Telephone: 207-622-3747.
Telecopier: 207-622-9732.
Brunswick, Maine Office: 167 Park Row.
Telephone: 207-729-1144.
Telecopier: 207-729-1140.
Camden, Maine Office: 7-9 Washington Street.
Telephone: 207-236-3325.
Telecopier: 207-236-8611.
Dover-Foxcroft, Maine Office: 30 East Main Street.
Telephone: 207-564-8378.
Telecopier: 207-564-7059.

Robert J. Eaton
Edward D. Leonard, III
Douglas M. Smith (Resident, Dover-Foxcroft and Augusta Offices)
Daniel G. McKay
John A. Cunningham (Resident, Brunswick Office)

OF COUNSEL

Donald A. Spear (Resident, Brunswick Office)

John M. Monahan (Resident, Dover-Foxcroft Office)
Jonathan B. Huntington (Resident, Dover-Foxcroft Office)
Lorena R. Rush

A List of Representative Clients available upon request.

For Complete List of Firm Personnel, See General Section

For full biographical listings, see the Martindale-Hubbell Law Directory

Gross, Minsky, Mogul & Singal, P.A. (AV)

Key Plaza, 23 Water Street, P.O. Box 917, 04402-0917
Telephone: 207-942-4644
Telecopier: 207-942-3699
Ellsworth, Maine Office: 26 State Street.
Telephone: 207-667-4611.
Telecopier: 207-667-6206.

Jules L. Mogul (1930-1994)
Norman Minsky
George Z. Singal
Louis H. Kornreich
George C. Schelling
Edward W. Gould
Steven J. Mogul
James R. Wholly

Wayne P. Libhart (Resident, Ellsworth, Maine Office)
Daniel A. Pileggi
Philip K. Clarke
Christopher R. Largay (Resident, Ellsworth Office)
Hans G. Huessy
William B. Entwisle
Sandra L. Rothera

OF COUNSEL

Edward I. Gross

Representative Clients: Merrill Merchants Bank; Union Trust Company of Ellsworth; Comprehensive Foreclosure Services, Inc.; Metropolitan Mortgage & Securities Co., Inc.

For full biographical listings, see the Martindale-Hubbell Law Directory

*PORTLAND,** Cumberland Co.

Jensen Baird Gardner & Henry (AV)

Ten Free Street, P.O. Box 4510, 04112
Telephone: 207-775-7271
Telecopier: 207-775-7935
York County Office: 419 Alfred Street, Biddeford, Maine.
Telephone: 207-282-5107.
Telecopier: 207-282-6301.

OF COUNSEL

Merton G. Henry

MEMBERS OF FIRM

John D. Bradford (Resident, York County Office)
Joan LaBrique Cook (Resident, York County Office)
F. Bruce Sleeper

Representative Clients: General Motors Acceptance Corp.; York Mutual Insurance Co.; Knutson Mortgage Corp.; Owens Corning Fiberglass.

For Complete List of Firm Personnel, See General Section

For full biographical listings, see the Martindale-Hubbell Law Directory

Pierce, Atwood, Scribner, Allen, Smith & Lancaster (AV)

One Monument Square, 04101
Telephone: 207-773-6411
Fax: 207-773-3419
Augusta, Maine Office: 77 Winthrop Street.
Telephone: 207-622-6311.
Camden, Maine Office: 36 Chestnut Street, P.O. Box 780.
Telephone: 207-236-4333.

MEMBERS OF FIRM

James B. Zimpritch
Richard P. Hackett
David J. Champoux

For Complete List of Firm Personnel, See General Section

For full biographical listings, see the Martindale-Hubbell Law Directory

Richardson & Troubh, A Professional Corporation (AV)

465 Congress Street, P.O. Box 9732, 04104-5032
Telephone: 207-774-5821
Telecopier: 207-761-2056
Bangor, Maine Office: Richardson Troubh & Badger, A Professional Corporation, 82 Columbia Street.
Telephone: 207-945-5900.
Telecopier: 207-945-0758.

William B. Troubh
Edwin A. Heisler
Michael P. Boyd
William K. McKinley
Paul S. Bulger

Linda L. Sears

Representative Client: Peoples Heritage Savings Bank.

For Complete List of Firm Personnel, See General Section

For full biographical listings, see the Martindale-Hubbell Law Directory

MARYLAND

*BALTIMORE,** (Independent City)

VENABLE, BAETJER AND HOWARD (AV)

A Partnership including Professional Corporations
1800 Mercantile Bank & Trust Building, 2 Hopkins Plaza, 21201
Telephone: 410-244-7400
Washington, D.C. Office: Venable, Baetjer, Howard & Civiletti. Suite 1000, 1201 New York Avenue, N.W.
Telephone: 202-962-4800.
McLean, Virginia Office: Suite 400, 2010 Corporate Ridge.
Telephone: 703-760-1600.
Rockville, Maryland Office: Suite 500, One Church Street, P. O. Box 1906.
Telephone: 301-217-5600.
Towson, Maryland Office: 210 Allegheny Avenue, P. O. Box 5517.
Telephone: 410-494-6200.

MEMBERS OF FIRM

William J. McCarthy (P.C.)
Russell Ronald Reno, Jr. (P.C.)
James A. Cole
Benjamin R. Civiletti (P.C.) (Also at Washington, D.C. and Towson, Maryland Offices)
David D. Downes (Resident, Towson, Maryland Office)
John Henry Lewin, Jr. (P.C.)
Lee M. Miller (P.C.)
Robert A. Shelton
Roger W. Titus (Resident, Rockville, Maryland Office)
Daniel O'C. Tracy, Jr. (Also at Rockville, Maryland Office)
Ronald R. Glancz (Not admitted in MD; Resident, Washington, D.C. Office)
David J. Levenson (Not admitted in MD; Resident, Washington, D.C. Office)
Joe A. Shull (Resident, Washington, D.C. Office)
Kenneth C. Bass, III (Not admitted in MD; Also at Washington, D.C. and McLean, Virginia Offices)
John H. Zink, III (Resident, Towson, Maryland Office)
Lars E. Anderson (Not admitted in MD; Resident, McLean, Virginia Office)
Joel Z. Silver (Not admitted in MD; Resident, Washington, D.C. Office)
William D. Dolan, III (P.C.) (Not admitted in MD; Resident, McLean, Virginia Office)
Joseph C. Wich, Jr. (Resident, Towson, Maryland Office)
Edward F. Glynn, Jr. (Not admitted in MD; Resident, Washington, D.C. Office)
Thomas B. Hudson (Also at Washington, D.C. Office)
Nell B. Strachan
Susan K. Gauvey (Also at Towson, Maryland Office)
James R. Myers (Not admitted in MD; Resident, Washington, D.C. Office)
Edward L. Wender (P.C.)
David M. Fleishman
Jeffrey A. Dunn (also at Washington, D.C. Office)
George F. Pappas (Also at Washington, D.C. Office)
Mitchell Kolkin
James L. Shea (Also at Washington, D.C. Office)
Ellen F. Dyke (Not admitted in MD; Resident, McLean, Virginia Office)
William D. Quarles (Also at Washington, D.C. and Towson, Maryland Offices)
Christopher R. Mellott
James A. Dunbar (Also at Washington, D.C. Office)
Elizabeth R. Hughes
Robert A. Cook
David J. Heubeck
J. Michael Brennan (Resident, Towson, Maryland Office)
Bruce H. Jurist (Also at Washington, D.C. Office)
Linda L. Lord (Not admitted in MD; Resident, Washington, D.C. Office)
Paul A. Serini (Also at Washington, D.C. Office)
Ariel Vannier
Michael H. Davis (Resident, Towson, Maryland Office)

OF COUNSEL

Thomas J. Cooper (Not admitted in MD; Resident, Washington, D. C. Office)
Mary T. Flynn (Not admitted in MD; Resident, McLean, Virginia Office)

ASSOCIATES

David S. Darland (Not admitted in MD; Resident, Washington, D.C. Office)
D. Brent Gunsalus (Not admitted in MD; Resident, Washington, D.C. Office)
Andrew R. Herrup (Resident, Washington, D.C. Office)
Mary-Dulany James (Resident, Towson, Maryland Office)
Gregory L. Laubach (Resident, Rockville, Maryland Office)
Jon M. Lippard (Not admitted in MD; Resident, McLean, Virginia Office)
Vicki Margolis
John A. McCauley
Mitchell Y. Mirviss
Michael J. Muller
Vadim A. Mzhen
Joseph C. Schmelter
J. Preston Turner

For Complete List of Firm Personnel, See General Section

For full biographical listings, see the Martindale-Hubbell Law Directory

*ROCKVILLE,** Montgomery Co.

VENABLE, BAETJER AND HOWARD (AV)

A Partnership including Professional Corporations
Suite 500, One Church Street, P.O. Box 1906, 20850-4129
Telephone: 301-217-5600
FAX: 301-217-5617
Baltimore, Maryland Office: 1800 Mercantile Bank & Trust Building, 2 Hopkins Plaza.
Telephone: 410-244-7400.
Washington, D.C. Office: Venable, Baetjer, Howard & Civiletti. Suite 1000, 1201 New York Avenue, N.W.
Telephone: 202-962-4800.
McLean, Virginia Office: Suite 400, 2010 Corporate Ridge.
Telephone: 703-760-1600.
Towson, Maryland, Office: 210 Allegheny Avenue, P. O. Box 5517.
Telephone: 410-494-6200.

MEMBERS OF FIRM

Daniel O'C. Tracy, Jr. (Also at Baltimore, Maryland Office)
Paul T. Glasgow
John A. Roberts (Also at Baltimore, Maryland Office)

ASSOCIATE

Gregory L. Laubach

For Complete List of Firm Personnel, See General Section

For full biographical listings, see the Martindale-Hubbell Law Directory

SILVER SPRING, Montgomery Co.

ALEXANDER, GEBHARDT, APONTE & MARKS, L.L.C. (AV)

Lee Plaza-Suite 805, 8601 Georgia Avenue, 20910
Telephone: 301-589-2222
Facsimile: 301-589-2523
Washington, D.C. Office: 1314 Nineteenth Street, N.W., 20036.
Telephone: 202-835-1555.
New York, New York Office: 330 Madison Avenue, 36th Floor.
Telephone: 212-808-0008.
Fax: 212-599-1028.

Koteles Alexander (Not admitted in MD)
James L. Bearden (Not admitted in MD)

J. Darrell Peterson
Adrienne P. Byrd

Reference: Riggs National Bank of Washington, D.C.

For full biographical listings, see the Martindale-Hubbell Law Directory

*TOWSON,** Baltimore Co.

VENABLE, BAETJER AND HOWARD (AV)

A Partnership including Professional Corporations
210 Allegheny Avenue, P.O. Box 5517, 21204
Telephone: 410-494-6200
FAX: 410-821-0147
Baltimore, Maryland Office: 1800 Mercantile Bank & Trust Building, 2 Hopkins Plaza.
Telephone: 410-244-7400.
Washington, D.C. Office: Venable, Baetjer, Howard & Civiletti. Suite 1000, 1201 New York Avenue, N.W.
Telephone: 202-962-4800.
McLean, Virginia Office: Suite 400, 2010 Corporate Ridge.
Telephone: 703-760-1600.
Rockville, Maryland Office: Suite 500, One Church Street, P. O. Box 1906.
Telephone: 301-217-5600.

PARTNERS

Benjamin R. Civiletti (P.C.) (Also at Washington, D.C. and Baltimore, Maryland Offices)
David D. Downes
John H. Zink, III
Joseph C. Wich, Jr.
J. Michael Brennan
Michael H. Davis

ASSOCIATE

Mary-Dulany James

For Complete List of Firm Personnel, See General Section

For full biographical listings, see the Martindale-Hubbell Law Directory

MASSACHUSETTS

*BOSTON,** Suffolk Co.

BARRON & STADFELD, P.C. (AV)

Two Center Plaza, 02108
Telephone: 617-723-9800
Telecopier: 617-523-8359
Hyannis, Massachusetts Office: 258 Winter Street.
Telephone: 617-778-6622.

Hertz N. Henkoff
Thomas V. Bennett
Kevin F. Moloney
Julie Taylor Moran

Alison L. Berman

For Complete List of Firm Personnel, See General Section

For full biographical listings, see the Martindale-Hubbell Law Directory

CRAIG AND MACAULEY, PROFESSIONAL CORPORATION (AV)

Federal Reserve Plaza, 600 Atlantic Avenue, 02210
Telephone: 617-367-9500
Telecopier: 617-742-1788; 617-248-0886

John C. Craig
William F. Macauley
David F. Hannon
Mary P. Brody

John G. Snyder
Mark W. Manning
Michael J. Degnan

For Complete List of Firm Personnel, See General Section

For full biographical listings, see the Martindale-Hubbell Law Directory

PALMER & DODGE (AV)

(Storey Thorndike Palmer & Dodge)
One Beacon Street, 02108
Telephone: 617-573-0100
Telecopier: 617-227-4420
Telex: 951104
Cable Address: "Storeydike," Boston

MEMBERS OF FIRM

Abigail A. Cheever
Matthew C. Dallett
Jerry V. Klima
John L. Whitlock

For Complete List of Firm Personnel, See General Section

For full biographical listings, see the Martindale-Hubbell Law Directory

SHERBURNE, POWERS & NEEDHAM, P.C. (AV)

One Beacon Street, 02108
Telephone: 617-523-2700
Fax: 617-523-6850

William D. Weeks
John T. Collins
Allan J. Landau
John L. Daly
Stephen A. Hopkins
Alan I. Falk
C. Thomas Swaim
James Pollock
William V. Tripp III
Stephen S. Young
William F. Machen
W. Robert Allison
Jacob C. Diemert
Philip J. Notopoulos
Richard J. Hindlian
Paul E. Troy
Harold W. Potter, Jr.
Dale R. Johnson
Philip S. Lapatin
Pamela A. Duckworth
Mark Schonfeld
James D. Smeallie
Paul Killeen
Gordon P. Katz
Joseph B. Darby, III
Richard M Yanofsky
James E. McDermott
Robert V. Lizza
Miriam Goldstein Altman
John J. Monaghan
Margaret J. Palladino
Mark C. Michalowski
David Scott Sloan
M. Chrysa Long
Lawrence D. Bradley
Miriam J. McKendall

Cynthia A. Brown
Cynthia M. Hern
Dianne R. Phillips
Paul M. James
Theodore F. Hanselman
Joshua C. Krumholz
Ieuan G. Mahony
Kenneth L. Harvey
Christopher J. Trombetta
Edwin F. Landers, Jr.
Amy J. Mastrobattista
William Howard McCarthy, Jr.
Douglas W. Clapp
Tamara E. Goulston
Nicholas J. Psyhogeos

COUNSEL

Haig Der Manuelian
Mason M. Taber, Jr.
Karl J. Hirshman
Benjamin Volinski
Kenneth P. Brier

OF COUNSEL

John Barr Dolan

For full biographical listings, see the Martindale-Hubbell Law Directory

WARNER & STACKPOLE (AV)

75 State Street, 02109
Telephone: 617-951-9000
Cable Address: "Warstack"
Telecopier: 617-951-9151
Telex: 940139

MEMBERS OF FIRM

John J. McCarthy
Stephen E. Moore
John C. Hutchins
Stanley V. Ragalevsky
Christopher E. Nolin
John A. Dziamba
Paul C. Bauer

ASSOCIATE

Richard R. Loewy

For Complete List of Firm Personnel, See General Section

For full biographical listings, see the Martindale-Hubbell Law Directory

*CAMBRIDGE,** Middlesex Co.

WILLIAM M. O'BRIEN (AV)

Suite 216, 186 Alewife Brook Parkway, 02138
Telephone: 617-661-2600
Fax: 617-864-0654

For full biographical listings, see the Martindale-Hubbell Law Directory

*SPRINGFIELD,** Hampden Co.

HENDEL, COLLINS & NEWTON, P.C. (AV)

101 State Street, 01103
Telephone: 413-734-6411
Fax: 413-734-8069

Philip J. Hendel
Joseph B. Collins
Carla W. Newton

Joseph H. Reinhardt
Jonathan R. Goldsmith
Henry E. Geberth, Jr.
George I. Roumeliotis

Representative Clients: Springfield Institution for Savings; Shawmut Bank, N.A.; United Cooperative Bank.
Approved Attorneys for: First American Title Insurance Co.; Commonwealth Land Title Ins. Co.
Reference: Shawmut Bank, N.A.

For full biographical listings, see the Martindale-Hubbell Law Directory

*WORCESTER,** Worcester Co.

MACCARTHY, POJANI & HURLEY (AV)

Worcester Plaza, 446 Main Street, 01608
Telephone: 508-798-2480
Fax: 508-797-9561

Philip J. MacCarthy
Dennis Pojani
John F. Hurley, Jr.
Howard E. Stempler
John Macuga, Jr.

ASSOCIATE

William J. Ritter

Representative Clients: Shawmut Bank N.A.; Melville Corp.; Travelers Insurance Co.; Liberty Mutual Co.; United States Fidelity & Guaranty Co.; Commerce Insurance Co.; Worcester Mutual Insurance Co.; Fleet Bank of Massachusetts, N.A.; Health Plans, Inc.; Marane Oil Corp.

For full biographical listings, see the Martindale-Hubbell Law Directory

MICHIGAN

*ADRIAN,** Lenawee Co.

WALKER, WATTS, JACKSON & MCFARLAND (AV)

160 North Winter Street, 49221
Telephone: 517-265-8138
Fax: 517-265-8286

MEMBERS OF FIRM

William H. Walker
Prosser M. Watts, Jr.
Mark A. Jackson
Michael McFarland

Attorneys for: Adrian State Bank; Bank of Lenawee.

For full biographical listings, see the Martindale-Hubbell Law Directory

*ANN ARBOR,** Washtenaw Co.

CONLIN, MCKENNEY & PHILBRICK, P.C. (AV)

700 City Center Building, 48104-1994
Telephone: 313-761-9000
Fax: 313-761-9001

(See Next Column)

CONLIN, MCKENNEY & PHILBRICK P.C., *Ann Arbor—Continued*

Edward F. Conlin (1902-1953)
John W. Conlin (1904-1972)
Albert J. Parker (1901-1970)
Chris L. McKenney
Karl R. Frankena
Allen J. Philbrick
Phillip J. Bowen
Richard E. Conlin
Michael D. Highfield
Bruce N. Elliott
Neil J. Juliar
Robert M. Brimacombe
David S. Swartz
James A. Schriemer
Elizabeth M. Petoskey
Bradley J. MeLampy
Joseph W. Phillips
William M. Sweet
Lori A. Buiteweg
Douglas G. McClure
Thomas B. Bourque
Marjorie M. Dixon
Bonnie H. Keen

OF COUNSEL

John W. Conlin

Representative Clients: Fingerle Lumber Co.; Ann Arbor Area Board of Realtors; Borders, Inc.; Society Bank, Michigan; Auto-Owners Insurance Co.; Wolverine Title Co.
Approved Attorneys for: American Title Insurance Co.; Ticor Title Insurance Co.

For full biographical listings, see the Martindale-Hubbell Law Directory

MILLER, CANFIELD, PADDOCK AND STONE, P.L.C. (AV)

A Professional Limited Liability Company
Founded in 1852 by Sidney Davy Miller
101 North Main Street, Seventh Floor, 48104-1400
Telephone: 313-663-2445
Fax: 313-747-7147
Detroit, Michigan Office: 150 West Jefferson, Suite 2500, 48226-4415.
Telephone: 313-963-6420.
Fax: 313-496-7500.
Cable Address: "Stem Detroit."
Bloomfield Hills, Michigan Office: Suite 100, Pinehurst Office Center, 1400 North Woodward, 48303-2014.
Telephone: 313-645-5000.
Fax: 313-645-1917.
Grand Rapids, Michigan Office: 1200 Campau Square Plaza, 99 Monroe, N.W., 49503-2639.
Telephone: 616-454-8656.
Fax: 616-776-6322.
Howell, Michigan Office: 121 South Barnard Street, Suite 4, 48843-2305.
Telephone: 517-546-7600.
Telecopier: 517-546-6974.
Kalamazoo, Michigan Office: 444 West Michigan Avenue, 49007-3752.
Telephone: 616-381-7030.
Fax: 616-382-0244.
Lansing, Michigan Office: One Michigan Avenue, Suite 900, 48933-1609.
Telephone: 517-487-2070.
Fax: 517-374-6304.
Monroe, Michigan Office: The Executive Centre, 214 East Elm Avenue, 48161-2682.
Telephone: 313-243-2000.
Fax: 313-243-0901.
Washington, D.C. Office: 1225 Nineteenth Street, N.W., Suite 400. 20036.
Telephone: 202-429-5575; 785-0600.
Fax: 202-331-1118; 785-1234.
Pensacola, Florida Office: 25 West Cedar, 32501.
Telephone: 904-469-1088.
Fax: 904-432-0677.
St. Petersburg, Florida Office: 100 Second Avenue S., Suite 7045, 33701.
Telephone: 813-982-6000.
Fax: 813-892-6002.
Gdansk, Poland Office: Suite 322, Dom Technika Building, Ul. Rajska 6, 80-850.
Telephone: 011-485-831-2808.
Fax: 011-485-831-4719.
Warsaw, Poland Office: Ul. Marszalkowska 82, Suite 561, 00-517.
Telephone: 011-482-623-6457 and 6458.
Fax: 011-482-623-6459.

RESIDENT PARTNER

Robert E. Gilbert

Representative Firm Clients: Chrysler Corp.; Comerica, Inc.; City of Detroit, Mich.; Detroit Tigers, Inc.; First of Michigan; Fretter, Inc.; Ford Motor Co.; Ford Motor Credit Co.; Great Lakes Bancorp; Henry Ford Hospital.

For Complete List of Firm Personnel, See General Section

For full biographical listings, see the Martindale-Hubbell Law Directory

PEAR SPERLING EGGAN & MUSKOVITZ, P.C. (AV)

Domino's Farms, 24 Frank Lloyd Wright Drive, 48105
Telephone: 313-665-4441
Fax: 313-665-8788
Ypsilanti, Michigan Offices: 5 South Washington Street.
Telephone: 313-483-3626 and 2164 Bellevue at Washtenaw.
Telephone: 313-483-7177.

(See Next Column)

Edwin L. Pear
Andrew M. Eggan
Joel F. Graziani
Helen Conklin Vick

Counsel For: Domino's Pizza, Inc.; Bank One, Ypsilanti, N.A.; The Credit Bureau of Ypsilanti.

For Complete List of Firm Personnel, See General Section

For full biographical listings, see the Martindale-Hubbell Law Directory

*BAY CITY,** Bay Co.

BRAUN KENDRICK FINKBEINER (AV)

201 Phoenix Building, P.O. Box 2039, 48708
Telephone: 517-895-8505
Telecopier: 517-895-8437
Saginaw, Michigan Office: 8th Floor Second National Bank Building.
Telephone: 517-753-3461.
Telecopier: 517-753-3951.

MEMBERS OF FIRM

Ralph J. Isackson
Patrick D. Neering
George F. Gronewold, Jr.
Frank M. Quinn
Gregory E. Meter
Daniel S. Opperman
Gregory T. Demers

Representative Clients: APV Chemical Machinery, Inc.; Bay Health Systems; Berger and Co.; Catholic Federal Credit Union; Charter Township of Bridgeport; City of Saginaw; City of Vassar; City of Zilwaukee; Corporate Service; Cox Cable.

For Complete List of Firm Personnel, See General Section

For full biographical listings, see the Martindale-Hubbell Law Directory

BIRMINGHAM, Oakland Co.

SIMPSON & BERRY, P.C. (AV)

260 East Brown, Suite 300, 48009
Telephone: 810-647-0200
Telecopier: 810-647-2776

Daniel F. Berry
Clark G. Doughty
Philip J. Goodman
James A. Simpson
Katheryne L. Zelenock

LEGAL SUPPORT PERSONNEL

Dwight Noble Baker, Jr.

Representative Clients: Rock Financial Corporation; World Wide Financial Services, Inc.; Equity Funding, Inc.; BSI-Banca della Svizzera Italiania.

For full biographical listings, see the Martindale-Hubbell Law Directory

BLOOMFIELD HILLS, Oakland Co.

HOWARD & HOWARD ATTORNEYS, P.C. (AV)

The Pinehurst Office Center, Suite 101, 1400 North Woodward Avenue, 48304-2856
Telephone: 810-645-1483
Telecopier: 810-645-1568
Kalamazoo, Michigan Office: The Kalamazoo Building, Suite 400, 107 West Michigan Avenue.
Telephone: 616-382-1483.
Telecopier: 616-382-1568.
Lansing, Michigan Office: The Phoenix Building, Suite 500, 222 Washington Square, North.
Telephone: 517-485-1483.
Telecopier: 517-485-1568.
Peoria, Illinois Office: Howard & Howard, P.C., The Creve Coeur Building, Suite 200, 321 Liberty Street.
Telephone: 309-672-1483.
Telecopier: 309-672-1568.

Gustaf R. Andreasen
Philip T. Carter
Paul Green
J. Michael Kemp
Timothy E. Kraepel
Claude Henry Miller
John E. Young

Representative Clients: For Representative Client list, see General Practice, Bloomfield Hills, MI.

For Complete List of Firm Personnel, See General Section

For full biographical listings, see the Martindale-Hubbell Law Directory

STROBL AND MANOOGIAN, P.C. (AV)

300 East Long Lake Road, Suite 200, 48304-2376
Telephone: 810-645-0306
Facsimile: 810-645-2690

Thomas J. Strobl
Brian C. Manoogian
John Sharp

James T. Dunn
Thomas H. Kosik

Representative Clients: Comerica Bank; Capitol Bancorp Ltd.; Chrysler Credit Corporation; Chrysler Financial Corporation; Deutsche Finance Corporation; First of America Bank; Michigan National Bank; Midwest Guar-

(See Next Column)

STROBL AND MANOOGIAN P.C.—*Continued*

anty Bank; Oakland Commerce Bank; TCF Bank Michigan; First Independence Bank.

For Complete List of Firm Personnel, See General Section

For full biographical listings, see the Martindale-Hubbell Law Directory

*CHEBOYGAN,** Cheboygan Co.

BODMAN, LONGLEY & DAHLING (AV)

229 Court Street, P.O. Box 405, 49721
Telephone: 616-627-4351
Fax: 616-627-2802
Detroit, Michigan Office: 34th Floor, 100 Renaissance Center.
Telephone: 313-259-7777.
Troy, Michigan Office: Suite 2020, 755 West Big Beaver Road.
Telephone: 810-362-2110.
Ann Arbor, Michigan Office: 110 Miller, Suite 300.
Telephone: 313-761-3780.

RESIDENT PARTNERS

James C. Conboy, Jr.
Lloyd C. Fell
Michael A. Stack
Kathleen A. Lieder
Lawrence P. Hanson
Linda J. Throne

RESIDENT ASSOCIATES

David W. Barton
Susan E. Conboy
A. Craig Klomparens

For full biographical listings, see the Martindale-Hubbell Law Directory

*DETROIT,** Wayne Co.

BODMAN, LONGLEY & DAHLING (AV)

34th Floor 100 Renaissance Center, 48243
Telephone: 313-259-7777
Fax: 313-393-7579
Troy, Michigan Office: Suite 2020, 755 West Big Beaver Road.
Telephone: 810-362-2110.
Ann Arbor, Michigan Office: 110 Miller, Suite 300.
Telephone: 313-761-3780.
Northern Michigan Office: 229 Court Street, P.O. Box 405, Cheboygan.
Telephone: 616-627-4351.

MEMBERS OF FIRM

Richard D. Rohr
Joseph A. Sullivan
Thomas A. Roach (Ann Arbor Office)
James T. Heimbuch
Herold McC. Deason
Joseph J. Kochanek
Randolph S. Perry (Ann Arbor Office)
David G. Chardavoyne
Larry R. Shulman
Thomas Van Dusen (Troy Office)
Robert J. Diehl, Jr.
James C. Conboy, Jr. (Northern Michigan Office)
Lloyd C. Fell (Northern Michigan Office)
Michael A. Stack (Northern Michigan Office)
Lawrence P. Hanson (Northern Michigan Office)
Christopher J. Dine (Troy Office)

Representative Clients: Abitibi Price Group; Archdiocese of Detroit; Comerica Bank; The Detroit Lions, Inc.; Ford Estates; General Motors Corporation; Charles Stewart Mott Foundation; Norfolk Southern Corporation; Panhandle Eastern Corporation; State Farm Mutual Automobile Insurance Company.

For Complete List of Firm Personnel, See General Section

For full biographical listings, see the Martindale-Hubbell Law Directory

BUTZEL LONG, A PROFESSIONAL CORPORATION (AV)

Suite 900, 150 West Jefferson, 48226
Telephone: 313-225-7000
Telecopier: 313-225-7080
Birmingham, Michigan Office: Suite 200, 32270 Telegraph Road.
Telephone: 810-258-1616.
Telecopier: 810-258-1439.
Lansing, Michigan Office: 118 West Ottawa Street.
Telephone: 517-372-6622.
Telecopier: 517-372-6672.
Ann Arbor, Michigan Office: Suite 400, 121 West Washington.
Telephone: 313-995-3110.
Telecopier: 313-995-1777.
Grosse Pointe Farms, Michigan Office: Suite 260, 21 Kercheval.
Telephone: 313-886-5446.
Telecopier: 313-886-2114.

Stephen A. Bromberg (Birmingham)
Robert B. Foster (Ann Arbor)
Philip J. Kessler
Edward M. Kalinka
Richard P. Saslow
Alan S. Levine

Representative Clients: National Bank of Detroit; D & N Bank; First of America; Nedbank of South America; Pontiac State Bank; National Marine Bankers Assn.; The National Bank of Chicago; Evans Assets Holding Company in Michigan; MCA Mortgate Corp.; Metlife Commercial Credit Corp.

(See Next Column)

For Complete List of Firm Personnel, See General Section

For full biographical listings, see the Martindale-Hubbell Law Directory

DICKINSON, WRIGHT, MOON, VAN DUSEN & FREEMAN (AV)

500 Woodward Avenue, Suite 4000, 48226-3425
Telephone: 313-223-3500
Facsimile: 313-223-3598
Bloomfield Hills, Michigan Office: 525 North Woodward Avenue, Suite 2000.
Telephone: 810-433-7200.
Facsimile: 810-433-7274.
Grand Rapids, Michigan Office: 200 Ottawa Avenue, N.W., Suite 900.
Telephone: 616-458-1300.
Facsimile: 616-458-6753.
Lansing, Michigan Office: Suite 200, 215 South Washington Square.
Telephone: 517-371-1730.
Facsimile: 517-487-4700.
Washington, D.C. Office: Suite 800, 1901 L Street, N.W.
Telephone: 202-457-0160.
Facsimile: 202-659-1559.
Chicago, Illinois Office: 225 West Washington, Suite 400.
Telephone: 312-220-0300.
Facsimile: 312-220-0021.
Warsaw, Poland Office: 46 Wilcza Street, 4th Floor, 00-679.
Telephone: (48-22) 299-241.
Facsimile: (48-2) 628-4107. Komertel Satellite Phone: (48-39) 121-510.

MEMBERS OF FIRM

Patrick J. Ledwidge
Ward Randol, Jr. (Bloomfield Hills Office)
Russell A. McNair, Jr.
Edgar C. Howbert
William J. Fisher, III (Grand Rapids Office)
Richard J. Meyers
John K. Lawrence
C. Beth DunCombe
James M. Tervo (Chicago, Illinois Office)
Stuart F. Cheney (Grand Rapids Office)
Richard M. Bolton
Jerome M. Schwartz
Bruce C. Thelen
Martin L. Greenberg (Chicago, Illinois Office)
Daniel M. Katlein
Mark R. High
Dwight D. Ebaugh (Lansing Office)
William P. Shield, Jr.
William T. Burgess
Judith E. Gowing (Bloomfield Hills Office)
Andrew S. Boyce
Steven H. Hilfinger

ASSOCIATES

Monica J. Labe
Mi Young Lee
Creighton R. Meland, Jr. (Chicago, Illinois Office)
Diane G. Schwartz
Colleen M. Shevnock
James M. Toner

Representative Clients: Federal-Mogul Corp.; Florists' Transworld Delivery Assn.; GMF Robotics Corp.; Kmart Corp.; Kuhlman Corp.; Michigan Consolidated Gas Co.; NBD Bank, N.A.

For Complete List of Firm Personnel, See General Section

For full biographical listings, see the Martindale-Hubbell Law Directory

MAGER, MERCER, SCOTT & ALBER, P.C. (AV)

2400 First National Building, 48226
Telephone: 313-965-1700
Facsimile: 313-965-3690
Macomb County Office: 18285 Ten Mile Road, Suite 100, Roseville, Michigan.
Telephone: 810-771-1100.

George J. Mager, Jr.
Phillip G. Alber
Lawrence M. Scott (Resident at Roseville Office)
George D. Mercer
Raymond C. McVeigh
Michael R. Alberty
Bruce H. Hoffman
Jeffrey M. Frank
Michael A. Schwartz

Representative Clients: ABB Flakt, Inc.; American States Insurance Co.; CEI Industries; Central Venture Corp.; CIGNA; Construction Management, Inc.

For full biographical listings, see the Martindale-Hubbell Law Directory

MILLER, CANFIELD, PADDOCK AND STONE, P.L.C. (AV)

A Professional Limited Liability Company
Founded in 1852 by Sidney Davy Miller
150 West Jefferson, Suite 2500, 48226-4415
Telephone: 313-963-6420
Fax: 313-496-7500
Cable Address: "Stem Detroit"
Detroit, Michigan Office: 150 West Jefferson, Suite 2500, 48226-4415.
Telephone: 313-963-6420.
Fax: 313-496-7500.
Cable Address: "Stem Detroit."
Ann Arbor, Michigan Office: 101 North Main Street, 7th Floor, 48104-1400.
Telephone: 313-663-2445.
Fax: 313-747-7147.

(See Next Column)

MILLER, CANFIELD, PADDOCK AND STONE P.L.C., *Detroit—Continued*

Bloomfield Hills, Michigan Office: Suite 100, Pinehurst Office Center, 1400 North Woodward, 48303-2014.
Telephone: 313-645-5000.
Fax: 313-645-1917.
Grand Rapids, Michigan Office: 1200 Campau Square Plaza, 99 Monroe, N.W., 49503-2639.
Telephone: 616-454-8656.
Fax: 616-776-6322.
Howell, Michigan Office: 121 South Barnard Street, Suite 4, 48843-2305.
Telephone: 517-546-7600.
Telecopier: 517-546-6974.
Kalamazoo, Michigan Office: 444 West Michigan Avenue, 49007-3752.
Telephone: 616-381-7030.
Fax: 616-382-0244.
Lansing, Michigan Office: One Michigan Avenue, Suite 900, 48933-1609.
Telephone: 517-487-2070.
Fax: 517-374-6304.
Monroe, Michigan Office: The Executive Centre, 214 East Elm Avenue, 48161-2682.
Telephone: 313-243-2000.
Fax: 313-243-0901.
Washington, D.C. Office: 1225 Nineteenth Street, N.W., Suite 400. 20036.
Telephone: 202-429-5575; 785-0600.
Fax: 202-331-1118; 785-1234.
Pensacola, Florida Office: 25 West Cedar, 32501.
Telephone: 904-469-1088.
Fax: 904-432-0677.
St. Petersburg, Florida Office: 100 Second Avenue S., Suite 7045, 33701.
Telephone: 813-982-6000.
Fax: 813-892-6002.
Gdansk, Poland Office: Suite 322, Dom Technika Building, Ul. Rajska 6, 80-850.
Telephone: 011-485-831-2808.
Fax: 011-485-831-4719.
Warsaw, Poland Office: Ul. Marszalkowska 82, Suite 561, 00-517.
Telephone: 011-482-623-6457 and 6458.
Fax: 011-482-623-6459.

MEMBERS OF FIRM

John W. Gelder
Richard A. Jones (P.C.) (Bloomfield Hills Office)
Rocque E. Lipford (P.C.) (Monroe Office)
David D. Joswick (P.C.)
John A. Marxer (P.C.) (Bloomfield Hills Office)
Ronald H. Riback (Bloomfield Hills Office)
Thomas W. Linn
Terrence M. Crawford
J. Kevin Trimmer (Bloomfield Hills Office)
Brad B. Arbuckle (Bloomfield Hills Office)
Karen Ann McCoy

OF COUNSEL

Richard B. Gushée
Henry R. Nolte, Jr. (Bloomfield Hills Office)

SENIOR ATTORNEYS

Elise Levasseur Rohn
David F. Dixon
Susan E. Juroe (Washington, D.C. Office)

ASSOCIATES

Ronald E. Hodess (Bloomfield Hills Office)
Terry Xiaotian Gao (Washington, D.C. Office)

Representative Firm Clients: Chrysler Corp.; Comerica, Inc.; City of Detroit, Mich.; Detroit Tigers, Inc.; First of Michigan; Fretter, Inc.; Ford Motor Co.; Ford Motor Credit Co.; Great Lakes Bancorp; Henry Ford Hospital.

For Complete List of Firm Personnel, See General Section

For full biographical listings, see the Martindale-Hubbell Law Directory

SHAHEEN, JACOBS & ROSS, P.C. (AV)

585 East Larned, Suite 200, 48226-4316
Telephone: 313-963-1301
Telecopier: 313-963-7123

Joseph Shaheen (1920-1984)
Michael A. Jacobs (1949-1992)
Steven P. Ross
Michael J. Thomas
Leslie Kujawski Carr
Margaret Conti Schmidt

OF COUNSEL

Mark A. Armitage, P.C.

For full biographical listings, see the Martindale-Hubbell Law Directory

*ESCANABA,** Delta Co.

BUTCH, QUINN, ROSEMURGY, JARDIS, BUSH, BURKHART & STROM, P.C. (AV)

816 Ludington Street, 49829
Telephone: 906-786-4422
Fax: 906-786-5128
Gladstone, Michigan Office: 201 First National Bank Building.
Telephone: 906-428-3123.
Marquette, Michigan Office: 300 South Front Street.
Telephone: 906-228-4440.
Iron Mountain, Michigan Office: 500 South Stephenson Avenue.
Telephone: 906-774-4460.

(See Next Column)

Marinette, Wisconsin Office: 2008 Ella Court.
Telephone: 715-732-4154.

Thomas L. Butch
Michael B. Quinn
Terry F. Burkhart
John A. Lewandowski
James E. Soderberg

Representative Clients: MFC First National Bank of Escanaba; Baybank; First Bank, Upper Michigan; First Northern National Bank of Manistique.

For Complete List of Firm Personnel, See General Section

For full biographical listings, see the Martindale-Hubbell Law Directory

*FLINT,** Genesee Co.

WINEGARDEN, SHEDD, HALEY, LINDHOLM & ROBERTSON (AV)

501 Citizens Bank Building, 48502-1983
Telephone: 810-767-3600
Telecopier: 810-767-8776

MEMBERS OF FIRM

William C. Shedd
Dennis M. Haley
John T. Lindholm
Donald H. Robertson
L. David Lawson
John R. Tucker

ASSOCIATES

Alan F. Himelhoch
Suellen J. Parker
Damion Frasier
Peter T. Mooney

Representative Clients: Citizens Commercial and Savings Bank; R. L. White Development Corporation; Interstate Traffic Consultants (Intracon) Inc.; Downtown Development Authority of Flint; Young Olds-Cadillac, Inc.; First American Title Insurance Co.; Sorensen Gross Construction Co.; Genesee County; Insight, Inc.; Modern Industries, Inc.

For Complete List of Firm Personnel, See General Section

For full biographical listings, see the Martindale-Hubbell Law Directory

*GRAND RAPIDS,** Kent Co.

MILLER, CANFIELD, PADDOCK AND STONE, P.L.C. (AV)

A Professional Limited Liability Company
Founded in 1852 by Sidney Davy Miller
1200 Campau Square Plaza, 99 Monroe, N.W., P.O. Box 329, 49503-2639
Telephone: 616-454-8656
Fax: 616-776-6322
Detroit, Michigan Office: 150 West Jefferson, Suite 2500, 48226-4415.
Telephone: 313-963-6420.
Fax: 313-496-7500.
Cable Address: "Stem Detroit."
Ann Arbor, Michigan Office: 101 North Main Street, 7th Floor, 48104-1400.
Telephone: 313-663-2445.
Fax: 313-747-7147.
Bloomfield Hills, Michigan Office: Suite 100, Pinehurst Office Center, 1400 North Woodward, 48303-2014.
Telephone: 313-645-5000.
Fax: 313-645-1917.
Howell, Michigan Office: 121 South Barnard Street, Suite 4, 48843-2305.
Telephone: 517-546-7600.
Telecopier: 517-546-6974.
Kalamazoo, Michigan Office: 444 West Michigan Avenue, 49007-3752.
Telephone: 616-381-7030.
Fax: 616-382-0244.
Lansing, Michigan Office: One Michigan Avenue, Suite 900, 48933-1609.
Telephone: 517-487-2070.
Fax: 517-374-6304.
Monroe, Michigan Office: The Executive Centre, 214 East Elm Avenue, 48161-2682.
Telephone: 313-243-2000.
Fax: 313-243-0901.
Washington, D.C. Office: 1225 Nineteenth Street, N.W., Suite 400. 20036.
Telephone: 202-429-5575; 785-0600;
Fax: 202-331-1118; 785-1234.
Pensacola, Florida Office: 25 West Cedar 32501.
Telephone: 904-469-1088.
Fax: 904-432-0677.
St. Petersburg Florida Office: 100 Second Avenue S., Suite 7045, 33701.
Telephone: 813-982-6000.
Fax: 813-892-6002.
Gdansk, Poland Office: Suite 322, Dom Technika Building, Ul. Rajska 6, 80-850.
Telephone: 011-485-831-2808.
Fax: 011-485-831-4719.
Warsaw, Poland Office: Ul. Marszalkowska 82, Suite 561, 00-517.
Telephone: 011-482-623-6457 and 6458.
Fax: 011-482-623-6459.

(See Next Column)

MILLER, CANFIELD, PADDOCK AND STONE P.L.C.—*Continued*

MEMBERS OF FIRM

Thomas J. Heiden (Resident)
Mark E. Putney (Resident)
Thomas C. Phillips
Richard A. Gaffin
Charles S. Mishkind (Detroit, Lansing and Kalamazoo Offices)
Stephen M. Tuuk (Resident)
Robert D. VanderLaan (Resident)
Michael G. Campbell (Resident)
Robert E. Lee Wright
Vernon Bennett III
Douglas W. Crim (Resident)

OF COUNSEL

George J. Slykhouse (Resident)

SENIOR ATTORNEYS

Charles E. Scholl (Resident)
David E. Hathaway (Resident)
Michael J. Taylor (Resident)
David J. Hasper (Resident)

ASSOCIATES

Gary E. Mitchell (Resident)
John C. Arndts (Resident)
Bradley C. White
Meg Hackett Carrier (Resident)

Representative Firm Clients: Chrysler Corp.; Comerica, Inc.; City of Detroit, Mich.; Detroit Tigers, Inc.; First of Michigan; Fretter, Inc.; Ford Motor Co.; Ford Motor Credit Co.; Great Lakes Bancorp; Henry Ford Hospital.

For full biographical listings, see the Martindale-Hubbell Law Directory

VARNUM, RIDDERING, SCHMIDT & HOWLETT (AV)

Bridgewater Place, P.O. Box 352, 49501-0352
Telephone: 616-336-6000
800-262-0011
Facsimile: 616-336-7000
Telex: 1561593 VARN
Lansing, Michigan Office: The Victor Center, Suite 810, 210 North Washington Square, 48933.
Telephone: 517-482-6237.
Facsimile: 517-482-6937.
Kalamazoo, Michigan Office: 350 East Michigan Avenue, 49007.
Telephone: 616-382-2300.
Facsimile: 616-382-2382.
Grand Haven, Michigan Office: 321 Washington Street, P.O. Box 288, 49417.
Telephone: 616-846-7100.
Facsimile: 616-846-7101.
Battle Creek, Michigan Office: 4950 West Dickman Road, Suite B-1, 49015.
Telephone: 616-962-7144.
Detroit, Michigan Office: 440 East Congress, Fourth Floor, 48226.
Telephone: 313-961-1600.
Facsimile: 313-961-1636.

MEMBERS OF FIRM

Donald L. Johnson
Timothy J. Curtin
Jeffrey L. Schad
Thomas G. Demling
Jeffrey R. Hughes
Thomas C. Clinton
Robert A. Hendricks
Michael G. Wooldridge
Joan E. Schleef

ASSOCIATES

Maureen Potter
Vicki S. Young

Counsel for: Eastern Michigan Financial Corp.; First Michigan Bank Corp.; Independent Bank Corp.; West Shore Bank Corp.
Special Counsel for: Comerica Bank, N.A.; Grand Bank; Michigan National Bank NA.

For Complete List of Firm Personnel, See General Section

For full biographical listings, see the Martindale-Hubbell Law Directory

WARNER, NORCROSS & JUDD (AV)

900 Old Kent Building, 111 Lyon Street, N.W., 49503-2489
Telephone: 616-752-2000
Fax: 616-752-2500
Muskegon, Michigan Office: 400 Terrace Plaza, P.O. Box 900.
Telephone: 616-727-2600.
Fax: 616-727-2699.
Holland, Michigan Office: Curtis Center, Suite 300, 170 College Avenue.
Telephone: 616-396-9800.
Fax: 616-396-3656.

MEMBERS OF FIRM

James H. Breay
Ernest M. Sharpe
Thomas H. Thornhill (Resident at Muskegon Office)
Rodney D. Martin

ASSOCIATES

Jeffrey A. Ott
Timothy L. Horner

Representative Clients: Michigan Bankers Assn.; Old Kent Financial Corp.; Shoreline Financial Corp.

For Complete List of Firm Personnel, See General Section

For full biographical listings, see the Martindale-Hubbell Law Directory

*KALAMAZOO,** Kalamazoo Co.

HOWARD & HOWARD ATTORNEYS, P.C. (AV)

The Kalamazoo Building, Suite 400, 107 West Michigan Avenue, 49007-3956
Telephone: 616-382-1483
Telecopier: 616-382-1568
Bloomfield Hills, Michigan Office: The Pinehurst Office Center, Suite 101, 1400 North Woodward Avenue.
Telephone: 810-645-1483.
Telecopier: 810-645-1568.
Lansing, Michigan Office: The Phoenix Building, Suite 500, 222 Washington Square North.
Telephone: 517-485-1483.
Telecopier: 517-485-1568.
Peoria, Illinois Office: Howard & Howard, P.C., The Creve Coeur Building, Suite 200, 321 Liberty Street.
Telephone: 309-672-1483.
Telecopier: 309-672-1568.

William A. Dornbos
Joseph B. Hemker

Representative Clients: For Representative Client list, see General Practice, Kalamazoo, MI.

For Complete List of Firm Personnel, See General Section

For full biographical listings, see the Martindale-Hubbell Law Directory

KREIS, ENDERLE, CALLANDER & HUDGINS, A PROFESSIONAL CORPORATION (AV)

One Moorsbridge, 49002
Telephone: 616-324-3000
Telecopier: 616-324-3010

Russell A. Kreis
Alan G. Enderle
C. Reid Hudgins III

For Complete List of Firm Personnel, See General Section

For full biographical listings, see the Martindale-Hubbell Law Directory

MILLER, CANFIELD, PADDOCK AND STONE, P.L.C. (AV)

A Professional Limited Liability Company
Founded in 1852 by Sidney Davy Miller
444 West Michigan Avenue, 49007-3752
Telephone: 616-381-7030
Fax: 616-382-0244
Detroit, Michigan Office: 150 West Jefferson, Suite 2500, 48226-4415.
Telephone: 313-963-6420.
Fax: 313-496-7500.
Cable Address: "Stem Detroit."
Ann Arbor, Michigan Office: 101 North Main Street, 7th Floor, 48104-1400.
Telephone: 313-663-2445.
Fax: 313-747-7147.
Bloomfield Hills, Michigan Office: Suite 100, Pinehurst Office Center, 1400 North Woodward, 48303-2014.
Telephone: 313-645-5000.
Fax: 313-645-1917.
Grand Rapids, Michigan Office: 1200 Campau Square Plaza, 99 Monroe, N.W., 49503-2639.
Telephone: 616-454-8656.
Fax: 616-776-6322.
Howell, Michigan Office: 121 South Barnard Street, Suite 4, 48843-2305.
Telephone: 517-546-7600.
Telecopier: 517-546-6974.
Lansing, Michigan Office: One Michigan Avenue, Suite 900, 48933-1609.
Telephone: 517-487-2070.
Fax: 517-374-6304.
Monroe, Michigan Office: The Executive Centre, 214 East Elm Avenue, 48161-2682.
Telephone: 313-243-2000.
Fax: 313-243-0901.
Washington, D.C. Office: 1225 Nineteenth Street, N.W., Suite 400. 20036.
Telephone: 202-429-5575; 785-0600.
Fax: 202-331-1118; 785-1234.
Pensacola, Florida Office: 25 West Cedar, 32501.
Telephone: 904-469-1088.
Fax: 904-432-0677.
St. Petersburg, Florida Office: 100 Second Avenue S., Suite 7045,33701.
Telephone: 813-982-6000.
Fax: 813-892-6002.
Gdansk, Poland Office: Suite 322, Dom Technika Building, Ul. Rajska 6, 80-850.
Telephone: 011-485-831-2808.
Fax: 011-485-831-4719.
Warsaw, Poland Office: Ul. Marszalkowska 82, Suite 561, 00-517.
Telephone: 011-482-623-6457 and 6458.
Fax: 011-482-623-6459.

(See Next Column)

MILLER, CANFIELD, PADDOCK AND STONE P.L.C., *Kalamazoo—Continued*

MEMBER OF FIRM
Eric V. Brown, Jr. (Resident)

Representative Firm Clients: Chrysler Corp.; Comerica, Inc.; City of Detroit, Mich.; Detroit Tigers, Inc.; First of Michigan; Fretter, Inc.; Ford Motor Co.; Ford Motor Credit Co.; Great Lakes Bancorp; Henry Ford Hospital.

For Complete List of Firm Personnel, See General Section

For full biographical listings, see the Martindale-Hubbell Law Directory

LANSING, Ingham Co.

FOSTER, SWIFT, COLLINS & SMITH, P.C. (AV)

313 South Washington Square, 48933-2193
Telephone: 517-371-8100
Telecopier: 517-371-8200
Farmington Hills, Michigan Office: 32300 Northwestern Highway, Suite 230.
Telephone: 810-851-7500.
Fax: 810-851-7504.

Richard B. Foster
Robert J. McCullen
James B. Jensen, Jr.
James B. Croom
Steven L. Owen
Brent A. Titus
Deanna Swisher
Michael W. Puerner
Mark J. Burzych

LEGAL SUPPORT PERSONNEL
LEGAL ASSISTANTS

Jeanne M. Phillips
Janice Underwood

Representative Clients: First of America Bank; M.S.U. Federal Credit Union, Community First Bank.

For Complete List of Firm Personnel, See General Section

For full biographical listings, see the Martindale-Hubbell Law Directory

FRASER TREBILCOCK DAVIS & FOSTER, P.C. (AV)

1000 Michigan National Tower, 48933
Telephone: 517-482-5800
Fax: 517-482-0887
Okemos, Michigan Office: 2188 Commons Parkway.
Telephone: 517-349-1300.
Fax: 517-349-0922.

Ronald R. Pentecost

Counsel for: Pioneer Bank; Northern Michigan Savings Bank; Bank One-East Lansing; Old Kent Bank; First National Bank of Michigan.

For Complete List of Firm Personnel, See General Section

For full biographical listings, see the Martindale-Hubbell Law Directory

HOWARD & HOWARD ATTORNEYS, P.C. (AV)

The Phoenix Building, Suite 500, 222 Washington Square, North, 48933-1817
Telephone: 517-485-1483
Telecopier: 517-485-1568
Kalamazoo, Michigan Office: The Kalamazoo Building, Suite 400, 107 West Michigan Avenue.
Telephone: 616-382-1483.
Telecopier: 616-382-1568.
Bloomfield Hills, Michigan Office: The Pinehurst Office Center, Suite 101, 1400 North Woodward Avenue.
Telephone: 810-645-1483.
Telecopier: 810-645-1568.
Peoria, Illinois Office: Howard & Howard, P.C., The Creve Coeur Building, Suite 200, 321 Liberty Street.
Telephone: 309-672-1483.
Telecopier: 309-672-1568.

Todd D. Chamberlain

Representative Clients: First of America Bank Corporation; W.R. Grace & Co.; Chrysler Corp.; Indian Head Industries; Cooper & Lybrand; United Technologies.
Local Counsel for: General Motors Corp.; American Cyanamid Co.

For Complete List of Firm Personnel, See General Section

For full biographical listings, see the Martindale-Hubbell Law Directory

MILLER, CANFIELD, PADDOCK AND STONE, P.L.C. (AV)

A Professional Limited Liability Company
Founded in 1852 by Sidney Davy Miller
Suite 900, One Michigan Avenue, 48933-1609
Telephone: 517-487-2070
Fax: 517-374-6304
Detroit, Michigan Office: 150 West Jefferson, Suite 2500, 48226-4415.
Telephone: 313-963-6420.
Fax: 313-496-7500.
Cable Address: "Stem Detroit."

(See Next Column)

Ann Arbor, Michigan Office: 101 North Main Street, 7th Floor, 48104-1400.
Telephone: 313-663-2445.
Fax: 313-747-7147.
Bloomfield Hills, Michigan Office: Suite 100, Pinehurst Office Center, 1400 North Woodward, 48303-2014.
Telephone: 313-645-5000.
Fax: 313-645-1917.
Grand Rapids, Michigan Office: 1200 Campau Square Plaza, 99 Monroe, N.W., 49503-2639.
Telephone: 616-454-8656.
Fax: 616-776-6322.
Howell, Michigan Office: 121 South Barnard Street, Suite 4, 48843-2305.
Telephone: 517-546-7600.
Telecopier: 517-546-6974.
Kalamazoo, Michigan Office: 444 West Michigan Avenue, 49007-3752.
Telephone: 616-381-7030.
Fax: 616-382-0244.
Monroe, Michigan Office: The Executive Centre, 214 East Elm Avenue, 48161-2682.
Telephone: 313-243-2000.
Fax: 313-243-0901.
Washington, D.C. Office: 1225 Nineteenth Street, N.W., Suite 400. 20036.
Telephone: 202-429-5575; 785-0600.
Fax: 202-331-1118; 785-1234.
Pensacola, Florida Office: 25 West Cedar, 32501.
Telephone: 904-469-1088.
Fax: 904-432-0677.
St. Petersburg Office: 100 Second Avenue S., Suite 7045, 33701.
Telephone: 813-982-6000.
Fax: 813-892-6002.
Gdansk, Poland Office: Suite 322, Dom Technika Building, UI. Rajska 6, 80-850.
Telephone: 011-485-831-2808.
Fax: 011-485-831-4719.
Warsaw, Poland Office: UI. Marszalkowska 82, Suite 561, 00-517.
Telephone: 011-482-623-6457 and 6458.
Fax: 011-482-623-6459.

MEMBER OF FIRM
William J. Danhof (Resident)

Representative Firm Clients: Chrysler Corp.; Comerica, Inc.; City of Detroit, Mich.; Detroit Tigers, Inc.; First of Michigan; Fretter, Inc.; Ford Motor Co.; Ford Motor Credit Co.; Great Lakes Bancorp; Henry Ford Hospital.

For Complete List of Firm Personnel, See General Section

For full biographical listings, see the Martindale-Hubbell Law Directory

*MIDLAND,** Midland Co.

CURRIE & KENDALL, P.C. (AV)

6024 Eastman Avenue, P.O. Box 1846, 48641-1846
Telephone: 517-839-0300
Fax: 517-832-0077

Gilbert A. Currie (1882-1960)
James A. Kendall
William C. Collins
Thomas L. Ludington
Ramon F. Rolf, Jr.
Daniel J. Cline
Peter A. Poznak
Julia A. Close
Peter J. Kendall
Jeffrey N. Dyer

OF COUNSEL

Gilbert A. Currie
I. Frank Harlow
William D. Schuette

LEGAL SUPPORT PERSONNEL
Barbara J. Byron

Counsel for: Chemical Financial Corp.; Chemical Bank & Trust Co.; Saginaw Valley State University; Northwood University; The Midland Foundation; Elsa U. Pardee Foundation; Rollin M. Gerstacker Foundation; Charles J. Strosacker Foundation.

For full biographical listings, see the Martindale-Hubbell Law Directory

*MUSKEGON,** Muskegon Co.

PARMENTER O'TOOLE (AV)

175 West Apple Street, P.O. Box 786, 49443-0786
Telephone: 616-722-1621
Telecopier: 616-728-2206; 722-7866

MEMBERS OF FIRM

Eric J. Fauri
John C. Schrier
Christopher L. Kelly

General Counsel for: FMB Lumberman's Bank; AmeriBank Federal Savings Bank; City of Muskegon; Quality Tool & Stamping Co., Inc.; Radiology Muskegon, P.C.
Local Counsel for: General Electric Capital Corp.; Paine-Webber; Teledyne Industries, Inc. (Continental Motors Division); Westinghouse Electric Corporation (Knoll Group).

For Complete List of Firm Personnel, See General Section

For full biographical listings, see the Martindale-Hubbell Law Directory

*SAGINAW,** Saginaw Co.

BRAUN KENDRICK FINKBEINER (AV)

8th Floor Second National Bank Building, 48607
Telephone: 517-753-3461
Telecopier: 517-753-3951
Bay City, Michigan Office: 201 Phoenix Building, P.O. Box 2039.
Telephone: 517-895-8505.
Telecopier: 517-895-8437.

MEMBERS OF FIRM

Hugo E. Braun, Jr.
Morton E. Weldy
Michael J. Sauer

Representative Clients: The Dow Chemical Co.; General Motors Corp.; Lobdell Emery Manufacturing Co.; Merrill, Lynch, Inc.; Saginaw General Hospital; Saginaw News; The Wickes Foundation.

For Complete List of Firm Personnel, See General Section

For full biographical listings, see the Martindale-Hubbell Law Directory

SOUTHFIELD, Oakland Co.

SOMMERS, SCHWARTZ, SILVER & SCHWARTZ, P.C. (AV)

2000 Town Center, Suite 900, 48075
Telephone: 810-355-0300
Telecopier: 810-746-4001
Plymouth, Michigan Office: 747 South Main Street.
Telephone: 313-455-4250.

Steven J. Schwartz
Paul Groffsky
Gary A. Taback
Victor A. Coen
David M. Black
Jon J. Birnkrant
Joseph H. Bourgon
Stephen S. Birnkrant

OF COUNSEL

Norman Samuel Sommers

General Counsel for: City of Taylor; Foodland Distributors; C.A. Muer Corporation; Vlasic & Company; Woodland Physicians; Midwest Health Centers, P.C.
Representative Clients: Michigan National Bank; Madison National Bank; Bank Hapoalim, B.M.; Beal Bank, S.A.

For Complete List of Firm Personnel, See General Section

For full biographical listings, see the Martindale-Hubbell Law Directory

*TRAVERSE CITY,** Grand Traverse Co.

MURCHIE, CALCUTT & BOYNTON (AV)

109 East Front Street, Suite 300, 49684
Telephone: 616-947-7190
Fax: 616-947-4341

Robert B. Murchie (1894-1975)
Harry Calcutt
Jack E. Boynton
William B. Calcutt
Mark A. Burnheimer
Dawn M. Rogers

ASSOCIATES

George W. Hyde, III
Ralph J. Dilley (Not admitted in MI)

General Counsel for: Old Kent Bank-Grand Traverse; Northwestern Savings Bank & Trust; Central-State Bancorp; Traverse City Record Eagle; WPNB-7 & WTOM-4; Emergency Consultants, Inc.; National Guardian Risk Retention Group, Inc.; Farmers Mutual Insurance Co.; Environmental Solutions, Inc.
Local Counsel For: Consumers Power Co.

For full biographical listings, see the Martindale-Hubbell Law Directory

MINNESOTA

*DULUTH,** St. Louis Co.

CRASSWELLER, MAGIE, ANDRESEN, HAAG & PACIOTTI, P.A. (AV)

1000 Alworth Building, P.O. Box 745, 55801
Telephone: 218-722-1411
Telecopier: 218-720-6817

Donald B. Crassweller
Robert H. Magie, III
Charles H. Andresen
Michael W. Haag
James P. Paciotti
Sandra E. Butterworth
Brian R. McCarthy
Bryan N. Anderson
Robert C. Barnes
Kurt D. Larson
Gerald T. Anderson

(See Next Column)

COUNSEL

John M. Donovan
Robert K. McCarthy (1915-1986)

Representative Clients: Inland Steel Co.; Allstate Insurance Co.; Liberty Mutual Insurance Co; State Farm Insurance Cos.; Great Lakes Gas Transmission Co.; Lakehead Pipe Line Co.; Trans-Canada Gas Pipeline, Ltd.

For full biographical listings, see the Martindale-Hubbell Law Directory

FRYBERGER, BUCHANAN, SMITH & FREDERICK, P.A. (AV)

700 Lonsdale Building, 302 West Superior Street, 55802
Telephone: 218-722-0861
Fax: 218-722-9568
St. Paul Office: Capitol Center, 386 N. Wabasha.
Telephone: 612-221-1044.

Bruce Buchanan
Nick Smith
Harold A. Frederick
Dexter A. Larsen
James H. Stewart
Robert E. Toftey
Michael K. Donovan
Neal J. Hessen
Joseph J. Mihalek
Shawn M. Dunlevy
Anne Lewis
David R. Oberstar
Abbot G. Apter
Michael Cowles
Martha M. Markusen

Daniel D. Maddy
Stephanie A. Ball
Paul B. Kilgore
Mary Frances Skala
Rolf A. Lindberg (Resident, St. Paul Office)
Kevin T. Walli (Resident, St. Paul Office)
Kevin J. Dunlevy (Resident, St. Paul Office)
Teresa M. O'Toole
Dean R. Borgh
James F. Voegeli (Resident, St. Paul Office)
James A. Lund
Mark D. Britton (Resident, St. Paul Office)
Judith A. Zollar

OF COUNSEL

Herschel B. Fryberger, Jr.

Representative Clients: North Shore Bank of Commerce; General Motors Acceptance Corp.; Western Lake Superior Sanitary District; City of Duluth; First Bank Minnesota (N.A.); Norwest Bank Minnesota North N.A.; Airport State Bank; Park State Bank; M & I First National Bank of Superior; St. Lukes Hospital Duluth.

For full biographical listings, see the Martindale-Hubbell Law Directory

*MANKATO,** Blue Earth Co.

MCLEAN PETERSON LAW FIRM, CHARTERED (AV)

Twin City Federal Building, 325 South Broad Street, P.O. Box 1360, 56002
Telephone: 507-387-3155
Fax: 507-387-3166
St. Clair, Minnesota Office: State Bank of St. Clair.
Telephone: 507-245-3785.
Lake Crystal, Minnesota Office: Highway 60.
Telephone: 507-726-2200.
Vernon Center, Minnesota Office:
Telephone: 507-549-3416.

Edward D. McLean
Charles T. Peterson
Thomas R. Sullivan
Howard F. Haugh
Bruce G. Miller (1943-1992)
John M. Riedy
Bradley C. Walker
John C. Peterson
Jeffrey D. Gednalske
Steven H. Fink

Representative Clients: CNA Insurance Co.; Katolight Corp.; The Family Bank F.S.B.; Robert W. Carlstrom Construction Co.; Condux International, Inc.; Independent School District #77 (Mankato); Immanuel-St. Joseph's Hospital of Mankato, Inc.; Jones Metal Products, Inc.; North Star Concrete Co.; Western National Insurance Company.

For Complete List of Firm Personnel, See General Section

For full biographical listings, see the Martindale-Hubbell Law Directory

MISSISSIPPI

*JACKSON,** Hinds Co.

ALLRED & DONALDSON (AV)

101 West Capitol Street, Suite 300, P.O. Box 3828, 39207-3828
Telephone: 601-948-2086
Telefax: 601-948-2175

MEMBERS OF FIRM

Michael S. Allred
John I. Donaldson

ASSOCIATES

Stephen M. Maloney
Kathleen H. Eiler

For full biographical listings, see the Martindale-Hubbell Law Directory

Jackson—Continued

WATKINS & EAGER (AV)

Suite 300 The Emporium Building, P.O. Box 650, 39205
Telephone: 601-948-6470
Facsimile: (601) 354-3623

MEMBERS OF FIRM

William F. Goodman, Jr.
Frank J. Hammond, III
George R. Fair
Paul J. Stephens
Jamie G. Houston, III
M. Binford Williams, Jr.

Representative Clients: Trustmark National Bank; Merchants & Marine Bank; Whitney National Bank; Hibernia National Bank.

For Complete List of Firm Personnel, See General Section

For full biographical listings, see the Martindale-Hubbell Law Directory

*OXFORD,** Lafayette Co.

FREELAND & FREELAND (AV)

1013 Jackson Avenue, P.O. Box 269, 38655
Telephone: 601-234-3414
Telecopier: 601-234-0604

MEMBERS OF FIRM

T. H. Freeland, III
T. H. Freeland, IV
J. Hale Freeland

ASSOCIATE

Paul W. Crutcher

Representative Clients: The Ohio Casualty Group; Crum & Forester.

For full biographical listings, see the Martindale-Hubbell Law Directory

*TUPELO,** Lee Co.

HOLLAND, RAY & UPCHURCH, P.A. (AV)

322 Jefferson Street, P.O. Drawer 409, 38802
Telephone: 601-842-1721
Facsimile: 601-844-6413

Sam E. Lumpkin (1908-1964)
Robert K. Upchurch
Ralph L. Holland
W. Reed Hillen, III
James Hugh Ray
Thomas A. Wicker

Michael D. Tapscott

Representative Clients: The Travelers; Continental Casualty Co.; South Central Bell Telephone Co.; The Greyhound Corp.; Mississippi Valley Gas Co.; Bryan-Rogers, Inc.; The Housing Authority of the City of Tupelo; Action Industries, Inc.; American Cable Systems, Inc.; American Funeral Assurance Co.

For full biographical listings, see the Martindale-Hubbell Law Directory

MONTANA

*BILLINGS,** Yellowstone Co.

CROWLEY, HAUGHEY, HANSON, TOOLE & DIETRICH (AV)

500 Transwestern II, 490 North 31st Street, P.O. Box 2529, 59103
Telephone: 406-252-3441
Fax: 406-259-4159
Helena, Montana Office: IBM Building, 100 North Park Avenue, Suite 300, 59601.
Telephone: 406-449-4165.
Fax: 406-449-5149.

MEMBERS OF FIRM

John M. Dietrich
William D. Lamdin, III
Gareld F. Krieg
Michael S. Dockery
Arthur F. Lamey, Jr.
Mary Scrim
Terry B. Cosgrove
Renee L. Coppock

Representative Clients: First Interstate Bancsystem of Montana, Inc.; First Interstate Bank of Commerce; Central Montana Bancorporation; Traders State Bank of Poplar; Security Richland Bancorporation; State Bank of Terry; The Bank of Baker; Richland National Bank & Trust.

For Complete List of Firm Personnel, See General Section

For full biographical listings, see the Martindale-Hubbell Law Directory

*BOZEMAN,** Gallatin Co.

KIRWAN & BARRETT, P.C. (AV)

215 West Mendenhall, P.O. Box 1348, 59771-1348
Telephone: 406-586-1553
Fax: 406-586-8971

Janice K. Whetstone
Stephen M. Barrett

(See Next Column)

Tom W. Stonecipher

Representative Clients: American Bank; First Citizens Bank of Bozeman; Big Sky Western Bank; Security Bank of Three Forks.

For full biographical listings, see the Martindale-Hubbell Law Directory

NEBRASKA

NORFOLK, Madison Co.

DOMINA & COPPLE, P.C. (AV)

2425 Taylor Avenue, P.O. Box 78, 68702-0078
Telephone: 402-371-4300
Fax: 402-371-0790
Omaha, Nebraska Office: 1065 North 115th Street, Suite 150.
Telephone: 402-493-4100.
FAX: 402-493-9782.

David A. Domina
David E. Copple

Kathleen K. Rockey
David H. Ptak
James G. Kube
Steven D. Sunde

For full biographical listings, see the Martindale-Hubbell Law Directory

*OMAHA,** Douglas Co.

FRASER, STRYKER, VAUGHN, MEUSEY, OLSON, BOYER & BLOCH, P.C. (AV)

500 Energy Plaza, 409 South 17th Street, 68102
Telephone: 402-341-6000
Telecopier: 402-341-8290

Thomas F. Flaherty
Robert W. Rieke
Robert M. Yates

For Complete List of Firm Personnel, See General Section

For full biographical listings, see the Martindale-Hubbell Law Directory

NEVADA

*LAS VEGAS,** Clark Co.

ALVERSON, TAYLOR, MORTENSEN & NELSON (AV)

3821 W. Charleston Boulevard, 89102
Telephone: 702-384-7000
FAX: 702-385-7000

MEMBERS OF FIRM

J. Bruce Alverson
Erven T. Nelson
Eric K. Taylor
LeAnn Sanders
David J. Mortensen
David R. Clayson

ASSOCIATES

Milton J. Eichacker
Kenneth M. Marias
Douglas D. Gerrard
Jeffrey H. Ballin
Marie Ellerton
Jeffrey W. Daly
James H. Randall
Kenneth R. Ivory
Peter Dubowsky
Edward D. Boyack
Hayley B. Chambers
Sandra Smagac
Michael D. Stevenson
Jill M. Chase
Cookie Lea Olshein
Francis F. Lin

Representative Clients: Citibank; First Interstate Bank; The CIT Group; Norwest Bank; Federal Deposit Insurance Corporation (FDIC); Resolution Trust Corporation (RTC); Countrywide Funding Corporation; Overseas Chinese Banking Corporation; Norwest Financial.

For full biographical listings, see the Martindale-Hubbell Law Directory

JOLLEY, URGA, WIRTH & WOODBURY (AV)

Suite 800 Bank of America Plaza, 300 South Fourth Street, 89101
Telephone: 702-385-5161
Telecopier: 702-382-6814
Boulder City, Nevada Office: Suite 105, 1000 Nevada Highway.
Telephone: 702-293-3674.

MEMBERS OF FIRM

R. Gardner Jolley
Jay Earl Smith

ASSOCIATE

Allen D. Emmel

Representative Clients: First Interstate Bank of Nevada; Nevada State Bank; Citicorp National Services, Inc.; Continental National Bank; First Nationwide Bank; PriMerit Bank.

(See Next Column)

JOLLEY, URGA, WIRTH & WOODBURY—*Continued*

For Complete List of Firm Personnel, See General Section

For full biographical listings, see the Martindale-Hubbell Law Directory

MILES & TIERNEY (AV)

3170 West Sahara Avenue Suite D-11, 89102
Telephone: 702-252-7120
FAX: 702-252-0916

MEMBERS OF FIRM

Charles H. Miles, Jr. | Keith J. Tierney

For full biographical listings, see the Martindale-Hubbell Law Directory

NEW HAMPSHIRE

*LACONIA,** Belknap Co.

NORMANDIN, CHENEY & O'NEIL (AV)

Normandin Square, 213 Union Avenue, P.O. Box 575, 03247-0575
Telephone: 603-524-4380

MEMBERS OF FIRM

Paul L. Normandin
John D. O'Shea, Jr.
Robert A. Dietz
James F. LaFrance

ASSOCIATE

Duncan J. Farmer

Counsel for: Laconia Savings Bank; Lakes Region Mental Health Center; Laconia Airport Authority; Community TV Corp.; Central New Hampshire Realty, Inc.; All Metals Industries, Inc.; Lakes Region Anesthesiology, P.A.; Cormier Corp.; Scotia Technology; Vemaline Products.

For Complete List of Firm Personnel, See General Section

For full biographical listings, see the Martindale-Hubbell Law Directory

NEW JERSEY

BERNARDSVILLE, Somerset Co.

SHAIN, SCHAFFER & RAFANELLO, A PROFESSIONAL CORPORATION (AV)

150 Morristown Road, 07924
Telephone: 908-953-9300
Fax: 908-953-2969

Joel L. Shain
Marguerite M. Schaffer
Richard A. Rafanello
Jeffrey A. Donner
Joyce Wilkins Pollison
Todd R. Staretz

OF COUNSEL

Elliott L. Katz

For full biographical listings, see the Martindale-Hubbell Law Directory

CHERRY HILL, Camden Co.

JUBANYIK, VARBALOW, TEDESCO, SHAW & SHAFFER (AV)

Commerce Atrium Building, 1701 Route 70 East, P.O. Box 2570, 08034
Telephone: 609-751-8500
Telefax: 609-751-9030
Philadelphia, Pennsylvania Office: The Fidelity Bank Building, 123 Broad Street, Thirteenth Floor.
Telephone: 215-732-8546.

Raymond J. Jubanyik (1910-1985)

MEMBERS OF FIRM

Richard J. Jubanyik
Michael D. Varbalow
Frank V. Tedesco
Barry N. Shaw
Hal Jonathan Shaffer
Arnold L. Bartfeld (Not admitted in NJ; Resident, Philadelphia, Pennsylvania Office)
Vincent D'Elia

Suzette D. Bonfiglio

ASSOCIATES

Francis P. Maneri
Gregg M. Wolff
Catherine M. Ward
Aimee L. Manocchio Nason
Francine G. Raichlen (Not admitted in NJ; Resident, Philadelphia, Pennsylvania Office)
William H. Karp
Sharon Goldin-Didinsky
Dean Stuart Reiche (Not admitted in NJ)

Representative Clients: Fidelity Bank; Continental Bank.

For full biographical listings, see the Martindale-Hubbell Law Directory

ELMWOOD PARK, Bergen Co.

ANDORA, PALMISANO & GEANEY, A PROFESSIONAL CORPORATION (AV)

303 Molnar Drive, P.O. Box 431, 07407-0431
Telephone: 201-791-0100
Fax: 201-791-8922

Anthony D. Andora
John P. Palmisano
John F. Geaney, Jr.
Vincent A. Siano
Joseph M. Andresini
Patrick J. Spina
Melissa A. Muilenburg
Joseph A. Venti

Representative Client: Interchange State Bank, Saddle Brook, New Jersey.

For full biographical listings, see the Martindale-Hubbell Law Directory

*HACKENSACK,** Bergen Co.

CONTANT, SCHERBY & ATKINS (AV)

33 Hudson Street, 07601
Telephone: 201-342-1070
Fax: 201-342-5213

MEMBERS OF THE FIRM

John M. Contant (1907-1988)
Richard J. Contant
Michael L. Scherby
Bruce L. Atkins
Daniel P. Greenstein
Matthew S. Rogers
Andrew T. Fede
Brian T. Keane

ASSOCIATES

Julie Grapin
Geraldine E. Beers
William J. Bailey
S. Y. Kim

OF COUNSEL

Michael S. Kopelman
Fenster & Weiss, , New City, New York

For full biographical listings, see the Martindale-Hubbell Law Directory

MAPLEWOOD, Essex Co.

FOYEN & PARTNERS (AV Ⓣ)

108 Baker Street, 07040
Telephone: 201-762-5800
Telefax: 212-762-5801
New York, N.Y. Office: 800 Third Avenue, 23rd Floor, NTC.
Telephone: 212-265-2555.
Telefax: 212-838-0374.
Affiliated Offices: Oslo, Norway Office: Advokatfirmaet Foyen & Co. ANS, Oscargate 52, N-0258 Olso 2.
Telephone: 02-44 46 40.
Telefax: 02-44 89 27.
Stockholm, Sweden Office: Advokatfirman Foyen & Partners, Nybrogatan 15, S-10246 Stockholm.
Telephone: 8-663-02-90.
Telefax: 8-662-15-90.

MEMBERS OF FIRM

Steven B. Peri | Michael T. Stewart

OF COUNSEL

Stein A. Føyen (Resident, Oslo, Norway Office)
Michael P. DiRaimondo (Resident, New York Office)

For full biographical listings, see the Martindale-Hubbell Law Directory

MONTVALE, Bergen Co.

BEATTIE PADOVANO (AV)

50 Chestnut Ridge Road, P.O. Box 244, 07645-0244
Telephone: 201-573-1810
Fax: (DEX) 201-573-9736

MEMBERS OF FIRM

James R. Beattie
Ralph J. Padovano
Roger W. Breslin, Jr.
Thomas W. Dunn
Martin W. Kafafian
Adolph A. Romei

Brian R. Martinotti

ASSOCIATES

Emery C. Duell
Brenda J. McAdoo
Kathleen Smyth Cook
Francis B. Sheehan
Susan Calabrese
Antimo A. Del Vecchio
Dean J. Obeidallah
Jeffrey L. Love
Steven A. Weisfeld
S. Joseph Oey
Edward S. Kiel
Christopher Heyer
JoAnne C. Gerber
Robert A. Blass

OF COUNSEL

John J. Lamb

Reference: United Jersey Bank.

For full biographical listings, see the Martindale-Hubbell Law Directory

MOORESTOWN, Burlington Co.

BRANDT, HAUGHEY, PENBERTHY, LEWIS, HYLAND & CLAYPOOLE, A PROFESSIONAL CORPORATION (AV)

240 West State Highway 38, P.O. Box 1002, 08057-0949
Telephone: 609-235-1111
Telecopier: 609-722-0357

S. David Brandt
Gerald E. Haughey
Edward A. Penberthy
Robert S. Lewis
William F. Hyland, Jr.
Susan L. Claypoole
Patrick F. McAndrew
Thomas J. DiPilla, Jr.
Steven A. Aboloff
Eileen K. Fahey

Representative Clients: City of Camden (Tax Matters); Davis Enterprises; Deptford Mall, Inc.; McDonald's Corp.; Mobil Oil Corp.; Chemical Bank; Continental Title Insurance Co.; Texaco; The Radner/Canuso Partnership.

For full biographical listings, see the Martindale-Hubbell Law Directory

*MORRISTOWN,** Morris Co.

SHANLEY & FISHER, A PROFESSIONAL CORPORATION (AV)

131 Madison Avenue, 07962-1979
Telephone: 201-285-1000
Telecopier: 1-201-285-1098
Telex: 475-4255 (I.T.T.)
Cable Address: "Shanley"
New York, N.Y. Office: 89th Floor, One World Trade Center.
Telephone: 212-321-1812.
Telecopier: 1-212-466-0569.

John Kandravy
Gerald W. Hull, Jr.
James H. Freis
Lydia C. Stefanowicz
Andrew V. Ballantine

Emily A. Schultz
Michael E. Helmer
Michael J. Nita
Ieva I. Rogers

For Complete List of Firm Personnel, See General Section

For full biographical listings, see the Martindale-Hubbell Law Directory

*NEWARK,** Essex Co.

CARPENTER, BENNETT & MORRISSEY (AV)

(Formerly Carpenter, Gilmour & Dwyer)
Three Gateway Center, 17th Floor, 100 Mulberry Street, 07102-4079
Telephone: 201-622-7711
New York City: 212-943-6530
Telex: 139405
Telecopier: 201-622-5314
EasyLink: 62827845
ABA/net: CARPENTERB

MEMBERS OF FIRM

Francis X. O'Brien
Edward F. Day, Jr.
John D. Goldsmith

ASSOCIATE

Hans G. Polak

Representative Clients: General Motors Corp.; E. I. du Pont de Nemours and Company; Texaco Inc.; AT&T; Litton Industries; ITT Corp.; International Flavors & Fragrances Inc.; New Jersey Hospital Association; Prudential Insurance Company of America; United Jersey Bank.

For Complete List of Firm Personnel, See General Section

For full biographical listings, see the Martindale-Hubbell Law Directory

FOX AND FOX (AV)

570 Broad Street, 07102
Telephone: 201-622-3624
Telecopier: 201-622-6220

MEMBERS OF FIRM

David I. Fox
Arthur D. Grossman
Paul I. Rosenberg
Kenneth H. Fast
Martin Kesselhaut
Dennis J. Alessi
Gabriel H. Halpern
Steven A. Holt
Nancy C. McDonald

OF COUNSEL

Jacob Fox (1898-1992)
Martin S. Fox
Robert J. Rohrberger
Robert S. Catapano-Friedman

ASSOCIATES

Robert P. Donovan
Stacey B. Rosenberg
Susan R. Fox
Virginia S. Ryan
Ronnie Ann Powell
Katherine J. Welsh
Craig S. Gumpel
Brett Alison Rosenberg
Alfred V. Acquaviva
Anthony F. Vitiello

For full biographical listings, see the Martindale-Hubbell Law Directory

GREENBERG DAUBER AND EPSTEIN, A PROFESSIONAL CORPORATION (AV)

Suite 600, One Gateway Center, 07102-5311
Telephone: 201-643-3700
Telecopier: 201-643-1218

Melvin Greenberg
Edward J. Dauber
Stanley A. Epstein
H. Glenn Tucker
Paul J. Dillon
Linda G. Harvey
Brenda J. Rediess-Hoosein
Adam W. Jacobs
Jeffrey S. Berkowitz
Kathryn Van Deusen Hatfield

For full biographical listings, see the Martindale-Hubbell Law Directory

MCCARTER & ENGLISH (AV)

Four Gateway Center, 100 Mulberry Street, P.O. Box 652, 07101-0652
Telephone: 201-622-4444
Telecopier: 201-624-7070
Cable Address: "McCarter" Newark
Cherry Hill, New Jersey Office: 1810 Chapel Avenue West.
Telephone: 609-662-8444.
Telecopier: 609-662-6203.
New York, New York Office: Suite 1519, One World Trade Center.
Telephone: 212-466-9018.
Telecopier: 212-432-6568.
Boca Raton, Florida Office: 2255 Glades Road, Suite 319-A.
Telephone: 407-994-6262.
Telecopier: 407-241-0798.
Wilmington, Delaware Office: Mellon Bank Center, 919 Market Street.
Telephone: 302-654-8010.
Telecopier: 302-654-0795.

MEMBERS OF FIRM

Michael M. Horn
Bart J. Colli
Todd M. Poland
Peter S. Twombly
David F. Broderick

For Complete List of Firm Personnel, See General Section

For full biographical listings, see the Martindale-Hubbell Law Directory

MCMANIMON & SCOTLAND (AV)

One Gateway Center, 18th Floor, 07102-5311
Telephone: 201-622-1800
Fax: 201-622-7333; 201-622-3744
Atlantic City, New Jersey Office: 26 South Pennsylvania Avenue.
Telephone: 609-347-0040.
Fax: 609-347-0866.
Trenton, New Jersey Office: 172 West State Street.
Telephone: 609-278-1800.
Fax: 609-278-9222.
Washington, D.C. Office: 1275 Pennsylvania Avenue, N.W.
Telephone: 202-638-3100.
Fax: 202-638-4222.

MEMBERS OF FIRM

Joseph P. Baumann, Jr.
Carla J. Brundage
John V. Cavaliere
Edward F. Clark
Christopher H. Falcon
Felicia L. Garland
James R. Gregory
John B. Hall
Thomas A. Hart, Jr. (Resident, Washington, D.C. Office)
Leah C. Healey
Ronald J. Ianoale
Andrea L. Kahn
Jeffrey G. Kramer
Michael A. Lampert
Joseph J. Maraziti, Jr.
Edward J. McManimon, III
Steven P. Natko
Martin C. Rothfelder
Steven Schaars (Resident, Washington, D.C. Office)
Glenn F. Scotland
Michael A. Walker

ASSOCIATES

Carl E. Ailara, Jr.
Diane Alexander-McCabe
Leslie G. London
Cheryl A. Maier
Daniel E. McManus
Sheryl L. Newman
Steven J. Reed
Erik F. Remmler
David J. Ruitenberg
Bradford M. Stern

OF COUNSEL

John R. Armstrong
Carl H. Fogler (Not admitted in NJ)

LEGAL SUPPORT PERSONNEL

Helen Lysaght

PARALEGALS

Jane Folmer
Zulmira Donahue

References: First Fidelity Bank, N.A., New Jersey; Midlantic National Bank.

For full biographical listings, see the Martindale-Hubbell Law Directory

MEYNER AND LANDIS (AV)

One Gateway Center, Suite 2500, 07102-5311
Telephone: 201-624-2800
Fax: 201-624-0356

(See Next Column)

MEYNER AND LANDIS—*Continued*

MEMBERS OF FIRM

Edwin C. Landis, Jr.
Jeffrey L. Reiner
John N. Malyska
William J. Fiore
Anthony F. Siliato
Francis R. Perkins
Geralyn A. Boccher
Howard O. Thompson
Robert B. Meyner (1908-1990)

ASSOCIATES

Kathryn Schatz Koles
Linda Townley Snyder
William H. Schmidt, Jr.
Scott T. McCleary
Maureen K Higgins
Richard A. Haws
Michael J. Palumbo
Theodore E. Lorenz

For full biographical listings, see the Martindale-Hubbell Law Directory

ROBINSON, ST. JOHN & WAYNE (AV)

Two Penn Plaza East, 07105-2249
Telephone: 201-491-3300
Fax: 201-491-3333
Rochester, New York Office: Robinson, St. John & Curtin. First Federal Plaza.
Telephone: 716-262-6780.
Fax: 716-262-6755.
New York, New York Office: 245 Park Avenue.
Telephone: 212-953-0700.
Fax: 212-880-6555.

MEMBERS OF FIRM

Bernard S. Davis
Paul D. Drobbin
John J. Oberdorf
Bryan G. Petkanics (Resident at New York, New York Office)
Robert A. Wayne (Resident, New York, New York Office)
E. Kenneth Williams, Jr.

For Complete List of Firm Personnel, See General Section

For full biographical listings, see the Martindale-Hubbell Law Directory

SAIBER SCHLESINGER SATZ & GOLDSTEIN (AV)

One Gateway Center, 13th Floor, 07102-5311
Telephone: 201-622-3333
Telecopier: 201-622-3349

MEMBERS OF FIRM

David M. Satz, Jr.
Bruce I. Goldstein
William F. Maderer
David J. D'Aloia
James H. Aibel
Sean R. Kelly
John L. Conover
Lawrence B. Mink
Michael L. Allen
Michael L. Messer
Jeffrey W. Lorell
Jeffrey M. Schwartz
David J. Satz
Joan M. Schwab
Jennine DiSomma
James H. Forte
Vincent F. Papalia

OF COUNSEL

Samuel S. Saiber
Norman E. Schlesinger

COUNSEL

Andrew Alcorn
Robin B. Horn
Randi Schillinger

ASSOCIATES

Audrey M. Weinstein
Robert B. Nussbaum
Michael J. Geraghty
Jonathan S. Davis
Paul S. DeGiulio
Diana L. Sussman
Deanna M. Beacham
Robert W. Geiger
William S. Gyves
Barry P. Kramer
Susan Rozman
Michelle Viola

LEGAL SUPPORT PERSONNEL
DIRECTOR OF FINANCE AND ADMINISTRATION

Ronald Henry

For full biographical listings, see the Martindale-Hubbell Law Directory

SILLS CUMMIS ZUCKERMAN RADIN TISCHMAN EPSTEIN & GROSS, A PROFESSIONAL CORPORATION (AV)

One Riverfront Plaza, 07102-5400
Telephone: 201-643-7000
Fax: 201-643-6500
Telex: 820630 Sillsbeck Nwk
Atlantic City, New Jersey Office: 17 Gordon's Alley.
Telephone: 609-344-2800.
New York, N.Y. Office: 250 Park Avenue.
Telephone: 212-643-7000.

Steven S. Radin
Michael B. Tischman
Steven E. Gross
Jeffrey J. Greenbaum
Morris Yamner
Gerald Span
Noah Bronkesh (Resident at Atlantic City, N.J. Office)
Steven M. Goldman
Ira A. Rosenberg
Robert Crane
Jack M. Zackin
Jerry Genberg
Margaret F. Black
Brian S. Coven
Trent S. Dickey

(See Next Column)

Joseph L. Buckley
David J. Rabinowitz
Ronald C. Rak
Victor H. Boyajian

Noel D. Humphreys
Steven B. Jackman (Not admitted in NJ)
Stuart Rosen
Stephen McNally
Mark E. Duckstein
Frederic M. Tudor
Jodi S. Brodsky
Robert W. Burke
Scott T. Gruber
Steven S. Katz
Ted Zangari
Lester Chanin
Patricia Brown Fugee
Paul F. Doda
Adam Kaiser
Garry Rogers

OF COUNSEL

Victor Futter (Resident at New York, N.Y. Office)

Representative Clients: Citibank, N.A.; Credit Lyonnais; Midlantic National Bank; First Fidelity Bancorporation; United Jersey Bank; Emigrant Savings Bank; National Community Bank (Bank of New York); Summit Bancorporation; Margaretten Financial Corp.; NatWest.

For Complete List of Firm Personnel, See General Section

For full biographical listings, see the Martindale-Hubbell Law Directory

TOMPKINS, MCGUIRE & WACHENFELD (AV)

A Partnership including a Professional Corporation
Four Gateway Center, 100 Mulberry Street, 07102-4070
Telephone: 201-622-3000
Telecopier: 201-623-7780

OF COUNSEL

Frances S. Margolis
William J. McGee

Representative Clients: Corbo Jewelers, Inc.; General Electric Co.; Hartford Insurance Group; Marriott Corp.; National Union Fire Insurance Co.; Summit Bank; Underwriters at Lloyd's, London.

For Complete List of Firm Personnel, See General Section

For full biographical listings, see the Martindale-Hubbell Law Directory

PARSIPPANY, Morris Co.

BARON, GALLAGHER, HERTZBERG & PERZLEY (AV)

Waterview Plaza, 2001 Route 46, 07054
Telephone: 201-335-7400
Telecopier: 201-335-8018

MEMBERS OF FIRM

Jack P. Baron
Jerome F. Gallagher, Jr.
Robert C. Hertzberg
Alan H. Perzley

ASSOCIATES

Kathleen Cavanaugh
Susan Burns
Philip A. Orsi
David A. Moss

For full biographical listings, see the Martindale-Hubbell Law Directory

PRINCETON, Mercer Co.

MCCARTHY AND SCHATZMAN, P.A. (AV)

228 Alexander Street, P.O. Box 2329, 08543-2329
Telephone: 609-924-1199
Fax: 609-683-5251

John F. McCarthy, Jr.
Richard Schatzman
G. Christopher Baker
John F. McCarthy, III
Michael A. Spero
Barbara Strapp Nelson
W. Scott Stoner

James A. Endicott
Angelo J. Onofri

Representative Clients: Trustees of Princeton University; The Linpro Co.; United Jersey Bank; Chemical Bank, New Jersey, N.A.; Carnegie Center Associates; Merrill Lynch Pierce Fenner & Smith, Inc.; Prudential Insurance Co.

For full biographical listings, see the Martindale-Hubbell Law Directory

RAMSEY, Bergen Co.

WEBER, MUTH & WEBER (AV)

One Cherry Lane, P.O. Box 912, 07446-0912
Telephone: 201-327-5000
Telecopier: 201-327-6848

MEMBERS OF FIRM

Walter W. Weber, Jr.
Clinton A. Poff

For Complete List of Firm Personnel, See General Section

For full biographical listings, see the Martindale-Hubbell Law Directory

ROSELAND, Essex Co.

BRACH, EICHLER, ROSENBERG, SILVER, BERNSTEIN, HAMMER & GLADSTONE, A PROFESSIONAL CORPORATION (AV)

101 Eisenhower Parkway, 07068
Telephone: 201-228-5700
Telecopier: 201-228-7852

Stuart M. Gladstone
Alan R. Hammer
Brian R. Lenker
Paul F. Rosenberg
Alexander J. Tafro

Vicki Sue Hull

Representative Clients: United Jersey Bank; Valley National Bank; Bank of New York; State Bank of South Orange; Palisade Savings Bank FSB; Oritani Savings & Loan Association; Intervest Bank; American Union Bank.

For Complete List of Firm Personnel, See General Section

For full biographical listings, see the Martindale-Hubbell Law Directory

HANNOCH WEISMAN, A PROFESSIONAL CORPORATION (AV)

4 Becker Farm Road, 07068-3788
Telephone: 201-535-5300
New York: 212-732-3262
Telecopier: 201-994-7198
Mailing Address: P.O. Box 1040, Newark, New Jersey, 07101-9819
Washington, D.C. Office: Suite 600, 1150 Seventeenth Street, N.W.
Telephone: 202-296-3432.

Albert G. Besser
Bernard J. D'Avella, Jr.
Robert C. Epstein
Sheldon M. Finkelstein
Joseph J. Fleischman
Stuart J. Glick
Howard A. Kantrowitz
Michael G. Keating
Ira B Marcus
Arlene Elgart Mirsky
Richard M. Slotkin
Ronald M. Sturtz

SPECIAL COUNSEL

Geralyn G. Humphrey
David P. Wadyka

Sheri Faith London
Jeffrey D. Mallinger

For Complete List of Firm Personnel, See General Section

For full biographical listings, see the Martindale-Hubbell Law Directory

LOWENSTEIN, SANDLER, KOHL, FISHER & BOYLAN, A PROFESSIONAL CORPORATION (AV)

65 Livingston Avenue, 07068
Telephone: 201-992-8700
Telefax: 201-992-5820
Somerville, New Jersey Office: 600 First Avenue. P.O. Box 1113.
Telephone: 201-526-3300.

Alan V. Lowenstein
Joseph LeVow Steinberg
John R. MacKay, 2nd
John D. Schupper
Allen B. Levithan
Peter H. Ehrenberg
Steven B. Fuerst (Resident at Somerville Office)
William S. Katchen
Alan Wovsaniker
William P. Munday
Daniel J. Barkin
George J. Mazin
Laura R. Kuntz
Linda Pickering
John D. Hogoboom

OF COUNSEL

Stuart S. Yusem (Resident at Somerville Office)

Phyllis F. Pasternak (Resident at Somerville Office)
Paul F. Koch, II
Jonathan T.K. Cohen
Susan Youdovin Leonard
Gary F. Eisenberg
Thomas M. FitzGibbon

For Complete List of Firm Personnel, See General Section

For full biographical listings, see the Martindale-Hubbell Law Directory

*SOMERVILLE,** Somerset Co.

OZZARD WHARTON, A PROFESSIONAL PARTNERSHIP (AV)

75-77 North Bridge Street, P.O. Box 938, 08876
Telephone: 908-526-0700
Telecopier: 908-526-2246

William E. Ozzard
William B. Savo
Edward M. Hogan
Michael V. Camerino

Arthur D. Fialk
Ellen M. Gillespie
Suzette Nanovic Berrios
Lori E. Salowe

OF COUNSEL

A. Arthur Davis, 3rd
Louis A. Imfeld
Mark F. Strauss

Representative Clients: New Jersey Savings Bank; First Community Bank; Somerset Valley Bank; Summit Bank.

(See Next Column)

For Complete List of Firm Personnel, See General Section

For full biographical listings, see the Martindale-Hubbell Law Directory

SUMMIT, Union Co.

BOURNE, NOLL & KENYON, A PROFESSIONAL CORPORATION (AV)

382 Springfield Avenue, 07901
Telephone: 908-277-2200
Telecopier: 908-277-6808

Donald Bourne (1903-1987)
Edward T. Kenyon
Cary R. Hardy
Charles R. Berman
Kenneth R. Johanson
Martin Rubashkin
David G. White
Roger Mehner
James R. Ottobre

OF COUNSEL

Robert B. Bourne
Clyde M. Noll (Retired)

Lauren K. Harris
Jaime A. O'Brien
Ellyn A. Draikiwicz
Dean T. Bennett
Craig M. Lessner
Michael O'B. Boldt
Christopher D. Boyman
Paul Ramirez
Timothy A. Kalas
Robert F. Moriarty
Mary E. Scrupski

For full biographical listings, see the Martindale-Hubbell Law Directory

*TRENTON,** Mercer Co.

BACKES & HILL (AV)

(Originally Backes & Backes)
(Formerly Backes, Waldron & Hill)
15 West Front Street, 08608-2098
Telephone: 609-396-8257
Telefax: 609-989-7323

Peter Backes (1858-1941)
Herbert W. Backes (1891-1970)
William Wright Backes (1904-1980)
Michael J. Nizolek (1950-1994)

OF COUNSEL

Robert Maddock Backes

PARTNERS

Harry R. Hill, Jr.
Robert C. Billmeier
Brenda Farr Engel

ASSOCIATES

Susan E. Bacso
Michele N. Siekerka
Henry A. Carpenter II
Lawrence A. Reisman

Representative Clients: New Jersey National Bank; Mercer Medical Center; Catholic Diocese of Trenton; Roller Bearing Company of America; New Jersey Manufacturers Insurance Co.; St. Francis Medical Center; The Trenton Savings Bank; Richie & Page Distributing Co., Inc.; Hill Refrigeration Corporation; General Sullivan Group, Inc.; A-1 Collections, Inc.

For full biographical listings, see the Martindale-Hubbell Law Directory

FOX, ROTHSCHILD, O'BRIEN & FRANKEL (AV)

Princeton Pike Corporate Center, 997 Lenox Drive, Building 3 (Lawrenceville), 08648-2311
Telephone: 609-896-3600
Telecopier: 609-896-1469
Philadelphia, Pennsylvania Office: 10th Floor, 2000 Market Street, 19103-3291.
Telephone: 215-299-2000.
Cable Address: "Frof".
Telecopier: 215-299-2150.
Exton, Pennsylvania Office: Eagleview Corporate Center, 717 Constitution Drive, Suite 111, P.O. Box 673, 19341-0673.
Telephone: 610-458-2100.
Telecopier: 610-458-2112.

Victor Walcoff
Richard M. Kohn
Phillip E. Griffin
Ezra D. Rosenberg
James F. X. Rudy

For Complete List of Firm Personnel, See General Section

For full biographical listings, see the Martindale-Hubbell Law Directory

WAYNE, Passaic Co.

WILLIAMS, CALIRI, MILLER & OTLEY, A PROFESSIONAL CORPORATION (AV)

1428 Route 23, P.O. Box 995, 07474-0995
Telephone: 201-694-0800
Telecopier: 201-694-0302

(See Next Column)

WILLIAMS, CALIRI, MILLER & OTLEY A PROFESSIONAL CORPORATION—*Continued*

Walter E. Williams (1904-1985)
David J. Caliri (Retired)
Richard S. Miller
Victor C. Otley, Jr.
Peter B. Eddy
William S. Robertson, III
David Golub
David C. Wigfield
Samuel G. Destito
John H. Hague
Stuart M. Geschwind
Steven A. Weisberger
Lawrence J. McDermott, Jr.
Darlene J. Pereksta
Hope M. Pomerantz
Cheryl H. Burstein
Joanne M. Sarubbi
Daniel Arent Colfax
David T. Miller

Representative Clients: Anchor Savings Bank, FSB; Federal Deposit Insurance Corporation (FDIC): The Hartford Accident and Indemnity Co.; The Ramapo Bank; Reliance Insurance Co.; Resolution Trust Corporation (RTC); Time-Warner Communications, Inc.; New Jersey Sports and Exposition Authority.

For full biographical listings, see the Martindale-Hubbell Law Directory

WEST ORANGE, Essex Co.

ZUCKER, FACHER AND ZUCKER, A PROFESSIONAL CORPORATION (AV)

100 Executive Drive, Third Floor, 07052
Telephone: 201-736-0444
Fax: 201-736-4011

Lionel P. Kristeller (1891-1956)
Melvin B. Cohen (1914-1966)
George R. Jackson (1895-1968)
Saul J. Zucker (1901-1984)
Morris R. Zucker
Irwin L. Facher
Roger C. Wilson
Paul J. Soderman

Judy L. Berberian
Brian Edward Tierney
James Kevin Haney

State Counsel for: Hobart; Becor Western.
Local Counsel for: United States Fidelity & Guaranty Co.; Kemper Insurance Group; Chubb & Son.

For full biographical listings, see the Martindale-Hubbell Law Directory

WEST PATERSON, Passaic Co.

EVANS HAND (AV)

One Garret Mountain Plaza, Interstate 80 at Squirrelwood Road, 07424-3396
Telephone: 201-881-1100
Fax: 201-881-1369

MEMBERS OF FIRM

Charles D. LaFiura
Thomas F. Craig, II

ASSOCIATES

William M. Sheehy
Lynda S. Korfmann

Representative Clients: Midlantic National Bank; The Bank of New York/National Community Division; The Prudential Insurance Co. of America; Connecticut General Life Insurance Co.; Travelers Insurance Co.; New Jersey Manufacturers Insurance Co.; Bell Atlantic; Algonquin Gas Transmission Co.; Tenneco, Inc.; Corning Glass Works.

For Complete List of Firm Personnel, See General Section

For full biographical listings, see the Martindale-Hubbell Law Directory

WOODBRIDGE, Middlesex Co.

WILENTZ, GOLDMAN & SPITZER, A PROFESSIONAL CORPORATION (AV)

90 Woodbridge Center Drive Suite 900, Box 10, 07095
Telephone: 908-636-8000
Telecopier: 908-855-6117
Eatontown, New Jersey Office: Meridian Center I, Two Industrial Way West, 07724.
Telephone: 908-493-1000.
Telecopier: 908-493-8387.
New York, New York Office: Wall Street Plaza, 88 Pine Street, 9th Floor, 10005.
Telephone: 212-267-3091.
Telecopier: 212-267-3828.

Stuart A. Hoberman
Sheldon E. Jaffe

Douglas Watson Lubic
Peter R. Herman
Eric S. Mandelbaum

Representative Clients: Amboy National Bank; United Jersey Bank; CoreStates/New Jersey National Bank; Bankers Savings; Midlantic National Bank; First Fidelity Bank, N.A., N.J.; The Trust Company of NJ.

For Complete List of Firm Personnel, See General Section

For full biographical listings, see the Martindale-Hubbell Law Directory

NEW MEXICO

*ALBUQUERQUE,** Bernalillo Co.

HINKLE, COX, EATON, COFFIELD & HENSLEY (AV)

Suite 800, 500 Marquette, N.W., P.O. Box 2043, 87103
Telephone: 505-768-1500
FAX: 505-768-1529
Roswell, New Mexico Office: Suite 700, United Bank Plaza, P.O. Box 10, 88202.
Telephone: 505-622-6510.
FAX: 505-623-9332.
Midland, Texas Office: 6 Desta Drive, Suite 2800, P.O. Box 3580, 79705.
Telephone: 915-683-4691.
FAX: 915-683-6518.
Amarillo, Texas Office: 1700 Bank One Center. P.O. Box 9238, 79105-9238.
Telephone: 806-372-5569.
FAX: 806-372-9761.
Santa Fe, New Mexico Office: 218 Montezuma, P.O. Box 2068, 87504.
Telephone: 505-982-4554.
FAX: 505-982-8623.
Austin, Texas Office: 401 West 15th Street, Suite 800, 78701.
Telephone: 512-476-7137.
FAX: 512-476-5431.
Associated Office: Hoffman & Stephens, P.C., 401 West 15th Street, Suite 800, 78701.
Telephone: 512-476-5434.
Fax: 512-476-5431.

Marshall G. Martin
Fred W. Schwendimann
Margaret Carter Ludewig

Representative Clients: Anadarko Petroleum Corp.; Atlantic Richfield Co.; Bass Enterprises Production Co.; BHP Petroleum; Caroon & Black Management, Inc.; Chevron, USA, Inc.; CIGNA; City of Albuquerque; Coastal Oil & Gas Corp. Co.; First Security Bank of Albuquerque, Pioneer Savings & Trust; Texas National Bank of Midland; Amarillo National Bank.

For Complete List of Firm Personnel, See General Section

For full biographical listings, see the Martindale-Hubbell Law Directory

KELLY, RAMMELKAMP, MUEHLENWEG, LUCERO & LEÓN, A PROFESSIONAL ASSOCIATION (AV)

Simms Tower, 400 Gold Avenue S.W., Suite 500, P.O. Box 25127, 87125-5127
Telephone: 505-247-8860
Fax: 505-247-8881

Henry A. Kelly
Robert J. Muehlenweg

Paige G. Leslie

Representative Clients: First Bank of Grants; Grants State Bank; Bank of America, New Mexico; United Companies Lending Corporation; Walt Arnold Commercial Properties.

For Complete List of Firm Personnel, See General Section

For full biographical listings, see the Martindale-Hubbell Law Directory

MILLER, STRATVERT, TORGERSON & SCHLENKER, P.A. (AV)

500 Marquette Avenue, N.W., Suite 1100, P.O. Box 25687, 87102
Telephone: 505-842-1950
Facsimile: 505-243-4408
Farmington, New Mexico Office: Suite 300, 300 West Arrington. P.O. Box 869.
Telephone: 505-326-4521.
Facsimile: 505-325-5474.
Las Cruces, New Mexico Office: Suite 300, 277 East Amador. P.O. Drawer 1231.
Telephone: 505-523-2481.
Facsimile: 505-526-2215.
Santa Fe, New Mexico Office: 125 Lincoln Avenue, Suite 221. P.O. Box 1986.
Telephone: 505-989-9614.
Facsimile: 505-989-9857.

Ranne B. Miller
Alan C. Torgerson
Kendall O. Schlenker
Alice Tomlinson Lorenz
Gregory W. Chase
Alan Konrad
Margo J. McCormick
Lyman G. Sandy
Stephen M. Williams
Stephan M. Vidmar
Robert C. Gutierrez
Seth V. Bingham (Resident at Farmington Office)
Michael H. Hoses
James B. Collins (Resident at Farmington Office)
Timothy Ray Briggs
Walter R. Parr (Resident at Santa Fe Office)
Rudolph A. Lucero
Daniel E. Ramczyk
Dean G. Constantine

(See Next Column)

MILLER, STRATVERT, TORGERSON & SCHLENKER P.A., *Albuquerque—Continued*

Deborah A. Solove
Gary L. Gordon
Lawrence R. White (Resident at Las Cruces Office)
Sharon P. Gross
Virginia Anderman
Marte D. Lightstone
Bradford K. Goodwin
John R. Funk (Resident at Las Cruces Office)
J. Scott Hall (Resident at Santa Fe Office)
Thomas R. Mack
Michael J. Happe (Resident at Farmington Office)
Denise Barela Shepherd
Nancy Augustus
Jill Burtram
Terri L. Sauer
Joel T. Newton (Resident at Las Cruces Office)
Judith K. Nakamura
Thomas M. Domme
David H. Thomas, III
C. Brian Charlton

COUNSEL

William K. Stratvert
Paul W. Robinson

Representative Clients: Dona Savings and Loan Assn.; Citizens Bank of Las Cruces; Ticor Title; First Federal Savings Bank of New Mexico; First Security Bank of New Mexico; White Sands Federal Credit Union.

For Complete List of Firm Personnel, See General Section

For full biographical listings, see the Martindale-Hubbell Law Directory

LAW OFFICES OF JOHN T. PORTER, P.A. (AV)

Suite 410, 20 First Plaza, N.W., 87102
Telephone: 505-243-6665
Fax: 505-764-9890

John T. Porter

Representative Clients: First Security Bank of New Mexico, N.A.

For full biographical listings, see the Martindale-Hubbell Law Directory

RODEY, DICKASON, SLOAN, AKIN & ROBB, P.A. (AV)

Albuquerque Plaza, Suite 2200, 201 Third Street, N.W., P.O. Box 1888, 87103-1888
Telephone: 505-765-5900
Fax: 505-768-7395
Santa Fe, New Mexico Office: Suite 101 Marcy Plaza, 123 East Marcy Street, P.O. Box 1357, 87504-1357.
Telephone: 505-984-0100.
Fax: 505-989-9542.

Robert M. St. John
John P. Burton (Resident, Santa Fe Office)
Catherine T. Goldberg
Jo Saxton Brayer
S. I. Betzer, Jr.
Nancy J. Appleby
Mark A. Smith

Jay D. Hill
Charles J. Vigil

For Complete List of Firm Personnel, See General Section

For full biographical listings, see the Martindale-Hubbell Law Directory

FARMINGTON, San Juan Co.

MILLER, STRATVERT, TORGERSON & SCHLENKER, P.A. (AV)

Suite 300, 300 West Arrington, P.O. Box 869, 87401
Telephone: 505-326-4521
Facsimile: 505-325-5474
Albuquerque, New Mexico Office: 500 Marquette Avenue, N.W., Suite 1100. P.O. Box 25687.
Telephone: 505-842-1950.
Facsimile: 505-243-4408.
Las Cruces, New Mexico Office: Suite 300, 277 East Amador. P.O. Drawer 1231.
Telephone: 505-523-2481.
Facsimile: 505-526-2215.
Santa Fe, New Mexico Office: 125 Lincoln Avenue, Suite 221. P.O. Box 1986.
Telephone: 505-989-9614.
Facsimile: 505-989-9857.

James B. Collins
Seth V. Bingham
Michael J. Happe

Representative Clients: St. Paul Insurance Cos.; State Farm Mutual Automobile Insurance Co.; The Travelers; United Resources Insurance Services; United States Fidelity & Guaranty Co.; New Mexico Physicians Mutual Liability Insurance Co.; Ticor Title Insurance Co.; Dona Ana Savings and Loan Assn.

For full biographical listings, see the Martindale-Hubbell Law Directory

*LAS CRUCES,** Dona Ana Co.

MILLER, STRATVERT, TORGERSON & SCHLENKER, P.A. (AV)

Suite 300, 277 East Amador, P.O. Drawer 1231, 88004
Telephone: 505-523-2481
Facsimile: 505-526-2215
Albuquerque, New Mexico Office: 500 Marquette Avenue, N.W., Suite 1100. P.O. Box 25687.
Telephone: 505-842-1950.
Facsimile: 505-243-4408.
Farmington, New Mexico Office: Suite 300, 300 West Arrington. P.O. Box 869.
Telephone: 505-326-4521.
Facsimile: 505-325-5474.
Santa Fe, New Mexico Office: 125 Lincoln Avenue, Suite 221. P.O. Box 1986.
Telephone: 505-989-9614.
Facsimile: 505-989-9857.

Lawrence R. White
John R. Funk
Joel T. Newton

Representative Clients: St. Paul Insurance Cos.; State Farm Mutual Automobile Insurance Co.; The Travelers; United States Fidelity & Guaranty Co.; New Mexico Physicians Mutual Liability Insurance Co.; Farmers Insurance Group; Citizens Bank of Las Cruces; Dona Ana Savings and Loan Assn.; Ticor Title Insurance Co.

For full biographical listings, see the Martindale-Hubbell Law Directory

WEINBRENNER, RICHARDS, PAULOWSKY & RAMIREZ, P.A. (AV)

8th Floor, First National Tower, P.O. Drawer O, 88004-1719
Telephone: 505-524-8624
Fax: 505-524-4252

David McNeill, Jr.

OF COUNSEL

Michael G. Paulowsky

General Counsel for: Stahmann Farms, Inc.; First National Bank of Dona Ana County.
Representative Clients: American General Cos.; Hartford Group; CNA Insurance; Fireman's Fund; United States Fidelity & Guaranty Co.; Travelers Insurance Co.; General Accident Group.

For Complete List of Firm Personnel, See General Section

For full biographical listings, see the Martindale-Hubbell Law Directory

*SANTA FE,** Santa Fe Co.

CATRON, CATRON & SAWTELL, A PROFESSIONAL ASSOCIATION (AV)

2006 Botulph Road, P.O. Box 788, 87504-0788
Telephone: 505-982-1947
Telecopier: 505-986-1013

Thomas B. Catron III
William A. Sawtell, Jr.
Fletcher R. Catron
W. Anthony Sawtell

LEGAL SUPPORT PERSONNEL

Peggy L. Feldt (Certified Public Accountant)

Attorneys for: Santa Fe Board of Education; American Express Co.; The Santa Fe Opera; Sunwest Bank of Santa Fe; VNS Health Services, Inc.

For Complete List of Firm Personnel, See General Section

For full biographical listings, see the Martindale-Hubbell Law Directory

SCHEUER, YOST & PATTERSON, A PROFESSIONAL CORPORATION (AV)

125 Lincoln Avenue, Suite 223, P.O. Drawer 9570, 87504
Telephone: 505-982-9911
Fax: 505-982-1621

Ralph H. Scheuer
Mel E. Yost
John N. Patterson
Holly A. Hart
Roger L. Prucino
Elizabeth A. Jaffe
Tracy Erin Conner
Ruth M. Fuess

OF COUNSEL

Melvin T. Yost

Representative Clients: Century Bank, FSB; Chicago Insurance Co.; GEICO; Los Alamos National Bank; Los Alamos Credit Union; Manufacturer's Hanover Trust Co.; Rocky Mountain Bankcard System; St. John's College; Sun Loan Companies; Territorial Abstract & Title Co.

For full biographical listings, see the Martindale-Hubbell Law Directory

NEW YORK

*BROOKLYN,** Kings Co.

WINGATE & CULLEN (AV)

142 Pierrepont Street, 11201
Telephone: 718-875-3652
Fax: 718-596-6750
Other Brooklyn Office: Bay Ridge, 8804 4th Avenue.
Telephone: 718-745-8844.
Fax: 718-680-0598.
Melville, New York Office: Fleet Financial Plaza, 290 Broad Hollow Road.
Telephone: 516-427-5400.
Fax: 516-427-5402.

MEMBERS OF FIRM

Thomas O. Rice
Peter N. Zogas
Richard H. Freeman
Jonathan R. Frank
Michael F. O'Shea
Robert P. Knapp, III

SENIOR COUNSEL

Claudia C. Conway
Calliope Manis

ASSOCIATES

Jani M. Foley
Kenneth V. Babi
Kevin G. Condon
Paula A. Miller
Marc A. Rapaport

For full biographical listings, see the Martindale-Hubbell Law Directory

*BUFFALO,** Erie Co.

BLOCK & COLUCCI, P.C. (AV)

1250 Statler Towers, 14202
Telephone: 716-854-4080; 1-800-388-2595
Telex: 919-186
Fax: 716-854-0059
Litigation Fax: 716-854-4070
Jupiter, Florida Office: 1001 N. U.S. Highway One, Suite 400.
Telephone: 407-747-0110.
Fax: 407-743-0046.
Albany, New York Office: 12 Century Hill Drive, P.O. Box 1160, (Latham).
Telephone: 518-783-0535.
Fax: 518-783-5670.
Binghamton, New York Office: The Press Building, 19 Chenago Street.
Telephone: 607-724-3138.
Fax: 607-724-6227.
Rochester, New York Office: 30 West Broad Street, Suite 200.
Telephone: 716-454-1660.
Fax: 716-454-7134.
Syracuse, New York Office: 5786 Widewaters Parkway.
Telephone: 315-445-1272.
Fax: 315-445-9530.

Ernest L. Colucci (1909-1989)
David Simon Brown
Steven S. Brown
Anthony J. Colucci, Jr.
Anthony J. Colucci, III
Mark K. Cramer
William P. Hessney, Jr. (Resident at Albany Office)
William T. Jebb, II
Cheryl A. Short

Elpiniki M. Bechakas
Frank M. Cassara
Dennis H. Cleary
Frank V. Fontana
Marie L. Gallagher
Kathleen M. Kaczor
Scott J. Leitten
John J. Marchese
John K. McAndrew
Kathleen F. McGovern (Resident, Albany Office)
Melanie C. Mecca
Natalie A. Napierala
Margaret Logan Noonan
Michael W. Schafer
Lawrence R. Schwach
Damon H. Serota
Debra A. Spellman
Maureen Tucker
Frederick R. Xlander (Resident Binghamton Office)

OF COUNSEL

Lester H. Block
Joseph F. Crangle

SPECIAL COUNSEL

Richard D. Nadel (Not admitted in NY; Resident, Jupiter, Florida Office)

References: Manufacturers & Traders Trust Co.; Palm Beach National Bank & Trust Co.

For full biographical listings, see the Martindale-Hubbell Law Directory

ELMSFORD, Westchester Co.

EISNER & LEVY (AV)

200 Clearbrook Road, 10523
Telephone: 914-345-3066
Fax: 914-345-3468

Lewis Eisner (1925-1987)
Roy G. Levy

(See Next Column)

ASSOCIATE

Donna F. Sheidlower

For full biographical listings, see the Martindale-Hubbell Law Directory

GARDEN CITY, Nassau Co.

ALBANESE, ALBANESE & FIORE LLP (AV)

1050 Franklin Avenue, 5th Floor, 11530
Telephone: 516-248-7000

MEMBERS OF FIRM

Vincent M. Albanese
Joseph R. Albanese
Joseph A. Fiore
Gary R. Steinberg
Thomas G. Sherwood
Arthur L. Colozzi

ASSOCIATES

Barry A. Oster
Richard H. Ferriggi
Rachel M. Harari
Laura Paglia Sikorski
Diana Centrella Prevete
Hyman Hacker
Vincent A. Albanese
Jack A. Horn

COUNSEL

Theodore D. Hoffmann
W. Hubert Plummer

LEGAL SUPPORT PERSONNEL

Linda Cristando
Deborah J. Dolan
Demitra Koliokotas Lynch
Florence M. McGoey

References: Apple Bank for Savings; Bank of New York; North Fork Bank; First American Title Insurance Company; American Title Insurance Company; Greater Jamaica Development Corp.; United Nations Plaza Tower Associates, Ltd.; Fidelity National Title Insurance Company of New York.

For full biographical listings, see the Martindale-Hubbell Law Directory

CULLEN AND DYKMAN (AV)

Garden City Center, 100 Quentin Roosevelt Boulevard, 11530-4850
Telephone: 516-357-3700
Telecopier: 516-357-3792
Brooklyn, New York Office: 177 Montague Street.
Telephone: 718-855-9000.
Telecopier: 718-855-4282.
Washington, D.C. Office: 1225 Nineteenth Street, N.W., Suite 320.
Telephone: 202-223-8890.
Telecopier: 202-457-1405.
Newark, New Jersey Office: One Riverfront Plaza, Suite 1410.
Telephone: 201-622-1545.
Telecopier: 201-622-4563.

MEMBERS OF FIRM

John J. Bishar, Jr.
Antonia M. Donohue
Thomas J. Douglas, Jr.
Joseph D. Simon
William P. Tucker

For Complete List of Firm Personnel, See General Section

For full biographical listings, see the Martindale-Hubbell Law Directory

REDMOND, POLLIO & PITTONI, P.C. (AV)

1461 Franklin Avenue, 11530
Telephone: 516-248-2500
Telecopier: 516-248-2348

Benedict J. Pollio
M. John Pittoni
Peter R. Bonchonsky

Mark E. Costello
Kathleen M. Galgano
Rachel Cohen Quaid
Stephen E. Zaino
Ronald A. Pollio

OF COUNSEL

Aldo A. Trabucchi
Leonard P. Marinello

Representative Clients: Bank of New York; Chemical Bank; NatWest Bank N.A.; Shawmut Bank.

For Complete List of Firm Personnel, See General Section

For full biographical listings, see the Martindale-Hubbell Law Directory

HUNTINGTON, Suffolk Co.

SMYTH & LACK (AV)

202 East Main Street, 11743
Telephone: 516-271-7500
Telecopier: 516-271-7504

MEMBERS OF FIRM

Vincent A. Smyth
James J. Lack

ASSOCIATES

Thomas P. Solferino
Dana M. Barberis
Stephen I. Witdorchic

Reference: Chemical Bank.

For full biographical listings, see the Martindale-Hubbell Law Directory

MELVILLE, Suffolk Co.

WINGATE & CULLEN (AV)

Fleet Financial Plaza, 290 Broad Hollow Road, 11747-4805
Telephone: 516-427-5400
Fax: 516-427-5402
Brooklyn, New York Office: 142 Pierrepont Street.
Telephone: 718-875-3652.
Fax: 718-596-6750.
Other Brooklyn Office: Bay Ridge, 8804 4th Avenue.
Telephone: 718-745-8844.
Fax: 718-680-0598.

MEMBERS OF FIRM

Thomas O. Rice
Peter N. Zogas
Richard H. Freeman
Jonathan R. Frank
Michael F. O'Shea
Robert P. Knapp, III

SENIOR COUNSEL

Claudia C. Conway
Calliope Manis

ASSOCIATES

Jani M. Foley
Kenneth V. Babi
Kevin G. Condon
Paula A. Miller
Marc A. Rapaport

For full biographical listings, see the Martindale-Hubbell Law Directory

MIDDLETOWN, Orange Co.

MACVEAN, LEWIS, SHERWIN & MCDERMOTT, P.C. (AV)

34 Grove Street, P.O. Box 310, 10940
Telephone: 914-343-3000
Fax: 914-343-3866

Kenneth A. MacVean
Kermit W. Lewis
Louis H. Sherwin
Paul T. McDermott
Jeffrey D. Sherwin

George F. Roesch, III
Michael F. McCusker
Thomas P. Clarke, Jr.

OF COUNSEL

V. Frank Cline

Counsel for: Orange County Trust Co.; Middletown Savings Bank; First Federal Savings & Loan Association of Middletown; Goshen Savings Bank; Advest Bank.

For Complete List of Firm Personnel, See General Section

For full biographical listings, see the Martindale-Hubbell Law Directory

*NEW CITY,** Rockland Co.

GRANIK SILVERMAN SANDBERG CAMPBELL NOWICKI RESNIK HEKKER (AV)

254 South Main Street, 10956
Telephone: 914-634-8822; 800-822-1238

MEMBERS OF FIRM

Joseph F. X. Nowicki (1922-1976)
Robert R. Granik (1922-1994)
David W. Silverman
Martin L. Sandberg
Patrick M. Campbell
Kenneth H. Resnik
John M. Hekker
Ricki Hollis Berger

ASSOCIATE

Catherine T. O'Toole Lauritano

OF COUNSEL

Morrie Slifkin

For full biographical listings, see the Martindale-Hubbell Law Directory

*NEW YORK,** New York Co.

BELLER & KELLER (AV)

415 Madison Avenue, 10017
Telephone: 212-754-2700
Facsimile: 212-754-2708

Barry Beller
Arthur Keller
Gary D. Roth
Jill D. Block
Roy H. Carlin (P.C.)
William E. Hammond
Robert S. Herbst
Jean Kim
Leonard D. Levin
Stephen A. Linde
Anna E. Panayotou
Elisabeth N. Radow
Harriet Rubin Roberts
Dan L. Rosenbaum
Bianca M. Scaramellino
Marc S. Shapiro
Paul S. Shapses
Richard S. Weisman

For full biographical listings, see the Martindale-Hubbell Law Directory

CHAPMAN & FENNELL (AV)

330 Madison Avenue, 10017
Telephone: 212-687-3600
Telex: WUI 880411 (ETOSHA NY)
Telefax: 212-972-5368
Stamford, Connecticut Office: Three Landmark Square.
Telephone: 203-353-8000.
Telefax: 203-353-8799.
Washington D.C. Office: 2000 L. Street, N.W., Suite 200.
Telephone: 202-822-9351.

MEMBERS OF FIRM

Darrell K. Fennell
Philip M. Chiappone

OF COUNSEL

Michael Winger
Carol E. Meltzer
Eric S. Kamisher

For full biographical listings, see the Martindale-Hubbell Law Directory

DEBEVOISE & PLIMPTON (AV)

875 Third Avenue, 10022
Telephone: 212-909-6000
Domestic Telex: 148377 DEBSTEVE NYK
Telecopier: (212) 909-6836
Los Angeles, California Office: 601 South Figueroa Street, Suite 3700, 90017.
Telephone: 213-680-8000.
Telecopier: 213-680-8100.
Washington, D.C. Office: 555 13th Street, N.W., 20004.
Telephone: 202-383-8000.
Telecopier: (202) 383-8118.
Paris, France Office: 21 Avenue George V 75008.
Telephone: (33-1) 40 73 12 12.
Telecopier: (33-1) 47 20 50 82.
Telex: 648141F DPPAR.
London, England Office: 1 Creed Court, 5 Ludgate Hill, EC4M 7AA.
Telephone: (44-171) 329-0779.
Telex: 88 4569 DPLON G.
Telecopier: (44-171) 329-0860.
Budapest, Hungary Office: 1065 Budapest, Révay Köz 2.III/2.
Telephone: (36-1)112-8067.
Telecopier: (36-1) 132-7995.
Hong Kong Office: 13/F Entertainment Building, 30 Queen's Road Central.
Telephone: (852) 2810-7918.
Fax: (852) 2810-9828.

MEMBERS OF FIRM

Bevis Longstreth
Stephen J. Friedman
Hans Bertram-Nothnagel
Eric D. Roiter (Washington, D.C. Office)
Darius Tencza
Marcia L. MacHarg (Washington, D.C. Office)
Thomas M. Kelly
Ivan E. Mattei

ASSOCIATES

Philomena A. Burke
Bonnie L. Martinolich
David P. Mason
Harold A. Neu
Peter W. Paulsen
Edmund H. Price (Washington, D.C. Office)

For Complete List of Firm Personnel, See General Section

For full biographical listings, see the Martindale-Hubbell Law Directory

EMMET, MARVIN & MARTIN, LLP (AV)

120 Broadway, 10271
Telephone: 212-238-3000
Cable Address: EMMARRO
Fax: 212-238-3100
Morristown, New Jersey Office: 10 Madison Avenue.
Telephone: 201-538-5600.
Fax: 201-538-6448.

MEMBERS OF FIRM

Thomas B. Fenlon
Thomas F. Noone (P.C.)
Lawrence B. Thompson
William A. Leet
David M. Daly
Peter B. Tisne
Michael C. Johansen
Robert W. Viets
Dennis C. Fleischmann
Eric M. Reuben
Jeffrey S. Chavkin
J. Christopher Eagan
Jesse Dudley B. Kimball
Stephen P. Cerow
Ellen J. Bickal
Edward P. Zujkowski
John P. Uehlinger
Irving C. Apar
Julian A. McQuiston
Maria-Liisa Lydon
Christine B. Cesare
Patrick A. McCartney
Matthew P. D'Amico
Brian D. Obergfell

OF COUNSEL

Guy B. Capel
Bernard F. Joyce (P.C.)
Richard P. Bourgerie
George H. P. Dwight

(See Next Column)

EMMET, MARVIN & MARTIN LLP—*Continued*

ASSOCIATES

Eunice M. O'Neill
Joseph M. Samulski
Sean M. Carlin
Alfred W. J. Marks
Eileen Chin-Bow
John M. Ryan
Francine M. Kors
Wendy E. Kramer
James C. Hughes, IV
Patricia C. Caputo
Bennett E. Josselsohn
Stephen I. Frank
Mildred Quinones
Anthony M. Harvin
Lynn D. Barsamian
Margaret H. Walker
Robert L. Morgan
Sally Shreeves
Michael Fotios Mavrides
Matthew A. Wieland
Eric E. Schneck (Resident, Morristown Office)
Lisa B. Lerner
Elizabeth K. Somers
Steven M. Berg
Michael E. Cavanaugh
Nancy J. Cohen
Peter L. Mancini
Stephen M. Ksenak

For full biographical listings, see the Martindale-Hubbell Law Directory

HUTTON INGRAM YUZEK GAINEN CARROLL & BERTOLOTTI (AV)

250 Park Avenue, 10177
Telephone: 212-907-9600
Facsimile: 212-907-9681

MEMBERS OF FIRM

Ernest J. Bertolotti
Daniel L. Carroll
Roger Cukras
Larry F. Gainen
G. Thompson Hutton
Samuel W. Ingram, Jr.
Paulette Kendler
Steven Mastbaum
Dean G. Yuzek
David G. Ebert
Shane O'Neill

ASSOCIATES

Warren E. Friss
Patricia Hewitt
Gail A. Buchman
Stuart A. Christie
Beth N. Green
Timish K. Hnateyko
Jeanne F. Pucci
Jane Drummey
Adam L. Sifre
Susan Ann Fennelly
Marc J. Schneider

For full biographical listings, see the Martindale-Hubbell Law Directory

KRASNER & CHEN (AV)

555 Madison Avenue, Suite 600, 10022
Telephone: 212-751-7100
Telefax: 212-371-4551

MEMBERS OF FIRM

Wesley Chen
Harvey I. Krasner

For full biographical listings, see the Martindale-Hubbell Law Directory

LOEB AND LOEB (AV)

A Partnership including Professional Corporations
345 Park Avenue, 10154-0037
Telephone: 212-407-4000
Facsimile: 212-407-4990
Los Angeles, California Office: Suite 1800, 1000 Wilshire Boulevard, 90017-2475.
Telephone: 213-688-3400.
Cable Address: "Loband LSA".
Telecopier: 213-688-3460; 688-3461; 688-3462.
Century City (Los Angeles), California Office: Suite 2200, 10100 Santa Monica Boulevard, Los Angeles, 90067-4164.
Telephone: 310-282-2000.
Telecopier: 310-282-2191; 282-2192.
Nashville, Tennessee Office: 45 Music Square West, 37203-3205.
Telephone: 615-749-8300.
Facsimile: 615-749-8308.
Rome, Italy Office: Piazza Digione 1, 00197.
Telephone: 011-396-808-8456.
Telecopier: 011-396-674-8223.

MEMBERS OF FIRM

Frank E. Feder (A P.C.)
Charles H. Miller
David S. Schaefer
Richard P. Streicher

For Complete List of Firm Personnel, See General Section

For full biographical listings, see the Martindale-Hubbell Law Directory

MILBANK, TWEED, HADLEY & MCCLOY (AV)

1 Chase Manhattan Plaza, 10005
Telephone: 212-530-5000
Cable Address: "Miltweed NYK"
Fax: 212-530-5219
MCI Mail: MilbankTweed ABA/net Milbank NY
Midtown Office: 50 Rockefeller Plaza, 10020.
Telephone: 212-530-5800.
Fax: 212-530-0158.

(See Next Column)

Los Angeles, California Office: 601 South Figueroa Street, 30th Floor, 90017.
Telephone: 213-892-4000.
Fax: 213-629-5063.
Telex: 678754. ABA/net: Milbank LA.
Washington, D.C. Office: International Square Building, Suite 1100, 1825 Eye Street, N.W., 20006.
Telephone: 202-835-7500.
Cable Address: "Miltweed Wsh". ITT 440667.
Fax: 202-835-7586. ABA/net: Milbank DC.
Tokyo, Japan Office: Nippon Press Center Building, 2-1, Uchisaiwai-cho 2-chome, Chiyoda-ku, Tokyo 100, Japan.
Telephone: 011-81-3-3504-1050.
Fax: 011-81-3-3595-2790, 011-81-3-3502-5192.
London, England Office: Ropemaker Place, 25 Ropemaker Street, EC2Y 9AS.
Telephone: 011-44-171-374-0423.
Cable Address: "Miltuk G."
Fax: 011-44-171-374-0912.
Hong Kong Office: 3007 Alexandra House, 16 Chater Road.
Telephone: 011-852-2526-5281.
Fax: 011-852-2840-0792; 011-852-2845-9046. ABA/net: Milbank HK.
Singapore Office: 14-02 Caltex House, 30 Raffles Place, 0104.
Telephone: 011-65-534-1700.
Fax: 011-65-534-2733. ABA/net: EDNANG.
Moscow, Russia Office: 24/27 Sadovaya-Samotyochnya, Moscow, 103051.
Telephone: 011-7-502-258-5015.
Fax: 011-7-502-258-5014.

MEMBERS OF FIRM

Richard S. Brach
Elliot Gewirtz
Richard M. Gray
Peter M. Mortimer
Robert S. O'Hara, Jr.
Frank C. Puleo
Elihu F. Robertson
Peter D. Rowntree
David C. Siegfried
Eric F. Silverman
David R. Slade
Robert E. Spring
Richard J. Wight

OF COUNSEL

David C. Stoller

For Complete List of Firm Personnel, See General Section

For full biographical listings, see the Martindale-Hubbell Law Directory

OTTERBOURG, STEINDLER, HOUSTON & ROSEN, P.C. (AV)

230 Park Avenue, 10169
Telephone: 212-661-9100
Cable Address: "Otlerton";
Telecopier: 212-682-6104
Telex: 960916

Kurt J. Wolff
William M. Silverman
Morton L. Gitter
Peter H. Stolzar
Alan R. Weiskopf
Bernard Beitel
Jonathan N. Helfat
Daniel Wallen
Glenn B. Rice
Albert F. Reisman
Kenneth J. Miller
Anthony M. Piccione
Steven B. Soll
Alan Kardon
Mitchell M. Brand
Stanley L. Lane, Jr.
David W. Morse
Peter L. Feldman

COUNSEL

Stephen B. Weissman

Diane B. Kaplan
Lloyd M. Green
Bruce P. Levine
Richard G. Haddad
Lauri Blum Regan
Stephen H. Alpert
Craig D. Zlotnick
Andrew M. Kramer

For Complete List of Firm Personnel, See General Section

For full biographical listings, see the Martindale-Hubbell Law Directory

PARKER CHAPIN FLATTAU & KLIMPL, L.L.P. (AV)

1211 Avenue of the Americas, 10036
Telephone: 212-704-6000
Telecopier: 212-704-6288
Cable Address: "Lawpark"
Telex: 640347
Great Neck, New York Office: 175 Great Neck Road.
Telephone: 516-482-4422.
Telecopier: 516-482-4469.

MEMBERS OF FIRM

Mark Abramowitz
Christopher Stewart Auguste
Aurora Cassirer
William D. Freedman
Mark S. Hirsch
Michael A. Leichtling
Mitchell P. Portnoy
Richard A. Rubin
Lawrence David Swift
Melvin Weinberg

OF COUNSEL

Raymond W. Dusch

(See Next Column)

PARKER CHAPIN FLATTAU & KLIMPL L.L.P., *New York—Continued*

ASSOCIATES

Amos Alter
Elyse J. Angelico
Sheon Karol

For Complete List of Firm Personnel, See General Section

For full biographical listings, see the Martindale-Hubbell Law Directory

WATSON, FARLEY & WILLIAMS (AV)

380 Madison Avenue, 10017
Telephone: 212-922-2200
Telex: 6790626 WFW NY
Fax: 212-922-1512
London, England Office: 15 Appold Street, London EC2A 2HB.
Telephone: (44 71) 814 8000.
Telex: 8955707 WFW LON G.
Fax: (44 71) 814 8141.
Paris, France Office: 19 rue de Marignan, 75008 Paris.
Telephone: (33 1) 45 63 15 15.
Telex: WFW PAR 651096 F.
Fax: (33 1) 45 61 09 01.
Oslo, Norway Office: Beddingen 8, Aker Brygge, 0250 Oslo.
Telephone: (47 22) 83 83 08.
Telex: 79209 WFW N.
Fax: (47 22) 83 83 13.
Athens, Greece Office: Alassia Building, Defteras Merarchias 13, 185-35 Piraeus.
Telephone: (30 1) 422 3660.
Telex: 24 1311 WFW GR.
Fax: (30 1) 422 3664.
Moscow, Russia Office: 36 Myaskovskovo Street, Moscow 121019.
Telephone: (7 502) 224 1700 (international only); (7 095) 291 8046/5968.
Fax: (7 502) 224 1701 (international only); (7 095) 202 9027.
Copenhagen, Denmark Office: Lille Kongensgade 20 DK-1074 Copenhagen K.
Telephone: (45 33) 91 33 03.
Fax: (45 33) 91 49 12.

MEMBERS OF FIRM

Derick W. Betts, Jr.
Leo Chang
John E. Nelson II
David N. Osborne
John S. Osborne, Jr.
Alfred E. Yudes, Jr.
Thatcher A. Stone
Joseph G. Braunreuther
Peter S. Smedresman
Philip H. Spector
R. Jay Fortin

For Complete List of Firm Personnel, See General Section

For full biographical listings, see the Martindale-Hubbell Law Directory

WINTHROP, STIMSON, PUTNAM & ROBERTS (AV)

One Battery Park Plaza, 10004-1490
Telephone: 212-858-1000
Telex: 62854 WINSTIM
Telefax: 212-858-1500
Stamford, Connecticut Office: Financial Centre, 695 East Main Street, P.O. Box 6760, 06904-6760.
Telephone: 203-348-2300.
Washington, D.C. Office: 1133 Connecticut Avenue, N.W., 20036.
Telephone: 202-775-9800.
Palm Beach, Florida Office: 125 Worth Avenue, 33480.
Telephone: 407-655-7297.
London Office: 2 Throgmorton Avenue, London EC2N 2AP, England.
Telephone: 011-4471-628-4931.
Brussels Office: Rue Du Taciturne 42, B-1040 Brussels, Belgium.
Telephone: 011-322-230-1392.
Tokyo, Japan Office: 608 Atagoyama Bengoshi Building 6-7, Atago 1-chome, Minato-ku, Tokyo 105 Japan.
Telephone: 011-813-3437-9740.
Hong Kong Office: 2505 Asia Pacific Finance Tower, Citibank Plaza, 3 Garden Road, Central.
Telephone: 011-852-530-3400.

MEMBERS OF FIRM

Kenneth E. Adelsberg
Takeo Akiyama
David W. Ambrosia
Mary Patricia Azevedo
Barton D. Ford
Robert W. Gray
Barton T. Jones
F. Joseph Owens, Jr.
Michael P. Schumaecker
James R. Silkenat
Jane Wallison Stein
Charles H. Vejvoda
Mark J. Volow
Robert D. Webster
Jonathan B. Whitney

COUNSEL

Glen R. Cuccinello
Charles S. Wassell

CONNECTICUT OFFICE
MEMBER OF FIRM

Frode Jensen, III

TOKYO OFFICE
MEMBER OF FIRM

Jeffrey L. Pote

(See Next Column)

HONG KONG OFFICE
MEMBER OF FIRM

William C. F. Kurz

ASSOCIATES

Ella W. Dodson
Vitaly Fiks
Jennifer E. Hochberg
Yong Hyun Kim
Helen F. R. Lawson
Scott J. Lorinsky
Ujwala Mahatme
J. Mark Pohl
Leslie E. Shigaki
Renée S. Zylberberg

For Complete List of Firm Personnel, See General Section

For full biographical listings, see the Martindale-Hubbell Law Directory

*POUGHKEEPSIE,** Dutchess Co.

CORBALLY, GARTLAND AND RAPPLEYEA (AV)

35 Market Street, 12601
Telephone: 914-454-1110
FAX: 914-454-4857
Millbrook, New York Office: Bank of Millbrook Building, Franklin Avenue.
Telephone: 914-677-5539.
Clearwater, Florida Office: Citizens Bank Building, Suite 250, 1130 Cleveland Street.
Telephone: 813-461-3144.

MEMBERS OF FIRM

John Hackett (Died 1916)
James L. Williams (Died 1908)
Charles J. Corbally (1888-1966)
John J. Gartland, Jr.
Allan E. Rappleyea
Daniel F. Curtin
Fred W. Schaeffer
Michael G. Gartland
Jon H. Adams
Vincent L. DeBiase
Paul O. Sullivan
William F. Bogle, Jr.

ASSOCIATES

Rena Muckenhoupt O'Connor
Allan B. Rappleyea, Jr.

OF COUNSEL

Joseph F. Hawkins (1916-1986)
Milton M. Haven
Edward J. Murtaugh

Representative Clients: Hudson Valley Farm Credit, A.C.A.; St. Francis Hospital; Marist College; Merritt-Meridian Construction Corp.
Counsel for: Poughkeepsie Savings Bank, F.S.B.; Bank of New York; Farm Credit Bank of Springfield; Equitable Life Assurance Society of the United States; McCann Foundation, Inc.
Reference: Bank of New York.

For full biographical listings, see the Martindale-Hubbell Law Directory

*ROCHESTER,** Monroe Co.

HARTER, SECREST & EMERY (AV)

700 Midtown Tower, 14604-2070
Telephone: 716-232-6500
Telecopier: 716-232-2152
Naples, Florida Office: Suite 400, 800 Laurel Oak Drive.
Telephone: 813-598-4444.
Telecopier: 813-598-2781.
Albany, New York Office: One Steuben Place.
Telephone: 518-434-4377.
Telecopier: 518-449-4025.
Syracuse, New York Office: 431 East Fayette Street.
Telephone: 315-474-4000.
Telecopier: 315-474-7789.

MEMBERS OF FIRM

W. Reynolds Bowers
Lawrence R. Palvino
James P. Burns, 3rd (Resident Partner, Syracuse Office)
James B. Gray, Jr.
John R. Weider
Timothy R. Parry (Not admitted in NY; Resident Partner, Naples, Florida Office)

SENIOR ATTORNEY

Russell W. Roberts

ASSOCIATES

Cathy Kaman Ryan
Jill M. Myers
Walter D. Bay
Kelly M. Braun (Resident Associate, Naples, Florida Office)

For Complete List of Firm Personnel, See General Section

For full biographical listings, see the Martindale-Hubbell Law Directory

SMITHTOWN, Suffolk Co.

MEYER, MEYER & METLI (AV)

28 Manor Road, 11787
Telephone: 516-265-4500
Telecopier: 516-265-4534

Bernard K. Meyer
Terence X. Meyer
Richard Metli
Joseph Patrick Keneally

(See Next Column)

MEYER, MEYER & METLI—*Continued*

ASSOCIATES

James E. Robinson | Mitchel A. Hill
Kara Cheeseman-Bak

Representative Clients: Chemical Bank; Commack Fire District; The Chase Manhattan Bank; The Bank of New York; United Artists; ITT Commercial Finance Corp.; Fleet Bank; EAB; Long Island Savings Bank; Crossland Savings Bank.

For full biographical listings, see the Martindale-Hubbell Law Directory

WOODBURY, Nassau Co.

STEBEL & PASELTINER, P.C. (AV)

7600 Jericho Turnpike, 11797
Telephone: 516-496-8117
Telecopier: 516-496-8112

Bernard Stebel | David E. Paseltiner

Mindy K. Smolevitz | Steven M. Gelfman

COUNSEL

Edwin H. Baker | Mitchell G. Mandell
Alan M. Pollack | Lori Samet Schwarz
Michael E. Greene | Scott A. Sommer

References: Chemical Bank; Fleet Bank.

For full biographical listings, see the Martindale-Hubbell Law Directory

NORTH CAROLINA

*CHARLOTTE,** Mecklenburg Co.

FENNEBRESQUE, CLARK, SWINDELL & HAY (AV)

NationsBank Corporate Center Suite 2900, 100 North Tryon Street, 28202-4011
Telephone: 704-347-3800
Facsimile: 704-347-3838

MEMBERS OF FIRM

John C. Fennebresque | Michael S. Marr
Bernard B. Clark | Mary B. Nutt
Gary W. Swindell | William W. Kohler
Jeffrey S. Hay | Jeffrey W. Glenney
Marvin L. Rogers, II | Patricia F. Hosmer
Michael L. Burt | Pamela L. Kopp
James K.L. (Lynn) Thorneburg | Deidre E. Holmes (Not admitted in NC)

LEGAL SUPPORT PERSONNEL

Laura L. Butz

For full biographical listings, see the Martindale-Hubbell Law Directory

WOMBLE CARLYLE SANDRIDGE & RICE (AV)

A Professional Limited Liability Company
3300 One First Union Center, 301 S. College Street, 28202-6025
Telephone: 704-331-4900
Telecopy: 704-331-4955
Telex: 853609
Winston-Salem, North Carolina Office: 1600 Southern National Financial Center.
Telephone: 919-721-3600.
Telecopy: 919-721-3660.
Telex: 806498.
Raleigh, North Carolina Office: 2100 First Union Capitol Center, 150 Fayetteville Street Mall, P.O. Box 831.
Telephone: 919-755-2100.
Telecopy: 919-755-2150.
Telex: 806498.
Atlanta, Georgia Office: One Ninety One Peachtree Tower, 191 Peachtree Street N.E., Suite 3250.
Telephone: 404-614-2580.
Fax: 404-614-2595.

MEMBERS OF FIRM

James R. Bryant, III | Gary D. Chamblee

Representative Clients: Childress Klein Properties, Inc.; Food Lion, Inc.; Fieldcrest Cannon, Inc.; J.A. Jones Construction Company; Parkdale Mills, Inc.; Duke Power Company; Bowles Hollowell Conner & Company; ALLTEL Carolina, Inc.; Belk Store Services, Inc.; Philip Holzmann A.G.

For Complete List of Firm Personnel, See General Section

For full biographical listings, see the Martindale-Hubbell Law Directory

*RALEIGH,** Wake Co.

* indicates certain Bar Register subscribers whose principal office is located elsewhere in the state and who have arranged for representation as a part of the state capital listings that follow

*** WOMBLE CARLYLE SANDRIDGE & RICE (AV)**

A Professional Limited Liability Company
2100 First Union Capitol Center, 150 Fayetteville Street Mall, P.O. Box 831, 27602
Telephone: 919-755-2100
Telecopy: 919-755-2150
Telex: 806498
Charlotte, North Carolina Office: 3300 One First Union Center, 301 South College Street.
Telephone: 704-331-4900.
Telecopy: 704-331-4955.
Telex: 853609.
Winston-Salem, North Carolina Office: 1600 Southern National Financial Center.
Telephone: 919-721-3600.
Telecopy: 919-721-3660.
Telex: 806498.
Atlanta, Georgia Office: One Ninety One Peachtree Tower, 191 Peachtree Street N.E., Suite 3250.
Telephone: 404-614-2580.
Fax: 404-614-2595.

RESIDENT PARTNERS

William Camp Matthews, Jr. | Stephen A. Yeagy

RESIDENT ASSOCIATE

Nicolas P. Robinson

Representative Clients: Aetna Casualty and Surety Co., Inc.; ALSCO/AmeriMark Building Products, Inc.; Aoki Corporation America, Inc.; Empire of Carolina, Inc.; Hackney Brothers, Inc.; Lawyers Mutual Liability Insurance Company of North Carolina; Meredith College; Monk-Austin, Inc.; Regency Park Corporation; Wachovia Bank of North Carolina, N.A.

For Complete List of Firm Personnel, See General Section

For full biographical listings, see the Martindale-Hubbell Law Directory

*WILMINGTON,** New Hanover Co.

KAUFMAN & GREEN, L.L.P. (AV)

Sea Towers Business Center, 2002 Eastwood Road, Suite 202, 28406-0038
Telephone: 910-256-5135
FAX: 910-256-6451
Syracuse, New York Office: Hancock & Estabrook, 1500 Mony Tower I, 13221.
Telephone: 315-471-3151.
Fax: 315-471-3167.

James J. Kaufman | Michael A. Green

Representative Clients: Holtz House of Vehicles; Import Automotive Specialists; D.G. Enterprises, Ltd.; Steven P. Braff, M.D. P.C.; Marine Motions; Scientific Medical Programs; Southeastern Telecom, Inc.; SRS Development Inc.; Stewart-Wrongall Builders, Inc.; T.F.S.I.; Paul Miller Parsche Audi Inc.

For full biographical listings, see the Martindale-Hubbell Law Directory

*WINSTON-SALEM,** Forsyth Co.

WOMBLE CARLYLE SANDRIDGE & RICE (AV)

A Professional Limited Liability Company
1600 Southern National Financial Center, P.O. Drawer 84, 27102
Telephone: 910-721-3600
Telecopy: 910-721-3660
Telex: 806498
Charlotte, North Carolina Office: 3300 One First Union Center, 301 South College Street.
Telephone: 704-331-4900.
Telecopy: 704-331-4955.
Telex: 853609.
Raleigh, North Carolina Office: 2100 First Union Capitol Center, 150 Fayetteville Street Mall, P.O. Box 831.
Telephone: 919-755-2100.
Telecopy: 919-755-2150.
Telex: 806498.
Atlanta, Georgia Office: One Ninety One Peachtree Tower, 191 Peachtree Street, N.E., Suite 3250.
Telephone: 404-614-2580.
Fax: 404-614-2595.

MEMBERS OF FIRM

Leslie E. Browder | Dennis W. McNames
Hardin Graham Halsey | Kenneth Allen Moser
James E. Lilly (Resident, Atlanta, Georgia Office) | W. Pendleton Sandridge, Jr.

(See Next Column)

WOMBLE CARLYLE SANDRIDGE & RICE, *Winston-Salem—Continued*

ASSOCIATE

Kimberly Kelly Mann

Representative Clients: Brad Ragan, Inc.; Brenner Companies; Food Lion, Inc.; Hanes Companies, Inc.; North Carolina Baptist Hospitals, Inc.; R.J. Reynolds Tobacco Company; Summit Communications Group, Inc.; Thomasville Furniture Industries, Inc.; Wachovia Corporation; Wake Forest University.

For Complete List of Firm Personnel, See General Section

For full biographical listings, see the Martindale-Hubbell Law Directory

NORTH DAKOTA

*BISMARCK,** Burleigh Co.

PETERSON, SCHMITZ, MOENCH & SCHMIDT, A PROFESSIONAL CORPORATION (AV)

Second Floor, Suite 200, 116 North Fourth Street, P.O. Box 2076, 58502-2076
Telephone: 701-224-0400
Fax: 701-224-0399

David L. Peterson
Orell D. Schmitz
Dale W. Moench
William D. Schmidt

OF COUNSEL

Gerald Glaser

LEGAL SUPPORT PERSONNEL

Vicki J. Kunz
Traci L. Albers

For full biographical listings, see the Martindale-Hubbell Law Directory

*FARGO,** Cass Co.

CONMY, FESTE, BOSSART, HUBBARD & CORWIN, LTD. (AV)

400 Norwest Center, Fourth Street and Main Avenue, 58126
Telephone: 701-293-9911
Fax: 701-293-3133

Charles A. Feste
David R. Bossart
Paul M. Hubbard
Wickham Corwin
Kim E. Brust
Lauris N. Molbert
Michael M. Thomas
Robert J. Schultz
Nancy J. Morris
Jiming Zhu

OF COUNSEL

E. T. Conmy, Jr.

State Counsel for: Metropolitan Life Insurance Company.
Representative Clients: Ford Motor Credit Co.; Norwest Corporation Region VII Banks (North Dakota & Minnesota West); U.S. Gypsum Co.
Insurance: American Hardware Insurance Group; Great American Insurance Companies; The Maryland.

For full biographical listings, see the Martindale-Hubbell Law Directory

NILLES, HANSEN & DAVIES, LTD. (AV)

1800 Radisson Tower, P.O. Box 2626, 58108
Telephone: 701-237-5544

Timothy Q. Davies
Robert L. Stroup, II
Gregory B. Selbo

Representative Clients: Metropolitan Federal Bank (fsb); First Bank of North Dakota (N.A.); First Trust Company of North Dakota.

For Complete List of Firm Personnel, See General Section

For full biographical listings, see the Martindale-Hubbell Law Directory

VOGEL, BRANTNER, KELLY, KNUTSON, WEIR & BYE, LTD. (AV)

502 First Avenue North, P.O. Box 1389, 58107
Telephone: 701-237-6983
Facsimile: 701-237-0847

David F. Knutson
H. Patrick Weir
Kermit Edward Bye
Jon R. Brakke

Representative Clients: Community First National Bank of Fargo; Ramsey National Bank & Trust Co.; Northwestern Savings Bank FSB; Northern Capital Management Co.; Farmers & Merchants Bank of Valley City; Federal Land Bank of St. Paul; First Trust Company of North Dakota; First International Bank & Trust, Fargo.

For Complete List of Firm Personnel, See General Section

For full biographical listings, see the Martindale-Hubbell Law Directory

OHIO

*CINCINNATI,** Hamilton Co.

DINSMORE & SHOHL (AV)

1900 Chemed Center, 255 East Fifth Street, 45202-3172
Telephone: 513-977-8200
FAX: 513-977-8141
Florence, Kentucky Office: Turfway Ridge Office Park, 7300 Turfway Road, Suite 430 41042-1355.
Telephone: 606-283-0515.
FAX: 606-283-6017.
Dayton, Ohio Office: 500 Courthouse Plaza, S.W., 10 N. Ludlow Street, 45402-1834.
Telephone: 513-228-8012.
FAX: 513-461-2543.
Columbus, Ohio Office: NBD Bank Building, Suite 330, 175 South Third Street, 43215-5134.
Telephone: 614-224-7887.
FAX: 614-224-7882.

MEMBERS OF FIRM

Clifford A. Roe, Jr.
Thomas J. Sherman
Jay A. Rosenberg
S. Richard Arnold
Charles F. Hertlein, Jr.
Joanne M. Schreiner
George H. Vincent
Steven H. Schreiber

ASSOCIATES

Harvey Jay Cohen
Lynn Marmer
John R. Glankler (Resident, Dayton, Ohio Office)
David M. Zuckerman
Susan B. Zaunbrecher
Gregory O. Long
Kent A. Shoemaker

For Complete List of Firm Personnel, See General Section

For full biographical listings, see the Martindale-Hubbell Law Directory

FROST & JACOBS (AV)

2500 PNC Center, 201 East Fifth Street, P.O. Box 5715, 45201-5715
Telephone: 513-651-6800
Cable Address: "Frostjac"
Telex: 21-4396 F & J CIN
Telecopier: 513-651-6981
Columbus, Ohio Office: One Columbus, 10 West Broad Street.
Telephone: 614-464-1211.
Telecopier: 614-464-1737.
Lexington, Kentucky Office: 1100 Vine Center Tower, 333 West Vine Street.
Telephone: 606-254-1100.
Telecopier: 606-253-2990.
Middletown, Ohio Office: 400 First National Bank Building, 2 North Main Street.
Telephone: 513-422-2001.
Telecopier: 513-422-3010.
Naples, Florida Office: 4001 Tamiami Trail North, Suite 220.
Telephone: 813-261-0582.
Telecopier: 813-261-2083.

MEMBERS OF FIRM

Edmund J. Adams
Richard J. Erickson
Jeffery R. Rush
Kathleen W. Carr
Joseph W. Plye
P. Reid Lemasters
Frederick W. Kindel

ASSOCIATES

John C. Krug
David S. Bence
Matthew S. Massarelli
Susan Mechley Lucci
Bryan S. Blade (Not admitted in OH)
Stuart B. Frankel

OF COUNSEL

Kimberly K. Mauer

COLUMBUS, OHIO OFFICE
MEMBER OF FIRM

John I. Cadwallader

LEXINGTON, KENTUCKY OFFICE
MEMBER OF FIRM

Greg E. Mitchell

MIDDLETOWN OFFICE
MEMBERS OF FIRM

Thomas A. Swope

SENIOR ATTORNEY

Daniel J. Picard

NAPLES, FLORIDA OFFICE
PARTNER

Roi E. Baugher, II

Representative Clients: Bank One, Cincinnati, N.A.; Cincinnati Bell, Inc.; Cincinnati Milacron, Inc.; Federated Department Stores; First National Bank of Southwestern Ohio; PNC Bank, Ohio, National Association; Society National Bank; Turner Construction Co.; The United States Shoe Corp.; University of Cincinnati.

(See Next Column)

FROST & JACOBS—*Continued*

For Complete List of Firm Personnel, See General Section

For full biographical listings, see the Martindale-Hubbell Law Directory

KEATING, MUETHING & KLEKAMP (AV)

1800 Provident Tower, One East Fourth Street, 45202
Telephone: 513-579-6400
Facsimile: 513-579-6457

MEMBERS OF FIRM

James R. Whitaker
J. David Rosenberg

Representative Clients: American Financial Corporation; BP America Inc.; Chiquita Brands International, Inc.; The Cincinnati Enquirer; Cintas Corporation; Comair Holdings, Inc.; Duke Associates; LSI Industries Inc.; Mosler Inc.; Provident Bankcorp, Inc.

For Complete List of Firm Personnel, See General Section

For full biographical listings, see the Martindale-Hubbell Law Directory

REISENFELD & STATMAN (AV)

Auburn Barrister House, 2355 Auburn Avenue, 45219
Telephone: 513-381-6810
FAX: 513-381-0255

Sylvan P. Reisenfeld
Alan J. Statman

John L. Day, Jr.
Melisa J. Richter
Bradley A. Reisenfeld
Rosemary E. Scollard
John Schmidt

For full biographical listings, see the Martindale-Hubbell Law Directory

*CLEVELAND,** Cuyahoga Co.

BAKER & HOSTETLER (AV)

3200 National City Center, 1900 East Ninth Street, 44114-3485
Telephone: 216-621-0200
Telecopier: 216-696-0740
TWX: 810 421 8375
RCA Telex: 215032
In Columbus, Ohio: Capitol Square, Suite 2100, 65 East State Street.
Telephone: 614-228-1541.
In Denver, Colorado: 303 East 17th Avenue, Suite 1100.
Telephone: 303-861-0600.
In Houston, Texas: 1000 Louisiana, Suite 2000.
Telephone: 713-751-1600.
In Long Beach, California: 300 Oceangate, Suite 620.
Telephone: 310-432-2827.
In Los Angeles, California: 600 Wilshire Boulevard.
Telephone: 213-624-2400.
In Orlando, Florida: SunBank Center, Suite 2300, 200 South Orange Avenue.
Telephone: 407-649-4000.
In Washington, D. C.: Washington Square, Suite 1100, 1050 Connecticut Avenue, N.W.
Telephone: 202-861-1500.
In College Park, Maryland: 9658 Baltimore Boulevard, Suite 206.
Telephone: 301-441-2781.
In Alexandria, Virginia: 437 North Lee Street.
Telephone: 703-549-1294.
In San Francisco, California: One Sansome Street, Suite 2000.
Telephone: 415-951-4705.

PARTNERS

Albert T. Adams
Susan B. Collins
Richard R. Hollington, Jr.
Norman S. Jeavons
Stephen A. Lenn

OF COUNSEL

Theodore W. Jones

For Complete List of Firm Personnel, See General Section

For full biographical listings, see the Martindale-Hubbell Law Directory

BERICK, PEARLMAN & MILLS A LEGAL PROFESSIONAL ASSOCIATION (AV)

1350 Eaton Center, 1111 Superior Avenue, 44114-2569
Telephone: 216-861-4900
Automatic Telecopier: 216-861-4929

James H. Berick
Samuel S. Pearlman
Osborne Mills, Jr.
Paul J. Singerman
Daniel G. Berick

Laura D. Nemeth

Representative Clients: Cleveland Browns Football Company, Inc.; The Equitable Life Assurance Society of the United States; The Huntington National Bank; National City Bank; The Provident Bank; Realty ReFund Trust; A. Schulman, Inc.; Society National Bank; Third Federal Savings; The Town and Country Trust.

(See Next Column)

For Complete List of Firm Personnel, See General Section

For full biographical listings, see the Martindale-Hubbell Law Directory

THOMPSON, HINE AND FLORY (AV)

1100 National City Bank Building, 629 Euclid Avenue, 44114-3070
Telephone: 216-566-5500
Fax: 216-566-5583
Telex: 980217
Cable Address: "Thomflor"
Akron, Ohio Office: 50 S. Main Street, Suite 502, 44308-1828.
Telephone: 216-376-8090.
Fax: 216-376-8386.
Cincinnati, Ohio Office: 312 Walnut Street, 14th Floor, 45202-4029.
Telephone: 513-352-6700.
Fax: 513-241-4771.
Telex: 938003.
Columbus, Ohio Office: One Columbus, 10 West Broad Street, 43215-3435.
Telephone: 614-469-3200.
Fax: 614-469-3361.
Dayton, Ohio Office: 2000 Courthouse Plaza, N.E., 45402-1706.
Telephone: 513-443-6600.
Fax: 513-443-6637; 443-6635.
Palm Beach, Florida Office: 125 Worth Avenue, Suite 117, 33480-4466.
Telephone: 407-833-5900.
Fax: 407-833-5951.
Washington, D.C. Office: 1920 N Street, N.W., 20036-1601.
Telephone: 202-331-8800.
Fax: 202-331-8330.
Telex: 904173.
Cable Address: "Caglaw".
Brussels, Belgium Office: Rue des Chevaliers, Ridderstraat 14 - B.10, B - 1050.
Telephone: 011(32-2) 511-9326.
Fax: 011(32-2) 513-9206.

MEMBERS OF FIRM

John H. Gherlein (Retired)
Craig R. Martahus
David J. Naftzinger
Thomas C. Stevens

ASSOCIATES

Katherine D. Brandt
Dean D. Gamin

For Complete List of Firm Personnel, See General Section

For full biographical listings, see the Martindale-Hubbell Law Directory

*COLUMBUS,** Franklin Co.

BRICKER & ECKLER (AV)

100 South Third Street, 43215-4291
Telephone: 614-227-2300
Telecopy: 614-227-2390
Cleveland, Ohio Office: 600 Superior Avenue East, Suite 800.
Telephone: 216-771-0720. Fax 216-771-7702.

Stephen K. Yoder
John C. Rosenberger
Gordon W. Johnston
John W. Cook, III
Charles H. McCreary, III
Kenneth C. Johnson
David K. Conrad
L. Brent Miller

Mark J. Palmer
Andrew A. Folkerth
Harry Wright, IV

Representative Clients: Bank One; Chemical Mortgage Company; County Savings Bank; First Indiana Federal Savings Bank; Huntington National Bank; National Bank of Detroit; National City Bank; Society Bank; Star Bank.

For Complete List of Firm Personnel, See General Section

For full biographical listings, see the Martindale-Hubbell Law Directory

EMENS, KEGLER, BROWN, HILL & RITTER (AV)

Capitol Square Suite 1800, 65 East State Street, 43215-4294
Telephone: 614-462-5400
Telecopier: 614-464-2634
Cable Address: "Law EKBHR"
Telex: 246671

J. Richard Emens
Allen L. Handlan
Larry J. McClatchey
Kevin L. Sykes
Beatrice E. Wolper

COUNSEL

John C. Deal
Chalmers P. Wylie

James M. Groner
David M. Johnson

Representative Clients: BancOhio National Bank; State Savings Bank.

For Complete List of Firm Personnel, See General Section

For full biographical listings, see the Martindale-Hubbell Law Directory

Columbus—Continued

PORTER, WRIGHT, MORRIS & ARTHUR (AV)

41 South High Street, 43215-6194
Telephone: 614-227-2000; (800-533-2794)
Telex: 6503213584 MCI
Fax: 614-227-2100
Dayton, Ohio Office: One Dayton Centre, One South Main Street, 45402.
Telephones: 513-228-2411; (800-533-4434).
Fax: 513-449-6820.
Cincinnati, Ohio Office: 250 E. Fifth Street, 45202-4166.
Telephones: 513-381-4700; (800-582-5813).
Fax: 513-421-0991.
Cleveland, Ohio Office: 925 Euclid Avenue, 44115-1483.
Telephones: 216-443-9000; (800-824-1980).
Fax: 216-443-9011.
Washington, D.C. Office: 1233 20th Street, N.W., 20036-2395.
Telephones: 202-778-3000; (800-456-7962).
Fax: 202-778-3063.
Naples, Florida Office: 4501 Tamiami Trail North, 33940-3060.
Telephones: 813-263-8898;(800-876-7962).
Fax: 813-436-2990.

MEMBERS OF FIRM
COLUMBUS, OHIO OFFICE

Michael J. Barren
James P. Botti
John E. Brady
Thomas E. Cavendish
S. Ronald Cook, Jr.
Robert E. Fultz
Timothy E. Grady
Polly J. Harris
John C. Hartranft
George M. Hauswirth
Donald W. Jordan
Robert C. Kiger
Jennifer T. Mills
Jack R. Pigman
James H. Prior
Teri G. Rasmussen
Norman T. Smith
H. Grant Stephenson
Richard G. Terapak
Nancy Belville Young

ASSOCIATES
COLUMBUS, OHIO OFFICE

Heather Lynn Guise
Megan V. Kent
Amy D. Klaben
Waymon B. McLeskey, II
Debra Ann Willet

OF COUNSEL
COLUMBUS, OHIO OFFICE

W. John Pritchard

DAYTON, OHIO OFFICE
RESIDENT MEMBERS

William G. Deas
Roland F. Eichner
Walter Reynolds

DAYTON, OHIO OFFICE
RESIDENT ASSOCIATE

Lawrence S. Walter

CINCINNATI, OHIO OFFICE
RESIDENT MEMBER

James R. Marlow

CINCINNATI, OHIO OFFICE
RESIDENT ASSOCIATES

Stephen P. Kenkel
Francine A. Wayman

CLEVELAND, OHIO OFFICE
RESIDENT MEMBERS

Jeffrey Baddeley
Thomas J. Talcott
John W. Waldeck, Jr.
William R. Weir

WASHINGTON, D.C. OFFICE
MEMBERS

E. Jay Finkel

WASHINGTON, D.C. OFFICE
RESIDENT ASSOCIATE

Matthew Steven Bergman

NAPLES, FLORIDA OFFICE
MEMBERS

W. Jeffrey Cecil (Resident)
James E. Willis (Resident)
Gary K. Wilson (Resident)

NAPLES, FLORIDA OFFICE
RESIDENT ASSOCIATE

Stuart A. Thompson

Representative Clients: Alco-Standard Corporation; American Electric Power Service Corporation; Bank One, Columbus, N.A.; Battelle Memorial Institute; Ford Motor Co.; Huntington Bancshares Incorporated; National City Bank, Columbus; Ohio State Medical Association; Society National Bank; Technical Rubber Co.

For Complete List of Firm Personnel, See General Section

For full biographical listings, see the Martindale-Hubbell Law Directory

VORYS, SATER, SEYMOUR AND PEASE (AV)

52 East Gay Street, P.O. Box 1008, 43216-1008
Telephone: 614-464-6400
Telex: 241348
Telecopier: 614-464-6350
Cable Address: "Vorysater"
Washington, D.C. Office: Suite 1111, 1828 L Street, N.W., 20036-5104.
Telephone: 202-467-8800.
Telex: 440693.
Telecopier: 202-467-8900.
Cleveland, Ohio Office: 2100 One Cleveland Center, 1375 East Ninth Street, 44114-1724.
Telephone: 216-479-6100.
Telecopier: 216-479-6060.
Cincinnati, Ohio Office: Suite 2100, 221 East Fourth Street, P.O. Box 0236, 45201-0236.
Telephone: 513-723-4000.
Telecopier: 513-723-4056.

MEMBERS OF FIRM

Roger A. Yurchuck (Resident, Cincinnati, Ohio Office)
Robert W. Werth
James H. Gross
Leon M. McCorkle, Jr.
Charles S. DeRousie
Frederick R. Reed (Resident, Cincinnati, Ohio Office)
James M. Ball
Roger E. Lautzenhiser
Reginald W. Jackson
Elizabeth Turrell Farrar
Terri Reyering Abare (Resident, Cincinnati, Ohio Office)
Anthony J. O'Malley

Cynthia A. Shafer (Resident, Cincinnati, Ohio Office)
Marianne E. Roche (Resident, Cincinnati, Ohio Office)

Representative Client: Honda of America Mfg., Inc.
Local Counsel: Abbott Laboratories; Anheuser-Busch, Inc.; Connecticut General Life Insurance Co.; Exxon Company U.S.A.; General Motors Corp.; Navistar International Corporation; Ohio Manufacturers Assn.; Ranco Inc.; Wendy's International, Inc.

For Complete List of Firm Personnel, See General Section

For full biographical listings, see the Martindale-Hubbell Law Directory

*DAYTON,** Montgomery Co.

THOMPSON, HINE AND FLORY (AV)

2000 Courthouse Plaza, N.E., 45402-1706
Telephone: 513-443-6600
Fax: 513-443-6637; 443-6635
Akron, Ohio Office: 50 S. Main Street, Suite 502, 44308-1828.
Telephone: 216-376-8090.
Fax: 216-376-8386.
Cincinnati, Ohio Office: 312 Walnut Street, 14th Floor, 45202-4029.
Telephone: 513-352-6700.
Fax: 513-241-4771.
Telex: 938003.
Cleveland, Ohio Office: 1100 National City Bank Building, 629 Euclid Avenue, 44114-3070.
Telephone: 216-566-5500.
Fax: 216-556-5583.
Telex: 980217.
Cable Address: "Thomflor".
Columbus, Ohio Office: One Columbus, 10 West Broad Street, 43215-3435.
Telephone: 614-469-3200.
Fax: 614-469-3361.
Palm Beach, Florida Office: 125 Worth Avenue, 33480-4466.
Telephone: 407-833-5900.
Fax: 407-833-5951.
Washington, D.C. Office: 1920 N Street, N.W., 20036-1601.
Telephone: 202-331-8800.
Fax: 202-331-8330.
Telex: 904173.
Cable Address: "Caglaw".
Brussels, Belgium Office: Rue des Chevaliers / Ridderstraat 14 - B.10, B - 1050.
Telephone: 011(32-2) 511-9326.
Fax: 011(32-2) 513-9206.

MEMBER OF FIRM

Arik A. Sherk

For Complete List of Firm Personnel, See General Section

For full biographical listings, see the Martindale-Hubbell Law Directory

*STEUBENVILLE,** Jefferson Co.

KINSEY, ALLEBAUGH & KING (AV)

200 Sinclair Building, P.O. Box 249, 43952
Telephone: 614-282-1900

MEMBERS OF FIRM

W. I. Kinsey (1876-1962)
Carl F. Allebaugh (1896-1970)
Robert P. King

ASSOCIATE

Robert C. Hargrave

(See Next Column)

KINSEY, ALLEBAUGH & KING—*Continued*

OF COUNSEL

Adam E. Scurti
Otto A. Jack, Jr.

Solicitors for: Consolidated Rail Corporation/Penn Central Transportation Co.
Attorneys for: Ohio Power Co.; Columbia Gas Company of Ohio; Ohio Bell Telephone Co.; Ohio Edison Co.; Continental Casualty Co.; Allstate Insurance Co.; Westfield Cos.; Federal Insurance Co.; Unibank.

For full biographical listings, see the Martindale-Hubbell Law Directory

*TOLEDO,** Lucas Co.

BARKAN AND ROBON (AV)

Suite 405 Spitzer Building, 43604-1302
Telephone: 419-244-5591
FAX: 419-244-8736

MEMBERS OF FIRM

William I. Barkan
Marvin A. Robon
Russell R. Miller
A. Thomas Christensen
Paul A. Radon
Gregory R. Elder

ASSOCIATES

Cynthia Godbey Tesznar
Marshall W. Guerin

For full biographical listings, see the Martindale-Hubbell Law Directory

EASTMAN & SMITH (AV)

One Seagate, Twenty-Fourth Floor, 43604
Telephone: 419-241-6000
Telecopier: 419-247-1777
Columbus, Ohio Office: 65 East State Street, Suite 1000, 43215.
Telephone: 614-460-3556.
Telecopier: 614-228-5371.

MEMBERS OF FIRM

Henry N. Heuerman
Kenneth C. Baker
Steven D. Reinbolt

ASSOCIATES

James L. Rogers
Michael W. Regnier

Representative Clients: The Huntington National Bank; Capital Bank, N.A.; Mid-American National Bank and Trust Co.; Bank One, Cleveland.

For Complete List of Firm Personnel, See General Section

For full biographical listings, see the Martindale-Hubbell Law Directory

SPENGLER NATHANSON (AV)

608 Madison Avenue, Suite 1000, 43604-1169
Telephone: 419-241-2201
FAX: 419-241-8599

MEMBERS OF FIRM

David A. Katz
Ralph Bragg
Theodore M. Rowen
Truman A. Greenwood
Richard E. Wolff
Michael S. Katz
Teresa L. Grigsby

Counsel for: Fifth-Third Bank of Northwestern Ohio, N.A.; Huntington Bank of Toledo; Society Bank & Trust; Citizens National Bank of Norwalk; Capital Bank, N.A.

For Complete List of Firm Personnel, See General Section

For full biographical listings, see the Martindale-Hubbell Law Directory

*YOUNGSTOWN,** Mahoning Co.

HARRINGTON HUXLEY SMITH MITCHELL & REED (AV)

1200 Mahoning Bank Building, 44503-1508
Telephone: 216-744-1111
Telecopier: 216-744-2029

MEMBERS OF FIRM

John C. Litty, Jr.
Robert A. Lenga
Patrick J. Coady

Counsel for: The Mahoning National Bank; WKBN Broadcasting Corp.; WYTV, Inc.
Representative Clients: Ohio Edison Co.; Ohio Bell Telephone Co.; Bank One Cleveland, N.A.

For Complete List of Firm Personnel, See General Section

For full biographical listings, see the Martindale-Hubbell Law Directory

OKLAHOMA

*DUNCAN,** Stephens Co.

ELLIS, LEONARD & BUCKHOLTS (AV)

Patterson Building, 929 West Willow, 73533-4921
Telephone: 405-252-3240
Fax: 405-252-9596

Thomas T. Ellis
Phillip H. Leonard
E. J. Buckholts, II

Reference: Security National Bank & Trust Co., Duncan, Oklahoma.

For full biographical listings, see the Martindale-Hubbell Law Directory

*OKLAHOMA CITY,** Oklahoma Co.

ANDREWS DAVIS LEGG BIXLER MILSTEN & PRICE, A PROFESSIONAL CORPORATION (AV)

500 West Main, 73102
Telephone: 405-272-9241
FAX: 405-235-8786

Carolyn C. Cummins
Alan C. Durbin

Barry Christopher Rooker

OF COUNSEL

John P. Roberts

Representative Clients: The Chase Manhattan Bank, N.A.; Local Federal Bank, N.A.; BancFirst; First National Bank of Bethany; United Bank Services; Sanwa Business Credit Corp.

For Complete List of Firm Personnel, See General Section

For full biographical listings, see the Martindale-Hubbell Law Directory

BRITTON AND ADCOCK (AV)

Suite 670, 101 Park Avenue, 73102
Telephone: 405-239-2393
Fax: 405-232-5135

James E. Britton

For full biographical listings, see the Martindale-Hubbell Law Directory

DAY, EDWARDS, FEDERMAN, PROPESTER & CHRISTENSEN, P.C. (AV)

Suite 2900 First Oklahoma Tower, 210 Park Avenue, 73102-5605
Telephone: 405-239-2121
Telecopier: 405-236-1012

Bruce W. Day
Joe E. Edwards
William B. Federman
Richard P. Propester
D. Wade Christensen
J. Clay Christensen
Kent A. Gilliland
Rodney J. Heggy
Ricki Valerie Sonders
Thomas Pitchlynn Howell, IV
John C. Platt

David R. Widdoes
Lori R. Roberts
Carolyn A. Romberg

OF COUNSEL

Herbert F. (Jack) Hewett
Jeanette Cook Timmons
Joel Warren Harmon
Jane S. Eulberg
Mark A. Cohen

Representative Clients: Aetna Life Insurance Co.; Boatmen's First National Bank of Oklahoma; Borg-Warner Chemicals, Inc.; City Bank & Trust; Federal Deposit Insurance Corp.; Bank One, Oklahoma City; Haskell Lemon Construction Co.; Merrill Lynch, Pierce, Fenner & Smith, Inc.; Prudential Securities, Inc.

For full biographical listings, see the Martindale-Hubbell Law Directory

HARTZOG CONGER & CASON, A PROFESSIONAL CORPORATION (AV)

1600 Bank of Oklahoma Plaza, 73102
Telephone: 405-235-7000
Facsimile: 405-235-7329

Larry D. Hartzog
J. William Conger
Len Cason
James C. Prince
Alan Newman
Steven C. Davis
Valerie K. Couch
Mark D. Dickey
Joseph P. Hogsett
John D. Robertson
Kurt M. Rupert
Laura Haag McConnell

Susan B. Shields
Ryan S. Wilson
Melanie J. Jester
Armand Paliotta
Julia Watson
J. Leslie LaReau

(See Next Column)

HARTZOG CONGER & CASON A PROFESSIONAL CORPORATION, *Oklahoma City—Continued*

OF COUNSEL

Kent F. Frates

For full biographical listings, see the Martindale-Hubbell Law Directory

HASTIE AND KIRSCHNER, A PROFESSIONAL CORPORATION (AV)

3000 Oklahoma Tower, 210 Park Avenue, 73102-5604
Telephone: 405-239-6404
Telecopier: 405-239-6403

Mark H. Bennett
Mitchell D. Blackburn
George W. Dahnke
John W. Funk
John D. Hastie
Michael Paul Kirschner
Ronald L. Matlock
Kieran D. Maye, Jr.
Robert D. McCutcheon
Kiran A. Phansalkar
Irwin H. Steinhorn
John W. Swinford, Jr.
Ruston C. Welch

OF COUNSEL

William S. Price

For Complete List of Firm Personnel, See General Section

For full biographical listings, see the Martindale-Hubbell Law Directory

MOCK, SCHWABE, WALDO, ELDER, REEVES & BRYANT, A PROFESSIONAL CORPORATION (AV)

Fifteenth Floor, One Leadership Square, 211 North Robinson Avenue, 73102
Telephone: 405-235-5500
Telecopy: 405-235-2875

James C. Elder
Gary A. Bryant

Representative Clients: Bank of Hydro; Bank of Oklahoma, N.A.; Central National Bank of Alva; Continental Bank, N.A.; Equity Bank for Savings, F.A.; Farm Credit Bank of Wichita; Federal Deposit Insurance Corporation; First United Bank & Trust Company of Holdenville; Hopeton State Bank; Kingfisher Bank & Trust Company; Bank of Oklahoma, N.A.

For Complete List of Firm Personnel, See General Section

For full biographical listings, see the Martindale-Hubbell Law Directory

PRINGLE & PRINGLE, A PROFESSIONAL CORPORATION (AV)

1601 N.W. Expressway, Suite 2100, 73118
Telephone: 405-848-4810
Fax: 405-848-4819

Lynn A. Pringle
Laura Nan Smith Pringle
Conni L. Allen
Stephen W. Elliott
James R. Martin, Jr.

OF COUNSEL

Alvin C. Harrell
Michael P. Sullivan

Representative Clients: Bankers Systems, Inc.; Central Oklahoma Clearing House Association; The Bankers Bank; Bank of Western Oklahoma, Elk City; The First National Bank and Trust Co., Chickasha; The First National Bank of Texhoma; The Citizens State Bank; Okemah; Oklahoma Home Bases Business Association; First State Bank, Idabel; The Farmers Bank, Carnagie.

For full biographical listings, see the Martindale-Hubbell Law Directory

SELF, GIDDENS & LEES, INC. (AV)

2725 Oklahoma Tower, 210 Park Avenue, 73102-5604
Telephone: 405-232-3001
Telecopier: 405-232-5553

Jared D. Giddens
C. Ray Lees
Shannon T. Self

Thomas J. Blalock
Christopher R. Graves
W. Shane Smithton
Bryan J. Wells

For full biographical listings, see the Martindale-Hubbell Law Directory

*SHAWNEE,** Pottawatomie Co.

DIAMOND, STUART & CLOVER (AV)

Formerly Miller, Peters, Diamond & Stuart
116 North Bell, P.O. Box 1925, 74802-1925
Telephone: 405-275-0700
Telecopy: 405-275-6805

MEMBERS OF FIRM

H. Jeffrey Diamond
James T. Stuart
Michael D. Clover

OF COUNSEL

Lindsay Peters

Representative Clients: Oklahoma Gas & Electric Co.; Shawnee Urban Renewal Authority; TDK Ferrites Corp.; Mobil Chemical Co.

(See Next Column)

General Counsel: BancFirst, Shawnee; Central Plastics Co.
Approved Examining Attorneys for: Southwest Title & Trust Co., Oklahoma City; Lawyers Title Insurance Corp.; American First Title & Trust Co., Oklahoma City.

For full biographical listings, see the Martindale-Hubbell Law Directory

*TULSA,** Tulsa Co.

BOESCHE, McDERMOTT & ESKRIDGE (AV)

Suite 800 Oneok Plaza, 100 West Fifth Street, 74103
Telephone: 918-583-1777
Fax: 918-592-5809
Muskogee, Oklahoma Office: 420 Broadway, 74101.
Telephone: 918-683-6100.

MEMBERS OF FIRM

David B. McKinney
Bradley K. Beasley

ASSOCIATE

Sheila M. Powers

Representative Clients: Bank of America; The Chase Manhattan Bank; Community Bank & Trust Co.; Federal Deposit Insurance Corp.; Resolution Trust Corp.; Superior Federal Bank; Union Bank, formerly Security Pacific National Bank; Vian State Bank.

For Complete List of Firm Personnel, See General Section

For full biographical listings, see the Martindale-Hubbell Law Directory

BOONE, SMITH, DAVIS, HURST & DICKMAN, A PROFESSIONAL CORPORATION (AV)

500 Oneok Plaza, 100 West 5th Street, 74103
Telephone: 918-587-0000
Fax: 918-599-9317

Byron V. Boone (1908-1988)
Royce H. Savage (1904-1993)
L. K. Smith
Reuben Davis
J. Jerry Dickman
Frederic N. (Nick) Schneider III
William C. Kellough
J Schaad Titus
John A. Burkhardt
Paul E. Swain III
Carol A. Grissom
Kimberly Lambert Love
Teresa Meinders Burkett
Paul J. Cleary

R. Tom Hillis
Barry G. Reynolds
Laura L. Gonsalves
Scott R. Rowland
Shane Egan
Nancy Lynn Davis

OF COUNSEL

Edwin S. Hurst
Lloyd G. Minter

Representative Clients: American Airlines; Chevron U.S.A., Inc.; The F & M Bank & Trust Co.; Hillcrest Medical Center; Boatmen's First National Bank of Oklahoma; Phillips Petroleum Co.; Rockwell International; Sears, Roebuck & Co.; Thrifty Rent-A-Car Systems, Inc.; World Publishing Co.

For full biographical listings, see the Martindale-Hubbell Law Directory

GABLE & GOTWALS (AV)

2000 Bank IV Center, 15 West Sixth Street, 74119-5447
Telephone: 918-582-9201
Facsimile: 918-586-8383

Teresa B. Adwan
Pamela S. Anderson
John R. Barker
David L. Bryant
Gene C. Buzzard
Dennis Clarke Cameron
Timothy A. Carney
Renee DeMoss
Elsie C. Draper
Sidney G. Dunagan
Theodore Q. Eliot
Richard W. Gable
Jeffrey Don Hassell
Patricia Ledvina Himes
Oliver S. Howard
Richard D. Koljack, Jr.
J. Daniel Morgan
Joseph W. Morris
Elizabeth R. Muratet
Richard B. Noulles
Ronald N. Ricketts
John Henry Rule
M. Benjamin Singletary
James M. Sturdivant
Patrick O. Waddel
Michael D. Hall
David Edward Keglovits
Stephen W. Lake
Kari S. McKee
Terry D. Ragsdale
Jeffrey C. Rambach

OF COUNSEL

G. Ellis Gable
Charles P. Gotwals, Jr.

For full biographical listings, see the Martindale-Hubbell Law Directory

HUFFMAN ARRINGTON KIHLE GABERINO & DUNN, A PROFESSIONAL CORPORATION (AV)

1000 ONEOK Plaza, 74103
Telephone: 918-585-8141
Telecopier: 918-588-7873
Oklahoma City Office: 2212 NW 50th Street, Suite 163.
Telephone: 405-840-4408.
Telecopier: 405-843-9090.

(See Next Column)

Huffman Arrington Kihle Gaberino & Dunn A Professional Corporation—*Continued*

John A. Gaberino, Jr. Sidney K. Swinson
Barry K. Beasley

General Counsel for: ONEOK Inc.; Oklahoma Natural Gas Co.; H W Allen Co.; ONEOK Exploration Co.; Woodland Bank; ONEOK Drilling Co.; ONEOK Resources Co.; Renberg's, Inc.

For Complete List of Firm Personnel, See General Section

For full biographical listings, see the Martindale-Hubbell Law Directory

James, Potts and Wulfers (AV)

Suite 705, 320 South Boston Avenue, 74103-3712
Telephone: 918-584-0881
FAX: 918-584-4521

MEMBERS OF FIRM

David F. James Thomas G. Potts
David W. Wulfers

For full biographical listings, see the Martindale-Hubbell Law Directory

Joyce and Pollard (AV)

Suite 300, 515 South Main Mall, 74103
Telephone: 918-585-2751
Fax: 918-582-9308

MEMBERS OF FIRM

J. C. Joyce Dwayne C. Pollard

Ted J. Nelson Sheila M. Bradley
John C. Joyce

A list of Representative Clients furnished upon request.

For full biographical listings, see the Martindale-Hubbell Law Directory

Sneed, Lang, Adams & Barnett, A Professional Corporation (AV)

2300 Williams Center Tower II, Two West Second Street, 74103
Telephone: 918-583-3145
Telecopier: 918-582-0410

James C. Lang
D. Faith Orlowski
Brian S. Gaskill
G. Steven Stidham
Stephen R. McNamara
Thomas E. Black, Jr.
Robbie Emery Burke
C. Raymond Patton, Jr.
Frederick K. Slicker
Richard D. Black
John D. Russell
Jeffrey S. Swyers

OF COUNSEL

James L. Sneed O. Edwin Adams
Howard G. Barnett, Jr.

Representative Clients: Amoco Production Company; Continental Bank; Deloitte & Touche; Enron Corporation; Halliburton Energy Services; Helmerich & Payne, Inc.; Lehman Brothers, Inc.; Shell Oil Company; Smith Barney, Inc.; State Farm Mutual Automobile Insurance Company.

For full biographical listings, see the Martindale-Hubbell Law Directory

OREGON

*PORTLAND,** Multnomah Co.

Black Helterline (AV)

1200 The Bank of California Tower, 707 S.W. Washington Street, 97205
Telephone: 503-224-5560
Telecopier: 503-224-6148

MEMBERS OF FIRM

John M. McGuigan Richard N. Roskie
Michael O. Moran David P. Roy

ASSOCIATES

Deneen M. Hubertin Donald L. Krahmer, Jr.

OF COUNSEL

Robert E. Glasgow

Representative Clients: The Bank of California, N.A.; Mitsubishi Bank, Ltd.; The Bank of Tokyo, Ltd.; Royal Bank of Canada.

For Complete List of Firm Personnel, See General Section

For full biographical listings, see the Martindale-Hubbell Law Directory

PENNSYLVANIA

BLUE BELL, Montgomery Co.

Lesser & Kaplin, Professional Corporation (AV)

350 Sentry Parkway, Bldg. 640, 19422-0757
Telephone: 610-828-2900; Telecopier: 610-828-1555
Marlton, New Jersey Office: Three Greentree Centre, Suite 104, Route 73, 08053-3215.
Telephone: 609-596-2400.
Telecopier: 609-596-8185.

Lawrence R. Lesser
Bruce R. Lesser
Harold G. Cohen (Resident, Marlton, New Jersey Office)
Anthony J. Krol
Katherine F. Bastian
Sara Lee Keller-Smith

Alan P. Fox (Resident, Marlton, New Jersey Office)
Richard Mark Zucker
Maulin S. Vidwans
Stephan A. Hartman

For full biographical listings, see the Martindale-Hubbell Law Directory

*EASTON,** Northampton Co.

Herster, Newton & Murphy (AV)

127 North Fourth Street, P.O. Box 1087, 18042
Telephone: 610-258-6219

MEMBERS OF FIRM

Andrew L. Herster, Jr. Henry R. Newton
William K. Murphy

General Counsel For: Valley Federal Savings & Loan Assn.; Lafayette Bank; Easton Printing Co.; Northampton Community College; Eisenhardt Mills, Inc.; Delaware Wood Products, Inc.; Panuccio Construction, Inc.
References: Merchants Bank, N.A.; Lafayette Bank; Valley Federal Savings and Loan.

*HARRISBURG,** Dauphin Co.

Mette, Evans & Woodside, A Professional Corporation (AV)

3401 North Front Street, P.O. Box 5950, 17110-0950
Telephone: 717-232-5000
Telecopier: 717-236-1816

Peter J. Ressler James A. Ulsh
Lloyd R. Persun Glen R. Grell
Elyse E. Rogers

Representative Clients: Commerce Bank; Community Banks, N.A.

For Complete List of Firm Personnel, See General Section

For full biographical listings, see the Martindale-Hubbell Law Directory

Nauman, Smith, Shissler & Hall (AV)

Eighteenth Floor, 200 North Third Street, P.O. Box 840, 17108-0840
Telephone: 717-236-3010
Telefax: 717-234-1925

MEMBERS OF FIRM

David C. Eaton John C. Sullivan
Spencer G. Nauman, Jr. J. Stephen Feinour
Craig J. Staudenmaier

ASSOCIATES

Benjamin Charles Dunlap, Jr. Stephen J. Keene

OF COUNSEL

Ralph W. Boyles, Jr.

Representative Clients: Mellon Bank, N.A.; PNC Bank, N.A.; General Motors Acceptance Corp.; Chrysler Credit Corp.; Capital Area Tax Collection Bureau.

For full biographical listings, see the Martindale-Hubbell Law Directory

Rhoads & Sinon (AV)

One South Market Square, 12th Floor, P.O. Box 1146, 17108-1146
Telephone: 717-233-5731
Fax: 717-232-1459
Boca Raton, Florida Affiliated Office: Suite 301, 299 West Camino Gardens Boulevard.
Telephone: 407-395-5595.
Fax: 407-395-9497.
Lancaster, Pennsylvania Office: 15 North Lime Street.
Telephone: 717-397-5127.
Fax: 717-397-5267.

(See Next Column)

RHOADS & SINON, *Harrisburg—Continued*

MEMBERS OF FIRM

Henry W. Rhoads
Sherill T. Moyer
J. Bruce Walter
Charles J. Ferry
Stanley A. Smith
Drake D. Nicholas
Dean H. Dusinberre
Donna M. J. Clark
Paul F. Wessell

ASSOCIATE

Virginia P. Henschel

For Complete List of Firm Personnel, See General Section

For full biographical listings, see the Martindale-Hubbell Law Directory

SHUMAKER WILLIAMS, A PROFESSIONAL CORPORATION (AV)

3425 Simpson Ferry Road (Camp Hill), P.O. Box 88, 17108-0088
Telephone: 717-763-1121
State College, PA: 814-234-3211
Maryland: 301-876-6190
Telecopier: 717-763-7419

Keith A. Clark
Paul A. Adams
Laurence W. Dague
Nicholas Bybel, Jr.
John J. Shumaker
Jerald P. Hurwitz
Glenn R. Davis
Michael L. Hund
Anthony J. Foschi
Raja G. Rajan
Robin M. Wilder
John D. Rigsby
Robert C. May

For full biographical listings, see the Martindale-Hubbell Law Directory

LANSDALE, Montgomery Co.

PEARLSTINE/SALKIN ASSOCIATES (AV)

1250 South Broad Street Suite 1000, P.O. Box 431, 19446
Telephone: 215-699-6000
Fax: 215-699-0231

MEMBERS OF FIRM

Philip Salkin
Ronald E. Robinson
Barry Cooperberg
Frederick C. Horn
Marc B. Davis
William R. Wanger
F. Craig La Rocca
Jeffrey T. Sultanik
Neal R. Pearlstine
Wendy G. Rothstein
Alan L. Eisen
Glenn D. Fox

Wilhelm L. Gruszecki
Brian E. Subers
Mark S. Cappuccio
James R. Hall
Michael S. Paul
David J. Draganosky
Lawrence P. Kempner

For full biographical listings, see the Martindale-Hubbell Law Directory

*PHILADELPHIA,** Philadelphia Co.

ANDERSON GREENFIELD & DOUGHERTY (AV)

1525 Penn Mutual Tower 510 Walnut Street, 19106-3610
Telephone: 215-627-0789
Fax: 215-627-0813
Wayne, Pennsylvania Office: First Fidelity Bank Building, 301 West Lancaster Avenue.
Telephone: 215-341-9010.

MEMBERS OF FIRM

Susan L. Anderson
Marjorie E. Greenfield
Donna Dougherty

ASSOCIATES

John Randolph Prince, III
Linda K. Hobkirk

For full biographical listings, see the Martindale-Hubbell Law Directory

BALLARD SPAHR ANDREWS & INGERSOLL (AV)

1735 Market Street, 51st Floor, 19103-7599
Telephone: 215-665-8500
Fax: 215-864-8999
Denver, Colorado Office: Seventeenth Street Plaza Building, Suite 2300, 1225 17th Street.
Telephone: 303-292-2400.
Fax: 303-296-3956.
Kaunas, Lithuania Office: Donelaicio g., 71-2, Kaunas 3000.
Telephone: (370-7) 20 56 66.
Fax: (370-7) 20 56 91.
Salt Lake City, Utah Office: One Utah Center, Suite 1200, 201 South Main Street.
Telephone: 801-531-3000.
Fax: 801-531-3001.
Washington, D.C. Office: Suite 900 East, 555 13th Street, N.W.
Telephone: 202-383-8800.
Fax: 202-383-8877; 383-8893.
Baltimore, Maryland Office: 300 East Lombard Street. 19th Floor.
Telephone: 410-528-5600.
Fax: 410-528-5650.

(See Next Column)

Camden, New Jersey Office: 800 Hudson Square, 5th Floor.
Telephone: 609-541-5577.
Fax: 609-541-8272.

E. Carolan Berkley
William H. Rheiner
Carl H. Fridy
Edward D. Slevin

Brian D. Doerner
Peter W. Laberee
Randall J. Towers

For Complete List of Firm Personnel, See General Section

For full biographical listings, see the Martindale-Hubbell Law Directory

BUCHANAN INGERSOLL, PROFESSIONAL CORPORATION (AV)

Two Logan Square Twelfth Floor, 18th & Arch Streets, 19103
Telephone: 215-665-8700
Telecopier: 215-569-2066
Pittsburgh, Pennsylvania Office: 5800 USX Tower, 600 Grant Street.
Telephone: 412-562-8800.
Harrisburg, Pennsylvania Office: Vartan Parc, 30 North Third Street.
Telephone: 717-237-4800.
Tampa, Florida Office: 101 East Kennedy Boulevard, Suite 1030.
Telephone: 813-222-8180.
North Miami Beach, Florida Office: 19495 Biscayne Boulevard.
Telephone: 305-933-5600.
Lexington, Kentucky Office: 1210 Vine Center Office Tower, 333 West Vine Street.
Telephone: 606-225-5333.
Princeton, New Jersey Office: Buchanan Ingersoll, A Partnership, College Centre, 500 College Road East.
Telephone: 609-452-2666.

Lawrence J. Lichtenstein

Stuart M. Brown

For Complete List of Firm Personnel, See General Section

For full biographical listings, see the Martindale-Hubbell Law Directory

FELLHEIMER EICHEN BRAVERMAN & KASKEY, A PROFESSIONAL CORPORATION (AV)

21st Floor, One Liberty Place, 19103-7334
Telephone: 215-575-3800
FAX: 215-575-3801
Camden, New Jersey Office: 519 Federal Street, Suite 503 Parkade Building, 08103-1147.
Telephone: 609-541-5323.
Fax: 609-541-5370.

Alan S. Fellheimer
David L. Braverman
Judith Eichen Fellheimer
John E. Kaskey
Kenneth S. Goodkind
Anna Hom
Peter E. Meltzer

Barbara Anisko
Maia R. Caplan
Jeffrey L. Eichen
Michael N. Feder
Jolie G. Kahn
George F. Newton
David B. Spitofsky
W. Thomas Tither, Jr.

For Complete List of Firm Personnel, See General Section

For full biographical listings, see the Martindale-Hubbell Law Directory

KLEHR, HARRISON, HARVEY, BRANZBURG & ELLERS (AV)

1401 Walnut Street, 19102
Telephone: 215-568-6060
Fax: 215-568-6603
Cherry Hill, New Jersey Office: Colwick-Suite 200, 51 Haddonfield Road.
Telephone: 609-486-7900.
Fax: 609-486-4875.
Allentown, Pennsylvania Office: Roma Corporate Center, Suite 501, 1605 North Cedar Crest Boulevard.
Telephone: 215-432-1803.
Fax: 215-433-4031.
Wilmington, Delaware Office: 222 Delaware Avenue, Suite 1101.
Telephone: 302-426-1189.
Fax: 302-426-9193.

MEMBERS OF FIRM

Donald M. Harrison
Robert C. Seiger, Jr.
John Spelman
Stephen T. Burdumy
Richard S. Roisman
Stuart K. Askot
Mark S. Kenney

ASSOCIATES

Marcy Newman Hart
Stewart Paley
Frederick J. Fisher

For Complete List of Firm Personnel, See General Section

For full biographical listings, see the Martindale-Hubbell Law Directory

Philadelphia—Continued

MANNINO GRIFFITH P.C. (AV)

2400 One Commerce Square, 19103
Telephone: 215-851-6300
Fax: 215-851-6315
Camden, New Jersey Office: 411 Cooper Street, Suite 3A, 08102.
Telephone: 609-964-3661.
Fax: 609-964-3626

James Lewis Griffith
Edward F. Mannino
Michael C. Hemsley
Virginia Lynn Hogben

OF COUNSEL

Richard T. Nassberg

Jack J. Bernstein
Charlotte E. Thomas
Amy L. Currier
Deborah Susan Baird-Diamond
Susan J. French
Peter A. Garcia
Johanna Smith
Martin J. Beck
Brett L. Messinger
David L. Comerford
Deirdre M. Richards
Michelle A. Fioravanti
William Christopher Duerr

For full biographical listings, see the Martindale-Hubbell Law Directory

PATTERSON & WEIR (AV)

Suite 1200, Land Title Building, 100 South Broad Street, 19110
Telephone: 215-665-8181
Telefax: 215-665-8464
Westmont, New Jersey Office: 216 Haddon Avenue, Suite 704, Sentry Office Plaza, 08108.
Telephone: 609-858-6100.
Telefax: 609-858-4606.

MEMBERS OF FIRM

Walter Weir, Jr.
Paul A. Patterson
Brent S. Gorey
Daniel S. Bernheim, III
Mark E. Herrera (Resident, Westmont, New Jersey Office)

ASSOCIATES

David J. Toll
Susan Verbonitz
Robert D. Sayre
Jonathan J. Bart
Scott C. Pyfer (Resident, Westmont, New Jersey Office)
Lee Ann M. Williams, Jr
Douglas J. McGill
Harry J. Giacometti

For full biographical listings, see the Martindale-Hubbell Law Directory

STRONG, STEVENS, BRISCOE & HAMILTON, P.C. (AV)

4000 Bell Atlantic Tower, 1717 Arch Street, 19103
Telephone: 215-563-5900
Fax: 215-563-2982
Blue Bell, Pennsylvania Office: 640 Sentry Parkway, First Floor.
Telephone: 215-832-5900.
Fax: 215-832-5914.

George V. Strong, Jr.
Richard K. Stevens, Jr.
James H. Stevens
Jack C. Briscoe
Jeffrey F. Janoski
Emory A. Wyant, Jr.
Thomas R. Kellogg
Ronald W. Fenstermacher, Jr.
Ralf W. Greenwood, Jr.
Mary K. Lemmon

COUNSEL

Samuel L. Sagendorph

For full biographical listings, see the Martindale-Hubbell Law Directory

*PITTSBURGH,** Allegheny Co.

BUCHANAN INGERSOLL, PROFESSIONAL CORPORATION (AV)

5800 USX Tower, 600 Grant Street, 15219
Telephone: 412-562-8800
Telecopier: 412-562-1041
Philadelphia, Pennsylvania Office: Two Logan Square, Twelfth Floor, 18th & Arch Streets.
Telephone: 215-665-8700.
Harrisburg, Pennsylvania Office: Vartan Parc, 30 North Third Street.
Telephone: 717-237-4800.
Tampa, Florida Office: 101 East Kennedy Boulevard, Suite 1030.
Telephone: 813-222-8180.
North Miami Beach, Florida Office: 19495 Biscayne Boulevard.
Telephone: 305-933-5600.
Lexington, Kentucky Office: 1210 Vine Center Office Tower, 333 West Vine Street.
Telephone: 606-225-5333.
Princeton, New Jersey Office: Buchanan Ingersoll, A Partnership, College Centre, 500 College Road East.
Telephone: 609-452-2666.

(See Next Column)

George L. Cass
Lewis U. Davis, Jr.
Calvin R. Harvey
Stephen W. Johnson
M. Bruce McCullough
Gary Philip Nelson
John M. Rumin
Michael A. Snyder
James R. Sweeny
Hugh G. Van der Veer
Paula A. Zawadzki

COUNSEL

Margaret B. Angel

SENIOR ATTORNEYS

Joan G. Dorgan
Reginald J. Weatherly

Jeffrey P. Bauman
Thomas S. Galey
Harrison S. Lauer
Donald E. Malecki
Daniel Alan O'Connor
Peter S. Russ
Joseph S. Sisca
Deborah B. Walrath
Pamela K. Wiles

For Complete List of Firm Personnel, See General Section

For full biographical listings, see the Martindale-Hubbell Law Directory

GACA, MATIS & HAMILTON, A PROFESSIONAL CORPORATION (AV)

300 Four PPG Place, 15222-5404
Telephone: 412-338-4750
Fax: 412-338-4742

Giles J. Gaca
Thomas A. Matis
Mark R. Hamilton
John W. Jordan, IV
Alan S. Baum
Thomas P. McGinnis
Bernard R. Rizza
Jeffrey A. Ramaley
Stephen J. Dalesio
John Timothy Hinton, Jr.
Shawn Lynne Reed

LEGAL SUPPORT PERSONNEL

PARALEGALS

Tina M. Shanafelt
Jill M. Peterson

For full biographical listings, see the Martindale-Hubbell Law Directory

TUCKER ARENSBERG, P.C. (AV)

1500 One PPG Place, 15222
Telephone: 412-566-1212
Telex: 902914
Fax: 412-594-5619
Harrisburg, Pennsylvania Office: 116 Pine Street.
Telephone: 717-238-2007.
Fax: 717-238-2242.
Pittsburgh Airport Area Office: Airport Professional Office Center, 1150 Thorn Run Road Ext., Moon Township, Pennsylvania, 15108.
Telephone: 412-262-3730.
Fax: 412-262-2576.

Charles F. C. Arensberg (1879-1974)
Frank R. S. Kaplan (1886-1957)
Donald L. Very (1933-1979)
Linda A. Acheson
W. Theodore Brooks
Matthew J. Carl
Richard W. Cramer
J. Kent Culley
Donald P. Eriksen
Paul F. Fagan
Gary J. Gushard
William T. Harvey
Joel M. Helmrich
Gary P. Hunt
Raymond M. Komichak
Jeffrey J. Leech
Beverly Weiss Manne
Garland H. McAdoo, Jr.
John M. McElroy
Robert L. McTiernan
John B. Montgomery
Stanley V. Ostrow
William A. Penrod
Daniel J. Perry
Henry S. Pool
Richard B. Tucker, III
Bradley S. Tupi
Charles J. Vater
Gary E. Wieczorek
G. Ashley Woolridge

Donald E. Ambrose
Robin K. Capozzi
Diane Hernon Chavis
Toni L. DiGiacobbe
Donna M. Donaher
John E. Graf
Mark L. Heleen
David P. Hvizdos
Timothy S. Johnson
Joni L. Landy
Jonathan S. McAnney
G. Ross Rhodes
Christopher J. Richardson
Eric M. Schumann
Steven H. Seel
Steven B. Silverman
Michael J. Tobak, III
Homer L. Walton

HARRISBURG OFFICE

J. Kent Culley

John G. Di Leonardo

SPECIAL COUNSEL

Richard S. Crone
Elliott W. Finkel
Michael J. Laffey
John P. Papuga
William J. Staley
Richard B. Tucker, Jr.

For full biographical listings, see the Martindale-Hubbell Law Directory

*READING,** Berks Co.

BINGAMAN, HESS, COBLENTZ & BELL, A PROFESSIONAL CORPORATION (AV)

660 Penn Square Center, 601 Penn Street, P.O. Box 61, 19603-0061
Telephone: 610-374-8377
Fax: 610-376-3105
Bernville, Pennsylvania Office: 331 Main Street.
Telephone: 610-488-0656.
Camden, New Jersey Office: 411 Cooper Street.
Telephone: 609-966-0117.
Fax: 609-965-0796.

James F. Bell (1921-1988)

OF COUNSEL

Llewellyn R. Bingaman
Raymond K. Hess
J. Wendell Coblentz
Ralph J. Althouse, Jr.
Gerald P. Sigal

David E. Turner
Clemson North Page, Jr.
Mark G. Yoder
Carl D. Cronrath, Jr.
Kurt Althouse
Harry D. McMunigal
Karen Feryo Longenecker
Shawn J. Lau

Lynne K. Beust
Elizabethanne D. McMunigal
Patrick T. Barrett
Susan N. Denaro
Daniel J. Poruban
Jill M. Scheidt

LEGAL SUPPORT PERSONNEL

Eric A. Barr (Office Administrator)

PARALEGALS

JoAnn Ruchlewicz
Laura I. Lehane
Louise E. Miller
Ruth Ann Sunderland
Kristine L. Krammes
Peter L. Torres

General Counsel for: Meridian Bank; Berks Products Corp.; Leighton Industries, Inc.; Utilities Employees Credit Union.
Local Counsel for: Erie Insurance Exchange; Liberty Mutual Insurance Co.; Old Guard Mutual Insurance Co.

For full biographical listings, see the Martindale-Hubbell Law Directory

MOGEL, SPEIDEL, BOBB & KERSHNER, A PROFESSIONAL CORPORATION (AV)

520 Walnut Street, P.O. Box 8581, 19603-8581
Telephone: 610-376-1515
Telecopier: 610-372-8710

George B. Balmer (1902-1969)
George A. Kershner (1907-1969)
Carl F. Mogel (1919-1994)
Donald K. Bobb
Edwin H. Kershner
Frederick R. Mogel
Samuel R. Fry II
Kathleen A. B. Kovach
Michael L. Mixell
George M. Lutz
Stephen H. Price
Kathryn K. Harenza

OF COUNSEL

Harry W. Speidel
Henry A. Gass

Representative Clients: Great Valley Savings Bank; Clover Farms Dairy Co.; National Penn Bank; Meridian Leasing, Inc.; Ducharme, McMillen & Associates; Edwards Business Machines, Inc.; Greater Berks Development Fund; Union Township, Berks County, Pennsylvania.

For full biographical listings, see the Martindale-Hubbell Law Directory

*WEST CHESTER,** Chester Co.

MACELREE, HARVEY, GALLAGHER, FEATHERMAN & SEBASTIAN, LTD. (AV)

17 West Miner Street, P.O. Box 660, 19381-0660
Telephone: 610-436-0100
Fax: 610-430-7885
Kennett Square, Pennsylvania Office: 211 E. State Street, P. O. Box 363.
Telephone 215-444-3180.
Fax: 215-444-3270.
Spring City, Pennsylvania Office: 3694 Schuylkill Road.
Telephone: 215-948-5700.

Lawrence E. MacElree
Dominic T. Marrone
William J. Gallagher
John A. Featherman, III
Randy L. Sebastian
Terry W. Knox
Michael G. Louis
Randall C. Schauer
Stacey W. McConnell
Frederick P. Kramer, II
John F. McKenna
C. Douglas Parvin
Harry J. DiDonato
Lance J. Nelson
Bernadette M. Walsh
Linda C. Tice
Joseph F. Harvey (1921-1985)
J. Barton Rettew, Jr. (1901-1981)
Richard Reifsnyder (1928-1974)

For full biographical listings, see the Martindale-Hubbell Law Directory

*WILLIAMSPORT,** Lycoming Co.

MCCORMICK, REEDER, NICHOLS, BAHL, KNECHT & PERSON (AV)

(Formerly McCormick, Herdic & Furst).
835 West Fourth Street, 17701
Telephone: 717-326-5131
Fax: 717-326-5529

OF COUNSEL

Henry Clay McCormick

MEMBERS OF FIRM

S. Dale Furst, Jr. (1904-1969)
Robert J. Sarno (1941-1982)
Paul W. Reeder
William E. Nichols
David R. Bahl
William L. Knecht
John E. Person, III
J. David Smith
Robert A. Eckenrode
Cynthia Ranck Person

ASSOCIATES

Joanne C. Ludwikowski
R. Matthew Patch
Sean P. Roman
Kenneth B. Young

General Counsel for: Northern Central Bank; Jersey Shore Steel Co.
Representative Clients: Pennsylvania Power & Light Co.; Consolidated Rail Corp.; Royal Insurance Co.; State Automobile Insurance Association.

For full biographical listings, see the Martindale-Hubbell Law Directory

MURPHY, BUTTERFIELD, HOLLAND & PRICE, P.C. (AV)

442 William Street, 17701
Telephone: 717-326-6505
Fax: 717-326-0437

Bertram S. Murphy
Jonathan E. Butterfield
Fred A. Holland
George R. Price, Jr.

Reference: Commonwealth Bank.

For full biographical listings, see the Martindale-Hubbell Law Directory

RHODE ISLAND

*PROVIDENCE,** Providence Co.

GOLDENBERG & MURI (AV)

15 Westminster Street, 02903
Telephone: 401-421-7300
Telecopier: 401-421-7352

MEMBERS OF FIRM

Michael R. Goldenberg
Anthony F. Muri
Barbara S. Cohen

ASSOCIATES

Douglas J. Emanuel
Susan M. Pepin

For full biographical listings, see the Martindale-Hubbell Law Directory

WILLIAM T. MURPHY (AV)

The Calart Tower, 400 Reservoir Avenue, Suite 3L, 02907
Telephone: 401-461-7740
Telecopier: 401-461-7753

ASSOCIATE

Sean P. Lardner

Reference: Fleet National Bank.

For full biographical listings, see the Martindale-Hubbell Law Directory

SOUTH CAROLINA

*COLUMBIA,** Richland Co.

* indicates certain Bar Register subscribers whose principal office is located elsewhere in the state and who have arranged for representation as a part of the state capital listings that follow

BARNES, ALFORD, STORK & JOHNSON, L.L.P. (AV)

1613 Main Street, P.O. Box 8448, 29202
Telephone: 803-799-1111
Telefax: 803-254-1335

Rudolph C. Barnes
William C. Stork
David G. Wolff

(See Next Column)

BARNES, ALFORD, STORK & JOHNSON L.L.P.—*Continued*

James R. Allen

Representative Clients: First Union National Bank of South Carolina; Aetna Casualty and Surety Co.; Kline Iron & Steel Co.

For Complete List of Firm Personnel, See General Section

For full biographical listings, see the Martindale-Hubbell Law Directory

*** HAYNSWORTH, MARION, MCKAY & GUÉRARD, L.L.P.** (AV)

Suite 2400 A T & T Building, 1201 Main Street, P.O. Drawer 7157, 29202
Telephone: 803-765-1818
Telecopier: 803-765-2399
Greenville, South Carolina Office: Two Insignia Financial Plaza, 75 Beattie Place, P.O. Box 2048, 29602.
Telephone: 803-240-3200.
Telecopier: 803-240-3300.
Charleston, South Carolina Office: #2 Prioleau Street, P.O. Box 1119, 29402.
Telephone: 803-722-7606.
Telecopier: 803-723-5263.

MEMBERS OF FIRM

William P. Simpson — Gary W. Morris

ASSOCIATES

Stephen F. McKinney — Edward G. Kluiters

Counsel for: St. Paul Insurance Group; Allstate Insurance Co.; Fluor-Daniel Corp.; South Carolina Jobs - Economic Development Authority; Anheuser Busch Company; CSX Transportation; Ernst & Young, LLP; Willis Corroon of South Carolina, Inc.; Westinghouse Savannah River Co.; Wachovia Bank of South Carolina, N.A.

For Complete List of Firm Personnel, See General Section

For full biographical listings, see the Martindale-Hubbell Law Directory

WOODWARD, LEVENTIS, UNGER, DAVES, HERNDON AND COTHRAN (AV)

(Formerly Woodward, Leventis, Unger, Herndon and Cothran)
1300 Sumter, P.O. Box 12399, 29211
Telephone: 803-799-9772
Fax: 803-779-3256

MEMBERS OF FIRM

James C. Leventis — Gary R. Daves
Richard M. Unger — Warren R. Herndon, Jr.
Darra Williamson Cothran

OF COUNSEL

Edward M. Woodward, Sr.

General Counsel for: The Columbia College.

For full biographical listings, see the Martindale-Hubbell Law Directory

*GREENVILLE,** Greenville Co.

HAYNSWORTH, MARION, MCKAY & GUÉRARD, L.L.P. (AV)

Two Insignia Financial Plaza, 75 Beattie Place, P.O. Box 2048, 29602
Telephone: 803-240-3200
Telecopier: 803-240-3300
Columbia, South Carolina Office: Suite 2400 A T & T Building, 1201 Main Street, P.O. Drawer 7157, 29202
Telephone: 803-765-1818.
Telecopier: 803-765-2399.
Charleston, South Carolina Office: #2 Prioleau Street, P.O. Box 1119, 29402.
Telephone: 803-722-7606.
Telecopier: 803-723-5263.

MEMBER OF FIRM

Jesse C. Belcher, Jr.

Counsel for: Duke Power Co.; Liberty Mutual Insurance Co.; Equitable Life Assurance Society of the United States; St. Paul Insurance Group; Allstate Insurance Co.; Fluor-Daniel Corp.; Snyalloy Corporation; Greenville Hospital System.

For Complete List of Firm Personnel, See General Section

For full biographical listings, see the Martindale-Hubbell Law Directory

WYCHE, BURGESS, FREEMAN & PARHAM, PROFESSIONAL ASSOCIATION (AV)

44 East Camperdown Way, P.O. Box 728, 29602-0728
Telephone: 803-242-8200
Telecopier: 803-235-8900

(See Next Column)

C. Thomas Wyche — William P. Crawford, Jr.

Counsel for: Multimedia, Inc.; Delta Woodside Industries, Inc.; Milliken & Company; Ryan's Family Steak Houses, Inc.; St. Francis Hospital; Span-America Medical Systems, Inc.; Carolina First Bank; KEMET Electronics Corp.; Builder Marts of America, Inc.; One Price Clothing, Inc.

For Complete List of Firm Personnel, See General Section

For full biographical listings, see the Martindale-Hubbell Law Directory

SOUTH DAKOTA

*ABERDEEN,** Brown Co.

BANTZ, GOSCH, CREMER, PETERSON & SOMMERS (AV)

305 Sixth Avenue, S.E., P.O. Box 970, 57402-0970
Telephone: 605-225-2232
Fax: 605-225-2497

MEMBERS OF FIRM

Douglas W. Bantz (1909-1983) — Greg L. Peterson
Kennith L. Gosch — Richard A. Sommers
James M. Cremer — Ronald A. Wager

General Counsel for: Dacotah Bank Holding Co.
Attorneys for: Northwestern Mutual Life Insurance Co.; Transamerica Insurance Group; Employers Mutual of Wausau; Employers Mutual Casualty Cos.; Farmers & Merchants Bank, Aberdeen; United Pacific Insurance Co.; Northwestern National Insurance Co.

For full biographical listings, see the Martindale-Hubbell Law Directory

*SIOUX FALLS,** Minnehaha Co.

DAVENPORT, EVANS, HURWITZ & SMITH (AV)

513 South Main Avenue, P.O. Box 1030, 57101-1030
Telephone: 605-336-2880
Telecopier: 605-335-3639

MEMBERS OF FIRM

David L. Knudson — Charles D. Gullickson
Robert E. Hayes — Catherine A. Tanck

Counsel for: American Society of Composers, Authors and Publishers (A.S.-C.A.P.); Burlington Northern, Inc.; Continental Insurance Cos.; The First National Bank in Sioux Falls; Ford Motor Credit Co.; General Motors Corp.; The St. Paul Cos.; The Travelers.

For Complete List of Firm Personnel, See General Section

For full biographical listings, see the Martindale-Hubbell Law Directory

TENNESSEE

*CHATTANOOGA,** Hamilton Co.

RAY & SIBLEY, P.C. (AV)

17 Cherokee Boulevard, 37405
Telephone: 615-265-2641
Fax: 615-265-2654

Thomas E. Ray — David M. Sibley

For full biographical listings, see the Martindale-Hubbell Law Directory

SPEARS, MOORE, REBMAN & WILLIAMS (AV)

8th Floor Blue Cross Building, 801 Pine Street, 37402
Telephone: 615-756-7000
Facsimile: 615-756-4801

MEMBERS OF FIRM

Thomas S. Kale — F. Scott LeRoy

Counsel for: Pioneer Bank; Chattanooga Gas Co.; South Central Bell Telephone Co.; Tennessee-American Water Co.; Blue Cross and Blue Shield of Tennessee; State Farm Mutual Automobile Insurance Cos.; Nationwide Insurance Co.; Siskin Steel & Supply Co., Inc.; CSX Transportation, Inc.; The McCallie School; Mueller Co.

For Complete List of Firm Personnel, See General Section

For full biographical listings, see the Martindale-Hubbell Law Directory

STOPHEL & STOPHEL, P.C. (AV)

500 Tallan Building, Two Union Square, 37402-2571
Telephone: 615-756-2333
Fax: 615-266-5032

(See Next Column)

STOPHEL & STOPHEL P.C., *Chattanooga—Continued*

Glenn C. Stophel Harry B. Ray
E. Stephen Jett C. Douglas Williams

Brian L. Woodward James C. Heartfield
John W. Rose

Representative Clients: Astec Industries, Inc.; McKenzie Leasing Corporation; The National Group, Inc.; Tennessee Temple University; HCA Valley Psychiatric Hospital Corporation; Chattanooga Armature Works, Inc.; Graco Children's Products, Inc.; American Manufacturing Co.; The Maclellan Foundation, Inc.; Roy H. Pack Broadcasting of Tennessee, Inc. (WDEF AM, FM & TV).

For Complete List of Firm Personnel, See General Section

For full biographical listings, see the Martindale-Hubbell Law Directory

*COLUMBIA,** Maury Co.

ROBIN S. COURTNEY (AV)

809 South Main Street, Suite 300, P.O. Box 1035, 38401
Telephone: 615-388-6031
Fax: 615-381-7317
(Of Counsel, Waller Lansden Dortch & Davis)

For full biographical listings, see the Martindale-Hubbell Law Directory

*JACKSON,** Madison Co.

RAINEY, KIZER, BUTLER, REVIERE & BELL (AV)

105 Highland Avenue South, P.O. Box 1147, 38302-1147
Telephone: 901-423-2414
Telecopier: 901-423-1386

MEMBERS OF FIRM

Thomas H. Rainey William C. Bell, Jr.
Laura A. Williams

ASSOCIATES

Charles C. Exum Clay M. McCormack

Attorneys for: First Tennessee Bank, Jackson, Tennessee; Union Planters National Bank; First American National Bank.

For Complete List of Firm Personnel, See General Section

For full biographical listings, see the Martindale-Hubbell Law Directory

KINGSPORT, Sullivan Co.

HUNTER, SMITH & DAVIS (AV)

1212 North Eastman Road, P.O. Box 3740, 37664
Telephone: 615-378-8800;
Johnson City: 615-282-4186;
Bristol: 615-968-7604
Telecopier: 615-378-8801
Johnson City, Tennessee Office: Suite 500 First American Center, 208 Sunset Drive, 37604.
Telephone: 615-283-6300.
Telecopier: 615-283-6301.

MEMBERS OF FIRM

T. Arthur Scott, Jr. William C. Argabrite
Mark S. Dessauer

ASSOCIATES

Cynthia S. Kessler Gary Dean Miller

Representative Clients: First National Bank; Bank of Tennessee; Banc Tenn Corp.; First Tennessee Bank National Association; NationsBank; Carter County Bank; Signet Bank/Virginia; Eastman Credit Union; Citizens Bank; First Union National Bank.

For Complete List of Firm Personnel, See General Section

For full biographical listings, see the Martindale-Hubbell Law Directory

*KNOXVILLE,** Knox Co.

EGERTON, MCAFEE, ARMISTEAD & DAVIS, P.C. (AV)

500 First American National Bank Center, P.O. Box 2047, 37901
Telephone: 615-546-0500
Fax: 615-525-5293

William W. Davis Lewis C. Foster, Jr.
M. W. Egerton, Jr. William W. Davis, Jr.
Joe M. McAfee Herbert H. Slatery III
William E. McClamroch, III

Representative Clients: First American National Bank of Knoxville; Home Federal Bank of Tennessee, F.S.B.; Bush Bros. & Co.; Johnson & Galyon Contractors; Baptist Hospital of East Tennessee; Revco D.S., Inc.; White Realty Corp.; Dick Broadcasting, Inc.

For Complete List of Firm Personnel, See General Section

For full biographical listings, see the Martindale-Hubbell Law Directory

MCCAMPBELL & YOUNG, A PROFESSIONAL CORPORATION (AV)

2021 Plaza Tower, P.O. Box 550, 37901-0550
Telephone: 615-637-1440
Telecopier: 615-546-9731

Herbert H. McCampbell, Jr. (1905-1974) Lindsay Young
F. Graham Bartlett (1920-1982) Robert S. Marquis
Robert S. Young Robert S. Stone
J. Christopher Kirk
Mark K. Williams

Janie C. Porter Tammy Kaousias
Gregory E. Erickson Benét S. Theiss
R. Scott Elmore Allen W. Blevins

For full biographical listings, see the Martindale-Hubbell Law Directory

WALKER & WALKER, P.C. (AV)

910 First American Center, P.O. Box 2774, 37901
Telephone: 615-523-0700
Telecopier: 615-523-4990

John A. Walker, Jr. Mary C. Walker

For full biographical listings, see the Martindale-Hubbell Law Directory

*MEMPHIS,** Shelby Co.

ARMSTRONG ALLEN PREWITT GENTRY JOHNSTON & HOLMES (AV)

80 Monroe Avenue Suite 700, 38103
Telephone: 901-523-8211
Telecopier: 901-524-4936
Jackson, Missippi Office: 1350 One Jackson Place, 188 East Capitol Street.
Telephone: 601-948-8020.
Telecopier: 601-948-8389.

MEMBERS OF FIRM

Elmore Holmes, III William A. Carson, II
Wm. Rowlett Scott James Rogers Hall, Jr.
Thomas W. Bell, Jr. James B. McLaren, Jr.
Charles R. Crawford

Sidney W. Farnsworth, III

For Complete List of Firm Personnel, See General Section

For full biographical listings, see the Martindale-Hubbell Law Directory

BAKER, DONELSON, BEARMAN & CALDWELL (AV)

20th Floor, First Tennessee Building, 165 Madison, 38103
Telephone: 901-526-2000
Telecopier: 901-577-2303
Nashville, Tennessee Office: 1700 Nashville City Center, 511 Union Street, 37219.
Telephone: 615-726-5600.
Telecopier: 615-726-0464.
Knoxville, Tennessee Office: 2200 Riverview Tower, 900 Gay Street, 37901.
Telephone: 615-549-7000.
Telecopier: 615-525-8569.
Chattanooga, Tennessee Office: 1800 Republic Centre, 633 Chestnut Street, 37450-1800.
Telephone: 615-752-4400.
Telecopier: 615-752-4410.
Huntsville, Tennessee Office: 3 Courthouse Square, 37756.
Telephone: 615-663-2321.
Telecopier: 615-663-2111.
Johnson City, Tennessee Office: Hamilton Bank Building, 207 Mockingbird Lane, 37604.
Telephone: 615-928-0181.
Telecopier: 615-928-5694; 615-928-3654; Kingsport: 615-246-6191.
Washington, D.C. Office: Market Square, 801 Pennsylvania Avenue, N.W., 20004.
Telephone: 202-508-3400.
Telecopier: 202-508-3402.

PARTNERS

David G. Williams Charles T. Tuggle, Jr.
Michael F. Pleasants Robert C. Liddon
Robert Walker Carla Peacher-Ryan
John C. Speer Linda M. Crouch

For Complete List of Firm Personnel, See General Section

For full biographical listings, see the Martindale-Hubbell Law Directory

GERRISH & MCCREARY, P.C. (AV)

Suite 200, 700 Colonial Road, P.O. Box 242120, 38124-2120
Telephone: 901-767-0900
Telecopier: 901-684-2339; 901-684-2338
Nashville, Tennessee Office: Washington Square, 222 Second Avenue North, Suite 424, 37201.
Telephone: 615-251-0900.
Telecopier: 615-251-0975.

(See Next Column)

GERRISH & MCCREARY P.C.—*Continued*

Jeffrey C. Gerrish
A. Neal Graham
Ann W. Langston
J. Franklin McCreary
P. Thomas Parrish
John S. Seabold
Philip K. Smith
Paul J. Dyar
(Not admitted in TN)
Harriet Hanlon Riser
(Not admitted in TN)

OF COUNSEL

David N. Burn

For full biographical listings, see the Martindale-Hubbell Law Directory

*NASHVILLE,** Davidson Co.

WHITE & REASOR (AV)

3305 West End Avenue, 37203
Telephone: 615-383-3345
Facsimile: 615-383-5534; 615-383-9390

MEMBERS OF FIRM

David J. White, Jr.
Charles B. Reasor, Jr.
Barrett B. Sutton, Jr.
John M. Baird
Dudley M. West
Van P. East, III
Steven L. West

For full biographical listings, see the Martindale-Hubbell Law Directory

TEXAS

*AMARILLO,** Potter Co.

HINKLE, COX, EATON, COFFIELD & HENSLEY (AV)

1700 Bank One Center, P.O. Box 9238, 79105-9238
Telephone: 806-372-5569
FAX: 806-372-9761
Roswell, New Mexico Office: 700 United Bank Plaza, P. O. Box 10, 88202.
Telephone: 505-622-6510.
FAX: 505-623-9332.
Midland, Texas Office: 6 Desta Drive, Suite 2800, P.O. Box 3580, 79702.
Telephone: 915-683-4691.
FAX: 915-683-6518.
Santa Fe, New Mexico Office: 218 Montezuma, P.O. Box 2068, 87504.
Telephone: 505-982-4554.
FAX: 505-982-8623.
Albuquerque, New Mexico Office: Suite 800, 500 Marquette, N.W., P.O. Box 2043, 87102.
Telephone: 505-768-1500.
FAX: 505-768-1529.
Austin, Texas Office: 401 West 15th Street, Suite 800, 78701.
Telephone: 512-476-7137.
FAX: 512-476-5431.
Associated Office: Hoffman & Stephens, P.C., 401 West 15th Street, Suite 800, 78701.
Telephone: 512-476-5434. Fax; 512-476-5431.

RESIDENT PARTNERS

Don L. Patterson
Jeffrey W. Hellberg
John C. Chambers

Representative Clients: Amarillo Diagnostic Clinic; Federated Mutual Insurance Company; The First National Bank of Amarillo; Natural Gas Pipeline Company of America; OXY USA Inc.; Pioneer General Contractors, Inc.; Pogo Producing Company; Southwestern Public Service Company; Utility Engineering Corp.; Viking General Agency, Inc.

For full biographical listings, see the Martindale-Hubbell Law Directory

*AUSTIN,** Travis Co.

BAKER & BOTTS, L.L.P. (AV)

1600 San Jacinto Center, 98 San Jacinto Boulevard, 78701
Telephone: 512-322-2500
Fax: 512-322-2501
Houston, Texas Office: One Shell Plaza, 910 Louisiana.
Telephone: 713-229-1234.
Dallas, Texas Office: 2001 Ross Avenue.
Telephone: 214-953-6500.
Washington, D.C. Office: The Warner, 1299 Pennsylvania Avenue, N.W.
Telephone: 202-639-7700.
New York, New York Office: 885 Third Avenue, Suite 2000.
Telephone: 212-705-5000.
Moscow, Russian Federation Office: 10 ul. Pushkinskaya, 103031.
Telephone: 7095/921-5300 (Local); 7501/929-7070 (International).

MEMBERS OF FIRM

Shelley W. Austin
William F. Stutts, Jr.

(See Next Column)

ASSOCIATE

Catherine M. Del Castillo

For Complete List of Firm Personnel, See General Section

For full biographical listings, see the Martindale-Hubbell Law Directory

FORD & FERRARO, L.L.P. (AV)

A Registered Limited Liability Partnership
98 San Jacinto Boulevard, Suite 2000, 78701-4286
Telephone: 512-476-2020
Telecopy: 512-477-5267

Joseph M. Ford (P.C.)
Peter E. Ferraro (P.C.)
Thomas D. Fritz
Daniel H. Byrne (P.C.)
William S. Rhea, IV
Lisa C. Fancher
Clint Hackney (P.C.)
John D. Head
Robert O. Renbarger

ASSOCIATES

Patricia A. Becker
Linda Cangelosi
Bruce Perkins
James A. Rodman
James V. Sylvester
Cari S. Young

SPECIAL COUNSEL

Clark Watts

OF COUNSEL

Salvatore F. Fiscina
(Not admitted in TX)
Lawrence H. Brenner
(Not admitted in TX)

For full biographical listings, see the Martindale-Hubbell Law Directory

HOHMANN, WERNER & TAUBE, L.L.P. (AV)

100 Congress Avenue, Suite 1600, 78701-4042
Telephone: 512-472-5997
Fax: 512-472-5248
Houston, Texas Office: 1300 Post Oak Boulevard, Suite 700.
Telephone: 713-961-3541.
Fax: 713-961-3542.

Guy M. Hohmann
Eric J. Taube
Paul Dobry Keeper

Nicholas S. Bressi
T. Wade Jefferies
Camille Johnson Mauldin
Sandra McFarland
Mitchell D. Savrick
Gary N. Schumann
Rachel J. Stroud

For full biographical listings, see the Martindale-Hubbell Law Directory

MCGINNIS, LOCHRIDGE & KILGORE, L.L.P. (AV)

1300 Capitol Center, 919 Congress Avenue, 78701
Telephone: 512-495-6000
Houston, Texas Office: 3200 One Houston Center, 1221 McKinney Street.
Telephone: 713-615-8500.

MEMBERS OF FIRM

Joe M. Kilgore
Shannon H. Ratliff
C. Morris Davis
William H. Bingham
William H. Daniel
Michael A. Wren
William A. Rogers, Jr.
Christine F. Miller
Jeff Bohm
Richard Kelley
Gregory S. Chanon

ASSOCIATE

Angela Chinn Woodbury

For Complete List of Firm Personnel, See General Section

For full biographical listings, see the Martindale-Hubbell Law Directory

*BROWNSVILLE,** Cameron Co.

RODRIGUEZ, COLVIN & CHANEY (AV)

1201 East Van Buren, P.O. Box 2155, 78520
Telephone: 210-542-7441
Fax: 210-541-2170

MEMBERS OF FIRM

Eduardo R. Rodriguez
Norton A. Colvin, Jr.
Mitchell C. Chaney
Marjory Colvin Batsell
Jaime A. Saenz

ASSOCIATES

Joseph A. (Tony) Rodriguez
Laura J. Urbis
Alison Kennamer
Lecia L. Chaney
Michael E. Rodriguez

OF COUNSEL

Benjamin S. Hardy
Neil E. Norquest
Chris A. Brisack

Division Attorneys for: Union Pacific Railroad.
Counsel for: Texas Commerce Bank-Rio Grande Valley, N.A.; Texas Commerce Bancshares, Inc.

For full biographical listings, see the Martindale-Hubbell Law Directory

*DALLAS,** Dallas Co.

JOE B. ABBEY (AV)

1717 Main Street, Suite 2220, 75201
Telephone: 214-748-0423
Fax: 214-748-0426

For full biographical listings, see the Martindale-Hubbell Law Directory

JOSEPH E. ASHMORE, JR., P.C. (AV)

Regency Plaza, 3710 Rawlins, Suite 1210, LB 84, 75219-4217
Telephone: 214-559-7202
Fax: 214-520-1550

Joseph E. Ashmore, Jr.

C. Gregory Shamoun
W. Charles Campbell
L. James Ashmore
Howard J. Klatsky

OF COUNSEL

B. Garfield Haynes
Mark S. Michael

For Complete List of Firm Personnel, See General Section

For full biographical listings, see the Martindale-Hubbell Law Directory

BAKER & BOTTS, L.L.P. (AV)

2001 Ross Avenue, 75201
Telephone: 214-953-6500
Fax: 214-953-6503
Houston, Texas Office: One Shell Plaza, 910 Louisiana.
Telephone: 713-229-1234.
Washington, D.C. Office: The Warner, 1299 Pennsylvania Avenue, N.W.
Telephone: 202-639-7700.
Austin, Texas Office: 1600 San Jacinto Center, 98 San Jacinto Boulevard.
Telephone: 512-322-2500.
New York, New York Office: 885 Third Avenue, Suite 2000.
Telephone: 212-705-5000.
Moscow, Russian Federation Office: 10 ul. Pushkinskaya, 103031.
Telephone: 7095/921-5300 (Local); 7095/929-7070.

MEMBER OF FIRM

Roderick A. Goyne

ASSOCIATES

Alison C. Glasstetter
Michelle White Suárez

For Complete List of Firm Personnel, See General Section

For full biographical listings, see the Martindale-Hubbell Law Directory

BARRETT BURKE WILSON CASTLE DAFFIN & FRAPPIER, L.L.P. (AV)

A Limited Liability Partnership including Professional Corporations
6750 Hillcrest Plaza Drive, Suite 313, 75230
Telephone: 214-386-5040
Fax: 214-386-7673
Houston, Texas Office: 24 Greenway Plaza, Suite 2001.
Telephone: 713-621-8673.
Denver, Colorado Affiliated Office: Burke & Castle, P.C. 1099 Eighteenth Street, Suite 2200.
Telephone: 303-299-1800.
Fax: 303-299-1808.
Little Rock, Arkansas Affiliated Office: Wilson & Associates, P.A. 425 West Capitol Avenue, Suite 1500.
Telephone: 501-375-1820.
San Antonio, Texas Office: 1100 Northwest Loop 410, Suite 700. 78213.
Telephone: 512-366-8793.
Fax: 512-366-0198.

Michael C. Barrett

For full biographical listings, see the Martindale-Hubbell Law Directory

CALHOUN & STACY (AV)

5700 NationsBank Plaza, 901 Main Street, 75202-3747
Telephone: 214-748-5000
Telecopier: 214-748-1421
Telex: 211358 CALGUMP UR

Mark Alan Calhoun
David W. Elrod
Steven D. Goldston
Parker Nelson
Roy L. Stacy

ASSOCIATES

Shannon S. Barclay
Robert A. Bragalone
Dennis D. Conder
Jane Elizabeth Diseker
Lawrence I. Fleishman
Thomas C. Jones
Katherine Johnson Knight
V. Paige Pace
Veronika Willard
Michael C. Wright

LEGAL CONSULTANT

Rees T. Bowen, III

For full biographical listings, see the Martindale-Hubbell Law Directory

GODWIN & CARLTON, A PROFESSIONAL CORPORATION (AV)

Suite 3300, 901 Main Street, 75202-3714
Telephone: 214-939-4400
Telecopier: 214-760-7332
Monterrey, Mexico Correspondent: Quintero y Quintero Abogodos. Martin De Zalva 840-3 Sur Esquinna Con Hidalgo.
Telephone: 44-07-74, 44-07-80, 44-06-56, 44-06-28.
Fax: 83-40-34-54.

David J. White
Thomas E. Rosen
John L. Hubble
Frank P. Skipper, Jr.
Marci L. Romick

Rodney L. Hubbard
Steven T. Polino

Kathleen Weidinger Foster
Michael K. Hurst

For Complete List of Firm Personnel, See General Section

For full biographical listings, see the Martindale-Hubbell Law Directory

HUGHES & LUCE, L.L.P. (AV)

A Registered Limited Liability Partnership including Professional Corporations
1717 Main Street, Suite 2800, 75201
Telephone: 214-939-5500
Fax: 214-939-6100
Telex: 730836
Austin, Texas Office: 111 Congress, Suite 900.
Telephone: 512-482-6800.
Fax: 512-482-6859.
Houston, Texas Office: Three Allen Center, 333 Clay Street, Suite 3800.
Telephone: 713-754-5200.
Fax: 713-754-5206.
Fort Worth, Texas Office: 2421 Westport Parkway, Suite 500A.
Telephone: 817-439-3000.
Fax: 817-439-4222.

MEMBERS OF FIRM

Paul A. Berry
James C. Chadwick
Larry A. Makel
Gary G. Null
James W. Sargent
Kenneth Mark Vesledahl

ASSOCIATES

Robert Jeffery Cole
Walter E. Evans

For Complete List of Firm Personnel, See General Section

For full biographical listings, see the Martindale-Hubbell Law Directory

JOHN P. KOONS (AV)

907 North Dallas Bank Tower, 12900 Preston Road, 75230
Telephone: 214-387-3788

Representative Clients: North Dallas Bank & Trust Co.; Dallas Wholesale Builders Supply, Inc.; Moore Lumber Co.; Sears, Roebuck & Co.

For full biographical listings, see the Martindale-Hubbell Law Directory

NOVAKOV, DAVIDSON & FLYNN, A PROFESSIONAL CORPORATION (AV)

2000 St. Paul Place, 750 North St. Paul, 75201-3286
Telephone: 214-922-9221
Telecopy: 214-969-7557

James Kevin Flynn
Charles N. Nye

For Complete List of Firm Personnel, See General Section

For full biographical listings, see the Martindale-Hubbell Law Directory

PALMER, ALLEN & MCTAGGART, L.L.P. (AV)

A Partnership including Professional Corporations
1900 St. Paul Place, 750 North St. Paul Street, 75201
Telephone: 214-969-0069
Telecopy: 214-720-0104
Austin, Texas Office: 6505 Lohmann's Crossing (Lago Vista).
Telephone: 512-267-1993. Mailing Address: P.O. Box 4345, Lago Vista, Texas, 78645.

Steven G. Palmer (P.C.)
Joe B. Allen III
Robert D. McTaggart (P.C.)
Guy Myrph Foote, Jr., (P.C.)
Brian G. Dicus (P.C.)

OF COUNSEL

Robert S. Leithiser (P.C.)
Dick P. Wood, Jr., (P.C.)

For full biographical listings, see the Martindale-Hubbell Law Directory

Dallas—Continued

THOMPSON & KNIGHT, A PROFESSIONAL CORPORATION (AV)

(Attorneys and Counselors)
1700 Pacific Avenue Suite 3300, 75201
Telephone: 214-969-1700
Telecopy: 214-969-1751
Cable Address: "Tomtex"
Telex: 732298
Austin, Texas Office: 1200 San Jacinto Center, 98 San Jacinto Boulevard, 78701.
Telephone: 512-469-6100.
Telecopy: 512-469-6180.
Fort Worth, Texas Office: 801 Cherry Street, Suite 1600, 76102.
Telephone: 817-347-1700.
Telecopy: 817-347-1799.
Houston, Texas Office: 1700 Texas Commerce Tower, 600 Travis, 77002.
Telephone: 713-217-2800.
Telecopy: 713-217-2828.
Monterrey, Mexico Office: Edificio Losoles PD-4, Av. Lázaro Cárdenas No. 2400 Pte., San Pedro Garza Garcia, Nuevo Léon C.P. 66220.
Telephone: (52-8) 363-0096.
Telecopy: (52-8) 363-3067.

SHAREHOLDERS

Dorothy H. Bjorck
O. Paul Corley, Jr.
James W. McKellar
John W. Rain

ASSOCIATES

Andrew P. Flint
Debra J. Villarreal

For Complete List of Firm Personnel, See General Section

For full biographical listings, see the Martindale-Hubbell Law Directory

*EL PASO,** El Paso Co.

EDWARDS, BELK, HUNTER & KERR (AV)

6070 Gateway East, Suite 102, P.O. Box 10058, 79991
Telephone: 915-779-6464
Fax: 915-772-0512

MEMBERS OF FIRM

Eugene T. Edwards (1889-1978)
Bates M. Belk
Frank H. Hunter
Crawford S. Kerr, Jr.
John William Welsh, Jr.
J. Crawford Kerr

Representative Clients: Nations Bank of Texas, El Paso, Texas; Montwood National Bank; Valley Bancorp, Inc.; Farah, Inc.; Texas & Pacific Land Trust; First National Bank of Fabens, Fabens, Texas

For full biographical listings, see the Martindale-Hubbell Law Directory

MAYFIELD AND PERRENOT, A PROFESSIONAL CORPORATION (AV)

Fifth Floor, First City National Bank Building, 79901
Telephone: 915-533-2468
Telecopier: 915-533-0620

Richard B. Perrenot
Steven Tredennick

OF COUNSEL

Ellis O. Mayfield
James B. McIntyre

For Complete List of Firm Personnel, See General Section

For full biographical listings, see the Martindale-Hubbell Law Directory

MOUNCE & GALATZAN, A PROFESSIONAL CORPORATION (AV)

7th Floor, Texas Commerce Bank Building, 79901-1334
Telephone: 915-532-3911
Fax: 915-541-1597

William J. Mounce
Wiley F. James, III
Risher Smith Gilbert
Timothy V. Coffey
John Steven Birkelbach
Harrel L. Davis III
Corey W. Haugland
Michael J. Hutson
Victor M. Firth
Bernard R. Given, II

Attorneys for: El Paso Natural Gas Co.; Texas Commerce Bank National Association; El Paso Independent School District; Commercial Union Assurance Cos.; State Farm Mutual Automobile Insurance Co.; Employers Insurance of Texas; Greater El Paso Association of Realtors; Bank of the West; State National Bank.

For Complete List of Firm Personnel, See General Section

For full biographical listings, see the Martindale-Hubbell Law Directory

FRISCO, Collin & Denton Cos.

WINIKATES & WINIKATES (AV)

Prosper State Bank Building, P.O. Box 249, 75034-0249
Telephone: 214-335-1122
Fax: 214-335-1125

(See Next Column)

MEMBERS OF FIRM

Charles J. Winikates
Charles J. Winikates, Jr.
Regina W. Mentesana

OF COUNSEL

Frances A. Fazio

For full biographical listings, see the Martindale-Hubbell Law Directory

*HOUSTON,** Harris Co.

BAKER & BOTTS, L.L.P. (AV)

One Shell Plaza, 910 Louisiana, 77002
Telephone: 713-229-1234
Cable Address: "Boterlove"
Fax: 713-229-1522
Washington, D.C. Office: The Warner, 1299 Pennsylvania Avenue, N.W.
Telephone: 202-639-7700.
New York, New York Office: 885 Third Avenue, Suite 2000.
Telephone: 212-705-5000.
Austin, Texas Office: 1600 San Jacinto Center, 98 San Jacinto Boulevard.
Telephone: 512-322-2500.
Dallas, Texas Office: 2001 Ross Avenue.
Telephone: 214-953-6500.
Moscow, Russian Federation Office: 10 ul. Pushkinskaya, 103031.
Telephone: 7095/921-5300 (Local); 7095/929-7070 (International).

MEMBERS OF FIRM

Michael S. Moehlman
David Alan Burns
Rufus Cormier, Jr.
Pamela B. Ewen
Stephen Krebs

ASSOCIATES

Bill Hart, Jr.
Marjorie A. Hirsch
Carol L. St. Clair
Dahl C. Thompson

For Complete List of Firm Personnel, See General Section

For full biographical listings, see the Martindale-Hubbell Law Directory

GILPIN, PAXSON & BERSCH (AV)

A Registered Limited Liability Partnership
1900 West Loop South, Suite 2000, 77027-3259
Telephone: 713-623-8800
Telecopier: 713-993-8451

MEMBERS OF FIRM

Gary M. Alletag
Timothy R. Bersch
Deborah J. Bullion
James L. Cornell, Jr.
George R. Diaz-Arrastia
Frank W. Gerold
John D. Gilpin
William T. Little
Darryl W. Malone
Michael W. McCoy
Michael J. Pappert
Stephen Paxson
Lionel M. Schooler
Mary E. Wilson
Kevin F. Risley

ASSOCIATES

Russell T. Abney
N. Terry Adams, Jr.
John W. Burchfield
Evan N. Kramer
Dale R. Mellencamp
P. Wayne Pickering
Susan M. Schwager

OF COUNSEL

Harless R. Benthul
Thomas F. Aubry

Representative Clients: Bank of America, N.A.; Charter Bancshares, Inc.; First Interstate Bank of Texas, N.A.; ICM Mortgage Corporation; MetroBanks, N.A.

For full biographical listings, see the Martindale-Hubbell Law Directory

HAYS, MCCONN, RICE & PICKERING (AV)

400 Two Allen Center, 1200 Smith Street, 77002
Telephone: 713-654-1111
Telecopier: 713-650-0027

MEMBERS OF FIRM

Michael S. Hays
James J. McConn, Jr.
B. Stephen Rice
Michael R. Pickering
Sharon Stagg
Frank Holcomb H.
Mark A. Padon
Bruce Clifford Gaible
Susan Crowley Stevenson
Allen Royce Till
Craig S. Wolcott
Don F. Russell
Rudy Cano
Naomi S. Ostfeld
Diana V. H. Shelby
Margaret Twomey Brenner
W. Michael Scott

ASSOCIATES

Jeffery Allen Addicks
Kevin Crawford
Steven M. Duble
Reid G. Gettys
J. Philip Griffis
Debra Donaldson Hovnatanian
Alan Scott Kidd
George A. Kurisky, Jr.
Michael W. Magee
Robert E. Purgatorio
Kathleen Reilly Richards
Lance K. Thomas
Troy A. Williams

For full biographical listings, see the Martindale-Hubbell Law Directory

Houston—Continued

WILSHIRE SCOTT & DYER, A PROFESSIONAL CORPORATION (AV)

4450 First City Tower, 1001 Fannin, 77002
Telephone: 713-651-1221
Telefax: 713-651-0020

Eugene B. Wilshire, Jr.
Patrick J. Dyer
Jacalyn D. Scott
Thomas E. Bilek
Kelly Cox Thornton

For full biographical listings, see the Martindale-Hubbell Law Directory

*MIDLAND,** Midland Co.

HINKLE, COX, EATON, COFFIELD & HENSLEY (AV)

6 Desta Drive, Suite 2800, P.O. Box 3580, 79702
Telephone: 915-683-4691
FAX: 915-683-6518
Roswell, New Mexico Office: 700 United Bank Plaza, P.O. Box 10.
Telephone: 505-622-6510.
FAX: 505-623-9332.
Amarillo, Texas Office: 1700 Bank One Center, P.O. Box 9238.
Telephone: 806-372-5569.
FAX: 806-372-9761.
Santa Fe, New Mexico Office: 218 Montezuma, P.O. Box 2068.
Telephone: 505-982-4554.
FAX: 505-982-8623.
Albuquerque, New Mexico Office: Suite 800, 500 Marquette, N.W., P.O. Box 2043.
Telephone: 505-768-1500.
FAX: 505-768-1529.
Austin, Texas Office: 401 West 15th Street, Suite 800, 78701.
Telephone: 512-476-7137.
FAX: 512-476-5431.
Associated Office: Hoffman & Stephens, P.C., 401 West 15th Street, Suite 800, 78701.
Telephone: 512-476-5434.
FAX: 512-476-5431.

RESIDENT PARTNERS

C. D. Martin
Jeffrey D. Hewett
James M. Hudson

Representative Clients: Atlantic Richfield Co.; Bass Enterprises Production Co.; BHP Petroleum; Devon Energy Corp.; Exxon Corp.; Midland National Bank; Mitchell Energy Corp.; Mobil Exploration and Producing U.S. Inc.; NationsBank of Texas, N.A.; OXY USA, Inc.; Parker & Parsley Petroleum Co.; Texas National Bank of Midland.

For full biographical listings, see the Martindale-Hubbell Law Directory

KERR, FITZ-GERALD & KERR, L.L.P. (AV)

Century Plaza Building, Suite 600, 310 West Wall Street, 79701
Telephone: 915-683-5291
FAX: 915-683-5257

William L. Kerr (1904-1978)
Theodore M. Kerr
Gerald Fitz-Gerald (1906-1980)
Harris E. Kerr
Wm. Monroe Kerr
William M. Kerr, Jr.

A. M. Nunley III
Brian T. McLaughlin
J. Devin Alsup

For full biographical listings, see the Martindale-Hubbell Law Directory

*SAN ANTONIO,** Bexar Co.

WHEATLEY, CAMPAGNOLO & SESSIONS, L.L.P. (AV)

100 West Houston, Suite 1200, 78205
Telephone: 210-227-5000
Fax: 210-225-1555

Seagal V. Wheatley
William Lewis Sessions
Theodore Campagnolo
John Frank Onion, III
Donald R. Philbin, Jr.

ASSOCIATES

Bradley S. Wilder
Katrina J. Carden
Julia W. Mann

For full biographical listings, see the Martindale-Hubbell Law Directory

UTAH

*PROVO,** Utah Co.

HOWARD, LEWIS & PETERSEN, P.C. (AV)

Delphi Building, 120 East 300 North Street, P.O. Box 778, 84603
Telephone: 801-373-6345
Fax: 801-377-4991

(See Next Column)

Jackson Howard
John L. Valentine
Don R. Petersen
D. David Lambert
Craig M. Snyder
Fred D. Howard
Leslie W. Slaugh

Richard W. Daynes
Phillip E. Lowry
Kenneth Parkinson

OF COUNSEL

S. Rex Lewis

LEGAL SUPPORT PERSONNEL

Mary Jackson
John O. Sump
Ray Winger

For full biographical listings, see the Martindale-Hubbell Law Directory

*SALT LAKE CITY,** Salt Lake Co.

CALLISTER, NEBEKER & McCULLOUGH, A PROFESSIONAL CORPORATION (AV)

800 Kennecott Building, 84133
Telephone: 801-530-7300
Telecopier: 801-364-9127

Louis H. Callister
Randall D Benson
Dorothy C. Pleshe
George E. Harris, Jr.
John A. Beckstead
John H. Rees
James R. Holbrook
Mark L. Callister

John B. Lindsay

Representative Clients: Zions First National Bank; Citicorp; Bank of America; Associates Commercial Corp.; Chrysler Credit Corp.; Western Farm Credit Bank; U.S. Bancorporation of Oregon.

For Complete List of Firm Personnel, See General Section
For full biographical listings, see the Martindale-Hubbell Law Directory

KIPP AND CHRISTIAN, P.C. (AV)

175 East 400 South 330 City Centre I, 84111
Telephone: 801-521-3773
Fax: 801-359-9004

Carman E. Kipp
J. Anthony Eyre
Michael F. Skolnick

Representative Client: Capital City Bank.

For Complete List of Firm Personnel, See General Section
For full biographical listings, see the Martindale-Hubbell Law Directory

PARSONS BEHLE & LATIMER, A PROFESSIONAL CORPORATION (AV)

One Utah Center, 201 South Main Street, Suite 1800, P.O. Box 45898, 84145-0898
Telephone: 801-532-1234
Telecopy: 801-536-6111

F. Robert Reeder
Robert C. Hyde
W. Jeffery Fillmore
Gary E. Doctorman

Representative Clients: Bank One, Utah, N.A.; Great Western Thrift and Loan.

For full biographical listings, see the Martindale-Hubbell Law Directory

RAY, QUINNEY & NEBEKER, A PROFESSIONAL CORPORATION (AV)

Suite 400 Deseret Building, 79 South Main Street, P.O. Box 45385, 84145-0385
Telephone: 801-532-1500
Telecopier: 801-532-7543
Provo, Utah Office: 210 First Security Bank Building, 92 North University Avenue.
Telephone: 801-226-7210.
Telecopier: 801-375-8379.

Alonzo W. Watson, Jr.
Brad D. Hardy
Don B. Allen
Larry G. Moore
James L. Wilde (Resident at Provo)
Douglas M. Monson
Craig Carlile (Resident at Provo)
Scott Hancock Clark
James M. Dester
Douglas Matsumori
Kevin G. Glade
Stephen C. Tingey

Elaine A. Monson
Katie A. Eccles

Representative Clients: First Security Bank of Utah, N.A.; Borden, Inc.; Southern Pacific Transportation; Utah Power & Light Co.; Travelers Insurance Co.; Greyhound Leasing & Financial; Holy Cross Hospital and Health System; Amoco Production Co.

(See Next Column)

Ray, Quinney & Nebeker A Professional Corporation—*Continued*

For Complete List of Firm Personnel, See General Section

For full biographical listings, see the Martindale-Hubbell Law Directory

Van Cott, Bagley, Cornwall & McCarthy, A Professional Corporation (AV)

Suite 1600, 50 South Main Street, P.O. Box 45340, 84145
Telephone: 801-532-3333
Telex: 453149
Telecopier: 801-534-0058
Ogden, Utah Office: Suite 900, 2404 Washington Boulevard.
Telephone: 801-394-5783.
Park City, Utah Office: 314 Main Street, Suite 205.
Telephone: 801-649-3889.
Reno, Nevada Office: Jeppson & Lee, 100 West Liberty, Suite 990.
Telephone: 702-333-6800.

David E. Salisbury
Stephen D. Swindle
Robert D. Merrill
Thomas T. Billings
Guy P. Kroesche

OF COUNSEL

Leonard J. Lewis

For Complete List of Firm Personnel, See General Section

For full biographical listings, see the Martindale-Hubbell Law Directory

VERMONT

*BURLINGTON,** Chittenden Co.

Burak & Anderson (AV)

Executive Square, 346 Shelburne Street, P.O. Box 64700, 05406-4700
Telephone: 802-862-0500
Telecopier: 802-862-8176

MEMBERS OF FIRM

Michael L. Burak
Thomas R. Melloni
David M. Hyman

ASSOCIATE

Julie D. M. Sovern

For Complete List of Firm Personnel, See General Section

For full biographical listings, see the Martindale-Hubbell Law Directory

Sheehey Brue Gray & Furlong, Professional Corporation (AV)

119 South Winooski Avenue, P.O. Box 66, 05402
Telephone: 802-864-9891
Facsimile: 802-864-6815

William B. Gray (1942-1994)
David T. Austin
R. Jeffrey Behm
Nordahl L. Brue
Michael G. Furlong
Ralphine Newlin O'Rourke
Donald J. Rendall, Jr.
Christina Schulz
Paul D. Sheehey
Peter H. Zamore

Rebecca L. Owen

Representative Client: Green Mountain Power Corp.

For full biographical listings, see the Martindale-Hubbell Law Directory

*RUTLAND,** Rutland Co.

Carroll, George & Pratt (AV)

64 & 66 North Main Street, P.O. Box 280, 05702-0280
Telephone: 802-775-7141
Telecopier: 802-775-6483
Woodstock, Vermont Office: The Mill - Route #4 E., P.O. Box 388, 05091.
Telephone: 802-457-1000.
Telecopier: 802-457-1874.

MEMBERS OF FIRM

Henry G. Smith (1938-1974)
James P. Carroll
Alan B. George
Robert S. Pratt
Neal C. Vreeland
Jon S. Readnour
Timothy U. Martin
Randall F. Mayhew (Resident Partner, Woodstock Office)
Richard S. Smith
Judy Godnick Barone
John J. Kennelly

ASSOCIATES

Thomas A. Zonay
Jeffrey P. White
Susan Boyle Ford (Resident, Woodstock Office)
Charles C. Humpstone

For full biographical listings, see the Martindale-Hubbell Law Directory

Hull, Webber & Reis (AV)

(Formerly Dick, Hackel & Hull)
60 North Main Street, P.O. Box 890, 05702-0890
Telephone: 802-775-2361
Fax: 802-775-0739

Donald H. Hackel (1925-1985)
John B. Webber
Robert K. Reis
John C. Holler
Lisa L. Chalidze

ASSOCIATES

Phyllis R. McCoy
Karen Abatiell Kalter

OF COUNSEL

Richard A. Hull (P.C.)
Steven D. Vogl

Representative Clients: Aetna Insurance Co.; Great American Insurance Cos.; Green Mountain Bank.

For full biographical listings, see the Martindale-Hubbell Law Directory

*ST. JOHNSBURY,** Caledonia Co.

Primmer & Piper, Professional Corporation (AV)

52 Summer Street, P.O. Box 159, 05819
Telephone: 802-748-5061
Facsimile: 802-748-3976
Montpelier, Vermont Office: 44 East State Street, 05602. Box 1309.
Telephone: 802-223-2102.
Fax: 802-223-2628.

John L. Primmer
William B. Piper
Denise J. Deschenes
Jeffrey P. Johnson
Robert W. Martin, Jr.
James E. Clemons

Trevor R. Lewis
James D. Huber

For full biographical listings, see the Martindale-Hubbell Law Directory

VIRGINIA

*ARLINGTON,** Arlington Co.

Bean, Kinney & Korman, A Professional Corporation (AV)

2000 North 14th Street, Suite 100, 22201
Telephone: 703-525-4000
Facsimile: 703-525-2207

James W. Korman
Jonathan C. Kinney
Frederick R. Taylor
Leo S. Fisher
James Bruce Davis
James R. Schroll
Carol Schrier-Polak
Joseph P. Corish

OF COUNSEL

L. Lee Bean (1916-1989)
Clifford A. Dougherty
Marilyn Tebor Shaw
David B. Kinney (Emeritus)
Barbara S. Kinosky

J. Carlton Howard, Jr.
Marbeth M. Spreyer
Charles E. Curran
Jennifer A. Brust
Karen L. Keyes
Eric H. D. Sahl
Dannon G. Williams

Counsel for: Nations Bank, N.A.
Reference: Nations Bank, N.A.

For full biographical listings, see the Martindale-Hubbell Law Directory

*FAIRFAX,** (Ind. City; Seat of Fairfax Co.)

Odin, Feldman & Pittleman, P.C. (AV)

9302 Lee Highway, Suite 1100, 22031
Telephone: 703-218-2100
Facsimile: 703-218-2160

David E. Feldman
James B. Pittleman
Thomas J. Shaughnessy
David A. Lawrence
Donald F. King

For Complete List of Firm Personnel, See General Section

For full biographical listings, see the Martindale-Hubbell Law Directory

Rust, Rust & Silver, A Professional Corporation (AV)

4103 Chain Bridge Road Fourth Floor, P.O. Box 460, 22030
Telephone: 703-591-7000
Telecopier: 703-591-7336

John H. Rust, Jr.
Glenn H. Silver
C. Thomas Brown

(See Next Column)

RUST, RUST & SILVER A PROFESSIONAL CORPORATION, *Fairfax—Continued*

James E. Kane
Paulo E. Franco, Jr.
Andrew W. White

RETIRED, EMERITUS

John H. Rust, Sr. (Retired)

Representative Clients: Crestar Bank; Commonwealth Land Title Insurance Co.; Patriot National Bank; Century Graphics Corp.

For full biographical listings, see the Martindale-Hubbell Law Directory

TYDINGS, BRYAN & ADAMS, P.C. (AV)

Suite 420 The Fairfax Bank & Trust Building, 4117 Chain Bridge Road, P.O. Box 250, 22030-0250
Telephone: 703-359-9100
Fax: 703-352-8913

Ronald W. Tydings
Kennon W. Bryan

Stuart L. Crenshaw, III

For Complete List of Firm Personnel, See General Section

For full biographical listings, see the Martindale-Hubbell Law Directory

MCLEAN, Fairfax Co.

VENABLE, BAETJER AND HOWARD (AV)

A Partnership including Professional Corporations
Suite 400, 2010 Corporate Ridge, 22102
Telephone: 703-760-1600
FAX: 703-821-8949
Baltimore, Maryland Office: 1800 Mercantile Bank & Trust Building, 2 Hopkins Plaza.
Telephone: 410-244-7400.
Washington, D.C. Office: Venable, Baetjer, Howard & Civiletti, Suite 1000, 1201 New York Avenue, N.W.
Telephone: 202-962-4800.
Rockville, Maryland Office: Suite 500, One Church Street, P.O. Box 1906.
Telephone: 301-217-5600.
Towson, Maryland Office: 210 Allegheny Avenue, P. O. Box 5517.
Telephone: 410-494-6200.

MEMBERS OF FIRM

Kenneth C. Bass, III (Also at Washington, D.C. Office)
Lars E. Anderson
William D. Dolan, III (P.C.)
Ellen F. Dyke

OF COUNSEL

Mary T. Flynn

For Complete List of Firm Personnel, See General Section

For full biographical listings, see the Martindale-Hubbell Law Directory

NORFOLK, (Independent City)

CRENSHAW, WARE AND MARTIN, P.L.C. (AV)

Suite 1200 NationsBank Center, One Commercial Place, 23510-2111
Telephone: 804-623-3000
FAX: 804-623-5735

Francis N. Crenshaw
Guilford D. Ware
Howard W. Martin, Jr.
Timothy A. Coyle
Ann K. Sullivan
James L. Chapman, IV
John T. Midgett
Martha M. Poindexter

Melanie Fix
David H. Sump
Donald C. Schultz
Kristen L. Hodeen

Representative Clients: Crestar Bank; First Virginia Bank of Tidewater.

For full biographical listings, see the Martindale-Hubbell Law Directory

STACKHOUSE, SMITH & NEXSEN (AV)

1600 First Virginia Tower, 555 Main Street, P.O. Box 3640, 23514
Telephone: 804-623-3555
FAX: 804-624-9245

MEMBERS OF FIRM

Robert C. Stackhouse
Peter W. Smith, IV
William W. Nexsen
R. Clinton Stackhouse, Jr.
Janice McPherson Doxey

ASSOCIATES

Mary Painter Opitz
Timothy P. Murphy
Carl J. Khalil

Representative Clients: Heritage Bank & Trust; The Atlantic Group, Inc.; Roughton Pontiac Corp; Federal National Mortgage Association; Kemper National Insurance Cos.; Shearson/American Express Mortgage Corp.; Harleysville Mutual Insurance Co.; Heritage Bankshares, Inc.; Presbyterian League of the Presbytery of Eastern Virginia, Inc.; Oakwood Acceptance Corp.

(See Next Column)

For full biographical listings, see the Martindale-Hubbell Law Directory

TAVSS, FLETCHER, EARLEY & KING, P.C. (AV)

Suite 100, Two Commercial Place, 23510
Telephone: 804-625-1214
Fax: 804-622-7295
Mailing Address: P.O. Box 3747, 23514

Richard J. Tavss
John R. Fletcher
Mark L. Earley
Ray W. King
Besianne Tavss Shilling

LEGAL SUPPORT PERSONNEL

Maurice J. O'Connor

Reference: Bank of the Commonwealth.

For full biographical listings, see the Martindale-Hubbell Law Directory

*RICHMOND,** (Ind. City; Seat of Henrico Co.)

MORRIS AND MORRIS, A PROFESSIONAL CORPORATION (AV)

1200 Ross Building, 801 East Main Street, 23201-0030
Telephone: 804-344-8300
FAX: 804-344-8359

James W. Morris, III
Philip B. Morris
R. Hunter Manson
Kirk D. McQuiddy

For Complete List of Firm Personnel, See General Section

For full biographical listings, see the Martindale-Hubbell Law Directory

WILLIAMS, MULLEN, CHRISTIAN & DOBBINS, A PROFESSIONAL CORPORATION (AV)

Two James Center, 1021 East Cary Street, P.O. Box 1320, 23210-1320
Telephone: 804-643-1991
Fax: 804-783-6456
Glen Allen, Virginia Office: 4401 Waterfront Drive, Suite 140.
Telephone: 804-965-9168.
Fax: 804-965-0955.
Washington, D.C. Office: 1575 Eye Street, N.W.
Telephone: 202-289-6200.
Fax: 202-289-4126.

Michael C. Buseck
Charles L. Cabell
Howard W. Dobbins
Hugh T. Harrison, II
Reginald N. Jones
John M. Mercer
G. Andrew Nea, Jr.
Warren E. Nowlin (Washington, D.C. Office)
Paul G. Saunders, II
William H. Schwarzschild, III
Wayne A. Whitham, Jr.

Henry C. Su

For Complete List of Firm Personnel, See General Section

For full biographical listings, see the Martindale-Hubbell Law Directory

VIENNA, Fairfax Co.

STAUFFER & ABRAHAM (AV)

Suite 1000, Tycon Tower, 8000 Towers Crescent Drive, 22182-2700
Telephone: 703-893-4670
Telecopier: 703-827-0545

MEMBERS OF FIRM

Mark S. Abraham
R. Grant Decker
T. Patrick Dulany
Thomas E. Helf
Ronald I. Hyatt (Not admitted in VA)
Kurt C. Rommel
William L. Stauffer, Jr.

Lora A. Brzezynski
Robert A. Harris, IV
Jeffrey M. Mervis

For full biographical listings, see the Martindale-Hubbell Law Directory

WASHINGTON

*SEATTLE,** King Co.

GAITÁN & CUSACK (AV)

30th Floor Two Union Square, 601 Union Street, 98101-2324
Telephone: 206-521-3000
Facsimile: 206-386-5259
Anchorage, Alaska Office: 425 G Street, Suite 760.
Telephone: 907-278-3001.
Facsimile: 907-278-6068.
San Francisco, California Office: 275 Battery Street, 20th Floor.
Telephone: 415-398-5562.
Fax: 415-398-4033.

(See Next Column)

GAITÁN & CUSACK—*Continued*

Washington, D.C. Office: 2000 L Street, Suite 200.
Telephone: 202-296-4637.
Fax: 202-296-4650.

MEMBERS OF FIRM

José E. Gaitán
Kenneth J. Cusack (Resident, Anchorage, Alaska Office)
William F. Knowles
Ronald L. Bozarth

OF COUNSEL

Howard K. Todd
Gary D. Gayton
Michel P. Stern (Also practicing alone, Bellevue, Washington)
Christopher A. Byrne
Patricia D. Ryan

ASSOCIATES

Mary F. O'Boyle
Bruce H. Williams
David J. Onsager
Diana T. Jimenez
Robert T. Mimbu
Cristina C. Kapela
Camilla M. Hedberg
John E. Lenker
Kathleen C. Healy

Representative Clients: Chemical Bank; Seafirst Bank; Federal Deposit Insurance Corporation; Resolution Trust Corporation; Fred Meyer Employees Credit Union; Great American Bank; Merabank; Federal Savings Bank; Safeway Employees Credit Union; West One Bank.

For full biographical listings, see the Martindale-Hubbell Law Directory

SMITH, SMART, HANCOCK, TABLER & SCHWENSEN (AV)

3800 Columbia Seafirst Center, 701 Fifth Avenue, 98104
Telephone: 206-624-7272
Telecopier: 206-624-5581

MEMBERS OF FIRM

J. Dimmitt Smith
Douglas J. Smart
David G. Hancock
Walter S. Tabler
Joyce S. Schwensen
Karen A. Willie

ASSOCIATES

Anne B. Tiura
Paul J. Battaglia
Oskar E. Rey
Craig A. Fielden

Reference: Seattle-First National Bank; Bank of America; Chemical Bank; Clise Properties, Inc.; Gentra Capital Corporation; Puget Sound Pilots; Aid Association for Lutherans; Citicorp Mortgage, Inc.; Lutheran Brotherhood; City of Tacoma.

For full biographical listings, see the Martindale-Hubbell Law Directory

WEST VIRGINIA

*CHARLESTON,** Kanawha Co.

JACKSON & KELLY (AV)

1600 Laidley Tower, P.O. Box 553, 25322
Telephone: 304-340-1000
Fax: 304-340-1130
Martinsburg, West Virginia Office: 300 Foxcroft Avenue, P.O. Box 1068.
Telephone: 304-263-8800.
Morgantown, West Virginia Office: 6000 Hampton Center, P.O. Box 619.
Telephone: 304-599-3000.
New Martinsville, West Virginia Office: 256 Russell Avenue, P.O. Box 68.
Telephone: 304-455-1751.
Charles Town, West Virginia Office: 700 East Washington Street, P.O. Box 983.
Telephone: 304-728-6088.
Clarksburg, West Virginia Office: 203 Main Street, P.O. Box 1587.
Telephone: 304-623-3002.
Lexington, Kentucky Office: 175 East Main Street, Suite 500, P.O. Box 2150.
Telephone: 606-255-9500.
Washington, D. C. Office: 2401 Pennsylvania Avenue, N.W., Suite 400.
Telephone: 202-973-0200.
Denver, Colorado Office: Suite 2710, 1660 Lincoln Street.
Telephone: 303-837-0003.

MEMBERS OF FIRM

James Knight Brown
John R. Lukens
Barry S. Settles (Resident Lexington, Kentucky Office)
Taunja Willis Miller
Ellen S. Cappellanti
Mary Clare Eros (Martinsburg and Charles Town, West Virginia Offices)
Charles D. Dunbar
Kevin M. McGuire (Resident, Lexington, Kentucky Office)
Charles W. Loeb, Jr.

ASSOCIATES

Eric H. London (Resident, Morgantown Office)
Elizabeth Osenton Lord
R. Scott Summers (Resident, Morgantown Office)

(See Next Column)

Representative Clients: One Valley Bancorp of West Virginia and Affiliates; United National Bank; First Empire Federal Savings & Loan Assn.; Mellon Bank, N.A.; Horizon Bancorp, Inc.; Potomac Bancshares, Inc.; Bank of Gassaway.

For Complete List of Firm Personnel, See General Section

For full biographical listings, see the Martindale-Hubbell Law Directory

*CLARKSBURG,** Harrison Co.

MCNEER, HIGHLAND & MCMUNN (AV)

Empire Building, P.O. Drawer 2040, 26301
Telephone: 304-623-6636
Facsimile: 304-623-3035
Morgantown Office: McNeer, Highland & McMunn, Baker & Armistead, 168 Chancery Row. P.O. Box 1615.
Telephone: 304-292-8473.
Fax: 304-292-1528.
Martinsburg, Office: 1446-1 Edwin Miller Boulevard. P.O. Box 2509.
Telephone: 304-264-4621.
Fax: 304-264-8623.

MEMBERS OF FIRM

C. David McMunn
J. Cecil Jarvis
James A. Varner
George B. Armistead (Resident, Morgantown Office)
Catherine D. Munster
Robert W. Trumble (Resident, Martinsburg Office)
Dennis M. Shreve
Geraldine S. Roberts
Harold M. Sklar
Jeffrey S. Bolyard
Steven R. Bratke
Michael J. Novotny (Resident, Martinsburg Office)

OF COUNSEL

James E. McNeer
Cecil B. Highland, Jr.
William L. Fury

Representative Clients: One Valley Bank of Clarksburg, National Association; Bruceton Bank; Harrison County Bank; Nationwide Mutual Insurance Cos.; Clarksburg Publishing Co.; C.I.T. Financial Services; State Automobile Mutual Insurance Co.; United Hospital Center, Inc.; West Virginia Coals, Inc.; Swanson Plating Company.

For Complete List of Firm Personnel, See General Section

For full biographical listings, see the Martindale-Hubbell Law Directory

*HUNTINGTON,** Cabell & Wayne Cos.

FRAZIER & OXLEY, L.C. (AV)

The St. James, 401 Tenth Street Mezzanine Level, P.O. Box 2808, 25727
Telephone: 304-697-4370
FAX: Available upon request

William M. Frazier
Leon K. Oxley
W. Michael Frazier

References: The Old National Bank; Commerce Bank, Huntington, N.A.

For full biographical listings, see the Martindale-Hubbell Law Directory

*PRINCETON,** Mercer Co.

GIBSON & ASSOCIATES (AV)

1345 Mercer Street, 24740
Telephone: 304-425-8276
800-742-3545

MEMBER OF FIRM

Michael F. Gibson

ASSOCIATES

Derrick Ward Lefler
Bill Huffman
Kelly R. Charnock

LEGAL SUPPORT PERSONNEL

SOCIAL SECURITY PARALEGALS

Nancy Belcher

PERSONAL INJURY PARALEGALS

Kathy Richards

WORKERS COMPENSATION PARALEGAL

Carol Hylton

MEDICAL NEGLIGENCE PARALEGAL

Deborah Fye

For full biographical listings, see the Martindale-Hubbell Law Directory

*WHEELING,** Ohio Co.

SCHRADER, RECHT, BYRD, COMPANION & GURLEY (AV)

1000 Hawley Building, 1025 Main Street, P.O. Box 6336, 26003
Telephone: 304-233-3390
Fax: 304-233-2769
Martins Ferry, Ohio Office: 205 North Fifth Street, P.O. Box 309.
Telephone: 614-633-8976.
Fax: 614-633-0400.

(See Next Column)

SCHRADER, RECHT, BYRD, COMPANION & GURLEY, *Wheeling—Continued*

PARTNERS

Henry S. Schrader (Retired)
Arthur M. Recht
Ray A. Byrd
James F. Companion
Terence M. Gurley
Frank X. Duff
Teresa Rieman-Camilletti
Yolonda G. Lambert
Patrick S. Casey
Sandra M. Chapman
Daniel P. Fry (Resident, Martins Ferry, Ohio Office)
James P. Mazzone

ASSOCIATES

Sandra K. Law
D. Kevin Coleman
Denise A. Jebbia
Edythe A. Nash
Robert G. McCoid
Denise D. Klug
Thomas E. Johnston

OF COUNSEL

James A. Byrum, Jr.

General Counsel: WesBanco Bank-Elm Grove.
Representative Clients: CIGNA Property and Casualty Cos.; Columbia Gas Transmission Corp.; Commercial Union Assurance Co.; Hazlett, Burt & Watson, Inc.; Stone & Thomas Department Stores; Transamerica Commercial Finance Corp.; Wheeling-Pittsburgh Steel Corp.

For full biographical listings, see the Martindale-Hubbell Law Directory

WISCONSIN

*MADISON,** Dane Co.

LAFOLLETTE & SINYKIN (AV)

One East Main, Suite 500, 53703
Telephone: 608-257-3911
Fax: 608-257-0609
Mailing Address: P.O. Box 2719, 53701-2719
Sauk City, Wisconsin Office: 603 Water Street.
Telephone: 608-643-2408.
Stoughton, Wisconsin Office: 113 East Main Street, P.O. Box 191.
Telephone: 608-873-9464.
Fax: 608-873-0781.

MEMBERS OF FIRM

Earl H. Munson
Christopher J. Wilcox
Howard A. Sweet
Thomas A. Hoffner
David E. McFarlane
Brady C. Williamson
Timothy J. Muldowney
Michael E. Skindrud
Jonathan C. Aked
Brett A. Thompson
Noreen J. Parrett
Eugenia G. Carter

ASSOCIATE

Timothy F. Nixon

Reference: M&I Madison Bank.

For Complete List of Firm Personnel, See General Section

For full biographical listings, see the Martindale-Hubbell Law Directory

*MILWAUKEE,** Milwaukee Co.

KOHNER, MANN & KAILAS, S.C. (AV)

1572 East Capitol Drive, P.O. Box 19982, 53211-0982
Telephone: 414-962-5110
Fax: 414-962-8725

Marvin L. Kohner (1908-1975)
Robert L. Mann
Steve Kailas
Mark R. Wolters
Jordan B. Reich
David S. Chartier

Roy Paul Roth
Gary P. Lantzy
Christopher C. Kailas
Robert E. Nailen
Matthew P. Gerdisch
Darrell R. Zall
Daniel J. Flynn
Timothy L. Zuberbier
Shawn G. Rice

Representative Clients: EcoLab, Inc.; Parker Pen Co.; Ray O Vac, Inc.

For full biographical listings, see the Martindale-Hubbell Law Directory

QUARLES & BRADY (AV)

411 East Wisconsin Avenue, 53202-4497
Telephone: 414-277-5000
Cable Address: "Lawdock"
Fax: 414-271-3552.
TWX: 910-262-3426
Madison, Wisconsin Office: Firstar Plaza, One South Pinckney Street, P.O. Box 2113.
Telephone: 608-251-5000.
Fax: 608-251-9166.
West Palm Beach, Florida Office: 222 Lakeview Avenue, 4th Floor.
Telephone: 407-653-5000.
Fax: 407-653-5333.

(See Next Column)

Naples, Florida Office: Barnett Center, 4501 Tamiami Trail North.
Telephone: 813-262-5959.
Fax: 813-434-4999.
Phoenix, Arizona Office: One Camelback Building, One East Camelback Road, Suite 400.
Telephone: 602-230-5500.
Fax: 602-230-5598.

MEMBERS OF FIRM

(ALPHABETICALLY BY YEAR OF ADMISSION TO BAR)

James Urdan
Jeremy C. Shea (Resident, Madison Office)
Arthur B. Harris
Patrick M. Ryan
James D. Friedman
F. Joseph McMackin, III (Resident, Naples, Florida Office)
Timothy G. Hains (Resident, Naples, Florida Office)
Andrew M. Barnes
Kenneth V. Hallett
Charles H. McMullen
Elizabeth A. Orelup

ASSOCIATES

John D. Humphreville (Resident, Naples, Florida Office)
John E. Dunn
Deborah L. Skurulsky

For Complete List of Firm Personnel, See General Section

For full biographical listings, see the Martindale-Hubbell Law Directory

REINHART, BOERNER, VAN DEUREN, NORRIS & RIESELBACH, S.C. (AV)

1000 North Water Street, P.O. Box 92900, 53202-0900
Telephone: 414-298-1000
Facsimile: 414-298-8097
Denver, Colorado Office: One Norwest Center, 1700 Lincoln Street, Suite 3725.
Telephone: 303-831-0909.
Fax: 303-831-4805.
Madison, Wisconsin Office: 7617 Mineral Point Road, 53701-2020.
Telephone: 608-283-7900.
Fax: 608-283-7919.
Washington, D.C. Office: 601 Pennsylvania Avenue, N.W., North Building, Suite 750.
Telephone: 202-393-3636.
Fax: 202-393-0796.

Richard H. Norris III
William F. Flynn

Jill M. Koch
Martin G. Flyke
Michael R. Miller

For Complete List of Firm Personnel, See General Section

For full biographical listings, see the Martindale-Hubbell Law Directory

WYOMING

*CASPER,** Natrona Co.

BROWN & DREW (AV)

Casper Business Center, Suite 800, 123 West First Street, 82601-2486
Telephone: 307-234-1000
800-877-6755
Telefax: 307-265-8025

MEMBERS OF FIRM

Morris R. Massey
W. Thomas Sullins, II
Donn J. McCall
Russell M. Blood

ASSOCIATES

Jon B. Huss
Courtney Robert Kepler

Attorneys for: First Interstate Bank of Wyoming, N.A.; Norwest Bank Wyoming, N.A.; Hilltop National Bank; The CIT Group/Industrial Financing; The CIT Group/Sales Financing; Chase Manhattan Bank, N.A.; Manufacturers Hanover Trust Co.; NationsBank; Key Lease Incorporated of Ohio; Wyoming Community Development Authority.

For Complete List of Firm Personnel, See General Section

For full biographical listings, see the Martindale-Hubbell Law Directory

*CHEYENNE,** Laramie Co.

HICKEY, MACKEY, EVANS, WALKER & STEWART (AV)

1712 Carey Avenue, P.O. Drawer 467, 82003
Telephone: 307-634-1525
Telecopier: 307-638-7335

MEMBERS OF FIRM

Paul J. Hickey
Terry W. Mackey
David F. Evans
John M. Walker
Mark R. Stewart III
Richard D. Tim Bush

(See Next Column)

HICKEY, MACKEY, EVANS, WALKER & STEWART—*Continued*

A List of Representative Clients will be furnished upon request.
Reference: Norwest Bank, Cheyenne, N.A.

For full biographical listings, see the Martindale-Hubbell Law Directory

PUERTO RICO

SAN JUAN, San Juan Dist.

FIDDLER, GONZÁLEZ & RODRÍGUEZ

Chase Manhattan Bank Building (Hato Rey), P.O. Box 363507, 00936-3507
Telephone: 809-753-3113
Telecopier: 809-759-3123

MEMBERS OF FIRM

Salvador E. Casellas
Rafael Cortés-Dapena
Antonio R. Sifre

Representative Clients: The Chase Manhattan Bank, N.A.; Banco Bilbao Vizcaya; The Bank & Trust Company of Puerto Rico; Shearson, Lehman, Hutton.

For Complete List of Firm Personnel, See General Section

For full biographical listings, see the Martindale-Hubbell Law Directory

GOLDMAN ANTONETTI & CÓRDOVA

American International Plaza Fourteenth & Fifteenth Floors, 250 Muñoz Rivera Avenue (Hato Rey), P.O. Box 70364, 00936-0364
Telephone: 809-759-8000
Telecopiers: 809-767-9333 (Main)
809-767-9177 (Litigation Department)
809-767-8660 (Labor & Corporate Law Departments)
809-767-9325 (Tax & Environmental Law Departments)

MEMBERS OF FIRM

Jorge Souss
Pedro Morell Losada
Thelma Rivera-Miranda
Francisco J. García-García

OF COUNSEL

Enrique Córdova Díaz

Representative Clients: Banco Bilbao Vizcaya; Banque Paribas; Ponce Federal Bank, F.S.B.; Banco Exterior de Espana, S.A.; The Bank of Nova Scotia; The Royal Bank of Canada; Scotiabank de Puerto Rico.

For Complete List of Firm Personnel, See General Section

For full biographical listings, see the Martindale-Hubbell Law Directory

GONZALEZ & BENNAZAR

Capital Center Building South Tower - 9th Floor, Arterial Hostos Avenue (Hato Rey), 00918
Telephone: 809-754-9191
Fax: 809-754-9325

MEMBERS OF FIRM

Raul E. González Díaz
A. J. Bennazar-Zequeira

Representative Clients: American Express Travel Related Services Co., Inc.; Federal Deposit Insurance Corp.; First Financial Caribbean; Troy Savings Bank; Bank of Miami; Resolution Trust Corp.; Banco Bilbao-Vizcaya.

For Complete List of Firm Personnel, See General Section

For full biographical listings, see the Martindale-Hubbell Law Directory

JORGE R. JIMENEZ

Suite 807 Bankers Finance Tower, 654 Muñoz Rivera Avenue (Hato Rey), 00918
Telephone: 809-763-0106
Fax: 809-763-0574

For full biographical listings, see the Martindale-Hubbell Law Directory

MÁRTINEZ ODELL & CALABRIA

Banco Popular Center, 16th Floor, (Hato Rey), P.O. Box 190998, 00919-0998
Telephone: 809-753-8914
Facsimile: 809-753-8402; 809-759-9075; 809-764-5664

MEMBERS OF FIRM

Lawrence Odell
Jose B. Diaz Asencio
Luis E. Lopez Correa

(See Next Column)

ASSOCIATES

Rafael Kodesh-Baragaño
Javier E. Ferrer-Canals
Maria del Carmen Garriga
Gary L. Leonard
Jose David Medina-Rivera
Ramón Eugenio-Meléndez
Victor Armando Lago
Gloria M. Sierra-Enriquez
Guillermo A. Somoza-Colombani
Lourdes M. Defendini-Rodriguez
Maria Teresa Rigau-Escudero
Luis J. Acevedo-Bengochea

Representative Clients: A.T. & T. Corp.; Pepsi-Cola P.R. Bottling Co.; Banco Popular de Puerto Rico; I.T.T. Financial Corp.; John H. Harland Company of Puerto Rico, Inc.; Lutron Electronics Co., Inc.; Paine Webber, Inc.; Lotus Development Corp.; Western Digital.

For Complete List of Firm Personnel, See General Section

For full biographical listings, see the Martindale-Hubbell Law Directory

VIRGIN ISLANDS

*CHARLOTTE AMALIE, ST. THOMAS,** St. Thomas

BIRCH, DE JONGH & HINDELS

Poinsettia House at Bluebeards Castle, P.O. Box 1197, 00804
Telephone: 809-774-1100
Telefax: 809-774-7300
Other St. Thomas Office: Palm Passage, Charlotte Amalie, 00802.

MEMBERS OF FIRM

Everett B. Birch (1922-1987)
John P. de Jongh
James H. Hindels

ASSOCIATE

Stanley L. de Jongh

OF COUNSEL

Richard P. Farrelly

Representative Clients: Barclays Bank PLC; The Chase Manhattan Bank, N.A.; Citibank, N.A.; Ernst & Young; Corestates First Pennsylvania Bank; FNMA/FHLMC (Regional Counsel); Westinghouse Foreign Sales Corp.; Hess Oil Virgin Islands Corp.; Peat, Marwick, V.I.

For Complete List of Firm Personnel, See General Section

For full biographical listings, see the Martindale-Hubbell Law Directory

GRUNERT STOUT BRUCH & MOORE

24-25 Kongensgade, P.O. Box 1030, 00804
Telephone: 809-774-1320
Fax: 809-774-7839

MEMBERS OF FIRM

John E. Stout
Susan Bruch Moorehead
Treston E. Moore

ASSOCIATES

Maryleen Thomas
Richard F. Taylor
H. Kevin Mart (Not admitted in VI)

OF COUNSEL

William L. Blum

For full biographical listings, see the Martindale-Hubbell Law Directory

CANADA ALBERTA

*CALGARY,** Calgary Jud. Dist.

BENNETT JONES VERCHERE (AV)

4500 Bankers Hall East, 855-2nd Street S.W., T2P 4K7
Telephone: (403) 298-3100
Facsimile: (403) 265-7219
Edmonton, Alberta Office: 1000, 10035-105 Street.
Telephone: (403) 421-8133.
Facsimile: (403) 421-7951.
Toronto, Ontario Office: 3400 1 First Canadian Place. P.O. Box 130.
Telephone: (416) 863-1200.
Facsimile: (416) 863-1716.
Ottawa, Ontario Office: Suite 1800. 350 Alberta Street, Box 25, K1R 1A4.
Telephone: (613) 230-4935.
Facsimile: (613) 230-3836.
Montreal, Quebec Office: Suite 1600, 1 Place Ville Marie.
Telephone: (514) 871-1200.
Facsimile: (514) 871-8115.

(See Next Column)

BENNETT JONES VERCHERE, *Calgary—Continued*

MEMBER OF FIRM

Walter B. O'Donoghue, Q.C.

For Complete List of Firm Personnel, See General Section

For full biographical listings, see the Martindale-Hubbell Law Directory

*EDMONTON,** Edmonton Jud. Dist.

LUCAS BOWKER & WHITE (AV)

Esso Tower - Scotia Place, 1201-10060 Jasper Avenue, T5J 4E5
Telephone: 403-426-5330
Telecopier: 403-428-1066

MEMBERS OF FIRM

Gerald A. I. Lucas, Q.C.
George E. Bowker, Q.C.
David J. Stratton, Q.C.
Cecilia I. Johnstone, Q.C.
John Reginald Day, Q.C.
E. James Kindrake
Elizabeth A. Johnson
Robert C. Dunseith
Douglas H. Shell
Robert A. Seidel
Robert P. Bruce

ASSOCIATES

Kevin J. Smith
Gordon V. Garside
Deborah L. Hughes
Douglas A. Bodner

COUNSEL

Joan C. Copp

Reference: Canadian Imperial Bank of Commerce.

For Complete List of Firm Personnel, See General Section

For full biographical listings, see the Martindale-Hubbell Law Directory

PARLEE MCLAWS (AV)

15th Floor Manulife Place, 10180 101st Street, T5J 4K1
Telephone: 403-423-8500
Telecopier: 403-423-2870
Calgary, Alberta Office: 3400, Western Canadian Place, 707 - 8th Avenue, S.W.
Telephone: 403-294-7000.
Telecopier: 403-265-8263.

MEMBERS OF FIRM

C. H. Kerr, Q.C.
M. D. MacDonald
K. F. Bailey, Q.C.
R. B. Davison, Q.C.
F. R. Haldane
P. E. J. Curran
D. G. Finlay
J. K. McFadyen
R. C. Secord
D. L. Kennedy
D. C. Rolf
D. F. Pawlowski
A. A. Garber
R. P. James
D. C. Wintermute
J. L. Cairns
R. A. Newton, Q.C.
T. A. Cockrall, Q.C.
H. D. Montemurro
F. J. Niziol
R. W. Wilson
I. L. MacLachlan
R. O. Langley
R. G. McBean
J. T. Neilson
E. G. Rice
J. F. McGinnis
J. H. H. Hockin
G. W. Jaycock
M. J. K. Nikel
B. J. Curial
S. L. May
M. S. Poretti

ASSOCIATES

C. R. Head
A.W. Slemko
L. H. Hamdon
K.A. Smith
K. D. Fallis-Howell
D. S. Tam
J.W. McClure
F.H. Belzil
R.A. Renz
J.G. Paulson
K. E. Buss
B. L. Andriachuk
P. E. S. J. Kennedy
R. Feraco
R.J. Billingsley
N.B.R. Thompson
P. A. Shenher
I. C. Johnson
K.G. Koshman
D.D. Dubrule
G. T. Lund
W.D. Johnston
G. E. Flemming
K. P. Nayyer

For full biographical listings, see the Martindale-Hubbell Law Directory

CANADA BRITISH COLUMBIA

*VANCOUVER,** Vancouver Co.

RUSSELL & DUMOULIN (AV)

2100-1075 West Georgia Street, V6E 3G2
Telephone: 604-631-3131
Fax: 604-631-3232
A Member of the national association of Borden DuMoulin Howard Gervais, comprising Russell & DuMoulin, Vancouver, British Columbia; Howard Mackie, Calgary, Alberta; Borden & Elliot, Toronto, Ontario; Mackenzie Gervais, Montreal, Quebec and Borden DuMoulin Howard Gervais, London, England.
Strategic Alliance with Perkins Coie with offices in Seattle, Spokane and Bellevue, Washington; Portland, Oregon; Anchorage, Alaska; Los Angeles, California; Washington, D.C.; Hong Kong and Taipei, Taiwan.
Represented in Hong Kong by Vincent T.K. Cheung, Yap & Co.

MEMBERS OF FIRM

Robert A. Goodrich
Donald J. Weaver

Representative Clients: Alcan Smelters & Chemicals Ltd.; The Bank of Nova Scotia; Canada Trust Co.; The Canada Life Assurance Co.; Forest Industrial Relations Ltd.; Honda Canada Inc.; IBM Canada Ltd.; Macmillan Bloedel Ltd.; Nissho Iwai Canada Ltd.; The Toronto-Dominion Bank.

For Complete List of Firm Personnel, See General Section

For full biographical listings, see the Martindale-Hubbell Law Directory

CANADA NEW BRUNSWICK

*SAINT JOHN,** Saint John Co.

CLARK, DRUMMIE & COMPANY (AV)

40 Wellington Row, P.O. Box 6850 Station "A", E2L 4S3
Telephone: 506-633-3800
Telecopier (Automatic): 506-633-3811

MEMBERS OF FIRM

Thomas B. Drummie, Q.C.
John M. McNair
Willard M. Jenkins
Patrick J. P. Ervin

OF COUNSEL

L. Paul Zed, M.P.

Reference: Royal Bank of Canada.

For Complete List of Firm Personnel, See General Section

For full biographical listings, see the Martindale-Hubbell Law Directory

CANADA NOVA SCOTIA

*HALIFAX,** Halifax Co.

MCINNES COOPER & ROBERTSON (AV)

1601 Lower Water Street, P.O. Box 730, B3J 2V1
Telephone: 902-425-6500
Fax: 902-425-6350
St. John's, Newfoundland Office: Suite 602, Scotia Centre, 235 Water Street, P.O. Box 547. A1C, 5K8.
Telephone: 709-726-9500.
Fax: 709-726-9550.

Harry E. Wrathall, Q.C.
Joseph A. F. Macdonald, Q.C.
Robert G. Belliveau, Q.C.
Linda Lee Oland
Peter M. S. Bryson
Lawrence J. Hayes, Q.C.
David H. Reardon, Q.C.
F. V. W. Penick
John D. Stringer
Karen Oldfield
Stephen J. Kingston

ASSOCIATE

Bernard F. Miller

Attorneys for: Bank of Nova Scotia; Imperial Oil, Limited; Frank B. Hall & Co., Inc. (New York); American Steamship Owners Protection & Indemnity Association, Inc.; Coca-Cola, Ltd.; Scott Worldwide Inc.; Hong Kong Bank of Canada.

For Complete List of Firm Personnel, See General Section

For full biographical listings, see the Martindale-Hubbell Law Directory

CANADA
ONTARIO

*TORONTO,** Regional Munic. of York

BORDEN & ELLIOT (AV)

Barristers & Solicitors
Scotia Plaza, 40 King Street West, M5H 3Y4
Telephone: 416-367-6000
Telecopier: 416-367-6749
Internet: @ borden.com
A Member of the national association of Borden DuMoulin Howard Gervais, comprising Borden & Elliot in Toronto, Ontario, Russell & DuMoulin in Vancouver, British Columbia, Howard, Mackie in Calgary, Alberta and Mackenzie Gervais in Montréal, Québec. Borden DuMoulin Howard Gervais also operates an office in London, England.

MEMBER AND ASSOCIATES

William S. Robertson

For Complete List of Firm Personnel, See General Section

For full biographical listings, see the Martindale-Hubbell Law Directory

CANADA
QUEBEC

*MONTREAL,** Montreal Dist.

BYERS CASGRAIN (AV)

A Member of McMillan Bull Casgrain
Suite 3900, 1 Place Ville-Marie, H3B 4M7
Telephone: 514-878-8800
Telecopier: 514-866-2241
Cable Address: "Magee"
Telex: 05-24195

Philippe Casgrain, Q.C.
Robert S. Carswell
Ray E. Lawson
Allan A. Mass
Michel A. Brunet
David McAusland
Louis Dumont
Nicolas Beaudin
Alain Roberge
André Racine
Charles R. Spector
Richard B. Epstein
Patrice Beaudin
Natali Boulva
Stéphane W. Miron

For Complete List of Firm Personnel, See General Section

For full biographical listings, see the Martindale-Hubbell Law Directory

GOLDSTEIN, FLANZ & FISHMAN (AV)

Suite 4100, 1250 René-Lévesque Boulevard West, H3B 4W8
Telephone: 514-932-4100
Cable Address: "Meybat"
Telex: 05-24593
Telecopier: 514-932-4170

MEMBERS OF FIRM

Yoine Goldstein
Leonard W. Flanz
Avram Fishman
Mark Schrager
Gilles Paquin
Mark E. Meland
Alain Daigle
Nancy Gross
Michael Gaon
Elyse Rosen
James D. Hughes

For full biographical listings, see the Martindale-Hubbell Law Directory

MCMASTER MEIGHEN (AV)

A General Partnership
7th Floor, 630 René-Lévesque Boulevard West, H3B 4H7
Telephone: 514-879-1212
Telecopier: 514-878-0605
Cable Address: "Cammerall"
Telex: "Cammerall MTL" 05-268637
Affiliated with Fraser & Beatty in Toronto, North York, Ottawa and Vancouver.

MEMBERS OF FIRM

Richard J. Riendeau, Q.C.
Elizabeth A. Mitchell
Pierre B. Côté
Chantal Béique
Norman A. Saibil
Benoît M. Provost
D. James Papadimitriou
J. Anthony Penhale

For Complete List of Firm Personnel, See General Section

For full biographical listings, see the Martindale-Hubbell Law Directory

CANADA
SASKATCHEWAN

*REGINA,** Regina Jud. Centre

MCDOUGALL, READY (AV)

700 Royal Bank Building, 2010-11th Avenue, S4P 0J3
Telephone: 306-757-1641
Telecopier: 306-359-0785
Saskatoon, Saskatchewan, Canada Office: 301 - 111 2nd Avenue South.
Telephone: 306-653-1641.
Telecopier: 306-665-8511.

MEMBERS OF FIRM

William F. Ready, Q.C.
R. Shawn Smith
Michael W. Milani
W. Randall Rooke (Resident, Saskatoon Office)
Ronald L. Miller (Resident, Saskatoon Office)

Catherine M. Wall

Representative Clients: Royal Bank of Canada.

For Complete List of Firm Personnel, See General Section

For full biographical listings, see the Martindale-Hubbell Law Directory

*SASKATOON,** Saskatoon Jud. Centre

MCKERCHER, MCKERCHER & WHITMORE (AV)

374 Third Avenue, South, S7K 1M5
Telephone: 306-653-2000
Fax: 306-244-7335
Regina, Saskatchewan Office: 1000 - 1783 Hamilton Street.
Telephone: 306-352-7661.
Fax: 306-781-7113.

MEMBERS OF FIRM

Peter A. Whitmore, Q.C. (Resident, Regina Office)
John R. Beckman, Q.C.
Leslie J. Dick Batten

ASSOCIATE

Gordon S. Wyant

For Complete List of Firm Personnel, See General Section

For full biographical listings, see the Martindale-Hubbell Law Directory

BANKRUPTCY LAW

ALABAMA

*BIRMINGHAM,** Jefferson Co.

BALCH & BINGHAM (AV)

1710 Sixth Avenue North, P.O. Box 306, 35201
Telephone: 205-251-8100
Facsimile: 205-226-8798
Other Birmingham, Alabama Office: 1901 Sixth Avenue North, 35203.
Telephone: 205-251-8100.
Facsimile: 205-226-8799.
Montgomery, Alabama Office: The Winter Building, 2 Dexter Avenue, 36101.
Telephone: 205-834-6500.
Facsimile: 205-269-3115.
Huntsville, Alabama Office: Suite 810, 200 West Court Square, 35801.
Telephone: 205-551-0171.
Facsimile: 205-551-0174.
Washington, D.C. Office: Suite 800, 1101 Connecticut Avenue, N.W., 20036.
Telephone: 202-296-0387.
Facsimile: 202-452-8180.

MEMBERS OF FIRM

Stanley M. Brock — Clark R. Hammond

ASSOCIATES

Jesse Stringer Vogtle, Jr. — Larry Stephen Logsdon

Counsel for: Alabama Power Co.; Blue Cross and Blue Shield of Alabama; The Boeing Company; Brasfield & Gorrie, Inc.; Compass Bancshares, Inc.; Harbert Corp.; Kimberly-Clark Corp.; Southern Company Services, Inc.; Southern Research Institute; Vesta Insurance Group, Inc.

For Complete List of Firm Personnel, See General Section

For full biographical listings, see the Martindale-Hubbell Law Directory

BRADLEY, ARANT, ROSE & WHITE (AV)

1400 Park Place Tower, 2001 Park Place, 35203
Telephone: 205-521-8000
Telex: 494-1324
Facsimile: 205-251-8611, 251-8665, 252-0264
Facsimile (Southtrust Office): 205-251-9915
Huntsville, Alabama Office: 200 Clinton Avenue West, Suite 900.
Telephone: 205-517-5100.
Facsimile: 205-533-5069.

MEMBER OF FIRM

John P. Whittington

ASSOCIATES

Sherri Tucker Freeman — J. Patrick Darby
J. Paul Compton, Jr. — Jay R. Bender

For Complete List of Firm Personnel, See General Section

For full biographical listings, see the Martindale-Hubbell Law Directory

CORLEY, MONCUS & WARD, P.C. (AV)

Suite 650, 2100 SouthBridge Parkway, 35209
Telephone: 205-879-5959
Telecopier: 205-879-5859

Ezra B. Perry, Jr.

For Complete List of Firm Personnel, See General Section

For full biographical listings, see the Martindale-Hubbell Law Directory

GORDON, SILBERMAN, WIGGINS & CHILDS, A PROFESSIONAL CORPORATION (AV)

1400 SouthTrust Tower, 420 North 20th Street, 35203
Telephone: 205-328-0640
Telecopier: 205-254-1500

Wilbur G. Silberman — Harvey L. Wachsman

Mark P. Williams

For Complete List of Firm Personnel, See General Section

For full biographical listings, see the Martindale-Hubbell Law Directory

PRITCHARD, MCCALL & JONES (AV)

800 Financial Center, 35203
Telephone: 205-328-9190

MEMBERS OF FIRM

William S. Pritchard (1890-1967) — Julian P. Hardy, Jr.
Alexander W. Jones (1914-1988) — Alexander W. Jones, Jr.
William S. Pritchard, Jr. — F. Hilton-Green Tomlinson
Madison W. O'Kelley, Jr. — James G. Henderson
William S. Pritchard, III

ASSOCIATES

Michael L. McKerley — Nina Michele LaFleur
Robert Bond Higgins — Mary W. Burge

Representative Clients: First National Bank of Columbiana; Central State Bank of Calera; Buffalo Rock-Pepsi-Cola Bottling Co.; Gillis Advertising, Inc.; Liberty Mutual Insurance Co.; Reliance Insurance Company; SouthTrust Bank, N.A.; Bromberg & Company, Inc.; Farmers Furniture Company; First Commercial Bank.

For full biographical listings, see the Martindale-Hubbell Law Directory

SCHOEL, OGLE, BENTON AND CENTENO (AV)

600 Financial Center, 505 North 20th Street, P.O. Box 1865, 35201-1865
Telephone: 205-521-7000
Telecopier: 205-521-7007

MEMBERS OF FIRM

Jerry W. Schoel — Melinda Murphy Dionne
Richard F. Ogle — Gilbert M. Sullivan, Jr.
Lee R. Benton — David O. Upshaw
Paul A. Liles — Paul Avron
Douglas J. Centeno — Lynn McCreery Shaw

Reference: National Bank of Commerce; First Alabama Bank.

For full biographical listings, see the Martindale-Hubbell Law Directory

SIROTE & PERMUTT, P.C. (AV)

2222 Arlington Avenue, South, P.O. Box 55727, 35255
Telephone: 205-933-7111
Facsimile: 205-930-5301
Huntsville, Alabama Office: 200 Clinton Avenue, N.W., Suite 1000.
Telephone: 205-536-1711.
Facsimile: 205-534-9650.
Mobile, Alabama Office: One St. Louis Centre, Suite 1000.
Telephone: 205-432-1671.
Facsimile: 205-434-0196.
Montgomery, Alabama Office: Colonial Commerce Center, Suite 305 One Commerce Street.
Telephone: 205-261-3400.
Facsimile: 205-261-3434.
Tuscaloosa, Alabama Office: 2216 14th Street.
Telephone: 205-752-2089.

Karl B. Friedman — Thomas G. Tutten, Jr.
Donald M. Wright — Stephen B. Porterfield

Representative Clients: International Business Machines (IBM); General Motors Corp.; Colonial Bank; Bruno's, Inc.; University of Alabama Hospitals; Westinghouse Electric Corp.; First Alabama Bank; Monsanto Chemical Company; South Central Bell; Prudential Insurance Company; American Home Products, Inc.; Minnesota Mining and Manufacturing, Inc. (3M).

For Complete List of Firm Personnel, See General Section

For full biographical listings, see the Martindale-Hubbell Law Directory

*GADSDEN,** Etowah Co.

FORD & HUNTER, P.C. (AV)

The Lancaster Building, 645 Walnut Street, Suite 5, P.O. Box 388, 35902
Telephone: 205-546-5432
Fax: 205-546-5435

George P. Ford — J. Gullatte Hunter, III

Richard M. Blythe

References: General Motors Acceptance Corp.; AmSouth Bank, N.A.

For Complete List of Firm Personnel, See General Section

For full biographical listings, see the Martindale-Hubbell Law Directory

*HUNTSVILLE,** Madison Co.

BERRY, ABLES, TATUM, LITTLE & BAXTER, P.C. (AV)

Legal Building, 315 Franklin Street, S.E., P.O. Box 165, 35804-0165
Telephone: 205-533-3740
Facsimile: 205-533-3751

William H. Blanton (1889-1973) — Loyd H. Little, Jr.
Joe M. Berry — James T. Baxter, III
L. Bruce Ables — Thomas E. Parker, Jr.
James T. Tatum, Jr. — Bill G. Hall

(See Next Column)

BERRY, ABLES, TATUM, LITTLE & BAXTER P.C., *Huntsville—Continued*

Representative Clients: AmSouth Bank, N.A.; First Alabama Bank; General Shale Products Co.; The Hartz Corp.; Litton Industries, Inc.; Farmers Tractor Co.; Colonial Bank; Farm Credit Bank of Texas; Resolution Trust Corp.
Reference: First Alabama Bank.

For full biographical listings, see the Martindale-Hubbell Law Directory

SIROTE & PERMUTT, P.C. (AV)

Suite 1000, 200 Clinton Avenue, N.W., 35801
Telephone: 205-536-1711
Facsimile: 205-534-9650
Birmingham, Alabama Office: 2222 Arlington Avenue, South, P.O. Box 55727.
Telephone: 205-933-7111.
Facsimile: 205-930-5301.
Mobile, Alabama Office: One St. Louis Centre, Suite 1000.
Telephone: 205-432-1671.
Facsimile: 205-434-0196.
Montgomery, Alabama Office: Colonial Commerce Center, Suite 305, One Commerce Street.
Telephone: 205-261-3400.
Facsimile: 205-261-3434.
Tuscaloosa, Alabama Office: 2216 14th Street.
Telephone: 205-752-2089.

George W. Royer, Jr. Roderic G. Steakley

For Complete List of Firm Personnel, See General Section

For full biographical listings, see the Martindale-Hubbell Law Directory

*MOBILE,** Mobile Co.

FEIBELMAN, SHULMAN AND TERRY (AV)

150 North Royal Street, Suite 1000, P.O. Box 2082, 36652
Telephone: 334-433-1597
Facsimile: 334-433-1613

MEMBERS OF FIRM

Herbert P. Feibelman, Jr. (1933-1983)
William S. Shulman
Russell S. Terry
Eric J. Breithaupt

Representative Clients: AmSouth Bank; Apex Corp.; Appraisal & Consultant Group, Inc.; Citizens' Bank; Engineered Textile Products, Inc.; First Alabama Bank; First Citizens Bank of Monroe County; ITT Commercial Finance Corp.; Julius Goldstein & Son, Inc..
Reference: First Alabama Bank.

For full biographical listings, see the Martindale-Hubbell Law Directory

FINKBOHNER AND LAWLER (AV)

169 Dauphin Street Suite 300, P.O. Box 3085, 36652
Telephone: 334-438-5871
Fax: 334-432-8052

MEMBERS OF FIRM

George W. Finkbohner, Jr. George W. Finkbohner, III
John L. Lawler Royce A. Ray, III

For full biographical listings, see the Martindale-Hubbell Law Directory

JOHNSTONE, ADAMS, BAILEY, GORDON AND HARRIS (AV)

Royal St. Francis Building, 104 St. Francis Street, P.O. Box 1988, 36633
Telephone: 334-432-7682
Facsimile: 334-432-2800
Telex: 782040

MEMBERS OF FIRM

I. David Cherniak William Alexander Gray, Jr.

General Counsel for: First Alabama Bank, Mobile; Infirmary Health System/Mobile Infirmary Medical Center/Rotary Rehabilitation Hospital (Multi-Hospital System).
Counsel for: Oil and Gas: Exxon Corp. Business and Corporate: Bell South Telecommunications, Inc.; Aluminum Co. of America; Michelin Tire Corp.; Metropolitan Life Insurance Co.; The Travelers Insurance Cos. Marine: The West of England Ship Owners Mutual Protection and Indemnity Association (Luxembourg); The Standard Steamship Owners' Protection and Indemnity Association (Bermuda) Ltd.

For Complete List of Firm Personnel, See General Section

For full biographical listings, see the Martindale-Hubbell Law Directory

LYONS, PIPES & COOK, P.C. (AV)

2 North Royal Street, P.O. Box 2727, 36652-2727
Telephone: 334-432-4481
Cable Address: "Lysea"
Telecopier: 334-433-1820

G. Sage Lyons W. David Johnson, Jr.
John C. Bell

Representative Clients: Chrysler Credit Corporation; Deere Credit Services; Mobile Airport Authority; SouthTrust Bank of Mobile.

(See Next Column)

For Complete List of Firm Personnel, See General Section

For full biographical listings, see the Martindale-Hubbell Law Directory

SIROTE & PERMUTT, P.C. (AV)

One St. Louis Centre, Suite 1000, P.O. Drawer 2025, 36652-2025
Telephone: 334-432-1671
Facsimile: 334-434-0196
Birmingham, Alabama Office: 2222 Arlington Avenue, South, P.O. Box 55727.
Telephone: 205-933-7111.
Facsimile: 205-930-5301.
Huntsville, Alabama Office: 200 Clinton Avenue, N.W., Suite 1000.
Telephone: 205-536-1711.
Facsimile: 205-534-9650.
Montgomery, Alabama Office: Colonial Commerce Center, Suite 305, One Commerce Street.
Telephone: 205-261-3400.
Facsimile: 205-261-3434.
Tuscaloosa, Alabama Office: 2216 14th Street.
Telephone: 205-752-2089.

Stephen R. Windom T. Julian Motes
M. Donald Davis, Jr. Steven L. Nicholas

For Complete List of Firm Personnel, See General Section

For full biographical listings, see the Martindale-Hubbell Law Directory

*MONTGOMERY,** Montgomery Co.

* indicates certain Bar Register subscribers whose principal office is located elsewhere in the state and who have arranged for representation as a part of the state capital listings that follow

*** BALCH & BINGHAM (AV)**

The Winter Building, 2 Dexter Avenue, P.O. Box 78, 36101
Telephone: 334-834-6500
Facsimile: 334-269-3115
Birmingham, Alabama Offices: 1710 Sixth Avenue North, 35203.
Telephone: 205-251-8100.
Facsimile: 205-226-8798. 1901 Sixth Avenue North, 35203.
Telephone: 205-251-8100.
Facsimile: 205-226-8799.
Huntsville, Alabama Office: Suite 810, 200 West Court Square, 35801.
Telephone: 205-551-0171.
Facsimile: 205-551-0174.
Washington, D.C. Office: Suite 800, 1101 Connecticut Avenue, N.W., 20036.
Telephone: 202-296-0387.
Facsimile: 202-452-8180.

RESIDENT MEMBER OF FIRM

W. Joseph McCorkle, Jr.

RESIDENT ASSOCIATES

Patricia Anne Hamilton John S. Bowman, Jr.

Counsel for: Alabama Power Co.; Blue Cross and Blue Shield of Alabama; The Boeing Company; Brasfield & Gorrie, Inc.; Compass Bancshares, Inc.; Harbert Corp.; Kimberly-Clark Corp.; Southern Company Services, Inc.; Southern Research Institute; Vesta Insurance Group, Inc.

For Complete List of Firm Personnel, See General Section

For full biographical listings, see the Martindale-Hubbell Law Directory

PARKER, BRANTLEY & WILKERSON, P.C. (AV)

323 Adams Avenue, P.O. Box 4992, 36103-4992
Telephone: 334-265-1500
Fax: 334-265-0319

Edward B. Parker, II Mark D. Wilkerson
Paul A. Brantley Leah Snell Stephens
Darla T. Furman

Representative Clients: Federated Rural Electric Insurance Corp.; Alabama Emergency Room Administrative Services, P.C.
Reference: SouthTrust Bank, N.A.

For full biographical listings, see the Martindale-Hubbell Law Directory

ARIZONA

*PHOENIX,** Maricopa Co.

BURCH & CRACCHIOLO, P.A. (AV)

702 East Osborn Road, Suite 200, 85014
Telephone: 602-274-7611
Fax: 602-234-0341
Mailing Address: P.O. Box 16882, Phoenix, AZ, 85011

(See Next Column)

BURCH & CRACCHIOLO P.A.—*Continued*

Thomas A. Longfellow

OF COUNSEL

Howard C. Meyers

Representative Clients: Bashas' Inc.; Farmers Insurance Group; U-Haul International, Inc.

For Complete List of Firm Personnel, See General Section

For full biographical listings, see the Martindale-Hubbell Law Directory

CARMICHAEL & POWELL, PROFESSIONAL CORPORATION (AV)

7301 North 16th Street, 85020-5224
Telephone: 602-861-0777
Facsimile: 602-870-0296

Ronald W. Carmichael
Laurence B. Stevens
Donald W. Powell
Sid A. Horwitz

Stephen Manes
Brian A. Hatch
Craig A. Raby
Richard C. Gramlich

Representative Clients: Kawasaki Motors Corp; Wendy's International, Inc.; Firstar Metropolitan Bank & Trust.

For full biographical listings, see the Martindale-Hubbell Law Directory

COOK, MEDA AND LANDE, A PROFESSIONAL CORPORATION (AV)

Tishman Biltmore Office Park, 2910 East Camelback Road, Suite 150, P.O. Box 32367, 85064-2367
Telephone: 602-957-2388
Fax: 602-957-2696
1-800-ROBERT M

Robert M. Cook
Alan A. Meda
Gail R. Lande

Representative Clients: Excel Country Fresh Meats, Phoenix, AZ; Gottsch Feeding Corp., Elkhorn, NE; Rufenacht Land & Cattle Co., Phoenix, AZ; Benedict Feeding Corp., Casa Grande, AZ; Norfolk Livestock Market, Norfolk, NE; Joplin Regional Stockyard, Joplin, MO; ; U.S. Airweld, Inc., Phoenix, AZ; Health Industry Business Communications Council, Phoenix, AZ; Chapter 7 Bankruptcy Trustees; Robin Yount.

For full biographical listings, see the Martindale-Hubbell Law Directory

DAVIS & LOWE, P.C. (AV)

Suite 722, Security Building, 234 North Central Avenue, 85004
Telephone: 602-253-2882
Fax: 602-253-3088

Edward E. Davis
Virginia S. Matte
Charles W. Lowe
Don A. Beskrone
Ilene J. Lashinsky
Alisa C. Lacey

Representative Clients: Citgo Petroleum Corporation; Sears Savings Bank; Mack Financial Corporation; DATAMAG Incorporated.
Reference: Firstar Metropolitan Bank.

For full biographical listings, see the Martindale-Hubbell Law Directory

FENNEMORE CRAIG, A PROFESSIONAL CORPORATION (AV)

Two North Central, Suite 2200, 85004
Telephone: 602-257-8700
Fax: 602-257-8527
Scottsdale, Arizona Office: 6263 North Scottsdale Road, Suite 290, 85250.
Telephone: 602-257-5400.
Fax: 602-945-4932.
Tucson, Arizona Office: One South Church Avenue, Suite 1030, 85701.
Telephone: 602-624-9312.
Fax: 602-882-7383.

C. Webb Crockett
David A. Weatherwax
Leland M. Jones
Cathy L. Reece
Bryan A. Albue

Gary H. Ashby
Tamra E. Walker
Paul Sala
Richard A. Bark
Elizabeth M. Behnke
Dewain D. Fox

Representative Clients: ASARCO Incorporated; AT&T Communications; Bridgestone/Firestone, Inc.; Catellus Development Corp.; Citibank (Arizona); First Interstate Bank of Arizona; GIANT Industries; Phelps Dodge Corporation; The Atchison, Topeka & Santa Fe Railway, Co.; US WEST Communications.

For Complete List of Firm Personnel, See General Section

For full biographical listings, see the Martindale-Hubbell Law Directory

GAMMAGE & BURNHAM (AV)

One Renaissance Square, Two North Central Avenue, Suite 1800, 85004
Telephone: 602-256-0566
Fax: 602-256-4475

MEMBERS OF FIRM

F. William Sheppard
Mary B. Fylstra
Michael R. King
Ellen Harris Hoff

Representative Clients: Resolution Trust Corp.; Canadian Imperial Bank of Commerce; American Bantrust Mortgage; Bank of America.

For Complete List of Firm Personnel, See General Section

For full biographical listings, see the Martindale-Hubbell Law Directory

JOHN C. HOVER, P.C. (AV)

2901 North Central Avenue, Suite 1150, 85012
Telephone: 602-230-8777
Fax: 602-230-8707

John C. Hover

LEGAL SUPPORT PERSONNEL

PARALEGAL

Diana G. Weeks

Representative Clients: First National Bank of Arizona; Bank of Hawaii; Buckeye Irrigation Co.; Linkletter-Perris Partnership.

For full biographical listings, see the Martindale-Hubbell Law Directory

JENNINGS, STROUSS AND SALMON, P.L.C. (AV)

A Professional Limited Liability Company
One Renaissance Square, Two North Central, 85004-2393
Telephone: 602-262-5911
Fax: 602-253-3255

Gary G. Keltner
Wendy D. Woodrow
Brian N. Spector

Margaret A. Gillespie

For Complete List of Firm Personnel, See General Section

For full biographical listings, see the Martindale-Hubbell Law Directory

LEWIS AND ROCA (AV)

A Partnership including Professional Corporations
40 North Central Avenue, 85004-4429
Telephone: 602-262-5311
Fax: 602-262-5747
Tucson, Arizona Office: One South Church Avenue, Suite 700.
Telephone: 602-622-2090.
Fax: 602-622-3088.

MEMBERS OF FIRM

Gerald K. Smith
Susan M. Freeman
Randolph J. Haines
Rob Charles (Resident, Tucson Office)
Brent C. Gardner
Cathy M. Holt
Bret A. Maidman

ASSOCIATES

John R. Worth
Juliet A. Lim
David D. Rodgers
Thel W. Casper

For Complete List of Firm Personnel, See General Section

For full biographical listings, see the Martindale-Hubbell Law Directory

MARISCAL, WEEKS, MCINTYRE & FRIEDLANDER, P.A. (AV)

2901 North Central Avenue Suite 200, 85012
Telephone: 602-285-5000
Fax: 602-279-2128; 264-0340

William L. Novotny

References: Northern Trust, Arizona; Rio Salado Bank.

For Complete List of Firm Personnel, See General Section

For full biographical listings, see the Martindale-Hubbell Law Directory

MEYER, HENDRICKS, VICTOR, OSBORN & MALEDON, A PROFESSIONAL ASSOCIATION (AV)

2929 North Central Avenue Suite 2100, 85012-2794
Telephone: 602-640-9000
Facsimile: (24 Hrs.) 602-640-9050
Mailing Address: P.O. Box 33449, 85067-3449,

Jeffrey L. Sellers
Thayne Lowe
C. Taylor Ashworth
Craig D. Hansen
Gary A. Gotto
Thomas J. Salerno

Christopher Graver
Laurie B. Shough

(See Next Column)

MEYER, HENDRICKS, VICTOR, OSBORN & MALEDON A PROFESSIONAL ASSOCIATION, *Phoenix—Continued*

CONSULTANTS

Myron M. Sheinfeld (Not admitted in AZ)

Reference: Bank One Arizona, NA.

For Complete List of Firm Personnel, See General Section

For full biographical listings, see the Martindale-Hubbell Law Directory

MYERS & JENKINS, A PROFESSIONAL CORPORATION (AV)

One Renaissance Square, Suite 1200, Two North Central Avenue, 85004
Telephone: 602-253-0440
Telecopier: 602-257-0527

William Scott Jenkins
Richard B. Murphy

Reference: First Interstate Bank of Arizona, N.A.

For full biographical listings, see the Martindale-Hubbell Law Directory

O'CONNOR, CAVANAGH, ANDERSON, WESTOVER, KILLINGSWORTH & BESHEARS, A PROFESSIONAL ASSOCIATION (AV)

One East Camelback Road, Suite 1100, 85012-1656
Telephone: 602-263-2400
FAX: 602-263-2900
Sun City, Arizona Office: 13250 North Del Webb Boulevard, Suite B, 85351.
Telephone: 602-263-2808.
FAX: 602-933-3100.
Tucson, Arizona Office: Suite 2200, One South Church Avenue, 85701.
Telephone: 602-882-8912.
FAX: 602-624-9564.
Nogales, Arizona Office: 1827 North Mastick Way, 85621.
Telephone: 602-761-4215.
FAX: 602-761-3505.

Henry L. Timmerman
Richard M. Lorenzen

Craig J. Bolton

Philip G. Mitchell

For Complete List of Firm Personnel, See General Section

For full biographical listings, see the Martindale-Hubbell Law Directory

ROBBINS & GREEN, A PROFESSIONAL ASSOCIATION (AV)

1800 CitiBank Tower, 3300 North Central Avenue, 85012-9826
Telephone: 602-248-7600
Fax: 602-266-5369

Wayne A. Smith
Jeffrey P. Boshes
Bradley J. Stevens
Michael S. Green

For Complete List of Firm Personnel, See General Section

For full biographical listings, see the Martindale-Hubbell Law Directory

SACKS TIERNEY P.A. (AV)

2929 North Central Avenue, Fourteenth Floor, 85012-2742
Telephone: 602-279-4900
Fax: 602-279-2027

Seymour Sacks
Marcia J. Busching
Peter W. Sorensen
Paul G. Johnson

Reference: M&I Thunderbird Bank.

For Complete List of Firm Personnel, See General Section

For full biographical listings, see the Martindale-Hubbell Law Directory

SNELL & WILMER (AV)

One Arizona Center, 85004-0001
Telephone: 602-382-6000
Fax: 602-382-6070
Tucson, Arizona Office: 1500 Norwest Tower, One South Church Avenue 85701-1612.
Telephone: 602-882-1200.
Fax: 602-884-1294.
Orange County Office: 1920 Main Street, Suite 1200, P.O. Box 19601, Irvine, California, 92714.
Telephone: 714-253-2700.
Fax: 714-955-2507.
Salt Lake City, Utah Office: Broadway Centre, 111 East Broadway, Suite 900, 84111.
Telephone: 801-237-1900.
Fax: 801-237-1950.

(See Next Column)

MEMBERS OF FIRM

Peter J. Rathwell
Patrick E. Hoog
Donald L. Gaffney
Christopher H. Bayley
Robert R. Kinas

ASSOCIATES

Jon S. Musial
Eugene F. O'Connor II

Representative Clients: Arizona Public Service Company; Ford Motor Credit Corp.; Executive Claimants as Member Official Unsecured Creditors Committee in MCorp; Graybar Electronic; Heron Financial Corporation; Mutual Life Insurance of New York; Official Unsecured Creditors Committee of American Continental Corp.; Travelers Insurance; Bank One, Arizona, NA.

For Complete List of Firm Personnel, See General Section

For full biographical listings, see the Martindale-Hubbell Law Directory

STREICH LANG, A PROFESSIONAL ASSOCIATION (AV)

Renaissance One, Two N. Central Avenue, 85004-2391
Telephone: 602-229-5200
Fax: 602-229-5690
Tucson, Arizona Office: One S. Church Avenue, Suite 1700.
Telephone: 602-770-8700.
Fax: 602-623-2518.
Las Vegas, Nevada Affiliated Office: Dawson & Associates, 3800 Howard Hughes Parkway, Suite 1500.
Telephone: 702-792-2727.
Fax: 702-792-2676.
Los Angeles, California Office: 444 S. Flower Street, Suite 1530.
Telephone: 213-896-0484.

John R. Clemency
John J. Dawson
Ronald E. Reinsel

Jeffrey D. Barlow
Scott B. Cohen
Russell O. Farr
John Anthony Harris
Robert P. Harris
Robert J. Miller
Brian Sirower

Representative Clients: General Electric Pension Trust; First Interstate Bank of Arizona, N.A.; Valley National Bank of Arizona; Goldriver Hotel and Gambling Casino; Travelers Insurance Company; American Stores, Inc.; Lucky Stores, Inc.; Grossman Company Properties; Great Western Bank; Admiral Insurance Company.

For Complete List of Firm Personnel, See General Section

For full biographical listings, see the Martindale-Hubbell Law Directory

SCOTTSDALE, Maricopa Co.

PESKIND HYMSON & GOLDSTEIN, P.C. (AV)

14595 North Scottsdale Road, Suite 14, 85254
Telephone: 602-991-9077
Fax: 602-443-8854

David B. Goldstein

Ronald Kanwischer
Alexis J. Stanton

For full biographical listings, see the Martindale-Hubbell Law Directory

*TUCSON,** Pima Co.

LEONARD FELKER ALTFELD & BATTAILE, P.C. (AV)

250 North Meyer Avenue, P.O. Box 191, 85702-0191
Telephone: 602-622-7733
Fax: 602-622-7967

David J. Leonard
Sidney L. Felker
Clifford B. Altfeld
John F. Battaile III
Judith B. Leonard
Denise Ann Faulk
Donna M. Aversa
Lynne M. Schwartz
Edward O. Comitz

For full biographical listings, see the Martindale-Hubbell Law Directory

O'CONNOR, CAVANAGH, ANDERSON, WESTOVER, KILLINGSWORTH & BESHEARS, A PROFESSIONAL ASSOCIATION (AV)

Suite 2200 One South Church Avenue, 85701-1621
Telephone: 602-882-8912
FAX: 602-624-9564
Phoenix, Arizona Office: One East Camelback Road, Suite 1100, 85012.
Telephone: 602-263-2400.
FAX: 602-263-2900.
Sun City, Arizona Office: 13250 North Del Webb Boulevard, Suite B, 85351.
Telephone: 602-263-2808.
FAX: 602-933-3100.
Nogales, Arizona Office: 1827 North Mastick Way, 85621.
Telephone: 602-761-4215.
FAX: 602-761-3505.

Scott D. Gibson

(See Next Column)

O'CONNOR, CAVANAGH, ANDERSON, WESTOVER, KILLINGSWORTH & BESHEARS A PROFESSIONAL ASSOCIATION—*Continued*

J. Matthew Derstine

Chris B. Nakamura

Representative Clients: Jeffco, Inc.
Reference: Citibank.

For Complete List of Firm Personnel, See General Section

For full biographical listings, see the Martindale-Hubbell Law Directory

RAVEN, KIRSCHNER & NORELL, P.C. (AV)

Suite 1600, One South Church Avenue, 85701-1612
Telephone: 602-628-8700
Telefax: 602-798-5200

Dennis J. Clancy
Sally M. Darcy
Stephen A. Thomas

Representative Clients: Pace American Bonding Company; Citibank (Arizona); Continental Medical Systems, Inc.; El Paso Natural Gas Co.; Norwest Bank Arizona; El Rio-Santa Cruz Neighborhood Health Center, Inc.; Resolution Trust Corp.; Sierra Vista Community Hospital; Southern Arizona Rehabilitation Hospital; Ford Motor Credit.

For Complete List of Firm Personnel, See General Section

For full biographical listings, see the Martindale-Hubbell Law Directory

SNELL & WILMER (AV)

1500 Norwest Tower, One South Church Avenue, 85701-1612
Telephone: 602-882-1200
Fax: 602-884-1294
Phoenix, Arizona Office: One Arizona Center, 85004-0001.
Telephone: 602-382-6000.
Fax: 602-382-6070.
Orange County Office: 1920 Main Street, Suite 1200, P.O. Box 19601, Irvine, California, 92714.
Telephone: 714-253-2700
Fax: 714-955-2507.
Salt Lake City, Utah Office: Broadway Centre, 111 East Broadway, Suite 900, 84111.
Telephone: 801-237-1900.
Fax: 801-237-1950.

MEMBER OF FIRM

Clague A. Van Slyke

Representative Clients: Arizona Public Service Company; Graybar Electronic; Heron Financial Corporation; Mutual Life Insurance of New York; Official Unsecured Creditors Committee of American Continental Corp.; Travelers Insurance; Bank One, Arizona, NA.

For full biographical listings, see the Martindale-Hubbell Law Directory

STREICH LANG, A PROFESSIONAL ASSOCIATION (AV)

One S. Church Avenue, Suite 1700, 85701-1621
Telephone: 602-770-8700
Fax: 602-623-2418
Phoenix, Arizona Office: Renaissance One, Two N. Central Avenue. 85004-2391.
Telephone: 602-229-5200.
Fax: 602-229-5690.
Las Vegas, Nevada Affiliated Office: Dawson & Associates, 3800 Howard Hughes Parkway, Suite 1500. 89109.
Telephone: 702-792-2727.
Fax: 702-792-2676.
Los Angeles California Office: 444 S. Flower Street, Suite 1530.
Telephone: 213-896-0484.

Susan G. Boswell
Steven R. Haydon

Nancy J. March
Steven Rand Owens

Representative Clients: Circle K. Corporation; First Interstate Bank of Arizona, N.A.; Valley National Bank of Arizona; John Hancock Life Insurance Co.; Travelers Insurance Co.; American Stores, Inc.; Lucky Stores, Inc.; Grossman Company Properties; Great Western Bank; Admiral Insurance Company.

For Complete List of Firm Personnel, See General Section

For full biographical listings, see the Martindale-Hubbell Law Directory

ARKANSAS

*LITTLE ROCK,** Pulaski Co.

ARNOLD, GROBMYER & HALEY, A PROFESSIONAL ASSOCIATION (AV)

875 Union National Plaza, 124 West Capitol Avenue, P.O. Box 70, 72203
Telephone: 501-376-1171
Fax: 501-375-3548

Benjamin F. Arnold
James F. Dowden
Richard L. Ramsay
Robert R. Ross

For Complete List of Firm Personnel, See General Section

For full biographical listings, see the Martindale-Hubbell Law Directory

HOOVER & STOREY (AV)

111 Center Street, 11th Floor, 72201-4445
Telephone: 501-376-8500
Facsimile: 501-372-3255

MEMBERS OF FIRM

Paul W. Hoover, Jr.
O. H. Storey, III
John Kooistra, III
Lawrence Joseph Brady
William P. Dougherty
Max C. Mehlburger
Joyce Bradley Babin
Herbert W. Kell, Jr.
Letty McAdams

For full biographical listings, see the Martindale-Hubbell Law Directory

ROSE LAW FIRM, A PROFESSIONAL ASSOCIATION (AV)

120 East Fourth Street, 72201
Telephone: 501-375-9131
Telecopy: 501-375-1309

Herbert C. Rule, III
Allen W. Bird, II
Garland J. Garrett
Thomas P. Thrash
Charles W. Baker
John T. Hardin
Stephen N. Joiner
Brian Rosenthal
J. Scott Schallhorn

Steven D. Durand
Stephen E. Snider

Representative Clients: Acxiom Corp.; Arkansas Freightways Corp.; The Equitable Life Assurance Society of the United States; Fairfield Communities, Inc.; Federal Deposit Insurance Corp.; General Electric Co.; General Motors Corp.; The Prudential Insurance Company of America; Stephens Inc.; J.A. Riggs Tractor Co.

For Complete List of Firm Personnel, See General Section

For full biographical listings, see the Martindale-Hubbell Law Directory

CALIFORNIA

*BAKERSFIELD,** Kern Co.

KLEIN, WEGIS, DENATALE, GOLDNER & MUIR (AV)

A Partnership including Professional Corporations
(Formerly Di Giorgio, Davis, Klein, Wegis, Duggan & Friedman)
ARCO Tower, 4550 California Avenue, Second Floor, P.O. Box 11172, 93389-1172
Telephone: 805-395-1000
Telecopier: 805-326-0418
Santa Ana, California Office: Park Tower Building #610, 200 W. Santa Ana Boulevard, 92701.
Telephone: 714-285-0711.
Fax: 714-285-9003.

MEMBERS OF FIRM

Anthony J. Klein (Inc.)
Claude P. Kimball

ASSOCIATE

Michael S. Abril

Representative Clients: Bank of America; Great Western Bank; Mojave Pipeline Co.; Transamerican Title Insurance Co.; Dean Whittier Reynolds, Inc.; California Republic Bank; San Joaquin Bank; Nahama & Weagant Energy Co.; Freymiller Trucking, Inc.; Westinghouse Electric Co.

For Complete List of Firm Personnel, See General Section

For full biographical listings, see the Martindale-Hubbell Law Directory

BEVERLY HILLS, Los Angeles Co.

SCHWARTZ, WISOT & RODOV, A PROFESSIONAL LAW CORPORATION (AV)

Suite 315, 315 South Beverly Drive, 90212
Telephone: 310-277-2323
Fax: 310-556-2308

Bruce Edward Schwartz
Valerie Wisot
Valentina Rodov

Reference: Home Savings of America (Century City Office, Los Angeles, California)

For full biographical listings, see the Martindale-Hubbell Law Directory

COSTA MESA, Orange Co.

RUTAN & TUCKER (AV)

A Partnership including Professional Corporations
611 Anton Boulevard, Suite 1400, P.O. Box 1950, 92626
Telephone: 714-641-5100; 213-625-7586
Telecopier: 714-546-9035

MEMBER OF FIRM

Lori Sarner Smith

ASSOCIATE

Michael K. Slattery

For Complete List of Firm Personnel, See General Section

For full biographical listings, see the Martindale-Hubbell Law Directory

*FRESNO,** Fresno Co.

DOWLING, MAGARIAN, AARON & HEYMAN, INCORPORATED (AV)

Suite 200, 6051 North Fresno Street, 93710
Telephone: 209-432-4500
Fax: 209-432-4590

Adolfo M. Corona

Reference: Wells Fargo Bank (Main).

For Complete List of Firm Personnel, See General Section

For full biographical listings, see the Martindale-Hubbell Law Directory

KIMBLE, MACMICHAEL & UPTON, A PROFESSIONAL CORPORATION (AV)

Fig Garden Financial Center, 5260 North Palm Avenue, Suite 221, P.O. Box 9489, 93792-9489
Telephone: 209-435-5500
Telecopier: 209-435-1500

Joseph C. Kimble (1910-1972)
Thomas A. MacMichael (1920-1990)
Jon Wallace Upton
Robert E. Bergin
Jeffrey G. Boswell
Steven D. McGee
Robert E. Ward
John P. Eleazarian
Robert H. Scribner
Michael E. Moss
David D. Doyle
Mark D. Miller
Michael F. Tatham
W. Richard Lee
D. Tyler Tharpe
Sylvia Halkousis Coyle

Michael J. Jurkovich
S. Brett Sutton
Douglas V. Thornton
Robert William Branch
Brian N. Folland
Christopher L. Wanger
Elise M. Krause
Donald J. Pool
Susan King Hatmaker

For full biographical listings, see the Martindale-Hubbell Law Directory

LANG, RICHERT & PATCH, A PROFESSIONAL CORPORATION (AV)

Fig Garden Financial Center, 5200 North Palm Avenue, 4th Floor, P.O. Box 40012, 93755
Telephone: 209-228-6700
Fax: 209-228-6727

Frank H. Lang
William T. Richert (1937-1993)
Robert L. Patch, II
Val W. Saldaña
Douglas E. Noll
Michael T. Hertz
Victoria J. Salisch
Bradley A. Silva
David R. Jenkins
Charles Trudrung Taylor
Mark L. Creede
Peter N. Zeitler
Charles L. Doerksen

Randall C. Nelson
Barbara A. McAuliffe
Laurie Quigley Cardot
Douglas E. Griffin
Nabil E. Zumout

(See Next Column)

References: Wells Fargo Bank (Fresno Main Office); First Interstate Bank (Fresno Main Office).

For full biographical listings, see the Martindale-Hubbell Law Directory

IRVINE, Orange Co.

STEVEN CASSELBERRY (AV)

5 Park Plaza, Suite 1440, 92714
Telephone: 714-476-9999
Fax: 714-476-0175

OF COUNSEL

Richard A. Harvey

Representative Clients: Chicago Title Insurance Company; Continental Lawyers Title Insurance Company; El Camino National Bank; First National Bank of Portsmouth; Huntington National Bank; Inland Empire National Bank; Landmark Bank; Omni Bank; Pioneer Savings and Loan Association; Queen City Bank.

For full biographical listings, see the Martindale-Hubbell Law Directory

ROBERT A. FISHER, INC. (AV)

(Formerly Craig, Weller & Laugharn)
Suite 980, 19800 MacArthur Boulevard, 92715
Telephone: 714-752-1229
Fax: 714-752-5407

Robert A. Fisher

LOBEL, WINTHROP & BROKER (AV)

Suite 1100, 19800 MacArthur Boulevard, P.O. Box 19588, 92713
Telephone: 714-476-7400
Fax: 714-476-7444
Santa Ana, California Office: 201 North Broadway, Suite 201.
Telephone: 714-543-4822.
Fax: 714-476-7444.

MEMBERS OF FIRM

William N. Lobel
Marc J. Winthrop
Todd C. Ringstad
Robert E. Opera
Lorie Dewhirst Porter

ASSOCIATES

Alan J. Friedman
Paul J. Couchot
Robert W. Pitts
Pamela Z. Karger
Whitney H. Leibow
Richard H. Golubow

For full biographical listings, see the Martindale-Hubbell Law Directory

*LOS ANGELES,** Los Angeles Co.

ADAMS, DUQUE & HAZELTINE (AV)

A Partnership including Professional Corporations
777 South Figueroa Street, Tenth Floor, 90017
Telephone: 213-620-1240
FAX: 213-896-5500
San Francisco, California Office: 500 Washington Street.
Telephone: 415-982-1240.
FAX: 415-982-0130.

MEMBERS OF FIRM

Kimler G. Casteel
Charles D. Schoor
Daniel H. Slate
Lauren T. Diehl

ASSOCIATES

Daren R. Brinkman
Susan G. Spira
Samuel A. Chuck
Sharon C. Sartorius

For Complete List of Firm Personnel, See General Section

For full biographical listings, see the Martindale-Hubbell Law Directory

BAKER & HOSTETLER (AV)

600 Wilshire Boulevard, 90017-3212
Telephone: 213-624-2400
FAX: 213-975-1740
In Cleveland, Ohio, 3200 National City Center, 1900 East Ninth Street.
Telephone: 216-621-0200.
In Columbus, Ohio, Capitol Square, Suite 2100, 65 East State Street.
Telephone: 614-228-1541.
In Denver, Colorado, 303 East 17th Avenue, Suite 1100. Telephone: 303-861-0600.
In Houston, Texas, 1000 Louisiana, Suite 2000. Telephone: 713-236-0020.
In Long Beach, California: 300 Oceangate, Suite 620.
Telephone: 310-432-2827.
In Orlando, Florida, SunBank Center, Suite 2300, 200 South Orange Avenue. Telephone: 407-649-4000.
In Washington, D. C., Washington Square, Suite 1100, 1050 Connecticut Avenue, N. W. Telephone: 202-861-1500.
In College Park, Maryland, 9658 Baltimore Boulevard, Suite 206.
Telephone: 301-441-2781.
In Alexandria, Virginia, 437 North Lee Street. Telephone: 703-549-1294.
In San Francisco, California: One Sansome Street, Suite 2000.
Telephone: 415-951-4705.

(See Next Column)

BAKER & HOSTETLER—*Continued*

PARTNER

Dean G. Rallis Jr.

ASSOCIATES

Edward T. Goines
Peggy A. Propper

For Complete List of Firm Personnel, See General Section

For full biographical listings, see the Martindale-Hubbell Law Directory

LAW OFFICES OF DAVID B. BLOOM A PROFESSIONAL CORPORATION (AV)

3325 Wilshire Boulevard, Ninth Floor, 90010
Telephone: 213-938-5248; 384-4088
Telecopier: 213-385-2009

David B. Bloom

Stephen S. Monroe (A Professional Corporation)
Raphael A. Rosemblat
James E. Adler
Bonni S. Mantovani
Martin A. Cooper
Roy A. Levun
Cherie S. Raidy
Jonathan Udell
Susan Carole Jay
Edward Idell
Sandra Kamenir
Steven Wayne Lazarus
Andrew Edward Briseno
Harold C. Klaskin
Shelley M. Gould
B. Eric Nelson
John C. Notti
Peter O. Israel
Anthony V. Seferian

For full biographical listings, see the Martindale-Hubbell Law Directory

BUCHALTER, NEMER, FIELDS & YOUNGER, A PROFESSIONAL CORPORATION (AV)

24th Floor, 601 South Figueroa Street, 90017
Telephone: 213-891-0700
Fax: 213-896-0400
Cable Address: "Buchnem"
Telex: 68-7485
New York, New York Office: 19th Floor, 237 Park Avenue.
Telephone: 212-490-8600.
Fax: 212-490-6022.
San Francisco, California Office: 29th Floor, 333 Market Street.
Telephone: 415-227-0900.
Fax: 415-227-0770.
San Jose, California Office: 12th Floor, 50 West San Fernando Street.
Telephone: 408-298-0350.
Fax: 408-298-7683.
Newport Beach, California Office: Suite 300, 620 Newport Center Drive.
Telephone: 714-760-1121.
Fax: 714-720-0182.
Century City, California Office: Suite 2400, 1801 Century Park East.
Telephone: 213-891-0700.
Fax: 310-551-0233.

Richard Jay Goldstein
Marvin D. Heileson
Pamela Kohlman Webster

OF COUNSEL

Ronald E. Gordon
Scott O. Smith
Randye B. Soref

Raymond H. Aver
Bernard D. Bollinger, Jr.
Julie A. Goren
Paul S. Arrow
William S. Brody
William P. Fong
Brett Michael Broderick
K. Todd Shollenbarger

References: City National Bank; Wells Fargo Bank; Metrobank.

For Complete List of Firm Personnel, See General Section

For full biographical listings, see the Martindale-Hubbell Law Directory

CLARK & TREVITHICK, A PROFESSIONAL CORPORATION (AV)

800 Wilshire Boulevard, 12th Floor, 90017
Telephone: 213-629-5700
Telecopier: 213-624-9441

John A. Lapinski
Leslie R. Horowitz

OF COUNSEL

Judith Ilene Bloom

References: Wells Fargo Bank (Los Angeles Main Office); National Bank of California.

For Complete List of Firm Personnel, See General Section

For full biographical listings, see the Martindale-Hubbell Law Directory

DANNING, GILL, DIAMOND & KOLLITZ (AV)

A Partnership Composed of Professional Corporations
2029 Century Park East, Suite 1900, 90067-3005
Telephone: 310-277-0077
FAX: 310-277-5735

(See Next Column)

MEMBERS OF FIRM

David A. Gill (A Professional Corporation)
Richard K. Diamond (A Professional Corporation)
Howard Kollitz (A Professional Corporation)
John J. Bingham, Jr., (A Professional Corporation)
Steven E. Smith (A Professional Corporation)
Michael S. Abrams (A Professional Corporation)
Eric P. Israel (A Professional Corporation)
David M. Poitras (A Professional Corporation)

ASSOCIATES

Robert A. Hessling
Jeffrey L. Sumpter
Kevin L. Hing
Barry Lurie
Kathy L. Bazoian
Daniel H. Gill

OF COUNSEL

Curtis B. Danning (A Professional Corporation)
James J. Joseph (A Professional Corporation)
Robert M. Ruben
Steven J. Kahn
Sandra W. Lavigna

For full biographical listings, see the Martindale-Hubbell Law Directory

GOLDMAN, GORDON & LIPSTONE (AV)

Suite 1920, 1801 Century Park East, 90067
Telephone: 310-277-7171
FAX: 310-277-1547

MEMBERS OF FIRM

A. S. Goldman (1895-1966)
Leonard A. Goldman
Robert P. Gordon
Ronald K. Lipstone

ASSOCIATE

Jerry A. Jacobson

References: Bank of America, Fourth and Spring Branch, Los Angeles; Bank of America, Wilshire-San Vincente Branch, Beverly Hills.

For full biographical listings, see the Martindale-Hubbell Law Directory

HONIGMAN MILLER SCHWARTZ AND COHN (AV)

A Partnership including Professional Corporations
Watt Plaza, Suite 2200, 1875 Century Park East, 90067-2799
Telephone: 310-789-3800
Fax: 310-789-3814
Detroit, Michigan Office: 2290 First National Building.
Telephone: 313-256-7800.
Lansing, Michigan Office: 222 North Washington Square, Suite 400.
Telephone: 517-484-8282.
West Palm Beach, Florida Office: Suite 800 Esperante Building, 222 Lakeview Avenue.
Telephone: 407-838-4500.
Tampa, Florida Office: 2700 Landmark Centre, 401 E. Jackson Street.
Telephone: 813-221-6600.
Orlando, Florida Office: 390 North Orange Avenue, Suite 1300.
Telephone: 407-648-0300.
Houston, Texas Office: 3100 First Interstate Bank Plaza, 1000 Louisiana.
Telephone: 713-650-2600.

MEMBERS OF FIRM

Daniel E. Martyn, Jr.
George E. Schulman

ASSOCIATES

Melanie J. Bingham
Adryane R. Omens

For Complete List of Firm Personnel, See General Section

For full biographical listings, see the Martindale-Hubbell Law Directory

HUFSTEDLER & KAUS (AV)

A Partnership including Professional Corporations
Thirty-Ninth Floor, 355 South Grand Avenue, 90071-3101
Telephone: 213-617-7070
Fax: 213-617-6170

MEMBERS OF FIRM

Leonard L. Gumport
Susan I. Schutzbank Montgomery

Reference: First Interstate Bank, 707 Wilshire.

For Complete List of Firm Personnel, See General Section

For full biographical listings, see the Martindale-Hubbell Law Directory

JONES, DAY, REAVIS & POGUE (AV)

555 West Fifth Street Suite 4600, 90013-1025
Telephone: 213-489-3939
Telex: 181439 UD
Telecopier: 213-243-2539
In Irvine, California: 2603 Main Street, Suite 900.
Telephone: 714-851-3939.
Telex: 194911 Lawyers LSA.
Telecopier: 714-553-7539.

(See Next Column)

JONES, DAY, REAVIS & POGUE, *Los Angeles—Continued*

In Atlanta, Georgia: 3500 One Peachtree Center, 303 Peachtree Street, N.E.
Telephone: 404-521-3939.
Cable Address: "Attorneys Atlanta".
Telex: 54-2711.
Telecopier: 404-581-8330.
In Brussels, Belgium: Avenue Louise 480, 7th Floor, B-1050 Brussels.
Telephone: 011-32-2-645-14-11.
Telecopier: 011-32-2-645-14-45.
In Chicago, Illinois: 77 West Wacker.
Telephone: 312-782-3939.
Telecopier: 312-782-8585.
In Cleveland, Ohio: North Point, 901 Lakeside Avenue.
Telephone: 216-586-3939.
Cable Address: "Attorneys Cleveland."
Telex: 980389.
Telecopier: 216-579-0212.
In Columbus, Ohio: 1900 Huntington Center.
Telephone: 614-469-3939.
Cable Address: "Attorneys Columbus."
Telecopier: 614-461-4198.
In Dallas, Texas: 2300 Trammell Crow Center, 2001 Ross Avenue.
Telephone: 214-220-3939.
Cable Address: "Attorneys Dallas."
Telex: 730852.
Telecopier: 214-969-5100.
In Frankfurt, Germany: Triton Haus, Bockenheimer Landstrasse 42, 60323 Frankfurt am Main.
Telephone: 49-69-9726-3939.
Telecopier: 49-69-9726-3993.
In Geneva, Switzerland: 20, rue de Candolle.
Telephone: 011-41-22-320-2339.
Telecopier: 011-41-22-320-1232.
In Hong Kong: 1501 One Exchange Square, 8 Connaught Place.
Telephone: 011-852-2526-6895.
Telecopier: 011-852-2810-5787.
In London England: One Mount Street.
Telephone: 011-44-71-493-9361.
Cable Address: "Surgoe London WI."
Telecopier: 011-44-71-493-9666.
In New York, New York: 599 Lexington Avenue.
Telephone: 212-326-3939.
Cable Address: "JONESDAY NEWYORK."
Telex: 237013 JDRP UR.
Telecopier: 212-755-7306.
In Paris, France: 62, rue du Faubourg Saint-Honore.
Telephone: 011-33-1-44-71-3939.
Cable Address: "Surgoe Paris."
Telex: 290156 Surgoe.
Telecopier: 011-33-1-49-24-0471.
In Pittsburgh, Pennsylvania: 500 Grant Street, 31st Floor.
Telephone: 412-391-3939.
Cable Address: "Attorneys Pittsburgh".
Telecopier: 412-394-7959.
In Riyadh, Saudi Arabia: Law Offices of Saud M.A. Shawwaf, P.O. Box 2700.
Telephones: 011 (966-1) 465-6543, 011 (966-1) 464-8534 or 011 (966-1) 464-8540.
Telex: 401831 SAUCON SJ.
Telecopier: (966-1) 464-8480.
In Taipei, Taiwan: 8th Floor, 2 Tun Hwa South Road, Section 2.
Telephone: 011 (886-2) 704-6808.
Telecopier: 011 (886-2) 704-6791.
In Tokyo, Japan: Toranomon MT Building, 4th Floor, 10-3, Toranomon 3-Chome, Minato-Ku, Tokyo 105, Japan.
Telephone: 011-81-3-3433-3939.
Telecopier: 011-81-3-5401-2725.
In Washington, D.C.: Metropolitan Square, 1450 G Street, N.W.
Telephone: 202-879-3939.
Cable Address: "Attorneys Washington."
Telex: 89-2410 ATTORNEYS WASH.
Telecopier: 202-737-2832.

MEMBERS OF FIRM IN LOS ANGELES

William G. Wilson
Howard J. Steinberg

ASSOCIATES

Thomas Botz
Craig H. Averch

For Complete List of Firm Personnel, See General Section

For full biographical listings, see the Martindale-Hubbell Law Directory

LEVENE & EISENBERG, A PROFESSIONAL CORPORATION (AV)

1901 Avenue of the Stars, 16th Floor, 90067-6080
Telephone: 310-551-1010
800-551-3339
Fax: 310-551-3059

David W. Levene
Joseph A. Eisenberg
Leslie A. Cohen
Richard L. Wynne
Scott C. Dew
Bennett L. Spiegel

(See Next Column)

Robbin Itkin Freeman
David L. Neale
Karen K. Carroll
Werner Disse
Ron Bender
Paul Halpern
Christopher W. Combs
Adam M. Reich
Debra I. Grassgreen

Reference: City National Bank (Commonwealth Branch).

For full biographical listings, see the Martindale-Hubbell Law Directory

LOEB AND LOEB (AV)

A Partnership including Professional Corporations
Suite 1800, 1000 Wilshire Boulevard, 90017-2475
Telephone: 213-688-3400
Telecopier: 213-688-3460; 688-3461; 688-3462
Century City, California Office: Suite 2200, 10100 Santa Monica Boulevard, Los Angeles, 90067-4164.
Telephone: 310-282-2000.
Telecopier: 310-282-2191; 282-2192.
New York, N.Y. Office: 345 Park Avenue, 10154-0037.
Telephone: 212-407-4000.
Facsimile: 212-407-4990.
Nashville, Tennessee Office: 45 Music Square West, 37203-3205.
Telephone: 615-749-8300;
Facsimile: 615-749-8308.
Rome, Italy Office: Piazza Digione 1, 00197.
Telephone: 011-396-808-8456.
Telecopier: 011-396-674-8223.

MEMBERS OF FIRM

Andrew S. Clare (A P.C.)
David B. Eizenman (New York City Office)
Lawrence B. Gutcho
Mary D. Lane
David M. Satnick (New York City Office)
Michael F. Sitzer
Ronald Weinstein (A P.C.)

ASSOCIATES

Scott L. Grossfeld
Karen Nielsen Higgins
Richard M. Johnson, Jr.
Lance N. Jurich
Paul J. Laurin

For Complete List of Firm Personnel, See General Section

For full biographical listings, see the Martindale-Hubbell Law Directory

PIZER & MICHAELSON INC. (AV)

2029 Century Park East, Suite 600, 90067
Telephone: 310-843-9729
Fax: 310-843-9619
Santa Ana, California Office: 2122 North Broadway, Suite 100, 92706.
Telephone: 714-558-0535.
Telecopier: 714-550-0841.

Bradley J. Pizer

For full biographical listings, see the Martindale-Hubbell Law Directory

ROBINSON, DIAMANT, BRILL & KLAUSNER, A PROFESSIONAL CORPORATION (AV)

Suite 1500, 1888 Century Park East (Century City), 90067
Telephone: 310-277-7400
Telecopier: 310-277-7584

Gilbert Robinson (1927-1991)
Elliott Lisnek (1939-1992)
Lawrence A. Diamant
Martin J. Brill
Edward M. Wolkowitz
Gary E. Klausner
Irving M. Gross
Douglas D. Kappler
Philip A. Gasteier
Karl E. Block
Uzzell S. Branson, III
Michael D. Warner

David T. Cohen
Judith E. Miller
Gregg D. Lundberg
Sandro F. Piedrahita
Brad Krasnoff
Leonard S. Perlman
Jeffrey A. Resler
Brian M. Grossman

References: Fidelity & Deposit Co.; Home Savings of America (Century City Office); Metrobank (Los Angeles Regional Office); Wells Fargo Bank (Century City Office).

For full biographical listings, see the Martindale-Hubbell Law Directory

RONALD P. SLATES A PROFESSIONAL CORPORATION (AV)

548 South Spring Street, Suite 1012, 90013-2309
Telephone: 213-624-1515; 213-654-1461
Fax: 213-624-7536; 213-654-1463

Ronald P. Slates

G. Michael Jackson

For full biographical listings, see the Martindale-Hubbell Law Directory

Los Angeles—Continued

STUTMAN, TREISTER & GLATT, PROFESSIONAL CORPORATION (AV)

3699 Wilshire Boulevard, Suite 900, 90010
Telephone: 213-251-5100
FAX: 213-251-5288

Jack Stutman (Retired Founder)
George M. Treister
Herman L. Glatt
Richard M. Neiter
Robert A. Greenfield
Charles D. Axelrod
Theodore B. Stolman
Isaac M. Pachulski
Kenneth N. Klee
Alan Pedlar
George C. Webster, II
Stephan M. Ray
Michael A. Morris
Jeffrey C. Krause
Bruce Bennett
Michael H. Goldstein
Lee R. Bogdanoff
Frank A. Merola
Jeffrey H. Davidson
Ronald L. Fein
Mark S. Wallace
Susan R. Purcell
K. John Shaffer
Mareta C. Hamre
Michael L. Tuchin
Eric D. Goldberg
Eve H. Karasik
Thomas R. Kreller
Martin R. Barash

For full biographical listings, see the Martindale-Hubbell Law Directory

SULMEYER, KUPETZ, BAUMANN & ROTHMAN, A PROFESSIONAL CORPORATION (AV)

300 South Grand Avenue, 14th Floor, 90071
Telephone: 213-626-2311
Fax: 213-629-4520

Irving Sulmeyer
Arnold L. Kupetz
Richard G. Baumann
Don Rothman
Alan G. Tippie
Israel Saperstein
Victor A. Sahn
Steven R. Wainess
David S. Kupetz
Howard M. Ehrenberg
Kathryn Kerfes

Nathan H. Harris
Chandler J. Coury
Suzanne L. Weakley
Susan Frances Moley
Matthew Rothman
Wesley Avery
Katherine Windler
Garrick Hollander
Moira Doherty

OF COUNSEL

Marilyn S. Scheer

Representative Clients: General Electric Capital Corp.; Continental Insurance Co.; Litton Industries; North American Phillips Corp.; Ventura Port District; Northwest Financial; Heller Financial Inc.; Transamerica Occidental Life Insurance Co.; Transamerica Realty Services, Inc.; Body Glove International.

For full biographical listings, see the Martindale-Hubbell Law Directory

MANHATTAN BEACH, Los Angeles Co.

STEINBERG, FOSTER & BARNESS (AV)

1334 Park View Avenue, Suite 100, 90266
Telephone: 310-546-5838
Telecopier: 310-546-5630

MEMBERS OF FIRM

Alex Steinberg
Douglas B. Foster
Daniel I. Barness

ASSOCIATE

William R. (Randy) Kirkpatrick

References: Home Bank; Imperial Bank; Citizens Commerical Trust & Savings Bank; Bank of America.

For full biographical listings, see the Martindale-Hubbell Law Directory

NEWPORT BEACH, Orange Co.

BUCHALTER, NEMER, FIELDS & YOUNGER, A PROFESSIONAL CORPORATION (AV)

Suite 300, 620 Newport Center Drive, 92660
Telephone: 714-760-1121
Fax: 714-720-0182
Los Angeles, California Office: 24th Floor, 601 South Figueroa Street.
Telephone: 213-891-0700.
Fax: 213-896-0400.
New York, New York Office: 19th Floor, 237 Park Avenue.
Telephone: 212-490-8600.
Fax: 212-490-6022.
San Francisco, California Office: 29th Floor, 333 Market Street.
Telephone: 415-227-0900.
Fax: 415-227-0770.
San Jose, California Office: 12th Floor, 50 West San Fernando Street.
Telephone: 408-298-0350.
Fax: 408-298-7683.

(See Next Column)

Century City, California Office: Suite 2400, 1801 Century Park East.
Telephone: 213-891-0700.
Fax: 310-551-0233.

Clifford John Meyer
Theodor C. Albert
Debra Solle Healy
Kirk S. Rense

OF COUNSEL

Marcus M. Kaufman

Bruce M. Boyd
Lori S. Ross
Jeffrey I. Golden
Mark M. Scott
Jennifer Ann Golison
David Mark Hershorin
Brian A. Kumamoto
Lori Suzanne Carver
Evan D. Smiley

References: City National Bank; Wells Fargo Bank; Metrobank.

For full biographical listings, see the Martindale-Hubbell Law Directory

GORDON & WOLF, A PROFESSIONAL CORPORATION (AV)

500 Newport Center Drive Suite 800, 92660
Telephone: 714-720-9200
Fax: 714-720-9250

Alan S. Wolf

Michael R. Pfeifer
Donald R. Davidson, III
Roland P. Reynolds
David Brian Lally
Steven M. Lawrence

OF COUNSEL

Stanley M. Gordon
Peter J. Marshall

For full biographical listings, see the Martindale-Hubbell Law Directory

*OAKLAND,** Alameda Co.

KORNFIELD, PAUL & BUPP, A PROFESSIONAL CORPORATION (AV)

Suite 800, Lake Merritt Plaza, 1999 Harrison Street, 94612
Telephone: 510-763-1000
Fax: 510-273-8669

Irving J. Kornfield
Aaron Paul
C. Randall Bupp
Merridith A. Schneider
Eric A. Nyberg

Charles D. Novack
Tavi Stanley McKay

For full biographical listings, see the Martindale-Hubbell Law Directory

NEAL & ASSOCIATES (AV)

Montclair Village, 6200 Antioch Street, Suite 202, P.O. Box 13314, 500, 94661-0314
Telephone: 510-339-0233
FAX: 510-339-6672

Howard D. Neal

Frank J. Gilbert
Steven S. Miyake

For full biographical listings, see the Martindale-Hubbell Law Directory

ORANGE, Orange Co.

WALSWORTH, FRANKLIN & BEVINS (AV)

1 City Boulevard West, Suite 308, 92668
Telephone: 714-634-2522
LAW-FAX: 714-634-0686
San Francisco, California Office: 580 California Street, Suite 1335.
Telephone: 415-781-7072.
Fax: 415-391-6258.

Jeffrey P. Walsworth
Ferdie F. Franklin
Ronald H. Bevins, Jr.
Michael T. McCall
Noel Edlin (Resident, San Francisco Office)
Lawrence E. Duffy, Jr.
Sheldon J. Fleming
J. Wayne Allen
James A. Anton
Ingrid K. Campagne (Resident, San Francisco Office)
Robert M. Channel (Resident, San Francisco Office)
Nicholas A. Cipiti
Sharon L. Clisham (Resident, San Francisco Office)
David W. Epps (Resident, San Francisco Office)
Richard M. Hills (Resident, San Francisco Office)
Sandra G. Kennedy
Randall J. Lee (Resident, San Francisco Office)
Kimberly K. Mays
Bruce A. Nelson (Resident, San Francisco Office)
Kevin Pegan
Allan W. Ruggles
Jonathan M. Slipp
Cyrian B. Tabuena (Resident, San Francisco Office)
John L. Trunko
Houston M. Watson, II
Mary A. Watson

For full biographical listings, see the Martindale-Hubbell Law Directory

OXNARD, Ventura Co.

NORDMAN, CORMANY, HAIR & COMPTON (AV)

1000 Town Center Drive, Sixth Floor, P.O. Box 9100, 93031-9100
Telephone: 805-485-1000
Ventura: 805-656-3304
Telecopier: 805-988-8387
805-988-7790
Westlake Village, California Office: 890 Hampshire Road, Suite A, 91361.
Telephone: 805-497-2795.

MEMBERS OF FIRM

Ronald H. Gill
William E. Winfield
Gerald M. Etchingham

Representative Clients: Bank of A. Levy; Real Estate Investment Trust of California; Berry Petroleum Company; Amgen; Kmart Corp.; Saticoy Lemon Association; The Procter & Gamble Paper Products Co.; Clairol, Inc.; Halliburton Services; Schlumberger.

For Complete List of Firm Personnel, See General Section

For full biographical listings, see the Martindale-Hubbell Law Directory

PASADENA, Los Angeles Co.

CAIRNS, DOYLE, LANS, NICHOLAS & SONI, A LAW CORPORATION (AV)

Ninth Floor, 225 South Lake Avenue, 91101
Telephone: 818-683-3111
Telecopier: 818-683-4999

Rohini Soni (1956-1994)
John C. Doyle
John D. Cairns
Stephen M. Lans
Francisco J. Nicholas

David M. Phillips

Representative Clients: Allstate Insurance Companies; Burger King Corporation; California Insurance Guarantee Association; California United Bank; CIGNA Insurance Companies; City of Pasadena; Cumis Insurance Society, Inc.; Employer's Mutual Insurance Companies; State Farm Insurance Companies; Tokio Marine Insurance.

For full biographical listings, see the Martindale-Hubbell Law Directory

LAGERLOF, SENECAL, BRADLEY & SWIFT (AV)

301 North Lake Avenue, 10th Floor, 91101-4107
Telephone: 818-793-9400
FAX: 818-793-5900

MEMBERS OF FIRM

Joseph J. Burris (1913-1980)
John F. Bradley
Stanley C. Lagerlof
Timothy J. Gosney
H. Melvin Swift, Jr.
William F. Kruse
H. Jess Senecal
Thomas S. Bunn, III
Jack T. Swafford
Andrew D. Turner
Rebecca J. Thyne

ASSOCIATES

Paul M. Norman
James D. Ciampa
John F. Machtinger
Ellen M. Burkhart

LEGAL SUPPORT PERSONNEL

Ronald E. Hagler

Representative Clients: Anchor Glass Container Corporation; Bethlehem Steel Corp.; Orthopaedic Hospital; Palmdale Water District; Public Water Agencies Group; Walnut Valley Water District.
Special Counsel: City of Redondo Beach, Calif.; Ventura Port Dist., Calif.

For full biographical listings, see the Martindale-Hubbell Law Directory

*REDDING,** Shasta Co.

DENNIS K. COWAN (AV)

280 Hemsted Drive, Suite B, P.O. Box 992090, 96099-2090
Telephone: 916-221-7300
Fax: 916-221-7389

For full biographical listings, see the Martindale-Hubbell Law Directory

*SACRAMENTO,** Sacramento Co.

JOHN D. BESSEY (AV)

CapitolBank Center, 300 Capitol Mall, Suite 1150, 95814
Telephone: 916-444-2400
Fax: 916-444-2708

ASSOCIATE

Bret R. Rossi

For full biographical listings, see the Martindale-Hubbell Law Directory

DOWNEY, BRAND, SEYMOUR & ROHWER (AV)

Suite 1050, 555 Capitol Mall, 95814
Telephone: 916-441-0131
FAX: 916-441-4021

MEMBERS OF FIRM

R. Dale Ginter
Dan L. Carroll
Lisa Lauritzen Ditora

ASSOCIATE

Lawrence T. Woodlock

Counsel for: Hyatt Corp.; Steelcase, Inc.; Bank of America, NT&SA; Business & Professional Bank; Raley's Inc.; CIGNA Corp.; Central California Power Agency No. 1; FDIC; Milgard Manufacturing, Inc.; Meadow Glen Farms, dba Jerseyland Cheese.

For Complete List of Firm Personnel, See General Section

For full biographical listings, see the Martindale-Hubbell Law Directory

MATHENY, POIDMORE & SEARS (AV)

2100 Northrop Avenue, Building 1200, P.O. Box 13711, 95853-4711
Telephone: 916-929-9271
Fax: 916-929-2458

MEMBERS OF FIRM

Henry G. Matheny (1933-1984)
James C. Damir
Anthony J. Poidmore
Michael A. Bishop
Douglas A. Sears
Ernest A. Long
Richard S. Linkert
Joann Georgallis
Kent M. Luckey

ASSOCIATES

Matthew C. Jaime
Ronald E. Enabnit
Jill P. Telfer
Cathy A. Reynolds
Robert B. Berrigan
Byron D. Damiani, Jr.
Daryl M. Thomas
Catherine Kennedy

OF COUNSEL

A. Laurel Bennett

LEGAL SUPPORT PERSONNEL

PARALEGALS

Karen D. Fisher
Lynell Rae Steed
Fran Studer
Jennifer Bachman
David Austin Boucher

For full biographical listings, see the Martindale-Hubbell Law Directory

WILKE, FLEURY, HOFFELT, GOULD & BIRNEY (AV)

A Partnership including Professional Corporations
400 Capitol Mall, Suite 2200, 95814-4408
Telephone: 916-441-2430
Telefax: 916-442-6664
Mailing Address: P.O. Box 15559, 95852-0559

MEMBERS OF FIRM

Richard H. Hoffelt (Inc.)
Ernest James Krtil
William A. Gould, Jr., (Inc.)
Robert R. Mirkin
Philip R. Birney (Inc.)
Matthew W. Powell
Thomas G. Redmon (Inc.)
Mark L. Andrews
Scott L. Gassaway
Stephen K. Marmaduke
Donald Rex Heckman II (Inc.)
David A. Frenznick
Alan G. Perkins
John R. Valencia
Bradley N. Webb
Angus M. MacLeod

ASSOCIATES

Paul A. Dorris
Anthony J. DeCristoforo
Kelli M. Kennaday
Rachel N. Kook
Tracy S. Hendrickson
Alicia F. From
Joseph G. De Angelis
Michael Polis
Jennifer L. Kennedy
Matthew J. Smith
Wayne L. Ordos

OF COUNSEL

Sherman C. Wilke
Anita Seipp Marmaduke
Benjamin G. Davidian

Representative Clients: NOR-CAL Mutual Insurance Co.; California Optometric Assn.; KPMG Peat Marwick; Glaxo, Inc.

For full biographical listings, see the Martindale-Hubbell Law Directory

*SAN BERNARDINO,** San Bernardino Co.

HANOVER & SCHNITZER (AV)

665 North Arrowhead Avenue, 92401
Telephone: 909-884-2147
Fax: 909-889-1828

MEMBERS OF FIRM

Norman L. Hanover
Mark C. Schnitzer

ASSOCIATES

Robert L. Goodrich
Michelle C. Araneta
Lazaro E. Fernandez

For full biographical listings, see the Martindale-Hubbell Law Directory

*SAN DIEGO,** San Diego Co.

CHRISTISON & MARTIN (AV)

402 West Broadway 23rd Floor, 92101
Telephone: 619-236-0305

Frederick Martin, Jr.
Perry T. Christison

For full biographical listings, see the Martindale-Hubbell Law Directory

HOVEY, KIRBY, THORNTON & HAHN, A PROFESSIONAL CORPORATION (AV)

101 West Broadway, Suite 1100, 92101-8297
Telephone: 619-685-4000
Fax: 619-685-4004

Dean T. Kirby, Jr.
Geraldine A. Valdez

For full biographical listings, see the Martindale-Hubbell Law Directory

LINDLEY, LAZAR & SCALES, A PROFESSIONAL CORPORATION (AV)

One America Plaza, 600 West Broadway, Suite 1400, 92101-3302
Telephone: 619-234-9181
Fax: 619-234-8475

John M. Seitman
Michael H. Wexler

For Complete List of Firm Personnel, See General Section

For full biographical listings, see the Martindale-Hubbell Law Directory

LUCE, FORWARD, HAMILTON & SCRIPPS (AV)

A Partnership including Professional Corporations
600 West Broadway, Suite 2600, 92101
Telephone: 619-236-1414
Fax: 619-232-8311
La Jolla, California Office: 4275 Executive Square, Suite 800, 92037.
Telephone: 619-535-2639.
Fax: 619-453-2812.
Los Angeles, California Office: 777 South Figueroa, 36th Floor, 90017.
Telephone: 213-892-4992.
Fax: 213-892-7731.
San Francisco, California Office: 100 Bush Street, 20th Floor, 94104.
Telephone: 415-395-7900.
Fax: 415-395-7949.
New York, N.Y. Office: Citicorp Center, 153 East 53rd Street, 26th Floor, 10022.
Telephone: 212-754-1414.
Fax: 212-644-9727.

MEMBERS OF FIRM

Edgar A. Luce, Jr.
Margaret M. Mann
Mikel R. Bistrow
Christopher Celentino

OF COUNSEL

Michael T. Andrew
Stephen R. Brown

ASSOCIATES

Teryl S. Murabayashi
Kathryn M. S. Catherwood

For Complete List of Firm Personnel, See General Section

For full biographical listings, see the Martindale-Hubbell Law Directory

MULVANEY, KAHAN & BARRY, A PROFESSIONAL CORPORATION (AV)

Seventeenth Floor, First National Bank Center, 401 West "A" Street, 92101-7994
Telephone: 619-238-1010
Fax: 619-238-1981
Los Angeles, California Office: Union Bank Plaza, 445 South Figueroa Street, Suite 2600.
Telephone: 213-612-7765.
La Jolla, California Office: Glendale Federal Building, 7911 Herschel, Suite 300, P.O Box 1885.
Telephone: 619-454-0142.
Fax: 619-454-7858.
Orange, California Office: The Koll Center, 500 North State College Boulevard, Suite 440.
Telephone: 714-634-7069.
Fax: 714-939-8000.

James F. Mulvaney
Lawrence Kahan
Everett G. Barry, Jr.
Donald G. Johnson, Jr.
Robert A. Linn
Maureen E. Markey
Paula Rotenberg
Melissa A. Blackburn
Rex B. Beatty
Julie A. Jones
Maureen H. Edwards
Greta C. Botka
Mark R. Raftery
Charles F. Bethel
Carrie L. Gleeson
Diane M. Racicot
John A. Mayers
Linda P. Lucal

(See Next Column)

Steven W. Pite
Patricia A. Sieveke (Resident, Los Angeles and Orange Offices)
Michael S. Umansky

OF COUNSEL

James P. McGowan, Jr. (Resident, La Jolla Office)
Derrick W. Samuelson (Not admitted in CA)

Representative Clients: Air Products & Chemicals, Inc.; Colonial National Bank; FCC National Bank; NationsBank; Revlon, Inc.; Rhône-Poulenc Rorer, Inc.; Union Bank; Wells Fargo Bank.

For full biographical listings, see the Martindale-Hubbell Law Directory

PAGE, POLIN, BUSCH & BOATWRIGHT, A PROFESSIONAL CORPORATION (AV)

350 West Ash Street, Suite 900, 92101-3404
Telephone: 619-231-1822
Fax: 619-231-1877
FAX: 619-231-1875

David C. Boatwright
Michael E. Busch
Robert K. Edmunds
Kathleen A. Cashman-Kramer
Richard L. Moskitis
Richard W. Page
Kenneth D. Polin
Steven G. Rowles

OF COUNSEL

Richard Edward Ball, Jr.

Rod S. Fiori
Christina B. Gamache
Dorothy A. Johnson
Theresa McCarthy
Jolene L. Parker
Deidre L. Schneider
Sandra L. Shippey

For full biographical listings, see the Martindale-Hubbell Law Directory

PROCOPIO, CORY, HARGREAVES AND SAVITCH (AV)

2100 Union Bank Building, 530 B Street, 92101
Telephone: 619-238-1900
Telecopier: 619-235-0398

MEMBERS OF FIRM

Jeffrey Isaacs
Raymond G. Wright
Philip J. Giacinti, Jr.
Steven J. Untiedt
Gerald P. Kennedy
Jeffrey D. Cawdrey

ASSOCIATE

Martina Mende

Representative Clients: Union Bank; Daley Corp. (highway construction); Associated General Contractors.

For Complete List of Firm Personnel, See General Section

For full biographical listings, see the Martindale-Hubbell Law Directory

*SAN FRANCISCO,** San Francisco Co.

BECKER LAW OFFICE (AV)

220 Montgomery Street, Suite 388, P.O. Box 192991, 94119-2991
Telephone: 415-434-8000
Telex: 6731234 BECKER SFO
Telecopier: 415-362-7411
WUW Cable: BECKER, CALIF

Stephen C. Becker

For full biographical listings, see the Martindale-Hubbell Law Directory

FELDMAN, WALDMAN & KLINE, A PROFESSIONAL CORPORATION (AV)

2700 Russ Building, 235 Montgomery Street, 94104
Telephone: 415-981-1300
Telex: 650-223-3204
Fax: 415-394-0121
Stockton, California Office: Sperry Building, 146-148 West Weber Avenue.
Telephone: 209-943-2004.
Fax: 209-943-0905.

Murry J. Waldman
Leland R. Selna, Jr.
Michael L. Korbholz
Howard M. Wexler
Patricia S. Mar
Kenneth W. Jones
Paul J. Dion
Vern S. Bothwell
L. J. Chris Martiniak
Kenneth A. Freed
Martha Jeanne Shaver (Resident, Stockton Office)
Robert Cedric Goodman
Steven K. Denebeim
Laura Grad
William F. Adams
William M. Smith
Elizabeth A. Thompson
Julie A. Jones
David L. Kanel

Abram S. Feuerstein
John R. Capron
Ted S. Storey
A. Todd Berman
Laura J. Dawson

(See Next Column)

FELDMAN, WALDMAN & KLINE A PROFESSIONAL CORPORATION, *San Francisco—Continued*

OF COUNSEL

Richard L. Jaeger
Malcolm Leader-Picone
Gerald A. Sherwin (Resident, Stockton Office)

For full biographical listings, see the Martindale-Hubbell Law Directory

GOLDBERG, STINNETT, MEYERS & DAVIS, A PROFESSIONAL CORPORATION (AV)

Suite 2900, 44 Montgomery Street, 94104
Telephone: 415-362-5045
Fax: 415-362-2392

Lawrence Goldberg
Terrance L. Stinnett
Merle C. Meyers
Dennis D. Davis
Daniel M. Linchey

Katherine D. Ray
Deborah L. Lavine
Joseph K. Falzon
Albert Flor, Jr.
Kenneth G. DeJarnette

Representative Clients: Alps Electric (USA) Inc.; Continental Illinois National Bank; Fremont Bank; Greyhound Leasing and Financing Corp.; K-Mart Corporation; Mitsubishi International Corp.; California Canners and Growers; States Steamship Co.; Pan-Pacific Properties; Hexcel Corp.

For full biographical listings, see the Martindale-Hubbell Law Directory

GRIFFINGER, FREED, HEINEMANN, COOK & FOREMAN (AV)

24th Floor, Steuart Street Tower, One Market Plaza, 94105
Telephone: 415-243-0300
Telecopier: 415-777-9366

MEMBERS OF FIRM

Theodore A. Griffinger, Jr.
Michael S. Freed
Peter M. Heinemann
Karen A. Cook
Stewart H. Foreman
Jonathan A. Funk
Peter S. Fishman

Dwight L. Monson
Eileen Trujillo
Robert L. Wishner
Marie C. Bendy
Eric C. Starr
Jonathan Polland

LEGAL SUPPORT PERSONNEL

LEGAL ADMINISTRATOR

Kathleen H. Hartley

PARALEGALS

Jeanne Diettinger
Jean Mahony
Irene E. Bernasconi
Janet L. Johnston

Representative Client: Smith Barney, Harris Upham Co., Inc.
Reference: Bank of America (Main Office).

For full biographical listings, see the Martindale-Hubbell Law Directory

*SAN JOSE,** Santa Clara Co.

SEYMOUR J. ABRAHAMS (AV)

Market Post Tower, Suite 1660, 55 South Market Street, 95113-2324
Telephone: 408-298-6337
Fax: 408-298-0302

For full biographical listings, see the Martindale-Hubbell Law Directory

CAMPEAU & THOMAS, A LAW CORPORATION (AV)

Market Post Tower, 55 South Market Street, Suite 1660, 95113
Telephone: 408-295-9555
Fax: 408-295-6606

Kenneth J. Campeau
Wayne H. Thomas
Scott L. Goodsell

Laura Basaloco-Lapo
Marcie E. Schaap
Kathryn J. Diemer

For full biographical listings, see the Martindale-Hubbell Law Directory

*SANTA ANA,** Orange Co.

LAW OFFICES OF WILLIAM M. BURD (AV)

200 East Sandpointe, Suite 620, 92707
Telephone: 714-708-3900

Karen Sue Naylor

LEGAL SUPPORT PERSONNEL

Patricia A. Britton (Paralegal)

For full biographical listings, see the Martindale-Hubbell Law Directory

PRENOVOST, NORMANDIN, BERGH & DAWE A PROFESSIONAL CORPORATION (AV)

2020 East First Street, Suite 500, 92705
Telephone: 714-547-2444
Fax: 714-835-2889

Thomas J. Prenovost, Jr.
Tom Roddy Normandin
Steven L. Bergh
Michael G. Dawe

Bruce T. Bauer
Kristen L. Welles Lanham
Kimberly D. Taylor
Nancy R. Tragarz

Reference: Marine National Bank.

For full biographical listings, see the Martindale-Hubbell Law Directory

SPERLING & PERGANDE (AV)

3 Hutton Centre, Suite 670, 92707
Telephone: 714-540-8500
Facsimile: 714-540-2599

MEMBERS OF FIRM

Dean P. Sperling
K. William Pergande

For full biographical listings, see the Martindale-Hubbell Law Directory

SANTA MONICA, Los Angeles Co.

STEINBERG, NUTTER & BRENT, LAW CORPORATION (AV)

501 Colorado Avenue, Suite 300, 90401
Telephone: 310-451-9714
Telecopier: 310-451-0929

Peter T. Steinberg
Guy B. Nutter
Paul M. Brent

James M. Buck

Reference: Santa Monica Bank.

For full biographical listings, see the Martindale-Hubbell Law Directory

*SANTA ROSA,** Sonoma Co.

BELDEN, ABBEY, WEITZENBERG & KELLY, A PROFESSIONAL CORPORATION (AV)

1105 North Dutton Avenue, P.O. Box 1566, 95402
Telephone: 707-542-5050
Telecopier: 707-542-2589

Thomas P. Kelly, Jr.
Richard W. Abbey
Candace H. Shirley
Timothy W. Hoffman

Representative Clients: Exchange Bank of Santa Rosa; Westamerica Bank; North Bay Title Co.; Northwestern Title Security Co.; Geyser Peak Winery; Arrowood Vineyards & Winery; Hansel Ford; Santa Rosa City School District.

For Complete List of Firm Personnel, See General Section

For full biographical listings, see the Martindale-Hubbell Law Directory

TORRANCE, Los Angeles Co.

FINER, KIM & STEARNS (AV)

An Association of Professional Corporations
City National Bank Building, 3424 Carson Street, Suite 500, 90503
Telephone: 310-214-1477
Telecopier: 310-214-0764

W. A. Finer (A Professional Corporation)

Robert B. Parsons
Mark Andrew Hooper

OF COUNSEL

Bennett A. Rheingold
Ryan E. Stearns

For Complete List of Firm Personnel, See General Section

For full biographical listings, see the Martindale-Hubbell Law Directory

COLORADO

*DENVER,** Denver Co.

BALLARD SPAHR ANDREWS & INGERSOLL (AV)

Seventeenth Street Plaza Building, Suite 2300, 1225 17th Street, 80202-5596
Telephone: 303-292-2400
Fax: 303-296-3956
Philadelphia, Pennsylvania Office: 1735 Market Street, 51st Floor.
Telephone: 215-665-8500.
Fax: 215-864-8999.

(See Next Column)

BALLARD SPAHR ANDREWS & INGERSOLL—*Continued*

Kaunas, Lithuania Office: Donelaičio 71-2, Kaunas 3000.
Telephone: (370-7) 20 56 66.
Fax: (370-7) 20 56 91.
Salt Lake City, Utah Office: One Utah Center, 201 South Main Street, Suite 1200.
Telephone: 801-531-3000.
Fax: 801-531-3001.
Washington, D.C. Office: Suite 900 East, 555 13th Street, N.W.
Telephone: 202-383-8800.
Fax: 202-383-8877; 383-8893.
Baltimore, Maryland Office: 300 East Lombard Street, 19th Floor.
Telephone: 410-528-5600.
Fax: 410-528-5650.
Camden, New Jersey Office: 800 Hudson Square, 5th Floor.
Telephone: 609-541-5577.
Fax: 609-541-8272.

OF COUNSEL
Claire E. Holmes

Jacquelyn Kilmer

For Complete List of Firm Personnel, See General Section

For full biographical listings, see the Martindale-Hubbell Law Directory

JON B. CLARKE, P.C. (AV)

Two DTC, Suite 150, 5290 DTC Parkway (Englewood), 80111-2721
Telephone: 303-779-0600
Fax: 303-850-7115

Jon B. Clarke

For full biographical listings, see the Martindale-Hubbell Law Directory

DUCKER, DEWEY & SEAWELL, P.C. (AV)

One Civic Center Plaza, Suite 1500, 1560 Broadway, 80202
Telephone: 303-861-2828
Telecopier: 303-861-4017
Frisco, Colorado Office: 179 Willow Lane, Suite A, P.O. Box 870, 80443.
Telephone: 303-668-3776. Direct Dial from Denver: 674-1783.

Bruce Ducker
Stephen Gurko (Resident, Frisco Office)
Michael J. Kelly
Robert C. Montgomery
Thomas C. Seawell
L. Bruce Nelson
Christopher J. Walsh

OF COUNSEL
Charles F. Dewey

For full biographical listings, see the Martindale-Hubbell Law Directory

DUFFORD & BROWN, P.C. (AV)

1700 Broadway, Suite 1700, 80290-1701
Telephone: 303-861-8013
Facsimile: 303-832-3804

David W. Furgason
Randall J. Feuerstein
Scott J. Mikulecky

Terry Jo Epstein
Thomas E. J. Hazard

SPECIAL COUNSEL
Morris B. Hecox, Jr.

Representative Clients: Bondholders' Committee-Wheeler Realty Company; Reorganized CF&I Steel Corporation; Amdura Corporation; United Steelworkers of America; Air Line Pilots Association; Graphics Information, Inc.; IDS Life Insurance Company; Hall & Hall Mortgage Corporation; Magic Chef; Unsecured Creditor's Committee-Sargent, Inc.

For Complete List of Firm Personnel, See General Section

For full biographical listings, see the Martindale-Hubbell Law Directory

HOLLAND & HART (AV)

Suite 2900, 555 Seventeenth Street, P.O. Box 8749, 80201
Telephone: 303-295-8000
Cable Address: "Holhart Denver"
Telecopier: 303-295-8261
TWX: 910-931-0568
Denver Tech Center, Colorado Office: Suite 1050, 4601 DTC Boulevard.
Telephone: 303-290-1600.
Telecopier: 303-290-1606.
Aspen, Colorado Office: 600 East Main Street.
Telephone: 303-925-3476.
Telecopier: 303-925-9367.
Boulder, Colorado Office: Suite 500, 1050 Walnut.
Telephone: 303-473-2700.
Telecopier: 303-473-2720.
Colorado Springs, Colorado Office: Suite 1000, 90 S. Cascade Avenue.
Telephone: 719-475-7730.
Telex: 82077 SHHTLX.
Telecopier: 719-634-2461.

(See Next Column)

Washington, D.C. Office: Suite 310, 1001 Pennsylvania Avenue, N.W.
Telephone: 202-638-5500.
Telecopier: 202-737-8998.
Boise, Idaho Office: Suite 1400, West One Plaza, 101 South Capitol Boulevard, P.O. Box 2527.
Telephone: 208-342-5000.
Telecopier: 208-343-8869.
Billings, Montana Office: Suite 1500, First Interstate Center, 401 North 31st Street, P.O. Box 639.
Telephone: 406-252-2166.
Telecopier: 406-252-1669.
Salt Lake City, Utah Office: Suite 880, 111 East Broadway.
Telephone: 801-578-6000.
FAX: 801-578-6010.
Cheyenne, Wyoming Office: Holland & Hart, A Partnership including Professional Corporations, Suite 500, 2020 Carey Avenue, P.O. Box 1347.
Telephone: 307-778-4200.
Telecopier: 307-778-8175.
Jackson, Wyoming Office: Holland & Hart, A Partnership including Professional Corporations, Suite 2, 175 South King Street, P.O. Box 68.
Telephone: 307-739-9741.
Telecopier: 307-739-9744.

MEMBERS OF FIRM
Jack L. Smith
Ronald M. Martin

OF COUNSEL
Howard R. Tallman

ASSOCIATES
R. Dana Cephas
Stephen Masciocchi
Risa L. Wolf-Smith

COLORADO SPRINGS, COLORADO PARTNER
Ronald M. Martin

BOISE, IDAHO RESIDENT PARTNER
Larry E. Prince

BOISE, IDAHO RESIDENT ASSOCIATE
Robert A. Faucher

BILLINGS, MONTANA RESIDENT ASSOCIATE
Bruce F. Fain

CHEYENNE, WYOMING RESIDENT ASSOCIATES
James R. Belcher
Bradley T. Cave

For Complete List of Firm Personnel, See General Section

For full biographical listings, see the Martindale-Hubbell Law Directory

HOLME ROBERTS & OWEN LLC (AV)

Suite 4100, 1700 Lincoln, 80203
Telephone: 303-861-7000
Telex: 45-4460
Telecopier: 303-866-0200
Boulder, Colorado Office: Suite 400, 1401 Pearl Street.
Telephone: 303-444-5955.
Telecopier: 303-444-1063.
Colorado Springs, Colorado Office: Suite 1300, 90 South Cascade Avenue.
Telephone: 719-473-3800.
Telecopier: 719-633-1518.
Salt Lake City, Utah Office: Suite 1100, 111 East Broadway.
Telephone: 801-521-5800.
Telecopier: 801-521-9639.
London, England Office: 4th Floor, Mellier House, 26a Albemarle Street.
Telephone: 44-171-499-8776.
Telecopier: 44-171-499-7769.
Moscow, Russia Office: 14 Krivokolenny Pr., Suite 30, 101000.
Telephone: 095-925-7816.
Telecopier: 095-923-2726.

MEMBERS OF FIRM
Stephen E. Snyder
Brent V. Manning (Salt Lake City Office)
Michael D. Strugar (Colorado Springs Office)
Eric E. Johnson

For Complete List of Firm Personnel, See General Section

For full biographical listings, see the Martindale-Hubbell Law Directory

LAW OFFICES OF NANCY D. MILLER, P.C. (AV)

1600 Broadway, Suite 2112, 80202
Telephone: 303-861-4404
Telecopier: 303-861-4133

Nancy D. Miller

Marianne Marshall Tims

OF COUNSEL
Sheila H. Meer (P.C.)

For full biographical listings, see the Martindale-Hubbell Law Directory

Denver—Continued

SKEEN & PEARLMAN, P.C. (AV)

Suite 3050, One Norwest Center 1700 Lincoln Street, 80203-4530
Telephone: 303-861-8400
Telecopier: 303-832-9002

Matthew D. Skeen
Philip A. Pearlman

OF COUNSEL

Cynthia V.R. Skeen

For full biographical listings, see the Martindale-Hubbell Law Directory

WELLER FRIEDRICH, LLC (AV)

One Civic Center, Suite 2000, 1560 Broadway, P.O. Box 989, 80201-0989
Telephone: 303-812-1200
FAX: 303-812-1212

David K. Kerr
Jerome M. Joseph
Dennis J. Bartlett

Representative Clients: Abbott Laboratories; Associated Aviation Underwriters; Commercial Union Insurance Companies.
Reference: Colorado State Bank of Denver.

For full biographical listings, see the Martindale-Hubbell Law Directory

CONNECTICUT

*HARTFORD,** Hartford Co.

HEBB & GITLIN, A PROFESSIONAL CORPORATION (AV)

One State Street, 06103-3178
Telephone: 203-240-2700
Telecopier: 203-278-8968

G. Eric Brunstad, Jr.
Richard F. Casher
Chester L. Fisher III
Douglas E. Fiske
Evan D. Flaschen
John J. Gillies, Jr.
Richard A. Gitlin
James Greenfield
Gary S. Hammersmith
Edwin Gordon Hebb, Jr.
Harold S. Horwich
Eric W. Johnson
William E. Kelly
Jeffery S. Kuperstock
Thomas J. Love, Jr.
George A. McKeon (Of Counsel)
M. Bree Nesbitt
Gregory W. Nye
Michael J. Reilly
R. Jeffrey Smith
Elliot N. Solomon
Lorraine Murphy Weil
Jeffrey L. Williams

Patti Lynn Boss
Claude M. Brouillard
Katherine A. Burroughs
Mark E. Chavey
Laura Gonzalez Ciabarra
Thomas H. Day
Jane M. Domboski
Scott A. Falk
Alison R. Faltersack
Christine E. Farrell
Deborah Samuels Freeman
Matthew F. Furlong
Elena M. Gervino
Jonathan A. Harris
John D. Inwood (Not admitted in CT)
Jeffrey A. Jones
James P. Juliano
James P. Maher
Theodore C. Morris
Thomas F. O'Connor
Thomas J. O'Shea
Joyce M. Resnick
Barry G. Russell
Joseph L. Scibilia
Patricia Ann Shackelford
James W. Shaughnessy
David Silber
Ronald J. Silverman
Robert C. Walsh, Jr.
Brian N. Watkins

For full biographical listings, see the Martindale-Hubbell Law Directory

*NEW HAVEN,** New Haven Co.

BERGMAN, HOROWITZ & REYNOLDS, P.C. (AV)

157 Church Street, 19th Floor, P.O. Box 426, 06502
Telephone: 203-789-1320
FAX: 203-785-8127
New York, New York Office: 499 Park Avenue, 26th Floor.
Telephone: 212-582-3580.

Melvin Ditman

David M. Spinner
Jeremy A. Mellitz
Richard M. Porter

For Complete List of Firm Personnel, See General Section

For full biographical listings, see the Martindale-Hubbell Law Directory

WETHERSFIELD, Hartford Co.

CHORCHES & NOVAK, P.C. (AV)

1260 Silas Deane Highway, 06109-4331
Telephone: 203-257-1980
Telecopier: 203-257-1988

Martin Chorches
Anthony S. Novak
Harry C. Blake

Ronald I. Chorches
Theresa A. Caldarone
Edward C. Taiman, Jr.

For full biographical listings, see the Martindale-Hubbell Law Directory

DELAWARE

*WILMINGTON,** New Castle Co.

POTTER ANDERSON & CORROON (AV)

350 Delaware Trust Building, P.O. Box 951, 19899-0951
Telephone: 302-658-6771
FAX: 658-1192; 655-1190; 655-1199

MEMBER OF FIRM

Laurie Selber Silverstein

ASSOCIATES

William R. Denny
Joanne Ceballos

Representative Clients: Meridian Oil Production, Inc.; Consolidated Rail Corporation; Travellers International; A.G.; ConAgra, Inc.; Swift Eckrich, Inc.; Beatrice Cheese, Inc.; Midlantic National Bank; Delaware Trust Company; DR Holdings Inc. of Delaware.

For Complete List of Firm Personnel, See General Section

For full biographical listings, see the Martindale-Hubbell Law Directory

SMITH, KATZENSTEIN & FURLOW (AV)

1220 Market Building, P.O. Box 410, 19899
Telephone: 302-652-8400
FAX: 302-652-8405

MEMBERS OF FIRM

Craig B. Smith
Anne E. Bookout

Stephen M. Miller
Joanne M. Shalk

For Complete List of Firm Personnel, See General Section

For full biographical listings, see the Martindale-Hubbell Law Directory

DISTRICT OF COLUMBIA

WASHINGTON, D.C. Co.

***** indicates certain Bar Register subscribers, in cities of comparable size and importance, who maintain an additional office in Washington, D.C. and who have arranged for representation as a part of the Washington, D.C. listings that follow

GEORGE FRANCIS BASON, JR. (AV)

4910 Massachusetts Avenue, N.W., Suite 18, 20016
Telephone: 202-537-0219
Telefax: 301-654-7917
Chevy Chase, Maryland Office: 4601 North Park Avenue, No. 110.
(Also Of Counsel to Michael J. Goergen)

For full biographical listings, see the Martindale-Hubbell Law Directory

DECKELBAUM OGENS & FISCHER, CHARTERED (AV)

1140 Connecticut Avenue, N.W., 20036
Telephone: 202-223-1474
Fax: 202-293-1471
Bethesda, Maryland Office: 6701 Democracy Boulevard.
Telephone: 301-564-5100.

Nelson Deckelbaum
Ronald L. Ogens
Lawrence H. Fischer
Arthur G. Kahn
Deborah E. Reiser
John B. Raftery
Charles A. Moster
Andrew J. Shedlock, III

Ronald G. Scheraga
Bryn Hope Sherman
Phyllis Lea Bean
Darryl Alan Feldman (Resident, Bethesda, Maryland Office)

(See Next Column)

DECKELBAUM OGENS & FISCHER CHARTERED—*Continued*

References: Franklin National Bank; Century National Bank.

For full biographical listings, see the Martindale-Hubbell Law Directory

LEONARD, RALSTON, STANTON & DANKS (AV)

Suite 609, Georgetown, 1000 Thomas Jefferson Street, N.W., 20007
Telephone: 202-342-3342
Fax: 202-298-7810
Fairfax, Virginia Office: Leonard, Ralston, Stanton & Danks, Sherwood Plaza, Suite 150, 9990 Lee Highway.
Telephone: 703-591-6200.
Fax: 703-591-6556.
Jackson, Mississippi Office: Keyes, Danks & Leonard, Suite 100, 213 South Lamar Street.
Telephone: 601-948-3100.
Fax: 601-948-1919.

MEMBERS OF FIRM

Jerris Leonard
David T. Ralston, Jr.
Thomas J. Stanton (Not admitted in DC)
Michael J. Remington
Mary Gayle Holden (Not admitted in DC)

ASSOCIATES

Roderick B. Williams
Rachel Danish Campbell
Karen M. Grane
Seanan B. Murphy
George Galt (Not admitted in DC)
Theodore Charles Curtin (Not admitted in DC)

OF COUNSEL

John D. Brosnan

For full biographical listings, see the Martindale-Hubbell Law Directory

SHAWN, MANN & NIEDERMAYER, L.L.P. (AV)

1850 M Street, N.W., Suite 280, 20036-5803
Telephone: 202-331-7900
Fax: 202-331-0726

MEMBERS OF FIRM

Joseph L. Steinfeld, Jr.
Robert B. Walker

For full biographical listings, see the Martindale-Hubbell Law Directory

*** VENABLE, BAETJER, HOWARD & CIVILETTI (AV)**

A Partnership including Professional Corporations
Suite 1000, 1201 New York Avenue, N.W., 20005
Telephone: 202-962-4800
Fax: 202-962-8300
Baltimore, Maryland Office: Venable, Baetjer and Howard, 1800 Mercantile Bank & Trust Building, 2 Hopkins Plaza.
Telephone: 410-244-7400.
McLean, Virginia Office: Venable, Baetjer and Howard, Suite 400, 2010 Corporate Ridge.
Telephone: 703-760-1600.
Rockville, Maryland Office: Venable, Baetjer and Howard, Suite 500, One Church Street, P. O. Box 1906.
Telephone: 301-217-5600.
Towson, Maryland Office: Venable, Baetjer and Howard, 210 Allegheny Avenue, P. O. Box 5517.
Telephone: 410-494-6200.

MEMBERS OF FIRM

Joe A. Shull
Kenneth C. Bass, III (Also at McLean, Virginia Office)
Joel Z. Silver
George F. Pappas (Also at Baltimore, Maryland Office)

For Complete List of Firm Personnel, See General Section

For full biographical listings, see the Martindale-Hubbell Law Directory

WILMER, CUTLER & PICKERING (AV)

2445 M Street, N.W., 20037-1420
Telephone: 202-663-6000
Facsimile: 202-663-6363
Internet: Law@Wilmer.Com
European Offices:
4 Carlton Gardens, London, SW1Y 5AA, England. Telephone: 011 (4471) 839-4466.
Facsimile: 011 (4471) 839-3537.
Rue de la Loi 15 Wetstraat, B-1040 Brussels, Belgium. Telephone: 011 (322) 231-0903.
Facsimile: 011 (322) 230-4322.
Friedrichstrasse 95, D-10117 Berlin, Germany. Telephone: 011 (4930) 2643-3601.
Facsimile: 011 (4930) 2643-3630.

(See Next Column)

MEMBERS OF FIRM

Louis R. Cohen
F. David Lake, Jr.
Stephen F. Black
Dr. Manfred Balz (Not admitted in the United States); (Resident, European Office, Berlin, Germany)
Mary Carolyn Cox
William J. Perlstein
Russell J. Bruemmer
William J. Wilkins
Thomas W. White
Duane D. Morse
Philip D. Anker
Anastasia D. Kelly
Bryan Slone (Not admitted in DC; Resident, European Office, Berlin, Germany)

For Complete List of Firm Personnel, See General Section

For full biographical listings, see the Martindale-Hubbell Law Directory

ZUCKERMAN, SPAEDER, GOLDSTEIN, TAYLOR & KOLKER (AV)

1201 Connecticut Avenue, N.W., 20036
Telephone: 202-778-1800
Fax: 202-822-8106
Miami, Florida Office: Zuckerman, Spaeder, Taylor & Evans. Suite 900, Miami Center, 201 South Biscayne Boulevard.
Telephones: 305-358-5000; 305-579-0110; Broward County: 305-523-0277.
Fax: 305-579-9749.
Ft. Lauderdale, Florida Office: Zuckerman, Spaeder, Taylor & Evans. One East Broward Boulevard, Suite 700.
Telephone: 305-356-0463.
Fax: 305-356-0406.
Baltimore, Maryland Office: Zuckerman, Spaeder, Goldstein, Taylor & Better. Suite 2440, 100 East Pratt Street.
Telephone: 410-332-0444.
Fax: 410-659-0436.
Tampa, Florida Office: Zuckerman, Spaeder, Taylor & Evans. 101 East Kennedy Boulevard, Suite 3140.
Telephone: 813-221-1010.
Fax: 813-223-7961.
New York, N.Y. Office: 1114 Avenue of the Americas, 45th Floor, Grace Building.
Telephone: 212-479-6500.
Fax: 212-479-6512.

MEMBERS OF FIRM

Bruce Goldstein
Nelson C. Cohen
Judith Sturtz Karp
Barbara Kramer Morgan
Barbara L. Ward

Reference: Sovran Bank/DC National.

For full biographical listings, see the Martindale-Hubbell Law Directory

FLORIDA

*JACKSONVILLE,** Duval Co.

FISCHETTE, OWEN & HELD (AV)

Suite 1916 Gulf Life Tower, 32207
Telephone: 904-398-7036
Fax: 904-398-4283

MEMBERS OF FIRM

James A. Fischette
Philip C. Owen
Edwin W. Held, Jr.
Charles W. McBurney, Jr.

ASSOCIATES

Donald M. DuFresne
Earl Warren (Chip) Parker, Jr.

LEGAL SUPPORT PERSONNEL

PARALEGALS

Susan S. Coleman
Carrie L. Smith

References: Sun Bank of Jacksonville; Enterprise National Bank of Jacksonville.

For full biographical listings, see the Martindale-Hubbell Law Directory

KIRSCHNER, MAIN, PETRIE, GRAHAM, TANNER & DEMONT, PROFESSIONAL ASSOCIATION (AV)

One Independent Drive, Suite 2000, P.O. Box 1559, 32201-1559
Telephone: 904-354-4141
Telecopier: 904-358-2199

Barry C. Averitt
Michael E. Demont
Curtis S. Fallgatter
T. Malcolm Graham
Lee Stathis Haramis
T. Geoffrey Heekin
Kenneth M. Kirschner
James L. Main
Gayle Petrie
Michael G. Tanner

(See Next Column)

KIRSCHNER, MAIN, PETRIE, GRAHAM, TANNER & DEMONT PROFESSIONAL ASSOCIATION, *Jacksonville—Continued*

Howard L. Alford
Karen Smith French
Deborah Greene
Reese J. Henderson, Jr.
Kenneth B. Jacobs
Julie Anne Luten
Charles S. McCall
Marsha Phillips Proctor
John T. Rogerson, III
Ann Krueger Vining
Alan S. Wachs

For full biographical listings, see the Martindale-Hubbell Law Directory

LAW OFFICE OF LANSING J. ROY, P.A. (AV)

Suite 1200, 200 West Forsyth Street, 32202
Telephone: 904-355-9960
Fax: 904-355-9963

Lansing J. Roy

References will be furnished upon request.

For full biographical listings, see the Martindale-Hubbell Law Directory

*MIAMI,** Dade Co.

MERSHON, SAWYER, JOHNSTON, DUNWODY & COLE (AV)

A Partnership including Professional Associations
Suite 4500 First Union Financial Center, 200 South Biscayne Boulevard, 33131-2387
Telephone: 305-358-5100
Cable Address: "Mercole"
Telex: 515705
Fax: 305-376-8654
Naples, Florida Office: Pelican Bay Corporate Centre, Suite 501, 5551 Ridgewood Drive.
Telephone: 813-598-1055.
Fax: 813-598-1868.
West Palm Beach, Florida Office: 777 South Flagler Drive, Suite 900.
Telephone: 407-659-5990.
Fax: 407-659-6313.
Key West, Florida Office: 3132 North Side Drive, Suite 102.
Telephone: 305-296-1774.
Fax: 305-296-1715
London, England Office: Blake Lodge, Bridge Lane, London SW11 3AD, England.
Telephone: 44-71-978-7748.
Fax: 44-71-350-0156.

MEMBERS OF FIRM

Dennis M. Campbell (P.A.)
Timothy J. Norris (P.A.)

ASSOCIATES

John D. Eaton
Natalie Scharf

Representative Clients: Arvida/JMB Partners; Bankers Trust Co.; Biscayne Kennel Club, Inc.; The Chase Manhattan Bank, N.A.; Lennar Corp.; Reynolds Metals Co.; United States Sugar Corp.; University of Miami.

For Complete List of Firm Personnel, See General Section

For full biographical listings, see the Martindale-Hubbell Law Directory

STEARNS WEAVER MILLER WEISSLER ALHADEFF & SITTERSON, P.A. (AV)

Suite 2200 Museum Tower, 150 West Flagler Street, 33130
Telephone: 305-789-3200
FAX: 305-789-3395
Tampa, Florida Office: Suite 2200 Landmark Centre, 401 East Jackson Street.
Telephone: 813-223-4800.
Fort Lauderdale, Florida Office: 200 East Broward Boulevard, Suite 1900.
Telephone: 305-462-9500.

E. Richard Alhadeff
Louise Jacowitz Allen
Stuart D. Ames
Thomas P. Angelo (Resident, Fort Lauderdale Office)
Lawrence J. Bailin (Resident, Tampa Office)
Patrick A. Barry (Resident, Fort Lauderdale Office)
Lisa K. Bennett (Resident, Fort Lauderdale Office)
Susan Fleming Bennett (Resident, Tampa Office)
Mark J. Bernet (Resident, Tampa Office)
Claire Bailey Carraway (Resident, Tampa Office)
Seth T. Craine (Resident, Tampa Office)
Piero Luciano Desiderio (Resident, Fort Lauderdale Office)
Mark P. Dikeman
Sharon Quinn Dixon
Alan H. Fein
Owen S. Freed
Dean M. Freitag
Robert E. Gallagher, Jr.
Alice R. Huneycutt (Resident, Tampa Office)
Theodore A. Jewell
Elizabeth J. Keeler
Teddy D. Klinghoffer
Robert T. Kofman
Thomas A. Lash (Resident, Tampa Office)
Joy Spillis Lundeen
Brian J. McDonough

(See Next Column)

Francisco J. Menendez
Antonio R. Menendez
Alison W. Miller
Vicki Lynn Monroe
Harold D. Moorefield, Jr.
John N. Muratides (Resident, Tampa Office)
John K. Olson (Resident, Tampa Office)
Robert C. Owens
Patricia A. Redmond
Carl D. Roston
Steven D. Rubin
Mark A. Schneider
Curtis H. Sitterson
Mark D. Solov
Eugene E. Stearns
Bradford Swing
Dennis R. Turner
Ronald L. Weaver (Resident, Tampa Office)
Robert I. Weissler
Patricia G. Welles
Martin B. Woods (Resident, Fort Lauderdale Office)

Shawn M. Bayne (Resident, Fort Lauderdale Office)
Lisa Berg
Hans C. Beyer (Resident, Tampa Office)
Dawn A. Carapella (Resident, Tampa Office)
Christina Maria Diaz
Robert I. Finvarb
Patricia K. Green
Marilyn D. Greenblatt
Richard B. Jackson
Aimee C. Jimenez
Cheryl A. Kaplan
Michael I. Keyes
Vernon L. Lewis
Kevin Bruce Love
Adam Coatsworth Mishcon
Elizabeth G. Rice (Resident, Tampa Office)
Glenn M. Rissman
Claudia J. Saenz
Richard E. Schatz
Robert P. Shantz (Resident, Tampa Office)
Martin S. Simkovic
Ronni D. Solomon
Jo Claire Spear (Resident, Tampa Office)
Gail Marie Stage (Resident, Fort Lauderdale Office)
Annette Torres
Barbara L. Wilhite

OF COUNSEL

Stephen A. Bennett

For full biographical listings, see the Martindale-Hubbell Law Directory

STUZIN AND CAMNER, PROFESSIONAL ASSOCIATION (AV)

25th Floor, 1221 Brickell Avenue, 33131-3260
Telephone: 305-577-0600

Charles B. Stuzin
Alfred R. Camner
Stanley A. Beiley
Marsha D. Bilzin
David S. Garbett
Nina S. Gordon
Barry D. Hunter
Nikki J. Nedbor
Neale J. Poller

Lisa R. Carstarphen
Maria E. Chang
Barry P. Gruher
Gustavo D. Llerena
Sherry D. McMillan
Roger A. Preziosi

OF COUNSEL

Anne Shari Camner

References: Citizens Federal Bank; City National Bank of Miami; Barnett Bank of South Florida, N.A.

For full biographical listings, see the Martindale-Hubbell Law Directory

ZIEGLER & GINSBURG, P.A. (AV)

370 Minorca Avenue, Suite 21 (Coral Gables), 33134
Telephone: 305-444-5676
Facsimile: 305-444-3937

Stuart Harvey Ziegler
Edwin M. Ginsburg

For full biographical listings, see the Martindale-Hubbell Law Directory

NORTH MIAMI BEACH, Dade Co.

BUCHANAN INGERSOLL, PROFESSIONAL CORPORATION (AV)

One Turnberry Place, 19495 Biscayne Boulevard, 33180
Telephone: 305-933-5600
Telecopier: 305-933-2350
Pittsburgh, Pennsylvania Office: 5800 USX Tower, 600 Grant Street.
Telephone: 412-562-8800.
Philadelphia, Pennsylvania Office: Two Logan Square, Twelfth Floor, 18th & Arch Streets.
Telephone: 215-665-8700.
Harrisburg, Pennsylvania Office: Vartan Parc, 30 North Third Street.
Telephone: 717-237-4800.
Tampa, Florida Office: Suite 1030, 101 East Kennedy Boulevard.
Telephone: 813-222-8180.
Princeton, New Jersey Office: Buchanan Ingersoll, A Partnership, College Centre, 500 College Road East.
Telephone: 609-452-2666.
Lexington, Kentucky Office: Suite 600, PNC Bank Plaza, 200 West Vine Street.
Telephone: 606-225-5333.

Dennis J. Eisinger
Barry A. Nelson

(See Next Column)

BUCHANAN INGERSOLL PROFESSIONAL CORPORATION—*Continued*

Richard N. Schermer

For Complete List of Firm Personnel, See General Section

For full biographical listings, see the Martindale-Hubbell Law Directory

*ORLANDO,** Orange Co.

JULES S. COHEN, P.A. (AV)

810 North Mills Avenue, 32803
Telephone: 407-896-4493

Jules S. Cohen

Miriam G. Suarez

Representative Clients: The American Bank of the South; First Federal Savings & Loan Association of Osceola County; Peoples State Bank; Aetna Bank; Swiss Bank Corporation; John Hancock Mutual Life Insurance Co.; Sony Corp.; Great American Insurance Co.
Reference: Sun Bank.

For full biographical listings, see the Martindale-Hubbell Law Directory

*SARASOTA,** Sarasota Co.

ABEL, BAND, RUSSELL, COLLIER, PITCHFORD & GORDON, CHARTERED (AV)

Barnett Bank Center, 240 South Pineapple Avenue, P.O. Box 49948, 34230-6948
Telephone: 813-366-6660
FAX: 813-366-3999
Fort Myers, Florida Office: The Tidewater Building, 1375 Jackson Street, Suite 201, 33901.
Telephone: 813-337-0062.
FAX: 813-337-0406.
Venice, Florida Office: Suite 199, 333 South Tamiami Trail, 34285.
Telephone: 813-485-8200.
Fax: 813-488-9436.

David S. Band
Jeffrey S. Russell
Ronald L. Collier
Malcolm J. Pitchford
Cheryl Lasris Gordon
Anthony J. Abate
Steven J. Chase
Kathryn Angell Carr
Michael S. Taaffe
Mark W. McFall
Jan Walters Pitchford

OF COUNSEL

Harvey J. Abel
Johnson S. Savary

Saralyn Abel
Douglas M. Bales
Gregory S. Band
John A. Garner
Mark D. Hildreth
Jane M. Kennedy
Christine Edwards Lamia
Bradley D. Magee
George H. Mazzarantani
Philip C. Zimmerman

References: Barnett Bank of Southwest Florida; Sun Bank/Gulf Coast.

For full biographical listings, see the Martindale-Hubbell Law Directory

*TALLAHASSEE,** Leon Co.

MARK FREUND, P.A. (AV)

227 North Bronough Street, Suite 1101, P.O. Box 10171, 32302
Telephone: 904-681-0066
FAX: 904-681-3798

Mark Freund

Laura Beth Faragasso

Representative Client: Abbey Color, Inc.; Cedar Concepts Corp.; Florida Commerce Federal Credit Union; Pride Resorts, Ltd.; Pride Resorts - Panama City Beach, Ltd.; Sport-Craft, Inc.; Tallahassee State Bank Corp.; Celwal Concepts Corp.
Reference: Tallahassee State Bank.

For full biographical listings, see the Martindale-Hubbell Law Directory

*TAMPA,** Hillsborough Co.

LANGFORD, HILL & TRYBUS, P.A. (AV)

Suite 800, Bayshore Place, 601 Bayshore Boulevard, 33606
Telephone: 813-251-5533
Telecopier: 813-251-1900
Wats: 1-800-277-2005

E. C. Langford
Edward A. Hill
Ronald H. Trybus
Ronald G. Hock
Catherine M. Catlin
Debra M. Kubicsek
William B. Smith

(See Next Column)

Fredrique B. Boire
Muriel Desloovere
Kevin H. O'Neill
Vicki L. Page
Frederick T. Reeves
Barbara A. Sinsley
Stephens B. Woodrough (Not admitted in FL)
Anthony G. Woodward

Representative Clients: Affiliated of Florida, Inc.; American Federation Insurance Co.; Armor Insurance; Bank of Tampa; Central Bank of Tampa; Cintas Corp.; Container Corporation of America; CU Financial Services; Farm Stores, Inc.; First Union Home Equity Bank.

For full biographical listings, see the Martindale-Hubbell Law Directory

RYDBERG, GOLDSTEIN & BOLVES, P.A. (AV)

Suite 200, 500 East Kennedy Boulevard, 33602
Telephone: 813-229-3900
Telecopier: 813-229-6101

Marsha Griffin Rydberg
Bruce S. Goldstein
Brian A. Bolves
Robert E. V. Kelley, Jr.
Homer Duvall, III
Richard Thomas Petitt
Donald Alan Workman
David M. Corry
Leenetta Blanton
Peter Baker
Jeffery R. Ward
Roy J. Ford, Jr.
John J. Dingfelder

For full biographical listings, see the Martindale-Hubbell Law Directory

STICHTER, RIEDEL, BLAIN & PROSSER, P.A. (AV)

110 East Madison Street, Suite 200, 33602-4700
Telephone: 813-229-0144
FAX: 813-229-1811

Don M. Stichter
Harley E. Riedel, II
Russell M. Blain
Richard C. Prosser
Charles A. Postler
Wanda Hagan Anthony
Scott A. Stichter
Lynn Pope Bikowitz
Alberto F. Gomez, Jr.
W. Gregory Golson
Stephen R. Leslie

For full biographical listings, see the Martindale-Hubbell Law Directory

TERRY & DITTMAR (AV)

Suite 2560, Barnett Plaza, 101 East Kennedy Boulevard, P.O. Box 20645, 33622-0645
Telephone: 813-222-8522
Fax: 813-222-8549

MEMBERS OF FIRM

William J. Terry
Charles H. Dittmar, Jr.

For full biographical listings, see the Martindale-Hubbell Law Directory

GEORGIA

*ALBANY,** Dougherty Co.

KELLEY & LOVETT, P.C. (AV)

504 North Jefferson, P.O. Box 1666, 31702
Telephone: 912-888-9128
Fax: 912-888-0966

Walter W. Kelley
Thomas D. Lovett

David P. Ward
Allen P. Turnage

Reference: 1st State Bank, Albany, Georgia

*ATLANTA,** Fulton Co.

FRANCIS M. BIRD, JR. (AV)

50 Hurt Plaza, Suite 730, 30303
Telephone: 404-525-0885
Fax: 404-523-2806

OF COUNSEL

Pamela L. Tremayne

For full biographical listings, see the Martindale-Hubbell Law Directory

BONDURANT, MIXSON & ELMORE (AV)

1201 W. Peachtree Street Suite 3900, 30309
Telephone: 404-881-4100
FAX: 404-881-4111

(See Next Column)

BONDURANT, MIXSON & ELMORE, *Atlanta—Continued*

MEMBERS OF FIRM

Emmet J. Bondurant II
H. Lamar Mixson
M. Jerome Elmore
Edward B. Krugman
James C. Morton
Jeffrey O. Bramlett
Dirk G. Christensen
Jane E. Fahey
Jeffrey D. Horst
John E. Floyd
Carolyn R. Gorwitz
Michael A. Sullivan

ASSOCIATES

Mary Jo Bradbury
P. Richard Game
Robin M. Hutchinson
J. Scott McClain
Keenan Rance Sephus Nix
Jill A. Pryor
Michael B. Terry
Joshua F. Thorpe

Representative Clients: The Aetna Casualty and Surety Company; Bottlers of Coca-Cola, U.S.A.; Brinks Home Security Systems, Inc.; Delta Air Lines, Inc.; Fina Oil and Chemical Company; The Florida Software Services, Inc.; JMB Realty Corp.; The Paradies Shops, Inc.; Sanifill, Inc.; Trammell Crow Co.

For Complete List of Firm Personnel, See General Section

For full biographical listings, see the Martindale-Hubbell Law Directory

DAVID G. CROCKETT, P.C. (AV)

1000 Equitable Building, 100 Peachtree Street, N.W., 30303
Telephone: 404-522-4280
Telecopier: 404-589-9891

David G. Crockett

Approved Attorney for: Chicago Title Insurance Co.
Reference: NationsBank, N.A.

For full biographical listings, see the Martindale-Hubbell Law Directory

KIRWAN, GOGER, CHESIN & PARKS, P.C. (AV)

2600 The Grand, 75 Fourteenth Street, 30309
Telephone: 404-873-8000
Facsimile: 404-873-8050

John J. Goger

Representative Client: Anheuser Busch Cos., Inc.
Reference: Trust Company Bank.

For full biographical listings, see the Martindale-Hubbell Law Directory

LAMBERTH, BONAPFEL, CIFELLI, WILLSON & STOKES, P.A. (AV)

Atlanta Financial Center, 3343 Peachtree Road, N.E. East Tower, Suite 550, 30326
Telephone: 404-262-7373

J. Michael Lamberth
James Craig Cifelli
William H. Willson, Jr.
Paul W. Bonapfel

G. Frank Nason, IV
Stuart F. Clayton, Jr.
Gregory D. Ellis
Donahue S. Silvis
A. Alexander Teel
Sharon K. Kacmarcik

Reference: The Chattahoochee Bank.

For full biographical listings, see the Martindale-Hubbell Law Directory

LONG ALDRIDGE & NORMAN (AV)

A Partnership including Professional Corporations
One Peachtree Center, Suite 5300, 303 Peachtree Street, 30308
Telephone: 404-527-4000
Telecopier: 404-527-4198
Washington, D.C. Office: Suite 950, 1615 L Street, 20036.
Telephone: 202-223-7033.
Telecopier: 202-223-7013.

MEMBERS OF FIRM

Evan Appel
Mark S. Kaufman
Bruce W. Moorhead, Jr.
Russell A. Tolley

ASSOCIATES

Gary W. Marsh
Laura Fink Nix
Kellie S. Raiford
Gregory Mark Simpson

For Complete List of Firm Personnel, See General Section

For full biographical listings, see the Martindale-Hubbell Law Directory

MACEY, WILENSKY, COHEN, WITTNER & KESSLER (AV)

Suite 700 Carnegie Building, 133 Carnegie Way, Northwest, 30303
Telephone: 404-584-1200
Telecopier: 404-681-4355
Other Atlanta, Georgia Office: 5784 Lake Forrest Drive, Suite 214, 30328.

MEMBERS OF FIRM

Morris W. Macey
Frank B. Wilensky
Neil C. Gordon

(See Next Column)

ASSOCIATES

James R. Sacca
David B. Kurzweil
Michael D. Pinsky
Shayna M. (Salomon) Steinfeld

For Complete List of Firm Personnel, See General Section

For full biographical listings, see the Martindale-Hubbell Law Directory

PARKER, HUDSON, RAINER & DOBBS (AV)

1500 Marquis Two Tower, 285 Peachtree Center Avenue, N.E., 30303
Telephone: 404-523-5300
FAX: 404-522-8409
Tallahassee, Florida Office: The Perkins House, 118 North Gadsden Street, 32301.
Telephone: 904-681-0191.
FAX: 904-681-9493.

MEMBERS OF FIRM

C. Edward Dobbs
Rufus Thomas Dorsey, IV

For full biographical listings, see the Martindale-Hubbell Law Directory

SCHREEDER, WHEELER & FLINT (AV)

1600 Candler Building, 127 Peachtree Street, N.E., 30303-1845
Telephone: 404-681-3450
Telecopy: 404-681-1046

MEMBERS OF FIRM

Warren O. Wheeler
John A. Christy

ASSOCIATE

Clifford A. Barshay

Reference: Fidelity National Bank; Wachovia Bank of Georgia, NA.

For full biographical listings, see the Martindale-Hubbell Law Directory

SCROGGINS & WILLIAMSON (AV)

Suite 750, East Tower Atlanta Financial Center, 3343 Peachtree Road, N.E., 30326
Telephone: 404-262-1440
Fax: 404-231-4192

MEMBERS OF FIRM

Frank W. Scroggins (P.C.)
J. Robert Williamson, Jr., (P.C.)

For full biographical listings, see the Martindale-Hubbell Law Directory

SUTHERLAND, ASBILL & BRENNAN (AV)

999 Peachtree Street, N.E., 30309-3996
Telephone: 404-853-8000
Facsimile: 404-853-8806
Washington, D.C. Office: 1275 Pennsylvania Avenue, N.W., 20004-2404.
Telephone: 202-383-0100.
New York, N.Y. Office: 1270 Avenue of the Americas, 10020-1700.
Telephone: 212-332-3000.
Austin, Texas Office: 111 Congress Avenue, 23rd Floor, 78701-4079.
Telephone: 512-469-3350.

Alfred G. Adams, Jr.
Thomas M. Byrne
H. Edward Hales, Jr.
James Bruce Jordan
Richard G. Murphy, Jr.
James R. Paulk, Jr.
Haynes R. Roberts

For Complete List of Firm Personnel, See General Section

For full biographical listings, see the Martindale-Hubbell Law Directory

WALLACE & DE MAYO, P.C. (AV)

5775-C Peachtree Dunwoody Road, Suite 250, 30342
Telephone: 404-843-0277
Fax: 404-252-5460

Richard T. De Mayo
Douglas W. Wallace

Paul J. Gallo
O. Byron Meredith, III

For full biographical listings, see the Martindale-Hubbell Law Directory

*AUGUSTA,** Richmond Co.

J. BENJAMIN KAY, III (AV)

808 First Union Bank Building, 30901
Telephone: 706-722-2008

Approved Attorney for: Lawyers Title Insurance Corp.
Reference: First Union National Bank of Georgia.

For full biographical listings, see the Martindale-Hubbell Law Directory

*MACON,** Bibb Co.

SELL & MELTON (AV)

A Partnership including a Professional Corporation
14th Floor, Charter Medical Building, P.O. Box 229, 31297-2899
Telephone: 912-746-8521
Telecopier: 912-745-6426

(See Next Column)

SELL & MELTON—*Continued*

Edward S. Sell, III | Brian J. Passante

General Counsel for: Macon Telegraph Publishing Co. (The Macon Telegraph); Macon-Bibb County Hospital Authority; County of Bibb; County of Twiggs; Smith & Sons Foods, Inc. (S & S Cafeterias); Macon Bibb County Industrial Authority; Burgess Pigment Co.

For Complete List of Firm Personnel, See General Section

For full biographical listings, see the Martindale-Hubbell Law Directory

*SAVANNAH,** Chatham Co.

INGLESBY, FALLIGANT, HORNE, COURINGTON & NASH, A PROFESSIONAL CORPORATION (AV)

300 Bull Street, Suite 302, P.O. Box 1368, 31402-1368
Telephone: 912-232-7000
Telecopier: 912-232-7300

Kathleen Horne | Dolly Chisholm

Representative Clients: Ford Motor Credit Co.; NationsBank of Georgia, N.A.; Chemical Financial Management Corp.; Resolution Trust Corp.; Federal Home Loan Mortgage Corp.; Georgia Federal Bank.

For Complete List of Firm Personnel, See General Section

For full biographical listings, see the Martindale-Hubbell Law Directory

HAWAII

*HONOLULU,** Honolulu Co.

DWYER IMANAKA SCHRAFF KUDO MEYER & FUJIMOTO ATTORNEYS AT LAW, A LAW CORPORATION (AV)

1800 Pioneer Plaza, 900 Fort Street Mall, 96813
Telephone: 808-524-8000
Telecopier: 808-526-1419
Mailing Address: P.O. Box 2727, 96803

John R. Dwyer, Jr.
Mitchell A. Imanaka
Paul A. Schraff
Benjamin A. Kudo (Atty. at Law, A Law Corp.)
William G. Meyer, III
Wesley M. Fujimoto
Ronald Van Grant
Jon M. H. Pang
Blake W. Bushnell
Kenn N. Kojima

Adelbert Green
Richard T. Asato, Jr.
Scott W. Settle
Darcie S. Yoshinaga
Tracy Timothy Woo
Lawrence I. Kawasaki
Douglas H. Inouye
Christine A. Low

OF COUNSEL

Randall Y. Iwase

For full biographical listings, see the Martindale-Hubbell Law Directory

IDAHO

*BOISE,** Ada Co.

ROSHOLT, ROBERTSON & TUCKER, CHARTERED (AV)

Suite 600, 1221 W. Idaho, P.O. Box 2139, 83701-2139
Telephone: 208-336-0700
Fax: 208-344-6034
Twin Falls, Idaho Office: 142 Third Avenue North, P.O. Box 1906.
Telephone: 208-734-0700.
Fax: 208-736-0041.

James C. Tucker

Jerry Jensen | Paul W. Samuelson

For full biographical listings, see the Martindale-Hubbell Law Directory

ILLINOIS

*CHICAGO,** Cook Co.

ADELMAN, GETTLEMAN & MERENS, LTD. (AV)

Suite 1050, 53 West Jackson Boulevard, 60604
Telephone: 312-435-1050
Fax: 312-435-1059

(See Next Column)

Howard L. Adelman | Chad H. Gettleman
Henry B. Merens

Brad A. Berish | Mark A. Carter
Kimberly L. Krawczyk | Kimberly J. Robinson
Michelle Greenberg

OF COUNSEL

Harry Adelman

For full biographical listings, see the Martindale-Hubbell Law Directory

WALINSKI & TRUNKETT, P.C. (AV)

25 East Washington Street, Suite 1927, 60602
Telephone: 312-704-0771
Fax: 312-704-8431

Robert J. Walinski | Kerry S. Trunkett

Lauren Newman | Michael R. Polk

Representative Clients: Edison Credit Union; Chicago Patrolmen's Federal Credit Union; Mid America National Bank; Paterno Imports, Ltd; Central Credit Union of Illinois; Trailmobile, Inc.; Bank of Indiana; Waste Management of the South Suburbs; American Construction Management, Inc.

For full biographical listings, see the Martindale-Hubbell Law Directory

*MOUNT VERNON,** Jefferson Co.

LAW OFFICE OF TERRY SHARP, P.C. (AV)

1115 Harrison Street, P.O. Box 906, 62864
Telephone: 618-242-0246
Fax: 618-242-1170
Benton, Illinois Office: 105 North Main Street.
Telephone: 618-435-5109.
FAX: 618-242-1170.

Terrell Lee Sharp

Marcus H. Herbert

For full biographical listings, see the Martindale-Hubbell Law Directory

INDIANA

CARMEL, Hamilton Co.

KNOWLES & ASSOCIATES (AV)

811 South Range Line Road, 46032
Telephone: 317-848-4360
Telecopier: 317-848-4363

William W. Knowles

Pamela Y. Rhine | D. Brandon Johnston

For full biographical listings, see the Martindale-Hubbell Law Directory

ELKHART, Elkhart Co.

THORNE, GRODNIK, RANSEL, DUNCAN, BYRON & HOSTETLER (AV)

228 West High Street, 46516-3176
Telephone: 219-294-7473
FAX: 219-294-5390
Mishawaka, Indiana Office: 310 Valley American Bank and Trust Building, 310 West McKinley Avenue. P.O. Box 1210.
Telephone: 219-256-5660.
FAX: 219-674-6835.

MEMBERS OF FIRM

William A. Thorne
Charles H. Grodnik
J. Richard Ransel
Glenn L. Duncan
James R. Byron
Steven L. Hostetler

ASSOCIATES

James H. Milstone | Michael A. Trippel

OF COUNSEL

F. Richard Kramer | Joseph C. Zakas

Counsel for: Witmer-McNease Music Co., Inc.; Valley American Bank and Trust Co., Mishawaka, Indiana.

For Complete List of Firm Personnel, See General Section

For full biographical listings, see the Martindale-Hubbell Law Directory

*EVANSVILLE,** Vanderburgh Co.

BAMBERGER, FOREMAN, OSWALD AND HAHN (AV)

7th Floor Hulman Building, P.O. Box 657, 47704-0657
Telephone: 812-425-1591
Fax: 812-421-4936

MEMBERS OF FIRM

William P. Foreman — Terry G. Farmer

ASSOCIATES

Douglas W. Patterson — Marjorie A. Meeks

Representative Clients: Citizens Bank of Central Indiana; Citizens Bank of Henderson County; CNB Bancshares, Inc.; CNB Bank of Kentucky; Dubois County Bank; Jasper State Bank; Peoples Bank & Trust Co.; Southern Indiana Gas and Electric Co.; The Citizens National Bank of Evansville; Valley Bank.

For Complete List of Firm Personnel, See General Section

For full biographical listings, see the Martindale-Hubbell Law Directory

BOWERS, HARRISON, KENT & MILLER (AV)

25 N.W. Riverside Drive, P.O. Box 1287, 47706-1287
Telephone: 812-426-1231
Fax: 812-464-3676

MEMBERS OF FIRM

Joseph H. Harrison — Gary R. Case
Paul E. Black — Paul J. Wallace

Representative Clients: Vantage Healthcare Corporation; International Steel Company; Mellon Bank N.A.; Champion Homes, Inc.

For Complete List of Firm Personnel, See General Section

For full biographical listings, see the Martindale-Hubbell Law Directory

FINE & HATFIELD (AV)

520 N.W. Second Street, P.O. Box 779, 47705-0779
Telephone: 812-425-3592
Telecopier: 812-421-4269

MEMBERS OF FIRM

James E. Marchand — Thomas H. Bryan
Danny E. Glass

For Complete List of Firm Personnel, See General Section

For full biographical listings, see the Martindale-Hubbell Law Directory

ZIEMER, STAYMAN, WEITZEL & SHOULDERS (AV)

(Formerly Early, Arnold & Ziemer)
1507 Old National Bank Building, P.O. Box 916, 47706
Telephone: 812-424-7575
Telecopier: 812-421-5089

MEMBERS OF FIRM

Robert F. Stayman — Marco L. DeLucio
Gregory G. Meyer

Reference: Old National Bank in Evansville.

For full biographical listings, see the Martindale-Hubbell Law Directory

*FORT WAYNE,** Allen Co.

BARRETT & MCNAGNY (AV)

215 East Berry Street, P.O. Box 2263, 46801-2263
Telephone: 219-423-9551
Telecopier: 219-423-8924
Huntington, Indiana Office: 429 Jefferson Park Mall, P.O. Box 5156.
Telephone: 219-356-7766.
Telecopier: 219-356-7782.

MEMBERS OF FIRM

Howard L. Chapman — Thomas P. Yoder
Michael P. O'Hara

Counsel For: Fort Wayne National Bank; N.B.D.; Union Federal Savings Bank of Indianapolis; Waterfield Mortgage Company, Incorporated.

For Complete List of Firm Personnel, See General Section

For full biographical listings, see the Martindale-Hubbell Law Directory

SHIPLEY & KOS (AV)

130 West Main Street, Suite 25, 46802
Telephone: 219-424-0025
Fax: 219-424-2960

Grant F. Shipley — Edmund P. Kos

ASSOCIATE

Martin E. Seifert

Representative Clients: NBD Bank, N.A.; Barclays Business Credit, Inc.; First National Bank, Portland (Indiana).

(See Next Column)

For full biographical listings, see the Martindale-Hubbell Law Directory

*INDIANAPOLIS,** Marion Co.

ANCEL & DUNLAP (AV)

Suite 1770 Market Square Center, 46204-2503
Telephone: 317-634-9052
FAX: 317-263-3871

MEMBERS OF FIRM

Steven H. Ancel — Timothy L. Black
David L. Dunlap — Paul T. Deignan
Sorelle J. Ancel — Jeffrey A. Hokanson
F. Jonathan Zusy — Mark C. Bainbridge

Reference: Ameritrust National Bank of Indianapolis.

For full biographical listings, see the Martindale-Hubbell Law Directory

BAKER & DANIELS (AV)

300 North Meridian Street, 46204
Telephone: 317-237-0300
FAX: 317-237-1000
Fort Wayne, Indiana Office: 2400 Fort Wayne National Bank Building.
Telephone: 219-424-8000.
South Bend, Indiana Office: First Bank Building, 205 West Jefferson Boulevard.
Telephone: 219-234-4149.
Elkhart, Indiana Office: 301 South Main Street, Suite 307,
Telephone: 219-296-6000.
Washington, D.C. Office: 1701 K Street, N.W., Suite 400.
Telephone: 202-785-1565.

MEMBERS OF FIRM

Stephen A. Claffey — Rebecca A. Richardson
James M. Carr — Jay Jaffe
Robert S. Wynne

ASSOCIATES

Wendy W. Ponader — Stephen L. Foutty
David V. Ceryak — Michael P. Bigelow

Representative Clients: Associated Insurance Companies, Inc.; Bank One, Indianapolis, N.A.; Borg-Warner Corp.; City of Indianapolis; Cummins Engine Co.; Eli Lilly and Company; General Motors Corp.; Indiana Bell; Indianapolis Public Schools; United Airlines.

For Complete List of Firm Personnel, See General Section

For full biographical listings, see the Martindale-Hubbell Law Directory

BOSE MCKINNEY & EVANS (AV)

2700 First Indiana Plaza, 135 North Pennsylvania Street, 46204
Telephone: 317-684-5000
Facsimile: 317-684-5173
Indianapolis North Office: Suite 1201, 8888 Keystone Crossing, 46240.
Telephone: 317-574-3700.
Facsimile: 317-574-3716.

MEMBERS OF FIRM

Leonard Opperman — Michael A. Trentadue
James E. Carlberg

ASSOCIATE

Thomas G. Burroughs

Representative Clients: Aetna Life Insurance Co.; Association of Indiana Life Insurance Cos.; Duke Realty Investments, Inc.; First Indiana Bank; Indiana League of Savings Institutions, Inc.; Prudential Life Insurance Co.; Metropolitan Insurance Co.; NBD Bank, N.A.; Farm Credit Services.

For Complete List of Firm Personnel, See General Section

For full biographical listings, see the Martindale-Hubbell Law Directory

BUSCHMANN, CARR & SHANKS, PROFESSIONAL CORPORATION (AV)

1020 Market Tower, 10 West Market Street, 46204-2963
Telephone: 317-636-5511
Fax: 317-636-3661
Franklin, Indiana Office: 160 Fairway Lakes Drive.
Telephone: 317-738-9540.
Fax: 317-738-9310.
Fishers, Indiana Office: 9093 Technology Drive, Suite 103.
Telephone: 317-577-0756.
Fax: 317-577-9910.

John R. Carr, Jr. — Stephen R. Buschmann
John R. Carr, III — Gary L. Dilk
Lisa T. Hamilton

Representative Clients: Archer-Daniels Midland Co.; Ball Corp.; Industrial Valley Title Insurance; Creative Risk Management, Inc.; Deflecto Corporation; Glenfed Mortgage Corp.; Gates McDonald; Merchants National Bank & Trust Company of Muncie; Monumental Life Insurance Co.; National Council on Compensation Insurance.

(See Next Column)

BUSCHMANN, CARR & SHANKS PROFESSIONAL CORPORATION—*Continued*

For Complete List of Firm Personnel, See General Section

For full biographical listings, see the Martindale-Hubbell Law Directory

FEIWELL & ASSOCIATES (AV)

251 North Illinois Street, Suite 1700, P.O. Box 44141, 46204
Telephone: 317-237-2727
Facsimile: 317-237-2722

Murray J. Feiwell

ASSOCIATE

Douglas J. Hannoy

Representative Clients: Fifth Third Bank; Lomas Mortgage USA, Inc.; Standard Federal Savings Bank; NBD Mortgage Company; Source One Mortgage Services Corp.; United Companies Lending Corp.; Ford Consumer Finance Company, Inc.; GMAC Mortgage Corp.; Barclays American Mortgage Corporation; Associates Financial Services.

For full biographical listings, see the Martindale-Hubbell Law Directory

HOPPER, WENZEL & GALLIHER, P.C. (AV)

Bank One Center/Circle, 111 Monument Circle, Suite 452, 46204-5170
Telephone: 317-635-5005
Facsimile: 317-634-2501

George W. Hopper
Mark R. Wenzel
Mark R. Galliher
Jeffrey E. Ramsey
David G. Pardo

Representative Clients: Bank One, Indianapolis, N.A.; National City Bank, Indiana; MetroBank; Mutual Guaranty Corporation; I.T.T. Financial Services, Commercial Division; ABC Supply Co., Inc.; Sholodge, Inc.; Purina Mills, Inc.

For full biographical listings, see the Martindale-Hubbell Law Directory

HOSTETLER & KOWALIK, P.C. (AV)

101 West Ohio Street Suite 2100, 46204
Telephone: 317-262-1001
Fax: 317-262-1010

Gary Lynn Hostetler
James S. Kowalik
David R. Krebs
J. Bradley Schooley

For full biographical listings, see the Martindale-Hubbell Law Directory

ICE MILLER DONADIO & RYAN (AV)

One American Square Box 82001, 46282-0002
Telephone: 317-236-2100
Fax: 317-236-2219

MEMBERS OF FIRM

John R. Thornburgh
Richard J. Thrapp
Henry A. Efroymson

OF COUNSEL

C. Daniel Motsinger

ASSOCIATES

Peggy J. Naile
Dominic F. Polizzotto
Timothy A. Brooks
Michael E. Schrader

Representative Clients: NBD Bank; National City Bank; Bank One, Indianapolis; Bargersville State Bank; Union County National Bank; Ameritrust National Bank; Rockwell International; Indiana Business Modernization and Technology Corp.; Eastman Kodak Co.; Perry Manufacturing Co.

For Complete List of Firm Personnel, See General Section

For full biographical listings, see the Martindale-Hubbell Law Directory

JOHNSON, SMITH, DENSBORN, WRIGHT & HEATH (AV)

One Indiana Square Suite 1800, 46204
Telephone: 317-634-9777
Telecopier: 317-636-9061

MEMBERS OF FIRM

Peter D. Cleveland
David R. Day
Thomas N. Eckerle

ASSOCIATES

Patricia L. Marshall
Bradley C. Morris

OF COUNSEL

Paul D. Gresk

For Complete List of Firm Personnel, See General Section

For full biographical listings, see the Martindale-Hubbell Law Directory

KROGER, GARDIS & REGAS (AV)

111 Monument Circle, Suite 900, 46204-3059
Telephone: 317-692-9000
Telecopier: 317-264-6832

(See Next Column)

MEMBERS OF FIRM

James A. Knauer
John J. Petr
James G. Lauck
Gary A. Schiffli
Jay P. Kennedy

ASSOCIATES

Marcia E. Roan
Mary Elizabeth Brames

LEGAL SUPPORT PERSONNEL

PARALEGALS

Rhonda K. Peterson
Debra K. Nix

Representative Clients: First of America Bank; Bank One, Indianapolis; Society National Bank; NBD Bank.

For full biographical listings, see the Martindale-Hubbell Law Directory

RUBIN & LEVIN, P.C. (AV)

500 Marott Center, 342 Massachusetts Avenue, 46204-2161
Telephone: 317-634-0300
Telecopier: 317-263-9411

Elliott D. Levin
Neil E. Shook
John W. Graub, II

Rodger K. Hendershot

OF COUNSEL

John C. Hoard

Representative Clients: Aetna Casualty & Surety; Browning Investments, Inc.; Chase Manhattan Bank of New York; General Electric Credit Corp.; Indiana Association of Credit Management; Indiana Farm Bureau Co-Operative Assn., Inc.; Sears, Roebuck & Co.; Xerox.

For full biographical listings, see the Martindale-Hubbell Law Directory

SOMMER & BARNARD, ATTORNEYS AT LAW, PC (AV)

4000 Bank One Tower, 111 Monument Circle, P.O. Box 44363, 46244-0363
Telephone: 317-630-4000
FAX: 317-236-9802
North Office: 8900 Keystone Crossing, Suite 1046, Indianapolis, Indiana, 46240-2134.
Telephone: 317-630-4000.
FAX: 317-844-4780.

Jerald I. Ancel
Marlene Reich
Richard C. Richmond, III

Gregory J. Seketa

Secured Creditor Representation: Bank One Bloomington, N.A.; Comerica Bank; Northwestern National Life Insurance Co.; PNC Realty Holding Corp;
Debtor Representation: Early-Daniel Company; Early-Daniel Industries; Indiana Grocery Company; Integrated Plastic Technology, Inc; Preston Safeway Foods.

For Complete List of Firm Personnel, See General Section

For full biographical listings, see the Martindale-Hubbell Law Directory

YARLING, ROBINSON, HAMMEL & LAMB (AV)

151 North Delaware, Suite 1535, P.O. Box 44128, 46204
Telephone: 317-262-8800
Fax: 317-262-3046

MEMBERS OF FIRM

Richard W. Yarling
Charles F. Robinson, Jr.
John W. Hammel
Linda Y. Hammel
Edgar H. Lamb
Douglas E. Rogers
Mark S. Gray

Representative Clients: Allstate Insurance Co.; American Family Mutual Insurance Company; Chrysler Credit Corporation; Fleet Financenter; General Motors Acceptance Corporation; Household Finance Corporation; Monroe Guaranty Insurance Company; Northbrook Property & Casualty Company; Pafco General Insurance Company; Security Pacific Finance Corporation.

For full biographical listings, see the Martindale-Hubbell Law Directory

*LAFAYETTE,** Tippecanoe Co.

HOFFMAN, LUHMAN & BUSCH (AV)

300 Main Street, Suite 700, P.O. Box 99, 47902
Telephone: 317-423-5404
Fax: 317-742-6448

MEMBERS OF FIRM

J. Frederick Hoffman
David W. Luhman
Thomas H. Busch

Representative Clients: Farm Bureau Mutual Insurance Co.; Bank of Wolcott; Bright National Bank; American States Insurance Co.
References: Lafayette Bank & Trust Co., Lafayette, Indiana; Farmers & Merchants Bank, Rochester, Indiana; Lafayette Savings Bank, Lafayette, Indiana.

(See Next Column)

HOFFMAN, LUHMAN & BUSCH, *Lafayette—Continued*

For Complete List of Firm Personnel, See General Section

For full biographical listings, see the Martindale-Hubbell Law Directory

*SOUTH BEND,** St. Joseph Co.

JOSEPH D. BRADLEY (AV)

105 East Jefferson Boulevard Suite 512, 46601
Telephone: 219-234-5091
Fax: Available Upon Request
Reference: Society Bank, Indiana.

For full biographical listings, see the Martindale-Hubbell Law Directory

JONES, OBENCHAIN, FORD, PANKOW, LEWIS & WOODS (AV)

1800 Valley American Bank Building, P.O. Box 4577, 46634
Telephone: 219-233-1194
Fax: 233-8957; 233-9675

Vitus G. Jones (1879-1951)
Francis Jones (1907-1988)
Roland Obenchain (1890-1961)
Roland Obenchain (Retired)
Milton A. Johnson (Retired)

MEMBERS OF FIRM

James H. Pankow
Robert W. Mysliwiec
Thomas F. Lewis, Jr.
Robert M. Edwards, Jr.
Timothy W. Woods
John B. Ford
John R. Obenchain
Mark J. Phillipoff
John W. Van Laere

ASSOCIATES

Patrick D. Murphy
Edward P. Benchik
Wendell G. Davis, Jr.

OF COUNSEL

G. Burt Ford

Representative Clients: South Bend Lathe, Inc.; Mallard Coach Co., Inc.; Uniroyal, Inc.; State Exchange Finance Co.; Commodore Corp.

For full biographical listings, see the Martindale-Hubbell Law Directory

*TERRE HAUTE,** Vigo Co.

WILKINSON, GOELLER, MODESITT, WILKINSON & DRUMMY (AV)

333 Ohio Street, P.O. Box 800, 47808-0800
Telephone: 812-232-4311
Fax: 812-235-5107

MEMBERS OF FIRM

Myrl O. Wilkinson
Kelvin L. Roots
David H. Goeller
John C. Wall
Raymond H. Modesitt
William M. Olah
B. Curtis Wilkinson
Craig M. McKee
William W. Drummy
Scott M. Kyrouac
Jeffrey A. Boyll

ASSOCIATES

David P. Friedrich
Anthony R. Jost

Representative Corporate Clients: Merchants National Bank; Owens Corning Fiberglass; CSX, Inc.; General Housewares Corp.; MAB Paints; Chicago Title Insurance Co.; Terre Haute Board of Realtors; Union Hospital; Associated Physicians and Surgeons Clinic, Inc.; PSI Energy, Inc.

For full biographical listings, see the Martindale-Hubbell Law Directory

IOWA

*COUNCIL BLUFFS,** Pottawattamie Co.

PERKINS, SACKS, HANNAN, REILLY AND PETERSEN (AV)

215 South Main Street, P.O. Box 1016, 51502-1016
Telephone: 712-328-1575
Fax: 712-328-1562

MEMBERS OF FIRM

Proctor R. Perkins (Retired)
C. R. Hannan
Kenneth Sacks (Retired)
Michael G. Reilly
Deborah L. Petersen

ASSOCIATE

Kellie Rae Taylor

References: First National Bank; Firstar Bank of Council Bluffs; State Bank and Trust.

For full biographical listings, see the Martindale-Hubbell Law Directory

TELPNER, SMITH & RUESCH (AV)

25 Main Place, Suite 200, P.O. Box 248, 51502-0248
Telephone: 712-325-9000
Fax: 712-328-1946

(See Next Column)

MEMBERS OF FIRM

Charles L. Smith
Jack E. Ruesch

Representative Clients: Firstar Bank; Houghton State Bank; City National Bank of Shenandoah; Oakland State Bank; Community National Bank; Resolution Trust Corporation; Federal Deposit Insurance Corporation; Bell Federal Credit Union; Mutual of Omaha Employees Credit Union.

For Complete List of Firm Personnel, See General Section

For full biographical listings, see the Martindale-Hubbell Law Directory

*SIOUX CITY,** Woodbury Co.

GILES AND GILES (AV)

322 Frances Building, 505 Fifth Street, 51101
Telephone: 712-252-4458
FAX: 712-252-3400
Crofton, Nebraska Office: P. O. Box 88.
Telephone: 402-388-4215.

MEMBER OF FIRM

W. Jefferson Giles, III

Representative Clients: Security National Bank, Firstar Bank, Boatmen's Bank, all in Sioux City, Iowa; Live Stock State Bank, Yankton, SD.

For Complete List of Firm Personnel, See General Section

For full biographical listings, see the Martindale-Hubbell Law Directory

KANSAS

*TOPEKA,** Shawnee Co.

WRIGHT, HENSON, SOMERS, SEBELIUS, CLARK & BAKER (AV)

Commerce Bank Building, 100 Southeast Ninth Street, 2nd Floor, P.O. Box 3555, 66601-3555
Telephone: 913-232-2200
FAX: 913-232-3344

MEMBERS OF FIRM

Dale L. Somers
Bruce J. Clark
Anne Lamborn Baker

For Complete List of Firm Personnel, See General Section

For full biographical listings, see the Martindale-Hubbell Law Directory

*WICHITA,** Sedgwick Co.

FOULSTON & SIEFKIN (AV)

(Formerly Foulston, Siefkin, Powers & Eberhardt)
700 Fourth Financial Center, Broadway at Douglas, 67202
Telephone: 316-267-6371
Facsimile: 316-267-6345
Topeka, Kansas Office: 1515 Bank IV Tower, 534 Kansas Avenue. 66603.
Telephone: 913-233-3600.
FAX: 913-233-1610.
Member: Lex Mundi, A Global Association of Independent Firms

MEMBERS OF FIRM

Terry C. Cupps
William R. Wood, II

For Complete List of Firm Personnel, See General Section

For full biographical listings, see the Martindale-Hubbell Law Directory

MORRIS, LAING, EVANS, BROCK & KENNEDY, CHARTERED (AV)

Fourth Floor, 200 West Douglas, 67202-3084
Telephone: 316-262-2671
FAX: 316-262-6226; 262-5991
Topeka Office: 800 S.W. Jackson, Suite 914. 66612-2214.
Telephone: 913-232-2662.
Fax: 913-232-9983.

David C. Adams
Karl R. Swartz
William B. Sorensen, Jr.
Richard F. Hayse (Resident, Topeka Office)
Robert E. Nugent

OF COUNSEL

Robert B. Morton

References: The Emprise Banks of Kansas; Mellon Bank; N.A.; The Merchants National Bank of Topeka; Southwest National Bank; Twin Lakes Bank & Trust.

For Complete List of Firm Personnel, See General Section

For full biographical listings, see the Martindale-Hubbell Law Directory

KENTUCKY

*BOWLING GREEN,** Warren Co.

ENGLISH, LUCAS, PRIEST & OWSLEY (AV)
1101 College Street, P.O. Box 770, 42102-0770
Telephone: 502-781-6500
Telecopier: 502-782-7782

MEMBERS OF FIRM

Charles E. English
James H. Lucas
Whayne C. Priest, Jr.
Michael A. Owsley
Keith M. Carwell
Murry A. Raines
Kurt W. Maier
Charles E. English, Jr.
Wade T. Markham, II

ASSOCIATES

D. Gaines Penn
Robert A. Young

General Counsel for: Medical Center at Bowling Green; Bowling Green Independent School District; Warren Rural Electric Cooperative Corporation; Trans Financial Bank, N.A.
Representative Clients: Commercial Union Insurance Cos.; Kemper Insurance Group; St. Paul Insurance Co.; Desa International; Kentucky Finance Co.; Sumitomo Electric Wiring Systems, Inc.

For Complete List of Firm Personnel, See General Section

For full biographical listings, see the Martindale-Hubbell Law Directory

HARLIN & PARKER, P.S.C. (AV)
519 East Tenth Street, P.O. Box 390, 42102-0390
Telephone: 502-842-5611
Telefax: 502-842-2607
Smiths Grove, Kentucky Office: Old Farmers Bank Building.
Telephone: 502-563-4701.

William Jerry Parker
Jerry A. Burns
Scott Charles Marks
Mark D. Alcott (Resident, Smith Grove Office)

Representative Clients: Jim Walter Corp.; Deere & Co.; Federal Deposit Insurance Corp.; Equitable Life Assurance Society of the United States.

For Complete List of Firm Personnel, See General Section

For full biographical listings, see the Martindale-Hubbell Law Directory

HUDDLESTON & HUDDLESTON (AV)
1032 College Street, P.O. Box 2130, 42102-2130
Telephone: 502-781-9870
Fax: 502-842-1659
Cave City, Kentucky: 210 Broadway; P.O. 810, 42127.
Telephone: 502-773-5511.
Fax: 502-773-5510.

MEMBERS OF FIRM

Philip I. Huddleston
Lee Huddleston

ASSOCIATE

Jeffrey A. Reed

Representative Clients: Dow Corning Corp.; Borg Warner Corp.; HFC Commercial Realty, Inc.; Transamerica Financial Services; South Central Banks; Autotruck Federal Credit Union.

For full biographical listings, see the Martindale-Hubbell Law Directory

*GLASGOW,** Barren Co.

GARMON & GOODMAN (AV)
139 North Public Square, P.O. Box 663, 42142-0663
Telephone: 502-651-8812
Telecopier: 502-651-8846

MEMBER OF FIRM

Charles A. Goodman III

Representative Clients: The New Farmers National Bank of Glasgow; United Farm Tools, Inc.; Dufour Petroleum, Inc.; Chrysler Credit Corp.
References: Trans Financial Bank, N.A., Glasgow, Ky.; South Central Bank of Barren County, Inc., Glasgow, Ky.; Farm Credit Services of Mid-America, ACA.

For Complete List of Firm Personnel, See General Section

For full biographical listings, see the Martindale-Hubbell Law Directory

*LEXINGTON,** Fayette Co.

BUNCH & BROCK (AV)
Suite 805 Security Trust Building, P.O. Box 2086, 40594
Telephone: 606-254-5522
Fax: 606-233-1434

(See Next Column)

MEMBERS OF FIRM

W. Thomas Bunch
Dan D. Brock, Jr.
Gail M. Bunch
W. Thomas Bunch II
Matthew B. Bunch

For full biographical listings, see the Martindale-Hubbell Law Directory

FOWLER, MEASLE & BELL (AV)
Kincaid Towers, 300 West Vine Street, Suite 650, 40507-1660
Telephone: 606-252-6700
Fax: 606-255-3735

MEMBERS OF FIRM

Taft A. McKinstry
John E. Hinkel, Jr.
Robert S. Ryan
Michael W. Troutman

Representative Clients: Bank One, Lexington, N.A.; PNC Bank, Kentucky, Inc.; Citizens Union Bank of Shelbyville; National City Bank & Trust Co.; Fifth Third Bank; Fifth Third Leasing; Liberty National Bank; Union Bank, CA.

For Complete List of Firm Personnel, See General Section

For full biographical listings, see the Martindale-Hubbell Law Directory

STOLL, KEENON & PARK (AV)
201 E. Main Street, Suite 1000, 40507-1380
Telephone: 606-231-3000
Telecopier: 606-253-1093; 606-253-1027
Frankfort, Kentucky Office: 326 West Main Street.
Telephone: 502-875-6000.
Telecopier: 502-875-6008.
Louisville, Kentucky Office: 400 West Market Street, Suite 2650, 40202.
Telephone: 502-568-9100.
Telecopier: 502-568-6340.

MEMBERS OF FIRM

Joseph M. Scott, Jr.
Harvie B. Wilkinson
Robert W. Kellerman
Dan M. Rose
Gregory D. Pavey

ASSOCIATES

Laura Day DelCotto
Lea Pauley Goff

For Complete List of Firm Personnel, See General Section

For full biographical listings, see the Martindale-Hubbell Law Directory

STURGILL, TURNER & TRUITT (AV)
155 East Main Street, 40507
Telephone: 606-255-8581
Fax: 606-231-0851

MEMBERS OF FIRM

Jerry D. Truitt
Stephen L. Barker
Gina S. McCann
Gene Lynn Humphreys

For Complete List of Firm Personnel, See General Section

For full biographical listings, see the Martindale-Hubbell Law Directory

VIMONT & WILLS (AV)
Suite 300, 155 East Main Street, 40507-1317
Telephone: 606-252-2202
Telecopier: 606-259-2927

MEMBER OF FIRM

Timothy C. Wills

ASSOCIATE

J. Thomas Rawlings

For Complete List of Firm Personnel, See General Section

For full biographical listings, see the Martindale-Hubbell Law Directory

*LOUISVILLE,** Jefferson Co.

GREENEBAUM DOLL & McDONALD (AV)
A Partnership including Professional Service Corporations
3300 National City Tower, 40202
Telephone: 502-589-4200
Fax: 502-587-3695
Lexington, Kentucky Office: 1400 Vine Center Tower.
Telephone: 606-231-8500.
Fax: 606-255-2742.
Covington, Kentucky Office: 50 East River Center Boulevard, P.O. Box 2050.
Telephone: 606-655-4200.
Fax: 606-655-4239.
Cincinnati, Ohio Office: 832 Main Street.
Telephone: 513-421-8087.
Fax: 513-421-8089.

(See Next Column)

GREENEBAUM DOLL & MCDONALD, *Louisville—Continued*

Michael G. Shaikun *
John S. Sawyer (Resident at Lexington, Kentucky)
Nicholas R. Glancy (Lexington and Covington, Kentucky)
John W. Ames
Margaret E. Keane
Tandy C. Patrick
Susan J. Hoffmann (Resident at Lexington, Kentucky)
Patrick J. Welsh

ASSOCIATES

Gregory R. Schaaf (Resident at Lexington, Kentucky)
Paul E. Porter

Representative Clients: Aetna Life Insurance Co.; ANDALEX Resources, Inc.; Ashland Oil, Inc.; A T & T Communications, Inc.; Bethlehem Steel Corp.; Brown-Forman Corp.; Humana, Inc.; Kentucky Kingdom, Inc.; KFC National Cooperative Advertising Program, Inc.

*A Professional Service Corporation

For Complete List of Firm Personnel, See General Section

For full biographical listings, see the Martindale-Hubbell Law Directory

LLOYD & MCDANIEL (AV)

700 Meidinger Tower, 460 South Fourth Avenue, 40202
Telephone: 502-585-1880
Fax: 502-585-3054
Lexington, Kentucky Office: Suite 102, 177 North Upper Street, 40507.
Telephone: 606-254-2102.
Jeffersonville, Indiana Office: 220 East Court Avenue, P.O. Box 934. 47131.
Telephone: 812-282-4380.

MEMBERS OF FIRM

Jeremiah A. Lloyd
James M. Lloyd
Michael V. Brodarick

ASSOCIATES

Anthony H. Ambrose
Deborah B. Simon
Julia M. Pike

OF COUNSEL

Gerald F. McDaniel

References: Liberty National Bank & Trust Co. of Kentucky; PNC Bank, Kentucky, Inc.; United Mercantile Agencies; National Association of Credit Management (NACM).

For full biographical listings, see the Martindale-Hubbell Law Directory

MAPOTHER & MAPOTHER (AV)

801 West Jefferson Street, 40202
Telephone: 502-587-5400
Fax: 502-587-5444
Lexington, Kentucky Office: 177 North Upper Street.
Telephone: 606-253-0003.
Fax: 606-255-3961.
Stanton, Kentucky Office: 209 Main Street.
Telephone: 606-663-9037.
Jeffersonville, Indiana Office: 505 East Seventh Street.
Telephone: 812-288-5059.
Fax: 502-587-5444.
Cincinnati, Ohio Office: Kroger Building, Suite 2220, 1014 Vine Street.
Telephone: 513-381-4888.
Fax: 513-381-3117.
Huntington, West Virginia Office: Morris Building, Suite 401, 845 Fourth Avenue.
Telephone: 304-525-1185.
Fax: 304-529-3764.
Evansville, Indiana Office: 329 Main Street.
Telephone: 812-421-9108.
Fax: 812-421-9109.

MEMBERS OF FIRM

Thomas C. Mapother (1907-1986)
William R. Mapother
Thomas L. Canary, Jr. (Resident, Lexington Office)
Elizabeth Lee Thompson (Resident, Lexington Office)
Charles M. Friedman

Brian P. Conaty
Andrea Fried Neichter
Kathryn Pry Coryell (Resident, Jeffersonville, Indiana Office)
Roberta S. Dunlap (Resident, Evansville, Indiana Office)
Terry Risner (Resident, Cincinnati, Ohio Office)
Lee W. Grace
Dean A. Langdon
T. Lawson McSwain, II
Charles Brent Robbins (Resident, Lexington Office)

Representative Clients: General Electric Capital Corp.; Ford Motor Credit Co.; General Motors Acceptance Corp.; Associates Commercial Corp.; Cuna Mutual Insurance Society; Bank One; National City Bank; PNC Bank BancOhio National Bank.

For full biographical listings, see the Martindale-Hubbell Law Directory

MIDDLETON & REUTLINGER, P.S.C. (AV)

2500 Brown and Williamson Tower, 40202-3410
Telephone: 502-584-1135
Fax: 502-561-0442
Jeffersonville, Indiana Office: 605 Watt Street, 47130.
Telephone: 812-282-4886.

(See Next Column)

Charles G. Middleton, III
James R. Higgins, Jr.
Thomas W. Frentz

Margaret E. Thorp

Counsel for: Chevron USA; Liberty National Bank; Logan Aluminum, Inc.; Louisville Gas & Electric Co.; MCI Telecommunications Corp.; Metropolitan Life Insurance Co.; Kosmos Cement Co.; Porcelain Metal Corp.; The Home Insurance Co.; The Kroger Co.; Demars Haka Development, Inc.

For Complete List of Firm Personnel, See General Section

For full biographical listings, see the Martindale-Hubbell Law Directory

MORGAN & POTTINGER, P.S.C. (AV)

601 West Main Street, 40202
Telephone: 502-589-2780
Telecopier: 502-585-3498
Lexington, Kentucky Office: 133 West Short Street.
Telephone: 606-253-1900.
Telecopier: 606-255-2038.
New Albany, Indiana Office: 400 Pearl Street, Suite 100.
Telephone: 812-948-0008.
Telecopier: 812-944-6215.

Patrick E. Morgan
John T. McGarvey
John A. Majors
Mark J. Sandlin
Scott T. Rickman (Resident, Lexington Office)

SENIOR COUNSEL

David C. Pottinger

For Complete List of Firm Personnel, See General Section

For full biographical listings, see the Martindale-Hubbell Law Directory

RUBIN HAYS & FOLEY (AV)

First Trust Centre 200 South Fifth Street, 40202
Telephone: 502-569-7550
Telecopier: 502-569-7555

MEMBERS OF FIRM

Wm. Carl Fust
Harry Lee Meyer
David W. Gray
Irvin D. Foley
Joseph R. Gathright, Jr.
Lisa Koch Bryant
Sharon C. Hardy
Charles S. Musson
W. Randall Jones
K. Gail Russell

ASSOCIATE

Christian L. Juckett

OF COUNSEL

James E. Fahey
Newman T. Guthrie

Representative Clients: J.C. Bradford & Co., Inc.; J.J.B. Hilliard, W.L. Lyons, Inc.; Huntington National Bank; Liberty National Bank and Trust Company; National City Bank; PNC Bank; Prudential Bache & Co., Inc.; Prudential Securities, Inc.; Society Bank; Stock Yards Bank and Trust Co.

For full biographical listings, see the Martindale-Hubbell Law Directory

SEILLER & HANDMAKER (AV)

2200 Meidinger Tower, 40202
Telephone: 502-584-7400
Telecopier: 502-583-2100
Paris, Kentucky Office: Seiller, Handmaker & Blevins, P.S.C., 1431 South Main Street.
Telephone: 606-987-3980.
Telecopier: 606-987-3982.
New Albany, Indiana Office: 204 Pearl Street, Suite 200.
Telephone: 812-948-8307.
Telecopier: 812-948-8383.

Edward F. Seiller (1897-1990)

MEMBERS OF FIRM

Stuart Allen Handmaker
Bill V. Seiller
David M. Cantor
Neil C. Bordy
Kyle Anne Citrynell
Maury D. Kommor
Cynthia Compton Stone

ASSOCIATES

Glenn A. Cohen
Pamela M. Greenwell
Tomi Anne Blevins Pulliam (Resident, Paris Office)
Linda Scholle Cowan
Mary Zeller Wing Ceridan
Michael C. Bratcher
John E. Brengle
Patrick R. Holland, II
Edwin Jon Wolfe
Donna F. Townsend
William C. Robinson

OF COUNSEL

Robert S. Frey

For full biographical listings, see the Martindale-Hubbell Law Directory

*OWENSBORO,** Daviess Co.

BAMBERGER & ABSHIER (AV)

111 West 2nd Street, 42303-4113
Telephone: 502-926-4545
Fax: 502-684-0064

(See Next Column)

BAMBERGER & ABSHIER—*Continued*

MEMBERS OF FIRM

Ronald J. Bamberger
Phillip G. Abshier

ASSOCIATES

Steven S. Crone
Angela L. Wathen

For full biographical listings, see the Martindale-Hubbell Law Directory

LOVETT & LAMAR (AV)

208 West Third Street, 42303-4121
Telephone: 502-926-3000
FAX: 502-685-2625

MEMBERS OF FIRM

Wells T. Lovett
John T. Lovett
Charles L. Lamar
Marty G. Jacobs

Representative Clients: Beaver Dam Deposit Bank; Carousel Nut Products, Inc.; Central Bank & Trust Co.; Farm Credit Services of Mid-America, ACA; ITT Commercial Finance Corp.; Navistar Financial Corp.; Sterett Construction Co.; The Wright Machine Co.

For full biographical listings, see the Martindale-Hubbell Law Directory

*PADUCAH,** McCracken Co.

WHITLOW, ROBERTS, HOUSTON & RUSSELL (AV)

Old National Bank Building, 300 Broadway, P.O. Box 995, 42001
Telephone: 502-443-4516
FAX: 502-443-4571

MEMBERS OF FIRM

Mark C. Whitlow
Randy L. Treece

Counsel for: Telmark, Inc.; Peoples First National Bank & Trust Co.; Chrysler Credit Corporation; Liberty National Bank & Trust Co.

For Complete List of Firm Personnel, See General Section

For full biographical listings, see the Martindale-Hubbell Law Directory

LOUISIANA

*BATON ROUGE,** East Baton Rouge Parish

KIZER, HOOD & MORGAN, L.L.P. (AV)

A Partnership including a Professional Corporation
748 Main Street, 70802-5526
Telephone: 504-387-3121
Fax: 504-387-5611

Roland C. Kizer (1899-1988)
Ralph E. Hood
Roland C. Kizer, Jr., (Ltd., A Law Corporation)
J. Donald Morgan
Walter N. O'Roark, III
Stacy G. Butler

Representative Clients: Hibernia National Bank; Premier Bank, National Association; The Dime Savings Bank of New York, FSB; G.E. Capital Asset Management Corp.; Bankers Systems, Inc.; United Companies Lending Corporation; Rabenhorst Life Insurance Co.; General Equipment, Inc. d/b/a Scott General; Old South Builders, Inc.; P.P.R., Inc.

For full biographical listings, see the Martindale-Hubbell Law Directory

*LAKE CHARLES,** Calcasieu Parish

JONES, TÊTE, NOLEN, HANCHEY, SWIFT & SPEARS, L.L.P. (AV)

First Federal Building, P.O. Box 910, 70602
Telephone: 318-439-8315
Telefax: 436-5606; 433-5536

MEMBERS OF FIRM

Sam H. Jones (1897-1978)
William R. Tête
William M. Nolen
James C. Hanchey
Carl H. Hanchey
William B. Swift
Kenneth R. Spears
Edward J. Fonti
Charles N. Harper
Gregory W. Belfour
Robert J. Tête
Yul D. Lorio

OF COUNSEL

John A. Patin
Edward D. Myrick

ASSOCIATES

Lilynn A. Cutrer
Lydia Ann Guillory-Lee
Clint David Bischoff

General Counsel for: First Federal Savings & Loan Association of Lake Charles; Beauregard Electric Cooperative, Inc.
Representative Clients: Atlantic Richfield Company; CITGO Petroleum Corp.; Conoco Inc.; HIMONT U.S.A., Inc.; ITT Hartford; Olin Corporation; OXY USA Inc.; Premier Bank, National Association; W.R. Grace & Co.

(See Next Column)

For full biographical listings, see the Martindale-Hubbell Law Directory

*MONROE,** Ouachita Parish

MCLEOD, VERLANDER, EADE & VERLANDER (AV)

A Partnership including Professional Law Corporations
1900 North 18th Street, Suite 610, P.O. Box 2270, 71207-2270
Telephone: 318-325-7000
Telecopier: 318-324-0580

MEMBERS OF FIRM

Robert P. McLeod (P.L.C.)
David E. Verlander, III (P.L.C.)
Ellen R. Eade
Paul J. Verlander
Rick W. Duplissey
Pamela G. Nathan

Representative Clients: FCS Servicing; Farm Credit Bank of Texas.

For full biographical listings, see the Martindale-Hubbell Law Directory

*NEW ORLEANS,** Orleans Parish

LANDWEHR & HOF (AV)

Suite 1100, Commerce Building, 821 Gravier Street, 70112
Telephone: 504-561-8086

MEMBERS OF FIRM

Merrill T. Landwehr
Ronald J. Hof
Darryl T. Landwehr

Reference: Bank of Louisiana, New Orleans, La.

For full biographical listings, see the Martindale-Hubbell Law Directory

NESSER, KING & LEBLANC (AV)

Suite 3800 Place St. Charles, 201 St. Charles Avenue, 70170
Telephone: 504-582-3800
Telecopier: 504-582-1233

John T. Nesser, III
Henry A. King
Joseph E. LeBlanc, Jr.
David S. Bland
Patricia Ann Krebs
Robert J. Burvant
Eric Earl Jarrell
Liane K. Hinrichs

Jeffrey M. Burmaster
Jeffrey A. Mitchell
Margaret M. Sledge
Josh M. Kantrow
Elton A. Foster
Elizabeth S. Wheeler
Robert J. Bergeron
Timothy S. Madden
Elizabeth A. Meek

OF COUNSEL

Clare P. Hunter
George B. Jurgens, III
J. Grant Coleman
Len R. Brignac
George Farber, Jr.

For full biographical listings, see the Martindale-Hubbell Law Directory

PREAUS, RODDY & KREBS (AV)

Suite 1650, 650 Poydras Street, 70130
Telephone: 504-523-2111
Telecopier: 504-523-2223

MEMBERS OF FIRM

Eugene R. Preaus
Virginia N. Roddy
David J. Krebs
Maura Zivalich Pelleteri

ASSOCIATES

Teresa Rose Young
Diane Lloyd Matthews
Krystil Borrouso Cook
Edward J. Parr, Jr.

Counsel for: American Society of Composers, Authors and Publishers; Fidelity and Deposit Company of Maryland; Metropolitan Life Insurance Co.; New York Life Insurance Co.; Reliance Insurance Co.; U.S. Home Corp.; Western Sizzlin, Inc.

For full biographical listings, see the Martindale-Hubbell Law Directory

*SHREVEPORT,** Caddo Parish

BODENHEIMER, JONES, KLOTZ & SIMMONS (AV)

509 Milam Street, 71101
Telephone: 318-221-1507
Fax: 318-221-4560

MEMBERS OF FIRM

J. W. Jones
Norman I. Lafargue

For full biographical listings, see the Martindale-Hubbell Law Directory

COOK, YANCEY, KING & GALLOWAY, A PROFESSIONAL LAW CORPORATION (AV)

1700 Commercial National Tower, 333 Texas Street, P.O. Box 22260, 71120-2260
Telephone: 318-221-6277
Telecopier: 318-227-2606

(See Next Column)

COOK, YANCEY, KING & GALLOWAY A PROFESSIONAL LAW CORPORATION, *Shreveport—Continued*

James Robert Jeter
Glenn L. Langley
Bernard S. Johnson
Curtis R. Shelton
Lance P. Havener

A list of representative clients will be furnished upon request.

For Complete List of Firm Personnel, See General Section

For full biographical listings, see the Martindale-Hubbell Law Directory

SIMON, FITZGERALD, COOKE, REED & WELCH (AV)

Suite 200, 4700 Line Avenue, 71106
Telephone: 318-868-2600
Telecopier: 318-868-8966

MEMBERS OF FIRM

Fred Simon (1904-1993)
Archie M. Simon
Thomas P. Fitzgerald (1914-1993)
Paul M. Cooke
Chatham H. Reed
Keith M. Welch
Kevin R. Molloy

A list of Representative Clients will be furnished upon request.

For full biographical listings, see the Martindale-Hubbell Law Directory

WIENER, WEISS, MADISON & HOWELL, A PROFESSIONAL CORPORATION (AV)

333 Texas Street, Suite 2350, P.O. Box 21990, 71120-1990
Telephone: 318-226-9100
Fax: 318-424-5128

James R. Madison
R. Joseph Naus

Representative Clients: Pioneer Bank & Trust Co.; Ford Motor Credit Corp.; CNA Insurance Companies; International Paper Companies; Louisiana Homebuilders Association Self Insurers Fund; LSU-Shreveport; Sealy Realty, Inc.; Palmer Petroleum, Inc.; Brookshire Grocery Company (Louisiana); Northwest Louisiana Production Credit Association.

For Complete List of Firm Personnel, See General Section

For full biographical listings, see the Martindale-Hubbell Law Directory

MAINE

*AUGUSTA,** Kennebec Co.

* indicates certain Bar Register subscribers whose principal office is located elsewhere in the state and who have arranged for representation as a part of the state capital listings that follow

*** PIERCE, ATWOOD, SCRIBNER, ALLEN, SMITH & LANCASTER (AV)**

77 Winthrop Street, 04330
Telephone: 207-622-6311
Fax: 207-623-9367
Portland, Maine Office: One Monument Square.
Telephone: 207-773-6411.
Camden, Maine Office: 36 Chestnut Street, P.O. Box 780.
Telephone: 207-236-4333.

MEMBERS OF FIRM

Warren E. Winslow, Jr.
Malcolm L. Lyons
Joseph M. Kozak
Michael D. Seitzinger
John C. Nivison

ASSOCIATES

Daniel J. Stevens
Benjamin P. Townsend
Christine F. Burke

For full biographical listings, see the Martindale-Hubbell Law Directory

*BANGOR,** Penobscot Co.

GROSS, MINSKY, MOGUL & SINGAL, P.A. (AV)

Key Plaza, 23 Water Street, P.O. Box 917, 04402-0917
Telephone: 207-942-4644
Telecopier: 207-942-3699
Ellsworth, Maine Office: 26 State Street.
Telephone: 207-667-4611.
Telecopier: 207-667-6206.

Jules L. Mogul (1930-1994)
Norman Minsky
George Z. Singal
Louis H. Kornreich
George C. Schelling
Edward W. Gould
Steven J. Mogul
James R. Wholly

(See Next Column)

Wayne P. Libhart (Resident, Ellsworth, Maine Office)
Daniel A. Pileggi
Philip K. Clarke
Christopher R. Largay (Resident, Ellsworth Office)
Hans G. Huessy
William B. Entwisle
Sandra L. Rothera

OF COUNSEL

Edward I. Gross

Representative Clients: Dahl Chase Pathology Associates; Superior Paper Products.
Local Counsel for: The St. Paul Insurance Cos.; Aetna Life & Casualty Co.; Imperial Casualty & Indemnity Co.

For full biographical listings, see the Martindale-Hubbell Law Directory

*PORTLAND,** Cumberland Co.

PIERCE, ATWOOD, SCRIBNER, ALLEN, SMITH & LANCASTER (AV)

One Monument Square, 04101
Telephone: 207-773-6411
Fax: 207-773-3419
Augusta, Maine Office: 77 Winthrop Street.
Telephone: 207-622-6311.
Camden, Maine Office: 36 Chestnut Street, P.O. Box 780.
Telephone: 207-236-4333.

MEMBERS OF FIRM

George J. Marcus
Jacob A. Manheimer

ASSOCIATES

Jennie L. Clegg
Richard P. Olson
Nancy V. Savage

For Complete List of Firm Personnel, See General Section

For full biographical listings, see the Martindale-Hubbell Law Directory

PRETI, FLAHERTY, BELIVEAU & PACHIOS (AV)

443 Congress Street, P.O. Box 11410, 04104-7410
Telephone: 207-791-3000
Telecopier: 207-791-3111
Augusta, Maine Office: 45 Memorial Circle, P.O. Box 1058, 04332-1058.
Telephone: 207-623-5300.
Telecopier: 207-623-2914.
Rumford, Maine Office: 150 Congress Street, P.O. Drawer L, 04276-2035.
Telephone: 207-364-4593.
Telecopier: 207-369-9421.

MEMBERS OF FIRM

Harold C. Pachios
Leonard M. Gulino
Estelle A. Lavoie
Michael Kaplan

ASSOCIATES

John P. McVeigh
Scott T. Rodgers

Representative Clients: Key Bank of Maine, Inc.; Peoples Heritage Savings Bank; RECOLL Management, Corp.; Meadowledge Associates; Southern Maine Medical Center; Colonial Supply Corp.; Fleet Bank of Maine.

For Complete List of Firm Personnel, See General Section

For full biographical listings, see the Martindale-Hubbell Law Directory

YORK, York Co.

ERWIN, OTT, CLARK & CAMPBELL (AV)

16A Woodbridge Road, P.O. Box 545, 03909
Telephone: 207-363-5208
Facsimile: 207-363-5322

MEMBERS OF FIRM

Frank E. Hancock (1923-1988)
James S. Erwin
John P. Campbell
David N. Ott
Jeffery J. Clark

For full biographical listings, see the Martindale-Hubbell Law Directory

MARYLAND

*BALTIMORE,** (Independent City)

GORDON, FEINBLATT, ROTHMAN, HOFFBERGER & HOLLANDER (AV)

The Garrett Building, 233 East Redwood Street, 21202
Telephone: 410-576-4000
Telex: 908041 BAL

MEMBERS OF FIRM

Lawrence D. Coppel (Chairman)
Jay A. Shulman
John Martin Klein II

(See Next Column)

GORDON, FEINBLATT, ROTHMAN, HOFFBERGER & HOLLANDER—*Continued*

ASSOCIATE

Karen M. Crabtree

For Complete List of Firm Personnel, See General Section

For full biographical listings, see the Martindale-Hubbell Law Directory

THIEBLOT, RYAN, MARTIN & FERGUSON, P.A. (AV)

4th Floor, The World Trade Center, 21202-3091
Telephone: 410-837-1140
Washington, D.C. Line: 202-628-8223
Fax: 410-837-3282

Robert J. Thieblot
Anthony W. Ryan
J. Edward Martin, Jr.
Robert L. Ferguson, Jr.
Bruce R. Miller
Robert D. Harwick, Jr.
Thomas J. Schetelich
Christopher J. Heffernan

M. Brooke Murdock
Anne M. Hrehorovich
Donna Marie Raffaele
Michael N. Russo, Jr.
Jodi K. Ebersole
Hamilton Fisk Tyler
Peter Joseph Basile

Representative Clients: Ford Motor Credit Co.; USF & G Co.; The American Road Insurance Co.; Fidelity Engineering Corp.; The North Charles Street Design Organization; Record Collections, Inc.; Toyota Motor Credit Co.

For full biographical listings, see the Martindale-Hubbell Law Directory

VENABLE, BAETJER AND HOWARD (AV)

A Partnership including Professional Corporations
1800 Mercantile Bank & Trust Building, 2 Hopkins Plaza, 21201
Telephone: 410-244-7400
Washington, D.C. Office: Venable, Baetjer, Howard & Civiletti. Suite 1000, 1201 New York Avenue, N.W.
Telephone: 202-962-4800.
McLean, Virginia Office: Suite 400, 2010 Corporate Ridge.
Telephone: 703-760-1600.
Rockville, Maryland Office: Suite 500, One Church Street, P. O. Box 1906.
Telephone: 301-217-5600.
Towson, Maryland Office: 210 Allegheny Avenue, P. O. Box 5517.
Telephone: 410-494-6200.

MEMBERS OF FIRM

Daniel O'C. Tracy, Jr. (Also at Rockville, Maryland Office)
Joe A. Shull (Resident, Washington, D.C. Office)
Kenneth C. Bass, III (Not admitted in MD; Also at Washington, D.C. and McLean, Virginia Offices)
Joel Z. Silver (Not admitted in MD; Resident, Washington, D.C. Office)
Paul T. Glasgow (Resident, Rockville, Maryland Office)
Joseph C. Wich, Jr. (Resident, Towson, Maryland Office)
Richard L. Wasserman (P.C.)
George F. Pappas (Also at Washington, D.C. Office)
Christopher R. Mellott
David Eugene Rice
John A. Roberts (Also at Rockville, Maryland Office)

OF COUNSEL

Mary T. Flynn (Not admitted in MD; Resident, McLean, Virginia Office)

ASSOCIATES

Gregory A. Cross
Ellen Berkow Feldman
Rochelle Block Fowler
Gregory L. Laubach (Resident, Rockville, Maryland Office)
Jon M. Lippard (Not admitted in MD; Resident, McLean, Virginia Office)
Myriam Judith Schmell
Brian R. Trumbauer

For Complete List of Firm Personnel, See General Section

For full biographical listings, see the Martindale-Hubbell Law Directory

BETHESDA, Montgomery Co.

DECKELBAUM OGENS & FISCHER, CHARTERED (AV)

6701 Democracy Boulevard, 20817
Telephone: 301-564-5100
Washington D.C. Office: 1140 Connecticut Avenue, N.W.
Telephone: 202-223-1474.

Nelson Deckelbaum
Ronald L. Ogens
Lawrence H. Fischer
Arthur G. Kahn
Deborah E. Reiser

Ronald G. Scheraga

LEGAL SUPPORT PERSONNEL

Shirley Mostow

References: First Liberty Bank; Sovran Bank, D.C.

For full biographical listings, see the Martindale-Hubbell Law Directory

*ROCKVILLE,** Montgomery Co.

KATZ, FROME AND BLEECKER, P.A. (AV)

6116 Executive Boulevard, Suite 200, 20852
Telephone: 301-230-5800
Facsimile: 301-230-5830

Steven M. Katz
Morton J. Frome
Lorin H. Bleecker
Gail B. Landau

Susan J. Rubin
Marilyn J. Brasier
Leslie Anne Sullivan
Seth B. Popkin
Richard O'Connor
Stanley A. Snyder

OF COUNSEL

Philip F. Finelli, Jr.

For full biographical listings, see the Martindale-Hubbell Law Directory

SILVER SPRING, Montgomery Co.

ALEXANDER, GEBHARDT, APONTE & MARKS, L.L.C. (AV)

Lee Plaza-Suite 805, 8601 Georgia Avenue, 20910
Telephone: 301-589-2222
Facsimile: 301-589-2523
Washington, D.C. Office: 1314 Nineteenth Street, N.W., 20036.
Telephone: 202-835-1555.
New York, New York Office: 330 Madison Avenue, 36th Floor.
Telephone: 212-808-0008.
Fax: 212-599-1028.

Koteles Alexander (Not admitted in MD)
S. Ricardo Narvaiz (Not admitted in MD)

Nihar R. Mohanty
John L. Machado (Not admitted in MD)

Reference: Riggs National Bank of Washington, D.C.

For full biographical listings, see the Martindale-Hubbell Law Directory

MASSACHUSETTS

*BOSTON,** Suffolk Co.

BINGHAM, DANA & GOULD (AV)

150 Federal Street, 02110
Telephone: 617-951-8000
Cable Address: "Blodgham Bsn"
Telex: 275147 BDGBSN UR
Telecopy: 617-951-8736
Hartford, Connecticut Office: 100 Pearl Street.
Telephone: 203-244-3770.
Telecopy: 203-527-5188.
London, England Office: 39 Victoria Street, SWIH 0EE.
Telephone: 011-44-71-799-2646.
Telecopy: 011-44-71-799-2654.
Telex: 888179 BDGLDN G.
Cable Address: "Blodgham Ldn".
Washington, D.C. Office: 1550 M Street, N.W.
Telephone: 202-822-9320.
Telecopy: 202-833-1506.

MEMBERS OF FIRM

Jonathan M. Albano
Joseph L. Kociubes
Paul J. Lambert (Resident in Washington, D.C. Office)
Guy B. Moss
Peter D. Schellie (Resident in Washington, D.C. Office)
Scott M. Schooley (Resident in Hartford, Connecticut Office)
Edwin E. Smith
Lee A. Spielman (Resident in Hartford, Connecticut Office)

For Complete List of Firm Personnel, See General Section

For full biographical listings, see the Martindale-Hubbell Law Directory

CRAIG AND MACAULEY, PROFESSIONAL CORPORATION (AV)

Federal Reserve Plaza, 600 Atlantic Avenue, 02210
Telephone: 617-367-9500
Telecopier: 617-742-1788; 617-248-0886

William F. Macauley
Stephen Wald
William R. Moorman, Jr.

Martin P. Desmery
Peter J. Roberts
Diane M. Crawford-Kelly

For Complete List of Firm Personnel, See General Section

For full biographical listings, see the Martindale-Hubbell Law Directory

Boston—Continued

HANIFY & KING, PROFESSIONAL CORPORATION (AV)

One Federal Street, 02110-2007
Telephone: 617-423-0400
Telefax: 617-423-0498

James Coyne King
John D. Hanify
Harold B. Murphy
David Lee Evans
Daniel J. Lyne
Donald F. Farrell, Jr.
Barbara Wegener Pfirrman
Gerard P. Richer
Timothy P. O'Neill

Gordon M. Jones, III
Kara L. Thornton
Jean A. Musiker
Ann M. Chiacchieri
Melissa J. Cassedy
Kara M. Lucciola
Philip C. Silverman
Michael R. Perry
Jeffrey S. Cedrone
Charles A. Dale, III
Joseph F. Cortellini
Hiram N. Pan
Amy Conroy
Michael S. Bloom
Andrew G. Lizotte
Peter D. Lee
Martin F. Gaynor, III

For full biographical listings, see the Martindale-Hubbell Law Directory

PALMER & DODGE (AV)

(Storey Thorndike Palmer & Dodge)
One Beacon Street, 02108
Telephone: 617-573-0100
Telecopier: 617-227-4420
Telex: 951104
Cable Address: "Storeydike," Boston

MEMBERS OF FIRM

Jeanne P. Darcey
Richard Hiersteiner
Raymond M. Murphy
John E. Rattigan, Jr.
Thomas G. Schnorr
Thomas M. Spera
George Ticknor
John L. Whitlock

For Complete List of Firm Personnel, See General Section

For full biographical listings, see the Martindale-Hubbell Law Directory

ROCHE, CARENS & DEGIACOMO (AV)

A Partnership including Professional Corporations
One Post Office Square, 02109
Telephone: 617-451-9300
Facsimile: 617-482-3868
Woburn, Massachusetts Office: 400 Unicorn Park Drive.
Telephone: 617-933-5505.
Saugus, Massachusetts Office: 605 Broadway.
Telephone: 617-233-4074.
Vineyard Haven, Massachusetts Office: P.O. Box 2165.
Telephone: 508-693-7333.
Braintree, Massachusetts Office: 51 Commercial Street.
Telephone: 617-356-4210.

MEMBERS OF FIRM

Frederick W. Roche (1914-1971)
James R. DeGiacomo
Robert J. Sherer
Michael T. Putziger (P.C.)
Judith K. Wyman (P.C.)
John C. Wyman (P.C.)
Richard J. Saletta
John W. Gahan, III
Frank M. Capezzera
Loring A. Cook, III
John J. O'Connor, Jr.
Thomas K. Zebrowski
Susan J. Baronoff
Johanna Smith
Mary S. Parker
Anne Hanford Stossel
Mark G. DeGiacomo
Joseph R. Tarby III (Resident, Woburn Office)
Lynne Callahan DeGiacomo
Joan P. Armstrong
Maury E. Lederman
Brian R. Cook
Tracie L. Longman
Jacqueline Holmes Haley
Francis A. DiLuna (Resident, Woburn Office)

ASSOCIATES

William M. Healy (Resident, Vineyard Haven Office)
Cynthia H.N. Post
Thomas S. Vangel
Elizabeth B. Ornstein
Mark J. Warner
James B. Pratt
John F. Brosnan
Rachel S. Gerny
Allen A. Lynch, III (Resident, Saugus Office)
David A. Kelly (Resident, Braintree Office)
Edward J. Rozmiarek
Nancy M. Harris
Timothy P. Cox
Peter Carbone, III (Resident, Woburn Office)

OF COUNSEL

Thomas J. Carens
Daniel J. Johnedis

For full biographical listings, see the Martindale-Hubbell Law Directory

SHERBURNE, POWERS & NEEDHAM, P.C. (AV)

One Beacon Street, 02108
Telephone: 617-523-2700
Fax: 617-523-6850

(See Next Column)

William D. Weeks
John T. Collins
Allan J. Landau
John L. Daly
Stephen A. Hopkins
Alan I. Falk
C. Thomas Swaim
James Pollock
William V. Tripp III
Stephen S. Young
William F. Machen
W. Robert Allison
Jacob C. Diemert
Philip J. Notopoulos
Richard J. Hindlian
Paul E. Troy
Harold W. Potter, Jr.
Dale R. Johnson
Philip S. Lapatin
Pamela A. Duckworth
Mark Schonfeld
James D. Smeallie
Paul Killeen
Gordon P. Katz
Joseph B. Darby, III
Richard M Yanofsky
James E. McDermott
Robert V. Lizza
Miriam Goldstein Altman
John J. Monaghan
Margaret J. Palladino
Mark C. Michalowski
David Scott Sloan
M. Chrysa Long
Lawrence D. Bradley
Miriam J. McKendall

Cynthia A. Brown
Cynthia M. Hern
Dianne R. Phillips
Paul M. James
Theodore F. Hanselman
Joshua C. Krumholz
Ieuan G. Mahony
Kenneth L. Harvey
Christopher J. Trombetta
Edwin F. Landers, Jr.
Amy J. Mastrobattista
William Howard McCarthy, Jr.
Douglas W. Clapp
Tamara E. Goulston
Nicholas J. Psyhogeos

COUNSEL

Haig Der Manuelian
Mason M. Taber, Jr.
Karl J. Hirshman
Benjamin Volinski
Kenneth P. Brier

OF COUNSEL

John Barr Dolan

For full biographical listings, see the Martindale-Hubbell Law Directory

SILVERMAN & KUDISCH, P.C. (AV)

Successor to Silverman & Kudisch.
One Longfellow Place, Suite 3608, 02114-2434
Telephone: 617-523-1711
Fax: 617-523-6037

William M. Silverman (1920-1981)
Clarence P. Kudisch (1936-1965)
Sumner Darman
Peter L. Zimmerman
Richard L. Blumenthal
Lisa B. Darman

For full biographical listings, see the Martindale-Hubbell Law Directory

*SPRINGFIELD,** Hampden Co.

HENDEL, COLLINS & NEWTON, P.C. (AV)

101 State Street, 01103
Telephone: 413-734-6411
Fax: 413-734-8069

Philip J. Hendel
Joseph B. Collins
Carla W. Newton

Joseph H. Reinhardt
Jonathan R. Goldsmith
Henry E. Geberth, Jr.
George I. Roumeliotis

Representative Clients: Springfield Institution for Savings; Shawmut Bank, N.A.; United Cooperative Bank.
Reference: Shawmut Bank, N.A.

For full biographical listings, see the Martindale-Hubbell Law Directory

KAMBERG, BERMAN, P.C. (AV)

One Monarch Place Twelfth Floor, 01144-1009
Telephone: 413-781-1300
Facsimile: 413-732-0860
ABA/net: KAMBERGB

Abraham Kamberg (1895-1981)
Eugene B. Berman
Richard G. Lemoine
Carolyn L. Burt
Mark W. Siegars
Kerry David Strayer

References: Shawmut Bank, N.A.; Fleet Bank of Massachusetts, N.A.; Baybank.

For full biographical listings, see the Martindale-Hubbell Law Directory

*WORCESTER,** Worcester Co.

SEDER & CHANDLER (AV)

Established 1918
Burnside Building, 339 Main Street, 01608
Telephone: 508-757-7721
Telecopiers: 508-798-1863; 831-0955

(See Next Column)

SEDER & CHANDLER—*Continued*

MEMBERS OF FIRM

Samuel Seder (1918-1964)
Harold Seder (1934-1988)
Burton Chandler
J. Robert Seder
Darragh K. Kasakoff
Marvin S. Silver
John Woodward
John L. Pfeffer, Jr.
Robert S. Adler
Dawn E. Caccavaro

ASSOCIATES

Kevin C. McGee
Paul J. O'Riordan
Jeffrey P. Greenberg
Lisa S. Sigel
Denise M. Tremblay

OF COUNSEL

Saul A. Seder
Gerald E. Norman

Reference: Shawmut Worcester County Bank N.A.

For full biographical listings, see the Martindale-Hubbell Law Directory

MICHIGAN

*ANN ARBOR,** Washtenaw Co.

CONLIN, MCKENNEY & PHILBRICK, P.C. (AV)

700 City Center Building, 48104-1994
Telephone: 313-761-9000
Fax: 313-761-9001

Edward F. Conlin (1902-1953)
John W. Conlin (1904-1972)
Albert J. Parker (1901-1970)
Chris L. McKenney
Karl R. Frankena
Allen J. Philbrick
Phillip J. Bowen
Richard E. Conlin
Michael D. Highfield
Bruce N. Elliott
Neil J. Juliar
Robert M. Brimacombe
David S. Swartz
James A. Schriemer
Elizabeth M. Petoskey
Bradley J. MeLampy
Joseph W. Phillips
William M. Sweet
Lori A. Buiteweg
Douglas G. McClure
Thomas B. Bourque
Marjorie M. Dixon
Bonnie H. Keen

OF COUNSEL

John W. Conlin

Representative Clients: Fingerle Lumber Co.; Ann Arbor Area Board of Realtors; Borders, Inc.; Society Bank, Michigan; Auto-Owners Insurance Co.; Wolverine Title Co.
Approved Attorneys for: American Title Insurance Co.; Ticor Title Insurance Co.

For full biographical listings, see the Martindale-Hubbell Law Directory

MILLER, CANFIELD, PADDOCK AND STONE, P.L.C. (AV)

A Professional Limited Liability Company
Founded in 1852 by Sidney Davy Miller
101 North Main Street, Seventh Floor, 48104-1400
Telephone: 313-663-2445
Fax: 313-747-7147
Detroit, Michigan Office: 150 West Jefferson, Suite 2500, 48226-4415.
Telephone: 313-963-6420.
Fax: 313-496-7500.
Cable Address: "Stem Detroit."
Bloomfield Hills, Michigan Office: Suite 100, Pinehurst Office Center, 1400 North Woodward, 48303-2014.
Telephone: 313-645-5000.
Fax: 313-645-1917.
Grand Rapids, Michigan Office: 1200 Campau Square Plaza, 99 Monroe, N.W., 49503-2639.
Telephone: 616-454-8656.
Fax: 616-776-6322.
Howell, Michigan Office: 121 South Barnard Street, Suite 4, 48843-2305.
Telephone: 517-546-7600.
Telecopier: 517-546-6974.
Kalamazoo, Michigan Office: 444 West Michigan Avenue, 49007-3752.
Telephone: 616-381-7030.
Fax: 616-382-0244.
Lansing, Michigan Office: One Michigan Avenue, Suite 900, 48933-1609.
Telephone: 517-487-2070.
Fax: 517-374-6304.
Monroe, Michigan Office: The Executive Centre, 214 East Elm Avenue, 48161-2682.
Telephone: 313-243-2000.
Fax: 313-243-0901.
Washington, D.C. Office: 1225 Nineteenth Street, N.W., Suite 400. 20036.
Telephone: 202-429-5575; 785-0600.
Fax: 202-331-1118; 785-1234.
Pensacola, Florida Office: 25 West Cedar, 32501.
Telephone: 904-469-1088.
Fax: 904-432-0677.

(See Next Column)

St. Petersburg, Florida Office: 100 Second Avenue S., Suite 7045, 33701.
Telephone: 813-982-6000.
Fax: 813-892-6002.
Gdansk, Poland Office: Suite 322, Dom Technika Building, Ul. Rajska 6, 80-850.
Telephone: 011-485-831-2808.
Fax: 011-485-831-4719.
Warsaw, Poland Office: Ul. Marszalkowska 82, Suite 561, 00-517.
Telephone: 011-482-623-6457 and 6458.
Fax: 011-482-623-6459.

RESIDENT PARTNER

Robert E. Gilbert

Representative Firm Clients: Chrysler Corp.; Comerica, Inc.; City of Detroit, Mich.; Detroit Tigers, Inc.; First of Michigan; Fretter, Inc.; Ford Motor Co.; Ford Motor Credit Co.; Great Lakes Bancorp; Henry Ford Hospital.

For Complete List of Firm Personnel, See General Section

For full biographical listings, see the Martindale-Hubbell Law Directory

*BAY CITY,** Bay Co.

BRAUN KENDRICK FINKBEINER (AV)

201 Phoenix Building, P.O. Box 2039, 48708
Telephone: 517-895-8505
Telecopier: 517-895-8437
Saginaw, Michigan Office: 8th Floor Second National Bank Building.
Telephone: 517-753-3461.
Telecopier: 517-753-3951.

MEMBERS OF FIRM

Ralph J. Isackson
Patrick D. Neering
George F. Gronewold, Jr.
Frank M. Quinn
Gregory E. Meter
Daniel S. Opperman
Gregory T. Demers

Representative Clients: APV Chemical Machinery, Inc.; Bay Health Systems; Berger and Co.; Catholic Federal Credit Union; Charter Township of Bridgeport; City of Saginaw; City of Vassar; City of Zilwaukee; Corporate Service; Cox Cable.

For Complete List of Firm Personnel, See General Section

For full biographical listings, see the Martindale-Hubbell Law Directory

BIRMINGHAM, Oakland Co.

CARSON FISCHER, P.L.C. (AV)

Third Floor, 300 East Maple Road, 48009-6317
Telephone: 810-644-4840
Facsimile: 810-644-1832

Joseph M. Fischer
Robert A. Weisberg
Sandra L. Labovitz
Stephen J. Carson

For full biographical listings, see the Martindale-Hubbell Law Directory

AUSTIN HIRSCHHORN, P.C. (AV)

251 East Merrill Street, 2nd Floor, 48009-6150
Telephone: 810-646-9944
FAX: 810-647-8596

Austin Hirschhorn

For full biographical listings, see the Martindale-Hubbell Law Directory

BLOOMFIELD HILLS, Oakland Co.

HOWARD & HOWARD ATTORNEYS, P.C. (AV)

The Pinehurst Office Center, Suite 101, 1400 North Woodward Avenue, 48304-2856
Telephone: 810-645-1483
Telecopier: 810-645-1568
Kalamazoo, Michigan Office: The Kalamazoo Building, Suite 400, 107 West Michigan Avenue.
Telephone: 616-382-1483.
Telecopier: 616-382-1568.
Lansing, Michigan Office: The Phoenix Building, Suite 500, 222 Washington Square, North.
Telephone: 517-485-1483.
Telecopier: 517-485-1568.
Peoria, Illinois Office: Howard & Howard, P.C., The Creve Coeur Building, Suite 200, 321 Liberty Street.
Telephone: 309-672-1483.
Telecopier: 309-672-1568.

Michael G. Cruse
Robert D. Mollhagen

Representative Clients: For Representative Client list, see General Practice, Bloomfield Hills, MI.

For Complete List of Firm Personnel, See General Section

For full biographical listings, see the Martindale-Hubbell Law Directory

Bloomfield Hills—Continued

STROBL AND MANOOGIAN, P.C. (AV)

300 East Long Lake Road, Suite 200, 48304-2376
Telephone: 810-645-0306
Facsimile: 810-645-2690

Thomas J. Strobl
John Sharp
Brian C. Manoogian
Kieran F. Cunningham

James T. Dunn
Keith S. King
Pamela S. Ritter

Representative Clients: Resolution Trust Corporation; Comerica Bank; Chrysler Credit Corporation; First of America Bank.

For Complete List of Firm Personnel, See General Section

For full biographical listings, see the Martindale-Hubbell Law Directory

*DETROIT,** Wayne Co.

ALLARD & FISH, A PROFESSIONAL CORPORATION (AV)

2600 Buhl Building, 535 Griswold Avenue, 48226
Telephone: 313-961-6141
Facsimile: 313-961-6142

David W. Allard
Deborah L. Fish

Ralph R. McKee
Rodney M. Glusac
Elias Themistocles Majoros
Gary A. Hansz

For full biographical listings, see the Martindale-Hubbell Law Directory

BODMAN, LONGLEY & DAHLING (AV)

34th Floor 100 Renaissance Center, 48243
Telephone: 313-259-7777
Fax: 313-393-7579
Troy, Michigan Office: Suite 2020, 755 West Big Beaver Road.
Telephone: 810-362-2110.
Ann Arbor, Michigan Office: 110 Miller, Suite 300.
Telephone: 313-761-3780.
Northern Michigan Office: 229 Court Street, P.O. Box 405, Cheboygan.
Telephone: 616-627-4351.

MEMBERS OF FIRM

David G. Chardavoyne
Lawrence P. Hanson (Northern Michigan Office)
Robert J. Diehl, Jr.
Ralph E. McDowell

ASSOCIATE

Marc M. Bakst

Representative Clients: Abitibi Price Group; Archdiocese of Detroit; Comerica Bank; The Detroit Lions, Inc.; Ford Estates; General Motors Corporation; Charles Stewart Mott Foundation; Norfolk Southern Corporation; Panhandle Eastern Corporation; State Farm Mutual Automobile Insurance Company.

For Complete List of Firm Personnel, See General Section

For full biographical listings, see the Martindale-Hubbell Law Directory

BUTZEL LONG, A PROFESSIONAL CORPORATION (AV)

Suite 900, 150 West Jefferson, 48226
Telephone: 313-225-7000
Telecopier: 313-225-7080
Birmingham, Michigan Office: Suite 200, 32270 Telegraph Road.
Telephone: 810-258-1616.
Telecopier: 810-258-1439.
Lansing, Michigan Office: 118 West Ottawa Street.
Telephone: 517-372-6622.
Telecopier: 517-372-6672.
Ann Arbor, Michigan Office: Suite 400, 121 West Washington.
Telephone: 313-995-3110.
Telecopier: 313-995-1777.
Grosse Pointe Farms, Michigan Office: Suite 260, 21 Kercheval.
Telephone: 313-886-5446.
Telecopier: 313-886-2114.

Stephen A. Bromberg (Birmingham)
D. Stewart Green (Birmingham)
Edward M. Kalinka
Thomas B. Radom (Birmingham)
Lawrence A. Lichtman

Daniel R. W. Rustmann
Eugene H. Boyle, Jr.

For Complete List of Firm Personnel, See General Section

For full biographical listings, see the Martindale-Hubbell Law Directory

CLARK, KLEIN & BEAUMONT (AV)

1600 First Federal Building, 1001 Woodward Avenue, 48226
Telephone: 313-965-8300
Facsimile: 313-962-4348
Bloomfield Hills Office: 1533 North Woodward Avenue, Suite 220, 48304.
Telephone: 810-258-2900.
Facsimile: 810-258-2949.

MEMBER OF FIRM

Michael S. Khoury

ASSOCIATES

Judith Greenstone Miller
Michael I. Conlon
David A. Foster

For Complete List of Firm Personnel, See General Section

For full biographical listings, see the Martindale-Hubbell Law Directory

DICKINSON, WRIGHT, MOON, VAN DUSEN & FREEMAN (AV)

500 Woodward Avenue, Suite 4000, 48226-3425
Telephone: 313-223-3500
Facsimile: 313-223-3598
Bloomfield Hills, Michigan Office: 525 North Woodward Avenue, Suite 2000.
Telephone: 810-433-7200.
Facsimile: 810-433-7274.
Grand Rapids, Michigan Office: 200 Ottawa Avenue, N.W., Suite 900.
Telephone: 616-458-1300.
Facsimile: 616-458-6753.
Lansing, Michigan Office: Suite 200, 215 South Washington Square.
Telephone: 517-371-1730.
Facsimile: 517-487-4700.
Washington, D.C. Office: Suite 800, 1901 L Street, N.W.
Telephone: 202-457-0160.
Facsimile: 202-659-1559.
Chicago, Illinois Office: 225 West Washington, Suite 400.
Telephone: 312-220-0300.
Facsimile: 312-220-0021.
Warsaw, Poland Office: 46 Wilcza Street, 4th Floor, 00-679.
Telephone: (48-22) 299-241.
Facsimile: (48-2) 628-4107. Komertel Satellite Phone: (48-39) 121-510.

MEMBERS OF FIRM

Douglas D. Roche
Richard M. Bolton
Edgar C. Howbert
Daniel M. Katlein
C. Beth DunCombe
Richard A. Wilhelm
Philip M. Frost
William P. Shield, Jr.

ASSOCIATES

Michael C. Hammer
James A. Plemmons

Representative Clients: Federal-Mogul Corp.; Florists' Transworld Delivery Assn.; GMF Robotics Corp.; Kmart Corp.; Kuhlman Corp.; Michigan Consolidated Gas Co.; NBD Bank, N.A.

For Complete List of Firm Personnel, See General Section

For full biographical listings, see the Martindale-Hubbell Law Directory

EAMES, WILCOX, MASTEJ, BRYANT, SWIFT & RIDDELL (AV)

1400 Buhl Building, 48226-3602
Telephone: 313-963-3750
Facsimile: 313-963-8485

MEMBERS OF FIRM

Leonard A. Wilcox, Jr.
Jerry R. Swift
Ronald J. Mastej
Neill T. Riddell
John W. Bryant
Elizabeth Roberto
Kevin N. Summers

ASSOCIATE

Keith M. Aretha

OF COUNSEL

Rex Eames
Robert E. Gesell
William B. McIntyre, Jr.

Representative Clients: Chrysler Credit Corp.

For full biographical listings, see the Martindale-Hubbell Law Directory

HONIGMAN MILLER SCHWARTZ AND COHN (AV)

A Partnership including Professional Corporations
2290 First National Building, 48226
Telephone: 313-256-7800
Telecopier: 313-962-0176
Telex: 235705
Lansing, Michigan Office: Phoenix Building, 222 North Washington Square, Suite 400.
Telephone: 517-484-8282.
West Palm Beach, Florida Office: Suite 800 Esperante Building, 222 Lakeview Avenue.
Telephone: 407-838-4500.
Tampa, Florida Office: 2700 Landmark Centre, 401 E. Jackson Street.
Telephone: 813-221-6600.
Orlando, Florida Office: 390 North Orange Avenue, Suite 1300.
Telephone: 407-648-0300.

(See Next Column)

HONIGMAN MILLER SCHWARTZ AND COHN—*Continued*

Houston, Texas Office: 3100 First Interstate Bank Plaza, 1000 Louisiana.
Telephone: 713-650-2600.
Los Angeles, California Office: McNeill Plaza, Suite 820, 15260 Ventura Boulevard, 91403.
Telephone: 818-784-2900.

MEMBERS OF FIRM

Donald F. Baty, Jr.
Judy B. Calton
Steven G. Howell
Theodore B. Sylwestrzak
Sheryl L. Toby
Sheldon S. Toll
Robert B. Weiss

ASSOCIATES

Seth D. Gould
Michelle Epstein Taigman

RESIDENT IN TAMPA, FLORIDA OFFICE

ASSOCIATE

Kevin M. Gilhool

RESIDENT IN HOUSTON, TEXAS OFFICE

OF COUNSEL

Asher Rabinowitz

RESIDENT IN LOS ANGELES, CALIFORNIA OFFICE

MEMBERS

Daniel E. Martyn, Jr.
George E. Schulman

ASSOCIATES

Melanie J. Bingham
Adryane R. Omens
Michael D. Schulman

Representative Clients: AT&T Commercial Finance Corp.; Barclays Business Credit, Inc.; First Wisconsin National Bank of Milwaukee; General Motors Corporation Legal Staff (General Motors Acceptance Corporation, General Motors Corporation); Hibernia National Bank; Hughes Aircraft Company Legal Staff; NBD Bank, N.A.; Security Pacific Automotive Financial Services Corp.; The Travelers Insurance Company and World Omni Leasing, Inc.

For Complete List of Firm Personnel, See General Section

For full biographical listings, see the Martindale-Hubbell Law Directory

JAFFE, RAITT, HEUER & WEISS, PROFESSIONAL CORPORATION (AV)

One Woodward Avenue, Suite 2400, 48226
Telephone: 313-961-8380
Telecopier: 313-961-8358
Cable Address: "Jafsni"
Southfield,Michigan Office: Travelers Tower, Suite 1520.
Telephone: 313-961-8380.
Monroe, Michigan Office: 212 East Front Street, Suite 3.
Telephone: 313-241-6470.
Telefacsimile: 313-241-3849.

Thomas E. Coughlin
Victor F. Ptasznik
Louis P. Rochkind
Linda C. Scheuerman
Jay L. Welford

Daniella Saltz
Jon A. Sherk
Wendy L Zabriskie

See General Practice Section for List of Representative Clients.

For Complete List of Firm Personnel, See General Section

For full biographical listings, see the Martindale-Hubbell Law Directory

MILLER, CANFIELD, PADDOCK AND STONE, P.L.C. (AV)

A Professional Limited Liability Company
Founded in 1852 by Sidney Davy Miller
150 West Jefferson, Suite 2500, 48226-4415
Telephone: 313-963-6420
Fax: 313-496-7500
Cable Address: "Stem Detroit"
Detroit, Michigan Office: 150 West Jefferson, Suite 2500, 48226-4415.
Telephone: 313-963-6420.
Fax: 313-496-7500.
Cable Address: "Stem Detroit."
Ann Arbor, Michigan Office: 101 North Main Street, 7th Floor, 48104-1400.
Telephone: 313-663-2445.
Fax: 313-747-7147.
Bloomfield Hills, Michigan Office: Suite 100, Pinehurst Office Center, 1400 North Woodward, 48303-2014.
Telephone: 313-645-5000.
Fax: 313-645-1917.
Grand Rapids, Michigan Office: 1200 Campau Square Plaza, 99 Monroe, N.W., 49503-2639.
Telephone: 616-454-8656.
Fax: 616-776-6322.
Howell, Michigan Office: 121 South Barnard Street, Suite 4, 48843-2305.
Telephone: 517-546-7600.
Telecopier: 517-546-6974.

(See Next Column)

Kalamazoo, Michigan Office: 444 West Michigan Avenue, 49007-3752.
Telephone: 616-381-7030.
Fax: 616-382-0244.
Lansing, Michigan Office: One Michigan Avenue, Suite 900, 48933-1609.
Telephone: 517-487-2070.
Fax: 517-374-6304.
Monroe, Michigan Office: The Executive Centre, 214 East Elm Avenue, 48161-2682.
Telephone: 313-243-2000.
Fax: 313-243-0901.
Washington, D.C. Office: 1225 Nineteenth Street, N.W., Suite 400. 20036.
Telephone: 202-429-5575; 785-0600.
Fax: 202-331-1118; 785-1234.
Pensacola, Florida Office: 25 West Cedar, 32501.
Telephone: 904-469-1088.
Fax: 904-432-0677.
St. Petersburg, Florida Office: 100 Second Avenue S., Suite 7045, 33701.
Telephone: 813-982-6000.
Fax: 813-892-6002.
Gdansk, Poland Office: Suite 322, Dom Technika Building, Ul. Rajska 6, 80-850.
Telephone: 011-485-831-2808.
Fax: 011-485-831-4719.
Warsaw, Poland Office: Ul. Marszalkowska 82, Suite 561, 00-517.
Telephone: 011-482-623-6457 and 6458.
Fax: 011-482-623-6459.

MEMBERS OF FIRM

Robert E. Lee Wright
Michael H. Traison
Jonathan S. Green

OF COUNSEL

Donald B. Lifton

ASSOCIATES

Donald J. Hutchinson
Lori L. Purkey
(Kalamazoo Office)
Lisa D. Pick

Representative Firm Clients: Chrysler Corp.; Comerica, Inc.; City of Detroit, Mich.; Detroit Tigers, Inc.; First of Michigan; Fretter, Inc.; Ford Motor Co.; Ford Motor Credit Co.; Great Lakes Bancorp; Henry Ford Hospital.

For Complete List of Firm Personnel, See General Section

For full biographical listings, see the Martindale-Hubbell Law Directory

FARMINGTON HILLS, Oakland Co.

COUZENS, LANSKY, FEALK, ELLIS, ROEDER & LAZAR, P.C. (AV)

33533 West Twelve Mile Road, Suite 150, P.O. Box 9057, 48333-9057
Telephone: 810-489-8600
Telecopier: 810-489-4156

Jerry M. Ellis
Phillip L. Sternberg
Mark S. Frankel

References: Comerica Bank-Southfield;
Representative Clients: Provided upon request.

For full biographical listings, see the Martindale-Hubbell Law Directory

*FLINT,** Genesee Co.

WINEGARDEN, SHEDD, HALEY, LINDHOLM & ROBERTSON (AV)

501 Citizens Bank Building, 48502-1983
Telephone: 810-767-3600
Telecopier: 810-767-8776

MEMBERS OF FIRM

William C. Shedd
Dennis M. Haley
John T. Lindholm
Donald H. Robertson
L. David Lawson
John R. Tucker

ASSOCIATES

Alan F. Himelhoch
Suellen J. Parker
Damion Frasier
Peter T. Mooney

Representative Clients: Citizens Commercial and Savings Bank; R.L. White Development Corporation; Interstate Traffic Consultants (Intracon) Inc.; Downtown Development Authority of Flint; Young Olds-Cadillac, Inc.; First American Title Insurance Co.; Sorensen Gross Construction Co.; Genesee County; Insight, Inc..; Flint Counsel, National Bank of Detroit.

For Complete List of Firm Personnel, See General Section

For full biographical listings, see the Martindale-Hubbell Law Directory

*GRAND RAPIDS,** Kent Co.

BORRE, PETERSON, FOWLER & REENS, P.C. (AV)

The Philo C. Fuller House, 44 Lafayette, N.E., P.O. Box 1767, 49501-1767
Telephone: 616-459-1971
FAX: 616-459-2393

(See Next Column)

BORRE, PETERSON, FOWLER & REENS P.C., *Grand Rapids—Continued*

Glen V. Borre | William C. Reens
Frank H. Johnson

Reference: Old Kent Bank & Trust Co.

For Complete List of Firm Personnel, See General Section

For full biographical listings, see the Martindale-Hubbell Law Directory

CLARY, NANTZ, WOOD, HOFFIUS, RANKIN & COOPER (AV)

500 Calder Plaza, 250 Monroe Avenue, N.W., 49503-2244
Telephone: 616-459-9487
Telecopier: 616-459-5121

MEMBERS OF FIRM

Harold E. Nelson | Daniel R. Kubiak

ASSOCIATE

Sandra S. Hamilton

Representative Clients: FMB First Michigan Bank, Grand Rapids; NBD Bank, N.A.; United Bank of Michigan;

For Complete List of Firm Personnel, See General Section

For full biographical listings, see the Martindale-Hubbell Law Directory

DAY & SAWDEY, A PROFESSIONAL CORPORATION (AV)

200 Monroe Avenue, Suite 500, 49503-2217
Telephone: 616-774-8121
Telefax: 616-774-0168

George B. Kingston (1889-1965)
John R. Porter (1915-1975)
Charles E. Day, Jr.
Robert W. Sawdey
William A. Hubble
C. Mark Stoppels
James B. Frakie
Larry A. Ver Merris
John Boyko, Jr.
Jonathan F. Thoits
John T. Piggins
Thomas A. DeMeester

John G. Grzybek | Theodore E. Czarnecki

Representative Clients: American National Bank & Trust Company of Chicago; Bank One Dayton, N.A.; Barclays Business Credit, Inc.; Chemical Bank, N.A.; Comerica Bank, N.A.; First of America Bank - West Michigan; Heller Financial, Inc.; Michigan National Bank; National Westminster Bank U.S.A.; Old Kent Bank and Trust Co.

For full biographical listings, see the Martindale-Hubbell Law Directory

DE GROOT, KELLER & VINCENT (AV)

300 Michigan Trust Building, 49503
Telephone: 616-459-6251
Fax: 616-459-6352

MEMBERS OF FIRM

Murray B. De Groot | James M. Keller
Brian D. Vincent

For full biographical listings, see the Martindale-Hubbell Law Directory

MILLER, CANFIELD, PADDOCK AND STONE, P.L.C. (AV)

A Professional Limited Liability Company
Founded in 1852 by Sidney Davy Miller
1200 Campau Square Plaza, 99 Monroe, N.W., P.O. Box 329, 49503-2639
Telephone: 616-454-8656
Fax: 616-776-6322
Detroit, Michigan Office: 150 West Jefferson, Suite 2500, 48226-4415.
Telephone: 313-963-6420.
Fax: 313-496-7500.
Cable Address: "Stem Detroit."
Ann Arbor, Michigan Office: 101 North Main Street, 7th Floor, 48104-1400.
Telephone: 313-663-2445.
Fax: 313-747-7147.
Bloomfield Hills, Michigan Office: Suite 100, Pinehurst Office Center, 1400 North Woodward, 48303-2014.
Telephone: 313-645-5000.
Fax: 313-645-1917.
Howell, Michigan Office: 121 South Barnard Street, Suite 4, 48843-2305.
Telephone: 517-546-7600.
Telecopier: 517-546-6974.
Kalamazoo, Michigan Office: 444 West Michigan Avenue, 49007-3752.
Telephone: 616-381-7030.
Fax: 616-382-0244.
Lansing, Michigan Office: One Michigan Avenue, Suite 900, 48933-1609.
Telephone: 517-487-2070.
Fax: 517-374-6304.
Monroe, Michigan Office: The Executive Centre, 214 East Elm Avenue, 48161-2682.
Telephone: 313-243-2000.
Fax: 313-243-0901.
Washington, D.C. Office: 1225 Nineteenth Street, N.W., Suite 400. 20036.
Telephone: 202-429-5575; 785-0600;
Fax: 202-331-1118; 785-1234.

(See Next Column)

Pensacola, Florida Office: 25 West Cedar 32501.
Telephone: 904-469-1088.
Fax: 904-432-0677.
St. Petersburg Florida Office: 100 Second Avenue S., Suite 7045, 33701.
Telephone: 813-982-6000.
Fax: 813-892-6002.
Gdansk, Poland Office: Suite 322, Dom Technika Building, Ul. Rajska 6, 80-850.
Telephone: 011-485-831-2808.
Fax: 011-485-831-4719.
Warsaw, Poland Office: Ul. Marszalkowska 82, Suite 561, 00-517.
Telephone: 011-482-623-6457 and 6458.
Fax: 011-482-623-6459.

MEMBERS OF FIRM

Thomas J. Heiden (Resident)
Mark E. Putney (Resident)
Thomas C. Phillips
Richard A. Gaffin
Charles S. Mishkind (Detroit, Lansing and Kalamazoo Offices)
Stephen M. Tuuk (Resident)
Robert D. VanderLaan (Resident)
Michael G. Campbell (Resident)
Robert E. Lee Wright
Vernon Bennett III
Douglas W. Crim (Resident)

OF COUNSEL

George J. Slykhouse (Resident)

SENIOR ATTORNEYS

Charles E. Scholl (Resident) | Michael J. Taylor (Resident)
David E. Hathaway (Resident) | David J. Hasper (Resident)

ASSOCIATES

Gary E. Mitchell (Resident) | Bradley C. White
John C. Arndts (Resident) | Meg Hackett Carrier (Resident)

Representative Firm Clients: Chrysler Corp.; Comerica, Inc.; City of Detroit, Mich.; Detroit Tigers, Inc.; First of Michigan; Fretter, Inc.; Ford Motor Co.; Ford Motor Credit Co.; Great Lakes Bancorp; Henry Ford Hospital.

For full biographical listings, see the Martindale-Hubbell Law Directory

VARNUM, RIDDERING, SCHMIDT & HOWLETT (AV)

Bridgewater Place, P.O. Box 352, 49501-0352
Telephone: 616-336-6000
800-262-0011
Facsimile: 616-336-7000
Telex: 1561593 VARN
Lansing, Michigan Office: The Victor Center, Suite 810, 210 North Washington Square, 48933.
Telephone: 517-482-6237.
Facsimile: 517-482-6937.
Kalamazoo, Michigan Office: 350 East Michigan Avenue, 49007.
Telephone: 616-382-2300.
Facsimile: 616-382-2382.
Grand Haven, Michigan Office: 321 Washington Street, P.O. Box 288, 49417.
Telephone: 616-846-7100.
Facsimile: 616-846-7101.
Battle Creek, Michigan Office: 4950 West Dickman Road, Suite B-1, 49015.
Telephone: 616-962-7144.
Detroit, Michigan Office: 440 East Congress, Fourth Floor, 48226.
Telephone: 313-961-1600.
Facsimile: 313-961-1636.

MEMBERS OF FIRM

Timothy J. Curtin
Thomas G. Demling
Jeffrey R. Hughes
Jeffrey D. Smith (Resident at Kalamazoo Office)
Thomas C. Clinton
Robert A. Hendricks
Michael S. McElwee (Resident at Kalamazoo Office)
Joan E. Schleef
Scott A. Huizenga

ASSOCIATES

Jinya Chen | Vicki S. Young
Maureen Potter | Thomas J. Augspurger

Counsel for: First Michigan Bank Corp.; Independent Bank Corp.
Special Counsel for: Comerica Bank, NA.; Michigan National Bank, N.A.; Great Lakes Bank Corp.

For Complete List of Firm Personnel, See General Section

For full biographical listings, see the Martindale-Hubbell Law Directory

WARNER, NORCROSS & JUDD (AV)

900 Old Kent Building, 111 Lyon Street, N.W., 49503-2489
Telephone: 616-752-2000
Fax: 616-752-2500
Muskegon, Michigan Office: 400 Terrace Plaza, P.O. Box 900.
Telephone: 616-727-2600.
Fax: 616-727-2699.
Holland, Michigan Office: Curtis Center, Suite 300, 170 College Avenue.
Telephone: 616-396-9800.
Fax: 616-396-3656.

MEMBERS OF FIRM

Charles E. McCallum | Kathleen M. Hanenburg
Timothy Hillegonds | Stephen B. Grow

(See Next Column)

WARNER, NORCROSS & JUDD—*Continued*

ASSOCIATE

Jeffrey S. Battershall

Representative Clients: Steelcase, Inc.; Bissell, Inc.; Old Kent Bank Financial Corporation; Haworth, Inc.; Country Fresh, Inc.; Challenge Machinery Company; Morbark Industries; Whirlpool Corporation; The Zondervan Corporation; Union Pump Company.

For Complete List of Firm Personnel, See General Section

For full biographical listings, see the Martindale-Hubbell Law Directory

*KALAMAZOO,** Kalamazoo Co.

HOWARD & HOWARD ATTORNEYS, P.C. (AV)

The Kalamazoo Building, Suite 400, 107 West Michigan Avenue, 49007-3956
Telephone: 616-382-1483
Telecopier: 616-382-1568
Bloomfield Hills, Michigan Office: The Pinehurst Office Center, Suite 101, 1400 North Woodward Avenue.
Telephone: 810-645-1483.
Telecopier: 810-645-1568.
Lansing, Michigan Office: The Phoenix Building, Suite 500, 222 Washington Square North.
Telephone: 517-485-1483.
Telecopier: 517-485-1568.
Peoria, Illinois Office: Howard & Howard, P.C., The Creve Coeur Building, Suite 200, 321 Liberty Street.
Telephone: 309-672-1483.
Telecopier: 309-672-1568.

Jeffrey P. Chalmers
William A. Dornbos
Bruce R. Grubb

Representative Clients: For Representative Client list, see General Practice, Kalamazoo, MI.

For Complete List of Firm Personnel, See General Section

For full biographical listings, see the Martindale-Hubbell Law Directory

KREIS, ENDERLE, CALLANDER & HUDGINS, A PROFESSIONAL CORPORATION (AV)

One Moorsbridge, 49002
Telephone: 616-324-3000
Telecopier: 616-324-3010

Russell A. Kreis
Thomas G. King
Robert B. Borsos
Daniel P. Mc Glinn

For Complete List of Firm Personnel, See General Section

For full biographical listings, see the Martindale-Hubbell Law Directory

MILLER, CANFIELD, PADDOCK AND STONE, P.L.C. (AV)

A Professional Limited Liability Company
Founded in 1852 by Sidney Davy Miller
444 West Michigan Avenue, 49007-3752
Telephone: 616-381-7030
Fax: 616-382-0244
Detroit, Michigan Office: 150 West Jefferson, Suite 2500, 48226-4415.
Telephone: 313-963-6420.
Fax: 313-496-7500.
Cable Address: "Stem Detroit."
Ann Arbor, Michigan Office: 101 North Main Street, 7th Floor, 48104-1400.
Telephone: 313-663-2445.
Fax: 313-747-7147.
Bloomfield Hills, Michigan Office: Suite 100, Pinehurst Office Center, 1400 North Woodward, 48303-2014.
Telephone: 313-645-5000.
Fax: 313-645-1917.
Grand Rapids, Michigan Office: 1200 Campau Square Plaza, 99 Monroe, N.W., 49503-2639.
Telephone: 616-454-8656.
Fax: 616-776-6322.
Howell, Michigan Office: 121 South Barnard Street, Suite 4, 48843-2305.
Telephone: 517-546-7600.
Telecopier: 517-546-6974.
Lansing, Michigan Office: One Michigan Avenue, Suite 900, 48933-1609.
Telephone: 517-487-2070.
Fax: 517-374-6304.
Monroe, Michigan Office: The Executive Centre, 214 East Elm Avenue, 48161-2682.
Telephone: 313-243-2000.
Fax: 313-243-0901.
Washington, D.C. Office: 1225 Nineteenth Street, N.W., Suite 400. 20036.
Telephone: 202-429-5575; 785-0600.
Fax: 202-331-1118; 785-1234.
Pensacola, Florida Office: 25 West Cedar, 32501.
Telephone: 904-469-1088.
Fax: 904-432-0677.

(See Next Column)

St. Petersburg, Florida Office: 100 Second Avenue S., Suite 7045,33701.
Telephone: 813-982-6000.
Fax: 813-892-6002.
Gdansk, Poland Office: Suite 322, Dom Technika Building, UI. Rajska 6, 80-850.
Telephone: 011-485-831-2808.
Fax: 011-485-831-4719.
Warsaw, Poland Office: UI. Marszalkowska 82, Suite 561, 00-517.
Telephone: 011-482-623-6457 and 6458.
Fax: 011-482-623-6459.

MEMBER OF FIRM

Eric V. Brown, Jr. (Resident)

RESIDENT ASSOCIATE

Lori L. Purkey

Representative Firm Clients: Chrysler Corp.; Comerica, Inc.; City of Detroit, Mich.; Detroit Tigers, Inc.; First of Michigan; Fretter, Inc.; Ford Motor Co.; Ford Motor Credit Co.; Great Lakes Bancorp; Henry Ford Hospital.

For Complete List of Firm Personnel, See General Section

For full biographical listings, see the Martindale-Hubbell Law Directory

LANSING, Ingham Co.

MILLER, CANFIELD, PADDOCK AND STONE, P.L.C. (AV)

A Professional Limited Liability Company
Founded in 1852 by Sidney Davy Miller
Suite 900, One Michigan Avenue, 48933-1609
Telephone: 517-487-2070
Fax: 517-374-6304
Detroit, Michigan Office: 150 West Jefferson, Suite 2500, 48226-4415.
Telephone: 313-963-6420.
Fax: 313-496-7500.
Cable Address: "Stem Detroit."
Ann Arbor, Michigan Office: 101 North Main Street, 7th Floor, 48104-1400.
Telephone: 313-663-2445.
Fax: 313-747-7147.
Bloomfield Hills, Michigan Office: Suite 100, Pinehurst Office Center, 1400 North Woodward, 48303-2014.
Telephone: 313-645-5000.
Fax: 313-645-1917.
Grand Rapids, Michigan Office: 1200 Campau Square Plaza, 99 Monroe, N.W., 49503-2639.
Telephone: 616-454-8656.
Fax: 616-776-6322.
Howell, Michigan Office: 121 South Barnard Street, Suite 4, 48843-2305.
Telephone: 517-546-7600.
Telecopier: 517-546-6974.
Kalamazoo, Michigan Office: 444 West Michigan Avenue, 49007-3752.
Telephone: 616-381-7030.
Fax: 616-382-0244.
Monroe, Michigan Office: The Executive Centre, 214 East Elm Avenue, 48161-2682.
Telephone: 313-243-2000.
Fax: 313-243-0901.
Washington, D.C. Office: 1225 Nineteenth Street, N.W., Suite 400. 20036.
Telephone: 202-429-5575; 785-0600.
Fax: 202-331-1118; 785-1234.
Pensacola, Florida Office: 25 West Cedar, 32501.
Telephone: 904-469-1088.
Fax: 904-432-0677.
St. Petersburg Office: 100 Second Avenue S., Suite 7045, 33701.
Telephone: 813-982-6000.
Fax: 813-892-6002.
Gdansk, Poland Office: Suite 322, Dom Technika Building, UI. Rajska 6, 80-850.
Telephone: 011-485-831-2808.
Fax: 011-485-831-4719.
Warsaw, Poland Office: UI. Marszalkowska 82, Suite 561, 00-517.
Telephone: 011-482-623-6457 and 6458.
Fax: 011-482-623-6459.

MEMBER OF FIRM

William J. Danhof (Resident)

Representative Firm Clients: Chrysler Corp.; Comerica, Inc.; City of Detroit, Mich.; Detroit Tigers, Inc.; First of Michigan; Fretter, Inc.; Ford Motor Co.; Ford Motor Credit Co.; Great Lakes Bancorp; Henry Ford Hospital.

For Complete List of Firm Personnel, See General Section

For full biographical listings, see the Martindale-Hubbell Law Directory

ROCHESTER, Oakland Co.

SHERMETA, CHIMKO AND KILPATRICK, P.C. (AV)

445 South Livernois, Suite 221, P.O. Box 5016, 48308
Telephone: 810-652-8200
Fax: 810-652-1292
Detroit, Michigan Office: Ford Building, 48226.
Telephone: 313-961-4848.
Fax: 313-961-4365.

(See Next Column)

SHERMETA, CHIMKO AND KILPATRICK P.C., *Rochester—Continued*

Grandville, Michigan Office: 4264 Turtle Bend Drive.
Telephone: 616-531-6980.
Fax: 616-531-7475.

Douglass H. Shermeta
Darryl J. Chimko
Richardo I. Kilpatrick
Barbara L. Adams
Karen E. Evangelista
Henry J. Mittelstaedt III
Thomas L. Beadle

Mariana J. Richmond
Robert D. Dzialo
Tammy L. Terry
Kelly L. Scola
Karen Lamoreaux Rice
John L. Burket
Christopher E. Mcneely
Richard L. McDonnell
Samuel D. Sweet
David R. Shook
Lisa E. Gocha
Sheryl S. Zamplas
Patrick (Casey) Coston
Krispen S. Carroll

For full biographical listings, see the Martindale-Hubbell Law Directory

*SAGINAW,** Saginaw Co.

BRAUN KENDRICK FINKBEINER (AV)

8th Floor Second National Bank Building, 48607
Telephone: 517-753-3461
Telecopier: 517-753-3951
Bay City, Michigan Office: 201 Phoenix Building, P.O. Box 2039.
Telephone: 517-895-8505.
Telecopier: 517-895-8437.

MEMBERS OF FIRM

J. Richard Kendrick
James V. Finkbeiner
Hugo E. Braun, Jr.
Morton E. Weldy
C. Patrick Kaltenbach
Harold J. Blanchet, Jr.
Kenneth W. Kable
E. Louis Ognisanti
Bruce L. Dalrymple
Michael H. Allen
Robert A. Kendrick
Charles A. Gilfeather
Thomas R. Luplow
John A. Decker
Michael J. Sauer
Timothy L Curtiss
Scott C. Strattard
Craig W. Horn
Francis J. Keating
Barry M. Levine
Brian F. Bauer

ASSOCIATES

Judith A. Lincoln
Irenna M. Garapetian
Carolyn Pollock Cary
Brian S. Makaric
William G. Tishkoff

OF COUNSEL

Thomas M. Murphy

Representative Clients: The Dow Chemical Co.; General Motors Corp.; Lobdell Emery Manufacturing Co.; Merrill, Lynch, Inc.; Saginaw General Hospital; Saginaw News; The Wickes Foundation.

For Complete List of Firm Personnel, See General Section

For full biographical listings, see the Martindale-Hubbell Law Directory

SOUTHFIELD, Oakland Co.

GOLDSTEIN, BERSHAD AND FRIED, PROFESSIONAL CORPORATION (AV)

4000 Town Center, Suite 1200, 48075
Telephone: 810-355-5300
Telefax: 810-355-4644

Charles L. Goldstein (1896-1986)
Alan P. Goldstein (Retired, 1988)
Stanley M. Bershad
Martin L. Fried

Michael D. Lieberman

Reference: The Comerica Bank.

For full biographical listings, see the Martindale-Hubbell Law Directory

*TRAVERSE CITY,** Grand Traverse Co.

MURCHIE, CALCUTT & BOYNTON (AV)

109 East Front Street, Suite 300, 49684
Telephone: 616-947-7190
Fax: 616-947-4341

Robert B. Murchie (1894-1975)
Harry Calcutt
Jack E. Boynton
William B. Calcutt
Mark A. Burnheimer
Dawn M. Rogers

ASSOCIATES

George W. Hyde, III
Ralph J. Dilley (Not admitted in MI)

General Counsel for: Old Kent Bank-Grand Traverse; Northwestern Savings Bank & Trust; Central-State Bancorp; Traverse City Record Eagle; WPNB-7 & WTOM-4; Emergency Consultants, Inc.; National Guardian Risk Retention Group, Inc.; Farmers Mutual Insurance Co.; Environmental Solutions, Inc.

(See Next Column)

Local Counsel For: Consumers Power Co.

For full biographical listings, see the Martindale-Hubbell Law Directory

TROY, Oakland Co.

JACOB & WEINGARTEN, PROFESSIONAL CORPORATION (AV)

2301 West Big Beaver Road, Suite 777, 48084
Telephone: 810-649-1900
Facsimile: 810-649-2920
West Palm Beach, Florida Office: 1555 Palm Beach Lake Boulevard, Suite 1510, 33401.
Telephone: 407-640-5600.
Facsimile: 407-683-0799.

Peter A. Nathan (Resident, West Palm Beach, Florida Office)
Steven P. Schubiner
Howard S. Sher
Phillip J. Neuman
Robert K. Siegel

Representative Clients: Afco Credit Corporation; IBM Credit Corp.; Michigan National Bank; State Bond and Mortgage Life Insurance Company.

For full biographical listings, see the Martindale-Hubbell Law Directory

MINNESOTA

*DULUTH,** St. Louis Co.

FRYBERGER, BUCHANAN, SMITH & FREDERICK, P.A. (AV)

700 Lonsdale Building, 302 West Superior Street, 55802
Telephone: 218-722-0861
Fax: 218-722-9568
St. Paul Office: Capitol Center, 386 N. Wabasha.
Telephone: 612-221-1044.

Bruce Buchanan
Nick Smith
Harold A. Frederick
Dexter A. Larsen
James H. Stewart
Robert E. Toftey
Michael K. Donovan
Neal J. Hessen
Joseph J. Mihalek
Shawn M. Dunlevy
Anne Lewis
David R. Oberstar
Abbot G. Apter
Michael Cowles
Martha M. Markusen

Daniel D. Maddy
Stephanie A. Ball
Paul B. Kilgore
Mary Frances Skala
Rolf A. Lindberg (Resident, St. Paul Office)
Kevin T. Walli (Resident, St. Paul Office)
Kevin J. Dunlevy (Resident, St. Paul Office)
Teresa M. O'Toole
Dean R. Borgh
James F. Voegeli (Resident, St. Paul Office)
James A. Lund
Mark D. Britton (Resident, St. Paul Office)
Judith A. Zollar

OF COUNSEL

Herschel B. Fryberger, Jr.

Representative Clients: North Shore Bank of Commerce; General Motors Acceptance Corp.; Western Lake Superior Sanitary District; City of Duluth; First Bank Minnesota (N.A.); Norwest Bank Minnesota North N.A.; Airport State Bank; Park State Bank; M & I First National Bank of Superior; St. Lukes Hospital Duluth.

For full biographical listings, see the Martindale-Hubbell Law Directory

*MINNEAPOLIS,** Hennepin Co.

HOLPER WELSH & MITCHELL, LTD. (AV)

750 Pillsbury Center, 200 South Sixth Street, 55402
Telephone: 612-373-2200
FAX: 612-373-2222

Richard D. Holper
Mary Ann Welsh
Ralph V. Mitchell, Jr.

John C. Holper
Karen M. Edwards

OF COUNSEL

David D. Hammargren

For full biographical listings, see the Martindale-Hubbell Law Directory

LOVETT & SMITH, LTD. (AV)

100 South Fifth Street, Suite 2250, 55402
Telephone: 612-339-4567

Thomas G. Lovett, Jr.
Glenn L. Smith
Larry B. Ricke

For full biographical listings, see the Martindale-Hubbell Law Directory

Minneapolis—Continued

MANSFIELD & TANICK, P.A. (AV)

International Centre, 900 Second Avenue South, 15th Floor, 55402
Telephone: 612-339-4295
Fax: 612-339-3161

Seymour J. Mansfield
Marshall H. Tanick
Earl H. Cohen
Robert A. Johnson
Teresa J. Ayling
Sholly A. Blustin
Catherine M. Klimek
Phillip J. Trobaugh
Richard J. Fuller

OF COUNSEL

Daniel S. Kleinberger

For full biographical listings, see the Martindale-Hubbell Law Directory

*ST. PAUL,** Ramsey Co.

BUCKLEY & JENSEN (AV)

1614 American National Bank Building, 101 East Fifth Street, 55101
Telephone: 612-224-3361
Fax: 612-297-6187

Sheridan J. Buckley
Mary Jo A. Jensen

For full biographical listings, see the Martindale-Hubbell Law Directory

STEIN & MOORE, P.A. (AV)

10th Floor, Minnesota Building, 55101
Telephone: 612-224-9683
Telecopier: 612-223-5212

Peter B. Stein
Ralph L. Moore
Jonathan (Jack) R. Fay
Peter R. Wilson

Reference: American National Bank of St. Paul.

For full biographical listings, see the Martindale-Hubbell Law Directory

MISSISSIPPI

*ABERDEEN,** Monroe Co.

HOLCOMB, DUNBAR, CONNELL, CHAFFIN & WILLARD, A PROFESSIONAL ASSOCIATION (AV)

109 1/2 West Commerce Street, P.O. Box 866, 39730
Telephone: 601-369-8800
Facsimile: 601-369-9404
Jackson, Mississippi Office: 111 East Capitol Street, Suite 290, P.O. Box 2990, 39207-2990.
Telephone: 601-948-0048.
Facsimile: 601-948-0050.
Clarksdale, Mississippi Office: 152 Delta Avenue, P.O. Box 368, 38614.
Telephone: 601-627-2241.
Facsimile: 601-627-9788.
Oxford, Mississippi Office: 1217 Jackson Avenue, P.O. Drawer 707, 38655.
Telephone: 601-234-8775.
Facsimile: 601-234-8638.
Southhaven, Mississippi Office: Suite 1, 8727 Northwest Drive, P.O. Box 190, 38671.
Telephone: 601-342-6806.
Facsimile: 601-342-6792.

Craig M. Geno
Robert H. Faulks

Counsel for: United Southern Bank; Mississippi Power & Light Co.; Mississippi Valley Gas Co.; Aetna Casualty & Surety Co.; Southern Farm Bureau Casualty Insurance Co.; South Central Bell Telephone Co.; State Farm Mutual Automobile Insurance Co.; Fireman's Fund Insurance Cos.; Deere & Co.; Navistar International Transportation Corp.

For Complete List of Firm Personnel, See General Section

For full biographical listings, see the Martindale-Hubbell Law Directory

PATTERSON & PATTERSON (AV)

304 East Jefferson Street, P.O. Box 663, 39730
Telephone: 601-369-2476
1-800-523-9975
FAX: 601-369-9806

MEMBERS OF FIRM

Robert D. Patterson
Jan P. Patterson

Local Counsel for: National Bank of Commerce of Mississippi; American Colloid Company; Vista Chemical Co.; Pruet Production Co.; Arco Oil & Gas Co.; Chemical Corporation; Unimin Corporation.

For Complete List of Firm Personnel, See General Section

For full biographical listings, see the Martindale-Hubbell Law Directory

*CLARKSDALE,** Coahoma Co.

HOLCOMB, DUNBAR, CONNELL, CHAFFIN & WILLARD, A PROFESSIONAL ASSOCIATION (AV)

152 Delta Avenue, P.O. Box 368, 38614
Telephone: 601-627-2241
Facsimile: 601-627-9788
Jackson, Mississippi Office: 111 East Capitol Street, Suite 290, P.O. Box 2990, 39207-2990.
Telephone: 601-948-0048.
Facsimile: 601-948-0050.
Aberdeen, Mississippi Office: 109 1/2 West Commerce Street, P.O. Box 866, 39730.
Telephone: 601-369-8800.
Facsimile: 601-369-9404.
Oxford, Mississippi Office: 1217 Jackson Avenue, P.O. Drawer 707, 38655.
Telephone: 601-234-8775.
Facsimile: 601-234-8638.
Southaven, Mississippi Office: Suite 1, 8727 Northwest Drive, 38671.
Telephone: 601-342-6806.
Facsimile: 601-342-6792.

William M. Chaffin
William A. Baskin

Counsel for: United Southern Bank; Mississippi Power & Light Co.; Mississippi Valley Gas Co.; Aetna Casualty & Surety Co.; Southern Farm Bureau Casualty Insurance Co.; South Central Bell Telephone Co.; State Farm Mutual Fire & Casualty Insurance Co.; Fireman's Fund Insurance Cos.; Deere & Co.; Navistar International Transportation Corp.

For Complete List of Firm Personnel, See General Section

For full biographical listings, see the Martindale-Hubbell Law Directory

*GULFPORT,** Harrison Co.

DUKES, DUKES, KEATING AND FANECA, P.A. (AV)

2308 East Beach Boulevard, P.O. Drawer W, 39501
Telephone: 601-868-1111
FAX: 601-863-2886

Hugh D. Keating
William H. Pettey, Jr.

Nick B. Roberts, Jr.

For full biographical listings, see the Martindale-Hubbell Law Directory

*JACKSON,** Hinds Co.

HOLCOMB, DUNBAR, CONNELL, CHAFFIN & WILLARD, A PROFESSIONAL ASSOCIATION (AV)

111 East Capitol Street, Suite 290, P.O. Box 2990, 39207-2990
Telephone: 601-948-0048
Facsimile: 601-948-0050
Clarksdale, Mississippi Office: 152 Delta Avenue, P.O. Box 368, 38614.
Telephone: 601-627-2241.
Facsimile: 601-627-9788.
Aberdeen, Mississippi Office: 109 1/2 West Commerce Street, P.O. Box 866, 39730.
Telephone: 601-369-8800.
Facsimile: 601-369-9404.
Oxford, Mississippi Office: 1217 Jackson Avenue, P.O. Drawer 707, 38655.
Telephone: 601-234-8775.
Facsimile: 601-234-8638.
Southaven, Mississippi Office: Suite 1, 8727 Northwest Drive, P.O. Box 190, 38671.
Telephone: 601-342-6806.
Facsimile: 601-342-6792.

Craig M. Geno
Thomas J. Suszek
John H. Dunbar
William A. Baskin
C. Michael Pumphrey
Robert H. Faulks
Jeffrey Kyle Tyree
Stephan L. McDavid
Barry C. Blackburn

Counsel for: United Southern Bank; Mississippi Power & Light Co.; Mississippi Valley Gas Co.; Aetna Casualty & Surety Co.; Southern Farm Bureau Casualty Insurance Co.; South Central Bell Telephone Co.; State Farm Fire & Casualty Insurance Co.; Fireman's Fund Insurance Cos.; Deere & Co.; Navistar International Transportation Corp.

For Complete List of Firm Personnel, See General Section

For full biographical listings, see the Martindale-Hubbell Law Directory

WATKINS & EAGER (AV)

Suite 300 The Emporium Building, P.O. Box 650, 39205
Telephone: 601-948-6470
Facsimile: (601) 354-3623

MEMBERS OF FIRM

John G. Corlew
Jamie G. Houston, III
Frank J. Hammond, III
Paul J. Stephens
J. Fred Spencer, Jr.

(See Next Column)

WATKINS & EAGER, *Jackson—Continued*

ASSOCIATE

Louis B. Lanoux

Representative Clients: Resolution Trust Corp.; Federal Deposit Insurance Corp.; Trustmark National Bank.

For Complete List of Firm Personnel, See General Section

For full biographical listings, see the Martindale-Hubbell Law Directory

*OXFORD,** Lafayette Co.

FREELAND & FREELAND (AV)

1013 Jackson Avenue, P.O. Box 269, 38655
Telephone: 601-234-3414
Telecopier: 601-234-0604

MEMBERS OF FIRM

T. H. Freeland, III
T. H. Freeland, IV
J. Hale Freeland

ASSOCIATE

Paul W. Crutcher

Representative Clients: The Ohio Casualty Group; Crum & Forester.

For full biographical listings, see the Martindale-Hubbell Law Directory

HOLCOMB, DUNBAR, CONNELL, CHAFFIN & WILLARD, A PROFESSIONAL ASSOCIATION (AV)

1217 Jackson Avenue P.O. Drawer 707, 38655
Telephone: 601-234-8775
Facsimile: 601-234-8638
Jackson, Mississippi Office: 111 East Capitol Street, Suite 290. P.O. Box 2990, 39207-2990.
Telephone: 601-948-0048.
Facsimile: 601-948-0050.
Clarksdale, Mississippi Office: 152 Delta Avenue, P.O. Box 368, 38614.
Telephone: 601-627-2241.
Facsimile: 601-627-9788.
Aberdeen, Mississippi Office: 109 1/2 West Commerce Street, P.O. Box 866, 39730.
Telephone: 601-369-8800.
Facsimile: 601-369-9404.
Southaven, Mississippi Office: Suite 1, 8727 Northwest Drive, P.O. Box 190, 38671.
Telephone: 601-342-6806.
Facsimile: 601-342-6792.

Craig M. Geno
Thomas J. Suszek
John H. Dunbar
Stephan L. McDavid

Counsel for: United Southern Bank; Mississippi Power & Light Co.; Mississippi Valley Gas Co.; Aetna Casualty & Surety Co.; Southern Farm Bureau Casualty Insurance Co.; South Central Bell Telephone Co.; State Farm Mutual Fire & Casualty Insurance Co.; Fireman's Fund Insurance Cos.; Deere & Co.; Navistar International Transportation Corp.

For Complete List of Firm Personnel, See General Section

For full biographical listings, see the Martindale-Hubbell Law Directory

SOUTHAVEN, De Soto Co.

HOLCOMB, DUNBAR, CONNELL, CHAFFIN & WILLARD, A PROFESSIONAL ASSOCIATION (AV)

Suite 1, 8727 Northwest Drive, P.O. Box 190, 38671
Telephone: 601-342-6806
Facsimile: 601-342-6792
Jackson, Mississippi Office: 111 East Capitol Street, Suite 290, P.O. Box 2990, 39207-2990.
Telephone: 601-948-0048.
Facsimile: 601-948-0050.
Clarksdale, Mississippi Office: 152 Delta Avenue, P.O. Box 368, 38614.
Telephone: 601-627-2241.
Facsimile: 601-627-9788.
Aberdeen, Mississippi Office: 109 1/2 West Commerce Street, P.O. Box 866, 39730.
Telephone: 601-369-8800.
Facsimile: 601-369-9404.
Oxford, Mississippi Office: 1217 Jackson Avenue, P.O. Drawer 707, 38655.
Telephone: 601-234-8775.
Facsimile: 601-234-8638.

William M. Chaffin
Thomas J. Suszek
William A. Baskin
Barry C. Blackburn

Counsel For: United Southern Bank; Trustmark National Bank; Sunburst National Bank; Deposit Guaranty National Bank; Mississippi Power & Light Co.; Mississippi Valley Gas Co.; South Central Bell Telephone Co.; Dunavant Enterprises, Inc.; Deere & Co.; Navistar International Transportation Corp.

For Complete List of Firm Personnel, See General Section

For full biographical listings, see the Martindale-Hubbell Law Directory

MISSOURI

KANSAS CITY, Jackson, Clay & Platte Cos.

BAKER, STERCHI & COWDEN (AV)

Suite 2100 Commerce Tower, 911 Main Street, P.O. Box 13566, 64199-3566
Telephone: 816-471-2121
FAX: 816-472-0288
Overland Park, Kansas Office: 51 Corporate Woods, 9393 West 110th Street, Suite 508.
Telephone: 913-451-6752.

MEMBERS OF FIRM

Thomas O. Baker
Thomas N. Sterchi
John W. Cowden
Thomas E. Rice, Jr.
Timothy S. Frets
Evan A. Douthit
Phillip C. Rouse
R. Douglas Gentile
James T. Seigfreid, Jr.
Robert A. Babcock
Peter F. Travis
John P. Poland

ASSOCIATES

Quentin L. Brown
James R. Jarrow
James S. Kreamer
Mary C. O'Connell
Randall L. Rhodes
D. Gregory Stonebarger
Kara Trouslot Stubbs
Robert M. Carroll
Stacy L. Cook
Patricia A. Sexton
Brent David Thomas

For full biographical listings, see the Martindale-Hubbell Law Directory

SWANSON, MIDGLEY, GANGWERE, KITCHIN & MCLARNEY, L.L.C. (AV)

1500 Commerce Trust Building, 922 Walnut, 64106-1848
Telephone: 816-842-6100
Overland Park, Kansas Office: The NCAA Building, Suite 350, 6201 College Boulevard.
Telephone: 816-842-6100.

Robert W. McKinley
Neil Loren Johnson

Counsel for: General Electric Co.; Chrysler Corp.; Conoco, Inc.; Yellow Freight System, Inc.; The Prudential Insurance Co. of America; Metropolitan Life Insurance Co.; National Collegiate Athletic Assn.; Land Title Insurance Co.; Safeway Stores, Inc.; The Lee Apparel Co.

For Complete List of Firm Personnel, See General Section

For full biographical listings, see the Martindale-Hubbell Law Directory

ST. LOUIS, (Independent City)

STONE, LEYTON & GERSHMAN, A PROFESSIONAL CORPORATION (AV)

7733 Forsyth Boulevard, Suite 500, 63105
Telephone: 314-721-7011
Telefax: 314-721-8660

Steven M. Stone
Steven H. Leyton
Jeffrey S. Gershman
Lynn G. Carey
Suzanne L. Zatlin
E. Rebecca Case
Thomas P. Rosenfeld
Paul J. Puricelli

Mary H. Moorkamp

OF COUNSEL

Sidney L. Stone

For full biographical listings, see the Martindale-Hubbell Law Directory

MONTANA

*BILLINGS,** Yellowstone Co.

CROWLEY, HAUGHEY, HANSON, TOOLE & DIETRICH (AV)

500 Transwestern II, 490 North 31st Street, P.O. Box 2529, 59103
Telephone: 406-252-3441
Fax: 406-259-4159
Helena, Montana Office: IBM Building, 100 North Park Avenue, Suite 300, 59601.
Telephone: 406-449-4165.
Fax: 406-449-5149.

(See Next Column)

CROWLEY, HAUGHEY, HANSON, TOOLE & DIETRICH—*Continued*

MEMBERS OF FIRM

William D. Lamdin, III
Malcolm H. Goodrich
Michael S. Dockery
Renee L. Coppock

Representative Clients: Farm Credit Bank; Northwest Farm Credit Services, ACA; First Interstate Bank of Commerce; General Motors Acceptance Corp.; Manufacturer's Hanover Trust; John Deere Co.; Mutual Life Insurance Co., N.Y.; Connecticut Mutual Life; PLM International; Country Kitchen International, Inc.

For Complete List of Firm Personnel, See General Section

For full biographical listings, see the Martindale-Hubbell Law Directory

WRIGHT, TOLLIVER AND GUTHALS A PROFESSIONAL SERVICE CORPORATION (AV)

Windsor Court, 10 North 27th Street, P.O. Box 1977, 59103-1977
Telephone: 406-245-3071
Telecopier: 406-245-3074

Kenneth D. Tolliver
Joel E. Guthals
Virginia A. Bryan

Susan Fisher Stevens
Jeffery A. Hunnes
J. Reuss
Kristin L. Omvig

For full biographical listings, see the Martindale-Hubbell Law Directory

NEBRASKA

*OMAHA,** Douglas Co.

BRASHEAR & GINN (AV)

800 Metropolitan Federal Plaza, 1623 Farnam Street, 68102-2106
Telephone: 402-348-1000; 800-746-4444
Telecopier: 402-348-1111

Robert V. Ginn
Julia L. Gold

Brad C. Epperly

Representative Clients: APX Mortgage Services, Palatine, Illinois; Federal Deposit Insurance Corporation, Washington, D.C.; The First National Bank of Sioux Center, Sioux Center, Iowa; Green Tree Financial Corporation, Sioux Falls, South Dakota; Nissan Motor Acceptance Corporation, Dallas, Texas; Resolution Trust Corporation, Washington, D.C.; TransAmerica Commercial Finance Corporation, Chicago, Illinois; Transportation Finance & Management, Inc., Omaha, Nebraska.

For Complete List of Firm Personnel, See General Section

For full biographical listings, see the Martindale-Hubbell Law Directory

DWYER, POHREN, WOOD, HEAVEY, GRIMM, GOODALL & LAZER (AV)

A Partnership including Professional Corporations
Suite 400, 8712 West Dodge Road, 68114
Telephone: 402-392-0101
Telefax: 402-392-1011

MEMBERS OF FIRM

Robert V. Dwyer, Jr.
Mark L. Goodall
Edward F. Pohren
Michael L. Lazer
W. Eric Wood (P.C.)
James D. Loerts
Michael W. Heavey (P.C.)
Lisa A. Sarver
Andrew E. Grimm
Shawn M. Ilg

Representative Clients: K-Products, Inc.; Deutsche Credit Corp.; Purina Mills, Inc.; Bishop Clarkson Memorial Hospital, Omaha, Nebraska; Nebraska Hospital Association; Strategic Air Command Federal Credit Union; Heller Financial, Inc.; Fordmotor Credit Company; National Medical Enterprises, Inc.; CETAC Technologies, Inc.

For full biographical listings, see the Martindale-Hubbell Law Directory

NEVADA

*LAS VEGAS,** Clark Co.

ALBRIGHT, STODDARD, WARNICK & ALBRIGHT, A PROFESSIONAL CORPORATION (AV)

Quail Park I, Building D-4, 801 South Rancho Drive, 89106
Telephone: 702-384-7111
FAX: 702-384-0605

(See Next Column)

G. Vern Albright
Whitney B. Warnick
William H. Stoddard
G. Mark Albright

Michael W. Brimley
Gavin C. Jangard
D. Chris Albright

Representative Clients: Tokio Marine and Fire Ins. Co.; INAPRO, a CIGNA Co.; Nevada Ready Mix; North American Health Care, Inc. (Nursing Home); Royal Insurance; First Security Bank of Utah; Nevada Community Bank; Nationwide Insurance Co.; Liberty Mutual Insurance; CB Commercial.

For full biographical listings, see the Martindale-Hubbell Law Directory

ALVERSON, TAYLOR, MORTENSEN & NELSON (AV)

3821 W. Charleston Boulevard, 89102
Telephone: 702-384-7000
FAX: 702-385-7000

MEMBERS OF FIRM

J. Bruce Alverson
Erven T. Nelson
Eric K. Taylor
LeAnn Sanders
David J. Mortensen
David R. Clayson

ASSOCIATES

Milton J. Eichacker
Kenneth M. Marias
Douglas D. Gerrard
Jeffrey H. Ballin
Marie Ellerton
Jeffrey W. Daly
James H. Randall
Kenneth R. Ivory
Peter Dubowsky
Edward D. Boyack
Hayley B. Chambers
Sandra Smagac
Michael D. Stevenson
Jill M. Chase
Cookie Lea Olshein
Francis F. Lin

Representative Clients: Citibank; First Interstate Bank; Federal Deposit Insurance Corporation (FDIC); Resolution Trust Corporation (RTC); Norwest Bank; Norwest Financial; The CIT Group; Countrywide Funding Corporation; Overseas Chinese Banking Corporation.

For full biographical listings, see the Martindale-Hubbell Law Directory

HALE, LANE, PEEK, DENNISON AND HOWARD (AV)

Suite 800, Nevada Financial Center, 2300 West Sahara Avenue, Box 8, 89102
Telephone: 702-362-5118
Fax: 702-365-6940
Reno, Nevada Office: Porsche Building, 100 West Liberty Street, Tenth Floor, P.O. Box 3237.
Telephone: 702-786-7900.
Telefax: 702-786-6179.

MEMBERS OF FIRM

Lenard E. Schwartzer
Donald L. Christensen

ASSOCIATE

Georganne W. Bradley

Representative Clients: Commonwealth Land Title Insurance Co.; Transamerica Insurance Co.

For Complete List of Firm Personnel, See General Section

For full biographical listings, see the Martindale-Hubbell Law Directory

JOLLEY, URGA, WIRTH & WOODBURY (AV)

Suite 800 Bank of America Plaza, 300 South Fourth Street, 89101
Telephone: 702-385-5161
Telecopier: 702-382-6814
Boulder City, Nevada Office: Suite 105, 1000 Nevada Highway.
Telephone: 702-293-3674.

MEMBERS OF FIRM

William R. Urga
Stephanie M. Smith
Donald E. Brookhyser

ASSOCIATES

Allen D. Emmel
Brian E. Holthus

Representative Clients: First Interstate Bank of Nevada; Nevada State Bank; First Nationwide Bank; PriMerit Bank; General Motors Acceptance Corp.; Ford Motor Credit Co.; Nissan Motor Acceptance Corp.; Toyota Motor Credit Corporation; Hyundai Motor Finance Co.

For Complete List of Firm Personnel, See General Section

For full biographical listings, see the Martindale-Hubbell Law Directory

JONES, JONES, CLOSE & BROWN, CHARTERED (AV)

Suite 700, Bank of America Plaza, 300 South Fourth Street, 89101-6026
Telephone: 702-385-4202
Telecopier: 702-384-2276
Reno, Nevada Office: 290 South Arlington.
Telephone: 702-322-3811.
Telecopier: 702-348-0886.

(See Next Column)

JONES, JONES, CLOSE & BROWN CHARTERED, *Las Vegas—Continued*

Janet L. Chubb (Resident, Reno Office)
Richard F. Holley

Representative Clients: Bank of America-Nevada; First Interstate Bank of Nevada; Lawyers Title; Chrysler Credit Corporation; Western Acceptance Corporation; Southern Farm Bureau; Life Insurance Company; Federal Deposit Insurance Corporation; Resolution Trust Corporation; Southwest Gas Corporation.

For Complete List of Firm Personnel, See General Section

For full biographical listings, see the Martindale-Hubbell Law Directory

JOHN PETER LEE, LTD. (AV)

830 Las Vegas Boulevard South, 89101
Telephone: 702-382-4044
Telecopy: 702-383-9950

John Peter Lee

Barney C. Ales
Nancy L. Allf
Theresa M. Dowling
Paul C. Ray

For Complete List of Firm Personnel, See General Section

For full biographical listings, see the Martindale-Hubbell Law Directory

LIONEL SAWYER & COLLINS (AV)

1700 Bank of America Plaza, 300 South Fourth Street, 89101
Telephone: 702-383-8888
Fax: 702-383-8845
Reno, Nevada Office: Suite 1100, Bank of America Plaza, 50 West Liberty Street.
Telephone: 702-788-8666.
Fax: 702-788-8682.

MEMBERS OF FIRM

Rodney M. Jean
Jennifer A. Smith (Resident, Reno Office)
Laurel Elizabeth Davis

Representative Clients: Heller Financial, Inc.; Home Federal Savings Bank; U.S. Bancorp Financial; City of Las Vegas Redevelopment Agency; California Federal Bank; ITT Federal Bank.

For Complete List of Firm Personnel, See General Section

For full biographical listings, see the Martindale-Hubbell Law Directory

SCHRECK, JONES, BERNHARD, WOLOSON & GODFREY, CHARTERED (AV)

600 East Charleston Boulevard, 89104
Telephone: 702-382-2101
Fax: 702-382-8135

Frank A. Schreck
Leslie Terry Jones
Peter C. Bernhard
Kenneth A. Woloson
John A. Godfrey
David D. Johnson
James R. Chamberlain
Michelle L. Morgando
Lance C. Earl
Thomas R. Canham
Sean T. McGowan
Dawn M. Cica
F. Edward Mulholland, II
Todd L. Bice
James J. Pisanelli
Ellen L. Schulhofer
John M. McManus

OF COUNSEL

Howard W. Cannon

For full biographical listings, see the Martindale-Hubbell Law Directory

*RENO,** Washoe Co.

HALE, LANE, PEEK, DENNISON AND HOWARD (AV)

Porsche Building, 100 West Liberty Street, Tenth Floor, P.O. Box 3237, 89501
Telephone: 702-786-7900
Telefax: 702-786-6179
Las Vegas, Nevada Office: Suite 800, Nevada Financial Center, 2300 West Sahara Avenue, Box 8.
Telephone: 702-362-5118.
Fax: 702-365-6940.

MEMBERS OF FIRM

Lenard E. Schwartzer
Donald L. Christensen

Representative Clients: Beneficial Mortgage Company of Nevada; First State Bank; NationsBank; Homes & Land Publishing Corp.; Bank of the West.

For Complete List of Firm Personnel, See General Section

For full biographical listings, see the Martindale-Hubbell Law Directory

JONES, JONES, CLOSE & BROWN, CHARTERED (AV)

290 South Arlington, Suite 200, 89504
Telephone: 702-322-3811
Telecopier: 702-348-0886
Las Vegas, Nevada Office: Suite 700, Bank of America Plaza. 300 South Fourth Street.
Telephone: 702-385-4202.
Telecopier: 702-384-2276.

Janet L. Chubb

M. Celeste Luce

Reference: Bank of America, Nevada.

For full biographical listings, see the Martindale-Hubbell Law Directory

NEW JERSEY

ATLANTIC CITY, Atlantic Co.

COOPER PERSKIE APRIL NIEDELMAN WAGENHEIM & LEVENSON, A PROFESSIONAL ASSOCIATION (AV)

1125 Atlantic Avenue, 08401-4891
Telephone: 609-344-3161
FAX: 609-344-0939
Northfield, New Jersey Office: 2111 New Road.
Telephone: 609-383-1300.
FAX: 609-383-1375.
Cherry Hill, New Jersey Office: 1415 Route 70 East, Cherry Hill Plaza, Suite 305.
Telephone: 609-795-9110.
FAX: 609-795-8641.
Wildwood, New Jersey Office: 3200 Pacific Avenue, P.O. Box 333.
Telephone: 609-729-1212.
FAX: 609-522-2544.

James L. Cooper
Lawrence M. Perskie (Retired)
Lewis B. April
Louis Niedelman
Ronald A. Wagenheim
Lloyd D. Levenson
Michael Jacobson (Resident, Northfield Office)
Frank A. Petro
Kenneth D. Wolfe
Charles A. Matison
Alan I. Gould (Resident, Wildwood Office)
Barry D. Cohen
Gerard W. Quinn
Russell L. Lichtenstein
Robert E. Salad
Steven D. Scherzer (Resident, Northfield Office)
Paul Tendler
Susan Petro
Eric A. Browndorf (Resident, Northfield Office)
John F. Collins
Rona Zucker Kaplan
Michael R. Litke

Arthur Korth
Anthony P. Monzo
William J. Kohler
Laura L. McAllister
Christine M. Coté
Christopher M. Baylinson
Scott R. Silverman
Joseph D. Deal (Resident, Cherry Hill Office)
Kevin S. Smith
Geralyn A. Furphy (Resident, Cherry Hill Office)
Pacifico S. Agnellini
James S. Weiss (Resident, Northfield Office)
Alan R. Angelo (Resident, Northfield Office)
Renata D. Lowenbraun
Lisa J. Abramson
Epiphany McGuigan

OF COUNSEL

Emanuel L. Levin
Liane P. Levenson

Representative Clients: Aetna Casualty Assurety Co.; Alexsis, Inc.; Commercial Union General Accident; Hartford Insurance Group; Prudential Insurance Co. of America; Reliance Insurance Co.

For full biographical listings, see the Martindale-Hubbell Law Directory

CHERRY HILL, Camden Co.

DAVIS, REBERKENNY & ABRAMOWITZ, A PROFESSIONAL CORPORATION (AV)

(Formerly Starr, Summerill & Davis and Hyland, Davis & Reberkenny, P.A. and Davis & Reberkenny, A Professional Corporation)
499 Cooper Landing Road, P.O. Box 5459, 08002
Telephone: 609-667-6000
Telecopier: 609-667-7434

William D. Hogan
Arthur J. Abramowitz
Harry A. Horwitz
Dean C. Waldt

David M. Brent
Andrew B. Altenburg, Jr.

OF COUNSEL

William Lipkin

For full biographical listings, see the Martindale-Hubbell Law Directory

FLORHAM PARK, Morris Co.

HACK, PIRO, O'DAY, MERKLINGER, WALLACE & MCKENNA, P.A. (AV)

30 Columbia Turnpike, P.O. Box 941, 07932-0941
Telephone: 201-301-6500
Fax: 201-301-0094

David L. Hack
John M. McKenna

Angela J. Mendelsohn
John F. Lanahan
Michelle M. Monte
Rosemarie Deehan Berard

Representative Clients: Cenlar Federal Savings Bank; County Mortgage Company, Inc.; First Fidelity Bank, N.A., N.J.; Citicorp Mortgage, Inc.; Aetna Life & Casualty Co.; Freddie Mac; Marine Midland Bank.

For Complete List of Firm Personnel, See General Section

For full biographical listings, see the Martindale-Hubbell Law Directory

*HACKENSACK,** Bergen Co.

SHAPIRO & SHAPIRO (AV)

Continental Plaza II, 411 Hackensack Avenue, 07601
Telephone: 201-488-3900
Fax: 201-488-9481

Robert P. Shapiro
Susan W. Shapiro (1943-1990)
John P. Di Iorio

ASSOCIATES

David O. Marcus
Robert F. Green

Reference: National Community Bank.

For full biographical listings, see the Martindale-Hubbell Law Directory

HADDONFIELD, Camden Co.

WEINBERG, MCCORMICK AND CHATZINOFF, A PROFESSIONAL ASSOCIATION (AV)

109 Haddon Avenue, 08033
Telephone: 609-795-1600
Telecopier: 609-795-9469

Joseph M. Weinberg
Joseph A. McCormick, Jr.
Barry Chatzinoff

Edward L. Paul
Donafaye Wilson Zoll
Antonieta M. Paiva
Stephanie Onorato

Representative Clients: Mobile Field Office Co.; Landress Computers; L & L Redi Mix; Aurora Financial Group, Inc.; Case Credit Corp.
Local Counsel For: John Deere Credit Services, Inc.; John Deere Company; John Deere Industrial Equipment Co.
Solicitor For: Berlin Township Planning Board.
Reference: United Jersey Bank/South.

For full biographical listings, see the Martindale-Hubbell Law Directory

*MORRISTOWN,** Morris Co.

SHANLEY & FISHER, A PROFESSIONAL CORPORATION (AV)

131 Madison Avenue, 07962-1979
Telephone: 201-285-1000
Telecopier: 1-201-285-1098
Telex: 475-4255 (I.T.T.)
Cable Address: "Shanley"
New York, N.Y. Office: 89th Floor, One World Trade Center.
Telephone: 212-321-1812.
Telecopier: 1-212-466-0569.

A. Dennis Terrell
Robert K. Malone

Lynn Ciolino Boyajian
Russell J. Passamano
Lawrence E. Behning
Stephen C. Hunt
Dawn R. SanFilippo

For Complete List of Firm Personnel, See General Section

For full biographical listings, see the Martindale-Hubbell Law Directory

*NEWARK,** Essex Co.

DEMARIA, ELLIS, HUNT, SALSBERG & FRIEDMAN (AV)

Suite 1400, 744 Broad Street, 07102
Telephone: 201-623-1699
Telecopier: 201-623-0954

MEMBERS OF FIRM

H. Reed Ellis
Paul A. Friedman
Ronald H. DeMaria
Brian N. Flynn
William J. Hunt
Richard H. Bauch
Richard M. Salsberg
Lee H. Udelsman

(See Next Column)

ASSOCIATES

Mitchell A. Schley
George W. Rettig
Joseph D. Olivieri
David S. Catuogno
Joanne M. Maxwell
Debra S. Friedman
Robyn L. Aversa
Kathryn A. Calista

For full biographical listings, see the Martindale-Hubbell Law Directory

CHARLES M. FORMAN & ASSOCIATES (AV)

Robert Treat Center, 50 Park Place, 07102
Telephone: 201-824-7222
Telefax: 201-824-1667

ASSOCIATES

Erin J. Kennedy
Nadine M. Alexander
Michael E. Holt

Reference: Bergen Commercial Bank.

For full biographical listings, see the Martindale-Hubbell Law Directory

HELLRING LINDEMAN GOLDSTEIN & SIEGAL (AV)

One Gateway Center, 07102-5386
Telephone: 201-621-9020
Telecopier: 201-621-7406

James A. Scarpone
Bruce S. Etterman
Richard B. Honig
Val Mandel
John A. Adler
Sarah Jane Jelin

For Complete List of Firm Personnel, See General Section

For full biographical listings, see the Martindale-Hubbell Law Directory

MCCARTER & ENGLISH (AV)

Four Gateway Center, 100 Mulberry Street, P.O. Box 652, 07101-0652
Telephone: 201-622-4444
Telecopier: 201-624-7070
Cable Address: "McCarter" Newark
Cherry Hill, New Jersey Office: 1810 Chapel Avenue West.
Telephone: 609-662-8444.
Telecopier: 609-662-6203.
New York, New York Office: Suite 1519, One World Trade Center.
Telephone: 212-466-9018.
Telecopier: 212-432-6568.
Boca Raton, Florida Office: 2255 Glades Road, Suite 319-A.
Telephone: 407-994-6262.
Telecopier: 407-241-0798.
Wilmington, Delaware Office: Mellon Bank Center, 919 Market Street.
Telephone: 302-654-8010.
Telecopier: 302-654-0795.

MEMBERS OF FIRM

Richard W. Hill
Theodore D. Moskowitz
Hayden Smith, Jr.
Joseph Lubertazzi, Jr.
Peter S. Twombly

COUNSEL

Curtis A. Johnson

ASSOCIATES

Edward S. Nathan
Edward J. Butler, Jr.
Lisa W.S. Bonsall
David J. Adler
William D. Wallach
Jennifer D. Subryan
Todd Mark Galante
Michael D. Siegel
Walter A. Effross
Melanie Leslie
Susan C.G. Ericksen
Bernadette Mary Wroblak
William P. Higgins, Jr.
Robert A. Schwartz
Nancy A. Washington

For Complete List of Firm Personnel, See General Section

For full biographical listings, see the Martindale-Hubbell Law Directory

SAIBER SCHLESINGER SATZ & GOLDSTEIN (AV)

One Gateway Center, 13th Floor, 07102-5311
Telephone: 201-622-3333
Telecopier: 201-622-3349

MEMBERS OF FIRM

David M. Satz, Jr.
Michael L. Allen
Bruce I. Goldstein
Michael L. Messer
William F. Maderer
Jeffrey W. Lorell
David J. D'Aloia
Jeffrey M. Schwartz
James H. Aibel
David J. Satz
Sean R. Kelly
Joan M. Schwab
John L. Conover
Jennine DiSomma
Lawrence B. Mink
James H. Forte
Vincent F. Papalia

OF COUNSEL

Samuel S. Saiber
Norman E. Schlesinger

COUNSEL

Andrew Alcorn
Robin B. Horn
Randi Schillinger

(See Next Column)

SAIBER SCHLESINGER SATZ & GOLDSTEIN, *Newark—Continued*

ASSOCIATES

Audrey M. Weinstein
Robert B. Nussbaum
Michael J. Geraghty
Jonathan S. Davis
Paul S. DeGiulio
Diana L. Sussman
Deanna M. Beacham
Robert W. Geiger
William S. Gyves
Barry P. Kramer
Susan Rozman
Michelle Viola

LEGAL SUPPORT PERSONNEL

DIRECTOR OF FINANCE AND ADMINISTRATION

Ronald Henry

For full biographical listings, see the Martindale-Hubbell Law Directory

SILLS CUMMIS ZUCKERMAN RADIN TISCHMAN EPSTEIN & GROSS, A PROFESSIONAL CORPORATION (AV)

One Riverfront Plaza, 07102-5400
Telephone: 201-643-7000
Fax: 201-643-6500
Telex: 820630 Sillsbeck Nwk
Atlantic City, New Jersey Office: 17 Gordon's Alley.
Telephone: 609-344-2800.
New York, N.Y. Office: 250 Park Avenue.
Telephone: 212-643-7000.

Steven S. Radin
Steven E. Gross
Steven M. Goldman
Alan E. Sherman
Ira A. Rosenberg
Robert Crane
Jack M. Zackin
Jerry Genberg
Margaret F. Black
Brian S. Coven
Victor H. Boyajian

Steven B. Jackman (Not admitted in NJ)
Stephen McNally
Frederic M. Tudor
Jodi S. Brodsky
Robert W. Burke
Scott T. Gruber
Patricia Brown Fugee

For Complete List of Firm Personnel, See General Section

For full biographical listings, see the Martindale-Hubbell Law Directory

ORADELL, Bergen Co.

NICOLETTE & PERKINS, P.A. (AV)

555 Kinderkamack Road, P.O. Box 549, 07649
Telephone: 201-261-9300
Telecopier: 201-261-8855

David A. Nicolette, Jr.
Eric R. Perkins

Evelyn J. Marose
Jeanette A. Odynski

For full biographical listings, see the Martindale-Hubbell Law Directory

ROSELAND, Essex Co.

RAVIN, GREENBERG & MARKS, A PROFESSIONAL CORPORATION (AV)

101 Eisenhower Parkway, 07068
Telephone: 201-226-1500
Telecopier: 201-226-6888

Morris M. Ravin (1900-1971)
Nathan Ravin
Howard S. Greenberg
Stephen B. Ravin
Gary N. Marks
Bruce J. Wisotsky

Allan M. Harris
Larry Lesnik
David Edelberg
Jay L. Lubetkin
Morris S. Bauer

Reference: Hudson United Bank.

For full biographical listings, see the Martindale-Hubbell Law Directory

*SOMERVILLE,** Somerset Co.

SCHACHTER, TROMBADORE, OFFEN, STANTON & PAVICS, A PROFESSIONAL CORPORATION (AV)

45 East High Street, P.O. Box 520, 08876-0520
Telephone: 908-722-5700
Fax: 908-722-8853

Timothy P. McKeown

References: Summit Bank; First National Bank of Central Jersey; New Jersey Savings Bank.

For full biographical listings, see the Martindale-Hubbell Law Directory

WOODBRIDGE, Middlesex Co.

GREENBAUM, ROWE, SMITH, RAVIN AND DAVIS (AV)

Metro Corporate Campus I, P.O. Box 5600, 07095-0988
Telephone: 908-549-5600
Cable Address: "Greelaw"
Telecopier: 908-549-1881
ABA Net: 2 529

MEMBERS OF FIRM

David L. Bruck
Marjorie F. Chertok

ASSOCIATES

Nancy Isaacson
Michael L. Konig

For Complete List of Firm Personnel, See General Section

For full biographical listings, see the Martindale-Hubbell Law Directory

NEW MEXICO

*ALBUQUERQUE,** Bernalillo Co.

FRANCIS & STARZYNSKI, P.A. (AV)

320 Gold Avenue S.W., Suite 800, 87102
Telephone: 505-242-2880
Fax: 505-242-7370

Douglas T. Francis
James S. Starzynski

For full biographical listings, see the Martindale-Hubbell Law Directory

GALLAGHER, CASADOS & MANN, P.C. (AV)

317 Commercial N.E., 2nd Floor, 87102
Telephone: 505-243-7848
Fax: 505-764-0153

James E. Casados
Nathan H. Mann
Michael P. Watkins
Gail S. Stewart
Doris W. Eng
Dawn T. (Penni) Adrian
Jack Carmody
Robert L. Hlady

OF COUNSEL

David R. Gallagher

For full biographical listings, see the Martindale-Hubbell Law Directory

HINKLE, COX, EATON, COFFIELD & HENSLEY (AV)

Suite 800, 500 Marquette, N.W., P.O. Box 2043, 87103
Telephone: 505-768-1500
FAX: 505-768-1529
Roswell, New Mexico Office: Suite 700, United Bank Plaza, P.O. Box 10, 88202.
Telephone: 505-622-6510.
FAX: 505-623-9332.
Midland, Texas Office: 6 Desta Drive, Suite 2800, P.O. Box 3580, 79705.
Telephone: 915-683-4691.
FAX: 915-683-6518.
Amarillo, Texas Office: 1700 Bank One Center. P.O. Box 9238, 79105-9238.
Telephone: 806-372-5569.
FAX: 806-372-9761.
Santa Fe, New Mexico Office: 218 Montezuma, P.O. Box 2068, 87504.
Telephone: 505-982-4554.
FAX: 505-982-8623.
Austin, Texas Office: 401 West 15th Street, Suite 800, 78701.
Telephone: 512-476-7137.
FAX: 512-476-5431.
Associated Office: Hoffman & Stephens, P.C., 401 West 15th Street, Suite 800, 78701.
Telephone: 512-476-5434.
Fax: 512-476-5431.

Stuart D. Shanor (Roswell Office)
Nancy S. Cusack (Roswell Office)
Mark C. Dow
William Paul Johnson (Roswell Office)
Martin P. Meyers
Andrew J. Cloutier (Roswell Office)

Representative Clients: Anadarko Petroleum Corp.; Atlantic Richfield Co.; Bass Enterprises Production Co.; BHP Petroleum; Caroon & Black Management, Inc.; Chevron, USA, Inc.; CIGNA; City of Albuquerque; Coastal Oil & Gas Corp. Co.; Ethicon Inc., A Johnson & Johnson, Co.; Diagnostik; Conoco; Texaco; Presbyterian Healthcare Services.

For Complete List of Firm Personnel, See General Section

For full biographical listings, see the Martindale-Hubbell Law Directory

Albuquerque—Continued

RODEY, DICKASON, SLOAN, AKIN & ROBB, P.A. (AV)
Albuquerque Plaza, Suite 2200, 201 Third Street, N.W., P.O. Box 1888, 87103-1888
Telephone: 505-765-5900
Fax: 505-768-7395
Santa Fe, New Mexico Office: Suite 101 Marcy Plaza, 123 East Marcy Street, P.O. Box 1357, 87504-1357.
Telephone: 505-984-0100.
Fax: 505-989-9542.

Jo Saxton Brayer
Debra Romero Thal

Paul C. Collins

For Complete List of Firm Personnel, See General Section

For full biographical listings, see the Martindale-Hubbell Law Directory

*ROSWELL,** Chaves Co.

HINKLE, COX, EATON, COFFIELD & HENSLEY (AV)
Suite 700, United Bank Plaza, P.O. Box 10, 88202
Telephone: 505-622-6510
FAX: 505-623-9332
Midland, Texas Office: 6 Desta Drive, Suite 2800, P.O. Box 3580, 79705.
Telephone: 915-683-4691.
FAX: 915-683-6518.
Amarillo, Texas Office: 1700 Bank One Center, P.O. Box 9238, 79105-9238.
Telephone: 806-372-5569.
FAX: 806-372-9761.
Santa Fe, New Mexico Office: 218 Montezuma, P.O. Box 2068, 87504.
Telephone: 505-982-4554.
FAX: 505-982-8623.
Albuquerque, New Mexico Office: Suite 800, 500 Marquette, N.W., P.O. Box 2043, 87103.
Telephone: 505-768-1500.
FAX: 505-768-1529.
Austin, Texas Office: 401 West 15th Street, Suite 800, 78701.
Telephone: 512-476-7137.
FAX: 512-476-5431.
Associated Office: Hoffman & Stephens, P.C., 401 West 15th Street, Suite 800, 78701.
Telephone: 512-476-5434.
Fax: 512-476-5431.

RESIDENT PARTNERS

Stuart D. Shanor
Nancy S. Cusack
William Paul Johnson
Andrew J. Cloutier

For full biographical listings, see the Martindale-Hubbell Law Directory

NEW YORK

*BUFFALO,** Erie Co.

HURWITZ & FINE, P.C. (AV)
1300 Liberty Building, 14202-3613
Telephone: 716-849-8900
Telecopier: 716-855-0874

James D. Gauthier
Ann E. Evanko

Diane E. Katz
Daniel R. Archilla
Paula Marie Eade Newcomb

For Complete List of Firm Personnel, See General Section

For full biographical listings, see the Martindale-Hubbell Law Directory

EAST MEADOW, Nassau Co.

CERTILMAN BALIN ADLER & HYMAN, LLP (AV)
90 Merrick Avenue, 11554
Telephone: 516-296-7000
Telecopier: 516-296-7111

MEMBERS OF FIRM

Ira J. Adler
Dale Allinson
Herbert M. Balin
Bruce J. Bergman
Michael D. Brofman
Morton L. Certilman
Murray Greenberg
David Z. Herman
Richard Herzbach
M. Allan Hyman
Bernard Hyman
Donna-Marie Korth
Steven J. Kuperschmid
Thomas J. McNamara
Fred S. Skolnik
Louis Soloway
Harold Somer
Howard M. Stein
Brian K. Ziegler

(See Next Column)

OF COUNSEL

Daniel S. Cohan
Norman J. Levy
Marilyn Price

ASSOCIATES

Howard B. Busch
Scott M. Gerber
Jodi S. Hoffman
Glenn Kleinbaum
Michael C. Manniello
Jaspreet S. Mayall
Stacey R. Miller
Lawrence S. Novak
Kim J. Radbell

For full biographical listings, see the Martindale-Hubbell Law Directory

GARDEN CITY, Nassau Co.

FISCHOFF, GELBERG & DIRECTOR (AV)
600 Old Country Road, Suite 410, 11530
Telephone: 516-228-4255
Facsimile: 516-228-4278

MEMBERS OF FIRM

Stuart P. Gelberg
Gary C. Fischoff
Michael C. Director

ASSOCIATES

Scott R. Schneider
Heath Berger

For full biographical listings, see the Martindale-Hubbell Law Directory

JASPAN, GINSBERG, SCHLESINGER, SILVERMAN & HOFFMAN (AV)
300 Garden City Plaza, 11530
Telephone: 516-746-8000
Telecopier: 516-746-0552

MEMBERS OF FIRM

Arthur W. Jaspan
Eugene S. Ginsberg
Steven R. Schlesinger
Kenneth P. Silverman
Carol M. Hoffman
Stanley A. Camhi
Eugene P. Cimini, Jr.
Holly Juster
Stephen P. Epstein
Gary F. Herbst
Allen Perlstein

For Complete List of Firm Personnel, See General Section

For full biographical listings, see the Martindale-Hubbell Law Directory

REDMOND, POLLIO & PITTONI, P.C. (AV)
1461 Franklin Avenue, 11530
Telephone: 516-248-2500
Telecopier: 516-248-2348

M. John Pittoni
Peter R. Bonchonsky

Kathleen M. Galgano
Stephen E. Zaino

For Complete List of Firm Personnel, See General Section

For full biographical listings, see the Martindale-Hubbell Law Directory

SHAW, LICITRA, PARENTE, ESERNIO & SCHWARTZ, P.C. (AV)
1010 Franklin Avenue, 11530
Telephone: 516-742-0610
Cable Address: Lawbanc.
Telex: 143227
Telecopier: 516-742-2670
New York City Office: 300 East 42nd Street.
Telephone: 212-338-0970.
Special Counsel: Holland & Knight 400 North Ashley, P.O. Box 1288, Tampa, Florida, 33602 and 2100 Pennsylvania Avenue, N.W., Washington, D.C., 20037.

Joseph Licitra (1930-1987)
J. Stanley Shaw
C. Albert Parente
George P. Esernio
Jeffrey L. Schwartz
Anton J. Borovina
Edward M. Flint
Stuart I. Gordon
Sarah M. Keenan
Frank J. Livoti
Alan E. Marder
Peter Marullo
Jeffrey M. Zalkin

Francesca Cellese
Caroline Leon Cona
Frank A. Cuoco
Michael C. DeLisa
David P. Gesser
John H. Hall, Jr.
Jeffrey A. Hill
Gaetana Liantonio-McBride
Bradley A. Max
Donald R. Shields
Roberta L. Slattery

SPECIAL COUNSEL

Edward D. Re
Louis D. Laurino

COUNSEL

Victor G. Beaudet (1919-1993)
Louis M. Laurino
Alan M. Parente
Frank Rossetti, III

For full biographical listings, see the Martindale-Hubbell Law Directory

HEMPSTEAD, Nassau Co.

Moritt, Hock & Hamroff (AV)

Hempstead Executive Plaza, 50 Clinton Street, 11550
Telephone: 516-489-7400
Fax: 516-489-0971
Garden City, New York Office: 600 Old Country Road.
Telephone: 516-489-7400.

MEMBERS OF FIRM

Neil J. Moritt
Alan S. Hock
Marc L. Hamroff
David H. Cohen

Robert S. Cohen
Robert M. Tils
Sharon I. Feder
Donna R. Ruggiero
Leslie A. Berkoff
Kenneth Paul Horowitz
Wendy Axelrod
(Not admitted in NY)
David A. Loglisci

For full biographical listings, see the Martindale-Hubbell Law Directory

HUNTINGTON, Suffolk Co.

Smyth & Lack (AV)

202 East Main Street, 11743
Telephone: 516-271-7500
Telecopier: 516-271-7504

MEMBERS OF FIRM

Vincent A. Smyth
James J. Lack

ASSOCIATES

Thomas P. Solferino
Dana M. Barberis
Stephen I. Witdorchic

Reference: Chemical Bank.

For full biographical listings, see the Martindale-Hubbell Law Directory

*NEW YORK,** New York Co.

Otterbourg, Steindler, Houston & Rosen, P.C. (AV)

230 Park Avenue, 10169
Telephone: 212-661-9100
Cable Address: "Otlerton";
Telecopier: 212-682-6104
Telex: 960916

Kurt J. Wolff
William M. Silverman
Morton L. Gitter
Peter H. Stolzar
Bernard Beitel
Jonathan N. Helfat
Daniel Wallen
Scott L. Hazan
Glenn B. Rice
Albert F. Reisman
Richard J. Rubin
Steven B. Soll
Mitchell M. Brand
Peter L. Feldman

Enid Nagler Stuart
Andrew M. Kramer
Jenette A. Barrow
Brett H. Miller
Matthew J. Miller
John J. Kenny
Richard L. Stehl
Gary G. Michael
Susan A. Joyce

For Complete List of Firm Personnel, See General Section

For full biographical listings, see the Martindale-Hubbell Law Directory

Parker Chapin Flattau & Klimpl, L.L.P. (AV)

1211 Avenue of the Americas, 10036
Telephone: 212-704-6000
Telecopier: 212-704-6288
Cable Address: "Lawpark"
Telex: 640347
Great Neck, New York Office: 175 Great Neck Road.
Telephone: 516-482-4422.
Telecopier: 516-482-4469.

MEMBERS OF FIRM

Charles P. Greenman
Joel Lewittes
Joel M. Wolosky

OF COUNSEL

Henry Condell

ASSOCIATES

John Carlson
E. Mark Gross
Andrew H. Sherman

For Complete List of Firm Personnel, See General Section

For full biographical listings, see the Martindale-Hubbell Law Directory

Siegel, Sommers & Schwartz (AV)

470 Park Avenue South, 16th Floor, 10016
Telephone: 212-889-7570
Fax: 212-889-0688

(See Next Column)

Lawrence C. Gottlieb
James A. Beldner
Jay Randall Indyke
Ronald R. Sussman
Robert A. Boghosian

ASSOCIATES

Eric J. Haber
Scott E. Rusczyk
Bryan W. Kishner

OF COUNSEL

Leonard Schwartz

For full biographical listings, see the Martindale-Hubbell Law Directory

Skadden, Arps, Slate, Meagher & Flom (AV)

919 Third Avenue, 10022
Telephone: 212-735-3000
Telex: 645899 SKARSLAW
Fax: 212-735-2000; 212-735-2001
Boston, Massachusetts Office: One Beacon Street, 02108.
Telephone: 617-573-4800.
Fax: 617-573-4822.
Washington, D.C. Office: 1440 New York Avenue, N.W., 20005.
Telephone: 202-371-7000.
Fax: 202-393-5760.
Wilmington, Delaware Office: One Rodney Square, 19899.
Telephone: 302-651-3000.
Fax: 302-651-3001.
Los Angeles, California Office: 300 South Grand Avenue, 90071.
Telephone: 213-687-5000.
Fax: 213-687-5600.
Chicago, Illinois Office: 333 West Wacker Drive, 60606.
Telephone: 312-407-0700.
Fax: 312-407-0411.
San Francisco, California Office: Four Embarcadero Center, 94111.
Telephone: 415-984-6400.
Fax: 415-984-2698.
Houston, Texas Office: 1600 Smith Street, Suite 4460, 77002.
Telephone: 713-655-5100.
Fax: 713-655-5181.
Newark, New Jersey Office: One Riverfront Plaza, 07102.
Telephone: 201-596-4440.
Fax: 201-596-4444.
Tokyo, Japan Office: 12th Floor, The Fukoku Seimei Building, 2-2-2, Uchisaiwaicho, Chiyoda-ku, 100.
Telephone: 011-81-3-3595-3850.
Fax: 011-81-3-3504-2780.
London, England Office: 25 Bucklersbury EC4N 8DA.
Telephone: 011-44-71-248-9929.
Fax: 011-44-71-489-8533.
Hong Kong Office: 30/F Peregrine Tower, Lippo Centre, 89 Queensway, Central.
Telephone: 011-852-820-0700.
Fax: 011-852-820-0727.
Sydney, New South Wales, Australia Office: Level 26-State Bank Centre, 52 Martin Place, 2000.
Telephone: 011-61-2-224-6000.
Fax: 011-61-2-224-6044.
Toronto, Ontario Office: Suite 1820, North Tower, P.O. Box 189, Royal Bank Plaza, M5J 2J4.
Telephone: 416-777-4700.
Fax: 416-777-4747.
Paris, France Office: 105 rue du Faubourg Saint-Honoré, 75008.
Telephone: 011-33-1-40-75-44-44.
Fax: 011-33-1-49-53-09-99.
Brussels, Belgium Office: 523 avenue Louise, Box 30, 1050.
Telephone: 011-32-2-648-7666.
Fax: 011-32-2-640-3032.
Frankfurt, Germany Office: MesseTurm, 27th Floor, 60308.
Telephone: 011-49-69-9757-3000.
Fax: 011-49-69-9757-3050.
Beijing, China Office: 1605 Capital Mansion Tower, No. 6 Xin Yuan Nan Road, Chao Yang District, 100004.
Telephone: 011-86-1-466-8800.
Fax: 011-86-1-466-8822.
Budapest, Hungary Office: Mahart Building, H-1052 Apáczai Csere János u.11, Vl.em.
Telephone: 011-36-1-266-2145.
Fax: 011-36-1-266-4033.
Prague, Czech Republic Office: Revolucni 16, 110 00.
Telephone: 011-42-2-231-75-18.
Fax: 011-42-2-231-47-33.
Moscow, Russia Office: Pleteshkovsky Pereulok 1, 107005.
Telephone: 011-7-501-940-2304.
Fax: 011-7-501-940-2511.

MEMBERS OF FIRM

Michael L. Cook
Alesia Ranney-Marinelli
Kayalyn A. Marafioti
George A. Zimmerman
Sally M. Henry

COUNSEL

Carlene J. Gatting

SPECIAL COUNSEL

Allen L. Weingarten

(See Next Column)

SKADDEN, ARPS, SLATE, MEAGHER & FLOM—*Continued*

CHICAGO, ILLINOIS OFFICE

PARTNERS

N. Lynn Hiestand
John Wm. Butler, Jr.

LOS ANGELES, CALIFORNIA OFFICE

COUNSEL

Peter W. Clapp

WILMINGTON, DELAWARE OFFICE

PARTNER

Anthony W. Clark

NEW YORK, N.Y. OFFICE

ASSOCIATES

Brad J. Axelrod
Steven L. Barnett
Stanley D. Brener
Dennis F. Dunne
Lawrence V. Gelber (Not admitted in NY)
Elihu Gordis
Mark Gross
Gilbert Hahn, III
Barbara K. Kelly
Jerome J. Lawton
David Alan Powar
Joseph H. Shaulson
Stefani J. Shavel
Rosa Anna Testani
Michael P. Trolman
Elizabeth H. Winchester

CHICAGO, ILLINOIS OFFICE

ASSOCIATES

Steven E. Boyce
Nicholas L. Giampietro
Robert W. Kadlec
Andrew S. Morrison
Maris M. Rodgon

LOS ANGELES, CALIFORNIA

ASSOCIATE

Robert J. Mrofka

WILMINGTON, DELAWARE

ASSOCIATES

Mark S. Chehi
Gregg M. Galardi

For Complete List of Firm Personnel, See General Section

For full biographical listings, see the Martindale-Hubbell Law Directory

STROOCK & STROOCK & LAVAN (AV)

Seven Hanover Square, 10004-2696
Telephone: 212-806-5400
Telecopier: (212) 806-6006
Telexes: Stroock, UT 177693 and Plastroock NYK 177077 (International)
Cable Address: "Plastroock, NYK"
New York Conference Center: 767 Third Avenue, 10017-2023.
Telephones: 212-806-5767; 5768; 5769; 5770.
Telecopier: (212) 421-6234.
Washington, D.C. Office: 1150 Seventeenth Street, N.W., Suite 600, 20036-4652.
Telephone: 202-452-9250.
Telecopier: (202) 421-6234.
Cable Address: "Plastroock, Washington."
Telex: 64238 STROOCK DC; 89401 STROOCK DC.
Los Angeles, California Office: 2029 Century Park East, Floors 16 & 18, 90067-3086.
Telephone: 310-556-5800.
Telecopier: (310) 556-5959.
Cable Address: "Plastroock L.A."
Telex: Plastroock LSA 677190 (Domestic and International).
Miami, Florida Office: 200 South Biscayne Boulevard, Suite 3000, First Union Financial Center, 33131-2385.
Telephone: 305-358-9900.
Telecopier: (305) 789-9302.
Telex: 803133 Stroock Mia (Domestic and International); Broward Line: 527-9900.
Budapest, Hungary Office: East-West Business Center, Rákóczi ut 1-3, H-1088.
Telephone: 011-361-266-9520; 011-361-266-7770.
Telecopier: 001-361-266-9279.

MEMBERS OF FIRM

Daniel H. Golden
Alan S. Halperin
Lawrence M. Handelsman
Fred S. Hodara
Robin E. Keller
Lewis Kruger
Mark A. Speiser

Lisa G. Beckerman
David H. Botter
Barbara G. Kaplan
Sherry J. Millman
Anthony H. N. Schnelling

For Complete List of Firm Personnel, See General Section

For full biographical listings, see the Martindale-Hubbell Law Directory

TOGUT, SEGAL & SEGAL (AV)

One Penn Plaza, 10119
Telephone: 212-594-5000
Telecopier: 212-967-4258

(See Next Column)

MEMBERS OF FIRM

Albert Togut
Bernard Segal (1932-1983)
Sidney Segal (1935-1968)

ASSOCIATES

Frank A. Oswald
James A. Sarna
Neil Berger

For full biographical listings, see the Martindale-Hubbell Law Directory

TRAUB, BONACQUIST & FOX (AV)

489 Fifth Avenue, 27th Floor, 10017
Telephone: 212-476-4770
Fax: 212-476-4787
Roseland, New Jersey Office: 103 Eisenhower Parkway, 07068.
Telephone: 201-567-1827.
Fax: 201-403-9021.

MEMBERS OF FIRM

Paul Traub
Harold F. Bonacquist
Michael S. Fox

ASSOCIATES

Fredrick J. Levy
Julie Gamache
Lisa J. Pollack
Susan F. Balaschak
Maura I. Russell

For full biographical listings, see the Martindale-Hubbell Law Directory

WINTHROP, STIMSON, PUTNAM & ROBERTS (AV)

One Battery Park Plaza, 10004-1490
Telephone: 212-858-1000
Telex: 62854 WINSTIM
Telefax: 212-858-1500
Stamford, Connecticut Office: Financial Centre, 695 East Main Street, P.O. Box 6760, 06904-6760.
Telephone: 203-348-2300.
Washington, D.C. Office: 1133 Connecticut Avenue, N.W., 20036.
Telephone: 202-775-9800.
Palm Beach, Florida Office: 125 Worth Avenue, 33480.
Telephone: 407-655-7297.
London Office: 2 Throgmorton Avenue, London EC2N 2AP, England.
Telephone: 011-4471-628-4931.
Brussels Office: Rue Du Taciturne 42, B-1040 Brussels, Belgium.
Telephone: 011-322-230-1392.
Tokyo, Japan Office: 608 Atagoyama Bengoshi Building 6-7, Atago 1-chome, Minato-ku, Tokyo 105 Japan.
Telephone: 011-813-3437-9740.
Hong Kong Office: 2505 Asia Pacific Finance Tower, Citibank Plaza, 3 Garden Road, Central.
Telephone: 011-852-530-3400.

MEMBERS OF FIRM

David W. Ambrosia
Richard L. Epling
Barton D. Ford
Robert W. Gray
William C. F. Kurz
F. Joseph Owens, Jr.
John F. Pritchard
Glenn E. Siegel
Charles H. Vejvoda

ASSOCIATES

Matthew J. Borger
Katarina V. Dimich
Erik W. Hepler
Jonathan B. Kim
Stacey E. Nadell

For Complete List of Firm Personnel, See General Section

For full biographical listings, see the Martindale-Hubbell Law Directory

*ROCHESTER,** Monroe Co.

SUTER DOYLE KESSELRING LAWRENCE & WERNER (AV)

Formerly Burns, Suter & Doyle
700 First Federal Plaza, 14614
Telephone: 716-325-6446
Fax: 716-262-5185
Canandaigua, New York Office: 23 Sly Street, 14424.
Telephone: 716-398-3400.
Fax: 716-398-2750.

Paul J. Suter (1918-1989)

OF COUNSEL

James B. Doyle

MEMBERS OF FIRM

Leo J. Kesselring
C. Bruce Lawrence
Christopher K. Werner
Colleen A. Brown
Steven H. Swartout

ASSOCIATE

Mary Jo S. Korona

Representative Clients: Ford Motor Credit Corp.; Wegmans Food Markets, Inc.; Johnny Antonelli Tire Company, Inc.; Grey Metal Products, Inc.; Rochester Plumbing Supply Company, Inc.; Hug-Langie Fuel Oil, Inc.; Brede Tool & Supply Company, Inc.; Sawyer's Industrial Fumigators; Lilac Laundry Company, Inc.; Hadlock Paint Company, Inc.

For full biographical listings, see the Martindale-Hubbell Law Directory

ROCKVILLE CENTRE, Nassau Co.

BATZAR & WEINBERG, A PROFESSIONAL CORPORATION (AV)

184 Sunrise Highway, P.O. Box 427, 11570
Telephone: 516-766-1860
Telecopier: 516-678-7801
Hoboken, New Jersey Office: Batzar, Weinberg & Levy, 86 Hudson Street.
Telephone: 201-653-1797.
Merion, Pennsylvania Office: 405 Andrew Road.
Telephone: 215-568-1060.
Haddonfield, New Jersey Office: Batzar, Weinberg & Levy, 36 Tanner Street.
Telephone: 609-795-9456.

Jules Shank (1908-1993)
Louis K. Batzar
Sanford I. Weinberg

Roger Levy (Hoboken and Haddonfield, New Jersey Offices)
Edward J. Damsky
John E. McLoughlin

OF COUNSEL

Norma R. Frank (Resident, Merion, Pennsylvania Office)

For full biographical listings, see the Martindale-Hubbell Law Directory

WESTBURY, Nassau Co.

PRYOR & MANDELUP, P.C. (AV)

675 Old Country Road, 11590
Telephone: 516-997-0999
Facsimile: 516-333-7333

Robert L. Pryor
A. Scott Mandelup
Randolph E. White

David J. Weiss
Jeanne Farnan
Eric J. Snyder
Adam H. Friedman
Gerard M. Bambrick

For full biographical listings, see the Martindale-Hubbell Law Directory

NORTH CAROLINA

CHAPEL HILL, Orange Co.

NORTHEN, BLUE, ROOKS, THIBAUT, ANDERSON & WOODS, L.L.P. (AV)

Suite 550, 100 Europa Center, P.O. Box 2208, 27515-2208
Telephone: 919-968-4441
Facsimile: 919-942-6603

MEMBERS OF FIRM

John A. Northen
Charles H. Thibaut
J. William Blue, Jr.
Charles T. L. Anderson
David M. Rooks, III
Jo Ann Ragazzo Woods
Carol J. Holcomb

ASSOCIATES

James C. Stanford
Gregory Herman-Giddens
Cheryl Y. Capron

References: Central Carolina Bank; The Village Bank; Investors Title Insurance Co.; First Union National Bank; Centura Bank; United Carolina Bank; BB&T; Balbirer & Coleman, CPA's.

For full biographical listings, see the Martindale-Hubbell Law Directory

*CHARLOTTE,** Mecklenburg Co.

DAVID R. BADGER, P.A. (AV)

Suite 1560 Carillon, 227 West Trade Street, 28202-1625
Telephone: 704-375-8875
FAX: 704-375-8835

David R. Badger

LEGAL SUPPORT PERSONNEL

Jane Patton
Wendy W. Fox

Representative Clients: Chase Manhattan Bank; First Charlotte Bank; Fycon Technologies, Inc.
References: First Charlotte Bank; Bank of Mecklenburg.

For full biographical listings, see the Martindale-Hubbell Law Directory

GRIER AND GRIER, P.A. (AV)

Suite 1240 One Independence Center, 101 North Tryon Street, 28246
Telephone: 704-375-3720
FAX: 704-332-0215

Joseph W. Grier, Jr.
Richard C. Belthoff, Jr.
Joseph W. Grier, III
Richard L. Robertson
Leigh A. Hobgood

J. Cameron Furr, Jr.
James L. Kiser
K. Lane Klotzberger

Approved Attorneys for: Lawyers Title Insurance Corp.
Reference: NationsBank.

For full biographical listings, see the Martindale-Hubbell Law Directory

LINDSEY AND SCHRIMSHER, P.A. (AV)

2316 Randolph Road, 28207
Telephone: 704-333-2141
Fax: 704-376-2562

Robert L. Lindsey, Jr.
Frank L. Schrimsher
B. Scott Schrimsher

Representative Clients: American General Finance; C.I.T. Group/Sales Financing, Inc.; Crestar Bank; Crestar Mortgage; Wachovia Bank of North Carolina, N.A.; Central Carolina Bank & Trust Co.; NationsBanc Financial Services; Lawyers Title Insurance Corp.; First Union Home Equity Corp.; Sunshine Mortgage Corp.; ContiMortgage Corp.

For full biographical listings, see the Martindale-Hubbell Law Directory

MITCHELL & RALLINGS (AV)

1800 Carillon, 227 West Trade Street, 28202
Telephone: 704-376-6574
FAX: 704-342-1531

MEMBERS OF FIRM

Richard M. Mitchell
Thomas B. Rallings, Jr.

ASSOCIATES

James L. Fretwell
James Dagoberto Concepcion
Joseph N. Tissue
John W. Taylor

COUNSEL

Alvin A. London

Representative Clients: Bonitz Contracting Co.; Captain D's. Inc.; Chemical Financial Services Corp.; Dorfio, Inc.; Dyke Industries, Inc.; Edgcomb Metals; Titan Building Products, Inc.; Fairfinish Corp.
References: Republic Bank & Trust Co.; N.C.N.B.

For full biographical listings, see the Martindale-Hubbell Law Directory

SMITH HELMS MULLISS & MOORE, L.L.P. (AV)

227 North Tryon Street, P.O. Box 31247, 28231
Telephone: 704-343-2000
Telecopier: 704-334-8467
Telex: 572460
Greensboro, North Carolina Office: Smith Helms Mulliss & Moore, Suite 1400 First Union Tower, 300 North Greene Street, P.O. Box 21927.
Telephone: 910-378-5200.
Telecopier: 910-379-9558.
Raleigh, North Carolina Office: 316 West Edenton Street, P.O. Box 27525.
Telephone: 919-755-8700.
Telecopier: 919-828-7938.

MEMBERS OF FIRM

Robert B. Cordle
Robert H. Pryor
Scott P. Vaughn

ASSOCIATE

Katherine T. Lange

For Complete List of Firm Personnel, See General Section

For full biographical listings, see the Martindale-Hubbell Law Directory

*GREENSBORO,** Guilford Co.

GERALD S. SCHAFER (AV)

220 Commerce Place, 27401
Telephone: 910-273-9309

Representative Clients: Snyder-Roberts Insurance Agency; Triad Wholesale Lumber, Inc.; Williamson Heating & Cooling, Inc.; Boren Clay Products Co.; Branch Banking & Trust Co.; Chase Home Mortgage Corp., Panel of Chapter 7 Trustees.
Reference: First Union National Bank.

For full biographical listings, see the Martindale-Hubbell Law Directory

Greensboro—Continued

SMITH HELMS MULLISS & MOORE, L.L.P. (AV)

Suite 1400 First Union Tower, 300 North Greene Street, P.O. Box 21927, 27420
Telephone: 910-378-5200
Telecopier: 910-379-9558
Charlotte, North Carolina Office: Smith Helms Mulliss & Moore, L.L.P., 227 North Tryon Street, P.O. Box 31247.
Telephone: 704-343-2000.
Telecopier: 704-334-8467.
Telex: 572460.
Raleigh, North Carolina Office: Smith Helms Mulliss & Moore, L.L.P., 316 West Edenton Street, P.O. Box 27525.
Telephone: 919-755-8700.
Telecopier: 919-828-7938.

MEMBERS OF FIRM

Benjamin F. Davis, Jr. Richard A. Leippe

ASSOCIATE

Jeffrey G. Weber

For Complete List of Firm Personnel, See General Section

For full biographical listings, see the Martindale-Hubbell Law Directory

*RALEIGH,** Wake Co.

*** indicates certain Bar Register subscribers whose principal office is located elsewhere in the state and who have arranged for representation as a part of the state capital listings that follow**

EVERETT, GASKINS, HANCOCK & STEVENS (AV)

The Professional Building, Suite 600, 127 West Hargett Street, P.O. Box 911, 27602
Telephone: 919-755-0025
Fax: 919-755-0009
Durham, North Carolina Office: Suite 300, 301 West Main Street, P.O. Box 586.
Telephone: 919-682-5691.
Fax: 919-682-5469.

MEMBER OF FIRM

Eura DuVal (Ed) Gaskins, Jr.

ASSOCIATES

Jeffrey B. Parsons Robert (Bob) H. Gourley, Jr.

LEGAL SUPPORT PERSONNEL

Allyson S. McNeill

Representative Clients: Chase Federal Bank; Lloyd's of London; Pawling Savings Bank; United Carolina Bank.

For Complete List of Firm Personnel, See General Section

For full biographical listings, see the Martindale-Hubbell Law Directory

SMITH DEBNAM HIBBERT & PAHL (AV)

Hedingham Oaks, 4700 New Bern Avenue, P.O. Box 26268, 27611-6268
Telephone: 919-250-2000
Facsimile: 919-250-2100

MEMBERS OF FIRM

Fred J. Smith, Jr.
W. Thurston Debnam, Jr.
Carl W. Hibbert
J. Larkin Pahl
John W. Narron
Bettie Kelley Sousa
Terri L. Gardner
Jerry T. Myers
Laura K. Howell
Elizabeth B. Godfrey
Rose H. Stout
Byron L. Saintsing
R. Jonathan Charleston
Franklin Drake

ASSOCIATES

Scott N. Johnson
Gerald H. Groon, Jr.
William G. Berggren
Terry M. Kilbride
R. Andrew Patty, II
Melanie J. Hogg
Caren Davis Enloe
Santiago M. Estrada
Jay P. Tobin
Clayton D. Morgan
Shannon Lowry Nagle
Michael D. Zetts, III
Martha L. Sewell
Philip R. Isley
Jeff D. Rogers
James Alan Flynt

For full biographical listings, see the Martindale-Hubbell Law Directory

*** SMITH HELMS MULLISS & MOORE, L.L.P. (AV)**

316 West Edenton Street, P.O. Box 27525, 27611-7525
Telephone: 919-755-8700
Telecopier: 919-828-7938
Charlotte, North Carolina Office: 227 North Tryon Street, P.O. Box 31247.
Telephone: 704-343-2000.
Telecopier: 704-334-8467.
Telex: 572460.
Greensboro, North Carolina Office: Smith Helms Mulliss & Moore, Suite 1400 First Union Tower, 300 North Greene Street, P.O. Box 21927.
Telephone: 910-378-5200.
Telecopier: 910-379-9558.

(See Next Column)

MEMBER OF FIRM

Charles N. Anderson, Jr.

For Complete List of Firm Personnel, See General Section

For full biographical listings, see the Martindale-Hubbell Law Directory

*WINSTON-SALEM,** Forsyth Co.

BLANCO TACKABERY COMBS & MATAMOROS, P.A. (AV)

215 Executive Park Boulevard, P.O. Drawer 25008, 27114-5008
Telephone: 910-768-1130
Facsimile: 910-765-4830

David B. Blanco
Neal E. Tackabery
Reginald F. Combs
Ronald A. Matamoros
John S. Harrison
Gene B. Tarr
Michael D. Hurst
Steven C. Garland
Peter J. Juran
Brian L. Herndon

Bowen C. Houff
George E. Hollodick
Marguerite Self
Charles D. Luckey
Barbara Fritz Tucker
John H. Hall, Jr.
David T. Watters
Julie M. Fisher
Mary Margaret Ogburn

Reference: Southern National Bank of North Carolina, Winston-Salem, North Carolina.

For full biographical listings, see the Martindale-Hubbell Law Directory

WOMBLE CARLYLE SANDRIDGE & RICE (AV)

A Professional Limited Liability Company
1600 Southern National Financial Center, P.O. Drawer 84, 27102
Telephone: 910-721-3600
Telecopy: 910-721-3660
Telex: 806498
Charlotte, North Carolina Office: 3300 One First Union Center, 301 South College Street.
Telephone: 704-331-4900.
Telecopy: 704-331-4955.
Telex: 853609.
Raleigh, North Carolina Office: 2100 First Union Capitol Center, 150 Fayetteville Street Mall, P.O. Box 831.
Telephone: 919-755-2100.
Telecopy: 919-755-2150.
Telex: 806498.
Atlanta, Georgia Office: One Ninety One Peachtree Tower, 191 Peachtree Street, N.E., Suite 3250.
Telephone: 404-614-2580.
Fax: 404-614-2595.

MEMBERS OF FIRM

Bonnie Kay Donahue William B. Sullivan

ASSOCIATES

James E. Vaughan Rory D. Whelehan

Representative Clients: Brad Ragan, Inc.; Brenner Companies; Food Lion, Inc.; Hanes Companies, Inc.; North Carolina Baptist Hospitals, Inc.; R.J. Reynolds Tobacco Company; Summit Communications Group, Inc.; Thomasville Furniture Industries, Inc.; Wachovia Corporation; Wake Forest University.

For Complete List of Firm Personnel, See General Section

For full biographical listings, see the Martindale-Hubbell Law Directory

NORTH DAKOTA

*FARGO,** Cass Co.

VOGEL, BRANTNER, KELLY, KNUTSON, WEIR & BYE, LTD. (AV)

502 First Avenue North, P.O. Box 1389, 58107
Telephone: 701-237-6983
Facsimile: 701-237-0847

David F. Knutson William A. Schlossman, Jr.
Jon R. Brakke

For Complete List of Firm Personnel, See General Section

For full biographical listings, see the Martindale-Hubbell Law Directory

OHIO

*CINCINNATI,** Hamilton Co.

DINSMORE & SHOHL (AV)

1900 Chemed Center, 255 East Fifth Street, 45202-3172
Telephone: 513-977-8200
FAX: 513-977-8141
Florence, Kentucky Office: Turfway Ridge Office Park, 7300 Turfway Road, Suite 430 41042-1355.
Telephone: 606-283-0515.
FAX: 606-283-6017.
Dayton, Ohio Office: 500 Courthouse Plaza, S.W., 10 N. Ludlow Street, 45402-1834.
Telephone: 513-228-8012.
FAX: 513-461-2543.
Columbus, Ohio Office: NBD Bank Building, Suite 330, 175 South Third Street, 43215-5134.
Telephone: 614-224-7887.
FAX: 614-224-7882.

MEMBERS OF FIRM

John W. Beatty
Lawrence R. Elleman
Jay A. Rosenberg
Patrick D. Lane
Joanne M. Schreiner
John D. Luken
Mark C. Bissinger

ASSOCIATES

Douglas W. Campbell
Rita A. Miller Altimari
Linda A. Cooper
Reuel D. Ash

For Complete List of Firm Personnel, See General Section

For full biographical listings, see the Martindale-Hubbell Law Directory

FAULKNER & TEPE (AV)

2200 Central Trust Tower, 5 West Fourth Street, 45202
Telephone: 513-421-7500
FAX: 513-421-7502

MEMBERS OF FIRM

R. Edward Tepe
John C. Scott
Christopher L. Moore
Anthony W. Brock

SENIOR COUNSEL

David P. Faulkner

OF COUNSEL

A. Norman Aubin

Reference: Fifth Third Bank.

For full biographical listings, see the Martindale-Hubbell Law Directory

FROST & JACOBS (AV)

2500 PNC Center, 201 East Fifth Street, P.O. Box 5715, 45201-5715
Telephone: 513-651-6800
Cable Address: "Frostjac"
Telex: 21-4396 F & J CIN
Telecopier: 513-651-6981
Columbus, Ohio Office: One Columbus, 10 West Broad Street.
Telephone: 614-464-1211.
Telecopier: 614-464-1737.
Lexington, Kentucky Office: 1100 Vine Center Tower, 333 West Vine Street.
Telephone: 606-254-1100.
Telecopier: 606-253-2990.
Middletown, Ohio Office: 400 First National Bank Building, 2 North Main Street.
Telephone: 513-422-2001.
Telecopier: 513-422-3010.
Naples, Florida Office: 4001 Tamiami Trail North, Suite 220.
Telephone: 813-261-0582.
Telecopier: 813-261-2083.

MEMBERS OF FIRM

Edmund J. Adams
Gerald L. Baldwin
Vincent E. Mauer
Kim Martin Lewis

SENIOR ATTORNEY

Fern E. Goldman

ASSOCIATES

Karen Johannes Bowman
Ronald E. Gold

Representative Clients: Champion International Corp.; Cincinnati Milacron, Inc.; Eagle Picher Industries, Inc.; Federated Department Stores; PNC Bank, Ohio, National Association; Society National Bank; Turner Construction Co.; The United States Shoe Corp.; University of Cincinnati.

For Complete List of Firm Personnel, See General Section

For full biographical listings, see the Martindale-Hubbell Law Directory

KATZ, GREENBERGER & NORTON (AV)

105 East Fourth Street, 9th Floor, 45202-4011
Telephone: 513-721-5151
FAX: 513-621-9285

Leonard H. Freiberg (1885-1954)
Alfred B. Katz
Mark Alan Greenberger
Louis H. Katz
Richard L. Norton
Steven M. Rothstein
Robert Gray Edmiston
Ellen Essig

ASSOCIATES

Scott P. Kadish
Stephen E. Imm
Stephen L. Robison
Jeffrey J. Greenberger

OF COUNSEL

Charles Weiner

For full biographical listings, see the Martindale-Hubbell Law Directory

LERNER, SAMPSON & ROTHFUSS A LEGAL PROFESSIONAL ASSOCIATION (AV)

120 East Fourth Street, Suite 800, 45202
Telephone: 513-241-3100
FAX: 513-241-4094

Rick D. De Blasis
J. Michael Debbeler

Representative Clients: Lomas Mortgage USA, Inc.; Chemical Mortgage Co.; PNC Mortgage Co.
Reference: Star Bank NA of Cincinnati.

For full biographical listings, see the Martindale-Hubbell Law Directory

REISENFELD & STATMAN (AV)

Auburn Barrister House, 2355 Auburn Avenue, 45219
Telephone: 513-381-6810
FAX: 513-381-0255

Sylvan P. Reisenfeld
Alan J. Statman

John L. Day, Jr.
Melisa J. Richter
Bradley A. Reisenfeld
Rosemary E. Scollard
John Schmidt

For full biographical listings, see the Martindale-Hubbell Law Directory

SANTEN & HUGHES A LEGAL PROFESSIONAL ASSOCIATION (AV)

Suite 3100, 312 Walnut Street, 45202
Telephone: 513-721-4450
FAX: 513-721-7644; 721-0109

Charles M. Meyer
Charles E. Reynolds
James P. Wersching
David M. Kothman
R. Mark Addy
Edward E. Santen
Charles J. Kubicki, Jr.

LEGAL SUPPORT PERSONNEL

Karen W. Crane (Corporate Paralegal)
Deborah M. McKinney (Trust/Estate Paralegal)
Karen L. Jansen (Litigation Paralegal)
Bobbie S. Ebbers (Paralegal)

For Complete List of Firm Personnel, See General Section

For full biographical listings, see the Martindale-Hubbell Law Directory

SLUTSKY & SLUTSKY CO., L.P.A. (AV)

Suite 206, 602 Main Street, 45202
Telephone: 513-421-0042
Fax: 513-421-5086

Norman L. Slutsky
June Clayton Slutsky

For full biographical listings, see the Martindale-Hubbell Law Directory

THOMPSON, HINE AND FLORY (AV)

312 Walnut Street, 14th Floor, 45202-4029
Telephone: 513-352-6700
Fax: 513-241-4771;
Telex: 938003
Akron, Ohio Office: 50 S. Main Street, Suite 502, 44308-1828.
Telephone: 216-376-8090.
Fax: 216-376-8386.
Cleveland, Ohio Office: 1100 National City Bank Building, 629 Euclid Avenue, 44114-3070.
Telephone: 216-566-5500.
Fax: 216-556-5583.
Telex: 980217.
Cable Address: "Thomflor".
Columbus, Ohio Office: One Columbus, 10 West Broad Street, 43215-3435.
Telephone: 614-469-3200.
Fax: 614-469-3361.
Dayton, Ohio Office: 2000 Courthouse Plaza, N.E., 45402-1706.
Telephone: 513-443-6600.
Fax: 513-443-6637; 443-6635.

(See Next Column)

THOMPSON, HINE AND FLORY—*Continued*

Palm Beach, Florida Office: 125 Worth Avenue, 33480-4466.
Telephone: 407-833-5900.
Fax: 407-833-5951.
Washington, D.C. Office: 1920 N Street, N.W., 20036-1601.
Telephone: 202-331-8800.
Fax: 202-331-8330.
Telex: 904173.
Cable Address: "Caglaw".
Brussels, Belgium Office: Rue des Chevaliers / Ridderstraat 14 - B.10, B - 1050.
Telephone: 011(32-2) 511-9326.
Fax: 011(-32-2) 513-9206.

MEMBER OF FIRM

Louis F. Solimine

ASSOCIATE

Philomena Saldanha Ashdown

For Complete List of Firm Personnel, See General Section

For full biographical listings, see the Martindale-Hubbell Law Directory

*CLEVELAND,** Cuyahoga Co.

BAKER & HOSTETLER (AV)

3200 National City Center, 1900 East Ninth Street, 44114-3485
Telephone: 216-621-0200
Telecopier: 216-696-0740
TWX: 810 421 8375
RCA Telex: 215032
In Columbus, Ohio: Capitol Square, Suite 2100, 65 East State Street.
Telephone: 614-228-1541.
In Denver, Colorado: 303 East 17th Avenue, Suite 1100.
Telephone: 303-861-0600.
In Houston, Texas: 1000 Louisiana, Suite 2000.
Telephone: 713-751-1600.
In Long Beach, California: 300 Oceangate, Suite 620.
Telephone: 310-432-2827.
In Los Angeles, California: 600 Wilshire Boulevard.
Telephone: 213-624-2400.
In Orlando, Florida: SunBank Center, Suite 2300, 200 South Orange Avenue.
Telephone: 407-649-4000.
In Washington, D. C.: Washington Square, Suite 1100, 1050 Connecticut Avenue, N.W.
Telephone: 202-861-1500.
In College Park, Maryland: 9658 Baltimore Boulevard, Suite 206.
Telephone: 301-441-2781.
In Alexandria, Virginia: 437 North Lee Street.
Telephone: 703-549-1294.
In San Francisco, California: One Sansome Street, Suite 2000.
Telephone: 415-951-4705.

PARTNERS

Susan B. Collins
Matthew R. Goldman
Wendy J. Gibson
John S. Hopkins, III
Thomas R. Lucchesi

ASSOCIATES

R. Timothy Coerdt
David B. Hathaway
Hilary Whipple Rule

For Complete List of Firm Personnel, See General Section

For full biographical listings, see the Martindale-Hubbell Law Directory

KELLEY, MCCANN & LIVINGSTONE (AV)

35th Floor, BP America Building, 200 Public Square, 44114-2302
Telephone: 216-241-3141
FAX: 216-241-3707

MEMBERS OF FIRM

Michael D. Schenker
Bruce L. Waterhouse, Jr.

ASSOCIATE

Peter K. Shelton

For Complete List of Firm Personnel, See General Section

For full biographical listings, see the Martindale-Hubbell Law Directory

RUBENSTEIN, NOVAK, EINBUND, PAVLIK & CELEBREZZE (AV)

Suite 270, Skylight Office Tower Tower City Center, 44113-1498
Telephone: 216-781-8700
Telecopier: 216-781-9227

MEMBERS OF FIRM

Ronald M. Rubenstein
Thomas C. Pavlik

ASSOCIATES

Christine A. Murphy
Scott H. Scharf

For full biographical listings, see the Martindale-Hubbell Law Directory

THOMPSON, HINE AND FLORY (AV)

1100 National City Bank Building, 629 Euclid Avenue, 44114-3070
Telephone: 216-566-5500
Fax: 216-566-5583
Telex: 980217
Cable Address: "Thomflor"
Akron, Ohio Office: 50 S. Main Street, Suite 502, 44308-1828.
Telephone: 216-376-8090.
Fax: 216-376-8386.
Cincinnati, Ohio Office: 312 Walnut Street, 14th Floor, 45202-4029.
Telephone: 513-352-6700.
Fax: 513-241-4771.
Telex: 938003.
Columbus, Ohio Office: One Columbus, 10 West Broad Street, 43215-3435.
Telephone: 614-469-3200.
Fax: 614-469-3361.
Dayton, Ohio Office: 2000 Courthouse Plaza, N.E., 45402-1706.
Telephone: 513-443-6600.
Fax: 513-443-6637; 443-6635.
Palm Beach, Florida Office: 125 Worth Avenue, Suite 117, 33480-4466.
Telephone: 407-833-5900.
Fax: 407-833-5951.
Washington, D.C. Office: 1920 N Street, N.W., 20036-1601.
Telephone: 202-331-8800.
Fax: 202-331-8330.
Telex: 904173.
Cable Address: "Caglaw".
Brussels, Belgium Office: Rue des Chevaliers, Ridderstraat 14 - B.10, B - 1050.
Telephone: 011(32-2) 511-9326.
Fax: 011(32-2) 513-9206.

MEMBERS OF FIRM

John H. Gherlein (Retired)
Alan R. Lepene
John F. Kostelnik, III
Craig R. Martahus
David J. Naftzinger

ASSOCIATES

Katherine D. Brandt
Dean D. Gamin

For Complete List of Firm Personnel, See General Section

For full biographical listings, see the Martindale-Hubbell Law Directory

ZIEGLER, METZGER & MILLER (AV)

2020 Huntington Building, 44115-1407
Telephone: 216-781-5470
FAX: 216-781-0714

MEMBER OF FIRM

Stephen M. Darlington

ASSOCIATES

Stephen M. Bales
Christopher W. Siemen

For Complete List of Firm Personnel, See General Section

For full biographical listings, see the Martindale-Hubbell Law Directory

*COLUMBUS,** Franklin Co.

* indicates certain Bar Register subscribers whose principal office is located elsewhere in the state and who have arranged for representation as a part of the state capital listings that follow

* BAKER & HOSTETLER (AV)

Capitol Square, Suite 2100, 65 East State Street, 43215-4260
Telephone: 614-228-1541
Telecopier: 614-462-2616
In Cleveland, Ohio: 3200 National City Center, 1900 East Ninth Street.
Telephone: 216-621-0200.
In Denver, Colorado: 303 East 17th Avenue, Suite 1100.
Telephone: 202-861-1500.
In Houston, Texas: 1000 Louisiana, Suite 2000.
Telephone: 713-751-1600.
In Long Beach, California: 300 Oceangate, Suite 620.
Telephone: 310-432-2827.
In Los Angeles, California: 600 Wilshire.
Telephone: 213-624-2400.
In Orlando, Florida: SunBank Center, Suite 2300, 200 South Orange Avenue.
Telephone: 407-649-4000.
In Washington, D. C.: Washington Square, Suite 1100, 1050 Connecticut Avenue, N.W.
Telephone: 202-861-1500.
In College Park, Maryland: 9658 Baltimore Boulevard, Suite 301.
Telephone: 301-441-2781.
In Alexandria, Virginia: 437 North Lee Street.
Telephone: 703-549-1294.
In San Francisco, California: One Sansome Street, Suite 2000.
Telephone: 415-951-4705.

(See Next Column)

BAKER & HOSTETLER, *Columbus—Continued*

PARTNERS

Henry P. Montgomery, IV
Alec Wightman

For Complete List of Firm Personnel, See General Section

For full biographical listings, see the Martindale-Hubbell Law Directory

EMENS, KEGLER, BROWN, HILL & RITTER (AV)

Capitol Square Suite 1800, 65 East State Street, 43215-4294
Telephone: 614-462-5400
Telecopier: 614-464-2634
Cable Address: "Law EKBHR"
Telex: 246671

John P. Brody
Robin Smith Hoke
Allen L. Handlan
Larry J. McClatchey

COUNSEL

John C. Deal

David M. Johnson
Nancy L. Koerner
Gregory D. May

Representative Clients: First Federal Savings & Loan of Galion; JMB Realty.

For Complete List of Firm Personnel, See General Section

For full biographical listings, see the Martindale-Hubbell Law Directory

LUPER, WOLINETZ, SHERIFF & NEIDENTHAL A LEGAL PROFESSIONAL ASSOCIATION (AV)

1200 LeVeque Tower, 50 West Broad Street, 43215-3374
Telephone: 614-221-7663
Telecopier: 614-464-2425

Frederick M. Luper
William B. Logan, Jr.
David M. Whittaker

Deborah Pitluk Ecker
Ruth Ann Hohl
Kenneth M. Richards

Representative Client: Bank One of Columbus.

For full biographical listings, see the Martindale-Hubbell Law Directory

PORTER, WRIGHT, MORRIS & ARTHUR (AV)

41 South High Street, 43215-6194
Telephone: 614-227-2000; (800-533-2794)
Telex: 6503213584 MCI
Fax: 614-227-2100
Dayton, Ohio Office: One Dayton Centre, One South Main Street, 45402.
Telephones: 513-228-2411; (800-533-4434).
Fax: 513-449-6820.
Cincinnati, Ohio Office: 250 E. Fifth Street, 45202-4166.
Telephones: 513-381-4700; (800-582-5813).
Fax: 513-421-0991.
Cleveland, Ohio Office: 925 Euclid Avenue, 44115-1483.
Telephones: 216-443-9000; (800-824-1980).
Fax: 216-443-9011.
Washington, D.C. Office: 1233 20th Street, N.W., 20036-2395.
Telephones: 202-778-3000; (800-456-7962).
Fax: 202-778-3063.
Naples, Florida Office: 4501 Tamiami Trail North, 33940-3060.
Telephones: 813-263-8898;(800-876-7962).
Fax: 813-436-2990.

MEMBERS OF FIRM
COLUMBUS, OHIO OFFICE

Michael J. Barren
James P. Botti
Thomas E. Cavendish
S. Ronald Cook, Jr.
Timothy E. Grady
Polly J. Harris
John C. Hartranft
George M. Hauswirth
Jennifer T. Mills
Jack R. Pigman
James H. Prior
Teri G. Rasmussen
H. Grant Stephenson
Richard G. Terapak

ASSOCIATES
COLUMBUS, OHIO OFFICE

Heather Lynn Guise
Waymon B. McLeskey, II
Debra Ann Willet

OF COUNSEL
COLUMBUS, OHIO OFFICE

W. John Pritchard

DAYTON, OHIO OFFICE
RESIDENT MEMBER

Walter Reynolds

DAYTON, OHIO OFFICE
RESIDENT ASSOCIATE

Lawrence S. Walter

CINCINNATI, OHIO OFFICE
RESIDENT ASSOCIATES

Stephen P. Kenkel
Francine A. Wayman

(See Next Column)

CLEVELAND, OHIO OFFICE
RESIDENT MEMBERS

Jeffrey Baddeley
Thomas J. Talcott

Representative Clients: Alco-Standard Corporation; American Electric Power Service Corporation; Battelle Memorial Institute; Ford Motor Co.; Huntington Bancshares Incorporated; National City Bank, Columbus; Ohio State Medical Association; Society National Bank; Technical Rubber Co.

For Complete List of Firm Personnel, See General Section

For full biographical listings, see the Martindale-Hubbell Law Directory

*** THOMPSON, HINE AND FLORY (AV)**

One Columbus, 10 West Broad Street, 43215-3435
Telephone: 614-469-3200
Fax: 614-469-3361
Akron, Ohio Office: 50 S. Main Street, Suite 502, 44308-1828.
Telephone: 216-376-8090.
Fax: 216-376-8386.
Cincinnati, Ohio Office: 312 Walnut Street, 14th Floor, 45202-4029.
Telephone: 513-352-6700.
Fax: 513-241-4771.
Telex: 938003.
Cleveland, Ohio Office: 1100 National City Bank Building, 629 Euclid Avenue, 44114-3070.
Telephone: 216-566-5500.
Fax: 216-556-5583.
Telex: 980217.
Cable Address: "Thomflor".
Dayton, Ohio Office: 2000 Courthouse Plaza, N.E., 45402-1706.
Telephone: 513-443-6600.
Fax: 513-443-6637; 443-6635.
Palm Beach, Florida Office: 125 Worth Avenue, 33480-4466.
Telephone: 407-833-5900.
Fax: 407-833-5951.
Washington, D.C. Office: 1920 N Street, N.W., 20036-1601.
Telephone: 202-331-8800.
Fax: 202-331-8330.
Telex: 904173.
Cable Address: "Caglaw".
Brussels, Belgium Office: Rue des Chevaliers / Ridderstraat 14 - B.10, B - 1050.
Telephone: 011(32-2) 511-9326.
Fax: 011(32-2) 513-9206.

MEMBERS OF FIRM

Thomas R. Allen
Daniel J. Hunter
Thomas E. Lodge
Thomas C. Scott (Partner-in-Charge in Columbus)

ASSOCIATES

Douglas L. Hertlein
Bonnie Irvin O'Neil
Susan L. Rhiel
Richard K. Stovall

OF COUNSEL

Charles B. Mills, Jr.

For Complete List of Firm Personnel, See General Section

For full biographical listings, see the Martindale-Hubbell Law Directory

VORYS, SATER, SEYMOUR AND PEASE (AV)

52 East Gay Street, P.O. Box 1008, 43216-1008
Telephone: 614-464-6400
Telex: 241348
Telecopier: 614-464-6350
Cable Address: "Vorysater"
Washington, D.C. Office: Suite 1111, 1828 L Street, N.W., 20036-5104.
Telephone: 202-467-8800.
Telex: 440693.
Telecopier: 202-467-8900.
Cleveland, Ohio Office: 2100 One Cleveland Center, 1375 East Ninth Street, 44114-1724.
Telephone: 216-479-6100.
Telecopier: 216-479-6060.
Cincinnati, Ohio Office: Suite 2100, 221 East Fourth Street, P.O. Box 0236, 45201-0236.
Telephone: 513-723-4000.
Telecopier: 513-723-4056.

MEMBERS OF FIRM

Robert W. Werth
Frederick R. Reed (Resident, Cincinnati, Ohio Office)
James M. Ball
Robert J. Sidman
Reginald W. Jackson
Terry M. Miller
Steven W. Mershon
Drew T. Parobek (Resident, Cleveland, Ohio Office)
Anthony J. O'Malley

Randall D. LaTour
Robert E. Bardwell, Jr.

Representative Client: Honda of America Mfg., Inc.
Local Counsel: Abbott Laboratories; Anheuser-Busch, Inc.; Connecticut General Life Insurance Co.; Exxon Company U.S.A.; General Motors Corp.; Navistar International Corporation; Ohio Manufacturers Assn.; Ranco Inc.; Wendy's International, Inc.

(See Next Column)

VORYS, SATER, SEYMOUR AND PEASE—*Continued*

For Complete List of Firm Personnel, See General Section

For full biographical listings, see the Martindale-Hubbell Law Directory

*DAYTON,** Montgomery Co.

ALTICK & CORWIN (AV)

1700 One Dayton Centre, One South Main Street, 45402
Telephone: 513-223-1201
Fax: 513-223-5100

MEMBERS OF FIRM

Robert N. Farquhar
Marshall D. Ruchman
R. Paul Perkins, Jr.
Thomas R. Noland
Thomas M. Baggott
Robert B. Berner
Dennis J. Adkins
Richard A. Boucher
Philip B. Herron
Deborah J. Adler

OF COUNSEL

Raymond J. Pikna, Jr.

ASSOCIATE

Donald K. Scott

RETIRED

Robert B. Brumbaugh
Robert K. Corwin
Ronald H. McDonnell, Jr.

Representative Clients: City of Beavercreek; City of Centerville; The Miami Conservancy District; Miami Valley Cable Council; Woodland Cemetery Assn.

For Complete List of Firm Personnel, See General Section

For full biographical listings, see the Martindale-Hubbell Law Directory

BOGIN, PATTERSON & BOHMAN (AV)

1200 Talbott Tower, 131 North Ludlow Street, 45402
Telephone: 513-226-1200
FAX: 513-226-1625

MEMBERS OF FIRM

Dennis L. Patterson
Jerome B. Bohman
James C. Ellis
Curtis F. Slaton
Randall L. Stump

OF COUNSEL

Asher Bogin

For full biographical listings, see the Martindale-Hubbell Law Directory

THOMPSON, HINE AND FLORY (AV)

2000 Courthouse Plaza, N.E., 45402-1706
Telephone: 513-443-6600
Fax: 513-443-6637; 443-6635
Akron, Ohio Office: 50 S. Main Street, Suite 502, 44308-1828.
Telephone: 216-376-8090.
Fax: 216-376-8386.
Cincinnati, Ohio Office: 312 Walnut Street, 14th Floor, 45202-4029.
Telephone: 513-352-6700.
Fax: 513-241-4771.
Telex: 938003.
Cleveland, Ohio Office: 1100 National City Bank Building, 629 Euclid Avenue, 44114-3070.
Telephone: 216-566-5500.
Fax: 216-556-5583.
Telex: 980217.
Cable Address: "Thomflor".
Columbus, Ohio Office: One Columbus, 10 West Broad Street, 43215-3435.
Telephone: 614-469-3200.
Fax: 614-469-3361.
Palm Beach, Florida Office: 125 Worth Avenue, 33480-4466.
Telephone: 407-833-5900.
Fax: 407-833-5951.
Washington, D.C. Office: 1920 N Street, N.W., 20036-1601.
Telephone: 202-331-8800.
Fax: 202-331-8330.
Telex: 904173.
Cable Address: "Caglaw".
Brussels, Belgium Office: Rue des Chevaliers / Ridderstraat 14 - B.10, B - 1050.
Telephone: 011(32-2) 511-9326.
Fax: 011(32-2) 513-9206.

MEMBERS OF FIRM

Lawrence T. Burick
Peter J. Donahue

For Complete List of Firm Personnel, See General Section

For full biographical listings, see the Martindale-Hubbell Law Directory

*TOLEDO,** Lucas Co.

BARKAN AND ROBON (AV)

Suite 405 Spitzer Building, 43604-1302
Telephone: 419-244-5591
FAX: 419-244-8736

(See Next Column)

MEMBERS OF FIRM

William I. Barkan
Marvin A. Robon
Russell R. Miller
A. Thomas Christensen
Paul A. Radon
Gregory R. Elder

ASSOCIATES

Cynthia Godbey Tesznar
Marshall W. Guerin

For full biographical listings, see the Martindale-Hubbell Law Directory

FREDERICKSON & HEINTSCHEL, CO., L.P.A. (AV)

1313 Fifth Third Center, 608 Madison Avenue, 43604
Telephone: 419-242-5100
FAX: 419-242-5556

Craig F. Frederickson
Thomas W. Heintschel

Douglas W. King

For full biographical listings, see the Martindale-Hubbell Law Directory

SPENGLER NATHANSON (AV)

608 Madison Avenue, Suite 1000, 43604-1169
Telephone: 419-241-2201
FAX: 419-241-8599

MEMBERS OF FIRM

Louis J. Hattner
Michael W. Bragg

Counsel for: Fifth-Third Bank of Northwestern Ohio, N.A.; Huntington Bank of Toledo; Society Bank & Trust; Seaway Food Town, Inc.; The University of Toledo; U.S. Fidelity & Guaranty Co.; Toledo Lucas County Port Authority; Toledo Board of Education; Great American Insurance Company.

For Complete List of Firm Personnel, See General Section

For full biographical listings, see the Martindale-Hubbell Law Directory

*YOUNGSTOWN,** Mahoning Co.

HARRINGTON HUXLEY SMITH MITCHELL & REED (AV)

1200 Mahoning Bank Building, 44503-1508
Telephone: 216-744-1111
Telecopier: 216-744-2029

MEMBERS OF FIRM

John C. Litty, Jr.
Frederick S. Coombs, III

Counsel for: The Mahoning National Bank; WKBN Broadcasting Corp.; WYTV, Inc.
Representative Clients: Ohio Edison Co.; Ohio Bell Telephone Co.; Bank One Cleveland, N.A.

For Complete List of Firm Personnel, See General Section

For full biographical listings, see the Martindale-Hubbell Law Directory

OKLAHOMA

*OKLAHOMA CITY,** Oklahoma Co.

DAY, EDWARDS, FEDERMAN, PROPESTER & CHRISTENSEN, P.C. (AV)

Suite 2900 First Oklahoma Tower, 210 Park Avenue, 73102-5605
Telephone: 405-239-2121
Telecopier: 405-236-1012

Bruce W. Day
Joe E. Edwards
William B. Federman
Richard P. Propester
D. Wade Christensen
J. Clay Christensen
Kent A. Gilliland
Rodney J. Heggy
Ricki Valerie Sonders
Thomas Pitchlynn Howell, IV
John C. Platt

David R. Widdoes
Lori R. Roberts
Carolyn A. Romberg

OF COUNSEL

Herbert F. (Jack) Hewett
Jeanette Cook Timmons
Joel Warren Harmon
Jane S. Eulberg
Mark A. Cohen

Representative Clients: Aetna Life Insurance Co.; Boatmen's First National Bank of Oklahoma; Borg-Warner Chemicals, Inc.; City Bank & Trust; Federal Deposit Insurance Corp.; Bank One, Oklahoma City; Haskell Lemon Construction Co.; Merrill Lynch, Pierce, Fenner & Smith, Inc.; Prudential Securities, Inc.

For full biographical listings, see the Martindale-Hubbell Law Directory

Oklahoma City—Continued

FULLER, TUBB & POMEROY (AV)

800 Bank of Oklahoma Plaza, 201 Robert S. Kerr Avenue, 73102-4292
Telephone: 405-235-2575
Fax: 405-232-8384

MEMBERS OF FIRM

G. M. Fuller
Jerry Tubb
L. David Pomeroy
Joe Heaton
Michael A. Bickford
Terry Stokes

OF COUNSEL

Thomas J. Kenan

LEGAL SUPPORT PERSONNEL

Sherie S. Adams (Legal Assistant)

Representative Clients: French Petroleum Corp.; Independent Insurance Agents of Oklahoma, Inc.; LTV Energy Products Co.; Northwestern National Life Insurance Co.; Purina Mills, Inc.; Sequa Corp.; Halliburton Oil Producing Co.; Chemical Bank/Chemical Financial Corporation; Pitney Bowes, Inc.; Norwest Banks.

For full biographical listings, see the Martindale-Hubbell Law Directory

HARTZOG CONGER & CASON, A PROFESSIONAL CORPORATION (AV)

1600 Bank of Oklahoma Plaza, 73102
Telephone: 405-235-7000
Facsimile: 405-235-7329

Larry D. Hartzog
J. William Conger
Len Cason
James C. Prince
Alan Newman
Steven C. Davis
Valerie K. Couch
Mark D. Dickey
Joseph P. Hogsett
John D. Robertson
Kurt M. Rupert
Laura Haag McConnell

Susan B. Shields
Ryan S. Wilson
Melanie J. Jester
Armand Paliotta
Julia Watson
J. Leslie LaReau

OF COUNSEL

Kent F. Frates

For full biographical listings, see the Martindale-Hubbell Law Directory

HASTIE AND KIRSCHNER, A PROFESSIONAL CORPORATION (AV)

3000 Oklahoma Tower, 210 Park Avenue, 73102-5604
Telephone: 405-239-6404
Telecopier: 405-239-6403

Mark H. Bennett
Mitchell D. Blackburn
George W. Dahnke
John W. Funk
John D. Hastie
Michael Paul Kirschner
Ronald L. Matlock
Kieran D. Maye, Jr.
Robert D. McCutcheon
Kiran A. Phansalkar
Irwin H. Steinhorn
John W. Swinford, Jr.
Ruston C. Welch

OF COUNSEL

William S. Price

For Complete List of Firm Personnel, See General Section

For full biographical listings, see the Martindale-Hubbell Law Directory

MOCK, SCHWABE, WALDO, ELDER, REEVES & BRYANT, A PROFESSIONAL CORPORATION (AV)

Fifteenth Floor, One Leadership Square, 211 North Robinson Avenue, 73102
Telephone: 405-235-5500
Telecopy: 405-235-2875

G. Blaine Schwabe, III
Gary A. Bryant
Steven L. Barghols
Kevin M. Coffey
Sarah Alexander Hall

Representative Clients: Bank Of Oklahoma, N.A.; Equity Bank for Savings, F.A.; Farm Credit Bank of Wichita; Financial Federal Credit, Inc.; Kingfisher Bank & Trust Company; LSB Industries; Metropolitan Life Insurance Co.; Orix Credit Alliance, Inc.; The Equitable Life Assurance Society of the United States; Liberty Bank & Trust Company of Oklahoma City.

For Complete List of Firm Personnel, See General Section

For full biographical listings, see the Martindale-Hubbell Law Directory

PRINGLE & PRINGLE, A PROFESSIONAL CORPORATION (AV)

1601 N.W. Expressway, Suite 2100, 73118
Telephone: 405-848-4810
Fax: 405-848-4819

(See Next Column)

Lynn A. Pringle
Laura Nan Smith Pringle
Conni L. Allen
Stephen W. Elliott
James R. Martin, Jr.

OF COUNSEL

Alvin C. Harrell
Michael P. Sullivan

Representative Clients: Bankers Systems, Inc.; Central Oklahoma Clearing House Association; The Bankers Bank; Bank of Western Oklahoma, Elk City; The Farmers Bank, Carnagie; The First National Bank and Trust Co., Chickasha; The First National Bank of Texhoma; Oklahoma Home Based Business Association; First State Bank, Idabel; Great Western Drilling, Co.

For full biographical listings, see the Martindale-Hubbell Law Directory

RAINEY, ROSS, RICE & BINNS (AV)

735 First National Center West, 73102-7405
Telephone: 405-235-1356
Telecopier: 405-235-2340

MEMBERS OF FIRM

H. D. Binns, Jr.
Robert J. Campbell, Jr.
Michael R. Perri

General Attorneys for Oklahoma: Santa Fe Pacific Corp.; Santa Fe Railway System.
Oklahoma Counsel for: Oklahoma Gas & Electric Co.
Attorneys for: Agristor Credit Corp.; AT&T Communications; Boatmen's First National Bank of Oklahoma; The Circle K Corp.; Continental Air Lines; Dover Elevator Co.; Dover Industries Acceptance, Inc.

For Complete List of Firm Personnel, See General Section

For full biographical listings, see the Martindale-Hubbell Law Directory

SELF, GIDDENS & LEES, INC. (AV)

2725 Oklahoma Tower, 210 Park Avenue, 73102-5604
Telephone: 405-232-3001
Telecopier: 405-232-5553

Jared D. Giddens
C. Ray Lees
Shannon T. Self

Thomas J. Blalock
Christopher R. Graves
W. Shane Smithton
Bryan J. Wells

For full biographical listings, see the Martindale-Hubbell Law Directory

*TULSA,** Tulsa Co.

BOESCHE, McDERMOTT & ESKRIDGE (AV)

Suite 800 Oneok Plaza, 100 West Fifth Street, 74103
Telephone: 918-583-1777
Fax: 918-592-5809
Muskogee, Oklahoma Office: 420 Broadway, 74101.
Telephone: 918-683-6100.

MEMBERS OF FIRM

David B. McKinney
Bradley K. Beasley

ASSOCIATE

Sheila M. Powers

Representative Clients: Bank of America; The Chase Manhattan Bank; Community Bank & Trust Co.; Federal Deposit Insurance Corp.; Resolution Trust Corp.; Superior Federal Bank; Union Bank, formerly Security Pacific National Bank; Vian State Bank.

For Complete List of Firm Personnel, See General Section

For full biographical listings, see the Martindale-Hubbell Law Directory

GABLE & GOTWALS (AV)

2000 Bank IV Center, 15 West Sixth Street, 74119-5447
Telephone: 918-582-9201
Facsimile: 918-586-8383

Teresa B. Adwan
Pamela S. Anderson
John R. Barker
David L. Bryant
Gene C. Buzzard
Dennis Clarke Cameron
Timothy A. Carney
Renee DeMoss
Elsie C. Draper
Sidney G. Dunagan
Theodore Q. Eliot
Richard W. Gable
Jeffrey Don Hassell
Patricia Ledvina Himes
Oliver S. Howard
Richard D. Koljack, Jr.
J. Daniel Morgan
Joseph W. Morris
Elizabeth R. Muratet
Richard B. Noulles
Ronald N. Ricketts
John Henry Rule
M. Benjamin Singletary
James M. Sturdivant
Patrick O. Waddel
Michael D. Hall
David Edward Keglovits
Stephen W. Lake
Kari S. McKee
Terry D. Ragsdale
Jeffrey C. Rambach

OF COUNSEL

G. Ellis Gable
Charles P. Gotwals, Jr.

For full biographical listings, see the Martindale-Hubbell Law Directory

Tulsa—Continued

HUFFMAN ARRINGTON KIHLE GABERINO & DUNN, A PROFESSIONAL CORPORATION (AV)

1000 ONEOK Plaza, 74103
Telephone: 918-585-8141
Telecopier: 918-588-7873
Oklahoma City Office: 2212 NW 50th Street, Suite 163.
Telephone: 405-840-4408.
Telecopier: 405-843-9090.

Sidney K. Swinson — William T. Walker

General Counsel for: ONEOK Inc.; Oklahoma Natural Gas Co.; H W Allen Co.; ONEOK Exploration Co.; Woodland Bank; ONEOK Drilling Co.; ONEOK Resources Co.; Renberg's, Inc.

For Complete List of Firm Personnel, See General Section

For full biographical listings, see the Martindale-Hubbell Law Directory

LIPE, GREEN, PASCHAL, TRUMP & BRAGG, A PROFESSIONAL CORPORATION (AV)

3700 First National Tower, 15 East Fifth Street, Suite 3700, 74103-4344
Telephone: 918-599-9400
Fax: 918-599-9404

Larry B. Lipe
James E. Green, Jr.
Richard A. Paschal
Timothy T. Trump
Patricia Dunmire Bragg

Melodie Freeman-Burney
Mark E. Dreyer
Constance L. Young
Leah Lowder Mills

For full biographical listings, see the Martindale-Hubbell Law Directory

SNEED, LANG, ADAMS & BARNETT, A PROFESSIONAL CORPORATION (AV)

2300 Williams Center Tower II, Two West Second Street, 74103
Telephone: 918-583-3145
Telecopier: 918-582-0410

James C. Lang
D. Faith Orlowski
Brian S. Gaskill
G. Steven Stidham
Stephen R. McNamara
Thomas E. Black, Jr.
Robbie Emery Burke
C. Raymond Patton, Jr.
Frederick K. Slicker
Richard D. Black
John D. Russell
Jeffrey S. Swyers

OF COUNSEL

James L. Sneed
O. Edwin Adams
Howard G. Barnett, Jr.

Representative Clients: Amoco Production Company; Continental Bank; Deloitte & Touche; Enron Corporation; Halliburton Energy Services; Helmerich & Payne, Inc.; Lehman Brothers, Inc.; Shell Oil Company; Smith Barney, Inc.; State Farm Mutual Automobile Insurance Company.

For full biographical listings, see the Martindale-Hubbell Law Directory

OREGON

*PORTLAND,** Multnomah Co.

BLACK HELTERLINE (AV)

1200 The Bank of California Tower, 707 S.W. Washington Street, 97205
Telephone: 503-224-5560
Telecopier: 503-224-6148

MEMBER OF FIRM

Ronald T. Adams

ASSOCIATES

James M. Baumgartner — Paul R. Rundle

Representative Client: The Bank of California, N.A.

For Complete List of Firm Personnel, See General Section

For full biographical listings, see the Martindale-Hubbell Law Directory

SUSSMAN SHANK WAPNICK CAPLAN & STILES (AV)

1000 S.W. Broadway Suite 1400, 97205
Telephone: 503-227-1111
Telecopier: 503-248-0130

MEMBERS OF FIRM

Norman Wapnick
Barry P. Caplan
John P. Davenport
Howard M. Levine
Stuart I. Teicher
Jeffrey C. Misley

(See Next Column)

ASSOCIATES

Robert L. Carlton
Michael G. Halligan
Thomas W. Stilley

OF COUNSEL

Jerome B. Shank

For Complete List of Firm Personnel, See General Section

For full biographical listings, see the Martindale-Hubbell Law Directory

PENNSYLVANIA

*ALLENTOWN,** Lehigh Co.

KARL E. FRIEND (AV)

Westfield Corporate Center, Suite 310, 4905 Tilghman Street, 18104
Telephone: 610-391-9878
Telecopier: 610-391-9879
Reading, Pennsylvania Office: 539 Court Street.
Telephone: 610-375-8979.

OF COUNSEL

Stephen J. Palopoli, II

For full biographical listings, see the Martindale-Hubbell Law Directory

BLUE BELL, Montgomery Co.

LESSER & KAPLIN, PROFESSIONAL CORPORATION (AV)

350 Sentry Parkway, Bldg. 640, 19422-0757
Telephone: 610-828-2900; Telecopier: 610-828-1555
Marlton, New Jersey Office: Three Greentree Centre, Suite 104, Route 73, 08053-3215.
Telephone: 609-596-2400.
Telecopier: 609-596-8185.

Lawrence R. Lesser
Bruce R. Lesser
Robert A. Kargen
Harold G. Cohen (Resident, Marlton, New Jersey Office)
David E. Stern
Gretchen M. Santamour
Leona Mogavero

Domenic E. Pacitti
Janet I. Moore
Richard L. Schepacarter (Resident, Marlton, New Jersey Office)
Maulin S. Vidwans

For full biographical listings, see the Martindale-Hubbell Law Directory

*HARRISBURG,** Dauphin Co.

McNEES, WALLACE & NURICK (AV)

100 Pine Street, P.O. Box 1166, 17108
Telephone: 717-232-8000
Fax: 717-237-5300

MEMBERS OF FIRM

Eric L. Brossman
David B. Disney
Michael A. Doctrow
Edward W. Rothman

ASSOCIATES

Brett D. Davis
Kathleen A. Dunst
P. Nicholas Guarneschelli

For Complete List of Firm Personnel, See General Section

For full biographical listings, see the Martindale-Hubbell Law Directory

NAUMAN, SMITH, SHISSLER & HALL (AV)

Eighteenth Floor, 200 North Third Street, P.O. Box 840, 17108-0840
Telephone: 717-236-3010
Telefax: 717-234-1925

MEMBERS OF FIRM

David C. Eaton
Spencer G. Nauman, Jr.
John C. Sullivan
J. Stephen Feinour
Craig J. Staudenmaier

ASSOCIATES

Benjamin Charles Dunlap, Jr. — Stephen J. Keene

OF COUNSEL

Ralph W. Boyles, Jr.

Representative Clients: Mellon Bank, N.A.; PNC Bank, N.A.; General Motors Acceptance Corp.; Enders Insurance Associates; Chrysler Credit Corp.; Capital Area Tax Collection Bureau.

For full biographical listings, see the Martindale-Hubbell Law Directory

*MEDIA,** Delaware Co.

KASSAB ARCHBOLD JACKSON & O'BRIEN (AV)

Lawyers-Title Building, 214 North Jackson Street, P.O. Box 626, 19063
Telephone: 610-565-3800
Telecopier: 610-892-6888
Wilmington, Delaware Office: 1326 King Street.
Telephone: 302-656-3393.
Fax: 302-656-1993.
Wildwood, New Jersey Office: 5201 New Jersey Avenue.
Telephone: 609-522-6559.

MEMBERS OF FIRM

Edward Kassab
William C. Archbold, Jr.
Robert James Jackson
Joseph Patrick O'Brien
Richard A. Stanko
Roy T. J. Stegena

OF COUNSEL

Matthew J. Ryan
John W. Nilon, Jr.

ASSOCIATES

Kevin William Gibson
Cynthia Kassab Larosa
Marc S. Stein
Terrance A. Kline
George C. McFarland, Jr.
Jill E. Aversa
Pamela A. La Torre
Kenneth D. Kynett

Representative Clients furnished upon request.

For full biographical listings, see the Martindale-Hubbell Law Directory

*NORRISTOWN,** Montgomery Co.

MANNING, KINKEAD, BROOKS & BRADBURY, A PROFESSIONAL CORPORATION (AV)

412 DeKalb Street, 19404-0231
Telephone: 610-279-1800
Fax: 610-279-8682

Franklin L. Wright (1880-1965)
William Perry Manning, Jr.
William H. Kinkead, III
William H. Bradbury, III

Cheri D. Andrews

Counsel for: The Philadelphia National Bank; John Deere Co.; The Rouse Co.; Consolidated Rail Corp.; Bethlehem Steel Co.; Royal Globe Insurance Co.; Nationwide Mutual Insurance Co.

For full biographical listings, see the Martindale-Hubbell Law Directory

*PHILADELPHIA,** Philadelphia Co.

ADELMAN LAVINE GOLD AND LEVIN, A PROFESSIONAL CORPORATION (AV)

Suite 1900, Two Penn Center Plaza, 19102-1799
Telephone: 215-568-7515
Telecopier: 215-557-7922

Lewis H. Gold
Robert H. Levin
Gary M. Schildhorn
Barry D. Kleban
Gary D. Bressler
Steven D. Usdin
Kevin W. Walsh
Raymond H. Lemisch

Robert M. Bovarnick
Douglas N. Candeub
Alan I. Moldoff
Kathleen E. Torbit
David L. Zive
Leon R. Barson
Matthew J. Swett
Douglas M. Leavitt

For full biographical listings, see the Martindale-Hubbell Law Directory

ASTOR WEISS KAPLAN & ROSENBLUM (AV)

The Bellevue, 6th Floor, Broad Street at Walnut, 19102
Telephone: 215-790-0100
Fax: 215-790-0509
Bala Cynwyd, Pennsylvania Office: Suite 100, Three Bala Plaza West, P.O. Box 1665.
Telephone: 610-667-8660.
Fax: 610-667-2783.
Cherry Hill, New Jersey Office: Woodland Falls Corporate Park, 210 Lake Drive East, Suite 201.
Telephone: 609-795-1113.
Fax: 609-795-7413.

MEMBERS OF FIRM

Paul C. Astor
Alvin M. Weiss (1936-1976)
G. David Rosenblum
Arthur H. Kaplan
Barbara Oaks Silver
Richard H. Martin
Allen B. Dubroff
David S. Workman
David S. Mandel
David Gutin (Resident at Bala Cynwyd Office)
Joseph B. Finlay, Jr.
Howard K. Goldstein
Steven W. Smith
Gerald J. Schorr
Jean M. Biesecker (Resident, Bala Cynwyd Office)

(See Next Column)

ASSOCIATES

Carol L. Vassallo
Thomas J. Maiorino
John R. Poeta
Bradley J. Begelman
Andrew S. Kessler
Marc S. Zamsky
Janet G. Felgoise (Resident, Bala Cynwyd Office)
Jacqueline G. Segal (Resident, Bala Cynwyd Office)

SPECIAL COUNSEL

Neil Hurowitz (Resident, Bala Cynwyd Office)

OF COUNSEL

Erwin L. Pincus
Edward W. Silver
Lloyd Zane Remick

For full biographical listings, see the Martindale-Hubbell Law Directory

BALLARD SPAHR ANDREWS & INGERSOLL (AV)

1735 Market Street, 51st Floor, 19103-7599
Telephone: 215-665-8500
Fax: 215-864-8999
Denver, Colorado Office: Seventeenth Street Plaza Building, Suite 2300, 1225 17th Street.
Telephone: 303-292-2400.
Fax: 303-296-3956.
Kaunas, Lithuania Office: Donelaicio g., 71-2, Kaunas 3000.
Telephone: (370-7) 20 56 66.
Fax: (370-7) 20 56 91.
Salt Lake City, Utah Office: One Utah Center, Suite 1200, 201 South Main Street.
Telephone: 801-531-3000.
Fax: 801-531-3001.
Washington, D.C. Office: Suite 900 East, 555 13th Street, N.W.
Telephone: 202-383-8800.
Fax: 202-383-8877; 383-8893.
Baltimore, Maryland Office: 300 East Lombard Street. 19th Floor.
Telephone: 410-528-5600.
Fax: 410-528-5650.
Camden, New Jersey Office: 800 Hudson Square, 5th Floor.
Telephone: 609-541-5577.
Fax: 609-541-8272.

Philip B. Korb
Vincent J. Marriott, III
William A. Slaughter

For Complete List of Firm Personnel, See General Section

For full biographical listings, see the Martindale-Hubbell Law Directory

BUCHANAN INGERSOLL, PROFESSIONAL CORPORATION (AV)

Two Logan Square Twelfth Floor, 18th & Arch Streets, 19103
Telephone: 215-665-8700
Telecopier: 215-569-2066
Pittsburgh, Pennsylvania Office: 5800 USX Tower, 600 Grant Street.
Telephone: 412-562-8800.
Harrisburg, Pennsylvania Office: Vartan Parc, 30 North Third Street.
Telephone: 717-237-4800.
Tampa, Florida Office: 101 East Kennedy Boulevard, Suite 1030.
Telephone: 813-222-8180.
North Miami Beach, Florida Office: 19495 Biscayne Boulevard.
Telephone: 305-933-5600.
Lexington, Kentucky Office: 1210 Vine Center Office Tower, 333 West Vine Street.
Telephone: 606-225-5333.
Princeton, New Jersey Office: Buchanan Ingersoll, A Partnership, College Centre, 500 College Road East.
Telephone: 609-452-2666.

Kenneth E. Aaron
Jerome N. Kline
Lawrence J. Lichtenstein

Stuart M. Brown
Robert Bruce Eyre
Sherry Kajdan Vetterlein

For Complete List of Firm Personnel, See General Section

For full biographical listings, see the Martindale-Hubbell Law Directory

LESLIE J. CARSON, JR. (AV)

42 South 15th Street, Suite 1150, 19102
Telephone: 215-568-1980
Fax: 215-568-6882

For full biographical listings, see the Martindale-Hubbell Law Directory

CIARDI & DIDONATO, P.C. (AV)

1900 Spruce Street, 19103
Telephone: 215-546-4370
Fax: 215-985-4175
Atlantic City, New Jersey Office: 30 South New York Avenue, 08401.
Telephone: 609-345-4080.
Telecopier: 609-348-2256.

(See Next Column)

CIARDI & DIDONATO P.C.—*Continued*

Albert A. Ciardi, Jr.
Edward J. DiDonato
Paul J. Winterhalter
Aris J. Karalis
Paul Brinton Maschmeyer
Camille Spinale

Donald Ethan Jeffery
Albert A. Ciardi, III
William P. Freeman

For full biographical listings, see the Martindale-Hubbell Law Directory

DUANE, MORRIS & HECKSCHER (AV)

Suite 4200 One Liberty Place, 19103-7396
Telephone: 215-979-1000
FAX: 215-979-1020
Harrisburg, Pennsylvania Office: 305 North Front Street, 5th Floor, P.O. Box 1003.
Telephone: 717-237-5500.
Fax: 717-232-4015.
Wilmington, Delaware Office: Suite 1500, 1201 Market Street.
Telephone: 302-571-5550.
Fax: 302-571-5560.
New York, N.Y. Office: 112 E. 42nd Street, Suite 2125.
Telephone: 212-499-0410.
Fax: 212-499-0420.
Wayne, Pennsylvania Office 735 Chesterbrook Boulevard, Suite 300.
Telephone: 610-647-3555.
Allentown, Pennsylvania Office: 968 Postal Road, Suite 200.
Telephone: 610-266-3650.
Fax: 610-640-2619.
Cherry Hill, New Jersey Office: 51 Haddonfield Road, Suite 340.
Telephone: 609-488-7300.
Fax: 609-488-7021.

MEMBERS OF FIRM

David T. Sykes
George E. Pierce, Jr.
Rudolph J. DiMassa, Jr.
Margery N. Reed
James L. Allison
John F. Horstmann, III
Richard C. Unger, Jr.
Peter S. Clark, II
Claudia Z. Springer
Mark J. Packel

ASSOCIATES

Diane E. Vuocolo
Richard W. Riley
James M. Keating, Jr.
David B. Smith
Matthew E. Tashman
Dianne A. Meyer
James J. Holman
Joanne M. Murray
Suzanne M. Mitchell
Linda M. Zimmermann
Andrew P. Hoppes

For Complete List of Firm Personnel, See General Section

For full biographical listings, see the Martindale-Hubbell Law Directory

FELLHEIMER EICHEN BRAVERMAN & KASKEY, A PROFESSIONAL CORPORATION (AV)

21st Floor, One Liberty Place, 19103-7334
Telephone: 215-575-3800
FAX: 215-575-3801
Camden, New Jersey Office: 519 Federal Street, Suite 503 Parkade Building, 08103-1147.
Telephone: 609-541-5323.
Fax: 609-541-5370.

Alan S. Fellheimer
David L. Braverman
Judith Eichen Fellheimer
John E. Kaskey
Kenneth S. Goodkind
Anna Hom
Peter E. Meltzer

Barbara Anisko
Maia R. Caplan
Jeffrey L. Eichen
Michael N. Feder
Jolie G. Kahn
George F. Newton
David B. Spitofsky
W. Thomas Tither, Jr.

For Complete List of Firm Personnel, See General Section

For full biographical listings, see the Martindale-Hubbell Law Directory

KLEHR, HARRISON, HARVEY, BRANZBURG & ELLERS (AV)

1401 Walnut Street, 19102
Telephone: 215-568-6060
Fax: 215-568-6603
Cherry Hill, New Jersey Office: Colwick-Suite 200, 51 Haddonfield Road.
Telephone: 609-486-7900.
Fax: 609-486-4875.
Allentown, Pennsylvania Office: Roma Corporate Center, Suite 501, 1605 North Cedar Crest Boulevard.
Telephone: 215-432-1803.
Fax: 215-433-4031.
Wilmington, Delaware Office: 222 Delaware Avenue, Suite 1101.
Telephone: 302-426-1189.
Fax: 302-426-9193.

(See Next Column)

MEMBERS OF FIRM

Morton R. Branzburg
Donald M. Harrison
Rona J. Rosen
Rosetta B. Packer
Alan M. Rosen
Carol Ann Slocum (Resident, Cherry Hill, New Jersey Office)
Jeffrey Kurtzman
Mark S. Kenney
Jill E. Jachera
Francis M. Correll, Jr.

ASSOCIATES

John J. Winter
Stewart Paley
Kevin W. Mahoney
John Keenan Fiorillo
Richard M. Beck
Michael J. Cordone
Joseph G. Gibbons

For Complete List of Firm Personnel, See General Section

For full biographical listings, see the Martindale-Hubbell Law Directory

PATTERSON & WEIR (AV)

Suite 1200, Land Title Building, 100 South Broad Street, 19110
Telephone: 215-665-8181
Telefax: 215-665-8464
Westmont, New Jersey Office: 216 Haddon Avenue, Suite 704, Sentry Office Plaza, 08108.
Telephone: 609-858-6100.
Telefax: 609-858-4606.

MEMBERS OF FIRM

Walter Weir, Jr.
Paul A. Patterson
Brent S. Gorey
Daniel S. Bernheim, III
Mark E. Herrera (Resident, Westmont, New Jersey Office)

ASSOCIATES

David J. Toll
Susan Verbonitz
Robert D. Sayre
Jonathan J. Bart
Scott C. Pyfer (Resident, Westmont, New Jersey Office)
Lee Ann M. Williams, Jr
Douglas J. McGill
Harry J. Giacometti

For full biographical listings, see the Martindale-Hubbell Law Directory

*PITTSBURGH,** Allegheny Co.

ADERSON, FRANK & STEINER, A PROFESSIONAL CORPORATION (AV)

2320 Grant Building, 15219
Telephone: 412-263-0500
Fax: 412-263-0565

Sanford M. Aderson
Bruce F. Rudoy

For full biographical listings, see the Martindale-Hubbell Law Directory

APPLE AND APPLE, A PROFESSIONAL CORPORATION (AV)

4650 Baum Boulevard, 15213
Telephone: 412-682-1466; 800-477-APPLE
Fax: 412-682-3138

Marvin J. Apple
James R. Apple

Charles F. Bennett
James S. Alter
Joel E. Hausman
Marylouise Wagner

Representative Clients: Boron Oil; N.A.C.M.; Associates Commercial Corp.; Hartford Insurance; Conrail; American Refinery; WRS Motion Picture and Video Laboratory.

For full biographical listings, see the Martindale-Hubbell Law Directory

BERNSTEIN AND BERNSTEIN, A PROFESSIONAL CORPORATION (AV)

1133 Penn Avenue, 15222
Telephone: 412-456-8100
Facsimile: 412-456-8135
Harrisburg, Pennsylvania Office: 204 State Street.
Telephone: 717-233-1000.
Fax: 717-233-8290.

Joseph J. Bernstein
Robert S. Bernstein
Owen W. Katz

Marlene J. Bernstein
Denise Simmons

Reference: Integra Bank.

For full biographical listings, see the Martindale-Hubbell Law Directory

Pittsburgh—Continued

BUCHANAN INGERSOLL, PROFESSIONAL CORPORATION (AV)
5800 USX Tower, 600 Grant Street, 15219
Telephone: 412-562-8800
Telecopier: 412-562-1041
Philadelphia, Pennsylvania Office: Two Logan Square, Twelfth Floor, 18th & Arch Streets.
Telephone: 215-665-8700.
Harrisburg, Pennsylvania Office: Vartan Parc, 30 North Third Street.
Telephone: 717-237-4800.
Tampa, Florida Office: 101 East Kennedy Boulevard, Suite 1030.
Telephone: 813-222-8180.
North Miami Beach, Florida Office: 19495 Biscayne Boulevard.
Telephone: 305-933-5600.
Lexington, Kentucky Office: 1210 Vine Center Office Tower, 333 West Vine Street.
Telephone: 606-225-5333.
Princeton, New Jersey Office: Buchanan Ingersoll, A Partnership, College Centre, 500 College Road East.
Telephone: 609-452-2666.

George L. Cass
Lewis U. Davis, Jr.
M. Bruce McCullough
Gary Philip Nelson
Michael A. Snyder
James R. Sweeny

SENIOR ATTORNEY
Joan G. Dorgan

Thomas S. Galey
Donald E. Malecki
Daniel Alan O'Connor
Peter S. Russ
Ronald W. Schuler
Joseph S. Sisca

For Complete List of Firm Personnel, See General Section

For full biographical listings, see the Martindale-Hubbell Law Directory

CAMPBELL & LEVINE (AV)
3100 Grant Building, 15219
Telephone: 412-261-0310
Fax: 412-261-5066

MEMBERS OF FIRM
Douglas A. Campbell
Stanley E. Levine
David P. Braun
David B. Salzman

ASSOCIATES
Roger M. Bould
Philip E. Milch

For full biographical listings, see the Martindale-Hubbell Law Directory

MARCUS & SHAPIRA (AV)
35th Floor, One Oxford Centre, 301 Grant Street, 15219-6401
Telephone: 412-471-3490
Telecopier: 412-391-8758

MEMBERS OF FIRM
Bernard D. Marcus
Daniel H. Shapira
George P. Slesinger
Robert L. Allman, II
Estelle F. Comay
Susan Gromis Flynn
Darlene M. Nowak
Glenn M. Olcerst
Elly Heller-Toig
Sylvester A. Beozzo

OF COUNSEL
John M. Burkoff

SPECIAL COUNSEL
Jane Campbell Moriarty

ASSOCIATES
Scott D. Livingston
Robert M. Barnes
Stephen S. Zubrow
David B. Rodes
Lori E. McMaster
Melody A. Pollock
James F. Rosenberg
Amy M. Gottlieb

For full biographical listings, see the Martindale-Hubbell Law Directory

PLOWMAN, SPIEGEL & LEWIS, P.C. (AV)
Grant Building, Suite 925, 15219-2201
Telephone: 412-471-8521
Fax: 412-471-4481

Jack W. Plowman
John L. Spiegel
Frank J. Kernan
Clifford L. Tuttle, Jr.
Kenneth W. Lee

Marshall J. Conn
David Raves

Reference: Pittsburgh National Bank.

For Complete List of Firm Personnel, See General Section

For full biographical listings, see the Martindale-Hubbell Law Directory

SABLE, MAKOROFF & GUSKY, P.C. (AV)
7th Floor, Frick Building, 15219-6002
Telephone: 412-471-4996
Fax: 412-281-2859

(See Next Column)

Robert G. Sable
Stanley G. Makoroff
Henry Gusky
Stephen J. Laidhold
David W. Lampl
Gregg M. Rosen
F. Scott Gray
Robert J. Blumling
Amy S. Cunningham
Alan B. Gordon
David P. Pusateri
Jeffrey T. Morris
Michael McGreal
M. Scott Zegeer
Jeffrey J. Ludwikowski
Mark S. Seewald
Michael Kaminski
K. Bradley Mellor
Thomas M. Ferguson
James C. Heneghan
David A. Levine
Alan K. Sable
Maureen E. Sweeney

OF COUNSEL
Jerome M. Libenson

For full biographical listings, see the Martindale-Hubbell Law Directory

STONECIPHER, CUNNINGHAM, BEARD & SCHMITT (AV)
125 First Avenue, 15222
Telephone: 412-391-8510
Telecopier: 412-391-8522

MEMBERS OF FIRM
Charles L. Cunningham (1889-1961)
C. W. Cunningham (1916-1962)
Philip E. Beard
Joseph E. Schmitt
Roger S. Cunningham
Norman E. Gilkey

ASSOCIATES
Paul R. Rennie
George T. Snyder
Philip E. Beard, II
Nathaniel Beaumont Beard

Reference: Integra Bank of Pittsburgh

For full biographical listings, see the Martindale-Hubbell Law Directory

THORP, REED & ARMSTRONG (AV)
One Riverfront Center, 15222
Telephone: 412-394-7711
Fax: 412-394-2555

MEMBERS OF FIRM
Edward B. Harmon
Thomas E. Lippard
Richard D. Rose
David A. Scott
Leonard F. Spagnolo

ASSOCIATE
Kimberly L. Wakim

For Complete List of Firm Personnel, See General Section

For full biographical listings, see the Martindale-Hubbell Law Directory

VOLLMER RULONG & ASSOCIATES, P.C. (AV)
Suite 1212, Grant Building, 15219
Telephone: 412-391-2121
Telecopier: 412-391-3578

Charles J. Vollmer

John R. Keating
Roger G. Rulong, Jr.

For full biographical listings, see the Martindale-Hubbell Law Directory

WEISMAN BOWEN & GROSS (AV)
310 Grant Street, Suite 420, 15219
Telephone: 412-566-2520
Fax: 412-566-1088

James L. Weisman
Alden Earl Bowen
Sanford P. Gross
Bradley S. Gelder
Barry J. Lipson
Christopher J. Klein
Laurel B. Diznoff
Robert L. Monks
Elliott I. Levenson

Reference: Pittsburgh National Bank.

For full biographical listings, see the Martindale-Hubbell Law Directory

*READING,** Berks Co.

BINGAMAN, HESS, COBLENTZ & BELL, A PROFESSIONAL CORPORATION (AV)
660 Penn Square Center, 601 Penn Street, P.O. Box 61, 19603-0061
Telephone: 610-374-8377
Fax: 610-376-3105
Bernville, Pennsylvania Office: 331 Main Street.
Telephone: 610-488-0656.
Camden, New Jersey Office: 411 Cooper Street.
Telephone: 609-966-0117.
Fax: 609-965-0796.

James F. Bell (1921-1988)

(See Next Column)

Bingaman, Hess, Coblentz & Bell A Professional Corporation—*Continued*

OF COUNSEL

Llewellyn R. Bingaman
Raymond K. Hess
J. Wendell Coblentz
Ralph J. Althouse, Jr.
Gerald P. Sigal

David E. Turner
Clemson North Page, Jr.
Mark G. Yoder
Carl D. Cronrath, Jr.
Kurt Althouse
Harry D. McMunigal
Karen Feryo Longenecker
Shawn J. Lau

Lynne K. Beust
Elizabethanne D. McMunigal
Patrick T. Barrett
Susan N. Denaro
Daniel J. Poruban
Jill M. Scheidt

LEGAL SUPPORT PERSONNEL

Eric A. Barr (Office Administrator)

PARALEGALS

JoAnn Ruchlewicz
Laura I. Lehane
Louise E. Miller
Ruth Ann Sunderland
Kristine L. Krammes
Peter L. Torres

General Counsel for: Meridian Bank; Berks Products Corp.; Leighton Industries, Inc.; Utilities Employees Credit Union.
Local Counsel for: Erie Insurance Exchange; Liberty Mutual Insurance Co.; Old Guard Mutual Insurance Co.

For full biographical listings, see the Martindale-Hubbell Law Directory

Karl E. Friend (AV)

539 Court Street, 19601
Telephone: 610-375-8979
Allentown, Pennsylvania Office: Westfield Corporate Center, Suite 310, 4905 Tilghman Street.
Telephone: 215-391-9878.
Telecopier: 215-391-9879.

For full biographical listings, see the Martindale-Hubbell Law Directory

*WILKES-BARRE,** Luzerne Co.

Rosenn, Jenkins & Greenwald (AV)

15 South Franklin Street, 18711-0075
Telephone: 717-826-5600
Fax: 717-826-5640

MEMBER OF FIRM

Bruce C. Rosenthal

ASSOCIATES

Steven P. Roth
Thomas B. Carpenter

Representative Clients: Allstate Insurance Co.; C-TEC Corporation; Chicago Title Insurance Co.; Franklin First Savings Bank; The Geisinger Medical Center; Guard Insurance Group; The Mays Department Stores Company; Student LoanMarketing Association (Sallie Mae); Subaru of America, Inc.

For Complete List of Firm Personnel, See General Section

For full biographical listings, see the Martindale-Hubbell Law Directory

RHODE ISLAND

JAMESTOWN, Newport Co.

Morneau & Murphy (AV)

77 Narragansett Avenue, 02835
Telephone: 401-423-0400
Telecopier: 401-423-7059
Providence, Rhode Island Office: 38 N. Court Street. 02903
Telephone: 401-453-0500.
Telecopier: 401-453-0505.

MEMBERS OF FIRM

John Austin Murphy
John B. Murphy (Resident at Providence Office)
Richard N. Morneau
Gloria C. Dahl

ASSOCIATES

Sheila M. Cooley
Stephen T. Morrissey
Anne Maxwell Livingston
Virginia Spaziano
Scott H. Moskol (Resident, Providence Office)

OF COUNSEL

Neale D. Murphy

For full biographical listings, see the Martindale-Hubbell Law Directory

SOUTH CAROLINA

*CHARLESTON,** Charleston Co.

Bernstein & Bernstein, P.A. (AV)

Maritime Building, 215 East Bay Street, Suite 203, P.O. Box 7, 29402-0007
Telephone: 803-723-3502
FAX: 803-723-3534

Charles S. Bernstein

Robert Alan Bernstein

For full biographical listings, see the Martindale-Hubbell Law Directory

Buist, Moore, Smythe & McGee, P.A. (AV)

Successors to Buist, Buist, Smythe and Smythe and Moore, Mouzon and McGee.
Five Exchange Street, P.O. Box 999, 29402
Telephone: 803-722-3400
Cable Address: "Conferees"
Telex: 57-6488
Telecopier: 803-723-7398
North Charleston, South Carolina Office: Atrium Northwood Office Building, 7301 Rivers Avenue, Suite 288. Zip: 29406-2859.
Telephone: 803-797-3000.
Telecopier: 803-863-5500.

Charles P. Summerall, IV

Robert A. Kerr, Jr.
Patricia L. Quentel

Counsel for: CSX Transportation; NationsBank; Metropolitan Life Insurance Co.; E. I. du Pont de Nemours & Co.; AIG Aviation, Inc.; Lamorte, Burns & Co., Inc.; Allstate Insurance Co.; General Dynamics Corp.; Independent Life & Accident Insurance Co.; Georgia-Pacific Corp.

For Complete List of Firm Personnel, See General Section

For full biographical listings, see the Martindale-Hubbell Law Directory

Haynsworth, Marion, McKay & Guérard, L.L.P (AV)

#2 Prioleau Street, P.O. Box 1119, 29402
Telephone: 803-722-7606
Telecopier: 803-723-5263
Columbia, South Carolina Office: Suite 2400 AT&T Building, 1201 Main Street, P.O. Drawer 7157, 29202.
Telephone: 803-765-1818.
Telecopier: 803-765-2399.
Greenville, South Carolina Office: Two Insignia Financial Plaza, 75 Beattie Place, P.O. Box 2048, 29602.
Telephone: 803-240-3200.
Telecopier: 803-240-3300.

MEMBER OF FIRM

W. E. Applegate, III

ASSOCIATE

J. Walker Coleman, IV

Counsel for: Bank of South Carolina; Baker Hospital; Healthsources of South Carolina; Allstate Insurance Co.; CSX Corporation; Lloyd's Underwriters; Coward-Hund Construction Co.; South Carolina Public Service Authority; South Carolina Jobs - Economic Development Authority; City of Hanahan.

For Complete List of Firm Personnel, See General Section

For full biographical listings, see the Martindale-Hubbell Law Directory

Rosen, Rosen & Hagood, P.A. (AV)

134 Meeting Street, Suite 200, P.O. Box 893, 29402
Telephone: 803-577-6726

Morris D. Rosen
Alice F. Paylor

Randy Horner

Reference: NationsBank of South Carolina, N.A.

For Complete List of Firm Personnel, See General Section

For full biographical listings, see the Martindale-Hubbell Law Directory

Wise & Cole, P.A. (AV)

Suite 200, 151 Meeting Street, P.O. Drawer O, 29402
Telephone: 803-727-2200
Telecopier: 803-727-2238

(See Next Column)

WISE & COLE P.A., *Charleston—Continued*

Thomas Dewey Wise
Michael T. Cole
E. Douglas Pratt-Thomas
W. Gregory Pearce
Andrew Kenneth Epting, Jr.
G. Trenholm Walker
Joseph S. Brockington
Bonum S. Wilson, III
W. Andrew Gowder, Jr.
D. Carlyle Rogers, Jr.
Jon L. Austen
Russell S. Stemke
Dennis J. Christensen

Robert B. Ransom
Robert S. Dodds
Allison Molony Carter
Gregg Meyers
D. Kay Tennyson
Paul A. James
Thomas H. Hesse

Reference: First Union National Bank.

For full biographical listings, see the Martindale-Hubbell Law Directory

*COLUMBIA,** Richland Co.

* indicates certain Bar Register subscribers whose principal office is located elsewhere in the state and who have arranged for representation as a part of the state capital listings that follow

FINKEL, GOLDBERG, SHEFTMAN & ALTMAN, P.A. (AV)

Suite 1800, 1201 Main Street, P.O. Box 1799, 29202
Telephone: 803-765-2935
Fax: 803-252-0786
Charleston, South Carolina Office: 12 Exchange Street, P.O. Box 225.
Telephone: 803-577-5460.
Fax: 803-577-5135.

Gerald M. Finkel
Harry L. Goldberg
Howard S. Sheftman
Charles S. Altman (Resident, Charleston South Carolina Office)
Elizabeth Henderson McCullough
Beverly J. Finkel

Richard R. Gleissner
Gilbert S. Bagnell
David E. Belding
Elizabeth Rhodes

COUNSEL

Ralph C. McCullough, II

Representative Clients: Hewitt-Robins; 1st Union National Bank; Banc One Mortgage Co.; Motorola Communications & Electronics Corp.

For full biographical listings, see the Martindale-Hubbell Law Directory

*** HAYNSWORTH, MARION, MCKAY & GUÉRARD, L.L.P. (AV)**

Suite 2400 A T & T Building, 1201 Main Street, P.O. Drawer 7157, 29202
Telephone: 803-765-1818
Telecopier: 803-765-2399
Greenville, South Carolina Office: Two Insignia Financial Plaza, 75 Beattie Place, P.O. Box 2048, 29602.
Telephone: 803-240-3200.
Telecopier: 803-240-3300.
Charleston, South Carolina Office: #2 Prioleau Street, P.O. Box 1119, 29402.
Telephone: 803-722-7606.
Telecopier: 803-723-5263.

MEMBERS OF FIRM

William P. Simpson
Gary W. Morris

ASSOCIATES

Stephen F. McKinney
Edward G. Kluiters

Counsel for: St. Paul Insurance Group; Allstate Insurance Co.; Fluor-Daniel Corp.; South Carolina Jobs - Economic Development Authority; Anheuser Busch Company; CSX Transportation; Ernst & Young, LLP; Willis Corroon of South Carolina, Inc.; Westinghouse Savannah River Co.; Wachovia Bank of South Carolina, N.A.

For Complete List of Firm Personnel, See General Section

For full biographical listings, see the Martindale-Hubbell Law Directory

*GREENVILLE,** Greenville Co.

HAYNSWORTH, MARION, MCKAY & GUÉRARD, L.L.P. (AV)

Two Insignia Financial Plaza, 75 Beattie Place, P.O. Box 2048, 29602
Telephone: 803-240-3200
Telecopier: 803-240-3300
Columbia, South Carolina Office: Suite 2400 A T & T Building, 1201 Main Street, P.O. Drawer 7157, 29202
Telephone: 803-765-1818.
Telecopier: 803-765-2399.
Charleston, South Carolina Office: #2 Prioleau Street, P.O. Box 1119, 29402.
Telephone: 803-722-7606.
Telecopier: 803-723-5263.

(See Next Column)

MEMBER OF FIRM

Andrew J. White, Jr.

Representative Clients: Wachovia Bank of South Carolina, N.A.; Vanderbilt Mortgage; M.S. Bailey and Sons, Bankers; Kubota Financial Corp.; Bergen Acceptance Corp.; General Electric Credit Corporation; First Citizens Bank & Trust Co.

For Complete List of Firm Personnel, See General Section

For full biographical listings, see the Martindale-Hubbell Law Directory

WYCHE, BURGESS, FREEMAN & PARHAM, PROFESSIONAL ASSOCIATION (AV)

44 East Camperdown Way, P.O. Box 728, 29602-0728
Telephone: 803-242-8200
Telecopier: 803-235-8900

D. Allen Grumbine
Marshall Winn

Counsel for: Multimedia, Inc.; Delta Woodside Industries, Inc.; Milliken & Company; Ryan's Family Steak Houses, Inc.; St. Francis Hospital; Span-America Medical Systems, Inc.; Carolina First Bank; KEMET Electronics Corp.; Builder Marts of America, Inc.; One Price Clothing, Inc.

For Complete List of Firm Personnel, See General Section

For full biographical listings, see the Martindale-Hubbell Law Directory

SOUTH DAKOTA

*SIOUX FALLS,** Minnehaha Co.

DAVENPORT, EVANS, HURWITZ & SMITH (AV)

513 South Main Avenue, P.O. Box 1030, 57101-1030
Telephone: 605-336-2880
Telecopier: 605-335-3639

MEMBERS OF FIRM

Robert E. Hayes
Monte R. Walz

Counsel for: American Society of Composers, Authors and Publishers (A.S.-C.A.P.); Burlington Northern, Inc.; Continental Insurance Cos.; The First National Bank in Sioux Falls; Ford Motor Credit Co.; General Motors Corp.; The St. Paul Cos.; The Travelers.

For Complete List of Firm Personnel, See General Section

For full biographical listings, see the Martindale-Hubbell Law Directory

TENNESSEE

*CHATTANOOGA,** Hamilton Co.

BROWN, DOBSON, BURNETTE & KESLER (AV)

713 Cherry Street, 37402
Telephone: 615-266-2121
Fax: 615-266-3324

MEMBERS OF FIRM

Scott N. Brown, Jr.
David B. Kesler
Richard R. Pettit

Reference: First Tennessee Bank.

For full biographical listings, see the Martindale-Hubbell Law Directory

CHAMBLISS & BAHNER (AV)

1000 Tallan Building, Two Union Square, 37402-2500
Telephone: 615-756-3000
Fax: 615-265-9574

MEMBERS OF FIRM

Bruce C. Bailey
Jay A. Young

ASSOCIATES

Benjamin Younger Pitts
Anthony A. Jackson

OF COUNSEL

William Crutchfield, Jr.

General Counsel for: McKee Foods Corporation; Porter Warner Inds., Inc.; SCT Yarns, Inc.; Stein Construction Co., Inc.
Representative Clients: BancBoston Financial Company; First American National Bank; Barclays Commercial; Goldome Credit Corporation; General Motors Acceptance Corporation.

For Complete List of Firm Personnel, See General Section

For full biographical listings, see the Martindale-Hubbell Law Directory

Chattanooga—Continued

KENNEDY, FULTON & KOONTZ (AV)

320 North Holtzclaw Avenue, 37404
Telephone: 615-622-4535
Facsimile: 615-622-4583

MEMBERS OF FIRM

Richard C. Kennedy | George E. Koontz
David J. Fulton | Jerrold D. Farinash

ASSOCIATES

James W. Clements, III | Kathryn R. Leiderman

OF COUNSEL

Richard T. Klingler

For full biographical listings, see the Martindale-Hubbell Law Directory

RAY & SIBLEY, P.C. (AV)

17 Cherokee Boulevard, 37405
Telephone: 615-265-2641
Fax: 615-265-2654

Thomas E. Ray | David M. Sibley

For full biographical listings, see the Martindale-Hubbell Law Directory

SHUMACKER & THOMPSON (AV)

Suite 500, First Tennessee Building, 701 Market Street, 37402-4800
Telephone: 615-265-2214
Telecopier: 615-266-1842
Branch Office: Suite 103, One Park Place, 6148 Lee Highway, Chattanooga, Tennessee, 37421-2900.
Telephone: 615-855-1814.
Telecopier: 615-899-1278.

MEMBERS OF FIRM

W. Neil Thomas, III | Harold L. North, Jr.
Everett L. Hixson, Jr.

For Complete List of Firm Personnel, See General Section

For full biographical listings, see the Martindale-Hubbell Law Directory

SPEARS, MOORE, REBMAN & WILLIAMS (AV)

8th Floor Blue Cross Building, 801 Pine Street, 37402
Telephone: 615-756-7000
Facsimile: 615-756-4801

MEMBERS OF FIRM

Thomas S. Kale | F. Scott LeRoy

Counsel for: Pioneer Bank; Chattanooga Gas Co.; South Central Bell Telephone Co.; Tennessee-American Water Co.; Blue Cross and Blue Shield of Tennessee; State Farm Mutual Automobile Insurance Cos.; Nationwide Insurance Co.; Siskin Steel & Supply Co., Inc.; CSX Transportation, Inc.; The McCallie School; Mueller Co.

For Complete List of Firm Personnel, See General Section

For full biographical listings, see the Martindale-Hubbell Law Directory

STOPHEL & STOPHEL, P.C. (AV)

500 Tallan Building, Two Union Square, 37402-2571
Telephone: 615-756-2333
Fax: 615-266-5032

Glenn C. Stophel | C. Douglas Williams

Ronald D. Gorsline | James C. Heartfield

Representative Clients: First American National Bank; First Tennessee Bank; Deere Credit Services, Inc.

For Complete List of Firm Personnel, See General Section

For full biographical listings, see the Martindale-Hubbell Law Directory

*COLUMBIA,** Maury Co.

ROBIN S. COURTNEY (AV)

809 South Main Street, Suite 300, P.O. Box 1035, 38401
Telephone: 615-388-6031
Fax: 615-381-7317

For full biographical listings, see the Martindale-Hubbell Law Directory

*JACKSON,** Madison Co.

RAINEY, KIZER, BUTLER, REVIERE & BELL (AV)

105 Highland Avenue South, P.O. Box 1147, 38302-1147
Telephone: 901-423-2414
Telecopier: 901-423-1386

MEMBERS OF FIRM

Thomas H. Rainey | William C. Bell, Jr.
Laura A. Williams

(See Next Column)

ASSOCIATES

Charles C. Exum | Clay M. McCormack

Representative Clients: First Tennessee Bank, Jackson, Tennessee; CIGNA Insurance Co.; State Farm Mutual Automobile Insurance Co.; Auto-Owners Insurance Co.; USF&G; CNA Group; Royal Insurance Co.; Great American Insurance Co.; ITT-Hartford; Union Planters National Bank.

For Complete List of Firm Personnel, See General Section

For full biographical listings, see the Martindale-Hubbell Law Directory

*KNOXVILLE,** Knox Co.

GENTRY, TIPTON, KIZER & LITTLE, P.C. (AV)

2610 Plaza Tower, 800 South Gay Street, 37929
Telephone: 615-525-5300
Telecopy: 615-523-7315

Mack A. Gentry | Timothy M. McLemore
James S. Tipton, Jr. | Mark Jendrek
W. Morris Kizer | Maurice K. Guinn
Lawrence E. Little | F. Scott Milligan

For full biographical listings, see the Martindale-Hubbell Law Directory

HODGES, DOUGHTY AND CARSON (AV)

617 Main Street, P.O. Box 869, 37901-0869
Telephone: 615-546-9611
Telecopier: 615-544-2014

MEMBERS OF FIRM

J. H. Hodges (1896-1983) | Roy L. Aaron
J. H. Doughty (1903-1987) | Dean B. Farmer
Richard L. Carson (1912-1980) | David Wedekind
John P. Davis, Jr. (1923-1977) | Julia Saunders Howard
Robert R. Campbell | Albert J. Harb
David E. Smith | Edward G. White, II
John W. Wheeler | Thomas H. Dickenson
Dalton L. Townsend | J. William Coley
Douglas L. Dutton | J. Michael Haynes
William F. Alley, Jr. | T. Kenan Smith
Wayne A. Kline

ASSOCIATES

James M. Cornelius, Jr. | W. Tyler Chastain

OF COUNSEL

Jonathan H. Burnett

Representative Clients: General Motors Corp.; Sears, Roebuck and Co.; Navistar International; Martin Marietta Energy Systems; Union Carbide Corp.; NationsBank of Tennessee; K-Mart Corporation; Aetna Life and Casualty Group; Fireman's Fund American Insurance Company; Safeco Insurance Group.

For full biographical listings, see the Martindale-Hubbell Law Directory

MCCAMPBELL & YOUNG, A PROFESSIONAL CORPORATION (AV)

2021 Plaza Tower, P.O. Box 550, 37901-0550
Telephone: 615-637-1440
Telecopier: 615-546-9731

Herbert H. McCampbell, Jr. (1905-1974) | Lindsay Young
F. Graham Bartlett (1920-1982) | Robert S. Marquis
Robert S. Young | Robert S. Stone
| J. Christopher Kirk
Mark K. Williams

Janie C. Porter | Tammy Kaousias
Gregory E. Erickson | Benét S. Theiss
R. Scott Elmore | Allen W. Blevins

For full biographical listings, see the Martindale-Hubbell Law Directory

WALKER & WALKER, P.C. (AV)

910 First American Center, P.O. Box 2774, 37901
Telephone: 615-523-0700
Telecopier: 615-523-4990

John A. Walker, Jr. | Mary C. Walker

For full biographical listings, see the Martindale-Hubbell Law Directory

*MEMPHIS,** Shelby Co.

ARMSTRONG ALLEN PREWITT GENTRY JOHNSTON & HOLMES (AV)

80 Monroe Avenue Suite 700, 38103
Telephone: 901-523-8211
Telecopier: 901-524-4936
Jackson, Missippi Office: 1350 One Jackson Place, 188 East Capitol Street.
Telephone: 601-948-8020.
Telecopier: 601-948-8389.

(See Next Column)

ARMSTRONG ALLEN PREWITT GENTRY JOHNSTON & HOLMES, *Memphis—Continued*

MEMBERS OF FIRM

Wm. Rowlett Scott
William A. Carson, II
Paul A. Matthews
Stephen P. Hale

H. Tucker Dewey

For Complete List of Firm Personnel, See General Section

For full biographical listings, see the Martindale-Hubbell Law Directory

BAKER, DONELSON, BEARMAN & CALDWELL (AV)

20th Floor, First Tennessee Building, 165 Madison, 38103
Telephone: 901-526-2000
Telecopier: 901-577-2303
Nashville, Tennessee Office: 1700 Nashville City Center, 511 Union Street, 37219.
Telephone: 615-726-5600.
Telecopier: 615-726-0464.
Knoxville, Tennessee Office: 2200 Riverview Tower, 900 Gay Street, 37901.
Telephone: 615-549-7000.
Telecopier: 615-525-8569.
Chattanooga, Tennessee Office: 1800 Republic Centre, 633 Chestnut Street, 37450-1800.
Telephone: 615-752-4400.
Telecopier: 615-752-4410.
Huntsville, Tennessee Office: 3 Courthouse Square, 37756.
Telephone: 615-663-2321.
Telecopier: 615-663-2111.
Johnson City, Tennessee Office: Hamilton Bank Building, 207 Mockingbird Lane, 37604.
Telephone: 615-928-0181.
Telecopier: 615-928-5694; 615-928-3654; Kingsport: 615-246-6191.
Washington, D.C. Office: Market Square, 801 Pennsylvania Avenue, N.W., 20004.
Telephone: 202-508-3400.
Telecopier: 202-508-3402.

PARTNER

Harris Patton Quinn

ASSOCIATES

Stephen William Ragland
R. Alan Pritchard, Jr.
Sean M. Haynes

For Complete List of Firm Personnel, See General Section

For full biographical listings, see the Martindale-Hubbell Law Directory

BOROD & KRAMER, P.C. (AV)

Brinkley Plaza, 80 Monroe Avenue, 5th Floor, P.O. Box 3504, 38173-0504
Telephone: 901-524-0200
Telecopier: 901-524-0242

Marx J. Borod
Bruce S. Kramer

Sharon Lee Petty
Jeffery D. Parrish

For full biographical listings, see the Martindale-Hubbell Law Directory

HANOVER, WALSH, JALENAK & BLAIR (AV)

Fifth Floor - Falls Building, 22 North Front Street, 38103-2109
Telephone: 901-526-0621
Telecopier: 901-521-9759

MEMBERS OF FIRM

Joseph Hanover (1888-1984)
David Hanover (1899-1963)
Jay Alan Hanover
William M. Walsh
James B. Jalenak
Allen S. Blair
Michael E. Goldstein
Edward J. McKenney, Jr.
James R. Newsom, III
John Kevin Walsh
James A. Johnson, Jr.
Donald S. Holm III
Barbara B. Lapides

Jennifer A. Sevier
Christina von Cannon Burdette
Jeffrey S. Rosenblum

OF COUNSEL

Helyn L. Keith

For full biographical listings, see the Martindale-Hubbell Law Directory

THOMASON, HENDRIX, HARVEY, JOHNSON & MITCHELL (AV)

Twenty-Ninth Floor, One Commerce Square, 38103
Telephone: 901-525-8721
Telecopier: 901-525-6722

MEMBER OF FIRM

Michael G. McLaren

For Complete List of Firm Personnel, See General Section

For full biographical listings, see the Martindale-Hubbell Law Directory

*NASHVILLE,** Davidson Co.

MANIER, HEROD, HOLLABAUGH & SMITH, A PROFESSIONAL CORPORATION (AV)

First Union Tower 2200 One Nashville Place, 150 Fourth Avenue North, 37219-2494
Telephone: 615-244-0030
Telecopier: 615-242-4203

Will R. Manier, Jr. (1885-1953)
Larkin E. Crouch (1882-1948)
Vincent L. Fuqua, Jr. (1930-1974)
J. Olin White (1907-1982)
Miller Manier (1897-1986)
William Edward Herod (1917-1992)
Lewis B. Hollabaugh
Don L. Smith
James M. Doran, Jr.
Stephen E. Cox
J. Michael Franks
Randall C. Ferguson
Terry L. Hill
James David Leckrone
Robert C. Evans
Tommy C. Estes
B. Gail Reese
Michael E. Evans
Laurence M. Papel
John M. Gillum
Gregory L. Cashion
Sam H. Poteet, Jr.
Samuel Arthur Butts III
David J. Deming
Mark S. LeVan
Richard McCallister Smith
Mary Paty Lynn Jetton
H. Rowan Leathers III
Jefferson C. Orr
William L. Penny

Lawrence B. Hammet II
John H. Rowland
Susan C. West
John E. Quinn
John F. Floyd
Paul L. Sprader
Lela M. Hollabaugh
J. Steven Kirkham
T. Richard Travis
Stephanie M. Jennings
Jerry W. Taylor
C. Benton Patton
Kenneth A. Weber
Phillip Robert Newman
Brett A. Oeser

General Counsel for: McKinnon Bridge Co., Inc.

For full biographical listings, see the Martindale-Hubbell Law Directory

TEXAS

*AMARILLO,** Potter Co.

CONANT WHITTENBURG WHITTENBURG & SCHACHTER, P.C. (AV)

1010 South Harrison, P.O. Box 31718, 79120
Telephone: 806-372-5700
Facsimile: 806-372-5757
Dallas, Texas Office: 2300 Plaza of the Americas, 600 North Pearl, LB 133,
Telephone: 214-999-5700.
Facsimile: 214-999-5747.

A. B. Conant, Jr.
George Whittenburg
Mack Whittenburg
Cary Ira Schachter
Susan Lynn Burnette
William B. Chaney
Charles G. White
Vikram K. D. Chandhok
J. Michael McBride

OF COUNSEL

Linda A. Hale

Karl L. Baumgardner
Raymond P. Harris, Jr.
Lewis Coppedge
Francis Hangarter, Jr.
Nanneska N. Magee
Stuart J. Ford
Shawn W. Phelan
Paul M. Saraceni

For full biographical listings, see the Martindale-Hubbell Law Directory

HINKLE, COX, EATON, COFFIELD & HENSLEY (AV)

1700 Bank One Center, P.O. Box 9238, 79105-9238
Telephone: 806-372-5569
FAX: 806-372-9761
Roswell, New Mexico Office: 700 United Bank Plaza, P. O. Box 10, 88202.
Telephone: 505-622-6510.
FAX: 505-623-9332.
Midland, Texas Office: 6 Desta Drive, Suite 2800, P.O. Box 3580, 79702.
Telephone: 915-683-4691.
FAX: 915-683-6518.
Santa Fe, New Mexico Office: 218 Montezuma, P.O. Box 2068, 87504.
Telephone: 505-982-4554.
FAX: 505-982-8623.
Albuquerque, New Mexico Office: Suite 800, 500 Marquette, N.W., P.O. Box 2043, 87102.
Telephone: 505-768-1500.
FAX: 505-768-1529.
Austin, Texas Office: 401 West 15th Street, Suite 800, 78701.
Telephone: 512-476-7137.
FAX: 512-476-5431.

(See Next Column)

HINKLE, COX, EATON, COFFIELD & HENSLEY—*Continued*

Associated Office: Hoffman & Stephens, P.C., 401 West 15th Street, Suite 800, 78701.
Telephone: 512-476-5434. Fax; 512-476-5431.

RESIDENT PARTNERS

Don L. Patterson | Coleman Young

Representative Clients: Motorola, Inc.; Bank One, Texas, N.A.; Ford Motor Credit Co.; Amarillo Federal Credit Union; Western National Life Insurance Co.; AT&T Commercial Capitol Corp.

For full biographical listings, see the Martindale-Hubbell Law Directory

*AUSTIN,** Travis Co.

BAKER & BOTTS, L.L.P. (AV)

1600 San Jacinto Center, 98 San Jacinto Boulevard, 78701
Telephone: 512-322-2500
Fax: 512-322-2501
Houston, Texas Office: One Shell Plaza, 910 Louisiana.
Telephone: 713-229-1234.
Dallas, Texas Office: 2001 Ross Avenue.
Telephone: 214-953-6500.
Washington, D.C. Office: The Warner, 1299 Pennsylvania Avenue, N.W.
Telephone: 202-639-7700.
New York, New York Office: 885 Third Avenue, Suite 2000.
Telephone: 212-705-5000.
Moscow, Russian Federation Office: 10 ul. Pushkinskaya, 103031.
Telephone: 7095/921-5300 (Local); 7501/929-7070 (International).

MEMBER OF FIRM

William F. Stutts, Jr.

For Complete List of Firm Personnel, See General Section

For full biographical listings, see the Martindale-Hubbell Law Directory

*DALLAS,** Dallas Co.

BAKER & BOTTS, L.L.P. (AV)

2001 Ross Avenue, 75201
Telephone: 214-953-6500
Fax: 214-953-6503
Houston, Texas Office: One Shell Plaza, 910 Louisiana.
Telephone: 713-229-1234.
Washington, D.C. Office: The Warner, 1299 Pennsylvania Avenue, N.W.
Telephone: 202-639-7700.
Austin, Texas Office: 1600 San Jacinto Center, 98 San Jacinto Boulevard.
Telephone: 512-322-2500.
New York, New York Office: 885 Third Avenue, Suite 2000.
Telephone: 212-705-5000.
Moscow, Russian Federation Office: 10 ul. Pushkinskaya, 103031.
Telephone: 7095/921-5300 (Local); 7095/929-7070.

MEMBERS OF FIRM

Jack L. Kinzie | Bobbie T. Shell

ASSOCIATES

Kenneth Arthur Hill | J. Gregory St. Clair

For Complete List of Firm Personnel, See General Section

For full biographical listings, see the Martindale-Hubbell Law Directory

CALHOUN & STACY (AV)

5700 NationsBank Plaza, 901 Main Street, 75202-3747
Telephone: 214-748-5000
Telecopier: 214-748-1421
Telex: 211358 CALGUMP UR

Mark Alan Calhoun | Steven D. Goldston
David W. Elrod | Parker Nelson

Roy L. Stacy

ASSOCIATES

Shannon S. Barclay | Thomas C. Jones
Robert A. Bragalone | Katherine Johnson Knight
Dennis D. Conder | V. Paige Pace
Jane Elizabeth Diseker | Veronika Willard
Lawrence I. Fleishman | Michael C. Wright

LEGAL CONSULTANT

Rees T. Bowen, III

For full biographical listings, see the Martindale-Hubbell Law Directory

CREEL & ATWOOD, A PROFESSIONAL CORPORATION (AV)

Suite 3100, 1600 Pacific Avenue, 75201-3566
Telephone: 214-720-0110
Telecopier: 214-720-2225

L. E. Creel, III | Robert D. White
John B. Atwood, III | Weldon L. Moore, III

OF COUNSEL

Dean M. Gandy

For full biographical listings, see the Martindale-Hubbell Law Directory

GODWIN & CARLTON, A PROFESSIONAL CORPORATION (AV)

Suite 3300, 901 Main Street, 75202-3714
Telephone: 214-939-4400
Telecopier: 214-760-7332
Monterrey, Mexico Correspondent: Quintero y Quintero Abogodos. Martin De Zalva 840-3 Sur Esquinna Con Hidalgo.
Telephone: 44-07-74, 44-07-80, 44-06-56, 44-06-28.
Fax: 83-40-34-54.

Marci L. Romick | Thomas S. Hoekstra

Micheal Wayne Bishop

For Complete List of Firm Personnel, See General Section

For full biographical listings, see the Martindale-Hubbell Law Directory

HUGHES & LUCE, L.L.P. (AV)

A Registered Limited Liability Partnership including Professional Corporations
1717 Main Street, Suite 2800, 75201
Telephone: 214-939-5500
Fax: 214-939-6100
Telex: 730836
Austin, Texas Office: 111 Congress, Suite 900.
Telephone: 512-482-6800.
Fax: 512-482-6859.
Houston, Texas Office: Three Allen Center, 333 Clay Street, Suite 3800.
Telephone: 713-754-5200.
Fax: 713-754-5206.
Fort Worth, Texas Office: 2421 Westport Parkway, Suite 500A.
Telephone: 817-439-3000.
Fax: 817-439-4222.

MEMBERS OF FIRM

William B. Finkelstein | David Weitman

ASSOCIATES

Craig W. Budner | Mark W. Steirer

For Complete List of Firm Personnel, See General Section

For full biographical listings, see the Martindale-Hubbell Law Directory

OLSON, GIBBONS, SARTAIN, NICOUD, BIRNE & SUSSMAN, L.L.P. (AV)

2600 Lincoln Plaza, 500 North Akard, 75201-3320
Telephone: 214-740-2600
Fax: 214-740-2601

Dennis O. Olson | Robert M. Nicoud, Jr.
Mark L. Gibbons | Robert E. Birne
Charles W. Sartain | Ronald L. Sussman

For full biographical listings, see the Martindale-Hubbell Law Directory

THOMPSON, COE, COUSINS & IRONS, L.L.P. (AV)

200 Crescent Court, Eleventh Floor, 75201-1840
Telephone: 214-871-8200 (Dallas)
512-480-8770 (Austin)
FAX: 214-871-8209

MEMBERS OF FIRM

Robert P. Franke | Beth D. Bradley

ASSOCIATES

James D. Cartier | Layne L. Anderson

Representative Clients: Hartford Insurance Group; Texas Automobile Insurance Service Office; Trinity Universal Insurance Company.

For Complete List of Firm Personnel, See General Section

For full biographical listings, see the Martindale-Hubbell Law Directory

THOMPSON & KNIGHT, A PROFESSIONAL CORPORATION (AV)

(Attorneys and Counselors)
1700 Pacific Avenue Suite 3300, 75201
Telephone: 214-969-1700
Telecopy: 214-969-1751
Cable Address: "Tomtex"
Telex: 732298
Austin, Texas Office: 1200 San Jacinto Center, 98 San Jacinto Boulevard, 78701.
Telephone: 512-469-6100.
Telecopy: 512-469-6180.
Fort Worth, Texas Office: 801 Cherry Street, Suite 1600, 76102.
Telephone: 817-347-1700.
Telecopy: 817-347-1799.
Houston, Texas Office: 1700 Texas Commerce Tower, 600 Travis, 77002.
Telephone: 713-217-2800.
Telecopy: 713-217-2828.

(See Next Column)

THOMPSON & KNIGHT A PROFESSIONAL CORPORATION, *Dallas—Continued*

Monterrey, Mexico Office: Edificio Losoles PD-4, Av. Lázaro Cárdenas No. 2400 Pte., San Pedro Garza Garcia, Nuevo Léon C.P. 66220.
Telephone: (52-8) 363-0096.
Telecopy: (52-8) 363-3067.

SHAREHOLDERS

David M. Bennett — Peter J. Riley
Robert W. Jones — Judith W. Ross

ASSOCIATES

James T. Anderson — G. Martin Green
James Prince

For Complete List of Firm Personnel, See General Section

For full biographical listings, see the Martindale-Hubbell Law Directory

*EL PASO,** El Paso Co.

LESLIE & SMITH, P.C. (AV)

300 East Main Street 7th Floor, 79901
Telephone: 915-544-4544
Fax: 915-533-4645

Donald S. Leslie — Nelson Smith

For full biographical listings, see the Martindale-Hubbell Law Directory

*FORT WORTH,** Tarrant Co.

CLIFFORD F. MCMASTER (AV)

1400 Oil & Gas Building, 309 West Seventh Street, 76102
Telephone: 817-335-8080
FAX: 817-429-3371

LEGAL SUPPORT PERSONNEL

Twalla J. Dupriest

For full biographical listings, see the Martindale-Hubbell Law Directory

*HOUSTON,** Harris Co.

BAKER & BOTTS, L.L.P. (AV)

One Shell Plaza, 910 Louisiana, 77002
Telephone: 713-229-1234
Cable Address: "Boterlove"
Fax: 713-229-1522
Washington, D.C. Office: The Warner, 1299 Pennsylvania Avenue, N.W.
Telephone: 202-639-7700.
New York, New York Office: 885 Third Avenue, Suite 2000.
Telephone: 212-705-5000.
Austin, Texas Office: 1600 San Jacinto Center, 98 San Jacinto Boulevard.
Telephone: 512-322-2500.
Dallas, Texas Office: 2001 Ross Avenue.
Telephone: 214-953-6500.
Moscow, Russian Federation Office: 10 ul. Pushkinskaya, 103031.
Telephone: 7095/921-5300 (Local); 7095/929-7070 (International).

MEMBER OF FIRM

Tony M. Davis

ASSOCIATES

Richard A. Brooks — Elizabeth M. Guffy
Mary Millwood Gregory — Dahl C. Thompson
Diane T. Weber

For Complete List of Firm Personnel, See General Section

For full biographical listings, see the Martindale-Hubbell Law Directory

RIECKE BAUMANN (AV)

1601 Westheimer, 77006
Telephone: 713-529-1600

Representative Clients: Sears Roebuck & Co.; Citibank South Dakota, N.A.; Montgomery Ward & Co.; General Electric Credit Corp.; Volvo Finance North America, Inc.; ITT Financial Services; Norwest Financial; Security Pacific Exec. Prof.; American Honda; Enterprise Leasing.

For full biographical listings, see the Martindale-Hubbell Law Directory

TEXARKANA, Bowie Co.

PATTON, HALTOM, ROBERTS, MCWILLIAMS & GREER, L.L.P. (AV)

A Registered Limited Liability Partnership including Professional Corporations
700 Texarkana National Bank Building, P.O. Box 1928, 75504-1928
Telephone: 903-794-3341
Fax: 903-792-6542; 903-792-0448

(See Next Column)

William B. Roberts — Phillip N. Cockrell

Representative Clients: Allstate Insurance Co.; Aetna Casualty & Surety Co.; Royal Insurance Group; Continental Insurance Group; Ranger/Pan American Insurance Cos.; The Hanover Insurance Group; American Mutual Liability Insurance Co.; American Hardware Mutual Insurance Co.; Kemper Insurance Co.; Texarkana National Bancshares, Inc.

For Complete List of Firm Personnel, See General Section

For full biographical listings, see the Martindale-Hubbell Law Directory

*TYLER,** Smith Co.

ROBERT M. BANDY, P.C. (AV)

NationsBank Plaza Tower, Suite 1122, 75702-7252
Telephone: 903-592-7333
800-374-2263
FAX: 903-592-7751
Dallas, Texas Office: University Tower, Suite 314, 6440 North Central Expressway.
Telephone: 214-480-8220.
Longview, Texas Office: 703 N. Green, 75606.
Telephone: 903-757-7506.
Fax: 903-592-7751.

Robert M. Bandy

William H. Lively, Jr.

For full biographical listings, see the Martindale-Hubbell Law Directory

UTAH

*SALT LAKE CITY,** Salt Lake Co.

CALLISTER, NEBEKER & MCCULLOUGH, A PROFESSIONAL CORPORATION (AV)

800 Kennecott Building, 84133
Telephone: 801-530-7300
Telecopier: 801-364-9127

H. Russell Hettinger — Steven E. Tyler
Jeffrey L. Shields — Andreś Diaz
Jan M. Bergeson

Representative Clients: Zions First National Bank; Western Farm Credit Bank; Chrysler Credit Corp.; Associates Commercial Corp.

For Complete List of Firm Personnel, See General Section

For full biographical listings, see the Martindale-Hubbell Law Directory

KRUSE, LANDA & MAYCOCK, L.L.C. (AV)

Eighth Floor, Valley Tower, 50 West Broadway (300 South), 84101
Telephone: 801-531-7090
Facsimile: 801-359-3954

Harriet E. Styler — Kevin R. Anderson
Steven G. Loosle

Reference: Bank One Utah.

For full biographical listings, see the Martindale-Hubbell Law Directory

PARSONS BEHLE & LATIMER, A PROFESSIONAL CORPORATION (AV)

One Utah Center, 201 South Main Street, Suite 1800, P.O. Box 45898, 84145-0898
Telephone: 801-532-1234
Telecopy: 801-536-6111

W. Jeffery Fillmore — E. Russell Vetter
Francis M. Wikstrom — J. Thomas Beckett
Craig B. Terry — James H. Woodall
Gary E. Doctorman — K. C. Jensen
Kent B. Alderman — Marji Hanson
Paul D. Veasy — John E. Diaz
Carolyn Montgomery — Barry N. Johnson

Representative Clients: American Honda Finance Corporation; American Honda Motor Company; Bank One, Utah, N.A.; PST Vans, Inc.; West One Bank.

For full biographical listings, see the Martindale-Hubbell Law Directory

Salt Lake City—Continued

RAY, QUINNEY & NEBEKER, A PROFESSIONAL CORPORATION (AV)

Suite 400 Deseret Building, 79 South Main Street, P.O. Box 45385, 84145-0385
Telephone: 801-532-1500
Telecopier: 801-532-7543
Provo, Utah Office: 210 First Security Bank Building, 92 North University Avenue.
Telephone: 801-226-7210.
Telecopier: 801-375-8379.

Herschel J. Saperstein
Weston L. Harris
Scott Hancock Clark
Steven H. Gunn
John P. Harrington
Douglas M. Monson
Steven T. Waterman
Steven W. Call

Representative Clients: First Security Bank of Utah, N.A.; Borden, Inc.; Southern Pacific Transportation; Utah Power & Light Co.; Travelers Insurance Co.; Greyhound Leasing & Financial; Holy Cross Hospital and Health System; Amoco Production Co.

For Complete List of Firm Personnel, See General Section

For full biographical listings, see the Martindale-Hubbell Law Directory

VAN COTT, BAGLEY, CORNWALL & McCARTHY, A PROFESSIONAL CORPORATION (AV)

Suite 1600, 50 South Main Street, P.O. Box 45340, 84145
Telephone: 801-532-3333
Telex: 453149
Telecopier: 801-534-0058
Ogden, Utah Office: Suite 900, 2404 Washington Boulevard.
Telephone: 801-394-5783.
Park City, Utah Office: 314 Main Street, Suite 205.
Telephone: 801-649-3889.
Reno, Nevada Office: Jeppson & Lee, 100 West Liberty, Suite 990.
Telephone: 702-333-6800.

Robert D. Merrill
William G. Fowler
Danny C. Kelly
Guy P. Kroesche
Gerald H. Suniville

Pamela Martinson

For Complete List of Firm Personnel, See General Section

For full biographical listings, see the Martindale-Hubbell Law Directory

VERMONT

*BURLINGTON,** Chittenden Co.

BURAK & ANDERSON (AV)

Executive Square, 346 Shelburne Street, P.O. Box 64700, 05406-4700
Telephone: 802-862-0500
Telecopier: 802-862-8176

MEMBERS OF FIRM

Michael L. Burak
David M. Hyman

For Complete List of Firm Personnel, See General Section

For full biographical listings, see the Martindale-Hubbell Law Directory

LISMAN & LISMAN, A PROFESSIONAL CORPORATION (AV)

84 Pine Street, P.O. Box 728, 05402-0728
Telephone: 802-864-5756
Fax: 802-864-3629

Carl H. Lisman
Allen D. Webster
Mary G. Kirkpatrick
E. William Leckerling, III
Douglas K. Riley

Judith Lillian Dillon
Richard W. Kozlowski

OF COUNSEL

Bernard Lisman
Louis Lisman

For full biographical listings, see the Martindale-Hubbell Law Directory

*RUTLAND,** Rutland Co.

CARROLL, GEORGE & PRATT (AV)

64 & 66 North Main Street, P.O. Box 280, 05702-0280
Telephone: 802-775-7141
Telecopier: 802-775-6483
Woodstock, Vermont Office: The Mill - Route #4 E., P.O. Box 388, 05091.
Telephone: 802-457-1000.
Telecopier: 802-457-1874.

(See Next Column)

MEMBERS OF FIRM

Henry G. Smith (1938-1974)
James P. Carroll
Alan B. George
Robert S. Pratt
Neal C. Vreeland
Jon S. Readnour
Timothy U. Martin
Randall F. Mayhew (Resident Partner, Woodstock Office)
Richard S. Smith
Judy Godnick Barone
John J. Kennelly

ASSOCIATES

Thomas A. Zonay
Jeffrey P. White
Susan Boyle Ford (Resident, Woodstock Office)
Charles C. Humpstone

For full biographical listings, see the Martindale-Hubbell Law Directory

VIRGINIA

ALEXANDRIA, (Independent City)

THOMAS, BALLENGER, VOGELMAN AND TURNER, P.C. (AV)

124 South Royal Street, 22314
Telephone: 703-836-3400
Fax: 703-836-3549

Jeffrey A. Vogelman

References: First Union National Bank of Virginia; Burke & Herbert Bank & Trust Co.

For Complete List of Firm Personnel, See General Section

For full biographical listings, see the Martindale-Hubbell Law Directory

ROY B. ZIMMERMAN (AV)

423 North Alfred Street, P.O. Box 185, 22313-0185
Telephone: 703-683-0130
Fax: 703-836-9287

ASSOCIATE

Laurie Pyne O'Reilly

Reference: Central Fidelity Bank.

For full biographical listings, see the Martindale-Hubbell Law Directory

*CHARLOTTESVILLE,** (Ind. City; Seat of Albemarle Co.)

ROBERT M. MUSSELMAN & ASSOCIATES (AV)

413 7th Street, N.E., P.O. Box 254, 22902
Telephone: 804-977-4500
Fax: 804-293-5727

ASSOCIATES

Carolyn C. Musselman
Douglas E. Little
Rose Marie Downs
Matthew A. Fass

For full biographical listings, see the Martindale-Hubbell Law Directory

NEWPORT NEWS, (Independent City)

ERWIN B. NACHMAN (AV)

708-C Thimble Shoals Boulevard, 23606
Telephone: 804-873-1840
FAX: 804-873-3028

Approved Attorneys for: Lawyers Title Insurance Corp.; Ticor Title Ins. Co.; American Title Ins. Co.; Chicago Title Ins. Co.
Reference: Crestar Bank.

For full biographical listings, see the Martindale-Hubbell Law Directory

PATTEN, WORNOM & WATKINS, L.C. (AV)

Patrick Henry Corporate Center Suite 360, 12350 Jefferson Avenue, 23602
Telephone: 804-249-1881
Facsimile: 804-249-3242; 804-249-1627

Joseph M. DuRant

Representative Clients: Commerce Bank; Janoff and Olshan, Inc.; Crestar Bank; First Union National Bank of Virginia; Central Fidelity National Bank.

For Complete List of Firm Personnel, See General Section

For full biographical listings, see the Martindale-Hubbell Law Directory

NORFOLK, (Independent City)

GOLDBLATT, LIPKIN & COHEN, P.C. (AV)

Suite 300, 415 St. Paul's Boulevard, P.O. Box 3505, 23514
Telephone: 804-627-6225
Telefax: 804-622-3698

(See Next Column)

GOLDBLATT, LIPKIN & COHEN P.C., *Norfolk—Continued*

Paul M. Lipkin
Robert S. Cohen
Steven M. Legum
Mary G. Commander
Beril M. Abraham
Larry W. Shelton

Approved Attorneys for: Lawyers Title Insurance Corp.

For full biographical listings, see the Martindale-Hubbell Law Directory

STACKHOUSE, SMITH & NEXSEN (AV)

1600 First Virginia Tower, 555 Main Street, P.O. Box 3640, 23514
Telephone: 804-623-3555
FAX: 804-624-9245

MEMBERS OF FIRM

Robert C. Stackhouse
Peter W. Smith, IV
William W. Nexsen
R. Clinton Stackhouse, Jr.
Janice McPherson Doxey

ASSOCIATES

Mary Painter Opitz
Timothy P. Murphy
Carl J. Khalil

Representative Clients: Heritage Bank & Trust; The Atlantic Group, Inc.; Roughton Pontiac Corp; Federal National Mortgage Association; Kemper National Insurance Cos.; Shearson/American Express Mortgage Corp.; Harleysville Mutual Insurance Co.; Heritage Bankshares, Inc.; Presbyterian League of the Presbytery of Eastern Virginia, Inc.; Oakwood Acceptance Corp.

For full biographical listings, see the Martindale-Hubbell Law Directory

VANDEVENTER, BLACK, MEREDITH & MARTIN (AV)

500 World Trade Center, 23510
Telephone: 804-446-8600
Cable Address: "Hughsvan"
Telex: 823-671
Telecopier: 446-8670
North Carolina, Kitty Hawk Office: 6 Juniper Trail.
Telephone: 919-261-5055.
Fax: 919-261-8444.
London, England Office: Suite 692, Level 6, Lloyd's, 1 Lime Street.
Telephone: (071) 623-2081.
Facsimile: (071) 929-0043.
Telex: 987321.

MEMBERS OF FIRM

Walter B. Martin, Jr.
Michael P. Cotter
Bryant C. McGann

For Complete List of Firm Personnel, See General Section

For full biographical listings, see the Martindale-Hubbell Law Directory

*RICHMOND,** (Ind. City; Seat of Henrico Co.)

WILLIAMS, MULLEN, CHRISTIAN & DOBBINS, A PROFESSIONAL CORPORATION (AV)

Two James Center, 1021 East Cary Street, P.O. Box 1320, 23210-1320
Telephone: 804-643-1991
Fax: 804-783-6456
Glen Allen, Virginia Office: 4401 Waterfront Drive, Suite 140.
Telephone: 804-965-9168.
Fax: 804-965-0955.
Washington, D.C. Office: 1575 Eye Street, N.W.
Telephone: 202-289-6200.
Fax: 202-289-4126.

Paul S. Bliley, Jr.
A. Peter Brodell
James J. Burns
Charles L. Cabell
Siran S. Faulders
Robert D. Perrow
William H. Schwarzschild, III

Henry C. Su

For Complete List of Firm Personnel, See General Section

For full biographical listings, see the Martindale-Hubbell Law Directory

WASHINGTON

*SEATTLE,** King Co.

BETTS, PATTERSON & MINES, P.S. (AV)

800 Financial Center, 1215 Fourth Avenue, 98161-1090
Telephone: 206-292-9988
Fax: 206-343-7053

John P. Braislin
John R. Rizzardi
Susan C. Hacker

(See Next Column)

Deborah A. Crabbe
Jonathan H. Burke

Representative Clients: Associated Grocers; Cape Fox Corporation; Chrysler Corporation; Key Bank of Washington; Lumberman's of Washington, Inc.; Supermarket Development Corp.; Sysco Food Services of Seattle, Inc.

For full biographical listings, see the Martindale-Hubbell Law Directory

LANE POWELL SPEARS LUBERSKY (AV)

A Partnership including Professional Corporations
1420 Fifth Avenue, Suite 4100, 98101-2338
Telephone: 206-223-7000
Cable Address: "Embe"
Telex: 32-8808
Telecopier: 206-223-7107
Other Offices at: Mount Vernon and Olympia, Washington; Los Angeles and San Francisco, California; Anchorage, Alaska; Portland, Oregon; London, England.

MEMBERS OF FIRM

Charles R. Ekberg (P.S.)
Douglas J. Shaeffer
John J. Mitchell
Bruce W. Leaverton

COUNSEL

Mary Jo Heston

Representative Clients: Associates Commercial Corp.; Blue Cross of Washington and Alaska; General Electric Capital Corp.; Greyhound Financial Corp.; Interwest Leasing, Inc.; Montgomery Ward & Co., Inc.; The Mutual Life Insurance Co. of New York; Pettit-Morry Co.; Safeco Credit Co., Inc.; Transamerica Commercial Finance Corp.

For Complete List of Firm Personnel, See General Section

For full biographical listings, see the Martindale-Hubbell Law Directory

*SPOKANE,** Spokane Co.

SOUTHWELL & O'ROURKE, P.S. (AV)

Suite 960, Paulsen Center, West 421 Riverside Avenue, 99201
Telephone: 509-624-0159
Fax: 509-624-9231

Robert A. Southwell (1929-1984)
Daniel O'Rourke

For full biographical listings, see the Martindale-Hubbell Law Directory

WEST VIRGINIA

*CHARLESTON,** Kanawha Co.

JACKSON & KELLY (AV)

1600 Laidley Tower, P.O. Box 553, 25322
Telephone: 304-340-1000
Fax: 304-340-1130
Martinsburg, West Virginia Office: 300 Foxcroft Avenue, P.O. Box 1068.
Telephone: 304-263-8800.
Morgantown, West Virginia Office: 6000 Hampton Center, P.O. Box 619.
Telephone: 304-599-3000.
New Martinsville, West Virginia Office: 256 Russell Avenue, P.O. Box 68.
Telephone: 304-455-1751.
Charles Town, West Virginia Office: 700 East Washington Street, P.O. Box 983.
Telephone: 304-728-6088.
Clarksburg, West Virginia Office: 203 Main Street, P.O. Box 1587.
Telephone: 304-623-3002.
Lexington, Kentucky Office: 175 East Main Street, Suite 500, P.O. Box 2150.
Telephone: 606-255-9500.
Washington, D. C. Office: 2401 Pennsylvania Avenue, N.W., Suite 400.
Telephone: 202-973-0200.
Denver, Colorado Office: Suite 2710, 1660 Lincoln Street.
Telephone: 303-837-0003.

MEMBERS OF FIRM

William F. Dobbs, Jr.
Ellen S. Cappellanti
Mary Clare Eros (Martinsburg and Charles Town, West Virginia Offices)

ASSOCIATES

Stanton L. Cave (Resident, Lexington, Kentucky Office)
Robert L. Johns

Representative Clients: One Valley Bancorp of West Virginia, Inc.; Navistar Financial Corp.; Orix Credit Alliance, Inc.; Westmoreland Coal Co.; F & M National of Winchester and its Affiliates; Pittston Coal Co.; Westvaco Corp.; Electric Fuels Corp.; Kentucky River Coal Corp.; Cypress-Amax Minerals Co.

For Complete List of Firm Personnel, See General Section

For full biographical listings, see the Martindale-Hubbell Law Directory

*CLARKSBURG,** Harrison Co.

McNEER, HIGHLAND & McMUNN (AV)

Empire Building, P.O. Drawer 2040, 26301
Telephone: 304-623-6636
Facsimile: 304-623-3035
Morgantown Office: McNeer, Highland & McMunn, Baker & Armistead, 168 Chancery Row. P.O. Box 1615.
Telephone: 304-292-8473.
Fax: 304-292-1528.
Martinsburg, Office: 1446-1 Edwin Miller Boulevard. P.O. Box 2509.
Telephone: 304-264-4621.
Fax: 304-264-8623.

MEMBERS OF FIRM

C. David McMunn
J. Cecil Jarvis
James A. Varner
George B. Armistead (Resident, Morgantown Office)
Catherine D. Munster
Robert W. Trumble (Resident, Martinsburg Office)
Dennis M. Shreve
Geraldine S. Roberts
Harold M. Sklar
Jeffrey S. Bolyard
Steven R. Bratke
Michael J. Novotny (Resident, Martinsburg Office)

OF COUNSEL

James E. McNeer
Cecil B. Highland, Jr.
William L. Fury

Representative Clients: One Valley Bank of Clarksburg, National Association; Bruceton Bank; Harrison County Bank; Nationwide Mutual Insurance Cos.; Clarksburg Publishing Co.; C.I.T. Financial Services; State Automobile Mutual Insurance Co.; United Hospital Center, Inc.; West Virginia Coals, Inc.; Swanson Plating Company.

For Complete List of Firm Personnel, See General Section

For full biographical listings, see the Martindale-Hubbell Law Directory

*WHEELING,** Ohio Co.

SCHRADER, RECHT, BYRD, COMPANION & GURLEY (AV)

1000 Hawley Building, 1025 Main Street, P.O. Box 6336, 26003
Telephone: 304-233-3390
Fax: 304-233-2769
Martins Ferry, Ohio Office: 205 North Fifth Street, P.O. Box 309.
Telephone: 614-633-8976.
Fax: 614-633-0400.

PARTNERS

Henry S. Schrader (Retired)
Arthur M. Recht
Ray A. Byrd
James F. Companion
Terence M. Gurley
Frank X. Duff
Teresa Rieman-Camilletti
Yolonda G. Lambert
Patrick S. Casey
Sandra M. Chapman
Daniel P. Fry (Resident, Martins Ferry, Ohio Office)
James P. Mazzone

ASSOCIATES

Sandra K. Law
D. Kevin Coleman
Denise A. Jebbia
Edythe A. Nash
Robert G. McCoid
Denise D. Klug
Thomas E. Johnston

OF COUNSEL

James A. Byrum, Jr.

General Counsel: WesBanco Bank-Elm Grove.
Representative Clients: CIGNA Property and Casualty Cos.; Columbia Gas Transmission Corp.; Commercial Union Assurance Co.; Hazlett, Burt & Watson, Inc.; Stone & Thomas Department Stores; Transamerica Commercial Finance Corp.; Wheeling-Pittsburgh Steel Corp.

For full biographical listings, see the Martindale-Hubbell Law Directory

WISCONSIN

*MILWAUKEE,** Milwaukee Co.

BIRD, MARTIN & SALOMON S.C. (AV)

735 North Water Street, Suite 1600, 53202-4104
Telephone: 414-276-7290
Facsimile: 414-276-7291

John D. Bird, Jr.
Frances H. Martin
Allen M. Salomon

References: Firstar Bank; Biltmore Investors Bank.

For full biographical listings, see the Martindale-Hubbell Law Directory

KOHNER, MANN & KAILAS, S.C. (AV)

1572 East Capitol Drive, P.O. Box 19982, 53211-0982
Telephone: 414-962-5110
Fax: 414-962-8725

(See Next Column)

Marvin L. Kohner (1908-1975)
Robert L. Mann
Steve Kailas
Mark R. Wolters
Jordan B. Reich
David S. Chartier

Roy Paul Roth
Gary P. Lantzy
Christopher C. Kailas
Robert E. Nailen
Matthew P. Gerdisch
Darrell R. Zall
Daniel J. Flynn
Timothy L. Zuberbier
Shawn G. Rice

Representative Clients: EcoLab, Inc.; Parker Pen Co.; Ray O Vac, Inc.

For full biographical listings, see the Martindale-Hubbell Law Directory

QUARLES & BRADY (AV)

411 East Wisconsin Avenue, 53202-4497
Telephone: 414-277-5000
Cable Address: "Lawdock"
Fax: 414-271-3552.
TWX: 910-262-3426
Madison, Wisconsin Office: Firstar Plaza, One South Pinckney Street, P.O. Box 2113.
Telephone: 608-251-5000.
Fax: 608-251-9166.
West Palm Beach, Florida Office: 222 Lakeview Avenue, 4th Floor.
Telephone: 407-653-5000.
Fax: 407-653-5333.
Naples, Florida Office: Barnett Center, 4501 Tamiami Trail North.
Telephone: 813-262-5959.
Fax: 813-434-4999.
Phoenix, Arizona Office: One Camelback Building, One East Camelback Road, Suite 400.
Telephone: 602-230-5500.
Fax: 602-230-5598.

MEMBERS OF FIRM

(ALPHABETICALLY BY YEAR OF ADMISSION TO BAR)

Roger P. Paulsen
Ned R. Nashban (Resident, West Palm Beach, Florida Office)
Andrew M. Barnes
Roy L. Prange, Jr. (Resident, Madison Office)
Charles H. McMullen
Elizabeth A. Orelup
Gerald L. Shelley (Resident, Phoenix, Arizona Office)

ASSOCIATES

Patrick J. Schoen
William G. Shofstall (Resident, West Palm Beach, Florida Office)
Jerome R. Kerkman
Stuart S. Mermelstein (Resident, West Palm Beach, Florida Office)
Nancy Berz Colman (Resident, West Palm Beach, Florida Office)
Louis D. D'Agostino (Resident, Naples, Florida Office)
Fran C. Windsor (Resident, Phoenix, Arizona Office)
Susan A. Cerbins
Sandra L. Tarver (Resident, Madison Office)
Valerie L. Bailey-Rihn (Resident, Madison Office)
Tracy D. Taylor (Resident, Phoenix, Arizona Office)

For Complete List of Firm Personnel, See General Section

For full biographical listings, see the Martindale-Hubbell Law Directory

WYOMING

*CASPER,** Natrona Co.

BROWN & DREW (AV)

Casper Business Center, Suite 800, 123 West First Street, 82601-2486
Telephone: 307-234-1000
800-877-6755
Telefax: 307-265-8025

MEMBERS OF FIRM

Donn J. McCall
Russell M. Blood

ASSOCIATES

P. Jaye Rippley
Courtney Robert Kepler
Drew A. Perkins

Attorneys for: First Interstate Bank of Wyoming, N.A.; Norwest Bank Wyoming, N.A.; Hilltop National Bank; The CIT Group/Industrial Financing; ITT Commercial Finance Corp.

For Complete List of Firm Personnel, See General Section

For full biographical listings, see the Martindale-Hubbell Law Directory

PUERTO RICO

SAN JUAN, San Juan Dist.

Fiddler, González & Rodríguez

Chase Manhattan Bank Building (Hato Rey), P.O. Box 363507, 00936-3507
Telephone: 809-753-3113
Telecopier: 809-759-3123

MEMBERS OF FIRM

Leopoldo J. Cabassa-Sauri Teodoro Peña-Garcia

Representative Clients: The Chase Manhattan Bank, N.A.; The Equitable Life Assurance Society of the U.S.; Pfizer, Inc.; Merck & Co., Inc.; American Cyanamid Co.; Bacardi Corp.; General Motor Acceptance Corp.; The Bank & Trust of Puerto Rico; Seaboard Surety Co.; Plaza Las Americas, Inc.

For Complete List of Firm Personnel, See General Section

For full biographical listings, see the Martindale-Hubbell Law Directory

Gonzalez & Bennazar

Capital Center Building South Tower - 9th Floor, Arterial Hostos Avenue (Hato Rey), 00918
Telephone: 809-754-9191
Fax: 809-754-9325

MEMBERS OF FIRM

Raul E. González Díaz A. J. Bennazar-Zequeira

Representative Clients: American Express Travel Related Services Co., Inc.; Federal Deposit Insurance Corp.; Resolution Trust Co.; M & M Mars; G-Tech Corporation; First Data Corporation.

For Complete List of Firm Personnel, See General Section

For full biographical listings, see the Martindale-Hubbell Law Directory

Indiano, Williams & Weinstein-Bacal

Hato Rey Tower, 21st Floor, 268 Muñoz Rivera Avenue (Hato Rey), 00918
Telephone: 809-754-2323; 763-0485
Fax: 809-766-3366
St. Thomas, Virgin Islands Office: Stuart A. Weinstein-Bacal, P.O. Box 9820, Charlotte Amalie, 00801.
Telephone: 809-776-2500.
Telecopier: 809-779-6918.

MEMBERS OF FIRM

Stuart A. Weinstein-Bacal David C. Indiano
Jeffrey M. Williams

ASSOCIATES

Javier A. Morales Ramos Madeline Garcia-Rodriguez

For full biographical listings, see the Martindale-Hubbell Law Directory

Mártinez Odell & Calabria

Banco Popular Center, 16th Floor, (Hato Rey), P.O. Box 190998, 00919-0998
Telephone: 809-753-8914
Facsimile: 809-753-8402; 809-759-9075; 809-764-5664

MEMBERS OF FIRM

Luis E. Lopez Correa Patrick D. O'Neill

ASSOCIATE

Jose Antonio Fernandez-Jaquete

Representative Clients: A.T. & T. Corp.; Pepsi-Cola P.R. Bottling Co.; Banco Popular de Puerto Rico; I.T.T. Financial Corp.; John H. Harland Company of Puerto Rico, Inc.; Lutron Electronics Co., Inc.; Paine Webber, Inc.; Lotus Development Corp.; Western Digital.

For Complete List of Firm Personnel, See General Section

For full biographical listings, see the Martindale-Hubbell Law Directory

O'Neill & Borges

10th Floor, Chase Manhattan Bank Building (Hato Rey), 254 Muñoz Rivera Avenue, 00918-1995
Telephone: 809-764-8181
Telecopier: 809-753-8944

MEMBERS OF FIRM

David P. Freedman Mario J. Pabón

Representative Clients: The First Boston Corp.; Ford Motor Co.; IBM Credit Corp.; Interpublic Group of Companies; Mitsubishi Motor Sales of Caribbean, Inc.; The Procter & Gamble Commercial Co.; Ralston Purina Co.; Thomson International Publishing; Tidewater, Inc.; Westinghouse Electric Corp.

For Complete List of Firm Personnel, See General Section

For full biographical listings, see the Martindale-Hubbell Law Directory

CANADA
ALBERTA

*EDMONTON,** Edmonton Jud. Dist.

Parlee McLaws (AV)

15th Floor Manulife Place, 10180 101st Street, T5J 4K1
Telephone: 403-423-8500
Telecopier: 403-423-2870
Calgary, Alberta Office: 3400, Western Canadian Place, 707 - 8th Avenue, S.W.
Telephone: 403-294-7000.
Telecopier: 403-265-8263.

MEMBERS OF FIRM

C. H. Kerr, Q.C. R. A. Newton, Q.C.
M. D. MacDonald T. A. Cockrall, Q.C.
K. F. Bailey, Q.C. H. D. Montemurro
R. B. Davison, Q.C. F. J. Niziol
F. R. Haldane R. W. Wilson
P. E. J. Curran I. L. MacLachlan
D. G. Finlay R. O. Langley
J. K. McFadyen R. G. McBean
R. C. Secord J. T. Neilson
D. L. Kennedy E. G. Rice
D. C. Rolf J. F. McGinnis
D. F. Pawlowski J. H. H. Hockin
A. A. Garber G. W. Jaycock
R. P. James M. J. K. Nikel
D. C. Wintermute B. J. Curial
J. L. Cairns S. L. May
M. S. Poretti

ASSOCIATES

C. R. Head P. E. S. J. Kennedy
A.W. Slemko R. Feraco
L. H. Hamdon R.J. Billingsley
K.A. Smith N.B.R. Thompson
K. D. Fallis-Howell P. A. Shenher
D. S. Tam I. C. Johnson
J.W. McClure K.G. Koshman
F.H. Belzil D.D. Dubrule
R.A. Renz G. T. Lund
J.G. Paulson W.D. Johnston
K. E. Buss G. E. Flemming
B. L. Andriachuk K. P. Nayyer

For full biographical listings, see the Martindale-Hubbell Law Directory

CANADA
BRITISH COLUMBIA

*VANCOUVER,** Vancouver Co.

Russell & DuMoulin (AV)

2100-1075 West Georgia Street, V6E 3G2
Telephone: 604-631-3131
Fax: 604-631-3232
A Member of the national association of Borden DuMoulin Howard Gervais, comprising Russell & DuMoulin, Vancouver, British Columbia; Howard Mackie, Calgary, Alberta; Borden & Elliot, Toronto, Ontario; Mackenzie Gervais, Montreal, Quebec and Borden DuMoulin Howard Gervais, London, England.
Strategic Alliance with Perkins Coie with offices in Seattle, Spokane and Bellevue, Washington; Portland, Oregon; Anchorage, Alaska; Los Angeles, California; Washington, D.C.; Hong Kong and Taipei, Taiwan.
Represented in Hong Kong by Vincent T.K. Cheung, Yap & Co.

MEMBERS OF FIRM

Michael A. Fitch Marcel J. Peerson

Representative Clients: Alcan Smelters & Chemicals Ltd.; The Bank of Nova Scotia; Canada Trust Co.; The Canada Life Assurance Co.; Forest Industrial Relations Ltd.; Honda Canada Inc.; IBM Canada Ltd.; Macmillan Bloedel Ltd.; Nissho Iwai Canada Ltd.; The Toronto-Dominion Bank.

For Complete List of Firm Personnel, See General Section

For full biographical listings, see the Martindale-Hubbell Law Directory

CANADA
NEW BRUNSWICK

*SAINT JOHN,** Saint John Co.

CLARK, DRUMMIE & COMPANY (AV)

40 Wellington Row, P.O. Box 6850 Station "A", E2L 4S3
Telephone: 506-633-3800
Telecopier (Automatic): 506-633-3811

MEMBERS OF FIRM

Thomas B. Drummie, Q.C.
Willard M. Jenkins
Patrick J. P. Ervin

Reference: Royal Bank of Canada.

For Complete List of Firm Personnel, See General Section

For full biographical listings, see the Martindale-Hubbell Law Directory

CANADA
NOVA SCOTIA

*HALIFAX,** Halifax Co.

McINNES COOPER & ROBERTSON (AV)

1601 Lower Water Street, P.O. Box 730, B3J 2V1
Telephone: 902-425-6500
Fax: 902-425-6350
St. John's, Newfoundland Office: Suite 602, Scotia Centre, 235 Water Street, P.O. Box 547. A1C, 5K8.
Telephone: 709-726-9500.
Fax: 709-726-9550.

Reginald A. Cluney, Q.C.
Robert G. Belliveau, Q.C.
David H. Reardon, Q.C.
John D. Stringer
Peter M. S. Bryson

ASSOCIATE

Bernard F. Miller

Attorneys for: Bank of Nova Scotia; Imperial Oil, Limited; Frank B. Hall & Co., Inc. (New York); American Steamship Owners Protection & Indemnity Association, Inc.; Coca-Cola, Ltd.; Scott Worldwide Inc.; Hong Kong Bank of Canada.

For Complete List of Firm Personnel, See General Section

For full biographical listings, see the Martindale-Hubbell Law Directory

CANADA
ONTARIO

KITCHENER, Regional Munic. of Waterloo

GIFFEN, LEE, WAGNER, MORLEY & GARBUTT (AV)

50 Queen Street North, P.O. Box 2396, N2H 6M3
Telephone: 519-578-4150
Fax: 519-578-8740

MEMBERS OF FIRM

Jeffrey J. Mansfield (1955-1991)
J. Peter Giffen, Q.C.
Bruce L. Lee
J. Scott Morley
Brian R. Wagner
Philip A. Garbutt

ASSOCIATES

Edward J. Vanderkloet
Keith C. Masterman
Daniel J. Fife
Jeffrey W. Boich

For full biographical listings, see the Martindale-Hubbell Law Directory

*TORONTO,** Regional Munic. of York

BORDEN & ELLIOT (AV)

Barristers & Solicitors
Scotia Plaza, 40 King Street West, M5H 3Y4
Telephone: 416-367-6000
Telecopier: 416-367-6749
Internet: @ borden.com
A Member of the national association of Borden DuMoulin Howard Gervais, comprising Borden & Elliot in Toronto, Ontario, Russell & DuMoulin in Vancouver, British Columbia, Howard, Mackie in Calgary, Alberta and Mackenzie Gervais in Montréal, Québec. Borden DuMoulin Howard Gervais also operates an office in London, England.

MEMBER AND ASSOCIATES

Geoffrey B. Morawetz

For Complete List of Firm Personnel, See General Section

For full biographical listings, see the Martindale-Hubbell Law Directory

KELLY AFFLECK GREENE (AV)

One First Canadian Place, Suite 840, P.O. Box 489, M5X 1E5
Telephone: 416-360-2800
FAX: 416-360-5960

MEMBERS OF FIRM

W. Anthony Kelly, Q.C.
Donald S. Affleck, Q.C.
Peter R. Greene
James H. Grout
James C. Orr
Robert I. Thornton
John L. Finnigan
Helen A. Daley

ASSOCIATES

Melissa J. Kennedy
D.J. Miller
Aida Van Wees

For full biographical listings, see the Martindale-Hubbell Law Directory

CANADA
QUEBEC

*MONTREAL,** Montreal Dist.

GOLDSTEIN, FLANZ & FISHMAN (AV)

Suite 4100, 1250 René-Lévesque Boulevard West, H3B 4W8
Telephone: 514-932-4100
Cable Address: "Meybat"
Telex: 05-24593
Telecopier: 514-932-4170

MEMBERS OF FIRM

Yoine Goldstein
Leonard W. Flanz
Avram Fishman
Mark Schrager
Gilles Paquin
Mark E. Meland
Alain Daigle
Nancy Gross
Michael Gaon
Elyse Rosen
James D. Hughes

For full biographical listings, see the Martindale-Hubbell Law Directory

McMASTER MEIGHEN (AV)

A General Partnership
7th Floor, 630 René-Lévesque Boulevard West, H3B 4H7
Telephone: 514-879-1212
Telecopier: 514-878-0605
Cable Address: "Cammerall"
Telex: "Cammerall MTL" 05-268637
Affiliated with Fraser & Beatty in Toronto, North York, Ottawa and Vancouver.

MEMBERS OF FIRM

Alexis P. Bergeron
Marc Duchesne
Luc Bëliveau
Michel A. Pinsonnault
Jacques Gauthier
Kurt A. Johnson

For Complete List of Firm Personnel, See General Section

For full biographical listings, see the Martindale-Hubbell Law Directory

CANADA
SASKATCHEWAN

*SASKATOON,** Saskatoon Jud. Centre

McKERCHER, McKERCHER & WHITMORE (AV)

374 Third Avenue, South, S7K 1M5
Telephone: 306-653-2000
Fax: 306-244-7335
Regina, Saskatchewan Office: 1000 - 1783 Hamilton Street.
Telephone: 306-352-7661.
Fax: 306-781-7113.

MEMBERS OF FIRM

John R. Beckman, Q.C.
Douglas B. Richardson
Joel A. Hesje

For Complete List of Firm Personnel, See General Section

For full biographical listings, see the Martindale-Hubbell Law Directory

BUSINESS LAW

ALABAMA

*BIRMINGHAM,** Jefferson Co.

BALCH & BINGHAM (AV)

1710 Sixth Avenue North, P.O. Box 306, 35201
Telephone: 205-251-8100
Facsimile: 205-226-8798
Other Birmingham, Alabama Office: 1901 Sixth Avenue North, 35203.
Telephone: 205-251-8100.
Facsimile: 205-226-8799.
Montgomery, Alabama Office: The Winter Building, 2 Dexter Avenue, 36101.
Telephone: 205-834-6500.
Facsimile: 205-269-3115.
Huntsville, Alabama Office: Suite 810, 200 West Court Square, 35801.
Telephone: 205-551-0171.
Facsimile: 205-551-0174.
Washington, D.C. Office: Suite 800, 1101 Connecticut Avenue, N.W., 20036.
Telephone: 202-296-0387.
Facsimile: 202-452-8180.

COUNSEL
John Bingham

MEMBERS OF FIRM
Walter M. Beale, Jr.
James F. Hughey, Jr.
Richard L. Pearson
William S. Wright
John F. Mandt
Timothy J. Tracy
Suzanne Ashe

ASSOCIATES
Gregory S. Curran
Colin H. Luke
Randall D. McClanahan

Counsel for: Alabama Power Co.; Blue Cross and Blue Shield of Alabama; The Boeing Company; Brasfield & Gorrie, Inc.; Compass Bancshares, Inc.; Harbert Corp.; Kimberly-Clark Corp.; Southern Company Services, Inc.; Southern Research Institute; Vesta Insurance Group, Inc.

For Complete List of Firm Personnel, See General Section

For full biographical listings, see the Martindale-Hubbell Law Directory

BERKOWITZ, LEFKOVITS, ISOM & KUSHNER, A PROFESSIONAL CORPORATION (AV)

1600 SouthTrust Tower, 420 North Twentieth Street, 35203
Telephone: 205-328-0480
Telecopier: 205-322-8007

Arnold K. Lefkovits
Harold B. Kushner
B. G. Minisman, Jr.
David A. Larsen
William R. Sylvester
D. J. Simonetti
David L. Silverstein
W. Clark Goodwin
Barry S. Marks
Ronald A. Levitt
Marvin T. Griff
Denise W. Killebrew
Thomas O. Kolb

J. Fred Kingren
Andrew J. Potts
Richard A. Pizitz, Jr.
Walton E. Williams III

Representative Clients: AlaTenn Resources, Inc.; AlaTenn Natural Gas Co.; B.A.S.S., Inc.; Hanna Steel Co., Inc.; Liberty Trouser Co. Inc.; McDonald's Corp.; Parisian, Inc.; Southern Pipe & Supply Co., Inc.; Supreme Beverage, Inc.

For Complete List of Firm Personnel, See General Section

For full biographical listings, see the Martindale-Hubbell Law Directory

BRADLEY, ARANT, ROSE & WHITE (AV)

1400 Park Place Tower, 2001 Park Place, 35203
Telephone: 205-521-8000
Telex: 494-1324
Facsimile: 205-251-8611, 251-8665, 252-0264
Facsimile (Southtrust Office): 205-251-9915
Huntsville, Alabama Office: 200 Clinton Avenue West, Suite 900.
Telephone: 205-517-5100.
Facsimile: 205-533-5069.

(See Next Column)

MEMBERS OF FIRM
Edward M. Selfe
Robert R. Reid, Jr.
John N. Wrinkle
Thomas Neely Carruthers, Jr.
Thad Gladden Long
William L. Hinds, Jr.
Charles Larimore Whitaker
P. Nicholas Greenwood
James E. Rotch
Laurence Duncan Vinson, Jr.
Walter H. Monroe, III
John K. Molen
Lant B. Davis
Carleta Roberts Hawley
M. Williams Goodwyn, Jr.
John B. Grenier
J. David Dresher
Paul S. Ware
Virginia Calvert Patterson

COUNSEL
Wm. Bew White, Jr.

ASSOCIATES
Denson Nauls Franklin III
L. Susan Doss
George Bryan Harris
Amy McNeer Tucker
Kevin J. Henderson
Christopher L. Howard
Hall B, Bryant III
Paul D. Gilbert
K. Wood Herren
Jennifer Byers McLeod

For Complete List of Firm Personnel, See General Section

For full biographical listings, see the Martindale-Hubbell Law Directory

BURR & FORMAN (AV)

3000 SouthTrust Tower, 420 North 20th Street, 35203
Telephone: 205-251-3000
Telecopier: 205-458-5100
Huntsville, Alabama Office: Suite 204, Regency Center, 400 Meridian Street.
Telephone: 205-551-0010.

MEMBERS OF FIRM
J. Fred Powell
Samuel W. Oliver, Jr.
Louis H. Anders, Jr.
Joseph G. Stewart
A. Brand Walton
Jack P. Stephenson, Jr.
Eric L. Carlton
George M. Taylor, III
Bruce A. Rawls
Dwight L. Mixson, Jr.
Gene T. Price
Henry Graham Beene
Deborah P. Fisher
Gail Livingston Mills
Marvin Glenn Perry, Jr.

ASSOCIATES
Jeffrey T. Baker
Jill Verdeyen Deer

For Complete List of Firm Personnel, See General Section

For full biographical listings, see the Martindale-Hubbell Law Directory

GORDON, SILBERMAN, WIGGINS & CHILDS, A PROFESSIONAL CORPORATION (AV)

1400 SouthTrust Tower, 420 North 20th Street, 35203
Telephone: 205-328-0640
Telecopier: 205-254-1500

Bruce L. Gordon
Ray D. Gibbons

Timothy D. Davis
Joseph H. Calvin, III
Linda J. Peacock

For Complete List of Firm Personnel, See General Section

For full biographical listings, see the Martindale-Hubbell Law Directory

HASKELL SLAUGHTER YOUNG & JOHNSTON, PROFESSIONAL ASSOCIATION (AV)

1200 AmSouth/Harbert Plaza, 1901 Sixth Avenue North, 35203
Telephone: 205-251-1000
Facsimile: 205-324-1133
Montgomery, Alabama Office: Haskell Slaughter Young Johnston & Gallion. Bailey Building, Suite 375, 400 South Union Street, P.O. Box 4660. 36104
Telephone: 205-265-8573.
Facsimile: 205-264-7945.

J. Brooke Johnston, Jr.
Beall D. Gary, Jr.
Ross N. Cohen
Gwen L. Windle

Louise Coker Wyman

Representative Clients: The Bradford Group, Inc.; Docucon, Incorporated; HEALTHSOUTH Rehabilitation Corporation/HEALTHSOUTH Medical Centers; Manpower Temporary Services (Alabama); Marshall Durbin Companies; MedPartners, Inc.; Psychiatric Healthcare Corporation; Revere Technology & Consulting Co., Inc.; Ridout's-Brown-Service Inc.; United Restaurants, Inc.

For Complete List of Firm Personnel, See General Section

For full biographical listings, see the Martindale-Hubbell Law Directory

PRITCHARD, MCCALL & JONES (AV)

800 Financial Center, 35203
Telephone: 205-328-9190

(See Next Column)

PRITCHARD, MCCALL & JONES, *Birmingham—Continued*

MEMBERS OF FIRM

William S. Pritchard (1890-1967)
Alexander W. Jones (1914-1988)
William S. Pritchard, Jr.
Madison W. O'Kelley, Jr.
Julian P. Hardy, Jr.
Alexander W. Jones, Jr.
F. Hilton-Green Tomlinson
James G. Henderson
William S. Pritchard, III

ASSOCIATES

Michael L. McKerley
Robert Bond Higgins
Nina Michele LaFleur
Mary W. Burge

Representative Clients: First National Bank of Columbiana; Central State Bank of Calera; Buffalo Rock-Pepsi-Cola Bottling Co.; Gillis Advertising, Inc.; Liberty Mutual Insurance Co.; Reliance Insurance Company; SouthTrust Bank, N.A.; Bromberg & Company, Inc.; Farmers Furniture Company; First Commercial Bank.

For full biographical listings, see the Martindale-Hubbell Law Directory

*HUNTSVILLE,** Madison Co.

BALCH & BINGHAM (AV)

Suite 810, 200 West Court Square, P.O. Box 18668, 35804-8668
Telephone: 205-551-0171
Facsimile: 205-551-0174
Birmingham, Alabama Offices: 1710 Sixth Avenue North, 35203.
Telephone: 205-251-8100.
Facsimile: 205-226-8798. 1901 Sixth Avenue North, 35203.
Telephone: 205-251-8100.
Facsimile: 205-226-8799.
Montgomery, Alabama Office: The Winter Building, 2 Dexter Avenue, 36101.
Telephone: 205-834-6500.
Facsimile: 205-269-3115.
Washington, D.C. Office: Suite 800, 1101 Connecticut Avenue, N.W., 20036.
Telephone: 202-296-0387.
Facsimile: 202-452-8180.

RESIDENT MEMBER OF FIRM

S. Revelle Gwyn

Counsel for: Alabama Power Co.; Blue Cross and Blue Shield of Alabama; The Boeing Company; Brasfield & Gorrie, Inc.; Compass Bancshares, Inc.; Harbert Corp.; Kimberly-Clark Corp.; Southern Company Services, Inc.; Southern Research Institute; Vesta Insurance Group, Inc.

For Complete List of Firm Personnel, See General Section

For full biographical listings, see the Martindale-Hubbell Law Directory

BERRY, ABLES, TATUM, LITTLE & BAXTER, P.C. (AV)

Legal Building, 315 Franklin Street, S.E., P.O. Box 165, 35804-0165
Telephone: 205-533-3740
Facsimile: 205-533-3751

William H. Blanton (1889-1973)
Joe M. Berry
L. Bruce Ables
James T. Tatum, Jr.
Loyd H. Little, Jr.
James T. Baxter, III
Thomas E. Parker, Jr.
Bill G. Hall

Representative Clients: AmSouth Bank, N.A.; First Alabama Bank; General Shale Products Co.; The Hartz Corp.; Litton Industries, Inc.; Farmers Tractor Co.; Colonial Bank; Farm Credit Bank of Texas; Resolution Trust Corp.
Reference: First Alabama Bank.

For full biographical listings, see the Martindale-Hubbell Law Directory

BURR & FORMAN (AV)

Suite 204, Regency Center, 400 Meridian Street, 35801
Telephone: 205-551-0010
Birmingham, Alabama Office: 3000 SouthTrust Tower, 420 North 20th Street.
Telephone: 205-251-3000.
Telecopier: 205-458-5100.

RESIDENT PARTNER

S. Dagnal Rowe

For full biographical listings, see the Martindale-Hubbell Law Directory

*JASPER,** Walker Co.

O'REAR & O'REAR (AV)

Suite B Bankhead-Byars Building, 1816 Third Avenue, P.O. Box 191, 35502-0191
Telephone: 205-387-2196
Fax: 205-387-2190

MEMBERS OF FIRM

Caine O'Rear, Jr.
Griff O'Rear
Mark A. McWhorter

Reference: First National Bank of Jasper.

For full biographical listings, see the Martindale-Hubbell Law Directory

*MOBILE,** Mobile Co.

JOHNSTONE, ADAMS, BAILEY, GORDON AND HARRIS (AV)

Royal St. Francis Building, 104 St. Francis Street, P.O. Box 1988, 36633
Telephone: 334-432-7682
Facsimile: 334-432-2800
Telex: 782040

MEMBERS OF FIRM

Charles B. Bailey, Jr.
Ben H. Harris, Jr.
William H. Hardie, Jr.
Joseph M. Allen, Jr.
I. David Cherniak
Wade B. Perry, Jr.
R. Gregory Watts

General Counsel for: First Alabama Bank, Mobile; Infirmary Health System/Mobile Infirmary Medical Center/Rotary Rehabilitation Hospital (Multi-Hospital System).
Counsel for: Oil and Gas: Exxon Corp. Business and Corporate: Bell South Telecommunications, Inc.; Aluminum Co. of America; Michelin Tire Corp.; Metropolitan Life Insurance Co.; The Travelers Insurance Cos. Marine: The West of England Ship Owners Mutual Protection and Indemnity Association (Luxembourg); The Standard Steamship Owners' Protection and Indemnity Association (Bermuda) Ltd.

For Complete List of Firm Personnel, See General Section

For full biographical listings, see the Martindale-Hubbell Law Directory

VICKERS, RIIS, MURRAY AND CURRAN (AV)

8th Floor, First Alabama Bank Building, P.O. Box 2568, 36652
Telephone: 334-432-9772
Fax: 334-432-9781

MEMBERS OF FIRM

J. Manson Murray
Edwin J. Curran, Jr.
Zebulon M. P. Inge, Jr.
Ronald P. Davis

Representative Clients: Dravo Natural Resources Co.; Midstream Fuel Services; John E. Graham & Sons; McPhillips Manufacturing Co.; Spring Hill College; Steiner Shipyard, Inc.; Homeowners Marketing Services, Inc.; Marine Office of America Corp.; Cummins Alabama, Inc.; Ben M. Radcliff Contractor, Inc.

For Complete List of Firm Personnel, See General Section

For full biographical listings, see the Martindale-Hubbell Law Directory

*MONTGOMERY,** Montgomery Co.

* indicates certain Bar Register subscribers whose principal office is located elsewhere in the state and who have arranged for representation as a part of the state capital listings that follow

*** BALCH & BINGHAM (AV)**

The Winter Building, 2 Dexter Avenue, P.O. Box 78, 36101
Telephone: 334-834-6500
Facsimile: 334-269-3115
Birmingham, Alabama Offices: 1710 Sixth Avenue North, 35203.
Telephone: 205-251-8100.
Facsimile: 205-226-8798. 1901 Sixth Avenue North, 35203.
Telephone: 205-251-8100.
Facsimile: 205-226-8799.
Huntsville, Alabama Office: Suite 810, 200 West Court Square, 35801.
Telephone: 205-551-0171.
Facsimile: 205-551-0174.
Washington, D.C. Office: Suite 800, 1101 Connecticut Avenue, N.W., 20036.
Telephone: 202-296-0387.
Facsimile: 202-452-8180.

RESIDENT MEMBER OF FIRM

Malcolm N. Carmichael

RESIDENT ASSOCIATES

Lois Smith Woodward
Patricia Anne Hamilton

Counsel for: Alabama Power Co.; Blue Cross and Blue Shield of Alabama; The Boeing Company; Brasfield & Gorrie, Inc.; Compass Bancshares, Inc.; Harbert Corp.; Kimberly-Clark Corp.; Southern Company Services, Inc.; Southern Research Institute; Vesta Insurance Group, Inc.

For Complete List of Firm Personnel, See General Section

For full biographical listings, see the Martindale-Hubbell Law Directory

CAPOUANO, WAMPOLD, PRESTWOOD & SANSONE, P.A. (AV)

350 Adams Avenue, P.O. Box 1910, 36102-1910
Telephone: 334-264-6401
Fax: 334-834-4954

Leon M. Capouano
Alvin T. Prestwood
Jerome D. Smith
Ellis D. Hanan
Joseph P. Borg
Joseph W. Warren

OF COUNSEL

Charles H. Wampold, Jr.

(See Next Column)

CAPOUANO, WAMPOLD, PRESTWOOD & SANSONE P.A.—*Continued*

Thomas B. Klinner
Linda Smith Webb
James M. Sizemore, Jr.

Counsel for: First Alabama Bank of Montgomery, N.A.; Union Bank and Trust Co.; Real Estate Financing, Inc.; SouthTrust Bank; AmSouth Bank; Central Bank; City Federal Savings & Loan Assoc.; Colonial Mortgage Co.; Lomas & Nettleton; First Bank of Linden.

For full biographical listings, see the Martindale-Hubbell Law Directory

*TUSCALOOSA,** Tuscaloosa Co.

PHELPS, JENKINS, GIBSON & FOWLER (AV)

1201 Greensboro Avenue, P.O. Box 020848, 35402-0848
Telephone: 205-345-5100
Fax: 205-758-4394
Fax: 205-391-6658

MEMBERS OF FIRM

Sam M. Phelps
James J. Jenkins
Johnson Russell Gibson, III
Randolph M. Fowler
Michael S. Burroughs
C. Barton Adcox
Farley A. Poellnitz

ASSOCIATES

K. Scott Stapp
Karen C. Welborn
Sandra C. Guin
Kimberly B. Glass
Stephen E. Snow

Attorneys for: Aetna Insurance Co.; Allstate Insurance Co.; Carolina Casualty Insurance Co.; Continental Insurance Cos.; Fireman's Fund-American Insurance Cos.; Great American Insurance Co.; Hanover Insurance Co.

For full biographical listings, see the Martindale-Hubbell Law Directory

ARIZONA

*FLAGSTAFF,** Coconino Co.

ASPEY, WATKINS & DIESEL (AV)

123 North San Francisco, 86001
Telephone: 602-774-1478
Facsimile: 602-774-1043
Sedona, Arizona Office: 120 Soldier Pass Road.
Telephone: 602-282-5955.
Facsimile: 602-282-5962.
Page, Arizona Office: 904 North Navajo.
Telephone: 602-645-9694.
Winslow, Arizona Office: 205 North Williamson.
Telephone: 602-289-5963.
Cottonwood, Arizona Office: 905 Cove Parkway, Unite 201.
Telephone: 602-639-1881.

MEMBERS OF FIRM

Frederick M. Fritz Aspey
Harold L. Watkins
Louis M. Diesel
Bruce S. Griffen
Donald H. Bayles, Jr.
Kaign N. Christy
John J. Dempsey

Zachary Markham
James E. Ledbetter
Whitney Cunningham
Holly S. Karris

LEGAL SUPPORT PERSONNEL

Deborah D. Roberts (Legal Assistant)
C. Denece Pruett (Legal Assistant)
Dominic M. Marino, Jr, (Paralegal Assistant)

Representative Clients: Farmer's Insurance Company of Arizona; Kelley-Moore Paint Co.; Pepsi-Cola Bottling Company of Northern Arizona; Bill Luke's Chrysler-Plymouth, Inc.; First American Title Insurance Company ; Transamerica Title Insurance Co.; Page Electric Utility; Comprehensive Access Health Plan, Inc.
Reference: First Interstate Bank-Arizona, N.A., Flagstaff, Arizona.

For full biographical listings, see the Martindale-Hubbell Law Directory

BONN, LUSCHER, PADDEN & WILKINS, CHARTERED (AV)

805 North Second Street, 85004
Telephone: 602-254-5557
Fax: 602-254-0656

Paul V. Bonn
Brian A. Luscher
Jeff C. Padden
Randall D. Wilkins
John H. Cassidy
D. Michael Hall
Samuel C. Wisotzkey

OF COUNSEL

Marvin Kantor

For full biographical listings, see the Martindale-Hubbell Law Directory

FENNEMORE CRAIG, A PROFESSIONAL CORPORATION (AV)

Two North Central, Suite 2200, 85004
Telephone: 602-257-8700
Fax: 602-257-8527
Scottsdale, Arizona Office: 6263 North Scottsdale Road, Suite 290, 85250.
Telephone: 602-257-5400.
Fax: 602-945-4932.
Tucson, Arizona Office: One South Church Avenue, Suite 1030, 85701.
Telephone: 602-624-9312.
Fax: 602-882-7383.

Edward C. LeBeau
C. Webb Crockett
Ronald L. Ballard
Stephen M. Savage
John R. Rawling
William L. Thorpe
David A. Weatherwax
Cathy L. Reece
Peter M. Gerstman
Karen Ciupak McConnell
J. Barry Shelley

Keith L. Hendricks
W. T. Eggleston, Jr.
Stephen A. Good
Richard A. Kasper

Representative Clients: ASARCO Incorporated; AT&T Communications; Bridgestone/Firestone, Inc.; Catellus Development Corp.; Citibank (Arizona); First Interstate Bank of Arizona; GIANT Industries; Phelps Dodge Corporation; The Atchison, Topeka & Santa Fe Railway, Co.; US WEST Communications.

For Complete List of Firm Personnel, See General Section

For full biographical listings, see the Martindale-Hubbell Law Directory

GOODSON & MANLEY, P.C. (AV)

The Brookstone Building, 2025 North 3rd Street, Suite 200, 85004-1471
Telephone: 602-252-5110
Fax: 602-257-1883

John F. Goodson
Colleen C. Manley
Richard E. Durfee, Jr.
Joel M. Klinge

A list of Representative Clients will be furnished upon request.
Reference: Caliber (Arizona).

For full biographical listings, see the Martindale-Hubbell Law Directory

JOHN S. LANCY & ASSOCIATES A PROFESSIONAL CORPORATION (AV)

Suite 600, 2425 East Camelback Road, 85016
Telephone: 602-381-6555
Fax: 602-381-6560

John S. Lancy
Steven W. Bienstock

For full biographical listings, see the Martindale-Hubbell Law Directory

LEWIS AND ROCA (AV)

A Partnership including Professional Corporations
40 North Central Avenue, 85004-4429
Telephone: 602-262-5311
Fax: 602-262-5747
Tucson, Arizona Office: One South Church Avenue, Suite 700.
Telephone: 602-622-2090.
Fax: 602-622-3088.

MEMBERS OF FIRM

Gerald K. Smith
Susan M. Freeman
Randolph J. Haines
Beth J. Schermer
Gabriel Beckmann (Resident, Tucson Office)
Scott DeWald
Richard N. Goldsmith
David E. Manch
Patrick Derdenger
Kevin L. Olson
David M. Bixby
Amy R. Porter
Bryant D. Barber

ASSOCIATES

J. Tyler Haahr
Michael G. Galloway
Barbara A. Anstey
Kevin G. Hunter

OF COUNSEL

Steven Marc Weinberg
Hope Leibsohn

Representative Clients: Arizona Hospital Association; Blood Systems, Inc.; The Dial Corp; The Industrial Development Authority of the City of Phoenix; MarkAir (General Counsel); Marcus J. Lawrence Medical Center; Phoenix Memorial Hospital; Rockford Corp.; Samaritan Health System; Skymall, Inc.

For Complete List of Firm Personnel, See General Section

For full biographical listings, see the Martindale-Hubbell Law Directory

LINZER, LANG & DITSCH, P.C. (AV)

3242 North Sixteenth Street, 85016
Telephone: 602-956-2525
Fax: 602-241-9885

Stephen P. Linzer

(See Next Column)

LINZER, LANG & DITSCH P.C., *Phoenix—Continued*

OF COUNSEL

Kenneth A. Linzer (Not admitted in AZ)

For full biographical listings, see the Martindale-Hubbell Law Directory

MEYER, HENDRICKS, VICTOR, OSBORN & MALEDON, A PROFESSIONAL ASSOCIATION (AV)

2929 North Central Avenue Suite 2100, 85012-2794
Telephone: 602-640-9000
Facsimile: (24 Hrs.) 602-640-9050
Mailing Address: P.O. Box 33449, 85067-3449,

Paul J. Meyer | William M. Hardin
David Victor | Michelle M. Matiski
Jones Osborn II | Lucia Fakonas Howard
Randall C. Nelson | Jay S. Ruffner
Jeffrey L. Sellers | Thayne Lowe
Thomas H. Curzon | Christopher D. Johnson
Gary A. Gotto | Michael A. Lechter
Catherine R. Hardwick

Bradley S. Paulson | Daniel J. Noblitt
Laurie B. Shough | Quentin T. Phillips
Evan Haglund | Laurel Finch
Cynthia P. Moehring | Christine A. Dupnik

CONSULTANTS

W. John Glancy (Not admitted in AZ)

Reference: Bank One Arizona, NA.

For Complete List of Firm Personnel, See General Section

For full biographical listings, see the Martindale-Hubbell Law Directory

STREICH LANG, A PROFESSIONAL ASSOCIATION (AV)

Renaissance One, Two N. Central Avenue, 85004-2391
Telephone: 602-229-5200
Fax: 602-229-5690
Tucson, Arizona Office: One S. Church Avenue, Suite 1700.
Telephone: 602-770-8700.
Fax: 602-623-2518.
Las Vegas, Nevada Affiliated Office: Dawson & Associates, 3800 Howard Hughes Parkway, Suite 1500.
Telephone: 702-792-2727.
Fax: 702-792-2676.
Los Angeles, California Office: 444 S. Flower Street, Suite 1530.
Telephone: 213-896-0484.

Douglas O. Guffey | Henry A. Perras
Thomas J. Lang | Kevin J. Tourek
Nancy L. White

OF COUNSEL

Matthew Mehr | Randall S. Theisen

Natalie A. Spencer | Michael B. Wixom (Resident, Las Vegas Office)

Representative Clients: Allied-Signal Aerospace Company; America West Airlines, Inc.; Atlantic Richfield Co.; Chicago Title; First Interstate Bank of Arizona, N.A.; Magma Copper Co.; Motorola, Inc.; Phelps Dodge Development Corp.; TRW Inc.; The Travelers Companies.

For Complete List of Firm Personnel, See General Section

For full biographical listings, see the Martindale-Hubbell Law Directory

VLASSIS & VLASSIS (AV)

1545 West Thomas Road, 85015
Telephone: 602-248-8811
Fax: 602-274-8983

George P. Vlassis | Elizabeth D. Vlassis

References: Bank One; Citibank.

For full biographical listings, see the Martindale-Hubbell Law Directory

SCOTTSDALE, Maricopa Co.

CARMICHAEL & TILKER (AV)

(An Association of Attorneys including a Professional Corporation)
6740 East Camelback Road Suite 100, 85251
Telephone: 602-949-7676
Fax: 602-945-2149

David H. Carmichael | James A. Tilker (P.C.)

For full biographical listings, see the Martindale-Hubbell Law Directory

PESKIND HYMSON & GOLDSTEIN, P.C. (AV)

14595 North Scottsdale Road, Suite 14, 85254
Telephone: 602-991-9077
Fax: 602-443-8854

Irving Hymson

Alexis J. Stanton | Eddie A. Pantiliat

OF COUNSEL

Marilee Miller Clarke | Jeffrey A. Leyton

For full biographical listings, see the Martindale-Hubbell Law Directory

*TUCSON,** Pima Co.

PETER T. GIANAS, P.C. (AV)

4400 East Broadway, Suite 800, 85711
Telephone: 602-795-6630
Fax: 602-327-1922

Peter T. Gianas

For full biographical listings, see the Martindale-Hubbell Law Directory

RAVEN, KIRSCHNER & NORELL, P.C. (AV)

Suite 1600, One South Church Avenue, 85701-1612
Telephone: 602-628-8700
Telefax: 602-798-5200

Benis E. Bernstein | Andrew Oldland Norell
Bradley G.A. Cloud | Mark B. Raven
Susan M. Freund | S. Leonard Scheff
Stephen A. Thomas

Representative Clients: Pace American Bonding Company; Citibank (Arizona); Continental Medical Systems, Inc.; El Paso Natural Gas Co.; Norwest Bank Arizona; El Rio-Santa Cruz Neighborhood Health Center, Inc.; Resolution Trust Corp.; Sierra Vista Community Hospital; Southern Arizona Rehabilitation Hospital; Ford Motor Credit.

For Complete List of Firm Personnel, See General Section

For full biographical listings, see the Martindale-Hubbell Law Directory

STOMPOLY, STROUD, GIDDINGS & GLICKSMAN, P.C. (AV)

1820 Citibank Tower, One South Church Avenue, 85702
Telephone: 602-628-8300
Telefax: 602-628-9948
Mailing Address: P.O. Box 190, Tucson, AZ, 85702-0190

John G. Stompoly | James L. Stroud
Charles E. Giddings

For Complete List of Firm Personnel, See General Section

For full biographical listings, see the Martindale-Hubbell Law Directory

ARKANSAS

*LITTLE ROCK,** Pulaski Co.

RICHARD C. DOWNING, P.A. (AV)

Lafayette Building, Suite 750, 523 South Louisiana, 72201
Telephone: 501-372-2066
FAX: 501-376-6420

Richard C. Downing

For full biographical listings, see the Martindale-Hubbell Law Directory

GILL LAW FIRM (AV)

3801 TCBY Tower, Capitol and Broadway, 72201
Telephone: 501-376-3800
Fax: 501-372-3359

John P. Gill | Victor A. Fleming
Charles C. Owen | Heartsill Ragon, III
W. W. Elrod, II | Joseph D. Calhoun, III

ASSOCIATES

Glenn E. Kelley | C. Tad Bohannon

OF COUNSEL

John A. Fogleman

For full biographical listings, see the Martindale-Hubbell Law Directory

HOOVER & STOREY (AV)

111 Center Street, 11th Floor, 72201-4445
Telephone: 501-376-8500
Facsimile: 501-372-3255

(See Next Column)

HOOVER & STOREY—*Continued*

MEMBERS OF FIRM

Paul W. Hoover, Jr.
O. H. Storey, III
John Kooistra, III
Lawrence Joseph Brady
William P. Dougherty
Max C. Mehlburger
Joyce Bradley Babin
Herbert W. Kell, Jr.
Letty McAdams

For full biographical listings, see the Martindale-Hubbell Law Directory

CALIFORNIA

*BAKERSFIELD,** Kern Co.

ELDON R. HUGIE A PROFESSIONAL CORPORATION (AV)

Suite 100, 1405 Commercial Way, 93309
Telephone: 805-328-0200
Telecopier: 805-328-0204

Eldon R. Hugie

Representative Clients: Tri-Fanucchi Farms, Inc.; Aquaculture Enterprises; Kern College Land Co.
References: Community First Bank (Bakersfield Main Branch).

For full biographical listings, see the Martindale-Hubbell Law Directory

BEVERLY HILLS, Los Angeles Co.

HOCHMAN, SALKIN AND DEROY, A PROFESSIONAL CORPORATION (AV)

9150 Wilshire Boulevard Suite 300, 90212-3414
Telephone: 310-281-3200; 273-1181
Fax: 310-859-1430

Bruce I. Hochman
Avram Salkin
Charles Rettig
Dennis Perez
Steven R. Toscher

OF COUNSEL

George DeRoy
James V. Looby

Michael W. Popoff
Joanna J. Tulio

Reference: Bank of California.

For full biographical listings, see the Martindale-Hubbell Law Directory

DANA B. TASCHNER, P.C. (AV(T))

9454 Wilshire Boulevard, Suite 550, 90212-2915
Telephone: 310-592-2600
Fax: 310-592-2640
Dallas, Texas Office: 350 St. Paul Street. 75201.
Liechtenstein Associated Office: DDr. Proksch & Partner. ITA P&A Bürotel Building. Landstrasse 161-163. FL 9494 Schaan.
Telephone: 41 75 2332303, 2322614, 2324121.
Facsimile: 41 75 2323562, 2324133, 2329181.
Telex: 899520 ita fl E-Mail:100415,1733 @ compuserve.com

Dana B. Taschner

OF COUNSEL

Reinhard J. Proksch (Not admitted in CA)

For full biographical listings, see the Martindale-Hubbell Law Directory

BURBANK, Los Angeles Co.

ALVIN N. LOSKAMP A LAW CORPORATION (AV)

290 East Verdugo Avenue, Suite 103, 91502
Telephone: 818-846-9000
Fax: 818-843-1441

Alvin N. Loskamp

References: Wells Fargo Bank, Glenoaks Branch, Burbank; Highland Savings & Loan, Burbank.

For full biographical listings, see the Martindale-Hubbell Law Directory

CORONA, Riverside Co.

CLAYSON, MANN, AREND & YAEGER, A PROFESSIONAL LAW CORPORATION (AV)

Clayson Law Building, 601 South Main Street, P.O. Box 1447, 91718-1447
Telephone: 909-737-1910
Riverside: 909-689-7241
Fax: 909-737-4384

(See Next Column)

Walter S. Clayson (1887-1972)
E. Spurgeon Rothrock (1918-1979)
Roy H. Mann
Erling C. Arend
Derrill E. Yaeger
Evan G. Evans
Gary K. Rosenzweig
Elisabeth Sichel
Kent A. Hansen
Roland C. Bainer
David R. Saunders
Sallie Barnett
Tambra L. Raush

Counsel for: Chino Valley Bank; Lee Lake Municipal Water District; Palo Verde Irrigation District; Loma Linda University.
Local Counsel: Minnesota Mining & Manufacturing Co.; Western Waste Industries.

For full biographical listings, see the Martindale-Hubbell Law Directory

COSTA MESA, Orange Co.

BALFOUR MACDONALD TALBOT MIJUSKOVIC & OLMSTED, A PROFESSIONAL CORPORATION (AV)

Suite 720, 611 Anton Boulevard, 92626
Telephone: 714-546-2400
Fax: 714-546-5008

Ralph E. Balfour
James B. MacDonald
R. Wayne Olmsted
Ruth Mijuskovic
M. D. Talbot

For full biographical listings, see the Martindale-Hubbell Law Directory

COULOMBE KOTTKE & KING, A PROFESSIONAL CORPORATION (AV)

Comerica Bank Tower, 611 Anton Boulevard, Suite 1260, P.O. Box 2410, 92628-2410
Telephone: 714-540-1234
Fax: 714-754-0808; 714-754-0707

Ronald B. Coulombe
Jon S. Kottke
Raymond King

COUNSEL

Mary J. Swanson
Roy B. Woolsey

LEGAL SUPPORT PERSONNEL

PARALEGALS

Karen M. Carrillo
Laura A. Bieser
Vicky M. Pearson

LEGAL ADMINISTRATOR

Sheila O. Elpern

For full biographical listings, see the Martindale-Hubbell Law Directory

MENKE, FAHRNEY & CARROLL, A PROFESSIONAL CORPORATION (AV)

650 Town Center Drive, Suite 1250, 92626
Telephone: 714-556-7111
Facsimile: 714-556-6426

Dennis V. Menke
Richard L. Fahrney II
Patrick D. Carroll

Vickie Lynn Bibro
Christopher R. Clark
Oakley C. Frost

For full biographical listings, see the Martindale-Hubbell Law Directory

RUTAN & TUCKER (AV)

A Partnership including Professional Corporations
611 Anton Boulevard, Suite 1400, P.O. Box 1950, 92626
Telephone: 714-641-5100; 213-625-7586
Telecopier: 714-546-9035

MEMBERS OF FIRM

Paul Frederic Marx
Ronald P. Arrington
Joseph D. Carruth
Thomas G. Brockington
Evridiki (Vicki) Dallas
Thomas J. Crane

For Complete List of Firm Personnel, See General Section

For full biographical listings, see the Martindale-Hubbell Law Directory

ENCINO, Los Angeles Co.

MARINO & DALLINGER (AV)

An Association including a Professional Corporation
17835 Ventura Boulevard, Suite 209, 91316
Telephone: 818-774-3636
FAX: 818-774-3635

Timothy G. Dallinger
J. Anthony Marino (A Professional Corporation)

For full biographical listings, see the Martindale-Hubbell Law Directory

*EUREKA,** Humboldt Co.

HARLAND LAW FIRM (AV)

622 H Street, 95501
Telephone: 707-444-9281
Fax: 707-445-2961
Fortuna, California Office: 954 Main Street.
Telephone: 707-725-4426.
Fax: 707-725-5738.
Crescent City, California Office: 1225 Marshall Street, Suite 6.
Telephone: 707-465-3894.
Fax: 707-465-4255.

MEMBERS OF FIRM

Gerald R. Harland
Richard A. Smith
David C. Moore
Thomas J. Becker
William T. Kay, Jr.
John W. Warren
Geri Anne Johnson

ASSOCIATES

Christine A. Doehle (Resident Associate, Crescent City Office)
Julia S. Gold

For full biographical listings, see the Martindale-Hubbell Law Directory

*FRESNO,** Fresno Co.

DOWLING, MAGARIAN, AARON & HEYMAN, INCORPORATED (AV)

Suite 200, 6051 North Fresno Street, 93710
Telephone: 209-432-4500
Fax: 209-432-4590

Michael D. Dowling
Richard M. Aaron
Philip David Kopp

Christopher A. Brown

Reference: Wells Fargo Bank (Main).

For Complete List of Firm Personnel, See General Section

For full biographical listings, see the Martindale-Hubbell Law Directory

JACKSON EMERICH PEDREIRA & NAHIGIAN, A PROFESSIONAL CORPORATION (AV)

7108 North Fresno Street, Suite 400, 93720-2938
Telephone: 209-261-0200
Facsimile: 209-261-0910

Donald A. Jackson
David R. Emerich
Thomas A. Pedreira
Eliot S. Nahigian
David A. Fike

John W. Phillips
John M. Cardot
Nicholas A. Tarjoman
Jeffrey B. Pape
David G. Hansen

Reference: Bank of California.

For full biographical listings, see the Martindale-Hubbell Law Directory

JORY, PETERSON, WATKINS & SMITH (AV)

555 West Shaw, Suite C-1, P.O. Box 5394, 93755
Telephone: 209-225-6700
Telecopier: 209-225-3416

MEMBERS OF FIRM

Jay V. Jory
John E. Peterson
Cal B. Watkins, Jr.
Michael Jens F. Smith

ASSOCIATES

William M. Woolman
Marcia A. Ross
Mark A. Pasculli

Reference: Valliwide Bank.

For full biographical listings, see the Martindale-Hubbell Law Directory

MCCORMICK, BARSTOW, SHEPPARD, WAYTE & CARRUTH (AV)

Five River Park Place East, 93720-1501
Telephone: 209-433-1300
Mailing Address: P.O. Box 28912, 93729-8912

MEMBERS OF FIRM

James H. Perkins
Andrew W. Wright
Steven G. Rau
W. F. Docker
Kenneth A. Baldwin
John A. Leonard

ASSOCIATE

Donald L. Mariotto

Counsel For: Bank of Fresno; Kings River State Bank; Penny Newman Grain Co.; Deniz Packing Inc.; Setton Pistachio Co., Inc.; Farmers Firebaugh Ginning Co.; Lewis C. Nelson Construction; Ranchwood Homes; Charles Tingey Associates (Brokerage); Trend Homes.

(See Next Column)

For Complete List of Firm Personnel, See General Section

For full biographical listings, see the Martindale-Hubbell Law Directory

PARICHAN, RENBERG, CROSSMAN & HARVEY, LAW CORPORATION (AV)

Suite 130, 2350 West Shaw Avenue, P.O. Box 9950, 93794-0950
Telephone: 209-431-6300
FAX: 209-432-1018

Harold A. Parichan
Charles L. Renberg
Richard C. Crossman
Ima Jean Harvey
Stephen T. Knudsen
Larry C. Gollmer
Robert G. Eliason
Steven M. McQuillan
Peter S. Bradley

Deborah A. Coe
Maureen P. Holford
Karen L. Lynch
Michael L. Renberg
Brady Kyle McGuinness

Reference: Bank of America, Commercial Banking Office, Fresno, California.

For full biographical listings, see the Martindale-Hubbell Law Directory

IRVINE, Orange Co.

CALLAHAN & GAUNTLETT (AV)

A Partnership including a Professional Corporation
Suite 800, 18500 Von Karman, 92715
Telephone: 714-553-1155
Fax: 714-553-0784

Daniel J. Callahan (A Professional Corporation)
David A. Gauntlett

ASSOCIATES

Stephen E. Blaine
David A. Stall
J. Craig Williams
Jim P. Mahacek
Leo E. Lundberg, Jr.
Michael J. Sachs
Michael Danton Richardson
Craig E. Lindberg
Edward Susolik
Carol L. Meedon
Andrew A. Smits

OF COUNSEL

Gary L. Hinman
Walt D. Mahaffa
Jose Zorrilla, Jr.
H. Thomas Hicks

For full biographical listings, see the Martindale-Hubbell Law Directory

PARILLA, MILITZOK & SHEDDEN (AV)

Suite 1250, 1 Park Plaza, 92714
Telephone: 714-263-1010
Telecopier: 714-263-1693

MEMBERS OF FIRM

Bradley N. Garber
Steven Militzok
Paul H. Parilla
Rhea S. Shedden

ASSOCIATES

Marc Ettinger
William A. Kozub

For full biographical listings, see the Martindale-Hubbell Law Directory

JACK L. SCHOELLERMAN (AV)

2030 Main Street, Suite 1600, 92714
Telephone: 714-660-7000
Fax: 714-660-6096

For full biographical listings, see the Martindale-Hubbell Law Directory

LARKSPUR, Marin Co.

WEINBERG, HOFFMAN & CASEY (AV)

A Partnership including a Professional Corporation
700 Larkspur Landing Circle, Suite 280, 94939
Telephone: 415-461-9666
Fax: 415-461-9681

Ivan Weinberg
Joseph Hoffman
A. Michael Casey

For full biographical listings, see the Martindale-Hubbell Law Directory

LONG BEACH, Los Angeles Co.

BENNETT & KISTNER (AV)

301 East Ocean Boulevard, Suite 800, 90802
Telephone: 310-435-6675
Fax: 310-437-8375
Riverside, California Office: 3403 Tenth Street, Suite 605. 92501-3676.
Telephone: 909-341-9360.
Fax: 909-341-9362.

Charles J. Bennett
Wayne T. Kistner

(See Next Column)

BENNETT & KISTNER—*Continued*

ASSOCIATES

Richard R. Bradbury
Todd R. Becker
Mary A. Estante (Resident, Riverside Office)
Karen H. Beckman (Resident, Riverside Office)

Representative Clients: The Hertz Corporation; Thrifty Oil Co.; Golden West Refining Co.; Standard Brands Paint Co.; Mattel, Inc.; Di Salvo Trucking Co.; County of Riverside; Southern California Rapid Transit District.
Reference: First Interstate Bank of California, The Market Place Office, Long Beach, California.

For full biographical listings, see the Martindale-Hubbell Law Directory

MADDEN, JONES & COLE, A PROFESSIONAL CORPORATION (AV)

Suite 1300, 111 W. Ocean Boulevard, 90802
Telephone: 310-435-6565
Fax: 310-590-7909

Philip M. Madden
Montgomery Cole
Steven A. Jones
Judith A. Rasmussen
Robert R. Johnson

John Vita
Carol Y. Adams
Mary Gillespie Frankart
John K. Fitle

Counsel for: Ameritone Paint Corporation; St. Mary Medical Center; St. Bernardine Medical Center; Farmers & Merchants Trust Co.; Wells Fargo Bank; Mack Truck, Inc.; Long Beach Public Transportation.

For Complete List of Firm Personnel, See General Section

For full biographical listings, see the Martindale-Hubbell Law Directory

LOS ALTOS, Santa Clara Co.

MALOVOS & KONEVICH (AV)

Los Altos Plaza, 5150 El Camino Real, Suite A-22, 94022
Telephone: 415-988-9700
Facsimile: 415-988-9639

Marian Malovos Konevich
Robert W. Konevich

RETIRED FOUNDING PARTNER

Kenneth R. Malovos

References: Bank of America, Mountain View, California Branch; First Interstate Bank, Mountain View and Los Altos, California Branches.

For full biographical listings, see the Martindale-Hubbell Law Directory

*LOS ANGELES,** Los Angeles Co.

BERGMAN & WEDNER, INC. (AV)

Suite 900, 10880 Wilshire Boulevard, 90024
Telephone: 310-470-6110
Fax: Available on Request

Gregory M. Bergman
Mark E. Fingerman
Gregory A. Wedner
Alan Harvey Mittelman
Robert M. Mason III

Kristi Anne Sjoholm-Sierchio
John V. Tamborelli
Keith A. Robinson
Blithe Ann Smith
John P. Dacey
Adrienne Elizabeth Nash
Lisa S. Shukiar

OF COUNSEL

Lloyd A. Bergman (1923-1994)
William L. Battles
Jacob A. Wedner

SPECIAL COUNSEL

Richard V. Godino

For full biographical listings, see the Martindale-Hubbell Law Directory

LAW OFFICES OF DAVID B. BLOOM A PROFESSIONAL CORPORATION (AV)

3325 Wilshire Boulevard, Ninth Floor, 90010
Telephone: 213-938-5248; 384-4088
Telecopier: 213-385-2009

David B. Bloom

Stephen S. Monroe (A Professional Corporation)
Jonathan Udell
Raphael A. Rosemblat
Susan Carole Jay
James E. Adler
Edward Idell
Bonni S. Mantovani
Sandra Kamenir
Martin A. Cooper
Steven Wayne Lazarus
Roy A. Levun
Andrew Edward Briseno
Cherie S. Raidy
Harold C. Klaskin
Shelley M. Gould

(See Next Column)

B. Eric Nelson
Peter O. Israel
John C. Notti
Anthony V. Seferian

For full biographical listings, see the Martindale-Hubbell Law Directory

CLARK & TREVITHICK, A PROFESSIONAL CORPORATION (AV)

800 Wilshire Boulevard, 12th Floor, 90017
Telephone: 213-629-5700
Telecopier: 213-624-9441

Donald P. Clark
Dean I. Friedman
Alexander C. McGilvray, Jr.
Michael K. Wofford
Kevin P. Fiore
Brent A. Reinke
James S. Arico

References: Wells Fargo Bank (Los Angeles Main Office); National Bank of California.

For Complete List of Firm Personnel, See General Section
For full biographical listings, see the Martindale-Hubbell Law Directory

CORINBLIT & SELTZER, A PROFESSIONAL CORPORATION (AV)

Suite 820 Wilshire Park Place, 3700 Wilshire Boulevard, 90010-3085
Telephone: 213-380-4200
Telecopier: 213-385-7503; 385-4560

Marc M. Seltzer

OF COUNSEL

Jack Corinblit
Earl P. Willens

Gretchen M. Nelson
Christina A. Snyder
George A. Shohet

Reference: Bank of America (Wilshire & Harvard Office).

For full biographical listings, see the Martindale-Hubbell Law Directory

DEMETRIOU, DEL GUERCIO, SPRINGER & MOYER (AV)

801 South Grand Avenue, 10th Floor, 90017
Telephone: 213-624-8407
Telecopy: 213-624-0174

MEMBERS OF FIRM

Ronald J. Del Guercio
Stephen A. Del Guercio
Angela Shanahan
Laurie E. Davis

Reference: Bank of America, L.A. Main Office, Los Angeles, Calif.

For full biographical listings, see the Martindale-Hubbell Law Directory

ECKARDT & KHOURY (AV)

Suite 700, 530 West Sixth Street, 90014-1298
Telephone: 213-626-5061
Cable Address: "Richeck"
Facsimile: 213-891-1590
ABA/Net: ABA 18857

Richard W. Eckardt

For full biographical listings, see the Martindale-Hubbell Law Directory

LEVINE & ASSOCIATES (AV)

Suite 710, 2049 Century Park East, 90067
Telephone: 310-553-8400
Fax: 310-553-8455
Seattle, Washington Office: 999 Third Avenue, Suite 3210, 98104.
Telephone: 206-626-5310.
Fax: 206-626-5318.

Jerome L. Levine

ASSOCIATES

Mary L. Prevost (Resident, Seattle, Washington Office)
Erin M. Copeland
Frank R. Lawrence

OF COUNSEL

Allan Albala

For full biographical listings, see the Martindale-Hubbell Law Directory

RONALD A. LITZ & ASSOCIATES (AV)

Suite 1901, 1901 Avenue of the Stars, 90067
Telephone: 310-201-0100
FAX: 310-201-0226

ASSOCIATE

Jennifer A. Litz

OF COUNSEL

Arnold W. Magasinn
Vicki Fisher Magasinn
Carl R. Waldman

For full biographical listings, see the Martindale-Hubbell Law Directory

MINTON, MINTON AND RAND (AV)

510 West Sixth Street, 90014
Telephone: 213-624-9394
Fax: 213-624-9323

MEMBERS OF FIRM

Carl W. Minton (1902-1974)
Carl Minton
David E. Rand

Reference: Bank of America National Trust & Savings Assn. (Seventh & Flower Office, Los Angeles, Calif.).

(See Next Column)

MINTON, MINTON AND RAND, *Los Angeles—Continued*

For full biographical listings, see the Martindale-Hubbell Law Directory

ROSENFELD & WOLFF, A PROFESSIONAL CORPORATION (AV)

2049 Century Park East, Suite 600, 90067
Telephone: 310-556-1221
Fax: 310-556-0401

Morton M. Rosenfeld
Steven G. Wolff
Alan D. Aronson

Yelena Yeruhim

For full biographical listings, see the Martindale-Hubbell Law Directory

RONALD P. SLATES A PROFESSIONAL CORPORATION (AV)

548 South Spring Street, Suite 1012, 90013-2309
Telephone: 213-624-1515; 213-654-1461
Fax: 213-624-7536; 213-654-1463

Ronald P. Slates

G. Michael Jackson

For full biographical listings, see the Martindale-Hubbell Law Directory

SULLIVAN, WALSH & WOOD (AV)

Wells Fargo Center, 333 South Grand Avenue, 37th Floor, 90071-1599
Telephone: 213-488-9200
Telecopier: 213-488-9664

MEMBERS OF FIRM

Michael R. Sullivan
E. Eugene Walsh

ASSOCIATES

Douglas G. Carroll
Richard J. Sestak

OF COUNSEL

Scott E. Wood
Martin J. Spear

For full biographical listings, see the Martindale-Hubbell Law Directory

WEHNER AND PERLMAN (AV)

A Partnership of Professional Corporations
11100 Santa Monica Boulevard, Suite 800, 90025-3302
Telephone: 310-478-3131
Facsimile: 310-312-0078

MEMBERS OF FIRM

Charles C. Wehner (P.C.)
Rodney M. Perlman (P.C.)

ASSOCIATES

Steven M. Cohen
Steven A. Berliner
David Eum
Stephen T. Hodge
Walter H. Kubelun
Dawne M. Macri

For full biographical listings, see the Martindale-Hubbell Law Directory

LOS GATOS, Santa Clara Co.

SWEENEY, MASON & WILSON, A PROFESSIONAL LAW CORPORATION (AV)

983 University Avenue, Suite 104C, 95030
Telephone: 408-356-3000
Fax: 408-354-8839

Joseph M. Sweeney
Roger M. Mason
Kurt E. Wilson
Bradley D. Bosomworth
Allan James Manzagol

For full biographical listings, see the Martindale-Hubbell Law Directory

MENLO PARK, San Mateo Co.

ROBERT E. MILLER, INC. A PROFESSIONAL CORPORATION (AV)

1550 El Camino Real, Suite 220, 94025-4111
Telephone: 415-326-6135
Fax: 415-326-6054

Robert E. Miller

Representative Clients: Allodyne, Inc.; Hussmann Corp.; LabLogix Inc.; Tiburon Systems, Inc.; Walt & Sommerhauser Communications, Inc.; Western Multiplex Corp.

For full biographical listings, see the Martindale-Hubbell Law Directory

*MODESTO,** Stanislaus Co.

RICHARD DOUGLAS BREW A PROFESSIONAL LAW CORPORATION (AV)

Suite 350 / Judge Frank C. Damrell Building, 1601 I Street, 95354-1110
Telephone: 209-572-3157
Telefax: 209-572-4641

(See Next Column)

Richard Douglas Brew

For full biographical listings, see the Martindale-Hubbell Law Directory

NEWPORT BEACH, Orange Co.

CAPRETZ & RADCLIFFE (AV)

5000 Birch Street, West Tower Suite 2500, 92660-2139
Telephone: 714-724-3000
Fax: 714-757-2635

James T. Capretz
Richard J. Radcliffe

LEGAL SUPPORT PERSONNEL

Rosanna S. Bertheola

For full biographical listings, see the Martindale-Hubbell Law Directory

DAVIS, PUNELLI, KEATHLEY & WILLARD (AV)

610 Newport Center Drive, Suite 1000, P.O. Box 7920, 92658-7920
Telephone: 714-640-0700
Telecopier: 714-640-0714
San Diego, California Office: 4370 La Jolla Village Drive, Suite 300.
Telephone: 619-558-2581.

MEMBERS OF FIRM

Robert E. Willard
S. Eric Davis
Frank Punelli, Jr.
H. James Keathley
Leonard R. Sager
Eric G. Anderson
Katherine D. O'Brian

OF COUNSEL

Lewis K. Uhler

For full biographical listings, see the Martindale-Hubbell Law Directory

JOHN C. LAUTSCH A PROFESSIONAL CORPORATION (AV)

4220 Von Karman, Suite 120, 92660
Telephone: 714-955-9095
Telefax: 714-955-2978

John C. Lautsch

Kurt E. English

For full biographical listings, see the Martindale-Hubbell Law Directory

NORTH HOLLYWOOD, Los Angeles Co.

F. BENTLEY MOONEY, JR. A LAW CORPORATION (AV)

4605 Lankershim Boulevard, Suite 718, 91602
Telephone: 818-769-4221
213-877-3902
FAX: 818-769-5002

F. Bentley Mooney, Jr.

For full biographical listings, see the Martindale-Hubbell Law Directory

*OAKLAND,** Alameda Co.

PEZZOLA & REINKE, A PROFESSIONAL CORPORATION (AV)

Suite 1300, Lake Merritt Plaza, 1999 Harrison Street, 94612
Telephone: 510-839-1350
Telecopier: 510-834-7440
San Francisco, California Office: 50 California Street, Suite 470. 94111.
Telephone: 415-989-9710.

Stephen P. Pezzola
Donald C. Reinke
Thomas A. Maier
Thomas C. Armstrong
Bruce D. Whitley

OF COUNSEL

Robert E. Krebs

LEGAL SUPPORT PERSONNEL

Loretta H. Hintz
Mary A. Fitzpatrick

For full biographical listings, see the Martindale-Hubbell Law Directory

HARVEY W. STEIN A PROFESSIONAL CORPORATION (AV)

Suite 600 Transpacific Centre, 1000 Broadway, 94607
Telephone: 510-763-6233
FAX: 510-832-0580

Harvey W. Stein

For full biographical listings, see the Martindale-Hubbell Law Directory

ORANGE, Orange Co.

WALSWORTH, FRANKLIN & BEVINS (AV)

1 City Boulevard West, Suite 308, 92668
Telephone: 714-634-2522
LAW-FAX: 714-634-0686
San Francisco, California Office: 580 California Street, Suite 1335.
Telephone: 415-781-7072.
Fax: 415-391-6258.

Jeffrey P. Walsworth
Ferdie F. Franklin
Ronald H. Bevins, Jr.
Michael T. McCall
Noel Edlin (Resident, San Francisco Office)
Lawrence E. Duffy, Jr.
Sheldon J. Fleming
J. Wayne Allen
James A. Anton
Ingrid K. Campagne (Resident, San Francisco Office)
Robert M. Channel (Resident, San Francisco Office)
Nicholas A. Cipiti
Sharon L. Clisham (Resident, San Francisco Office)
David W. Epps (Resident, San Francisco Office)
Richard M. Hills (Resident, San Francisco Office)
Sandra G. Kennedy
Randall J. Lee (Resident, San Francisco Office)
Kimberly K. Mays
Bruce A. Nelson (Resident, San Francisco Office)
Kevin Pegan
Allan W. Ruggles
Jonathan M. Slipp
Cyrian B. Tabuena (Resident, San Francisco Office)
John L. Trunko
Houston M. Watson, II
Mary A. Watson

For full biographical listings, see the Martindale-Hubbell Law Directory

PALM SPRINGS, Riverside Co.

SCHLECHT, SHEVLIN & SHOENBERGER, A LAW CORPORATION (AV)

Suite 100, 801 East Tahquitz Canyon Way, P.O. Box 2744, 92263-2744
Telephone: 619-320-7161
Facsimile: 619-323-1758; 619-325-4623

James M. Schlecht
John C. Shevlin
Jon A. Shoenberger
Daniel T. Johnson

Bonnie Garland Guss
Karen S. Helmuth
R. Brad Sevier
David Darrin
Elizabeth A. Harreus

OF COUNSEL

Donald B. McNelley
Allen O. Perrier (Retired)

Representative Clients: Outdoor Resorts of America; The Escrow Connection; Wells Fargo Bank; Canyon Country Club; Waste Management Co.

For full biographical listings, see the Martindale-Hubbell Law Directory

PALO ALTO, Santa Clara Co.

FLICKER & KERIN (AV)

Suite 460, 285 Hamilton, P.O. Box 840, 94302
Telephone: 415-321-0947
Fax: 415-326-9722

MEMBERS OF FIRM

Michael R. Flicker
Anthony J. Kerin, III

ASSOCIATE

Rhesa C. Rubin

For full biographical listings, see the Martindale-Hubbell Law Directory

CHRISTOPHER REAM (AV)

1717 Embarcadero Road, 94303
Telephone: 415-424-0821
Facsimile: 415-857-1288

For full biographical listings, see the Martindale-Hubbell Law Directory

PASADENA, Los Angeles Co.

ALAN R. TALT (AV)

Suite 710, 790 East Colorado Boulevard, 91101
Telephone: 818-356-0853
Telecopier: 818-356-0731

Reference: Northern Trust of California.

For full biographical listings, see the Martindale-Hubbell Law Directory

TAYLOR KUPFER SUMMERS & RHODES (AV)

301 East Colorado Boulevard, Suite 407, 91101
Telephone: 818-304-0953; 213-624-7877
Fax: 818-795-6375

MEMBERS OF FIRM

John D. Taylor
Robert C. Summers
Stephen F. Peters

(See Next Column)

COUNSEL

Kenneth O. Rhodes

Reference: Citizens Bank (Pasadena).

For Complete List of Firm Personnel, See General Section

For full biographical listings, see the Martindale-Hubbell Law Directory

*SACRAMENTO,** Sacramento Co.

DIEPENBROCK, WULFF, PLANT & HANNEGAN (AV)

Suite 1700, 300 Capitol Mall, P.O. Box 3034, 95812-3034
Telephone: 916-444-3910
Telecopier: 916-446-1696

MEMBERS OF FIRM

Forrest A. Plant
James T. Freeman
Steven H. Felderstein
Cary M. Adams
Brian T. Regan
Patricia J. Hartman
Suzanne E. Hennessy
Donald E. Brodeur
Jeffrey W. Curcio

ASSOCIATES

Donna Taylor Parkinson
Katherine Andritsakis Kaminski
Gary N. Challburg
Harold J. Marcus

Representative Clients: California Public Employees Retirement System; Catholic Healthcare West; Bank of California; Fibreboard Corp.

For full biographical listings, see the Martindale-Hubbell Law Directory

HANSEN, BOYD, CULHANE & WATSON (AV)

A Partnership including Professional Corporations
Central City Centre, 1331 Twenty-First Street, 95814
Telephone: 916-444-2550
Telecopier: 916-444-2358

Hartley T. Hansen (Inc.)
Kevin R. Culhane (Inc.)
David E. Boyd
Lawrence R. Watson
John J. Rueda
James J. Banks

OF COUNSEL

Betsy S. Kimball

Lorraine M. Pavlovich
Thomas L. Riordan
D. Jeffery Grimes
Joseph Zuber
James O. Moses

For full biographical listings, see the Martindale-Hubbell Law Directory

WILKE, FLEURY, HOFFELT, GOULD & BIRNEY (AV)

A Partnership including Professional Corporations
400 Capitol Mall, Suite 2200, 95814-4408
Telephone: 916-441-2430
Telefax: 916-442-6664
Mailing Address: P.O. Box 15559, 95852-0559

MEMBERS OF FIRM

Richard H. Hoffelt (Inc.)
William A. Gould, Jr., (Inc.)
Philip R. Birney (Inc.)
Thomas G. Redmon (Inc.)
Scott L. Gassaway
Donald Rex Heckman II (Inc.)
Alan G. Perkins
Bradley N. Webb
Ernest James Krtil
Robert R. Mirkin
Matthew W. Powell
Mark L. Andrews
Stephen K. Marmaduke
David A. Frenznick
John R. Valencia
Angus M. MacLeod

ASSOCIATES

Paul A. Dorris
Kelli M. Kennaday
Tracy S. Hendrickson
Joseph G. De Angelis
Jennifer L. Kennedy
Anthony J. DeCristoforo
Rachel N. Kook
Alicia F. From
Michael Polis
Matthew J. Smith
Wayne L. Ordos

OF COUNSEL

Sherman C. Wilke
Anita Seipp Marmaduke
Benjamin G. Davidian

Representative Clients: NOR-CAL Mutual Insurance Co.; California Optometric Assn.; KPMG Peat Marwick; Glaxo, Inc.

For full biographical listings, see the Martindale-Hubbell Law Directory

SAN CLEMENTE, Orange Co.

SAM HILL INC. (AV)

2119 Via Gavilan, P.O. Box 5105, 92674-5105
Telephone: 714-498-8666
Fax: 714-498-5124

(See Next Column)

SAM HILL INC., *San Clemente—Continued*

Sam Hill

*SAN DIEGO,** San Diego Co.

BARNHORST, SCHREINER & GOONAN, A PROFESSIONAL CORPORATION (AV)

550 West C Street, Suite 1350, 92101-3532
Telephone: 619-544-0900
Fax: 619-544-0703

Howard J. Barnhorst, II
Stephen L. Schreiner
Gregory P. Goonan
Brian A. Wright
John J. Freni
Niles Rice Sharif
Brian W. DeWitt

Representative Clients: Alex. Brown Kleinwort Benson Realty Advisors; Amron International Diving Supply; Continental American Properties; James Hardie Industries (USA), Inc.; Montrose Chemical Corp. of California; The Price Company; SeaQuest, Inc.; United Pacific Insurance Company; Anne Winton & Associates; InaCom Corp.

For full biographical listings, see the Martindale-Hubbell Law Directory

DETISCH, CHRISTENSEN & WOOD (AV)

444 West C Street, Suite 200, 92101
Telephone: 619-236-9343
Fax: 619-236-8307

MEMBERS OF FIRM

Charles B. Christensen
Donald W. Detisch
John W. Wood

ASSOCIATE

Lydia L. Brashear

For full biographical listings, see the Martindale-Hubbell Law Directory

FERRIS & BRITTON, A PROFESSIONAL CORPORATION (AV)

1600 First National Bank Center, 401 West A Street, 92101
Telephone: 619-233-3131
Fax: 619-232-9316

Alfred G. Ferris
Harry J. Proctor
Tamara K. Fogg
Pauline H. G. Getz
Gary T. Moyer

OF COUNSEL

William M. Winter

Representative Clients: Allstate Insurance Co.; Cox Communications, Inc.; Enterprise Rent-a-Car; Exxon; Immuno Pharmaceutics, Inc.; Invitrogen Corporation; Teleport Communications Group; Southwest Airlines; Times-Mirror Cable Television.

For Complete List of Firm Personnel, See General Section

For full biographical listings, see the Martindale-Hubbell Law Directory

HILLYER & IRWIN, A PROFESSIONAL CORPORATION (AV)

550 West C Street, 16th Floor, 92101
Telephone: 619-234-6121
Telecopier: 619-595-1313

Henry J. Klinker
Gary S. Hardke
Murray T. S. Lewis
John C. O'Neill

For full biographical listings, see the Martindale-Hubbell Law Directory

HYDE AND CANOFF (AV)

401 West "A" Street, Suite 1200, 92101
Telephone: 619-696-6911
Telecopier: 619-696-6919

MEMBERS OF FIRM

Laurel Lee Hyde
Karen H. Canoff

Representative Clients: HomeFed Bank; San Diego Trust & Savings Bank; Union Bank; The Resolution Trust Corp.; American Pacific Contractors & Builders; San Diego Gas & Electric Co.; The Hahn Company ; The Regents of the University of California; San Diego Metropolitan Transit Development Board; Kmart Corporation.

For full biographical listings, see the Martindale-Hubbell Law Directory

LINDLEY, LAZAR & SCALES, A PROFESSIONAL CORPORATION (AV)

One America Plaza, 600 West Broadway, Suite 1400, 92101-3302
Telephone: 619-234-9181
Fax: 619-234-8475

(See Next Column)

Luke R. Corbett
John M. Seitman
Robert M. McLeod
William E. Johns
Stephen F. Treadgold
Michael H. Wexler
Richard J. Pekin, Jr.
George C. Lazar
Raymond L. Heidemann
James Henry Fox
Kenneth C. Jones

Representative Clients: McGraw-Hill Broadcasting Co.; City Chevrolet; Metro Imports; Shapell Industries, Inc.; George Wimpey, Inc.; Dura Pharmaceuticals; Driscoll, Inc.

For Complete List of Firm Personnel, See General Section

For full biographical listings, see the Martindale-Hubbell Law Directory

LUCE, FORWARD, HAMILTON & SCRIPPS (AV)

A Partnership including Professional Corporations
600 West Broadway, Suite 2600, 92101
Telephone: 619-236-1414
Fax: 619-232-8311
La Jolla, California Office: 4275 Executive Square, Suite 800, 92037.
Telephone: 619-535-2639.
Fax: 619-453-2812.
Los Angeles, California Office: 777 South Figueroa, 36th Floor, 90017.
Telephone: 213-892-4992.
Fax: 213-892-7731.
San Francisco, California Office: 100 Bush Street, 20th Floor, 94104.
Telephone: 415-395-7900.
Fax: 415-395-7949.
New York, N.Y. Office: Citicorp Center, 153 East 53rd Street, 26th Floor, 10022.
Telephone: 212-754-1414.
Fax: 212-644-9727.

MEMBERS OF FIRM

Robert G. Steiner
William M. McKenzie, Jr.
John W. Brooks
Charles A. Bird
G. Edward Arledge
Mark L. Mann
John B. McNeece III
Darryl L. Steinhause
Richard R. Spirra
R. William Bowen
Dennis J. Doucette
Terrence L. Bingman
Otto E. Sorensen
Robert H. Roe, Jr.
Phillip L. Jelsma

OF COUNSEL

William L. Hoese

SPECIAL COUNSEL

Richard T. Forsyth

ASSOCIATES

Dan Lawton
Robert B. Clark
Charles A. Danaher
John P. Cooley
Michael G. Fraunces
Nancy Fuller-Jacobs
Peter K. Hahn
James A. Mercer III
John T. Brooks

For Complete List of Firm Personnel, See General Section

For full biographical listings, see the Martindale-Hubbell Law Directory

PAGE, POLIN, BUSCH & BOATWRIGHT, A PROFESSIONAL CORPORATION (AV)

350 West Ash Street, Suite 900, 92101-3404
Telephone: 619-231-1822
Fax: 619-231-1877
FAX: 619-231-1875

David C. Boatwright
Michael E. Busch
Robert K. Edmunds
Kathleen A. Cashman-Kramer
Richard L. Moskitis
Richard W. Page
Kenneth D. Polin
Steven G. Rowles

OF COUNSEL

Richard Edward Ball, Jr.

Rod S. Fiori
Christina B. Gamache
Dorothy A. Johnson
Theresa McCarthy
Jolene L. Parker
Deidre L. Schneider
Sandra L. Shippey

For full biographical listings, see the Martindale-Hubbell Law Directory

*SAN FRANCISCO,** San Francisco Co.

ERLACH & ERLACH (AV)

4 Embarcadero Center, Seventeenth Floor, 94111
Telephone: 415-788-3322
FAX: 415-788-8613

Raymond N. Erlach
Gregory J. Erlach
Stephen Peter U. Erlach

For full biographical listings, see the Martindale-Hubbell Law Directory

San Francisco—Continued

FELDMAN, WALDMAN & KLINE, A PROFESSIONAL CORPORATION (AV)

2700 Russ Building, 235 Montgomery Street, 94104
Telephone: 415-981-1300
Telex: 650-223-3204
Fax: 415-394-0121
Stockton, California Office: Sperry Building, 146-148 West Weber Avenue.
Telephone: 209-943-2004.
Fax: 209-943-0905.

Murry J. Waldman
Leland R. Selna, Jr.
Michael L. Korbholz
Howard M. Wexler
Patricia S. Mar
Kenneth W. Jones
Paul J. Dion
Vern S. Bothwell
L. J. Chris Martiniak
Kenneth A. Freed
Martha Jeanne Shaver (Resident, Stockton Office)
Robert Cedric Goodman
Steven K. Denebeim
Laura Grad
William F. Adams
William M. Smith
Elizabeth A. Thompson
Julie A. Jones
David L. Kanel

Abram S. Feuerstein
John R. Capron
Ted S. Storey
A. Todd Berman
Laura J. Dawson

OF COUNSEL

Richard L. Jaeger
Malcolm Leader-Picone
Gerald A. Sherwin (Resident, Stockton Office)

For full biographical listings, see the Martindale-Hubbell Law Directory

LAW OFFICE OF KEVIN W. FINCK (AV)

601 Montgomery Street, Suite 1900, 94111
Telephone: 415-296-9100
Facsimile: 415-394-6446

Marla Raucher Osborn

For full biographical listings, see the Martindale-Hubbell Law Directory

FLEISCHMANN & FLEISCHMANN (AV)

650 California Street, Suite 2550, 94108-2606
Telephone: 415-981-0140
FAX: 415-788-6234

MEMBERS OF FIRM

Hartly Fleischmann
Roger Justice Fleischmann

Stella J. Kim
Mark S. Molina

OF COUNSEL

Grace C. Shohet

LEGAL SUPPORT PERSONNEL

Lissa Dirrim

For full biographical listings, see the Martindale-Hubbell Law Directory

FURTH, FAHRNER & MASON (AV)

Furth Building, Suite 1000, 201 Sansome Street, 94104
Telephone: 415-433-2070
Telecopier: 415-982-2076
Healdsburg, California Office: 10300 Chalk Hill Road.
Telephone: 707-838-4379.
FAX: 707-838-9685.

MEMBERS OF FIRM

Frederick P. Furth
Daniel S. Mason
Thomas R. Fahrner
Bruce J. Wecker
Michael P. Lehmann
Craig C. Corbitt
Michele C. Jackson
George F. Bishop
Scott R. Campbell
Joseph W. Bell

Brett L. Raven
Christopher T. Micheletti
Wesley E. Overson, Jr.
Steven S. Lubliner
Emily Platt
David A. Hoskins
Valerie M. Wagner

For full biographical listings, see the Martindale-Hubbell Law Directory

GRIFFINGER, FREED, HEINEMANN, COOK & FOREMAN (AV)

24th Floor, Steuart Street Tower, One Market Plaza, 94105
Telephone: 415-243-0300
Telecopier: 415-777-9366

MEMBERS OF FIRM

Theodore A. Griffinger, Jr.
Michael S. Freed
Peter M. Heinemann
Karen A. Cook
Stewart H. Foreman
Jonathan A. Funk
Peter S. Fishman

(See Next Column)

Dwight L. Monson
Eileen Trujillo
Robert L. Wishner
Marie C. Bendy
Eric C. Starr
Jonathan Polland

LEGAL SUPPORT PERSONNEL

LEGAL ADMINISTRATOR

Kathleen H. Hartley

PARALEGALS

Jeanne Diettinger
Jean Mahony
Irene E. Bernasconi
Janet L. Johnston

Representative Client: Smith Barney, Harris Upham Co., Inc.
Reference: Bank of America (Main Office).

For full biographical listings, see the Martindale-Hubbell Law Directory

MANWELL & MILTON (AV)

101 California Street, 37th Floor, 94111
Telephone: 415-362-2375
Telecopier: 415-362-1010

Edmund R. Manwell
Denise B. Milton

ASSOCIATES

Mari C. Siebold
Kevin M. Walsh
Matthew M. Ogburn

For full biographical listings, see the Martindale-Hubbell Law Directory

TERAOKA & ASSOCIATES, A LAW CORPORATION (AV)

Spear Street Tower, 41st Floor, One Market Plaza, 94105
Telephone: 415-981-3100
Telecopier: 415-777-9898

Steven G. Teraoka

Catherine M. Gormley
William D. Rauch, Jr.

Representative Clients: Japan Travel Bureau International, Inc.; Kikkoman International, Inc.; JFC International, Inc.; Inabata America Corporation; Viz Communications, Inc. (Shogajukan, Inc.); Sumida Trading & Co., Ltd.; Sunflower Bus Lines; Tokyo Television and Broadcasting Corp.; Goldilocks Heavy Industries, Inc. (Korea).

For full biographical listings, see the Martindale-Hubbell Law Directory

*SAN JOSE,** Santa Clara Co.

FERRARI, ALVAREZ, OLSEN & OTTOBONI, A PROFESSIONAL CORPORATION (AV)

333 West Santa Clara Street, Suite 700, 95113
Telephone: 408-280-0535
Fax: 408-280-0151
Palo Alto, California Office: 550 Hamilton Avenue.
Telephone: 415-327-3233.

Clarence J. Ferrari, Jr.
Kent E. Olsen
John M. Ottoboni
Richard S. Bebb
James J. Eller
Robert C. Danneskiold
Terence M. Kane
Emma Peña Madrid
John P. Thurau
Roger D. Wintle
Christopher E. Cobey

Michael D. Brayton
Lisa Intrieri Caputo
Jil Dalesandro
Gregory R. Dietrich
J. Timothy Maximoff
Joseph W. Mell, Jr.
George P. Mulcaire
Eleanor C. Schuermann
Melva M. Vollersen

OF COUNSEL

Edward M. Alvarez

For full biographical listings, see the Martindale-Hubbell Law Directory

McPHARLIN & SPRINKLES (AV)

Fairmont Plaza, 50 West San Fernando, Suite 810, 95113
Telephone: 408-293-1900
Fax: 408-293-1999

MEMBERS OF FIRM

Linda Hendrix McPharlin
Catherine C. Sprinkles

ASSOCIATES

Timothy B. McCormick
Mary Lee Malysz

For full biographical listings, see the Martindale-Hubbell Law Directory

THE SKORNIA LAW FIRM (AV)

160 West Santa Clara Street, Suite 1500, 95113
Telephone: 408-280-2820
FAX: 408-977-0129

Thomas A. Skornia

(See Next Column)

THE SKORNIA LAW FIRM, *San Jose—Continued*

ASSOCIATE
Ronald S. Kramer
LEGAL SUPPORT PERSONNEL
Sharii E. Rey
Paula K. Gray
R. Marissa Gonzales

For full biographical listings, see the Martindale-Hubbell Law Directory

*SAN RAFAEL,** Marin Co.

MCNEIL, SILVEIRA & RICE (AV)

A Partnership including Professional Corporations
55 Professional Center Parkway, Suite A, 94903
Telephone: 415-472-3434
FAX Telecopier: 415-472-1298

Patrick J. McNeil (A Professional Corporation)
Ronald A. Silveira (A Professional Corporation)
Mark J. Rice

For full biographical listings, see the Martindale-Hubbell Law Directory

*SANTA ANA,** Orange Co.

LANCASTER & ASSOCIATES (AV)

313 North Birch Street, P.O. Box 22021, 92701-2021
Telephone: 714-836-1411
Fax: 714-836-9930

Michael J. Lancaster
ASSOCIATE
Dieter Zacher

For full biographical listings, see the Martindale-Hubbell Law Directory

*SANTA BARBARA,** Santa Barbara Co.

SCHRAMM & RADDUE (AV)

15 West Carrillo Street, P.O. Box 1260, 93102
Telephone: 805-963-2044
Fax: 805-564-4181

MEMBERS OF FIRM
Edward W. Schramm (1913-1982)
Ralph C. Raddue (1906-1986)
Lawrence M. Parma (1911-1957)
Paul W. Hartloff, Jr.
Dale E. Hanst
Charles H. Jarvis
Douglas E. Schmidt
Kurt H. Pyle
Daniel A. Reicker
Weldon U. Howell, Jr.
Frederick W. Clough
Brian G. Gough
Richard F. Lee
Michael E. Pfau
Edward C. Thoits

ASSOCIATES
Judith E. Koper
Marjorie F. Allen
Christine M. Sontag
Diana Jessup Lee

OF COUNSEL
Howard M. Simon
Bruce W. McRoy

Representative Clients: Berkus Group Architects; Circon Corp.; LaArcada Investment Corp.; Michael Towbes Construction and Development Co.; Santa Barbara Bank & Trust; Santa Barbara Medical Foundation Clinic.

For full biographical listings, see the Martindale-Hubbell Law Directory

SANTA MONICA, Los Angeles Co.

CRANE & MCCANN (AV)

530 Wilshire Boulevard, Suite 400, 90401-1423
Telephone: 310-917-9277
Fax: 310-393-7338

MEMBERS OF FIRM
Richard P. Crane, Jr.
Joseph J. McCann, Jr.

ASSOCIATES
Lawrence J. Lennemann
John Benedict
Brian D. McMahon
Daniel P. Ayala

For full biographical listings, see the Martindale-Hubbell Law Directory

LAW OFFICES OF GARY FREEDMAN (AV)

725 Arizona Avenue, Suite 100, 90401
Telephone: 310-576-2444
Telecopier: 310-576-2440

MEMBER OF FIRM
Gary A. Freedman

Emily F. Bresler
Rosemary Jackovic Schwimmer

OF COUNSEL
Paul H. Samuels

For full biographical listings, see the Martindale-Hubbell Law Directory

SACKS & ZWEIG (AV)

A Partnership of Professional Corporations
100 Wilshire Building, Suite 1300, 100 Wilshire Boulevard, 90401
Telephone: 310-451-3113
Facsimile: 310-451-0089

Lee Sacks
Michael K. Zweig
Filomena E. Meyer

OF COUNSEL
Dennis Holahan

For full biographical listings, see the Martindale-Hubbell Law Directory

*SANTA ROSA,** Sonoma Co.

BELDEN, ABBEY, WEITZENBERG & KELLY, A PROFESSIONAL CORPORATION (AV)

1105 North Dutton Avenue, P.O. Box 1566, 95402
Telephone: 707-542-5050
Telecopier: 707-542-2589

Thomas P. Kelly, Jr.
Richard W. Abbey

Lewis R. Warren

Representative Clients: Exchange Bank of Santa Rosa; Westamerica Bank; North Bay Title Co.; Northwestern Title Security Co.; Geyser Peak Winery; Arrowood Vineyards & Winery; Hansel Ford; Santa Rosa City School District.

For Complete List of Firm Personnel, See General Section

For full biographical listings, see the Martindale-Hubbell Law Directory

UNIVERSAL CITY, Los Angeles Co.

DAVID W. FLEMING, P.C. (AV)

10 Universal City Plaza, Suite 2570, 91608
Telephone: 818-753-8141
Fax: 818-753-5657

David W. Fleming

For full biographical listings, see the Martindale-Hubbell Law Directory

WALNUT CREEK, Contra Costa Co.

JACKL & KATZEN (AV)

2033 North Main Street, Suite 700, 94596
Telephone: 510-932-8500
Fax: 510-932-1961

MEMBERS OF FIRM
V. James Jackl
Linda R. Katzen

Christopher J. Joy
David W. Walters
James M. Sitkin
Andrew N. Contopoulos
David A. Schuricht

For full biographical listings, see the Martindale-Hubbell Law Directory

LAW OFFICES OF JOHN F. MARTIN A PROFESSIONAL CORPORATION (AV)

Station Plaza, 3100 Oak Road, Suite 230, P.O. Box 5331, 94596
Telephone: 510-937-5433
Telecopier: 510-938-5567

John F. Martin

Mara Beth Berman
Jennifer L. Sipes

OF COUNSEL
Carl N. Sandvik
Douglas G. Cowan

Representative Clients: Safeway Stores, Inc.; Marine World Africa USA; BMW of North America, Inc.; Oliver De Silva, Inc.; Interlake Packaging Corp.; Overland Construction Company, Inc.; Wendland Trucking Inc.

For full biographical listings, see the Martindale-Hubbell Law Directory

WOODLAND HILLS, Los Angeles Co.

FELDMAN, KARP & FELDMAN, A PROFESSIONAL CORPORATION (AV)

5959 Topanga Canyon Boulevard, Suite 275, 91367
Telephone: 818-992-0357
Facsimile: 818-992-0537

Deborah L. Feldman
David I. Karp
Yacoba Ann Feldman

Douglas A. Bordner

(See Next Column)

FELDMAN, KARP & FELDMAN A PROFESSIONAL CORPORATION—*Continued*

LEGAL SUPPORT PERSONNEL

Debra Kay "BJ" Philben (Paralegal)

For full biographical listings, see the Martindale-Hubbell Law Directory

WALLECK, SHANE, STANARD & BLENDER (AV)

5959 Topanga Canyon Boulevard, Suite 200, 91367
Telephone: 818-346-1333
Fax: 818-702-8939

MEMBERS OF FIRM

David L. Shane — David L. Blender
Roger L. Stanard — Gary N. Schwartz

Representative Clients: San Fernando Valley Board of Realtors; Keffco, Inc.; Fuller-Jeffrey Broadcasting; Lynn Simay-Key Centers, Inc.; DA/PRO Rubber, Inc.; Pinnacle Estate Properties, Inc.; Comet Electric, Inc.; Wausau Insurance Company; Western States Imports Co., Inc.; California Coast Escrow, Inc.

For full biographical listings, see the Martindale-Hubbell Law Directory

COLORADO

*BOULDER,** Boulder Co.

DOTY & SHAPIRO, P.C. (AV)

1720 Fourteenth Street, Suite 100, 80302-6353
Telephone: 303-443-3234
Telecopier: 303-443-3438

H. McGregor Doty, II — Mark R. Shapiro

For full biographical listings, see the Martindale-Hubbell Law Directory

*COLORADO SPRINGS,** El Paso Co.

DANIEL P. EDWARDS, P.C. (AV)

Suite 310, 128 South Tejon, 80903
Telephone: 719-634-6620
Fax: 719-634-3142

Daniel P. Edwards

Representative Clients: AMI Industries, Inc.; Analytical Surveys, Inc.; A.C. Israel Enterprises, Inc.; Boddington Lumber Co., Inc.; Cardiovascular Surgeons of Colorado Springs, P.C.; Colorado Springs Radiologists, P.C.; Digital, Inc.; Music Semiconductors, Inc.; Schlage Lock Co.; Texas Instruments.

For full biographical listings, see the Martindale-Hubbell Law Directory

*DENVER,** Denver Co.

BROWNSTEIN HYATT FARBER & STRICKLAND, P.C. (AV)

Twenty-Second Floor, 410 Seventeenth Street, 80202-4437
Telephone: 303-534-6335
Telecopier: 303-623-1956

Norman Brownstein — Michael J. Sternick
Steven W. Farber — Gary M. Reiff
Edward N. Barad — Michael R. McGinnis
John R. Call — Bruce A. James
Steven M. Sommers — Brian Hoffmann
Ronald B. Merrill — Nesa E. Hassanein
Lynda A. McNeive — Jeffrey M. Knetsch (Not admitted in CO)
Laura Jean Christman
Wayne H. Hykan — Hubert A. Farbes, Jr.

OF COUNSEL

Jack N. Hyatt — Ann B. Riley
Susan F. Hammerman

Robert Kaufmann — Gregory A. Vallin
Brent T. Slosky — Jill E. Murray
Jay F. Kamlet — Gregory W. Berger
Ana Lazo Tenzer — Marquitte C. Starkey
David M. Brown — Howard J. Pollack (Not admitted in CO)
Kyle M. Hall (Not admitted in CO)

Representative Clients: Blue Cross and Blue Shield of Colorado; Boston Chicken, Inc.; Celestial Seasonings, Inc.; Donaldson Lufkin & Jenrette Securities Corp.; John Elway Auto Dealerships; Liberty Media Corporation; M.D.C. Holdings, Inc.; Manville Corporation; The Prudential Insurance Co. of America; SunAmerica, Inc.

For Complete List of Firm Personnel, See General Section

For full biographical listings, see the Martindale-Hubbell Law Directory

BURNS WALL SMITH AND MUELLER, A PROFESSIONAL CORPORATION (AV)

Suite 800, 303 East Seventeenth Avenue, 80203-1260
Telephone: 303-830-7000
Telecopier: 303-830-6708
Telex: 650-278-8717 (MCI UW)

Peter J. Wall — James E. Bosik
Gregory J. Smith — Steven F. Mueller
George W. Mueller — Robert T. Cosgrove

James P. Rouse — Donald D. Farlow
Gretchen L. Aultman — Mark D. Masters

OF COUNSEL

Thomas M. Burns — Darrell C. Miller
Frank H. Houck — Anthony van Westrum

SPECIAL COUNSEL

John D. Amen — Robert Neece
Jack M. Merritts

Representative Clients: IBM Credit Corporation; PIPTO Holdings, Inc.; Coopers & Lybrand; Colorado Chapter of the American Physical Therapy Association; QC Data Inc.; Ford Motor Company; Altro Medical Corp.; Advance Geophysical Corporation; Meteor Industries, Inc.; In-Situ, Inc.

For full biographical listings, see the Martindale-Hubbell Law Directory

GLEN B. CLARK, JR., P.C. (AV)

Mile High Center, 1700 Broadway, Suite 1217, 80290
Telephone: 303-832-3000
Fax: 303-832-3044

Glen B. Clark, Jr.

Representative Clients: Citadel Bank, Colorado Springs; Cyclo Manufacturing Co.; Camp Coast to Coast, Inc.; Charter Bank & Trust, Inc.; Corporate Air, Inc.; Vacation Matrix, Inc.

For full biographical listings, see the Martindale-Hubbell Law Directory

DUCKER, DEWEY & SEAWELL, P.C. (AV)

One Civic Center Plaza, Suite 1500, 1560 Broadway, 80202
Telephone: 303-861-2828
Telecopier: 303-861-4017
Frisco, Colorado Office: 179 Willow Lane, Suite A, P.O. Box 870, 80443.
Telephone: 303-668-3776. Direct Dial from Denver: 674-1783.

Bruce Ducker — Robert C. Montgomery
Stephen Gurko (Resident, Frisco Office) — Thomas C. Seawell
L. Bruce Nelson
Michael J. Kelly — Christopher J. Walsh

OF COUNSEL

Charles F. Dewey

For full biographical listings, see the Martindale-Hubbell Law Directory

DUFFORD & BROWN, P.C. (AV)

1700 Broadway, Suite 1700, 80290-1701
Telephone: 303-861-8013
Facsimile: 303-832-3804

Thomas G. Brown — Randall J. Feuerstein
Beverly J. Quail — Edward D. White

Thomas E. J. Hazard

SPECIAL COUNSEL

Marc A. Chorney — James E. Carpenter

Representative Clients: CF&I Steel, L.P.; Colorado Permanente Medical Group, Inc.; Equilease Corporation; General Electric Company; Hall and Hall Mortgage Corporation; Metallurgy International Inc.; Hewlett-Packard; Hong Kong & Shanghai Banking Corporation; Ingersoll-Rand Financial Company; The Lincoln National Life Insurance Company.

For Complete List of Firm Personnel, See General Section

For full biographical listings, see the Martindale-Hubbell Law Directory

FRIEDLOB SANDERSON RASKIN PAULSON & TOURTILLOTT (AV)

A Partnership of Professional Corporations
1400 Glenarm Place, 80202-5099
Telephone: 303-571-1400
Fax: 303-595-3159; 303-595-3970

Raymond L. Friedlob — Christopher R. Paulson
James W. Sanderson — Herrick K. Lidstone, Jr.
Gerald Raskin — Mary M. Maikoetter

John W. Kellogg — Colleen R. Belak

(See Next Column)

FRIEDLOB SANDERSON RASKIN PAULSON & TOURTILLOTT, *Denver—Continued*

OF COUNSEL

Jack D. Feuer

For full biographical listings, see the Martindale-Hubbell Law Directory

HAMILTON AND FAATZ, A PROFESSIONAL CORPORATION (AV)

Suite 600 Colorado State Bank Building, 1600 Broadway, 80202-4988
Telephone: 303-830-0500
Facsimile: 303-860-7855

Pierpont Fuller (1906-1983)
John M. Evans (1911-1984)
Dwight Alan Hamilton
Clyde A. Faatz, Jr.
John T. Willson
James H. Marlow
Jan E. Montgomery
Gregory W. Smith

Robert L. Bartholic

SPECIAL COUNSEL

Michael E. Gurley

OF COUNSEL

Kenneth W. Caughey

Representative Clients: PPG Industries, Inc.; Public Employees Retirement Association of Colorado; Masonic Temple Association of Denver; Lockton Silversmith, Inc.; Muller, Sirhall and Associates, Inc.; South Denver Cardiology Associates, P.C.; Landmark Reclamation, Inc.; Stone's Farm Supply, Inc.; Heather Gardens Association; DCX, Inc.

For full biographical listings, see the Martindale-Hubbell Law Directory

HOLME ROBERTS & OWEN LLC (AV)

Suite 4100, 1700 Lincoln, 80203
Telephone: 303-861-7000
Telex: 45-4460
Telecopier: 303-866-0200
Boulder, Colorado Office: Suite 400, 1401 Pearl Street.
Telephone: 303-444-5955.
Telecopier: 303-444-1063.
Colorado Springs, Colorado Office: Suite 1300, 90 South Cascade Avenue.
Telephone: 719-473-3800.
Telecopier: 719-633-1518.
Salt Lake City, Utah Office: Suite 1100, 111 East Broadway.
Telephone: 801-521-5800.
Telecopier: 801-521-9639.
London, England Office: 4th Floor, Mellier House, 26a Albemarle Street.
Telephone: 44-171-499-8776.
Telecopier: 44-171-499-7769.
Moscow, Russia Office: 14 Krivokolenny Pr., Suite 30, 101000.
Telephone: 095-925-7816.
Telecopier: 095-923-2726.

MEMBERS OF FIRM

James C. Owen Jr.
Richard G. Wohlgenant
Joseph W. Morrisey, Jr.
G. Kevin Conwick
Paul D. Holleman
W. Dean Salter
Frank Erisman
Thomas A. Richardson
William D. Watson
Bruce R. Kohler (Resident Managing Member, London, England Office; Co-Director, Moscow, Russia Office)
Bruce L. Likoff
William R. Roberts (Boulder Office)
Phillip R. Clark
Randy G. Bobier (Colorado Springs Office)
Martha Traudt Collins
David K. Detton (Salt Lake City Office)
Thomas F. Cope
Lynn Parker Hendrix
Nick Nimmo
Douglas R. Wright
Francis R. Wheeler
Jan N. Steiert
Marla J. Williams
David D. Kleinkopf
Steven B. Richardson
McKay Marsden (Salt Lake City Office)
Martha Dugan Rehm
John F. Knoeckel
Kay M. Small (Boulder Office)
Michael D. Strugar (Colorado Springs Office)
Jill K. Rood (Boulder Office)
P. Christian Anderson (Salt Lake City Office)
David Harold Little (Salt Lake City Office)
Robert H. Bach
Garth B. Jensen
Mary L. Groves
Thomas M. James (Colorado Springs Office)
Manuel L. Martinez
Paul V. Timmins

OF COUNSEL

Harold S. Bloomenthal
Nancy J. Severson

SPECIAL COUNSEL

David Akers Weinstein
David K. Schollenberger (London, England Office)
Diane S. Barrett
Lawrence A. Leporte (London, England Office)
John P. Babb
Stephen P. Ward

SENIOR COUNSEL

Kathryn B. Stoker

(See Next Column)

ASSOCIATES

Kristen L. Alleman
William H. Auerswald, Jr.
John Adams Barrett, Jr. (On Leave of Absence)
Diane D. Card (Salt Lake City Office)
Steven A. Cohen
James F. Cress
Paul V. Franke
Staunton L. T. Golding
Mary C. Gordon (Salt Lake City Office)
Lisa A. Hawkins
Rhonda R. Johnson
Kelvin D. Jones III
Robert J. Kaukol (Colorado Springs Office)
Kevin H. Kelley
Susana E. Laos Konon (Not admitted in CO)
Maria Mashenka Lundberg
Margaret B. McLean (Resident Managing Lawyer, Moscow, Russia Office)
Sandra Orihuela
Patrick K. Perrin (Boulder Office)
Timothy G. Pfeifer (Not admitted in CO; Colorado Springs Office)
Alan Romero (Salt Lake City Office)
Susanne D. Roubidoux
Rashid Sharipov (Resident, Moscow, Russia Office)
Steven B. Smith (Colorado Springs Office)
David E. Tenzer (Boulder Office)
Paul G. Thompson
Christopher T. Toll
Alexander Udovenko (Moscow, Russia Office)

For Complete List of Firm Personnel, See General Section

For full biographical listings, see the Martindale-Hubbell Law Directory

HOPPER AND KANOUFF, A PROFESSIONAL CORPORATION (AV)

Suite 200, 1610 Wynkoop Street, 80202
Telephone: 303-892-6000
Fax: 303-892-0457

George W. Hopper (1930-1986)
John P. Kanouff
Thomas S. Smith
Alan W. Peryam
Ward E. Terry, Jr.
Kim I. McCullough
Dennis A. Graham
Cameron J. Syke
Douglas R. Ferguson
Gene R. Thornton
James Rollin Miller, Jr.
Michael L. Glaser

Victor M. Morales
Randy E. Dunn
Paul R. Wood
Annita M. Menogan
Harold R. Bruno, III
K. Harsha Krishnan
Lynne M. Hanson
Michael D. Murphy
Garrett M. Tuttle
Darren J. Warner (Not admitted in CO)

OF COUNSEL

Jan B. Delbridge-Graham
Joseph P. Benkert

Reference: Colorado National Bank.

For full biographical listings, see the Martindale-Hubbell Law Directory

LOHF, SHAIMAN & JACOBS, P.C. (AV)

900 Cherry Tower, 950 South Cherry Street, 80222
Telephone: 303-753-9000
Telecopier: 303-753-9997

Neil E. Ayervais
Charles H. Jacobs
Moshe Luber
Robert Shaiman

Reference: Professional Bank.

For full biographical listings, see the Martindale-Hubbell Law Directory

MYER, SWANSON & ADAMS, P.C. (AV)

The Colorado State Bank Building, 1600 Broadway, Suite 1850, 80202-4918
Telephone: 303-866-9800
Facsimile: 303-866-9818

Rendle Myer
Allan B. Adams
Robert K. Swanson
Thomas J. Wolf

Kevin M. Brady

OF COUNSEL

Robert Swanson
Fred E. Neef (1910-1986)

Representative Clients: The Oppenheimer Funds; Daily Cash Accumulation Fund; The Centennial Trusts; Mile High Chapter of American Red Cross; Master Lease; Heartland Management Company; Kan-Build of Colorado, Inc.
Reference: The Colorado State Bank of Denver.

For full biographical listings, see the Martindale-Hubbell Law Directory

NETZORG & McKEEVER, PROFESSIONAL CORPORATION (AV)

5251 DTC Parkway (Englewood) Penthouse One, 80111
Telephone: 303-770-8200
Fax: 303-770-8342

(See Next Column)

NETZORG & MCKEEVER PROFESSIONAL CORPORATION—*Continued*

Gordon W. Netzorg
J. Nicholas McKeever, Jr.
Susan Bernhardt
Cecil E. Morris, Jr.

For full biographical listings, see the Martindale-Hubbell Law Directory

H. F. RIEBESELL, JR., P.C. (AV)

5290 DTC Parkway, Suite 150 (Englewood), P.O. Box 4715, 80155-4715
Telephone: 303-721-1180
Telecopier: 303-850-7115

H. F. Riebesell, Jr.

For full biographical listings, see the Martindale-Hubbell Law Directory

*GREELEY,** Weld Co.

BREGA & WINTERS, P.C. (AV)

1100 Tenth Street, Suite 402, 80631
Telephone: 303-352-4805
Fax: 303-352-6547
Denver, Colorado Office: One United Bank Center. 1700 Lincoln Street, Suite 2222 Street.
Telephone: 303-866-9400.
FAX: 303-861-9109.

Jerry D. Winters
Pamela A. Shaddock

Bradley D. Laue

For full biographical listings, see the Martindale-Hubbell Law Directory

CONNECTICUT

*BRIDGEPORT,** Fairfield Co.

ELSTEIN AND ELSTEIN, P.C. (AV)

Suite 400 1087 Broad Street, 06604-4231
Telephone: 203-367-4421
Telecopier: 203-366-8615

Henry Elstein
Bruce L. Elstein

For full biographical listings, see the Martindale-Hubbell Law Directory

CHESHIRE, New Haven Co.

WINTERS & FORTE (AV)

Waverly Professional Park, 315 Highland Avenue, Suite 102, P.O. Box 844, 06410
Telephone: 203-272-2927
Fax: 203-271-1222

MEMBERS OF FIRM

David Wayne Winters
Michael C. Forte

A List of Representative Clients will be furnished upon request.
Re ferences: Bank of Boston, Connecticut; Centerbank; American National Bank.

For full biographical listings, see the Martindale-Hubbell Law Directory

*HARTFORD,** Hartford Co.

SOROKIN SOROKIN GROSS HYDE & WILLIAMS P.C. (AV)

One Corporate Center, 06103
Telephone: 203-525-6645
Fax: 203-522-1781
Simsbury, Connecticut Office: 730 Hopmeadow Street.
Telephone: 203-651-9348.
Rocky Hill, Connecticut Office: 2360 Main Street.
Telephone: 203-563-9305.
Fax: 203-529-6931.
Glastonbury, Connecticut Office: 124 Hebron Avenue.
Telephone: 203-659-8801.

Morris W. Banks
Richard G. Convicer
Andrew C. Glassman
Charles R. Moore, Jr.
Richard D. Tulisano (Resident, Rocky Hill Office)

Brian S. Becker
Sharon Kowal Freilich

OF COUNSEL

Milton Sorokin

For Complete List of Firm Personnel, See General Section

For full biographical listings, see the Martindale-Hubbell Law Directory

MERIDEN, New Haven Co.

BROWN & WELSH, P.C. (AV)

100 Hanover Street, P.O. Box 183, 06450-0183
Telephone: 203-235-1651
Telecopier: 203-235-9600
Internet: 71561.1601@Compuserve.Com

David Brown
Thomas J. Welsh
Houston Putnam Lowry
Charles D. Houlihan, Jr.

Thomas P. Malnati
Bart F. Peters

OF COUNSEL

Dr. Michael T.W. Arnheim

For full biographical listings, see the Martindale-Hubbell Law Directory

*NEW HAVEN,** New Haven Co.

HOGAN & RINI, P.C. (AV)

Gold Building, 8th Floor 234 Church Street, 06510
Telephone: 203-787-4191
Telecopier: 203-777-4032

John W. Hogan, Jr.
Joseph L. Rini
Sue A. Cousineau

OF COUNSEL

Mark S. Cousineau

For full biographical listings, see the Martindale-Hubbell Law Directory

SUSMAN, DUFFY & SEGALOFF, P.C. (AV)

55 Whitney Avenue, 06510-1300
Telephone: 203-624-9830
Telecopier: 203-562-8430
Mailing Address: P.O. Box 1684, New Haven, Connecticut, 06507-1684

Allen H. Duffy (1931-1986)
Michael Susman
James H. Segaloff
David A. Reif
Joseph E. Faughnan
Susan W. Wolfson
Laura M. Sklaver
Andrew R. Lubin
James J. Perito
Matthew C. Susman
Thomas E. Katon

Charles J. Filardi, Jr.
Jennifer L. Schancupp
Donna Decker Morris
Peter G. Kruzynski
Joshua W. Cohen

OF COUNSEL

Diana C. Ballard

For full biographical listings, see the Martindale-Hubbell Law Directory

ORANGE, New Haven Co.

SCHINE & JULIANELLE, P.C. (AV)

Suite 28, 477 Boston Post Road, P.O. Box 905, 06477-3548
Telephone: 203-795-3563
FAX: 203-799-9655
Westport, Connecticut Office: Suite 100, 830 Post Road East.
Telephone: 203-226-6861.
FAX: 203-226-6866.

Leonard A. Schine (1943-1982)
Robert L. Julianelle

Mary D. Mix
Patrick W. Frazier, Jr.
Natale V. Di Natale

OF COUNSEL

Lawrence W. Kanaga

Representative Client: Sacred Heart University.

For full biographical listings, see the Martindale-Hubbell Law Directory

SOUTHPORT, Fairfield Co.

BRODY AND OBER, P.C. (AV)

135 Rennell Drive, 06490
Telephone: 203-259-7405
Fax: 203-255-8572

Charles S. Brody (1894-1976)
Seth O. L. Brody
Stanley B. Garrell
Frank F. Ober
S. Giles Payne
William J. Britt
James M. Thorburn
Barbara S. Miller
Ronald B. Noren

Stephen L. Lichtman
Diane F. Martucci
Richard W. Mather

For full biographical listings, see the Martindale-Hubbell Law Directory

Southport—Continued

SEELEY & BERGLASS (AV)

3695 Post Road, P.O. Box 858, 06490
Telephone: 203-256-3250
Fax: 203-562-9365
New Haven, Connecticut Office: 121 Whitney Avenue.
Telephone: 203-562-5888.
Fax: 203-562-9365.

W. Parker Seeley, Jr. | Teresa E. Cichucki

OF COUNSEL

Leonard S. Paoletta

For full biographical listings, see the Martindale-Hubbell Law Directory

WESTPORT, Fairfield Co.

LEVETT, ROCKWOOD & SANDERS, PROFESSIONAL CORPORATION (AV)

33 Riverside Avenue, P.O. Box 5116, 06881
Telephone: 203-222-0885
Telecopier: 203-226-8025

David R. Levett
William O. Rockwood, Jr.
John Sanders
Gregory Griffin
Madeleine F. Grossman
Judy A. Rabkin
Dorit Schutzengel Heimer
Sharon M. Schweitzer
Barbara A. Young
Steven M. Siegelaub
Marc J. Kurzman
Suzanne B. Albani
Alfred U. Pavlis
Peter H. Struzzi

OF COUNSEL

John W. Auchincloss, II

Ellen S. Aho
Edward B. Chansky
Margaret H DeSaussure
Cheryl L. Johnson
Ernest C. Mysogland
Robert W. Riordan
Patricia D. Weitzman

Representative Clients: Advantage Health Corporation; Business Express, Inc.; Cannondale Corporation; Caradon, Inc.; Fabrique de Fer de Charleroi (USA), Inc.; Heyman Properties; Hospital of Saint Raphael; Marketing Corporation of America; St. Vincent's Medical Center; Shawmut Bank, N.A.

For full biographical listings, see the Martindale-Hubbell Law Directory

WILLIAM L. SCHEFFLER (AV(T))

315 Post Road West, 06880
Telephone: 203-226-6600; 212-795-7800
Telecopier: 203-227-1873

For full biographical listings, see the Martindale-Hubbell Law Directory

RONALD L. SHEIMAN (AV)

1804 Post Road East, 06880
Telephone: 203-259-0599
Telex: 238198 TLXAUR
Telecopier: 203-255-2570

For full biographical listings, see the Martindale-Hubbell Law Directory

WAKE, SEE, DIMES & BRYNICZKA (AV)

27 Imperial Avenue, P.O. Box 777, 06881
Telephone: 203-227-9545
Telecopier: 203-226-1641

MEMBERS OF FIRM

Hereward Wake (1905-1977)
Edgar T. See
Edwin K. Dimes
Jacob P. Bryniczka
Amy L. Y. Day
Ira W. Bloom
Ernest Michael Dichele
Jonathan A. Flatow

ASSOCIATES

Douglas E. LoMonte | Rosamond A. Koether

OF COUNSEL

Richard S. Gibbons

General Counsel for: L.H. Gault & Son, Inc.; M.B.I., Inc.; The Danbury Mint; Beta Shim, Co.; Easton Press; Coverbind Corp.; D.L. Ryan Companies, Ltd.;
Approved Attorneys for: Lawyers Title Insurance Corporation of Richmond, Va.; Chicago Title Insurance Co.; Old Republic National Title Insurance Co.

For full biographical listings, see the Martindale-Hubbell Law Directory

DELAWARE

*WILMINGTON,** New Castle Co.

CONNOLLY, BOVE, LODGE & HUTZ (AV)

1220 Market Street, P.O. Box 2207, 19899-2207
Telephone: 302-658-9141
Telecopier: 302-658-5614
Cable Address: "Artcon"
Telex: 83-5477

James M. Mulligan, Jr.
Arthur G. Connolly, Jr.
Henry E. Gallagher, Jr.
Richard David Levin
Jeffrey B. Bove
Collins J. Seitz, Jr.
Charles J. Durante
F. L. Peter Stone
John C. Kairis
Arthur G. Connolly, III
James D. Heisman
Anne Love Barnett (Not admitted in DE)

For Complete List of Firm Personnel, See General Section
For full biographical listings, see the Martindale-Hubbell Law Directory

SCHLUSSER, REIVER, HUGHES & SISK (AV)

1700 West 14th Street, 19806
Telephone: 302-655-8181
Fax: 302-655-8190

MEMBERS OF FIRM

Robert E. Schlusser
Joanna Reiver
Mark D. Sisk
Bryan E. Keenan
Brian P. Glancy

OF COUNSEL

Thomas G. Hughes

ASSOCIATES

Theresa P. Wilson (Not admitted in DE) | John A. Ciccarone

For full biographical listings, see the Martindale-Hubbell Law Directory

SMITH, KATZENSTEIN & FURLOW (AV)

1220 Market Building, P.O. Box 410, 19899
Telephone: 302-652-8400
FAX: 302-652-8405

MEMBERS OF FIRM

Craig B. Smith | Anne E. Bookout

Stephen M. Miller

For Complete List of Firm Personnel, See General Section

For full biographical listings, see the Martindale-Hubbell Law Directory

DISTRICT OF COLUMBIA

WASHINGTON, D.C. Co.

* indicates certain Bar Register subscribers, in cities of comparable size and importance, who maintain an additional office in Washington, D.C. and who have arranged for representation as a part of the Washington, D.C. listings that follow

*** BAKER & BOTTS, L.L.P. (AV)**

A Registered Limited Liability Partnership
The Warner, 1299 Pennsylvania Avenue, N.W., 20004-2400
Telephone: 202-639-7700
Fax: 202-639-7832
Houston, Texas Office: One Shell Plaza, 910 Louisiana.
Telephone: 713-229-1234.
Austin, Texas Office: 1600 San Jacinto Center, 98 San Jacinto Boulevard.
Telephone: 512-322-2500.
Dallas, Texas Office: 2001 Ross Avenue.
Telephone: 214-953-6500.
New York, New York Office: 805 Third Avenue, Suite 2000.
Telephone: 212-705-5000.
Moscow, Russian Federation Office: 10 ul. Pushkinskaya, 103031.
Telephone: 7095/921-5300 (Local); 7501/929-7070 (International).

MEMBERS OF FIRM

James R. Doty
David N. Powers
Hugh Tucker

(See Next Column)

BAKER & BOTTS L.L.P.—*Continued*

ASSOCIATES

Ruby D'andrea Ceaser
Kevin B. Dent
Leslie Anne Freiman

For Complete List of Firm Personnel, See General Section

For full biographical listings, see the Martindale-Hubbell Law Directory

CAPLIN & DRYSDALE, CHARTERED (AV)

One Thomas Circle, N.W., 20005
Telephone: 202-862-5000
Cable Address: "Capdale"
Telex: 904001 CAPL UR WSH
Fax: 202-429-3301
New York, N.Y. Office: 399 Park Avenue.
Telephone: 212-319-7125.
Fax: 212-644-6755.

Mortimer M. Caplin
Robert A. Klayman
Ralph A. Muoio
Elihu Inselbuch (Resident, New York Office)
Ronald B. Lewis
Richard W. Skillman
Patricia G. Lewis
Bernard S. Bailor
Stafford Smiley
Sally A. Regal
Julie W. Davis
Carl S. Kravitz
Robert A. Boisture
Charles T. Plambeck
Beth Shapiro Kaufman
Craig A. Sharon
James E. Salles
Paul G. Cellupica
Michael Doran (Not admitted in DC)
Dorothy L. Foley
Matthew W. Frank
Elizabeth M. Sellers (Not admitted in DC)
Douglas D. Drysdale
Thomas A. Troyer
David N. Webster
H. David Rosenbloom
Peter Van N. Lockwood
Cono R. Namorato
Daniel B. Rosenbaum
Richard E. Timbie
Graeme W. Bush
Albert G. Lauber, Jr.
Scott D. Michel
Kent A. Mason
Trevor W. Swett III
James Sottile, IV
Harry J. Hicks, III
C. Sanders McNew (Resident, New York Office)
Ann C. McMillan
Catherine E. Livingston
Christian R. Pastore (Resident, New York Office)
Nathan D. Finch
Jessica L. Goldstein

OF COUNSEL

Robert H. Elliott, Jr.
Milton Cerny
Myron C. Baum
Vivian L. Cavalieri

For full biographical listings, see the Martindale-Hubbell Law Directory

DE MARTINO FINKELSTEIN ROSEN & VIRGA (AV)

A Partnership including Professional Corporations
Suite 400, 1818 N Street, N.W., 20036
Telephone: 202-659-0494
Telecopier: 202-659-1290
New York, N.Y. Office: Suite 1700, 90 Broad Street.
Telephone: 212-363-2500.
Telecopier: 212-363-2723.

MEMBERS OF FIRM

Kathleen L. Cerveny (Resident)
Ralph V. De Martino (Resident)
Steven R. Finkelstein (Not admitted in DC; Resident, New York, N.Y. Office)
Jeffrey S. Rosen (Resident)
Gerard A. Virga (Not admitted in DC; Resident, New York, N.Y. Office)

Keith H. Peterson (Not admitted in DC; Resident, New York, N.Y. Office)
Victoria A. Baylin (Not admitted in DC; Resident)
Hal B. Perkins (Resident)
Lee W. Cassidy (Resident)

LEGAL SUPPORT PERSONNEL

J. Keoni Robinson (Paralegal)

For full biographical listings, see the Martindale-Hubbell Law Directory

KENNETH R. FEINBERG & ASSOCIATES (AV)

1120 20th Street, N.W. Suite 740 South, 20036
Telephone: 202-371-1110
Fax: 202-962-9290
New York, N.Y. Office: 780 3rd Avenue, Suite 2202.
Telephone: 212-527-9600.
Fax: 212-527-9611.

ASSOCIATES

Deborah E. Greenspan
Michael K. Rozen (Not admitted in DC)
Peter H. Woodin (Not admitted in DC)

For full biographical listings, see the Martindale-Hubbell Law Directory

MIDLEN & GUILLOT, CHARTERED (AV)

3238 Prospect Street, N.W., 20007-3214
Telephone: 202-333-1500
Facsimile: 202-333-6852
Internet: MGCG@delphi.com

John H. Midlen, Jr.
Gregory H. Guillot (Not admitted in DC)

For full biographical listings, see the Martindale-Hubbell Law Directory

SUTHERLAND, ASBILL & BRENNAN (AV)

1275 Pennsylvania Avenue, N.W., 20004-2404
Telephone: 202-383-0100
Cable Address: "Sutab Wash"
Telex: 89-501
Facsimile: 202-637-3593
Atlanta, Georgia Office: 999 Peachtree Street, N. E., 30309-3996.
Telephone: 404-853-8000.
New York, N.Y. Office: 1270 Avenue of the Americas, 10020-1700.
Telephone: 212-332-3000.
Austin, Texas Office: 111 Congress Avenue, 23rd Floor, 78701-4079.
Telephone: 512-469-3350.

Frederick R. Bellamy
Steven B. Boehm
James M. Cain
James D. Darrow
Paul J. Mason
Stephen E. Roth
David Schwinger

For Complete List of Firm Personnel, See General Section

For full biographical listings, see the Martindale-Hubbell Law Directory

* THOMPSON, HINE AND FLORY (AV)

1920 N Street, N.W., 20036-1601
Telephone: 202-331-8800
Fax: 202-331-8330
Telex: 904173
Cable Address: "Caglaw"
Akron, Ohio Office: 50 S. Main Street, Suite 502, 44308-1828.
Telephone: 216-376-8090.
Fax: 216-376-8386.
Cincinnati, Ohio Office: 312 Walnut Street, 14th Floor, 45202-4029.
Telephone: 513-352-6700.
Fax: 513-241-4771.
Telex: 938003.
Cleveland, Ohio Office: 1100 National City Bank Building, 629 Euclid Avenue, 44114.
Telephone: 216-566-5500.
Fax: 216-566-5583.
Telex: 980217. Cable Address "Thomflor".
Columbus, Ohio Office: One Columbus, 10 West Broad Street, 43215-34353.
Telephone: 614-469-3200.
Fax: 614-469-3361.
Dayton, Ohio Office: 2000 Courthouse Plaza, N.E., 45402-1706.
Telephone: 513-443-6600.
Fax: 513-443-6637, 513-443-6635.
Palm Beach, Florida Office: 125 Worth Avenue, 33480-4466.
Telephone: 407-833-5900.
Fax: 407-833-5951.
Brussels, Belgium Office: Rue Des Chevaliers, Ridderstraat 14 - B.10, B-1050.
Telephone: 011-32-2-511-9326.
Fax: 011-32-2-513-9206.

MEMBER OF FIRM

Michael Wm. Sacks

For Complete List of Firm Personnel, See General Section

For full biographical listings, see the Martindale-Hubbell Law Directory

* VENABLE, BAETJER, HOWARD & CIVILETTI (AV)

A Partnership including Professional Corporations
Suite 1000, 1201 New York Avenue, N.W., 20005
Telephone: 202-962-4800
Fax: 202-962-8300
Baltimore, Maryland Office: Venable, Baetjer and Howard, 1800 Mercantile Bank & Trust Building, 2 Hopkins Plaza.
Telephone: 410-244-7400.
McLean, Virginia Office: Venable, Baetjer and Howard, Suite 400, 2010 Corporate Ridge.
Telephone: 703-760-1600.
Rockville, Maryland Office: Venable, Baetjer and Howard, Suite 500, One Church Street, P. O. Box 1906.
Telephone: 301-217-5600.
Towson, Maryland Office: Venable, Baetjer and Howard, 210 Allegheny Avenue, P. O. Box 5517.
Telephone: 410-494-6200.

(See Next Column)

VENABLE, BAETJER, HOWARD & CIVILETTI, *Washington—Continued*

MEMBERS OF FIRM

Benjamin R. Civiletti (P.C.) (Also at Baltimore and Towson, Maryland Offices)
Anthony M. Carey (Not admitted in DC; Also at Baltimore, Maryland Office)
Neal D. Borden (Not admitted in DC; Also at Baltimore, Maryland Office)
Jan K. Guben (Not admitted in DC; Also at Baltimore, Maryland Office)
David J. Levenson
Joe A. Shull
Robert E. Madden (Also at Baltimore, Maryland and McLean, Virginia Offices)
Kenneth C. Bass, III (Also at McLean, Virginia Office)
Joseph G. Block
Bryson L. Cook (P.C.) (Not admitted in DC; Also at Baltimore, Maryland Office)
Jeffrey D. Knowles
William D. Coston
Maurice Baskin
Robert J. Bolger, Jr. (Not admitted in DC; Also at Baltimore, Maryland Office)
Bruce H. Jurist (Also at Baltimore, Maryland Office)
Linda L. Lord
John M. Gurley
Paul A. Serini (Not admitted in DC; Also at Baltimore, Maryland Office)

OF COUNSEL

Fred W. Hathaway

ASSOCIATES

Donald P. Creston
D. Brent Gunsalus
Fernand A. Lavallee
Traci H. Mundy (Not admitted in DC)

For Complete List of Firm Personnel, See General Section

For full biographical listings, see the Martindale-Hubbell Law Directory

WILMER, CUTLER & PICKERING (AV)

2445 M Street, N.W., 20037-1420
Telephone: 202-663-6000
Facsimile: 202-663-6363
Internet: Law@Wilmer.Com
European Offices:
4 Carlton Gardens, London, SW1Y 5AA, England. Telephone: 011 (4471) 839-4466.
Facsimile: 011 (4471) 839-3537.
Rue de la Loi 15 Wetstraat, B-1040 Brussels, Belgium. Telephone: 011 (322) 231-0903.
Facsimile: 011 (322) 230-4322.
Friedrichstrasse 95, D-10117 Berlin, Germany. Telephone: 011 (4930) 2643-3601.
Facsimile: 011 (4930) 2643-3630.

MEMBERS OF FIRM

Louis R. Cohen
Michael R. Klein
Richard W. Cass
Stephen P. Doyle
Russell J. Bruemmer
Thomas W. White
Anastasia D. Kelly

COUNSEL

Roger J. Patterson

For Complete List of Firm Personnel, See General Section

For full biographical listings, see the Martindale-Hubbell Law Directory

ZUCKERMAN, SPAEDER, GOLDSTEIN, TAYLOR & KOLKER (AV)

1201 Connecticut Avenue, N.W., 20036
Telephone: 202-778-1800
Fax: 202-822-8106
Miami, Florida Office: Zuckerman, Spaeder, Taylor & Evans. Suite 900, Miami Center, 201 South Biscayne Boulevard.
Telephones: 305-358-5000; 305-579-0110; Broward County: 305-523-0277.
Fax: 305-579-9749.
Ft. Lauderdale, Florida Office: Zuckerman, Spaeder, Taylor & Evans. One East Broward Boulevard, Suite 700.
Telephone: 305-356-0463.
Fax: 305-356-0406.
Baltimore, Maryland Office: Zuckerman, Spaeder, Goldstein, Taylor & Better. Suite 2440, 100 East Pratt Street.
Telephone: 410-332-0444.
Fax: 410-659-0436.
Tampa, Florida Office: Zuckerman, Spaeder, Taylor & Evans. 101 East Kennedy Boulevard, Suite 3140.
Telephone: 813-221-1010.
Fax: 813-223-7961.
New York, N.Y. Office: 1114 Avenue of the Americas, 45th Floor, Grace Building.
Telephone: 212-479-6500.
Fax: 212-479-6512.

MEMBERS OF FIRM

Mark W. Foster
Arthur K. Mason
Anthony Thompson
Edward C. Berkowitz
Eric F. Facer
Marshall S. Wolff
Michael Steven Greene (Resident, Miami, Florida Office)

(See Next Column)

Reference: Sovran Bank/DC National.

For full biographical listings, see the Martindale-Hubbell Law Directory

FLORIDA

*FORT LAUDERDALE,** Broward Co.

BERGER, SHAPIRO & DAVIS, P.A. (AV)

Suite 400, 100 N.E. 3rd Avenue, 33301
Telephone: 305-525-9900
Fax: 305-523-2872

James L. Berger
Mitchell W. Berger
James B. Davis
Manuel Kushner
Leonard K. Samuels
Laz L. Schneider

Thomas L. Abrams
Melissa P. Anderson
Lawrence C. Callaway, III
Nick Jovanovich
Robert B. Judd
Brent L. Moody
Terri E. Tuchman

OF COUNSEL

Franklin H. Caplan
Kenneth W. Shapiro

For full biographical listings, see the Martindale-Hubbell Law Directory

LARRY V. BISHINS, P.A. (AV)

4548 North Federal Highway, 33308-5271
Telephone: Broward: 305-772-7900
Palm Beach: 407-732-5809
Facsimile: 305-772-7924
National Watts Line: 1-800-940-4TAX

Larry V. Bishins

Reference: NationsBank of Florida, N.A.

For full biographical listings, see the Martindale-Hubbell Law Directory

*KISSIMMEE,** Osceola Co.

POHL & BROWN, P.A.

(See Winter Park)

*MIAMI,** Dade Co.

BREIER AND SEIF, P.A. (AV)

1320 South Dixie Highway (Coral Gables), 33146-2986
Telephone: 305-667-0046; 667-0065
Telecopier: 305-667-3071

Robert G. Breier
Evan D. Seif

For full biographical listings, see the Martindale-Hubbell Law Directory

SPARBER, KOSNITZKY, TRUXTON, DE LA GUARDIA SPRATT & BROOKS, P.A. (AV)

1401 Brickell Avenue Suite 700, 33131
Telephone: Dade: 305-379-7200; Broward: 305-760-9133
Fax: 305-379-0800

Byron L. Sparber
Michael Kosnitzky
Gregg S. Truxton
Oscar G. de la Guardia
Marc H. Auerbach

Jorge A. Gonzalez
Thomas O. Wells
Deborah R. Mayo

For Complete List of Firm Personnel, See General Section

For full biographical listings, see the Martindale-Hubbell Law Directory

STEARNS WEAVER MILLER WEISSLER ALHADEFF & SITTERSON, P.A. (AV)

Suite 2200 Museum Tower, 150 West Flagler Street, 33130
Telephone: 305-789-3200
FAX: 305-789-3395
Tampa, Florida Office: Suite 2200 Landmark Centre, 401 East Jackson Street.
Telephone: 813-223-4800.
Fort Lauderdale, Florida Office: 200 East Broward Boulevard, Suite 1900.
Telephone: 305-462-9500.

E. Richard Alhadeff
Louise Jacowitz Allen
Stuart D. Ames
Thomas P. Angelo (Resident, Fort Lauderdale Office)
Lawrence J. Bailin (Resident, Tampa Office)
Patrick A. Barry (Resident, Fort Lauderdale Office)

(See Next Column)

STEARNS WEAVER MILLER WEISSLER ALHADEFF & SITTERSON P.A.—*Continued*

Lisa K. Bennett (Resident, Fort Lauderdale Office)
Susan Fleming Bennett (Resident, Tampa Office)
Mark J. Bernet (Resident, Tampa Office)
Claire Bailey Carraway (Resident, Tampa Office)
Seth T. Craine (Resident, Tampa Office)
Piero Luciano Desiderio (Resident, Fort Lauderdale Office)
Mark P. Dikeman
Sharon Quinn Dixon
Alan H. Fein
Owen S. Freed
Dean M. Freitag
Robert E. Gallagher, Jr.
Alice R. Huneycutt (Resident, Tampa Office)
Theodore A. Jewell
Elizabeth J. Keeler
Teddy D. Klinghoffer
Robert T. Kofman
Thomas A. Lash (Resident, Tampa Office)
Joy Spillis Lundeen
Brian J. McDonough
Francisco J. Menendez
Antonio R. Menendez
Alison W. Miller
Vicki Lynn Monroe
Harold D. Moorefield, Jr.
John N. Muratides (Resident, Tampa Office)
John K. Olson (Resident, Tampa Office)
Robert C. Owens
Patricia A. Redmond
Carl D. Roston
Steven D. Rubin
Mark A. Schneider
Curtis H. Sitterson
Mark D. Solov
Eugene E. Stearns
Bradford Swing
Dennis R. Turner
Ronald L. Weaver (Resident, Tampa Office)
Robert I. Weissler
Patricia G. Welles
Martin B. Woods (Resident, Fort Lauderdale Office)

Shawn M. Bayne (Resident, Fort Lauderdale Office)
Lisa Berg
Hans C. Beyer (Resident, Tampa Office)
Dawn A. Carapella (Resident, Tampa Office)
Christina Maria Diaz
Robert I. Finvarb
Patricia K. Green
Marilyn D. Greenblatt
Richard B. Jackson
Aimee C. Jimenez
Cheryl A. Kaplan
Michael I. Keyes
Vernon L. Lewis
Kevin Bruce Love
Adam Coatsworth Mishcon
Elizabeth G. Rice (Resident, Tampa Office)
Glenn M. Rissman
Claudia J. Saenz
Richard E. Schatz
Robert P. Shantz (Resident, Tampa Office)
Martin S. Simkovic
Ronni D. Solomon
Jo Claire Spear (Resident, Tampa Office)
Gail Marie Stage (Resident, Fort Lauderdale Office)
Annette Torres
Barbara L. Wilhite

OF COUNSEL

Stephen A. Bennett

For full biographical listings, see the Martindale-Hubbell Law Directory

*NAPLES,** Collier Co.

WILLIAM B. ROBERTS (AV)

4532 Tamiami Trail, East Suite 303, 33962-6783
Telephone: 813-774-6778
Fax: 813-774-6286

For full biographical listings, see the Martindale-Hubbell Law Directory

NORTH MIAMI, Dade Co.

KLEIN AND ASSOCIATES, P.A. (AV)

901 Northeast 125th Street, 33161
Telephone: 305-891-6100
Fax: 305-891-6104

Ronald G. Klein

For full biographical listings, see the Martindale-Hubbell Law Directory

*ORLANDO,** Orange Co.

POHL & BROWN, P.A.

(See Winter Park)

*SARASOTA,** Sarasota Co.

ABEL, BAND, RUSSELL, COLLIER, PITCHFORD & GORDON, CHARTERED (AV)

Barnett Bank Center, 240 South Pineapple Avenue, P.O. Box 49948, 34230-6948
Telephone: 813-366-6660
FAX: 813-366-3999
Fort Myers, Florida Office: The Tidewater Building, 1375 Jackson Street, Suite 201, 33901.
Telephone: 813-337-0062.
FAX: 813-337-0406.
Venice, Florida Office: Suite 199, 333 South Tamiami Trail, 34285.
Telephone: 813-485-8200.
Fax: 813-488-9436.

(See Next Column)

David S. Band
Jeffrey S. Russell
Ronald L. Collier
Malcolm J. Pitchford
Cheryl Lasris Gordon
Anthony J. Abate
Steven J. Chase
Kathryn Angell Carr
Michael S. Taaffe
Mark W. McFall
Jan Walters Pitchford

OF COUNSEL

Harvey J. Abel
Johnson S. Savary

Saralyn Abel
Douglas M. Bales
Gregory S. Band
John A. Garner
Mark D. Hildreth
Jane M. Kennedy
Christine Edwards Lamia
Bradley D. Magee
George H. Mazzarantani
Philip C. Zimmerman

References: Barnett Bank of Southwest Florida; Sun Bank/Gulf Coast.

For full biographical listings, see the Martindale-Hubbell Law Directory

WILSON, JOHNSON & JAFFER, P.A. (AV)

27 South Orange Avenue, P.O. Box 1298, 34230-1298
Telephone: 813-955-5800
FAX: 813-955-7353

Clyde H. Wilson (1908-1994)
Robert M. Johnson
Clyde H. Wilson, Jr.
John S. Jaffer

James M. Kunick

For full biographical listings, see the Martindale-Hubbell Law Directory

*TAMPA,** Hillsborough Co.

GOLD, RESNICK & SEGALL, P.A. (AV)

704 West Bay Street, 33606
Telephone: 813-254-2071
FAX: (813) 251-0616

Aaron J. Gold
Eddy R. Resnick
Larry M. Segall

Nancy J. Cass

Reference: Barnett Bank of Tampa.

For full biographical listings, see the Martindale-Hubbell Law Directory

KALISH & WARD, PROFESSIONAL ASSOCIATION (AV)

4100 Barnett Plaza, 101 East Kennedy Boulevard, P.O. Box 71, 33601-0071
Telephone: 813-222-8700
Facsimile: 813-222-8701

William Kalish
Alton C. Ward
Richard A. Schlosser
Roger J. Rovell
Michael A. Bedke
William T. Harrison, III
Thomas P. McNamara
Robert Reid Haney
Charles H. Carver
Kelley A. Bosecker

For full biographical listings, see the Martindale-Hubbell Law Directory

WINTER PARK, Orange Co.

POHL & BROWN, P.A. (AV)

280 West Canton Avenue, Suite 410, P.O. Box 3208, 32789
Telephone: 407-647-7645; 407-647-POHL
Telefax: 407-647-2314

Frank L. Pohl
Usher L. Brown
Houston E. Short
Dwight I. Cool
William W. Pouzar
Mary B. Van Leuven

OF COUNSEL

Frederick W. Peirsol

Representative Clients: Orange County Comptroller; Osceola County; School Board of Osceola County, Florida; Osceola Tourist Development Council; NationsBank of Florida, N.A.; SunBank, N.A.; The Bank of Winter Park; Bekins Moving and Storage Co., Inc.; Champion Boats, Inc.; KeyCom Telephone Systems, Inc.

For full biographical listings, see the Martindale-Hubbell Law Directory

GEORGIA

*ATLANTA,** Fulton Co.

ALEMBIK, FINE & CALLNER, P.A. (AV)

Marquis One Tower, Fourth Floor, 245 Peachtree Center Avenue, N.E., 30303
Telephone: 404-688-8800
Telecopier: 404-420-7191

(See Next Column)

ALEMBIK, FINE & CALLNER P.A., *Atlanta—Continued*

Michael D. Alembik (1936-1993)
Lowell S. Fine
Bruce W. Callner
Kathy L. Portnoy
Ronald T. Gold
G. Michael Banick
Mark E. Bergeson
Russell P. Love

Z. Ileana Martinez
Kevin S. Green
Susan M. Lieppe
T. Kevin Mooney
Bruce R. Steinfeld
Janet Lichiello Franchi

For full biographical listings, see the Martindale-Hubbell Law Directory

BIVENS, HOFFMAN & FOWLER (AV)

A Partnership of Professional Corporations
5040 Roswell Road, N.E., 30342
Telephone: 404-256-6464
FAX: 404-256-1422

MEMBERS OF FIRM

Clifford G. Hoffman (P.C.)
Michael C. Fowler (P.C.)

For full biographical listings, see the Martindale-Hubbell Law Directory

CARTER & ANSLEY (AV)

Suite 1000 One Ninety One Peachtree Tower, 191 Peachtree Street, 30303-1747
Telephone: 404-658-9220
FAX: 404-658-9726

MEMBERS OF FIRM

Shepard Bryan (1871-1970)
W. Colquitt Carter (1904-1988)
Ben Kingree, III
Tommy T. Holland
H. Sanders Carter, Jr.
A. Terry Sorrells
Robert A. Barnaby, II
Thomas E. Magill
Robert O. McCloud, Jr.
Anthony J. McGinley
Christopher N. Shuman
Elizabeth J. Bondurant

ASSOCIATES

Michael A. Coval
Rebecca J. Schmidt
Keith L. Lindsay
Burke B. Johnson
Kenton J. Coppage
John H. Zwald
A. Louise Tanner
David M. Atkinson

For Complete List of Firm Personnel, See General Section

For full biographical listings, see the Martindale-Hubbell Law Directory

CASHIN, MORTON & MULLINS (AV)

Two Midtown Plaza - Suite 1900, 1360 Peachtree Street, N.E., 30309-3214
Telephone: 404-870-1500
Telecopier: 404-870-1529

MEMBERS OF FIRM

Harry L. Cashin, Jr.
C. Read Morton, Jr.
A. L. Mullins, Jr.
Richard A. Fishman
William T. McKenzie
James Dean Spratt, Jr.
David W. Cranshaw
Richard Gerakitis
Robert Hunt Dunlap, Jr.
Robert O. Ball, III
Steven R. Glasscock
David Tully Hazell

ASSOCIATES

Lisa S. Street
Noel B. McDevitt, Jr.
James Marx Sherman
Kara E. Albert (Not admitted in GA)
Gibson T. Hess

Representative Clients: Alex Brown Realty, Inc.; ARA Food Services; Bank South, N.A.; Carey Paul Cos.; Central Life Insurance Company; Diversified Shelter Group, Ltd.; Dymetrol Co., Inc.; Edwards-Warren Tire Co.; First Union National Bank; Flournoy Development Co.

For full biographical listings, see the Martindale-Hubbell Law Directory

FRANKEL, HARDWICK, TANENBAUM & FINK, P.C. (AV)

359 East Paces Ferry Road, N.E., 30305
Telephone: 404-266-2930
Fax: 404-231-3362

Samuel N. Frankel
Allan J. Tanenbaum
Neal J. Fink
Pepi Friedman

Representative Clients: America's Favorite Chicken Co. (Church's and Popeye's); Buffalo's Franchise Concepts, Inc.; CISU, Inc.; Combustion Engineering, Inc.; Commerical Bank of Georgia; South Trust Bank of Georgia, N.A.; Hank Aaron Enterprises, Inc.; Venture Construction Company; Nursecare (Nursing Homes); Patients Pharmacies; Sobstad Corp.

For Complete List of Firm Personnel, See General Section

For full biographical listings, see the Martindale-Hubbell Law Directory

GLASS, MCCULLOUGH, SHERRILL & HARROLD (AV)

1409 Peachtree Street, N.E., 30309
Telephone: 404-885-1500
Telecopier: 404-892-1801
Buckhead Office: Monarch Plaza, 3414 Peachtree Road, N.E., Suite 450, Atlanta, Georgia, 30326-1162.
Telephone: 404-885-1500.
Telecopier: 404-231-1978.
Washington, D.C. Office: 1155 15th Street, N.W., Suite 400, Washington, D.C., 20005.
Telephone: 202-785-8118.
Telecopier: 202-785-0128.

T. Kennerly Carroll, Jr.
Ugo F. Ippolito
S. Andrew McKay

For Complete List of Firm Personnel, See General Section

For full biographical listings, see the Martindale-Hubbell Law Directory

GOMEL & DAVIS (AV)

812 Peachtree Center Harris Tower, 233 Peachtree Street, N.E., 30303-1506
Telephone: 404-223-5900
Telecopier: 404-524-4755

MEMBERS OF FIRM

Walter E. Gomel
Ronald J. Davis
Jed Steven Beardsley
Gregory A. Sanderson

ASSOCIATES

David L. Watson
Timothy R. Brown
Marie K. Evans

OF COUNSEL

Edward O. C. Ord (Not admitted in GA)
William K. Norman (Not admitted in GA)

References: Trust Company Bank; Merrill Lynch.

For full biographical listings, see the Martindale-Hubbell Law Directory

HARMAN, OWEN, SAUNDERS & SWEENEY, A PROFESSIONAL CORPORATION (AV)

1900 Peachtree Center Tower, 230 Peachtree Street, N.W., 30303
Telephone: 404-688-2600
Telecopier: 404-525-4347

H. Andrew Owen
Frederick F. Saunders, Jr.
Timothy J. Sweeney

For full biographical listings, see the Martindale-Hubbell Law Directory

HICKS, MALOOF & CAMPBELL, A PROFESSIONAL CORPORATION (AV)

Suite 2200 Marquis Two Tower, 285 Peachtree Center Avenue, 30303-1234
Telephone: 404-588-1100
Telecopy: 404-420-7474

Robert E. Hicks
Maurice Ted Maloof
Charles E. Campbell
Robert A. Bartlett
Charles E. Wilson, III
Robert E. Tritt
J. David Dantzler, Jr.
Steven K. Bender
Michael S. Bradley
Lisa W. Wannamaker

James E. Meadows
Edward D. Hirsch
James A. Harvey
Andrew M. Hepburn, Jr.
Karl J. Forrest

For full biographical listings, see the Martindale-Hubbell Law Directory

HISHON & BURBAGE (AV)

Suite 2000 Eleven Hundred Peachtree Building, 1100 Peachtree Street, 30309
Telephone: 404-898-9880
Telecopier: 404-898-9890

MEMBERS OF FIRM

Robert H. Hishon
Jesse S. Burbage, III
Bruce B. Weddell
R. Bradley Carr

ASSOCIATE

Mike Bothwell

OF COUNSEL

James G. Killough

For full biographical listings, see the Martindale-Hubbell Law Directory

HOLT, NEY, ZATCOFF & WASSERMAN (AV)

A Partnership including Professional Corporations
100 Galleria Parkway, Suite 600, 30339
Telephone: 404-956-9600
Facsimile Number: 404-956-1490

(See Next Column)

HOLT, NEY, ZATCOFF & WASSERMAN—*Continued*

MEMBERS OF FIRM

Robert G. Holt (P.C.)
Michael G. Wasserman (P.C.)
Charles D. Vaughn

Representative Clients: AmeriHealth, Inc.; Cummins South, Inc.; Georgia Scientific and Technical Research Foundation, Inc.; Hen Co., Inc. (Georgia); Trammell Crow Residential; Citicorp Real Estate, Inc.; The Vinings Club, Inc.; Sterling Trust.

For Complete List of Firm Personnel, See General Section

For full biographical listings, see the Martindale-Hubbell Law Directory

JOHNSON AND MONTGOMERY (AV)

One Buckhead Plaza, 3060 Peachtree Road, N.W., Suite 400, 30305
Telephone: 404-262-1000
Telecopier: 404-262-1222

MEMBERS OF FIRM

Thomas E. Jones, Jr.
William D. Montgomery
C. Talbot Nunnally, III

ASSOCIATE

Andrew Parks Kaiser

For full biographical listings, see the Martindale-Hubbell Law Directory

JOHNSON & WARD (AV)

2100 The Equitable Building, 100 Peachtree Street N.W., 30303-1962
Telephone: 404-524-5626
Facsimile: 404-524-1769

MEMBERS OF FIRM

John C. Dabney, Jr.
Baxter P. Jones
William D. deGolian

For full biographical listings, see the Martindale-Hubbell Law Directory

JAMES P. KELLY & ASSOCIATES, P.C. (AV)

200 Galleria Parkway, Suite 1510, 30339
Telephone: 404-955-2770
Telecopier: 404-859-0831

James P. Kelly
Robert E. DeWitt
H. Carol Saul

For full biographical listings, see the Martindale-Hubbell Law Directory

LAMBERTH, BONAPFEL, CIFELLI, WILLSON & STOKES, P.A. (AV)

Atlanta Financial Center, 3343 Peachtree Road, N.E. East Tower, Suite 550, 30326
Telephone: 404-262-7373

J. Michael Lamberth
Paul W. Bonapfel
James Craig Cifelli
Gary D. Stokes
William H. Willson, Jr.
Carter L. Stout

G. Frank Nason, IV
Donahue S. Silvis
Stuart F. Clayton, Jr.
A. Alexander Teel
Gregory D. Ellis
Sharon K. Kacmarcik

Reference: The Chattahoochee Bank.

For full biographical listings, see the Martindale-Hubbell Law Directory

LONG ALDRIDGE & NORMAN (AV)

A Partnership including Professional Corporations
One Peachtree Center, Suite 5300, 303 Peachtree Street, 30308
Telephone: 404-527-4000
Telecopier: 404-527-4198
Washington, D.C. Office: Suite 950, 1615 L Street, 20036.
Telephone: 202-223-7033.
Telecopier: 202-223-7013.

MEMBERS OF FIRM

Stephen L. Camp
David M. Ivey
F. T. Davis, Jr., (P.C.)
Clay C. Long
Jeffrey K. Haidet
Philip H. Moise
W. Stell Huie
Jesse J. Spikes

ASSOCIATES

Wayne N. Bradley
Roy E. Hadley, Jr.
Susan E. Dignan
H. Franklin Layson
Deborah Stone Grossman
Briggs L. Tobin

OF COUNSEL

William J. Carney
Martin R. Tilson, Jr.

For Complete List of Firm Personnel, See General Section

For full biographical listings, see the Martindale-Hubbell Law Directory

MOZLEY, FINLAYSON & LOGGINS (AV)

One Premier Plaza, Suite 900, 5605 Glenridge Drive, 30342
Telephone: 404-256-0700
Telecopier: 404-250-9355

MEMBERS OF FIRM

Robert M. Finlayson II
Sewell K. Loggins

For full biographical listings, see the Martindale-Hubbell Law Directory

PARKER, HUDSON, RAINER & DOBBS (AV)

1500 Marquis Two Tower, 285 Peachtree Center Avenue, N.E., 30303
Telephone: 404-523-5300
FAX: 404-522-8409
Tallahassee, Florida Office: The Perkins House, 118 North Gadsden Street, 32301.
Telephone: 904-681-0191.
FAX: 904-681-9493.

MEMBERS OF FIRM

Paul L. Hudson, Jr.
Mitchell M. Purvis

For full biographical listings, see the Martindale-Hubbell Law Directory

MORETON ROLLESTON, JR. (AV)

Suite 1870, Riverwood 100, 3350 Cumberland Circle, N.W., 30339
Telephone: 404-988-9300

Reference: Wachovia Bank of Georgia, Private Banking Department.

SCHULTEN & WARD (AV)

Suite 930 The Hurt Building, 50 Hurt Plaza, 30303
Telephone: 404-688-6800
Fax: 404-688-6840

MEMBERS OF FIRM

Wm. Scott Schulten
Kevin L. Ward

ASSOCIATES

David L. Turner
Susan Kastan Murphey
Erik V. Huey

Reference: NationsBank of Georgia, N.A.

For full biographical listings, see the Martindale-Hubbell Law Directory

LAW OFFICE OF THOMAS PATY STAMPS (AV)

314 Buckhead Avenue, 30305
Telephone: 404-364-9200
Telecopier: 404-364-9202

Reference: Trust Company Bank.

For full biographical listings, see the Martindale-Hubbell Law Directory

SUTHERLAND, ASBILL & BRENNAN (AV)

999 Peachtree Street, N.E., 30309-3996
Telephone: 404-853-8000
Facsimile: 404-853-8806
Washington, D.C. Office: 1275 Pennsylvania Avenue, N.W., 20004-2404.
Telephone: 202-383-0100.
New York, N.Y. Office: 1270 Avenue of the Americas, 10020-1700.
Telephone: 212-332-3000.
Austin, Texas Office: 111 Congress Avenue, 23rd Floor, 78701-4079.
Telephone: 512-469-3350.

F. Louise Adams
Thomas B. Hyman, Jr.
Reginald J. Clark
Edward W. Kallal, Jr.
George L. Cohen
Mark D. Kaufman
N. Jerold Cohen
Bennett Lexon Kight
Peter H. Dean
Cada T. Kilgore, III
B. Knox Dobbins
James R. Paulk, Jr.
Barrett K. Hawks
Herbert J. Short, Jr.
Thomas C. Herman
C. Christopher Trower
James H. Wilson, Jr.

COUNSEL OF THE FIRM
IN ATLANTA, GEORGIA

S. Elaine McChesney

For Complete List of Firm Personnel, See General Section

For full biographical listings, see the Martindale-Hubbell Law Directory

THRASHER, WHITLEY, HAMPTON & MORGAN, A PROFESSIONAL CORPORATION (AV)

Suite 2150, Five Concourse Parkway, 30328
Telephone: 404-804-8000
Telecopier: 404-804-5555

H. Grady Thrasher, III
Robert E. Whitley

Representative Clients: Georgia Dental Assn.; Kearney National, Inc.; Middle Bay Oil Company, Inc.; Nova Information Systems, Inc.; Perry & Co.; Smallwood, Reynold, Stewart, Stewart & Assoc., Inc.; Sunchase Holdings, Ltd.; Touch Industries, Inc.

For full biographical listings, see the Martindale-Hubbell Law Directory

Atlanta—Continued

WAGNER & JOHNSTON, P.C. (AV)

Suite 800, East Tower Atlanta Financial Center, 3343 Peachtree Road, N.E., 30326-1044
Telephone: 404-261-0500
Facsimile: 404-261-6779

Craig A. Wagner
C. David Johnston
Benjamin Cade Abney
Adam J. Conti

John R. Thornburgh

OF COUNSEL

Robert E. Altenbach

For full biographical listings, see the Martindale-Hubbell Law Directory

WEISZ & ASSOCIATES (AV)

Suite 900 Live Oak Center, 3475 Lenox Road, N.E., 30326-1232
Telephone: 404-233-7888
Facsimile: 404-261-1925

Peter R. Weisz

ASSOCIATE

Cathy Rae Nash

LEGAL SUPPORT PERSONNEL

PARALEGALS

Jo Anne Gunn

For full biographical listings, see the Martindale-Hubbell Law Directory

*AUGUSTA,** Richmond Co.

HULL, TOWILL, NORMAN & BARRETT, A PROFESSIONAL CORPORATION (AV)

Seventh Floor, Trust Company Bank Building, P.O. Box 1564, 30903-1564
Telephone: 706-722-4481
Fax: 706-722-9779

James M. Hull (1885-1975)
George B. Barrett (1894-1942)
Julian J. Willingham (1887-1963)
John Bell Towill (1907-1991)
Robert C. Norman (Retired, 1991)
W. Hale Barrett
Lawton Jordan, Jr.
Patrick J. Rice
Douglas D. Batchelor, Jr.
David E. Hudson
Neal W. Dickert
John W. Gibson
William F. Hammond
Mark S. Burgreen
George R. Hall
James B. Ellington
F. Michael Taylor

Robert A. Mullins
William J. Keogh, III
Edward J. Tarver
J. Noel Schweers, III
Michael S. Carlson
Ralph Emerson Hanna, III
Susan D. Barrett
Timothy Moses

Counsel for: Trust Company Bank of Augusta, N.A.; Georgia Federal Bank, FSB, Augusta Division; Southeastern Newspapers Corp.; Georgia Power Co.; Southern Bell Telephone & Telegraph Co.; St. Joseph Hospital, Augusta, Georgia, Inc.; Norfolk Southern Corp.; Merry Land & Investment Co., Inc.; Housing Authority of the City of Augusta; Georgia Press Association.

For full biographical listings, see the Martindale-Hubbell Law Directory

*CARROLLTON,** Carroll Co.

TISINGER, TISINGER, VANCE & GREER, A PROFESSIONAL CORPORATION (AV)

100 Wagon Yard Plaza, P.O. Box 2069, 30117
Telephone: 404-834-4467
FAX: 404-834-5426

Richard G. Tisinger
J. Thomas Vance
C. David Mecklin, Jr.
G. Gregory Shadrix
Stacey L. Blackmon
Steven T. Minor
Edith Freeman Rooks

Representative Clients: Carrollton Federal Bank-Federal Savings Bank; Pinnacle Financial Group, Inc.; Richards & Malloy Manufacturing, Inc.; Southwire Company; Tanner Medical Center, Inc.

For Complete List of Firm Personnel, See General Section

For full biographical listings, see the Martindale-Hubbell Law Directory

*DECATUR,** De Kalb Co.

SIMMONS, WARREN & SZCZECKO, PROFESSIONAL ASSOCIATION (AV)

315 West Ponce de Leon Avenue, Suite 850, 30030
Telephone: 404-378-1711
Fax: 404-377-6101

(See Next Column)

Wesley B. Warren, Jr.
William C. McFee, Jr.

Representative Clients: David Hocker & Associates (Shopping Center Development); Julian LeCraw & Company (Real Estate); Royal Oldsmobile,; Cotter & Co.; Atlanta Neurosurgical Associates, P.A.; Villager Lodge, Inc.; Troncalli Motors, Inc.

For Complete List of Firm Personnel, See General Section

For full biographical listings, see the Martindale-Hubbell Law Directory

*GRIFFIN,** Spalding Co.

JOHN M. COGBURN, JR. (AV)

115 North Sixth Street, P.O. Box 907, 30224
Telephone: 404-228-2148
Telecopier: 404-228-5018
McDonough, Georgia Office: Suite 300E, First Community Bank Building, 12 North Cedar Street.
Telephone: 404-954-9004.
Fax: 404-228-5018.

ASSOCIATE

R. Michelle Denton

Representative Clients: Griffin-Spalding County Hospital Authority; Allstar Knitwear Co., Inc. (Textiles); Atlanta Tees, Inc. (Sportswear Distribution); Industrial Refrigeration Enterprises, Inc. (Refrigeration Engineers and Contractors); Spauchus Associates, Inc. (Chemical Engineering Consultants).

For full biographical listings, see the Martindale-Hubbell Law Directory

*LAWRENCEVILLE,** Gwinnett Co.

ANDERSEN, DAVIDSON & TATE, P.C. (AV)

324 West Pike Street, Suite 200, P.O. Box 265, 30246-0265
Telephone: 404-822-0900
Telecopier: 404-822-9680

Thomas J. Andersen
Jeffrey R. Mahaffey

William M. Ray, II

References: Trust Company Bank; The Bank of Gwinnett County; Chicago Title Insurance Co.; Title Insurance Company of Minnesota.

For Complete List of Firm Personnel, See General Section

For full biographical listings, see the Martindale-Hubbell Law Directory

WEBB, TANNER & POWELL (AV)

Suite 300 Gwinnett Federal Building, 750 South Perry Street, P.O. Box 27, 30246
Telephone: 404-962-8545; 963-3423
Fax: 404-963-3424

MEMBERS OF FIRM

Jones Webb
William G. Tanner
Anthony O. L. Powell

Attorneys for: Gwinnett Federal Savings & Loan Assn.; City of Lawrenceville, Ga.; Water and Sewer Authority of Gwinnett County; Federal Land Bank of Columbia; Georgia Power Co.; Lawyers Title Insurance Corp.; Young Harris College, Young Harris, Georgia; Chicago Title Insurance Co.

For Complete List of Firm Personnel, See General Section

For full biographical listings, see the Martindale-Hubbell Law Directory

*MACON,** Bibb Co.

HALL, BLOCH, GARLAND & MEYER (AV)

1500 Charter Medical Building, P.O. Box 5088, 31213-3199
Telephone: 912-745-1625
Telecopier: 912-741-8822

MEMBERS OF FIRM

Benjamin M. Garland
J. Steven Stewart
Duncan D. Walker, III
Mark E. Toth

Counsel for: Wachovia Bank of Georgia, N.A.; Charter Medical Corporation; South Georgia Natural Gas Co.; Helena Chemical Corp.; American Druggist Insurance Cop.; Fickling & Walker Asset and Property Management, Inc.; Navistar International Corporation.

For Complete List of Firm Personnel, See General Section

For full biographical listings, see the Martindale-Hubbell Law Directory

SELL & MELTON (AV)

A Partnership including a Professional Corporation
14th Floor, Charter Medical Building, P.O. Box 229, 31297-2899
Telephone: 912-746-8521
Telecopier: 912-745-6426

(See Next Column)

SELL & MELTON—*Continued*

E. S. Sell, Jr. Joseph W. Popper, Jr.
Buckner F. Melton Brian J. Passante

General Counsel for: Macon Telegraph Publishing Co. (The Macon Telegraph); Macon-Bibb County Hospital Authority; County of Bibb; County of Twiggs; Smith & Sons Foods, Inc. (S & S Cafeterias); Macon Bibb County Industrial Authority; Burgess Pigment Co.

For Complete List of Firm Personnel, See General Section

For full biographical listings, see the Martindale-Hubbell Law Directory

*MARIETTA,** Cobb Co.

W. R. ROBERTSON, III (AV)

244 Roswell Street, Suite 600, 30060-2000
Telephone: 404-422-0200
Fax: 404-424-1322

For full biographical listings, see the Martindale-Hubbell Law Directory

*NEWNAN,** Coweta Co.

GLOVER & DAVIS, P.A. (AV)

10 Brown Street, P.O. Box 1038, 30264
Telephone: 404-253-4330;
Atlanta: 404-463-1100
Fax: 404-251-7152
Peachtree City, Georgia Office: Suite 130, 200 Westpark Drive.
Telephone: 404-487-5834.
Fax: 404-487-3492.

J. Littleton Glover, Jr. Alan W. Jackson

Representative Clients: Newnan Savings Bank; Pike Transfer Co.; Batson-Cook Company, General Corporate and Construction Divisions; Coweta County, Georgia; Book Warehouse of Georgia, Inc.; Bailey & Associates; J. Smith.
Local Counsel for: International Latex Corp.; First Union National Bank of Georgia; Lanler & Co.

For Complete List of Firm Personnel, See General Section

For full biographical listings, see the Martindale-Hubbell Law Directory

HAWAII

*HONOLULU,** Honolulu Co.

DAVID F. DAY (AV)

Amfac Center, Hawaii Building, Suite 1840, 745 Fort Street, 96813
Telephone: 808-531-8020
Fax: 808-521-0962

For full biographical listings, see the Martindale-Hubbell Law Directory

FOLEY MAEHARA NIP & CHANG (AV)

2700 Grosvenor Center, 737 Bishop Street, 96813
Telephone: 808-526-3011
Telecopier: 808-523-1171, 808-526-0121, 808-533-4814

MEMBERS OF FIRM

Thomas M. Foley Edward R. Brooks
Eric T. Maehara Arlene S. Kishi
Renton L. K. Nip Susan M. Ichinose
Wesley Y. S. Chang Robert F. Miller
Carl Tom Christian P. Porter

ASSOCIATES

Paula W. Chong Jordan D. Wagner
Lenore H. Lee Donna H. Yamamoto
Leanne A. N. Nikaido Mark J. Bernardin
Jenny K. T. Wakayama

OF COUNSEL

Elizabeth A. Ivey

References: First Hawaiian Bank; Bank of Honolulu; Bank of Hawaii.

For full biographical listings, see the Martindale-Hubbell Law Directory

KOBAYASHI, SUGITA & GODA (AV)

A Partnership including Professional Corporations
8th Floor, Hawaii Tower, 745 Fort Street, 96813
Telephone: 808-539-8700
Telecopier: 808-539-8799
Telex: 6502396585 MCI
MCI Mail: 23 96585
ABA/Net: ABA2281

(See Next Column)

OF COUNSEL

Bert T. Kobayashi, Sr.

Reference: First Hawaiian Bank.

For Complete List of Firm Personnel, See General Section

For full biographical listings, see the Martindale-Hubbell Law Directory

MCCORRISTON MIHO MILLER MUKAI (AV)

Five Waterfront Plaza, 4th Floor, 500 Ala Moana Boulevard, 96813
Telephone: 808-529-7300
Facsimile: 808-524-8293
Cable: Attorneys, Honolulu

MEMBERS OF FIRM

Jon T. Miho David N. Kuriyama
Clifford J. Miller Eric T. Kawatani
Franklin K. Mukai Keith K. Suzuka
Calvert G. Chipchase, III Randal Keiji Nagatani

ASSOCIATES

Andrew W. Char Randall F. Sakumoto
Alexander R. Jampel

OF COUNSEL

Stanley Y. Mukai

For Complete List of Firm Personnel, See General Section

For full biographical listings, see the Martindale-Hubbell Law Directory

PITLUCK & KIDO (AV)

701 Bishop Street, 96813
Telephone: 808-523-5030
Telecopier: 808-545-4015

MEMBERS OF FIRM

Wayne Marshall Pitluck Alan Takashi Kido
Dana Kiyomi Nalani Sato

James Mauliola Keaka Stone, Jr. Margaret Ann Leong

Reference: Bank of Hawaii.

For full biographical listings, see the Martindale-Hubbell Law Directory

IDAHO

*BOISE,** Ada Co.

ROSHOLT, ROBERTSON & TUCKER, CHARTERED (AV)

Suite 600, 1221 W. Idaho, P.O. Box 2139, 83701-2139
Telephone: 208-336-0700
Fax: 208-344-6034
Twin Falls, Idaho Office: 142 Third Avenue North, P.O. Box 1906.
Telephone: 208-734-0700.
Fax: 208-736-0041.

James C. Tucker

Jerry Jensen Patrick D. Madigan
Paul W. Samuelson

For full biographical listings, see the Martindale-Hubbell Law Directory

*POCATELLO,** Bannock Co.

MERRILL & MERRILL, CHARTERED (AV)

Key Bank Building, P.O. Box 991, 83204
Telephone: 208-232-2286
Fax: 208-232-2499

Wesley F. Merrill Dave R. Gallafent
N. Randy Smith

Representative Clients: Idaho Central Credit Union; West One Bank of Idaho; J.R. Simplot Co.; School District #25, Bannock County, Idaho; First American Title Co.; Pocatello Dental Group, P.L.L.C.; Jackson State Bank; Eastern Idaho Development Corp.; American Land Title Co.

For Complete List of Firm Personnel, See General Section

For full biographical listings, see the Martindale-Hubbell Law Directory

*TWIN FALLS,** Twin Falls Co.

ROSHOLT, ROBERTSON & TUCKER, CHARTERED (AV)

142 Third Avenue North, P.O. Box 1906, 83303-1906
Telephone: 208-734-0700
Fax: 208-736-0041
Boise, Idaho Office: Suite 600, 1221 W. Idaho, P.O. Box 2139.
Telephone: 208-336-0700.
Fax: 208-344-6034.

(See Next Column)

ROSHOLT, ROBERTSON & TUCKER CHARTERED, *Twin Falls—Continued*

John A. Rosholt
J. Evan Robertson
Gary D. Slette

Thomas J. Ryan

For full biographical listings, see the Martindale-Hubbell Law Directory

ILLINOIS

*CHICAGO,** Cook Co.

BOWLES, KEATING, HERING & LOWE, CHARTERED (AV)

135 South La Salle Street, Suite 1040, 60603-4295
Telephone: 312-263-6300
Fax: 312-263-0415
Italy Office: 10, Via Pietro Verri, 20121 Milan, Italy.
Telephone: 2-798609.
Fax: 276001473.
European Associated Offices:
Italy Office: Studio Legale Ippolito, viale Astichello, 6, 36100 Vicenza, Italy.
Telephone: 444-300957.
Fax: 444-300827..
Sweden Office: Advokatgruppen i Stockholm AB, Kommendorsgatan 26,114 48 Stockholm, Sweden.
Telephone: 8-667-0765.
Fax: 8-660-9827.
France Office: Allain - Kaltenbach - Plaisant - Raimon, 14 Rue Lejemptel, 94302 Vincennes (Paris), France.
Telephone: 1-4374 7494.
Fax: 1-4374 3222.
Asian Cooperative Offices:
China Offices: Liaoning Law Office For Foreign Affairs, 11 Liaohe Street, Shenyang Liaoning 110032, China.
Telephone: 652125.
Telex: 808305 LCPIT CN.
FAX: (24) 664791. Dalian Foreign Economic Law Office: No. 2 S. Square, Dalian, Liaoning, China.
Telephone: 332532.
FAX: 332532. Shenyang Foreign Economic Law Office, 230-3, Quingnian Street, Shenhe District, Shenyang Liaoning 110014, China.
Telephone: 290123.

Clyde O. Bowles, Jr. (Chicago Office)
Mario Bruno
Roberto N. Bruno
Nicola Fiordalisi (Chicago Office)
Glenn Z. Hering (Chicago Office)
Kathryn R. Ingrim (Chicago Office)
Christopher L. Ingrim (Chicago Office)
Thomas M. Keating (Chicago Office)
Jung Y. Lowe (Chicago Office)
Lynne R. Ostfeld (Chicago Office)
Arnold A. Silvestri (Chicago Office)

COUNSEL

Malcolm A. Chandler (Chicago Office)

For full biographical listings, see the Martindale-Hubbell Law Directory

COWEN, CROWLEY & NORD, P.C. (AV)

Xerox Centre, 55 West Monroe Street, Suite 500, 60603
Telephone: 312-641-0060
Fax: 312-641-6959

Richard A. Cowen
Wilbert F. Crowley, Jr.
Donald C. Nord

For full biographical listings, see the Martindale-Hubbell Law Directory

GORDON & EINSTEIN, LTD. (AV)

224 East Ontario, 60611
Telephone: 312-280-7766
Telecopier: 312-280-9599

Raymond P. Gordon
Jean M. Einstein

LEGAL SUPPORT PERSONNEL

Laura A. Kozicki

For full biographical listings, see the Martindale-Hubbell Law Directory

GORDON & GLICKSON, P.C. (AV)

36th Floor, 444 North Michigan Avenue, 60611-3903
Telephone: 312-321-1700
FAX: 312-321-9324
Springfield, Illinois Office: 600 South Second Street.
Telephone: 217-789-1040.
FAX: 217-789-1077.

(See Next Column)

Richard L. Fogel
Scott L. Glickson
Mark L. Gordon
Michael E.C. Moss

For full biographical listings, see the Martindale-Hubbell Law Directory

ARAM A. HARTUNIAN AND ASSOCIATES (AV)

122 South Michigan Avenue, Suite 1850, 60603
Telephone: 312: 427-3600
FAX: 312-427-1850

Aram A. Hartunian

ASSOCIATE

Steven Paul Schneck

For full biographical listings, see the Martindale-Hubbell Law Directory

HOWARD GORDON KAPLAN, LTD. (AV)

180 North La Salle Street, 28th Floor, 60601
Telephone: 312-641-2555
Facsimile No.: 312-641-6265
Telex No.: 5101010213

Howard Gordon Kaplan

Leonard J. Brenner
Earl L. Simon
Rhonda D. Kaplan-Katz
Michael J. Kerschner

For full biographical listings, see the Martindale-Hubbell Law Directory

THE LAW OFFICES OF MARC J. LANE A PROFESSIONAL CORPORATION (AV)

Suite 2100 180 North La Salle Street, 60601-2701
Telephone: 312-372-1040
Fax: 312-346-1040

Marc J. Lane

Gregory A. Papiernik

For full biographical listings, see the Martindale-Hubbell Law Directory

McBRIDE BAKER & COLES (AV)

500 West Madison Street 40th Floor, 60661
Telephone: 312-715-5700
Cable Address: "Chilaw"
Telex: 270258
Telecopier: 312-993-9350

MEMBERS OF FIRM

David Ackerman
Michael J. Boland
Martin J. Campanella
William J. Cooney
Lola Miranda Hale
Thomas J. Kinasz
Evan M. Kjellenberg
Sidney C. Kleinman
David S. Mann
Morgan J. Ordman
Elizabeth S. Perdue
G. Gale Roberson, Jr.
Anne Hamblin Schiave
Robert I. Schwimmer
Thomas J. Smedinghoff
Michael L. Weissman

OF COUNSEL

Robert O. Case
Lawrence A. Coles, Jr.

ASSOCIATE

Jerald Holisky

For Complete List of Firm Personnel, See General Section

For full biographical listings, see the Martindale-Hubbell Law Directory

PRETZEL & STOUFFER, CHARTERED (AV)

One South Wacker Drive Suite 2500, 60606-4673
Telephone: 312-346-1973
FAX: 312-346-8242; 346-8060

Richard William Austin
Glen R. Bernfield
Michael G. Bruton
Neil K. Quinn
Lewis M. Schneider
Robert D. Tuerk

Representative Clients: Allstate Insurance Co.; St. Paul Insurance Companies.

For Complete List of Firm Personnel, See General Section

For full biographical listings, see the Martindale-Hubbell Law Directory

WILDMAN, HARROLD, ALLEN & DIXON (AV)

225 West Wacker Drive, 30th Floor, 60606-1229
Telephone: 312-201-2000
Cable Address: "Whad"
Fax: 312-201-2555
Aurora, Illinois Office: 1851 W. Galena Boulevard, Suite 210.
Telephone: 708-892-7021.
Fax: 708-892-7158.
Waukegan, Illinois Office: 404 West Water, P. O. Box 890.
Telephone: 708-623-0700.
Fax: 708-244-5273.
Lisle, Illinois Office: 4300 Commerce Court.
Telephone: 708-955-0555.
Libertyville, Illinois Office: 611 South Milwaukee Avenue.
Telephone: 708-680-3030.

(See Next Column)

WILDMAN, HARROLD, ALLEN & DIXON—*Continued*

New York, New York Office: Wildman, Harrold, Allen, Dixon & Smith. The International Building, 45 Rockefeller Plaza, Suite 353.
Telephone: 212-632-3850.
Fax: 212-632-3858.
Toronto, Ontario affiliated Office: Keel Cottrelle. 36 Toronto Street, Ninth Floor, Suite 920.
Telephone: 416-367-2900.
Telefax: 416-367-2791.
Telex: 062-18660.
Mississauga, Ontario affiliated Office: Keel Cottrelle. 100 Matatson Avenue East, Suite 104.
Telephone: 416-890-7700.
Fax: 416-890-8006.

MEMBERS OF FIRM

Paul S. Chervin (Waukegan and Libertyville Offices)
Stewart S. Dixon
Thomas P. Duffy
John L. Eisel
Jerald P. Esrick
Roger G. Fein
Donald E. Figliulo
David J. Fischer
Mark W. Hianik
Young Kim
R. Henry Kleeman
John E. McGovern, Jr.
Sheldon P. Migdal
George S. Rosic
Alan B. Roth

COUNSEL

Howard Arvey
Marshall L. Burman

Kathryn S. Bedward
Troy M. Brethauer
Ira S. Friedrich
Cheryl A. Kettler
Brad L. Peterson

For Complete List of Firm Personnel, See General Section

For full biographical listings, see the Martindale-Hubbell Law Directory

*DECATUR,** Macon Co.

TENNEY & TENNEY (AV)

1264 First of America Center, P.O. Box 355, 62525
Telephone: 217-423-1800
Fax: 217-423-0524

MEMBERS OF FIRM

Harold F. Tenney
Carl J. Tenney

Representative Client: The Travelers Insurance Companies: Design Professional Insurance Company (DPIC Companies); Shelter Insurance Companies; Right Recreation, Inc.; Lucas Meyer, Inc. (lecithin products); Miles Chevrolet, Inc.; Crown Oldsmobile-Toyota, Inc.; Bob Brady Dodge, Inc.; Sims Lumber Company; Heinkel's Packing Co., Inc.

For full biographical listings, see the Martindale-Hubbell Law Directory

*PEORIA,** Peoria Co.

BEHRENDS & GENTRY (AV)

700 River Valley Plaza, 331 Fulton Street, 61602
Telephone: 309-676-0475
Telecopier: 309-676-0126

F. Louis Behrends
Richard N. Gentry, Jr.

Frank A. Hess
L. Paige Miller

For full biographical listings, see the Martindale-Hubbell Law Directory

INDIANA

*BLOOMINGTON,** Monroe Co.

BUNGER & ROBERTSON (AV)

226 South College Square, P.O. Box 910, 47402-0910
Telephone: 812-332-9295
Fax: 812-331-8808

MEMBERS OF FIRM

Len E. Bunger, Jr. (1921-1993)
Don M. Robertson
James L. Whitlatch

OF COUNSEL

Philip C. Hill

Representative Clients: Aetna Insurance Companies; Bloomington Hospital; Commercial Union Group; Indiana Insurance Co.; Liberty Mutual Insurance; Medical Protective Co.; Monroe County Community School Corp.; Professional Golf Car, Inc.; Prudential Insurance Company of America; State Farm Automobile Insurance Co.

For Complete List of Firm Personnel, See General Section

For full biographical listings, see the Martindale-Hubbell Law Directory

CARMEL, Hamilton Co.

KNOWLES & ASSOCIATES (AV)

811 South Range Line Road, 46032
Telephone: 317-848-4360
Telecopier: 317-848-4363

William W. Knowles

Pamela Y. Rhine
D. Brandon Johnston

For full biographical listings, see the Martindale-Hubbell Law Directory

ELKHART, Elkhart Co.

CHESTER, PFAFF & BROTHERSON (AV)

317 West Franklin Street, P.O. Box 507, 46515-0507
Telephone: 219-294-5421
Telecopier: 219-522-1476

MEMBERS OF FIRM

Robert A. Pfaff
James R. Brotherson
Glenn E. Killoren

For Complete List of Firm Personnel, See General Section

For full biographical listings, see the Martindale-Hubbell Law Directory

*EVANSVILLE,** Vanderburgh Co.

BOWERS, HARRISON, KENT & MILLER (AV)

25 N.W. Riverside Drive, P.O. Box 1287, 47706-1287
Telephone: 812-426-1231
Fax: 812-464-3676

MEMBERS OF FIRM

David V. Miller
George C. Barnett, Jr.

Division Counsel in Indiana for: Southern Railway Co.
District Attorneys for the Southern District of Indiana: CSX Transportation, Inc.
Representative Clients: Permanent Federal Savings Bank; Citizens Realty & Insurance, Inc.

For Complete List of Firm Personnel, See General Section

For full biographical listings, see the Martindale-Hubbell Law Directory

LAW OFFICES OF RANDALL K. CRAIG (AV)

Reed Building Suite 5, 2709 Washington Avenue, 47714
Telephone: 812-477-3337
Telefax: 812-477-3658

For full biographical listings, see the Martindale-Hubbell Law Directory

FINE & HATFIELD (AV)

520 N.W. Second Street, P.O. Box 779, 47705-0779
Telephone: 812-425-3592
Telecopier: 812-421-4269

MEMBERS OF FIRM

James E. Marchand
Thomas R. Fitzsimmons
Stephen S. Lavallo

ASSOCIATE

Shannon Scholz Frank

For Complete List of Firm Personnel, See General Section

For full biographical listings, see the Martindale-Hubbell Law Directory

ZIEMER, STAYMAN, WEITZEL & SHOULDERS (AV)

(Formerly Early, Arnold & Ziemer)
1507 Old National Bank Building, P.O. Box 916, 47706
Telephone: 812-424-7575
Telecopier: 812-421-5089

MEMBERS OF FIRM

Stephan E. Weitzel
Marco L. DeLucio

Reference: Old National Bank in Evansville.

For full biographical listings, see the Martindale-Hubbell Law Directory

*INDIANAPOLIS,** Marion Co.

DUTTON OVERMAN GOLDSTEIN PINKUS, A PROFESSIONAL CORPORATION (AV)

710 Century Building, 36 South Pennsylvania Street, 46204
Telephone: 317-633-4000
Telecopier: 317-633-1494

C. B. Dutton
Carl D. Overman

(See Next Column)

DUTTON OVERMAN GOLDSTEIN PINKUS A PROFESSIONAL CORPORATION, *Indianapolis—Continued*

Diane Hubbard Kennedy D. Bryan Weese

Representative Clients: Central Supply Co., Inc.; Huber, Hunt & Nichols, Inc.; The Hunt Paving Co., Inc.; Laughner Brothers, Inc.; The Howard E. Nyhart Co., Inc.; Starkes Tarzian, Inc.; The Dalton Foundries, Inc.; Central Indiana Hardware Co., Inc.; MCM Enterprises, Inc.; Fink, Roberts & Petrie, Inc.

For full biographical listings, see the Martindale-Hubbell Law Directory

GOODIN & KRAEGE (AV)

8888 Keystone Crossing Suite 820, 46240-4616
Telephone: 317-843-2606
FAX: 317-574-3095

James A. Goodin
Richard C. Kraege
Jon C. Abernathy
Amy Loraine White
Patrick L. Miller
James W. Johnson, III

OF COUNSEL

Wilson S. Stober

Representative Clients: Allstate Insurance Companies; American National Property and Casualty Co.; Bituminous Insurance Company; Builder's Square; Commercial Union Insurance Companies; Continental Loss Adjusting Service; Construction Associates, Inc.; Continental Western Insurance Company; Economy Fire & Casualty; General Casualty Companies.

For full biographical listings, see the Martindale-Hubbell Law Directory

JOHNSON, HALL AND LAWHEAD, PROFESSIONAL CORPORATION (AV)

Suite 940, 8900 Keystone Crossing, 46240-2162
Telephone: 317-848-5808
FAX: 317-574-3429

G. Weldon Johnson
Richard M. Hall
Lawrence E. Lawhead

Gregory L. Padgett
Annette T. Brogden

For full biographical listings, see the Martindale-Hubbell Law Directory

KATZMAN KATZMAN & PYLITT, A PROFESSIONAL CORPORATION (AV)

3905 Vincennes Road, Suite 100, 46268
Telephone: 317-872-5700
Telecopier: 317-872-5769

Alvin J. Katzman
Mariellen Katzman
Bernard L. Pylitt

Jeffrey A. Hearn

OF COUNSEL

Daniel B. Altman

A list of representative clients will be furnished upon request.

For full biographical listings, see the Martindale-Hubbell Law Directory

KROGER, GARDIS & REGAS (AV)

111 Monument Circle, Suite 900, 46204-3059
Telephone: 317-692-9000
Telecopier: 317-264-6832

MEMBERS OF FIRM

James A. Knauer
Jay P. Kennedy
Brian C. Bosma

ASSOCIATES

Gregory P. Cafouros
William Bock, III

Representative Clients: Waffle House; Kova Fertilizer, Inc.

For full biographical listings, see the Martindale-Hubbell Law Directory

MILLER MULLER MENDELSON & KENNEDY (AV)

8900 Keystone Crossing Suite 1250, 46240
Telephone: 317-574-4500
1-800-394-3094
Fax: 317-574-4501

MEMBER OF FIRM

Tilden Mendelson

For full biographical listings, see the Martindale-Hubbell Law Directory

MITCHELL HURST JACOBS & DICK (AV)

152 East Washington Street, 46204
Telephone: 317-636-0808
1-800-636-0808
Fax: 317-633-7680

(See Next Column)

MEMBERS OF FIRM

Marvin H. Mitchell
William W. Hurst
Samuel L. Jacobs
Richard J. Dick
Marshall S. Hanley
Steven K. Huffer
Robert W. Strohmeyer, Jr.

ASSOCIATES

Danielle A. Takla
John M. Reames
Michael T. McNelis
Michael P. Kilkenny

LEGAL SUPPORT PERSONNEL

L. Kathleen Hughes Brown, R.N.

General Counsel for: Premium Optical Co.; Calderon Bros. Vending Machines, Inc.; Grocers Supply Co., Inc.; Power Train Services, Inc.; Frank E. Irish, Inc.; Bedding Liquidators; Galyan's Trading Co.; Harcourt Management Co., Inc.; Kosene & Kosene Mgt. & Dev. Co., Inc.; Hasten Bancorp.

For full biographical listings, see the Martindale-Hubbell Law Directory

SOMMER & BARNARD, ATTORNEYS AT LAW, PC (AV)

4000 Bank One Tower, 111 Monument Circle, P.O. Box 44363, 46244-0363
Telephone: 317-630-4000
FAX: 317-236-9802
North Office: 8900 Keystone Crossing, Suite 1046, Indianapolis, Indiana, 46240-2134.
Telephone: 317-630-4000.
FAX: 317-844-4780.

James K. Sommer
Eric R. Johnson
Julianne S. Lis-Milam
Robert J. Hicks

Thomas R. DeVoe

OF COUNSEL

Glenn Scolnik
Philip L. McCool
Charles E. Valliere

Representative Clients: Comerica Bank; Excel Industries; Federal Express; Kimball International; Monsanto; Renault Automation; Repport International; TRW, Inc.

For Complete List of Firm Personnel, See General Section

For full biographical listings, see the Martindale-Hubbell Law Directory

MUNSTER, Lake Co.

PINKERTON AND FRIEDMAN, PROFESSIONAL CORPORATION (AV)

The Fairmont, 9245 Calumet Avenue Suite 201, 46321
Telephone: 219-836-3050
Fax: 219-836-2955

Kirk A. Pinkerton
Stuart J. Friedman
Jeffrey F. Gunning
Gail Oosterhof

For full biographical listings, see the Martindale-Hubbell Law Directory

*SOUTH BEND,** St. Joseph Co.

DIAMOND AND DIAMOND (AV)

405 West Wayne Street, P.O. Box 1875, 46634-1875
Telephone: 219-232-6918

Arthur M. Diamond
Eric L. Diamond
Jeffrey M. Jankowski

Representative Clients: Creed Excavating Co., Inc.; Eslinger Furniture & Appliances, Inc.; Ideal Consolidated, Inc.; International Bakers Service, Inc.; Lithotone Inc.; Louie's Tux Shop, Inc.; Portage Realty Corp.; Radiology, Inc.; Van Overberghe Builders, Inc.
References: Norwest Bank Indiana, N.A., South Bend.

For full biographical listings, see the Martindale-Hubbell Law Directory

*WARSAW,** Kosciusko Co.

ROCKHILL, PINNICK, PEQUIGNOT, HELM & LANDIS (AV)

105 East Main Street, 46580-2742
Telephone: 219-267-6116
Telecopier: 219-269-9264

MEMBERS OF FIRM

Brooks C. Pinnick
Stanley E. Pequignot
Richard K. Helm
Vern K. Landis
Jay A. Rigdon
Jeanne A. Rondot

ASSOCIATE

Jamelyn E. Casbon

OF COUNSEL

Alvin T. Rockhill

Representative Clients: First National Bank of Warsaw, Warsaw, Indiana; Warsaw Times-Union Newspaper and WRSW Radio and Broadcast Station; State Farm Insurance Cos.; Warsaw Chemical Co., Inc.; Little Crow Milling Co., Inc.; Farmers State Bank; C & D Foods, Inc.; Maple Leaf Farms, Inc.; United Farm Bureau Mutual Insurance Co.

For full biographical listings, see the Martindale-Hubbell Law Directory

IOWA

*COUNCIL BLUFFS,** Pottawattamie Co.

Smith Peterson Law Firm (AV)
35 Main Place, Suite 300, P.O. Box 249, 51502
Telephone: 712-328-1833
Fax: 712-328-8320
Omaha, Nebraska Office: 9290 West Dodge Road, Suite 205.
Telephone: 402-397-8500.
Fax: 402-397-5519.

MEMBERS OF FIRM

Raymond A. Smith (1892-1977)
John LeRoy Peterson (1895-1969)
Harold T. Beckman
Robert J. Laubenthal
Richard A. Heininger
Lawrence J. Beckman
Gregory G. Barntsen
W. Curtis Hewett
Steven H. Krohn
Randy R. Ewing
Joseph D. Thornton

ASSOCIATES

Trent D. Reinert (Not admitted in IA)
T. J. Pattermann

Representative Clients: Aetna Life and Casualty Co.; Employers Mutual Co.; First National Bank of Council Bluffs; IMT Insurance Co.; Monsanto Co.; United Fire & Casualty Co.; U.S. Fidelity and Guaranty.

For full biographical listings, see the Martindale-Hubbell Law Directory

*DES MOINES,** Polk Co.

Roxanne B. Conlin and Associates, P.C. (AV)
The Plaza, 300 Walnut Street - Suite 5, 50309-2239
Telephone: 515-282-3333
Fax: 515-282-0318

Roxanne B. Conlin

For full biographical listings, see the Martindale-Hubbell Law Directory

Finley, Alt, Smith, Scharnberg, May & Craig, P.C. (AV)
Fourth Floor Equitable Building, 50309
Telephone: 515-288-0145
Telecopier: 515-288-2724

Glenn L. Smith
David C. Craig

Representative Clients: Aetna Casualty & Surety Co.; Aetna Life Insurance Co.; ALAS; American Society of Composers, Authors and Publishers; Equitable Life Assurance Society of the U.S.; Federated Insurance Co.; Meredith Corp.
Iowa Attorneys for: Midwest Medical Insurance Co.
District Attorneys for: Norfolk & Southern Railroad; CP Rail Systems.

For Complete List of Firm Personnel, See General Section

For full biographical listings, see the Martindale-Hubbell Law Directory

The Rosenberg Law Firm (AV)
1010 Insurance Exchange Building, 505 Fifth Avenue, 50309
Telephone: 515-243-7600

MEMBERS OF FIRM

Raymond Rosenberg
Paul H. Rosenberg

ASSOCIATES

Dean A. Stowers
Brent D. Rosenberg

Reference: Firstar Bank, Des Moines, Iowa.

For full biographical listings, see the Martindale-Hubbell Law Directory

*WATERLOO,** Black Hawk Co.

Swisher & Cohrt (AV)
528 West Fourth Street, P.O. Box 1200, 50704
Telephone: 319-232-6555
FAX: 319-232-4835

MEMBERS OF FIRM

Benjamin F. Swisher (1878-1959)
L. J. Cohrt (1898-1974)
Charles F. Swisher (1919-1986)
Eldon R. McCann
Steven A. Weidner
Larry J. Cohrt
J. Douglas Oberman
Stephen J. Powell
Jim D. DeKoster
Jeffrey J. Greenwood
Samuel C. Anderson
Robert C. Griffin
Kevin R. Rogers

ASSOCIATES

Beth E. Hansen
Mark F. Conway
Natalie Williams Burr

Firm is Counsel for: Koehring Corp.; Clay Equipment; Chamberlain Manufacturing Co.; Waterloo Courier.

(See Next Column)

Local Counsel for: Allied Group; John Deere Insurance; Liberty Mutual Insurance Co.

For full biographical listings, see the Martindale-Hubbell Law Directory

KANSAS

PRAIRIE VILLAGE, Johnson Co.

Holman, McCollum & Hansen, P.C. (AVⓉ)
9400 Mission Road Suite 205, 66206
Telephone: 913-648-7272
Fax: 913-383-9596
Kansas City, Missouri Office: 644 West 57th Terrace.
Telephone: 816-333-8522.
Fax: 913-383-9596.

Joseph Y. Holman
Frank B. W. McCollum
Eric L. Hansen
Dana L. Parks
Nancy Merrill Wilson
Amy L. Brown
E. John Edwards III (Not admitted in KS)
Katherine E. Rich

For full biographical listings, see the Martindale-Hubbell Law Directory

*TOPEKA,** Shawnee Co.

Foulston & Siefkin (AV)
(Formerly Foulston, Siefkin, Powers & Eberhardt)
1515 Bank IV Tower, 534 Kansas Avenue, 66603
Telephone: 913-233-3600
FAX: 913-233-1610
Wichita, Kansas Office: 700 Fourth Financial Center, Broadway at Douglas. 67202.
Telephone: 316-267-6371.
Facsimile: 316-267-6345.
Member: Lex Mundi, A Global Association of Independent Firms

MEMBERS OF FIRM

James P. Rankin
Benjamin C. Langel (Resident, Wichita Office)
Stanley G. Andeel (Resident, Wichita Office)
Harvey R. Sorensen (Resident, Wichita Office)
James D. Oliver (Resident, Wichita Office)
William R. Wood, II (Resident, Wichita Office)

SPECIAL COUNSEL

James L. Grimes, Jr.

For full biographical listings, see the Martindale-Hubbell Law Directory

*WICHITA,** Sedgwick Co.

Foulston & Siefkin (AV)
(Formerly Foulston, Siefkin, Powers & Eberhardt)
700 Fourth Financial Center, Broadway at Douglas, 67202
Telephone: 316-267-6371
Facsimile: 316-267-6345
Topeka, Kansas Office: 1515 Bank IV Tower, 534 Kansas Avenue. 66603.
Telephone: 913-233-3600.
FAX: 913-233-1610.
Member: Lex Mundi, A Global Association of Independent Firms

MEMBERS OF FIRM

Benjamin C. Langel
Stanley G. Andeel
Harvey R. Sorensen
James D. Oliver
William R. Wood, II

For Complete List of Firm Personnel, See General Section

For full biographical listings, see the Martindale-Hubbell Law Directory

KENTUCKY

*BOWLING GREEN,** Warren Co.

Campbell, Kerrick & Grise (AV)
1025 State Street, P.O. Box 9547, 42102-9547
Telephone: 502-782-8160
FAX: 502-782-5856

MEMBERS OF FIRM

Joe Bill Campbell
Thomas N. Kerrick
John R. Grise
Gregory N. Stivers
H. Brent Brennenstuhl
Deborah Tomes Wilkins

(See Next Column)

CAMPBELL, KERRICK & GRISE, *Bowling Green—Continued*

ASSOCIATES

H. Harris Pepper, Jr. Lanna Martin Kilgore
Laura Hagan

Representative Clients: Dollar General Corp.; Greenview Hospital; Hospital Corporation of America; Hardin Memorial Hospital; Monarch Environmental, Inc.; Mid-South Management Group, Inc.; Western Kentucky University; Service One Credit Union; Trans Financial Bank; TKR Cable.

For full biographical listings, see the Martindale-Hubbell Law Directory

CATRON, KILGORE & BEGLEY (AV)

918 State Street, P.O. Box 280, 42102-0280
Telephone: 502-842-1050
Fax: 502-842-4720

Stephen B. Catron J. Patrick Kilgore
Ernest Edward Begley, II

For full biographical listings, see the Martindale-Hubbell Law Directory

COVINGTON, Kenton Co.

GREENEBAUM DOLL & MCDONALD (AV)

A Partnership including Professional Service Corporations
50 East Rivercenter Boulevard, P.O. Box 2050, 41012-2050
Telephone: 606-655-4200
Telecopier: 606-655-4239
Louisville, Kentucky Office: 3300 National City Tower.
Telephone: 502-589-4200.
Fax: 502-587-3695.
Lexington, Kentucky Office: 1400 Vine Center Tower.
Telephone: 606-231-8500.
Fax: 606-255-2742.
Cincinnati, Ohio Office: 832 Main Street.
Telephone: 513-421-8087.
Fax: 513-421-8089.

MEMBERS OF FIRM

Wm. T. Robinson, III P. Richard Anderson, Jr.
Edwin H. Perry Hiram Ely, III
Michael M. Fleishman * Peggy B. Lyndrup
Phillip D. Scott Nicholas R. Glancy
Charles Fassler William L. Montague
Jeffrey A. McKenzie

OF COUNSEL

Edward B. Weinberg *

Representative Clients: Aetna Life Insurance Co.; ANDALEX Resources, Inc.; Ashland Oil, Inc.; A T & T Communications, Inc.; Bethlehem Steel Corp.; Brown-Forman Corp.; Citizens Fidelity Bank & Trust Co.; Columbia/HCA Health Care Corp.; Humana, Inc.; KFC National Cooperative Advertising Program, Inc.
*A Professional Service Corporation

For Complete List of Firm Personnel, See General Section

For full biographical listings, see the Martindale-Hubbell Law Directory

*LEXINGTON,** Fayette Co.

GREENEBAUM DOLL & MCDONALD (AV)

A Partnership including Professional Service Corporations
1400 Vine Center Tower, 40508
Telephone: 606-231-8500
Telecopier: 606-255-2742
Telex: 213029
Louisville, Kentucky Office: 3300 National City Tower.
Telephone: 502-589-4200.
Fax: 502-587-3695.
Covington, Kentucky Office: 50 East River Center Boulevard, P.O. Box 2050.
Telephone: 606-655-4200.
Fax: 606-655-4239.
Cincinnati, Ohio Office: 832 Main Street.
Telephone: 513-421-8087.
Fax: 513-421-8089.

MEMBERS OF FIRM

Phillip D. Scott Charles Fassler
A. Robert Doll * Robert C. Stilz, Jr. (Resident)
Edwin H. Perry Job D. Turner, III (Resident)
Ivan M. Diamond John S. Sawyer (Resident)
Michael M. Fleishman * Hiram Ely, III
Lawrence K. Banks * Peggy B. Lyndrup
Wm. T. Robinson, III Nicholas R. Glancy
Stephen W. Switzer (Resident)

ASSOCIATE

D. Barry Stilz (Resident)

Representative Clients: Aetna Life Insurance Co.; ANDALEX Resources, Inc.; Ashland Oil, Inc.; AT&T Communications, Inc.; Bethlehem Steel Corp.; Brown-Forman Corp.; Columbia Gas & Transmission Co.; Columbia/HCA Healthcare Corp.; Commonwealth Aluminum Corp.; Consolidation Coal Co.; Costain Coal, Inc.
*A Professional Service Corporation

(See Next Column)

For Complete List of Firm Personnel, See General Section

For full biographical listings, see the Martindale-Hubbell Law Directory

LANDRUM & SHOUSE (AV)

106 West Vine Street, P.O. Box 951, 40588-0951
Telephone: 606-255-2424
Facsimile: 606-233-0308
Louisville, Kentucky Office: 400 West Market Street, Suite 1550, 40202.
Telephone: 502-589-7616.
Facsimile: 502-589-2119.

MEMBERS OF FIRM

John H. Burrus Mark L. Moseley
William C. Shouse Jack E. Toliver

ASSOCIATES

David G. Hazlett Charles E. Christian
(Resident, Louisville Office)

District Attorneys: CSX Transportation, Inc.
Special Trial Counsel: Ford Motor Co. and Affiliates (Eastern Kentucky); Clark Equipment Co.
Representative Clients: The Continental Insurance Cos.; U.S. Insurance Group; U.S. Fidelity & Guaranty Co.; Ohio Casualty Insurance Co.; CIGNA; Royal Insurance Cos.

For Complete List of Firm Personnel, See General Section

For full biographical listings, see the Martindale-Hubbell Law Directory

MARTIN, OCKERMAN & BRABANT (AV)

200 North Upper Street, 40507
Telephone: 606-254-4401

MEMBERS OF FIRM

Hogan Yancey (1881-1960) Thomas C. Brabant
William B. Martin (1895-1975) Foster Ockerman, Jr.
Madeleine B. Eldred

OF COUNSEL

Foster Ockerman

Counsel for: Lexington Federal Savings Bank; Good Samaritan Hospital; Newmarket Bloodstock Agency, Ltd.; Equity Property and Development Co.; Park Communications of KY (WTVQ); AAA Blue Grass/Kentucky; Good Samaritan Foundation.
Reference: Bank One, Lexington, N.A.

For full biographical listings, see the Martindale-Hubbell Law Directory

STOLL, KEENON & PARK (AV)

201 E. Main Street, Suite 1000, 40507-1380
Telephone: 606-231-3000
Telecopier: 606-253-1093; 606-253-1027
Frankfort, Kentucky Office: 326 West Main Street.
Telephone: 502-875-6000.
Telecopier: 502-875-6008.
Louisville, Kentucky Office: 400 West Market Street, Suite 2650, 40202.
Telephone: 502-568-9100.
Telecopier: 502-568-6340.

MEMBERS OF FIRM

William L. Montague Herbert A. Miller, Jr.
Robert M. Watt, III Robert W. Kellerman
J. Peter Cassidy, Jr. J. David Smith, Jr.
Samuel D. Hinkle, IV Dan M. Rose
Gary L. Stage John Wesley Walters, Jr.

ASSOCIATES

Mary Beth Griffith Richard A. Nunnelley
Culver V. Halliday William L. Montague, Jr.
Robert E. Wier

Representative Clients: Bank One, Lexington, NA; Farmers Capital Bank Corp.; The Tokai Bank Ltd.; Link Belt Construction Equipment Co.; General Motors Corp.; International Business Machines Corp.; Ohbayashi Corp.; R. J. Reynolds Tobacco Co.; Rockwell International Corp.; Square D Co.

For Complete List of Firm Personnel, See General Section

For full biographical listings, see the Martindale-Hubbell Law Directory

STURGILL, TURNER & TRUITT (AV)

155 East Main Street, 40507
Telephone: 606-255-8581
Fax: 606-231-0851

MEMBERS OF FIRM

Don S. Sturgill Ann D. Sturgill
Jerry D. Truitt Douglas L. McSwain
Stephen L. Barker Kevin G. Henry

For Complete List of Firm Personnel, See General Section

For full biographical listings, see the Martindale-Hubbell Law Directory

*LOUISVILLE,** Jefferson Co.

GREENEBAUM DOLL & McDONALD (AV)

A Partnership including Professional Service Corporations
3300 National City Tower, 40202
Telephone: 502-589-4200
Fax: 502-587-3695
Lexington, Kentucky Office: 1400 Vine Center Tower.
Telephone: 606-231-8500.
Fax: 606-255-2742.
Covington, Kentucky Office: 50 East River Center Boulevard, P.O. Box 2050.
Telephone: 606-655-4200.
Fax: 606-655-4239.
Cincinnati, Ohio Office: 832 Main Street.
Telephone: 513-421-8087.
Fax: 513-421-8089.

A. Robert Doll *
Edwin H. Perry
Michael G. Shaikun *
Ivan M. Diamond
Michael M. Fleishman *
Lawrence K. Banks *
Phillip D. Scott (Covington and Lexington, Kentucky)
Wm. T. Robinson, III
Charles Fassler
John H. Stites, III
Robert C. Stilz, Jr. (Resident at Lexington, Kentucky)
P. Richard Anderson, Jr.
Mark S. Ament *
Job D. Turner, III (Resident at Lexington, Kentucky)
John S. Sawyer (Resident at Lexington, Kentucky)
Hiram Ely, III
Peggy B. Lyndrup
Nicholas R. Glancy (Lexington and Covington, Kentucky)
Carmin D. Grandinetti
Janet P. Jakubowicz
Tandy C. Patrick
William L. Montague (Covington, Kentucky and Cincinnati, Ohio Offices)
Patrick J. Welsh
Holland N. McTyeire, V
Jeffrey A. McKenzie
Stephen W. Switzer (Resident at Lexington, Kentucky)
Daniel E. Fisher

ASSOCIATES

D. Barry Stilz (Resident at Lexington, Kentucky)
Mark F. Sommer
Daniel L. Waddell
John P. Fendig
John S. Lueken

OF COUNSEL

Edward B. Weinberg *

Representative Clients: Aetna Life Insurance Co.; ANDALEX Resources, Inc.; Ashland Oil, Inc.; A T & T Communications, Inc.; Bethlehem Steel Corp.; Brown-Forman Corp.; Columbia/HCA Healthcare Corp.; Humana, Inc.; Kentucky Kingdom, Inc.; KFC National Cooperative Advertising Program, Inc.

*A Professional Service Corporation

For Complete List of Firm Personnel, See General Section

For full biographical listings, see the Martindale-Hubbell Law Directory

LANDRUM & SHOUSE (AV)

400 West Market Street Suite 1550, 40202
Telephone: 502-589-7616
Facsimile: 502-589-2119
Lexington, Kentucky Office: 106 West Vine Street, P.O. Box 951.
Telephone: 606-255-2424.
Facsimile: 606-233-0308.

RESIDENT MEMBERS OF THE FIRM

George P. Parker
John R. Martin, Jr.
Delores Hill Pregliasco
Michael J. O'Connell
R. Kent Westberry
J. Denis Ogburn

RESIDENT ASSOCIATES

David G. Hazlett
Thomas E. Roma, Jr.
Dave Whalin
G. Bruce Stigger
Courtney T. Baxter
D. Sean Nilsen

OF COUNSEL

Frank J. Dougherty, Jr.

For Complete List of Firm Personnel, See General Section

For full biographical listings, see the Martindale-Hubbell Law Directory

MULLOY, WALZ, WETTERER, FORE & SCHWARTZ (AV)

First Trust Centre, Suite 700N, 200 South Fifth Street, 40202
Telephone: 502-589-5250
Fax: 502-589-1637

MEMBERS OF FIRM

William P. Mulloy
Karl M. Walz
William S. Wetterer, Jr.
F. Larkin Fore
Dan T. Schwartz
B. Mark Mulloy
Mary Anne Wetterer Watkins
William S. Wetterer, III
Bryan J. Dillon
J. Gregory Clare
Ronda Hartlage
T. Lee Sisney

(See Next Column)

OF COUNSEL

Stephen H. Miller

Reference: American States Insurance Co.; Crawford & Company; Paragon Group, Inc.; Queens Group; Southeastern Dairies, Inc.; Ticor Title Co.; First National Bank of Louisville; Stockyards Bank; Arrow Electric Co.

For full biographical listings, see the Martindale-Hubbell Law Directory

OGDEN NEWELL & WELCH (AV)

1200 One Riverfront Plaza, 40202-2973
Telephone: 502-582-1601
Fax: 502-581-9564

MEMBERS OF FIRM

Richard F. Newell
James S. Welch
Joseph C. Oldham
James L. Coorssen
John G. Treitz, Jr.
Ernest W. Williams
Robert E. Thieman
James B. Martin, Jr.
Lisa Ann Vogt
Turney P. Berry

ASSOCIATES

Lynn H. Wangerin
John Wade Hendricks
James G. Campbell
Teresa C. Buchheit
Lady Evelyn Booth
Thomas E. Rutledge

Counsel for: KU Energy Corp.; Kentucky Utilities Co.; Brown-Forman Corp.; B. F. Goodrich Co.; Brown & Williamson Tobacco Corp.; J.J.B. Hilliard, W.L. Lyons, Inc.; Interlock Industries, Inc.; Akzo Coatings, Inc.; United Medical Corp.; Bank of Louisville.

For Complete List of Firm Personnel, See General Section

For full biographical listings, see the Martindale-Hubbell Law Directory

SEILLER & HANDMAKER (AV)

2200 Meidinger Tower, 40202
Telephone: 502-584-7400
Telecopier: 502-583-2100
Paris, Kentucky Office: Seiller, Handmaker & Blevins, P.S.C., 1431 South Main Street.
Telephone: 606-987-3980.
Telecopier: 606-987-3982.
New Albany, Indiana Office: 204 Pearl Street, Suite 200.
Telephone: 812-948-8307.
Telecopier: 812-948-8383.

Edward F. Seiller (1897-1990)

MEMBERS OF FIRM

Stuart Allen Handmaker
Bill V. Seiller
David M. Cantor
Neil C. Bordy
Kyle Anne Citrynell
Maury D. Kommor
Cynthia Compton Stone

ASSOCIATES

Glenn A. Cohen
Pamela M. Greenwell
Tomi Anne Blevins Pulliam (Resident, Paris Office)
Linda Scholle Cowan
Mary Zeller Wing Ceridan
Michael C. Bratcher
John E. Brengle
Patrick R. Holland, II
Edwin Jon Wolfe
Donna F. Townsend
William C. Robinson

OF COUNSEL

Robert S. Frey

For full biographical listings, see the Martindale-Hubbell Law Directory

TAUSTINE, POST, SOTSKY, BERMAN, FINEMAN & KOHN (AV)

8th Floor Marion E. Taylor Building, 40202
Telephone: 502-589-5760
Telecopier: 502-584-5927

MEMBERS OF FIRM

Hugo Taustine (1899-1987)
Edward M. Post (1929-1986)
Marvin M. Sotsky
Jerome D. Berman
Joseph E. Fineman
Robert A. Kohn
Alex Berman
H. Philip Grossman
Stanley W. Whetzel, Jr.
Maria A. Fernandez

ASSOCIATE

Sandra Sotsky Harrison

OF COUNSEL

W. David Shearer, Jr.
David A. Friedman
Martin R. Snyder
Jerald R. Steinberg (Also Practicing individually as Steinberg & Steinberg)
Craig I. Lustig

For full biographical listings, see the Martindale-Hubbell Law Directory

*OWENSBORO,** Daviess Co.

CONNOR, NEAL & STEVENSON (AV)

613 Frederica Street, 42301
Telephone: 502-926-9911
Fax: 502-686-7905

(See Next Column)

CONNOR, NEAL & STEVENSON, *Owensboro—Continued*

MEMBERS OF FIRM

Sidney A. Neal (1927-1987) Thomas E. Neal
Jack A. Connor John W. Stevenson
James A. Wethington, II

ASSOCIATE

William A. Mitchell

Representative Client: Grange Mutual Casualty Co.
Approved Attorneys for: Farmers Home Administration.

For full biographical listings, see the Martindale-Hubbell Law Directory

RUMMAGE, KAMUF, YEWELL, PACE & CONDON (AV)

Great Financial Federal Building, 322 Frederica Street, 42301
Telephone: 502-685-3901
FAX: 502-926-2005

MEMBERS OF FIRM

William E. Rummage David L. Yewell
Charles J. Kamuf Patrick D. Pace
David C. Condon

ASSOCIATE

John M. Mischel

Representative Clients: Owensboro Municipal Utilities Commission; Lincoln Service Corp.; Hancock County Planning Commission; Daviess County Board of Education; Barmet Aluminum Corp.; Owensboro Sewer Commission; TICOR Title Insurance Co.; Chicago Title Insurance Co.; Owensboro Riverport Authority; Housing Authority of Owensboro.

For full biographical listings, see the Martindale-Hubbell Law Directory

LOUISIANA

*ALEXANDRIA,** Rapides Parish

CROWELL & OWENS (AV)

601 Hibernia National Bank Building, P.O. Box 330, 71309-0330
Telephone: 318-445-1488
Fax: 318-445-9098

MEMBERS OF FIRM

Richard L. Crowell William B. Owens
Richard B. Crowell W. Brent Pearson

Counsel For: Empire Construction Company; Hixson Brothers Funeral Home; KALB-TV; Louisiana College; Provine School Pictures; Southern Chevrolet-Geo; Ratcliff Construction Company.
References: Rapides Bank and Trust Company, Alexandria, La.; Whitney National Bank, New Orleans, La.; Hibernia National Bank, Alexandria, La.

For full biographical listings, see the Martindale-Hubbell Law Directory

*BATON ROUGE,** East Baton Rouge Parish

JAMES S. HOLLIDAY, JR. (AV)

5236 Corporate Boulevard, P.O. Box 80739, 70898
Telephone: 504-926-5899
Fax: 504-926-6698

ASSOCIATE

Susan Wall Griffin

For full biographical listings, see the Martindale-Hubbell Law Directory

POWERS, CLEGG & WILLARD (AV)

7967 Office Park Boulevard, P.O. Box 15948, 70895
Telephone: 504-928-1951
Telecopier: 504-929-9834

MEMBERS OF FIRM

John Dale Powers Michael V. Clegg
William E. Willard

ASSOCIATES

Neil H. Mixon Troy J. Charpentier
Mary A. Cazes

General Counsel for: Audubon Insurance Co.
Louisiana Counsel for: Hancock Bank & Trust Co.; Hertz Corp.; Ciba-Geigy Corp.; Utica Mutual Insurance Co.

For full biographical listings, see the Martindale-Hubbell Law Directory

BERT K. ROBINSON (AV)

10357 Old Hammond Highway, 70816-8261
Telephone: 504-924-0296
Fax: 504-924-5288

ASSOCIATE

Johanna R. Landreneau

(See Next Column)

OF COUNSEL

Charles C. Holbrook

For full biographical listings, see the Martindale-Hubbell Law Directory

*LAFAYETTE,** Lafayette Parish

HILL & BEYER, A PROFESSIONAL LAW CORPORATION (AV)

101 LaRue France, Suite 502, P.O. Box 53006, 70505-3006
Telephone: 318-232-9733
Fax: 1-318-237-2566

John K. Hill, Jr. Eugene P. Matherne
Bret C. Beyer Robert B. Purser
David R. Rabalais Erin J. Sherburne
Lisa C. McCowen Harold Adam Lawrence

For full biographical listings, see the Martindale-Hubbell Law Directory

*NEW ORLEANS,** Orleans Parish

SLATER LAW FIRM, A PROFESSIONAL CORPORATION (AV)

650 Poydras Street Suite 2400, 70130-6101
Telephone: 504-523-7333
Fax: 504-528-1080

Benjamin R. Slater, Jr. Mark E. Van Horn
Benjamin R. Slater, III Kevin M. Wheeler

Anne Elise Brown Donald J. Miester, Jr.

OF COUNSEL

Michael O. Waguespack

Representative Clients: Norfolk Southern Corporation; New Orleans Steamship Association; Anheuser-Busch, Inc.; The Quaker Oats Company; Primerica Financial Services, Inc.; Primerica Life Insurance Company; Electric Mutual Liability Insurance Company; Diversified Foods and Seasonings; American International Gaming Association, Inc.

For full biographical listings, see the Martindale-Hubbell Law Directory

*SHREVEPORT,** Caddo Parish

BARLOW AND HARDTNER L.C. (AV)

Tenth Floor, Louisiana Tower, 401 Edwards Street, 71101-3289
Telephone: 318-227-1131
Telecopier: 318-227-1141
Mailing Address: P.O. Box 8, Shreveport, Louisiana, 71161-0008

Ray A. Barlow David R. Taggart
Quintin T. Hardtner, III Clair F. White
Malcolm S. Murchison Philip E. Downer, III
Joseph L. Shea, Jr. Michael B. Donald
Jay A. Greenleaf

OF COUNSEL

Cecil E. Ramey, Jr.

Representative Clients: Kelley Oil Corporation; NorAm Energy Corp. (formerly Arkla, Inc.); Central and South West; Panhandle Eastern Corp.; Pennzoil Producing Co.; Johnson Controls, Inc.; Ashland Oil, Inc.; Southwestern Electric Power Company; Brammer Engineering, Inc.; The Brinkmann Corporation.

For Complete List of Firm Personnel, See General Section

For full biographical listings, see the Martindale-Hubbell Law Directory

ROBERT U. GOODMAN, P.L.C. (AV)

Mid South Towers, 416 Travis Street, Suite 1105, 71101-5514
Telephone: 318-221-1601
Fax: 318-221-1749

Robert U. Goodman

OF COUNSEL

James E. Clark Nancy Kay Fox-Reiter

Representative Clients: Dealers Truck & Equipment Co.; Transworld Life Insurance Co.; Graham Brothers Entertainment, Inc.; Integrated Exploration.

For full biographical listings, see the Martindale-Hubbell Law Directory

SOCKRIDER, BOLIN & ANGLIN, A PROFESSIONAL LAW CORPORATION (AV)

327 Crockett Street, 71101
Telephone: 318-221-5503
Fax: 318-221-3849

John R. Pleasant (1905-1983) James E. Bolin, Jr.
H. F. Sockrider, Jr. D. Rex Anglin
Gregory H. Batte

For full biographical listings, see the Martindale-Hubbell Law Directory

MAINE

*BANGOR,** Penobscot Co.

EATON, PEABODY, BRADFORD & VEAGUE, P.A. (AV)

Fleet Center-Exchange Street, P.O. Box 1210, 04402-1210
Telephone: 207-947-0111
Telecopier: 207-942-3040
Augusta, Maine Office: 2 Central Plaza.
Telephone: 207-622-3747.
Telecopier: 207-622-9732.
Brunswick, Maine Office: 167 Park Row.
Telephone: 207-729-1144.
Telecopier: 207-729-1140.
Camden, Maine Office: 7-9 Washington Street.
Telephone: 207-236-3325.
Telecopier: 207-236-8611.
Dover-Foxcroft, Maine Office: 30 East Main Street.
Telephone: 207-564-8378.
Telecopier: 207-564-7059.

Malcolm E. Morrell, Jr.
Daniel G. McKay
Michael B. Trainor
George Franklin Eaton, II
Gregory A. Brodek

Judy A.S. Metcalf (Resident, Brunswick Office)
Allison C. Lucy
Michael A. Duddy

A List of Representative Clients available upon request.

For Complete List of Firm Personnel, See General Section

For full biographical listings, see the Martindale-Hubbell Law Directory

*PORTLAND,** Cumberland Co.

PIERCE, ATWOOD, SCRIBNER, ALLEN, SMITH & LANCASTER (AV)

One Monument Square, 04101
Telephone: 207-773-6411
Fax: 207-773-3419
Augusta, Maine Office: 77 Winthrop Street.
Telephone: 207-622-6311.
Camden, Maine Office: 36 Chestnut Street, P.O. Box 780.
Telephone: 207-236-4333.

MEMBERS OF FIRM

Jeremiah D. Newbury
Bruce A. Coggeshall
James B. Zimpritch
George J. Marcus
Richard P. Hackett
Christopher E. Howard
Gregory D. Woodworth
David J. Champoux
Gloria A. Pinza

ASSOCIATE

Foster A. Stewart, Jr

For Complete List of Firm Personnel, See General Section

For full biographical listings, see the Martindale-Hubbell Law Directory

PRETI, FLAHERTY, BELIVEAU & PACHIOS (AV)

443 Congress Street, P.O. Box 11410, 04104-7410
Telephone: 207-791-3000
Telecopier: 207-791-3111
Augusta, Maine Office: 45 Memorial Circle, P.O. Box 1058, 04332-1058.
Telephone: 207-623-5300.
Telecopier: 207-623-2914.
Rumford, Maine Office: 150 Congress Street, P.O. Drawer L, 04276-2035.
Telephone: 207-364-4593.
Telecopier: 207-369-9421.

MEMBERS OF FIRM

John J. Flaherty
Harold C. Pachios
Michael J. Gentile (Augusta Office)
Richard H. Spencer, Jr.
Eric P. Stauffer
Jonathan S. Piper
Randall B. Weill
James C. Pitney, Jr. (Augusta Office)
Leonard M. Gulino
Dennis C. Sbrega
Estelle A. Lavoie
Susan E. LoGiudice
Michael Kaplan
Michael L. Sheehan

ASSOCIATES

James E. Phipps
Jeanne T. Cohn-Connor
John P. McVeigh
Marilyn E. Mistretta
Scott T. Rodgers

Representative Clients: Key Bank of Maine; Guy Gannett Publishing Co.; Peoples Heritage Savings Bank; Liberty Group, Inc.; RECOLL Management Cor;.; NRG Barriers, Inc.; Hussey Corp.; Northeast Air Group; The Woodlands Club; P.H. Chadbourne and Co.

For Complete List of Firm Personnel, See General Section

For full biographical listings, see the Martindale-Hubbell Law Directory

MARYLAND

*BALTIMORE,** (Independent City)

KOLLMAN & SHEEHAN, P.A. (AV)

Sun Life Building, 20 South Charles Street, 21201
Telephone: 410-727-4300
Telecopier: 410-727-4391

Frank L. Kollman
David M. Sheehan
Peter S. Saucier

Charles J. Morton, Jr.
Jessica V. Carter
Clifford B. Geiger

For full biographical listings, see the Martindale-Hubbell Law Directory

VENABLE, BAETJER AND HOWARD (AV)

A Partnership including Professional Corporations
1800 Mercantile Bank & Trust Building, 2 Hopkins Plaza, 21201
Telephone: 410-244-7400
Washington, D.C. Office: Venable, Baetjer, Howard & Civiletti. Suite 1000, 1201 New York Avenue, N.W.
Telephone: 202-962-4800.
McLean, Virginia Office: Suite 400, 2010 Corporate Ridge.
Telephone: 703-760-1600.
Rockville, Maryland Office: Suite 500, One Church Street, P. O. Box 1906.
Telephone: 301-217-5600.
Towson, Maryland Office: 210 Allegheny Avenue, P. O. Box 5517.
Telephone: 410-494-6200.

MEMBERS OF FIRM

Jacques T. Schlenger (P.C.)
William J. McCarthy (P.C.)
Thomas P. Perkins, III (P.C.)
Benjamin R. Civiletti (P.C.) (Also at Washington, D.C. and Towson, Maryland Offices)
John B. Howard (Resident, Towson, Maryland Office)
Anthony M. Carey (Also at Washington, D.C. Office)
Lee M. Miller (P.C.)
Alan D. Yarbro (P.C.)
Neal D. Borden (Also at Washington, D.C. Office)
Robert A. Shelton
Roger W. Titus (Resident, Rockville, Maryland Office)
Daniel O'C. Tracy, Jr. (Also at Rockville, Maryland Office)
Jan K. Guben (Also at Washington, D. C Office)
David J. Levenson (Not admitted in MD; Resident, Washington, D.C. Office)
Joe A. Shull (Resident, Washington, D.C. Office)
Robert E. Madden (Not admitted in MD; also at Washington, D.C. and McLean, Virginia Offices)
Kenneth C. Bass, III (Not admitted in MD; Also at Washington, D.C. and McLean, Virginia Offices)
John H. Zink, III (Resident, Towson, Maryland Office)
Paul T. Glasgow (Resident, Rockville, Maryland Office)
Joseph G. Block (Not admitted in MD; Resident, Washington, D.C. Office)
Sondra Harans Block (Resident, Rockville, Maryland Office)
Bryson L. Cook (P.C.) (Also at Washington, D.C. Office)
Susan K. Gauvey (Also at Towson, Maryland Office)
H. Russell Frisby, Jr.
Jeffrey D. Knowles (Not admitted in MD; Resident, Washington, D.C. Office)
F. Dudley Staples, Jr. (Also at Towson, Maryland Office)
David M. Fleishman
Jana Howard Carey (P.C.)
William D. Coston (Not admitted in MD; Resident, Washington, D.C. Office)
Nathaniel E. Jones, Jr.
Maurice Baskin (Resident, Washington, D.C. Office)
W. Robert Zinkham
Elizabeth R. Hughes
Robert J. Bolger, Jr. (Also at Washington, D.C. Office)
J. Michael Brennan (Resident, Towson, Maryland Office)
Bruce H. Jurist (Also at Washington, D.C. Office)
Linda L. Lord (Not admitted in MD; Resident, Washington, D.C. Office)
John M. Gurley (Not admitted in MD; Resident, Washington, D.C. Office)
Paul A. Serini (Also at Washington, D.C. Office)
Ariel Vannier

OF COUNSEL

Arthur W. Machen, Jr. (P.C.)
Herbert R. O'Conor, Jr. (Resident, Towson, Maryland Office)
Emried D. Cole, Jr.
Joyce K. Becker
Fred W. Hathaway (Not admitted in MD; Resident, Washington, D.C. Office)

ASSOCIATES

Michael J. Baader
Wallace E. Christner (Not admitted in MD)
Christine J. Collins
Kevin B. Collins
Michael W. Conron
Donald P. Creston (Not admitted in MD; Resident, Washington, D.C. Office)
John P. Edgar
Newton B. Fowler, III
Francis X. Gallagher, Jr. (Not admitted in MD)
Robert H. Geis, Jr.
Jeffrey K. Gonya
D. Brent Gunsalus (Not admitted in MD; Resident, Washington, D.C. Office)

(See Next Column)

VENABLE, BAETJER AND HOWARD, *Baltimore—Continued*

ASSOCIATES (Continued)

Lisa H. Rice Hayes
Mary-Dulany James (Resident, Towson, Maryland Office)
Gregory L. Laubach (Resident, Rockville, Maryland Office)
Fernand A. Lavallee (Not admitted in MD; Resident, Washington, D. C. Office)
Jon M. Lippard (Not admitted in MD; Resident, McLean, Virginia Office)
Wingrove S. Lynton
John A. McCauley
Michael J. Muller
Traci H. Mundy (Not admitted in MD; Resident, Washington, D.C. Office)
Vadim A. Mzhen
Joseph C. Schmelter
Davis V. R. Sherman
Todd K. Snyder
Neal H. Strum
Linda Marotta Thomas
Brian R. Trumbauer
Robin L. Zimelman

For Complete List of Firm Personnel, See General Section

For full biographical listings, see the Martindale-Hubbell Law Directory

*BEL AIR,** Harford Co.

STARK & KEENAN, A PROFESSIONAL ASSOCIATION (AV)

30 Office Street, 21014
Telephone: 410-838-5522
Baltimore: 410-879-2222
Fax: 410-879-0688

Elwood V. Stark, Jr.
Charles B. Keenan, Jr.
Thomas E. Marshall
Edwin G. Carson
Judith C. H. Cline
Gregory A. Szoka
Robert S. Lynch

Claire Prin Blomquist
Kimberly Kahoe Muenter
Paul W. Ishak

For full biographical listings, see the Martindale-Hubbell Law Directory

COLUMBIA, Howard Co.

LAW OFFICES OF GUY B. MASERITZ (AV)

Hobbit's Glen, 5040 Rushlight Path, 21044
Telephone: 410-997-9400
Fax: 410-997-3116

Reference: First National Bank of Maryland.

*ROCKVILLE,** Montgomery Co.

KATZ, FROME AND BLEECKER, P.A. (AV)

6116 Executive Boulevard, Suite 200, 20852
Telephone: 301-230-5800
Facsimile: 301-230-5830

Steven M. Katz
Morton J. Frome
Lorin H. Bleecker
Gail B. Landau

Susan J. Rubin
Marilyn J. Brasier
Leslie Anne Sullivan
Seth B. Popkin
Richard O'Connor
Stanley A. Snyder

OF COUNSEL

Philip F. Finelli, Jr.

For full biographical listings, see the Martindale-Hubbell Law Directory

STEIN, SPERLING, BENNETT, DE JONG, DRISCOLL, GREENFEIG & METRO, P.A. (AV)

25 West Middle Lane, 20850
Telephone: 301-340-2020; 800-435-5230
Telecopier: 301-340-8217

Millard S. Bennett
David S. De Jong
Jack A. Garson
Ann G. Jakabcin
A. Howard Metro
Donald N. Sperling

Beth H. McIntosh
Kieyasien K. Moore

For Complete List of Firm Personnel, See General Section

For full biographical listings, see the Martindale-Hubbell Law Directory

VENABLE, BAETJER AND HOWARD (AV)

A Partnership including Professional Corporations
Suite 500, One Church Street, P.O. Box 1906, 20850-4129
Telephone: 301-217-5600
FAX: 301-217-5617
Baltimore, Maryland Office: 1800 Mercantile Bank & Trust Building, 2 Hopkins Plaza.
Telephone: 410-244-7400.
Washington, D.C. Office: Venable, Baetjer, Howard & Civiletti. Suite 1000, 1201 New York Avenue, N.W.
Telephone: 202-962-4800.

(See Next Column)

McLean, Virginia Office: Suite 400, 2010 Corporate Ridge.
Telephone: 703-760-1600.
Towson, Maryland, Office: 210 Allegheny Avenue, P. O. Box 5517.
Telephone: 410-494-6200.

MEMBERS OF FIRM

Roger W. Titus
Daniel O'C. Tracy, Jr. (Also at Baltimore, Maryland Office)
Paul T. Glasgow

ASSOCIATE

Gregory L. Laubach

For Complete List of Firm Personnel, See General Section

For full biographical listings, see the Martindale-Hubbell Law Directory

SILVER SPRING, Montgomery Co.

ALEXANDER, GEBHARDT, APONTE & MARKS, L.L.C. (AV)

Lee Plaza-Suite 805, 8601 Georgia Avenue, 20910
Telephone: 301-589-2222
Facsimile: 301-589-2523
Washington, D.C. Office: 1314 Nineteenth Street, N.W., 20036.
Telephone: 202-835-1555.
New York, New York Office: 330 Madison Avenue, 36th Floor.
Telephone: 212-808-0008.
Fax: 212-599-1028.

Kenneth H. Marks, Jr. (Not admitted in MD)

Y. Kris Oh (Ms.) (Not admitted in MD)
Suzette Wynn Blackwell

Reference: Riggs National Bank of Washington, D.C.

For full biographical listings, see the Martindale-Hubbell Law Directory

*TOWSON,** Baltimore Co.

VENABLE, BAETJER AND HOWARD (AV)

A Partnership including Professional Corporations
210 Allegheny Avenue, P.O. Box 5517, 21204
Telephone: 410-494-6200
FAX: 410-821-0147
Baltimore, Maryland Office: 1800 Mercantile Bank & Trust Building, 2 Hopkins Plaza.
Telephone: 410-244-7400.
Washington, D.C. Office: Venable, Baetjer, Howard & Civiletti. Suite 1000, 1201 New York Avenue, N.W.
Telephone: 202-962-4800.
McLean, Virginia Office: Suite 400, 2010 Corporate Ridge.
Telephone: 703-760-1600.
Rockville, Maryland Office: Suite 500, One Church Street, P. O. Box 1906.
Telephone: 301-217-5600.

PARTNERS

Benjamin R. Civiletti (P.C.) (Also at Washington, D.C. and Baltimore, Maryland Offices)
John B. Howard
John H. Zink, III
F. Dudley Staples, Jr. (Also at Baltimore, Maryland Office)
J. Michael Brennan

OF COUNSEL

Herbert R. O'Conor, Jr.

ASSOCIATE

Mary-Dulany James

For Complete List of Firm Personnel, See General Section

For full biographical listings, see the Martindale-Hubbell Law Directory

MASSACHUSETTS

AMESBURY, Essex Co.

HAMEL, DESHAIES & GAGLIARDI (AV)

Five Market Square, P.O. Box 198, 01913
Telephone: 508-388-3558
Telecopier: 508-388-0441

MEMBERS OF FIRM

Richard P. Hamel
Robert J. Deshaies
Paul J. Gagliardi

ASSOCIATES

H. Scott Haskell
Peter R. Ayer, Jr.
Roger D. Turgeon
Charles E. Schissel

Representative Clients: Essex County Gas Co., Amesbury, MA; First and Ocean National Bank, Newburyport, MA; Amesbury Co-Operative Bank, Amesbury, MA.
Approved Attorneys for: Chicago Title Insurance; Old Republic Title Insurance Co.

(See Next Column)

HAMEL, DESHAIES & GAGLIARDI—*Continued*

For full biographical listings, see the Martindale-Hubbell Law Directory

BEVERLY, Essex Co.

GLOVSKY & GLOVSKY (AV)

8 Washington Street, 01915
Telephone: 508-922-5000
FAX: 508-921-7809

MEMBER OF FIRM

C. Henry Glovsky

Representative Clients: Warren Five Cents Savings Bank; Rose's Oil Service, Inc.; Medical Group, Inc.; Associates in OBGYN, Inc.; Pewter Pot, Inc.; Leslie S. Ray Insurance Agency, Inc.; Professional Relations and Research Institute, Inc.
Reference: Beverly National Bank.

For Complete List of Firm Personnel, See General Section

For full biographical listings, see the Martindale-Hubbell Law Directory

*BOSTON,** Suffolk Co.

CHERWIN & GLICKMAN (AV)

A Partnership including Professional Corporations
One International Place, 02110-2622
Telephone: 617-330-1625
FAX: 617-330-1642

Stanley A. Glickman (1937-1994)
Joel I. Cherwin (P.C.)
Marshall D. Stein
Douglas L. Jones
Alfred D. Ellis (P.C.)
Emilie F. Athanasoulis
Lisa Lee Foster
Elizabeth J. McGlynn

OF COUNSEL

Jay F. Theise (P.C.)

For full biographical listings, see the Martindale-Hubbell Law Directory

CRAIG AND MACAULEY, PROFESSIONAL CORPORATION (AV)

Federal Reserve Plaza, 600 Atlantic Avenue, 02210
Telephone: 617-367-9500
Telecopier: 617-742-1788; 617-248-0886

John C. Craig
David F. Hannon
Mary P. Brody
A. Van C. Lanckton

John G. Snyder
Christopher J. Panos
Mark W. Manning
Christopher S. Dalton

For Complete List of Firm Personnel, See General Section

For full biographical listings, see the Martindale-Hubbell Law Directory

CUDDY BIXBY (AV)

One Financial Center, 02111
Telephone: 617-348-3600
Telecopier: 617-348-3643
Wellesley, Massachusetts Office: 60 Walnut Street.
Telephone: 617-235-1034.

Francis X. Cuddy (Retired)
Wayne E. Hartwell
Brian D. Bixby
Anthony M. Ambriano
William E. Kelly
Paul G. Boylan
Robert A. Vigoda
Paul J. Murphy
Alexander L. Cataldo
Duncan S. Payne
Stephen T. Kunian
Arthur P. Menard
Joseph H. Walsh
Michael J. Owens
Robert J. O'Regan
Andrew R. Menard
David F. Hendren
Glenn B. Asch
Timothy E. McAllister
William R. Moriarty
Kevin P. Sweeney
Denise I. Murphy

For full biographical listings, see the Martindale-Hubbell Law Directory

HEMENWAY & BARNES (AV)

60 State Street, 02109
Telephone: 617-227-7940
Fax: 617-227-0781

MEMBERS OF FIRM

Alfred Hemenway (1863-1927)
Charles B. Barnes (1893-1956)
George H. Kidder
David H. Morse
Roy A. Hammer
Lawrence T. Perera
John J. Madden
George T. Shaw
Timothy F. Fidgeon
Ruth R. Budd
Michael B. Elefante
Michael J. Puzo
Thomas L. Guidi
Edward Notis-McConarty
Diane C. Tillotson
Susan Hughes Banning
Frederic J. Marx
Deborah J. Hall
Kurt F. Somerville
Stephen W. Kidder
Teresa A. Belmonte

(See Next Column)

COUNSEL

Michael L. Leshin

ASSOCIATES

Andrea H. Maislen
Barbara Zicht Richmond
Marsha K. Zierk
Charles Fayerweather
Christopher Denn
James P. Warner
Brian C. Broderick

OF COUNSEL

Guido R. Perera

For full biographical listings, see the Martindale-Hubbell Law Directory

PALMER & DODGE (AV)

(Storey Thorndike Palmer & Dodge)
One Beacon Street, 02108
Telephone: 617-573-0100
Telecopier: 617-227-4420
Telex: 951104
Cable Address: "Storeydike," Boston

MEMBERS OF FIRM

F. Andrew Anderson
F. Kingston Berlew
Abigail A. Cheever
Matthew C. Dallett
Jeanne P. Darcey
Robert Duggan
Lynnette C. Fallon
Steven N. Farber
Nathaniel S. Gardiner
Leon J. Glazerman
Richard Hiersteiner
George M. Hughes
Stanley Keller
Ronald H. Kessel
Jerry V. Klima
Michael Lytton
Maureen P. Manning
Robert P. Moncreiff
David R. Pokross, Jr.
Richard S. Rosenstein
James L. Terry
George Ticknor
William T. Whelan
John L. Whitlock
John Taylor Williams
Peter Wirth

COUNSEL

David J. Corrsin
Richard L. Farr (Not admitted in MA)
Zick Rubin

OF COUNSEL

John P. Weitzel

For Complete List of Firm Personnel, See General Section

For full biographical listings, see the Martindale-Hubbell Law Directory

POWERS & HALL, PROFESSIONAL CORPORATION (AV)

(Powers, Hall & Jones 1897-1903)
(Powers & Hall 1903-1957).
(Powers Hall, Montgomery & Weston 1957-1970)
100 Franklin Street, 02110
Telephone: 617-728-9600
Facsimile: 617-728-9633

DIRECTORS

Richard A. Wiley
Walter G. Van Dorn
William Williams II
Douglas A. Nadeau
Gene A. Blumenreich
John V. Woodard
Robert W. Holmes, Jr.
Gregory J. Englund
Andrew D. Frieze
Sydelle Pittas
Pamela J. Anderson
Benjamin W. Moulton
Stephen J. Small
Philip S. Mehall
David A. Broadwin

OF COUNSEL

John Clarke Kane

COUNSEL

Robert L. Nessen

Philip R. Reilly
Richard W. Mable
Michael K. Barron
Kathleen M. Bildzok
Marc C. Laredo
James T. Barrett
Mark G. Maher
Marcia Beth Stairman Wagner
David L. McEvoy
Gail Eagan
Eileen Smith Ewing (Not admitted in MA)

For full biographical listings, see the Martindale-Hubbell Law Directory

RACKEMANN, SAWYER & BREWSTER, PROFESSIONAL CORPORATION (AV)

One Financial Center, 02111
Telephone: 617-542-2300
Telecopier: 617-542-7437

William B. Tyler
George V. Anastas
Henry H. Thayer
Stephen Carr Anderson
Albert M. Fortier, Jr.
Michael F. O'Connell
Stuart T. Freeland
Raymond J. Brassard
Alan B. Rubenstein
Martin R. Healy
James R. Shea, Jr.
Brian M. Hurley

(See Next Column)

RACKEMANN, SAWYER & BREWSTER PROFESSIONAL CORPORATION, *Boston—Continued*

Janet M. Smith
Peter Friedenberg
Richard S. Novak
J. David Leslie
Alexander H. Spaulding
Sanford M. Matathia
Anne P. Zebrowski

OF COUNSEL

Albert B. Wolfe
August R. Meyer
Richard H. Lovell

COUNSEL

Ronald S. Duby
Ross J. Hamlin

Margaret L. Hayes
Daniel J. Ossoff
Mary B. Freeley
Gordon M. Orloff
Donald R. Pinto, Jr.
Lucy West Behymer
Richard J. Gallogly
Melissa Langer Ellis
James A. Wachta
Susan Dempsey Baer
Daniel J. Bailey, III
Michael S. Giaimo
Maura E. Murphy
Mary L. Gallant
Peter A. Alpert
Lauren D. Armstrong
Robert B. Foster
Elizabeth A. Gibbons

For full biographical listings, see the Martindale-Hubbell Law Directory

RICH, MAY, BILODEAU & FLAHERTY, P.C. (AV)

The Old South Building, 294 Washington Street, 02108-4675
Telephone: 617-482-1360
FAX: 617-556-3889

John F. Rich (1908-1987)
Thomas H. Bilodeau (1915-1987)
Gerald May
Harold B. Dondis
Walter L. Landergan, Jr.
Edwin J. Carr
Arthur F. Flaherty
Franklin M. Hundley
Michael F. Donlan
Joseph F. Sullivan, Jr.
Owen P. Maher
Nicolas A. Kensington
Daniel T. Clark
Gerald V. May, Jr.
Eric J. Krathwohl
Michael J. McHugh
James M. Behnke
James M. Avery
Stephen M. Kane
Mark C. O'Connor
Walter A. Wright, III
Emmett E. Lyne

Nicholas F. Kourtis
James T. Finnigan
Carol E. Kazmer
Robert P. Snell

For full biographical listings, see the Martindale-Hubbell Law Directory

ROCHE, CARENS & DEGIACOMO (AV)

A Partnership including Professional Corporations
One Post Office Square, 02109
Telephone: 617-451-9300
Facsimile: 617-482-3868
Woburn, Massachusetts Office: 400 Unicorn Park Drive.
Telephone: 617-933-5505.
Saugus, Massachusetts Office: 605 Broadway.
Telephone: 617-233-4074.
Vineyard Haven, Massachusetts Office: P.O. Box 2165.
Telephone: 508-693-7333.
Braintree, Massachusetts Office: 51 Commercial Street.
Telephone: 617-356-4210.

MEMBERS OF FIRM

Frederick W. Roche (1914-1971)
James R. DeGiacomo
Robert J. Sherer
Michael T. Putziger (P.C.)
Judith K. Wyman (P.C.)
John C. Wyman (P.C.)
Richard J. Saletta
John W. Gahan, III
Frank M. Capezzera
Loring A. Cook, III
John J. O'Connor, Jr.
Thomas K. Zebrowski
Susan J. Baronoff
Johanna Smith
Mary S. Parker
Anne Hanford Stossel
Mark G. DeGiacomo
Joseph R. Tarby III (Resident, Woburn Office)
Lynne Callahan DeGiacomo
Joan P. Armstrong
Maury E. Lederman
Brian R. Cook
Tracie L. Longman
Jacqueline Holmes Haley
Francis A. DiLuna (Resident, Woburn Office)

ASSOCIATES

William M. Healy (Resident, Vineyard Haven Office)
Cynthia H.N. Post
Thomas S. Vangel
Elizabeth B. Ornstein
Mark J. Warner
James B. Pratt
John F. Brosnan
Rachel S. Gerny
Allen A. Lynch, III (Resident, Saugus Office)
David A. Kelly (Resident, Braintree Office)
Edward J. Rozmiarek
Nancy M. Harris
Timothy P. Cox
Peter Carbone, III (Resident, Woburn Office)

OF COUNSEL

Thomas J. Carens
Daniel J. Johnedis

For full biographical listings, see the Martindale-Hubbell Law Directory

RUBIN AND RUDMAN (AV)

50 Rowes Wharf, 02110
Telephone: 617-330-7000
Telecopier: 617-439-9556

Milton Bordwin
Robert S. Walker
Jacob Aaron Esher

David C. Fixler
Edward R. Hill, Jr.

For Complete List of Firm Personnel, See General Section

For full biographical listings, see the Martindale-Hubbell Law Directory

SHERBURNE, POWERS & NEEDHAM, P.C. (AV)

One Beacon Street, 02108
Telephone: 617-523-2700
Fax: 617-523-6850

William D. Weeks
John T. Collins
Allan J. Landau
John L. Daly
Stephen A. Hopkins
Alan I. Falk
C. Thomas Swaim
James Pollock
William V. Tripp III
Stephen S. Young
William F. Machen
W. Robert Allison
Jacob C. Diemert
Philip J. Notopoulos
Richard J. Hindlian
Paul E. Troy
Harold W. Potter, Jr.
Dale R. Johnson
Philip S. Lapatin
Pamela A. Duckworth
Mark Schonfeld
James D. Smeallie
Paul Killeen
Gordon P. Katz
Joseph B. Darby, III
Richard M Yanofsky
James E. McDermott
Robert V. Lizza
Miriam Goldstein Altman
John J. Monaghan
Margaret J. Palladino
Mark C. Michalowski
David Scott Sloan
M. Chrysa Long
Lawrence D. Bradley
Miriam J. McKendall

Cynthia A. Brown
Cynthia M. Hern
Dianne R. Phillips
Paul M. James
Theodore F. Hanselman
Joshua C. Krumholz
Ieuan G. Mahony
Kenneth L. Harvey
Christopher J. Trombetta
Edwin F. Landers, Jr.
Amy J. Mastrobattista
William Howard McCarthy, Jr.
Douglas W. Clapp
Tamara E. Goulston
Nicholas J. Psyhogeos

COUNSEL

Haig Der Manuelian
Mason M. Taber, Jr.
Karl J. Hirshman
Benjamin Volinski
Kenneth P. Brier

OF COUNSEL

John Barr Dolan

For full biographical listings, see the Martindale-Hubbell Law Directory

SHERIN AND LODGEN (AV)

100 Summer Street, 02110
Telephone: 617-426-5720
Telecopier: 617-542-5186
Los Angeles, California Office: 11300 W. Olympic Boulevard, Suite 700.
Telephone: 310-914-7891.
Fax: 310-552-5327.
Nashua New Hampshire Office: One Indian Head Plaza.
Telephone: 603-595-4511.
Fax: 603-595-4968.
Providence, Rhode Island Office: 55 Pine Street.
Telephone: 401-274-8060.

MEMBERS OF FIRM

Arthur L. Sherin (1946-1964)
George E. Lodgen (1946-1971)
Morton B. Brown
George Waldstein
John M. Reed
Robert J. Muldoon, Jr.
Alette E. Reed
Edward M. Bloom
Thomas J. Raftery
Joshua M. Alper
Gary M. Markoff
Bryan G. Killian
David A. Guberman
Kenneth R. Berman
Frank J. Bailey
Thomas P. Gorman
Dorothy Nelson Stookey
Mark A. Nowak
Ronald W. Ruth
Steven D. Eimert
Daniel B. Winslow
Barbara A. O'Donnell
Brian C. Levey
A. Neil Hartzell
Kenneth J. Mickiewicz
Craig M. Brown
Andrew Royce
Daniel O. Gaquin
Thomas A. Hippler
Rhonda B. Parker
John J. Slater, III (Resident)

ASSOCIATES

Joanna E. Scannell
Nereyda Garcia
John C. La Liberte
Karen Elise Berman
Margaret H. Leeson
Joseph M. Kerwin
Christopher A. Kenney
David Benfield
Michael C. Giardiello

(See Next Column)

SHERIN AND LODGEN—*Continued*

OF COUNSEL

Paul Melrose | Michael S. Strauss

LEGAL SUPPORT PERSONNEL

Marilyn Stewart

For full biographical listings, see the Martindale-Hubbell Law Directory

SILVERMAN & KUDISCH, P.C. (AV)

Successor to Silverman & Kudisch.
One Longfellow Place, Suite 3608, 02114-2434
Telephone: 617-523-1711
Fax: 617-523-6037

William M. Silverman (1920-1981)
Clarence P. Kudisch (1936-1965)
Sumner Darman
Peter L. Zimmerman
Richard L. Blumenthal
Lisa B. Darman

For full biographical listings, see the Martindale-Hubbell Law Directory

CONCORD, Middlesex Co.

LAW OFFICE OF HENRY J. DANE (AV)

37 Main Street, P.O. Box 540, 01742
Telephone: 508-369-8333
Fax: 508-369-3106
Cable Address: Danelaw

ASSOCIATE

Trevor A. Haydon, Jr.

OF COUNSEL

Mark D. Shuman

For full biographical listings, see the Martindale-Hubbell Law Directory

LOWELL, Middlesex Co.

PETER B. ROBINSON (AV)

Nine Central Street, 01852-1927
Telephone: 508-452-5130
Telefax: 508-452-4136

For full biographical listings, see the Martindale-Hubbell Law Directory

*SPRINGFIELD,** Hampden Co.

ELY & KING (AV)

One Financial Plaza, 1350 Main Street, 01103
Telephone: 413-781-1920
Telecopier: 413-733-3360

MEMBERS OF FIRM

Joseph Buell Ely (1905-1956)
Raymond T. King (1919-1971)
Frederick M. Kingsbury (1924-1968)
Hugh J. Corcoran (1938-1992)
Richard S. Milstein
Donald A. Beaudry
Richard F. Faille
Leland B. Seabury
Gregory A. Schmidt
Pamela Manson
Anthony T. Rice
Russell J. Mawdsley

ASSOCIATE

Donna M. Brown

Representative Clients: Hartford Accident & Indemnity Co.; Albert Steiger Cos.; Shawmut Bank N.A.; Springfield Institution for Savings; St. Paul Fire & Marine Insurance Co.; The Rouse Co.; Tighe & Bond, Inc.; Northeast Utilities.

For full biographical listings, see the Martindale-Hubbell Law Directory

GABERMAN & PARISH, P.C. (AV)

32 Hampden Street, 01103
Telephone: 413-781-5066
Fax: 413-732-5439

Richard M. Gaberman | Ronda G. Parish

Richard D. Keough

OF COUNSEL

Leonard Judelson

For full biographical listings, see the Martindale-Hubbell Law Directory

*WORCESTER,** Worcester Co.

SEDER & CHANDLER (AV)

Established 1918
Burnside Building, 339 Main Street, 01608
Telephone: 508-757-7721
Telecopiers: 508-798-1863; 831-0955

(See Next Column)

MEMBERS OF FIRM

Samuel Seder (1918-1964)
Harold Seder (1934-1988)
Burton Chandler
J. Robert Seder
Darragh K. Kasakoff
Marvin S. Silver
John Woodward
John L. Pfeffer, Jr.
Robert S. Adler
Dawn E. Caccavaro

ASSOCIATES

Kevin C. McGee
Paul J. O'Riordan
Jeffrey P. Greenberg
Lisa S. Sigel
Denise M. Tremblay

OF COUNSEL

Saul A. Seder | Gerald E. Norman

Reference: Shawmut Worcester County Bank N.A.

For full biographical listings, see the Martindale-Hubbell Law Directory

MICHIGAN

*ANN ARBOR,** Washtenaw Co.

HOOPER, HATHAWAY, PRICE, BEUCHE & WALLACE (AV)

126 South Main Street, 48104
Telephone: 313-662-4426
Fax: 313-662-9559

James R. Beuche | Charles W. Borgsdorf
Bruce C. Conybeare, Jr.

Representative Clients: Chem-Trend, Inc.; Dundee Cement Co.; Ervin Industries, Inc.; First Martin Corp.; Group 243 Design, Inc.; Honeywell; Microwave Sensors, Inc.; Shearson Lehman Hutton; O'Neal Construction Co.; Pittsfield Products, Inc.

For Complete List of Firm Personnel, See General Section

For full biographical listings, see the Martindale-Hubbell Law Directory

BINGHAM FARMS, Oakland Co.

MEISNER AND HODGDON, P.C. (AV)

Suite 467, 30200 Telegraph Road, 48025-4506
Telephone: 810-644-4433
Fax: 810-644-2941

Robert M. Meisner | Samuel K. Hodgdon

Reference: Comerica Bank.

For full biographical listings, see the Martindale-Hubbell Law Directory

SOTIROFF ABRAMCZYK & RAUSS, P.C. (AV)

30400 Telegraph Road, Suite 444, 48025-4541
Telephone: 810-642-6000
Facsimile: 810-642-9001

Philip Sotiroff
Lawrence R. Abramczyk
Dennis M. Rauss
Lawrence A. Tower
Robert B. Goldi
Keith A. Sotiroff
Edward S. Toth

OF COUNSEL

John N. Kaspers

For full biographical listings, see the Martindale-Hubbell Law Directory

BIRMINGHAM, Oakland Co.

LOUIS J. BURNETT, P.C. (AV)

555 South Woodward, Suite 755, 48009-6782
Telephone: 810-642-4345
Fax: 810-642-2005

Louis J. Burnett

Reference: Comerica, Detroit, Michigan.

For full biographical listings, see the Martindale-Hubbell Law Directory

CARSON FISCHER, P.L.C. (AV)

Third Floor, 300 East Maple Road, 48009-6317
Telephone: 810-644-4840
Facsimile: 810-644-1832

Robert M. Carson
Joseph M. Fischer
Peter L. Wanger
William C. Edmunds
Todd M. Fink

For full biographical listings, see the Martindale-Hubbell Law Directory

AUSTIN HIRSCHHORN, P.C. (AV)

251 East Merrill Street, 2nd Floor, 48009-6150
Telephone: 810-646-9944
FAX: 810-647-8596

(See Next Column)

AUSTIN HIRSCHHORN, P.C., *Birmingham—Continued*

Austin Hirschhorn

For full biographical listings, see the Martindale-Hubbell Law Directory

HYMAN AND LIPPITT, P.C. (AV)

185 Oakland Avenue, Suite 300, P.O. Box 1750, 48009
Telephone: 810-646-8292
Facsimile: 810-646-8375

J. Leonard Hyman
Norman L. Lippitt
Douglas A. Hyman
Brian D. O'Keefe
H. Joel Newman
Nazli G. Sater
Kenneth F. Neuman
Terry S. Givens
Paul J. Fischer
Sanford Plotkin
John A. Sellers
Robert H. Lippitt
Roger L. Myers

COUNSEL

Alice L. Gilbert

For full biographical listings, see the Martindale-Hubbell Law Directory

MACDONALD AND GOREN, P.C. (AV)

Suite 200, 260 East Brown Street, 48009
Telephone: 810-645-5940
Fax: 810-645-2490

Harold C. MacDonald
Kalman G. Goren
Cindy Rhodes Victor
Amy L. Glenn
David D. Marsh
Glenn G. Ross
Miriam Blanks-Smart
John T. Klees

Representative Clients: Bay Corrugated Container, Inc.; Miles Fox Company; Orlandi Gear Company, Inc.; Bing Steel, Inc.; Superb Manufacturing, Inc.; Spring Engineering, Inc.; Adrian Steel Company; Southfield Radiology Associates, P.C.; Blockbuster Entertainment Corporation; E.N.U.F. Internationale, Inc.

For full biographical listings, see the Martindale-Hubbell Law Directory

PIERCE & PIERCE, P.C. (AV)

255 S. Woodward Avenue, Suite 205, 48009
Telephone: 810-647-0404
Fax: 810-647-0849

Robert B. Pierce
Mark C. Pierce

For full biographical listings, see the Martindale-Hubbell Law Directory

SIMPSON & BERRY, P.C. (AV)

260 East Brown, Suite 300, 48009
Telephone: 810-647-0200
Telecopier: 810-647-2776

Daniel F. Berry
Clark G. Doughty
Philip J. Goodman
James A. Simpson
Katheryne L. Zelenock

LEGAL SUPPORT PERSONNEL

Dwight Noble Baker, Jr.

Representative Clients: Automation Services Equipment, Inc.; BSI-Banca della Svizzera Italiana; Brown Tire Co.; Detroit Public Schools; Dupuis & Ryden, Accountants; Edw. C. Levy Co.; Ferndale School District; Filter Engineering Corp.; General Electric Capital Corp.

For full biographical listings, see the Martindale-Hubbell Law Directory

WEINGARDEN & HAUER, P.C. (AV)

30100 Telegraph Road, Suite 221, 48025
Telephone: 810-258-0800
Telecopier: 810-258-2750

Larry A. Weingarden

Reference: Security Bank & Trust.

For full biographical listings, see the Martindale-Hubbell Law Directory

BLOOMFIELD HILLS, Oakland Co.

CLARK, KLEIN & BEAUMONT (AV)

1533 North Woodward Avenue, Suite 220, 48304
Telephone: 810-258-2900
Facsmile: 810-258-2949
Detroit, Michigan Office: 1600 First Federal Building. 1001 Woodward Avenue.
Telephone: 313-965-8300.
Facsimile: 313-962-4348.

MEMBERS OF FIRM

Edward C. Dawda
Curtis J. Mann

Representative Clients: R.P. Scherer; Budd Company; LCI International; CDI Corporation; Booth Communications, Inc.; First Federal of Michigan; Horizon Health Systems; Michigan Manufacturers Association; The Skillman Foundation; Hudson-Weber Foundation.

(See Next Column)

For Complete List of Firm Personnel, See General Section

For full biographical listings, see the Martindale-Hubbell Law Directory

GOOGASIAN, HOPKINS, HOHAUSER & FORHAN, P.C. (AV)

6895 Telegraph Road, 48301-3138
Telephone: 810-540-3333
Fax: 810-540-7213

George A. Googasian
Stephen J. Hopkins
Michael S. Hohauser
Craig G. Forhan
Craig Weber
Steven G. Googasian

For full biographical listings, see the Martindale-Hubbell Law Directory

HARDIG & PARSONS (AV)

2000 North Woodward Avenue, Suite 100, 48304
Telephone: 313-642-3500
Facsimile: 313-645-1128
Charlevoix, Michigan Office: 212 Bridge Street.
Telephone: 616-547-1200.
Facsimile: 616-547-1026.
Pawley's Island, South Carolina Office: 216 Highway 17, P.O. Box 1607, 29585.
Telephone: 803-237-9219.
Facsimile: 803-237-9530.
West Palm Beach, Florida Office: Suite 1450, 515 North Flagler.
Telephone: 407-833-1622.
Facsimile: 407-833-6933.
Charlotte Amalie, St. Thomas, Virgin Islands Office: International Plaza, 22 Dronningens Gade.
Telephone: 809-776-7650.
Facsimile: 809-774-2729.

MEMBERS OF FIRM

Joseph L. Hardig, Jr.
Donald H. Parsons
Joseph L. Hardig, III

ASSOCIATES

Bradley S. Stout
Kevin M. O'Connell

OF COUNSEL

Frederick Wm. Heath

MEMBER IN FLORIDA

Charles Ryan Hickman

MEMBER IN SOUTH CAROLINA

John C. Benso

OF COUNSEL

Preston Bennett Haines, III

MEMBER IN CHARLOTTE AMALIE, ST. THOMAS, VIRGIN ISLANDS

Arthur Pomerantz

ASSOCIATE

Marcia B. Resnick

For full biographical listings, see the Martindale-Hubbell Law Directory

HOWARD & HOWARD ATTORNEYS, P.C. (AV)

The Pinehurst Office Center, Suite 101, 1400 North Woodward Avenue, 48304-2856
Telephone: 810-645-1483
Telecopier: 810-645-1568
Kalamazoo, Michigan Office: The Kalamazoo Building, Suite 400, 107 West Michigan Avenue.
Telephone: 616-382-1483.
Telecopier: 616-382-1568.
Lansing, Michigan Office: The Phoenix Building, Suite 500, 222 Washington Square, North.
Telephone: 517-485-1483.
Telecopier: 517-485-1568.
Peoria, Illinois Office: Howard & Howard, P.C., The Creve Coeur Building, Suite 200, 321 Liberty Street.
Telephone: 309-672-1483.
Telecopier: 309-672-1568.

Gustaf R. Andreasen
Robert L. Biederman
Walter J. Borda
Thomas R. Curran, Jr.
Mark A. Davis
Paul Green
Timothy E. Kraepel
D. Craig Martin
Claude Henry Miller
James C. Wickens
Timothy M. Wittebort
John E. Young

Representative Clients: For Representative Client list, see General Practice, Bloomfield Hills, MI.

For Complete List of Firm Personnel, See General Section

For full biographical listings, see the Martindale-Hubbell Law Directory

MAY, SIMPSON & STROTE, A PROFESSIONAL CORPORATION (AV)

100 West Long Lake Road Suite 200, P.O. Box 541, 48303-0541
Telephone: 810-646-9500

(See Next Column)

MAY, SIMPSON & STROTE A PROFESSIONAL CORPORATION—*Continued*

Richard H. May
Thomas C. Simpson
Ronald P. Strote
Steven M. Raymond
John A. Forrest
David K. McDonnell

Steven F. Alexsy
Marilynn K. Arnold
Michele A. Lerner

Representative Clients: Aamco Transmission; American Annuity Life Insurance; Container Corporation of America; Citicorp Financial Center; Century 21 Real Estate Corp.; Oak Hills Mortgage Corp.; Ziebart International Corp.
Reference: NBD Bank, N.A.

For full biographical listings, see the Martindale-Hubbell Law Directory

MEYER, KIRK, SNYDER & SAFFORD (AV)

Suite 100, 100 West Long Lake Road, 48304
Telephone: 810-647-5111
Telecopier: 810-647-6079
Detroit, Michigan Office: 2500 Penobscot Building.
Telephone: 313-961-1261.

George H. Meyer
John M. Kirk
George E. Snyder
Ralph R. Safford
Donald H. Baker, Jr.
Patrick K. Rode

ASSOCIATES

Christopher F. Clark
Boyd C. Farnam
Debra S. Meier

OF COUNSEL

Mark R. Solomon

Representative Clients: Chemical Waste Management; Ervin Advertising; The Michigan and S.E. Michigan McDonald's Operators Assn.; The Southland Corp. (7-Eleven Food Stores); Stauffer Chemical Co.; Techpoint, Inc.

For full biographical listings, see the Martindale-Hubbell Law Directory

DAVID D. PATTON & ASSOCIATES, P.C. (AV)

100 Bloomfield Hills Parkway, Suite 110, 48304
Telephone: 810-258-6020
Fax: 810-258-6052

David D. Patton

Ellen Bartman Jannette
James A. Reynolds, Jr.
Patricia C. White
David H. Patton (1912-1993)

For full biographical listings, see the Martindale-Hubbell Law Directory

SILLS, LAW, ESSAD, FIEDLER & CHARBONEAU, P.C. (AV)

1550 Woodward Avenue, Suite 200, 48304
Telephone: 810-646-1310
Fax: 810-901-4842
Lansing, Michigan Office: 412 West Ionia.
Telephone: 517-372-1717.
Fax: 517-372-0209.
Flint, Michigan Office: 1000 Beach Street, 48502.
Telephone: 313-233-0484.
Fax: 313-233-5415.
Traverse City, Michigan Office: 900 East Front Street, Suite 300.
Telephone: 616-941-2218.
Fax: 616-941-8958.

John D. Sills
Robert C. Law
Ernest J. Essad, Jr.
Charles Arthur Fiedler
Thomas R. Charboneau, Jr.
Victor A. Zambardi
David W. Geiss
Scott J. Rynearson
Christopher L. Buday

For full biographical listings, see the Martindale-Hubbell Law Directory

STROBL AND MANOOGIAN, P.C. (AV)

300 East Long Lake Road, Suite 200, 48304-2376
Telephone: 810-645-0306
Facsimile: 810-645-2690

Thomas J. Strobl
Brian C. Manoogian
John Sharp
James A. Rocchio
Kieran F. Cunningham
Michael E. Thoits
James D. Wilson

James T. Dunn
Sara S. Lisznyai
Brian M. Gottry
Thomas H. Kosik
Keith S. King
Pamela S. Ritter
Robert F. Boesiger
Douglas Young

Representative Clients: American Speedy Printing Centers, Inc.; Bohn Aluminum Corporation; Consulting Resource Associates, Inc.; Crown Boring, Inc.; Engineered Products Sales Company, Inc.; Masco Corporation; MascoTech; Metrostaff Health Care Services; Michigan Marine Terminal, Inc.; Modern Vending Service Co.

(See Next Column)

For Complete List of Firm Personnel, See General Section

For full biographical listings, see the Martindale-Hubbell Law Directory

BRIGHTON, Livingston Co.

BURCHFIELD, PARK & ASSOCIATES, P.C. (AV)

225 E. Grand River, Suite 203, 48116
Telephone: 810-227-3100
Facsimile: 810-227-2996

Kenneth E. Burchfield
David L. Park

Shari L. Heddon
Gregory C. Burkart

LEGAL SUPPORT PERSONNEL

Janet M. Schillinger

For full biographical listings, see the Martindale-Hubbell Law Directory

*DETROIT,** Wayne Co.

ABBOTT, NICHOLSON, QUILTER, ESSHAKI & YOUNGBLOOD, P.C. (AV)

19th Floor, One Woodward Avenue, 48226
Telephone: 313-963-2500
Telecopier: 313-963-7882

C. Richard Abbott
John R. Nicholson
Thomas R. Quilter III
Gene J. Esshaki
John F. Youngblood
Donald E. Conley
James B. Perry
Carl F. Jarboe
Jay A. Kennedy
Timothy A. Stoepker
Timothy J. Kramer
Norbert T. Madison, Jr.
William D. Gilbride, Jr.

Mary P. Nelson
Michael R. Blum
Thomas Ferguson Hatch
Anne D. Warren Bagno
Mark E. Mueller
Eric J. Girdler

OF COUNSEL

Thomas C. Shumaker
Roy R. Hunsinger

For full biographical listings, see the Martindale-Hubbell Law Directory

BODMAN, LONGLEY & DAHLING (AV)

34th Floor 100 Renaissance Center, 48243
Telephone: 313-259-7777
Fax: 313-393-7579
Troy, Michigan Office: Suite 2020, 755 West Big Beaver Road.
Telephone: 810-362-2110.
Ann Arbor, Michigan Office: 110 Miller, Suite 300.
Telephone: 313-761-3780.
Northern Michigan Office: 229 Court Street, P.O. Box 405, Cheboygan.
Telephone: 616-627-4351.

MEMBERS OF FIRM

Richard D. Rohr
Theodore Souris
Joseph A. Sullivan
Walter O. Koch (Troy Office)
Michael B. Lewiston
George D. Miller, Jr.
Thomas A. Roach (Ann Arbor Office)
Kenneth R. Lango (Troy Office)
James T. Heimbuch
Herold McC. Deason
James R. Buschmann
Joseph J. Kochanek
David G. Chardavoyne
Terrence B. Larkin (Troy Office)
Robert J. Diehl, Jr.
Martha Bedsole Goodloe (Troy Office)
Harvey W. Berman (Ann Arbor Office)
Barbara Bowman Bluford
Christopher J. Dine (Troy Office)

COUNSEL

Lewis A. Rockwell

Representative Clients: Abitibi Price Group; Archdiocese of Detroit; Comerica Bank; The Detroit Lions, Inc.; Ford Estates; General Motors Corporation; Charles Steward Mott Foundation; Norfolk Southern Corporation; Panhandle Eastern Corporation; State Farm Mutual Automobile Insurance Company.

For Complete List of Firm Personnel, See General Section

For full biographical listings, see the Martindale-Hubbell Law Directory

BUTZEL LONG, A PROFESSIONAL CORPORATION (AV)

Suite 900, 150 West Jefferson, 48226
Telephone: 313-225-7000
Telecopier: 313-225-7080
Birmingham, Michigan Office: Suite 200, 32270 Telegraph Road.
Telephone: 810-258-1616.
Telecopier: 810-258-1439.
Lansing, Michigan Office: 118 West Ottawa Street.
Telephone: 517-372-6622.
Telecopier: 517-372-6672.
Ann Arbor, Michigan Office: Suite 400, 121 West Washington.
Telephone: 313-995-3110.
Telecopier: 313-995-1777.

(See Next Column)

BUTZEL LONG A PROFESSIONAL CORPORATION, *Detroit—Continued*

Grosse Pointe Farms, Michigan Office: Suite 260, 21 Kercheval.
Telephone: 313-886-5446.
Telecopier: 313-886-2114.

Harold A. Ruemenapp
Morris Milmet
Frank B. Vecchio
William R. Ralls (Lansing)
C. Peter Theut
Robert B. Foster (Ann Arbor)
Philip J. Kessler
Thomas E. Sizemore
James C. Bruno
Mark S. Smallwood
Justin G. Klimko
Barbara S. Kendzierski
Mark R. Lezotte
Michael F. Golab
James L. Hughes
Arthur Dudley II
Gary J. Abraham (Birmingham)
James Y. Stewart
Brian P. Henry (Birmingham and Lansing)

COUNSEL

Oscar H. Feldman
Ralph S. Rumsey (Ann Arbor)

OF COUNSEL

Erwin S. Simon

Brian J. Miles
Joshua A. Sherbin

Representative Clients: American Tape Co.; William Beaumont Hospital; Dunham's Athleisure, Inc.; The Evening News Assn.; Fruehauf Corp.; Hanac Acquisition Co.; Harvard Industries; Jackson National Life Insurance Co.; The Stroh Brewery Co.

For Complete List of Firm Personnel, See General Section

For full biographical listings, see the Martindale-Hubbell Law Directory

CLARK, KLEIN & BEAUMONT (AV)

1600 First Federal Building, 1001 Woodward Avenue, 48226
Telephone: 313-965-8300
Facsimile: 313-962-4348
Bloomfield Hills Office: 1533 North Woodward Avenue, Suite 220, 48304.
Telephone: 810-258-2900.
Facsimile: 810-258-2949.

MEMBERS OF FIRM

D. Kerry Crenshaw
John F. Burns
Robert L. Weyhing, III
David E. Nims, III
Edward C. Dawda (Resident Bloomfield Hills, Michigan Office)
Curtis J. Mann (Resident Bloomfield Hills, Michigan Office)
Duane L. Tarnacki
Michael S. Khoury
John J. Hern, Jr.
Andrea M. Kanski

ASSOCIATES

Michael I. Conlon
David A. Foster
Patrice A. Villani
Georgette Borrego Dulworth

Representative Clients: R. P. Scherer; The Budd Co.; LCI International; CDI Corporation; Booth Communications, Inc.; First Federal of Michigan; Horizon Health Systems; Michigan Manufacturers Association; The Skillman Foundation; Hudson-Weber Foundation.

For Complete List of Firm Personnel, See General Section

For full biographical listings, see the Martindale-Hubbell Law Directory

DENARDIS, MCCANDLESS & MULLER, P.C. (AV)

800 Buhl Building, 48226-3602
Telephone: 313-963-9050
Fax: 313-963-4553

Ronald F. DeNardis
William McCandless
Gregory J. Muller
Mark F. Miller
Lawrence M. Hintz
Michael D. Dolenga

Representative Clients: Acustar; American Medical Systems, Inc.; Bettcher Industries, Inc.; Cargill, Inc.; Chrysler Corporation; The Doctors Company; Emro Marketing Company; Marathon Oil Company; MedMarc; Parker Hannifin Corporation.

For full biographical listings, see the Martindale-Hubbell Law Directory

EGGENBERGER, EGGENBERGER, MCKINNEY, WEBER & HOFMEISTER, P.C. (AV)

42nd Floor Penobscot Building, 48226
Telephone: 313-961-9722

William J. Eggenberger (1900-1984)
William D. Eggenberger
Robert E. Eggenberger
John P. McKinney
Stephen L. Weber
Paul D. Hofmeister

R. Scott Mills
Mary T. Humbert
James B. Eggenberger

Representative Clients: Amoco Oil Co.; Central National Insurance Group of Omaha; City of Wayne, Michigan; Clark Oil & Refining Corp.; Country Mutual Casualty Co.; Auto Club Insurance Assn.; General Accident Assurance Co., Ltd.; Great Central Insurance Co.; Inland Mutual Insurance Co.; Midwest Mutual Insurance Co.

(See Next Column)

For full biographical listings, see the Martindale-Hubbell Law Directory

JAFFE, RAITT, HEUER & WEISS, PROFESSIONAL CORPORATION (AV)

One Woodward Avenue, Suite 2400, 48226
Telephone: 313-961-8380
Telecopier: 313-961-8358
Cable Address: "Jafsni"
Southfield,Michigan Office: Travelers Tower, Suite 1520.
Telephone: 313-961-8380.
Monroe, Michigan Office: 212 East Front Street, Suite 3.
Telephone: 313-241-6470.
Telefacsimile: 313-241-3849.

Judith Lowitz Adler
Penny L. Carolan
Wallace H. Glendening
Robert J. Gordon
Jeffrey G. Heuer
Blair B. Hysni
Ira J. Jaffe
Robin H. Krueger
Mark P. Krysinski
Joel J. Morris
Stephen G. Schafer
Elliot A. Spoon
David D. Warner
Arthur A. Weiss
Richard A. Zussman

Derek S. Adolf
Lesley A. Gaber
Gerald F. Reinhart
Jeffrey M. Weiss

See General Practice Section for list of Representative Clients.

For Complete List of Firm Personnel, See General Section

For full biographical listings, see the Martindale-Hubbell Law Directory

JOHNSON & VALENTINE (AV)

4372 Penobscot Building, 48226
Telephone: 313-961-4700

MEMBERS OF FIRM

Edward C. Johnson
Glenn L. Valentine

ASSOCIATE

Dale T. McPherson

OF COUNSEL

Jarvis J. Schmidt

Representative Clients: First of America Bank-Southeast Michigan, N.A., Corp. Tr. Dpt.; Sun Bank-Miami, N.A., Coral Gables, Tr.Dpt.; Fifth Third Bank of Toledo, N.A.; Cozadd Rotary Foundation Trust; Colonial Hockey League; National Transportation Counsellors.
References: First of America Bank; Southeast Michigan, N.A.

For full biographical listings, see the Martindale-Hubbell Law Directory

R.H. PYTELL & ASSOCIATES, P.C. (AV)

18580 Mack Avenue, 48236
Telephone: 313-343-9200
Fax: 313-343-0207

R. H. Pytell
Henry C. Pytell (1903-1988)
Paul E. Varchetti

OF COUNSEL

Lewis M. Slater

For full biographical listings, see the Martindale-Hubbell Law Directory

RICKEL & BAUN, A PROFESSIONAL CORPORATION (AV)

Suite 1400, 600 Renaissance Center, 48243
Telephone: 313-259-3500
Telecopier Group 3, 2, 1 313-886-0405
Grosse Pointe Farms
Grosse Pointe Farms, Michigan Office: 63 Kercheval.
Telephone: 313-886-0000.
Telecopier: Group 3, 2, 1 313-886-0405.

John M. Rickel
Mark A. Baun

Representative Clients: Alexander & Alexander of Michigan, Inc.; American Box Co.; Farm House Foods; French Trade Commission, Detroit; Grosse Pointe Cable TV, Inc.; Grosse Pointe War Memorial Assn.

For full biographical listings, see the Martindale-Hubbell Law Directory

DAVID M. THOMS & ASSOCIATES, P.C. (AV)

400 Renaissance Center, Suite 950, 48243
Telephone: 313-259-6333
Facsimile: 313-259-7037
Bloomfield Hills, Office: 1500 Woodward Avenue, Suite 100.
Telephone: 313-259-6333.
Fax: 313-259-7037.
Grosse Pointe Office: 377 Fisher Road.
Telephone: 313-259-6333.
Fax: 313-259-7037.

David M. Thoms

(See Next Column)

DAVID M. THOMS & ASSOCIATES, P.C.—*Continued*

Audrey R. Holley | Duane B. Brown

OF COUNSEL

Allan G. Meganck | Thomas V. Trainer

Representative Clients: Avion Concepts, Inc.; Fowler Agency Corp.; Gibbs World Wide Wines, Inc.; deBary Travel, Inc.; North Management, Inc.; St. Jude Children's Research Hospital.
References: Comerica Bank-Detroit, National Bank of Detroit.

For full biographical listings, see the Martindale-Hubbell Law Directory

TIMMIS & INMAN (AV)

300 Talon Centre, 48207
Telephone: 313-396-4200
Telecopier: 313-396-4228

MEMBERS OF FIRM

Michael T. Timmis
Wayne C. Inman
Robert E. Graziani
George A. Peck
Charles W. Royer
Richard L. Levin
Henry J. Brennan, III
Mark W. Peyser
Richard M. Miettinen
Lisa R. Gorman

ASSOCIATES

Bradley J. Knickerbocker
George M. Malis
Amy Lynn Ryntz
Mark Robert Adams
Daniel G. Kielczewski
Michael F. Wais
Kevin S. Kendall
John P. Kanan
David J. Galbenski

OF COUNSEL

William B. Fitzgerald | W. Clark Durant, III

Representative Clients: F & M Distributors; Deneb Robotics; Combine International; Chateau Estates.

For full biographical listings, see the Martindale-Hubbell Law Directory

WISE & MARSAC, PROFESSIONAL CORPORATION (AV)

11th Floor Buhl Building, 48226-3681
Telephone: 313-962-0643
Telecopier: 313-962-0688
Cable: "DYWI-DET"
Telex: 810-221-5371
Ann Arbor, Michigan Office: 24 Frank Lloyd Wright Drive.
Telephone: 313-930-4405.
Birmingham, Michigan Office: 555 South Woodward, Suite 755.
Telephone: 810-642-4345.

John A. Wise
Robert A. Marsac
Stephen M. Fleming
Darrell M. Grams
Eric H. Lipsitt
John M. Pollock (Resident, Birmingham Office)
Edward V. Keelean
Guy P. Hoadley
Robert A. Feldman
James F. Kamp

OF COUNSEL

Louis J. Burnett (Resident, Birmingham Office)
Robert E. Day
Albert L. Lieberman
William D. Maroney (Not admitted in MI)
Elijah Poxson

Karen E. Bridges
Lisa A. Robinson
Gary A. Kendra
Howard M. Klausmeier
Scott A. Steinhoff (Resident, Birmingham Office)
Amy E. Anderson
Michael S. Thomas
Mark V. Heusel
Jerry L. Ashford

Representative Clients: Aon Corporation; BASF Corp.; Bell Atlantic TriCon Leasing Corp.; Camp, Dresser & McKee, Inc.; The Detroit Edison Co.; The Dow Chemical Co.; Seaboard Surety Co.; Suburban Communications Corp.; Texaco, Inc.; Union Carbide Corp.

For full biographical listings, see the Martindale-Hubbell Law Directory

EAST LANSING, Ingham Co.

FARHAT, STORY & KRAUS, P.C. (AV)

Beacon Place, 4572 South Hagadorn Road, Suite 3, 48823
Telephone: 517-351-3700
Fax: 517-332-4122

Leo A. Farhat
James E. Burns (1925-1979)
Monte R. Story
Richard C. Kraus
Max R. Hoffman Jr.
Chris A. Bergstrom
Kitty L. Groh
Charles R. Toy
David M. Platt
Lawrence P. Schweitzer
Jeffrey J. Short
Kathy A. Breedlove
Thomas L. Sparks

Representative Clients: Big L. Corp.; Michigan Automotive Wholesalers Association; Hartman-Fabco, Inc.; Lansing Electric Motors, Inc.; Mike Miller Lincoln Mercury; GTE Sprint Communications; GTE Directories Service Corp.; Central Transport, Inc.; American Medical Malpractice, Inc.; Jackson National Life Ins. Co.; State Farm Life Ins. Co.
Reference: Capitol National Bank, Old City Bank, Old Kent Bank & Trust.

For full biographical listings, see the Martindale-Hubbell Law Directory

*ESCANABA,** Delta Co.

BUTCH, QUINN, ROSEMURGY, JARDIS, BUSH, BURKHART & STROM, P.C. (AV)

816 Ludington Street, 49829
Telephone: 906-786-4422
Fax: 906-786-5128
Gladstone, Michigan Office: 201 First National Bank Building.
Telephone: 906-428-3123.
Marquette, Michigan Office: 300 South Front Street.
Telephone: 906-228-4440.
Iron Mountain, Michigan Office: 500 South Stephenson Avenue.
Telephone: 906-774-4460.
Marinette, Wisconsin Office: 2008 Ella Court.
Telephone: 715-732-4154.

Thomas L. Butch
Terry F. Burkhart
Peter W. Strom
John A. Lewandowski

Representative Clients: Champion, Inc.; St. Francis Hospital; Bresnan Cable Communications Co.; Valmet Logging Americas, Inc.; Alger-Delta Cooperative Electric Association; Northern Motors Ford; Champion International Corporation; Soo Line Railroad; Upper Peninsula Association of Realtors.

For Complete List of Firm Personnel, See General Section

For full biographical listings, see the Martindale-Hubbell Law Directory

FARMINGTON HILLS, Oakland Co.

COUZENS, LANSKY, FEALK, ELLIS, ROEDER & LAZAR, P.C. (AV)

33533 West Twelve Mile Road, Suite 150, P.O. Box 9057, 48333-9057
Telephone: 810-489-8600
Telecopier: 810-489-4156

Sheldon A. Fealk
Jack S. Couzens, II
Jerry M. Ellis
Donald M. Lansky
Bruce J. Lazar
Alan C. Roeder
Alan J. Ferrara
Renard J. Kolasa
Kathryn Gilson Sussman
Jeffrey A. Levine
Stephen M. Feldman
Phillip L. Sternberg
Marc L. Prey
Lisa J. Walters
Michael P. Witzke
Stephen Scapelliti
Cyrus Raamin Kashef
William P. Lyshak
Gregg A. Nathanson
Aaron H. Sherbin
Mark S. Frankel
Lynette M. Sheldon

References: Comerica Bank-Southfield;
Representative Clients: Provided upon request.

For full biographical listings, see the Martindale-Hubbell Law Directory

DAGUANNO AND ACCETTURA (AV)

Arboretum Office Park, 34705 West Twelve Mile Road, Suite 311, 48331
Telephone: 810-489-1444
Fax: 810-489-1453

MEMBERS OF FIRM

Richard Daguanno | P. Mark Accettura

ASSOCIATES

Robert J. Constan | Harry P. Bugeja

OF COUNSEL

John A. Zick | Robert E. Miller

References: Comerica Bank; Michigan Chamber of Commerce.

For full biographical listings, see the Martindale-Hubbell Law Directory

KAUFMAN AND PAYTON (AV)

200 Northwestern Financial Center, 30833 Northwestern Highway, 48334
Telephone: 810-626-5000
Telefacsimile: 810-626-2843
Grand Rapids, Michigan Office: 420 Trust Building.
Telephone: 616-459-4200.
Fax: 616-459-4929.
Traverse City, Michigan Office: 122 West State Street.
Telephone: 616-947-4050.
Fax: 616-947-7321.

(See Next Column)

KAUFMAN AND PAYTON, *Farmington Hills—Continued*

Alan Jay Kaufman
Donald L. Payton
Kenneth C. Letherwood
Stephen R. Levine
Thomas L. Vitu
Ralph C. Chapa, Jr.
Raymond I. Foley, II
Jeffrey K. Van Hattum
Leo D. Neville

For full biographical listings, see the Martindale-Hubbell Law Directory

*FLINT,** Genesee Co.

HICKS, SCHMIDLIN & BANCROFT, P.C. (AV)

2300 Austin Parkway, Suite 120, 48507
Telephone: 810-232-5038
Fax: 810-232-5538

L. James Hicks
Randall R. Schmidlin
Robert H. Bancroft
Carolyn S. Pringle
David J. Ledermann

Representative Clients: Atlas Technologies, Inc.; J. Austin Oil Company; Contour Fabricators, Inc.; Erickson Lindstrom Construction Co.; Eugene Welding Co.; Industrial Mutual Association of Flint; McLaren Regional Medical Center; Muffler Man Supply Co., Inc.; Shively Brothers, Inc.
Reference: Citizens Commercial & Savings Bank.

For full biographical listings, see the Martindale-Hubbell Law Directory

WINEGARDEN, SHEDD, HALEY, LINDHOLM & ROBERTSON (AV)

501 Citizens Bank Building, 48502-1983
Telephone: 810-767-3600
Telecopier: 810-767-8776

MEMBERS OF FIRM

William C. Shedd
Dennis M. Haley
John T. Lindholm
Donald H. Robertson
L. David Lawson
John R. Tucker

ASSOCIATES

Alan F. Himelhoch
Suellen J. Parker
Damion Frasier
Peter T. Mooney

OF COUNSEL

Howard R. Grossman

Representative Clients: Citizens Commercial and Savings Bank; R. L. White Development Corporation; Interstate Traffic Consultants (Intracon) Inc.; Downtown Development Authority of Flint; Young Olds-Cadillac, Inc.; First American Title Insurance Co.; Sorensen Gross Construction Co.; Genesee County; Insight, Inc.; Modern Industries, Inc.

For Complete List of Firm Personnel, See General Section

For full biographical listings, see the Martindale-Hubbell Law Directory

*GRAND RAPIDS,** Kent Co.

CLARY, NANTZ, WOOD, HOFFIUS, RANKIN & COOPER (AV)

500 Calder Plaza, 250 Monroe Avenue, N.W., 49503-2244
Telephone: 616-459-9487
Telecopier: 616-459-5121

MEMBERS OF FIRM

Leonard M. Hoffius
Harold E. Nelson

OF COUNSEL

Richard J. Rankin, Jr.

ASSOCIATE

Dale R. Rietberg

Representative Clients: United Bank of Michigan; D&W Food Centers, Inc.; FMB First Michigan Bank-Grand Rapids; Goodrich Theatres & Radio, Inc.; S. Abraham & Sons, Inc.; Garb-Ko, Inc., d/b/a 7-Eleven; Weather Shield Mfg., Inc.; JET Electronics & Technology, Inc.; Westinghouse Credit Corp.

For Complete List of Firm Personnel, See General Section

For full biographical listings, see the Martindale-Hubbell Law Directory

RHOADES, MCKEE, BOER, GOODRICH & TITTA (AV)

161 Ottawa N.W., Suite 600, 49503-2793
Telephone: 616-235-3500
Fax: 616-459-5102
Affiliated Offices: De Francesco & De Francesco, The Shepard House, 903 Main Street, P.O. Box 769, St. Joseph, Michigan, 49085.
Telephone: 616-983-7712.
Fax: 616-983-6901.
De Francesco & De Francesco, 139 North Whittaker Street, New Buffalo, Michigan, 49117. Telephone: 616-469-0537.
Fax: 616-649-4603.

(See Next Column)

Edward B. Goodrich
Peter A. Titta
Richard G. Leonard
Arthur C. Spalding
Robert J. Dugan
Terrence L. Groesser
Thomas P. Hogan
Kurt D. Hassberger
James M. Flaggert
Mary Ann Cartwright
Joel S. Huyser
Daniel L. Elve
Laurie M. Strong
Stephen A. Hilger
Gregory G. Timmer

Mary Lynette Williams
Scott J. Steiner
Charles A. Pearce
Robert C. Shaver
Jeff A. Moyer
Kevin A. Hansen

Reference: First Michigan Bank.

For full biographical listings, see the Martindale-Hubbell Law Directory

VARNUM, RIDDERING, SCHMIDT & HOWLETT (AV)

Bridgewater Place, P.O. Box 352, 49501-0352
Telephone: 616-336-6000
800-262-0011
Facsimile: 616-336-7000
Telex: 1561593 VARN
Lansing, Michigan Office: The Victor Center, Suite 810, 210 North Washington Square, 48933.
Telephone: 517-482-6237.
Facsimile: 517-482-6937.
Kalamazoo, Michigan Office: 350 East Michigan Avenue, 49007.
Telephone: 616-382-2300.
Facsimile: 616-382-2382.
Grand Haven, Michigan Office: 321 Washington Street, P.O. Box 288, 49417.
Telephone: 616-846-7100.
Facsimile: 616-846-7101.
Battle Creek, Michigan Office: 4950 West Dickman Road, Suite B-1, 49015.
Telephone: 616-962-7144.
Detroit, Michigan Office: 440 East Congress, Fourth Floor, 48226.
Telephone: 313-961-1600.
Facsimile: 313-961-1636.

COUNSEL

William J. Halliday, Jr.
H. Raymond Andrews, Jr.

MEMBERS OF FIRM

James N. DeBoer, Jr.
Hilary F. Snell
John C. Carlyle (Resident at Grand Haven Office)
Donald L. Johnson
Daniel C. Molhoek
Thomas T. Huff (Resident at Kalamazoo Office)
J. Terry Moran
Robert D. Kullgren
Robert P. Cooper
Frank G. Dunten
Robert L. Diamond
Lawrence P. Burns
Carl Oosterhouse
William J. Lawrence III
Kaplin S. Jones
Michael G. Wooldridge
Jeffrey W. Beswick (Resident at Grand Haven Office)
Scott A. Huizenga

ASSOCIATES

Kathleen P. Fochtman
Jinya Chen
Patrick A. Miles, Jr.
Steven J. Morren
Randy A. Bridgeman
Joseph B. Levan

Counsel For: Donnelly Corporation; First Michigan Bank Corporation ; Gainey Corporation; Gentex Corporation; Grand Rapids Association of Realtors; Harrow Products, Inc.; Herman Miller, Inc.; Holland Hitch Co.; S-2 Yachts, Inc.; X-Rite Corporation.

For Complete List of Firm Personnel, See General Section

For full biographical listings, see the Martindale-Hubbell Law Directory

WHEELER UPHAM, A PROFESSIONAL CORPORATION (AV)

Second Floor, Trust Building, 40 Pearl Street, N.W., 49503
Telephone: 616-459-7100
Fax: 616-459-6366

Gordon B. Wheeler (1904-1986)
Buford A. Upham (Retired)
Robert H. Gillette
Geoffrey L. Gillis
John M. Roels
Gary A. Maximiuk
Timothy J. Orlebeke
Kenneth E. Tiews
Jack L. Hoffman
Janet C. Baxter
Peter Kladder, III
James M. Shade
Thomas A. Kuiper

Counsel for: Travelers Insurance Co.; Prudential Insurance Co. of America; Farmers Insurance Group; Metropolitan Life Insurance Co.; Conrail Trans.; Monsanto Co.; Firestone Tire & Rubber Co.; Navistar, Inc.; Medtronic, Inc.; Westdale Better Homes and Gardens.

For full biographical listings, see the Martindale-Hubbell Law Directory

GROSSE POINTE FARMS, Wayne Co.

RICKEL & BAUN, A PROFESSIONAL CORPORATION (AV)

63 Kercheval, Suite 100, 48236-3627
Telephone: 313-886-0000
Telecopier: Group 3, 2, 1 313-886-0405
Detroit, Michigan Office: Suite 1400, 600 Renaissance Center.
Telephone: 313-259-3500.
Telecopier: Group 3, 2, 1 313-886-0405.

John M. Rickel
Mark A. Baun

For full biographical listings, see the Martindale-Hubbell Law Directory

*KALAMAZOO,** Kalamazoo Co.

DEMING, HUGHEY, LEWIS, ALLEN & CHAPMAN, P.C. (AV)

800 Old Kent Bank Building, 49007
Telephone: 616-349-6601
Fax: 616-349-3831

Ned W. Deming
Richard M. Hughey
Dean S. Lewis
W. Fred Allen, Jr.
Ross E. Chapman
Winfield J. Hollander
John A. Scott
Bruce W. Martin (Resident)
Daniel L. Conklin
William A. Redmond
Stephen M. Denenfeld
Thomas C. Richardson
Gregory G. St. Arnauld
Roger G. Allen (Retired)
Anne McGregor Fries
Amy J. Glass
Richard M. Hughey, Jr.
Richard J. Bosch
Thomas P. Lewis
Christopher T. Haenicke

LEGAL SUPPORT PERSONNEL

Dorothy B. Kelly

General Counsel for: The Old Kent Bank of Kalamazoo; Gilmore Brothers, Inc.; Root Spring Scraper Co.; Kalamazoo County Road Commission; Loftenberg Educational Scholarship Trust; Farm Credit Services of West Michigan; Irving S. Gilmore Foundation; National Meals on Wheels Foundation; Irving S. Gilmore International Keyboard Festival.

For full biographical listings, see the Martindale-Hubbell Law Directory

EARLY, LENNON, PETERS & CROCKER, P.C. (AV)

900 Comerica Building, 49007-4752
Telephone: 616-381-8844
Fax: 616-349-8525

George H. Lennon, III
James E. Beck
Lawrence M. Brenton
Gordon C. Miller
Robert M. Taylor
Andrew J. Vorbrich

Attorneys for: General Motors Corp.; Wal-Mart Stores; Borgess Medical Center; Aetna Insurance: Kemper Group; Medical Protective Co.; Zurich Insurance; AAA; Liberty Mutual; Home Insurance.

For Complete List of Firm Personnel, See General Section

For full biographical listings, see the Martindale-Hubbell Law Directory

HOWARD & HOWARD ATTORNEYS, P.C. (AV)

The Kalamazoo Building, Suite 400, 107 West Michigan Avenue, 49007-3956
Telephone: 616-382-1483
Telecopier: 616-382-1568
Bloomfield Hills, Michigan Office: The Pinehurst Office Center, Suite 101, 1400 North Woodward Avenue.
Telephone: 810-645-1483.
Telecopier: 810-645-1568.
Lansing, Michigan Office: The Phoenix Building, Suite 500, 222 Washington Square North.
Telephone: 517-485-1483.
Telecopier: 517-485-1568.
Peoria, Illinois Office: Howard & Howard, P.C., The Creve Coeur Building, Suite 200, 321 Liberty Street.
Telephone: 309-672-1483.
Telecopier: 309-672-1568.

Jeffrey P. Chalmers
David L. Holmes
John C. Howard
Peter J. Livingston
D. Craig Martin
Shamra M. Van Wagoner

Representative Clients: First of America Bank Corp.; Simpson Paper Company; W.R. Grace & Co.; Stryker Corp.; Kalamazoo Valley Community College.
Local Counsel for: Chrysler Motors Corp.
International Counsel for: Sony Corp.

For Complete List of Firm Personnel, See General Section

For full biographical listings, see the Martindale-Hubbell Law Directory

LANSING, Ingham Co.

HOWARD & HOWARD ATTORNEYS, P.C. (AV)

The Phoenix Building, Suite 500, 222 Washington Square, North, 48933-1817
Telephone: 517-485-1483
Telecopier: 517-485-1568
Kalamazoo, Michigan Office: The Kalamazoo Building, Suite 400, 107 West Michigan Avenue.
Telephone: 616-382-1483.
Telecopier: 616-382-1568.
Bloomfield Hills, Michigan Office: The Pinehurst Office Center, Suite 101, 1400 North Woodward Avenue.
Telephone: 810-645-1483.
Telecopier: 810-645-1568.
Peoria, Illinois Office: Howard & Howard, P.C., The Creve Coeur Building, Suite 200, 321 Liberty Street.
Telephone: 309-672-1483.
Telecopier: 309-672-1568.

Todd D. Chamberlain
D. Craig Martin

Representative Clients: First of America Bank Corporation; W.R. Grace & Co.; Chrysler Corp.; Indian Head Industries; Cooper & Lybrand; United Technologies.
Local Counsel for: General Motors Corp.; American Cyanamid Co.

For Complete List of Firm Personnel, See General Section

For full biographical listings, see the Martindale-Hubbell Law Directory

HUBBARD, FOX, THOMAS, WHITE & BENGTSON, P.C. (AV)

5801 West Michigan Avenue, 48917
Telephone: 517-886-7176
Fax: 517-886-1080

Jonathon R. White
Thomas A. Bengtson
Michael G. Woodworth
Donald B. Lawrence, Jr.
Harold Kirby Albright
Peter A. Teholiz
Geoffrey H. Seidlein
Ryan M. Wilson
Bruce W. Brown
Mark W. Geschwendt
Thomas L. Lapka
Janice K. Cunningham
Joseph M. Stewart
Mark E. Hills
William R. Thiel

OF COUNSEL

Allison K. Thomas

General Counsel for: Avisco, Inc.; The Beneicke Group; Capistar, Inc.; Coldwell Banker Hacker Co.; Mooney Oil Corp.; Sir Pizza of Michigan, Inc.; Spartan International, Inc.
Local Counsel for: Agribank, FCB.
Reference: Michigan National Bank.

For full biographical listings, see the Martindale-Hubbell Law Directory

STREET & GRUA (AV)

2401 East Grand River, 48912
Telephone: 517-487-8300
Fax: 517-487-8306

MEMBERS OF FIRM

Victor C. Anderson (1904-1981)
Cassius E. Street, Jr.
Remo Mark Grua

Representative Clients: Applegate Insulation Manufacturing; General Aviation, Inc.; Classic Aircraft Corp.; General White GMC; Old Kent Bank of Lansing.
References: First of America-Central; Old Kent Bank of Lansing, N.A.

For full biographical listings, see the Martindale-Hubbell Law Directory

*PONTIAC,** Oakland Co.

BOOTH, PATTERSON, LEE, NEED & ADKISON, P.C. (AV)

1090 West Huron Street, 48328
Telephone: 810-681-1200
FAX: 810-681-1754

Douglas W. Booth (1918-1992)
Calvin E. Patterson (1913-1987)
Parvin Lee, Jr.
J. Timothy Patterson
David J. Lee
Gregory K. Need
Phillip G. Adkison
Martin L. Kimmel
Allan T. Motzny
Ann DeCaminada Christ
Kathryn Niazy Nichols

For full biographical listings, see the Martindale-Hubbell Law Directory

BASSEY AND SELESKO, P.C. (AV)

1400 American Center, 27777 Franklin Road, 48034-2379
Telephone: 810-355-5000
Telecopier: 810-355-2119

Ronald D. Bassey
John D. Selesko
John N. Thomson
Dennis C. Modzelewski
Robert C. Zack
Eric T. Weiss
Drake D. Hill
Mark Merlanti
Andrew J. Goldberg

OF COUNSEL

George G. Romas

For full biographical listings, see the Martindale-Hubbell Law Directory

Southfield—Continued

De Vine & Kohn (AV)

29800 Telegraph Road, 48034
Telephone: 810-353-6500

Clifford J. De Vine
Sheldon B. Kohn

For full biographical listings, see the Martindale-Hubbell Law Directory

Robert B. Labe, P.C. (AV)

260 Franklin Center, 29100 Northwestern Highway, 48034
Telephone: 810-354-3100
Telecopier: 810-351-0487

Robert B. Labe

Reference: NBD Bank, N.A.

For full biographical listings, see the Martindale-Hubbell Law Directory

Maddin, Hauser, Wartell, Roth, Heller & Pesses, P.C. (AV)

Third Floor Essex Center, 28400 Northwestern Highway, P.O. Box 215, 48037
Telephone: 810-354-4030, 355-5200
Telefax: 810-354-1422

Milton M. Maddin (1902-1984)
Michael W. Maddin
Mark R. Hauser
C. Robert Wartell
Richard J. Maddin
Richard F. Roth
Harvey R. Heller
Ian D. Pesses
Michael S. Leib
Robert D. Kaplow
William E. Sigler
Stewart C. W. Weiner
Charles M. Lax
Stuart M. Bordman
Steven D. Sallen
Joseph M. Fazio

Gregory J. Gamalski
Julie Chenot Mayer
Nathaniel H. Simpson
Ronald A. Sollish
Lisa Schatz Broder
Mark H. Fink
Brian J. Simmons
Gayle L. Landrum
Gary E. Perlmuter
Lowell D. Salesin
Jeffrey B. Hollander

Reference: Comerica Bank.

For full biographical listings, see the Martindale-Hubbell Law Directory

Sommers, Schwartz, Silver & Schwartz, P.C. (AV)

2000 Town Center, Suite 900, 48075
Telephone: 810-355-0300
Telecopier: 810-746-4001
Plymouth, Michigan Office: 747 South Main Street.
Telephone: 313-455-4250.

Steven J. Schwartz
Paul Groffsky
Donald R. Epstein
Patrick B. McCauley
Gary A. Taback
James J. Vlasic
Jon J. Birnkrant
Joseph H. Bourgon
Stephen S. Birnkrant

General Counsel For: City of Taylor; Foodland Distributors; C.A. Muer Corporation; Vlasic & Company; Nederlander Corporation; Woodland Physicians; Midwest Health Centers, P.C.
Representative Clients: Huffy Corporation; City of Pontiac; Michigan National Bank; Perry Drugs.

For Complete List of Firm Personnel, See General Section

For full biographical listings, see the Martindale-Hubbell Law Directory

TROY, Oakland Co.

Barlow & Lange, P.C. (AV)

3290 West Big Beaver Road Suite 310, 48084
Telephone: 810-649-3150
Facsimile: 810-649-3175

Thomas W. H. Barlow
Craig W. Lange
Paul W. Coughenour
Craig S. Schwartz
Donna A. Lavoie
Matthew S. Derby
Julie Benson Valice
John K. Ausdemore

For full biographical listings, see the Martindale-Hubbell Law Directory

Campbell, O'Brien & Mistele, P.C. (AV)

850 Stephenson Highway Suite 410, 48083-1163
Telephone: 810-588-5800
Fax: 810-588-6669

Edwin G. O'Brien (1907-1983)
Dale C. Campbell
Henry E. Mistele
Arthur R. Spears, Jr.
Paul W. Loock
Robert J. Figa
Curtis H. Mistele

References: First of America, Comerica Bank.

For full biographical listings, see the Martindale-Hubbell Law Directory

Driggers, Schultz, Herbst & Paterson, A Professional Corporation (AV)

2600 West Big Beaver Road, Suite 550, 48084
Telephone: 810-649-6000
Telecopier: 810-649-6442

Nathan B. Driggers
Laurence S. Schultz
Jay A. Herbst
Andrew A. Paterson, Jr.
Richard B. Tomlinson
Daniel R. Boynton
Joseph W. Thomas
Gene S. Davis
Raymond J. Sterling
Mary C. O'Donnell

Paul A. DePorre
Rebecca Salminen Witt
Suzanne M. Miklos
Judith F. Fertel

OF COUNSEL

Robert A. Straub

Representative Clients: Anthony J. Amaradio & Associates; Applied Dynamics International, Inc.; Automotive Industries, Inc.; Autotek Sealants; Peter A. Basile Sons, Inc.; Chrysler Corp.; C & I Mechanical Contractors; Dunn Blue Print Co.;
Reference: National Bank of Detroit.

For full biographical listings, see the Martindale-Hubbell Law Directory

Hainer & Demorest, P.C. (AV)

100 West Big Beaver, Suite 665, 48084-5283
Telephone: 810-680-8866
Fax: 810-680-0313

Michael J. Hainer
Mark S. Demorest

James D. Zazakis
Paul S. Miller
Leonard K. Berman
Bradley D. Gorman

OF COUNSEL

John P. Charters
Michael A. Heck
Michael A. Kus
Douglas W. Mires

Representative Clients: American Empire Surplus Lines Insurance Co.; Central Distributors of Beer, Inc.; Century 21 Premier Real Estate; City Management Corp.; Clarklift of Detroit, Inc.; Federal Reserve Bank of Chicago; Mid-West Instrument, Inc.; Rockwell International Corp.; Zurich Insurance Co.; Hotel Investment Services, Inc.

For full biographical listings, see the Martindale-Hubbell Law Directory

Keywell and Rosenfeld (AV)

Suite 600, 2301 West Big Beaver Road, 48084
Telephone: 810-649-3200
Fax: 810-649-0454

MEMBERS OF FIRM

Frederic I. Keywell
Gary A. Goldberg
Jimm F. White
Norman E. Greenfield
Lucy R. Benham
Jerrold M. Bigelman

ASSOCIATE

Kelly M. Hayes

Reference: National Bank of Detroit.

For full biographical listings, see the Martindale-Hubbell Law Directory

Poling, McGaw & Poling, P.C. (AV)

Suite 275, 5435 Corporate Drive, 48098
Telephone: 810-641-0500
Telecopier: 810-641-0506

Benson T. Buck (1926-1989)
Richard B. Poling
D. Douglas McGaw
Richard B. Poling, Jr.
David W. Moore
Gregory C. Hamilton
Veronica B. Winter
James R. Parker

OF COUNSEL

Ralph S. Moore

Representative Clients: County of Oakland; City of Troy; United States Fidelity & Guaranty Co.; Sentry Insurance Co.; Admiral Insurance; DeMaria Construction Co.; Leo Corporation; Aetna Casualty and Surety Co.; Concord Design; Pneumo-Abex.

For full biographical listings, see the Martindale-Hubbell Law Directory

WEST BLOOMFIELD, Oakland Co.

Stephen K. Valentine, Jr., P.C. (AV)

5767 West Maple Road, Suite 400, 48322
Telephone: 810-851-3010
Troy, Michigan Office: 600 Columbia Center. 201 West Big Beaver Road.
Telephone: 810-851-3010.

Stephen K. Valentine, Jr.

(See Next Column)

STEPHEN K. VALENTINE, JR., P.C.—*Continued*

OF COUNSEL

Philip G. Meyer

For full biographical listings, see the Martindale-Hubbell Law Directory

MINNESOTA

*MINNEAPOLIS,** Hennepin Co.

ABDO AND ABDO, P.A. (AV)

710 Northstar West, 625 Marquette Avenue, 55402
Telephone: 612-333-1526
Fax: 612-342-2608

Robert P. Abdo
Keith J. Broady
Steven R. Hedges
Kenneth J. Abdo
Timothy C. Matson

Representative Clients: ADT Security Systems, Inc.; Cold Spring Brewing Co., Cold Spring, Minn.

For Complete List of Firm Personnel, See General Section

For full biographical listings, see the Martindale-Hubbell Law Directory

ARNOLD & McDOWELL (AV)

5881 Cedar Lake Road, 55416-1492
Telephone: 612-545-9000
Minnesota Wats Line: 800-343-4545
Fax: 612-545-1793
Princeton, Minnesota Office: 501 South Fourth Street.
Telephone: 612-389-2214.
Hutchinson, Minnesota Office: 101 Park Place.
Telephone: 612-587-7575.

MEMBERS OF FIRM

David B. Arnold
Steven S. Hoge
Gary D. McDowell
Paul D. Dove
Steven A. Anderson
David A. Brueggemann

ASSOCIATES

Gina M. Brandt
Brett D. Arnold

For Complete List of Firm Personnel, See General Section

For full biographical listings, see the Martindale-Hubbell Law Directory

BRENNER & GLASSMAN, LTD. A PROFESSIONAL ASSOCIATION (AV)

Suite 170, 2001 Killebrew Drive, 55425-1822
Telephone: 612-854-7600
Telecopier: 612-854-0502

Louis W. Brenner, Sr.
Richard A. Glassman

William D. Turkula
Michael J. Orme
Thomas W. Larkin

OF COUNSEL

John J. Todd

For full biographical listings, see the Martindale-Hubbell Law Directory

FOSTER, WALDECK, LIND & GRIES, LTD. (AV)

Suite 2300 Metropolitan Centre, 333 South Seventh Street, 55402
Telephone: 612-375-1550
Facsimilie: 612-375-0647
St. Michael, Minnesota Office: 100 East Central, P.O. Box 35, 55376.
Telephone: 612-497-3099. Facsimilie: 612-497-3639.

Thomas A. Foster
Rolf E. Sonnesyn
Timothy W. Waldeck
David J. Lenhardt
Peter E. Lind
Byron M. Peterson
John R. Gries
Steven E. Tomsche

Gregory J. Van Heest
Jennifer L. Kjos
Philip J. Danen

Reference: Firstar Bank of Minnesota, N.A.

For full biographical listings, see the Martindale-Hubbell Law Directory

FROMMELT & EIDE, LTD. (AV)

580 International Centre, 900 Second Avenue South, 55402
Telephone: 612-332-2200; 800-332-2296
FAX: 612-342-2761

(See Next Column)

Roger H. Frommelt
James W. Rude
David B. Eide
Jean M. Davis
John R. Dorgan
Fredrick R. Krietzman
Randy J. Sparling
Douglas M. Ramler

For full biographical listings, see the Martindale-Hubbell Law Directory

LOMMEN, NELSON, COLE & STAGEBERG, P.A. (AV)

1800 IDS Center, 80 South 8th Street, 55402
Telephone: 612-339-8131
Fax: 612-339-8064
Hudson, Wisconsin Office: Grandview Professional Building, 400 South Second Street, Suite 210.
Telephones: 715-386-8217 and 612-436-8085.

W. Wyman Smith (1914-1994)
J. Christopher Cuneo
John P. Lommen (1927-1988)
Thomas F. Dougherty
Michael P. Shroyer (1953-1993)
Stacey A. DeKalb
Leonard T. Juster
Kay N. Hunt
Alvin S. Malmon
Richard L. Plagens
Ronald L. Haskvitz
Ehrich L. Koch
Phillip A. Cole
Margie R. Bodas
Roger V. Stageberg
James M. Lockhart
Glenn R. Kessel
Stephen C. Rathke
Thomas R. Jacobson (Resident, Hudson, Wisconsin Office)
James C. Searls
Linc S. Deter
John M. Giblin
Paul L. Dinger
John R. McBride
Sherri D. Ulland
Reid R. Lindquist

Jill G. Doescher
Marc A. Johannsen
James R. Johnson (Resident, Hudson, Wisconsin Office)
Angela W. Allen
Adam Levitsky
Terrance W. Moore
Barry A. O'Neil
Lynn M. Starkovich
Mary I. King
Sheila A. Bjorklund

OF COUNSEL

V. Owen Nelson
Henry H. Feikema

Representative Clients: Mutual Service Insurance Co.; Employers Mutual Companies; Economy Fire and Casualty Co.

For full biographical listings, see the Martindale-Hubbell Law Directory

WIESE LAW FIRM, P.A. (AV)

4100 Multifoods Tower, 33 South Sixth Street, 55402
Telephone: 612-339-3818
Fax: 612-339-7661

Donald E. Wiese
Thomas J. Brown Wiese
Michael J. Wiese

LuAnn M. Petricka

For full biographical listings, see the Martindale-Hubbell Law Directory

ZAMANSKY PROFESSIONAL ASSOCIATION (AV)

4924 IDS Tower, 55402
Telephone: 612-340-9720
Fax: 612-340-9662
St. Paul, Minnesota Office: 6 West 5th Street.
Telephone: 612-297-6400.

Ronald A. Zamansky

Scott A. Weaver
Glen F. Meyer

Reference: Norwest Bank Minneapolis.

For full biographical listings, see the Martindale-Hubbell Law Directory

MISSISSIPPI

*GREENWOOD,** Leflore Co.

JOHN P. HENSON (AV)

105 West Market Street, P.O. Box 494, 38930
Telephone: 601-453-6227
Telefax: 601-453-6228

For full biographical listings, see the Martindale-Hubbell Law Directory

*GULFPORT,** Harrison Co.

DUKES, DUKES, KEATING AND FANECA, P.A. (AV)

2308 East Beach Boulevard, P.O. Drawer W, 39501
Telephone: 601-868-1111
FAX: 601-863-2886

(See Next Column)

DUKES, DUKES, KEATING AND FANECA P.A., *Gulfport—Continued*

Hugh D. Keating | Cy Faneca
William H. Pettey, Jr.

Nick B. Roberts, Jr.

For full biographical listings, see the Martindale-Hubbell Law Directory

*JACKSON,** Hinds Co.

DRISDALE & LINDSTROM, P.A. (AVⓣ)

302 Banner Hall, 4465 I-55 North, P.O. Box 13329, 39236-3329
Telephone: 601-982-5599
Telecopier: 601-982-3005
MS Wats 1-800-710-7833

John K. Drisdale, Jr. | Eric E. Lindstrom, Jr.

For full biographical listings, see the Martindale-Hubbell Law Directory

PRICE & ZIRULNIK (AV)

Suite 1150 Capital Towers, 125 South Congress Street, P.O. Box 3439, 39207-3439
Telephone: 601-353-3000
Telecopier: 601-353-3007

John H. Price, Jr. | Barry S. Zirulnik

ASSOCIATE

William G. Cheney, Jr.

Representative Clients: Yellow Freight System, Inc.; Mississippi Dairy Products Association, Inc.; LuVel Dairy Products, Inc.; Mississippi Farm Bureau Federation; Mississippi Department of Transportation; Mississippi High School Activities Association, Inc.; Variety Wholesalers, Inc.; Mississippi Bankers Association; Metal Rolling, Inc.

For full biographical listings, see the Martindale-Hubbell Law Directory

*TUPELO,** Lee Co.

WEBB, SANDERS, DEATON, BALDUCCI & SMITH (AV)

363 North Broadway, P.O. Box 496, 38802-0496
Telephone: 601-844-2137
Facsimile: 601-842-3863
Oxford, Mississippi Office: 2154 South Lamar Boulevard, P.O. Box 148.
Telephone: 601-236-5700.
Facsimile: 601-236-5800.

MEMBERS OF FIRM

Dan W. Webb | Timothy R. Balducci
Benjamin H. Sanders | Kent E. Smith
Dana Gail Deaton | Danny P. Hall, Jr.
Chris H. Deaton | B. Wayne Williams

OF COUNSEL

Rachael Howell Webb

Representative Clients: Allstate Insurance Company; Georgia Casualty & Surety Company; GAB Business Services, Inc.; The Kroger Company; Ohio Casualty Insurance Company; Phillips and Associates; State Auto Insurance Company; State Farm Fire & Casualty Company; Transport Life Insurance Company; United States Fidelity & Guaranty Company.

For full biographical listings, see the Martindale-Hubbell Law Directory

MISSOURI

CAPE GIRARDEAU, Cape Girardeau Co.

DICKERSON, RICE, SPAETH, HEISSERER & SUMMERS, L.C. (AV)

Fourth Floor Commerce Bank Building, 160 South Broadview at Route K, P.O. Box 1568, 63702
Telephone: 314-334-6061
Facsimile: 314-334-0979

Donald L. Dickerson | Kevin B. Spaeth
Joe Perry Rice, III | John P. Heisserer
David B. Summers

Kathleen A. Wolz | Kevin L. Wibbenmeyer

Representative Clients: Health Services Corporation of America; Health Careers Foundation; Family Practice Specialty Center; Neurologic Associates; Cape Neurosurgical Associates, P.C.; SEMO Otolaryngology.
Reference: Boatmen's Bank of Cape Girardeau.

For full biographical listings, see the Martindale-Hubbell Law Directory

KANSAS CITY, Jackson, Clay & Platte Cos.

SHERWIN L. EPSTEIN & ASSOCIATES (AV)

Suite 1700, 1006 Grand Avenue, 64106
Telephone: 816-421-6200
FAX: 816-421-6201

John W. Roe

ASSOCIATE

Mark H. Epstein

LEGAL SUPPORT PERSONNEL

Amy L. Edwards | Christine Marie Leete

For full biographical listings, see the Martindale-Hubbell Law Directory

DETLEF G. LEHNARDT (AVⓣ)

911 Main Street, Suite 1322, 64105
Telephone: 816-221-2440
Facsimile: 816-221-5665
New York, New York Office: 90 Park Avenue, 17th Floor.
Telephone: 212-972-4263.
Facsimile: 212-972-4264.

LEGAL SUPPORT PERSONNEL

Stephen K. Lehnardt

For full biographical listings, see the Martindale-Hubbell Law Directory

LEE'S SUMMIT, Jackson Co.

CARL CHINNERY & ASSOCIATES, P.C. (AV)

200 South Douglas, 64063
Telephone: 816-525-2050

Carl L. Chinnery

Nancy E. Blackwell

OF COUNSEL

Elizabeth Unger Carlyle

LEGAL SUPPORT PERSONNEL

PARALEGALS

Jean Wehner Chinnery | Elaine K. Hanrahan
Janice Sue Hancock | Alicia Hodges
Susan Breitenbach

For full biographical listings, see the Martindale-Hubbell Law Directory

ST. LOUIS, (Independent City)

JEROME R. MANDELSTAMM (AV)

Suite 1600, 1010 Market Street, 63101
Telephone: 314-621-2261

For full biographical listings, see the Martindale-Hubbell Law Directory

MOLINE & SHOSTAK (AV)

The Berkley Building, 8015 Forsyth Boulevard, 63105
Telephone: 314-725-3200
Fax: 314-725-3275

Harry O. Moline | Donald J. Mehan, Jr.
Burton H. Shostak | Deborah J. Westling
Sherri Cranmore Strand | Michael S. Ghidina

For full biographical listings, see the Martindale-Hubbell Law Directory

PEPER, MARTIN, JENSEN, MAICHEL AND HETLAGE (AV)

720 Olive Street, Twenty-Fourth Floor, 63101
Telephone: 314-421-3850
Fax: 314-621-4834
Fort Myers, Florida Office: 2080 McGregor Boulevard, Third Floor.
Telephone: 813-337-3850.
Fax: 813-337-0970.
Punta Gorda, Florida Office: 1625 West Marion Avenue, Suite 2.
Telephone: 813-637-1955.
Fax: 813-637-8485.
Naples, Florida Office: 850 Park Shore Drive, Suite 202.
Telephone: 813-261-6525.
Fax: 813-649-1805.
Belleville, Illinois Office: 720 West Main Street, Suite 140.
Telephone: 618-234-9574.
Fax: 618-234-9846.

MEMBERS OF FIRM

Lewis R. Mills | John W. Brickler
John R. Short | Kathleen S. Schoene
Marshall D. Hier | Terry L. Lister
Ronald O. Schowalter | Andrew T. Hoyne

COUNSEL

Cleon L. Burt | Christian B. Peper
Malcolm W. Martin | Thomas F. Schlafly

(See Next Column)

PEPER, MARTIN, JENSEN, MAICHEL AND HETLAGE—*Continued*

ASSOCIATES

Craig A. Adoor
Stuart E. Funderburg
Stephen T. Bee
Benjamin H. Hulsey
Thomas A. A. Cook
Thomas E. Proost
David Lee Fleisher, Jr.
Sally Herr Townsley
M. Celeste Vossmeyer

For Complete List of Firm Personnel, See General Section

For full biographical listings, see the Martindale-Hubbell Law Directory

SCHRAMM & PINES, L.L.C. (AV)

Suite 1404 Chromalloy Plaza, 120 South Central Avenue, 63105
Telephone: 314-721-5321
Telecopier: 314-721-0790

MEMBERS OF FIRM

Paul H. Schramm
M. Harvey Pines
Daniel R. Schramm

Norman S. Newmark
Dean A. Schramm
Peter L. Hoffman

Reference: The Boatmen's National Bank of St. Louis.

For full biographical listings, see the Martindale-Hubbell Law Directory

WITTNER, POGER, ROSENBLUM & SPEWAK, P.C. (AV)

Suite 400, 7700 Bonhomme Avenue, 63105
Telephone: 314-862-3535
Fax: 314-862-5741

Gerald M. Poger
Steven B. Spewak
Howard A. Wittner
David S. Spewak
N. Scott Rosenblum
Jean H. Maylack

Ramona L. Marten
Barbara Greenberg
Jane M. Carriker
Vanessa C. Antoniou
Gary M. Siegel
Joseph L. Green

For full biographical listings, see the Martindale-Hubbell Law Directory

MONTANA

*BILLINGS,** Yellowstone Co.

CROWLEY, HAUGHEY, HANSON, TOOLE & DIETRICH (AV)

500 Transwestern II, 490 North 31st Street, P.O. Box 2529, 59103
Telephone: 406-252-3441
Fax: 406-259-4159
Helena, Montana Office: IBM Building, 100 North Park Avenue, Suite 300, 59601.
Telephone: 406-449-4165.
Fax: 406-449-5149.

MEMBERS OF FIRM

John M. Dietrich
Daniel N. McLean
Gareld F. Krieg
Robert G. Michelotti, Jr.
Arthur F. Lamey, Jr.
John R. Alexander
Myles J. Thomas
William D. Lamdin, III
David L. Johnson
Michael S. Dockery
Terry B. Cosgrove
Malcolm H. Goodrich
Allan L. Karell
Mary Scrim
James P. Sites
Eric K. Anderson
Laura A. Mitchell
Renee L. Coppock

ASSOCIATES

John R. Lee
Scott M. Heard

Representative Clients: General Motors Acceptance Corporation; Deaconess Medical Center of Billings; Billings Clinic; John Deere Co.; First Interstate Bank of Commerce; Aetna; Montana Livestock Ag Credit, Inc.; Turner Enterprises, Inc.

For Complete List of Firm Personnel, See General Section

For full biographical listings, see the Martindale-Hubbell Law Directory

EDWARDS LAW FIRM (AV)

1601 Lewis Avenue, Suite 206, P.O. Box 20039, 59104
Telephone: 406-256-8155
Fax: 406-256-8159
Toll Free: 1-800-556-8155

MEMBERS OF FIRM

A. Clifford Edwards
Charles P. Myers
Kevin M. Funyak
Roger W. Frickle

For full biographical listings, see the Martindale-Hubbell Law Directory

*BOZEMAN,** Gallatin Co.

KIRWAN & BARRETT, P.C. (AV)

215 West Mendenhall, P.O. Box 1348, 59771-1348
Telephone: 406-586-1553
Fax: 406-586-8971

Peter M. Kirwan
Stephen M. Barrett

Tom W. Stonecipher

Representative Clients: Boyne USA, Inc.; Kenyon Noble Lumber Company; Video Lottery Technologies, Inc.

For full biographical listings, see the Martindale-Hubbell Law Directory

*HELENA,** Lewis and Clark Co.

BROWNING, KALECZYC, BERRY & HOVEN, P.C. (AV)

139 North Last Chance Gulch, P.O. Box 1697, 59624
Telephone: 406-449-6220
Telefax: 406-443-0700

Stanley T. Kaleczyc

Katharine S. Donnelley
Ken C. Crippen
Sharon A. O'Leary

Reference: First Bank Helena, Helena, Montana.

For Complete List of Firm Personnel, See General Section

For full biographical listings, see the Martindale-Hubbell Law Directory

NEBRASKA

*LINCOLN,** Lancaster Co.

DEMARS, GORDON, OLSON, RECKNOR & SHIVELY (AV)

Suite 400 Centre Terrace Building, 1225 L Street, P.O. Box 81607, 68501-1607
Telephone: 402-438-2500
Fax: 402-438-6329

MEMBERS OF FIRM

James J. DeMars
John F. Recknor
James E. Gordon
Robert W. Shively
William E. Olson, Jr.
James C. Zalewski
Danene J. Tushar

ASSOCIATE

Bruce A. Smith

For full biographical listings, see the Martindale-Hubbell Law Directory

*OMAHA,** Douglas Co.

BRASHEAR & GINN (AV)

800 Metropolitan Federal Plaza, 1623 Farnam Street, 68102-2106
Telephone: 402-348-1000; 800-746-4444
Telecopier: 402-348-1111

Kermit A. Brashear
Mark J. Daly
Robert V. Ginn
Mitchell L. Pirnie

Paul J. Halbur
Kermit A. Brashear III

Representative Clients: Aero-Colours, Inc., Danville, California; Bay Enterprises, Inc., Los Angeles, California; Guild Cooperative, Danville, California; Lutheran Ministry Foundation, Omaha, Nebraska; Omniflight Helicopters, Inc., Dallas, Texas; SmithKline Beecham Corporation, Westchester, Pennsylvania; Transportation Finance & Management, Inc., Omaha, Nebraska; TransWood Carriers, Inc., Omaha, Nebraska.

For Complete List of Firm Personnel, See General Section

For full biographical listings, see the Martindale-Hubbell Law Directory

NEVADA

*ELKO,** Elko Co.

LAW OFFICES GOICOECHEA & DI GRAZIA, LTD. A PROFESSIONAL CORPORATION (AV)

In Association with
Vaughan & Hull, Ltd.
A Professional Corporation
P.O. Box 1358, 89803
Telephone: 702-738-8091
Fax: 702-738-4220

Robert B. Goicoechea
Gary E. Di Grazia

Thomas J. Coyle, Jr.

Representative Clients: G & T Construction, Inc.; Alpark Petroleum, Inc.; Nevada Bank & Trust; Metropolitan Life Ins.

For full biographical listings, see the Martindale-Hubbell Law Directory

*LAS VEGAS,** Clark Co.

ALVERSON, TAYLOR, MORTENSEN & NELSON (AV)

3821 W. Charleston Boulevard, 89102
Telephone: 702-384-7000
FAX: 702-385-7000

MEMBERS OF FIRM

J. Bruce Alverson
Eric K. Taylor
David J. Mortensen
Erven T. Nelson
LeAnn Sanders
David R. Clayson

ASSOCIATES

Milton J. Eichacker
Douglas D. Gerrard
Marie Ellerton
James H. Randall
Peter Dubowsky
Hayley B. Chambers
Michael D. Stevenson
Cookie Lea Olshein
Kenneth M. Marias
Jeffrey H. Ballin
Jeffrey W. Daly
Kenneth R. Ivory
Edward D. Boyack
Sandra Smagac
Jill M. Chase
Francis F. Lin

Representative Clients: Citibank; First Interstate Bank; General Electric; Southwest Gas Corporation; The CIT Group; Kentucky Fried Chicken; Norwest Bank; Federal Deposit Insurance Corporation (FDIC); Resolution Trust Corporation (RTC); Yellow Cab Company.

For full biographical listings, see the Martindale-Hubbell Law Directory

CROCKETT & MYERS, LTD. A PROFESSIONAL CORPORATION (AV)

700 South Third Street, 89101
Telephone: 702-382-6711
Fax: 702-384-8102

J. R. Crockett, Jr.
Richard W. Myers
James V. Lavelle III
Eleissa C. Lavelle
Michael P. Villani

Laura E. Wunsch Stubberud

Reference: Sun State Bank.

For full biographical listings, see the Martindale-Hubbell Law Directory

KEEFER, O'REILLY & FERRARIO (AV)

An Association including a Professional Corporation
Nevada Professional Center, 325 South Maryland Parkway, Suite One, 89101
Telephone: 702-382-2660; 384-8944
Fax: 702-387-6978

Milton W. Keefer
John F. O'Reilly (A Professional Corporation)
Mark E. Ferrario
Edward C. Lubbers

Anita A. Webster
Kevin E. Helm
Jon M. Okazaki
Maribeth Jo Stock
James R. Sweetin

Representative Clients: Associates Commercial Corp.; Bailey & McGah; Chism Homes, Inc.; Cole Travel Service; Greentree Acceptance Co.; Hartford Insurance Co.; Holiday Inns, Inc.; Home Ins. Co.; Legal Protective Life Ins. Co.; Maryland Casualty Co.

For full biographical listings, see the Martindale-Hubbell Law Directory

LEAVITT, SULLY & RIVERS (AV)

An Association of Professional Corporations
601 East Bridger Avenue, 89101
Telephone: 702-382-5111
Telecopier: 702-382-2892

K. Michael Leavitt (Chartered)
W. Leslie Sully, Jr. (Chartered)
David J. Rivers, II (Chartered)

For full biographical listings, see the Martindale-Hubbell Law Directory

LAURENCE A. SPEISER, LTD. (AV)

2133 Industrial Road, 89102
Telephone: 702-384-6156
Telecopier: 702-471-0592

Laurence A. Speiser

For full biographical listings, see the Martindale-Hubbell Law Directory

WOODBURN AND WEDGE (AV)

Suite 620 Bank of America Plaza, 300 South Fourth Street, 89101
Telephone: 702-387-1000
Reno, Nevada Office: 16th Floor, First Interstate Bank Building. P.O. Box 2311.
Telephone: 702-688-3000.
Telecopier: 702-688-3088.

MEMBERS OF FIRM

James J. Halley
Richard O. Kwapil, Jr.
Casey Woodburn Vlautin
John F. Murtha
Charles A. Jeannes
Kirk S. Schumacher
Harry J. Schlegelmilch

ASSOCIATE

Gregg P. Barnard

Representative Clients: Atlantic Richfield Co.; Sierra Pacific Power Co.; The Union Pacific Railroad Co.; Western Union Telegraph Co.; Cyprus Minerals Corp.; The Roman Catholic Bishop of Reno, A Corporation Sole.

For full biographical listings, see the Martindale-Hubbell Law Directory

*RENO,** Washoe Co.

WOODBURN AND WEDGE (AV)

16th Floor, First Interstate Bank Building, One East First Street, P.O. Box 2311, 89505
Telephone: 702-688-3000
Telecopier: 702-688-3088
Las Vegas, Nevada Office: Suite 620 Bank of American Plaza, 300 South Court Street.
Telephone: 702-387-1000.

MEMBERS OF FIRM

James J. Halley
Richard O. Kwapil, Jr.
Casey Woodburn Vlautin
John F. Murtha
Charles A. Jeannes
Kirk S. Schumacher
Harry J. Schlegelmilch

ASSOCIATE

Gregg P. Barnard

Representative Clients: Atlantic Richfield Co.; Sierra Pacific Power Co.; The Union Pacific Railroad Co.; Western Union Telegraph Co.; Bank of America; Cyprus Minerals Corp.; The Roman Catholic Bishop of Reno, A Corporation Sole.

For full biographical listings, see the Martindale-Hubbell Law Directory

NEW HAMPSHIRE

*CONCORD,** Merrimack Co.

RANSMEIER & SPELLMAN, PROFESSIONAL CORPORATION (AV)

One Capitol Street, P.O. Box 600, 03302-0600
Telephone: 603-228-0477
Telecopier: 603-224-2780

Joseph S. Ransmeier
John C. Ransmeier
Jeffrey J. Zellers
Timothy E. Britain

R. Stevenson Upton

For Complete List of Firm Personnel, See General Section

For full biographical listings, see the Martindale-Hubbell Law Directory

NEW JERSEY

*HACKENSACK,** Bergen Co.

DEENER, FEINGOLD & STERN, A PROFESSIONAL CORPORATION (AV)

2 University Plaza, Suite 602, 07601
Telephone: 201-343-8788
Fax: 201-343-4640

Jerome A. Deener
Cal R. Feingold
Robert A. Stern

Debra T. Hirsch
David M. Edelblum
Anthony M. Vizzoni
James J. Costello, Jr. (Not admitted in NJ)

References: United Jersey Bank; Midlantic Bank; Midland Bank and Trust Co. (Trust Department); Fidelity Bank; Hudson United Bank.

For full biographical listings, see the Martindale-Hubbell Law Directory

HEIN, SMITH, BEREZIN, MALOOF & ROGERS (AV)

Court Plaza East, 19 Main Street, 07601-7023
Telephone: 201-487-7400
Telecopier: 201-487-4228

MEMBER OF FIRM

Alan A. Davidson

OF COUNSEL

Seymour A. Smith

Representative Clients: National Community Bank of New Jersey; Savings Bank of Rockland County; Phoenix Financial Group; National Westminster Bank of N.J.; The Bank of Tokyo.
Reference: United Jersey Bank.

For Complete List of Firm Personnel, See General Section

For full biographical listings, see the Martindale-Hubbell Law Directory

KAPS & BARTO (AV)

15 Warren Street, 07601
Telephone: 201-489-5277
Telecopier: 201-489-0477

Warren J. Kaps
Raymond Barto

Concetta R. De Lucia
Brenda P. Rosenberg

Representative Clients: Continental Baking Co.; Mayflower Vapor Seal Co.; The Society of American Magicians.
Reference: United Jersey Bank.

For full biographical listings, see the Martindale-Hubbell Law Directory

SHAPIRO & SHAPIRO (AV)

Continental Plaza II, 411 Hackensack Avenue, 07601
Telephone: 201-488-3900
Fax: 201-488-9481

Robert P. Shapiro
Susan W. Shapiro (1943-1990)
John P. Di Iorio

ASSOCIATES

David O. Marcus
Robert F. Green

Reference: National Community Bank.

For full biographical listings, see the Martindale-Hubbell Law Directory

MARLTON, Burlington Co.

FLASTER, GREENBERG, WALLENSTEIN, RODERICK, SPIRGEL, ZUCKERMAN, SKINNER & KIRCHNER, P.C. (AV)

Suite 200, Five Greentree Centre, 08053
Telephone: 609-983-7200
Telecopier: 609-983-7877
Philadelphia, Pennsylvania Office: 1710-12 Spruce Street.
Telephone: 215-731-1490.

Richard J. Flaster
Stephen M. Greenberg
Laura B. Wallenstein
Allen P. Fineberg
Markley S. Roderick
Peter R. Spirgel
Alan H. Zuckerman
William S. Skinner
J. Philip Kirchner

E. Richard Dressel
Paul J. Russoniello
Elizabeth J. Hampton
Deborah H. Bjornstad

For full biographical listings, see the Martindale-Hubbell Law Directory

*NEWARK,** Essex Co.

SILLS CUMMIS ZUCKERMAN RADIN TISCHMAN EPSTEIN & GROSS, A PROFESSIONAL CORPORATION (AV)

One Riverfront Plaza, 07102-5400
Telephone: 201-643-7000
Fax: 201-643-6500
Telex: 820630 Sillsbeck Nwk
Atlantic City, New Jersey Office: 17 Gordon's Alley.
Telephone: 609-344-2800.
New York, N.Y. Office: 250 Park Avenue.
Telephone: 212-643-7000.

Michael B. Tischman
Steven E. Gross
Jeffrey J. Greenbaum
Simon Levin
Noah Bronkesh (Resident at Atlantic City, N.J. Office)
Steven M. Goldman
Ira A. Rosenberg
Robert Crane
Jack M. Zackin
Jerry Genberg
Brian S. Coven
Richard J. Schulman (Not admitted in NJ)
Bernard I. Flateman
Stanley U. North, III
Victor H. Boyajian

Steven B. Jackman (Not admitted in NJ)
Frederic M. Tudor
Jodi S. Brodsky
Robert W. Burke
Scott T. Gruber
Garry Rogers
Lorraine M. Potenza

Representative Clients: Margaretten Financial Corporation; Sorin Biomedical Inc.; FIAT (USA); O'Brien Environmental Energy; DiGiorgio Corporation; T.J. Cinnamons; White Rose Foods, Inc.; Rag Shops, Inc.; New Jersey Nets; Bally Manufacturing Corp.

For Complete List of Firm Personnel, See General Section

For full biographical listings, see the Martindale-Hubbell Law Directory

PRINCETON, Mercer Co.

BUCHANAN INGERSOLL (AV)

A Partnership
College Centre, 500 College Road East, 08540-6615
Telephone: 609-452-2666
Telecopier: 609-520-0360
Pittsburgh, Pennsylvania Office: Buchanan Ingersoll, Professional Corporation, 5800 USX Tower, 600 Grant Street.
Telephone: 412-562-8800.
Philadelphia, Pennsylvania Office: Buchanan Ingersoll, Professional Corporation, Two Logan Square, Twelfth Floor, 18th & Arch Streets.
Telephone: 215-665-8700.
Harrisburg, Pennsylvania Office: Buchanan Ingersoll, Professional Corporation, Vartan Parc, 30 North Third Street.
Telephone: 717-237-4800.
Tampa, Florida Office: Buchanan Ingersoll, Professional Corporation, 101 East Kennedy Boulevard, Suite 1030.
Telephone: 813-222-8180.
North Miami Beach, Florida Office: Buchanan Ingersoll, Professional Corporation, 19495 Biscayne Boulevard.
Telephone: 305-933-5600.
Lexington, Kentucky Office: Buchanan Ingersoll, Professional Corporation, 1210 Vine Center Office Tower, 333 West Vine Street.
Telephone: 606-225-5333.

David J. Sorin

SENIOR ATTORNEY

William J. Thomas

Catherine M. Verna

For Complete List of Firm Personnel, See General Section

For full biographical listings, see the Martindale-Hubbell Law Directory

ROSELAND, Essex Co.

CLANCY, CALLAHAN & SMITH (AV)

103 Eisenhower Parkway, 07068-1090
Telephone: 201-403-8300
Fax: 201-403-8355

MEMBERS OF FIRM

John J. Clancy (1922-1979)
Edward M. Callahan, Jr.
Dennis J. Smith

ASSOCIATES

James J. Cronin
Beth A. Callahan

For full biographical listings, see the Martindale-Hubbell Law Directory

UNION, Union Co.

O'BRIEN, LIOTTA & MANDEL (AV)

Liberty Hall Corporate Center, 1085 Morris Avenue, P.O. Box 3180, 07083-1980
Telephone: 908-354-7530
Telecopier: 908-354-7531

MEMBERS OF FIRM

Stephen L. Ritz
Carmine J. Liotta
Richard M. Mandel
David M. Kupfer

ASSOCIATES

John R. Poirier
Kenneth R. Rush
Leslie A. Santora
James S. Richter
Marie Seitz
Laura J. Sinnott

OF COUNSEL

Raymond D. O'Brien

Representative Clients: The Penn Central Corp.
Reference: United Jersey Bank/Central.

For full biographical listings, see the Martindale-Hubbell Law Directory

WEST ORANGE, Essex Co.

BURSIK, KURITSKY & GIASULLO (AV)

443 Northfield Avenue, 07052
Telephone: 201-325-7800
Telecopier: 201-325-7930

MEMBERS OF FIRM

David H. E. Bursik
Stuart M. Kuritsky
Robert J. Giasullo

ASSOCIATES

Amy Bard
John Messina
Barbara Koerner Craig

For full biographical listings, see the Martindale-Hubbell Law Directory

WESTWOOD, Bergen Co.

BARRY G. LEVEEN (AV)

99 Kinderkamack Road, P.O. Box 977, 07675
Telephone: 201-666-3232
Telefax: 201-666-6993

Reference: Citizens First National Bank of New Jersey.

For full biographical listings, see the Martindale-Hubbell Law Directory

NEW MEXICO

*ALBUQUERQUE,** Bernalillo Co.

CAMPBELL, PICA, OLSON & SEEGMILLER (AV)

6565 Americas Parkway, N.E., Suite 800, P.O. Box 35459, 87176
Telephone: 505-883-9110
Fax: 505-884-3882

MEMBERS OF FIRM

Lewis O. Campbell
Nicholas R. Pica
David C. Olson
Douglas Seegmiller

ASSOCIATES

Brad Vaughn
Roger A. Stansbury
Philip Craig Snyder
Arthur J. G. Lacerte, Jr.
Jeffrey C. Gilmore

Representative Clients: Phelps Dodge Corporation; Chino Mines Company; Large Power Users Coalition; Sara Lee Corporation; New Mexico Retail Association; Compania Minera Ojos Del Salado S.A.; General Electric Capital Corporation; Lectrosonics, Inc.

For full biographical listings, see the Martindale-Hubbell Law Directory

HINKLE, COX, EATON, COFFIELD & HENSLEY (AV)

Suite 800, 500 Marquette, N.W., P.O. Box 2043, 87103
Telephone: 505-768-1500
FAX: 505-768-1529
Roswell, New Mexico Office: Suite 700, United Bank Plaza, P.O. Box 10, 88202.
Telephone: 505-622-6510.
FAX: 505-623-9332.
Midland, Texas Office: 6 Desta Drive, Suite 2800, P.O. Box 3580, 79705.
Telephone: 915-683-4691.
FAX: 915-683-6518.
Amarillo, Texas Office: 1700 Bank One Center. P.O. Box 9238, 79105-9238.
Telephone: 806-372-5569.
FAX: 806-372-9761.

(See Next Column)

Santa Fe, New Mexico Office: 218 Montezuma, P.O. Box 2068, 87504.
Telephone: 505-982-4554.
FAX: 505-982-8623.
Austin, Texas Office: 401 West 15th Street, Suite 800, 78701.
Telephone: 512-476-7137.
FAX: 512-476-5431.
Associated Office: Hoffman & Stephens, P.C., 401 West 15th Street, Suite 800, 78701.
Telephone: 512-476-5434.
Fax: 512-476-5431.

Marshall G. Martin
Fred W. Schwendimann
Margaret Carter Ludewig

Representative Clients: Anadarko Petroleum Corp.; Atlantic Richfield Co.; Bass Enterprises Production Co.; BHP Petroleum; Caroon & Black Management, Inc.; Chevron, USA, Inc.; CIGNA; City of Albuquerque; Coastal Oil & Gas Corp. Co.; Diagnostek.

For Complete List of Firm Personnel, See General Section

For full biographical listings, see the Martindale-Hubbell Law Directory

MILLER, STRATVERT, TORGERSON & SCHLENKER, P.A. (AV)

500 Marquette Avenue, N.W., Suite 1100, P.O. Box 25687, 87102
Telephone: 505-842-1950
Facsimile: 505-243-4408
Farmington, New Mexico Office: Suite 300, 300 West Arrington. P.O. Box 869.
Telephone: 505-326-4521.
Facsimile: 505-325-5474.
Las Cruces, New Mexico Office: Suite 300, 277 East Amador. P.O. Drawer 1231.
Telephone: 505-523-2481.
Facsimile: 505-526-2215.
Santa Fe, New Mexico Office: 125 Lincoln Avenue, Suite 221. P.O. Box 1986.
Telephone: 505-989-9614.
Facsimile: 505-989-9857.

Ranne B. Miller
Alan C. Torgerson
Kendall O. Schlenker
Alice Tomlinson Lorenz
Gregory W. Chase
Alan Konrad
Margo J. McCormick
Lyman G. Sandy
Stephen M. Williams
Stephan M. Vidmar
Robert C. Gutierrez
Seth V. Bingham (Resident at Farmington Office)
Michael H. Hoses
James B. Collins (Resident at Farmington Office)
Timothy Ray Briggs
Walter R. Parr (Resident at Santa Fe Office)
Rudolph A. Lucero
Daniel E. Ramczyk
Dean G. Constantine
Deborah A. Solove
Gary L. Gordon
Lawrence R. White (Resident at Las Cruces Office)
Sharon P. Gross
Virginia Anderman
Marte D. Lightstone
Bradford K. Goodwin
John R. Funk (Resident at Las Cruces Office)
J. Scott Hall (Resident at Santa Fe Office)
Thomas R. Mack
Michael J. Happe (Resident at Farmington Office)
Denise Barela Shepherd
Nancy Augustus
Jill Burtram
Terri L. Sauer
Joel T. Newton (Resident at Las Cruces Office)
Judith K. Nakamura
Thomas M. Domme
David H. Thomas, III
C. Brian Charlton

COUNSEL

William K. Stratvert
Paul W. Robinson

Representative Clients: St. Paul Insurance Cos.; State Farm Mutual Automobile Insurance Co.; The Travelers; United States Fidelity & Guaranty Co.; New Mexico Physicians Mutual Liability Insurance Co.; Farmers Insurance Group; Ticor Title; Dona Ana Savings and Loan Assn.; Citizens Bank of Las Cruces.

For Complete List of Firm Personnel, See General Section

For full biographical listings, see the Martindale-Hubbell Law Directory

RODEY, DICKASON, SLOAN, AKIN & ROBB, P.A. (AV)

Albuquerque Plaza, Suite 2200, 201 Third Street, N.W., P.O. Box 1888, 87103-1888
Telephone: 505-765-5900
Fax: 505-768-7395
Santa Fe, New Mexico Office: Suite 101 Marcy Plaza, 123 East Marcy Street, P.O. Box 1357, 87504-1357.
Telephone: 505-984-0100.
Fax: 505-989-9542.

Robert M. St. John
Mark K. Adams
John P. Burton (Resident, Santa Fe Office)
Catherine T. Goldberg
Jo Saxton Brayer
S. I. Betzer, Jr.
Nancy J. Appleby
Debra Romero Thal
Patricia M. Taylor
DeWitt Michael Morgan
Mark A. Smith
Theresa W. Parrish

(See Next Column)

RODEY, DICKASON, SLOAN, AKIN & ROBB P.A.—*Continued*

Jay D. Hill
Paul C. Collins

For Complete List of Firm Personnel, See General Section

For full biographical listings, see the Martindale-Hubbell Law Directory

FARMINGTON, San Juan Co.

MILLER, STRATVERT, TORGERSON & SCHLENKER, P.A. (AV)

Suite 300, 300 West Arrington, P.O. Box 869, 87401
Telephone: 505-326-4521
Facsimile: 505-325-5474
Albuquerque, New Mexico Office: 500 Marquette Avenue, N.W., Suite 1100. P.O. Box 25687.
Telephone: 505-842-1950.
Facsimile: 505-243-4408.
Las Cruces, New Mexico Office: Suite 300, 277 East Amador. P.O. Drawer 1231.
Telephone: 505-523-2481.
Facsimile: 505-526-2215.
Santa Fe, New Mexico Office: 125 Lincoln Avenue, Suite 221. P.O. Box 1986.
Telephone: 505-989-9614.
Facsimile: 505-989-9857.

James B. Collins
Seth V. Bingham
Michael J. Happe

Representative Clients: St. Paul Insurance Cos.; State Farm Mutual Automobile Insurance Co.; The Travelers; United States Fidelity & Guaranty Co.; New Mexico Physicians Mutual Liability Insurance Co.; Farmers Insurance Group; Ticor Title Insurance Company; Sunrise Healthcare.

For full biographical listings, see the Martindale-Hubbell Law Directory

NEW YORK

*ALBANY,** Albany Co.

ROWLEY, FORREST, O'DONNELL & HITE, P.C. (AV)

90 State Street Suite 729, 12207-1715
Telephone: 518-434-6187
Fax: 518-434-1287

Richard R. Rowley
Thomas J. Forrest
Brian J. O'Donnell
Robert S. Hite
John H. Beaumont
Mark S. Pelersi
David C. Rowley

James J. Seaman
David P. Miranda
Kevin S. Casey
Richard W. Bader
Daniel W. Coffey
Thomas D. Spain

OF COUNSEL

Rush W. Stehlin

Reference: Norstar Bank.

For full biographical listings, see the Martindale-Hubbell Law Directory

GARDEN CITY, Nassau Co.

REDMOND, POLLIO & PITTONI, P.C. (AV)

1461 Franklin Avenue, 11530
Telephone: 516-248-2500
Telecopier: 516-248-2348

Benedict J. Pollio
M. John Pittoni
Peter R. Bonchonsky

Mark E. Costello
Kathleen M. Galgano
Rachel Cohen Quaid
Stephen E. Zaino
Ronald A. Pollio

OF COUNSEL

Aldo A. Trabucchi
Frederick Arthur Ross
John T. Redmond
Leonard P. Marinello

For full biographical listings, see the Martindale-Hubbell Law Directory

MELVILLE, Suffolk Co.

SPANTON, PARSOFF & SIEGEL, P.C. (AV)

425 Broad Hollow Road, Route 110, 11747
Telephone: 516-777-3200
Fax: 516-777-3204
New York, N.Y. Office: 790 Madison Avenue, 10021.
Telephone: 212-717-5948.

(See Next Column)

Donald M. Spanton
Neil M. Parsoff
Lawrence A. Siegel

Pamela G. Weiss

OF COUNSEL

Murray D. Schwartz

For full biographical listings, see the Martindale-Hubbell Law Directory

*NEW YORK,** New York Co.

BAKER & BOTTS, L.L.P. (AV)

885 Third Avenue Suite 2000, 10022
Telephone: 212-705-5000
Fax: 212-705-5125
Washington, D.C. Office: The Warner, 1299 Pennsylvania Avenue, N.W.
Telephone: 202-639-7700.
Austin, Texas Office: 1600 San Jacinto Center, 98 San Jacinto Boulevard.
Telephone: 512-322-2500.
Dallas, Texas Office: 2001 Ross Avenue.
Telephone: 214-953-6500.
Houston, Texas Office: One Shell Plaza, 910 Louisiana.
Telephone: 713-229-1234.
Moscow, Russian Federation Office: 10 ul. Pushkinskaya, 103031.
Telephone: 7095/921-5300 (Local); 7095/929-7070 (International).

MEMBERS OF FIRM

Jerome H. Kern
Karen Leslye Wolf
(Not admitted in NY)
Elizabeth M. Markowski
Frederick H. McGrath
Robert W. Murray Jr.
Kenneth S. Siegel

OF COUNSEL

Marc A. Leaf
Ronald D. Sernau

ASSOCIATES

Lee D. Charles
Thomas V. D'Ambrosio
Nancy E. Field
(Not admitted in NY)
Laura S. Franco
John L. Graham
(Not admitted in NY)
Alice W. Turinas
(Not admitted in NY)

For Complete List of Firm Personnel, See General Section

For full biographical listings, see the Martindale-Hubbell Law Directory

BECKMAN & MILLMAN, P.C. (AV)

116 John Street, 10038
Telephone: 212-227-6777
Telecopier: 212-227-1486
Midtown Office: 666 Fifth Avenue, New York, New York 10103.

Michael Beckman
Debra J. Millman

For full biographical listings, see the Martindale-Hubbell Law Directory

BRESLOW & WALKER (AV)

875 Third Avenue, 10022-7597
Telephone: 212-832-1930
Fax: 212-888-4955

Joel M. Walker
Howard S. Breslow
Gary T. Moomjian

Leslie S. Luft
Brendan T. Guastella
Jennifer A. O'Hare

For full biographical listings, see the Martindale-Hubbell Law Directory

CAPLIN & DRYSDALE, CHARTERED (AV)

399 Park Avenue, 10022
Telephone: 212-319-7125
Fax: 212-644-6755
Washington, D.C. Office: One Thomas Circle, N.W.
Telephone: 202-862-5000.
Fax: 202-429-3301.

Elihu Inselbuch
C. Sanders McNew
Christian R. Pastore

For full biographical listings, see the Martindale-Hubbell Law Directory

EDMONDS & BEIER, P.C. (AV)

21st Floor, 475 Fifth Avenue, 10017-6220
Telephone: 212-696-9191
Facsimile: 212-696-1164; 212-696-4167

Robert C. Edmonds
David L. Beier
Sharon Blau
Marc E. Elliott
Eugenia S. Nathanson
Lisa Paolella

For full biographical listings, see the Martindale-Hubbell Law Directory

New York—Continued

HAYTHE & CURLEY (AV)

237 Park Avenue, 10017
Telephone: 212-880-6000
Telex: 662184
Facsimile: (212) 682-0200
London, England Office: 11/12 Pall Mall, London SWIY 5LU, England.
Telephone: 71-930-0061.
Facsimile: 71-930-0083.
Beijing, China Office: Beijing Lufthansa Center Offices, Suite 306, 50 Liangmaqiao Road, Beijing, China 100016.
Telephone: 861-465-1265.
Facsimile: 861-465-1965.

MEMBERS OF FIRM

Leonard S. Baum
Andrew J. Beck
Susan W. Berson
Kimberly S. Blanchard
Richard H. Block
John J. Butler
Justine M. Clark
Bradley P. Cost
Stephen C. Curley
Charles E. Dorkey III
Miroslav M. Fajt
Clinton B. Fisher
Nathan Hale
Thomas M. Haythe
Charles B. Hughes, III
Roger Hall Lloyd (Resident Partner, European Office)
Jerry E. Muntz
Robert A. Ouimette
Thomas I. Sheridan, III
Adam A. Veltri
David W. R. Wawro

PRINCIPALS

Henry H. Liu
Jun Wei

ASSOCIATES

Mark K Beesley
Andrew J. Bernstein
Michael G. Boyd
Kenneth Allen Brown
Karen B. Burrows
John D. Burton
Dean T. Cho
Jeffrey L. Coploff
Erin T. Cornyn
Nora Jean Dahlman
Carol L. Divine
Darren R. Fortunato
Allison Greenhut
Vernadette L. Hart
Edward J. Henderson
Lee J. Hirsch
Jeffrey C. House
Peter J. Keenan
Gary S. Litke
James P. Lynn
Gina M. Mazzarulli
Suzanne O. Mills
Ronald J. Prague
Joseph J. Romagnoli
Ediberto Román
Todd L. Schleifstein
Steven R. Schoenfeld
Christine P. Shields
Marshall A. Sklar
H. William Smith III (Not admitted in NY)
John P. Stokke
Mark B Waldstein

For full biographical listings, see the Martindale-Hubbell Law Directory

HUTTON INGRAM YUZEK GAINEN CARROLL & BERTOLOTTI (AV)

250 Park Avenue, 10177
Telephone: 212-907-9600
Facsimile: 212-907-9681

MEMBERS OF FIRM

Ernest J. Bertolotti
Daniel L. Carroll
Roger Cukras
Larry F. Gainen
G. Thompson Hutton
Samuel W. Ingram, Jr.
Paulette Kendler
Steven Mastbaum
Dean G. Yuzek
David G. Ebert
Shane O'Neill

ASSOCIATES

Warren E. Friss
Patricia Hewitt
Gail A. Buchman
Stuart A. Christie
Beth N. Green
Timish K. Hnateyko
Jeanne F. Pucci
Jane Drummey
Adam L. Sifre
Susan Ann Fennelly
Marc J. Schneider

For full biographical listings, see the Martindale-Hubbell Law Directory

BUREAU FRANCIS LEFEBVRE (AV)

712 Fifth Avenue, 10019
Telephone: (1.212) 246.80.45
Fax: (1.212) 246.29.51
Paris, France Office: 3, Villa Emile Bergerat, 92522 Neuilly-Sur-Seine, Cedex.
Telephone: (33.1) 47 38 55 00.
Telex: 620971 LEFEB A.
Fax: (33.1) 47 38 55 55.

RESIDENT PARTNERS

Carina Levintoff
Pierre-Sébastien Thill (Not admitted in NY)

RESIDENT ASSOCIATES

Clotilde Fournier
Edouard Milhac (Not admitted in NY)

For full biographical listings, see the Martindale-Hubbell Law Directory

MALONEY, GERRA, MEHLMAN & KATZ (AV)

Chrysler Building, 405 Lexington Avenue, 10174
Telephone: 212-973-6900
Fax: 212-973-6097

MEMBERS OF FIRM

Ralph A. Gerra, Jr.
Melvin Katz
Thomas J. Maloney
Barry T. Mehlman

ASSOCIATES

Philip H. Sheehan, Jr.
Kenneth J. Zinghini

For full biographical listings, see the Martindale-Hubbell Law Directory

OTTERBOURG, STEINDLER, HOUSTON & ROSEN, P.C. (AV)

230 Park Avenue, 10169
Telephone: 212-661-9100
Cable Address: "Otlerton";
Telecopier: 212-682-6104
Telex: 960916

Kurt J. Wolff
Donald N. Gellert
William M. Silverman
Morton L. Gitter
Peter H. Stolzar
Alan R. Weiskopf
Bernard Beitel
Jonathan N. Helfat
Daniel Wallen
Scott L. Hazan
Glenn B. Rice
Albert F. Reisman
Kenneth J. Miller
Richard J. Rubin
Anthony M. Piccione
Steven B. Soll
Alan Kardon
Eugene V. Kokot
Mitchell M. Brand
Stanley L. Lane, Jr.
David W. Morse
Peter L. Feldman

COUNSEL

Lawrence B. Milling
Stephen B. Weissman

Diane B. Kaplan
Lloyd M. Green
Bruce P. Levine
Richard G. Haddad
Lauri Blum Regan
Enid Nagler Stuart
Stephen H. Alpert
Craig D. Zlotnick
Andrew M. Kramer
Jeanne-Marie Marziliano
Jenette A. Barrow
Brett H. Miller
Matthew J. Miller
John J. Kenny
Steven H. Weitzen
Richard L. Stehl
Gary G. Michael
Marc E. Schneider
Susan A. Joyce
Howard M. Sendrovitz

For full biographical listings, see the Martindale-Hubbell Law Directory

PILIERO GOLDSTEIN JENKINS & HALL (AV)

292 Madison Avenue, 10017
Telephone: 212-213-8200
Fax: 212-685-2028
Carlstadt, New Jersey Office: One Palmer Terrace.
Telephone: 201-507-5157.
FAX: 201-507-5221.
Washington, D.C. Office: 888 17th Street, N.W., Suite 1100.
Telephone: 202-467-6991.
FAX: 202-467-6703.

MEMBERS OF FIRM

Edward J. Goldstein
Christopher P. Hall
Jon Mark Jenkins
Robert D. Piliero

ASSOCIATES

John William LaRocca
Juliana M. Moday
Elaine B. Michetti (Not admitted in NY)

OF COUNSEL

Ricardo J. Davila

For full biographical listings, see the Martindale-Hubbell Law Directory

SHACK & SIEGEL, P.C. (AV)

530 Fifth Avenue, 10036
Telephone: 212-782-0700
Fax: 212-730-1964

Charles F. Crames
Pamela E. Flaherty
Paul S. Goodman
Ronald S. Katz
Donald D. Shack
Jeffrey N. Siegel
Jeffrey B. Stone

Paul A. Lucido
Steven M. Lutt
Ruby S. Teich
Keith D. Wellner
Adam F. Wergeles (Not admitted in NY)

For full biographical listings, see the Martindale-Hubbell Law Directory

New York—Continued

SIEGEL, MANDELL & DAVIDSON, P.C. (AV)

1515 Broadway One Astor Plaza, 10036
Telephone: 212-944-7900
Telecopier: 212-944-8497
Washington, D.C. Office: 1990 M Street, N.W., Suite 340, 20036.
Telephone: 202-223-8304.
Telecopier: 202-223-8305.

Samuel T. Siegel (1882-1948)
Sidney Mandell (1889-1969)
Joshua M. Davidson (1911-1981)
Harvey A. Isaacs
Brian S. Goldstein
Steven S. Weiser
Louis S. Shoichet
Ellen E. Rosenberg
Edward B. Ackerman
Robert T. Stack

Paul A. Horowitz
Arthur W. Bodek
Laurence M. Friedman
David A. Eisen
Amy J. Johannesen
Maytee Pereira
Brett Harris

For full biographical listings, see the Martindale-Hubbell Law Directory

TRAUB, BONACQUIST & FOX (AV)

489 Fifth Avenue, 27th Floor, 10017
Telephone: 212-476-4770
Fax: 212-476-4787
Roseland, New Jersey Office: 103 Eisenhower Parkway, 07068.
Telephone: 201-567-1827.
Fax: 201-403-9021.

MEMBERS OF FIRM

Paul Traub
Harold F. Bonacquist
Michael S. Fox

ASSOCIATES

Fredrick J. Levy
Julie Gamache
Lisa J. Pollack
Susan F. Balaschak
Maura I. Russell

For full biographical listings, see the Martindale-Hubbell Law Directory

*ROCHESTER,** Monroe Co.

HARRIS & CHESWORTH (AV)

1820 East Avenue, 14607
Telephone: 716-242-2400
Fax: 716-242-2424

MEMBERS OF FIRM

Wayne M. Harris
Donald O. Chesworth
Edward M. O'Brien

ASSOCIATES

David J. Gutmann
Michael A. Damia
David Mayer
Timothy P. Blodgett

SPECIAL COUNSEL

Melvin Bressler

For full biographical listings, see the Martindale-Hubbell Law Directory

*WHITE PLAINS,** Westchester Co.

GREENE & ZINNER, P.C. (AV)

202 Mamaroneck Avenue, 10601
Telephone: 914-948-4800
FAX: 914-948-4936

Andrew Greene
Stanley S. Zinner

Jeffrey P. Rogan
Robert J. Bellinson
Daniel E. Schnapp (Not admitted in NY)

For full biographical listings, see the Martindale-Hubbell Law Directory

WOODBURY, Nassau Co.

STEBEL & PASELTINER, P.C. (AV)

7600 Jericho Turnpike, 11797
Telephone: 516-496-8117
Telecopier: 516-496-8112

Bernard Stebel
David E. Paseltiner

Mindy K. Smolevitz
Steven M. Gelfman

COUNSEL

Edwin H. Baker
Alan M. Pollack
Michael E. Greene
Mitchell G. Mandell
Lori Samet Schwarz
Scott A. Sommer

References: Chemical Bank; Fleet Bank.

For full biographical listings, see the Martindale-Hubbell Law Directory

NORTH CAROLINA

*ASHEBORO,** Randolph Co.

JOHN N. OGBURN, JR. (AV)

Suite 201, Triad Bank Building, 261 North Fayetteville Street, Drawer 4067, 27204-4067
Telephone: 910-629-3345
Facsimile: 910-629-1882

Representative Clients: Bossong Mill, Inc.; Asheboro Hosiery Mill; Shaw Furniture Galleries; City of Randleman; Vestal Motors; Mid-State Motors; Weeks Construction Co.; The North Carolina One-Call Center; Triad Bank; Hospice of Randolph, Inc.

For full biographical listings, see the Martindale-Hubbell Law Directory

CHAPEL HILL, Orange Co.

NORTHEN, BLUE, ROOKS, THIBAUT, ANDERSON & WOODS, L.L.P. (AV)

Suite 550, 100 Europa Center, P.O. Box 2208, 27515-2208
Telephone: 919-968-4441
Facsimile: 919-942-6603

MEMBERS OF FIRM

John A. Northen
J. William Blue, Jr.
David M. Rooks, III
Charles H. Thibaut
Charles T. L. Anderson
Jo Ann Ragazzo Woods
Carol J. Holcomb

ASSOCIATES

James C. Stanford
Gregory Herman-Giddens
Cheryl Y. Capron

References: Central Carolina Bank; The Village Bank; Investors Title Insurance Co.; First Union National Bank; Centura Bank; United Carolina Bank; BB&T; Balbirer & Coleman, CPA's.

For full biographical listings, see the Martindale-Hubbell Law Directory

*CHARLOTTE,** Mecklenburg Co.

CULP ELLIOTT & CARPENTER, P.L.L.C. (AV)

A Partnership including a Professional Association
227 West Trade Street Suite 1500, 28202-1675
Telephone: 704-372-6322
Telefax: 704-372-1474

William R. Culp, Jr., (P.A.)
W. Curtis Elliott, Jr.
John Joseph Carpenter
Margaret R. K. Leinbach
Jonathan E. Gopman
Christopher Hannum
Stefan R. Latorre

For full biographical listings, see the Martindale-Hubbell Law Directory

NEWITT & BRUNY (AV)

417 East Boulevard, Suite 104, 28203
Telephone: 704-372-6181
Fax: 704-377-0535

MEMBERS OF FIRM

John G. Newitt, Sr. (1897-1973)
John G. Newitt, Jr.
Roger H. Bruny

ASSOCIATE

Todd A. Stewart

For full biographical listings, see the Martindale-Hubbell Law Directory

RAYBURN, MOON & SMITH, P.A. (AV)

The Carillon, 227 West Trade Street, Suite 1200, 28202
Telephone: 704-334-0891
FAX: 704-377-1897; 704-358-8866

Albert F. Durham
Travis W. Moon
C. Richard Rayburn, Jr.
James C. Smith
W. Scott Cooper
Matthew R. Joyner
James L. Bagwell
Cynthia D. Lewis
Patricia B. Edmondson
Paul R. Baynard
Laura D. Fennell
G. Kirkland Hardymon

For full biographical listings, see the Martindale-Hubbell Law Directory

WOMBLE CARLYLE SANDRIDGE & RICE (AV)

A Professional Limited Liability Company
3300 One First Union Center, 301 S. College Street, 28202-6025
Telephone: 704-331-4900
Telecopy: 704-331-4955
Telex: 853609
Winston-Salem, North Carolina Office: 1600 Southern National Financial Center.
Telephone: 919-721-3600.
Telecopy: 919-721-3660.
Telex: 806498.

(See Next Column)

WOMBLE CARLYLE SANDRIDGE & RICE, *Charlotte—Continued*

Raleigh, North Carolina Office: 2100 First Union Capitol Center, 150 Fayetteville Street Mall, P.O. Box 831.
Telephone: 919-755-2100.
Telecopy: 919-755-2150.
Telex: 806498.
Atlanta, Georgia Office: One Ninety One Peachtree Tower, 191 Peachtree Street N.E., Suite 3250.
Telephone: 404-614-2580.
Fax: 404-614-2595.

MEMBERS OF FIRM

Garza Baldwin, III
Cyrus M. Johnson, Jr.
Joe B. Cogdell, Jr.
David E. Johnston
J. Carlton Fleming
J. Alexander Salisbury

RESIDENT ASSOCIATES

David W. Dabbs
Jane Jeffries Jones

Representative Clients: Childress Klein Properties, Inc.; Food Lion, Inc.; Fieldcrest Cannon, Inc.; J.A. Jones Construction Company; Parkdale Mills, Inc.; Duke Power Company; Bowles Hollowell Conner & Company; ALLTEL Carolina, Inc.; Belk Store Services, Inc.; Philip Holzmann A.G.

For Complete List of Firm Personnel, See General Section

For full biographical listings, see the Martindale-Hubbell Law Directory

*GREENSBORO,** Guilford Co.

FORMAN, MARTH, BLACK & ANGLE, P.A. (AV)

235 North Greene Street, P.O. Drawer 2020, 27402-2020
Telephone: 910-378-0172; 272-5591
FAX: 910-378-0015

Richard C. Forman
T. Keith Black
Paul E. Marth
Robert B. Angle, Jr.
Jeffrey S. Iddings

Reference: Wachovia Bank & Trust Co., N.A.; Triad Bank.

For full biographical listings, see the Martindale-Hubbell Law Directory

ISAACSON ISAACSON & GRIMES (AV)

Suite 400 NationsBank Building, 101 West Friendly Avenue, P.O. Box 1888, 27402
Telephone: 910-275-7626
FAX: 910-273-7293

MEMBERS OF FIRM

Henry H. Isaacson
Marc L. Isaacson
L. Charles Grimes

ASSOCIATE

Thomas B. Kobrin

For full biographical listings, see the Martindale-Hubbell Law Directory

MOREHEAD CITY, Carteret Co.

BENNETT, MCCONKEY, THOMPSON & MARQUARDT, P.A. (AV)

1007 Shepard Street, P.O. Drawer 189, 28557
Telephone: 919-726-4114
FAX: 919-726-7975

Thomas S. Bennett
James W. Thompson, III
Samuel A. McConkey, Jr.
Dennis M. Marquardt

Approved Attorneys For: Lawyers Title Insurance Corp.
Reference: First Citizens Bank & Trust Co.

For full biographical listings, see the Martindale-Hubbell Law Directory

*RALEIGH,** Wake Co.

* indicates certain Bar Register subscribers whose principal office is located elsewhere in the state and who have arranged for representation as a part of the state capital listings that follow

THE LAW OFFICES OF PAUL E. CASTELLOE (AV)

Carolina Place, Suite 500, 2626 Glenwood Avenue, P.O. Box 31603, 27622-1603
Telephone: 919-571-9876
Fax: 919-571-9476

Paul E. Castelloe
Deborah A. Malizia
Walter N. Rak

For full biographical listings, see the Martindale-Hubbell Law Directory

THARRINGTON, SMITH & HARGROVE (AV)

209 Fayetteville Street Mall, P.O. Box 1151, 27602
Telephone: 919-821-4711
Telecopier: 919-829-1583

(See Next Column)

MEMBERS OF FIRM

Carlisle W. Higgins (1887-1980)
Carlyn G. Poole
J. Harold Tharrington
Douglas E. Kingsbery
Roger W. Smith
Randall M. Roden
Wade M. Smith
Michael Crowell
George T. Rogister, Jr.
Ann L. Majestic
C. Allison Brown Schafer

ASSOCIATES

Melissa Hill
Debra R. Nickels
Daniel W. Clark
Rod Malone
Jonathan A. Blumberg
E. Hardy Lewis
Jaye Powell Meyer

LEGAL SUPPORT PERSONNEL

Michael M. Cogswell

Representative Clients: North Carolina Association of Broadcasters; AT&T Communications; ABC-TV Network Affiliates Assn.; North Carolina Cable Television Assn.; Associated Press; Time-Warner Communications; Public Service Company of N.C.; The Hearst Corp.; Capitol Broadcasting.

For full biographical listings, see the Martindale-Hubbell Law Directory

* WOMBLE CARLYLE SANDRIDGE & RICE (AV)

A Professional Limited Liability Company
2100 First Union Capitol Center, 150 Fayetteville Street Mall, P.O. Box 831, 27602
Telephone: 919-755-2100
Telecopy: 919-755-2150
Telex: 806498
Charlotte, North Carolina Office: 3300 One First Union Center, 301 South College Street.
Telephone: 704-331-4900.
Telecopy: 704-331-4955.
Telex: 853609.
Winston-Salem, North Carolina Office: 1600 Southern National Financial Center.
Telephone: 919-721-3600.
Telecopy: 919-721-3660.
Telex: 806498.
Atlanta, Georgia Office: One Ninety One Peachtree Tower, 191 Peachtree Street N.E., Suite 3250.
Telephone: 404-614-2580.
Fax: 404-614-2595.

RESIDENT PARTNER

Deborah Hylton Hartzog

RESIDENT ASSOCIATES

Jennifer E. Bennett Overton
Kathleen Nowack Worm

Representative Clients: Aetna Casualty and Surety Co., Inc.; ALSCO/AmeriMark Building Products, Inc.; Aoki Corporation America, Inc.; Empire of Carolina, Inc.; Hackney Brothers, Inc.; Lawyers Mutual Liability Insurance Company of North Carolina; Meredith College; Monk-Austin, Inc.; Regency Park Corporation; Wachovia Bank of North Carolina, N.A.

For Complete List of Firm Personnel, See General Section

For full biographical listings, see the Martindale-Hubbell Law Directory

*WINSTON-SALEM,** Forsyth Co.

WOMBLE CARLYLE SANDRIDGE & RICE (AV)

A Professional Limited Liability Company
1600 Southern National Financial Center, P.O. Drawer 84, 27102
Telephone: 910-721-3600
Telecopy: 910-721-3660
Telex: 806498
Charlotte, North Carolina Office: 3300 One First Union Center, 301 South College Street.
Telephone: 704-331-4900.
Telecopy: 704-331-4955.
Telex: 853609.
Raleigh, North Carolina Office: 2100 First Union Capitol Center, 150 Fayetteville Street Mall, P.O. Box 831.
Telephone: 919-755-2100.
Telecopy: 919-755-2150.
Telex: 806498.
Atlanta, Georgia Office: One Ninety One Peachtree Tower, 191 Peachtree Street, N.E., Suite 3250.
Telephone: 404-614-2580.
Fax: 404-614-2595.

MEMBERS OF FIRM

Zeb E. Barnhardt, Jr.
William Allison Davis, II
Kenneth G. Carroll
John L. W. Garrou
Linwood Layfield Davis
Murray C. Greason, Jr.
Jeffrey C. Howland

ASSOCIATE

Heather A. King

Representative Clients: Brad Ragan, Inc.; Brenner Companies; Food Lion, Inc.; Hanes Companies, Inc.; North Carolina Baptist Hospitals, Inc.; R.J. Reynolds Tobacco Company; Summit Communications Group, Inc.; Thom-

(See Next Column)

WOMBLE CARLYLE SANDRIDGE & RICE—*Continued*

asville Furniture Industries, Inc.; Wachovia Corporation; Wake Forest University.

For Complete List of Firm Personnel, See General Section

For full biographical listings, see the Martindale-Hubbell Law Directory

OHIO

ASHTABULA, Ashtabula Co.

WARREN AND YOUNG (AV)

134 West 46th Street, P.O. Box 2300, 44004-6951
Telephone: (216) 997-6175
Facsimile: (216) 992-9114

MEMBER OF FIRM
Stuart W. Cordell
OF COUNSEL
E. Terry Warren

Representative Clients: Ashtabula County Medical Center; Ashtabula Rubber Co.; Bank One; Carlisle Retailers; Iten Industries; Molded Fiber Glass Cos.; Peoples Savings; Premix; Plasticolors.

For Complete List of Firm Personnel, See General Section

For full biographical listings, see the Martindale-Hubbell Law Directory

*BOWLING GREEN,** Wood Co.

SPITLER, VOGTSBERGER & HUFFMAN (AV)

131 East Court Street, 43402-2495
Telephone: 419-352-2535
FAX: 419-353-8728
Rossford, Ohio Office: 932 Dixie Highway.
Telephone: 419-666-7130.

MEMBERS OF FIRM

Emmett V. Spitler
Daniel T. Spitler
Robert E. Spitler
Thomas H. Vogtsberger
Rex H. Huffman
Diane Rausch Huffman

Representative Clients: First Federal Savings & Loan Association of Wood County; Prudential Insurance Company of America; The Mutual Benefit Life Insurance Co.; John Hancock Mutual Life Insurance Co.; Equitable Life Assurance Society of the U.S.; Minnesota Mutual Life Insurance Co.

For full biographical listings, see the Martindale-Hubbell Law Directory

*CANTON,** Stark Co.

DAY, KETTERER, RALEY, WRIGHT & RYBOLT (AV)

800 William R. Day Building, 121 Cleveland Avenue, South, 44702-1921
Telephone: 216-455-0173
Telecopier: 216-455-2633
Columbus, Ohio Office: Suite 1602, 50 West Broad Street.
Telephone: 614-228-3611.
Telecopier: 614-228-3663

MEMBERS OF FIRM

David B. Day (1863-1947)
John G. Ketterer (1901-1973)
Donald W. Raley (1905-1986)
Clyde H. Wright (1909-1991)
Robert M. Rybolt (Retired)
Robert P. Eshelman (Retired)
Robert E. Levitt (Retired)
Louis A. Boettler
John R. Werren
William B. Badger
James K. Brooker
E. Lang D'Atri
J. Sean Keenan
Sheila M. Markley
Fred H. Zollinger, Jr.
James R. Blake
John H. Brannen
Richard A. Princic
Tim A. Powell
Richard E. Davis, II
Douglas J. Maser (Resident, Columbus Office)
Michael S. Gruber
Alicia M. Wyler
William S. Cline
Daniel A. Minkler
Matthew Yackshaw
Raymond T. Bules
John A. Murphy, Jr.
Merle D. Evans, III
Craig G. Pelini
Darrell N. Markijohn
Robert E. Roland
Jill Freshley Otto
Sara E. Lioi

ASSOCIATES

Mark F. Fischer
J. Curtis Werren
James F. Contini, II
Thomas E. Hartnett
Andrew M. McIlvaine
Cari Fusco Evans

OF COUNSEL

John F. Buchman
Stephen A. Reilly (Resident, Columbus Office)
David M. Thomas

Representative Clients: The Timken Co.; Bank One, Akron; National City Bank; Detroit Diesel Corp.; Canton Drop Forge.

For full biographical listings, see the Martindale-Hubbell Law Directory

*CINCINNATI,** Hamilton Co.

BROWN, CUMMINS & BROWN CO., L.P.A. (AV)

3500 Carew Tower, 441 Vine Street, 45202
Telephone: 513-381-2121
Fax: 513-381-2125

J. W. Brown (Retired)
Robert S Brown
James R. Cummins
Donald S. Mendelsohn
Lynne Skilken
Melanie S. Corwin

Counsel for: Midwest Group of Funds; Eastgate Health Care Center, Inc.; Highlands Health Care Center, Inc.; Clarke Detroit Diesel-Allison; Benson, Inc.
Reference: State Bank of Cincinnatti.

For full biographical listings, see the Martindale-Hubbell Law Directory

CASH, CASH, EAGEN & KESSEL (AV)

1000 Tri State Building, 432 Walnut Street, 45202
Telephone: 513-621-4443
FAX: 513-621-5231

MEMBERS OF FIRM

Albert D. Cash
Michael J. Stegman

ASSOCIATE
Jeffrey G. Stagnaro

Representative Clients: Future Healthcare, Inc.; The Armrel Byrnes Company; Mio's, Inc.; Tiger Machinery Co., Inc.; Byrnes-Conway Company; Hamilton Distributing Co.; Charles F. Shiels & Co., Inc.; Pest-All, Inc.; Queen City Packaging Co.; International Managed Care Strategies, Inc.

For full biographical listings, see the Martindale-Hubbell Law Directory

DINSMORE & SHOHL (AV)

1900 Chemed Center, 255 East Fifth Street, 45202-3172
Telephone: 513-977-8200
FAX: 513-977-8141
Florence, Kentucky Office: Turfway Ridge Office Park, 7300 Turfway Road, Suite 430 41042-1355.
Telephone: 606-283-0515.
FAX: 606-283-6017.
Dayton, Ohio Office: 500 Courthouse Plaza, S.W., 10 N. Ludlow Street, 45402-1834.
Telephone: 513-228-8012.
FAX: 513-461-2543.
Columbus, Ohio Office: NBD Bank Building, Suite 330, 175 South Third Street, 43215-5134.
Telephone: 614-224-7887.
FAX: 614-224-7882.

MEMBERS OF FIRM

John E. McDowell
Jerome H. Kearns
Wiley Dinsmore
Clifford A. Roe, Jr.
Thomas J. Sherman
James H. Stethem
William H. Seall (Resident, Dayton, Ohio Office)
Paul R. Mattingly
J. Michael Cooney
Richard J. Beckmann (Resident, Dayton, Ohio Office)
Edward J. Buechel (Resident, Florence, Kentucky Office)
Paul A. Ose
S. Richard Arnold
Charles F. Hertlein, Jr.
Joanne M. Schreiner
George H. Vincent
C. Christopher Muth
Steven H. Schreiber
Calvin D. Buford

ASSOCIATES

G. Franklin Miller
Christine L. McBroom
Harvey Jay Cohen
Lynn Marmer
Douglas W. Campbell
John R. Glankler (Resident, Dayton, Ohio Office)
Richard L. Schuster
Deborah Price Rambo
David M. Zuckerman
John H. Wendeln
Susan B. Zaunbrecher
Moira J. Squier
Gregory O. Long
Kent A. Shoemaker
Phillip A. Rotman, II
Merideth A. Trott (Resident, Dayton, Ohio Office)

For Complete List of Firm Personnel, See General Section

For full biographical listings, see the Martindale-Hubbell Law Directory

EICHEL & KRONE CO., L.P.A. (AV)

508 Atlas Bank Building, 524 Walnut Street, 45202
Telephone: 513-241-1234
Fax: 513-241-2731

Lawrence E. Eichel (1908-1981)
Paul W. Krone
Bruce A. Krone

References: Star Bank N.A.; PNC Bank N.A.

For full biographical listings, see the Martindale-Hubbell Law Directory

Cincinnati—Continued

KATZ, GREENBERGER & NORTON (AV)

105 East Fourth Street, 9th Floor, 45202-4011
Telephone: 513-721-5151
FAX: 513-621-9285

Leonard H. Freiberg (1885-1954)
Alfred B. Katz
Mark Alan Greenberger
Louis H. Katz
Richard L. Norton
Steven M. Rothstein
Robert Gray Edmiston
Ellen Essig

ASSOCIATES

Scott P. Kadish
Stephen E. Imm
Stephen L. Robison
Jeffrey J. Greenberger

OF COUNSEL

Charles Weiner

For full biographical listings, see the Martindale-Hubbell Law Directory

KATZ, TELLER, BRANT & HILD A LEGAL PROFESSIONAL ASSOCIATION (AV)

2400 Chemed Center, 255 East Fifth Street, 45202-4724
Telephone: 513-721-4532
Telecopier: 513-721-7120

Reuven J. Katz
Jerome S. Teller
Joseph A. Brant
Guy M. Hild
Robert A. Pitcairn, Jr.
Robert E. Brant
Ronald J. Goret
Stephen C. Kisling
Andrew R. Berger
Mark J. Jahnke
William F. Russo
John R. Gierl
Bruce A. Hunter
Gregory E. Land
Bradley G. Haas
Daniel P. Utt
Brent G. Houk
Cynthia Loren Gibson
Suzanne Prieur Land
Tedd H. Friedman

Representative Clients: Eagle Picher Industries, Inc.; F & C International, Inc.; Jewish Hospitals of Cincinnati; Johnny Bench; Texo Corporation; University of Cincinnati Medical Associates, Inc.

For full biographical listings, see the Martindale-Hubbell Law Directory

KEPLEY, MACCONNELL & EYRICH A LEGAL PROFESSIONAL ASSOCIATION (AV)

Formerly Clark & Eyrich
2200 Ameritrust Center, 525 Vine Street, 45202
Telephone: 513-241-5540; 621-1045
FAX: 513-241-8111; 621-0038

K. Gregory Kepley
David J. Eyrich
James J. Ryan
Michael E. Neiheisel
T. Scott Gilligan
C. Thomas Dupuis
Richard K. Graham
Paul D. Rattermann
Jane Elizabeth Fink

Representative Clients and References furnished upon request.

For full biographical listings, see the Martindale-Hubbell Law Directory

KLAINE, WILEY, HOFFMANN & MEURER A LEGAL PROFESSIONAL ASSOCIATION (AV)

Suite 1850, 105 East Fourth Street, 45202-4080
Telephone: 513-241-0202
Fax: 513-241-9322

Franklin A. Klaine, Jr.
Donald L. Wiley
Gary R. Hoffmann
Gregory J. Meurer
James P. Minutolo

For Complete List of Firm Personnel, See General Section

For full biographical listings, see the Martindale-Hubbell Law Directory

SCHWARTZ, MANES & RUBY A LEGAL PROFESSIONAL ASSOCIATION (AV)

2900 Carew Tower, 441 Vine Street, 45202
Telephone: 513-579-1414
Telecopier: 513-579-1418

Richard M. Schwartz
Dennis L. Manes
Stanley L. Ruby
Scott M. Slovin
Howard L. Richshafer
Kenneth R. Thompson, II

For Complete List of Firm Personnel, See General Section

For full biographical listings, see the Martindale-Hubbell Law Directory

STRAUSS & TROY A LEGAL PROFESSIONAL ASSOCIATION (AV)

2100 PNC Center, 201 East Fifth Street, 45202-4186
Telephone: 513-621-2120
Telecopier: 513-241-8259
Northern Kentucky Office: Suite 1400, 50 East Rivercenter Boulevard, Covington, Kentucky, 41011.
Telephone: 513-621-8900; 513-621-2120.
Telecopier: 513-629-9444.

Samuel M. Allen (Resident, Covington, Kentucky Office)
Gordon H. Hood (Resident, Covington, Kentucky Office)
Alan Comstock Rosser
William R. Jacobs
James G. Heldman
Charles Jay Postow
Stuart C. Brinn
Ann W. Gerwin
Timothy B. Theissen (Resident, Covington, Kentucky Office)
Charles C. Ashdown

Shawn M. Young
Eric H. Kearney
Thomas H. Stewart

OF COUNSEL

Paul J. Theissen (Resident, Covington, Kentucky Office)

Representative Clients: PNC Bank, N.A. (Ohio and Kentucky); Corporex Companies, Inc.; Mercantile Stores Company, Inc.; Star Bank, N.A. (Ohio and Kentucky).

For Complete List of Firm Personnel, See General Section

For full biographical listings, see the Martindale-Hubbell Law Directory

THOMPSON, HINE AND FLORY (AV)

312 Walnut Street, 14th Floor, 45202-4029
Telephone: 513-352-6700
Fax: 513-241-4771;
Telex: 938003
Akron, Ohio Office: 50 S. Main Street, Suite 502, 44308-1828.
Telephone: 216-376-8090.
Fax: 216-376-8386.
Cleveland, Ohio Office: 1100 National City Bank Building, 629 Euclid Avenue, 44114-3070.
Telephone: 216-566-5500.
Fax: 216-556-5583.
Telex: 980217.
Cable Address: "Thomflor".
Columbus, Ohio Office: One Columbus, 10 West Broad Street, 43215-3435.
Telephone: 614-469-3200.
Fax: 614-469-3361.
Dayton, Ohio Office: 2000 Courthouse Plaza, N.E., 45402-1706.
Telephone: 513-443-6600.
Fax: 513-443-6637; 443-6635.
Palm Beach, Florida Office: 125 Worth Avenue, 33480-4466.
Telephone: 407-833-5900.
Fax: 407-833-5951.
Washington, D.C. Office: 1920 N Street, N.W., 20036-1601.
Telephone: 202-331-8800.
Fax: 202-331-8330.
Telex: 904173.
Cable Address: "Caglaw".
Brussels, Belgium Office: Rue des Chevaliers / Ridderstraat 14 - B.10, B - 1050.
Telephone: 011(32-2) 511-9326.
Fax: 011(-32-2) 513-9206.

MEMBERS OF FIRM

William T. Bahlman, Jr.
Daniel O. Berger
William H. Cordes
Robert W. Crawford
C. Jackson Cromer
Stephen M. King
Leonard S. Meranus
Michael H. Neumark
Michael R. Oestreicher (Partner-in-Charge in Cincinnati; Brussels Office Liaison Partner)
Richard J. Ruebel
Robert A. Selak
Louis F. Solimine

ASSOCIATES

Paul Allaer
Philomena Saldanha Ashdown

For Complete List of Firm Personnel, See General Section

For full biographical listings, see the Martindale-Hubbell Law Directory

*CLEVELAND,** Cuyahoga Co.

BERICK, PEARLMAN & MILLS A LEGAL PROFESSIONAL ASSOCIATION (AV)

1350 Eaton Center, 1111 Superior Avenue, 44114-2569
Telephone: 216-861-4900
Automatic Telecopier: 216-861-4929

James H. Berick
Samuel S. Pearlman
Osborne Mills, Jr.
William M. Mills
Paul J. Singerman
Gary S. Desberg
Daniel G. Berick

COUNSEL

Joseph G. Berick
Joan M. Gross

(See Next Column)

BERICK, PEARLMAN & MILLS A LEGAL PROFESSIONAL ASSOCIATION—*Continued*

Arthur J. Tassi — Laura D. Nemeth
Edmund G. Kauntz — Robert G. Marischen

Representative Clients: Cleveland Browns Football Company, Inc.; The Equitable Life Assurance Society of the United States; The Town and Country Trust; Republic Savings Bank; The Huntington National Bank; Realty Re-Fund Trust; Retail Apparel Group, Inc.; A. Schulman, Inc.; Society National Bank; The Tranzonic Companies.

For full biographical listings, see the Martindale-Hubbell Law Directory

JAMES J. BRANAGAN (AV)
1100 National City Bank Building, 44114-3070
Telephone: 216-566-5888
Fax: 216-566-8527
Telex: 980217

For full biographical listings, see the Martindale-Hubbell Law Directory

GOLDFARB & REZNICK (AV)
Suite 1800, 55 Public Square, 44113
Telephone: 216-781-0383
Telecopier: 216-781-0393

MEMBERS OF FIRM

Bernard S. Goldfarb — Morris M. Reznick
Mark V. Webber

ASSOCIATES

Carl E. Cormany — Sergio A. Carano

For full biographical listings, see the Martindale-Hubbell Law Directory

GOODMAN WEISS MILLER FREEDMAN (AV)
100 Erieview Plaza, 27th Floor, 44114-1824
Telephone: 216-696-3366
Telecopier: 216-363-5835

MEMBERS OF FIRM

Robert A. Goodman — Steven J. Miller
Ronald I. Weiss — Glenn S. Hansen
John F. Ballard — Richard S. Mitchell

Daniel D. Domozick — James E. Goodrich
Jay Faeges — Wendy N. Weigand

OF COUNSEL

Howard J. Freedman — Roger J. Weiss
Michael D. Goler

For full biographical listings, see the Martindale-Hubbell Law Directory

KADISH & BENDER A LEGAL PROFESSIONAL ASSOCIATION (AV)
2112 East Ohio Building, 44114
Telephone: 216-696-3030
Telecopier: 216-696-3492

Stephen L. Kadish — Kevin M. Hinkel
J. Timothy Bender — David G. Weibel

Aaron H. Bulloff — William A. Duncan
Joseph P. Alexander — Mary Beth Duffy
David G. Lambert — James H. Rownd

For full biographical listings, see the Martindale-Hubbell Law Directory

KAUFMAN & CUMBERLAND CO., L.P.A. (AV)
Third Floor, 1404 East 9th Street, 44114-1779
Telephone: 216-861-0707
Telefax: 216-694-6883
TDD: 216-694-6891
Columbus, Ohio Office: 300 South Second Street, 43215.
Telephone: 614-224-0717.
Telefax: 614-229-4111.

Steven S. Kaufman — Robert A. Blattner
Frank J. Cumberland, Jr. — Hollis A. Selvaggi

OF COUNSEL

James A. Scott — Anthony R. Troia

Representative Clients: CertainTeed Corp.; Teledyne Inc.

For Complete List of Firm Personnel, See General Section

For full biographical listings, see the Martindale-Hubbell Law Directory

KELLEY, McCANN & LIVINGSTONE (AV)
35th Floor, BP America Building, 200 Public Square, 44114-2302
Telephone: 216-241-3141
FAX: 216-241-3707

(See Next Column)

MEMBERS OF FIRM

James P. Oliver — M. Patricia Oliver
Michael D. Schenker — Bruce L. Waterhouse, Jr.

ASSOCIATES

Peter K. Shelton — Halle Fine Terrion

For Complete List of Firm Personnel, See General Section

For full biographical listings, see the Martindale-Hubbell Law Directory

SELKER & FURBER (AV)
1111 Ohio Savings Plaza, 1801 East Ninth Street, 44114
Telephone: 216-781-8686
FAX: 216-781-8688

MEMBERS OF FIRM

Eugene I. Selker — Philip C. Furber
Harlan Daniel Karp

For full biographical listings, see the Martindale-Hubbell Law Directory

THOMPSON, HINE AND FLORY (AV)
1100 National City Bank Building, 629 Euclid Avenue, 44114-3070
Telephone: 216-566-5500
Fax: 216-566-5583
Telex: 980217
Cable Address: "Thomflor"
Akron, Ohio Office: 50 S. Main Street, Suite 502, 44308-1828.
Telephone: 216-376-8090.
Fax: 216-376-8386.
Cincinnati, Ohio Office: 312 Walnut Street, 14th Floor, 45202-4029.
Telephone: 513-352-6700.
Fax: 513-241-4771.
Telex: 938003.
Columbus, Ohio Office: One Columbus, 10 West Broad Street, 43215-3435.
Telephone: 614-469-3200.
Fax: 614-469-3361.
Dayton, Ohio Office: 2000 Courthouse Plaza, N.E., 45402-1706.
Telephone: 513-443-6600.
Fax: 513-443-6637; 443-6635.
Palm Beach, Florida Office: 125 Worth Avenue, Suite 117, 33480-4466.
Telephone: 407-833-5900.
Fax: 407-833-5951.
Washington, D.C. Office: 1920 N Street, N.W., 20036-1601.
Telephone: 202-331-8800.
Fax: 202-331-8330.
Telex: 904173.
Cable Address: "Caglaw".
Brussels, Belgium Office: Rue des Chevaliers, Ridderstraat 14 - B.10, B - 1050.
Telephone: 011(32-2) 511-9326.
Fax: 011(32-2) 513-9206.

MEMBERS OF FIRM

Thomas A. Aldrich — Alan L. Hyde
Malvin E. Bank — Donald H. Messinger (Partner-in-Charge)
James R. Carlson — Raymond T. Sawyer
Betsey Brewster Case — Thomas C. Stevens
John L. Dampeer — Richard E. Streeter
Oliver C. Henkel, Jr.
Roy L. Turnell

ASSOCIATES

F. Howard Mandel — Peter J. Muñiz
Ronda R. Mascaro — Michelle Lafond Potter
Gregory A. Smith

For Complete List of Firm Personnel, See General Section

For full biographical listings, see the Martindale-Hubbell Law Directory

ULMER & BERNE (AV)
Ninth Floor, Bond Court Building, 1300 East Ninth Street, 44114-1583
Telephone: 216-621-8400
Telex: 201999 UBLAW
Telecopier: 216-621-7488
Columbus, Ohio Office: 88 East Broad Street, Suite 1980.
Telephone: 614-228-8400.
Telecopier: 614-228-8561.

MEMBERS OF FIRM

Robert L. Lewis (Retired) — Robert A. Fein
Jordan C. Band (Retired) — Christopher C. McCracken
Morton L. Stone — Richard G. Hardy
Harold E. Friedman — Ruth Anna Carlson
Albert B. Glickman — Stephen Rowan
Donald E. Heiser — Peter A. Rome
Stuart A. Laven — Stanley T. Koenig
Jeffrey S. Gray

For Complete List of Firm Personnel, See General Section

For full biographical listings, see the Martindale-Hubbell Law Directory

*COLUMBUS,** Franklin Co.

* indicates certain Bar Register subscribers whose principal office is located elsewhere in the state and who have arranged for representation as a part of the state capital listings that follow

EMENS, KEGLER, BROWN, HILL & RITTER (AV)

Capitol Square Suite 1800, 65 East State Street, 43215-4294
Telephone: 614-462-5400
Telecopier: 614-464-2634
Cable Address: "Law EKBHR"
Telex: 246671

John F. Allevato
Jack A. Bjerke
Larry K. Carnahan
J. Richard Emens
Allen L. Handlan
Edward C. Hertenstein
Charles J. Kegler
Paul D. Ritter, Jr.
Steven R. Russi
Kevin L. Sykes
John R. Thomas
Beatrice E. Wolper

COUNSEL

John L. Gray

Holly Robinson Fischer
James M. Groner
Paul R. Hess
Shelley A. McBride
Amy M. Shepherd
Shawnell Williams

Representative Clients: Abrasive Technology, Inc.; Access Energy Corp.; Donato's Pizza, Inc.; Drug Emporium, Inc.; The Fishel Co.; Spenley Newspapers, Inc.; Warner Cable Communications, Inc.

For Complete List of Firm Personnel, See General Section

For full biographical listings, see the Martindale-Hubbell Law Directory

*** THOMPSON, HINE AND FLORY (AV)**

One Columbus, 10 West Broad Street, 43215-3435
Telephone: 614-469-3200
Fax: 614-469-3361
Akron, Ohio Office: 50 S. Main Street, Suite 502, 44308-1828.
Telephone: 216-376-8090.
Fax: 216-376-8386.
Cincinnati, Ohio Office: 312 Walnut Street, 14th Floor, 45202-4029.
Telephone: 513-352-6700.
Fax: 513-241-4771.
Telex: 938003.
Cleveland, Ohio Office: 1100 National City Bank Building, 629 Euclid Avenue, 44114-3070.
Telephone: 216-566-5500.
Fax: 216-556-5583.
Telex: 980217.
Cable Address: "Thomflor".
Dayton, Ohio Office: 2000 Courthouse Plaza, N.E., 45402-1706.
Telephone: 513-443-6600.
Fax: 513-443-6637; 443-6635.
Palm Beach, Florida Office: 125 Worth Avenue, 33480-4466.
Telephone: 407-833-5900.
Fax: 407-833-5951.
Washington, D.C. Office: 1920 N Street, N.W., 20036-1601.
Telephone: 202-331-8800.
Fax: 202-331-8330.
Telex: 904173.
Cable Address: "Caglaw".
Brussels, Belgium Office: Rue des Chevaliers / Ridderstraat 14 - B.10, B - 1050.
Telephone: 011(32-2) 511-9326.
Fax: 011(32-2) 513-9206.

MEMBERS OF FIRM

Thomas J. Bonasera
William S. Fein
Barry L. Lubow
Robert P. Mone
Susan A. Petersen
Raymond T. Sawyer (In Columbus and Cleveland, Ohio)

ASSOCIATE

Charles E. Ticknor, III

For Complete List of Firm Personnel, See General Section

For full biographical listings, see the Martindale-Hubbell Law Directory

*DAYTON,** Montgomery Co.

BOGIN, PATTERSON & BOHMAN (AV)

1200 Talbott Tower, 131 North Ludlow Street, 45402
Telephone: 513-226-1200
FAX: 513-226-1625

MEMBERS OF FIRM

Dennis L. Patterson
Jerome B. Bohman
James C. Ellis
Curtis F. Slaton
Randall L. Stump

(See Next Column)

OF COUNSEL

Asher Bogin

For full biographical listings, see the Martindale-Hubbell Law Directory

LOUIS & FROELICH A LEGAL PROFESSIONAL ASSOCIATION (AV)

1812 Kettering Tower, 45423
Telephone: 513-226-1776
FAX: 513-226-1945
Trotwood, Ohio Office: 101 East Main Street.
Telephone: 513-226-1776.

Herbert M. Louis
Gary L. Froelich
Jeffrey E. Froelich
Jeffrey A. Winwood
Marybeth W. Rutledge

F. Ann Crossman
James I. Weprin

Reference: Society Bank, N.A. of Dayton, Ohio.

For full biographical listings, see the Martindale-Hubbell Law Directory

ROGERS & GREENBERG (AV)

2160 Kettering Tower, 45423
Telephone: 513-223-8171
Fax: 513-223-1649

MEMBERS OF FIRM

William A. Rogers, Jr.
Stanley Z. Greenberg
John M. Cloud
Barry W. Mancz
Keith R. Kearney

Richard L. Carr, Jr.
James G. Kordik
Carl D. Sherrets
L. Anthony Lush
Dawn S. Garrett

General Counsel for: Heartland Federal Credit Union; National Management Association; Moraine Materials Co.; Techway Industries, Inc.; Washington Township Park Board.

For full biographical listings, see the Martindale-Hubbell Law Directory

SEBALY, SHILLITO & DYER (AV)

1300 Courthouse Plaza, NE, P.O. Box 220, 45402-0220
Telephone: 513-222-2500
Telefax: 513-222-6554; 222-8279
Springfield, Ohio Office: National City Bank Building, 4 West Main Street, Suite 530, P.O. Box 1346, 45501-1346.
Telephone: 513-325-7878.
Telefax: 513-325-6151.

MEMBERS OF FIRM

James A. Dyer
Gale S. Finley
William W. Lambert
Michael P. Moloney
Mary Lynn Readey
Jon M. Sebaly
Beverly F. Shillito
Jeffrey B. Shulman
Karl R. Ulrich
Robert A. Vaughn (Resident, Springfield Office)

Martin A. Beyer
Daniel A. Brown
Anne L. Rhoades
Orly R. Rumberg
Juliana M. Spaeth
Kendra F. Thompson

For full biographical listings, see the Martindale-Hubbell Law Directory

STOECKLEIN, KOVERMAN & SMITH (AV)

1300 Hulman Building, 45402
Telephone: 513-222-6926
Fax: 513-222-6901

Robert J. Stoecklein (1917-1990)
John R. Koverman, Jr.
Patrick K. Smith
James E. Fox

For full biographical listings, see the Martindale-Hubbell Law Directory

THOMPSON, HINE AND FLORY (AV)

2000 Courthouse Plaza, N.E., 45402-1706
Telephone: 513-443-6600
Fax: 513-443-6637; 443-6635
Akron, Ohio Office: 50 S. Main Street, Suite 502, 44308-1828.
Telephone: 216-376-8090.
Fax: 216-376-8386.
Cincinnati, Ohio Office: 312 Walnut Street, 14th Floor, 45202-4029.
Telephone: 513-352-6700.
Fax: 513-241-4771.
Telex: 938003.
Cleveland, Ohio Office: 1100 National City Bank Building, 629 Euclid Avenue, 44114-3070.
Telephone: 216-566-5500.
Fax: 216-556-5583.
Telex: 980217.
Cable Address: "Thomflor".

(See Next Column)

THOMPSON, HINE AND FLORY—*Continued*

Columbus, Ohio Office: One Columbus, 10 West Broad Street, 43215-3435.
Telephone: 614-469-3200.
Fax: 614-469-3361.
Palm Beach, Florida Office: 125 Worth Avenue, 33480-4466.
Telephone: 407-833-5900.
Fax: 407-833-5951.
Washington, D.C. Office: 1920 N Street, N.W., 20036-1601.
Telephone: 202-331-8800.
Fax: 202-331-8330.
Telex: 904173.
Cable Address: "Caglaw".
Brussels, Belgium Office: Rue des Chevaliers / Ridderstraat 14 - B.10, B - 1050.
Telephone: 011(32-2) 511-9326.
Fax: 011(32-2) 513-9206.

MEMBERS OF FIRM

Barry M. Block
Richard F. Carlile
Peter J. Donahue
Stanley A. Freedman
Sharen Swartz Gage
J. Michael Herr
David A. Neuhardt
Joseph M. Rigot (Partner-in-Charge in Dayton)
Arik A. Sherk
Howard N. Thiele, Jr.

For Complete List of Firm Personnel, See General Section

For full biographical listings, see the Martindale-Hubbell Law Directory

*LANCASTER,** Fairfield Co.

STEBELTON, ARANDA & SNIDER A LEGAL PROFESSIONAL ASSOCIATION (AV)

One North Broad Street, P.O. Box 130, 43130
Telephone: 614-654-4141;
Columbus Direct Line: 614-837-1212;
1-800-543-Laws
Fax: 614-654-2521

Gerald L. Stebelton
James C. Aranda
Rick L. Snider
John M. Snider

Sandra W. Davis
Jason A. Price

LEGAL SUPPORT PERSONNEL

Sandra J. Steinhauser
Rose M. Sels
Sandra K. Hillyard
Michelle K. Garlinger

For full biographical listings, see the Martindale-Hubbell Law Directory

*TOLEDO,** Lucas Co.

EASTMAN & SMITH (AV)

One Seagate, Twenty-Fourth Floor, 43604
Telephone: 419-241-6000
Telecopier: 419-247-1777
Columbus, Ohio Office: 65 East State Street, Suite 1000, 43215.
Telephone: 614-460-3556.
Telecopier: 614-228-5371.

MEMBERS OF FIRM

Frank D. Jacobs
Bruce L. Smith
Henry N. Heuerman
John H. Boggs
David L. Kuhl
Kenneth C. Baker
Ronald J. Tice
Gary M. Harden
Roger Paul Klee
Mark C. Abramson
Steven D. Reinbolt

ASSOCIATES

Bryan K. Prosek
John M. Kirsner
Oksana M. Ludd
Bryan M. Bach
David C. Krock

OF COUNSEL

Howard M. Friedman
Ralph S. Boggs
Gerald P. Moran

Counsel for: Marathon Oil Co.; Borg Warner Corp.; McDonalds Corp.; A P Parts Co.; 21 International Holdings, Inc. (f/k/a Knoll International Holdings, Inc.); Master Chemical Co.; Glasstech, Inc.; Omnisource Corporation; Stateline Steel Corporation; Commonwealth Construction Corp.

For Complete List of Firm Personnel, See General Section

For full biographical listings, see the Martindale-Hubbell Law Directory

OKLAHOMA

*OKLAHOMA CITY,** Oklahoma Co.

BRITTON AND ADCOCK (AV)

Suite 670, 101 Park Avenue, 73102
Telephone: 405-239-2393
Fax: 405-232-5135

James E. Britton
J. Michael Adcock

For full biographical listings, see the Martindale-Hubbell Law Directory

DAY, EDWARDS, FEDERMAN, PROPESTER & CHRISTENSEN, P.C. (AV)

Suite 2900 First Oklahoma Tower, 210 Park Avenue, 73102-5605
Telephone: 405-239-2121
Telecopier: 405-236-1012

Bruce W. Day
Joe E. Edwards
William B. Federman
Richard P. Propester
D. Wade Christensen
J. Clay Christensen
Kent A. Gilliland
Rodney J. Heggy
Ricki Valerie Sonders
Thomas Pitchlynn Howell, IV
John C. Platt

David R. Widdoes
Lori R. Roberts
Carolyn A. Romberg

OF COUNSEL

Herbert F. (Jack) Hewett
Jeanette Cook Timmons
Joel Warren Harmon
Jane S. Eulberg
Mark A. Cohen

Representative Clients: Aetna Life Insurance Co.; Boatmen's First National Bank of Oklahoma; Borg-Warner Chemicals, Inc.; City Bank & Trust; Federal Deposit Insurance Corp.; Bank One, Oklahoma City; Haskell Lemon Construction Co.; Merrill Lynch, Pierce, Fenner & Smith, Inc.; Prudential Securities, Inc.

For full biographical listings, see the Martindale-Hubbell Law Directory

*TULSA,** Tulsa Co.

BOND & BALMAN (AV)

800 Beacon Building, 406 South Boulder, 74103
Telephone: 918-583-0303
Facsimile: 918-583-5577

MEMBERS OF FIRM

Patterson Bond
Steven K. Balman

For full biographical listings, see the Martindale-Hubbell Law Directory

GABLE & GOTWALS (AV)

2000 Bank IV Center, 15 West Sixth Street, 74119-5447
Telephone: 918-582-9201
Facsimile: 918-586-8383

Teresa B. Adwan
Pamela S. Anderson
John R. Barker
David L. Bryant
Gene C. Buzzard
Dennis Clarke Cameron
Timothy A. Carney
Renee DeMoss
Elsie C. Draper
Sidney G. Dunagan
Theodore Q. Eliot
Richard W. Gable
Jeffrey Don Hassell
Patricia Ledvina Himes
Oliver S. Howard
Richard D. Koljack, Jr.
J. Daniel Morgan
Joseph W. Morris
Elizabeth R. Muratet
Richard B. Noulles
Ronald N. Ricketts
John Henry Rule
M. Benjamin Singletary
James M. Sturdivant
Patrick O. Waddel
Michael D. Hall
David Edward Keglovits
Stephen W. Lake
Kari S. McKee
Terry D. Ragsdale
Jeffrey C. Rambach

OF COUNSEL

G. Ellis Gable
Charles P. Gotwals, Jr.

For full biographical listings, see the Martindale-Hubbell Law Directory

JAMES, POTTS AND WULFERS (AV)

Suite 705, 320 South Boston Avenue, 74103-3712
Telephone: 918-584-0881
FAX: 918-584-4521

MEMBERS OF FIRM

David F. James
Thomas G. Potts
David W. Wulfers

For full biographical listings, see the Martindale-Hubbell Law Directory

Tulsa—Continued

JOHNSON, ALLEN, JONES & DORNBLASER (AV)

900 Petroleum Club Building, 601 South Boulder, 74119
Telephone: 918-584-6644
FAX: 918-584-6645

MEMBERS OF FIRM

Mark H. Allen
W. Thomas Coffman
Kenneth E. Dornblaser
John B. Johnson, Jr.
C. Robert Jones
Richard D. Jones
Randy R. Shorb

ASSOCIATE

Frances F. Hillsman

For full biographical listings, see the Martindale-Hubbell Law Directory

JONES, GIVENS, GOTCHER & BOGAN, A PROFESSIONAL CORPORATION (AV)

3800 First National Tower, 74103
Telephone: 918-581-8200
Fax: 918-583-1189 or 918-583-6652

Neil E. Bogan (1945-1990)
William B. Jones
Jack R. Givens
Roy C. Breedlove
David C. Cameron
Vaden F. Bales
James E. Weger
Thomas L. Vogt
Ronald O. Ray, Jr.
Ira L. Edwards, Jr.

C. Michael Copeland

OF COUNSEL

Deryl Lee Gotcher
Dan A. Rogers
Richard C. Honn
Judi E. Beaumont
Gregory G. Meier

Representative Clients: Financial Services: Boatmen's First National Bank of Oklahoma. Insurance: Aetna Insurance Co.; Oklahoma Bar Professional Liability Insurance Co.; Physicians Liability Insurance Co.; Travelers Insurance Co.; Employers Casualty Insurance Co.; Government Employees Insurance Co. Professional Services: KPMG, Peat Marwick. Manufacturing & Commerce: Ciba-Geigy Chemical Co.; Clear Channel Communications.

For full biographical listings, see the Martindale-Hubbell Law Directory

JOYCE AND POLLARD (AV)

Suite 300, 515 South Main Mall, 74103
Telephone: 918-585-2751
Fax: 918-582-9308

MEMBERS OF FIRM

J. C. Joyce
Dwayne C. Pollard

Ted J. Nelson
Sheila M. Bradley
John C. Joyce

A list of Representative Clients furnished upon request.

For full biographical listings, see the Martindale-Hubbell Law Directory

OREGON

*PORTLAND,** Multnomah Co.

COONEY & CREW, P.C. (AV)

Pioneer Tower, Suite 890, 888 S.W. Fifth Avenue, 97204
Telephone: 503-224-7600
FAX: 503-224-6740

Paul A. Cooney
Thomas E. Cooney
Thomas M. Cooney
Brent M. Crew
Michael D. Crew
Kelly T. Hagan
Raymond F. Mensing, Jr.
Robert S. Perkins

LEGAL SUPPORT PERSONNEL

Alma Weber (Paralegal)

For full biographical listings, see the Martindale-Hubbell Law Directory

GRENLEY, ROTENBERG EVANS & BRAGG, P.C. (AV)

30th Floor, Pacwest Center, 1211 S.W. Fifth Avenue, 97204
Telephone: 503-241-0570
Facsimile: 503-241-0914

Gary I. Grenley
Stan N. Rotenberg
Lawrence Evans
Michael J. Bragg
Steven D. Adler
Michael S. Evans
Michael C. Zusman
Jeffrey C. Bodie

OF COUNSEL

Sol Siegel
Robert C. Laskowski
Norman A. Rickles

(See Next Column)

Ann M. Lane

Reference: Key Bank of Oregon.

For full biographical listings, see the Martindale-Hubbell Law Directory

HAGEN, DYE, HIRSCHY & DILORENZO, P.C. (AV)

19th Floor Benj. Franklin Plaza, One S.W. Columbia Street, 97258-2087
Telephone: 503-222-1812
FAX: 503-274-7979

Joseph T. Hagen
Jeffrey L. Dye
John A. Hirschy
John A. DiLorenzo, Jr.
Dana R. Taylor
Mark A. Golding
Kenneth A. Williams

Blanche I. Sommers
Timothy J. Wachter
Annie T. Buell
Adam S. Rittenberg
Michael E. Farnell
John D. Parsons

LEGAL SUPPORT PERSONNEL

Carol A. R. Wong
Flora L. Wade

For full biographical listings, see the Martindale-Hubbell Law Directory

O'DONNELL, RAMIS, CREW, CORRIGAN & BACHRACH (AV)

Ballow & Wright Building, 1727 N.W. Hoyt Street, 97209
Telephone: 503-222-4402
FAX: 503-243-2944
Clackamas County Office: Suite 202, 181 N. Grant, Canby.
Telephone: 503-266-1149.

MEMBERS OF FIRM

Mark P. O'Donnell
Stephen F. Crew
Charles E. Corrigan

ASSOCIATES

Mark L. Busch
William J. Stalnaker

LEGAL SUPPORT PERSONNEL

Dawna S. Shattuck (Legal Assistant)

For full biographical listings, see the Martindale-Hubbell Law Directory

SUSSMAN SHANK WAPNICK CAPLAN & STILES (AV)

1000 S.W. Broadway Suite 1400, 97205
Telephone: 503-227-1111
Telecopier: 503-248-0130

MEMBERS OF FIRM

Norman Wapnick
Barry P. Caplan
William N. Stiles
John P. Davenport
Jeffrey R. Spere

ASSOCIATES

Gary E. Enloe
William S. Manne

SPECIAL COUNSEL

Aaron Jay Besen
John E. McCormick

For Complete List of Firm Personnel, See General Section

For full biographical listings, see the Martindale-Hubbell Law Directory

PENNSYLVANIA

BALA CYNWYD, Montgomery Co.

KANIA, LINDNER, LASAK AND FEENEY (AV)

Suite 525, Two Bala Plaza, 19004
Telephone: 610-667-3240
Fax: 610-668-9676

Arthur J. Kania
Albert A. Lindner
John Lasak
Thomas J. Feeney, III
Robert A. Griffiths

ASSOCIATE

Michael F. Merlie

A list of Representative Clients for which the firm serves as General Counsel or Local Counsel will be supplied upon request.

For full biographical listings, see the Martindale-Hubbell Law Directory

*DOYLESTOWN,** Bucks Co.

ANTHEIL NICHOLAS MASLOW & MACMINN (AV)

95 North Broad Street, P.O. Box 50, 18901
Telephone: 215-230-7500
Telecopier: 215-230-7796

(See Next Column)

ANTHEIL NICHOLAS MASLOW & MACMINN—*Continued*

William L. Antheil, III
Jeffrey H. Nicholas
Susan A. Maslow
William T. MacMinn

Emma Crowder Brown
Warren A. Wilbur, III
Patricia A. Wenger

OF COUNSEL

Frank C. Nicholas

For full biographical listings, see the Martindale-Hubbell Law Directory

*EASTON,** Northampton Co.

BROSE, POSWISTILO & ELLIOTT (AV)

Suite 201, 1101 Building, 1101 Northampton Street, 18042
Telephone: 610-258-2374
Telex: 847461
(Answer Back: BP&L EAT)
Facsimile: 610-258-8363

MEMBERS OF FIRM

E. Jerome Brose
Frank S. Poswistilo
Thomas R. Elliott, Jr.
James F. Brose

General Counsel for: Lehigh Valley Title Co.; SI Handling Systems, Inc.; Harvel Plastics, Inc.; Follett Corp.; Aetna Casualty Insurance Co.; Lehigh & New England Development Corp.; Clark Equipment Credit Corp.; Selective Insurance Co.; Shand Morahan & Co., Inc.

For full biographical listings, see the Martindale-Hubbell Law Directory

HERSTER, NEWTON & MURPHY (AV)

127 North Fourth Street, P.O. Box 1087, 18042
Telephone: 610-258-6219

MEMBERS OF FIRM

Andrew L. Herster, Jr.
Henry R. Newton
William K. Murphy

General Counsel For: Valley Federal Savings & Loan Assn.; Lafayette Bank; Easton Printing Co.; Northampton Community College; Eisenhardt Mills, Inc.; Delaware Wood Products, Inc.; Panuccio Construction, Inc.
References: Merchants Bank, N.A.; Lafayette Bank; Valley Federal Savings and Loan.

ELKINS PARK, Montgomery Co.

DAVID E. WASSERSTROM (AV)

Elkins Park House, 7900 Old York Road, 19027
Telephone: 215-635-3770
Fax: 215-635-4690

For full biographical listings, see the Martindale-Hubbell Law Directory

*GREENSBURG,** Westmoreland Co.

DAVID J. MILLSTEIN (AV)

218 South Maple Avenue, 15601
Telephone: 412-837-3333
Fax: 412-837-8344

For full biographical listings, see the Martindale-Hubbell Law Directory

*HARRISBURG,** Dauphin Co.

BOSWELL, SNYDER, TINTNER & PICCOLA (AV)

315 North Front Street, P.O. Box 741, 17108-0741
Telephone: 717-236-9377
Telecopier: 717-236-9316

MEMBERS OF FIRM

William D. Boswell
Donn L. Snyder
Leonard Tintner
Jeffrey E. Piccola
Jeffrey R. Boswell
Brigid Q. Alford
Mark R. Parthemer
Charles J. Hartwell

OF COUNSEL

Richard B. Wickersham

Representative Clients: Bramalea Inc.; Iceland Seafood Corp.; Industrial Motor Supply, Inc.; Space Petroleum & Chemical Co., Inc.; Hartman Motor Cars Co.; Union Quanies, Inc.; United Restaurant Equipment.

For full biographical listings, see the Martindale-Hubbell Law Directory

BUCHANAN INGERSOLL, PROFESSIONAL CORPORATION (AV)

Vartan Parc, 30 North Third Street, 17101
Telephone: 717-237-4800
Telecopier: 717-233-0852
Pittsburgh, Pennsylvania Office: 5800 USX Tower, 600 Grant Street.
Telephone: 412-562-8800.
Philadelphia, Pennsylvania Office: Two Logan Square, Twelfth Floor, 18th & Arch Streets.
Telephone: 215-665-8700.
Tampa, Florida Office: 101 East Kennedy Boulevard, Suite 1030.
Telephone: 813-222-8180.

(See Next Column)

North Miami Beach, Florida Office: 19495 Biscayne Boulevard.
Telephone: 305-933-5600.
Lexington, Kentucky Office: 1210 Vine Center Office Tower, 333 West Vine Street.
Telephone: 606-225-5333.
Princeton, New Jersey Office: Buchanan Ingersoll, A Partnership, College Centre, 500 College Road East.
Telephone: 609-452-2666.

Bradley J. Gunnison
Mary Hannah Leavitt
Gerald K. Morrison

COUNSEL

Evelyn S. Harris

SENIOR ATTORNEY

Michael L. Solomon

Arbelyn Elizabeth Wolfe

For Complete List of Firm Personnel, See General Section

For full biographical listings, see the Martindale-Hubbell Law Directory

GOLDBERG, KATZMAN & SHIPMAN, P.C. (AV)

320 Market Street - Strawberry Square, P.O. Box 1268, 17108-1268
Telephone: 717-234-4161
Telecopier: 717-234-6808; 717-234-6810

Ronald M. Katzman
Neil Hendershot
Jesse Jay Cooper
Michael A. Finio

Arnold B. Kogan

Representative Clients: Pennsylvania Supply, Inc.; Elco Concrete Products, Inc.; Hirsch Valuation Group; Lemoyne Sleeper; E.N. Dunlap, Inc.; Herre Brothers, Inc.; Memorial Eye Institute; E.I. Associates; Tressler Lutheran Services.
Reference: Fulton Bank.

For Complete List of Firm Personnel, See General Section

For full biographical listings, see the Martindale-Hubbell Law Directory

HEPFORD, SWARTZ & MORGAN (AV)

111 North Front Street, P.O. Box 889, 17108-0889
Telephone: 717-234-4121
Fax: 717-232-6802
Lewistown, Pennsylvania Office: 12 South Main Street, P.O. Box 867.
Telephone: 717-248-3913.

MEMBERS OF FIRM

H. Joseph Hepford
Lee C. Swartz
James G. Morgan, Jr.
Sandra L. Meilton
Stephen M. Greecher, Jr.
Dennis R. Sheaffer

COUNSEL

Stanley H. Siegel (Resident, Lewistown Office)

ASSOCIATES

Richard A. Estacio
Michael H. Park
Andrew K. Stutzman

For full biographical listings, see the Martindale-Hubbell Law Directory

HAVERFORD, Montgomery & Delaware Cos.

BENJAMIN S. OHRENSTEIN (AV)

354 West Lancaster Avenue, Suite 212, 19041
Telephone: 610-649-1268; 215-473-6900
Fax: 610-642-6553

For full biographical listings, see the Martindale-Hubbell Law Directory

*INDIANA,** Indiana Co.

BONYA AND DOUGLASS (AV)

134 South Sixth Street, 15701
Telephone: 412-465-5535
Fax: 412-465-9685

MEMBERS OF FIRM

John A. Bonya
Stanley P. DeGory
Robert D. Douglass
Beverly A. Gazza
Nicholas J. Mikesic
David M. Zimmerman

Reference: S & T Bank, of Indiana, Pennsylvania.

For full biographical listings, see the Martindale-Hubbell Law Directory

*LANCASTER,** Lancaster Co.

APPEL & YOST (AV)

33 North Duke Street, 17602-2886
Telephone: 717-394-0521
Telecopier: 717-299-9781 ABA NET NUMBER 1556
New Holland, Pennsylvania Office: 142 East Main Street.
Telephone: 717-354-4117.

(See Next Column)

APPEL & YOST, *Lancaster—Continued*

Strasburg, Pennsylvania Office: 39 East Main Street.
Telephone: 717-687-7871.
Quarryville, Pennsylvania Office: 201 East State Street.
Telephone: 717-786-3172.
Ephrata, Pennsylvania Office: 123 East Main Street, 17522.
Telephone: 717-733-2104.

MEMBERS OF FIRM

T. Roberts Appel, II
Harry B. Yost
James W. Appel
John L. Sampson
Kenneth H. Howard
William R. Wheatly
William J. Cassidy, Jr.
Greta R. Aul
Matthew G. Guntharp
Peter M. Schannauer

Julia G. Vanasse
Elaine G. Ugolnik
David W. Mersky

OF COUNSEL

Paul F. McKinsey
J. Marlin Shreiner

Counsel for: School Lane Hills, Inc.; Wickersham, Inc. (Construction & Development).

For full biographical listings, see the Martindale-Hubbell Law Directory

LANSDALE, Montgomery Co.

PEARLSTINE/SALKIN ASSOCIATES (AV)

1250 South Broad Street Suite 1000, P.O. Box 431, 19446
Telephone: 215-699-6000
Fax: 215-699-0231

MEMBERS OF FIRM

Philip Salkin
Ronald E. Robinson
Barry Cooperberg
Frederick C. Horn
Marc B. Davis
William R. Wanger
F. Craig La Rocca
Jeffrey T. Sultanik
Neal R. Pearlstine
Wendy G. Rothstein
Alan L. Eisen
Glenn D. Fox

Wilhelm L. Gruszecki
Brian E. Subers
Mark S. Cappuccio
James R. Hall
Michael S. Paul
David J. Draganosky
Lawrence P. Kempner

For full biographical listings, see the Martindale-Hubbell Law Directory

*NORRISTOWN,** Montgomery Co.

GERBER & GERBER (AV)

Suite 500, One Montgomery Plaza, 19401
Telephone: 610-279-6700
Fax: 610-279-7126

MEMBERS OF FIRM

Morris Gerber
A. Richard Gerber

ASSOCIATE

Parke H. Ulrich

For full biographical listings, see the Martindale-Hubbell Law Directory

MANNING, KINKEAD, BROOKS & BRADBURY, A PROFESSIONAL CORPORATION (AV)

412 DeKalb Street, 19404-0231
Telephone: 610-279-1800
Fax: 610-279-8682

Franklin L. Wright (1880-1965)
William Perry Manning, Jr.
William H. Kinkead, III
William H. Bradbury, III

Cheri D. Andrews

Counsel for: The Philadelphia National Bank; John Deere Co.; The Rouse Co.; Consolidated Rail Corp.; Bethlehem Steel Co.; Royal Globe Insurance Co.; Nationwide Mutual Insurance Co.

For full biographical listings, see the Martindale-Hubbell Law Directory

*PHILADELPHIA,** Philadelphia Co.

ANDERSON GREENFIELD & DOUGHERTY (AV)

1525 Penn Mutual Tower 510 Walnut Street, 19106-3610
Telephone: 215-627-0789
Fax: 215-627-0813
Wayne, Pennsylvania Office: First Fidelity Bank Building, 301 West Lancaster Avenue.
Telephone: 215-341-9010.

MEMBERS OF FIRM

Susan L. Anderson
Marjorie E. Greenfield
Donna Dougherty

(See Next Column)

ASSOCIATES

John Randolph Prince, III
Linda K. Hobkirk

For full biographical listings, see the Martindale-Hubbell Law Directory

ASTOR WEISS KAPLAN & ROSENBLUM (AV)

The Bellevue, 6th Floor, Broad Street at Walnut, 19102
Telephone: 215-790-0100
Fax: 215-790-0509
Bala Cynwyd, Pennsylvania Office: Suite 100, Three Bala Plaza West, P.O. Box 1665.
Telephone: 610-667-8660.
Fax: 610-667-2783.
Cherry Hill, New Jersey Office: Woodland Falls Corporate Park, 210 Lake Drive East, Suite 201.
Telephone: 609-795-1113.
Fax: 609-795-7413.

MEMBERS OF FIRM

Paul C. Astor
Alvin M. Weiss (1936-1976)
G. David Rosenblum
Arthur H. Kaplan
Barbara Oaks Silver
Richard H. Martin
Allen B. Dubroff
David S. Workman
David S. Mandel
David Gutin (Resident at Bala Cynwyd Office)
Joseph B. Finlay, Jr.
Howard K. Goldstein
Steven W. Smith
Gerald J. Schorr
Jean M. Biesecker (Resident, Bala Cynwyd Office)

ASSOCIATES

Carol L. Vassallo
Thomas J. Maiorino
John R. Poeta
Bradley J. Begelman
Andrew S. Kessler
Marc S. Zamsky
Janet G. Felgoise (Resident, Bala Cynwyd Office)
Jacqueline G. Segal (Resident, Bala Cynwyd Office)

SPECIAL COUNSEL

Neil Hurowitz (Resident, Bala Cynwyd Office)

OF COUNSEL

Erwin L. Pincus
Edward W. Silver
Lloyd Zane Remick

For full biographical listings, see the Martindale-Hubbell Law Directory

BALDWIN RENNER & CLARK (AV)

1201 Chestnut Street, Tenth Floor, 19107
Telephone: 215-563-1950
Fax: 215-563-2014
Wayne, Pennsylvania Office: The Woods Suite 905. 992 Old Eagle School Road.
Telephone: 610-687-4664.
Fax: 610-687-4640.

Frank B. Baldwin, III

For full biographical listings, see the Martindale-Hubbell Law Directory

BUCHANAN INGERSOLL, PROFESSIONAL CORPORATION (AV)

Two Logan Square Twelfth Floor, 18th & Arch Streets, 19103
Telephone: 215-665-8700
Telecopier: 215-569-2066
Pittsburgh, Pennsylvania Office: 5800 USX Tower, 600 Grant Street.
Telephone: 412-562-8800.
Harrisburg, Pennsylvania Office: Vartan Parc, 30 North Third Street.
Telephone: 717-237-4800.
Tampa, Florida Office: 101 East Kennedy Boulevard, Suite 1030.
Telephone: 813-222-8180.
North Miami Beach, Florida Office: 19495 Biscayne Boulevard.
Telephone: 305-933-5600.
Lexington, Kentucky Office: 1210 Vine Center Office Tower, 333 West Vine Street.
Telephone: 606-225-5333.
Princeton, New Jersey Office: Buchanan Ingersoll, A Partnership, College Centre, 500 College Road East.
Telephone: 609-452-2666.

Kenneth E. Aaron
Thomas J. Bender, Jr.
Stephen C. Braverman
Alan C. Kessler
Jerome N. Kline
Lawrence J. Lichtenstein
George F. Nagle
Antoinette R. Stone
Thomas L. VanKirk
Marguerite S. Walsh

COUNSEL

Richard W. Hayden
Nathaniel Metz

SENIOR ATTORNEYS

Ralph E. Arpajian
Mary Ellen Krober

Andrew W. Allison
Mary Kay Brown
Stuart M. Brown
Kristine Grady Derewicz
Robert Bruce Eyre
Nancy Sabol Frantz
Paul B. Halligan
Sherry Kajdan Vetterlein
Lawrence J. Kotler
Raymond McGarry

(See Next Column)

Buchanan Ingersoll Professional Corporation—*Continued*

Fern L. McGovern
Mark Andrew Polemeni
Robert W. Scott
Sherman W. Smith III
Noreen M. Walsh
Thomas G. Wolpert
DonnaMarie Zotter

For full biographical listings, see the Martindale-Hubbell Law Directory

Fellheimer Eichen Braverman & Kaskey, A Professional Corporation (AV)

21st Floor, One Liberty Place, 19103-7334
Telephone: 215-575-3800
FAX: 215-575-3801
Camden, New Jersey Office: 519 Federal Street, Suite 503 Parkade Building, 08103-1147.
Telephone: 609-541-5323.
Fax: 609-541-5370.

Alan S. Fellheimer
David L. Braverman
Judith Eichen Fellheimer
John E. Kaskey
Kenneth S. Goodkind
Anna Hom
Peter E. Meltzer

Barbara Anisko
Maia R. Caplan
Jeffrey L. Eichen
Michael N. Feder
Jolie G. Kahn
George F. Newton
David B. Spitofsky
W. Thomas Tither, Jr.

For Complete List of Firm Personnel, See General Section

For full biographical listings, see the Martindale-Hubbell Law Directory

Gallagher, Reilly and Lachat, P.C. (AV)

Suite 1300, 2000 Market Street, 19103
Telephone: 215-299-3000
FAX: 215-299-3010
Pennsauken, New Jersey Office: Kevon Office Center, Suite 130, 2500 McClellan Boulevard, 08109.
Telephone: 609-663-8200.

Stanley S. Frazee, Jr.
Paul F. X. Gallagher
Thomas F. Reilly
Frederick T. Lachat, Jr.
Richard K. Hohn
James Emerson Egbert
Stephen A. Scheuerle
Elizabeth F. Walker

David Scott Morgan
Wilfred T. Mills, Jr.
Maureen Rowan
Charles L. McNabb
Thomas O'Neill
Laurence I. Gross
Sean F. Kennedy
Milica Novakovic
John A. Livingood, Jr.

SPECIAL COUNSEL

Dolores Rocco Kulp

For full biographical listings, see the Martindale-Hubbell Law Directory

Klehr, Harrison, Harvey, Branzburg & Ellers (AV)

1401 Walnut Street, 19102
Telephone: 215-568-6060
Fax: 215-568-6603
Cherry Hill, New Jersey Office: Colwick-Suite 200, 51 Haddonfield Road.
Telephone: 609-486-7900.
Fax: 609-486-4875.
Allentown, Pennsylvania Office: Roma Corporate Center, Suite 501, 1605 North Cedar Crest Boulevard.
Telephone: 215-432-1803.
Fax: 215-433-4031.
Wilmington, Delaware Office: 222 Delaware Avenue, Suite 1101.
Telephone: 302-426-1189.
Fax: 302-426-9193.

MEMBERS OF FIRM

Morton R. Branzburg
William A. Harvey
Leonard M. Klehr
Mark L. Alderman
John Spelman
Stephen T. Burdumy
Richard S. Roisman
Stuart K. Askot
William R. Thompson
Gary W. Levi (Resident, Cherry Hill, New Jersey Office)
M. Norman Goldberger
Jason M. Shargel
Michael C. Forman
Brian J. Sisko
Michael K. Coran

ASSOCIATES

Wayne D. Bloch
Denise M. Day
Todd L. Silverberg
Frederick J. Fisher
Stephen P. Lieske

For Complete List of Firm Personnel, See General Section

For full biographical listings, see the Martindale-Hubbell Law Directory

Melvin B. Miller, Ltd. (AV)

Suite 750 Curtis Center, 6th & Walnut Streets, 19106
Telephone: 215-923-8626
Telecopier: 215-574-9510

(See Next Column)

Melvin B. Miller

Representative Clients: Berkshire Investment Corp.; Asbell & Associates; Delaire Nursing Home, Inc.; Berkeley Heights Convalescent Center, Inc.; Hospicomm, Inc.; Metropolitan Management Corp.; First Winthrop Corporation.

For full biographical listings, see the Martindale-Hubbell Law Directory

Patterson & Weir (AV)

Suite 1200, Land Title Building, 100 South Broad Street, 19110
Telephone: 215-665-8181
Telefax: 215-665-8464
Westmont, New Jersey Office: 216 Haddon Avenue, Suite 704, Sentry Office Plaza, 08108.
Telephone: 609-858-6100.
Telefax: 609-858-4606.

MEMBERS OF FIRM

Walter Weir, Jr.
Paul A. Patterson
Brent S. Gorey
Daniel S. Bernheim, III
Mark E. Herrera (Resident, Westmont, New Jersey Office)

ASSOCIATES

David J. Toll
Susan Verbonitz
Robert D. Sayre
Jonathan J. Bart
Scott C. Pyfer (Resident, Westmont, New Jersey Office)
Lee Ann M. Williams, Jr
Douglas J. McGill
Harry J. Giacometti

For full biographical listings, see the Martindale-Hubbell Law Directory

Spector Gadon & Rosen, Attorneys at Law, P.C. (AV)

29th Floor, 1700 Market Street, 19103-3913
Telephone: 215-241-8888
Fax: 215-241-8844
Moorestown, New Jersey Office: Spector, Gadon & Rosen, P.C. 307 Fellowship Road. P.O. Box 550.
Telephone: 609-778-8100.
Fax: 609-722-5344.

Paul R. Rosen
Steven F. Gadon
Samuel L. Hirshland
Edward G. Fitzgerald, Jr.
Albert E. Janke, Jr.
Lary I. Zucker
James B. Kozloff
Niels Korup
Daniel J. Dugan
Alan H. Wallen

OF COUNSEL

Sanders D. Newman
Sidney Margulies

Leslie Beth Baskin
Jill M. Bellak
Debra Malone Berger
Christopher P. Flannery (Not admitted in PA)
Shona K. Gibson
Amy B. Goldstein
Jeffrey M. Goldstein
Robert L. Grundlock, Jr.
Jane E. Herman (Not admitted in PA)
Stanley Peter Jaskiewicz
Kenneth J. LaFiandra
Marilou Lombardi
Brooke Caroline Madonna
P. Dara Marcozzi
Bruce S. Marks
Ann Miller
Frank J. Perch, III
Steven J. Polansky
George M. Vinci, Jr.

For full biographical listings, see the Martindale-Hubbell Law Directory

Strong, Stevens, Briscoe & Hamilton, P.C. (AV)

4000 Bell Atlantic Tower, 1717 Arch Street, 19103
Telephone: 215-563-5900
Fax: 215-563-2982
Blue Bell, Pennsylvania Office: 640 Sentry Parkway, First Floor.
Telephone: 215-832-5900.
Fax: 215-832-5914.

George V. Strong, Jr.
Richard K. Stevens, Jr.
James H. Stevens
Jack C. Briscoe
Jeffrey F. Janoski
Emory A. Wyant, Jr.
Thomas R. Kellogg
Ronald W. Fenstermacher, Jr.
Ralf W. Greenwood, Jr.
Mary K. Lemmon

COUNSEL

Samuel L. Sagendorph

For full biographical listings, see the Martindale-Hubbell Law Directory

*PITTSBURGH,** Allegheny Co.

Buchanan Ingersoll, Professional Corporation (AV)

5800 USX Tower, 600 Grant Street, 15219
Telephone: 412-562-8800
Telecopier: 412-562-1041
Philadelphia, Pennsylvania Office: Two Logan Square, Twelfth Floor, 18th & Arch Streets.
Telephone: 215-665-8700.
Harrisburg, Pennsylvania Office: Vartan Parc, 30 North Third Street.
Telephone: 717-237-4800.
Tampa, Florida Office: 101 East Kennedy Boulevard, Suite 1030.
Telephone: 813-222-8180.

(See Next Column)

BUCHANAN INGERSOLL PROFESSIONAL CORPORATION, *Pittsburgh—Continued*

North Miami Beach, Florida Office: 19495 Biscayne Boulevard.
Telephone: 305-933-5600.
Lexington, Kentucky Office: 1210 Vine Center Office Tower, 333 West Vine Street.
Telephone: 606-225-5333.
Princeton, New Jersey Office: Buchanan Ingersoll, A Partnership, College Centre, 500 College Road East.
Telephone: 609-452-2666.

Bruce A. Americus
Ronald Basso
Bruce I. Booken
A. Bruce Bowden
Sheryl Atkinson Clark
Carl A. Cohen
Lewis U. Davis, Jr.
Vincent C. Deluzio
Robert G. Devlin
Christopher F. Farrell
Michael J. Flinn
Carole C. Gori
Stephen W. Johnson
William R. Newlin
Gregory A. Pearson
Larry E. Phillips
John R. Previs
Carl E. Rothenberger, Jr.
Hugh G. Van der Veer
Thomas L. VanKirk
Paula A. Zawadzki

COUNSEL

Margaret B. Angel

SENIOR ATTORNEYS

Cristopher Charles Hoel
Gary R. Walker
Reginald J. Weatherly

James J. Barnes
Thomas G. Buchanan
Susan M. Hartman
Harrison S. Lauer
S. Bryan Lawrence III
JoEllen Lyons
Frances Magovern O'Connor
Timothy J. Reynolds
Ronald W. Schuler
Deborah B. Walrath
Pamela K. Wiles

For Complete List of Firm Personnel, See General Section

For full biographical listings, see the Martindale-Hubbell Law Directory

DICKIE, MCCAMEY & CHILCOTE, A PROFESSIONAL CORPORATION (AV)

Suite 400, Two PPG Place, 15222-5402
Telephone: 412-281-7272
Fax: 412-392-5367
Wheeling, West Virginia Office: Suite 2002, 1233 Main Street, 26003-2839.
Telephone: 304-233-1022.
Facsimile: 304-233-1026.

Clayton A. Sweeney
Thomas P. Lutz
Robert F. Wagner
Steven B. Larchuk
John W. Lewis, II
George Randal Fox, III

David S. Horvitz
Christopher A. Brodman
Donald E. Evans

For Complete List of Firm Personnel, See General Section

For full biographical listings, see the Martindale-Hubbell Law Directory

FELDSTEIN GRINBERG STEIN & MCKEE, A PROFESSIONAL CORPORATION (AV)

428 Boulevard of the Allies, 15219
Telephone: 412-471-0677
Fax: 412-263-6129
Elizabeth, Pennsylvania Office: 400 Second Street.
Telephone: 412-384-6111.
Wexford, Pennsylvania Office: 12300 Perry Highway.
Telephone: 412-935-5540.

Edwin I. Grinberg
Robert E. McKee, Jr.
Joan Singh

Jeffrey B. Balicki
David G. Henry
Jeffrey B. Yao

For full biographical listings, see the Martindale-Hubbell Law Directory

MOLLICA, MURRAY & HOGUE (AV)

3400 Gulf Tower, 15219
Telephone: 412-263-5200
Fax: 412-263-5220

MEMBERS OF FIRM

James A. Mollica, Jr.
Dr. John E. Murray, Jr.
Jon Geoffrey Hogue
Blaine A. Lucas
Cathy Ann Chromulak
Timothy Murray
Sandra L. Lannis
William J. Moorhead, Jr.
Jeannine A. Schuster
Steven M. Nolan
Benjamin J. Viloski

For full biographical listings, see the Martindale-Hubbell Law Directory

WICK, STREIFF, MEYER, METZ & O'BOYLE, P.C. (AV)

1450 Two Chatham Center, 15219
Telephone: 412-765-1600
Telecopier: 412-261-3783

Henry M. Wick, Jr.
Charles J. Streiff
Carl F. Meyer
LeRoy L. Metz, II
David M. O'Boyle
Vincent P. Szeligo
Patricia J. Liptak-McGrail

Lucille N. Wick
Ronald Joseph Rademacher
Roger A. Isla
Donna Lynn Miller

Reference: PNC Bank.

For full biographical listings, see the Martindale-Hubbell Law Directory

WITTLIN GOLDSTON & CAPUTO, P.C. (AV)

213 Smithfield Street, Suite 200, 15222
Telephone: 412-261-4200
Telecopier: 412-261-9137

Charles E. Wittlin
Linda Leebov Goldston
Robert Simcox Adams
John H. Iannucci
Laurence R. Landis

For Complete List of Firm Personnel, See General Section

For full biographical listings, see the Martindale-Hubbell Law Directory

YUKEVICH, BLUME & ZANGRILLI (AV)

Sixth Floor, One Gateway Center, 15222
Telephone: 412-261-6777
Fax: 412-261-6789

MEMBERS OF FIRM

Michael Yukevich, Jr.
Peter K. Blume
Albert J. Zangrilli, Jr.

Mark Fischer

For full biographical listings, see the Martindale-Hubbell Law Directory

*READING,** Berks Co.

MOGEL, SPEIDEL, BOBB & KERSHNER, A PROFESSIONAL CORPORATION (AV)

520 Walnut Street, P.O. Box 8581, 19603-8581
Telephone: 610-376-1515
Telecopier: 610-372-8710

George B. Balmer (1902-1969)
George A. Kershner (1907-1969)
Carl F. Mogel (1919-1994)
Donald K. Bobb
Edwin H. Kershner
Frederick R. Mogel
Samuel R. Fry II
Kathleen A. B. Kovach
Michael L. Mixell
George M. Lutz
Stephen H. Price
Kathryn K. Harenza

OF COUNSEL

Harry W. Speidel
Henry A. Gass

Representative Clients: Great Valley Savings Bank; Clover Farms Dairy Co.; National Penn Bank; Meridian Leasing, Inc.; Ducharme, McMillen & Associates; Edwards Business Machines, Inc.; Greater Berks Development Fund; Union Township, Berks County, Pennsylvania.

For full biographical listings, see the Martindale-Hubbell Law Directory

*WASHINGTON,** Washington Co.

GREENLEE, DERRICO, POSA & RODGERS (AV)

325 Washington Trust Building, 15301
Telephone: 412-225-7660; Pittsburgh: 412-344-9400
Fax: 412-228-1704

MEMBER OF FIRM

Gaylord W. Greenlee

For full biographical listings, see the Martindale-Hubbell Law Directory

PEACOCK, KELLER, YOHE, DAY & ECKER (AV)

East Beau Building, 70 East Beau Street, 15301
Telephone: 412-222-4520
Telefax: 412-222-3318 ABA/NET ABA 34517
Waynesburg, Pennsylvania Office: 102 East High Street.
Telephone: 412-627-8331.
Telefax: 412-627-8025.

MEMBERS OF FIRM

Charles C. Keller
Reed B. Day
Roger J. Ecker
Robert T. Crothers
Kenneth L. Baker
Mary Drake Korsmeyer
Richard J. Amrhein
Barbara A. Rizzo

(See Next Column)

PEACOCK, KELLER, YOHE, DAY & ECKER—*Continued*

Representative Clients: Consolidation Coal Co.; Monogahela Valley Hospital, Inc.; Family Health Council, Inc.; Cal-Ed Federal Credit Union; Marianna & Scenery Hill Telephone Co.; Maternal & Family Health Services, Inc.; Sensory Devices, Inc.; Air Products and Chemicals, Inc.

For Complete List of Firm Personnel, See General Section

For full biographical listings, see the Martindale-Hubbell Law Directory

WAYNE, Delaware Co.

BALDWIN RENNER & CLARK (AV)

The Woods Suite 905, 992 Old Eagle School Road, 19087
Telephone: 610-687-4664
Fax: 610-687-4640
Philadelphia, Pennsylvania Office: 1201 Chestnut Street, Tenth Floor.
Telephone: 215-563-1950.
Fax: 215-563-2014.

Frank B. Baldwin, III
Michael D. Renner
Francis X. Clark
Mara L. Stratt

For full biographical listings, see the Martindale-Hubbell Law Directory

*WEST CHESTER,** Chester Co.

BUCKLEY, NAGLE, GENTRY, McGUIRE & MORRIS (AV)

304 North High Street, P.O. Box 133, 19380
Telephone: 610-436-4400
Telecopier: 610-436-8305
Thorndale, Pennsylvania Office: 3532 East Lincoln Highway.
Telephone: 215-383-5666.

MEMBERS OF FIRM

C. Barry Buckley
Ronald C. Nagle
W. Richard Gentry
Stephen P. McGuire
Anthony Morris
John J. Teti, Jr.
Jeffrey R. Sommer
Isabel M. Albuquerque

OF COUNSEL

R. Curtis Schroder

For full biographical listings, see the Martindale-Hubbell Law Directory

CRAWFORD, WILSON, RYAN & AGULNICK, P.C. (AV)

220 West Gay Street, 19380
Telephone: 610-431-4500
Fax: 610-430-8718
Radnor, Pennsylvania Office: 252 Radnor-Chester Road, P. O. Box 8333, 19087.
Telephone: 215-688-1205.
Fax: 215-688-7802.

Ronald M. Agulnick
Fronefield Crawford, Jr.
Thomas R. Wilson
Kevin J. Ryan

John J. Mahoney
Kim Denise Morton
Steven L. Mutart
Rita Kathryn Borzillo
Patricia T. Brennan
Richard H. Morton
Patricia J. Kelly
Charles W. Tucker

Reference: First National Bank of West Chester.

For full biographical listings, see the Martindale-Hubbell Law Directory

RHODE ISLAND

*PROVIDENCE,** Providence Co.

GOLDENBERG & MURI (AV)

15 Westminster Street, 02903
Telephone: 401-421-7300
Telecopier: 401-421-7352

MEMBERS OF FIRM

Michael R. Goldenberg
Anthony F. Muri
Barbara S. Cohen

ASSOCIATES

Douglas J. Emanuel
Susan M. Pepin

For full biographical listings, see the Martindale-Hubbell Law Directory

SOUTH CAROLINA

*CHARLESTON,** Charleston Co.

HAYNSWORTH, MARION, McKAY & GUÉRARD, L.L.P (AV)

#2 Prioleau Street, P.O. Box 1119, 29402
Telephone: 803-722-7606
Telecopier: 803-723-5263
Columbia, South Carolina Office: Suite 2400 AT&T Building, 1201 Main Street, P.O. Drawer 7157, 29202.
Telephone: 803-765-1818.
Telecopier: 803-765-2399.
Greenville, South Carolina Office: Two Insignia Financial Plaza, 75 Beattie Place, P.O. Box 2048, 29602.
Telephone: 803-240-3200.
Telecopier: 803-240-3300.

OF COUNSEL

Theodore B. Guérard

MEMBERS OF FIRM

W. E. Applegate, III
J. Paul Trouche
Samuel W. Howell, IV
Donald Bancroft Meyer
Carol L. Clark

ASSOCIATES

Paul M. Lynch
J. Walker Coleman, IV

Counsel for: Bank of South Carolina; Baker Hospital; Healthsources of South Carolina; Allstate Insurance Co.; CSX Corporation; Lloyd's Underwriters; Coward-Hund Construction Co.; South Carolina Public Service Authority; South Carolina Jobs - Economic Development Authority; City of Hanahan.

For Complete List of Firm Personnel, See General Section

For full biographical listings, see the Martindale-Hubbell Law Directory

ROBERTSON & SEEKINGS (AV)

First Union Center, 177 Meeting Street, Suite 300, 29401
Telephone: 803-723-6470
FAX: 803-853-9045

MEMBERS OF FIRM

Claron A. Robertson, III
Michael S. Seekings

ASSOCIATES

Dunn D. Hollingsworth
R. Patrick Flynn

For full biographical listings, see the Martindale-Hubbell Law Directory

*COLUMBIA,** Richland Co.

* indicates certain Bar Register subscribers whose principal office is located elsewhere in the state and who have arranged for representation as a part of the state capital listings that follow

*** HAYNSWORTH, MARION, McKAY & GUÉRARD, L.L.P. (AV)**

Suite 2400 A T & T Building, 1201 Main Street, P.O. Drawer 7157, 29202
Telephone: 803-765-1818
Telecopier: 803-765-2399
Greenville, South Carolina Office: Two Insignia Financial Plaza, 75 Beattie Place, P.O. Box 2048, 29602.
Telephone: 803-240-3200.
Telecopier: 803-240-3300.
Charleston, South Carolina Office: #2 Prioleau Street, P.O. Box 1119, 29402.
Telephone: 803-722-7606.
Telecopier: 803-723-5263.

MEMBERS OF FIRM

William P. Simpson
Samuel W. Howell, IV
Gary W. Morris

ASSOCIATE

Edward G. Kluiters

Counsel for: St. Paul Insurance Group; Allstate Insurance Co.; Fluor-Daniel Corp.; South Carolina Jobs - Economic Development Authority; Anheuser Busch Company; CSX Transportation; Ernst & Young, LLP; Willis Corroon of South Carolina, Inc.; Westinghouse Savannah River Co.; Wachovia Bank of South Carolina, N.A.

For Complete List of Firm Personnel, See General Section

For full biographical listings, see the Martindale-Hubbell Law Directory

ISAACS, ALLEY & HARVEY, L.L.P. (AV)

900 Elmwood Avenue, Suite 103, P.O. Box 8596, 29202-8596
Telephone: 803-252-6323
Telecopier: 803-779-5220

W. Joseph Isaacs

Representative Clients: NationsBank of South Carolina, N.A.; GATX Corporation; First Financial Corp.; Zurich-American Insurance Group; Wetterau Incorp.; Southland Log Homes, Inc.; Thompson Dental Co.; Dairymen Credit Union; Modern Exterminating, Inc.; Elizabeth Arden Co.; J.L. Todd

(See Next Column)

ISAACS, ALLEY & HARVEY L.L.P., *Columbia—Continued*

Auction, Inc.; Continental Cards Co., Inc.; Norton-Senn Corporation; Eastern Flatbed Systems, Inc.; Valk Brokerage, Inc.; Snipes Electric, Inc.; The Loan Pros, Inc.; Palmetto Restorations, Inc.; Palmer & Cay/Carswell, Inc.; Plastitech Products, Inc.; Marek Brothers, Inc.; Ferillo & Associates, Inc.; Jacon Associates, Inc.; Blue Ridge Log Cabins, Inc.; Jones & Frank Corp.

For full biographical listings, see the Martindale-Hubbell Law Directory

RICHARDSON, PLOWDEN, GRIER AND HOWSER, P.A. (AV)

1600 Marion Street, P.O. Drawer 7788, 29202
Telephone: 803-771-4400
Telecopy: 803-779-0016
Myrtle Beach, South Carolina Office: Southern National Bank Building, Suite 202, 601 21st Avenue North, P.O. Box 3646, 29578.
Telephone: 803-448-1008.
FAX: 803-448-1533.

Frank E. Robinson, II
Frederick A. Crawford
Samuel F. Crews, III

Douglas C. Baxter
S. Nelson Weston Jr.
Harley D. Ruff

Representative Clients: First Union Bank; Boozer Lumber Co., Inc.; National Bank of South Carolina; Southern Wine & Spirits, Inc.

For Complete List of Firm Personnel, See General Section

For full biographical listings, see the Martindale-Hubbell Law Directory

TOMPKINS AND MCMASTER (AV)

Palmetto Building, Fourth Floor, 1400 Main Street, P.O. Box 7337, 29202
Telephone: 803-799-4499
Telefax: 803-252-2240

MEMBERS OF FIRM

Frank G. Tompkins (1874-1956)
Frank G. Tompkins, Jr. (1908-1973)
Elizabeth Eldridge (1895-1976)
John Gregg McMaster
Henry Dargan McMaster
Frank Barnwell McMaster
Joseph Dargan McMaster

OF COUNSEL

George Hunter McMaster

For full biographical listings, see the Martindale-Hubbell Law Directory

WOODWARD, LEVENTIS, UNGER, DAVES, HERNDON AND COTHRAN (AV)

(Formerly Woodward, Leventis, Unger, Herndon and Cothran)
1300 Sumter, P.O. Box 12399, 29211
Telephone: 803-799-9772
Fax: 803-779-3256

MEMBERS OF FIRM

James C. Leventis
Richard M. Unger
Gary R. Daves
Warren R. Herndon, Jr.
Darra Williamson Cothran

ASSOCIATE

Frances G. Smith

OF COUNSEL

Edward M. Woodward, Sr.
Gwendelyn Geidel
James S. Guignard

General Counsel for: The Columbia College.

For full biographical listings, see the Martindale-Hubbell Law Directory

*GREENVILLE,** Greenville Co.

HAYNSWORTH, MARION, MCKAY & GUÉRARD, L.L.P. (AV)

Two Insignia Financial Plaza, 75 Beattie Place, P.O. Box 2048, 29602
Telephone: 803-240-3200
Telecopier: 803-240-3300
Columbia, South Carolina Office: Suite 2400 A T & T Building, 1201 Main Street, P.O. Drawer 7157, 29202
Telephone: 803-765-1818.
Telecopier: 803-765-2399.
Charleston, South Carolina Office: #2 Prioleau Street, P.O. Box 1119, 29402.
Telephone: 803-722-7606.
Telecopier: 803-723-5263.

MEMBERS OF FIRM

Jesse C. Belcher, Jr.
Maye R. Johnson, Jr.
Andrew J. White, Jr.
Joseph J. Blake, Jr.
David L. McMurray
Knox H. White

ASSOCIATES

Arthur Frazier McLean, III
Donna S. Kivett

Representative Clients: Wachovia Bank of South Carolina, N.A.; A T & T Credit Corporation; The B F Goodrich Company; TNA Mills, Inc.; Stone Manufacturing Co.; Willis Corroon Corp. of South Carolina.

(See Next Column)

For Complete List of Firm Personnel, See General Section

For full biographical listings, see the Martindale-Hubbell Law Directory

SOUTH DAKOTA

*ABERDEEN,** Brown Co.

BANTZ, GOSCH, CREMER, PETERSON & SOMMERS (AV)

305 Sixth Avenue, S.E., P.O. Box 970, 57402-0970
Telephone: 605-225-2232
Fax: 605-225-2497

MEMBERS OF FIRM

Douglas W. Bantz (1909-1983)
Kennith L. Gosch
James M. Cremer
Greg L. Peterson
Richard A. Sommers
Ronald A. Wager

General Counsel for: Dacotah Bank Holding Co.
Attorneys for: Northwestern Mutual Life Insurance Co.; Transamerica Insurance Group; Employers Mutual of Wausau; Employers Mutual Casualty Cos.; Farmers & Merchants Bank, Aberdeen; United Pacific Insurance Co.; Northwestern National Insurance Co.

For full biographical listings, see the Martindale-Hubbell Law Directory

*BROOKINGS,** Brookings Co.

LEWAYNE M. ERICKSON, P.C. (AV)

517 Sixth Street, 57006-1436
Telephone: 605-692-6158
Fax: 605-692-7734

Lewayne M. Erickson

For full biographical listings, see the Martindale-Hubbell Law Directory

*RAPID CITY,** Pennington Co.

GUNDERSON, PALMER, GOODSELL & NELSON (AV)

440 Mount Rushmore Road, 4th Floor, P.O. Box 8045, 57709-8045
Telephone: 605-342-1078
Fax: 605-342-9503

MEMBERS OF FIRM

Wynn A. Gunderson
J. Crisman Palmer
G. Verne Goodsell
James S. Nelson
Daniel E. Ashmore
Donald P. Knudsen
Patrick G. Goetzinger
Talbot J. Wieczorek
Paul S. Swedlund
Mark J. Connot

Representative Clients: Norwest Bank South Dakota, N.A.; Sodak Gaming, Inc.; Bally Gaming, Inc.; SEGA of America; United States Fidelity & Guaranty Co.; Aetna Life and Casualty Co.; Homestake Mining Company; Wal-Mart Stores, Inc.; Dain Bosworth, Inc.; Underwriters Counsel/Norwest Investment Services.

For full biographical listings, see the Martindale-Hubbell Law Directory

*SIOUX FALLS,** Minnehaha Co.

DAVENPORT, EVANS, HURWITZ & SMITH (AV)

513 South Main Avenue, P.O. Box 1030, 57101-1030
Telephone: 605-336-2880
Telecopier: 605-335-3639

MEMBERS OF FIRM

Richard A. Cutler
P. Daniel Donohue
David L. Knudson
Robert E. Hayes
Charles D. Gullickson
Monte R. Walz
Edward J. Leahy
Jonathan P. Brown
Catherine A. Tanck

ASSOCIATES

Jean H. Bender
Scott Bradley Anderson

Counsel for: American Society of Composers, Authors and Publishers (A.S.C.A.P.); Burlington Northern, Inc.; Continental Insurance Cos.; The First National Bank in Sioux Falls; Ford Motor Credit Co.; General Motors Corp.; The St. Paul Cos.; The Travelers.

For Complete List of Firm Personnel, See General Section

For full biographical listings, see the Martindale-Hubbell Law Directory

TENNESSEE

*CHATTANOOGA,** Hamilton Co.

GEARHISER, PETERS & HORTON (AV)

320 McCallie Avenue, 37402-2007
Telephone: 615-756-5171
Fax: 615-266-1605

MEMBERS OF FIRM

Charles J. Gearhiser
R. Wayne Peters
William H. Horton
Roy C. Maddox, Jr.
Robert L. Lockaby, Jr.
Ralph E. Tallant, Jr.
Terry Atkin Cavett
Sam D. Elliott
Lane C. Avery
Michael A. Anderson
Wade K. Cannon

ASSOCIATE

Robin L. Miller

References: First Tennessee Bank; Pioneer Bank.

For full biographical listings, see the Martindale-Hubbell Law Directory

*MEMPHIS,** Shelby Co.

EUGENE BERNSTEIN, SR. (AV)

5050 Poplar, Suite 2410, 38157
Telephone: 901-684-1652
Telecopier: 901-761-5505

For full biographical listings, see the Martindale-Hubbell Law Directory

*NASHVILLE,** Davidson Co.

DORAMUS & TRAUGER (AV)

Southern Turf Building, 222 Fourth Avenue North, 37219
Telephone: 615-256-8585
Fax: 615-256-7444

MEMBERS OF FIRM

Byron R. Trauger
James V. Doramus
Paul C. Ney, Jr.

ASSOCIATES

David L. Kleinfelter
Gregory Mitchell
Jane H. Allen
Anne Sumpter Arney
Todd J. Campbell

For full biographical listings, see the Martindale-Hubbell Law Directory

RANDOLPH B. JONES (AV)

3200 West End Avenue, Suite 500, 37203
Telephone: 615-783-1705

MANIER, HEROD, HOLLABAUGH & SMITH, A PROFESSIONAL CORPORATION (AV)

First Union Tower 2200 One Nashville Place, 150 Fourth Avenue North, 37219-2494
Telephone: 615-244-0030
Telecopier: 615-242-4203

Will R. Manier, Jr. (1885-1953)
Larkin E. Crouch (1882-1948)
Vincent L. Fuqua, Jr. (1930-1974)
J. Olin White (1907-1982)
Miller Manier (1897-1986)
William Edward Herod (1917-1992)
Lewis B. Hollabaugh
Don L. Smith
James M. Doran, Jr.
Stephen E. Cox
J. Michael Franks
Randall C. Ferguson
Terry L. Hill
James David Leckrone
Robert C. Evans
Tommy C. Estes
B. Gail Reese
Michael E. Evans
Laurence M. Papel
John M. Gillum
Gregory L. Cashion
Sam H. Poteet, Jr.
Samuel Arthur Butts III
David J. Deming
Mark S. LeVan
Richard McCallister Smith
Mary Paty Lynn Jetton
H. Rowan Leathers III
Jefferson C. Orr
William L. Penny

Lawrence B. Hammet II
John H. Rowland
Susan C. West
John E. Quinn
John F. Floyd
Paul L. Sprader
Lela M. Hollabaugh
J. Steven Kirkham
T. Richard Travis
Stephanie M. Jennings
Jerry W. Taylor
C. Benton Patton
Kenneth A. Weber
Phillip Robert Newman
Brett A. Oeser

General Counsel for: McKinnon Bridge Co., Inc.

For full biographical listings, see the Martindale-Hubbell Law Directory

TEXAS

*AUSTIN,** Travis Co.

* indicates certain Bar Register subscribers whose principal office is located elsewhere in the state and who have arranged for representation as a part of the state capital listings that follow

BAKER & BOTTS, L.L.P. (AV)

1600 San Jacinto Center, 98 San Jacinto Boulevard, 78701
Telephone: 512-322-2500
Fax: 512-322-2501
Houston, Texas Office: One Shell Plaza, 910 Louisiana.
Telephone: 713-229-1234.
Dallas, Texas Office: 2001 Ross Avenue.
Telephone: 214-953-6500.
Washington, D.C. Office: The Warner, 1299 Pennsylvania Avenue, N.W.
Telephone: 202-639-7700.
New York, New York Office: 885 Third Avenue, Suite 2000.
Telephone: 212-705-5000.
Moscow, Russian Federation Office: 10 ul. Pushkinskaya, 103031.
Telephone: 7095/921-5300 (Local); 7501/929-7070 (International).

MEMBERS OF FIRM

Shelley W. Austin
William F. Stutts, Jr.

ASSOCIATES

Catherine M. Del Castillo
Polly F. Powell

For Complete List of Firm Personnel, See General Section

For full biographical listings, see the Martindale-Hubbell Law Directory

DAVIS & DAVIS, P.C. (AV)

Arboretum Plaza One, 9th Floor, 9442 Capitol of Texas Highway, P.O. Box 1588, 78767
Telephone: 512-343-6248
Fax: 512-343-0121

C. Dean Davis
Fred E. Davis
Alexis J. Fuller, Jr.
Francis A. (Tony) Bradley
Ruth Russell-Schafer

Bill Cline, Jr.
Robert L. Hargett
Michael L. Neely
Brian Gregory Jackson
A. A. Jack Ross, IV
Kevin Wayde Morse
Mark Alan Keene
Kenda B. Dalrymple

For Complete List of Firm Personnel, See General Section

For full biographical listings, see the Martindale-Hubbell Law Directory

JOHN MCDUFF, P.C. A PROFESSIONAL CORPORATION (AV)

100 Congress Avenue Suite 1817, 78701
Telephone: 512-469-6360
Fax: 512-469-5505

John McDuff

For full biographical listings, see the Martindale-Hubbell Law Directory

*** THOMPSON & KNIGHT, A PROFESSIONAL CORPORATION (AV)**

(Attorneys and Counselors)
1200 San Jacinto Center, 98 San Jacinto Boulevard, 78701
Telephone: 512-469-6100
Telecopy: 512-469-6180
Dallas, Texas Office: 1700 Pacific Avenue, Suite 3300, 75201.
Telephone: 214-969-1700.
Telecopy: 512-969-1751.
Cable Address: "Tomtex."
Telex: 732298.
Fort Worth, Texas Office: 801 Cherry Street, Suite 1600, 76102.
Telephone: 817-347-1700.
Telecopy: 817-347-1799.
Houston, Texas Office: 1700 Texas Commerce Tower, 600 Travis, 77002.
Telephone: 713-217-2800.
Telecopy: 713-217-2828; 713-217-2882.
Monterrey, Mexico Office: Edificio Losoles PD-4, Av. Lázaro Cárdenas No. 2400 Pte., San Pedro Garza Garcia, Nuevo Léon C.P. 66220.
Telephone: (52-8) 363-0096.
Telecopy: (52-8) 363-3067.

SHAREHOLDERS

Carrie Parker Tiemann

OF COUNSEL

Richard J. Wieland

For Complete List of Firm Personnel, See General Section

For full biographical listings, see the Martindale-Hubbell Law Directory

*BEAUMONT,** Jefferson Co.

GERMER & GERTZ, L.L.P. (AV)

805 Park Street, P.O. Box 3728, 77704
Telephone: 409-838-2080
Fax: 409-838-4050

MEMBERS OF FIRM

Lawrence L. Germer
Paul W. Gertz

ASSOCIATES

Karen R. Bennett
Larry J. Simmons, Jr.
Catherine P. Waites

For full biographical listings, see the Martindale-Hubbell Law Directory

*DALLAS,** Dallas Co.

BAKER & BOTTS, L.L.P. (AV)

2001 Ross Avenue, 75201
Telephone: 214-953-6500
Fax: 214-953-6503
Houston, Texas Office: One Shell Plaza, 910 Louisiana.
Telephone: 713-229-1234.
Washington, D.C. Office: The Warner, 1299 Pennsylvania Avenue, N.W.
Telephone: 202-639-7700.
Austin, Texas Office: 1600 San Jacinto Center, 98 San Jacinto Boulevard.
Telephone: 512-322-2500.
New York, New York Office: 885 Third Avenue, Suite 2000.
Telephone: 212-705-5000.
Moscow, Russian Federation Office: 10 ul. Pushkinskaya, 103031.
Telephone: 7095/921-5300 (Local); 7095/929-7070.

MEMBERS OF FIRM

Richard C. Johnson
James A. Taylor
Karen Leslye Wolf
Kerry C. L. North
Andrew M. Baker
Jonathan W. Dunlay
Patricia M. Stanton
John W. Martin
Carlos A. Fierro
Geoffrey L. Newton

ASSOCIATES

Julie A. Gregory
Susan Nethery Hogan
Shelley LaGere
Tamara Gail Mattison
David G. Monk
Douglass Michael Rayburn
Brenda Levine Sutherland

For Complete List of Firm Personnel, See General Section

For full biographical listings, see the Martindale-Hubbell Law Directory

LAW OFFICES OF FRANK L. BRANSON, P.C. (AV)

18th Floor, Highland Park Place, 4514 Cole Avenue, 75205
Telephone: 214-522-0200;
Metro: 817-263-7452
Fax: 214-521-5485

Frank L. Branson
Debbie D. Branson
George A. Quesada, Jr.
Jerry M. White
J. Stephen King
Christopher A. Payne
Michael L. Parham
Joel M. Fineberg

OF COUNSEL

Ted Z. Robertson
J. Hadley Edgar, Jr.

For full biographical listings, see the Martindale-Hubbell Law Directory

CALHOUN & STACY (AV)

5700 NationsBank Plaza, 901 Main Street, 75202-3747
Telephone: 214-748-5000
Telecopier: 214-748-1421
Telex: 211358 CALGUMP UR

Mark Alan Calhoun
David W. Elrod
Steven D. Goldston
Parker Nelson
Roy L. Stacy

ASSOCIATES

Shannon S. Barclay
Robert A. Bragalone
Dennis D. Conder
Jane Elizabeth Diseker
Lawrence I. Fleishman
Thomas C. Jones
Katherine Johnson Knight
V. Paige Pace
Veronika Willard
Michael C. Wright

LEGAL CONSULTANT

Rees T. Bowen, III

For full biographical listings, see the Martindale-Hubbell Law Directory

HUGHES & LUCE, L.L.P. (AV)

A Registered Limited Liability Partnership including Professional Corporations
1717 Main Street, Suite 2800, 75201
Telephone: 214-939-5500
Fax: 214-939-6100
Telex: 730836
Austin, Texas Office: 111 Congress, Suite 900.
Telephone: 512-482-6800.
Fax: 512-482-6859.
Houston, Texas Office: Three Allen Center, 333 Clay Street, Suite 3800.
Telephone: 713-754-5200.
Fax: 713-754-5206.
Fort Worth, Texas Office: 2421 Westport Parkway, Suite 500A.
Telephone: 817-439-3000.
Fax: 817-439-4222.

MEMBERS OF FIRM

David N. Guedry
John E. Howell
David H. Judson
Thomas W. Luce, III

ASSOCIATE

Bernard Lau

For Complete List of Firm Personnel, See General Section

For full biographical listings, see the Martindale-Hubbell Law Directory

NOVAKOV, DAVIDSON & FLYNN, A PROFESSIONAL CORPORATION (AV)

2000 St. Paul Place, 750 North St. Paul, 75201-3286
Telephone: 214-922-9221
Telecopy: 214-969-7557

Steven D. Davidson
James Kevin Flynn
Gary C. Morgan
Daniel P. Novakov
Charles N. Nye

For Complete List of Firm Personnel, See General Section

For full biographical listings, see the Martindale-Hubbell Law Directory

PALMER, ALLEN & MCTAGGART, L.L.P. (AV)

A Partnership including Professional Corporations
1900 St. Paul Place, 750 North St. Paul Street, 75201
Telephone: 214-969-0069
Telecopy: 214-720-0104
Austin, Texas Office: 6505 Lohmann's Crossing (Lago Vista).
Telephone: 512-267-1993. Mailing Address: P.O. Box 4345, Lago Vista, Texas, 78645.

Steven G. Palmer (P.C.)
Joe B. Allen III
Robert D. McTaggart (P.C.)
Guy Myrph Foote, Jr., (P.C.)
Brian G. Dicus (P.C.)

OF COUNSEL

Robert S. Leithiser (P.C.)
Dick P. Wood, Jr., (P.C.)

For full biographical listings, see the Martindale-Hubbell Law Directory

DANA B. TASCHNER, P.C. (AV Ⓣ)

350 St. Paul Street, 75201
Telephone: 1-800-448-5800
Fax: 818-583-8825
Pasadena, California Office: 1115 East Cordova, Suite 404. 91106.
Telephone: 818-583-8500.
Fax: 818-583-8825.
Beverly Hills, California Office: 9454 Wilshire Boulevard, Suite 550. 90212-2915.
Telephone: 310-275-5077; 800-448-5800.

Dana B. Taschner (Not admitted in TX)

For full biographical listings, see the Martindale-Hubbell Law Directory

THOMPSON, COE, COUSINS & IRONS, L.L.P. (AV)

200 Crescent Court, Eleventh Floor, 75201-1840
Telephone: 214-871-8200 (Dallas)
512-480-8770 (Austin)
FAX: 214-871-8209

MEMBERS OF FIRM

Emory L. White, Jr.
Richard S. Geiger
Jack M. Cleaveland, Jr.
Jon G. Petersen
Robert P. Franke
Rodney D. Bucker
Ronald G. Houdyshell
Michael A. McClelland
Beth D. Bradley
Ronald D. Horner

ASSOCIATES

Michael W. Jones
James D. Cartier
Layne L. Anderson
James L. Sowder
Bradley D. Broberg

Representative Clients: Bank One Texas, N.A.; Amresco Management, Inc.; Federal Deposit Insurance Corporation; J. E. Robert Company; Atlantic Asset Management Company; Compass Bank; PSM International, Inc.; Revco D.S., Inc.; Rigg Group, Inc.; Star Automotive Warehouse, Inc.

(See Next Column)

THOMPSON, COE, COUSINS & IRONS L.L.P.—*Continued*

For Complete List of Firm Personnel, See General Section

For full biographical listings, see the Martindale-Hubbell Law Directory

THOMPSON & KNIGHT, A PROFESSIONAL CORPORATION (AV)

(Attorneys and Counselors)
1700 Pacific Avenue Suite 3300, 75201
Telephone: 214-969-1700
Telecopy: 214-969-1751
Cable Address: "Tomtex"
Telex: 732298
Austin, Texas Office: 1200 San Jacinto Center, 98 San Jacinto Boulevard, 78701.
Telephone: 512-469-6100.
Telecopy: 512-469-6180.
Fort Worth, Texas Office: 801 Cherry Street, Suite 1600, 76102.
Telephone: 817-347-1700.
Telecopy: 817-347-1799.
Houston, Texas Office: 1700 Texas Commerce Tower, 600 Travis, 77002.
Telephone: 713-217-2800.
Telecopy: 713-217-2828.
Monterrey, Mexico Office: Edificio Losoles PD-4, Av. Lázaro Cárdenas No. 2400 Pte., San Pedro Garza Garcia, Nuevo Léon C.P. 66220.
Telephone: (52-8) 363-0096.
Telecopy: (52-8) 363-3067.

SHAREHOLDERS

Michael L. Bengtson
Sam P. Burford, Jr.
Frederick W. Burnett, Jr.
Robert D. Campbell
Steven K. Cochran
Richard L. Covington
Joseph Dannenmaier
James L. Irish
Paul M. Johnston
Harold F. Kleinman
C. Neel Lemon III
Jack M. Little
Peter A. Lodwick
Don J. McDermett, Jr.
David E. Morrison
James R. Peacock III
Norman R. Rogers
William J. Schuerger
Kenn W. Webb
Jeffrey A. Zlotky

ASSOCIATES

Craig N. Adams
Ann Marie Bixby
Priscilla Lynn Dunckel
David L. Emmons
Mark C. Gunnin
John F. Sterling

For Complete List of Firm Personnel, See General Section

For full biographical listings, see the Martindale-Hubbell Law Directory

*EL PASO,** El Paso Co.

C. MICHAEL GINNINGS (AV)

303 Texas Avenue, Suite 902, 79901
Telephone: 915-532-5929
FAX: 915-532-7073

For full biographical listings, see the Martindale-Hubbell Law Directory

*FORT WORTH,** Tarrant Co.

H. ELDRIDGE DICKEY, JR. (AV)

Sundance Courtyard, 115 West Second Street, Suite 204, 76102
Telephone: 817-336-3006
FAX: 817-336-3211

For full biographical listings, see the Martindale-Hubbell Law Directory

MICHENER, LARIMORE, SWINDLE, WHITAKER, FLOWERS, SAWYER, REYNOLDS & CHALK, L.L.P. (AV)

3500 City Center Tower II, 301 Commerce Street, 76102
Telephone: 817-335-4417
Telecopy: 817-335-6935

MEMBERS OF FIRM

John W. Michener, Jr.
Tom L. Larimore
Mack Ed Swindle
Wayne M. Whitaker
H. David Flowers
Jerry K. Sawyer
James G. Reynolds
John Allen Chalk

Thomas S. Brandon, Jr.
Matthew P. McDonald
Clark R. Cowley
Thomas F. Harkins, Jr.
Geno E. Borchardt
John A. Chalk, Jr.
Leslie Combs
Suzanne S. Miskin
Robert G. West
Theresa Brewton Lyons
Jonathan K. Henderson
David R. Childress

OF COUNSEL

Jerry D. Minton

For full biographical listings, see the Martindale-Hubbell Law Directory

THOMPSON & KNIGHT, A PROFESSIONAL CORPORATION (AV)

(Attorneys and Counselors)
801 Cherry Street, Suite 1600, 76102
Telephone: 817-347-1700
Telecopy: 817-347-1799
Dallas, Texas Office: 1700 Pacific Avenue, Suite 3300, 75201.
Telephone: 214-969-1700.
Telecopy: 214-969-1751.
Cable Address: "Tomtex."
Telex: 732298.
Austin, Texas Office: 1200 San Jacinto Center, 98 San Jacinto Boulevard, 78701.
Telephone: 512-469-6100.
Telecopy: 512-469-6180.
Houston, Texas Office: 1700 Texas Commerce Tower, 600 Travis, 77002.
Telephone: 713-217-2800.
Telecopy: 713-217-2828; 713-2882.
Monterrey, Mexico Office: Edificio Losoles PD-4, Av. Lázaro Cárdenas No. 2400 Pte., San Pedro Garza Garcia, Nuevo Léon C.P. 66220.
Telephone: (52-8) 363-0096.
Telecopy: (52-8) 363-3067.

SHAREHOLDERS

Stephen B. Norris

For Complete List of Firm Personnel, See General Section

For full biographical listings, see the Martindale-Hubbell Law Directory

*HOUSTON,** Harris Co.

BAKER & BOTTS, L.L.P. (AV)

One Shell Plaza, 910 Louisiana, 77002
Telephone: 713-229-1234
Cable Address: "Boterlove"
Fax: 713-229-1522
Washington, D.C. Office: The Warner, 1299 Pennsylvania Avenue, N.W.
Telephone: 202-639-7700.
New York, New York Office: 885 Third Avenue, Suite 2000.
Telephone: 212-705-5000.
Austin, Texas Office: 1600 San Jacinto Center, 98 San Jacinto Boulevard.
Telephone: 512-322-2500.
Dallas, Texas Office: 2001 Ross Avenue.
Telephone: 214-953-6500.
Moscow, Russian Federation Office: 10 ul. Pushkinskaya, 103031.
Telephone: 7095/921-5300 (Local); 7095/929-7070 (International).

MEMBERS OF FIRM

Moulton Goodrum, Jr.
Robert L. Stillwell
James D. Randall
John M. Huggins
Thad T. Hutcheson, Jr.
Frank W. R. Hubert, Jr.
Lewis Proctor Thomas, III
Wade H. Whilden
James L. Leader
Roy L. Nolen
John P. Cogan, Jr.
J. Patrick Garrett
Fred H. Dunlop
Joseph A. Cialone, II
R. Joel Swanson
Walter J. Smith
C. Michael Watson
Stephen A. Massad
Charles Szalkowski
Robert P. Wright
Marley Lott
Joe S. Poff
J. David Kirkland, Jr.
Louise A. Shearer
Paul B. Landen
Gene J. Oshman
Margo S. Scholin
David F. Asmus
Darrell W. Taylor
Kenneth S. Culotta
Joshua Davidson

ASSOCIATES

Frederick William Backus
Marian L. Brancaccio
Karen Skeens Caldwell
William R. Caldwell
Janet Chambers
Shane Robert DeBeer
Jennifer J. De La Rosa
Victoria Donnenberg
Katherine P. Ellis
Nicolas J. Evanoff
Brian P. Fenske
Nancy E. Field
John D. Geddes
Sten L. Gustafson
Henry Havre
Rosalind M. Lawton
Victoria V. Lazar
Jennifer S. McGinty
Peter M. Oxman
Theodore William Paris
James LeGrand Read
Kelly Brunetti Rose
Richard S. Roth
Jeffrey Alan Schlegel
W. Lance Schuler
Nancy E. Siegal
Timothy S. Taylor
Robert M. White

For Complete List of Firm Personnel, See General Section

For full biographical listings, see the Martindale-Hubbell Law Directory

FARNSWORTH & VONBERG (AV)

A Partnership of Professional Corporations
333 North Sam Houston Parkway, Suite 300, 77060
Telephone: 713-931-8902
Telecopy: 713-931-6032

T Brooke Farnsworth (P.C.)
Mary Frances vonBerg (P.C.)

ASSOCIATES

Diane B. Gould
Bennett S. Bartlett

(See Next Column)

FARNSWORTH & VONBERG, *Houston—Continued*

LEGAL SUPPORT PERSONNEL

Lucille P. Poole

For full biographical listings, see the Martindale-Hubbell Law Directory

WAYNE C. FOX (AV)

700 Louisiana, Suite 3990, 77002
Telephone: 713-224-0123
Fax: 713-224-7112

For full biographical listings, see the Martindale-Hubbell Law Directory

CHARLES H. PUCKETT, III (AV)

2390 Five Post Oak Park, 77027
Telephone: 713-871-8881
Fax: 713-871-8898

For full biographical listings, see the Martindale-Hubbell Law Directory

REYNOLDS & SYDOW, L.L.P. (AV)

One Riverway, Suite 1950, 77056
Telephone: 713-840-9600
Fax: 713-840-9605

Michael D. Sydow
Kelli McDonald Sydow
Paula S. Elliott
Kay K. Morgan

OF COUNSEL

Joe H. Reynolds

For full biographical listings, see the Martindale-Hubbell Law Directory

SCHWARTZ & CAMPBELL, L.L.P. (AV)

1221 McKinney, Suite 1000, 77010
Telephone: 713-752-0017
Telecopier: 713-752-0327

Richard A. Schwartz
Marshall S. Campbell

Monica F. Oathout
Stephen A. Mendel
Samuel E. Dunn
Harold W. Hargis
Phillip W. Bechter
Laura M. Taylor
Michael D. Hudgins

LEGAL SUPPORT PERSONNEL

PARALEGALS

Nannette Koger
Bettye Vaughan Johnson
Lenore Chomout
Maria Pinillos

For full biographical listings, see the Martindale-Hubbell Law Directory

THOMPSON & KNIGHT, A PROFESSIONAL CORPORATION (AV)

(Attorneys and Counselors)
1700 Texas Commerce Tower, 600 Travis, 77002
Telephone: 713-217-2800
Telecopy: 713-217-2828; 713-217-2882
Dallas, Texas Office: 1700 Pacific Avenue, Suite 3300, 75201.
Telephone: 214-969-1700.
Telecopy: 214-969-1751.
Cable Address: "Tomtex."
Telex: 732298.
Austin, Texas Office: 1200 San Jacinto Center, 98 San Jacinto Boulevard, 78701.
Telephone: 512-469-6100.
Telecopy: 512-469-6180.
Fort Worth, Texas Office: 801 Cherry Street, Suite 1600, 76102.
Telephone: 817-347-1700.
Telecopy: 817-347-1799.
Monterrey, Mexico Office: Edificio Losoles PD-4, Av. Lázaro Cárdenas No. 2400 PTE., San Pedro Garza Garcia, Nuevo Léon C.P. 66220.
Telephone: (52-8) 363-0096.
Telecopy: (52-8) 363-3067.

SHAREHOLDERS

Mary Margaret Bearden
Daniel J. Hayes
Debbi M. Johnstone
Michael K. Pierce

For Complete List of Firm Personnel, See General Section

For full biographical listings, see the Martindale-Hubbell Law Directory

*SAN ANTONIO,** Bexar Co.

SCHOENBAUM, CURPHY & SCANLAN, P.C. (AV)

NationsBank Plaza, Suite 1775, 300 Convent Street, 78205-3744
Telephone: 210-224-4491
Fax: 210-224-7983

(See Next Column)

Stanley Schoenbaum
R. James Curphy
William Scanlan, Jr.
Alfred G. Holcomb
Banks M. Smith
R. Bradley Oxford
Darin N. Digby

Patricia Flora Sitchler
Emily Harrison Liljenwall
Susan L. Saeger

For full biographical listings, see the Martindale-Hubbell Law Directory

WHEATLEY, CAMPAGNOLO & SESSIONS, L.L.P. (AV)

100 West Houston, Suite 1200, 78205
Telephone: 210-227-5000
Fax: 210-225-1555

Seagal V. Wheatley
Theodore Campagnolo
William Lewis Sessions
John Frank Onion, III
Donald R. Philbin, Jr.

ASSOCIATES

Bradley S. Wilder
Katrina J. Carden
Julia W. Mann

For full biographical listings, see the Martindale-Hubbell Law Directory

UTAH

*SALT LAKE CITY,** Salt Lake Co.

CALLISTER, NEBEKER & MCCULLOUGH, A PROFESSIONAL CORPORATION (AV)

800 Kennecott Building, 84133
Telephone: 801-530-7300
Telecopier: 801-364-9127

Louis H. Callister
Leland S. McCullough
Dorothy C. Pleshe
John A. Beckstead
Jeffrey N. Clayton
Charles M. Bennett
W. Waldan Lloyd
Craig F. McCullough
Damon E. Coombs
Lynda Cook
John H. Rees

John B. Lindsay
Douglas K. Cummings

Representative Clients: Zions Bancorporation; Utah Automobile Dealers Association; Sinclair Oil (Little America); Keystone Communications; Central Valley Water Reclamation Facility Board; Children's Miracle Network (Osmond Foundation); American Stores; Utah Resources International; WordPerfect Corporation; Novell, Inc.

For Complete List of Firm Personnel, See General Section

For full biographical listings, see the Martindale-Hubbell Law Directory

DURHAM, EVANS, JONES & PINEGAR (AV)

Key Bank Tower 50 South Main, Suite 850, 84144
Telephone: 801-538-2424
Fax: 801-363-1835
Telluride, Colorado Office: 126 West Colorado Avenue, Suite 102-C, P.O. Box 3153, 81435.
Telephone: 303-728-5775.
Fax: 303-728-5898.

Jeffrey M. Jones
Richard W. Evans
Paul M. Durham
Kevin R. Pinegar
Douglas R. Tueller (Resident, Telluride, Colorado Office)
G. Richard Hill
Pamela B. Slater (Resident, Telluride, Colorado Office)

For full biographical listings, see the Martindale-Hubbell Law Directory

KESLER & RUST, A PROFESSIONAL CORPORATION (AV)

2000 Beneficial Life Tower, 36 South State Street, 84111
Telephone: 801-355-9333
Telecopier: 801-531-7965

Joseph C. Rust
Scott O. Mercer
Douglas E. Griffith
Lester A. Perry

Ian A. Forrest

OF COUNSEL

Vibert L. Kesler, Jr.
Francis M. Gibbons

Reference: First Security Bank of Utah, N.A.

For full biographical listings, see the Martindale-Hubbell Law Directory

Salt Lake City—Continued

PARSONS BEHLE & LATIMER, A PROFESSIONAL CORPORATION (AV)

One Utah Center, 201 South Main Street, Suite 1800, P.O. Box 45898, 84145-0898
Telephone: 801-532-1234
Telecopy: 801-536-6111

James B. Lee
J. Gordon Hansen
W. Jeffery Fillmore
Val R. Antczak
Robert C. Hyde
Craig B. Terry
Gary E. Doctorman
William D. Holyoak
Robert C. Delahunty
Stuart A. Fredman
Jonathan K. Butler
Scott R. Carpenter
Shawn C. Ferrin

Representative Clients: Alta Gold; American Barrick Resources Corporation; Bank One, Utah, N.A.; Kennecott Corporation; Solaray, Inc.

For full biographical listings, see the Martindale-Hubbell Law Directory

RICHARDS, BRANDT, MILLER & NELSON, A PROFESSIONAL CORPORATION (AV)

Suite 700 50 South Main Street, P.O. Box 2465, 84110
Telephone: 801-531-2000
Fax: 801-532-5506

Robert W. Brandt
Robert W. Miller (1940-1983)
P. Keith Nelson
Gary D. Stott
Robert L. Stevens
David L. Barclay
John L. Young
Brett F. Paulsen
David K. Lauritzen
Lynn S. Davies
Robert G. Gilchrist
Russell C. Fericks
Michael K. Mohrman
Michael N. Emery
Michael P. Zaccheo
Gary L. Johnson
Curtis J. Drake
George T. Naegle
Craig C. Coburn
Lloyd A. Hardcastle

JoAnn E. Carnahan
Brad C. Betebenner
Robert G. Wright
Barbara K. Berrett
Nathan R. Hyde
Christian W. Nelson
Craig Aramaki
Elizabeth A. Hruby-Mills
Bret M. Hanna (Not admitted in UT)

OF COUNSEL

William S. Richards
Wallace R. Lauchnor

Reference: Key Bank of Utah.

For full biographical listings, see the Martindale-Hubbell Law Directory

STRONG & HANNI, A PROFESSIONAL CORPORATION (AV)

Sixth Floor Boston Building, 9 Exchange Place, 84111
Telephone: 801-532-7080
Fax: 801-596-1508

Gordon R. Strong (1909-1969)
Glenn C. Hanni
Henry E. Heath
Philip R. Fishler
Roger H. Bullock
Robert A. Burton
R. Scott Williams
Dennis M. Astill (Managing Partner)
S. Baird Morgan
Stuart H. Schultz
Paul M. Belnap
Stephen J. Trayner
Joseph J. Joyce
Bradley Wm. Bowen

Robert L. Janicki
Elizabeth L. Willey
Peter H. Christensen
H. Burt Ringwood
David R. Nielson
Adam Trupp
Catherine M. Larson

Representative Clients: State Farm Mutual Automobile Insurance Co.; Standard Accident Insurance Co.; United Services Automobile Assn.; Western Casualty & Surety Co.; Government Employees Insurance Co.; Guaranty Mutual Life Co.

For full biographical listings, see the Martindale-Hubbell Law Directory

VAN COTT, BAGLEY, CORNWALL & MCCARTHY, A PROFESSIONAL CORPORATION (AV)

Suite 1600, 50 South Main Street, P.O. Box 45340, 84145
Telephone: 801-532-3333
Telex: 453149
Telecopier: 801-534-0058
Ogden, Utah Office: Suite 900, 2404 Washington Boulevard.
Telephone: 801-394-5783.
Park City, Utah Office: 314 Main Street, Suite 205.
Telephone: 801-649-3889.
Reno, Nevada Office: Jeppson & Lee, 100 West Liberty, Suite 990.
Telephone: 702-333-6800.

(See Next Column)

David E. Salisbury
M. Scott Woodland
Norman S. Johnson
Stephen D. Swindle
Alan F. Mecham
Brent J. Giauque
Maxilian A. Farbman
Arthur B. Ralph
Thomas T. Billings
Danny C. Kelly
Richard H. Johnson, II
Brent Christensen
Thomas Berggren
Ervin R. Holmes
Ronald G. Moffitt
S. Robert Bradley
Jon C. Christiansen
Guy P. Kroesche
Wayne D. Swan
Gregory N. Barrick
Douglas A. Taggart (Resident, Ogden, Utah Office)

OF COUNSEL

Leonard J. Lewis
John Crawford, Jr.

Susan Pierce Lawrence
Nathan W. Jones
David E. Allen
Daniel P. McCarthy
Preston C. Regehr

For Complete List of Firm Personnel, See General Section

For full biographical listings, see the Martindale-Hubbell Law Directory

VERMONT

*BURLINGTON,** Chittenden Co.

BURAK & ANDERSON (AV)

Executive Square, 346 Shelburne Street, P.O. Box 64700, 05406-4700
Telephone: 802-862-0500
Telecopier: 802-862-8176

MEMBERS OF FIRM

Michael L. Burak
Thomas R. Melloni

ASSOCIATE

Julie D. M. Sovern

For Complete List of Firm Personnel, See General Section

For full biographical listings, see the Martindale-Hubbell Law Directory

*RUTLAND,** Rutland Co.

CARROLL, GEORGE & PRATT (AV)

64 & 66 North Main Street, P.O. Box 280, 05702-0280
Telephone: 802-775-7141
Telecopier: 802-775-6483
Woodstock, Vermont Office: The Mill - Route #4 E., P.O. Box 388, 05091.
Telephone: 802-457-1000.
Telecopier: 802-457-1874.

MEMBERS OF FIRM

Henry G. Smith (1938-1974)
James P. Carroll
Alan B. George
Robert S. Pratt
Neal C. Vreeland
Jon S. Readnour
Timothy U. Martin
Randall F. Mayhew (Resident Partner, Woodstock Office)
Richard S. Smith
Judy Godnick Barone
John J. Kennelly

ASSOCIATES

Thomas A. Zonay
Jeffrey P. White
Susan Boyle Ford (Resident, Woodstock Office)
Charles C. Humpstone

For full biographical listings, see the Martindale-Hubbell Law Directory

VIRGINIA

ALEXANDRIA, (Independent City)

GRAD, LOGAN & KLEWANS, P.C. (AV)

112 North Columbus Street, P.O. Box 1417-A44, 22313
Telephone: 703-548-8400
Facsimile: 703-836-6289

John D. Grad
Michael P. Logan
Samuel N. Klewans

Sean C. E. McDonough
Claire R. Pettrone
David A. Damiani

OF COUNSEL

Jeanne F. Franklin

For full biographical listings, see the Martindale-Hubbell Law Directory

Alexandria—Continued

E. Michael Paturis (AV)

Lee Street Square, 431 North Lee Street, 22314-2301
Telephone: 703-836-2501
Facsimile: 703-836-4487

For full biographical listings, see the Martindale-Hubbell Law Directory

Stauffer & Abraham

(See Vienna)

*FAIRFAX,** (Ind. City; Seat of Fairfax Co.)

Rust, Rust & Silver, A Professional Corporation (AV)

4103 Chain Bridge Road Fourth Floor, P.O. Box 460, 22030
Telephone: 703-591-7000
Telecopier: 703-591-7336

John H. Rust, Jr.
Glenn H. Silver
C. Thomas Brown

James E. Kane
Paulo E. Franco, Jr.
Andrew W. White

RETIRED, EMERITUS

John H. Rust, Sr. (Retired)

Representative Clients: Crestar Bank; Commonwealth Land Title Insurance Co.; Patriot National Bank; Century Graphics Corp.

For full biographical listings, see the Martindale-Hubbell Law Directory

*MANASSAS,** Prince William Co.

Allen & Harold, P.L.C. (AV)

10610-A Crestwood Drive, P.O. Box 2126, 22110
Telephone: 703-361-2278
Facsimile: 703-361-0594
Washington, D.C. Office: Suite 200, 2000 L Street, N.W.
Telephone: 202-452-7872; 1-800-433-2636.
Telex: 373-0708.
Facsimile: 202-833-3843.
Shenandoah Valley Office: 5413 Main Street. Stephens City, Virginia 22655.
Telephone: 703-869-0040.
Fax: 703-869-0041.

Robert G. Allen
Douglas W. Harold, Jr.

Robert A. Harris, II

For full biographical listings, see the Martindale-Hubbell Law Directory

MCLEAN, Fairfax Co.

Michael Horwatt & Associates, P.C. (AV)

1501 Farm Credit Drive, Suite 3600, 22102
Telephone: 703-790-7790
Fax: 703-790-7796

Michael S. Horwatt

Charles F. Wright

OF COUNSEL

Frances A. Scibelli
Lawrence W. Koltun (Not admitted in VA)

For full biographical listings, see the Martindale-Hubbell Law Directory

NORFOLK, (Independent City)

Boyd & Boyd, P.C. (AV)

Fourteenth Floor, NationsBank Center, One Commercial Place, 23510
Telephone: 804-622-3611

Robert Friend Boyd
James M. Boyd

Representative Clients: Virginia Wesleyan College; Mary Jane Bakeries; Day Spring Productions; Belanga Construction Corp.; Olympic Enterprises; Quality Irrigation Company; Battlefield Group; Harris Tire, Inc.; W.I. McKendree Co.; Fields Construction; J.D. Law & Son; Wynn's Auto; PhotoMemories.

For full biographical listings, see the Martindale-Hubbell Law Directory

Stackhouse, Smith & Nexsen (AV)

1600 First Virginia Tower, 555 Main Street, P.O. Box 3640, 23514
Telephone: 804-623-3555
FAX: 804-624-9245

MEMBERS OF FIRM

Robert C. Stackhouse
William W. Nexsen
Peter W. Smith, IV
R. Clinton Stackhouse, Jr.
Janice McPherson Doxey

(See Next Column)

ASSOCIATES

Mary Painter Opitz
Timothy P. Murphy
Carl J. Khalil

Representative Clients: Heritage Bank & Trust; The Atlantic Group, Inc.; Roughton Pontiac Corp; Federal National Mortgage Association; Kemper National Insurance Cos.; Shearson/American Express Mortgage Corp.; Harleysville Mutual Insurance Co.; Heritage Bankshares, Inc.; Presbyterian League of the Presbytery of Eastern Virginia, Inc.; Oakwood Acceptance Corp.

For full biographical listings, see the Martindale-Hubbell Law Directory

*RICHMOND,** (Ind. City; Seat of Henrico Co.)

Williams, Mullen, Christian & Dobbins, A Professional Corporation (AV)

Two James Center, 1021 East Cary Street, P.O. Box 1320, 23210-1320
Telephone: 804-643-1991
Fax: 804-783-6456
Glen Allen, Virginia Office: 4401 Waterfront Drive, Suite 140.
Telephone: 804-965-9168.
Fax: 804-965-0955.
Washington, D.C. Office: 1575 Eye Street, N.W.
Telephone: 202-289-6200.
Fax: 202-289-4126.

Ralph L. Axselle, Jr.
David George Ball (Resident, Washington, D.C. Office)
R. Brian Ball
Charles L. Cabell
Theodore L. Chandler, Jr.
Alexander C. Graham, Jr.
A. Brooks Hock
David R. Johnson
Reginald N. Jones
Randolph H. Lickey
Thomas B. McVey (Not admitted in VA; Resident, Washington, D.C. Office)
Robert L. Musick, Jr.
Warren E. Nowlin (Washington, D.C. Office)
Craig L. Rascoe
Malcolm E. Ritsch, Jr.
Walter H. Ryland
Paul G. Saunders, II
William H. Schwarzschild, III
Julious P. Smith, Jr.
Robert E. Spicer, Jr.
Robin Robertson Starr
Andrea Rowse Stiles
W. Scott Street, III
C. William Waechter, Jr.
Wayne A. Whitham, Jr.
Fielding L. Williams, Jr.
Russell Alton Wright

Naila Townes Ahmed
Wyatt S. Beazley, IV
William J. Benos
David L. Dallas, Jr.
William L. Pitman
Ian D. Titley
Charles E. Wall

For Complete List of Firm Personnel, See General Section

For full biographical listings, see the Martindale-Hubbell Law Directory

ROANOKE, (Independent City)

Bersch & Rhodes, P.C. (AV)

640 Crestar Plaza, P.O. Box 1529, 24007
Telephone: 703-345-7400
Facsimile: 703-345-7353

Robert S. Bersch
Harry S. Rhodes

William C. Leach
Scott A. Butler

For full biographical listings, see the Martindale-Hubbell Law Directory

Glenn, Flippin, Feldmann & Darby, A Professional Corporation (AV)

200 First Campbell Square, P.O. Box 2887, 24001
Telephone: 703-224-8000
Telecopier: 703-224-8050

Robert E. Glenn
G. Franklin Flippin
Mark E. Feldmann
Harwell M. Darby, Jr.
Maryellen F. Goodlatte
Claude M. Lauck
Robert A. Ziogas
Charles E. Troland, Jr.
David E. Perry
Paul G. Beers
Phillip R. Lingafelt
James Peyton Cargill
Sarah Elizabeth Powell

Representative Clients: Liberty Mutual Insurance Co.; Grand Piano & Furniture Co.; Sears, Roebuck and Co.
References: NationsBank; Crestar Bank.

For full biographical listings, see the Martindale-Hubbell Law Directory

SPRINGFIELD, Fairfax Co.

Madigan & Scott, Inc. (AV)

7880 Backlick Road, 22150-2288
Telephone: 703-455-1800; 451-2080
Fax: 703-451-4121
Manassas, Virginia Office: 9100 Church Street, Suite 107.
Telephone: 703-361-0185. Metro: 631-9193.
Fax: 703-631-9633.

(See Next Column)

MADIGAN & SCOTT INC.—*Continued*

Robert J. Madigan
Paul A. Scott
Scott H. Donovan (Resident, Manassas Office)
Mitchell Komaroff

Richard G. Hornig (1958-1994)

For full biographical listings, see the Martindale-Hubbell Law Directory

VIENNA, Fairfax Co.

BORING, PARROTT & PILGER, P.C. (AV)

307 Maple Avenue West, Suite D, 22180-4368
Telephone: 703-281-2161
FAX: 703-281-9464

W. Thomas Parrott, III
Thomas J. Sawyer

Representative Clients: Balmar, Inc.; Hewlett-Packard Co.; Toshiba America Information Systems, Inc.; King Wholesale, Inc.; FSM Leasing, Inc.; KDI Sylvan Pools, Inc.; Brobst International, Inc.; Telematics, Inc.; Northern Virginia Surgical Associates, P.C.; Rainbow Industries, Inc.

For full biographical listings, see the Martindale-Hubbell Law Directory

PETERSON & BASHA, P.C. (AV)

Tysons Square Office Park, 8214-C Old Courthouse Road, 22182-3855
Telephone: 703-442-3890
Fax: 703-448-1834

Gary G. Peterson
Leigh-Alexandra Basha

Alison K. Markell
Cynthia L. Gausvik
Ki Jun Sung

OF COUNSEL

Daniel J. O'Connell

For full biographical listings, see the Martindale-Hubbell Law Directory

REES, BROOME & DIAZ, P.C. (AV)

Ninth Floor, 8133 Leesburg Pike, 22182
Telephone: 703-790-1911
Telecopier: 703-848-2530

Joel M. Birken
John F. Boland
Michael L. O'Reilly
Michael M. Mannix
Andrew B. Golkow

Richard M. Ware, Jr.

OF COUNSEL

John F. Lefevere

For full biographical listings, see the Martindale-Hubbell Law Directory

WASHINGTON

*OLYMPIA,** Thurston Co.

BEAN & GENTRY (AV)

Columbia Square, 320 North Columbia, P.O. Box 2317, 98507
Telephone: 206-943-8040
Fax: 206-786-6943

MEMBERS OF FIRM

Stephen J. Bean
Fred D. Gentry

ASSOCIATES

Mary G. Gentry
Cecilia Marie Clynch

Reference: Key Bank of Puget Sound.

For full biographical listings, see the Martindale-Hubbell Law Directory

*SEATTLE,** King Co.

BETTS, PATTERSON & MINES, P.S. (AV)

800 Financial Center, 1215 Fourth Avenue, 98161-1090
Telephone: 206-292-9988
Fax: 206-343-7053

Donald L. Thoreson
Bruce H. Hurst
John P. Braislin
Livingston Wernecke
John R. Rizzardi
Charles W. Davis
Thomas F. Peterson

(See Next Column)

Ronald D. Allen
Deborah A. Crabbe
Stephen A. Crandall

Representative Clients; Associated Grocers; Cape Fox Corporation: Chrysler Corporation; Great Lakes Chemical Corp.; Key Bank of Washington; Minnesota Mining and Manufacturing Company; Pankratz Forest Industries, Inc.; Pfizer, Inc.; State Farm Fire & Casualty Co.; Supermarket Development Corp.

For full biographical listings, see the Martindale-Hubbell Law Directory

GAITÁN & CUSACK (AV)

30th Floor Two Union Square, 601 Union Street, 98101-2324
Telephone: 206-521-3000
Facsimile: 206-386-5259
Anchorage, Alaska Office: 425 G Street, Suite 760.
Telephone: 907-278-3001.
Facsimile: 907-278-6068.
San Francisco, California Office: 275 Battery Street, 20th Floor.
Telephone: 415-398-5562.
Fax: 415-398-4033.
Washington, D.C. Office: 2000 L Street, Suite 200.
Telephone: 202-296-4637.
Fax: 202-296-4650.

MEMBERS OF FIRM

José E. Gaitán
Kenneth J. Cusack (Resident, Anchorage, Alaska Office)
William F. Knowles
Ronald L. Bozarth

OF COUNSEL

Howard K. Todd
Gary D. Gayton
Michel P. Stern (Also practicing alone, Bellevue, Washington)
Christopher A. Byrne
Patricia D. Ryan

ASSOCIATES

Mary F. O'Boyle
Bruce H. Williams
David J. Onsager
Diana T. Jimenez
Robert T. Mimbu
Cristina C. Kapela
Camilla M. Hedberg
John E. Lenker
Kathleen C. Healy

Representative Clients: Cummins Great Plains Diesel; Sears, Roebuck & Company; National Insurance Professional Corporation; Nabisco; Pillsbury Company; Harvest Software; Trevino Foods; Hosho America; HFI Foods.

For full biographical listings, see the Martindale-Hubbell Law Directory

J. RICHARD MANNING (AV)

925 Logan Building, 98101
Telephone: 206-623-6302
Fax: 206-624-3865
Reference: West One Bank, Ranier Square, Seattle, Washington.

For full biographical listings, see the Martindale-Hubbell Law Directory

SIRIANNI & YOUTZ (AV)

1700 Westlake Center, 1601 Fifth Avenue, 98101-1625
Telephone: 206-223-0303
Telecopier: 206-223-0246

MEMBERS OF FIRM

Stephen J. Sirianni
Chris Robert Youtz

ASSOCIATES

Ann E. Merryfield
Btian W. Esler

Reference: Pacific Northwest Bank.

For full biographical listings, see the Martindale-Hubbell Law Directory

STOKES, EITELBACH & LAWRENCE, P.S. (AV)

800 Fifth Avenue, Suite 4000, 98104-3199
Telephone: 206-626-6000
Fax: 206-464-1496

Sarah Butler Eitelbach
James H. Feldman
Phillip H. Ginsberg
Byron E. Springer, Jr.
Robert J. Thomas

For full biographical listings, see the Martindale-Hubbell Law Directory

*SPOKANE,** Spokane Co.

CHASE, HAYES & KALAMON, P.S. (AV)

1000 Seafirst Financial Center, 99201
Telephone: 509-456-0333
FAX: 509-838-9826

Roger F. Chase
Hedley W. Greene

Nancy A. Pohlman
Brent T. Stanyer
Gerald Kobluk

(See Next Column)

CHASE, HAYES & KALAMON P.S., *Spokane—Continued*

OF COUNSEL

W. Kenneth Jones

Representative Clients: Albertson's Inc.; Key Tronic Corp.; Volvo of America, Inc.; Security Management; Familian Northwest; Tidyman's Inc.; Farmers Insurance Group; Sacred Heart Medical Center; Farm Credit Bank of Spokane.

For Complete List of Firm Personnel, See General Section

For full biographical listings, see the Martindale-Hubbell Law Directory

WEST VIRGINIA

*CLARKSBURG,** Harrison Co.

MCNEER, HIGHLAND & MCMUNN (AV)

Empire Building, P.O. Drawer 2040, 26301
Telephone: 304-623-6636
Facsimile: 304-623-3035
Morgantown Office: McNeer, Highland & McMunn, Baker & Armistead, 168 Chancery Row. P.O. Box 1615.
Telephone: 304-292-8473.
Fax: 304-292-1528.
Martinsburg, Office: 1446-1 Edwin Miller Boulevard. P.O. Box 2509.
Telephone: 304-264-4621.
Fax: 304-264-8623.

MEMBERS OF FIRM

C. David McMunn
J. Cecil Jarvis
James A. Varner
George B. Armistead (Resident, Morgantown Office)
Catherine D. Munster
Robert W. Trumble (Resident, Martinsburg Office)
Dennis M. Shreve
Geraldine S. Roberts
Harold M. Sklar
Jeffrey S. Bolyard
Steven R. Bratke
Michael J. Novotny (Resident, Martinsburg Office)

OF COUNSEL

James E. McNeer
Cecil B. Highland, Jr.
William L. Fury

Representative Clients: One Valley Bank of Clarksburg, National Association; Bruceton Bank; Harrison County Bank; Nationwide Mutual Insurance Cos.; Clarksburg Publishing Co.; C.I.T. Financial Services; State Automobile Mutual Insurance Co.; United Hospital Center, Inc.; West Virginia Coals, Inc.; Swanson Plating Company.

For Complete List of Firm Personnel, See General Section

For full biographical listings, see the Martindale-Hubbell Law Directory

WISCONSIN

*APPLETON,** Outagamie Co.

MENN, NELSON, SHARRATT, TEETAERT & BEISENSTEIN, LTD. (AV)

(Formerly, Fulton, Menn & Nehs, Ltd.)
222 North Oneida Street, P.O. Box 785, 54912-0785
Telephone: 414-731-6631
FAX: 414-734-0981

Homer H. Benton (1886-1957)
Alfred C. Bosser (1890-1965)
Franklin L. Nehs (1922-1979)
David L. Fulton (1911-1985)
Glenn L. Sharratt (Retired)
John B. Menn
Peter S. Nelson
John R. Teetaert
Joseph J. Beisenstein
Mark R. Feldmann
Joseph A. Bielinski
Jonathan M. Menn
Douglas D. Hahn
Keith W. Kostecke
Robert N. Duimstra

LEGAL SUPPORT PERSONNEL

Kathy J. Krause

Representative Clients: Bank One Appleton, NA; Time Warner Entertainment Company LP.

For full biographical listings, see the Martindale-Hubbell Law Directory

*GREEN BAY,** Brown Co.

SCHOBER & ULATOWSKI, S.C. (AV)

414 East Walnut Street, Suite 150, 54305-1780
Telephone: 414-432-5355
Facsimile: 414-432-5967

Adrian T. Ulatowski

(See Next Column)

Mark A. Bartels
Timothy A. Cisler

For full biographical listings, see the Martindale-Hubbell Law Directory

*MADISON,** Dane Co.

NEIDER & BOUCHER, S.C. (AV)

7617 Mineral Point Road, 53717
Telephone: 608-829-1400
Facsimile: 608-829-2080

F. Anthony Brewster
Charles E. Neider
Joseph W. Boucher
Steven C. Underwood
Ronald C. Berman
Susan M. De Groot
Kent L. Schlienger
Jeffrey J. Bartzen
Annemarie G. Pace

OF COUNSEL

Ralph M. Cagle

For full biographical listings, see the Martindale-Hubbell Law Directory

*MILWAUKEE,** Milwaukee Co.

DAVIS & KUELTHAU, S.C. (AV)

111 East Kilbourn Avenue, Suite 1400, 53202-6613
Telephone: 414-276-0200
Facsimile: 414-276-9369
Cable Address: "Shiplaw"

James A. Brindley
Scott E. Fiducci
James H. Gormley, Jr.
Norman J. Matar
Erich Mildenberg
Daniel J. Minahan
Michael C. Runde
Robert K. Steuer

OF COUNSEL

Peter J. Ruud

Maurice D. Jones
Kenneth A. Kirley
Victor A. Lazzaretti
Lesli K. Hosford McLinden
Brett K. Miller
Dana E. Roberts

For full biographical listings, see the Martindale-Hubbell Law Directory

EHLINGER & KRILL, S.C. (AV)

316 North Milwaukee Street, Suite 410, 53202-5803
Telephone: 414-272-8085
Facsimile: 414-272-8290

Ralph J. Ehlinger
R. Jeffrey Krill

For full biographical listings, see the Martindale-Hubbell Law Directory

FIORENZA & HAYES, S.C. (AV)

Kildeer Court, 3900 West Brown Deer Road, 53209
Telephone: 414-355-3600
Fax: 414-355-8080

John A. Fiorenza
Clare L. Fiorenza
Richard D. Moake
Daniel J. Miske
William J. Mantyh
Lawrence G. Wickert
Jeffrey M. Leggett
Lisa A. Dziadulewicz
Timothy M. Hughes

Representative Clients: M & I Marshall & Ilsley Bank, Silver Spring Division; Valley Bank; Miller-Bradford & Risberg, Inc.; Magnetek, Inc.; Litton Industries, Inc.; Centel Communications, Inc.; FJA Christiansen Roofing Co.; North American Van Lines; Kendor Corp.; Todd Equipment, Inc.

For full biographical listings, see the Martindale-Hubbell Law Directory

KOHNER, MANN & KAILAS, S.C. (AV)

1572 East Capitol Drive, P.O. Box 19982, 53211-0982
Telephone: 414-962-5110
Fax: 414-962-8725

Marvin L. Kohner (1908-1975)
Robert L. Mann
Steve Kailas
Mark R. Wolters
Jordan B. Reich
David S. Chartier

Roy Paul Roth
Gary P. Lantzy
Christopher C. Kailas
Robert E. Nailen
Matthew P. Gerdisch
Darrell R. Zall
Daniel J. Flynn
Timothy L. Zuberbier
Shawn G. Rice

Representative Clients: EcoLab, Inc.; Parker Pen Co.; Ray O Vac, Inc.

For full biographical listings, see the Martindale-Hubbell Law Directory

MEISSNER & TIERNEY, S.C. (AV)

The Milwaukee Center, 111 East Kilbourn Avenue, 19th Floor, 53202-6622
Telephone: 414-273-1300
Facsimile: 414-273-5840

(See Next Column)

MEISSNER & TIERNEY S.C.—*Continued*

Paul F. Meissner	Todd J. Mitchell
Joseph E. Tierney III	Thomas J. Nichols
Dennis L. Fisher	Randal J. Brotherhood

Michael J. Cohen

Eric J. Klumb	Steven R. Glaser
Kenneth A. Iwinski	Catherine M. Priebe Hertzberg

OF COUNSEL

Thomas E. Whipp

For full biographical listings, see the Martindale-Hubbell Law Directory

QUARLES & BRADY (AV)

411 East Wisconsin Avenue, 53202-4497
Telephone: 414-277-5000
Cable Address: "Lawdock"
Fax: 414-271-3552.
TWX: 910-262-3426
Madison, Wisconsin Office: Firstar Plaza, One South Pinckney Street, P.O. Box 2113.
Telephone: 608-251-5000.
Fax: 608-251-9166.
West Palm Beach, Florida Office: 222 Lakeview Avenue, 4th Floor.
Telephone: 407-653-5000.
Fax: 407-653-5333.
Naples, Florida Office: Barnett Center, 4501 Tamiami Trail North.
Telephone: 813-262-5959.
Fax: 813-434-4999.
Phoenix, Arizona Office: One Camelback Building, One East Camelback Road, Suite 400.
Telephone: 602-230-5500.
Fax: 602-230-5598.

MEMBERS OF FIRM
(ALPHABETICALLY BY YEAR OF ADMISSION TO BAR)

Arthur H. Laun, Jr.	James D. Friedman
John S. Sammond (Resident, West Palm Beach, Florida Office)	John R. Maynard
	Quinn W. Martin
	John W. Daniels, Jr.
David L. MacGregor	Timothy G. Hains (Resident, Naples, Florida Office)
James Urdan	
Jackson M. Bruce, Jr.	Phillip E. Recht
Robert J. Kalupa	Patrick J. Goebel
Jeremy C. Shea (Resident, Madison Office)	Molly K. Martin (Resident, Madison Office)
Donald S. Taitelman	Nicholas J. Seay (Resident, Madison Office)
John A. Hazelwood	
John S. Holbrook, Jr. (Resident, Madison Office)	Joseph D. Masterson
	Peter A. Terry (Resident, Phoenix, Arizona Office)
Peter J. Lettenberger	
Henry J. Loos	Kimberly Leach Johnson (Resident, Naples, Florida Office)
Michael J. Spector	
Robert H. Diaz, Jr.	
Anthony W. Asmuth, III	Daniel L. Muchow (Resident, Phoenix, Arizona Office)
Thomas W. O'Brien	
Jeffrey B. Bartell (Resident, Madison Office)	Thomas A. Simonis
	David D. Wilmoth
Steven R. Duback	Paul M. Gales (Resident, Phoenix, Arizona Office)
Conrad G. Goodkind	
Lawrence J. Jost	Michael A. Levey
Patrick M. Ryan	Elizabeth G. Nowakowski
Bruce C. Davidson	William J. Toman (Resident, Madison Office)
P. Robert Moya (Resident, Phoenix, Arizona Office)	
	Michael K. Bresson
Stephen E. Richman	Michael D. Zeka

Fredrick G. Lautz

OF COUNSEL

A. William Asmuth, Jr.	Elwin J. Zarwell

Neal E. Madisen

ASSOCIATES

Jerome R. Kerkman	Susan A. Cerbins
Robert S. Bornhoft (Resident, Phoenix, Arizona Office)	Andra J. Palmer (Resident, Madison Office)
Kathryn M. Coates	Charles M. Weber
Jeffrey L. Elverman	Walter J. Skipper
Kenneth J. Hansen (Resident, Madison Office)	Deborah L. Skurulsky
	Valerie L. Bailey-Rihn (Resident, Madison Office)
Jennifer Vogel Powers	
David L. Bourne	Kurt A. Johnson (Resident, Phoenix, Arizona Office)
N. (Norrie) Daroga	
Lorraine J. Koeper	Lisa A. Lyons

Harold O.M. Rocha

For Complete List of Firm Personnel, See General Section

For full biographical listings, see the Martindale-Hubbell Law Directory

NEENAH, Winnebago Co.

DI RENZO AND BOMIER (AV)

231 East Wisconsin Avenue, P.O. Box 788, 54957-0788
Telephone: 414-725-8464
Fax: 414-725-8568

MEMBERS OF FIRM

Robert C. Di Renzo	Roy N. Fine

ASSOCIATE

Ross A. Sharkey

Representative Clients: Kimberly-Clark Corporation, Neenah, WI; Banta Publishing Co., Inc., Menasha, WI; Phillips Plastics Corp., Phillips, WI; Kennedy Center for the Hip and Knee, S.C., Neenah, Wi.; Great Northern Corporation, Appleton, WI; Bank One, Neenah, WI; Geo. A. Whiting Paper Co., Menasha, WI; Bergstrom Chevrolet-Buick-Cadillac, Inc., Neenah and Appleton, WI; Paper Valley Hotel and Conference Center, Inc., Appleton, WI.

For Complete List of Firm Personnel, See General Section

For full biographical listings, see the Martindale-Hubbell Law Directory

WYOMING

*CASPER,** Natrona Co.

BROWN & DREW (AV)

Casper Business Center, Suite 800, 123 West First Street, 82601-2486
Telephone: 307-234-1000
800-877-6755
Telefax: 307-265-8025

MEMBERS OF FIRM

Morris R. Massey	John A. Warnick
Harry B. Durham, III	Thomas F. Reese
W. Thomas Sullins, II	Russell M. Blood
Donn J. McCall	J. Kenneth Barbe

ASSOCIATES

Jon B. Huss	Courtney Robert Kepler
Carol Warnick	Drew A. Perkins

Attorneys for: First Interstate Bank of Wyoming, N.A.; Norwest Bank Wyoming, N.A.; The CIT Group/Industrial Financing; Aetna Casualty & Surety Co.; The Doctor's Co.; MEDMARC; WOTCO, Inc.; Chevron USA; Kerr-McGee Corp.; Chicago and NorthWestern Transportation Company.

For Complete List of Firm Personnel, See General Section

For full biographical listings, see the Martindale-Hubbell Law Directory

SCHWARTZ, BON, WALKER & STUDER (AV)

141 South Center, Suite 505, 82601
Telephone: 307-235-6681
Fax: 307-234-5099

William T. Schwartz	Cameron S. Walker
William S. Bon	Judith A. W. Studer

ASSOCIATES

Patrick T. Holscher	Peter J. Young

Kathleen J. Doyle

Representative Clients: Key Bank of Casper; Equitable Life Assurance Society; ANR Production; Union Carbide Corp.; Hill Top Shopping Center; Exxon Co., U.S.A.; Armco Steel Corp.; USF&G; American Insurance Cos.

For full biographical listings, see the Martindale-Hubbell Law Directory

*WORLAND,** Washakie Co.

DAVIS, DONNELL, WORRALL & BANCROFT, P.C. (AV)

718 Big Horn Avenue, P.O. Box 552, 82401
Telephone: 307-347-9801
Fax: 307-347-2859

John W. Davis	John P. Worrall
Jeffrey A. Donnell	Thomas C. Bancroft

Michael D. Greear

Reference: First National Bank.

For full biographical listings, see the Martindale-Hubbell Law Directory

VIRGIN ISLANDS

*CHARLOTTE AMALIE, ST. THOMAS,** St. Thomas

GRUNERT STOUT BRUCH & MOORE

24-25 Kongensgade, P.O. Box 1030, 00804
Telephone: 809-774-1320
Fax: 809-774-7839

MEMBERS OF FIRM

John E. Stout
Susan Bruch Moorehead
Treston E. Moore

ASSOCIATES

Maryleen Thomas
H. Kevin Mart (Not admitted in VI)
Richard F. Taylor

OF COUNSEL

William L. Blum

For full biographical listings, see the Martindale-Hubbell Law Directory

CANADA
ALBERTA

*CALGARY,** Calgary Jud. Dist.

BENNETT JONES VERCHERE (AV)

4500 Bankers Hall East, 855-2nd Street S.W., T2P 4K7
Telephone: (403) 298-3100
Facsimile: (403) 265-7219
Edmonton, Alberta Office: 1000, 10035-105 Street.
Telephone: (403) 421-8133.
Facsimile: (403) 421-7951.
Toronto, Ontario Office: 3400 1 First Canadian Place. P.O. Box 130.
Telephone: (416) 863-1200.
Facsimile: (416) 863-1716.
Ottawa, Ontario Office: Suite 1800. 350 Alberta Street, Box 25, K1R 1A4.
Telephone: (613) 230-4935.
Facsimile: (613) 230-3836.
Montreal, Quebec Office: Suite 1600, 1 Place Ville Marie.
Telephone: (514) 871-1200.
Facsimile: (514) 871-8115.

MEMBER OF FIRM

Walter B. O'Donoghue, Q.C.

For Complete List of Firm Personnel, See General Section

For full biographical listings, see the Martindale-Hubbell Law Directory

*EDMONTON,** Edmonton Jud. Dist.

PARLEE McLAWS (AV)

15th Floor Manulife Place, 10180 101st Street, T5J 4K1
Telephone: 403-423-8500
Telecopier: 403-423-2870
Calgary, Alberta Office: 3400, Western Canadian Place, 707 - 8th Avenue, S.W.
Telephone: 403-294-7000.
Telecopier: 403-265-8263.

MEMBERS OF FIRM

C. H. Kerr, Q.C.
R. A. Newton, Q.C.
M. D. MacDonald
T. A. Cockrall, Q.C.
K. F. Bailey, Q.C.
H. D. Montemurro
R. B. Davison, Q.C.
F. J. Niziol
F. R. Haldane
R. W. Wilson
P. E. J. Curran
I. L. MacLachlan
D. G. Finlay
R. O. Langley
J. K. McFadyen
R. G. McBean
R. C. Secord
J. T. Neilson
D. L. Kennedy
E. G. Rice
D. C. Rolf
J. F. McGinnis
D. F. Pawlowski
J. H. H. Hockin
A. A. Garber
G. W. Jaycock
R. P. James
M. J. K. Nikel
D. C. Wintermute
B. J. Curial
J. L. Cairns
S. L. May
M. S. Poretti

ASSOCIATES

C. R. Head
P. E. S. J. Kennedy
A.W. Slemko
R. Feraco
L. H. Hamdon
R.J. Billingsley
K.A. Smith
N.B.R. Thompson
K. D. Fallis-Howell
P. A. Shenher
D. S. Tam
I. C. Johnson
J.W. McClure
K.G. Koshman
F.H. Belzil
D.D. Dubrule
R.A. Renz
G. T. Lund

(See Next Column)

ASSOCIATES (Continued)

J.G. Paulson
G. E. Flemming
W.D. Johnston
B. L. Andriachuk
K. E. Buss
K. P. Nayyer

For full biographical listings, see the Martindale-Hubbell Law Directory

CANADA
BRITISH COLUMBIA

*VANCOUVER,** Vancouver Co.

LAWSON LUNDELL LAWSON & McINTOSH (AV)

1600 Cathedral Place, 925 West Georgia Street, V6C 3L2
Telephone: 604-685-3456
Facsimile: 604-669-1620
Yellowknife. Northwest Territories Office: Suite 204, 4817 - 49th Street, Yellowknife Northwest Territories, X1A 3S7. Telephone (403) 669-9990.
Facsimile: (403)669-9991. Toronto, Ontario Affiliate: Tory Tory DesLauriers & Binnington, Suite 3000, Aetna Tower, Toronto-Dominion Centre, P.O. Box 270, Toronto, Ontario, M5K 1N2.
Telephone: (416) 865-0040.
Facsimile: (416) 865-7398.
London, England Affiliate: Tory Tory DesLauriers & Binnington, 44/45 Chancery Lane, London, WC2A 1JB, England.
Telephone: (171) 831-8155.
Facsimile: (171) 831-1812.
Hong Kong Affiliate: Tory Tory DesLauriers & Binnington, Suite 1705, One Exchange Square, 8 Connaught Place, Central, Hong Kong.
Telephone: (852) 2868-3099.
Facsimile: (852) 2523-8140.
Montreal Affiliate: Desjardins Ducharme Stein Monast, 600 rue de la Gauchetière Ouest, Montréal, Québec, H3B 4L8.
Telephone: (514) 878-9411.
Facsimile: (514) 878-9092.
Quebec City Affiliate: Desjardins Ducharme Stein Monast, Bureau 300, 1150 rue de Claire Fontaine, Quebec, Québec, G1R 5G4.
Telephone: (418) 529-6531.
Facsimile: (418) 523-5391.

James H. Lawson, Q.C. (1955)
Oscar F. Lundell, Q.C. (1982)
David A. Lawson (1975)
G. Buchan McIntosh, Q.C. (Retired 1992)
John M. Tennant
David J. Smith
Robert J. Mair, Q.C.
John O.E. Lundell
Lorne D. Peterson
John G. Trueman
Brian J. Wallace, Q.C.
William F. Dickson
Gregory T. W. Bowden
Alastair G. Miller
David L. Rice
William M. Everett, Q.C.
Douglas F. Robinson
Stephen McCullough
John H. Fraser
Anthony W. Ryan
Paul D. Bradley
Christopher G. Baldwin
J. Martin Kyle
Chris W. Sanderson
Gordon M. Craig
J. Edward Gouge, Q.C.
Kelly R. Doyle
Brian D. Fulton
L. Neil Marshall
Gordon C. Weatherill
S. Bradley Armstrong
David L. Adderley
John Smith
Edward L. Wilson
Gail P. Black
Peter D. Feldberg
Rodney L. Hayley
Margaret J. O'Brien
Murray T. A. Campbell
A.W. Carpenter
Irving D. Laskin
Randolph G. Klarenbach
Gordon R. Chambers
Jerrold W. Schramm
K. Alan Blair
Maureen E. Baird
Lise Bertrand
Gwen A. Benjamin
Karen L. Rix
David A. Allard
Ron A. Skolrood
Ian C. MacLeod
Thomas S. Woods
H. Jane Murdoch
C. Kelly Oehlschlager
David E. Venour
E. Sigurd Ruud
Rita C. Andreone
Barbara Cornish
Melanie C. Samuels
Clifford Proudfoot
Leslee J. Warren (Not admitted in BC)
Craig A. B. Ferris
Michael J. Low
Caroline A. Longcroft
Cecilia A. Low
John T.C. Christian
Valerie C. Mann
Clara Y.K. Tsang
Donald R. Collie
Gregory W. Hollingsworth
James D. Fraser
Reinhold G. Krahn
Christine MacLean
Bryan C. Haynes
Desiree Skutshek
Jeff Christian
Peter A. Goldthorpe

For full biographical listings, see the Martindale-Hubbell Law Directory

Vancouver—Continued

RUSSELL & DUMOULIN (AV)

2100-1075 West Georgia Street, V6E 3G2
Telephone: 604-631-3131
Fax: 604-631-3232
A Member of the national association of Borden DuMoulin Howard Gervais, comprising Russell & DuMoulin, Vancouver, British Columbia; Howard Mackie, Calgary, Alberta; Borden & Elliot, Toronto, Ontario; Mackenzie Gervais, Montreal, Quebec and Borden DuMoulin Howard Gervais, London, England.
Strategic Alliance with Perkins Coie with offices in Seattle, Spokane and Bellevue, Washington; Portland, Oregon; Anchorage, Alaska; Los Angeles, California; Washington, D.C.; Hong Kong and Taipei, Taiwan.
Represented in Hong Kong by Vincent T.K. Cheung, Yap & Co.

MEMBERS OF FIRM

Donald M. Dalik
John S. McKercher
Peter H. Stafford

Representative Clients: Alcan Smelters & Chemicals Ltd.; The Bank of Nova Scotia; Canada Trust Co.; The Canada Life Assurance Co.; Forest Industrial Relations Ltd.; Honda Canada Inc.; IBM Canada Ltd.; Macmillan Bloedel Ltd.; Nissho Iwai Canada Ltd.; The Toronto-Dominion Bank.

For Complete List of Firm Personnel, See General Section

For full biographical listings, see the Martindale-Hubbell Law Directory

CANADA MANITOBA

*WINNIPEG,** Eastern Jud. Dist.

AIKINS, MACAULAY & THORVALDSON (AV)

Thirtieth Floor, Commodity Exchange Tower, 360 Main Street, R3C 4G1
Telephone: 204-957-0050
Fax: 204-957-0840

MEMBERS OF FIRM

A. Lorne Campbell, O.C., C.D., Q.C., LL.D.
A.J. Mercury, Q.C.
J. Timothy Samson
Bryan D. Klein
Thomas P. Dooley
E. Bruce Parker
Barbara M. Hamilton, Q.C.
G. Bruce Taylor
Robert G. Siddall
Herbert J. Peters
Lisa M. Collins
J. Douglas Sigurdson
Kathleen M.T. Craton
James C.R. Ludlow
Michael E. Guttormson
Robert L. Tyler
Jacqueline N. Freedman
Roger J. Hansell, Q.C.
Michael J. Mercury, Q.C.
Martin H. Freedman, Q.C.
Larry R. Crane, Q.C.
Charles L. Chappell
Joel A. Weinstein
S. Jane Evans, Q.C.
David L. Voechting
Richard L. Yaffe
Frank Lavitt
David M. Carrick
Barbara R. Hochman
John R. Braun
Brian D. Lerner
Anita R. Wortzman
Carmele N. Peter
Lori A. Lavoie
Francis J. St.Hilaire

Representative Clients: Bank of Montreal; Canada Safeway Ltd.; Co-Operative Credit Society; Federal Industries; Great-West Life; Greater Winnipeg Cablevision; National Bank of Canada; New Flyer Industries; Standard Aero Limited; Winnipeg Jets.

For Complete List of Firm Personnel, See General Section

For full biographical listings, see the Martindale-Hubbell Law Directory

CANADA NEW BRUNSWICK

*SAINT JOHN,** Saint John Co.

GILBERT, MCGLOAN, GILLIS (AV)

Suite 710, Mercantile Centre, 55 Union Street P.O. Box 7174, Station "A", E2L 4S6
Telephone: 506-634-3600
Telecopier: 506-634-3612

T. Louis McGloan, Q.C. (1896-1986)
Adrian B. Gilbert, Q.C. (1895-1986)

MEMBERS OF FIRM

Donald M. Gillis, Q.C.
Thomas L. McGloan, Q.C.
A. G. Warwick Gilbert, Q.C.
Rodney J. Gillis, Q.C.
Douglas A. M. Evans, Q.C.
Brenda J. Lutz
David N. Rogers

(See Next Column)

ASSOCIATES

Paulette C. Garnett, Q.C.
Edward Veitch
Hugh J. Flemming, Q.C.
Anne F. MacNeill
Nancy E. Forbes
Marie T. Bérubé
Guy C. Spavold
Claire B.N. Porter
Michael J. Murphy
Mark A. Canty

Representative Clients: Bank of Montreal; Canada Packers Ltd.; McCain Foods Ltd.; The Sunderland Steamship Protecting & Indemnity Association; Steamship Mutual Underwriting Association (Bermuda) Limited; Royal Insurance Co.; Wawanesa Mutual Insurance Co.; Dominion of Canada General Insurance Co.; Canadian General Insurance Co.

For full biographical listings, see the Martindale-Hubbell Law Directory

CANADA NOVA SCOTIA

*HALIFAX,** Halifax Co.

MCINNES COOPER & ROBERTSON (AV)

1601 Lower Water Street, P.O. Box 730, B3J 2V1
Telephone: 902-425-6500
Fax: 902-425-6350
St. John's, Newfoundland Office: Suite 602, Scotia Centre, 235 Water Street, P.O. Box 547. A1C, 5K8.
Telephone: 709-726-9500.
Fax: 709-726-9550.

Stewart McInnes, P.C., Q.C.
Joseph A. F. Macdonald, Q.C.
David H. Reardon, Q.C.
Linda Lee Oland
Marcia L. Brennan
Lawrence J. Hayes, Q.C.
George T. H. Cooper, Q.C.
F. V. W. Penick
John D. Stringer
Fae J. Shaw
Karen Oldfield

COUNSEL

Hector McInnes, Q.C.

Attorneys for: Bank of Nova Scotia; Imperial Oil, Limited; Frank B. Hall & Co., Inc. (New York); American Steamship Owners Protection & Indemnity Association, Inc.; Coca-Cola, Ltd.; Scott Worldwide Inc.; Hong Kong Bank of Canada.

For Complete List of Firm Personnel, See General Section

For full biographical listings, see the Martindale-Hubbell Law Directory

CANADA ONTARIO

KITCHENER, Regional Munic. of Waterloo

GIFFEN, LEE, WAGNER, MORLEY & GARBUTT (AV)

50 Queen Street North, P.O. Box 2396, N2H 6M3
Telephone: 519-578-4150
Fax: 519-578-8740

MEMBERS OF FIRM

Jeffrey J. Mansfield (1955-1991)
J. Peter Giffen, Q.C.
Bruce L. Lee
J. Scott Morley
Brian R. Wagner
Philip A. Garbutt

ASSOCIATES

Edward J. Vanderkloet
Keith C. Masterman
Daniel J. Fife
Jeffrey W. Boich

For full biographical listings, see the Martindale-Hubbell Law Directory

*TORONTO,** Regional Munic. of York

BORDEN & ELLIOT (AV)

Barristers & Solicitors
Scotia Plaza, 40 King Street West, M5H 3Y4
Telephone: 416-367-6000
Telecopier: 416-367-6749
Internet: @ borden.com
A Member of the national association of Borden DuMoulin Howard Gervais, comprising Borden & Elliot in Toronto, Ontario, Russell & DuMoulin in Vancouver, British Columbia, Howard, Mackie in Calgary, Alberta and Mackenzie Gervais in Montréal, Québec. Borden DuMoulin Howard Gervais also operates an office in London, England.

MEMBER AND ASSOCIATES

William T. Pashby

For Complete List of Firm Personnel, See General Section

For full biographical listings, see the Martindale-Hubbell Law Directory

CANADA
PRINCE EDWARD ISLAND

*CHARLOTTETOWN,** Queen's Co.

CAMPBELL, LEA, MICHAEL, MCCONNELL & PIGOT (AV)

15 Queen Street, P.O. Box 429, C1A 7K7
Telephone: 902-566-3400
Telecopier: 902-566-9266

MEMBERS OF FIRM

Paul D. Michael, Q.C.
Robert A. McConnell
Ross D. Pigot
Kenneth L. Godfrey

General Counsel in Prince Edward Island for: Canadian Imperial Bank of Commerce; Maritime Electric Co., Ltd.; Michelin Tires (Canada) Ltd.; Newsco Investments Ltd. (Dundas Farms); Queen Elizabeth Hospital Inc.; Imperial Oil Limited; General Motors of Canada; Co-op Atlantic; Liberty Mutual; Employers Reinsurance Group.

For Complete List of Firm Personnel, See General Section

For full biographical listings, see the Martindale-Hubbell Law Directory

CANADA
QUEBEC

*MONTREAL,** Montreal Dist.

LENGVARI BRAMAN BARBACKI MOREAU, S.E.N.C. (AV)

Suite 2707, One Place Ville Marie, H3B 4G4
Telephone: 514-871-9770
Telecopier: 514-866-4773

George F. Lengvari, Jr., Q.C.
Frederick A. Braman
Richard Barbacki
Bernard Moreau
Albert Zoltowski
Pascale Houde
Daniela L. Villatora
Jean-Bertrand Giroux
Seti K. Hamalian
Nathalie Marchand

OF COUNSEL

Jacques Marchessault, Q.C.
Seymour D. Steinman
Harold Dizgun

For full biographical listings, see the Martindale-Hubbell Law Directory

CANADA
SASKATCHEWAN

*REGINA,** Regina Jud. Centre

MACPHERSON LESLIE & TYERMAN (AV)

1500-1874 Scarth Street, S4P 4E9
Telephone: 306-347-8000
Telecopier: 306-352-5250
Saskatoon, Saskatchewan Office: 1500-410 22nd Street East, S7K 5T6.
Telephone: 306-975-7100.
Telecopier: 306-975-7145.

MEMBERS OF FIRM

Carl A. P. Wagner
Donald K. Wilson
Alain J. Gaucher (Resident Saskatoon Office)
James S. Kerby (Resident, Saskatoon Office)
Robert B. Pletch, Q.C.
Garret J. Oledzki
Douglas A. Ballou
Danny R. Anderson (Resident, Saskatoon Office)

For Complete List of Firm Personnel, See General Section

For full biographical listings, see the Martindale-Hubbell Law Directory

MEXICO

MONTERREY, NUEVO LEÓN,

Monterrey, Nuevo León

THOMPSON & KNIGHT, A PROFESSIONAL CORPORATION

(Attorneys and Counselors)
Edificio Losoles PD-4, Av. Lázaro Cárdenas No. 2400 PTE San Pedro Garza Garcia, Monterrey, Nuevo León 66220
Telephone: (52-8) 363-0096
Telecopy: (52-8) 363-3067
Dallas, Texas Office: 1700 Pacific Avenue, Suite 3300, 75201.
Telephone: 214-969-1700.
Telecopy: 214-969-1751.
Cable Address: "Tomtex."
Telex: 732298.
Austin, Texas Office: 1200 San Jacinto Center, 98 San Jacinto Boulevard, 78701.
Telephone: 512-469-6100.
Telecopy: 512-469-6180.
Fort Worth, Texas Office: 801 Cherry Street, Suite 1600, 76102.
Telephone: 817-347-1700.
Telecopy: 817-347-1799.
Houston, Texas Office: 1700 Texas Commerce Tower, 600 Travis, 77002.
Telephone: 713-217-2800.
Telecopy: 713-217-2828; 713-217-2882.

SHAREHOLDERS

Michael C. Titens

For Complete List of Firm Personnel, See General Section

For full biographical listings, see the Martindale-Hubbell Law Directory

CIVIL TRIAL PRACTICE

ALABAMA

ALBERTVILLE, Marshall Co.

GULLAHORN & HARE, P.C. (AV)
310 West Main Street, P.O. Box 1669, 35950
Telephone: 205-878-1891
FAX: 205-878-1965

Charles R. Hare, Jr. — John C. Gullahorn

Representative Clients: First Bank of Boaz; The Home Bank; Bank of Albertville; Peoples Independent Bank of Boaz; AmSouth Bank; Compass Bank of the South; Albertville Industrial Development Board; Boaz Industrial Development Board; Marshall-Dekalb Electric Cooperative; Olympia Construction, Inc.

For full biographical listings, see the Martindale-Hubbell Law Directory

*ANNISTON,** Calhoun Co.

BURNHAM, KLINEFELTER, HALSEY, JONES & CATER, P.C. (AV)
South Trust Bank Building, Suite 401, P.O. Box 1618, 36202
Telephone: 205-237-8515
Fax: 205-236-5150

H. R. Burnham
J. L. Klinefelter
William S. Halsey
Richard H. Cater
Patrick S. Burnham
Thomas M. Sowa
J. Thomas Corbett
C. David Stubbs
Cynthia M. Calhoun
Polly D. Enger (Not admitted in AL)

Representative Clients: Alfa Insurance Cos.; American International Insurance Group; Alabama Municipal Insurance Corp.; Fireman's Fund; SouthTrust Bank of Calhoun County, N.A.; America's First Credit Union; First South Production Credit; Calhoun County, Anniston City and City of Jacksonville Boards of Education; Calhoun County Commission; Coca-Cola Enterprises, Inc.

For Complete List of Firm Personnel, See General Section

For full biographical listings, see the Martindale-Hubbell Law Directory

*BIRMINGHAM,** Jefferson Co.

BAINBRIDGE, MIMS & ROGERS (AV)
The Luckie Building, Suite 415, 600 Luckie Drive, P.O. Box 530886, 35253
Telephone: 205-879-1100
Fax: 205-879-4300

MEMBERS OF FIRM

Walter L. Mims (1910-1993)
Frank M. Bainbridge
Bruce F. Rogers

For Complete List of Firm Personnel, See General Section

For full biographical listings, see the Martindale-Hubbell Law Directory

BALCH & BINGHAM (AV)
1710 Sixth Avenue North, P.O. Box 306, 35201
Telephone: 205-251-8100
Facsimile: 205-226-8798
Other Birmingham, Alabama Office: 1901 Sixth Avenue North, 35203.
Telephone: 205-251-8100.
Facsimile: 205-226-8799.
Montgomery, Alabama Office: The Winter Building, 2 Dexter Avenue, 36101.
Telephone: 205-834-6500.
Facsimile: 205-269-3115.
Huntsville, Alabama Office: Suite 810, 200 West Court Square, 35801.
Telephone: 205-551-0171.
Facsimile: 205-551-0174.
Washington, D.C. Office: Suite 800, 1101 Connecticut Avenue, N.W., 20036.
Telephone: 202-296-0387.
Facsimile: 202-452-8180.

(See Next Column)

MEMBERS OF FIRM

James O. Spencer, Jr.
Michael L. Edwards
Marshall Timberlake
John P. Scott, Jr.
S. Allen Baker, Jr.
Steven F. Casey
James A. Bradford
Alan T. Rogers
M. Stanford Blanton
Will Hill Tankersley, Jr.
Cavender Crosby Kimble

ASSOCIATES

Julia S. McIntyre
Michael D. Freeman
Suzanne Alldredge
Gregory Carl Cook
Debra Carter White
David B. Block
Leigh Anne Hodge

Counsel for: Alabama Power Co.; Blue Cross and Blue Shield of Alabama; The Boeing Company; Brasfield & Gorrie, Inc.; Compass Bancshares, Inc.; Harbert Corp.; Kimberly-Clark Corp.; Southern Company Services, Inc.; Southern Research Institute; Vesta Insurance Group, Inc.

For Complete List of Firm Personnel, See General Section

For full biographical listings, see the Martindale-Hubbell Law Directory

BARNETT, NOBLE, HANES, O'NEAL & DUFFEE (AV)
Suite 1600 City Federal Building, 2026 Second Avenue North, 35203
Telephone: 205-322-0471; 205-322-0484

MEMBERS OF FIRM

Robert C. Barnett
G. William Noble
Thomas B. Hanes
James P. O'Neal
Cecil G. Duffee
Frederick Mott Garfield, Jr.
Janice G. Formato

OF COUNSEL

Arthur J. Hanes

Counsel for: City of Gardendale; State of Alabama Highway Department.
Approved Attorneys for: Alabama Title Co., Inc.

For full biographical listings, see the Martindale-Hubbell Law Directory

BERKOWITZ, LEFKOVITS, ISOM & KUSHNER, A PROFESSIONAL CORPORATION (AV)
1600 SouthTrust Tower, 420 North Twentieth Street, 35203
Telephone: 205-328-0480
Telecopier: 205-322-8007

Lee H. Zell
Henry I. Frohsin
Susan S. Wagner
Patricia Clotfelter
Frank S. James III
Wesley C. Redmond

Lisa Wright Borden
Vincent R. Ledlow
Michael R. Silberman
Lisa B. Singer

Representative Clients: AlaTenn Resources, Inc.; AlaTenn Natural Gas Co.; B.A.S.S., Inc.; Hanna Steel Co., Inc.; Liberty Trouser Co., Inc.; McDonald's Corp.; Parisian, Inc.; Southern Pipe & Supply Co., Inc.

For Complete List of Firm Personnel, See General Section

For full biographical listings, see the Martindale-Hubbell Law Directory

BRADLEY, ARANT, ROSE & WHITE (AV)
1400 Park Place Tower, 2001 Park Place, 35203
Telephone: 205-521-8000
Telex: 494-1324
Facsimile: 205-251-8611, 251-8665, 252-0264
Facsimile (Southtrust Office): 205-251-9915
Huntsville, Alabama Office: 200 Clinton Avenue West, Suite 900.
Telephone: 205-517-5100.
Facsimile: 205-533-5069.

MEMBERS OF FIRM

John H. Morrow
Hobart A. McWhorter, Jr.
Macbeth Wagnon, Jr.
Thad Gladden Long
A. H. Gaede, Jr.
James W. Gewin
Brittin Turner Coleman
E. Mabry Rogers
Walter H. Monroe, III
Andrew J. Noble, III
Walter J. Sears, III
Linda A. Friedman
Robert K. Spotswood
Joseph B. Mays, Jr.
Scott M. Phelps
Norman Jetmundsen, Jr.
Joseph S. Bird, III
John D. Watson, III
Jay D. St. Clair
Patricia Trott Mandt
G. Edward Cassady, III
Michael R. Pennington
Michael D. McKibben
David Glenn Hymer
Sid J. Trant
Stewart M. Cox
Axel Bolvig III

COUNSEL

Stanley D. Bynum

ASSOCIATES

Forrest K. Covington
Philip J. Carroll III
James S. Christie, Jr.
John E. Goodman
T. Michael Brown
Michael S. Denniston
George Bryan Harris
Susan Donovan Josey
J. Patrick Darby
Frank M. Caprio (Resident, Huntsville Office)
Denise Avery Dodson

(See Next Column)

BRADLEY, ARANT, ROSE & WHITE, *Birmingham—Continued*

ASSOCIATES (Continued)

Matthew H. Lembke
Richard H. Monk III
Amy K. Myers
John W. Smith T
James W. Davis
James F. Archibald, III
Justin T. McDonald
Douglas E. Eckert
Kenneth M. Perry

Representative Clients: Ford Motor Co.; Volkswagen of America; Chrysler Corp.; The Firestone Tire & Rubber Co.; The Goodyear Tire & Rubber Co.; Torchmark Corp.; Lincoln National Life Insurance Co.; J. I. Case Co.; Monsanto Co.; A. H. Robins Co.

For Complete List of Firm Personnel, See General Section

For full biographical listings, see the Martindale-Hubbell Law Directory

BURR & FORMAN (AV)

3000 SouthTrust Tower, 420 North 20th Street, 35203
Telephone: 205-251-3000
Telecopier: 205-458-5100
Huntsville, Alabama Office: Suite 204, Regency Center, 400 Meridian Street.
Telephone: 205-551-0010.

MEMBERS OF FIRM

C. V. Stelzenmuller
Robert G. Tate
J. Fredric Ingram
William C. Knight, Jr.
John D. Clements
John F. DeBuys, Jr.
James Ross Forman, III
D. Frank Davis
William F. Murray, Jr.
James J. Robinson
Joseph W. Letzer
T. Thomas Cottingham, III
J. Patrick Logan
Gary M. London
F. A. Flowers, III
Michael L. Lucas
J. Hunter Phillips, III
Carol H. Stewart
Robert H. Rutherford, Jr.
Henry Graham Beene
Richard A. Freese
John C. Morrow
Victor L. Hayslip
E. Clayton Lowe, Jr.
Robert S. W. Given
Mark McCarroll Lawson
Dent M. Morton
Sue Ann Willis

OF COUNSEL

A. Jackson Noble, Jr.

ASSOCIATES

Paul P. Bolus
David A. Elliott
Harri J. Haikala
Frank Hampton McFadden, Jr.
Christopher W. Weller
Jennifer M. Busby
James A. Taylor, Jr.
Gerald P. Gillespy
Timothy M. Lupinacci
Edwin O. Rogers

For Complete List of Firm Personnel, See General Section

For full biographical listings, see the Martindale-Hubbell Law Directory

CABANISS, JOHNSTON, GARDNER, DUMAS & O'NEAL (AV)

Park Place Tower, 2001 Park Place North, Suite 700, P.O. Box 830612, 35283-0612
Telephone: 205-252-8800
Telecopier: 205-716-5389
Mobile, Alabama Office: 700 AmSouth Center, P.O. Box 2906.
Telephone: 205-433-6961.
Telecopier: 205-433-1060.

MEMBERS OF FIRM

William F. Gardner
Crawford S. McGivaren, Jr.
Sydney F. Frazier, Jr.
William A. Robinson
William K. Thomas
R. Carlton Smyly
Steve A. Tucker
R. Taylor Abbot, Jr.

COUNSEL

L. Murray Alley

ASSOCIATE

Cecil H. Macoy, Jr.

Counsel for: Alabaster Industries, Inc.; Schuler Industries, Inc.; Carraway Methodist Hospitals of Alabama; Doster Construction Co., Inc.; Liberty Mutual Insurance Co.; John Alden Life Insurance Co.; MacMillan Bloedel Inc.; Norfolk Southern Corp.; O'Neal Steel, Inc.

For Complete List of Firm Personnel, See General Section

For full biographical listings, see the Martindale-Hubbell Law Directory

COOPER, MITCH, CRAWFORD, KUYKENDALL & WHATLEY (AV)

1100 Financial Center, 505 20th Street North, 35203-2605
Telephone: 205-328-9576
Telecopier: 205-328-9669

MEMBERS OF FIRM

Jerome A. Cooper
William E. Mitch
Thomas N. Crawford, Jr.
Frederick T. Kuykendall, III
Joe R. Whatley, Jr.
John D. Saxon
Glen M. Connor
Patricia Guthrie Fraley
Jay Smith
(On Leave of Absence)

(See Next Column)

ASSOCIATES

Candis A. McGowan
Andrew C. Allen
William Z. Cullen
Samuel H. Heldman
Hilary E. Ball-Walker
Patrick F. Clark
G. Patterson Keahey
Maureen Kane Berg
Gerald B. Taylor, Jr.
Rebecca Higgins Hunt
Marcel L. Debruge
Peter H. Burke

Counsel for: United Steelworkers of America, AFL-CIO; United Mine Workers of America, District 20; Birmingham Plumbers & Steamfitters Local Union No. 91 Pension Fund.
Reference: AMSouth Bank of Birmingham.

For full biographical listings, see the Martindale-Hubbell Law Directory

DOMINICK, FLETCHER, YEILDING, WOOD & LLOYD, P.A. (AV)

2121 Highland Avenue, 35205
Telephone: 205-939-0033

J. Fred Wood, Jr.
Harold L. Ferguson, Jr.
Sammye Oden Kok
B. Boozer Downs, Jr.
J. Mitchell Frost, Jr.

John W. Dodson

Counsel for: Citizens Federal Savings Bank; Title Insurance Corporation; St. Vincent's Hospital; Birmingham-Southern College; Castle Mortgage Corporation; Methodist Homes for the Aging.

For Complete List of Firm Personnel, See General Section

For full biographical listings, see the Martindale-Hubbell Law Directory

HARDIN & HAWKINS (AV)

A Partnership including a Professional Corporation
2201 Arlington Avenue, 35205
Telephone: 205-930-6900
1-800-368-1960
Telecopier: 205-930-6910
Mailing Address: P.O. Box 55705, 35255-5705

Edward L. Hardin, Jr. (P.C.)
Kevin John Hawkins

ASSOCIATES

Belinda Masdon Kimble
W. Lee Gresham, III
Jill T. Karle

OF COUNSEL

Hubert A. Grissom, Jr.

For full biographical listings, see the Martindale-Hubbell Law Directory

HARRIS, EVANS, BERG & ROGERS, P.C. (AV)

Historic 2007 Building, 2007 Third Avenue North, 35203-2366
Telephone: 205-328-2366
Telecopier: 205-328-0013

Lyman H. Harris
Judy Whalen Evans
Lonette Lamb Berg
Susan Rogers

Matthew J. Dougherty
David L. Selby, II
Jeffrey K. Hollis
Stephen J. Bumgarner

For full biographical listings, see the Martindale-Hubbell Law Directory

HASKELL SLAUGHTER YOUNG & JOHNSTON, PROFESSIONAL ASSOCIATION (AV)

1200 AmSouth/Harbert Plaza, 1901 Sixth Avenue North, 35203
Telephone: 205-251-1000
Facsimile: 205-324-1133
Montgomery, Alabama Office: Haskell Slaughter Young Johnston & Gallion. Bailey Building, Suite 375, 400 South Union Street, P.O. Box 4660. 36104
Telephone: 205-265-8573.
Facsimile: 205-264-7945.

William M. Slaughter
Frank M. Young, III
Thomas T. Gallion, III (Resident, Montgomery Office)
James C. Huckaby, Jr.
Stephen L. Poer
Beverly P. Baker
Richard H. Walston
Charles A. McCallum, III
Constance A. Caldwell (Resident, Montgomery Office)

Michael K. K. Choy
Carter H. Dukes
R. Scott Williams
Barry D. Woodham

Representative Clients: Beech Aircraft Corp.; The Equitable Life Assurance Society of the United States; Exxon Corporation; Federal Deposit Insurance Corporation/Resolution Trust Corporation; Fireman's Fund Insurance Companies; Jones Plumbing Systems, Inc.; Marshall Durbuin Companies; Montgomery County, Alabama; Ridout's-Brown-Service Inc.; Shoney's, Inc.

For Complete List of Firm Personnel, See General Section

For full biographical listings, see the Martindale-Hubbell Law Directory

LIGHTFOOT, FRANKLIN, WHITE & LUCAS (AV)

300 Financial Center, 505 20th Street North, 35203-2706
Telephone: 205-581-0700
Facsimile: 205-581-0799

(See Next Column)

LIGHTFOOT, FRANKLIN, WHITE & LUCAS—*Continued*

MEMBERS OF FIRM

Warren B. Lightfoot
Samuel H. Franklin
Jere F. White, Jr.
William R. Lucas, Jr.
Mac M. Moorer
John M. Johnson
M. Christian King
E. Glenn Waldrop, Jr.
Adam K. Peck
Harlan I. Prater, IV

ASSOCIATES

Michael L. Bell
William S. Cox, III
William H. King, III
Sabrina A. Simon
Madeline H. Haikala
Sarah Bruce Jackson
William H. Brooks
S. Douglas Williams, Jr.
J. Banks Sewell, III
Lee M. Hollis
Kim A. Craddock
Wynn M. Shuford
John P. Dulin, Jr.

Counsel for: AT&T; Ford Motor Co.; Emerson Electric Co.; Monsanto Co.; Chrysler Corp.; Unocal Corp.; The Upjohn Co.; Bristol-Myers Squibb Co.; The Goodyear Tire & Rubber Co.; Mitsubishi Motor Sales of America, Inc.

For full biographical listings, see the Martindale-Hubbell Law Directory

PATRICK & LACY, P.C. (AV)

1201 Financial Center, 35203
Telephone: 205-323-5665
Telecopier: 205-324-6221

J. Vernon Patrick, Jr.
Alex S. Lacy
William M. Acker, III
Elizabeth N. Pitman
Joseph A. Cartee

For full biographical listings, see the Martindale-Hubbell Law Directory

PORTERFIELD, HARPER & MILLS, P.A. (AV)

22 Inverness Center Parkway, Suite 600, P.O. Box 530790, 35253-0790
Telephone: 205-980-5000
Fax: 205-980-5001

Jack B. Porterfield, Jr.
Larry W. Harper
William T. Mills, II
William Dudley Motlow, Jr.
Stanley K. Smith
Philip F. Hutcheson
H. C. "Trey" Ireland, III
Keith Pflaum

Connie Shaw Granata
Michael L. Haggard

Representative Clients: CIGNA; Equitable Life Assurance Society of the U.S.; Figge International; The Hanover Insurance Co.; Ingersoll-Rand Co.; New York Life Insurance Co.; The St. Paul Insurance Co.; Terex Corp.; The Travelers.

For Complete List of Firm Personnel, See General Section

For full biographical listings, see the Martindale-Hubbell Law Directory

PRITCHARD, MCCALL & JONES (AV)

800 Financial Center, 35203
Telephone: 205-328-9190

MEMBERS OF FIRM

William S. Pritchard (1890-1967)
Alexander W. Jones (1914-1988)
William S. Pritchard, Jr.
Madison W. O'Kelley, Jr.
Julian P. Hardy, Jr.
Alexander W. Jones, Jr.
F. Hilton-Green Tomlinson
James G. Henderson
William S. Pritchard, III

ASSOCIATES

Michael L. McKerley
Robert Bond Higgins
Nina Michele LaFleur
Mary W. Burge

Representative Clients: First National Bank of Columbiana; Central State Bank of Calera; Buffalo Rock-Pepsi-Cola Bottling Co.; Gillis Advertising, Inc.; Liberty Mutual Insurance Co.; Reliance Insurance Company; SouthTrust Bank, N.A.; Bromberg & Company, Inc.; Farmers Furniture Company; First Commercial Bank.

For full biographical listings, see the Martindale-Hubbell Law Directory

REDDEN, MILLS & CLARK (AV)

940 First Alabama Bank Building, 35203
Telephone: 205-322-0457
Fax: 205-322-8481

MEMBERS OF FIRM

L. Drew Redden
William H. Mills
William N. Clark
Gerald L. Miller
Stephen W. Shaw

ASSOCIATES

Maxwell H. Pulliam, Jr.
Joseph H. Hilley

References: SouthTrust Bank; First Alabama Bank.

For full biographical listings, see the Martindale-Hubbell Law Directory

SCHOEL, OGLE, BENTON AND CENTENO (AV)

600 Financial Center, 505 North 20th Street, P.O. Box 1865, 35201-1865
Telephone: 205-521-7000
Telecopier: 205-521-7007

MEMBERS OF FIRM

Jerry W. Schoel
Richard F. Ogle
Lee R. Benton
Paul A. Liles
Douglas J. Centeno
Melinda Murphy Dionne
Gilbert M. Sullivan, Jr.
David O. Upshaw
Paul Avron
Lynn McCreery Shaw

Reference: National Bank of Commerce; First Alabama Bank.

For full biographical listings, see the Martindale-Hubbell Law Directory

SIROTE & PERMUTT, P.C. (AV)

2222 Arlington Avenue, South, P.O. Box 55727, 35255
Telephone: 205-933-7111
Facsimile: 205-930-5301
Huntsville, Alabama Office: 200 Clinton Avenue, N.W., Suite 1000.
Telephone: 205-536-1711.
Facsimile: 205-534-9650.
Mobile, Alabama Office: One St. Louis Centre, Suite 1000.
Telephone: 205-432-1671.
Facsimile: 205-434-0196.
Montgomery, Alabama Office: Colonial Commerce Center, Suite 305 One Commerce Street.
Telephone: 205-261-3400.
Facsimile: 205-261-3434.
Tuscaloosa, Alabama Office: 2216 14th Street.
Telephone: 205-752-2089.

Jerry E. Held
J. Mason Davis
C. Lee Reeves
David M. Wooldridge
Rodney A. Max
George M. (Jack) Neal, Jr.
John R. Chiles
Charles R. Driggars
Kaye Houser Turberville
Greggory M. Deitsch
Daniel J. Burnick
Rodney E. Nolen
Robert R. Baugh
J. Rushton McClees
Thomas G. Tutten, Jr.
W. McCollum Halcomb
C. Randal Johnson
Jeffrey H. Wertheim
Donna Bowling Nathan
David W. Long
James Sarven Williams

Representative Clients: International Business Machines (IBM); General Motors Corp.; Colonial Bank; Bruno's, Inc.; University of Alabama Hospitals; Westinghouse Electric Corp.; First Alabama Bank; Monsanto Chemical Company; South Central Bell; Prudential Insurance Company; American Home Products, Inc.; Minnesota Mining and Manufacturing, Inc. (3M).

For Complete List of Firm Personnel, See General Section

For full biographical listings, see the Martindale-Hubbell Law Directory

SPAIN, GILLON, GROOMS, BLAN & NETTLES (AV)

The Zinszer Building, 2117 2nd Avenue North, 35203
Telephone: 205-328-4100
Telecopier: 205-324-8866

MEMBERS OF FIRM

H. Hobart Grooms, Jr.
Ollie L. Blan, Jr.
Bert S. Nettles
Allwin E. Horn, III
Eugene P. Stutts
Alton B. Parker, Jr.
Charles D. Stewart
Elizabeth Ann McMahan
J. Mark Hart
Thomas M. Eden, III
James A. Kee, Jr.

General Counsel for: Liberty National Life Insurance Co.; United States Fidelity & Guaranty Co.; Piggly Wiggly Alabama Distributing Co.; AmSouth Mortgage Co., Inc.; Alabama Insurance Guaranty Association; Alabama Life and Disability Insurance Guaranty Association; Alabama Insurance Underwriters Association.
Counsel for: The Prudential Insurance Company of America; Government Employees Insurance Co.; Massachusetts Mutual Life Insurance Co.

For Complete List of Firm Personnel, See General Section

For full biographical listings, see the Martindale-Hubbell Law Directory

STARNES & ATCHISON (AV)

100 Brookwood Place, P.O. Box 598512, 35259-8512
Telephone: 205-868-6000
Telecopier: 205-868-6099

MEMBERS OF FIRM

W. Stancil Starnes
W. Michael Atchison
William Anthony Davis, III
Michael A. Florie
L. Graves Stiff, III
E. Martin Bloom
J. Bentley Owens, III
Walter William Bates
Michael K. Wright
Michael K. Beard
Robert P. Mackenzie, III
Jeffrey E. Friedman

(See Next Column)

STARNES & ATCHISON, *Birmingham—Continued*

ASSOCIATES

Steven T. McMeekin
Joe L. Leak
Mark W. Macoy

Representative Clients: Drummond Co., Inc.; Mobile Infirmary Medical Center; National Bank of Commerce; Hoffman-La Roche, Inc.; International Playtex, Inc.; Honda North America, Inc.; TLT Babcock; Business Council of Alabama; Weyerhauser, Inc.; AIG Aviation.

For full biographical listings, see the Martindale-Hubbell Law Directory

*CHATOM,** Washington Co.

TURNER, ONDERDONK, KIMBROUGH & HOWELL, P.A. (AV)

100 Central Avenue, P.O. Drawer 1389, 36518
Telephone: 334-847-2237
Fax: 334-847-3115
Mobile, Alabama Office: 1359 Dauphin Street, P.O. Box 2821.
Telephone: 205-432-2855.
Fax: 205-432-2863.

Edward P. Turner, Jr.
A. Michael Onderdonk
William A. Kimbrough, Jr. (Resident, Mobile Office)
Gordon K. Howell
Marc E. Bradley (Resident, Mobile Office)

Halron W. Turner
Frank Woodson (Resident, Mobile Office)
David M. Huggins (Resident, Mobile Office)
E. Tatum Turner

For full biographical listings, see the Martindale-Hubbell Law Directory

*CULLMAN,** Cullman Co.

ST. JOHN & ST. JOHN (AV)

108 Third Street South East, P.O. Drawer K, 35055
Telephone: 205-734-3542; 734-3543
Fax: 205-734-3544

MEMBERS OF FIRM

F. E. St. John (1874-1943)
Finis E. St. John (1909-1984)
Finis E. St. John, III (1933-1984)
Juliet G. St. John
Finis E. St. John, IV

Attorneys for: CSX Transportation, Inc.; U.S. Fidelity & Guaranty Co.; Alabama Power Co.; Golden-Rod Broilers, Inc.; Travelers Insurance Cos.; South Central Bell Telephone Co.; Liberty Mutual Insurance Cos.; ALFA Mutual Insurance Co.; First Federal Savings & Loan.

For Complete List of Firm Personnel, See General Section

For full biographical listings, see the Martindale-Hubbell Law Directory

*DOTHAN,** Houston Co.

COBB & SHEALY, P.A. (AV)

206 North Lena Street, P.O. Box 6346, 36302
Telephone: 334-794-8526
Fax: 334-677-0030

Herman W. Cobb
Steadman S. Shealy, Jr.
Brad E. Mendheim
Julie Sorrells

OF COUNSEL

Joey Hornsby

Representative Clients: Travelers Insurance; Nationwide Insurance; Auto-Owners, Ins.; Employers Casualty of Texas; Safeco Insurance; Federated Insurance; Universal Underwriters; National Security Ins.; Great Central Ins.
Approved Title Attorneys for: Lawyers Title Insurance Corp.

For full biographical listings, see the Martindale-Hubbell Law Directory

LEE & MCINISH (AV)

238 West Main Street, P.O. Box 1665, 36302
Telephone: 334-792-4156
Facsimile: 334-794-8342

MEMBERS OF FIRM

W. L. Lee (1873-1944)
Alto V. Lee, III (1915-1987)
William L. Lee, III
Alan C. Livingston
William C. Carn, III
Peter A. McInish
Jerry M. White

OF COUNSEL

H. Dwight McInish

Counsel for: Seaboard Coast Line Railroad Co.; Atlanta & St. Andrews Bay Railroad Co.; ALFA; U. S. F. & G. Co.; Maryland Casualty Co.; Continental Insurance Cos.; Royal-Globe Group; Slocomb National Bank; The Federal Land Bank of Jackson; GTE South.

For full biographical listings, see the Martindale-Hubbell Law Directory

RUFUS R. SMITH JR. & ASSOCIATES (AV)

103 South St. Andrews Street, P.O. Box 6629, 36302
Telephone: 334-671-7959
Fax: 334-671-7957

ASSOCIATE

William C. Maddox

For full biographical listings, see the Martindale-Hubbell Law Directory

ENTERPRISE, Coffee Co.

CASSADY, FULLER & MARSH (AV)

203 East Lee Avenue, P.O. Box 780, 36331
Telephone: 334-347-2626
Telecopier: 334-393-1396

MEMBERS OF FIRM

Joe C. Cassady
Kenneth T. Fuller
M. Dale Marsh
Joe C. Cassady, Jr.
Mark E. Fuller

Representative Clients: First Alabama Bank; Enterprise Hospital Board; Sessions Co., Inc.; Allstate; State Farm Mutual Insurance Co.; Coffee County Bank.
Approved Attorneys for: First American Title Insurance Co.

For full biographical listings, see the Martindale-Hubbell Law Directory

J. E. SAWYER, JR. (AV)

203 South Edwards Street, P.O. Box 720, 36331-0720
Telephone: 334-347-6447
Fax: 334-347-8217

For full biographical listings, see the Martindale-Hubbell Law Directory

FAIRHOPE, Baldwin Co.

THE FOSTER LAW FIRM, P.A. (AV)

101 North Section Street, P.O. Box 1499, 36533-1499
Telephone: 334-928-8855
Fax: 334-928-4224
Foley, Alabama Office: 315 E. Laurel Avenue, Suite 314 A.
Telephone: 205-943-4500.
Fax: 205-943-6100.

J. Don Foster

OF COUNSEL

Elizabeth C. Campbell

For full biographical listings, see the Martindale-Hubbell Law Directory

*FLORENCE,** Lauderdale Co.

SELF & SELF (AV)

408 West Dr. Hicks Boulevard, P.O. Box 1062, 35631
Telephone: 205-767-2570; 1-800-336-2574
Fax: 205 767-2632

MEMBERS OF FIRM

Henry (Hank) H. Self, Jr.
Gilbert P. Self

OF COUNSEL

Barry Mansell

Reference: Bank Independent; AmSouth Bank; Central Bank of the South.

For full biographical listings, see the Martindale-Hubbell Law Directory

*FORT PAYNE,** De Kalb Co.

SCRUGGS, JORDAN & DODD, P.A. (AV)

207 Alabama Avenue, South, P.O. Box 1109, 35967
Telephone: 205-845-5932
Fax: 205-845-4325

William D. Scruggs, Jr.
Robert K. Jordan
David Dodd
E. Allen Dodd, Jr.

Representative Clients: State Farm Insurance Company; Allstate Insurance Co., Inc.; USF&G Insurance Co.; Nucor, Inc.; Ladd Engineering, Inc.; ALABAMA Band; First Federal Savings & Loan Association of Dekalb County; Fritz Structural Steel, Inc.; Williamson Oil Co., Inc.

For full biographical listings, see the Martindale-Hubbell Law Directory

*GADSDEN,** Etowah Co.

DORTCH, WRIGHT & WRIGHT (AV)

239 College Street, P.O. Box 405, 35902
Telephone: 205-546-4616

MEMBERS OF FIRM

Curtis Wright
Curtis Wright, II

Attorneys for: St. Paul Insurance Cos.; Employers Insurance of Wausau; Mutual Assurance Society of Alabama; State Farm Insurance Cos.; Alabama Hospital Association Trust; Mutual Savings Life Insurance Co.; Lawyers Title Insurance Corp.; Nationwide Mutual Insurance Co.; Government Employees Insurance Co.; CSX Transportation Systems.

(See Next Column)

DORTCH, WRIGHT & WRIGHT—*Continued*

For Complete List of Firm Personnel, See General Section

For full biographical listings, see the Martindale-Hubbell Law Directory

FLOYD, KEENER, CUSIMANO & ROBERTS, P.C. (AV)

816 Chestnut Street, P.O. Box 49, 35902
Telephone: 205-547-6328
Fax: 205-546-8173

Jack Floyd
Gregory S. Cusimano
Larry H. Keener
Michael L. Roberts
David A. Kimberley

Mary Ann Ross Stackhouse
John D. Floyd

For Complete List of Firm Personnel, See General Section

For full biographical listings, see the Martindale-Hubbell Law Directory

FORD & HUNTER, P.C. (AV)

The Lancaster Building, 645 Walnut Street, Suite 5, P.O. Box 388, 35902
Telephone: 205-546-5432
Fax: 205-546-5435

George P. Ford
J. Gullatte Hunter, III

Richard M. Blythe

References: General Motors Acceptance Corp.; AmSouth Bank, N.A.

For Complete List of Firm Personnel, See General Section

For full biographical listings, see the Martindale-Hubbell Law Directory

INZER, STIVENDER, HANEY & JOHNSON, P.A. (AV)

(Inzer, Suttle, Swann & Stivender)
(Lusk, Swann, Burns & Stivender)
(Inzer, Suttle & Inzer)
Second Floor, Compass Bank Building, 601 Broad Street, P.O. Drawer 287, 35999-0287
Telephone: 205-546-1656
Telecopier: 205-546-1093

James C. Stivender
James C. Inzer, III
W. Roscoe Johnson, III
F. Michael Haney
Robert D. McWhorter, Jr.

James W. McGlaughn

Assistant Division Counsel for: Southern Railway System.
Attorneys for: L & N Railroad; General Motors Corp.; Goodyear Tire & Rubber Corp.; Alabama Power Co.; Insurance Company of North America; Allstate Insurance Co.; Travelers Insurance Co.; Liberty Mutual Insurance Co.; Home Insurance Co.

For Complete List of Firm Personnel, See General Section

For full biographical listings, see the Martindale-Hubbell Law Directory

SIMMONS, BRUNSON, SASSER AND CALLIS, ATTORNEYS, P.A. (AV)

1411 Rainbow Drive, P.O. Box 1189, 35902
Telephone: 205-546-9206
Telecopier: 205-546-8091

Clarence Simmons, Jr.
Steve P. Brunson
James T. Sasser

Rebecca A. Walker

Attorneys for: Preferred Risk Mutual Insurance Co.; ALFA Mutual Insurance Co.; Royal Insurance Cos.
Approved Attorneys for: Lawyers Title Insurance Corp.; Mississippi Valley Title Insurance Co.

For Complete List of Firm Personnel, See General Section

For full biographical listings, see the Martindale-Hubbell Law Directory

HALEYVILLE, Winston Co.

JAMES, LOWE & MOBLEY (AV)

1210-21st Street, P.O. Box 576, 35565
Telephone: 205-486-5296
Fax: 205-486-4531

MEMBERS OF FIRM

Walter Joe James, Jr. (1923-1990)
John W. Lowe
Jeffery A. Mobley
Robert B. Aderholt

Representative Clients: Traders & Farmers Bank; Burdick-West Memorial Hospital.

(See Next Column)

Approved Attorneys for: Lawyers Title Insurance Corp.

For full biographical listings, see the Martindale-Hubbell Law Directory

*HUNTSVILLE,** Madison Co.

BRADLEY, ARANT, ROSE & WHITE (AV)

200 Clinton Avenue West, Suite 900, 35801
Telephone: 205-517-5100
Facsimile: 205-533-5069
Birmingham, Alabama Office: 1400 Park Place Tower, 2001 Park Place.
Telephone: 205-521-8000.
Telex: 494-1324.
Facsimile: 205-251-8611, 251-8665, 252-0264. Facsimile (Southtrust Office): 205-251-9915.

RESIDENT PARTNERS

Gary C. Huckaby
Patrick H. Graves, Jr.
E. Cutter Hughes, Jr.
G. Rick Hall

RESIDENT ASSOCIATES

Warne S. Heath
Frank M. Caprio
H. Knox McMillan
James Tassin
Carolyn Reed Douglas

For Complete List of Firm Personnel, See General Section

For full biographical listings, see the Martindale-Hubbell Law Directory

HORNSBY, WATSON & MEGINNISS (AV)

1110 Gleneagles Drive, 35801
Telephone: 205-650-5500
Fax: 205-650-5504

Ralph W. Hornsby
David H. Meginniss
S. A. "Bud" Watson, Jr.
Ralph W. Hornsby, Jr.

For full biographical listings, see the Martindale-Hubbell Law Directory

MORRIS, CLOUD AND CONCHIN, P.C. (AV)

521 Madison Street, P.O. Box 248, 35804
Telephone: 205-534-0065
Fax: 205-539-0741

Harvey B. Morris (P.C.)
Joseph M. Cloud
Gary V. Conchin

Maureen "Mike" Kelley

For full biographical listings, see the Martindale-Hubbell Law Directory

SIROTE & PERMUTT, P.C. (AV)

Suite 1000, 200 Clinton Avenue, N.W., 35801
Telephone: 205-536-1711
Facsimile: 205-534-9650
Birmingham, Alabama Office: 2222 Arlington Avenue, South, P.O. Box 55727.
Telephone: 205-933-7111.
Facsimile: 205-930-5301.
Mobile, Alabama Office: One St. Louis Centre, Suite 1000.
Telephone: 205-432-1671.
Facsimile: 205-434-0196.
Montgomery, Alabama Office: Colonial Commerce Center, Suite 305, One Commerce Street.
Telephone: 205-261-3400.
Facsimile: 205-261-3434.
Tuscaloosa, Alabama Office: 2216 14th Street.
Telephone: 205-752-2089.

Julian D. Butler
John P. Burbach
George W. Royer, Jr.
Fred L. Coffey, Jr.
Roderic G. Steakley
J. Jeffery Rich

For Complete List of Firm Personnel, See General Section

For full biographical listings, see the Martindale-Hubbell Law Directory

SPURRIER, RICE, WOOD & HALL (AV)

3226 Bob Wallace Avenue, 35805
Telephone: 205-533-5015
Fax: 205-536-0105

MEMBERS OF FIRM

Donald N. Spurrier
Robert V. Wood, Jr.
Benjamin R. Rice
Ruth Ann Hall

ASSOCIATES

Clint W. Butler
Anthony B. Johnson

Representative Clients: Alabama Hospital Association Trust Fund; Alfa Insurance Co.; Allstate Insurance Co.; Atlanta Casualty; Auto-Owners Insurance Co.; Balboa Property & Casualty Co.; Bruno's; Casualty Indemnity Exchange; Chubb Group of Insurance Cos.; CIGNA Insurance Cos.

For full biographical listings, see the Martindale-Hubbell Law Directory

Huntsville—Continued

STEPHENS, MILLIRONS, HARRISON & WILLIAMS, P.C. (AV)

333 Franklin Street, P.O. Box 307, 35801
Telephone: 205-533-7711
Telecopier: 205-536-9388

Arthur M. Stephens
Paul L. Millirons
James G. Harrison
Bruce E. Williams
Vicki Ann Bell

Attorneys for: Lomas Mortgage USA, Inc.; AmSouth Mortgage Co., Inc.

For full biographical listings, see the Martindale-Hubbell Law Directory

WATSON, GAMMONS & FEES, P.C. (AV)

200 Clinton Avenue, N.W., Suite 800, P.O. Box 46, 35804
Telephone: 205-536-7423
Telecopier: 205-536-2689

Herman Watson, Jr.
Robert C. Gammons
Michael L. Fees
Joseph A. Jimmerson
J. Barton Warren
Charles H. Pullen
Billie B. Line, Jr.

OF COUNSEL

George K. Williams

LEGAL SUPPORT PERSONNEL

James W. Lowery, Jr. (Administrator)

For full biographical listings, see the Martindale-Hubbell Law Directory

*JASPER,** Walker Co.

O'REAR & O'REAR (AV)

Suite B Bankhead-Byars Building, 1816 Third Avenue, P.O. Box 191, 35502-0191
Telephone: 205-387-2196
Fax: 205-387-2190

MEMBERS OF FIRM

Caine O'Rear, Jr.
Griff O'Rear
Mark A. McWhorter

Reference: First National Bank of Jasper.

For full biographical listings, see the Martindale-Hubbell Law Directory

*MOBILE,** Mobile Co.

ARMBRECHT, JACKSON, DEMOUY, CROWE, HOLMES & REEVES (AV)

1300 AmSouth Center, P.O. Box 290, 36601
Telephone: 334-432-6751
Facsimile: 334-432-6843; 433-3821

MEMBERS OF FIRM

Marshall J. DeMouy
Wm. H. Armbrecht, III
Rae M. Crowe
Broox G. Holmes
W. Boyd Reeves
E. B. Peebles III
William B. Harvey
Kirk C. Shaw
Norman E. Waldrop, Jr.
Conrad P. Armbrecht
Edward G. Hawkins
Grover E. Asmus II
David A. Bagwell
Douglas L. Brown
Donald C. Radcliff
Christopher I. Gruenewald
James Donald Hughes
M. Kathleen Miller
Dabney Bragg Foshee
Edward A. Dean
David E. Hudgens
Ray Morgan Thompson
James Dale Smith
Duane A. Graham
Robert J. Mullican
Wm. Steele Holman, II
Coleman F. Meador
Broox G. Holmes, Jr.

ASSOCIATES

James E. Robertson, Jr.
Scott G. Brown
Clifford C. Brady
Richard W. Franklin
Stephen Russell Copeland
Tara T. Bostick

Representative Clients: AmSouth Bank N.A. (Regional Counsel); Burlington Northern Railroad Co. (District Counsel); Ryan-Walsh, Inc.; Scott Paper Co.; Travelers Insurance Co.

For Complete List of Firm Personnel, See General Section

For full biographical listings, see the Martindale-Hubbell Law Directory

BRISKMAN & BINION, P.C. (AV)

205 Church Street, P.O. Box 43, 36601
Telephone: 334-433-7600
Fax: 334-433-4485

Donald M. Briskman
Mack B. Binion

Donna Ward Black
Alex F. Lankford, IV
Christ N. Coumanis

A List of Representative Clients will be furnished upon request.
References: First Alabama Bank; AmSouth Bank, N.A.; Southtrust Bank of Mobile.

(See Next Column)

For full biographical listings, see the Martindale-Hubbell Law Directory

BURNS, CUNNINGHAM & MACKEY, P.C. (AV)

50 St. Emanuel Street, P.O. Box 1583, 36633
Telephone: 334-432-0612

Peter F. Burns
William M. Cunningham, Jr.
Peter S. Mackey

Max Cassady

For full biographical listings, see the Martindale-Hubbell Law Directory

CABANISS, JOHNSTON, GARDNER, DUMAS & O'NEAL (AV)

700 AmSouth Center, P.O. Box 2906, 36652
Telephone: 334-433-6961
Telecopier: 334-433-1060
Birmingham, Alabama Office: Park Place Tower. 2001 Park Place North, Suite 700. P.O. Box 830612.
Telephone: 205-252-8800.
Telecopier: 205-716-5389.

MEMBERS OF FIRM

Benjamen T. Rowe (Resident)
Patrick H. Sims (Resident)
Donald J. Stewart (Resident)
David L. Kane (Resident)
R. Boyd Miller (Resident)

Representative Clients: American Marine Underwriters, Inc.; Liberty Mutual Insurance Co.; Union Carbide Corp.; Rohr, Inc.

For Complete List of Firm Personnel, See General Section

For full biographical listings, see the Martindale-Hubbell Law Directory

CUNNINGHAM, BOUNDS, YANCE, CROWDER & BROWN (AV)

1601 Dauphin Street, P.O. Box 66705, 36660
Telephone: 334-471-6191
Fax: 334-479-1031

Richard Bounds
James A. Yance
John T. Crowder, Jr.
Robert T. Cunningham, Jr.
Joseph M. Brown, Jr.
Gregory B. Breedlove
Andrew T. Citrin
Michael A. Worel

David G. Wirtes, Jr.
Randolph B. Walton
Toby D. Brown
Mitchell K. Shelly

OF COUNSEL

Robert T. Cunningham
Valentino D. B. Mazzia

References: First Alabama Bank; AmSouth Bank, N.A.

For full biographical listings, see the Martindale-Hubbell Law Directory

FINKBOHNER AND LAWLER (AV)

169 Dauphin Street Suite 300, P.O. Box 3085, 36652
Telephone: 334-438-5871
Fax: 334-432-8052

MEMBERS OF FIRM

George W. Finkbohner, Jr.
John L. Lawler
George W. Finkbohner, III
Royce A. Ray, III

For full biographical listings, see the Martindale-Hubbell Law Directory

HELMSING, LYONS, SIMS & LEACH, P.C. (AV)

The Laclede Building, 150 Government Street, P.O. Box 2767, 36652
Telephone: 334-432-5521
Telecopy: 334-432-0633

Larry U. Sims
Champ Lyons, Jr.
Frederick G. Helmsing
John N. Leach, Jr.
Warren C. Herlong, Jr.
James B. Newman
Robert H. Rouse
Charles H. Dodson, Jr.
Sandy Grisham Robinson
Richard E. Davis
Joseph P. H. Babington
John J. Crowley, Jr.
Joseph D. Steadman

Todd S. Strohmeyer
William R. Lancaster
Robin Kilpatrick Fincher

For full biographical listings, see the Martindale-Hubbell Law Directory

INGE, TWITTY & DUFFY (AV)

1410 First Alabama Bank Building, P.O. Box 1109, 36633
Telephone: 334-433-3200
Facsimile: 334-433-3444

MEMBERS OF FIRM

James J. Duffy, Jr.
James J. Duffy, III

Francis H. Inge (1902-1959)
Thos. E. Twitty (1901-1975)
Richard H. Inge (1912-1980)

For full biographical listings, see the Martindale-Hubbell Law Directory

Mobile—Continued

JOHNSTONE, ADAMS, BAILEY, GORDON AND HARRIS (AV)

Royal St. Francis Building, 104 St. Francis Street, P.O. Box 1988, 36633
Telephone: 334-432-7682
Facsimile: 334-432-2800
Telex: 782040

MEMBERS OF FIRM

Brock B. Gordon
Ben H. Harris, Jr.
William H. Hardie, Jr.
I. David Cherniak
David C. Hannan
Wade B. Perry, Jr.
Thomas S. Rue
Alan C. Christian
Gregory C. Buffalow
Celia J. Collins

ASSOCIATE

Tracy P. Turner

General Counsel for: First Alabama Bank, Mobile; Infirmary Health System/Mobile Infirmary Medical Center/Rotary Rehabilitation Hospital (Multi-Hospital System).
Counsel for: Oil and Gas: Exxon Corp. Business and Corporate: Bell South Telecommunications, Inc.; Aluminum Co. of America; Michelin Tire Corp.; Metropolitan Life Insurance Co.; The Travelers Insurance Cos. Marine: The West of England Ship Owners Mutual Protection and Indemnity Association (Luxembourg); The Standard Steamship Owners' Protection and Indemnity Association (Bermuda) Ltd.

For Complete List of Firm Personnel, See General Section

For full biographical listings, see the Martindale-Hubbell Law Directory

LOVELESS, BANKS & LYONS (AV)

28 North Florida Street, 36607
Telephone: 334-476-7857
Fax: 334-476-8510

MEMBERS OF FIRM

Ralph P. Loveless
J. Donald Banks

For Complete List of Firm Personnel, See General Section

For full biographical listings, see the Martindale-Hubbell Law Directory

LYONS, PIPES & COOK, P.C. (AV)

2 North Royal Street, P.O. Box 2727, 36652-2727
Telephone: 334-432-4481
Cable Address: "Lysea"
Telecopier: 334-433-1820

Wesley Pipes
Norton W. Brooker, Jr.
Cooper C. Thurber
Marion A. Quina, Jr.
Walter M. Cook, Jr.
John Patrick Courtney, III
Charles L. Miller, Jr.
Joseph J. Minus, Jr.
William E. Shreve, Jr.
Dan S. Cushing
Richard D. Morrison

General Counsel: Alabama State Docks Department (an agency of the State of Alabama).
Counsel: McKenzie Tank Lines, Inc.; SCNO Barge Lines, Inc.; Scott Paper Co.; Shell Oil Corp.
Trial Counsel: Aetna Life & Casualty Co.; Chubb Group of Insurance Companies.

For Complete List of Firm Personnel, See General Section

For full biographical listings, see the Martindale-Hubbell Law Directory

AUGUSTINE MEAHER, III, P.C. (AV)

Suite 2118, First National Bank Building, 36602
Telephone: 334-432-9971
FAX: 334-432-9978

Augustine Meaher, III

References: Bank of Mobile, Mobile, Alabama; AmSouth Bank, Mobile, Alabama.

For full biographical listings, see the Martindale-Hubbell Law Directory

MILLER, HAMILTON, SNIDER & ODOM, L.L.C. (AV)

254-256 State Street, P.O. Box 46, 36601
Telephone: 334-432-1414
Telecopier: 334-433-4106
Montgomery, Alabama Office: Suite 802, One Commerce Street.
Telephone: 205-834-5550.
Telecopier: 205-265-4533.
Washington, D.C. Office: Miller, Hamilton, Snider, Odom & Bridgeman, L.L.C., Suite 1150, 1747 Pennsylvania Avenue, N.W.
Telephone: 202-429-9223.
Telecopier: 202-293-2068.

(See Next Column)

MEMBERS OF FIRM

Thomas Troy Zieman, Jr.
Bradley R. Byrne
George A. LeMaistre, Jr.
Lester M. Bridgeman
Louis T. Urbanczyk (Not admitted in AL; Washington, D.C. Office)
Christopher G. Hume, III
Richard A. Wright
M. Kathryn Knight
Matthew C. McDonald
Susan Russ Walker (Resident, Montgomery Office)

OF COUNSEL

Lewis G. Odom, Jr.

ASSOCIATES

Robert G. Jackson, Jr.
Christopher Kern
James Rebarchak
Michael M. Shipper
M. Stephen Dampier
Anthony Michael Hoffman
Elizabeth Barry Johnson

Representative Clients: The Colonial BancGroup, Inc.; Colonial Mortgage Co.; Chase Manhattan Bank, N.A.; The Mitchell Co.; Poole Truck Line, Inc.; Brittania Airways, Ltd. (U.K.); Air Europe (Italy); K-Mart Corporation; K & B Alabama Corp.; Ford Consumer Finance Company, Inc.

For Complete List of Firm Personnel, See General Section

For full biographical listings, see the Martindale-Hubbell Law Directory

PIERCE, CARR & ALFORD, P.C. (AV)

Suite 900 Montlimar Place Office Building, 1110 Montlimar Drive, P.O. Box 16046, 36616
Telephone: 334-344-5151
FAX: 334-344-9696

Donald F. Pierce
Davis Carr
Helen Johnson Alford
Goodman G. Ledyard
Forrest S. Latta
H. William Wasden
Andrew C. Clausen

James W. Lampkin II
John Chas. S. Pierce
Pamela Kirkwood Millsaps
Mignon Mestayer DeLashmet
Rachel D. Sanders
C. William Daniels, Jr.

Representative Clients: Grove Worldwide; Beloit Corp.; Koehring Cranes & Excavators; Winnebago; Toyota Motor Sales Corp.; Blue Cross and Blue Shield; Charter Medical Corp.; Connecticut Mutual Life Ins. Co.; Nationwide Insurance Cos.

For full biographical listings, see the Martindale-Hubbell Law Directory

SIROTE & PERMUTT, P.C. (AV)

One St. Louis Centre, Suite 1000, P.O. Drawer 2025, 36652-2025
Telephone: 334-432-1671
Facsimile: 334-434-0196
Birmingham, Alabama Office: 2222 Arlington Avenue, South, P.O. Box 55727.
Telephone: 205-933-7111.
Facsimile: 205-930-5301.
Huntsville, Alabama Office: 200 Clinton Avenue, N.W., Suite 1000.
Telephone: 205-536-1711.
Facsimile: 205-534-9650.
Montgomery, Alabama Office: Colonial Commerce Center, Suite 305, One Commerce Street.
Telephone: 205-261-3400.
Facsimile: 205-261-3434.
Tuscaloosa, Alabama Office: 2216 14th Street.
Telephone: 205-752-2089.

William H. McDermott
Stephen R. Windom
Richard H. Sforzini, Jr.
Joseph P. Jones, Jr.
T. Julian Motes
Steven L. Nicholas
Michael A. Youngpeter

For Complete List of Firm Personnel, See General Section

For full biographical listings, see the Martindale-Hubbell Law Directory

*MONTGOMERY,** Montgomery Co.

***** indicates certain Bar Register subscribers whose principal office is located elsewhere in the state and who have arranged for representation as a part of the state capital listings that follow

*** BALCH & BINGHAM (AV)**

The Winter Building, 2 Dexter Avenue, P.O. Box 78, 36101
Telephone: 334-834-6500
Facsimile: 334-269-3115
Birmingham, Alabama Offices: 1710 Sixth Avenue North, 35203.
Telephone: 205-251-8100.
Facsimile: 205-226-8798. 1901 Sixth Avenue North, 35203.
Telephone: 205-251-8100.
Facsimile: 205-226-8799.
Huntsville, Alabama Office: Suite 810, 200 West Court Square, 35801.
Telephone: 205-551-0171.
Facsimile: 205-551-0174.

(See Next Column)

BALCH & BINGHAM, *Montgomery—Continued*

Washington, D.C. Office: Suite 800, 1101 Connecticut Avenue, N.W., 20036.
Telephone: 202-296-0387.
Facsimile: 202-452-8180.

RESIDENT MEMBERS OF FIRM

Maury D. Smith
Charles M. Crook
Sterling G. Culpepper, Jr.
William P. Cobb, II
W. Joseph McCorkle, Jr.

RESIDENT ASSOCIATES

Donald R. Jones, Jr.
John S. Bowman, Jr.
Leslie M. Allen
Cynthia Anne Holland

Counsel for: Alabama Power Co.; Blue Cross and Blue Shield of Alabama; The Boeing Company; Brasfield & Gorrie, Inc.; Compass Bancshares, Inc.; Harbert Corp.; Kimberly-Clark Corp.; Southern Company Services, Inc.; Southern Research Institute; Vesta Insurance Group, Inc.

For Complete List of Firm Personnel, See General Section

For full biographical listings, see the Martindale-Hubbell Law Directory

BALL, BALL, MATTHEWS & NOVAK, P.A. (AV)

1100 Union Bank Tower, P.O. Drawer 2148, 36102-2148
Telephone: 334-834-7680
Fax: 334-265-3222

Fred S. Ball (1866-1942)
Charles A. Ball (1904-1969)
Fred S. Ball, Jr. (1896-1974)
Richard A. Ball (1906-1983)
John R. Matthews, Jr.
Richard A. Ball, Jr.
Tabor R. Novak, Jr.
Clyde C. Owen, Jr.
C. Winston Sheehan, Jr.
William H. Brittain II
Joana S. Ellis
E. Hamilton Wilson, Jr.
Richard E. Broughton
T. Cowin Knowles
Gerald C. Swann, Jr.

Mark T. Davis
James A. Rives
Fred B. Matthews
Allison L. Alford

Counsel for: Bell Helicopter Co.; John Deere Co.; Government Employees Insurance Co.; Chubb & Son; Cigna Co.; Chrysler Corp.; Associated Aviation Underwriters.

For full biographical listings, see the Martindale-Hubbell Law Directory

CAPOUANO, WAMPOLD, PRESTWOOD & SANSONE, P.A. (AV)

350 Adams Avenue, P.O. Box 1910, 36102-1910
Telephone: 334-264-6401
Fax: 334-834-4954

Leon M. Capouano
Alvin T. Prestwood
Jerome D. Smith
Ellis D. Hanan
Joseph P. Borg
Joseph W. Warren

OF COUNSEL

Charles H. Wampold, Jr.

Thomas B. Klinner
Linda Smith Webb
James M. Sizemore, Jr.

Counsel for: First Alabama Bank of Montgomery, N.A.; Union Bank and Trust Co.; Real Estate Financing, Inc.; SouthTrust Bank; AmSouth Bank; Central Bank; City Federal Savings & Loan Assoc.; Colonial Mortgage Co.; Lomas & Nettleton; First Bank of Linden.

For full biographical listings, see the Martindale-Hubbell Law Directory

HASKELL SLAUGHTER YOUNG JOHNSTON & GALLION, PROFESSIONAL ASSOCIATION (AV)

Suite 375 Bailey Building, 400 South Union Street, P.O. Box 4660, 36104
Telephone: 334-265-8573
Facsimile: 334-264-7945
Birmingham, Alabama Office: Haskell Slaughter Young & Johnston. 1200 AmSouth/Harbert Plaza, 1901 Sixth Avenue North. 35203
Telephone: 205-251-1000.
Facsimile: 205-324-1133.

Thomas T. Gallion, III
Constance A. Caldwell

Barry D. Woodham

Representative Clients: Beech Aircraft Corp.; The Equitable Life Assurance Society of the United States; Exxon Corporation; Federal Deposit Insurance Corporation/Resolution Trust Corporation; Fireman's Fund Insurance Companies; Jones Plumbing Systems, Inc.; Marshall Durbuin Companies; Montgomery County, Alabama; Ridout's-Brown-Service Inc.; Shoney's, Inc.

For full biographical listings, see the Martindale-Hubbell Law Directory

HILL, HILL, CARTER, FRANCO, COLE & BLACK, P.C. (AV)

425 South Perry Street, P.O. Box 116, 36101-0116
Telephone: 334-834-7600
Fax: 334-263-5969

(See Next Column)

Thomas B. Hill, Jr. (1903-1984)
James T. Stovall (1905-1972)
James J. Carter (1913-1985)
William A. Oldacre (1932-1973)
Wm. Inge Hill
Ralph A. Franco
T. Bowen Hill, III
Harry Cole
Robert C. Black, Sr.
William I. Hill, II
John M. Milling, Jr.
William Inge Hill, Jr.
Gerald W. Hartley
Randall Morgan
Robert W. Bradford, Jr.
David E. Allred
Laura L. Crum
Charles A. Stewart, III
Mark A. Franco
Terry A. Sides
John R. Bradwell

H. Byron Carter, III
William C. McGowin
Robert C. Black, Jr.
David E. Avery, III
R. Rainer Cotter, III
Susan E. Kennedy
Pamela Pelekis Swan

Representative Clients: The Aetna Group; The State Farm Group; ALFA; General Electric Co.; General Motors Corp; Blue Cross and Blue Shield of Alabama; Allstate Insurance Co.; Winn-Dixie Stores, Inc.; Scottsdale Insurance Co.; National Casualty Co.

For full biographical listings, see the Martindale-Hubbell Law Directory

PARKER, BRANTLEY & WILKERSON, P.C. (AV)

323 Adams Avenue, P.O. Box 4992, 36103-4992
Telephone: 334-265-1500
Fax: 334-265-0319

Edward B. Parker, II
Paul A. Brantley
Mark D. Wilkerson
Leah Snell Stephens
Darla T. Furman

Representative Clients: AlaTenn Resources, Inc.; ALLTEL; Contel Cellular, Inc.; Telephone and Data Systems, Inc.; Construction Claims Management, Inc.; Federated Rural Electric Insurance Corp.; Alabama Emergency Room Administrative Services, P.C.
Reference: South Trust Bank, N.A.

For full biographical listings, see the Martindale-Hubbell Law Directory

RUSHTON, STAKELY, JOHNSTON & GARRETT, P.A. (AV)

184 Commerce Street, P.O. Box 270, 36104
Telephone: 334-834-8480
Fax: 334-262-6277

Charles A. Stakely
Nicholas T. Braswell, III
Henry C. Chappell, Jr.
James W. Garrett, Jr.
Robert A. Huffaker
Thomas H. Keene
Richard B. Garrett
Dennis R. Bailey
Ronald G. Davenport
Fred W. Tyson
Robert C. Brock
F. Chadwick Morriss
T. Kent Garrett
Frank J. Stakely
William S. Haynes
Jack B. Hinton, Jr.
Amy Catherine Vibbart
Paul M. James, Jr
N. Wayne Simms, Jr.
D. Mitchell Henry

OF COUNSEL

William B. Moore, Jr.

General Counsel for: Automobile Dealers Association of Alabama, Inc.; Alabama Rural Electric Association Cooperative; Alabama Roadbuilders Association.
Representative General Clients: Sears Roebuck & Co.; Dow Chemical U.S.A.; The Advertiser Co.
Representative Insurance Clients: United States Fidelity and Guaranty Co.; The Travelers Insurance Co.; The Continental National American Group.

For Complete List of Firm Personnel, See General Section

For full biographical listings, see the Martindale-Hubbell Law Directory

SIROTE & PERMUTT, P.C. (AV)

Colonial Commerce Center, Suite 305, One Commerce Street, 36104
Telephone: 334-261-3400
Facsimile: 334-261-3434
Birmingham, Alabama Office: 2222 Arlington Avenue, South, P.O. Box 55727.
Telephone: 205-933-7111.
Facsimile: 205-930-5301.
Huntsville, Alabama Office: 200 Clinton Avenue, N.W., Suite 1000.
Telephone: 205-536-1711.
Facsimile: 205-534-9650.
Mobile, Alabama Office: One St. Louis Centre, Suite 1000.
Telephone: 205-432-1671.
Facsimile: 205-434-0196.
Tuscaloosa, Alabama Office: 2216 14th Street.
Telephone: 205-752-2089.

Susan B. Anderson

For Complete List of Firm Personnel, See General Section

For full biographical listings, see the Martindale-Hubbell Law Directory

PELL CITY, St. Clair Co.

BLAIR, HOLLADAY AND PARSONS (AV)

St. Clair Land Title Building, 1711 Cogswell Avenue, 35125
Telephone: 205-884-3440
Fax: 205-884-3442

MEMBERS OF FIRM

A. Dwight Blair
Hugh E. Holladay
Elizabeth S. Parsons

Representative Clients: Colonial Bank; Metro Bank; St. Clair Federal Savings Bank; State Farm Mutual Insurance Cos; ALFA Mutual Insurance Co.; Allstate Insurance Co.; St. Paul Insurance Cos.; Auto Owners Insurance Co.; Reliance Insurance Cos.; St. Clair Land Title Co., Inc.

For full biographical listings, see the Martindale-Hubbell Law Directory

*SCOTTSBORO,** Jackson Co.

LIVINGSTON, PORTER & PAULK, P.C. (AV)

123 East Laurel Street, P.O. Box 1108, 35768
Telephone: 205-259-1919
Telecopier: 205-259-1189

Jack Livingston
John F. Porter, III
Gerald R. Paulk

Counsel for: Jackson County, Alabama; Jackson County Board of Education; Jackson County Health Care Authority; Scottsboro Electric Power Board; First National Bank of Stevenson, Alabama; Jacobs Bank.
Local Counsel for: State Farm Insurance Cos.; The Travelers Insurance Cos.; Liberty Mutual Insurance Co.; The Hartford Insurance Co.

For full biographical listings, see the Martindale-Hubbell Law Directory

*TALLADEGA,** Talladega Co.

BARRY N. MCCRARY (AV)

223 West North Street, 35160
Telephone: 205-362-2190
Telecopier: 205-362-8280
Mailing Address: P.O. Drawer 56,

References: First National Bank of Talladega; Talladega Federal Savings and Loan Assn.

For full biographical listings, see the Martindale-Hubbell Law Directory

*TROY,** Pike Co.

CALHOUN, FAULK, WATKINS & CLOWER (AV)

78 South Court Square, P.O. Box 489, 36081
Telephone: 334-566-7200
Fax: 334-566-7584

Richard F. Calhoun
William Keith Watkins
Joseph E. Faulk
James G. Clower

General Counsel for: City of Troy; City of Brundidge; First Alabama Bank, Troy; First National Bank of Brundidge; Troy City Board of Education; Pike County Board of Education; South Alabama Electric Cooperative, Inc.; B & D Plastics, Inc.; Battery Marketing Corporation.

For full biographical listings, see the Martindale-Hubbell Law Directory

*TUSCALOOSA,** Tuscaloosa Co.

DAVIDSON, WIGGINS & CROWDER, P.C. (AV)

2625 Eighth Street, P.O. Box 1939, 35403
Telephone: 205-759-5771
Fax: 205-752-8259

M. McCoy Davidson
Courtney Crowder
G. Stephen Wiggins
David Ryan

OF COUNSEL

Hugh W. Roberts, Jr.

Attorneys for: Aetna Life & Casualty Co.; Canal Insurance Co.; Government Employees Insurance Co.; The Travelers Group; Auto-Owners Insurance Co.; Continental National American Group; Federated Insurance; Lynn Insurance Group; The Trinity Cos.; The PMA Group.

For full biographical listings, see the Martindale-Hubbell Law Directory

PHELPS, JENKINS, GIBSON & FOWLER (AV)

1201 Greensboro Avenue, P.O. Box 020848, 35402-0848
Telephone: 205-345-5100
Fax: 205-758-4394
Fax: 205-391-6658

MEMBERS OF FIRM

Sam M. Phelps
Randolph M. Fowler
James J. Jenkins
Michael S. Burroughs
Johnson Russell Gibson, III
C. Barton Adcox
Farley A. Poellnitz

(See Next Column)

ASSOCIATES

K. Scott Stapp
Sandra C. Guin
Karen C. Welborn
Kimberly B. Glass
Stephen E. Snow

Attorneys for: Aetna Insurance Co.; Allstate Insurance Co.; Carolina Casualty Insurance Co.; Continental Insurance Cos.; Fireman's Fund-American Insurance Cos.; Great American Insurance Co.; Hanover Insurance Co.

For full biographical listings, see the Martindale-Hubbell Law Directory

ZEANAH, HUST, SUMMERFORD & DAVIS, L.L.C. (AV)

Seventh Floor, AmSouth Bank Building, P.O. Box 1310, 35403
Telephone: 205-349-1383
Fax: 205-391-1319

MEMBERS OF FIRM

Olin W. Zeanah (1922-1987)
Kenneth D. Davis
Wilbor J. Hust, Jr.
Christopher H. Jones
E. Clark Summerford
Beverly A. Smith

OF COUNSEL

Marvin T. Ormond

Representative Clients: Alfa Insurance Cos.; Hartford Insurance Group; Home Insurance Co.; Nationwide Insurance Co.; Alabama Power Co.; Liberty Mutual Ins. Co.; The Uniroyal Goodrich Tire Co.

For full biographical listings, see the Martindale-Hubbell Law Directory

*TUSCUMBIA,** Colbert Co.

SELF & SELF

(See Florence)

ALASKA

*ANCHORAGE,** Third Judicial District

YOUNG, SANDERS & FELDMAN, INC. (AV)

Suite 400, 500 L Street, 99501
Telephone: 907-272-3538
Telecopier: 907-274-0819

Joseph L. Young
Eric T. Sanders
Jeffrey M. Feldman

Reference: Key Bank of Alaska.

For full biographical listings, see the Martindale-Hubbell Law Directory

*JUNEAU,** First Judicial District

RUDDY, BRADLEY & KOLKHORST, A PROFESSIONAL CORPORATION (AV)

Jordan Creek Center, 8800 Glacier Highway, Suite 223, P.O. Box 34338, 99801
Telephone: 907-789-0047
FAX: 907-789-0783

William G. Ruddy
J. B. Bradley
Kathryn Kolkhorst

For full biographical listings, see the Martindale-Hubbell Law Directory

ARIZONA

*FLAGSTAFF,** Coconino Co.

ASPEY, WATKINS & DIESEL (AV)

123 North San Francisco, 86001
Telephone: 602-774-1478
Facsimile: 602-774-1043
Sedona, Arizona Office: 120 Soldier Pass Road.
Telephone: 602-282-5955.
Facsimile: 602-282-5962.
Page, Arizona Office: 904 North Navajo.
Telephone: 602-645-9694.
Winslow, Arizona Office: 205 North Williamson.
Telephone: 602-289-5963.
Cottonwood, Arizona Office: 905 Cove Parkway, Unite 201.
Telephone: 602-639-1881.

MEMBERS OF FIRM

Frederick M. Fritz Aspey
Bruce S. Griffen
Harold L. Watkins
Donald H. Bayles, Jr.
Louis M. Diesel
Kaign N. Christy
John J. Dempsey

(See Next Column)

ASPEY, WATKINS & DIESEL, *Flagstaff—Continued*

Zachary Markham
James E. Ledbetter
Whitney Cunningham
Holly S. Karris

LEGAL SUPPORT PERSONNEL

Deborah D. Roberts (Legal Assistant)
C. Denece Pruett (Legal Assistant)
Dominic M. Marino, Jr, (Paralegal Assistant)

Representative Clients: Farmer's Insurance Company of Arizona; Kelley-Moore Paint Co.; Pepsi-Cola Bottling Company of Northern Arizona; Bill Luke's Chrysler-Plymouth, Inc.; First American Title Insurance Company ; Transamerica Title Insurance Co.; Page Electric Utility; Comprehensive Access Health Plan, Inc.
Reference: First Interstate Bank-Arizona, N.A., Flagstaff, Arizona.

For full biographical listings, see the Martindale-Hubbell Law Directory

MANGUM, WALL, STOOPS & WARDEN, P.L.L.C. (AV)

222 East Birch Avenue, P.O. Box 10, 86002
Telephone: 602-779-6951
Fax: 602-773-1312

OF COUNSEL

Douglas J. Wall
Robert W. Warden

MEMBERS OF FIRM

Daniel J. Stoops
Jon W. Thompson

ASSOCIATE

David W. Rozema

Representative Clients: United States Automobile Assn.; Federated Insurance; Hartford Insurance Co.; State Farm Fire & Casualty Insurance Co.; Cincinnati Insurance Co.; Canal Insurance Co.; Economy Fire & Casualty Co.; Guaranty National Insurance Co.; Progressive Insurance Co.; Transamerica Insurance Co.

For Complete List of Firm Personnel, See General Section

For full biographical listings, see the Martindale-Hubbell Law Directory

GREEN VALLEY, Pima Co.

DUFFIELD, MILLER, YOUNG, ADAMSON & ALFRED, P.C. (AV)

101-65 South La Canada, Green Valley Mall, 85614
Telephone: 602-625-4404
Tucson, Arizona Office: Suite 711, Transamerica Building, 177 North Church Avenue.
Telephone: 602-792-1181.
LaPaloma Office: LaPaloma Corporate Center, 3573 East Sunrise Drive, Suite 115, Tucson, Arizona.
Telephone: 602-577-1135.

Richard Duffield
Michael C. Young
Larry R. Adamson
K. Alexander Hobson
Eugene C. Gieseler

Representative Clients: San Xavier Rock & Materials, Inc.; Mobat-Adamson Tire Co.
Insurance Company Clientele: State Farm Mutual Insurance Cos.; Automobile Club Insurance Co.; Colonial Penn Insurance Co.; Crum & Forster Group.

For full biographical listings, see the Martindale-Hubbell Law Directory

*NOGALES,** Santa Cruz Co.

O'CONNOR, CAVANAGH, ANDERSON, WESTOVER, KILLINGSWORTH & BESHEARS, A PROFESSIONAL ASSOCIATION (AV)

1827 North Mastick Way, 85621
Telephone: 602-761-4215
FAX: 602-761-3505
Phoenix, Arizona Office: One East Camelback Road, Suite 1100, 85012.
Telephone: 602-263-2400.
FAX: 602-263-2900.
Tucson, Arizona Office: Suite 2200, One South Church Avenue, 85701.
Telephone: 602-882-8912.
FAX: 602-624-9564.
Sun City, Arizona Office: 13250 North Del Webb Boulevard, Suite B, 85351.
Telephone: 602-263-2808.
FAX: 602-933-3100.

Kimberly A. Howard Arana

Representative Clients: Omega Produce Co.; Frank's Distributing, Inc.; City of Nogales; Collectron of Ariz., Inc.; James K. Wilson Produce Co.; Agricola Bon, S. de R.L. de C.V.; Angel Demerutis E.; Rene Carrillo C.; Arturo Lomeli; Theojary Crisantes E.

For Complete List of Firm Personnel, See General Section

For full biographical listings, see the Martindale-Hubbell Law Directory

*PHOENIX,** Maricopa Co.

APKER, APKER, HAGGARD & KURTZ, P.C. (AV)

2111 East Highland Avenue, Suite 230, 85016
Telephone: 602-381-0085
Telecopier: 602-956-3457

Burton M. Apker
Jerry L. Haggard
David B. Apker
Gerrie Apker Kurtz

Cynthia M. Chandley
Kevin M. Moran

Representative Clients: ASARCO Incorporated; Douglas Land Corp.; Frito-Lay, Inc.; Lawyers Title Insurance Corp.; Nevada Power Company; The North West Life Assurance Co.; Phelps Dodge Corporation; Santa Fe Pacific Gold Corporation; Santa Fe Pacific Industrials; Western Federal Savings & Loan Assn.

For full biographical listings, see the Martindale-Hubbell Law Directory

BEGAM, LEWIS, MARKS, WOLFE & DASSE A PROFESSIONAL ASSOCIATION OF LAWYERS (AV)

111 West Monroe Street, Suite 1400, 85003-1787
Telephone: 602-254-6071
Fax: 602-252-0042

Robert G. Begam
Frank Lewis
Stanley J. Marks
Elliot G. Wolfe
Thomas F. Dasse
Cora Perez
Kelly J. McDonald
Daniel J. Adelman
Lisa Kurtz
Dena Rosen Epstein

Reference: National Bank of Arizona.

For full biographical listings, see the Martindale-Hubbell Law Directory

BESS & DYSART, P.C. (AV)

7210 North 16th Street, 82020-5201
Telephone: 602-331-4600
Telecopier: 602-331-8600

Leon D. Bess
Robert L. Dysart
Donald R. Kunz
Timothy R. Hyland
William M. Demlong
Connie Totorica Gould

For full biographical listings, see the Martindale-Hubbell Law Directory

BONN, LUSCHER, PADDEN & WILKINS, CHARTERED (AV)

805 North Second Street, 85004
Telephone: 602-254-5557
Fax: 602-254-0656

Paul V. Bonn
Brian A. Luscher
Randall D. Wilkins
John H. Cassidy
D. Michael Hall

For full biographical listings, see the Martindale-Hubbell Law Directory

BONNETT, FAIRBOURN, FRIEDMAN, HIENTON, MINER & FRY, P.C. (AV)

4041 North Central Avenue Suite 1100, 85012
Telephone: 602-274-1100
Fax: 602-274-1199

Jerry C. Bonnett
William G. Fairbourn
Andrew S. Friedman
Joseph P. Hienton
James R. Hienton
Don J. Miner
Gary H. Fry
Joe Keilp
Francis J. Balint, Jr.
H. Sullivan Bunch
Michael N. Widener
Robert J. Spurlock
C. Kevin Dykstra
Elaine Ryan
Tara L. Jackson
Laurence G. Christopher
Wendy J. Harrison
Scott A. Erickson
John S. Keating

For full biographical listings, see the Martindale-Hubbell Law Directory

CHARLES M. BREWER, LTD. (AV)

5500 North 24th Street, P.O. Box 10720, 85064
Telephone: 602-381-8787
Fax: 602-381-1152

Charles M. Brewer

Mark S. O'Connor

For full biographical listings, see the Martindale-Hubbell Law Directory

BROENING, OBERG & WOODS, P.C. (AV)

1122 East Jefferson Street, P.O. Box 20527, 85036
Telephone: 602-271-7700
Telecopier: 602-258-7785

(See Next Column)

BROENING, OBERG & WOODS P.C.—*Continued*

James R. Broening
Terrence P. Woods
John W. Oberg
Donald Wilson, Jr.
Vincent A. Cass
Kenneth C. Miller
Neal B. Thomas
Wesley S. Loy
Gregg A. Thurston
Michael M. Haran
Jerry T. Collen
Cynthia van R. Cheney
Bruce M. Preston
Robert M. Moore
James G. McElwee, Jr.
Deborah E. Solliday
Martha Masteller Burns
Gary A. Fadell
R. Jeffrey Woodburn
Kathleen Fawcett Collins
David S. Shughart, II
David C. Donohue
Barbara A. Hamner
Joel P. Borowiec
Marilyn D. Cage

Representative Clients: Farmers Insurance Group; Home Insurance Co.; Chubb Group of Insurance Cos.; St. Paul Fire and Marine Insurance Cos.; Ohio Casualty Insurance Group.

For full biographical listings, see the Martindale-Hubbell Law Directory

BROWN & BAIN, A PROFESSIONAL ASSOCIATION (AV)

2901 North Central Avenue, P.O. Box 400, 85001-0400
Telephone: 602-351-8000
Cable: TWX 910-951-0646
Telecopier: 602-351-8516
Palo Alto, California Affiliated Office: Brown & Bain, 600 Hansen Way.
Telephone: 415-856-9411.
Telecopier: 415-856-6061.
Tucson, Arizona Affiliated Office: Brown & Bain, A Professional Association. One South Church Avenue, Nineteenth Floor, P.O. Box 2265.
Telephone: 602-798-7900
Telecopier: 602-798-7945.

Lynne Christensen Adams
Robert E. B. Allen
Michael F. Bailey
C. Randall Bain
Eddward P. Ballinger, Jr.
Daniel C. Barr
Alan H. Blankenheimer
Jack E. Brown
John A. Buttrick
Howard Ross Cabot
H. Michael Clyde
Richard Calvin Cooledge
Paul F. Eckstein
Terry E. Fenzl
Jodi Knobel Feuerhelm
Douglas Gerlach (On leave)
Amy J. Gittler
Philip R. Higdon (Resident at Tucson Office)
Joseph E. Mais
Joseph W. Mott
Joel W. Nomkin
Michael W. Patten
Charles S. Price
Daniel P. Quigley
John W. Rogers
Lawrence G. D. Scarborough
Lex J. Smith
Craig W. Soland
Antonio T. Viera
Kim E. Williamson

Charles A. Blanchard
David P. Brooks
Chad S. Campbell
Timothy J. Franks
Jonathan M. James
Shirley Ann Kaufman
Todd R. Kerr
Jeanean Kirk
C. Mark Kittredge
Grant A. Koppelman
Deborah Henscheid Lyon
Anthony L. Marks
Kelly A. O'Connor
Lane D. Oden (Resident at Tucson Office)
Peter J. Osetek
Christopher J. Raboin
Jane L. Rodda (Resident at Tucson Office)
Lee Stein

For Complete List of Firm Personnel, See General Section

For full biographical listings, see the Martindale-Hubbell Law Directory

BURCH & CRACCHIOLO, P.A. (AV)

702 East Osborn Road, Suite 200, 85014
Telephone: 602-274-7611
Fax: 602-234-0341
Mailing Address: P.O. Box 16882, Phoenix, AZ, 85011

Daniel Cracchiolo
Stephen E. Silver
Brian Kaven
Daryl Manhart
Ian Neale
David G. Derickson
Andrew Abraham
Donald W. Lindholm
F. Michael Carroll
Daniel R. Malinski
Edwin D. Fleming
Ralph D. Harris

Josephine Cuccurullo
Paul F. Dowdell
Stephen M. Hart
Theodore (Todd) Julian
Thomas A. Longfellow
Steven M. Serrano
David M. Villadolid
J. Brent Welker

Representative Clients: Bashas' Inc.; Farmers Insurance Group; U-Haul International, Inc.

For Complete List of Firm Personnel, See General Section

For full biographical listings, see the Martindale-Hubbell Law Directory

COHEN AND COTTON, A PROFESSIONAL CORPORATION (AV)

One Arizona Center, Suite 400, 400 East Van Buren Street, 85004
Telephone: 602-252-8400
FAX: 602-252-5339

Ronald Jay Cohen
John H. Cotton
Laura Hartigan Kennedy
Daniel G. Dowd
David W. Smith
Scott L. Long
Paula M. DeMore
Darlene M. Wauro
Joshua R. Woodard
Samantha Gail Masters-Brown
Robert N. Mann
John Maston O'Neal

Representative Clients: Amex Life Assurance Co.; Coopers & Lybrand; Del Webb Corp.; Fireman's Fund; Grubb & Ellis Realty Co.; Talley Industries, Inc.; U-Haul International, Inc.; United States Fidelity and Guaranty Co.; Accuvanc Mortgage Co.; Express America Mortgage Co.

For full biographical listings, see the Martindale-Hubbell Law Directory

DUSHOFF MCCALL, A PROFESSIONAL CORPORATION (AV)

Two Renaissance Square, 40 North Central, 14th Floor, 85004
Telephone: 602-254-3800
Fax: 602-258-2551

Jay Dushoff
Jack E. McCall
Michael J. McGivern
Denise J. Henslee
Jean Weaver Rice
Janice Sloan Feinberg Massey

OF COUNSEL

Dawn Stoll Zeitlin (P.C.)

LEGAL SUPPORT PERSONNEL

Thomas M. Flynn

For full biographical listings, see the Martindale-Hubbell Law Directory

FENNEMORE CRAIG, A PROFESSIONAL CORPORATION (AV)

Two North Central, Suite 2200, 85004
Telephone: 602-257-8700
Fax: 602-257-8527
Scottsdale, Arizona Office: 6263 North Scottsdale Road, Suite 290, 85250.
Telephone: 602-257-5400.
Fax: 602-945-4932.
Tucson, Arizona Office: One South Church Avenue, Suite 1030, 85701.
Telephone: 602-624-9312.
Fax: 602-882-7383.

Calvin H. Udall
James Powers
Kenneth J. Sherk
John D. Everroad
F. Pendleton Gaines, III
Donald R. Gilbert
Roger T. Hargrove
David T. Maddox (Not admitted in AZ)
John G. Ryan
Leland M. Jones
David A. Weatherwax
Graeme E. M. Hancock
Kaye L. McCarthy
Scott M. Finical
William T. Burghart
Andrew M. Federhar
Christopher L. Callahan
Loral Deatherage
Christopher P. Staring
Janet W. Lord

James J. Trimble
Mark H. Brain
Jon R. Hulburd
Ann-Martha Andrews
Polly S. Rapp
Douglas J. Grier
Marc H. Lamber
Richard A. Kasper

Representative Clients: ASARCO Incorporated; AT&T Communications; Bridgestone/Firestone, Inc.; Catellus Development Corp.; Citibank (Arizona); First Interstate Bank of Arizona; GIANT Industries; Phelps Dodge Corporation; The Atchison, Topeka & Santa Fe Railway, Co.; US WEST Communications.

For Complete List of Firm Personnel, See General Section

For full biographical listings, see the Martindale-Hubbell Law Directory

GALBUT & ASSOCIATES, A PROFESSIONAL CORPORATION (AV)

Camelback Esplanade, Suite 1020, 2425 East Camelback Road, 85016
Telephone: 602-955-1455
Fax: 602-955-1585

Martin R. Galbut
Paul A. Conant
Brian J. Schulman

For full biographical listings, see the Martindale-Hubbell Law Directory

GOLDSTEIN, KINGSLEY & MCGRODER, LTD. A PROFESSIONAL CORPORATION (AV)

Professional Arts Building, 1110 East McDowell Road, 85006-2678
Telephone: 602-254-5581
Fax: 602-258-7390
Other Phoenix Office: 2200 East Camelback Road, Suite 221, 85016-3456.
Telephone: 602-957-1500.
Telecopier: 602-956-9294.

(See Next Column)

GOLDSTEIN, KINGSLEY & MCGRODER LTD. A PROFESSIONAL CORPORATION, *Phoenix—Continued*

Philip T. Goldstein
Pamela L. Kingsley
Patrick J. McGroder, III
(East Camelback Road Office)
Kathleen Delarosa
Suzanne P. Clarke

For full biographical listings, see the Martindale-Hubbell Law Directory

HORNE, KAPLAN AND BISTROW, P.C. (AV)

Renaissance Two, 40 North Central, Suite 2800, 85004
Telephone: 602-253-9700
Fax: 602-258-4805

Thomas C. Horne
Martha Bachner Kaplan
Eric J. Bistrow
Michael S. Dulberg
Kimball J. Corson
Mark D. Zuckerman

For full biographical listings, see the Martindale-Hubbell Law Directory

JOHN C. HOVER, P.C. (AV)

2901 North Central Avenue, Suite 1150, 85012
Telephone: 602-230-8777
Fax: 602-230-8707

John C. Hover

LEGAL SUPPORT PERSONNEL

PARALEGAL

Diana G. Weeks

Representative Clients: First National Bank of Arizona; Bank of Hawaii; Buckeye Irrigation Co.; Linkletter-Perris Partnership.

For full biographical listings, see the Martindale-Hubbell Law Directory

JENNINGS & HAUG (AV)

2800 North Central Avenue Suite Eighteen Hundred, 85004-1019
Telephone: 602-234-7800
Fax: 602-277-5595
Irvine, California Office: 1920 Main Street, Suite 830.
Telephone: 714-250-7800.
Fax: 602-250-4913.

MEMBERS OF FIRM

Curtis A. Jennings
William F. Haug
Robert A. Scheffing
Robert O. Dyer
Jack R. Cunningham
Jay M. Mann
Carolyn M. Kaluzniacki
Dean Kim Lough
Chad L. Schexnayder
Mark E. Barker

James L. Csontos

ASSOCIATES

J. Daniel Shell
Jeff R. Wilhelm
Julianne C. Wheeler
Edward Rubacha
Robert J. Berens
Judy J. Shell
Russell C. Brown
Paul D. Kramer (Resident, Irvine, California Office)
Paul S. Ruderman
Laurence R. Sharlot
John G. Sinodis

For full biographical listings, see the Martindale-Hubbell Law Directory

JENNINGS, STROUSS AND SALMON, P.L.C. (AV)

A Professional Limited Liability Company
One Renaissance Square, Two North Central, 85004-2393
Telephone: 602-262-5911
Fax: 602-253-3255

William T. Birmingham
Gary G. Keltner
T. Patrick Flood
W. Michael Flood
Ronald H. Moore
Gary L. Stuart
M. Byron Lewis
Douglas G. Zimmerman
Michael A. Beale
Gerald W. Alston
David L. White
John B. Weldon, Jr.
James D. Vieregg
John G. Sestak, Jr.
Kenneth C. Sundlof, Jr.
Rita A. Meiser
Diane K. Geimer
Gary L. Lassen
Richard N. Morrison
John A. Micheaels
Barry E. Lewin
Jay A. Fradkin
Michael R. Palumbo
Joseph A. Drazek
Glenn J. Carter
H. Christian Bode
Stephen E. Crofton
James M. Ackerman
Preston H. Longino, Jr.
Ernest Calderon
Jon D. Schneider
Frederick M. Cummings
Wendy D. Woodrow
Brian N. Spector
Michael J. O'Connor
Katherine M. Cooper
John J. Egbert
Matthew D. Kleifield

Lisa M. McKnight

OF COUNSEL

Nicholas Udall

(See Next Column)

Tracy A. Gromer
Charles D. Onofry
J. Matthew Powell
Robert D. Haws
James D. Shook
Jennifer M. Bligh
K. Thomas Slack
Kim D. Steinmetz
Cody M. Hall
Elizabeth C. Painter
Mark A. McGinnis
David B. Earl
Brian D. Wallace
Brian C. Silbernagel
Lisa A. Frey
Gordon Lewis
Stephanie McRae
Martin A. Tetreault

For Complete List of Firm Personnel, See General Section

For full biographical listings, see the Martindale-Hubbell Law Directory

JONES, SKELTON & HOCHULI (AV)

2901 North Central, Suite 800, 85012
Telephone: 602-263-1700
Telefax: 602-263-1784

MEMBERS OF FIRM

William R. Jones, Jr.
J. Russell Skelton
Edward G. Hochuli
A. Melvin McDonald, Jr.
Peter G. Kline
Donald L. Myles, Jr.
William D. Holm
Ronald W. Collett
Mark D. Zukowski
Bruce D. Crawford
Jeffrey Boyd Miller
Georgia A. Staton
William J. Schrank
Gary H. Burger
Michael E. Hensley
Kathleen L. Wieneke

Kevin D. Neal

ASSOCIATES

Daniel P. Struck
Lori A. Shipley
Robert R. Berk
John T. Masterson
David C. Lewis
Brian W. LaCorte
Angela K. Sinner
Jeffrey T. Bergin

For full biographical listings, see the Martindale-Hubbell Law Directory

KIMERER, LAVELLE, HAY & HOOD, P.L.C. (AV)

2715 North Third Street, 85004
Telephone: 602-279-5900
FAX: 602-264-5566

Richard B. Hood
Michael J. LaVelle

Merrick B. Firestone

For Complete List of Firm Personnel, See General Section

For full biographical listings, see the Martindale-Hubbell Law Directory

LEWIS AND ROCA (AV)

A Partnership including Professional Corporations
40 North Central Avenue, 85004-4429
Telephone: 602-262-5311
Fax: 602-262-5747
Tucson, Arizona Office: One South Church Avenue, Suite 700.
Telephone: 602-622-2090.
Fax: 602-622-3088.

MEMBERS OF FIRM

John P. Frank
Jeremy E. Butler
Douglas L. Irish
Tom Galbraith
R. Kent Klein
Barry Fish
Patricia K. Norris
Dale A. Danneman
Thomas H. Campbell
Geoffrey H. Walker
David J. Cantelme
Newman R. Porter
George L. Paul
Thomas G. Ryan
Steven J. Labensky
Edward M. Mansfield
Barbara J. Muller
Jesse B. Simpson
James K. Kloss
Robert F. Roos
Mary Ellen Simonson
Steven J. Hulsman
Carl F. Mariano
Robert H. Mc Kirgan
James J. Belanger
L. Keith Beauchamp
Joseph E. McGarry
Peter D. Baird
Merton E. Marks (P.C.)
Marty Harper
Richard S. Cohen
Judith E. Sirkis
José A. Cárdenas
Foster Robberson
Michael J. Holden
John N. Iurino (Resident, Tucson Office)
Sheila Carmody
James L. Hohnbaum
Betty L. Hum
Stephen M. Bressler
Thomas Klinkel
Allen R. Clarke
Jessica Jeanne Youle
Michael Owen Miller (Resident, Tucson Office)
James T. Acuff, Jr.
Rosemarie Christofolo
Christopher J. Brelje
Steven J. Burr
Pamela B. Petersen
Jane E. Reddin

ASSOCIATES

Charles W. Steese
Kim C. Stanger
Greg S. Como
Stephen R. Winkelman
Deborah A. Nye
Barbara A. Anstey
Bradley P. Balson
David A. Kelly

(See Next Column)

LEWIS AND ROCA—*Continued*

ASSOCIATES (Continued)

R. Neil Taylor, III
Richard A. Halloran
Michael L. Burke
Christine Ann Hartland
Deanna Salazar
Karl C. Eppich
Margaret R. Russell

OF COUNSEL

Thomas V. Rawles

Representative Clients: Blood Systems, Inc.; Bristol-Myers Squibb Company; Del Webb Corp.; The Dial Corp; E.I. de Pont de Nemours and Company; MCI Communications Corporation; The Prudential Insurance Company of America; Southwest Risk Services; Zurich Insurance Company.

For Complete List of Firm Personnel, See General Section

For full biographical listings, see the Martindale-Hubbell Law Directory

LIEBERMAN, DODGE, SENDROW & GERDING, LTD. (AV)

First Interstate Tower, Suite 1801 3550 North Central Avenue, 85012-2114
Telephone: 602-277-3000
Fax: 602-277-7478
Chicago, Illinois Office: LaSalle Bank Building, Suite 1407, 135 South La Salle Street.
Telephone: 312-541-8510.
Fax: 312-845-2902.

David D. Dodge
Paul S. Gerding
Marc R. Lieberman
Susan G. Sendrow

Mary K. Farrington-Lorch
Paul S. Gerding, Jr. (Not admitted in AZ; Resident, Chicago, Illinois Office)

OF COUNSEL

Terence D. Woolston
Karen L. Kothe
Robert G. Anderson

For full biographical listings, see the Martindale-Hubbell Law Directory

LINZER, LANG & DITSCH, P.C. (AV)

3242 North Sixteenth Street, 85016
Telephone: 602-956-2525
Fax: 602-241-9885

Stephen P. Linzer
Kent A. Lang
Brian E. Ditsch

Mark S. Diekemper
David L. O'Daniel

OF COUNSEL

James A. Ullman

For full biographical listings, see the Martindale-Hubbell Law Directory

MEYER, HENDRICKS, VICTOR, OSBORN & MALEDON, A PROFESSIONAL ASSOCIATION (AV)

2929 North Central Avenue Suite 2100, 85012-2794
Telephone: 602-640-9000
Facsimile: (24 Hrs.) 602-640-9050
Mailing Address: P.O. Box 33449, 85067-3449,

Ed Hendricks
William J. Maledon
Larry A. Hammond
Andrew D. Hurwitz
Robert L. Palmer
R. Douglas Dalton
Don Bivens
Ron Kilgard
Donald M. Peters
David G. Campbell
Brett L. Dunkelman
Helen Perry Grimwood
David B. Rosenbaum
Diane M. Johnsen
W. Scott Bales
Bruce E. Meyerson
Robert V. Kerrick
Mark D. Samson
Shane R. Swindle
Mary E. Berkheiser
G. Murray Snow
Brent Ghelfi
David K. Duncan
Clark M. Porter
Mark Andrew Fuller
Debra A. Hill
Sigmund G. Popko

Dawn L. Dauphine
Scott W. Rodgers
Ronald R. Gallegos
Trevor A. Brown
Geoffrey M.T. Sturr
Joan S. Burke
Susan Ann Cannata
Douglas C. Anderson

Reference: Bank One Arizona, NA.

For Complete List of Firm Personnel, See General Section

For full biographical listings, see the Martindale-Hubbell Law Directory

MILLER & MILLER, LTD. (AV)

Suite 2250, 3200 North Central Avenue, 85012
Telephone: 602-266-8440
Fax: 602-266-8453

Murray Miller
Richard K. Miller
Robert M. Miller
Marcus Westervelt

For full biographical listings, see the Martindale-Hubbell Law Directory

MYERS & JENKINS, A PROFESSIONAL CORPORATION (AV)

One Renaissance Square, Suite 1200, Two North Central Avenue, 85004
Telephone: 602-253-0440
Telecopier: 602-257-0527

Stephen W. Myers
William Scott Jenkins
Teresa Dawn Farrison
Richard B. Murphy

Reference: First Interstate Bank of Arizona, N.A.

For full biographical listings, see the Martindale-Hubbell Law Directory

O'CONNOR, CAVANAGH, ANDERSON, WESTOVER, KILLINGSWORTH & BESHEARS, A PROFESSIONAL ASSOCIATION (AV)

One East Camelback Road, Suite 1100, 85012-1656
Telephone: 602-263-2400
FAX: 602-263-2900
Sun City, Arizona Office: 13250 North Del Webb Boulevard, Suite B, 85351.
Telephone: 602-263-2808.
FAX: 602-933-3100.
Tucson, Arizona Office: Suite 2200, One South Church Avenue, 85701.
Telephone: 602-882-8912.
FAX: 602-624-9564.
Nogales, Arizona Office: 1827 North Mastick Way, 85621.
Telephone: 602-761-4215.
FAX: 602-761-3505.

Harry J. Cavanagh
John H. Westover
Robert G. Beshears
Ralph E. Hunsaker
Thomas A. McGuire, Jr.
George H. Mitchell
Richard J. Woods
Jeffrey B. Smith
Jolyon Grant
Harding B. Cure
Steven D. Smith
J. Victor Stoffa
Henry L. Timmerman
Philip C. Gerard
Franzula M. Bacher
Michael W. Carnahan
Charles L. Fine
Carol N. Cure
Scott A. Salmon
Paul J. Roshka, Jr.
John E. DeWulf
David L. Kurtz
Stephen E. Richman
David A. Van Engelhoven
Paul J. Giancola
Pamela M. Overton
Frank M. Fox
Raymond S. Heyman
Christina S. Hamilton
Lisa M. Sommer

Michael R. Altaffer
Lucas J. Narducci
Janet E. Kornblatt
Steven M. Rudner

Jeffrey R. Hovik
Robert L. Ehmann
R. Corey Hill
Steven G. Biddle
Timothy F. Bolden
Mark J. DePasquale
Troy B. Froderman
John A. Felix
Ashley D. Adams
Carla A. Wortley
Carl O. Wortley, III
Janet M. Walsh
Mark D. Dillon
Frank W. Moskowitz
Eric A. Mark
Kent S. Berk
Jamal F. Allen
Steven J. German
Peter C. Prynkiewicz

Representative Clients: Coldwell Banker Real Estate; Karsten Manufacturing Co.; The Dial Corp; M&I Thunderbird Bank; State Farm Mutual Automobile Insurance Co.; Chicago Title Insurance Co.; Samsung Electronics; Hartford Insurance Group.

For Complete List of Firm Personnel, See General Section

For full biographical listings, see the Martindale-Hubbell Law Directory

RIDENOUR, SWENSON, CLEERE & EVANS, P.C. (AV)

302 North First Avenue, Suite 900, 85003
Telephone: 602-254-2143
Fax: 602-254-8670

Harold H. Swenson
James W. Evans
Robert R. Beltz
Lloyd J. Andrews
Michael J. Frazelle
John W. Storer, III
Richard H. Oplinger
Tamalyn E. Lewis
John T. Moshier
Joseph A. Kendhammer
Peter S. Spaw
Alan R. Costello

OF COUNSEL

Ronald A. Schlosser

(See Next Column)

RIDENOUR, SWENSON, CLEERE & EVANS P.C., *Phoenix—Continued*

Robert R. Byrne
David M. Reaves
Philip Simon
Jeffrey A. Bernick
Scott A. Holden
Gregory P. Gillis

Representative Clients: State Farm Insurance Co.; Travelers Insurance Co.; Allstate Insurance Co.; Transamerica Insurance Co.; St. Paul Fire & Marine Insurance Co.

For full biographical listings, see the Martindale-Hubbell Law Directory

ROBBINS & GREEN, A PROFESSIONAL ASSOCIATION (AV)

1800 CitiBank Tower, 3300 North Central Avenue, 85012-9826
Telephone: 602-248-7600
Fax: 602-266-5369

Philip A. Robbins
Richard W. Abbuhl
Wayne A. Smith
Joe M. Romley
Edmund F. Richardson
William H. Sandweg III
Jack N. Rudel
Jeffrey P. Boshes
Brian Imbornoni
Janet B. Hutchison
Bradley J. Stevens
Ronald G. Wilson
Dwayne Ross
Alfred W. Ricciardi
K. Leonard Judson
Dorothy Baran
Austin D. Potenza, II
Sarah McGiffert
Michael S. Green
Kenneth A. Hodson
Daniel L. Brown

For full biographical listings, see the Martindale-Hubbell Law Directory

SACKS TIERNEY P.A. (AV)

2929 North Central Avenue, Fourteenth Floor, 85012-2742
Telephone: 602-279-4900
Fax: 602-279-2027

Marvin S. Cohen
David C. Tierney
Lawrence J. Rosenfeld
Robert J. DuComb, Jr.
Scot C. Stirling
Randall S. Yavitz
Peter W. Sorensen
Sharon Brook Shively
James W. Armstrong
Paul G. Johnson

Reference: M&I Thunderbird Bank.

For Complete List of Firm Personnel, See General Section

For full biographical listings, see the Martindale-Hubbell Law Directory

SHIMMEL, HILL, BISHOP & GRUENDER, P.C. (AV)

3700 North 24th Street, 85016
Telephone: 602-224-9500
Telecopier: 602-955-6176

Daniel F. Gruender
Richard B. Kelly
David N. Farren
Keith F. Overholt
Scott J. Richardson
Joseph Wm. Kruchek
Margaret L. Steiner
Michael V. Perry
Susan M. Swick
S. Gregory Jones

OF COUNSEL

Charles A. Finch

James C. Paul
James H. Hazlewood
Glenn B. Hotchkiss
C. Peter Delgado, Jr.
Judith M. Dworkin

Representative Clients: Berry's Appliances; Harkins Amusement Enterprises, Inc.

For Complete List of Firm Personnel, See General Section

For full biographical listings, see the Martindale-Hubbell Law Directory

SNELL & WILMER (AV)

One Arizona Center, 85004-0001
Telephone: 602-382-6000
Fax: 602-382-6070
Tucson, Arizona Office: 1500 Norwest Tower, One South Church Avenue 85701-1612.
Telephone: 602-882-1200.
Fax: 602-884-1294.
Orange County Office: 1920 Main Street, Suite 1200, P.O. Box 19601, Irvine, California, 92714.
Telephone: 714-253-2700.
Fax: 714-955-2507.
Salt Lake City, Utah Office: Broadway Centre, 111 East Broadway, Suite 900, 84111.
Telephone: 801-237-1900.
Fax: 801-237-1950.

OF COUNSEL

Mark Wilmer

(See Next Column)

MEMBERS OF FIRM

John J. Bouma
George H. Lyons
Daniel J. McAuliffe
Douglas W. Seitz
Barry D. Halpern
James R. Condo
Vaughn A. Crawford
Suzanne McCann
Arthur T. Anderson
Richard W. Shapiro
Katherine M. Harmeyer
James J. Sienicki
George J. Coleman, III
Heidi L. McNeil
Stephen M. Hopkins
Donald H. Smith
Steven S. Guy
Warren E. Platt
Peter J. Rathwell
Donald D. Colburn
Robert B. Hoffman
Joel P. Hoxie
Lonnie J. Williams, Jr.
Arthur P. Greenfield
Donald L. Gaffney
Patrick E. Hoog
Martha E. Gibbs
Jeffrey Messing
E. Jeffrey Walsh
Timothy G. O'Neill
Janet E. Barton
Kevin J. Parker
Peter M. Wittekind
Christopher H. Bayley
Robert R. Kinas

SENIOR ATTORNEYS

Bruce P. White
Shirley J. Wahl
Lisa M. Coulter

ASSOCIATES

Patrick G. Byrne
Timothy J. Casey
Barbara J. Dawson
Patrick X. Fowler
Joseph C. Kreamer
Jon S. Musial
Loren A. Piel
Scott D. Sherman
Prithviraj S. Sivananthan
Brian J. Campbell
Jeffrey Webb Crockett
Brian J. Foster
Charles P. Keller
Bob J. McCullough
Eugene F. O'Connor II
GinaMarie Rossano
Thea Foglietta Silverstein
Randall C. Urbom
Jonathan F. Weisbard

Representative Clients: Arizona Public Service Company; Cigna Healthplan of Arizona; Del Webb Corporation; Emerson Electric Co.; Ford Motor Co.; Honeywell; Mardian Construction; McCarthy Western; Price-Waterhouse; Bank One, Arizona, NA.

For Complete List of Firm Personnel, See General Section

For full biographical listings, see the Martindale-Hubbell Law Directory

STREICH LANG, A PROFESSIONAL ASSOCIATION (AV)

Renaissance One, Two N. Central Avenue, 85004-2391
Telephone: 602-229-5200
Fax: 602-229-5690
Tucson, Arizona Office: One S. Church Avenue, Suite 1700.
Telephone: 602-770-8700.
Fax: 602-623-2518.
Las Vegas, Nevada Affiliated Office: Dawson & Associates, 3800 Howard Hughes Parkway, Suite 1500.
Telephone: 702-792-2727.
Fax: 702-792-2676.
Los Angeles, California Office: 444 S. Flower Street, Suite 1530.
Telephone: 213-896-0484.

Dan M. Durrant
William Shepard Hawgood, II
Douglas W. Holly
Charles W. Jirauch
Craig H. Kaufman (Resident, Tucson Office)
Don P. Martin
Robert E. Miles
Deana S. Peck
Karen A. Potts
James A. Ryan
Louis A. Stahl
Timothy J. Thomason
Edwin Baird Wainscott
Jeffrey Willis (Partner-in-Charge, Tucson Office)

OF COUNSEL

Raymond R. Cusack (Resident, Tucson Office)
Laurence J. De Respino

Thomas D. Arn
David Bray
Leigh Lani Taylor Brown
Linda B. Dubnow
Lisa Dibbern Duran
Michael R. Hall (Resident, Tucson Office)
Joy E. Herr-Cardillo (Resident, Tucson Office)
Elliot S. Isaac
Scott A. Klundt
Stephen R. Mick (Resident, Los Angeles Office)
David V. Millard (Resident, Tucson Office)
Debra A. Stanton

Representative Clients: American West Airlines, Inc.; Arthur Andersen & Co.; Atlantic Richfield Co.; Chicago Title; Eli Lilly & Company; First Interstate Bank of Arizona, N.A.; Motorola, Inc.; Prudential-Bache Securities, Inc.; TRW Inc.; The Travelers Companies.

For Complete List of Firm Personnel, See General Section

For full biographical listings, see the Martindale-Hubbell Law Directory

ULRICH, THOMPSON & KESSLER, P.C. (AV)

Suite 1000, 3030 North Central Avenue, 85012-2717
Telephone: 602-248-9465
Fax: 602-248-0165

(See Next Column)

ULRICH, THOMPSON & KESSLER P.C.—*Continued*

Paul G. Ulrich — Nancy C. Thompson
Donn G. Kessler

For full biographical listings, see the Martindale-Hubbell Law Directory

*PRESCOTT,** Yavapai Co.

FAVOUR, MOORE, WILHELMSEN & SCHUYLER, A PROFESSIONAL ASSOCIATION (AV)

1580 Plaza West Drive, P.O. Box 1391, 86302
Telephone: 602-445-2444
Fax: 602-771-0450

John B. Schuyler, Jr. — David K. Wilhelmsen
Mark M. Moore — Lance B. Payette
Clifford G. Cozier

OF COUNSEL

John M. Favour — Richard G. Kleindienst

Representative Clients: Yavapai Regional Medical Center; Yavapai Title Co.; Father Wasson's Orphans; Hidden Valley Ranch; Bank of America; Employers Mutual Co.; Lawyers Title Insurance Co.; Farmers Insurance Group; Inter-Cal Corp.; Arroyo Seco Development.

For full biographical listings, see the Martindale-Hubbell Law Directory

MURPHY, LUTEY, SCHMITT & BECK (AV)

Elks Building, 117 East Gurley Street, 86301
Telephone: 602-445-6860
Fax: 602-445-6488
Yuma, Arizona Office: Valley Professional Plaza. 1763 West Twenty-Fourth Street, Suite 200.
Telephone: 602-726-0314.
Fax: 602-341-1079.

MEMBERS OF FIRM

Thelton D. Beck — Michael R. Murphy
Selmer D. Lutey

ASSOCIATES

Dan A. Wilson — Bruce E. Rosenberg

OF COUNSEL

Keith F. Quail

Northern Arizona Counsel for: State Farm Mutual Automobile Insurance Co.; Transamerica Title Insurance Co.; Allstate Insurance Co.
Local Counsel for: Bank One Arizona, N.A.; General Motors Corp.
Representative Clients: Chino Valley Irrigation District; Prescott College; Galpin Ford, Inc.; Yavapai Medical Center, P.C.

For Complete List of Firm Personnel, See General Section

For full biographical listings, see the Martindale-Hubbell Law Directory

SCOTTSDALE, Maricopa Co.

CARMICHAEL & TILKER (AV)

(An Association of Attorneys including a Professional Corporation)
6740 East Camelback Road Suite 100, 85251
Telephone: 602-949-7676
Fax: 602-945-2149

David H. Carmichael — James A. Tilker (P.C.)

For full biographical listings, see the Martindale-Hubbell Law Directory

JEFFREY A. MATZ A PROFESSIONAL CORPORATION (AV㊉)

6711 East Camelback Road, Suite 8, 85251
Telephone: 602-955-0900
Fax: 602-955-1885

Jeffrey A. Matz (Not admitted in AZ)

PESKIND HYMSON & GOLDSTEIN, P.C. (AV)

14595 North Scottsdale Road, Suite 14, 85254
Telephone: 602-991-9077
Fax: 602-443-8854

E. J. Peskind — David B. Goldstein

Ronald Kanwischer — Alexis J. Stanton

OF COUNSEL

Marilee Miller Clarke — Jeffrey A. Leyton

For full biographical listings, see the Martindale-Hubbell Law Directory

*TUCSON,** Pima Co.

EDWARD P. BOLDING (AV)

110 South Church Avenue, Suite 9300, 85701
Telephone: 602-884-9221
Fax: 602-629-0197

For full biographical listings, see the Martindale-Hubbell Law Directory

CHANDLER, TULLAR, UDALL & REDHAIR (AV)

1700 Bank of America Plaza, 33 North Stone Avenue, 85701
Telephone: 602-623-4353
Telefax: 602-792-3426

MEMBERS OF FIRM

Thomas Chandler — Edwin M. Gaines, Jr.
D. B. Udall — Dwight M. Whitley, Jr.
Jack Redhair — E. Hardy Smith
Joe F. Tarver, Jr. — John J. Brady
Steven Weatherspoon — Christopher J. Smith
S. Jon Trachta — Charles V. Harrington
Bruce G. MacDonald

ASSOCIATES

Margaret A. Barton — Mark Fredenberg
Joel T. Ireland — Mariann T. Shinoskie
Kurt Kroese

Representative Clients: Arizona Electric Power Cooperative, Inc.; Atlantic & Richfield Co.; Northwestern Mutual Life Insurance Co.; Rex Broadcasting Co.; Citizen Auto Stage Company; Grayline Tours.

For full biographical listings, see the Martindale-Hubbell Law Directory

COREY & FARRELL, P.C. (AV)

Suite 830, Norwest Tower, One South Church Avenue, 85701-1620
Telephone: 602-882-4994
Telefax: 602-884-7757

Barry M. Corey — Barrett L. Kime
Patrick J. Farrell — Kristen B. Klotz

Representative Clients: Amphitheater Public School District; Civil Service Commission of the City of Tucson; La Quinta Homes, Inc.; Pima County Merit System Commission; DANKA-Uni-Copy Corp.; Introspect Health Care Corp.

For full biographical listings, see the Martindale-Hubbell Law Directory

JACK A. ETTINGER, P.C. (AV)

4301 East 5th Street, Suite 201, 85711
Telephone: 602-795-3516
Facsimile: 602-323-1080

Jack A. Ettinger — Cynthia D. Ettinger

Reference: First Interstate Bank of Arizona, N.A. (Downtown Branch, Tucson).

For full biographical listings, see the Martindale-Hubbell Law Directory

GABROY, ROLLMAN & BOSSÉ, P.C. (AV)

Suite 201, 2195 E. River Road, 85718
Telephone: 602-577-1300
Telefax: 602-577-0717

Richard M. Rollman — Ronald M. Lehman
John Gabroy — Lyle D. Aldridge

Ronna Lee Fickbohm — Richard A. Brown

For Complete List of Firm Personnel, See General Section

For full biographical listings, see the Martindale-Hubbell Law Directory

HARALSON, KINERK & MOREY, P.C. (AV)

82 South Stone Avenue, 85701
Telephone: 602-792-4330
Fax: 602-623-9568

Bob Barber (1903-1978) — Burton J. Kinerk
Dale Haralson — Carter Morey

Kenneth Lee — Daniel C. Gloria
R. Douglas Holt — Linda S. Sherrill
Gregory G. Wasley — Colleen L. Kinerk

For full biographical listings, see the Martindale-Hubbell Law Directory

KIMBLE, GOTHREAU & NELSON, P.C. (AV)

5285 East Williams Circle, Suite 3500, 85711-7411
Telephone: 602-748-2440
Fax: 602-748-2469

(See Next Column)

KIMBLE, GOTHREAU & NELSON P.C., *Tucson—Continued*

Darwin J. Nelson
Daryl A. Audilett
Stephen E. Kimble
Lawrence McDonough
David F. Toone
Michael P. Morrison
Michelle T. Lopez
Negatu Molla
Carroll E. Mizelle

OF COUNSEL

William Kimble

Representative Clients: State of Arizona; General Motors Corp.; Procter & Gamble Co.; St. Paul Fire and Marine Insurance Co.; City of Tucson; Tucson Electric Power Co.; United States Fidelity & Guaranty Co.; Industrial Indemnity Insurance Co.; Allstate Insurance Co.

For Complete List of Firm Personnel, See General Section

For full biographical listings, see the Martindale-Hubbell Law Directory

LEONARD FELKER ALTFELD & BATTAILE, P.C. (AV)

250 North Meyer Avenue, P.O. Box 191, 85702-0191
Telephone: 602-622-7733
Fax: 602-622-7967

David J. Leonard
Sidney L. Felker
Clifford B. Altfeld
John F. Battaile III
Judith B. Leonard
Denise Ann Faulk
Donna M. Aversa
Lynne M. Schwartz
Edward O. Comitz

For full biographical listings, see the Martindale-Hubbell Law Directory

MILLER, PITT & MCANALLY, P.C. (AV)

111 South Church Avenue, 85701-1680
Telephone: 602-792-3836
Telecopier: 602-624-5080
Nogales, Arizona Office: 272 West View Point, 85621.
Telephone: 602-281-1361.
Correspondent Office: Lizarraga, Robles, Savinon & Tapia, S.C. Boulevard Hidalgo 64, Colonia Centenario. CP 83000 Hermosillo, Sonora, Mexico.
Telephone: (62) 17-27-28, 12-79-89, 13-47-10, 12-79-18, 13-33-25, 12-77-70.

Barry N. Akin (1939-1988)
G. Eugene Isaak
Gerald Maltz
Janice A. Wezelman
Philip J. Hall
Grace McIlvain
Thomas G. Cotter
Lindsay E. Brew
Armando Rivera
Gus Aragón, Jr.
Eugene N. Goldsmith

Denneen L. Peterson
Jonathan Reich
Carole A. Summers

OF COUNSEL

Richard L. McAnally

Representative Clients: Bell Atlantic Metro Mobile; Evergreen International Aviation; Farmers Investment Co.; Forest City Enterprises; Vince Granatelli Racing; KVOA Channel 4 TV; Newmont Mining Corp.; S.L. Industries, Inc.; Tucson Unified School District; University of Arizona Foundation.

For Complete List of Firm Personnel, See General Section

For full biographical listings, see the Martindale-Hubbell Law Directory

MURPHY, GOERING, ROBERTS & BERKMAN, P.C. (AV)

Suite 302, 1840 East River Road, 85718
Telephone: 602-577-9300
FAX: 602-577-0848

James M. Murphy
Thomas M. Murphy
Scott Goering
Howard T. Roberts, Jr.
David L. Berkman
William L. Rubin
Carmine A. Brogna

Representative Clients: Roman Catholic Church Diocese of Tucson; Fireman's Fund Insurance; Safeco Insurance; Royal Insurance; Sentry Insurance; INA; Carondelet Health Services, Inc.; County of Pima; State Farm Insurance.
Reference: Bank One.

For full biographical listings, see the Martindale-Hubbell Law Directory

O'CONNOR, CAVANAGH, ANDERSON, WESTOVER, KILLINGSWORTH & BESHEARS, A PROFESSIONAL ASSOCIATION (AV)

Suite 2200 One South Church Avenue, 85701-1621
Telephone: 602-882-8912
FAX: 602-624-9564
Phoenix, Arizona Office: One East Camelback Road, Suite 1100, 85012.
Telephone: 602-263-2400.
FAX: 602-263-2900.
Sun City, Arizona Office: 13250 North Del Webb Boulevard, Suite B, 85351.
Telephone: 602-263-2808.
FAX: 602-933-3100.

(See Next Column)

Nogales, Arizona Office: 1827 North Mastick Way, 85621.
Telephone: 602-761-4215.
FAX: 602-761-3505.

Ted A. Schmidt
Bruce R. Heurlin
Peter Akmajian

Jenne S. Forbes
Drue A. Morgan-Birch

Amy M. Samberg
James D. Campbell

Representative Clients: Jeffco, Inc.
Reference: Citibank.

For Complete List of Firm Personnel, See General Section

For full biographical listings, see the Martindale-Hubbell Law Directory

RAVEN, KIRSCHNER & NORELL, P.C. (AV)

Suite 1600, One South Church Avenue, 85701-1612
Telephone: 602-628-8700
Telefax: 602-798-5200

Donald T. Awerkamp
Dennis J. Clancy
Sally M. Darcy
L. Anthony Fines
Barry Kirschner
Karen B. Tavolaro

Representative Clients: Pace American Bonding Company; Citibank (Arizona); Continental Medical Systems, Inc.; El Paso Natural Gas Co.; Norwest Bank Arizona; El Rio-Santa Cruz Neighborhood Health Center, Inc.; Resolution Trust Corp.; Sierra Vista Community Hospital; Southern Arizona Rehabilitation Hospital; Ford Motor Credit.

For Complete List of Firm Personnel, See General Section

For full biographical listings, see the Martindale-Hubbell Law Directory

SHULTZ & ROLLINS, LTD. (AV)

St. Philip's Plaza, 4280 North Campbell Avenue, Suite 214, 85718-6580
Telephone: 602-577-7777

Silas H. Shultz
Michael F. Rollins

Gerald T. Barton

For full biographical listings, see the Martindale-Hubbell Law Directory

SLUTES, SAKRISON, EVEN, GRANT & PELANDER, P.C. (AV)

33 North Stone Avenue, Suite 1100, 85701-1489
Telephone: 602-624-6691
Fax: 602-791-9632

Tom Slutes
James M. Sakrison
John R. Even
Philip H. Grant
A. John Pelander
David E. Hill
Christopher C. Browning
Mark D. Rubin
Jerome J. Bromiel
Alphus R. Christensen
Michael B. Smith
Mary Beth Joublanc
Neil H. Ashley

Representative Clients: Allstate Insurance Co.; St. Paul Insurance Co.; Aetna Casualty and Surety Co.; Montgomery Ward & Co.; Northbrook Insurance Co.; Farmers Insurance Group; Jim Click Auto Group; Beneficial Corp.

For full biographical listings, see the Martindale-Hubbell Law Directory

STOMPOLY, STROUD, GIDDINGS & GLICKSMAN, P.C. (AV)

1820 Citibank Tower, One South Church Avenue, 85702
Telephone: 602-628-8300
Telefax: 602-628-9948
Mailing Address: P.O. Box 190, Tucson, AZ, 85702-0190

John G. Stompoly
James L. Stroud
Charles E. Giddings
Elliot A. Glicksman
George Erickson

For full biographical listings, see the Martindale-Hubbell Law Directory

STREICH LANG, A PROFESSIONAL ASSOCIATION (AV)

One S. Church Avenue, Suite 1700, 85701-1621
Telephone: 602-770-8700
Fax: 602-623-2418
Phoenix, Arizona Office: Renaissance One, Two N. Central Avenue. 85004-2391.
Telephone: 602-229-5200.
Fax: 602-229-5690.
Las Vegas, Nevada Affiliated Office: Dawson & Associates, 3800 Howard Hughes Parkway, Suite 1500. 89109.
Telephone: 702-792-2727.
Fax: 702-792-2676.
Los Angeles California Office: 444 S. Flower Street, Suite 1530.
Telephone: 213-896-0484.

Craig H. Kaufman
Jeffrey Willis (Partner-in-Charge)

(See Next Column)

STREICH LANG A PROFESSIONAL ASSOCIATION—*Continued*

OF COUNSEL

Raymond R. Cusack

Michael R. Hall
Joy E. Herr-Cardillo
David V. Millard

Representative Clients: Granite Construction Co.; KFC Corporation; First Interstate Bank of Arizona, N.A.; Chicago Title Insurance Co.; Allied-Signal Aerospace Co.; Circle K Corp.; Burr-Brown Corporation; Valley National Bank of Arizona; Del Webb Corporation.

For Complete List of Firm Personnel, See General Section

For full biographical listings, see the Martindale-Hubbell Law Directory

ARKANSAS

*BENTON,** Saline Co.

ELLIS LAW FIRM (AV)

126 North Main Street, P.O. Box 1259, 72015
Telephone: 501-776-3916; Little Rock: 375-5210
FAX: 501-776-2278

MEMBER OF FIRM

George D. Ellis

LEGAL SUPPORT PERSONNEL

Rhonda Beck Malone (Legal Assistant and Office Manager)

References: The Union Bank of Benton; Benton State Bank.

For full biographical listings, see the Martindale-Hubbell Law Directory

*FAYETTEVILLE,** Washington Co.

BASSETT LAW FIRM (AV)

221 North College Avenue, P.O. Box 3618, 72702-3618
Telephone: 501-521-9996
Fax: 501-521-9600

MEMBERS OF FIRM

Woodson W. Bassett, Jr.
Woodson W. Bassett, III
Tod C. Bassett
Wm. Robert Still, Jr.
Walker Dale Garrett
Curtis L. Nebben
Earl Buddy Chadick, Jr.
Angela M. Doss
Gary V. Weeks
J. David Wall
Shawn David Twing
Vincent O. Chadick
Michael W. Langley

Representative Clients: The Home Insurance Co.; Hartford Insurance Group; Tyson Foods, Inc.; Farmers Insurance Group; CIGNA; Commercial Union Insurance Co.; St. Paul Fire and Marine Insurance Co.; AIG Aviation Ins. Co.; WAUSAU; USAA.

For full biographical listings, see the Martindale-Hubbell Law Directory

DAVIS, COX & WRIGHT (AV)

19 East Mountain Street, P.O. Drawer 1688, 72702-1688
Telephone: 501-521-7600
Fax: 501-521-7661

MEMBERS OF FIRM

Sidney P. Davis, Jr.
Walter B. Cox
Tilden P. Wright, III
Constance G. Clark
William Jackson Butt, II
Kelly P. Carithers
Tim E. Howell
Don A. Taylor
Paul H. Taylor

ASSOCIATES

Laura J. Andress
John G. Trice

Representative Clients: Aetna Casualty & Surety Co.; Arkansas Farm Bureau Insurance Cos.; Fireman's Fund Insurance Group; United States Fidelity and Guaranty Co.; St. Paul Insurance Cos; Chrysler Motors Corp.; Kemper Insurance Group; Kawasaki Motors Corp.; CIGNA.

For full biographical listings, see the Martindale-Hubbell Law Directory

NIBLOCK LAW FIRM (AV)

20 East Mountain Street, P.O. Drawer 818, 72701
Telephone: 501-521-5510
1-800-446-3314 Toll Free (Ark. only)
Fax: 501-444-7608

MEMBERS OF FIRM

Walter R. Niblock
Mima Cazort Wallace
George H. Niblock

For full biographical listings, see the Martindale-Hubbell Law Directory

ODOM, ELLIOTT, WINBURN AND WATSON (AV)

No. 1 East Mountain Street, P.O. Drawer 1868, 72702
Telephone: 501-442-7575
FAX: 501-442-9008

MEMBERS OF FIRM

Bobby Lee Odom
Don R. Elliott, Jr.
Russell B. Winburn
Jason L. Watson

J. Timothy Smith
Conrad T. Odom
Timothy J. Myers

Reference: Bank of Fayetteville, Fayetteville, Arkansas.

For full biographical listings, see the Martindale-Hubbell Law Directory

*FORT SMITH,** Sebastian Co.

BETHELL, CALLAWAY, ROBERTSON, BEASLEY & COWAN (AV)

615 North "B" Street, P.O. Box 23, 72902
Telephone: 501-782-7911
FAX: 501-782-7964

MEMBERS OF FIRM

Donald P. Callaway (1935-1984)
Thomas E. Robertson, Jr.
John R. Beasley
Kenneth W. Cowan
J. Michael Fitzhugh

ASSOCIATE

Matthew J. Ketcham

OF COUNSEL

Edgar E. Bethell

Representative Clients: The Aetna Casualty & Surety Co.; James River - Dixie Cup; Arkansas-Oklahoma Gas Corp.; Beverage Products Corp. (Pepsi-Cola); The Prudential Insurance Company of America; Sentry - Dairyland Insurance Co; General Tire and Rubber; Quanex Corp.; The Fort Smith Municipal Airport Commission; Southern Steel & Wire Co.

For full biographical listings, see the Martindale-Hubbell Law Directory

DAILY, WEST, CORE, COFFMAN & CANFIELD (AV)

Stephens Office Building, 623 Garrison Avenue, P.O. Box 1446, 72902
Telephone: 501-782-0361
Fax: 501-782-6160

MEMBERS OF FIRM

Ben Core
Eldon F. Coffman
Jerry L. Canfield
Thomas A. Daily
Wyman R. Wade, Jr.
Stanley A. Leasure
Douglas M. Carson
Michael C. Carter
Robert W. Bishop

OF COUNSEL

James E. West

Counsel for: Claims Management, Inc. (Wal-Mart); Arkla, Inc.; City of Fort Smith; Commercial Union Insurance Cos.; Pennzoil Exploration and Production Co.; Silvey Cos., Inc.; CIGNA; Metropolitan Life Insurance Co.; Chevron U.S.A., Inc.

For full biographical listings, see the Martindale-Hubbell Law Directory

JONES, GILBREATH, JACKSON & MOLL (AV)

401 North Seventh Street, P.O. Box 2023, 72902
Telephone: 501-782-7203
Fax: 501-782-9460

MEMBERS OF FIRM

Robert L. Jones, Jr.
E. C. Gilbreath
Robert L. Jones, III
Randolph C. Jackson
Kendall B. Jones
Mark A. Moll

ASSOCIATES

Charles R. Garner, Jr.
Daniel W. Gilbreath
Lynn M. Flynn
Christina Dawn Ferguson

Insurance Counsel for: Argonaut Insurance Cos.; Farmers Insurance Group; Maryland-American General Insurance Cos.; Shelter Insurance Cos.; Travelers Insurance Co.; Continental Insurance Cos.
Counsel for: Merchants National Bank, Fort Smith, Ar.; Ryder Truck Rental, Inc.; Whirlpool Corp.

For full biographical listings, see the Martindale-Hubbell Law Directory

WARNER AND SMITH (AV)

214 North Sixth Street, P.O. Box 1626, 72901
Telephone: 501-782-6041
Fax: 501-782-0841

MEMBERS OF FIRM

Harry Preston Warner (1885-1969)
Cecil Randolph Warner (1890-1955)
Thomas G. Graves (1939-1971)
Douglas O. Smith, Jr.
C. Wayne Harris
Gerald L. DeLung
Patrick Neill Moore
Lillard Cody Hayes
G. Alan Wooten
James Melvin Dunn

(See Next Column)

WARNER AND SMITH, *Fort Smith—Continued*

MEMBERS OF FIRM (Continued)

John Alan Lewis
Gary W. Udouj
Joel D. Johnson
J. Randall McGinnis
Kathryn A. Stocks

Matthew H. P. Warner

OF COUNSEL

C. R. Warner, Jr.

District Attorneys for: Burlington Northern Railroad Co.
Counsel for: Fairfield Communities, Inc.; River Valley Bank.
Local Counsel for: Planters Division, Nabisco Brands, Inc.; Gerber Products Co.; United States Fidelity & Guaranty Co.; Aetna Group; Fireman's Fund-American Insurance Cos.; Hiram Walker & Sons, Inc.; Continental National American Group.

For full biographical listings, see the Martindale-Hubbell Law Directory

*JONESBORO,** Craighead Co.

BARRETT & DEACON (AV)

Mercantile Bank Building, 300 South Church Street, P.O. Box 1700, 72403
Telephone: 501-931-1700
FAX: 501-931-1800

MEMBERS OF FIRM

Joe C. Barrett (1897-1980)
John C. Deacon
J. Barry Deacon
David W. Cahoon
Ralph W. Waddell
Paul D. Waddell

ASSOCIATES

D. Price Marshall, Jr.
James D. Bradbury (Not admitted in AR)
Kevin W. Cole

For full biographical listings, see the Martindale-Hubbell Law Directory

*LITTLE ROCK,** Pulaski Co.

ALLEN LAW FIRM, A PROFESSIONAL CORPORATION (AV)

950 Centre Place, 212 Center Street, 72201
Telephone: 501-374-7100
Telecopier: 501-374-1611

H. William Allen

Sandra E. Jackson

Representative Clients: Worthen National Bank of Arkansas; Colonia Insurance Co.; Shoney's Inc.; Miller Brewing Co.; Garlock, Inc.

For full biographical listings, see the Martindale-Hubbell Law Directory

ANDERSON & KILPATRICK (AV)

The First Commercial Building, 400 West Capitol Avenue, Suite 2640, 72201
Telephone: 501-372-1887
Fax: 501-372-7706

MEMBERS OF FIRM

Overton S. Anderson, II
Joseph E. Kilpatrick, Jr.
Michael E. Aud
Aylmer Gene Williams
Randy P. Murphy
Frances E. Scroggins

ASSOCIATES

Mariam T. Hopkins
Michael P. Vanderford

For full biographical listings, see the Martindale-Hubbell Law Directory

ARNOLD, GROBMYER & HALEY, A PROFESSIONAL ASSOCIATION (AV)

875 Union National Plaza, 124 West Capitol Avenue, P.O. Box 70, 72203
Telephone: 501-376-1171
Fax: 501-375-3548

Benjamin F. Arnold
James F. Dowden
John H. Haley
David H. Pennington
Richard L. Ramsay
Robert R. Ross

For Complete List of Firm Personnel, See General Section

For full biographical listings, see the Martindale-Hubbell Law Directory

CEARLEY LAW FIRM (AV)

Suite 350 Gans Building, 217 West Second Street, 72201
Telephone: 501-375-9451
Fax: 501-374-3463

Robert M. Cearley, Jr.

Counsel for: Arkansas Bankers Association; Greyhound Lines, Inc.

For full biographical listings, see the Martindale-Hubbell Law Directory

DAVIDSON, HORNE & HOLLINGSWORTH, A PROFESSIONAL ASSOCIATION (AV)

401 West Capitol, Suite 501, P.O. Box 3363, 72203
Telephone: 501-376-4731
FAX: 501-372-7142

Walter W. Davidson (Retired)
Allan W. Horne
Cyril Hollingsworth
Michael O. Parker
Garland W. Binns, Jr.
James P. Beachboard
Mark H. Allison
Judy P. McNeil

William S. Roach

Representative Clients: Associated Industries of Arkansas, Inc.; Arkansas Blue Cross and Blue Shield; Worthen National Bank of Arkansas; J.B. Hunt Transport, Inc.; American Insurance Association; Arkansas Kraft Corp.; Gaylord Container Corp.; American Pioneer Life Insurance Co.; Robinette-Burnett Construction Co.

For full biographical listings, see the Martindale-Hubbell Law Directory

DUNCAN & RAINWATER TRIAL LAWYERS A PROFESSIONAL ASSOCIATION (AV)

Suite 500 Three Financial Centre, 900 South Shackleford, P.O. Box 25938, 72221-5938
Telephone: 501-228-7600
FAX: 501-228-7664

Phillip J. Duncan (P.A.)
Michael R. Rainwater (P.A.)
Robert A. Russell, Jr.
Neil Ray Chamberlin

For full biographical listings, see the Martindale-Hubbell Law Directory

FRIDAY, ELDREDGE & CLARK (AV)

A Partnership including Professional Associations
Formerly, Smith, Williams, Friday, Eldredge & Clark
2000 First Commercial Building, 400 West Capitol, 72201-3493
Telephone: 501-376-2011
Telecopier: 501-376-2147; 376-6369

MEMBERS OF FIRM

William H. Sutton (P.A.)
John Dewey Watson (P.A.)
Paul B. Benham, III, (P.A.)
Larry W. Burks (P.A.)
James M. Simpson, Jr., (P.A.)
Elizabeth J. Robben (P.A.)
Kevin A. Crass (P.A.)
William A. Waddell, Jr., (P.A.)
Jerry L. Malone (P.A.)

ASSOCIATES

Tonia P. Jones
David D. Wilson
Jeffrey H. Moore
Jonann C. Roosevelt
Tony L. Wilcox

Counsel for: Union Pacific System; St. Paul Insurance Co.; Liberty Mutual Insurance Co.; Cigna Property & Casualty Co.; Arkansas Power & Light Co.; Dillard Department Stores, Inc.; First Commercial Corp.; Browning Arms Co.; Phillips Petroleum Co.; Aetna Casualty & Surety Co.

For Complete List of Firm Personnel, See General Section

For full biographical listings, see the Martindale-Hubbell Law Directory

HILBURN, CALHOON, HARPER, PRUNISKI & CALHOUN, LTD. (AV)

P.O. Box 1256, 72203-1256
Telephone: 501-372-0110
FAX: 501-372-2029
North Little Rock, Arkansas Office: Eighth Floor, The Twin City Bank Building, One Riverfront Place, P.O. Box 5551, 72119.
Telephone: 501-372-0110.
FAX: 501-372-2029.

Sam Hilburn
John E. Pruniski, III
John C. Calhoun, Jr.
David M. Fuqua
James M. McHaney, Jr.
Phillip W. Campbell
J. Maurice Rogers
Scott E. Daniel
Scott Thomas Vaughn

Dorcy Kyle Corbin
James D. Lawson
Graham F. Sloan
Dean L. Worley

Representative Clients: The Twin City Bank; Merril Lynch Pierce Fenner & Smith, Inc.; Central Arkansas Risk Management Association; Smith Barney Shearson, Inc.; Deere & Co.

For Complete List of Firm Personnel, See General Section

For full biographical listings, see the Martindale-Hubbell Law Directory

HOOVER & STOREY (AV)

111 Center Street, 11th Floor, 72201-4445
Telephone: 501-376-8500
Facsimile: 501-372-3255

(See Next Column)

HOOVER & STOREY—*Continued*

MEMBERS OF FIRM

Paul W. Hoover, Jr.
O. H. Storey, III
John Kooistra, III
Lawrence Joseph Brady
William P. Dougherty
Max C. Mehlburger
Joyce Bradley Babin
Herbert W. Kell, Jr.
Letty McAdams

For full biographical listings, see the Martindale-Hubbell Law Directory

HUCKABAY, MUNSON, ROWLETT & TILLEY, P.A. (AV)

First Commercial Building, Suite 1900, 400 West Capitol, 72201
Telephone: 501-374-6535
FAX: 501-374-5906

Mike Huckabay
Bruce E. Munson
Beverly A. Rowlett
James W. Tilley
John E. Moore
Tim Boone
Rick Runnells
Sarah Ann Presson

Lizabeth Lookadoo
Valerie Denton
Edward T. Oglesby
D. Michael Huckabay, Jr.
Carol Lockard Worley
Mark S. Breeding
Elizabeth Fletcher Rogers
Jeffrey A. Weber

Representative Clients: Allstate Insurance Company; American International Group; American Medical International; Farmers Insurance Group; General Electric Company; Nationwide Insurance Company; Safeco Insurance Company; State Farm Mutual Automobile Insurance Company; State Farm Fire and Casualty Company; United States Fidelity and Guaranty Company.

For full biographical listings, see the Martindale-Hubbell Law Directory

LASER, SHARP, WILSON, BUFFORD & WATTS, P.A. (AV)

101 S. Spring Street, Suite 300, 72201-2488
Telephone: 501-376-2981
Telecopier: 501-376-2417

Dan F. Bufford
Brian A. Brown
Karen J. Hughes

Representative Clients: Allstate Insurance Co.; American International Insurance Group; Continental Insurance Cos.; Farm Bureau Insurance Cos. (Casualty & Fire); Farmers Insurance Group; GAB Business Services, Inc.; St. Paul Insurance Cos.; Scottsdale Insurance Co.; State Farm Auto (Fire) Insurance Cos.

For Complete List of Firm Personnel, See General Section

For full biographical listings, see the Martindale-Hubbell Law Directory

THE MCMATH LAW FIRM, P.A. (AV)

711 West Third Street, P.O. Box 1401, 72203
Telephone: 501-376-3021
FAX: 501-374-5118

Sidney S. McMath
Leland F. Leatherman
Sandy S. McMath
Phillip H. McMath
James Bruce McMath
Mart Vehik
Winslow Drummond
Paul E. Harrison
Sandra L. Sanders

For full biographical listings, see the Martindale-Hubbell Law Directory

WILLIAM L. OWEN (AV)

The Fones House, 902 West Second, P.O. Box 989, 72203
Telephone: 501-372-1655
Fax: 501-372-7884

For full biographical listings, see the Martindale-Hubbell Law Directory

THE PERRONI LAW FIRM, P.A. (AV)

Stewart Building, 801 West Third Street, 72201
Telephone: 501-372-6555
Fax: 501-372-6333

Samuel A. Perroni
Rita S. Looney
Mona J. McNutt

LEGAL SUPPORT PERSONNEL

Sherry Joyce

References: First Commercial Bank, Little Rock, Ark.; Bank of Little Rock, Ark.

For full biographical listings, see the Martindale-Hubbell Law Directory

ROSE LAW FIRM, A PROFESSIONAL ASSOCIATION (AV)

120 East Fourth Street, 72201
Telephone: 501-375-9131
Telecopy: 501-375-1309

(See Next Column)

Phillip Carroll
Kenneth Robert Shemin
Jerry C. Jones
James H. Druff
Jess Askew, III
Amy Lee Stewart

Representative Clients: Aluminum Company of America; The Equitable Life Assurance Society of the United States; Federal Deposit Insurance Corp.; Bridgestone/Firestone, Inc.; General Motors Corp.; Kemper Insurance Group; New York Life Insurance Co.; The Prudential Insurance Company of America; TCBY Enterprises.

For Complete List of Firm Personnel, See General Section

For full biographical listings, see the Martindale-Hubbell Law Directory

WILLIAMS & ANDERSON (AV)

Twenty-Second Floor, 111 Center Street, 72201
Telephone: 501-372-0800
FAX: 501-372-6453

MEMBERS OF FIRM

W. Jackson Williams
Philip S. Anderson
Peter G. Kumpe
David F. Menz
Steven W. Quattlebaum
James E. Hathaway III
John E. Tull, III
Rush B. Deacon
J. Leon Holmes

Thomas G. Williams
J. Madison Barker
Jeanne L. Seewald
Sarah J. Heffley

Representative Clients: Arkansas Development Finance Authority; Coregis; Dean Witter Reynolds Inc.; Entergy Power, Inc.; Little Rock Newspapers, Inc. d/b/a/ Arkansas Democrat-Gazette; Texaco, Inc.; Transport Indemnity Insurance Co.; Wal-Mart Stores, Inc.

For Complete List of Firm Personnel, See General Section

For full biographical listings, see the Martindale-Hubbell Law Directory

WILSON, ENGSTROM, CORUM, DUDLEY & COULTER (AV)

809 West Third Street, P.O. Box 71, 72203
Telephone: 501-375-6453
FAX: 501-375-5914

MEMBERS OF FIRM

Roxanne Wilson (1947-1992)
Stephen Engstrom
Gary D. Corum
Timothy O. Dudley
Nate Coulter

For full biographical listings, see the Martindale-Hubbell Law Directory

*RUSSELLVILLE,** Pope Co.

RICHARD L. PEEL, P.A. (AV)

120 South Glenwood, P.O. Box 986, 72811
Telephone: 501-968-4000
Fax: 501-968-4388

Richard L. Peel

Representative Clients: First Bank of Arkansas; West Central Solid Waste Board; Valley Motors Inc.; Ridout Lumber Company; Russellville School District; Russellville Housing Authority; City of Ola, Arkansas; City of Russellville, Arkansas.
Agents for: TRW Title Insurance Co.
Reference: First Bank of Arkansas, Russellville, Arkansas.

For full biographical listings, see the Martindale-Hubbell Law Directory

SILOAM SPRINGS, Benton Co.

ELROD LAW FIRM (AV)

123 South Broadway, P.O. Box 460, 72761
Telephone: 501-524-8191
FAX: 501-524-3550

MEMBERS OF FIRM

Russell Elrod (1904-1985)
John R. Elrod
Georgia Elrod
Daniel R. Elrod

ASSOCIATE

Martha L. Londagin

General Counsel for: First National Bank, Siloam Springs and Gentry, Ark.; John Brown University; Northwest Arkansas Regional Airport Authority.
Representative Clients: Simmons Industries, Inc.; Gates Rubber Co.

For full biographical listings, see the Martindale-Hubbell Law Directory

SPRINGDALE, Washington Co.

CYPERT, CROUCH, CLARK & HARWELL (AV)

111 Holcomb Street, P.O. Box 869, 72764-1400
Telephone: 501-751-5222
Fax: 501-751-5777

(See Next Column)

CYPERT, CROUCH, CLARK & HARWELL, *Springdale—Continued*

Courtney C. Crouch (1912-1975) William M. Clark, Jr.
James D. Cypert Charles L. Harwell
James E. Crouch Brian L. Spaulding
R. Jeffrey Reynerson

OF COUNSEL

Leslie L. Reid Stanley W. Ludwig

General Counsel for: First National Bank of Springdale; Springdale Memorial Hospital; Springdale School District.
Representative Clients: Purina Mills, Inc.; Swift-Eckrich, Inc.
Insurance Clients: Western Casualty & Surety Co.; The John Hancock Cos.; Home Ins. Co.; Liberty Mutual; Fireman's Fund.

For full biographical listings, see the Martindale-Hubbell Law Directory

LISLE LAW FIRM, P.C. (AV)

210 South Thompson Street, Suite 6, P.O. Box 6877, 72766-6877
Telephone: 501-750-4444
Fax: 501-751-6792

John Lisle

Joe B. Reed Christopher James Lisle
Donnie W. Rutledge, II

For full biographical listings, see the Martindale-Hubbell Law Directory

*TEXARKANA,** Miller Co.

LAVENDER, ROCHELLE, BARNETTE & PICKETT (AV)

507 Hickory Street, P.O. Box 1938, 75504
Telephone: 501-773-3187
Telecopier: 501-773-3181

MEMBERS OF FIRM

G. William Lavender Charles Decker Barnette
Jerry A. Rochelle John M. Pickett

ASSOCIATE

Shannon Tuckett

Counsel for: Southwestern Electric Power Co.; Prudential Insurance Company of America; E.I. DuPont De Nemours & Company, Inc.; John Hancock Mutual Life Insurance Co.; Federal Deposit Insurance Corp.; Farmers Insurance Group of Cos.; New York Life Insurance Co.; Commercial National Bank of Texarkana; Builders Transport, Inc., Resolution Trust Corp.

For full biographical listings, see the Martindale-Hubbell Law Directory

SMITH, STROUD, McCLERKIN, DUNN & NUTTER (AV)

State Line Plaza, Box 8030, 75502-5945
Telephone: 501-773-5651
Telecopier: 501-772-2037

MEMBERS OF FIRM

Hayes C. McClerkin Nelson V. Shaw
Winford L. Dunn, Jr. R. David Freeze
R. Gary Nutter Demaris A. Hart
William David Carter

ASSOCIATE

Carol Cannedy Dalby

LEGAL SUPPORT PERSONNEL

LEGAL ASSISTANTS

Myra J. Conaway Sonja L. Oliver

Representative Clients: North American Energy Corporation (NorAm); The State First National Bank of Texarkana; CNA Insurance Cos.; First Federal Savings & Loan Assn.; St. Michael Hospital; Shelter Insurance Cos.; CIGNA Insurance Cos.; Sentry Insurance.

For Complete List of Firm Personnel, See General Section

For full biographical listings, see the Martindale-Hubbell Law Directory

WEST MEMPHIS, Crittenden Co.

RIEVES & MAYTON (AV)

304 East Broadway, P.O. Box 1359, 72303
Telephone: 501-735-3420
Telecopier: 501-735-4678

MEMBERS OF FIRM

Elton A. Rieves, Jr. (1909-1984) Michael R. Mayton
Elton A. Rieves, III Elton A. Rieves, IV

ASSOCIATES

Martin W. Bowen William J. Stanley

For full biographical listings, see the Martindale-Hubbell Law Directory

CALIFORNIA

APTOS, Santa Cruz Co.

DENNIS J. KEHOE A LAW CORPORATION (AV)

311 Bonita Drive, 95003
Telephone: 408-662-8444
Fax: 408-662-0227

Dennis J. Kehoe

For full biographical listings, see the Martindale-Hubbell Law Directory

RUMMONDS, WILLIAMS & MAIR (AV)

311 Bonita Drive, P.O. Box 1870, 95001
Telephone: 408-688-2911
Sacramento, California Office: 6991 Garden Highway. 95837.
Telephone: 916-927-4610.

MEMBERS OF FIRM

James S. Rummonds Sally Ann Williams

OF COUNSEL

Peter K. Mair Patrick J. Waltz
(Resident, Sacramento Office)

For full biographical listings, see the Martindale-Hubbell Law Directory

*BAKERSFIELD,** Kern Co.

BUNKER, SAGHATELIAN & GIBBS (AV)

A Law Partnership
2821 "H" Street, 93301-1913
Telephone: 805-634-1144
Telecopier: 805-327-1923

Bruce F. Bunker Tommi R. Saghatelian
Steven G. Gibbs

ASSOCIATE

Timothy L. Kleier

For full biographical listings, see the Martindale-Hubbell Law Directory

KLEIN, WEGIS, DENATALE, GOLDNER & MUIR (AV)

A Partnership including Professional Corporations
(Formerly Di Giorgio, Davis, Klein, Wegis, Duggan & Friedman)
ARCO Tower, 4550 California Avenue, Second Floor, P.O. Box 11172, 93389-1172
Telephone: 805-395-1000
Telecopier: 805-326-0418
Santa Ana, California Office: Park Tower Building #610, 200 W. Santa Ana Boulevard, 92701.
Telephone: 714-285-0711.
Fax: 714-285-9003.

MEMBERS OF FIRM

Anthony J. Klein (Inc.) Gregory A. Muir
Ralph B. Wegis (Inc.) Barry L. Goldner
Thomas V. DeNatale, Jr. Jay L. Rosenlieb
David J. Cooper

Representative Clients: Bank of America; Great Western Bank; Mojave Pipeline Co.; Transamerican Title Insurance Co.; Dean Whittier Reynolds, Inc.; California Republic Bank; San Joaquin Bank; Nahama & Weagant Energy Co.; Freymiller Trucking, Inc.; Westinghouse Electric Co.

For Complete List of Firm Personnel, See General Section

For full biographical listings, see the Martindale-Hubbell Law Directory

KUHS, PARKER & STANTON (AV)

Suite 200, 1200 Truxtun Avenue, P.O. Box 2205, 93303
Telephone: 805-322-4004
FAX: 805-322-2906

William C. Kuhs James R. Parker, Jr.
David B. Stanton

Lorraine G. Adams John P. Doering, III
Robert G. Kuhs

Reference: First Interstate Bank (Bakersfield Main Branch).

For full biographical listings, see the Martindale-Hubbell Law Directory

ROBINSON, PALMER & LOGAN (AV)

Suite 150, 3434 Truxtun Avenue, 93301
Telephone: 805-323-8277
Fax: 805-323-4205

(See Next Column)

ROBINSON, PALMER & LOGAN—*Continued*

MEMBERS OF FIRM

Oliver U. Robinson
William D. Palmer
Gary L. Logan

For Complete List of Firm Personnel, See General Section

For full biographical listings, see the Martindale-Hubbell Law Directory

THOMAS M. STANTON (AV)

1430 Truxtun Avenue, Suite 900, 93301
Telephone: 805-861-8655
Fax: 805-322-3508

For full biographical listings, see the Martindale-Hubbell Law Directory

WARREN C. WETTEROTH (AV)

Park Plaza, 1801 Oak Street, Suite 166, 93301
Telephone: 805-334-2780
Fax: 805-326-1628

For full biographical listings, see the Martindale-Hubbell Law Directory

LAW OFFICES OF YOUNG WOOLDRIDGE (AV)

1800 30th Street, Fourth Floor, 93301
Telephone: 805-327-9661
Facsimile: 805-327-1087

MEMBERS OF FIRM

G. Neil Farr
Steve W. Nichols
Larry R. Cox
Scott K. Kuney

ASSOCIATE

Russell B. Hicks

Representative Clients: Arvin-Edison Water Storage District; Motor City Truck Sales and Service.
References: Wells Fargo Bank; First Interstate Bank; California Republic Bank.

For Complete List of Firm Personnel, See General Section

For full biographical listings, see the Martindale-Hubbell Law Directory

BERKELEY, Alameda Co.

GILLIN, JACOBSON, ELLIS, LARSEN & DOYLE (AV)

Seventh Floor, 2030 Addison Street, P.O. Box 523, 94701-0523
Telephone: 510-841-7820
Fax: 510-848-0266
San Francisco Office: One Sutter Street, 10th Floor.
Telephone: 415-986-4777.

Andrew R. Gillin
Ralph L. Jacobson
Luke Ellis
James Paul Larsen
Richard P. Doyle, Jr.
Susan Hunt
Mitchell S. Rosenfeld

For full biographical listings, see the Martindale-Hubbell Law Directory

BEVERLY HILLS, Los Angeles Co.

FRIEDMAN & FRIEDMAN (AV)

9454 Wilshire Boulevard, Suite 313, 90212-2904
Telephone: 310-273-2800
Fax: 310-273-3642

Ira M. Friedman
Abby B. Friedman

Representative Clients: Gursey Schneider & Co.; Harvey Capital Corp.; Christensen, White, Miller, Fink & Jacobs; Jeffer, Mangels, Butler & Marmaro; Key Bank of Maine; Southern California Bank.

For full biographical listings, see the Martindale-Hubbell Law Directory

NORMINTON & WIITA (AV)

A Partnership including Professional Corporations
433 North Camden Drive Twelfth Floor, 90210
Telephone: 310-205-2077
Facsimile: 310-205-2078

Thomas M. Norminton (P.C.)
Douglas P. Wiita (P.C.)
Kathleen Dority Fuster

For full biographical listings, see the Martindale-Hubbell Law Directory

SCHWARTZ, WISOT & RODOV, A PROFESSIONAL LAW CORPORATION (AV)

Suite 315, 315 South Beverly Drive, 90212
Telephone: 310-277-2323
Fax: 310-556-2308

(See Next Column)

Bruce Edward Schwartz
Valerie Wisot
Valentina Rodov

Reference: Home Savings of America (Century City Office, Los Angeles, California)

For full biographical listings, see the Martindale-Hubbell Law Directory

TURNER, GERSTENFELD, WILK, TIGERMAN & YOUNG (AV)

Formerly, Turner, Gerstenfeld & Wilk. . . est. 1972
Suite 510, 8383 Wilshire Boulevard, 90211
Telephone: 213-653-3900
Facsimile: 213-653-3021

MEMBERS OF FIRM

Bert Z. Tigerman
Steven E. Young
Edward Friedman
Linda Wight Mazur

ASSOCIATES

Joan R. Isaacs
Dortha Larene Pyles
Steven A. Morris
Vicki L. Cresap

For Complete List of Firm Personnel, See General Section

For full biographical listings, see the Martindale-Hubbell Law Directory

CARLSBAD, San Diego Co.

GATZKE, MISPAGEL & DILLON (AV)

A Partnership including a Professional Law Corporation
Suite 200, 1921 Palomar Oaks Way, P.O. Box 1636, 92009
Telephone: 619-431-9501
Fax: 619-431-9512

MEMBERS OF FIRM

Michael Scott Gatzke (A Professional Law Corporation)
Mark F. Mispagel
Mark J. Dillon
Lori D. Ballance

ASSOCIATES

David P. Hubbard
Kristin Beth White

For full biographical listings, see the Martindale-Hubbell Law Directory

LODGE & HELLER (AV)

A Partnership including a Professional Corporation
1901 Camino Vida Roble, Suite 110, 92008
Telephone: 619-931-9700
Fax: 619-931-1155
Pauma Valley, California Office: The Pauma Building, Suite 403, 16160 Highway 76, P.O. Box 600.
Telephone: 619-749-3199.

MEMBERS OF FIRM

Eric T. Lodge (P.C.)
Richard A. Heller

William R. Baber

For full biographical listings, see the Martindale-Hubbell Law Directory

WEIL & WRIGHT (AV)

1921 Palomar Oaks Way, Suite 301, 92008
Telephone: 619-438-1214
Telefax: 619-438-2666

Paul M. Weil
James T. Reed, Jr.
David A. Ebersole

For full biographical listings, see the Martindale-Hubbell Law Directory

CLAREMONT, Los Angeles Co.

JOHN C. MCCARTHY (AV)

401 Harvard Avenue, 91711
Telephone: 909-621-4984
Telecopier: 909-621-5757

Reference: Bank of America, Claremont Branch.

For full biographical listings, see the Martindale-Hubbell Law Directory

CORONA DEL MAR, Orange Co.

GERALD M. SHAW A PROFESSIONAL CORPORATION (AV)

1111 Bayside Drive, Suite 270, 92625
Telephone: 714-759-5600
Telefax: 714-759-5656

Gerald M. Shaw

References: Marine National Bank, Irvine; Western Financial Savings Bank, Orange.

For full biographical listings, see the Martindale-Hubbell Law Directory

COSTA MESA, Orange Co.

BALFOUR MACDONALD TALBOT MIJUSKOVIC & OLMSTED, A PROFESSIONAL CORPORATION (AV)

Suite 720, 611 Anton Boulevard, 92626
Telephone: 714-546-2400
Fax: 714-546-5008

R. Wayne Olmsted

For Complete List of Firm Personnel, See General Section

For full biographical listings, see the Martindale-Hubbell Law Directory

COULOMBE KOTTKE & KING, A PROFESSIONAL CORPORATION (AV)

Comerica Bank Tower, 611 Anton Boulevard, Suite 1260, P.O. Box 2410, 92628-2410
Telephone: 714-540-1234
Fax: 714-754-0808; 714-754-0707

Ronald B. Coulombe
Jon S. Kottke
Raymond King

COUNSEL

Mary J. Swanson
Roy B. Woolsey

LEGAL SUPPORT PERSONNEL

PARALEGALS

Karen M. Carrillo
Laura A. Bieser
Vicky M. Pearson

LEGAL ADMINISTRATOR

Sheila O. Elpern

For full biographical listings, see the Martindale-Hubbell Law Directory

MCCAULEY & ASSOCIATES (AV)

Bank of the West, 611 Anton Boulevard, Suite 1240, 92626
Telephone: 714-957-3710
Fax: 714-957-3718

MEMBER OF FIRM

John J. McCauley

For full biographical listings, see the Martindale-Hubbell Law Directory

MURTAUGH, MILLER, MEYER & NELSON (AV)

A Partnership including Professional Corporations
3200 Park Center Drive, 9th Floor, P.O. Box 5023, 92628-5023
Telephone: 714-513-6800
Facsimile: 714-513-6899

Michael J. Murtaugh (A Professional Corporation)
Bradford H. Miller (A Professional Corporation)
Richard E. Meyer
Michael J. Nelson
Robert T. Lemen
Mark S. Himmelstein
Harry A. Halkowich
Madelyn A. Enright
James A. Murphy, IV
Lawrence A. Treglia, Jr.

Roberta A. Evans
Debra Lynn Braasch
Thomas J. Skane
Lydia R. Bouzaglou
David C. Holt
Robin L. More
Lawrence J. DiPinto
Debra L. Reilly
Susan Westover
Lawrence D. Marks
Carrie E. Phelan
Robert A. Fisher, II
John R. Browning
Eric J. Dubin
Stacey Sarowatz
Daniel E. Roston

OF COUNSEL

Susan W. Menkes
Gary M. Pohlson

Representative Clients: Continental Insurance Cos. (Continental Loss Adjusting Services); Design Professionals Insurance Co.
Reference: Wells Fargo Bank.

For full biographical listings, see the Martindale-Hubbell Law Directory

RUTAN & TUCKER (AV)

A Partnership including Professional Corporations
611 Anton Boulevard, Suite 1400, P.O. Box 1950, 92626
Telephone: 714-641-5100; 213-625-7586
Telecopier: 714-546-9035

MEMBERS OF FIRM

Leonard A. Hampel, Jr.
John B. Hurlbut, Jr.
Milford W. Dahl, Jr.
Theodore I. Wallace, Jr., (P.C.)
Robert C. Braun
Edward D. Sybesma, Jr., (P.C.)
Thomas S. Salinger (P.C.)
David C. Larsen (P.C.)
Clifford E. Frieden
Michael D. Rubin
Ira G. Rivin (P.C.)
Jeffrey M. Oderman (P.C.)
Robert S. Bower
William M. Marticorena
William J. Caplan
Michael T. Hornak
Philip D. Kohn
Joel D. Kuperberg
Steven A. Nichols
William W. Wynder

(See Next Column)

MEMBERS OF FIRM (Continued)

Philip M. Prince
Mark B. Frazier
M. Katherine Jenson
Duke Wahlquist
Richard Montevideo
Ernest W. Klatte, III
Jayne Taylor Kacer

ASSOCIATE

Michael K. Slattery

OF COUNSEL

Garvin F. Shallenberger

For Complete List of Firm Personnel, See General Section

For full biographical listings, see the Martindale-Hubbell Law Directory

ENCINO, Los Angeles Co.

ALLAN F. GROSSMAN (AV)

Suite 304 Encino Law Center, 15915 Ventura Boulevard, 91436
Telephone: 818-990-8200
FAX: 818-990-4616

Reference: First Los Angeles Bank, Woodland Hills.

For full biographical listings, see the Martindale-Hubbell Law Directory

MARINO & DALLINGER (AV)

An Association including a Professional Corporation
17835 Ventura Boulevard, Suite 209, 91316
Telephone: 818-774-3636
FAX: 818-774-3635

Timothy G. Dallinger
J. Anthony Marino (A Professional Corporation)

For full biographical listings, see the Martindale-Hubbell Law Directory

*FRESNO,** Fresno Co.

DOWLING, MAGARIAN, AARON & HEYMAN, INCORPORATED (AV)

Suite 200, 6051 North Fresno Street, 93710
Telephone: 209-432-4500
Fax: 209-432-4590

Kent F. Heyman
Adolfo M. Corona
Philip David Kopp

Francine Marie Kanne
John G. Kerkorian
Richard E. Heatter
James C. Sherwood
Mark D. Magarian

Reference: Wells Fargo Bank (Main).

For Complete List of Firm Personnel, See General Section

For full biographical listings, see the Martindale-Hubbell Law Directory

JACKSON EMERICH PEDREIRA & NAHIGIAN, A PROFESSIONAL CORPORATION (AV)

7108 North Fresno Street, Suite 400, 93720-2938
Telephone: 209-261-0200
Facsimile: 209-261-0910

Donald A. Jackson
David R. Emerich
Thomas A. Pedreira
Eliot S. Nahigian
David A. Fike

John W. Phillips
John M. Cardot
Nicholas A. Tarjoman
Jeffrey B. Pape
David G. Hansen

Reference: Bank of California.

For full biographical listings, see the Martindale-Hubbell Law Directory

JORY, PETERSON, WATKINS & SMITH (AV)

555 West Shaw, Suite C-1, P.O. Box 5394, 93755
Telephone: 209-225-6700
Telecopier: 209-225-3416

MEMBERS OF FIRM

Jay V. Jory
John E. Peterson
Cal B. Watkins, Jr.
Michael Jens F. Smith

ASSOCIATES

William M. Woolman
Marcia A. Ross
Mark A. Pasculli

Reference: Valliwide Bank.

For full biographical listings, see the Martindale-Hubbell Law Directory

Fresno—Continued

KIMBLE, MACMICHAEL & UPTON, A PROFESSIONAL CORPORATION (AV)

Fig Garden Financial Center, 5260 North Palm Avenue, Suite 221, P.O. Box 9489, 93792-9489
Telephone: 209-435-5500
Telecopier: 209-435-1500

Joseph C. Kimble (1910-1972)
Thomas A. MacMichael (1920-1990)
Jon Wallace Upton
Robert E. Bergin
Jeffrey G. Boswell
Steven D. McGee
Robert E. Ward
John P. Eleazarian
Robert H. Scribner
Michael E. Moss
David D. Doyle
Mark D. Miller
Michael F. Tatham
W. Richard Lee
D. Tyler Tharpe
Sylvia Halkousis Coyle

Michael J. Jurkovich
S. Brett Sutton
Douglas V. Thornton
Robert William Branch
Brian N. Folland
Christopher L. Wanger
Elise M. Krause
Donald J. Pool
Susan King Hatmaker

For full biographical listings, see the Martindale-Hubbell Law Directory

LANG, RICHERT & PATCH, A PROFESSIONAL CORPORATION (AV)

Fig Garden Financial Center, 5200 North Palm Avenue, 4th Floor, P.O. Box 40012, 93755
Telephone: 209-228-6700
Fax: 209-228-6727

Frank H. Lang
William T. Richert (1937-1993)
Robert L. Patch, II
Val W. Saldaña
Douglas E. Noll
Michael T. Hertz
Victoria J. Salisch
Bradley A. Silva
David R. Jenkins
Charles Trudrung Taylor
Mark L. Creede
Peter N. Zeitler
Charles L. Doerksen

Randall C. Nelson
Barbara A. McAuliffe
Laurie Quigley Cardot
Douglas E. Griffin
Nabil E. Zumout

References: Wells Fargo Bank (Fresno Main Office); First Interstate Bank (Fresno Main Office).

For full biographical listings, see the Martindale-Hubbell Law Directory

MILES, SEARS & EANNI, A PROFESSIONAL CORPORATION (AV)

2844 Fresno Street, P.O. Box 1432, 93716
Telephone: 209-486-5200
Fax: 209-486-5240

Wm. M. Miles (1909-1991)
Robert E. Sears (1918-1992)
Carmen A. Eanni
Richard C. Watters
Gerald J. Maglio
William J. Seiler
Douglas L. Gordon

For full biographical listings, see the Martindale-Hubbell Law Directory

PARICHAN, RENBERG, CROSSMAN & HARVEY, LAW CORPORATION (AV)

Suite 130, 2350 West Shaw Avenue, P.O. Box 9950, 93794-0950
Telephone: 209-431-6300
FAX: 209-432-1018

Harold A. Parichan
Charles L. Renberg
Richard C. Crossman
Ima Jean Harvey
Stephen T. Knudsen
Larry C. Gollmer
Robert G. Eliason
Steven M. McQuillan
Peter S. Bradley

Deborah A. Coe
Maureen P. Holford
Karen L. Lynch
Michael L. Renberg
Brady Kyle McGuinness

Reference: Bank of America, Commercial Banking Office, Fresno, California.

For full biographical listings, see the Martindale-Hubbell Law Directory

STAMMER, MCKNIGHT, BARNUM & BAILEY (AV)

2540 West Shaw Lane, Suite 110, P.O. Box 9789, 93794-9789
Telephone: 209-449-0571
Fax: 209-432-2619

(See Next Column)

W. H. Stammer (1891-1969)
James K. Barnum (1918-1987)
Dean A. Bailey (Retired)
Galen McKnight (1904-1991)
James N. Hays
Carey H. Johnson
Jan M. Biggs
Frank D. Maul
Daniel O. Jamison
Craig M. Mortensen
Jerry D. Jones
Michael P. Mallery
M. Bruce Smith

ASSOCIATES

A. John Witkowski
Thomas J. Georgouses
Steven R. Stoker
M. Jaqueline Yates
Bruce J. Berger

OF COUNSEL

Donald D. Pogoloff

Representative Clients: Pacific Bell; Chevron, U.S.A.; Fresno Irrigation District; The Travelers Insurance Group; State Farm Insurance Cos.; Farmers Insurance Group.
Reference: Bank of America National Trust & Savings Assn. (Fresno Main Office).

For full biographical listings, see the Martindale-Hubbell Law Directory

GLENDALE, Los Angeles Co.

IRSFELD, IRSFELD & YOUNGER (AV)

A Partnership including Professional Corporations
Suite 900, 100 West Broadway, 91210-1296
Telephone: 818-242-6859
Fax: 818-240-7728

MEMBERS OF FIRM

James B. Irsfeld (1880-1966)
John H. Brink (P.C.)
Peter J. Irsfeld (P.C.)
James J. Waldorf (P.C.)
C. Phillip Jackson (P.C.)
Ross R. Hart (P.C.)
Norman H. Green (P.C.)
Diane L. Walker (P.C.)

ASSOCIATES

Peter C. Wright
Andrew J. Thomas
Kathryn E. Van Houten

RETIRED

James B. Irsfeld, Jr.
Kenneth C. Younger

Representative Clients: Lear Sieglar, Inc.; Chrysler Credit Corp.
References: First Interstate Bank (Glendale Main Office); Bank of Hollywood.

For full biographical listings, see the Martindale-Hubbell Law Directory

O'ROURKE, ALLAN & FONG (AV)

3rd Floor, 104 North Belmont, P.O. Box 10220, 91209-3220
Telephone: 818-247-4303
Fax: 818-247-1451

MEMBERS OF FIRM

Denis M. O'Rourke
Joan H. Allan
Roderick D. Fong

ASSOCIATE

Robert G. Mindess

Reference: Verdugo Banking Company (Glendale, California); Community Bank (Glendale, California).

For full biographical listings, see the Martindale-Hubbell Law Directory

IRVINE, Orange Co.

CHAPMAN, FULLER & BOLLARD (AV)

2010 Main Street, Suite 400, 92714
Telephone: 714-752-1455
Telecopier: 714-752-1485

William D. Chapman
H. Daniel Fuller
William C. Bollard
Dirk O. Julander
Edward (Ted) B. Paulson

OF COUNSEL

Bruce H. Haglund
Paul A. Wensel
Robert V. Gibson

For full biographical listings, see the Martindale-Hubbell Law Directory

LAW OFFICES OF WILLIAM C. HOLZWARTH (AV)

2600 Michelson Drive, Suite 780, 92715
Telephone: 714-851-0550
Fax: 714-252-1514

William C. Holzwarth (P.C.)

For full biographical listings, see the Martindale-Hubbell Law Directory

PIVO & HALBREICH (AV)

1920 Main Street, Suite 800, 92714
Telephone: 714-253-2000; 213-688-7311

(See Next Column)

PIVO & HALBREICH, *Irvine—Continued*

Kenneth R. Pivo
Eva S. Halbreich
Douglas A. Amo
Richard O. Schwartz

ASSOCIATES

Mona Z. Hanna
Karin H. Ota
Charles A. Palmer
Jeffrey S. Schroer
Victoria E. Moss

Representative Clients: Physicians and Surgeons Underwriters Corp.; Fremont Indemnity; American Continental Insurance Co.; AKROS Medico Enterprises; Kaiser Foundation Healthplan, Inc.; Caronia Corp.; The Doctor's Company; Harbor Regional Center; Developmental Disabilities Regional Center; South Central Los Angeles Regional Center.

For full biographical listings, see the Martindale-Hubbell Law Directory

STEPONOVICH & ASSOCIATES, A PROFESSIONAL LAW CORPORATION (AV)

Koll Center Irvine - Transamerica Tower, 18201 Von Karman Avenue, Suite 650, 92715
Telephone: 714-852-1073
Fax: 714-852-1276

Michael J. Steponovich, Jr.

For full biographical listings, see the Martindale-Hubbell Law Directory

WATT, TIEDER & HOFFAR (AV Ⓣ)

3 Park Plaza, Suite 1530, 92714
Telephone: 714-852-6700
Telecopier: 714-261-0771
McLean Virginia Office: 7929 Westpark Drive, Suite 400,
Telephone: 703-749-1000.
Telex: 248797 WATTR.
Telecopier: 703-893-8029.
Washington, D.C. Office: 601 Pennsylvania Avenue, N.W. Suite 900,
Telephone: 202-462-4697.

MEMBERS OF FIRM

John B. Tieder, Jr. (Not admitted in CA)
Robert M. Fitzgerald (Not admitted in CA)
Michael G. Long

ASSOCIATE

Christopher P. Pappas

For full biographical listings, see the Martindale-Hubbell Law Directory

WESIERSKI & ZUREK (AV)

Suite 1500, 5 Park Plaza, 92714
Telephone: 714-975-1000
Telecopier: 714-756-0517
Glendale, California Office: Suite 250, 800 North Brand Boulevard.
Telephone: 818-543-6100.
Telecopier: 818-543-6101.

PARTNERS

Christopher P. Wesierski
Ronald Zurek (Resident, Glendale Office)
Daniel J. Ford, Jr.
Terence P. Carney
James E. Siepler
Thomas G. Wianecki
Marilyn M. Smith
Jolynn L. Bumiller
Stephen M. Ziemann
Peter A. Saporito
Mark E. Brubaker

ASSOCIATES

Christopher M. Fisher
Kimberly M. Kopchick
K. Scott Dwyer (Not admitted in CA)
Mark J. Giannamore
Paul J. Lipman
David F. Mastan
David A. Clinton
Mark D. Holmes

For full biographical listings, see the Martindale-Hubbell Law Directory

LA JOLLA, San Diego Co.

LAW OFFICES OF MAURILE C. TREMBLAY A PROFESSIONAL CORPORATION (AV)

4180 La Jolla Village Drive, Suite 210, 92037
Telephone: 619-558-3030
FAX: 619-558-2502

Maurile C. Tremblay

Mark D. Estle
Ted A. Connor

OF COUNSEL

David R. Endres

For full biographical listings, see the Martindale-Hubbell Law Directory

LARKSPUR, Marin Co.

KATZ, BIERER & BRADY, INC. (AV)

101 Larkspur Landing Circle, Suite 223, 94939
Telephone: 415-925-1600
FAX: 415-925-0940

Richard L. Katz
Joel D. Bierer
Steven J. Brady

OF COUNSEL

Alvin J. Schifrin

For full biographical listings, see the Martindale-Hubbell Law Directory

LONG BEACH, Los Angeles Co.

BENNETT & KISTNER (AV)

301 East Ocean Boulevard, Suite 800, 90802
Telephone: 310-435-6675
Fax: 310-437-8375
Riverside, California Office: 3403 Tenth Street, Suite 605. 92501-3676.
Telephone: 909-341-9360.
Fax: 909-341-9362.

Charles J. Bennett
Wayne T. Kistner

ASSOCIATES

Richard R. Bradbury
Mary A. Estante (Resident, Riverside Office)
Todd R. Becker
Karen H. Beckman (Resident, Riverside Office)

Representative Clients: The Hertz Corporation; Thrifty Oil Co.; Golden West Refining Co.; Standard Brands Paint Co.; Mattel, Inc.; Di Salvo Trucking Co.; County of Riverside; Southern California Rapid Transit District.
Reference: First Interstate Bank of California, The Market Place Office, Long Beach, California.

For full biographical listings, see the Martindale-Hubbell Law Directory

CAMERON, MADDEN, PEARLSON, GALE & SELLARS (AV)

One World Trade Center Suite 1600, 90831-1600
Telephone: 310-436-3888
Telecopier: 310-437-1967

MEMBERS OF THE FIRM

Timothy C. Cameron
Charles M. Gale
Patrick T. Madden
Paul R. Pearlson
James D. Sellars

ASSOCIATE

Lillian D. Salinger

For full biographical listings, see the Martindale-Hubbell Law Directory

CAYER, KILSTOFTE & CRATON, A PROFESSIONAL LAW CORPORATION (AV)

Suite 700, 444 West Ocean Boulevard, 90802
Telephone: 310-435-6008
Fax: 310-435-3704

John J. Cayer
Stephen R. Kilstofte
Curt R. Craton

Stephen B. Clemmer

For full biographical listings, see the Martindale-Hubbell Law Directory

LAW OFFICES OF WILLIAM D. EVANS A PROFESSIONAL CORPORATION (AV)

200 Oceangate, Suite 380, 90802
Telephone: 310-435-4499
Facsimile: 310-495-4299

William D. Evans

For full biographical listings, see the Martindale-Hubbell Law Directory

FLYNN, DELICH & WISE (AV)

One World Trade Center, Suite 1800, 90831-1800
Telephone: 310-435-2626
Fax: 310-437-7555
San Francisco, California Office: Suite 1750, 580 California Street.
Telephone: 415-693-5566.
Fax: 415-693-0410.

Erich P. Wise
Nicholas S. Politis

Representative Clients: American Hawaii Cruises; Holland America Line; Through Transport Mutual Insurance Association, Ltd.; The Britannia Steam Ship Insurance Association Limited; The Steamship Mutual Underwriting Association (Bermuda) Ltd.; General Steamship Corp., Ltd.; Commodore Cruise Line, Ltd.; Interocean Steamship Corporation; Sea-Land Service, Inc.; Hatteras Yachts.

For full biographical listings, see the Martindale-Hubbell Law Directory

Long Beach—Continued

FORD, WALKER, HAGGERTY & BEHAR, PROFESSIONAL LAW CORPORATION (AV)

One World Trade Center, Twenty Seventh Floor, 90831
Telephone: 310-983-2500
Telecopier: 310-983-2555

G. Richard Ford
Timothy L. Walker
William C. Haggerty
Jeffrey S. Behar
Mark Steven Hennings
Donna Rogers Kirby
Tina Ivankovic Mangarpan
Jamiel G. Dave
Susan D. Berger
Joseph A. Heath
Robert J. Chavez
J. Michael McClure

Arthur W. Schultz
Jon T. Moseley
Maxine J. Lebowitz
Timothy P. McDonald
K. Michele Williams
Kevin P. Bateman
Stephen Ward Moore
James D. Savage
Todd D. Pearl
Patrick J. Gibbs
James O. Miller
David Huchel
Sheila Anne Alexander
Heidi M. Yoshioka
Robert Reisinger
Theodore A. Clapp
Stanley L. Scarlett
Scott A. Ritsema
Michael Guy Martin
Colleen A. Strong
Kristin L. Jervis
Thomas L. Gourde
Patrick J. Stark
Shayne L. Wulterin

OF COUNSEL

Theodore P. Shield, P.L.C.

For full biographical listings, see the Martindale-Hubbell Law Directory

EDWARD P. GEORGE, JR., INC. A PROFESSIONAL CORPORATION (AV)

Suite 430, 5000 East Spring Street, 90815
Telephone: 310-497-2900
Facsimile: 310-497-2904

Edward P. George, Jr.
Timothy L. O'Reilly

OF COUNSEL

Albert C. S. Ramsey

Reference: Harbor Bank, Long Beach.

For full biographical listings, see the Martindale-Hubbell Law Directory

JOE LING (AV)

200 Oceangate, Suite 380, 90802
Telephone: 310-435-4499

For full biographical listings, see the Martindale-Hubbell Law Directory

MADDEN, JONES & COLE, A PROFESSIONAL CORPORATION (AV)

Suite 1300, 111 W. Ocean Boulevard, 90802
Telephone: 310-435-6565
Fax: 310-590-7909

Philip M. Madden
Steven A. Jones
Montgomery Cole
Judith A. Rasmussen
Robert R. Johnson

John Vita
Mary Gillespie Frankart
Carol Y. Adams
John K. Fitle

Counsel for: Ameritone Paint Corporation; St. Mary Medical Center; St. Bernardine Medical Center; Farmers & Merchants Trust Co.; Wells Fargo Bank; Mack Truck, Inc.; Long Beach Public Transportation.

For Complete List of Firm Personnel, See General Section

For full biographical listings, see the Martindale-Hubbell Law Directory

RUSSELL & MIRKOVICH (AV)

One World Trade Center, Suite 1450, 90831-1450
Telephone: 310-436-9911
FAX: 310-436-1897

Carlton E. Russell
Joseph N. Mirkovich

For Complete List of Firm Personnel, See General Section

For full biographical listings, see the Martindale-Hubbell Law Directory

STOLPMAN, KRISSMAN, ELBER, MANDEL & KATZMAN (AV)

A Partnership including Professional Corporations
Nineteenth Floor, 111 West Ocean Boulevard, 90802-4649
Telephone: 310-435-8300
Telecopier: 310-435-8304
Los Angeles (Westwood) Office: Suite 1800, 10880 Wilshire Boulevard.
Telephone: 213-470-8011.

(See Next Column)

MEMBERS OF FIRM

Thomas G. Stolpman (Inc.)
Leonard H. Mandel (Inc.)
Bernard Katzman (Inc.)
Joel Krissman
Mary Nielsen Abbott
Donna Silver
Dennis M. Elber

ASSOCIATES

Edwin Silver
Lynne Rasmussen
Marilyn S. Heise
Elaine Mandel

OF COUNSEL

Richard L. McWilliams (Inc.)

For full biographical listings, see the Martindale-Hubbell Law Directory

TAUBMAN, SIMPSON, YOUNG & SULENTOR (AV)

Suite 700 Home Savings Building, 249 East Ocean Boulevard, P.O. Box 22670, 90801
Telephone: 310-436-9201
FAX: 310-590-9695

E. C. Denio (1864-1952)
Geo. A. Hart (1881-1967)
Geo. P. Taubman, Jr. (1897-1970)
Matthew C. Simpson (1900-1988)
Richard G. Wilson (1928-1993)
Roger W. Young
William J. Sulentor
Peter M. Williams
Scott R. Magee
Valerie K. de Martino
Maria M. Rohaidy

Attorneys for: Bixby Land Co.; Renick Cadillac, Inc.; Oil Operators Incorporated.
Local Counsel: Crown Cork & Seal Co., Inc.

For full biographical listings, see the Martindale-Hubbell Law Directory

WILLIAMS WOOLLEY COGSWELL NAKAZAWA & RUSSELL (AV)

111 West Ocean Boulevard, Suite 2000, 90802-4614
Telephone: 310-495-6000
Telecopier: 310-435-1359
Telex: ITT: 4933872; WU: 984929

MEMBERS OF FIRM

Reed M. Williams
David E. R. Woolley
Forrest R. Cogswell
Alan Nakazawa
Blake W. Larkin
Thomas A. Russell

ASSOCIATES

B. Alexander Moghaddam
Dennis R. Acker

For full biographical listings, see the Martindale-Hubbell Law Directory

WISE, WIEZOREK, TIMMONS & WISE, A PROFESSIONAL CORPORATION (AV)

3700 Santa Fe Avenue, Suite 300, 90810
Telephone: 310-834-5028
Facsimile: 310-834-8018
Mailing Address: P.O. Box 2190, 90801
Los Angeles, California Office: 888 South Figueroa Street, Suite 840.
Telephone: 213-628-3717.
Redding, California Office: 280 Hemsted Drive, Suite 115.
Telephone: 916-221-7632.

George E. Wise
Duane H. Timmons
Anthony F. Wiezorek
Susan E. Anderson Wise
Albert F. Padley, III (Resident at Los Angeles)
Michael J. Pearce
Mark C. Allen, III
Richard P. Dieffenbach
Steven C. Rice
Stephen M. Smith (Resident at Los Angeles)
Thomas J. Yocis
James M. Cox
Mathew J. Vande Wydeven (Resident at Los Angeles)
Bailey J. Farrin
William P. Bennett
Tae J. Im (Resident at Los Angeles)

OF COUNSEL

John W. Nelson
Brownell Merrell, Jr.

For full biographical listings, see the Martindale-Hubbell Law Directory

*LOS ANGELES,** Los Angeles Co.

ADAMS, DUQUE & HAZELTINE (AV)

A Partnership including Professional Corporations
777 South Figueroa Street, Tenth Floor, 90017
Telephone: 213-620-1240
FAX: 213-896-5500
San Francisco, California Office: 500 Washington Street.
Telephone: 415-982-1240.
FAX: 415-982-0130.

MEMBERS OF FIRM

Bruce A. Beckman
Richard R. Terzian
Lonnie E. Woolverton (P.C.)
Kimler G. Casteel
James R. Willcox (San Francisco Office)
Frederick A. Clark
David L. Bacon
Richard T. Davis, Jr.
C. Forrest Bannan
John A. Blue
Margaret Levy
Charles D. Schoor
Jeffrey P. Smith

(See Next Column)

ADAMS, DUQUE & HAZELTINE, *Los Angeles—Continued*

MEMBERS OF FIRM (Continued)

Catherine Hunt Ruddy
Joseph M. Rimac, Jr. (San Francisco Office)
Paul M. Smith
James J. Moak
John L. Viola
Ward D. Smith
Lauren T. Diehl
Cristina L. Sierra
Ronald F. Frank
Lesley C. Green
Berna Warner-Fredman
Kevin P. Farmer
David R. Shane (San Francisco Office)
Margaret Lynn Oldendorf
G. Andrew Jones
Thomas Myers
Remy Kessler

ASSOCIATES

Rande Sherman Sotomayor
Cheryl A. De Bari
Peter James Bado
Gordon N. Kojima
Sara Anne Culp
Daren R. Brinkman
Stephen P. Pfahler
Thomas J. Kearney
Terry L. Tron
Tamarra T. Rennick
Kristin Pelletier
Thomas B. Croke IV

For Complete List of Firm Personnel, See General Section

For full biographical listings, see the Martindale-Hubbell Law Directory

AGAPAY, LEVYN & HALLING, A PROFESSIONAL CORPORATION (AV)

Fourth Floor, 10801 National Boulevard, 90064
Telephone: 310-470-1700
Fax: 310-470-2602
Orange, California Office: One City Boulevard West, Suite 707, 92668.
Telephone: 714-634-1744.
Fax: 714-634-0417.

Joe M. Agapay, Jr.
Thomas S. Levyn
Chris W. Halling

Glen R. Segal (Resident Member, Orange Office)
Peter J. Krupinsky
Laurie J. Leckband
Tracey P. Hom

OF COUNSEL

Alan B. Grass
Glen Dresser

For full biographical listings, see the Martindale-Hubbell Law Directory

BAKER & HOSTETLER (AV)

600 Wilshire Boulevard, 90017-3212
Telephone: 213-624-2400
FAX: 213-975-1740
In Cleveland, Ohio, 3200 National City Center, 1900 East Ninth Street. Telephone: 216-621-0200.
In Columbus, Ohio, Capitol Square, Suite 2100, 65 East State Street. Telephone: 614-228-1541.
In Denver, Colorado, 303 East 17th Avenue, Suite 1100. Telephone: 303-861-0600.
In Houston, Texas, 1000 Louisiana, Suite 2000. Telephone: 713-236-0020.
In Long Beach, California: 300 Oceangate, Suite 620. *Telephone:* 310-432-2827.
In Orlando, Florida, SunBank Center, Suite 2300, 200 South Orange Avenue. Telephone: 407-649-4000.
In Washington, D. C., Washington Square, Suite 1100, 1050 Connecticut Avenue, N. W. Telephone: 202-861-1500.
In College Park, Maryland, 9658 Baltimore Boulevard, Suite 206. Telephone: 301-441-2781.
In Alexandria, Virginia, 437 North Lee Street. Telephone: 703-549-1294.
In San Francisco, California: One Sansome Street, Suite 2000. *Telephone:* 415-951-4705.

PARTNERS

Patrick J. Cain
David A. Destino
Jack D. Fudge
Emil W. Herich
Judd L. Jordan
Howard J. Privett
Diane C. Stanfield
Penny M. Costa
G. Richard Doty
Richard A. Goette
Peter W. James
Larry W. McFarland
Bill E. Schroeder
Ralph Zarefsky

ASSOCIATES

Angela C. Agrusa
Richard A. Deeb
Rebecca Lobl
Gregg A. Rapoport
Barry Bookbinder
Marcia T. Law
Lynn S. Loeb
Brooke K. Richter
Dennis L. Wilson

OF COUNSEL

Richard Clark
Meri A. deKelaita
Franklin H. Wilson

For Complete List of Firm Personnel, See General Section

For full biographical listings, see the Martindale-Hubbell Law Directory

BERMAN, BLANCHARD, MAUSNER & KINDEM, A LAW CORPORATION (AV)

4727 Wilshire Boulevard, Suite 500, 90010
Telephone: 213-965-1200
Telecopier: 213-965-1919

Laurence M. Berman
Lonnie C. Blanchard, III
Jeffrey N. Mausner
Peter R. Dion-Kindem

Paul A. Hoffman
Eric Levinrad
Cary P. Ocon

For full biographical listings, see the Martindale-Hubbell Law Directory

BLECHER & COLLINS, A PROFESSIONAL CORPORATION (AV)

611 West Sixth Street, 20th Floor, 90017
Telephone: 213-622-4222
Telecopier: 213-622-1656

Maxwell M. Blecher
Harold R. Collins, Jr.
Douglas H. Altschuler
Mark D. Baute
Florence F. Cameron
Ralph C. Hofer
William C. Hsu
Jinna Kim
Benjamin D. Nieberg
James Robert Noblin
Donald R. Pepperman
Alicia G. Rosenberg

OF COUNSEL

John J. McCauley

For full biographical listings, see the Martindale-Hubbell Law Directory

LAW OFFICES OF DAVID B. BLOOM A PROFESSIONAL CORPORATION (AV)

3325 Wilshire Boulevard, Ninth Floor, 90010
Telephone: 213-938-5248; 384-4088
Telecopier: 213-385-2009

David B. Bloom

Stephen S. Monroe (A Professional Corporation)
Raphael A. Rosemblat
James E. Adler
Bonni S. Mantovani
Martin A. Cooper
Roy A. Levun
Cherie S. Raidy
Jonathan Udell
Susan Carole Jay
Edward Idell
Sandra Kamenir
Steven Wayne Lazarus
Andrew Edward Briseno
Harold C. Klaskin
Shelley M. Gould
B. Eric Nelson
John C. Notti
Peter O. Israel
Anthony V. Seferian

For full biographical listings, see the Martindale-Hubbell Law Directory

BODKIN, MCCARTHY, SARGENT & SMITH (AV)

Fifty-First Floor, First Interstate Bank Building, 707 Wilshire Boulevard, 90017
Telephone: 213-620-1000
Facsimile: 213-623-5224
Cable Address: "Bolindy"

MEMBERS OF FIRM

Henry G. Bodkin, Jr.
J. Thomas McCarthy
Edward B. Smith, III
Gordon F. Sausser
Michael A. Branconier
Robert H. Berkes
Donna D. Melby
Barbara S. Hodous
James F. Boyle

ASSOCIATES

Joseph T. Teglovic
William Balderrama
Richard P. Kinnan
Michael T. Ohira
Mark W. Lau
Jacqueline A. Armstrong
Judith G. Belsito
William G. Lieb
Marco P. Ferreira
Angela M. Brown
Anna Orlowski
Charise A. Fong
Thomas M. Phillips
Gayle L. Wilder
Ty Shimoguchi

Reference: First Interstate Bank (Los Angeles Main Office, Los Angeles, California).

For Complete List of Firm Personnel, See General Section

For full biographical listings, see the Martindale-Hubbell Law Directory

BRONSON, BRONSON & MCKINNON (AV)

A Partnership including Professional Corporations
444 South Flower Street, 24th Floor, 90071
Telephone: 213-627-2000
Fax: 213-627-2277
San Francisco, California Office: 505 Montgomery Street. *Telephone:* 415-986-4200.
Santa Rosa, California Office: 100 B Street, Suite 400. *Telephone:* 707-527-8110.
San Jose, California Office: 10 Almaden Boulevard, Suite 600. *Telephone:* 408-293-0599.

(See Next Column)

BRONSON, BRONSON & MCKINNON—*Continued*

RESIDENT PARTNERS

Charles N. Bland, Jr.
Thomas T. Carpenter
Sheldon J. Warren
Stephen L. Backus
John D. Boyle
Donna P. Arlow
Ralph S. LaMontagne, Jr.
James H. Fox
Elizabeth A. Erskine

RESIDENT ASSOCIATES

Janet T. Andrea
M. Guadalupe Valencia
Manuel Saldaña
Eric A. Amador

For Complete List of Firm Personnel, See General Section

For full biographical listings, see the Martindale-Hubbell Law Directory

---

BUCHALTER, NEMER, FIELDS & YOUNGER, A PROFESSIONAL CORPORATION (AV)

24th Floor, 601 South Figueroa Street, 90017
Telephone: 213-891-0700
Fax: 213-896-0400
Cable Address: "Buchnem"
Telex: 68-7485
New York, New York Office: 19th Floor, 237 Park Avenue.
Telephone: 212-490-8600.
Fax: 212-490-6022.
San Francisco, California Office: 29th Floor, 333 Market Street.
Telephone: 415-227-0900.
Fax: 415-227-0770.
San Jose, California Office: 12th Floor, 50 West San Fernando Street.
Telephone: 408-298-0350.
Fax: 408-298-7683.
Newport Beach, California Office: Suite 300, 620 Newport Center Drive.
Telephone: 714-760-1121.
Fax: 714-720-0182.
Century City, California Office: Suite 2400, 1801 Century Park East.
Telephone: 213-891-0700.
Fax: 310-551-0233.

Murray M. Fields
Michael J. Cereseto
Jay R. Ziegler
Bernard E. Le Sage

Stephen K. Lubega
Cheryl Croteau Orr

References: City National Bank; Wells Fargo Bank; Metrobank.

For Complete List of Firm Personnel, See General Section

For full biographical listings, see the Martindale-Hubbell Law Directory

---

CLARK & TREVITHICK, A PROFESSIONAL CORPORATION (AV)

800 Wilshire Boulevard, 12th Floor, 90017
Telephone: 213-629-5700
Telecopier: 213-624-9441

Philip W. Bartenetti
Leonard Brazil
Dolores Cordell
Leslie R. Horowitz
Vincent Tricarico
Arturo Santana Jr.
Kerry T. Ryan

OF COUNSEL

Judith Ilene Bloom

References: Wells Fargo Bank (Los Angeles Main Office); National Bank of California.

For Complete List of Firm Personnel, See General Section

For full biographical listings, see the Martindale-Hubbell Law Directory

---

COLEMAN & MARCUS, A PROFESSIONAL CORPORATION (AV)

Suite 810, 1801 Avenue of the Stars (Century City), 90067
Telephone: 310-277-2700

Richard M. Coleman
Michael D. Marcus
Laurie J. Richards

For full biographical listings, see the Martindale-Hubbell Law Directory

---

LAW OFFICES OF ROBERT L. CORBIN, P.C. (AV)

601 South Figueroa Street, Suite 3715, 90017-5742
Telephone: 213-680-8220
Facsimile: 213-614-8666

Robert L. Corbin

James Bird
Kevin F. Ruf

For full biographical listings, see the Martindale-Hubbell Law Directory

---

CORINBLIT & SELTZER, A PROFESSIONAL CORPORATION (AV)

Suite 820 Wilshire Park Place, 3700 Wilshire Boulevard, 90010-3085
Telephone: 213-380-4200
Telecopier: 213-385-7503; 385-4560

(See Next Column)

Marc M. Seltzer

OF COUNSEL

Jack Corinblit
Earl P. Willens

Gretchen M. Nelson
Christina A. Snyder
George A. Shohet

Reference: Bank of America (Wilshire & Harvard Office).

For full biographical listings, see the Martindale-Hubbell Law Directory

---

DANIELS, BARATTA & FINE (AV)

A Partnership including a Professional Corporation
1801 Century Park East, 9th Floor, 90067
Telephone: 310-556-7900
Telecopier: 310-556-2807

MEMBERS OF FIRM

John P. Daniels (Inc.)
Mary Hulett
James M. Baratta
Michael B. Geibel
Paul R. Fine
James I. Montgomery, Jr.
Nathan B. Hoffman
Lance D. Orloff
Mark R. Israel

ASSOCIATES

Deborah Kaplan Galer
Scott Ashford Brooks
Ilene Wendy Nebenzahl
Craig A. Laidig
Heidi Susan Hart
Paul E. Blevins
Janet Sacks
Joan T. Lind
Michael N. Schonbuch
Rodi F. Rispone
Linda A. Schweitz
Stephanie J. Berman
Christine S. Chu
Michelle C. Hopkins
Glenn T. Rosenblatt
Robin A. Webb
Scott M. Leavitt
Ronda Lynn Crowley
Karen Ann Holloway
Scott A. Spungin
Mark A. Vega
Theodore L. Wilson
Patricio Esquivel
Daniel Joseph Kolodziej
Robert B. Gibson
Craig Momita
Brett S. Markson
Spencer A. Schneider
Michelle R. Press
Angelo A. DuPlantier, III

OF COUNSEL

Timothy J. Hughes
Drew T. Hanker

For full biographical listings, see the Martindale-Hubbell Law Directory

---

DEMETRIOU, DEL GUERCIO, SPRINGER & MOYER (AV)

801 South Grand Avenue, 10th Floor, 90017
Telephone: 213-624-8407
Telecopy: 213-624-0174

MEMBERS OF FIRM

Jeffrey Z. B. Springer
Kermit D. Marsh
Regina Liudzius Cobb
Leslie M. Smario
Jennifer M. Burman
Kelly A. Sakir

Reference: Bank of America, L.A. Main Office, Los Angeles, Calif.

For full biographical listings, see the Martindale-Hubbell Law Directory

---

ECKARDT & KHOURY (AV)

Suite 700, 530 West Sixth Street, 90014-1298
Telephone: 213-626-5061
Cable Address: "Richeck"
Facsimile: 213-891-1590
ABA/Net: ABA 18857

Richard W. Eckardt
Robert P. Khoury

For full biographical listings, see the Martindale-Hubbell Law Directory

---

RICK EDWARDS, INC. (AV)

20th Floor, 1925 Century Park East, 90067
Telephone: 310-277-6464
Telecopier: 310-286-9501

Rick Edwards

William R. Bishin
Ken Yuwiler

Reference: Union Bank, 445 South Figueroa Street, Los Angeles, California 90071.

For full biographical listings, see the Martindale-Hubbell Law Directory

---

GAIMS, WEIL, WEST & EPSTEIN (AV)

A Partnership including a Professional Corporation
1875 Century Park East, Twelfth Floor, 90067
Telephone: 310-553-6666
Fax: 310-277-2133
Answer Back: Wild West
Telex: 910678746

(See Next Column)

GAIMS, WEIL, WEST & EPSTEIN, *Los Angeles—Continued*

MEMBERS OF FIRM

John Gaims
Barry G. West
Alan Jay Weil
Marc Epstein (P.C.)
Steven S. Davis
Jeffrey B. Ellis
Amy L. Rice
Corey E. Klein

ASSOCIATES

Gerald M. Fujii
Peter L. Steinman
Scott A. Schneider
Jason H. Gipstein

For full biographical listings, see the Martindale-Hubbell Law Directory

GALTON & HELM (AV)

500 South Grand Avenue, Suite 1200, 90071
Telephone: 213-629-8800
Telecopier: 213-629-0037

MEMBERS OF FIRM

Stephen H. Galton
Hugh H. Helm
Michael F. Bell
Daniel W. Maguire
David A. Lingenbrink

ASSOCIATES

Nancy A. Jerian
Keith A. Jacoby
Michael Hoffman
Cori Gayle Stockman
Susan G. Wells
Chris D. Olsen

For full biographical listings, see the Martindale-Hubbell Law Directory

GOLDMAN, GORDON & LIPSTONE (AV)

Suite 1920, 1801 Century Park East, 90067
Telephone: 310-277-7171
FAX: 310-277-1547

MEMBERS OF FIRM

A. S. Goldman (1895-1966)
Leonard A. Goldman
Robert P. Gordon
Ronald K. Lipstone

ASSOCIATE

Jerry A. Jacobson

References: Bank of America, Fourth and Spring Branch, Los Angeles; Bank of America, Wilshire-San Vincente Branch, Beverly Hills.

For full biographical listings, see the Martindale-Hubbell Law Directory

GRAY, YORK, DUFFY & RATTET (AV)

15760 Ventura Boulevard, 16th Floor (Encino), 91436
Telephone: 818-907-4000; 310-553-0445
FAX: 818-783-4551

MEMBERS OF FIRM

Gary S. Gray
James R. York
John J. Duffy
Gary S. Rattet
James C. Mavridis (Retired)
Arlene A. Colman

ASSOCIATES

Amalia L. Taylor
Kenneth A. Hearn
Gabriel H. Wainfeld
James B. Sanborn
Stephen Coopersmith
John L. Barber
Vincent F. Bennett
Miloslav Khadilkar
Michael S. Eisenbaum
Kevin S. Wattles
Frank J. Ozello, Jr.
Marc E. Carlson

Reference: Marathon National Bank, Los Angeles, California.

For full biographical listings, see the Martindale-Hubbell Law Directory

HALSTEAD, BAKER & OLSON (AV)

Suite 500, 1000 Wilshire Boulevard, 90017
Telephone: 213-622-0200
Telecopier: 213-623-3836

MEMBERS OF FIRM

Harry M. Halstead
Sheldon S. Baker
Eric Olson
John J. Jacobson
Charles L. LeCroy, III
William C. Hansen
Arsen Danielian

ASSOCIATES

Michael S. Simon
Andrea L. Esterson
Donald J. Gary, Jr.

For full biographical listings, see the Martindale-Hubbell Law Directory

HAMRICK, GARROTTO, BRISKIN & PENE, A PROFESSIONAL CORPORATION (AV)

3580 Wilshire Boulevard, 10th Floor, 90010
Telephone: 213-252-0041
Fax: 213-386-5414
Long Beach, California Office: 300 Oceangate, Suite 600.
Telephone: 310-435-4553.
Fax: 310-435-6442.

(See Next Column)

Robert S. Hamrick (A P.C.)
Greg W. Garrotto
Jeffrey F. Briskin (Resident, Long Branch Office)
Katherine B. Pene
John J. Latzanich, II

Craig A. McDougall (Resident, Long Beach Office)
Marla (Beth) Shah
Terry Porvin
Jana L. Gordon
Peter E. Garrell (Resident, Long Beach Office)
Roman Y. Nykolyshyn
Lori M. Levine
Nancy J. Lemkin (Resident, Long Beach Office)
Norman Goldman
Maureen A. McKinley
Linda L. Hamlin (Resident, Long Beach Office)

For full biographical listings, see the Martindale-Hubbell Law Directory

HANNA AND MORTON (AV)

A Partnership including Professional Corporations
Seventeenth Floor, Wilshire-Grand Building, 600 Wilshire Boulevard, 90017
Telephone: 213-628-7131

MEMBERS OF FIRM

Edward S. Renwick (A Professional Corporation)
James P. Lower
Robert M. Newell, Jr.
James P. Modisette
David A. Ossentjuk

OF COUNSEL

Bela G. Lugosi (A Professional Corporation)
Milo V. Olson
David A. Thomas

ASSOCIATES

Stephen G. Mason
Thomas N. Campbell
Robert J. Roche
Michael P. Wippler
Allison L. Malin

For Complete List of Firm Personnel, See General Section

For full biographical listings, see the Martindale-Hubbell Law Directory

LAW OFFICES OF DAVID M. HARNEY (AV)

Suite 1300 Figueroa Plaza, 201 North Figueroa Street, 90012-2636
Telephone: 213-482-0881
Fax: 213-250-4042

SPECIAL COUNSEL

Thomas Kallay

ASSOCIATES

Carl A. McMahan
Julie A. Harney
David T. Harney
Andrew J. Nocas
Vincent McGowan
Peter J. Polos
Thomas A. Schultz
Christopher P. Leyel
Jeffrey B. Smith
Robert H. Pourvali
C. Michael Alder
Daniel S. Glaser

OF COUNSEL

Gert K. Hirschberg

Reference: Bank of America.

For full biographical listings, see the Martindale-Hubbell Law Directory

HAWKINS, SCHNABEL, LINDAHL & BECK (AV)

660 South Figueroa Street, Suite 1500, 90017
Telephone: 213-488-3900
Telecopier: 213-486-9883
Cable Address: "Haslin"

MEMBERS OF FIRM

Roger E. Hawkins
Laurence H. Schnabel
George M. Lindahl
Kelley K. Beck
Jon P. Kardassakis
William E. Keitel
Timothy A. Gonzales
R. Timothy Stone
Richard C. Weston

For full biographical listings, see the Martindale-Hubbell Law Directory

HONIGMAN MILLER SCHWARTZ AND COHN (AV)

A Partnership including Professional Corporations
Watt Plaza, Suite 2200, 1875 Century Park East, 90067-2799
Telephone: 310-789-3800
Fax: 310-789-3814
Detroit, Michigan Office: 2290 First National Building.
Telephone: 313-256-7800.
Lansing, Michigan Office: 222 North Washington Square, Suite 400.
Telephone: 517-484-8282.
West Palm Beach, Florida Office: Suite 800 Esperante Building, 222 Lakeview Avenue.
Telephone: 407-838-4500.
Tampa, Florida Office: 2700 Landmark Centre, 401 E. Jackson Street.
Telephone: 813-221-6600.
Orlando, Florida Office: 390 North Orange Avenue, Suite 1300.
Telephone: 407-648-0300.

(See Next Column)

HONIGMAN MILLER SCHWARTZ AND COHN—*Continued*

Houston, Texas Office: 3100 First Interstate Bank Plaza, 1000 Louisiana.
Telephone: 713-650-2600.

MEMBERS OF FIRM

Daniel E. Martyn, Jr.
George E. Schulman

ASSOCIATES

Melanie J. Bingham
Adryane R. Omens

For Complete List of Firm Personnel, See General Section

For full biographical listings, see the Martindale-Hubbell Law Directory

HORNBERGER & CRISWELL (AV)

444 South Flower, 31st Floor, 90071
Telephone: 213-488-1655
Facsimile: 213-488-1255

MEMBERS OF FIRM

Nicholas W. Hornberger
Leslie E. Criswell
Carla J. Feldman
Ann M. Ghazarians
Michael A. Brewer

ASSOCIATES

Scott Alan Freedman
Marlin E. Howes
Christopher T. Olsen
Scott B. Cloud
Celeste S. Makuta
John Shaffery
Charles I. Karlin
K. Christopher Branch
David F. Berry
James M. Slominski
Gina T. Sponzilli

For full biographical listings, see the Martindale-Hubbell Law Directory

HUFSTEDLER & KAUS (AV)

A Partnership including Professional Corporations
Thirty-Ninth Floor, 355 South Grand Avenue, 90071-3101
Telephone: 213-617-7070
Fax: 213-617-6170

MEMBERS OF FIRM

Seth M. Hufstedler (Professional Corporation)
Shirley M. Hufstedler (Professional Corporation)
Otto M. Kaus
John Sobieski
Burton J. Gindler
Jerome H. Craig (Professional Corporation)
Thomas J. Ready (Professional Corporation)
Patricia Dominis Phillips
John P. Olson
Dennis M. Perluss
Margot A. Metzner
Leonard L. Gumport
Dan Marmalefsky
Gary Plessman
Michael V. Toumanoff
Susan I. Schutzbank Montgomery
Mark R. McDonald

ASSOCIATES

John W. (Jack) Alden Jr.
David K. Barrett
Eliot F. Krieger
Steven M. Haines
Ann Haberfelde
Elayna J. Youchah

Reference: First Interstate Bank, 707 Wilshire.

For Complete List of Firm Personnel, See General Section

For full biographical listings, see the Martindale-Hubbell Law Directory

KANANACK, MURGATROYD, BAUM & HEDLUND, A PROFESSIONAL CORPORATION (AV)

Suite 650, 12100 Wilshire Boulevard, 90025
Telephone: 310-207-3233; 800-827-0087
Facsimile: 310-820-7444
Washington, D.C. Office: 1250 24th Street, N.W., Suite 300.
Telephone: 202-466-0513; 800-827-0097.
Facsimile: 202-466-0527.

Michael L. Baum
Paul J. Hedlund
Robert E. Guilford
J. Clark Aristei
William J. Downey III

OF COUNSEL

Michael J. Kananack
George W. Murgatroyd III

John A. Greaves
Cara L. Belle (Not admitted in CA)
Denise K. Tomaiko
Robert F. Foss

Reference: Union Bank.

For full biographical listings, see the Martindale-Hubbell Law Directory

KINDEL & ANDERSON (AV)

A Partnership including Professional Corporations
Twenty-Ninth Floor, 555 South Flower Street, 90071
Telephone: 213-680-2222
Cable Address: "Kayanda"
Telex: 67-7497
FAX: 213-688-7564
Irvine, California Office: 5 Park Plaza, Suite 1000.
Telephone: 714-752-0777.

(See Next Column)

Woodland Hills, California Office: Suite 244, 5959 Topanga Canyon Boulevard.
Telephone: 818-712-0036.
San Francisco, California Office: 580 California Street, 15th Floor.
Telephone: 415-398-0110.

MEMBERS OF FIRM

Robert K. Baker
Dale S. Fischer
Manuel S. Klausner (P.C.)
Jon L. Rewinski
Carlos Solis

ASSOCIATES

Steven M. Friedman
Paul W. Poareo

OF COUNSEL

Paul L. Freese

For Complete List of Firm Personnel, See General Section

For full biographical listings, see the Martindale-Hubbell Law Directory

KINSELLA, BOESCH, FUJIKAWA & TOWLE (AV)

A Partnership including Professional Corporations
1901 Avenue of the Stars, Seventh Floor, 90067
Telephone: 310-201-2000
Fax: 310-284-6018

MEMBERS OF FIRM

Dale F. Kinsella (Professional Corporation)
Philip W. Boesch, Jr., (Professional Corporation)
Ronald K. Fujikawa (Professional Corporation)
Edmund J. Towle, III, (Professional Corporation)
Michael C. Denison
Mark F. Katz (Professional Corporation)
David T. Stowell
Catherine H. Coleman
Mark K. Brown
Michael J. Kump
Michael Howald
Jack G. Cairl, Jr.
David Andrew Pash
Donald L. Zachary
Cathleen Collins
Charles G. Smith
Gregory J. Aldisert

ASSOCIATES

Todd T. Alberstone
Michael Kerry Burke
Alan R. Kossoff
Michelle Ben-yehuda
David A. De Jute
Bruce Bolkin
Joseph P. Bartlett
Catherine E. Haltom
Helene E. Pretsky
Suzanne M. Madison
Jill Rosenthal

For full biographical listings, see the Martindale-Hubbell Law Directory

KOSLOV & CADY (AV)

Suite 650 Roosevelt Building, 727 West Seventh Street, 90017
Telephone: 213-629-2647
FAX: 213-689-9628

MEMBERS OF FIRM

John Koslov
Eurus Cady

ASSOCIATES

Judy L. McKelvey
Melina J. Burns
William P. Medlen

For full biographical listings, see the Martindale-Hubbell Law Directory

LA FOLLETTE, JOHNSON, DE HAAS, FESLER & AMES, A PROFESSIONAL CORPORATION (AV)

865 South Figueroa Street, Suite 3100, 90017-5443
Telephone: 213-426-3600
Fax: 213-426-3650
San Francisco, California Office: 50 California Street, Suite 3350.
Telephone: 415-433-7610.
Telecopier: 415-392-7541.
Santa Ana, California Office: 2677 North Main Street, Suite 901.
Telephone: 714-558-7008.
Telecopier: 714-972-0379.
Riverside, California Office: 3403 Tenth Street, Suite 820.
Telephone: 714-275-9192.
Fax: 714-275-9249.

John T. La Follette (1922-1990)
Daren T. Johnson
Louis H. De Haas
Donald C. Fesler
Dennis K. Ames (Resident, Santa Ana Office)
Alfred W. Gerisch, Jr.
Brian W. Birnie
Peter J. Zomber
Robert E. Kelly, Jr.
Leon A. Zallen
G. Kelley Reid, Jr. (Resident, San Francisco Office)
Dennis J. Sinclitico
Christopher C. Cannon (Resident, Santa Ana Office)
Dorothy B. Reyes
Steven R. Odell (Santa Ana and Riverside Offices)
Christopher L. Thomas (Santa Ana and Riverside Offices)
Robert K. Warford (Resident, Riverside Office)
John L. Supple (Resident, San Francisco Office)
Vincent D. Lapointe
Steven J. Joffe
Mark M. Stewart
Bradley J. McGirr (Resident, Santa Ana Office)
Sydney La Branche Merritt

(See Next Column)

La Follette, Johnson, De Haas, Fesler & Ames A Professional Corporation, *Los Angeles—Continued*

Peter R. Bing
Larry P. Nathenson
Donald R. Beck (Resident, Santa Ana Office)
Donna R. Evans
David J. Ozeran
Mark B. Guterman
Terry A. Woodward (Resident, Santa Ana Office)
Stephen C. Dreher (Resident, Santa Ana Office)
Tatiana M. Schultz (Resident, San Francisco Office)
Peter E. Theophilos (Resident, San Francisco Office)
Deborah A. Cowley
Thomas S. Alch
Kenton E. Moore
Kent T. Brandmeyer
Garry O. Moses
Jeffery R. Erickson (Resident, Riverside Office)
Michael J. O'Connor
Elizabeth Anne Scherer (Resident, Santa Ana Office)
Hugh R. Burns
Stephen K. Hiura
James G. Wold
Eileen S. Lemmon (Resident, Riverside, Office)
David M. Wright
Larry E. White (Resident, Riverside Office)
Laurie Miyamoto Johnson
David James Reinard
Michelle Louise McCoy
Duane A. Newton (Resident, Riverside Office)
Adriaan F. van der Capellen (Resident, Santa Ana Office)
William T. Gray (Resident, Santa Ana Office)
Thomas J. Lo (Resident, Santa Ana Office)
Daniel D. Sorenson (Resident, Riverside Office)
Joanne Rosendin (Resident, San Francisco Office)
Henry P. Canvel (Resident, San Francisco Office)
Peter D. Busciglio (Resident, Santa Ana Office)
Mark S. Rader (Resident, Riverside Office)
Jay B. Lake
Erin L. Muellenberg (Resident, Riverside Office)
Phyllis M. Winston (Resident, Riverside Office)
John Calfee Mulvana (Resident, Santa Ana Office)
David L. Bell
Brian T. Chu (Resident, Santa Ana Office)
John Hammond
Laurent C. Vonderweidt
David Peim
Daniel V. Kohls (Resident, San Francisco Office)
Joel E. D. Odou
Robert T. Bergsten
Marcelo A. D'Asero
Natasha M. Riggs
Henry M. Su
Richard K. Kay
Annette A. Apperson

A list of References will be furnished upon request.

For full biographical listings, see the Martindale-Hubbell Law Directory

Lagerlof, Senecal, Bradley & Swift

(See Pasadena)

Langberg, Leslie & Gabriel (AV)

An Association including a Professional Corporation
2049 Century Park East Suite 3030, 90067
Telephone: 310-286-7700
Telecopier: 310-284-8355

Barry B. Langberg (A Professional Corporation)
Jody R. Leslie
Joseph M. Gabriel

Eileen M. Cohn
Deborah Drooz
Richard J. Wynne
Beatrice L. Hoffman
Michael M. Baranov
Beth F. Dumas
Dwayne A. Watts
Mitchell J. Langberg

LEGAL SUPPORT PERSONNEL

PARALEGALS

Patricia Urban
Patricia Ann Essig
Jeanne A. Logé

For full biographical listings, see the Martindale-Hubbell Law Directory

Lebovits & David, A Professional Corporation (AV)

Suite 3100, Two Century Plaza, 2049 Century Park East, 90067
Telephone: 310-277-0200
FAX: 310-552-1028

Moses Lebovits
Deborah A. David

OF COUNSEL

Joseph J. M. Lange

Reference: City National Bank (Main Office - Beverly Hills).

For full biographical listings, see the Martindale-Hubbell Law Directory

Leib, Alton (AV)

1801 Century Park East, Suite 2500, 90067-2326
Telephone: 310-286-0880
Fax: 310-286-1633

Alton Leib

Representative Clients: Western Dye House, Inc.; Cal-Pacific Dying & Finishing; Ideal Textile Co., Inc.

(See Next Column)

For full biographical listings, see the Martindale-Hubbell Law Directory

Leopold, Petrich & Smith, A Professional Corporation (AV)

(Formerly Youngman, Hungate & Leopold)
Suite 3110, 2049 Century Park East (Century City), 90067
Telephone: 310-277-3333
Telecopier: 310-277-7444

Gordon E. Youngman (1903-1983)
A. Fredric Leopold
Louis P. Petrich
Joel McCabe Smith
Edward A. Ruttenberg
Vincent Cox
Donald R. Gordon
Walter R. Sadler
Daniel M. Mayeda

OF COUNSEL

Richard Hungate

Paul M. Krekorian
David Aronoff
Gary M. Grossenbacher
Robert S. Gutierrez

For full biographical listings, see the Martindale-Hubbell Law Directory

Ronald A. Litz & Associates (AV)

Suite 1901, 1901 Avenue of the Stars, 90067
Telephone: 310-201-0100
FAX: 310-201-0226

ASSOCIATE

Jennifer A. Litz

OF COUNSEL

Arnold W. Magasinn
Vicki Fisher Magasinn
Carl R. Waldman

For full biographical listings, see the Martindale-Hubbell Law Directory

Loeb and Loeb (AV)

A Partnership including Professional Corporations
Suite 1800, 1000 Wilshire Boulevard, 90017-2475
Telephone: 213-688-3400
Telecopier: 213-688-3460; 688-3461; 688-3462
Century City, California Office: Suite 2200, 10100 Santa Monica Boulevard, Los Angeles, 90067-4164.
Telephone: 310-282-2000.
Telecopier: 310-282-2191; 282-2192.
New York, N.Y. Office: 345 Park Avenue, 10154-0037.
Telephone: 212-407-4000.
Facsimile: 212-407-4990.
Nashville, Tennessee Office: 45 Music Square West, 37203-3205.
Telephone: 615-749-8300;
Facsimile: 615-749-8308.
Rome, Italy Office: Piazza Digione 1, 00197.
Telephone: 011-396-808-8456.
Telecopier: 011-396-674-8223.

MEMBERS OF FIRM

Debra J. Albin-Riley
Harold A. Barza
Carol Laurene Belfield
David B. Eizenman (New York City Office)
Howard I. Friedman (A P.C.)
Robert A. Holtzman (A P.C.)
John F. Lang (New York City Office)
Robert A. Meyer
Charles H. Miller (New York City Office)
Douglas E. Mirell
Martin R. Pollner (New York City Office)
David M. Satnick (New York City Office)
Peter S. Selvin
David B. Shontz (New York City Office)
Alan W. Wilken
Michael P. Zweig (New York City Office)

OF COUNSEL

Harry First (New York City Office)
Alfred I. Rothman (A P.C.)
Albert F. Smith (A P.C.)

ASSOCIATES

Matthew Clark Bures
Charlene A. Busch
Paula K. Colbath (New York City Office)
Bert C. Cozart
Kathryn Lee Crawford (New York City Office)
David P. Crochetiere
Brant H. Dveirin
Daniel J. Friedman
Helen Gavaris (New York City Office)
Kurtiss Lee Grossman
Robert B. Rosen (New York City Office)
Roni Schneider (New York City Office)
Terri J. Seligman (New York City Office)
Robert N. Treiman
Rebecca E. White (New York City Office)
Nena W. Wong

For Complete List of Firm Personnel, See General Section

For full biographical listings, see the Martindale-Hubbell Law Directory

Los Angeles—Continued

LYNBERG & WATKINS, A PROFESSIONAL CORPORATION (AV)

Sixteenth Floor International Tower Plaza, 888 South Figueroa Street, 90017-2516
Telephone: 213-624-8700
Fax: 213-627-3732
Santa Ana, California Office: Suite 101, 2020 E. 1st Street.
Telephone: 714-973-1220.
Fax: 714-973-1002.

Charles A. Lynberg
Judith Gold
Norman J. Watkins
R. Jeff Carlisle
Dana J. McCune
Michael J. Larin
Randall J. Peters
Ric C. Ottaiano **
Dana A. Fox
Stephen M. Harber

Ruth Segal
Catherine L. Ferro
Christine H. Gosney
Heller-Ann C. Hancock
Louis E.. Marino, Jr.
Douglas G. MacKay
William F. Bernard **
Michael A. Cartelli
Sharon P. McAleenan
Pamela H. Roth
Peter B. Langbord **
Claudia H. Hanzlick
Peggy Kolkey
Wendy E. Schultz
Sue Ann Salmon
Jamie L. Busching
David K. Morrison
Timothy F. Rivers
David C. Pierce
Robert McLaughlin **
Aaron Bowers
Andrew Ira Selman
Sharyn G. Alcaraz
Monique M. Hanno
Mark F. Gamboa
Nicholas R. Andrea
Brian J. Gladstone
Dina M. De Laurentis
Caroline M. Albert
Antonia M. Chan

OF COUNSEL

Martin D. Kaplan
Lisa T. Mathies

Representative Clients: Fireman's Fund Insurance Co.; American International Cos.; Allstate Insurance Co.; American Mutual Insurance Co.; California Federal Savings & Loan.
**Santa Ana Office

For full biographical listings, see the Martindale-Hubbell Law Directory

MCNICHOLAS & MCNICHOLAS (AV)

10866 Wilshire Boulevard, 90024
Telephone: 310-474-1582
FAX: 310-475-7871

MEMBERS OF FIRM

John P. McNicholas
Patrick McNicholas
David M. Ring

For full biographical listings, see the Martindale-Hubbell Law Directory

O'MELVENY & MYERS (AV)

400 South Hope Street, 90071-2899
Telephone: 213-669-6000
Cable Address: "Moms"
Facsimile: 213-669-6407
Century City, California Office: 1999 Avenue of the Stars, 7th Floor, 90067-6035.
Telephone: 310-553-6700.
Facsimile: 310-246-6779.
Newport Beach, California Office: 610 Newport Center Drive, Suite 1700, 92660.
Telephone: 714-760-9600.
Cable Address: "Moms".
Facsimile: 714-669-6994.
San Francisco, California Office: Embarcadero Center West Tower, 275 Battery Street, Suite 2600, 94111.
Telephone: 415-984-8700.
Facsimile: 415-984-8701.
New York, N.Y. Office: Citicorp Center, 153 East 53rd Street, 54th Floor, 10022-4611.
Telephone: 212-326-2000.
Facsimile: 212-326-2061.
Washington, D.C. Office: 555 13th Street, N.W., Suite 500 West, 20004-1109.
Telephone: 202-383-5300.
Cable Address: "Moms".
Facsimile: 202-383-5414.
Newark, New Jersey Office: One Gateway Center, 7th Floor, 07102.
Telephone: 201-639-8600.
Facsimile: 201-639-8630.
London, England Office: 10 Finsbury Square, London, EC2A 1LA.
Telephone: 011-44-171-256 8451.
Facsimile: 011-44-171-638-8205.
Tokyo, Japan Office: Sanbancho KB-6 Building, 6 Sanbancho, Chiyoda-ku, Tokyo 102, Japan.
Telephone: 011-81-3-3239-2800.
Facsimile: 011-81-3-3239-2432.
Hong Kong Office: 1104 Lippo Tower, Lippo Centre, 89 Queensway, Central Hong Kong.
Telephone: 011-852-523-8266.
Facsimile: 011-852-522-1760.

(See Next Column)

MEMBERS OF FIRM

Douglas W. Abendroth (Newport Beach Office)
Wallace M. Allan
John L. Altieri, Jr. (New York, N.Y. Office)
Seth Aronson
James R. Asperger
Richard E. Ayres (Not admitted in CA; Washington, D.C. Office)
John H. Beisner (Washington, D.C. Office)
Charles W. Bender
Donald T. Bliss, Jr. (Not admitted in CA; Washington, D.C. Office)
Daniel H. Bookin (San Francisco Office)
Dale M. Cendali (Not admitted in CA; New York, N.Y. Office)
Martin S. Checov (San Francisco Office)
Alan M. Cohen (Not admitted in CA; New York, N.Y. Office)
James W. Colbert, III
William T. Coleman, Jr. (Not admitted in CA; Washington, D.C. Office)
Bertrand M. Cooper
Michael A. Curley (New York, N.Y. Office)
Brian S. Currey
Ralph W. Dau
John F. Daum (Washington, D.C. Office)
Charles P. Diamond (Century City Office)
Robert S. Draper
Scott H. Dunham
Richard N. Fisher
Cliff H. Fonstein (New York, N.Y. Office)
Andrew J. Frackman (Not admitted in CA; New York, N.Y. Office)
Martin Glenn (New York, N.Y. Office)
Richard B. Goetz
Catherine Burcham Hagen (Newport Beach Office)
Stephen J. Harburg (Not admitted in CA; Washington, D.C. Office)
B. Boyd Hight
Bruce A. Hiler (Washington, D.C. Office)
Tom A. Jerman
Phillip R. Kaplan (Newport Beach Office)
Holly E. Kendig
David E. Killough
Louis B. Kimmelman (Not admitted in CA; New York, N.Y. Office)
F. Curt Kirschner, Jr. (San Francisco Office)
Paul R. Koepff (New York, N.Y. Office)
Jeffrey I. Kohn (Not admitted in CA; New York, N.Y. Office)
Gordon E. Krischer
Charles C. Lifland
Patrick Lynch
Joseph M. Malkin (San Francisco Office)
Cheryl White Mason
Thomas Michael McCoy
Julie A. McMillan (San Francisco Office)
Paul G. McNamara
John G. Niles
M. Randall Oppenheimer (Century City Office)
Kenneth R. O'Rourke
Richard G. Parker (Washington, D.C. Office)
Stephen P. Pepe
Alan Rader (Century City Office)
Charles C. Read
George A. Riley (San Francisco Office)
Mark A. Samuels
Carl R. Schenker, Jr. (Washington, D.C. Office)
Patricia Ann Schmiege (San Francisco Office)
Robert M. Schwartz (Century City Office)
James V. Selna (Newport Beach Office)
Ralph J. Shapira
Robert A. Siegel
Linda Jane Smith
Steven L. Smith (San Francisco Office)
John W. Stamper
Victoria Dagy Stratman
Henry C. Thumann
Debra A. Valentine (Not admitted in CA; Washington, D.C. Office)
Robert C. Vanderet
William W. Vaughn
Framroze M. Virjee
Kim McLane Wardlaw
Richard C. Warmer (San Francisco Office)
Robert E. Willett
W. Mark Wood
Michael G. Yoder (Newport Beach Office)

OF COUNSEL

Charles G. Bakaly, Jr.
Everett B. Clary

SPECIAL COUNSEL

Peter B. Ackerman
Brian C. Anderson (Washington, D.C. Office)
David T. Beddow (Not admitted in CA; Washington, D.C. Office)
Rosemary B. Boller (New York, N.Y. Office)
Joseph E. Boury (Newark, N.J. Office)
Brian David Boyle (Washington, D.C. Office)
Thomas K. Braun
Richard W. Buckner
Cormac J. Carney (Newport Beach Office)
Thomas G. Carruthers (New York, N.Y. Office)
John A. Crose, Jr.
Douglas E. Dexter (San Francisco Office)
Suzanne F. Duff
Charles W. Fournier (New York, N.Y. Office)
Kathleen A. Gallagher (New York, N.Y. Office)
H. Douglas Galt
David R. Garcia
Karen R. Growdon
Kenneth E. Johnson
Abigail A. Jones
Michael G. McGuinness
Daniel M. Mansueto
Gregory R. Oxford
Diane E. Pritchard
Thomas H. Reilly (Newport Beach Office)
Glenn W. Trost
Dana K. Welch (San Francisco Office)
Alfred M. Wurglitz (Washington, D.C. Office)

(See Next Column)

O'MELVENY & MYERS, *Los Angeles—Continued*

ASSOCIATES

Gregory N. Albright (Century City Office)
Paul M. Alfieri (New York, N.Y. Office)
Mary Amilea Anderson (Washington, D.C. Office)
James D. Arbogast (New York, N.Y. Office)
Linda A. Bagley (San Francisco Office)
Patrick J. Bannon (San Francisco Office)
Alec M. Barinholtz
Bernard C. Barmann, Jr.
Steven Basileo
Evelyn Becker
Kathleen L. Beiermeister (Newark, N.J. Office)
Diane Wasil Biagianti (Newport Beach Office)
Stanley Blumenfeld
Michael G. Bosko (Newport Beach Office)
John M. Bowers
Debra L. Boyd
Laura C. Bremer (San Francisco Office)
Renée Turkell Brook
William R. Burford (San Francisco Office)
John R. Call
Viola I. Canales (San Francisco Office)
Apalla U. Chopra
Carla J. Christofferson (Century City Office)
Peggy Ann Clarke (Not admitted in CA; Washington, D.C. Office)
Steven M. Cooper
Craig A. Corman (Century City Office)
Ira A. Daves, III
Elizabeth A. Delaney (Washington, D.C. Office)
Ralph P. DeSanto (New York, N.Y. Office)
Elena Bocca Dietrich (San Francisco Office)
Thomas J. Di Resta (New York, N.Y. Office)
Erica K. Doran (Not admitted in CA; New York, N.Y. Office)
Paul F. Douglas
Kate W. Duchene
David P. Enzminger
Marcia A. Fay (Washington, D.C. Office)
Marc F. Feinstein
Aaron F. Fishbein (New York, N.Y. Office)
Randy J. Funk
James H. Gianninoto (Newark, N.J. Office)
Kenneth A. Goldberg (Not admitted in CA; New York, N.Y. Office)
Lawrence M. Gordon
Edward Gregory
Greg Groeneveld
Karin Lyn Gustafson (Century City Office)
Lawrence M. Hadley
Eugene P. Hanson (New York, N.Y. Office)
Kevin M. Harr
J. Michael Harty (New York, N.Y. Office)
Hilary R. Hegener (Washington, D.C. Office)
Peter R. Herman (Not admitted in CA; New York, N.Y. Office)
David L. Herron
John E. Hoffman
Chris Hollinger
Jennifer L. Isenberg (San Francisco Office)
Bruce Gen Iwasaki
Gloria Ching-hua Jan (New York, N.Y. Office)
Jeffrey M. Judd (San Francisco Office)
M. Flynn Justice, III (Newport Beach Office)
Thomas J. Karr (Not admitted in CA; Washington, D. C. Office)
Kevin M. Kelcourse (Not admitted in CA; Washington, D.C. Office)
Jeffrey W. Kilduff (Not admitted in CA; Washington, D.C. Office)
Patricia H. Kim (Not admitted in CA; New York, N.Y. Office)
Kathleen E. Kinney (Newport Beach Office)
Stephen V. Kovarik (New York, N.Y. Office)
Robert F. Kramer (Not admitted in CA; New York, N.Y. Office)
Paul A. Leodori (Newark, N.J. Office)
Sharon G. Levin (Not admitted in CA; Washington, D.C. Office)
Michael Cary Levine
Lisa Litwiller (Newport Beach Office)
Monique Janelle London (San Francisco Office)
Michele Logan Lynch
Michael M. Maddigan
David A. Marcus
Maria Rose Mazur (Washington, D.C. Office)
Marion K. McDonald (Washington, D.C. Office)
Darren S. McNally (Newark, N.J. Office)
Susan M. McNeill (New York, N.Y. Office)
Linda M. Mealey-Lohmann
Karen M. Mendalka (Newark, N.J. Office)
Kathleen A. Mishkin (Newark, N.J. Office)
Vicki A. Nash (Newport Beach Office)
Matthew B. Pachman (Washington, D.C. Office)
Lynn E. Parseghian (Not admitted in CA; Washington, D.C. Office)
Achilles M. Perry (Not admitted in CA; New York, N.Y. Office)
George R. Phillips, Jr.
M. Catherine Powell
Katherine W. Pownell
Claudia E. Ray (New York, N.Y. Office)
Anthony W. Rayburn
David J. Reis (San Francisco Office)
Patrick R. Rizzi (Not admitted in CA; Washington, D.C. Office)
James Gerard Rizzo (New York, N.Y. Office)
Gregory Roer (Newark, N.J. Office)
Pamela D. Samuels
Philip C. Scheurer (Washington, D.C. Office)
Tancred V. Schiavoni, III (New York, N.Y. Office)
Scott Schrader (New York Office)
Darrel M. Seife (New York, N.Y. Office)
Mary Louise Serafine (Century City Office)
Sam S. Shaulson (New York, N.Y. Office)
Craig W. Smith

ASSOCIATES (Continued)

(See Next Column)

Sandra E. Smith
Darin W. Snyder (San Francisco Office)
Albert J. Solecki, Jr. (Not admitted in CA; New York, N.Y. Office)
Irene E. Stewart
Michael I. Stockman
Nancy E. Sussman (Century City Office)
Janet I. Swerdlow
Edward J. Szczepkowski
Frieda A. Taylor
Gloria Trattles (New York, N.Y. Office)
Scott Treanor (San Francisco Office)
Kenneth J. Turnbull (Not admitted in CA; New York, N.Y. Office)
Karen Mary Wahle (Washington, D.C. Office)
William M. Walker
Larry A. Walraven (Newport Beach Office)
Brett J. Williamson (Newport Beach Office)
David A. Wimmer
Mary Catherine Wirth
Todd R. Wulffson (Newport Beach Office)
Scott N. Yamaguchi

For Complete List of Firm Personnel, See General Section

For full biographical listings, see the Martindale-Hubbell Law Directory

PILLSBURY MADISON & SUTRO (AV)

Citicorp Plaza, 725 South Figueroa Street, Suite 1200, 90017-2513
Telephone: 213-488-7100
Fax: 213-629-1033
Costa Mesa, California Office: Plaza Tower, 600 Anton Boulevard, Suite 1100, 92626.
Telephone: 714-436-6800.
Fax: 714-662-6999.
Menlo Park, California Office: 2700 Sand Hill Road, 94025.
Telephone: 415-233-4500.
Fax: 415-233-4545.
Sacramento, California Office: 400 Capitol Mall, Suite 1700, 95814.
Telephone: 916-329-4700.
Fax: 916-441-3583.
San Diego, California Office: 101 West Broadway, Suite 1800, 92101.
Telephone: 619-234-5000.
Fax: 619-236-1995.
San Francisco, California Office: 225 Bush Street, 94104.
Telephone: 415-983-1000.
Fax: 415-398-2096.
San Jose, California Office: Ten Almaden Boulevard, 95113.
Telephone: 408-947-4000.
Fax: 408-287-8341.
Washington, D. C. Office: 1667 K Street, N.W., Suite 1100, Suite 20006.
Telephone: 202-887-0300.
Fax: 202-296-7605.
New York, New York Office: One Liberty Plaza, 165 Broadway, 51st Floor.
Telephone: 212-374-1890.
Fax: 212-374-1852.
Hong Kong Office: 6/F Asia Pacific Finance Tower, Citibank Plaza, 3 Garden Road, Central.
Telephone: 011-852-509-7100.
Fax: 011-852-509-7188.
Tokyo, Japan Office: Churchill and Shimazaki, Gaiko-Jimo-Bengoshi Jimusho, 11-12, Toranomon, 5-chome Minato-ku, Tokyo 105, Japan.
Telephone: 800-729-9830; 011-81-3-5472-6561.
Fax: 011-81-3-5472-5761.

MEMBERS OF FIRM

Lawrence D. Bradley, Jr.
Kenneth R. Chiate
Robert A. Gutkin
Sidney K. Kanazawa
John Y. Liu
Catherine D. Meyer
William E. Stoner
John R. Cadarette, Jr.
Kent B. Goss
Amy D. Hogue
Ralph D. Kirwan
James A. Magee
Faisal Shah
David B. Van Etten

SENIOR COUNSEL

Susan S. Grover

ASSOCIATE

Jeffrey A. Rich

For Complete List of Firm Personnel, See General Section

For full biographical listings, see the Martindale-Hubbell Law Directory

QUINN, KULLY AND MORROW, A PROFESSIONAL LAW CORPORATION (AV)

Eighth Floor 520 South Grand Avenue, 90071
Telephone: 213-622-0300
Telecopier: 213-622-3799

John J. Quinn
Margaret M. Morrow
Laurence J. Hutt
J. David Oswalt
Lawrence A. Cox
Polly Horn
Eric L. Dobberteen
David S. Eisen
James I. Ham

For Complete List of Firm Personnel, See General Section

For full biographical listings, see the Martindale-Hubbell Law Directory

Los Angeles—Continued

SCHWARTZ, STEINSAPIR, DOHRMANN & SOMMERS (AV)

Suite 1820, 3580 Wilshire Boulevard, 90010
Telephone: 213-487-5700
Fax: 213-487-5548

MEMBERS OF FIRM

Laurence D. Steinsapir
Robert M. Dohrmann
Richard D. Sommers
Stuart Libicki
Michael R. Feinberg
Michael D. Four
Margo A. Feinberg
Henry M. Willis
Dennis J. Murphy
D. William Heine, Jr.
Claude Cazzulino
Dolly M. Gee
William T. Payne

ASSOCIATES

Kathy A. Finn
Brenda E. Sutton

For full biographical listings, see the Martindale-Hubbell Law Directory

STEVEN J. STANWYCK (AV)

1800 Century Park East, Suite 512, 90067-1508
Telephone: 310-557-8390
Telecopier: 310-557-8391

Reference: Western Bank.

For full biographical listings, see the Martindale-Hubbell Law Directory

SULLIVAN, WALSH & WOOD (AV)

Wells Fargo Center, 333 South Grand Avenue, 37th Floor, 90071-1599
Telephone: 213-488-9200
Telecopier: 213-488-9664

MEMBERS OF FIRM

Michael R. Sullivan
E. Eugene Walsh

ASSOCIATES

Douglas G. Carroll
Richard J. Sestak

OF COUNSEL

Scott E. Wood
Martin J. Spear

For full biographical listings, see the Martindale-Hubbell Law Directory

TALCOTT, LIGHTFOOT, VANDEVELDE, WOEHRLE & SADOWSKY (AV)

Thirteenth Floor 655 South Hope Street, 90017
Telephone: 213-622-4750
Fax: 213-622-2690

MEMBERS OF FIRM

Robert M. Talcott
Michael J. Lightfoot
John D. Vandevelde
Carla M. Woehrle
Stephen B. Sadowsky
John S. Crouchley
John P. Martin

OF COUNSEL

Quin Denvir

ASSOCIATES

Melissa N. Widdifield
James H. Locklin
Patricia Lea Peckham

Reference: Sterling Bank, Los Angeles, California.

For full biographical listings, see the Martindale-Hubbell Law Directory

VEATCH, CARLSON, GROGAN & NELSON (AV)

A Partnership including a Professional Corporation
3926 Wilshire Boulevard, 90010
Telephone: 213-381-2861
Telefax: 213-383-6370

MEMBERS OF FIRM

Wayne Veatch
Henry R. Thomas (1905-1963)
James R. Nelson (1925-1987)
James C. Galloway, Jr. (A Professional Corporation)
C. Snyder Patin
Anthony D. Seine
Mark A. Weinstein
John A. Peterson

ASSOCIATES

Michael Eric Wasserman
Richard A. Wood
Michael A. Kramer
Mark M. Rudy
André S. Goodchild
Lyn A. Woodward
Kevin L. Henderson
Betty Rubin-Elbaz
John B. Loomis
Judith Randel Cooper
Karen J. Travis
Amy W. Lyons
Wayne Rozenberg
Gilbert A. Garcia
Judy Lew
James A. Jinks

OF COUNSEL

Robert C. Carlson (A Professional Corporation)
Stephen J. Grogan
David J. Aisenson

For full biographical listings, see the Martindale-Hubbell Law Directory

VITTAL AND STERNBERG (AV)

2121 Avenue of the Stars, 22nd Floor, 90067-5010
Telephone: 310-551-0900
Facsimile: 310-551-2710

J. Anthony Vittal
Terence M. Sternberg

For full biographical listings, see the Martindale-Hubbell Law Directory

ROBERT D. WALKER A PROFESSIONAL CORPORATION (AV)

Suite 1208, One Park Plaza, 3250 Wilshire Boulevard, 90010-1606
Telephone: 213-382-8010
Fax: 213-388-1033

Robert D. Walker

Delia Flores
René M. Faucher

Reference: Bank of America (Los Angeles Main Office)

For full biographical listings, see the Martindale-Hubbell Law Directory

LOS OSOS, San Luis Obispo Co.

GEORGE, GALLO & SULLIVAN, A LAW CORPORATION (AV)

2238 Bayview Heights Drive, P.O. Box 6129, 93402
Telephone: 805-528-3351
Cable: SLOLAW
Telecopier: 805-528-5598
San Luis Obispo, California Office: 694 Santa Rosa, P.O. Box 12710.
Telephone: 805-544-3351.
Facsimile: 805-528-5598.

J. K. George
Ray A. Gallo
Shaunna L. Sullivan
Todd A. Porter

Anne C. Cyr

Reference: Mid State Bank, Los Osos, California.

For full biographical listings, see the Martindale-Hubbell Law Directory

MALIBU, Los Angeles Co.

LAW OFFICES OF TODD M. SLOAN (AV)

22601 Pacific Coast Highway, Suite 240, 90265
Telephone: 310-456-7900
Facsimile: 310-456-7906

For full biographical listings, see the Martindale-Hubbell Law Directory

MANHATTAN BEACH, Los Angeles Co.

STEINBERG, FOSTER & BARNESS (AV)

1334 Park View Avenue, Suite 100, 90266
Telephone: 310-546-5838
Telecopier: 310-546-5630

MEMBERS OF FIRM

Alex Steinberg
Douglas B. Foster
Daniel I. Barness

ASSOCIATE

William R. (Randy) Kirkpatrick

References: Home Bank; Imperial Bank; Citizens Commerical Trust & Savings Bank; Bank of America.

For full biographical listings, see the Martindale-Hubbell Law Directory

MENLO PARK, San Mateo Co.

O'REILLY & COLLINS, A PROFESSIONAL CORPORATION (AV)

2500 Sand Hill Road, Suite 201, 94025
Telephone: 415-854-7700
Fax: 415-854-8350

Terry O'Reilly
James P. Collins

James P. Tessier

For full biographical listings, see the Martindale-Hubbell Law Directory

LAW OFFICES OF JOHN C. SHAFFER, JR. A PROFESSIONAL LAW CORPORATION (AV)

750 Menlo Avenue, Suite 250, 94025
Telephone: 415-324-0622
Fax: 415-321-0198

John C. Shaffer, Jr.
Douglas N. Thomason

For full biographical listings, see the Martindale-Hubbell Law Directory

MISSION VIEJO, Orange Co.

ROBINSON, PHILLIPS & CALCAGNIE, A PROFESSIONAL CORPORATION (AV)

Incorporated 1986
26722 Plaza Street, Suite 230, 92690
Telephone: 714-582-6901
Fax: 714-582-3923
San Diego, California Office: 110 Laurel Street.
Telephone: 619-338-4060.
FAX: 619-338-0423.

Mark P. Robinson, Jr.
Gordon G. Phillips, Jr.
Kevin F. Calcagnie

Allan F. Davis
Susan Lee Guinn
Jeoffrey L. Robinson

For full biographical listings, see the Martindale-Hubbell Law Directory

*MODESTO,** Stanislaus Co.

BRUNN & FLYNN, A PROFESSIONAL CORPORATION (AV)

928 12th Street, P.O. Box 3366, 95353
Telephone: 209-521-2133
Fax: 209-521-7584

Charles K. Brunn
Gerald E. Brunn
Timothy T. Flynn
Roger S. Matzkind

Reference: Pacific Valley Bank.

For full biographical listings, see the Martindale-Hubbell Law Directory

DAMRELL, NELSON, SCHRIMP, PALLIOS & LADINE, A PROFESSIONAL CORPORATION (AV)

1601 I Street, Fifth Floor, 95354
Telephone: 209-526-3500
Fax: 209-526-3534
Sacramento, California Office: Suite 200, 1100 K Street.
Telephone: 916-447-2909.
Fax: 916-447-0552.
Oakdale, California Office: 703 West "F" Street, P.O. Drawer C.
Telephone: 209-848-3500.
Fax: 209-848-3400.

Frank C. Damrell (1898-1988)
Steven G. Pallios
Frank C. Damrell, Jr.
Wray F. Ladine
Duane L. Nelson
Matthew O. Pacher
Roger M. Schrimp
Susan D. Siefkin
Fred A. Silva

Craig W. Hunter
Wendelin Z. Warwick
Anthony J. Sarkis
Elizabeth T. Clayton
John K. Peltier
Christopher G. Daniel
James F. Lewis
Debra L. Klevatt
Jefferey A. Wooten
Lisa L. Gillispie
Robert F. Pomper

OF COUNSEL

Ann M. Veneman
Cressey H. Nakagawa

Representative Clients: American Honda Motor Co., Inc.; Bronco Wine Co.; E. & J. Gallo Winery; Gallo Glass Co.; The Luckey Co.; Norfolk Southern Corp.; Pep Boys of California, Inc.; W. R. Grace & Co.; National Medical Enterprises, Inc.; Ogden Corp.

For full biographical listings, see the Martindale-Hubbell Law Directory

MONTEREY, Monterey Co.

HARRAY, PIERCE & MASUDA (AV)

80 Garden Court, Suite 260, 93940
Telephone: 408-373-3101
Fax: 408-373-6712

Richard K. Harray
Jacqueline M. Pierce
Michael P. Masuda

ASSOCIATE

Stan L. Linker

For full biographical listings, see the Martindale-Hubbell Law Directory

MURPHY, THOMPSON & GUNTER, A PROFESSIONAL LAW PARTNERSHIP (AV)

580 Calle Principal, 93940-2818
Telephone: 408-646-1221
Fax: 408-646-0953

Ralph W. Thompson, III
Roy C. Gunter, III

For full biographical listings, see the Martindale-Hubbell Law Directory

GEORGE R. WALKER (AV)

215 West Franklin Street, 5th Floor, Professional Building, P.O. Box Law, 93940
Telephone: 408-649-1100
Fax: 408-649-6805

ASSOCIATE

Ute M. Isbill

Representative Clients: A. F. Victor Foundation, Carmel, California; The Carmel Foundation, Carmel, California; Robert Louis Stevenson School, Pebble Beach, California; Brintons Consolidated, Inc.; C & E Farms, Inc.; The Mildred Hitchcock Huff Charitable Trust.

For full biographical listings, see the Martindale-Hubbell Law Directory

LAW OFFICES OF CHARLES G. WARNER (AV)

631 Abrego Street, 93940
Telephone: 408-375-0203
Facsimile: 408-375-4159

For full biographical listings, see the Martindale-Hubbell Law Directory

MOUNTAIN VIEW, Santa Clara Co.

SCHNEIDER, LUCE, QUILLINAN & MORGAN (AV)

A Partnership including a Professional Corporation
444 Castro Street, Suite 900, 94041-2073
Telephone: 415-969-4000
FAX: 415-969-6953

MEMBERS OF FIRM

Michael E. Schneider (A P.C.)
James V. Quillinan
James G. Luce
Michael R. Morgan

ASSOCIATES

Richard Posilippo
Melissa C. Johnson

For full biographical listings, see the Martindale-Hubbell Law Directory

NEWPORT BEACH, Orange Co.

BUCHALTER, NEMER, FIELDS & YOUNGER, A PROFESSIONAL CORPORATION (AV)

Suite 300, 620 Newport Center Drive, 92660
Telephone: 714-760-1121
Fax: 714-720-0182
Los Angeles, California Office: 24th Floor, 601 South Figueroa Street.
Telephone: 213-891-0700.
Fax: 213-896-0400.
New York, New York Office: 19th Floor, 237 Park Avenue.
Telephone: 212-490-8600.
Fax: 212-490-6022.
San Francisco, California Office: 29th Floor, 333 Market Street.
Telephone: 415-227-0900.
Fax: 415-227-0770.
San Jose, California Office: 12th Floor, 50 West San Fernando Street.
Telephone: 408-298-0350.
Fax: 408-298-7683.
Century City, California Office: Suite 2400, 1801 Century Park East.
Telephone: 213-891-0700.
Fax: 310-551-0233.

Clifford John Meyer
Debra Solle Healy
Theodor C. Albert
Kirk S. Rense

OF COUNSEL

Marcus M. Kaufman

Bruce M. Boyd
Jennifer Ann Golison
Lori S. Ross
David Mark Hershorin
Jeffrey I. Golden
Brian A. Kumamoto
Mark M. Scott
Lori Suzanne Carver
Evan D. Smiley

References: City National Bank; Wells Fargo Bank; Metrobank.

For full biographical listings, see the Martindale-Hubbell Law Directory

CALL, CLAYTON & JENSEN, A PROFESSIONAL CORPORATION (AV)

Suite 700, 610 Newport Center Drive, 92660
Telephone: 714-760-8711
FAX: 714-759-3637

Wayne W. Call
Troy L. Tate
L. Whitney Clayton, III
Seth L. Liebman

Michael R. Overly
James A. Durant
Maryam Shokrai
Jeffrey A. Blackie

For full biographical listings, see the Martindale-Hubbell Law Directory

Newport Beach—Continued

Capretz & Radcliffe (AV)

5000 Birch Street, West Tower Suite 2500, 92660-2139
Telephone: 714-724-3000
Fax: 714-757-2635

James T. Capretz
Richard J. Radcliffe

LEGAL SUPPORT PERSONNEL

Rosanna S. Bertheola

For full biographical listings, see the Martindale-Hubbell Law Directory

Davis, Punelli, Keathley & Willard (AV)

610 Newport Center Drive, Suite 1000, P.O. Box 7920, 92658-7920
Telephone: 714-640-0700
Telecopier: 714-640-0714
San Diego, California Office: 4370 La Jolla Village Drive, Suite 300.
Telephone: 619-558-2581.

MEMBERS OF FIRM

Robert E. Willard
S. Eric Davis
Frank Punelli, Jr.
H. James Keathley
Leonard R. Sager
Eric G. Anderson
Katherine D. O'Brian

OF COUNSEL

Lewis K. Uhler

For full biographical listings, see the Martindale-Hubbell Law Directory

John C. Lautsch A Professional Corporation (AV)

4220 Von Karman, Suite 120, 92660
Telephone: 714-955-9095
Telefax: 714-955-2978

John C. Lautsch

Kurt E. English

For full biographical listings, see the Martindale-Hubbell Law Directory

Ronald K. Van Wert A Professional Corporation (AV)

One Newport Place, Suite 900, 1301 Dove Street, 92660
Telephone: 714-752-7964

Ronald K. Van Wert

For full biographical listings, see the Martindale-Hubbell Law Directory

The Walker Law Firm A Professional Corporation (AV)

Suite 450, 1301 Dove Street, 92660-2464
Telephone: 714-752-2522
Telecopier: 714-752-0439
Temecula, California Office: 41877 Enterprise Circle North, Suite 100.
Telephone: 909-676-1314.
Telecopier: 909-676-5325.

Joseph A. Walker

OF COUNSEL

Duff S. McEvers
Ronald R. Sikes (Resident, Temecula, California Office)
David T. Sanford
Wendy Patricia Coleman

Reference: Liberty National Bank.

For full biographical listings, see the Martindale-Hubbell Law Directory

*OAKLAND,** Alameda Co.

Haims, Johnson, MacGowan & McInerney (AV)

490 Grand Avenue, 94610
Telephone: 510-835-0500
Facsimile: 510-835-2833

MEMBERS OF FIRM

Arnold B. Haims
Gary R. Johnson
Clyde L. MacGowan
Thomas McInerney
Lawrence A. Baker
Randy M. Marmor
John K. Kirby
Robert J. Frassetto
Caroline N. Valentino

ASSOCIATES

Joseph Y. Ahn
Edward D. Baldwin
Kathleen B. Boehm
Marc P. Bouret
Anne M. Michaels
Dianne D. Peebles
Michelle D. Perry
Edward C. Schroeder, Jr.

For full biographical listings, see the Martindale-Hubbell Law Directory

Hardin, Cook, Loper, Engel & Bergez (AV)

1999 Harrison Street, 18th Floor, 94612-3541
Telephone: 510-444-3131
Telecopier: 510-839-7940

(See Next Column)

MEMBERS OF FIRM

J. Marcus Hardin (1905-1993)
L. S. Fletcher (1905-1964)
Herman Cook (1914-1982)
John C. Loper
Barrie Engel
Raymond J. Bergez
George S. Peyton, Jr.
Ralph A. Lombardi
Sandra F. Wagner
Willard L. Alloway
Gennaro A. Filice, III
Stephen McKae
Bruce P. Loper
Bruce E. McLeod
Eugene Brown, Jr.
Linda C. Roodhouse
Matthew S. Conant
Chris P. Lavdiotis
Robert D. Eassa
Peter O. Glaessner

Amber L. Kelly
Owen T. Rooney
John A. De Pasquale
Nicholas D. Kayhan
William H. Curtis
Elsa M. Baldwin
Rodney Ian Headington
Marshall A. Johnson
Diane R. Stanton
Jennifer M. Walker
Margaret L. Kotzebue
Amee A. Mikacich
Peter A. Strotz
Timothy J. McCaffery
Stephen J. Valen
Troy D. McMahan
Lisa L. Hillegas
GayLynn Renee Kirn
Richard V. Normington III
Kevin J. Chechak

OF COUNSEL

Ronald A. Wagner
Lydia T. Van't Rood

Representative Clients: Firemans Fund Insurance Cos.; City of Piedmont; The Dow Chemical Co.; Nissan Motor Corp.; Subaru of America; Weyerhauser Co.; Bay Area Rapid Transit District; Diamond Shamrock; Home Indemnity Co.; Rhone-Poulenc.

For Complete List of Firm Personnel, See General Section

For full biographical listings, see the Martindale-Hubbell Law Directory

Kazan, McClain, Edises, Simon & Abrams, A Professional Law Corporation (AV)

Suite 300, 171 Twelfth Street, 94607
Telephone: 510-465-7728; 893-7211
TDD: (510) 763-8808
Fax: 510-835-4913
Internet: Kazan@kmes.com

Steven Kazan
David M. McClain
Aaron H. Simon
Denise Abrams

Francis E. Fernandez
Anne M. Landwehr
Dianna J. Lyons
Frances C. Schreiberg
Simona A. Farrise

LEGAL SUPPORT PERSONNEL

Elizabeth C. Johnson (Director of Administration and Finance)

Reference: Union Bank (Oakland Main Branch).

For full biographical listings, see the Martindale-Hubbell Law Directory

Martin, Ryan & Andrada, A Professional Corporation (AV)

Twenty-Second Floor, Ordway Building, One Kaiser Plaza, 94612
Telephone: 510-763-6510
Fax: 510-763-3921

Gerald P. Martin, Jr.
Joseph D. Ryan, Jr.
J. Randall Andrada
Jill J. Lifter
Jolie Krakauer
Glenn Gould
Michael J. Daley
Charles E. Kallgren
Rhonda D. Shelton
Betty J. Jones
Lora N. Vail
Vikki L. Barron-Jennings

Representative Clients: Alameda Contra Costa County Transit District; Continental Insurance Cos.; Commercial Union Insurance Group; Liberty Mutual Insurance Co.; Safeway Stores, Inc.

For full biographical listings, see the Martindale-Hubbell Law Directory

Van Blois & Knowles (AV)

Suite 2245 Ordway Building, One Kaiser Plaza, 94612
Telephone: 510-444-1906
Contra Costa County 510-947-1055
Fax: 510-444-1294
Livermore, California Office: 2109 Fourth Street.
Telephone: 510-455-0193.

MEMBERS OF FIRM

R. Lewis Van Blois
Thomas C. Knowles
Ellen R. Schwartz
Richard J. Baskin

For full biographical listings, see the Martindale-Hubbell Law Directory

ORANGE, Orange Co.

WALSWORTH, FRANKLIN & BEVINS (AV)

1 City Boulevard West, Suite 308, 92668
Telephone: 714-634-2522
LAW-FAX: 714-634-0686
San Francisco, California Office: 580 California Street, Suite 1335.
Telephone: 415-781-7072.
Fax: 415-391-6258.

Jeffrey P. Walsworth
Ferdie F. Franklin
Ronald H. Bevins, Jr.
Michael T. McCall
Noel Edlin (Resident, San Francisco Office)
Lawrence E. Duffy, Jr.
Sheldon J. Fleming
J. Wayne Allen
James A. Anton
Ingrid K. Campagne (Resident, San Francisco Office)
Robert M. Channel (Resident, San Francisco Office)
Nicholas A. Cipiti
Sharon L. Clisham (Resident, San Francisco Office)
David W. Epps (Resident, San Francisco Office)
Richard M. Hills (Resident, San Francisco Office)
Sandra G. Kennedy
Randall J. Lee (Resident, San Francisco Office)
Kimberly K. Mays
Bruce A. Nelson (Resident, San Francisco Office)
Kevin Pegan
Allan W. Ruggles
Jonathan M. Slipp
Cyrian B. Tabuena (Resident, San Francisco Office)
John L. Trunko
Houston M. Watson, II
Mary A. Watson

For full biographical listings, see the Martindale-Hubbell Law Directory

*OROVILLE,** Butte Co.

HENDREN LAW OFFICES (AV)

19 Nelson Avenue, P.O. Box 1822, 95965
Telephone: 916-533-0661
Fax: 916-533-3956

Ed W. Hendren

Reference: Butte Community Bank.

For full biographical listings, see the Martindale-Hubbell Law Directory

PALO ALTO, Santa Clara Co.

BLASE, VALENTINE & KLEIN, A PROFESSIONAL CORPORATION (AV)

1717 Embarcadero Road, P.O. Box 51050, 94303
Telephone: 415-857-1717
Telecopier: 415-857-1288

Lawrence A. Klein
Peter A. Whitman
George C. Fisher
Craig S. Ritchey
Ellen B. Turbow
Jean K. McCown
Martha Corcoran Luemers
Karen E. Wentzel
John G. Hursh
Terence M. Kelly
Gillian G. Hays
David A. Kays
Anne Marie Flaherty
Terrence H. Cross

COUNSEL

C. Grant Spaeth
Guy Blase
Paul C. Valentine

For Complete List of Firm Personnel, See General Section

For full biographical listings, see the Martindale-Hubbell Law Directory

FTHENAKIS & VOLK (AV)

540 University Avenue, Suite 300, 94301
Telephone: 415-326-1397
Telecopier: 415-326-3203

MEMBERS OF FIRM

Basil P. Fthenakis
John D. Volk

ASSOCIATE

Oliver P. Colvin

For full biographical listings, see the Martindale-Hubbell Law Directory

CHRISTOPHER REAM (AV)

1717 Embarcadero Road, 94303
Telephone: 415-424-0821
Facsimile: 415-857-1288

For full biographical listings, see the Martindale-Hubbell Law Directory

PASADENA, Los Angeles Co.

BARKER & ASSOCIATES, A PROFESSIONAL CORPORATION (AV)

301 East Colorado Boulevard Suite 200, 91101-1977
Telephone: 818-578-1970; 213-617-3112
Facsimile: 818-578-0768

(See Next Column)

Lee Barker
Steven G. Harman
Timothy M. Howett
Kelly G. Richardson
John J. Isaza
Blaine Jay Wanke

Reference: Union Bank.

For full biographical listings, see the Martindale-Hubbell Law Directory

COLLINS, COLLINS, MUIR & TRAVER (AV)

Successor to Collins & Collins
Suite 300, 265 North Euclid, 91101
Telephone: 818-793-1163
Los Angeles: 213-681-2773
FAX: 818-793-5982

MEMBERS OF FIRM

James E. Collins (1910-1987)
John J. Collins
Samuel J. Muir
Robert J. Traver

ASSOCIATES

John B. Foss
Frank J. D'Oro
Paul L. Rupard
Brian K. Stewart
Robert H. Stellwagen, Jr.
Tomas A. Guterres
Karen B. Sharp
Amina R. Merritt
Christine E. Drage

For full biographical listings, see the Martindale-Hubbell Law Directory

FRANSCELL, STRICKLAND, ROBERTS & LAWRENCE, A PROFESSIONAL CORPORATION (AV)

Penthouse, 225 South Lake Avenue, 91101-3005
Telephone: 818-304-7830; 213-684-7830; 800-303-5503 (CA Only)
Fax: 818-795-7460
Santa Ana, California Office: Suite 800, 401 Civic Center Drive West.
Telephone: 714-543-6511.
Fax: 714-543-6711.
Riverside, California Office: Suite 670, 3801 University Avenue.
Telephone: 909-686-1000.
Fax: 909-686-2565.

George J. Franscell
Tracy Strickland (Resident, Santa Ana Office)
Barbara E. Roberts (Resident, Riverside Office)
David D. Lawrence
Carol Ann Rohr
Scott D. MacLatchie
W. Charles Bradley (Resident, Riverside Office)
S. Frank Harrell (Resident, Santa Ana Office)
Conrad R. Clark (Resident, Riverside Office)
Jeri Tabback Thompson
Olaf W. Hedberg (Resident, Santa Ana Office)
Spencer Krieger
Jack D. Hoskins

For full biographical listings, see the Martindale-Hubbell Law Directory

FREEBURG, JUDY, MACCHIAGODENA & NETTELS (AV)

600 South Lake Avenue, 91106
Telephone: 818-585-4150
FAX: 818-585-0718
Santa Ana, California Office: Xerox Centre. 1851 East First Street, Suite 120. 92705-4017.
Telephone: 714-569-0950.
Facsimile: 714-569-0955.

Steven J. Freeburg
J. Lawrence Judy
Marina A. Macchiagodena
Charles F. Nettels

ASSOCIATES

Ingall W. Bull, Jr.
Richard B. Castle
Cynthia B. Schaldenbrand (Resident, Santa Ana Office)
Robert S. Brody
Sheral A. Hyde
Holly A. McNulty
Karen S. Freeburg
Jennifer D. Helsel
James P. Habel
Marianne L. Offermans

For full biographical listings, see the Martindale-Hubbell Law Directory

LAGERLOF, SENECAL, BRADLEY & SWIFT (AV)

301 North Lake Avenue, 10th Floor, 91101-4107
Telephone: 818-793-9400
FAX: 818-793-5900

MEMBERS OF FIRM

Joseph J. Burris (1913-1980)
Stanley C. Lagerlof
H. Melvin Swift, Jr.
H. Jess Senecal
Jack T. Swafford
John F. Bradley
Timothy J. Gosney
William F. Kruse
Thomas S. Bunn, III
Andrew D. Turner
Rebecca J. Thyne

ASSOCIATES

Paul M. Norman
John F. Machtinger
James D. Ciampa
Ellen M. Burkhart

(See Next Column)

LAGERLOF, SENECAL, BRADLEY & SWIFT—*Continued*

LEGAL SUPPORT PERSONNEL

Ronald E. Hagler

Representative Clients: Anchor Glass Container Corporation; Bethlehem Steel Corp.; Orthopaedic Hospital; Palmdale Water District; Public Water Agencies Group; Walnut Valley Water District.
Special Counsel: City of Redondo Beach, Calif.; Ventura Port Dist., Calif.

For full biographical listings, see the Martindale-Hubbell Law Directory

KEVIN MEENAN (AV)

790 East Colorado Boulevard Ninth Floor Penthouse, 91101-2105
Telephone: 818-398-0000
FAX: 818-585-0999

For full biographical listings, see the Martindale-Hubbell Law Directory

ROBMAN & SEELEY (AV)

225 South Lake Avenue, 9th Floor, 91101
Telephone: 818-788-8494
Fax: 818-683-0755

MEMBERS OF FIRM

Louis Robman
Ronald J. Seeley

For full biographical listings, see the Martindale-Hubbell Law Directory

THROCKMORTON, BECKSTROM, OAKES & TOMASSIAN (AV)

A Partnership including Professional Corporations
Corporate Center Pasadena, 225 South Lake Avenue, Suite 500, 91101-3005
Telephone: 818-568-2500; 213-681-2321
Fax: 818-405-0786
Newport Beach, California Office: Suite 1200, 4695 Macarthur Court.
Telephone: 714-955-2280.
Fax: 714-467-8081.

MEMBERS OF FIRM

A. Robert Throckmorton (A Professional Corporation)
Spencer S. Beckstrom (A Professional Corporation)
George A. Oakes
Serge Tomassian
Alan Stanfill
David Alan Huffaker

References Available Upon Request.

For full biographical listings, see the Martindale-Hubbell Law Directory

*REDWOOD CITY,** San Mateo Co.

CODDINGTON, HICKS & DANFORTH, A PROFESSIONAL CORPORATION (AV)

Suite 300, 555 Twin Dolphin Drive, Paragon Center, Redwood Shores, 94065
Telephone: 415-592-5400
Facsimile: 415-592-5027

Clinton H. Coddington
Randolph S. Hicks
Lee J. Danforth
David M. King
Richard G. Grotch

Edward A. Heinlein
David W. Wessel
R. Wardell Loveland
Jo Saxe Kerlinsky
Pamela Ann Smith
David B. Burnett
Peter L. Candy
David K. Levine

OF COUNSEL

William G. Tucker
Arnold I Bennigson

For full biographical listings, see the Martindale-Hubbell Law Directory

*SACRAMENTO,** Sacramento Co.

BOLLING, WALTER & GAWTHROP, A PROFESSIONAL CORPORATION (AV)

8880 Cal Center Drive, Suite 400, P.O. Box 255200, 95865-5200
Telephone: 916-369-0777
Telecopier: 916-369-2698

Laurence L. Angelo
Theodore D. Bolling, Jr.
Kathy Christopher Breining
John P. Coleman
Michael J. Conlan
Alfred Gawthrop, Jr.
Charlotte E. Hemker-Smith
Michael F. Keddy
Bruce A. Kilday
Carolee Kilduff
Marjorie E. Manning
Bruno D. Marraccini
J. Brian Powers
Thomas A. Tweedy
Donald S. Walter
John A. Whitesides

Timothy L. Fall
David W. Ford
Gerald C. Hicks
Glenn M. Holley
Glenn V. Lawson
Christine Green Sanfilippo
Barbara L. Sheldon
Allison K. Smith
Wendy C. York

(See Next Column)

OF COUNSEL

Gerald K. Petersen
Marion H. Pothoven

LEGAL SUPPORT PERSONNEL

Susan M. Jarboe (Paralegal-Law Librarian)
Karen M. Murphy
Sharon Ericksen

Representative Clients: Aetna Casualty & Surety; Cal-Farm Insurance; California State Auto Assn.; Fireman's Fund American Co.; Gallagher Bassett Insurance Services; General Adjustment Bureau; Industrial Indemnity Co.; Nationwide Insurance Co.; Royal Insurance Co.; St. Paul Insurance Co.
Reference: River City Bank.

For full biographical listings, see the Martindale-Hubbell Law Directory

BOUTIN • GIBSON (AV)

455 Capitol Mall, Suite 300, 95814-4406
Telephone: 916-321-4444
Telecopier: 916-441-7597

MEMBERS OF FIRM

Stephen F. Boutin
Chris Gibson

ASSOCIATES

Robert D. Swanson
Ned M. Gelhaar
Deborah L. Maddux
Carol A. Salvagione

For full biographical listings, see the Martindale-Hubbell Law Directory

DIEPENBROCK, WULFF, PLANT & HANNEGAN (AV)

Suite 1700, 300 Capitol Mall, P.O. Box 3034, 95812-3034
Telephone: 916-444-3910
Telecopier: 916-446-1696

MEMBERS OF FIRM

John S. Gilmore
David A. Riegels
Dennis M. Campos
Jack V. Lovell
David Rosenberg
John E. Fischer
Charity Kenyon
Francis M. Goldsberry, II
Raymond M. Cadei
Forrest A. Plant, Jr.
Jeffery Owensby
William J. Coyne
Frank P. Fedor
Felicita S. Fields
David L. Ditora
P. John Swanson

ASSOCIATES

V. Blair Shahbazian
Melinda Guzman Moore
Sean O. Sheridan
Richard K. Voss
Holly B. Armstrong
Michael R. O'Neil
James F. Curran

Representative Clients: Southern Pacific Transportation Co.; Chevron Corp.; Metropolitan Life Insurance Co.; Aerojet-General Corp.; Farmers Insurance Group; Sears, Roebuck and Co.

For full biographical listings, see the Martindale-Hubbell Law Directory

DONAHUE LAMBERT & WOOD (AV)

83 Scripps Drive, Suite 200, 95825
Telephone: 916-648-7444
Fax: 916-648-7447

MEMBERS OF FIRM

James E. Donahue
Gerrit W. Wood
Walter H. Loving, III
Jeffrey W. Lambert
Michael E. Myers
Barry Vogel

William K. Blakemore
Thomas P. Connolly III
David E. Erickson
Stephen J. Mackey
Doug Winter
Eric M. Bonzell
Jean M. O'Sullivan
Mark A. Bates
Michele M. Campos
Aleshia M. Poole

For full biographical listings, see the Martindale-Hubbell Law Directory

HANSEN, BOYD, CULHANE & WATSON (AV)

A Partnership including Professional Corporations
Central City Centre, 1331 Twenty-First Street, 95814
Telephone: 916-444-2550
Telecopier: 916-444-2358

Hartley T. Hansen (Inc.)
Kevin R. Culhane (Inc.)
David E. Boyd
Lawrence R. Watson
John J. Rueda
James J. Banks

OF COUNSEL

Betsy S. Kimball

Lorraine M. Pavlovich
Thomas L. Riordan
D. Jeffery Grimes
Joseph Zuber
James O. Moses

For full biographical listings, see the Martindale-Hubbell Law Directory

Sacramento—Continued

JOHNSON, SCHACHTER, LEWIS & COLLINS, A PROFESSIONAL CORPORATION (AV)

701 University Avenue, Suite 150, 95825
Telephone: 916-921-5800
Telecopier: 916-921-0247
Walnut Creek, California Office: 500 Ygnacio Valley Road #490.
Telephone: 510-947-0100.
Fax: 510-947-0111.
Chico, California Office: 515 Wall Street.
Telephone: 916-895-1623.

Robert H. Johnson
Alesa M. Schachter
Luther R. Lewis
Kim H. Collins

George W. Holt
Timothy P. Dailey
James B. Walker
R. James Miller

OF COUNSEL

Ford R. Smith
Carolyn M. Wood
Susanne M. Shelley
James W. Rushford

Representative Clients: Fireman's Fund Insurance Cos; GAB Business Services; Jonsson Communications Corp.; McClatchy Newspapers and Broadcasting; State Farm Fire & Casualty Co.; State Farm Mutual Automobile Insurance Co.
Reference: Business & Professional Bank, Sacramento.

For full biographical listings, see the Martindale-Hubbell Law Directory

JOHN B. LEWIS (AV)

1006 Fourth Street, 10th Floor, 95814
Telephone: 916-443-2051

For full biographical listings, see the Martindale-Hubbell Law Directory

MASON & THOMAS (AV)

2151 River Plaza Drive, Suite 100, P.O. Box 868, 95812-0868
Telephone: 916-567-8211
Fax: 916-567-8212

MEMBERS OF FIRM

Stephen A. Mason
Bradley S. Thomas
Robert L. Moore

ASSOCIATES

Douglas W. Brown
Robert G. Kruse
David S. Yost
Patrick J. Hehir
Kevin L. Elder
Tina L. Izen

OF COUNSEL

John D. Stumbos, Jr.

For full biographical listings, see the Martindale-Hubbell Law Directory

MATHENY, POIDMORE & SEARS (AV)

2100 Northrop Avenue, Building 1200, P.O. Box 13711, 95853-4711
Telephone: 916-929-9271
Fax: 916-929-2458

MEMBERS OF FIRM

Henry G. Matheny (1933-1984)
Anthony J. Poidmore
Douglas A. Sears
Richard S. Linkert
James C. Damir
Michael A. Bishop
Ernest A. Long
Joann Georgallis
Kent M. Luckey

ASSOCIATES

Matthew C. Jaime
Jill P. Telfer
Robert B. Berrigan
Daryl M. Thomas
Ronald E. Enabnit
Cathy A. Reynolds
Byron D. Damiani, Jr.
Catherine Kennedy

OF COUNSEL

A. Laurel Bennett

LEGAL SUPPORT PERSONNEL

PARALEGALS

Karen D. Fisher
Fran Studer
Lynell Rae Steed
Jennifer Bachman
David Austin Boucher

For full biographical listings, see the Martindale-Hubbell Law Directory

MCDONALD, SAELTZER, MORRIS, CREEGGAN & WADDOCK (AV)

555 Capitol Mall, Suite 700, 95814
Telephone: 916-444-5706
Fax: 916-444-8529

MEMBERS OF FIRM

Eugene W. Saeltzer
William O. Morris
Richard C. Creeggan
Thomas P. Waddock
Gregory R. Madsen

(See Next Column)

ASSOCIATES

Paul J. Wagstaffe
Ronald Craig Schwarzkopf
Hank G. Greenblatt
Jon S. Allin
Scott W. DePeel
Jonathan M. Cohen
Robert S. Brunelli
Gretchen K. Mello

OF COUNSEL

Douglas B. McDonald

Reference: Wells Fargo Bank.

For full biographical listings, see the Martindale-Hubbell Law Directory

MCKINLEY & SMITH (AV)

3425 American River Drive, Suite B, 95864
Telephone: 916-972-1333
Fax: 916-972-1335

William C. McKinley
Timothy M. Smith

For full biographical listings, see the Martindale-Hubbell Law Directory

MOORE, MEEGAN, HANSCHU & KASSENBROCK (AV)

1545 River Park Drive, Suite 550, 95815
Telephone: 916-925-1800

MEMBERS OF FIRM

John M. Moore
David M. Meegan
James L. Hanschu
Mark R. Kassenbrock

Roberta Lindsey-Scott
Mary Clarke Ver Hoef
Peter J. Pullen

For full biographical listings, see the Martindale-Hubbell Law Directory

PORTER, SCOTT, WEIBERG & DELEHANT, A PROFESSIONAL CORPORATION (AV)

350 University Avenue, Suite 200, 95825
Telephone: 916-929-1481
Fax: 916-927-3706

Russell G. Porter
A. Irving Scott, Jr.
Edwin T. Weiberg
John W. Delehant
Anthony S. Warburg
Ned P. Telford
James K. Mirabell
Craig A. Caldwell
Terence J. Cassidy
Tom H. Bailey
Carl J. Calnero
Russ J. Wunderli
Nancy J. Sheehan
Norman V. Prior
Timothy M. Blaine
Stephen E. Horan

Amanda R. Lowe
Mark L. Hardy
John R. Thacker
David R. Lane
Clay A. Jackson
Elisa Ungerman
Jesse Cardenas
Fred G. Wiesner
John Carl Padrick
Dennis M. Beaty
Molly Geremia Wiese
David E. Faliszek
Michael J. LeVangie
Carissa A. Shubb
Erik Z. Revai
Karen Beth Ebel
Carl L. Fessenden
Shannon I. Sutherland
Grant Collins Woodruff
Dana K. Astrachan
Paul William Naso

For full biographical listings, see the Martindale-Hubbell Law Directory

WILKE, FLEURY, HOFFELT, GOULD & BIRNEY (AV)

A Partnership including Professional Corporations
400 Capitol Mall, Suite 2200, 95814-4408
Telephone: 916-441-2430
Telefax: 916-442-6664
Mailing Address: P.O. Box 15559, 95852-0559

MEMBERS OF FIRM

Richard H. Hoffelt (Inc.)
William A. Gould, Jr., (Inc.)
Philip R. Birney (Inc.)
Thomas G. Redmon (Inc.)
Scott L. Gassaway
Donald Rex Heckman II (Inc.)
Alan G. Perkins
Bradley N. Webb
Ernest James Krtil
Robert R. Mirkin
Matthew W. Powell
Mark L. Andrews
Stephen K. Marmaduke
David A. Frenznick
John R. Valencia
Angus M. MacLeod

ASSOCIATES

Paul A. Dorris
Kelli M. Kennaday
Tracy S. Hendrickson
Joseph G. De Angelis
Jennifer L. Kennedy
Anthony J. DeCristoforo
Rachel N. Kook
Alicia F. From
Michael Polis
Matthew J. Smith
Wayne L. Ordos

OF COUNSEL

Sherman C. Wilke
Anita Seipp Marmaduke
Benjamin G. Davidian

Representative Clients: NOR-CAL Mutual Insurance Co.; California Optometric Assn.; KPMG Peat Marwick; Glaxo, Inc.

(See Next Column)

WILKE, FLEURY, HOFFELT, GOULD & BIRNEY—*Continued*

For full biographical listings, see the Martindale-Hubbell Law Directory

*SAN BERNARDINO,** San Bernardino Co.

FURNESS, MIDDLEBROOK, KAISER & HIGGINS, A PROFESSIONAL CORPORATION (AV)

1411 North "D" Street, P.O. Box 1319, 92402-1319
Telephone: 909-888-5751
Fax: 909-888-7360
Palm Springs, California Office: 3001 East Tahquitz Canyon Way, Suite 109.
Telephone: 619-322-0806.
Fax: 619-322-8979.

John W. Furness
Greg C. Middlebrook
Michael R. Kaiser (Resident, Palm Springs Office)
James A. Higgins

Floyd F. Fishell
Thomas J. Mullen
Jeffrey A. Weaver (Resident, Palm Springs Office)
Jeffrey Mark Yoss (Resident, Palm Springs Office)
Robert F. Wilson
Cheryl A. Shaw (Resident, Palm Springs Office)

References: First Interstate Bank; Dun & Bradstreet.

For full biographical listings, see the Martindale-Hubbell Law Directory

GRESHAM, VARNER, SAVAGE, NOLAN & TILDEN (AV)

Suite 300, 600 North Arrowhead Avenue, 92401
Telephone: 909-884-2171
Fax: 909-888-2120
Victorville, California Office: 14011 Park Avenue, Suite 140.
Telephone: 619-243-2889.
Fax: 619-243-3057.
Riverside, California Office: 3737 Main Street, Suite 420.
Telephone: 714-274-7777.
Fax: 714-274-7770.

MEMBERS OF FIRM

Allen B. Gresham
John C. Nolan
Thomas N. Jacobson
Stephan G. Saleson
Robin Bramlett Cochran
Duke D. Rouse
Michael Duane Davis (Resident, Victorville Office)
Bart W. Brizzee
Richard D. Marca

Representative Clients: Kaiser Steel Resources, Inc.; California Steel Industries, Inc.; Southern California Edison Co.; General Telephone Company of California; Southern California Gas Co.; General Motors Corp.; Stater Bros. Markets; North American Chemical Co.; Kerr-McGee Chemical Corp.; TTX Co.

For Complete List of Firm Personnel, See General Section

For full biographical listings, see the Martindale-Hubbell Law Directory

MAC LACHLAN, BURFORD & ARIAS, A LAW CORPORATION (AV)

560 East Hospitality Lane, Fourth Floor, 92408
Telephone: 909-885-4491
Fax: 909-888-6866
Rancho Cucamonga, California Office: 8280 Utica Avenue, Suite 200. 909-989-4481.
Palm Springs, California Office: 255 North El Cielo Road, Suite 470. 619-320-5761.
Victorville, California Office: 14011 Park Avenue, Suite 410. 619-243-7933.

Bruce D. Mac Lachlan
Ronald A. Burford
Joseph Arias
Michael W. Mugg
Dennis G. Popka
Leigh O. Harper (Resident, Palm Springs Office)
Clifford R. Cunningham (Resident, Rancho Cucamonga Office)
Dennis R. Stout
Sharon K. Burchett (Resident, Rancho Cucamonga Office)
Christopher D. Lockwood
Vernon C. Lauridsen (Resident, Rancho Cucamonga Office)
John G. Evans (Resident, Palm Springs Office)
Richard R. Hegner (Resident, Victorville Office)
Dennis J. Mahoney
Kathleen M. Keefe
Toni R. Fullerton
Mark R. Harris
Diana J. Carloni (Resident, Victorville Office)
Jean M. Landry
Frank M. Loo

Representative Clients: Aetna Life & Casualty; Automobile Club of Southern California; California State Automobile Association; City of San Bernardino; Reliance Insurance; Republic Insurance; Southern Pacific Transportation Co.; State Farm Fire and Casualty Co.; State Farm Mutual Automobile Insurance Co.; County of San Bernardino.

For full biographical listings, see the Martindale-Hubbell Law Directory

WILSON, BORROR, DUNN, SCOTT & DAVIS (AV)

Suite 307, The Bank of California Building, 255 North D Street, P.O. Box 540, 92401
Telephone: 909-884-8855
Fax: 909-884-5161

MEMBERS OF FIRM

Fred A. Wilson (1886-1973)
Wm. H. Wilson (1915-1981)
Caywood J. Borror
James R. Dunn
Richard L. Scott
Thomas M. Davis
Keith D. Davis

ASSOCIATES

Timothy P. Prince
Sarah L. Overton

Representative Clients: Travelers Insurance Co.; Rockwell International; Westinghouse Air Brake Co.; Goodyear Tire and Rubber Co.; Home Insurance Co.; Cities of: Redlands, Chino, Colton, San Bernardino and Upland; The Canadian Insurance Co.

For full biographical listings, see the Martindale-Hubbell Law Directory

*SAN DIEGO,** San Diego Co.

BUTZ, LUCAS, DUNN & ENRIGHT, A PROFESSIONAL CORPORATION (AV)

101 West Broadway, Suite 1700, 92101-8289
Telephone: 619-233-4777
Fax: 619-231-0341

Douglas M. Butz
Stephen D. Lucas
K. Elizabeth Dunn
Kevin A. Enright
Richard L. Boyer

Kevin V. DeSantis
Kevin A. Park
Linda Hunt Mullany
Albert E. Haverkamp
Roger P. Bingham

OF COUNSEL

J. Lawrence Irving

For full biographical listings, see the Martindale-Hubbell Law Directory

CASEY, GERRY, CASEY, WESTBROOK, REED & SCHENK (AV)

A Partnership including Professional Law Corporations
110 Laurel Street, 92101
Telephone: 619-238-1811
Fax: 619-544-9232

MEMBERS OF FIRM

David S. Casey (A Professional Law Corporation)
Richard F. Gerry (A Professional Law Corporation)
David S. Casey, Jr.
T. Michael Reed
Frederick Schenk

ASSOCIATES

Robert J. Francavilla
Gayle Meryl Blatt
Thomas D. Penfield
Michael P. Montgomery
Suzanne C. Etpison
Bonnie E. Kane

Reference: San Diego Trust & Savings Bank.

For full biographical listings, see the Martindale-Hubbell Law Directory

CHAPIN, FLEMING & WINET, A PROFESSIONAL CORPORATION (AV)

1320 Columbia Street, 92101
Telephone: 619-232-4261
Telefax: 619-232-4840
Vista, California Office: 410 South Melrose Drive, Suite 101.
Telephone: 619-758-4261.
Telefax: 619-758-6420.
Los Angeles, California Office: 12121 Wilshire Boulevard, Suite 401.
Telephone: 310-826-4834.
Telefax: 310-207-4236.

Edward D. Chapin
George E. Fleming
Randall L. Winet (Resident, Vista Office)
Peter C. Ward
Roger L. Popeney
Lawrence W. Shea, II
Gregory S. Tavill
Aaron H. Katz
Maria C. Roberts
Shirley A. Gauvin
Kennett L. Patrick (Resident, Vista Office)
Terence L. Greene
Amy B. Vandeveld
Victor M. Barr, Jr.
Elizabeth J. Koumas
Leslie A. Greathouse
Kelli Jean Brooks
John F. Sahhar (Resident, Vista Office)
Andrew Nicholas Kohn
Frank L. Tobin
Shawn M. Robinson
Katherine M. Green
Dean G. Chandler (Resident, Vista Office)
Joseph A. Solomon
Victoria Chen
Jane Mobaldi
Dean A. Gonsonski
Daniel P. Murphy
Steven S. Richter
Gregory Kevin Hansen

(See Next Column)

CHAPIN, FLEMING & WINET A PROFESSIONAL CORPORATION, *San Diego—Continued*

OF COUNSEL

James Michael Zimmerman

For full biographical listings, see the Martindale-Hubbell Law Directory

COUGHLAN, SEMMER & LIPMAN (AV)

A Partnership including Professional Corporations
501 West Broadway, Suite 400, 92101
Telephone: 619-232-0800
Fax: 619-232-0107

MEMBERS OF FIRM

R. J. (Jerry) Coughlan, Jr. (A P.C.)
Robert F. Semmer (A P.C.)
Michael L. Lipman

ASSOCIATES

Cathleen Gilliland Fitch
Sheryl S. King
Duane Tyler
Carol A. Ensalaco
Angela L. Baxter

OF COUNSEL

Alexandra M. Kwoka

Representative Clients: Ernst & Young; U.S. Air; Wells Fargo Bank; Lawyers Mutual Insurance Co.; Prudential-Bache Securities, Inc.; CAMICO; Shell Oil; IBP, Inc.; UST Inc.; San Diego National Bank.

For full biographical listings, see the Martindale-Hubbell Law Directory

DETISCH, CHRISTENSEN & WOOD (AV)

444 West C Street, Suite 200, 92101
Telephone: 619-236-9343
Fax: 619-236-8307

MEMBERS OF FIRM

Charles B. Christensen
Donald W. Detisch
John W. Wood

ASSOCIATE

Lydia L. Brashear

For full biographical listings, see the Martindale-Hubbell Law Directory

EDWARDS, WHITE & SOOY, A PROFESSIONAL CORPORATION (AV)

101 West Broadway, Ninth Floor, 92101
Telephone: 619-231-1500
Fax: 619-231-1588

Michael M. Edwards
Daniel M. White
Richard R. Sooy
Charles R. Bongard
Thomas W. Byron
Glen M. Rasmussen
Karen Anderson Holmes
John A. Simpson
Stephen A. Gentes
William P. Harris, III
John D. Marino

Marc D. Cleavinger
Lisa G. Shemonsky
Robyn S. McClain
Paul J. Delmore
Eulalio J. Garcia
Erich J. Lidl
William L. Pettingill
Michael J. Orzel
Robert F. Tyson, Jr.
Elaine L. Heine
Michael W. Barrett
Derek J. Emge
Susan L. Oliver
John J. Philpott
Timothy S. Noon
Patrick L. Hosey
Veronica M. Aguilar
Keith C. Cramer

OF COUNSEL

Stanley J. Wezelman

For full biographical listings, see the Martindale-Hubbell Law Directory

FERRIS & BRITTON, A PROFESSIONAL CORPORATION (AV)

1600 First National Bank Center, 401 West A Street, 92101
Telephone: 619-233-3131
Fax: 619-232-9316

Christopher Q. Britton
Steven J. Pynes
Michael R. Weinstein

OF COUNSEL

Allan J. Reniche

Representative Clients: Allstate Insurance Co.; Cox Communications, Inc.; Enterprise Rent-a-Car; Exxon; Immuno Pharmaceutics, Inc.; Invitrogen Corporation; Teleport Communications Group; Southwest Airlines; Times-Mirror Cable Television.

For Complete List of Firm Personnel, See General Section

For full biographical listings, see the Martindale-Hubbell Law Directory

FRANCO BRADLEY & MARTORELLA (AV)

A Partnership of Professional Corporations
8880 Rio San Diego Drive, Suite 800, 92108
Telephone: 619-688-0080
Fax: 619-688-0081
Oakland, California Office: Suite 600, 1300 Clay Street.
Telephone: 510-466-6310.

MEMBERS OF THE FIRM

Elizabeth Franco Bradley (APC)
Daniel A. Martorella (APC)

OF COUNSEL

Charles A. Viviano (APC)

ASSOCIATES

Kerry Don Alexander
Elizabeth Leigh Bradley (Resident, Oakland, California)
Kathryn S. Clenney
Madeline Moriyama Clogston
Zoë G. Gruber
Kim Karels Resnick
Kenneth D. Richard
Daniel L. Rodriguez
Mary Crenshaw Tyler

For full biographical listings, see the Martindale-Hubbell Law Directory

LAW OFFICES OF LOUIS E. GOEBEL, P.C. (AV)

Suite 6000, McClintock Plaza, 1202 Kettner Boulevard, 92101
Telephone: 619-239-2611
FAX: 619-239-4269

Louis E. Goebel

For full biographical listings, see the Martindale-Hubbell Law Directory

HAASIS, POPE & CORRELL, A PROFESSIONAL CORPORATION (AV)

550 West "C" Street, 9th Floor, 92101-3509
Telephone: 619-236-9933
Fax: 619-236-8961
Voice Mail: 619-236-8955

Steven R. Haasis
A. Mark Pope
Harvey C. Berger
William A. Calders
Denis Long

Michael J. Wijas
A. David Mongan
Nelson J. Goodin
Steven B. Bitter

For full biographical listings, see the Martindale-Hubbell Law Directory

HIGGS, FLETCHER & MACK (AV)

2000 First National Bank Building, 401 West "A" Street, 92101
Telephone: 619-236-1551
ABA Net: 9011
Telex: 382028 HFM UD
Telecopier: 619-696-1410
North County Office: 613 West Valley Parkway, Suite 345. Escondido, California, 92025-2552.
Telephone: 619-743-1201.
Telecopier: 619-743-9926.

MEMBERS OF FIRM

Henry Pitts Mack (1909-1974)
David D. Randolph
John W. Netterblad
Joe N. Turner
Craig D. Higgs
Harry L. Carter
Michael F. Boyle
Steven B. Davis
Bruce D. Jaques, Jr. (Resident Partner, Escondido Office)
John Morris
John L. Morrell
Steven H. Kruis
Gregory Y. Lievers (Resident Partner, Escondido Office)
Jeanne S. Gallagher
M. Cory Brown
Patricia P. Hollenbeck
Thomas P. Sayer, Jr.
Helen H. Peak (Resident Partner, Escondido Office)
James M. Peterson
James A. Cunningham

OF COUNSEL

DeWitt A. Higgs
Ferdinand T. Fletcher

ASSOCIATES

Greg A. McAtee
Susan D. Moriarty

Representative Clients: Frazee Industries; Kawasaki Motors Corp.; Rohr Industries; Allstate Insurance Co.; Associated Aviation Underwriters; Physicians & Surgeons Insurance Exchange.

For Complete List of Firm Personnel, See General Section

For full biographical listings, see the Martindale-Hubbell Law Directory

HILLYER & IRWIN, A PROFESSIONAL CORPORATION (AV)

550 West C Street, 16th Floor, 92101
Telephone: 619-234-6121
Telecopier: 619-595-1313

(See Next Column)

HILLYER & IRWIN A PROFESSIONAL CORPORATION—*Continued*

Norman R. Allenby
Brown B. Smith
James G. Ehlers
Peter J. Ippolito
Howard A. Allen
Robert J. Hanna
Jonathan S. Dabbieri
Howard E. Susman
Murray T. S. Lewis
Robert L. Zajac
Michael F. Millerick
Steven M. Hill
Lesa Christenson

For full biographical listings, see the Martindale-Hubbell Law Directory

HOVEY, KIRBY, THORNTON & HAHN, A PROFESSIONAL CORPORATION (AV)

101 West Broadway, Suite 1100, 92101-8297
Telephone: 619-685-4000
Fax: 619-685-4004

Gregg B. Hovey
Dean T. Kirby, Jr.
Cynthia K. Thornton
M. Leslie Hovey
Jane Hahn
Patrick R. Kitchin

For full biographical listings, see the Martindale-Hubbell Law Directory

HYDE AND CANOFF (AV)

401 West "A" Street, Suite 1200, 92101
Telephone: 619-696-6911
Telecopier: 619-696-6919

MEMBERS OF FIRM

Laurel Lee Hyde
Karen H. Canoff

Representative Clients: HomeFed Bank; San Diego Trust & Savings Bank; Union Bank; The Resolution Trust Corp.; Stewart Title; San Diego Gas & Electric Co.; The Hahn Company; The Regents of the University of California; San Diego Metropolitan Transit Development Board; Kmart Corporation.

For full biographical listings, see the Martindale-Hubbell Law Directory

CHARLES S. LIMANDRI (AV)

2120 San Diego Avenue, Suite 100, 92110-2997
Telephone: 619-497-0091
Telefax: 619-497-0386

ASSOCIATE

R. Timothy Ireland

Representative Clients: The Standard Steamship Owners Protection and Indemnity Association, Ltd. (London); Caribbean Marine Service Co., Inc. (San Diego); Calfon Construction, Inc.
Reference: Wells Fargo Bank.

For full biographical listings, see the Martindale-Hubbell Law Directory

LINDLEY, LAZAR & SCALES, A PROFESSIONAL CORPORATION (AV)

One America Plaza, 600 West Broadway, Suite 1400, 92101-3302
Telephone: 619-234-9181
Fax: 619-234-8475

Luke R. Corbett
John M. Seitman
Robert M. McLeod
Michael H. Wexler
Richard J. Pekin, Jr.
George C. Lazar
R. Gordon Huckins

Donna C. Looper
William A. Larkin

Representative Clients: Commonwealth Land Title Insurance Company; Bank of Commerce; Resolution Trust Corp.; Palomar Savings & Loan Association; FDIC; Southern California Soil & Testing, Inc.; Chicago Title Insurance Company.

For Complete List of Firm Personnel, See General Section

For full biographical listings, see the Martindale-Hubbell Law Directory

MCCLELLAN & ASSOCIATES, A PROFESSIONAL CORPORATION (AV)

1144 State Street, 92101
Telephone: 619-231-0505
Fax: 619-544-0540

Craig R. McClellan

LaMar B. Brown
Andrew Phillip Greenfield

For full biographical listings, see the Martindale-Hubbell Law Directory

MULVANEY, KAHAN & BARRY, A PROFESSIONAL CORPORATION (AV)

Seventeenth Floor, First National Bank Center, 401 West "A" Street, 92101-7994
Telephone: 619-238-1010
Fax: 619-238-1981
Los Angeles, California Office: Union Bank Plaza, 445 South Figueroa Street, Suite 2600.
Telephone: 213-612-7765.
La Jolla, California Office: Glendale Federal Building, 7911 Herschel, Suite 300, P.O Box 1885.
Telephone: 619-454-0142.
Fax: 619-454-7858.
Orange, California Office: The Koll Center, 500 North State College Boulevard, Suite 440.
Telephone: 714-634-7069.
Fax: 714-939-8000.

James F. Mulvaney
Lawrence Kahan
Everett G. Barry, Jr.
Donald G. Johnson, Jr.
Robert A. Linn
Maureen E. Markey
Paula Rotenberg
Melissa A. Blackburn
Rex B. Beatty
Julie A. Jones
Maureen H. Edwards
Greta C. Botka
Mark R. Raftery
Charles F. Bethel
Carrie L. Gleeson
Diane M. Racicot
John A. Mayers
Linda P. Lucal
Steven W. Pite
Patricia A. Sieveke (Resident, Los Angeles and Orange Offices)
Michael S. Umansky

OF COUNSEL

James P. McGowan, Jr. (Resident, La Jolla Office)
Derrick W. Samuelson (Not admitted in CA)

Representative Clients: Air Products & Chemicals, Inc.; Revlon, Inc.; Rhône-Poulenc Rorer, Inc.; Union Bank; Union Land Title Co.; Wells Fargo Bank-;Esselte Pendaflex Corp.

For full biographical listings, see the Martindale-Hubbell Law Directory

PAGE, POLIN, BUSCH & BOATWRIGHT, A PROFESSIONAL CORPORATION (AV)

350 West Ash Street, Suite 900, 92101-3404
Telephone: 619-231-1822
Fax: 619-231-1877
FAX: 619-231-1875

David C. Boatwright
Michael E. Busch
Robert K. Edmunds
Kathleen A. Cashman-Kramer
Richard L. Moskitis
Richard W. Page
Kenneth D. Polin
Steven G. Rowles

OF COUNSEL

Richard Edward Ball, Jr.

Rod S. Fiori
Christina B. Gamache
Dorothy A. Johnson
Theresa McCarthy
Jolene L. Parker
Deidre L. Schneider
Sandra L. Shippey

For full biographical listings, see the Martindale-Hubbell Law Directory

PROCOPIO, CORY, HARGREAVES AND SAVITCH (AV)

2100 Union Bank Building, 530 B Street, 92101
Telephone: 619-238-1900
Telecopier: 619-235-0398

MEMBERS OF FIRM

Jeffrey Isaacs
Robert G. Russell, Jr.
James G. Sandler
Thomas R. Laube
Philip J. Giacinti, Jr.
Steven M. Strauss
Kenneth J. Rose
Gerald P. Kennedy
Lynne R. Lasry
Edward I. Silverman
Jeffrey D. Cawdrey
Stephen R. Robinson

ASSOCIATES

Kenneth J. Witherspoon
Matthew W. Argue
Jeffrey M. Byer
Richard M. Valdez
Kathryn M. Otto
Martina Mende

Counsel for: Union Bank.
Representative Clients: Daley Corp.; Associated General Contractors; GEA Power Cooling Systems, Inc.; Mobil Oil Corporation; County of San Diego (Citizens Law Enforcement Review Board).

For Complete List of Firm Personnel, See General Section
For full biographical listings, see the Martindale-Hubbell Law Directory

SELTZER CAPLAN WILKINS & MCMAHON, A PROFESSIONAL CORPORATION (AV)

2100 Symphony Towers, 750 B Street, 92101
Telephone: 619-685-3003
Fax: 619-685-3100

(See Next Column)

SELTZER CAPLAN WILKINS & MCMAHON A PROFESSIONAL CORPORATION, *San Diego—Continued*

Gerald L. McMahon
Reginald A. Vitek
James B. Franklin
Elizabeth A. Smith
Julie P. Dubick
Joyce A. McCoy
Dennis J. Wickham
Bruce H. Fagan
Donald A. English
Michael H. Riney
James P. Delphey
Craig E. Courter
Michael G. Nardi
Neal P. Panish
Janice Patrice Brown
Vera P. Pardee
David J. Zubkoff
Virginia C. Pearson
Cynthia B. Chapman
Patricia Garcia

OF COUNSEL

Bonnie Nelson Reading

Representative Clients: Girard Savings Bank; W.R. Grace & Co--Conn.; McDonnell-Douglas Corp.; McMillin Communities; Philip Morris Incorporated; Taco Bell Corp.; Western Financial Savings Bank.

For Complete List of Firm Personnel, See General Section

For full biographical listings, see the Martindale-Hubbell Law Directory

THORSNES, BARTOLOTTA, MCGUIRE & PADILLA (AV)

A Partnership including Professional Corporations
Fifth Avenue Financial Center, 11th Floor, 2550 Fifth Avenue, 92103
Telephone: 619-236-9363
Fax: 619-236-9653

Michael T. Thorsnes (P.C.)
Vincent J. Bartolotta, Jr., (P.C.)
John F. McGuire (P.C.)
Michael D. Padilla (P.C.)
Kevin F. Quinn (P.C.)
C. Brant Noziska (P.C.)
Mitchell S. Golub (P.C.)
Frederic L. Gordon (P.C.)
Palma Cesar Hooper (P.C.)
Neal H. Rockwood (P.C.)
Daral B. Mazzarella (P.C.)

ASSOCIATES

R. Christian Hulburt
Jeffrey F. LaFave
Stephen D. Lipkin
Rhonda J. Holmes
Martin W. Hagan
John J. Rice
Robert E. Bright
B. James Pantone
Douglas J. Billings

For full biographical listings, see the Martindale-Hubbell Law Directory

WINGERT, GREBING, ANELLO & BRUBAKER (AV)

A Partnership including Professional Corporations
One America Plaza, Seventh Floor, 600 West Broadway, 92101-3370
Telephone: 619-232-8151
Facsimile: 619-232-4665

MEMBERS OF FIRM

John R. Wingert (A Professional Corporation)
Charles R. Grebing (A Professional Corporation)
Michael M. Anello (A Professional Corporation)
Alan K. Brubaker (A Professional Corporation)
Norman A. Ryan
James Goodwin
Robert M. Caietti
Eileen Mulligan Marks
Christopher W. Todd
Robert L. Johnson
Douglas J. Simpson
Shawn D. Morris
Robert M. Juskie

ASSOCIATES

Julie E. Saake
Michael Sullivan
John S. Addams
Carolyn P. Gallinghouse
Michael S. Burke
Kimberly I. Cary
Terie M. Theis
James P. Broder
James J. Brown, Jr.
Sara A. Henry
Sarah F. Burke
Beverly A. Kalasky
Craig Gross

OF COUNSEL

William L. Todd, Jr.

Representative Clients: California Casualty Insurance Co.; Farmers Insurance Group; The Ohio Casualty Group; United Services Automobile Assn.; Transamerica Insurance Group; United States Fidelity & Guaranty Co.

For full biographical listings, see the Martindale-Hubbell Law Directory

*SAN FRANCISCO,** San Francisco Co.

BERG, ZIEGLER, ANDERSON & PARKER (AV)

4 Embarcadero Center, Suite 1400, 94111
Telephone: 415-397-6000
Telecopier: 415-397-9449
Portland, Oregon Office: 1211 S.W. Fifth Avenue, Suite 2900, 97204.
Telephone: 503-245-0989.
Telecopier: 503-228-5799.

MEMBERS OF FIRM

James M. Berg
William J. Ziegler, Jr.
Robert L. Anderson
Robert Ted Parker
David B. Franklin
David L. Monetta
Ivan M. Gold

(See Next Column)

Douglas A. Applegate
F. Gale Connor
Mark W. Epstein
Michael A. Gardiner
Jill Meier Garvey (Resident, Portland, Oregon Office)
Jeffrey B. Kirschenbaum
Jennifer S. Malloy
Patrick J. O'Brien
Luis V. Garcia

PARALEGALS

David A. Dunbar
Diane E. Gresham
Sharon L. Gostlin
Lizabeth N. Uhlmann

For full biographical listings, see the Martindale-Hubbell Law Directory

BOSTWICK & TEHIN (AV)

A Partnership including Professional Corporations
Bank of America Center, 555 California Street, 33rd Floor, 94104-1609
Telephone: 415-421-5500
Fax: 415-421-8144
Honolulu, Hawaii Office: Suite 900, 333 Queen Street.
Telephone: 808-536-7771.

MEMBERS OF FIRM

James S. Bostwick (Professional Corporation)
Nikolai Tehin (Professional Corporation)
Pamela J. Stevens

ASSOCIATES

James J. O'Donnell
Sara A. Smith
Baron J. Drexel

For full biographical listings, see the Martindale-Hubbell Law Directory

BUCHALTER, NEMER, FIELDS & YOUNGER, A PROFESSIONAL CORPORATION (AV)

29th Floor, 333 Market Street, 94105
Telephone: 415-227-0900
Fax: 415-227-0770
Los Angeles, California Office: 24th Floor, 601 South Figueroa Street.
Telephone: 213-891-0700.
Fax: 213-896-0400.
New York, New York Office: 19th Floor, 237 Park Avenue.
Telephone: 212-490-8600.
Fax: 212-490-6022.
San Jose, California Office: 12th Floor, 50 West San Fernando Street.
Telephone: 408-298-0350.
Fax: 408-298-7683.
Newport Beach, California Office: Suite 300, 620 Newport Center Drive.
Telephone: 714-760-1121.
Fax: 714-720-0182.
Century City, California Office: Suite 2400, 1801 Century Park East.
Telephone: 213-891-0700.
Fax: 310-551-0233.

NORTHERN CALIFORNIA RESIDENTS IN CHARGE

Roxani M. Gillespie
Richard de Saint Phalle (Resident)
William McC. Wright (Resident)
Gary Nemer
Robert E. Izmirian (Resident)
James B. Wright
Peter G. Bertrand
W. David Campagne
Shawn M. Christianson (Resident)

OF COUNSEL

Robert A. Zadek

Stephen W. Sommerhalter (Resident)
Jared A. Goldin
Mary P. McCurdy (Resident)
Mary E. Jameson (Resident)
Kimberly A. Fanady
Ronald S. Beacher
Dennis D. Miller
Jeffrey L. Fazio
David Sturgeon-Garcia
Aron Mark Oliner
Mark C. Goodman
Marie G. Quashnock
Barbara Mikalson
David M. Serepca

References: City National Bank; Wells Fargo Bank; Metrobank.

For full biographical listings, see the Martindale-Hubbell Law Directory

BUELL & BERNER (AV)

A Partnership of Professional Corporations
101 California Street, 22nd Floor, 94111
Telephone: 415-391-5011
Fax: 415-391-7383

MEMBERS OF FIRM

E. Rick Buell, II, (P.C.)
Curtis William Berner (P.C.)

For full biographical listings, see the Martindale-Hubbell Law Directory

CARR & MUSSMAN, A PROFESSIONAL CORPORATION (AV)

3 Embarcadero Center, Suite 1060, 94111
Telephone: 415-391-7112
Telecopier: 415-391-7124

(See Next Column)

CARR & MUSSMAN A PROFESSIONAL CORPORATION—*Continued*

Timothy E. Carr
William E. Mussman
William E. Mussman, III

Michael T. Healy

For full biographical listings, see the Martindale-Hubbell Law Directory

CYRIL & CROWLEY (AV)

17th Floor, 456 Montgomery Street, 94104
Telephone: 415-989-1100
Facsimile: 415-421-6651

MEMBERS OF FIRM

John W. Crowley
David L. Sandborg
Robert B. Stringer
David W. Gordon
Michael W. Field
Carol P. Rohwer
Wendy J. Hannum

OF COUNSEL

Paul H. Cyril (A Professional Corporation)

ASSOCIATES

Elizabeth L. Dolter
Mark D. Skilling
Mark D. Fenske

For full biographical listings, see the Martindale-Hubbell Law Directory

ERLACH & ERLACH (AV)

4 Embarcadero Center, Seventeenth Floor, 94111
Telephone: 415-788-3322
FAX: 415-788-8613

Raymond N. Erlach
Gregory J. Erlach
Stephen Peter U. Erlach

For full biographical listings, see the Martindale-Hubbell Law Directory

EWELL & LEVY (AV)

351 California Street, 94104-2501
Telephone: 415-788-6600
Fax: 415-433-7311

Arthur D. Levy
Gary Ewell

OF COUNSEL

Scott H. Miller
Theresa R. Owens

For full biographical listings, see the Martindale-Hubbell Law Directory

FELDMAN, WALDMAN & KLINE, A PROFESSIONAL CORPORATION (AV)

2700 Russ Building, 235 Montgomery Street, 94104
Telephone: 415-981-1300
Telex: 650-223-3204
Fax: 415-394-0121
Stockton, California Office: Sperry Building, 146-148 West Weber Avenue.
Telephone: 209-943-2004.
Fax: 209-943-0905.

Murry J. Waldman
Leland R. Selna, Jr.
Michael L. Korbholz
Howard M. Wexler
Patricia S. Mar
Kenneth W. Jones
Paul J. Dion
Vern S. Bothwell
L. J. Chris Martiniak
Kenneth A. Freed
Martha Jeanne Shaver (Resident, Stockton Office)
Robert Cedric Goodman
Steven K. Denebeim
Laura Grad
William F. Adams
William M. Smith
Elizabeth A. Thompson
Julie A. Jones
David L. Kanel

Abram S. Feuerstein
John R. Capron
Ted S. Storey
A. Todd Berman
Laura J. Dawson

OF COUNSEL

Richard L. Jaeger
Malcolm Leader-Picone
Gerald A. Sherwin (Resident, Stockton Office)

For full biographical listings, see the Martindale-Hubbell Law Directory

FLEISCHMANN & FLEISCHMANN (AV)

650 California Street, Suite 2550, 94108-2606
Telephone: 415-981-0140
FAX: 415-788-6234

MEMBERS OF FIRM

Hartly Fleischmann
Roger Justice Fleischmann

Stella J. Kim
Mark S. Molina

OF COUNSEL

Grace C. Shohet

(See Next Column)

LEGAL SUPPORT PERSONNEL

Lissa Dirrim

For full biographical listings, see the Martindale-Hubbell Law Directory

FLYNN, DELICH & WISE (AV)

Suite 1750, 580 California Street, 94104
Telephone: 415-693-5566
Fax: 415-693-0410
Long Beach, California Office: 1 World Trade Center, Suite 1800.
Telephone: 310-435-2626.
Fax: 310-437-7555.

John Allen Flynn
Sam D. Delich
James B. Nebel

Representative Clients: American Hawaii Cruises; Holland America Line; Through Transport Mutual Insurance Association, Ltd.; The Britannia Steam Ship Insurance Association Limited; The Steamship Mutual Underwriting Association (Bermuda) Ltd.; General Steamship Corp., Ltd.; Commodore Cruise Line, Ltd.; Interocean Steamship Corporation; Sea-Land Service, Inc.; Hatteras Yachts.

For full biographical listings, see the Martindale-Hubbell Law Directory

FRIEDMAN, ROSS & HERSH, A PROFESSIONAL CORPORATION (AV)

One Maritime Plaza, Suite 1040, 94111
Telephone: 415-788-2200
Telecopier: 415-394-0222

Jeffrey S. Ross
Jill Hersh

David M. Fried
Michael J. Kass
Wendi Temkin-Nadel
Ellen L. Winick

OF COUNSEL

Stanley J. Friedman

For full biographical listings, see the Martindale-Hubbell Law Directory

GRIFFINGER, FREED, HEINEMANN, COOK & FOREMAN (AV)

24th Floor, Steuart Street Tower, One Market Plaza, 94105
Telephone: 415-243-0300
Telecopier: 415-777-9366

MEMBERS OF FIRM

Theodore A. Griffinger, Jr.
Michael S. Freed
Peter M. Heinemann
Karen A. Cook
Stewart H. Foreman
Jonathan A. Funk
Peter S. Fishman

Dwight L. Monson
Eileen Trujillo
Robert L. Wishner
Marie C. Bendy
Eric C. Starr
Jonathan Polland

LEGAL SUPPORT PERSONNEL

LEGAL ADMINISTRATOR

Kathleen H. Hartley

PARALEGALS

Jeanne Diettinger
Jean Mahony
Irene E. Bernasconi
Janet L. Johnston

Representative Client: Smith Barney, Harris Upham Co., Inc.
Reference: Bank of America (Main Office).

For full biographical listings, see the Martindale-Hubbell Law Directory

ROBERT A. HARLEM, INC. & ASSOCIATES A PROFESSIONAL CORPORATION (AV)

120 Montgomery Street, Suite 2410, 94104
Telephone: 415-981-1801
Fax: 415-981-5815

Robert A. Harlem

B. Mark Fong

OF COUNSEL

Patricia Knight
Jack Miller

For full biographical listings, see the Martindale-Hubbell Law Directory

HINES & THOMAS (AV)

Suite 835 Russ Building, 235 Montgomery Street, 94104
Telephone: 415-981-2623
Fax: 415-981-4904
Twain Harte, California Office: 22984 Twain Harte Drive.
Telephone: 209-586-1104.

Franklin Dean Thomas

Timothy J. Arneson

(See Next Column)

HINES & THOMAS, *San Francisco—Continued*

OF COUNSEL

Robert L. Hines

For full biographical listings, see the Martindale-Hubbell Law Directory

HORNING JANIN & HARVEY (AV)

Suite 720, 555 Montgomery Street, 94111-2543
Telephone: 415-434-1081
Telex: 284998
Telecopier: 415-982-8931

MEMBERS OF FIRM

D. Peter Harvey
Richard Allan Horning
Blaine Covington Janin

For full biographical listings, see the Martindale-Hubbell Law Directory

JUDD C. IVERSEN A PROFESSIONAL CORPORATION (AV)

Penthouse, 1231 Market Street, 94103-1488
Telephone: 415-552-6500
Fax: 415-552-1806
Burlingame, California Office: 500 Airport Boulevard, Suite 230.

Judd C. Iversen

Daniel S. Frankston

OF COUNSEL

George F. Camerlengo (Resident at Burlingame, California Office)
C. Judith Johnson (Resident at Burlingame, California Office)

For full biographical listings, see the Martindale-Hubbell Law Directory

KEKER & VAN NEST (AV)

A Partnership including Professional Corporations
710 Sansome Street, 94111-1704
Telephone: 415-391-5400
Fax: 415-397-7188

MEMBERS OF FIRM

John W. Keker (P.C.)
Robert A. Van Nest (P.C.)
Jeffrey R. Chanin
Henry C. Bunsow
Gary M. Cohen
Susan J. Harriman
Jan Nielsen Little
Kathryn E. Ma
Karin Kramer
Christopher C. Kearney
Elliot R. Peters
Stuart L. Gasner

ASSOCIATES

Helene M. Linker
Michael J. Proctor
Loretta Lynch
Vernon C. Grigg, III
Ethan Allen Miller
Susan C. Moon
Daralyn Jeannine Durie
Wendy J. Thurm
Steven A. Hirsch
Jon S. Tigar
James M. Emery
Denise M. DeMory
Ragesh K. Tangri
Michelle K. Lee

For full biographical listings, see the Martindale-Hubbell Law Directory

LASKY, HAAS & COHLER, PROFESSIONAL CORPORATION (AV)

Two Transamerica Center, 505 Sansome Street, 12th Floor, 94111-3183
Telephone: 415-788-2700
Facsimile: 415-981-4025

Moses Lasky
Charles B. Cohler
William A. Logan, Jr.
Kevin C. McCann
David M. Rosenberg-Wohl

Jeffrey F. Silverman
Deborah E. Beck
Christopher S. Yates
Stacey M. Sklar

For full biographical listings, see the Martindale-Hubbell Law Directory

LEACH & ENGLISH (AV(T))

601 Montgomery Street, Suite 1150, 94111
Telephone: 415-249-4800
Fax: 415-249-4806
Washington, D.C. Office: Capitol Hill, 516 C Street, N.E., 20002.
Telephone: 202-546-0050.
Fax: 202-546-0092.

Daniel E. Leach
James L. English
Martin H. Goyette
Greta Siegel
Melissa A. Korber
Paula K. Bauer
Brian J. Finn

OF COUNSEL

Harvey M. Katz (Resident, Washington, D.C. Office)

For full biographical listings, see the Martindale-Hubbell Law Directory

LOVITT & HANNAN, INC. (AV)

900 Front Street, Suite 300, 94111
Telephone: 415-362-8769
Facsimile: 415-362-7528

Ronald Lovitt
J. Thomas Hannan

OF COUNSEL

Henry I. Bornstein

For full biographical listings, see the Martindale-Hubbell Law Directory

KATHLEEN M. LUCAS (AV)

Suite 500, 530 Bush Street, 94108
Telephone: 415-433-6166
FAX: 415-433-6517

ASSOCIATES

David S. Schwartz
Erika A. Zucker

For full biographical listings, see the Martindale-Hubbell Law Directory

GEORGE C. MARTINEZ (AV)

Russ Building, 235 Montgomery Street, Suite 1160, 94104-3004
Telephone: 415-989-0751
FAX: 415-989-2730

For full biographical listings, see the Martindale-Hubbell Law Directory

DEAN W. MCPHEE (AV)

100 Pine Street, 21st Floor, 94111
Telephone: 415-398-8220
Telecopier: 415-421-0320

For full biographical listings, see the Martindale-Hubbell Law Directory

MOLLIGAN, COX & MOYER, A PROFESSIONAL CORPORATION (AV)

703 Market Street, Suite 1800, 94103
Telephone: 415-543-9464
Fax: 415-777-1828

Ingemar E. Hoberg (1903-1971)
John H. Finger (1913-1991)
Phillip E. Brown (Retired)
Peter N. Molligan
Stephen T. Cox
David W. Moyer

John C. Hentschel
Guy D. Loranger
Nicholas J. Piediscazzi

OF COUNSEL

Kenneth W. Rosenthal
Barbara A. Zuras

For full biographical listings, see the Martindale-Hubbell Law Directory

MORGENSTEIN & JUBELIRER (AV)

A Partnership including a Professional Corporation
One Market Plaza, Spear Street Tower, 32nd Floor, 94105
Telephone: 415-896-0666
Fax: 415-896-5592

MEMBERS OF FIRM

Marvin D. Morgenstein (P.C.)
Eliot S. Jubelirer
Lee Ann Huntington
Jean L. Bertrand
Jeffrey R. Williams
James R. Balich
Rocky N. Unruh
Laurie K. Anger
Larry C. Lowe
James L. McGinnis

Wendi J. Berkowitz
David H. Bromfield
Randi Covin
Roberta Nicol Dempster
Stephen M. Hankins
Robert B. Mullen
John J. Petry
Margaret E. Schaus
Samantha J. Smith
Bruce A. Wagman
John S. Worden

For full biographical listings, see the Martindale-Hubbell Law Directory

MORTON & LACY (AV)

Suite 2280, Three Embarcadero Center, 94111-3614
Telephone: 415-296-9000
Facsimile: 415-398-3295

Thomas E. Morton
Alan E. Lacy

ASSOCIATES

Jeremy Sugerman
David H. Bennett
Deborah M. Hall

For full biographical listings, see the Martindale-Hubbell Law Directory

San Francisco—Continued

MURPHY, PEARSON, BRADLEY & FEENEY, A PROFESSIONAL CORPORATION (AV)

88 Kearny Street, 11th Floor, 94108
Telephone: 415-788-1900
Telecopier: 415-393-8087
Sacramento, California Office: Suite 200, 3600 American River Drive, 95864.
Telephone: 916-483-6074.
Telecopier: 916-483-6088.

James A. Murphy
Arthur V. Pearson
Michael P. Bradley
John H. Feeney
Gregory A. Bastian (Resident, Sacramento Office)
Timothy J. Halloran
Karen M. Goodman (Resident, Sacramento Office)
Mark S. Perelman
Mark Ellis (Resident, Sacramento Office)
William S. Kronenberg

Peter L. Isola
Gregg Anthony Thornton
Anne F. Marchant
Antoinette Waters Farrell
Tomislav (Tom) Peraic
Douglas L. Johnson (Resident, Sacramento Office)
Michael K. Pazdernik (Resident, Sacramento Office)
Reed R. Johnson (Resident, Sacramento Office)
Alexander J. Berline
Alec Hunter Boyd
Amy Bisson Holloway (Resident, Sacramento Office)
Peter W. Thompson (Resident, Sacramento Office)
Gregory S. Maple
Rita K. Johnson
Jane L. O'Hara Gamp
Joseph E. Addiego, III
Kevin T. Burton (Resident at Sacramento, California Office)
Stacy Marie Howard (Resident, Sacramento Office)

LEGAL SUPPORT PERSONNEL

Wilfred A. Fregeau

For full biographical listings, see the Martindale-Hubbell Law Directory

O'CONNOR, COHN, DILLON & BARR, A LAW CORPORATION (AV)

The Folger Coffee Building, 101 Howard Street, Fifth Floor, 94105-1619
Telephone: 415-281-8888
Fax: 415-281-8890

Joseph T. O'Connor (Deceased, 1959)
Harold H. Cohn (1910-1992)
James L. Dillon
Duncan Barr
Janet L. Grove
Mark Oium
Jerald W. F. Jamison
Lisa T. Ungerer
Joel C. Lamp
Michael J. FitzSimons

Thomas G. Manning
Susan Reifel Goins
Dexter B. Louie
Deborah L. Panter
Marirose Piciucco
Keith Reyen
Deems A. Fishman
Jeanine M. Donohue
Karen K. Smith
Daniel J. Herp
James A. Beltzer (Not admitted in CA)

For full biographical listings, see the Martindale-Hubbell Law Directory

HERMAN D. PAPA (AV)

Suite 333, 22 Battery Street, 94111
Telephone: 415-391-4903
Fax: 415-392-3729

For full biographical listings, see the Martindale-Hubbell Law Directory

J. MICHAEL PHELPS (AV)

One Maritime Plaza, Suite 1600, 94111
Telephone: 415-433-3733
Voicemail: 415-433-3739
Fax: 415-781-1034

Representative Clients: Heinz, U.S.A.; Continental Insurance Cos.; Farmers Insurance Group; Leader National Insurance Co.; Travelers Insurance Co.

For full biographical listings, see the Martindale-Hubbell Law Directory

ROGERS, JOSEPH, O'DONNELL & QUINN, A PROFESSIONAL CORPORATION (AV)

311 California Street, 94104
Telephone: 415-956-2828
Fax: 415-956-6457

(See Next Column)

Allan J. Joseph
Martin Quinn
Neil H. O'Donnell
Margot Wenger
Pamela Phillips
Anna M. Rossi
Kyra A. Subbotin
Linda R. Koenig
Connie M. Teevan
Allen Samelson
Suzanne M. Mellard
John G. Heller
David Nied
Neil H. Weinstein
Patricia A. Meagher

OF COUNSEL

Joseph W. Rogers
William Bennett Turner

Joelle Tobin
Valerie Ackerman
Merri A. Baldwin
David F. Innis

For full biographical listings, see the Martindale-Hubbell Law Directory

ROSEN, BIEN & ASARO (AV)

Eighth Floor, 155 Montgomery Street, 94104
Telephone: 415-433-6830
Fax: 415-433-7104

Sanford Jay Rosen
Michael W. Bien
Andrea G. Asaro

Stephen M. Liacouras
Hilary A. Fox
Thomas Nolan
Mary Ann Cryan (Not admitted in CA)
Donna Petrine

For full biographical listings, see the Martindale-Hubbell Law Directory

SCADDEN, HAMILTON & RYAN (AV)

580 California Street, Suite 1400, 94104
Telephone: 415-362-5116
Facsimile: 415-362-4214

James G. Scadden
Robert P. Hamilton
Robert J. Ryan

James P. Cunningham
James F. Hetherington
Julie M. Sinclair
Charles O. Thompson
Eileen Santana Wright

For full biographical listings, see the Martindale-Hubbell Law Directory

STEEFEL, LEVITT & WEISS, A PROFESSIONAL CORPORATION (AV)

29th Floor, One Embarcadero Center, 94111
Telephone: 415-788-0900
Telecopier: 415-397-7802; 415-788-2019

Lenard G. Weiss
Richard A. Kramer
Michael J. Lawson
Leonard R. Stein
Michael D. Early
Marc A. Lackner
Barry W. Lee

For Complete List of Firm Personnel, See General Section

For full biographical listings, see the Martindale-Hubbell Law Directory

LAW FIRM OF ROBERT A. SUSK (AV)

101 California Street, Suite 3550, 94111-5847
Telephone: 415-982-3950
Fax: 415-982-6143

Robert A. Susk
Leslie J. Mann
Phillip H. Kalsched

For full biographical listings, see the Martindale-Hubbell Law Directory

VOGL & MEREDITH (AV)

456 Montgomery Street, 20th Floor, 94104
Telephone: 415-398-0200
Facsimile: 415-398-2820

Samuel E. Meredith
David R. Vogl
Bryan A. Marmesh
John P. Walovich
Jean N. Yeh
Janet Brayer
Thomas S. Clifton (Resident)

George C. Leal

For full biographical listings, see the Martindale-Hubbell Law Directory

*SAN JOSE,** Santa Clara Co.

THE ALEXANDER LAW FIRM (AV)

55 South Market Street, Suite 1080, 95113
Telephone: 408-289-1776
Fax: 408-287-1776
Cincinnati, Ohio Office: 1300 Mercantile Library Building, 414 Walnut Street.
Telephone: 513-723-1776.
Fax: 513-421-1776.

Richard Alexander

ASSOCIATES

Mark P. Rapazzini
Jeffrey W. Rickard
Michael T. Alexander (Resident, Cincinnati, Ohio Office)
M. Elizabeth Graham
Jotham S. Stein

For full biographical listings, see the Martindale-Hubbell Law Directory

CRAIG M. BROWN, INC. (AV)

Suite 618 Pacific Valley Building, 333 West Santa Clara Street, 95113
Telephone: 408-286-8844
Fax: 408-286-6699

Craig M. Brown

For full biographical listings, see the Martindale-Hubbell Law Directory

JAN CHAMPION (AV)

4 North Second Street, Suite 860, 95113
Telephone: 408-286-5550
Fax: 408-286-5597

For full biographical listings, see the Martindale-Hubbell Law Directory

FERRARI, ALVAREZ, OLSEN & OTTOBONI, A PROFESSIONAL CORPORATION (AV)

333 West Santa Clara Street, Suite 700, 95113
Telephone: 408-280-0535
Fax: 408-280-0151
Palo Alto, California Office: 550 Hamilton Avenue.
Telephone: 415-327-3233.

Clarence J. Ferrari, Jr.
Kent E. Olsen
John M. Ottoboni
Richard S. Bebb
James J. Eller
Robert C. Danneskiold
Terence M. Kane
Emma Peña Madrid
John P. Thurau
Roger D. Wintle
Christopher E. Cobey

Michael D. Brayton
Lisa Intrieri Caputo
Jil Dalesandro
Gregory R. Dietrich
J. Timothy Maximoff
Joseph W. Mell, Jr.
George P. Mulcaire
Eleanor C. Schuermann
Melva M. Vollersen

OF COUNSEL

Edward M. Alvarez

For full biographical listings, see the Martindale-Hubbell Law Directory

HINSHAW, WINKLER, DRAA, MARSH & STILL (AV)

152 North Third Street, Suite 300, P.O. Box 15030, 95115-0030
Telephone: 408-293-5959
Fax: 408-280-0966

MEMBERS OF FIRM

Edward A. Hinshaw
Tyler G. Draa
Gerhard O. Winkler
Barry C. Marsh
Thomas E. Still

ASSOCIATES

Lynne Thaxter Brown
Bradford J. Hinshaw
Jennifer H. Still
Megan A. Smith

For full biographical listings, see the Martindale-Hubbell Law Directory

LAW OFFICES OF THOMAS R. HOGAN (AV)

60 South Market Street Suite 1125, 95113-2332
Telephone: 408-292-7600
Facsimile: 408-292-7611

PARALEGAL

Leslie Holmes

For full biographical listings, see the Martindale-Hubbell Law Directory

MCPHARLIN & SPRINKLES (AV)

Fairmont Plaza, 50 West San Fernando, Suite 810, 95113
Telephone: 408-293-1900
Fax: 408-293-1999

(See Next Column)

MEMBERS OF FIRM

Linda Hendrix McPharlin
Catherine C. Sprinkles

ASSOCIATES

Timothy B. McCormick
Mary Lee Malysz

For full biographical listings, see the Martindale-Hubbell Law Directory

MORGAN, RUBY, SCHOFIELD, FRANICH & FREDKIN (AV)

A Partnership of Law Corporations
99 Almaden Boulevard, Suite 1000, 95113
Telephone: 408-288-8288
Fax: 408-288-8325

MEMBERS OF FIRM

Mark B. Fredkin (L.C.)
Glen W. Schofield (L.C.)
Allen Ruby (L.C.)
Anthony E. Marsh (L.C.)
Brian P. Preston (L.C.)
Robert E. Dunne (L.C.)

ASSOCIATE

Linda M. Bertolucci

For Complete List of Firm Personnel, See General Section

For full biographical listings, see the Martindale-Hubbell Law Directory

TREPEL & CLARK (AV)

50 West San Fernando Street, 13th Floor, 95113
Telephone: 408-275-0501
Fax: 408-293-3369

Anthony J. Trepel
Daniel Clark

For full biographical listings, see the Martindale-Hubbell Law Directory

VAN LOUCKS & HANLEY (AV)

First American Building, 160 West Santa Clara Street, Suite 1050, 95113
Telephone: 408-287-2773
Fax: 408-297-5480

Geoffrey Van Loucks
Anthony L. Hanley

Michael K. Budra
Laura Uddenberg

Reference: San Jose National Bank.

For full biographical listings, see the Martindale-Hubbell Law Directory

*SAN LUIS OBISPO,** San Luis Obispo Co.

GEORGE, GALLO & SULLIVAN, A LAW CORPORATION (AV)

694 Santa Rosa, P.O. Box 12710, 93406
Telephone: 805-544-3351
Facsimile: 805-528-5598
Los Osos, California Office: 2238 Bayview Heights Drive, P.O. Box 6129.
Telephone: 805-528-3351.
Telecopier: 805-528-5598.

J. K. George
Ray A. Gallo
Todd A. Porter

Reference: Mid State Bank, Los Osos, California.

For full biographical listings, see the Martindale-Hubbell Law Directory

SMITH, HELENIUS & HAYES, A LAW CORPORATION (AV)

Railroad Square, P.O. Box 1446, 93406
Telephone: 805-544-8100
Facsimile: 805-544-4381

J. Edmund Smith
Christopher A. Helenius
Carl E. Hayes
Linda D. Hurst
A. David Medeiros
Kevin J. Smith
Christopher J. Duenow
Shae Kolby

For full biographical listings, see the Martindale-Hubbell Law Directory

SAN MARINO, Los Angeles Co.

LAW OFFICES OF LILLIAN TOMICH (AV)

2460 Huntington Drive, 91108-2657
Telephone: 818-287-1248
Fax: 818-287-7111

References: Home Savings & Loan, San Marino, Calif.; Bank of America, San Gabriel, Calif.; First Interstate Bank, San Gabriel, Calif.

For full biographical listings, see the Martindale-Hubbell Law Directory

SAN MATEO, San Mateo Co.

ANDERLINI, GUHEEN, FINKELSTEIN, EMERICK & MCSWEENEY, A PROFESSIONAL CORPORATION (AV)

400 South El Camino Real, Suite 700, 94402
Telephone: 415-348-0102
Fax: 415-348-0962

(See Next Column)

ANDERLINI, GUHEEN, FINKELSTEIN, EMERICK & MCSWEENEY A PROFESSIONAL CORPORATION—*Continued*

P. Terry Anderlini
John J. Guheen
David G. Finkelstein
Merrill G. Emerick
Brian J. McSweeney

A. James Scholz
John P. Antonakos
Paul J. Smoot
Jennifer Gustafson

OF COUNSEL

Daniel J. Monaco (Inc.)

A list of Representative Clients will be furnished upon request.

For full biographical listings, see the Martindale-Hubbell Law Directory

STUBBS & STUBBS (AV)

Borel Estate Building, Suite 505, 1700 South El Camino Real, 94402-3051
Telephone: 415-345-4350
Telecopier: 415-345-6748

MEMBERS OF FIRM

Barry Stubbs
Brian P. Stubbs

Reference: Wells Fargo Bank.

For full biographical listings, see the Martindale-Hubbell Law Directory

*SANTA ANA,** Orange Co.

THOMAS A. CULBERTSON (AV)

1851 East First Street, Suite 1100, 92705-4017
Telephone: 714-541-4454; 310-379-7298
Fax: 714-558-0967

For full biographical listings, see the Martindale-Hubbell Law Directory

HAIGHT, BROWN & BONESTEEL (AV)

A Partnership including Professional Corporations
Suite 900, 5 Hutton Centre Drive, 92707
Telephone: 714-754-1100
Telecopier: 714-754-0826
Santa Monica, California Office: 1620 26th Street, Suite 4000 North, P.O. Box 680.
Telephone: 310-449-6000.
Telecopier: 310-829-5117.
Telex: 705837.
Riverside, California Office: 3750 University Avenue, Suite 650.
Telephone: 909-341-8300.
Fax: 909-341-8309.

RESIDENT MEMBERS

Ronald C. Kline (A Professional Corporation)
Bruce L. Cleeland
Jay T. Thompson

ASSOCIATES

Paul N. Jacobs
Laura M. Knox (Resident)
Jeffrey S. Gerardo (Resident)

Counsel for: Orange County: Aetna Casualty and Surety Co.; Zurich-American Insurance Cos.; Industrial Indemnity Co.; Professional Liability Claims Managers; Maryland Casualty Insurance Co.; Royal Insurance Company of America.

For Complete List of Firm Personnel, See General Section

For full biographical listings, see the Martindale-Hubbell Law Directory

KLEIN, WEGIS, DENATALE, GOLDNER & MUIR (AV)

Park Tower Building #610, 200 W. Santa Ana Boulevard, 92701
Telephone: 714-285-0711
Fax: 714-285-9003
Bakersfield, California Office: Arco Tower, 4550 California Avenue, Second Floor, P.O. Box 11172.
Telephone: 805-395-1000.
Telecopier: 805-326-0418.

RESIDENT PARTNER

Laurence C. Hall

For full biographical listings, see the Martindale-Hubbell Law Directory

RICKS & ANDERSON, A LAW CORPORATION (AV)

Suite 970, Griffin Towers, 5 Hutton Centre Drive, 92707-5754
Telephone: 714-966-9190

Cecil E. Ricks, Jr.
Annette L. Anderson

For full biographical listings, see the Martindale-Hubbell Law Directory

*SANTA BARBARA,** Santa Barbara Co.

ARCHBALD & SPRAY (AV)

505 Bath Street, 93101
Telephone: 805-564-2070
Telecopier: 805-564-2081

(See Next Column)

MEMBERS OF FIRM

Joseph L. Spray (1927-1985)
Kenneth L. Moes
J. William McLafferty
Douglas B. Large
James P. Gazdecki
Karen T. Burgett
Edwin K. Loskamp
Wm. Brennan Lynch
Michael A. Colton
Ann Gormican Anderson

SENIOR ATTORNEYS

Peri Maziarz
Katherine H. Bower

ASSOCIATE

Emmet J. Hawkes

OF COUNSEL

Malcolm Archbald

Representative Clients: Caterpillar Inc.; General Motors Corp.; Lawyers Mutual; City of Lompoc; Nissan Motor Corp.; St. Paul Fire & Marine Insurance Co.; State Farm Insurance Cos.; Volkswagen of America, Inc.; Nationwide Insurance Co.; Travelers Insurance Co.

For full biographical listings, see the Martindale-Hubbell Law Directory

HOLLISTER & BRACE, A PROFESSIONAL CORPORATION (AV)

1126 Santa Barbara Street, P.O. Box 630, 93101
Telephone: 805-963-6711
FAX: 805-965-0329

William A. Brace (Retired)
J. James Hollister, III (Retired)
John S. Poucher
Richard C. Monk
George A. Rempe, III
Steven Evans Kirby
Bradford F. Ginder
John G. Busby
Susan H. McCollum
Richard G. Kravetz
Robert L. Brace
Janean Acevedo Daniels
Marcus Scott Bird

OF COUNSEL

Julie A. Turner

Attorneys for: First American Title Insurance Co.; Celite Corp.; Chevron, U.S.A., Inc.; Mission Industries; Gaviota Marine Terminal Co.; Hyatt Hotels; Occidential Petroleum Corp.; Great Universal Capital Corp; Mobil Oil Corp.; Texaco Trading & Transportation Inc.

For full biographical listings, see the Martindale-Hubbell Law Directory

MULLEN & HENZELL (AV)

A Partnership including Professional Corporations
112 East Victoria Street, Post Office Drawer 789, 93102-0789
Telephone: 805-966-1501
FAX: 805-966-9204

MEMBERS OF FIRM

Thomas M. Mullen (1915-1991)
Arthur A. Henzell (Retired)
Philip S. Wilcox
J. Robert Andrews
James W. Brown
Dennis W. Reilly
Jeffrey C. Nelson
Charles S. Bargiel
Joseph F. Green
Gary W. Robinson
Joel C. Baiocchi
Lawrence T. Sorensen
Gregory F. Faulkner
Richard G. Battles
William E. Degen

OF COUNSEL

Kim A. Harley Seefeld

ASSOCIATES

Adam Brooks Firestone
Andrew M. Polinsky
Holly S. Bander
Michael E. Cage
Catherine Perlman
Paul K. Wilcox
Maria May Foulke

Representative Clients: Goleta Sanitary District; Interinsurance Exchange of the Automobile Club of Southern California; State Farm Fire & Casualty Co.; State Farm Mutual Automobile Insurance Co.

For full biographical listings, see the Martindale-Hubbell Law Directory

*SANTA CRUZ,** Santa Cruz Co.

ATCHISON, ANDERSON, HURLEY & BARISONE, A PROFESSIONAL CORPORATION (AV)

333 Church Street, 95060
Telephone: 408-423-8383
Fax: 408-423-9401
Salinas, California Office: 137 Central Avenue, Suite 6. 93901.
Telephone: 408-755-7833.
Fax: 408-753-0293.

Rodney R. Atchison
Neal R. Anderson (1947-1986)
Vincent P. Hurley
John G. Barisone

Justin B. Lighty
Mitchell A. Jackman
David Y. Imai
Anthony P. Condotti
Mary C. Logan

Counsel for: City of Santa Cruz.

For full biographical listings, see the Martindale-Hubbell Law Directory

Santa Cruz—Continued

DUNLAP, BURDICK AND MCCORMACK, A PROFESSIONAL LAW CORPORATION (AV)

121 Jewell Street, 95060
Telephone: 408-426-7040
FAX: 408-426-1095

Michael E. Dunlap
Paul P. Burdick

OF COUNSEL

Sandra C. McCormack

For full biographical listings, see the Martindale-Hubbell Law Directory

SANTA MONICA, Los Angeles Co.

BIENSTOCK & CLARK (AV)

A Partnership including Professional Associations
3340 Ocean Park Boulevard, Suite 3075, 90405
Telephone: 310-314-8660
Telecopier: 310-314-8662
Miami, Florida Office: First Union Financial Center. 200 South Biscayne Boulevard, Suite 3160.
Telephone: 305-373-1100.
Telecopier: 305-358-1226.
Washington, D.C.: Bienstock Clark & Carmel, 1555 Connecticut Avenue, NW, Suite 500.
Telephone: 202-785-2900.
Telecopier: 202-785-2760.

Terry S. Bienstock (P.A.) (Not admitted in CA)
Roger W. Clark

Robert D. Goldberg
Ira I. Hershkowitz
Christopher L. Mass

Reference: First Union National Bank.

For full biographical listings, see the Martindale-Hubbell Law Directory

CRANE & MCCANN (AV)

530 Wilshire Boulevard, Suite 400, 90401-1423
Telephone: 310-917-9277
Fax: 310-393-7338

MEMBERS OF FIRM

Richard P. Crane, Jr.
Joseph J. McCann, Jr.

ASSOCIATES

Lawrence J. Lennemann
Brian D. McMahon
John Benedict
Daniel P. Ayala

For full biographical listings, see the Martindale-Hubbell Law Directory

DICKSON, CARLSON & CAMPILLO (AV)

120 Broadway, Suite 300, P.O. Box 2122, 90407-2122
Telephone: 310-451-2273
Telecopier: 310-451-9071

Robert L. Dickson
Jeffery J. Carlson
Ralph A. Campillo
William B. Fitzgerald
Hall R. Marston
Debra E. Pole
Roxanne M. Wilson
David J. Fleming
George E. Berry
Charles R. Messer
Kathryn C. Grogman
Mark S. Geraghty
William A. Hanssen
Mario Horwitz
Frederick J. Ufkes
Aylene M. Geringer
Daniel D. Rodarte

Karen S. Bril
Mark C. Riedel
Stephen H. Turner
Brian A. Cardoza
Pamela J. Yates
Robert C. Bohner
Deborah A. Lee-Germain
Jean A. Hobart
Thomas M. Madruga
James K. Lee

For Complete List of Firm Personnel, See General Section

For full biographical listings, see the Martindale-Hubbell Law Directory

FOGEL, FELDMAN, OSTROV, RINGLER & KLEVENS, A LAW CORPORATION (AV)

1620 26th Street, Suite 100 South, 90404-4040
Telephone: 310-453-6711
Fax: 310-828-2191

Daniel Fogel (1923-1991)
Lester G. Ostrov
Larry R. Feldman
Joel N. Klevens
Robert M. Turner
Jerome L. Ringler
Richard L. Rosett
Jon H. Levenstein

Gerald J. Miller
Stephen D. Rothschild
Leighanne Lake
Thomas H. Peters

(See Next Column)

OF COUNSEL

Carol S. May

Reference: Republic Bank of California, Beverly Hills, California.

For full biographical listings, see the Martindale-Hubbell Law Directory

LAW OFFICES OF GARY FREEDMAN (AV)

725 Arizona Avenue, Suite 100, 90401
Telephone: 310-576-2444
Telecopier: 310-576-2440

MEMBER OF FIRM

Gary A. Freedman

Emily F. Bresler
Rosemary Jackovic Schwimmer

OF COUNSEL

Paul H. Samuels

For full biographical listings, see the Martindale-Hubbell Law Directory

HAIGHT, BROWN & BONESTEEL (AV)

A Partnership including Professional Corporations
1620 26th Street, Suite 4000 North, P.O. Box 680, 90404
Telephone: 310-449-6000
Telecopier: 310-829-5117
Telex: 705837
Santa Ana, California Office: Suite 900, 5 Hutton Centre Drive.
Telephone: 714-754-1100.
Telecopier: 714-754-0826.
Riverside, California Office: 3750 University Avenue, Suite 650.
Telephone: 909-341-8300.
Fax: 909-341-8309.
San Francisco, California Office: Suite 300, 201 Sansome Street.
Telephone: 415-986-7700.
Fax: 415-986-6945.

MEMBERS OF FIRM

Fulton Haight (A Professional Corporation)
Harold Hansen Brown (A Professional Corporation)
Michael J. Bonesteel (A Professional Corporation)
Gary C. Ottoson (A Professional Corporation)
Roy G. Weatherup
William K. Koska (A Professional Corporation)
Peter Q. Ezzell (A Professional Corporation)
Dennis K. Wheeler (A Professional Corporation)
Steven L. Hoch (A Professional Corporation)
John W. Sheller (A Professional Corporation)
William G. Baumgaertner (A Professional Corporation)
Bruce A. Armstrong (A Professional Corporation)
Wayne E. Peterson (A Professional Corporation)
Morton Rosen
Peter A. Dubrawski
Michael J. Leahy
Lori R. Behar
David F. Peterson
Robert L. Kaufman
William J. Sayers
Michael McCarthy
Barry Z. Brodsky
Gary A. Bague
Kathryn M. Forgie
J. R. Seashore
Kevin R. Crisp
Lee Marshall
Donald S. Ralphs
George Christensen
Steven E. Moyer
Denis J. Moriarty
Desmond J. Hinds, Jr.
Jules Solomon Zeman
Frank Kendo Berfield (Resident, San Francisco Office)
David L. Jones
Thomas N. Charchut
Neil G. McNiece
Thomas M. Moore
Rita (Sucharita) Gunasekaran
Kenneth G. Anderson
Victor Anderson III
William O. Martin, Jr.
Theresa M. Marchlewski
Jennifer K. Saunders
Timothy B. Bradford
Amor A. Esteban
William E. Ireland
Lisa L. Oberg (Resident, San Francisco Office)

ASSOCIATES

Ted J. Duffy
David C. McGovern
Kelly C. McSpadden
Cynthia A. Robins
Marsha L. Palmer
Valerie A. Moore
Jon M. Kasimov
Lisa K. Sepe
Alicia E. Taylor
Stephen M. Caine (Resident, San Francisco Office)
Jeffrey B. Margulies
Dorothy B. Ceccon
Tammy L. Andrews
Tamara Equals Holmes
Zēb F. Gleason
Margaret Johnson Wiley
Jodi L. Girten
Holly M. Teel
Marti E. Longo
Armando M. Galvan
Elizabeth A. Livesay
S. Christian Stouder
Michael J. Sipos
Cary D. Glassner
Barry J. Thompson
Caroline E. Chan
Nancy W. Carman
Caroline S. Craddock
Celeste Elig
Michael H. Gottschlich
Jennifer A. Ellis
Caroline Kelley Hunt
Stacey R. Konkoff
Farah Sohaili Nicol
Amy C. Weinreich

(See Next Column)

HAIGHT, BROWN & BONESTEEL—*Continued*

OF COUNSEL

William M. Fitzhugh
Richard F. Runkle
Ira E. Bilson
R. Roy Finkle

For Complete List of Firm Personnel, See General Section

For full biographical listings, see the Martindale-Hubbell Law Directory

MAURICE HARWICK (AV)

Suite 600, Penthouse, 2001 Wilshire Boulevard, 90403
Telephone: 310-829-0231
Cable Address: "Harlaw Los Angeles"

Reference: Union Bank, Santa Monica Office.

For full biographical listings, see the Martindale-Hubbell Law Directory

MALONEY & MULLEN, A PROFESSIONAL CORPORATION (AV)

520 Broadway, Suite 300, 90401
Telephone: 310-393-0175
Fax: 310-394-9323

J. William Maloney
Jack M. Panagiotis
Dennis M. Mullen
Charles A. Gruber, Jr.
Christine M. Arden

Reference: Santa Monica Bank.

For full biographical listings, see the Martindale-Hubbell Law Directory

O'NEILL, LYSAGHT & SUN (AV)

A Partnership including Professional Corporations
100 Wilshire Boulevard, Suite 700, 90401
Telephone: 310-451-5700
Telecopier: 310-399-7201

Brian O'Neill (A Professional Corporation)
Frederick D. Friedman
Brian A. Sun
Brian C. Lysaght (A Professional Corporation)
Yolanda Orozco
John M. Moscarino

Harriet Beegun Leva
J. Andrew Coombs
David E. Rosen
Ellyn S. Garofalo
Lisa Newman Tucker
Edward A. Klein
Robert L. Meylan

OF COUNSEL

J. Joseph Connolly
Arn H. Tellem (P.C.)

Reference: Santa Monica Bank, Santa Monica.

For full biographical listings, see the Martindale-Hubbell Law Directory

SACKS & ZWEIG (AV)

A Partnership of Professional Corporations
100 Wilshire Building, Suite 1300, 100 Wilshire Boulevard, 90401
Telephone: 310-451-3113
Facsimile: 310-451-0089

Lee Sacks
Michael K. Zweig
Filomena E. Meyer

OF COUNSEL

Dennis Holahan

For full biographical listings, see the Martindale-Hubbell Law Directory

*SANTA ROSA,** Sonoma Co.

ACHOR, MILLER, CULVER & MAILLIARD (AV)

A Partnership including a Professional Corporation
100 B Street, Suite 200, P.O. Box 5257, 95402
Telephone: 707-571-8112
Fax: 707-575-9116

Christopher R. Miller (P.C.)
Michael E. Kinney
David C. Culver
Laura G. Drenning
William S. Mailliard, Jr.
R. W. Achor (P.C.) (Retired)

Representative Clients: Warrack Medical Center Hospital; WD-40 Co.
Representative Insurance Client: Farmers/Truck Insurance Exchange.

For full biographical listings, see the Martindale-Hubbell Law Directory

BELDEN, ABBEY, WEITZENBERG & KELLY, A PROFESSIONAL CORPORATION (AV)

1105 North Dutton Avenue, P.O. Box 1566, 95402
Telephone: 707-542-5050
Telecopier: 707-542-2589

Thomas P. Kelly, Jr.
W. Barton Weitzenberg
Candace H. Shirley

(See Next Column)

Wayne R. Wolski
Lewis R. Warren

Representative Clients: Exchange Bank of Santa Rosa; Westamerica Bank; North Bay Title Co.; Northwestern Title Security Co.; Geyser Peak Winery; Arrowood Vineyards & Winery; Hansel Ford; Santa Rosa City School District.

For Complete List of Firm Personnel, See General Section

For full biographical listings, see the Martindale-Hubbell Law Directory

CLEMENT, FITZPATRICK & KENWORTHY, INCORPORATED (AV)

3333 Mendocino Avenue, P.O. Box 1494, 95402
Telephone: 707-523-1181
Telecopier: 707-546-1360

Clayton E. Clement
Peter C. De Golia
Paul J. Fitzpatrick
Anthony Cohen
K. Randall Kenworthy
Stephen K. Butler
Christopher W. Silva

References: Exchange Bank; Sonoma National Bank.

For full biographical listings, see the Martindale-Hubbell Law Directory

*STOCKTON,** San Joaquin Co.

DIEHL, STEINHEIMER, RIGGIO, HAYDEL & MORDAUNT, A PROFESSIONAL LAW CORPORATION (AV)

400 East Main Street, Suite 600, 95290
Telephone: 209-464-8732
Fax: 209-464-9165
Mailing Address: P.O. Box 201072, Stockton, California, 95201-3022
Sonora, California Office: 38 North Washington Street, Suite A.
Telephone: 209-532-1424.
Fax: 209-532-4233.

M. Max Steinheimer
Kevin M. Seibert
Donald M. Riggio
Scott A. Ginns
Douglas A. Haydel
Tamara M. Polley
Michael R. Mordaunt
Edward S. Maxwell
Peter J. Kelly
David W. Culp
P. Gary Cassel
Kay E. Gorman
Scott Malm
Elizabeth R. Bogart
Mark F. Ornellas
Darin T. Judd
Joseph H. Fagundes
Frank R. Perrott
William D. Johnson
Lance Burtis Smith
Frank J. Enright
Rachelle C. Sanchez
Kate Powell Segerstrom (Resident, Sonora Office)

OF COUNSEL

Joseph W. Diehl

Counsel for: Pacific Gas and Electric Co.; Kleinfelder Inc.; Turlock Irrigation District.
Insurance Clients: Allied Insurance Group; Design Professional Insurance Co.; The Doctors Co.; Kemper Insurance Co.; Norcal Mutual Insurance Co.; The Travelers.

For full biographical listings, see the Martindale-Hubbell Law Directory

TARZANA, Los Angeles Co.

WASSERMAN, COMDEN & CASSELMAN (AV)

5567 Reseda Boulevard, Suite 330, P.O. Box 7033, 91357-7033
Telephone: 818-705-6800; 213-872-0995
Fax: 818-345-0162; 818-996-8266

MEMBERS OF FIRM

Steve K. Wasserman
Rebecca J. Schroer
Leonard J. Comden
Jay N. Rosenwald
David B. Casselman
Daniel E. Lewis
Clifford H. Pearson
Crystal A. Zarpas
Mark S. Roth
Gary S. Soter

ASSOCIATES

Joel Fischman
Ted G. Schwartz
Jeffrey K. Jayson
Richard A. Brownstein
Catherine Stevenson Garcia
Albert G. Turner, Jr.
Glenn A. Brown, Jr.
Kenneth M. Jones
Robin F. Genchel
Sharon Zemel
Lloyd S. Mann
Robert T. Leonard
J. Christopher Bennington
Stephen D. Adler
Paul H. Lasky
Keith Nussbaum
Norman L. Pearl
L. Stephen Albright
Todd A. Chamberlain
John A. Raymond
Howard S. Blum
Penny L. Wheat
Caroline S. Manankichian

OF COUNSEL

Cecilia S. Wu
John P. Doyle

Representative Clients: Toplis & Harding; Appalachian Insurance; Lumbermens Mutual Insurance Co.; State Farm Fire and Casualty Co.; Factory Mutual Engineering; Cravens, Dargan & Co.; Lloyd's of London.

For full biographical listings, see the Martindale-Hubbell Law Directory

UPLAND, San Bernardino Co.

ALTHOUSE & BAMBER (AV)

Second Floor, Home Federal Savings & Loan Building, 188 North Euclid Avenue, P.O. Box 698, 91785
Telephone: 909-985-9828
Telecopier: 909-985-3282

Charles S. Althouse
Sherril L. Alexander
Elizabeth A. McDonough

References: Security Pacific National Bank, Upland Branch; First National Bank & Trust Company, Upland Branch.

For Complete List of Firm Personnel, See General Section

For full biographical listings, see the Martindale-Hubbell Law Directory

*VENTURA,** Ventura Co.

BENTON, ORR, DUVAL & BUCKINGHAM, A PROFESSIONAL CORPORATION (AV)

39 North California Street, P.O. Box 1178, 93002
Telephone: 805-648-5111; 656-1166
Fax: 805-648-7218

James T. Sherren
Ronald L. Colton
Robert A. Davidson
Thomas E. Olson
Dean W. Hazard
Brenda L. DeHart

Mark S. Borrell

Counsel for: American Commercial Bank; Petoseed Co., Inc.
Trial Counsel for: Southern California Edison Co.; Shell Oil Co.; Automobile Club of Southern California; Southern California Physicians Insurance Exchange.

For full biographical listings, see the Martindale-Hubbell Law Directory

FERGUSON, CASE, ORR, PATERSON & CUNNINGHAM (AV)

1050 South Kimball Road, 93004
Telephone: 805-659-6800
Telecopier: 805-659-6818

Thomas R. Ferguson
Michael W. Case
John C. Orr
William E. Paterson
David L. Cunningham
Lou Carpiac
Joseph L. Strohman, Jr.
Allen F. Camp
Robert L. Gallaway
Sandra M. Robertson
William B. Smith

Annette M. Lercel
Ramon L. Guizar
Gisele Goetz
Gregory W. Herring
Douglas E. Kulper

Representative Clients: First American Title Insurance Company; Wells Fargo Bank; Lincoln Title Insurance Co.; The Hahn Company (Oaks Regional Shopping Center); Area Housing Authority of the County of Ventura; Buenaventura Medical Clinic, Inc.; H.F. Ahmanson Company; Southern Pacific Milling Company; USA Petroleum Corporation; Cellular One.

For full biographical listings, see the Martindale-Hubbell Law Directory

TAYLOR McCORD, A LAW CORPORATION (AV)

721 East Main Street, P.O. Box 1477, 93002
Telephone: 805-648-4700
Fax: 805-653-6124

Richard L. Taylor
Robert L. McCord, Jr.
Ellen G. Conroy
David L. Praver

Patrick Cherry
Susan D. Siple

For full biographical listings, see the Martindale-Hubbell Law Directory

VICTORVILLE, San Bernardino Co.

LYNN E. ZUMBRUNN A LAW CORPORATION (AV)

14335 Park Avenue, Suite A, 92392-6072
Telephone: 619-245-5333
Fax: 619-245-2000

Lynn Edward Zumbrunn

James Bruce Minton
Gregory L. Zumbrunn

Representative Clients: H.D. Medical Home Care Supply, Inc.; Rammar Painting, Inc.; Sunland Ford, Inc.; T.L. Timmerman Construction, Inc.

For full biographical listings, see the Martindale-Hubbell Law Directory

WALNUT CREEK, Contra Costa Co.

HYDE & HOLCOMB (AV)

An Association including a Professional Corporation
1646 N. California Boulevard Suite 550, 94596
Telephone: 510-939-7700
Fax: 510-939-2248

Patrick M. Hyde (P.C.)
David J. Holcomb

For full biographical listings, see the Martindale-Hubbell Law Directory

JACKL & KATZEN (AV)

2033 North Main Street, Suite 700, 94596
Telephone: 510-932-8500
Fax: 510-932-1961

MEMBERS OF FIRM

V. James Jackl
Linda R. Katzen

Christopher J. Joy
David W. Walters
James M. Sitkin
Andrew N. Contopoulos
David A. Schuricht

For full biographical listings, see the Martindale-Hubbell Law Directory

WHITTIER, Los Angeles Co.

BEWLEY, LASSLEBEN & MILLER (AV)

A Law Partnership including Professional Corporations
Suite 510 Whittier Square, 13215 East Penn Street, 90602
Telephone: 310-698-9771; 723-8062; 714-994-5131
Telecopier: 310-696-6357

MEMBERS OF FIRM

Thomas W. Bewley (1903-1986)
William M. Lassleben, Jr. (A Professional Corporation)
Edward L. Miller (A Professional Corporation)
J. Terrence Mooschekian
Richard A. Hayes (A Professional Corporation)
Ernie Zachary Park (A Professional Corporation)
Robert H. Dewberry (A Professional Corporation)
Richard L. Dewberry (A Professional Corporation)
Jeffrey S. Baird
Kevin P. Duthoy
Joseph A. Vinatieri
Jason C. Demille

Representative Clients: Quaker City Federal Savings & Loan Assn.; Whittier College; Presbyterian Intercommunity Hospital; Bank of Whittier; Circuit Systems, Inc.; Lockhart Industries, Inc.; Subdivided Land, Inc.; United Ad-Label Co., Inc.
References: Bank of America National Trust & Savings Assn. (Whittier Main Office); Southern California Bank.

For Complete List of Firm Personnel, See General Section

For full biographical listings, see the Martindale-Hubbell Law Directory

WOODLAND HILLS, Los Angeles Co.

FELDMAN, KARP & FELDMAN, A PROFESSIONAL CORPORATION (AV)

5959 Topanga Canyon Boulevard, Suite 275, 91367
Telephone: 818-992-0357
Facsimile: 818-992-0537

Deborah L. Feldman
David I. Karp
Yacoba Ann Feldman

Douglas A. Bordner

LEGAL SUPPORT PERSONNEL

Debra Kay "BJ" Philben (Paralegal)

For full biographical listings, see the Martindale-Hubbell Law Directory

WALLECK, SHANE, STANARD & BLENDER (AV)

5959 Topanga Canyon Boulevard, Suite 200, 91367
Telephone: 818-346-1333
Fax: 818-702-8939

MEMBERS OF FIRM

David L. Shane
Roger L. Stanard
Gary N. Schwartz
Stephen A. DiGiuseppe
Christopher F. Johnson

Representative Clients: San Fernando Valley Board of Realtors; Keffco, Inc.; Fuller-Jeffrey Broadcasting; Lynn Simay-Key Centers, Inc.; DA/PRO Rubber, Inc.; Pinnacle Estate Properties, Inc.; Comet Electric, Inc.; Wausau Insurance Company; Western States Imports Co., Inc.; California Coast Escrow, Inc.

For full biographical listings, see the Martindale-Hubbell Law Directory

COLORADO

*ALAMOSA,** Alamosa Co.

LUCERO, LESTER & SIGMOND (AV)

311 San Juan Avenue, P.O. Box 1270, 81101-1270
Telephone: 719-589-6626
Telecopier: 719-589-5555

Carlos F. Lucero
James K. Lester
Helen Sigmond

David A. Rooney
Erich Schwiesow

OF COUNSEL

Richard A. Kadinger

For full biographical listings, see the Martindale-Hubbell Law Directory

ARVADA, Jefferson Co.

THE ELLIOTT LAW OFFICES (AV)

7884 Ralston Road, 80002
Telephone: 303-424-5319
Fax: 303-424-6130

James E. Elliott, Jr.
Mark D. Elliott

LEGAL SUPPORT PERSONNEL

James R. Elliott

Reference: Vectra Bank of Lakewood, N.A.

For full biographical listings, see the Martindale-Hubbell Law Directory

*ASPEN,** Pitkin Co.

AUSTIN, PEIRCE & SMITH, P.C. (AV)

Suite 205, 600 East Hopkins Avenue, 81611
Telephone: 303-925-2600
FAX: 303-925-4720

Ronald D. Austin
Frederick F. Peirce
Thomas Fenton Smith

Rhonda J. Bazil

Counsel for: Clark's Market; Coates, Reid & Waldron Realtors; Crystal Palace Corp.; Snowmass Shopping Center; Coldwell Banker; William Poss & Assoc., Architects; Snowmass Resort Association; Real Estate Affiliates, Inc.; Raleigh Enterprises.

For full biographical listings, see the Martindale-Hubbell Law Directory

J. NICHOLAS MCGRATH, P.C. (AV)

Suite 203, 600 East Hopkins Avenue, 81611
Telephone: 303-925-2612
Telecopier: 303-925-4402

J. Nicholas McGrath

Cynthia C. Tester
Susan W. Laatsch (Not admitted in CO)

Representative Clients: Aspen Center for Physics; Aspen Chamber Resort Association.; The Gant Condominium Association; Mt. States Communications, Inc.; Gerald D. Hines Interests; Marty Stouffer Productions, Ltd.; Steak Pit, Inc.; UCB Services, Inc.; Hotel Jerome Associates, Ltd. Partners.

For full biographical listings, see the Martindale-Hubbell Law Directory

OATES, HUGHES & KNEZEVICH, P.C. (AV)

Aspen Plaza Building, 3rd Floor, 533 East Hopkins Avenue, 81611
Telephone: 303-920-1700
Telecopier: 303-920-1121

Leonard M. Oates
Richard A. Knezevich
Robert W. Hughes
Ted D. Gardenswartz

OF COUNSEL

John Thomas Kelly

Counsel for: Stapleton Insurance Agency; Silvertree Hotel; Pitkin County Title, Inc.

For full biographical listings, see the Martindale-Hubbell Law Directory

*BOULDER,** Boulder Co.

HOWARD BITTMAN (AV)

1406 Pearl Street, Suite 200, 80302
Telephone: 303-443-2281
Fax: 303-443-2862

For full biographical listings, see the Martindale-Hubbell Law Directory

COOK & LEE, P.C. (AV)

Canyonside Office Park, 100 Arapahoe Avenue, Suite 9, 80302-5862
Telephone: 303-444-9700
Fax: 303-444-9691
Denver, Colorado Office: Sherman Street Plaza, 1888 Sherman Street, Suite 375, 80203-1158.
Telephone: 303-831-8008.

Stephen H. Cook
Larry D. Lee

Patti L. Holt
Daniel E. Bronstein

For full biographical listings, see the Martindale-Hubbell Law Directory

LAW OFFICES OF MICHAEL R. ENWALL (AV)

720 Pearl Street, 80302
Telephone: 303-449-3891
FAX: 303-449-3992

ASSOCIATE

Barbara K. Grant

For full biographical listings, see the Martindale-Hubbell Law Directory

PURVIS, GRAY, SCHUETZE & GORDON (AV)

The Exeter Building, Suite 501, 1050 Walnut Street, 80302
Telephone: 303-442-3366
Fax: 303-440-3688
Denver, Colorado Office: 303 East 17th Avenue, Suite 700.
Telephone: 303-860-1888.

MEMBERS OF FIRM

William R. Gray
Robert A. Schuetze
John A. Purvis
Glen F. Gordon

For full biographical listings, see the Martindale-Hubbell Law Directory

WILLIAMS & TRINE, P.C. (AV)

1435 Arapahoe Avenue, 80302-6390
Telephone: 303-442-0173
Fax: 303-443-7677

William A. Trine
J. Conard Metcalf
Joel H. Greenstein (1933-1984)
Mari C. Bush
Michael A. Patrick

OF COUNSEL

Charles E. Williams

Reference: Norwest Bank of Boulder.

For full biographical listings, see the Martindale-Hubbell Law Directory

*COLORADO SPRINGS,** El Paso Co.

CROSS, GADDIS, KIN, HERD & KELLY, P.C. (AV)

118 South Wahsatch, 80903
Telephone: 719-471-3848
Fax: 719-471-0317

Thomas R. Cross
David L. Quicksall (1950-1991)
Larry R. Gaddis
Thomas J. Herd
James W. Kin
Debra L. Kelly

OF COUNSEL

James B. Turner

Reference: Norwest Bank of Colorado Springs.

For full biographical listings, see the Martindale-Hubbell Law Directory

HANES & SCHUTZ, P.C. (AV)

7222 Commerce Center Drive Suite 243, 80916
Telephone: 719-260-7900
Denver Line: 303-740-9694
Fax: 719-260-7904

Richard W. Hanes
Tim Schutz

For full biographical listings, see the Martindale-Hubbell Law Directory

KANE, DONLEY & SHAFFER (AV)

90 South Cascade Avenue, Suite 1100, P.O. Box 1119, 80901
Telephone: 719-471-1650
Fax: 719-471-1663

MEMBERS OF FIRM

Jerry A. Donley
Thomas Kelly Kane
E. William Shaffer, Jr.
Mark H. Kane
Jack E. Donley

ASSOCIATES

William A. Palmer
Hayden W. Kane, II

OF COUNSEL

Hayden W. Kane

Representative Clients: American States Insurance Co.; Hawkeye-Security Insurance Co.

(See Next Column)

KANE, DONLEY & SHAFFER, *Colorado Springs—Continued*

Reference: Norwest Bank of Colorado Springs.

For full biographical listings, see the Martindale-Hubbell Law Directory

MELAT, PRESSMAN, EZELL & HIGBIE (AV)

711 South Tejon Street, 80903-4041
Telephone: 719-475-0304
Fax: 719-475-0242

MEMBERS OF FIRM

Justin R. Melat
Glenn S. Pressman
E. Steven Ezell
Alanson Higbie

ASSOCIATES

Robert J. Frank
Rebecca A. Lorenz

OF COUNSEL

Bernard R. Baker

References: Colorado Springs National Bank; Colorado Bank-Exchange.

RETHERFORD, MULLEN, JOHNSON & BRUCE (AV)

A Partnership including Professional Corporations
415 South Sahwatch, P.O. Box 1580, 80901
Telephone: 719-475-2014
Fax: 719-630-1267
Pueblo, Colorado Office: Suite 510, 201 West 8th Street, 81003.
Telephone: 719-543-7181.
Fax: 719-543-5650.

MEMBERS OF FIRM

Jerry A. Retherford
J. Stephen Mullen (P.C.)
Anthony A. Johnson (P.C.)
Neil C. Bruce
Thomas J. Barton (P.C.)
Patrick R. Salt
J. Ronald Voss

ASSOCIATES

Lori M. Moore
Amelia L. Klemme
Chad J. Hessel
M. James Zendejas

Representative Clients: State Farm Insurance; The Home Insurance; Farmers Insurance, USAA; Travelers Insurance; Case Corporation; AllState Insurance; City of Colorado Springs Memorial Hospital; Harnishfeger Corp; ITT Hartford.

For full biographical listings, see the Martindale-Hubbell Law Directory

SEARS, ANDERSON & SWANSON, P.C. (AV)

The Holly Sugar Building, Suite 1250 2 North Cascade Avenue, 80903
Telephone: 719-471-1984
FAX: 719-577-4356
Denver, Colorado Office: 3900 East Mexico Avenue, Denver Centerpoint, Suite 810.
Telephone: 303-759-1963.
Fax: 303-759-2760.

Lance M. Sears
Leland P. Anderson (Resident, Denver, Colorado)
Victoria C. Swanson

OF COUNSEL

Stephanie H. Yukawa

Reference: Norwest Bank of Colorado Springs, N.A.

For full biographical listings, see the Martindale-Hubbell Law Directory

VAGLICA & CARLSON (AV)

105 East Moreno, Suite 100, 80903
Telephone: 719-635-0041
Telefax: 719-634-8592

MEMBERS OF FIRM

Phillip A. Vaglica
Kathleen A. Carlson

OF COUNSEL

Brian T. Borders

Representative Clients: Continental Loss Adjusting Co.; El Paso County, Colorado.

For full biographical listings, see the Martindale-Hubbell Law Directory

J. GREGORY WALTA, P.C. (AV)

Suite 101 - Cascade Station, 620 South Cascade Avenue, 80903-4039
Telephone: 719-578-8888
FAX: 719-578-8931

J. Gregory Walta
Celeste Lisanne Crizer Gerber

Reference: Norwest Bank of Colorado Springs.

For full biographical listings, see the Martindale-Hubbell Law Directory

THE WILLS LAW FIRM (AV)

Holly Sugar Building, 2 North Cascade Avenue, Suite 1000, 80903-1651
Telephone: 719-633-8500
Telecopier: 719-471-7750

(See Next Column)

MEMBERS OF FIRM

Lee R. Wills
Wm. Andrew Wills, II

For full biographical listings, see the Martindale-Hubbell Law Directory

*DENVER,** Denver Co.

ALEXANDER LAW FIRM, P.C. (AV)

216 16th Street, Suite 1300, 80202
Telephone: 303-825-7307
Fax: 303-595-3202

C. Scott Crabtree

For full biographical listings, see the Martindale-Hubbell Law Directory

BADER & VILLANUEVA, P.C. (AV)

Suite 1100, 1660 Wynkoop Street, 80202
Telephone: 303-534-1700
Telecopier: 303-534-0725

Gerald L. Bader, Jr.
Jeffrey M. Villanueva

Randolph S. Dement
Steven M. Feder
Renée Beth Taylor

LEGAL SUPPORT PERSONNEL

Colette Poeppel (Paralegal)

Reference: The Bank of Denver.

For full biographical listings, see the Martindale-Hubbell Law Directory

BAKER & HOSTETLER (AV)

303 East 17th Avenue, Suite 1100, 80203-1264
Telephone: 303-861-0600
FAX: 303-861-7805
In Cleveland, Ohio: 3200 National City Center, 1900 East Ninth Street.
Telephone: 216-621-0200.
In Columbus, Ohio: Capitol Square, Suite 2100, 65 East State Street.
Telephone: 614-228-1541.
In Houston, Texas: 1000 Louisiana, Suite 2000.
Telephone: 713-751-1600.
In Long Beach, California: 300 Oceangate, Suite 620.
Telephone: 310-432-2827.
In Los Angeles, California: 600 Wilshire Boulevard. Telephone 213-624-2400.
In Orlando, Florida: SunBank Center, Suite 2300, 200 South Orange Avenue,
Telephone: 305-841-1111.
In Washington, D. C.: Washington Square, Suite 1100, 1050 Connecticut Avenue, N.W.
Telephone: 202-861-1500.
In College Park, Maryland: 9658 Baltimore Boulevard, Suite 206.
Telephone: 301-441-2781.
In Alexandria, Virginia: 437 North Lee Street.
Telephone: 703-549-1294.
In San Francisco, California: One Sansome Street, Suite 2000.
Telephone: 415-951-4705.

MEMBER OF FIRM IN DENVER, COLORADO

James A. Clark (Managing Partner-Denver Office)

PARTNERS

Timothy R. Beyer
Kathryn A. Elzi
Marc D. Flink
Todd L. Lundy
John B. Moorhead

ASSOCIATES

Mary Price Birk
Stephen D. Gurr
Peter J. Korneffel, Jr.
Michael G. Martin
Michael J. Roche
Marjorie N. Sloan

OF COUNSEL

Winchester Cooley, III (Not admitted in CO)
Fred M. Winner

For Complete List of Firm Personnel, See General Section

For full biographical listings, see the Martindale-Hubbell Law Directory

ARTHUR BOSWORTH & ASSOCIATES, P.C. (AV)

Suite 2500, 1775 Sherman Street, 80203-4322
Telephone: 303-839-5400
Fax: 303-839-8009

Arthur H. Bosworth, II

Janet T. Ward

For full biographical listings, see the Martindale-Hubbell Law Directory

Denver—Continued

Brega & Winters, P.C. (AV)

One Norwest Center, 1700 Lincoln Street, Suite 2222, 80203
Telephone: 303-866-9400
FAX: 303-861-9109
Greeley, Colorado Office: 1100 Tenth Street, Suite 402, 80631.
Telephone: 303-352-4805.
Fax: 303-352-6547.

James W. Bain
Thomas D. Birge
Charles F. Brega
Robert R. Dormer
Robert C. Kaufman
Ronald S. Loser
Brian A. Magoon
Loren L. Mall
Pamela A. Shaddock (Resident, Greeley Office)
Jay John Schnell
Jerry D. Winters (Resident, Greeley Office)

Mark J. Appleton
Wesley B. Howard, Jr.
Jennifer G. Krolik
Bradley D. Laue (Resident, Greeley Office)
Cathryn B. Mayers
Carla B. Minckley
Nathan D. Simmons
Scott L. Terrell

OF COUNSEL

Mark Spitalnik

For full biographical listings, see the Martindale-Hubbell Law Directory

Brownstein Hyatt Farber & Strickland, P.C. (AV)

Twenty-Second Floor, 410 Seventeenth Street, 80202-4437
Telephone: 303-534-6335
Telecopier: 303-623-1956

Mark F. Leonard
Andrew W. Loewi
Charles B. White
Stanley L. Garnett
Lisa A. Hogan
Wayne F. Forman
Hubert A. Farbes, Jr.

Anne M. Murphy
Terence C. Gill
Robert C. Troyer
Patrick F Carrigan
Beth Morrison Klein
Mark J. Mathews
Peter Q. Murphy

Representative Clients: Air Line Pilots Association; Citicorp North America, Inc.; Louisiana-Pacific Corporation; Metro Taxi, Inc.; Metropolitan Life Insurance Co. of America; Owens-Corning Fiberglas Corporation; PCL Construction Services, Inc.; The Prudential Insurance Co. of America; Rose Medical Center/Rose Health Care Systems; Trammell Crow Company.

For Complete List of Firm Personnel, See General Section

For full biographical listings, see the Martindale-Hubbell Law Directory

Burg & Eldredge, P.C. (AV)

Suite 900 Regency Plaza One, 4643 South Ulster, 80237-2866
Telephone: 303-779-5595
Fax: 303-779-0527
Albuquerque, New Mexico Office: 20 First Plaza, Suite 508, 87102.
Telephone: 505-242-7020.
Fax: 505-242-7247.

Michael S. Burg
Peter W. Burg
Scott J. Eldredge
David P. Hersh
David M. Houliston
R. Hunter Ellington

Thomas Willard Henderson, IV
Janet R. Spies
Tom Van Buskirk
Matthew R. Giacomini
Kerry N. Jardine
Andrew M. Ominsky
Ashley Rea Kilroy
Brendan O'Rourke Powers
Jack D. Robinson
Kirstin G. Lindberg
Willie E. Shepherd, Jr.
John J. Mattey
Bradley W. Howard (Resident, Albuquerque, New Mexico Office)
Christian C. Doherty (Resident, Albuquerque, New Mexico Office)
Gillian Cooley Morrison
Christina Gratke Nason (Resident, Albuquerque, New Mexico Office)
Rosemary Orsini
Kathleen H. Bridges

OF COUNSEL

Gregory E. Bunker
Dale J. Coplan

Reference: Norwest Colorado, Inc.

For full biographical listings, see the Martindale-Hubbell Law Directory

Canges, Iwashko & Bethke, A Professional Corporation (AV)

303 East 17th Avenue Suite 400, 80203-1261
Telephone: 303-860-1900
Fax: 303-860-1665

E. Michael Canges
Nina A. Iwashko
Erich L. Bethke

(See Next Column)

Stephen R. Fatzinger
James S. Bailey

Reference: Norwest Bank Denver.

For full biographical listings, see the Martindale-Hubbell Law Directory

Clanahan, Tanner, Downing and Knowlton, P.C. (AV)

Suite 2400, 1600 Broadway, 80202
Telephone: 303-830-9111
Telecopier: 303-830-0299

David C. Knowlton
Thomas C. McKee
Denis B. Clanahan
Michael J. Wozniak
James M. Colosky
J. David Arkell
James T. Ayers, Jr.
Janet N. Harris
Sheryl L. Howe
Jack D. Henderson
Peter T. Moore
Judith M. Matlock
C. Kevin Cahill
Gary P. LaPlante
Richard L. Shearer
David M. Rich
Langdon J. Jorgensen
Brian D. Fitzgerald

Robert J. Bricmont, Jr.
Dino A. Ross
Robert M. O'Hayre
Richard J. Gognat

SPECIAL COUNSEL

Joseph K. Reynolds
Leslie Abrams Pizzi

OF COUNSEL

Barkley L. Clanahan
Ira E. Tanner, Jr.
Richard Downing, Jr.

Representative Clients: Amoco Production Co.; Ampol (U.S.A.), Inc.; Apache Corporation; Celebrity Homes, Inc.; Farmers Reservoir & Irrigation Company; KN Production Company; Maxus Exploration, Inc.; Oryx Energy Company; Pace Membership Warehouse, Inc.; Snyder Oil Corporation.

For Complete List of Firm Personnel, See General Section

For full biographical listings, see the Martindale-Hubbell Law Directory

Cook & Lee, P.C. (AV)

Sherman Street Plaza, 1888 Sherman Street, Suite 375, 80203-1158
Telephone: 303-831-8008
Fax: 303-860-1844
Boulder, Colorado Office: Canyonside Office Park, 100 Arapahoe Avenue, Suite 9, 80302-5862.
Telephone: 303-444-9700.
Fax: 303-444-9691.

Stephen H. Cook
Larry D. Lee

Patti L. Holt
Daniel E. Bronstein

For full biographical listings, see the Martindale-Hubbell Law Directory

Dufford & Brown, P.C. (AV)

1700 Broadway, Suite 1700, 80290-1701
Telephone: 303-861-8013
Facsimile: 303-832-3804

Philip G. Dufford
David W. Furgason
Beverly J. Quail
Phillip D. Barber
Gregory A. Ruegsegger
S. Kirk Ingebretsen
Douglas P. Ruegsegger
Peggy J. Anderson
Craig B. Shaffer
Scott J. Mikulecky
Terry Jo Epstein

Representative Clients: CF&I Steel, L.P.; The Colorado and Wyoming Railway Co.; Echo Bay-Sunnyside Gold; Hewlett-Packard Co.; Ingersoll Rand Financial Co.; Peabody Holding Company, Inc.; Reorganized CF&I Steel Corporation; Stewart& Stevenson Services, Inc.; Tenneco Oil Co.

For Complete List of Firm Personnel, See General Section

For full biographical listings, see the Martindale-Hubbell Law Directory

Eiberger, Stacy, Smith & Martin (AV)

A Partnership including Professional Corporations
3500 Republic Plaza, 370 Seventeenth Street, 80202-5635
Telephone: 303-534-3500
Telecopier: 303-595-9554

MEMBERS OF FIRM

Carl F. Eiberger
David H. Stacy (P.C.)
Rodney L. Smith (P.C.)
Raymond W. Martin (P.C.)
Lawrence D. Stone (P.C.)

ASSOCIATES

Paul F. Hodapp
Susan M. Schaecher
David M. Bost
Kim L. Ritter

Representative Clients: U.S. West, Inc.; Super Valu, Inc.; The Denver Post Corp.; Cub Foods; Rocky Mountain Motorist d/b/a/ AAA; Enterprise Rent-A-Car Co.; Times Mirror Corp.; Service Merchandise, Inc.; Wright-McGill/Eagle Claw; EG&G - Rocky Flats.

(See Next Column)

EIBERGER, STACY, SMITH & MARTIN, *Denver—Continued*

For full biographical listings, see the Martindale-Hubbell Law Directory

FAIRFIELD AND WOODS, P.C. (AV)

One Norwest Center, Suite 2400, 1700 Lincoln Street, 80203-4524
Telephone: 303-830-2400
Telecopier: 303-830-1033

Peter F. Breitenstein	John J. Silver
Charlton H. Carpenter	Thomas P. Kearns
Howard Holme	Rocco A. Dodson
Robert S. Slosky	Mary E. Moser
James L. Stone	Christine K. Truitt
Michael M. McKinstry	Brent T. Johnson
Jac K. Sperling	Craig A. Umbaugh
Robert L. Loeb, Jr.	Stephen H. Leonhardt
Daniel R. Frost	Caroline C. Fuller
Stephen W. Seifert	John M. Frew
Mary Jo Gross	Gregory C. Smith
Robert A. Holmes	John M. Tanner

Neil T. Duggan

OF COUNSEL

George C. Keely (Retired)

Douglas J. Becker	Mary Sommerville Welch
Brent A. Waite	Lisa A. D'Ambrosia (Not admitted in CO)
Thomas M. Pierce	
Suzanne R. Kalutkiewicz	Jacalyn W. Peter
Philip J. Roselli	David L. Joeris

Representative Clients: IBM Credit Corp.; ITT Commercial Finance Corp.; Olivetti Office U.S.A., Inc.; PaineWebber, Incorporated.

For full biographical listings, see the Martindale-Hubbell Law Directory

FEDER, MORRIS, TAMBLYN & GOLDSTEIN, P.C. (AV)

150 Blake Street Building, 1441 Eighteenth Street, 80202
Telephone: 303-292-1441
FAX: 303-292-1126

Harry A. Feder (1905-1967)	Stephen B. Schuyler
Harold A. Feder	John B. Carraher
Leonard M. Goldstein	Barbara Salomon
Denise K. Mills	Mark D. Thompson

Gina B. Weitzenkorn

OF COUNSEL

Milton Morris	Katherine Tamblyn

Reference: Guaranty Bank & Trust Co., Denver, Colorado.

For full biographical listings, see the Martindale-Hubbell Law Directory

FRIEDLOB SANDERSON RASKIN PAULSON & TOURTILLOTT (AV)

A Partnership of Professional Corporations
1400 Glenarm Place, 80202-5099
Telephone: 303-571-1400
Fax: 303-595-3159; 303-595-3970

Richard H. Goldberg	Michael J. Norton

For full biographical listings, see the Martindale-Hubbell Law Directory

HAMILTON AND FAATZ, A PROFESSIONAL CORPORATION (AV)

Suite 600 Colorado State Bank Building, 1600 Broadway, 80202-4988
Telephone: 303-830-0500
Facsimile: 303-860-7855

Pierpont Fuller (1906-1983)	John T. Willson
John M. Evans (1911-1984)	James H. Marlow
Dwight Alan Hamilton	Jan E. Montgomery
Clyde A. Faatz, Jr.	Gregory W. Smith

Robert L. Bartholic

SPECIAL COUNSEL

Michael E. Gurley

OF COUNSEL

Kenneth W. Caughey

Representative Clients: PPG Industries, Inc.; Public Employees Retirement Association of Colorado; Masonic Temple Association of Denver; Lockton Silversmith, Inc.; Muller, Sirhall and Associates, Inc.; South Denver Cardiology Associates, P.C.; Landmark Reclamation, Inc.; Stone's Farm Supply, Inc.; Heather Gardens Association; DCX, Inc.

For full biographical listings, see the Martindale-Hubbell Law Directory

HANSEN AND HOLMES, A PROFESSIONAL CORPORATION (AV)

Lincoln Center, 1660 Lincoln Street, Suite 2750, 80264
Telephone: 303-830-8008
Fax: 303-830-8531

(See Next Column)

Robert W. Hansen	Judith H. Holmes

Sharon E. Smith

For full biographical listings, see the Martindale-Hubbell Law Directory

HOLLAND & HART (AV)

Suite 2900, 555 Seventeenth Street, P.O. Box 8749, 80201
Telephone: 303-295-8000
Cable Address: "Holhart Denver"
Telecopier: 303-295-8261
TWX: 910-931-0568
Denver Tech Center, Colorado Office: Suite 1050, 4601 DTC Boulevard.
Telephone: 303-290-1600.
Telecopier: 303-290-1606.
Aspen, Colorado Office: 600 East Main Street.
Telephone: 303-925-3476.
Telecopier: 303-925-9367.
Boulder, Colorado Office: Suite 500, 1050 Walnut.
Telephone: 303-473-2700.
Telecopier: 303-473-2720.
Colorado Springs, Colorado Office: Suite 1000, 90 S. Cascade Avenue.
Telephone: 719-475-7730.
Telex: 82077 SHHTLX.
Telecopier: 719-634-2461.
Washington, D.C. Office: Suite 310, 1001 Pennsylvania Avenue, N.W.
Telephone: 202-638-5500.
Telecopier: 202-737-8998.
Boise, Idaho Office: Suite 1400, West One Plaza, 101 South Capitol Boulevard, P.O. Box 2527.
Telephone: 208-342-5000.
Telecopier: 208-343-8869.
Billings, Montana Office: Suite 1500, First Interstate Center, 401 North 31st Street, P.O. Box 639.
Telephone: 406-252-2166.
Telecopier: 406-252-1669.
Salt Lake City, Utah Office: Suite 880, 111 East Broadway.
Telephone: 801-578-6000.
FAX: 801-578-6010.
Cheyenne, Wyoming Office: Holland & Hart, A Partnership including Professional Corporations, Suite 500, 2020 Carey Avenue, P.O. Box 1347.
Telephone: 307-778-4200.
Telecopier: 307-778-8175.
Jackson, Wyoming Office: Holland & Hart, A Partnership including Professional Corporations, Suite 2, 175 South King Street, P.O. Box 68.
Telephone: 307-739-9741.
Telecopier: 307-739-9744.

MEMBERS OF FIRM

Warren L. Tomlinson (Retired)	W. Harold Flowers, Jr.
Patrick M. Westfeldt (Retired)	Peter C. Houtsma
William C. McClearn	John M. Husband
Harry L. Hobson	John M. Vaught
Gordon G. Greiner	Brian Muldoon
William E. Murane	Jeffrey T. Johnson
John S. Castellano	Scott S. Barker
Robert E. Benson	Timothy M. Rastello
Stephen H. Foster (Not admitted in CO)	John C. Tredennick, Jr.
	Maureen Reidy Witt
Jack L. Smith	Jack M. Englert, Jr.
R. Brooke Jackson	A. Bruce Jones
Wiley E. Mayne, Jr.	Daniel W. Patterson
Gregory A. Eurich	Geraldine A. Brimmer
Ronald M. Martin	Sandra R. Goldman
Gregory Russell Piché	Harry Shulman
Jane Michaels	Christopher H. Toll
James E. Hartley	Steven C. Choquette

SPECIAL COUNSEL

James J. Gonzales	Brian M. Mumaugh

ASSOCIATES

Margaret Althoff	Eric L. Hilty
Judith A. (Jude) Biggs	Sunhee Juhon
Steven W. Black	Ian S. Karpel
J. Kevin Bridston	Robert H. Kelly (Not admitted in CO)
Elizabeth Carney	
R. Dana Cephas	Stephen Masciocchi
Steven E. Christoffersen	Jane Lowell Montgomery
Donald A. Degnan	Fiona W. Ong
Robert P. Detrick	Lee R. Osman
Lynn Bolinske Dolven	David D. Powell, Jr.
Jimmy Goh	Carlos A. Samour, Jr.
Heather R. Hanneman	Alan N. Stern
Charles Henson	Craig E. Stewart

Stephanie D. Welsh

DENVER TECH CENTER, COLORADO RESIDENT PARTNERS

William W. Maywhort	Perry L. Glantz
Michael S. Beaver	Todd W. Miller

DENVER TECH CENTER RESIDENT OF COUNSEL

Mary D. Metzger

DENVER TECH CENTER, COLORADO RESIDENT ASSOCIATE

Rachel A. Yates

(See Next Column)

HOLLAND & HART—*Continued*

BOULDER, COLORADO PARTNERS

William E. Mooz, Jr.
Scott Havlick

BOULDER, COLORADO ASSOCIATE

Judith A. (Jude) Biggs

COLORADO SPRINGS, COLORADO PARTNERS

Ronald M. Martin
Edward H. Flitton (Resident)

COLORADO SPRINGS, COLORADO RESIDENT ASSOCIATE

David Scott Prince

BOISE, IDAHO RESIDENT PARTNERS

Walter H. Bithell
J. Frederick Mack
Larry E. Prince
B. Newal Squyres, Jr.
Steven B. Andersen

BOISE, IDAHO RESIDENT OF COUNSEL

Debra K. Ellers

BOISE, IDAHO RESIDENT ASSOCIATES

Kim J. Dockstader
Robert A. Faucher
Dana Lieberman Hofstetter
Kurt D. Holzer

BILLINGS, MONTANA PARTNERS

Stephen H. Foster
Paul D. Miller
Jeanne Matthews Bender
James M. Ragain

BILLINGS, MONTANA SPECIAL COUNSEL

Kyle A. Gray

BILLINGS, MONTANA RESIDENT ASSOCIATES

Bruce F. Fain
Patricia D. Peterman

CHEYENNE, WYOMING PARTNERS

Donald I. Schultz (P.C.)
Patrick R. Day (P.C.)
Edward W. Harris

CHEYENNE, WYOMING RESIDENT ASSOCIATES

Bradley T. Cave
Susan E. Laser-Bair
Richard Schneebeck

JACKSON, WYOMING RESIDENT PARTNER

Marilyn S. Kite (P.C.)

JACKSON RESIDENT OF COUNSEL

Stephen R. Duerr

SALT LAKE CITY UTAH RESIDENT PARTNER

Lawrence J. Jensen

For Complete List of Firm Personnel, See General Section

For full biographical listings, see the Martindale-Hubbell Law Directory

HOLME ROBERTS & OWEN LLC (AV)

Suite 4100, 1700 Lincoln, 80203
Telephone: 303-861-7000
Telex: 45-4460
Telecopier: 303-866-0200
Boulder, Colorado Office: Suite 400, 1401 Pearl Street.
Telephone: 303-444-5955.
Telecopier: 303-444-1063.
Colorado Springs, Colorado Office: Suite 1300, 90 South Cascade Avenue.
Telephone: 719-473-3800.
Telecopier: 719-633-1518.
Salt Lake City, Utah Office: Suite 1100, 111 East Broadway.
Telephone: 801-521-5800.
Telecopier: 801-521-9639.
London, England Office: 4th Floor, Mellier House, 26a Albemarle Street.
Telephone: 44-171-499-8776.
Telecopier: 44-171-499-7769.
Moscow, Russia Office: 14 Krivokolenny Pr., Suite 30, 101000.
Telephone: 095-925-7816.
Telecopier: 095-923-2726.

MEMBERS OF FIRM

Donald K. Bain
Lawrence L. Levin
Charles J. Kall
Edward J. McGrath
Richard R. Young (Managing Member, Colorado Springs Office)
Glenn E. Porzak (Managing Member, Boulder Office)
John R. Webb
Spencer T. Denison
Stephen E. Snyder
Jeffrey A. Chase
Brent V. Manning (Salt Lake City Office)
Richard L. Nagl (Colorado Springs Office)
Michael F. Browning (Boulder Office)
Charlotte Louise Neitzel
David S. Steefel
Henry W. Ipsen
Daniel J. Dunn
Kevin Michael Shea
Raymond L. Petros
Linnea Brown
Boyd N. Boland
John Leonard Watson
LeGrand R. Curtis, Jr. (Salt Lake City Office)
Robert Tuchman
Katherine Jean Peck
Bruce F. Black
Brent E. Rychener (Colorado Springs Office)
Susan E. Duffey Campbell (Colorado Springs Office)
Richard A. Johnson (Boulder Office)
David B. Wilson
James R. Ghiselli (Boulder Office)
Alan C. Bradshaw (Salt Lake City Office)
Patricia C. Tisdale
John D. McCarthy

(See Next Column)

MEMBERS OF FIRM (Continued)

James W. Spensley
Eric E. Johnson
Duncan E. Barber
Richard L. Gabriel

OF COUNSEL

A. Edgar Benton
Richard L. Schrepferman

SPECIAL COUNSEL

Thomas F. Dixon

ASSOCIATES

Jon Bernhardt
Michael W. Bruzga
Colin G. Harris
Kenneth W. Lund
Lawrence M. Zavadil

For Complete List of Firm Personnel, See General Section

For full biographical listings, see the Martindale-Hubbell Law Directory

IRELAND, STAPLETON, PRYOR & PASCOE, P.C. (AV)

Suite 2600, 1675 Broadway, 80202
Telephone: 303-623-2700
Telecopier: 303-623-2062

D. Monte Pascoe
Margaret L. Toal-Rossi
Lawrence P. Terrell

Representative Clients: Bank of Denver; Mountain States Bank; Central Bank of Denver, N.A.: Freeport-McMoran, Inc.; Price Waterhouse; Shaw Construction Co.

For Complete List of Firm Personnel, See General Section

For full biographical listings, see the Martindale-Hubbell Law Directory

JOHNSON, RUDDY, NORMAN & MCCONATY, A PROFESSIONAL CORPORATION (AV)

Ptarmigan Place - Suite 801, 3773 Cherry Creek Drive North, 80209-3866
Telephone: 303-388-7711
Telecopier: 303-388-1749

Roger F. Johnson
Robert Ruddy
Brian G. McConaty
Collie E. Norman

Thomas H. Anderson
Phil C. Pearson
Marci L. Laddusaw
Craig A. Sargent

OF COUNSEL

Gary H. Hemminger
Christine Ann Mullen

For full biographical listings, see the Martindale-Hubbell Law Directory

KENNEDY & CHRISTOPHER, P.C. (AV)

1616 Wynkoop Street, Suite 900, 80202
Telephone: 303-825-2700
Fax: 303-825-0434

Frank R. Kennedy
Daniel R. Christopher
Kim B. Childs
Elizabeth A. Starrs
Richard B. Caschette
Mark A. Fogg
Michael T. Mihm
Charles R. Ledbetter
Lisa B. Heintz
Ronald H. Nemirow
Barbara H. Glogiewicz
Dawn E. Mitzner
John R. Mann
Daniel R. McCune

OF COUNSEL

Paul E. Scott

Douglas J. Cox
Dean A. McConnell
Matthew S. Feigenbaum
Catherine O'Brien-Crum
Steven J. Picardi
Cheryl K. Hara
Nancy Hart-Edwards

Representative Clients: AETNA Casualty and Surety Co.; American Medical International; Blue Cross/Blue Shield of Colorado; COPIC; The Doctors Co.; Hartford Insurance Co.; Home Insurance Co.; St. Paul Fire and Marine Insurance Co.; PRMS, Colorado Insurance Guaranty Association.

For full biographical listings, see the Martindale-Hubbell Law Directory

LEVENTHAL AND BOGUE, P.C. (AV)

950 South Cherry Street, Suite 600, 80222
Telephone: 303-759-9945
Fax: 303-759-9692

Jim Leventhal
Jeffrey A. Bogue
Bruce J. Kaye
Natalie Brown
Victoria J. Koury
Kelly P. Roberts

Reference: Omni Bank.

For full biographical listings, see the Martindale-Hubbell Law Directory

LONG & JAUDON, P.C. (AV)

The Bailey Mansion, 1600 Ogden Street, 80218-1414
Telephone: 303-832-1122
FAX: 303-832-1348

(See Next Column)

LONG & JAUDON P.C., *Denver—Continued*

Lawrence A. Long (1908-1992)	Cecelia A. Fleischner
Joseph C. Jaudon, Jr.	Walter N. Houghtaling
David B. Higgins	Ellen Rubright Ivy
Frederick W. Long	Christine Anne Craigmile
Gary B. Blum	Carla M. LaRosa
Michael T. McConnell	Sheri Lyn Hood
Stephen P. Hopkins	Thomas C. Kearns, Jr.
Robert M. Baldwin	Michael Shaefer Drew
Dennis Woodfin Brown	Margaret J. Walton
Alan D. Avery	David H. Yun

OF COUNSEL

Michael T. DePinto

Representative Clients: St. Joseph Hospital, Inc.; King Soopers, Inc.; Aetna Casualty & Surety Co.; COPIC; The Doctors Co.; Home Insurance Company; Montgomery Wards.

For Complete List of Firm Personnel, See General Section

For full biographical listings, see the Martindale-Hubbell Law Directory

LOWERY AND LOWERY, P.C. (AV)

1999 Broadway, Suite 3800, 80202
Telephone: 303-296-1456
Telefax: 303-296-8538
Tempe, Arizona Office: 1707 E. Southern Avenue, Suite B, 85282.
Telephone: 602-831-1550.
Telefax: 602-838-5005.

Philip E. Lowery	Philip Scott Lowery

Marcella T. Clark	Spero A. Leon
Terri B. Cohen	Maria J. Murray

David L. Michael

References: Colorado State Bank; Bank of Denver; Jefferson Bank & Trust.

For full biographical listings, see the Martindale-Hubbell Law Directory

JOHN O. MARTIN, P.C. (AV)

5445 DTC Parkway, Suite 800 (Englewood), 80111
Telephone: 303-771-7010
Fax: 303-793-0692

John O. Martin

For full biographical listings, see the Martindale-Hubbell Law Directory

MONTGOMERY, GREEN, JARVIS, KOLODNY AND MARKUSSON, A PROFESSIONAL CORPORATION (AV)

Suite 2300, 1050 Seventeenth Street, 80265
Telephone: 303-534-4800
Fax: 303-595-3780
Fort Collins Office: 323 South College Avenue, Suite 2.
Telephone: 303-221-2800.
FAX: 303-221-0271.

C. Michael Montgomery	John W. Grund
James K. Green	John T. Van Voorhis
H. Keith Jarvis	Kevin F. Amatuzio
Joel A. Kolodny	Scott A. McGath
Dennis H. Markusson	Peter S. Dusbabek (Resident, Fort Collins Office)

Joyce L. Jenkins	James L. Gillies
Christopher J. Roberts	Christopher J. Kuelling
Jeffrey S. Greenblatt	Robert N. Clark (Resident, Fort Collins Office)
Thomas E. Napp	
Marc G. Lassman	Lorraine E. Parker

Representative Clients: Club Mediterranean; The Coca-Cola Co.; Commercial Union Insurance Cos.; Dow Chemical Co.; Dow Corning Corp.; Owens Corning Fiberglass Corp.; Sherwin-Williams; Target Stores, a division of Dayton Hudson Corp.; Travelers Insurance Cos.; Vulcan Materials Co.

For full biographical listings, see the Martindale-Hubbell Law Directory

MONTGOMERY LITTLE & MCGREW, P.C. (AV)

The Quadrant, 5445 DTC Parkway, Suite 800 (Englewood), 80111
Telephone: 303-773-8100
Telecopier: 303-220-0412

Roy E. Montgomery (1907-1986)	David A. Burlage
	Robert J. Beattie
Robert R. Montgomery	David L. Kelble, Jr.
David C. Little	Michael H. Smith
Dan McGrew	William H. ReMine, III
James J. Soran, III	Thomas C. Deline
Richard L. Murray, Jr.	Craig A. Adams
Kevin J. Kuhn	Robert J. Bruce
Brian K. Stutheit	Karen B. Best

(See Next Column)

John R. Riley	Christopher B. Little
Zion Avdi	Melinda L. Sanders
Rebecca B. Givens	Timothy M. Schulte
Theresa A. Raynor	Carole Salamaha
Daniel P. Murphy	James P. Campbell

James X. Quinn

OF COUNSEL

J. Bayard Young

Representative Clients: Amoco Oil Co.; Bristol-Myers Squibb; Colorado Medical Society; Chrysler Corporation; Cyprus Minerals; Dillon Cos., Inc., d/b/a King Soopers; The St. Paul Insurance Cos.; University of Colorado Health Sciences Center.

For Complete List of Firm Personnel, See General Section

For full biographical listings, see the Martindale-Hubbell Law Directory

MUSGRAVE & THEIS, P.C. (AV)

Mellon Financial Center, 1775 Sherman Street, Suite 2950, 80203
Telephone: 303-863-8686
Facsimile: 303-863-0423

B. Lawrence Theis	Bobbee J. Musgrave

Jane G. Ebisch	Nancy Lynne Bauer

OF COUNSEL

Thomas P. McMahon

Representative Clients: Anheuser-Busch Companies; City and County of Denver; Schuller International; Sashco, Inc.; Tri-County Cablevision, Inc.
Reference: Norwest Bank of Buckingham Square.

For full biographical listings, see the Martindale-Hubbell Law Directory

MYER, SWANSON & ADAMS, P.C. (AV)

The Colorado State Bank Building, 1600 Broadway, Suite 1850, 80202-4918
Telephone: 303-866-9800
Facsimile: 303-866-9818

Rendle Myer	Robert K. Swanson
Allan B. Adams	Thomas J. Wolf

Kevin M. Brady

OF COUNSEL

Robert Swanson	Fred E. Neef (1910-1986)

Representative Clients: The Oppenheimer Funds; Daily Cash Accumulation Fund; The Centennial Trusts; Mile High Chapter of American Red Cross; Master Lease; Heartland Management Company; Kan-Build of Colorado, Inc.
Reference: The Colorado State Bank of Denver.

For full biographical listings, see the Martindale-Hubbell Law Directory

NETZORG & MCKEEVER, PROFESSIONAL CORPORATION (AV)

5251 DTC Parkway (Englewood) Penthouse One, 80111
Telephone: 303-770-8200
Fax: 303-770-8342

Gordon W. Netzorg	Susan Bernhardt
J. Nicholas McKeever, Jr.	Cecil E. Morris, Jr.

For full biographical listings, see the Martindale-Hubbell Law Directory

OPPERMAN & ASSOCIATES, P.C. (AV)

Suite 410 Kittredge Building, 511 16th Street, 80202
Telephone: 303-623-1970
Telecopier: 303-893-9328

Marlin D. Opperman

William M. Schell	Timothy L. Goddard

Douglas S. Widlund

Representative Clients: Denver Urban Renewal Authority; City of Denver, Denver International Airport; City of Boulder, Colo.; City of Westminster, Colo.; City of Telluride, Colorado; City of Central City, Colorado; American Society of Farm Managers and Rural Appraisers, Inc.; City of Thornton.
Reference: Colorado National Bank.

For full biographical listings, see the Martindale-Hubbell Law Directory

PRYOR, CARNEY AND JOHNSON, A PROFESSIONAL CORPORATION (AV)

Carrara Place, Suite 400, 6200 South Syracuse Way (Englewood), P.O. Box 22003, 80222-0003
Telephone: 303-771-6200
Facsimile: 303-779-0740

(See Next Column)

PRYOR, CARNEY AND JOHNSON A PROFESSIONAL CORPORATION—*Continued*

Peter W. Pryor	Arlene V. Dykstra
Robert W. Carney	JoAnne M. Zboyan
Irving G. Johnson	Peggy S. Ball
W. Randolph Barnhart	Marilee E. Langhoff
Thomas L. Roberts	Michael J. McNally
Rodney R. Patula	Elizabeth C. Moran
David D. Karr	C. Gregory Tiemeier
Christopher N. Mammel	Todd E. Kastetter
Edward D. Bronfin	Daniel M. Hubbard
John L. Wheeler	Steven G. York
Scott S. Nixon	Nick S. Kaluk, Jr.
Bruce A. Montoya	Teresa L. Thraikill

Representative Clients: Olin Corp.; Hartford Accident & Indemnity Co.; State Mutual Companies; First Commercial Corp.; Big O Tire, Co.; Merrell-Dow Pharmaceuticals; Kaiser Foundation Health Plan of Colorado; Great West Life Assurance Co.; Nash-Finch Co.; National Medical Enterprises, Inc.

For Complete List of Firm Personnel, See General Section

For full biographical listings, see the Martindale-Hubbell Law Directory

PURVIS, GRAY, SCHUETZE & GORDON (AV)

303 East 17th Avenue, Suite 700, 80203
Telephone: 303-860-1888
Boulder, Colorado Office: The Exeter Building, Suite 501, 1050 Walnut Street.
Telephone: 303-442-3366.
Fax: 303-440-3688.

MEMBERS OF FIRM

William R. Gray	Robert A. Schuetze
John A. Purvis	Glen F. Gordon

For full biographical listings, see the Martindale-Hubbell Law Directory

REIMAN & ASSOCIATES, P.C. (AV)

1600 Broadway, Suite 1640, 80202
Telephone: 303-860-1500
Fax: 303-839-4380

Jeffrey Reiman

Marcie K. Bayaz	James Birch

For full biographical listings, see the Martindale-Hubbell Law Directory

REINHART, BOERNER, VAN DEUREN, NORRIS & RIESELBACH, P.C. (AV)

One Norwest Center, 1700 Lincoln Street, Suite 3725, 80203
Telephone: 303-831-0909
Fax: 303-831-4805
Milwaukee, Wisconsin Office: 1000 North Water Street.
Telephone: 414-298-1000.
Facsimile: 414-298-8097.
Madison, Wisconsin Office: 7617 Mineral Point Road, 53701-2020.
Telephone: 608-283-7900.
Fax: 608-283-7919.
Washington, D.C. Office: 601 Pennsylvania Avenue, N.W., North Building, Suite 750.
Telephone: 202-393-3636.
Fax: 202-393-0796.

Timothy G. Atkinson	Herbert A. Delap

Stephen C. Peters

David D. Pavek

Representative Clients: OnGuard Systems, Inc.; Club Sports International, Inc.

For full biographical listings, see the Martindale-Hubbell Law Directory

JOHN M. RICHILANO P.C. (AV)

1660 Wynkoop Suite 1160, 80202
Telephone: 303-893-8000
Telecopier: 303-893-8055

John M. Richilano

For full biographical listings, see the Martindale-Hubbell Law Directory

SHERMAN & HOWARD L.L.C. (AV)

Attorneys at Law
633 Seventeenth Street, Suite 3000, 80202
Telephone: 303-297-2900
Telecopier: 303-298-0940
Colorado Springs, Colorado Office: Suite 1500, 90 South Cascade Avenue, 80903.
Telephone: 719-475-2440.

(See Next Column)

Las Vegas, Nevada Office: Swendseid & Stern a member in Sherman & Howard L.L.C., 317 Sixth Street, 89101.
Telephone: 702-387-6073.
Reno, Nevada Office: Swendseid & Stern, a member in Sherman & Howard L.L.C., 50 West Liberty Street, Suite 660, 89501.
Telephone: 702-323-1980.

Christopher Lane	Kenneth B. Siegel
Hugh J. McClearn	Joseph J. Bronesky
Mark L. Fulford	Leanne B. DeVos

Cynthia P. Delaney

COUNSEL

Raymond J. Turner

Representative Clients: AT&T Corp.; Eastman Kodak Co.; Hathaway Corp.; Newmont Gold Corp.; Tele-Communications, Inc.

For Complete List of Firm Personnel, See General Section

For full biographical listings, see the Martindale-Hubbell Law Directory

TREECE, ALFREY & MUSAT, P.C. (AV)

Denver Place, 999 18th Street, Suite 1600, 80202
Telephone: 303-292-2700
Facsimile: 303-295-0414

Robert S. Treece	Thomas N. Alfrey

L. Richard Musat

Nancy L. Pearl	Evan M. Zuckerman
Kim D. Poletto	David T. Wexler
Alison F. Kyles	Robert N. Trigg
Michael L. Hutchinson	Paul E. Collins

Andrew S. Ford

OF COUNSEL

Duncan W. Cameron

For full biographical listings, see the Martindale-Hubbell Law Directory

EDWARD L. VOLPE, P.C. (AV)

Suite 780 Seventeenth and Grant Building, 303 East 17th Avenue, 80203
Telephone: 303-861-7800
Fax: 303-860-9364

Edward L. Volpe

For full biographical listings, see the Martindale-Hubbell Law Directory

WALLER AND MARK, P.C. (AV)

Penthouse 200, 1777 South Harrison Street, 80210
Telephone: 303-691-2922
Fax: 303-756-2815

William C. Waller, Jr.	Denis H. Mark

For full biographical listings, see the Martindale-Hubbell Law Directory

WALTERS & JOYCE, P.C. (AV)

2015 York Street, 80205
Telephone: 303-322-1404
FAX: 303-377-5668

William E. Walters, III	Craig D. Joyce

Anne Baudino Holton

Reference: Norwest Bank of Buckingham Square.

For full biographical listings, see the Martindale-Hubbell Law Directory

WELLER FRIEDRICH, LLC (AV)

One Civic Center, Suite 2000, 1560 Broadway, P.O. Box 989, 80201-0989
Telephone: 303-812-1200
FAX: 303-812-1212

Geoffrey S. Race	Mary A. Wells
David K. Kerr	James C. Tienken
Andrew J. Friedrich	Sheryl Lynn Anderson
Marc R. Brosseau	Jerome M. Joseph

Dennis J. Bartlett

OF COUNSEL

W. Robert Ward

Suanne Marie Dell	Kelly Koepp Robinson
Gregory E. Sopkin	Karen Martinson Girard

Fermin G. Montoya

Representative Clients: Abbott Laboratories; Associated Aviation Underwriters; Chrysler Corp.; Connaught Laboratories, Inc.; Great American Insurance Companies; Industrial Indemnity Co.; Maryland Casualty Co.; Royal Insurance Companies; State Farm Fire and Casualty Co.; Travelers Insurance Companies.

For full biographical listings, see the Martindale-Hubbell Law Directory

Denver—Continued

White and Steele, Professional Corporation (AV)

1225 17th Street, Suite 2800, 80202
Telephone: 303-296-2828
Telecopier: 303-296-3131
Cheyenne, Wyoming Office: 1912 Capital Avenue, Suite 404, 82003.
Telephone: 307-778-4160.

Lowell White (1897-1983)
Walter A. Steele
R. Eric Peterson
Stephen K. Gerdes
Michael W. Anderson
James M. Dieterich
Glendon L. Laird
John M. Lebsack
Stephen G. Sparr
John P. Craver
David J. Nowak
Sandra Spencer
John M. Palmeri
Frederick W. Klann
William F. Campbell, Jr.
Richard M. Kaudy
Peter W. Rietz
Kurt A. Horton
Stewart J. Rourke
Allan Singer
Michael J. Daugherty
Robert R. Carlson

Thomas B. Quinn
George A. Codding, III
Christopher P. Kenney
June Baker
Robert H. D. Coate
Monty L. Barnett
Joseph R. King

OF COUNSEL

Fred L. Witsell

Colorado Tort Counsel for: Goodyear Tire and Rubber Co.; The Dow Chemical Co.; Celotex.
Insurance Clients: Allied Insurance Co.; CNA; Kemper Insurance Group; Massachusetts Mutual Life Insurance Co.; U.S.A.A.; Underwriters at Lloyds; Farmers Insurance Group.

For Complete List of Firm Personnel, See General Section

For full biographical listings, see the Martindale-Hubbell Law Directory

Wood, Ris & Hames, Professional Corporation (AV)

1775 Sherman Street, Suite 1600, 80203-4317
Telephone: 303-863-7700
Telecopier: 303-830-8772

Edward L. Wood (1899-1974)
Stephen E. Connor
F. Michael Ludwig
Charles E. Weaver
Clayton B. Russell
Christopher M. Brandt
Mark R. Davis
Colin C. Campbell
Christian M. Lind
Jeffrey Clay Ruebel
Clifton J. Latiolais, Jr.
Mary E. Kanan
William H. Short
Dennis A. Hanson
Jennifer L. Veiga
Michel P. Williams
William A. Rogers, III

OF COUNSEL

William K. Ris
Eugene S. Hames

SPECIAL COUNSEL

E. Gregory Martin
Donald B. Gentry

Counsel for: American Family Insurance Company; American International Companies; Continental Insurance Companies; Equitable Life Assurance Society of the United States; Fireman's Fund Insurance Company; Home Insurance Company; Maryland Casualty Company; Metropolitan Life Insurance Company; Prudential Insurance Co. of America; Safeco Insurance Company.

For Complete List of Firm Personnel, See General Section

For full biographical listings, see the Martindale-Hubbell Law Directory

*DURANGO,** La Plata Co.

Shand, McLachlan & Newbold, P.C. (AV)

124 East Ninth Street, P.O. Drawer I, 81302-2790
Telephone: 303-247-3091
Fax: 303-247-3100

E. Bentley Hamilton (1918-1981)
J. Douglas Shand
Michael E. McLachlan
Keith Newbold

David A. Bode
A. Michael Chapman (Resident)
Sheryl Rogers

For full biographical listings, see the Martindale-Hubbell Law Directory

ENGLEWOOD, Arapahoe Co.

Banta, Hoyt, Greene & Everall, P.C. (AV)

Suite 555, 6300 South Syracuse Way, 80111
Telephone: 303-220-8000
Fax: 303-220-0153

Richard J. Banta
Stephen G. Everall

(See Next Column)

OF COUNSEL

Richard D. Greene
Craig E. Wagner

Representative Clients: American Institute of Timber Construction; Cherry Creek School District No. 5; City of Greenwood Village; Colorado School District Self Insurance Pool; Intermountain Rural Electric Association; Kiewit Western Co.; Littleton Public Schools; National Union Fire Insurance Co. (local); Southgate Sanitation and Water Districts.

For Complete List of Firm Personnel, See General Section

For full biographical listings, see the Martindale-Hubbell Law Directory

Thomas J. Tomazin, P.C. (AV)

Suite 200, 5655 South Yosemite, 80111
Telephone: 303-771-1900
FAX: 303-793-0923

Thomas J. Tomazin

Reference: Key Bank.

For full biographical listings, see the Martindale-Hubbell Law Directory

*GOLDEN,** Jefferson Co.

Bradley, Campbell, Carney & Madsen, Professional Corporation (AV)

1717 Washington Avenue, 80401-1994
Telephone: 303-278-3300
Fax: 303-278-3379

Leo N. Bradley
Victor F. Boog
Thomas A. Nolan
Jim Michael Hansen
Shelly M. Rowan
Dennis L. Arfmann

Counsel for: Adolph Coors Co.; Coors Brewing Co.; Evergreen National Bank, Evergreen, Colorado; Coors Ceramics Co.; Clear Creek National Bank, Georgetown, Colorado; ASARCO, Inc.; Morrison-Knudsen; Westinghouse Electric Corp.
Local Counsel for: Public Service Company of Colorado.
Reference: Colorado National Bank, Denver, Colorado.

For Complete List of Firm Personnel, See General Section

For full biographical listings, see the Martindale-Hubbell Law Directory

Holley, Albertson & Polk, P.C. (AV)

Suite 100, 1667 Cole Boulevard, 80401
Telephone: 303-233-7838
Fax: 303-233-2860

George Alan Holley
Scott D. Albertson
Dennis B. Polk

Eric E. Torgersen
Thomas A. Walsh
Howard R. Stone

Reference: First Bank of Wheat Ridge.

For full biographical listings, see the Martindale-Hubbell Law Directory

*GRAND JUNCTION,** Mesa Co.

Reams, Reams & Coff (AV)

660 White Avenue, P.O. Box 118, 81502
Telephone: 303-242-7847
Fax: 303-242-7849

Warren F. Reams
Charles F. Reams
Harry E. Coff, Jr.
Kevin R. Kennedy

Representative Clients: American States Insurance Co.; Amwest Surety Ins. Co.; Farmer's Group of Ins. Cos.; National Farmers' Union; Pafco General Insurance Co.; Union Insurance Co.; United Fire & Casualty Co.; State Farm National Auto. Ins. Co.

For full biographical listings, see the Martindale-Hubbell Law Directory

*GREELEY,** Weld Co.

Brega & Winters, P.C. (AV)

1100 Tenth Street, Suite 402, 80631
Telephone: 303-352-4805
Fax: 303-352-6547
Denver, Colorado Office: One United Bank Center. 1700 Lincoln Street, Suite 2222 Street.
Telephone: 303-866-9400.
FAX: 303-861-9109.

Jerry D. Winters
Pamela A. Shaddock

Bradley D. Laue

For full biographical listings, see the Martindale-Hubbell Law Directory

LAKEWOOD, Jefferson Co.

PLAUT LIPSTEIN MORTIMER PC (AV)

Suite C-400, 12600 West Colfax Avenue, 80215
Telephone: 303-232-5151
Fax: 303-232-5161
Denver, Colorado Office: 2750 Lincoln Center. 1660 Lincoln Street, 80264.
Telephone: 303-232-5154.

Frank Plaut | Evan S. Lipstein
Charles E. Mortimer, Jr.

For full biographical listings, see the Martindale-Hubbell Law Directory

POLIDORI, GEROME, FRANKLIN AND JACOBSON (AV)

Suite 300, 550 South Wadsworth Boulevard, 80226
Telephone: 303-936-3300
Fax: 303-936-0125

Gary L. Polidori | Dennis J. Jacobson
R. Jerold Gerome | Peter L. Franklin

Lesleigh S. Monahan | Barry J. Seidenfeld

Representative Clients: Lakewood City Center; Treeforms, Inc.; Lakewood Chrysler-Plymouth, Inc.; Western Fasteners U.S.A., Inc.; Horizon Glass and Glazing Co., Inc.; Grif-Fab Corp.; Fred Schmid Appliance and TV Co., Inc.; Commercial Architectural Products, Inc.; Voyaguers International, Inc.; 1st Bank, Villa Italia.

For full biographical listings, see the Martindale-Hubbell Law Directory

*LAMAR,** Prowers Co.

JOHN GEHLHAUSEN, P.C. (AV)

200 South Fifth Street, Drawer 1079, 81052
Telephone: 719-336-9071
Fax: Available Upon Request

John Gehlhausen

Darla Scranton Specht

For full biographical listings, see the Martindale-Hubbell Law Directory

*MONTROSE,** Montrose Co.

EDWARD D. DURHAM (AV)

524 South First Street, P.O. Box 1721, 81402
Telephone: 303-249-2274
Fax: 303-249-6482

Reference: Norwest Bank of Montrose.

For full biographical listings, see the Martindale-Hubbell Law Directory

VAIL, Eagle Co.

DUNN, ABPLANALP & CHRISTENSEN, P.C. (AV)

Suite 300 Vail National Bank Building, 108 South Frontage Road West, 81657-5087
Telephone: 303-476-0300
Telecopier: 303-476-4765

John W. Dunn | Allen C. Christensen
Diane L. Herman

SPECIAL COUNSEL

Jerry W. Hannah

Representative Clients: Towns of Avon, Minturn and Red Cliff, Colorado.

For Complete List of Firm Personnel, See General Section

For full biographical listings, see the Martindale-Hubbell Law Directory

CONNECTICUT

*BRIDGEPORT,** Fairfield Co.

BAI, POLLOCK AND DUNNIGAN, P.C. (AV)

Park City Plaza, 10 Middle Street, P.O. Box 1978, 06604
Telephone: 203-366-7991
Fax: 203-366-4723

Arnold J. Bai (1931-1992) | Jeffrey A. Blueweiss
Paul E. Pollock | Garie J. Mulcahey
Keith D. Dunnigan | Raymond J. Plouffe, Jr.
James E. Coyne | Philip F. von Kuhn
Madonna A. Sacco

(See Next Column)

Michael S. Lynch | Gaileen A. Kaufman
Susan M. Wood | Kevin S. Coyne
David J. Robertson | Colleen D. Fries
Edward P. Brady III | Neal P. Rogan
Andrew S. Turret | Corrine H. Canace

For full biographical listings, see the Martindale-Hubbell Law Directory

GLADSTONE, SCHWARTZ, BLUM, WOODS, L.L.C. (AV)

1087 Broad Street, P.O. Box 1900, 06604
Telephone: 203-368-6746
Telecopier: 203-576-8847

MEMBERS OF FIRM

Lawrence B. Schwartz (1929-1993) | Louis I. Gladstone
Leonard C. Blum
Matthew B. Woods

ASSOCIATES

Arthur E. Miller | Jason P. Gladstone
Roberta S. Schwartz | Stacey M. Daves-ohlin

OF COUNSEL

Peter L. Leepson | Edward N. Lerner
Arthur A. Lunin

Counsel for: Baker Companies, Inc.; D'Addario Industries, Inc.; Connecticut Jai Alai, Inc.; McNeil Brothers, Inc.; IMG & Associates Ltd., Partnership.

For full biographical listings, see the Martindale-Hubbell Law Directory

WILLIAMS, COONEY & SHEEHY (AV)

One Lafayette Circle, 06604
Telephone: 203-331-0888
Telecopier: 203-331-0896

MEMBERS OF FIRM

Ronald D. Williams | Peter J. Dauk
Robert J. Cooney | Dion W. Moore
Edward Maum Sheehy | Ronald D. Williams, Jr.
Peter D. Clark | Francis A. Smith, Jr. (1951-1989)

Lawrence F. Reilly | Michael P. Bowler
Michael Cuff Deakin

Representative Clients: Aetna Life & Casualty Co.; Nationwide Insurance Co.; Connecticut Medical Insurance Co.; ; Zimmer Manufacturing Co.; Textron-Lycoming; The Stop & Shop Companies, Inc.; Shawmut Bank Connecticut, N.A.; Allied Van Lines, Inc.; Podiatary Insurance Company of America; Town of Easton, Conn.

For full biographical listings, see the Martindale-Hubbell Law Directory

CHESHIRE, New Haven Co.

DODD, LESSACK, RANANDO & DALTON, L.L.C. (AV)

700 West Johnson Avenue, Suite 305, 06410
Telephone: 203-272-1883
FAX: 203-272-2077

MEMBERS OF FIRM

Edward T. Dodd, Jr. | Paul S. Ranando
Ross T. Lessack | Mary-Margaret Dalton
Charles F. Senich

Jack Senich

For full biographical listings, see the Martindale-Hubbell Law Directory

GREENWICH, Fairfield Co.

ALBERT, WARD & JOHNSON, P.C. (AV)

125 Mason Street, P.O. Box 1668, 06836
Telephone: 203-661-8600
Telecopier: 203-661-8051

OF COUNSEL

David Albert

Tom S. Ward, Jr. | Jane D. Hogeman
Scott R. Johnson | Howard R. Wolfe

Christopher A. Kristoff

For full biographical listings, see the Martindale-Hubbell Law Directory

IVEY, BARNUM & O'MARA (AV)

Meridian Building, 170 Mason Street, P.O. Box 1689, 06830
Telephone: 203-661-6000
Telecopier: 203-661-9462

(See Next Column)

IVEY, BARNUM & O'MARA, *Greenwich—Continued*

MEMBERS OF FIRM

Michael J. Allen
Robert C. Barnum, Jr.
Edward D. Cosden, Jr.
James W. Cuminale
Wilmot L. Harris, Jr.
William I. Haslun, II
Edward T. Krumeich, Jr.
Donat C. Marchand
Miles F. McDonald, Jr.
Edwin J. O'Mara, Jr.
Remy A. Rodas
Gregory A. Saum
Lorraine Slavin

ASSOCIATES

Juerg A. Heim
Melissa Townsend Klauberg
Nicole Barrett Lecher
Alan S. Rubenstein

OF COUNSEL

Philip R. McKnight

For full biographical listings, see the Martindale-Hubbell Law Directory

*HARTFORD,** Hartford Co.

GORDON, MUIR AND FOLEY (AV)

Hartford Square North, Ten Columbus Boulevard, 06106-1944
Telephone: 203-525-5361
Telecopier: 203-525-4849

MEMBERS OF FIRM

William S. Gordon, Jr. (1946-1956)
George Muir (1939-1976)
Edward J. Foley (1955-1983)
Peter C. Schwartz
John J. Reid
John H. Goodrich, Jr.
R. Bradley Wolfe
Jon Stephen Berk
William J. Gallitto
Gerald R. Swirsky
Robert J. O'Brien
Philip J. O'Connor
Kenneth G. Williams
Chester J. Bukowski
Mary Ann Santacroce

ASSOCIATES

J. Lawrence Price
Mary Anne Alicia Charron
James G. Kelly
Kevin F. Morin
Claudia A. Baio
Patrick T. Treacy
Andrew J. Hern
Eileen Geel
Christopher L. Slack
Renee W. Dwyer
David B. Heintz

OF COUNSEL

Stephen M. Riley

Reference: Fleet Bank.

For full biographical listings, see the Martindale-Hubbell Law Directory

THOMAS P. HESLIN (AV)

40 Russ Street, 06106
Telephone: 203-549-3750

For full biographical listings, see the Martindale-Hubbell Law Directory

JACKSON, O'KEEFE AND PHELAN (AV)

36 Russ Street, 06106-1571
Telephone: 203-278-4040
Fax: 203-527-2500
West Hartford, Connecticut Office: 62 LaSalle Road.
Telephone: 203-521-7500.
Fax: 203-561-5399.
Bethlehem, Connecticut Office: 423 Munger Lane.
Telephone: 203-266-5255.

MEMBERS OF FIRM

Jay W. Jackson
Andrew J. O'Keefe
Denise Martino Phelan
Matthew J. O'Keefe
Peter K. O'Keefe
Philip R. Dunn, Jr.
Michael J. Walsh
Anna M. Carbonaro
Denise Rodosevich

OF COUNSEL

Maureen Sullivan Dinnan

Representative Clients: Aetna Casualty & Surety Co.; ITT Hartford; Liberty Mutual Insurance Co.; Connecticut Medical Insurance Co.

For full biographical listings, see the Martindale-Hubbell Law Directory

REGNIER, TAYLOR, CURRAN & EDDY (AV)

CityPlace, 06103-4402
Telephone: 203-249-9121
FAX: 203-527-4343

MEMBERS OF FIRM

J. Ronald Regnier (1906-1987)
Robert F. Taylor (1930-1994)
Edmund T. Curran
Ralph G. Eddy
Jack D. Miller

(See Next Column)

ASSOCIATES

Lawrence L. Connelli
A. Patrick Alcarez
Robert B. McLaughlin
Sandra L. Connelli
A. Alan Sheffy
Robert A. Byers
Jay F. Huntington
John D. Palermo
Frederick M. O'Brien
Keith Mccabe
Margaret H. Ralphs

Representative Clients: Atlantic Mutual Insurance Co.; Government Employees Insurance Co.; Hartford Accident & Indemnity Co.; Hartford Fire Insurance Co.; Pioneer Co-operative Fire; United Services Automobile Assn.

For full biographical listings, see the Martindale-Hubbell Law Directory

RISCASSI AND DAVIS, P.C. (AV)

131 Oak Street, P.O. Box 260550, 06126-0550
Telephone: 203-522-1196
FAX: 203-246-5847

William R. Davis

James D. Bartolini
Andrew S. Groher
Michael C. Jainchill
John J. Houlihan, Jr.
David W. Cooney
Eugene K. Swain
Kathryn Calibey
Douglas W. Hammond
Everett Howard Madin, Jr.
Paul M. Iannaccone

For full biographical listings, see the Martindale-Hubbell Law Directory

SOROKIN SOROKIN GROSS HYDE & WILLIAMS P.C. (AV)

One Corporate Center, 06103
Telephone: 203-525-6645
Fax: 203-522-1781
Simsbury, Connecticut Office: 730 Hopmeadow Street.
Telephone: 203-651-9348.
Rocky Hill, Connecticut Office: 2360 Main Street.
Telephone: 203-563-9305.
Fax: 203-529-6931.
Glastonbury, Connecticut Office: 124 Hebron Avenue.
Telephone: 203-659-8801.

John J. Bracken III
Clifford J. Grandjean
Jeffrey R. Martin
Lewis Rabinovitz
Richard C. Robinson

Jeffery P. Apuzzo
Jamie N. Cody

For Complete List of Firm Personnel, See General Section

For full biographical listings, see the Martindale-Hubbell Law Directory

*NEW HAVEN,** New Haven Co.

WILLIAM H. CLENDENEN, JR. A PROFESSIONAL CORPORATION (AV)

400 Orange Street, P.O. Box 301, 06502-0301
Telephone: 203-787-1183
Fax: 203-787-2847

William H. Clendenen, Jr.

James E. Clifford
Nancy L. Walker

For full biographical listings, see the Martindale-Hubbell Law Directory

DEL SOLE & DEL SOLE (AV)

Suite 410, 900 Chapel Street, P.O. Box 405, 06502-0405
Telephone: 203-785-8500
Fax: 203-777-4485

MEMBERS OF FIRM

Dominic P. Del Sole
Stephen P. Del Sole
Michael P. Del Sole
Lawrence A. Ouellette, Jr.
Janine W. Hodgson
Denise D. Kennedy

ASSOCIATES

Edward F. Piazza
Gregory P. Patti
Caroline C. Musmanno
Charles M. Fresher
Rene Gerard Martineau
Paula S. Giles

For full biographical listings, see the Martindale-Hubbell Law Directory

GALLAGHER GALLAGHER & CALISTRO (AV)

1377 Boulevard, P.O. Box 1925, 06509
Telephone: 203-624-4165
Fax: 203-865-5598

William F. Gallagher
Elizabeth A. Gallagher
Roger B. Calistro
Cynthia C. Bott
Barbara L. Cox

Approved Attorneys For: Chicago Title Insurance Co.; Security Title and Guaranty Co.; American Title Insurance Co.; Connecticut Savings Bank; Dime Savings Bank of Wallingford; New Haven Savings Bank; Essex Savings

(See Next Column)

GALLAGHER GALLAGHER & CALISTRO—*Continued*

Bank; Branford Savings Bank; First Federal Savings & Loan of Madison; First Constitution Bank.

For Complete List of Firm Personnel, See General Section

For full biographical listings, see the Martindale-Hubbell Law Directory

GREENFIELD AND MURPHY (AV)

234 Church Street, P.O. Box 1103, 06504-1103
Telephone: 203-787-6711
Telecopier: 203-777-6442

MEMBERS OF FIRM

James R. Greenfield
Helen D. Murphy
Maureen M. Murphy

Reference: Union Trust Co.

For full biographical listings, see the Martindale-Hubbell Law Directory

HOGAN & RINI, P.C. (AV)

Gold Building, 8th Floor 234 Church Street, 06510
Telephone: 203-787-4191
Telecopier: 203-777-4032

John W. Hogan, Jr.
Joseph L. Rini
Sue A. Cousineau

OF COUNSEL

Mark S. Cousineau

For full biographical listings, see the Martindale-Hubbell Law Directory

PAUL A. SCHOLDER ATTORNEY AT LAW, P.C. (AV)

2 Whitney Avenue, P.O. Box 1722, 06507
Telephone: 203-777-7218
Fax: 203-772-2672

Paul A. Scholder

John J. Morgan

References: Peoples Bank; Lafayette American Bank.

For full biographical listings, see the Martindale-Hubbell Law Directory

SHAY, SLOCUM & DEWEY (AV)

234 Church Street, P.O. Box 1921, 06509
Telephone: 203-772-3600
Fax: 203-787-4581

MEMBERS OF FIRM

Edward N. Shay
Shaun M. Slocum
Earl F. Dewey, II

ASSOCIATE

Kathryn J. Coassin

Representative Clients: Hartford Accident and Indemnity Co.; United Services Automobile Association; Commercial Union Insurance Co.; Atlantic Mutual Insurance Co.; Northbrook Insurance Co.; Safeco Insurance Co.; Andover Insurance Co.; National Interstate Transportation Insurance Specialists; First Financial Insurance Co.; Burlington Insurance Group.

For full biographical listings, see the Martindale-Hubbell Law Directory

SUSMAN, DUFFY & SEGALOFF, P.C. (AV)

55 Whitney Avenue, 06510-1300
Telephone: 203-624-9830
Telecopier: 203-562-8430
Mailing Address: P.O. Box 1684, New Haven, Connecticut, 06507-1684

Allen H. Duffy (1931-1986)
Michael Susman
James H. Segaloff
David A. Reif
Joseph E. Faughnan
Susan W. Wolfson
Laura M. Sklaver
Andrew R. Lubin
James J. Perito
Matthew C. Susman
Thomas E. Katon

Charles J. Filardi, Jr.
Jennifer L. Schancupp
Donna Decker Morris
Peter G. Kruzynski
Joshua W. Cohen

OF COUNSEL

Diana C. Ballard

For full biographical listings, see the Martindale-Hubbell Law Directory

WIGGIN & DANA (AV)

One Century Tower, 06508-1832
Telephone: 203-498-4400
Telefax: 203-782-2889
Hartford, Connecticut Office: One CityPlace.
Telephone: 203-297-3700.
FAX: 203-525-9380.

(See Next Column)

Stamford, Connecticut Office: Three Stamford Plaza, 301 Tresser Boulevard.
Telephone: 203-363-7600.
Telefax: 203-363-7676.

MEMBERS OF FIRM

S. Robert Jelley
William J. Doyle
William J. Egan
Shaun S. Sullivan
Jeremy G. Zimmermann
William H. Prout, Jr.
Mark R. Kravitz
Edward Wood Dunham
Alan G. Schwartz
Penny Quinn Seaman
Patrick J. Monahan, II (Resident at Hartford)
Robert M. Langer (Resident at Hartford)

ASSOCIATES

Jennifer S. Aniskovich
Jeffrey R. Babbin
Nancy A. Beatty
Penelope I. Bellamy
Ian E. Bjorkman
Joaquina L. Borges
Thomas L. Casagrande
Isabel E. Chenoweth
Tanya F. Clark
John F. Conway
Michelle Wilcox DeBarge
Eleanor Stuart Devane
Elizabeth P. Gilson
Gerald Lewis Harmon
Marcella Ann Hourihane
Kevin M. Kennedy
Andrea C. Kramer
Keith M. Krom
Eric P. Neff (Resident at Hartford)
Susan M. Neilson
Phyllis M. Pari
Bonnie Lynne Patten
Charles P. Reed
Kevin Christopher Shea
Harry M. Stokes
Littleton Waller Tazewell
Robert Tilewick
Janis Lynn Warrecker
Thomas J. Witt (Resident at Hartford)

For Complete List of Firm Personnel, See General Section

For full biographical listings, see the Martindale-Hubbell Law Directory

LAW OFFICES OF JOHN R. WILLIAMS (AV)

51 Elm Street, 06510
Telephone: 203-562-9931
Fax: 203-776-9494

ASSOCIATES

Diane Polan
Katrena Engstrom
Norman A. Pattis
Denise A. Bailey-Garris

Reference: Founders Bank.

For full biographical listings, see the Martindale-Hubbell Law Directory

NEW LONDON, New London Co.

FAULKNER & BOYCE, P.C. (AV)

216 Broad Street, P.O. Box 66, 06320
Telephone: 203-442-9900
Fax: 203-443-6428

MEMBERS OF FIRM

Dale Patrick Faulkner
Thomas W. Boyce, Jr.
Humbert J. Polito, Jr.

ASSOCIATES

Lucia M. Mercurio
Michael J. Quinn
Jane Richardson
Nicholas W. Burlingham

Reference: Shawmut Bank Connecticut.

For full biographical listings, see the Martindale-Hubbell Law Directory

WALLER, SMITH & PALMER, P.C. (AV)

52 Eugene O'Neill Drive, P.O. Box 88, 06320
Telephone: 203-442-0367
Telecopier: 203-447-9915
Old Lyme, Connecticut Office: 103-A Halls Road.
Telephone: 203-434-8063.

Edward B. O'Connell

Tracy M. Collins

General Counsel for: Colotone Group.
Counsel for: Union Trust Co.; Coastal Savings Bank; Cash Home Center, Inc.
Local Counsel for: Metropolitan Insurance Co.; Connecticut General Life Insurance Co.

For Complete List of Firm Personnel, See General Section

For full biographical listings, see the Martindale-Hubbell Law Directory

ORANGE, New Haven Co.

SCHINE & JULIANELLE, P.C. (AV)

Suite 28, 477 Boston Post Road, P.O. Box 905, 06477-3548
Telephone: 203-795-3563
FAX: 203-799-9655
Westport, Connecticut Office: Suite 100, 830 Post Road East.
Telephone: 203-226-6861.
FAX: 203-226-6866.

(See Next Column)

SCHINE & JULIANELLE P.C., *Orange—Continued*

Leonard A. Schine (1943-1982)
Robert L. Julianelle

Mary D. Mix
Patrick W. Frazier, Jr.
Natale V. Di Natale

OF COUNSEL

Lawrence W. Kanaga

Representative Client: Sacred Heart University.

For full biographical listings, see the Martindale-Hubbell Law Directory

SOUTHPORT, Fairfield Co.

BRODY AND OBER, P.C. (AV)

135 Rennell Drive, 06490
Telephone: 203-259-7405
Fax: 203-255-8572

Charles S. Brody (1894-1976)
Seth O. L. Brody
Stanley B. Garrell
Frank F. Ober
S. Giles Payne
William J. Britt
James M. Thorburn
Barbara S. Miller
Ronald B. Noren

Stephen L. Lichtman
Diane F. Martucci
Richard W. Mather

For full biographical listings, see the Martindale-Hubbell Law Directory

STAMFORD, Fairfield Co.

CHAPMAN & FENNELL (AV)

Three Landmark Square, 06901
Telephone: 203-353-8000
Telecopier: 203-353-8799
New York, New York Office: 330 Madison Avenue.
Telephone: 212-687-3600.
Washington, D.C. Office: 2000 L Street, N.W., Suite 200.
Telephone: 202-822-9351.

MEMBERS OF FIRM

John Haven Chapman
Philip M. Chiappone (Resident, New York, N.Y. Office)
Darrell K. Fennell (Resident, New York, N.Y. Office)
Peter S. Gummo
D. Seeley Hubbard
Eric S. Kamisher (Resident, New York, N.Y. Office)
Brian E. Moran
Victor L. Zimmermann, Jr.

ASSOCIATE

Barton Meyerhoff (Not admitted in CT)

OF COUNSEL

Kevin T. Hoffman
Carol E. Meltzer (Resident, New York, N.Y. Office)
Brainard S. Patton
E. Gabriel Perle (Not admitted in CT)
Victor J. Toth (Resident, Washington, D.C. Office)
Michael Winger (Resident, New York, N.Y. Office)

For full biographical listings, see the Martindale-Hubbell Law Directory

ROSENBLUM & FILAN (AV Ⓣ)

One Landmark Square, 06901
Telephone: 203-358-9200
Fax: 203-969-6140
White Plains, New York Office: 50 Main Street. 10606.
Telephone: 914-686-6100.
Fax: 914-686-6140.
New York, New York Office: 400 Madison Avenue. 10017.
Telephone: 212-888-8001.
Fax: 212-888-3331.

MEMBERS OF FIRM

Patrick J. Filan
James B. Rosenblum

Jeannine M. Foran
James F. Walsh
Kate E. Maguire
M. Karen Noble
James Newfield

OF COUNSEL

Lee Judy Johnson (Not admitted in CT)
Katherine Benesch (Not admitted in CT)
Theodore J. Greene
Jack L. Most
Richard M. Schwartz (Not admitted in CT)

For full biographical listings, see the Martindale-Hubbell Law Directory

RYAN, RYAN, JOHNSON, CLEAR & DELUCA (AV)

80 Fourth Street, P.O. Box 3057, 06905
Telephone: 203-357-9200
FAX: 203-357-7915
New York, New York Office: Park Avenue Atrium, 237 Park Avenue.
Telephone: 212-949-0722.

(See Next Column)

MEMBERS OF FIRM

Daniel E. Ryan, Jr.
W. Patrick Ryan
Jon Paul Johnson
Michael Gene Clear
Charles A. Deluca
Daniel E. Ryan, III
Michael T. Ryan
Charles M. McCaghey
John W. Mullin

ASSOCIATES

Elizabeth W. Carter
Beverly J. Hunt
Holly K. Dustin
Gary R. Khachian
Joan P. Freydberg
Laureen V. Holland
Richard P. Colbert
John F. Leydon, Jr.
Barbara J. Pulaski
Thomas J. O'Neill
Robert C.E. Laney

For full biographical listings, see the Martindale-Hubbell Law Directory

SILVER, GOLUB & TEITELL (AV)

184 Atlantic Street, P.O. Box 389, 06904
Telephone: 203-325-4491
FAX: 203-325-3769

MEMBERS OF FIRM

Richard A. Silver
David S. Golub
Ernest F. Teitell
Elaine T. Silver

John D. Josel
Mario DiNatale
Jonathan M. Levine
Marilyn J. Ramos
Jack Zaremski (Not admitted in CT)

For Complete List of Firm Personnel, See General Section

For full biographical listings, see the Martindale-Hubbell Law Directory

WOFSEY, ROSEN, KWESKIN & KURIANSKY (AV)

600 Summer Street, 06901
Telephone: 203-327-2300
FAX: 203-967-9273

MEMBERS OF FIRM

Abraham Wofsey (1915-1944)
Michael Wofsey (1927-1951)
David M. Rosen (1926-1967)
Julius B. Kuriansky (1910-1992)
Monroe Silverman
Emanuel Margolis
Howard C. Kaplan
Anthony R. Lorenzo
Edward M. Kweskin
David M. Cohen
Marshall Goldberg
Stephen A. Finn
Judith Rosenberg
Robert L. Teicher
Mark H. Henderson

Steven D. Grushkin

OF COUNSEL

Saul Kwartin
Sydney C. Kweskin (Retired)

ASSOCIATES

Brian Bandler
John J.L. Chober
Steven M. Frederick
Eric M. Higgins
James A. Lenes
Valerie E. Maze
Maurice K. Segall
Randall M. Skigen
Gregory J. Williams

Representative Clients: Benenson Realty; Cellular Information Systems, Inc.; Gateway Bank; Hartford Provision Company; Louis Dreyfus Corp.; Norwalk Federation of Teachers; Patient Care, Inc.; People's Bank; Ridgeway Shopping Center and Stamford Housing Authority.

For full biographical listings, see the Martindale-Hubbell Law Directory

WATERBURY, New Haven Co.

TINLEY, NASTRI & RENEHAN (AV)

161 North Main Street, 06702
Telephone: 203-596-9030
Fax: 203-596-9036

Jeffrey J. Tinley
Robert Nastri, Jr.
Richard P. Renehan
Mary Piscatelli Brigham
William T. Blake, Jr.

Representative Clients: Center Capital Corporation; Citizens Fidelity Bank & Trust Co.; Gar-San Corporation; General Electric Capital Commercial Automotive Finance Inc.; Mahler Financial Group Inc.; Mobil Oil Corporation; St. Mary's Hospital; Teikyo Post University.

For full biographical listings, see the Martindale-Hubbell Law Directory

WEST HARTFORD, Hartford Co.

ADINOLFI, O'BRIEN & HAYES, P.C. (AV)

Corporate Center West, 433 South Main Street, 06110-1692
Telephone: 203-561-5020
Facsimile: 203-561-0229

Joseph Adinolfi, Jr.
Joseph A. O'Brien
Valentino D. Clementino
Edward W. Case
Stephen H. Minich

(See Next Column)

ADINOLFI, O'BRIEN & HAYES P.C.—*Continued*

Representative Clients: Aetna Casualty & Surety Co.; Olivetti Corporation of America; Viking Glass Co. (Manufacturing); Associated Construction Co. (General Contractors); Cummings Insulation Co. (Sub-Contractors); Adwst Bank; Shawmut Manufacturing Co.
Reference: Fleet Bank, N.A.

For full biographical listings, see the Martindale-Hubbell Law Directory

WESTPORT, Fairfield Co.

ANDREW B. BOWMAN (AV)

1804 Post Road East, 06880
Telephone: 203-259-0599
Fax: 203-255-2570

Reference: Peoples Bank.

For full biographical listings, see the Martindale-Hubbell Law Directory

LAWRENCE W. KANAGA (AV)

830 Post Road East, 06880-5291
Telephone: 203-221-0696
Fax: 203-226-6866
(Also Of Counsel to Schine, Julianelle & De Barbieri, P.C.)

For full biographical listings, see the Martindale-Hubbell Law Directory

STUART A. MCKEEVER (AV)

155 Post Road, East, 06880
Telephone: 203-227-4756
Fax: 203-454-2031

Reference: Fleet Bank.

For full biographical listings, see the Martindale-Hubbell Law Directory

ALAN NEIGHER (AV)

1804 Post Road East, 06880
Telephone: 203-259-0599
Fax: 203-255-2570
Telex: 238198 TLXAUR

OF COUNSEL

Judith M. Trutt

For full biographical listings, see the Martindale-Hubbell Law Directory

LAW OFFICES OF PAUL J. PACIFICO (AV)

12 Avery Place, Second Floor, 06880
Telephone: 203-221-8066
Fax: 203-221-8076

LEGAL SUPPORT PERSONNEL

Karen L. Kosinski

For full biographical listings, see the Martindale-Hubbell Law Directory

WEISMAN & LUBELL (AV)

5 Sylvan Road South, P.O. Box 3184, 06880
Telephone: 203-226-8307
Telecopier: 203-221-7279

MEMBERS OF FIRM

Lawrence P. Weisman
Ellen B. Lubell

Andrew R. Tarshis

For full biographical listings, see the Martindale-Hubbell Law Directory

DELAWARE

*DOVER,** Kent Co.

BARROS, MCNAMARA, SCANLON, MALKIEWICZ & TAYLOR, PROFESSIONAL ASSOCIATION (AV)

State & Loockerman Streets, P.O. Box 1298, 19903-1298
Telephone: 302-734-8400
Telefax: 302-734-4349

A. Richard Barros
Edward R. McNamara
Patrick Scanlon
Michael J. Malkiewicz
Robert J. Taylor
James J. Lazzeri

Bradley S. Eaby
Elizabeth Y. Olsen

Representative Clients: Delaware State Music Teachers Assn.; Sears Roebuck & Co.

For full biographical listings, see the Martindale-Hubbell Law Directory

PARKOWSKI, NOBLE & GUERKE, PROFESSIONAL ASSOCIATION (AV)

116 West Water Street, P.O. Box 598, 19903
Telephone: 302-678-3262
Telecopier: 302-678-9415

F. Michael Parkowski
John W. Noble
I. Barry Guerke
Clay T. Jester
Jeremy W. Homer
John C. Andrade
Jonathan Eisenberg
Donald R. Kinsley

Dana J. Schaefer

OF COUNSEL

George F. Gardner, III

Representative Clients: Delaware Solid Waste Authority; Cabe Associates (Consulting Engineers).
Approved Attorneys for: Ticor Title Insurance Co.
Reference: First National Bank of Wyoming.

For full biographical listings, see the Martindale-Hubbell Law Directory

*WILMINGTON,** New Castle Co.

ASHBY & GEDDES (AV)

One Rodney Square, P.O. Box 1150, 19899
Telephone: 302-654-1888
FAX: 302-654-2067

MEMBERS OF FIRM

Lawrence C. Ashby
James McC. Geddes
Stephen E. Jenkins
Randall E. Robbins
Steven J. Balick

ASSOCIATES

Regina A. Iorii
William P. Bowden
Richard D. Heins
Philip Trainer, Jr.
Amy Arnott Quinlan
Steven T. Margolin
Christopher S. Sontchi
John S. Grimm

For full biographical listings, see the Martindale-Hubbell Law Directory

BIGGS AND BATTAGLIA (AV)

1800 Mellon Bank Center, P.O. Box 1489, 19899-1489
Telephone: 302-655-9677

MEMBERS OF FIRM

Victor F. Battaglia
Alan W. Behringer
Francis S. Babiarz
Robert D. Goldberg
Robert K. Beste, Jr.
Jeffrey S. Marlin
Philip B. Bartoshesky
Victor F. Battaglia, Jr.
Christopher J. Battaglia
David L. Finger
Linda F. Shopland

OF COUNSEL

John Biggs, III
Gerard P. Kavanaugh, Sr.
S. Bernard Ableman

For full biographical listings, see the Martindale-Hubbell Law Directory

CASARINO, CHRISTMAN & SHALK (AV)

Suite 1220, 222 Delaware Avenue, P.O. Box 1276, 19899
Telephone: 302-594-4500
Telecopier: 302-594-4509

MEMBERS OF FIRM

Stephen P. Casarino
Colin M. Shalk
Beth H. Christman

Donald M. Ransom
Kenneth M. Doss

For full biographical listings, see the Martindale-Hubbell Law Directory

KIMMEL, WEISS & CARTER, P.A. (AV)

12th Floor, 913 Market Street, P.O. Box 272, 19899-0272
Telephone: 302-571-0800

Morton Richard Kimmel
Michael Weiss
Edward B. Carter, Jr.

Thomas J. Roman
William Peltz
Michael D. Bednash
Matthew M. Bartkowski

Reference: Wilmington Trust Co.; Delaware Trust Co.

For full biographical listings, see the Martindale-Hubbell Law Directory

EUGENE J. MAURER, JR., P.A. (AV)

1201-A King Street, 19801
Telephone: 302-652-7900
Fax: 302-652-2173

(See Next Column)

EUGENE J. MAURER, JR., P.A., *Wilmington—Continued*

Eugene J. Maurer, Jr. Marilou A. Szymanski

For full biographical listings, see the Martindale-Hubbell Law Directory

MORRIS, JAMES, HITCHENS & WILLIAMS (AV)

222 Delaware Avenue, P.O. Box 2306, 19899-2306
Telephone: 302-888-6800
Telecopier: 302-571-1750
Dover, Delaware Office: Suite 202, 32 West Loockerman Street, 19904.
Telephone: 302-678-8815.
Telecopier: 302-678-9063.

MEMBERS OF FIRM

Henry N. Herndon, Jr. P. Clarkson Collins, Jr.
George C. Hering, III Richard Galperin
Alfred M. Isaacs Steven R. Director
Grover C. Brown Barbara D. Crowell
William R. Hitchens, Jr. Richard D. Kirk
Richard P. Beck Lewis H. Lazarus
Glenn E. Hitchens (Resident at Dover) Francis J. Jones, Jr.
Daniel P. McCollom
Edward M. McNally Barbara MacDonald
Norris P. Wright Joanne B. Wills
James W. Semple Kent A. Jordan
David H. Williams Robert L. Symonds, Jr.
John D. Demmy

ASSOCIATES

Maureen M. Blanding Peter A. Pietra
Mary M. Culley Bruce Charles Doeg
Sherry C. McReynolds Walter Hamberg, III
Joseph R. Slights, III Janet M. Burris
Neal C. Belgam (Not admitted in DE)
Norman M. Powell Joseph C. Schoell
Eileen K. Andersen Eric D. Schwartz
Gretchen S. Knight John T. Meli, Jr.
Matthew J. O'Toole

OF COUNSEL

Howard L. Williams William F. Lynch, II

For full biographical listings, see the Martindale-Hubbell Law Directory

POTTER ANDERSON & CORROON (AV)

350 Delaware Trust Building, P.O. Box 951, 19899-0951
Telephone: 302-658-6771
FAX: 658-1192; 655-1190; 655-1199

MEMBERS OF FIRM

Charles S. Crompton, Jr. Gregory A. Inskip
Robert K. Payson David J. Baldwin
Richard E. Poole John E. James
Michael D. Goldman W. Harding Drane, Jr.
James F. Burnett Richard L. Horwitz
Daniel F. Wolcott, Jr. William J. Marsden, Jr.
David B. Brown Kathleen Furey McDonough
Somers S. Price, Jr. Laurie Selber Silverstein
Donald J. Wolfe, Jr. Peter J. Walsh, Jr.
Stephen C. Norman

ASSOCIATES

Arthur L. Dent Lewis C. Ledyard, III
David L. Baumberger Joanne Ceballos
William R. Denny Eric T. Kirschner
Peter L. Tracey Gayle P. Lafferty
Jennifer G. Gimler Wendy K. Voss

Representative Clients: Monsanto Company; North American Philips Corporation; KAO Corporation; Delmarva Power & Light Company; General Motors Corporation; Chrysler Corporation; Delaware Trust Company; University of Delaware; Conrail; Hercules, Incorporated.

For Complete List of Firm Personnel, See General Section

For full biographical listings, see the Martindale-Hubbell Law Directory

ROSENTHAL, MONHAIT, GROSS & GODDESS, P.A. (AV)

Suite 214 First Federal Plaza, P.O. Box 1070, 19899-1070
Telephone: 302-656-4433
Telecopier: 302-658-7567

Joseph A. Rosenthal Norman M. Monhait
Kevin Gross Jeffrey S. Goddess

Carmella Piscopo Keener

Counsel for: Delaware Incorporating Company.

For full biographical listings, see the Martindale-Hubbell Law Directory

SMITH, KATZENSTEIN & FURLOW (AV)

1220 Market Building, P.O. Box 410, 19899
Telephone: 302-652-8400
FAX: 302-652-8405

(See Next Column)

MEMBERS OF FIRM

Craig B. Smith Anne E. Bookout
Clark W. Furlow Susan L. Parker
Robert J. Katzenstein Vicki A. Hagel
David A. Jenkins Laurence V. Cronin

Brett D. Fallon Kathleen M. Miller
Michele C. Gott Patricia A. Garthwaite

For Complete List of Firm Personnel, See General Section

For full biographical listings, see the Martindale-Hubbell Law Directory

TRZUSKOWSKI, KIPP, KELLEHER & PEARCE, P.A. (AV)

1020 North Bancroft Parkway, P.O. Box 429, 19899-0429
Telephone: 302-571-1782
Fax: 302-571-1638

Francis J. Trzuskowski Robert K. Pearce
James F. Kipp Edward F. Kafader
Daniel F. Kelleher Francis J. Schanne

For full biographical listings, see the Martindale-Hubbell Law Directory

TYBOUT, REDFEARN & PELL (AV)

Suite 1100, PNC Bank Building, 300 Delaware Avenue, P.O. Box 2092, 19899
Telephone: 302-658-6901
FAX: 658-4018

F. Alton Tybout Anne L. Naczi
B. Wilson Redfearn Nancy E. Chrissinger
Richard W. Pell David G. Culley

ASSOCIATES

Sherry Ruggiero Fallon Michael I. Silverman
Sean A. Dolan Bernadette M. Plaza
Elizabeth Daniello Maron Joel R. Brown
Francis X. Nardo John J. Klusman, Jr.
Todd M. Finchler

Representative Clients: CIGNA Ins., Co.; Liberty Mutual Ins., Co.; Hartford Ins., Co.; Universal Underwriters; PHICO; State of Delaware; GAB Business Services Inc.; State Farm Ins., Co.; Alliance of American Insurers; Insurance Guarantee Assn.

For full biographical listings, see the Martindale-Hubbell Law Directory

DISTRICT OF COLUMBIA

WASHINGTON, D.C. Co.

* indicates certain Bar Register subscribers, in cities of comparable size and importance, who maintain an additional office in Washington, D.C. and who have arranged for representation as a part of the Washington, D.C. listings that follow

THE ABELSON LAW FIRM (AV)

Suite 300, 1000 Sixteenth Street, N.W., 20036
Telephone: 202-331-0600
Fax: 202-429-9088

Michael A. Abelson

For full biographical listings, see the Martindale-Hubbell Law Directory

*** ANDERSON KILL OLICK & OSHINSKY (AV)**

2000 Pennsylvania Avenue, N.W. Suite 7500, 20006
Telephone: 202-728-3100
Telecopier: 202-728-3199
New York, N.Y. Office: Anderson Kill Olick & Oshinsky, P.C., 1251 Avenue of the Americas.
Telephone: 212-278-1000.
Fax: 212-278-1733 and 212-953-7249.
Philadelphia, Pennsylvania Office: Anderson Kill Olick & Oshinsky, P.C. 1600 Market Street.
Telephone: 215-568-4202.
Telecopier: 215-568-4573.
Newark, New Jersey Office: Anderson Kill Olick & Oshinsky, P.C. One Gateway Center, Suite 901.
Telephone: 201-642-5858.
Telecopier: 201-621-6361.
San Francisco, California Office: Anderson Kill Olick & Oshinsky, P.C., One Sansome Street, Suite 1610.
Telephone: 415-677-1450.
Telecopier: 415-677-1475.
New Haven, Connecticut Office: Anderson Kill Olick & Oshinsky, P.C., 59 Elm Street.
Telephone: 203-777-2230.
Telecopier: 203-777-9717.

(See Next Column)

ANDERSON KILL OLICK & OSHINSKY—*Continued*

Phoenix, Arizona Office: Anderson Kill Olick & Oshinsky, P.C., One Renaissance Square, Two North Central, Suite 1250.
Telephone: 602-252-0002.
Telecopier: 602-252-0003.

Karen L. Bush
Robert L. Carter, Jr.
Suzan F. Charlton
Dana M. Dicarlo
Neal Dittersdorf (Not admitted in DC)
David L. Elkind
Barry J. Fleishman
Eric Taylor Gormsen (Not admitted in DC)
Gerald S. Hartman
Gregory W. Homer
Joseph V. Jest
Leon B. Kellner (Not admitted in DC)
Mark H. Kolman
Lorelie S. Masters
Karen L. Meengs
John E. Menditto
Mark E. Miller (Not admitted in DC)
Michael A. Nardolilli
Rhonda D. Orin
Jerold Oshinsky
Andrew M. Reidy
Dirk R. Rountree
Murray D. Sacks
Catherine J. Serafin (Not admitted in DC)
Joseph D. Tydings
James R. Wagner
Stephan G. Weil
Kent T. Withycombe (Not admitted in DC)

For Complete List of Firm Personnel, See General Section

For full biographical listings, see the Martindale-Hubbell Law Directory

ANDERSON & QUINN (AV)

1220 L Street, N.W., Suite 540, 20005
Telephone: 202-371-1245
Rockville, Maryland Office: Adams Law Center, 25 Wood Lane.
Telephone: 301-762-3303.
FAX: 301-762-3776.

MEMBERS OF FIRM

Charles C. Collins (1900-1973)
Robert E. Anderson (Retired)
Francis X. Quinn
William Ray Scanlin
Donald P. Maiberger

ASSOCIATE

Richard L. Butler

Representative Clients: C & P Telephone; Commercial Union Insurance Cos.; Allstate Insurance Co.; State Farm Mutual Automobile Insurance Co.; Northbrook Insurance Cos.; Travelers Insurance Co.; National General Insurance Co.; American International Adjustment Co.; Marriott Corp.

For Complete List of Firm Personnel, See General Section

For full biographical listings, see the Martindale-Hubbell Law Directory

ASBILL, JUNKIN & MYERS, CHTD. (AV)

1615 New Hampshire Avenue, N.W., 20009
Telephone: 202-234-9000
Facsimile: 202-332-6480
Alexandria, Virginia Office: 317 South Patrick Street.
Telephone: 703-684-7900.
Rockville, Maryland Office: Suite 315, 200-A Monroe Street.
Telephone: 301-294-0460.

Henry W. Asbill
Timothy deForest Junkin
Matthew L. Myers
Lenard B. Boss
Terrance G. Reed

Lauren Clingan

For full biographical listings, see the Martindale-Hubbell Law Directory

*** BAKER & BOTTS, L.L.P. (AV)**

A Registered Limited Liability Partnership
The Warner, 1299 Pennsylvania Avenue, N.W., 20004-2400
Telephone: 202-639-7700
Fax: 202-639-7832
Houston, Texas Office: One Shell Plaza, 910 Louisiana.
Telephone: 713-229-1234.
Austin, Texas Office: 1600 San Jacinto Center, 98 San Jacinto Boulevard.
Telephone: 512-322-2500.
Dallas, Texas Office: 2001 Ross Avenue.
Telephone: 214-953-6500.
New York, New York Office: 805 Third Avenue, Suite 2000.
Telephone: 212-705-5000.
Moscow, Russian Federation Office: 10 ul. Pushkinskaya, 103031.
Telephone: 7095/921-5300 (Local); 7501/929-7070 (International).

MEMBERS OF FIRM

Bruce F. Kiely
Charles M. Darling, IV
Randolph Quaile McManus
Thomas J. Eastment
Steven R. Hunsicker
Kirk K. Van Tine
John B. Veach, III

(See Next Column)

ASSOCIATES

Jesse R. Adams, III
Drew J. Fossum
Jacqueline R. Helmberger (Not admitted in DC)
Wendy J. Lang
Jennifer S. Leete (Not admitted in DC)
Mark K. Lewis
Martin Schaefermeier
David A. Super
Cheryl J. Walker

For Complete List of Firm Personnel, See General Section

For full biographical listings, see the Martindale-Hubbell Law Directory

BAKER & HOSTETLER (AV)

Washington Square, Suite 1100, 1050 Connecticut Avenue, N.W., 20036-5304
Telephone: 202-861-1500
In Cleveland, Ohio: 3200 National City Center, 1900 East Ninth Street.
Telephone: 216-621-0200.
In Columbus, Ohio: Capitol Square, Suite 2100, 65 East State Street.
Telephone: 614-228-1541.
In Denver, Colorado: 303 East 17th Avenue, Suite 1100.
Telephone: 303-861-0600.
In Houston, Texas: 1000 Louisiana, Suite 2000.
Telephone: 713-751-1600.
In Long Beach, California: 300 Oceangate, Suite 620.
Telephone: 310-432-2827.
In Los Angeles, California: 600 Wilshire Boulevard.
Telephone: 213-624-2400.
In Orlando, Florida: SunBank Center, Suite 2300, 200 South Orange Avenue.
Telephone: 305-841-1111.
In College Park, Maryland: 9658 Baltimore Boulevard, Suite 206.
Telephone: 301-441-2781.
In Alexandria, Virginia: 437 North Lee Street.
Telephone: 703-549-1294.
In San Francisco, California: One Sansome Street, Suite 2000.
Telephone: 415-951-4705.

MEMBER OF FIRM IN WASHINGTON, D.C.

William H. Schweitzer (Managing Partner, Washington, D.C. Office)

PARTNERS

Frederick W. Chockley, III
Mark A. Cymrot
Lee T. Ellis, Jr.
Leonard C. Greenebaum
Thomas Hylden
Richard J. Leon
Marshall Lee Miller
Bruce W. Sanford
Belinda Jayne Scrimenti

ASSOCIATES

Ralph G. Blasey, III
Margaret E. Goss
Robert D. Lystad
Kent W. McAllister (Not admitted in DC)
M. Tracy McPherson
Beth Elise Morrow
Gregory A. Paw

For Complete List of Firm Personnel, See General Section

For full biographical listings, see the Martindale-Hubbell Law Directory

*** BELL, BOYD & LLOYD (AV)**

1615 L Street, N.W., 20036
Telephone: 202-466-6300
FAX: 202-463-0678
Chicago, Illinois Office: Three First National Plaza, Suite 3300, 70 West Madison Street.
Telephone: 312-372-1121.
FAX: 312-372-2098.

RESIDENT PARTNERS

Raymond C. Fay
Thomas R. Gibbon
Neal A. Jackson

RESIDENT ASSOCIATE

Hillary L. Pettegrew

For Complete List of Firm Personnel, See General Section

For full biographical listings, see the Martindale-Hubbell Law Directory

BOOTHBY & YINGST (AV)

4545 42nd Street, N.W., 20016
Telephone: 202-363-1773
Fax: 202-363-0304
Berrien Springs, Michigan Office: 9047-4 US 31 North. P.O. Box 268.
Telephone: 616-471-7787.
Fax: 616-471-7400.

Lee Boothby
Robert A. Yingst

ASSOCIATE

Holly F. Underwood (Not admitted in DC)

For full biographical listings, see the Martindale-Hubbell Law Directory

Washington—Continued

BRAUDE & MARGULIES, P.C. (AV)

Suite 200, 1025 Connecticut Avenue, N.W., 20036
Telephone: 202-293-2993
Fax: 202-331-7916
Baltimore, Maryland Office: 1206 St. Paul Street.
Telephone: 410-234-0202.
Fax: 410-625-2872.
San Francisco, California Office: William R. Delaney, Citicorp Center, One Sansome Street, Suite 2000.
Telephone: 415-951-4709.
Fax: 415-951-4754.
Riyadh, Saudi Arabia Office: Mohammed A. Al-Abdullah, P.O. Box 59446, Nuzha Building, Sixth Floor, 11525.
Telephone: 966-1-405-1291.
Fax: 966-1-405-1291.
Abu Dhabi, United Arab Emirates Office: P.O. Box 43908.
Telephone: (971-2) 787222.
Fax: (971-2) 784001.

Herman M. Braude
William M. Huddles (Resident, Baltimore, Maryland Office)
Roger C. Jones (Not admitted in DC; Resident, Baltimore, Maryland Office)
Howard A. Pollack (Resident, Baltimore, Maryland Office)

Samuel M. Morrison, Jr.
Robert D. Windus
John P. McGowan, Jr. (Not admitted in DC; Resident, Abu Dhabi, U.A.E. Office)
Chuncheng Lian
Kenneth Knut Sorteberg (Resident, Baltimore, Maryland Office)

OF COUNSEL

J. Richard Margulies
William R. Delaney (Resident, San Francisco, California Office)

For full biographical listings, see the Martindale-Hubbell Law Directory

BRAULT, GRAHAM, SCOTT & BRAULT (AV)

1906 Sunderland Place, N.W., 20036
Telephone: 202-785-1200
Fax: 202-785-4301
Rockville, Maryland Office: 101 South Washington Street.
Telephone: 301-424-1060.
FAX: 301-424-7991.
Arlington, Virginia Office: Suite 1201, 2300 North Clarendon Boulevard, Courthouse Plaza.
Telephone: 703-522-1781.

OF COUNSEL

Laurence T. Scott

MEMBERS OF FIRM

Denver H. Graham (1922-1987)
Albert E. Brault (Retired)
Albert D. Brault (Resident, Rockville, Maryland Office)
Leo A. Roth, Jr.
James S. Wilson (Resident, Rockville, Maryland Office)
Ronald G. Guziak (Resident, Rockville, Maryland Office)
Daniel L. Shea (Resident, Rockville, Maryland Office)
Keith M. Bonner
M. Kathleen Parker (Resident, Rockville, Maryland Office)
Regina Ann Casey (Resident, Rockville, Maryland Office)
James M. Brault (Resident, Rockville, Maryland Office)

ASSOCIATES

David G. Mulquin (Not admitted in DC; Resident, Rockville, Maryland Office)
Sanford A. Friedman
Holly D. Shupert (Not admitted in DC; Resident, Rockville, Maryland Office)
Eric A. Spacek
Joan F. Brault (Resident, Rockville, Maryland Office)

Representative Clients: American Oil Co.; Crum & Forster Group; Fireman's Fund American Insurance Cos.; Kemper Group; Reliance Insurance Cos.; Safeco Group; Government Employees Insurance Co.; Medical Mutual Society of Maryland; Legal Mutual Liability Insurance Society of Maryland.

For Complete List of Firm Personnel, See General Section

For full biographical listings, see the Martindale-Hubbell Law Directory

BUTSAVAGE & ASSOCIATES, P.C. (AV)

1150 Connecticut Avenue, N.W., Ninth Floor, 20036
Telephone: 202-862-4355
Fax: 202-828-4130

Carey R. Butsavage
George Wiszynski
Dianna Marie Louis (Not admitted in DC)
Marc A. Stefan

For full biographical listings, see the Martindale-Hubbell Law Directory

CAPLIN & DRYSDALE, CHARTERED (AV)

One Thomas Circle, N.W., 20005
Telephone: 202-862-5000
Cable Address: "Capdale"
Telex: 904001 CAPL UR WSH
Fax: 202-429-3301
New York, N.Y. Office: 399 Park Avenue.
Telephone: 212-319-7125.
Fax: 212-644-6755.

Mortimer M. Caplin
Robert A. Klayman
Ralph A. Muoio
Elihu Inselbuch (Resident, New York Office)
Ronald B. Lewis
Richard W. Skillman
Patricia G. Lewis
Bernard S. Bailor
Stafford Smiley
Sally A. Regal
Julie W. Davis
Carl S. Kravitz
Robert A. Boisture
Charles T. Plambeck
Beth Shapiro Kaufman
Craig A. Sharon
James E. Salles
Paul G. Cellupica
Michael Doran (Not admitted in DC)
Dorothy L. Foley
Matthew W. Frank
Elizabeth M. Sellers (Not admitted in DC)
Douglas D. Drysdale
Thomas A. Troyer
David N. Webster
H. David Rosenbloom
Peter Van N. Lockwood
Cono R. Namorato
Daniel B. Rosenbaum
Richard E. Timbie
Graeme W. Bush
Albert G. Lauber, Jr.
Scott D. Michel
Kent A. Mason
Trevor W. Swett III
James Sottile, IV
Harry J. Hicks, III
C. Sanders McNew (Resident, New York Office)
Ann C. McMillan
Catherine E. Livingston
Christian R. Pastore (Resident, New York Office)
Nathan D. Finch
Jessica L. Goldstein

OF COUNSEL

Robert H. Elliott, Jr.
Milton Cerny
Myron C. Baum
Vivian L. Cavalieri

For full biographical listings, see the Martindale-Hubbell Law Directory

MARK A. COHEN & ASSOCIATES, P.A. (AV)

Homer Building, 601 Thirteenth Street, N.W., Suite 440 North, 20005
Telephone: 202-347-2000
Facsimile: 202-347-2002
Miami, Florida Office: 1221 Brickell Avenue, Suite 1780, 33131.
Telephone: 305-375-9292.
Facsimile: 305-381-6799.

Mark A. Cohen
Roger S. Kobert (Not admitted in DC)
Todd R. Legon (Not admitted in DC)

SENIOR COUNSEL

David J. Federbush

For full biographical listings, see the Martindale-Hubbell Law Directory

JOSEPH FRANCIS CUNNINGHAM & ASSOCIATES (AV)

Two Connecticut Place, 5039 Connecticut Avenue, N.W., 20008
Telephone: 202-364-0872
Fax: 202-364-6142
Alexandria, Virginia Office: 115 South St. Asaph Street.
Telephone: 703-684-0069.
Fax: 703-548-5220.

ASSOCIATES

Valerie L. Tetro (Not admitted in DC)
Thomas C. Swiers
Gregory James Dumark (Not admitted in DC)
Kathleen A. Chapman (Not admitted in DC)

For full biographical listings, see the Martindale-Hubbell Law Directory

DECKELBAUM OGENS & FISCHER, CHARTERED (AV)

1140 Connecticut Avenue, N.W., 20036
Telephone: 202-223-1474
Fax: 202-293-1471
Bethesda, Maryland Office: 6701 Democracy Boulevard.
Telephone: 301-564-5100.

Nelson Deckelbaum
Ronald L. Ogens
Lawrence H. Fischer
Arthur G. Kahn
Deborah E. Reiser
John B. Raftery
Charles A. Moster
Andrew J. Shedlock, III

Ronald G. Scheraga
Bryn Hope Sherman
Phyllis Lea Bean
Darryl Alan Feldman (Resident, Bethesda, Maryland Office)

References: Franklin National Bank; Century National Bank.

For full biographical listings, see the Martindale-Hubbell Law Directory

Washington—Continued

The Falk Law Firm A Professional Limited Company (AV)

Suite 260 One Westin Center, 2445 M Street, N.W., 20037
Telephone: 202-833-8700
Telecopier: 202-872-1725

James H. Falk, Sr.
James H. Falk, Jr.
John M. Falk
Rose Burks Emery (Not admitted in DC)
Robert K. Tompkins (Not admitted in DC)

OF COUNSEL

Pierre E. Murphy

For full biographical listings, see the Martindale-Hubbell Law Directory

Kenneth R. Feinberg & Associates (AV)

1120 20th Street, N.W. Suite 740 South, 20036
Telephone: 202-371-1110
Fax: 202-962-9290
New York, N.Y. Office: 780 3rd Avenue, Suite 2202.
Telephone: 212-527-9600.
Fax: 212-527-9611.

ASSOCIATES

Deborah E. Greenspan
Michael K. Rozen (Not admitted in DC)
Peter H. Woodin (Not admitted in DC)

For full biographical listings, see the Martindale-Hubbell Law Directory

Foret & Thompson (AV)

1275 K Street, N.W., Suite 1101, 20005
Telephone: 202-408-4700
Facsimile: 202-408-4708

MEMBERS OF FIRM

L. Palmer Foret
Mark R. Thompson

ASSOCIATE

Craig L. Davitian

For full biographical listings, see the Martindale-Hubbell Law Directory

Ifshin & Friedman (AV)

888 16th Street N.W., Suite 300, 20006
Telephone: 202-293-4175
Fax: 202-296-8791

MEMBERS OF FIRM

David M. Ifshin
Philip S. Friedman

For full biographical listings, see the Martindale-Hubbell Law Directory

Kananack, Murgatroyd, Baum & Hedlund, A Professional Corporation (AV)

1250 24th Street, N.W., Suite 300, 20037
Telephone: 202-466-0513; 800-827-0097
Fax: 202-466-0527
Los Angeles, California Office: Suite 650, 12100 Wilshire Boulevard.
Telephones: 310-207-3233; 800-827-0087.
Facsimile: 310-820-7444.

Cara L. Belle

For full biographical listings, see the Martindale-Hubbell Law Directory

Leonard, Ralston, Stanton & Danks (AV)

Suite 609, Georgetown, 1000 Thomas Jefferson Street, N.W., 20007
Telephone: 202-342-3342
Fax: 202-298-7810
Fairfax, Virginia Office: Leonard, Ralston, Stanton & Danks, Sherwood Plaza, Suite 150, 9990 Lee Highway.
Telephone: 703-591-6200.
Fax: 703-591-6556.
Jackson, Mississippi Office: Keyes, Danks & Leonard, Suite 100, 213 South Lamar Street.
Telephone: 601-948-3100.
Fax: 601-948-1919.

MEMBERS OF FIRM

Jerris Leonard
David T. Ralston, Jr.
Thomas J. Stanton (Not admitted in DC)
Michael J. Remington
Mary Gayle Holden (Not admitted in DC)

ASSOCIATES

Roderick B. Williams
Rachel Danish Campbell
Karen M. Grane
Seanan B. Murphy
George Galt (Not admitted in DC)
Theodore Charles Curtin (Not admitted in DC)

(See Next Column)

OF COUNSEL

John D. Brosnan

For full biographical listings, see the Martindale-Hubbell Law Directory

Mary A. McReynolds, P.C. (AV)

Suite 400, 888 Sixteenth Street, N.W., 20006
Telephone: 202-775-1996
Telecopier: 202-296-8791

Mary A. McReynolds

For full biographical listings, see the Martindale-Hubbell Law Directory

Miller, Cassidy, Larroca & Lewin (AV)

2555 M Street, N.W., 20037
Telephone: 202-293-6400
Telecopier: 202-293-1827

MEMBERS OF FIRM

Herbert J. Miller, Jr.
John J. Cassidy
Raymond G. Larroca
Nathan Lewin
Martin D. Minsker
William H. Jeffress, Jr.
R. Stan Mortenson
Thomas B. Carr
James E. Rocap, III
Randall J. Turk
Stephen L. Braga
Joe R. Caldwell, Jr.
Scott L. Nelson
Julia Evans Guttman
Niki Kuckes
Jay L. Alexander
Cynthia Thomas Calvert
Paul F. Enzinna

ASSOCIATES

Cathy J. Burdette
Douglas F. Curtis
Michael J. Barta
Stuart A. Levey
David S. Cohen
David R. Fontaine
James B. Bennett
Ellen Fels Berkman
Hugh P. Quinn
Nancy E. Friedman
Barry J. Pollack
James R. Heavner, Jr.
Mathew S. Nosanchuk (Not admitted in DC)
Kirsten D. Levingston
John T. Bentivoglio (Not admitted in DC)
Katherine L. Pringle (Not admitted in DC)
Robert J. McGahan (Not admitted in DC)

OF COUNSEL

Courtney A. Evans
William W. Greenhalgh (1927-1994)

For full biographical listings, see the Martindale-Hubbell Law Directory

Nelson & Nelson (AV)

1050 17th Street, N.W., Suite 830, 20036
Telephone: 202-659-0815
Bethesda, Maryland Office: 3 Bethesda Metro Center, Suite 750.
Telephone: 301-961-1958.

MEMBERS OF FIRM

William E. Nelson
Sherlee Stanford Nelson

For full biographical listings, see the Martindale-Hubbell Law Directory

Paulson, Nace & Norwind (AV)

1814 N Street, N.W., 20036
Telephone: 202-463-1999
Fax: 202-223-6824

MEMBERS OF FIRM

Richard S. Paulson (1928-1986)
Barry J. Nace
Edward L. Norwind

ASSOCIATES

John S. Lopatto, III
Mark R. Lightfoot

OF COUNSEL

Irving R. M. Panzer

For full biographical listings, see the Martindale-Hubbell Law Directory

Reichler, Milton & Medel (AV)

Suite 1200, 1747 Pennsylvania Avenue, N.W., 20006-4604
Telephone: 202-223-1200
Telex: 494-3588
Fax: 202-785-6687

Paul S. Reichler
Kathleen M. Milton
Arthur V. Medel

ASSOCIATES

Janis H. Brennan
Padideh Ala'i
Traci Duvall Humes
Alima Joned (Not admitted in DC)

For full biographical listings, see the Martindale-Hubbell Law Directory

The Robinson Law Firm (AV)

Market Square, 717 D Street, N.W., 4th Floor, 20004
Telephone: 202-347-6100
Fax: 202-347-0081

(See Next Column)

THE ROBINSON LAW FIRM, *Washington—Continued*

MEMBERS OF FIRM

Kenneth Michael Robinson
Lars H. Liebeler
Nicholas H. Hantzes
Paul S. Thaler
Daniel E. Ellenbogen

ASSOCIATE

Randall W. Roy (Not admitted in DC)

OF COUNSEL

Dennis M. Hart

For full biographical listings, see the Martindale-Hubbell Law Directory

ROSS, DIXON & MASBACK (AV)

601 Pennsylvania Avenue, N.W., North Building, 20004-2688
Telephone: 202-662-2000
Orange County, California Office: 5 Park Plaza, Suite 1200, Irvine, California, 92714.
Telephone: 714-622-2700.
Fax: 714-622-2739.

MEMBERS OF FIRM

Stuart Philip Ross
Gary V. Dixon
Wallace A. Christensen
John R. Gerstein
Cathy Ann Simon
David M. Gische
Richard A. Simpson
Lee Levine
Sean M. Hanifin
Peter G. Thompson
Elizabeth Sarah Gere
Barbara E. Etkind
Rebecca L. Ross
Robert M. Pozin (Resident, Orange County, California Office)
Michael D. Sullivan
Kevin M. LaCroix
Lewis K. Loss
William H. Briggs, Jr.
James E. Grossberg (Resident, Orange County, California Office)
Charles I. Hadden
William E. O'Brian, Jr.
Lona Triplett Perry
Andrew L. Shapiro
Celeste Phillips (Not admitted in DC; Resident, Orange County, California Office)
Elizabeth C. Koch
Merril Jay Hirsh

Leslie S. Ahari
Seth D. Berlin
Charles T. Blair
Gregory W. Brown (Not admitted in DC)
Jay Ward Brown
Lisa A. Burns
Vincent J. Columbia, Jr.
R. Darryl Cooper
John W. Duchelle (Not admitted in DC)
David R. Dwares
Jeffrey H. Dygert (Not admitted in DC)
Stephen W. Funk
John R. Griffiths (Not admitted in DC)
Garrick P. Grobler
Martin G. Hacala
Thomas H. Howlett
Eric M. Jaffe (Not admitted in DC)
John W. Jensen
Jason R. Karp
Thomas T. Locke (Not admitted in DC)
Stacey L. McGraw (Not admitted in DC)
Terrence R. McInnis
Douglas R. M. Nazarian
David L. Perry (Not admitted in DC)
Richard J. Pratt
Erik Jorma Salovaara (Not admitted in DC)
Roland G. Schroeder
Daniel J. Standish
Susan M. Camp Stocks
Joel Scott Townsend
Jennifer S. Young (Not admitted in DC)

OF COUNSEL

Harold E. Masback, III
William D. Hopkins

For full biographical listings, see the Martindale-Hubbell Law Directory

SCHWALB, DONNENFELD, BRAY & SILBERT, A PROFESSIONAL CORPORATION (AV)

1025 Thomas Jefferson Street, N.W. Suite 300 East, 20007
Telephone: 202-965-7910
Telecopier: 202-337-0676

Burton A. Schwalb
Charles R. Donnenfeld
John M. Bray
Earl J. Silbert
David J. Curtin
Charles B. Wayne
Steven Sarfatti
Lucinda J. Bach
Cary M. Feldman
Joseph M. Jones
Adam S. Hoffinger
Kevin M. Dinan
Patricia L. Maher

Debra Ornstein
Robert A. Salerno
Carmen R. Kelley
Richard J. Oparil
James T. Phalen
James P. Kennedy (Not admitted in DC)
Robert J. McAuliffe
Anthony W. Verran (Not admitted in DC)
Jeffrey D. Clark

For full biographical listings, see the Martindale-Hubbell Law Directory

SHAWN, MANN & NIEDERMAYER, L.L.P. (AV)

1850 M Street, N.W., Suite 280, 20036-5803
Telephone: 202-331-7900
Fax: 202-331-0726

MEMBERS OF FIRM

William H. Shawn
Roy I. Niedermayer
Jeffrey L. Squires

For full biographical listings, see the Martindale-Hubbell Law Directory

SUTHERLAND, ASBILL & BRENNAN (AV)

1275 Pennsylvania Avenue, N.W., 20004-2404
Telephone: 202-383-0100
Cable Address: "Sutab Wash"
Telex: 89-501
Facsimile: 202-637-3593
Atlanta, Georgia Office: 999 Peachtree Street, N. E., 30309-3996.
Telephone: 404-853-8000.
New York, N.Y. Office: 1270 Avenue of the Americas, 10020-1700.
Telephone: 212-332-3000.
Austin, Texas Office: 111 Congress Avenue, 23rd Floor, 78701-4079.
Telephone: 512-469-3350.

Nicholas T. Christakos
Hamilton P. Fox, III
Karen L. Grimm
Robert G. Levy (Not admitted in DC)
Kenneth G. Starling
Steuart H. Thomsen

COUNSEL

Lovida H. Coleman, Jr.

For Complete List of Firm Personnel, See General Section

For full biographical listings, see the Martindale-Hubbell Law Directory

*** THOMPSON, HINE AND FLORY (AV)**

1920 N Street, N.W., 20036-1601
Telephone: 202-331-8800
Fax: 202-331-8330
Telex: 904173
Cable Address: "Caglaw"
Akron, Ohio Office: 50 S. Main Street, Suite 502, 44308-1828.
Telephone: 216-376-8090.
Fax: 216-376-8386.
Cincinnati, Ohio Office: 312 Walnut Street, 14th Floor, 45202-4029.
Telephone: 513-352-6700.
Fax: 513-241-4771.
Telex: 938003.
Cleveland, Ohio Office: 1100 National City Bank Building, 629 Euclid Avenue, 44114.
Telephone: 216-566-5500.
Fax: 216-566-5583.
Telex: 980217. Cable Address "Thomflor".
Columbus, Ohio Office: One Columbus, 10 West Broad Street, 43215-34353.
Telephone: 614-469-3200.
Fax: 614-469-3361.
Dayton, Ohio Office: 2000 Courthouse Plaza, N.E., 45402-1706.
Telephone: 513-443-6600.
Fax: 513-443-6637, 513-443-6635.
Palm Beach, Florida Office: 125 Worth Avenue, 33480-4466.
Telephone: 407-833-5900.
Fax: 407-833-5951.
Brussels, Belgium Office: Rue Des Chevaliers, Ridderstraat 14 - B.10, B-1050.
Telephone: 011-32-2-511-9326.
Fax: 011-32-2-513-9206.

MEMBERS OF FIRM

Steven D. Cundra
Paul R. Webber, IV

ASSOCIATES

Michele D. Lynch
Patricia L. Taylor

For Complete List of Firm Personnel, See General Section

For full biographical listings, see the Martindale-Hubbell Law Directory

*** VENABLE, BAETJER, HOWARD & CIVILETTI (AV)**

A Partnership including Professional Corporations
Suite 1000, 1201 New York Avenue, N.W., 20005
Telephone: 202-962-4800
Fax: 202-962-8300
Baltimore, Maryland Office: Venable, Baetjer and Howard, 1800 Mercantile Bank & Trust Building, 2 Hopkins Plaza.
Telephone: 410-244-7400.
McLean, Virginia Office: Venable, Baetjer and Howard, Suite 400, 2010 Corporate Ridge.
Telephone: 703-760-1600.
Rockville, Maryland Office: Venable, Baetjer and Howard, Suite 500, One Church Street, P. O. Box 1906.
Telephone: 301-217-5600.

(See Next Column)

VENABLE, BAETJER, HOWARD & CIVILETTI—*Continued*

Towson, Maryland Office: Venable, Baetjer and Howard, 210 Allegheny Avenue, P. O. Box 5517.
Telephone: 410-494-6200.

MEMBERS OF FIRM

Benjamin R. Civiletti (P.C.) (Also at Baltimore and Towson, Maryland Offices)
Thomas J. Madden
Ronald R. Glancz
David J. Levenson
Douglas D. Connah, Jr. (P.C.) (Also at Baltimore, Maryland Office)
Kenneth C. Bass, III (Also at McLean, Virginia Office)
Max Stul Oppenheimer (P.C.) (Also at Baltimore and Towson, Maryland Offices)
Edward F. Glynn, Jr.
Robert G. Ames (Also at Baltimore, Maryland Office)
Michael Schatzow (Also at Baltimore and Towson, Maryland Offices)
N. Frank Wiggins
James K. Archibald (Also at Baltimore and Towson, Maryland Offices)
Judson W. Starr (Also at Baltimore and Towson, Maryland Offices)
James R. Myers
Jeffrey A. Dunn (Also at Baltimore, Maryland Office)
George F. Pappas (Also at Baltimore, Maryland Office)
James L. Shea (Not admitted in DC; also at Baltimore, Maryland Office)
William D. Coston
Maurice Baskin
Amy Berman Jackson
William D. Quarles (Also at Towson, Maryland Office)
James A. Dunbar (Also at Baltimore, Maryland Office)
Mary E. Pivec (Not admitted in DC; Also at Baltimore, Maryland Office)
Thomas J. Kelly, Jr.
Patrick J. Stewart (Also at Baltimore, Maryland Office)
Gary M. Hnath

OF COUNSEL

Geoffrey R. Garinther (Not admitted in DC; Also at Baltimore, Maryland Office)
Fred W. Hathaway

ASSOCIATES

Carla Draluck Craft
Fred Joseph Federici, III
David W. Goewey
Edward Brendan Magrab (Not admitted in DC)
Samuel T. Morison
Traci H. Mundy (Not admitted in DC)
Melissa Landau Steinman (Not admitted in DC)
Paul N. Wengert

For Complete List of Firm Personnel, See General Section

For full biographical listings, see the Martindale-Hubbell Law Directory

* VINSON & ELKINS L.L.P. (AV)

A Registered Limited Liability Partnership
The Willard Office Building, 1455 Pennsylvania Avenue, N.W., 20004-1008
Telephone: 202-639-6500
Fax: 202-639-6604
Cable Address: Vinelkins
Houston, Texas Office: 1001 Fannin, Suite 2300.
Telephone: 713-758-2222.
Fax: 713-758-2346. International
Telex: 6868314.
Cable Address: Vinelkins
Austin, Texas Office: One American Center, 600 Congress Avenue.
Telephone: 512-495-8400.
Fax: 512-495-8612.
Dallas, Texas Office: 3700 Trammell Crow Center, 2001 Ross Avenue.
Telephone: 214-220-7700.
Fax: 214-220-7716.
London Office: 47 Charles Street, Berkeley Square, London, W1X 7PB, England.
Telephone: 011 (441-71) 491-7236.
Fax: 011 (44-171) 499-5320.
Cable Address: VinelkinsLondon W.1.
Moscow, Russia Federation Office: 16 Alexey Tolstoy Street, Second Floor, Moscow, 103001 Russia Federation.
Telephone: 011 (70-95) 956-1995.
Telecopy: 011 (70-95) 956-1996.
Mexico City, Mexico Office: Aristóteles 77, 5°Piso, Colonia Chapultepec Polanco, 11560 Mexico, D.F.
Telephone: (52-5) 280-7828.
Fax: (52-5) 280-9223.
Singapore Office: 50 Raffles Place, #19-05 Shell Tower, 0104. U.S. Voice Mailbox: 713-758-3500.
Telephone: (65) 536-8300.
Fax: (65) 536-8311.

RESIDENT PARTNERS

Alden L. Atkins
C. Michael Buxton
Ky P. Ewing, Jr.
Michael J. Henke
Neil W. Imus
John D. Taurman
Charles D. Tetrault

RESIDENT OF COUNSEL

Roderick Glen Ayers, Jr.

(See Next Column)

RESIDENT ASSOCIATES

Alex J. Bourelly (Not admitted in DC)
Robert H. Cox
Tegan M. Flynn
Mary H. Hirth (Not admitted in DC)
Jonathan M. Zeitler (Not admitted in DC)

For Complete List of Firm Personnel, See General Section

For full biographical listings, see the Martindale-Hubbell Law Directory

WATT, TIEDER & HOFFAR (AV)

601 Pennsylvania Avenue, N.W., Suite 900, 20004
Telephone: 202-462-4697
Telecopier: 703-893-8029
McLean Virginia Office: 7929 Westpark Drive, Suite 400,
Telephone: 703-749-1000.
Telecopier: 703-893-8029.
Irvine California Office: 3 Park Plaza, Suite 1530.
Telephone: 714-852-6700.

MEMBERS OF FIRM

John B. Tieder, Jr.
Robert K. Cox
David C. Romm

For full biographical listings, see the Martindale-Hubbell Law Directory

WILLIAMS & CONNOLLY (AV)

725 Twelfth Street, N.W., 20005
Telephone: 202-434-5000

MEMBERS OF FIRM

Vincent J. Fuller
Raymond W. Bergan
Jeremiah C. Collins
Robert L. Weinberg
David Povich
Steven M. Umin
John W. Vardaman
Paul Martin Wolff
J. Alan Galbraith
John G. Kester
William E. McDaniels
Brendan V. Sullivan, Jr.
Aubrey M. Daniel, III
Richard M. Cooper
Gerald A. Feffer
Robert P. Watkins
Jerry L. Shulman
Lawrence Lucchino
Lewis H. Ferguson, III
Robert B. Barnett
David E. Kendall
Gregory B. Craig
John J. Buckley, Jr.
Douglas R. Marvin
John K. Villa
Barry S. Simon
Kevin T. Baine
Stephen L. Urbanczyk
Philip J. Ward
Frederick Whitten Peters
Peter J. Kahn
Lon S. Babby
Michael S. Sundermeyer
James T. Fuller, III
David D. Aufhauser
Bruce R. Genderson
Carolyn H. Williams
Frank Lane Heard III
Steven R. Kuney
Gerson A. Zweifach
Paul Mogin
Howard W. Gutman
Nancy F. Lesser
Richard S. Hoffman
Paula Michele Ellison
Steven A. Steinbach
Mark S. Levinstein
Mary Greer Clark
Daniel F. Katz
Nicole K. Seligman
Robert M. Krasne
Kathleen L. Beggs
Sven Erik Holmes
William R. Murray, Jr.
Eva Petko Esber
Stephen D. Raber
John D. Cline

David C. Kiernan
Nancy A. Bard
Lon E. Musslewhite
Robin E. Jacobsohn
Charles A. Sweet
Elizabeth D. Collery
Glenn J. Pfadenhauer
George A. Borden
Robert J. Shaughnessy
Jonathan P. Graham
Allen P. Waxman
William M. Wiltshire
J. Roger Williams, Jr.
Eric M. Braun
David S. Blatt
Betsy K. Wanger
Ari S. Zymelman
Joseph D. Piorkowski, Jr.
Philip B. Busch
H. Douglas Owens
Laurence Shore
Dane H. Butswinkas
Laurie S. Fulton

OF COUNSEL

Lyman G. Friedman

For Complete List of Firm Personnel, See General Section

For full biographical listings, see the Martindale-Hubbell Law Directory

WILMER, CUTLER & PICKERING (AV)

2445 M Street, N.W., 20037-1420
Telephone: 202-663-6000
Facsimile: 202-663-6363
Internet: Law@Wilmer.Com
European Offices:
4 Carlton Gardens, London, SW1Y 5AA, England. Telephone: 011 (4471) 839-4466.
Facsimile: 011 (4471) 839-3537.
Rue de la Loi 15 Wetstraat, B-1040 Brussels, Belgium. Telephone: 011 (322) 231-0903.
Facsimile: 011 (322) 230-4322.

(See Next Column)

WILMER, CUTLER & PICKERING, *Washington—Continued*

Friedrichstrasse 95, D-10117 Berlin, Germany. Telephone: 011 (4930) 2643-3601.
Facsimile: 011 (4930) 2643-3630.

MEMBERS OF FIRM

Max O. Truitt, Jr.
Howard P. Willens
Daniel K. Mayers
Stephen H. Sachs
Arthur F. Mathews
Dennis M. Flannery
James Robertson
Louis R. Cohen
Michael R. Klein
Paul J. Mode, Jr.
Stephen F. Black
Gary D. Wilson
James A. Rogers
Michael L. Burack
Robert B. McCaw
A. Douglas Melamed
William J. Kolasky, Jr.
Arthur L. Marriott (Resident, European Office, London, England)
A. Stephen Hut, Jr.
John Rounsaville, Jr.
Roger M. Witten
David M. Becker
Christopher R. Lipsett
William J. Perlstein
Andrew B. Weissman
Lynn Bregman
James E. Coleman, Jr.
Juanita A. Crowley
John Payton
Bruce M. Berman
Thomas F. Connell
Charles E. Davidow
Gary B. Born (Resident, European Office, London, England)
Philip D. Anker
Joseph K. Brenner
Carol Clayton
Thomas P. Olson
Patrick J. Carome
Jane C. Sherburne
David P. Donovan
Stephen M. Cutler
Roger W. Yoerges
Mark D. Cahn
Randolph D. Moss

SPECIAL COUNSEL

Joseph E. Killory, Jr.

For Complete List of Firm Personnel, See General Section

For full biographical listings, see the Martindale-Hubbell Law Directory

ZUCKERMAN, SPAEDER, GOLDSTEIN, TAYLOR & KOLKER (AV)

1201 Connecticut Avenue, N.W., 20036
Telephone: 202-778-1800
Fax: 202-822-8106
Miami, Florida Office: Zuckerman, Spaeder, Taylor & Evans. Suite 900, Miami Center, 201 South Biscayne Boulevard.
Telephones: 305-358-5000; 305-579-0110; Broward County: 305-523-0277.
Fax: 305-579-9749.
Ft. Lauderdale, Florida Office: Zuckerman, Spaeder, Taylor & Evans. One East Broward Boulevard, Suite 700.
Telephone: 305-356-0463.
Fax: 305-356-0406.
Baltimore, Maryland Office: Zuckerman, Spaeder, Goldstein, Taylor & Better. Suite 2440, 100 East Pratt Street.
Telephone: 410-332-0444.
Fax: 410-659-0436.
Tampa, Florida Office: Zuckerman, Spaeder, Taylor & Evans. 101 East Kennedy Boulevard, Suite 3140.
Telephone: 813-221-1010.
Fax: 813-223-7961.
New York, N.Y. Office: 1114 Avenue of the Americas, 45th Floor, Grace Building.
Telephone: 212-479-6500.
Fax: 212-479-6512.

MEMBERS OF FIRM

Roger E. Zuckerman
Mark W. Foster
Roger C. Spaeder
William W. Taylor, III
Peter R. Kolker
Stephen H. Glickman
Michael R. Smith
Herbert Better (Resident, Baltimore, Maryland Office)
Ronald B. Ravikoff (Resident, Miami, Florida Office)
Donald J. McCartney (Resident, Baltimore, Maryland Office)
Blair G. Brown
Martin S. Himeles, Jr. (Resident, Baltimore, Maryland Office)
Edward J. M. Little (Resident, New York, N.Y. Office)
Thomas J. Meeks (Resident, Miami, Florida Office)
Deborah J. Jeffrey
Thomas B. Mason

ASSOCIATES

Leslie M. Berger
Cyril V. Smith (Resident, Baltimore, Maryland Office)

Reference: Sovran Bank/DC National.

For full biographical listings, see the Martindale-Hubbell Law Directory

FLORIDA

*BARTOW,** Polk Co.

BOSWELL, STIDHAM, PURCELL, CONNER, WILSON & BREWER, P.A. (AV)

150 East Davidson Street, P.O. Box 1578, 33830-1578
Telephone: 813-533-0866
Telecopier: 813-533-7255

Wofford Hampton Stidham
Dabney L. Conner
Jonathan Stidham
Claude M. Harden, III

For full biographical listings, see the Martindale-Hubbell Law Directory

FROST, O'TOOLE & SAUNDERS, P.A. (AV)

395 South Central Avenue, P.O. Box 2188, 33830
Telephone: 813-533-0314; 800-533-0967
Telecopier: 813-533-8985

John W. Frost, II
Neal L. O'Toole
Thomas C. Saunders
Richard E. "Rick" Dantzler
Robert A. Carr
Robert H. Van Hart
James R. Franklin
John Marc Tamayo

Reference: Community National Bank, Bartow.

For full biographical listings, see the Martindale-Hubbell Law Directory

BOCA RATON, Palm Beach Co.

CARTER & CONNOLLY, P.A. (AV)

Suite 312, 1200 North Federal Highway, 33432
Telephone: 407-368-9900

John Edward Carter
Andrew James Connolly

OF COUNSEL

Robert T. Carlile

For full biographical listings, see the Martindale-Hubbell Law Directory

WEISS & HANDLER, P.A. (AV)

Suite 218A, One Boca Place, 2255 Glades Road, 33431-7313
Telephone: 407-997-9995
Broward: 305-421-5101
Palm Beach: 407-734-8008
Telecopier: 407-997-5280

Howard I. Weiss
Henry B. Handler
Donald Feldman
Walter M. Cooperstein
Carol A. Kartagener
Bruce A. Harris
David K. Friedman
William M. Franz
Mia Lucas

OF COUNSEL

Malcolm L. Stein (Not admitted in FL)
Raoul Lionel Felder (Not admitted in FL)

For full biographical listings, see the Martindale-Hubbell Law Directory

*BRADENTON,** Manatee Co.

LANE, TROHN, CLARKE, BERTRAND, VREELAND & JACOBSEN, P.A. (AV)

233 15th Street, West, P.O. Box 551, 34206
Telephone: 813-747-1871
Telecopier: 813-745-2866
Lakeland, Florida Office: One Lake Morton Drive, P.O. Box 3.
Telephone: 813-284-2200.

Robert J. Bertrand
Lynn H. Groseclose
Patrick J. Murphy
John V. Quinlan
Gary S. Rabin
Robert L. Trohn

Andrew R. McCumber
Nancy C. Harrison

For Complete List of Firm Personnel, See General Section

For full biographical listings, see the Martindale-Hubbell Law Directory

*CLEARWATER,** Pinellas Co.

R. TIMOTHY PETERS, P.A. (AV)

587 South Duncan Avenue, P.O. Box 6316, 34618
Telephone: 813-447-4585

R. Timothy Peters

Reference: Fortune Savings Bank.

For full biographical listings, see the Martindale-Hubbell Law Directory

CRYSTAL RIVER, Citrus Co.

BEST & ANDERSON, P.A. (AV)

7655 West Gulf to Lake Highway, Suite 6, 34429
Telephone: 904-795-1107
Orlando, Florida Office: 20 North Orange Avenue, Suite 505.
Telephone: 407-425-2985.

David R. Best
George H. "Dutch" Anderson, III

Mark S. Walker
G. Clay Morris
Perry M. Nardi
Lawrence I. Hauser

For full biographical listings, see the Martindale-Hubbell Law Directory

DAYTONA BEACH, Volusia Co.

FINK & SWEET (AV)

149 East International Speedway Boulevard, P.O. Box 5386, 32118
Telephone: 904-252-7653
FAX: 904-238-3604

Wesley A. Fink
Jeffrey C. Sweet

Representative Client: Sun Bank of Volusia County.
Approved Attorneys for: Attorneys' Title Insurance Fund; Title Insurance Company of Minnesota; Chicago Title Insurance Co.
Reference: Sun Bank of Volusia County.

For full biographical listings, see the Martindale-Hubbell Law Directory

*FORT LAUDERDALE,** Broward Co.

BERGER, SHAPIRO & DAVIS, P.A. (AV)

Suite 400, 100 N.E. 3rd Avenue, 33301
Telephone: 305-525-9900
Fax: 305-523-2872

James L. Berger
Mitchell W. Berger
James B. Davis
Manuel Kushner
Leonard K. Samuels
Laz L. Schneider

Thomas L. Abrams
Melissa P. Anderson
Lawrence C. Callaway, III
Nick Jovanovich
Robert B. Judd
Brent L. Moody
Terri E. Tuchman

OF COUNSEL

Franklin H. Caplan
Kenneth W. Shapiro

For full biographical listings, see the Martindale-Hubbell Law Directory

BYRD & MURPHY (AV)

Suite 200N Justice Building, 524 South Andrews Avenue, 33301
Telephone: 305-463-1423
FAX: 305-463-5428

MEMBERS OF FIRM

Thomas E. Byrd
James O. Murphy, Jr.

Approved Attorneys for: Attorneys' Title Insurance Fund.

For Complete List of Firm Personnel, See General Section

For full biographical listings, see the Martindale-Hubbell Law Directory

CONRAD, SCHERER, JAMES & JENNE (AV)

A Partnership of Professional Associations
Eighth Floor, 633 South Federal Highway, P.O. Box 14723, 33302
Telephone: 305-462-5500
Facsimile: 305-463-9244
Miami, Florida Office: 2180 Southwest 12th Avenue, P.O. Box 450888, 33245-0888.
Telephone: 305-856-9920.
Facsimile: 305-856-4546.

MEMBERS OF FIRM

William R. Scherer, Jr., (P.A.)
Gordon James, III, (P.A.)
Kenneth C. Jenne, II (P.A.)
Gary S. Genovese (P.A.)
Valerie Shea (P.A.)
William V. Carcioppolo (P.A.)

OF COUNSEL

Rex Conrad

ASSOCIATES

Linda Rae Spaulding
Lynn Futch Cooney
Kimberly A. Kisslan
Reid A. Cocalis
Albert L. Frevola, Jr.

Local Counsel for: American Home Assurance Group; Caterpillar Tractor Co.; Division of Risk Management, State of Florida; Florida East Coast Railway; Fort Motor Co.; Liberty Mutual Insurance Co.; Ryder Truck Lines; Unigard Insurance Group.
Approved Attorneys for: Attorneys' Title Insurance Fund.
Reference: Barnett Bank of Fort Lauderdale.

(See Next Column)

For Complete List of Firm Personnel, See General Section

For full biographical listings, see the Martindale-Hubbell Law Directory

ESLER PETRIE & SALKIN, P.A. (AV)

Suite 300 The Advocate Building, 315 S.E. Seventh Street, 33301
Telephone: 305-764-5400
FAX: 305-764-5408

Gary A. Esler
C. Daniel Petrie, Jr.
Sonya L. Salkin

Laurie S. Moss

Representative Clients: The Chubb Group of Insurance Cos.; Fireman's Fund Insurance Co.; State of Florida-Department of Risk Management; Marriott Corp.; Gregson Furniture Industries, Inc.; Loewenstein, Inc.; Richfield Hotel Management, Inc.; Mobile America Insurance Group, Inc.; Colonial Penn Insurance Co.
References: Capital Bank.

For full biographical listings, see the Martindale-Hubbell Law Directory

HEINRICH GORDON BATCHELDER HARGROVE & WEIHE (AV)

A Partnership including Professional Associations
500 East Broward Boulevard, Suite 1000, 33394-3092
Telephone: 305-527-2800
Telecopier: 305-524-9481

MEMBERS OF FIRM

Mark R. Boyd
Richard G. Gordon (P.A.)
John R. Hargrove (P.A.)
Eugene L. Heinrich (P.A.)
Jeffrey A. O'Keefe
Bruce A. Weihe (P.A.)

ASSOCIATES

William Kent Brown
Kandice L. Kilkelly
Paula Revene
Jodi R. Stone
Kenneth W. Waterway
Eric M. Zivitz

OF COUNSEL

Gerald M. Morris
Gilbert E. Theissen

Representative Clients: Aetna Life Insurance Company; Allstate Insurance Company; Amerisure Companies; The BellSouth Companies; Blackfin Yacht Corporation, Inc.; First Union National Bank of Florida; First Westinghouse Equities Corporation; Schindler Elevator Corporation; Sears, Roebuck and Co.; Westinghouse Electric Corporation.

For Complete List of Firm Personnel, See General Section

For full biographical listings, see the Martindale-Hubbell Law Directory

KRUPNICK CAMPBELL MALONE ROSELLI BUSER & SLAMA, P.A. (AV)

700 Southeast 3rd Avenue, 33316
Telephone: 305-763-8181
FAX: 305-763-8292

Jon E. Krupnick
Walter G. Campbell, Jr.
Kevin A. Malone
Richard J. Roselli
Thomas E. Buser
Joseph J. Slama
Kelly D. Hancock
Lisa A. McNelis

Kelley Badger Gelb
Elaine P. Krupnick
Scott S. Liberman
Robert J. McKee
Adria E. Quintela

Reference: Citizens and Southern Bank.

For full biographical listings, see the Martindale-Hubbell Law Directory

KENNETH R. MIKOS, P.A. (AV)

2780 East Oakland Park Boulevard, 33306
Telephone: 305-566-7200
Facsimile: 305-566-1568

Kenneth R. Mikos

Special Counsel to: Fort Lauderdale Civil Service Board.

For Complete List of Firm Personnel, See General Section

For full biographical listings, see the Martindale-Hubbell Law Directory

PETERSON, BERNARD, VANDENBERG, ZEI, GEISLER & MARTIN (AV)

707 Southeast Third Avenue, P.O. Drawer 14126, 33302
Telephone: 305-763-3200
Fax: 305-728-9019
West Palm Beach, Florida Office: 1550 Southern Boulevard.
Telephone: 407-686-5005.
Fax: 407-471-5603.
Stuart, Florida Office: 2100 E. Ocean Boulevard, Suite 202.
Telephone: 407-286-9881.
Naples, Florida Office: 3400 Bailey Lane, Suite 190.
Telephone: 813-263-6444.

(See Next Column)

PETERSON, BERNARD, VANDENBERG, ZEI, GEISLER & MARTIN, *Fort Lauderdale—Continued*

William M. Martin
Eric A. Peterson
William Zei

Alexander Clark
Michael A. Acker
Clifford Gorman
Kindy K. Coogler

OF COUNSEL

Leonard M. Bernard, Jr.

For full biographical listings, see the Martindale-Hubbell Law Directory

LAW OFFICES PRINCE, GLICK & MCFARLANE, P.A. (AV)

1112 Southeast 3rd Avenue, 33316
Telephone: Broward: 305-525-1112
Dade: 305-940-6414
FAX: 305-462-1243

Charles M. Prince
Joseph Glick
William J. McFarlane, III

For full biographical listings, see the Martindale-Hubbell Law Directory

PYSZKA, KESSLER, MASSEY, WELDON, CATRI, HOLTON & DOUBERLEY, P.A. (AV)

110 Tower, Twentieth Floor, 110 Southeast Sixth Street, 33301
Telephone: 305-463-8593
Miami, Florida Office: Fifth Floor, Grand Bay Plaza, 2665 South Bayshore Drive.
Telephone: 305-858-6614.

Charles T. Kessler (Resident)
Albert P. Massey, III (Resident)
Wesley L. Catri (Resident)
Raymond O. Holton, Jr. (Resident)
Paula C. Kessler (Resident)
Gregory G. Coican (Resident)
Andrea L. Kessler (Resident)
Kenneth A. Cutler (Resident)
Edward D. Schuster (Resident)

J. Michael Magee (Resident)

For Complete List of Firm Personnel, See General Section

For full biographical listings, see the Martindale-Hubbell Law Directory

WEAVER & WEAVER, P.A. (AV)

500 Southeast Sixth Street, P.O. Box 14663, 33302-4663
Telephone: 305-763-2511
Miami: 305-944-4452
West Palm Beach: 407-655-6012
FAX: 305-764-3590

Ben J. Weaver
Dianne Jay Weaver

For full biographical listings, see the Martindale-Hubbell Law Directory

*FORT MYERS,** Lee Co.

ALDERMAN & AHLBRAND, P.A. (AV)

Suite 200, The Historic Edison Theater Building, 1533 Hendry Street, P.O. Box 1530, 33902
Telephone: 813-334-7899
FAX: 813-334-0770

Frank C. Alderman, III
Mark W. Ahlbrand

For full biographical listings, see the Martindale-Hubbell Law Directory

AVERY, WHIGHAM & WINESETT, P.A. (AV)

Corner of First and Hendry Streets, 2248 First Street, P.O. Drawer 610, 33902-0610
Telephone: 813-334-7040
FAX: 813-334-6258

Richard W. Winesett
Sherra Winesett
Dwight A. Whigham
Dennis L. Avery
Robert A. Winesett
James M. Costello

For full biographical listings, see the Martindale-Hubbell Law Directory

HENDERSON, FRANKLIN, STARNES & HOLT, PROFESSIONAL ASSOCIATION (AV)

1715 Monroe Street, P.O. Box 280, 33902-0280
Telephone: 813-334-4121
Telecopier: 813-332-4494

Stephen L. Helgemo
John A. Noland
Gerald W. Pierce
J. Terrence Porter
Michael J. Corso
Vicki L. Sproat
John W. Lewis
Craig Ferrante
James L. Nulman
Harold N. Hume, Jr.
Bruce M. Stanley
Daniel W. Sheppard
Jack E. Lundy
Steven G. Koeppel

(See Next Column)

Douglas B. Szabo
Andrew L. Ringers, Jr.
John F. Potanovic, Jr.
Robert C. Shearman
Kevin D. Cooper
Jeffrey D. Kottkamp
Gregory D. Whitworth

Representative Clients: Aetna Life & Casualty Group; CIGNA Group; CSX Transportation, Inc.; Fireman's Fund Insurance Cos.; Barnett Bank of Lee County, N.A.; Northern Trust Bank of Florida, N.A.; The Hartford Insurance Group; Travelers Group; United Telephone Company of Florida.

For Complete List of Firm Personnel, See General Section

For full biographical listings, see the Martindale-Hubbell Law Directory

SMOOT ADAMS EDWARDS & GREEN, P.A. (AV)

One University Park Suite 600, 12800 University Drive, P.O. Box 60259, 33906-6259
Telephone: 813-489-1776
(800) 226-1777 (in Florida)
Fax: 813-489-2444

J. Tom Smoot, Jr.
Hal Adams
Franklyn A. (Chip) Johnson (1947-1991)
Charles B. Edwards
Bruce D. Green
Steven I. Winer
Mark R. Komray
Thomas P. Clark

Lynne E. Denneler
Clayton W. Crevasse
M. Brian Cheffer
Robert S. Forman
Thomas M. Howell
Plutarco M. Villalobos

C. Berk Edwards, Jr.

For Complete List of Firm Personnel, See General Section

For full biographical listings, see the Martindale-Hubbell Law Directory

*FORT PIERCE,** St. Lucie Co.

BRENNAN, HAYSKAR, JEFFERSON, GORMAN, WALKER & SCHWERER, PROFESSIONAL ASSOCIATION (AV)

515 and 519 South Indian River Drive, P.O. Box 3779, 34948-3779
Telephone: 407-461-2310
FAX: 407-468-6580

John T. Brennan
Thad H. Carlton (1906-1965)
Robert J. Gorman
Stephen G. Hayskar
Bradford L. Jefferson
Robert V. Schwerer
James T. Walker

William F. Gallese
Garrison M. Dundas

Representative Clients: Allstate Insurance Co.; Auto Owners Insurance Co.; Canal Insurance Co.; Florida Farm Bureau Insurance Group; Kemper Insurance Group; First Union National Bank of Fla.; Scottsdale Insurance Group; USF&G; Gallagher Bassett.

For full biographical listings, see the Martindale-Hubbell Law Directory

FEE, BRYAN & KOBLEGARD, P.A. (AV)

401 A South Indian River Drive, P.O. Box 1000, 34950
Telephone: 407-461-5020
FAX: 407-468-8461

Frank Fee (1913-1983)
Frank H. Fee, III
Benjamin L. Bryan, Jr.
Rupert N. Koblegard, III

Robert E. Maloney, Jr.

General Counsel: Harbor Federal Savings; North St. Lucie River Water Control District; Fort Pierce Farms Water Control District; Fort Pierce Utilities Authority; Capron Trail Community Development District.
Representative Clients: Adams Ranch, Inc.; Callaway Land & Cattle Co., Inc., McArthur Farms, Inc.
Approved Attorneys for: Equitable Life Assurance Society of the United States; Equitable Agri-Business, Inc.

For Complete List of Firm Personnel, See General Section

For full biographical listings, see the Martindale-Hubbell Law Directory

MELVILLE & FOWLER, P.A. (AV)

Laurel Professional Park, 2940 South 25th Street, 34981
Telephone: 407-464-7900
FAX: 407-464-8220

Harold G. Melville
Michael D. Fowler

David N. Sowerby
Richard M. Carnell, Jr.

OF COUNSEL

Charles R. P. Brown

For full biographical listings, see the Martindale-Hubbell Law Directory

NEILL GRIFFIN JEFFRIES & LLOYD, CHARTERED (AV)

311 South Second Street, P.O. Box 1270, 34954
Telephone: 407-464-8200
Fax: 407-464-2566

(See Next Column)

NEILL GRIFFIN JEFFRIES & LLOYD CHARTERED—*Continued*

Richard V. Neill
Michael Jeffries
J. Stephen Tierney, III
Richard V. Neill, Jr.

Local Counsel for: Sun Bank Treasure Coast, N.A., (Commercial and Trust Departments); St. Paul Fire and Marine Insurance Co.; Chubb Group of Insurances Co.; Becker Holding Corp.
Approved Attorneys for: Attorneys' Title Insurance Fund; Commonwealth Land Title Insurance Co.
Reference: Sun Bank Treasure Coast, N.A., Fort Pierce, Florida (Commercial and Trust Departments).

For full biographical listings, see the Martindale-Hubbell Law Directory

*GAINESVILLE,** Alachua Co.

STRIPLING, MCMICHAEL & STRIPLING, P.A. (AV)

102 N.W. Second Avenue, P.O. Box 1287, 32602
Telephone: 904-376-8888
FAX: 904-376-4645

Robert O. Stripling, Jr.
Alan E. McMichael
Sylvia A. K. Stripling

For full biographical listings, see the Martindale-Hubbell Law Directory

HOLLYWOOD, Broward Co.

ELLIS, SPENCER AND BUTLER (AV)

Emerald Hills Executive Plaza I, 4601 Sheridan Street, Suite 505, 33021
Telephone: Broward: 305-986-2291
Dade Line: 305-947-0620
Facsimile: 305-986-2778

MEMBERS OF FIRM

Robert B. Butler
W. Tinsley Ellis
William S. Spencer
Mark F. Butler
Robert Paul Keeley
Jonathan E. Brody
Chapman L. Smith, Jr.

OF COUNSEL

Sherwood Spencer (Retired)
E. Paige Drummond Brody

General Counsel for: American Bank of Hollywood.
Representative Clients: American Bank of Hollywood; Bank of North America; State Farm Fire & Casualty Company; Banaszak Concrete Corp.; Peakload, Inc. of America; Doby Building Supply, Inc.; Michael Swerdlow Companies; Construction Management Services, Inc.; Raintree Golf Club.

For full biographical listings, see the Martindale-Hubbell Law Directory

*JACKSONVILLE,** Duval Co.

ALLEN, BRINTON & SIMMONS, P.A. (AV)

One Independent Drive, Suite 3200, 32202
Telephone: 904-353-8800
Fax: 904-353-8770

A. Graham Allen
William D. Brinton
Sidney S. Simmons, II

Edward McCarthy, III
Lisa Lloyd Pickert
Joelle J. Dillard

For full biographical listings, see the Martindale-Hubbell Law Directory

BLEDSOE, SCHMIDT, LIPPES & ADAMS, P.A. (AV)

One Independent Drive, Suite 2501, 32202
Telephone: 904-356-2501
Fax: 904-356-6341

James A. Bledsoe, Jr.
Terrance E. Schmidt
Harold S. Lippes
Adam G. Adams, III
Stephen K. Moonly
Cheryl A. Roberson
Julie Hills Tucker
Courtney Kneece Grimm

For full biographical listings, see the Martindale-Hubbell Law Directory

BOYER, TANZLER & BOYER (AV)

200 East Forsyth Street, 32202
Telephone: 904-358-3030
Fax: 904-634-0036

MEMBERS OF FIRM

Tyrie A. Boyer
Tyrie W. Boyer
Herbert T. Sussman

ASSOCIATES

Richard C. Watson
Daryl C. Jaquette

Reference: American National Bank of Jacksonville.

For full biographical listings, see the Martindale-Hubbell Law Directory

BROWN, TERRELL, HOGAN, ELLIS, MCCLAMMA & YEGELWEL, P.A. (AV)

Suite 804 Blackstone Building, 233 East Bay Street, 32202
Telephone: 904-632-2424

Thomas R. Brown
James T. Terrell
Wayne Hogan
Timothy D. Ellis
T. Edward McClamma
Evan J. Yegelwel

Thomas E. Duffy, Jr.
Annette J. Ritter
Anita Pryor
Christopher G. Burns
Carroll Cayer
Michael S. Sharrit
Alan M. Pickert

Reference: NCNB.

For full biographical listings, see the Martindale-Hubbell Law Directory

JOHN F. CALLENDER (AV)

2105 Gulf Life Tower, 32207
Telephone: 904-398-8833
Fax: 904-396-4457

Reference: First Union National Bank.

For full biographical listings, see the Martindale-Hubbell Law Directory

FANNIN, TYLER & HAMILTON, P.A. (AV)

Park Pointe, Suite D, 4741 Atlantic Boulevard, 32207-2127
Telephone: 904-398-9999
Facsimile: 904-398-0806

John F. Fannin
H. Tyrone Tyler
J. Clark Hamilton, Jr.
Jay C. Floyd

For full biographical listings, see the Martindale-Hubbell Law Directory

GABEL & HAIR (AV)

76 South Laura Street, Suite 1600, 32202-3421
Telephone: 904-353-7329
Cable Address: "Wahlgabel"
Fax: 904-358-1637

MEMBERS OF FIRM

George D. Gabel, Jr.
Mattox S. Hair
Joel B. Toomey
Robert M. Dees
Sheldon Boney Forte
Timothy J. Conner
Suzanne Meyer Schnabel

ASSOCIATES

Christine S. Mayo
Michael L. Berry, Jr.
Karen Harris Hildebrand

Scott M. Loftin (1878-1953)
Harold B. Wahl (1907-1993)

Representative Clients: Florida Publishing Co.; Southern Bell Telephone & Telegraph Co.; Florida East Coast Railway Co.; Florida Hotel-Motel Self Insurers Fund; The Steamship Mutual Underwriting Association, Ltd.; The Standard Steamship Owners Protection & Indemnity Association, Ltd.; The Japan Ship Owners Mutual Protection & Indemnity Association; Liverpool & London Steamship Protection & Indemnity Association; Exxon Corp.; U.S. Fidelity and Guaranty Co.

For full biographical listings, see the Martindale-Hubbell Law Directory

LILES, GAVIN & COSTANTINO (AV)

One Enterprise Center, Suite 1500, 225 Water Street, 32202
Telephone: 904-634-1100
Fax: 904-634-1234

Rutledge R. Liles
R. Kyle Gavin
R. Scott Costantino
F. Bay Neal III

For full biographical listings, see the Martindale-Hubbell Law Directory

PENLAND & BLOCK, P.A. (AV)

Suite 1113 Blackstone Building, 32202
Telephone: 904-632-2100
Fax: 904-353-3756

S. Perry Penland

Eric S. Block

For full biographical listings, see the Martindale-Hubbell Law Directory

*KISSIMMEE,** Osceola Co.

POHL & BROWN, P.A.

(See Winter Park)

Kissimmee—Continued

TROUTMAN, WILLIAMS, IRVIN, GREEN & HELMS, PROFESSIONAL ASSOCIATION (AV)

Suite 206, 120 Broadway, 34741
Telephone: 407-933-8834
FAX: 407-933-8253
Winter Park, Florida Office: 311 West Fairbanks Avenue.
Telephone: 407-647-2277.
FAX: 407-628-2986.

Russell Troutman
Jack E. Bowen

For full biographical listings, see the Martindale-Hubbell Law Directory

LAKELAND, Polk Co.

LANE, TROHN, CLARKE, BERTRAND, VREELAND & JACOBSEN, P.A. (AV)

One Lake Morton Drive, P.O. Box 3, 33802-0003
Telephone: 813-284-2200
Telecopier: 813-688-0310
Bradenton, Florida Office: 233 15th Street, West, P.O. Box 551.
Telephone: 813-747-1871.

A. H. Lane (Retired)
Robert L. Trohn
Thomas L. Clarke, Jr.
Robert J. Bertrand
John K. Vreeland
Donald G. Jacobsen
Christopher M. Fear
Gary S. Rabin
Lynn H. Groseclose
Robert M. Brush
Kingswood Sprott, Jr.
John V. Quinlan
John A. Attaway, Jr.
Hank B. Campbell
Judith J. Flanders
Patrick J. Murphy
Mitchell D. Franks

Jonathan B. Trohn
Edwin A. Scales, III
Andrew R. McCumber
Nancy C. Harrison
Mia L. McKown
Deborah Laux Slowik

Counsel for: Ewell Industries, Inc.
Local Counsel for: Auto Owners Insurance Co.; Liberty Mutual Insurance Co.; St. Paul Fire & Marine Insurance Cos.; U.S. Fidelity & Guaranty Co.; State Farm Insurance Cos.
Approved Attorneys for: Attorneys' Title Insurance Fund; Chicago Title Insurance Co.

For Complete List of Firm Personnel, See General Section

For full biographical listings, see the Martindale-Hubbell Law Directory

PETERSON, MYERS, CRAIG, CREWS, BRANDON & PUTERBAUGH, P.A. (AV)

100 East Main Street, P.O. Box 24628, 33802-4628
Telephone: 813-683-6511; 676-6934
Telecopier: 813-682-8031
Lake Wales, Florida Office: 130 East Central Avenue, P.O. Box 1079.
Telephones: 813-676-7611; 683-8942.
Winter Haven, Florida Office: Suite 300, 141 5th Street, N.W., P.O. Drawer 7608.
Telephone: 813-294-3360

Jack P. Brandon
Beach A Brooks, Jr.
J. Davis Connor
Roy A. Craig, Jr.
Jacob C. Dykxhoorn
Dennis P. Johnson
Kevin C. Knowlton
Douglas A. Lockwood, III
Corneal B. Myers
Cornelius B. Myers, III
Robert E. Puterbaugh
Abel A. Putnam
Thomas B. Putnam, Jr.
Deborah A. Ruster
Stephen R. Senn
Andrea Teves Smith
Kerry M. Wilson

General Counsel For: Barnett Bank of Polk County.
Representative Clients: Mutual Wholesale Co.; Sun Bank/Mid-Florida, N.A.; Chase Commercial Corp.; Barnett Banks, Inc.; Ben Hill Griffin, Inc.; Alcoma Association, Inc.
Approved Attorneys For: Equitable Life Assurance Society of the United States; Federal Land Bank of Columbia, S.C.; Attorneys' Title Insurance Fund.

For full biographical listings, see the Martindale-Hubbell Law Directory

LAKE WALES, Polk Co.

PETERSON, MYERS, CRAIG, CREWS, BRANDON & PUTERBAUGH, P.A. (AV)

130 East Central Avenue, P.O. Box 1079, 33853
Telephone: 813-676-7611; 683-8942
Telecopier: 813-676-0643
Lakeland, Florida Office: 100 East Main Street, P.O. Box 24628.
Telephones: 813-683-6511; 676-6934.
Winter Haven, Florida Office: Suite 300, 141 5th Street, N.W., P.O. Drawer 7608.
Telephone: 813-294-3360.

(See Next Column)

Jack P. Brandon
Beach A Brooks, Jr.
Beach A Brooks, Jr.
J. Davis Connor
Roy A. Craig, Jr.
Jacob C. Dykxhoorn
Dennis P. Johnson
Kevin C. Knowlton
Douglas A. Lockwood, III
Corneal B. Myers
Cornelius B. Myers, III
Robert E. Puterbaugh
Robert E. Puterbaugh
Abel A. Putnam
Thomas B. Putnam, Jr.
Deborah A. Ruster
Stephen R. Senn
Andrea Teves Smith
Kerry M. Wilson

General Counsel for: Barnett Bank of Polk County.
Representative Clients: Mutual Wholesale Co.; Sun Bank/Mid-Florida, N.A.; Chase Commercial Corp.; Barnett Banks, Inc.; Ben Hill Griffin, Inc.; Alcoma Association, Inc.
Approved Attorneys for: Equitable Life Assurance Society of the United States; Federal Land Bank of Columbia, S.C.; Attorneys' Title Insurance Fund.

For full biographical listings, see the Martindale-Hubbell Law Directory

LAKE WORTH, Palm Beach Co.

RENICK, SINGER, KAMBER & FISCHER (AV)

1530 North Federal Highway, 33460
Telephone: 407-582-6644
Fax: 407-533-7975

Kenneth H. Renick
Leonard I. Singer
Cathy L. Kamber
Brian Scott Fischer

ASSOCIATE

Darryl P. Figueroa

For full biographical listings, see the Martindale-Hubbell Law Directory

LEESBURG, Lake Co.

AUSTIN & PEPPERMAN (AV)

Suite C 1321 West Citizens Boulevard, P.O. Drawer 490200, 34749-0200
Telephone: 904-728-1020
FAX: 904-728-0595

Robert E. Austin, Jr.
Carla R. Pepperman

ASSOCIATE

Robin L. Hoyle

Representative Clients: Allstate Insurance Co.; American Excess Insurance Co.; American Re-Insurance Co.; Florida Rock Industries, Inc.; Goodyear Tire & Rubber Co.; Great American Insurance Co.

For full biographical listings, see the Martindale-Hubbell Law Directory

LONGWOOD, Seminole Co.

JAMES B. BYRNE, JR., P.A. (AV)

Crown Oak Centre, 370 Crown Oak Centre Drive, 32750
Telephone: 407-831-0450
Fax: 407-339-0542
Orange City, Florida Office: 815 South Volusia Avenue, Suite 3.
Telephone: 904-775-0038.

James B. Byrne, Jr.

For full biographical listings, see the Martindale-Hubbell Law Directory

MELBOURNE, Brevard Co.

GLEASON, BARLOW & BOHNE, P.A. (AV)

121-123 Fifth Avenue (Indialantic), P.O. Box 3648, 32903
Telephone: 407-723-5121
Fax: 407-984-5426

William H. Gleason
T. Mitchell Barlow, Jr. (Resident)
Karl W. Bohne, Jr.

Reference: First Union National Bank of Florida, Melbourne, Florida.

For full biographical listings, see the Martindale-Hubbell Law Directory

KRASNY AND DETTMER (AV)

A Partnership of Professional Associations
780 South Apollo Boulevard, P.O. Box 428, 32902-0428
Telephone: 407-723-5646
Telecopier: 407-768-1147

Myron S. (Mike) Krasny (P.A.)
Dale A. Dettmer (P.A.)

Scott Krasny

Representative Clients: Security National Bank; The Coy A. Clark Co.

For full biographical listings, see the Martindale-Hubbell Law Directory

Melbourne—Continued

NANCE, CACCIATORE, SISSERSON, DURYEA AND HAMILTON (AV)

525 North Harbor City Boulevard, 32935
Telephone: 407-254-8416
Fax: 407-259-8243

MEMBERS OF FIRM

James H. Nance
Sammy Cacciatore
James A. Sisserson
Ronald G. Duryea
John N. Hamilton
Charles G. Barger, Jr.

Reference: Reliance Bank, Melbourne.

For full biographical listings, see the Martindale-Hubbell Law Directory

*MIAMI,** Dade Co.

ADAMS & ADAMS (AV)

5th Floor, Concord Building, 66 West Flagler Street, 33130
Telephone: 305-371-3333
Broward: 305-728-8770
Telecopier: 305-372-3987

Richard B. Adams (1926-1983)
Richard B. Adams, Jr.
R. Wade Adams

ASSOCIATES

Mai-Ling E. Castillo
Anthony P. Strasius

For full biographical listings, see the Martindale-Hubbell Law Directory

ANGONES, HUNTER, MCCLURE, LYNCH & WILLIAMS, P.A. (AV)

Ninth Floor-Concord Building, 66 West Flagler Street, 33130
Telephone: 305-371-5000
Fort Lauderdale: 305-728-9112
FAX: 305-371-3948

Frank R. Angones
Steven Kent Hunter
John McClure
Christopher J. Lynch
Stewart D. Williams
B. Scott Hunter

Leopoldo Garcia, Jr.
Thomas W. Paradise
Donna Joy Hunter
Lourdes Alfonsin Ruiz
Matthew K. Mitchell
Kara D. Phinney
C. David Durkee

Insurance Clients: Allstate Insurance Co.; Prudential Property & Casualty Insurance Company; State Farm Fire & Casualty Insurance Company; Rollins Hudig Hall Healthcare Risk, Inc.

For full biographical listings, see the Martindale-Hubbell Law Directory

ARAGON, MARTIN, BURLINGTON & CROCKETT, P.A. (AV)

Office in the Grove - Penthouse, 2699 South Bayshore Drive, 33133
Telephone: 305-858-2900
Telefax: 305-858-5261

Rudolph F. Aragon
Robert K. Burlington
Jeffrey B. Crockett
Gregory A. Martin
Carla M. Barrow
Daniel F. Blonsky
Kevin C. Kaplan
Mark A. Salzberg
Paul J. Schwiep

For full biographical listings, see the Martindale-Hubbell Law Directory

CLARK, SPARKMAN, ROBB, NELSON & MASON (AV)

Suite 1003 Biscayne Building, 19 West Flagler Street, 33130
Telephone: 305-374-0033
Broward: 305-522-0045
Fax: 305-539-0767
Fort Lauderdale, Florida Office: Suite 1210, 110 Tower, 110 S.E. Sixth Street.
Telephones: 305-463-3590; Dade: 305-945-4461.
West Palm Beach, Florida Office: 324 Datura Street, Suite 303. Telephone 407-659-6933.
Fax: 407-659-4328.

MEMBERS OF FIRM

James K. Clark
James T. Sparkman
Michael A. Robb
Richard M. Nelson
Donald Edward Mason
Marc S. Buschman
Paul S. Ginsburg
Frances Fernandez Guasch
Dan Kaufman
Valerie Kiffin Lewis

For full biographical listings, see the Martindale-Hubbell Law Directory

MARK A. COHEN & ASSOCIATES, P.A. (AV)

1221 Brickell Avenue, Suite 1780, 33131-3260
Telephone: 305-375-9292
Facsimile: 305-381-6799
Washington, D.C. Office: Mark A. Cohen & Associates, P.C. Homer Building, 601 Thirteenth Street, N.W., Suite 440 North, 20005.
Telephone: 202-347-2000.
Facsimile: 202-347-2002.

(See Next Column)

Mark A. Cohen
Roger S. Kobert
Todd R. Legon

SENIOR COUNSEL

David J. Federbush

Fred Goldberg
Neil L. Potash
Michael P. Rainerman
Douglas P. Fremont
Karen G. Morton

For full biographical listings, see the Martindale-Hubbell Law Directory

PETER A. COHEN, P.A. (AV)

Penthouse One, 155 South Miami Avenue, 33130
Telephone: 305-358-9251
Fax: 305-358-3412

Peter A. Cohen

For full biographical listings, see the Martindale-Hubbell Law Directory

CORLETT KILLIAN, A PROFESSIONAL ASSOCIATION (AV)

116 West Flagler Street, 33130
Telephone: 305-377-8931
Cable Address: "Advocot"
Telefax: 305-372-9306

Edward S. Corlett, III
A. Dan Killian, Jr.
Donna G. Levi
Andrew E. Grigsby
Rene E. Lamar
Charles S. Rowley, Jr.

Representative Clients: CSX Transportation, Inc.; Florida East Coast Railway Co.; Great West Casualty Co.; Hartz Mountain Corp.; Leach Company; National Railroad Passeger Corp.; Nationwide Insurance Co.; Northland Insurance Co.; Travelers Insurance Co.; Utica Mutual Insurance Co.

For full biographical listings, see the Martindale-Hubbell Law Directory

DEUTSCH & BLUMBERG, P.A. (AV)

Suite 2802 New World Tower, 100 North Biscayne Boulevard, 33132
Telephone: 305-358-6329
Fax: 305-358-9304

Steven K. Deutsch
Edward R. Blumberg
Louis Thaler

For full biographical listings, see the Martindale-Hubbell Law Directory

LAW OFFICES OF DUBÉ AND WRIGHT, P.A. (AV)

Suite 2608 New World Tower, 100 North Biscayne Boulevard, 33132
Telephone: 305-374-7472
Fax: 305-374-3219

Robert L. Dubé
Wilkinson D. Wright, III

OF COUNSEL

Richard M. Gale

For full biographical listings, see the Martindale-Hubbell Law Directory

DUNN, LODISH & WIDOM, P.A. (AV)

24th Floor One Biscayne Tower, Two South Biscayne Boulevard, 33131
Telephone: 305-374-4401
Fax: 305-374-6401

Richard M. Dunn
Alvin D. Lodish
Mitchell E. Widom
Barbara A. Eagan
Scott D. Kravetz
Michael G. Srebnick
Dana Corbo
Ronnie R. Savar
Sherril M. Colombo

For full biographical listings, see the Martindale-Hubbell Law Directory

FERRELL & FERTEL, P.A. (AV)

Suite 1920 Miami Center, 201 South Biscayne Boulevard, 33131-2305
Telephone: 305-371-8585
Telecopier: 305-371-5732

Milton M. Ferrell, Jr.
Alan K. Fertel

Reference: City National Bank of Florida.

For full biographical listings, see the Martindale-Hubbell Law Directory

FLOYD PEARSON RICHMAN GREER WEIL BRUMBAUGH & RUSSOMANNO, P.A. (AV)

Miami Center, Tenth Floor, 201 South Biscayne Boulevard, 33131
Telephone: 305-373-4000
Fax: 305-373-4099

Robert L. Floyd
Ray H. Pearson
Gerald F. Richman
Alan G. Greer
Kenneth J. Weil
John M. Brumbaugh
Herman J. Russomanno
Andrew J. Mirabito
Bruce A. Christensen
Scott D. Sheftall

(See Next Column)

FLOYD PEARSON RICHMAN GREER WEIL BRUMBAUGH & RUSSOMANNO P.A., *Miami—Continued*

Charles H. Johnson
Gary S. Betensky
Diane Wagner Katzen
Robert C. Levine
Robert J. Fiore
Robert J. Borrello
Manuel A. Garcia-Linares
Carroll J. Kelly
Mark Anthony Romance
Richard C. Alvarez
Steven M Brady

OF COUNSEL

Paul M. Bunge
James W. Middleton

Representative Clients: AT&T Information Systems, Inc.; Shriners Hospitals for Crippled Children; Motorola, Inc.; Minnesota Mining and Manufacturing Co.; South Florida Hotel and Motel Assn.; The Lubrizol Corp.; Republic of Panama; Hallmark.

For full biographical listings, see the Martindale-Hubbell Law Directory

HADDAD, JOSEPHS, JACK, GAEBE & MARKARIAN (AV)

1493 Sunset Drive (Coral Gables), P.O. Box 345118, 33114
Telephone: Dade County: 305-666-6006
Broward County: 305-463-6699
Telecopier: 305-662-9931

MEMBERS OF FIRM

Gil Haddad
Michael R. Josephs
Lewis N. Jack, Jr.
John S. Gaebe
David K. Markarian

ASSOCIATES

Amarillys E. Garcia-Perez
Elisabeth M. McClosky

For full biographical listings, see the Martindale-Hubbell Law Directory

HALL AND O'BRIEN, P.A. (AV)

Penthouse, 1428 Brickell Avenue, 33131
Telephone: 305-374-5030
Fax: 305-374-5033

Andrew C. Hall
Richard F. O'Brien, III

Leana Marie Vastine
Christopher M. David
Philippe Lieberman

For full biographical listings, see the Martindale-Hubbell Law Directory

HARDY, BISSETT & LIPTON, P.A. (AV)

501 Northeast First Avenue, 33132
Telephone: 305-358-6200
Broward: 305-462-6377
Fax: 305-577-8230
Boca Raton, Florida Office: 2201 Corporate Boulevard, N.W., Suite 205.
Telephone: 407-998-9202.
Telecopier: 407-998-9693.

G. Jack Hardy
G. William Bissett
Stephen N. Lipton (Resident, Boca Raton Office)

Howard K. Cherna
Lee Philip Teichner
Matthew Kennedy
H. Dane Mottlau

Representative Clients: International Paper Co.; Masonite Corp.; Bridgestone/Firestone Inc.; American International Underwriters; American International Group, Inc.; Pennsylvania National Insurance Cos.; Crown Equipment Corp.; The Coleman Co., Inc.; Interamerican Car Rental, Inc.; York International Corp.

For full biographical listings, see the Martindale-Hubbell Law Directory

HOFFMAN & HERTZIG, P.A. (AV)

Suite 900, 241 Sevilla Avenue (Coral Gables), 33134
Telephone: 305-445-3100

Carl H. Hoffman
David Hertzig

For full biographical listings, see the Martindale-Hubbell Law Directory

KELLY, BLACK, BLACK, BYRNE & BEASLEY, PROFESSIONAL ASSOCIATION (AV)

1400 Alfred I. du Pont Building, 169 East Flagler Street, 33131
Telephone: 305-358-5700

Hugo L. Black, Jr.
Robert Carleton Byrne
Joseph W. Beasley
Bonnie J. Losak-Jimenez
Eric L. Lundt

Representative Clients: Credit Suisse; Multi-Media Entertainment, Inc.; Japan Development Company; Israel Discount Bank; Bank of North America; EquityLine Securities, Inc.; Bacardi Imports, Inc.; Safecard Services, Inc.; Peoples Telephone Co.
Reference: United National Bank.

For full biographical listings, see the Martindale-Hubbell Law Directory

KENNY NACHWALTER SEYMOUR ARNOLD CRITCHLOW & SPECTOR, PROFESSIONAL ASSOCIATION (AV)

1100 Miami Center, 201 South Biscayne Boulevard, 33131-4327
Telephone: 305-373-1000
Facsimile: 305-372-1861
ABA/net: 18338
Rogersville, Tennessee Office: 107 East Main Street, Suite 301, 37857-3347.
Telephone: 615-272-5300.
Facsimile: 615-272-4961.

James J. Kenny
Michael Nachwalter
Thomas H. Seymour
Richard Alan Arnold
Richard H. Critchlow
Brian F. Spector
Kevin J. Murray
William J. Blechman
Harry R. Schafer
Deborah A. Sampieri
David H. Lichter
Scott E. Perwin
Jeffrey T. Foreman
Lauren C. Ravkind
Katherine Clark Silverglate
Amanda M. McGovern
Paul C. Huck, Jr.
Tara M. Higgins

Representative Clients: Albertson's, Inc.; American Bankers; Cartier, Inc.; Ethan Allen; Federated Department Stores, Inc.; The Florida Bar; General Telephone Company of Florida; GTE Directories Corp.; Health Trust, Inc.; Hospital Corporation of America.

For full biographical listings, see the Martindale-Hubbell Law Directory

KLUGER, PERETZ, KAPLAN & BERLIN, P.A. (AV)

1970 Miami Center, 201 South Biscayne Boulevard, 33131
Telephone: Dade: 305-379-9000
Broward: 305-728-8100
Fax: 305-379-3428

Alan J. Kluger
Abbey L. Kaplan
Steven I. Peretz
Howard J. Berlin
Jay A. Steinman
Steve I. Silverman
Bruce A. Katzen
Marcia Soto
Andrew P. Gold

Alyne Wrubel Kaplan
Karen Evans
Paul L. Orshan
Michael David Ehrenstein
Kimberly D. Kolback
Michael B. Chesal
Craig T. Galle
Donna E. Miller
Ronny J. Halperin
Gary A. Levinson
Todd A. Levine
Deborah Berlin Talenfeld
Michael S. Perse
Beth Cohen Besner
Michael Jeffrey Feuerman

OF COUNSEL

James R. Longacre (Not admitted in FL)

LEGAL SUPPORT PERSONNEL

PARALEGALS

Vernia Contrearas
Cathy A. Davis
Diane M. Payne
Maria A. Tucci

For full biographical listings, see the Martindale-Hubbell Law Directory

KUBICKI DRAPER (AV)

Penthouse City National Bank Building, 25 West Flagler Street, 33130
Telephone: 305-374-1212
Fax: 305-374-7846
West Palm Beach, Florida Office: Suite 1100 United National Bank Tower, 1675 Palm Beach Lakes Boulevard, 33401.
Telephone: 407-640-0303.
Fax: 407-640-0524.
Fort Lauderdale, Florida Office: Suite 1600, One East Broward Boulevard, 33301.
Telephone: 305-768-0011.
Fax: 305-768-0514.

Gene Kubicki
Daniel Draper, Jr.
Robert F. Bouchard
Robert Baldwin Brown, III
Virginia Easley Johnson
Joseph J. Kalbac, Jr.
Elwood T. Lippincott, Jr.

Betsy Ellwanger Gallagher
Dennis J. Murphy
Charles Mustell
Anthony L. Pietrofesa
Carol A. Scott
Martin Van Haasteren

OF COUNSEL

Aubrey L. Talburt

For Complete List of Firm Personnel, See General Section

For full biographical listings, see the Martindale-Hubbell Law Directory

KUTNER, RUBINOFF & BUSH (AV)

501 N.E. 1st Avenue, 33132
Telephone: 305-358-6200; Broward: 305-462-6377

Arno Kutner
Edward G. Rubinoff
Kenneth J. Bush

(See Next Column)

KUTNER, RUBINOFF & BUSH—*Continued*

ASSOCIATE

Susan Scrivani Lerner

For full biographical listings, see the Martindale-Hubbell Law Directory

LEESFIELD, LEIGHTON, RUBIO & HILLENCAMP, P.A. (AV)

2350 South Dixie Highway, 33133
Telephone: 305-854-4900/1-800-836-6400 (toll free)
Fax: 305-854-8266
Key West, Florida Office: 615 1/2 Whitehead Street.
Telephone: 305-296-1342.
Fax: 305-294-1793.

Ira H. Leesfield
John Elliott Leighton
Maria L. Rubio
Ibis J. Hillencamp
Robert S. Glazier
Alex Alvarez
Sally Gross-Farina

For full biographical listings, see the Martindale-Hubbell Law Directory

THOMAS W. MCALILEY, P.A. (AV)

3260 Miami Center, 201 South Biscayne Boulevard, 33131
Telephone: 305-373-6551
Telecopier: 305-358-3404

Thomas W. McAliley

For full biographical listings, see the Martindale-Hubbell Law Directory

MERSHON, SAWYER, JOHNSTON, DUNWODY & COLE (AV)

A Partnership including Professional Associations
Suite 4500 First Union Financial Center, 200 South Biscayne Boulevard, 33131-2387
Telephone: 305-358-5100
Cable Address: "Mercole"
Telex: 515705
Fax: 305-376-8654
Naples, Florida Office: Pelican Bay Corporate Centre, Suite 501, 5551 Ridgewood Drive.
Telephone: 813-598-1055.
Fax: 813-598-1868.
West Palm Beach, Florida Office: 777 South Flagler Drive, Suite 900.
Telephone: 407-659-5990.
Fax: 407-659-6313.
Key West, Florida Office: 3132 North Side Drive, Suite 102.
Telephone: 305-296-1774.
Fax: 305-296-1715
London, England Office: Blake Lodge, Bridge Lane, London SW11 3AD, England.
Telephone: 44-71-978-7748.
Fax: 44-71-350-0156.

MEMBERS OF FIRM

Aubrey V. Kendall (P.A.)
William J. Dunaj (P.A.)
James M. McCann, Jr. (Resident, West Palm Beach Office)
Robert T. Wright, Jr.
Dennis M. Campbell (P.A.)
Timothy J. Norris (P.A.)
Harvey W. Gurland, Jr.
Jeffrey D. Fridkin (Resident, Naples Office)
Carlos M. Sires
Thomas E. Streit (Resident, West Palm Beach Office)
John C. Shawde
Jack A. Falk, Jr
Mary Ellen Valletta

OF COUNSEL

Alexander Penelas

ASSOCIATES

Lawrence P. Rochefort
Rona F. Morrow
Nancy A. Romfh (Resident, West Palm Beach Office)
John D. Eaton
Mario David Carballo
Elizabeth Cassidy Barber
Natalie Scharf
Gregg Metzger

Representative Clients: Arvida/JMB Partners; Bankers Trust Co.; Biscayne Kennel Club, Inc.; The Chase Manhattan Bank, N.A.; Lennar Corp.; Reynolds Metals Co.; United States Sugar Corp.; University of Miami.

For Complete List of Firm Personnel, See General Section

For full biographical listings, see the Martindale-Hubbell Law Directory

MURAI, WALD, BIONDO & MORENO, P.A. (AV)

9th Floor Ingraham Building, 25 Southeast 2nd Avenue, 33131
Telephone: 305-358-5900
Fax: 305-358-9490

Rene V. Murai
Gerald B. Wald
Gerald J. Biondo
M. Cristina Moreno
William E. Davis

Cristina Echarte Brochin
Ana Maria Escagedo
Manuel Kadre
Lynette Ebeoglu McGuinness
Mary Leslie Smith

(See Next Column)

Reference: Republic National Bank of Miami.

For full biographical listings, see the Martindale-Hubbell Law Directory

NICKLAUS, VALLE, CRAIG & WICKS (AV)

15th Floor New World Tower, 100 North Biscayne Boulevard, 33132
Telephone: 305-358-2888
Facsimile: 305-358-5501
Fort Lauderdale, Florida Office: Suite 101N, Justice Building, 524 South Andrews Avenue, 33301.
Telephone: 305-523-1858.
Facsimile: 305-523-8068.

MEMBERS OF FIRM

Edward R. Nicklaus
Laurence F. Valle
Lawrance B. Craig, III
William R. Wicks, III
James W. McCready, III
Michael W. Whitaker

ASSOCIATES

Richard D. Settler
Kevin M. Fitzmaurice
Timothy Maze Hartley
Keith S. Grybowski
Patricia Blanco
Michael J. Lynott

For full biographical listings, see the Martindale-Hubbell Law Directory

PATTERSON, CLAUSSEN, SANTOS & HUME (AV)

A Partnership of Professional Associations
18th Floor, Courthouse Tower, 44 West Flagler Street, 33130-1808
Telephone: 305-350-9000
Fax: 305-372-3940

John H. Patterson (P.A.)
Kenneth F. Claussen (P.A.)
Jose A. Santos, Jr. (P.A.)
John H. Patterson, Jr. (P.A.)
Charles Lea Hume (P.A.)

OF COUNSEL

James H. Sweeny, III (P.A.)

For Complete List of Firm Personnel, See General Section

For full biographical listings, see the Martindale-Hubbell Law Directory

PODHURST, ORSECK, JOSEFSBERG, EATON, MEADOW, OLIN & PERWIN, P.A. (AV)

Suite 800 City National Bank Building, 25 West Flagler Street, 33130-1780
Telephone: 305-358-2800; Fort Lauderdale: 305-463-4346
Fax: 305-358-2382

Aaron Podhurst
Robert Orseck (1934-1978)
Robert C. Josefsberg
Joel D. Eaton
Barry L. Meadow
Michael S. Olin
Joel S. Perwin
Steven C. Marks
Victor M. Diaz, Jr.
Katherine W. Ezell

Karen B. Podhurst

OF COUNSEL

Walter H. Beckham, Jr.

Representative Clients: Burger King Corp.; Ryder System, Inc.; Ernst & Young; Lennar Corporation; The Continental Companies.
Reference: United National Bank of Miami; City National Bank of Miami.

For full biographical listings, see the Martindale-Hubbell Law Directory

PROENZA, WHITE & ROBERTS, P.A. (AV)

Grove Plaza, 2900 Middle Street, 33133
Telephone: 305-442-1700
Telecopier: 305-442-2559

Morris C. Proenza
David J. White
H. Clay Roberts
H. Mark Vieth
Robert C. Tilghman

For Complete List of Firm Personnel, See General Section

For full biographical listings, see the Martindale-Hubbell Law Directory

PYSZKA, KESSLER, MASSEY, WELDON, CATRI, HOLTON & DOUBERLEY, P.A. (AV)

Fifth Floor, Grand Bay Plaza, 2665 South Bayshore Drive, 33133
Telephone: 305-858-6614
Fort Lauderdale, Florida Office: 110 Tower, Twentieth Floor, 110 Southeast Sixth Street.
Telephone: 305-463-8593.

Gerard E. Pyszka
Malcolm W. "Mac" Weldon
William M. Douberley
Phillip D. Blackmon, Jr.
Benjamin D. Levy
L.H. Steven Savola
Jordan J. Lewis

(See Next Column)

PYSZKA, KESSLER, MASSEY, WELDON, CATRI, HOLTON & DOUBERLEY P.A., *Miami—Continued*

OF COUNSEL

Donald E. Stone

For Complete List of Firm Personnel, See General Section

For full biographical listings, see the Martindale-Hubbell Law Directory

RICHEY, MUNROE, RODRIGUEZ & DIAZ, P.A. (AV)

3100 First Union Financial Center, 200 South Biscayne Boulevard, 33131-2327
Telephone: 305-372-8808
Telefax: 305-372-3669; 374-4652
Telex: 4932891 RAMPA

Kirk W. Munroe
Juan J. Rodriguez
William L. Richey
Michael Diaz, Jr.

Tamara R. Piety

For full biographical listings, see the Martindale-Hubbell Law Directory

STANLEY M. ROSENBLATT PROFESSIONAL ASSOCIATION (AV)

12th Floor, Concord Building, 66 West Flagler Street, 33130
Telephone: 305-374-6131
Fax: 305-381-8818

Stanley M. Rosenblatt

Susan Rosenblatt
Mary Margaret Schneider
David C. Rash

For full biographical listings, see the Martindale-Hubbell Law Directory

ROSSMAN, BAUMBERGER & REBOSO, A PROFESSIONAL ASSOCIATION (AV)

23rd Floor, Courthouse Tower, 44 West Flagler Street, 33130
Telephone: 305-373-0708
Fax: 305-577-4370

Charles H. Baumberger
Stephen F. Rossman

Manuel A. Reboso
David A. Sierra

Reference: United National Bank of Miami.

For full biographical listings, see the Martindale-Hubbell Law Directory

SAMS, MARTIN & LISTER, P.A. (AV)

The Atrium, Suite 200, 1500 San Remo Avenue (Coral Gables), 33146
Telephone: 305-666-3181
Fax: 305-666-5867
Fort Lauderdale, Florida Office: Sams, Spier, Hoffman and Hastings, P.A., 500 Southeast Sixth Street, Suite 101, 33301.
Telephone: 305-467-3181.
Fax: 305-523-5462.
Jacksonville, Florida Office: Sams, Spier, Hoffman and Hastings, P.A., 1301 Gulf Life Drive, Suite 2010, 32207.
Telephone: 904-399-5546.
Fax: 904-354-0182.

Murray Sams, Jr.
Timothy M. Martin
David P. Lister

Julianne K. Lara

For full biographical listings, see the Martindale-Hubbell Law Directory

SINCLAIR, LOUIS, HEATH, NUSSBAUM & ZAVERTNIK, P.A. (AV)

11th Floor Alfred I. Du Pont Building, 33131
Telephone: 305-374-0544
FAX: 305-381-6869

Henry M. Sinclair (1908-1977)
Bayard E. Heath
Paul A. Louis
Frank Nussbaum
John L. Zavertnik

OF COUNSEL

Leonard H. Rubin
Steven I. Weissman

For full biographical listings, see the Martindale-Hubbell Law Directory

SPARBER, KOSNITZKY, TRUXTON, DE LA GUARDIA SPRATT & BROOKS, P.A. (AV)

1401 Brickell Avenue Suite 700, 33131
Telephone: Dade: 305-379-7200; Broward: 305-760-9133
Fax: 305-379-0800

Gary S. Brooks

(See Next Column)

Alan G. Geffin
Komal J. Bhojwani

For Complete List of Firm Personnel, See General Section

For full biographical listings, see the Martindale-Hubbell Law Directory

SPENCER AND KLEIN, PROFESSIONAL ASSOCIATION (AV)

Suite 1901, 801 Brickell Avenue, 33131
Telephone: 305-374-7700
Telecopier: 305-374-4890

Thomas R. Spencer, Jr.

Samuel B. Reiner, II
Jose M. Companioni
Stephen L. Vinson, Jr.

Representative Clients: America Publishing Group; Amerivend Corp.; Buen Hogar Magazine; Editorial America; Gold Star Medical Management, Inc.; Grupo Anaya, S.A.; Independent Living Care, Inc.; Lourdes Health Services, Inc.; Managed Care of America, Inc.

For Complete List of Firm Personnel, See General Section

For full biographical listings, see the Martindale-Hubbell Law Directory

LELAND E. STANSELL, JR., P.A. (AV)

903 Biscayne Building, 19 West Flagler Street, 33130
Telephone: 305-374-5911

ASSOCIATE

Charles L. Balli

For full biographical listings, see the Martindale-Hubbell Law Directory

STEARNS WEAVER MILLER WEISSLER ALHADEFF & SITTERSON, P.A. (AV)

Suite 2200 Museum Tower, 150 West Flagler Street, 33130
Telephone: 305-789-3200
FAX: 305-789-3395
Tampa, Florida Office: Suite 2200 Landmark Centre, 401 East Jackson Street.
Telephone: 813-223-4800.
Fort Lauderdale, Florida Office: 200 East Broward Boulevard, Suite 1900.
Telephone: 305-462-9500.

E. Richard Alhadeff
Louise Jacowitz Allen
Stuart D. Ames
Thomas P. Angelo (Resident, Fort Lauderdale Office)
Lawrence J. Bailin (Resident, Tampa Office)
Patrick A. Barry (Resident, Fort Lauderdale Office)
Lisa K. Bennett (Resident, Fort Lauderdale Office)
Susan Fleming Bennett (Resident, Tampa Office)
Mark J. Bernet (Resident, Tampa Office)
Claire Bailey Carraway (Resident, Tampa Office)
Seth T. Craine (Resident, Tampa Office)
Piero Luciano Desiderio (Resident, Fort Lauderdale Office)
Mark P. Dikeman
Sharon Quinn Dixon
Alan H. Fein
Owen S. Freed
Dean M. Freitag
Robert E. Gallagher, Jr.
Alice R. Huneycutt (Resident, Tampa Office)
Theodore A. Jewell
Elizabeth J. Keeler
Teddy D. Klinghoffer
Robert T. Kofman
Thomas A. Lash (Resident, Tampa Office)
Joy Spillis Lundeen
Brian J. McDonough
Francisco J. Menendez
Antonio R. Menendez
Alison W. Miller
Vicki Lynn Monroe
Harold D. Moorefield, Jr.
John N. Muratides (Resident, Tampa Office)
John K. Olson (Resident, Tampa Office)
Robert C. Owens
Patricia A. Redmond
Carl D. Roston
Steven D. Rubin
Mark A. Schneider
Curtis H. Sitterson
Mark D. Solov
Eugene E. Stearns
Bradford Swing
Dennis R. Turner
Ronald L. Weaver (Resident, Tampa Office)
Robert I. Weissler
Patricia G. Welles
Martin B. Woods (Resident, Fort Lauderdale Office)

Shawn M. Bayne (Resident, Fort Lauderdale Office)
Lisa Berg
Hans C. Beyer (Resident, Tampa Office)
Dawn A. Carapella (Resident, Tampa Office)
Christina Maria Diaz
Robert I. Finvarb
Patricia K. Green
Marilyn D. Greenblatt
Richard B. Jackson
Aimee C. Jimenez
Cheryl A. Kaplan
Michael I. Keyes
Vernon L. Lewis
Kevin Bruce Love
Adam Coatsworth Mishcon
Elizabeth G. Rice (Resident, Tampa Office)
Glenn M. Rissman
Claudia J. Saenz
Richard E. Schatz
Robert P. Shantz (Resident, Tampa Office)
Martin S. Simkovic
Ronni D. Solomon

(See Next Column)

STEARNS WEAVER MILLER WEISSLER ALHADEFF & SITTERSON P.A.—*Continued*

Jo Claire Spear (Resident, Tampa Office)
Gail Marie Stage (Resident, Fort Lauderdale Office)
Annette Torres
Barbara L. Wilhite

OF COUNSEL

Stephen A. Bennett

For full biographical listings, see the Martindale-Hubbell Law Directory

STEWART TILGHMAN FOX & BIANCHI, P.A. (AV)

Suite 1900, 44 West Flagler Street, 33130-1808
Telephone: 305-358-6644
Fax: 305-358-4707

Larry S. Stewart
James B. Tilghman, Jr.
Gary D. Fox
David W. Bianchi

Stuart N. Ratzan

For full biographical listings, see the Martindale-Hubbell Law Directory

STUZIN AND CAMNER, PROFESSIONAL ASSOCIATION (AV)

25th Floor, 1221 Brickell Avenue, 33131-3260
Telephone: 305-577-0600

Charles B. Stuzin
Alfred R. Camner
Stanley A. Beiley
Marsha D. Bilzin
David S. Garbett
Nina S. Gordon
Barry D. Hunter
Nikki J. Nedbor
Neale J. Poller

Lisa R. Carstarphen
Maria E. Chang
Barry P. Gruher
Gustavo D. Llerena
Sherry D. McMillan
Roger A. Preziosi

OF COUNSEL

Anne Shari Camner

References: Citizens Federal Bank; City National Bank of Miami; Barnett Bank of South Florida, N.A.

For full biographical listings, see the Martindale-Hubbell Law Directory

TAYLOR, BRION, BUKER & GREENE (AV)

Fourteenth Floor, 801 Brickell Avenue, 33131-2900
Telephone: 305-377-6700
Telex: 153653 Taybri
Telecopier: 305-371-4578; 371-4579
Tallahassee, Florida Office: Suite 250, 225 South Adams Street.
Telephone: 904-222-7717.
Telecopier: 904-222-3494.
Key West, Florida Office: 500 Fleming Street.
Telephone: 305-292-1776.
Telecopier: 305-292-1982.
Fort Lauderdale, Florida Office: Barnett Bank Plaza, 12th Floor, One East Broward Boulevard.
Telephone: 305-522-6700.
Telecopier: 305-522-6711.
Coral Gables, Florida Office: 2801 Ponce De Leon Boulevard, Suite 707.
Telephone: 305-445-7577.
Telecopier: 305-446-9944.

John S. Andrews (Fort Lauderdale)
Peter C. Bianchi, Jr.
David S. Bowman (Fort Lauderdale)
Wilbur E. Brewton (Tallahassee)
Harold L. Greene
W. Douglas Moody, Jr. (Tallahassee)
James W. Moore
I. Ed Pantaleon (Tallahassee)
Robert J. Paterno
Anthony F. Sanchez
Robert S. Singer
Arnaldo Velez
R. Bruce Wallace

OF COUNSEL

Burton Harrison

For list of Representative Clients, see General Section.

For Complete List of Firm Personnel, See General Section

For full biographical listings, see the Martindale-Hubbell Law Directory

THORNTON, DAVIS & MURRAY, P.A. (AV)

World Trade Center, 80 Southwest 8th Street Suite 2900, 33130
Telephone: 305-446-2646
Fax: 305-441-2374

John M. Murray
Barry L. Davis
J. Thompson Thornton
Gregory P. Sreenan

(See Next Column)

Frederick J. Fein
Ana Maria Marin
Kathleen M. O'Connor

For Complete List of Firm Personnel, See General Section

For full biographical listings, see the Martindale-Hubbell Law Directory

WALLACE, ENGELS, PERTNOY, SOLOWSKY & ALLEN, P.A. (AV)

International Place, 100 Southeast 2nd Street, 21st Floor, 33131
Telephone: 305-371-2223
Fax: 305-373-2073

Milton J. Wallace
Martin Engels
Sidney M. Pertnoy
Jay Solowsky
Richard Lewis Allen
Joseph J. Gersten
Bryan W. Bauman
Todd A. Fodiman

Steven H. Brotman
Alfred I. Hopkins
Michael G. Shannon
Darin S. Engelhardt
Adam B. Leichtling
Mark D. Wallace

For full biographical listings, see the Martindale-Hubbell Law Directory

WELBAUM, ZOOK & JONES (AV)

Penthouse Suite, 901 Ponce de Leon Boulevard (Coral Gables), 33134-3009
Telephone: 305-441-8900
Fax: 305-441-2255

MEMBERS OF FIRM

D. Lloyd Zook (1922-1990)
R. Earl Welbaum
Peter C. Jones
Dan B. Guernsey
Robert A. Hingston
W. Frank Greenleaf
John H. Gregory

ASSOCIATES

Kenn W. Goff
Michael Yates
Mark D. Greenwell

OF COUNSEL

René Sacasas

For full biographical listings, see the Martindale-Hubbell Law Directory

ZUCKERMAN, SPAEDER, TAYLOR & EVANS (AV)

Miami Center, 201 South Biscayne Boulevard, Suite 900, 33131
Telephone: 305-358-5000; 305-579-0110
Broward County: 305-523-0277
Fax: 305-579-9749
Tampa, Florida Office: 101 East Kennedy Boulevard, Suite 3140.
Telephone: 813-221-1010.
Fax: 813-223-7961.
Ft. Lauderdale, Florida Office: One East Broward Boulevard, Suite 700.
Telephone: 305-356-0463.
Fax: 305-356-0406.
Washington, D.C. Office: Zuckerman, Spaeder, Goldstein, Taylor & Kolker, 1201 Connecticut Avenue, N.W.
Telephone: 202-778-1800.
Fax: 202-822-8106.
Baltimore, Maryland Office: Zuckerman, Spaeder, Goldstein, Taylor & Better, Suite 2440, 100 East Pratt Street.
Telephone: 410-332-0444.
Fax: 410-659-0436.
New York, N.Y. Office: Zuckerman, Spaeder, Goldstein, Taylor & Kolker, 1114 Avenue of the Americas, 45th Floor, Grace Building.
Telephone: 212-479-6500.
Fax: 212-479-6512.

MEMBERS OF FIRM

Ronald B. Ravikoff (Resident)
Michael S. Pasano
Morris Weinberg, Jr. (Resident, Tampa, Florida Office)
Humberto J. Peña
Sharon L. Kegerreis
Thomas J. Meeks

ASSOCIATES

Guy A. Rasco
Bryan R. Cleveland
Melissa Hammersley Clark (Not admitted in FL; Resident, Tampa, Florida Office)
Jennifer Rae Coberly
Laura L. Vaughan (Resident, Tampa, Florida Office)
Teresa Halligan (Resident, Tampa Florida Office)

For full biographical listings, see the Martindale-Hubbell Law Directory

*NAPLES,** Collier Co.

HARDT & STEWART (AV)

Suite 705 Sun Bank Building, 801 Laurel Oak Drive, 33963
Telephone: 813-598-2900
Fax: 813-598-3785

MEMBERS OF FIRM

Frederick R. Hardt
Joseph D. Stewart
John D. Kehoe

References: Northern Trust Bank of Florida/Naples, N.A.; U.S. Trust Company of Florida; Sun Bank/Naples, N.A.

(See Next Column)

McDonnell Law Offices (AV)

Suite 304, The Commons, 720 Goodlette Road North, 33940
Telephone: 813-434-7711; Fort Myers: 860-873-8060
Fax: 813-434-5629

Michael McDonnell

Melissa A. Vasquez
Eric J. Vasquez
Lori Hamilton

For full biographical listings, see the Martindale-Hubbell Law Directory

Vega, Brown, Stanley, Martin & Zelman, P.A. (AV)

2660 Airport Road, South, 33962
Telephone: 813-774-3333
Fax: 813-774-6420

George Vega, Jr.
John F. Stanley
Lawrence D. Martin
Theodore W. Zelman

Thomas J. Wood
Paula J. Rhoads
John G. Vega
Sharon M. Hanlon

General Counsel for: Lely Estates; Naples Community Hospital.
Local Counsel: Fleischmann Trust; Quail Creek Developments.

For Complete List of Firm Personnel, See General Section

For full biographical listings, see the Martindale-Hubbell Law Directory

NEW PORT RICHEY, Pasco Co.

Martin, Figurski & Harrill (AV)

A Partnership of Professional Associations
Suite B-1, 8406 Massachusetts Avenue, P.O. Box 786, 34653
Telephone: 813-842-8439
Clearwater, Florida Office: 28059 U.S. Highway 19, Suite 202.
Telephone: 813-796-3259.
Fax: 813-796-3598.

MEMBERS OF FIRM

Daniel N. Martin (P.A.)
Gerald A. Figurski (P.A.)
James Benjamin Harrill (P.A.)

Representative Clients: Regency Communities, Inc., formerly Minieri Communities of Florida, Inc.; Greene Builders, Inc.; Mobil Oil Corp.; Barnett Bank of Pasco County; Hospital Corporation of America; U.S. Home Corp.
Approved Attorneys For: Attorneys' Title Insurance Fund; First American Title Insurance Co.; Commonwealth Land Title Insurance Company.
Reference: Barnett Bank of Pasco County.

For full biographical listings, see the Martindale-Hubbell Law Directory

NORTH MIAMI, Dade Co.

Klein and Associates, P.A. (AV)

901 Northeast 125th Street, 33161
Telephone: 305-891-6100
Fax: 305-891-6104

Ronald G. Klein

For full biographical listings, see the Martindale-Hubbell Law Directory

NORTH MIAMI BEACH, Dade Co.

Buchanan Ingersoll, Professional Corporation (AV)

One Turnberry Place, 19495 Biscayne Boulevard, 33180
Telephone: 305-933-5600
Telecopier: 305-933-2350
Pittsburgh, Pennsylvania Office: 5800 USX Tower, 600 Grant Street.
Telephone: 412-562-8800.
Philadelphia, Pennsylvania Office: Two Logan Square, Twelfth Floor, 18th & Arch Streets.
Telephone: 215-665-8700.
Harrisburg, Pennsylvania Office: Vartan Parc, 30 North Third Street.
Telephone: 717-237-4800.
Tampa, Florida Office: Suite 1030, 101 East Kennedy Boulevard.
Telephone: 813-222-8180.
Princeton, New Jersey Office: Buchanan Ingersoll, A Partnership, College Centre, 500 College Road East.
Telephone: 609-452-2666.
Lexington, Kentucky Office: Suite 600, PNC Bank Plaza, 200 West Vine Street.
Telephone: 606-225-5333.

Jeremy A. Koss
Wayne M. Pathman
Gary S. Phillips

(See Next Column)

Kenneth P. Kerr

For Complete List of Firm Personnel, See General Section

For full biographical listings, see the Martindale-Hubbell Law Directory

NORTH PALM BEACH, Palm Beach Co.

Law Offices of Patrick C. Massa, P.A. (AV)

11891 U.S. Highway One, Suite 110, 33408-2864
Telephone: 407-694-1800
Facsimile: 407-694-1833

Patrick C. Massa

For full biographical listings, see the Martindale-Hubbell Law Directory

ORANGE PARK, Clay Co.

Head, Smith, Metcalf, Aguilar, Moss & Sieron, P.A. (AV)

1329A Kingsley Avenue, P.O. Box 855, 32073
Telephone: 904-264-6000
Fax: 904-264-9223

Robert J. Head, Jr.
Larry Smith
Frank B. Metcalf
Robert Aguilar
John B. Moss
Mark A. Sieron

Holly Fulton Perritt

For full biographical listings, see the Martindale-Hubbell Law Directory

*ORLANDO,** Orange Co.

Baker & Hostetler (AV)

SunBank Center, Suite 2300, 200 South Orange Avenue, 32802-3432
Telephone: 407-649-4000
In Cleveland, Ohio: 3200 National City Center, 1900 East Ninth Street.
Telephone: 216-621-0200.
In Columbus, Ohio: Capitol Square, Suite 2100, 65 East State Street.
Telephone: 614-228-1541.
In Denver, Colorado: 303 East 17th Avenue, Suite 1100.
Telephone: 303-861-0600.
In Houston, Texas: 1000 Louisiana, Suite 2000.
Telephone: 713-751-1600.
In Long Beach, California: 300 Oceangate, Suite 620.
Telephone: 310-432-2827.
In Los Angeles, California: 600 Wilshire Boulevard.
Telephone: 213-624-2400.
In Washington, D.C.: Washington Square, Suite 1100, 1050 Connecticut Avenue, N.W., Suite 1100.
Telephone: 202-861-1500.
In College Park, Maryland: 9658 Baltimore Boulevard, Suite 206.
Telephone: 301-441-2781.
In Alexandria, Virginia: 437 North Lee Street.
Telephone: 703-549-1294.
In San Francisco, California: One Sansome Street, Suite 2000.
Telephone: 415-951-4705.

PARTNERS

John W. Foster, Sr.
Jerry R. Linscott

For Complete List of Firm Personnel, See General Section

For full biographical listings, see the Martindale-Hubbell Law Directory

Best & Anderson, P.A. (AV)

20 North Orange Avenue, Suite 505, 32801
Telephone: 407-425-2985
Crystal River, Florida Office: 7655 West Gulf to Lake Highway, Suite 6.
Telephone: 904-795-1107.

David R. Best
George H. "Dutch" Anderson, III

Mark S. Walker
Perry M. Nardi
Jeffrey B. Sexton
G. Clay Morris
Lawrence I. Hauser

For full biographical listings, see the Martindale-Hubbell Law Directory

Bobo, Spicer, Ciotoli, Fulford, Bocchino, DeBevoise & Le Clainche, P.A. (AV)

Landmark Center One, Suite 510, 315 East Robinson Street, 32801-1949
Telephone: 407-849-1060
Fax: 407-843-4751
West Palm Beach, Florida Office: Esperante, Sixth Floor, 222 Lakeview Avenue, 33401.
Telephone: 407-684-6600.
FAX: 407-684-3828.

(See Next Column)

BOBO, SPICER, CIOTOLI, FULFORD, BOCCHINO, DEBEVOISE & LE CLAINCHE P.A.—*Continued*

John W. Bocchino
D. Andrew DeBevoise

Christopher C. Curry
J. Clancey Bounds
Robert R. Saunders
Sharon A. Chapman
Keith A. Scott
Sophia B. Ehringer
Tyler S. McClay

For full biographical listings, see the Martindale-Hubbell Law Directory

COBB COLE & BELL (AV)

Suite 1428 SunBank Center, 200 South Orange Avenue, 32801
Telephone: 407-843-3337
Fax: 407-843-0553
Daytona Beach, Florida Office: 150 Magnolia Avenue.
Telephone: 904-255-8171.
Fax: 904-258-5068.
Maitland, Florida Office: 900 Winderley Place, Suite 122.
Telephone: 407-661-1123.
Fax: 407-661-5743.
Tallahassee, Florida Office: 131 North Gadsden Street.
Telephone: 904-681-3233.
Fax: 904-681-3241.
Palm Coast, Florida Office: Sun Bank Building, 1 Florida Park Drive South, Suite 350.
Telephone: 904-446-2622.
Fax: 904-446-2654.

Samuel P. Bell, III
James M. Barclay
Jay D. Bond, Jr.
C. Allen Watts
Jonathan D. Kaney Jr.
Kevin X. Crowley
J. Lester Kaney
Kenneth R. Artin
John J. Upchurch
Michael D. Williams

General Counsel for: Daytona Beach Racing & Recreational Facilities District; News Journal Corporation.
Local Counsel for: Canal Insurance Co.; First Union National Bank of Florida; Southern Bell Telephone & Telegraph Co.; United States Fidelity & Guaranty Co.
Approved Attorneys for: American Pioneer Title Insurance Co.; Attorneys' Title Insurance Fund.

For full biographical listings, see the Martindale-Hubbell Law Directory

DEMPSEY & ASSOCIATES, P.A. (AV)

605 East Robinson Street, P.O. Box 1980, 32802-1980
Telephone: 407-422-5166
Mailing Address: 1031 West Morse Boulevard, Suite 200, Winter Park, Florida, 32789
Winter Park, Florida Office: 1031 West Morse Boulevard, Suite 200, 32789.
Telephone: 407-740-7778.
Telecopier: 407-740-0911.

Bernard H. Dempsey, Jr.
Michael C. Sasso

M. Susan Sacco
Daniel N. Brodersen
William P. Weatherford, Jr.
Lori R. Benton
Barbara B. Smithers

OF COUNSEL

Gary S. Salzman

Reference: First Union National Bank of Florida.

For full biographical listings, see the Martindale-Hubbell Law Directory

DEWOLF, WARD, O'DONNELL & HOOFMAN, P.A. (AV)

Suite 2000, 111 North Orange Avenue, 32801-4800
Telephone: 407-841-7000
Telecopy: 407-843-6035

Thomas B. DeWolf
Robert S. Hoofman
John H. Ward
A. Clifton Black
John L. O'Donnell, Jr.
James E. Glatt, Jr.,

Michael W. O. Holihan
Victor A. Diaz

Representative Clients: Walt Disney World, Co.; The Walt Disney Co.; Buena Vista Pictures Distribution Co.; Fleetwood Enterprises, Inc.; Roadway Express; Lockheed Missiles & Space Company, Inc.; Deutsche Credit Corp.; Chicago Title Insurance Co.; Massachusetts Mutual Life Insurance Co.; Employers Insurance of Wausau.

For full biographical listings, see the Martindale-Hubbell Law Directory

LAW OFFICES OF JACK F. (JAY) DURIE, JR. (AV)

1000 East Robinson Street, 32801
Telephone: 407-841-6000; 1-800-940-0442
Fax: 407-841-2425

Jack F. (Jay) Durie, Jr.

(See Next Column)

ASSOCIATE

Jean Marie Steedley

For full biographical listings, see the Martindale-Hubbell Law Directory

GATTIS, HALLOWES & CARPENTER, PROFESSIONAL ASSOCIATION (AV)

130 Hillcrest Street, P.O. Box 3109, 32802
Telephone: 407-843-8470
Fax: 407-843-4436

Donald L. Gattis, Jr.
Walton B. Hallowes, Jr.
Darrell F. Carpenter

For full biographical listings, see the Martindale-Hubbell Law Directory

GRAY, HARRIS AND ROBINSON, PROFESSIONAL ASSOCIATION (AV)

Suite 1200 Southeast Bank Building, 201 East Pine Street, P.O. Box 3068, 32802
Telephone: 407-843-8880
Telecopier: 407-244-5690
Cocoa Beach, Florida Office: Gray, Harris, Robinson, Kirschenbaum & Peeples. Glass Bank Building, 4th Floor, 505 North Orlando Avenue, P.O. Box 320757.
Telephone: 407-783-2218.
Telecopier: 407-783-2297.

Gordon H. "Stumpy" Harris
J. Mason Williams III
James F. Page, Jr.
G. Robertson Dilg
Charles W. Sell

Representative Clients: California Public Employees Retirement System; Florida Land Company; Hard Rock International PLC; McDonnell Douglas Corp.; Pleasurama PLC; Southeast Bank, N.A.; Telesat Cablevision, Inc.

For Complete List of Firm Personnel, See General Section

For full biographical listings, see the Martindale-Hubbell Law Directory

GURNEY & HANDLEY, P.A. (AV)

225 E. Robinson, Suite 450, 32801
Telephone: 407-843-9500

Leon H. Handley
W. Marvin Hardy, III
Richard W. Lassiter
Ronald L. Harrop
John L. Sewell
Francis E. Pierce, III
David W. Roquemore, Jr.
Michael F. Sutton
Robert S. Green
Peter N. Smith
Dennis R. O'Connor

David Brian Falstad
Michael J. Maloney
J. Brian Baird
Michael V. Barszcz
Steven H. Preston

LEGAL SUPPORT PERSONNEL

Charles J. Brackett, Jr. (Claims Analyst)

Representative Clients: Atlanta Casualty Company; Beneficial Mortgage Corp.; Ford Consumer Finance Co., Inc.; Government Employees Insurance Co.; Home Savings of America, FSB; John Hancock Mutual Life Insurance Co.; Meritor Credit Corp.; Orlando Utilities Commission; Phoenix Home Life Mutual Insurance Co.; Vistana Resort Development, Inc.

For full biographical listings, see the Martindale-Hubbell Law Directory

HARTLEY & WALL (AV)

200 South Orange Avenue, Suite 2810, P.O. Box 2168, 32802
Telephone: 407-422-7992
Fax: 407-425-2182

MEMBERS OF FIRM

Carl W. Hartley, Jr.
Richard F. Wall

ASSOCIATES

Robert G. Clements
Jeffrey S. Dawson

Reference: Sun Bank, N.A.

For full biographical listings, see the Martindale-Hubbell Law Directory

HILL AND PONTON, PROFESSIONAL ASSOCIATION (AV)

Suite 500, 605 East Robinson Street, P.O. Box 2673, 32802
Telephone: 407-422-4665

Brian D. Hill
Carol J. Ponton

Rebecca Jean Alexander
Maria T. Fabré
Silvia R. Sanders
Maria D. Santana (Not admitted in FL)

For full biographical listings, see the Martindale-Hubbell Law Directory

Orlando—Continued

MARTINEZ & DALTON, PROFESSIONAL ASSOCIATION (AV)

719 Vassar Street, 32804
Telephone: 407-425-0712
Fax: 407-425-1856

Mel R. Martinez
Robert H. Dellecker
Roy B. Dalton, Jr.
Brian T. Wilson

Yvonne M. Yegge
Leticia Marques

For full biographical listings, see the Martindale-Hubbell Law Directory

MATHEWS SMITH RAILEY & DECUBELLIS, P.A. (AV)

Suite 801, Citrus Center, 255 South Orange Avenue, P.O. Box 4976, 32802-4976
Telephone: 407-872-2200
Telecopier: 407-423-1038

Lawrence G. Mathews, Jr.
Daniel L. DeCubellis
Maura T. Smith
Frank M. Bedell
Lilburn R. Railey, III
Mary Meeks Wills
W. Edward (Ned) McLeod

Representative Clients: American Telephone and Telegraph; Design Professional Insurance Corp.; Florida Lawyers Mutual Insurance Corp.; Great Southwest Corp.; International Game Technology, Inc.; Jennings Environmental Services, Inc.; Mader Southeast, Inc.; Orange County; PGA Tour, Inc.; Sun Banks, Inc.

For full biographical listings, see the Martindale-Hubbell Law Directory

O'NEILL, CHAPIN, MARKS, LIEBMAN, COOPER & CARR (AV)

A Partnership including Professional Associations
865 Eola Park Center, 200 East Robinson Street, 32801
Telephone: 407-425-2751
Telex: 407-423-1192

Bernard C. O'Neill, Jr. (P.A.)
John B. Liebman (P.A.)
Bruce E. Chapin (P.A.)
Mark O. Cooper (P.A.)
Robert O. Marks (P.A.)
George E. Carr

ASSOCIATES

Lisa M. Cvetic
Rod C. Lundy

Reference: First Union National Bank.

For full biographical listings, see the Martindale-Hubbell Law Directory

OSBORNE AND AIKIN, P.A. (AV)

538 East Washington Street, 32801-1996
Telephone: 407-843-5211
Fax: 407-425-1383

William G. Osborne
Wendy L. Aikin

For full biographical listings, see the Martindale-Hubbell Law Directory

PLEUS, ADAMS, DAVIS & SPEARS, P.A. (AV)

940 Highland Avenue, P.O. Box 3627, 32802
Telephone: 407-422-8116
Fax: 407-648-1044

Robert J. Pleus, Jr.
Douglas C. Spears
Richard H. Adams, Jr.
Richard D. Connor, Jr.
Bradley J. Davis
Paul L. SanGiovanni

Jennifer S. Eden
Deborah B. Ansbro
Reinhard G. Stephan
Kevin E. Mangum

General Counsel for: Lochaven Federal Savings & Loan; Independence Mortgage Corporation of America; Roman Catholic Diocese of Orlando.
Representative Clients: Ensign Property Group, Inc.; Herman J. Heidrich & Sons; Deere Credit Services.

For full biographical listings, see the Martindale-Hubbell Law Directory

POHL & BROWN, P.A.

(See Winter Park)

ROBERTSON, WILLIAMS & McDONALD, P.A. (AV)

538 East Washington Street, 32801
Telephone: 407-425-1606
Fax: 407-872-1341
Other Orlando Office: 20 North Eola Drive.

John M. Robertson
Hubert W. Williams (1937-1986)
J. Stephen McDonald

Beth S. Schick

Reference: First Union Bank.

For full biographical listings, see the Martindale-Hubbell Law Directory

LAW OFFICES OF JAMES M. RUSS, P.A. (AV)

Tinker Building, 18 West Pine Street, 32801
Telephone: 407-849-6050
Fax: 407-849-6059

James M. Russ

Reference: First Union National Bank of Orlando.

For full biographical listings, see the Martindale-Hubbell Law Directory

RUSSELL & HULL, P.A. (AV)

537 North Magnolia Avenue, P.O. Box 2751, 32802
Telephone: 407-422-1234

Rodney Laird Russell
Norman L. Hull

Reference: First Union National Bank, N.A.

For full biographical listings, see the Martindale-Hubbell Law Directory

ZIMMERMAN, SHUFFIELD, KISER & SUTCLIFFE, P.A. (AV)

Landmark Center One, Suite 600, 315 East Robinson Street, P.O. Box 3000, 32802
Telephone: 407-425-7010
Telecopier: 407-425-2747

Bernard J. Zimmerman
Robert E. Mansbach, Jr.
W. Charles Shuffield
Robert L. Dietz
Wendell J. Kiser
Stephen B. Hatcher
Roland A. Sutcliffe Jr.
Robert W. Peacock, Jr.
Ultima Degnan Morgan
Clement L. Hyland
J. Timothy Schulte

Melissa Dubina Kaplan
Vivian M. Reeves
John C. Bachman
Joseph A. Regnery
Pamela Lynn Foels
John V. Colvin
Paul A. Kelley
Kraig N. Johnson
Edward M. Kuhn III
Gene E. Crick, Jr.
Eric P. Gibbs
Charles B. Costar III
Joseph C. L. Wettach
Kevin G. Malchow
Edward C. Duncan, III
Thomas Warren Sculco
Derrick E. Cox
Kevin L. Lienard
Trent W. Ling
Daniel R. Murphy
Charles H. Leo
Michael C. Tyson

LEGAL SUPPORT PERSONNEL

W. Raymond Herod

For full biographical listings, see the Martindale-Hubbell Law Directory

PALM BEACH, Palm Beach Co.

MINTMIRE & ASSOCIATES (AV)

265 Sunrise Avenue, Suite 204, 33480
Telephone: 407-832-5696
Fax: 407-659-5371

Donald F. Mintmire

ASSOCIATES

Jeffrey A. Shaffer
Timothy D. Friedman

OF COUNSEL

Paul Safran, Jr.

For full biographical listings, see the Martindale-Hubbell Law Directory

ROZELLE, SULLIVAN AND CALL (AV)

223 Sunset Avenue, Suite 200, P.O. Box 229, 33480
Telephone: 407-655-8585
Fax: 407-655-8663

MEMBERS OF FIRM

Douglas D. Rozelle, Jr.
Paul M. Sullivan, Jr.
John S. Call, Jr.

ASSOCIATE

Stephen W. Stoll, Jr.

Representative Clients: Wal-Mart Stores, Inc.; Motors Insurance Corp.; American Contractors Insurance Group, Inc.; Continental Loss Adjusting Co.; The Equitable Life Assurance Society; Connecticut General Life Insurance Co.; Safeco Insurance Co.; Phar-Mor of Florida, Inc.; World Wide Insurance Group; Chrysler Insurance Co.

For full biographical listings, see the Martindale-Hubbell Law Directory

PALM BEACH GARDENS, Palm Beach Co.

MARJORIE GADARIAN GRAHAM, P.A. (AV)

Suite D 129, 11211 Prosperity Farms Road, 33410
Telephone: 407-775-1204

Marjorie Gadarian Graham

For full biographical listings, see the Martindale-Hubbell Law Directory

Palm Beach Gardens—Continued

SCOTT, ROYCE, HARRIS, BRYAN, BARRA & JORGENSEN, PROFESSIONAL ASSOCIATION (AV)

4400 PGA Boulevard, Suite 900, 33410
Telephone: 407-624-3900
Fax: 407-524-3533

John L. Bryan, Jr. John M. Jorgensen
Donna A. Nadeau

Representative Clients: First Union National Bank of Florida, N.A.; Barnett Banks, Inc.; North Palm Beach County Association of Realtors, Inc.; Lost Tree Village; Jupiter Hills, Pappalardo Contractors, Inc.; Art Moran Pontiac, Inc.; Admiralty Bank; Enterprise National Bank of Palm Beach, N.A.; Alandco, Inc.; Northern Trust Bank of Florida, N.A.

For Complete List of Firm Personnel, See General Section

For full biographical listings, see the Martindale-Hubbell Law Directory

SLAWSON & GLICK (AV)

Harbour Financial Center, 2401 PGA Boulevard, Suite 140, 33410
Telephone: 407-625-6260
Facsimile: 407-625-6269
Boca Raton, Florida Office: The Plaza, Suite 801, 5355 Town Center Road.
Telephone: 407-391-4900.
Facsimile: 407-368-9274.

Richard W. Slawson (P.A.) Fred A. Cunningham
Brian J. Glick (P.A.) Patrick St. George Cousins

For full biographical listings, see the Martindale-Hubbell Law Directory

*PENSACOLA,** Escambia Co.

FULLER, JOHNSON & FARRELL, P.A. (AV)

Quayside Quarters, 700 South Palafox, Suite 300, P.O. Box 12219, 32581
Telephone: 904-434-8845
Fax: 904-432-6667
Tallahassee, Florida Office: 111 North Calhoun Street, P.O. Box 1739, 32302-1739.
Telephone: 904-224-4663.
Fax: 904-561-8839.

Belinda Barnes deKozan (Resident) Michael W. Kehoe (Resident)
Alan R. Horky (Resident)

Representative Clients: Aetna Life & Casualty; Amoco Oil Co.; Anesthesiologists' Professional Assurance Trust; CIGNA; Crum & Forster Insurance Cos.; Fireman's Fund; Florida Physicians Insurance Reciprocal; Ford Motor Co.; GEICO; Toyota Motor Corp.

For full biographical listings, see the Martindale-Hubbell Law Directory

B. RICHARD YOUNG, P.A. (AV)

309B South Palafox Place, 32501
Telephone: 904-432-2222
Fax: 904-432-1444

B. Richard Young

For full biographical listings, see the Martindale-Hubbell Law Directory

PLANTATION, Broward Co.

FENSTER AND FAERBER, PROFESSIONAL ASSOCIATION (AV)

Suite 307, The Gulfstream Building, 8751 West Broward Boulevard, 33324
Telephone: 305-473-1500; Miami: 305-949-9998
Mailing Address: P.O. Box 16688, 33318

Jeffrey M. Fenster Jesse S. Faerber
Stacie L. Cohen

OF COUNSEL

Elizabeth Anne Beavers

For full biographical listings, see the Martindale-Hubbell Law Directory

ST. PETERSBURG, Pinellas Co.

CARTER, STEIN, SCHAAF & TOWZEY (AV)

270 First Avenue South, Suite 300, 33701-4306
Telephone: 813-894-4333
Fax: 813-894-0175

Victoria Hunt Carter Gary M. Schaaf
Henry A. Stein Phyllis J. Towzey

For full biographical listings, see the Martindale-Hubbell Law Directory

KALEEL & KALEEL, P.A. (AV)

3819 Central Avenue, P.O. Box 14333, 33713
Telephone: 813-321-0744

(See Next Column)

Wm. C. Kaleel, Sr. (1903-1976) H. Shelton Philips
William C. Kaleel, Jr. Robert L. Kaleel

Representative Clients: State Farm Mutual Automobile Insurance Co.; Auto Owners Insurance Co.
Reference: First Union National Bank of Florida.

For full biographical listings, see the Martindale-Hubbell Law Directory

MARTIN ERROL RICE, P.A. (AV)

696 First Avenue North, Suite 400, P.O. Box 205, 33701
Telephone: 813-821-4884
Fax: 813-821-4987

Martin Errol Rice

For full biographical listings, see the Martindale-Hubbell Law Directory

LAW OFFICE OF GLENN WOODWORTH, P.A. (AV)

Orange Park Center, 696 First Avenue North, Suite 400, 33701
Telephone: 813-892-2499
Fax: 813-822-6611

Glenn M. Woodworth

For full biographical listings, see the Martindale-Hubbell Law Directory

*SANFORD,** Seminole Co.

THOMAS A. SPEER, P.A. (AV)

Speer Building, P.O. Box 1364, 32772
Telephone: 407-322-0681
Fax: 407-322-2674

Thomas A. Speer

For full biographical listings, see the Martindale-Hubbell Law Directory

STENSTROM, MCINTOSH, JULIAN, COLBERT, WHIGHAM & SIMMONS, P.A. (AV)

Suite 22 Sun Bank-Downtown, P.O. Box 4848, 32772-4848
Telephone: 407-322-2171
Fax: 407-330-2379

Thomas E. Whigham (1952-1988) William L. Colbert
Douglas Stenstrom (Retired) Franklin C. Whigham
Kenneth W. McIntosh Clayton D. Simmons
Ned N. Julian, Jr. Robert K. McIntosh
Donna L. Surratt-McIntosh

William E. Reischmann, Jr. Catherine D. Reischmann
Martha H. McIntosh

Representative Clients: City of Sanford; Seminole County School Board; City of Oviedo; City of Casselberry; Seminole Community College; City of Lake Mary.

For full biographical listings, see the Martindale-Hubbell Law Directory

*SARASOTA,** Sarasota Co.

ABEL, BAND, RUSSELL, COLLIER, PITCHFORD & GORDON, CHARTERED (AV)

Barnett Bank Center, 240 South Pineapple Avenue, P.O. Box 49948, 34230-6948
Telephone: 813-366-6660
FAX: 813-366-3999
Fort Myers, Florida Office: The Tidewater Building, 1375 Jackson Street, Suite 201, 33901.
Telephone: 813-337-0062.
FAX: 813-337-0406.
Venice, Florida Office: Suite 199, 333 South Tamiami Trail, 34285.
Telephone: 813-485-8200.
Fax: 813-488-9436.

David S. Band Anthony J. Abate
Jeffrey S. Russell Steven J. Chase
Ronald L. Collier Kathryn Angell Carr
Malcolm J. Pitchford Michael S. Taaffe
Cheryl Lasris Gordon Mark W. McFall
Jan Walters Pitchford

OF COUNSEL

Harvey J. Abel Johnson S. Savary

Saralyn Abel Jane M. Kennedy
Douglas M. Bales Christine Edwards Lamia
Gregory S. Band Bradley D. Magee
John A. Garner George H. Mazzarantani
Mark D. Hildreth Philip C. Zimmerman

References: Barnett Bank of Southwest Florida; Sun Bank/Gulf Coast.

For full biographical listings, see the Martindale-Hubbell Law Directory

Sarasota—Continued

DICKINSON & GIBBONS, P.A. (AV)
1750 Ringling Boulevard, P.O. Box 3979, 34230
Telephone: 813-366-4680
FAX: 813-953-3136

G. Hunter Gibbons
Ward E. Dahlgren
Lewis F. Collins, Jr.
Gary H. Larsen
Camden T. French
Ralph L. Marchbank, Jr.
A. James Rolfes
Burwell J. Jones
Richard R. Garland
Stephen G. Brannan
Deborah J. Blue
Mark A. Haskins
Jeffrey D. Peairs
Kim Carlton Bonner
Douglas R. Wight
Stephen R. Kanzer
David S. Preston
Mary Gall Jack
John A. Yanchek

OF COUNSEL

Patrick H. Dickinson

Representative Clients: Allstate Insurance Co.; Liberty Mutual; Nationwide Insurance Co.; St. Paul Fire & Marine Insurance Co.; Cincinnati Insurance Co.; Ohio Casualty Insurance Co.; Florida Physicians Insurance Co.; Travelers Insurance Co.; Prudential Insurance Co.; State Farm Insurance Company.

For Complete List of Firm Personnel, See General Section

For full biographical listings, see the Martindale-Hubbell Law Directory

NELSON HESSE CYRIL SMITH WIDMAN HERB CAUSEY & DOOLEY (AV)
2070 Ringling Boulevard, P.O. Box 2524, 34230
Telephone: 813-366-7550
FAX: 813-955-3708

MEMBERS OF FIRM

Richard E. Nelson
Ronald Alexander Cyril (1938-1988)
Richard L. Smith
Robert C. Widman
F. Steven Herb
Omer S. Causey
William A. Dooley
Michael S. Drews
Frederick J. Elbrecht

ASSOCIATES

Gary W. Peal
Philip Sypula
J. Kal Gibron
J. Neal Mobley

OF COUNSEL

Robert L. Hesse

General Counsel for: Enterprise National Bank; Dooley Mack Construction Co.;
Representative Clients: Wellcraft Marine; Attorneys Title Insurance Fund; Crum & Forster Insurance Co.; Radiology, Inc.; The Carlton Ranch, Inc.
References: Southtrust Bank; Enterprise National Bank.

For full biographical listings, see the Martindale-Hubbell Law Directory

WILLIAMS, PARKER, HARRISON, DIETZ & GETZEN, PROFESSIONAL ASSOCIATION (AV)
1550 Ringling Boulevard, 34230-3258
Telephone: 813-366-4800
Telecopier: 813-366-5109
Mailing Address: P.O. Box 3258, Sarasota, Florida, 34230-3258

John V. Cannon, III
Frank Strelec
David A. Wallace
Mark A. Schwartz
Kimberly J. Page

OF COUNSEL

Frazer F. Hilder
Elvin W. Phillips

Counsel for: Sarasota-Manatee Airport Authority; Sarasota County Public Hospital Board; William G. & Marie Selby Foundation; Taylor Woodrow Homes Ltd.; The School Board of Sarasota County.
Local Counsel for: NationsBank of Florida; Arvida/JMB Partners.

For Complete List of Firm Personnel, See General Section

For full biographical listings, see the Martindale-Hubbell Law Directory

*STUART,** Martin Co.

MCCARTHY, SUMMERS, BOBKO, MCKEY & BONAN, P.A. (AV)
2081 East Ocean Boulevard, Suite 2-A, 34996
Telephone: 407-286-1700
FAX: 407-283-1803

Terence P. McCarthy
Robert P. Summers
Noel A. Bobko
John D. McKey, Jr.
W. Martin Bonan

Representative Clients: American Bank of Martin County; First National Bank and Trust Company of the Treasure Coast; Great Western Bank; Hydratech Utilities; Lost Lake at Hobe Sound; Taylor Creek Marina, Inc.; GBS Excavating, Inc.; Seaboard Savings Bank; The Stuart News; Gary Player Design Group.

For full biographical listings, see the Martindale-Hubbell Law Directory

*TALLAHASSEE,** Leon Co.

COLLINS & TRUETT, P.A. (AV)
2804 Remington Green Circle, Suite 4, Post Office Drawer 12429, 32317-2429
Telephone: 904-386-6060
Telecopier: 904-385-8220

Richard B. Collins
Gary A. Shipman

Brett Q. Lucas (Resident)
Dawn D. Caloca
Joseph E. Brooks
C. Timothy Gray
Rogelio Fontela
Charles N. Cleland, Jr.
Clifford W. Rainey

OF COUNSEL

Edgar C. Booth
James A. Dixon, Jr.

Representative Clients: Agency Rent-A-Car; Agricultural Excess and Surplus Insurance Co.; AIG Life Insurance Co.; Alliance Insurance Group; Allstate Insurance Co.; American Empire Surplus Lines Insurance Co.; American International Underwriters Inc.; Atlanta Casualty Insurance Co.; Avis Rent-A-Car; Bankers and Shippers Insurance Co.

For full biographical listings, see the Martindale-Hubbell Law Directory

COOPER, COPPINS & MONROE, P.A. (AV)
3303 Thomasville Road, Suite 301 P.O. Drawer 14447, 32317-4447
Telephone: 904-422-2420
Facsimile: 904-422-2730

John C. Cooper
Michael F. Coppins
D. Lloyd Monroe, IV

Gwendolyn P. Adkins
Floy M. Busby
David B. Switalski
Betsy L. Stupski

Reference: Barnett Bank of Tallahassee.

For full biographical listings, see the Martindale-Hubbell Law Directory

DAVIS & TAFF (AV)
210 East College Avenue, Suite 200, P.O. Box 37190, 32315-7190
Telephone: 904-222-6026
Telecopier: 904-224-1039

MEMBERS OF FIRM

Ken Davis
Angus Broward Taff, Jr.

For full biographical listings, see the Martindale-Hubbell Law Directory

FULLER, JOHNSON & FARRELL, P.A. (AV)
111 North Calhoun Street, P.O. Box 1739, 32302-1739
Telephone: 904-224-4663
Fax: 904-561-8839
Pensacola, Florida Office: Quayside Quarters, 700 South Palafox, Suite 300, P.O. Box 12219, 32581.
Telephone: 904-434-8845.
FAX: 904-432-6667.

Ben A. Andrews
Jeannette M. Andrews
Marjorie M. Cain
M. Elizabeth Chesser
Robert C. Crabtree
Patrick J. Farrell, Jr.
S. William Fuller, Jr.
Beverly H. Heckler
Alan R. Horky (Resident, Pensacola Office)
Fred M. Johnson
Michael W. Kehoe (Resident, Pensacola Office)
J. Craig Knox
Belinda Barnes deKozan (Resident, Pensacola Office)
William R. Mabile, III
P. Scott Mitchell
Steven Michael Puritz
Cynthia D. Simmons
Michael J. Thomas
Robert W. Ritsch
Sidney M. McCrackin

Representative Clients: Aetna Life & Casualty; CIGNA Companies; Cotton States Insurance; Crum & Forster Insurance Companies; Ford Motor Company; Gallagher Bassett Services, Inc.; MMI Companies; The St. Paul Insurance Companies, Inc.; Toyota Motor Sales, U.S.A., Inc.

For full biographical listings, see the Martindale-Hubbell Law Directory

HENRY, BUCHANAN, MICK, HUDSON & SUBER, P.A. (AV)
117 South Gadsden Street P.O. Drawer 1049, 32302
Telephone: 904-222-2920
Telecopier: 904-224-0034

Bryan W. Henry (1925-1986)
John D. Buchanan, Jr.
Robert A. Mick
Edwin R. Hudson
Jesse F. Suber
Harriet W. Williams
J. Steven Carter

Reference: Barnett Bank of Tallahassee, Inc.

For full biographical listings, see the Martindale-Hubbell Law Directory

Tallahassee—Continued

McConnaughhay, Roland, Maida & Cherr, P.A. (AV)

Suite 900, 101 North Monroe Street, P.O. Drawer 229, 32302-0229
Telephone: 904-222-8121
Telecopier: 904-222-4359
Pensacola, Florida Office: 316 South Baylen Street, Suite 500.
Telephone: 904-434-7122.
Telecopier: 904-435-0924.
Panama City, Florida Office: 825 Jenks Avenue.
Telephone: 904-784-2599.
Telecopier: 904-769-5461.
Jacksonville, Florida Office: 4811 Beach Boulevard, Suite 100.
Telephone: 904-348-0903.
Telecopier: 904-348-0908.
Sarasota, Florida Office: 1800 Second Street, Suite 954.
Telephone: 813-955-6141.
Telecopier: 813-955-6244.

James N. McConnaughhay
R. William Roland
Thomas J. Maida
Gordon D. Cherr
Gus V. Soto
Patricia Hart Malono
Christopher John duBois
Michael J. Rudicell (Resident at Pensacola Office)
Mary Lalley Wakeman
Cecil L. Davis, Jr.
R. Stephen Coonrod
Patrick E. Weaver (Resident at Panama City)
Stephen M. Masterson (Resident at Pensacola Office)
Mary Ellen Ingley
Joe G. Durrett
Michael C. Crumpler (Resident at Jacksonville Office)
Brian S. Duffy
M. Kemmerly Thomas
Robert D. Pope (Resident at Jacksonville Office)
Robert C. Palmer, III (Resident at Pensacola Office)
E. Louis Stern (Resident at Sarasota Office)
Mary E. Cruickshank
Elizabeth L. Feathers (Resident at Jacksonville Office)
Laurel A. Hajek (Resident at Sarasota Office)
Peter P. Sledzik (Resident at Jacksonville Office)
Jana E. Black
Michael James Valen (Resident at Pensacola Office)
Herschel C. Minnis
Sarah M. Stokes
Clyde W. (Billy) Galloway, Jr.
James A. Tucker (Resident at Sarasota Office)
Austin B. Neal
Tracey J. Brunyansky (Resident at Panama City Office)

OF COUNSEL

Roderic G. Magie (Resident at Pensacola Office)

For full biographical listings, see the Martindale-Hubbell Law Directory

McFarlain, Wiley, Cassedy & Jones, Professional Association (AV)

215 South Monroe Street, Suite 600, P.O. Box 2174, 32316-2174
Telephone: 904-222-2107
Telecopier: 904-222-8475

Richard C. McFarlain
William B. Wiley
Marshall R. Cassedy
Douglas P. Jones
Charles A. Stampelos
Linda McMullen
H. Darrell White, Jr.
Christopher Barkas

Harold R. Mardenborough, Jr.
Katherine Hairston LaRosa
J. Robert Griffin

OF COUNSEL

Betty J. Steffens

For full biographical listings, see the Martindale-Hubbell Law Directory

Radey Hinkle Thomas & McArthur (AV)

Suite 1000 Monroe-Park Tower, 101 North Monroe Street, P.O. Drawer 11307, 32302
Telephone: 904-681-7766
Telecopier: 904-681-0506

John Radey
Robert L. Hinkle
Harry O. Thomas
Elizabeth Waas McArthur
Ricky L. Polston
Jeffrey L. Frehn
Leslie G. Street

Representative Clients: Electronic Data Systems Corp.; Ringling Bros. Barnum-Bailey Combined Shows; Johnson & Johnson; Columbia/HCA Healthcare Corp.; Tallahassee Community Hospital; Tampa General Hospital; State Mutual Life Assurance Co. of America; Commonwealth Land Title Insurance Co.

For full biographical listings, see the Martindale-Hubbell Law Directory

Wadsworth & Davis (AV)

Suite 1, 203 North Gadsden Street, P.O. Box 10529, 32302-2529
Telephone: 904-224-9037
FAX: 904-561-6119

MEMBERS OF FIRM

Murray M. Wadsworth
William H. Davis

(See Next Column)

ASSOCIATE

James J. Dean

Reference: Capital City First National Bank.

For full biographical listings, see the Martindale-Hubbell Law Directory

*TAMPA,** Hillsborough Co.

Adkins & Kise, P.A. (AV)

2175 Barnett Plaza, 101 East Kennedy Boulevard, 33602
Telephone: 813-221-2200
Fax: 813-221-8850

Edward C. Adkins
Christopher M. Kise

For full biographical listings, see the Martindale-Hubbell Law Directory

Allen, Dell, Frank & Trinkle (AV)

1240 Barnett Plaza, 101 East Kennedy Boulevard, P.O. Box 2111, 33601
Telephone: 813-223-5351
Telecopier: 813-229-6682

MEMBERS OF FIRM

Ralph C. Dell
Roderick K. Shaw, Jr.
Stewart C. Eggert
Gary M. Witters
Joseph G. Heyck, Jr.
Michael N. Brown
Lynn H. Cole
Marian Priest McCulloch
Robert A. Mora
Benjamin G. Morris
A. Christopher Kasten, II
Richard A. Harrison
James S. Eggert

Representative Clients: CSX Transportation; Bank of Tampa; Florida Citrus Processors Assn.; Florida Steel Corp.; The Coca Cola Co., Foods Division; Montgomery Elevator Co.; Seminole Electric Cooperative Inc.; Hillsborough County Hospital Authority; Tampa General Healthcare f/k/a Tampa General Hospital; Tampa Greyhound Track.

For Complete List of Firm Personnel, See General Section

For full biographical listings, see the Martindale-Hubbell Law Directory

Alley and Alley, Chartered (AV)

205 Brush Street, P.O. Box 1427, 33601
Telephone: 813-229-6481
Fax: 813-223-7029
Miami, Florida Office: 612 Ingraham Building, 25 S.E. 2nd Avenue.
Telephone: 305-371-6753.

Granville M. Alley, Jr. (1929-1976)
John-Edward Alley
Robert D. Hall, Jr.

Representative Clients: Buford Television, Inc.; K-mart Corp.; The Miami Herald Publishing Co./Knight-Ridder Newspapers, Inc.; Pasco County School Board; Pinellas County, Florida; Publix Super Markets, Inc.; Southern Bakeries, Inc.; Sysco Corp.; The Wackenhut Corp. and subsidiaries; TJX Cos. (T.J. Maxx).

For full biographical listings, see the Martindale-Hubbell Law Directory

Alpert, Josey & Hughes, P.A. (AV)

100 South Ashley Drive, Suite 2000 (33602), P.O. Box 3270, 33601-3270
Telephone: 813-223-4131
Fax: 813-228-9612

Jonathan L. Alpert
William S. Josey
Linda Renate Hughes

Catherine A. Kyres
Patrick B. Calcutt
R. Christopher Rodems
Chris A. Barker
Kirsten K. Ullman
Gregory Joseph Blackburn
David D. Ferrentino
William J. Cook
Suzanne P. Tortorice
Matthew J. Jowanna
Daniel J. Mathis

OF COUNSEL

Stanley T. Padgett

Representative Clients: AABCO Mortgage & Investments, Inc.; Alexander & Alexander, Inc.; AMI Memorial Hospital; Georgia-Pacific Corp.; Hospital Underwriting Group; Maryland Casualty Co.; National Reinsurance Corp.; Professional Service Industries; RLI Insurance Co.

For full biographical listings, see the Martindale-Hubbell Law Directory

Buchanan Ingersoll, Professional Corporation (AV)

Suite 1030, 101 East Kennedy Boulevard, 33602
Telephone: 813-222-8180
Telecopier: 813-222-8189
Pittsburgh, Pennsylvania Office: 5800 USX Tower, 600 Grant Street.
Telephone: 412-562-8800.
Philadelphia, Pennsylvania Office: Two Logan Square, Twelfth Floor, 18th & Arch Streets.
Telephone: 215-665-8700.
Harrisburg, Pennsylvania Office: Vartan Parc, 30 North Third Street.
Telephone: 717-237-4800.

(See Next Column)

BUCHANAN INGERSOLL PROFESSIONAL CORPORATION, *Tampa—Continued*

North Miami Beach, Florida Office: 19495 Biscayne Boulevard.
Telephone: 305-933-5600.
Princeton, New Jersey Office: Buchanan Ingersoll, A Partnership, College Centre, 500 College Road East.
Telephone: 609-452-2666.
Lexington, Kentucky Office: Suite 600, PNC Bank Plaza, 200 West Vine Street.
Telephone: 606-225-5333.

James J. Kennedy III

For Complete List of Firm Personnel, See General Section

For full biographical listings, see the Martindale-Hubbell Law Directory

RAY CALAFELL, JR., P.A. (AV)

105 South Armenia Avenue, 33609
Telephone: 813-871-3890
Fax: Available upon Request

Ray Calafell

For full biographical listings, see the Martindale-Hubbell Law Directory

CLARK, CHARLTON & MARTINO, A PROFESSIONAL ASSOCIATION (AV)

Westshore Center, Suite 700, 1715 North Westshore Boulevard, P.O. Box 24268, 33623-4268
Telephone: 813-289-0700
Fax: 813-289-5498

Scott T. Borders
Scott Charlton
James W. Clark
Anthony T. Martino

Reference: Southtrust Bank of Tampa.

For full biographical listings, see the Martindale-Hubbell Law Directory

CUNNINGHAM LAW GROUP, P.A. (AV)

100 Ashley Drive, South, Suite 100, 33602
Telephone: 813-228-0505
Telefax: 813-229-7982

Anthony W. Cunningham
Donald G. Greiwe
James D. Clark

For full biographical listings, see the Martindale-Hubbell Law Directory

PATRICK H. DEKLE, P.A. (AV)

808 Landmark Building, 412 Madison Street, 33602-4640
Telephone: 813-223-2300

Patrick H. Dekle

For full biographical listings, see the Martindale-Hubbell Law Directory

GLENN RASMUSSEN & FOGARTY (AV)

1300 First Union Center, 100 South Ashley Drive, P.O. Box 3333, 33601-3333
Telephone: 813-229-3333
Fax: 813-229-5946

Rod Anderson
David E. Arroyo
Robert W. Bivins
Sharon Docherty Danco
Richard E. Fee
David S. Felman
Michael A. Fogarty
Robert B. Glenn
Donald S. Hart, Jr.
Michael S. Hooker
Erin C. Keleher
Bradford D. Kimbro
Guy P. McConnell
Robert C. Rasmussen
Edwin G. Rice
Steven W. Vazquez

Representative Clients: AMCA International Finance Corp.; Electronic Data Systems Corp.; Ford Motor Co.; Ford Motor Credit Co.; Southeast Toyota Distributors, Inc.; Tampa Electronic Co.; The Citizens and Southern National Bank of Florida; Turner Development Corp.

For full biographical listings, see the Martindale-Hubbell Law Directory

GUNN, OGDEN & SULLIVAN, PROFESSIONAL ASSOCIATION (AV)

201 East Kennedy Boulevard, Suite 1850, P.O. Box 1006, 33601
Telephone: 813-223-5111
FAX: 813-229-2336

Timon V. Sullivan
Randy J. Ogden
Lee D. Gunn, IV

Bradley J. Goewert
Andrea L. Hairelson
Michael F. Hancock
Brian Thompson
Charles E. Mckeon
Kelly K. Griffin
Daneil M. McAuliffe

For full biographical listings, see the Martindale-Hubbell Law Directory

HILL, WARD & HENDERSON, A PROFESSIONAL ASSOCIATION (AV)

101 East Kennedy Boulevard, Suite 3700, P.O. Box 2231, 33601
Telephone: 813-221-3900
FAX: 813-221-2900

Thomas W. Black
Martin L. Garcia
Thomas N. Henderson, III
Benjamin H. Hill, III
John L. Holcomb
Stephen M. Hudoba
Timothy A. Hunt
David T. Knight
Andrew J. Lubrano
Douglas P. McClurg
Brett J. Preston
R. James Robbins, Jr.
W. Lawrence Smith
Jeanne Trudeau Tate
David R. Tyrrell
Dennis P. Waggoner
David E. Ward, Jr.

Marie A. Borland
Phillip S. Dingle
S. Katherine Frazier
Troy A. Fuhrman
Robert B. Gough, III
John B. Grandoff III
Pamela Schmitt Herman
Jonathan P. Jennewein
Jeffrey D. Murphy
Karen E. Ross
Seth M. Schimmel
D. Keith Wickenden

Representative Clients: Allstate Insurance Co.; Aetna Casualty and Surety Co.; Bridgestone/Firestone, Inc.; Busch Entertainment Corp.; Cargill Fertilizer, Inc.; Chrysler Motors Corp.; City of Tampa; Citibank, N.A; Ch2M Hill; Fidelity and Deposit Company of Maryland.

For full biographical listings, see the Martindale-Hubbell Law Directory

HONIGMAN MILLER SCHWARTZ AND COHN (AV)

A Partnership including Professional Corporations
2700 Landmark Centre, 401 E. Jackson Street, 33602
Telephone: 813-221-6600
Telecopier: 813-223-4410
West Palm Beach, Florida Office: Suite 800 Esperante Building, 222 Lakeview Avenue.
Telephone: 407-838-4500.
Orlando, Florida Office: 390 North Orange Avenue, Suite 1300.
Telephone: 407-648-0300.
Detroit, Michigan Office: 2290 First National Building.
Telephone: 313-256-7800.
Lansing, Michigan Office: 222 North Washington Square, Suite 400.
Telephone: 517-484-8282.
Houston, Texas Office: 3100 First Interstate Bank Plaza, 1000 Louisiana.
Telephone: 713-650-2600.
Los Angeles, California Office: Watt Plaza, Suite 2200, 1875 Century Park East.
Telephone: 310-789-3800.
Fax: 310-789-3814.

MEMBERS

Robert W. Boos (P.A.)
Harry Christopher Goplerud (P.A.)
Gregory G. Jones (P.A.)

ASSOCIATES

Kevin M. Gilhool
Dennis Hernandez
Susan M. Salvatore

Representative Clients: Commonwealth Land Title Insurance Co.; First American Title Insurance Co.; General Host Corp.; Pulte Home Corp.; The Sembler Co.; Trammel Crow Co.; Wilma South Corp.

For Complete List of Firm Personnel, See General Section

For full biographical listings, see the Martindale-Hubbell Law Directory

HOYT, COLGAN & ANDREU, P.A. (AV)

2900 Barnett Plaza, 101 East Kennedy Boulevard, 33602
Telephone: 813-229-6688
Facsimile: 813-229-3331

Brooks P. Hoyt
Michael B. Colgan
Timothy A. Andreu

Stacey Marantz Stabile

OF COUNSEL

Louis J. Beltrami

For full biographical listings, see the Martindale-Hubbell Law Directory

LANGFORD, HILL & TRYBUS, P.A. (AV)

Suite 800, Bayshore Place, 601 Bayshore Boulevard, 33606
Telephone: 813-251-5533
Telecopier: 813-251-1900
Wats: 1-800-277-2005

E. C. Langford
Edward A. Hill
Ronald H. Trybus
Ronald G. Hock
Catherine M. Catlin
Debra M. Kubicsek
William B. Smith

(See Next Column)

LANGFORD, HILL & TRYBUS P.A.—*Continued*

Fredrique B. Boire
Muriel Desloovere
Kevin H. O'Neill
Vicki L. Page
Frederick T. Reeves
Barbara A. Sinsley
Stephens B. Woodrough (Not admitted in FL)
Anthony G. Woodward

Representative Clients: Affiliated of Florida, Inc.; American Federation Insurance Co.; Armor Insurance; Bank of Tampa; Central Bank of Tampa; Cintas Corp.; Container Corporation of America; CU Financial Services; Farm Stores, Inc.; First Union Home Equity Bank.

For full biographical listings, see the Martindale-Hubbell Law Directory

LEVINE, HIRSCH, SEGALL & NORTHCUTT, P.A. (AV)

First Union Center, 100 South Ashley Drive, Suite 1600, P.O. Box 3429, 33601-3429
Telephone: 813-229-6585
Telecopier: 813-229-7210

Arnold D. Levine
Richard A. Hirsch
Stephen L. Segall
Stevan T. Northcutt

Edward M. Brennan

Representative Clients: Bank Societe Generale (Paris and Stockholm); Payment Systems for Credit Unions, Inc.

For full biographical listings, see the Martindale-Hubbell Law Directory

MANEY, DAMSKER, HARRIS & JONES, P.A. (AV)

606 Madison Street, P.O. Box 172009, 33672-0009
Telephone: 813-228-7371
Fax: 813-223-4846

Lee S. Damsker
David A. Maney

Lorena L. Kiely

For full biographical listings, see the Martindale-Hubbell Law Directory

PIPPINGER, TROPP & MATASSINI, P.A. (AV)

101 East Kennedy Boulevard, Suite 3305, 33602
Telephone: 813-225-1611

Richard G. Pippinger
Robert A. Tropp
Nicholas M. Matassini

For full biographical listings, see the Martindale-Hubbell Law Directory

RYWANT, ALVAREZ, JONES & RUSSO, PROFESSIONAL ASSOCIATION (AV)

Suite 500 Perry Paint & Glass Building, 109 North Brush Street, P.O. Box 3283, 33601
Telephone: 813-229-7007
Fax: 813-223-6544
Ocala, Florida Office: 3300 S.W. 34th Avenue, Suite 124C, 32674.
Telephone: 904-237-8810.
FAX: 904-237-2022.

Manuel J. Alvarez
Jill M. Deziel
Darrell D. Dirks
Matthew D. Emerson
John A.C. Guyton, III
Gregory D. Jones
Burke G. Lopez
Kerry C. McGuinn, Jr.
Andrew F. Russo
Michael S. Rywant
Scott M. Whitley
James R. Wilson
Susan M. Zwiesler

LEGAL SUPPORT PERSONNEL

Traci D. Tew
Bradley Hugh Holt
Stephanie Dickinson Neal (Paralegal)

Representative Clients: Peerless Insurance Co.; Gulf Insurance Group; Employers Casualty Co.; Landmark Insurance Co.

For full biographical listings, see the Martindale-Hubbell Law Directory

CHARLES F. SANSONE (AV)

Suite 200, 701 North Franklin Street, 33602
Telephone: 813-223-9282
FAX: 813-229-0595

For full biographical listings, see the Martindale-Hubbell Law Directory

SCHROPP, BUELL & ELLIGETT, PROFESSIONAL ASSOCIATION (AV)

Landmark Centre, Suite 2600, 401 East Jackson Street, 33602-5226
Telephone: 813-221-2600
FAX: 813-221-1760

Charles P. Schropp
Mark P. Buell
Raymond T. Elligett, Jr.

William R. Daniel
Amy S. Farrior
Bonnie A. Glober
Maria Lara Peet

For full biographical listings, see the Martindale-Hubbell Law Directory

SMITH, WILLIAMS & BOWLES, P.A. (AV)

Old Hyde Park, 712 South Oregon Avenue, 33606
Telephone: 813-253-5400
Fax: 813-254-3459
Orlando, Florida Office: Smith, Williams & Humphries, P.A., Southeast Bank Building, Suite 700, 201 East Pine Street.
Telephone: 407-849-5151.
St. Cloud, Florida Office: 1700-13th Street, Suite 2, 34769.
Telephone: 407-892-5545.

David Lisle Smith
Gregory L. Williams
Margaret E. Bowles
Jana P. Andrews
Jeffrey A. Aman
J. Gregory Humphries (Resident, Orlando Office)
James A. Muench
Dale K. Bohner
Neal A. Sivyer
Robert L. Harding (Resident, Orlando Office)
Daniel William King
Rebecca H. Forest (Resident, Orlando Office)

For full biographical listings, see the Martindale-Hubbell Law Directory

SOMERS & ASSOCIATES (AV)

3333 Henderson Boulevard, Suite 110, 33609-2913
Telephone: 813-872-7322
Fax: 813-872-8614

MEMBERS OF FIRM

Clifford L. Somers
Barbara B. Somers
R. Elliott Dunn, Jr.

Representative Clients: Caronia; CIGNA; Florida Physicians Insurance Co.; The Hartford Insurance Group; United States Fidelity & Guaranty Co.; Gulf Atlantic Insurance Co.; Alexander & Alexander; Florida Lawyers Indemnity Group; Cubic Corp.; Osteopathic Mutual Insurance Co.

For full biographical listings, see the Martindale-Hubbell Law Directory

STUART & STRICKLAND, P.A. (AV)

605 South Boulevard, 33606
Telephone: 813-251-8081
Fax: 813-254-2459
Brooksville, Florida Office: 217 Howell Avenue.
Telephone: 904-796-6733.
Fax: 904-799-7506.

Stephen K. Stuart
Steven A. Strickland (Resident)

Jeffrey A. Caglianone
Francis Anthony Miller

Reference: City Bank of Tampa.

For full biographical listings, see the Martindale-Hubbell Law Directory

TERRY & DITTMAR (AV)

Suite 2560, Barnett Plaza, 101 East Kennedy Boulevard, P.O. Box 20645, 33622-0645
Telephone: 813-222-8522
Fax: 813-222-8549

MEMBERS OF FIRM

William J. Terry
Charles H. Dittmar, Jr.

For full biographical listings, see the Martindale-Hubbell Law Directory

WAGNER, VAUGHAN & MCLAUGHLIN, P.A. (AV)

708 Jackson Street (Corner of Jefferson), and 601 Bayshore Boulevard, Suite 910, 33602
Telephone: 813-223-7421; 813-225-4000
FAX: 813-221-0254; 813-225-4010

Bill Wagner (Resident, Bayshore Boulevard Office)
Roger A. Vaughan, Jr.
John J. McLaughlin

Alan F. Wagner (Resident, Bayshore Boulevard Office)
Ruth Whetstone Wagner (Resident, Bayshore Boulevard Office)
Denise E. Vaughan
Weldon "Web" Earl Brennan (Resident, Bayshore Boulevard Office)
Bob Vaughan

For full biographical listings, see the Martindale-Hubbell Law Directory

ZUCKERMAN, SPAEDER, TAYLOR & EVANS (AV)

101 East Kennedy Boulevard, Suite 3140, 33602
Telephone: 813-221-1010
Fax: 813-223-7961
Miami, Florida Office: Suite 900, Miami Center, 201 South Biscayne Boulevard.
Telephones: 305-358-5000; 305-579-0110; Broward County: 305-523-0277.
Fax: 305-579-9749.
Ft. Lauderdale, Florida Office: One East Broward Boulevard, Suite 700.
Telephone: 305-356-0463.
Fax: 305-356-0406.

(See Next Column)

ZUCKERMAN, SPAEDER, TAYLOR & EVANS, *Tampa—Continued*

Washington, D.C. Office: Zuckerman, Spaeder, Goldstein, Taylor & Kolker, 1201 Connecticut Avenue, N.W.
Telephone: 202-778-1800.
Fax: 202-822-8106.
Baltimore, Maryland Office: Zuckerman, Spaeder, Goldstein, Taylor & Better, Suite 2440, 100 East Pratt Street.
Telephone: 410-332-0444.
Fax: 410-659-0436.
New York, N.Y. Office: Zuckerman, Spaeder, Goldstein, Taylor & Kolker, 1114 Avenue of the Americas, 45th Floor, Grace Building.
Telephone: 212-479-6500.
Fax: 212-479-6512.

MEMBERS OF FIRM

Morris Weinberg, Jr.
Ronald B. Ravikoff (Resident, Miami, Florida Office)
Michael S. Pasano (Miami, Florida and Ft. Lauderdale, Florida Offices)
Humberto J. Peña (Resident, Miami, Florida Office)
Sharon L. Kegerreis (Resident, Miami, Florida Office)
Thomas J. Meeks (Resident, Miami, Florida Office)

ASSOCIATES

Laura L. Vaughan
Teresa Halligan
Guy A. Rasco (Resident, Miami, Florida Office)
Bryan R. Cleveland (Resident, Miami, Florida Office)
Melissa Hammersley Clark (Not admitted in FL)
Jennifer Rae Coberly (Resident, Miami, Florida Office)

For full biographical listings, see the Martindale-Hubbell Law Directory

VENICE, Sarasota Co.

SNYDER, GRONER & SCHIEB (AV)

A Partnership including Professional Associations
355 West Venice Avenue, 34285
Telephone: 813-485-9626; 800-260-9626
Telecopier: 813-485-8163
Sarasota, Florida Office: 2033 Main Street, Suite 403.
Telephone: 813-951-1333; 800-448-0721.
Telecopier: 813-953-9685.

W. Russell Snyder (P.A.)
Richard W. Groner
Scott A. Schieb
W. Andrew Clayton, Jr.
Stanley M. Krawetz

Reference: Community National Bank of Sarasota

For full biographical listings, see the Martindale-Hubbell Law Directory

*VERO BEACH,** Indian River Co.

CLEM, POLACKWICH & VOCELLE (AV)

A Partnership including Professional Associations
Univest Building-Suite 501, 2770 North Indian River Boulevard, 32960
Telephone: 407-562-8111
Fax: 407-562-2870

MEMBERS OF FIRM

Chester Clem (P.A.)
Alan S. Polackwich, Sr. (P.A.)
Louis B. Vocelle, Jr., (P.A.)
James A. Taylor, III

ASSOCIATE

Paul Richard Berg

OF COUNSEL

Robert Golden

References: Barnett Bank of The Treasure Coast; Beach Bank of Vero Beach; Indian River National Bank; Riverside National Bank of Florida.

For full biographical listings, see the Martindale-Hubbell Law Directory

COLLINS, BROWN & CALDWELL, CHARTERED (AV)

756 Beachland Boulevard, P.O. Box 3686, 32964
Telephone: 407-231-4343
FAX: 407-234-5213

George G. Collins, Jr.
Calvin B. Brown
William W. Caldwell
Bruce D. Barkett
Bradley W. Rossway
Michael J. Garavaglia
John E. Moore, III

Reference: First Union Bank of Indian River County, Vero Beach, Florida.

For full biographical listings, see the Martindale-Hubbell Law Directory

GOULD, COOKSEY, FENNELL, BARKETT, O'NEILL & MARINE, PROFESSIONAL ASSOCIATION (AV)

979 Beachland Boulevard, 32963
Telephone: 407-231-1100
Fax: 407-231-2020

(See Next Column)

John R. Gould (1921-1988)
Byron T. Cooksey
Darrell Fennell
Lawrence A. Barkett
Eugene J. O'Neill
Christopher H. Marine

David M. Carter

Counsel for: Barnett Bank of Indian River County; Indian River National Bank; Citrus Bank, N.A..
Approved Attorneys for: Attorneys' Title Insurance Fund; Commonwealth Land Title Insurance Company; Lawyers Title Insurance Corp.; Federal Land Bank of Columbia.
Local Counsel for: Los Angeles Dodgers, Inc.

For full biographical listings, see the Martindale-Hubbell Law Directory

MOSS, HENDERSON, VAN GAASBECK, BLANTON & KOVAL, P.A. (AV)

817 Beachland Boulevard, P.O. Box 3406, 32964-3406
Telephone: 407-231-1900
Fax: 407-231-4387

George H. Moss, II
Steve L. Henderson
Everett J. Van Gaasbeck
Robin A. Blanton
Thomas A. Koval
Clinton W. Lanier
Kevin S. Doty

Donald E. Feuerbach
Fred L. Kretschmer, Jr.
Margaret Sue Lyon
Lisa D. Harpring
Kathleen W. Stratton
Lewis W. Murphy, Jr.
E. Clayton Yates
Judith Goodman Hill

OF COUNSEL

Charles E. Garris
Ford J. Fegert

Representative Clients: Aetna Life & Casualty; Alcoa Florida, Inc.; Florida Power & Light Co.; Insurance Company of North America; Liberty Mutual Insurance Co.; Sears, Roebuck & Co.; Sugar Cane Growers Cooperative of Florida.

For full biographical listings, see the Martindale-Hubbell Law Directory

O'HAIRE, QUINN, CANDLER & O'HAIRE (AV)

3111 Cardinal Drive, P.O. Box 4375, 32964
Telephone: 407-231-6900
FAX: 407-231-9729

MEMBERS OF FIRM

Michael O'Haire
Jerome D. Quinn
Richard Boyer Candler
Sean M. O'Haire

References: Barnett Bank of Indian River County; The Beach Bank of Vero Beach.

For full biographical listings, see the Martindale-Hubbell Law Directory

PAXTON, CROW, BRAGG, SMITH & KEYSER, P.A. (AV)

1717 Indian River Boulevard Suite 202C, 32960
Telephone: 407-778-1755
FAX: 407-778-2433
West Palm Beach, Florida Office: Barristers Building, Suite 501, 1615 Forum Place.
Telephone: 407-684-2121.
FAX: 407-684-6855.

David F. Crow
Robert A. Hawley, Jr.

For full biographical listings, see the Martindale-Hubbell Law Directory

SMITH & SMITH (AV)

Citrus Financial Center, Suite 301, 1717 Indian River Boulevard, 32960
Telephone: 407-567-4351
FAX: 407-567-4298

MEMBERS OF FIRM

Sherman N. Smith, Jr.
Sherman N. Smith, III

References: Barnett Bank of Indian River County; The Beach Bank of Vero Beach.

For full biographical listings, see the Martindale-Hubbell Law Directory

*WEST PALM BEACH,** Palm Beach Co.

ADAMS, COOGLER, WATSON & MERKEL, P.A. (AV)

Suite 1600, 1555 Palm Beach Lakes Boulevard, P.O. Box 2069, 33402
Telephone: 407-478-4500
Fax: 407-684-7346

Samuel H. Adams (1913-1981)
Monroe A. Coogler, Jr.
Roy R. Watson
Robert G. Merkel
Keith R. Pallo
James C. Barry
Reed W. Kellner
Catherine Lynn Kasten
Louis P. Pfeffer

(See Next Column)

ADAMS, COOGLER, WATSON & MERKEL P.A.—*Continued*

Daniel J. DeMay
David M. Gaspari
Patricia A. Judge
Faith L. Connor
Scott S. Warburton
William Scott Hamilton
Karen J. Valente
Andrea D. McMillan
Kathryn L. Tignor
Michael D. Kiner
Eric M. Price
Peter A. Cooke
Esther A. Zapata
Carlos J. Hernandez

OF COUNSEL

L. C. Shepard, Jr.

Representative Clients: Auto-Owners Insurance; Liberty Mutual Insurance Co.

For full biographical listings, see the Martindale-Hubbell Law Directory

BABBITT, HAZOURI AND JOHNSON, P.A. (AV)

1801 Australian Avenue South, Suite 200, P.O. Drawer 024426, 33402
Telephone: 407-684-2500
Fax: 407-684-6308

Theodore Babbitt
Fred A. Hazouri
Joseph R. Johnson

For full biographical listings, see the Martindale-Hubbell Law Directory

BEVERLY & TITTLE, P.A. (AV)

823 North Olive Avenue, 33401
Telephone: 407-655-6022
Fax: 407-655-6044

Don Beverly
James D. Tittle, Jr.

Reference: Barnett Bank, West Palm Beach, Florida.

For full biographical listings, see the Martindale-Hubbell Law Directory

BOBO, SPICER, CIOTOLI, FULFORD, BOCCHINO, DEBEVOISE & LE CLAINCHE, P.A. (AV)

Esperante, Sixth Floor, 222 Lakeview Avenue, 33401
Telephone: 407-684-6600
Fax: 407-684-3828
Orlando, Florida Office: Landmark Center One, Suite 510, 315 East Robinson Street, 32801-1949.
Telephone: 407-849-1060.
Fax: 407-843-4751.

A. Russell Bobo
David W. Spicer
Eugene L. Ciotoli
Jeffrey C. Fulford
John W. Bocchino (Resident, Orlando Office)
D. Andrew DeBevoise (Resident, Orlando Office)
Stephan A. Le Clainche

Christopher C. Curry (Resident, Orlando Office)
Patti A. Haber
Paul A. Nugent
Joseph A. Osborne
Richard B. Schwamm
Michael S. Smith
Paul M. Adams
Robert A. Zimmerman
Neil A. Deleon
Sharon A. Chapman (Resident, Orlando Office)
J. Clancey Bounds (Resident, Orlando Office)
Robert R. Saunders (Resident, Orlando Office)
Keith A. Scott (Resident, Orlando Office)
Sophia B. Ehringer (Resident, Orlando Office)
Tyler S. McClay (Resident, Orlando Office)
Michael D. Burt
Dominic John "Jack" Scalera, III
Casey D. Shomo
Armando T. Lauritano

For full biographical listings, see the Martindale-Hubbell Law Directory

CARUSO, BURLINGTON, BOHN & COMPIANI, P.A. (AV)

Suite 3A Barristers Building, 1615 Forum Place, 33401
Telephone: 407-686-8010
Fax: 407-686-8663

Edna L. Caruso
Philip M. Burlington
Russell S. Bohn
Barbara J. Compiani

For full biographical listings, see the Martindale-Hubbell Law Directory

LAWRENCE U. L. CHANDLER (AV)

1555 Palm Beach Lakes Boulevard, Suite 1520
Telephone: 407-478-1478
Fax: 407-478-1498

For full biographical listings, see the Martindale-Hubbell Law Directory

CHRISTIANSEN & JACKNIN (AV)

Suite 1010, NationsBank Tower, 1555 Palm Beach Lakes Boulevard, P.O. Box 3346, 33402
Telephone: 407-689-1888
Fax: 407-689-0586

(See Next Column)

MEMBERS OF FIRM

John T. Christiansen
Jay R. Jacknin
Neil B. Jagolinzer

Clients and References Furnished by Request.

For full biographical listings, see the Martindale-Hubbell Law Directory

DAMSEL & GELSTON, P.A. (AV)

601B North Dixie Highway Post Office Drawer 4507, 33402-4507
Telephone: 407-832-6455
FAX: 407-832-5773

Charles H. Damsel, Jr.
Fred H. Gelston

Stuart M. Silverman

LEGAL SUPPORT PERSONNEL

Linda M. Colombo (Legal Assistant/Group Health Insurance Administrator)

For full biographical listings, see the Martindale-Hubbell Law Directory

EASLEY & WILLITS, P.A. (AV)

Suite 800 Forum III, 1655 Palm Beach Lakes Boulevard, 33401
Telephone: 407-684-7300
Facsimile: 407-684-8711

H. Michael Easley
Richard H. Willits
M. Christopher Edwards

For full biographical listings, see the Martindale-Hubbell Law Directory

FARISH, FARISH & ROMANI (AV)

316 Banyan Boulevard, P.O. Box 4118, 33402
Telephone: 407-659-3500
Fax: 407-655-3158

MEMBERS OF FIRM

Joseph D. Farish (1892-1977)
Joseph D. Farish, Jr.
Robert V. Romani

References: 1st Union Bank; Clewiston National Bank; Barnett Bank of Palm Beach County.

For Complete List of Firm Personnel, See General Section

For full biographical listings, see the Martindale-Hubbell Law Directory

FREEMAN & ROSS, P.A. (AV)

811 North Olive Avenue, 33401-3709
Telephone: 407-655-6025
Fax: 407-655-5759
Palatka Office: 415 St. Johns Avenue.
Telephone: 904-325-6239.
Fax: 904-329-9626.

Terry N. Freeman
Robert C. Ross

OF COUNSEL

Henry P. Ruffolo

LEGAL SUPPORT PERSONNEL

Debra J. McPherson
E.I. "Chuck" Engelking

For full biographical listings, see the Martindale-Hubbell Law Directory

DANIEL H. JAMES (AV)

Suite 1603 Northbridge Centre, 515 North Flagler Drive, P.O. Box 3246, 33402
Telephone: 407-659-4000
Deerfield Beach: 305-426-5588
FAX: 407-659-0527

LEGAL SUPPORT PERSONNEL

Monica Sessa

Representative Clients: Six L's Corp.; David C. Brown Farms Inc.; Dubois Farms Inc.

For full biographical listings, see the Martindale-Hubbell Law Directory

JONES, FOSTER, JOHNSTON & STUBBS, P.A. (AV)

Flagler Center Tower, 505 South Flagler Drive, P.O. Box 3475, 33402-3475
Telephone: 407-659-3000
Fax: 407-832-1454

Sidney A. Stubbs, Jr.
John Blair McCracken
John C. Randolph
Herbert Adams Weaver, Jr.
Larry B. Alexander
Thornton M. Henry
Margaret L. Cooper
D. Culver Smith III (P.A.)
Allen R. Tomlinson
Peter S. Holton
Michael P. Walsh
Peter A. Sachs
Michael T. Kranz
John S. Trimper

(See Next Column)

JONES, FOSTER, JOHNSTON & STUBBS P.A., *West Palm Beach—Continued*

Mark B. Kleinfeld
Andrew R. Ross
Scott Gardner Hawkins
Steven J. Rothman
Rebecca G. Doane

Joyce A. Conway
Stephen J. Aucamp
Christopher S. Duke
Scott L. McMullen
John C. Rau
Tracey Biagiotti
Edward Diaz

Counsel For: U.S. Trust Co.; NationsBank of Florida, N.A.; Island National Bank; Bankers Trust Company of Florida; Sun Bank/South Florida, N.A.; General Motors Acceptance Corp.

For full biographical listings, see the Martindale-Hubbell Law Directory

LEWIS KAPNER, P.A. (AV)

Suite 1402, One Clearlake Centre, 250 Australian Avenue South, P.O. Box 1428, 33402
Telephone: 407-655-3000;
Delray/Ft. Lauderdale: 305-930-9191
Fax: 407-655-8899
Boca Raton, Florida Office: 621 Northwest 53rd Street.
Telephone: 305-930-9191.

Lewis Kapner
Victoria A. Calebrese

For full biographical listings, see the Martindale-Hubbell Law Directory

THOMAS E. KINGCADE PROFESSIONAL ASSOCIATION (AV)

209 South Olive Avenue, 33401
Telephone: 407-659-7300
FAX: 407-655-1593

Thomas E. Kingcade

William W. Booth

For full biographical listings, see the Martindale-Hubbell Law Directory

STUART E. KOCHA, P.A. (AV)

118 Clematis Street, P.O. Box 1427, 33402
Telephone: 407-659-5611
Fax: 407-659-5636

Stuart E. Kocha

LEGAL SUPPORT PERSONNEL

David L. Halderman (Chief Investigator)
Steve L. Sheehy (Investigator)

References: NationsBank; Admiralty Bank.

For full biographical listings, see the Martindale-Hubbell Law Directory

JANE KREUSLER-WALSH (AV)

Suite 503 Flagler Center, 501 South Flagler Drive, 33401
Telephone: 407-659-5455
Fax: 407-820-8762

For full biographical listings, see the Martindale-Hubbell Law Directory

ALFRED A. LASORTE, JR. (AV)

Suite 1000, United National Bank Tower, 1645 Palm Beach Lakes Boulevard, 33401
Telephone: 407-684-3000
FAX: 407-684-3004

For full biographical listings, see the Martindale-Hubbell Law Directory

MONTGOMERY & LARMOYEUX (AV)

1016 Clearwater Place, Drawer 3086, 33402-3086
Telephone: 407-832-2880
Fax: 407-832-0887

MEMBERS OF FIRM

Robert M. Montgomery, Jr.
Christopher M. Larmoyeux

ASSOCIATES

Rebecca L. Larson
Todd Cash Alofs
Odette Marie Bendeck

For full biographical listings, see the Martindale-Hubbell Law Directory

NASON, GILDAN, YEAGER, GERSON & WHITE, P.A. (AV)

Penthouse Suite United National Bank Tower, 1645 Palm Beach Lakes Boulevard, 33401
Telephone: 407-686-3307
Fax: 407-686-5442

(See Next Column)

Herbert L. Gildan
Thomas J. Yeager
Gary N. Gerson
John White, II
Phillip C. Gildan
Nathan E. Nason
M. Richard Sapir
Kenneth A. Marra
Gregory L. Scott
Domenick R. Lioce
Alan I. Armour, II
Mark A. Pachman
Elaine Johnson James

John M. McDivitt
Howard J. Falcon, III
Susan Fleischner Kornspan

For full biographical listings, see the Martindale-Hubbell Law Directory

PAXTON, CROW, BRAGG, SMITH & KEYSER, P.A. (AV)

Barristers Building, Suite 500, 1615 Forum Place, 33401
Telephone: 407-684-2121
Fax: 407-684-6855
Vero Beach, Florida Office: 1717 Indian River Boulevard.
Telephone: 407-778-1755.
FAX: 407-778-2433.

Ralph B. Paxton (Retired)
David F. Crow
Morgan S. Bragg
Clark W. Smith
Gregory M. Keyser
Michele I. Nelson
Robert A. Hawley, Jr. (Resident, Vero Beach Office)

John E. Peterson
Thomas Brown Miller
F. Neal Colvin, Jr.
Michael B. Davis
Peter W. Wildman
Canda L. Brown

OF COUNSEL

Stephen C. McAliley

For full biographical listings, see the Martindale-Hubbell Law Directory

PRUITT & PRUITT, P.A. (AV)

Suite 400 Flagler Tower, 505 South Flagler Drive, 33401
Telephone: 407-655-8080
Fax: 407-655-4134

William H. Pruitt
William E. Pruitt

Reference: Flagler National Bank.

For full biographical listings, see the Martindale-Hubbell Law Directory

ANTHONY E. PUCILLO, P.A. (AV)

222 Piccadilly Street, P.O. Box 3131, 33402
Telephone: 407-659-5050
FAX: 407-833-3541

Anthony E. Pucillo

For full biographical listings, see the Martindale-Hubbell Law Directory

RICCI, HUBBARD & LEOPOLD ATTORNEYS AT LAW, P.A. (AV)

United National Bank Building, 1645 Palm Beach Lakes Boulevard, P.O. Box 2946, 33402
Telephone: 407-684-6500
Fax: 407-697-2383

Edward M. Ricci
James R. Hubbard
Theodore J. Leopold
Theresa A. DiPaola
Scott C. Murray

LEGAL SUPPORT PERSONNEL

Robert V. Pautsch (Automotive Engineer)
Janice C. Develle (Paralegal)
Lisa B. Simone (Paralegal)
Joseph L. Vaccaro (Paralegal)
Linda J. Hermans (Paralegal)

For full biographical listings, see the Martindale-Hubbell Law Directory

RONALD SALES, LAWYER, P.A. (AV)

Suite 300 F, 1551 Forum Place, 33402
Telephone: 407-686-2333

Ronald Sales

Reference: Palm Beach National Bank & Trust Co., Palm Beach, Florida.

For full biographical listings, see the Martindale-Hubbell Law Directory

SEARCY DENNEY SCAROLA BARNHART & SHIPLEY, PROFESSIONAL ASSOCIATION (AV)

2139 Palm Beach Lakes Boulevard, P.O. Drawer 3626, 33402-3626
Telephone: 407-686-6300
800-780-8607
Fax: 407-478-0754

(See Next Column)

SEARCY DENNEY SCAROLA BARNHART & SHIPLEY PROFESSIONAL ASSOCIATION—*Continued*

Christian D. Searcy, Sr.
Earl L. Denney, Jr.
John Scarola
F. Gregory Barnhart
John A. Shipley
Lois J. Frankel
David K. Kelley, Jr.
Lawrence J. Block, Jr.
C. Calvin Warriner, III
William A. Norton
David J. Sales

James N. Nance
Katherine Ann Martinez
T. Michael Kennedy
Todd S. Stewart
Christopher K. Speed

LEGAL SUPPORT PERSONNEL

Deane L. Cady (Paralegal/Investigator)
James E. Cook (Paralegal/Investigator)
Emilio Diamantis (Paralegal/Investigator)
David W. Gilmore (Paralegal/Investigator)
John C. Hopkins (Paralegal/Investigator)
Thaddeus E. Kulesa (Paralegal/Investigator)
J. Peter Love (Paralegal/Investigator)
Marjorie A. Morgan (Paralegal)
Joel C. Padgett (Paralegal/Investigator)
William H. Seabold (Paralegal/Investigator)
Kathleen Simon (Paralegal)
Steve M. Smith (Paralegal/Investigator)
Judson Whitehorn (Paralegal/Investigator)
Marcia Yarnell Dodson (Not admitted in FL; Law Clerk)
Kelly Lynn Hopkins (Paralegal/Investigator)
Frank Cotton (Paralegal/Investigator)

For full biographical listings, see the Martindale-Hubbell Law Directory

LAW OFFICES OF LOUIS M. SILBER, P.A. (AV)

Reflections II, Suite 855, 400 Australian Avenue, South, 33401
Telephone: 407-655-6640
Fax: 407-659-3345

Louis M. Silber

Philip L. Valente, Jr.

For full biographical listings, see the Martindale-Hubbell Law Directory

PAUL A. TURK, JR., P.A. (AV)

Suite 1000, United National Bank Building, 1645 Palm Beach Lakes Boulevard, 33401
Telephone: 407-684-0098
Facsimile: 407-684-3004

Paul A. Turk, Jr.

Reference: Great Southern Bank, West Palm Beach, Fla.

For full biographical listings, see the Martindale-Hubbell Law Directory

WAGNER, NUGENT, JOHNSON & MCAFEE, P.A. (AV)

Commerce Pointe, Suite 450, 1818 South Australian Avenue, P.O. Box 3466, 33402
Telephone: 407-686-5200; 1-800-899-5200
FAX: 407-686-6710

Ward Wagner, Jr.
Robert R. Johnson
Helen Wagner McAfee
William J. McAfee
Julia A. Wagner

Michael G. Bodik

OF COUNSEL

Charles A. Nugent, Jr.

References: Sunbank/South Florida, N.A.; Fidelity Federal Savings & Loan Association of West Palm Beach.

For full biographical listings, see the Martindale-Hubbell Law Directory

JAMES E. WEBER, P.A. (AV)

Suite 502 The Flagler Center, 501 South Flagler Drive, 33401
Telephone: 407-832-2266
Fax: 407-833-3816

James E. Weber

For full biographical listings, see the Martindale-Hubbell Law Directory

WIEDERHOLD, MOSES, BULFIN & RUBIN, P.A. (AV)

Northbridge Centre, Suite 800, 515 North Flagler Drive, P.O. Box 3918, 33401
Telephone: 407-659-2296;
Broward: 305-763-5630
FAX: 407-659-2865

John P. Wiederhold
Robert D. Moses
John J. Bulfin
Kenneth M. Rubin

(See Next Column)

Lawrence I. Bass
Kay Seeber Hoff
Marc S. Ruderman
Bruce R. Katzell

Reference: Florida National Bank of Palm Beach Co.

For full biographical listings, see the Martindale-Hubbell Law Directory

WINTER HAVEN, Polk Co.

PETERSON, MYERS, CRAIG, CREWS, BRANDON & PUTERBAUGH, P.A. (AV)

Suite 300, 141 5th Street N.W., P.O. Drawer 7608, 33883-7608
Telephone: 813-294-3360
Lake Wales, Florida Office: 130 East Central Avenue, P.O. Box 1079.
Telephones: 813-676-7611; 683-8942.
Lakeland, Florida Office: 100 East Main Street, P.O. Box 24628.
Telephones: 813-683-6511; 676-6934.

Jack P. Brandon
Beach A Brooks, Jr.
J. Davis Connor
Michael S. Craig
Roy A. Craig, Jr.
Jacob C. Dykxhoorn
Dennis P. Johnson
Kevin C. Knowlton
Douglas A. Lockwood, III
Corneal B. Myers
Cornelius B. Myers, III
Robert E. Puterbaugh
Abel A. Putnam
Thomas B. Putnam, Jr.
Deborah A. Ruster
Stephen R. Senn
Andrea Teves Smith
Kerry M. Wilson

General Counsel for: Barnett Bank of Polk County.
Representative Clients: Mutual Wholesale Co.; Sun Bank/Mid-Florida, N.A.; Chase Commercial Corp.; Barnett Banks, Inc.; Ben Hill Griffin, Inc.; Alcoma Association, Inc.
Approved Attorneys for: Attorneys' Title Insurance Fund; Federal Land Bank, Columbia, South Carolina; Equitable Life Assurance Society of the United States.

For full biographical listings, see the Martindale-Hubbell Law Directory

WINTER PARK, Orange Co.

GRAHAM, CLARK, JONES, PRATT & MARKS (AV)

Third Floor, NationsBank Building, 369 North New York Avenue, P.O. Drawer 1690, 32790
Telephone: 407-647-4455
Telefax: 407-740-7063
Orlando, Florida Office: 111 North Orlando Avenue, Suite 1075, 32801.
Telephone: 407-648-5740.

MEMBERS OF FIRM

Jesse E. Graham
Scott D. Clark
Frederick W. Jones
James R. Pratt
Howard S. Marks
Geoffrey D. Withers
J. Gary Miller
John L. DiMasi
Mary W. Christian
Laura L. Jacobs
Jesse E. Graham, Jr.

Approved Attorneys for: Chicago Title Insurance Co.
Reference: NationsBank of Florida.

For full biographical listings, see the Martindale-Hubbell Law Directory

POHL & BROWN, P.A. (AV)

280 West Canton Avenue, Suite 410, P.O. Box 3208, 32789
Telephone: 407-647-7645; 407-647-POHL
Telefax: 407-647-2314

Frank L. Pohl
Usher L. Brown
Houston E. Short
Dwight I. Cool
William W. Pouzar
Mary B. Van Leuven

OF COUNSEL

Frederick W. Peirsol

Representative Clients: Orange County Comptroller; Osceola County; School Board of Osceola County, Florida; Osceola Tourist Development Council; NationsBank of Florida, N.A.; SunBank, N.A.; The Bank of Winter Park; Bekins Moving and Storage Co., Inc.; Champion Boats, Inc.; KeyCom Telephone Systems, Inc.

For full biographical listings, see the Martindale-Hubbell Law Directory

TROUTMAN, WILLIAMS, IRVIN, GREEN & HELMS, PROFESSIONAL ASSOCIATION (AV)

311 West Fairbanks Avenue, 32789
Telephone: 407-647-2277
FAX: 407-628-2986
Kissimmee, Florida Office: Suite 206, 120 Broadway, 34741.
Telephone: 407-933-8834.
FAX: 407-933-8253.

(See Next Column)

TROUTMAN, WILLIAMS, IRVIN, GREEN & HELMS PROFESSIONAL ASSOCIATION, *Winter Park—Continued*

Russell Troutman
Joseph H. Williams
Paul B. Irvin
Robert F. Green
Roger D. Helms
Joseph J. Polich, Jr.
Jack E. Bowen
David M. Giard
Kim Michael Cullen

For full biographical listings, see the Martindale-Hubbell Law Directory

GEORGIA

*ALBANY,** Dougherty Co.

CANNON, MEYER VON BREMEN & MEIER (AV)

2417 Westgate Drive, P.O. Box 70909, 31708-0909
Telephone: 912-435-1470
Telefax: 912-888-2156

MEMBERS OF FIRM

William E. Cannon, Jr.
Michael S. Meyer von Bremen
John A. Meier, II
Timothy O. Davis

For full biographical listings, see the Martindale-Hubbell Law Directory

*ATHENS,** Clarke Co.

BLASINGAME, BURCH, GARRARD & BRYANT, P.C. (AV)

440 College Avenue North, P.O. Box 832, 30603
Telephone: 706-354-4000
Telecopier: 706-353-0673

J. Ralph Beaird
Gary B. Blasingame
E. Davison Burch
Henry G. Garrard, III
Everett Clay Bryant
M. Steven Heath
Andrew J. Hill, III
Michael A. Morris
Thomas H. Rogers, Jr.
William D. Harvard
Rikard L. Bridges
William S. Cowsert
Ivan A. Gustafson
Michael C. Daniel
David S. Thomson
Gregory Alexander Daniels
Milton F. Eisenberg
Stephen E.B. Smith
J. David Felt, Jr.
Wayne R. Allen
Amy Lou King

Representative Clients: NationsBank of Georgia, N.A.; Georgia Power Co.; Georgia Natural Gas Co.; Pittsburgh Corning Corp.; Downtown Athens Development Authority; Georgia National Bank; Fowler Products Co., Inc.; St. Paul Fire & Marine Insurance Co.; Athens Newspapers, Inc.; First Commerce Bancorp, Inc.

For full biographical listings, see the Martindale-Hubbell Law Directory

MCLEOD, BENTON, BEGNAUD & MARSHALL (AV)

8th Floor, NationsBank Building, P.O. Box 8108, 30603
Telephone: 706-549-9400
Fax: 706-549-9406

MEMBERS OF FIRM

Larry V. McLeod
Terrell W. Benton, Jr.
Jeanette S. Scott
Darrel Begnaud
Andrew H. Marshall
Malcolm C. McArthur
William C. Berryman, Jr.
Daniel C. Haygood
Hilary N. Shuford
David K. Linder
Richard L. Brittain

OF COUNSEL

Robert E. Gibson

Counsel for: NationsBank; Athens First Bank & Trust Company; Georgia Power Company; CSX Transportation, Inc.; St. Mary's Hospital; Benson's Inc.

For full biographical listings, see the Martindale-Hubbell Law Directory

*ATLANTA,** Fulton Co.

ALEMBIK, FINE & CALLNER, P.A. (AV)

Marquis One Tower, Fourth Floor, 245 Peachtree Center Avenue, N.E., 30303
Telephone: 404-688-8800
Telecopier: 404-420-7191

Michael D. Alembik (1936-1993)
Lowell S. Fine
Bruce W. Callner
Kathy L. Portnoy
Ronald T. Gold
G. Michael Banick
Mark E. Bergeson
Russell P. Love

Z. Ileana Martinez
Kevin S. Green
Susan M. Lieppe
T. Kevin Mooney
Bruce R. Steinfeld
Janet Lichiello Franchi

For full biographical listings, see the Martindale-Hubbell Law Directory

ALSTON & BIRD (AV)

A Partnership including Professional Corporations
One Atlantic Center, 1201 West Peachtree Street, 30309-3424
Telephone: 404-881-7000
Telecopier: 404-881-7777
Cable Address: AMGRAM GA
Telex: 54-2996
Easylink: 62985848
Washington, D.C. Office: 700 Thirteenth Street, Suite 350 20005-3960.
Telephone: 202-508-3300.
Telecopier: 202-508-3333.

MEMBERS OF FIRM

G. Conley Ingram
Michael A. Doyle
Ronald L. Reid
C. David Butler
R. Neal Batson
Oscar N. Persons
Benjamin F. Johnson III
William C. Humphreys, Jr.
James S. Stokes
Dow N. Kirkpatrick II
W. Terence Walsh
Robert D. McCallum, Jr.
Jack H. Senterfitt
Peter Q. Bassett
Judson Graves
Peter M. Degnan
Lee A. DeHihns III
Jay D. Bennett
J. William Boone
Steven M. Collins
John C. Weitnauer
Nill V. Toulme
R. Wayne Thorpe
John I. Spangler III
Grant T. Stein
Theodore E. G. Pound
Bernard Taylor
Richard T. Fulton
Mary C. Gill
William H. Hughes, Jr.
Donna Potts Bergeson
Gerald L. Mize, Jr.
Robert P. Riordan
John E. Stephenson, Jr.
Dennis J. Connolly
Todd R. David
Elizabeth A. Gilley
Richard R. Hays
Jennifer Brown Moore

COUNSEL

Lawrie E. Demorest
Sydney S. Cleland

ASSOCIATES

Lori G. Baer
Holly B. Barnett
Lonnie T. Brown, Jr.
Jay B. Bryan
Linda G. Carpenter
Bradley L. Cooper
Alston D. Correll III
Cynthia L. Counts
Robert L. Crewdson
Kristen K. Darnell
Jo C. Dearing
Susan B. Devitt
Lance P. Dunnings
A. McCampbell Gibson
James C. Grant
Ernest LaMont Greer
James W. Hagan
Jennifer Gimer Hays
H. Douglas Hinson
W. Hunter Holliday
Lori P. Hughes
Susan E. Hurd
Clifton M. Iler
John A. Jordak, Jr.
Daniel A. Kent
Rebecca McLemore Lamberth
Matthew W. Levin
David M. Maxwell
Robin Goff Mayer
William S. Mayfield
Scott A. McLaren
R. Clay Milling
Robert D. Mowrey
Laura Lewis Owens
Vionnette Reyes
Daniel L. Rikard
Thomas S. Robinson III
Candace N. Smith
Robyn Ice Sosebee
K. David Steele
Paul F. Wellborn III
Karen K. Wolter

OF COUNSEL

Sidney O. Smith, Jr.

Representative Clients: Bristol-Myers Co.; Chrysler Corp.; CSX Transportation, Inc.; E.I. du Pont de Nemours and Company; Exxon Corporation; NationsBank Corporation; Prudential Insurance Company of America; Sears, Roebuck and Co.

For Complete List of Firm Personnel, See General Section

For full biographical listings, see the Martindale-Hubbell Law Directory

E. ALAN ARMSTRONG (AV)

Building 5, 2900 Chamblee-Tucker Road, 30341
Telephone: 404-451-0313
FAX: 404-451-0317
(Also Of Counsel, Kellogg & Saccoccia)

OF COUNSEL

Edward H. Kellogg, Jr., P.C.

LEGAL SUPPORT PERSONNEL

Jane Maxwell

Representative Clients: Brock Candy Company; Airline Transport Professionals, Inc.
Reference: NationsBank; Aircraft Owners and Pilots Association.

For full biographical listings, see the Martindale-Hubbell Law Directory

BELTRAN & ASSOCIATES (AV)

One Atlantic Center, Suite 3095, 1201 West Peachtree Street, 30309
Telephone: 404-892-3100
Facsimile: 404-892-1222

(See Next Column)

BELTRAN & ASSOCIATES—*Continued*

Frank J. Beltran
Simone R. Siex
Ralph Perales

Reference: NationsBank.

For full biographical listings, see the Martindale-Hubbell Law Directory

BLACKWOOD & MATTHEWS (AV)

Monarch Plaza, 3414 Peachtree Road Suite 660, 30326
Telephone: 404-237-5050
Toll Free: 800-776-0098
Fax: 404-233-3910

B. Randall Blackwood
James B. Matthews, III
John D. Steel
John B. Briggs
H. Craig Stafford

For full biographical listings, see the Martindale-Hubbell Law Directory

BONDURANT, MIXSON & ELMORE (AV)

1201 W. Peachtree Street Suite 3900, 30309
Telephone: 404-881-4100
FAX: 404-881-4111

MEMBERS OF FIRM

Emmet J. Bondurant II
H. Lamar Mixson
M. Jerome Elmore
Edward B. Krugman
James C. Morton
Jeffrey O. Bramlett
Dirk G. Christensen
Jane E. Fahey
Jeffrey D. Horst
John E. Floyd
Carolyn R. Gorwitz
Michael A. Sullivan

ASSOCIATES

Mary Jo Bradbury
P. Richard Game
Robin M. Hutchinson
Frank M. Lowrey, IV
J. Scott McClain
Keenan Rance Sephus Nix
Jill A. Pryor
Michael B. Terry
Joshua F. Thorpe

Representative Clients: The Aetna Casualty and Surety Company; Bottlers of Coca-Cola, U.S.A.; Brinks Home Security Systems, Inc.; Delta Air Lines, Inc.; Fina Oil and Chemical Company; JMB Realty Corp.; The Paradies Shops, Inc.; Sanifill, Inc.; Trammell Crow Co.

For Complete List of Firm Personnel, See General Section

For full biographical listings, see the Martindale-Hubbell Law Directory

BUTLER, WOOTEN, OVERBY & CHEELEY (AV)

2719 Buford Highway, 30324
Telephone: 404-321-1700
WATS 1-800-242-2962
FAX: 404-321-1713
Columbus, Georgia Office: 1500 Second Avenue, P.O. Box 2766.
Telephone: 706-322-1990; National Wats: 1-800-233-4086.
FAX: 706-323-2962.

MEMBERS OF FIRM

James E. Butler, Jr.
Joel O. Wooten, Jr.
C. Frederick Overby
Robert D. Cheeley
Albert M. Pearson, III
George W. Fryhofer, III

ASSOCIATES

Peter J. Daughtery
J. Frank Myers, III
Patrick A. Dawson
Lee Tarte
Jason L. Crawford
Keith A. Pittman

Reference: Columbus Bank and Trust, Columbus, Ga.

For full biographical listings, see the Martindale-Hubbell Law Directory

CARTER & ANSLEY (AV)

Suite 1000 One Ninety One Peachtree Tower, 191 Peachtree Street, 30303-1747
Telephone: 404-658-9220
FAX: 404-658-9726

MEMBERS OF FIRM

Shepard Bryan (1871-1970)
W. Colquitt Carter (1904-1988)
Ben Kingree, III
Tommy T. Holland
H. Sanders Carter, Jr.
A. Terry Sorrells
Robert A. Barnaby, II
Thomas E. Magill
Robert O. McCloud, Jr.
Anthony J. McGinley
Christopher N. Shuman
Elizabeth J. Bondurant

ASSOCIATES

Michael A. Coval
Rebecca J. Schmidt
Keith L. Lindsay
Burke B. Johnson
Kenton J. Coppage
John H. Zwald
A. Louise Tanner
David M. Atkinson

For Complete List of Firm Personnel, See General Section

For full biographical listings, see the Martindale-Hubbell Law Directory

COOPER, HEWITT & KATZ (AV)

Resurgens Plaza Suite 1700, 945 East Paces Ferry Road, 30326
Telephone: 404-814-0000
Fax: 404-816-8900

MEMBERS OF FIRM

Lawrence A. Cooper
A. Kenneth Hewitt, III
Robert Neal Katz

ASSOCIATE

Julie Ann Hauge

For full biographical listings, see the Martindale-Hubbell Law Directory

DAVID G. CROCKETT, P.C. (AV)

1000 Equitable Building, 100 Peachtree Street, N.W., 30303
Telephone: 404-522-4280
Telecopier: 404-589-9891

David G. Crockett

Approved Attorney for: Chicago Title Insurance Co.
Reference: NationsBank, N.A.

For full biographical listings, see the Martindale-Hubbell Law Directory

DAVIS, MATTHEWS & QUIGLEY, P.C. (AV)

Fourteenth Floor, Lenox Towers II, 3400 Peachtree Road, 30326
Telephone: 404-261-3900
Telecopier: 404-261-0159

Baxter L. Davis
Ron L. Quigley
Richard W. Schiffman, Jr.
Frank A. DeVincent
John Charles Olderman

Approved Attorneys for: Lawyers Title Insurance Corp.

For Complete List of Firm Personnel, See General Section

For full biographical listings, see the Martindale-Hubbell Law Directory

DENNIS, CORRY, PORTER & GRAY (AV)

3300 One Atlanta Plaza, 950 East Paces Ferry Road, P.O. Box 18640, 30326
Telephone: 404-240-6900
Wats: 800-735-0838
Fax: 404-240-6909
Telex: 4611041

MEMBERS OF FIRM

Robert E. Corry, Jr.
R. Clay Porter
William E. Gray, II
James S. Strawinski
Grant B. Smith

OF COUNSEL

Douglas Dennis

ASSOCIATES

Frederick D. Evans, III
Virginia M. Greer
Robert G. Ballard
Matthew J. Jewell
Pamela Jean Gray
Ronald G. Polly, Jr.
Thomas D. Trask
J. Steven Fisher
Stephanie F. Goff
Alison Roberts Solomon
Robert David Schoen
Brian DeVoe Rogers

Representative Clients: Farmers Insurance Group; Roadway Services, Inc.

For full biographical listings, see the Martindale-Hubbell Law Directory

DREW ECKL & FARNHAM (AV)

880 West Peachtree Street, P.O. Box 7600, 30357
Telephone: 404-885-1400
Facsimile: 404-876-0992

MEMBERS OF FIRM

Charles L. Drew
W. Wray Eckl
Clayton H. Farnham
Arthur H. Glaser
James M. Poe
John A. Ferguson, Jr.
Theodore Freeman
John P. Reale
Stevan A. Miller
H. Michael Bagley
Hall F. McKinley III
G. Randall Moody
B. Holland Pritchard
T. Bart Gary
David A. Smith
Kenneth A. Hindman
Paul W. Burke
Daniel C. Kniffen
John C. Bruffey, Jr.
Benton J. Mathis, Jr.
John G. Blackmon, Jr.
Dennis M. Hall
J. William Haley
Donald R. Andersen
Gary R. Hurst

ASSOCIATES

Anne M. Landrum
Nena K. Puckett
Nicole D. Tifverman
Jerry C. Carter, Jr.
Phillip E. Friduss
L. Lee Bennett, Jr.
Christopher J. Culp
Katherine D. Dixon
William T. Mitchell
J. Robb Cruser
Philip Wade Savrin
Lucian Gillis, Jr.
Peter H. Schmidt, II
Brooks von Biberstein Powers
April Rich
Maureen M. Middleton

(See Next Column)

DREW ECKL & FARNHAM, *Atlanta—Continued*

ASSOCIATES (Continued)

Robert L. Welch
Julie Young John
Jeffrey B. Grimm
Suzanne VonHarten Sanders
Leigh Lawson Reeves
Bruce A. Taylor, Jr.
Douglas T. Lay
Elizabeth B. Luzuriaga

Representative Clients: American International Adjustment Co.; Chicago Title Insurance Co.; CIGNA; Crum & Forster Commercial Insurance; Ford Motor Co.; Frito-Lay, Inc.; General Motors; Georgia Pacific Corp.; Liberty Mutual Insurance Co.; Parthenon/Hospital Corporation of America.

For Complete List of Firm Personnel, See General Section

For full biographical listings, see the Martindale-Hubbell Law Directory

EIDSON & ASSOCIATES, P.C. (AV)

Suite 201, 600 South Central Avenue (Hapeville), 30354
Telephone: 404-763-3401
FAX: 404-763-3404

James A. Eidson

Penni A. Dudley

Reference: First Bank of Georgia.

For full biographical listings, see the Martindale-Hubbell Law Directory

ENGLAND & MCKNIGHT (AV)

Suite 410 River Ridge, 9040 Roswell Road, 30350
Telephone: 404-641-6010
FAX: 404-641-6003

MEMBERS OF FIRM

J. Melvin England
Robert H. McKnight, Jr.

Reference: Bank South, N.A.

For full biographical listings, see the Martindale-Hubbell Law Directory

FRANKEL, HARDWICK, TANENBAUM & FINK, P.C. (AV)

359 East Paces Ferry Road, N.E., 30305
Telephone: 404-266-2930
Fax: 404-231-3362

Samuel N. Frankel
Martha J. Kuckleburg
James J. Brissette
Joel S. Arogeti

Susan L. Shaver

Representative Clients: America's Favorite Chicken Co. (Church's and Popeye's); Basic, Inc.; Bridan Industries; Capitol Materials, Inc.; Combustion Engineering, Inc.; Commercial Bank of Georgia; Homart Development; Market Place Shopping Center, L.P.; Sundance Products, Inc.; Venture Construction Company; Chicago Title Insurance Company.

For Complete List of Firm Personnel, See General Section

For full biographical listings, see the Martindale-Hubbell Law Directory

FREEMAN & HAWKINS (AV)

4000 One Peachtree Center, 303 Peachtree Street, N.E., 30308-3243
Telephone: 404-614-7400
Fax: 404-614-750
CompuServe address: 73541,1626
Internet address: 73451.1626@compuserve.com

MEMBERS OF FIRM

Joe C. Freeman, Jr.
Paul M. Hawkins
J. Bruce Welch
Albert H. Parnell
A. Timothy Jones
Alan F. Herman
Howell Hollis, III
Michael J. Goldman
H. Lane Young, II
Joseph R. Cullens
Frank C. Bedinger, III
Julia Bennett Jagger
Stephen M. Lore
William H. Major, III
Edward M. Newsom
T. Ryan Mock, Jr.
Lawrence J. Myers
Jack N. Sibley
Warner S. Fox
Robert U. Wright
Thomas F. Wamsley, Jr.

OF COUNSEL

J. R. Cullens

ASSOCIATES

Kimberly Houston Ridley
Ollie M. Harton
Michael E. Hutchins
Barry S. Noeltner
Kevin J. Bahr
Joanne Beauvoir Brown
Edwin L. Hall, Jr.
Kenan G. Loomis
Roger M. Goode
Robert Rache Elarbee
Charles R. Beans
Louis E. Bridges III
Dennis J. Manganiello
Peter R. York
Kathryn Anne Thurman
Cullen Christie Wilkerson, Jr.
Allen W. Nelson

(See Next Column)

Representative Clients: The Coca-Cola Company; Ashland Oil Company; Eli Lilly and Co.; American International Group; Chrysler Corporation; Tenneco Oil Co.; Goodyear Tire & Rubber Co.; Georgia Pacific Corp.; Monsanto; American Suzuki Motor Corp.

For Complete List of Firm Personnel, See General Section

For full biographical listings, see the Martindale-Hubbell Law Directory

GARLAND, SAMUEL & LOEB, P.C. (AV)

3151 Maple Drive, N.E., 30305
Telephone: 404-262-2225
FAX: 404-365-5041

Edward T. M. Garland
Donald F. Samuel
Robin N. Loeb
Patrick J. Geheren

For full biographical listings, see the Martindale-Hubbell Law Directory

GLASS, MCCULLOUGH, SHERRILL & HARROLD (AV)

1409 Peachtree Street, N.E., 30309
Telephone: 404-885-1500
Telecopier: 404-892-1801
Buckhead Office: Monarch Plaza, 3414 Peachtree Road, N.E., Suite 450, Atlanta, Georgia, 30326-1162.
Telephone: 404-885-1500.
Telecopier: 404-231-1978.
Washington, D.C. Office: 1155 15th Street, N.W., Suite 400, Washington, D.C., 20005.
Telephone: 202-785-8118.
Telecopier: 202-785-0128.

MEMBERS OF FIRM

Peter B. Glass
Kenneth R. McCullough
Mark A. Block
William D. Brunstad
T. Kennerly Carroll, Jr.
Geoffrey H. Cederholm
Luther C. Curtis
C. Walker Ingraham
Ugo F. Ippolito
James H. Kaminer, Jr.
John A. Sherrill
Thomas J. Harrold, Jr.
Ross P. Kendall
James W. King
S. Andrew McKay
Jerry A. Shaifer
R. Phillip Shinall, III
John M. Stuckey, Jr.
Bradley J. Taylor
Robert M. Trusty

ASSOCIATES

Deborah L. Britt
Allen W. Groves
Betsy Birns McCall

For Complete List of Firm Personnel, See General Section

For full biographical listings, see the Martindale-Hubbell Law Directory

GOLDNER, SOMMERS, SCRUDDER & BASS (AV)

2839 Paces Ferry Road, Suite 800, 30339-3774
Telephone: 404-436-4777
Facsimile: 404-436-8777

Stephen L. Goldner
Susan V. Sommers
Henry E. Scrudder, Jr.
Glenn S. Bass
C. G. Jester, Jr.

For Complete List of Firm Personnel, See General Section

For full biographical listings, see the Martindale-Hubbell Law Directory

GREENE, BUCKLEY, JONES & MCQUEEN (AV)

P.O. Box 56446, 30343
Telephone: 404-522-3541
Telecopier: 404-522-3677

Harry L. Greene (1896-1974)

MEMBERS OF FIRM

John David Jones
C. Richard McQueen
John E. Talmadge
James C. Frenzel
Harold S. White, Jr.
Daniel A. Angelo
Francis Carl Schenck
F. Taylor Putney, Jr.
Edward D. Buckley, III
Margaret L. Milroy
J. Russell Phillips

ASSOCIATES

William D. Matthews
B. Kyle Childress
H. Lee Pruett
Leslie C. Ruiter
Rose E. Goff
Henry M. Perlowski

OF COUNSEL

Ferdinand Buckley
Jack F. Williams (Not admitted in GA)

Counsel for: Graybar Electric Co.; Pennsylvania National Mutual Casualty Insurance Co.; Reliance Insurance Co.; Roadway Services, Inc.

For full biographical listings, see the Martindale-Hubbell Law Directory

Atlanta—Continued

HARMON, SMITH, BRIDGES & WILBANKS (AV)

1795 Peachtree Street, N.E., 30309
Telephone: 404-881-1200
Fax: 404-881-8523

MEMBERS OF FIRM

Archer D. Smith, III
Tyrone M. Bridges
Marlan B. Wilbanks

ASSOCIATE

Fred Paul Anthony, Jr.

OF COUNSEL

Nolan B. (Joe) Harmon
Mark C. Walker
Lynn M. Wilson

For full biographical listings, see the Martindale-Hubbell Law Directory

HISHON & BURBAGE (AV)

Suite 2000 Eleven Hundred Peachtree Building, 1100 Peachtree Street, 30309
Telephone: 404-898-9880
Telecopier: 404-898-9890

MEMBERS OF FIRM

Robert H. Hishon
Bruce B. Weddell
Jesse S. Burbage, III
R. Bradley Carr

ASSOCIATE

Mike Bothwell

OF COUNSEL

James G. Killough

For full biographical listings, see the Martindale-Hubbell Law Directory

HOLT, NEY, ZATCOFF & WASSERMAN (AV)

A Partnership including Professional Corporations
100 Galleria Parkway, Suite 600, 30339
Telephone: 404-956-9600
Facsimile Number: 404-956-1490

MEMBERS OF FIRM

J. Scott Jacobson
Stephen C. Greenberg

ASSOCIATES

David S. O'Quinn
Jay Frank Castle

Representative Clients: Cummins South, Inc.; First American Title Insurance Co.; Lincoln Property Co.; Old Republic National Title Insurance Co.; Safety-Kleen Corp.; Trammell Crow Residential Cos.; John Wieland Homes, Inc.; Childress Klein Properties.

For Complete List of Firm Personnel, See General Section

For full biographical listings, see the Martindale-Hubbell Law Directory

JONES, DAY, REAVIS & POGUE (AV)

3500 One Peachtree Center, 303 Peachtree Street, N.E., 30308-3242
Telephone: 404-521-3939
Cable Address: "Attorneys Atlanta"
Telex: 54-2711
Telecopier: 404-581-8330
In Brussels, Belgium: Avenue Louise 480, 7th Floor, B-1050 Brussels.
Telephone: 011-32-2-645-14-11.
Telecopier: 011-32-2-645-14-45.
In Chicago, Illinois: 77 West Wacker.
Telephone: 312-782-3939.
Telecopier: 312-782-8585.
In Cleveland, Ohio: North Point. 901 Lakeside Avenue.
Telephone: 216-586-3939.
Cable Address: "Attorneys Cleveland".
Telex: 980389.
Telecopier: 216-579-0212.
In Columbus, Ohio: 1900 Huntington Center.
Telephone: 614-469-3939.
Cable Address: "Attorneys Columbus".
Telecopier: 614-461-4198.
In Dallas, Texas: 2300 Trammell Crow Center, 2001 Ross Avenue.
Telephone: 214-220-3939.
Cable Address: "Attorneys Dallas."
Telex: 730852.
Telecopier: 214-969-5100.
In Frankfurt, Germany: Westendstrasse 41, 60325 Frankfurt am Main.
Telephone: 011-49-69-7438-3939.
Telecopier: 011-49-69-741-1686.
In Geneva, Switzerland: 20, rue de Candolle.
Telephone: 011-41-22-320-2339.
Telecopier: 011-41-22-320-1232.
In Hong Kong: 1501 One Exchange Square, 8 Connaught Place.
Telephone: 011-852-526-6895.
Telecopier: 011-852-810-5787.
In Irvine, California: 2603 Main Street, Suite 900.
Telephone: 714-851-3939.
Telex: 194911 Lawyers LSA.
Telecopier: 714-553-7539.

(See Next Column)

In London, England: One Mount Street.
Telephone: 011-44-71-493-9361.
Cable Address: "Surgoe London WI."
Telecopier: 011-44-71-493-9666.
In Los Angeles, California: 555 West Fifth Street, Suite 4600.
Telephone: 213-489-3939.
Telex: 181439 UD.
Telecopier: 213-243-2539.
In New York, New York: 599 Lexington Avenue.
Telephone: 212-326-3939.
Cable Address: "JONESDAY NEWYORK."
Telex: 237013 JDRP UR.
Telecopier: 212-755-7306.
In Paris, France: 62, rue du Faubourg Saint-Honore.
Telephone: 011-33-1-44-71-3939.
Cable Address: "Surgoe Paris."
Telex: 290156 Surgoe.
Telecopier: 011-33-1-49-24-0471.
In Pittsburgh, Pennsylvania: 500 Grant Street, 31st Floor.
Telephone: 412-391-3939.
Cable Address: "Attorneys Pittsburgh".
Telecopier: 412-394-7959.
In Riyadh, Saudi Arabia: Law Offices of Saud M.A. Shawwaf, P.O. Box 2700.
Telephones: 011 (966-1) 465-6543, 011 (966-1) 464-8534 or 011 (966-1) 464-8540.
Telex: 401831 SAUCON SJ.
Telecopier: (966-1) 464-8480.
In Taipei, Taiwan: 7th Floor, 2 Tun Hwa South Road, Section 2.
Telephone: 011 (886-2) 704-6808 and 704-6809.
Telecopier: 011 (886-2) 704-6791.
In Tokyo, Japan: Shiroyama JT Mori Bldg., 15th Floor, 3-1, Toranomon 4-chome Minato-ku.
Telephone: 011-81-3-3433-3939.
Telecopier: 011-81-3-5401-2725.
In Washington, D.C.: Metropolitan Square, 1450 G Street, N.W.
Telephone: 202-879-3939.
Cable Address: "Attorneys Washington."
Telex: 89-2410 ATTORNEYS WASH.
Telecopier: 202-737-2832. 2-737-2832.

MEMBERS OF FIRM IN ATLANTA

W. Rhett Tanner
Richard M. Kirby
Girard E. Boudreau, Jr.
G. Lee Garrett, Jr.
W. Lyman Dillon
James R. Johnson
Dorothy Yates Kirkley
R. Dal Burton
David J. Bailey
William B. B. Smith
R. Matthew Martin

For Complete List of Firm Personnel, See General Section

For full biographical listings, see the Martindale-Hubbell Law Directory

KING & CROFT (AV)

191 Peachtree Street, N.E. 20th Floor, 30303-1741
Telephone: 404-577-8400
Facsimile: 404-577-8401

MEMBERS OF FIRM

Terrence Lee Croft
Thomas A. Croft
F. Carlton King, Jr.

For full biographical listings, see the Martindale-Hubbell Law Directory

LIPSHUTZ, GREENBLATT & KING (AV)

2300 Harris Tower-Peachtree Center, 233 Peachtree Street, N.E., 30043
Telephone: 404-688-2300
Fax: 404-588-0648
Washington, D.C. Office: Suite 950, 1275 K Street, N.W.
Telephone: 202-898-4800.

MEMBERS OF FIRM

Robert J. Lipshutz
Edward L. Greenblatt
Randall M. Lipshutz

OF COUNSEL

William R. King
Tito Mazzetta

ASSOCIATES

Paula B. Smith
Timothy L. S. Sitz

For full biographical listings, see the Martindale-Hubbell Law Directory

LONG ALDRIDGE & NORMAN (AV)

A Partnership including Professional Corporations
One Peachtree Center, Suite 5300, 303 Peachtree Street, 30308
Telephone: 404-527-4000
Telecopier: 404-527-4198
Washington, D.C. Office: Suite 950, 1615 L Street, 20036.
Telephone: 202-223-7033.
Telecopier: 202-223-7013.

(See Next Column)

LONG ALDRIDGE & NORMAN, *Atlanta—Continued*

MEMBERS OF FIRM

Phillip A. Bradley
Bruce P. Brown
Deborah S. Ebel
J. James Johnson
J. Allen Maines
Barbara A. McIntyre
James J. Thomas II
Jack H. Watson, Jr. (Resident, Washington, D.C. Office)

ASSOCIATES

David L. Balser
Lynn Gavin
Eric Charles Lang
Carole A. Loftin
Paula Rafferty Miller
Andrew R. Pachman
J. Michell Philpott
Johnathan H. Short
Sheryl L. Thomson

OF COUNSEL

Carl W. Mullis, III
John L. Watkins

For Complete List of Firm Personnel, See General Section

For full biographical listings, see the Martindale-Hubbell Law Directory

LONG, WEINBERG, ANSLEY AND WHEELER (AV)

A Partnership including Professional Corporations
999 Peachtree Street, N.E., Suite 2700, 30309
Telephone: 404-876-2700
Facsimile: 404-875-9433

MEMBERS OF FIRM

Thomas J. Long (1898-1965)
Palmer H. Ansley (1927-1991)
Ben L. Weinberg, Jr., (P.C.)
Sidney F. Wheeler
J. Kenneth Moorman
John M. Hudgins, IV, (P.C.)
Robert G. Tanner
Joseph W. Watkins
James H. Fisher, II
M. Diane Owens
Robert D. Roll
Kenneth Marc Barré, Jr.
Alan L. Newman
Marvin A. Devlin
Earl W. Gunn
C. Bradford Marsh
Arnold E. Gardner
Lance D. Lourie
Milton B. Satcher, III
David A. Sapp
Stephen H. Sparwath
Kathryn S. Whitlock

ASSOCIATES

Ronald R. Coleman Jr.
Mark E. Robinson
Frederick N. Sager, Jr.
Debra E. LeVorse
Quinton S. Seay
Charles K. Reed
Sharon B. Austin
Patricia M. Peters
Carol P. Michel
John K. Train, IV
Johnathan T. Krawcheck
John C. Bonnie
Emily J. Brantley
Paul L. Weisbecker
Daniel W. Sweat
Margie M. Eget
Joseph N. Crosswhite
William P. Langdale, III
J. Calhoun Harris, Jr.
Laura V. Semonche
Michele L. Davis
Dennis J. Webb, Jr.
Jacquelyn D. Van Tuyl

OF COUNSEL

Meade Burns

Representative Clients: Aetna Casualty & Surety Corp.; Chrysler Motors Corp.; Emory University; Dow Corning Corp.; Ford Motor Co.; Freuhauf Trailer Corp.; Merck; Otis Elevator Co.; St. Paul Fire & Marine Insurance Co.; Toyota Motor Sales U.S.A., Inc.

For Complete List of Firm Personnel, See General Section

For full biographical listings, see the Martindale-Hubbell Law Directory

MACEY, WILENSKY, COHEN, WITTNER & KESSLER (AV)

Suite 700 Carnegie Building, 133 Carnegie Way, Northwest, 30303
Telephone: 404-584-1200
Telecopier: 404-681-4355
Other Atlanta, Georgia Office: 5784 Lake Forrest Drive, Suite 214, 30328.

MEMBERS OF FIRM

Morris W. Macey
Frank B. Wilensky
H. William Cohen
Richard P. Kessler, Jr.
Mark L. Golder
Neil C. Gordon
Susan L. Howick
M. Todd Westfall

ASSOCIATES

James R. Sacca
David B. Kurzweil
Michael D. Pinsky
Shayna M. (Salomon) Steinfeld
Robert A. Winter
Pamela Gronauer Hill
Rachel Anderson Snider

For Complete List of Firm Personnel, See General Section

For full biographical listings, see the Martindale-Hubbell Law Directory

MILLS & MORAITAKIS (AV)

Resurgens Plaza, Suite 2515 945 East Paces Ferry Road, Northeast, 30326
Telephone: 404-261-0016
Facsimile: 404-261-0024

(See Next Column)

Roger Mills
Nicholas C. Moraitakis
Glenn E. Kushel

For full biographical listings, see the Martindale-Hubbell Law Directory

MOZLEY, FINLAYSON & LOGGINS (AV)

One Premier Plaza, Suite 900, 5605 Glenridge Drive, 30342
Telephone: 404-256-0700
Telecopier: 404-250-9355

MEMBERS OF FIRM

J. Arthur Mozley
Robert M. Finlayson II
Sewell K. Loggins
William D. Harrison
Eric D. Griffin, Jr.
C. David Hailey
Deborah A. Finnerty
D. Keith Calhoun
Richard D. Hall
R. Ann Grier

ASSOCIATES

Lawrence B. Domenico
Edward C. Bresee, Jr.
Amberly A. Warner
J. Marcus Howard

For full biographical listings, see the Martindale-Hubbell Law Directory

LAW OFFICES OF J. WAYNE PIERCE, P.A. (AV)

Two Paces West, Suite 1700 4000 Cumberland Parkway, 30339
Telephone: 404-435-0500
Telecopier: 404-435-0362

J. Wayne Pierce

Dargan Scott Cole
Thomas L. Schaefer

For full biographical listings, see the Martindale-Hubbell Law Directory

POPE, MCGLAMRY, KILPATRICK & MORRISON (AV)

A Partnership including Professional Corporations
83 Walton Street, N.W., P.O. Box 1733, 30303
Telephone: 404-523-7706;
Phenix City, Alabama: 205-298-7354
Columbus, Georgia Office: 318 11th Street, 2nd Floor, P.O. Box 2128, 31902-2128.
Telephone: 706-324-0050.

MEMBERS OF FIRM

C. Neal Pope (P.C.)
Max R. McGlamry (P.C.) (Resident, Columbus, Georgia Office)
Paul V. Kilpatrick, Jr. (Resident, Columbus, Georgia Office)
R. Timothy Morrison
Michael L. McGlamry
Earle F. Lasseter
William J. Cornwell
Jay F. Hirsch
Daniel W. Sigelman
Wade H. Tomlinson, III
William Usher Norwood, III

RESIDENT ASSOCIATE

C. Elizabeth Pope

Reference: Columbus Bank & Trust Co.

For full biographical listings, see the Martindale-Hubbell Law Directory

REYNOLDS & MCARTHUR (AV)

A Partnership including a Professional Corporation
Suite 1010, One Buckhead Plaza, 3060 Peachtree Road, N.W., 30305
Telephone: 404-240-0265
Fax: 404-262-3557
Macon, Georgia Office: 850 Walnut Street.
Telephone: 912-741-6000.
Fax: 912-742-0750.
Asheville, North Carolina Office: The Jackson Building, 22 South Pack Square, Suite 1200.
Telephone: 704-254-8523.
Fax: 704-254-3038.

MEMBERS OF FIRM

W. Carl Reynolds (P.C.)
Katherine L. McArthur
Steve Ray Warren (Not admitted in GA)
Charles M. Cork, III
O. Wendell Horne, III
Bradley J. Survant
Laura D. Hogue

For full biographical listings, see the Martindale-Hubbell Law Directory

ANDREW M. SCHERFFIUS, P.C. (AV)

3166 Mathieson Drive, P.O. Box 53299, 30355
Telephone: 404-261-3562; 1-800-521-2867
Fax: 404-841-0861

Andrew M. Scherffius

Tamara McDowell Ayres

For full biographical listings, see the Martindale-Hubbell Law Directory

Atlanta—Continued

SCHREEDER, WHEELER & FLINT (AV)

1600 Candler Building, 127 Peachtree Street, N.E., 30303-1845
Telephone: 404-681-3450
Telecopy: 404-681-1046

MEMBERS OF FIRM

David H. Flint
Lawrence S. Burnat
John A. Christy
Mark W. Forsling
Timothy C. Batten

ASSOCIATES

J. Christopher Desmond
Alexander J. Simmons, Jr.
Lynn C. Stewart
Debra A. Wilson

Reference: Fidelity National Bank; Wachovia Bank of Georgia, NA.

For full biographical listings, see the Martindale-Hubbell Law Directory

SCHULTEN & WARD (AV)

Suite 930 The Hurt Building, 50 Hurt Plaza, 30303
Telephone: 404-688-6800
Fax: 404-688-6840

MEMBERS OF FIRM

Wm. Scott Schulten
Kevin L. Ward

ASSOCIATES

David L. Turner
Susan Kastan Murphey
Erik V. Huey

Reference: NationsBank of Georgia, N.A.

For full biographical listings, see the Martindale-Hubbell Law Directory

LAW OFFICE OF THOMAS PATY STAMPS (AV)

314 Buckhead Avenue, 30305
Telephone: 404-364-9200
Telecopier: 404-364-9202

Reference: Trust Company Bank.

For full biographical listings, see the Martindale-Hubbell Law Directory

SULLIVAN, HALL, BOOTH & SMITH, A PROFESSIONAL CORPORATION (AV)

One Midtown Plaza, 1360 Peachtree Street, N.E., Suite 800, 30309
Telephone: 404-870-8000
FAX: 404-870-8020

Terrance C. Sullivan
John E. Hall, Jr.
Alexander H. Booth
Rush S. Smith, Jr.
Henry D. Green, Jr.
Jack G. Slover, Jr.
Timothy H. Bendin
Michael A. Pannier
Brynda Sue Rodriguez
Roger S. Sumrall

David V. Johnson
Jeffrey T. Wise
Eleanor L. Martel
A. Spencer McManes, Jr.
David G. Goodchild, Jr.
Robert L. Shannon, Jr.
T. Andrew Graham
Earnest Redwine
Melanie P. Simon (Not admitted in GA)

Reference: Wachovia Bank of Georgia.

For full biographical listings, see the Martindale-Hubbell Law Directory

SUMNER & HEWES (AV)

Suite 700, The Hurt Building, 50 Hurt Plaza, 30303
Telephone: 404-588-9000

PARTNERS

William E. Sumner
Nancy Becker Hewes
Stephen J. Anderson
David A. Webster

ASSOCIATES

Rosemary Smith
Andrew A. Davenport
Marguerite Patrick Bryan
Michelle Harris Jordan
Edith M. Shine

For full biographical listings, see the Martindale-Hubbell Law Directory

SUTHERLAND, ASBILL & BRENNAN (AV)

999 Peachtree Street, N.E., 30309-3996
Telephone: 404-853-8000
Facsimile: 404-853-8806
Washington, D.C. Office: 1275 Pennsylvania Avenue, N.W., 20004-2404.
Telephone: 202-383-0100.
New York, N.Y. Office: 1270 Avenue of the Americas, 10020-1700.
Telephone: 212-332-3000.
Austin, Texas Office: 111 Congress Avenue, 23rd Floor, 78701-4079.
Telephone: 512-469-3350.

Peter J. Anderson
William D. Barwick
John W. Bonds, Jr.
Thomas M. Byrne
John A. Chandler
Thomas A. Cox
David Robert Cumming, Jr.
Carey P. DeDeyn

(See Next Column)

J. D. Fleming, Jr.
John H. Fleming
James P. Groton
C. Christopher Hagy
Charles T. Lester, Jr.
Alfred A. Lindseth
James R. McGibbon
Richard G. Murphy, Jr.
Judith A. O'Brien
James A. Orr
Richard L. Robbins
George Anthony Smith
Elizabeth Vranicar Tanis

COUNSEL OF THE FIRM IN ATLANTA, GEORGIA

Patricia Bayer Cunningham
Louise B. Matte
S. Lawrence Polk
R. Michael Robinson

For Complete List of Firm Personnel, See General Section
For full biographical listings, see the Martindale-Hubbell Law Directory

CHARLES L. WEATHERLY (AV)

3151 Maple Drive, N.E., 30305
Telephone: 404-365-5045
Fax: 404-365-5041

For full biographical listings, see the Martindale-Hubbell Law Directory

WEBB, CARLOCK, COPELAND, SEMLER & STAIR (AV)

A Partnership including Professional Corporations
2600 Marquis Two Tower, 285 Peachtree Center Avenue, P.O. Box 56770, 30343-0770
Telephone: 404-522-8220
FAX: 404-523-2345

MEMBERS OF FIRM

Dennis J. Webb (P.C.)
Thomas S. Carlock (P.C.)
Robert C. Semler (P.C.)
Wade K. Copeland (P.C.)
Kent T. Stair (P.C.)
Douglas W. Smith
David F. Root
William E. Zschunke
Wayne D. McGrew, III
Douglas A. Wilde
Frederick M. Valz, III
E. Alan Miller
Johannes S. Kingma
Dennis G. Lovell, Jr.
Pat M. Anagnostakis

ASSOCIATES

Brian R. Neary
William T. Clark
Marvin D. Dikeman
Robert W. Browning
Philip P. Taylor
David D. Cookson
James T. Brieske
Todd M. Yates
Adam L. Appel
R. Michael Ethridge
Daniel J. Huff
Nora Beth Dorsey
Scott D. Huray
Gregory H. Wheeler
Christopher A. Whitlock
John W. Sandifer
Craig A. Brookes
Mary Katherine Smith
William G. Pike, Jr.
Daniel R. Ketchum, II

Counsel for: Allstate Insurance Co.

For full biographical listings, see the Martindale-Hubbell Law Directory

*AUGUSTA,** Richmond Co.

RICHARD E. ALLEN (AV)

440 Greene Street, 30901
Telephone: 706-724-4466

For full biographical listings, see the Martindale-Hubbell Law Directory

BELL & PANNELL (AV)

619 Greene Street, P.O. Box 1547, 30903-1547
Telephone: 706-722-2014
FAX: 706-722-7552

Harry H. Bell, Jr. (1911-1992)
John C. Bell, Jr.
William A. Pannell
Pamela S. James

References: First Atlanta Bank & Trust Company; Citizens & Southern National Bank & Trust Co.

For full biographical listings, see the Martindale-Hubbell Law Directory

BURNSIDE, WALL, DANIEL, ELLISON & REVELL (AV)

A Partnership including Professional Corporations
454 Greene Street, P.O. Box 2125, 30903
Telephone: 706-722-0768
FAX: 706-722-5984

MEMBERS OF FIRM

Thomas R. Burnside, Jr. (P.C.)
James B. Wall (P.C.)
James W. Ellison
Harry D. Revell

Representative Clients: CSRA Regional Development Commission; City of Harlem, Georgia; Liquid Carbonic Corp.; Richmond County, Georgia; Southern Machine & Tool Co.; Jefferson EMC; Southeastern Equipment Co.; SECO Aviation, Inc.; SECO Parts & Equipment, Inc.

For Complete List of Firm Personnel, See General Section
For full biographical listings, see the Martindale-Hubbell Law Directory

Augusta—Continued

CAPERS, DUNBAR, SANDERS & BRUCKNER (AV)

Fifteenth Floor, First Union Bank Building, 30901-1454
Telephone: 706-722-7542
Telecopier: 706-724-7776

MEMBERS OF FIRM

John D. Capers
Paul H. Dunbar, III
E. Frederick Sanders
Ziva P. Bruckner

ASSOCIATE

Carl P. Dowling

For full biographical listings, see the Martindale-Hubbell Law Directory

DYE, TUCKER, EVERITT, WHEALE & LONG, A PROFESSIONAL ASSOCIATION (AV)

453 Greene Street, P.O. Box 2426, 30903
Telephone: 706-722-0771
Fax: 706-722-7028

A. Rowland Dye
Thomas W. Tucker
A. Zachry Everitt
Duncan D. Wheale
John B. Long
Benjamin H. Brewton

OF COUNSEL

A. Montague Miller

Representative Clients: State Farm Insurance Cos.; The Travelers Insurance Co.; Georgia Power Co.; Wachovia National Bank (Augusta Division); Chubb Group; Montgomery Ward; Augusta Board of Realtors; Ryder Truck Rental, Inc.; Canal Insurance Company; K Mart.

For Complete List of Firm Personnel, See General Section

For full biographical listings, see the Martindale-Hubbell Law Directory

FULCHER, HAGLER, REED, HANKS & HARPER (AV)

A Partnership including Professional Corporations
520 Greene Street, P.O. Box 1477, 30903-1477
Telephone: 706-724-0171
Telecopier: 706-724-4573

MEMBERS OF FIRM

William M. Fulcher (1902-1993)
Gould B. Hagler (Retired)
William C. Reed (Retired)
David H. Hanks (P.C.)
John I. Harper (P.C.)
Robert C. Hagler (P.C.)
Michael B. Hagler (P.C.)
James W. Purcell (P.C.)
J. Arthur Davison (P.C.)
Mark C. Wilby (P.C.)
Ronald C. Griffeth
N. Staten Bitting, Jr. (P.C.)

ASSOCIATES

David P. Dekle
Sharon R. Blair
J. Edward Enoch, Jr.
Elizabeth McLeod Kitchens
Barry A. Fleming

General Counsel for: GIW Industries, Inc.
Division Counsel for: CSX Transportation; Textron, Inc. (E-Z Go Car Division).
Counsel for: NationsBank; Georgia Natural Gas Co. (a division of Atlanta Gas Light Co.); Champion International Corp.; Aetna Life and Casualty; Liberty Mutual Insurance Company; St. Paul Fire & Marine Insurance Co.; Kimberly Clark Corporation.

For Complete List of Firm Personnel, See General Section

For full biographical listings, see the Martindale-Hubbell Law Directory

HULL, TOWILL, NORMAN & BARRETT, A PROFESSIONAL CORPORATION (AV)

Seventh Floor, Trust Company Bank Building, P.O. Box 1564, 30903-1564
Telephone: 706-722-4481
Fax: 706-722-9779

Robert C. Norman (Retired, 1991)
W. Hale Barrett
Lawton Jordan, Jr.
Patrick J. Rice
Douglas D. Batchelor, Jr.
David E. Hudson
Neal W. Dickert
John W. Gibson
William F. Hammond
Mark S. Burgreen
George R. Hall
James B. Ellington
F. Michael Taylor

Robert A. Mullins
William J. Keogh, III
Edward J. Tarver
J. Noel Schweers, III
Michael S. Carlson
Ralph Emerson Hanna, III
Susan D. Barrett
Timothy Moses

Counsel for: Trust Company Bank of Augusta, N.A.; Georgia Federal Bank, FSB, Augusta Division; Southeastern Newspapers Corp.; Georgia Power Co.; Southern Bell Telephone & Telegraph Co.; St. Joseph Hospital, Augusta, Georgia, Inc.; Norfolk Southern Corp.; Merry Land & Investment Co., Inc.; Housing Authority of the City of Augusta; Georgia Press Association.

(See Next Column)

For Complete List of Firm Personnel, See General Section

For full biographical listings, see the Martindale-Hubbell Law Directory

KILPATRICK & CODY (AV)

Suite 1400, First Union Bank Building, P.O. Box 2043, 30903
Telephone: 706-724-2622
Telephone Copier: 706-722-0219
Atlanta, Georgia Office: Suite 2800, 1100 Peachtree Street.
Telephone: 404-815-6500.
Telecopier: 404-815-6555.
Washington, D.C. Office: Suite 800, 700 13th Street, N.W., 20005.
Telephone: 202-508-5800. Telephone Copier: 202-508-5858.
Brussels, Belgium Office: Avenue Louise 65, BTE 3, 1050 Brussels.
Telephone: (32) (2) 533-03-00.
Telecopier: (32) (2) 534-86-38.
London, England Office: 68 Pall Mall, London, SW1Y 5ES, England.
Telephone: (44) (71) 321 0477.
Telecopier: (44) (71) 930 9733.

Wyck A. Knox, Jr.
Raymond G. Chadwick, Jr.
James E. Blanchard
Ted H. Clarkson
Gregg E. McDougal

R. Perry Sentell, III
Joseph H. Huff
W. Craig Smith

Representative Clients: University Health Services, Inc.; National Cardiovascular Network, Inc.; Atlanta Cardiology, P.C.; First Union National Bank of Georgia; A.A. Friedman Co.; Blanchard & Calhoun Real Estate Co., Inc.; Boardman Petroleum, Inc.; Castleberry's Food Co., Inc.; DSM Chemicals North America, Inc.; Westinghouse Savannah River Company.

For full biographical listings, see the Martindale-Hubbell Law Directory

SAMUEL F. MAGUIRE (AV)

448 Telfair Street, 30901
Telephone: 706-722-4341
Fax: 706-724-8300

ASSOCIATE

James C. Walker

Representative Clients: Utilities of Augusta; Electrical Equipment Co.; Bilbub, Inc.; Hospital Authority of the City of Augusta; Residential Care Facilities for the Elderly Authority.
Approved Attorney For: First American Title Insurance Co.

For full biographical listings, see the Martindale-Hubbell Law Directory

WILEY S. OBENSHAIN, III, P.C. (AV)

511 Courthouse Lane, 30901
Telephone: 706-722-1789
Fax: 706-722-7145

Wiley S. Obenshain, III

For full biographical listings, see the Martindale-Hubbell Law Directory

WARLICK, TRITT & STEBBINS (AV)

15th Floor, First Union Bank Building, 30901
Telephone: 706-722-7543
Fax: 706-722-1822
Columbia County Office: 119 Davis Road, Martinez, Georgia 30907.
Telephone: 706-860-7595.
Fax: 705-860-7597.

MEMBERS OF FIRM

William Byrd Warlick
Roy D. Tritt (Resident, Martinez Office)
Charles C. Stebbins, III
E. L. Clark Speese
Michael W. Terry
D. Scott Broyles
Ross S. Snellings
C. Gregory Bryan

OF COUNSEL

Richard E. Miley

For full biographical listings, see the Martindale-Hubbell Law Directory

BRUNSWICK, Glynn Co.*

FENDIG, MCLEMORE, TAYLOR & WHITWORTH, P.C. (AV)

Suite 200 Trust Company Bank Building, P.O. Box 1996, 31521
Telephone: 912-264-4126
Telecopier: 912-264-0591

Albert Fendig, Jr.
Gilbert C. McLemore, Jr.
Philip R. Taylor
David T. Whitworth
James B. Durham

Donna L. Crossland
Beth B. Mason-O'Neal

Counsel for: Trust Company Bank of S.E. Georgia, N.A.; First Federal Savings Bank; Sea Island Property Owners Assn.; Calsilite Manufacturing Co.; Continental Insurance Cos.; Crum & Forster; Fireman's Fund Insurance Cos.; The Hertz Corp.; Insurance Company of North America; United States Fidelity & Guaranty Co.

For full biographical listings, see the Martindale-Hubbell Law Directory

GILBERT, HARRELL, GILBERT, SUMERFORD & MARTIN, P.C. (AV)

Suite 200 First Federal Plaza, 31521
Telephone: 912-265-6700
Fax: 912-264-3917

Wallace E. Harrell
James B. Gilbert, Jr.
Rees M. Sumerford
M. Fleming Martin, III
Monroe Lynn Frey, III
Jameson L. Gregg
Wallace E. Harrell, III

Charles G. Spalding
Lisa Godbey
Kristi E. Harrison
Mark D. Johnson

OF COUNSEL

James B. Gilbert
Joseph A. Whittle
Ralph T. Skelton, Jr.

Attorneys for: Sea Island Co.; American National Bank; Georgia-Pacific Corp.; Atlanta Gas Light Co.; Sea Harvest Packing Co.; Zurich General Accident & Liability Insurance Co.; Lumbermens Mutual Casualty Co.; BMW of North America.
Assistant Division Counsel for: Southern Railway Co.
Counsel for: Hercules Inc.

For full biographical listings, see the Martindale-Hubbell Law Directory

JORDAN & O'DONNELL (AV)

1528 Ellis Street, P.O. Box 2115, 31521
Telephone: 912-262-9200
Fax: 912-262-0277

Randall A. Jordan
Christopher J. O'Donnell
Rita C. Spalding
Steven P. Bristol

For full biographical listings, see the Martindale-Hubbell Law Directory

WHELCHEL, BROWN, READDICK & BUMGARTNER (AV)

5 Glynn Avenue, P.O. Box 220, 31521-0220
Telephone: 912-264-8544
Telecopier: 912-264-9667

MEMBERS OF FIRM

J. Thomas Whelchel
Richard A. Brown, Jr.
Terry L. Readdick
John E. Bumgartner
B. Kaye Katz

ASSOCIATES

G. Todd Carter
Richard K. Strickland
Joseph R. Odachowski

Representative Clients: Georgia Power Co.; Sears, Roebuck & Co.; Allstate Insurance Co.; Commercial Union Insurance Co.; Georgia Farm Bureau Mutual Insurance Co.; Government Employees Insurance Co.; Nationwide Insurance Co.; State Farm Insurance Cos.; Wausau Insurance Cos.

For full biographical listings, see the Martindale-Hubbell Law Directory

*CEDARTOWN,** Polk Co.

MUNDY & GAMMAGE, P.C. (AV)

216 Main Street, P.O. Box 930, 30125-0930
Telephone: 706-748-3870
706-688-9416 (Atlanta)
Fax: 706-748-2489
Rome, Georgia Office: The Carnegie Building, 607 Broad Street.
Telephone: 706-290-5180.

Emil Lamar Gammage, Jr.
William D. Sparks
(Mrs.) Gerry E. Holmes
George E. Mundy
Miles L. Gammage
John S. Husser
B. Jean Crane

For Complete List of Firm Personnel, See General Section

For full biographical listings, see the Martindale-Hubbell Law Directory

*COLUMBUS,** Muscogee Co.

BUTLER, WOOTEN, OVERBY & CHEELEY (AV)

1500 Second Avenue, P.O. Box 2766, 31902
Telephone: 706-322-1990;
National Wats: 1-800-233-4086
FAX: 706-323-2962
Atlanta, Georgia Office: 2719 Buford Highway, 30324.
Telephone: 404-321-1700.
FAX: 404-321-1713. Wats Line: 1-800-242-2962.

MEMBERS OF FIRM

James E. Butler, Jr.
Joel O. Wooten, Jr.
C. Frederick Overby
Robert D. Cheeley
Albert M. Pearson, III
George W. Fryhofer, III

(See Next Column)

ASSOCIATES

Peter J. Daughtery
J. Frank Myers, III
Patrick A. Dawson
Lee Tarte
Jason L. Crawford
Keith A. Pittman

For full biographical listings, see the Martindale-Hubbell Law Directory

POPE, McGLAMRY, KILPATRICK & MORRISON (AV)

A Partnership including Professional Corporations
318 11th Street, 2nd Floor, P.O. Box 2128, 31902-2128
Telephone: 706-324-0050;
Phenix City, Alabama: 205-298-7354
Atlanta, Georgia Office: 83 Walton Street, N.W., P.O. Box 1733, 30303.
Telephone: 404-523-7706.

MEMBERS OF FIRM

C. Neal Pope (P.C.)
Max R. McGlamry (P.C.) (Resident)
Paul V. Kilpatrick, Jr. (Resident)
R. Timothy Morrison (Resident, Atlanta, Georgia Office)
Michael L. McGlamry
Earle F. Lasseter
William J. Cornwell
Jay F. Hirsch
Daniel W. Sigelman
Wade H. Tomlinson, III (Resident, Atlanta Office)
William Usher Norwood, III (Resident, Atlanta Office)

RESIDENT ASSOCIATES

Joan S. Redmond
Teresa Pike Majors

Reference: Columbus Bank & Trust Co.

For full biographical listings, see the Martindale-Hubbell Law Directory

TAYLOR, HARP & CALLIER (AV)

Suite 900 The Corporate Center, P.O. Box 2645, 31902-2645
Telephone: 706-323-7711
National WATS: 1-800-422-3352
Fax: 706-323-7544

MEMBERS OF FIRM

J. Sherrod Taylor
J. Anderson Harp
Jefferson C. Callier

For full biographical listings, see the Martindale-Hubbell Law Directory

CORNELIA, Habersham Co.

CATHEY & STRAIN (AV)

6 Irvin Street, P.O. Box 689, 30531
Telephone: 706-778-2601
Fax: 706-776-2899

MEMBERS OF FIRM

Dennis T. Cathey
Edward E. Strain, III

ASSOCIATE

J. Edward Staples

For full biographical listings, see the Martindale-Hubbell Law Directory

*DALTON,** Whitfield Co.

MITCHELL & MITCHELL, P.C. (AV)

101 North Thornton Avenue, 30720
Telephone: 706-278-2040
Fax: 706-278-3040

D. Wright Mitchell (1895-1970)
Douglas W. Mitchell (1921-1984)
Erwin Mitchell
Neil Wester
James H. Bisson, III
Terry L. Miller
Michael C. Cherof
Susan Williams Bisson
Christine Clark Taylor
William J. Kimsey

Counsel for: The City of Dalton, Georgia; Galaxy Carpet Mills, Inc.
Local Counsel for: Bituminous Casualty Corp.; CSX Corp.; NationsBank of Dalton, Georgia.
Reference: Nations Bank of Dalton, Georgia.

For full biographical listings, see the Martindale-Hubbell Law Directory

*DECATUR,** De Kalb Co.

WILLIAM G. QUINN, III (AV)

Suite 480 One Decatur Town Center, 150 East Ponce De Leon Avenue, 30030
Telephone: 404-377-9254
Fax: 404-377-5776

For full biographical listings, see the Martindale-Hubbell Law Directory

SIMMONS, WARREN & SZCZECKO, PROFESSIONAL ASSOCIATION (AV)

315 West Ponce de Leon Avenue, Suite 850, 30030
Telephone: 404-378-1711
Fax: 404-377-6101

(See Next Column)

SIMMONS, WARREN & SZCZECKO PROFESSIONAL ASSOCIATION, *Decatur—Continued*

M. T. Simmons, Jr. Joseph Szczecko
Wesley B. Warren, Jr. William C. McFee, Jr.

Representative Clients: David Hocker & Associates (Shopping Center Development); Julian LeCraw & Company (Real Estate); Royal Oldsmobile,; Cotter & Co.; Atlanta Neurosurgical Associates, P.A.; Villager Lodge, Inc.; Troncalli Motors, Inc.

For full biographical listings, see the Martindale-Hubbell Law Directory

*GAINESVILLE,** Hall Co.

HULSEY, OLIVER & MAHAR (AV)

200 E.E. Butler Parkway, P.O. Box 1457, 30503
Telephone: 404-532-6312
Fax: 404-531-9230

MEMBERS OF FIRM

Julius M. Hulsey R. David Syfan
Samuel L. Oliver Jane A. Range
James E. Mahar, Jr. Joseph D. Cooley, III
Thomas L. Fitzgerald

ASSOCIATES

Thomas D. Calkins B. Chan Caudell

Counsel for: United Cities Gas Co.; Continental Insurance Cos.; Underwriters Adjusting Co.; Ralston Purina Co.; Carolina Casualty Insurance Co.; Hall County; Lake Lanier Islands Development Authority; Winn-Dixie Stores, Inc.; Gainesville Bank and Trust.

For Complete List of Firm Personnel, See General Section

For full biographical listings, see the Martindale-Hubbell Law Directory

*GRIFFIN,** Spalding Co.

ROBERT H. SMALLEY, JR. PROFESSIONAL CORPORATION (AV)

115 North Sixth Street, P.O. Box 907, 30224
Telephone: 404-228-2125
Telecopier: 404-228-5018

Robert H. Smalley, Jr. Thomas E. Baynham, III

Representative Clients: The Bank of Spalding County; Griffin Spalding County Development Authority; Masada Communications, Ltd. (CATV); Union Camp Corp. (Local Counsel).

For full biographical listings, see the Martindale-Hubbell Law Directory

*HARTWELL,** Hart Co.

WALTER JAMES GORDON (AV)

Gordon Building, P.O. Box 870, 30643
Telephone: 706-376-5418
FAX: 706-376-5416

ASSOCIATE

Eleanor Patat Cotton

LEGAL SUPPORT PERSONNEL

Flo W. Brown

References: NationsBank of Georgia, N.A.; The Bank of Hartwell; Athens First Bank & Trust Company.

For full biographical listings, see the Martindale-Hubbell Law Directory

*JESUP,** Wayne Co.

ROBERT B. SMITH (AV)

356 East Cherry Street, P.O. Box 285, 31545
Telephone: 912-427-4779; 427-4629
FAX: 912-427-9203

References: Trust Company Bank of Southeast Georgia; Barnett Bank.

For full biographical listings, see the Martindale-Hubbell Law Directory

*JONESBORO,** Clayton Co.

DRIEBE & DRIEBE, P.C. (AV)

6 Courthouse Way, P.O. Box 975, 30237
Telephone: 404-478-8894
FAX: 404-478-9606
Atlanta, Georgia Office: 152 Nassau Street, N.W.
Telephone: 404-688-5500.

Charles J. Driebe Charles J. Driebe, Jr.
J. Ron Stegall

Approved Attorneys for: First American Title Insurance Co.; Attorney's Title Guaranty Fund.
Representative Clients: Atlanta International Records, Inc.; Henry County Airport, Inc.; Clayton News/Daily; Atlanta Beach Sports & Entertainment Park, Inc.

For full biographical listings, see the Martindale-Hubbell Law Directory

OLIVER, DUCKWORTH, SPARGER & WINKLE, P.C. (AV)

146 McDonough Street, P.O. Box 37, 30236
Telephone: 404-478-8883
Fax: 404-473-0872

G. Robert Oliver Kevin W. Sparger
David P. Winkle

Richard Lord Kathy Brown Valencia

OF COUNSEL

William H. Duckworth, Jr.

Local Counsel for: Department of Transportation, State of Georgia.
Representative Clients: Clayton County Hospital Authority; Clayton County Water Authority; Clayton College Foundation, Inc.; Clayton County Development Authority; Low Temp Industries, Inc.; Medical Association of Georgia Mutual Insurance Co.

For full biographical listings, see the Martindale-Hubbell Law Directory

*LAWRENCEVILLE,** Gwinnett Co.

ANDERSEN, DAVIDSON & TATE, P.C. (AV)

324 West Pike Street, Suite 200, P.O. Box 265, 30246-0265
Telephone: 404-822-0900
Telecopier: 404-822-9680

Gerald Davidson, Jr. Thomas T. Tate

William M. Ray, II Johnathan D. Crumly

References: Trust Company Bank; The Bank of Gwinnett County; Commercial Bank of Gwinnett; Madison Ventures, Ltd.; Network Publications, Inc.

For Complete List of Firm Personnel, See General Section

For full biographical listings, see the Martindale-Hubbell Law Directory

*MACON,** Bibb Co.

CHAMBLESS, HIGDON & CARSON (AV)

Suite 200 Ambrose Baber Building, 577 Walnut Street, P.O. Box 246, 31298-5399
Telephone: 912-745-1181
Telecopier: 912-746-9479

MEMBERS OF FIRM

Joseph H. Davis Thomas F. Richardson
Joseph H. Chambless Mary Mendel Katz
David B. Higdon Emmitte H. Griggs
James F. Carson, Jr. Marc T. Treadwell

ASSOCIATES

Kim H. Stroup Christopher Balch
Jon Christopher Wolfe

Local Counsel for: Atlanta Gas Light Co.; First Union National Bank of Georgia; Security National Bank.

For full biographical listings, see the Martindale-Hubbell Law Directory

HALL, BLOCH, GARLAND & MEYER (AV)

1500 Charter Medical Building, P.O. Box 5088, 31213-3199
Telephone: 912-745-1625
Telecopier: 912-741-8822

MEMBERS OF FIRM

J. E. Hall (1876-1945) Benjamin M. Garland
Charles J. Bloch (1893-1974) J. Patrick Meyer, Jr.
Ellsworth Hall, Jr. (1908-1984) J. Steven Stewart
J. René Hawkins (1924-1971) J. Burton Wilkerson, Jr.
Ellsworth Hall, III Duncan D. Walker, III
F. Kennedy Hall Mark E. Toth

ASSOCIATES

Ramsey T. Way, Jr. Todd C. Brooks

F. Kennedy Hall, Division Counsel (Georgia): Norfolk Southern Corporation; Norfolk Southern Railway Company.
Counsel for: Wachovia Bank of Georgia, N.A.; Charter Medical Corporation; South Georgia Natural Gas Co.; United States Fidelity and Guaranty Company; Fina Oil and Chemical Company; Helena Chemical Corporation; Ear, Nose & Throat Medical Group, P.A.; Fickling & Walker Asset and Property Management, Inc.

For full biographical listings, see the Martindale-Hubbell Law Directory

JONES, CORK & MILLER (AV)

435 Second Street, Fifth Floor, P.O. Box 6437, 31201-2724
Telephone: 912-745-2821
Telecopier: 912-743-9609

MEMBERS OF FIRM

C. Baxter Jones (1895-1968) John C. Cork
Charles M. Cork (1908-1982) H. Jerome Strickland
Charles M. Cork, Jr. Hubert C. Lovein, Jr.
Carr G. Dodson W. Warren Plowden, Jr.
Timothy K. Adams Rufus D. Sams, III

(See Next Column)

JONES, CORK & MILLER—*Continued*

MEMBERS OF FIRM (Continued)

Thomas C. James, III
Steve L. Wilson
James M. Elliott, Jr.
Thomas C. Alexander
C. Ashley Royal
Robert C. Norman, Jr.
Jerry A. Lumley
John T. Mitchell, Jr.
W. Carter Bates III
Timothy Harden, III
Howard J. Strickland, Jr.
Cater C. Thompson
Thomas W. Joyce
Brandon A. Oren

ASSOCIATES

W. Kerry Howell
David A. Pope
William T. Prescott
Shawn Marie Story
James E. Messer, Jr.
Timothy K. Hall

OF COUNSEL

Wallace Miller, Jr.
John W. Smith

General Counsel for: The Bibb Co.; Trust Company Bank of Middle Georgia, N.A.; First Liberty Bank; Wesleyan College; Bibb County Board of Education.
Division Counsel for: Georgia Power Co.
Represent Locally: Southern Bell Telephone & Telegraph Co.; Allstate Insurance Co.; The City of Macon; St. Paul Fire & Marine Insurance Co.

For full biographical listings, see the Martindale-Hubbell Law Directory

REYNOLDS & MCARTHUR (AV)

A Partnership including a Professional Corporation
850 Walnut Street, 31201
Telephone: 912-741-6000
Fax: 912-742-0750
Atlanta, Georgia Office: Suite 1010, One Buckhead Plaza, 3060 Peachtree Road, N.W.
Telephone: 404-240-0265.
Fax: 404-262-3557.
Asheville, North Carolina Office: The Jackson Building, 22 South Pack Square, Suite 1200.
Telephone: 704-254-8523.
Fax: 704-254-3038.

MEMBERS OF FIRM

W. Carl Reynolds (P.C.)
Katherine L. McArthur
Steve Ray Warren (Not admitted in GA)
Charles M. Cork, III
O. Wendell Horne, III
Bradley J. Survant
Laura D. Hogue

For full biographical listings, see the Martindale-Hubbell Law Directory

SELL & MELTON (AV)

A Partnership including a Professional Corporation
14th Floor, Charter Medical Building, P.O. Box 229, 31297-2899
Telephone: 912-746-8521
Telecopier: 912-745-6426

Andrew W. McKenna (1918-1981)
E. S. Sell, Jr.
John D. Comer
Buckner F. Melton
Mitchel P. House, Jr.
Joseph W. Popper, Jr.
Doye E. Green
Edward S. Sell, III
John A. Draughon
R. (Chix) Miller
Russell M. Boston (P.C.)
Brian J. Passante

ASSOCIATES

Doye E. Green, Jr.
Jeffrey B. Hanson
Robert D. McCullers
Michelle W. Johnson

General Counsel for: Macon Telegraph Publishing Co. (The Macon Telegraph); Macon-Bibb County Hospital Authority; County of Bibb; County of Twiggs; Smith & Sons Foods, Inc. (S & S Cafeterias); Macon Bibb County Industrial Authority; Burgess Pigment Co.

For Complete List of Firm Personnel, See General Section

For full biographical listings, see the Martindale-Hubbell Law Directory

*MARIETTA,** Cobb Co.

AWTREY AND PARKER, P.C. (AV)

211 Roswell Street, P.O. Box 997, 30061
Telephone: 404-424-8000
Fax: 404-424-1594

L. M. Awtrey, Jr. (1915-1986)
George L. Dozier, Jr.
Harvey D. Harkness
Mike Harrison
Dana L. Jackel
Donald A. Mangerie (1924-1988)
Barbara H. Martin
A. Sidney Parker
Toby B. Prodgers
J. Lynn Rainey
Annette M. Risse (Mrs.)
Robert B. Silliman

OF COUNSEL

J. Ben Moore

General Counsel for: Kennesaw Finance Co.; Cobb Electric Membership Corporation; Development Authority of Cobb County.
Local Counsel for: Coats & Clark; Bell South Mobility; Lockheed-Georgia Corp.; Post Properties, Inc.; CSX Transportation, Inc.

(See Next Column)

For Complete List of Firm Personnel, See General Section

For full biographical listings, see the Martindale-Hubbell Law Directory

DOWNEY & CLEVELAND (AV)

288 Washington Avenue, 30060
Telephone: 404-422-3233
Fax: 404-423-4199

OF COUNSEL

Lynn A. Downey

MEMBERS OF FIRM

Robert H. Cleveland (1940-1989)
Joseph C. Parker
Y. Kevin Williams
Russell B. Davis
G. Lee Welborn

ASSOCIATE

Rodney S. Shockley

Representative Clients: Allstate Insurance Co.; St. Paul Insurance Cos.; Georgia Farm Bureau Mutual Insurance Co.; State Farm Insurance Cos.; Cotton States Mutual Insurance Co.; Colonial Insurance Co. of California; Ed Voyles Oldsmobile, Honda and Chrysler-Plymouth; Chuck Clancy Ford; City of Acworth; Lockheed Aeronautical Systems Company, a Division of Lockheed Corporation.

For Complete List of Firm Personnel, See General Section

For full biographical listings, see the Martindale-Hubbell Law Directory

MOORE & ROGERS (AV)

192 Anderson Street, P.O. Box 3305, 30060
Telephone: 404-429-1499
Telecopier: 404-429-8631

MEMBERS OF FIRM

John H. Moore
Stephen C. Steele
William R. Johnson
Robert D. Ingram
G. Phillip Beggs
Eldon L. Basham

ASSOCIATES

Sara J. Murphree
Diane Matassino Busch
Jere C. Smith
Jeffrey A. Watkins
Elizabeth E. DeBauche
Ross E. Longood

Representative Client: C.W. Matthews Contracting Co., Inc.
Approved Attorneys for: Chicago Title Insurance Co.; Ticor Title Insurance Company of California.
References: Charter Bank and Trust Co.; First Alliance Bank.

For full biographical listings, see the Martindale-Hubbell Law Directory

*MCDONOUGH,** Henry Co.

SMITH, WELCH & STUDDARD (AV)

41 Keys Ferry Street, P.O. Box 31, 30253
Telephone: 404-957-3937
Fax: 404-957-9165
Stockbridge, Georgia Office: 1231-A Eagle's Landing Parkway.
Telephone: 404-389-4864.
FAX: 404-389-5157.

MEMBERS OF FIRM

Ernest M. Smith (1911-1992)
A. J. Welch, Jr.
Ben W. Studdard, III
J. Mark Brittain (Resident, Stockbridge Office)

ASSOCIATES

Patrick D. Jaugstetter
E. Gilmore Maxwell
J.V. Dell, Jr. (Resident, Stockbridge Office)

Representative Clients: Alliance Corp.; Atlanta Motor Speedway, Inc.; Bellamy-Strickland Chevrolet, Inc.; Ceramic and Metal Coatings Corp.; City of Hampton; City of Locust Grove; City of Stockbridge.

For full biographical listings, see the Martindale-Hubbell Law Directory

*NEWNAN,** Coweta Co.

GLOVER & DAVIS, P.A. (AV)

10 Brown Street, P.O. Box 1038, 30264
Telephone: 404-253-4330;
Atlanta: 404-463-1100
Fax: 404-251-7152
Peachtree City, Georgia Office: Suite 130, 200 Westpark Drive.
Telephone: 404-487-5834.
Fax: 404-487-3492.

J. Littleton Glover, Jr.
Delia T. Crouch
Asa M. Powell, Jr.

Representative Clients: Newnan Savings Bank; Pike Transfer Co.; Batson-Cook Company, General Corporate and Construction Divisions; Coweta County, Georgia; Heard County, Georgia; Bailey & Associates; Book Warehouse of Georgia, Inc.; West Georgia Farm Credit, ACA.
Local Counsel for: International Latex Corp.; First Union National Bank of Georgia.

(See Next Column)

GLOVER & DAVIS P.A., *Newnan—Continued*

For Complete List of Firm Personnel, See General Section

For full biographical listings, see the Martindale-Hubbell Law Directory

ROSENZWEIG, JONES & MACNABB, P.C. (AV)

32 South Court Square, P.O. Box 220, 30264
Telephone: 404-253-3282;
(Atlanta) 404-577-5376
FAX: 404-251-7262

George C. Rosenzweig
Sidney Pope Jones, Jr.
Joseph P. MacNabb

Douglas L. Dreyer

Approved Attorneys for: Lawyers Title Insurance Corp.; Commonwealth Land Title Insurance Co.; St. Paul Title Insurance Co.; Chicago Title Insurance Co.

For Complete List of Firm Personnel, See General Section

For full biographical listings, see the Martindale-Hubbell Law Directory

*OCILLA,** Irwin Co.

WALTERS, DAVIS, MEEKS & PUJADAS, P.C. (AV)

South Cherry Street, P.O. Box 247, 31774
Telephone: 912-468-7472; 468-9433
Fax: 912-468-9022

W. Emory Walters
W. Edward Meeks, Jr.
J. Harvey Davis
Thomas E. Pujadas
C. Vinson Walters, II

Attorneys for: Irwin County Board of Education; First State Bank of Ocilla; Irwin County; Wilcox County.
Local Counsel for: Georgia Farm Bureau Mutual Insurance Co.
Approved Attorneys for: Kaiser Aluminum & Chemical Sales, Inc.; Lawyers Title Insurance Corp.; Ticor Title Insurance Co.; Farmers Home Administration; Federal Land Bank of Columbia.

For Complete List of Firm Personnel, See General Section

For full biographical listings, see the Martindale-Hubbell Law Directory

*ROME,** Floyd Co.

BRINSON, ASKEW, BERRY, SEIGLER, RICHARDSON & DAVIS (AV)

A Partnership including Professional Corporations
Omberg House, 615 West First Street, P.O. Box 5513, 30162-5513
Telephone: 706-291-8853;
Atlanta: 404-521-0908
Telecopier: 706-234-3574

MEMBERS OF FIRM

Robert M. Brinson (P.C.)
Joseph M. Seigler, Jr.
C. King Askew (P.C.)
Thomas D. Richardson
Robert L. Berry
J. Anderson Davis
Hendrick L. Cromartie, III

OF COUNSEL

Wright W. Smith

ASSOCIATES

Mark M. J. Webb
Joseph B. Atkins
I. Stewart Duggan, Jr.

Representative Clients: City of Rome; Georgia Power Co.; NationsBank of Georgia, N.A.; News Publishing Company (Rome News Tribune); Redmond Regional Medical Center; Oglethorpe Power Corp.; Suhner Manufacturing, Inc.; The Federal Land Bank of Columbia; AmSouth Bank of Georgia; United States Fidelity & Guaranty Co.

For full biographical listings, see the Martindale-Hubbell Law Directory

SHAW, MADDOX, GRAHAM, MONK & BOLING (AV)

Trust Company Bank Building, P.O. Box 29, 30162-0029
Telephone: 706-291-6223
Telecopier: 706-291-7429

MEMBERS OF FIRM

Charles C. Shaw
Jo H. Stegall, III
James D. Maddox
David F. Guldenschuh
John M. Graham, III
Daniel M. Roper
C. Wade Monk
Jule W. Peek, Jr.
William H. Boling, Jr.
Virginia B. Harman

ASSOCIATES

Scott M. Smith
David Tomlin
Thomas H. Manning
Mather D. Graham

(See Next Column)

OF COUNSEL

Oscar M. Smith

Representative Clients: Trust Company Bank of Northwest Georgia; Bagby Transfer Co.; Inland-Rome Inc.; Southern Railway Co.; Aetna Casualty & Surety Co.; American Mutual Liability Insurance; Commercial Union Assurance Cos.; Hartford Accident & Indemnity Co.

For full biographical listings, see the Martindale-Hubbell Law Directory

*SAVANNAH,** Chatham Co.

BRANNEN, SEARCY & SMITH (AV)

22 East Thirty-Fourth Street, P.O. Box 8002, 31412
Telephone: 912-234-8875
Fax: 912-232-1792

Perry Brannen (1903-1984)
David R. Smith
Frank P. Brannen
Daniel C. Cohen
William N. Searcy
Wayne L. Durden

OF COUNSEL

William T. Daniel, Jr.

ASSOCIATES

Robert L. Jenkins
Bernard F. Kistler, Jr.
Fonda L. Jackson

Counsel for: Continental Insurance Co.

For full biographical listings, see the Martindale-Hubbell Law Directory

MCCALLAR AND ASSOCIATES (AV)

115 Oglethorpe Avenue West, P.O. Box 9026, 31412
Telephone: 912-234-1215
Telecopier: 912-236-7549

C. James McCallar, Jr.

Mark Bulovic
Todd E. Schwartz (Not admitted in GA)

For full biographical listings, see the Martindale-Hubbell Law Directory

WOODALL AND MACKENZIE, P.C. (AV)

327 Tattnall Street, P.O. Box 10166, 31412
Telephone: 912-238-9999

John T. Woodall
Malcolm Mackenzie, III

Peter A. Giusti

Reference: Trust Company Bank.

For full biographical listings, see the Martindale-Hubbell Law Directory

ZIPPERER & LORBERBAUM, P.C. (AV)

200 E. St. Julian Street, P.O. Box 9147, 31412
Telephone: 912-232-3770
FAX: 912-232-0643

Alex L. Zipperer
Janet Shedd Foerster
Ralph R. Lorberbaum
Steven L. Beauvais

For full biographical listings, see the Martindale-Hubbell Law Directory

*STATESBORO,** Bulloch Co.

EDENFIELD, STONE & COX (AV)

201 South Main Street, P.O. Box 1700, 30459
Telephone: 912-764-8600
FAX: 912-764-8862

MEMBERS OF FIRM

Gerald M. Edenfield
R. Kenny Stone
Susan W. Cox

ASSOCIATES

E. Lee Davis
Ben Kirbo

For full biographical listings, see the Martindale-Hubbell Law Directory

*SUMMERVILLE,** Chattooga Co.

COOK & PALMOUR (AV)

128 South Commerce Street, P.O. Box 370, 30747
Telephone: 706-857-3421
Fax: 706-857-1520

MEMBERS OF FIRM

Bobby Lee Cook
L. Branch S. Connelly
A. Cecil Palmour (1913-1980)
Todd Johnson

For full biographical listings, see the Martindale-Hubbell Law Directory

*TOCCOA,** Stephens Co.

McClure, Ramsay & Dickerson (AV)

400 Falls Road, P.O. Drawer 1408, 30577
Telephone: 706-886-3178
Fax: 706-886-1150

MEMBERS OF FIRM

Clyde M. McClure (1892-1976)
George B. Ramsay, Jr.
John A. Dickerson
Allan R. Ramsay
Martha B. Sikes
Marlin R. Escoe

ASSOCIATES

Alice D. Hayes
Elizabeth Felton Moore
Leon Jourolmon

OF COUNSEL

Knox Bynum

Counsel for: Coats and Clark, Inc.; Stephens Federal Savings & Loan Assn.; St. Paul Insurance Cos.; State Farm Insurance Cos.; Cotton States Insurance Cos.; City of Toccoa; Citizens Bank; Habersham Plantation Corp.; Patterson Pump Co.

For full biographical listings, see the Martindale-Hubbell Law Directory

*VALDOSTA,** Lowndes Co.

Dodd & Turner, P.C. (AV)

613 N. Patterson Street, P.O. Box 1066, 31603-1066
Telephone: 912-242-4470
Telecopier: 912-245-7731

Roger J. Dodd
L. Warren Turner, Jr.

James A. Kiger

Reference: First Union Bank.

For full biographical listings, see the Martindale-Hubbell Law Directory

Tillman, McTier, Coleman, Talley, Newbern & Kurrie (AV)

910 North Patterson Street, P.O. Box 5437, 31603-5437
Telephone: 912-242-7562
Fax: 912-333-0885

MEMBERS OF FIRM

John T. McTier
Wade H. Coleman
George T. Talley
C. George Newbern
Thompson Kurrie, Jr.
Richard L. Coleman
Edward F. Preston
William E. Holland
Clay Powell

OF COUNSEL

Dona Scott Laskey

Attorneys for: NationsBank; Georgia Power Company; Atlanta Gas Company; Griffin Agricultural Chemicals Group; SAFT America Inc.; Sears; The Park Avenue Bank; Liberty Mutual Insurance Company; USF&G Company; MAG Mutual Insurance Company.

For Complete List of Firm Personnel, See General Section

For full biographical listings, see the Martindale-Hubbell Law Directory

HAWAII

*HONOLULU,** Honolulu Co.

Ashford & Nakamura (AV)

2910 Pacific Tower, 1001 Bishop Street, 96813
Telephone: 808-528-0444
Telex: 723-8158
Telecopier: (808) 533-0761
Cable Address: Justlaw

George W. Ashford, Jr.
Lee T. Nakamura

Ann C. Kemp
Francis T. O'Brien

Representative Clients: Baker Industries, Inc.; Burns International Security Services; Clark Equipment Co.; Great Lakes Chemical Corporation; California Union Insurance Co.; Fireman's Fund Insurance Companies; Great American Insurance Companies; Guaranty National Companies; Horace Mann Insurance Company; Marine Office of America Corp.

For full biographical listings, see the Martindale-Hubbell Law Directory

Ayabe, Chong, Nishimoto, Sia & Nakamura (AV)

A Partnership including a Professional Corporation
3000 Grosvenor Center, 737 Bishop Street, 96813
Telephone: 808-537-6119
Telecopier: 808-526-3491

MEMBERS OF FIRM

Sidney K. Ayabe (P.C.)
Robert A. Chong
John S. Nishimoto
Richard Nakamura
Jeffrey H. K. Sia
Kenneth T. Goya
Francis M. Nakamoto
Calvin E. Young
Diane W. Wong
Rodney S. Nishida
Patricia T. Fujii
Rhonda Nishimura
Gail M. Kang

Ann H. Aratani
Philip S. Uesato
Ronald M. Shigekane
Robin R. Horner
Nicole Jung-Shin Rhee
Stephen G. Dyer
Steven L. Goto
Daria Ann Loy
Virgil B. Prieto
Kelley G.A. Nakano

Representative Clients: Travelers Insurance Co.; St. Paul Fire and Marine Insurance Co.; The Employers Group of Insurance Companies; TIG Insurance Co.; Pacific Insurance Co.; Hartford Accident and Indemnity Co.; Continental Casualty Co.; First Insurance Company of Hawaii, Ltd.

For full biographical listings, see the Martindale-Hubbell Law Directory

Cades Schutte Fleming & Wright (AV)

Formerly Smith, Wild, Beebe & Cades
1000 Bishop Street, P.O. Box 939, 96808
Telephone: 808-521-9200
Telex: 7238589
Telecopier: 808-531-8738
Affiliated Law Firm: Udom-Prok Associates Law Offices, 105/36 Tharinee Mansion, Borom Raj Chananee Road Bangkoknoi, Bangkok, Thailand, 10700.
Telephone: 011 660 435-4146.
Kailua-Kona, Hawaii Office: Hualalai Center, Suite B-303, 75-170 Hualalai Road.
Telephone: 808-329-5811.
Telecopier: 808-326-1175.

MEMBERS OF FIRM

Robert B. Bunn
William M. Swope
Douglas E. Prior
E. Gunner Schull
Michael P. Porter
Donald E. Scearce
Richard A. Hicks
Roger H. Epstein
Jeffrey S. Portnoy
Bernice Littman
Nicholas C. Dreher
Mark A. Hazlett
Philip J. Leas
David C. Larsen
Stephen B. MacDonald
Larry T. Takumi
William A. Cardwell
C. Michael Hare
Richard R. Clifton
Roy A. Vitousek, III (Resident, Kona Office)
Nelson N. S. Chun
Darryl H. W. Johnston
Vito Galati
Cary S. Matsushige
David Schulmeister
Thomas E. Crowley, III
Lorraine H. Akiba
Milton M. Yasunaga
Susan Oki Mollway
Gino L. Gabrio
Colin O. Miwa
Martin E. Hsia
Stewart J. Martin
Peter W. Olson
Rhonda L. Griswold
Gail M. Tamashiro
Grace Nihei Kido
Donna Y. L. Leong
David F.E. Banks
Dennis J. Gaughan

ASSOCIATES

Patricia J. McHenry
K. James Steiner, Jr.
Blane T. Yokota
Jeffrey D. Watts
Eric N. Roose
Marjorie A. Lau
Laurie A. Kuribayashi
James H. Ashford
Michele M. Sunahara
Nani Lee (Resident, Kona Office)
Cynthia M. Johiro
John P. Powell (Resident, Kona Office)
Dennis W. Chong Kee
Carlito P. Caliboso
Catherine A. Carey
Daniel H. Devaney IV
Allen R. Wolff
Mark D. Lofstrom
Karen Wong
Michael H. Shikuma
Jeffrey K. Natori
Eric S.T. Young
Dean T. Yamamoto
Lynn Higashi Hiatt (Resident, Kona Office)
Johnnel L. Nakamura (Not admitted in HI)
Kimberly A. O'Neill (Not admitted in HI; Resident, Kona Office)

Arthur G. Smith (1882-1966)
Urban Earl Wild (1891-1952)
Eugene H. Beebe (1889-1966)
Charles A. Gregory (1902-1972)
C. Frederick Schutte (1921-1988)
Milton Cades (1903-1992)
A. Singleton Cagle (1923-1994)
Edward deL. Boyle (1942-1994)

(See Next Column)

CADES SCHUTTE FLEMING & WRIGHT, *Honolulu—Continued*

OF COUNSEL

J. Russell Cades
William L. Fleming
Harold S. Wright
James S. Campbell

Counsel for: Amfac, Inc.; First Hawaiian Bank; Bishop Trust Co., Ltd.; Alexander & Baldwin, Inc.; Theo. H. Davies & Co., Ltd.; C. Brewer & Company, Ltd.; Bank of America, FSB; The Bank of Tokyo, Ltd.; Haseko (Hawaii), Inc.; The Industrial Bank of Japan, Ltd.

For full biographical listings, see the Martindale-Hubbell Law Directory

CASE & LYNCH (AV)

A Partnership including Professional Corporations
(Formerly Pratt, Moore, Bortz & Case - 1967 to 1971)
(Formerly Case, Kay & Lynch - 1979 to 1986)
2600 Grosvenor Center, Mauka Tower, 737 Bishop Street, 96813
Telephone: 808-547-5400
Cable Address: "Loio"
Telex: 7238523
Telecopier: 808-523-1920
Lihue, Kauai, Hawaii Office: Watumull Plaza, Suite 202, 4334 Rice Street.
Telephone: 808-245-4705.
Kahului, Maui, Hawaii Office: The Kahului Building, Suite 470, 33 Lono Avenue.
Telephone: 808-871-8351.
Kilauea, Kauai, Hawaii Office: Kong Lung Center, Kilauea Lighthouse Road, P.O. Box 988.
Telephone: 808-828-2890.
Hilo, Hawaii Office: Case & Lynch Business Center, 460 Kilauea Avenue.
Telephone: 808-961-6611.
Kailua-Kona, Hawaii Office: Hanama Place, Suite 101, 75-5706 Kuakini Highway.
Telephone: 808-329-4421.

Caroline Peters Egli (Resident at Kahului, Maui Office)
David C. Farmer
Wesley W. Ichida (A Law Corporation)
Lyle Minoru Ishida
Nenad Krek
Paul A. Lynch (A Law Corporation)
Michael R. Marsh
John R. Myrdal (A Law Corporation)
David W. Proudfoot (A Law Corporation)
Frederick R. Troncone

ASSOCIATES

David F. Andrew
Jerilynn Ono Hall
Steven J. Kim
Stephen M. Teves

COUNSEL

Dianne G. Jagmin

OF COUNSEL

Allen M. Stack

Representative Clients: Alexander & Baldwin, Inc.; Architects Hawaii, Ltd.; Chevron Corp.; Del Monte Fresh Produce (Hawaii), Inc.; Ford Motor Company; London Steamship Owners' Mutual Insurance Assn., Ltd.; Marsh & McLennan, Inc.; Mitsubishi International Corporation; Murphy Construction Co., Inc.; Long & Melone, Ltd. (Agents for First American Title Insurance Co.).

For Complete List of Firm Personnel, See General Section

For full biographical listings, see the Martindale-Hubbell Law Directory

DWYER IMANAKA SCHRAFF KUDO MEYER & FUJIMOTO ATTORNEYS AT LAW, A LAW CORPORATION (AV)

1800 Pioneer Plaza, 900 Fort Street Mall, 96813
Telephone: 808-524-8000
Telecopier: 808-526-1419
Mailing Address: P.O. Box 2727, 96803

John R. Dwyer, Jr.
Mitchell A. Imanaka
Paul A. Schraff
Benjamin A. Kudo (Atty. at Law, A Law Corp.)
William G. Meyer, III
Wesley M. Fujimoto
Ronald Van Grant
Jon M. H. Pang
Blake W. Bushnell
Kenn N. Kojima

Adelbert Green
Richard T. Asato, Jr.
Scott W. Settle
Darcie S. Yoshinaga
Tracy Timothy Woo
Lawrence I. Kawasaki
Douglas H. Inouye
Christine A. Low

OF COUNSEL

Randall Y. Iwase

For full biographical listings, see the Martindale-Hubbell Law Directory

GREELEY WALKER & KOWEN (AV)

A Partnership including a Law Corporation
Suite 1300 Pauahi Tower, 1001 Bishop Street, 96813
Telephone: 808-526-2211
Telecopier: 808-528-4690

(See Next Column)

MEMBERS OF FIRM

Burnham H. Greeley (A Law Corporation)
Susan P. Walker
Richard J. Kowen
Janice T. Futa

ASSOCIATES

Frank P. Richardson
Kimberly Ann Greeley (Not admitted in HI)
Andrew D. Smith
George H. Keller

For full biographical listings, see the Martindale-Hubbell Law Directory

DAVID W. HALL ATTORNEY AT LAW, A LAW CORPORATION (AV)

735 Bishop Street Dillingham Transportation Building, Suite 237, 96813
Telephone: 808-526-0402
FAX: 808-526-0404

David W. Hall

For full biographical listings, see the Martindale-Hubbell Law Directory

LEE, KIM, WONG, YEE & LAU ATTORNEYS AT LAW, A LAW CORPORATION (AV)

Suite 700 The Queen Street Building, 345 Queen Street, 96813
Telephone: 808-536-4421
Telecopier: 808-521-3566

Douglas T. Y. Lee
Wayson W. S. Wong
Edmund K. U. Yee
Eric T. W. Kim
Gene K. Lau

Arthur H. Kuwahara
Walter E. Hebelethwaite

For full biographical listings, see the Martindale-Hubbell Law Directory

MATSUBARA, LEE & KOTAKE ATTORNEYS AT LAW, A LAW CORPORATION (AV)

Charles R. Kendall Building, 888 Mililani Street, Eighth Floor, 96813-2918
Telephone: 808-526-9566
Facsimile: 808-538-3840

Benjamin M. Matsubara
Gary B. K. T. Lee
Mervyn M. Kotake

Howard M. Nobunaga
Jason M. Yoshida
Curtis T. Tabata

For full biographical listings, see the Martindale-Hubbell Law Directory

MCCORRISTON MIHO MILLER MUKAI (AV)

Five Waterfront Plaza, 4th Floor, 500 Ala Moana Boulevard, 96813
Telephone: 808-529-7300
Facsimile: 808-524-8293
Cable: Attorneys, Honolulu

MEMBERS OF FIRM

William C. McCorriston
Michael D. Tom
William K. Meheula
Kenneth G. K. Hoo
Jerrold Y. Chun
Mark J. Bennett
Nadine Y. Ando
Darolyn Hatsuko Lendio
Richard B. Miller
Randall K. Schmitt
John Y. Yamano
Brad S. Petrus

ASSOCIATES

Thomas E. Bush
Lisa M. Ginoza
Mark D. Clement
Leslie H. Kondo
Carrie K. Okinaga
Joel D. Kam

For Complete List of Firm Personnel, See General Section

For full biographical listings, see the Martindale-Hubbell Law Directory

PERKIN & HOSODA (AV)

2440 Mauka Tower, Grosvenor Center, 737 Bishop Street, 96813
Telephone: 808-523-2300
FAX: 808-531-8898

John Francis Perkin
Lyle S. Hosoda

For full biographical listings, see the Martindale-Hubbell Law Directory

LAW OFFICE OF KENNETH S. ROBBINS ATTORNEY AT LAW, A LAW CORPORATION (AV)

Suite 2220 Davies Pacific Center, 841 Bishop Street, 96813
Telephone: 808-524-2355
Fax: 808-526-0290

Kenneth S. Robbins

(See Next Column)

LAW OFFICE OF KENNETH S. ROBBINS ATTORNEY AT LAW, A LAW CORPORATION—*Continued*

Vincent A. Rhodes	Shinken Naitoh

For full biographical listings, see the Martindale-Hubbell Law Directory

DAVID C. SCHUTTER & ASSOCIATES (AV)

Suite 300 Ocean View Center, 707 Richards Street, 96813
Telephone: 808-524-4600
Facsimile: 808-521-2870

ASSOCIATES

Emlyn H. Higa	James R. Veary
Karen Kightlinger	Mitchell S. Wong
Paul V. Smith	Gary M. Levitt

For full biographical listings, see the Martindale-Hubbell Law Directory

WATANABE, ING & KAWASHIMA (AV)

A Partnership including Professional Corporations
Hawaii Tower, 5th & 6th Floors, 745 Fort Street, 96813
Telephone: 808-544-8300
Facsimile: 808-544-8399
Telex: 6502396585 MCI
MCI Mail: 23 96585
ABA/Net: ABA2281

MEMBERS OF FIRM

Jeffrey N. Watanabe (Atty. at Law, A Law Corp.)	Cynthia Winegar (Atty. at Law, A Law Corp.)
James Kawashima (Atty. at Law, A Law Corp.)	Randall Y. Yamamoto (Atty. at Law, A Law Corp.)
J. Douglas Ing (Atty. at Law, A Law Corp.)	Lyle Y. Harada (Atty. at Law, A Law Corp.)
Wray H. Kondo (Atty. at Law, A Law Corp.)	Michael A. Lorusso (Atty. at Law, A Law Corp.)
John T. Komeiji (Atty. at Law, A Law Corp.)	Pamela J. Larson (Atty. At Law, A Law Corp.)
Ronald Y. K. Leong (Atty. at Law, A Law Corp.)	William H. Gilardy, Jr.
Robert T. Takamatsu (Atty. at Law, A Law Corp.)	John R. Aube (Atty. at Law, A Law Corp.)
	Jan M.L.Y. Amii (Atty. at Law, A Law Corp.)

ASSOCIATES

Donna Y. Kanemaru	LLoyd S. Yoshioka
George B. Apter	Curtis C. Kim
Marcus B. Sierra	Beth K. Fujimoto
Lani Narikiyo	Patsy H. Kirio
Seth M. Reiss	Kevin H. Oda
George D. Quillin	Michael C. Bird
Charlene K. Ikeda	Brian Y. Hiyane
Peter L. Fritz	Dennis J. Hwang
Elena J. Onaga	Teri Y. Kondo

Jeff N. Miyashiro

OF COUNSEL

George R. Ariyoshi

ASIA PACIFIC CONSULTANT

Victor Hao Li (Not admitted in HI)

LEGAL SUPPORT PERSONNEL

GOVERNMENT AFFAIRS ADVISORS

Jon T. Okudara	Millicent M. Y. H. Kim

References: First Hawaiian Bank; American Savings Bank.

For full biographical listings, see the Martindale-Hubbell Law Directory

WEINBERG & BELL ATTORNEYS AT LAW, A LAW CORPORATION (AV)

Suite 1200, 1164 Bishop Street, 96813
Telephone: 808-523-9477
FAX: 808-521-4681

Jan M. Weinberg	Roy J. Bell, III

For full biographical listings, see the Martindale-Hubbell Law Directory

KAILUA-KONA, Hawaii Co.

CADES SCHUTTE FLEMING & WRIGHT (AV)

Hualalai Center, Suite B-303, 75-170 Hualalai Road, 96740
Telephone: 808-329-5811
Telecopier: 808-326-1175
Honolulu, Hawaii Office: 1000 Bishop Street, P. O. Box 939.
Telephone: 808-521-9200.
Affiliated Law Firm: Udom-Prok Associates Law Offices, 105/36 Tharinee Mansion, Bormo Raj Chananee Road Bangkoknoi, Bangkok, Thailand, 10700.
Telephone: 011 662 435-4146.

(See Next Column)

RESIDENT ASSOCIATES

Kimberly A. O'Neill (Not admitted in HI)

For Complete List of Firm Personnel, See General Section

For full biographical listings, see the Martindale-Hubbell Law Directory

IDAHO

*BOISE,** Ada Co.

EBERLE, BERLIN, KADING, TURNBOW & MCKLVEEN, CHARTERED (AV)

Capitol Park Plaza, 300 North Sixth Street, P.O. Box 1368, 83701
Telephone: 208-344-8535
Facsimile: 208-344-8542

R.B. Kading, Jr.	Scott D. Hess
Warren Eugene Jones	Bradley G. Andrews
Mark S. Geston	William A. Fuhrman

General Counsel: Key Bank of Idaho; Key Trust Company of the West; Key Mortgage Funding; IdaWest Energy Company; Diamond Sports.
Representative Clients: Key Bank of Idaho; U.S. West Communications; Cessna Aircraft Co.

For Complete List of Firm Personnel, See General Section

For full biographical listings, see the Martindale-Hubbell Law Directory

ELAM & BURKE, A PROFESSIONAL ASSOCIATION (AV)

Key Financial Center, 702 West Idaho Street, P.O. Box 1539, 83701
Telephone: 208-343-5454
Telecopier: 208-384-5844

Carl P. Burke	John Magel
M. Allyn Dingel, Jr.	James D. LaRue

Representative Clients: Morrison-Knudsen, Inc.; Texas Instruments, Inc.; Prudential Securities, Inc.; Pechiney Corp.; Dow Corning Corporation; U.S. West Communications; State Farm Insurance Cos.; Sinclair Oil Company d/b/a Sun Valley Company; Farmers Insurance Group; Hecla Mining Company.

For Complete List of Firm Personnel, See General Section

For full biographical listings, see the Martindale-Hubbell Law Directory

HALL, FARLEY, OBERRECHT & BLANTON (AV)

Key Financial Center, 702 West Idaho Street, Suite 700, P.O. Box 1271, 83701-1271
Telephone: 208-336-0404
Facsimile: 208-336-5193

Richard E. Hall	Candy Wagahoff Dale
Donald J. Farley	Robert B. Luce
Phillip S. Oberrecht	J. Kevin West
Raymond D. Powers	Bart W. Harwood

J. Charles Blanton	Thorpe P. Orton
John J. Burke	Ronald S. Best
Steven J. Hippler	(Not admitted in ID)

References: Boise State University; Farm Bureau Mutual Insurance Company of Idaho; Medical Insurance Exchange of California; The St. Paul Cos.

For full biographical listings, see the Martindale-Hubbell Law Directory

MOFFATT, THOMAS, BARRETT, ROCK & FIELDS, CHARTERED (AV)

First Security Building, 911 West Idaho Street, Suite 300, P.O. Box 829, 83701
Telephone: 208-345-2000
FAX: 208-385-5384
Idaho Falls Office: 525 Park Avenue, Suite 2D, P.O. Box 1367, 83403.
Telephone: 208-522-6700.
FAX: 208-522-5111.
Pocatello, Idaho Office: 1110 Call Creek Drive, P.O. Box 4941, 83201.
Telephone: 208-233-2001.

R. B. Rock	Larry C. Hunter

Stephen R. Thomas

Representative Clients: BMC West Corporation; Chevron, U.S.A.; First Security Bank of Idaho, N.A.; General Motors Corp.; Idaho Potato Commission; Intermountain Gas Co.; John Alden Life Insurance Co.; Micron, Inc.; Royal Insurance Cos.; St. Luke's Regional Medical Center & Mountain States Tumor Institute.

For Complete List of Firm Personnel, See General Section

For full biographical listings, see the Martindale-Hubbell Law Directory

Boise—Continued

WILSON, CARNAHAN & MCCOLL, CHARTERED (AV)

420 Washington Street, P.O. Box 1544, 83701
Telephone: 208-345-9100
FAX: 208-384-0442

Jeffrey M. Wilson
Debrha Jo Carnahan
Brian F. McColl
Stephanie Jo Williams

Representative Clients: A & J Construction, Inc.; Pure-gro Company; Transamerica Commercial Finance Corp.; John H. Crowther, Inc.; Jess W. Swan Insurance Agency; Higgins and Rutledge Insurance Co., Inc.; Communication Workers of America, Local # 8103.

For full biographical listings, see the Martindale-Hubbell Law Directory

*POCATELLO,** Bannock Co.

MERRILL & MERRILL, CHARTERED (AV)

Key Bank Building, P.O. Box 991, 83204
Telephone: 208-232-2286
Fax: 208-232-2499

Dave R. Gallafent
Stephen S. Dunn
D. Russell Wight
N. Randy Smith
David C. Nye

Representative Clients: Western States Equipment Co.; J. R. Simplot Co.

For Complete List of Firm Personnel, See General Section

For full biographical listings, see the Martindale-Hubbell Law Directory

ILLINOIS

*BELLEVILLE,** St. Clair Co.

DONOVAN, ROSE, NESTER & SZEWCZYK, P.C. (AV)

8 East Washington Street, 62220
Telephone: 618-235-2020
Telecopier: 618-235-9632

Harold A. Donovan, Sr.
Michael J. Nester
Dennis E. Rose
Edward J. Szewczyk
Charles L. Joley

OF COUNSEL

Vincent J. Hatch (Retired)

Douglas R. Heise
Georgiann Oliver
Kenneth M. Nussbaumer
Bret A. Cohen

Representative Clients: State Farm Mutual Auto & Life Co.; Travelers Insurance Co.; Liberty Mutual Insurance Co.; Government Employees Insurance Co.; Great American Insurance Co.; Aetna Casualty & Surety Co.; Royal Globe Insurance Co.; Illinois Founders Insurance Co.; INA (Insurance Company of North America).

For full biographical listings, see the Martindale-Hubbell Law Directory

THE DUCEY LAW FIRM, P.C. (AV)

Richland Executive Plaza II, Suite 201, 521 West Main Street, 62220
Telephone: 618-233-1358; 271-0826
Telecopier: 618-234-9560
St. Louis, Missouri Office: 906 Olive Street.
Telephone: 314-621-5581.

Cornelius T. Ducey, Sr.
Cornelius T. Ducey, Jr.
C. Patout Ducey

Timothy L. Donaho, Jr.

For full biographical listings, see the Martindale-Hubbell Law Directory

GEORGE RIPPLINGER & ASSOCIATES (AV)

2215 West Main Street, 62223
Telephone: 618-234-2440; 800-733-8333
Telecopier: 618-234-6728
St. Louis, Missouri Office: 4144 Lindell Boulevard.

George R. Ripplinger, Jr.

ASSOCIATES

Thomas L. Zimmer
Lisa M. Pennock

A list of Representative Clients provided on request.
Reference: First National Bank of Belleville, Illinois.

For full biographical listings, see the Martindale-Hubbell Law Directory

THOMPSON & MITCHELL (AV)

525 West Main Street, 62220
Telephone: 618-277-4700; 314-271-1800
Telecopier: 618-236-3434
St. Louis, Missouri Office: One Mercantile Center, Suite 3300.
Telephone: 314-231-7676.
Telecopier: 314-342-1717.
St. Charles, Missouri Office: 200 North Third Street.
Telephone: 314-946-7717.
Telecopier: 314-946-4938.
Washington, D.C. Office: 700 14th Street, N.W., Suite 900.
Telephone: 202-508-1000.
Telecopier: 202-508-1010.

MEMBERS OF FIRM

W. Thomas Coghill, Jr.
Michael D. O'Keefe
Thomas W. Alvey, Jr.
Karl D. Dexheimer
Raymond L. Massey
Gary Mayes
Allan McD. Goodloe, Jr.
Thomas F. Hennessy, III
William A. Schmitt
Robert H. Brownlee
Thomas R. Jayne
Mary M. Bonacorsi
Allen D. Allred
Dan H. Ball
William R. Bay
Mark Sableman
Edward S. Bott, Jr.
Bradley A. Winters
Edward A. Cohen
Nicholas J. Lamb
Kurt E. Reitz

ASSOCIATES

Conny Davinroy Beatty
D. Kimberly Brown
Tom R. Burcham III
David S. Corwin
Mary Sue Juen
Crystal M. Kennedy
Cherie K. Harpole MacDonald
William J. Niehoff
Donald K. Schoemaker
Mark S. Schuver
David A. Stratmann
David F. Szewczyk
Roman P. Wuller

Representative Clients: General Motors Corp.; Illinois Central Railroad Co.; S. C. Johnson & Sons, Inc.; Joy Technologies Inc.; Memorial Hospital of Belleville; Nissan Motor Corporation in U.S.A.; Norfolk Southern Corp. & affiliates; Peabody Coal Company; U-Haul International Inc.; Union Electric Co.

For Complete List of Firm Personnel, See General Section

For full biographical listings, see the Martindale-Hubbell Law Directory

*BENTON,** Franklin Co.

HART AND HART (AV)

602 West Public Square, P.O. Box 937, 62812-0937
Telephone: 618-435-8123
Telecopier: 618-435-2962

William W. Hart, Jr. (Retired)
Richard O. Hart
Murphy C. Hart
A. Courtney Cox
Pamela Sue Lacey

Representative Clients: Boatmen's Bank of Franklin County; State Bank of Whittington; Magna Bank of Southern Illinois; Benton Park District; Benton Public Library District; HHL Financial Services; Barnes Hospital (St. Louis); St. Lukes Hospital (St. Louis); St. Mary's Hospital (Centralia); Credit Bureau Systems, Inc.

For Complete List of Firm Personnel, See General Section

For full biographical listings, see the Martindale-Hubbell Law Directory

*CARLINVILLE,** Macoupin Co.

PHELPS, KASTEN, RUYLE & BURNS (AV)

130 East Main Street, 62626
Telephone: 217-854-3283
FAX: 217-854-9527

MEMBERS OF FIRM

Carl E. Kasten
Nancy L. Ruyle
Thomas P. Burns

ASSOCIATE

Byron J. Sims

Representative Clients: Carlinville National Bank; Blackburn University; Area Diesel Service, Inc.; Farmers and Merchants Bank; H & H Construction Services, Inc.

For Complete List of Firm Personnel, See General Section

For full biographical listings, see the Martindale-Hubbell Law Directory

*CHICAGO,** Cook Co.

ABRAMSON & FOX (AV)

One East Wacker Drive, 60601
Telephone: 312-644-8500
FAX: 644-0798
Evergreen, Colorado Office: 1202 Highway 74.
Telephone: 303-674-1328.
FAX: 303-674-0437.

(See Next Column)

ABRAMSON & FOX—*Continued*

MEMBERS OF FIRM

Floyd H. Abramson
Renato L. Amponin
Thomas Brejcha
William D. Brejcha
Donald P. Colleton
John K. Eggers (1936-1991)
James L. Fox
Joseph C. Grayson
Richard S. Hartford
Anthony P. Janik
John J. Jawor
Peter J. Karabas
Carol A. Seelig

John M. Brosnan
Elizabeth E. Fiesman

OF COUNSEL

John J. Alioto
Robert J. Amedeo (Resident, Evergreen, Colorado Office)
Jacob N. Gross (Ltd.)
Martin S. Hall
Richard Hirschtritt
Anthony R. Hofeld
Malcolm S. Kamin
Juris Kins
Marc R. Kromelow

For full biographical listings, see the Martindale-Hubbell Law Directory

ANESI, OZMON & RODIN, LTD. (AV)

161 North Clark Street, 21st Floor, 60601
Telephone: 312-372-3822
Fax: 312-372-3833

Nat P. Ozmon
Charles E. Anesi
Richard A. Lewin (1925-1985)
Curt N. Rodin
Mark Novak
Arnold G. Rubin
Richard L. Rumsey
Bruce M. Kohen
Richard A. Kimnach
Joseph J. Miroballi
Douglas A. Colby
David J. Comeau
James J. Morici, Jr.
Alain Leval
Stephen S. Phalen
Marc A. Taxman
Scott H. Rudin
John A. Salzeider
David Figlioli
Martin J. Lucas
Christopher J. Dallavo
Daniel V. O'Connor
Micaela M. Cassidy
John M. Popelka
Telly C. Nakos
Michelle Dekalb
Mark Murnane

OF COUNSEL

Noel C. Lindenmuth
Irving D. Fasman

For full biographical listings, see the Martindale-Hubbell Law Directory

BAILEY, BORLACK, NADELHOFFER & CARROLL (AV)

Suite 2000, 135 South La Salle Street, 60603
Telephone: 312-629-2700
Telecopier: 312-629-0174

Robert C. Bailey
Alan R. Borlack
Clement J. Carroll, Jr.
Sarah K. Nadelhoffer
Eric G. Grossman

For full biographical listings, see the Martindale-Hubbell Law Directory

BATES MECKLER BULGER & TILSON (AV)

8300 Sears Tower, 233 South Wacker, 60606
Telephone: 312-474-7900
Facsimile: 312-474-7898

MEMBERS OF FIRM

Robert J. Bates, Jr.
Brian W. Bulger
Scott L. Carey
Patrick J. Foley
J. Stuart Garbutt
Paul R. Garry
Maryann C. Hayes
Mari Henry Leigh
Michael M. Marick
Bruce R. Meckler
Steven D. Pearson
Joseph E. Tilson

ASSOCIATES

Dina L. Brantman
Catherine M. Crisham
Robin Edelstein
Maria G. Enriquez
Stanley V. Figura
Judith Y. Gaston
Mary E. Gootjes
Michael J. Gray
Robert C. Heist
Julie Marie Hextell
Darlene M. Jarzyna
Kathleen H. Jensen
Michael I. Leonard
Mary F. Licari
James A. Lupo, Jr.
Susan M. Narimatsu
Brett G. Rawitz
John E. Rodewald
Scott M. Seaman
Mark G. Sheridan
Frederick W. Stein
Monica T. Sullivan
Timothy A. Wolfe

For full biographical listings, see the Martindale-Hubbell Law Directory

LAW OFFICES OF THEODORE M. BECKER, P.C. (AV)

30 North La Salle Street Suite 3400, 60602
Telephone: 312-332-5000
Fax: 312-332-4663

Theodore M. Becker

For full biographical listings, see the Martindale-Hubbell Law Directory

BELL, BOYD & LLOYD (AV)

Three First National Plaza Suite 3300, 70 West Madison Street, 60602
Telephone: 312-372-1121
FAX: 312-372-2098
Washington, D.C. Office: 1615 L Street, N.W.
Telephone: 202-466-6300.
FAX: 202-463-0678.

MEMBERS OF FIRM

Michael J. Abernathy
D. Daniel Barr
William L. Barr, Jr.
Paul M. Bauch
William R. Carney
James W. Collins
Randy J. Curato
Nicholas J. Etten
Lawrence M. Gavin
Frank K. Heap
Francis J. Higgins
Ellen S. Kornichuk
Daniel Lawler
Brian E. Martin
Brigid M. McGrath
Rebecca C. Meriwether
David M. Novak
Stephen J. O'Neil
Kenneth E. Rechtoris
James A. Romanyak
John W. Rotunno
Peter G. Rush
John P. Scotellaro
Robert V. Shannon
Edwin C. Thomas, III
Larry L. Thompson
John J. Verscaj

OF COUNSEL

Richard L. Curry

ASSOCIATES

Douglas M. Chalmers
David D. Cleary
Carol A. Genis
Kathleen M. Meyers-Grabemann
Ari J. Rosenthal
Stuart A. Shanus
James P. Tutaj

For Complete List of Firm Personnel, See General Section

For full biographical listings, see the Martindale-Hubbell Law Directory

BOWLES, KEATING, HERING & LOWE, CHARTERED (AV)

135 South La Salle Street, Suite 1040, 60603-4295
Telephone: 312-263-6300
Fax: 312-263-0415
Italy Office: 10, Via Pietro Verri, 20121 Milan, Italy.
Telephone: 2-798609.
Fax: 276001473.
European Associated Offices:
Italy Office: Studio Legale Ippolito, viale Astichello, 6, 36100 Vicenza, Italy.
Telephone: 444-300957.
Fax: 444-300827..
Sweden Office: Advokatgruppen i Stockholm AB, Kommendorsgatan 26,114 48 Stockholm, Sweden.
Telephone: 8-667-0765.
Fax: 8-660-9827.
France Office: Allain - Kaltenbach - Plaisant - Raimon, 14 Rue Lejemptel, 94302 Vincennes (Paris), France.
Telephone: 1-4374 7494.
Fax: 1-4374 3222.
Asian Cooperative Offices:
China Offices: Liaoning Law Office For Foreign Affairs, 11 Liaohe Street, Shenyang Liaoning 110032, China.
Telephone: 652125.
Telex: 808305 LCPIT CN.
FAX: (24) 664791. Dalian Foreign Economic Law Office: No. 2 S. Square, Dalian, Liaoning, China.
Telephone: 332532.
FAX: 332532. Shenyang Foreign Economic Law Office, 230-3, Quingnian Street, Shenhe District, Shenyang Liaoning 110014, China.
Telephone: 290123.

Clyde O. Bowles, Jr. (Chicago Office)
Mario Bruno
Roberto N. Bruno
Nicola Fiordalisi (Chicago Office)
Glenn Z. Hering (Chicago Office)
Kathryn R. Ingrim (Chicago Office)
Christopher L. Ingrim (Chicago Office)
Thomas M. Keating (Chicago Office)
Jung Y. Lowe (Chicago Office)
Lynne R. Ostfeld (Chicago Office)
Arnold A. Silvestri (Chicago Office)

COUNSEL

Malcolm A. Chandler (Chicago Office)

For full biographical listings, see the Martindale-Hubbell Law Directory

CORBOY • DEMETRIO • CLIFFORD, P.C. (AV)

33 North Dearborn Street 21st Floor, 60602
Telephone: 312-346-3191
FAX: 312-346-5562
TDD: 312-236-3191

Philip H. Corboy
Thomas A. Demetrio
Robert A. Clifford
Philip Harnett Corboy, Jr.

(See Next Column)

CORBOY • DEMETRIO • CLIFFORD P.C., *Chicago—Continued*

Robert J. Bingle
Kevin G. Burke
Michael K. Demetrio
Kevin P. Durkin
Keith A. Hebeisen
Francis Patrick Murphy
Susan J. Schwartz

Thomas F. Boleky
Richard F. Burke, Jr.
Susan A. Capra
Patricia J. Carlson
Timothy J. Cavanagh
Barry R. Chafetz
G. Grant Dixon III
Mary E. Doherty
J. Matthew Dudley
Shawn S. Kasserman
Jeffrey J. Kroll
Michael G. Mahoney
Michael K. Muldoon
Margaret M. Power
Thomas K. Prindable
Richard L. Pullano
Michael Flinn Roe
Robert P. Walsh, Jr.
Edward G. Willer
David C. Wise

OF COUNSEL

Robert P. Sheridan
Phillip Taxman

Reference: The American National Bank & Trust Company, Chicago, Illinois.

For full biographical listings, see the Martindale-Hubbell Law Directory

COWEN, CROWLEY & NORD, P.C. (AV)

Xerox Centre, 55 West Monroe Street, Suite 500, 60603
Telephone: 312-641-0060
Fax: 312-641-6959

Richard A. Cowen
Wilbert F. Crowley, Jr.

For full biographical listings, see the Martindale-Hubbell Law Directory

DEUTSCH, LEVY & ENGEL, CHARTERED (AV)

Suite 1700, 225 West Washington Street, 60606
Telephone: 312-346-1460
Boynton, Beach Florida Office: 3C Westgate Lane.
Telephone: 407-737-6003.
Wheaton, Illinois Office: Suite B2, 620 West Roosevelt Road.
Telephone: 312-665-9112.

Paul M. Levy
Michael J. Devine
Stuart Berks
LaDonna M. Loitz
Michael B. Kahane

Phillip J. Zisook
Stephen A. Viz
Thomas W. Goedert

For Complete List of Firm Personnel, See General Section

For full biographical listings, see the Martindale-Hubbell Law Directory

DOWD & DOWD, LTD. (AV)

Suite 1000, 55 West Wacker Drive, 60601
Telephone: 312-704-4400
Telecopier: 312-704-4500

Joseph V. Dowd
Michael E. Dowd
Kenneth Gurber
Robert C. Yelton III
Patrick C. Dowd

S. Robert Depke
Robert J. Golden
Kevin J. Kane
Jeffrey Edward Kehl
Joseph J. Leonard
Ronald J. Lukes
Donald G. Machalinski
John M. McAndrews
Martha A. Niles
Michael G. Patrizio
Patrick J. Ruberry
Anthony R. Rutkowski
Karen W. Worsek

LEGAL SUPPORT PERSONNEL

Carrie J. Julian
Jill A. Weiseman

OF COUNSEL

Guenther Ahlf
Joel S. Ostrow

Reference: Central National Bank in Chicago.

For full biographical listings, see the Martindale-Hubbell Law Directory

THE LAW OFFICES OF EDNA SELAN EPSTEIN (AV)

321 South Plymouth Court Suite 800, 60603
Telephone: 312-408-2750
FAX: 312-408-2760

Edna Selan Epstein

For full biographical listings, see the Martindale-Hubbell Law Directory

FOX & GROVE, CHARTERED (AV)

311 South Wacker Drive Suite 6200, 60606
Telephone: 312-876-0500
Telecopier: 312-362-0700
St. Petersburg, Florida Office: Fox, Grove, Abbey, Adams, Reynolds, Byclick & Kiernan, Eleventh Floor, 360 Central Avenue.
Telephone: 813-821-2080.
Tampa, Florida Office: Fox, Grove, Abbey, Adams, Reynolds, Byclick & Kiernan, 500 East Kennedy Boulevard, Suite 200.
Telephone: 813-253-0745.
San Francisco, California Office: 240 Stockton Street, Suite 900.
Telephone: 415-956-1360.

Shayle P. Fox
Lawrence M. Cohen
S. Richard Pincus
Russell M. Kofoed
Jeffrey S. Goldman
Marty Denis
Steven L. Gillman
William Henry Barrett
Allison C. Blakley
Jeffrey E. Beeson

OF COUNSEL

Kalvin M. Grove
Joseph M. Kehoe, Jr.

Tamra S. Domeyer
Jill J. Gladney
Mari Rose Hatzenbuehler
Davi L. Hirsch
Joshua D. Holleb
Diane Kristen
Steven H. Kuh
Steven I. Locke
Daniel R. Madock
Robert M. Mintz
Paul A. Olsen
Michael Paull
Joel W. Rice
Peter S. Rukin
Kerry Evan Saltzman
Michael L. Sullivan
Douglas M. Werman

Labor Counsel for: Sears Roebuck and Co.; National Association of Independent Insurers; Alliance of American Insurers.
Representative Labor Client: Liberty Mutual Insurance Co.

For full biographical listings, see the Martindale-Hubbell Law Directory

GESSLER, FLYNN, FLEISCHMANN, HUGHES & SOCOL, LTD. (AV)

Three First National Plaza, Suite 2200, 60602
Telephone: 312-580-0100
Telecopy: 312-580-1994

Mark S. Dym
Michael J. Flaherty
Thomas J. Fleischmann
Terence E. Flynn
George W. Gessler
John K. Hughes
William P. Jones
Peter M. Katsaros
Mark A. LaRose
Terence J. Moran
Matthew J. Piers
David J. Pritchard
Kalman D. Resnick
Jonathan A. Rothstein
Donna Kaner Socol

Eric Berg
Benjamin P. Beringer
Anjali Dayal
Ruth M. Dunning
Jennifer Fischer
Charles J. Holley
Laura C. Liu
Kimberley Marsh
Alex W. Miller
Paul A. Reasoner
Michael P. Simkus
Marci S. Sperling
Maria L. Venturo
Vanessa J. Weathersby
Mark B. Weiner
Charles H. Winterstein

OF COUNSEL

James T. Derico, Jr.
Susan R. Gzesh
Foster Marshall, Jr.

For full biographical listings, see the Martindale-Hubbell Law Directory

GLEASON, MCGUIRE & SHREFFLER (AV)

160 North Wacker Drive, 60606
Telephone: 312-641-0580
Fax: 312-641-0380
Roseland, New Jersey Office: Three A.D.P. Boulevard.
Telephone: 201-533-1334.
Fax: 201-533-1339.

MEMBERS OF FIRM

Nancy J. Gleason
Judith A. Gleason
Philip J. McGuire
David E. Schroeder
Douglas G. Shreffler
Virginia M. Vermillion

ASSOCIATES

Bonnie F. Bagdon
Cynthia L. Bordelon
Maryterese Ceko
Henry T. French Jr.
Edward W. Gleason
Joanne Gleason
Richard E. Gottlieb
Patricia M. Kelly
Robert Nils Lane
John S. Lindemann
Anthony J. Madormo
Linda L. McCarty
Timothy M. Nolan
Michael R. Orlando
Robert C. Thurston
Hugh C. Welsh (Resident, Roseland, New Jersey Office)
J. Richard West
Vincent S. Ziccolella (Resident, Roseland, New Jersey Office)

LEGAL SUPPORT PERSONNEL

Ronald E. Feret

(See Next Column)

GLEASON, MCGUIRE & SHREFFLER—*Continued*

Stacy M. Boyle
Josephine J. Campagna
Jane W. Grimme
Monica M. Brace
Christine E. Houska
Susan E. Kelly
Kathleen A. Wrobel
Sally S. Tuxhorn

Representative Clients: Allstate Insurance Co.; Employer's Mutual Casualty Co.; Northbrook Property & Casualty; Mutual Marine Office; American Home Assurance Co.; Lexington Insurance Co.; Pacific Mutual Marine; Utica Mutual; New York Marine & General Insurance Co.

For full biographical listings, see the Martindale-Hubbell Law Directory

MICHAEL T. HANNAFAN & ASSOCIATES, LTD. (AV)

Suite 4040 Three First National Plaza, 60602
Telephone: 312-782-7490
FAX: 312-782-9440

Michael T. Hannafan

William E. Blais
Cory A. Johnson

Reference: The Northern Trust Co.

For full biographical listings, see the Martindale-Hubbell Law Directory

WILLIAM J. HARTE, LTD. (AV)

Suite 1100, 111 West Washington Street, 60602
Telephone: 312-726-5015
Fax: 312-641-1288

William J. Harte

Sylvia A. Sotiras
Erik D. Gruber
Stephen L. Garcia

OF COUNSEL

David J. Walker

For full biographical listings, see the Martindale-Hubbell Law Directory

JOHN PATRICK HEALY (AV)

29 South La Salle - Suite 640, 60603
Telephone: 312-332-7950
FAX: 312-782-4502

ASSOCIATE

Sheryl E. Healy

For full biographical listings, see the Martindale-Hubbell Law Directory

JOHNSON & BELL, LTD. (AV)

Suite 2200, 222 North La Salle Street, 60601
Telephone: 312-372-0770
Facsimile: 312-372-9818
Wheaton, Illinois Office: Suite 1640, 2100 Manchester Road.
Telephone: 708-510-0880.
Facsimile: 780-510-0939.

William V. Johnson
John W. Bell
Jack T. Riley, Jr.
Brian C. Fetzer
Thomas H. Fegan
Thomas W. Murphy
Pamela L. Gellen
Thomas J. Andrews
William G. Beatty
John A. Childers
Robert L. Nora
Margaret A. Unger
Timothy J. McKay
Howard Patrick Morris
Scott W. Hoyne
James S. Stickles, Jr.
Frederick S. Mueller
Joseph R. Marconi
Frederick H. Branding
Robert M. Burke
Cornelius J. Harrington, III
Thomas W. Murphy
Michael B. Gunzburg
Charles W. Planek
Edward D. D'Arcy, Jr.
Debra A. DiMaggio
Michael P. Siavelis
William A. Geiser
Thomas J. Koch
Kurt C. Meihofer
Kevin G. Owens
Steven I. Rapaport
Dennis C. Cusack
Emilio E. Machado
Charles P. Rantis
Dean M. Athans
Robert J. Comfort
Alan Jay Goldstein
Susan Marzec Hannigan
Daniel C. Murray
Thomas F. Poelking

William J. Anaya
Frank S. Capuani
Michael A. Chabraja
Gregory D. Conforti
Larry A. Crotser
Christopher M. Daddino
Jeffrey W. Deer
Maria S. Doughty
Nancy G. Enderby
Patrick T. Garvey
Laura B. Glaser
Kevin J. Greenwood
Sean J. Hardy
Mark D. Johnson
Robert Johnson
Janet A. Kachoyeanos
Mindy L. Kallus
Andrea H. Kott
Genevie F. Labuda
Bruce M. Lichtcsien
Steven E. Lieb
Kathryn K. Loft
Mary E. Lopez
Michael J. Lynch

(See Next Column)

David M. Macksey
Robert J. Malmrose
Robert R. McNamara
Peter A. Nicholson
Eric G. Patt
Richard C. Perna
Brendan S. Power
Marilyn McCabe Reidy
Joseph D. Ryan
Ann M. Smith
Robert Spitkovsky, Jr.
Terry Takash
Paul A. Tanzillo
Kelly N. Warnick
Douglas B. Wexler
Steven F. Wittman

References available upon request.

For full biographical listings, see the Martindale-Hubbell Law Directory

LAW OFFICES KOMIE AND ASSOCIATES (AV)

Suite 3500 Avondale Centre, 20 North Clark Street, 60602-5002
Telephone: 312-263-4383
Fax: 312-263-2803

Stephen M. Komie
Michael T. van der Veen

OF COUNSEL

Douglas W. Godfrey

LEGAL SUPPORT PERSONNEL

Paul J. Ciolino

For full biographical listings, see the Martindale-Hubbell Law Directory

KRALOVEC, MARQUARD, DOYLE & GIBBONS, CHARTERED (AV)

122 South Michigan Avenue, Suite 1720, 60603
Telephone: 312-939-4455
Fax: 312-939-8923
Wheaton, Illinois Office: 211 South Wheaton Avenue, Suite 303.
Telephone: 708-665-9750.
Fax: 708-665-9772.

John C. Doyle
Michael J. Gibbons
Philip W. Domagalski
Michael T. Sprengnether
William E. Spizzirri
Nancy Jo Arnold
Michael J. Mullen
James F. Donovan
David T. Nani

Linda C. Abens
Michael T. Clarke
James V. Creen
Daniel J. Donnelly
Lawrence J. Drabot
Kathleen A. Johnson
Timothy E. Takash
Sara T. Wiggs

OF COUNSEL

Henry J. Marquard
Austin J. Gibbons
Sam L. Miller

Representative Clients: American Mutual Liability Insurance Co.; Mutual of Omaha Insurance Co.; Royal Insurance Cos.; Safeco Insurance Group; United States Fidelity & Guaranty Co.; American Risk Management, Inc.; American States Insurance; American Mutual Insurance Co.; Babcock Industries, Inc.; Banker's Life & Casualty.

For full biographical listings, see the Martindale-Hubbell Law Directory

LAWRENCE, KAMIN, SAUNDERS & UHLENHOP (AV)

208 South La Salle Street, Suite 1750, 60604
Telephone: 312-372-1947
Telecopier: 312-372-2389

MEMBERS OF FIRM

Howard P. Kamin
Raymond E. Saunders
Paul B. Uhlenhop
Kent Lawrence
Robert J. Lawrence
Kenneth S. Perlman
David E. Muschler
Charles J. Risch
Lawrence A. Rosen
Michael Wise
Randall B. Gold

OF COUNSEL

Patricia Brosterhous

ASSOCIATE

David L. Reich

For full biographical listings, see the Martindale-Hubbell Law Directory

MANDEL, LIPTON AND STEVENSON LIMITED (AV)

Suite 2900, 120 North La Salle Street, 60602
Telephone: 312-236-7080
Facsimile: 312-236-0781

Richard L. Mandel
Leonard M. Malkin
R. Peter Carey
Kathleen Roseborough
Richard A. Lifshitz
Terry Yale Feiertag
Kathleen Hogan Morrison
Uve R. Jerzy
Carolyn E. Winter

Audrey L. Gaynor
Goldie C. Domingue

OF COUNSEL

Nicholas Stevenson

(See Next Column)

MANDEL, LIPTON AND STEVENSON LIMITED, *Chicago—Continued*

LEGAL SUPPORT PERSONNEL

Jacqueline Steffens (Paralegal)

References: Northern Trust Co.; American National Bank of Chicago.

For Complete List of Firm Personnel, See General Section

For full biographical listings, see the Martindale-Hubbell Law Directory

MARTIN, BROWN & SULLIVAN, LTD. (AV)

321 South Plymouth Court 10th Floor, 60604
Telephone: 312-360-5000
Fax: 312-360-5026

Royal B. Martin
Steven S. Brown
William G. Sullivan
Leigh D. Roadman

Daniel T. Hartnett
Michael D. Cotton
Robert S. Grabemann
William K. Kane

For full biographical listings, see the Martindale-Hubbell Law Directory

MCANDREWS, HELD & MALLOY, LTD. (AV)

Northwestern Atrium Center Suite 3400, 500 West Madison Street, 60661
Telephone: 312-707-8889
Telecopier: 312-707-9155
Telex: 650-388-1248

George P. McAndrews
John J. Held
Timothy J. Malloy
William M. Wesley
Lawrence M. Jarvis
Robert C. Ryan
Gregory J. Vogler
Jean Dudek Kuelper
Herbert D. Hart III
Robert W. Fieseler
D. David Hill
Thomas J. Wimbiscus
Steven J. Hampton
Alejandro Menchaca
Priscilla F. Gallagher
Stephen F. Sherry
Patrick J. Arnold, Jr.
Robert B. Polit
George Wheeler
Christopher C. Winslade
Edward A. Mas, II
Gregory C. Schodde
John S. Artz
David D. Headrick
Sharon A. Hwang
Phyllis T. Turner Brim
Jeff D. Wheeler

OF COUNSEL

S. Jack Sauer
Donald P. Reynolds

For full biographical listings, see the Martindale-Hubbell Law Directory

BERNARD R. NEVORAL AND ASSOCIATES LTD. (AV)

150 North Wacker Drive, Suite 2450, 60606
Telephone: 312 263-7058
FAX: 312-263-4566

Bernard R. Nevoral

Paul W. Pasche
John L. Malevitis
Maurice E. Dusky

For full biographical listings, see the Martindale-Hubbell Law Directory

NOVACK AND MACEY (AV)

303 West Madison Street, Suite 1500, 60606
Telephone: 312-419-6900
Fax: 312-419-6928

MEMBERS OF FIRM

Bruce E. Braverman
P. Andrew Fleming
Karen Levine
Eric N. Macey
Mitchell L. Marinello
Timothy J. Miller
Stephen Novack
Donald A. Tarkington
Michael A. Weinberg

ASSOCIATES

James E. Bayles, Jr.
Timothy G. Compall
Pauline Levy
Nancy K. Linnerooth
Sandra Raitt
Stephen J. Siegel

OF COUNSEL

Kenneth S. Schlesinger

For full biographical listings, see the Martindale-Hubbell Law Directory

O'BRIEN, O'ROURKE & HOGAN (AV)

135 South La Salle Street, 60603
Telephone: 312-372-1462
Fax: 312-372-8029
Orlando, Florida Office: Moye, O'Brien, O'Rourke, Hogan & Pickert, 201 East Pine Street, Suite 710.
Telephone: 407-843-3341.

(See Next Column)

MEMBERS OF FIRM

William J. Cotter
William T. Dwyer, Jr.
W. Craig Fowler
Michael A. Gilman
Frederic G. Hogan
Gregory R. Meeder
James Elton Moye (Resident at Orlando, Florida Office)
Donald V. O'Brien
John C. O'Rourke, Jr.
Stephen W. Pickert (Resident at Orlando, Florida Office)

OF COUNSEL

William E. McNulty

For full biographical listings, see the Martindale-Hubbell Law Directory

PAVALON & GIFFORD (AV)

Two North La Salle Street, Suite 1600, 60602
Telephone: 312-419-7400
FAX: 312-419-7408
Rockford, Illinois Office: 501 Seventh Street, Suite 501, 61104.
Telephone: 815-968-5100.

MEMBERS OF FIRM

Eugene I. Pavalon
Geoffrey L. Gifford
Gary K. Laatsch
Frank C. Marino

Kathleen A. Russell
Jodi L. Habush
Richard S. Goode

OF COUNSEL

Henry Phillip Gruss

For full biographical listings, see the Martindale-Hubbell Law Directory

POWER ROGERS & SMITH, P.C. (AV)

35 West Wacker Drive, Suite 3700, 60601
Telephone: 312-236-9381
Fax: 312-236-0920

Joseph A. Power, Jr.
Larry R. Rogers
Todd A. Smith
Thomas G. Siracusa
Paul L. Salzetta
Thomas M. Power

Larry R. Rogers, Jr.
Ruth M. Degnan

For full biographical listings, see the Martindale-Hubbell Law Directory

PRETZEL & STOUFFER, CHARTERED (AV)

One South Wacker Drive Suite 2500, 60606-4673
Telephone: 312-346-1973
FAX: 312-346-8242; 346-8060

Gemma B. Allen
Richard William Austin
David M. Bennett
Richard L. Berdelle
Audrey A. Berish
Glen R. Bernfield
Paula Meyer Besler
William B. Bower
Michael G. Bruton
Barbara Condit Canning
Maryanne H. Capron
Robert Marc Chemers
Michael A. Clarke
Elizabeth Conkin
Suzanne Marie Crowley
Jeffery W. Davis
Marilyn Brock Doig
Joseph M. Dooley, III
Matthew J. Egan
Marc I. Fenton
David B. Gelman
Timothy J. Gillick (1940-1984)
Michael D. Goodman
Richard J. Gorman
Joyce M. Greene
Sally Oxley Hagerty
Brian T. Henry
Robert J. Heyne
William E. Kenny
Donald J. Kindwald
James A. Knox, Jr.
Marlene A. Kurilla
James A. LaBarge
Ronald S. Ladden
Steven M. Laduzinsky
Donald B. Lenderman
David J. Loughnane
Patrick Foran Lustig
Steven John Martin
William P. McGowen, III
Daniel B. Mills
James P. Moran
Edward H. Nielsen
Donald J. O'Meara, Jr.
Molly M. O'Reilly
Gary Arthur Peters
Paul L. Price
Neil K. Quinn
Charles F. Redden
Lynn M. Reid
Catherine Coyne Reiter
Mark D. Roth
Roger A. Rubin
Edward B. Ruff, III
Lewis M. Schneider
Betty-Jane Schrum
Alan J. Schumacher
Peter G. Skiko
John V. Smith, II
Christine Hough Speranza
Mark P. Standa
Leo M. Tarpey, Jr.
Robert D. Tuerk
Anthony J. Tunney
Stephen C. Veltman
John J. Walsh, III
Richard M. Waris
Timothy A. Weaver
Michael J. Weber
William P. White III
Richard S. Wisner

OF COUNSEL

Joseph B. Lederleitner
Paul W. Pretzel (1906-1987)
Ralph E. Stouffer, Jr.

Representative Clients: Allstate Insurance Co.; St. Paul Insurance Companies.

For Complete List of Firm Personnel, See General Section

For full biographical listings, see the Martindale-Hubbell Law Directory

Chicago—Continued

ROSENTHAL AND SCHANFIELD, PROFESSIONAL CORPORATION (AV)

46th Floor, Mid Continental Plaza, 55 East Monroe Street, 60603
Telephone: 312-236-5622
Telecopier: 312-236-7274

Joseph A. Baldi
Francis A. Beninati
Martin K. Blonder
Steven H. Blumenthal
David T. Brown
Marvin Cohn
James M. Dash
I. Walter Deitch
Rochelle Secemsky Dyme
Jay Russell Goldberg
David A. Golin
David E. Gordon
William H. Kelly, Jr.
Stephen P. Kikoler
Richard F. Lee
Ira M. Levin
Joel C. Levin
Mark S. Lieberman
Thomas I. Matyas
Henry M. Morris
Gerald B. Mullin
Joseph R. Podlewski, Jr.
Donald A. Robinson
Lester Rosen
Robert O. Rosenman
William P. Rosenthal
Norman L. Rothenbaum
Suzanne M. Soltan
Blooma Stark
Ronald K. Szopa
Michael Viner
Sheri E. Warsh
Mary Prus Wasik
Stanley R. Weinberger
David L. Weinstein

OF COUNSEL

Alex Elson
Richard E. Friedman
Maynard I. Wishner

For Complete List of Firm Personnel, See General Section

For full biographical listings, see the Martindale-Hubbell Law Directory

---

SAUNDERS & MONROE (AV)

Suite 4201, 205 North Michigan Avenue, 60601
Telephone: 312-946-9000
Facsimile: 312-946-0528

MEMBERS OF FIRM

George L. Saunders, Jr.
Lee A. Monroe
Thomas F. Bush, Jr.
Matthew E. Van Tine

Thomas A. Doyle
Christina J. Norton
Gwen A. Niedbalski

For full biographical listings, see the Martindale-Hubbell Law Directory

---

SCARIANO, KULA, ELLCH AND HIMES, CHARTERED (AV)

Two Prudential Plaza 180 North Stetson Suite 3100, 60601-6224
Telephone: 312-565-3100
Facsimile: 312-565-0000
Chicago Heights, Illinois Office: 1450 Aberdeen.
Telephone: 708-755-1900.
Facsimile: 708-755-0000.

Anthony G. Scariano
David P. Kula
Robert H. Ellch
Alan T. Sraga
A. Lynn Himes
Justino D. Petrarca
Lawrence Jay Weiner
Kathleen Field Orr
John M. Izzo
Raymond A. Hauser

OF COUNSEL

Max A. Bailey
G. Robb Cooper
Teri E. Engler
John B. Kralovec

Daniel M. Boyle
Patrick J. Broncato
Sarah R. Carlin
Diane S. Cohen
Jon G. Crawford
Douglas D. Danielson
Anthony Ficarelli
Kelly A. Hayden
Todd K. Hayden
David A. Hemenway
Kathleen Roche Hirsman
Jonathan A. Pearl
Lisa Ann Rapacz
Shelia C. Riley
Joanne W. Schochat

For full biographical listings, see the Martindale-Hubbell Law Directory

---

SCHAFFENEGGER, WATSON & PETERSON, LTD. (AV)

Suite 3504, One East Wacker Drive, 60601-1802
Telephone: 312-527-5566
Fax: 312-527-5540

J. V. Schaffenegger (1914-1986)
Jack L. Watson
Donald G. Peterson
Jay Scott Nelson
Michael A. Strom

James L. McKnight

Reference: American National Bank & Trust Co.

For full biographical listings, see the Martindale-Hubbell Law Directory

PETER R. SONDERBY, P.C. (AV)

135 South La Salle Street Suite 1420, 60603
Telephone: 312-201-0999
Fax: 312-201-0749;
Fax: 312-641-1930

Peter R. Sonderby

For full biographical listings, see the Martindale-Hubbell Law Directory

---

SWANSON, MARTIN & BELL (AV)

One IBM Plaza, Suite 2900, 60611
Telephone: 312-321-9100
Fax: 312-321-0990
Wheaton, Illinois Office: 605 East Roosevelt Road.
Telephone: 708-653-2266.
Fax: 708-653-2292.

MEMBERS OF FIRM

Lenard C. Swanson
Kevin T. Martin
Brian W. Bell
Stanley V. Boychuck
Kay L. Schichtel
David J. Cahill (Resident, Wheaton Office)
Lawrence Helms
Joseph P. Switzer
George F. Fitzpatrick, Jr.
David E. Kawala
Bruce S. Terlep

ASSOCIATES

Kevin V. Boyle
Matthew D. Jacboson
Joseph P. Kincaid
Patricia S. Kocour
Robert J. Meyer
Sheryl A. Pethers
Barbara N. Petrungaro
Aaron T. Shepley
William Blake Weiler

For full biographical listings, see the Martindale-Hubbell Law Directory

---

TRIBLER & ORPETT, A PROFESSIONAL CORPORATION (AV)

30 North La Salle Street, Suite 2200, 60602
Telephone: 312-201-6400
Fax: 312-201-6401

Willis R. Tribler
Mitchell A. Orpett
Douglas C. Crone
Dion J. Sartorio
Janet R. Davis
Philip R. King
Michael J. Meyer
Steven R. McMannon

H. Wesley Sunu
Jean Donath Franke
Panos T. Topalis
John W. Carver
Stanley D. Sterna
David M. Menditto

OF COUNSEL

Daniel D. Drew

For full biographical listings, see the Martindale-Hubbell Law Directory

---

WATT & SAWYIER (AV)

Amalgamated Bank Annex Building, 55 West Van Buren Street, Suite 500, 60605
Telephone: 312-663-1440
Telecopier: 312-663-1410

MEMBERS OF FIRM

Garland W. Watt
Michael T. Sawyier

Representative Clients: First National Bank of Chicago; Chicago Title & Trust Company; North Carolina Mutual Life Insurance Company (Durham, North Carolina); Supreme Life Insurance Company of America; Illinois/Service Federal Savings and Loan Association of Chicago; Sonicraft, Inc.; Universal Casket Company (Cassopolis, Michigan).

For full biographical listings, see the Martindale-Hubbell Law Directory

---

WILLIAMS AND MONTGOMERY, LTD. (AV)

20 North Wacker Drive Suite 2100, 60606
Telephone: 312-443-3200
Telex: 206598
Facsimile: 312-443-1323
Waukegan, Illinois Office: 33 North County Street.
Telephone: 708-360-1220.
Wheaton, Illinois Office: 310 S. County Farm Road.
Telephone: 708-690-3200.
Joliet, Illinois Office: 81 North Chicago Avenue.
Telephone: 815-727-2653.
Miami, Florida Office: Williams, Montgomery & Thompson, Ltd., 25 Southeast Second Avenue.
Telephone: 305-373-7611.
Facsimile: 305-358-1251.

Lloyd E. Williams, Jr.
C. Barry Montgomery
Barry L. Kroll
Thomas H. Neuckranz
Anthony P. Katauskas
David E. Morgans
Craig A. Tomassi
Nunzio C. Radogno
Anthony J. Kiselis
Edward J. Murphy
Alton C. Haynes
James K. Horstman
Patrick F. Klunder
David E. Stevenson

(See Next Column)

WILLIAMS AND MONTGOMERY LTD., *Chicago—Continued*

Michael R. La Barge
Kevin Campbell
David P. Boyd
Rodney E. VanAusdal
Lori E. Iwan
Lawrence K. Rynning
Jeffrey H. Lipe
Bruce W. Lyon
Thomas F. Cameli
Manya A. Pastalan Grant
Michael D. Huber

OF COUNSEL

Robert D. McHugh

Lawrence A. Szymanski
Walter S. Calhoun
Gregory J. Bird
Mary Anne Sliwinski
Thomas J. Pontikis
Mark J. Vogg
Brigid E. Kennedy
Perry W. Hoag
Mark R. Misiorowski
Peter J. Szatkowski
Douglas A. Miller
Hall Adams, III
Stephen W. Heil
Thomas J. Popovich
Edward R. Moor
Michael J. Pacer
J. Calvin Downing, III
David E. Neumeister
Sheila M. Reilly
Mark D. Brent
Shimon B. Kahan
Jennifer M. Lundy
Mark E. Winters
Brian J. Hunt
Amy McKeever Toman
Bradley C. Nahrstadt
Charles D. Stone
Brian W. Troglia
Karen M. Talty
Elizabeth Felt Wakeman
Edward O. Pacer
Ralph J. Kooy
Gregory W. Beihl
Douglas W. Lohmar, Jr.

For full biographical listings, see the Martindale-Hubbell Law Directory

WILSON & MCILVAINE (AV)

500 West Madison, Suite 3700, 60661-2511
Telephone: 312-715-5000
Telecopier: 312-715-5155

John P. Wilson (1867-1922)
Wm. B. McIlvaine (1888-1943)

PARTNERS

C. John Anderson
Walter W. Bell
Cynthia A. Bergmann
Richard P. Blessen
Thomas E. Chomicz
Michael F. Csar
Thomas G. Draths
Carrie A. Durkin
Robert F. Forrer
James J. Gatziolis
Douglas R. Hoffman
Richard L. Horn
Jerry D. Jones
Gary H. Kline
Sarah M. Linsley
Thomas J. Magill
Daniel C. McKay
Kendall R. Meyer
Dennis J. O'Hara
Dwight B. Palmer, Jr.
Thomas A. Polachek
John J. Quinlisk
Janice E. Rodgers
Peter A. Sarasek
Quinton F. Seamons
Stephanie B. Shellenback
Leonard S. Shifflett
Steven A. Smith
Alexander Terras
John P. Vail
Brian J. Wanca

ASSOCIATES

Cynthia J. Barnes
Patrick J. Bitterman
Marie K. Eitrheim
Timothy S. Harris
William T. McCormick
Alison L. Paul
Anne S. Quinn
Todd A. Rowden
David S. Schaffer, Jr.
Clinton J. Wesolik

OF COUNSEL

Charles W. Boand
Kent Chandler, Jr.
Frank A. Reichelderfer
Kenneth F. Montgomery
Vernon T. Squires

For full biographical listings, see the Martindale-Hubbell Law Directory

*DANVILLE,** Vermilion Co.

GUNN & HICKMAN, P.C. (AV)

220 North Vermilion Street, P.O. Box 706, 61832
Telephone: 217-446-0880
Fax: 217-442-3901

John B. Jenkins
James L. Brougher
Fred L. Hubbard
Michael C. Upperman, Jr.

OF COUNSEL

Robert Z. Hickman

Representative Clients: Insurance Company of North America (INA); Ranger Insurance Co.; ESIS Risk Management; Carolina Casualty Co.; Providence Washington Insurance Group; CNA Insurance Co.; First Midwest Bank/-Danville and Foremost Insurance Group; CIGNA Insurance Cos.; The Prudential Insurance Co.

For Complete List of Firm Personnel, See General Section

For full biographical listings, see the Martindale-Hubbell Law Directory

HUTTON, LAURY, HESSER, LIETZ & WILCOX (AV)

16 West Madison Street, P.O. Box 1128, 61832
Telephone: 217-446-9436
FAX: 217-446-9462

(See Next Column)

MEMBERS OF FIRM

Everett L. Laury
Gary D. Hesser
Gregory G. Lietz
Roy G. Wilcox

Representative Clients: Pekin Insurance; Prudential Insurance Company; Metropolitan Life Insurance Company; Illinois State Medical Insurance Services, Inc.; Associated Physicians Insurance Company; Employers Reinsurance Corp.; Northwestern National Insurance Company; St. Paul Insurance Companies; Clarendon National Insurance Company; General Motors Corporation.

For Complete List of Firm Personnel, See General Section

For full biographical listings, see the Martindale-Hubbell Law Directory

SEBAT, SWANSON, BANKS, GARMAN & TOWNSLEY (AV)

139 North Vermilion, 61832
Telephone: 217-443-0255
Fax: 217-443-0263

MEMBERS OF FIRM

Walter J. Grant (1874-1962)
Paul F. Jones (1898-1953)
John E. Sebat (Retired)
Ralph J. Swanson
Robert J. Banks, Jr.
Gill M. Garman
William L. Townsley
Randall P. Ray
Arthur J. Kapella

ASSOCIATE

Kristin R. Solberg

Representative Clients: Allied Chemical Co.; First Savings & Loan Assn.; Crows Hybrid Corn Co.; Missouri Pacific Railroad; Argonaut Insurance Co.; Ohio Casualty Co.; Liberty Mutual Insurance Co.; St. Paul-Mercury; U. S. F. & G. Co.; Zurich Insurance Group.

For full biographical listings, see the Martindale-Hubbell Law Directory

*DECATUR,** Macon Co.

ERICKSON, DAVIS, MURPHY, GRIFFITH & WALSH, LTD. (AV)

Suite 200, 225 South Main Street, P.O. Box 25138, 62525-5138
Telephone: 217-428-0948
FAX: 217-428-0996

Frederick P. Erickson
Garry E. Davis
W. Scott Murphy
Thomas E. Griffith
Michael A. Walsh

Representative Clients: American Family Insurance Company; Commercial Union Insurance Company; General Casualty Insurance Company; Great Central Insurance Company; Illinois State Medical Insurance Services; Nationwide Insurance Company; Ohio Casualty Insurance Company; Armstrong-Pirelli Tire; Proctor & Gamble Company; Transamerica Insurance Group.

For Complete List of Firm Personnel, See General Section

For full biographical listings, see the Martindale-Hubbell Law Directory

TENNEY & TENNEY (AV)

1264 First of America Center, P.O. Box 355, 62525
Telephone: 217-423-1800
Fax: 217-423-0524

MEMBERS OF FIRM

Harold F. Tenney
Carl J. Tenney

Representative Client: The Travelers Insurance Companies: Design Professional Insurance Company (DPIC Companies); Shelter Insurance Companies; Right Recreation, Inc.; Lucas Meyer, Inc. (lecithin products); Miles Chevrolet, Inc.; Crown Oldsmobile-Toyota, Inc.; Bob Brady Dodge, Inc.; Sims Lumber Company; Heinkel's Packing Co., Inc.

For full biographical listings, see the Martindale-Hubbell Law Directory

*EDWARDSVILLE,** Madison Co.

LUCCO BROWN & MUDGE (AV)

224 St. Louis Street, P.O. Box 539, 62025
Telephone: 618-656-2321
FAX: 618-656-2363

Dick H. Mudge, Jr. (1919-1978)
J. William Lucco
Joseph R. Brown, Jr.
William A. Mudge

Reference: Bank of Edwardsville, Edwardsville, Illinois.

For full biographical listings, see the Martindale-Hubbell Law Directory

REED, ARMSTRONG, GORMAN, COFFEY, THOMSON, GILBERT & MUDGE, PROFESSIONAL CORPORATION (AV)

One Mark Twain Plaza, Suite 300, P.O. Box 368, 62025
Telephone: 618-656-0257; 656-2244
Facsimile: 618-692-4416
Other Edwardsville Office: 125 North Buchanan.
Telephone: 618-656-2244.
Fax: 618-658-1307.

(See Next Column)

REED, ARMSTRONG, GORMAN, COFFEY, THOMSON, GILBERT & MUDGE PROFESSIONAL CORPORATION—*Continued*

Springfield, Illinois Office: One West Old State Capital Plaza, Suite 400, Myers Building.
Telephone: 217-525-1366.
Fax: 217-525-0986.

James L. Reed (Retired)
Harry C. Armstrong
James E. Gorman
Gary R. Coffey
Stephen W. Thomson
John L. Gilbert
Stephen C. Mudge
Charles C. Compton
Martin K. Morrissey

Debra J. Meadows
Kevin J. Babb
Richard J. Behr
Michael J. Bedesky
Rodney W. Phillipe
Mitchell B. Stoddard
David Laurent
Gregory W. Coffey
Bryan L. Skelton

Representative Clients: State Farm Insurance Cos.; Country Companies; Standard Mutual Casualty Co.; General Casualty Company of Wisconsin; Western States Mutual Insurance Co.; Hawkeye-Security Insurance Co.; Shelter Insurance Co.; New Hampshire Insurance Group; Heritage Insurance Co.; Southern Illinois University of Edwardsville.

For full biographical listings, see the Martindale-Hubbell Law Directory

FAIRVIEW HEIGHTS, St. Clair Co.

KEEFE & DEPAULI, P.C. (AV)

2 Executive Drive, P.O. Box 3190, 62208
Telephone: 618-624-2444
Fax: 618-624-6031

Thomas Q. Keefe
Frank E. DePauli
William L. Rogers
Thomas H. Kuergeleis
James K. Keefe

William L. Hanks
William Lemp
Andrew T. Nalefski
Kevin M. Hazlett
Patrick M. Keefe
Richard H. Risse
Dennis O. Douglas
Scott A. White
Darren K. Short

Reference: Magna Bank.

For full biographical listings, see the Martindale-Hubbell Law Directory

GRANITE CITY, Madison Co.

BERNARD & DAVIDSON (AV)

3600 Nameoki Road, 62040
Telephone: 618-452-6100
Telecopier: 618-451-2051
St. Louis, Missouri Office: 314 N. Broadway.
Telephone: 314-231-4181.

MEMBERS OF FIRM

Joseph R. Davidson
Ronald A. Roth
David L. Antognoli

ASSOCIATES

Mervin W. Warren, Jr.
Gary L. Smith
Peter M. Gannott

A list of Representative Clients will be furnished upon request.

For Complete List of Firm Personnel, See General Section

For full biographical listings, see the Martindale-Hubbell Law Directory

*HARRISBURG,** Saline Co.

JELLIFFE, FERRELL & MORRIS (AV)

108 East Walnut Street, 62946
Telephone: 618-253-7153; 253-7647
Telecopier: 618-252-1843

OF COUNSEL

Charles R. Jelliffe

MEMBERS OF FIRM

DeWitt Twente (1904-1976)
Donald V. Ferrell
Walden E. Morris

ASSOCIATES

Michal Doerge
Thomas J. Foster
Timothy L. Fornes

Representative Clients: Auto-Owners Insurance; Country Cos; Metropolitan Life Insurance; Ohio Casualty Group; Standard Mutual Insurance Co.; State Farm Cos.; Redland Insurance Co.; Aetna Casualty & Surety Co.; Kerr-McGee Coal Corp.; Sahara Coal Co.

For full biographical listings, see the Martindale-Hubbell Law Directory

*JOLIET,** Will Co.

MCKEOWN, FITZGERALD, ZOLLNER, BUCK, HUTCHISON & RUTTLE (AV)

2455 Glenwood Avenue, 60435
Telephone: 815-729-4800
FAX: 815-729-4711
Frankfort, Illinois Office: 28 Kansas Street.
Telephone: 815-469-2176.
FAX: 815-469-0295.

MEMBERS OF FIRM

Charles J. McKeown (1908-1985)
Paul O. McKeown (1913-1982)
Richard T. Buck (1936-1992)
Joseph C. Fitzgerald
Max E. Zollner
Douglas P. Hutchison
David L. Ruttle
Theodore J. Jarz
Douglas J. McKeown
Timothy J. Rathbun
James B. Harvey
Kenneth A. Grey
Michael R. Lucas

ASSOCIATES

Christopher N. Wise
Gary S. Mueller
Frank S. Cservenyak, Jr.
William P Mullarkey
Arthur J. Wilhelmi

OF COUNSEL

Stewart C. Hutchison

Representative Clients: Caterpillar Tractor Co.; First National Bank of Lockport; Homart Development Co.; First Midwest Bank, N.A.; Silver Cross Hospital; Joliet Township High School District; Villages of: Plainfield and Mokena; Southwest Agency for Risk Management; Joliet Junior College Foundation; Health Service Systems, Inc.

For full biographical listings, see the Martindale-Hubbell Law Directory

*KANKAKEE,** Kankakee Co.

ACKMAN, MAREK, BOYD & SIMUTIS, LTD. (AV)

Suite 400, One Dearborn Square, 60901
Telephone: 815-933-6681
FAX: 815-933-9985
Watseka, Illinois Office: 123 South Fourth Street.
Telephone: 815-432-5215.
FAX: 815-432-3186.
Gilman, Illinois Office: 201 S. Crescent.
Telephone: 815-265-4533.

Richard L. Ackman
J. Dennis Marek
Robert W. Boyd
Frank J. Simutis (Watseka and Gilman Offices)
Deborah A. Woodruff

James A. Devine
Jack L. Haan

Representative Clients: American States Insurance Co.; Auto Owners Insurance Co.; Country Mutual Insurance Co.; Farmers Insurance Group; Hartford Accident & Indemnity Co.; Kankakee Water Co.; Medical Protective Co.; State Farm Insurance Co.; Watseka First National Bank; Economy Fire & Casualty Co.

For full biographical listings, see the Martindale-Hubbell Law Directory

*LAWRENCEVILLE,** Lawrence Co.

GOSNELL, BORDEN & ENLOE, LTD. (AV)

815 12th Street, P.O. Box 737, 62439-0737
Telephone: 618-943-2338
Fax: 618-943-2080

John F. Borden
Douglas A. Enloe

Representative Clients: Aetna Casualty & Surety Co.; Bituminous Casualty Co.; Country Mutual Insurance Co.; Hartford Accident & Indemnity Co.; Liberty Mutual Insurance Co.; State Farm Insurance Co.; First Bank of Lawrence County, N.A.; Peoples National Bank in Lawrenceville; Texaco, Inc.

For Complete List of Firm Personnel, See General Section

For full biographical listings, see the Martindale-Hubbell Law Directory

MATTOON, Coles Co.

CRAIG & CRAIG (AV)

1807 Broadway, P.O. Box 689, 61938-0689
Telephone: 217-234-6481
Telecopier: 217-234-6486
Mount Vernon, Illinois Office: 227 1/2 South 9th Street.
Telephone: 618-244-7511.

MEMBERS OF FIRM

John H. Armstrong
John P. Ewart
Richard F. Record, Jr.
Stephen L. Corn
Richard Charles Hayden
Robert G. Grierson
Gregory C. Ray
Paul R. Lynch (Resident, Mount Vernon Office)
Kenneth F. Werts (Resident, Mount Vernon Office)
John L. Barger
James M. Dion

(See Next Column)

CRAIG & CRAIG, *Mattoon—Continued*

ASSOCIATES

Mark R. Karpus
Beverly J. Ring
Joshua N. Rosen (Resident, Mount Vernon Office)
Kathleen M. Kattner

OF COUNSEL

Jack E. Horsley

Representative Clients: Zeigler Coal Co.; Marathon Oil Co.; Illinois Central Railroad Co.; Okaw Building & Loan Association; Travelers Insurance Co.; The Medical Protective Co.; Lloyds Underwriters at London; Aetna Life & Casualty Insurance Co.; Scattering Fork Drainage District of Douglas, Illinois; Mattoon Township Park District of Coles County, Illinois.

For Complete List of Firm Personnel, See General Section

For full biographical listings, see the Martindale-Hubbell Law Directory

HELLER, HOLMES & ASSOCIATES, P.C. (AV)

1101 Broadway, P.O. Box 889, 61938-0889
Telephone: 217-235-2700
FAX: 217-235-0743

Harlan Heller
Brent D. Holmes
H. Kent Heller
Mitchell K. Shick

Teresa K. Righter
Rodney L. Smith
Maria C. Dunn
Matthew P. Garland
William R. Tapella

Representative Clients: Quantum Chemical Co.; First National Bank of Effingham.
References: First National Bank, Mattoon, Ill.; Central National Bank of Mattoon.

For full biographical listings, see the Martindale-Hubbell Law Directory

RYAN, BENNETT & RADLOFF (AV)

300 Richmond East, P.O. Box 629, 61938-0629
Telephone: 217-234-2000
Fax: 217-234-2001

MEMBERS OF FIRM

James A. Bennett
Stephen R. Ryan
Michael D. Ryan
Michael K. Radloff
Christopher A. Koester
Brien J. O'Brien

Counsel For: State Farm Insurance Cos.; American States Insurance Co.; Auto-Owners Insurance Co.; Country Cos.; Economy Fire and Casualty Co.; Bituminous Insurance Cos.; Farmland Insurance; Millers Mutual Insurance; Horace Mann Insurance Co.
Reference: First Mid-Illinois Bank & Trust, Mattoon, Ill.

For Complete List of Firm Personnel, See General Section

For full biographical listings, see the Martindale-Hubbell Law Directory

*MOUNT CARROLL,** Carroll Co.

LEEMON, WEINSTINE, SHIRK & MELLOTT (AV)

102 1/2 East Market Street, P.O. Box 112, 61053
Telephone: 815-244-3422
Fax: 815-244-3900
Weinstine, Shirk, Mellott & Leemon: 301 East Main Street, Morrison, Illinois, 61270.
Telephone: 815-772-7211.
Fax: 815-772-4599.

MEMBERS OF FIRM

John A. Leemon
Lester S. Weinstine
William R. Shirk
Michael A. Mellott

Representative Clients: First State Bank of Shannon, Shannon, Ill.; Savanna State Bank; Farm Credit Bank of St. Louis; Mt. Carroll Mutual Fire Insurance Co.; Country Mutual Insurance Co.

For full biographical listings, see the Martindale-Hubbell Law Directory

*MOUNT VERNON,** Jefferson Co.

CAMPBELL, BLACK, CARNINE & HEDIN, P.C. (AV)

P.O. Drawer C, 62864
Telephone: 618-242-3310
Fax: 618-242-3735

David A. Campbell
Terry R. Black
Roy L. Carnine
Craig R. Hedin
Mark J. Ballard
Jerome E. McDonald
Carl L. Favreau
Howard W. Campbell (1911-1980)
John E. Jacobsen (1922-1985)
Glenn E. Moore (1911-1991)
David E. Furnall (1905-1993)

Fred R. Mann

Representative Clients: Kerr-McGee Coal Corp.; Good Samaritan Hospital; Country Mutual Insurance Co.; Southern Illinois Stone Co; Rend Lake Conservancy District; King City Federal Savings Bank; Consolidation Coal Co.;

(See Next Column)

Illinois State Medical Insurance Services; State Farm Automobile Insurance Co.; John Hancock Mutual Life Insurance Co.

For full biographical listings, see the Martindale-Hubbell Law Directory

OAK BROOK, Du Page Co.

BOTTI, MARINACCIO & TAMELING, LTD. (AV)

720 Enterprise Drive, 60521
Telephone: 708-573-8585
Fax: 708-573-8586
Wheaton, Illinois Office: Suite 401 The Ticor Title Building, 330 Naperville Road.
Telephone: 708-653-2100.

Aldo E. Botti
Stephen R. Botti
Andrew Y. Acker
Carlo F. Cavallaro
Peter M. DeLongis
Terry W. Huebner
Lee A. Marinaccio
Ronald D. Menna
Mark W. Salkeld
Eva W. Tameling
Peter M. Tumminaro
Frank J. Wesolowski

For full biographical listings, see the Martindale-Hubbell Law Directory

*OREGON,** Ogle Co.

WILLIAMS & McCARTHY, A PROFESSIONAL CORPORATION (AV)

607 Washington Street, P.O. Box 339, 61061
Telephone: 815-732-2101
Fax: 815-732-2289
Rockford, Illinois Office: 321 West State Street, P.O. Box 219.
Telephone: 815-987-8900.
Fax: 815-968-0019. ABANET: ABA 5519.

Kim D. Krahenbuhl
Clayton L. Lindsey
Wendy S. Howarter

Representative Clients: Anderson Industries, Inc.; Liberty Mutual Insurance Co.; Atwood Industries, Inc.; The Travelers; American Mutual Insurance Co.; Rockford Memorial Hospital; Chrysler Corp.

For full biographical listings, see the Martindale-Hubbell Law Directory

*PEORIA,** Peoria Co.

CASSIDY & MUELLER (AV)

1510 First Financial Plaza, 61602
Telephone: 309-676-0591
FAX: 309-676-8036

MEMBERS OF FIRM

John E. Cassidy (1896-1984)
John E. Cassidy, Jr.
David B. Mueller
John E. Cassidy, III
Timothy J. Cassidy
Timothy J. Newlin

ASSOCIATE

Andrew D. Cassidy

Representative Clients: Aetna Casualty & Surety Co.; Dow Corning, Inc.; E.I. DuPont-DeNemours & Company; Economy Fire & Casualty Co.; Hartford Insurance Group; Liberty Mutual Insurance Co.; St. Paul Fire and Casualty; Warner-Lambert Company; Squibb & Sons, Inc.; Parke Davis Company; Merrell Dow Pharmaceuticals, Inc.; The Upjohn Company.

For full biographical listings, see the Martindale-Hubbell Law Directory

KAVANAGH, SCULLY, SUDOW, WHITE & FREDERICK, P.C. (AV)

301 S.W. Adams Street, Suite 700, 61602
Telephone: 309-676-1381
FAX: 309-676-0324

Julian E. Cannell
Charles G. Roth
David J. Dubicki
Phillip B. Lenzini
Douglas S. Slayton
James W. Springer
Mark W. Marlott
Michael A. Kraft

Counsel for: First of America Bank - Illinois, N.A.; Farm Credit Bank of St. Louis; Construction Equipment Federal Credit Union; Travelers Insurance Co.; Phoenix Mutual Life Insurance Co.; United States Fidelity & Guaranty Co.; Equitable Life Assurance Society of the U.S.; The Pleasure Driveway and Park District of Peoria; Board of Education of the City of Peoria School District, 150; Anderson State Bank.

For Complete List of Firm Personnel, See General Section

For full biographical listings, see the Martindale-Hubbell Law Directory

KINGERY DURREE WAKEMAN & RYAN, ASSOC. (AV)

915 Commerce Bank Building, 61602
Telephone: 309-676-3612
FAX: 309-676-1329

Arthur R. Kingery
Edward R. Durree
Steven A. Wakeman
Christopher P. Ryan
Lindsay W. Wright
Craig J. Reiser

(See Next Column)

KINGERY DURREE WAKEMAN & RYAN ASSOC.—*Continued*

Reference: Commerce Bank of Peoria.

For full biographical listings, see the Martindale-Hubbell Law Directory

QUINN, JOHNSTON, HENDERSON & PRETORIUS, CHARTERED (AV)

(Formerly McConnell, Kennedy, Quinn & Johnston)
227 N. E. Jefferson Street, 61602
Telephone: 309-674-1133
Telecopier: 309-674-6503
Springfield, Illinois Office: Three North, Old State Capitol Plaza, 62701.
Telephone: 217-753-1133.

W. Thomas Johnston
R. Michael Henderson
Murvel Pretorius, Jr.
Bradley W. Dunham
Robert H. Jennetten
Charles D. Knell
Gregory A. Cerulo
Paul P. Gilfillan
John P. Fleming
Mary W. McDade
Stephen P. Kelly

Jeanne L. Wysocki
Joseph J. Bembenek, Jr.

Representative Clients: Allstate Insurance Co.; American International Group; Bituminous Insurance Co.; City of Peoria; General Motors; Illinois State Medical Insurance Services, Inc.; Pekin Insurance; Peoria Journal Star, Inc.; St. Paul Insurance Co.

For Complete List of Firm Personnel, See General Section

For full biographical listings, see the Martindale-Hubbell Law Directory

ROBERT C. STRODEL, LTD. (AV)

927 Commerce Bank Building, 61602
Telephone: 309-676-4500
Fax: 309-676-4566

Robert C. Strodel

For full biographical listings, see the Martindale-Hubbell Law Directory

WINGET & KANE (AV)

807 Commerce Bank Building, 61602
Telephone: 309-674-2310
Fax: 309-674-9722

Walter W. Winget
James F. Kane

Representative Clients: National Hampshire Swine Registry; Davison-Fulton Ltd.
References: Commerce Bank; Bank One - Peoria.

For full biographical listings, see the Martindale-Hubbell Law Directory

PERU, La Salle Co.

ANTHONY C. RACCUGLIA & ASSOCIATES (AV)

1200 Maple Drive, 61354
Telephone: 815-223-0230
Ottawa, Illinois Office: 633 La Salle Street.
Telephone: 815-434-2003.

ASSOCIATES

James A. McPhedran
Louis L. Bertrand

References: La Salle National Bank; Citizens First National Bank of Peru, Illinois.

For full biographical listings, see the Martindale-Hubbell Law Directory

*QUINCY,** Adams Co.

SCHMIEDESKAMP, ROBERTSON, NEU & MITCHELL (AV)

525 Jersey, P.O. Box 1069, 62306
Telephone: 217-223-3030
Telecopier: 217-223-1005

MEMBERS OF FIRM

Delmer R. Mitchell, Jr.
Jonathan H. Barnard
Mark A. Drummond
Gena J. Awerkamp

Representative Clients: Mercantile Trust & Savings Bank; Moorman Manufacturing Co.; Travelers Insurance Co.; Hartford Accident & Indemnity Co.; Aetna Casualty & Surety Co.; Knapheide Mfg. Co.; Harris Corp.; Bituminous Casualty Corp.; Quincy Compressor Division of Colt Industries, Inc.

For Complete List of Firm Personnel, See General Section

For full biographical listings, see the Martindale-Hubbell Law Directory

*ROCKFORD,** Winnebago Co.

HALDEMAN & ASSOCIATES (AV)

200 Pioneer Centre, 303 North Main Street, 61101
Telephone: 815-965-8840
Fax: 815-965-8355

(See Next Column)

Richard R. Haldeman

ASSOCIATE

Michael J. Hedeen

Representative Clients: Pioneer Life Insurance Company of Illinois, Rockford, Ill.; E.D. Etnyre & Co., Rockford, ILL.

For full biographical listings, see the Martindale-Hubbell Law Directory

RENO, ZAHM, FOLGATE, LINDBERG & POWELL (AV)

Camelot Tower, 1415 East State Street, 61104
Telephone: 815-987-4050
FAX: 815-987-4092

Robert A. Fredrickson
Jack D. Ward
Jan H. Ohlander

Representative Clients: Amcore Bank N.A., Rockford; HomeBanc; Amerock Corp.; Elco Industries, Inc.; Rockford Division of Borg-Warner Corp.; Roper Whitney Inc.; Cherry Valley and North Park Fire Protection Districts; Firemen's Fund-American; Kemper; U.S.F. & G.; Traveler's; Crum & Forster.

For Complete List of Firm Personnel, See General Section

For full biographical listings, see the Martindale-Hubbell Law Directory

WILLIAMS & MCCARTHY, A PROFESSIONAL CORPORATION (AV)

321 West State Street, P.O. Box 219, 61105-0219
Telephone: 815-987-8900
Fax: 815-968-0019 ABANET: ABA 5519
Oregon, Illinois Office: 607 Washington Street. P.O. Box 339.
Telephone: 815-732-2101.
Fax: 815-732-2289.

John R. Kinley
Elmer C. Rudy
Thomas S. Johnson
Edward R. Telling, III
Russell D. Anderson
John E. Pfau
Richard A. Berman
John W. Rosenbloom
John W. France
John L. Shepherd
Terry D. Anderson
Kim D. Krahenbuhl (Resident Partner, Oregon, Illinois Office)
Scott C. Sullivan
Carol H. Hallock
Jane E. Durgom-Powers
James P. Devine
J. Mark Doherty
John J. Holevas
Timothy J. Rollins

Stephen E. Balogh
Robert E. Luedke
Marc C. Gravino
Thomas P. Sandquist
Carl A. Ecklund
Wendy S. Howarter (Resident, Oregon, Illinois Office)
Ronald A. Barch

OF COUNSEL

John C. McCarthy

Representative Clients: Anderson Industries, Inc.; Liberty Mutual Insurance Co.; Atwood Industries, Inc.; The Travelers; American Mutual Insurance Co.; Rockford Memorial Hospital; Chrysler Corp.; USF&G, West Bend.

For Complete List of Firm Personnel, See General Section

For full biographical listings, see the Martindale-Hubbell Law Directory

*ROCK ISLAND,** Rock Island Co.

KATZ, MCANDREWS, BALCH, LEFSTEIN & FIEWEGER, P.C. (AV)

200 Plaza Office Building, 1705 Second Avenue, P.O. Box 3250, 61204-3250
Telephone: 309-788-5661
Facsimile: 309-788-5688

Stuart R. Lefstein
Martin H. Katz
Peter C. Fieweger
Robert T. Park
Samuel S. McHard
Dale G. Haake
Linda E. Frischmeyer
John A. Hoekstra
Brian S. Nelson
Stephen T. Fieweger

Attorneys for: Roy E. Roth Co.; Augustana College.
Local Attorneys for: Aetna Casualty & Surety Co.; Maryland Casualty Co.; Liberty Mutual Insurance Co.; CIGNA Cos.; Country Mutual Insurance Co.; Cincinnati Insurance Co.

For Complete List of Firm Personnel, See General Section

For full biographical listings, see the Martindale-Hubbell Law Directory

WINSTEIN, KAVENSKY & WALLACE (AV)

4th Floor, Rock Island Bank Building, 224 18th Street, P.O. Box 4298, 61201
Telephone: 309-794-1515; 800-747-1527
FAX: 309-794-9929

MEMBERS OF FIRM

Stewart R. Winstein
Harrison H. Kavensky
Franklin S. Wallace
Craig L. Kavensky

(See Next Column)

WINSTEIN, KAVENSKY & WALLACE, *Rock Island—Continued*

John Allan Hartsock
James H. Schultz (Not admitted in IL)
Arthur R. Winstein
David L. Cunningham
Christine A. Hunter-Keys
Brett Andrew Nelson

Local Regional Counsel for: United Auto Workers.
Reference: First National Bank of Quad Cities.

For full biographical listings, see the Martindale-Hubbell Law Directory

*SPRINGFIELD,** Sangamon Co.

GIFFIN, WINNING, COHEN & BODEWES, P.C. (AV)

1 West Old State Capitol Plaza, Suite 600 Myers Building, P.O. Box 2117, 62705
Telephone: 217-525-1571
Facsimile: 217-525-1710

Carol Hansen Fines
R. Mark Mifflin
Thomas P. Schanzle-Haskins, III
Gregory K. Harris

Representative Clients: Illinois Municipal League Risk Management Association; Alliance of American Insurers; Board of Regents of Regency Universities; Allstate Insurance Co.; Grinnell Mutual Reinsurance Company; Horace Mann Insurance Company; Ohio Casualty Insurance Company; Transamerica Insurance Company; Associated Beer Distributors of Illinois Risk Management Association.

For Complete List of Firm Personnel, See General Section

For full biographical listings, see the Martindale-Hubbell Law Directory

METNICK, WISE, CHERRY & FRAZIER (AV)

Fourth Floor, Myers Building, 1 West Old State Capitol Plaza, P.O. Box 12140, 62791
Telephone: 217-753-4242
Telefax: 217-753-4642

MEMBERS OF FIRM

Michael B. Metnick
D. Peter Wise
Richard D. Frazier

ASSOCIATE

Frederick J. Schlosser

For full biographical listings, see the Martindale-Hubbell Law Directory

*VANDALIA,** Fayette Co.

BURNSIDE DEES JOHNSTON & CHOISSER (AV)

First National Bank Building, 62471
Telephone: 618-283-3260
FAX: 618-283-2851

MEMBERS OF FIRM

J. G. Burnside (1873-1969)
Robert G. Burnside
Joe Dees
Jack B. Johnston
Dale F. Choisser

General Counsel for: The First National Bank of Vandalia; The First State Bank of St. Peter; State Bank of Farina; S&S Urethane, Inc.
Local Counsel for: Pekin Insurance Co.

For full biographical listings, see the Martindale-Hubbell Law Directory

*WAUKEGAN,** Lake Co.

DIVER, GRACH, QUADE & MASINI (AV)

First Federal Savings and Loan Building, 111 North County Street, 60085
Telephone: 708-662-8611
FAX: 708-662-2960

MEMBERS OF FIRM

Clarence W. Diver (1883-1962)
Thomas W. Diver
Brian S. Grach
David R. Quade
Robert J. Masini
Sarah P. Lessman

Heidi J. Aavang
Donna-Jo Rodden Vorderstrasse

A list of Representative Clients will be furnished upon request.
Reference: First Midwest Bank of Waukegan.

For full biographical listings, see the Martindale-Hubbell Law Directory

*WHEATON,** Du Page Co.

DONOVAN & ROBERTS, P.C. (AV)

104 East Roosevelt Road, Suite 202, P.O. Box 417, 60189-0417
Telephone: 708-668-4211
Fax: 708-668-2076

Keith E. Roberts, Sr.
Keith E. (Chuck) Roberts, Jr.
Robert R. Verchota
James J. Konetski

(See Next Column)

Marie F. Leach
Mark J. Lyons
Andrew L. Dryjanski
Robert M. Skutt
Robert J. Lentz
Rosemarie Calandra

For full biographical listings, see the Martindale-Hubbell Law Directory

O'REILLY, CUNNINGHAM, NORTON & MANCINI, PROFESSIONAL CORPORATION (AV)

109 North Hale Street, P.O. Box 846, 60189
Telephone: 708-668-9440
FAX: 708-668-9489
Chicago, Illinois Office: 111 West Washington Street, Suite 850.
Telephone: 312-807-4999.
FAX: 312-807-4998.

Roger K. O'Reilly
William F. Cunningham
John E. Norton
Lorenzo A. Mancini
Patricia L. Argentati
Thomas R. Weiler
James L. DeAno

Mark C. Meyer
Thomas J. Long
Kevin J. Vedrine
Denis K. Sheehan
Ian R. Stevenson
Robert J. Cap
Maura S. Weidner
Sandra Wright
Craig D. Queen
Jonathan S. Gunn
Harry E. Bartosiak

OF COUNSEL

William E. Corrigan
Adrianna K. Liber

Representative Clients: Aetna Life & Casualty; Allstate Insurance Company; Chicago Motor Club Insurance Company; County of DuPage; CNA Insurance Company; The Doctors' Company; Hartford Insurance Company; Illinois State Medical Insurance Services, Inc.; St. Paul Insurance Company; Wausau Insurance Companies.

For full biographical listings, see the Martindale-Hubbell Law Directory

*WOODSTOCK,** McHenry Co.

THEODORE A. E. POEHLMANN (AV)

205 East South Street, P.O. Box 271, 60098-0271
Telephone: 815-337-3337
Fax: 815-337-3340

ASSOCIATE

Dona S. Lowrimore

For full biographical listings, see the Martindale-Hubbell Law Directory

INDIANA

*BEDFORD,** Lawrence Co.

STEELE, STEELE, MCSOLEY & MCSOLEY (AV)

Bank One Building, Suite One, 1602 I Street, 47421
Telephone: 812-279-3513
Fax: 812-275-3504

MEMBERS OF FIRM

Byron W. Steele
Brent E. Steele
Patrick S. McSoley
Darlene Steele McSoley

Representative Clients: Bank One; The First National Bank of Mitchell; The Times Mail (newspaper); Ralph Rogers & Co., Inc.; Indiana Bell Telephone Co.; Texas Gas Transmission Corporation; Edgewood Clinic, Inc. (Medical Professional Corporation); U.S. Gypsum Company and Druthers Restaurant of Mitchell, Inc.

For Complete List of Firm Personnel, See General Section

For full biographical listings, see the Martindale-Hubbell Law Directory

*BLOOMINGTON,** Monroe Co.

BARNHART, STURGEON & SPENCER (AV)

313 North Lincoln, P.O. Box 1234, 47402-1234
Telephone: 812-332-9476
Fax: 812-331-8819

MEMBERS OF FIRM

Frank A. Barnhart
Suzanne Sturgeon
Michael J. Spencer

OF COUNSEL

Robert L. Ralston

Local Attorneys for: Home Insurance Co.; Westinghouse Electric Corp.; General Electric Co.; Government Employees Insurance Co.; Bloomington Board of Realtors; The Peoples State Bank, Ellettsville, Indiana; Hawkeye-Security Insurance Co.
Approved Attorney for: Lawyers Title Insurance Corp.

(See Next Column)

BARNHART, STURGEON & SPENCER—*Continued*

For Complete List of Firm Personnel, See General Section

For full biographical listings, see the Martindale-Hubbell Law Directory

THOMAS A. BERRY & ASSOCIATES (AV)

701 North Walnut Street, 47404
Telephone: 812-336-8300
Fax: 812-336-2343

ASSOCIATES

P. Mason Clark
Michelle Berry Domer

For full biographical listings, see the Martindale-Hubbell Law Directory

BUNGER & ROBERTSON (AV)

226 South College Square, P.O. Box 910, 47402-0910
Telephone: 812-332-9295
Fax: 812-331-8808

MEMBERS OF FIRM

Len E. Bunger, Jr. (1921-1993)
Thomas Bunger
Don M. Robertson
James L. Whitlatch
Samuel R. Ardery

ASSOCIATE

William J. Beggs

Representative Clients: Aetna Insurance Companies; Bloomington Hospital; Commercial Union Group; Indiana Insurance Co.; Liberty Mutual Insurance; Medical Protective Co.; Monroe County Community School Corp.; Professional Golf Car, Inc.; Prudential Insurance Company of America; State Farm Automobile Insurance Co.

For Complete List of Firm Personnel, See General Section

For full biographical listings, see the Martindale-Hubbell Law Directory

KELLEY, BELCHER & BROWN, A PROFESSIONAL CORPORATION (AV)

301 West Seventh Street, P.O. Box 3250, 47402-3250
Telephone: 812-336-9963
Telecopier: 812-336-4588

William H. Kelley
Thomas J. Belcher
Barry Spencer Brown

Shannon L. Robinson
Darla Sue Brown

For full biographical listings, see the Martindale-Hubbell Law Directory

CARMEL, Hamilton Co.

COOTS, HENKE & WHEELER, PROFESSIONAL CORPORATION (AV)

255 East Carmel Drive, 46032
Telephone: 317-844-4693
Fax: 317-573-5385

E. Davis Coots
Jeffrey O. Meunier
Steven H. Henke
James D. Crum
James K. Wheeler
Jeffrey S. Zipes

Representative Clients: Freightliner Corp.; Landmark Development Co.; MPH Industries, Inc.; Volvo GM Heavy Truck Corp.

For Complete List of Firm Personnel, See General Section

For full biographical listings, see the Martindale-Hubbell Law Directory

KNOWLES & ASSOCIATES (AV)

811 South Range Line Road, 46032
Telephone: 317-848-4360
Telecopier: 317-848-4363

William W. Knowles

Pamela Y. Rhine
D. Brandon Johnston

For full biographical listings, see the Martindale-Hubbell Law Directory

CLARKSVILLE, Clark Co.

HANGER, ENGEBRETSON, MAYER & VOGT (AV)

501 Eastern Boulevard, 47129
Telephone: 812-288-1235
Louisville, Kentucky: 502-584-5800
Fax: 812-288-1240

MEMBERS OF FIRM

William F. Engebretson
Samuel H. Vogt, Jr.
John M. Mayer, Jr.
Steven K. Palmquist

(See Next Column)

ASSOCIATES

Cara Wells Stigger
Susan Wagner Hynes
Kerstin Ann Schuhmann

Representative Clients: First Federal Savings and Loan Association of Clark County; Ticor Title Insurance Company; Old Republic National Title Insurance Company.
Approved Attorneys for: Commonwealth Land Title Insurance Co.
Reference: First Federal Savings and Loan Association of Clark County; PNC Bank Indiana, Inc.

For Complete List of Firm Personnel, See General Section

For full biographical listings, see the Martindale-Hubbell Law Directory

*COLUMBUS,** Bartholomew Co.

JONES PATTERSON BOLL & TUCKER, PROFESSIONAL CORPORATION (AV)

330 Franklin Street, P.O. Box 67, 47202
Telephone: 812-376-8266
Fax: 812-376-0981

Harold V. Jones, Jr.
Cynthia A. Boll
Dan A. Patterson
J. Grant Tucker

For full biographical listings, see the Martindale-Hubbell Law Directory

SHARPNACK, BIGLEY, DAVID & RUMPLE (AV)

321 Washington Street, P.O. Box 310, 47202-0310
Telephone: 812-372-1553
Fax: 812-372-1567

MEMBERS OF FIRM

Thomas C. Bigley, Jr.
John A. Stroh
Timothy J. Vrana
Joan Tupin Crites

Representative Clients: Irwin Union Bank and Trust Co.; PSI Energy, Inc.; State Farm Mutual Insurance Cos.; American States Insurance Co.; Home News Enterprises; Cummins Federal Credit Union; Richards Elevator, Inc.

For Complete List of Firm Personnel, See General Section

For full biographical listings, see the Martindale-Hubbell Law Directory

EAST CHICAGO, Lake Co.

SMITH & DEBONIS (AV)

Professional Office Building, Suite 411, 4320 Fir Street, 46312
Telephone: 219-398-3900
Fax: 219-398-4324
La Porte, Indiana Office: First of America Bank Building, Suite 302, 800 Lincolnway.
Telephone: 219-326-7527.
Munster, Indiana Office: 1640 45th Street.
Telephone: 219-836-9900.
Wanatah, Indiana office: 105 North Main Street.
Telephone: 219-733-2184.
Hobart, Indiana Office: 600 West Old Ridge Road.
Telephone: 219-947-1692.

MEMBERS OF FIRM

Terrance L. Smith
Anthony DeBonis, Jr.
Dennis F. Smith

ASSOCIATES

Julie R. Fouts
Patricia A. Rees

LEGAL SUPPORT PERSONNEL

PARALEGAL ASSISTANTS

Linda A Phillips
Judith S. Evans

For full biographical listings, see the Martindale-Hubbell Law Directory

ELKHART, Elkhart Co.

CHESTER, PFAFF & BROTHERSON (AV)

317 West Franklin Street, P.O. Box 507, 46515-0507
Telephone: 219-294-5421
Telecopier: 219-522-1476

OF COUNSEL

Willard H. Chester

ASSOCIATE

Robert C. Whippo

For Complete List of Firm Personnel, See General Section

For full biographical listings, see the Martindale-Hubbell Law Directory

Elkhart—Continued

THORNE, GRODNIK, RANSEL, DUNCAN, BYRON & HOSTETLER (AV)

228 West High Street, 46516-3176
Telephone: 219-294-7473
FAX: 219-294-5390
Mishawaka, Indiana Office: 310 Valley American Bank and Trust Building, 310 West McKinley Avenue. P.O. Box 1210.
Telephone: 219-256-5660.
FAX: 219-674-6835.

MEMBERS OF FIRM

William A. Thorne
Charles H. Grodnik
J. Richard Ransel
Glenn L. Duncan
James R. Byron
Steven L. Hostetler

ASSOCIATES

James H. Milstone
Michael A. Trippel
W. Douglas Thorne (Not admitted in IN)

OF COUNSEL

F. Richard Kramer
Joseph C. Zakas

Counsel for: Witmer-McNease Music Co., Inc.; Valley American Bank and Trust Co., Mishawaka, Indiana.

For full biographical listings, see the Martindale-Hubbell Law Directory

*EVANSVILLE,** Vanderburgh Co.

BAMBERGER, FOREMAN, OSWALD AND HAHN (AV)

7th Floor Hulman Building, P.O. Box 657, 47704-0657
Telephone: 812-425-1591
Fax: 812-421-4936

OF COUNSEL

Charles E. Oswald, Jr.

MEMBERS OF FIRM

Frederick P. Bamberger (1903-1983)
William P. Foreman
Robert H. Hahn
Jeffrey R. Kinney
George A. Porch
Robert M. Becker
Fred S. White
R. Thomas Bodkin
George Montgomery
Terry G. Farmer
Roderick W. Clutter, Jr.

ASSOCIATES

Michele S. Bryant
Douglas W. Patterson
David D. Bell
J. Herbert Davis
Marjorie A. Meeks

General Counsel for: North Park Shopping Center; Southern Indiana Gas and Electric Co.; The Citizens National Bank of Evansville; Welborn Clinic; Welborn HMO.
Representative Clients: Aetna Life and Casualty Group; Medical Protective Insurance Co.; State Farm Mutual Automobile Insurance Co.; The Travelers Insurance Co.; Transamerica Insurance Co.

For Complete List of Firm Personnel, See General Section

For full biographical listings, see the Martindale-Hubbell Law Directory

BERGER AND BERGER (AV)

313 Main Street, 47708-1485
Telephone: 812-425-8101;
Indiana Only: 800-622-3604;
Outside Indiana: 800-327-0182
Fax: 812-421-5909

MEMBERS OF FIRM

Sydney L. Berger (1917-1988)
Charles L. Berger
Sheila M. Corcoran
Mark W. Rietman
Robert J. Pigman

References: Citizens National Bank of Evansville; Old National Bank in Evansville.

For full biographical listings, see the Martindale-Hubbell Law Directory

BOWERS, HARRISON, KENT & MILLER (AV)

25 N.W. Riverside Drive, P.O. Box 1287, 47706-1287
Telephone: 812-426-1231
Fax: 812-464-3676

MEMBERS OF FIRM

F. Wesley Bowers
David V. Miller
Paul E. Black
Arthur D. Rutkowski
George C. Barnett, Jr.
James P. Casey
Thomas A. Massey
Greg A. Granger
Joseph H. Harrison, Jr.

Representative Clients: Ameritech Publishing, Inc.; CSX Transportation, Inc.; Southern Railway Company; Bootz Manufacturing Company; Indiana Bell Telephone: Company; Black Beauty Resources, Inc.

For Complete List of Firm Personnel, See General Section

For full biographical listings, see the Martindale-Hubbell Law Directory

FINE & HATFIELD (AV)

520 N.W. Second Street, P.O. Box 779, 47705-0779
Telephone: 812-425-3592
Telecopier: 812-421-4269

MEMBERS OF FIRM

Thomas H. Bryan
Danny E. Glass
D. Timothy Born
Patricia Kay Woodring

ASSOCIATES

William H. Mullis
Debra S. McGowan

For Complete List of Firm Personnel, See General Section

For full biographical listings, see the Martindale-Hubbell Law Directory

GERLING LAW OFFICES, PROFESSIONAL CORPORATION (AV)

519 Main Street Walkway, P.O. Box 3203, 47731
Telephone: 812-423-5251
Fax: 812-423-9928

Gary L. Gerling
Daniel J. McGinn
Edward B. Anderson
David G. Hatfield
Christian M. Lenn
Barbara S. Barrett
Gayle Gerling Pettinga

For full biographical listings, see the Martindale-Hubbell Law Directory

KAHN, DEES, DONOVAN & KAHN (AV)

P.O. Box 3646, 47735-3646
Telephone: 812-423-3183
Fax: 812-423-3841

MEMBERS OF FIRM

Alan N. Shovers
Thomas O. Magan
Wm. Michael Schiff
Robert H. Brown
Jon D. Goldman
Brian P. Williams
David L. Clark
Jeffrey A. Wilhite
Jeffrey W. Ahlers
Mary Lee Franke

ASSOCIATE

Richard O. Hawley, Jr.

Representative Clients: Atlas Van Lines, Inc.; Sterling Boiler & Mechanical, Inc.: WATS/800, Inc.; University of Southern Indiana; Cresline Plastic Pipe Co., Inc.; Perdue Farms Incorporated; Deaconess Hospital, Inc.

For Complete List of Firm Personnel, See General Section

For full biographical listings, see the Martindale-Hubbell Law Directory

LOCKYEAR & KORNBLUM (AV)

555 Sycamore Street, P.O. Box 3515, 47734
Telephone: 812-422-1199
Fax: 812-426-0799

MEMBERS OF FIRM

Theodore Lockyear
James A. Kornblum

Reference: Citizens National Bank.

For full biographical listings, see the Martindale-Hubbell Law Directory

STATHAM, JOHNSON & MCCRAY (AV)

215 North West Martin Luther King Jr. Boulevard, P.O. Box 3567, 47734-3567
Telephone: 812-425-5223
Facsimile: 812-421-4238

MEMBERS OF FIRM

William E. Statham
Michael McCray
Stephen Hensleigh Thomas
Gerald F. Allega
Douglas V. Jessen

ASSOCIATES

Brent Alan Raibley
Bryan S. Rudisill

Representative Clients: ALCOA; Coca-Cola Bottler's Assn.; Cooper Industries, Inc.; Dresser Industries, Inc.; General Motors Corporation; Kraft General Foods; McDonald's Corporation; O. F. Mossberg & Sons, Inc.; The Ohio River Company; White Consolidated Industries, Inc.

For Complete List of Firm Personnel, See General Section

For full biographical listings, see the Martindale-Hubbell Law Directory

WRIGHT, EVANS AND DALY (AV)

425 Main Street, 47708
Telephone: 812-424-3300
Fax: 812-421-5588

MEMBERS OF FIRM

Donald R. Wright
R. Lawrence Daly

ASSOCIATE

Keith M. Wallace

Representative Clients: Allstate Insurance Company; Browning-Ferris Industries of Indiana, Inc.; Castle Contracting Co., Inc.; Chrysler Corporation; Home Insurance Companies; Liberty Mutual Insurance Company; Manpower Incorporated of Evansville; The Mortgage Connection of Evansville,

(See Next Column)

WRIGHT, EVANS AND DALY—*Continued*

Inc.; Orkin Exterminating Company; United Farm Bureau Mutual Insurance Company.

For Complete List of Firm Personnel, See General Section

For full biographical listings, see the Martindale-Hubbell Law Directory

*FORT WAYNE,** Allen Co.

BARRETT & McNAGNY (AV)

215 East Berry Street, P.O. Box 2263, 46801-2263
Telephone: 219-423-9551
Telecopier: 219-423-8924
Huntington, Indiana Office: 429 Jefferson Park Mall, P.O. Box 5156.
Telephone: 219-356-7766.
Telecopier: 219-356-7782.

MEMBERS OF FIRM

J. Michael O'Hara
Ted S. Miller (Resident, Huntington Office)
John M. Clifton, Jr.
Robert S. Walters
John F. Lyons
William L. Sweet, Jr.
Gary J. Rickner
John D. Walda
James P. Fenton
Alan VerPlanck
Thomas M. Kimbrough
Thomas A. Herr

ASSOCIATES

Anthony M. Stites
Kevin K. Fitzharris

Counsel For: Aetna Group; Allen County Motors, Inc.; Fort Wayne National Bank; Northern Indiana Public Service Co.; Omni-Source Corp.; Phelps Dodge Magnet; The Journal-Gazette.
Representative Clients: Kemper Insurance Co.; State Farm Mutual Automobile Co.

For Complete List of Firm Personnel, See General Section

For full biographical listings, see the Martindale-Hubbell Law Directory

GALLUCCI, HOPKINS & THEISEN, P.C. (AV)

229 West Berry Street, Suite 400, P.O. Box 12663, 46864-2663
Telephone: 219-424-3800
Telecopier: 219-420-1260

William T. Hopkins, Jr.
John C. Theisen
John T. Menzie
M. Scott Hall
Loren K. Allison

Michael A. Scheer
Thomas N. O'Malley
Mark S. Kittaka
Tonya S. Shea
Kristen L. Maly
Eric H. J. Stahlhut
Jeffrey S. Schafer
Anthony G. Genakos (Not admitted in IN)
Frank L. Gallucci

For full biographical listings, see the Martindale-Hubbell Law Directory

HUNT, SUEDHOFF, BORROR & EILBACHER (AV)

900 Courtside, 803 South Calhoun Street, 46802-2399
Telephone: 219-423-1311
Telecopier: 219-424-5396

RETIRED

Carl J. Suedhoff, Jr.

MEMBERS OF FIRM

Leigh L. Hunt (1899-1975)
William E. Borror (1932-1989)
Leonard E. Eilbacher
Robert E. Kabisch
Arthur G. Surguine, Jr.
Thomas C. Ewing
Carolyn White Spengler
Thomas W. Belleperche
Mark W. Baeverstad
Michael D. Mustard
Branch R. Lew
Carla J. Baird
James J. Shea
Scott L. Bunnell

ASSOCIATES

Dane L. Tubergen
David M. Lutz
Carolyn M. Trier
Kathleen A. Kilar
Daniel J. Palmer
Brian L. England
Craig J. Bobay

For full biographical listings, see the Martindale-Hubbell Law Directory

ROBY & HOOD (AV)

Standard Federal Plaza, Suite 520, 200 East Main, 46802
Telephone: 219-423-3366
Fax: 219-423-3367
Anderson, Indiana Office: One Citizens Plaza, Suite 305.
Telephone: 317-642-2402.

MEMBERS OF FIRM

Daniel A. Roby
G. Stanley Hood
Kathryn J. Roudebush
Thomas A. Manges

(See Next Column)

ASSOCIATE

Theodore T. Storer

References: Norwest Bank; NBD Bank.

For full biographical listings, see the Martindale-Hubbell Law Directory

SHAMBAUGH, KAST, BECK & WILLIAMS (AV)

600 Standard Federal Plaza, 46802-2405
Telephone: 219-423-1430
FAX: 219-422-9038

MEMBERS OF FIRM

Michael H. Kast (Semi-Active)
Stephen J. Williams
Edward E. Beck
Daniel E. Serban
John B. Powell
Timothy L. Claxton
James D. Streit

Counsel for: Hagerman Construction Corp.; Rogers Markets, Inc.; K & H Realty Corp.; Olive B. Cole Foundation; M. E. Raker Foundation, Inc.; Associates Financial Services Co., of Indiana, Inc.; Professional Federal Credit Union; Fort Wayne Education Association; American Ambassador Casualty Company; CBT Credit Services, Inc.

For Complete List of Firm Personnel, See General Section

For full biographical listings, see the Martindale-Hubbell Law Directory

*FOWLER,** Benton Co.

BARCE & RYAN (AV)

103 North Jackson Avenue, P.O. Box 252, 47944
Telephone: 317-884-0383
Fax: 317-884-0445
Kentland, Indiana Office: 301 East Graham Street, P.O. Box 338.
Telephone: 219-474-5158.
Fax: 219-474-6610.

MEMBER OF FIRM

John W. Barce

For Complete List of Firm Personnel, See General Section

For full biographical listings, see the Martindale-Hubbell Law Directory

GARY, Lake Co.

STULTS, STULTS, FORSZT & PAWLOWSKI, A PROFESSIONAL ASSOCIATION (AV)

3637 Grant Street, P.O. Box 15050, 46409-5050
Telephone: 219-887-7000
Fax: 219-884-1179

Fred M. Stults, Jr.
Frederick M. Stults, III
Robert P. Forszt
David R. Pawlowski

Representative Clients: American Road Insurance Co.; Employers Casualty Co.; Indiana Insurance Co.; SAFECO Insurance Co.

For full biographical listings, see the Martindale-Hubbell Law Directory

GREENWOOD, Johnson Co.

VAN VALER WILLIAMS & HEWITT (AV)

Suite 400 National City Bank Building, 300 South Madison Avenue, P.O. Box 405, 46142
Telephone: 317-888-1121
Fax: 317-887-4069

MEMBERS OF FIRM

Joe N. Van Valer
Jon E. Williams
Brian C. Hewitt

ASSOCIATES

J. Lee Robbins
William M. Waltz
John M. White
Kim Van Valer Shilts
Mark E. Need

For full biographical listings, see the Martindale-Hubbell Law Directory

HAMMOND, Lake Co.

ABRAHAMSON, REED & ADLEY (AV)

5231 Hohman Avenue, 46320
Telephone: 219-937-1500
Fax: 219-937-3174

MEMBERS OF FIRM

Harold Abrahamson
Kenneth D. Reed
Michael C. Adley

ASSOCIATES

Scott R. Bilse
Christopher R. Karsten
Joseph L. Curosh

References: Calumet National Bank, Hammond; Mercantile National Bank, Hammond.

For full biographical listings, see the Martindale-Hubbell Law Directory

Hammond—Continued

BECKMAN, KELLY & SMITH (AV)

5920 Hohman Avenue, 46320
Telephone: 219-933-6200
Telecopier: 219-933-6201

MEMBERS OF FIRM

Richard P. Tinkham (1902-1973)
Daniel F. Kelly (1914-1978)
J. B. Smith
Andrew J. Fetsch
Randall J. Nye
Robert F. Parker
Daniel W. Glavin

ASSOCIATES

Larry L. Chubb
Melanie Morgan Dunajeski
Scott A. Bearby
Christine Hajduch Curosh

OF COUNSEL

Eric L. Kirschner
John F. Beckman, Jr.

Representative Clients: Waste Management of North America, Inc.; The Travelers Companies; Bethlehem Steel Corp.; ITT Finance; Northwest Indiana Public Broadcasting, Inc.; Signal Capital Corporation; CIGNA Companies; Sears Roebuck and Co.

For full biographical listings, see the Martindale-Hubbell Law Directory

GALVIN, GALVIN & LEENEY (AV)

5231 Hohman Avenue, 46320
Telephone: 219-933-0380
Fax: 219-933-0471

MEMBERS OF FIRM

Edmond J. Leeney (1897-1978)
Timothy P. Galvin, Sr. (1894-1993)
Francis J. Galvin, Sr. (Retired)
Carl N. Carpenter
John E. Chevigny
Timothy P. Galvin, Jr.
Patrick J. Galvin
W. Patrick Downes

Brian L. Goins
William G. Crabtree II
John H. Lloyd, IV

Attorneys for: Mercantile National Bank of Indiana; Citizens Federal Savings & Loan Association; Auto Owners Insurance Co.; CIGNA; Pepsi-Cola General Bottlers, Inc.; St. Margaret Mercy Healthcare Centers, Inc.; St. Anthony Hospital and Health Centers (Michigan City); Calumet Construction Corp.; Chicago Title Insurance Company.

For full biographical listings, see the Martindale-Hubbell Law Directory

MCHIE, MYERS, MCHIE & ENSLEN (AV)

53 Muenich Court, 46320
Telephone: 219-931-1707
Telecopier: 219-932-2417

MEMBERS OF FIRM

G. Edward McHie
Charles A. Myers
James E. McHie
Charles Endicott Enslen

ASSOCIATES

Carol M. Green
Richard A. Hanning
Carolyn N. Fehring

Representative Clients: USX Corp.; Ronwal Transportation, Inc.; Hammond Redevelopment Commission; Raytrans, Inc.; La Salle Steel Co.; The Budd Co.; Emro Marketing Co., A Division of Marathon Oil.

For full biographical listings, see the Martindale-Hubbell Law Directory

*INDIANAPOLIS,** Marion Co.

BAKER & DANIELS (AV)

300 North Meridian Street, 46204
Telephone: 317-237-0300
FAX: 317-237-1000
Fort Wayne, Indiana Office: 2400 Fort Wayne National Bank Building.
Telephone: 219-424-8000.
South Bend, Indiana Office: First Bank Building, 205 West Jefferson Boulevard.
Telephone: 219-234-4149.
Elkhart, Indiana Office: 301 South Main Street, Suite 307,
Telephone: 219-296-6000.
Washington, D.C. Office: 1701 K Street, N.W., Suite 400.
Telephone: 202-785-1565.

MEMBERS OF FIRM

Virgil L. Beeler
Norman P. Rowe
Terrill D. Albright
Wendell R. Tucker
Thomas G. Stayton
James H. Ham, III
Brian K. Burke
David K. Herzog
Christopher G. Scanlon
John R. Schaibley, III
Robert Kirk Stanley
Alan L. McLaughlin
Brent D. Taylor
Joseph H. Yeager, Jr.
Byron K. Mason
Ronald D. Gifford
Kevin M. Toner

(See Next Column)

ASSOCIATES

David A. Given
John Joseph Tanner
Scott D. Himsel
Andrew Z. Soshnick
Nancy G. Bollinger
Ellen E. Boshkoff
Cynthia M. Cormany
Mark A. Voigtmann
Carl R. Pebworth
Michael P. Bigelow
Melissa S. Barnes

Representative Clients: Associated Insurance Companies, Inc.; Bank One, Indianapolis, N.A.; Borg-Warner Corp.; City of Indianapolis; Cummins Engine Co.; Eli Lilly and Company; General Motors Corp.; Indiana Bell; Indianapolis Public Schools; United Airlines.

For Complete List of Firm Personnel, See General Section

For full biographical listings, see the Martindale-Hubbell Law Directory

BOBERSCHMIDT, MILLER, O'BRYAN, TURNER & ABBOTT, A PROFESSIONAL ASSOCIATION (AV)

Bank One Center/Circle, 111 Monument Circle, Suite 302, 46204-5169
Telephone: 317-632-5892
Telecopier: 317-686-3423

Jerald L. Miller
Berton W. O'Bryan
L. Craig Turner

A List of Representative Clients will be furnished upon request.

For Complete List of Firm Personnel, See General Section

For full biographical listings, see the Martindale-Hubbell Law Directory

BOSE MCKINNEY & EVANS (AV)

2700 First Indiana Plaza, 135 North Pennsylvania Street, 46204
Telephone: 317-684-5000
Facsimile: 317-684-5173
Indianapolis North Office: Suite 1201, 8888 Keystone Crossing, 46240.
Telephone: 317-574-3700.
Facsimile: 317-574-3716.

MEMBERS OF FIRM

Wayne C. Ponader
James P. Seidensticker, Jr.
Theodore J. Nowacki
Ronald E. Elberger
Daniel C. Emerson
Leonard Opperman
Stephen E. Arthur
George E. Purdy
Keith E. White
C. Joseph Russell
Michael A. Trentadue
J. Greg Easter
Roderick H. Morgan
V. Samuel Laurin III

ASSOCIATES

George Thomas Patton, Jr.
Debra Linn Burns
Thomas G. Burroughs
Jeffrey S. Koehlinger
William C. Ahrbecker

Representative Clients: Chicago Title Insurance Co.; Duke Construction and Development Cos.; Emmis Broadcasting Corp.; First Indiana Bank; Metropolitan Life Insurance Co.; The Prudential Insurance Company of America; The Travelers Insurance Co.; Indianapolis Colts, Inc.; United Parcel Service, Inc.

For Complete List of Firm Personnel, See General Section

For full biographical listings, see the Martindale-Hubbell Law Directory

BUSCHMANN, CARR & SHANKS, PROFESSIONAL CORPORATION (AV)

1020 Market Tower, 10 West Market Street, 46204-2963
Telephone: 317-636-5511
Fax: 317-636-3661
Franklin, Indiana Office: 160 Fairway Lakes Drive.
Telephone: 317-738-9540.
Fax: 317-738-9310.
Fishers, Indiana Office: 9093 Technology Drive, Suite 103.
Telephone: 317-577-0756.
Fax: 317-577-9910.

John R. Carr, III
Stephen R. Buschmann

Representative Clients: Archer-Daniels Midland Co.; Ball Corp.; Industrial Valley Title Insurance; Creative Risk Management, Inc.; Deflecto Corporation; Glenfed Mortgage Corp.; Gates McDonald; Merchants National Bank & Trust Company of Muncie; Monumental Life Insurance Co.; National Council on Compensation Insurance.

For Complete List of Firm Personnel, See General Section

For full biographical listings, see the Martindale-Hubbell Law Directory

CONOUR • DOEHRMAN (AV)

Suite 1725, One Indiana Square, 46204
Telephone: 317-269-3550
Fax: 317-269-3564

MEMBERS OF FIRM

William F. Conour
Thomas C. Doehrman

ASSOCIATES

Rex E. Baker
Daniel S. Chamberlain
Daniel J. Mages

For full biographical listings, see the Martindale-Hubbell Law Directory

Indianapolis—Continued

DALE & EKE, PROFESSIONAL CORPORATION (AV)

Suite 400, 9100 Keystone Crossing, 46240
Telephone: 317-844-7400
FAX: 317-574-9426

Joseph W. Eke
Catherine Chambers Kennedy
Deborah J. Caruso
A. Robert Lasich
Dawn Michelle Snow

For full biographical listings, see the Martindale-Hubbell Law Directory

DUTTON OVERMAN GOLDSTEIN PINKUS, A PROFESSIONAL CORPORATION (AV)

710 Century Building, 36 South Pennsylvania Street, 46204
Telephone: 317-633-4000
Telecopier: 317-633-1494

Alan H. Goldstein
Craig Pinkus
Susan Rogers Brooke

Donna J. Bays
Stephen P. Ullrich

Representative Clients: Huber, Hunt & Nichols, Inc.; The Hunt Paving Co., Inc.; Baldwin & Lyons, Inc.; The Dalton Foundries, Inc.; Roosevelt Building Products Company, Inc.; Polaris Amphitheater Limited Partnership.

For full biographical listings, see the Martindale-Hubbell Law Directory

HOLLAND & HOLLAND (AV)

Two Market Square Center, Suite 1011, 251 East Ohio Street, 46204
Telephone: 317-637-4400
Fax: Available Upon Request

C. Warren Holland
Michael W. Holland

ASSOCIATE

Gretchen Holland Elling

OF COUNSEL

Charles G. Reeder

Reference: The Indiana National Bank.

For full biographical listings, see the Martindale-Hubbell Law Directory

HUGHES AND HUGHES (AV)

(Not a Partnership)
Two Meridian Plaza, Suite 202, 10401 North Meridian Street, 46290
Telephone: 317-573-2255
Telecopier: 317-573-2266

David B. Hughes
Gary D. Sallee

For full biographical listings, see the Martindale-Hubbell Law Directory

ICE MILLER DONADIO & RYAN (AV)

One American Square Box 82001, 46282-0002
Telephone: 317-236-2100
Fax: 317-236-2219

MEMBERS OF FIRM

James V. Donadio
Alan H. Lobley
Jim A. O'Neal
Evan E. Steger
Ralph A. Cohen
Arthur P. Kalleres
G. Daniel Kelley, Jr.
David M. Mattingly
James R. Fisher
Cory Brundage
W. C. Blanton
David J. Mallon, Jr.
Phillip R. Scaletta, III
James L. Petersen
Gary J. Dankert
Philip A. Whistler
John F. Prescott, Jr.
Fred R. Biesecker
Mary Nold Larimore
Richard A. Smikle
L. Alan Whaley
Bonnie L. Gallivan
John T. Murphy
Debra Hanley Miller
Michael A. Wukmer
Michael J. Lewinski
Michael D. Marine

OF COUNSEL

Bradley L. Williams
Nancy Menard Riddle
Gloria A. Aplin
Kathleen K. Shortridge
Bruce J. Alvarado
Diana Lynn Wann

ASSOCIATES

Terri Ann Czajka
Sherry A. Fabina-Abney
Kelly Bauman Pitcher
Donald M. Snemis
Edward P. Steegmann
Michael A. Wilkins
Kristin L. Altice
Michael R. Kerr
James Scott Fanzini
Laure V. Flaniken
Gerald B. Coleman
John J. Morse
Judy Starobin Okenfuss
Stephanie Alden Smithey
Angela K. Wade
Barbara J. Weigel
Curtis W. McCauley
Laura B. Daghe
Jodie L. Miner
Thomas E. Mixdorf

(See Next Column)

Counsel for: Amax, Inc.; American Cyanamid Co.; Chrysler Corp.; Community Hospitals of Indiana, Inc.; Ford Motor Company; Howard Needles, Tammen & Bergendoff; Indiana Department of Insurance; Parke-Davis; Proctor & Gamble Co.; Liberty Mutual Ins. Co.

For Complete List of Firm Personnel, See General Section

For full biographical listings, see the Martindale-Hubbell Law Directory

JOHNSON, SMITH, DENSBORN, WRIGHT & HEATH (AV)

One Indiana Square Suite 1800, 46204
Telephone: 317-634-9777
Telecopier: 317-636-9061

MEMBERS OF FIRM

John F. Joyce (1948-1994)
Wayne O. Adams, III
Thomas A. Barnard
David J. Carr
Peter D. Cleveland
David R. Day
Donald K. Densborn
Thomas N. Eckerle
Mark W. Ford
G. Ronald Heath
Robert B. Hebert
John David Hoover
Andrew W. Hull
Dennis A. Johnson
Richard L. Johnson
Michael J. Kaye
John R. Kirkwood
David Williams Russell
James T. Smith
David E. Wright

ASSOCIATES

Robert C. Wolf (1949-1993)
Carolyn H. Andretti
David G. Blachly
Robert T. Buday
Jeffrey S. Cohen
Patricia L. Marshall
David D. Robinson
Ronald G. Sentman
Sally Franklin Zweig

OF COUNSEL

Paul D. Gresk
William T. Lawrence
Mark A. Palmer
Catherine A. Singleton

For Complete List of Firm Personnel, See General Section

For full biographical listings, see the Martindale-Hubbell Law Directory

KATZMAN KATZMAN & PYLITT, A PROFESSIONAL CORPORATION (AV)

3905 Vincennes Road, Suite 100, 46268
Telephone: 317-872-5700
Telecopier: 317-872-5769

Alvin J. Katzman
Mariellen Katzman
Bernard L. Pylitt

Jeffrey A. Hearn

OF COUNSEL

Daniel B. Altman

A list of representative clients will be furnished upon request.

For full biographical listings, see the Martindale-Hubbell Law Directory

KIGHTLINGER & GRAY (AV)

Market Square Center, Suite 660, 151 North Delaware Street, 46204
Telephone: 317-638-4521
Telecopier: 317-636-5917
Evansville, Indiana Office: One Riverfront Place, Suite 210, 20 N.W. First Street, 47708.
Telephone: 812-464-9508.
Telecopier: 812-464-9511.
New Albany, Indiana Office: Pinnacle Centre, Suite 200, 3317 Grant Line Road, P.O. Box 6727, 46151.
Telephone: 812-949-2300.
Telecopier: 812-949-8556.

MEMBERS OF FIRM

Vayne M. Armstrong (1894-1959)
Harry L. Gause (1898-1964)
Paul B. Hudson (1907-1970)
Aribert L. Young (1923-1980)
Mark William Gray
Robert J. Wampler
Donald L. Dawson
Peter G. Tamulonis
Richard A. Young
J. Randall Aikman
Michael E. Brown
Mark D. Gerth
Steven E. Springer
Joan Fullam Irick
Richard T. Mullineaux (Resident, New Albany Office)
Robert M. Kelso
Brent R. Weil (Resident, Evansville Office)
Philip Linnemeier
John B. Drummy
James W. Roehrdanz
Peter A. Velde
Thomas B. Blackwell
Briane M. House
Thomas J. Jarzyniecki, Jr.
Jeffrey A. Doty
Thomas E. Wheeler II
Rodney L. Scott (Resident, New Albany Office)

OF COUNSEL

Erle A. Kightlinger

(See Next Column)

KIGHTLINGER & GRAY, *Indianapolis—Continued*

ASSOCIATES

S. Michael Woodard
Troy A. Reynolds (Resident, Evansville Office)
Jill Reifinger Marcrum (Resident, Evansville Office)
Mary M. Nord (Resident, New Albany Office)
John K. Baird
William L. O'Connor
Van T. Willis (Resident, New Albany Office)
Scott L. Tyler (Resident, New Albany Office)
Laura E. Moenning
Paul F. Lottes

Representative Clients: American Family Mutual Insurance Co.; American International Group; American States; Associated Aviation Underwriters; Black & Decker (U.S., Inc.); Government Employees Insurance Co.; Mack Trucks, Inc.; Reliance Insurance Group.
Reference: INB National Bank.

For Complete List of Firm Personnel, See General Section

For full biographical listings, see the Martindale-Hubbell Law Directory

LEWIS & WAGNER (AV)

500 Place, 501 Indiana Avenue, Suite 200, 46202-3199
Telephone: 317-237-0500
Fax: 317-630-2790

Judith Trevor Kirtland (1947-1990)
Edward D. Lewis
Robert F. Wagner
David Konnersman
John C. Trimble
Thomas C. Hays
R. Robert Stommel
Kenneth P. Reese
Michael S. Huntine
Susan E. Mehringer
Daun A. Weliever
Robert K. Cowles
Richard K. Shoultz
William Owen Harrington

OF COUNSEL

Felson Bowman
Thomas P. Weliever

For full biographical listings, see the Martindale-Hubbell Law Directory

LOCKE REYNOLDS BOYD & WEISELL (AV)

1000 Capital Center South, 201 North Illinois Street, 46204
Telephone: 317-237-3800
Telecopier: 317-237-3900

Hugh E. Reynolds, Jr.
Lloyd H. Milliken, Jr.
William V. Hutchens
David S. Allen
David M. Haskett
Michael A. Bergin
David T. Kasper
Steven J. Strawbridge
Thomas L. Davis
Robert A. Fanning
Randall R. Riggs
Alan S. Brown
Mark J. Roberts
Kevin Charles Murray
Julia M. Blackwell
Kim F. Ebert
Terrence L. Brookie
Richard A. Huser
Thomas J. Campbell
Diane L. Parsons
Burton M. Harris
Charles B. Baldwin
Thomas W. Farlow
Karl M. Koons, III
Julia F. Crowe
James Dimos

Stephen L. Vaughan
Kristen K. Rollison
Thomas R. Schultz
Todd J. Kaiser
Eric A. Riegner
Kevin C. Schiferl
Ariane Schallwig Johnson
Peter H. Pogue
John H. Daerr
John K. McDavid
Robert W. Wright
Robert T. Dassow
Jeffrey J. Mortier
Kevin M. Boyle
Nicholas C. Pappas
Mary A. Schopper
Susan E. Cline
Jerrilyn Powers Ramsey
Katherine Coble Dassow
Lisa A. McCallum
Charles S. Eberhardt, II
Kathryn Weymouth Williams
Mary Margaret Ruth Feldhake

OF COUNSEL

William H. Vobach
Robert C. Riddell

Representative Clients: American Honda Motor Co., Inc; Center for Claims Resolution; Citizens Insurance Company of America; CNA Insurance Cos.; General Motors Corp.; PEPSICO, Inc.; PSI Energy, Inc.; St. Francis Hospital; U.S. Aircraft Insurance Group; Wal-Mart Stores, Inc.

For Complete List of Firm Personnel, See General Section

For full biographical listings, see the Martindale-Hubbell Law Directory

MCTURNAN & TURNER (AV)

2070 Market Tower, 10 West Market Street, 46204
Telephone: 317-464-8181
Telecopier: 317-464-8131

Lee B. McTurnan
Wayne C. Turner
Judy L. Woods
Jacqueline Bowman Ponder
Steven M. Badger
Matthew W. Foster

Representative Clients: Indiana Bell Telephone Company, Incorporated (Ameritech Indiana); Indiana Bell Communications, A Division of Ameritech Information Systems, Inc.; The Dow Chemical Company; Coopers &

(See Next Column)

Lybrand; IPALCO Enterprises Inc.; Prudential Securities Incorporated; National City Bank, Indiana; Western Newspaper Publishing Company; McGraw-Hill Broadcasting Co., Inc., (WRTV-6); CSX Transportation, Inc.

For full biographical listings, see the Martindale-Hubbell Law Directory

MILLER MULLER MENDELSON & KENNEDY (AV)

8900 Keystone Crossing Suite 1250, 46240
Telephone: 317-574-4500
1-800-394-3094
Fax: 317-574-4501

MEMBERS OF FIRM

Michael S. Miller
John Muller
Tilden Mendelson
Timothy J. Kennedy
Faith L. Pottschmidt

For full biographical listings, see the Martindale-Hubbell Law Directory

MITCHELL HURST JACOBS & DICK (AV)

152 East Washington Street, 46204
Telephone: 317-636-0808
1-800-636-0808
Fax: 317-633-7680

MEMBERS OF FIRM

Marvin H. Mitchell
William W. Hurst
Samuel L. Jacobs
Richard J. Dick
Marshall S. Hanley
Steven K. Huffer
Robert W. Strohmeyer, Jr.

ASSOCIATES

Danielle A. Takla
John M. Reames
Michael T. McNelis
Michael P. Kilkenny

LEGAL SUPPORT PERSONNEL

L. Kathleen Hughes Brown, R.N.

General Counsel for: Premium Optical Co.; Calderon Bros. Vending Machines, Inc.; Grocers Supply Co., Inc.; Power Train Services, Inc.; Frank E. Irish, Inc.; Bedding Liquidators; Galyan's Trading Co.; Harcourt Management Co., Inc.; Kosene & Kosene Mgt. & Dev. Co., Inc.; Hasten Bancorp.

For full biographical listings, see the Martindale-Hubbell Law Directory

OSBORN HINER & LISHER P.C. (AV)

Suite 380, One Woodfield, 8330 Woodfield Crossing Boulevard, 46240
Telephone: 317-469-2100
Fax: 317-469-9011

John R. Hiner (1920-1986)
John L. Lisher

Donald G. Orzeske
Donald K. Broad

OF COUNSEL

William M. Osborn
Edward A. Straith-Miller
Janet K. Storer

For full biographical listings, see the Martindale-Hubbell Law Directory

LAW OFFICES OF LINDA L. PENCE (AV)

2300 First Indiana Plaza, 135 North Pennsylvania Street, 46204
Telephone: 317-264-5555
Fax: 317-264-5564

ASSOCIATES

David J. Hensel
Anthony J. Rose
Jane Ann Himsel

LEGAL SUPPORT PERSONNEL

Penny S. Bloemker
Teresa L. Zembrycki
Rachel I. Lamb

For full biographical listings, see the Martindale-Hubbell Law Directory

PRICE & BARKER (AV)

The Hammond Block Building, 301 Massachusetts Avenue, 46204
Telephone: 317-633-8787
Telecopier: 317-633-8797

PARTNERS

Henry J. Price
Robert G. Barker
Mary Arlien Findling
Jennifer L. Graham
Jerry A. Garau
Mary J. Hoeller

ASSOCIATES

H. Dean Bowman
Melissa A. Clark
Stephanie L. Franco
Barbara J. Germano
Larry R. Jackson
Deborah K. Pennington

For full biographical listings, see the Martindale-Hubbell Law Directory

Indianapolis—Continued

SOMMER & BARNARD, ATTORNEYS AT LAW, PC (AV)

4000 Bank One Tower, 111 Monument Circle, P.O. Box 44363, 46244-0363
Telephone: 317-630-4000
FAX: 317-236-9802
North Office: 8900 Keystone Crossing, Suite 1046, Indianapolis, Indiana, 46240-2134.
Telephone: 317-630-4000.
FAX: 317-844-4780.

William C. Barnard
James E. Hughes
Edward W. Harris, III
Gordon L. Pittenger
Michael C. Terrell
Richard C. Richmond, III
Steven C. Shockley
Debra McVicker Lynch

Gayle A. Reindl

Representative Clients: Comerica Bank; Federal Express; Renault Automation; Reppert International; Kimball International; TRW, Inc.

For Complete List of Firm Personnel, See General Section

For full biographical listings, see the Martindale-Hubbell Law Directory

STEWART DUE MILLER & PUGH (AV)

55 Monument Circle, 900 Circle Tower, 46204-5900
Telephone: 317-635-7700
Fax: 317-636-2408

MEMBERS OF FIRM

Kent O. Stewart
Danford R. Due
Charles F. Miller, Jr.
Larry S. Pugh
Robert J. Doyle

ASSOCIATES

Catharine Stewart
Mark A. Metzger

Representative Clients: American States Insurance; Wausau Insurance Company; B.F. Goodrich; Carr Metal Products, Inc.; Rockwood Insurance Co.; Capital Enterprise Insurance Group; Risk Management; The Huntington National Bank of Indiana; Protective Insurance Co.; Auto Owners Insurance Company.

For full biographical listings, see the Martindale-Hubbell Law Directory

TOWNSEND, HOVDE & MONTROSS (AV)

230 East Ohio Street, 46204
Telephone: 317-264-4444
FAX: 317-264-2080

F. Boyd Hovde
John F. Townsend, Jr.
W. Scott Montross
Frederick R. Hovde

OF COUNSEL

John F. Townsend

Reference: The Indiana National Bank of Indianapolis.

For full biographical listings, see the Martindale-Hubbell Law Directory

YARLING, ROBINSON, HAMMEL & LAMB (AV)

151 North Delaware, Suite 1535, P.O. Box 44128, 46204
Telephone: 317-262-8800
Fax: 317-262-3046

MEMBERS OF FIRM

Richard W. Yarling
Charles F. Robinson, Jr.
John W. Hammel
Linda Y. Hammel
Edgar H. Lamb
Douglas E. Rogers
Mark S. Gray

Representative Clients: Allstate Insurance Co.; American Family Mutual Insurance Company; Chrysler Credit Corporation; Fleet Financenter; General Motors Acceptance Corporation; Household Finance Corporation; Monroe Guaranty Insurance Company; Northbrook Property & Casualty Company; Pafco General Insurance Company; Security Pacific Finance Corporation.

For full biographical listings, see the Martindale-Hubbell Law Directory

YOSHA, LADENDORF & TODD (AV)

2220 North Meridian Street, 46208
Telephone: 317-925-9200
FAX: 317-923-5759

MEMBERS OF FIRM

Louis Buddy Yosha
William Levy
Mark C. Ladendorf
Teresa L. Todd

ASSOCIATE

David C. Krahulik

OF COUNSEL

Irwin J. Prince
Irving L. Fink
Theodore F. Smith, Jr.

References: NBD Indiana; Bank One, Indianapolis.

For full biographical listings, see the Martindale-Hubbell Law Directory

*KENTLAND,** Newton Co.

BARCE & RYAN (AV)

301 East Graham Street, P.O. Box 338, 47951
Telephone: 219-474-5158
Fax: 219-474-6610
Fowler, Indiana Office: 103 North Jackson Avenue, P.O. Box 252.
Telephone: 317-884-0383.
Fax: 317-884-0445.

MEMBERS OF FIRM

John W. Barce
R. Steven Ryan
J. Edward Barce (Resident at Fowler Office)

Representative Clients: USX Corporation; Metropolitan Life Insurance Company; Goodland State Bank; Bank of Oxford; DeMotte State Bank; Newton County Stone; Northern Indiana Public Service Company; DeMeter, Inc; Town of Boswell; Town of Brook.

For full biographical listings, see the Martindale-Hubbell Law Directory

*KOKOMO,** Howard Co.

BAYLIFF, HARRIGAN, CORD & MAUGANS, P.C. (AV)

The Security Building, 123 North Buckeye, P.O. Box 2249, 46904-2249
Telephone: 317-459-3941
Fax: 317-459-3974

Edgar W. Bayliff
Daniel J. Harrigan
C. Michael Cord
J. Conrad Maugans

Mark A. Scott

Reference: Society National Bank, Indiana; First Federal Savings Bank of Kokomo, Indiana.

For full biographical listings, see the Martindale-Hubbell Law Directory

*LAFAYETTE,** Tippecanoe Co.

HANNA, GERDE & BURNS (AV)

Fifth Floor Bank & Trust Building, P.O. Box 1098, 47902
Telephone: 317-742-5005

Charles H. Robertson (1902-1982)

MEMBERS OF FIRM

George L. Hanna
Cy Gerde
Eric H. Burns

Reference: Lafayette Bank & Trust Co.

For full biographical listings, see the Martindale-Hubbell Law Directory

STUART & BRANIGIN (AV)

The Life Building, 300 Main Street, Suite 800, 47902
Telephone: 317-423-1561
Telecopier: 317-742-8175

MEMBERS OF FIRM

Allison Ellsworth Stuart (1886-1950)
Roger D. Branigin (1902-1975)
Russell H. Hart
James V. McGlone
Larry R. Fisher
Stephen R. Pennell
Anthony S. Benton
William E. Emerick
John C. Duffey
Thomas B. Parent
Laura L. Bowker
Kevin D. Nicoson

COUNSEL

George A. Rinker

ASSOCIATES

Susan K. Holtberg
John M. Stuckey
Deborah B. Trice
Brent W. Huber

General Counsel for: The Lafayette Life Insurance Co.; INB National Bank, N.W.; Lafayette Home Hospital, Inc.
State Counsel for: Norfolk & Western Railway Co.
Mr. Ryan is Counsel to: The Trustees of Purdue University.
Representative Clients: Aluminum Company of America; Liberty Mutual Insurance Group.

For Complete List of Firm Personnel, See General Section

For full biographical listings, see the Martindale-Hubbell Law Directory

*LA PORTE,** La Porte Co.

NEWBY, LEWIS, KAMINSKI & JONES (AV)

916 Lincoln Way, 46350
Telephone: 219-362-1577
Direct Line Michigan City: 219-879-6300
Fax: 219-362-2106
Mailing Address: P.O. Box 1816, La Porte, Indiana, 46352-1816

(See Next Column)

NEWBY, LEWIS, KAMINSKI & JONES, *La Porte—Continued*

MEMBERS OF FIRM

John E. Newby (1916-1990)
Daniel E. Lewis, Jr.
Gene M. Jones
John W. Newby
Perry F. Stump, Jr.
Edward L. Volk
Mark L. Phillips
Martin W. Kus
Marsha Schatz Volk
Mark A. Lienhoop
James W. Kaminski

ASSOCIATES

John F. Lake
William S. Kaminski
Christine A. Sulewski
David P. Jones

SENIOR COUNSEL

Leon R. Kaminski

OF COUNSEL

Daniel E. Lewis

Counsel for: U. S. F. & G. Co.; State Farm Mutual Insurance Co.; Auto Owners Insurance Co.; La Porte Bank & Trust Co.; Liberty Mutual Insurance Co.; Sullair Corp.; La Porte Community School Corp.; United Farm Bureau Mutual Insurance Co.; Physicians Insurance of Indiana.

For full biographical listings, see the Martindale-Hubbell Law Directory

*MARION,** Grant Co.

BROWNE, SPITZER, HERRIMAN, STEPHENSON, HOLDEREAD & MUSSER (AV)

One Twenty Two East Fourth Street, P.O. Box 927, 46952-0927
Telephone: 317-664-7307
Fax: 317-662-0574

MEMBERS OF FIRM

James R. Browne (1940-1993)
John R. Browne, Jr.
Herbert A. Spitzer, Jr.
Charles E. Herriman
Phillip E. Stephenson
Jerome T. Holderead
Josef D. Musser
Michael D. Conner

ASSOCIATE

Mark E. Spitzer

OF COUNSEL

Jerry W. Torrance (Semi-Retired)

Representative Clients: State Farm Mutual Insurance Company; United Farm Bureau Mutual Insurance Company; Star Financial Group; Ford Motor Company; Tulox Plastics Corp.

For full biographical listings, see the Martindale-Hubbell Law Directory

MERRILLVILLE, Lake Co.

BURKE, MURPHY, COSTANZA & CUPPY (AV)

Suite 600 8585 Broadway, 46410
Telephone: 219-769-1313
Telecopier: 219-769-6806
East Chicago, Indiana Office: First National Bank Building. 720 W. Chicago Avenue.
Telephone: 219-397-2401.
Telecopier: 219-397-0506.
Palm Harbor, Florida Office: Suite 280, 33920 U.S. Highway 19 North.
Telephone: 813-787-7799.
Telecopier: 813-787-7237.

MEMBERS OF FIRM

Lester F. Murphy (East Chicago, Indiana and Palm Harbor, Florida Offices)
Frederick M. Cuppy
David K. Ranich
Kathryn D. Schmidt
David Cerven

ASSOCIATE

Craig R. Van Schouwen

Representative Clients: NBD/Gainer N.A.; Centier Bank; Town of Merrillville; Whiteco Industries; Continental Machine & Engineering Co., Inc.; Gary Steel Products Corp.; Superior Construction Co., Inc.; Federal National Mortgage Association; Morrison Construction Co.; St. Catherine Hospital of East Chicago, Indiana.

For Complete List of Firm Personnel, See General Section

For full biographical listings, see the Martindale-Hubbell Law Directory

HODGES & DAVIS, P.C. (AV)

5525 Broadway, 46410
Telephone: 219-981-2557
Fax: 219-980-7090
Portage, Indiana Office: 6508 U.S. Highway 6.
Telephone: 219-762-9129.
Fax: 219-762-2826.

Clyde D. Compton
William B. Davis
Earle F. Hites
R. Lawrence Steele
Gregory A. Sobkowski
Bonnie C. Coleman
Jill M. Madajczyk
Laura B. Brown
David H. Kreider

(See Next Column)

OF COUNSEL

Edward J. Hussey

Representative Clients: The Associated Group; Metropolitan Life Insurance Co.

For Complete List of Firm Personnel, See General Section

For full biographical listings, see the Martindale-Hubbell Law Directory

SPANGLER, JENNINGS & DOUGHERTY, P.C. (AV)

8396 Mississippi Street, 46410-6398
Telephone: 219-769-2323
Facsimile: 219-769-5007
Valparaiso, Indiana Office: 150 Lincolnway, Suite 3001.
Telephone: 219-462-6151.
FAX: 219-477-4935.

Ronald T. Spangler
Harry J. Jennings
Patrick J. Dougherty (Valparaiso Office)
Samuel J. Furlin
Richard A. Mayer
Jay A. Charon
John P. McQuillan
Samuel J. Bernardi, Jr. (Valparaiso Office)
Jon F. Schmoll
Robert D. Hawk
Joseph E. McDonald
Peter G. Koransky
David J. Hanson
Robert P. Kennedy
Allen B. Zaremba
James T. McNiece
Daniel A. Gioia
James D. McQuillan
David L. Abel, II
Harold G. Hagberg
Lawrence A. Kalina
Robert P. Stoner (Valparaiso Office)
Theresa Lazar Springmann

Gregory J. Tonner
Kathleen M. Maicher
Paul B. Poracky
Robert D. Brown
Robert J. Dignam
David R. Phillips
Kristin A. Mulholland
Feisal Amin Istrabadi
Anthony F. Tavitas
Lloyd P. Mullen
Kisti Good Risse
Jeff J. Shaw
Tammy S. Sestak

Representative Clients: Allstate Insurance Cos.; Bank One, Merriville, N.A.; First National Bank of Valparaiso; Ford Motor Credit Co.; Inland Steel Co.; Munster Calumet Shopping Center; School Town of Munster; St. Paul Insurance Cos.; State Farm Cos.; Volkswagen of America.

For Complete List of Firm Personnel, See General Section

For full biographical listings, see the Martindale-Hubbell Law Directory

MUNSTER, Lake Co.

LAW OFFICES OF EUGENE M. FEINGOLD (AV)

707 Ridge Road, Suite 204, 46321
Telephone: 219-836-8800
Fax: 219-836-8944

ASSOCIATES

Steven P. Kennedy
Barbara Richards Campbell

For full biographical listings, see the Martindale-Hubbell Law Directory

LAW OFFICES OF TIMOTHY F. KELLY (AV)

Suite 2A, 9250 Columbia Avenue, 46321
Telephone: 219-836-4062
Telecopier: 219-836-0167

MEMBERS OF FIRM

Timothy F. Kelly
Karl K. Vanzo

ASSOCIATE

Harvey Karlovac

For Complete List of Firm Personnel, See General Section

For full biographical listings, see the Martindale-Hubbell Law Directory

*NEW ALBANY,** Floyd Co.

DAVID V. SCOTT (AV)

409 Bank Street, P.O. Box 785, 47150
Telephone: 812-945-9151

Reference: PNC Bank, Indiana.

For full biographical listings, see the Martindale-Hubbell Law Directory

PORTAGE, Porter Co.

HODGES & DAVIS, P.C. (AV)

6508 U.S. Highway 6, 46368
Telephone: 219-762-9129
Fax: 219-762-2826
Merrillville, Indiana Office: 5525 Broadway.
Telephone: 219-981-2557.
Fax: 219-980-7090.

(See Next Column)

HODGES & DAVIS P.C.—*Continued*

Clyde D. Compton | R. Lawrence Steele
Earle F. Hites | Gregory A. Sobkowski
Bonnie C. Coleman

Representative Clients: The Associated Group; Metropolitan Life Insurance Co.

For full biographical listings, see the Martindale-Hubbell Law Directory

*SOUTH BEND,** St. Joseph Co.

DORAN BLACKMOND READY HAMILTON & WILLIAMS (AV)

1700 Valley American Bank Building, 211 W. Washington Street, 46601
Telephone: 219-288-1800
Fax: 219-236-4265

MEMBERS OF FIRM

John E. Doran | David T. Ready
Don G. Blackmond | John C. Hamilton
A. Howard Williams

For full biographical listings, see the Martindale-Hubbell Law Directory

HARDIG, LEE AND GROVES, PROFESSIONAL ASSOCIATION (AV)

Suite 502, First Bank Building, 205 West Jefferson Boulevard, 46601
Telephone: 219-232-5923
Fax: 219-232-5942

Edward W. Hardig | Robert D. Lee
James F. Groves

William T. Webb

Representative Client: South Bend-Mishawaka New Car Dealers Assn.
Reference: First Interstate Bank of South Bend.

For full biographical listings, see the Martindale-Hubbell Law Directory

JONES, OBENCHAIN, FORD, PANKOW, LEWIS & WOODS (AV)

1800 Valley American Bank Building, P.O. Box 4577, 46634
Telephone: 219-233-1194
Fax: 233-8957; 233-9675

Vitus G. Jones (1879-1951) | Francis Jones (1907-1988)
Roland Obenchain (1890-1961) | Roland Obenchain (Retired)
Milton A. Johnson (Retired)

MEMBERS OF FIRM

James H. Pankow | Robert W. Mysliwiec
Thomas F. Lewis, Jr. | Robert M. Edwards, Jr.
Timothy W. Woods | John B. Ford
John R. Obenchain | Mark J. Phillipoff
John W. Van Laere

ASSOCIATES

Patrick D. Murphy | Edward P. Benchik
Wendell G. Davis, Jr.

OF COUNSEL

G. Burt Ford

Attorneys for: American Family Insurance; The Equitable Life Assurance Society of the United States; Ohio Casualty Co.; Holy Cross Health Systems; Saint Joseph's Care Group; Koontz-Wagner Electric Co.; Old Kent Bank-Southwest; The Travelers Insurance Co.; H.G. Christman Construction Co., Inc.; Automatic Technologies.

For full biographical listings, see the Martindale-Hubbell Law Directory

EDWARD N. KALAMAROS & ASSOCIATES PROFESSIONAL CORPORATION (AV)

129 North Michigan Avenue, P.O. Box 4156, 46634
Telephone: 219-232-4801
Telecopier: 219-232-9736

Edward N. Kalamaros | Patrick J. Hinkle
Timothy J. Walsh | Bernard E. Edwards
Thomas F. Cohen | Philip E. Kalamaros
Joseph M. Forte | Sally P. Norton
Robert Deane Woods | Kevin W. Kearney
Peter J. Agostino | Lynn E. Arnold

Representative Clients: Liberty Mutual Insurance Co.; Employers Mutual of Wausau; Fireman's Fund American Insurance Group; U.S.F. & G.; Cincinnati Insurance Co.; Kemper Group; St. Paul Insurance Companies; Continental Loss Adjusting Services, Inc.; Orion Group.

For full biographical listings, see the Martindale-Hubbell Law Directory

ROWE, FOLEY & GARDNER (AV)

Suite 900 Society Bank Building, 46601
Telephone: 219-233-8200

R. Kent Rowe | Edmond W. Foley
R. Kent Rowe, III | Martin J. Gardner

(See Next Column)

ASSOCIATES

Gregory J. Haines | Steven D. Groth
Timothy J. Maher | Evan S. Roberts
Lee Korzan | William James O'Mahony

For full biographical listings, see the Martindale-Hubbell Law Directory

*TERRE HAUTE,** Vigo Co.

COX, ZWERNER, GAMBILL & SULLIVAN (AV)

511 Wabash Avenue, P.O. Box 1625, 47808-1625
Telephone: 812-232-6003
Fax: 812-232-6567

MEMBERS OF FIRM

Ernest J. Zwerner (1918-1980) | David W. Sullivan
Benjamin G. Cox (1915-1988) | Robert L. Gowdy
Gilbert W. Gambill, Jr. | Louis F. Britton
James E. Sullivan | Robert D. Hepburn
Benjamin G. Cox, Jr. | Carroll D. Smeltzer
Jeffry A. Lind

ASSOCIATE

Ronald E. Jumps

Counsel for: Terre Haute First National Bank; Farmers Insurance Group; Indiana-American Water Co.; Indiana State University; Merchants National Bank of Terre Haute; Rose-Hulman Institute of Technology; Tribune-Star Publishing Co., Inc.; Weston Paper & Manufacturing Co.; Equitable Life Assurance Society of U.S.; Federated Mutual Insurance Co.; Fireman's Fund; General Accident Group; Guaranty National Insurance; Milwaukee Mutual Insurance Co.; Ohio Casualty Insurance Co.; Hartford Insurance; The Travelers Co.; United Services Auto Assn.; Vernon Insurance Co.

For full biographical listings, see the Martindale-Hubbell Law Directory

LEWIS AND LEWIS (AV)

629 Cherry Street, P.O. Box 1506, 47808
Telephone: 812-232-2382
Fax: 812-232-2383

MEMBERS OF FIRM

Jerdie D. Lewis (1904-1993) | Michael J. Lewis
Jordan D. Lewis | Elizabeth Lewis Rodway

Representative Clients: United Farm Bureau Mutual Insurance Companies; Consolidated Rail Corp.; The Statesman Group; Sentry Insurance Co.; General Casualty Cos.; Inter-Insurance Exchange of the Chicago Motor Club.
Reference: The Merchants National Bank of Terre Haute, Indiana.

For full biographical listings, see the Martindale-Hubbell Law Directory

WILKINSON, GOELLER, MODESITT, WILKINSON & DRUMMY (AV)

333 Ohio Street, P.O. Box 800, 47808-0800
Telephone: 812-232-4311
Fax: 812-235-5107

MEMBERS OF FIRM

Myrl O. Wilkinson | John C. Wall
Raymond H. Modesitt | Craig M. McKee
B. Curtis Wilkinson | Scott M. Kyrouac
William W. Drummy | Jeffrey A. Boyll

ASSOCIATES

David P. Friedrich | Anthony R. Jost

Representative Clients: State Farm Mutual Automobile Insurance Company; State Farm Fire & Casualty Co.; Nationwide Insurance Company; Fireman's Fund Insurance Companies; The Country Companies; The Medical Protective Company; Physician's Insurance Company; Indiana Insurance Companies; United Farm Bureau Mutual Insurance Company; St. Paul Insurance Companies.

For Complete List of Firm Personnel, See General Section

For full biographical listings, see the Martindale-Hubbell Law Directory

*VALPARAISO,** Porter Co.

BLACHLY, TABOR, BOZIK & HARTMAN (AV)

Suite 401 Indiana Federal Building, 46383
Telephone: 219-464-1041

MEMBERS OF FIRM

Quentin A. Blachly | David L. Hollenbeck
Glenn J. Tabor | David L. DeBoer
James S. Bozik | Thomas F. Macke
Duane W. Hartman | Randall J. Zromkoski
Richard J. Rupcich

ASSOCIATE

Roger A. Weitgenant

Reference: First National Bank.

For Complete List of Firm Personnel, See General Section

For full biographical listings, see the Martindale-Hubbell Law Directory

Valparaiso—Continued

DOUGLAS, ALEXA, KOEPPEN & HURLEY (AV)

14 Indiana Avenue, P.O. Box 209, 46384-0209
Telephone: 219-462-2126
Fax: 219-477-4408

MEMBERS OF FIRM

Herbert K. Douglas
William E. Alexa
R. Bradley Koeppen
Brian J. Hurley

ASSOCIATE

Mark A. Gland

OF COUNSEL

George W. Douglas
Leo J. Clifford

Attorneys for: Urschel Laboratories, Inc.; Northern Indiana Public Service Co.; Midwest Steel Division, National Steel; McGill Manufacturing Co., Inc.; Park District, City of Valparaiso.

For full biographical listings, see the Martindale-Hubbell Law Directory

LAW OFFICES OF JAMES V. TSOUTSOURIS (AV)

Five Lincolnway, 46383
Telephone: 219-462-4148
Fax: 219-477-4932

ASSOCIATES

Joann Tsoutsouris
G. Anthony Bertig
John Edward Martin
Lori L. Ferngren

A list of Representative Clients and References will be furnished upon request.

For full biographical listings, see the Martindale-Hubbell Law Directory

*VERSAILLES,** Ripley Co.

EATON & ROMWEBER (AV)

123 South Main Street, P.O. Box 275, 47042
Telephone: 812-689-5111
Fax: 812-689-5165
Batesville, Indiana Office: 13 East George Street. Telephone 812-934-5735. *Fax:* 812-934-6041.

MEMBERS OF FIRM

Larry L. Eaton
Anthony A. Romweber

ASSOCIATE

W. Gregory Coy

For full biographical listings, see the Martindale-Hubbell Law Directory

*WARSAW,** Kosciusko Co.

LEMON, REED, ARMEY, HEARN & LEININGER (AV)

210 North Buffalo Street, P.O. Box 770, 46581-0770
Telephone: 219-268-9111
Telecopier: 219-267-8647

MEMBERS OF FIRM

Thomas R. Lemon
Rex L. Reed
Michael E. Armey
R. Steven Hearn
Daniel K. Leininger

ASSOCIATES

Jane L. Kauffman
Katharine Mull Carter

OF COUNSEL

Robert L. Rasor

Representative Clients: Lake City Bank; Zimmer Inc.; The Dalton Foundries, Inc.; Grace Schools, Inc.; Kosciusko Community Hospital, Inc.; Othy, Inc.

For full biographical listings, see the Martindale-Hubbell Law Directory

ROCKHILL, PINNICK, PEQUIGNOT, HELM & LANDIS (AV)

105 East Main Street, 46580-2742
Telephone: 219-267-6116
Telecopier: 219-269-9264

MEMBERS OF FIRM

Brooks C. Pinnick
Stanley E. Pequignot
Richard K. Helm
Vern K. Landis
Jay A. Rigdon
Jeanne A. Rondot

ASSOCIATE

Jamelyn E. Casbon

OF COUNSEL

Alvin T. Rockhill

Representative Clients: First National Bank of Warsaw, Warsaw, Indiana; Warsaw Times-Union Newspaper and WRSW Radio and Broadcast Station; State Farm Insurance Cos.; Warsaw Chemical Co., Inc.; Little Crow Milling Co., Inc.; Farmers State Bank; C & D Foods, Inc.; Maple Leaf Farms, Inc.; United Farm Bureau Mutual Insurance Co.

For full biographical listings, see the Martindale-Hubbell Law Directory

IOWA

CEDAR FALLS, Black Hawk Co.

REDFERN, MASON, DIETER, LARSEN & MOORE (AV)

315 Clay Street, P.O. Box 627, 50613
Telephone: 319-277-6830
Facsimile: 319-277-3531

MEMBERS OF FIRM

David R. Mason
Robert J. Dieter
John C. Larsen
Steven D. Moore
Donald B. Redfern
Mark W. Fransdal
Mark S. Rolinger

ASSOCIATE

Susan Bernau Staudt

Representative Clients: Norwest Bank Iowa, N.A.; The National Bank of Waterloo; Sartori Memorial Hospital; Cedar Falls Utilities; University of Northern Iowa Foundation; Cedar Falls Community School District; United States Fidelity & Guaranty Co.; The Travelers Insurance Cos.; Fireman's Fund Insurance Cos.; Control-o-fax Corp.

For Complete List of Firm Personnel, See General Section

For full biographical listings, see the Martindale-Hubbell Law Directory

*CEDAR RAPIDS,** Linn Co.

LYNCH, DALLAS, SMITH & HARMAN, P.C. (AV)

526 Second Avenue SE, P.O. Box 2457, 52406-2457
Telephone: 319-365-9101
Facsimile: 319-365-9512

Donald G. Ribble
Scott E. McLeod
Robert R. Rush
Edward J. Krug
Wilford H. Stone
Sean W. McPartland
Matthew J. Nagle

Jana L. Happel

Representative Clients: American States Insurance Co.; Blue Cross and Blue Shield of Iowa; Chicago Central & Pacific Railroad Co.; Connecticut General Life Insurance Company; Deere & Co.; Electric Mutual Insurance Company; Farm Credit Bank of Omaha; Rockwell International Corp.; State Farm Insurance Cos.; The Travelers Insurance Cos.

For Complete List of Firm Personnel, See General Section

For full biographical listings, see the Martindale-Hubbell Law Directory

PICKENS, BARNES & ABERNATHY (AV)

Tenth Floor American Building, P.O. Box 74170, 52407-4170
Telephone: 319-366-7621
Fax: 319-366-3158

MEMBERS OF FIRM

Minor Barnes
Terry J. Abernathy
Mark H. Ogden
Matthew G. Novak

ASSOCIATE

JoAnne M. Lilledahl

OF COUNSEL

James F. Pickens

A list of Representative Clients furnished upon request.

For full biographical listings, see the Martindale-Hubbell Law Directory

SHUTTLEWORTH & INGERSOLL, P.C. (AV)

500 Firstar Bank Building, P.O. Box 2107, 52406-2107
Telephone: 319-365-9461
Fax: 319-365-8443

John M. Bickel
Robert D. Houghton
Richard S. Fry
Richard C. Garberson
Steven J. Pace
Glenn L. Johnson
Thomas P. Peffer
Kevin H. Collins
Diane Kutzko
Mark L. Zaiger
Douglas R. Oelschlaeger
Constance M. Alt
Kurt L. Kratovil

Christine L. McLaughlin
William H. Courter

OF COUNSEL

Ralph W. Gearhart

COUNSEL

James D. Hodges, Jr.

Representative Clients: Archer-Daniels-Midland Co.; Cargill, Inc.; CIGNA Companies; CNA Insurance Companies; Fireman's Fund Insurance Companies; Firstar Bank Cedar Rapids, N.A.; General Casualty Company of Wisconsin; General Motors Corp.; Grinnell Mutual Insurance Company; IMT Insurance Company.

(See Next Column)

SHUTTLEWORTH & INGERSOLL P.C.—*Continued*

For Complete List of Firm Personnel, See General Section

For full biographical listings, see the Martindale-Hubbell Law Directory

SIMMONS, PERRINE, ALBRIGHT & ELLWOOD, L.L.P. (AV)

A Partnership including a Professional Corporation
115 Third Street S.E. Suite 1200, 52401
Telephone: 319-366-7641
Telecopier: 319-366-1917 (I,II,III)

PARTNERS

James R. Snyder
James E. Shipman
Stephen J. Holtman
Robert M. Jilek (P.C.)
Iris E. Muchmore
Gregory M. Lederer
James A. Gerk
Richard G. Hileman, Jr.
Roger W. Stone
David A. Hacker
Matthew J. Petrzelka
James M. Peters

Representative Clients: Amana Refrigeration, Inc.; Norwest Bank Iowa, N.A.; Sheaffer Pen; Weyerhaeuser Co.; Grand Wood Area Education Agency; Howard R. Green Co.; Varied Investments, Inc.; Norand Corp.; Universal Gym Equipment Co.; Hall Foundation.

For Complete List of Firm Personnel, See General Section

For full biographical listings, see the Martindale-Hubbell Law Directory

*COUNCIL BLUFFS,** Pottawattamie Co.

PETERS LAW FIRM, P.C. (AV)

233 Pearl Street, P.O. Box 1078, 51502-1078
Telephone: 712-328-3157
FAX: 712-328-9092

Dennis Leu
Dennis M. Gray
Lyle W. Ditmars
Scott H. Peters
John M. McHale
Jacob J. Peters

Representative Clients: Hawkeye Bank & Trust; Grinnell Mutual Reinsurance Co.; Iowa West Racing Association; Rockwell International; Shelter Insurance; State Farms Insurance; Midlands Mall; Kemper Group; The Pillsbury Co.; The Cities of Crescent.

For Complete List of Firm Personnel, See General Section

For full biographical listings, see the Martindale-Hubbell Law Directory

*DES MOINES,** Polk Co.

AHLERS, COONEY, DORWEILER, HAYNIE, SMITH & ALLBEE, P.C. (AV)

100 Court Avenue, Suite 600, 50309-2231
Telephone: 515-243-7611
Fax: 515-243-2149

H. Richard Smith
Robert G. Allbee
L. W. Rosebrook
Richard G. Santi
David H. Luginbill

Representative Clients: Drake University; Insurance Company of North America; West Des Moines State Bank; Koss Construction Co.; Pittsburgh-Des Moines Steel Co.; Sears, Roebuck & Co.; Iowa Association of Municipal Utilities; Iowa State Board of Regents; Kirke Van Orsdel, Inc.; Travelers Insurance Group; WestBank.

For Complete List of Firm Personnel, See General Section

For full biographical listings, see the Martindale-Hubbell Law Directory

BELIN HARRIS LAMSON MCCORMICK, A PROFESSIONAL CORPORATION (AV)

2000 Financial Center, 50309
Telephone: 515-243-7100
Telecopier: 515-282-7615

Mark McCormick
Roger T. Stetson
Charles D. Hunter
Quentin R. Boyken
Charles F. Becker
Mark E. Weinhardt
Dennis P. Ogden
Margaret C. Callahan
Robert D. Sharp
Timothy P. Willcockson

For Complete List of Firm Personnel, See General Section

For full biographical listings, see the Martindale-Hubbell Law Directory

NICHOLAS CRITELLI ASSOCIATES, P.C. (AV)

Suite 500, 317 Sixth Avenue, 50309-4128
Telephone: 515-243-3122
Telecopier: (FAX) 515-243-3121
London, England Office: 11 Stone Buildings, Lincoln's Inn.
Telephone: 011-44-71-404-5055.
FAX: 011-44-71-405-1551.

(See Next Column)

Nick Critelli, Jr.
Lylea Dodson Critelli
Connie L. Diekema
Joseph B. Saluri

References: Boatmen's Bank of Des Moines, N.A.; Iowa State Bar Association.

For full biographical listings, see the Martindale-Hubbell Law Directory

FINLEY, ALT, SMITH, SCHARNBERG, MAY & CRAIG, P.C. (AV)

Fourth Floor Equitable Building, 50309
Telephone: 515-288-0145
Telecopier: 515-288-2724

Thomas A. Finley
Steven K. Scharnberg

Representative Clients: Aetna Casualty & Surety Co.; Aetna Life Insurance Co.; ALAS; American Society of Composers, Authors and Publishers; Equitable Life Assurance Society of the U.S.; Federated Insurance Co.; Meredith Corp.
Iowa Attorneys for: Midwest Medical Insurance Co.
District Attorneys for: Norfolk & Southern Railroad; CP Rail Systems.

For Complete List of Firm Personnel, See General Section

For full biographical listings, see the Martindale-Hubbell Law Directory

GREFE & SIDNEY (AV)

2222 Grand Avenue, P.O. Box 10434, 50306
Telephone: 515-245-4300
Fax: 515-245-4452

MEMBERS OF FIRM

Ross H. Sidney
Henry A. Harmon
Claude H. Freeman
Stephen D. Hardy
John Werner
Patrick J. McNulty
Iris J. Post
Mark W. Thomas
Guy R. Cook

ASSOCIATES

Ken A. Winjum
David C. Duncan
Andrew D. Hall
Kevin W. Techau
Stephanie L. Glenn

Representative Clients: Easter Stores; Freeman Decorating Co.; Iowa-Nebraska Farm Equipment Association, Inc.; Pella Corp.; State Farm Mutual Insurance Companies of Bloomington, Ill.; Liberty Mutual Insurance Co.; United States Fidelity and Guaranty Co.; Koehring Co.

For Complete List of Firm Personnel, See General Section

For full biographical listings, see the Martindale-Hubbell Law Directory

HERRICK, LANGDON & LANGDON (AV)

1800 Financial Center, Seventh and Walnut, 50309
Telephone: 515-282-8150
Telecopier: 515-282-8226

MEMBERS OF FIRM

Allan A. Herrick (1896-1989)
Herschel G. Langdon
Richard G. Langdon
William R. Clark, Jr.
Richard N. Winders
Richard A. Steffen
Eric F. Turner
Kermit B. Anderson
Kathleen L. Nutt

ASSOCIATE

Michael B. O'Meara

Representative Clients: Norwest Bank Iowa N.A.; The Principal Financial Group; Hy-Vee Food Stores, Inc.; Des Moines Independent Community School District; Mercedes Benz; MAPCO, Inc.; Continental Insurance Healthcare; CIGNA Property and Casualty Co.; Crum and Forster Manager's Corp.

For full biographical listings, see the Martindale-Hubbell Law Directory

PATTERSON, LORENTZEN, DUFFIELD, TIMMONS, IRISH, BECKER & ORDWAY (AV)

729 Insurance Exchange Building, 50309
Telephone: 515-283-2147
Fax: 515-283-1002

MEMBERS OF FIRM

G. O. Patterson (1914-1982)
James A. Lorentzen
Theodore T. Duffield
William E. Timmons
Roy M. Irish
Gary D. Ordway
Robin L. Hermann
Harry Perkins, III
Michael F. Lacey, Jr.
Jeffrey A. Boehlert
Douglas A. Haag
Charles E. Cutler
Ronald M. Rankin
Michael D. Huppert
William A. Wickett

ASSOCIATES

Jeffrey A. Baker
Janice M. Herfkens
Coreen K. Bezdicek
Scott S. Bellis

(See Next Column)

PATTERSON, LORENTZEN, DUFFIELD, TIMMONS, IRISH, BECKER & ORDWAY, *Des Moines—Continued*

OF COUNSEL

F. H. Becker

Representative Clients: Allied Mutual Insurance Company; CNA Insurance Company; Chubb Insurance Group; Continental Western Insurance Co.; Farmers Insurance Group; Farmland Insurance Company; Grinnell Mutual Reinsurance Company; Hawkeye Security Insurance Company; Iowa Insurance Institute, St. Paul Fire & Marine Insurance Company.

For Complete List of Firm Personnel, See General Section

For full biographical listings, see the Martindale-Hubbell Law Directory

WASKER, DORR, WIMMER & MARCOUILLER, P.C. (AV)

801 Grand Avenue, Suite 3100, 50309-8036
Telephone: 515-283-1801
Facsimile: 515-283-1802

Fred L. Dorr

Jennifer Ann Tyler
Matthew D. Kern

For Complete List of Firm Personnel, See General Section

For full biographical listings, see the Martindale-Hubbell Law Directory

WHITFIELD & EDDY, P.L.C. (AV)

317 6th Avenue, Suite 1200 Locust at 6th, 50309-4110
Telephone: 515-288-6041
Fax: 515-246-1474

A. Roger Witke
Timothy J. Walker
David L. Phipps
Benjamin B. Ullem
Robert M. Kreamer
Robert L. Fanter
Bernard L. Spaeth, Jr.
Rodney P. Kubat
William L. Fairbank
Robert G. Bridges
Jaki K. Samuelson
Kevin M. Reynolds
Thomas H. Burke
Thomas Henderson
George H. Frampton
Megan Manning Antenucci
Wendy L. Carlson
Robert J. Blink
Gary A. Norton
Mark V. Hanson
Maureen Roach Tobin

Jeffrey William Courter
August B. Landis
Kent Thomas Kelsey
Richard J. Kirschman
John F. Fatino
Jason M. Casini
Nancy P. O'Brien

OF COUNSEL

Dean Dutton

General Counsel for: American Life and Casualty Co.; The Statesman Group, Inc.; United Security Insurance Co.; Crum & Forster; General Motors Corp.; Old Republic Surety; Royal Insurance Co.; Tudor Insurance Co.; Western World Insurance Co.

For Complete List of Firm Personnel, See General Section

For full biographical listings, see the Martindale-Hubbell Law Directory

*HAMPTON,** Franklin Co.

HOBSON, CADY & CADY (AV)

9 First Street S.W., 50441
Telephone: 515-456-2555
Fax: 515-456-3315

MEMBERS OF FIRM

A. J. Hobson (1903-1972)
G. Arthur Cady
G. A. Cady, III

General Counsel for: Ag Services of America, Inc.
A list of Representative Clients will be furnished upon request.
References: First National Bank of Hampton; Liberty Bank & Trust.

For full biographical listings, see the Martindale-Hubbell Law Directory

*IOWA CITY,** Johnson Co.

MEARDON, SUEPPEL, DOWNER & HAYES P.L.C. (AV)

122 South Linn Street, 52240
Telephone: 319-338-9222
Fax: 319-338-7250

William L. Meardon
James P. Hayes
James D. McCarragher
Thomas D. Hobart
Paul J. McAndrew, Jr.

Charles A. Meardon
Steven A. Michalek

Representative Clients: United Technologies-Automotive; Perpetual Savings Bank; Farmers Savings Bank of Kalona; Metro Pavers, Inc.; League of Iowa Municipalities; Hills Bank and Trust Co.; J.M. Swank Co.; City of Muscatine; McComas-Lacina Construction Co., Inc.; Diamond Dave's Taco Company, Inc.

(See Next Column)

For Complete List of Firm Personnel, See General Section

For full biographical listings, see the Martindale-Hubbell Law Directory

*MARENGO,** Iowa Co.

HARNED & MCMEEN (AV)

888 Court Avenue, P.O. Box 267, 52301
Telephone: 319-642-5521

MEMBERS OF FIRM

F. Paul Harned (1892-1973)
L. C. McMeen

ASSOCIATE

Edward D. Jorgensen

Representative Clients: Benton County State Bank; Boatmen's Bank of Marengo; I.M.T. Insurance Co.; Iowa Valley Community School District.
References: Boatmen's Bank of Marengo; Benton County State Bank, Blairstown, Iowa.

For full biographical listings, see the Martindale-Hubbell Law Directory

*SIOUX CITY,** Woodbury Co.

EIDSMOE, HEIDMAN, REDMOND, FREDREGILL, PATTERSON & SCHATZ (AV)

A Partnership including Professional Corporations
701 Pierce Street, Suite 200, P.O. Box 3086, 51102
Telephone: 712-255-8838
Fax: 712-258-6714

MEMBERS OF FIRM

Marvin F. Heidman
James W. Redmond
Alan E. Fredregill (P.C.)
Charles T. Patterson
Kenneth C. Schatz (P.C.)
Thomas M. Plaza
Daniel D. Dykstra
Lance D. Ehmcke
Margaret M. Prahl
John Ackerman
Gregg E. Williams
Judith A. Higgs
John C. Gray
Daniel B. Shuck

ASSOCIATES

Rita C. Grimm
Ryan K. Crayne
Charles E. Trullinger
John W. Gleysteen (Retired)
Robert R. Eidsmoe (Retired)
Jacob C. Gleysteen (1883-1943)
H. Clifford Harper (1891-1959)

Representative Clients: Aetna Casualty & Surety Co.; Irving F. Jensen Co., Inc.; Marian Health Center; Medical Protective Co.; John Morrell & Co.; Pig Improvement Co.; State Farm Mutual Insurance Co.; Terra International, Inc.; The Security National Bank of Sioux City; Wal-Mart Stores, Inc.

For full biographical listings, see the Martindale-Hubbell Law Directory

*WATERLOO,** Black Hawk Co.

GALLAGHER, LANGLAS & GALLAGHER, P.C. (AV)

Law Building, 405 East Fifth Street, P.O. Box 2615, 50704
Telephone: 319-233-6163
Fax: 319-233-6435

Edward J. Gallagher, Jr.
Thomas W. Langlas
Edward J. Gallagher, III
George L. Weilein
Timothy C. Boller
Cynthia A. Scherrman
Thomas C. Verhulst

Jeffrey C. Peterzalek
David A. Roth

References: The National Bank of Waterloo; The Waterloo Savings Bank; Norwest Bank Iowa NA, Waterloo, Iowa.

For full biographical listings, see the Martindale-Hubbell Law Directory

SWISHER & COHRT (AV)

528 West Fourth Street, P.O. Box 1200, 50704
Telephone: 319-232-6555
FAX: 319-232-4835

MEMBERS OF FIRM

Benjamin F. Swisher (1878-1959)
L. J. Cohrt (1898-1974)
Charles F. Swisher (1919-1986)
Eldon R. McCann
Steven A. Weidner
Larry J. Cohrt
J. Douglas Oberman
Stephen J. Powell
Jim D. DeKoster
Jeffrey J. Greenwood
Samuel C. Anderson
Robert C. Griffin
Kevin R. Rogers

ASSOCIATES

Beth E. Hansen
Mark F. Conway
Natalie Williams Burr

Firm is Counsel for: Koehring Corp.; Clay Equipment; Chamberlain Manufacturing Co.; Waterloo Courier.
Local Counsel for: Allied Group; John Deere Insurance; Liberty Mutual Insurance Co.

For full biographical listings, see the Martindale-Hubbell Law Directory

KANSAS

*KANSAS CITY,** Wyandotte Co.

HOLBROOK, HEAVEN & FAY, P.A. (AV)

757 Armstrong, P.O. Box 171927, 66117
Telephone: 913-342-2500
Fax: 913-342-0603
Merriam, Kansas Office: 6700 Antioch Street.
Telephone: 913-677-1717.
Fax: 913-677- 0403.

Reid F. Holbrook
Lewis A. Heaven, Jr. (Resident, Merriam Office)
Ted F. Fay, Jr. (Resident, Merriam Office)
Thomas E. Osborn
Robert L. Kennedy
Janet M. Simpson
John D. Tongier (Resident, Merriam Office)
Thomas M. Sutherland
Thomas S. Busch (Resident, Merriam Office)
Vincent K. Snowbarger (Resident, Merriam Office)
Kurt S. Brack
Sally A. Howard
Brent G. Wright

For Complete List of Firm Personnel, See General Section

For full biographical listings, see the Martindale-Hubbell Law Directory

McANANY, VAN CLEAVE & PHILLIPS, P.A. (AV)

Fourth Floor, 707 Minnesota Avenue, P.O. Box 1300, 66117
Telephone: 913-371-3838
Facsimile: 913-371-4722
Lenexa, Kansas Office: Suite 200, 11900 West 87th Street Parkway.
Telephone: 913-888-9000.
Facsimile: 913-888-7049.
Kansas City, Missouri Office: Suite 304, 819 Walnut Street.
Telephone: 816-556-9417.

John J. Jurcyk, Jr.
Robert D. Benham
Clifford T. Mueller (Resident, Lenexa Office)
Patrick D. McAnany (Resident, Lenexa Office)
Frank D. Menghini
David M. Druten (Resident, Lenexa Office)
Daniel B. Denk
Charles A. Getto
William P. Coates, Jr. (Resident, Lenexa Office)
Jeanne Gorman Rau
Robert F. Rowe, Jr. (Resident, Lenexa Office)
Lawrence D. Greenbaum
Douglas M. Greenwald
Daniel F. Church
Terri L. Savely Bezek
Gregory S. Brown

Reference: UMB Commercial National Bank.

For Complete List of Firm Personnel, See General Section

For full biographical listings, see the Martindale-Hubbell Law Directory

OVERLAND PARK, Johnson Co.

FISHER, PATTERSON, SAYLER & SMITH (AV)

Suite 210, 11050 Roe Street, 66211
Telephone: 913-339-6757
FAX: 913-339-6187
Topeka, Kansas Office: 534 Kansas Avenue, Suite 400. 66603-3463.
Telephone: 913-232-7761.
Fax: 913-232-6604.

MEMBERS OF FIRM

Edwin Dudley Smith (Resident)
Michael K. Seck (Resident)
David P. Madden (Resident)

ASSOCIATE

Kurt A. Level (Resident)

For full biographical listings, see the Martindale-Hubbell Law Directory

SHAMBERG, JOHNSON, BERGMAN & MORRIS, CHARTERED (AV)

Suite 355, 4551 West 107th Street, 66207
Telephone: 913-642-0600
Fax: 913-642-9629
Kansas City, Kansas Office: Suite 860, New Brotherhood Building, 8th and State Streets.
Telephone: 913-281-1900.
Kansas City, Missouri Office: Suite 205, Scarritt Arcade Building, 819 Walnut.
Telephone: 816-556-9431.

Lynn R. Johnson
Victor A. Bergman
David R. Morris
John M. Parisi

Steven G. Brown
John E. Rogers
Steve N. Six
Anthony L. DeWitt (Not admitted in KS)
Patrick A. Hamilton

(See Next Column)

OF COUNSEL

John E. Shamberg

For full biographical listings, see the Martindale-Hubbell Law Directory

PRAIRIE VILLAGE, Johnson Co.

HOLMAN, McCOLLUM & HANSEN, P.C. (AV(T))

9400 Mission Road Suite 205, 66206
Telephone: 913-648-7272
Fax: 913-383-9596
Kansas City, Missouri Office: 644 West 57th Terrace.
Telephone: 816-333-8522.
Fax: 913-383-9596.

Joseph Y. Holman
Frank B. W. McCollum
Eric L. Hansen
Dana L. Parks
Nancy Merrill Wilson
Amy L. Brown
E. John Edwards III (Not admitted in KS)
Katherine E. Rich

For full biographical listings, see the Martindale-Hubbell Law Directory

*SALINA,** Saline Co.

NORTON, WASSERMAN, JONES & KELLY (AV)

215 South Santa Fe, P.O. Box 2388, 67402-2388
Telephone: 913-827-3646
Fax: 913-827-0538

MEMBERS OF FIRM

Frank C. Norton
Kenneth W. Wasserman
Robert S. Jones
Norman R. Kelly

ASSOCIATES

Robert A. Martin
Timothy M. Henderson

Reference: Gypsum Valley Bank.

For full biographical listings, see the Martindale-Hubbell Law Directory

*TOPEKA,** Shawnee Co.

BENNETT & DILLON (AV)

1605 Southwest 37th Street, 66611
Telephone: 913-267-5063
Fax: 913-267-2652

MEMBERS OF FIRM

Mark L. Bennett, Jr.
Wilburn Dillon, Jr.
Ann L. Hoover

Representative Clients: Southern Pacific Transportation Co.; St. Louis Southwestern Railway Co.; Denver and Rio Grande Western Railroad Co.; American Insurance Association; Sears Roebuck and Company; Zenith Inc.; St. Paul Insurance Co.; Kansas Medical Mutual Insurance Co.
References: Silver Lake State Bank; Columbian National Bank and Trust.

For Complete List of Firm Personnel, See General Section

For full biographical listings, see the Martindale-Hubbell Law Directory

DAVIS, UNREIN, HUMMER, McCALLISTER & BUCK (AV)

100 East Ninth Street, Third Floor, P.O. Box 3575, 66601-3575
Telephone: 913-354-1100
Fax: 913-354-1113

MEMBERS OF FIRM

Byron M. Gray (1901-1986)
Maurice D. Freidberg (1902-1965)
Charles L. Davis, Jr. (1921-1992)
Michael J. Unrein
J. Franklin Hummer
Mark A. Buck
James B. Biggs
Christopher M. Rohrer
Brenda L. Head

OF COUNSEL

Gary D. McCallister

Representative Clients: Adams Business Forms; Bettis Asphalt Co., Inc.; Blue Cross & Blue Shield of Kansas; Cooper Tire & Rubber Co.; Deere & Co.; Famous Brands; Jostens, Inc.; Kansas Association of Realtors; McElroys, Inc.; McPherson Contractors.

For full biographical listings, see the Martindale-Hubbell Law Directory

FISHER, PATTERSON, SAYLER & SMITH (AV)

534 Kansas Avenue, Suite 400, 66603-3463
Telephone: 913-232-7761
Fax: 913-232-6604
Overland Park, Kansas Office: Suite 210, 11050 Roe Street. 66211.
Telephone: 913-339-6757.
Fax: 913-339-6187.

(See Next Column)

FISHER, PATTERSON, SAYLER & SMITH, *Topeka—Continued*

MEMBERS OF FIRM

Donald Patterson
Charles Keith Sayler
Edwin Dudley Smith (Resident, Overland Park Office)
Larry G. Pepperdine
James P. Nordstrom
Justice B. King
J. Steven Pigg
Steve R. Fabert
Ronald J. Laskowski
Michael K. Seck (Resident, Overland Park Office)
David P. Madden (Resident, Overland Park Office)
Steven K. Johnson

ASSOCIATES

Kristine A. Larscheid
Michael L. Bennett
Kurt A. Level (Resident, Overland Park Office)
Betty J. Mick

OF COUNSEL

David H. Fisher

Representative Clients: Gage Shopping Center, Inc.; Fireman's Fund-American Insurance Cos.; United States Fidelity and Guaranty Co.; Hartford Insurance Group.; The Procter & Gamble Company; American Cyanamid Company; Commercial Union Insurance Companies; Kansas Fire & Casualty Co.; National Casualty/Scottsdale Insurance Co.

For full biographical listings, see the Martindale-Hubbell Law Directory

GOODELL, STRATTON, EDMONDS & PALMER (AV)

515 South Kansas Avenue, 66603-3999
Telephone: 913-233-0593
Telecopier: 913-233-8870

MEMBERS OF FIRM

Gerald L. Goodell
Wayne T. Stratton
Arthur E. Palmer
Harold S. Youngentob
Charles R. Hay
Patrick M. Salsbury
Les E. Diehl
David E. Bruns
Daniel J. Gronniger
N. Larry Bork
John D. Ensley

ASSOCIATES

Curtis J. Waugh
Catherine Walberg

SPECIAL COUNSEL

Marta Fisher Linenberger

Local Counsel for: Farm Bureau Mutual Insurance Co.; Metropolitan Life Insurance Co.; St. Paul Fire & Marine Insurance Co.
General Counsel for: American Home Life Insurance Co.; Columbian National Title Insurance Co.; The Menninger Foundation; Stauffer Communications, Inc.; Kansas Association of Realtors; Kansas Medical Society; Kansas Hospital Association.

For Complete List of Firm Personnel, See General Section

For full biographical listings, see the Martindale-Hubbell Law Directory

PORTER, FAIRCHILD, WACHTER & HANEY, P.A. (AV)

Suite 1000, Bank IV Tower, 534 South Kansas Avenue, P.O. Box 1833, 66601-1833
Telephone: 913-235-2200
Facsimile: 913-235-8950

James W. Porter
Ronald W. Fairchild
John H. Wachter
Thomas D. Haney

Douglas F. Martin
Sheldon J. Moss

For full biographical listings, see the Martindale-Hubbell Law Directory

WRIGHT, HENSON, SOMERS, SEBELIUS, CLARK & BAKER (AV)

Commerce Bank Building, 100 Southeast Ninth Street, 2nd Floor, P.O. Box 3555, 66601-3555
Telephone: 913-232-2200
FAX: 913-232-3344

MEMBERS OF FIRM

Thomas E. Wright
K. Gary Sebelius
Bruce J. Clark
Anne Lamborn Baker

ASSOCIATES

Catherine A. Walter
Evelyn Zabel Wilson

Representative Clients: Continental Insurance Companies; American Family Insurance Companies; Shelter Insurance Companies; Newtek, Inc.; Phico Group; Insurance Co.; Kansas Bankers Association; Western Resources, Inc.; KPL/Gas Service Co.; Payless ShoeSource, Inc.

For Complete List of Firm Personnel, See General Section

For full biographical listings, see the Martindale-Hubbell Law Directory

*WICHITA,** Sedgwick Co.

DEPEW & GILLEN (AV)

151 North Main, Suite 700, 67202-1408
Telephone: 316-265-9621
Facsimile: 316-265-3819

(See Next Column)

MEMBERS OF FIRM

Spencer L. Depew
Dennis L. Gillen
Jack Scott McInteer
David W. Nickel
Nicholas S. Daily
David E. Rogers
Charles Christian Steincamp

For full biographical listings, see the Martindale-Hubbell Law Directory

FLEESON, GOOING, COULSON & KITCH, L.L.C. (AV)

125 North Market Street, Suite 1600, P.O. Box 997, 67201-0997
Telephone: 316-267-7361
Telecopier: 316-267-1754

Gerrit H. Wormhoudt
Richard I. Stephenson
Thomas D. Kitch
Stephen M. Joseph
Stephen E. Robison
Mark F. Anderson
Ronald Campbell
Charles E. Millsap
William P. Tretbar
Susan P. Selvidge
Thomas J. Lasater
David G. Seely
Lyndon W. Vix

John T. Steere
William Townsley
Jordan Clay
John E. Rees, II

OF COUNSEL

Dale M. Stucky
Donald R. Newkirk

Attorneys for: Bank IV, Wichita, N.A; Intrust Bank, N.A.; Wichita Eagle and Beacon Publishing Co., Inc.; Southwest Kansas Royalty Owners Assn.; Liberty Mutual Insurance Co.; Grant Thornton; The Law Company; Vulcan Materials Co.; The Wichita State University Board of Trustees.

For Complete List of Firm Personnel, See General Section

For full biographical listings, see the Martindale-Hubbell Law Directory

FOULSTON & SIEFKIN (AV)

(Formerly Foulston, Siefkin, Powers & Eberhardt)
700 Fourth Financial Center, Broadway at Douglas, 67202
Telephone: 316-267-6371
Facsimile: 316-267-6345
Topeka, Kansas Office: 1515 Bank IV Tower, 534 Kansas Avenue. 66603.
Telephone: 913-233-3600.
FAX: 913-233-1610.
Member: Lex Mundi, A Global Association of Independent Firms

MEMBERS OF FIRM

Robert L. Howard
Mikel L. Stout
Richard D. Ewy
Darrell L. Warta
James M. Armstrong
Mary Kathleen Babcock
Gary L. Ayers
Wyatt M. Wright
J. Steven Massoni
Jeffery A. Jordan
Trisha A. Thelen
Craig W. West
Carol A. Beier

For Complete List of Firm Personnel, See General Section

For full biographical listings, see the Martindale-Hubbell Law Directory

HERSHBERGER, PATTERSON, JONES & ROTH, L.C. (AV)

600 Hardage Center, 100 South Main, 67202-3779
Telephone: 316-263-7583
Fax: 316-263-7595

Jerome E. Jones
Robert J. Roth
William R. Smith
Greer Gsell
J. Michael Kennalley
Evan J. Olson
John A. Vetter
Jeffrey A. Roth
David J. Morgan
Ken W. Dannenberg

Tracy A. Applegate
Marc P. Clements

OF COUNSEL

H. E. Jones
John L. Kratzer, Jr.

Counsel For: First National Bank in Wichita; Andarko Petroleum Corporation; Chinese Industries; Mobil Oil Corp.; CNA Insurance; Royal Exchange Group; Central National Insurance Group; Transamerica Insurance Group; Northwestern National Insurance Group.

For Complete List of Firm Personnel, See General Section

For full biographical listings, see the Martindale-Hubbell Law Directory

KAHRS, NELSON, FANNING, HITE & KELLOGG (AV)

Suite 630, 200 West Douglas Street, 67202-3089
Telephone: 316-265-7761
Telecopier: 316-267-7803

MEMBERS OF FIRM

Richard C. Hite
Richard L. Honeyman
Larry A. Withers
Steven D. Gough
Scott J. Gunderson
Randy Troutt
Arthur S. Chalmers
Marc A. Powell
Forrest James Robinson, Jr.

(See Next Column)

KAHRS, NELSON, FANNING, HITE & KELLOGG—*Continued*

ASSOCIATE
J. Scott Pohl
OF COUNSEL
H. W. Fanning

Representative Clients: Advance Chemical Dist., Inc.; Learjet Corp.; Hahner, Foreman & Harness, Contractors; New York Life Ins. Co.; United States Fidelity & Guaranty Co; General Motors Corp.; St. Paul Ins. Cos.; Ruffin Hotel Corp.; Central Detroit Diesel Allison, Inc.

For Complete List of Firm Personnel, See General Section

For full biographical listings, see the Martindale-Hubbell Law Directory

MORRIS, LAING, EVANS, BROCK & KENNEDY, CHARTERED (AV)

Fourth Floor, 200 West Douglas, 67202-3084
Telephone: 316-262-2671
FAX: 316-262-6226; 262-5991
Topeka Office: 800 S.W. Jackson, Suite 914. 66612-2214.
Telephone: 913-232-2662.
Fax: 913-232-9983.

Joseph W. Kennedy
Ken M. Peterson
Richard D. Greene
Dennis M. Feeney
Jeffery L. Carmichael
Robert W. Coykendall
Susan R. Schrag
Robert E. Nugent
Michael Lennen
Jana Deines Abbott
Richard F. Hayse (Resident, Topeka Office)
Thomas R. Docking
Gerald N. Capps
Diane S. Worth
Tim J. Moore
Bruce A. Ney

References: The Emprise Banks of Kansas; Mellon Bank; N.A.; The Merchants National Bank of Topeka; Southwest National Bank; Twin Lakes Bank & Trust.

For Complete List of Firm Personnel, See General Section

For full biographical listings, see the Martindale-Hubbell Law Directory

YOUNG, BOGLE, MCCAUSLAND, WELLS & CLARK, P.A. (AV)

106 West Douglas, Suite 923, 67202
Telephone: 316-265-7841
Facsimile: 316-265-3956

Glenn D. Young, Jr.
Jerry D. Bogle
Paul S. McCausland
William A. Wells
Kenneth M. Clark
Patrick C. Blanchard

Mark R. Maloney
OF COUNSEL
Orlin L. Wagner

Representative Clients: Bridgestone/Firestone, Inc.; Deere & Co.; GAF Corp.; Sears Roebuck & Co.; Deere Credit Services, Inc.; Horace Mann Insurance, Co.; Straightline Manufacturing, Inc.; Lida Advertising.

For full biographical listings, see the Martindale-Hubbell Law Directory

KENTUCKY

ASHLAND, Boyd Co.

MARTIN, PICKLESIMER, JUSTICE & VINCENT (AV)

431 Sixteenth Street, P.O. Box 2528, 41105-2528
Telephone: 606-329-8338
Fax: 606-325-8199

Richard W. Martin
Max D. Picklesimer
David Justice
John F. Vincent

ASSOCIATES

Thomas Wade Lavender, II
P. Kimberly Watson

Representative Clients: City of Ashland; FIVCO Area Development District; Boyd County Sanitation District No. 2; Mid-America Distributors, Inc.
Insurance Counsel for: State Farm Mutual Automobile Insurance Co.; State Farm Fire and Casualty Co.; Aetna Casualty Insurance Co.; Grange Mutual Insurance Co.; Great American Insurance Co.

For full biographical listings, see the Martindale-Hubbell Law Directory

*BOWLING GREEN,** Warren Co.

BELL, ORR, AYERS & MOORE, P.S.C. (AV)

1010 College Street, P.O. Box 738, 42102-0738
Telephone: 502-781-8111
Telecopier: 502-781-9027

(See Next Column)

Chas. R. Bell (1891-1976)
Joe B. Orr (1914-1987)
Reginald L. Ayers
Ray B. Buckberry, Jr.
Quinten B. Marquette
George E. Strickler, Jr.
Kevin C. Brooks
Timothy L. Mauldin
Barton D. Darrell
Timothy L. Edelen

James S. Weisz

General Counsel for: First American National Bank of Kentucky; Farm Credit Services of Mid-America, ACA.; Houchens Industries, Inc. (Food Markets and Shopping Centers); Warren County Board of Education; Bowling Green Municipal Utilities.
Representative Clients: Chicago Title Insurance Co.; Commonwealth Land Title Insurance Co.; Kentucky Farm Bureau Mutual Insurance Co.; Martin Automotive Group; Home Insurance Group.

For full biographical listings, see the Martindale-Hubbell Law Directory

CAMPBELL, KERRICK & GRISE (AV)

1025 State Street, P.O. Box 9547, 42102-9547
Telephone: 502-782-8160
FAX: 502-782-5856

MEMBERS OF FIRM

Joe Bill Campbell
Thomas N. Kerrick
John R. Grise
Gregory N. Stivers
H. Brent Brennenstuhl
Deborah Tomes Wilkins

ASSOCIATES

H. Harris Pepper, Jr.
Lanna Martin Kilgore
Laura Hagan

Representative Clients: Dollar General Corp.; Greenview Hospital; Hospital Corporation of America; Monarch Environmental, Inc.; Western Kentucky University; Aetna Casualty & Surety Co.; Cincinnati Insurance Co.; Kentucky Hospital Association Trust; Kentucky Medical Insurance Co.; Nationwide Insurance Co.

For full biographical listings, see the Martindale-Hubbell Law Directory

CATRON, KILGORE & BEGLEY (AV)

918 State Street, P.O. Box 280, 42102-0280
Telephone: 502-842-1050
Fax: 502-842-4720

Stephen B. Catron
J. Patrick Kilgore
Ernest Edward Begley, II

Representative Clients: Kentucky Farm Bureau Mutual Insurance Company; Adriatic Insurance Company; Puritan Insurance Company; General Growth Management Corporation; Kentucky Transportation Cabinet; International Paper Company; Convention Center Authority; Camping World, Inc.; National Corvette Museum; Minit Mart Foods, Inc.

For full biographical listings, see the Martindale-Hubbell Law Directory

COLE, MOORE & MCCRACKEN (AV)

921 College Street-Phoenix Place, P.O. Box 10240, 42102-7240
Telephone: 502-782-6666
FAX: 502-782-8666

MEMBERS OF FIRM

John David Cole
Frank Hampton Moore, Jr.
John H. McCracken
Matthew J. Baker

ASSOCIATES

Howard E. Frasier, Jr.
Douglas W. Gott
Dov Moore
C. Terrell Miller
Michael D. Lindsey

OF COUNSEL

Frank R. Goad

Counsel for: Western Kentucky Cola-Cola Bottling Co.; Clark Distributing Co., Inc.; Scotty's Contracting & Stone Co.
Local Counsel for: General Electric Co.; Bucyrus-Erie Company; Wal-Mart Stores, Inc.; Kroger/Country Oven.
Representative Insurance Clients: Liberty Mutual Insurance Co.; Travelers Insurance Co.; Wausau Insurance Co.

For full biographical listings, see the Martindale-Hubbell Law Directory

ENGLISH, LUCAS, PRIEST & OWSLEY (AV)

1101 College Street, P.O. Box 770, 42102-0770
Telephone: 502-781-6500
Telecopier: 502-782-7782

MEMBERS OF FIRM

Charles E. English
James H. Lucas
Whayne C. Priest, Jr.
Michael A. Owsley
Keith M. Carwell
Murry A. Raines
Kurt W. Maier
Charles E. English, Jr.
Wade T. Markham, II

(See Next Column)

ENGLISH, LUCAS, PRIEST & OWSLEY, *Bowling Green—Continued*

ASSOCIATES

D. Gaines Penn
W. Cravens Priest, III
Robert A. Young
Marc Allen Lovell

General Counsel for: Medical Center at Bowling Green; Bowling Green Independent School District; Warren Rural Electric Cooperative Corporation; Trans Financial Bank, N.A.

Representative Clients: Commercial Union Insurance Cos.; Kemper Insurance Group; St. Paul Insurance Co.; Eaton Corp.; Desa International; Sumitomo Electric Wiring Systems, Inc.

For Complete List of Firm Personnel, See General Section

For full biographical listings, see the Martindale-Hubbell Law Directory

HARLIN & PARKER, P.S.C. (AV)

519 East Tenth Street, P.O. Box 390, 42102-0390
Telephone: 502-842-5611
Telefax: 502-842-2607
Smiths Grove, Kentucky Office: Old Farmers Bank Building.
Telephone: 502-563-4701.

William Jerry Parker
Max B. Harlin, III
James David Bryant
Jerry A. Burns
James D. Harris, Jr.
Scott Charles Marks
Michael K. Bishop
Mark D. Alcott (Resident, Smith Grove Office)

OF COUNSEL

Maxey B. Harlin
Jo T. Orendorf

Representative Clients: General Motors Corp.; Ford Motor Co.; Chrysler Corp.; The Goodyear Tire and Rubber Co.; CSX Transportation, Inc.; South Central Bell Telephone Co.; CNA Insurance Companies; Maryland Casualty Company; American International Group; Sears Roebuck & Company.

For full biographical listings, see the Martindale-Hubbell Law Directory

HUDDLESTON & HUDDLESTON (AV)

1032 College Street, P.O. Box 2130, 42102-2130
Telephone: 502-781-9870
Fax: 502-842-1659
Cave City, Kentucky: 210 Broadway; P.O. 810, 42127.
Telephone: 502-773-5511.
Fax: 502-773-5510.

MEMBERS OF FIRM

Philip I. Huddleston
Lee Huddleston

ASSOCIATE

Jeffrey A. Reed

Representative Clients: Dow Corning Corp.; Borg Warner Corp.; HFC Commercial Realty, Inc.; South Central Banks; Autotruck Federal Credit Union; Acceptance Insurance Company.

For full biographical listings, see the Martindale-Hubbell Law Directory

MILLIKEN LAW FIRM (AV)

426 East Main Street, P.O. Box 1640, 42102-1640
Telephone: 502-843-0800
Fax: 502-842-1237

W. Currie Milliken
Morris Lowe

Reference: Trans Financial Bank, Bowling Green, Kentucky.

For full biographical listings, see the Martindale-Hubbell Law Directory

RUDLOFF, GOLDEN & EVANS (AV)

553 East Main Street, 42101-2256
Telephone: 502-781-7754; 781-7762

MEMBERS OF FIRM

William J. Rudloff
J. Dale Golden
R. Brian Evans

Reference: National City Bank, Bowling Green, Ky.

For full biographical listings, see the Martindale-Hubbell Law Directory

COVINGTON, Kenton Co.

ADAMS, BROOKING, STEPNER, WOLTERMANN & DUSING (AV)

421 Garrard Street, P.O. Box 861, 41012
Telephone: 606-291-7270
FAX: 606-291-7902
Florence, Kentucky Office: 8100 Burlington Pike, Suite 400, 41042.
Telephone: 606-371-6220.
FAX: 606-371-8341.

(See Next Column)

Charles S. Adams (1906-1971)
John R. S. Brooking
Donald L. Stepner
James G. Woltermann (Resident at Florence Office)
Gerald F. Dusing (Resident at Florence Office)
Michael M. Sketch (Resident at Florence Office)
Dennis R. Williams (Resident at Florence Office)
James R. Kruer
Jeffrey C. Mando

ASSOCIATES

Marc D. Dietz (Resident at Florence Office)
Gregory S. Shumate
John S. "Brook" Brooking (Resident at Florence Office)
Stacey L. Graus

Representative Clients: CSX Transportation; Balluff, Inc., Wampler, Inc., Kisters, Inc., Krauss-Maffei, Inc., A group of German companies; State Automobile Mutual Insurance Co.; Chevron of California; Great American Insurance Co.; Grange Mutual Insurance Co.; Meridian Mutual Insurance Co.; Fifth-Third Bank of Northern Ky.; Northern Kentucky University.

For Complete List of Firm Personnel, See General Section

For full biographical listings, see the Martindale-Hubbell Law Directory

ROBERT C. CETRULO, P.S.C. (AV)

The Cetrulo Building, 620 Washington Street, 41011
Telephone: 606-491-6200
FAX: 606-491-6201

Robert C. Cetrulo

Representative Clients: Atlanta Casualty Insurance Co.; Celina Insurance Group; Commercial Union Assurance Cos.; Fireman's Fund; Dairyland Insurance Co.; Gates Rubber Co.; Greyhound Lines, Inc.; Kentucky Insurance Guaranty Assn.; Universal Underwriters Insurance Co.; Zurich-American Insurance Cos.

For full biographical listings, see the Martindale-Hubbell Law Directory

GREENEBAUM DOLL & MCDONALD (AV)

A Partnership including Professional Service Corporations
50 East Rivercenter Boulevard, P.O. Box 2050, 41012-2050
Telephone: 606-655-4200
Telecopier: 606-655-4239
Louisville, Kentucky Office: 3300 National City Tower.
Telephone: 502-589-4200.
Fax: 502-587-3695.
Lexington, Kentucky Office: 1400 Vine Center Tower.
Telephone: 606-231-8500.
Fax: 606-255-2742.
Cincinnati, Ohio Office: 832 Main Street.
Telephone: 513-421-8087.
Fax: 513-421-8089.

MEMBERS OF FIRM

Wm. T. Robinson, III
Phillip D. Scott
Eric L. Ison
Hiram Ely, III
Roger N. Braden (Resident)

ASSOCIATE

Sheryl E. Heeter

Representative Clients: Aetna Life Insurance Co.; ANDALEX Resources, Inc.; Ashland Oil, Inc.; A T & T Communications, Inc.; Bethlehem Steel Corp.; Brown-Forman Corp.; Citizens Fidelity Bank & Trust Co.; Humana, Inc.; KFC National Cooperative Advertising Program, Inc.

For Complete List of Firm Personnel, See General Section

For full biographical listings, see the Martindale-Hubbell Law Directory

O'HARA, RUBERG, TAYLOR, SLOAN AND SERGENT (AV)

Suite 209 C, Thomas More Park, P.O. Box 17411, 41017-0411
Telephone: 606-331-2000
Fax: 606-578-3365

MEMBERS OF FIRM

John J. O'Hara
Robert E. Ruberg
Arnold S. Taylor
Donald J. Ruberg
David B. Sloan
Gary J. Sergent
Michael K. Ruberg
Michael O'Hara

ASSOCIATES

Lisa Kalker
Anne Marie Mielech
Suzanne Cassidy

Representative Clients: Union Light, Heat & Power Co., Legal Dept.; American States Insurance Co.; American Hardware Mutual Indemnity Co.; Hartford Insurance Co.; Ohio Casualty Co.; Kenton County Board of Education; Zurich-American Insurance Co.; Celina Insurance Co.; The Huntington National Bank of Covington, Ky.; Jefferson Insurance Co.

For full biographical listings, see the Martindale-Hubbell Law Directory

ROBERT E. SANDERS AND ASSOCIATES, P.S.C. (AV)

The Charles H. Fisk House, 1017 Russell Street, 41011
Telephone: 606-491-3000
FAX: 606-655-4642

(See Next Column)

ROBERT E. SANDERS AND ASSOCIATES, P.S.C.—*Continued*

Robert E. Sanders

Julie Lippert Duncan

LEGAL SUPPORT PERSONNEL

Shirley L. Sanders | Harry E. Holtkamp
Sandra A. Head | Joseph E. Schmiade, Sr.

For full biographical listings, see the Martindale-Hubbell Law Directory

SMITH, WOLNITZEK, SCHACHTER & ROWEKAMP, P.S.C. (AV)

502 Greenup Street, P.O. Box 352, 41012-0352
Telephone: 606-491-4444
Fax: 606-491-1001
Fort Mitchell, Kentucky Office: 250 Grandview Avenue., Suite 500.
Telephone: 606-578-4444.
Fax: 606-578-4440.

Thomas C. Smith | Leonard G. Rowekamp
Stephen D. Wolnitzek | J. David Bender
Paul J. Schachter | Barbara Dahlenburg Bonar

Penny Unkraut Hendy | Timothy B. Schenkel
John J. Garvey, III | David A. Shearer

Representative Clients: Hartford Insurance Co.; Nationwide Insurance Co.

For full biographical listings, see the Martindale-Hubbell Law Directory

TALIAFERRO AND MEHLING (AV)

1005 Madison Avenue, P.O. Box 468, 41012-0468
Telephone: 606-291-9900
Fax: 606-291-3014

MEMBERS OF FIRM

Philip Taliaferro, III | Christopher J. Mehling

ASSOCIATES

Lucinda C. Shirooni | Alice G. Keys
C. Houston Ebert | J. David Brittingham

OF COUNSEL

Robert W. Carran | Norbert J. Bischoff

For full biographical listings, see the Martindale-Hubbell Law Directory

WARE, BRYSON, WEST & KUMMER (AV)

157 Barnwood Drive, 41017
Telephone: 606-341-0255
FAX: 606-341-1876

MEMBERS OF FIRM

Rodney S. Bryson | Mark W. Howard
Larry C. West | Greg D. Voss
John R. Kummer | Robert B. Cetrulo

ASSOCIATES

Susanne M. Cetrulo | Orie S. Ware (1882-1974)
W. L. (Skip) Hammons, Jr. | William O. Ware (1908-1961)
James M. West | James C. Ware (1913-1991)

Attorneys for: First National Bank of Northern Ky.; State Farm Insurance Co.; Reliance Insurance Group; Maryland Casualty Insurance Co.; Kemper Insurance Co.; Prudential Insurance Co.; State Farm Fire & Casualty Insurance Co.; Shelby Mutual Insurance Co.; Cincinnati Insurance Co.

For full biographical listings, see the Martindale-Hubbell Law Directory

FLORENCE, Boone Co.

ADAMS, BROOKING, STEPNER, WOLTERMANN & DUSING (AV)

8100 Burlington Pike, Suite 400, 41042-0576
Telephone: 606-371-6220
FAX: 606-371-8341
Covington, Kentucky Office: 421 Garrard Street.
Telephone: 606-291-7270.
FAX: 606-291-7902.

Donald L. Stepner | Gerald F. Dusing (Resident)
James G. Woltermann (Resident) | Michael M. Sketch (Resident)
Dennis R. Williams (Resident)

Representative Clients: CSX Transportation; State Automobile Mutual Insurance Co.; Standard Oil Co. (Ky.); Great American Insurance Co.; Grange Mutual Insurance Co.; Meridian Mutual Insurance Co.; Fifth-Third Bank of Boone County; Northern Kentucky University.

For Complete List of Firm Personnel, See General Section

For full biographical listings, see the Martindale-Hubbell Law Directory

FORT THOMAS, Campbell Co.

DON JOHNSON, P.S.C. (AV)

20 North Grand Avenue, Suite 15, 41075
Telephone: 606-441-3900
Telecopier: 606-441-3018

Donald L. Johnson

Richard G. Johnson

Reference: Northern Kentucky Bank & Trust Co.; Alexandria IGA; D. Schneider Const. Co.; Bluegrass Carryout, Inc.; Kees Medical Speciality Co.; Ralph Long Concrete Pumping, Inc.; El Jiroto Enterprises; HASCO, Inc.; West Side Baber Cab Co.

For full biographical listings, see the Martindale-Hubbell Law Directory

*FRANKLIN,** Simpson Co.

STEERS & STEERS, P.S.C. (AV)

211 South College Street, P.O. Box 447, 42135-0447
Telephone: 502-586-4466
Telecopier: 502-586-4467

Roy L. Steers (1917-1980) | R. Lee Steers, Jr.

William Scott Crabtree | Gregory R. Vincent

Reference: Simpson County Bank.

For full biographical listings, see the Martindale-Hubbell Law Directory

*GLASGOW,** Barren Co.

HERBERT & HERBERT (AV)

135 North Public Square, P.O. Box 1000, 42141
Telephone: 502-651-9000
FAX: 502-651-3317

MEMBERS OF FIRM

H. Jefferson Herbert, Jr. | Betty Reece Herbert

Representative Clients: Eaton Corp.; Fireman's Fund Insurance Companies; Glasgow Foods, Inc.; Alliance Corp. (Construction); Indiana Insurance Co.; Kentucky Hospital Association Trust; Wininger Oil Co.; Supreme Mills, Inc.; T.J. Samson Community Hospital, Inc.; Travelers Insurance Co.

For full biographical listings, see the Martindale-Hubbell Law Directory

*HENDERSON,** Henderson Co.

DEEP & WOMACK (AV)

790 Bob Posey Street, P.O. Box 50, 42420
Telephone: 502-827-2522
FAX: 502-826-2870

MEMBERS OF FIRM

Charles David Deep | Zack N. Womack
James G. Womack

For full biographical listings, see the Martindale-Hubbell Law Directory

KING, DEEP AND BRANAMAN (AV)

127 North Main Street, P.O. Box 43, 42420
Telephone: 502-827-1852
FAX: 502-826-7729

MEMBERS OF FIRM

Leo King (1893-1982) | Harry L. Mathison, Jr.
William M. Deep (1920-1990) | W. Mitchell Deep, Jr.
William Branaman | H. Randall Redding
Dorin E. Luck

ASSOCIATES

Leslie M. Newman | Robert Khuon Wiederstein
Greg L. Gager

Counsel for: Allstate Insurance; MMI; Community United Methodist Hospital; Thompson International; Reynolds Metals Co.; Scott Lumber Co., Inc.; Westerfield Insurance Cos.; Grange Mutual Insurance Co.; Indiana Lumbermen.

For full biographical listings, see the Martindale-Hubbell Law Directory

*LEXINGTON,** Fayette Co.

BOEHL STOPHER & GRAVES (AV)

444 West Second Street, 40508
Telephone: 606-252-6721
FAX: 606-253-1445
Louisville, Kentucky Office: Suite 2300, Providian Center, 400 West Market Street.
Telephone: 502-589-5980.
Fax: 502-561-9400.

(See Next Column)

BOEHL STOPHER & GRAVES, *Lexington—Continued*

Paducah, Kentucky Office: Suite 340 Executive Inn Riverfront, One Executive Boulevard.
Telephone: 502-442-4369.
Fax: 502-442-4689.
Prestonsburg, Kentucky Office: 125 Court Street.
Telephone: 606-886-8004.
Fax: 606-886-9579.
New Albany, Indiana Office: Elsby East, Suite 204, 400 Pearl Street.
Telephone: 812-948-5053.
Fax: 812-948-9233.

RESIDENT PARTNERS

W. T. Adkins
Nolan Carter, Jr.
Gregory K. Jenkins
Ronald L. Green
Steven G. Kinkel
Kim Martin Wilkie
Guillermo A. Carlos

RESIDENT ASSOCIATES

James B. Cooper
Michael J. Cox
Garry R. Kaplan

Counsel for: Ford Motor Co.; Texas Eastern Transmission Corp.; Coca-Cola Bottling Co.; National Collegiate Athletic Assn.; Hartford Accident and Indemnity Co.; Continental Insurance Group; St. Paul Fire & Marine Insurance Co.; Lloyds of London; Old Republic Insurance Co.

For full biographical listings, see the Martindale-Hubbell Law Directory

BROCK, BROCK & BAGBY (AV)

190 Market Street, P.O. Box 1630, 40592-1630
Telephone: 606-255-7795
Fax: 606-255-6198

MEMBERS OF FIRM

Walter L. Brock, Jr.
Daniel N. Brock
Glen S. Bagby
J. Robert Lyons, Jr.
Beverly Benton Polk

ASSOCIATE

Bruce A. Rector

LEGAL SUPPORT PERSONNEL

PARALEGALS

Pamela H. Brown
Freda Greer Grubbs

For full biographical listings, see the Martindale-Hubbell Law Directory

FOWLER, MEASLE & BELL (AV)

Kincaid Towers, 300 West Vine Street, Suite 650, 40507-1660
Telephone: 606-252-6700
Fax: 606-255-3735

MEMBERS OF FIRM

Taft A. McKinstry
Guy R. Colson
E. Patrick Moores
John E. Hinkel, Jr.
Robert S. Ryan
T. Bruce Bell
Michael W. Troutman
Elizabeth S. Feamster
R. Craig Reinhardt

ASSOCIATES

Barry M. Miller
Dianne P. Allison
Brendan M. Turney
Michael E. Liska

OF COUNSEL

Walter C. Cox, Jr.

Representative Clients: General Electric Co.; Kentucky Farm Bureau Mutual Ins. Co.; Liberty Mutual Ins. Co.; State Farm Ins. Co.; Allstate Ins. Co.; Progressive Casualty Ins. Co.; Prudential Property & Casualty Insurance Co.; Federated Insurance Co.; Universal Underwriters Ins. Co.; EIMCO Coal Machinery, Inc.; Pfizer, Inc.

For Complete List of Firm Personnel, See General Section

For full biographical listings, see the Martindale-Hubbell Law Directory

GREENEBAUM DOLL & MCDONALD (AV)

A Partnership including Professional Service Corporations
1400 Vine Center Tower, 40508
Telephone: 606-231-8500
Telecopier: 606-255-2742
Telex: 213029
Louisville, Kentucky Office: 3300 National City Tower.
Telephone: 502-589-4200.
Fax: 502-587-3695.
Covington, Kentucky Office: 50 East River Center Boulevard, P.O. Box 2050.
Telephone: 606-655-4200.
Fax: 606-655-4239.
Cincinnati, Ohio Office: 832 Main Street.
Telephone: 513-421-8087.
Fax: 513-421-8089.

(See Next Column)

MEMBERS OF FIRM

Phillip D. Scott
Wm. T. Robinson, III
Eric L. Ison
James G. LeMaster (Resident)
Hiram Ely, III
V. Thomas Fryman, Jr. (Resident)
Bruce E. Cryder
Mark T. Hayden (Resident)

ASSOCIATES

Anne A. Chesnut (Resident)
D. Barry Stilz (Resident)
Benjamin D. Crocker

Representative Clients: Aetna Life Insurance Co.; ANDALEX Resources, Inc.; Ashland Oil, Inc.; AT&T Communications, Inc.; Bethlehem Steel Corp.; Brown-Forman Corp.; Columbia Gas & Transmission Co.; Commonwealth Aluminum Corp.; Consolidation Coal Co.; Costain Coal, Inc.
*A Professional Service Corporation

For Complete List of Firm Personnel, See General Section

For full biographical listings, see the Martindale-Hubbell Law Directory

LANDRUM & SHOUSE (AV)

106 West Vine Street, P.O. Box 951, 40588-0951
Telephone: 606-255-2424
Facsimile: 606-233-0308
Louisville, Kentucky Office: 400 West Market Street, Suite 1550, 40202.
Telephone: 502-589-7616.
Facsimile: 502-589-2119.

MEMBERS OF FIRM

John H. Burrus
George P. Parker (Resident, Louisville Office)
Thomas M. Cooper
William C. Shouse
Pierce W. Hamblin
Mark L. Moseley
Leslie Patterson Vose
John R. Martin, Jr. (Resident, Louisville Office)
James W. Smirz
Larry C. Deener
Sandra Mendez Dawahare
Mark J. Hinkel
Delores Hill Pregliasco (Resident, Louisville Office)
Benjamin Cowgill, Jr.
John Garry McNeill
Jack E. Toliver
Michael J. O'Connell (Resident, Louisville Office)
R. Kent Westberry (Resident, Louisville Office)
J. Denis Ogburn (Resident, Louisville Office)
Jane Durkin Samuel

ASSOCIATES

Stephen D. Milner
Stephen R. Chappell
David G. Hazlett (Resident, Louisville Office)
Thomas E. Roma, Jr. (Resident, Louisville Office)
Virginia W. Gregg
Douglas L. Hoots
Dave Whalin (Resident, Louisville Office)
G. Bruce Stigger (Resident, Louisville Office)
Daniel E. Murner
Courtney T. Baxter (Resident, Louisville Office)
Julie A. Butcher
Frank M. Jenkins, III

OF COUNSEL

Weldon Shouse

District Attorneys: CSX Transportation, Inc.
Special Trial Counsel: Ford Motor Co. and Affiliates (Eastern Kentucky); Clark Equipment Co.
Representative Clients: The Continental Insurance Cos.; U.S. Insurance Group; U.S. Fidelity & Guaranty Co.; Ohio Casualty Insurance Co.; CIGNA; Royal Insurance Cos.

For Complete List of Firm Personnel, See General Section

For full biographical listings, see the Martindale-Hubbell Law Directory

PETER PERLMAN LAW OFFICES, P.S.C. (AV)

388 South Broadway, 40508
Telephone: 606-253-3919
FAX: 606-259-0493

Peter Perlman

Bryce D. Franklin, Jr.
Pamela D. Perlman

For full biographical listings, see the Martindale-Hubbell Law Directory

PIPER, WELLMAN & BOWERS (AV)

200 North Upper Street, 40507
Telephone: 606-231-1012
FAX: 606-231-7367

MEMBERS OF FIRM

George C. Piper
Dean T. Wellman
Barbara J. Bowers

ASSOCIATE

Johann F. Herklotz

Representative Clients: Kentucky Hospital Assn. Trust; Woodford Hospital; Garrard Memorial Hospital; Century American Insurance Co.; Guaranty National Ins. Co.; Rhone Pharmaceuticals; Glaxo; Hillhaven Corp.; Sisters of Charity of Nazareth Health System, Inc.; Ky. River Medical Center; St. Josephs Hospital.

(See Next Column)

PIPER, WELLMAN & BOWERS—*Continued*

For Complete List of Firm Personnel, See General Section

For full biographical listings, see the Martindale-Hubbell Law Directory

GEORGE F. RABE (AV)

Suite 1004 First National Building, Main and Upper Streets, 40507-1708
Telephone: 606-255-2313

References: Liberty National Bank of Lexington; Bank One Lexington, N.A.

For full biographical listings, see the Martindale-Hubbell Law Directory

SAVAGE, GARMER & ELLIOTT, P.S.C. (AV)

Opera House Office Building, 141 North Broadway, 40507
Telephone: 606-254-9351
Fax: 606-233-9769

Joe C. Savage
William R. Garmer
Robert L. Elliott

For full biographical listings, see the Martindale-Hubbell Law Directory

STOLL, KEENON & PARK (AV)

201 E. Main Street, Suite 1000, 40507-1380
Telephone: 606-231-3000
Telecopier: 606-253-1093; 606-253-1027
Frankfort, Kentucky Office: 326 West Main Street.
Telephone: 502-875-6000.
Telecopier: 502-875-6008.
Louisville, Kentucky Office: 400 West Market Street, Suite 2650, 40202.
Telephone: 502-568-9100.
Telecopier: 502-568-6340.

MEMBERS OF FIRM

William E. Johnson
Leslie W. Morris, II
Lindsey W. Ingram, Jr.
Bennett Clark
Spencer D. Noe
Joseph M. Scott, Jr.
Michael L. Judy
Charles E. Shivel, Jr.
Robert M. Watt, III
J. Peter Cassidy, Jr.
Robert F. Houlihan, Jr.
William M. Lear, Jr.
Donald P. Wagner
Robert W. Kellerman
Lizbeth Ann Tully
Eileen M. O'Brien
David C. Schwetschenau
Anita M. Britton
Diane M. Carlton
Larry A. Sykes
P. Douglas Barr
Perry M. Bentley
Dan M. Rose
J. Guthrie True
Denise Kirk Ash
Bonnie Hoskins
Gregory D. Pavey
J. Mel Camenisch, Jr.
Richard M. Guarnieri

ASSOCIATES

Laura Day DelCotto
James L. Thomerson
David E. Fleenor
Melissa Anne Stewart
William L. Montague, Jr.
Robert E. Wier

Representative Clients: Ashland Oil, Inc.; Fireman's Fund Insurance Group; Bank One, Lexington, NA; International Business Machines Corp.; Keeneland Assn.; Kentucky-American Water Co.; Kentucky Utilities Co.; Lexington Herald-Leader Inc.; Sisters of Charity of Nazareth Health Corp.; Wausau Insurance Co.

For Complete List of Firm Personnel, See General Section

For full biographical listings, see the Martindale-Hubbell Law Directory

STURGILL, TURNER & TRUITT (AV)

155 East Main Street, 40507
Telephone: 606-255-8581
Fax: 606-231-0851

MEMBERS OF FIRM

Don S. Sturgill
Gardner L. Turner
Stephen L. Barker
Donald P. Moloney, II
Phillip M. Moloney
Douglas L. McSwain
Kevin G. Henry

For Complete List of Firm Personnel, See General Section

For full biographical listings, see the Martindale-Hubbell Law Directory

*LONDON,** Laurel Co.

FARMER, KELLEY & FARMER (AV)

502 West Fifth Street, Drawer 490, 40743
Telephone: 606-878-7640
Fax: 606-878-2364
Lexington Office: 121 Prosperous Place, Suite 13 B, 40509-1834.
Telephone: 606: 263-2567.
Facsimile: 606: 263-2567.

MEMBERS OF FIRM

F. Preston Farmer
John F. Kelley, Jr.
Michael P. Farmer

(See Next Column)

ASSOCIATES

Martha L. Brown
Jeffrey T. Weaver

References: The First National Bank; Cumberland Valley National Bank & Trust Company of London, Ky.; London Bank & Trust Co.

For full biographical listings, see the Martindale-Hubbell Law Directory

TAYLOR, KELLER & DUNAWAY (AV)

802 North Main Street, P.O. Box 905, 40743-0905
Telephone: 606-878-8844
Facsimile: 606-878-5547

Boyd F. Taylor
J. Warren Keller
Bridget L. Dunaway

OF COUNSEL

Pamela Adams Chesnut

LEGAL SUPPORT PERSONNEL

Berneda Baker (Paralegal)

Representative Clients: Chubb Group; Coronet Insurance Group; ITT Hartford; Mutual of Omaha; American General Property Ins. Co.; State Farm Fire & Casualty; State Farm Mutual Automobile Insurance Co.
Local Counsel for: Kentucky Utilities Co.
References: The First National Bank; Cumberland Valley National Bank & Trust Company of London, Kentucky.

For full biographical listings, see the Martindale-Hubbell Law Directory

TOOMS & HOUSE (AV)

310 West Fifth Street, P.O. Box 520, 40743-0520
Telephone: 606-864-4145
FAX: 606-864-4279

MEMBERS OF FIRM

Murray L. Brown (1894-1980)
Roy E. Tooms (1917-1986)
R. William Tooms
Brian C. House

ASSOCIATE

Amy V. Barker

Representative Clients: State Auto Mutual Insurance Co.; Grange Mutual Casualty Co.; Kentucky Farm Bureau Mutual Insurance Co.

For full biographical listings, see the Martindale-Hubbell Law Directory

*LOUISVILLE,** Jefferson Co.

BOEHL STOPHER & GRAVES (AV)

Suite 2300 Providian Center, 400 West Market Street, 40202-3354
Telephone: 502-589-5980
FAX: 502-561-9400
Lexington, Kentucky Office: 444 West Second Street.
Telephone: 606-252-6721.
Fax: 606-253-1445.
Paducah, Kentucky Office: Suite 340 Executive Inn Riverfront, One Executive Boulevard.
Telephone: 502-442-4369.
Fax: 502-442-4689.
Prestonsburg, Kentucky Office: 125 Court Street.
Telephone: 606-886-8004.
Fax: 606-886-9579.
New Albany, Indiana Office: Elsby East, Suite 204, 400 Pearl Street.
Telephone: 812-948-5053.
Fax: 812-948-9233.

OF COUNSEL

Joseph E. Stopher
George R. Effinger (Resident at Paducah)

MEMBERS OF FIRM

Herbert F. Boehl (1894-1986)
Arthur J. Deindoerfer (1907-1990)
Raymond O. Harmon (1918-1990)
William O. Guethlein
Galen J. White, Jr.
William P. Swain
Larry L. Johnson
W. T. Adkins (Resident at Lexington)
Edward H. Stopher
Nolan Carter, Jr. (Resident at Lexington)
Jefferson K. Streepey
Wesley G. Gatlin
George R. Carter
Robert E. Stopher
Philip J. Reverman, Jr.
Jonathan Freed (Resident at Paducah)
Peter J. Glauber
Gregory K. Jenkins (Resident at Lexington)
Raymond G. Smith
Walter E. Harding
William M. Newman, Jr.
Thomas M. Smith (Resident at Prestonsburg)
Robert M. Brooks
John W. Phillips
Susan D. Phillips
Ronald L. Green (Resident at Lexington)
Richard L. Walter (Resident at Paducah)
Douglas A. U'Sellis
Steven G. Kinkel (Resident at Lexington)
John P. Rall (Resident at Paducah)
Kim Martin Wilkie (Resident at Lexington)
John Harlan Callis, III (Resident at Prestonsburg)
Charles D. Walter (Resident at Paducah)
Janie C. McKenzie (Resident at Prestonsburg)

(See Next Column)

BOEHL STOPHER & GRAVES, *Louisville—Continued*

MEMBERS OF FIRM (Continued)

Guillermo A. Carlos (Resident at Lexington)
William B. Orberson
John F. Parker Jr.
Jeffrey L. Hansford (Not admitted in KY; Resident at New Albany, Indiana)
Matthew Hunter Jones (Resident at New Albany, Indiana)

ASSOCIATES

James B. Cooper (Resident at Lexington)
Martin H. Kinney, Jr.
Mary Ann Kiwala
Richard W. Edwards
Frank Miller, Jr.
Teresa M. Groves (Resident at Paducah)
John B. Moore
Kimberly S. May-Downey (Resident at Prestonsburg)
Robert D. McClure
Michael J. Cox (Resident at Lexington)
William J. Crowe
Denise Bashford Askin
Garry R. Kaplan (Resident at Lexington)

Counsel for: Ford Motor Co.; Texas Eastern Transmission Corp.; Coca-Cola Bottling Co.; Hartford Accident and Indemnity Co.; Continental Insurance Group; St. Paul Fire & Marine Insurance Co.; Lloyds of London; Old Republic Insurance Co.

For Complete List of Firm Personnel, See General Section

For full biographical listings, see the Martindale-Hubbell Law Directory

EWEN, HILLIARD & BUSH (AV)

The Starks Building Suite 1090, 455 S. 4th Street, 40202
Telephone: 502-584-1090
Fax: 502-584-4707

MEMBERS OF FIRM

Victor W. Ewen (1924-1989)
A. Campbell Ewen
Frank P. Hilliard
John M. Bush

ASSOCIATES

Kevin P. Kinney
Scott F. Scheynost
Lawrence W. Cook
Richard G. Sloan

For full biographical listings, see the Martindale-Hubbell Law Directory

FRANKLIN AND HANCE, P.S.C. (AV)

The Speed House, 505 West Ormsby Avenue, 40203
Telephone: 502-637-6000
Fax: 502-637-1413

Larry B. Franklin
Michael R. Hance

David B. Gray

Reference: First National Bank.

For full biographical listings, see the Martindale-Hubbell Law Directory

GOLDBERG & SIMPSON, P.S.C. (AV)

3000 National City Tower, 40202
Telephone: 502-589-4440
Telefax: 502-581-1344
Washington, D.C. Office: 1200 G Street, N.W. - Suite 800, 20005.
Telephone: 202-434-8968.
Telefax: 202-737-5822.

Fred M. Goldberg
David B. Ratterman
Jonathan D. Goldberg
James S. Goldberg
Mitchell A. Charney
Steven A. Goodman
A. Courtney Guild, Jr.
Edward L. Schoenbaechler
Samuel H. DeShazer
R. Thomas Carter
Cathy S. Pike
Gerald L. Stovall
Stephen E. Smith
Mary Alice Maple
Marva M. Gay
Douglas S. Haynes
Scott P. Zoppoth
Cynthia Buss Maddox
Jan M. West
Charles H. Cassis

OF COUNSEL

Ronald V. Simpson
David A. Brill
Kenneth G. Lee (Not admitted in KY; Resident, Washington, D.C. Office)

Representative Clients: First National Bank; Liberty Mutual Insurance Co.; Jewish Hospital Healthcare Services, Inc.; Louisville & Jefferson County Board of Health; Capital Holding Corp.

For full biographical listings, see the Martindale-Hubbell Law Directory

GREENEBAUM DOLL & McDONALD (AV)

A Partnership including Professional Service Corporations
3300 National City Tower, 40202
Telephone: 502-589-4200
Fax: 502-587-3695
Lexington, Kentucky Office: 1400 Vine Center Tower.
Telephone: 606-231-8500.
Fax: 606-255-2742.

(See Next Column)

Covington, Kentucky Office: 50 East River Center Boulevard, P.O. Box 2050.
Telephone: 606-655-4200.
Fax: 606-655-4239.
Cincinnati, Ohio Office: 832 Main Street.
Telephone: 513-421-8087.
Fax: 513-421-8089.

Phillip D. Scott (Covington and Lexington, Kentucky)
Wm. T. Robinson, III
R. Van Young
Eric L. Ison
James G. LeMaster (Resident at Lexington, Kentucky)
Hiram Ely, III
V. Thomas Fryman, Jr. (Resident at Lexington, Kentucky)
Bruce E. Cryder (Lexington, Kentucky and Cincinnati, Ohio)
Janet P. Jakubowicz
Margaret E. Keane
Roger N. Braden (Resident at Covington, Kentucky)
Mark S. Riddle
Holland N. McTyeire, V
Mark T. Hayden (Resident at Lexington, Kentucky)

ASSOCIATES

Anne A. Chesnut (Resident at Lexington, Kentucky)
J. Mark Grundy
D. Barry Stilz (Resident at Lexington, Kentucky)
Daniel P. Cherry
Thomas M. Williams
Angela McCormick Bisig
Nora J. Clevenger
Benjamin D. Crocker (Resident, Lexington Office)
Sheryl E. Heeter (Covington and Cincinnati Offices)
J. Kent Wicker
Paul E. Porter
Brent R. Baughman

Representative Clients: AT & T; Ashland Oil, Inc; Courtaulds Coatings Inc. (Porter Paint Co.); Hillerich & Bradsby; Federal Deposit Insurance Corp.; Humana Inc.; NTS Development Co.; Toyota Motor Manufacturing, U.S.A., Inc; United States Gypsum Co.; University of Louisville, Inc.

For Complete List of Firm Personnel, See General Section

For full biographical listings, see the Martindale-Hubbell Law Directory

FRANK E. HADDAD, JR. (AV)

Kentucky Home Life Building, 239 South Fifth Street, Fifth Floor, 40202
Telephone: 502-583-4881
Fax: 502-589-1058

Reference: Citizens Fidelity Bank & Trust Co.

For full biographical listings, see the Martindale-Hubbell Law Directory

HIRN DOHENY REED & HARPER (AV)

A Partnership including a Professional Service Corporation
2000 Meidinger Tower, 40202
Telephone: 502-585-2450
Telecopiers: 502-585-2207; 585-2529

MEMBERS OF FIRM

Marvin J. Hirn
Frank P. Doheny, Jr.
John S. Reed
James R. Cox
John E. Selent
Lisabeth Hughes Abramson

B. Todd Thompson

ASSOCIATES

Steven A. Edwards
Michael A. Valenti
Mary R. Harville
Michael W. Oyler

Benjamin C. Fultz

Representative Clients: Humana, Inc.; Louisville Gas and Electric Co.; Presbyterian Church (U.S.A.); Mid-America Bank of Louisville; Indiana United Bancorp; National City Bank Kentucky; PNC Bank; Costain Coal Inc.; Ser-Vend International Inc.; J.J.B. Hilliard, W.L. Lyons, Inc.

For Complete List of Firm Personnel, See General Section

For full biographical listings, see the Martindale-Hubbell Law Directory

MIDDLETON & REUTLINGER, P.S.C. (AV)

2500 Brown and Williamson Tower, 40202-3410
Telephone: 502-584-1135
Fax: 502-561-0442
Jeffersonville, Indiana Office: 605 Watt Street, 47130.
Telephone: 812-282-4886.

O. Grant Bruton
Kenneth S. Handmaker
James N. Williams, Jr.
Charles G. Middleton, III
Charles D. Greenwell
John W. Bilby
Stewart L. Prather
D. Randall Gibson
G. Kennedy Hall, Jr.
Mark S. Fenzel
Kathiejane Oehler
William Jay Hunter, Jr.
James E. Milliman
David J. Kellerman

John M. Franck II

Amy B. Berge
Dennis D. Murrell

For Complete List of Firm Personnel, See General Section

For full biographical listings, see the Martindale-Hubbell Law Directory

Louisville—Continued

J. Bruce Miller Law Group (AV)

621 West Main Street, Third Floor, 40202
Telephone: 502-587-0900
Telecopier: 502-587-9008

J. Bruce Miller
Evan G. Perkins
Norma C. Miller
Anthony L. Schnell
Denis B. Fleming, Jr.
Michael J. Kitchen

Representative Clients: Anson Machine Mfg. Co.; Biddinger Investment Capital Corp. (Indiana); Carneal Enterprises, Inc. (Kentucky/Florida); Jefferson County, Kentucky; MPD Inc. (Owensboro, Kentucky); Motion Picture Association of America; Packaging Unlimited Group (Kentucky/North Carolina); Paducah Medical Supply, Inc. (Kentucky/Tennessee/Florida); Sun Group Broadcasting, Inc. (Indiana/Tennessee); Thurman Development Co. (Kentucky/Florida).

For full biographical listings, see the Martindale-Hubbell Law Directory

Mosley, Clare & Townes (AV)

Fifth Floor, Hart Block Building, 730 West Main Street, 40202
Telephone: 502-583-7400
Telecopier: 502-589-4997

MEMBERS OF FIRM

Eugene L. Mosley
W. Waverley Townes
Larry C. Ethridge
Victor L. Baltzell, Jr.
William J. Nold
Judith E. McDonald-Burkman

ASSOCIATE

E. Jeffrey Mosley

For full biographical listings, see the Martindale-Hubbell Law Directory

Ogden Newell & Welch (AV)

1200 One Riverfront Plaza, 40202-2973
Telephone: 502-582-1601
Fax: 502-581-9564

MEMBERS OF FIRM

John T. Ballantine
Stephen F. Schuster
Scott T. Wendelsdorf
David A. Harris
Gregory J. Bubalo
D. Brian Rattliff
W. Gregory King

ASSOCIATES

Susan C. Bybee
Douglas C. Ballantine
Tracy S. Prewitt
Jennifer J. Hall

Counsel for: KU Energy Corp.; Kentucky Utilities Co.; Brown-Forman Corp.; B.F. Goodrich Co.; Brown & Williamson Tobacco Corp.; J.J.B. Hilliard, W.L. Lyons, Inc.; Interlock Industries, Inc.; Akzo Coatings, Inc.; United Medical Corp.; Bank of Louisville.

For Complete List of Firm Personnel, See General Section

For full biographical listings, see the Martindale-Hubbell Law Directory

Oldfather & Morris (AV)

One Mezzanine The Morrissey Building, 304 West Liberty Street, 40202
Telephone: 502-589-5500
Fax: 502-589-5338

Ann B. Oldfather
Douglas H. Morris, II
William F. McMurry
James Barrett
Teresa A. Talbott

For full biographical listings, see the Martindale-Hubbell Law Directory

W. R. (Pat) Patterson, Jr. (AV)

Suite 408, 310 West Liberty Street, 40202
Telephone: 502-583-1122
FAX: 502-583-3520

For full biographical listings, see the Martindale-Hubbell Law Directory

Pedley, Ross, Zielke & Gordinier (AV)

1150 Starks Building, 455 South Fourth Avenue, 40202
Telephone: 502-589-4600
Fax: 502-584-0422

MEMBERS OF FIRM

Lawrence L. Pedley
Robert P. Ross
Laurence J. Zielke
John K. Gordinier
William W. Stodghill
Schuyler J. Olt
P. Stephen Gordinier
Frank G. Simpson, III
Charles F. Merz

OF COUNSEL

William C. Stone
J. Chester Porter

(See Next Column)

ASSOCIATES

William H. Mooney
William J. Shreffler
John H. Dwyer, Jr.

Representative Clients: Kentucky Independent Community Bankers Assoc.; Louisville and Jefferson County Metropolitan Sewer District; Storer Communications of Jefferson County; Gannet Co.; Hitachi Consumer Products of America; Service Painting Co.; Irwin H. Whitehouse & Sons, Inc.; American Marine Service Barge Lines; Aetna Life & Casualty Co.

For full biographical listings, see the Martindale-Hubbell Law Directory

Ronald D. Ray (AV)

1012 South Fourth Street, 40203
Telephone: 502-584-8300; 241-5552
Cable Address: "Victory"
FAX: 502-584-1948; 241-1552

Representative Clients: Abel Construction Co., Inc.; Adams Dominion, Inc.; Appolo Fuels, Inc.; Christian Brotherhood Newsletter, Inc.; Center Heritage Center; Humphries Mortgage Co.; Institute for Media Education, Inc.; Komo Machine, Inc.; MagneTek, Inc.; Naval Aviation Foundation, Inc.; University of Louisville.

For full biographical listings, see the Martindale-Hubbell Law Directory

Rubin Hays & Foley (AV)

First Trust Centre 200 South Fifth Street, 40202
Telephone: 502-569-7550
Telecopier: 502-569-7555

MEMBERS OF FIRM

Wm. Carl Fust
Harry Lee Meyer
David W. Gray
Irvin D. Foley
Joseph R. Gathright, Jr.
Lisa Koch Bryant
Sharon C. Hardy
Charles S. Musson
W. Randall Jones
K. Gail Russell

ASSOCIATE

Christian L. Juckett

OF COUNSEL

James E. Fahey
Newman T. Guthrie

Representative Clients: J.C. Bradford & Co., Inc.; J.J.B. Hilliard, W.L. Lyons, Inc.; Huntington National Bank; Liberty National Bank and Trust Company; National City Bank; PNC Bank; Prudential Bache & Co., Inc.; Prudential Securities, Inc.; Society Bank; Stock Yards Bank and Trust Co.

For full biographical listings, see the Martindale-Hubbell Law Directory

Seiller & Handmaker (AV)

2200 Meidinger Tower, 40202
Telephone: 502-584-7400
Telecopier: 502-583-2100
Paris, Kentucky Office: Seiller, Handmaker & Blevins, P.S.C., 1431 South Main Street.
Telephone: 606-987-3980.
Telecopier: 606-987-3982.
New Albany, Indiana Office: 204 Pearl Street, Suite 200.
Telephone: 812-948-8307.
Telecopier: 812-948-8383.

Edward F. Seiller (1897-1990)

MEMBERS OF FIRM

Stuart Allen Handmaker
Bill V. Seiller
David M. Cantor
Neil C. Bordy
Kyle Anne Citrynell
Maury D. Kommor
Cynthia Compton Stone

ASSOCIATES

Glenn A. Cohen
Pamela M. Greenwell
Tomi Anne Blevins Pulliam (Resident, Paris Office)
Linda Scholle Cowan
Mary Zeller Wing Ceridan
Michael C. Bratcher
John E. Brengle
Patrick R. Holland, II
Edwin Jon Wolfe
Donna F. Townsend
William C. Robinson

OF COUNSEL

Robert S. Frey

For full biographical listings, see the Martindale-Hubbell Law Directory

Weiss & Frederick (AV)

1425 Citizens Plaza, 40202
Telephone: 502-583-1000
FAX: 502-583-4478

MEMBERS OF FIRM

Gary M. Weiss
Carl D. Frederick
Howard H. Swartz
Janice M. Weiss

OF COUNSEL

Henry M. Burt

For full biographical listings, see the Martindale-Hubbell Law Directory

Louisville—Continued

WOODWARD, HOBSON & FULTON (AV)

2500 National City Tower, 101 South Fifth Street, 40202
Telephone: 502-581-8000
Fax: 502-581-8111
Lexington, Kentucky Office: National City Plaza, 301 East Main Street, Suite 650.
Telephone: 606-244-7100.
Telecopier: 606-244-7111.

MEMBERS OF FIRM

Kenneth L. Anderson
William D. Grubbs
Harry K. Herren
David R. Monohan
Will H. Fulton
Bradley R. Hume
Richard H. C. Clay
Mary Jo Wetzel
Gregory L. Smith
Gregory A. Bölzle
Elizabeth Ullmer Mendel
Jann B. Logsdon
Linsey W. West (Resident, Lexington, Kentucky Office)

Representative Clients: CSX Transportation; Fischer Packing-Wilson Foods; Ford Motor Co.; General Motors Corp.; Ralston Purina Co.; Sears Roebuck Co.

For Complete List of Firm Personnel, See General Section

For full biographical listings, see the Martindale-Hubbell Law Directory

WYATT, TARRANT & COMBS (AV)

Citizens Plaza, 40202
Telephone: 502-589-5235
Telecopier: 502-589-0309
Lexington, Kentucky Office: 1700 Lexington Financial Center.
Telephone: 606-233-2012.
Telecopier: 606-259-0649.
Frankfort, Kentucky Office: The Taylor-Scott Building, 311 West Main Street.
Telephone: 502-223-2104.
Telecopier: 502-227-7681.
New Albany, Indiana Office: The Elsby Building, 117 East Spring Street,
Telephone: 812-945-3561.
Telecopier: 812-949-2524.
Nashville, Tennessee Office: 1500 Nashville City Center, 511 Union Street.
Telephone: 615-244-0020.
Telecopier: 615-256-1726.
Music Row, Nashville Office: 29 Music Square East.
Telephone: 615-255-6161.
Telecopier: 615-254-4490.
Hendersonville, Tennessee Office: 313 E. Main Street, Suite 1.
Telephone: 615-822-8822.
Telecopier: 615-824-4684.

MEMBERS OF FIRM

Edgar A. Zingman
Richard W. Iler
Robert C. Ewald
Samuel G. Bridge, Jr.
Robert I. Cusick
John P. Reisz
Jon L. Fleischaker
K. Gregory Haynes
M. Stephen Pitt
Walter M. Jones
Frank F. Chuppe, Jr.
Merrill S. Schell
Virginia Hamilton Snell
Byron E. Leet
Mary Ann Main
Holliday Hopkins Thacker

Representative Clients: Ashland Oil, Inc.; Brown & Williamson Tobacco Corp.; Churchill Downs, Inc.; E. I. du Pont de Nemours and Company; Ford Motor Co.; Gannett Co., Inc./The Courier-Journal/Louisville Times; General Electric Co.; Kentucky Hospital Assn.; Metropolitan Life Insurance Co.; PNC Bank, Kentucky, Inc. and its affiliates.

For Complete List of Firm Personnel, See General Section

For full biographical listings, see the Martindale-Hubbell Law Directory

*OWENSBORO,** Daviess Co.

LOVETT & LAMAR (AV)

208 West Third Street, 42303-4121
Telephone: 502-926-3000
FAX: 502-685-2625

MEMBERS OF FIRM

Wells T. Lovett
Charles L. Lamar
John T. Lovett
Marty G. Jacobs

Representative Clients: Athlone Industries, Inc.; Beaver Dam Deposit Bank; Carousel Nut Products, Inc.; Central Bank & Trust Co.; Fern Terrace Rest Homes, Inc.; Green River District Health Dept.; Pullman Power Products, Inc.; Sterett Construction Co.; Willamette Industries, Inc.

For full biographical listings, see the Martindale-Hubbell Law Directory

RUMMAGE, KAMUF, YEWELL, PACE & CONDON (AV)

Great Financial Federal Building, 322 Frederica Street, 42301
Telephone: 502-685-3901
FAX: 502-926-2005

(See Next Column)

MEMBERS OF FIRM

William E. Rummage
Charles J. Kamuf
David L. Yewell
Patrick D. Pace
David C. Condon

ASSOCIATE

John M. Mischel

Representative Clients: Owensboro Municipal Utilities Commission; Lincoln Service Corp.; Hancock County Planning Commission; Daviess County Board of Education; Barmet Aluminum Corp.; Owensboro Sewer Commission; TICOR Title Insurance Co.; Chicago Title Insurance Co.; Owensboro Riverport Authority; Housing Authority of Owensboro.

For full biographical listings, see the Martindale-Hubbell Law Directory

*OWINGSVILLE,** Bath Co.

BYRON & ROBERTS (AV)

112 Court Street, 40360
Telephone: 606-674-2911

MEMBERS OF FIRM

Roger A. Byron
Winifred Byron Roberts

General Counsel for: Farmers Bank, Owingsville, Kentucky.
Local Counsel for: Delta Natural Gas Co.
Approved Attorney for: Lawyers Title Insurance Corp.

For full biographical listings, see the Martindale-Hubbell Law Directory

*PADUCAH,** McCracken Co.

BOEHL STOPHER & GRAVES (AV)

Suite 340 Executive Inn Riverfront, One Executive Boulevard, 42001
Telephone: 502-442-4369
FAX: 502-442-4689
Louisville, Kentucky Office: Providian Center, Suite 2300, 400 West Market Street.
Telephone: 502-589-5980.
Fax: 502-561-9400.
Lexington, Kentucky Office: 444 West Second Street.
Telephone: 606-252-6721.
Fax: 606-253-1445.
Prestonsburg, Kentucky Office: 125 Court Street.
Telephone: 606-886-8004.
Fax: 606-886-9579.
New Albany, Indiana Office: Elsby East, Suite 204, 400 Pearl Street.
Telephone: 812-948-5053.
Fax: 812-948-9233.

RESIDENT PARTNERS

Jonathan Freed
Richard L. Walter
John P. Rall
Charles D. Walter

RESIDENT ASSOCIATE

Teresa M. Groves

Counsel for: Ford Motor Co.; Texas Eastern Transmission Corp.; Coca-Cola Bottling Co.; National Collegiate Athletic Assn.; Hartford Accident and Indemnity Co.; Continental Insurance Group; St. Paul Fire & Marine Insurance Co.; Lloyds of London; Old Republic Insurance Co.

For Complete List of Firm Personnel, See General Section

For full biographical listings, see the Martindale-Hubbell Law Directory

WHITLOW, ROBERTS, HOUSTON & RUSSELL (AV)

Old National Bank Building, 300 Broadway, P.O. Box 995, 42001
Telephone: 502-443-4516
FAX: 502-443-4571

MEMBERS OF FIRM

Richard C. Roberts
Thomas B. Russell
Mark C. Whitlow
E. Frederick Straub, Jr.
Mark S. Medlin
R. Christion Hutson

ASSOCIATE

Ronald F. Kupper

Representative Clients: State Farm Mutual Insurance Cos.; Liberty Mutual Insurance; Aetna Life and Casualty; Kentucky Medical Insurance Co.; The Medical Protective Co.; Elf Atochem North America, Inc.; Westvaco Corp.; Peoples First National Bank & Trust Co.; The B.F. Goodrich Co.; Martin Marietta Energy Systems, Inc.

For Complete List of Firm Personnel, See General Section

For full biographical listings, see the Martindale-Hubbell Law Directory

LOUISIANA

*ALEXANDRIA,** Rapides Parish

NEBLETT, BEARD & ARSENAULT (AV)

A Registered Limited Liability Partnership including Law Corporations
2220 Bonaventure Court, P.O. Box 1190, 71301
Telephone: 318-487-9874; 1-800-256-1050
FAX: 318-443-7887

Robert B. Neblett (1927-1991)
Richard W. Beard (1955-1988)
Richard J. Arsenault (Law Corporation)
C. Michael Bollinger
David O. Walker (Law Corporation)
Paul J. Tellarico
William S. Neblett

ASSOCIATES

Michael S. Koch
Allen A. Krake
Galen (Allen) W. McBride
Douglas L. Bryan
Wesley J. Gralapp
Troy R. Keller

Reference: Guaranty Bank & Trust Co.

For full biographical listings, see the Martindale-Hubbell Law Directory

STAFFORD, STEWART & POTTER (AV)

3112 Jackson Street, P.O. Box 1711, 71309
Telephone: 318-487-4910
Fax: 318-487-9417

MEMBERS OF FIRM

Grove Stafford, Jr.
Larry A. Stewart
Russell L. Potter
Paul Boudreaux, Jr.
Bradley J. Gadel
James D. Kirk
Andrew P. Texada
Mark Alan Watson
Gary B. Tillman

ASSOCIATES

Mark Pearce
Randall B. Keiser

Representative Clients: Admiral Insurance Co.; Allied Insurance Co.; Asplundh Manufacturing Company; Bankers & Shippers Insurance Company of New York; Bic Corporation; John Deere Insurance Company; Government Employees Insurance Co.; Sentry Insurance Co.; Trinity Universal Insurance Company; U.S. Fidelity & Guaranty Co.

For full biographical listings, see the Martindale-Hubbell Law Directory

*BATON ROUGE,** East Baton Rouge Parish

BREAZEALE, SACHSE & WILSON, L.L.P. (AV)

Twenty-Third Floor, One American Place, P.O. Box 3197, 70821-3197
Telephone: 504-387-4000
Fax: 504-387-5397
New Orleans, Louisiana Office: Place St. Charles, Suite 4214, 201 St. Charles Avenue.
Telephone: 504-582-1170.
Fax: 504-582-1164.

MEMBERS OF FIRM

Victor A. Sachse, III
Gordon A. Pugh
Paul M. Hebert, Jr.
Claude F. Reynaud, Jr.
Christine Lipsey
Robert L. Atkinson
John F. Whitney (Resident, New Orleans Office)
John W. Barton, Jr.
Michael R. Hubbell
Jude C. Bursavich

ASSOCIATES

James R. Chastain, Jr.
Gwen P. Harmon

Counsel for: Hibernia National Bank; South Central Bell Telephone Co.; Allied-Signal Corp.; Reynolds Metal Co.; Illinois Central Railroad Co.; The Continental Insurance Cos.; Fireman's Fund American Group; Chicago Bridge & Iron Co.; Montgomery Ward & Co.

For Complete List of Firm Personnel, See General Section

For full biographical listings, see the Martindale-Hubbell Law Directory

KANTROW, SPAHT, WEAVER & BLITZER, A PROFESSIONAL LAW CORPORATION (AV)

Suite 300, City Plaza, 445 North Boulevard, P.O. Box 2997, 70821-2997
Telephone: 504-383-4703
Fax: 504-343-0630; 343-0637

Byron R. Kantrow
Carlos G. Spaht
Geraldine B. Weaver
Sidney M. Blitzer, Jr.
Paul H. Spaht
Lee C. Kantrow
John C. Miller
Vincent P. Fornias
David S. Rubin
Diane L. Crochet
Richard F. Zimmerman, Jr.
Bob D. Tucker
Martin E. Golden
Joseph A. Schittone, Jr.

S. Layne Lee
J. Michael Robinson, Jr.
Connell L. Archey
Richard D. Moreno
Randal J. Robert

(See Next Column)

Representative Clients: CNA Insurance Cos.; Federal Deposit Insurance Corp.; Hartford Insurance Group; Air Products and Chemicals, Inc.; CF Industries, Inc.; AT&T; United Companies Financial Corp.

For full biographical listings, see the Martindale-Hubbell Law Directory

KEAN, MILLER, HAWTHORNE, D'ARMOND, MCCOWAN & JARMAN, L.L.P. (AV)

22nd Floor, One American Place, P.O. Box 3513, 70821
Telephone: 504-387-0999
Fax: 504-388-9133
New Orleans, Louisiana Office: Energy Centre, Suite 1470, 1100 Poydras Street.
Telephone: 504-585-3050.
Fax: 504-585-3051.

MEMBERS OF FIRM

William R. D'Armond
Charles S. McCowan, Jr.
G. William Jarman
Leonard L. Kilgore III
Gary A. Bezet
Michael C. Garrard
Vance A. Gibbs
James R. Lackie
David K. Nelson
J. Carter Wilkinson
Sandra Louise Edwards
Bradley C. Myers
Melanie M. Hartmann
Linda Sarradet Akchin
Erich P. Rapp
Charles L. Patin, Jr.
Mathile W. Abramson
Cynthia M. Chemay

Kelly Wilkinson
Gregg R. Kronenberger
Charles S. McCowan III
Linda G. Rodrigue
Theresa R. Hagen
Glenn M. Farnet
Esteban Herrera, Jr.
Susan Knight Carter (Resident, New Orleans Office)
Gary P. Graphia

Representative Clients: BASF Corporation, Parsippany, N.J.; Exxon Company, U.S.A., Baton Rouge, La.; Georgia Gulf Corporation, Atlanta, Ga.; Hancock Bank of Louisiana, Baton Rouge, La.; Georgia-Pacific Corporation, Atlanta, Ga.; Insurance Corporation of America, Houston, Tx.; Louisiana Medical Mutual Insurance Company, Metairie, La.; Metropolitan Life Insurance Company, New York, N.Y.; Texaco, Inc., White Plains, N.Y.

For Complete List of Firm Personnel, See General Section

For full biographical listings, see the Martindale-Hubbell Law Directory

KLEINPETER & KLEINPETER (AV)

1680 South Lobdell Avenue, Suite E, P.O. Box 66443, 70896
Telephone: 504-926-5093

MEMBERS OF FIRM

Robert L. Kleinpeter
R. Loren Kleinpeter

Representative Clients: Argonaut Insurance Co.; American Indemnity Co.; All American Assurance Co.; American Southern Insurance Co.; Louisiana Underwriters of American Indemnity Co.; American Surety Company of New York; Tri-State General Agency; State Fire & Casualty Co.; Early American Insurance Co.; Members Mutual Insurance Co.

For full biographical listings, see the Martindale-Hubbell Law Directory

PHELPS DUNBAR, L.L.P. (AV)

Suite 701, City National Bank Building, P.O. Box 4412, 70821-4412
Telephone: 504-346-0285
Telecopier: 504-381-9197
New Orleans, Louisiana Office: Texaco Center, 400 Poydras Street.
Telephone 504-566-1311.
Telecopier: 504-568-9130; 504-568-9007.
Cable Address: "Howspencer."
Telex: 584125 WU.
Telex: 6821155 WUI.
Jackson, Mississippi Office: Suite 500, Security Centré North, 200 South Lamar Street, P.O. Box 23066.
Telephone: 601-352-2300.
Telecopier: 601-360-9777.
Tupelo, Mississippi Office: Seventh Floor, One Mississippi Plaza, P.O. Box 1220.
Telephone: 601-842-7907.
Telecopier: 601-842-3873.
Houston, Texas Office: Suite 501, 4 Houston Center, 1331 Lamar Street.
Telephone: 713-659-1386.
Telecopier: 713-659-1388.
London, England Office: Suite 976, Level 9, Lloyd's, 1 Lime Street, London EC3M 7DQ England.
Telephone: 011-44-71-929-4765.
Telecopier: 011-44-71-929-0046.
Telex: 987321.

RESIDENT PARTNERS

H. Alston Johnson, III
Michael D. Hunt
Jennifer Bowers Zimmerman
F. Scott Kaiser
Steven J. Levine
Allen D. Darden
Thomas H. Kiggans
Marshall M. Redmon

COUNSEL

E. Jane Sherman

(See Next Column)

PHELPS DUNBAR L.L.P., *Baton Rouge—Continued*

RESIDENT ASSOCIATES

Jane H. Barney
Susan W. Furr
Michael David Ferachi
Darrell J. Loup
Patricia Hill Wilton

Representative Clients: American National Insurance Co.; Argonaut Insurance Co.; Belvedere Insurance Company; Capitol American Life Insurance Co.; City National Bank; Louisiana Companies; New England Insurance Co.; The Travelers Insurance Co.

For Complete List of Firm Personnel, See General Section

For full biographical listings, see the Martindale-Hubbell Law Directory

POWERS, CLEGG & WILLARD (AV)

7967 Office Park Boulevard, P.O. Box 15948, 70895
Telephone: 504-928-1951
Telecopier: 504-929-9834

MEMBERS OF FIRM

John Dale Powers
Michael V. Clegg
William E. Willard

ASSOCIATES

Neil H. Mixon
Troy J. Charpentier
Mary A. Cazes

General Counsel for: Audubon Insurance Co.
Louisiana Counsel for: Hancock Bank & Trust Co.; Hertz Corp.; Ciba-Geigy Corp.; Utica Mutual Insurance Co.

For full biographical listings, see the Martindale-Hubbell Law Directory

BERT K. ROBINSON (AV)

10357 Old Hammond Highway, 70816-8261
Telephone: 504-924-0296
Fax: 504-924-5288

ASSOCIATE

Johanna R. Landreneau

OF COUNSEL

Charles C. Holbrook

For full biographical listings, see the Martindale-Hubbell Law Directory

SEALE, SMITH, ZUBER & BARNETTE (AV)

Two United Plaza, Suite 200, 8550 United Plaza Boulevard, 70809
Telephone: 504-924-1600
Telecopier: 504-924-6100

Armbrust Gordon Seale (1913-1989)
Robert W. Smith (1922-1989)
Donald S. Zuber
Kenneth E. Barnette
William C. Kaufman III
John W. L. Swanner
James H. Morgan III
Ronald A. Seale
Brent E. Kinchen
Charles K. Watts
Myron A. Walker, Jr.
Daniel A. Reed
Kenner O. Miller, Jr.
William C. Rowe, Jr.
Lawrence R. Anderson, Jr.

ASSOCIATES

Richard T. Reed
Barbara G. Chatelain
Anthony J. Russo, Jr.
Catherine S. Nobile

Representative Clients: Farmers Insurance Group; St. Paul Fire and Marine Insurance Company; United Services Automobile Association; General Motors Acceptance Corporation.
Reference: City National Bank, Baton Rouge, Louisiana.

For full biographical listings, see the Martindale-Hubbell Law Directory

*HOMER,** Claiborne Parish

SHAW AND SHAW, A PROFESSIONAL LAW CORPORATION (AV)

522 East Main Street, P.O. Box 420, 71040
Telephone: 318-927-6149

William M. Shaw

Reference: Homer National Bank.

*LAFAYETTE,** Lafayette Parish

DAVIDSON, MEAUX, SONNIER, McELLIGOTT & SWIFT (AV)

810 South Buchanan Street, P.O. Drawer 2908, 70502
Telephone: 318-237-1660
Fax: 318-237-3676

MEMBERS OF FIRM

James J. Davidson, Jr. (1904-1990)
V. Farley Sonnier (1942-1988)
Richard C. Meaux, Sr.
James J. Davidson, III
John E. McElligott, Jr.
John G. Swift
Jeffrey A. Rhoades
Philip A. Fontenot
Kyle L. Gideon
Theodore G. Edwards, IV
Stacey L. Knight

(See Next Column)

ASSOCIATES

Jhan C. Boudreaux Beaullieu
Tracy P. Curtis

Representative Clients: Southern Pacific Transportation Co., Wal-Mart Stores, Inc.; Power Rig Drilling Co., Inc.; Southwest Louisiana Electric Membership Corp.; Macro Oil Company; Highlands Insurance Company; United Services Automobile Association; Sears, Roebuck & Company; Lawyers Title Insurance Corporation; Wal-Mart Stores, Inc.; USAA.

For Complete List of Firm Personnel, See General Section

For full biographical listings, see the Martindale-Hubbell Law Directory

DOMENGEAUX, WRIGHT, MOROUX & ROY, A PROFESSIONAL LAW CORPORATION (AV)

556 Jefferson Street, Suite 500, P.O. Box 3668, 70502-3668
Telephone: 318-233-3033; 1-800-375-3106
Fax: 318-232-8213
Hammond, Louisiana Office: Magnolia Plaza, Suite K, 1007 West Thomas Street, P. O. Box 1558.
Telephone: 504-542-4963; 1-800-423-1160.

James Domengeaux (1907-1988)
Anthony D. Moroux (1948-1993)
Bob F. Wright (A Professional Law Corporation)
James Parkerson Roy (A Professional Law Corporation)
Robert K. Tracy (A Professional Law Corporation)
Thomas R. Edwards (A Professional Law Corporation)
Frank Edwards (Resident, Hammond Office)
James Wattigny
James H. Domengeaux
R. Hamilton Davis
Gilbert Hennigan Dozier
Carla Marie Perron
Tyron D. Picard

OF COUNSEL

Jerome E. Domengeaux

Reference: Mid-South National Bank; Advocate Financial, L.L.C.

For full biographical listings, see the Martindale-Hubbell Law Directory

HILL & BEYER, A PROFESSIONAL LAW CORPORATION (AV)

101 LaRue France, Suite 502, P.O. Box 53006, 70505-3006
Telephone: 318-232-9733
Fax: 1-318-237-2566

John K. Hill, Jr.
Bret C. Beyer
David R. Rabalais
Lisa C. McCowen
Eugene P. Matherne
Robert B. Purser
Erin J. Sherburne
Harold Adam Lawrence

For full biographical listings, see the Martindale-Hubbell Law Directory

RICHARD R. KENNEDY A PROFESSIONAL LAW CORPORATION (AV)

309 Polk Street, P.O. Box 3243, 70502-3243
Telephone: 318-232-1934
Fax: 318-232-9720

Richard R. Kennedy

For full biographical listings, see the Martindale-Hubbell Law Directory

MANGHAM, DAVIS AND OGLESBEE (AV)

Suite 1400 First National Bank Towers, 600 Jefferson Street, P.O. Box 93110, 70509-3110
Telephone: 318-233-6200
Fax: 318-233-6521

Michael R. Mangham
Louis R. Davis
Michael G. Oglesbee
Herman E. Garner, Jr.

ASSOCIATES

Dawn Mayeux Fuqua
Lisa Hanchey Sevier

SPECIAL COUNSEL

Michael J. O'Shee

OF COUNSEL

George W. Hardy, III
Robert E. Rowe

Reference: The First National Bank of Lafayette, Lafayette, Louisiana.

For full biographical listings, see the Martindale-Hubbell Law Directory

ONEBANE, DONOHOE, BERNARD, TORIAN, DIAZ, McNAMARA & ABELL (AV)

Suite 600, Versailles Centre, 102 Versailles Boulevard, P.O. Box 3507, 70502
Telephone: 318-237-2660
Telecopier: 318-266-1232
Cable Address: "Ondob"
Telex: 311283

(See Next Column)

ONEBANE, DONOHOE, BERNARD, TORIAN, DIAZ, MCNAMARA & ABELL—*Continued*

Joseph Onebane (1917-1987)
John G. Torian, II (1936-1991)
Lawrence E. Donohoe, Jr.
John Allen Bernard
James E. Diaz
Timothy J. McNamara
Edward C. Abell, Jr.
Helen Onebane Mendell
Lawrence L. Lewis, III
Robert M. Mahony
Daniel G. Fournerat
Douglas W. Truxillo
Randall C. Songy
Chris G. Robbins
Michael G. Durand
Greg Guidry
Joseph L. Lemoine, Jr.
Mark L. Riley
Graham N. Smith
Gordon T. Whitman
Gary P. Kraus
Richard J. Petre, Jr.
Thomas G. Smart
James E. Diaz, Jr.
Roger E. Ishee
R. Thomas Jorden, Jr.
Kevin R. Rees
John W. Penny, Jr.
John A. Keller

Jennifer McDaniel Kleinpeter
Steven C. Lanza
Christopher H. Hebert
John W. Kolwe
Sue Nations
Joel P. Babineaux
Michael W. Landry
Ted M. Anthony
Carolyn Trahan Bertrand
Alison M. Brumley

Representative Clients: Allstate Insurance Co.; CIGNA; Continental Insurance Co.; Employers-Commercial; Fireman's Fund American Insurance Co.; Highlands Insurance Co.; Travelers Insurance Co.

For full biographical listings, see the Martindale-Hubbell Law Directory

*LAKE CHARLES,** Calcasieu Parish

BERGSTEDT & MOUNT (AV)

Second Floor, Magnolia Life Building, P.O. Drawer 3004, 70602-3004
Telephone: 318-433-3004
Facsimile: 318-433-8080

MEMBERS OF FIRM

Thomas M. Bergstedt
Benjamin W. Mount

ASSOCIATES

Van C. Seneca
Thomas J. Gayle
Gregory P. Marceaux

OF COUNSEL

Charles S. Ware

Representative Clients: Armstrong World Industries; Ashland Oil Co.; CIGNA Property & Casualty Companies; Homequity; Lake Area Medical Center; Leach Company; Olin Corporation; Terra Corporation; Town of Iowa; R. D. Werner Company.

For Complete List of Firm Personnel, See General Section

For full biographical listings, see the Martindale-Hubbell Law Directory

JONES, TÊTE, NOLEN, HANCHEY, SWIFT & SPEARS, L.L.P. (AV)

First Federal Building, P.O. Box 910, 70602
Telephone: 318-439-8315
Telefax: 436-5606; 433-5536

MEMBERS OF FIRM

Sam H. Jones (1897-1978)
William R. Tête
William M. Nolen
James C. Hanchey
Carl H. Hanchey
William B. Swift
Kenneth R. Spears
Edward J. Fonti
Charles N. Harper
Gregory W. Belfour
Robert J. Tête
Yul D. Lorio

OF COUNSEL

John A. Patin
Edward D. Myrick

ASSOCIATES

Lilynn A. Cutrer
Lydia Ann Guillory-Lee
Clint David Bischoff

General Counsel for: First Federal Savings & Loan Association of Lake Charles; Beauregard Electric Cooperative, Inc.
Representative Clients: Atlantic Richfield Company; CITGO Petroleum Corp.; Conoco Inc.; HIMONT U.S.A., Inc.; ITT Hartford; Olin Corporation; OXY USA Inc.; Premier Bank, National Association; W.R. Grace & Co.

For full biographical listings, see the Martindale-Hubbell Law Directory

PLAUCHÉ SMITH & NIESET, A PROFESSIONAL LAW CORPORATION (AV)

1123 Pithon Street, P.O. Drawer 1705, 70602
Telephone: 318-436-0522
Facsimile: 318-436-9637

(See Next Column)

S. W. Plauché (1889-1952)
S. W. Plauché, Jr. (1915-1966)
A. Lane Plauché
Allen L. Smith, Jr.
James R. Nieset
Frank M. Walker, Jr.
Michael J. McNulty, III
Jeffrey M. Cole
Andrew R. Johnson, IV
Charles V. Musso, Jr.
Christopher P. Ieyoub
H. David Vaughan, II
Rebecca S. Young
Stephanie A. Landry

Representative Clients: CIGNA; CNA Insurance Cos.; Commercial Union Insurance Cos.; Crum & Forster; General Motors Corp.; Reliance Insurance Cos.; Royal Insurance Group; State Farm; U.S. Insurance Group.

For full biographical listings, see the Martindale-Hubbell Law Directory

RAGGIO, CAPPEL, CHOZEN & BERNIARD (AV)

500 Magnolia Life Building, P.O. Box 820, 70601
Telephone: 318-436-9481
Fax: 318-436-9499

MEMBERS OF FIRM

Thomas L. Raggio
Richard B. Cappel
Frederick L. Cappel
Richard A. Chozen
Stephen A. Berniard, Jr.
Christopher M. Trahan
L. Paul Foreman
M. Keith Prudhomme

Counsel for: Aetna Casualty & Surety Co.; Allstate Insurance Co.; Hercules Incorporated; Liberty Mutual Insurance Co.; Southern Pacific Co.; United States Fidelity and Guaranty Co.; Crowley Maritime Corp.; General Motors Corp.; Sabine Towing & Transportation Co.; E. I. duPont de Nemours & Co., Inc.

For Complete List of Firm Personnel, See General Section

For full biographical listings, see the Martindale-Hubbell Law Directory

SCOFIELD, GERARD, VERON, SINGLETARY & POHORELSKY, A PROFESSIONAL LAW CORPORATION (AV)

1114 Ryan Street, P.O. Drawer 3028, 70601
Telephone: 318-433-9436
Telefax: 318-436-0306

John B. Scofield
Richard E. Gerard, Jr.
J. Michael Veron
C. Eston Singletary
John R. Pohorelsky
Scott J. Scofield
Patrick D. Gallaugher, Jr.
Robert E. Landry
Russell J. Stutes, Jr.

Representative Clients: Admiral Insurance Co.; Amoco Production Co.; Browning-Ferris Industries, Inc.; Cosmos Broadcasting Corp.; Ford Motor Co.; Dresser Industries, Inc.; Kansas City Southern Railway Co.; Mobil Exploration & Producing U.S., Inc.; Phillips Petroleum Co.; Premier Bank, N.A.

For full biographical listings, see the Martindale-Hubbell Law Directory

METAIRIE, Jefferson Parish

KIEFER & RUDMAN, A PROFESSIONAL LAW CORPORATION (AV)

One Galleria Boulevard, Suite 1212, 70001
Telephone: 504-838-2250
Telefax: 504-838-2251
New Orleans, Louisiana Office: One Seine Court, Suite 112.
Telephone: 504-368-2220.
Fax: 504-368-2278.

John B. Kiefer
Laurence D. Rudman
Roger B. Jacobs
Bruce M. Danner
Philip Schoen Brooks
Harry L. Cahill, III
Terri Bankston Stirling
Pierre V. Miller II
Gregory G. Faia
Scott B. Kiefer

References: First National Bank of Commerce; First National Bank of Commerce of Jefferson Parish; Hibernia National Bank; Jefferson Guaranty Bank; Whitney National Bank of New Orleans.

For full biographical listings, see the Martindale-Hubbell Law Directory

*MONROE,** Ouachita Parish

HAYES, HARKEY, SMITH & CASCIO, L.L.P. (AV)

2811 Kilpatrick Boulevard, P.O. Box 8032, 71211-8032
Telephone: 318-387-2422
FAX: 318-388-5809

Haynes L. Harkey, Jr.
Louis D. Smith
Joseph D. Cascio, Jr.
Charles S. Smith
Thomas M. Hayes, III
Bruce McKamy Mintz
C. Joseph Roberts, III

OF COUNSEL

Thomas M. Hayes, Jr.

John B. Saye
Karen L. Hayes

Representative Clients: Ford Motor Co.; Cigna-Ina; St. Francis Medical Center, Inc.; St. Paul Insurance Group; Cooper Industries, Inc.; Dresser Industries, Inc.; State Farm Insurance Cos.; CNA Insurance Co.; Travelers Insurance Cos.; Riverwood International Corp.

For full biographical listings, see the Martindale-Hubbell Law Directory

McLeod, Verlander, Eade & Verlander (AV)

A Partnership including Professional Law Corporations
1900 North 18th Street, Suite 610, P.O. Box 2270, 71207-2270
Telephone: 318-325-7000
Telecopier: 318-324-0580

MEMBERS OF FIRM

Robert P. McLeod (P.L.C.) | Paul J. Verlander
David E. Verlander, III (P.L.C.) | Rick W. Duplissey
Ellen R. Eade | Pamela G. Nathan

For full biographical listings, see the Martindale-Hubbell Law Directory

Snellings, Breard, Sartor, Inabnett & Trascher (AV)

1503 North 19th Street, P.O. Box 2055, 71207-2055
Telephone: 318-387-8000
Fax: 318-387-8200

MEMBERS OF FIRM

George M. Snellings, Jr. (1910-1984)
E. Frank Snellings
L. Kent Breard, Jr.
Daniel Ryan Sartor, Jr.
Clara Moss Sartor
Carrick R. Inabnett
William Brooks Watson
Charles C. Trascher, III
David C. McMillin

ASSOCIATES

Jon Keith Guice | Carrick B. Inabnett

Representative Clients: Central Bank; Delta Air Lines, Inc.; Federal Deposit Insurance Co.; Glenwood Regional Medical Center; John Hancock Mutual Life Insurance Company; Kemper Insurance Group; Horace Mann Insurance Cos.; Resolution Trust Corp.

For Complete List of Firm Personnel, See General Section

For full biographical listings, see the Martindale-Hubbell Law Directory

*NEW ORLEANS,** Orleans Parish

The Godfrey Firm A Professional Law Corporation (AV)

2500 Energy Centre, 1100 Poydras Street, 70163-2500
Telephone: 504-585-7538
Fax: 504-585-7535

Jarrell E. Godfrey, Jr. | Glenn J. Reames
Jacob S. Capraro | Paul F. Guarisco

For full biographical listings, see the Martindale-Hubbell Law Directory

House, Golden, Kingsmill & Riess, L.L.P. (AV)

Suite 2100 The Energy Centre, 1100 Poydras Street, 70163-2100
Telephone: 504-582-2110
Telecopier: 504-582-2120
Houston, Texas Office: Suite 4750, Texas Commerce Tower, 600 Travis Street, 77002.
Telephone: 713-250-4745.
Telecopier: 713-250-4747.
Singapore Office: B. RAO & K.S. RAJAH. 8 Robinson Road, #04-00. Singapore 0104.
New Delhi, India Office: O.P. KHAITAN & CO., Tolstoy House, Flat No. 1102 & 1103. 11th Floor, 15-17 Tolstoy Marg, New Delhi 110 001.

MEMBERS OF FIRM

W. Richard House, Jr. | Marguerite K. Kingsmill
John M. Golden | Michael R.C. Riess
Charles F. Seabolt

COUNSEL

Murray A. Calhoun | Seth J. Riklin (Resident, Houston, Texas Office)

ASSOCIATES

Michael S. Haddad | Thomas H. Huval
Jeffrey E. Combes | Randal R. Cangelosi
Stephen S. Hall | Avery Griffin Abadie

For full biographical listings, see the Martindale-Hubbell Law Directory

Leake & Andersson (AV)

1700 Energy Centre, 1100 Poydras Street, 70163-1701
Telephone: 504-585-7500
Telecopier: 504-585-7775

MEMBERS OF FIRM

Robert E. Leake, Jr. | Marta-Ann Schnabel O'Bryon
W. Paul Andersson | Kevin O'Bryon
Lawrence A. Mann | George D. Fagan
Donald E. McKay, Jr.

(See Next Column)

ASSOCIATES

Stanton E. Shuler, Jr. | Rebecca Olivier Hand
Guy D. Perrier

Representative Clients: Commercial Credit Services Corp.; First Financial Insurance Co.; Government Employees Insurance Co.; National Union Fire Insurance Co.; National Food Processors, Inc.; Nationwide Insurance Co.; Professional Construction Services, Inc.

For full biographical listings, see the Martindale-Hubbell Law Directory

Nesser, King & LeBlanc (AV)

Suite 3800 Place St. Charles, 201 St. Charles Avenue, 70170
Telephone: 504-582-3800
Telecopier: 504-582-1233

John T. Nesser, III | Patricia Ann Krebs
Henry A. King | Robert J. Burvant
Joseph E. LeBlanc, Jr. | Eric Earl Jarrell
David S. Bland | Liane K. Hinrichs

Jeffrey M. Burmaster | Elton A. Foster
Jeffrey A. Mitchell | Elizabeth S. Wheeler
Margaret M. Sledge | Robert J. Bergeron
Josh M. Kantrow | Timothy S. Madden
Elizabeth A. Meek

OF COUNSEL

Clare P. Hunter | J. Grant Coleman
George B. Jurgens, III | Len R. Brignac
George Farber, Jr.

For full biographical listings, see the Martindale-Hubbell Law Directory

Phelps Dunbar, L.L.P. (AV)

Texaco Center, 400 Poydras Street, 70130-3245
Telephone: 504-566-1311
Telecopier: 504-568-9130, 504-568-9007
Cable Address: "Howspencer"
Telex: 584125 WU
Telex: 6821155 WUI
Baton Rouge, Louisiana Office: Suite 701, City National Bank Building, P.O. Box 4412.
Telephone: 504-346-0285.
Telecopier: 504-381-9197.
Jackson, Mississippi Office: Suite 500, Security Centré North, 200 South Lamar Street, P.O. Box 23066.
Telephone: 601-352-2300.
Telecopier: 601-360-9777.
Tupelo, Mississippi Office: Seventh Floor, One Mississippi Plaza, P.O. Box 1220.
Telephone: 601-842-7907.
Telecopier: 601-842-3873.
Houston, Texas Office: Suite 501, 4 Houston Center, 1331 Lamar Street.
Telephone: 713-659-1386.
Telecopier: 713-659-1388.
London, England Office: Suite 976, Level 9, Lloyd's, 1 Lime Street, London EC3M 7DQ England.
Telephone: 011-44-71-929-4765.
Telecopier: 011-44-71-929-0046.
Telex: 987321.

MEMBERS OF FIRM

Harry Rosenberg | William D. Aaron, Jr.
Roy C. Cheatwood | Nancy Scott Degan
Danny G. Shaw | M. Nan Alessandra
Brent B. Barriere | Mary Ellen Roy
Bruce V. Schewe | Sessions Ault Hootsell III
Paul L. Peyronnin

ASSOCIATES

Gerardo R. Barrios | James M. Jacobs
Robert S. Eitel | Danatus N. King
N. Eleanor Graham | David M. Korn
L. Tiffany Hawkins | Kent A. Lambert
Ronald J. White

Representative Clients: Fidelity Investments; First National Bank of Commerce; Freeport-McMoRan Inc.; General Electric Company and Subsidiaries; Hibernia National Bank; Hilton Hotels Corp.; Lawyers Title Insurance Company; Louisiana Gas Service Co., Inc.; The Travelers Companies; Witco Corp.

For Complete List of Firm Personnel, See General Section

For full biographical listings, see the Martindale-Hubbell Law Directory

Preaus, Roddy & Krebs (AV)

Suite 1650, 650 Poydras Street, 70130
Telephone: 504-523-2111
Telecopier: 504-523-2223

MEMBERS OF FIRM

Eugene R. Preaus | David J. Krebs
Virginia N. Roddy | Maura Zivalich Pelleteri

(See Next Column)

PREAUS, RODDY & KREBS—*Continued*

ASSOCIATES

Teresa Rose Young
Krystil Borrouso Cook
Diane Lloyd Matthews
Edward J. Parr, Jr.

Counsel for: American Society of Composers, Authors and Publishers; Fidelity and Deposit Company of Maryland; Metropolitan Life Insurance Co.; New York Life Insurance Co.; Reliance Insurance Co.; U.S. Home Corp.; Western Sizzlin, Inc.

For full biographical listings, see the Martindale-Hubbell Law Directory

*OPELOUSAS,** St. Landry Parish

DAUZAT, FALGOUST, CAVINESS, BIENVENU & STIPE (AV)
510 S. Court Street, P.O. Box 1450, 70571
Telephone: 318-942-5811
Fax: 318-948-9512

MEMBERS OF FIRM

Jimmy L. Dauzat
Peter F. Caviness
Jerry J. Falgoust
Steven J. Bienvenu
Jeigh L. Stipe

For full biographical listings, see the Martindale-Hubbell Law Directory

*SHREVEPORT,** Caddo Parish

TROY E. BAIN (AV)
1540 Irving Place, 71101
Telephone: 318-221-0076
Fax: 318-227-8290

Reference: Commercial National Bank of Shreveport.

For full biographical listings, see the Martindale-Hubbell Law Directory

BARLOW AND HARDTNER L.C. (AV)
Tenth Floor, Louisiana Tower, 401 Edwards Street, 71101-3289
Telephone: 318-227-1131
Telecopier: 318-227-1141
Mailing Address: P.O. Box 8, Shreveport, Louisiana, 71161-0008

Ray A. Barlow
David R. Taggart
Malcolm S. Murchison
Clair F. White
Kay Cowden Medlin
Philip E. Downer, III
Joseph L. Shea, Jr.
Michael B. Donald
Jay A. Greenleaf

Representative Clients: Anderson Oil & Gas, Inc.; Beaird Industries, Inc.; Goodrich Oil Company; Kelley Oil Corporation; NorAm Energy Corp. (formerly Arkla, Inc.); Panhandle Eastern Corp.; Southwestern Electric Power Company; Central and South West; Pennzoil Producing Co.; Johnson Controls, Inc.

For Complete List of Firm Personnel, See General Section

For full biographical listings, see the Martindale-Hubbell Law Directory

BODENHEIMER, JONES, KLOTZ & SIMMONS (AV)
509 Milam Street, 71101
Telephone: 318-221-1507
Fax: 318-221-4560

MEMBERS OF FIRM

G. M. Bodenheimer, Jr.
F. John Reeks, Jr.
J. W. Jones
Mary Louise Coon Blackley
David B. Klotz
James P. Bodenheimer
Harry D. Simmons
Norman I. Lafargue
C. Gary Mitchell
Claude W. Bookter, Jr.

ASSOCIATE

David A. Szwak

For full biographical listings, see the Martindale-Hubbell Law Directory

COOK, YANCEY, KING & GALLOWAY, A PROFESSIONAL LAW CORPORATION (AV)
1700 Commercial National Tower, 333 Texas Street, P.O. Box 22260, 71120-2260
Telephone: 318-221-6277
Telecopier: 318-227-2606

Edwin L. Blewer, Jr.
Sidney E. Cook, Jr.
Herschel E. Richard, Jr.
Eskridge E. Smith, Jr.
Samuel W. Caverlee
Timothy B. Burnham
F. Drake Lee, Jr.
Curtis R. Shelton
Charles G. Tutt
Kenneth Mascagni
Albert M. Hand, Jr.
James R. Sterritt
Jerald R. Harper
Leland H. Ayres
Cynthia C. Anderson
Bryce J. Denny
Brian A. Homza
Lance P. Havener
Bernard S. Johnson
S. Price Barker
Glenn L. Langley
Lisa Dunn Folsom

(See Next Column)

S. Curtis Mitchell
Julia E. Blewer
Gregg A. Wilkes
Tracy A. Burch
Mary D. Bicknell

Counsel for: Aetna Life and Casualty Co.; AllState Insurance Co.; Caddo Bossier Port Commission; Commercial National Bank in Shreveport; Specialty Oil Co.; International Paper Co.; Hartford Insurance Co.; Maryland-American General Insurance Co.; State Farm Fire & Casualty Insurance Co.; Missouri Pacific Railroad Co.

For Complete List of Firm Personnel, See General Section

For full biographical listings, see the Martindale-Hubbell Law Directory

ROBERT U. GOODMAN, P.L.C. (AV)
Mid South Towers, 416 Travis Street, Suite 1105, 71101-5514
Telephone: 318-221-1601
Fax: 318-221-1749

Robert U. Goodman

OF COUNSEL

James E. Clark
Nancy Kay Fox-Reiter

Representative Clients: Dealers Truck & Equipment Co.; Transworld Life Insurance Co.; Graham Brothers Entertainment, Inc.; Integrated Exploration.

For full biographical listings, see the Martindale-Hubbell Law Directory

MAYER, SMITH & ROBERTS, L.L.P. (AV)
1550 Creswell, 71101
Telephone: 318-222-2135, 222-2268
Fax: 318-222-6420

MEMBERS OF FIRM

Caldwell Roberts
Richard G. Barham
Walter O. Hunter, Jr.
David Butterfield
Mark A. Goodwin
Vicki C. Warner
Ben Marshall, Jr.
Henry N. Bellamy
Alexander S. Lyons
John C. Turnage
Kim Purdy Thomas
Paul R. Mayer, Jr.
Steven E. Soileau

ASSOCIATES

Deborah Shea Baukman
Frank K. Carroll
Caldwell Roberts, Jr.
Dalton Roberts Ross

STAFF ATTORNEY

J. Thomas Butler

OF COUNSEL

Charles L. Mayer
Paul R. Mayer

Representative Clients: CNA Insurance Companies; Liberty Mutual Insurance Company; The St. Paul Companies; United States Fidelity and Guaranty Company; Schumpert Medical Center; Travelers Insurance Company; Great American Insurance Company; Insurance Corporation of America; Highlands Insurance Company; Ohio Casualty Group of Insurance Companies.

For full biographical listings, see the Martindale-Hubbell Law Directory

WEEMS, WRIGHT, SCHIMPF, HAYTER & CARMOUCHE, A PROFESSIONAL LAW CORPORATION (AV)
912 Kings Highway, 71104
Telephone: 318-222-2100
Telecopier: 318-227-0136

Carey T. Schimpf
Paul J. Carmouche
John O. Hayter, III
Mark W. Odom
Mark A. Perkins

Representative Clients: Royal Insurance Co.; Lutheran Benevolent Ins. Co.; National Union Life; Patterson Ins. Co.; Louisiana Indemnity; Louisiana Insurance Guaranty Association; State of Louisiana; Louisiana State University Medical Center; Hibernia National Bank.

For full biographical listings, see the Martindale-Hubbell Law Directory

WIENER, WEISS, MADISON & HOWELL, A PROFESSIONAL CORPORATION (AV)
333 Texas Street, Suite 2350, P.O. Box 21990, 71120-1990
Telephone: 318-226-9100
Fax: 318-424-5128

John M. Madison, Jr.
Larry Feldman, Jr.
James Fleet Howell
Katherine Clark Hennessey
James R. Madison
Jeffrey W. Weiss
Neil T. Erwin
R. Joseph Naus
Lawrence Russo, III
Mark L. Hornsby
Susie Morgan
Donald B. Wiener

Representative Clients: Pioneer Bank & Trust Co.; Ford Motor Credit Corp.; CNA Insurance Companies; International Paper Companies; Louisiana Homebuilders Association Self Insurers Fund; LSU-Shreveport; Sealy Realty, Inc.; Palmer Petroleum, Inc.; Brookshire Grocery Company (Louisiana); Northwest Louisiana Production Credit Association.

(See Next Column)

WIENER, WEISS, MADISON & HOWELL A PROFESSIONAL CORPORATION, *Shreveport—Continued*

For Complete List of Firm Personnel, See General Section

For full biographical listings, see the Martindale-Hubbell Law Directory

WILKINSON, CARMODY & GILLIAM (AV)

1700 Beck Building, 400 Travis Street, P.O. Box 1707, 71166
Telephone: 318-221-4196
Telecopier: 318-221-3705

MEMBERS OF FIRM

John D. Wilkinson (1867-1929)
William Scott Wilkinson (1895-1985)
Arthur R. Carmody, Jr.
Bobby S. Gilliam
Mark E. Gilliam
Penny D. Sellers
Brian D. Landry

Representative Clients: Farmers Insurance Group; Home Federal Savings & Loan Association of Shreveport; The Kansas City Southern Railway Co.; KTAL-TV; Lincoln National Life Insurance Co.; Mobil Oil Co.; Schumpert Medical Center; Sears, Roebuck & Co.; Southern Pacific Transportation Co.; Southwestern Electric Power Co.

For full biographical listings, see the Martindale-Hubbell Law Directory

MAINE

*AUGUSTA,** Kennebec Co.

* indicates certain Bar Register subscribers whose principal office is located elsewhere in the state and who have arranged for representation as a part of the state capital listings that follow

LAW OFFICES OF PHILLIP E. JOHNSON (AV)

160 Capitol Street, P.O. Box 29, 04332-0029
Telephone: 207-623-5110
Fax: 207-622-4160

David G. Webbert

Representative Clients: Agway, Inc.; American Eagle Group; Associated Aviation Underwriters; Aviation Underwriting Specialists; AVEMCO; Central Maine Power Co.; The Doctors Company; Loss Management Services, Inc.; Progressive Casualty Insurance Co.; Shand, Morahan & Co.

For full biographical listings, see the Martindale-Hubbell Law Directory

LIPMAN & KATZ, P.A. (AV)

227 Water Street, 04330
Telephone: 207-622-3711
Telecopier: 207-622-7415

Sumner H. Lipman
David M. Lipman
Roger J. Katz
Robert J. Stolt
Peter B. Bickerman
Steven T. Blackwell
Keith R. Varner
Kathryn L. Vezina

OF COUNSEL

Joseph B. Campbell

LEGAL SUPPORT PERSONNEL

Jeannine M. Tarrio

For full biographical listings, see the Martindale-Hubbell Law Directory

*** PIERCE, ATWOOD, SCRIBNER, ALLEN, SMITH & LANCASTER (AV)**

77 Winthrop Street, 04330
Telephone: 207-622-6311
Fax: 207-623-9367
Portland, Maine Office: One Monument Square.
Telephone: 207-773-6411.
Camden, Maine Office: 36 Chestnut Street, P.O. Box 780.
Telephone: 207-236-4333.

MEMBERS OF FIRM

Malcolm L. Lyons
Joseph M. Kozak
Michael D. Seitzinger
John C. Nivison

ASSOCIATES

Daniel J. Stevens
Benjamin P. Townsend

For Complete List of Firm Personnel, See General Section

For full biographical listings, see the Martindale-Hubbell Law Directory

*BANGOR,** Penobscot Co.

EATON, PEABODY, BRADFORD & VEAGUE, P.A. (AV)

Fleet Center-Exchange Street, P.O. Box 1210, 04402-1210
Telephone: 207-947-0111
Telecopier: 207-942-3040
Augusta, Maine Office: 2 Central Plaza.
Telephone: 207-622-3747.
Telecopier: 207-622-9732.
Brunswick, Maine Office: 167 Park Row.
Telephone: 207-729-1144.
Telecopier: 207-729-1140.
Camden, Maine Office: 7-9 Washington Street.
Telephone: 207-236-3325.
Telecopier: 207-236-8611.
Dover-Foxcroft, Maine Office: 30 East Main Street.
Telephone: 207-564-8378.
Telecopier: 207-564-7059.

Thomas M. Brown
Bernard J. Kubetz
Stephen G. Morrell (Resident, Brunswick Office)
Glen L. Porter
Gordon H. S. Scott (Resident, Augusta Office)
Martin L. Wilk (Resident, Brunswick Office)
William B. Devoe
Terry W. Calderwood (Resident, Camden Office)
Paul L. Gibbons (Resident, Camden Office)

Laurie A. Dart
Jonathan B. Huntington (Resident, Dover-Foxcroft Office)
Judy A.S. Metcalf (Resident, Brunswick Office)
David C. Webb
Thad B. Zmistowski
Dorisann B. W. Wagner (Resident, Augusta Office)

A List of Representative Clients available upon request.

For Complete List of Firm Personnel, See General Section

For full biographical listings, see the Martindale-Hubbell Law Directory

GROSS, MINSKY, MOGUL & SINGAL, P.A. (AV)

Key Plaza, 23 Water Street, P.O. Box 917, 04402-0917
Telephone: 207-942-4644
Telecopier: 207-942-3699
Ellsworth, Maine Office: 26 State Street.
Telephone: 207-667-4611.
Telecopier: 207-667-6206.

Jules L. Mogul (1930-1994)
Norman Minsky
George Z. Singal
Louis H. Kornreich
George C. Schelling
Edward W. Gould
Steven J. Mogul
James R. Wholly

Wayne P. Libhart (Resident, Ellsworth, Maine Office)
Daniel A. Pileggi
Philip K. Clarke
Christopher R. Largay (Resident, Ellsworth Office)
Hans G. Huessy
William B. Entwisle
Sandra L. Rothera

OF COUNSEL

Edward I. Gross

Representative Clients: Dahl Chase Pathology Associates; Superior Paper Products.
Local Counsel for: The St. Paul Insurance Cos.; Aetna Life & Casualty Co.; Imperial Casualty & Indemnity Co.

For full biographical listings, see the Martindale-Hubbell Law Directory

RICHARDSON, TROUBH & BADGER, A PROFESSIONAL CORPORATION (AV)

82 Columbia Street, P.O. Box 2429, 04402-2429
Telephone: 207-945-5900
Telecopier: 207-945-0758
Portland, Maine Office: Richardson & Troubh, A Professional Corporation, 465 Congress Street. P.O. Box, 9732.
Telephone: 207-774-5821.
Telecopier: 207-761-2056.

Frederick J. Badger, Jr. (Resident)
Frederick F. Costlow (Resident)
Ann M. Murray (Resident)
John B. Lucy (Resident)

Representative Clients: CIGNA; General Motors Corp.; Hanover Insurance; Liberty Mutual Insurance; Fireman's Fund American; Concord Group Insurance Cos.; DuPont Company.
Local Counsel for: General Motors Corp.; Beloit Corp./Harnischfeger; Winnebago Industries.

For full biographical listings, see the Martindale-Hubbell Law Directory

Bangor—Continued

VAFIADES, BROUNTAS & KOMINSKY (AV)

Key Plaza, 23 Water Street, P.O. Box 919, 04402-0919
Telephone: 207-947-6915
Telecopier: 207-941-0863

MEMBERS OF FIRM

Nicholas P. Brountas
Marvin H. Glazier
Susan R. Kominsky
Eugene C. Coughlin, III

OF COUNSEL

Lewis V. Vafiades

For Complete List of Firm Personnel, See General Section

For full biographical listings, see the Martindale-Hubbell Law Directory

BAR HARBOR, Hancock Co.

FENTON, CHAPMAN, FENTON, SMITH & KANE, P.A. (AV)

109 Main Street, P.O. Box B, 04609
Telephone: 207-288-3331
FAX: 207-288-9326

Douglas B. Chapman
Nathaniel R. Fenton
Chadbourn H. Smith

Reference: Bar Harbor Banking and Trust Co.

For Complete List of Firm Personnel, See General Section

For full biographical listings, see the Martindale-Hubbell Law Directory

*BATH,** Sagadahoc Co.

CONLEY, HALEY & O'NEIL (AV)

Thirty Front Street, 04530
Telephone: 207-443-5576
Telefax: 207-443-6665

J. Michael Conley
Constance P. O'Neil
Mark L. Haley
Arlyn H. Weeks
Laura M. O'Hanlon

Representative Clients: Bath Iron Works Corporation; Central Maine Power Company; Saco Defense, Inc.; Sugarloaf Mountain Corporation.
References: Casco Northern Bank, N.A.; First Federal Savings & Loan Association of Bath; Shawmut Bank.

For full biographical listings, see the Martindale-Hubbell Law Directory

BRIDGTON, Cumberland Co.

BERMAN & SIMMONS, P.A. (AV)

Route 302, Portland Street, 04009
Telephone: 207-647-3125
Fax: 207-647-3134
Lewiston, Maine Office: 129 Lisbon Street, P.O. Box 961, 04243-0961.
Telephone: 207-784-3576.
Fax: 207-784-7699.
Portland, Maine Office: 178 Middle Street.
Telephone: 207-774-5277.
Fax: 207-774-0166.
South Paris, Maine Office: 4 Western Avenue.
Telephone: 207-743- 8775.
Fax: 207-743-8559.

C. Martin Berman
Julian L. Sweet
David W. Grund

For full biographical listings, see the Martindale-Hubbell Law Directory

*ELLSWORTH,** Hancock Co.

HALE & HAMLIN (AV)

10 State Street, P.O. Box 729, 04605
Telephone: 207-667-2561
Telefax: 207-667-8790

MEMBER OF FIRM

Barry K. Mills

Approved Attorneys for: Commonwealth Title Insurance Company; American Title Insurance Company.

For Complete List of Firm Personnel, See General Section

For full biographical listings, see the Martindale-Hubbell Law Directory

LEWISTON, Androscoggin Co.

BERMAN & SIMMONS, P.A. (AV)

129 Lisbon Street, P.O. Box 961, 04243-0961
Telephone: 207-784-3576
Fax: 207-784-7699
Portland, Maine Office: 178 Middle Street.
Telephone: 207-774-5277.
Fax: 207-774-0166.

(See Next Column)

South Paris, Maine Office: 4 Western Avenue.
Telephone: 207-743- 8775.
Fax: 207-743-8559.
Bridgton, Maine Office: Route 302, Portland Street.
Telephone: 207-647-3125.
Fax: 207-647-3134.

C. Martin Berman
Steven D. Silin
Jack H. Simmons
Valerie Stanfill
John E. Sedgewick
Tyler N. Kolle
William D. Robitzek
Glenn S. Eddy
Julian L. Sweet
David J. Van Dyke
Jeffrey Rosenblatt
David W. Grund
Paul F. Macri
Daniel G. Kagan
Jeffrey A. Thaler
Joy C. Cantrell
Ivy L. Frignoca

For full biographical listings, see the Martindale-Hubbell Law Directory

PLATZ & THOMPSON, P.A. (AV)

95 Park Street, P.O. Box 960, 04243
Telephone: 207-783-8558
Telecopier: 207-783-9487

J. Peter Thompson
Roger J. O'Donnell, III
Philip K. Hargesheimer
Robert V. Hoy
Paul S. Douglass
Michael J. LaTorre
James B. Main

Representative Clients: State Farm Mutual Automobile Insurance Co.; Peerless Insurance Co.; Farm Family Mutual Insurance Co.; State Farm Fire & Casualty Co.; Patrons-Oxford Mutual Insurance Co.; New England Guaranty Insurance Co.; Home Insurance Co.; Patrons-Oxford Mutual Insurance Co.; Concord General Insurance Co.; Union Mutual Insurance Co.

For Complete List of Firm Personnel, See General Section

For full biographical listings, see the Martindale-Hubbell Law Directory

*PORTLAND,** Cumberland Co.

AMERLING & BURNS, A PROFESSIONAL ASSOCIATION (AV)

193 Middle Street, 04101
Telephone: 207-775-3581
Facsimile: 207-775-3814
Affiliated St. Croix Office: Coon & Sanford, P.O. Box 25918, Six Chandlers's Wharf, Suite 202, 00824-0918.

W. John Amerling
Arnold C. Macdonald
George F. Burns
Mary DeLano
David P. Ray
Joanne F. Cole
John R. Coon
A. Robert Ruesch

OF COUNSEL

Bruce M. Jervis

Representative Clients: H.E. Sargent, Inc. (construction); Merrill Trust; J.M. Huber, Inc.; Jackson Laboratories; Hague International (engineering); Aetna Life & Casualty Co.; The Hartford; Great American Insurance Co.; Wausau Insurance Co.

For full biographical listings, see the Martindale-Hubbell Law Directory

HERBERT H. BENNETT AND ASSOCIATES, P.A. (AV)

Suite 300, 121 Middle Street, P.O. Box 7799, 04112-7799
Telephone: 207-773-4775
Telecopier: 207-774-2366

Herbert H. Bennett (1928-1992)
Frederick B. Finberg
Peter Bennett
Melinda J. Caterine
Jeffrey Bennett
Hilary A. Rapkin

Counsel for: Associated Grocers of New England; Casco Northern Bank, N.A.; Coca Cola Bottling Company of Northern New England, Inc.; Northern Utilities/Bay State Gas; Pratt & Whitney (Division of United Technologies); Primerica Financial Services; Sprague Energy (C.H. Sprague & Son); Perrier Group of America, Inc.; Lepage Bakeries, Inc. (Country Kitchen); Table Talk Pies, Inc.; Texaco, Inc.

For full biographical listings, see the Martindale-Hubbell Law Directory

BERMAN & SIMMONS, P.A. (AV)

178 Middle Street, 04101
Telephone: 207-774-5277
Fax: 207-774-0166
Lewiston, Maine Office: 129 Lisbon Street.
Telephone: 207-784-3576.
Fax: 207-784-7699.
South Paris, Maine Office: 4 Western Avenue.
Telephone: 207-743-8775.
Fax: 207-743-8559.
Bridgton, Maine Office: Route 302, Portland Street.
Telephone: 207-647-3125.
Fax: 207-647-3134.

William D. Robitzek

For full biographical listings, see the Martindale-Hubbell Law Directory

Portland—Continued

FRIEDMAN & BABCOCK (AV)

Suite 400, Six City Center, P.O. Box 4726, 04112-4726
Telephone: 207-761-0900
Telecopier: 207-761-0186

MEMBERS OF FIRM

Harold J. Friedman
Ernest J. Babcock
Martha C. Gaythwaite
Gregory W. Powell
Thomas A. Cox
Karen Frink Wolf
Jennifer S. Begel
Laurence H. Leavitt

ASSOCIATES

Theodore H. Irwin, Jr.
Lee H. Bals
Michelle A. Landmann
Arthur J. Lamothe
Brian L. Champion
Laurie B. Perzley
Elizabeth A. Germani
Tracey G. Burton
Jonathan Marc Dunitz
Lori A. Desjardins

For full biographical listings, see the Martindale-Hubbell Law Directory

JENSEN BAIRD GARDNER & HENRY (AV)

Ten Free Street, P.O. Box 4510, 04112
Telephone: 207-775-7271
Telecopier: 207-775-7935
York County Office: 419 Alfred Street, Biddeford, Maine.
Telephone: 207-282-5107.
Telecopier: 207-282-6301.

MEMBERS OF FIRM

Michael A. Nelson
Joseph H. Groff, III
Deborah M. Mann
Keith R. Jacques (Resident, York County Office)

ASSOCIATES

Emily A. Bloch
Anne H. Jordan (Resident, York County Office)
Karen McGee Hurley

Representative Clients: General Motors Acceptance Corp.; York Mutual Insurance Co.; Knutson Mortgage Corp.; Owens Corning Fiberglass; Sedgwick James.

For Complete List of Firm Personnel, See General Section

For full biographical listings, see the Martindale-Hubbell Law Directory

PERKINS, THOMPSON, HINCKLEY & KEDDY, P.A. (AV)

One Canal Plaza, P.O. Box 426, 04112-0426
Telephone: 207-774-2635

Thomas Schulten
Bruce E. Leddy
Owen W. Wells
Douglas S. Carr
Andrew A. Cadot
Thomas B. Wheatley
John R. Opperman
Philip C. Hunt
John S. Upton
Peggy L. McGehee
Melissa Hanley Murphy
John H. Rich III
John A. Ciraldo
John A. Hobson
Helen I. Muther
Timothy P. Benoit

Fred W. Bopp III
Craig N. Denekas
Mark P. Snow

For Complete List of Firm Personnel, See General Section

For full biographical listings, see the Martindale-Hubbell Law Directory

PETRUCCELLI & MARTIN (AV)

50 Monument Square, P.O. Box 9733, 04104-5033
Telephone: 207-775-0200
Telecopier: 207-775-2360

MEMBERS OF FIRM

Gerald F. Petruccelli
Joel C. Martin
Daniel W. Bates

ASSOCIATES

Michael K. Martin
James B. Haddow
Linda C. Russell
Kenneth D. Keating
Thomas C. Bradley

Representative Clients: Bangor Hydro-Electric Co.; Chubb Insurance Co.; Coopers & Lybrand; Cumberland Farms; General Electric Capital Corp.; Maine Medical Center; Pine Tree Telephone & Telegraph Co.; KPMG Peat Marwick; Union Mutual Fire Insurance Co.; Vermont Mutual Insurance Co.

For full biographical listings, see the Martindale-Hubbell Law Directory

PIERCE, ATWOOD, SCRIBNER, ALLEN, SMITH & LANCASTER (AV)

One Monument Square, 04101
Telephone: 207-773-6411
Fax: 207-773-3419
Augusta, Maine Office: 77 Winthrop Street.
Telephone: 207-622-6311.

(See Next Column)

Camden, Maine Office: 36 Chestnut Street, P.O. Box 780.
Telephone: 207-236-4333.

MEMBERS OF FIRM

Ralph I. Lancaster, Jr.
Jotham D. Pierce, Jr.
Malcolm L. Lyons (Resident, Augusta Office)
John O'Leary
Peter W. Culley
Jeffrey M. White
Louise K. Thomas
Michael D. Seitzinger (Resident, Augusta Office)
Daniel M. Snow
William J. Kayatta, Jr.
James R. Erwin, II
Scott T. Maker
John C. Nivison (Resident, Augusta Office)
John J. Aromando
Catherine R. Connors
David E. Barry

ASSOCIATES

Stephen G. Grygiel
Gisele M. Nadeau
Daniel J. Stevens (Resident, Augusta Office)
Michael N. Ambler, Jr.
Kate L. Geoffroy
Michael S. Wilson
Deborah L. Shaw
Jared S. des Rosiers
Barney Simeon Goldstein
William L. Worden
Debra L. Brown
Christine F. Burke (Resident, Augusta Office)

For Complete List of Firm Personnel, See General Section

For full biographical listings, see the Martindale-Hubbell Law Directory

PRETI, FLAHERTY, BELIVEAU & PACHIOS (AV)

443 Congress Street, P.O. Box 11410, 04104-7410
Telephone: 207-791-3000
Telecopier: 207-791-3111
Augusta, Maine Office: 45 Memorial Circle, P.O. Box 1058, 04332-1058.
Telephone: 207-623-5300.
Telecopier: 207-623-2914.
Rumford, Maine Office: 150 Congress Street, P.O. Drawer L, 04276-2035.
Telephone: 207-364-4593.
Telecopier: 207-369-9421.

MEMBERS OF FIRM

John J. Flaherty
Albert J. Beliveau, Jr. (Rumford Office)
Severin M. Beliveau (Augusta Office)
Keith A. Powers
Christopher D. Nyhan
Jonathan S. Piper
Daniel Rapaport
Bruce C. Gerrity (Augusta Office)
Jeffrey T. Edwards
Michael G. Messerschmidt
Randall B. Weill
Evan M. Hansen
Edward R. Benjamin, Jr.
Geoffrey K. Cummings
Michael Kaplan

ASSOCIATES

Nelson J. Larkins
Stephen E. F. Langsdorf (Augusta Office)
John P. McVeigh
Elizabeth A. Olivier
Jeffrey M. Sullivan
Kevin J. Beal
Penny St. Louis
Jeffrey P. Russell (Augusta Office)

Representative Clients: Crum & Forster; United States Fidelity Guaranty Co.; St. Paul Fire & Marine Insurance Co.; American International Group; PHICO Insurance Company; Dunlap Corp.; Maine Municipal Association; Liberty Group; Key Bank of Maine.

For Complete List of Firm Personnel, See General Section

For full biographical listings, see the Martindale-Hubbell Law Directory

RICHARDSON & TROUBH, A PROFESSIONAL CORPORATION (AV)

465 Congress Street, P.O. Box 9732, 04104-5032
Telephone: 207-774-5821
Telecopier: 207-761-2056
Bangor, Maine Office: Richardson Troubh & Badger, A Professional Corporation, 82 Columbia Street.
Telephone: 207-945-5900.
Telecopier: 207-945-0758.

Harrison L. Richardson
Robert J. Piampiano
Richard J. Kelly
Wendell G. Large
Frederick J. Badger, Jr. (Resident, Bangor Office)
Kevin M. Gillis
Thomas E. Getchell
Michael Richards
William K. McKinley
Elizabeth G. Stouder
Barri Bloom
Daniel F. Gilligan
Ann M. Murray (Resident, Bangor Maine)

Frederick F. Costlow (Resident, Bangor Office)
John B. Lucy (Resident, Bangor Office)
John G. Richardson

Representative Clients: Fireman's Fund American Insurance Companies; Ford Motor Company; Great American Insurance Co.; CIGNA; Kemper Insurance Group; Liberty Mutual Insurance Co.; Norfolk & Dedham Mutual Fire Insurance Co.; Security Insurance Group; Scott Paper Co.; United Parcel Service.

For Complete List of Firm Personnel, See General Section

For full biographical listings, see the Martindale-Hubbell Law Directory

Portland—Continued

THOMPSON & BOWIE (AV)

Three Canal Plaza, P.O. Box 4630, 04112
Telephone: 207-774-2500
Telecopier: 207-774-3591

MEMBERS OF FIRM

Roy E. Thompson, Jr.
James M. Bowie
Daniel R. Mawhinney
Rebecca H. Farnum
Glenn H. Robinson
Frank W. DeLong, III
Michael E. Saucier
Mark V. Franco

ASSOCIATES

Elizabeth G. Knox
Cathy S. Roberts
Paul C. Catsos

Representative Clients: Aetna Life & Casualty; Chrysler Corp.; W.R. Grace & Co.; Hertz; Chubb Group; Abbott Laboratories.

For full biographical listings, see the Martindale-Hubbell Law Directory

SACO, York Co.

SMITH ELLIOTT SMITH & GARMEY, P.A. (AV)

199 Main Street, P.O. Box 1179, 04072
Telephone: 207-282-1527
Telefax: 207-283-4412
Sanford Telephone: 207-324-1560
Portland Telephone: 207-774-3199
Wells Telephone: 207-646-0970
Kennebunk, Maine Office: Route One South, P.O. Box 980.
Telephone: 207-985-4464.
Telefax: 207-985-3946.
Portland, Maine Office: 100 Commercial Street, Suite 304.
Telephone: 207-774-3199.
Telefax: 207-774-2235.

Randall E. Smith
Charles W. Smith, Jr.
Terrence D. Garmey
Peter W. Schroeter
Richard P. Romeo
Robert H. Furbish
John H. O'Neil, Jr.
Harry B. Center, II
David S. Abramson

Robert M. Nadeau
Michael J. Waxman

Representative Clients: Towns of Waterboro and Kennebunk, Maine; City of Biddeford; Saco and Biddeford Savings Institution; Ocean Communities Federal Credit Union.
Local Counsel for: Mutual Fire Insurance Company.
References: Casco Northern Bank, N.A. (Saco Branch); Saco & Biddeford Savings Institution.

For Complete List of Firm Personnel, See General Section

For full biographical listings, see the Martindale-Hubbell Law Directory

*SKOWHEGAN,** Somerset Co.

WRIGHT & MILLS, P.A. (AV)

218 Water Street, P.O. Box 9, 04976
Telephone: 207-474-3324
Telefax: 207-474-3609

Carl R. Wright
S. Peter Mills, III
Paul P. Sumberg
Kenneth A. Lexier
Dale F. Thistle

Representative Clients: Design Professionals Insurance Company, New Jersey; Solon Manufacturing Company, Solon, Maine; Kleinschmidt Associates-Engineers, Pittsfield, Maine; Acheron Engineering, Newport, Maine; E.W. Littlefield-Contractors, Hartland, Maine; WBRC-Architects, Bangor, Maine.

For full biographical listings, see the Martindale-Hubbell Law Directory

*SOUTH PARIS,** Oxford Co.

BERMAN & SIMMONS, P.A. (AV)

4 Western Avenue, 04281
Telephone: 207-743-8775
Fax: 207-743-8559
Lewiston, Maine Office: 129 Lisbon Street, P.O. Box 961.
Telephone: 207-284-3576.
Fax: 207-784-7699.
Portland, Maine Office: 178 Middle Street.
Telephone: 207-774-5277.
Fax: 207-774-0166.
Bridgton, Maine Office: Route 302, Portland Street.
Telephone: 207-647-3125.
Fax: 207-647-3134.

Jack H. Simmons
Glenn S. Eddy

For full biographical listings, see the Martindale-Hubbell Law Directory

YORK, York Co.

ERWIN, OTT, CLARK & CAMPBELL (AV)

16A Woodbridge Road, P.O. Box 545, 03909
Telephone: 207-363-5208
Facsimile: 207-363-5322

MEMBERS OF FIRM

Frank E. Hancock (1923-1988)
James S. Erwin
John P. Campbell
David N. Ott
Jeffery J. Clark

For full biographical listings, see the Martindale-Hubbell Law Directory

MARYLAND

*BALTIMORE,** (Independent City)

ALLEN, JOHNSON, ALEXANDER & KARP, P.A. (AV)

Suite 1540, 100 East Pratt Street, 21202
Telephone: 410-727-5000
Fax: 410-727-0861
Washington, D.C. Office: 1707 L Street, N.W., Suite 1050.
Telephone: 202-828-4141.

Donald C. Allen
John D. Alexander, Jr.
Daniel Karp
D'Ana E. Johnson (Resident, Washington, D.C. Office)

Anne Marie McGinley (Resident, Washington, D.C. Office)
Denise Ramsburg Stanley
George B. Breen (Not admitted in MD; Resident, Washington, D.C. Office)
Robert G. McGinley (Resident, Washington, D.C. Office)
James X. Crogan, Jr.
Yvette M. Bryant
Kevin Bock Karpinski
Brett A. Balinsky

Representative Clients: Scottsdale Insurance Co.; Nautilus Insurance Co.; Jefferson Insurance Co.; Liberty Mutual Insurance Co.; Avis Rent-A-Car; Otis Elevator Co.; Montgomery Elevator Co.; Admiral Insurance Co.; Local Government Insurance Trust; Lancer Insurance Co.

For full biographical listings, see the Martindale-Hubbell Law Directory

BRAUDE & MARGULIES, P.C. (AV)

1206 St. Paul Street, 21202-2706
Telephone: 410-234-0202
Fax: 410-625-2872
Washington, D.C. Office: Suite 200, 1025 Connecticut Ave., N.W.
Telephone: 202-293-2993.
Fax: 202-331-7916.
San Francisco, California Office: William R. Delaney, Citicorp Center, One Sansome Street, Suite 2000.
Telephone: 415-951-4709.
Fax: 415-951-4754.
Riyadh, Saudi Arabia Office: Mohammed A. Al-Abdullah, P.O. Box 59446, Nuzha Building, Sixth Floor, 11525.
Telephone: 966-1-405-1291.
Fax: 966-1-405-1291.
Abu Dhabi, United Arab Emirates Office: P.O. Box 43908.
Telephone: (971-2) 787222.
Fax: (971-2) 784001.

Herman M. Braude
William M. Huddles (Resident)
Roger C. Jones (Not admitted in MD; Resident, District of Columbia Office)
Howard A. Pollack (Resident)

Kenneth Knut Sorteberg (Resident)

For full biographical listings, see the Martindale-Hubbell Law Directory

ELLIN AND BAKER (AV)

Second Floor, 1101 St. Paul Street, 21202
Telephone: 410-727-1787
FAX: 410-752-4838

MEMBER OF FIRM

Marvin Ellin
LaVonna Lee Vice

Jack David Lebowitz
Michael P. Smith

For full biographical listings, see the Martindale-Hubbell Law Directory

FREISHTAT & SANDLER (AV)

Suite 1500, One Calvert Plaza, 201 E. Baltimore Street, 21202
Telephone: 410-727-7740
FAX: 410-727-7356

(See Next Column)

FREISHTAT & SANDLER, *Baltimore—Continued*

MEMBERS OF FIRM

David Freishtat
Paul Mark Sandler
Raymond F. Altman
Raymond Daniel Burke
William M. Mullen

Lloyd J. Snow
Lynn Weinberg
Stacie F. Dubnow
T. Allen Mott

For full biographical listings, see the Martindale-Hubbell Law Directory

GORDON, FEINBLATT, ROTHMAN, HOFFBERGER & HOLLANDER (AV)

The Garrett Building, 233 East Redwood Street, 21202
Telephone: 410-576-4000
Telex: 908041 BAL

MEMBERS OF FIRM

Donald N. Rothman
Allan J. Malester
Lawrence S. Greenwald
Robert E. Sharkey
Nancy E. Paige
Sheila K. Sachs
Robert W. Katz
Jerrold A. Thrope (Chairman)
Thomas X. Glancy, Jr.
Michael C. Powell
Michael J. Jack

ASSOCIATES

Claire A. Smearman
Caroline G. Ellis
David W. Lease
John R. Severino
Catherine A. Bledsoe
Nancy M. Juda
Gregory S. Reynolds
Jonathan J. Biedron
Rebecca L. Dietz

For Complete List of Firm Personnel, See General Section

For full biographical listings, see the Martindale-Hubbell Law Directory

HYLTON & GONZALES (AV)

Suite 418 Equitable Building, 10 North Calvert Street, 21202
Telephone: 410-547-0900
Telecopier: 410-625-1560

MEMBER OF FIRM

William A. Hylton, Jr.

For Complete List of Firm Personnel, See General Section

For full biographical listings, see the Martindale-Hubbell Law Directory

ISRAELSON, SALSBURY, CLEMENTS & BEKMAN (AV)

300 West Pratt Street, Suite 450, 21201
Telephone: 410-539-6633
FAX: 410-625-9554

MEMBERS OF FIRM

Stuart Marshall Salsbury
Paul D. Bekman
Daniel M. Clements
Matthew Zimmerman
Laurence A. Marder

Suzanne K. Farace
Scott R. Scherr
Carol J. Glover

COUNSEL TO THE FIRM

Max R. Israelson

OF COUNSEL

Samuel Omar Jackson, Jr. (Semi-Retired)

For full biographical listings, see the Martindale-Hubbell Law Directory

E. FREMONT MAGEE, P.A. (AV)

The Legg Mason Tower, 111 South Calvert Street, Suite 2700, 21202
Telephone: 410-385-5295; 410-625-7540
FAX: 410-385-5201

E. Fremont Magee

Lynn K. Edwards

For full biographical listings, see the Martindale-Hubbell Law Directory

PHILLIPS P. O'SHAUGHNESSY, P.A. (AV)

22 East Fayette Street, 7th Floor, 21202-1706
Telephone: 410-685-0300
FAX: 410-659-6945

Phillips P. O'Shaughnessy

For full biographical listings, see the Martindale-Hubbell Law Directory

PIERSON, PIERSON & NOLAN (AV)

Suite 1600 Redwood Tower, 217 East Redwood Street, 21202
Telephone: 410-727-7733
FAX: 410-625-0253

(See Next Column)

MEMBERS OF FIRM

W. Michel Pierson
James J. Nolan, Jr.
Robert L. Pierson

OF COUNSEL

David S. Sykes

For Complete List of Firm Personnel, See General Section

For full biographical listings, see the Martindale-Hubbell Law Directory

ROBINETTE, DUGAN & JAKUBOWSKI, P.A. (AV)

The Robinette-Dugan Building, 801 St. Paul Street, 21202
Telephone: 410-659-6700
FAX: 410-752-0456

Gilbert H. Robinette
Henry E. Dugan, Jr.
Ruth A. Jakubowski
Bruce J. Babij

Pamela S. Foresman
George S. Tolley, III

OF COUNSEL

Marian V. Fleming

For full biographical listings, see the Martindale-Hubbell Law Directory

ROLLINS, SMALKIN, RICHARDS & MACKIE (AV)

401 North Charles Street, 21201
Telephone: 410-727-2443
Fax: 410-727-8390

MEMBERS OF FIRM

H. Beale Rollins (1898-1985)
Samuel S. Smalkin (1906-1982)
T. Benjamin Weston (1913-1980)
Thomas G. Andrew (1910-1973)
Edward C. Mackie
John F. Linsenmeyer
Thomas C. Gentner
Glenn W. Trimmer
Patrick G. Cullen
James P. O'Meara
Dennis J. Sullivan

ASSOCIATES

Francis B. Buckley
Elaine R. Wilford
Paul G. Donoghue
Ralph E. Wilson III
Kenneth G. Macleay
Donna Lynn Kolakowski-Hollen

OF COUNSEL

Raymond A. Richards (Retired)
Hartman J. Miller

For full biographical listings, see the Martindale-Hubbell Law Directory

SCHOCHOR, FEDERICO AND STATON, P.A. (AV)

The Paulton, 1211 St. Paul Street, 21202
Telephone: 410-234-1000
FAX: 410-234-1010
Washington D.C. Office: 777 North Capitol Street, N.E., Suite 910.
Telephone: 202-408-3300.
Fax: 202-408-3304.

Jonathan Schochor
Philip C. Federico
Kerry D. Staton

Louis G. Close, III
Diane M. Littlepage
Christopher P. Kennedy

For full biographical listings, see the Martindale-Hubbell Law Directory

THIEBLOT, RYAN, MARTIN & FERGUSON, P.A. (AV)

4th Floor, The World Trade Center, 21202-3091
Telephone: 410-837-1140
Washington, D.C. Line: 202-628-8223
Fax: 410-837-3282

Robert J. Thieblot
Anthony W. Ryan
J. Edward Martin, Jr.
Robert L. Ferguson, Jr.
Bruce R. Miller
Robert D. Harwick, Jr.
Thomas J. Schetelich
Christopher J. Heffernan

M. Brooke Murdock
Anne M. Hrehorovich
Donna Marie Raffaele
Michael N. Russo, Jr.
Jodi K. Ebersole
Hamilton Fisk Tyler
Peter Joseph Basile

Representative Clients: Ford Motor Credit Co.; USF & G Co.; The American Road Insurance Co.; Fidelity Engineering Corp.; The North Charles Street Design Organization; Record Collections, Inc.; Toyota Motor Credit Co.

For full biographical listings, see the Martindale-Hubbell Law Directory

VENABLE, BAETJER AND HOWARD (AV)

A Partnership including Professional Corporations
1800 Mercantile Bank & Trust Building, 2 Hopkins Plaza, 21201
Telephone: 410-244-7400
Washington, D.C. Office: Venable, Baetjer, Howard & Civiletti. Suite 1000, 1201 New York Avenue, N.W.
Telephone: 202-962-4800.

(See Next Column)

VENABLE, BAETJER AND HOWARD—*Continued*

McLean, Virginia Office: Suite 400, 2010 Corporate Ridge.
Telephone: 703-760-1600.
Rockville, Maryland Office: Suite 500, One Church Street, P. O. Box 1906.
Telephone: 301-217-5600.
Towson, Maryland Office: 210 Allegheny Avenue, P. O. Box 5517.
Telephone: 410-494-6200.

MEMBERS OF FIRM

Benjamin R. Civiletti (P.C.) (Also at Washington, D.C. and Towson, Maryland Offices)
George Cochran Doub (P.C.)
John Henry Lewin, Jr. (P.C.)
Stanley Mazaroff (P.C.)
Roger W. Titus (Resident, Rockville, Maryland Office)
N. Peter Lareau (P.C.)
Thomas J. Madden (Not admitted in MD; Resident, Washington, D.C. Office)
Ronald R. Glancz (Not admitted in MD; Resident, Washington, D.C. Office)
David J. Levenson (Not admitted in MD; Resident, Washington, D.C. Office)
Douglas D. Connah, Jr. (P.C.) (Also at Washington, D.C. Office)
David T. Stitt (Not admitted in MD; Resident, McLean, Virginia Office)
Kenneth C. Bass, III (Not admitted in MD; Also at Washington, D.C. and McLean, Virginia Offices)
John H. Zink, III (Resident, Towson, Maryland Office)
Bruce E. Titus (Resident, McLean, Virginia Office)
Paul F. Strain (P.C.)
Max Stul Oppenheimer (P.C.) (Also at Washington, D.C. and Towson, Maryland Offices)
William D. Dolan, III (P.C.) (Not admitted in MD; Resident, McLean, Virginia Office)
Paul T. Glasgow (Resident, Rockville, Maryland Office)
Joseph C. Wich, Jr. (Resident, Towson, Maryland Office)
Sondra Harans Block (Resident, Rockville, Maryland Office)
Edward F. Glynn, Jr. (Not admitted in MD; Resident, Washington, D.C. Office)
Craig E. Smith
Robert G. Ames (Also at Washington, D.C. Office)
Michael Schatzow (Also at Washington, D.C. and Towson, Maryland Offices)
Nell B. Strachan
David G. Lane (Resident, McLean, Virginia Office)
N. Frank Wiggins (Resident, Washington, D.C. Office)
L. Paige Marvel
Susan K. Gauvey (Also at Towson, Maryland Office)
James K. Archibald (Also at Washington, D.C. and Towson, Maryland Offices)
G. Stewart Webb, Jr.
George W. Johnston (P.C.)
Judson W. Starr (Not admitted in MD; Also at Washington, D.C. and Towson, Maryland Offices)
James R. Myers (Not admitted in MD; Resident, Washington, D.C. Office)
Jana Howard Carey (P.C.)
Jeffrey A. Dunn (also at Washington, D.C. Office)
George F. Pappas (Also at Washington, D.C. Office)
William D. Coston (Not admitted in MD; Resident, Washington, D.C. Office)
James L. Shea (Also at Washington, D.C. Office)
Jeffrey P. Ayres (P.C.)
Elizabeth C. Honeywell
Maurice Baskin (Resident, Washington, D.C. Office)
Amy Berman Jackson (Not admitted in MD; Resident, Washington, D.C. Office)
William D. Quarles (Also at Washington, D.C. and Towson, Maryland Offices)
C. Carey Deeley, Jr. (Also at Towson, Maryland Office)
Kathleen Gallogly Cox (Resident, Towson, Maryland Office)
Christopher R. Mellott
Cynthia M. Hahn (Resident, Towson, Maryland Office)
M. King Hill, III (Resident, Towson, Maryland Office)
James A. Dunbar (Also at Washington, D.C. Office)
Ronald W. Taylor
Mary E. Pivec (Also at Washington, D.C. Office)
Thomas J. Kelly, Jr. (Not admitted in MD; Resident, Washington, D. C. Office)
David J. Heubeck
Herbert G. Smith, II (Not admitted in MD; Resident, McLean, Virginia Office)
Patrick J. Stewart (Also at Washington, D.C. Office)
Gary M. Hnath (Resident, Washington, D.C. Office)
Michael H. Davis (Resident, Towson, Maryland Office)
Darrell R. VanDeusen

OF COUNSEL

A. Samuel Cook (P.C.) (Resident, Towson, Maryland Office)
Joyce K. Becker
Geoffrey R. Garinther (Also at Washington, D.C. Office)
Mary T. Flynn (Not admitted in MD; Resident, McLean, Virginia Office)
Fred W. Hathaway (Not admitted in MD; Resident, Washington, D.C. Office)

ASSOCIATES

Paul D. Barker, Jr.
Elizabeth Marzo Borinsky
Julian Sylvester Brown (Not admitted in MD; Resident, McLean, Virginia Office)
Daniel William China
Patricia Gillis Cousins (Resident, Rockville, Maryland Office)
Carla Draluck Craft (Resident, Washington, D.C. Office)
Royal W. Craig (Resident, Washington, D.C. Office)
Gregory A. Cross
Marina Lolley Dame (Resident, Towson, Maryland Office)
J. Van L. Dorsey (Resident, Towson, Maryland Office)
Fred Joseph Federici, III (Resident, Washington, D.C. Office)

(See Next Column)

ASSOCIATES (Continued)

David W. Goewey (Not admitted in MD; Resident, Washington, D.C. Office)
E. Anne Hamel
David R. Hodnett (Not admitted in MD; Resident, McLean, Virginia Office)
J. Scott Hommer, III (Not admitted in MD; Resident, McLean, Virginia Office)
Todd J. Horn
Maria F. Howell
Mary-Dulany James (Resident, Towson, Maryland Office)
Paula Titus Laboy (Resident, Rockville, Maryland Office)
Gregory L. Laubach (Resident, Rockville, Maryland Office)
Jon M. Lippard (Not admitted in MD; Resident, McLean, Virginia Office)
Edward Brendan Magrab (Resident, Washington, D.C. Office)
Patricia A. Malone (Resident, Towson, Maryland Office)
Vicki Margolis
Christine M. McAnney (Not admitted in MD; Resident, McLean, Virginia Office)
John A. McCauley
Timothy J. McEvoy
Mitchell Y. Mirviss
Samuel T. Morison (Not admitted in MD; Resident, Washington, D.C. Office)
Traci H. Mundy (Not admitted in MD; Resident, Washington, D.C. Office)
Valerie Floyd Portner
John T. Prisbe
Lawrence C. Renbaum
Michael W. Robinson (Not admitted in MD; Resident, McLean, Virginia Office)
John Peter Sarbanes
Catherine L. Schuster
Robert A. Schwinger
Nathan E. Siegel
Todd K. Snyder
Melissa Landau Steinman (Resident, Washington, D.C. Office)
J. Preston Turner
Terri L. Turner
Paul N. Wengert (Not admitted in MD; Resident, Washington, D.C. Office)

For Complete List of Firm Personnel, See General Section

For full biographical listings, see the Martindale-Hubbell Law Directory

---

VERDERAIME & DU BOIS, P.A. (AV)

1231 North Calvert Street, 21202
Telephone: 410-752-8888
FAX: 301-752-0425

Robert C. Verderaime
A. Harold Du Bois
William D. Kurtz
Elizabeth Jesukiewicz Frey
Neil J. Bixler

Reference: Maryland National Bank, Baltimore, Maryland.

For full biographical listings, see the Martindale-Hubbell Law Directory

---

ROBIN PAGE WEST (AV)

110 St. Paul Street, Suite 301, 21202
Telephone: 410-244-0400
Fax: 410-244-0402

For full biographical listings, see the Martindale-Hubbell Law Directory

---

ZUCKERMAN, SPAEDER, GOLDSTEIN, TAYLOR & BETTER (AV)

Suite 2440, 100 East Pratt Street, 21202
Telephone: 410-332-0444
Fax: 410-659-0436
Washington, D.C. Office: Zuckerman, Spaeder, Goldstein, Taylor & Kolker. 1201 Connecticut Avenue, N.W.
Telephone: 202-778-1800.
Fax: 202-822-8106.
Miami, Florida Office: Zuckerman, Spaeder, Taylor & Evans. Suite 900, Miami Center, 201 South Biscayne Boulevard.
Telephones: 305-358-5000; 305-579-0110; Broward County: 305-523-0277.
Fax: 305-579-9749.
Ft. Lauderdale, Florida Office: Zuckerman, Spaeder, Taylor & Evans. One East Broward Boulevard, Suite 700.
Telephone: 305-356-0463.
Fax: 305-356-0406.
Tampa, Florida Office: Zuckerman, Spaeder, Taylor & Evans. 101 East Kennedy Boulevard, Suite 3140.
Telephone: 813-221-1010.
Fax: 813-223-7961.
New York, N.Y. Office: Zuckerman, Spaeder, Goldstein, Taylor & Kolker, 1114 Avenue of the Americas, 45th Floor, Grace Building.
Telephone: 212-479-6500.
Fax: 212-479-6512.

RESIDENT MEMBERS

Herbert Better
Donald J. McCartney

RESIDENT ASSOCIATE

Cyril V. Smith

For full biographical listings, see the Martindale-Hubbell Law Directory

---

*BEL AIR,** Harford Co.

STARK & KEENAN, A PROFESSIONAL ASSOCIATION (AV)

30 Office Street, 21014
Telephone: 410-838-5522
Baltimore: 410-879-2222
Fax: 410-879-0688

(See Next Column)

STARK & KEENAN A PROFESSIONAL ASSOCIATION, *Bel Air—Continued*

Elwood V. Stark, Jr.
Charles B. Keenan, Jr.
Thomas E. Marshall
Edwin G. Carson
Judith C. H. Cline
Gregory A. Szoka
Robert S. Lynch

Claire Prin Blomquist
Kimberly Kahoe Muenter
Paul W. Ishak

For full biographical listings, see the Martindale-Hubbell Law Directory

BETHESDA, Montgomery Co.

DECKELBAUM OGENS & FISCHER, CHARTERED (AV)

6701 Democracy Boulevard, 20817
Telephone: 301-564-5100
Washington D.C. Office: 1140 Connecticut Avenue, N.W.
Telephone: 202-223-1474.

Nelson Deckelbaum
Ronald L. Ogens
Lawrence H. Fischer
Arthur G. Kahn
Deborah E. Reiser

Ronald G. Scheraga

LEGAL SUPPORT PERSONNEL

Shirley Mostow

References: First Liberty Bank; Sovran Bank, D.C.

For full biographical listings, see the Martindale-Hubbell Law Directory

NELSON & NELSON (AV)

3 Bethesda Metro Center Suite 750, 20814
Telephone: 301-961-1958
Washington, D.C. Office: 1050 17th Street, N.W., Suite 830.
Telephone: 202-659-0815.

MEMBERS OF FIRM

William E. Nelson
Sherlee Stanford Nelson (Not admitted in MD)

For full biographical listings, see the Martindale-Hubbell Law Directory

OCEAN CITY, Worcester Co.

COURTLAND K. TOWNSEND, JR. CHARTERED (AV)

The Executive Building, Suite 101, 7200 Coastal Highway, 21842
Telephone: 410-524-4300
FAX: 410-524-4953

Courtland K. Townsend, Jr.

For full biographical listings, see the Martindale-Hubbell Law Directory

RIVERDALE, Prince Georges Co.

MEYERS, BILLINGSLEY, SHIPLEY, RODBELL & ROSENBAUM, P.A. (AV)

Suite 400 Berkshire Building, 6801 Kenilworth Avenue, 20737-1385
Telephone: 301-699-5800
Fax: 301-779-5746

Lance W. Billingsley
Robert H. Rosenbaum
Joseph B. Chazen
Leslie A. Pladna
Rita Kaufman Grindle
Juliane Corroon Miller
Gina Marie Smith

Reference: First National Bank of Maryland.

For Complete List of Firm Personnel, See General Section

For full biographical listings, see the Martindale-Hubbell Law Directory

*ROCKVILLE,** Montgomery Co.

ANDERSON & QUINN (AV)

The Adams Law Center, 25 Wood Lane, 20850
Telephone: 301-762-3303
FAX: 301-762-3776
Washington, D.C. Office: 1220 L Street, N.W., Suite 540.
Telephone: 202-371-1245.

MEMBERS OF FIRM

Charles C. Collins (1900-1973)
Robert E. Anderson (Not admitted in MD; Retired)
Francis X. Quinn
William Ray Scanlin (Resident, Washington, D.C. Office)
Donald P. Maiberger
Robert P. Scanlon (Resident, Washington, D.C. Office)
James G. Healy

ASSOCIATES

John A. Rego
Richard L. Butler (Resident, Washington, D.C. Office)
Marie M. Gavigan (Mrs.)
Donald J. Urgo, Jr.
Laura A. Garufi

(See Next Column)

Representative Clients: C & P Telephone; Commercial Union Insurance Cos.; Allstate Insurance Co.; State Farm Mutual Automobile Insurance Co.; Liberty Mutual Insurance Co.; Northbrook Insurance Cos.; Travelers Insurance Co.; National General Insurance Co.; American International Adjustment Co.; Marriott Corp.

For Complete List of Firm Personnel, See General Section

For full biographical listings, see the Martindale-Hubbell Law Directory

ARMSTRONG, DONOHUE & CEPPOS, CHARTERED (AV)

Suite 101, 204 Monroe Street, 20850
Telephone: 301-251-0440
Telecopier: 301-279-5929

Larry A. Ceppos
H. Patrick Donohue
H. Kenneth Armstrong
Benjamin S. Vaughan
John C. Monahan

Kirk S. Burgee
Oya S. Oner
Pamela Barrow Kincheloe
Maura J. Condon
Richard S. Schrager
Sharon A. Marcial
J. Eric Rhoades

For full biographical listings, see the Martindale-Hubbell Law Directory

BRAULT, GRAHAM, SCOTT & BRAULT (AV)

101 South Washington Street, 20850
Telephone: 301-424-1060
Fax: 301-424-7991
Washington, D.C. Office: 1906 Sunderland Place, N.W.
Telephone: 202-785-1200.
FAX: 202-785-4301.
Arlington, Virginia Office: Suite 1201, 2300 North Clarendon Boulevard, Courthouse Plaza.
Telephone: 703-522-1781.

OF COUNSEL

Laurence T. Scott

MEMBERS OF FIRM

Denver H. Graham (1922-1987)
Albert E. Brault (Retired)
Albert D. Brault (Resident)
Leo A. Roth, Jr.
James S. Wilson (Resident)
Ronald G. Guziak (Resident)
Daniel L. Shea (Resident)
Keith M. Bonner
M. Kathleen Parker (Resident)
Regina Ann Casey (Resident)
James M. Brault (Resident)

ASSOCIATES

David G. Mulquin (Resident)
Sanford A. Friedman
Holly D. Shupert (Resident)
Eric A. Spacek (Not admitted in MD)
Rhonda Ann Hurwitz (Resident)
Joan F. Brault (Resident)

Representative Clients: American Oil Co.; Crum & Forster Group; Fireman's Fund American Insurance Cos.; Kemper Group; Reliance Insurance Cos.; Safeco Group; Government Employees Insurance Co.; Medical Mutual Insurance Society of Maryland; Legal Mutual Liability Insurance Society of Maryland.

For full biographical listings, see the Martindale-Hubbell Law Directory

KATZ, FROME AND BLEECKER, P.A. (AV)

6116 Executive Boulevard, Suite 200, 20852
Telephone: 301-230-5800
Facsimile: 301-230-5830

Steven M. Katz
Morton J. Frome
Lorin H. Bleecker
Gail B. Landau

Susan J. Rubin
Marilyn J. Brasier
Leslie Anne Sullivan
Seth B. Popkin
Richard O'Connor
Stanley A. Snyder

OF COUNSEL

Philip F. Finelli, Jr.

For full biographical listings, see the Martindale-Hubbell Law Directory

PAULSON, NACE, NORWIND & SELLINGER (AV)

31 Wood Lane, 20850
Telephone: 301-294-8060
Washington, D.C. Office: 1814 N Street, N.W.
Telephone: 202-463-1999.
Fax: 202-223-6824.

John J. Sellinger

For full biographical listings, see the Martindale-Hubbell Law Directory

ROWAN & QUIRK (AV)

The Adams Law Center, 27 Wood Lane, 20850
Telephone: 301-762-4050
FAX: 301-762-9189

(See Next Column)

ROWAN & QUIRK—*Continued*

MEMBERS OF FIRM

William J. Rowan, III
Joseph M. Quirk

ASSOCIATE

John G. Nalls

For full biographical listings, see the Martindale-Hubbell Law Directory

SHULMAN, ROGERS, GANDAL, PORDY & ECKER, P.A. (AV)

Third Floor, 11921 Rockville Pike, 20852-2743
Telephone: 301-230-5200
Telecopier: 301-230-2891
Washington, D.C. Office: 1120-19th Street, N.W., Eighth Floor.
Telephone: 202-872-0400.

Lawrence A. Shulman
Donald R. Rogers
Larry N. Gandal
Karl L. Ecker
David A. Pordy
David D. Freishtat
Martin P. Schaffer
Christopher C. Roberts
Edward M. Hanson, Jr.
David M. Kochanski
Walter A. Oleniewski
Lawrence L. Bell
James M. Kefauver
Rebecca Oshoway
Robert B. Canter
Edward F. Schiff
Philip J. McNutt
Daniel S. Krakower
Kevin P. Kennedy
Ashley Joel Gardner
Alan B. Sternstein
Nancy P. Regelin

OF COUNSEL

Martin Levine

Michael J. Froehlich
James M. Hoffman
William C. Davis, III
Elizabeth N. Shomaker
Michael V. Nakamura
Paul A. Bellegarde
Gregory J. Rupert
Douglas K. Hirsch

Reference: Maryland National Bank, Montgomery County Regional Office.

For Complete List of Firm Personnel, See General Section

For full biographical listings, see the Martindale-Hubbell Law Directory

STEIN, SPERLING, BENNETT, DE JONG, DRISCOLL, GREENFEIG & METRO, P.A. (AV)

25 West Middle Lane, 20850
Telephone: 301-340-2020; 800-435-5230
Telecopier: 301-340-8217

David C. Driscoll, Jr.
Stuart S. Greenfeig
Jeffrey M. Schwaber
Paul T. Stein

James D. Dalrymple
Jeffrey D. Goldstein

For Complete List of Firm Personnel, See General Section

For full biographical listings, see the Martindale-Hubbell Law Directory

VENABLE, BAETJER AND HOWARD (AV)

A Partnership including Professional Corporations
Suite 500, One Church Street, P.O. Box 1906, 20850-4129
Telephone: 301-217-5600
FAX: 301-217-5617
Baltimore, Maryland Office: 1800 Mercantile Bank & Trust Building, 2 Hopkins Plaza.
Telephone: 410-244-7400.
Washington, D.C. Office: Venable, Baetjer, Howard & Civiletti. Suite 1000, 1201 New York Avenue, N.W.
Telephone: 202-962-4800.
McLean, Virginia Office: Suite 400, 2010 Corporate Ridge.
Telephone: 703-760-1600.
Towson, Maryland, Office: 210 Allegheny Avenue, P. O. Box 5517.
Telephone: 410-494-6200.

MEMBERS OF FIRM

Roger W. Titus
Sondra Harans Block

ASSOCIATES

Patricia Gillis Cousins
Paula Titus Laboy
Gregory L. Laubach

For Complete List of Firm Personnel, See General Section

For full biographical listings, see the Martindale-Hubbell Law Directory

SEABROOK, Prince Georges Co.

FOSSETT & BRUGGER, CHARTERED (AV)

The Aerospace Building, 10210 Greenbelt Road, 20706
Telephone: 301-794-6900
Telecopy: 301-794-7638
La Plata, Maryland Office: 105 LaGrange Avenue, P.O. Box F.
Telephone: 301-934-4200. Washington Line: 301-753-9600.
FAX: 301-870-2884.

(See Next Column)

George A. Brugger
Clarence L. Fossett
Jonathan I. Kipnis
Nancy L. Slepicka
Diane O. Leasure
Midgett S. Parker, Jr.
William M. Shipp
John C. Fredrickson
Lorraine J. Webb (Resident, La Plata Office)
Michael A. Faerber
Michael F. Canning, Jr.
Harold Gregory Martin
Mary A. Liano

LEGAL SUPPORT PERSONNEL

Dean Armstrong

Representative Clients: Banyan Management Corp.; Capital Office Park; Coscan Washington, Inc.; Citizens Bank & Trust Company of Maryland; Greenhorne & O'Mara, Inc.; Kettler Brothers; Michael T. Rose Cos.; The Mutual Life Insurance Company of New York; Richmond-American Homes; Winchester Homes, Inc.

For full biographical listings, see the Martindale-Hubbell Law Directory

SILVER SPRING, Montgomery Co.

ALEXANDER, GEBHARDT, APONTE & MARKS, L.L.C. (AV)

Lee Plaza-Suite 805, 8601 Georgia Avenue, 20910
Telephone: 301-589-2222
Facsimile: 301-589-2523
Washington, D.C. Office: 1314 Nineteenth Street, N.W., 20036.
Telephone: 202-835-1555.
New York, New York Office: 330 Madison Avenue, 36th Floor.
Telephone: 212-808-0008.
Fax: 212-599-1028.

Joseph D. Gebhardt
Glenn K. Garnes

Gregory E. Gaskins
Adrian Van Nelson II
Nihar R. Mohanty
John L. Machado (Not admitted in MD)

Reference: Riggs National Bank of Washington, D.C.

For full biographical listings, see the Martindale-Hubbell Law Directory

GARTRELL & ASSOCIATES (AV)

Lee Plaza, Suite 900, 8601 Georgia Avenue, 20910
Telephone: 301-589-8855
Facsimile: 301-589-8866

MEMBERS OF FIRM

Bernadette Gartrell
Vernon S. Lynch III
Stephanie Y. Bradley

ASSOCIATES

Randall J. Craig, Jr.
Sharon D. Nelson
Woong (Thomas) Yi
Serene D. Charles (Not admitted in MD)
Darlene E. Townsend
Peyton S. Isaac

OF COUNSEL

Ruthann Aron

Representative Clients: Allstate Insurance Company; Washington Suburban Sanitary Commission; Baltimore City Police Department; Resolution Trust Corporation; American Telephone & Telegraph.

For full biographical listings, see the Martindale-Hubbell Law Directory

*TOWSON,** Baltimore Co.

HOWELL, GATELY, WHITNEY & CARTER (AV)

401 Washington Avenue, Twelfth Floor, 21204
Telephone: 410-583-8000
FAX: 410-583-8031

MEMBERS OF FIRM

H. Thomas Howell
William F. Gately
Benjamin R. Goertemiller
Daniel W. Whitney
David A. Carter
William R. Levasseur

ASSOCIATES

Una M. Perez
John S. Bainbridge, Jr.
George D. Bogris
Wendy A. Lassen
Kathleen D. Leslie

For full biographical listings, see the Martindale-Hubbell Law Directory

NOLAN, PLUMHOFF & WILLIAMS, CHARTERED (AV)

Suite 700 Court Towers, 210 West Pennsylvania Avenue, 21204
Telephone: 410-823-7800
Fax: 410-296-2765

William P. Englehart, Jr.
Stephen J. Nolan
Robert L. Hanley, Jr.
Stephen M. Schenning
Robert E. Cahill, Jr.
J. Joseph Curran, III

Representative Clients: Anne Arundel County, Maryland; Baltimore County, Maryland; Board of Education of Anne Arundel County; Board of Education of Baltimore County (Special Counsel in Environmental Cost Recovery Litigation); Bituminous Insurance Companies; Carolina Freight Carriers Corporation; Keystone Insurance Company; Maryland Automobile Insurance Fund; Rossville Vending Machine Corporation.

(See Next Column)

NOLAN, PLUMHOFF & WILLIAMS CHARTERED, *Towson—Continued*

For Complete List of Firm Personnel, See General Section

For full biographical listings, see the Martindale-Hubbell Law Directory

VENABLE, BAETJER AND HOWARD (AV)

A Partnership including Professional Corporations
210 Allegheny Avenue, P.O. Box 5517, 21204
Telephone: 410-494-6200
FAX: 410-821-0147
Baltimore, Maryland Office: 1800 Mercantile Bank & Trust Building, 2 Hopkins Plaza.
Telephone: 410-244-7400.
Washington, D.C. Office: Venable, Baetjer, Howard & Civiletti. Suite 1000, 1201 New York Avenue, N.W.
Telephone: 202-962-4800.
McLean, Virginia Office: Suite 400, 2010 Corporate Ridge.
Telephone: 703-760-1600.
Rockville, Maryland Office: Suite 500, One Church Street, P. O. Box 1906.
Telephone: 301-217-5600.

PARTNERS

Benjamin R. Civiletti (P.C.) (Also at Washington, D.C. and Baltimore, Maryland Offices)
John H. Zink, III
Max Stul Oppenheimer (P.C.) (Also at Baltimore, Maryland and Washington, D.C. offices)
Joseph C. Wich, Jr.
Michael Schatzow (Also at Baltimore, Maryland and Washington, D.C. Offices)
Susan K. Gauvey (Also at Baltimore, Maryland Office)
James K. Archibald (Also at Baltimore, Maryland and Washington, D.C. Offices)
William D. Quarles (Also at Washington, D.C. Office)
C. Carey Deeley, Jr. (Also at Baltimore, Maryland Office)
Kathleen Gallogly Cox
Cynthia M. Hahn
M. King Hill, III
Michael H. Davis

ASSOCIATES

Marina Lolley Dame
J. Van L. Dorsey
Mary-Dulany James
Patricia A. Malone

For Complete List of Firm Personnel, See General Section

For full biographical listings, see the Martindale-Hubbell Law Directory

MASSACHUSETTS

*BOSTON,** Suffolk Co.

ATWOOD & CHERNY (AV)

Mason House 211 Commonwealth Avenue, 02116
Telephone: 617-262-6400
Telecopier: 617-421-9482

Jacob M. Atwood
David E. Cherny
Susan G. Lillis
Pasquale DeSantis

For full biographical listings, see the Martindale-Hubbell Law Directory

BARRON & STADFELD, P.C. (AV)

Two Center Plaza, 02108
Telephone: 617-723-9800
Telecopier: 617-523-8359
Hyannis, Massachusetts Office: 258 Winter Street.
Telephone: 617-778-6622.

Bernard A. Dwork
Hertz N. Henkoff
Peter P. Myerson
Enid M. Starr
Thomas V. Bennett
Edward E. Kelly
Kevin F. Moloney
David P. Dwork
John J. Yagjian
Julie Taylor Moran
Mitchell J. Notis
Robert J. Hoffer
Joseph G. Butler
Denise L. Page
Mark W. Roberts
Rosemary Purtell

Dorothy M. Bickford
Alison L. Berman
Roger T. Manwaring
Donna M. Pisciotta
Warren E. Agin
Christine Ann Gardner
Shawn P. O'Rourke

For Complete List of Firm Personnel, See General Section

For full biographical listings, see the Martindale-Hubbell Law Directory

BURNS & LEVINSON (AV)

125 Summer Street, 02110-1624
Telephone: 617-345-3000
Telecopier: 617-345-3299
Rockland, Massachusetts Office: 1001 Hingham Street.
Telephone: 617-749-1023; 982-4100.
Telecopier: 617-982-4141.

(See Next Column)

MEMBERS OF FIRM

Thomas D. Burns
William H. Clancy
John A. Donovan
Charles Mark Furcolo
Traver Clinton Smith, Jr.
Paul E. Stanzler
Chester A. Janiak
Michael Weinberg
John J. McGivney
David P. Rosenblatt
Barbara S. Hamelburg
Michael Ross Gottfried
Dennis J. Kelly
Michael G. Tracy
Darrell Mook
Robin Patrick Daniels
Gary Wm. Smith
Richard L. Wulsin

ASSOCIATES

Kevin G. Kenneally
Elizabeth J. Maillett
Ralph G. Picardi
Mark C. DiVincenzo
Mark Ventola
Ann M. Donovan
Maria-Eugenia Recalde
Dennis J. Bannon
Henry T.A. Moniz
Frank C. Muggia

For Complete List of Firm Personnel, See General Section

For full biographical listings, see the Martindale-Hubbell Law Directory

COGAVIN AND WAYSTACK (AV)

2 Center Plaza, 02108
Telephone: 617-742-3340
Telecopier: 617-723-7563

MEMBERS OF FIRM

John J. Cogavin
Edward W. Waystack
John P. Fitzgerald
Gerard A. Butler
Kevin J. McGinty

ASSOCIATES

David T. Donnelly
John J. Jarosak
Thomas M. Franco
Mark A. Darling
Audrey Lewchik Bradley
Daniel S. McInnis
William P. Hurley
Laura E. Iannetta
Thomas G. Leonard, Jr.
John A. Dolan

For full biographical listings, see the Martindale-Hubbell Law Directory

CORNELL AND GOLLUB (AV)

75 Federal Street, 02110
Telephone: 617-482-8100
Telecopier: 617-482-3917

MEMBERS OF FIRM

Robert W. Cornell (1910-1988)
Karl L. Gollub (1934-1985)
David H. Sempert
Philip J. Foley
Peter M. Durney
Paul F. Lynch

ASSOCIATES

Susan Geyer Malloy
Jane Treen Brand
Hugh M. Coxe
Janet J. Bobit
Thomas A. Pursley
David W. McGough
Susan M. Donaldson
Marie E. Chadeayne
Bruce E. Hopper
Thomas H. Dolan
Eric B. Goldberg
Kelly L. Wilkins
Martha Jane Dickey

For full biographical listings, see the Martindale-Hubbell Law Directory

CUDDY BIXBY (AV)

One Financial Center, 02111
Telephone: 617-348-3600
Telecopier: 617-348-3643
Wellesley, Massachusetts Office: 60 Walnut Street.
Telephone: 617-235-1034.

Francis X. Cuddy (Retired)
Wayne E. Hartwell
Brian D. Bixby
Anthony M. Ambriano
William E. Kelly
Paul G. Boylan
Robert A. Vigoda
Paul J. Murphy
Alexander L. Cataldo
Duncan S. Payne
Stephen T. Kunian
Arthur P. Menard
Joseph H. Walsh
Michael J. Owens
Robert J. O'Regan
Andrew R. Menard
David F. Hendren
Glenn B. Asch
Timothy E. McAllister
William R. Moriarty
Kevin P. Sweeney
Denise I. Murphy

For full biographical listings, see the Martindale-Hubbell Law Directory

DENNIS J. CURRAN (AV)

One State Street, Suite 410, 02109
Telephone: 617-742-3010
Fax: 617-742-1799

For full biographical listings, see the Martindale-Hubbell Law Directory

Boston—Continued

DEUTSCH WILLIAMS BROOKS DERENSIS HOLLAND & DRACHMAN, P.C. (AV)

99 Summer Street, 02110-1235
Telephone: 617-951-2300
Fax: 617-951-2323
Nantucket, Massachusetts Office: 5 Gladlands Avenue.
Telephone: 508-228-8725.
Fax: 508-325-5860.

Burton L. Williams
Steven J. Brooks
Paul R. DeRensis
Robert E. Holland
Allan W. Drachman
Roland Gray, III
Richard D. Bickelman
Valerie Swett
John Foskett
Barry L. Mintzer
Roger K. Soderberg
Neil R. Schauer
Kenneth N. Margolin
Eric I. Zucker
Mary Jo Hollender
Alice E. Richmond
Morris L. Deutsch
John M. Carey

Rodney G. Hoffman
Daniel R. Deutsch
Richard S. Blank
Virginia N. H. Dodge
Michael P. Ridulfo
Laurie W. Engdahl
Kurt W. Terwilliger
Marnie Wortzman
Lawrence R. Holland
Stephen K. Ault
R. Scott Cooper
Frank J. Weiner
Loren Callan Rosenzweig
Peter J. Berry
Susan A. Moniz
Tristin Beard
Catherine Skahan Reidy
Robert D. Hillman
Janet L. Maloof

OF COUNSEL

Jack Green (P.C.)
Kenneth B. Gould

For full biographical listings, see the Martindale-Hubbell Law Directory

FRIEDMAN & ATHERTON (AV)

(Formerly Friedman, Atherton, King & Turner)
(Formerly Friedman, Atherton, Sisson & Kozol)
Exchange Place, 53 State Street, 02109-2803
Telephone: 617-227-5540
Telecopier: 617-523-1559

Lee M. Friedman (1895-1957)
Percy A. Atherton (1903-1940)
Frank L. Kozol (1927-1993)

OF COUNSEL

Frank H. Shapiro

MEMBERS OF FIRM

Joel A. Kozol
Lee H. Kozol
William I. Cowin
Robert D. Kozol
Richard M. Zinner
Matthew S. Kozol
Alan M. Spiro
David L. Kelston
Victor Bass

ASSOCIATES

Thomas C. Bailey
Andrew D. Cummings
Paula F. Donahue
John J. Ellis
Michele L. King
David M. Kozol
Penny Kozol
Joseph B. Lichtblau
David A. Rich
Marie C. Vaccarelli
Herbert Weinberg

COUNSEL

Paul Bork

For full biographical listings, see the Martindale-Hubbell Law Directory

GADSBY & HANNAH (AV)

125 Summer Street, 02110
Telephone: 617-345-7000
Telex: 6817512 GADHAN BSN
Telefax: 617-345-7050
Washington, D.C. Office: 1747 Pennsylvania Avenue, N.W., Suite 800.
Telephone: 202-429-9600.

PARTNERS

Richard K. Allen
Ronald G. Busconi
Robert J. Kaler
Daniel J. Kelly
Stanley A. Martin
James J. Myers
Michael N. Sheetz
William A. Zucker

ASSOCIATES

Peter M. Coppinger
Michael W. Dingle
Leigh A. Gilligan
John R. Hallal
Rosa C. Hallowell
Michael T. McInerny
Richard P. Quinn
Linda A. Surdacki
Peter F. Trotter

WASHINGTON, D.C. OFFICE

RESIDENT PARTNERS

Robert S. Brams (Not admitted in MA)
Michael A. Hordell
Paul F. Kilmer (Not admitted in MA)
Carol L. B. Matthews (Not admitted in MA)

(See Next Column)

RESIDENT ASSOCIATES

Thomas W. Brooke (Not admitted in MA)
Robert F. Garcia, Jr. (Not admitted in MA)

RESIDENT OF COUNSEL

Jeffrey B. Mulhall (Not admitted in MA)

For Complete List of Firm Personnel, See General Section

For full biographical listings, see the Martindale-Hubbell Law Directory

GLOVSKY & ASSOCIATES (AV)

Suite 810, 31 Milk Street, 02109
Telephone: 617-423-7100
Telecopier: 617-482-8034
Washington, D.C. Office: 1101 17th Street, N.W.
Telephone: 202-659-9119.

Richard D. Glovsky

ASSOCIATES

Melinda Milberg
Daniel S. Tarlow
Loretta A. Healy
Peter M. Kelley
John F. Tocci
Debra L. Feldstein

OF COUNSEL

Lynne K. Zusman (Not admitted in MA; Resident, Washington, D.C. Office)
Paul S. Davis

For full biographical listings, see the Martindale-Hubbell Law Directory

HANIFY & KING, PROFESSIONAL CORPORATION (AV)

One Federal Street, 02110-2007
Telephone: 617-423-0400
Telefax: 617-423-0498

James Coyne King
John D. Hanify
Harold B. Murphy
David Lee Evans
Daniel J. Lyne
Donald F. Farrell, Jr.
Barbara Wegener Pfirrman
Gerard P. Richer
Timothy P. O'Neill

Gordon M. Jones, III
Kara L. Thornton
Jean A. Musiker
Ann M. Chiacchieri
Melissa J. Cassedy
Kara M. Lucciola
Philip C. Silverman
Michael R. Perry
Jeffrey S. Cedrone
Charles A. Dale, III
Joseph F. Cortellini
Hiram N. Pan
Amy Conroy
Michael S. Bloom
Andrew G. Lizotte
Peter D. Lee
Martin F. Gaynor, III

For full biographical listings, see the Martindale-Hubbell Law Directory

KOPELMAN AND PAIGE, P.C. (AV)

101 Arch Street, 02110
Telephone: 617-951-0007
Cable Address: "Lawkope"
Fax: 617-951-2735

Leonard Kopelman
Donald G. Paige
Elizabeth A. Lane
Joyce F. Frank
John W. Giorgio
Barbara J. Saint Andre
Joel B. Bard
Everett Joseph Marder
Patrick J. Costello

William Hewig, III
Judith Chanoux Cutler
Anne-Marie M. Hyland
Richard Bowen
Cheryl Ann Banks
Brian W. Riley

For Complete List of Firm Personnel, See General Section

For full biographical listings, see the Martindale-Hubbell Law Directory

MINTZ, LEVIN, COHN, FERRIS, GLOVSKY AND POPEO, P.C. (AV)

One Financial Center, 02111
Telephone: 617-542-6000
FAX: 617-542-2241
Washington, D.C. Office: 701 Pennsylvania Avenue, N.W. Suite 900.
Telephone: 202-434-7300.
Fax: 202-434-7400.

R. Robert Popeo
Thomas R. Murtagh
Stephen M. Leonard
Robert M. Gault
John K. Markey
Michael S. Gardener
Cameron F. Kerry
Patrick J. Sharkey
Elizabeth B. Burnett
Kenneth M. Bello
Peter A. Biagetti
H. Joseph Hameline
Bruce F. Metge
Jeffrey S. Robbins
David E. Lurie
Henry A. Sullivan
Tracy A. Miner
Rosemary M. Allen

(See Next Column)

MINTZ, LEVIN, COHN, FERRIS, GLOVSKY AND POPEO P.C., *Boston—Continued*

John C. Plotkin
Joanne A. Robbins
Michael F. Connolly
Beth I. Z. Boland
Joseph P. Crawford-Kelly
John F. Sylvia

For Complete List of Firm Personnel, See General Section

For full biographical listings, see the Martindale-Hubbell Law Directory

PALMER & DODGE (AV)

(Storey Thorndike Palmer & Dodge)
One Beacon Street, 02108
Telephone: 617-573-0100
Telecopier: 617-227-4420
Telex: 951104
Cable Address: "Storeydike," Boston

MEMBERS OF FIRM

Acheson H. Callaghan, Jr.
Ralph A. Child
David R. Friedman
Ralph D. Gants
Michael T. Gass
Laurie S. Gill
Jeffrey F. Jones
Michael J. Lacek
William L. Lahey
Scott P. Lewis
Francis C. Lynch
Peter M. Saparoff
Steven L. Schreckinger
Thane D. Scott
Craig E. Stewart
Robert E. Sullivan
Jeffrey Swope
Peter S. Terris
Tamara S. Wolfson

COUNSEL

Stephen J. Abarbanel
Charles E. DeWitt, Jr.
Jay E. Gruber
Kevin R. McNamara
Alan S. Musgrave
Russell B. Swapp
Cassandra Warshowsky

For Complete List of Firm Personnel, See General Section

For full biographical listings, see the Martindale-Hubbell Law Directory

RACKEMANN, SAWYER & BREWSTER, PROFESSIONAL CORPORATION (AV)

One Financial Center, 02111
Telephone: 617-542-2300
Telecopier: 617-542-7437

William B. Tyler
George V. Anastas
Henry H. Thayer
Stephen Carr Anderson
Albert M. Fortier, Jr.
Michael F. O'Connell
Stuart T. Freeland
Raymond J. Brassard
Alan B. Rubenstein
Martin R. Healy
James R. Shea, Jr.
Brian M. Hurley
Janet M. Smith
Peter Friedenberg
Richard S. Novak
J. David Leslie
Alexander H. Spaulding
Sanford M. Matathia
Anne P. Zebrowski

OF COUNSEL

Albert B. Wolfe
August R. Meyer
Richard H. Lovell

COUNSEL

Ronald S. Duby
Ross J. Hamlin

Margaret L. Hayes
Daniel J. Ossoff
Mary B. Freeley
Gordon M. Orloff
Donald R. Pinto, Jr.
Lucy West Behymer
Richard J. Gallogly
Melissa Langer Ellis
James A. Wachta
Susan Dempsey Baer
Daniel J. Bailey, III
Michael S. Giaimo
Maura E. Murphy
Mary L. Gallant
Peter A. Alpert
Lauren D. Armstrong
Robert B. Foster
Elizabeth A. Gibbons

For full biographical listings, see the Martindale-Hubbell Law Directory

RICH, MAY, BILODEAU & FLAHERTY, P.C. (AV)

The Old South Building, 294 Washington Street, 02108-4675
Telephone: 617-482-1360
FAX: 617-556-3889

John F. Rich (1908-1987)
Thomas H. Bilodeau (1915-1987)
Gerald May
Harold B. Dondis
Walter L. Landergan, Jr.
Edwin J. Carr
Arthur F. Flaherty
Franklin M. Hundley
Michael F. Donlan
Joseph F. Sullivan, Jr.
Owen P. Maher
Nicolas A. Kensington
Daniel T. Clark
Gerald V. May, Jr.
Eric J. Krathwohl
Michael J. McHugh
James M. Behnke
James M. Avery
Stephen M. Kane
Mark C. O'Connor
Walter A. Wright, III
Emmett E. Lyne

(See Next Column)

Nicholas F. Kourtis
James T. Finnigan
Carol E. Kazmer
Robert P. Snell

For full biographical listings, see the Martindale-Hubbell Law Directory

ROPES & GRAY (AV)

One International Place, 02110
Telephone: 617-951-7000
Fax: 617-951-7050
Washington, D.C. Office: Suite 1200, 1001 Pennsylvania Avenue, N.W.
Telephone: 202-626-3900.
Telecopy: 202-626-3961.
Providence, Rhode Island Office: 30 Kennedy Plaza.
Telephone: 401-455-4400.
Telecopy: 401-455-4401.

MEMBERS OF FIRM

George C. Caner, Jr.
A. Lane McGovern
George H. Lewald
George T. Finnegan
Jerome M. Leonard
Thomas G. Dignan, Jr.
Paul B. Galvani
William G. Meserve
G. Marshall Moriarty
William L. Patton
John C. Kane, Jr.
Robert K. Gad, III
Roscoe Trimmier, Jr.
Kenneth W. Erickson
Harvey J. Wolkoff
Jeffrey B. Storer
James L. Sigel
Thomas H. Hannigan, Jr.
John C. Bartenstein
Douglas H. Meal
Steven A. Kaufman
John D. Donovan, Jr.
Martin J. Newhouse
Mark P. Szpak
Michael K. Fee

ASSOCIATES

Kathryn Selleck Shea
Paul J. O'Donnell
Lee C. Rubin
Ann Pauly
Michael R. Pontrelli
David A. Martland
Andrew C. Pickett
Jeffrey P. Trout
Jay B. Smith
Howard J. Castleman
Peter M. DelVecchio
John R. Baraniak, Jr.
David A. Brown

For Complete List of Firm Personnel, See General Section

For full biographical listings, see the Martindale-Hubbell Law Directory

RUBIN AND RUDMAN (AV)

50 Rowes Wharf, 02110
Telephone: 617-330-7000
Telecopier: 617-439-9556

Stanley H. Rudman
Howard Rubin
Milton Bordwin
Myrna Putziger
Charles J. Speleotis
W. Bradley Ryan
Peter B. Finn
Andrew J. Newman
Harold Stahler
Michael R. Coppock
J. Robert Casey
John D. Kalish
Raymond M. Kwasnick
Jason A. Sokolov
Robert S. Walker
Dana F. Rodin
Lawrence E. Uchill
Kenneth M. Barna
Selig A. Saltzman
Edward R. Zaval
Peter F. Granoff
Gene T. Barton, Jr.
Jonathan D. Canter
Alan K. Posner
Philip L. Sussler
Jacob Aaron Esher
James H. Greene
John A. DeTore

Michael L. Altman
Stephen C. Flashenberg
Alan D. Mandl
Robert D. Shapiro
Jane Elizabeth Jones
Leonard M. Davidson
Dale Ann Kaiser
Donald J. Quill
Robert J. Mack
Michael K. Crossen
Mark W. Corner
David C. Fixler
Suzanne L. King
Diedre T. Lawrence
Helen E. Morgan
Susan A. Bernstein
Margaret A. Robbins
Edward R. Hill, Jr.
Donna C. Sharkey
Michael C. Bainum
Susan M. Caruso

For full biographical listings, see the Martindale-Hubbell Law Directory

SALLY & FITCH (AV)

225 Franklin Street, 02110-2804
Telephone: 617-542-5542
Telecopy: 617-542-1542

MEMBERS OF FIRM

Francis J. Sally
Jonathan W. Fitch
James B. Re
Thomas P. Billings

ASSOCIATES

Andrea Peraner-Sweet
Paul M. McDermott
Samuel J. Gesten
Rory A. Valas
John J. Pentz
Kathleen A. O'Neill

For full biographical listings, see the Martindale-Hubbell Law Directory

Boston—Continued

SCHNEIDER, REILLY, ZABIN & COSTELLO, P.C. (AV)

Three Center Plaza, Suite 430, 02108
Telephone: 617-227-7500

Joseph Schneider (1924-1985)	E. L. Schneider (1931-1973)
Joseph E. Reilly (1930-1951)	Marcia J. Allar
Albert P. Zabin	Jeffrey D. Woolf
Robert V. Costello	Joanne D'Alcomo

References: The National Shawmut Bank of Boston; State Street Bank & Trust Co.; Norfolk County Trust Co.; United States Trust Co.

For full biographical listings, see the Martindale-Hubbell Law Directory

SHERIN AND LODGEN (AV)

100 Summer Street, 02110
Telephone: 617-426-5720
Telecopier: 617-542-5186
Los Angeles, California Office: 11300 W. Olympic Boulevard, Suite 700.
Telephone: 310-914-7891.
Fax: 310-552-5327.
Nashua New Hampshire Office: One Indian Head Plaza.
Telephone: 603-595-4511.
Fax: 603-595-4968.
Providence, Rhode Island Office: 55 Pine Street.
Telephone: 401-274-8060.

MEMBERS OF FIRM

Arthur L. Sherin (1946-1964)	Thomas P. Gorman
George E. Lodgen (1946-1971)	Dorothy Nelson Stookey
Morton B. Brown	Mark A. Nowak
George Waldstein	Ronald W. Ruth
John M. Reed	Steven D. Eimert
Robert J. Muldoon, Jr.	Daniel B. Winslow
Alette E. Reed	Barbara A. O'Donnell
Edward M. Bloom	Brian C. Levey
Thomas J. Raftery	A. Neil Hartzell
Joshua M. Alper	Kenneth J. Mickiewicz
Gary M. Markoff	Craig M. Brown
Bryan G. Killian	Andrew Royce
David A. Guberman	Daniel O. Gaquin
Kenneth R. Berman	Thomas A. Hippler
Frank J. Bailey	Rhonda B. Parker

John J. Slater, III (Resident)

ASSOCIATES

Joanna E. Scannell	Margaret H. Leeson
Nereyda Garcia	Joseph M. Kerwin
John C. La Liberte	Christopher A. Kenney
Karen Elise Berman	David Benfield

Michael C. Giardiello

OF COUNSEL

Paul Melrose	Michael S. Strauss

LEGAL SUPPORT PERSONNEL

Marilyn Stewart

For full biographical listings, see the Martindale-Hubbell Law Directory

SWARTZ & SWARTZ (AV)

10 Marshall Street, 02108
Telephone: 617-742-1900
Fax: 617-367-7193

Edward M. Swartz	Joan E. Swartz
Alan L. Cantor	James A. Swartz
Joseph A. Swartz	Robert S. Berger
Victor A. Denaro	Harold David Levine

OF COUNSEL

Fredric A. Swartz

For full biographical listings, see the Martindale-Hubbell Law Directory

TAYLOR, ANDERSON & TRAVERS (AV)

75 Federal Street, 02110
Telephone: 617-654-8200
Fax: 617-482-5350
Providence, Rhode Island Office: The Wilcox Building, 42 Weybosset Street.
Telephone: 401-273-7171.
Fax: 401-273-2904.

MEMBERS OF FIRM

Allan E. Taylor	John J. Barton
James H. Anderson	Susan H. Williams
Margaret S. Travers	Ellen Epstein Cohen
James J. Duane, III	Pamela Slater Gilman
Sidney W. Adler	Alexandra B. Harvey

(See Next Column)

ASSOCIATES

Edward D. Shoulkin	A. Bernard Guekguezian
Jennifer Ellis Burke	Francis A. Connor, III
Melanie J. Gargas	Gina Witalec Verdi

Robert C. Shindell

For full biographical listings, see the Martindale-Hubbell Law Directory

WARNER & STACKPOLE (AV)

75 State Street, 02109
Telephone: 617-951-9000
Cable Address: "Warstack"
Telecopier: 617-951-9151
Telex: 940139

MEMBERS OF FIRM

Samuel Adams	Janice Kelley Rowan
Ronald F. Kehoe	Judith G. Dein
Joseph J. Leghorn	Linda A. Ouellette
Ralph T. Lepore, III	Antoinette D. Hubbard
Christopher E. Nolin	Keith C. Long
John A. Dziamba	Douglas F. Seaver

ASSOCIATES

Deborah K. Blum-Shore	Ellen S. Rosenberg
Gilbert R. Hoy, Jr.	Laurie C. Buck
Robert A. Whitney	Alexis L. Smith
Deborah E. Barnard	Geoffrey E. Proulx
Peter T. Wechsler	William P. Corbett, Jr.

COUNSEL

Andrew F. Lane

OF COUNSEL

Norman A. Hubley

For Complete List of Firm Personnel, See General Section

For full biographical listings, see the Martindale-Hubbell Law Directory

WILLCOX, PIROZZOLO AND MCCARTHY, PROFESSIONAL CORPORATION (AV)

50 Federal Street, 02110
Telephone: 617-482-5470
Telecopier: 617-423-1572
Worcester, Massachusetts Office: 421 Main Street.
Telephone: 508-799-7446.

Harold M. Willcox (1925-1975)	Jack R. Pirozzolo

Richard F. McCarthy

Richard L. Binder	Judith Seplowitz Ziss
Richard E. Bennett	Kelly M. Bird

OF COUNSEL

Richard P. Crowley	Thomas A. Kahrl

For full biographical listings, see the Martindale-Hubbell Law Directory

BROCKTON, Plymouth Co.

VINCENT P. CAHALANE, P.C. (AV)

478 Torrey Street, 02401
Telephone: 508-588-1222
Fax: 508-584-4748

Vincent P. Cahalane	Robert J. Zullas

Julie A. Cahalane

LEGAL SUPPORT PERSONNEL

PARALEGALS

Joan C. Cahalane	Kristopher S. Stefani

For full biographical listings, see the Martindale-Hubbell Law Directory

FITCHBURG, Worcester Co.

O'CONNOR AND RYAN, P.C. (AV)

61 Academy Street, 01420
Telephone: 508-345-4166
Fax: 508-343-8416

John M. O'Connor	Edward P. Ryan, Jr.

John Markham O'Connor

For full biographical listings, see the Martindale-Hubbell Law Directory

FRANKLIN, Norfolk Co.

ROCHE AND MURPHY (AV)

Franklin Office Park West, 38 Pond Street, Suite 308, P.O. Box 267, 02038
Telephone: 508-528-8300
FAX: 508-528-8889

MEMBERS OF FIRM

Neil J. Roche	Paul G. Murphy

(See Next Column)

ROCHE AND MURPHY, *Franklin—Continued*

ASSOCIATE

John J. Roche

For full biographical listings, see the Martindale-Hubbell Law Directory

MEDFORD, Middlesex Co.

DAVID BERMAN (AV)

100 George P. Hassett Drive, 02155
Telephone: 617-395-7520

Reference: Bay Bank

For full biographical listings, see the Martindale-Hubbell Law Directory

*NANTUCKET,** Nantucket Co.

DEUTSCH WILLIAMS BROOKS DERENSIS HOLLAND & DRACHMAN, P.C. (AV)

5 Gladlands Avenue, 02554
Telephone: 508-228-8725
Fax: 508-325-5860
Boston, Massachusetts Office: 99 Summer Street.
Telephone: 617-951-2300.
Fax: 617-951-2323.

Paul R. DeRensis

For full biographical listings, see the Martindale-Hubbell Law Directory

NEW BEDFORD, Bristol Co.

BEAUREGARD & BURKE (AV)

13 Hamilton Street, P.O. Box B-952, 02741
Telephone: 508-993-0333
Fax: 508-990-2045

MEMBERS OF FIRM

Philip N. Beauregard
Richard E. Burke, Jr.

For full biographical listings, see the Martindale-Hubbell Law Directory

MCLAUGHLIN & FOLAN, P.C. (AV)

448 County Street, P.O. Box 2095, 02741-2095
Telephone: 508-992-9800
Fax: 508-992-9730

David A. McLaughlin
Mary Alice S. McLaughlin
John F. Folan
Michael J. McGlone
Frank H. Spillane

OF COUNSEL

John J. Kinsley, Jr.
John H. Solomito

For full biographical listings, see the Martindale-Hubbell Law Directory

*NORTHAMPTON,** Hampshire Co.

GREEN, MILES, LIPTON, WHITE & FITZ-GIBBON (AV)

The Plaza Building, 77 Pleasant Street, P.O. Box 210, 01061-0210
Telephone: 413-586-8218
Fax: 413-584-6278

MEMBERS OF FIRM

John J. Green, Jr.
Harry L. Miles
Roger P. Lipton
Geoffrey B. White
John H. Fitz-Gibbon

ASSOCIATE

Susan L. Herzberg

Representative Clients: Gazette Printing Co.; Shumway and Sons Tree and Landscaping Corp.; Schneider Plumbing and Heating, Inc.

For full biographical listings, see the Martindale-Hubbell Law Directory

*SPRINGFIELD,** Hampden Co.

ROBERT ARONSON (AV)

101 State Street, 01103
Telephone: 413-733-2600
Fax: 413-737-4318

For full biographical listings, see the Martindale-Hubbell Law Directory

ELY & KING (AV)

One Financial Plaza, 1350 Main Street, 01103
Telephone: 413-781-1920
Telecopier: 413-733-3360

(See Next Column)

MEMBERS OF FIRM

Joseph Buell Ely (1905-1956)
Raymond T. King (1919-1971)
Frederick M. Kingsbury (1924-1968)
Hugh J. Corcoran (1938-1992)
Richard S. Milstein
Donald A. Beaudry
Richard F. Faille
Leland B. Seabury
Gregory A. Schmidt
Pamela Manson
Anthony T. Rice
Russell J. Mawdsley

ASSOCIATE

Donna M. Brown

Representative Clients: Hartford Accident & Indemnity Co.; Albert Steiger Cos.; Shawmut Bank N.A.; Springfield Institution for Savings; St. Paul Fire & Marine Insurance Co.; The Rouse Co.; Tighe & Bond, Inc.; Northeast Utilities.

For full biographical listings, see the Martindale-Hubbell Law Directory

MORIARTY, DONOGHUE & LEJA, P.C. (AV)

1331 Main Street, 01103
Telephone: 413-737-4319
Fax: 413-732-8767

James P. Moriarty (1878-1973)
Thomas J. Donoghue
Edward V. Leja
Patricia A. Barbalunga

Robert F. Connelly
John B. Stewart
Bernard Romani, III

Local Counsel for: Insurance Company of North America; United Community Insurance Company; Transamerica Insurance Co.; Preferred Mutual Insurance Co.; Utica Mutual Insurance Co.; Spalding & Evenflo Cos. Inc.; St. Paul Insurance Co.; Cigna Insurance Co.; Ina Pro; Ford Motor Co.

For full biographical listings, see the Martindale-Hubbell Law Directory

PELLEGRINI & SEELEY, P.C. (AV)

1145 Main Street, 01103
Telephone: 413-785-5300
Fax: 413-731-0626

Gilbert W. Baron (1911-1987)
Gerard L. Pellegrini
Earlon L. Seeley, Jr.
Donald W. Blakesley
Phyllis P. Ryan
Paul F. Schneider

Steven D. Rose
Michael J. Chieco
Charles R. Casartello, Jr.
Thomas E. Casartello
Patrick C. Gable
Catherine L. Watson

For full biographical listings, see the Martindale-Hubbell Law Directory

ROBINSON DONOVAN MADDEN & BARRY, P.C. (AV)

Suite 1600, Baybank Tower, 1500 Main Street, 01115
Telephone: 413-732-2301
Fax: 413-785-4658

Homans Robinson (1894-1973)
Lawrence M. Sinclair (1942-1986)

OF COUNSEL

Milton J. Donovan
John H. Madden, Jr.
Edward J. Barry

Gordon H. Wentworth
James H. Tourtelotte
Charles K. Bergin, Jr.
Victor Rosenberg
Ronald C. Kidd
Jeffrey W. Roberts
Jeffrey L. McCormick
James M. Rabbitt
James F. Martin
Robert P. Cunningham
John C. Sikorski
Nancy Frankel Pelletier
Paul S. Weinberg
Frederica H. McCarthy
Matthew J. King

James K. Bodurtha
Douglas F. Boyd
Susan L. Cooper
Kimberly Davis Crear
Russell F. Denver
Edmund J. Gorman
Keith A. Minoff
Patricia M. Rapinchuk
Jonathan P. Rice
Neva Kaufman Rohan

Counsel for: Shawmut Bank, N.A.; The First National Bank of Boston; United Cooperative Bank; Sunshine Art Studios.
Representative Clients: American Policyholders' Insurance Co.; C.N.A.; Commercial Union Insurance Co.; Hanover Insurance Co.

For full biographical listings, see the Martindale-Hubbell Law Directory

RYAN, MARTIN, COSTELLO, ALLISON & LEITER, P.C. (AV)

Suite 2500, BayBank Tower, 1500 Main Street, P.O. Box 15629, 01115-5629
Telephone: 413-739-6971
Fax: 413-739-1441

(See Next Column)

RYAN, MARTIN, COSTELLO, ALLISON & LEITER P.C.—*Continued*

Charles V. Ryan | Bruce L. Leiter
Philip J. Ryan | Joan C. Steiger
Bradford R. Martin, Jr. | Timothy J. Ryan
Mary K. Downey Costello | William J. Cass
Donald J. Allison | Michael P. Ryan

For full biographical listings, see the Martindale-Hubbell Law Directory

WELLESLEY, Norfolk Co.

NICHOLAS B. SOUTTER (AV)

One Washington Street, Suite 208, 02181
Telephone: 617-237-6300
Fax: 617-237-6143

ASSOCIATE
Paul S. McGovern

For full biographical listings, see the Martindale-Hubbell Law Directory

WESTBOROUGH, Worcester Co.

GREENWALD, GREENWALD & POWERS (AV)

33 Lyman Street, 01581-1404
Telephone: 508-366-6094
Fax: 508-366-6159
Milford, Massachusetts Office: 409 Fortune Boulevard, Granite Park.
Telephone: 508-478-8611.
Fax: 508-634-3959; 478-5937.

Alan Greenwald | Sarah Orlov
Steven A. Greenwald | Stephen A. Gould
John D. Powers | Patricia J. Flynn
Jacqueline Nastro Hathaway | Stefani Jill Saitow
Sean W. Melville

For full biographical listings, see the Martindale-Hubbell Law Directory

*WORCESTER,** Worcester Co.

CHRISTOPHER & LEDOUX (AV)

370 Main Street, 01608
Telephone: 508-792-2800
FAX: 508-792-6224

MEMBERS OF FIRM
William J. LeDoux | David A. Wojcik
William W. Hays | John A. Mavricos

OF COUNSEL
Christopher Christopher

Reference: Mechanics Bank.

For full biographical listings, see the Martindale-Hubbell Law Directory

FULLER, ROSENBERG, PALMER & BELIVEAU (AV)

14 Harvard Street, P.O. Box 764, 01613
Telephone: 508-755-5225
Telecopier: 508-757-1039

MEMBERS OF FIRM
Albert E. Fuller | Peter A. Palmer
Kenneth F. Rosenberg | Thomas W. Beliveau

ASSOCIATES
Robert W. Towle | Mark C. Darling
Julie Bednarz Russell | William J. Mason
Timothy O. Ribley | Antoinette J. Yitchinsky
Mark W. Murphy | Michael I. Mutter
Lisa R. Bertonazzi | Brian F. Welsh
John J. Finn

For full biographical listings, see the Martindale-Hubbell Law Directory

GLICKMAN, SUGARMAN & KNEELAND (AV)

11 Harvard Street, P.O. Box 2917, 01613
Telephone: 508-756-6206
Fax: 508-831-0443

MEMBERS OF FIRM
Melvyn Glickman | David W. Sugarman
David J. Kneeland, Jr.

ASSOCIATES
Joe Boynton | Wayne M. LeBlanc

Representative Clients: Country Bank for Savings; Clinton Savings Bank.
References: Country Bank for Savings; Shawmut Worcester County Bank N.A.

For full biographical listings, see the Martindale-Hubbell Law Directory

MACCARTHY, POJANI & HURLEY (AV)

Worcester Plaza, 446 Main Street, 01608
Telephone: 508-798-2480
Fax: 508-797-9561

(See Next Column)

Philip J. MacCarthy | John F. Hurley, Jr.
Dennis Pojani | Howard E. Stempler
John Macuga, Jr.

ASSOCIATE
William J. Ritter

Representative Clients: Shawmut Bank N.A.; Melville Corp.; Travelers Insurance Co.; Liberty Mutual Co.; United States Fidelity & Guaranty Co.; Commerce Insurance Co.; Worcester Mutual Insurance Co.; Fleet Bank of Massachusetts, N.A.; Health Plans, Inc.; Marane Oil Corp.

For full biographical listings, see the Martindale-Hubbell Law Directory

MCGUIRE & MCGUIRE, P.C. (AV)

340 Main Street, Suite 910, 01608
Telephone: 508-754-3291
Fax: 508-752-0553

John K. McGuire (1952-1985) | Joseph E. McGuire
John K. McGuire, Jr.

Penelope A. Kathiwala | Paul Durkee
Christine Griggs Narcisse | Teresa Brooks

For full biographical listings, see the Martindale-Hubbell Law Directory

REARDON & REARDON (AV)

One Exchange Place, 01608
Telephone: 508-754-1111
Fax: 508-797-6176
Boston, Massachusetts Office: 69 Beacon Street.
Telephone: 617-248-6998.

MEMBERS OF FIRM
James G. Reardon | Edward P. Reardon
Frank S. Puccio, Jr.

ASSOCIATES
Austin M. Joyce | James G. Reardon, Jr.
James G. Haddad | Julie E. Reardon
Margaret Reardon Suuberg | Michael J. Akerson
Francis J. Duggan

References: Mechanics National Bank; Shawmut Worcester County Bank N.A.; Bank of New England, Worcester.

For full biographical listings, see the Martindale-Hubbell Law Directory

SEDER & CHANDLER (AV)

Established 1918
Burnside Building, 339 Main Street, 01608
Telephone: 508-757-7721
Telecopiers: 508-798-1863; 831-0955

MEMBERS OF FIRM
Samuel Seder (1918-1964) | Marvin S. Silver
Harold Seder (1934-1988) | John Woodward
Burton Chandler | John L. Pfeffer, Jr.
J. Robert Seder | Robert S. Adler
Darragh K. Kasakoff | Dawn E. Caccavaro

ASSOCIATES
Kevin C. McGee | Jeffrey P. Greenberg
Paul J. O'Riordan | Lisa S. Sigel
Denise M. Tremblay

OF COUNSEL
Saul A. Seder | Gerald E. Norman

Reference: Shawmut Worcester County Bank N.A.

For full biographical listings, see the Martindale-Hubbell Law Directory

MICHIGAN

*ANN ARBOR,** Washtenaw Co.

BLASKE AND BLASKE (AV)

320 North Main, Suite 303, 48104
Telephone: 313-747-7055
Battle Creek, Michigan Office: 1509 Comerica Building, 25 West Michigan Mall.
Telephone: 616-964-9491.

Edmund R. Blaske (1911-1982) | Thomas H. Blaske
E. Robert Blaske

Reference: Comerica Bank-Battle Creek.

For full biographical listings, see the Martindale-Hubbell Law Directory

Ann Arbor—Continued

BOOTHMAN, HEBERT & ELLER, P.C. (AV)

300 N. Fifth Avenue, Suite 140, 48108
Telephone: 313-995-9050
Fax: 313-995-8966
Detroit, Michigan Office: One Kennedy Square, Suite 2006.
Telephone: 313-964-0150.
Fax: 313-964-2226.

Richard C. Boothman (Resident)

For full biographical listings, see the Martindale-Hubbell Law Directory

DAVIS AND FAJEN, P.C. (AV)

Suite 400, 320 North Main Street, 48104
Telephone: 313-995-0066
Facsimile: 313-995-0184
Grand Haven, Michigan Office: Davis, Fajen & Miller. Harbourfront Place, 41 Washington Street, Suite 260.
Telephone: 616-846-9875.
Facsimile: 616-846-4920.

Peter A. Davis
James A. Fajen
Nelson P. Miller
Richard B. Bailey
Catherine G. Tennant

Reference: First of America Bank-Ann Arbor.

For full biographical listings, see the Martindale-Hubbell Law Directory

HOOPER, HATHAWAY, PRICE, BEUCHE & WALLACE (AV)

126 South Main Street, 48104
Telephone: 313-662-4426
Fax: 313-662-9559

Joseph C. Hooper (1899-1980)
Alan E. Price
James R. Beuche
Bruce T. Wallace
Charles W. Borgsdorf
Mark R. Daane
Gregory A. Spaly
Robert W. Southard
William J. Stapleton
Bruce C. Conybeare, Jr.
Anthony P. Patti
Marcia J. Major

OF COUNSEL

James A. Evashevski
Roderick K. Daane

Representative Clients: Chem-Trend, Inc.; Dundee Cement Co.; Ervin Industries, Inc.; First Martin Corp.; Group 243 Design, Inc.; Honeywell; Microwave Sensors, Inc.; Shearson Lehman Hutton; O'Neal Construction Co.; Pittsfield Products, Inc.

For Complete List of Firm Personnel, See General Section

For full biographical listings, see the Martindale-Hubbell Law Directory

HURBIS, CMEJREK & CLINTON (AV)

Fifth Floor, City Center Building, 48104
Telephone: 313-761-8358
Fax: 313-761-3134

Charles J. Hurbis
James R. Cmejrek
Mary F. Clinton

Robert Lipnik

Representative Clients: General Motors Corp.; ITT Hartford; Insurance Company of North America; The University of Michigan; North Oakland Medical Center; City of Pontiac; Sears Roebuck and Co.; Montgomery Ward and Co., Inc.; Sedjwick-James, Inc.; Michigan State Accident Fund.

For full biographical listings, see the Martindale-Hubbell Law Directory

MILLER, CANFIELD, PADDOCK AND STONE, P.L.C. (AV)

A Professional Limited Liability Company
Founded in 1852 by Sidney Davy Miller
101 North Main Street, Seventh Floor, 48104-1400
Telephone: 313-663-2445
Fax: 313-747-7147
Detroit, Michigan Office: 150 West Jefferson, Suite 2500, 48226-4415.
Telephone: 313-963-6420.
Fax: 313-496-7500.
Cable Address: "Stem Detroit."
Bloomfield Hills, Michigan Office: Suite 100, Pinehurst Office Center, 1400 North Woodward, 48303-2014.
Telephone: 313-645-5000.
Fax: 313-645-1917.
Grand Rapids, Michigan Office: 1200 Campau Square Plaza, 99 Monroe, N.W., 49503-2639.
Telephone: 616-454-8656.
Fax: 616-776-6322.
Howell, Michigan Office: 121 South Barnard Street, Suite 4, 48843-2305.
Telephone: 517-546-7600.
Telecopier: 517-546-6974.
Kalamazoo, Michigan Office: 444 West Michigan Avenue, 49007-3752.
Telephone: 616-381-7030.
Fax: 616-382-0244.

(See Next Column)

Lansing, Michigan Office: One Michigan Avenue, Suite 900, 48933-1609.
Telephone: 517-487-2070.
Fax: 517-374-6304.
Monroe, Michigan Office: The Executive Centre, 214 East Elm Avenue, 48161-2682.
Telephone: 313-243-2000.
Fax: 313-243-0901.
Washington, D.C. Office: 1225 Nineteenth Street, N.W., Suite 400. 20036.
Telephone: 202-429-5575; 785-0600.
Fax: 202-331-1118; 785-1234.
Pensacola, Florida Office: 25 West Cedar, 32501.
Telephone: 904-469-1088.
Fax: 904-432-0677.
St. Petersburg, Florida Office: 100 Second Avenue S., Suite 7045, 33701.
Telephone: 813-982-6000.
Fax: 813-892-6002.
Gdansk, Poland Office: Suite 322, Dom Technika Building, UI. Rajska 6, 80-850.
Telephone: 011-485-831-2808.
Fax: 011-485-831-4719.
Warsaw, Poland Office: UI. Marszalkowska 82, Suite 561, 00-517.
Telephone: 011-482-623-6457 and 6458.
Fax: 011-482-623-6459.

RESIDENT PARTNERS

Robert E. Gilbert
Allyn D. Kantor
David A. French

SENIOR ATTORNEY

Marta A. Manildi

Representative Firm Clients: Chrysler Corp.; Comerica, Inc.; City of Detroit, Mich.; Detroit Tigers, Inc.; First of Michigan; Fretter, Inc.; Ford Motor Co.; Ford Motor Credit Co.; Great Lakes Bancorp; Henry Ford Hospital.

For Complete List of Firm Personnel, See General Section

For full biographical listings, see the Martindale-Hubbell Law Directory

O'BRIEN AND O'BRIEN (AV)

300 North Fifth Avenue, 48104
Telephone: 313-996-0550
Fax: 313-996-5555

MEMBERS OF FIRM

Thomas C. O'Brien
Darlene A. O'Brien

OF COUNSEL

Francis L. O'Brien (1907-1991)

Reference: Society Bank.

For full biographical listings, see the Martindale-Hubbell Law Directory

PEAR SPERLING EGGAN & MUSKOVITZ, P.C. (AV)

Domino's Farms, 24 Frank Lloyd Wright Drive, 48105
Telephone: 313-665-4441
Fax: 313-665-8788
Ypsilanti, Michigan Offices: 5 South Washington Street.
Telephone: 313-483-3626 and 2164 Bellevue at Washtenaw.
Telephone: 313-483-7177.

Edwin L. Pear
Lawrence W. Sperling
Andrew M. Eggan
Melvin J. Muskovitz
Thomas E. Daniels
Joel F. Graziani
Paul R. Fransway
Francyne Stacey
Helen Conklin Vick
Scott H. Mandel
David E. Kempner

Counsel for: Domino's Pizza, Inc.; Technical Engineering Consultants, Inc.; Victory Lane Quick Oil Change, Inc.; Bank One Ypsilanti, N.A.; The Credit Bureau of Ypsilanti; Meadowbrook Insurance Group; Michigan Municipal Liability & Property Pool.

For full biographical listings, see the Martindale-Hubbell Law Directory

BATTLE CREEK, Calhoun Co.

BLASKE AND BLASKE (AV)

1509 Comerica Building, 25 West Michigan Mall, 49017
Telephone: 616-964-9491
Ann Arbor, Michigan Office: 320 North Main, Suite 303.
Telephone: 313-747-7055.

Edmund R. Blaske (1911-1982)
E. Robert Blaske
Thomas H. Blaske

Reference: Comerica Bank-Battle Creek.

For full biographical listings, see the Martindale-Hubbell Law Directory

SULLIVAN, HAMILTON, SCHULZ, LETZRING, SIMONS, KRETER, TOTH & LEBEUF (AV)

Tenth Floor Comerica Building 25 West Michigan Mall, 49017
Telephone: 616-965-3216

(See Next Column)

SULLIVAN, HAMILTON, SCHULZ, LETZRING, SIMONS, KRETER, TOTH & LEBEUF—*Continued*

Maxwell B. Allen (1884-1942)
John M. Allen (1914-1985)
Ronald H. Ryan (1901-1988)
James M. Sullivan
Robert P. Hamilton
Bert W. Schulz
Kurt F. Letzring
Stephen L. Simons
Mark E. Kreter
Michael J. Toth
Ronald A. Lebeuf

OF COUNSEL

Raymond R. Allen

General Counsel for: Michigan Woodwork and Specialties.
Local Counsel for: The Medical Protective Co.; Gannett, Inc.; Automobile Club of Michigan Insurance Group and Insurance Assn. (AAA); Michigan Physicians Mutual Liability Co.; State Farm Mutual Insurance Co.; Auto Owners Ins. Co.; Cincinnati Ins. Co.; Nationwide Ins. Co.

For full biographical listings, see the Martindale-Hubbell Law Directory

VARNUM, RIDDERING, SCHMIDT & HOWLETT (AV)

4950 West Dickman Road, Suite B-1, 49015
Telephone: 616-962-7144
Grand Rapids, Michigan Office: Bridgewater Place, P.O. Box 352, 49501-0352.
Telephone: 616-336-6000; 800-262-0011.
Facsimile: 616-336-7000.
Telex: 1561593 VARN.
Lansing, Michigan Office: The Victor Center, Suite 810, 201 North Washington Square, 48933.
Telephone: 517-482-6237.
Facsimile: 517-482-6937.
Kalamazoo, Michigan Office: 350 East Michigan Avenue, 49007.
Telephone: 616-382-2300.
Facsimile: 616-382-2382.
Grand Haven, Michigan Office: 321 Washington Street, P.O. Box 288, 49417.
Telephone: 616-846-7100.
Facsimile: 616-846-7101.
Detroit, Michigan Office: 440 East Congress, Fourth Floor, 48226.
Telephone: 313-961-1600.
Facsimile: 313-961-1636.

MEMBER OF FIRM

Carl E. Ver Beek

For full biographical listings, see the Martindale-Hubbell Law Directory

BERRIEN SPRINGS, Berrien Co.

BOOTHBY & YINGST (AV)

9047-4 US 31 North, P.O. Box 268, 49103
Telephone: 616-471-7787
Fax: 616-471-7400
Washington, D.C. Office: 4545 42nd Street, N.W.
Telephone: 202-363-1773.
Fax: 202-363-0304.

MEMBERS OF FIRM

Lee Boothby
Robert A. Yingst

ASSOCIATE

Holly F. Underwood

For full biographical listings, see the Martindale-Hubbell Law Directory

*BIG RAPIDS,** Mecosta Co.

WALZ & WARBA, P.C. (AV)

115 Ives, 49307
Telephone: 616-796-5887
Fax: 616-796-5949
Traverse City, Michigan Office: 13983 West Bayshore Drive.
Telephone: 616-947-0313.
Fax: 616-947-8811.

Kenneth P. Walz
Mark J. Warba

For full biographical listings, see the Martindale-Hubbell Law Directory

BINGHAM FARMS, Oakland Co.

MEISNER AND HODGDON, P.C. (AV)

Suite 467, 30200 Telegraph Road, 48025-4506
Telephone: 810-644-4433
Fax: 810-644-2941

Robert M. Meisner
Samuel K. Hodgdon

Reference: Comerica Bank.

For full biographical listings, see the Martindale-Hubbell Law Directory

SMALL, TOTH, BALDRIDGE & VAN BELKUM, P.C. (AV)

30100 Telegraph Road Suite 250, 48025-4516
Telephone: 810-647-9595
Facsimile: 810-647-9599

(See Next Column)

Richard L. Small
John M. Toth
David M. Baldridge
Thomas G. Van Belkum

Representative Clients: The Medical Protective Co.; Michigan Physicians Mutual Liability Insurance Co.; Physicians Insurance Company of Michigan; Shelby Insurance Group; Kemper Insurance Group; Michigan Society of Oral and Maxillofacial Surgeons; Michigan Association of Orthodontists; Michigan Association of Endodontists; AAMOS Mutual; Mt Vernon Insurance Company.

For full biographical listings, see the Martindale-Hubbell Law Directory

BIRMINGHAM, Oakland Co.

CARSON FISCHER, P.L.C. (AV)

Third Floor, 300 East Maple Road, 48009-6317
Telephone: 810-644-4840
Facsimile: 810-644-1832

Joseph M. Fischer
Anne Cole Pierce
Kathleen A. Stibich
George M. Head
Stephen J. Carson

For full biographical listings, see the Martindale-Hubbell Law Directory

AUSTIN HIRSCHHORN, P.C. (AV)

251 East Merrill Street, 2nd Floor, 48009-6150
Telephone: 810-646-9944
FAX: 810-647-8596

Austin Hirschhorn

For full biographical listings, see the Martindale-Hubbell Law Directory

HYMAN AND LIPPITT, P.C. (AV)

185 Oakland Avenue, Suite 300, P.O. Box 1750, 48009
Telephone: 810-646-8292
Facsimile: 810-646-8375

J. Leonard Hyman
Norman L. Lippitt
Douglas A. Hyman
Brian D. O'Keefe
H. Joel Newman
Nazli G. Sater
Kenneth F. Neuman
Terry S. Givens
Paul J. Fischer
Sanford Plotkin
John A. Sellers
Robert H. Lippitt
Roger L. Myers

COUNSEL

Alice L. Gilbert

For full biographical listings, see the Martindale-Hubbell Law Directory

KELL & LYNCH, P.C. (AV)

300 East Maple Road, Suite 200, 48009
Telephone: 810-647-2333
Fax: 810-647-2781

Michael V. Kell
Margaret A. Lynch

Lissa M. Cinat
Jose L. Patino

For full biographical listings, see the Martindale-Hubbell Law Directory

LACEY & JONES (AV)

600 South Adams Road, Suite 300, 48009-6827
Telephone: 810-433-1414
Fax: 810-433-1241
Grand Rapids, Michigan Office: Suite 330, Ledyard Building, 125 Ottawa Avenue, N.W.
Telephone: 616-776-3641.
FAX: 616-776-3516.

Ralph B. Lacey (1885-1966)
William J. Jones (1908-1991)
Robert B. Lacey (1912-1976)
Francis L. Sylvester (Retired)
Paul Van Hartesveldt (Retired)
John A. Hilgendorf (Retired)

MEMBERS OF FIRM

Theodore A. Lughezzani
Steve N. Yardley
John Hayes
Charles E. Mann
Larry P. Beidelman
Bruce C. Roberts
Lawrence G. Kozaruk
David J. Duthie (Resident, Grand Rapids)
Dennis E. Zacharski
Gerald M. Marcinkoski
Kathleen McNichol Behn

ASSOCIATES

Michael Thomas Reinholm
Johnnie B. Rambus
Sean J. Powers
Timothy M. McAree (Resident, Grand Rapids)
Timothy D. Finegan
Robert H. Orlowski, Jr.
J. Patrick O'Neill
Dawn M. Sutkiewicz

(See Next Column)

LACEY & JONES, *Birmingham—Continued*

OF COUNSEL

Walter F. Reebel
Michele Kilar Kemler
Thomas J. Sullivan

Representative Clients: Alexsis, Inc.; Ameritech; Chrysler Corporation; CIGNA; Liberty Mutual Insurance Company; Meijer, Inc.; Metropolitan Prop. & Casualty; Michigan Hospital Association; Penn General Services; Travelers Insurance Company.

For full biographical listings, see the Martindale-Hubbell Law Directory

MACDONALD AND GOREN, P.C. (AV)

Suite 200, 260 East Brown Street, 48009
Telephone: 810-645-5940
Fax: 810-645-2490

Harold C. MacDonald
Kalman G. Goren
Cindy Rhodes Victor
Amy L. Glenn
David D. Marsh
Glenn G. Ross
Miriam Blanks-Smart
John T. Klees

Representative Clients: Bay Corrugated Container, Inc.; Miles Fox Company; Orlandi Gear Company, Inc.; Bing Steel, Inc.; Superb Manufacturing, Inc.; Spring Engineering, Inc.; Adrian Steel Company; Southfield Radiology Associates, P.C.; Blockbuster Entertainment Corporation; E.N.U.F. Internationale, Inc.

For full biographical listings, see the Martindale-Hubbell Law Directory

SIMPSON & BERRY, P.C. (AV)

260 East Brown, Suite 300, 48009
Telephone: 810-647-0200
Telecopier: 810-647-2776

Daniel F. Berry
Clark G. Doughty
Philip J. Goodman
James A. Simpson
Katheryne L. Zelenock

LEGAL SUPPORT PERSONNEL

Dwight Noble Baker, Jr.

Representative Clients: Anthony S. Brown Development Co., Inc.; Automation Services Equipment, Inc.; Brown Tire Co.; Chenoweth Construction Co.; Detroit Public Schools; Dupuis & Ryden, Accountants; Hall Financial Group, Trizec Properties, Inc.; NBD Bancorp, Inc.

For full biographical listings, see the Martindale-Hubbell Law Directory

BLOOMFIELD HILLS, Oakland Co.

BAUM & ASSOCIATES (AV)

200 East Long Lake Road Suite 180, 48304
Telephone: 810-647-6890

Martin S. Baum

ASSOCIATE

Margo S. Horwitz

For full biographical listings, see the Martindale-Hubbell Law Directory

FEENEY KELLETT & WIENNER, PROFESSIONAL CORPORATION (AV)

950 N. Hunter Boulevard, Third Floor, 48304-3927
Telephone: 810-258-1580
Fax: 810-258-0421

James P. Feeney
S. Thomas Wienner
Peter M. Kellett
Cheryl A. Bush
Linda M. Galante
Deborah F. Collins
David N. Goltz
G. Gregory Schuetz
Tracy D. Knox (Not admitted in MI)
Patrick G. Seyferth
Mark A. Fisher

For full biographical listings, see the Martindale-Hubbell Law Directory

HARDIG & PARSONS (AV)

2000 North Woodward Avenue, Suite 100, 48304
Telephone: 313-642-3500
Facsimile: 313-645-1128
Charlevoix, Michigan Office: 212 Bridge Street.
Telephone: 616-547-1200.
Facsimile: 616-547-1026.
Pawley's Island, South Carolina Office: 216 Highway 17, P.O. Box 1607, 29585.
Telephone: 803-237-9219.
Facsimile: 803-237-9530.
West Palm Beach, Florida Office: Suite 1450, 515 North Flagler.
Telephone: 407-833-1622.
Facsimile: 407-833-6933.
Charlotte Amalie, St. Thomas, Virgin Islands Office: International Plaza, 22 Dronningens Gade.
Telephone: 809-776-7650.
Facsimile: 809-774-2729.

(See Next Column)

MEMBERS OF FIRM

Joseph L. Hardig, Jr.
Donald H. Parsons
Joseph L. Hardig, III

ASSOCIATES

Bradley S. Stout
Kevin M. O'Connell

OF COUNSEL

Frederick Wm. Heath

MEMBER IN FLORIDA

Charles Ryan Hickman

MEMBER IN SOUTH CAROLINA

John C. Benso

OF COUNSEL

Preston Bennett Haines, III

MEMBER IN CHARLOTTE AMALIE, ST. THOMAS, VIRGIN ISLANDS

Arthur Pomerantz

ASSOCIATE

Marcia B. Resnick

For full biographical listings, see the Martindale-Hubbell Law Directory

HOWARD & HOWARD ATTORNEYS, P.C. (AV)

The Pinehurst Office Center, Suite 101, 1400 North Woodward Avenue, 48304-2856
Telephone: 810-645-1483
Telecopier: 810-645-1568
Kalamazoo, Michigan Office: The Kalamazoo Building, Suite 400, 107 West Michigan Avenue.
Telephone: 616-382-1483.
Telecopier: 616-382-1568.
Lansing, Michigan Office: The Phoenix Building, Suite 500, 222 Washington Square, North.
Telephone: 517-485-1483.
Telecopier: 517-485-1568.
Peoria, Illinois Office: Howard & Howard, P.C., The Creve Coeur Building, Suite 200, 321 Liberty Street.
Telephone: 309-672-1483.
Telecopier: 309-672-1568.

Philip T. Carter
Kevin M. Chudler
Roger M. Groves
Wade E. Haddad
Jon H. Kingsepp
Jeffrey G. Raphelson
Thomas J. Tallerico
Donald F. Tucker
Jacqueline K. Vestevich
Marla Gottlieb Zwas

Representative Clients: For Representative Client list, see General Practice, Bloomfield Hills, MI.

For Complete List of Firm Personnel, See General Section

For full biographical listings, see the Martindale-Hubbell Law Directory

MAY, SIMPSON & STROTE, A PROFESSIONAL CORPORATION (AV)

100 West Long Lake Road Suite 200, P.O. Box 541, 48303-0541
Telephone: 810-646-9500

Richard H. May
Thomas C. Simpson
Ronald P. Strote
Steven M. Raymond
John A. Forrest
David K. McDonnell

Steven F. Alexsy
Marilynn K. Arnold
Michele A. Lerner

Representative Clients: Aamco Transmission; American Annuity Life Insurance; Container Corporation of America; Citicorp Financial Center; Century 21 Real Estate Corp.; Oak Hills Mortgage Corp.; Ziebart International Corp.
Reference: NBD Bank, N.A.

For full biographical listings, see the Martindale-Hubbell Law Directory

MEYER, KIRK, SNYDER & SAFFORD (AV)

Suite 100, 100 West Long Lake Road, 48304
Telephone: 810-647-5111
Telecopier: 810-647-6079
Detroit, Michigan Office: 2500 Penobscot Building.
Telephone: 313-961-1261.

George H. Meyer
John M. Kirk
George E. Snyder
Ralph R. Safford
Donald H. Baker, Jr.
Patrick K. Rode

ASSOCIATES

Christopher F. Clark
Boyd C. Farnam
Debra S. Meier

OF COUNSEL

Mark R. Solomon

Representative Clients: Chemical Waste Management; Ervin Advertising; The Michigan and S.E. Michigan McDonald's Operators Assn.; The Southland Corp. (7-Eleven Food Stores); Stauffer Chemical Co.; Techpoint, Inc.

For full biographical listings, see the Martindale-Hubbell Law Directory

Bloomfield Hills—Continued

DAVID D. PATTON & ASSOCIATES, P.C. (AV)

100 Bloomfield Hills Parkway, Suite 110, 48304
Telephone: 810-258-6020
Fax: 810-258-6052

David D. Patton

Ellen Bartman Jannette
James A. Reynolds, Jr.
Patricia C. White
David H. Patton (1912-1993)

For full biographical listings, see the Martindale-Hubbell Law Directory

PORTNOY, PIDGEON & ROTH, P.C. (AV)

3883 Telegraph, Suite 103, 48302
Telephone: 810-647-4242
Fax: 810-647-8251

Bernard N. Portnoy
James M. Pidgeon
Robert P. Roth
Marc S. Berlin
Berton K. May

Representative Clients: North Oakland Medical Center, Pontiac General Hospital Division; Hurley Medical Center, Flint, Michigan; McLaren Regional Medical Center, Flint, Michigan; William Beaumont Hospital, Royal Oak, Michigan; Crittenton Hospital, Rochester, Michigan; Detroit Osteopathic Hospital, Detroit, Michigan; City of Pontiac; City of Troy; Honda North America, Inc.; Honda Motor Co., Ltd.

For full biographical listings, see the Martindale-Hubbell Law Directory

STROBL AND MANOOGIAN, P.C. (AV)

300 East Long Lake Road, Suite 200, 48304-2376
Telephone: 810-645-0306
Facsimile: 810-645-2690

Brian C. Manoogian
John Sharp
Kieran F. Cunningham
Michael E. Thoits
James D. Wilson

James T. Dunn
Sara S. Lisznyai
Keith S. King
Pamela S. Ritter
Douglas Young

Representative Clients: Resolution Trust Corporation; American Speedy Printing Centers, Inc.; Scibal Insurance Group; Capitol Bancorp Ltd.; Chrysler Credit Corporation; Chrysler Financial Corporation; Deutsche Finance Corporation; Masco Corporation.

For Complete List of Firm Personnel, See General Section

For full biographical listings, see the Martindale-Hubbell Law Directory

LAW OFFICES OF THOMAS J. TRENTA, P.C. (AV)

33 Bloomfield Hills Parkway Suite 145, 48304-2945
Telephone: 810-258-9610
Fax: 810-258-5132

Thomas J. Trenta

Richard A. Joslin, Jr.

OF COUNSEL

James F. Jordan

Representative Clients: American International Group (A.I.G.); National Union Fire Insurance Company; Caronia Corporation; Secura Insurance Co.; National Guardian Risk Retention Group; Hutzel Hospital; Mt. Clemens General Hospital; United States Professional Ski Tour; Beverly Enterprises Nursing Homes; Havenwyck Hospital.

For full biographical listings, see the Martindale-Hubbell Law Directory

BRIGHTON, Livingston Co.

BURCHFIELD, PARK & ASSOCIATES, P.C. (AV)

225 E. Grand River, Suite 203, 48116
Telephone: 810-227-3100
Facsimile: 810-227-2996

Kenneth E. Burchfield
David L. Park

Shari L. Heddon
Gregory C. Burkart

LEGAL SUPPORT PERSONNEL

Janet M. Schillinger

For full biographical listings, see the Martindale-Hubbell Law Directory

DEARBORN, Wayne Co.

ROBERT F. RILEY, P.C. (AV)

Garrison Place East 19855 W. Outer Drive, Suite E-109, 48124
Telephone: 313-565-1330
Facsimile: 313-565-1318

Robert F. Riley

Laura L. Nordberg

For full biographical listings, see the Martindale-Hubbell Law Directory

*DETROIT,** Wayne Co.

ABBOTT, NICHOLSON, QUILTER, ESSHAKI & YOUNGBLOOD, P.C. (AV)

19th Floor, One Woodward Avenue, 48226
Telephone: 313-963-2500
Telecopier: 313-963-7882

C. Richard Abbott
John R. Nicholson
Thomas R. Quilter III
Gene J. Esshaki
John F. Youngblood
Donald E. Conley
James B. Perry
Carl F. Jarboe
Jay A. Kennedy
Timothy A. Stoepker
Timothy J. Kramer
Norbert T. Madison, Jr.
William D. Gilbride, Jr.

Mary P. Nelson
Michael R. Blum
Thomas Ferguson Hatch
Anne D. Warren Bagno
Mark E. Mueller
Eric J. Girdler

OF COUNSEL

Thomas C. Shumaker
Roy R. Hunsinger

For full biographical listings, see the Martindale-Hubbell Law Directory

BARRIS, SOTT, DENN & DRIKER, P.L.L.C. (AV)

211 West Fort Street, Fifteenth Floor, 48226-3281
Telephone: 313-965-9725
Telecopier: 313-965-2493
313-965-5398

MEMBERS OF FIRM

Donald E. Barris
Herbert Sott
David L. Denn
Eugene Driker
William G. Barris
Sharon M. Woods
Stephen E. Glazek
Robert E. Kass
Daniel M. Share
Elaine Fieldman
Morley Witus
John A. Libby
James S. Fontichiaro
Daniel J. LaCombe

COUNSEL

Leon S. Cohan

OF COUNSEL

Stanley M. Weingarden
Robert E. Epstein

ASSOCIATES

Dennis M. Barnes
Gary Schwarcz
Matthew J. Boettcher
Barry R. Powers
Thomas F. Cavalier
Bonita R. Gardner
C. David Bargamian
Michael J. Reynolds
John Christopher Clark

Representative Clients: Avis Rent A Car System, Inc.; Borman's, Inc.; Consumers Power Co.; County of Wayne, Michigan; Ford Motor Co.; The Great Atlantic & Pacific Tea Company, Inc.; Henry Ford Health System; Michigan Consolidated Gas Co.; NBD Bank, N.A.; Textron, Inc.

For full biographical listings, see the Martindale-Hubbell Law Directory

BENDURE & THOMAS (AV)

577 East Larned, Suite 210, 48226-4392
Telephone: 313-961-1525
Fax: 313-961-1553

MEMBERS OF FIRM

Mark R. Bendure
Marc E. Thomas

ASSOCIATES

J. Christopher Caldwell
Victor S. Valenti
Sidney A. Klingler

OF COUNSEL

Nancy L. Bosh
John A. Lydick

For full biographical listings, see the Martindale-Hubbell Law Directory

BODMAN, LONGLEY & DAHLING (AV)

34th Floor 100 Renaissance Center, 48243
Telephone: 313-259-7777
Fax: 313-393-7579
Troy, Michigan Office: Suite 2020, 755 West Big Beaver Road.
Telephone: 810-362-2110.

(See Next Column)

BODMAN, LONGLEY & DAHLING, *Detroit—Continued*

Ann Arbor, Michigan Office: 110 Miller, Suite 300.
Telephone: 313-761-3780.
Northern Michigan Office: 229 Court Street, P.O. Box 405, Cheboygan.
Telephone: 616-627-4351.

MEMBERS OF FIRM

Theodore Souris
Joseph A. Sullivan
Carson C. Grunewald
James A. Smith
George G. Kemsley
James J. Walsh
David G. Chardavoyne
Robert G. Brower
Charles N. Raimi
Thomas Van Dusen (Troy Office)
John C. Cashen (Troy Office)
Martha Bedsole Goodloe (Troy Office)
Harvey W. Berman (Ann Arbor Office)

Representative Clients: Abitibi Price Group; Archdiocese of Detroit; Comerica Bank; The Detroit Lions, Inc.; Ford Estates; General Motors Corporation; Charles Stewart Mott Foundation; Norfolk Southern Corporation; Panhandle Eastern Corporation; State Farm Mutual Automobile Insurance Company.

For Complete List of Firm Personnel, See General Section

For full biographical listings, see the Martindale-Hubbell Law Directory

BOOTHMAN, HEBERT & ELLER, P.C. (AV)

One Kennedy Square, Suite 2006 719 Griswold, 48226
Telephone: 313-964-0150; 1-800-572-8022
Fax: 313-964-2226
Ann Arbor, Michigan Office: 300 N. Fifth Avenue, Suite 140.
Telephone: 313-995-9050.
Fax: 313-995-8966.

Dale L. Hebert
Richard C. Boothman (Resident, Ann Arbor Office)
Gary S. Eller

George D. Moustakas
Roy A. Luttmann
Marta J. Hoffman
Sharon E. Hollins
Joyce E. Taylor

OF COUNSEL

L. Stewart Hastings, Jr.
Kathryn A. Kerka

Representative Clients: University of Michigan; CNA Insurance Companies; Michigan Physicians Mutual Liability Co.; Emergency Physicians Medical Group; Kaiser Permanente; Physicians Insurance Co. of Michigan.
Reference: Comerica Bank-Detroit.

For full biographical listings, see the Martindale-Hubbell Law Directory

BRADY HATHAWAY, PROFESSIONAL CORPORATION (AV)

1330 Buhl Building, 48226-3602
Telephone: 313-965-3700
Telecopier: 313-965-2830

Thomas M. J. Hathaway

Representative Clients: Beam Stream, Inc.; Bundy Tubing Company; Century 21 Real Estate Corp.; Datamedia Corporation; Energy Conversion Devices, Inc.; Michigan Gas Utilities; Pony Express Courier Corp.; Schering Corporation; Warner-Lambert; Wolverine Technologies.

For Complete List of Firm Personnel, See General Section

For full biographical listings, see the Martindale-Hubbell Law Directory

BUTZEL LONG, A PROFESSIONAL CORPORATION (AV)

Suite 900, 150 West Jefferson, 48226
Telephone: 313-225-7000
Telecopier: 313-225-7080
Birmingham, Michigan Office: Suite 200, 32270 Telegraph Road.
Telephone: 810-258-1616.
Telecopier: 810-258-1439.
Lansing, Michigan Office: 118 West Ottawa Street.
Telephone: 517-372-6622.
Telecopier: 517-372-6672.
Ann Arbor, Michigan Office: Suite 400, 121 West Washington.
Telephone: 313-995-3110.
Telecopier: 313-995-1777.
Grosse Pointe Farms, Michigan Office: Suite 260, 21 Kercheval.
Telephone: 313-886-5446.
Telecopier: 313-886-2114.

William M. Saxton
Harold A. Ruemenapp
Stephen A. Bromberg (Birmingham)
Morris Milmet
Douglas G. Graham
Robert J. Battista
Frank B. Vecchio
Allan Nachman (Birmingham)
William R. Ralls (Lansing)
John P. Williams
Xhafer Orhan
John B. Weaver
George H. Zinn, Jr.
C. Peter Theut
John Henry Dudley, Jr.
Robert M. Vercruysse
Richard E. Rassel
Abba I. Friedman (Birmingham)
Edward D. Gold (Birmingham)

(See Next Column)

Robert B. Foster (Ann Arbor)
Paul L. Triemstra (Birmingham)
Jack D. Shumate
Edward M. Kronk
Philip J. Kessler
Thomas E. Sizemore
Donald B. Miller
John P. Hancock, Jr.
James E. Stewart
Virginia F. Metz
Frederick G. Buesser, III (Birmingham)
Leonard F. Charla
T. Gordon Scupholm II (Birmingham)
James C. Bruno
Mark S. Smallwood
David W. Sommerfeld (Birmingham, Grosse Pointe Farms and Ann Arbor)
Michael M. Jacob (Birmingham)
Thomas B. Radom (Birmingham)
David W. Berry (Birmingham)
Carl Rashid, Jr.
D. Stewart Green (Birmingham)
Dennis B. Schultz
Gregory V. Murray
Mark T. Nelson
Daniel P. Malone
Keefe A. Brooks
Justin G. Klimko
Michael D. Guzick
James E. Wynne
Barbara S. Kendzierski
Raymond J. Carey
David B. Calzone
Mark R. Lezotte
Michael J. Lavoie
Michael F. Golab
Edward M. Kalinka
Gordon J. Walker (Birmingham)
James L. Hughes
Arthur Dudley II
E. William S. Shipman
Richard P. Saslow
Gordon W. Didier
Dennis K. Egan
Jack J. Mazzara
Bruce L. Sendek
Lynne E. Deitch
Peter D. Holmes
Diane M. Soubly
Daniel B. Tukel
Susan Carino Nystrom
Alan S. Levine
Darlene M. Domanik
Leonard M. Niehoff
Carey A. DeWitt
Gary J. Abraham (Birmingham)
James Y. Stewart
Eric J. Flessland (Birmingham)
Lawrence A. Lichtman
Brian P. Henry (Birmingham and Lansing)
Lynn Abraham Sheehy
Robert A. Boonin
Sheldon H. Klein
Andrea Roumell Dickson

COUNSEL

Oscar H. Feldman
David F. DuMouchel
John F. McCuen, Jr. (Ann Arbor)
Robert F. Magill, Jr. (Ann Arbor)
Ralph S. Rumsey (Ann Arbor)

INTERNATIONAL PRACTICE ADVISOR

Akira Hara (Not admitted United States)

OF COUNSEL

George E. Brand, Jr.
Sidney L. Cohn (Birmingham)
Martha Ellen Dennis (Ann Arbor)
Jere D. Johnston
John J. Kuhn
William A. Penner, Jr.
Robin S. Phillips (Ann Arbor)
Erwin S. Simon
Malcolm J. Sutherland
James M. Wienner (Birmingham)

William D. Vanderhoef
J. Michael Huget
Barbara T. Pichan
Katherine B. Albrecht (Birmingham)
Anthony J. Saulino, Jr. (Birmingham)
James S. Rosenfeld
David K. Tillman
Brian J. Miles
Clara DeMatteis Mager
Patrick A. Karbowski (Birmingham)
Ronald E. Reynolds
Kenneth H. Adamczyk
Phillip C. Korovesis
Jordan S. Schreier
Richard T. Hewlett
Robert P. Perry (Birmingham)
Michael R. Poterala
Joshua A. Sherbin
Nicholas J. Stasevich
Susan Klein Friedlaender (Birmingham)
James J. Urban (Lansing)
Leland R. Rosier (Lansing)
Daniel R. W. Rustmann
Eugene H. Boyle, Jr.
Bernice M. Tatarelli
Jeffrey S. Wilke
Guglielmo A. Pezza
Debra Auerbach Clephane
Timothy M. Labadie
Paul S. Lewandowski
Susan Hartmus Hiser
Elizabeth A. Dumouchelle
Stacy D. Holloman
Robert E. Norton II
James J. Giszczak
Lois E. Walker
Maria T. Harshe
Sherri A. Krause
Robin K. Luce
Patricia E. Nessel
Ann M. Kelly
Barbara L. McQuade
Laurie J. Michelson
Barbara Dodenhoff Urlaub
Herbert C. Donovan (Not admitted in MI)
Caridad Pastor-Klucens
Timothy E. Galligan (Not admitted in MI)
Wendel Vincent Hall (Lansing)

Representative Clients: Bridgestone/Firestone, Inc.; The Detroit News, Inc.; Detroit Diesel Corp.; Kelly Services; Kelsey Hayes Co.; Merrill Lynch & Co., Inc.; Stroh Brewery Co.; Takata Corp.; United Parcel Services of America, Inc.; The University of Michigan.

For Complete List of Firm Personnel, See General Section

For full biographical listings, see the Martindale-Hubbell Law Directory

Detroit—Continued

Clark, Klein & Beaumont (AV)

1600 First Federal Building, 1001 Woodward Avenue, 48226
Telephone: 313-965-8300
Facsimile: 313-962-4348
Bloomfield Hills Office: 1533 North Woodward Avenue, Suite 220, 48304.
Telephone: 810-258-2900.
Facsimile: 810-258-2949.

MEMBERS OF FIRM

Patrick J. Keating
Laurence M. Scoville, Jr.
J. Walker Henry
David M. Hayes
Richard C. Marsh
P. Robert Brown, Jr.
Dennis G. Bonucchi
James E. Baiers
Suanne Tiberio Trimmer
Jonathan T. Walton, Jr.
Susan J. Sadler (Resident Bloomfield Hills, Michigan Office)
Michael S. Khoury
Mark L. McAlpine
Michael J. Sullivan
Tyler D. Tennent (Resident, Bloomfield Hills, Michigan Office)
Rachelle G. Silberberg
Cynthia L.M. Johnson
Sherwin E. Zamler (Resident Bloomfield Hills, Michigan Office)
Paul E. Scheidemantel
John E. Berg

ASSOCIATES

Thomas M. Dixon
Thomas D. Dyze
Judith Greenstone Miller
Edward J. Hood
Keith James
Michael I. Conlon
David A. Foster
Patricia Bordman
Katrina I. Crawley
David A. Breuch
Joseph K. Hart, Jr. (Resident, Bloomfield Hills, Michigan Office)
Laura S. Stafford
M. Maureen McHugh

Representative Clients: American Red Cross; BASF; Bechtel Corporation; Booth Communications, Inc.; The Budd Co.; Coopers & Lybrand; First Federal of Michigan; R.E. Dailey & Co.; Rouge Steel Company; Scot Ladd Foods; Trammell Crow Co.

For Complete List of Firm Personnel, See General Section

For full biographical listings, see the Martindale-Hubbell Law Directory

DeNardis, McCandless & Muller, P.C. (AV)

800 Buhl Building, 48226-3602
Telephone: 313-963-9050
Fax: 313-963-4553

Ronald F. DeNardis
William McCandless
Gregory J. Muller
Mark F. Miller
Lawrence M. Hintz
Michael D. Dolenga

Representative Clients: Acustar; American Medical Systems, Inc.; Bettcher Industries, Inc.; Cargill, Inc.; Chrysler Corporation; The Doctors Company; Emro Marketing Company; Marathon Oil Company; MedMarc; Parker Hannifin Corporation.

For full biographical listings, see the Martindale-Hubbell Law Directory

Dickinson, Wright, Moon, Van Dusen & Freeman (AV)

500 Woodward Avenue, Suite 4000, 48226-3425
Telephone: 313-223-3500
Facsimile: 313-223-3598
Bloomfield Hills, Michigan Office: 525 North Woodward Avenue, Suite 2000.
Telephone: 810-433-7200.
Facsimile: 810-433-7274.
Grand Rapids, Michigan Office: 200 Ottawa Avenue, N.W., Suite 900.
Telephone: 616-458-1300.
Facsimile: 616-458-6753.
Lansing, Michigan Office: Suite 200, 215 South Washington Square.
Telephone: 517-371-1730.
Facsimile: 517-487-4700.
Washington, D.C. Office: Suite 800, 1901 L Street, N.W.
Telephone: 202-457-0160.
Facsimile: 202-659-1559.
Chicago, Illinois Office: 225 West Washington, Suite 400.
Telephone: 312-220-0300.
Facsimile: 312-220-0021.
Warsaw, Poland Office: 46 Wilcza Street, 4th Floor, 00-679.
Telephone: (48-22) 299-241.
Facsimile: (48-2) 628-4107. Komertel Satellite Phone: (48-39) 121-510.

MEMBERS OF FIRM

Selden S. Dickinson (1892-1964)
Edward P. Wright (1894-1962)
Richard C. Van Dusen (1925-1991)
Fred W. Freeman
Patrick J. Ledwidge
Verne C. Hampton II
Ward Randol, Jr. (Bloomfield Hills Office)
Charles F. Clippert (Bloomfield Hills Office)
Russell A. McNair, Jr.
John E. S. Scott
Herbert G. Sparrow, III
John Corbett O'Meara
Judson Werbelow (Lansing Office)
Charles R. Kinnaird
Michael T. Platt (Washington, D.C. Office)
John A. Krsul, Jr.
Douglas D. Roche
John A. Everhardus

(See Next Column)

MEMBERS OF FIRM (Continued)

Robert V. Peterson (Bloomfield Hills Office)
Edgar C. Howbert
Peter S. Sheldon (Lansing Office)
Robert S. Krause
Frank G. Pollock (Bloomfield Hills Office)
Robert E. Neiman (Chicago, Illinois Office)
Joseph A. Fink (Lansing Office)
Joyce Q. Lower (Bloomfield Hills Office)
Robert P. Hurlbert (Chicago, Illinois Office)
Thomas G. Kienbaum
Lawrence G. Campbell
Charles T. Harris (Bloomfield Hills Office)
David L. Turner
John H. Norris (Bloomfield Hills Office)
Ronald B. Grais (Chicago, Illinois Office)
William J. Fisher, III (Grand Rapids Office)
James N. Candler, Jr.
Kenneth J. McIntyre
Julia Donovan Darlow
J. Bryan Williams
Stephen E. Dawson (Bloomfield Hills Office)
Richard J. Meyers
Edward H. Pappas (Bloomfield Hills Office)
Jeffrey M. Petrash (Washington, D.C. Office)
Michael Gary Vartanian
Henry W. Saad (Bloomfield Hills Office)
John K. Lawrence
C. Beth DunCombe
James A. Samborn
Philip M. Frost
Timothy H. Howlett
James M. Tervo (Chicago, Illinois Office)
Terence M. Donnelly
Thomas D. Carney
Roger H. Cummings
Stuart F. Cheney (Grand Rapids Office)
Richard L. Braun, II
Joseph C. Marshall, III
Richard M. Bolton
Steven C. Nadeau
Jerome M. Schwartz
Richard A. Glaser (Grand Rapids Office)
George R. Ashford (Bloomfield Hills Office)
Henry M. Grix
James W. Bliss (Lansing Office)
Erik J. Stone (Bloomfield Hills Office)
Gregory L. McClelland (Lansing Office)
Richard W. Paul
David R. Bruegel (Bloomfield Hills Office)
Bruce C. Thelen
Peter H. Ellsworth (Lansing Office)
Noel D. Massie
Richard L. Caretti
Theodore R. Opperwall
Kirk Howard Betts (Washington, D.C. Office)
Margaret A. Coughlin
William E. Elwood (Washington, D.C. Office)
Martin L. Greenberg (Chicago, Illinois Office)
Keith J. Lerminiaux
Kester K. So (Lansing Office)
John M. Lichtenberg (Grand Rapids Office)
Francis R. Ortiz
Thomas J. Manganello
W. Anthony Jenkins
Larry J. Stringer
Robert E. Kinchen
Daniel M. Katlein
Robert W. Powell
Thomas D. Hammerschmidt, Jr.
Thomas V. Yates
Mark R. High
Richard A. Wilhelm
Peter Swiecicki (Warsaw, Poland Office)
Paul M. Wyzgoski
Barbara Hughes Erard
Maureen H. Burke (Bloomfield Hills Office)
Dwight D. Ebaugh (Lansing Office)
Samuel D. Littlepage (Washington, D.C. Office)
Conrad J. Clark (Washington, D.C. Office)
Stephen S. Herseth (Chicago, Illinois Office)
Jon Robert Steiger (Bloomfield Hills Office)
Kenneth T. Brooks (Lansing Office)
Kathleen A. Lang
Tomoaki Ikenaga
Daniel F. Gosch (Chicago, Illinois Office)
William P. Shield, Jr.
Brian K. Cullin
Thomas G. McNeill
Elizabeth Phelps Hardy
William T. Burgess
Zan M. Nicolli (Bloomfield Hills Office)
Jeffery V. Stuckey (Lansing Office)
Deborah L. Grace (Bloomfield Hills Office)
Gail A. Anderson (Lansing Office)
Andrea Andrews Larkin (Lansing Office)
Robert A. LaBelle (Bloomfield Hills Office)
Christopher L. Rizik
Elizabeth M. Pezzetti (Bloomfield Hills Office)
Judith E. Gowing (Bloomfield Hills Office)
Cynthia A. Moore (Bloomfield Hills Office)
Claudia Rast
David E. Pierson (Lansing Office)
Linda V. Parker
Johanna H. Armstrong
Dustin P. Ordway (Grand Rapids Office)
Mary Elizabeth Kelly
Danna Marie Kozerski
Andrew S. Boyce
Eric J. Pelton
Mark K. Riashi
Daniel M. Brinks (Bloomfield Hills Office)
Cynthia M. York
Steven H. Hilfinger
Joel M. Shere
Thea D. Dunmire (Chicago, Illinois Office)
Krzysztof Wierzbowski (Warsaw, Poland Office)
Joseph W. DeLave (Bloomfield Hills Office)
Jerry L. Johnson
Mary A. Pearson (Bloomfield Hills Office)
Brian K. Zahra
Margaret Van Meter (Bloomfield Hills Office)

CONSULTING PARTNERS

Charles R. Moon
Ernest Getz
W. Gerald Warren
Grady Avant, Jr.

(See Next Column)

DICKINSON, WRIGHT, MOON, VAN DUSEN & FREEMAN, *Detroit—Continued*

OF COUNSEL

Lucien N. Nedzi (Washington, D.C. Office)
Bruce A. Tassan (Washington, D.C. Office)
Thomas D. McLennan (Bloomfield Hills Office)
T. R. Knecht (Grand Rapids Office)
Steven V. Napolitano (Chicago, Illinois Office)
Douglas L. Mann (Bloomfield Hills Office)
Vivian Perry-Johnston (Bloomfield Hills Office)
Piotr J. Strawa (Warsaw, Poland Office)
John A. Ziegler, Jr.
Bethany E. Hawkins (Bloomfield Hills Office)
Douglas J. Van Der Aa (Grand Rapids Office)
Allan G. Sweig (Chicago, Illinois Office)
Mitchell J. Rapp (Lansing Office)
Marc A. Bergsman (Washington, D.C. Office)
Jill M. Barker (Washington, D.C. Office)

ASSOCIATES

Michelle Stahl Ausdemore (Bloomfield Hills Office)
Terrence A. Barr (Bloomfield Hills Office)
William R. Beekman (Lansing Office)
William C. Bertrand, Jr. (Lansing Office)
Jeffrey J. Brown (Bloomfield Hills Office)
Bruce R. Byrd
Robert E. Carr (Bloomfield Hills Office)
Kim D. Crooks (Lansing Office)
Michael S. Daar
Stephanie Dawkins Davis
Mark Alan Densmore
David R. Deromedi
Andrew S. Doctoroff
Julie T. Emerick
Sara Anne Engle (Bloomfield Hills Office)
Christine R. Essique
James P. Evans (Lansing Office)
Sherisse Eddy Fiorvento
Michelle Thurber Freese
Todd K. Garvelink
Kirk E. Grable (Lansing Office)
Nanci J. Grant (Bloomfield Hills Office)
Erin E. Gravelyn (Grand Rapids Office)
Melissa A. Hagen (Lansing Office)
K. Scott Hamilton
Michael C. Hammer
Craig W. Hammond
Douglas D. Hampton
Jana L. Henkel-Benjamin
Robert B. Hotchkiss (Bloomfield Hills Office)
Deborah A. Hulse (Not admitted in MI; Bloomfield Hills Office)
Lauren M. Hurwitz (Bloomfield Hills Office)
Kyle M. H. Jones
Mary Keizer Kalmink
Kelli L. Kerbawy (Bloomfield Hills Office)
Monica J. Labe
Douglas P. Lane
Deborah A. Lee (Lansing Office)
Mi Young Lee
Sandra J. LeFevre
Randi S. Lipin (Chicago, Illinois Office)
Edwin J. Lukas
Elizabeth Virginia Main
Sean D. Major (Chicago, Illinois Office)
Linda S. McAlpine
Clara Scholla McCarthy
Mark A. McDowell (Lansing Office)
Richard R. McGill, Jr. (Chicago, Illinois Office)
Sarah A. McLaren
Richard D. McNulty (Lansing Office)
Creighton R. Meland, Jr. (Chicago, Illinois Office)
Karen Raitt Modell (Bloomfield Hills Office)
Sharon R. Newlon
James Gavan O'Connor (Grand Rapids Office)
Richard W. Paige
John T. Panourgias (Bloomfield Hills Office)
Gregory J. Parry (Bloomfield Hills Office)
Matthew V. Piwowar (Warsaw, Poland Office)
James A. Plemmons
Daniel D. Quick
Henryk Romanczuk (Not admitted in United States) (Warsaw, Poland Office)
Jeffrey S. Ruprich
Diane G. Schwartz
Marian Keidan Seltzer
Daniel James Sheridan (Chicago, Illinois Office)
Colleen M. Shevnock
Delmas A. Szura (Lansing Office)
John L. Teeples (Grand Rapids Office)
Louis Theros (Chicago, Illinois Office)
Jeffrey E. Thompson (Lansing Office)
Andrew H. Thorson (Bloomfield Hills Office)
James M. Toner
Linda J. Truitt
Rock A. Wood (Grand Rapids Office)
Jennifer A. Zinn

LEGAL SUPPORT PERSONNEL

COMPUTER LITIGATION SUPPORT

Valerie L. Hanafee

JAPANESE CLIENT SUPPORT

Yukiko Sato

Representative Clients: American Yazaki Corp.; Ameritech International; Ameritech Publishing Inc.; Arthur Andersen & Co.; Ashland Petroleum Co.; Automobile Club of Michigan; Barden Cablevision; Baxter International, Inc.; Chrysler Corp.; Chrysler Realty Corp.

For full biographical listings, see the Martindale-Hubbell Law Directory

DISE & GUREWITZ, P.C. (AV)

3600 Cadillac Tower, 48226
Telephone: 313-963-8155
Telefax: 313-963-8438

(See Next Column)

John H. Dise, Jr.
Harold Gurewitz

Gina Ursula Puzzuoli
Margaret Sind Raben
G. Gus Morris
Elizabeth M. Malone

OF COUNSEL

Timothy Downs
Gene A. Farber

For full biographical listings, see the Martindale-Hubbell Law Directory

DYKEMA GOSSETT (AV)

400 Renaissance Center, 48243-1668
Telephone: 313-568-6800
Cable Address: "Dyke-Detroit"
Telex: 23-0121
Fax: 313-568-6594
Ann Arbor, Michigan Office: 315 East Eisenhower Parkway, Suite 100, 48108-3306.
Telephone: 313-747-7660.
Fax: 313-747-7696.
Bloomfield Hills, Michigan Office: 1577 North Woodward Avenue, Suite 300, 48304-2820.
Telephone: 810-540-0700.
Fax: 810-540-0763.
Grand Rapids, Michigan Office: 200 Oldtown Riverfront Building, 248 Louis Campau Promenade, N.W., 49503-2668.
Telephone: 616-776-7500.
Fax: 616-776-7573.
Lansing, Michigan Office: 800 Michigan National Tower, 48933-1707.
Telephone: 517-374-9100.
Fax: 517-374-9191.
Washington, D.C. Office: Franklin Square, Suite 300 West Tower, 1300 I Street, N.W., 20005-3306.
Telephone: 202-522-8600.
Fax: 202-522-8669.
Chicago, Illinois Office: Three First National Plaza, Suite 1400, 70 W. Madison, 60602-4270.
Telephone: 312-214-3380.
Fax: 312-214-3441.

MEMBERS OF FIRM

Ted T. Amsden
Susan Artinian
Joseph C. Basta
Richard B. Baxter (Resident at Grand Rapids Office)
William J. Brennan (Resident at Grand Rapids Office)
James M. Cameron, Jr. (Resident at Ann Arbor Office)
Laurence D. Connor
Michael P. Cooney
John B. Curcio (Resident at Lansing Office)
J. Terrance Dillon (Resident at Grand Rapids Office)
J. Bruce Donaldson (Resident at Bloomfield Hills Office)
John A. Ferroli (Resident at Grand Rapids Office)
Robert J. Franzinger
Barbara L. Goldman
Alan M. Greene (Resident at Bloomfield Hills Office)
Dennis M. Haffey (Resident at Bloomfield Hills Office)
Mark E. Hauck
Patrick F. Hickey
E. Edward Hood (Resident at Ann Arbor Office)
Kathryn J. Humphrey
Craig L. John (Resident at Bloomfield Hills Office)
Sharon M. Kelly (Resident at Ann Arbor Office)
Gregory M. Kopacz
Richard J. Landau (Resident at Ann Arbor Office)
J. Thomas Lenga
Kathleen McCree Lewis
Bonnie L. Mayfield
Richard J. McClear
Debra M. McCulloch
Derek I. Meier
Stephen S. Muhich (Resident at Grand Rapids Office)
Howard E. O'Leary, Jr. (Resident at Washington, D.C. Office)
Marilyn A. Peters
Thomas W. B. Porter
Jack C. Radcliffe, Jr. (Resident at Ann Arbor Office)
Jonathan D. Rowe (Resident at Ann Arbor Office)
Mary Elizabeth Royce (Resident at Bloomfield Hills Office)
Suzanne Sahakian
Daniel J. Scully, Jr.
Lori M. Silsbury (Resident at Lansing Office)
Wilfred A. Steiner, Jr.
Daniel J. Stephenson (Resident at Ann Arbor Office)
Mark H. Sutton (Resident at Bloomfield Hills Office)
Roger K. Timm
Stephen D. Winter
Fred L. Woodworth (Resident at Washington, D.C. Office)
Daniel G. Wyllie
Donald S. Young

OF COUNSEL

Donald E. Shely

RETIRED PARTNER

Robert N. Hammond (Resident at Grand Rapids Office)

ASSOCIATES

Michael J. Brown (Resident at Lansing Office)
Margaret A. Costello
Krishna S. Dighe
Cheryl Anne Fletcher
Lee S. Fruman
Kevin P. Fularczyk
Grant P. Gilezan
Margaret M. Gillis
Zora E. Johnson
Jeffrey S. Jones
Jerome I. Maynard (Resident at Chicago, Illinois Office)
Ava K. Ortner
Mark W. Osler
Thomas M. Pastore

(See Next Column)

DYKEMA GOSSETT—*Continued*

Paul W. Ritsema (Resident at Grand Rapids Office)
Rosemary G. Schikora
John F. Smart (Resident at Grand Rapids Office)
Thomas R. Stevick (Resident at Ann Arbor Office)
Sally A. York (Resident at Bloomfield Hills Office)

For Complete List of Firm Personnel, See General Section

For full biographical listings, see the Martindale-Hubbell Law Directory

EAMES, WILCOX, MASTEJ, BRYANT, SWIFT & RIDDELL (AV)

1400 Buhl Building, 48226-3602
Telephone: 313-963-3750
Facsimile: 313-963-8485

MEMBERS OF FIRM

Leonard A. Wilcox, Jr.
Ronald J. Mastej
John W. Bryant
Jerry R. Swift
Neill T. Riddell
Elizabeth Roberto
Kevin N. Summers

ASSOCIATE

Keith M. Aretha

OF COUNSEL

Rex Eames
Robert E. Gesell
William B. McIntyre, Jr.

Representative Clients: ABF Freight System, Inc.; Chrysler Credit Corp.; City Transfer Co.; Engineered Heat Treat, Inc.; Fetz Engineering Co.; I E & E Industries, Inc.; Schneider Transport; Tank Carrier Employers Association of Michigan; TNT Transport Group, Inc.; Waste Management of Michigan.

For full biographical listings, see the Martindale-Hubbell Law Directory

EGGENBERGER, EGGENBERGER, MCKINNEY, WEBER & HOFMEISTER, P.C. (AV)

42nd Floor Penobscot Building, 48226
Telephone: 313-961-9722

William J. Eggenberger (1900-1984)
William D. Eggenberger
Robert E. Eggenberger
John P. McKinney
Stephen L. Weber
Paul D. Hofmeister

R. Scott Mills
Mary T. Humbert
James B. Eggenberger

Representative Clients: Amoco Oil Co.; Central National Insurance Group of Omaha; City of Wayne, Michigan; Clark Oil & Refining Corp.; Country Mutual Casualty Co.; Auto Club Insurance Assn.; General Accident Assurance Co., Ltd.; Great Central Insurance Co.; Inland Mutual Insurance Co.; Midwest Mutual Insurance Co.

For full biographical listings, see the Martindale-Hubbell Law Directory

FEIKENS, VANDER MALE, STEVENS, BELLAMY & GILCHRIST, P.C. (AV)

One Detroit Center Suite 3400, 500 Woodward Avenue, 48226-3406
Telephone: 313-962-5909
Fax: 313-962-3125

Jack E. Vander Male
L. Neal Kennedy

Roger L. Wolcott
Richard G. Koefod
Joseph E. Kozely, Jr.
Jeffrey Feikens
Michael B. Barey
Gary T. Tandberg
Susan Tillotson Mills

For Complete List of Firm Personnel, See General Section

For full biographical listings, see the Martindale-Hubbell Law Directory

FILDEW, HINKS, MILLER, TODD & WANGEN (AV)

3600 Penobscot Building, 48226-4291
Telephone: 313-961-9700
Telecopier: 313-961-0754

MEMBERS OF FIRM

Stanley L. Fildew (1896-1978)
Frank T. Hinks (1887-1974)
Richard E. Hinks (1916-1990)
John H. Fildew
Alan C. Miller
Charles D. Todd III
Randall S. Wangen
Mary Jane Ruffley
Robert D. Welchli
William P. Thorpe
Colleen A. Kramer
Stephen J. Pokoj

ASSOCIATES

Charles S. Kennedy, III
Gerald M. Swiacki

References: First of America Bank-Detroit, N.A.; Comerica Bank-Detroit; National Bank of Detroit.

For full biographical listings, see the Martindale-Hubbell Law Directory

GARAN, LUCOW, MILLER, SEWARD, COOPER & BECKER, P.C. (AV)

1000 Woodbridge Place, 48207-3192
Telephone: 313-446-1530
Fax: 313-259-0450
Grand Blanc, Michigan Office: 8332 Office Park Drive.
Telephone: 810-695-3700.
Fax: 810-695-6488.
Port Huron, Michigan Office: Port Huron Office Center, 511 Fort Street, Suite 505.
Telephone: 810-985-4400.
Fax: 810-985-4107.
Ann Arbor, Michigan Office: 101 North Main Street, Suite 801.
Telephone: 313-930-5600.
Fax: 313-930-0043.
Troy, Michigan Office: 2301 West Big Beaver Road, Suite 212.
Telephone: 810-649-7600.
Fax: 810-649-5438.
Mount Clemens Office: Towne Square Development, 10 S. Main Street, Suite 307.
Telephone: 810-954-3800.
Fax: 810-954-3803.

Matthew A. Seward
David J. Cooper
James L. Borin
Thomas F. Myers
Dennis P. Partridge
John E. McSorley
Lamont E. Buffington
Thomas L. Misuraca
Rosalind Rochkind
James J. Hayes, Jr.
Thomas W. Emery
Joseph Crystal
Boyd E. Chapin, Jr.
Mark C. Smiley

Ian C. Simpson
Patricia L. Patterson
Daniel S. Saylor
Peter B. Worden, Jr.
Charlotte H. Johnson
David M. Shafer
Lloyd G. Johnson
John J. Gillooly
Robert D. Goldstein
Michael J. Paolucci
Michael J. Severyn
Michael J. DePolo
C. David Miller, II
Robert J. Squiers, Jr.
David J. Langford
Anne K. Newcomer
Robert A. Obringer
Eun (Ellen) G. Ha

OF COUNSEL

Daniel L. Garan
Albert A. Miller
Roy E. Castetter
Beth A. Andrews
Nancy J. Bourget

Counsel for: Allstate Insurance Co.; Sears, Roebuck & Co.; Liberty Mutual Insurance Co.; Continental Insurance Companies.

For Complete List of Firm Personnel, See General Section

For full biographical listings, see the Martindale-Hubbell Law Directory

HAISCH & BOYDA (AV)

100 Renaissance Center, Suite 1750, 48243
Telephone: 313-259-4370
Facsimile: 313-259-6487

Anthony A. Haisch
John M. Boyda

ASSOCIATE

Donald C. Wheaton, Jr.

Representative Clients: AT&T Corp.; AT&T Universal Card Services Corp.; Amoco Corp.; North American Philips Corp.; Empire Blue Cross & Blue Shield; Lyon Financial Services, Inc.; Schwans' Sales Enterprises; Marshalls, Inc.; Access America Inc.; Grant Industries, Inc.

For full biographical listings, see the Martindale-Hubbell Law Directory

HAYDUK, ANDREWS & HYPNAR, P.C. (AV)

444 Penobscot Building, 48226
Telephone: 313-962-4500
Fax: 313-964-6577

Mark S. Hayduk
Robin K. Andrews
Mark A. Hypnar
Paul J. Ellison
Sean Angus McPhillips
Robert J. Heimbuch

Representative Clients: Farmers Insurance Group; GameTime, Inc.; Admiral Insurance Co.; Safeco Insurance Cos.; Heritage Insurance; Prudential-LMI ; Perkins Great Lakes, Inc.; Meijer, Inc.; Alexis Condon & Forsyth; Pinkerton's Inc.

For full biographical listings, see the Martindale-Hubbell Law Directory

HONIGMAN MILLER SCHWARTZ AND COHN (AV)

A Partnership including Professional Corporations
2290 First National Building, 48226
Telephone: 313-256-7800
Telecopier: 313-962-0176
Telex: 235705
Lansing, Michigan Office: Phoenix Building, 222 North Washington Square, Suite 400.
Telephone: 517-484-8282.

(See Next Column)

HONIGMAN MILLER SCHWARTZ AND COHN, *Detroit—Continued*

West Palm Beach, Florida Office: Suite 800 Esperante Building, 222 Lakeview Avenue.
Telephone: 407-838-4500.
Tampa, Florida Office: 2700 Landmark Centre, 401 E. Jackson Street.
Telephone: 813-221-6600.
Orlando, Florida Office: 390 North Orange Avenue, Suite 1300.
Telephone: 407-648-0300.
Houston, Texas Office: 3100 First Interstate Bank Plaza, 1000 Louisiana.
Telephone: 713-650-2600.
Los Angeles, California Office: McNeill Plaza, Suite 820, 15260 Ventura Boulevard, 91403.
Telephone: 818-784-2900.

MEMBERS OF FIRM

Peter M. Alter
Norman C. Ankers
Frederick M. Baker, Jr. (Lansing, Michigan Office)
Richard Bisio
Jay E. Brant
Lee W. Brooks
Robert A. Fineman
Herschel P. Fink
William F. Frey
Mark A. Goldsmith
Michael A. Gruskin
Raymond W. Henney
Norman Hyman
Robert M. Jackson
Sandra L. Jasinski (Lansing, Michigan Office)
Timothy Sawyer Knowlton (Lansing, Michigan Office)
Ronald S. Longhofer
Gerard Mantese
Mark Morton (Lansing, Michigan Office)
David B. Nelson
John D. Pirich (Lansing, Michigan Office)
William D. Sargent
John Sklar
Mark A. Stern
Stuart H. Teger
Gary A. Trepod (Lansing, Michigan Office)
Stephen Wasinger
Mark R. Werder
I. W. Winsten
Ruth E. Zimmerman (Lansing, Michigan Office)
Richard E. Zuckerman

ASSOCIATES

Ann L. Andrews (Lansing, Michigan Office)
Gary K. August
Cameron J. Evans
Gregory D. Hanley (Not admitted in MI)
Andrea Hansen (Lansing, Michigan Office)
Daniel G. Helton
John S. Kane (Lansing, Michigan Office)
Lawrence J. Murphy
Steven M. Ribiat
Cynthia G. Thomas

OF COUNSEL

Milton J. Miller

RESIDENT IN WEST PALM BEACH, FLORIDA OFFICE

MEMBERS

Carla L. Brown
Steven L. Schwarzberg (P.A.)
Lloyd R. Schwed

ASSOCIATE

Jose O. Diaz

OF COUNSEL

Delmer C. Gowing, III, (P.A.)

RESIDENT IN TAMPA, FLORIDA OFFICE

MEMBERS

Robert W. Boos (P.A.)
Harry Christopher Goplerud (P.A.)
Gregory G. Jones (P.A.)

ASSOCIATES

Kevin M. Gilhool
Dennis Hernandez

RESIDENT IN ORLANDO, FLORIDA OFFICE

MEMBERS

Charles V. Choyce, Jr.
David S. Oliver (P.A.)

ASSOCIATES

Brian Stuart Chilton
Roseanna J. Lee
Paul W. Moses II
Vincent J. Profaci

RESIDENT IN HOUSTON, TEXAS OFFICE

MEMBERS

Louis Karl Bonham (P.C.)
John T. Klug (P.C.)
Sid Leach (P.C.)

ASSOCIATES

Anne E. Brookes
John G. Flaim
Joy Jacobson
Paul N. Katz

RESIDENT IN LOS ANGELES, CALIFORNIA OFFICE

MEMBER

George E. Schulman

ASSOCIATE

Michael D. Schulman

Representative Clients: Consumers Power Co.; The Detroit Edison Co.; The Detroit Free Press; Ford Motor Co.; General Motors Corporation, Legal Staff (General Motors Corporation and General Motors Acceptance Corporation); Michigan Bell Telephone Co.; Michigan Hospital Association; The Taubman Company, Inc.; ThornApple Valley, Inc.; Walbridge Aldinger Co.

For Complete List of Firm Personnel, See General Section

For full biographical listings, see the Martindale-Hubbell Law Directory

HOUGHTON, POTTER, SWEENEY & BRENNER, A PROFESSIONAL CORPORATION (AV)

The Guardian Building, 500 Griswold Street, Suite 3300, 48226-3806
Telephone: 313-964-0050
Facsimile: 313-964-4005

William C. Potter, Jr.
James E. Brenner
Mark W. McInerney

Mary C. Dirkes

LEGAL SUPPORT PERSONNEL

LEGAL ASSISTANTS

Ann E. Adams
Janet C. Driver

Representative Clients: Bell Sports, Inc.; Wynn's International, Inc.; Metropolitan Life Insurance Co.; Phoenix Mutual Life Insurance Company; New England Mutual Life Insurance Co.; Village of Grosse Pointe Shores; Wayne Center; Molded Materials, Inc.; Greenfield Construction Company, Inc.; Harding Tube Corporation.

For full biographical listings, see the Martindale-Hubbell Law Directory

JAFFE, RAITT, HEUER & WEISS, PROFESSIONAL CORPORATION (AV)

One Woodward Avenue, Suite 2400, 48226
Telephone: 313-961-8380
Telecopier: 313-961-8358
Cable Address: "Jafsni"
Southfield,Michigan Office: Travelers Tower, Suite 1520.
Telephone: 313-961-8380.
Monroe, Michigan Office: 212 East Front Street, Suite 3.
Telephone: 313-241-6470.
Telefacsimile: 313-241-3849.

Christopher A. Andreoff
Julia Blakeslee
R. Christopher Cataldo
Wallace H. Glendening
Jeffrey G. Heuer
Sharon J. LaDuke
Melanie LaFave
Eric A. Linden
Steven C. Powell
Michael A. Rajt
Brian G. Shannon
Joseph J. Shannon
Lawrence R. Shoffner
George A. Sumnik
Jeffrey D. Weisserman
Thomas H. Williams

David P. Armstrong
Susan Michelle Bakst
Harolyn D. Beverly
Susan S. Lichterman
Thomas L. Shaevsky
Nancy L. Waldmann

See General Practice Section for List of Representative Clients.

For Complete List of Firm Personnel, See General Section

For full biographical listings, see the Martindale-Hubbell Law Directory

JOHNSON & VALENTINE (AV)

4372 Penobscot Building, 48226
Telephone: 313-961-4700

MEMBERS OF FIRM

Edward C. Johnson
Glenn L. Valentine

ASSOCIATE

Dale T. McPherson

OF COUNSEL

Jarvis J. Schmidt

Representative Clients: First of America Bank-Southeast Michigan, N.A., Corp. Tr. Dpt.; Sun Bank-Miami, N.A., Coral Gables, Tr.Dpt.; Fifth Third Bank of Toledo, N.A.; Cozadd Rotary Foundation Trust; Colonial Hockey League; National Transportation Counsellors.
References: First of America Bank; Southeast Michigan, N.A.

For full biographical listings, see the Martindale-Hubbell Law Directory

KELLER, THOMA, SCHWARZE, SCHWARZE, DUBAY & KATZ, P.C. (AV)

440 E. Congress, 5th Floor, 48226
Telephone: 313-965-7610
Bloomfield Hills, Michigan Office: Suite 122, 100 West Long Lake Road.
Telephone: 313-647-3114.

Thomas H. Schwarze
Thomas L. Fleury
Terrence J. Miglio
Donna R. Nuyen
Robert A. Lusk
Linda M. Foster
Carl F. Schwarze
George P. Butler, III
Christopher M. Murray
Brian A. Kreucher

Counsel For: H & H Tube & Manufacturing; Howard Plating Industries, Inc.; Livonia Public Schools; Ludington News Company, Inc.; Northville Public Schools; Ryco Engineering, Inc.; Sign of the Beefcarver, Inc.
Representative Clients: General: Baxter Healthcare Corp.; Borg-Warner Corp.; Detrex Industries, Inc.

(See Next Column)

KELLER, THOMA, SCHWARZE, SCHWARZE, DUBAY & KATZ P.C.—*Continued*

For Complete List of Firm Personnel, See General Section

For full biographical listings, see the Martindale-Hubbell Law Directory

KERR, RUSSELL AND WEBER (AV)

One Detroit Center, 500 Woodward Avenue, Suite 2500, 48226-3406
Telephone: 313-961-0200
Telecopier: 313-961-0388
Bloomfield Hills, Michigan Office: 3883 Telegraph Road.
Telephone: 810-649-5990.
East Lansing, Michigan Office: 1301 North Hagadorn Road.
Telephone: 517-336-6767.

Richard D. Weber
Roy H. Christiansen
William A. Sankbeil
Patrick McLain
Daniel G. Beyer
James R. Case
Stephen D. McGraw
Edward C. Cutlip, Jr.
Mark M. Cunningham
Robert J. Pineau
Catherine Bonczak Edwards
David E. Sims
Christopher A. Cornwall
Dennis A. Martin
Patrick J. Haddad
Eric I. Lark
James E. DeLine

OF COUNSEL

Robert G. Russell

For Complete List of Firm Personnel, See General Section

For full biographical listings, see the Martindale-Hubbell Law Directory

KITCH, DRUTCHAS, WAGNER & KENNEY, P.C. (AV)

One Woodward, Tenth Floor, 48226-3412
Telephone: 313-965-7900
Fax: 313-965-7403
Lansing, Michigan Office: 120 Washington Square, North, Suite 805, One Michigan Avenue, 48933-1609.
Telephone: 517-372-6430.
Fax: 517-372-0441.
Macomb County Office: Towne Square Development, 10 South Main Street, Suite 301, Mount Clemens, 48043-7903.
Telephone: 810-463-9770.
Fax: 810-463-8994.
Toledo, Ohio Office: 405 Madison Avenue, Suite 1500, 43604-1235.
Telephone: 419-243-4006.
Fax: 419-243-7333.
Troy, Michigan Office: 3001 West Big Beaver Road, Suite 200, 48084-3103.
Telephone: 810-637-3500.
Fax: 810-637-6630.
Ann Arbor, Michigan Office: 303 Detroit Street, Suite 400, P.O. Box 8610, 48107-8610.
Telephone: 313-994-7600.
Fax: 313-994-7626.

Richard A. Kitch
Ronald E. Wagner
Jeremiah J. Kenney (Managing Principal)
Ralph F. Valitutti, Jr.
Richard R. DeNardis
Mona K. Majzoub
Harry J. Sherbrook
Anthony G. Arnone
Mark D. Willmarth (Principal)
Charles W. Fisher
Clyde M. Metzger, III (Principal, Ann Arbor Office)
Thomas J. Foley
Victor J. Abela (Principal, Troy Office)
Jeffrey H. Chilton
James H. Hughesian
John P. Ryan (Principal, Lansing Office)
William D. Chaklos
Steve N. Cheolas (Principal, Macomb County Office)
Richard S. Baron
Susan Healy Zitterman
William Vertes (Principal, Lansing Office)
William A. Tanoury (Principal, Ann Arbor Office)
R. Michael O'Boyle (Associate Principal, Troy Office)
John J. Ramar
John Stephen Wasung (Principal, Toledo, Ohio Office)
Bruce R. Shaw
Karen Bernard Berkery (Associate Principal)
Susan M. Ramage (Associate Principal, Lansing Office)
Pamela Hobbs
Daniel R. Corbet
Brian R. Garves
Daniel R. Shirey
Daniel J. Niemann (Associate Principal, Ann Arbor Office)
John M. Sier (Associate Principal)
Philip Cwagenberg (Troy Office)
William P. O'Leary
David M. Kraus
Verlin R. Nafziger
Robert A. Fehniger (Macomb County Office)
Christopher P. Dinverno
Kenneth M. Essad
Steven Waclawski
Gregory P. Sweda (Troy Office)
Ronald S. Bowling
Sara Mae Gerbitz
Linda M. Garbarino
Antonio Mauti
Lawrence David Rosenstock
Thomas R. Shimmel
Elizabeth I. Huldin
Susan Marie Beutel
Carole S. Empey (Ann Arbor Office)
Debra S. Hirsch (Lansing Office)
David R. Nauts
Richard T. Counsman

(See Next Column)

Karen Ann Smyth
Robert J. Bradfield III
Mark A. Wisniewski
Julia Kelly McNelis
J. Mark Trimble (Toledo, Ohio Office)
Sharon A. DeWaele
Arthur F. Brandt
Dean A. Etsios
Michael K. McCoy
Stephen R. Brzezinski
Kent Riesen (Toledo, Ohio Office)
Joseph P. McGill
Paula M. Burgess (Toledo, Ohio Office)
Lisa M. Iulianelli
Fred J. Fresard
Maureen Rouse-Ayoub
Matthew M. Walton (Mount Clemens Office)
Barbara A. Martin
Carol S. Allis (Ann Arbor Office)
Terese L. Farhat
Christopher J. Valeriote
Richard P. Cuneo
Kim J. Sveska

For Complete List of Firm Personnel, See General Section

For full biographical listings, see the Martindale-Hubbell Law Directory

LEWIS, WHITE & CLAY, A PROFESSIONAL CORPORATION (AV)

1300 First National Building, 660 Woodward Avenue, 48226-3531
Telephone: 313-961-2550
Washington, D.C. Office: 1250 Connecticut Avenue, N.W., Suite 630, 20036.
Telephone: 202-835-0616.
Fax: 202-833-3316.

David Baker Lewis
Richard Thomas White
Eric Lee Clay
Reuben A. Munday
Ulysses Whittaker Boykin
S. Allen Early, III
Carl F. Stafford
Helen Francine Strong
Derrick P. Mayes
Frank E. Barbee
Camille Stearns Miller
Melvin J. Hollowell, Jr.
Michael T. Raymond
Jacqueline H. Sellers
Thomas R. Paxton
Kathleen Miles (Resident, Washington, D.C. Office)
David N. Zacks

Karen Kendrick Brown (Resident, Washington, D.C. Office)
J. Taylor Teasdale
Wade Harper McCree
Tyrone A. Powell
Blair A. Person
Susan D. Hoffman
Stephon E. Johnson
John J. Walsh
Andrea L. Powell
Teresa N. Gueyser
Hans J. Massaquoi, Jr.
Werten F. W. Bellamy, Jr. (Resident, Washington, D.C. Office)
Akin O. Akindele
Regina P. Freelon-Solomon
Calita L. Elston
Nancy C. Borland
Terrence Randall Haugabook
Lynn R. Westfall
Lance W. Mason

OF COUNSEL

Otis M. Smith (1922-1994)
Inez Smith Reid (Resident, Washington, D.C. Office)

Representative Clients: Omnicare Health Plan; Aetna Life & Casualty Co.; Chrysler Motors Corp.; Chrysler Financial Corp.; MCI Communications Corp.; City of Detroit; City of Detroit Building Authority; City of Detroit Downtown Development Authority; Consolidated Rail Corp. (Conrail); Equitable Life Assurance Society of the United States.

For full biographical listings, see the Martindale-Hubbell Law Directory

LIZZA, MULCAHY & CASEY, P.C. (AV)

1700 Buhl Building, 48226
Telephone: 313-963-3123

John B. Lizza
James H. Mulcahy
Brian J. Casey
Thomas M. Lizza
Patrick F. Mulcahy

OF COUNSEL

Emil D. Berg

Representative Clients: Safeco Insurance Cos.; Lincoln Mutual Casualty Co.; L.J. Griffin Funeral Homes; Fidelity & Guarantee Internatl. Ltd; Admiral Insurance Co.; Foremost Insurance Cos.; Frankenmuth Mutual.
References: First of America Bank; National Bank of Detroit.

For full biographical listings, see the Martindale-Hubbell Law Directory

LOPATIN, MILLER, FREEDMAN, BLUESTONE, HERSKOVIC & HEILMANN, A PROFESSIONAL CORPORATION (AV)

1301 East Jefferson, 48207
Telephone: 313-259-7800

Albert Lopatin
Sheldon L. Miller
Stuart G. Freedman
Saul Bluestone
Maurice Herskovic
Michael G. Heilmann

Michael A. Gantz (1939-1990)
David F. Dickinson
Richard E. Shaw
Ronald Robinson
Jeffrey A. Danzig
B. J. Belcoure
David R. Berndt
Stephen I. Kaufman
Jeffrey S. Cook
Robert J. Boyd, III
Patrick M. Horan
Richard R. Mannausa
Alan Wittenberg

(See Next Column)

LOPATIN, MILLER, FREEDMAN, BLUESTONE, HERSKOVIC & HEILMANN A PROFESSIONAL CORPORATION, *Detroit—Continued*

OF COUNSEL

Harry Okrent (1912-1990)
Lee R. Franklin (Ms.)
Bernard L. Humphrey

For full biographical listings, see the Martindale-Hubbell Law Directory

MAGER, MERCER, SCOTT & ALBER, P.C. (AV)

2400 First National Building, 48226
Telephone: 313-965-1700
Facsimile: 313-965-3690
Macomb County Office: 18285 Ten Mile Road, Suite 100, Roseville, Michigan.
Telephone: 810-771-1100.

George J. Mager, Jr.
Phillip G. Alber
Lawrence M. Scott
(Resident at Roseville Office)
George D. Mercer
Raymond C. McVeigh
Michael R. Alberty
Bruce H. Hoffman
Jeffrey M. Frank
Michael A. Schwartz

Representative Clients: ABB Flakt, Inc.; American States Insurance Co.; CEI Industries; Central Venture Corp.; CIGNA; Construction Management, Inc.

For full biographical listings, see the Martindale-Hubbell Law Directory

MILLER, CANFIELD, PADDOCK AND STONE, P.L.C. (AV)

A Professional Limited Liability Company
Founded in 1852 by Sidney Davy Miller
150 West Jefferson, Suite 2500, 48226-4415
Telephone: 313-963-6420
Fax: 313-496-7500
Cable Address: "Stem Detroit"
Detroit, Michigan Office: 150 West Jefferson, Suite 2500, 48226-4415.
Telephone: 313-963-6420.
Fax: 313-496-7500.
Cable Address: "Stem Detroit."
Ann Arbor, Michigan Office: 101 North Main Street, 7th Floor, 48104-1400.
Telephone: 313-663-2445.
Fax: 313-747-7147.
Bloomfield Hills, Michigan Office: Suite 100, Pinehurst Office Center, 1400 North Woodward, 48303-2014.
Telephone: 313-645-5000.
Fax: 313-645-1917.
Grand Rapids, Michigan Office: 1200 Campau Square Plaza, 99 Monroe, N.W., 49503-2639.
Telephone: 616-454-8656.
Fax: 616-776-6322.
Howell, Michigan Office: 121 South Barnard Street, Suite 4, 48843-2305.
Telephone: 517-546-7600.
Telecopier: 517-546-6974.
Kalamazoo, Michigan Office: 444 West Michigan Avenue, 49007-3752.
Telephone: 616-381-7030.
Fax: 616-382-0244.
Lansing, Michigan Office: One Michigan Avenue, Suite 900, 48933-1609.
Telephone: 517-487-2070.
Fax: 517-374-6304.
Monroe, Michigan Office: The Executive Centre, 214 East Elm Avenue, 48161-2682.
Telephone: 313-243-2000.
Fax: 313-243-0901.
Washington, D.C. Office: 1225 Nineteenth Street, N.W., Suite 400. 20036.
Telephone: 202-429-5575; 785-0600.
Fax: 202-331-1118; 785-1234.
Pensacola, Florida Office: 25 West Cedar, 32501.
Telephone: 904-469-1088.
Fax: 904-432-0677.
St. Petersburg, Florida Office: 100 Second Avenue S., Suite 7045, 33701.
Telephone: 813-982-6000.
Fax: 813-892-6002.
Gdansk, Poland Office: Suite 322, Dom Technika Building, Ul. Rajska 6, 80-850.
Telephone: 011-485-831-2808.
Fax: 011-485-831-4719.
Warsaw, Poland Office: Ul. Marszalkowska 82, Suite 561, 00-517.
Telephone: 011-482-623-6457 and 6458.
Fax: 011-482-623-6459.

MEMBERS OF FIRM

Gilbert E. Gove
Carl H. von Ende
Allyn D. Kantor
(Ann Arbor Office)
Gregory L. Curtner
Joseph F. Galvin
Clarence L. Pozza, Jr.
Michael W. Hartmann
Larry J. Saylor
James G. Vantine, Jr.
(Kalamazoo and Grand Rapids Offices)
Marjory G. Basile
Michael P. Coakley
James E. Spurr
(Kalamazoo Office)
Mark T. Boonstra
David A. French
(Ann Arbor Office)
Le Roy L. Asher, Jr.
Richard T. Urbis
Steven A. Roach

(See Next Column)

OF COUNSEL

George E. Bushnell, Jr.

SENIOR ATTORNEYS

Abigail Elias
Lawrence M. Dudek
Marta A. Manildi
(Ann Arbor Office)
Gary W. Faria

ASSOCIATES

Ellen M. Tickner
Gary E. Mitchell
(Grand Rapids Office)
Ballard Jay Yelton III
(Kalamazoo Office)
Thomas R. Cox
Frederick A. Acomb
A. Michael Palizzi
Jeffrey S. Starman
Meg Hackett Carrier
(Grand Rapids Office)

Representative Firm Clients: Chrysler Corp.; Comerica, Inc.; City of Detroit, Mich.; Detroit Tigers, Inc.; First of Michigan; Fretter, Inc.; Ford Motor Co.; Ford Motor Credit Co.; Great Lakes Bancorp; Henry Ford Hospital.

For Complete List of Firm Personnel, See General Section

For full biographical listings, see the Martindale-Hubbell Law Directory

PATTERSON, PHIFER & PHILLIPS, P.C. (AV)

L. B. King Building, 1274 Library Street, Suite 500, 48226
Telephone: 313-964-2360

Michael D. Patterson
Randolph D. Phifer
Dwight W. Phillips

Nancy M. Rade
Joseph M. White
Wendy Z. Linehan

Representative Clients: Detroit Board of Education; Fireman's Fund Insurance Co.; General Motors Corp.; Home Federal Savings Bank; Liberty Mutual Insurance Co.; Metropolitan Life Insurance Co.; Michigan Basic Property Insurance Assn.; New York Life Insurance Co.; Wayne State University.
Reference: First of American Bank-Detroit, N.A.

For full biographical listings, see the Martindale-Hubbell Law Directory

PRATHER & ASSOCIATES, P.C. (AV)

3800 Penobscot Building, 48226-4220
Telephone: 313-962-7722
Facsimile: 313-962-2653

Kenneth E. Prather

Jan Rewers McMillan

For full biographical listings, see the Martindale-Hubbell Law Directory

SCHUREMAN, FRAKES, GLASS & WULFMEIER (AV)

440 East Congress, Fourth Floor, 48226
Telephone: 313-961-1500
Telecopier: 313-961-1087
Harbor Springs, Michigan Office: One Spring Street Sq., 49740.
Telephone: 616-526-1145.
Telecopier: 616-526-9343.

MEMBERS OF FIRM

Jeptha W. Schureman
John C. Frakes, Jr.
Charles F. Glass
LeRoy H. Wulfmeier, III
Cheryl L. Chandler
David M. Ottenwess

ASSOCIATES

Daniel J. Dulworth
John J. Moran
Paul A. Salyers
Erane C. Washington

Representative Clients: Michigan Physicians' Mutual Liability Co.; The Medical Protective Co.; Physicians' Insurance Company of Michigan; Michigan Health Care Corp.; Pontiac Osteopathic Hospital; JP Bender & Associates; Insurance Equities Corporation.

For full biographical listings, see the Martindale-Hubbell Law Directory

SIEMION, HUCKABAY, BODARY, PADILLA, MORGANTI & BOWERMAN, P.C. (AV)

1700 Penobscot Building, 48226
Telephone: 313-962-1700

Robert P. Siemion
Charles A. Huckabay
James W. Bodary
Gerald V. Padilla
Raymond W. Morganti
Cathy Rogers Bowerman
Michael J. Rinkel
Mark A. Roberts
Barbara Ann Rush
Arnold J. Matusz
Steven B. Sinkoff

Eugene Kelly Cullen
Thomas M. Caplis
Karen M. Leonetti
Donna Montano Severyn

For full biographical listings, see the Martindale-Hubbell Law Directory

Detroit—Continued

STRINGARI, FRITZ, KREGER, AHEARN & CRANDALL, P.C. (AV)

650 First National Building, 48226-3538
Telephone: 313-961-6474
Fax: 313-961-5688

Richard J. Fritz
Conrad W. Kreger
Brian S. Ahearn
Martin E. Crandall
Kenneth S. Wilson

Dallas G. Moon
John C. Dickinson

OF COUNSEL

Karl R. Bennett, Jr.
Matt W. Zeigler

For full biographical listings, see the Martindale-Hubbell Law Directory

TIMMIS & INMAN (AV)

300 Talon Centre, 48207
Telephone: 313-396-4200
Telecopier: 313-396-4228

MEMBERS OF FIRM

Robert E. Graziani
George A. Peck
Mark W. Peyser

ASSOCIATES

Bradley J. Knickerbocker
George M. Malis
Amy Lynn Ryntz
Daniel G. Kielczewski
Michael F. Wais
David J. Galbenski

Representative Clients: Wash/Blount; Talon, Inc.; F & M Distributors, Inc.; Certain Underwriters at Lloyds of London; Gay & Taylor.

For Complete List of Firm Personnel, See General Section

For full biographical listings, see the Martindale-Hubbell Law Directory

VANDEVEER GARZIA, PROFESSIONAL CORPORATION (AV)

Suite 1600, 333 West Fort Street, 48226
Telephone: 313-961-4880
Fax: 313-961-3822
Oakland County Office: 220 Park Street, Suite 300, Birmingham, Michigan.
Telephone: 810-645-0100.
Fax: 810-645-2430.
Macomb County Office: 50 Crocker Boulevard, Mount Clemens, Michigan.
Telephone: 810-468-4880.
Fax: 810-465-7159.
Kent County Office: 510 Grand Plaza Place, 220 Lyon Square, Grand Rapids, Michigan.
Telephone: 616-366-8600.
Fax: 616-786-9095.
Holland, Michigan Office: 1121 Ottawa Beach Road, Suite 140.
Telephone: 616-399-8600.
Fax: 616-786-9095.

Thomas P. Rockwell
James A. Sullivan
Michael M. Hathaway
John J. Lynch, III (Resident, Oakland County Office)
Thomas M. Peters
James K. Thome (Resident, Oakland County Office)
Cecil F. Boyle, Jr. (Resident, Oakland County Office)
Ronald L. Cornell (Resident, Macomb County Office)
William J. Heaphy (Kent County and Holland Offices)
Gary Alan Miller
William L. Kiriazis
Cynthia E. Merry
Dennis B. Cotter
Daniel P. Steele
Shelley K. Miller (Resident, Oakland County Office)
Terrance P. Lynch

OF COUNSEL

John M. Heaphy
Roy C. Hebert

Representative Clients: Aetna Casualty and Surety Co.; Bic Corp.; CNA Insurance Group; Travelers Insurance Co.; United States Aviation Underwriters; Goodyear Tire & Rubber Co.

For Complete List of Firm Personnel, See General Section

For full biographical listings, see the Martindale-Hubbell Law Directory

WISE & MARSAC, PROFESSIONAL CORPORATION (AV)

11th Floor Buhl Building, 48226-3681
Telephone: 313-962-0643
Telecopier: 313-962-0688
Cable: "DYWI-DET"
Telex: 810-221-5371
Ann Arbor, Michigan Office: 24 Frank Lloyd Wright Drive.
Telephone: 313-930-4405.
Birmingham, Michigan Office: 555 South Woodward, Suite 755.
Telephone: 810-642-4345.

(See Next Column)

John A. Wise
Robert A. Marsac
Stephen M. Fleming
Darrell M. Grams
Eric H. Lipsitt
John M. Pollock (Resident, Birmingham Office)
Edward V. Keelean
Guy P. Hoadley
Robert A. Feldman
James F. Kamp

OF COUNSEL

Louis J. Burnett (Resident, Birmingham Office)
Robert E. Day
Albert L. Lieberman
William D. Maroney (Not admitted in MI)
Elijah Poxson

Karen E. Bridges
Lisa A. Robinson
Gary A. Kendra
Howard M. Klausmeier
Scott A. Steinhoff (Resident, Birmingham Office)
Amy E. Anderson
Michael S. Thomas
Mark V. Heusel
Jerry L. Ashford

Representative Clients: Aon Corporation; BASF Corp.; Bell Atlantic TriCon Leasing Corp.; Camp, Dresser & McKee, Inc.; The Detroit Edison Co.; The Dow Chemical Co.; Seaboard Surety Co.; Suburban Communications Corp.; Texaco, Inc.; Union Carbide Corp.

For full biographical listings, see the Martindale-Hubbell Law Directory

ZEFF AND ZEFF, P.C. (AV)

The Zeff Building, 607 Shelby, 48226
Telephone: 313-962-3825
Fax: 313-962-6007

Louis Zeff (1896-1966)
A. Robert Zeff

Sheryl L. Berenbaum
Paul Broschay
Edward J. Kreski

For full biographical listings, see the Martindale-Hubbell Law Directory

EAST LANSING, Ingham Co.

FARHAT, STORY & KRAUS, P.C. (AV)

Beacon Place, 4572 South Hagadorn Road, Suite 3, 48823
Telephone: 517-351-3700
Fax: 517-332-4122

Leo A. Farhat
James E. Burns (1925-1979)
Monte R. Story
Richard C. Kraus
Max R. Hoffman Jr.
Chris A. Bergstrom
Kitty L. Groh
Charles R. Toy
David M. Platt

Lawrence P. Schweitzer
Jeffrey J. Short
Kathy A. Breedlove
Thomas L. Sparks

Representative Clients: Big L. Corp.; Michigan Automotive Wholesalers Association; Hartman-Fabco, Inc.; Lansing Electric Motors, Inc.; Mike Miller Lincoln Mercury; Edward Rose Realty, Inc.; Squires School and Commercial Sales; CBI Copy Products.
Reference: Capitol National Bank.

For full biographical listings, see the Martindale-Hubbell Law Directory

*ESCANABA,** Delta Co.

BUTCH, QUINN, ROSEMURGY, JARDIS, BUSH, BURKHART & STROM, P.C. (AV)

816 Ludington Street, 49829
Telephone: 906-786-4422
Fax: 906-786-5128
Gladstone, Michigan Office: 201 First National Bank Building.
Telephone: 906-428-3123.
Marquette, Michigan Office: 300 South Front Street.
Telephone: 906-228-4440.
Iron Mountain, Michigan Office: 500 South Stephenson Avenue.
Telephone: 906-774-4460.
Marinette, Wisconsin Office: 2008 Ella Court.
Telephone: 715-732-4154.

Robert S. Rosemurgy
Terrill S. Jardis
Allen S. Bush
Paul L. Strom
Steven C. Parks
Bonnie Lee Hoff

Representative Clients: Aetna Life & Casualty Co.; Transamerica Insurance Co.; Fireman's Fund Insurance Co.; United State Fidelity & Guaranty Co.; Liberty Mutual Insurance Co.; CNA Insurance Companies; Maryland Casualty Co.; Farm Bureau Insurance Co.; Michigan Hospital Association Mutual Insurance Co.; Farmers Insurance Co.

For Complete List of Firm Personnel, See General Section

For full biographical listings, see the Martindale-Hubbell Law Directory

FARMINGTON HILLS, Oakland Co.

COUZENS, LANSKY, FEALK, ELLIS, ROEDER & LAZAR, P.C. (AV)

33533 West Twelve Mile Road, Suite 150, P.O. Box 9057, 48333-9057
Telephone: 810-489-8600
Telecopier: 810-489-4156

Sheldon A. Fealk
Jerry M. Ellis
Bruce J. Lazar
Phillip L. Sternberg
Stephen Scapelliti
Mark S. Frankel

References: Comerica Bank-Southfield;
Representative Clients: Provided upon request.

For full biographical listings, see the Martindale-Hubbell Law Directory

MICHAEL H. GOLOB (AV)

30300 Northwestern Highway, Suite 300, 48334
Telephone: 810-855-2626
Fax: 810-932-4009

For full biographical listings, see the Martindale-Hubbell Law Directory

KAUFMAN AND PAYTON (AV)

200 Northwestern Financial Center, 30833 Northwestern Highway, 48334
Telephone: 810-626-5000
Telefacsimile: 810-626-2843
Grand Rapids, Michigan Office: 420 Trust Building.
Telephone: 616-459-4200.
Fax: 616-459-4929.
Traverse City, Michigan Office: 122 West State Street.
Telephone: 616-947-4050.
Fax: 616-947-7321.

Alan Jay Kaufman
Donald L. Payton
Kenneth C. Letherwood
Stephen R. Levine
Thomas L. Vitu
Ralph C. Chapa, Jr.
Raymond I. Foley, II
Jeffrey K. Van Hattum
Leo D. Neville

For full biographical listings, see the Martindale-Hubbell Law Directory

*FLINT,** Genesee Co.

DEAN, DEAN, SEGAR, HART & SHULMAN, P.C. (AV)

1616 Genesee Towers, One East First Street, 48502
Telephone: 810-235-5631
Fax: 810-235-8983

Max Dean
Robert L. Segar
Clifford H. Hart
Leonard B. Shulman

Representative Clients: Flint Industrial Sales & Equipment Co.; P&H Plumbing & Heating, Inc.; Genesee County Dental Society; City of Montrose; Royalite Electric Co.; King of All Manufacturing, Inc.; Executive Travel Service.
Local Counsel for: Auto Club Insurance Association; Newkirk Electric Co.
References: Genesee Merchants Bank & Trust Co.; Citizens Commercial & Savings Bank.

For Complete List of Firm Personnel, See General Section

For full biographical listings, see the Martindale-Hubbell Law Directory

GROVES, DECKER & WYATT, PROFESSIONAL CORPORATION (AV)

2357 Stone Bridge Drive, 48532
Telephone: 810-732-6920
Fax: 810-732-9015
East Lansing, Michigan Office: 2760 East Lansing Drive, Suite 4.
Telephone: 517-332-7715.
Facsimile: 517-332-4405.

Harvey R. Groves
Lee A. Decker
George H. Wyatt III
William L. Meuleman III
Thomas J. Ruth
Cameron D. Reddy

Representative Clients: American International Group; Ameritech; Crawford & Co.; General Motors Corp.; Hastings Mutual Insurance Co.; Kmart Corp.; Johnson Controls; MASCO Corp.; Weyerhauser Co.; Zurich Insurance Co.

For full biographical listings, see the Martindale-Hubbell Law Directory

LAW OFFICES OF PATRICK M. KIRBY A PROFESSIONAL CORPORATION (AV)

G1335 South Linden Road, Suite G, 48532
Telephone: 810-230-0833
Fax: 810-230-8222

Patrick M. Kirby

(See Next Column)

Todd O. Pope

Representative Clients: Brotherhood Mutual Insurance Co.; City of Flint; K&K Insurance Group; Merchants and Medical Credit Corp.; Nero Plastics; Rent-A-Center.

For full biographical listings, see the Martindale-Hubbell Law Directory

NEAL, NEAL & STEWART, P.C. (AV)

Old Elks Building, Suite 102, 142 West Second Street, 48502
Telephone: 1-810-767-8800
Fax: 810-767-8958

Jack Neal
Stephanie A. Neal
David M. Stewart

Wendy J. Maxfield
Warren A. Hampton
Richard R. Bachelder
Brian C. Titus

For full biographical listings, see the Martindale-Hubbell Law Directory

O'ROURKE & JOSEPH, P.C. (AV)

727 South Grand Traverse Street, 48502
Telephone: 810-239-3165
Fax: 810-239-5965

Edward P. Joseph (1927-1987)
Jerome F. O'Rourke

Reference: Citizens Commercial and Savings Bank.

For full biographical listings, see the Martindale-Hubbell Law Directory

WINEGARDEN, SHEDD, HALEY, LINDHOLM & ROBERTSON (AV)

501 Citizens Bank Building, 48502-1983
Telephone: 810-767-3600
Telecopier: 810-767-8776

MEMBERS OF FIRM

William C. Shedd
Dennis M. Haley
John T. Lindholm
L. David Lawson
John R. Tucker

ASSOCIATES

Alan F. Himelhoch
Suellen J. Parker
Damion Frasier
Peter T. Mooney

OF COUNSEL

Howard R. Grossman

Representative Clients: Citizens Commercial and Savings Bank; R.L. White Development Corporation; Interstate Traffic Consultants (Intracon) Inc.; Downtown Development Authority of Flint; Young Olds-Cadillac, Inc.; First American Title Insurance Co.; Sorensen Gross Construction Co.; Genesee County; Insight, Inc..; Flint Counsel, National Bank of Detroit.

For Complete List of Firm Personnel, See General Section

For full biographical listings, see the Martindale-Hubbell Law Directory

*GAYLORD,** Otsego Co.

BENSINGER, COTANT, MENKES & AARDEMA, P.C. (AV)

308 West Main Street, P.O. Box 1000, 49735
Telephone: 517-732-7536
Fax: 517-732-4922
Grand Rapids, Michigan Office: 983 Spaulding Avenue, S.E.
Telephone: 616-949-7963.
Fax: 616-949-5264.
Marquette, Michigan Office: 122 West Bluff.
Telephone: 906-225-1000.
Fax: 906-225-0818.

Richard G. Bensinger
James C. Cotant
Michael E. Menkes
Patrick J. Michaels
James F. Pagels
Steven C. Byram
Michael J. Harrelson
William M. Fury
Brian P. McMahon

Representative Clients: Accident Fund of Michigan; Auto-Owner Insurance Co.; Citizens/Hanover Insurance Co.; Farm Bureau Mutual Insurance Co.; Employers Reinsurance Co,; Lake State Mutual Insurance Co.; Michigan Hospital Association; Michigan Licensed Beverage Association; Physicians Insurance Co. of Michigan; State Farm Mutual Insurance Co.

For full biographical listings, see the Martindale-Hubbell Law Directory

*GRAND RAPIDS,** Kent Co.

ALLABEN, MASSIE, VANDER WEYDEN & TIMMER (AV)

Suite 850, Commerce Building, 5 Lyon Street, N.W., 49503
Telephone: 616-774-2182
Fax: 616-774-0602

MEMBERS OF FIRM

Fred Roland Allaben (1901-1985)
Sam F. Massie, Jr.
Keith A. Vander Weyden
John J. Timmer
Robert W. Bandeen

(See Next Column)

ALLABEN, MASSIE, VANDER WEYDEN & TIMMER—*Continued*

Representative Clients: Auto Club Insurance Association; American States Insurance Co.; Michigan Mutual Liability Co.; Fidelity & Casualty Company of New York; U.S. Aircraft Insurance Group; Security Mutual Casualty Co.; Nationwide Mutual Insurance Co.; Security Mutual Casualty Co.; Nationwide Mutual Insurance Co.; Union Insurance Co.

For Complete List of Firm Personnel, See General Section

For full biographical listings, see the Martindale-Hubbell Law Directory

BORRE, PETERSON, FOWLER & REENS, P.C. (AV)

The Philo C. Fuller House, 44 Lafayette, N.E., P.O. Box 1767, 49501-1767
Telephone: 616-459-1971
FAX: 616-459-2393

Glen V. Borre
James B. Peterson
Ben A. Fowler
William C. Reens
Frank H. Johnson
Mark D. Sevald
William R. Vander Sluis
William G. Krupar

Reference: Old Kent Bank & Trust Co.

For full biographical listings, see the Martindale-Hubbell Law Directory

BREMER, WADE, NELSON, LOHR & COREY (AV)

600 Three Mile Road, N.W., 49504-1601
Telephone: 616-784-4434
Fax: 616-784-7322

MEMBERS OF FIRM

William M. Bremer
Michael D. Wade
Phillip J. Nelson
James H. Lohr
Michael J. Corey

ASSOCIATES

Michael S. Dantuma
J. Mark Cooney
Cheryl L. Bart
Barbara L. Olafsson

LEGAL SUPPORT PERSONNEL

Kathleen A. Fitzpatrick

For full biographical listings, see the Martindale-Hubbell Law Directory

BUCHANAN & BOS (AV)

300 Ottawa N.W., Suite 800, 49503
Telephone: 616-458-1224
Fax: 616-458-0608

MEMBERS OF FIRM

John C. Buchanan
Carole D. Bos
Bradley K. Glazier
Lee T. Silver

ASSOCIATES

Raymond S. Kent
Jane M. Beckering
Richard A. Stevens
Susan Wilson Keener
Gwen E. Buday
Anne M. Frye
Brian K. Lawson
Nancy K. Haynes

Representative Clients: Baker Book House Co.; Chrysler Corp.; Cigna Group of Insurance Companies (INA); Clark Equipment Co.; Colt's Manufacturing Company, Inc. (National Defense Counsel); Commercial Union Insurance Companies; Corning Glass; Cranford Insurance; Excam, Inc.; F.I.E. Corp.

For full biographical listings, see the Martindale-Hubbell Law Directory

CHOLETTE, PERKINS & BUCHANAN (AV)

900 Campau Square Plaza Building, 99 Monroe Avenue, N.W., 49503
Telephone: 616-774-2131
Fax: 616-774-7016

MEMBERS OF FIRM

Calvin R. Danhof
Frederick W. Bleakley
Reynolds A. Brander, Jr.
Bruce M. Bieneman
William J. Warren
Donald C. Exelby
Thomas H. Cypher
William A. Brengle
Alfred J. Parent
Charles H. Worsfold
Michael P. McCasey
Marc A. Kidder
Michael C. Mysliwiec
Evan L. MacFarlane
John A. Quinn
Albert J. Engel, III
Stephen C. Oldstrom
William E. McDonald, Jr.
Mark E. Fatum
Richard K. Grover, Jr.
David J. DeGraw

ASSOCIATES

Kenneth L. Block
William J. Yob
Robert E. Attmore
Martin W. Buschle
Miles J. Murphy, III
Martha P. Forman
Kathrine M. West
Robert A. Kamp

Counsel for: Aetna Casualty & Surety Co.; Argonaut Insurance Co.; Auto-Owners Insurance Co.; Employers Mutual; Liberty Mutual Insurance Co.; Sentry Group; State Farm Insurance; Eastern Aviation and Marine Underwriters; Home Insurance Co.; Nationwide Insurance.

For Complete List of Firm Personnel, See General Section

For full biographical listings, see the Martindale-Hubbell Law Directory

CLARY, NANTZ, WOOD, HOFFIUS, RANKIN & COOPER (AV)

500 Calder Plaza, 250 Monroe Avenue, N.W., 49503-2244
Telephone: 616-459-9487
Telecopier: 616-459-5121

MEMBERS OF FIRM

Jack R. Clary
Philip W. Nantz
Philip F. Wood
Leonard M. Hoffius
Robert P. Cooper
Robert L. DeJong
Richard A. Wendt
Stephen J. Mulder
Leo H. Litowich
Harold E. Nelson
Stanley J. Stek
John H. Gretzinger
Edward J. Inman
Daniel R. Kubiak
Scott G. Smith
Mark R. Smith
Marshall W. Grate
Steven K. Girard
Jeffrey VanHorne Sluggett

OF COUNSEL

Richard J. Rankin, Jr.

ASSOCIATES

Mark D. Pakkala
Dale R. Rietberg
Douglas H. Wiegerink
Jack C. Clary
Sandra S. Hamilton
Peter H. Peterson
Thomas J. Dempsey (Not admitted in MI)
Philip G. Henderson
Fred J. Posont
Michael J. Distel
Terry E. Tobias
Kathryn Kraus Nunzio

Representative Clients: United Bank of Michigan; FMB First Michigan Bank-Grand Rapids; Goodrich Theatres & Radio, Inc.; S. Abraham & Sons, Inc.; Garb-Ko, Inc., d/b/a 7-Eleven; Weather Shield Manufacturing Co.; JET Electronics & Technology, Inc.; Westinghouse Credit Corp.

For Complete List of Firm Personnel, See General Section

For full biographical listings, see the Martindale-Hubbell Law Directory

DAY & SAWDEY, A PROFESSIONAL CORPORATION (AV)

200 Monroe Avenue, Suite 500, 49503-2217
Telephone: 616-774-8121
Telefax: 616-774-0168

George B. Kingston (1889-1965)
John R. Porter (1915-1975)
Charles E. Day, Jr.
Robert W. Sawdey
William A. Hubble
C. Mark Stoppels
James B. Frakie
Larry A. Ver Merris
John Boyko, Jr.
Jonathan F. Thoits
John T. Piggins
Thomas A. DeMeester

John G. Grzybek
Theodore E. Czarnecki

Representative Clients: Blodgett Construction and Home Improvement Co.; C.M.S.-North America, Inc.; Heath Mfg. Co.; Heller Financial, Inc.; Michigan National Bank; National Westminster Bank, U.S.A.; Old Kent Bank and Trust Co.; Zurn Industries.

For full biographical listings, see the Martindale-Hubbell Law Directory

FARR & OOSTERHOUSE (AV)

Suite 400, Ledyard Building, 125 Ottawa Avenue, N.W., 49503
Telephone: 616-459-3355
Fax: 616-235-3350

MEMBERS OF FIRM

William S. Farr
Kenneth R. Oosterhouse
Joel E. Krissoff
John R. Oostema
Charles E. Chamberlain, Jr.

ASSOCIATE

Michelene B. Pattee

Representative Clients: Aetna Casualty & Surety Co.; Alliance Group Insurance Co.; Citizens Insurance Company of America; Grand Rapids Community College; Hartford Insurance Co.; J. W. Messner, Inc.; Michigan Lawyers Mutual Insurance Co.; K-Mart Corp.; New England Insurance co.; VASA North Atlantic Insurance Co.; General Star Indemnity Co.; Select Insured Risk Services.

For full biographical listings, see the Martindale-Hubbell Law Directory

GRUEL, MILLS, NIMS AND PYLMAN (AV)

50 Monroe Place, Suite 700 West, 49503
Telephone: 616-235-5500
Fax: 616-235-5550

MEMBERS OF FIRM

Grant J. Gruel
William F. Mills
J. Clarke Nims
Norman H. Pylman, II
Scott R. Melton
Brion J. Brooks
Thomas R. Behm
J. Paul Janes

Representative Clients: Aquinas College; Bell Helmet Co.; Blodgett Memorial Medical Center; Butterworth Hospital; Chem Central, Inc.; Cook Pump Co.; Grove, Inc.; NBDC; Heim Corp.

For full biographical listings, see the Martindale-Hubbell Law Directory

Grand Rapids—Continued

LINSEY, STRAIN & WORSFOLD, P.C. (AV)

1200 Michigan National Bank Building, 77 Monroe Center, N.W., 49503
Telephone: 616-456-1661
Fax: 616-456-5027

Dale M. Strain
Alan R. Smith
Patrick D. Murphy
Larry D. Vander Wal
David J. Buter
Peter D. Bosch

Joseph P. Vander Veen
William D. Howard
Kurt R. Killman

Representative Clients: American States Insurance Co.; TransAmerica Insurance Co.; Auto Owners Insurance Co.; Ohio Casualty Insurance Co.; West American Insurance Co.; Fremont Mutual Insurance Co.; American Home Insurance Co.; American Intl. Adjustment Cos.; Lincoln Mutual Insurance Co.; Royal Indemnity Insurance Co.

For full biographical listings, see the Martindale-Hubbell Law Directory

ROBERTS, BETZ & BLOSS, P.C. (AV)

555 Riverfront Plaza Building, 55 Campau, 49503
Telephone: 616-235-9955
Telecopier: 616-235-0404

Michael J. Roberts
Michael W. Betz
David J. Bloss
Gregory A. Block
Michael T. Small
Ralph M. Reisinger
Elena C. Cardenas
Henry S. Emrich

For full biographical listings, see the Martindale-Hubbell Law Directory

SMITH, HAUGHEY, RICE & ROEGGE, P.C. (AV)

200 Calder Plaza Building, 250 Monroe Avenue, N.W., 49503-2251
Telephone: 616-774-8000
Telecopier: 616-774-2461
East Lansing, Michigan Office: 1301 North Hagadorn, 48823-2320.
Telephone: 517-332-3030.
Telecopier: 517-332-3468.
Traverse City, Michigan Office: 241 East State Street, P.O. Box 848, 49685-0804.
Telephone: 616-929-4878.
Telecopier: 616-929-4182.

Clifford A. Mitts (1902-1962)
Laurence D. Smith (1913-1980)
Robert V.V. Rice (1899-1982)
Michael S. Barnes (1944-1989)
L. Roland Roegge
Thomas F. Blackwell
P. Laurence Mulvihill
Lawrence P. Mulligan
Thomas R. Tasker
Paul H. Reinhardt
Lance R. Mather
Charles F. Behler
Gary A. Rowe
William W. Jack, Jr.
William J. Hondorp
Thomas M. Weibel
James G. Black
E. Thomas Mc Carthy, Jr.
Glenn W. House, Jr.
Thomas R. Wurst
Craig R. Noland
Paul M. Oleniczak
Craig S. Neckers
Thomas E. Kent
Leonard M. Hickey
David N. Campos
Anthony J. Quarto
Bruce P. Rissi
John C. O'Loughlin
John M. Kruis
Paul G. Van Oostenburg
Dale Ann Iverson
William R. Jewell
Jon D. Vander Ploeg
Patrick F. Geary
Terence J. Ackert
Brian J. Kilbane
Dan C. Porter
Brian J. Plachta
Phillip K. Mowers
Carol D. Carlson

Kay L. Griffith Hammond
Ann M. Stuursma
Richard E. Holmes, Jr.
Marilyn S. Nickell
Christopher R. Genther
Beth Suzanne Kromer
Lois Marie Ens
Paul D. Fox
Robert M. Kruse
Harriet M. Hageman
John B. Combs
Aileen M. Simet
Scott W. Morgan
Matthew L. Meyer
Bret M. Hanna
Carine J. Joachim
Todd W. Millar
Elizabeth Roberts VerHey
Jennifer Jane Nasser

OF COUNSEL

A. B. Smith, Jr.
David O. Haughey
Susan Bradley Jakubowski
Thomas P. Scholler

Representative Clients: Chevron; Cincinnati Insurance Co.; General Motors Corp.; Kemper Insurance Group; Michigan Hospital Assn.; Navistar International; St. Paul Insurance Cos.; Steelcase, Inc.; Sears Roebuck & Co.; Dow Elanco.

For full biographical listings, see the Martindale-Hubbell Law Directory

PETER W. STEKETEE (AV)

660 Cascade West Parkway, S.E., Suite 65, 49546
Telephone: 616-949-6551
Fax: 616-949-8817

For full biographical listings, see the Martindale-Hubbell Law Directory

TOLLEY, VANDENBOSCH & WALTON, P.C. (AV)

5650 Foremost Drive, S.E., 49546
Telephone: 616-942-8090
Facsimile: 616-942-4677

Peter R. Tolley
Lynwood P. VandenBosch
Michael C. Walton
Lawrence Korolewicz
Todd R. Dickinson
Paul L. Nelson
David A. Malson, Jr.
James B. Doezema
David L. Harrison
Richard J. Durden
Robert C. Greene
Miles J. Postema
James K. Schepers
Susan Jasper Stein
Mark J. Colon
Mark A. VandenBosch
Robert J. Nolan
Scott H. Hogan

Representative Clients: Brunswick Corp.; Citadel Corp.; Meijer, Inc.; Ford Consumer Finance; Gordon Food Service; First Michigan Bank; Society Bank; State Farm Insurance Co.; Sentry Insurance Co.; Fremont Mutual Insurance Co.

For full biographical listings, see the Martindale-Hubbell Law Directory

VARNUM, RIDDERING, SCHMIDT & HOWLETT (AV)

Bridgewater Place, P.O. Box 352, 49501-0352
Telephone: 616-336-6000
800-262-0011
Facsimile: 616-336-7000
Telex: 1561593 VARN
Lansing, Michigan Office: The Victor Center, Suite 810, 210 North Washington Square, 48933.
Telephone: 517-482-6237.
Facsimile: 517-482-6937.
Kalamazoo, Michigan Office: 350 East Michigan Avenue, 49007.
Telephone: 616-382-2300.
Facsimile: 616-382-2382.
Grand Haven, Michigan Office: 321 Washington Street, P.O. Box 288, 49417.
Telephone: 616-846-7100.
Facsimile: 616-846-7101.
Battle Creek, Michigan Office: 4950 West Dickman Road, Suite B-1, 49015.
Telephone: 616-962-7144.
Detroit, Michigan Office: 440 East Congress, Fourth Floor, 48226.
Telephone: 313-961-1600.
Facsimile: 313-961-1636.

COUNSEL

Terrance R. Bacon

MEMBERS OF FIRM

Peter Armstrong
Robert J. Eleveld
Thomas J. Mulder
Richard A. Kay
Bruce A. Barnhart
Peter A. Smit
Bruce G. Hudson (Resident at Lansing Office)
Teresa S. Decker
William E. Rohn
Jeffrey D. Smith (Resident at Kalamazoo Office)
Stephen P. Afendoulis
Perrin Rynders
Mark S. Allard
Timothy E. Eagle
Michael S. McElwee (Resident at Kalamazoo Office)
Jacqueline D. Scott
N. Stevenson Jennette III
Elizabeth Joy Fossel

ASSOCIATES

Jeffery S. Crampton
Ronald G. DeWaard
Eric J. Guerin (Kalamazoo Office)
Kevin Abraham Rynbrandt
Thomas J. Augspurger
Michael X. Hidalgo
Jon M. Bylsma

Representative Clients: Celotex Corporation; Foremost Insurance Co.; Alvey Corporation; Progressive Engineering.

For Complete List of Firm Personnel, See General Section

For full biographical listings, see the Martindale-Hubbell Law Directory

WARNER, NORCROSS & JUDD (AV)

900 Old Kent Building, 111 Lyon Street, N.W., 49503-2489
Telephone: 616-752-2000
Fax: 616-752-2500
Muskegon, Michigan Office: 400 Terrace Plaza, P.O. Box 900.
Telephone: 616-727-2600.
Fax: 616-727-2699.
Holland, Michigan Office: Curtis Center, Suite 300, 170 College Avenue.
Telephone: 616-396-9800.
Fax: 616-396-3656.

(See Next Column)

WARNER, NORCROSS & JUDD—*Continued*

MEMBERS OF FIRM

Charles E. McCallum
John D. Tully
William K. Holmes
Roger M. Clark
John H. Logie
Jack B. Combs
Peter L. Gustafson
J. A. Cragwall, Jr.
Eugene E. Smary
Douglas E. Wagner
Jeffrey O. Birkhold
Paul T. Sorensen
Rodney D. Martin
F. William McKee
Louis C. Rabaut
Douglas A. Dozeman
Stephen B. Grow
Daniel R. Gravelyn
Robert J. Jonker
Devin S. Schindler

ASSOCIATES

Valerie Pierre Simmons
James Moskal
Robert J. Buchanan
Kenneth W. Vermeulen
Mark R. Lange
Jeffrey A. Ott

General Counsel for: Bissell Inc.; Blodgett Memorial Medical Center; Guardsman Products, Inc.; Haworth, Inc.; Kysor Industrial Corp.; Michigan Bankers Assn.; Old Kent Financial Corp.; Steelcase Inc.; Wolverine World Wide, Inc.

For Complete List of Firm Personnel, See General Section

For full biographical listings, see the Martindale-Hubbell Law Directory

WHEELER UPHAM, A PROFESSIONAL CORPORATION (AV)

Second Floor, Trust Building, 40 Pearl Street, N.W., 49503
Telephone: 616-459-7100
Fax: 616-459-6366

Gordon B. Wheeler (1904-1986)
Buford A. Upham (Retired)
Robert H. Gillette
Geoffrey L. Gillis
John M. Roels
Gary A. Maximiuk
Timothy J. Orlebeke
Kenneth E. Tiews
Jack L. Hoffman
Janet C. Baxter
Peter Kladder, III
James M. Shade
Thomas A. Kuiper

Counsel for: Travelers Insurance Co.; Prudential Insurance Co. of America; Farmers Insurance Group; Metropolitan Life Insurance Co.; Conrail Trans.; Monsanto Co.; Firestone Tire & Rubber Co.; Navistar, Inc.; Medtronic, Inc.; Westdale Better Homes and Gardens.

For full biographical listings, see the Martindale-Hubbell Law Directory

GROSSE POINTE WOODS, Wayne Co.

BARBIER & BARBIER, P.C. (AV)

19251 Mack Avenue, Suite 200, 48236-2800
Telephone: 313-882-9500
Fax: 313-882-0919

Ralph W. Barbier, Jr.
Tara J. Hanley

For full biographical listings, see the Martindale-Hubbell Law Directory

HANCOCK, Houghton Co.

WISTI & JAASKELAINEN, P.C. (AV)

101 Quincy Street, 49930
Telephone: 906-482-5220
Iron Mountain, Michigan Office: 623 Stephenson Avenue.
Telephone: 906-779-1280.
Marquette, Michigan Office: 117 South Front Street.
Telephone: 906-228-8204.

Andrew H. Wisti
Mark Wisti
Daniel J. Wisti

David M. Gemignani

OF COUNSEL

Gordon J. Jaaskelainen

References: Superior National Bank & Trust Company of Hancock, Michigan; Houghton National Bank, Houghton, Michigan.

For full biographical listings, see the Martindale-Hubbell Law Directory

*HOWELL,** Livingston Co.

PETER B. VAN WINKLE, P.C. (AV)

105 East Grand River, 48843
Telephone: 517-546-2680

William P. Van Winkle (1858-1920)
Don W. Van Winkle (1887-1971)
Charles K. Van Winkle (Retired)
Peter B. Van Winkle

Reference: First National Bank in Howell, Howell, Mich.

For full biographical listings, see the Martindale-Hubbell Law Directory

*KALAMAZOO,** Kalamazoo Co.

DIETRICH, ZODY, HOWARD & VANDERROEST, P.C. (AV)

834 King Highway, Suite 110, 49001
Telephone: 616-344-9236
Fax: 616-344-0412

G. Philip Dietrich
Richard J. Howard
James W. Smith
James E. VanderRoest
Brenda Wheeler Zody

Barbara S. Weintraub

Representative Clients: Amplimedical S.P.A.; Arvco Container Corp; Consolidated Rail Corporation; Day's Molding & Machinery, Inc.; The Deaccelerator Corp.; Do-It Corp.; Engineered Stadium Systems, Inc.; Langeland Memorial Chapel, Inc.; Jonan, Ltd.; Partnership; Trinity Development Corp.

For full biographical listings, see the Martindale-Hubbell Law Directory

HOWARD & HOWARD ATTORNEYS, P.C. (AV)

The Kalamazoo Building, Suite 400, 107 West Michigan Avenue, 49007-3956
Telephone: 616-382-1483
Telecopier: 616-382-1568
Bloomfield Hills, Michigan Office: The Pinehurst Office Center, Suite 101, 1400 North Woodward Avenue.
Telephone: 810-645-1483.
Telecopier: 810-645-1568.
Lansing, Michigan Office: The Phoenix Building, Suite 500, 222 Washington Square North.
Telephone: 517-485-1483.
Telecopier: 517-485-1568.
Peoria, Illinois Office: Howard & Howard, P.C., The Creve Coeur Building, Suite 200, 321 Liberty Street.
Telephone: 309-672-1483.
Telecopier: 309-672-1568.

John W. Allen
Robert C. Beck
James H. Geary
Myra L. Willis

Representative Clients: First of America Bank Corp.; Simpson Paper Company; W.R. Grace & Co.; Stryker Corp.; Kalamazoo Valley Community College.
Local Counsel for: Chrysler Motors Corp.
International Counsel for: Sony Corp.

For Complete List of Firm Personnel, See General Section

For full biographical listings, see the Martindale-Hubbell Law Directory

KREIS, ENDERLE, CALLANDER & HUDGINS, A PROFESSIONAL CORPORATION (AV)

One Moorsbridge, 49002
Telephone: 616-324-3000
Telecopier: 616-324-3010

Douglas L. Callander
Jeffrey C. O'Brien
Stephen J. Hessen
Thomas G. King
Raymond C. Schultz
Jeffrey D. Swenarton
Julie A. Sullivan

For Complete List of Firm Personnel, See General Section

For full biographical listings, see the Martindale-Hubbell Law Directory

LILLY & LILLY, P.C. (AV)

505 South Park Street, 49007
Telephone: 616-381-7763
Fax: 616-344-6880

Charles M. Lilly (1990-1903)
Terrence J. Lilly

For full biographical listings, see the Martindale-Hubbell Law Directory

MILLER, CANFIELD, PADDOCK AND STONE, P.L.C. (AV)

A Professional Limited Liability Company
Founded in 1852 by Sidney Davy Miller
444 West Michigan Avenue, 49007-3752
Telephone: 616-381-7030
Fax: 616-382-0244
Detroit, Michigan Office: 150 West Jefferson, Suite 2500, 48226-4415.
Telephone: 313-963-6420.
Fax: 313-496-7500.
Cable Address: "Stem Detroit."
Ann Arbor, Michigan Office: 101 North Main Street, 7th Floor, 48104-1400.
Telephone: 313-663-2445.
Fax: 313-747-7147.
Bloomfield Hills, Michigan Office: Suite 100, Pinehurst Office Center, 1400 North Woodward, 48303-2014.
Telephone: 313-645-5000.
Fax: 313-645-1917.

(See Next Column)

MILLER, CANFIELD, PADDOCK AND STONE P.L.C., *Kalamazoo—Continued*

Grand Rapids, Michigan Office: 1200 Campau Square Plaza, 99 Monroe, N.W., 49503-2639.
Telephone: 616-454-8656.
Fax: 616-776-6322.
Howell, Michigan Office: 121 South Barnard Street, Suite 4, 48843-2305.
Telephone: 517-546-7600.
Telecopier: 517-546-6974.
Lansing, Michigan Office: One Michigan Avenue, Suite 900, 48933-1609.
Telephone: 517-487-2070.
Fax: 517-374-6304.
Monroe, Michigan Office: The Executive Centre, 214 East Elm Avenue, 48161-2682.
Telephone: 313-243-2000.
Fax: 313-243-0901.
Washington, D.C. Office: 1225 Nineteenth Street, N.W., Suite 400. 20036.
Telephone: 202-429-5575; 785-0600.
Fax: 202-331-1118; 785-1234.
Pensacola, Florida Office: 25 West Cedar, 32501.
Telephone: 904-469-1088.
Fax: 904-432-0677.
St. Petersburg, Florida Office: 100 Second Avenue S., Suite 7045,33701.
Telephone: 813-982-6000.
Fax: 813-892-6002.
Gdansk, Poland Office: Suite 322, Dom Technika Building, Ul. Rajska 6, 80-850.
Telephone: 011-485-831-2808.
Fax: 011-485-831-4719.
Warsaw, Poland Office: Ul. Marszalkowska 82, Suite 561, 00-517.
Telephone: 011-482-623-6457 and 6458.
Fax: 011-482-623-6459.

MEMBERS OF FIRM

Eric V. Brown, Jr. (Resident)
James G. Vantine, Jr. (Resident)
James E. Spurr (Resident)

RESIDENT ASSOCIATE

Ballard Jay Yelton, III

Representative Firm Clients: Chrysler Corp.; Comerica, Inc.; City of Detroit, Mich.; Detroit Tigers, Inc.; First of Michigan; Fretter, Inc.; Ford Motor Co.; Ford Motor Credit Co.; Great Lakes Bancorp; Henry Ford Hospital.

For Complete List of Firm Personnel, See General Section

For full biographical listings, see the Martindale-Hubbell Law Directory

LANSING, Ingham Co.

* indicates certain Bar Register subscribers whose principal office is located elsewhere in the state and who have arranged for representation as a part of the state capital listings that follow

CHURCH, KRITSELIS, WYBLE & ROBINSON, P.C. (AV)

3939 Capital City Boulevard, 48906-9962
Telephone: 517-323-4770

William N. Kritselis
J. Richard Robinson
James T. Heos
David S. Mittleman

D. Michael Dudley
Catherine Groll
James M. Hofer

For full biographical listings, see the Martindale-Hubbell Law Directory

DENFIELD, TIMMER, JAMO & O'LEARY (AV)

521 Seymour Avenue, 48933
Telephone: 517-371-3500
Fax: 517-371-4514

George H. Denfield
James A. Timmer
James S. Jamo
James S. O'Leary
Kathleen A. Lopilato

Representative Clients: Auto-Owners Insurance Co.; National Indemnity Insurance Co.; Pennsylvania Insurance Co.; Travelers Insurance Co.; Ohio Farmers Insurance Co.; Bankers Life & Casualty Co.; Western Casualty & Surety Co.; Indiana Insurance Group; Western Surety Co.; United States Aviation Underwriters, Inc.

For full biographical listings, see the Martindale-Hubbell Law Directory

DUNNINGS & FRAWLEY, P.C. (AV)

Duncan Building, 530 South Pine Street, 48933-2299
Telephone: 517-487-8222
Fax: 517-487-2026

Stuart J. Dunnings, Jr.
John J. Frawley

Stuart J. Dunnings, III
Steven D. Dunnings

Representative Clients: Lansing Board of Education; Lansing Housing Commission; Ford Motor Co.

(See Next Column)

References: First of America; Michigan National Bank.

For full biographical listings, see the Martindale-Hubbell Law Directory

FOSTER, SWIFT, COLLINS & SMITH, P.C. (AV)

313 South Washington Square, 48933-2193
Telephone: 517-371-8100
Telecopier: 517-371-8200
Farmington Hills, Michigan Office: 32300 Northwestern Highway, Suite 230.
Telephone: 810-851-7500.
Fax: 810-851-7504.

Theodore W. Swift
John L. Collins
William K. Fahey
Stephen O. Schultz
William R. Schulz
David H. Aldrich
Scott A. Storey
Charles A. Janssen
Charles E. Barbieri
James B. Jensen, Jr.
Scott L. Mandel
James B. Croom
Michael D. Sanders
David J. Houston
Frank A. Fleischmann
Kevin T. McGraw
Michael J. Bommarito
Brian G. Goodenough
Robert L. Knechtel

LEGAL SUPPORT PERSONNEL

LEGAL ASSISTANTS

Laurie A. Delaney
Nancy O'Shea
Theresa G. Solberg

General Counsel: First of America Bank - Central; Michigan Milk Producers Assn.; Story, Inc.; Edward W. Sparrow Hospital; St. Lawrence Hospital; Michigan Financial Corp.; The State Journal; Peninsular Products; Demmer Corp.; Spartan Motors; North Community Health Care.

For Complete List of Firm Personnel, See General Section

For full biographical listings, see the Martindale-Hubbell Law Directory

FRASER TREBILCOCK DAVIS & FOSTER, P.C. (AV)

1000 Michigan National Tower, 48933
Telephone: 517-482-5800
Fax: 517-482-0887
Okemos, Michigan Office: 2188 Commons Parkway.
Telephone: 517-349-1300.
Fax: 517-349-0922.

Ronald R. Pentecost
Peter L. Dunlap
Michael E. Cavanaugh
C. Mark Hoover
Ronald R. Sutton
Brett Jon Bean
Gary C. Rogers
Mark A. Bush
Michael H. Perry

Mark R. Fox
Michael S. Ashton
Michael James Reilly
Patrick K. Thornton
Charyn K. Hain
Michael J. Laramie

Counsel for: Amtrak; Auto Club Insurance Assn. (A.A.A.); Auto Owners Insurance Co.; Farm Bureau, Inc.; Federated Insurance Co.; State Farm Insurance Companies.

For Complete List of Firm Personnel, See General Section

For full biographical listings, see the Martindale-Hubbell Law Directory

* HONIGMAN MILLER SCHWARTZ AND COHN (AV)

A Partnership including Professional Corporations
222 North Washington Square, Suite 400, 48933
Telephone: 517-484-8282
Telecopier: 517-484-8286
Detroit, Michigan Office: 2290 First National Building.
Telephone: 313-256-7800.
West Palm Beach, Florida Office: Suite 800 Esperante Building, 222 Lakeview Avenue.
Telephone: 407-838-4500.
Tampa, Florida Office: Suite 350 One Harbour Place, 777 South Harbour Island Boulevard.
Telephone: 813-221-6600.
Orlando, Florida Office: 390 North Orange Avenue, Suite 1300.
Telephone: 407-648-0300.
Houston, Texas Office: 3100 First Interstate Bank Plaza, 1000 Louisiana.
Telephone: 713-650-2600.
Los Angeles, California Office: McNeill Plaza, Suite 820, 15260 Ventura Boulevard, 91403.
Telephone: 818-784-2900.

MEMBERS

Richard J. Aaron
Frederick M. Baker, Jr.
Sandra L. Jasinski
Timothy Sawyer Knowlton
Mark Morton
John D. Pirich
Gary A. Trepod
William C. Whitbeck
Ruth E. Zimmerman

(See Next Column)

HONIGMAN MILLER SCHWARTZ AND COHN—*Continued*

ASSOCIATES

Ann L. Andrews — Andrea Hansen

Representative Clients: American Society of Composers, Authors and Publishers (ASCAP); Garb-Ko, Inc. (7-Eleven Stores); Granger Land Development Co.; Greater Detroit Resource Recovery Authority; Lawyers Title Insurance Company; Michigan Bell Telephone Co.; Michigan Gas Utilities, a division of UtiliCorp United, Inc.; Michigan Hospital Association; ThornApple Valley, Inc.

For Complete List of Firm Personnel, See General Section

For full biographical listings, see the Martindale-Hubbell Law Directory

HOWARD & HOWARD ATTORNEYS, P.C. (AV)

The Phoenix Building, Suite 500, 222 Washington Square, North, 48933-1817
Telephone: 517-485-1483
Telecopier: 517-485-1568
Kalamazoo, Michigan Office: The Kalamazoo Building, Suite 400, 107 West Michigan Avenue.
Telephone: 616-382-1483.
Telecopier: 616-382-1568.
Bloomfield Hills, Michigan Office: The Pinehurst Office Center, Suite 101, 1400 North Woodward Avenue.
Telephone: 810-645-1483.
Telecopier: 810-645-1568.
Peoria, Illinois Office: Howard & Howard, P.C., The Creve Coeur Building, Suite 200, 321 Liberty Street.
Telephone: 309-672-1483.
Telecopier: 309-672-1568.

David C. Coey
Matthew J. Coffey
Thomas L. Cooper
Patrick D. Hanes
Ellen M. Harvath
James E. Lozier

Representative Clients: First of America Bank Corporation; W.R. Grace & Co.; Chrysler Corp.; Indian Head Industries; Cooper & Lybrand; United Technologies.
Local Counsel for: General Motors Corp.; American Cyanamid Co.

For Complete List of Firm Personnel, See General Section

For full biographical listings, see the Martindale-Hubbell Law Directory

HUBBARD, FOX, THOMAS, WHITE & BENGTSON, P.C. (AV)

5801 West Michigan Avenue, 48917
Telephone: 517-886-7176
Fax: 517-886-1080

Jonathon R. White
Thomas A. Bengtson
Michael G. Woodworth
Donald B. Lawrence, Jr.
Harold Kirby Albright
Peter A. Teholiz
Geoffrey H. Seidlein
Ryan M. Wilson
Bruce W. Brown
Mark W. Geschwendt
Thomas L. Lapka
Janice K. Cunningham
Joseph M. Stewart
Mark E. Hills
William R. Thiel

OF COUNSEL

Allison K. Thomas

General Counsel for: Adams Outdoor Advertising Co.; Farm Credit Services of Michigan's Heartland; Lansing Community Credit Union; Midwest Business Corp.; Mooney Oil Corp.
Local Counsel for: Equitable Life Assurance Society of the United States, FCB.
Reference: First of America Bank-Central; Michigan National Bank.

For full biographical listings, see the Martindale-Hubbell Law Directory

RAYMOND JOSEPH (AV)

1602 Michigan National Tower, 48933
Telephone: 517-372-4410
Fax: 517-372-2137

OF COUNSEL

George R. Sidwell (1899-1983)
Michael Bowman
Bruce C. Blanton

Representative Clients: Ashland Oil, Inc.; Complete Auto Transit, Inc.; Employers Insurance of Wausau; Evans Products Co.; Grain Dealers Mutl.; Harbor Insurance Co.; Interstate Motor Freight System; Lansing Symphony Assn., Inc.; RCA Service Co.; West American Insurance Co.

For full biographical listings, see the Martindale-Hubbell Law Directory

STREET & GRUA (AV)

2401 East Grand River, 48912
Telephone: 517-487-8300
Fax: 517-487-8306

(See Next Column)

MEMBERS OF FIRM

Victor C. Anderson (1904-1981)
Cassius E. Street, Jr.
Remo Mark Grua

Representative Clients: Applegate Insulation Manufacturing; General Aviation, Inc.; Classic Aircraft Corp.; General White GMC; Old Kent Bank of Lansing.
References: First of America-Central; Old Kent Bank of Lansing, N.A.

For full biographical listings, see the Martindale-Hubbell Law Directory

*MARQUETTE,** Marquette Co.

WEBER, SWANSON & DETTMANN (AV)

Marquette Professional Building, 148 West Washington Street, 49855
Telephone: 906-228-7355
Fax: 906-228-7357

MEMBERS OF FIRM

John R. Weber
Keith E. Swanson
Darrell R. Dettmann

Representative Clients: Kemper Insurance Cos.; USF&G Insurance Co.; SETSEG, Inc.; Gallagher Bassett Insurance Service; North Pointe Insurance Co.; Auto Owners Insurance Co.; CoreSource, Inc.; USAA; Upper Peninsula Health Education Corp.
Reference: First of America Bank-Marquette, N.A.

For full biographical listings, see the Martindale-Hubbell Law Directory

*MIDLAND,** Midland Co.

CURRIE & KENDALL, P.C. (AV)

6024 Eastman Avenue, P.O. Box 1846, 48641-1846
Telephone: 517-839-0300
Fax: 517-832-0077

Gilbert A. Currie (1882-1960)
James A. Kendall
William C. Collins
Thomas L. Ludington
Ramon F. Rolf, Jr.
Daniel J. Cline
Peter A. Poznak
Julia A. Close
Peter J. Kendall
Jeffrey N. Dyer

OF COUNSEL

Gilbert A. Currie
I. Frank Harlow
William D. Schuette

LEGAL SUPPORT PERSONNEL

Barbara J. Byron

Counsel for: Chemical Financial Corp.; Chemical Bank & Trust Co.; Saginaw Valley State University; Northwood University; The Midland Foundation; Elsa U. Pardee Foundation; Rollin M. Gerstacker Foundation; Charles J. Strosacker Foundation.

For full biographical listings, see the Martindale-Hubbell Law Directory

*MUSKEGON,** Muskegon Co.

PARMENTER O'TOOLE (AV)

175 West Apple Street, P.O. Box 786, 49443-0786
Telephone: 616-722-1621
Telecopier: 616-728-2206; 722-7866

MEMBERS OF FIRM

G. Thomas Johnson
W. Brad Groom
Timothy G. Hicks
John C. Schrier

ASSOCIATE

Shawn P. Davis

OF COUNSEL

Arthur M. Rude
Thomas J. O'Toole

General Counsel for: FMB Lumberman's Bank; AmeriBank Federal Savings Bank; City of Muskegon; Quality Tool & Stamping Co., Inc.; Radiology Muskegon, P.C.
Local Counsel for: General Electric Capital Corp.; Paine-Webber; Teledyne Industries, Inc. (Continental Motors Division); Westinghouse Electric Corporation (Knoll Group).

For Complete List of Firm Personnel, See General Section

For full biographical listings, see the Martindale-Hubbell Law Directory

PLYMOUTH, Wayne Co.

DRAUGELIS & ASHTON (AV)

843 Penniman Avenue, 48170-1690
Telephone: 313-453-4044
Clawson, Michigan Office: 380 North Main Street.
Telephone: 313-810-7704.

MEMBERS OF FIRM

Edward F. Draugelis
John A. Ashton
Donald S. Scully
Richard T. Haynes
Lamberto DiStefano
David T. Rogers

(See Next Column)

DRAUGELIS & ASHTON, *Plymouth—Continued*

ASSOCIATES

Debra Clancy
Dawn E. Clancy
Joseph R. Conte
Timothy M. O'Connor
Steven O. Ashton
Floyd C. Virant
Taras P. Jarema
Deborah A. Tonelli
Timothy M. McKercher
Anne K. Mayer
Sally S. Stauffer
Robert D. Wilkins
Darlene M. Germaine
Joel B. Ashton

Representative Clients: State Farm Mutual Automobile Insurance Co.; State Farm Fire and Casualty Co.; Secura Insurance Co.; Westfield Insurance Co.; United States Fidelity and Guaranty Co.; RLI Insurance Co.; United States Automobile Association; Michigan Automobile Insurance Placement Facility; Northville Downs; Charter Township of Plymouth.

For full biographical listings, see the Martindale-Hubbell Law Directory

SEMPLINER, THOMAS AND BOAK (AV)

711 West Ann Arbor Trail, 48170
Telephone: 313-453-6220, 455-4560

MEMBERS OF FIRM

William Sempliner (1908-1985)
John E. Thomas
Stephen H. Boak

ASSOCIATES

Mark D. Lang
Tracy S. Thomas

OF COUNSEL

Robert P. Tiplady

For full biographical listings, see the Martindale-Hubbell Law Directory

*PONTIAC,** Oakland Co.

BOOTH, PATTERSON, LEE, NEED & ADKISON, P.C. (AV)

1090 West Huron Street, 48328
Telephone: 810-681-1200
FAX: 810-681-1754

Douglas W. Booth (1918-1992)
Calvin E. Patterson (1913-1987)
Parvin Lee, Jr.
J. Timothy Patterson
David J. Lee
Gregory K. Need
Phillip G. Adkison
Martin L. Kimmel
Allan T. Motzny
Ann DeCaminada Christ
Kathryn Niazy Nichols

For full biographical listings, see the Martindale-Hubbell Law Directory

CHARTRAND & BADGLEY (AV)

1401 NBD Building, 48342
Telephone: 810-333-2210
Fax: 810-332-7487
Bloomfield Hills, Michigan Office: 1760 South Telegraph Road, Suite 102.
Telephone: 810-332-8900.
Fax: 810-332-7487.

Douglas Chartrand

Reference: NBD Bank, NA.

For full biographical listings, see the Martindale-Hubbell Law Directory

HACKETT, MAXWELL & PHILLIPS, P.L.L.C. (AV)

The Riker Building, Suite 902, 35 West Huron Street, 48342
Telephone: 810-335-0404
Facsimile: 810-335-0581

Patrick E. Hackett
Phillip B. Maxwell
Dawn L. Phillips

Mark T. Butler
Jill Tilton Silverman

For full biographical listings, see the Martindale-Hubbell Law Directory

*PORT HURON,** St. Clair Co.

NICHOLSON, FLETCHER & DEGROW (AV)

522 Michigan Street, 48060-3893
Telephone: 810-987-8444
Facsimile: 810-987-8149

MEMBERS OF FIRM

David C. Nicholson
Gary A. Fletcher

ASSOCIATE

Mark G. Clark

Representative Clients: Fremont Mutual Insurance Co.; Westfield Insurance Co.; Michigan Municipal Risk Management Authority; City of Port Huron; City of Marysville; Port Huron Area School District; Marysville Public Schools; Wirtz Manufacturing Co.; Raymond Excavating; Relleum Real Estate Development Co.

For Complete List of Firm Personnel, See General Section

For full biographical listings, see the Martindale-Hubbell Law Directory

ROYAL OAK, Oakland Co.

CARDELLI, SCHAEFER & MASON, P.C. (AV)

306 South Washington Avenue, Suite 500, 48067
Telephone: 810-544-1100
Telecopier: 810-544-1191

Thomas G. Cardelli
William C. Schaefer
Laura D. Mason
Cheryl A. Cardelli
Deborah A. Hebert
Mary Ann J. O'Neil
Shelly M. Lee

Representative Clients: Allianz Insurance Company; Coltec Industries (Garlock Inc); Dana Corporation; Duchossois Industries, Inc.; Fruehauf Trailer Corporation; NBD Bancorp, Inc; Otis Elevator Company; Raymond Corporation; Robert Bosch Power Tool Corporation; Ryobi Power Tool Corporation.

For full biographical listings, see the Martindale-Hubbell Law Directory

*SAGINAW,** Saginaw Co.

SMITH & BROOKER, P.C. (AV)

3057 Davenport Avenue, 48602
Telephone: 517-799-1891
Bay City, Michigan Office: 703 Washington Avenue.
Telephone: 517-892-2595.
Flint, Michigan Office: 3506 Lennon Road.
Telephone: 810-733-0140.

RESIDENT ATTORNEYS

Francis B. Drinan
Michael J. Huffman

BAY CITY, MICHIGAN OFFICE

Carl H. Smith, Jr.
Albert C. Hicks
Glenn F. Doyle
Richard C. Sheppard
George B. Mullison
Charles T. Hewitt

FLINT, MICHIGAN OFFICE

Thomas A. Connolly
Peter L. Diesel

Representative Clients: CIGNA; Citizens Insurance Co.; City of Saginaw; General Motors Corp.; Saginaw Township Community Schools; Saginaw Intermediate School District; State Farm Mutual Automobile Insurance Co.; Tri-City Airport Commission; CSX Transportation; Tittabawasee Township.

For full biographical listings, see the Martindale-Hubbell Law Directory

*ST. JOSEPH,** Berrien Co.

GLOBENSKY, GLEISS, BITTNER & HYRNS, P.C. (AV)

610 Ship Street, P.O. Box 290, 49085
Telephone: 616-983-0551
FAX: 616-983-5858

H. S. Gray (1867-1961)
Luman H. Gray (1902-1952)
John L. Globensky
Henry W. Gleiss
Rodger V. Bittner
Randy S. Hyrns

J. Joseph Daly
Charles T. LaSata

LEGAL SUPPORT PERSONNEL

Robin J. Jollay

General Counsel for: Inter-City Bank; Southern Michigan Cold Storage Co.; Pearson Construction Co., Inc.
Approved Attorneys for: Lawyers Title Insurance Corp.
Reference: Inter-City Bank of Benton Harbor.

For full biographical listings, see the Martindale-Hubbell Law Directory

*SAULT STE. MARIE,** Chippewa Co.

MOHER & CANNELLO, P.C. (AV)

150 Water Street, P.O. Box 538, 49783
Telephone: 906-632-3397
FAX: 906-632-0479
Newberry, Michigan Office: 200 East John.
Telephone: 906-293-3600.

Thomas G. Moher
Steven J. Cannello
Timothy S. Moher

Representative Clients: City of Sault Ste. Marie, Michigan; Sault Bank; Sault Ste. Marie Economic Development Corp.; State of Michigan; Michigan Department of Transportation; Tendercare Nursing Homes of Michigan; Chippewa County, Village of De Tour; Pickford Township.

For full biographical listings, see the Martindale-Hubbell Law Directory

SOUTHFIELD, Oakland Co.

FIEGER, FIEGER & SCHWARTZ, A PROFESSIONAL CORPORATION (AV)

19390 West Ten Mile Road, 48075-2463
Telephone: 810-355-5555
FAX: 810-355-5148

(See Next Column)

FIEGER, FIEGER & SCHWARTZ A PROFESSIONAL CORPORATION—*Continued*

Bernard J. Fieger (1922-1988)
Geoffrey N. Fieger
Michael Alan Schwartz
Dennis Fuller
Pamela A. Hamway
Dean W. Amburn
Ronald S. Glaser
Gary S. Fields
Todd J. Weglarz

OF COUNSEL

Barry Fayne
Stephen L. Witenoff
Beverly Hires Brode

For full biographical listings, see the Martindale-Hubbell Law Directory

GORDON, CUTLER AND HOFFMAN, P.C. (AV)

18411 West Twelve Mile Road, 48076
Telephone: 810-443-1500

Arnold M. Gordon
Joel L. Hoffman
Donald M. Cutler
Michael H. Cutler
John M. Callahan

Reference: Michigan National Bank-Oakland.

O'LEARY, O'LEARY, JACOBS, MATTSON, PERRY & MASON, P.C. (AV)

26777 Central Park Boulevard, Suite 275, 48076
Telephone: 810-799-8260

John Patrick O'Leary
Thomas M. O'Leary
John P. Jacobs
Kenneth M. Mattson
C. Kenneth Perry, Jr.
Larry G. Mason
D. Jennifer Andreou
Kevin P. Hanbury
Debra A. Reed

For full biographical listings, see the Martindale-Hubbell Law Directory

SCHWARTZ & JALKANEN, P.C. (AV)

Suite 200, 24400 Northwestern Highway, 48075
Telephone: 810-352-2555
Facsimile: 810-352-5963

Melvin R. Schwartz
Arthur W. Jalkanen
Karl Eric Hannum

Anne Loridas Randall
Deborah L. Laura
Lisa M. Green

For full biographical listings, see the Martindale-Hubbell Law Directory

SOMMERS, SCHWARTZ, SILVER & SCHWARTZ, P.C. (AV)

2000 Town Center, Suite 900, 48075
Telephone: 810-355-0300
Telecopier: 810-746-4001
Plymouth, Michigan Office: 747 South Main Street.
Telephone: 313-455-4250.

Stanley S. Schwartz
Leonard B. Schwartz
Lawrence Warren
Jeffrey N. Shillman
Jeremy L. Winer
David R. Getto
Robert H. Darling
Paul W. Hines
Donald J. Gasiorek
Patrick B. McCauley
Justin C. Ravitz
David L. Nelson
Joseph A. Golden
Richard D. Fox
Frank Mafrice
James J. Vlasic
Richard L. Groffsky
David J. Winter
David M. Black
Daniel D. Swanson
Jon J. Birnkrant
David A. Kotzian
Patricia A. Stamler
David J. Shea
Alan B. Koenig

General Counsel for: City of Taylor; Foodland Distributors; C.A. Muer Corporation; Vlasic & Company; Nederlander Corporation; Woodland Physicians; Midwest Health Centers, P.C.
Representative Clients: Crum & Forster Insurance Company; City of Pontiac; Michigan National Bank; Perry Drugs.

For Complete List of Firm Personnel, See General Section

For full biographical listings, see the Martindale-Hubbell Law Directory

YOUNG & ASSOCIATES, P.C. (AV)

Suite 305 Westview Office Center, 26200 American Drive, 48034
Telephone: 810-353-8620
Telecopier: 810-353-6559

Rodger D. Young

Anthony Cho
Michael J. Fergestrom

Representative Clients: ADT; Commtract Corp.; GTE; Phillips Service Industries, NC. (PSI); Regal Plastics; Siemens; The Virtual Group

For full biographical listings, see the Martindale-Hubbell Law Directory

*TRAVERSE CITY,** Grand Traverse Co.

MURCHIE, CALCUTT & BOYNTON (AV)

109 East Front Street, Suite 300, 49684
Telephone: 616-947-7190
Fax: 616-947-4341

Robert B. Murchie (1894-1975)
Harry Calcutt
Jack E. Boynton
William B. Calcutt
Mark A. Burnheimer
Dawn M. Rogers

ASSOCIATES

George W. Hyde, III
Ralph J. Dilley (Not admitted in MI)

General Counsel for: Old Kent Bank-Grand Traverse; Northwestern Savings Bank & Trust; Central-State Bancorp; Traverse City Record Eagle; WPNB-7 & WTOM-4; Emergency Consultants, Inc.; National Guardian Risk Retention Group, Inc.; Farmers Mutual Insurance Co.; Environmental Solutions, Inc.
Local Counsel For: Consumers Power Co.

For full biographical listings, see the Martindale-Hubbell Law Directory

THOMPSON, PARSONS & O'NEIL (AV)

309 East Front Street, P.O. Box 429, 49685
Telephone: 616-929-9700; 1-800-678-1307
Fax: 616-929-7262

MEMBERS OF FIRM

George R. Thompson
Grant W. Parsons
Daniel P. O'Neil

William J. Brooks

For full biographical listings, see the Martindale-Hubbell Law Directory

WALTON, SMITH, PHILLIPS & DIXON, P.C. (AV)

216 Cass Street, P.O. Box 549, 49685
Telephone: 616-947-7410
Fax: 616-947-5112

Geoff G. Smith
L. Kent Walton
Thomas L. Phillips

OF COUNSEL

David S. Dixon

Representative Clients: The Travelers Insurance Cos.; Farm Bureau Insurance Group; First Of America-Northern Michigan; State Farm Insurance;
Reference: First of America-Northern Michigan.

For full biographical listings, see the Martindale-Hubbell Law Directory

WALZ & WARBA, P.C. (AV)

13983 West Bayshore Drive, 49684
Telephone: 616-947-0313
Fax: 616-947-8811
Big Rapids, Michigan Office: 115 Ives.
Telephone: 616-796-5887.
Fax: 616-796-5949.

Kenneth P. Walz
Mark J. Warba

For full biographical listings, see the Martindale-Hubbell Law Directory

TROY, Oakland Co.

HOLAHAN, MALLOY, MAYBAUGH & MONNICH (AV)

Suite 100, 2690 Crooks Road, 48084-4700
Telephone: 810-362-4747
Fax: 810-362-4779
East Tawas, Michigan Office: 910 East Bay Street.
Telephone: 517-362-4747.
Fax: 517-362-7331.

MEMBERS OF FIRM

J. Michael Malloy, III
James D. Maybaugh
John R. Monnich
David L. Delie, Jr.
William J. Kliffel

OF COUNSEL

Thomas H. O'Connor
Maureen Holahan (Retired; Resident, East Tawas Office)

Representative Clients: Johnson & Higgens; Employers Reinsurance; Chubb Companies; American States Insurance Co.; Travelers Insurance; Pontiac Osteopathic Hospital; Michigan Health Care Corporation.

For full biographical listings, see the Martindale-Hubbell Law Directory

HUTSON, SAWYER, CHAPMAN & REILLY (AV)

292 Town Center Drive, 48084-1799
Telephone: 810-689-5700
Fax: 810-689-5741

(See Next Column)

HUTSON, SAWYER, CHAPMAN & REILLY, *Troy—Continued*

MEMBERS OF FIRM

Thomas G. Sawyer
Michael W. Hutson
Ronald A. Chapman
Michael J. Reilly

Representative Clients: Advanced Friction Materials Co.; Atina Construction Co.; Security Bank of Commerce; Birmingham Chrysler-Plymouth Co.; Century 21-Advantage Design Fabrications, Inc.; Four Seasons Air Conditioning Co.; The John Christian Co., Inc.; Hawtal-Whiting, Inc.; Jason Tool & Engineering, Inc.; Oakland County Medical Society.

For full biographical listings, see the Martindale-Hubbell Law Directory

KEYWELL AND ROSENFELD (AV)

Suite 600, 2301 West Big Beaver Road, 48084
Telephone: 810-649-3200
Fax: 810-649-0454

MEMBERS OF FIRM

Frederic I. Keywell
Jimm F. White
Elaine A. Parson

ASSOCIATES

Marjorie L. Kolin
Julie D. Abear
Jennifer L. Lord
Jill R. Hart

Reference: National Bank of Detroit.

For full biographical listings, see the Martindale-Hubbell Law Directory

POLING, McGAW & POLING, P.C. (AV)

Suite 275, 5435 Corporate Drive, 48098
Telephone: 810-641-0500
Telecopier: 810-641-0506

Benson T. Buck (1926-1989)
Richard B. Poling
D. Douglas McGaw
Richard B. Poling, Jr.
David W. Moore
Gregory C. Hamilton
Veronica B. Winter

Representative Clients: County of Oakland; City of Troy; United States Fidelity & Guaranty Co.; Sentry Insurance Co.; Admiral Insurance; DeMaria Construction Co.; Leo Corporation; Aetna Casualty and Surety Co.; Concord Design; Pneumo-Abex.

For full biographical listings, see the Martindale-Hubbell Law Directory

REYNOLDS, BEEBY & MAGNUSON, P.C. (AV)

50 West Big Beaver Road Suite 400, 48084
Telephone: 810-740-9860
FAX: 810-740-9870
Detroit, Michigan Office: Ford Building.
Telephone: 810-740-9860.
Fax: 810-740-9870.

Gregory A. Reynolds
Thomas D. Beeby
Arnold N. Magnuson, Jr.
Kenneth M. Zorn
Thomas G. Grubba
Frank K. Mandlebaum

Elizabeth A. Fellows
Michael K. Sheehy
Joseph J. Wright

Representative Clients: Chrysler Corp.; General Motors Corp.; Emerson Electric Co.; Michelin Tire Co.; Federation Internationale Automotive; Goody; Nissan Automotive; First Brand, Inc.

For full biographical listings, see the Martindale-Hubbell Law Directory

STEPHEN K. VALENTINE, JR., P.C. (AV)

600 Columbia Center, 201 West Big Beaver Road, 48084
Telephone: 810-851-3010
West Bloomfield, Michigan Office: Suite 400, 5767 West Maple Road.
Telephone: 810-851-3010.

Stephen K. Valentine, Jr.

For full biographical listings, see the Martindale-Hubbell Law Directory

WEST BLOOMFIELD, Oakland Co.

CHEATHAM ACKER & SHARP, P.C. (AV)

5777 West Maple Road, Suite 130, P.O. Box 255002, 48325-5002
Telephone: 810-932-2000

Charles C. Cheatham
Lawrence J. Acker
Gary D. Sharp

William E. Osantowski
Tracy A. Leahy
Jody D. Klask
John M. Mooney
Mary E. Hollman
Adam K. Gordon

COUNSEL

Lynn L. Lower
Kyle B. Mansfield (Not admitted in MI)

For full biographical listings, see the Martindale-Hubbell Law Directory

STEPHEN K. VALENTINE, JR., P.C. (AV)

5767 West Maple Road, Suite 400, 48322
Telephone: 810-851-3010
Troy, Michigan Office: 600 Columbia Center. 201 West Big Beaver Road.
Telephone: 810-851-3010.

Stephen K. Valentine, Jr.

OF COUNSEL

Philip G. Meyer

For full biographical listings, see the Martindale-Hubbell Law Directory

YPSILANTI, Washtenaw Co.

PEAR SPERLING EGGAN & MUSKOVITZ, P.C. (AV)

5 South Washington Street, 48197
Telephone: 313-483-3626
Fax: 313-483-1107
Ann Arbor, Michigan Office: Domino's Farms, 24 Frank Lloyd Wright Drive.
Telephone: 313-665-4441
Other Ypsilanti, Michigan Office: 2164 Bellevue at Washtenaw.
Telephone: 313-483-7177.

Lawrence W. Sperling
Andrew M. Eggan
Thomas E. Daniels
Helen Conklin Vick

Counsel for: Domino's Pizza, Inc.; Bank One, Ypsilanti, N.A.; Townsend and Bottum, Inc.; Ann Arbor Housing Commission; The Credit Bureau of Ypsilanti; City of Ypsilanti (Labor Counsel); Michigan Municipal Worker's Compensation; Self-Insurance Fund.
Approved Attorneys for: Lawyers Title Insurance Corp.

For full biographical listings, see the Martindale-Hubbell Law Directory

MINNESOTA

*AUSTIN,** Mower Co.

HOVERSTEN, STROM, JOHNSON & RYSAVY (AV)

807 West Oakland Avenue, 55912
Telephone: 507-433-3483
Fax: 507-433-7889

MEMBERS OF FIRM

Kermit F. Hoversten
Craig W. Johnson
Donald E. Rysavy
David V. Hoversten
John S. Beckmann
Fred W. Wellmann
Steven J Hovey

ASSOCIATE

Mary Carroll Leahy

OF COUNSEL

Kenneth M. Strom

Representative Clients: Hartford Insurance Co.; Allied Insurance Group; Travelers Insurance; American States Insurance; Royal Milbank Insurance; Prudential Insurance Co.; Independent School District 756; St. Olaf Hospital; Austin Medical Clinic; Norwest Bank, Austin.

For Complete List of Firm Personnel, See General Section

For full biographical listings, see the Martindale-Hubbell Law Directory

*BEMIDJI,** Beltrami Co.

POWELL, POWELL & AAMODT (AV)

713 Beltrami Avenue, P.O. Box 908, 56601
Telephone: 218-751-5650
FAX: 218-751-5658

MEMBERS OF FIRM

Romaine R. Powell
Charles R. Powell
Paul R. Aamodt

Representative Clients: The State Farm Insurance Companies; American Family Mutual Insurance Co..

For full biographical listings, see the Martindale-Hubbell Law Directory

*DULUTH,** St. Louis Co.

CLURE, EATON, BUTLER, MICHELSON, FERGUSON & MUNGER, P.A. (AV)

Suite 200 222 West Superior Street, 55802-1907
Telephone: 218-722-0528
Cable Address: "MCVanEV"
Telex: (RCA) 251857 VECB UR
FAX: 218-720-6722
800-488-8278

(See Next Column)

CLURE, EATON, BUTLER, MICHELSON, FERGUSON & MUNGER P.A.—*Continued*

Thomas A. Clure
Robert F. Eaton
Kenneth D. Butler
David R. Michelson
Joseph V. Ferguson, III
Mark A. Munger

Philip Eckman

OF COUNSEL

William P. Van Evera
Arthur M. Clure (1900-1956)
Thomas M. McCabe (1896-1970)

Representative Clients: Prudential Insurance Company of America; The Congdon Office; West of England Steam Ship Owners Protection and Indemnity Assn., Ltd.

For full biographical listings, see the Martindale-Hubbell Law Directory

CRASSWELLER, MAGIE, ANDRESEN, HAAG & PACIOTTI, P.A. (AV)

1000 Alworth Building, P.O. Box 745, 55801
Telephone: 218-722-1411
Telecopier: 218-720-6817

Donald B. Crassweller
Robert H. Magie, III
Charles H. Andresen
Michael W. Haag
James P. Paciotti
Sandra E. Butterworth
Brian R. McCarthy
Bryan N. Anderson
Robert C. Barnes
Kurt D. Larson
Gerald T. Anderson

COUNSEL

John M. Donovan
Robert K. McCarthy (1915-1986)

Representative Clients: Inland Steel Co.; Allstate Insurance Co.; Liberty Mutual Insurance Co; State Farm Insurance Cos.; Great Lakes Gas Transmission Co.; Lakehead Pipe Line Co.; Trans-Canada Gas Pipeline, Ltd.

For full biographical listings, see the Martindale-Hubbell Law Directory

FRYBERGER, BUCHANAN, SMITH & FREDERICK, P.A. (AV)

700 Lonsdale Building, 302 West Superior Street, 55802
Telephone: 218-722-0861
Fax: 218-722-9568
St. Paul Office: Capitol Center, 386 N. Wabasha.
Telephone: 612-221-1044.

Bruce Buchanan
Nick Smith
Harold A. Frederick
Dexter A. Larsen
James H. Stewart
Robert E. Toftey
Michael K. Donovan
Neal J. Hessen
Joseph J. Mihalek
Shawn M. Dunlevy
Anne Lewis
David R. Oberstar
Abbot G. Apter
Michael Cowles
Martha M. Markusen

Daniel D. Maddy
Stephanie A. Ball
Paul B. Kilgore
Mary Frances Skala
Rolf A. Lindberg (Resident, St. Paul Office)
Kevin T. Walli (Resident, St. Paul Office)
Kevin J. Dunlevy (Resident, St. Paul Office)
Teresa M. O'Toole
Dean R. Borgh
James F. Voegeli (Resident, St. Paul Office)
James A. Lund
Mark D. Britton (Resident, St. Paul Office)
Judith A. Zollar

OF COUNSEL

Herschel B. Fryberger, Jr.

Representative Clients: North Shore Bank of Commerce; General Motors Acceptance Corp.; Western Lake Superior Sanitary District; City of Duluth; First Bank Minnesota (N.A.); Norwest Bank Minnesota North N.A.; Airport State Bank; Park State Bank; M & I First National Bank of Superior; St. Lukes Hospital Duluth.

For full biographical listings, see the Martindale-Hubbell Law Directory

HANFT, FRIDE, O'BRIEN, HARRIES, SWELBAR & BURNS, P.A. (AV)

1000 First Bank Place, 130 West Superior Street, 55802-2094
Telephone: 218-722-4766
Fax: 218-720-4920

Gaylord W. Swelbar
John D. Kelly
Richard J. Leighton
John R. Baumgarth
J. Kent Richards
Tim A. Strom
R. Thomas Torgerson
Cheryl M. Prince
Robin C. Merritt

(See Next Column)

Kathleen Small Bray

Counsel for: Canadian National Railways; Great American Insurance Cos.; Minnesota Power; Northern Minnesota Utilities; Oglebay Norton Co.; United States Fidelity & Guaranty Co.; U.S. Insurance Group; American International Adjustment Companies; Duluth Transit Authority; LTV Corporation.

For Complete List of Firm Personnel, See General Section

For full biographical listings, see the Martindale-Hubbell Law Directory

*HALLOCK,** Kittson Co.

BRINK, SOBOLIK, SEVERSON, VROOM & MALM, P.A. (AV)

217 South Birch Avenue, P.O. Box 790, 56728
Telephone: 218-843-3686
FAX: 218-843-2724

Dennis M. Sobolik
Robert K. Severson
Ronald C. Vroom
Roger C. Malm
Robert M. Albrecht
Blake S. Sobolik

Representative Clients: Northwestern State Bank, Hallock, Minn.; Karlstad State Bank, Karlstad, Minn.; Argyle State Bank, Argyle, Minn.; City of Hallock; American Federal Savings & Loan Assn.; State Farm Insurance Co.; Minnesota Rice Growers, Inc.

For Complete List of Firm Personnel, See General Section

For full biographical listings, see the Martindale-Hubbell Law Directory

*HASTINGS,** Dakota Co.

SIEBEN, POLK, LAVERDIERE, JONES & HAWN, A PROFESSIONAL ASSOCIATION (AV)

999 Westview Drive, 55033
Telephone: 612-437-3148
Fax: 612-437-2732
St. Paul, Minnesota Office: Galtier Plaza, Suite 550, Box 45, 175 Fifth Street East.
Telephone: 612-222-4146.
Fax: 612-223-8279.

Michael R. Sieben
Michael S. Polk
Harvey N. Jones
Richard A. LaVerdiere
Steven D. Hawn (Resident, St. Paul Office)

Thomas R. Longfellow (Resident, St. Paul Office)
Bernie M. Dusich
Mark J. Fellman (Resident, St. Paul Office)
Michael R. Strom
John P. Sieben (Resident, St. Paul Office)
Scott J. Hertogs
Sara M. Hulse

For full biographical listings, see the Martindale-Hubbell Law Directory

*MANKATO,** Blue Earth Co.

BLETHEN, GAGE & KRAUSE (AV)

127 South Second Street, P.O. Box 3049, 56001
Telephone: 507-345-1166
Fax: 507-345-8003

OF COUNSEL

Kelton Gage

MEMBERS OF FIRM

Raymond C. Krause (Retired)
Bailey W. Blethen
Randall C. Berkland
James H. Turk
Stephen P. Rolfsrud
Michael C. Karp
Kevin M. Connelly
Wm. David Taylor III

General Counsel For: Mankato Citizens Telephone Co.; Norwest Bank Minnesota South Central, N.A.: Waseca Mutual Insurance Co.; Hickory Tech Corporation; Winco, Inc.
Local Counsel For: American States Insurance Co.; ConAgra Fertilizer Co.; Northern Natural Gas Co., a division of Enron Corp.; General Motors Corp.; Millers Mutual Insurance Co.

For Complete List of Firm Personnel, See General Section

For full biographical listings, see the Martindale-Hubbell Law Directory

FARRISH, JOHNSON & MASCHKA (AV)

200 Union Square Business Center, 201 North Broad Street, P.O. Box 550, 56002-0550
Telephone: 507-387-3002
Fax: 507-625-4002

MEMBERS OF FIRM

Robert G. Johnson
Gerald L. Maschka
Scott V. Kelly
William S. Partridge
Kenneth R. White
Mary Anne Wray
Paul J. Simonett

Representative Clients: Travelers Insurance Co.; American State Bank of Mankato, Mankato, Minn.; Hartford Insurance Group; St. Paul Insurance Cos.; Employers Mutual of Wausau; State Farm Co.; Federated Insurance

(See Next Column)

FARRISH, JOHNSON & MASCHKA, *Mankato—Continued*

Co.; Firemen's Fund American Insurance Co.; Maryland Casualty Co.; American Family Insurance Group.

For Complete List of Firm Personnel, See General Section

For full biographical listings, see the Martindale-Hubbell Law Directory

GISLASON, DOSLAND, HUNTER AND MALECKI (AV)

A Partnership including a Professional Association
75 Teton Lane, P.O. Box 4157, 56002-4157
Telephone: 507-387-1115
FAX: 507-387-4413
New Ulm, Minnesota Office: State and Center Streets, P.O. Box 458.
Telephone: 507-354-3111.
Telecopier: 507-354-8447.
Minneapolis, Minnesota Office: Opus Center, Suite 215E. 9900 Bren Road East, P.O. Box 5297.
Telephone: 612-933-9900.
Telecopier: 612-933-0242.
Chanhassen, Minnesota Office: Americana Community Bank Building, 600 West 79th Street, P.O. Box 950.
Telephone: 612-934-7754.
Fax: 612-934-7793.

James H. Malecki

ASSOCIATES

John C. Hottinger
Andrew A. Willaert

Regional Counsel for: Associated Milk Producers, Inc.
Representative Clients: Travelers Insurance Co.; CIGNA; St. Paul Insurance Cos.; Farmers Insurance Group; Auto-Owners Insurance Co.; Midwest Medical Insurance Co.; Minnesota Lawyers Mutual Insurance Co.; Wausau Insurance Co.; Wal-Mart.

For full biographical listings, see the Martindale-Hubbell Law Directory

*MINNEAPOLIS,** Hennepin Co.

ARNOLD & McDOWELL (AV)

5881 Cedar Lake Road, 55416-1492
Telephone: 612-545-9000
Minnesota Wats Line: 800-343-4545
Fax: 612-545-1793
Princeton, Minnesota Office: 501 South Fourth Street.
Telephone: 612-389-2214.
Hutchinson, Minnesota Office: 101 Park Place.
Telephone: 612-587-7575.

MEMBERS OF FIRM

David B. Arnold
Gary D. McDowell
G. Barry Anderson
Steven S. Hoge
Laura K. Fretland

ASSOCIATES

Richard G. McGee
Cathryn D. Reher
Gina M. Brandt
Brett D. Arnold

For Complete List of Firm Personnel, See General Section

For full biographical listings, see the Martindale-Hubbell Law Directory

ARTHUR, CHAPMAN, McDONOUGH, KETTERING & SMETAK, P.A. (AV)

500 Young Quinlan Building, 81 South Ninth Street, 55402
Telephone: 612-339-3500
Fax: 612-339-7655

Lindsay G. Arthur, Jr.
John T. Chapman
Michael P. McDonough
Robert W. Kettering, Jr.
Theodore J. Smetak
Donna D. Geck
Patrick C. Cronan
Thomas A. Pearson
Colby B. Lund
Michael R. Quinlivan
Sally J. Ferguson
James S. Pikala
Jeremiah P. Gallivan
Katherine L. MacKinnon
Blake W. Duerre
Karen Melling van Vliet
Richard C. Nelson
Eugene C. Shermoen, Jr.
Paul J. Rocheford
Lee J. Keller
Gregory J. Johnson
Paula Duggan Vraa
Joseph W. Waller

Representative Clients: American International Group; American States; Bristol Myers-Squibb, Inc.; Continental Insurance Co.; General Casualty; Home Insurance Co.; Metropolitan Property & Liability Insurance Co.; Navistar International; Safeco Insurance Co.; USAA.

For Complete List of Firm Personnel, See General Section

For full biographical listings, see the Martindale-Hubbell Law Directory

AUSTIN & ABRAMS, A PROFESSIONAL ASSOCIATION (AV)

700 Northstar West, 55402
Telephone: 612-332-4273; 800-659-2679
FAX: 612-342-2107

(See Next Column)

Robert M. Austin
Jerome B. Abrams
Paul R. Smith
Lauris Heyerdahl
Keith J. Goar
Paul V. Kieffer
Timothy J. Wilson

Representative Clients: Hawkeye Security Ins. Co.; CNA Insurance; Employer's Mutual Ins. Co.

For Complete List of Firm Personnel, See General Section

For full biographical listings, see the Martindale-Hubbell Law Directory

BASSFORD, LOCKHART, TRUESDELL & BRIGGS, P.A. (AV)

(Formerly Richards, Montgomery, Cobb & Bassford, P.A.)
3550 Multifoods Tower, 55402-3787
Telephone: 612-333-3000
Telecopier: 612-333-8829

Fred B. Snyder (1859-1951)
Edward C. Gale (1862-1943)
Frank A. Janes (1908-1959)
Nathan A. Cobb, Sr. (1905-1976)
Bergmann Richards (1888-1978)
Edmund T. Montgomery (1904-1987)
Charles A. Bassford (1914-1990)
Greer E. Lockhart
Lynn G. Truesdell
Jerome C. Briggs
Frederick E. Finch
John M. Degnan
Lewis A. Remele, Jr.
Kevin P. Keenan
James O. Redman
Rebecca Egge Moos
John M. Anderson
Charles E. Lundberg
Gregory P. Bulinski
Donna J. Blazevic
Mary E. Steenson
Mark P. Hodkinson
Thomas J. Niemiec
Andrew L. Marshall
Michael A. Klutho
Kathryn H. Davis
Gregory W. Deckert

Kevin P. Hickey
John P. Buckley
Bradley J. Betlach
Mark Whitmore
Christopher R. Morris
Kelly Christensen

Representative Clients: American States Insurance Co.; Austin Mutual Insurance Co.; Midwest Family Mutual Insurance Co.; Minnesota Lawyers Mutual; St. Paul Insurance Cos.; The Travelers Insurance Co.; United States Fidelity & Guaranty Co.; Wausau Insurance.

For full biographical listings, see the Martindale-Hubbell Law Directory

BENNETT, INGVALDSON & COATY, P.A. (AV)

Suite 1640, 8500 Normandale Lake Boulevard, 55437
Telephone: 612-921-8350
Telecopier: 612-921-8351

Robert Bennett
Eric W. Ingvaldson
Michael P. Coaty

For full biographical listings, see the Martindale-Hubbell Law Directory

BOWMAN AND BROOKE (AV)

Suite 2600 Fifth Street Towers, 150 South Fifth Street, 55402
Telephone: 612-339-8682
Fax: 612-672-3200
Phoenix, Arizona Office: Phoenix Plaza, Suite 1700, 2929 North Central Avenue.
Telephone: 602-248-0899.
Fax: 602-248-0947.
Detroit, Michigan Office: 1800 Fisher Building, 3011 West Grand Boulevard.
Telephone: 313-871-3000.
Fax: 313-871-3006.
San Jose, California Office: Suite 1150, 160 West Santa Clara Street.
Telephone: 408-279-5393.
Fax: 408-279-5845.
Torrance, California Office: Suite 1000, 19191 South Vermont Avenue.
Telephone: 310-768-3068.
Fax: 310-719-1019.

MEMBERS OF FIRM

Richard A. Bowman
John Q. McShane
David R. Kelly
David W. Graves, Jr.
George W. Soule
Hildy Bowbeer
Kent B. Hanson
Wayne D. Struble
Thomas B. Heffelfinger
Matthew J. Valitchka, II
Kenneth Ross
Robert E. Pederson (Not admitted in MN)
Robert K. Miller
Marcia M. Kull
Mickey W. Greene
Cynthia J. Atsatt
Lezlie Ott Marek
James W. Halbrooks, Jr.
Mary E. Bolkcom
Timothy J. Mattson

ASSOCIATES

Daniel C. Adams
Kim M. Schmid
David N. Lutz
Sheryl A. Bjork
John D. Sear
Anton J. van der Merwe
Steven L. Reitenour
Cortney G. Sylvester
Darin D. Smith
Bard D. Borkon
C. Paul Carver
Jacqueline M. Moen

(See Next Column)

BOWMAN AND BROOKE—*Continued*

OF COUNSEL

Michael G. Fiergola (Not admitted in MN)

For full biographical listings, see the Martindale-Hubbell Law Directory

FRED BURSTEIN & ASSOCIATES, P.A. (AV)

5450 Norwest Center, 90 South Seventh Street, 55402
Telephone: 612-339-6561
Fax: 612-337-5572

Fred Burstein

Dylan J. McFarland
Eric J. Olsen

Reference: Firstar Bank of Minnesota, N.A.

For full biographical listings, see the Martindale-Hubbell Law Directory

CHESTNUT & BROOKS, PROFESSIONAL ASSOCIATION (AV)

3700 Piper Jaffray Tower, 222 South Ninth Street, 55402
Telephone: 612-339-7300
Fax: 612-336-2940
Suburban Office: 4661 Highway 61, NorthStar Bank Building, Suite 204, White Bear Lake, Minnesota, 55110.
Telephone: 612-653-0990.

Jack L. Chestnut
Richard C. Jones (1926-1969)
Karl L. Cambronne
Cort C. Holten
Craig A. Erickson
Dennis B. Johnson (Resident, White Bear Lake Office)
Alan B. Demmer

Janet Waller
Robert A. LaFleur
Jeanette A. Frederickson
Stuart C. Bear
Sandra J. McGoldrick-Kendall
Jeffrey D. Bores
Timothy P. McCarthy

Representative Clients: Minnesota Mining and Manufacturing Co.; Minnesota Judges Assn.

For full biographical listings, see the Martindale-Hubbell Law Directory

COSGROVE, FLYNN & GASKINS (AV)

29th Floor, Metropolitan Centre, 333 South Seventh Street, 55402
Telephone: 612-333-9500
Fax: 612-333-9579

MEMBERS OF FIRM

Hugh J. Cosgrove
George W. Flynn
Steve Gaskins
Robert J. Terhaar
Jeannine L. Lee
Douglas R. Archibald
Barbara Jean D'Aquila
Susan D. Hall
Steven J. Pfefferle
Thomas Klosowski

ASSOCIATES

Randall J. Pattee
Bradley J. Ayers
Hal A. Shillingstad
David A. Wikoff
Gary D. Ansel
Laurie A. Willard
Sarah L. Brew
Lisa R. Griebel
Thomas F. Ascher
Lynn M. Meyer
Scott M. Rusert
Jennifer F. Rosemark
Anthony J. Kane

For full biographical listings, see the Martindale-Hubbell Law Directory

COX & GOUDY (AV)

600A Butler Square, 100 North Sixth Street, 55403-1592
Telephone: 612-338-1414
Fax: 612-338-6754

MEMBERS OF FIRM

Charles A. Cox
Craig A. Goudy
Charles A. Cox, III

For full biographical listings, see the Martindale-Hubbell Law Directory

CULLEN LAW FIRM, LTD. (AV)

Suite 2500, One Financial Plaza, 120 South Sixth Street, 55402
Telephone: 612-349-5208

James P. Cullen

Kathleen Rusler O'Connor

For full biographical listings, see the Martindale-Hubbell Law Directory

DUNKLEY, BENNETT & CHRISTENSEN, P.A. (AV)

Suite 700, 701 Fourth Avenue South, 55415
Telephone: 612-339-1290
FAX: 612-339-9545

(See Next Column)

Jay L. Bennett
William M. Dunkley
Robert P. Christensen
John Harper, III
Thomas J. Hunziker
Daniel W. Hergott (P.A.)
Steven B. Nosek
James E. Betz
Richard M. Dahl
T. Chris Stewart
William G. Selman
Terrance J. Wagener

For full biographical listings, see the Martindale-Hubbell Law Directory

FETTERLY & GORDON, P.A. (AV)

808 Nicollet Mall, Suite 800, 55402
Telephone: 612-333-2003
Fax: 612-333-5950

James L. Fetterly
Gary J. Gordon
Keith A. Hanson

Stephen G. Lickteig
Diane B. Bratvold
Timothy J. Fetterly

Reference: National City Bank.

For full biographical listings, see the Martindale-Hubbell Law Directory

WILLIAM D. FOSTER & ASSOCIATES (AV)

2124 Dupont Avenue South, 55405
Telephone: 612-897-0749
Fax: 612-879-0059

ASSOCIATES

Janet M. McCutcheon
Miaja L. Gunewitz

For full biographical listings, see the Martindale-Hubbell Law Directory

FOSTER, WALDECK, LIND & GRIES, LTD. (AV)

Suite 2300 Metropolitan Centre, 333 South Seventh Street, 55402
Telephone: 612-375-1550
Facsimilie: 612-375-0647
St. Michael, Minnesota Office: 100 East Central, P.O. Box 35, 55376.
Telephone: 612-497-3099. Facsimilie: 612-497-3639.

Thomas A. Foster
Timothy W. Waldeck
Peter E. Lind
John R. Gries
Rolf E. Sonnesyn
David J. Lenhardt
Byron M. Peterson
Steven E. Tomsche

Gregory J. Van Heest
Jennifer L. Kjos
Philip J. Danen

Reference: Firstar Bank of Minnesota, N.A.

For full biographical listings, see the Martindale-Hubbell Law Directory

GILMORE, AAFEDT, FORDE, ANDERSON & GRAY, P.A. (AV)

150 South Fifth Street, Suite 3100, 55402
Telephone: 612-339-8965
Fax: 612-349-6839

Curtis C. Gilmore (Retired)
John R. de Lambert (Retired)
Michael D. Aafedt
Michael Forde
Donald W. Anderson
James R. Gray
Jay T. Hartman
Roderick C. Cosgriff
Janet Monson
Steven C. Gilmore
Mary Marvin Hager

Peter M. Banovetz
Robin D. Simpson
Kirk C. Thompson
Kathy A. Endres
Miriam P. Rykken
Janet Scheel Stellpflug
Lawrence C. Miller
Adam S. Wolkoff
David J. Klaiman
David Brian Kempston
Charles S. Bierman
Sheryl A. Zaworski
Kathryn M. Hipp

Representative Clients: Aetna Casualty and Surety Company; CIGNA Companies; Crawford Risk Management Service; Kemper Insurance Group; Liberty Mutual Insurance Group; Sentry Insurance Company; St. Paul Companies; United States Fidelity and Guaranty; U.S. Insurance Group/Crum and Forster Commercial Insurance; Western National Insurance Group.

For full biographical listings, see the Martindale-Hubbell Law Directory

GISLASON, DOSLAND, HUNTER AND MALECKI (AV)

A Partnership including a Professional Association
Opus Center, Suite 215E, 9900 Bren Road East, P.O. Box 5297, 55343-2297
Telephone: 612-933-9900
Telecopier: 612-933-0242
New Ulm, Minnesota Office: State and Center Streets, P.O. Box 458.
Telephone: 507-354-3111.
Telecopier: 507-354-8447.
Mankato, Minnesota Office: 75 Teton Lane, P.O. Box 4157.
Telephone: 507-387-1115.
Fax: 507-387-4413.

(See Next Column)

GISLASON, DOSLAND, HUNTER AND MALECKI, *Minneapolis—Continued*

Chanhassen, Minnesota Office: Americana Community Bank Building, 600 West 79th Street, P.O. Box 950.
Telephone: 612-934-7754.
Fax: 612-934-7793.

MEMBERS OF FIRM

Donald F. Hunter (P.A.)
Timothy P. Tobin
David D. Alsop
Roger H. Gross
Barry G. Vermeer
R. Stephen Tillitt
Wade R. Wacholz

RESIDENT ASSOCIATES

Beverly Babcock Kranz
Anne T. Johnson
Laura L. Myslis
Elliot L. Olsen
Daniel A. Beckman
Craig P. Goldman
Gregory A. Wohletz

OF COUNSEL

Daniel B. Ventres, Jr.

Regional Counsel for: Associated Milk Producers, Inc.
Representative Clients: Travelers Insurance Co.; CIGNA; St. Paul Insurance Cos.; Farmers Insurance Group; Auto-Owners Insurance Co.; Midwest Medical Insurance Co.; Minnesota Lawyers Mutual Insurance Co.; Wausau Insurance Co.; Wal-Mart.

For full biographical listings, see the Martindale-Hubbell Law Directory

HUNEGS, STONE, KOENIG & DOLAN, P.A. (AV)

565 Northstar East, 608 Second Avenue South, 55402
Telephone: 612-339-4511; 800-328-4340
Fax: 612-339-5150

William H. DeParcq (1905-1988)
Robert N. Stone
Richard Gene Hunegs
Ralph E. Koenig
Robert T. Dolan

Frances S. P. Li
Lawrence Alan Thomas

Reference: First Bank of Minneapolis.

For full biographical listings, see the Martindale-Hubbell Law Directory

HVASS, WEISMAN & KING, CHARTERED (AV)

Suite 450, 100 South Fifth Street, 55402
Telephone: 612-333-0201
FAX: 612-342-2606

Charles T. Hvass (Retired)
Richard A. Williams, Jr.
Si Weisman (1912-1992)
Charles T. Hvass, Jr.
Robert J. King
Robert J. King, Jr.
Frank J. Brixius
Michael W. Unger

John E. Daly
John M. Dornik
Mark T. Porter

For full biographical listings, see the Martindale-Hubbell Law Directory

KELLY & BERENS, P.A. (AV)

Suite 3720 IDS Center, 80 South Eighth Street, 55402
Telephone: 612-349-6171
Telecopier: 612-349-6416

Timothy D. Kelly
Jeffrey L. Levy
Michael Berens
Thomas H. Gunther
Wendy A. Snyder
Celeste E. Culberth
Erin K. Fogarty

For full biographical listings, see the Martindale-Hubbell Law Directory

LOMMEN, NELSON, COLE & STAGEBERG, P.A. (AV)

1800 IDS Center, 80 South 8th Street, 55402
Telephone: 612-339-8131
Fax: 612-339-8064
Hudson, Wisconsin Office: Grandview Professional Building, 400 South Second Street, Suite 210.
Telephones: 715-386-8217 and 612-436-8085.

W. Wyman Smith (1914-1994)
J. Christopher Cuneo
John P. Lommen (1927-1988)
Thomas F. Dougherty
Michael P. Shroyer (1953-1993)
Stacey A. DeKalb
Leonard T. Juster
Kay N. Hunt
Alvin S. Malmon
Richard L. Plagens
Ronald L. Haskvitz
Ehrich L. Koch
Phillip A. Cole
Margie R. Bodas
Roger V. Stageberg
James M. Lockhart
Glenn R. Kessel
Stephen C. Rathke
Thomas R. Jacobson (Resident, Hudson, Wisconsin Office)
James C. Searls
Linc S. Deter
John M. Giblin
Paul L. Dinger
John R. McBride
Sherri D. Ulland
Reid R. Lindquist

(See Next Column)

Jill G. Doescher
Marc A. Johannsen
James R. Johnson (Resident, Hudson, Wisconsin Office)
Angela W. Allen
Adam Levitsky
Terrance W. Moore
Barry A. O'Neil
Lynn M. Starkovich
Mary I. King
Sheila A. Bjorklund

OF COUNSEL

V. Owen Nelson
Henry H. Feikema

Representative Clients: Mutual Service Insurance Co.; Employers Mutual Companies; Economy Fire and Casualty Co.

For full biographical listings, see the Martindale-Hubbell Law Directory

MAHONEY, DOUGHERTY AND MAHONEY, PROFESSIONAL ASSOCIATION (AV)

801 Park Avenue, 55404-1189
Telephone: 612-339-5863; (800)-328-4827 Ext. 1318
Fax: 612-339-1529

Richard P. Mahoney
Patrick E. Mahoney
John (Jack) M. Miller
James M. Lehman
James M. Mahoney
Thomas Scott McEachron
Kenneth P. Gleason
Gregory A. Zinn
Dale B. Lindman
Kelley R. Lorix
Gary C. Reiter
Victor E. Lund
Randee S. Held
Sandra J. Grove
Mark J. Manderfeld
Philip Sieff
Gay B. Urness (Mr.)
Terry J. Battaglia
Mary R. Watson
Lisa A. Dittmann

Representative Insurance Clients: Armour & Co.; Fireman's Fund Group; General Accident Group; Great American Insurance Company.
Reference: Norwest Bank of Minneapolis.

For full biographical listings, see the Martindale-Hubbell Law Directory

MANSFIELD & TANICK, P.A. (AV)

International Centre, 900 Second Avenue South, 15th Floor, 55402
Telephone: 612-339-4295
Fax: 612-339-3161

Seymour J. Mansfield
Teresa J. Ayling
Marshall H. Tanick
Sholly A. Blustin
Earl H. Cohen
Catherine M. Klimek
Robert A. Johnson
Phillip J. Trobaugh
Richard J. Fuller

OF COUNSEL

Daniel S. Kleinberger

For full biographical listings, see the Martindale-Hubbell Law Directory

MASLON EDELMAN BORMAN & BRAND (AV)

3300 Norwest Center, 90 South Seventh Street, 55402-4140
Telephone: 612-672-8200
Fax: 612-672-8397

MEMBERS OF FIRM

Samuel H. Maslon (1901-1988)
Richard G. Wilson
Hyman Edelman (1905-1993)
Leon I. Steinberg
Sidney J. Kaplan (1909-1962)
Lawrence M. Shapiro
Roger E. Joseph (1917-1966)
Howard B. Tarkow
Irving R. Brand (1918-1990)
William M. Mower
Marvin Borman
Larry A. Koch
Charles Quaintance, Jr.
Virginia Ann Bell
Neil I. Sell
Justin H. Perl
Martin G. Weinstein
Cooper S. Ashley
William E. Mullin
Sally Stolen Grossman
William Z. Pentelovitch
Terri Krivosha
Joseph Alexander
Mary R. Vasaly
Gary J. Haugen
Edwin Chanin
Thomas H. Borman
Clark T. Whitmore
Rebecca A. Palmer
Wayne S. Moskowitz
Mark Eric Baumann
Mallory K. Mullins
David F. Herr
Susan D. Holappa
R. Lawrence Purdy
Charles A. Hoffman
James Duffy O'Connor
Russell F. Lederman

ASSOCIATES

Richard A. Kempf
Jeanmarie T. Sales
Mark W. Lee
David T. Quinby
Lorrie L. Salzl
Kevin M. Koepke
Susan E. Oliphant
Douglas T. Holod
Alain Marc Baudry
Carleton B. Crutchfield
Patricia I. Reding
John D. Darling (Not admitted in MN)
Anna L. Korinko
Jonathan S. Parritz
Neil P. Ayotte
Brian J. Klein
Rachel U. Gibbs
James F. Killian
Brenda J. Arndt
James F. Hanneman
Laurie K. Fett
Cynthia F. Gilbertson

(See Next Column)

MASLON EDELMAN BORMAN & BRAND—*Continued*

OF COUNSEL

Robert A. Engelke
Michael L. Snow

Reference: National City Bank, Minneapolis, Minnesota.

For full biographical listings, see the Martindale-Hubbell Law Directory

MESHBESHER & SPENCE, LTD. (AV)

1616 Park Avenue, 55404
Telephone: 612-339-9121
Fax: 612-339-9188
St. Paul, Minnesota Office: World Trade Center.
Telephone: 612-227-0799.
St. Cloud, Minnesota Office: 400 Zapp Bank Plaza.
Telephone: 612-656-0484.

Kenneth Meshbesher
Ronald I. Meshbesher
Russell M. Spence (Resident, St. Paul Office)
James H. Gilbert
John P. Clifford
Dennis R. Johnson
Jack Nordby
Paul W. Bergstrom (Resident, St. Paul Office)
Patrick K. Horan (Resident, St. Paul Office)
Daniel J. Boivin
Michael C. Snyder
James A. Wellner
John P. Sheehy
Mark D. Streed
Randall Spence
Howard I. Bass
Daniel C. Guerrero
Katherine S. Flom
Pamela R. Finney
Jeffrey P. Oistad (Resident, St. Cloud Office)
Daniel E. Meshbesher

For Complete List of Firm Personnel, See General Section

For full biographical listings, see the Martindale-Hubbell Law Directory

PARSINEN BOWMAN & LEVY, A PROFESSIONAL ASSOCIATION (AV)

100 South 5th Street Suite 1100, 55402
Telephone: 612-333-2111
FAX: 612-333-6798

Dennis A. Bowman
John Parsinen
Robert A. Levy
Jack A. Rosberg
John F. Bonner, III
David A. Gotlieb
Karen Ciegler Hansen
Jeffrey C. Robbins
E. Burke Hinds, III
Howard J. Rubin
David A. Orenstein
Diane L. Kroupa
Jeanne K. Stretch
John C. Levy
Joseph M. Sokolowski
Randy B. Evans
Brian R. Martens
Steven R. Katz

Rebecca McDaniel
Ann Marks Sanford
Timothy R. Ring
Robert A. Hill
W. James Vogl, Jr.
Bradley Allen Kletscher
John R. Bedosky
Roben D. Hunter
Jeffrey R. Johnson (Not admitted in MN)

OF COUNSEL

Bruce B. James

For full biographical listings, see the Martindale-Hubbell Law Directory

SIEGEL, BRILL, GREUPNER & DUFFY, P.A. (AV)

1300 Washington Square, 100 Washington Avenue South, 55401
Telephone: 612-339-7131
Telecopier: 612-339-6591

Richard Siegel
Josiah E. Brill, Jr.
James R. Greupner
Gerald S. Duffy
Wood R. Foster, Jr.
Thomas H. Goodman
John S. Watson
Wm. Christopher Penwell
Susan M. Voigt
Anthony James Gleekel
Joel H. Jensen

Sherri L. Rohlf
Brian E. Weisberg
Rosemary Tuohy
Jordan M. Lewis
James A. Yarosh

RETIRED

Maurice L. Grossman (P.A.)
Sheldon D. Karlins (P.A.)

Representative Clients: Champion Auto Stores, Inc.; Holiday Inns; Ron-Vik, Inc.; Super America Stations, Inc.; Ashland Oil, Inc.; Aveda Corporation; Applied Spectrum Technology, Inc.; Richard Manufacturing Co.; Mann Theaters; Homecraft Builders, Inc.

For full biographical listings, see the Martindale-Hubbell Law Directory

ZELLE & LARSON (AV)

33 South Sixth Street, City Center, Suite 4400, 55402
Telephone: 612-339-2020
Telecopier: 612-336-9100
Waltham, Massachusetts Office: 3 University Office Park, 95 Sawyer Road, Suite 500.
Telephone: 617-891-7020.
Dallas, Texas Office: 1201 Main Street, Suite 3000.
Telephone: 214-742-3000.
San Francisco, California Office: One Market Plaza, Steuart Street Tower, 15th Floor.
Telephone: 415-978-9788.

MEMBERS OF FIRM

Lowry Barfield (Resident, Dallas, Texas Office)
Stanley G. DeLaHunt
Alex M. Duarte (Resident, San Francisco, California Office)
Mark J. Feinberg
H. Jerome Gette (Resident, Dallas, Texas Office)
Rolf E. Gilbertson
Paul L. Gingras
Richard M. Hagstrom
John T. Harding, Jr. (Resident, Waltham, Massachusetts Office)
Lawrence T. Hofmann
Philip C. Hunsucker (Resident, San Francisco, California Office)
Dale I. Larson
David S. Markun (Resident, San Francisco, California Office)
John Buck Massopust
William Gerald McElroy, Jr. (Resident, Waltham, Massachusetts Office)
Terrence C. McRea (Resident, Dallas, Texas Office)
Steven D. Meier (Resident, San Francisco, California Office)
Janet L. R. Menna (Resident Waltham, Massachusetts Office)
Michael S. Quinn (Resident, Dallas, Texas Office)
James S. Reece
Timothy W. Regan
Jeff Ross
Patricia St. Peter
Lyle B. Sinell (Resident, San Francisco, California Office)
James E. Speier (Resident, Dallas, Texas Office)
Richard L. Voelbel
Sandra Wallace
Robert M. Wattson
Anthony R. Zelle (Resident, Waltham, Massachusetts Office)
Lawrence Zelle

ASSOCIATES

Steven J. Badger (Resident, Dallas, Texas Office)
Bryan M. Barber (Resident, San Francisco, California Office)
Michelle R. Bernard (Resident, San Francisco, California Office)
Karen Ann Brandstrader (Resident, San Francisco, California Office)
Brad E. Brewer (Resident, Dallas, Texas Office)
Kerry K. Brown (Resident, Dallas, Texas Office)
Michael R. Cashman
Thomas B. Caswell, III
Catherine M. Colinvaux (Resident, Waltham, Massachusetts Office)
Thomas H. Cook, Jr. (Resident, Dallas, Texas Office)
Veronica Czuchna (Resident, Dallas, Texas Office)
Thomas M. Darden
Matthew K. Davis (Resident, Dallas, Texas Office)
Keith A. Dotseth
Michelle Kathleen Enright
Greg S. Farnik (Resident, Dallas, Texas Office)
Rosemary A. Frazel
Felicia F. Goldstein (Resident, San Francisco, California Office)
Robert L. Gonser (Resident, San Francisco, California Office)
John C. Goodnow
Lisa F. Graul (Resident, San Francisco, California Office)
Andrea J. Greenberg (Resident, San Francisco, California Office)
Colleen C. Hammer (Resident, San Francisco, California Office)
Lesley M. James
Jonathan D. Jay
Mark C. Kareken
Ronald S. Kravitz (Resident, San Francisco, California Office)
David C. Linder (Not admitted in MN)
Brian E. Mahoney (Resident, San Francisco, California Office)
Robert D. Martinez (Resident, Dallas, Texas Office)
Kristin E. McIntosh (Resident, Waltham, Massachusetts Office)
Robert F. McKenna (Resident, San Francisco, California Office)
Daniel J. Millea
Natalie S. Monroe (Resident, Waltham, Massachusetts Office)
Joanne Munro (Resident, Dallas, Texas Office)
Kathleen B. O'Neill (Resident, Waltham, Massachusetts Office)
Joseph P. Pozen
Ranjani Ramakrishna (Resident, San Francisco, California Office)
Brian L. Ripperger
Andrew H. Roberts (Resident, Dallas, Texas Office)
Charles J. Rothstein
Scott J. Ryskoski (Not admitted in MN)
Denise Schardein (Resident, San Francisco, California Office)
Dana Shelhimer (Resident, Dallas, Texas Office)
Scott A. Slomiak (Resident, San Francisco, California Office)
Gillian Small, G.M. (Resident, San Francisco, California Office)
Paul K. Smith
T. Joe Snodgrass
L. Kimberly Steele (Resident, Dallas, Texas Office)
Michael J. Steinlage
Karl S. Vasiloff (Resident, Waltham, Massachusetts Office)
Terese S. Wallschlaeger
Daniel S. Weiss

For full biographical listings, see the Martindale-Hubbell Law Directory

*MOORHEAD,** Clay Co.

GUNHUS, GRINNELL, KLINGER, SWENSON & GUY, LTD. (AV)

512 Center Avenue, P.O. Box 1077, 56561-1077
Telephone: 218-236-6462
Telecopier: 218-236-9873
Fargo, North Dakota Office: 514 Gate City Building, P.O. Box 2783.
Telephone: 701-235-2506.
Telecopier: 701-235-9862.

ATTORNEYS

Gunder Gunhus
Paul E. Grinnell
Edward F. Klinger
Robert H. Swenson
William L. Guy, III
Dean A. Hoistad
Craig R. Campbell
Jon E. Strinden
Bernard E. Reynolds
Eric K. Fosaaen
Gregory P. Hammes
Bruce A. Schoenwald
Mary C. Locken
David M. Petrocchi (Not admitted in MN)

Insurance Clients: Aetna Life and Casualty Co.; Crum & Forster; Home Insurance Co.; Royal Insurance—USTU; St. Paul Cos.; United States Fidelity and Guaranty Co.
Representative Clients: Certainteed Corp.; Farm Credit Services; Heartland Medical Center; U.S. West Communications.

For full biographical listings, see the Martindale-Hubbell Law Directory

*NEW ULM,** Brown Co.

GISLASON, DOSLAND, HUNTER AND MALECKI (AV)

A Partnership including a Professional Association
State and Center Streets, P.O. Box 458, 56073-0458
Telephone: 507-354-3111
Telecopier: 507-354-8447
Minneapolis, Minnesota Office: Opus Center, Suite 215E. 9900 Bren Road East, P.O. Box 5297.
Telephone: 612-933-9900.
Telecopier: 612-933-0242.
Mankato, Minnesota Office: 75 Teton Lane, P.O. Box 4157.
Telephone: 507-387-1115.
Fax: 507-387-4413.
Chanhassen, Minnesota Office: Americana Community Bank Building, 600 West 79th Street, P.O. Box 950.
Telephone: 612-934-7754.
Fax: 612-934-7793.

MEMBERS OF FIRM

Sidney P. Gislason (1908-1985)
C. Allen Dosland
Daniel A. Gislason
C. Thomas Wilson
Ruth Ann Webster
Gary W. Koch
William A. Moeller
Kurt D. Johnson
Reed H. Glawe
Noel L. Phifer
Jeffry C. Braegelmann

ASSOCIATES

David W. Sturges (Not admitted in MN)
Mark S. Ullery
Michael S. Dove

Regional Counsel for: Associated Milk Producers, Inc.
Representative Clients: Travelers Insurance Co.; CIGNA; St. Paul Insurance Cos.; Farmers Insurance Group; Auto-Owners Insurance Co.; Midwest Medical Insurance Co.; Minnesota Lawyers Mutual Insurance Co.; Wausau Insurance Co.; Wal-Mart.

For Complete List of Firm Personnel, See General Section

For full biographical listings, see the Martindale-Hubbell Law Directory

*ST. CLOUD,** Stearns, Benton & Sherburne Cos.

HUGHES, MATHEWS & DIDIER, P.A. (AV)

110 South Sixth Avenue, Suite 200, P.O. Box 548, 56302-0548
Telephone: 612-251-4397
Fax: 612-251-5781

Kevin J. Hughes
Jean M. Didier

Paul R. Harris
Timothy S. Murphy

Representative Clients: The First American National Bank of St. Cloud; The St. Cloud Hospital; St. John's University; College of St. Benedict; Tanner Systems, Inc.; Anderson Trucking Service, Inc.

For Complete List of Firm Personnel, See General Section

For full biographical listings, see the Martindale-Hubbell Law Directory

HUGHES, THOREEN & KNAPP, P.A. (AV)

110 South Sixth Avenue, Suite 200, P.O. Box 1718, 56302-1718
Telephone: 612-251-6175
Fax: 612-251-6857

(See Next Column)

Keith F. Hughes
Gerald L. Thoreen
Thomas P. Knapp
Jerry O. Relph
Bradley W. Hanson

Representative Clients: The First American Bank of St. Cloud; North American State Bank of Belgrade, Minnesota; Holiday Inn of St. Cloud, Inc.; Catholic Charities of the Diocese of St. Cloud; Central Minnesota Mental Health Center; Central Minnesota Community Foundation; D.H. Blattner & Sons, Inc.; St. John's Abbey and University; College of St. Benedict; Sisters of the Order of St. Benedict.

For full biographical listings, see the Martindale-Hubbell Law Directory

*ST. PAUL,** Ramsey Co.

BANNIGAN & KELLY, P.A. (AV)

Suite 1750, North Central Life Tower, 445 Minnesota Street, 55101
Telephone: 612-224-3781
FAX: 612-223-8019

John F. Bannigan, Jr.
Patrick J. Kelly
James J. Hanton
Janet M. Wilebski
John W. Quarnstrom

For full biographical listings, see the Martindale-Hubbell Law Directory

BRIGGS AND MORGAN, PROFESSIONAL ASSOCIATION (AV)

2200 First National Bank Building, 55101
Telephone: 612-223-6600
Telecopier: 612-223-6450
Minneapolis, Minnesota Office: 2400 IDS Center, 80 South Eighth Street.
Telephone: 612-334-8400.
Telecopier: 612-334-8650.

RESIDENT PERSONNEL

David C. Forsberg
Alan H. Maclin
Jeffrey F. Shaw
Michael H. Streater
John B. Van de North, Jr.

MINNEAPOLIS OFFICE

Samuel L. Hanson
Jeffrey J. Keyes
Richard G. Mark
J. Patrick McDavitt
Timothy R. Thornton

For Complete List of Firm Personnel, See General Section

For full biographical listings, see the Martindale-Hubbell Law Directory

GERAGHTY, O'LOUGHLIN & KENNEY, PROFESSIONAL ASSOCIATION (AV)

One Capital Centre Plaza, Suite 1400, 55102-1308
Telephone: 612-291-1177
Fax: 612-297-6901

Terence J. O'Loughlin
James R. Gowling
Robert M. Mahoney
David C. Hutchinson
Timothy R. Murphy
William H. Leary, III
Richard J. Thomas
Patrick H. O'Neill, Jr
Mary H. Alcorn
Patricia Rosvold
Daniel R. Fritz
Matthew J. Hanzel
Ann D. Bray
Jean B. Rudolph
Bryon Ascheman

OF COUNSEL

James H. Geraghty
James W. Kenney (Retired)

Representative Clients: St. Paul Fire & Marine Insurance Cos.; Midwest Medical Insurance Co.; Minnesota Lawyers Mutual Insurance Co.; University of Minnesota Hospitals; American National Bank and Trust Co.; Continental National American Group; Commercial State Bank; MMI Co.; Hammel Green Abrahamson, Inc.; Lunda Construction Co.

For full biographical listings, see the Martindale-Hubbell Law Directory

JARDINE, LOGAN & O'BRIEN (AV)

2100 Piper Jaffray Plaza, 444 Cedar Street, 55101
Telephone: 612-290-6500
Fax: 612-223-5070

MEMBERS OF FIRM

Donald M. Jardine
John R. O'Brien
Gerald M. Linnihan
Alan R. Vanasek
John M. Kennedy, Jr.
Eugene J. Flick
Charles E. Gillin
James J. Galman
Pierre N. Regnier
Mark A. Fonken
Gregory G. Heacox
George W. Kuehner
James A. Jardine
Patti J. Skoglund
Sean E. Hade
Gregg A. Johnson
Timothy S. Crom
Lawrence M. Rocheford

ASSOCIATES

Thomas M. Countryman
James G. Golembeck
Kerry C. Koep
David J. Hoekstra
James K. Helling
Thomas A. Harder
Marsha E. Devine
Leonard J. Schweich
Kimberly K. Hobert
Katherine E. Sprague
Michael A. Rayer
Marlene S. Garvis

(See Next Column)

JARDINE, LOGAN & O'BRIEN—*Continued*

ASSOCIATES (Continued)

Mary Patricia Rowe
Karen R. Cote
Randall S. Lane
Jane Lanoue Binzak
Nathan W. Hart
Joseph E. Flynn
Ronald R. Envall
William R. Hauck

Representative Clients: American Hardware Mutual Insurance Co.; Ohio-Casualty Group; Farmers Insurance Group; Maryland-Casualty Co; CIGNA; Federated Insurance Co.; American International Group; Lumbermen's Underwriting Alliance; Dodson Insurance Group; Safeco Insurance Co.

For Complete List of Firm Personnel, See General Section

For full biographical listings, see the Martindale-Hubbell Law Directory

STRINGER & ROHLEDER, LTD. (AV)

1200 Norwest Center Tower, 55 East Fifth Street, 55101-1788
Telephone: 612-227-7784
Fax: 612-227-0044

Richard A. Rohleder
Harry T. Neimeyer
A. James Dickinson
Owen L. Sorenson
Suzanne Wolbeck Kvas
Bradley D. Hauswirth
Arthur J. Donnelly (1902-1988)
Philip Stringer (1899-1990)

Representative Clients: Farm Bureau Mutual Insurance Co.; MacArthur Co.; State Farm Insurance Cos.; American Cancer Society, Minnesota Division, Inc.; Norfolk Southern Corp.; Manville Sales Corp.
References: Norwest Bank Minnesota, N.A.; First Bank of Saint Paul, National Association; First Trust National Association.

For full biographical listings, see the Martindale-Hubbell Law Directory

WAYZATA, Hennepin Co.

CHAMBERLAIN, NEATON & JOHNSON (AV)

445 Lake, Suite 303, 55391
Telephone: 612-473-8444
FAX: 612-473-3501

MEMBERS OF FIRM

Paul W. Chamberlain
Scott A. Johnson
Todd M. Johnson
Patrick J. Neaton

For full biographical listings, see the Martindale-Hubbell Law Directory

*WILLMAR,** Kandiyohi Co.

SCHMIDT, THOMPSON, JOHNSON & MOODY, P.A. (AV)

707 Litchfield Avenue, S.W., Suite 100, P.O. Box 913, 56201-0913
Telephone: 612-235-1980; 1-800-733-7057

Henry W. Schmidt
Joe E. Thompson
William W. Thompson
Thomas G. Johnson
David C. Moody

Bradley J. Schmidt
Kathryn N. Smith

Representative Clients: First American Bank of Willmar; First Bank Central, N.A.; Willmar School District # 347; Holiday Inn of Willmar; Hormel Foods Corp.; Roth Chevrolet, Inc.; Auto Owners Insurance Co.; American Hardware Mutual Insurance Co.; American Family Insurance Co.

For full biographical listings, see the Martindale-Hubbell Law Directory

SCHNEIDER LAW FIRM, A PROFESSIONAL ASSOCIATION (AV)

706 South First Street, P.O. Box 776, 56201
Telephone: 612-235-1850
WATS: 800-840-1850
Fax: 612-235-3611

Ronald H. Schneider (P.A.)

Reference: First Bank Willmar.

For full biographical listings, see the Martindale-Hubbell Law Directory

MISSISSIPPI

*ABERDEEN,** Monroe Co.

HOLCOMB, DUNBAR, CONNELL, CHAFFIN & WILLARD, A PROFESSIONAL ASSOCIATION (AV)

109 1/2 West Commerce Street, P.O. Box 866, 39730
Telephone: 601-369-8800
Facsimile: 601-369-9404
Jackson, Mississippi Office: 111 East Capitol Street, Suite 290, P.O. Box 2990, 39207-2990.
Telephone: 601-948-0048.
Facsimile: 601-948-0050.

(See Next Column)

Clarksdale, Mississippi Office: 152 Delta Avenue, P.O. Box 368, 38614.
Telephone: 601-627-2241.
Facsimile: 601-627-9788.
Oxford, Mississippi Office: 1217 Jackson Avenue, P.O. Drawer 707, 38655.
Telephone: 601-234-8775.
Facsimile: 601-234-8638.
Southhaven, Mississippi Office: Suite 1, 8727 Northwest Drive, P.O. Box 190, 38671.
Telephone: 601-342-6806.
Facsimile: 601-342-6792.

Jack F. Dunbar
Craig M. Geno
Guy T. Gillespie, III
John H. Dunbar
David C. Dunbar
Robert H. Faulks

OF COUNSEL

Ralph E. Pogue

Representative Clients: Mississippi Power & Light Co.; Mississippi Valley Gas Co.; South Central Bell Telephone Co.; Cooper Tire & Rubber Co.; Navistar International; Volkswagen; Garan, Inc.; J.I. Case Co.; Farm Credit Bank of Texas; Keller Industries, Inc.

For Complete List of Firm Personnel, See General Section

For full biographical listings, see the Martindale-Hubbell Law Directory

PATTERSON & PATTERSON (AV)

304 East Jefferson Street, P.O. Box 663, 39730
Telephone: 601-369-2476
1-800-523-9975
FAX: 601-369-9806

MEMBERS OF FIRM

Robert D. Patterson
Jan P. Patterson

Local Counsel for: National Bank of Commerce of Mississippi; American Colloid Company; Vista Chemical Co.; Pruet Production Co.; Arco Oil & Gas Co.; Chemical Corporation; Unimin Corporation.

For Complete List of Firm Personnel, See General Section

For full biographical listings, see the Martindale-Hubbell Law Directory

BILOXI, Harrison Co.

MINOR AND GUICE (AV)

A Partnership including a Professional Association
160 Main Street, Drawer 1388, 39533
Telephone: 601-374-5151
FAX: 601-374-6630

Paul S. Minor (P.A.)
Judy M. Guice

Mark D. Lumpkin
Michael Bruffey

For full biographical listings, see the Martindale-Hubbell Law Directory

RUSHING & GUICE (AV)

683 Water Street, P.O. Box 1925, 39533-1925
Telephone: 601-374-2313
Telecopier: 601-374-8155

MEMBERS OF FIRM

Charles L. Rushing (1881-1923)
William L. Guice (1887-1971)
William Lee Guice III

OF COUNSEL

Jacob D. Guice

ASSOCIATES

Edgar F. Maier
R. Scott Wells

LEGAL SUPPORT PERSONNEL

Antonia Strong

For full biographical listings, see the Martindale-Hubbell Law Directory

*CLARKSDALE,** Coahoma Co.

HOLCOMB, DUNBAR, CONNELL, CHAFFIN & WILLARD, A PROFESSIONAL ASSOCIATION (AV)

152 Delta Avenue, P.O. Box 368, 38614
Telephone: 601-627-2241
Facsimile: 601-627-9788
Jackson, Mississippi Office: 111 East Capitol Street, Suite 290, P.O. Box 2990, 39207-2990.
Telephone: 601-948-0048.
Facsimile: 601-948-0050.
Aberdeen, Mississippi Office: 109 1/2 West Commerce Street, P.O. Box 866, 39730.
Telephone: 601-369-8800.
Facsimile: 601-369-9404.
Oxford, Mississippi Office: 1217 Jackson Avenue, P.O. Drawer 707, 38655.
Telephone: 601-234-8775.
Facsimile: 601-234-8638.

(See Next Column)

HOLCOMB, DUNBAR, CONNELL, CHAFFIN & WILLARD A PROFESSIONAL ASSOCIATION, *Clarksdale—Continued*

Southaven, Mississippi Office: Suite 1, 8727 Northwest Drive, 38671.
Telephone: 601-342-6806.
Facsimile: 601-342-6792.

William M. Chaffin
William G. Willard, Jr.
William A. Baskin
Jeffrey S. Dilley
David A. Burns

Representative Clients: Mississippi Power & Light Co.; Mississippi Valley Gas Co.; South Central Bell Telephone Co.; Cooper Tire & Rubber Co.; Volkswagen; Navistar International; Garan, Inc.; J.I. Case Co.; Farm Credit Bank of Texas; Keller Industries, Inc.

For Complete List of Firm Personnel, See General Section

For full biographical listings, see the Martindale-Hubbell Law Directory

MERKEL & COCKE, A PROFESSIONAL ASSOCIATION (AV)

30 Delta Avenue, P.O. Box 1388, 38614
Telephone: 601-627-9641
Fax: 601-627-3592

Charles M. Merkel
John H. Cocke
Walter Stephens Cox
Cynthia I. Mitchell
William B. Raiford, III
Jack R. Dodson, Jr.

Reference: United Southern Bank, Clarksdale, Miss.

For full biographical listings, see the Martindale-Hubbell Law Directory

*CLEVELAND,** Bolivar Co.

W. ALLEN PEPPER, JR., P.A. (AV)

The Gallery Building, 301 West Sunflower Road, P.O. Box 187, 38732
Telephone: 601-843-2724

W. Allen Pepper, Jr.

References: Sunburst Bank; Cleveland State Bank; Federal Land Bank of New Orleans; Farmers Home Administration; Mississippi Valley Title Insurance Co.

For full biographical listings, see the Martindale-Hubbell Law Directory

*COLUMBIA,** Marion Co.

AULTMAN, TYNER, MCNEESE & RUFFIN, LTD., A PROFESSIONAL LAW CORPORATION (AV)

329 Church Street, P.O. Drawer 707, 39429
Telephone: 601-736-2222
Hattiesburg, Mississippi Office: 315 Hemphill Street, P.O. Drawer 750.
Telephone: 601-583-2671.
Gulfport, Mississippi Office: 1201 25th Avenue, Suite 300, P.O. Box 607.
Telephone: 601-863-6913.

Thomas D. McNeese
Richard F. Yarborough, Jr.

Lawrence E. Hahn

OF COUNSEL

Ernest Ray Duff

Representative Clients: Hercules, Inc.; United States Steel Corp.; Ford Motor Co.; International Paper Co.; Phillips Petroleum Co.; Aetna Casualty & Surety Co.; CNA Group; Liberty Mutual Insurance Co.; St. Paul Fire & Marine Insurance Co.; Fireman's Fund.

For full biographical listings, see the Martindale-Hubbell Law Directory

*COLUMBUS,** Lowndes Co.

J. RANDOLPH LIPSCOMB (AV)

223 Sixth Street North, 39701
Telephone: 601-328-2100
Facsimile: 601-328-1067

For full biographical listings, see the Martindale-Hubbell Law Directory

*GREENWOOD,** Leflore Co.

UPSHAW, WILLIAMS, BIGGERS, PAGE & KRUGER (AV)

309 Fulton Street, P.O. Drawer 8230, 38930
Telephone: 601-455-1613
Facsimile: 601-453-9245
Jackson, Mississippi Office: One Jackson Place, 188 East Capitol Street, Suite 600. P.O. Drawer 1163, 39215.
Telephone: 601-944-0005.
Facsimile: 601-355-4269.

MEMBERS OF FIRM

James E. Upshaw
Tommie G. Williams
Marc A. Biggers
Thomas Y. Page (Resident, Jackson Office)
Stephen P. Kruger (Resident, Jackson Office)
Glenn F. Beckham
James D. Holland (Resident, Jackson Office)

(See Next Column)

MEMBERS OF FIRM (Continued)

F. Ewin Henson, III
Lonnie D. Bailey
Robert S. Upshaw
Clinton M. Guenther
Roger C. Riddick (Resident, Jackson Office)
Edley H. Jones, III (Resident, Jackson Office)
C. Richard Benz, Jr.
Richard C. Williams, Jr.
Wes Peters (Resident, Jackson Office)

ASSOCIATES

Brent E. Southern (Resident, Jackson Office)
R.H. Burress, III
Kathleen S. Gordon (Resident, Jackson Office)
W. Hugh Gillon, IV (Resident, Jackson Office)
William C. Helm (Resident, Jackson Office)
Bryan H. Callaway
Mark C. Carroll (Resident, Jackson Office)
Paul L. Goodman
Walter C. Morrison, IV (Resident, Jackson Office)
Patrick C. Malouf (Resident, Jackson Office)
David C. Meadors
Stuart B. Harmon (Resident, Jackson Office)

OF COUNSEL

B. L. Riddick (Resident, Jackson Office)
John R. Countiss, III (Resident, Jackson Office)

Representative Clients: U.S.F. & G. Co.; State Farm Mutual Automobile Ins. Co.; ; Continental Insurance Co.; St. Paul Fire & Marine Insurance Co.; Aetna Casualty & Surety Co.; Kemper Insurance Co.; Zurich-American Ins. Group; Home Ins. Co.; Illinois Central Railroad Co.; Allstate Insurance Co.

For full biographical listings, see the Martindale-Hubbell Law Directory

*GRENADA,** Grenada Co.

LISTON/LANCASTER

(See Winona)

*GULFPORT,** Harrison Co.

ALLEN, VAUGHN, COBB & HOOD, P.A. (AV)

One Hancock Plaza, Suite 1209, P.O. Drawer 4108, 39502-4108
Telephone: 601-864-4011
Fax: 601-864-4852

Harry R. Allen
Thomas E. Vaughn
David L. Cobb
Billy W. Hood
Robert W. Atkinson
Benjamin U. Bowden
Richard B. Tubertini
Rodney Douglas Robinson

Steven Johnson Allen (Resident)
E. Colette Towles
David W. Crane
John A. Foxworth, Jr.
H. Gray Laird, III
W. Wright Hill

OF COUNSEL

D. Knox White

For full biographical listings, see the Martindale-Hubbell Law Directory

AULTMAN, TYNER, MCNEESE & RUFFIN, LTD., A PROFESSIONAL LAW CORPORATION (AV)

1201 25th Avenue, Suite 300, P.O. Box 607, 39502
Telephone: 601-863-6913
Hattiesburg, Mississippi Office: 315 Hemphill Street, P.O. Drawer 750.
Telephone: 601-583-2671.
Columbia, Mississippi Office: 329 Church Street, P.O. Drawer 707.
Telephone: 601-736-2222.

Ben E. Sheely
Paul J. Delcambre, Jr.
Dorrance (Dee) Aultman, Jr.

For full biographical listings, see the Martindale-Hubbell Law Directory

DUKES, DUKES, KEATING AND FANECA, P.A. (AV)

2308 East Beach Boulevard, P.O. Drawer W, 39501
Telephone: 601-868-1111
FAX: 601-863-2886

William F. Dukes
Walter W. Dukes
Hugh D. Keating
Cy Faneca
William H. Pettey, Jr.
Phillip W. Jarrell

Horace Simon Scruggs
Helen C. Werby
David Charles Goff

For full biographical listings, see the Martindale-Hubbell Law Directory

FRANKE, RAINEY & SALLOUM (AV)

2605 14th Street, P.O. Drawer 460, 39502
Telephone: 601-868-7070
Telecopier: 601-868-7090

MEMBERS OF FIRM

Paul M. Franke, Jr.
William M. Rainey
Richard P. Salloum
Paul B. Howell
Ronald T. Russell
Fredrick B. Feeney, II
Traci M. Castille

(See Next Column)

FRANKE, RAINEY & SALLOUM—*Continued*

ASSOCIATES

Kaleel G. Salloum, Jr.
Ruth E. Bennett
Donald P. Moore
Roland F. Samson, III
Jeffrey S. Bruni
Stefan G. Bourn

For full biographical listings, see the Martindale-Hubbell Law Directory

BOYCE HOLLEMAN A PROFESSIONAL CORPORATION (AV)

1913 15th Street, P.O. Drawer 1030, 39502
Telephone: 601-863-3142
Telecopier: 601-863-9829

Boyce Holleman

Michael B. Holleman
Timothy C. Holleman
Leslie Dean Holleman
David J. White

References: Hancock Bank, Gulfport; Merchants Bank & Trust Co., Gulfport; Bank of Wiggins, Wiggins, Mississippi.

For full biographical listings, see the Martindale-Hubbell Law Directory

HOPKINS, DODSON, CRAWLEY, BAGWELL, UPSHAW & PERSONS (AV)

2701 24th Avenue, P.O. Box 1510, 39502-1510
Telephone: 601-864-2200
Mississippi & USA Wats: 1-800-421-3629
Fax: 601-868-9358; 601-863-4227

MEMBERS OF FIRM

Alben N. Hopkins
Lisa P. Dodson
Timothy D. Crawley
Douglas Bagwell
Jessica Sibley Upshaw
James B. Persons

ASSOCIATES

Perre M. Cabell
Christopher Anthony Davis
James Robert Reeves, Jr.
Ottis B. Crocker, III
Kaye Johnson Persons (Not admitted in MS)
Matthew G. Mestayer
Regina A. Lightsey
Mary Benton-Shaw (Not admitted in MS)
K. Douglas Lee (Not admitted in MS)
Thomas A. Waller
M. Amanda Baucum (Not admitted in MS)

LEGAL SUPPORT PERSONNEL

PARALEGALS

Cherri Nickoles
Penny W. West
Jennifer Susan Regan
Justina M. Tillman
Jayme L. Evans
Tracey L. Owen
Marcia P. Henry
Anne B. Parks

Representative Clients: Avondale Shipyards; Employers Insurance of Wausau; Fireman's Fund Insurance Company; General Cable Company; Hartford Insurance Company and Its Affiliates; Insurance Company of North America; Libery Mutual Group; Reliance Insurance; USX Corporation.

For full biographical listings, see the Martindale-Hubbell Law Directory

MEADOWS, RILEY, KOENENN AND TEEL, P.A. (AV)

1720 23rd Avenue, P.O. Box 550, 39502
Telephone: 601-864-4511
Telecopier: 601-868-2178

Joseph R. Meadows
Donnie D. Riley
Alfred R. Koenenn
Walter W. Teel
Jerry D. Riley
Karen J. Young

Representative Clients: Bubba Oustalat Lincoln Mercury, Inc.; Lee Tractor Co. of Mississippi.
Reference: Hancock Bank.

For full biographical listings, see the Martindale-Hubbell Law Directory

*HATTIESBURG,** Forrest Co.

AULTMAN, TYNER, MCNEESE & RUFFIN, LTD., A PROFESSIONAL LAW CORPORATION (AV)

315 Hemphill Street, P.O. Drawer 750, 39403-0750
Telephone: 601-583-2671
Columbia, Mississippi Office: 329 Church Street, P.O. Drawer 707.
Telephone: 601-736-2222.
Gulfport, Mississippi Office: 1201 25th Avenue, Suite 300, P.O. Box 607.
Telephone: 601-863-6913.

Dorrance Aultman
Thomas W. Tyner
Thomas D. McNeese (Resident, Columbia Office)
Louie F. Ruffin
Richard F. Yarborough, Jr. (Resident, Columbia Office)
Ben E. Sheely (Resident, Gulfport Office)
Patrick H. Zachary
Paul J. Delcambre, Jr. (Resident, Gulfport Office)
Robert J. Dambrino, III
Vicki R. Leggett
R. Curtis Smith, II
Dorrance (Dee) Aultman, Jr. (Resident, Gulfport Office)
William Nelson Graham

(See Next Column)

James L. Quinn
Walter J. Eades
Lawrence E. Hahn (Resident, Columbia Office)
Carol Ann Estes
Victor A. DuBose

OF COUNSEL

Ernest Ray Duff (Resident, Columbia Office)

Representative Clients: Hercules, Inc.; U.S. Steel Corp.; Ford Motor Co.; Phillips Petroleum Co.; Aetna Casualty & Surety Co.; CNA Group; Liberty Mutual Insurance Co.; St. Paul Fire & Marine Insurance Co.; Fireman's Fund.

For full biographical listings, see the Martindale-Hubbell Law Directory

*JACKSON,** Hinds Co.

* indicates certain Bar Register subscribers whose principal office is located elsewhere in the state and who have arranged for representation as a part of the state capital listings that follow

ALLRED & DONALDSON (AV)

101 West Capitol Street, Suite 300, P.O. Box 3828, 39207-3828
Telephone: 601-948-2086
Telefax: 601-948-2175

MEMBERS OF FIRM

Michael S. Allred
John I. Donaldson

ASSOCIATES

Stephen M. Maloney
Kathleen H. Eiler

For full biographical listings, see the Martindale-Hubbell Law Directory

ALSTON, RUTHERFORD, TARDY & VAN SLYKE (AV)

121 North State Street, P.O. Drawer 1532, 39215-1532
Telephone: 601-948-6882
Fax: 601-948-6902

MEMBERS OF FIRM

Alex A. Alston, Jr.
Kenneth A. Rutherford
Thomas W. Tardy, III
Barry H. Powell
Julie E. Chaffin
Patrick D. McMurtray
Terryl K. Rushing
C. Jackson Williams

ASSOCIATES

Denise Foster Schreiber
Richard L. Jones
Terry S. Williamson
David M. Loper

Counsel for: Ford Motor Co.; E.I. DuPont de Nemours Co.; Gannett Co., Inc.; Conoco, Inc.; General Electric Company; Jostens, Inc.; Georgia-Pacific Corp.; Dean Witter Reynolds, Inc.; Transcontinental Gas Pipeline, Inc.; Piccadilly Cafeterias.

For Complete List of Firm Personnel, See General Section

For full biographical listings, see the Martindale-Hubbell Law Directory

COPELAND COOK TAYLOR & BUSH (AV)

17th Floor, Capital Towers Building, 125 South Congress Street, P.O. Drawer 2132, 39225-2132
Telephone: 601-354-0123
Facsimile: 601-352-6714

MEMBERS OF FIRM

Charles G. Copeland
Thomas A. Cook
Glenn G. Taylor
C. Glen Bush, Jr.
Thomas C. Gerity
Harry E. Neblett, Jr.
James R. Moore, Jr.
Suzanna Baker
J. Tucker Mitchell
Robert P. Thompson
Thomas R. Hudson
Michael W. Baxter
Keith David Obert
James F. Noble III
Lee Howell, III
Monte L. Barton, Jr.
W. Shan Thompson
Gregory L. Kennedy
John M. Breland
C. Dale Shearer

For full biographical listings, see the Martindale-Hubbell Law Directory

HOLCOMB, DUNBAR, CONNELL, CHAFFIN & WILLARD, A PROFESSIONAL ASSOCIATION (AV)

111 East Capitol Street, Suite 290, P.O. Box 2990, 39207-2990
Telephone: 601-948-0048
Facsimile: 601-948-0050
Clarksdale, Mississippi Office: 152 Delta Avenue, P.O. Box 368, 38614.
Telephone: 601-627-2241.
Facsimile: 601-627-9788.
Aberdeen, Mississippi Office: 109 1/2 West Commerce Street, P.O. Box 866, 39730.
Telephone: 601-369-8800.
Facsimile: 601-369-9404.
Oxford, Mississippi Office: 1217 Jackson Avenue, P.O. Drawer 707, 38655.
Telephone: 601-234-8775.
Facsimile: 601-234-8638.

(See Next Column)

HOLCOMB, DUNBAR, CONNELL, CHAFFIN & WILLARD A PROFESSIONAL ASSOCIATION, *Jackson—Continued*

Southaven, Mississippi Office: Suite 1, 8727 Northwest Drive, P.O. Box 190, 38671.
Telephone: 601-342-6806.
Facsimile: 601-342-6792.

Jack F. Dunbar
William M. Chaffin
William G. Willard, Jr.
Craig M. Geno
Guy T. Gillespie, III
Edward A. Moss
Thomas J. Suszek
John H. Dunbar
David C. Dunbar
Michael N. Watts
Janet G. Arnold
William A. Baskin
Thomas T. Dunbar
Robert H. Faulks
Jeffrey S. Dilley
David A. Burns
T. Swayze Alford
Nancy M. Maddox
Robert S. Mink
Jeffrey Kyle Tyree
Stephan L. McDavid
Barry C. Blackburn

OF COUNSEL

Ralph E. Pogue

Representative Clients: Mississippi Power & Light Co.; Mississippi Valley Gas Co.; South Central Bell Telephone Co.; Cooper Tire & Rubber Co.; Navistar International; Garan, Inc.; J.I. Case Co.; Farm Credit Bank of Texas; Keller Industries, Inc.; Deere & Co.

For Complete List of Firm Personnel, See General Section

For full biographical listings, see the Martindale-Hubbell Law Directory

JOEL W. HOWELL, III (AV)

5446 Executive Place, P.O. Box 16772, 39236
Telephone: 601-362-8129
Telecopier: 601-362-8419

Reference: Deposit Guaranty National Bank, Jackson, Mississippi.

For full biographical listings, see the Martindale-Hubbell Law Directory

LILLY & WISE (AV)

Suite 2180 Deposit Guaranty Plaza, 210 East Capitol Street, 39201-2305
Telephone: 601-354-4040; 601-354-0078
Fax: DATA 601-354-2244

Thomas G. Lilly
Joseph P. Wise

For full biographical listings, see the Martindale-Hubbell Law Directory

MCDAVID, NOBLIN & WEST (AV)

Suite 1000, Security Centre North, 200 South Lamar Street, 39201
Telephone: 601-948-3305
Telecopier: 601-354-4789

MEMBERS OF FIRM

John Land McDavid
William C. Noblin, Jr.
W. Eric West
John Sanford McDavid
John C. Robertson

OF COUNSEL

Lowell F. Stephens

For full biographical listings, see the Martindale-Hubbell Law Directory

MCNAMARA, KELLY & WELSH (AV)

4273 I-55 North, Suite 200, 39206
Telephone: 601-362-6700
Telecopier: 601-362-4888

MEMBERS OF FIRM

J. Leray (Ray) McNamara
Ann H. Kelly
Jennifer L. Welsh

Representative Clients: Deposit Guaranty National Bank; Sears, Roebuck and Co.; Wal-Mart Stores, Inc.; Chubb and Son, Inc.; Kawasaki Motors Corp., U.S.A.; Medical Assurance Company of Mississippi; Mississippi Hospital Association.
References: Deposit Guaranty National Bank; Sunburst Bank.

For full biographical listings, see the Martindale-Hubbell Law Directory

PHELPS DUNBAR, L.L.P. (AV)

Suite 500, Security Centré North, 200 South Lamar Street, P.O. Box 23066, 39225-3066
Telephone: 601-352-2300
Telecopier: 601-360-9777
New Orleans, Louisiana Office: Texaco Center, 400 Poydras Street.
Telephone: 504-566-1311.
Telecopier: 504-568-9130; 504-568-9007.
Cable Address: "Howspencer."
Telex: 584125 WU.
Telex: 6821155 WUI.
Baton Rouge, Louisiana Office: Suite 701, City National Bank Building, P.O. Box 4412.
Telephone: 504-346-0285.
Telecopier: 504-381-9197.

(See Next Column)

Tupelo, Mississippi Office: Seventh Floor, One Mississippi Plaza, P.O. Box 1220.
Telephone: 601-842-7907.
Telecopier: 601-842-3873.
Houston, Texas Office: Suite 501, 4 Houston Center, 1331 Lamar Street.
Telephone: 713-659-1386.
Telecopier: 713-659-1388.
London, England Office: Suite 976, Level 9, Lloyd's, 1 Lime Street, London EC3M 7DQ England.
Telephone: 011-44-171-929-4765.
Telecopier: 011-44-171-929-0046.
Telex: 987321.

MEMBERS OF FIRM

Fred M. Bush, Jr. (Also at Tupelo, Mississippi Office)
F. M. Bush, III (Also at Tupelo, Mississippi Office)
Walker W. (Bill) Jones, III (Also at Tupelo, Mississippi Office)
David W. Mockbee
Ross F. Bass, Jr.
E. Clifton Hodge, Jr.
Reuben V. Anderson
Frank W. Trapp
Arthur F. Jernigan, Jr.
Luther T. Munford
Michael B. Wallace
John P. Sneed
William C. Brabec
Charles D. Porter

COUNSEL

Mary Elizabeth Hall
G. Kay L. Trapp (Also at Tupelo, Mississippi Office)

ASSOCIATES

Chuck D. Barlow
Scott W. Bates
Sheryl Bey
Danny A. Drake
Gregory D. Guida
Robert T. Higginbotham Jr.
Angela M. McLain
John A. Meynardie
Julie Sneed Muller
Carlton W. Reeves
Todd C. Richter
William F. Selph III
William Carter Smallwood, III (Also at Tupelo, Mississippi Office)
Joseph A. Ziemianski

Representative Clients: AMCA International Limited (Jesco Division); Bank of Mississippi; Blue Cross & Blue Shield of Mississippi; CBI Equifax; General Motors Corporation; The Kroger Co.; Mississippi Municipal Liability Plan; North Mississippi Medical Center, Inc. (and affiliated hospitals); Philip Morris Incorporated; Underwriters at Lloyd's, London.

For Complete List of Firm Personnel, See General Section

For full biographical listings, see the Martindale-Hubbell Law Directory

PRICE & ZIRULNIK (AV)

Suite 1150 Capital Towers, 125 South Congress Street, P.O. Box 3439, 39207-3439
Telephone: 601-353-3000
Telecopier: 601-353-3007

John H. Price, Jr.
Barry S. Zirulnik

ASSOCIATE

William G. Cheney, Jr.

Representative Clients: Yellow Freight System, Inc.; Mississippi Dairy Products Association, Inc.; LuVel Dairy Products, Inc.; Mississippi Farm Bureau Federation; Mississippi Department of Transportation; Mississippi High School Activities Association, Inc.; Variety Wholesalers, Inc.; Mississippi Bankers Association; Metal Rolling, Inc.

For full biographical listings, see the Martindale-Hubbell Law Directory

SHELL, BUFORD, BUFKIN, CALLICUTT & PERRY (AV)

920 Trustmark Building, P.O. Box 157, 39205
Telephone: 601-948-2291
Facsimile: 601-352-6968

MEMBERS OF FIRM

Dan H. Shell (1918-1976)
Frank T. Williams (1904-1977)
J. Dudley Buford (1920-1991)
Cary E. Bufkin
K. Hayes Callicutt
Kenneth G. Perry
Douglas R. Duke
Crane D. Kipp
James F. Mixson
James N. Bullock
Ken R. Adcock
D. Collier Graham, Jr.
Eugene R. Naylor

ASSOCIATES

E. Frank Goodman
R. Scott Sellers (Not admitted in MS)

Representative Clients: Mississippi Baptist Medical Center; Mississippi Chemical Corp.; Aetna Casualty and Surety Co.; American International Group; Atlantic Mutual Insurance Co.; Commercial Union Insurance Co.; United States Fidelity and Guaranty Co.; Home Insurance Co.; The Chubb Group; Trustmark National Bank.

For full biographical listings, see the Martindale-Hubbell Law Directory

STEEN REYNOLDS DALEHITE & CURRIE (AV)

Mississippi Valley Title Building, 315 Tombigbee Street, P.O. Box 900, 39205
Telephone: 601-969-7054
Telecopier: 601-969-5120

(See Next Column)

STEEN REYNOLDS DALEHITE & CURRIE—*Continued*

MEMBERS OF FIRM

Jimmie B. Reynolds, Jr.
William M. Dalehite, Jr.
Edward J. Currie, Jr.
Whitman B. Johnson, III
William C. Griffin
Philip W. Gaines
Michael F. Myers

ASSOCIATES

Frances R. Shields
William H. Creel, Jr.
James C. Smallwood, III
F. Keith Ball
Shannon S. Clark
Lisa L. Williams
Le Robinson Brown

OF COUNSEL

Jerome B. Steen

Mississippi Counsel for: State Farm Insurance Co.
Representative Clients include: Allstate Insurance Co.; St. Paul Insurance Cos.; Indiana Lumbermens Mutual Insurance Co.; United Services Automobile Assn.; Empire Fire & Marine Ins.; Sears Roebuck & Co.
References: Trustmark National Bank, Jackson, Mississippi.

For full biographical listings, see the Martindale-Hubbell Law Directory

*** UPSHAW, WILLIAMS, BIGGERS, PAGE & KRUGER (AV)**

One Jackson Place, 188 East Capitol Street, Suite 600, P.O. Drawer 1163, 39215
Telephone: 601-944-0005
Facsimile: 601-355-4269
Greenwood, Mississippi Office: 309 Fulton Street, P.O. Drawer 8230, 38930.
Telephone: 601-455-1613.
Facsimile: 601-453-9245.

RESIDENT MEMBERS

Thomas Y. Page
Stephen P. Kruger
James D. Holland
Roger C. Riddick
Edley H. Jones, III
Wes Peters

RESIDENT ASSOCIATES

Brent E. Southern
Kathleen S. Gordon
W. Hugh Gillon, IV
William C. Helm
Mark C. Carroll
Walter C. Morrison, IV
Patrick C. Malouf
Stuart B. Harmon

OF COUNSEL

B. L. Riddick
John R. Countiss, III

Representative Clients: U.S.F. & G. Co.; State Farm Mutual Automobile Ins. Co.; Continental Insurance Co.; St. Paul Fire & Marine Insurance Co.; Aetna Casualty & Surety Co.; Kemper Insurance Co.; Zurich-America Ins. Group; Home Ins. Co.; Illinois Central Railroad Co.; Allstate Insurance Co.

For full biographical listings, see the Martindale-Hubbell Law Directory

WATKINS & EAGER (AV)

Suite 300 The Emporium Building, P.O. Box 650, 39205
Telephone: 601-948-6470
Facsimile: (601) 354-3623

MEMBERS OF FIRM

William H. Cox, Jr.
P. Nicholas Harkins, III
John G. Corlew
John L. Low, IV
Paul H. Stephenson, III
William F. Goodman, III
Douglas J. Gunn
William F. Ray

Representative Clients: Armco, Inc.; Caterpillar Tractor Co.; Ford Motor Co.; Ingersoll-Rand Co.; International Paper Co.; Shell Oil Co.; Toyota Motor Sales, U.S.A., Inc.

For Complete List of Firm Personnel, See General Section

For full biographical listings, see the Martindale-Hubbell Law Directory

WELLS MARBLE & HURST (AV)

Suite 400, Lamar Life Building, 317 East Capitol Street, P.O. Box 131, 39205-0131
Telephone: 601-355-8321
Telecopier: 601-355-4217

William Calvin Wells (1844-1914)
Major W. Calvin Wells (1878-1957)
William Calvin Wells, Jr. (1908-1988)

MEMBERS OF FIRM

Erskine W. Wells
Roland D. Marble
Joe Jack Hurst
J. Jerry Langford
John Edward Hughes, III
James S. Armstrong
William H. Glover, Jr.
Wendell H. Cook, Jr.
Kenna L. Mansfield, Jr.
Steven H. Begley
Daniel H. Fairly
Roy H. Liddell
Walter D. Willson

(See Next Column)

ASSOCIATES

Kelly D. Simpkins
Lana Edwards Gillon

Counsel for: General Motors Corp.; United States Steel Corp.; International Business Machines Corp.; Illinois Central Railroad Co.; Lamar Life Insurance Co.; Metropolitan Life Insurance Co.; Prudential Insurance Company of America; Southern Natural Gas Co.; Trustmark National Bank of Jackson.

For full biographical listings, see the Martindale-Hubbell Law Directory

WISE CARTER CHILD & CARAWAY, PROFESSIONAL ASSOCIATION (AV)

600 Heritage Building, 401 East Capitol Street, P.O. Box 651, 39205
Telephone: 601-968-5500
FAX: 601-968-5519

Natie P. Caraway
James L. Robertson
George Q. Evans
A. Spencer Gilbert III
Charles T. Ozier
W. McDonald Nichols
Richard D. Gamblin
David W. Clark
John D. Price
Douglas E. Levanway
F. Hall Bailey
Clifford K. Bailey, III
Andrew D. Sweat
Mark P. Caraway
George H. Ritter
R. Mark Hodges
Charles E. Ross

John W. Robinson, III.
Ronald J. Artigues, Jr.
Rachael Hetherington Lenoir

Representative Clients: General Motors Corp.; Sanderson Farms, Inc.; Sunburst Bank; Energy Operations, Inc.; Illinois Central Railroad Co.; McCaw Cellular Communications, Inc.; Mississippi Power & Light Co.; Mississippi Hospital Assn.; St. Paul Cos.

For Complete List of Firm Personnel, See General Section

For full biographical listings, see the Martindale-Hubbell Law Directory

*MERIDIAN,** Lauderdale Co.

BOURDEAUX AND JONES (AV)

505 Constitution Avenue, P.O. Box 2009, 39302-2009
Telephone: 601-693-2393
Fax: 601-693-0226

Thomas D. Bourdeaux
Thomas R. Jones
William C. Hammack
Thomas L. Webb
J. Richard Barry
E. Gregory Snowden
Michael D. Herrin
Lee Thaggard

General Counsel for: Dixie Oil Co. of Alabama; Great Southern National Bank; Meridian Housing Authority; Mississippi Loggers Purchasing Group, Inc.; New South Communications, Inc.; City of Meridian; Lauderdale County Board of Supervisors.
Local Counsel for: Chrysler Corporation; Louisiana-Pacific Corp.; Hartford Insurance Group; Fireman's Fund American Insurance Cos.; Mississippi Loggers Assn., S.I.F.; United States Fidelity and Guaranty Co.

For full biographical listings, see the Martindale-Hubbell Law Directory

EPPES, WATTS & SHANNON (AV)

4805 Poplar Springs Drive, P.O. Box 3787, 39303-3787
Telephone: 601-483-3968
Telecopier: 601-693-0416

MEMBERS OF FIRM

Walter W. Eppes, Jr.
T. Kenneth Watts
John Rex Shannon
Grace Watts Mitts
William B. Carter

Representative Clients: Allstate Insurance Co.; American International Adjusting Co.; CIGNA; Liberty Mutual Insurance Co.; Royal Globe Insurance Co.; St. Paul Insurance Cos.; State Farm Insurance Co.; General Motors Corporation; Medical Assurance Corp.; Sears, Roebuck and Co.

For full biographical listings, see the Martindale-Hubbell Law Directory

*NATCHEZ,** Adams Co.

MULHEARN & MULHEARN (AV)

202 South Wall Street, P.O. Box 967, 39120
Telephone: 601-442-4808
Fax: 601-446-6224

MEMBERS OF FIRM

John E. Mulhearn (1910-1981)
John E. Mulhearn, Jr.

LEGAL SUPPORT PERSONNEL

Eva Ruth Seale
Norma Joyce Beasley

Representative Client: Natchez Electric & Supply Co., Inc.
Approved Attorneys for: Mississippi Valley Title Insurance Co.; American Title Insurance Co.

For full biographical listings, see the Martindale-Hubbell Law Directory

*NEW ALBANY,** Union Co.

TALMADGE D. LITTLEJOHN (AV)

108 East Main Street, P.O. Box 869, 38652
Telephone: 601-534-6835; 534-6215
FAX: 601-534-6215

References: First National Bank, New Albany, Miss.; Bank of New Albany.

For full biographical listings, see the Martindale-Hubbell Law Directory

OLIVE BRANCH, De Soto Co.

WOODS AND SNYDER (AV)

8925 E. Goodman Road, P.O. Box 456, 38654
Telephone: 601-895-2996
Memphis Direct Line: 901-526-1312
Fax: 601-895-5480

MEMBERS OF FIRM

James E. Woods
Gary P. Snyder

For full biographical listings, see the Martindale-Hubbell Law Directory

*OXFORD,** Lafayette Co.

FREELAND & FREELAND (AV)

1013 Jackson Avenue, P.O. Box 269, 38655
Telephone: 601-234-3414
Telecopier: 601-234-0604

MEMBERS OF FIRM

T. H. Freeland, III
T. H. Freeland, IV
J. Hale Freeland

ASSOCIATE

Paul W. Crutcher

Representative Clients: The Ohio Casualty Group; Crum & Forester.

For full biographical listings, see the Martindale-Hubbell Law Directory

HOLCOMB, DUNBAR, CONNELL, CHAFFIN & WILLARD, A PROFESSIONAL ASSOCIATION (AV)

1217 Jackson Avenue P.O. Drawer 707, 38655
Telephone: 601-234-8775
Facsimile: 601-234-8638
Jackson, Mississippi Office: 111 East Capitol Street, Suite 290. P.O. Box 2990, 39207-2990.
Telephone: 601-948-0048.
Facsimile: 601-948-0050.
Clarksdale, Mississippi Office: 152 Delta Avenue, P.O. Box 368, 38614.
Telephone: 601-627-2241.
Facsimile: 601-627-9788.
Aberdeen, Mississippi Office: 109 1/2 West Commerce Street, P.O. Box 866, 39730.
Telephone: 601-369-8800.
Facsimile: 601-369-9404.
Southaven, Mississippi Office: Suite 1, 8727 Northwest Drive, P.O. Box 190, 38671.
Telephone: 601-342-6806.
Facsimile: 601-342-6792.

Jack F. Dunbar
Guy T. Gillespie, III
Edward A. Moss
Thomas J. Suszek
John H. Dunbar
Michael N. Watts
Janet G. Arnold
Thomas T. Dunbar
T. Swayze Alford
Nancy M. Maddox
Stephan L. McDavid
Louis H. Watson, Jr.

Representative Clients: Mississippi Power & Light Co.; Mississippi Valley Gas Co.; South Central Bell Telephone Co.; Cooper Tire & Rubber Co.; Navistar International; Garan, Inc.; J.I. Case Co.; Farm Credit Bank of Texas; Keller Industries, Inc.; Deere & Co.

For Complete List of Firm Personnel, See General Section

For full biographical listings, see the Martindale-Hubbell Law Directory

*PASCAGOULA,** Jackson Co.

BRYAN, NELSON, SCHROEDER, CASTIGLIOLA & BANAHAN (AV)

1103 Jackson Avenue, P.O. Drawer 1529, 39568-1529
Telephone: 601-762-6631
Fax: 601-769-6392

MEMBERS OF FIRM

Ernest R. Schroeder
Vincent J. Castigliola, Jr.
John A. Banahan

ASSOCIATES

H. Benjamin Mullen
Melinda O. Johnson
E. Russell Turner

Representative Clients: Allstate Insurance Company; American Tobacco Company; Bethlehem Steel Corporation; Citizens National Bank; Colle Tug & Towing Company, Inc.; Medical Assurance Co. of Mississippi; RYOBI Motor Products Corporation; SAIA Motor Reight Lines, Inc.; State Farm Insurance Companies; United Services Automobile Association.

(See Next Column)

For full biographical listings, see the Martindale-Hubbell Law Directory

*POPLARVILLE,** Pearl River Co.

WILLIAMS, WILLIAMS AND MONTGOMERY, P.A. (AV)

109 Erlanger Street, P.O. Box 113, 39470
Telephone: 601-795-4572
FAX: 601-795-8382
Picayune, Mississippi Office: 900 Highway 11 South, P.O. Box 1058.
Telephone: 601-798-0480.
FAX: 601-798-5481.

E. B. Williams (1890-1976)
E. B. Williams, Jr. (1917-1990)
Lampton O'Neal Williams
Joseph H. Montgomery
E. Bragg Williams, III
L. O'Neal Williams, Jr.

Michael E. Patten
Anne M. Parker

Representative Clients: Hancock Bank, Bank of Commerce Branch; Wesley's Fertilizer Plant, Inc.; Wesley Oil and Gas Co., Inc.; Garrett Industries, Inc.; Bass Pecan Co., Lumberton, Miss.; Joe N. Miles & Sons Lumber Co., Inc., Lumberton and Silver Creek, Miss. and Bogalusa, La.

Reference: Hancock Bank, Bank of Commerce Branch, Poplarville, Mississippi.

For full biographical listings, see the Martindale-Hubbell Law Directory

*SENATOBIA,** Tate Co.

NAT G. TROUTT (AV)

210 South Ward Street, 38668
Telephone: 601-562-4426
FAX: 601-562-8653

For full biographical listings, see the Martindale-Hubbell Law Directory

SOUTHAVEN, De Soto Co.

HOLCOMB, DUNBAR, CONNELL, CHAFFIN & WILLARD, A PROFESSIONAL ASSOCIATION (AV)

Suite 1, 8727 Northwest Drive, P.O. Box 190, 38671
Telephone: 601-342-6806
Facsimile: 601-342-6792
Jackson, Mississippi Office: 111 East Capitol Street, Suite 290, P.O. Box 2990, 39207-2990.
Telephone: 601-948-0048.
Facsimile: 601-948-0050.
Clarksdale, Mississippi Office: 152 Delta Avenue, P.O. Box 368, 38614.
Telephone: 601-627-2241.
Facsimile: 601-627-9788.
Aberdeen, Mississippi Office: 109 1/2 West Commerce Street, P.O. Box 866, 39730.
Telephone: 601-369-8800.
Facsimile: 601-369-9404.
Oxford, Mississippi Office: 1217 Jackson Avenue, P.O. Drawer 707, 38655.
Telephone: 601-234-8775.
Facsimile: 601-234-8638.

Jack F. Dunbar
Thomas J. Suszek
Michael N. Watts
William A. Baskin

Representative Clients: Mississippi Power & Light Co.; Mississippi Valley Gas Co.; South Central Bell Telephone Co.; Cooper Tire & Rubber Co.; Dunavant Enterprises: Volkswagen; Navistar International; Garan, Inc.; J.I. Case Co.; Keller Industries, Inc.

For Complete List of Firm Personnel, See General Section

For full biographical listings, see the Martindale-Hubbell Law Directory

TAYLOR, JONES, ALEXANDER, SORRELL & MCFALL, LTD. (AV)

961 State Line Road, West, P.O. Box 188, 38671
Telephone: 601-342-1300
Telecopier: 601-342-1312

Ronald L. Taylor
Jack R. Jones, III
Keith M. Alexander
Mark K. Sorrell
George McFall

Approved Attorneys for: Mississippi Valley Title Insurance Co.; First American Title, Insurance.

Reference: Sunburst Bank, Southaven, Miss.

For full biographical listings, see the Martindale-Hubbell Law Directory

*TUPELO,** Lee Co.

PHELPS DUNBAR, L.L.P. (AV)

Seventh Floor, One Mississippi Plaza, P.O. Box 1220, 38802-1220
Telephone: 601-842-7907
Telecopier: 601-842-3873
New Orleans, Louisiana Office: Texaco Center, 400 Poydras Street.
Telephone: 504-566-1311.
Telecopier: 504-568-9130; 504-568-9007.
Cable Address: "Howspencer."
Telex: 584125 WU.
Telex: 6821155 WUI.
Baton Rouge, Louisiana Office: Suite 701, City National Bank Building, P.O. Box 4412.
Telephone: 504-346-0285.
Telecopier: 504-381-9197.
Jackson, Mississippi Office: Suite 500, Security Centré North, 200 South Lamar Street, P.O. Box 23066.
Telephone: 601-352-2300.
Telecopier: 601-360-9777.
Houston, Texas Office: Suite 501, 4 Houston Center, 1331 Lamar Street.
Telephone: 713-659-1386.
Telecopier: 713-659-1388.
London, England Office: Suite 976, Level 9, Lloyd's, 1 Lime Street, London EC3M 7DQ England.
Telephone: 011-44-171-929-4765.
Telecopier: 011-44-171-929-0046.
Telex: 987321.

MEMBERS OF FIRM

Fred M. Bush, Jr.
F. M. Bush, III (Also at Jackson, Mississippi Office)
Walker W. (Bill) Jones, III (Also at Jackson, Mississippi Office)

COUNSEL

G. Kay L. Trapp

ASSOCIATE

William Carter Smallwood, III

Representative Clients: AMCA International Limited (Jesco Division); Bank of Mississippi; Blue Cross & Blue Shield of Mississippi; CBI Equifax; General Motors Corporation; The Kroger Co.; Mississippi Municipal Liability Plan; North Mississippi Medical Center, Inc. (and affiliated hospitals); Philip Morris Incorporated; Underwriters at Lloyd's, London.

For Complete List of Firm Personnel, See General Section

For full biographical listings, see the Martindale-Hubbell Law Directory

WEBB, SANDERS, DEATON, BALDUCCI & SMITH (AV)

363 North Broadway, P.O. Box 496, 38802-0496
Telephone: 601-844-2137
Facsimile: 601-842-3863
Oxford, Mississippi Office: 2154 South Lamar Boulevard, P.O. Box 148.
Telephone: 601-236-5700.
Facsimile: 601-236-5800.

MEMBERS OF FIRM

Dan W. Webb
Benjamin H. Sanders
Dana Gail Deaton
Chris H. Deaton
Timothy R. Balducci
Kent E. Smith
Danny P. Hall, Jr.
B. Wayne Williams

OF COUNSEL

Rachael Howell Webb

Representative Clients: Allstate Insurance Company; Georgia Casualty & Surety Company; GAB Business Services, Inc.; The Kroger Company; Ohio Casualty Insurance Company; Phillips and Associates; State Auto Insurance Company; State Farm Fire & Casualty Company; Transport Life Insurance Company; United States Fidelity & Guaranty Company.

For full biographical listings, see the Martindale-Hubbell Law Directory

WAVELAND, Hancock Co.

LUCIEN M. GEX, JR. (AV)

229 Coleman Avenue, Drawer 47, 39576-0047
Telephone: 601-467-5426
Telefax: 601-467-3258

Representative Clients: City of Waveland; Waveland Housing Authority; Merchants Bank and Trust Co.; Charles H. Johnson, Inc.; Universal Warehouses, Inc.; Bay St. Louis Housing Authority; Bay St. Louis-Waveland Municipal School District; Island Utilities Inc.; Bay Waveland Yacht Club; Waveland Regional Wastewater Management District.

For full biographical listings, see the Martindale-Hubbell Law Directory

*WINONA,** Montgomery Co.

LISTON/LANCASTER (AV)

126 North Quitman Avenue, P.O. Box 645, 38967
Telephone: 601-283-2132
Fax: 601-283-3742

(See Next Column)

William H. Liston
Alan D. Lancaster
William Liston, III
Lee B. Hazlewood

For full biographical listings, see the Martindale-Hubbell Law Directory

MISSOURI

CAPE GIRARDEAU, Cape Girardeau Co.

DICKERSON, RICE, SPAETH, HEISSERER & SUMMERS, L.C. (AV)

Fourth Floor Commerce Bank Building, 160 South Broadview at Route K, P.O. Box 1568, 63702
Telephone: 314-334-6061
Facsimile: 314-334-0979

Donald L. Dickerson
Joe Perry Rice, III
Kevin B. Spaeth
John P. Heisserer
David B. Summers

Kathleen A. Wolz
Kevin L. Wibbenmeyer

Representative Clients: Health Services Corporation of America; Health Careers Foundation; Family Practice Specialty Center; Neurologic Associates; Cape Neurosurgical Associates, P.C.; SEMO Otolaryngology.
Reference: Boatmen's Bank of Cape Girardeau.

For full biographical listings, see the Martindale-Hubbell Law Directory

OLIVER, OLIVER & WALTZ, P.C. (AV)

400 Broadway, P.O. Box 559, 63702-0559
Telephone: 314-335-8278
Fax: 314-334-6375

R. B. Oliver (1850-1934)
R. B. Oliver, Jr. (1880-1971)
Allen Laws Oliver (1886-1970)
John (Jack) L. Oliver (1916-1978)
John L. Oliver, Jr.
James Frederick Waltz
Richard K. Kuntze
Jeffrey P. Hine

J. Michael Ponder
Jonah Ted Yates

Representative Clients: Mercantile Bank of Cape Girardeau; Union Electric Co.; Soutwestern Bell Corp.; Ford Motor Co.; Consolidated Drainage District No. 1; City of Charleston; MOMEDICO; CNA; The Travelers; The Hartford.

For Complete List of Firm Personnel, See General Section

For full biographical listings, see the Martindale-Hubbell Law Directory

THOMASSON, GILBERT, COOK, REMLEY & MAGUIRE (AV)

715 Clark Avenue, P.O. Box 1180, 63702-1180
Telephone: 314-335-6651
Fax: 314-335-6182

MEMBERS OF FIRM

Donald P. Thomasson
John L. Cook
David M. Remley
Jeffrey S. Maguire

Representative Clients: Aetna Life & Casualty; Allstate Insurance Cos.; American Family Insurance; Cameron Mutual Insurance Co.; Farmers Insurance Group; Hospital Services Group; John Deere Insurance Co.; St. Paul Insurance Co.; State Farm Insurance Cos.

For Complete List of Firm Personnel, See General Section

For full biographical listings, see the Martindale-Hubbell Law Directory

*HILLSBORO,** Jefferson Co.

THURMAN, HOWALD, WEBER, BOWLES & SENKEL (AV)

One Thurman Court, 63050
Telephone: 314-789-2601, 797-2601
Telecopier: 314-797-2904

MEMBERS OF FIRM

John W. Howald
Louis J. Weber
James E. Bowles
David P. Senkel
Floyd T. Norrick

For Complete List of Firm Personnel, See General Section

For full biographical listings, see the Martindale-Hubbell Law Directory

KANSAS CITY, Jackson, Clay & Platte Cos.

BAKER, STERCHI & COWDEN (AV)

Suite 2100 Commerce Tower, 911 Main Street, P.O. Box 13566, 64199-3566
Telephone: 816-471-2121
FAX: 816-472-0288
Overland Park, Kansas Office: 51 Corporate Woods, 9393 West 110th Street, Suite 508.
Telephone: 913-451-6752.

MEMBERS OF FIRM

Thomas O. Baker
Thomas N. Sterchi
John W. Cowden
Thomas E. Rice, Jr.
Timothy S. Frets
Evan A. Douthit
Phillip C. Rouse
R. Douglas Gentile
James T. Seigfreid, Jr.
Robert A. Babcock
Peter F. Travis
John P. Poland

ASSOCIATES

Quentin L. Brown
James R. Jarrow
James S. Kreamer
Mary C. O'Connell
Randall L. Rhodes
D. Gregory Stonebarger
Kara Trouslot Stubbs
Robert M. Carroll
Stacy L. Cook
Patricia A. Sexton
Brent David Thomas

Representative Clients: American Home Products; General Motors Corp.; Chrysler Motors Corp.; Honda North America, Inc.; Johnson & Johnson, Minnesota; Mining & Manufacturing Co.; Sears Roebuck & Co; Tele-Communications, Inc.; TransWorld Airlines, Inc.; Square D Company.

For full biographical listings, see the Martindale-Hubbell Law Directory

BLACKWELL SANDERS MATHENY WEARY & LOMBARDI L.C. (AV)

Suite 1100, Two Pershing Square, 2300 Main Street, 64108
Telephone: 816-274-6800
Telecopier: 816-274-6914
Overland Park, Kansas Office: 40 Corporate Woods, Suite 1200, 9401 Indian Creek Parkway.
Telephone: 913-345-8400.
Telecopier: 913-344-6375.

MEMBERS OF FIRM

Jeffrey D. Ayers
Timothy M. Aylward
James Bandy
James Borthwick
Floyd R. Finch, Jr.
Allan V. Hallquist
Robert A. Horn
Martin M. Loring
William A. Lynch
Larry L. McMullen
Peter T. Niosi
Leslie J. Parrette, Jr.
William H. Sanders, Jr.
William H. Sanders, Sr.
Randy P. Scheer
Roger W. Slead
Peter B. Sloan
Sally B. Surridge
Michael J. Thompson
Thomas W. Wagstaff
Karl Zobrist

SENIOR COUNSEL

Katharine S. Bunn

ASSOCIATES

Michael J. Furlong
Gregory J. Minana
David B. Raymond
Dora E. Reid
William W. Richerson, Jr.
Shelley Ann Runion
Roger Warren

Representative Clients: Associated Wholesale Grocers; Commerce Bancshares; Fireman's Fund; Kansas City Power & Light; Puritan-Bennett Corp.; St. Paul Fire & Marine; UtiliCorp United Inc.

For Complete List of Firm Personnel, See General Section

For full biographical listings, see the Martindale-Hubbell Law Directory

SHERWIN L. EPSTEIN & ASSOCIATES (AV)

Suite 1700, 1006 Grand Avenue, 64106
Telephone: 816-421-6200
FAX: 816-421-6201

John W. Roe

ASSOCIATE

Mark H. Epstein

LEGAL SUPPORT PERSONNEL

Amy L. Edwards
Christine Marie Leete

For full biographical listings, see the Martindale-Hubbell Law Directory

JACKSON, LILLA & MCFERRIN, P.C. (AV)

800 Bryant Building, 1102 Grand Avenue, 64106
Telephone: 816-474-1900
Fax: 816-474-0217

John M. Lilla
Lindsay K. McFerrin (Bates)

Brian A. Snyder

(See Next Column)

OF COUNSEL

Don M. Jackson
Jesse L. Childers

LEGAL SUPPORT PERSONNEL

Rebecca S. Wortman (Legal Assistant/Investigator)

References: Available upon request.

For full biographical listings, see the Martindale-Hubbell Law Directory

NIEWALD, WALDECK & BROWN, A PROFESSIONAL CORPORATION (AV)

One Kansas City Place, 1200 Main, Suite 4100, 64105
Telephone: 816-471-7000
Telecopier: 816-474-0872
Overland Park, Kansas Office: Suite 550 Corporate Woods Building #40. 9401 Indian Creek Parkway. P.O. Box 25790, 66225.
Telephone: 913-451-1717.

Paul H. Niewald
Michael E. Waldeck
Stephen S. Brown
Kenton C. Granger
William J. DeBauche
Randa Rawlins
Michael D. Matteuzzi
Alice G. Amick
Vincent F. O'Flaherty

Jill Frost

For Complete List of Firm Personnel, See General Section

For full biographical listings, see the Martindale-Hubbell Law Directory

SHUGHART THOMSON & KILROY, A PROFESSIONAL CORPORATION (AV)

Twelve Wyandotte Plaza, 120 West 12th Street, 64105
Telephone: 816-421-3355
Overland Park, Kansas Office: Suite 1100, 32 Corporate Woods, 9225 Indian Creek Parkway 66210.
Telephone: 913-451-3355.

John M. Kilroy
Thomas J. Leittem
R. Lawrence Ward
Robert R. Raymond
George E. Leonard
William V. North
Thomas F. Fisher
Thomas G. Kokoruda
Jack L. Campbell
John M. Kilroy, Jr.
W. James Foland
Timothy D. O'Leary
Roy Bash
Donald H. Loudon
Dennis D. Palmer
William E. Quirk
Jennifer Gille Bacon
W. Terrence Kilroy
William L. Yocum
Steven D. Ruse
Robert A. Henderson
John S. Conner
P. John Brady
Russell S. Jones, Jr.
Bradley J. Baumgart
James P. O'Hara
Kirk J. Goza
Joel R. Mosher
Gregory M. Bentz
Philip W. Bledsoe
Anthony F. Rupp
Ted R. Osburn
Claudia J. York
Gregory L. Musil
Michael J. Gorman
Joseph J. Roper
Dean Kuckelman
G. William Quatman
Lisa D. Eckold
Sheryl Feutz-Harter
Roger P. Wright
David E. Shay
Thomas A. Sheehan
Mary A. Schmitt
Mark A. Olthoff
Michael P. Allen
Bradley D. Honnold
Ralph K. Phalen
Joseph Conrad Smith
Mary Owensby Thompson
Karen R. Glickstein
James C. Sullivan
Andrew L. McMullen
Ellen S. Martin
Charles J. Hyland
Michael S. Ketchmark
Bradley D. Holmstrom
Randall W. Schroer
James D. George
Michael D. Moeller
Brett Davis
Adam P. Sachs
Leah M. Gagne

OF COUNSEL

William C. Nulton
David E. Pierce (Not admitted in MO)

For Complete List of Firm Personnel, See General Section

For full biographical listings, see the Martindale-Hubbell Law Directory

SPENCER FANE BRITT & BROWNE (AV)

1400 Commerce Bank Building, 1000 Walnut Street, 64106-2140
Telephone: 816-474-8100
Overland Park, Kansas Office: Suite 500, 40 Corporate Woods, 9401 Indian Creek Parkway.
Telephone: 913-345-8100.
Washington, D.C. Office: 1133 Connecticut Avenue, N.W., Suite 1000.
Telephone: 202-775-2376.

MEMBERS OF FIRM

J. Nick Badgerow (Resident, Overland Park, Kansas Office)
James G. Baker
Russell W. Baker, Jr.
Paul D. Cowing
Stanley E. Craven
Gardiner B. Davis
Michael F. Delaney
Donald W. Giffin
Michael D. Hockley

(See Next Column)

SPENCER FANE BRITT & BROWNE—*Continued*

MEMBERS OF FIRM (Continued)

Elaine Drodge Koch
William C. Martucci
James T. Price
Michael F. Saunders
Terry W. Schackmann
Sandra L. Schermerhorn
Lowell L. Smithson
James A. Snyder
Mark A. Thornhill
Michaela M. Warden (Resident, Overland Park, Kansas Office)
David L. Wing
Jack L. Whitacre
Jerome T. Wolf
Curtis E. Woods
Teresa A. Woody

Representative Clients: Allsop Venture Partners; AT&T Technologies, Inc.; Baird Kurtz & Dobson; Bedford Properties; Builders Association of Missouri; City of Kansas City, Missouri; Daniels-McCray Lumber Co.; Heavy Constructors Assn.; Kansas City Power & Light Co.; Missouri Hospital Assn.

For Complete List of Firm Personnel, See General Section

For full biographical listings, see the Martindale-Hubbell Law Directory

SPRADLEY & RIESMEYER, A PROFESSIONAL CORPORATION (AV)

Boatmen's Center Suite 1900, 920 Main Street, 64105
Telephone: 816-474-6006
Telecopier: 816-474-1803

Ronald C. Spradley
Frederick H. Riesmeyer, II
Douglas D. Silvius

J. Dale Youngs
Derron D. Gunderman

OF COUNSEL

Robert M. Landman

LEGAL SUPPORT PERSONNEL

SENIOR LEGAL ASSISTANTS

Staci Holcom
Keenan J. Barker

For full biographical listings, see the Martindale-Hubbell Law Directory

SWANSON, MIDGLEY, GANGWERE, KITCHIN & MCLARNEY, L.L.C. (AV)

1500 Commerce Trust Building, 922 Walnut, 64106-1848
Telephone: 816-842-6100
Overland Park, Kansas Office: The NCAA Building, Suite 350, 6201 College Boulevard.
Telephone: 816-842-6100.

George H. Gangwere, Jr.
John J. Kitchin
James H. McLarney
Robert W. McKinley
C. W. Crumpecker, Jr.
John S. Black
Lawrence M. Maher
Rodney V. Hipp
Richard N. Bien
Neil Loren Johnson
W. Ann Hansbrough

Craig T. Kenworthy
Linda J. Salfrank
James A. Durbin
Tedrick A. Housh, III

OF COUNSEL

Daniel V. Hiatt

Counsel for: General Electric Co.; Chrysler Corp.; Conoco, Inc.; Yellow Freight System, Inc.; The Prudential Insurance Co. of America; Metropolitan Life Insurance Co.; National Collegiate Athletic Assn.; Land Title Insurance Co.; Safeway Stores, Inc.; The Lee Apparel Co.

For Complete List of Firm Personnel, See General Section

For full biographical listings, see the Martindale-Hubbell Law Directory

WYRSCH ATWELL MIRAKIAN LEE & HOBBS, P.C. (AV)

1300 Mercantile Tower 1101 Walnut, 64106-2122
Telephone: 816-221-0080
Fax: 816-221-3280

James R. Wyrsch
Stephen G. Mirakian
Ronald D. Lee
Charles E. Atwell
James R. Hobbs
Keith E. Drill
Michael P. Joyce
Marilyn B. Keller
Cheryl A. Pilate
W. Brian Gaddy

LEGAL SUPPORT PERSONNEL

Phillip A. Thompson (Investigative and Paralegal)
Darlene Wyrsch (Paralegal)
Dru A. Colhour (Paralegal)
Al Tolentino (Paralegal and Videographer/Photographer)
Kathy Vetsch (Paralegal)

For full biographical listings, see the Martindale-Hubbell Law Directory

*KIRKSVILLE,** Adair Co.

OSWALD & COTTEY, A PROFESSIONAL CORPORATION (AV)

Suite A, 210 North Elson, P.O. Box K, 63501
Telephone: 816-665-5628
Fax: 816-665-6035

(See Next Column)

Thomas R. Oswald
Louis F. Cottey

Brenda Wall-Swedberg
Scott L. Templeton

Representative Clients: State Farm Insurance Co.; Shelter Insurance Co.; General Casualty Cos.; American States Insurance; American Family Insurance Group; Federated Insurance; Wausau Insurance Cos.; The Bar Plan; The Medical Protective Company; Fireman's Fund.

For Complete List of Firm Personnel, See General Section

For full biographical listings, see the Martindale-Hubbell Law Directory

*MEXICO,** Audrain Co.

SEIGFREID, RUNGE, LEONATTI, POHLMEYER & SEIGFREID, P.C. (AV)

123 East Jackson Street, 65265
Telephone: 314-581-2211
Telecopier: 314-581-6577

Louis J. Leonatti
Paul A. Seigfreid

Counsel for: Commerce Bank N.A.; Aetna Casualty & Surety Co.; State Farm Mutual Insurance Cos.; National Refractories and Minerals Corp.; City of Mexico, Mo.; Central Electric Co.; U. S. Fidelity & Guaranty Co; Audrain Medical Center.

For Complete List of Firm Personnel, See General Section

For full biographical listings, see the Martindale-Hubbell Law Directory

ST. LOUIS, (Independent City)

ANDERSON & GILBERT (AV)

The Boatmen's Bank Building, Sixth Floor, 7800 Forsyth Boulevard (Clayton), 63105
Telephone: 314-721-2777
Telecopier: 314-721-3515

MEMBERS OF FIRM

Robert G. Burridge
Francis X. Duda
Joel D. Monson
D. Paul Myre

Representative Clients: Medical Defense Associates, Ltd.; St. Paul Insurance Co.; Risk Control Associates; Foremost Insurance Co; Symons Int'l; Schneider Nat'l, Inc.; American Specialty Claims Service.

For Complete List of Firm Personnel, See General Section

For full biographical listings, see the Martindale-Hubbell Law Directory

ARMSTRONG, TEASDALE, SCHLAFLY & DAVIS (AV)

A Partnership including Professional Corporations
One Metropolitan Square, 63102-2740
Telephone: 314-621-5070
Facsimile: 314-621-5065
Twx: 910 761-2246
Cable: ATKV LAW
Kansas City, Missouri Office: 1700 City Center Square. 1100 Main Street, 64105.
Telephone: 816-221-3420.
Facsimile: 816-221-0786.
Belleville, Illinois Office: 23 South First Street, 62220.
Telephone: 618-397-4411.
Olathe, Kansas Office: 100 East Park, 66061.
Telephone: 913-345-0706.

MEMBERS OF FIRM

Kenneth F. Teasdale (P.C.)
Frank N. Gundlach (P.C.)
Justin C. Cordonnier (P.C.)
James J. Virtel
Thomas Cummings (P.C.)
Richard B. Scherrer (P.C.)
Jay A. Summerville
Edwin L. Noel (P.C.)
Byron E. Francis (P.C.)
John H. Quinn III, (P.C.)
Steven P. Sanders
Theodore J. Williams, Jr.
Timothy K. Kellett (P.C.)
Thomas B. Weaver (P.C.)
Wilbur L. Tomlinson (P.C.)
Raymond R. Fournie
Clark H. Cole
Paul N. Venker
Jordan B. Cherrick
John F. Cowling
Ann E. Buckley
Glenn E. Davis
George M. von Stamwitz
Mary C. Kickham
Joan Z. Cohen
Gary L. Rutledge
Mark D. Sophir
William M. Corrigan, Jr.

ASSOCIATES

David G. Loseman
Deirdre C. Gallagher
John S. Metzger
Andrew B. Mayfield
Michelle Suzanne House
Michael L. Skinner
James L. Stockberger
James G. Nowogrocki
Thomas L. Orris
Lisa M. Wood
Susan B. Knowles
Richard L. Saville, Jr.
Douglas R. Sprong
Karen A. Menghini
James E. Mello
Timothy J. Prosser
Petree A. Eastman
Matthew R. Byer

(See Next Column)

ARMSTRONG, TEASDALE, SCHLAFLY & DAVIS, *St. Louis—Continued*

OF COUNSEL

John J. Cole (P.C.)
Frederick H. Mayer (P.C.)
John P. Emde (P.C.)

Representative Clients: McDonald's Corporation; Anheuser-Busch Companies, Inc.; United Missouri Bank; McCarthy Brothers; Lincoln National Life Insurance Company; Avon Products, Inc.; Eli Lilly & Co.; The Coca-Cola Co.; Union Pacific Railroad Company; Merrill Lynch.

For Complete List of Firm Personnel, See General Section

For full biographical listings, see the Martindale-Hubbell Law Directory

C. MARSHALL FRIEDMAN A PROFESSIONAL CORPORATION (AV)

Thirteenth Floor, 1010 Market Street, 63101
Telephone: 314-621-8400
FAX: 314-621-8843

C. Marshall Friedman
Kenneth E. Rudd
Patrick S. O'Brien
Douglas K. Rush
Thomas P. McDermott
Mark Thomas Rudder

Bret E. Taylor

For full biographical listings, see the Martindale-Hubbell Law Directory

GALLOP, JOHNSON & NEUMAN, L.C. (AV)

Interco Corporate Tower, 101 S. Hanley, 63105
Telephone: 314-862-1200
Telecopier: 314-862-1219

MEMBERS OF FIRM

Stephen W. Skrainka
Edwin D. Akers, Jr.
David W. Harlan
David T. Hamilton
Thomas M. Newmark
Michael A. Kahn
Jason M. Rugo
Peter D. Kerth
Patrick M. Sanders
Cawood K. Bebout
Kurtis B. Reeg
Thomas P. Hohenstein

Todd J. Aschbacher
Tod J. O'Donoghue
Timothy J. Sarsfield
Lucy A. Singer
David A. Streubel
Daniel G. Vogel
John T. Walsh
Rebecca Epstein Walsh
Patricia S. Williams

COUNSEL

Kay R. Sherman

Representative Clients: Data Research Associates, Inc.; Falcon Products, Inc.; KV Pharmaceutical Co.; Ciba Giegy Corp.; Magna Group, Inc. and subsidiary banks; Medicine Shoppe International, Inc.; Missouri Research Laboratories, Inc.; Raskas Foods, Inc.; Paric Corp.; Safeco and General Insurance Companies of America.

For Complete List of Firm Personnel, See General Section

For full biographical listings, see the Martindale-Hubbell Law Directory

LEWIS, RICE & FINGERSH (AV)

A Partnership including Partnerships and Individuals
500 North Broadway, Suite 2000, 63102-2147
Telephone: 314-444-7600
Telecopier: 314-241-6056
Clayton, Missouri Office: Suite 400, 8182 Maryland Avenue.
Telephone: 314-444-7600.
Belleville, Illinois Office: 325 South High Street.
Telephone: 618-234-8636.
Hays, Kansas Office: 201 W. 11th St.
Telephone: 913-625-3997.
Leawood, Kansas Office: Suite 375, 8900 State Line.
Telephone: 913-381-8898.
Kansas City, Missouri Office: 1010 Walnut, Suite 500.
Telephone: 816-421-2500.

RESIDENT PARTNERS

Robert Smith Allen
Robert B. Hoemeke
James W. Herron
Michael P. Casey
Allen S. Boston
Barry A. Short
Mark T. Keaney
Andrew Rothschild
John J. Gazzoli, Jr.
Richard A. Ahrens
John J. Moellering
John M. Hessel
Richard A. Wunderlich
James V. O'Brien
Joseph J. Trad
Joseph E. Martineau
Curtis C. Calloway
David L. Coffman
Richard B. Walsh, Jr.
Jeffrey B. Hunt

ASSOCIATES

Daniel E. Claggett
John E. Hall
Mary B. Schultz
Cordell P. Schulten
Duane L. Coleman
Thomas L. Caradonna
Robert J. Golterman
Robert J. Will
Ronald A. Norwood
Eric D. Paulsrud

(See Next Column)

ASSOCIATES (Continued)

Theodore H. Lucas
Jon A. Santangelo
Elizabeth Webster Lane
Mary L. Frontczak
Benjamin A. Lipman
Robert S. Moore
Gary M. Smith
Neal F. Perryman

For Complete List of Firm Personnel, See General Section

For full biographical listings, see the Martindale-Hubbell Law Directory

DENNIS T. MCCUBBIN (AV)

165 North Meramec, Suite 300 (Clayton), 63105
Telephone: 314-721-5030
Fax: 314-721-6767

For full biographical listings, see the Martindale-Hubbell Law Directory

MOLINE & SHOSTAK (AV)

The Berkley Building, 8015 Forsyth Boulevard, 63105
Telephone: 314-725-3200
Fax: 314-725-3275

Harry O. Moline
Burton H. Shostak
Sherri Cranmore Strand
Donald J. Mehan, Jr.
Deborah J. Westling
Michael S. Ghidina

For full biographical listings, see the Martindale-Hubbell Law Directory

MOSER AND MARSALEK, P.C. (AV)

Suite 700, St. Louis Place, 200 North Broadway, 63102-2730
Telephone: 314-421-5364
Telecopier: 314-421-5640

Joseph H. Mueller
F. Douglas O'Leary
John J. Horgan
William L. Davis
David L. Zwart
Michael R. Noakes
Jerome C. Simon
Peter F. Spataro
Brian R. Plegge
Philip L. Willman
Thomas Carter, II
Thomas J. Magee
J. Steven Erickson
Doreen G. Powell
Kevin M. Leahy

Robyn G. Fox
Kimberly A. Maschmeyer
Seth G. Gausnell
Laurie S. Wright
Terry L. Pijut
Brian D. Winer
Ann Gaylor Rucker
Gregory T. Mueller
Jill M. Young
Patrick J. Horgan
John F. Padberg
Karie E. Casey
Robert G. Pennell
Mark A. Cordes
Mark D. Madden
Thomas Edward Fagan
Bradlee L. Blake
Sherry Alisa Gutnick (Not admitted in MO)

Representative Clients: Aetna Casualty & Surety; American Ind. Group; American International Group; Chubb Group Insurance Cos.; Fireman's Fund Insurance Co.; Goodyear Tire & Rubber Co.; Jewish Hospital; Lancer Claims; Medical Protective Ins. Co.

For Complete List of Firm Personnel, See General Section

For full biographical listings, see the Martindale-Hubbell Law Directory

PADBERG, MCSWEENEY, SLATER & MERZ, A PROFESSIONAL CORPORATION (AV)

Suite 800, 1015 Locust Street, 63101
Telephone: 314-621-3787
Telecopier: 314-621-7396

Godfrey P. Padberg
Edward P. McSweeney
R. J. Slater
Charles L. Merz

Richard J. Burke, Jr.
Matthew J. Padberg
James P. Leonard
Anthony J. Soukenik
Thomas C. Simon
Mary K. Munroe
Marty Daesch

For full biographical listings, see the Martindale-Hubbell Law Directory

PEPER, MARTIN, JENSEN, MAICHEL AND HETLAGE (AV)

720 Olive Street, Twenty-Fourth Floor, 63101
Telephone: 314-421-3850
Fax: 314-621-4834
Fort Myers, Florida Office: 2080 McGregor Boulevard, Third Floor.
Telephone: 813-337-3850.
Fax: 813-337-0970.
Punta Gorda, Florida Office: 1625 West Marion Avenue, Suite 2.
Telephone: 813-637-1955.
Fax: 813-637-8485.
Naples, Florida Office: 850 Park Shore Drive, Suite 202.
Telephone: 813-261-6525.
Fax: 813-649-1805.
Belleville, Illinois Office: 720 West Main Street, Suite 140.
Telephone: 618-234-9574.
Fax: 618-234-9846.

(See Next Column)

PEPER, MARTIN, JENSEN, MAICHEL AND HETLAGE—*Continued*

MEMBERS OF FIRM

William A. Richter
Lewis R. Mills
Robert C. Johnson
Arthur L. Smith
John C. Rasp
Richard P. Sher
Stephen H. Rovak
Kenneth A. Jones (At Fort Myers, Punta Gorda and Naples, Florida Offices)
Michael D. Hart
Jeffrey J. Kalinowski
Richard J. Pautler
Joanne D. Martin
Mark S. Packer
Gary D. McConnell
Michael A. Clithero
Ian P. Cooper
Robert L. Jackstadt (At Belleville, Illinois Office)
Mark Steinbeck (At Fort Myers, Florida Office)

SENIOR ATTORNEY

Robert Schultz

ASSOCIATES

Catherine Hope Johnson
James R. Myers (At Fort Myers and Punta Gorda, Florida Offices)
Stephen J. O'Brien
David L. Schenberg
Diana M. Schmidt
B. Michelle Ward

For Complete List of Firm Personnel, See General Section

For full biographical listings, see the Martindale-Hubbell Law Directory

---

SCHRAMM & PINES, L.L.C. (AV)

Suite 1404 Chromalloy Plaza, 120 South Central Avenue, 63105
Telephone: 314-721-5321
Telecopier: 314-721-0790

MEMBERS OF FIRM

Paul H. Schramm
M. Harvey Pines
Daniel R. Schramm

Norman S. Newmark
Dean A. Schramm
Peter L. Hoffman

Reference: The Boatmen's National Bank of St. Louis.

For full biographical listings, see the Martindale-Hubbell Law Directory

---

THOMPSON & MITCHELL (AV)

One Mercantile Center, Suite 3300, 63101
Telephone: 314-231-7676
Telecopier: 314-342-1717
Belleville, Illinois Office: 525 West Main Street.
Telephone: 618-277-4700; 314-271-1800.
Telecopier: 618-236-3434.
St. Charles, Missouri Office: 200 North Third Street.
Telephone: 314-946-7717.
Telecopier: 314-946-4938.
Washington, D.C. Office: 700 14th Street, N.W., Suite 900.
Telephone: 202-508-1000.
Telecopier: 202-508-1010.

MEMBERS OF FIRM

William G. Guerri
W. Stanley Walch
James J. Raymond
Michael D. O'Keefe
David Wells
Charles A. Newman
Gordon L. Ankney
Raymond L. Massey
Gary Mayes
Robert H. Brownlee
James W. Erwin
Thomas R. Jayne
Mary M. Bonacorsi
Allen D. Allred
Dan H. Ball
Kenton E. Knickmeyer
William R. Bay
Mark Sableman
Bradley A. Winters
Michael J. Morris
Edward A. Cohen
Nicholas J. Lamb
Lawrence C. Friedman

OF COUNSEL

Michael Jos. Hart

ASSOCIATES

Mike W. Bartolacci
Conny Davinroy Beatty
Mark V. Bossi
John J. Carey
J. Powell Carman
David S. Corwin
Tracy J. Cowan
Joseph P. Danis
Matthew J. Fairless
Lorna L. Frahm
William D. Hakes
Jennifer J. Herner
Diane M. Hoelzl
Bettina Lynn Joist
Roger A. Keller, Jr.
Crystal M. Kennedy
A. Laurie Koller
Robert L. Norton
Linda Carroll Reisner
T. Evan Schaeffer
Anthony G. Simon
Martin B. Sipple
David A. Stratmann
Bryan L. Sutter
David F. Szewczyk
Stephen R. Welby
Roman P. Wuller

BELLEVILLE, ILLINOIS OFFICE
RESIDENT MEMBERS OF FIRM

W. Thomas Coghill, Jr.
Thomas W. Alvey, Jr.
Karl D. Dexheimer
Allan McD. Goodloe, Jr.
Thomas F. Hennessy, III
William A. Schmitt
Edward S. Bott, Jr.
Kurt E. Reitz

(See Next Column)

RESIDENT ASSOCIATES

D. Kimberly Brown
Tom R. Burcham, III
Karen A. Carr
Mary Sue Juen
CHERIE K. HARPOLE MACDONALD
William J. Niehoff
Donald K. Schoemaker
Mark S. Schuver
Michael J. Scotti, III

ST. CHARLES, MISSOURI OFFICE
MEMBER OF FIRM

Rollin J. Moerschel

ASSOCIATE

V. Scott Williams

Representative Clients: American Commercial Lines, Inc.; Chrysler Corp.; General American Life Insurance Co.; General Motors Corp.; Joy Technologies Inc.; Mercantile Bancorporation Inc.; Norfolk Southern Corp.; Peabody Coal Company; St. Anthony's Medical Center; Union Pacific Railroad Company.

For Complete List of Firm Personnel, See General Section

For full biographical listings, see the Martindale-Hubbell Law Directory

---

WITTNER, POGER, ROSENBLUM & SPEWAK, P.C. (AV)

Suite 400, 7700 Bonhomme Avenue, 63105
Telephone: 314-862-3535
Fax: 314-862-5741

Gerald M. Poger
Howard A. Wittner
N. Scott Rosenblum
Steven B. Spewak
David S. Spewak
Jean H. Maylack

Ramona L. Marten
Jane M. Carriker
Gary M. Siegel
Barbara Greenberg
Vanessa C. Antoniou
Joseph L. Green

For full biographical listings, see the Martindale-Hubbell Law Directory

---

SIKESTON, Scott Co.

DRUMM, WINCHESTER & GLEASON (AV)

113 West North Street, P.O. Box 40, 63801
Telephone: 314-471-1207
Fax: 314-971-1050

MEMBERS OF FIRM

Manuel Drumm
William H. Winchester, III

Representative Clients: Aetna Casualty & Surety Co.; Cameron Mutual Insurance Co.; Boyer Construction Co.; Risk Control Associates; Missouri Medical Insurance Co.

For Complete List of Firm Personnel, See General Section

For full biographical listings, see the Martindale-Hubbell Law Directory

---

*SPRINGFIELD,** Greene Co.

DORR, BAIRD AND LIGHTNER, A PROFESSIONAL CORPORATION (AV)

Suite 2-202 Two Corporate Centre, 1949 East Sunshine Street, 65804
Telephone: 417-887-0133
Fax: 417-887-8740

Richard E. Dorr
C. Ronald Baird
John R. Lightner

Mark J. Millsap
James Michael Bridges

Reference: First City National Bank of Springfield.

For full biographical listings, see the Martindale-Hubbell Law Directory

---

FARRINGTON & CURTIS, P.C. (AV)

750 North Jefferson, 65802
Telephone: 417-862-6726
Telecopier: 417-862-6948

Lincoln J. Knauer
Debra Mallonee Shantz

District Attorneys for: Union Pacific Railroad Co.
Attorneys for: Boatmen's Bank of Southern Missouri; Paul Mueller Co.; Montgomery Ward & Co.; Acme Structural, Inc.; Silver Dollar City, Inc.; Drury College; Meek Building Centers; Walmart Stores, Inc.

For Complete List of Firm Personnel, See General Section

For full biographical listings, see the Martindale-Hubbell Law Directory

---

MILLER & SANFORD, A PROFESSIONAL CORPORATION (AV)

1845 South National Avenue, P.O. Box 4288, 65808-4288
Telephone: 417-886-2000
Fax: 417-886-9126

(See Next Column)

MILLER & SANFORD A PROFESSIONAL CORPORATION, *Springfield—Continued*

John Weston Miller (1900-1981)
John F. Carr (1911-1990)
Wm. P. Sanford
Vincent Tyndall
Frank M. Evans, III
James F. McLeod
Craig R. Oliver
Douglas R. Nickell
Mark A. Powell
Ed. L. Payton
Cynthia B. McGinnis
Jerry A. Harmison, Jr.

Daniel R. Wichmer
Bob Lawson, Jr.

OF COUNSEL

James H. Arneson

Counsel for: ITT Hartford; Home Insurance Co.; Boatmen's National Bank Springfield, N.A.; Liberty Mutual Insurance Co.; St. John's Regional Health Center; Maryland Casualty Co.; Great West Casualty Co.; American International Group.

For Complete List of Firm Personnel, See General Section

For full biographical listings, see the Martindale-Hubbell Law Directory

TURNER, REID, DUNCAN, LOOMER & PATTON, P.C. (AV)

Suite A, 1355 East Bradford Parkway, P.O. Box 4043, 65808
Telephone: 417-883-2102
FAX: 417-883-5024

Meredith B. Turner (1913-1993)
Kenneth H. Reid
Donald R. Duncan
Rodney E. Loomer
Michael J. Patton
M. Sean McGinnis
Sherry Ann Rozell
Gregory W. Aleshire
Joseph P. Winget
Christopher A. Hazelrigg
Eric M. Belk
Wallace S. Squibb

Representative Clients: General Motors Corp.; Ryder Truck Rental, Inc.; St. John's Regional Health Center; Royal Insurance; CIGNA Ins. Co.; The St. Paul Insurance Cos.; Shelter Insurance Cos; The Cameron Cos.; Zurich-American Insurance Group.

For full biographical listings, see the Martindale-Hubbell Law Directory

WOOLSEY, FISHER, WHITEAKER & MCDONALD, A PROFESSIONAL CORPORATION (AV)

300 S. Jefferson, Suite 600, P.O. Box 1245, 65801
Telephone: 417-869-0581
Telecopier: 417-831-7852

Clarence O. Woolsey (1911-1984)
Harold J. Fisher (Retired)
Raymond E. Whiteaker
William H. McDonald
Bradley J. Fisher
John E. Price
Virginia L. Fry
David A. Childers
Richard C. Miller
Thomas Y. Auner
Richard E. Davis
William G. Todd
Joseph Dow Sheppard, III
William Craig Hosmer
Brent S. Bothwell

Lee Ann Miller

OF COUNSEL

Richard K. Wilson

Rana L. Faaborg
Carol Taylor Aiken
Stuart H. King
William R. Robb
James R. Royce
William G. Petrus, Jr.

Representative Clients: AT&T/Paradyne/MRAC, Inc.; Bass Pro Shops/-Tracker Marine, Inc.; Emerson Electric Companies; Enron Liquid Fuels; Unisys; American States Insurance Company; Kemper Insurance Group; Wausau Insurance Group; Zurich-American Insurance Company.

For Complete List of Firm Personnel, See General Section

For full biographical listings, see the Martindale-Hubbell Law Directory

MONTANA

*BILLINGS,** Yellowstone Co.

CROWLEY, HAUGHEY, HANSON, TOOLE & DIETRICH (AV)

500 Transwestern II, 490 North 31st Street, P.O. Box 2529, 59103
Telephone: 406-252-3441
Fax: 406-259-4159
Helena, Montana Office: IBM Building, 100 North Park Avenue, Suite 300, 59601.
Telephone: 406-449-4165.
Fax: 406-449-5149.

OF COUNSEL

Bruce R. Toole

(See Next Column)

MEMBERS OF FIRM

George C. Dalthorp
Herbert I. Pierce, III
Terry B. Cosgrove
Ronald R. Lodders
Charles R. Cashmore
Lawrence B. Cozzens
James P. Sites
Carolyn S. Ostby
Steven J. Lehman
Donald L. Harris
William J. Mattix
Peter F. Habein
Jon T. Dyre
Bruce A. Fredrickson
Renee L. Coppock
Janice L. Rehberg

Joe C. Maynard, Jr.

ASSOCIATES

Steven Robert Milch
Leonard H. Smith
Neil G. Westesen
Michael S. Lahr

Robert T. Bell

Representative Clients: Montana Power Company; MDU Resources Group, Inc.; R.J. Reynolds Tobacco Co., Inc.; United Parcel Service; Noranda Minerals Corp.; Connecticut Mutual Life; Metropolitan Life Insurance Co.; Prudential Insurance Co.; Equitable Life Assurance Society of the United States; Washington National Insurance.

For Complete List of Firm Personnel, See General Section

For full biographical listings, see the Martindale-Hubbell Law Directory

*BOZEMAN,** Gallatin Co.

KIRWAN & BARRETT, P.C. (AV)

215 West Mendenhall, P.O. Box 1348, 59771-1348
Telephone: 406-586-1553
Fax: 406-586-8971

Peter M. Kirwan
Stephen M. Barrett

Tom W. Stonecipher

For full biographical listings, see the Martindale-Hubbell Law Directory

*GREAT FALLS,** Cascade Co.

JAMES, GRAY & MCCAFFERTY, P.C. (AV)

615 Second Avenue North, P.O. Box 2885, 59403
Telephone: 406-454-5700
Fax: 406-727-0287

Orville Gray (1920-1993)
Dennis C. McCafferty
Randall H. Gray
Robert F. James
Leslie S. Waite, III
Darcy M. Crum
William O. Bronson
Gorham E. Swanberg

Bert A. Fairclough

Matthew K. Hutchison

RETIRED

Ted James

Reference: Norwest Bank.

For full biographical listings, see the Martindale-Hubbell Law Directory

*HELENA,** Lewis and Clark Co.

KELLER, REYNOLDS, DRAKE, JOHNSON & GILLESPIE, P.C. (AV)

38 South Last Chance Gulch, 59601
Telephone: 406-442-0230

P. Keith Keller
Thomas Q. Johnson
Richard E. Gillespie
G. Curt Drake
Jacqueline Terrell Lenmark
Robert R. Throssell

Charles J. Seifert

OF COUNSEL

Glen L. Drake

Representative Clients: Fireman's Fund American Insurance Cos.; Northwestern National Insurance Group; Government Employees Insurance Co.; Hartford Accident and Indemnity Co.; Commercial Union Assurance Cos.; Kemper Insurance Group; Crum and Forster Group; The Home Insurance Co.; CNA Insurance Cos.; Safeco Insurance.

For full biographical listings, see the Martindale-Hubbell Law Directory

WHITEFISH, Flathead Co.

MORRISON AND MORRISON (AV)

236 Wisconsin Avenue, 59937-1090
Telephone: 406-862-9600
Fax: 406-862-9611

Frank B. Morrison, Jr.
Sharon M. Morrison

OF COUNSEL

Frank B. Morrison, Sr.

For full biographical listings, see the Martindale-Hubbell Law Directory

NEBRASKA

*LINCOLN,** Lancaster Co.

Barlow, Johnson, Flodman, Sutter, Guenzel & Eske (AV)

1227 Lincoln Mall, P.O. Box 81686, 68501-1686
Telephone: 402-475-4240
Fax: 402-475-0329

MEMBERS OF FIRM

Robert A. Barlow (1921-1986) William D. Sutter
Kile W. Johnson Steven E. Guenzel
Steven J. Flodman James A. Eske

ASSOCIATE

Mark T. Gokie

OF COUNSEL

Gene D. Watson

Special Counsel: Nebraska Public Power District.
Representative Clients: Allied Group; Chubb/Pacific Indemnity Group; Citizens State Bank, Polk, Nebraska; Crum & Foster; Federated Rural Electric Insurance Corp.; Runza Drive-Inns of America; United States Fidelity & Guaranty Co.; Viking Insurance Company of Wisconsin.

For Complete List of Firm Personnel, See General Section

For full biographical listings, see the Martindale-Hubbell Law Directory

Erickson & Sederstrom, P.C. (AV)

Suite 400, Cornhusker Plaza, 301 South 13th Street, 68508
Telephone: 402-476-1000
Fax: 402-476-6167
Omaha, Nebraska Office: Regency Westpointe, 10330 Regency Parkway Drive.
Telephone: 402-397-2200.
Fax: 402-390-7137.

Charles D. Humble Douglas L. Curry
Linda W. Rohman

Representative Clients: Lincoln Electric System; Lincoln General Hospital; Southeast Nebraska Community College; Builders, Inc.; Kingery Construction Co.; American Honda Motor Co., Inc.; Lincoln Welding Co.

For Complete List of Firm Personnel, See General Section

For full biographical listings, see the Martindale-Hubbell Law Directory

NORFOLK, Madison Co.

Domina & Copple, P.C. (AV)

2425 Taylor Avenue, P.O. Box 78, 68702-0078
Telephone: 402-371-4300
Fax: 402-371-0790
Omaha, Nebraska Office: 1065 North 115th Street, Suite 150.
Telephone: 402-493-4100.
FAX: 402-493-9782.

David A. Domina David E. Copple

Kathleen K. Rockey David H. Ptak
James G. Kube Steven D. Sunde

For full biographical listings, see the Martindale-Hubbell Law Directory

*OMAHA,** Douglas Co.

Brashear & Ginn (AV)

800 Metropolitan Federal Plaza, 1623 Farnam Street, 68102-2106
Telephone: 402-348-1000; 800-746-4444
Telecopier: 402-348-1111

Kermit A. Brashear Mark J. Daly
Julia L. Gold Craig A. Knickrehm
Richard A. Drews

Donald J. Straka Kermit A. Brashear III
Brad C. Epperly

OF COUNSEL

MaryBeth Frankman

Representative Clients: ABF Freight Systems, Inc., Fort Smith, Arkansas; American International Group, New York, New York; Chemtool, Incorporated, Crystal Lake, Illinois; Crawford & Company, Dallas, Texas; Federal Deposit Insurance Corporation, Washington, D.C.; John Deere Company, Kansas City, Missouri; New Hampshire Insurance Company, Manchester, New Hampshire; Scottsdale Insurance Company, Scottsdale, Arizona; Sears, Roebuck & Co., Chicago, Illinois; TransWood Carriers, Inc., Omaha, Nebraska.

(See Next Column)

For Complete List of Firm Personnel, See General Section

For full biographical listings, see the Martindale-Hubbell Law Directory

Cassem, Tierney, Adams, Gotch & Douglas (AV)

Suite 300, 8805 Indian Hills Drive, 68114
Telephone: 402-390-0300
Telecopier: 402-390-9676

MEMBERS OF FIRM

Edwin Cassem (1902-1980) Michael F. Kinney
Lawrence J. Tierney Terry J. Grennan
Robert K. Adams Patrick B. Donahue
Charles F. Gotch Ronald F. Krause
John R. Douglas Dennis R. Riekenberg
Daniel J. Duffy David A. Blagg
Theodore J. Stouffer Brien M. Welch
Michael K. Huffer

ASSOCIATES

Michael F. Scahill Helarie H. Hollenbeck
Leif D. Erickson Melany S. Chesterman

OF COUNSEL

Edward Shafton

Representative Clients: Aetna Casualty & Surety Co.; Chrysler Corp.; Eli Lilly & Co.; G. D. Searle & Co.; Hartford Accident & Indemnity Co.; Johnson & Johnson; Litigation Management Specialists; Merck & Co., Inc.; Safeco Insurance Co.; Travelers Insurance Co.

For full biographical listings, see the Martindale-Hubbell Law Directory

Dwyer, Pohren, Wood, Heavey, Grimm, Goodall & Lazer (AV)

A Partnership including Professional Corporations
Suite 400, 8712 West Dodge Road, 68114
Telephone: 402-392-0101
Telefax: 402-392-1011

MEMBERS OF FIRM

Robert V. Dwyer, Jr. Michael W. Heavey (P.C.)
Edward F. Pohren Mark L. Goodall
W. Eric Wood (P.C.) Michael L. Lazer

Representative Clients: K-Products, Inc.; Purina Mills, Inc.; SAC Federal Credit Union; Heller Financial Corporation; Deutsche Credit Corporation; Ford Motor Credit Company; Bishop Clarkson Memorial Hospital; National Hospital Association; Omaha Police Federal Credit Union; Walkers, Inc.

For Complete List of Firm Personnel, See General Section

For full biographical listings, see the Martindale-Hubbell Law Directory

Erickson & Sederstrom, P.C. (AV)

Regency Westpointe, 10330 Regency Parkway Drive, 68114
Telephone: 402-397-2200
Fax: 402-390-7137
Lincoln, Nebraska Office: Suite 400, Cornhusker Plaza, 301 South 13th Street.
Telephone: 402-476-1000.
Fax: 402-476-6167.

Donald H. Erickson Thomas J. Culhane
John C. Brownrigg Richard J. Gilloon
Jerald L. Rauterkus

OF COUNSEL

Leo Eisenstatt

Representative Clients: Applied Communications, Inc.; Cornhusker Casualty Co.; Hartford Accident & Indemnity Co.; Imperial Casualty & Indemnity Co.; J I Case Co.; Lueder Construction Co.; National American Insurance Company of Nebraska; Pepsico, Inc.; West Telemarketing Corp.

For Complete List of Firm Personnel, See General Section

For full biographical listings, see the Martindale-Hubbell Law Directory

Katskee, Henatsch & Suing (AV)

10404 Essex Court, Suite 100, 68114
Telephone: 402-391-1697
Fax: 402-391-8932

MEMBERS OF FIRM

Milton A. Katskee Dean F. Suing
Jerry W. Katskee

ASSOCIATES

Francis T. Belsky John B. Henley
David A. Castello Kristine K. Kluck

OF COUNSEL

Harry R. Henatsch

References: Mid-City Bank; FirsTier Bank N.A., Omaha.

For full biographical listings, see the Martindale-Hubbell Law Directory

Omaha—Continued

LAUGHLIN, PETERSON & LANG (AV)

11306 Davenport Street, 68154
Telephone: 402-330-1900
Fax: 402-330-0936

MEMBERS OF FIRM

Mark L. Laughlin
Robert F. Peterson
James E. Lang

Representative Clients: Andersen Electric Co.; General Electric Capital Corp.; Sears, Roebuck & Co.; Dodge Land Co.; Security Mutual Life Insurance Co. of Lincoln, NE; Century Development Co.

For full biographical listings, see the Martindale-Hubbell Law Directory

McGILL, GOTSDINER, WORKMAN & LEPP, P.C. (AV)

Suite 500 - First National Plaza, 11404 West Dodge Road, 68154
Telephone: 402-492-9200
Telecopier: 402-492-9222

Robert Lepp
Michael S. Mostek
Paul R. Elofson

Representative Clients: Norwest Bank Nebraska N.A.; Metz Baking Company; Vetter Health Services, Inc.; Behlen Mfg. Co.; Mutual of Omaha.

For Complete List of Firm Personnel, See General Section

For full biographical listings, see the Martindale-Hubbell Law Directory

McGRATH, NORTH, MULLIN & KRATZ, P.C. (AV)

Suite 1400, One Central Park Plaza, 68102
Telephone: 402-341-3070
Telecopy: 402-341-0216
Telex: 797122 MNMKOM

John E. North
Robert D. Mullin, Sr.
Bruce C. Rohde
James P. Fitzgerald
Leo A. Knowles
Terrence D. O'Hare
John F. Thomas
John P. Passarelli
Mark F. Enenbach
Roger J. Miller
Timothy J. Pugh
Robert D. Mullin, Jr.
Thomas C. McGowan
A. Stevenson Bogue
William F. Hargens
Robert J. Bothe
Michael G. Mullin
Patrick J. Barrett
Steven P. Case
James G. Powers
Ronald L. Comes
Gary F. Wence
Douglas E. Quinn
J. Scott Paul

Representative Clients: ConAgra, Inc.; Valmont Industries, Inc.; Physicians Mutual Insurance Company; Omaha Airport Authority; American Family Insurance Group; Dow Chemical; Lloyds of London; Mutual of Omaha; The Pacesetter Corporation.

For Complete List of Firm Personnel, See General Section

For full biographical listings, see the Martindale-Hubbell Law Directory

NEVADA

*ELKO,** Elko Co.

LAW OFFICES GOICOECHEA & DI GRAZIA, LTD. A PROFESSIONAL CORPORATION (AV)

In Association with
Vaughan & Hull, Ltd.
A Professional Corporation
P.O. Box 1358, 89803
Telephone: 702-738-8091
Fax: 702-738-4220

Robert B. Goicoechea
Gary E. Di Grazia

Thomas J. Coyle, Jr.

Representative Clients: Independence Minning Co., Inc.; Alpark Petroleum, Inc.; Nevada Bank & Trust; Metropolitan Life Ins.

For full biographical listings, see the Martindale-Hubbell Law Directory

*LAS VEGAS,** Clark Co.

ALVERSON, TAYLOR, MORTENSEN & NELSON (AV)

3821 W. Charleston Boulevard, 89102
Telephone: 702-384-7000
FAX: 702-385-7000

MEMBERS OF FIRM

J. Bruce Alverson
Eric K. Taylor
David J. Mortensen
Erven T. Nelson
LeAnn Sanders
David R. Clayson

(See Next Column)

ASSOCIATES

Milton J. Eichacker
Douglas D. Gerrard
Marie Ellerton
James H. Randall
Peter Dubowsky
Hayley B. Chambers
Michael D. Stevenson
Cookie Lea Olshein
Kenneth M. Marias
Jeffrey H. Ballin
Jeffrey W. Daly
Kenneth R. Ivory
Edward D. Boyack
Sandra Smagac
Jill M. Chase
Francis F. Lin

Representative Clients: Citibank; General Electric Corporation; Kentucky Fried Chicken; Federal Deposit Insurance Corporation (FDIC); Resolution Trust Corporation (RTC); American Bonding Company; Southwest Gas Corporation; Kendall Healthcare Company; Decratrend Corporation; ETEC Testing Laboratories; Yellow Cab Company.

For full biographical listings, see the Martindale-Hubbell Law Directory

BARKER, GILLOCK, KONING & BROWN, A PROFESSIONAL CORPORATION (AV)

430 South Third Street, 89101
Telephone: 702-386-1086
Fax: 702-384-5386

William S. Barker
Gerald I. Gillock
Michael A. Koning
Janice J. Brown
Jerry S. Busby
Thomas D. Sutherland
James P. Chrisman
David L. Thomas

Janet S. Markley
Antonia C. Killebrew
Terry W. Riedy
Julie A. Mersch
Lewisjohn Gazda
Robert A. Winner
Robert D. Tarte (Not admitted in NV)
Susan Arlene Winters
Stephen P. Ellis

Representative Clients: American International Group; Ford Motor Co.; National Food Processors; Sta-Rite Industries; Albertsons, Inc.; Combustion Engineering; Charter Medical Corp.; Caterpillar, Inc.; Smith's Management Corp.; Humana, Inc.

For full biographical listings, see the Martindale-Hubbell Law Directory

THOMAS D. BEATTY (AV)

601 East Bridger Avenue, 89101
Telephone: 702-382-5111
Telecopier: 702-382-2892

ASSOCIATES

Geoffrey A. Potts
Rena G. Benefield

Representative Clients: Liberty Mutual Insurance Co.; Aetna Casualty & Surety Co.; Bayliner Marine Corporation; Clark County Association of School Administrators.
Reference: First Interstate Bank of Nevada.

For full biographical listings, see the Martindale-Hubbell Law Directory

BECKLEY, SINGLETON, DE LANOY, JEMISON & LIST, CHARTERED, A PROFESSIONAL LAW CORPORATION (AV)

530 Las Vegas Boulevard South, 89101
Telephone: 702-385-3373
Telecopier: 702-385-9447
Reno, Nevada Office: 100 West Liberty Street, Suite 700.
Telephone: 702-323-8866.
Telecopier: 702-323-5523.

Rex A. Jemison
J. Mitchell Cobeaga
Daniel F. Polsenberg
Carol Davis Zucker
Philip M. Hymanson
Norman Patrick Flanagan, III (Resident, Reno Office)

Kwasi Nyamekye

OF COUNSEL

Drake De Lanoy

For Complete List of Firm Personnel, See General Section

For full biographical listings, see the Martindale-Hubbell Law Directory

BELL, DAVIDSON & MYERS (AV)

601 East Bridger Avenue, 89101
Telephone: 702-382-5111

MEMBERS OF FIRM

Stewart L. Bell
Michael D. Davidson
Andrew S. Myers

Representative Client: Jack Kent Cooke.

For full biographical listings, see the Martindale-Hubbell Law Directory

DENTON & DENTON, LTD. (AV)

626 South Seventh Street, 89101
Telephone: 702-384-1723
Fax: 702-384-8019

(See Next Column)

DENTON & DENTON LTD.—*Continued*

Ralph L. Denton
Mark R. Denton
Joseph A. Lopez, IV

Representative Clients: Shetakis Wholesalers, Inc.; TRW, Inc.; Leprechaun Mining & Chemical, Inc.
Reference: Bank of America.

For full biographical listings, see the Martindale-Hubbell Law Directory

---

DICKERSON, DICKERSON, LIEBERMAN & CONSUL (AV)

Suite 1130, 330 South Third Street, 89101
Telephone: 702-388-8600
Fax: 702-388-0210

MEMBERS OF FIRM

George M. Dickerson
Robert P. Dickerson
Barry L. Lieberman
Vincent A. Consul
Richard J. Pocker

ASSOCIATES

Douglass A. Mitchell
Luke Puschnig
Paul J. Lal
Bryce C. Duckworth

Reference: Nevada State Bank.

For full biographical listings, see the Martindale-Hubbell Law Directory

---

GREENMAN, GOLDBERG, RABY & MARTINEZ, PROFESSIONAL CORPORATION (AV)

601 South Ninth Street, 89101-7012
Telephone: 702-384-1616
FAX: 702-384-2990

John A. Greenman
Aubrey Goldberg
Paul E. Raby
Gabriel A. Martinez

Eduardo G. San Miguel
Daniel S. Simon

Reference: First Interstate Bank.

For full biographical listings, see the Martindale-Hubbell Law Directory

---

HALE, LANE, PEEK, DENNISON AND HOWARD (AV)

Suite 800, Nevada Financial Center, 2300 West Sahara Avenue, Box 8, 89102
Telephone: 702-362-5118
Fax: 702-365-6940
Reno, Nevada Office: Porsche Building, 100 West Liberty Street, Tenth Floor, P.O. Box 3237.
Telephone: 702-786-7900.
Telefax: 702-786-6179.

MEMBERS OF FIRM

Steve Lane
J. Stephen Peek
Richard L. Elmore
Alex J. Flangas
Donald L. Christensen
Robert D. Martin

ASSOCIATE

I. Scott Bogatz

OF COUNSEL

Gary B. Gelfand

Representative Clients: Perini Building Company; Bank of America Nevada; Chicago Title Insurance Co.; Commonwealth Land Title Insurance Co.; Design Professional Insurance Co.; United Gaming, Inc.; United Coin Machine Co.; Transamerica Title Insurance Co.

For Complete List of Firm Personnel, See General Section

For full biographical listings, see the Martindale-Hubbell Law Directory

---

JOLLEY, URGA, WIRTH & WOODBURY (AV)

Suite 800 Bank of America Plaza, 300 South Fourth Street, 89101
Telephone: 702-385-5161
Telecopier: 702-382-6814
Boulder City, Nevada Office: Suite 105, 1000 Nevada Highway.
Telephone: 702-293-3674.

MEMBERS OF FIRM

R. Gardner Jolley
William R. Urga
Roger A. Wirth
Bruce L. Woodbury
Jay Earl Smith
Stephanie M. Smith
Kathryn Elizabeth Stryker
Mark A. James
Donald E. Brookhyser

ASSOCIATES

Allen D. Emmel
Troy E. Peyton
Brian E. Holthus

Representative Clients: First Interstate Bank of Nevada; Nevada State Bank; Citicorp National Services, Inc.; Chicago Title Insurance Co.; National Title Company; Fidelity National Title; Continental National Bank; General Motors Acceptance Corp.; Ford Motor Credit Co.; Toyota Motor Credit Corporation.

(See Next Column)

For Complete List of Firm Personnel, See General Section

For full biographical listings, see the Martindale-Hubbell Law Directory

---

JONES, JONES, CLOSE & BROWN, CHARTERED (AV)

Suite 700, Bank of America Plaza, 300 South Fourth Street, 89101-6026
Telephone: 702-385-4202
Telecopier: 702-384-2276
Reno, Nevada Office: 290 South Arlington.
Telephone: 702-322-3811.
Telecopier: 702-348-0886.

Melvin D. Close, Jr.
Gary R. Goodheart
Douglas M. Cohen
Kirk B. Lenhard

Representative Clients: Bank of America-Nevada; First Interstate Bank of Nevada; Lawyers Title; Chrysler Credit Corporation; Western Acceptance Corporation; Southern Farm Bureau; Life Insurance Company; Federal Deposit Insurance Corporation; Resolution Trust Corporation; Southwest Gas Corporation.

For Complete List of Firm Personnel, See General Section

For full biographical listings, see the Martindale-Hubbell Law Directory

---

KEEFER, O'REILLY & FERRARIO (AV)

An Association including a Professional Corporation
Nevada Professional Center, 325 South Maryland Parkway, Suite One, 89101
Telephone: 702-382-2660; 384-8944
Fax: 702-387-6978

Milton W. Keefer
John F. O'Reilly (A Professional Corporation)
Mark E. Ferrario
Edward C. Lubbers

Anita A. Webster
Kevin E. Helm
Jon M. Okazaki
Maribeth Jo Stock
James R. Sweetin

Representative Clients: Associates Commercial Corp.; Bailey & McGah; Chism Homes, Inc.; Cole Travel Service; Greentree Acceptance Co.; Hartford Insurance Co.; Holiday Inns, Inc.; Home Ins. Co.; Legal Protective Life Ins. Co.; Maryland Casualty Co.

For full biographical listings, see the Martindale-Hubbell Law Directory

---

LEAVITT, SULLY & RIVERS (AV)

An Association of Professional Corporations
601 East Bridger Avenue, 89101
Telephone: 702-382-5111
Telecopier: 702-382-2892

K. Michael Leavitt (Chartered)
W. Leslie Sully, Jr. (Chartered)
David J. Rivers, II (Chartered)

For full biographical listings, see the Martindale-Hubbell Law Directory

---

JOHN PETER LEE, LTD. (AV)

830 Las Vegas Boulevard South, 89101
Telephone: 702-382-4044
Telecopy: 702-383-9950

John Peter Lee

Barney C. Ales
Nancy L. Allf
Theresa M. Dowling
Paul C. Ray

For Complete List of Firm Personnel, See General Section

For full biographical listings, see the Martindale-Hubbell Law Directory

---

LIONEL SAWYER & COLLINS (AV)

1700 Bank of America Plaza, 300 South Fourth Street, 89101
Telephone: 702-383-8888
Fax: 702-383-8845
Reno, Nevada Office: Suite 1100, Bank of America Plaza, 50 West Liberty Street.
Telephone: 702-788-8666.
Fax: 702-788-8682.

MEMBERS OF FIRM

Samuel S. Lionel
Grant Sawyer
Paul Hejmanowski
Robert D. Faiss
David N. Frederick
Dennis L. Kennedy
Richard W. Horton (Resident, Reno Office)
Dan C. Bowen (Resident, Reno Office)
Mark A. Solomon
Evan J. Wallach
Todd M. Touton
Cam Ferenbach
Lynda Sue Mabry
John R. Bailey
Dan R. Reaser (Resident, Reno Office)

OF COUNSEL

Robert M. Buckalew

(See Next Column)

LIONEL SAWYER & COLLINS, *Las Vegas—Continued*

ASSOCIATES

Jeffrey D. Menicucci (Resident, Reno Office)
Gordon H. Warren
Louis E. Garfinkel
Donald L. Soderberg (Resident, Reno Office)
Deborah L. Earl
Ellen F. Whittemore
Paul E. Larsen
Christopher R. Hooper (Resident, Reno Office)
Suvinder S. Ahluwalia

Representative Clients: Caesars Palace; Humana Inc.; General Motors Corporation; Kerr McGee Corporation; Lewis Homes of Nevada; Citicorp; Hilton Hotels Corporation; Sprint/Central Telephone-Nevada; Republic Insurance; Columbia Healthcare Corp.

For Complete List of Firm Personnel, See General Section

For full biographical listings, see the Martindale-Hubbell Law Directory

McDONALD, CARANO, WILSON, McCUNE, BERGIN, FRANKOVICH & HICKS (AV)

Suite 1000, 2300 West Sahara Avenue, 89102
Telephone: 702-873-4100
Telecopier: 702-873-9966
Reno, Nevada Office: 241 Ridge Street.
Telephone: 702-322-0635.
Telecopier: 702-786-9532.

MEMBERS OF FIRM

David W. Huston (Resident)
Thomas R. C. Wilson, II
John J. McCune
Leo P. Bergin, III
John J. Frankovich
Larry R. Hicks
William A. S. Magrath, II
James W. Bradshaw
Lenard T. Ormsby
Deborah E. Schumacher
Sylvia L. Harrison
George F. Ogilvie III (Resident)

ASSOCIATES

Pat Lundvall
Matthew C. Addison
James P. Stefflre
Andrew P. Gordon (Resident)
Bryan R. Clark

OF COUNSEL

William S. Boyd (Resident)
Charles E. Huff (Resident)

Representative Clients: AT&T Communications of Nevada; Bally Gaming, Inc.; Boomtown, Inc.; Boyd Gaming Corporation; First Interstate Bank of Nevada; Jackpot Enterprises, Inc.; Primadonna Resorts, Inc.; Shaver Construction.

For Complete List of Firm Personnel, See General Section

For full biographical listings, see the Martindale-Hubbell Law Directory

MORSE & MOWBRAY, A PROFESSIONAL CORPORATION (AV)

Suite 1400 Bank of America Plaza, 300 South Fourth Street, 89101
Telephone: 702-384-6340
Telecopier: 702-384-4596
London, England Office: Lamb Building, Temple.
Telephone: 071-353-6701.

William R. Morse
Harold M. Morse
John H. Mowbray
Christopher H. Byrd
Steven R. Scow
Marsha H. Tarte

Allan P. Capps

For full biographical listings, see the Martindale-Hubbell Law Directory

JOHN D. O'BRIEN, LTD. (AV)

1409 Bank of America Plaza, 300 South Fourth Street, 89101
Telephone: 702-382-5222
Fax: 702-382-0540

John D. O'Brien

For full biographical listings, see the Martindale-Hubbell Law Directory

PICO & MITCHELL (AV)

2000 South Eastern Avenue, 89104
Telephone: 702-457-9099
FAX: 702-457-8451

MEMBERS OF FIRM

James F. Pico
Bert O. Mitchell
Christy Brad Escobar

ASSOCIATES

James R. Rosenberger
Gary L. Myers
E. Breen Arntz
Robert W. Cottle
Cory Hilton
Lawrence Davidson
Thomas A. Ericsson
Linda M. Graham

Representative Clients: Home Insurance Co.; State Farm Mutual Insurance Co.; Industrial Indemnity Ins. Co.; Great American Insurance Co.; Argonaut Insurance Cos.; Clark County Medical Society; Rose de Lima Hospital; Fairway Chevrolet; American States Insurance Co.; Hartford Ins.

For full biographical listings, see the Martindale-Hubbell Law Directory

RAWLINGS, OLSON & CANNON, A PROFESSIONAL CORPORATION (AV)

301 East Clark Avenue, Suite 1000, 89101
Telephone: 702-384-4012
Telecopier: 702-383-0701

Henry H. Rawlings, Jr.
James R. Olson
Walter R. Cannon
John D. Nitz
John E. Gormley
Richard E. Desruisseaux
Dana Jonathon Nitz
Janice Hodge Jensen
Brian C. Whitaker

Melissa Collins
Yvette D. Robichaud
Peter M. Angulo
Don F. Shreve, Jr.
Kenneth A. Cardone
Larry Lee Ketzenberger
Bryan W. Lewis
Michael C. Mills
Michelle D. Mullins
Michael E. Stoberski
Craig B. Friedberg
Bryan K. Scott
Joseph J. Purdy
Bradley M. Ballard

For full biographical listings, see the Martindale-Hubbell Law Directory

THORNDAL, BACKUS, ARMSTRONG & BALKENBUSH, A PROFESSIONAL CORPORATION (AV)

1100 East Bridger Avenue, P.O. Box 2070, 89125-2070
Telephone: 702-366-0622
Fax: 702-366-0327
Reno, Nevada Office: Suite 200, 888 West Second Street.
Telephone: 702-786-2882.
Fax: 702-786-8004.

John L. Thorndal
Leland Eugene Backus
James G. Armstrong
Craig R. Delk
Peggy A. Leen
Stephen C. Balkenbush (Resident, Reno Office)
Paul F. Eisinger
Charles Lee Burcham (Resident, Reno Office)
Brian K. Terry
Brent Thomas Kolvet (Resident, Reno Office)

Blair C. Parker
Ginger R. James
William R. Killip, Jr.
Carrie McCrea Hanlon
Sara Kathryn Anderson
Janiece S. Marshall
Stephanie K. Newman
Michael E. Sullivan
David W. Mincavage

Representative Clients: Circus Circus Enterprises, Inc.; EG&G, Inc.; First Interstate Bank of Nevada; Westinghouse Electric Corporation; NCAA; Farmers Insurance Group; CIGNA Property & Casualty Companies; Travelers Indemnity Company; Nationwide Insurance Company; California Casualty Company.

For full biographical listings, see the Martindale-Hubbell Law Directory

WOODBURN AND WEDGE (AV)

Suite 620 Bank of America Plaza, 300 South Fourth Street, 89101
Telephone: 702-387-1000
Reno, Nevada Office: 16th Floor, First Interstate Bank Building. P.O. Box 2311.
Telephone: 702-688-3000.
Telecopier: 702-688-3088.

MEMBERS OF FIRM

Virgil H. Wedge
Richard O. Kwapil, Jr.
Casey Woodburn Vlautin
Gordon H. DePaoli
Suellen Fulstone
William E. Peterson
John F. Murtha
W. Chris Wicker
Charles A. Jeannes
Shawn B Meador
Lynne K. Jones
John E. Leach
Harry J. Schlegelmilch

ASSOCIATE

David G. Johnson

Representative Clients: Atlantic Richfield Co.; Sierra Pacific Power Co.; The Union Pacific Railroad Co.; Western Union Telegraph Co.; Cyprus Minerals Corp.; The Roman Catholic Bishop of Reno, A Corporation Sole.

For full biographical listings, see the Martindale-Hubbell Law Directory

WRIGHT, JUDD & WINCKLER (AV)

Third Floor, First Interstate Bank Building, 302 East Carson Avenue, 89101
Telephone: 702-382-4004
FAX: 702-382-4800

MEMBERS OF FIRM

Richard A. Wright
Bruce M. Judd
Karen C. Winckler

For full biographical listings, see the Martindale-Hubbell Law Directory

*RENO,** Washoe Co.

BIBLE, HOY, TRACHOK, WADHAMS & ZIVE, A PROFESSIONAL CORPORATION (AV)

232 Court Street, 89501-1808
Telephone: 702-786-8000
Telecopier: 702-786-7426
Las Vegas, Nevada Office: 2110 E. Flamingo R. Ste. 325.
Telephone: 702-369-6690.
Telecopier: 702-733-8198.

Paul A. Bible
David R. Hoy
Richard M. Trachok, II
James L. Wadhams (Resident, Las Vegas Office)
Gregg W. Zive

Michael D. Hoy
Constance L. Akridge (Resident, Las Vegas Office)
Mark S. Sertic
Jon M. Ludwig
Mark F. Bruce

References: First Interstate Bank of Nevada; Bank of America.

For full biographical listings, see the Martindale-Hubbell Law Directory

ERICKSON, THORPE & SWAINSTON, LTD. (AV)

601 S. Arlington Avenue, P.O. Box 3559, 89505
Telephone: 702-786-3930
Fax: 702-786-4160

Roger L. Erickson
Donald A. Thorpe
George W. Swainston
William G. Cobb
James L. Lundemo
Gary A. Cardinal
Thomas Peter Beko
John A. Aberasturi

Representative Clients: Albertson's, Inc.; Allstate Insurance Co.; Avis Rent-A-Car System; Chrysler Corp.; Airport Authority of Washoe County; Dow Corning; Reno-Sparks Convention and Visitors Authority; Nevada Public Agency Insurance Pool; Airport Authority of Washoe County; Bank of America Nevada.

For full biographical listings, see the Martindale-Hubbell Law Directory

GUILD, RUSSELL, GALLAGHER & FULLER, LTD. (AV)

100 West Liberty, Suite 800, P.O. Box 2838, 89505
Telephone: 702-786-2366
Telecopier: 702-322-9105

Clark J. Guild (1887-1971)
Clark J. Guild, Jr.
C. David Russell
John K. Gallagher
Gary M. Fuller
Craig M. Burkett

OF COUNSEL

Reese H. Taylor, Jr.

Representative Clients: City of Los Angeles Department of Water & Power; Southwest Gas Corporation; Fred H. Dressler; Security Pacific Bank; Teachers Insurance & Annuity Assoc.-College Retirement Equities Fund; Federal Deposit Insurance Corp.

For full biographical listings, see the Martindale-Hubbell Law Directory

HALE, LANE, PEEK, DENNISON AND HOWARD (AV)

Porsche Building, 100 West Liberty Street, Tenth Floor, P.O. Box 3237, 89501
Telephone: 702-786-7900
Telefax: 702-786-6179
Las Vegas, Nevada Office: Suite 800, Nevada Financial Center, 2300 West Sahara Avenue, Box 8.
Telephone: 702-362-5118.
Fax: 702-365-6940.

MEMBERS OF FIRM

J. Stephen Peek
Richard L. Elmore
Alex J. Flangas
Donald L. Christensen

ASSOCIATES

Tracy L. Chase
Jeremy J. Nork
Kimberly A. Chatlin

OF COUNSEL

Gary B. Gelfand

Representative Clients: Bank of America Nevada; Chicago Title Insurance Co.; Commonwealth Land Title Insurance Co.; Crawford and Company; Design Professional Insurance Co.; First California Mortgage; Scolari's Markets; United Gaming, Inc.; United Coin Machine Co.; Transamerica Title Insurance Co.

For Complete List of Firm Personnel, See General Section

For full biographical listings, see the Martindale-Hubbell Law Directory

MCDONALD, CARANO, WILSON, MCCUNE, BERGIN, FRANKOVICH & HICKS (AV)

241 Ridge Street, 89505
Telephone: 702-322-0635
Telecopier: 702-786-9532
Las Vegas, Nevada Office: Suite 1000, 2300 West Sahara Avenue.
Telephone: 702-873-4100.
Telecopier: 702-873-9966.

MEMBERS OF FIRM

John J. McCune
Thomas R. C. Wilson, II
Leo P. Bergin, III
John J. Frankovich
Larry R. Hicks
Alvin J. (Bud) Hicks
William A. S. Magrath, II
Timothy E. Rowe
James W. Bradshaw
Lenard T. Ormsby
Deborah E. Schumacher
Sylvia L. Harrison

ASSOCIATES

James C. Giudici
Matthew C. Addison
James P. Stefflre

OF COUNSEL

Donald L. Carano
William S. Boyd (Resident, Las Vegas Office)
Charles E. Huff (Resident, Las Vegas Office)

Representative Clients: AT&T Communications of Nevada; Associated General Contractors of America; Boyd Gaming Corporation; Eldorado Hotel & Casino; First Interstate Bank of Nevada; Intermountain Federal Land Bank Association; James Hardie (USA), Inc.; Scolari's Warehouse Markets; Shaver Construction; Time Oil Company (Nevada Counsel).

For Complete List of Firm Personnel, See General Section

For full biographical listings, see the Martindale-Hubbell Law Directory

MORTIMER SOURWINE MOUSEL & SLOANE, LTD. (AV)

333 Marsh Avenue, P.O. Box 460, 89504
Telephone: 702-323-8633
Facsimile: 702-323-8668

Julien G. Sourwine
Douglas A. Sloane

Representative Clients: American International Group; Bradford White Corporation; California Casualty; Capital Ford; General Motors Corp.; Holcomb Construction Co.; Martin Iron Works, Inc.; United States Fidelity and Guaranty Co.
Reference: First Interstate Bank of Nevada.

For Complete List of Firm Personnel, See General Section

For full biographical listings, see the Martindale-Hubbell Law Directory

VARGAS & BARTLETT (AV)

201 West Liberty Street, P.O. Box 281, 89504
Telephone: 702-786-5000
Cable Address: "Varbadix"
Fax: 702-786-1177

MEMBERS OF FIRM

George L. Vargas (1909-1985)
John C. Bartlett (1910-1982)
James P. Logan (1920-1984)
Louis Mead Dixon (1919-1993)
Albert F. Pagni
Frederic R. Starich
Phillip W. Bartlett
Scott A. Glogovac
Michael R. Kealy
Michael P. Lindell
Karen M. Ayarbe
J. William Ebert

ASSOCIATES

Debra B. Robinson
Michael G. Alonso
Stacey A. Upson

For Complete List of Firm Personnel, See General Section

For full biographical listings, see the Martindale-Hubbell Law Directory

WOODBURN AND WEDGE (AV)

16th Floor, First Interstate Bank Building, One East First Street, P.O. Box 2311, 89505
Telephone: 702-688-3000
Telecopier: 702-688-3088
Las Vegas, Nevada Office: Suite 620 Bank of American Plaza, 300 South Court Street.
Telephone: 702-387-1000.

MEMBERS OF FIRM

Virgil H. Wedge
Richard O. Kwapil, Jr.
Casey Woodburn Vlautin
Gordon H. DePaoli
Suellen Fulstone
William E. Peterson
John F. Murtha
W. Chris Wicker
Charles A. Jeannes
Shawn B Meador
Lynne K. Jones
John E. Leach
Harry J. Schlegelmilch

(See Next Column)

WOODBURN AND WEDGE, *Reno—Continued*

ASSOCIATE

David G. Johnson

Representative Clients: Atlantic Richfield Co.; Sierra Pacific Power Co.; The Union Pacific Railroad Co.; Western Union Telegraph Co.; Bank of America; Cyprus Minerals Corp.; The Roman Catholic Bishop of Reno, A Corporation Sole.

For full biographical listings, see the Martindale-Hubbell Law Directory

NEW HAMPSHIRE

*CONCORD,** Merrimack Co.

DOUGLAS & DOUGLAS (AV)

6 Loudon Road Suite 502, 03301
Telephone: 603-224-1988
Fax: 603-229-1988

Charles G. Douglas, III
Caroline G. Douglas
James B. Kazan
Robert J. Rabuck
Susanna G. Robinson
C. Kevin Leonard
Carolyn Garvey

For full biographical listings, see the Martindale-Hubbell Law Directory

ORR & RENO, PROFESSIONAL ASSOCIATION (AV)

One Eagle Square, P.O. Box 3550, 03302-3550
Telephone: 603-224-2381
Fax: 603-224-2318

Ronald L. Snow
Richard B. Couser
William L. Chapman

Representative Clients: Beach Aircraft Corporation; Chubb Life America; Fleet Bank; Dartmouth-Hitchcock Medical Center; EnergyNorth, Inc.; National Grange Mutual Co.; New England College; New England Electric System Co.; Newspapers of New England, Inc.; St. Paul's School.

For Complete List of Firm Personnel, See General Section

For full biographical listings, see the Martindale-Hubbell Law Directory

*KEENE,** Cheshire Co.

BELL, FALK & NORTON, P.A. (AV)

8 Middle Street, P.O. Box F, 03431
Telephone: 603-352-5950
FAX: 603-352-5930

Ernest L. Bell, Jr. (1925-1961)
Ernest L. Bell
Arnold R. Falk
John C. Norton

William James Robinson

For full biographical listings, see the Martindale-Hubbell Law Directory

*LACONIA,** Belknap Co.

NORMANDIN, CHENEY & O'NEIL (AV)

Normandin Square, 213 Union Avenue, P.O. Box 575, 03247-0575
Telephone: 603-524-4380

MEMBERS OF FIRM

A. Gerard O'Neil
A.G. O'Neil, Jr.
James F. LaFrance

ASSOCIATE

Duncan J. Farmer

Counsel for: Laconia Savings Bank; Lakes Region Mental Health Center; Laconia Airport Authority; Community TV Corp.; Central New Hampshire Realty, Inc.; All Metals Industries, Inc.; Lakes Region Anesthesiology, P.A.; Cormier Corp.; Scotia Technology; Vemaline Products.

For Complete List of Firm Personnel, See General Section

For full biographical listings, see the Martindale-Hubbell Law Directory

*MANCHESTER,** Hillsborough Co.

McLANE, GRAF, RAULERSON & MIDDLETON, PROFESSIONAL ASSOCIATION (AV)

City Hall Plaza, 900 Elm Street, P.O. Box 326, 03105
Telephone: 603-625-6464
Telecopier: 603-625-5650
Concord, New Hampshire Office: Bicentennial Square, 15 North Main Street.
Telephone: 603-226-0400.
Portsmouth, New Hampshire Office: 30 Penhallow Street.
Telephone: 603-436-2818.

(See Next Column)

Arthur A. Greene, Jr. (Retired)
Jack B. Middleton
James R. Muirhead
Arthur G. Greene
R. David DePuy
Bruce W. Felmly
Robert E. Jauron
Thomas J. Donovan
Wilbur A. Glahn, III
Ralph F. Holmes
Peter D. Anderson
David Wolowitz (Resident Partner, Portsmouth Office)

Alice K. Page (Resident, Portsmouth Office)
Kevin M. Leach
Suzanne M. Gorman
Mark C. Rouvalis
Anne M. Edwards
J. Kirk Trombley (Resident, Portsmouth Office)

Representative Clients: Action Equipment Co., Inc.; Agfa Gavaert, Inc.; BankEast Corp.; Child & Family Services of New Hampshire; EnergyNorth Inc.; Hitchner Manufacturing; Manchester Water Works; New England Telephone & Telegraph Co.; New Hampshire Automobile Dealers Assn.; Shearson, Lehman/American Express, Inc.

For Complete List of Firm Personnel, See General Section

For full biographical listings, see the Martindale-Hubbell Law Directory

PORTSMOUTH, Rockingham Co.

GERALD F. GILES (AV)

70 Heritage Avenue, P.O. Box 4190, 03082-4190
Telephone: 603-436-7400
Fax: 603-436-2924

NEW JERSEY

BLOOMFIELD, Essex Co.

KENNEDY & KENNEDY (AV)

Bloomfield Plaza Building, 650 Bloomfield Avenue, 07003
Telephone: 201-429-7091
Fax: 201-743-5853

MEMBERS OF FIRM

William V. Kennedy
John J. Kennedy

For full biographical listings, see the Martindale-Hubbell Law Directory

BRICK, Ocean Co.

STARKEY, KELLY, BLANEY & WHITE (AV)

522 Brick Boulevard, P.O. Box 610, 08723
Telephone: 908-477-1610
Fax: 908-477-2225

MEMBERS OF FIRM

Charles E. Starkey
William V. Kelly
James M. Blaney

ASSOCIATES

Natalie Pouch
Anthony Mancuso
Therese A. Nestor
Robert A. Bauer
Christopher J. Carkhuff

Representative Clients: Hartford Insurance Co.; New Jersey Education Assn.; New Jersey Psychiatric Assn.; Ocean County Utilities Authority; Prudential Property & Casualty Insurance Co.; Hanover Insurance Co.; Westinghouse Corp.; John Hancock Insurance Co.

For full biographical listings, see the Martindale-Hubbell Law Directory

BURLINGTON, Burlington Co.

SMITH, GOLDSTEIN & MAGRAM, A PROFESSIONAL CORPORATION (AV)

415 High Street, P.O. Box 603, 08016-0603
Telephone: 609-386-2633
Fax: 609-386-8674

Louis A. Smith
Jeffrey N. Goldstein
Edward J. Magram

Elizabeth D. Berenato

Reference: First Fidelity Bank of South Jersey, Burlington, New Jersey.

For full biographical listings, see the Martindale-Hubbell Law Directory

*CAMDEN,** Camden Co.

BROWN & CONNERY (AV)

518 Market Street, P.O. Box 1449, 08101
Telephone: 609-365-5100
Facsimile: 609-858-4967
Westmont, New Jersey Office: 360 Haddon Avenue. P.O. Box 539.
Telephone: 609-854-8900.

(See Next Column)

BROWN & CONNERY—*Continued*

MEMBERS OF FIRM

Thomas F. Connery, Jr.
Michael J. Vassalotti
William J. Cook
John J. Mulderig
Warren W. Faulk
William M. Tambussi
Steven G. Wolschina
Bruce H. Zamost
Paul Mainardi
Mark P. Asselta
John L. Conroy, Jr.
Stephen J. DeFeo
Dennis P. Blake
Jane A. Lorber

ASSOCIATES

Isabel C. Balboa
Michael J. Fagan
Joseph A. Zechman
Karen A. Peterson
Jeffrey E. Ugoretz

Representative Clients: Delaware River Port Authority; Underwood-Memorial Hospital; Garden State Water Company; Honeywell, Inc.; Philadelphia Newspapers, Inc.; Port Authority Transit Co.; Resolution Trust Corp.; General Electric; Mercedes-Benz Credit Corp.; American Red Cross.

For Complete List of Firm Personnel, See General Section

For full biographical listings, see the Martindale-Hubbell Law Directory

CHATHAM, Morris Co.

ARSENEAULT, DONOHUE, SORRENTINO & FASSETT (AV)

560 Main Street, 07928-2119
Telephone: 201-635-3366
FAX: 201-635-0855

MEMBERS OF FIRM

Jack Arseneault
Joan Sorrentino
Timothy M. Donohue
David W. Fassett
Frank P. Arleo

ASSOCIATES

David G. Tomeo
William Strazza

For full biographical listings, see the Martindale-Hubbell Law Directory

O'CONNOR & RHATICAN, A PROFESSIONAL CORPORATION (AV)

383 Main Street, 07928
Telephone: 201-635-2210
FAX: 201-635-2622

Gerald B. O'Connor
Peter E. Rhatican
Vivian Demas

Paul A. O'Connor, III

OF COUNSEL

Patricia J. Cooney

For full biographical listings, see the Martindale-Hubbell Law Directory

CHERRY HILL, Camden Co.

FORKIN, MCSHANE & ROTZ, A PROFESSIONAL ASSOCIATION (AV)

750 Kings Highway North, 08034-1581
Telephone: 609-779-8500
Fax: 609-779-8030

Thomas S. Forkin
Richard B. Rotz
Joseph Patrick McShane, III
George W. Stevenson, III

For full biographical listings, see the Martindale-Hubbell Law Directory

GARRIGLE & PALM (AV)

Suite 204, 1415 State Highway 70 East, 08034
Telephone: 609-427-9300
Fax: 609-427-9590

MEMBERS OF FIRM

William A. Garrigle
John M. Palm

ASSOCIATES

Harold H. Thomasson
James J. Law
Paul F Kulinski
Eleanore A. Rogalski

Representative Clients: Crum & Forster Group; Kemper Insurance Group; Atlantic Mutual Group; American Hardware Mutual; National General Insurance Co.; Transamerica Group; State Farm Fire Insurance Co.; Progressive Insurance Co.; United Southern Insurance Co.; New Jersey Market Transition Facility and Joint Underwriting Association.

For full biographical listings, see the Martindale-Hubbell Law Directory

KENNEY & KEARNEY (AV)

Woodland Falls Corporate Park, Suite 210, 220 Lake Drive East, P.O. Box 5034, 08034-0421
Telephone: 609-779-7000
Telecopier: 609-779-1342

(See Next Column)

Joseph H. Kenney
Allen A. Etish
John B. Kearney
Michele Mareschi Fox
John A. Miller, Jr.
William J. DeSantis
Mark Schwartz
Charles J. Connery

ASSOCIATES

Richard J. Sexton
Ralph R. Smith, 3rd
Margaret J. Quinn
Kevin Walker
Thomas A. Whelihan

Representative Clients: American Cyanamid; Eastman Kodak Co.; The Hanover Insurance Co.; Hospital of the University of Pennsylvania; Lederle Labs., Inc.; Mellon Bank (DE), N.A.; Ryder Truck Rental, Inc.; Stone & Webster; The Travelers Insurance Co.; Wheaton, Inc.

For full biographical listings, see the Martindale-Hubbell Law Directory

MCCARTER & ENGLISH (AV)

1810 Chapel Avenue West, 08002
Telephone: 609-662-8444
Telecopier: 609-662-6203
Newark, New Jersey Office: Four Gateway Center, 100 Mulberry Street. P.O. Box 652.
Telephone: 201-622-4444.
Telecopier: 201-624-7070.
Cable Address: "McCarter" Newark.
New York, New York Office: Suite 1519, One World Trade Center.
Telephone: 212-466-9018.
Telecopier: 212-432-6568.
Boca Raton, Florida Office: 2255 Glades Road, Suite 319-A.
Telephone: 407-994-6262.
Telecopier: 407-241-0798.
Wilmington, Delaware Office: Mellon Bank Center, 919 Market Street.
Telephone: 302-654-8010
Telecopier: 302-654-0795

RESIDENT PARTNERS

James F. Hammill
Therese M. Keeley
Nathan A. Schachtman

For Complete List of Firm Personnel, See General Section

For full biographical listings, see the Martindale-Hubbell Law Directory

MONTANO, SUMMERS, MULLEN, MANUEL, OWENS AND GREGORIO, A PROFESSIONAL CORPORATION (AV)

Two Executive Campus, Suite 400, Route 70 and Cuthbert Boulevard, 08002
Telephone: 609-665-9400
Fax: 609-665-0006
Northfield, New Jersey Office: The Executive Plaza, 2111 New Road, Suite 105.
Telephone: 609-383-8900.
Philadelphia, Pennsylvania Office: 1700 Market Street - Suite 2628.
Telephone: 215-732-3900.

Carl Kisselman (1899-1975)
Gary L. Jakob
James A. Mullen, Jr.
Lawrence D. Lally
G. Wesley Manuel, Jr.
Paul F. Gilligan, Jr.
F. Herbert Owens, III
David D. Duffin
Carl J. Gregorio
Michael G. B. David

Craig W. Summers
Arthur E. Donnelly, III
Mary C. Brennan
Bruce C. Truesdale
James A. Nolan, Jr.
Ronald S. Collins, Jr.
Alfred J. Quasti, Jr.
Matthew P. Lyons
Robert H. Ayik
William J. Rudnik (Resident, Northfield Office)
Stephen D. Holtzman (Resident, Northfield Office)

OF COUNSEL

Arthur Montano
William W. Summers

Local Counsel for: Indemnity Insurance Company of North America; Royal Group; General Motors Corp.
Reference: Midlantic National Bank, Cherry Hill, New Jersey.

For full biographical listings, see the Martindale-Hubbell Law Directory

PARKER, MCCAY & CRISCUOLO, P.A. (AV)

Commerce Atrium, Suite 500, 1701 Route 70 East, P.O. Box 1806, 08034
Telephone: 609-424-4300
Telecopier: 609-424-1006
Marlton, New Jersey Office: Suite 401 Three Greentree Center, Route 73 & Greentree Road.
Telephone: 609-596-8900.
Telecopier: 609-596-9631.
Philadelphia, Pennsylvania Office: 3700 Bell Atlantic Tower, 1717 Arch Street.
Telephone: 215-994-5315.
Telecopier: 215-994-3100.

Robert C. Beck

(See Next Column)

PARKER, MCCAY & CRISCUOLO P.A., *Cherry Hill—Continued*

Richard M. Berman

Local Counsel for: Aetna Casualty & Surety Co.; U.S. Fidelity & Guaranty Co.; Keystone Insurance Co.; Eagle Dyeing & Finishing Co.; Zurich-American Insurance Co.; Commerce Bank, N.A.; First Fidelity Bank; Midlantic Bank.

For Complete List of Firm Personnel, See General Section

For full biographical listings, see the Martindale-Hubbell Law Directory

CLIFTON, Passaic Co.

CELENTANO, STADTMAUER & WALENTOWICZ (AV)

1035 Route 46 East, P.O. Box 2594, 07015-2594
Telephone: 201-778-1771
Telecopier: 201-778-4136

MEMBERS OF FIRM

John A. Celentano, Jr.
Arnold L. Stadtmauer
Henry Walentowicz

Ellen M. Seigerman

Representative Clients: Jefferson National Bank (N.A.); Clifton Savings Bank, S.L.A.; The General Hospital Center at Passaic (commercial); Passaic Boys Club; Smith Sondy Asphalt Construction Co., Inc.; Boro Lumber Co., Inc.; Castle Arms Condominium; ADX Copy Corp.; Country Club Towers.
References: Jefferson National Bank (N.A.), Passaic, New Jersey; Commonwealth Land Title Insurance Co., Paterson, New Jersey.

For full biographical listings, see the Martindale-Hubbell Law Directory

CRANFORD, Union Co.

MCCREEDY AND COX (AV)

Second Floor, Six Commerce Drive, 07016-3509
Telephone: 908-709-0400
Fax: 908-709-0405

MEMBERS OF FIRM

Edwin J. McCreedy
Robert F. Cox

ASSOCIATE

Patrick J. Hermesmann

Reference: United Counties Trust Co.

For full biographical listings, see the Martindale-Hubbell Law Directory

ENGLEWOOD, Bergen Co.

CHAZEN & CHAZEN (AV)

75 Grand Avenue, P.O. Box 470, 07631
Telephone: 201-567-5500
Telefax: 201-567-4282

Bernard Chazen
David K. Chazen

For full biographical listings, see the Martindale-Hubbell Law Directory

FAIR LAWN, Bergen Co.

MUSCARELLA, BOCHET, LAHIFF, PECK & EDWARDS, P.C. (AV)

0-100 28th Street, P.O. Box 2770, 07410
Telephone: 201-796-3100; 201-791-9666
Telecopier: 201-791-0350

William C. Bochet
Dennis P. LaHiff
H. Shepard Peck, Jr.
Barbara Anne Edwards
James P. D'Alessandro

For full biographical listings, see the Martindale-Hubbell Law Directory

FLORHAM PARK, Morris Co.

HACK, PIRO, O'DAY, MERKLINGER, WALLACE & MCKENNA, P.A. (AV)

30 Columbia Turnpike, P.O. Box 941, 07932-0941
Telephone: 201-301-6500
Fax: 201-301-0094

David L. Hack
Peter A. Piro
William J. O'Day
M. Richard Merklinger
Joseph V. Wallace
Peter T. Melnyk
Patrick M. Sages

Bonny G. Rafel
Darlene D. Steinhart
Robert G. Alencewicz
John T. West
Scott D. Samansky
Douglas J. Olcott
John J. Petrizzo
William F. Murphy
Thomas M. Madden

Representative Clients: Aetna Life & Casualty Co.; Avis Rent-a-Car Systems; Eastman Kodak Co.; State Farm Insurance Cos.; Trans World Airlines, Inc.; Travelers Insurance Co.; Westinghouse Electric Co.; Weyerhauser Co.

(See Next Column)

For Complete List of Firm Personnel, See General Section

For full biographical listings, see the Martindale-Hubbell Law Directory

*HACKENSACK,** Bergen Co.

BRESLIN AND BRESLIN, P.A. (AV)

41 Main Street, 07601
Telephone: 201-342-4014; 342-4015
Fax: 201-342-0068; 201-342-3077

John J. Breslin, Jr. (1899-1987)
James A. Breslin, Sr. (1900-1980)
Charles Rodgers
E. Carter Corriston
Donald A. Caminiti

Michael T. Fitzpatrick
Angelo A. Bello
Terrence J. Corriston
Kevin C. Corriston
Karen Boe Gatlin
Lawrence Farber
E. Carter Corriston, Jr.

Representative Clients: Bergen County Housing Authority; Phillips Fuel Co.; Prudential Insurance Co.; Rent Leveling Board of Township of North Bergen; Housing Authority of Passaic.
Reference: United Jersey Bank.

For Complete List of Firm Personnel, See General Section

For full biographical listings, see the Martindale-Hubbell Law Directory

CUCCIO AND CUCCIO (AV)

45 Essex Street, 07601
Telephone: 201-487-7411
Fax: 201-487-6574
Mailing Address: P.O. Box 2223, South Hackensack, New Jersey, 07606

MEMBERS OF FIRM

Frank J. Cuccio
Emil S. Cuccio

ASSOCIATE

Pamela Beth Keitz

Representative Clients: TCI of Northern New Jersey; Huffman Koos, Inc.; The Actors Fund of America; Blue Circle-Raia, Inc.; Zimpro, Inc., Division of Sterling Drug; Honig Chemical and Processing Corp.; Napp Technologies, Inc.; River Terrace Gardens Assoc.; Franklin Lakes P.B.A. Local 150.

For full biographical listings, see the Martindale-Hubbell Law Directory

DUNN, PASHMAN, SPONZILLI, SWICK & FINNERTY (AV)

411 Hackensack Avenue, 07601
Telephone: 201-489-1500; 845-4000
Fax: 201-489-1512

COUNSEL

Morris Pashman
Murray L. Cole
Paul D. Rosenberg

MEMBERS OF FIRM

Joseph Dunn
Louis Pashman
John E. Finnerty
Edward G. Sponzilli
Daniel A. Swick
Robert E. Rochford
Warren S. Robins

ASSOCIATES

Nicholas F. Pellitta
Laura S. Kirsch
Danya A. Grunyk
Richard P. Jacobson
Jeffrey M. Shapiro
Deborah L. Ustas
Mark E. Lichtblau
Edward B. Stevenson
Stephen F. Roth

References: United Jersey Bank; Valley National Bank.

For full biographical listings, see the Martindale-Hubbell Law Directory

HARWOOD LLOYD (AV)

130 Main Street, 07601
Telephone: 201-487-1080
Facsimile: 487-4758; 487-8410
East Brunswick, New Jersey Office: Two Tower Center, 10th Floor.
Telephone: 908-214-1010.
Facsimile: 908-214-1818.
Ridgewood, New Jersey Office: 41 Oak Street.
Telephone: 201-447-1422.
Facsimile: 201-447-1926.

MEMBERS OF FIRM

Victor C. Harwood, III
Frank V. D. Lloyd
Brian J. Coyle
Michael B. Oropollo
Richard J. Ryan
Leonard P. Rosa
John D. Allen, III
Frank Holahan
Russell A. Pepe
Gregory J. Irwin
Anthony M. Carlino
Thomas B. Hanrahan
Brian R. Ade
Brian C. Gallagher
Bernadette N. Gordon
Edward Zampino
Jonathan Bubrow

(See Next Column)

HARWOOD LLOYD—*Continued*

OF COUNSEL

David F. McBride
Theodore W. Trautwein
August Schedler
Francis V. D. Lloyd (1896-1974)
John W. Griggs (1929-1980)
Charles C. Shenier (1905-1970)
Emil M. Wulster (1907-1978)
Daniel Gilady (1927-1975)
George A. Brown (1913-1986)

Reference: Midlantic National Bank/North.

For Complete List of Firm Personnel, See General Section

For full biographical listings, see the Martindale-Hubbell Law Directory

HEIN, SMITH, BEREZIN, MALOOF & ROGERS (AV)

Court Plaza East, 19 Main Street, 07601-7023
Telephone: 201-487-7400
Telecopier: 201-487-4228

MEMBERS OF FIRM

Robert J. Maloof
Sidney Berezin
Allan H. Rogers
Robert L. Baum
Lawrence H. Jacobs

ASSOCIATES

John L. Shanahan
Ellen W. Smith
Carla H. Madnick
Marian H. Speid

Representative Clients: Aetna Insurance Co.; Commercial Union of New York; Employers of Wausau; Great American Insurance Cos.; Hanover Insurance Co.; Health Care Insurance Co.; Merchants Mutual Insurance Co.; St. Paul Fire & Marine Insurance Co.; U.S. Fidelity & Guaranty Co.
Reference: United Jersey Bank.

For Complete List of Firm Personnel, See General Section

For full biographical listings, see the Martindale-Hubbell Law Directory

LAW OFFICES OF DONALD HOROWITZ (AV)

24 Bergen Street, 07601
Telephone: 201-343-0100
FAX: 201-343-3321
New York, New York Office: 2 Park Avenue, Suite 2100.
Telephone: 212-349-1150.

For full biographical listings, see the Martindale-Hubbell Law Directory

KAPS & BARTO (AV)

15 Warren Street, 07601
Telephone: 201-489-5277
Telecopier: 201-489-0477

Warren J. Kaps
Raymond Barto

Concetta R. De Lucia
Brenda P. Rosenberg

Representative Clients: Continental Baking Co.; Mayflower Vapor Seal Co.; The Society of American Magicians.
Reference: United Jersey Bank.

For full biographical listings, see the Martindale-Hubbell Law Directory

LITWIN & HOLSINGER (AV)

Two University Plaza, 07601
Telephone: 201-487-9000
Telecopier: 201-487-9070

MEMBERS OF FIRM

John R. Holsinger
Gerald H. Litwin

OF COUNSEL

Bernard J. Koster (Not admitted in NJ)

For full biographical listings, see the Martindale-Hubbell Law Directory

HAWTHORNE, Passaic Co.

JEFFER, HOPKINSON, VOGEL, COOMBER & PEIFFER (AV)

(Formerly Jeffer, Walter, Tierney, DeKorte, Hopkinson & Vogel)
Law Building, 1600 Route 208N, P.O. Box 507, 07507
Telephone: 201-423-0100
Fax: 201-423-5614
Tequesta, Florida Office: 250 Tequesta Drive.
Telephone: 407-747-6000.
Fax: 407-575-9167.
New York, N.Y. Office: Suite 2206, 150 Broadway.
Telephone: 212-406-7260.

MEMBERS OF FIRM

Peter Hofstra (1886-1961)
George Tierney (1895-1976)
Joseph V. Fumagalli (1901-1965)
Richard W. DeKorte (1936-1975)
Robert Walter (1908-1990)
Herman M. Jeffer
Reginald F. Hopkinson
Jerome A. Vogel
Donald J. Coomber
Gary D. Peiffer

(See Next Column)

ASSOCIATES

Melinda B. Maidens
Peter E. Riccobene
Darryl W. Siss
I. Barbara Cecere

Counsel for: Brioschi, Inc.; Opici Wine Co.; Gas Pumpers of America Corp.; The Paterson Market Growers Assn.; Jupiter Tequesta National Bank; Dowling Fuel Oil Co.

For Complete List of Firm Personnel, See General Section

For full biographical listings, see the Martindale-Hubbell Law Directory

*JERSEY CITY,** Hudson Co.

MILLER & GALDIERI (AV)

32 Jones St., 07306
Telephone: 201-653-4543; 653-1830
Fax: 201-653-0130

MEMBERS OF FIRM

Spencer N. Miller
James A. Galdieri

ASSOCIATE

Charles P. Daglian

Reference: Midlantic National Bank/North.

For full biographical listings, see the Martindale-Hubbell Law Directory

LINDEN, Union Co.

KAPLOWITZ AND WISE, A PROFESSIONAL CORPORATION (AV)

923 North Wood Avenue, 07036
Telephone: 908-925-2468
Fax: 908-925-6849

Leo Kaplowitz
Steven Wise
Warren L. Fink

References: United Counties Trust Co.; Columbia Savings and Loan Assn.

For full biographical listings, see the Martindale-Hubbell Law Directory

LIVINGSTON, Essex Co.

GENOVA, BURNS, TRIMBOLI & VERNOIA (AV)

Eisenhower Plaza II, 354 Eisenhower Parkway, 07039
Telephone: 201-533-0777
Facsimile: 201-533-1112
Trenton, New Jersey Office: Suite One, 160 West State Street.
Telephone: 609-393-1131.

MEMBERS OF FIRM

Angelo J. Genova
James M. Burns
Stephen E. Trimboli
Francis J. Vernoia

ASSOCIATES

Meryl G. Nadler
John C. Petrella
James J. McGovern, III
Kathleen M. Connelly
Joseph Licata
Elaine M. Reyes
Lynn S. Degen
James J. Gillespie
T. Sean Jackson

For full biographical listings, see the Martindale-Hubbell Law Directory

KRONISCH, SCHKEEPER AND LESSER, A PROFESSIONAL CORPORATION (AV)

139 East McClellan Avenue, 07039
Telephone: 201-994-1016
Fax: 201-994-3903

Myron W. Kronisch
Marc E. Lesser
Elizabeth Kronisch
Katherine V. Dresdner
William E. Schkeeper (1949-1985)

References: Summit Trust Co.; National Westminster Bank.

For full biographical listings, see the Martindale-Hubbell Law Directory

PHILIP M. LUSTBADER & DAVID LUSTBADER A PROFESSIONAL CORPORATION (AV)

615 West Mount Pleasant Avenue, 07039
Telephone: 201-740-1000
Fax: 201-740-1520

Philip M. Lustbader
David Lustbader

John N. Holly
John L. Riordan, Jr.

OF COUNSEL

Robert J. McKenna

For full biographical listings, see the Martindale-Hubbell Law Directory

Livingston—Continued

MORGAN, MELHUISH, MONAGHAN, ARVIDSON, ABRUTYN & LISOWSKI (AV)

(Formerly Schneider and Morgan)
651 West Mount Pleasant Avenue, 07039
Telephone: 201-994-2500
Fax: 201-994-3375
New York, N.Y. Office: 39 Broadway, 35th Floor.
Telephone: 212-809-1111.
Fax: 212-509-3422.

MEMBERS OF FIRM

Jacob Schneider (1910-1949)
Louis Schneider (1921-1965)
Henry G. Morgan
James L. Melhuish
Robert E. Monaghan
William F. Perry
Richard E. Arvidson
John I. Lisowski
Elliott Abrutyn
Jeffrey M. Kadish
Paul A. Tripodo
John J. Agostini
Robert J. Aste
Mary Adele Hornish
Richard E. Snyder
David M. Welt
Michael A. Sicola
Joseph DeDonato
Robert A. Assuncao

Richard Micliz
Roger C. Schechter
Richard J. Hull
Leonard C. Leicht
Nina Lynn Caroselli
Anthony M. Santoro, Jr.
Robert J. Machi
Michael H. Cohen
Timothy K. Saia
Mary Ellen Scalera
Robert G. Klinck
Linda G. O'Connell

OF COUNSEL

Vincent J. Cirlin

Represent: The Home Insurance Co.; The Insurance Company of North American Cos.; General Accident Fire & Life Assurance Corp., Ltd.; Zurich Insurance Co.; Trans America Insurance Group; Allstate Insurance Co.; Penn Mutual Insurance Co.; State Farm Insurance; Ohio Casualty Co.; American Mutual Liability Insurance Co.

For Complete List of Firm Personnel, See General Section

For full biographical listings, see the Martindale-Hubbell Law Directory

SCHWARTZ, SIMON, EDELSTEIN, CELSO & KESSLER (AV)

(A Partnership including a Professional Corporation)
Presidential Center Suite 300, 293 Eisenhower Parkway, 07039
Telephone: 201-740-1600
Telecopier: 201-740-0891

Lawrence S. Schwartz (P.C.)
Stephen J. Edelstein
Nathanya Guritzky Simon
Nicholas Celso, III
Donald A. Kessler

Michael S. Rubin
David L. Rosenberg
Denise Pamela Coleman
Alan R. Niedz
Joel G. Scharff
Andrew B. Brown
John B. Mariano, Jr.
Joyce A. Brauer-Weston
Wendi F. Weill
Jeffrey A. Bennett
Alison C. Leonard
Joseph P. Kreoll
Pamela T. Hanback
Thomas Russo

OF COUNSEL

Miguel A. Maza

For full biographical listings, see the Martindale-Hubbell Law Directory

SKOLOFF & WOLFE (AV)

293 Eisenhower Parkway, 07039
Telephone: 201-992-0900
Fax: 201-992-0301
Morristown, New Jersey Office: 10 Park Place.
Telephone: 201-267-3511.

Saul A. Wolfe
Gary N. Skoloff
Francis W. Donahue
Richard H. Singer, Jr. (Resident at Morristown Office)
Stephen P. Haller
Cary B. Cheifetz
Robert F. Giancaterino
Edward J. O'Donnell
Stephanie Frangos Hagan
Michael R. Pallarino
Phyllis S. Klein
Beatrice E. Kandell
Heather A. Turnbull
Maryanne Fantalis
Garry J. Roettger

OF COUNSEL

Bertram Polow

For full biographical listings, see the Martindale-Hubbell Law Directory

MARLTON, Burlington Co.

PARKER, MCCAY & CRISCUOLO, P.A. (AV)

Suite 401 Three Greentree Centre, Route 73 & Greentree Road, 08053
Telephone: 609-596-8900
Telecopier: 609-596-9631
Cherry Hill, New Jersey Office: Commerce Atrium, Suite 500, 1701 Route 70 East, P.O. Box 1806.
Telephone: 609-424-4300.
Telecopier: 609-424-1006.
Philadelphia, Pennsylvania Office: 3700 Bell Atlantic Tower, 1717 Arch Street.
Telephone: 215-994-5315.
Telecopier: 215-994-3100.

Harold T. Parker (1903-1983)
Albert McCay (1901-1969)
Robert W. Criscuolo (1909-1977)
Barry T. Parker
Robert C. Beck (Resident at Cherry Hill, New Jersey Office)
David A. Parker
Robert J. Partlow
John Michael Devlin
Yves C. Veenstra
Thomas M. Masick
Marc M. Baldwin
Ronald C. Morgan
Jeffrey P. Heppard
Timothy J. Hinlicky
Stacy L. Moore, Jr.
Drew J. Parker
Thomas D. Romando
Thomas M. Walsh
Gary F. Piserchia
Philip A. Norcross
Suzanne M. Kourlesis

Robert D. Bernardi
Irving G. Finkel
Mary Ann C. O'Brien
Richard M. Berman (Resident at Cherry Hill, New Jersey Office)
Brian M. Brodowski
Thomas S. Harty
Lynn S. Besancon
Thomas J. Coleman, III
Thomas J. Walls, Jr.
Emily M. Clay (Not admitted in NJ)
John D. Borbi
Robert C. Beck, Jr.
J. Brooks DiDonato
Michael C. Cascio

OF COUNSEL

William V. Webster, Jr.
Richard J. Dill
John P. Lippincott

Local Counsel for: Aetna Casualty & Surety Co.; U.S. Fidelity & Guaranty Co.; Keystone Insurance Co.; Eagle Dyeing & Finishing Co.; Zurich-American Insurance Co.; Rider Insurance Co.; Continental Insurance Co.; Commerce Bank, N.A.

For Complete List of Firm Personnel, See General Section

For full biographical listings, see the Martindale-Hubbell Law Directory

MILLBURN, Essex Co.

KUTTNER LAW OFFICES (AV)

24 Lackawanna Plaza, P.O. Box 745, 07041-0745
Telephone: 201-467-8300
Fax: 201-467-4333

Bernard A. Kuttner
Robert D. Kuttner

Reference: Summit Bank, Millburn, New Jersey.

For full biographical listings, see the Martindale-Hubbell Law Directory

MCDERMOTT & MCGEE (AV)

64 Main Street, P.O. Box 192, 07041-0192
Telephone: 201-467-8080
FAX: 201-467-0012

MEMBERS OF FIRM

John L. McDermott
John P. McGee
Richard P. Maggi
Thomas A. Wester
Richard A. Tango
Frank P. Leanza
John L. McDermott, Jr.

ASSOCIATES

Lawrence G. Tosi
David J. Dickinson
A. Charles Lorenzo
Robert A. McDermott
Kevin John McGee

OF COUNSEL

Daniel K. Van Dorn

Representative Clients: Allstate Insurance Co.; American Hardware Mutual Insurance Co.; Argonaut Insurance Cos.; Continental Insurance Cos.; Commercial Union Insurance Cos.; General Accident Group; Maryland-American General Group; Zurich-American Insurance Co.; P.C.M. Intermediaries, Ltd.; The Hanover Insurance Cos.

For full biographical listings, see the Martindale-Hubbell Law Directory

MONTVALE, Bergen Co.

BEATTIE PADOVANO (AV)

50 Chestnut Ridge Road, P.O. Box 244, 07645-0244
Telephone: 201-573-1810
Fax: (DEX) 201-573-9736

(See Next Column)

BEATTIE PADOVANO—*Continued*

MEMBERS OF FIRM

Ralph J. Padovano
Roger W. Breslin, Jr.
Martin W. Kafafian
Brian R. Martinotti

ASSOCIATES

Emery C. Duell
Brenda J. McAdoo
Susan Calabrese

Reference: United Jersey Bank.

For Complete List of Firm Personnel, See General Section

For full biographical listings, see the Martindale-Hubbell Law Directory

MOORESTOWN, Burlington Co.

CHIERICI & WRIGHT, A PROFESSIONAL CORPORATION (AV)

Blason Campus - III, 509 South Lenola Road Building Six, 08057-1561
Telephone: 609-234-6300
Fax: 609-234-9490

Donald R. Chierici, Jr.
David B. Wright
Elizabeth Coleman Chierici
Julie C. Smith
Sheri Nelson Oliano
Jaunice M. Canning
Rhonda J. Eiger
Michael A. Foresta
Linda M. Novosel

For full biographical listings, see the Martindale-Hubbell Law Directory

ESTELLA S. GOLD (AV)

Blason II, 505 South Lenola Road, 08057
Telephone: 609-234-1004
Telecopier: 609-234-7836

Representative Clients: South Jersey Processing, Inc.; J. S. Hovnanian and Sons; American Communication Installations.

For full biographical listings, see the Martindale-Hubbell Law Directory

MORRIS PLAINS, Morris Co.

VOORHEES & ACCIAVATTI (AV)

Powder Mill Plaza, 101 Gibraltar Drive, 07950
Telephone: 201-267-6677
Fax: 201-267-9152
Mailing Address: P.O. Box 1236, Morristown, New Jersey, 07962-1236
Atlantic City, New Jersey Office: 1624 Pacific Avenue, P.O. Box 1801, 08401.
Telephone: 609-348-6698.

MEMBERS OF FIRM

William Wolverton Voorhees, Jr.
Diane M. Acciavatti
Robert W. McAndrew

ASSOCIATES

Thomas C. Pluciennik
Ana Linda Day

For full biographical listings, see the Martindale-Hubbell Law Directory

*MORRISTOWN,** Morris Co.

CLEMENTE, DICKSON & MUELLER, P.A. (AV)

218 Ridgedale Avenue, P.O. Box 1296, 07962-1296
Telephone: 201-455-8008
Fax: 201-455-8118

William F. Mueller
Jonathan D. Clemente
Joseph A. Dickson
Patrick D. Tobia
Daniel E. Somers
Kathleen Kane Morrison
Jeffrey H. Clott
Christina A. Luancing

For full biographical listings, see the Martindale-Hubbell Law Directory

MASKALERIS & ASSOCIATES (AV)

30 Court Street, 07960
Telephone: 201-267-0222
Newark, New Jersey Office: Federal Square Station, P.O. Box 20207.
Telephone: 201-622-4300.
Far Hills, New Jersey Office: Route 202 Station Plaza.
Telephone: 201-234-0600.
New York, New York Office: 123 Bank Street.
Telephone: 212-724-8669.
Athens, Greece Office: Stadio 28, Fourth Floor.
Telephone: 322-6790.

Stephen N. Maskaleris

ASSOCIATES

Peter C. Ioannou
Christopher P. Luongo

For full biographical listings, see the Martindale-Hubbell Law Directory

MCELROY, DEUTSCH AND MULVANEY (AV)

1300 Mount Kemble Avenue, P.O. Box 2075, 07962-2075
Telephone: 201-993-8100
Fax: 201-425-0161
Denver, Colorado Office: 1099 18th Street, Suite 3120.
Telephone: 303-293-8800.
Fax: 303-293-3116.

MEMBERS OF FIRM

Lorraine M. Armenti (Resident Partner, Denver Colorado Office)
Grace C. Bertone
John P. Beyel
William C. Carey
Margaret F. Catalano
Stephen H. Cohen (1938-1992)
Kevin T. Coughlin
Edward B. Deutsch
Timothy I. Duffy
Robert J. Kelly
Joseph P. La Sala
Paul A. Lisovicz
Fred A. Manley, Jr.
Michael J. Marone
William T. McElroy
Laurence M. McHeffey
Joseph P. McNulty, Jr.
James M. Mulvaney
Moira E. O'Connell
Loren L. Pierce
Warren K. Racusin
John H. Suminski
Kevin E. Wolff

OF COUNSEL

Richard G. McCarty (Not admitted in NJ)
John F. Whitteaker

ASSOCIATES

Caroline L. Beers
Christopher Robert Carroll
Edward V. Collins
Billy J. Cooper (Resident, Denver, Colorado Office)
John Thomas Coyne
Nada Leslie Wolff Culver (Resident, Denver, Colorado Office)
John J. Cummings
Anthony J. Davis
John Paul Gilfillan
Kevin M. Haas
Gary S. Kull
Matthew J. Lodge
Tracey L. Matura
Nancy McDonald
Robert McGuire
Suzanne Cocco Midlige
Robert W. Muilenburg
Gary Potters
Kathleen M. Quinn
Vincent E. Reilly
Agnes A. Reiss
Barbara C. Zimmerman Robertson
Samuel J. Samaro
Laura A. Sanom
Thomas P. Scrivo
Dennis T. Smith
Patricia Leen Sullivan
Pamela A. Tanis
Christine L. Thieman
Catharine Acker Vaughan

Representative Clients: ADT Security Systems, Inc.; Yale Materials Handling Corp; Crum & Forster Insurance Co.; Eaton Corp.; Fireman's Fund Insurance Cos.; New Jersey Manufacturers Insurance Co.; The Home Indemnity Co.; Ingersol l-Rand Company; The Pittston Company; Security Pacific Finance Corporation.

For full biographical listings, see the Martindale-Hubbell Law Directory

MCKIRDY AND RISKIN, A PROFESSIONAL CORPORATION (AV)

136 South Street, 07962-2379
Telephone: 201-539-8900
Fax: 201-984-5529

Edward D. McKirdy
Harry J. Riskin
John H. Buonocore, Jr.
Thomas M. Olson

For full biographical listings, see the Martindale-Hubbell Law Directory

PITNEY, HARDIN, KIPP & SZUCH (AV)

Park Avenue at Morris County, P.O. Box 1945, 07962-1945
Telephone: 201-966-6300
New York City: 212-926-0331
Telex: 642014
Telecopier: 201-966-1550

MEMBERS OF FIRM

Clyde A. Szuch
Murray J. Laulicht
Richard L. Plotkin
Robert L. Hollingshead
Frederick L. Whitmer
Robert G. Rose
James E. Tyrrell, Jr.
Anthony J. Marchetta
Paul E. Graham
J. Michael Nolan, Jr.
Dennis R. LaFiura
Dennis T. Kearney
Donald W. Kiel
Elizabeth J. Sher
Stephen G. Traflet
Hope S. Cone
John C. Maloney, Jr.

OF COUNSEL

Philip G. Barber (Not admitted in NJ)

Representative Clients: AlliedSignal Inc.; AT&T; Base Ten Systems, Inc.; Exxon Corp.; Ford Motor Co.; Midlantic National Bank; Sony Electronics, Inc.; Union Carbide Corp.; United Parcel Services, Inc.; Warner-Lambert Co.

For Complete List of Firm Personnel, See General Section

For full biographical listings, see the Martindale-Hubbell Law Directory

Morristown—Continued

PORZIO, BROMBERG & NEWMAN, A PROFESSIONAL CORPORATION (AV)

163 Madison Avenue, 07962-1997
Telephone: 201-538-4006
Facsimile: 201-538-5146
New York, New York Office: 655 Third Avenue, 10017-5617.
Telephone: 212-986-0600.
Facsimile: 212-986-6491.

Steven P. Benenson
Robert J. Brennan
Lisa Murtha Bromberg
Myron J. Bromberg
D. Jeffrey Campbell
Thomas R. Chesson
Roy Alan Cohen
Alexander J. Drago (Resident, New York Office)
Lauren E. Handler
Edward A. Hogan
Anita Hotchkiss
Kenneth R. Meyer
John M. Newman
Howard J. Schwartz

COUNSEL

Stewart A. Cunningham
Charles E. Erway, III
Thomas Spiesman

Maura E. Blau
Howard P. Davis
Christopher P. DePhillips
Garineh S. Dovletian
Peter A. Drucker
Frank Fazio
Karen A. Kaplan
Vanessa M. Kelly
Jonathan M. Korn
William A. Krais
Jonathan R. Kuhlman
Coleen McCaffery
Jay R. McDaniel
Nancy Gail Minikes
Dean M. Monti (Resident Associate, New York Office)
Randi N. Pomerantz
Robert T. Quackenboss
Cynthia D. Richardson
Gregory J. Schwartz
Diane M. Siana
Charles J. Stoia
Janet A. Sullivan
Morna L. Sweeney
Stephen L. Willis

Representative Clients: American Cyanamid Co.; American Home Products Corp.; ASARCO Inc.; Ayerst Laboratories; Johnson & Johnson; Pfizer Inc.; Warner-Lambert Co.

For full biographical listings, see the Martindale-Hubbell Law Directory

SHANLEY & FISHER, A PROFESSIONAL CORPORATION (AV)

131 Madison Avenue, 07962-1979
Telephone: 201-285-1000
Telecopier: 1-201-285-1098
Telex: 475-4255 (I.T.T.)
Cable Address: "Shanley"
New York, N.Y. Office: 89th Floor, One World Trade Center.
Telephone: 212-321-1812.
Telecopier: 1-212-466-0569.

L. Bruce Puffer, Jr.
William G. Becker, Jr.
Raymond M. Tierney, Jr.
Arthur R. Schmauder
Thomas F. Campion
John J. Francis, Jr.
A. Dennis Terrell
Richard E. Brennan
Thomas J. Alworth
William K. Lewis, II
Jeffrey A. Peck
Matthew Farley
Daniel F. O'Connell
Richard A. Levao
Ronald Gould
John D. Clemen
Charles A. Reid, III
Paul G. Nittoly
Robert A. Boutillier
Walter J. Fleischer, Jr.
Susan M. Sharko
Stephen R. Long
Mary E. Tracey
Brian F. McDonough
James M. Altieri
Patrick M. Stanton
Robert M. Leonard
Theodore S. Smith
Michael O. Adelman

COUNSEL

Charles D. Donohue, Jr. (Resident, New York, N.Y. Office)
Stephanie C. Rosen

Peter O. Hughes
Bruce L. Shapiro
Kenneth J. Wilbur
Arthur P. Havighorst, II
Thomas A. Roberts (Resident, New York, N.Y. Office)
Sheila G. Gruber
Mark Diana
Joseph M. Cerra
Kathleen H. Dooley
William R. Brown, Sr.
Kathleen B. Harden
Maureen L. Nesbitt
Andrew S. Turkish
Douglas S. Zucker
Robert A. Burke
Carole A. Hafferty
Jeffrey S. Lipkin
Lisa M. Plinio
Nicholas J. Taldone
Carla Marie Mascaro
Rita C. Burghardt
Suzanne Cerra
Stephen R. Fitzpatrick
William J. Mendrzycki
Mary Jane Armstrong (Resident, New York, N.Y. Office)
Michael R. Clarke

For Complete List of Firm Personnel, See General Section

For full biographical listings, see the Martindale-Hubbell Law Directory

STEPHEN S. WEINSTEIN A PROFESSIONAL CORPORATION (AV)

20 Park Place, Suite 301, 07960
Telephone: 201-267-5200
FAX: 201-538-1779

Stephen S. Weinstein

Gail S. Boertzel
Peter N. Gilbreth
William A. Johnson
Melissa H. Luce

For full biographical listings, see the Martindale-Hubbell Law Directory

*NEWARK,** Essex Co.

BARRY & MCMORAN, A PROFESSIONAL CORPORATION (AV)

One Newark Center, 07102
Telephone: 201-624-6500
Telecopier: 201-624-4052

John J. Barry
Bruce P. McMoran
Salvatore T. Alfano
Mark Falk
John A. Avery
John P. Flanagan

Mark F. Kluger
Madeline E. Cox
Joann K. Dobransky
Adam N. Saravay
Thomas F. Doherty
Judson L. Hand
Carmen J. Di Maria

For full biographical listings, see the Martindale-Hubbell Law Directory

ALAN DEXTER BOWMAN, P.A. (AV)

One Gateway Center, Suite 510, 07102
Telephone: 201-622-2225

Alan Dexter Bowman

For full biographical listings, see the Martindale-Hubbell Law Directory

BROWN & BROWN, P.C. (AV)

One Gateway Center, Fifth Floor, 07102
Telephone: 201-622-1846
Fax: 201-622-2223
Jersey City, New Jersey Office:
Telephone: 201-656-2381.

Raymond A. Brown
Raymond M. Brown

Reference: National Westminster Bank, NJ.

For full biographical listings, see the Martindale-Hubbell Law Directory

CARPENTER, BENNETT & MORRISSEY (AV)

(Formerly Carpenter, Gilmour & Dwyer)
Three Gateway Center, 17th Floor, 100 Mulberry Street, 07102-4079
Telephone: 201-622-7711
New York City: 212-943-6530
Telex: 139405
Telecopier: 201-622-5314
EasyLink: 62827845
ABA/net: CARPENTERB

MEMBERS OF FIRM

John C. Heavey
John E. Keale
Edward F. Ryan
James J. Crowley, Jr.
John P. Dwyer
Michael S. Waters
James G. Gardner
John F. Lynch, Jr.
Donald A. Romano
Francis X. Dee
Rudy B. Coleman
Irving L. Hurwitz
Rosemary J. Bruno
William A. Carpenter, Jr.
John J. Peirano
Linda B. Celauro
John K. Bennett
Patrick G. Brady
Louis M. DeStefano
Thomas F. McGuane
Joseph D. Rasnek
Robert J. Stickles
Robert M. Goodman
Lynn D. Healy
Robert L. Heugle, Jr.
Jane Andrews
Thomas M. Moore
James E. Patterson
Scott J. Sheldon

OF COUNSEL

Thomas L. Morrissey

ASSOCIATES

Jane A. Rigby
Jennifer L. Kapell
James Peter Lidon
Lois H. Goodman
Dennis M. Helewa
Jeffrey Bernstein
Joseph Gerard Lee
Patrick J. McNamara
Daniel J. O'Hern, Jr.
Matthew Q. Berge
Margaret R. Bennett
C. Brian Kornbrek
Judith A. Eisenberg

Representative Clients: General Motors Corp.; E. I. du Pont de Nemours and Company; Texaco Inc.; Johnson & Johnson; Litton Industries; ITT Corp.; International Flavors & Fragrances Inc.; The Boeing Co.; Caterpillar, Inc.; Hartford Insurance Co.

(See Next Column)

CARPENTER, BENNETT & MORRISSEY—*Continued*

For Complete List of Firm Personnel, See General Section

For full biographical listings, see the Martindale-Hubbell Law Directory

CRUMMY, DEL DEO, DOLAN, GRIFFINGER & VECCHIONE, A PROFESSIONAL CORPORATION (AV)

One Riverfront Plaza, 07102
Telephone: 201-596-4500
Telecopier: 201-596-0545
Cable-Telex: 138154
Brussels, Belgium Office: Crummy, Del Deo, Dolan, Griffinger & Vecchione. Avenue Louise 475, BTE. 8, B-1050.
Telephone: 011-322-646-0019.
Telecopier: 011-322-646-0152.

Ralph N. Del Deo
John T. Dolan
Michael R. Griffinger
Michael D. Loprete
John A. Ridley
David J. Sheehan (Managing Partner)
Richard S. Zackin
David M. Hyman
Arnold B. Calmann
John H. Klock
Ann G. McCormick
Brian J. McMahon
Philip W. Crawford
Ira J. Hammer
Susanne Peticolas
Kerry M. Parker
Michael F. Quinn
Anthony P. La Rocco
Gary F. Werner
Stephen R. Reynolds

Representative Clients: American Telephone & Telegraph Co.; Hoffmann-La Roche Inc.; McGraw-Hill, Inc.; Mitsubishi Electric Corp.; Mobile Oil Corp.; Emerson Electric Corp. (Skil); Makita Corp.; Suzuki Motor Corp.; Interbank Card (Mastercard); Data General Carnival Cruise Lines, Inc.

For Complete List of Firm Personnel, See General Section

For full biographical listings, see the Martindale-Hubbell Law Directory

DEMARIA, ELLIS, HUNT, SALSBERG & FRIEDMAN (AV)

Suite 1400, 744 Broad Street, 07102
Telephone: 201-623-1699
Telecopier: 201-623-0954

MEMBERS OF FIRM

H. Reed Ellis
Ronald H. DeMaria
William J. Hunt
Richard M. Salsberg
Paul A. Friedman
Brian N. Flynn
Richard H. Bauch
Lee H. Udelsman

ASSOCIATES

Mitchell A. Schley
Joseph D. Olivieri
Joanne M. Maxwell
Robyn L. Aversa
George W. Rettig
David S. Catuogno
Debra S. Friedman
Kathryn A. Calista

For full biographical listings, see the Martindale-Hubbell Law Directory

GOLDSTEIN TILL & LITE (AV)

Suite 800, 744 Broad Street, 07102-3803
Telephone: 201-623-3000
FAX: 201-623-0858
Telex: 262320 USA UR

MEMBERS OF FIRM

Andrew J. Goldstein
Peter W. Till
Allyn Z. Lite
Joseph J. DePalma

Nancy Lem

For full biographical listings, see the Martindale-Hubbell Law Directory

GREENBERG DAUBER AND EPSTEIN, A PROFESSIONAL CORPORATION (AV)

Suite 600, One Gateway Center, 07102-5311
Telephone: 201-643-3700
Telecopier: 201-643-1218

Melvin Greenberg
Edward J. Dauber
Paul J. Dillon
Linda G. Harvey
Brenda J. Rediess-Hoosein
Jeffrey S. Berkowitz
Kathryn Van Deusen Hatfield

For Complete List of Firm Personnel, See General Section

For full biographical listings, see the Martindale-Hubbell Law Directory

HELLRING LINDEMAN GOLDSTEIN & SIEGAL (AV)

One Gateway Center, 07102-5386
Telephone: 201-621-9020
Telecopier: 201-621-7406

(See Next Column)

Philip Lindeman, II
Joel D. Siegal
Jonathan L. Goldstein
Margaret Dee Hellring
Richard D. Shapiro
Charles Oransky
Richard B. Honig
Richard K. Coplon
Robert S. Raymar
Ronny Jo Greenwald Siegal
Stephen L. Dreyfuss
John A. Adler
Judah I. Elstein
Ronnie F. Liebowitz
Bruce S. Etterman
Matthew E. Moloshok
Rachel N. Davidson
Sarah Jane Jelin
Eric A. Savage
David N. Narciso
Sheryl E. Koomer

For Complete List of Firm Personnel, See General Section

For full biographical listings, see the Martindale-Hubbell Law Directory

KENNY & STEARNS (AV)

56 Park Place, 07102
Telephone: 201-624-7779
New York, N.Y. Office: 26 Broadway.
Telephone: 212-422-6111.
FAX: 212-422-6544.

PARTNERS IN CHARGE

James M. Kenny
Joseph T. Stearns

For full biographical listings, see the Martindale-Hubbell Law Directory

MATTSON, MADDEN & POLITO (AV)

One Gateway Center, 10th Floor, 07102-5311
Telephone: 201-621-7000
Fax: 201-621-7065

MEMBERS OF FIRM

Le Roy H. Mattson
Edward G. Madden, Jr.
John R. Leith
Mark L. Czyz
Joseph M. Soriano

OF COUNSEL

Andrew S. Polito
Francis T. Giuliano

ASSOCIATES

Charles J. Hayden
Raymond S. Gurak
Angelo A. Cuonzo

Representative Clients: New Jersey Manufacturers Insurance Co.; Chubb & Son, Inc.; Shell Oil Co.; Ford Motor Co.; North American Van Lines.

For full biographical listings, see the Martindale-Hubbell Law Directory

MCCARTER & ENGLISH (AV)

Four Gateway Center, 100 Mulberry Street, P.O. Box 652, 07101-0652
Telephone: 201-622-4444
Telecopier: 201-624-7070
Cable Address: "McCarter" Newark
Cherry Hill, New Jersey Office: 1810 Chapel Avenue West.
Telephone: 609-662-8444.
Telecopier: 609-662-6203.
New York, New York Office: Suite 1519, One World Trade Center.
Telephone: 212-466-9018.
Telecopier: 212-432-6568.
Boca Raton, Florida Office: 2255 Glades Road, Suite 319-A.
Telephone: 407-994-6262.
Telecopier: 407-241-0798.
Wilmington, Delaware Office: Mellon Bank Center, 919 Market Street.
Telephone: 302-654-8010.
Telecopier: 302-654-0795.

MEMBERS OF FIRM

Eugene M. Haring
Thomas F. Daly
Andrew T. Berry
John L. McGoldrick
Richard C. Cooper
William H. Horton
Richard M. Eittreim
John E. Flaherty
Gita F. Rothschild
David R. Kott
Lanny S. Kurzweil
John F. Brenner
Frank E. Ferruggia
Richard P. O'Leary
Theodore D. Moskowitz
Seth T. Taube
Lisa M. Goldman

OF COUNSEL

Julius B. Poppinga

COUNSEL

Joseph F. Falgiani
Steven A. Beckelman
Jerry P. Sattin

For Complete List of Firm Personnel, See General Section

For full biographical listings, see the Martindale-Hubbell Law Directory

MEDVIN & ELBERG (AV)

One Gateway Center, 16th Floor, 07102
Telephone: 201-642-1300
Fax: 201-642-8613

MEMBERS OF FIRM

Philip Elberg
Alan Y. Medvin

(See Next Column)

MEDVIN & ELBERG, *Newark—Continued*

Robert A. Jones
Edna Y. Baugh

For full biographical listings, see the Martindale-Hubbell Law Directory

MEYNER AND LANDIS (AV)

One Gateway Center, Suite 2500, 07102-5311
Telephone: 201-624-2800
Fax: 201-624-0356

MEMBERS OF FIRM

Edwin C. Landis, Jr.
Jeffrey L. Reiner
John N. Malyska
William J. Fiore
Anthony F. Siliato
Francis R. Perkins
Geralyn A. Boccher
Howard O. Thompson
Robert B. Meyner (1908-1990)

ASSOCIATES

Kathryn Schatz Koles
Linda Townley Snyder
William H. Schmidt, Jr.
Scott T. McCleary
Maureen K Higgins
Richard A. Haws
Michael J. Palumbo
Theodore E. Lorenz

For full biographical listings, see the Martindale-Hubbell Law Directory

ROBINSON, ST. JOHN & WAYNE (AV)

Two Penn Plaza East, 07105-2249
Telephone: 201-491-3300
Fax: 201-491-3333
Rochester, New York Office: Robinson, St. John & Curtin. First Federal Plaza.
Telephone: 716-262-6780.
Fax: 716-262-6755.
New York, New York Office: 245 Park Avenue.
Telephone: 212-953-0700.
Fax: 212-880-6555.

MEMBERS OF FIRM

Bruce S. Edington
Mark F. Hughes, Jr.
Steven L. Lapidus
Donald A. Robinson
Peter B. Van Deventer, Jr.

For Complete List of Firm Personnel, See General Section

For full biographical listings, see the Martindale-Hubbell Law Directory

SAIBER SCHLESINGER SATZ & GOLDSTEIN (AV)

One Gateway Center, 13th Floor, 07102-5311
Telephone: 201-622-3333
Telecopier: 201-622-3349

MEMBERS OF FIRM

David M. Satz, Jr.
Bruce I. Goldstein
William F. Maderer
David J. D'Aloia
James H. Aibel
Sean R. Kelly
John L. Conover
Lawrence B. Mink
Michael L. Allen
Michael L. Messer
Jeffrey W. Lorell
Jeffrey M. Schwartz
David J. Satz
Joan M. Schwab
Jennine DiSomma
James H. Forte
Vincent F. Papalia

OF COUNSEL

Samuel S. Saiber
Norman E. Schlesinger

COUNSEL

Andrew Alcorn
Robin B. Horn
Randi Schillinger

ASSOCIATES

Audrey M. Weinstein
Robert B. Nussbaum
Michael J. Geraghty
Jonathan S. Davis
Paul S. DeGiulio
Diana L. Sussman
Deanna M. Beacham
Robert W. Geiger
William S. Gyves
Barry P. Kramer
Susan Rozman
Michelle Viola

LEGAL SUPPORT PERSONNEL

DIRECTOR OF FINANCE AND ADMINISTRATION

Ronald Henry

For full biographical listings, see the Martindale-Hubbell Law Directory

SILLS CUMMIS ZUCKERMAN RADIN TISCHMAN EPSTEIN & GROSS, A PROFESSIONAL CORPORATION (AV)

One Riverfront Plaza, 07102-5400
Telephone: 201-643-7000
Fax: 201-643-6500
Telex: 820630 Sillsbeck Nwk
Atlantic City, New Jersey Office: 17 Gordon's Alley.
Telephone: 609-344-2800.
New York, N.Y. Office: 250 Park Avenue.
Telephone: 212-643-7000.

(See Next Column)

Clive S. Cummis
Steven S. Radin
Morton S. Bunis
Stanley Tannenbaum
Barry M. Epstein
Thomas J. Demski
Charles J. Walsh
Jeffrey J. Greenbaum
Jeffrey Barton Cahn
Lester Aron
Kenneth F. Oettle
Robert J. Alter
Marc S. Klein
Philip R. Sellinger
Thomas S. Novak
Stuart M. Feinblatt
Robert M. Axelrod
Trent S. Dickey
Richard J. Schulman (Not admitted in NJ)
Joseph L. Buckley
Kathleen Gengaro
James D. Toll (Resident at Atlantic City, N.J. Office)
James M. Hirschhorn
Ronald C. Rak
Mark S. Olinsky
Richard J. Sapinski
Philip R. White
Alan J. Cohen (Resident at Atlantic City, N.J. Office)
Mark J. Blunda
Lori G. Singer

Cherie L. Maxwell
Stuart Rosen
Steven R. Rowland
Jack Wenik
Eric D. Mann (Resident at Atlantic City, N.J. Office)
Stephen McNally
Mark E. Duckstein
Beth S. Rose
Scott N. Rubin
Kenneth L. Moskowitz
Alma Lutjen Abrams
A. Ross Pearlson (Not admitted in NJ)
Jeffrey M. Pollock
Bennet Susser
Steven S. Katz
Linda Badash Katz
N. Lynne Hughes (Resident at Atlantic City Office)
Lester Chanin
Paul P. Josephson
Douglas R. Weider
Paul F. Doda
Lora L. Fong
Joshua D. Goodman
Helen E. Kleiner
Rhonda Sobral
Jeffrey M. Weinhaus
Adam Kaiser
Alissa Pyrich
Keith J. Weingold
Gayle N. Wolkenberg
Jennifer L. Borofsky
Joseph D. Glazer
Vaughn L. McKoy
Gwen L. Posner
Susanne K. Rosenzweig
Michele-Lee Berko

Representative Clients: Bristol-Myers Squibb Corporation; Citibank, N.A.; BMW of North America; Circuit City Stores, Inc.; Hechinger Company; Bellcore; Shortline Bus; Midlantic National Bank; Six Flags Corporation; WWOR-TV.

For Complete List of Firm Personnel, See General Section

For full biographical listings, see the Martindale-Hubbell Law Directory

TOMPKINS, MCGUIRE & WACHENFELD (AV)

A Partnership including a Professional Corporation
Four Gateway Center, 100 Mulberry Street, 07102-4070
Telephone: 201-622-3000
Telecopier: 201-623-7780

MEMBERS OF FIRM

William F. Tompkins (1913-1989)
William B. McGuire (P.A.)
Howard G. Wachenfeld
Francis X. Crahay
William J. Prout, Jr.
Rex K. Harriott
Michael F. Nestor
James F. Flanagan, III
Christopher James Carey
Marianne M. De Marco
Patrick M. Callahan
John J. Henschel
Michael S. Miller
Douglas E. Motzenbecker

ASSOCIATES

Evelyn A. Donegan
Joseph K. Cobuzio
George G. Campion
Leonore C. Lewis
Richard F. Connors, Jr.
Richard A. Ulsamer
Anthony E. Bush
Gina G. Milestone
John R. Watkins, II
Angelo Giacchi
Nadia M. Walker
Diane E. Sugrue
Brian M. English
Cynthia K. Stroud
Lisa W. Santola
David S. Blatteis
Whitney W. Bremer
Carol J. Gismondi
Albert Wesley McKee

OF COUNSEL

William T. Wachenfeld
Paul B. Thompson
Frances S. Margolis
William J. McGee

COUNSEL

Ellen Nunno Corbo
Evelyn R. Storch
William H. Trousdale

Representative Clients: Corbo Jewelers, Inc.; General Electric Co.; Hartford Insurance Group; Marriott Corp.; National Union Fire Insurance Co.; Underwriters at Lloyd's, London.

For Complete List of Firm Personnel, See General Section

For full biographical listings, see the Martindale-Hubbell Law Directory

Newark—Continued

ZAZZALI, ZAZZALI, FAGELLA & NOWAK, A PROFESSIONAL CORPORATION (AV)

One Riverfront Plaza, 07102-5410
Telephone: 201-623-1822
Telecopier: 201-623-2209
Trenton, New Jersey Office: 150 West State Street.
Telephone: 609-392-8172.
Telecopier: 609-392-8933.

Andrew F. Zazzali (1925-1969)
Andrew F. Zazzali, Jr.
James R. Zazzali
Robert A. Fagella
Kenneth I. Nowak

Paul L. Kleinbaum
Richard A. Friedman
Kathleen Anne Naprstek
Michael J. Buonoaguro
Aileen M. O'Driscoll
Charles J. Farley, Jr.
Edward H. O'Hare

For full biographical listings, see the Martindale-Hubbell Law Directory

*NEW BRUNSWICK,** Middlesex Co.

HOAGLAND, LONGO, MORAN, DUNST & DOUKAS (AV)

40 Paterson Street, P.O. Box 480, 08903
Telephone: 908-545-4717
Fax: 908-545-4579

MEMBERS OF FIRM

John J. Hoagland
Bartholomew A. Longo
James B. Moran
Alan I. Dunst
Kenneth J. Doukas, Jr.
Michael John Stone
Donald D. Davidson
Thaddeus J. Hubert, III
Joan Alster Weisblatt
Karen M. Buerle
Robert G. Kenny
Michael J. Baker
Robert J. Young
Andrew J. Carlowicz, Jr.
Gary J. Hoagland
Jeffrey S. Intravatola
Jamie D. Happas
Thomas J. Walsh
Robert S. Helwig
Michael F. Dolan
Douglas M. Fasciale
Carol Lonergan Perez
Marc S. Gaffrey

ASSOCIATES

John Charles Simons
Susan K. O'Connor
Stephen G. Perrella
Jacquelyn L. Poland
Gary S. Shapiro
Douglas Susan
Anne M. Weidenfeller
Edward Hoagland, Jr.
Patrick J. McDonald
Susan M. Pierce
Andrew N. Kessler
Ashley C. Paul
R. Michael Keefe
Robert B. Rogers
Carleen M. Steward
Claire N. Gallagher
Dennis P. Liloia
John P. Barnes
Daniel J. Cogan
Judith B. Moor
Kevin Nerwinski

Representative Clients: CNA/Continental Casualty; National Indemnity Co.; Providence Washington Insurance Co.; Underwriters Adjusting Co.; INA-PRO/CIGNA; Shand, Morahan & Co.; Imperial Casualty and Indemnity Co.; CSC Insurance Services; American International Group.

For Complete List of Firm Personnel, See General Section

For full biographical listings, see the Martindale-Hubbell Law Directory

LUTZ, SHAFRANSKI, GORMAN AND MAHONEY, P.A. (AV)

77 Livingston Avenue, P.O. Box 596, 08903
Telephone: 908-249-0444
Fax: 908-249-0834

Francis J. Lutz
James A. Shafranski
John R. Gorman
John L. Mahoney

Reference: National Westminster Bank.

For full biographical listings, see the Martindale-Hubbell Law Directory

NEW PROVIDENCE, Union Co.

TAFARO & FLYNN (AV)

571 Central Avenue Suite 108, 07974
Telephone: 908-508-0100
Fax: 908-508-0599

Stephen J. Tafaro
Catherine J. Flynn

Eric L. Grogan
Jill M. Frazee
William J. Buckley

For full biographical listings, see the Martindale-Hubbell Law Directory

NORTH BRUNSWICK, Middlesex Co.

BORRUS, GOLDIN, FOLEY, VIGNUOLO, HYMAN & STAHL, A PROFESSIONAL CORPORATION (AV)

2875 U.S. Highway 1, Route 1 & Finnigans Lane, P.O. Box 1963, 08902
Telephone: 908-422-1000
Fax: 908-422-1016

Jack Borrus
Martin S. Goldin
David M. Foley
Anthony B. Vignuolo
Jeffrey M. Hyman
James E. Stahl
James F. Clarkin III
Anthony M. Campisano
Aphrodite C. Koscelansky
Robert C. Nisenson
Michael L. Marcus
Eileen Mary Foley
Rosalind Westlake

Representative Clients: United Jersey Bank/Franklin State; R. J. Reynolds Tobacco Co.; N.J. Aluminum Co.; K. Hovnanian Enterprises, Inc.; Chicago Title Insurance Co.; Transamerica Title Insurance Co.

For Complete List of Firm Personnel, See General Section

For full biographical listings, see the Martindale-Hubbell Law Directory

NUTLEY, Essex Co.

STRASSER & ASSOCIATES, A PROFESSIONAL CORPORATION (AV)

391 Franklin Avenue, P.O. Box 595, 07110-0107
Telephone: 201-661-5000
Fax: 201-661-0056
Saddle River, New Jersey Office: 70 East Allendale Road, 07458.
Telephone: 201-236-1861.
Fax: 201-236-1863.

William I. Strasser

Robert J. Bavagnoli
Stephen J. Morrone

For full biographical listings, see the Martindale-Hubbell Law Directory

PARAMUS, Bergen Co.

STERN STEIGER CROLAND, A PROFESSIONAL CORPORATION (AV)

One Mack Centre Drive, Mack Centre II, 07652
Telephone: 201-262-9400
Telecopier: 201-262-6055

Howard Stern
Joel J. Steiger
Barry I. Croland
Gerald Goldman
Donald R. Sorkow (1930-1985)
Norman Tanenbaum
Barry L. Baime
Jay Rubenstein
Frank L. Brunetti
Kenneth S. Goldrich
Bruce J. Ackerman
Thomas Loikith
John J. Stern
Stuart Reiser
William J. Heimbuch
Edward P. D'Alessio
E. Drew Britcher
Meridith J. Bronson
Valerie D. Solimano

William R. Kugelman
Mindy Michaels Roth
Neil E. Kozek
Lizabeth Sarakin
Joanne T. Nowicki
Armand Leone, Jr.
Craig P. Caggiano
Jeffrey P. Gardner
David Torchin

OF COUNSEL

Harvey R. Sorkow

Representative Clients: K Mart Corp.; Meyer Brothers Department Stores.

For full biographical listings, see the Martindale-Hubbell Law Directory

PARSIPPANY, Morris Co.

CUYLER, BURK & MATTHEWS (AV)

Parsippany Corporate Center, Four Century Drive, 07054-4663
Telephone: 201-734-3200
Telex: 429071
Telecopier: 201-734-3201
E Mail main@cuyler.mhs.compuserve.com
New York, New York Office: 350 Fifth Avenue, Suite 3304. 10018.
Telephone: 212-312-6352.

MEMBERS OF FIRM

Stephen D. Cuyler
Jo Ann Burk
Edwin R. Matthews
Stefano Calogero
Allen E. Molnar
David L. Menzel
Peter Petrou
Richard A. Crooker
Nancy Giacumbo
Michael J. Jones
Gregg S. Sodini

COUNSEL

Anne M. Mohan

(See Next Column)

CUYLER, BURK & MATTHEWS, *Parsippany—Continued*

ASSOCIATES

Ellen C. Williams
Mary Fran Farley
William M. Fischer
J. Scott MacKay
Jan C. Walker
Kathleen Jane Olear
Cherie A. Hiller
Julie A. Sutton
Robert B. Flynn
Edward K. Rodgers
Ronald D. Puhala
Robert J. Pansulla
David F. Guido
Paul B. Hyman
Daniel J. Bonner
Drew D. Krause
Darin J. Winick
Kimberly A. Paw
Robert P. Lesko

LEGAL SUPPORT PERSONNEL

Frederick M. H. Currie, Jr.

For full biographical listings, see the Martindale-Hubbell Law Directory

GENNET, KALLMANN, ANTIN & ROBINSON, A PROFESSIONAL CORPORATION (AV)

6 Campus Drive, 07054-4406
Telephone: 201-285-1919
Fax: 201-285-1177

Stanley W. Kallmann
Mark L. Antin
Harry Robinson, III
Richard S. Nichols

OF COUNSEL

Samuel A. Gennet

Michael Margello
William Gary Hanft
Alan E. Burkholz
Thomas J. Olsen

Representative Clients: Aetna Insurance Co.; Hartford Fire; Lloyds of London; New England Mutuals.
Reference: United Jersey Bank.

For full biographical listings, see the Martindale-Hubbell Law Directory

KUMMER, KNOX, NAUGHTON & HANSBURY (AV)

Lincoln Centre, 299 Cherry Hill Road, 07054
Telephone: 201-335-3900
Telecopier: 201-335-9577

MEMBERS OF FIRM

Richard E. Kummer
Stephen R. Knox
Michael J. Naughton
Stephan C. Hansbury

ASSOCIATES

Gail H. Fraser
Kurt W. Krauss
Linda M. DeVenuto

For full biographical listings, see the Martindale-Hubbell Law Directory

PHILLIPSBURG, Warren Co.

JOHN J. COYLE, JR., P.C. (AV)

Memorial Parkway at 2nd Street, P.O. Box 5270, 08865
Telephone: 908-454-3300
Telecopier: 908-454-9367

John J. Coyle, Jr.

James S. DeBosh

Reference: Phillipsburg National Bank.

For full biographical listings, see the Martindale-Hubbell Law Directory

PRINCETON, Mercer Co.

BERGMAN & BARRETT (AV)

9 Tamarack Circle, Montgomery Knoll, U. S. Highway 206 North, P.O. Box 1273, 08542
Telephone: 609-921-1502
Fax: 609-683-0288

Edward J. Bergman
Michael T. Barrett

For full biographical listings, see the Martindale-Hubbell Law Directory

MCCARTHY AND SCHATZMAN, P.A. (AV)

228 Alexander Street, P.O. Box 2329, 08543-2329
Telephone: 609-924-1199
Fax: 609-683-5251

John F. McCarthy, Jr.
Richard Schatzman
G. Christopher Baker
John F. McCarthy, III
Michael A. Spero
Barbara Strapp Nelson
W. Scott Stoner

(See Next Column)

James A. Endicott
Angelo J. Onofri

Representative Clients: Trustees of Princeton University; The Linpro Co.; United Jersey Bank; Chemical Bank, New Jersey, N.A.; Carnegie Center Associates; Merrill Lynch Pierce Fenner & Smith, Inc.; Prudential Insurance Co.

For full biographical listings, see the Martindale-Hubbell Law Directory

PELLETTIERI, RABSTEIN AND ALTMAN (AV)

100 Nassau Park Boulevard Suite 111, 08540
Telephone: 609-520-0900
Fax: 609-452-8796
Mount Holly, New Jersey Office: Tarnsfield & Woodlane Roads.
Telephone: 609-267-3390.

MEMBERS OF FIRM

George Pellettieri (1903-1980)
Richard M. Altman
Ira C. Miller
John A. Hartmann, III
Andrew M. Rockman
Bruce P. Miller
Edward Slaughter, Jr.
Anne P. McHugh
Neal S. Solomon
Gary E. Adams
Mel Narol
E. Elizabeth Sweetser
Arthur Penn
Thomas R. Smith
George Louis Pellettieri (1961-1973)

ASSOCIATES

Christine McHugh
James Lazzaro
Jed S. Kadish
Martin S. Pappaterra
Daniel S. Sweetser
Lydia Fabbro Keephart
Kenneth W. Lozier
John K. Semler, Jr.
Nicole J. Huckerby
Elyse Genek
Mark K. Smith

OF COUNSEL

Ruth Rabstein

For full biographical listings, see the Martindale-Hubbell Law Directory

RAMSEY, Bergen Co.

FRANCIS T. GIULIANO (AV)

102 Hilltop Road, P.O. Box 340, 07446
Telephone: 201-825-7675
Fax: 201-825-2672

For full biographical listings, see the Martindale-Hubbell Law Directory

DONALD C. OHNEGIAN (AV)

88 West Main Street, P.O. Box 360, 07446
Telephone: 201-327-7000
Telefax: 201-327-6651

ASSOCIATE

Diane K. Gaylinn

Representative Clients: Upon Request.

For full biographical listings, see the Martindale-Hubbell Law Directory

RED BANK, Monmouth Co.

PHILIP G. AUERBACH A PROFESSIONAL CORPORATION (AV)

231 Maple Avenue, P.O. Box Y, 07701
Telephone: 908-842-6660

Philip G. Auerbach

Edward A. Genz
John J. Ryan

For full biographical listings, see the Martindale-Hubbell Law Directory

ROCHELLE PARK, Bergen Co.

BARRY D. EPSTEIN, P.A. (AV)

340 West Passaic Street, 07662
Telephone: 201-845-5962

Barry D. Epstein

Bruno K. Brunini
Edward P. Drummond

For full biographical listings, see the Martindale-Hubbell Law Directory

ROSELAND, Essex Co.

BRACH, EICHLER, ROSENBERG, SILVER, BERNSTEIN, HAMMER & GLADSTONE, A PROFESSIONAL CORPORATION (AV)

101 Eisenhower Parkway, 07068
Telephone: 201-228-5700
Telecopier: 201-228-7852

(See Next Column)

BRACH, EICHLER, ROSENBERG, SILVER, BERNSTEIN, HAMMER & GLADSTONE A PROFESSIONAL CORPORATION—*Continued*

Alan H. Bernstein
William L. Brach
James T. Davis, II
Richard J. Driver
Burton L. Eichler
Charles X. Gormally
Joseph M. Gorrell
Alan S. Pralgever
Harris R. Silver

David J. Klein
Thomas M. Badenhausen
David S. Bernstein
Regina A. McGuire
Kelly A. Waters
Daniel L. Schmutter
Melissa E. Flax
Michael S. Zicherman
Carl J. Soranno

OF COUNSEL

Lance A. Posner

Representative Clients: Saint Barnabas Medical Center; Ohio Casualty Insurance Group; Broan Associates General Contractors, Inc.; Gebroe-Hammer Associates; M. Epstein, Inc.; United Jersey Bank; Radiological Society of New Jersey; Coastal Group, Inc.; R & S Strauss, Inc.; Palisade Savings Bank, F.S.B.

For Complete List of Firm Personnel, See General Section

For full biographical listings, see the Martindale-Hubbell Law Directory

CONNELL, FOLEY & GEISER (AV)

85 Livingston Avenue, 07068
Telephone: 201-535-0500
Telefax: 201-535-9217

MEMBERS OF FIRM

George W. Connell
Adrian M. Foley, Jr.
Theodore W. Geiser
John B. Lavecchia
George J. Kenny
Samuel Darrow Lord
Richard D. Catenacci
Richard J. Badolato
Peter D. Manahan
Mark L. Fleder
Jerome M. Lynes
Linda A. Palazzolo
John F. Neary
Thomas S. Cosma
Kathleen S. Murphy
Patrick J. McAuley
Peter J. Pizzi
Kevin R. Gardner
Robert E. Ryan
Michael X. McBride
Jeffrey W. Moryan
Donald S. Maclachlan
Patricia J. Pindar
Peter J. Smith
Brian G. Steller
Frank A. Lattal
Judith A. Wahrenberger
Karen Munster Cassidy
Stephen D. Kinnard
Karen Painter Randall
Liza M. Walsh

ASSOCIATES

Maureen A. Mahoney-Madarasz
Timothy E. Corriston
Ernest W. Schoellkopff
Heidi Willis Currier

OF COUNSEL

Margaret L. Moses

Representative Clients: Bethlehem Steel Corp.; Borden Inc.; Chase Manhattan Bank; CNA Insurance; Conrail; Hilton Hotels Corp.; Merrill Lynch; Microsoft; New Jersey Manufacturers Insurance.

For Complete List of Firm Personnel, See General Section

For full biographical listings, see the Martindale-Hubbell Law Directory

HANNOCH WEISMAN, A PROFESSIONAL CORPORATION (AV)

4 Becker Farm Road, 07068-3788
Telephone: 201-535-5300
New York: 212-732-3262
Telecopier: 201-994-7198
Mailing Address: P.O. Box 1040, Newark, New Jersey, 07101-9819
Washington, D.C. Office: Suite 600, 1150 Seventeenth Street, N.W.
Telephone: 202-296-3432.

Shirley L. Berger
Albert G. Besser
Eric R. Breslin
Robert C. Epstein
Sheldon M. Finkelstein
Joseph J. Fleischman
Dean A. Gaver
Stuart J. Glick
William J. Heller
Carmine A. Iannaccone
Theodore Margolis
Lawrence T. Neher
William W. Robertson
Todd M. Sahner
James J. Shrager
Ronald M. Sturtz
Diane P. Sullivan

SPECIAL COUNSEL

David P. Wadyka

Mary Jane McNicholas Dobbs
James P. Flynn
Christopher W. Nanos

For Complete List of Firm Personnel, See General Section

For full biographical listings, see the Martindale-Hubbell Law Directory

HOCHBERG, KRIEGER, DANZIG & GARUBO (AV)

75 Livingston Avenue, 07068
Telephone: 201-535-5700
Telecopier: 201-535-6293

MEMBERS OF FIRM

George S. Hochberg
Lewis L. Krieger
Howard Danzig
Angelo G. Garubo

OF COUNSEL

David M. Kaye

For full biographical listings, see the Martindale-Hubbell Law Directory

LOWENSTEIN, SANDLER, KOHL, FISHER & BOYLAN, A PROFESSIONAL CORPORATION (AV)

65 Livingston Avenue, 07068
Telephone: 201-992-8700
Telefax: 201-992-5820
Somerville, New Jersey Office: 600 First Avenue. P.O. Box 1113.
Telephone: 201-526-3300.

Matthew P. Boylan
Stephen N. Dermer
Gregory B. Reilly
Theodore V. Wells, Jr.
Gerald Krovatin
Richard D. Wilkinson
David L. Harris
Kevin Kovacs
(Resident at Somerville Office)
David W. Field
Terry E. Thornton
Jeffrey J. Wild

OF COUNSEL

Robert L. Krakower
Harvey Smith

Phyllis F. Pasternak
(Resident at Somerville Office)
Marc B. Kramer
John M. Nolan
(Resident at Somerville Office)
Eileen M. Clark
(Resident at Somerville Office)
Allen P. Langjahr
John B. McCusker
Paul F. Koch, II
Bruce S. Rosen
Samuel B. Santo, Jr.
Paul F. Carvelli
Rosemary E. Ramsay
Vincent P. Browne
Lawrence M. Rolnick
Karim G. Kaspar
Robert M. Lapinsky
Henry M. Price
Andrew E. Anselmi
Richard C. Szuch
Stephen R. Buckingham
Stephanie Wilson
Virginia A. Lazala
Geoffrey A. Price
Peter L. Skolnik
Neslihan S. Montag
Alex Moreau
William J. VonDerHeide
Edward T. Arnold
Joyce A. Davis
Howard A. Matalon
Amy C. Grossman
Maureen E. Montague
(Resident at Somerville Office)
Gavin J. Rooney

For Complete List of Firm Personnel, See General Section

For full biographical listings, see the Martindale-Hubbell Law Directory

ORLOFF, LOWENBACH, STIFELMAN & SIEGEL, A PROFESSIONAL CORPORATION (AV)

101 Eisenhower Parkway, 07068
Telephone: 201-622-6200
Telecopier: 201-622-3073

Laurence B. Orloff
Jeffrey M. Garrod
Samuel Feldman
Michael S. Haratz
Eileen A. Lindsay

David B. Katz
Linda B. Lewinter
Laura Valenti Studwell
Linda S. Moore

For Complete List of Firm Personnel, See General Section

For full biographical listings, see the Martindale-Hubbell Law Directory

POST, POLAK, GOODSELL & MACNEILL, P.A. (AV)

65 Livingston Avenue, 07068
Telephone: 201-994-1100
Telecopier: 201-994-1705
New York, New York Office: Suite 1006, 575 Madison Avenue.
Telephone: 212-486-1455.

John N. Post
Frederick B. Polak
Robert A. Goodsell
Jay Scott MacNeill
Charles R. Church
Mary H. Post
David L. Epstein

Allison D. B. Liebowitz
G. Alexander Crispo
Peter A. Bogaard
Lauren F. Koffler
Robert P. Merenich

For full biographical listings, see the Martindale-Hubbell Law Directory

SELLAR, RICHARDSON, STUART & CHISHOLM, P.C. (AV)

Six Becker Farm Road, 07068
Telephone: 201-535-1400
Fax: 201-535-6522

(See Next Column)

SELLAR, RICHARDSON, STUART & CHISHOLM P.C., *Roseland—Continued*

James P. Richardson
Richard M. Chisholm
James P. Lisovicz
Wendy H. Smith
John M. Kearney

Denise M. Luckenbach
Chris William Kemprowski
Andrew M. Wolfenson
John B. D'Alessandro
Jonathan S. Fabricant
Robert P. Hoag
Shawn R. Stowell
Ian C. Doris

OF COUNSEL

Alastair J. Sellar
Anthony C. Stuart

For full biographical listings, see the Martindale-Hubbell Law Directory

WALDER, SONDAK & BROGAN, A PROFESSIONAL CORPORATION (AV)

5 Becker Farm Road, 07068
Telephone: 201-992-5300
Telecopier: 201-992-1505; 992-1006

Justin P. Walder
John A. Brogan
Thomas J. Spies
Barry A. Kozyra
James A. Plaisted
Heather Grasz Suarez
Michael J. Faul, Jr.
Jeffrey A. Walder
Shalom D. Stone
Judith A. Hartz
David Paige

OF COUNSEL

Joel Sondak
John H. Skarbnik

Representative Clients: Hartz Mountain Industries; NEC America, Inc.; American Brands, Inc.; Bally Manufacturing Corp.; Six Flags Corp.; U.S. Cable Corp.; Goldome Credit Corp.; Old Republic Insurance Co.; North Atlantic Insurance Co.; Chicago Underwriting Group.

For full biographical listings, see the Martindale-Hubbell Law Directory

WOLFF & SAMSON, P.A. (AV)

280 Corporate Center, 5 Becker Farm Road, 07068
Telephone: 201-740-0500
Fax: 201-740-1407

David Samson
Ronald E. Wiss
Arthur S. Goldstein
Armen Shahinian
Gage Andretta
Daniel D. Caldwell
Kenneth N. Laptook

John M. Simon
Thomas W. Sabino

Representative Clients: International Fidelity Insurance Co.; Celentano Brothers, Inc.; Chicago Title Insurance Co.; Hartz Mountain Industries; The Hillier Group; Foster Wheeler Corp.

For Complete List of Firm Personnel, See General Section

For full biographical listings, see the Martindale-Hubbell Law Directory

SADDLE RIVER, Bergen Co.

LEWIS & McKENNA (AV)

82 East Allendale Road, 07458
Telephone: 201-934-9800
Telecopier: 201-934-8681
New York, N.Y. Office: 230 Park Avenue, Suite 2240.
Telephone: 212-772-0943.
Tallahassee, Florida Office: 820 E East Park Avenue, P.O. Box 10475.
Telephone: 904-681-3813
Telecopier: 904-222-1732.

MEMBERS OF FIRM

Paul Z. Lewis
Michael F. McKenna
Geoffrey McC. Johnson

ASSOCIATES

Sherry L. Foley
John A. Napolitano
Mariangela Chiaravalloti
Colin M. Quinn
David B. Beal
Timothy J. Foley

OF COUNSEL

Robert J. Bennett
James W. Anderson (Not admitted in NJ; Resident, Tallahassee, Florida Office)

For full biographical listings, see the Martindale-Hubbell Law Directory

STRASSER & ASSOCIATES, A PROFESSIONAL CORPORATION (AV)

70 East Allendale Rd., 07458
Telephone: 201-236-1861
Fax: 201-236-1863
Nutley, New Jersey Office: 391 Franklin Avenue, 07110-0107.
Telephone: 201-661-5000.
Fax: 201-661-0056.

(See Next Column)

William I. Strasser

SECAUCUS, Hudson Co.

WATERS, McPHERSON, McNEILL, P.C. (AV)

300 Lighting Way, 7th Floor, 07096
Telephone: 201-863-4400
Telecopy: 201-863-2866
Trenton, New Jersey Office: 224 West State Street.
Telephone: 609-599-1000.
New York, N.Y. Office: The Woolworth Building, 233 Broadway, Suite 970.
Telephone: 212-227-7878.

David A. Waters
Kenneth D. McPherson
John J. Kot
Gregory J. Castano
George T. Imperial
James A. Kosch
Frank J. Zazzaro

Representative Clients: American Institute of Certified Public Accountants; Bally Gaming International, Inc.; Cablevision Systems Corp.; The Edward J. DeBartolo Corporation; Hartz Mountain Industries, Inc.; Jones, Lang, Wootton U.S.A.; Liberty Mutual Insurance Co.; Tropicana Products, Inc.

For Complete List of Firm Personnel, See General Section

For full biographical listings, see the Martindale-Hubbell Law Directory

*SOMERVILLE,** Somerset Co.

LOWENSTEIN, SANDLER, KOHL, FISHER & BOYLAN, A PROFESSIONAL CORPORATION (AV)

600 First Avenue, P.O. Box 1113, 08876
Telephone: 908-526-3300
Roseland, New Jersey Office: 65 Livingston Avenue.
Telephone: 201-992-8700.
Telefax: 201-992-5820.

Steven B. Fuerst
Kevin Kovacs

Phyllis F. Pasternak
John M. Nolan
Eileen M. Clark
Vincent P. Browne
Maureen E. Montague

For Complete List of Firm Personnel, See General Section

For full biographical listings, see the Martindale-Hubbell Law Directory

OZZARD WHARTON, A PROFESSIONAL PARTNERSHIP (AV)

75-77 North Bridge Street, P.O. Box 938, 08876
Telephone: 908-526-0700
Telecopier: 908-526-2246

William E. Ozzard
Victor A. Rizzolo
George A. Mauro, Jr.
Michael V. Camerino
Alan Bart Grant

Arthur D. Fialk
Kam S. Minhas
Suzette Nanovic Berrios
Frederick H. Allen, III
Wendy L. Wiebalk
Lori E. Salowe
Denise M. Marra

Representative Clients: American Cyanamid; Science Management Corp.; New Jersey Manufacturers Insurance Co.; Travelers Insurance Co.; New Jersey Savings Bank, Middlesex County, Somerset County.

For Complete List of Firm Personnel, See General Section

For full biographical listings, see the Martindale-Hubbell Law Directory

SCHACHTER, TROMBADORE, OFFEN, STANTON & PAVICS, A PROFESSIONAL CORPORATION (AV)

45 East High Street, P.O. Box 520, 08876-0520
Telephone: 908-722-5700
Fax: 908-722-8853

Richard J. Schachter
John J. Trombadore
Stephen M. Offen
Michael J. Stanton
Thomas A. Pavics

William D. Alden
Mary Ann Bauer
Timothy P. McKeown

LEGAL SUPPORT PERSONNEL

Joan V. Shaw (Office Manager)

References: Summit Bank; First National Bank of Central Jersey; New Jersey Savings Bank.

For full biographical listings, see the Martindale-Hubbell Law Directory

Somerville—Continued

Raymond R. and Ann W. Trombadore A Professional Corporation (AV)

33 East High Street, 08876
Telephone: 908-722-7555
Fax: 908-722-6269

Raymond R. Trombadore

Megan C. Seel

OF COUNSEL

Ann W. Trombadore

References: Summit Bank; New Jersey Savings Bank; Somerset Savings & Loan Assn.

For full biographical listings, see the Martindale-Hubbell Law Directory

SPRINGFIELD, Union Co.

Bumgardner, Hardin & Ellis, A Professional Corporation (AV)

673 Morris Avenue, 07081
Telephone: 201-564-6500
Fax: 201-564-6527; 201-912-9847

William R. Bumgardner
George R. Hardin
Roger G. Ellis
Robert L. Polifroni
Janet L. Poletto
Mark S. Kundla
John F. McKeon
M. Christie Wise
James R. Greene
John Samuel Favate

Laurie A. Villano
Nicea J. D'Annunzio
Patricia L. Noll
Kieran P. Hughes
Nicholas J. Lombardi
Russel V. Mancino
Edward M. Suarez, Jr.
Patrick J. Clare
Charles T. McCook, Jr.
Marybeth Scriven
Anna Marie Strand
Edward Walsh
Jeffrey A. Oshin
Janice G. Meola
Ethan Jesse Sheffet
Cheryl A. McAvaddy
Francine M. Chillemi
Leona C. McFadden
Mark A. Edwards
Jennifer Zima
Jared P. Kingsley
Michael A. Swimmer
Charles M. Fisher
Joseph A. DeFuria
John G. Kilbride
Deborah J. Metzger-Mulvey
Elizabeth E. Groisser
Joseph R. Lowicky
Tracy C. Forsyth
Michael J. Rant
Emmanuel Abongwa

Representative Clients: Crum & Forster Corp.; St. Paul Fire and Marine Insurance Co.; Wausau Insurance Cos.; A.M. Best Company; Chrysler Corp.; Continental Insurance Co.; The Home Insurance Co.; McDonald's Corp.; Pepsico; Xerox Corp.

For full biographical listings, see the Martindale-Hubbell Law Directory

Javerbaum Wurgaft & Hicks (AV)

Park Place Legal Center, 959 South Springfield Avenue, 07081-3555
Telephone: 201-379-4200
Fax: 201-379-7872
Newark, New Jersey Office: 233 Lafayette Street, 07105.
Telephone: 201-623-8754.

Kenneth S. Javerbaum
Jack Wurgaft
Robert G. Hicks

Anthony P. Valenti
Karen Lee
John M. Pinho

For full biographical listings, see the Martindale-Hubbell Law Directory

Kraemer, Burns, Mytelka & Lovell, P.A. (AV)

673 Morris Avenue, 07081
Telephone: 201-912-8700
Telecopier: 201-912-8602

Daniel G. Kasen (1905-1990)
William E. Lovell (1914-1994)
Waldron Kraemer
Arnold K. Mytelka
Douglas E. Burns
Joan A. Lovell
Wayne D. Greenfeder
Eleonore Kessler Cohen
Scott B. Stolbach

OF COUNSEL

Gerard S. Doyle, Jr.

For full biographical listings, see the Martindale-Hubbell Law Directory

McDonough, Korn & Eichhorn, A Professional Corporation (AV)

Park Place Legal Center, 959 South Springfield Avenue, P.O. Box 712, 07081-0712
Telephone: 201-912-9099
Fax: 201-912-8604

(See Next Column)

Peter L. Korn
R. Scott Eichhorn
James R. Korn
William S. Mezzomo

Timothy J. Jaeger
Dona Feeney
Karen M. Lerner
Wilfred P. Coronato
Gail R. Arkin
Nancy Crosta Landale
Christopher K. Costa

OF COUNSEL

Robert P. McDonough

Representative Clients: Chubb Insurance Co.; The Travelers; Medical Inter-Insurance Exchange of New Jersey; GRE Insurance; New Jersey Property-Liability Insurance Guaranty Association; Medical Liability Mutual Insurance Co.; University of Medicine, Dentistry of New Jersey; Columbia Presbyterian Medical Center; Greater New York Blood Center; Wausau Insurance; Cigna.
Reference: United Counties Trust Company.

For full biographical listings, see the Martindale-Hubbell Law Directory

SUMMIT, Union Co.

Cooper Rose & English (AV)

480 Morris Avenue, 07901-1527
Telephone: 908-273-1212
Fax: 908-273-8922
Rumson, New Jersey Office: 20 Bingham Avenue. 07760.
Telephone: 908-741-7777.
Fax: 908-758-1879.

MEMBERS OF FIRM

John W. Cooper
Frederick W. Rose
Jerry Fitzgerald English
Joseph E. Imbriaco
Roger S. Clapp
Arthur H. Garvin, III
Peter M. Burke
Gary F. Danis
John J. DeLaney, Jr.
David G. Hardin

OF COUNSEL

Harrison F. Durand
Russell T. Kerby, Jr.
Ronald J. Tell

ASSOCIATES

Fredi L. Pearlmutter
Kristi Bragg
Stephen R. Geller
Peter W. Ulicny
Thomas J. Sateary
Gianfranco A. Pietrafesa
Donna M. Russo
J. Andrew Kinsey
Jonathan S. Chester
Daniel Jon Kleinman
Holly English
Margaret R. Kalas
Mary T. Zdanowicz
Robert A. Meyers
Richard F. Iglar

Counsel for: Ciba-Geigy Corp.; Witco Corp.; New Jersey American Water Co.; Mikropul Corp.; AT&T Bell Laboratories; Aircast.

For full biographical listings, see the Martindale-Hubbell Law Directory

Haggerty, Donohue & Monaghan, A Professional Association (AV)

One Springfield Avenue, 07901
Telephone: 908-277-2600
Fax: 908-273-1641

James C. Haggerty
George J. Donohue
Walter E. Monaghan

Rose Ann Haggerty
Thomas J. Haggerty
Alfred F. Carolonza, Jr.
William A. Wenzel
Mahlon H. Ortman
Michael A. Conway
James C. Haggerty, Jr.

OF COUNSEL

Joseph D. Haggerty

Representative Clients: American International Group; Chubb/Pacific Indemnity Co.; Crawford & Co.; Kemper Insurance Group; New Jersey Manufacturers; Royal Insurance Co.; Selective Insurance Co., Inc.; Sun Oil Co.; Transamerica Insurance Group; Marsh & McLennan, Inc.

For Complete List of Firm Personnel, See General Section

For full biographical listings, see the Martindale-Hubbell Law Directory

*TOMS RIVER,** Ocean Co.

Lomell, Muccifori, Adler, Ravaschiere, Amabile & Pehlivanian, A Professional Corporation (AV)

250 Washington Street, P.O. Box 787, 08754
Telephone: 908-349-2443
Fax: 908-349-6917

Howard Ewart (1890-1961)
A. Thomas Amabile (1936-1993)
Herman A. Adler
Dominic Ravaschiere
John S. Pehlivanian
Ronald E. Prusek
Jeffrey R. Surenian
James M. McKenna
Teresa K. Gierla

(See Next Column)

LOMELL, MUCCIFORI, ADLER, RAVASCHIERE, AMABILE & PEHLIVANIAN A PROFESSIONAL CORPORATION, *Toms River—Continued*

Marc S. Galella
Robyn A. Belluardo
Ann M. Dougherty
Janet Zaorski Kalapos
Arthur F. Leyden, III
Carla Patricia Aldarelli

OF COUNSEL

Leonard G. Lomell
Thomas J. Muccifori
Alfred J. Napier

For full biographical listings, see the Martindale-Hubbell Law Directory

NOVINS, YORK & PENTONY, A PROFESSIONAL CORPORATION (AV)

202 Main Street, 08753
Telephone: 908-349-7100

Robert F. Novins
Kenneth R. Pentony
Ann K. Haskell
S. Karl Mohel
Michael S. Paduano

Barry K. Odell

Counsel for: Allstate Insurance Co.; Motor Club of America.

For Complete List of Firm Personnel, See General Section

For full biographical listings, see the Martindale-Hubbell Law Directory

*TRENTON,** Mercer Co.

BACKES & HILL (AV)

(Originally Backes & Backes)
(Formerly Backes, Waldron & Hill)
15 West Front Street, 08608-2098
Telephone: 609-396-8257
Telefax: 609-989-7323

Peter Backes (1858-1941)
Herbert W. Backes (1891-1970)
William Wright Backes (1904-1980)
Michael J. Nizolek (1950-1994)

OF COUNSEL

Robert Maddock Backes

PARTNERS

Harry R. Hill, Jr.
Robert C. Billmeier
Brenda Farr Engel

ASSOCIATES

Susan E. Bacso
Michele N. Siekerka
Henry A. Carpenter II
Lawrence A. Reisman

Representative Clients: New Jersey National Bank; Mercer Medical Center; Catholic Diocese of Trenton; Roller Bearing Company of America; New Jersey Manufacturers Insurance Co.; St. Francis Medical Center; The Trenton Savings Bank; Richie & Page Distributing Co., Inc.; Hill Refrigeration Corporation; General Sullivan Group, Inc.; A-1 Collections, Inc.

For full biographical listings, see the Martindale-Hubbell Law Directory

DESTRIBATS, CAMPBELL, DESANTIS & MAGEE (AV)

247 White Horse Avenue, 08610
Telephone: 609-585-2443
Telefax: 609-585-9508

MEMBERS OF FIRM

Jay G. Destribats
Bernard A. Campbell, Jr.
Dennis M. DeSantis
Michael H. Magee

ASSOCIATE

Daniel J. O'Donnell

OF COUNSEL

Henry F. Gill

For full biographical listings, see the Martindale-Hubbell Law Directory

LENOX, SOCEY, WILGUS, FORMIDONI & CASEY (AV)

3131 Princeton Pike, 08648
Telephone: 609-896-2000
Fax: 609-895-1693

MEMBERS OF FIRM

Samuel D. Lenox (1897-1975)
Rudolph A. Socey, Jr.
George Wilgus, III
Roland R. Formidoni
Robert P. Casey
Thomas M. Brown
Gregory J. Giordano

ASSOCIATE

Elizabeth L. Tolkach
Denise M. Mariani

Representative Clients: Royal-Globe Insurance Cos.; New Jersey Bell Telephone Co.; Government Employees Insurance Co.; Pennsylvania Manufacturers Association Casualty Insurance Cos.; General Motors Corp.; Travelers Insurance Co.

For full biographical listings, see the Martindale-Hubbell Law Directory

NEEDELL & MCGLONE, A PROFESSIONAL CORPORATION (AV)

Quakerbridge Commons, 2681 Quakerbridge Road, 08619-1625
Telephone: 609-584-7700
Fax: 609-584-0123

Stanley H. Needell
Patricia Hart McGlone

Michael W. Krutman
Anthony P. Castellani
Barbara Brosnan
Douglas R. D'Antonio

For full biographical listings, see the Martindale-Hubbell Law Directory

STERNS & WEINROTH (AV)

50 West State Street, Suite 1400, P.O. Box 1298, 08607-1298
Telephone: 609-392-2100
Fax: 609-392-7956
Atlantic City, New Jersey Office: 2901 Atlantic Avenue, Suite 201, 08401.
Telephone: 609-340-8300.
Fax: 609-340-8722.
Washington, D.C. Office: 1150 Seventeenth Street, N.W., Suite 600, 20036.
Telephone: 202-296-3432.

William J. Bigham
Vincent J. Paluzzi
Jeffrey S. Posta
Michael L. Rosenberg
David M. Roskos
Mark D. Schorr
Susan Stryker
Robert Paul Zoller

Karen A. Confoy
Brian J. Mulligan
Edgar Alden Dunham, IV
Marshall D. Bilder
Michael S. Stein
Richard J. Van Wagner
C. Lauren Graham

For Complete List of Firm Personnel, See General Section

For full biographical listings, see the Martindale-Hubbell Law Directory

VINELAND, Cumberland Co.

EISENSTAT, GABAGE, BERMAN & FURMAN, A PROFESSIONAL CORPORATION (AV)

1179 East Landis Avenue, P.O. Box O, 08360
Telephone: 609-691-1200
Telecopier: 609-691-0414

Gerald (Jere) M. Eisenstat
Charles W. Gabage
Mitchell S. Berman
Harry Furman

For Complete List of Firm Personnel, See General Section

For full biographical listings, see the Martindale-Hubbell Law Directory

JAY H. GREENBLATT & ASSOCIATES A PROFESSIONAL CORPORATION (AV)

200 North Eighth Street, P.O. Box 883, 08360-0883
Telephone: 609-691-0424
Facsimile: 609-696-1010

M. Joseph Greenblatt (1896-1992)
Jay H. Greenblatt

Bonnie L. Laube
Nicholas Kierniesky
Charles S. Epstein
John M. Amorison

Counsel for: Newcomb Medical Center; Ware's Van & Storage Co., Inc.
Local Counsel for: A. O. Smith Corp.; Vik Brothers Insurance Group; Chance Industries, Inc.; Coca Cola Bottlers' Association; Fireman's Fund Insurance Co.; Ford Motor Co.; Thermadyne Industries; The West Bend Company.

For full biographical listings, see the Martindale-Hubbell Law Directory

GRUCCIO, PEPPER, GIOVINAZZI, DESANTO & FARNOLY, P.A., A PROFESSIONAL CORPORATION (AV)

817 Landis Avenue, P.O. Box CN 1501, 08360
Telephone: 609-691-0100
Fax: 609-692-4095
Associated with: Stradley, Ronon, Stevens & Young, a Philadelphia Law Firm.
Woodbury, New Jersey Office: 21 Delaware Street.
Telephone: 609-848-5558.
Fax: 609-384-1181.
Avalon, New Jersey Office: 2878 Dune Drive.
Telephone: 609-967-4040.
Other New Jersey Offices:
Atlantic City Area: 609-347- 0909.
Salem Area: 609-935-3559.

James J. Gruccio
Robert A. DeSanto
Thomas P. Farnoly
Walter F. Gavigan
E. Edward Bowman

(See Next Column)

GRUCCIO, PEPPER, GIOVINAZZI, DESANTO & FARNOLY P.A., A PROFESSIONAL CORPORATION—*Continued*

Representative Clients: State Farm Mutual Automobile Insurance Cos.; United States Fidelity & Guaranty Co.; Atlantic City Expressway Authority; County of Salem; County of Cape May; CNA Insurance Co.; Cumberland Mutual Fire Insurance Co.; Cumberland County Guidance Center; Pizza Hut Inc.; Farmers and Merchants National Bank of Bridgeton.

For Complete List of Firm Personnel, See General Section

For full biographical listings, see the Martindale-Hubbell Law Directory

RIESENBURGER & KIZNER, P.C. (AV)

190 South Main Road, P.O. Box 640, 08360
Telephone: 609-691-6200
Telecopier: 609-696-8150

Franklin J. Riesenburger
Mitchell H. Kizner

Teresa Marie Munson
William C. Mills, IV
Jeffrey R. Owens

For full biographical listings, see the Martindale-Hubbell Law Directory

WAYNE, Passaic Co.

DEYOE, HEISSENBUTTEL & MATTIA (AV)

401 Hamburg Turnpike, P.O. Box 2449, 07474-2449
Telephone: 201-595-6300
Fax: 201-595-0146; 201-595-9262

MEMBERS OF FIRM

Charles P. DeYoe (1923-1973)
Wood M. DeYoe
Frederick C. Heissenbuttel
Philip F. Mattia
Gary R. Matano
Scott B. Piekarsky

ASSOCIATES

Anne Hutton
Glenn Z. Poosikian
Jo Ann G. Durr
Frank D. Samperi
Frank A. Campana
John E. Clarke
Jason T. Shafron

Representative Clients: INA/Aetna Insurance Co. (Cigna); Medical Inter-Insurance Companies; Hanover-Amgro, Inc.; Maryland Casualty Co.; Ohio Casualty Insurance Co.; Motor Club of America; Selected Insurance Co.

For Complete List of Firm Personnel, See General Section

For full biographical listings, see the Martindale-Hubbell Law Directory

FELDMAN & FIORELLO (AV)

Suite 301, 57 Willowbrook Boulevard, 07470
Telephone: 201-890-9222
Fax: 201-890-7068

William A. Feldman
John Fiorello

OF COUNSEL

Avram S. Eule

ASSOCIATES

Linda Couso Puccio
Jacqueline I. Heath
Melissa A. Feldman

Reference: First Fidelity Bank, N.A.; Valley National Bank (Willowbrook Branch).

For full biographical listings, see the Martindale-Hubbell Law Directory

WEST CALDWELL, Essex Co.

RONALD REICHSTEIN (AV)

West Caldwell Office Park, 195 Fairfield Avenue, Suite 4C, 07006
Telephone: 201-228-8818
Fax: 201-228-5730

References: National Community Bank; Chemical Bank.

For full biographical listings, see the Martindale-Hubbell Law Directory

WESTFIELD, Union Co.

DWYER & CANELLIS, P.A. (AV)

150 Elm Street, 07090
Telephone: 908-233-2000
Fax: 908-233-2041

George W. Canellis

Brian M. Adams
Barbara Ann Canellis

OF COUNSEL

Thomas F. Dwyer

Reference: Summit Bank; Midlantic Bank.

For full biographical listings, see the Martindale-Hubbell Law Directory

LINDABURY, MCCORMICK & ESTABROOK, A PROFESSIONAL CORPORATION (AV)

53 Cardinal Drive, P.O. Box 2369, 07091
Telephone: 908-233-6800
Fax: 908-233-5078

Richard R. Width
Anthony J. LaRusso
Edward J. Frisch
John H. Schmidt, Jr.
Donald F. Nicolai
Bruce P. Ogden
James D. DeRose
Barry J. Donohue
David R. Pierce
Jay Lavroff

Marlene Browne Berg
Raymond A. Grimes
Timothy D. Lyons
Lisa A. Freidenrich

OF COUNSEL

Kenneth L. Estabrook

Representative Clients: Alfa Romeo Distributors of N.A.; American Brands, Inc.; BMW of North America, Inc.; Great American Insurance Co.; Handex Environmental Recovery, Inc.; Kuehne Chemical Co., Inc.; Mechanical Contractors Association of New Jersey; Saxon Construction and Management Corp.; USF&G; Western Industries, Inc.

For Complete List of Firm Personnel, See General Section

For full biographical listings, see the Martindale-Hubbell Law Directory

WESTMONT, Camden Co.

BROWN & CONNERY (AV)

360 Haddon Avenue, P.O. Box 539, 08108
Telephone: 609-854-8900
Facsimile: 609-858-4967
Camden, New Jersey Office: 518 Market Street, P.O. Box 1449.
Telephone: 609-365-5100.
Telecopier: 609-858-4967.

MEMBERS OF FIRM

Thomas F. Connery, Jr.
William J. Cook
Warren W. Faulk
Steven G. Wolschina
Paul Mainardi
John L. Conroy, Jr.
Dennis P. Blake
Michael J. Vassalotti
John J. Mulderig
William M. Tambussi
Bruce H. Zamost
Mark P. Asselta
Stephen J. DeFeo
Jane A. Lorber

ASSOCIATES

Isabel C. Balboa
Joseph A. Zechman
Michael J. Fagan
Karen A. Peterson
Jeffrey E. Ugoretz
Christine O'Hearn
Christine A. Campbell
Joseph T. Carney

Representative Clients: Delaware River Port Authority; Underwood-Memorial Hospital; Garden State Water Company; Honeywell, Inc.; Philadelphia Newspapers, Inc.; Port Authority Transit Co.; Resolution Trust Corp.; General Electric; Mercedez-Benz Credit Corp.; American Red Cross.

For full biographical listings, see the Martindale-Hubbell Law Directory

WEST ORANGE, Essex Co.

BURSIK, KURITSKY & GIASULLO (AV)

443 Northfield Avenue, 07052
Telephone: 201-325-7800
Telecopier: 201-325-7930

MEMBERS OF FIRM

David H. E. Bursik
Stuart M. Kuritsky
Robert J. Giasullo

ASSOCIATES

Amy Bard
John Messina
Barbara Koerner Craig

For full biographical listings, see the Martindale-Hubbell Law Directory

ALAN L. ZEGAS (AV)

20 Northfield Avenue, 07052
Telephone: 201-736-1011
Fax: 201-325-2248

For full biographical listings, see the Martindale-Hubbell Law Directory

WEST PATERSON, Passaic Co.

EVANS HAND (AV)

One Garret Mountain Plaza, Interstate 80 at Squirrelwood Road, 07424-3396
Telephone: 201-881-1100
Fax: 201-881-1369

MEMBERS OF FIRM

Douglas C. Borchard, Jr.
Roy J. Evans
Harry D. Norton, Jr.
Douglas E. Arpert

(See Next Column)

EVANS HAND, *West Paterson—Continued*

ASSOCIATES

Janet Connery
Florence Amato Scrivo
Karen Santo Tracy
Deirdre Rafferty Thompson

Representative Clients: Midlantic National Bank; The Bank of New York/ National Community Division; The Prudential Insurance Co. of America; Connecticut General Life Insurance Co.; Travelers Insurance Co.; New Jersey Manufacturers Insurance Co.; Bell Atlantic; Algonquin Gas Transmission Co.; Tenneco, Inc.; Corning Glass Works.

For Complete List of Firm Personnel, See General Section

For full biographical listings, see the Martindale-Hubbell Law Directory

WOODBRIDGE, Middlesex Co.

GREENBAUM, ROWE, SMITH, RAVIN AND DAVIS (AV)

Metro Corporate Campus I, P.O. Box 5600, 07095-0988
Telephone: 908-549-5600
Cable Address: "Greelaw"
Telecopier: 908-549-1881
ABA Net: 2 529

MEMBERS OF FIRM

Paul A. Rowe
David L. Bruck
Michael B. Himmel
Dennis A. Estis
William D. Grand
Alan S. Naar
Harriet Farber Klein
Mark H. Sobel
Barry S. Goodman
Margaret Goodzeit
Robert J. Kipnees
Bruce D. Greenberg
Carlton T. Spiller
Jeffrey L. Kantowitz
Sabrina A. Kogel
Jacqueline M. Printz
Lawrence H. Wertheim

ASSOCIATES

Nancy Isaacson
Tyrone M. McDonnell
Gary Keith Wolinetz
Michael L. Konig
Matthew E. Power
Jessica R. Mayer
Richard L. Hertzberg
Ellen Ann Silver
Andrea J. Sullivan
Christine F. Marks
Andrew J. Rothman
Shirleen A. Roberts
Kathleen Meehan DalCortivo
Marc Jonathan Gross
Nigel I. Farinha
Stephanie Kay Austin
Luke John Kealy
Christopher S. Porrino
Mary Jean Pizza

For Complete List of Firm Personnel, See General Section

For full biographical listings, see the Martindale-Hubbell Law Directory

WILENTZ, GOLDMAN & SPITZER, A PROFESSIONAL CORPORATION (AV)

90 Woodbridge Center Drive Suite 900, Box 10, 07095
Telephone: 908-636-8000
Telecopier: 908-855-6117
Eatontown, New Jersey Office: Meridian Center I, Two Industrial Way West, 07724.
Telephone: 908-493-1000.
Telecopier: 908-493-8387.
New York, New York Office: Wall Street Plaza, 88 Pine Street, 9th Floor, 10005.
Telephone: 212-267-3091.
Telecopier: 212-267-3828.

Warren W. Wilentz
Morris Brown
Harold G. Smith
Frederic K. Becker
Robert J. Cirafesi
Alan M. Darnell
Gordon J. Golum
Frank M. Ciuffani
Marvin J. Brauth
Nicholas Willard Mc Clear
Richard R. Bonamo
Christine D. Petruzzell
Roger B. Kaplan
Philip A. Pahigian
Randall J. Richards
Frederick J. Dennehy
Christopher M. Placitella
Maureen S. Binetti
Michael J. Barrett
Angelo J. Cifaldi
Kevin M. Berry (Resident, New York, New York, Office)

Jon G. Kupilik
Robert Watson Smith
Frank M. Ortiz (Resident, New York, New York Office)
Edward T. Kole
Ruth D. Marcus (Not admitted in NJ; Resident New York, New York Office)
Lynne M. Kizis
Richard J. Byrnes
Georgia C. Haglund
Mark F. Curley
Robert T. Haefele
Donald E. Taylor
John E. Keefe, Jr.
Steven P. Knowlton
Barry R. Sugarman
Melissa L. Klipp
Andrea I. Bazer
Anita J. Dupree
Alfred Michael Anthony
Richard B. Becker
Jean M. Shanley

Representative Clients: Amerada Hess Corp.; Caesars World, Inc.; Chevron, U.S.A.; Constellation Bancorp; Cumberland Farms, Inc.; Middlesex County Utilities Authority; New Jersey Automobile Dealers Assn.; Raritan River Steel Co.; The Rouse Co.

(See Next Column)

For Complete List of Firm Personnel, See General Section

For full biographical listings, see the Martindale-Hubbell Law Directory

*WOODBURY,** Gloucester Co.

ANGELO J. FALCIANI, P.A. A PROFESSIONAL CORPORATION (AV)

35 South Broad Street, P.O. Box 379, 08096
Telephone: 609-845-8333
Fax: 609-845-9441

Angelo J. Falciani

Scott J. Lewis
Angelo John Falciani
Antoinette L. Falciani
Carol Tenney

For full biographical listings, see the Martindale-Hubbell Law Directory

NEW MEXICO

*ALBUQUERQUE,** Bernalillo Co.

PETER J. ADANG, P.C. (AV)

500 Marquette N.W., Suite 630, 87102
Telephone: 505-242-3999
Fax: 505-242-3939

Peter J. Adang

For full biographical listings, see the Martindale-Hubbell Law Directory

BUTT, THORNTON & BAEHR, P.C. (AV)

7000 CityPlace, 2155 Louisiana Boulevard, N.E., P.O. Box 3170, 87190
Telephone: 505-884-0777
FAX: 505-889-8870

Paul L. Butt
J. Duke Thornton
Raymond A. Baehr
Carlos G. Martinez
Norman L. Gagne
John A. Klecan
Alfred L. Green, Jr.
James H. Johansen
Martin Diamond
J. Douglas Compton
Donald E. Lepley, Jr.
John S. Stiff
David N. Whitham
Emily A. Franke
James P. Lyle
Jane A. Laflin
Paul T. Yarbrough
Glenna Hayes

Sherrill K. Filter
Michael P. Clemens
Agnes Fuentevilla Padilla

Representative Clients: Ford Motor Co.; Home Insurance Co.; Reliance Insurance Cos.; Royal Insurance Co.; International Harvester/Navistar; FMC Corp.; American Honda Motor; CIGNA; General Tire Company; ARA Spectrum Emergency Care Services.

For Complete List of Firm Personnel, See General Section

For full biographical listings, see the Martindale-Hubbell Law Directory

CAMPBELL, PICA, OLSON & SEEGMILLER (AV)

6565 Americas Parkway, N.E., Suite 800, P.O. Box 35459, 87176
Telephone: 505-883-9110
Fax: 505-884-3882

MEMBERS OF FIRM

Lewis O. Campbell
Nicholas R. Pica
David C. Olson
Douglas Seegmiller

ASSOCIATES

Brad Vaughn
Roger A. Stansbury
Philip Craig Snyder
Arthur J. G. Lacerte, Jr.
Jeffrey C. Gilmore

For full biographical listings, see the Martindale-Hubbell Law Directory

CARPENTER & CHÁVEZ, LTD. (AV)

1600 University Boulevard, N.E., Suite B, 87102-1711
Telephone: 505-243-1336
Facsimile: 505-243-1339

William H. Carpenter
Edward L. Chávez
David J. Stout

Reference: First Security Bank, Albuquerque, New Mexico.

For full biographical listings, see the Martindale-Hubbell Law Directory

CIVEROLO, WOLF, GRALOW & HILL, A PROFESSIONAL ASSOCIATION (AV)

500 Marquette, N.W., Suite 1400, P.O. Drawer 887, 87103
Telephone: 505-842-8255
Telecopier: 505-764-6099

(See Next Column)

CIVEROLO, WOLF, GRALOW & HILL A PROFESSIONAL ASSOCIATION—*Continued*

Richard C. Civerolo
Wayne C. Wolf
William P. Gralow
Lawrence H. Hill
Kathleen Davison Lebeck
Dennis E. Jontz
W. R. Logan
Roberto C. Armijo
Paul L. Civerolo
Ross L. Crown
Julia C. Roberts
Ellen M. Kelly
R. Thomas Dawe
Thomas P. Gulley
Robert James Curtis
Clinton W. Thute
Kathleen Schaechterle
Gary J. Cade
M. Clea Gutterson
Judith M. O'Neil
Lisa Entress Pullen
Leslie McCarthy Apodaca

General Counsel for: Western Bank.
Counsel for: Home Insurance Co.; Hartford Accident and Indemnity Co.; Farmers Insurance Group; Transamerica Insurance Co.; St. Joseph Hospital.
Representative Clients: AMREP Corp.; St. Vincent Hospital; Risk Management, State of New Mexico; G.D. Searle.

For Complete List of Firm Personnel, See General Section

For full biographical listings, see the Martindale-Hubbell Law Directory

EAVES, BARDACKE & BAUGH, P.A. (AV)

6400 Uptown Boulevard N.E., Suite 110-W, P.O. Box 35670, 87176
Telephone: 505-888-4300
Facsimile: 505-883-4406

John M. Eaves
Paul Bardacke
John G. Baugh
Kerry Kiernan
Peter S. Kierst
David V. Halliburton
David A. Garcia
Lisabeth L. Occhialino

OF COUNSEL

Marianne Woodard
Jennifer J. Pruett
Susan C. Kery

For full biographical listings, see the Martindale-Hubbell Law Directory

THE FARLOW LAW FIRM (AV)

Suite 1020, 6501 Americas Parkway, NE, 87110
Telephone: 505-883-4975
Fax: 505-883-4992

LeRoi Farlow
Suzanne Guest

Representative Clients: Allstate Insurance Co.; Commercial Insurance Co.; Sentry Insurance Co.; National Farmers Union Insurance Co.; Preferred Risk Mutual Insurance Co.; Guaranty National Insurance Co.
Reference: Bank of New Mexico.

For full biographical listings, see the Martindale-Hubbell Law Directory

FREEDMAN, BOYD, DANIELS, PEIFER, HOLLANDER, GUTTMANN & GOLDBERG, P.A. (AV)

Suite 700, 20 First Plaza, 200 Third Street, N.W., 87102
Telephone: 505-842-9960
Fax: 505-842-0761

David A. Freedman
John W. Boyd
Charles W. Daniels
K. Lee Peifer
J. Michele Guttmann
Joseph Goldberg

For full biographical listings, see the Martindale-Hubbell Law Directory

GALLAGHER, CASADOS & MANN, P.C. (AV)

317 Commercial N.E., 2nd Floor, 87102
Telephone: 505-243-7848
Fax: 505-764-0153

James E. Casados
Nathan H. Mann
Michael P. Watkins
Gail S. Stewart
Doris W. Eng
Dawn T. (Penni) Adrian
Jack Carmody
Robert L. Hlady

OF COUNSEL

David R. Gallagher

Representative Clients: Great American Insurance Co.; Mutual of Omaha; Safeco Insurance Co.; Amica Insurance Co.; American International Adjustment Co.; Progressive Insurance Co.; Maryland Casualty Co.; Sentry-Dairyland; Stonewall Insurance Co.; Scottsdale Insurance Co.

For full biographical listings, see the Martindale-Hubbell Law Directory

GUEBERT & YEOMANS, P.C. (AV)

4308 Carlisle Boulevard N.E., Suite 207, 87107
Telephone: 505-883-1606
Telefax: 505-883-1691

(See Next Column)

Terry R. Guebert
Richard D. Yeomans
Donald G. Bruckner, Jr.
RaMona G. Bootes
Robert A. Corchine

For full biographical listings, see the Martindale-Hubbell Law Directory

HINKLE, COX, EATON, COFFIELD & HENSLEY (AV)

Suite 800, 500 Marquette, N.W., P.O. Box 2043, 87103
Telephone: 505-768-1500
FAX: 505-768-1529
Roswell, New Mexico Office: Suite 700, United Bank Plaza, P.O. Box 10, 88202.
Telephone: 505-622-6510.
FAX: 505-623-9332.
Midland, Texas Office: 6 Desta Drive, Suite 2800, P.O. Box 3580, 79705.
Telephone: 915-683-4691.
FAX: 915-683-6518.
Amarillo, Texas Office: 1700 Bank One Center. P.O. Box 9238, 79105-9238.
Telephone: 806-372-5569.
FAX: 806-372-9761.
Santa Fe, New Mexico Office: 218 Montezuma, P.O. Box 2068, 87504.
Telephone: 505-982-4554.
FAX: 505-982-8623.
Austin, Texas Office: 401 West 15th Street, Suite 800, 78701.
Telephone: 512-476-7137.
FAX: 512-476-5431.
Associated Office: Hoffman & Stephens, P.C., 401 West 15th Street, Suite 800, 78701.
Telephone: 512-476-5434.
Fax: 512-476-5431.

Eric D. Lanphere
Marshall G. Martin
Thomas J. McBride
Mark C. Dow
Stanley K. Kotovsky, Jr.
Howard R. Thomas

Representative Clients: Anadarko Petroleum Corp.; Atlantic Richfield Co.; Bass Enterprises Production Co.; BHP Petroleum; Caroon & Black Management, Inc.; Chevron, USA, Inc.; CIGNA; City of Albuquerque; Coastal Oil & Gas Corp. Co.; Diagnostek.

For Complete List of Firm Personnel, See General Section

For full biographical listings, see the Martindale-Hubbell Law Directory

KELLY, RAMMELKAMP, MUEHLENWEG, LUCERO & LEÓN, A PROFESSIONAL ASSOCIATION (AV)

Simms Tower, 400 Gold Avenue S.W., Suite 500, P.O. Box 25127, 87125-5127
Telephone: 505-247-8860
Fax: 505-247-8881

David A. Rammelkamp
Robert J. Muehlenweg
Alberto A. León

Todd M. Stafford
Paige G. Leslie

Representative Clients: Basis International, Ltd.; Resolution Trust Corp.; First Bank of Grants; Bank of America, New Mexico; John L. Rust Co. (Caterpillar); Bridgers & Paxton Consulting Engineers, Inc.; Newman Newsom, Inc.; D.W.B.H., Inc. (Nissan, Mitsubishi and Hyundai); Underwriters at Lloyd's, London; Reliance National Insurance.

For Complete List of Firm Personnel, See General Section

For full biographical listings, see the Martindale-Hubbell Law Directory

MILLER, STRATVERT, TORGERSON & SCHLENKER, P.A. (AV)

500 Marquette Avenue, N.W., Suite 1100, P.O. Box 25687, 87102
Telephone: 505-842-1950
Facsimile: 505-243-4408
Farmington, New Mexico Office: Suite 300, 300 West Arrington. P.O. Box 869.
Telephone: 505-326-4521.
Facsimile: 505-325-5474.
Las Cruces, New Mexico Office: Suite 300, 277 East Amador. P.O. Drawer 1231.
Telephone: 505-523-2481.
Facsimile: 505-526-2215.
Santa Fe, New Mexico Office: 125 Lincoln Avenue, Suite 221. P.O. Box 1986.
Telephone: 505-989-9614.
Facsimile: 505-989-9857.

Ranne B. Miller
Alan C. Torgerson
Kendall O. Schlenker
Alice Tomlinson Lorenz
Gregory W. Chase
Alan Konrad
Margo J. McCormick
Lyman G. Sandy
Stephen M. Williams
Stephan M. Vidmar
Robert C. Gutierrez
Seth V. Bingham (Resident at Farmington Office)
Michael H. Hoses
James B. Collins (Resident at Farmington Office)
Timothy Ray Briggs
Walter R. Parr (Resident at Santa Fe Office)
Rudolph A. Lucero

(See Next Column)

MILLER, STRATVERT, TORGERSON & SCHLENKER P.A., *Albuquerque—Continued*

Daniel E. Ramczyk
Dean G. Constantine
Deborah A. Solove
Gary L. Gordon
Lawrence R. White (Resident at Las Cruces Office)
Sharon P. Gross
Virginia Anderman
Marte D. Lightstone
Bradford K. Goodwin
John R. Funk (Resident at Las Cruces Office)
J. Scott Hall (Resident at Santa Fe Office)
Thomas R. Mack
Michael J. Happe (Resident at Farmington Office)
Denise Barela Shepherd
Nancy Augustus
Jill Burtram
Terri L. Sauer
Joel T. Newton (Resident at Las Cruces Office)
Judith K. Nakamura
Thomas M. Domme
David H. Thomas, III
C. Brian Charlton

COUNSEL

William K. Stratvert
Paul W. Robinson

Representative Clients: Dona Ana Savings and Loan Assn.; Medical Protective Co.; Mesa Limited Partnership; New Mexico Physicians Mutual Liability Insurance Co.; St. Paul Insurance Cos.; State Farm Fire and Casualty Insurance Co.; State Farm Mutual Automobile Insurance Co.; Ticor Title Insurance Co.; The Travelers; United States Fidelity & Guaranty Co.

For Complete List of Firm Personnel, See General Section

For full biographical listings, see the Martindale-Hubbell Law Directory

SHEEHAN, SHEEHAN & STELZNER, P.A. (AV)

Suite 300, 707 Broadway, N.E., P.O. Box 271, 87103
Telephone: 505-247-0411
Fax: 505-842-8890

Craig T. Erickson
Juan L. Flores
Kim A. Griffith
Philip P. Larragoite
Susan C. Little
Maria O'Brien
Judith D. Schrandt
Timothy M. Sheehan
Luis G. Stelzner
Elizabeth Newlin Taylor
Robert P. Warburton

OF COUNSEL

Briggs F. Cheney
Charles T. DuMars
Thomas J. Horan
Pat Sheehan

For full biographical listings, see the Martindale-Hubbell Law Directory

SUTIN, THAYER & BROWNE, A PROFESSIONAL CORPORATION (AV)

Two Park Square, Suite 1000, 6565 Americas Parkway, N.E., P.O. Box 1945, 87103
Telephone: 505-883-2500
Fax: 505-888-6565
Santa Fe, New Mexico Office: 300 First Interstate Plaza, 150 Washington, P.O. Box 2187, 87504.
Telephone: 505-988-5521.
Fax: 505-982-5297.

Saul Cohen (Resident at Santa Fe Office)
Norman S. Thayer, Jr.
Jonathan B. Sutin
Ronald Segel
Jay D. Hertz
Mary E. McDonald (Resident at Santa Fe Office)
Gail Gottlieb
Frank C. Salazar
Suann Hendren
Jeffery L. Graves

Representative Clients: Eastern New Mexico University; Employers National Insurance Co.; Ford Motor Credit Co.; General Electric Co.; General Motors Acceptance Corp.; General Electric Co.; Levi Strauss & Co.; Trammell Crow Co.; United New Mexico Financial Corp.; University of New Mexico; Walgreen Co.

For Complete List of Firm Personnel, See General Section

For full biographical listings, see the Martindale-Hubbell Law Directory

FARMINGTON, San Juan Co.

TANSEY, ROSEBROUGH, GERDING & STROTHER, P.C. (AV)

621 West Arrington Street, P.O. Box 1020, 87499
Telephone: 505-325-1801
Telecopier: 505-325-4675

Haskell D. Rosebrough
Austin E. Roberts (1921-1983)
Richard L. Gerding
Robin D. Strother
Douglas A. Echols
James B. Payne
Michael T. O'Loughlin
Tommy Roberts
Karen L. Townsend

OF COUNSEL

Charles M. Tansey, Jr.

Representative Clients: American International Adjustment Co.; New Mexico Newspapers, Inc.; CIGNA Insurance Co.; Commercial Union Insurance Cos.; United Indian Traders Association, Inc.; Farmington Municipal Schools; Risk Management Division, State of New Mexico; San Juan Regional Medical Center; Merrion Oil & Gas Co; Giant Exploration and Production Co.

(See Next Column)

For full biographical listings, see the Martindale-Hubbell Law Directory

*LAS CRUCES,** Dona Ana Co.

LAW OFFICE OF T. A. SANDENAW (AV)

545 South Melendres, Suite C, 88005
Telephone: 505-523-7500
Fax: 505-523-5600

Thomas A. Sandenaw, Jr.

Mary T. Torres
Richard L. Musick

For full biographical listings, see the Martindale-Hubbell Law Directory

*ROSWELL,** Chaves Co.

HINKLE, COX, EATON, COFFIELD & HENSLEY (AV)

Suite 700, United Bank Plaza, P.O. Box 10, 88202
Telephone: 505-622-6510
FAX: 505-623-9332
Midland, Texas Office: 6 Desta Drive, Suite 2800, P.O. Box 3580, 79705.
Telephone: 915-683-4691.
FAX: 915-683-6518.
Amarillo, Texas Office: 1700 Bank One Center, P.O. Box 9238, 79105-9238.
Telephone: 806-372-5569.
FAX: 806-372-9761.
Santa Fe, New Mexico Office: 218 Montezuma, P.O. Box 2068, 87504.
Telephone: 505-982-4554.
FAX: 505-982-8623.
Albuquerque, New Mexico Office: Suite 800, 500 Marquette, N.W., P.O. Box 2043, 87103.
Telephone: 505-768-1500.
FAX: 505-768-1529.
Austin, Texas Office: 401 West 15th Street, Suite 800, 78701.
Telephone: 512-476-7137.
FAX: 512-476-5431.
Associated Office: Hoffman & Stephens, P.C., 401 West 15th Street, Suite 800, 78701.
Telephone: 512-476-5434.
Fax: 512-476-5431.

RESIDENT PARTNERS

Harold L. Hensley, Jr.
Stuart D. Shanor
Richard E. Olson
Albert L. Pitts
Thomas D. Haines, Jr.
Rebecca Nichols Johnson
William Paul Johnson
Andrew J. Cloutier

Representative Clients: ARCO; BTA; The Citizens Bank of Clovis; Exxon; Natural Gas Pipeline Company of America; Pennzoil; Phillips Petroleum Co.; Southwestern Public Service Co.; Texaco; Transwestern Pipeline Co.; United New Mexico Bank at Roswell.

For full biographical listings, see the Martindale-Hubbell Law Directory

*SANTA FE,** Santa Fe Co.

CAMPBELL, CARR, BERGE & SHERIDAN, P.A. (AV)

110 North Guadalupe, P.O. Box 2208, 87504-2208
Telephone: 505-988-4421
Telecopier: 505-983-6043

Michael B. Campbell
William F. Carr
Bradford C. Berge
Mark F. Sheridan

Michael H. Feldewert
Tanya M. Trujillo
Nancy A. Rath

For Complete List of Firm Personnel, See General Section

For full biographical listings, see the Martindale-Hubbell Law Directory

CARPENTER, COMEAU, MALDEGEN, BRENNAN, NIXON & TEMPLEMAN (AV)

Coronado Building, 141 East Palace Avenue, P.O. Box 669, 87504-0669
Telephone: 505-982-4611
Telecopier: 505-988-2987

MEMBERS OF FIRM

Richard N. Carpenter
Michael R. Comeau
Larry D. Maldegen
Michael W. Brennan
Sunny J. Nixon
William P. Templeman
Jon J. Indall
Stephen J. Lauer
Paula Ann Cook
Grey Handy
Joseph E. Manges

Representative Clients: Homestake Mining Co.; First National Bank of Santa Fe; N. M. Electric Cooperatives; Plains Electric G & T Cooperative; United Nuclear Corp.; Uranium Producers of America; BHP Minerals; Great American Insurance Co.; GTE Corp.; State of New Mexico.

For full biographical listings, see the Martindale-Hubbell Law Directory

Santa Fe—Continued

Patrick A. Casey, P.A. (AV)

1421 Luisa Street, Suite Q, P.O. Box 2436, 87504
Telephone: 505-982-3639
Fax: 505-989-9181

Patrick A. Casey

David C. Ruyle

References: First Interstate Bank of Santa Fe; Sunwest Bank.

For full biographical listings, see the Martindale-Hubbell Law Directory

Catron, Catron & Sawtell, A Professional Association (AV)

2006 Botulph Road, P.O. Box 788, 87504-0788
Telephone: 505-982-1947
Telecopier: 505-986-1013

John S. Catron
W. Anthony Sawtell
Michael T. Pottow
Kathrin M. Kinzer-Ellington

Attorneys for: Santa Fe Board of Education; American Express Co.; The Santa Fe Opera; Sunwest Bank of Santa Fe; VNS Health Services, Inc.; Santa Maria El Mirador Rehabilitation Services, Inc.; Diamond Shamrock Refining & Marketing Company.

For Complete List of Firm Personnel, See General Section

For full biographical listings, see the Martindale-Hubbell Law Directory

Gallegos Law Firm, P.C. (AV)

141 East Palace Avenue, 87501
Telephone: 505-983-6686
Telefax: 505-986-0741

J. E. Gallegos
Mary E. Walta
Michael J. Condon
David Sandoval
Glenn Theriot

Representative Clients: Doyle Hartman Oil Operator; Cuesta Production Co.; Graham Royalty Ltd.; Windward Energy and Marketing Co.; The Northern Trust Co.; San Rio Oil & Gas Co.

For full biographical listings, see the Martindale-Hubbell Law Directory

Hinkle, Cox, Eaton, Coffield & Hensley (AV)

218 Montezuma, P.O. Box 2068, 87504
Telephone: 505-982-4554
FAX: 505-982-8623
Roswell, New Mexico Office: Suite 700 United Bank Plaza, P.O. Box 10, 88202.
Telephone: 505-622-6510.
FAX: 505-623-9332.
Midland, Texas Office: 6 Desta Drive, Suite 2800, P.O. Box 3580, 79705.
Telephone: 915-683-4691.
FAX: 915-683-6518.
Amarillo, Texas Office: 1700 Bank One Center, P.O. Box 9238, 79105-9238.
Telephone: 806-372-5569.
FAX: 806-372-9761.
Albuquerque, New Mexico Office: Suite 800, 500 Marquette, N.W., P.O. Box 2043, 87103.
Telephone: 505-768-1500.
FAX: 505-768-1529.
Austin, Texas Office: 401 West 15th Street, Suite 800, 78701.
Telephone: 512-476-7137.
FAX: 512-476-5431.
Associated Office: Hoffman & Stephens, P.C., 401 West 15th Street, Suite 800, 78701.
Telephone: 512-476-5434.
Fax: 512-476-5431.

RESIDENT PARTNERS

Jeffrey L. Fornaciari
James Bruce
Thomas M. Hnasko

Representative Clients: Pennzoil; Southwestern Public Service; W.R. Grace & Co.

For full biographical listings, see the Martindale-Hubbell Law Directory

Jones, Snead, Wertheim, Rodriguez & Wentworth, P.A. (AV)

215 Lincoln Avenue, P.O. Box 2228, 87504-2228
Telephone: 505-982-0011
Fax: 505-989-6288

O. Russell Jones (1912-1978)
James E. Snead
Jerry Wertheim
Manuel J. Rodriguez
John Wentworth
Arturo L. Jaramillo
Peter V. Culbert
James G. Whitley
Francis J. Mathew

(See Next Column)

Jerry Todd Wertheim
Carol A. Clifford

LEGAL SUPPORT PERSONNEL

PARALEGALS

Linda A. Zieba

For full biographical listings, see the Martindale-Hubbell Law Directory

Montgomery & Andrews, Professional Association (AV)

325 Paseo de Peralta, P.O. Box 2307, 87504-2307
Telephone: 505-982-3873
Albuquerque, New Mexico Office: Suite 1300 Albuquerque Plaza, 201 Third Street, N.W., P.O. Box 26927.
Telephone: 505-242-9677.
FAX: 505-243-2542.

Victor R. Ortega
John B. Pound
Walter J. Melendres
Bruce Herr
Sarah Michael Singleton
Stephen S. Hamilton
R. Michael Shickich
Paul S. Grand

Representative Clients: Meridian Oil, Inc.; El Paso Natural Gas Co.; LAC Minerals (USA) Inc.; State of Kansas; State of New Mexico, Risk Management Division; St. Vincent Hospital; Travelers Insurance Co.; United States Fidelity and Guaranty Co.; US WEST Communications; Catholic Mutual Relief Society of America.

For Complete List of Firm Personnel, See General Section

For full biographical listings, see the Martindale-Hubbell Law Directory

Rose, Kohl & Davenport, Ltd. (AV)

1516 Paseo De Peralta, 87501
Telephone: 505-982-0080
Fax: 505-982-0081

Filmore E. Rose
Bruce R. Kohl
Beth R. Davenport
Robert J. Dodds, III
Marie A. Cioth (Not admitted in NM)

Reference: The First National Bank of Santa Fe.

For full biographical listings, see the Martindale-Hubbell Law Directory

Roth, Van Amberg, Gross, Rogers & Ortiz (AV)

347 East Palace Avenue, P.O. Box 1447, 87501
Telephone: 505-983-7319; 988-8979
Fax: 505-983-7508

F. Joel Roth
Ronald J. Van Amberg
Michael P. Gross
Carl Bryant Rogers
Raymond Z. Ortiz

Reference: First Interstate Bank.

For full biographical listings, see the Martindale-Hubbell Law Directory

Rothstein, Donatelli, Hughes, Dahlstrom, Cron & Schoenburg (AV)

Sanbusco Center, 500 Montezuma Avenue, Suite 101, P.O. Box 8180, 87504-8180
Telephone: 505-988-8004
Fax: 505-982-0307
Albuquerque, New Mexico Office: 320 Central S.W., Suite 30, 87102.
Telephone: 505-243-1443.
Fax: 505-242-7845.
Phoenix, Arizona Office: 234 North Central, Suite 722, 85004.
Telephone: 602-252-3226.
Fax: 602-253-3088.

MEMBERS OF FIRM

Robert R. Rothstein
Mark H. Donatelli
Richard W. Hughes
Eric N. Dahlstrom (Not admitted in NM; Resident, Phoenix, Arizona Office)
Dan Cron
Peter Schoenburg (Resident, Albuquerque, New Mexico Office)

ASSOCIATES

Michael C. Shiel (Not admitted in NM; Resident, Phoenix, Arizona Office)
Tina S. Boradiansky
Lisa Chau

For full biographical listings, see the Martindale-Hubbell Law Directory

Scheuer, Yost & Patterson, A Professional Corporation (AV)

125 Lincoln Avenue, Suite 223, P.O. Drawer 9570, 87504
Telephone: 505-982-9911
Fax: 505-982-1621

(See Next Column)

SCHEUER, YOST & PATTERSON A PROFESSIONAL CORPORATION, *Santa Fe—Continued*

Ralph H. Scheuer
Mel E. Yost
John N. Patterson
Holly A. Hart
Roger L. Prucino
Elizabeth A. Jaffe
Tracy Erin Conner
Ruth M. Fuess

OF COUNSEL

Melvin T. Yost

Representative Clients: Cyprus-AMAX, Inc.; Century Bank, FSB; Chicago Insurance Co.; GEICO; Pepsico, Inc.; Rocky Mountain Bankcard System; State Farm Insurance Company; St. John's College; Sun Loan Companies; Territorial Abstract & Title Co.

For full biographical listings, see the Martindale-Hubbell Law Directory

NEW YORK

*ALBANY,** Albany Co.

CARTER, CONBOY, CASE, BLACKMORE, NAPIERSKI AND MALONEY, P.C. (AV)

20 Corporate Woods Boulevard, 12211-2350
Telephone: 518-465-3484
Fax: 518-465-1843

J. S. Carter (1920-1954)
M. James Conboy (1920-1969)
James S. Carter
James M. Conboy
Forrest N. Case, Jr.
James C. Blackmore
Eugene E. Napierski
John T. Maloney
Gregory S. Mills
Edward D. Laird, Jr.
Susanna L. Martin
Brian P. Krzykowski
Terence S. Hannigan

John W. VanDenburgh
William J. Greagan
Anne M. Hurley
John J. Gable
Susan DiBella Harvey
Shirley Clouser Greagan
James Anthony Resila
James P. Trainor
David A. Rikard
Nancy E. May-Skinner
Christopher Lyons
Eugene Daniel Napierski
Joseph T. Perkins
Colleen H. Whalen
Paul C. Marthy

Reference: Key Bank of New York.

For Complete List of Firm Personnel, See General Section

For full biographical listings, see the Martindale-Hubbell Law Directory

DONOHUE, SABO, VARLEY & ARMSTRONG, P.C. (AV)

18 Computer Drive East, P.O. Box 15056, 12212-5056
Telephone: 518-458-8922
Telecopier: 518-438-4349

Paul F. Donohue, Sr. (Retired)
Alvin O. Sabo
Kenneth Varley, Jr.
Robert J. Armstrong
Fred J. Hutchison
Bruce S. Huttner
Kathleen L. Werther

Christine M. D'Addio
Walter M.B. Spiro

Representative Clients: CNA Insurance Cos.; Continental Loss Adjusting Services; Electric Insurance Co.; Electric Mutual Insurance Co.; General Accident Assurance Co.; General Electric Co.; NY Central Mutual Fire Insurance Co.; Preferred Mutual Insurance Co.; State Insurance Fund; Zurich-American Insurance Co.

For full biographical listings, see the Martindale-Hubbell Law Directory

DREYER, BOYAJIAN & TUTTLE (AV)

75 Columbia Street, 12210
Telephone: 518-463-7784
Telecopier: 518-463-4039

William J. Dreyer
Donald W. Boyajian
James B. Tuttle
Daniel J. Stewart
Brian W. Devane
Christopher M. Scaringe
Damon J. Stewart
Jill A. Dunn

For full biographical listings, see the Martindale-Hubbell Law Directory

HARVEY AND HARVEY HARVEY & MUMFORD (AV)

29 Elk Street, 12207
Telephone: 518-463-4491
Telecopier: 518-463-5665

Arthur J. Harvey (1903-1986)

MEMBERS OF FIRM

Jack D. Harvey
Jonathan P. Harvey
Brian F. Mumford

(See Next Column)

ASSOCIATE

Eva Lynn M. Hayko

Reference: Chemical Bank.

For full biographical listings, see the Martindale-Hubbell Law Directory

ISEMAN, CUNNINGHAM, RIESTER & HYDE (AV)

9 Thurlow Terrace, 12203
Telephone: 518-462-3000
Telecopier: 518-462-4199

MEMBERS OF FIRM

Frederick C. Riester
Michael J. Cunningham
Robert Hall Iseman
Carol Ann Hyde
Michael J. McNeil

Brian M. Culnan
Linda J. Clark

For full biographical listings, see the Martindale-Hubbell Law Directory

O'CONNELL AND ARONOWITZ, P.C. (AV)

100 State Street, 12207-1885
Telephone: 518-462-5601
Telecopier: 518-462-2670
Plattsburgh, New York Office: Grand Plaza Building, Suite 204, 159 Margaret Street.
Telephone: 518-562-0600.
Fax: 518-562-0657.
Saratoga Springs, New York Office: Suite 202, 358 Broadway.
Telephone: 518-587-0425.
Fax: 518-587-0565.

Stephen R. Coffey
Thomas J. Di Novo

For Complete List of Firm Personnel, See General Section

For full biographical listings, see the Martindale-Hubbell Law Directory

ROWLEY, FORREST, O'DONNELL & HITE, P.C. (AV)

90 State Street Suite 729, 12207-1715
Telephone: 518-434-6187
Fax: 518-434-1287

Richard R. Rowley
Thomas J. Forrest
Brian J. O'Donnell
Robert S. Hite
John H. Beaumont
Mark S. Pelersi
David C. Rowley

James J. Seaman
David P. Miranda
Kevin S. Casey
Richard W. Bader
Daniel W. Coffey
Thomas D. Spain

OF COUNSEL

Rush W. Stehlin

Reference: Norstar Bank.

For full biographical listings, see the Martindale-Hubbell Law Directory

THORN AND GERSHON (AV)

5 Wembley Court, New Karner Road, P.O. Box 15054, 12212
Telephone: 518-464-6770
Fax: 518-464-6778

MEMBERS OF FIRM

Richard M. Gershon
Arthur H. Thorn
Jeffrey J. Tymann
Maureen Sullivan Bonanni
Robin Bartlett Phelan

ASSOCIATES

Murry S. Brower
Noreen J. Eaton
Paul J. Catone
Nancy Nicholson Bogan
Sheila Toborg
John C. Garvey
Paul D. Jureller
Mario D. Cometti
Robert S. Bruschini

OF COUNSEL

Robert F. Doran

For full biographical listings, see the Martindale-Hubbell Law Directory

THUILLEZ, FORD, GOLD & CONOLLY (AV)

90 State Street, Suite 1500, 12207-1797
Telephone: 518-455-9952
Facsimile: 518-462-4031

MEMBERS OF FIRM

Dale M. Thuillez
Donald P. Ford, Jr.
Barry A. Gold
Henry Neal Conolly

ASSOCIATES

Jonathan B. Summers
Ann C. Crowell

OF COUNSEL

Thomas A. Ford

(See Next Column)

THUILLEZ, FORD, GOLD & CONOLLY—*Continued*

SPECIAL COUNSEL

Michael J. Hutter, Jr. | Susan L. Lore

Representative Clients: Kemper Insurance Group; Hospital Underwriters Mutual Insurance Co.; Government Employees Insurance Co.; Ellis Hospital; Exchange Insurance Co.; Crum & Forster; Hartford Insurance Co.; Worcester Insurance Co.; Sofco-Mead, Inc.; United States Fidelity & Guaranty Co.

For Complete List of Firm Personnel, See General Section

For full biographical listings, see the Martindale-Hubbell Law Directory

WHITEMAN OSTERMAN & HANNA (AV)

One Commerce Plaza, 12260
Telephone: 518-487-7600
Telecopier: 518-487-7777
Cable Address: "Advocate Albany"
Buffalo, New York Office: 1700 Liberty Building.
Telephone: 716-854-4420.
Telecopier: 716-854-4428.

MEMBERS OF FIRM

Michael Whiteman
Melvin H. Osterman
John Hanna, Jr.
Joel L. Hodes
Philip H. Gitlen
Scott N. Fein
Alice J. Kryzan (Resident, Buffalo Office)
Daniel A. Ruzow
Philip H. Dixon
Günter Dully
James W. Lytle
Richard E. Leckerling
Margaret J. Gillis
Jonathan P. Nye
Heather D. Diddel
Neil L. Levine
Mary Jane Bendon Couch
John T. Kolaga (Resident, Buffalo Office)

SENIOR COUNSEL

Howard T. Sprow

COUNSEL

John R. Dunne | Thomas H. Lynch

OF COUNSEL

Leslie K. Thiele

ASSOCIATES

Kenneth S. Ritzenberg
Jean F. Gerbini
Jeffrey S. Baker
Terresa M. Bakner
Elizabeth M. Morss
Carla E. Hogan
Paul C. Rapp
D. Scott Bassinson
Alan J. Goldberg (Not admitted in NY)
James H. Hoeksema, Jr.
Mary Walsh Snyder
Maria E. Villa
Beth A. Bourassa
Boty McDonald
Martin J. Ricciardi
Alicia C. Rood (Resident, Buffalo Office)
Sonya Kumari Del Peral
Carolyn Dick
David R. Everett
Michael G. Sterthous
John J. Henry
Lisa S. Kwong
Ellen M. Bach
Molly M.A. Brown
Judith Gaies Kahn
Ana-Maria Galeano
Alexandra J. Streznewski
Wayne Barr, Jr.

For full biographical listings, see the Martindale-Hubbell Law Directory

*AUBURN,** Cayuga Co.

MICHAELS & BELL, P.C. (AV)

71 South Street, P.O. Box 308, 13021
Telephone: 315-253-3293
Fax: 315-252-6970

Lee S. Michaels | John V. Bell
Jan M. Smolak

Paul C. Campbell | Stephanie Viscelli

Reference: Security Norstar, Auburn, N.Y.

For full biographical listings, see the Martindale-Hubbell Law Directory

*BINGHAMTON,** Broome Co.

HINMAN, HOWARD & KATTELL (AV)

700 Security Mutual Building, 80 Exchange Street, 13901
Telephone: 607-723-5341
Fax: 607-723-6605
Norwich, New York Office: 600 South Broad Street, Suite 200.
Telephone: 607-334-5896.
Fax: 607-336-6240.

MEMBERS OF FIRM

John M. Keeler
John S. Davidge
N. Theodore Sommer
James L. Chivers
James M. Hayes
James S. Gleason
James F. Lee
Albert J. Millus, Jr.
Paul T. Sheppard

(See Next Column)

ASSOCIATE

Leslie Prechtl Guy

Representative Clients: First-City Division, Chase Lincoln First Bank, N.A.; Binghamton Savings Bank; International Business Machines Corp.; Universal Instruments Corp.; Security Mutual Life Insurance Company of New York; New York Telephone Co.; Travelers Insurance Co.; New York State Electric & Gas Corp.; Exxon Corp.; Columbia Gas System, Inc.

For Complete List of Firm Personnel, See General Section

For full biographical listings, see the Martindale-Hubbell Law Directory

*BRONX,** Bronx Co.

MAXWELL S. PFEIFER (AV)

714 East 241st Street, 10470
Telephone: 718-325-5000
Fax: 718-324-0333
Hallandale, Florida Office: 1920 East Hallandale Beach Boulevard, Suite 606.
Telephone: 305-454-1550.

ASSOCIATES

Steven E. Millon | Robert S. Summer

OF COUNSEL

Hon. Alexander A. Dellecese | Sandra Krevitsky Janin
Anthony J. Hatab

LEGAL SUPPORT PERSONNEL

Jay S. Zwerling

For full biographical listings, see the Martindale-Hubbell Law Directory

*BROOKLYN,** Kings Co.

BONINA & BONINA, P.C. (AV)

Suite 1608, 16 Court Street, 11241
Telephone: 718-522-1786
Fax: 718-243-0414

John Anthony Bonina
John Bonina, III
Elizabeth Bonina
Andrea E. Bonina

Deborah A. Trerotola | Michael Campanile
Louise Gleason

OF COUNSEL

Sandra Krevitsky Janin

LEGAL SUPPORT PERSONNEL

Pedro Cintron | Inez M. Diaz
Shari Resnick

Reference: Republic Bank of New York.

For full biographical listings, see the Martindale-Hubbell Law Directory

*BUFFALO,** Erie Co.

ALBRECHT, MAGUIRE, HEFFERN & GREGG, P.C. (AV)

2100 Main Place Tower, 14202
Telephone: 716-853-1521
Fax: 716-852-2609

Charles H. Dougherty | Alan J. Bozer
John M. Curran

William P. Keefer

For Complete List of Firm Personnel, See General Section

For full biographical listings, see the Martindale-Hubbell Law Directory

BROWN & KELLY (AV)

1500 Liberty Building, 14202
Telephone: 716-854-2620
Telecopier: 716-854-0082

MEMBERS OF FIRM

Mark N. Turner (1897-1985)
Thomas J. Kelly
James T. Duggan
Frederick D. Turner
Paul Michael Hassett
Peter E. Klaasesz
Donald B. Eppers
Andrew D. Merrick
Gordon D. Tresch
William E. Nitterauer
William P. Wiles
William D. Harrington
Rodney O. Personius
Paula L. Feroleto
Daniel J. Marren
Lisa T. Sofferin

COUNSEL

Ogden R. Brown | Charles F. Harrington
Roland R. Benzow

ASSOCIATES

Raymond C. Stilwell
Carlton K. Brownell, III
David S. Zygaj
Kathleen F. Smith
Karen L. Cook
Colleen P. Doyle
Aileen M. Mcnamara

(See Next Column)

BROWN & KELLY, *Buffalo—Continued*

Representative Clients: Exchange Insurance Co.; Aetna Life & Casualty Co.; Fidelity & Deposit Company of Maryland; Consolidated Freightways, Inc.; United States Aviation Underwriters; Maryland Casualty Co.; Frontier Insurance Co.; Crum & Forster.

For Complete List of Firm Personnel, See General Section

For full biographical listings, see the Martindale-Hubbell Law Directory

CONNORS & VILARDO (AV)

1020 Liberty Building, 420 Main Street, 14202
Telephone: 716-852-5533
Fax: 716-852-5649
Dunkirk, New York Office: 401 Central Avenue, P.O. Box 706.
Telephone: 716-366-0606.

MEMBERS OF FIRM

Terrence M. Connors
Lawrence J. Vilardo
Kevin A. Ricotta

ASSOCIATES

Randall D. White
John T. Loss
Vincent E. Doyle III
Nancy M. Langer
Michael J. Roach

For full biographical listings, see the Martindale-Hubbell Law Directory

J. MICHAEL HAYES (AV)

69 Delaware Avenue, Suite 1201, 14202
Telephone: 716-852-2027
Fax: 716-852-0711

ASSOCIATE

R. Colin Campbell

For full biographical listings, see the Martindale-Hubbell Law Directory

HODGSON, RUSS, ANDREWS, WOODS & GOODYEAR (AV)

A Partnership including Professional Associations
Suite 1800, One M & T Plaza, 14203
Telephone: 716-856-4000
Cable Address: "Magna Carta" Buffalo, N.Y.
Telecopier: 716-849-0349
Albany, New York Office: Three City Square.
Telephone: 518-465-2333.
Telecopier: 518-465-1567.
Rochester, New York Office: 400 East Avenue.
Telephone: 716-454-6950.
Telecopier: 716-454-4698.
Boca Raton, Florida Office: Suite 400, Nations Bank Building, 2000 Glades Road.
Telephone: 407-394-0500.
Telecopier: 305-427-4303.
Mississauga, Ontario, Canada Office: Suite 880, 3 Robert Speck Parkway.
Telephone: 905-566-5061.
Telecopier: 905-566-2049.
New York, New York Office: 330 Madison Avenue, 11th Floor. Telephone 212-297-3370.
Telecopier: 212-972-6521.

MEMBERS OF FIRM

(ALPHABETICALLY BY YEAR OF ADMISSION TO BAR)

Victor T. Fuzak
William H. Gardner
H. Kenneth Schroeder, Jr.
Michael H. Gora (P.A.) (Boca Raton, Florida Office)
Robert W. Keller
Robert B. Conklin
Richard A. Goetz (P.A.) (Boca Raton, Florida Office)
Jerome D. Schad
Allen H. Beroza
Garry M. Graber
Richard L. Weisz (Albany Office)
Paul I. Perlman
Larry Corman (P.A.) (Boca Raton, Florida Office)
Rick W. Kennedy
Robert J. Lane, Jr.
Benjamin M. Zuffranieri, Jr.
Patrick J. Maxwell
Kevin A. Szanyi
Kevin M. Kearney
Hugh M. Russ, III
Cheryl R. Storie
Peter A. Muth
Douglas R. Edwards
Suzanne P. Stern
John F. Donogher
Deborah L. Kelly (Albany Office)
Michael E. Maxwell
Paul D. Meosky
Lisa C. Saurer

COUNSEL

John E. Dickinson

ASSOCIATES

(ALPHABETICALLY BY YEAR OF ADMISSION TO BAR)

Anna L. Case
Theresa J. Puleo (Albany Office)
Amy J. Vigneron
John C. Krenitsky
Diane H. Nowak
R. Anthony Rupp III
Timothy P. Sheehan (Rochester Office)
Charles E. Graney
Daniel A. Spitzer

For Complete List of Firm Personnel, See General Section

For full biographical listings, see the Martindale-Hubbell Law Directory

LIPSITZ, GREEN, FAHRINGER, ROLL, SALISBURY & CAMBRIA (AV)

42 Delaware Avenue, Suite 300, 14202
Telephone: 716-849-1333
Fax: 716-855-1580
New York, N.Y. Office: 110 East 59th Street.
Telephone: 212-909-9670.
East Aurora, New York Office: 164 Quaker Road.
Telephone: 716-652-4290.
Alden, New York Office: 1472 Exchange Street.
Telephone: 716-937-9494.

MEMBERS OF FIRM

Carl A. Green
James T. Scime
Laraine Kelley
William M. Feigenbaum
Michael A. Ponterio
Sharon M. Heim
Richard P. Weisbeck, Jr.
John A. Collins

Jeremy M. Schnurr
Robert L. Voltz

SPECIAL COUNSEL

Gerard R. Fornes
James W. Kirkpatrick

Representative Clients: Buffalo Bills; Marine Midland Bank, N.A.
Reference: Marine Midland Bank.

For Complete List of Firm Personnel, See General Section

For full biographical listings, see the Martindale-Hubbell Law Directory

MALONEY, GALLUP, ROACH, BROWN & MCCARTHY, P.C. (AV)

1620 Liberty Building, 14202
Telephone: 716-852-0400
Fax: 716-852-2535

Arthur J. Maloney
John Y. Gallup
Daniel T. Roach
Edmund S. Brown, Jr.
T. Alan Brown
Joseph V. McCarthy
J. Mark Gruber
Donald P. Chiari
Brian Sutter
J. Gregory Hoelscher
Colleen P. Cartonia
Mary J. Murray
John P. Danieu

Elizabeth G. Redmond

Local Attorneys for: American International Group; Chubb Group of Insurance Co.; Healthcare Underwriters Mutual Insurance Co.; Peter J. McBreen and Associates; Medical Liability Mutual Insurance Co.; Medical Malpractice Insurance Association; Merrill Dow; Reliance Insurance Group; Travelers Group.

For full biographical listings, see the Martindale-Hubbell Law Directory

MCGEE & GELMAN (AV)

200 Summer Street, 14222
Telephone: 716-883-7272
Fax: 716-883-7084

MEMBERS OF FIRM

Michael R. McGee
Warren B. Gelman
F. Brendan Burke, Jr.
James P. Giambrone, Jr.
Laura A. Colca

For full biographical listings, see the Martindale-Hubbell Law Directory

RODGERS, MENARD & COPPOLA (AV)

1630 Liberty Building, 420 Main Street, 14202-3616
Telephone: 716-852-4100
Facsimile: 716-852-0002

MEMBERS OF FIRM

Douglas S. Coppola
Michael Menard
Mark C. Rodgers

ASSOCIATES

Patricia S. Stroman
Patricia S. Ciccarelli

For full biographical listings, see the Martindale-Hubbell Law Directory

SMITH, KELLER, MINER & O'SHEA (AV)

69 Delaware Avenue Suite 1212, 14202-3891
Telephone: 716-855-3611
Fax: 716-855-3250

MEMBERS OF FIRM

Terry D. Smith
Robert E. Keller
R. Charles Miner
Philip J. O'Shea, Jr.
Deborah Bergeron O'Shea
Carrie L. Smith

For full biographical listings, see the Martindale-Hubbell Law Directory

SMITH, MURPHY & SCHOEPPERLE (AV)

786 Ellicott Square, 14203
Telephone: 716-852-1544
Telecopier: 716-852-3559

(See Next Column)

SMITH, MURPHY & SCHOEPPERLE—*Continued*

MEMBERS OF FIRM

Clayton M. Smith (1884-1967)
Esmond D. Murphy (1903-1960)
Richard K. Schoepperle
Frank G. Godson
Peter M. Collard
Lynn D. Gates
Bonnie T. Hager
Janice A. Barber
Linda J. Marsh
Robert A. Baker, Jr.
Norton T. Lowe
Edward J. Murphy, III
Dennis P. Mescall
Stephen P. Brooks

SPECIAL COUNSEL

Dennis C. Vacco

ASSOCIATES

Daniel H. Dillon
Ross J. Runfola
Susan W. Schoepperle
Michael T. Glascott

LEGAL SUPPORT PERSONNEL

LEGAL ADMINISTRATOR

Marybeth Cerrone

PARALEGALS

Michelle M. Wojciechowicz
Janice M. Beyer
Tamara Montaldi
Laurie A. Tripp

Representative Clients: Hartford Insurance Group; Dominion of Canada General Insurance Co.; Casualty Company of Canada; Royal Insurance Cos.; Chrysler Corp.; Merchants Inc., Group; Associated Aviation Underwriters; U.S. Aviation Underwriters.

For full biographical listings, see the Martindale-Hubbell Law Directory

CARLE PLACE, Nassau Co.

DOLLINGER, GONSKI, GROSSMAN, PERMUT & HIRSCHHORN (AV)

One Old Country Road, 11514
Telephone: 516-747-1010
Telecopier: 516-747-2494

MEMBERS OF FIRM

Matthew Dollinger
Dennis M. Gonski
Floyd G. Grossman
Michael Permut
Alan K. Hirschhorn

ASSOCIATES

Leslie Ann Foodim
Michael J. Spithogiannis
Jessica M. Seidman
Bruce N. Roberts
Alicia B. Devins
Bryan J. Holzberg
Mindy Anne Wallach
Rachel L. Hollander

Reference: Marine Midland National Bank, Carle Place, New York.

For full biographical listings, see the Martindale-Hubbell Law Directory

EAST MEADOW, Nassau Co.

CERTILMAN BALIN ADLER & HYMAN, LLP (AV)

90 Merrick Avenue, 11554
Telephone: 516-296-7000
Telecopier: 516-296-7111

MEMBERS OF FIRM

Ira J. Adler
Dale Allinson
Herbert M. Balin
Bruce J. Bergman
Michael D. Brofman
Morton L. Certilman
Murray Greenberg
David Z. Herman
Richard Herzbach
M. Allan Hyman
Bernard Hyman
Donna-Marie Korth
Steven J. Kuperschmid
Thomas J. McNamara
Fred S. Skolnik
Louis Soloway
Harold Somer
Howard M. Stein
Brian K. Ziegler

OF COUNSEL

Daniel S. Cohan
Norman J. Levy
Marilyn Price

ASSOCIATES

Howard B. Busch
Scott M. Gerber
Jodi S. Hoffman
Glenn Kleinbaum
Michael C. Manniello
Jaspreet S. Mayall
Stacey R. Miller
Lawrence S. Novak
Kim J. Radbell

For full biographical listings, see the Martindale-Hubbell Law Directory

GARDEN CITY, Nassau Co.

ALBANESE, ALBANESE & FIORE LLP (AV)

1050 Franklin Avenue, 5th Floor, 11530
Telephone: 516-248-7000

MEMBERS OF FIRM

Vincent M. Albanese
Joseph A. Fiore
Thomas G. Sherwood

ASSOCIATES

Barry A. Oster
Rachel M. Harari
Diana Centrella Prevete
Hyman Hacker

(See Next Column)

COUNSEL

W. Hubert Plummer

References: Apple Bank for Savings; Bank of New York; North Fork Bank; First American Title Insurance Company; American Title Insurance Company; Greater Jamaica Development Corp.; United Nations Plaza Tower Associates, Ltd.; Fidelity National Title Insurance Company of New York.

For Complete List of Firm Personnel, See General Section

For full biographical listings, see the Martindale-Hubbell Law Directory

FISCHOFF, GELBERG & DIRECTOR (AV)

600 Old Country Road, Suite 410, 11530
Telephone: 516-228-4255
Facsimile: 516-228-4278

MEMBERS OF FIRM

Stuart P. Gelberg
Gary C. Fischoff
Michael C. Director

ASSOCIATES

Scott R. Schneider
Heath Berger

For full biographical listings, see the Martindale-Hubbell Law Directory

GALLAGHER GOSSEEN & FALLER (AV)

1010 Franklin Avenue, Suite 400, 11530-2927
Telephone: 516-742-2500
Fax: 516-742-2516
Cable: COMPROAIR
New York, New York Office: 350 Fifth Avenue.
Telephone: 212-947-5800.
FAX: 212-967-4965.

MEMBERS OF FIRM

James A. Gallagher, Jr.
Robert I. Gosseen (Resident, New York City Office)
Robert A. Faller
Alan D. Kaplan
Michael J. Crowley
William E. Vita

ASSOCIATES

David H. Arnsten
William A. Bales, Jr.
Jeanne M. Gonsalves-Lloyd
Brian P. Morrissey
Robert A. Sparer (Resident, New York City Office)

OF COUNSEL

Edward M. O'Brien (Resident, New York City Office)
Peter F. Vetro
Daniel F. Hayes
John P. Coogan

For Complete List of Firm Personnel, See General Section

For full biographical listings, see the Martindale-Hubbell Law Directory

L'ABBATE, BALKAN, COLAVITA & CONTINI, L.L.P. (AV)

1050 Franklin Avenue, 11530
Telephone: 516-294-8844
Telecopier: 516-294-8202; 742-6563

MEMBERS OF FIRM

Donald R. L'Abbate
Kenneth J. Balkan
Anthony P. Colavita
Peter L. Contini
Monte E. Sokol
Douglas L. Pintauro
Richard P. Byrne
Ronald C. Burke
Harry Makris
Marie Ann Hoenings
Jane M. Myers
Dean L. Milber
James Plousadis

OF COUNSEL

Paula M. Gart

ASSOCIATES

Anna M. DiLonardo
David B. Kosakoff
Lewis A. Bartell
Ralph A. Catalano
Gay B. Levine
Victoria Roberts Drogin
Douglas R. Halstrom
Joseph A. Barra
Stephane Jasmin
Lawrence A. Kushnick
Diane H. Miller
Barbara Jean Romaine
Joseph V. Cambareri
Christine Andreoli

Representative Clients: Chicago Underwriting Group, Inc.; CNA; DPIC Insurance Cos.; Evanston Insurance Co.; General Accident Insurance Co.; The Home Insurance Co.; Imperial Casualty and Indemnity Co.; Markel American Insurance Co.; Shand, Morahan & Co., Inc.; Utica Mutual Insurance Co.

For full biographical listings, see the Martindale-Hubbell Law Directory

MONTFORT, HEALY, MCGUIRE & SALLEY (AV)

1140 Franklin Avenue, 11530
Telephone: 516-747-4082
Telecopier: 516-746-0748

MEMBERS OF FIRM

E. Richard Rimmels, Jr.
Frank J. Cafaro
Philip J. Catapano
Fredric C. Montfort
Donald S. Neumann, Jr.
James J. Keefe, Jr.
Michael A. Baranowicz
James Michael Murphy

(See Next Column)

MONTFORT, HEALY, MCGUIRE & SALLEY, *Garden City—Continued*

OF COUNSEL

Fredric H. Montfort
Edward M. Salley, Jr.
David J. Fleming

ASSOCIATES

Raymond J. Geoghegan
Robert J. Mettalia
Henry J. Wheller
Claudia C. Glacken
Marcie K. Glasser
Bruce A. Cook
Jeffrey D. Present
Joan E. Resnik
Susan H. Dempsey
Camille L. Hansen
Joseph F. Ferrette
Pui C. Cheng
Kathleen Dumont
Christopher T. Cafaro
Edward R. Rimmels
Jeffrey B. Siler

For full biographical listings, see the Martindale-Hubbell Law Directory

SAWYER, DAVIS & HALPERN (AV)

600 Old Country Road, 11530
Telephone: 516-222-4567
Telecopier: 516-222-4585

MEMBER OF FIRM

James Sawyer

ASSOCIATE

Adam C. Demetri

For Complete List of Firm Personnel, See General Section

For full biographical listings, see the Martindale-Hubbell Law Directory

BENJAMIN VINAR (AV)

1050 Franklin Avenue, 11530
Telephone: 516-746-0241
Telecopier: 516-747-9759

For full biographical listings, see the Martindale-Hubbell Law Directory

GREAT NECK, Nassau Co.

MARTIN, VAN DE WALLE, DONOHUE, MANDRACCHIA & McGAHAN (AV)

17 Barstow Road, P.O. Box 222074, 11022
Telephone: 516-482-6100
Telecopier: 516-482-6969

MEMBERS OF FIRM

Jules Martin
Charles R. Van de Walle
Nicholas J. Donohue
Stephen P. Mandracchia
James M. McGahan

ASSOCIATE

Ted J. Feldman

Representative Clients: Fidelity National Title Insurance Company of New York; Bancker Construction Corp.; Biener Pontiac-Nissan, Inc.; Festo Corp.; First Investors Corp.; Lighting Horizons, Inc.; Prime Realty Holdings Co.; First Financial Savings Bank, S.L.A.; Chaminade High School; Oppenheimer Management Corp.

For Complete List of Firm Personnel, See General Section

For full biographical listings, see the Martindale-Hubbell Law Directory

PEGALIS & WACHSMAN, P.C. (AV)

175 East Shore Road, 11023
Telephone: 718-895-7492; 212-936-2662; 516-487-1990
Outside New York: 1-800-522-0170
Telecopier: 516-487-4304
Philadelphia, Pennsylvania Office: 1601 Market Street, Suite 1040.
Telephone: 215-564-6838.
FAX: 215-564-6840.

Steven E. Pegalis
Harvey F. Wachsman

Kathryn M. Wachsman
Alice F. Collopy
Annamarie Bondi-Stoddard
Michael A. Carlucci
Gilbert G. Spencer, Jr.
James B. Baydar
Sanford Nagrotsky
Rhonda L. Meyer
Glenn C. McCarthy (Not admitted in NY)
Michael Aronoff
Daniel Albert Thomas

For full biographical listings, see the Martindale-Hubbell Law Directory

HARRISON, Westchester Co.

CLUNE, HAYES, FREY, BENTZEN & CLUNE, P.C. (AV)

480 Mamaroneck Avenue, 10528
Telephone: 914-698-8200
Telecopier: 914-698-8248
Garden City, New York Office: 350 Old Country Road, Suite 103.
Telephone: 516-248-6600. Greenwich, Connecticut Office: 55 Old Field Point Road.
Telephone: 203-629-8313.
Fax: 203-629-8216.

(See Next Column)

J. Russell Clune
Edward A. Frey
Alfred E. Page, Jr.
Richard D. Bentzen
Martin F. Hayes
Kevin P. Clune
James H. O'Brien, Jr.

Rafael Otero
Robert P. Kelly
Sharon Ann Scanlan
Kenneth E. Mangano
Stephen J. Lo Presti
Nicholas P. Barone
Michael P. Farley

For full biographical listings, see the Martindale-Hubbell Law Directory

HAUPPAUGE, Suffolk Co.

ERIC H. HOLTZMAN (AV)

330 Vanderbilt Motor Parkway, P.O. Box 11005, 11788-0903
Telephone: 516-435-8800
Fax: 516-435-8832

Richard E. Trachtenberg

Reference: European-American Bank & Trust Co.

For full biographical listings, see the Martindale-Hubbell Law Directory

HEMPSTEAD, Nassau Co.

FUREY, FUREY, LAPPING, DEMARIA & PETROZZO, P.C. (AV)

A Partnership including a Professional Corporation
600 Front Street, 11550
Telephone: 516-538-2500
Telecopier: 516-489-5056

James M. Furey
James M. Furey, Jr.
Robert K. Lapping
William D. Demaria
Vincent J. Petrozzo

Susan B. Williams
Susan W. Darlington
Patricia M. Meisenheimer
Jane Himelfarb
Thomas G. Leverage
Judith Pilatsky
Garyn Gdanian
Stuart J. Manzione
Linda A. Henninger
Michael T. Colavecchio
Elena R. Lanza
Christina A. Marotto
Lydia J. Keenan
Joseph M. Nador
David Stephen Wilck
Adam B. Rosen
James W. Jankowski

Reference: Fleet Bank, Hempstead.

For full biographical listings, see the Martindale-Hubbell Law Directory

JOSEPH R. MADDALONE, JR. (AV)

230 Hilton Avenue, 11550
Telephone: 516-486-3577
Telecopier: 516-486-3934

For full biographical listings, see the Martindale-Hubbell Law Directory

MORITT, HOCK & HAMROFF (AV)

Hempstead Executive Plaza, 50 Clinton Street, 11550
Telephone: 516-489-7400
Fax: 516-489-0971
Garden City, New York Office: 600 Old Country Road.
Telephone: 516-489-7400.

MEMBERS OF FIRM

Neil J. Moritt
Alan S. Hock
Marc L. Hamroff
David H. Cohen

Robert S. Cohen
Robert M. Tils
Sharon I. Feder
Donna R. Ruggiero
Leslie A. Berkoff
Kenneth Paul Horowitz
Wendy Axelrod (Not admitted in NY)
David A. Loglisci

For full biographical listings, see the Martindale-Hubbell Law Directory

LAKE SUCCESS, Nassau Co.

IVONE, DEVINE & JENSEN (AV)

2001 Marcus Avenue-Suite N100, 11042
Telephone: 516-326-2400
Telecopier: 516-352-4952

MEMBERS OF FIRM

Michael T. Ivone
Robert Devine
Richard C. Jensen
Brian E. Lee
Michael Ferguson

(See Next Column)

IVONE, DEVINE & JENSEN—*Continued*

ASSOCIATES

James C. Brady
Amy S. Barash
Ann-Marie Fassl Hartline
Debora G. Nobel
Charles Costas

For full biographical listings, see the Martindale-Hubbell Law Directory

LIBERTY, Sullivan Co.

APPELBAUM, EISENBERG, BAUMAN & APPELBAUM (AV)

6 North Main Street, 12754
Telephone: 914-292-4444

MEMBERS OF FIRM

Sidney Appelbaum
Bertram W. Eisenberg
Harold J. Bauman
Joel R. Appelbaum

ASSOCIATES

Steven M. Pivovar
Michael Frey

Representative Clients: Public Service Mutual Insurance Co.; Aetna Life and Casualty Co.; Allstate Insurance Co.; State Farm Mutual Insurance Co.; Employers-Commercial Union Insurance Group; Royal Globe Indemnity Co.; Pearl Assurance Co.; National Grange Insurance Co.
Reference: Marine Midland Bank.

For full biographical listings, see the Martindale-Hubbell Law Directory

MERRICK, Nassau Co.

CURTIS, ZAKLUKIEWICZ, VASILE, DEVINE & MCELHENNY (AV)

2174 Hewlett Avenue, P.O. Box 801, 11566-0801
Telephone: 516-623-1111
Riverhead, New York Office: 80 W. Main Street.
Telephone: 516-727-1111.

MEMBERS OF FIRM

Reid A. Curtis (1911-1987)
Francis E. Zaklukiewicz
Roy W. Vasile
Paul S. Devine
Brian W. McElhenny

ASSOCIATES

Eugene Zimbalist (1926-1989)
James J. Morris
Michael G. Mehary
Thomas M. Quinn
Eugene Patrick Devany
Dominick A. Piccininni, Jr.
William E. Morrissey
Marijane McQueeney
Thomas P. Lalor
Joseph M. Puzo
Stephen J. Molinelli
Amelia T. Walsh
Dennis J. Brady
Thomas J. Foley

OF COUNSEL

Raymond F. Condon (1910-1980)

Representative Clients: General Accident Fire & Life Assurance Co.; Kemper Insurance Cos.; The Royal Insurance Cos.; Allstate Insurance Co.; American International Group; Exxon Company, U.S.A.; Hertz Corp.; Metropolitan Suburban Bus Authority; Long Island Railroad.

For full biographical listings, see the Martindale-Hubbell Law Directory

MIDDLETOWN, Orange Co.

MACVEAN, LEWIS, SHERWIN & MCDERMOTT, P.C. (AV)

34 Grove Street, P.O. Box 310, 10940
Telephone: 914-343-3000
Fax: 914-343-3866

Kenneth A. MacVean
Kermit W. Lewis
Louis H. Sherwin
Paul T. McDermott
Jeffrey D. Sherwin

George F. Roesch, III
Michael F. McCusker
Thomas P. Clarke, Jr.

OF COUNSEL

V. Frank Cline

Counsel for: Orange County Trust Co.; Middletown Savings Bank; First Federal Savings & Loan Association of Middletown; Goshen Savings Bank; Advest Bank.

For Complete List of Firm Personnel, See General Section

For full biographical listings, see the Martindale-Hubbell Law Directory

MINEOLA,* Nassau Co.

JONES & JONES (AV)

286 Old Country Road, 11501
Telephone: 516-747-1141

MEMBERS OF FIRM

C. H. Tunnicliffe Jones (1900-1991)
Lawrence T. Jones

(See Next Column)

OF COUNSEL

Howard L. DeMott

Reference: Bank of New York, Long Island Region.

For full biographical listings, see the Martindale-Hubbell Law Directory

MURPHY, BARTOL & O'BRIEN (AV)

Formerly Murphy & Bartol
22 Jericho Turnpike, 11501
Telephone: 516-294-5100
Telecopier: 516-294-5385

MEMBERS OF FIRM

Patrick M. Murphy, Jr. (1938-1991)
Ernest T. Bartol
Kevin J. O'Brien

ASSOCIATES

Jeffrey P. Sharkey
Kathleen Godfrey Oldak
Jeffrey Robert D'Amico

OF COUNSEL

Gary F. Musiello (1952-1993)
William L. Maher
Robert M. Stein

Reference: Chemical Bank, Hempstead, N.Y.

For full biographical listings, see the Martindale-Hubbell Law Directory

NICOLINI & PARADISE (AV)

114 Old Country Road Suite 500, 11501
Telephone: 516-741-6355

MEMBERS OF FIRM

Anthony J. Nicolini
Vincent J. Paradise

Representative Clients: Long Island Railroad; NYS Liquidation Bureau; Avis Rent-A-Car System, Inc.; County of Nassau; Continental Excess & Select.

For full biographical listings, see the Martindale-Hubbell Law Directory

NEW YORK,* New York Co.

ANDERSON KILL OLICK & OSHINSKY, P.C. (AV)

1251 Avenue of the Americas, 10020-1182
Telephone: 212-278-1000
Cable Address: "Neweralaw New York"
Telex: WU 12-7022; WUI 66513.
Fax: 212-278-1733
Washington, D.C. Office: Anderson Kill Olick & Oshinsky, 2000 Pennsylvania Avenue, N.W., Suite 7500.
Telephone: 202-728-3100.
Fax: 202-728-3199.
Philadelphia, Pennsylvania Office: 1600 Market Street.
Telephone: 215-568-4202.
Fax: 215-568-4573.
Newark, New Jersey Office: One Gateway Center, Suite 0901.
Telephone: 201-642-5858.
Fax: 201-621-6361.
San Francisco, California Office: Citicorp Center, One Samsone Street, Suite 1610.
Telephone: 415-677-1450.
Fax: 415-677-1475.
New Haven, Connecticut Office: 59 Elm Street.
Telephone: 203-777-2230.
Fax: 203-777-9717.
Phoenix, Arizona Office: One Renaissance Square, Two North Central, Suite 1250.
Telephone: 602-252-0002.
Fax: 601-252-0003.

Edward P. Abbot
Lisa M. Anastos (Not admitted in NY)
Eugene R. Anderson
Peter J. Andrews
John B. Berringer
Chaim B. Book
Amy G. Borress-Glass
Stefan R. Boshkov
Martin F. Brecker
Ronald S. Brody
Mark M. Brown (Not admitted in NY)
Anna S. Chacko
Jordan M. Cohen
Leonard A. Cohen
Robin L. Cohen
Steven Cooper
Howard E. Cotton
Samantha S. Daniels
Jennifer W. Darger
Duncan N. Darrow
Risa F. Davis
Steven J. Dolmanisth
John H. Doyle, III
Stephen A. Dvorkin
David J. Egidi
David A. Einhorn
Bennett Ellenbogen
Jean M. Farrell
Wendy Ferber
Gloria J. Frank
John W. Fried
Karen L. Illuzzi Gallinari
John P. Gasior
Linda Gerstel
Ann S. Ginsberg
Jeffrey L. Glatzer
Michael S. Gordon
M. Beth Gorrie
Telma M. Grayson
Tara A. Griffin
John H. Gross
Michael Gurland
Philippa M. Haggar
Finley T. R. Harckham
Richard L. Hartz
Mary Angela Hawke
Sarah B. Hechtman
Robert M. Horkovich

(See Next Column)

ANDERSON KILL OLICK & OSHINSKY P.C., *New York—Continued*

Leslie Sue Howard
Shahan Islam
Raymond A. Joao
T. Michael Johnson
Laura V. Jones
Gabriella Jordan
Edward M. Joyce
Robert A. Karin
John H. Kazanjian
Michael J. Keane
R. Mark Keenan
Thomas L. Kent
Lawrence Kill
Mark E. Klein
Ann V. Kramer
Joan L. Lewis
Diane E. Lifton
Henry A. Lowet
Nestor P. Maddatu
Tracy Ellen Makow
Steven M. Manket
Susan M. Marotta
Raj Mehra
Jeffrey A. Moross
Avraham C. Moskowitz
Frank S. Occhipinti
Arthur S. Olick
Randy Paar
Susan G. Papano
William G. Passannante
Amalia Gisela Pena
Michelle Perez
Bennett Pine
Mayda Prego
Anthony Princi
J. Andrew Rahl, Jr.
Jane Revellino
David Garfield Roland
Harry Rothenberg
Lia B. Royle
Melvin Salberg
Seth B. Schafler
David M. Schlecker
David J. Schwartz
Lori C. Seegers
Edan Dawn Segal
Irving Shafran
Jordan W. Siev
Mark D. Silverschotz
James Walker Smith
Neal S. Smolar
Erik T. Sorensen
A. Thomas Southwick
Jay B. Spievack
Michael W. Stamm
Kevin N. Starkey
Eric D. Statman
Robert J. Stevens
Charles Addison Stewart, III
Catherine M. (Kay) Stockwell
Irene C. Warshauer
Margaret Armstrong Weiner
Mark L. Weyman
John P. Winsbro
Judith A. Yavitz
Nazim Zilkha
Jean E. Zimmerman
Nicholas J. Zoogman

OF COUNSEL

Roy Babitt
Richard W. Collins
Dona Seeman Kahn
Melvin S. Slade
David Toren

For full biographical listings, see the Martindale-Hubbell Law Directory

ARKIN SCHAFFER & SUPINO (AV)

1370 Avenue of the Americas, 10019
Telephone: 212-333-0200
Fax: 212-333-2350
Los Angeles, California Office: 10940 Wilshire Blvd., Suite 700. 90024-3902.
Telephone: 310-443-7689.
Fax: 310-443-7599.

Stanley S. Arkin
Hyman L. Schaffer
Anthony M. Supino

OF COUNSEL

Jeffrey M. Kaplan

ASSOCIATES

Katherine E. Hargrove
Joseph Lee Matalon
Barry S. Pollack (Resident, Los Angeles, California Office)
Harry B. Feder
Marc S. Ullman

For full biographical listings, see the Martindale-Hubbell Law Directory

GLENN BACKER (AV)

292 Madison Avenue, 10017
Telephone: 212-686-7644
Fax: 212-683-1394

For full biographical listings, see the Martindale-Hubbell Law Directory

BAER MARKS & UPHAM (AV)

A Partnership including a Professional Corporation
805 Third Avenue, 10022
Telephone: 212-702-5700
Fax: 212-702-5941
Cable Address: "Julibaer"; "Sellew"

Howard Graff
Eugene R. Scheiman

For Complete List of Firm Personnel, See General Section

For full biographical listings, see the Martindale-Hubbell Law Directory

BAKER & BOTTS, L.L.P. (AV)

885 Third Avenue Suite 2000, 10022
Telephone: 212-705-5000
Fax: 212-705-5125
Washington, D.C. Office: The Warner, 1299 Pennsylvania Avenue, N.W.
Telephone: 202-639-7700.
Austin, Texas Office: 1600 San Jacinto Center, 98 San Jacinto Boulevard.
Telephone: 512-322-2500.

(See Next Column)

Dallas, Texas Office: 2001 Ross Avenue.
Telephone: 214-953-6500.
Houston, Texas Office: One Shell Plaza, 910 Louisiana.
Telephone: 713-229-1234.
Moscow, Russian Federation Office: 10 ul. Pushkinskaya, 103031.
Telephone: 7095/921-5300 (Local); 7095/929-7070 (International).

MEMBERS OF FIRM

Kenneth M. Bialo
Henry B. Gutman
Kerry L. Konrad

OF COUNSEL

Bertram Perkel

ASSOCIATES

Karen F. Conway
C. Ben Garren
Michael A. Lippert
Jeffrey E. Ostrow

For Complete List of Firm Personnel, See General Section

For full biographical listings, see the Martindale-Hubbell Law Directory

PAUL A. BATISTA A PROFESSIONAL CORPORATION (AV)

950 Third Avenue, Suite 3200, 10022
Telephone: 212-980-0070
Telecopier: 212-758-2809

Paul A. Batista

For full biographical listings, see the Martindale-Hubbell Law Directory

BEATIE, KING & ABATE (AV)

599 Lexington Avenue, Suite 1300, 10022
Telephone: 212-888-9000
Fax: 212-888-9664

Russel H. Beatie, Jr.
Kenneth J. King
Samuel J. Abate, Jr.

ASSOCIATES

Susan Kelty Law
Charna L. Gerstenhaber
Eric J. Gruber
Philip J. Miller
Peter S. Liaskos
W.H. Ramsay Lewis

For full biographical listings, see the Martindale-Hubbell Law Directory

BECKMAN & MILLMAN, P.C. (AV)

116 John Street, 10038
Telephone: 212-227-6777
Telecopier: 212-227-1486
Midtown Office: 666 Fifth Avenue, New York, New York 10103.

Michael Beckman
Debra J. Millman

For full biographical listings, see the Martindale-Hubbell Law Directory

BELDOCK LEVINE & HOFFMAN (AV)

99 Park Avenue, 10016-1502
Telephone: 212-490-0400
Cable Address: "Telhofflaw, N.Y."
Telecopier: 212-557-0565

MEMBERS OF FIRM

Lee F. Bantle
Myron Beldock
Karen L. Dippold
Elliot L. Hoffman
Lawrence S. Levine
Jon B. Levison
Brian E. Maas
Melvin L. Wulf

Daniel M. Kummer
James Rielly

OF COUNSEL

Cynthia Rollings

For full biographical listings, see the Martindale-Hubbell Law Directory

BIGHAM ENGLAR JONES & HOUSTON (AV)

14 Wall Street, 10005-2140
Telephone: 212-732-4646
Cable: "Kedge"
RCA Telex: 235332 BEJHUR
Telefax: 2126190781 GR I II III; 2122279491 GR I II III
London, England Office: Lloyd's Suite 699, 1 Lime Street.
Telephone: 71-283-9541.
Telex: 893323 BEJH G.
Telefax: 016262382 GR I II III.
Newark, New Jersey Office: One Gateway Center.
Telephone: 201-643-1303.
Telecopier: 201-643-1124.
Washington, D.C. Office: 1919 Pennsylvania Avenue, N.W., Suite 300.
Telephone: 202-736-2150.
Telefax: 202-223-6739.
Long Beach, California Office: 301 Ocean Boulevard, Suite 800.
Telephone: 310-437-5155.
Telefax: 310-495-3273.

(See Next Column)

BIGHAM ENGLAR JONES & HOUSTON—*Continued*

MEMBERS OF FIRM

Douglas A. Jacobsen
Joseph A. Kilbourn
James J. Taylor
James B. McQuillan
James S. McMahon, Jr.
John T. Kochendorfer
Louis G. Juliano
Jay Levine
George R. Daly
John E. Cone, Jr.
John MacCrate, III
Francis A. Montbach
Robert J. Phillips, Jr.
Stephen M. Marcusa
William R. Connor, III
Robert E. Hirsch
Thomas R. Pattison
Marilyn L. Lytle
Peter I. Broeman
Donald T. Rave, Jr.
William C. Brown, III
Adrian Mecz (Resident, London, England Office)
Helen M. Benzie
Chris Christofides
Paul Ambos
Lawrence B. Brennan
Martin J. Flannery, Jr.
John V. Coulter, Jr.
Karin A. Schlosser
Martin J. Nilsen

COUNSEL

Laurence W. Levine
William P. Sullivan, Jr.

ASSOCIATES

George S. Evans, Jr.
Aileen J. Fox
Frederick A. Lovejoy
Frank G. Sinatra
Stacey Tranchina

For Complete List of Firm Personnel, See General Section

For full biographical listings, see the Martindale-Hubbell Law Directory

BROWN RAYSMAN & MILLSTEIN (AV)

120 West Forty-Fifth Street, 10036
Telephone: 212-944-1515
Fax: 212-840-2429
Los Angeles, California Office: 550 South Hope Street, 20th Floor.
Telephone: 213-624-1616.
Fax: 213-624-4663.
Hartford, Connecticut Office: City Place I, 185 Asylum Street.
Telephone: 203-769-6810.
Fax: 203-769-6816.
Newark, New Jersey Office: One Gateway Center.
Telephone: 201-596-1480.
Fax: 201-622-3317.

MEMBERS OF FIRM

Richard Raysman
Peter Brown
Julian S. Millstein
Michael Hirschberg
Barry G. Felder
Sylvia Khatcherian
Jeffrey B. Steiner
Robert M. Unger
Edward A. Pisacreta
Scott A. Steinberg
Gerard R. Boyce
Kenneth M. Block
Catherine M. McGrath
John H. Reid (Resident, Los Angeles, California)
Dan C. Aardal (Resident, Los Angeles, California)
Thomas C. Clark (Resident, Hartford, Connecticut)

COUNSEL

Michael A. Gerber
Michael I. Chakansky
Gabriela P. Cacuci

ASSOCIATES

John J. Lynch
John S. Rosania (Resident, Hartford, Connecticut)
George S. Trisciuzzi
James K. Landau
Paul J. Pollock
Kenneth A. Adler
Rand G. Boyers
Bruce A. Levy
Jeffrey D. Neuburger
Andrew L. Kramer
Melanie Finkel
Scott A. Weinberg
Robert Anthony Miller
Dov H. Scherzer
Nicholas Tanelli
Jeffrey P. Weingart
John C. Eichenberger
Nanette Claire Heide
David P. Stich
Robert R. Kiesel
Joseph William Chouinard
Susan B. Kalman (Resident, Los Angeles Office)
John C. Ohman
Martin Hillery
T. Anthony Howell
Catherine Termini
Horace H. Ng
Morlan Ty Rogers

For full biographical listings, see the Martindale-Hubbell Law Directory

CALLAN, REGENSTREICH, KOSTER & BRADY (AV)

One Whitehall Street 10th Floor, 10004
Telephone: 212-248-8800
Fax: 212-248-6815
Shrewsbury, New Jersey Office: 179 Avenue of the Common, P.O. Box 7413.
Telephone: 908-389-8400.

MEMBERS OF FIRM

Paul F. Callan
Bruce N. Regenstreich
Warren S. Koster
Bruce M. Brady
Angela M. Zito
William L. Brennan
Richard D. Meadow

(See Next Column)

ASSOCIATES

Jennifer M. Woodward
Scott W. Bermack
Kenneth S. Merber
Dorothy Spinelli (Not admitted in NY)
Michael P. Kandler
Neva M. Hoffmaier
Kathleen A. Ianno
Elyse Cohen Wolfe
Walter Paterson Burrell
Raymond G. H. Waugh, Jr.
Lisa R. DeMarzo (Not admitted in NY)
Beth S. Block
Kurt E. Reinheimer (Not admitted in NY)
Vincent A. Nagler
Melissa A. Cohn
Michael I. Braverman

For full biographical listings, see the Martindale-Hubbell Law Directory

CAPLIN & DRYSDALE, CHARTERED (AV)

399 Park Avenue, 10022
Telephone: 212-319-7125
Fax: 212-644-6755
Washington, D.C. Office: One Thomas Circle, N.W.
Telephone: 202-862-5000.
Fax: 202-429-3301.

Elihu Inselbuch
C. Sanders McNew
Christian R. Pastore

For full biographical listings, see the Martindale-Hubbell Law Directory

JACQUES CATAFAGO (AV)

Suite 4710, 350 5th Avenue, 10018
Telephone: 212-239-9669
Facsimile: 212-239-9688

ASSOCIATES

George E. Sermier (Not admitted in NY)
Thomas Coppola
Lawrence R. Lonergan

OF COUNSEL

Nadienne Vincent Catafago

For full biographical listings, see the Martindale-Hubbell Law Directory

COSTELLO, SHEA & GAFFNEY (AV)

One Battery Park Plaza, 10004
Telephone: 212-483-9600
Fax: 212-344-7680

MEMBERS OF FIRM

Joseph M. Costello
Mortimer C. Shea
Frederick N. Gaffney
Steven E. Garry
William A. Goldstein
Donald J. Scialabba
Paul E. Blutman
Alan T. Blutman

ASSOCIATES

Robert R. Arena
Edward S. Benson
J Mcgarry Costello
Mario J. DiRe
Leo V. Duval, III
Cathy Ann Gallagher
Jozef K. Goscilo
Adam Charles Kandell
Timothy M. McCann
Kevin B. McHugh
Samuel Mark Mizrahi
Margaret Sullivan O'Connell
Manuel Ortega
John F. Parker
Neil B. Ptashnik
David Schrager
Lydia P. Shure
David N. Zane
Craig F. Wilson
Brian G. Winter

OF COUNSEL

James F. Corcoran

For full biographical listings, see the Martindale-Hubbell Law Directory

CURTIS, MALLET-PREVOST, COLT & MOSLE (AV)

101 Park Avenue, 10178
Telephone: 212-696-6000
Telecopier: 212-697-1559
Cable Address: "Migniar d New York"
Telex: 12-6811 Migniard; ITT 422127 MGND
Washington, D.C. Office: Suite 1205 L, 1801 K Street, N.W.
Telephone: 202-452-7373.
Telecopier: 202-452-7333.
Telex: ITT 440379 CMPUI.
Newark, New Jersey Office: One Gateway Center, Suite 403.
Telephone: 201-622-0605.
Telecopier: 201-622-5646.
Houston, Texas Office: 2 Houston Center, 909 Fannin Street, Suite 3725.
Telephone: 713-759-9555.
Telecopier: 713-759-0712.
Mexico City, D.F., Mexico Office: Torre Chapultepec, Ruben Dario 281, Col. Bosques de Chapultepec, 11530 Mexico, D.F.
Telephone: 525-282-0444.
Telecopier: 525-282-0637.
Paris, France Office: 8 Avenue Victor Hugo.
Telephone: 45-00-99-68.
Telecopier: 45-00-84-06.
London, England Office: Two Throgmorton Avenue, EC2N 2DL.
Telephone: 71-638-7957.
Telecopier: 71-638-5512.

(See Next Column)

CURTIS, MALLET-PREVOST, COLT & MOSLE, *New York—Continued*

Frankfurt am Main 1 Office: Staufenstrasse 42.
Telephone: 069-971-4420.
Telecopier: 69-17 33 99.

MEMBERS OF FIRM

Peter E. Fleming, Jr.
T. Barry Kingham
Eliot Lauer
Robert S. Lipton
Joseph D. Pizzurro
Benard V. Preziosi, Jr.
Turner P. Smith
Martin Wendel (Resident Partner, Newark, New Jersey Office)

SPECIAL COUNSEL

Jan Marcantonio

ASSOCIATES

Harold J. Bacon
Joseph F. Clyne
Michelle A. Rice

For Complete List of Firm Personnel, See General Section

For full biographical listings, see the Martindale-Hubbell Law Directory

D'AMATO & LYNCH (AV)

70 Pine Street, 10270
Telephone: 212-269-0927
Cable Address: "Damcosh"
Telex: 960085 DCOS UI NYK
Telefax: 212-269-3559

MEMBERS OF FIRM

George G. D'Amato
Luke D. Lynch
Peter J. Thumser
Robert M. Makla
Kenneth A. Sagat
Howard Wildman
John J. Cullen
Luke D. Lynch, Jr.
Richard George
Richard F. Russell
Robert E. Kushner
Robert W. Lang
Neal M. Glazer
John P. Higgins
Andrew R. Simmonds
Thomas F. Breen
Alfred A. D'Agostino, Jr.
Mary Jo Barry
David A. Boyar
Barbara R. Seymour
John H. FitzSimons
Thomas Ward Hanlon, Jr.
Bill V. Kakoullis
William P. Larsen, III
Ronald H. Alenstein
Harry J. Arnold, Jr.
Philip J. Bergan

ASSOCIATES

Timothy C. Baldwin
Michael V. Baronio
Laurie P. Beatus
Frances Buckley
Nancy M. Cagan
Carla S. Caliendo
Kevin P. Carroll
Liza A. Chafiian
James D. Christo
Deborah M. Collins
Mary Lee Cunningham
Theodore Deliyannis
Michael J. Devereaux
Jeffrey J. Diecidue
John R. Edwards
Terri Green Fagan
Paul A. Ferrillo
Jeffrey R. Gaylord
John A. Goldenberg
Lloyd J. Herman
Donna Marie Hughes
Stephen Hymes
Susanne Mast Murray
Sharon A. McCloskey
Kenneth David Milbauer
Marie L. Monaco
Neil R. Morrison
Samuel F. Paniccia
Polly Schiavone
Gino D. Serpe
Lisa L. Shrewsberry
James I. Stempel
Peter A. Stroili
Maryann Taylor
Stephen F. Willig
Kevin J. Windels
Robert M. Yellen

COUNSEL

Robert E. Gilroy
Jerome Murray
Harvey Barrison
James M. Condon
Charles H. Witherwax
Richard G. McGahren

For full biographical listings, see the Martindale-Hubbell Law Directory

DEBEVOISE & PLIMPTON (AV)

875 Third Avenue, 10022
Telephone: 212-909-6000
Domestic Telex: 148377 DEBSTEVE NYK
Telecopier: (212) 909-6836
Los Angeles, California Office: 601 South Figueroa Street, Suite 3700, 90017.
Telephone: 213-680-8000.
Telecopier: 213-680-8100.
Washington, D.C. Office: 555 13th Street, N.W., 20004.
Telephone: 202-383-8000.
Telecopier: (202) 383-8118.
Paris, France Office: 21 Avenue George V 75008.
Telephone: (33-1) 40 73 12 12.
Telecopier: (33-1) 47 20 50 82.
Telex: 648141F DPPAR.
London, England Office: 1 Creed Court, 5 Ludgate Hill, EC4M 7AA.
Telephone: (44-171) 329-0779.
Telex: 88 4569 DPLON G.
Telecopier: (44-171) 329-0860.

(See Next Column)

Budapest, Hungary Office: 1065 Budapest, Révay Köz 2.III/2.
Telephone: (36-1)112-8067.
Telecopier: (36-1) 132-7995.
Hong Kong Office: 13/F Entertainment Building, 30 Queen's Road Central.
Telephone: (852) 2810-7918.
Fax: (852) 2810-9828.

MEMBERS OF FIRM

Andrew C. Hartzell, Jr.
Judah Best (Washington, D.C. Office)
Robert L. King (Los Angeles, California Office)
Standish Forde Medina, Jr.
John H. Hall
John G. Koeltl
Ralph C. Ferrara (Washington, D.C. Office)
Martin Frederic Evans
Roger E. Podesta
Loren Kieve (Washington, D.C. Office)
Bruce G. Merritt (Los Angeles, California Office)
Robert N. Shwartz
Steven Klugman
Michael E. Wiles
Daniel M. Abuhoff
Bruce P. Keller
John S. Kiernan
David W. Rivkin
Edwin G. Schallert
Joseph P. Moodhe
Donald Francis Donovan
Lorna G. Schofield
Anne E. Cohen
Bruce E. Yannett

OF COUNSEL

Robert B. von Mehren

RETIRED PARTNER

Robert J. Geniesse (Washington, D.C. Office)

For Complete List of Firm Personnel, See General Section

For full biographical listings, see the Martindale-Hubbell Law Directory

DEBLASIO & ALTON, P.C. (AV)

Woolworth Building, 233 Broadway, 10279
Telephone: 212-732-2620
Fax: 212-571-2045

Peter E. DeBlasio
Walter G. Alton, Jr.
Steven A. Epstein
Rhoda Grossberg Faller
Stephen S. La Rocca

For full biographical listings, see the Martindale-Hubbell Law Directory

DANIEL DONNELLY (AV)

521 Fifth Avenue Suite 1740, 10175
Telephone: 212-757-6454
Garrison, New York Office: Garrison's Landing, P.O. Box 253. 10524.
Telephone: 914-424-3877.
Facsimile: 914-424-3968

For full biographical listings, see the Martindale-Hubbell Law Directory

DUKER & BARRETT (AV)

1585 Broadway, 10036
Telephone: 212-969-5600
Telecopy: 212-969-5650
Albany, New York Office: 100 State Street.
Telephone: 518-434-0600.
Telecopy: 518-434-0665.

David A. Barrett
William F. Duker
Richard L. Crisona
Rodney L. Stenlake
George F. Carpinello
Nicholas A. Gravante, Jr.

OF COUNSEL

Gary K. Harris (Not admitted in NY)
Robert B. Silver
Michael Straus
Jack G. Stern
Karen Caudill Dyer (Not admitted in NY)
Tracey Lynn Altman

Christopher Allegaert
Cynthia Goldman
Kenneth G. Alberstadt
Richard S. Laudor
David A. Berger
Laura A. Hastings
Richard A. Schwartz
Janine Marie Gargiulo
Michael S. Vogel
Scott W. Dales
Rebecca L. Fine

For full biographical listings, see the Martindale-Hubbell Law Directory

EMMET, MARVIN & MARTIN, LLP (AV)

120 Broadway, 10271
Telephone: 212-238-3000
Cable Address: EMMARRO
Fax: 212-238-3100
Morristown, New Jersey Office: 10 Madison Avenue.
Telephone: 201-538-5600.
Fax: 201-538-6448.

MEMBERS OF FIRM

Thomas B. Fenlon
Thomas F. Noone (P.C.)
Lawrence B. Thompson
William A. Leet
David M. Daly
Peter B. Tisne
Michael C. Johansen
Robert W. Viets

(See Next Column)

EMMET, MARVIN & MARTIN LLP—*Continued*

MEMBERS OF FIRM (Continued)

Dennis C. Fleischmann
Eric M. Reuben
Jeffrey S. Chavkin
J. Christopher Eagan
Jesse Dudley B. Kimball
Stephen P. Cerow
Ellen J. Bickal
Edward P. Zujkowski
John P. Uehlinger
Irving C. Apar
Julian A. McQuiston
Maria-Liisa Lydon
Christine B. Cesare
Patrick A. McCartney
Matthew P. D'Amico
Brian D. Obergfell

OF COUNSEL

Guy B. Capel
Bernard F. Joyce (P.C.)
Richard P. Bourgerie
George H. P. Dwight

ASSOCIATES

Eunice M. O'Neill
Joseph M. Samulski
Sean M. Carlin
Alfred W. J. Marks
Eileen Chin-Bow
John M. Ryan
Francine M. Kors
Wendy E. Kramer
James C. Hughes, IV
Patricia C. Caputo
Bennett E. Josselsohn
Stephen I. Frank
Mildred Quinones
Anthony M. Harvin
Lynn D. Barsamian
Margaret H. Walker
Robert L. Morgan
Sally Shreeves
Michael Fotios Mavrides
Matthew A. Wieland
Eric E. Schneck (Resident, Morristown Office)
Lisa B. Lerner
Elizabeth K. Somers
Steven M. Berg
Michael E. Cavanaugh
Nancy J. Cohen
Peter L. Mancini
Stephen M. Ksenak

For full biographical listings, see the Martindale-Hubbell Law Directory

EVANS, ORR, LAFFAN, TORRES & DEMAGGIO, P.C. (AV)

225 Broadway, Suite 1405, 10007-3001
Telephone: 212-267-1800
FAX: 212-964-0958
Long Island Office: 25 Jackson Avenue, Syosset, 11791.
Telephone: 516-364-0300.

Walter G. Evans (1886-1981)
William F. Laffan, Jr.
Frank Torres
David DeMaggio

Seymour I. Yanofsky
Eugene Guarneri
Angelantonio Bianchi
Cari E. Pepkin
Maura V. Laffan
Christian A. Rofrano
Paula T. Amsterdam
Donald G. Derrico
Patricia Ann Cavagnaro
Thomas P. Ryan, Jr.
Lambert C Sheng
Richard Fama

OF COUNSEL

Steven DeMaggio

OF COUNSEL EMERITUS

Alexander Orr, Jr.
Alfred V. Norton, Jr.
Edward J. Pacelli

LEGAL SUPPORT PERSONNEL

PARALEGALS

Alicia Carrano
Susan Dunphy
Damian L. Calemmo
Diana L. Cohen

For full biographical listings, see the Martindale-Hubbell Law Directory

SANDOR FRANKEL, P.C. (AV)

230 Park Avenue, 10169
Telephone: 212-661-5000
Fax: 212-661-5007

Sandor Frankel
Stuart E. Abrams
Al J. Daniel, Jr.

For full biographical listings, see the Martindale-Hubbell Law Directory

FRIEDMAN & KAPLAN (AV)

875 Third Avenue, 10022-6225
Telephone: 212-833-1100
Telecopier: 212-355-6401

MEMBERS OF FIRM

Bruce S. Kaplan
Edward A. Friedman
Eric Seiler
Robert D. Kaplan
Gary D. Friedman
Andrew W. Goldwater
Lisa Gersh Hall
Robert J. Lack
Daniel M. Taitz
Hal Neier

ASSOCIATES

Philippe Adler
Marilyn Woroner Fisch
Lance J. Gotko
Matthew S. Haiken
Ellen A. Harnick
Edward Rubin
Katharine L. Sonnenberg
Cameron A. Stracher
Barry E. Warner
Marla J. Wasserman
Daniel R. Zenkel

For full biographical listings, see the Martindale-Hubbell Law Directory

AEGIS J. FRUMENTO (AV)

805 Third Avenue Suite 2800, 10022
Telephone: 212-888-8288
TeleFax: 212-759-7080
(Also Member, Flott Rosner & O'Brien)

For full biographical listings, see the Martindale-Hubbell Law Directory

GAIR, GAIR, CONASON, STEIGMAN & MACKAUF (AV)

80 Pine Street, 10005
Telephone: 212-943-1090

MEMBERS OF FIRM

Harry A. Gair (1894-1975)
Robert L. Conason
Herbert H. Hirschhorn
Seymour Boyers
Herman Schmertz
Ernest R. Steigman
Stephen H. Mackauf
Warren J. Willinger
Ronald Berson
Jerome I. Katz
David G. Miller
Candice Singer Ram
Jeffrey B. Bloom
Anthony H. Gair
Mary Nicholls
Gayle F. Bertoldo
Vincent F. Maher
Robert E. Godosky
Rick S. Conason
Ben B. Rubinowitz
Rhonda E. Kay

COUNSEL

Harriet E. Gair

For full biographical listings, see the Martindale-Hubbell Law Directory

GINSBERG & BROOME (AV)

225 Broadway, Suite 3105, 10007
Telephone: 212-227-4225

Robert M. Ginsberg
Alvin H. Broome

ASSOCIATE

Michael Finkelstein

For full biographical listings, see the Martindale-Hubbell Law Directory

MAX E. GREENBERG, TRAGER, TOPLITZ & HERBST (AV)

100 Church Street, 10007
Telephone: 212-267-5700
Telecopier: 212-267-5814
West Orange, New Jersey Office: 200 Executive Drive West.
Telephone: 201-641-3110.
Fax: 201-731-0163.
Staten Island, New York Office: 1688 Victory Boulevard.
Telephone: 718-981-6335.
Fax: 718-981-6386.

Max E. Greenberg (1894-1980)
Murray B. Trayman (1903-1988)

MEMBERS OF FIRM

David A. Trager
George N. Toplitz
Leonard Shabasson
Todd L. Herbst
Kalvin Kamien
Mark A. Rosen
John M. Cilmi

ASSOCIATES

Regina C. Saat
Ira C. Wellen
Robert H. Schlosser
Allison Essner
Joseph G. Portela

For full biographical listings, see the Martindale-Hubbell Law Directory

GUSRAE, KAPLAN & BRUNO (AV)

120 Wall Street, 10005
Telephone: 212-269-1400

MEMBERS OF FIRM

Mark J. Astarita
Cirino M. Bruno
Melvyn J. Falis
Martin H. Kaplan
Robert Perez

ASSOCIATES

Richard A. Friedman
Bradford L. Jacobowitz
Shirley Kaplan
Thomas A. Rigilano

OF COUNSEL

David Greene
Bert L. Gusrae

For full biographical listings, see the Martindale-Hubbell Law Directory

HARLEY & BROWNE (AV)

18 East 41st Street, 10017
Telephone: 212-545-7900

MEMBERS OF FIRM

J. Austin Browne
Robert G. Harley
Bridget Asaro

Robert E. Fein

(See Next Column)

HARLEY & BROWNE, *New York—Continued*

OF COUNSEL

Richard H. Dreyfuss

Reference: Chemical Bank.

For full biographical listings, see the Martindale-Hubbell Law Directory

HUTTON INGRAM YUZEK GAINEN CARROLL & BERTOLOTTI (AV)

250 Park Avenue, 10177
Telephone: 212-907-9600
Facsimile: 212-907-9681

MEMBERS OF FIRM

Ernest J. Bertolotti
Daniel L. Carroll
Roger Cukras
Larry F. Gainen
G. Thompson Hutton
Samuel W. Ingram, Jr.
Paulette Kendler
Steven Mastbaum
Dean G. Yuzek
David G. Ebert
Shane O'Neill

ASSOCIATES

Warren E. Friss
Patricia Hewitt
Gail A. Buchman
Stuart A. Christie
Beth N. Green
Timish K. Hnateyko
Jeanne F. Pucci
Jane Drummey
Adam L. Sifre
Susan Ann Fennelly
Marc J. Schneider

For full biographical listings, see the Martindale-Hubbell Law Directory

JACOBSON & TRIGGS (AV)

52 Duane Street, 10007
Telephone: 212-791-3600
Telecopier: 212-791-3607

MEMBERS OF FIRM

John F. Triggs
Gary S. Jacobson
Kristine M. Reddington

OF COUNSEL

Susan C. Lushing

For full biographical listings, see the Martindale-Hubbell Law Directory

JOHNSTON & MCSHANE, P.C. (AV)

Graybar Building, 420 Lexington Avenue, 10170
Telephone: 212-972-5252
Facsimilie: 212-697-2737

William R. Johnston
Bruce W. McShane
Peter F. Breheny

Dennis W. Grogan
Arthur J. Smith
Kenneth E. Moffett, Jr.
Andrew Ross
Robert D. Donahue
James M. Carman

OF COUNSEL

Charles A. Miller, II (Not admitted in NY)

For full biographical listings, see the Martindale-Hubbell Law Directory

BONNIE P. JOSEPHS (AV)

1414 Avenue of the Americas, 10019
Telephone: 212-644-5712

For full biographical listings, see the Martindale-Hubbell Law Directory

JULIEN & SCHLESINGER, P.C. (AV)

150 William Street, 19th Floor, 10038
Telephone: 212-962-8020

Alfred S. Julien (1910-1989)
Stuart A. Schlesinger
Denise Mortner Kranz
Ira M. Newman
David B. Turret

OF COUNSEL

Louis Fusco, Jr.

Mary Elizabeth Burns
Richard A. Robbins
Michael J. Taub
Marla L. Schiff
Alvin Craig Gordon
Adam Schlesinger
Robert J. Epstein

For full biographical listings, see the Martindale-Hubbell Law Directory

KENNY & STEARNS (AV)

26 Broadway, 10004
Telephone: 212-422-6111
FAX: 212-422-6544
Newark, New Jersey Office: 56 Park Place.
Telephone: 201-624-7779.

(See Next Column)

MEMBERS OF FIRM

James M. Kenny
Joseph T. Stearns
Stephen J. Buckley

William J. Manning, Jr.
Gino A. Zonghetti
Matthew Patrick McCloskey

For full biographical listings, see the Martindale-Hubbell Law Directory

KING, PAGANO & HARRISON (AV)

425 Park Avenue, 10022
Telephone: 212-223-4000
FAX: 212-223-4134
Washington, D.C. Office: 901 Fifteenth Street, N.W.
Telephone: 202-371-6550.
FAX: 202-371-6770.

MEMBERS OF FIRM

Jeffrey W. King (Not admitted in NY)
Jeffrey W. Pagano
Keith J. Harrison
James E. Kellett
Steven Schaars (Not admitted in NY; Resident, Washington, D.C. Office)

ASSOCIATES

Herbert I. Meyer
Ira M. Saxe
Sharyn L. Bernstein
Bethany A. Cook

Representative Clients: Brink's Inc.; Burlington Air Express; The Pittston Co.; The Union Corp.; Philadelphia National Bank; Kaiser Permanente; Medica; Del Laboratories; E-Systems; Renaissance International Hotels and Resorts; Group Health Association of America; Capital Credit Corp.

For full biographical listings, see the Martindale-Hubbell Law Directory

KOPFF, NARDELLI & DOPF (AV)

440 Ninth Avenue, 10001
Telephone: 212-244-2999
Telecopier: 212-643-0862

MEMBERS OF FIRM

Peter C. Kopff
Camillo Nardelli (1936-1987)
Glenn W. Dopf
Scott F. Morgan
Charles K. Faillace
Joseph R. Cammarosano
Victoria A. Lombardi
Michael L. Manci
Martin B. Adams

ASSOCIATES

Eugene A. Ward
Mary E. Pearson
Joseph T. Belevich
Catherine R. Richter
Susan D. Noble
John A. Orbon
Denise D. Sapanara
Ronnie Michelle Grill
Richard J. Valent
Edward J. Arevalo
Edward A. Flores
Peter S. Williams
Tara K. Curcillo
Jonathan Adam Judd

Representative Clients: Aetna Casualty and Surety Co.; American International Group; Citicorp, U.S.A.; County of Nassau, State of New York; Franklin Hospital Medical Center; Guarantee National Insurance Co.; Lenox Hill Hospital; The May Department Stores Co.; Medical Inter-Insurance Exchange of New Jersey; Medical Liability Mutual Insurance Co.

For full biographical listings, see the Martindale-Hubbell Law Directory

KRAMER, LEVIN, NAFTALIS, NESSEN, KAMIN & FRANKEL (AV)

919 Third Avenue, 10022
Telephone: 212-715-9100
Cable Address: "Nickral"
TWX: 710 581-5340
Telex: 645041
Telecopier: 212-688-2119

MEMBERS OF FIRM

Arthur H. Aufses III
Michael J. Dell
Charlotte Moses Fischman
David S. Frankel
Marvin E. Frankel
Alan R. Friedman
Robert M. Heller
Arthur B. Kramer
Thomas H. Moreland
Ellen R. Nadler
Gary P. Naftalis
Maurice N. Nessen
Michael S. Oberman
Jeffrey S. Trachtman
Harold P. Weinberger

SPECIAL COUNSEL

Debora K. Grobman
Jonathan M. Wagner

ASSOCIATES

Philip Bentley
Jeffrey W. Davis
Ronald S. Greenberg
Mark J. Headley

For Complete List of Firm Personnel, See General Section

For full biographical listings, see the Martindale-Hubbell Law Directory

New York—Continued

LAVIN, COLEMAN, FINARELLI & GRAY (AV Ⓣ)

780 Third Avenue Suite 1401, 10017
Telephone: 212-319-6898
Fax: 212-319-6932
Philadelphia, Pennsylvania Office: 12th Floor, Penn Mutual Tower, 510 Walnut Street.
Telephone: 215-627-0303.
Fax: 215-627-2551.
Mount Laurel, New Jersey Office: 10000 Midlantic Drive, Suite 300 West.
Telephone: 609-778-5544.
Fax: 609-778-3383.

William J. Ricci (Not admitted in NY)
Edward A. Gray (Not admitted in NY)
Joseph A. McGinley
Michael D. Brophy

John Kieran Daly
Steven R. Kramer
Joseph F. Dunne

For full biographical listings, see the Martindale-Hubbell Law Directory

LEVENTHAL SLADE & KRANTZ (AV)

777 Third Avenue, 10017
Telephone: 212-935-0800
Fax: 212-207-8256

MEMBERS OF FIRM

Melvyn R. Leventhal
Jeffrey C. Slade
Larry H. Krantz

ASSOCIATES

Laura F. Dukess
Marjorie E. Berman
Maryanne Yen
Thomas Bartlett Wilinsky

For full biographical listings, see the Martindale-Hubbell Law Directory

LIDDLE, ROBINSON & SHOEMAKER (AV)

685 Third Avenue, 10017
Telephone: 212-687-8500
Telecopier: 212-687-1505

MEMBERS OF FIRM

Samuel Finkelstein (Retired)
Jeffrey L. Liddle
Miriam M. Robinson
Paul T. Shoemaker
Laurence S. Moy
W. Dan Boone

ASSOCIATES

James A. Batson
Blaine H. Bortnick
Ethan A. Brecher
Linda A. Danovitch
Jeffrey A. Koslowsky
Douglas A. Lopp

For full biographical listings, see the Martindale-Hubbell Law Directory

LITMAN, ASCHE, LUPKIN, GIOIELLA & BASSIN (AV)

45 Broadway Atrium, 10006
Telephone: 212-809-4500
Telecopier: GP II, III (212) 509-8403

MEMBERS OF FIRM

Richard M. Asche
Jack T. Litman
Stanley N. Lupkin
Russell M. Gioiella
Steven Jay Bassin

ASSOCIATES

Mary Lou Chatterton
Frederick L. Sosinsky

OF COUNSEL

Alan C. Rothfeld
Ronald S. Pohl

For full biographical listings, see the Martindale-Hubbell Law Directory

LOEB AND LOEB (AV)

A Partnership including Professional Corporations
345 Park Avenue, 10154-0037
Telephone: 212-407-4000
Facsimile: 212-407-4990
Los Angeles, California Office: Suite 1800, 1000 Wilshire Boulevard, 90017-2475.
Telephone: 213-688-3400.
Cable Address: "Loband LSA".
Telecopier: 213-688-3460; 688-3461; 688-3462.
Century City (Los Angeles), California Office: Suite 2200, 10100 Santa Monica Boulevard, Los Angeles, 90067-4164.
Telephone: 310-282-2000.
Telecopier: 310-282-2191; 282-2192.
Nashville, Tennessee Office: 45 Music Square West, 37203-3205.
Telephone: 615-749-8300.
Facsimile: 615-749-8308.
Rome, Italy Office: Piazza Digione 1, 00197.
Telephone: 011-396-808-8456.
Telecopier: 011-396-674-8223.

(See Next Column)

MEMBERS OF FIRM

John F. Lang
Charles H. Miller
Martin R. Pollner
David M. Satnick
David B. Shontz
Michael P. Zweig

OF COUNSEL

Harry First

ASSOCIATES

Paula K. Colbath
Robert B. Rosen
Laurie S. Ruckel
Roni Schneider
Terri J. Seligman
Rebecca E. White

For Complete List of Firm Personnel, See General Section

For full biographical listings, see the Martindale-Hubbell Law Directory

LONDON FISCHER (AV)

375 Park Avenue, 10152
Telephone: 212-888-3636
Facsimile: 212-888-3974

MEMBERS OF FIRM

Bernard London
James L. Fischer
John W. Manning
Daniel Zemann, Jr.
John E. Sparling

ASSOCIATES

Richard S. Endres
Nicholas Kalfa
Evan D. Lieberman
Amy M. Kramer
Robert S. Sunshine
Robert M. Vecchione
John P. Bruen
Christina M. Ambrosio
William C. Nanis
Michael P. Mezzacappa
Douglas W. Hammond
Michael S. Leavy
Robert L. Honig

For full biographical listings, see the Martindale-Hubbell Law Directory

MCALOON & FRIEDMAN, P.C. (AV)

116 John Street, 10038
Telephone: 212-732-8700

Edward H. McAloon (1908-1986)
Stanley D. Friedman
Gunther H. Kilsch
Theodore B. Rosenzweig
Gary A. Greenfield
Brendan J. Lantier
Lawrence W. Mumm
Laura R. Shapiro

Rose Candeloro
Regina E. Schneller
Lisa B. Goldstein
John Langell
Barbara A. Dalton
Michelle E. Just
Eleanor M. Kanzler
Paul Nasta
Kim R. Kleppel
Kenneth Gordon Ellison
Evette E. Harrison
Thomas Medardo Oliva
Adam R. Goldsmith
Christopher B. O'Malley
Arlene Bergman

For full biographical listings, see the Martindale-Hubbell Law Directory

MENDES & MOUNT (AV)

750 Seventh Avenue, 10019
Telephone: 212-261-8000
Telecopier: 212-261-8750
Cable Address: "Menmount"
Telex: WUI 620392; 620332
Los Angeles, California Office: Citicorp Plaza, 725 South Figueroa Street, Nineteenth Floor.
Telephone: 213-955-7700.
Telecopy: 213-955-7725.
Telex: 6831520.
Cable Address: "MNDMT."
Newark, New Jersey Office: 1 Newark Center.
Telephone: 201-639-7300.
Fax: 201-639-7350.

MEMBERS OF FIRM

William Blanc Mendes (1891-1957)
Russell Theodore Mount (1881-1962)
John R. Arscott
Joseph J. Asselta
Daniel M. Bianca
Mark F. Bruckmann
Warren D. Cheesman
Frank J. Chiarchiaro
William R. Continanza
Mary Ann D'Amato
James J. Finnerty, Jr.
Donald K. Fitzpatrick (Resident, Los Angeles, California Office)
Garrett J. Fitzpatrick
James M. FitzSimons (Resident, Los Angeles, California Office)
Robert M. Flannery
Leo W. Fraser, III
Ronald R. Houdlett
James W. Hunt (Resident, Los Angeles, California Office)
John F. Larkin, III
George C. Lock
Edward M. Manganiello
John G. McAndrews
William J. McAndrews
James A. McGuire
Edward J. McMurrer
Thomas J. Quinn
Stephen Tucker
Arthur J. Washington, III

(See Next Column)

MENDES & MOUNT, *New York—Continued*

Charles G. Carluccio, III (Resident, Los Angeles, California Office)
John A. Catania
Kevin F. Cook
Catherine A. Gerspach
Michael C. Giordano
William G. Goldsmith
John A. Guarascio
Robert M. Mangino, Jr.
George L. Maniatis
Eileen T. McCabe
William A. Meehan
Mary D. Melvin
Richard C. Milazzo
Paul E. Moran
Dennis R. Mullins
Elizabeth Nelson
Richard R. Nelson (Resident, Los Angeles, California Office)
Edward G. Spacek
Robert B. Wall
Bruce R. Wildermuth
Joseph J. Winowiecki

OF COUNSEL

Arthur C. Muller, Jr.

ASSOCIATES

Steven P. Agosta
Barbara Agulnek
Christine Ardita
Glenn M. Bieler
Colleen Marie Browne
Kathleen Browne-Pindilli (Resident, Newark, New Jersey Office)
William J. Cleary
Joan E. Cochran (Resident, Los Angeles, California Office)
Robert E. Cook
Joseph M. Coppola
Olympia Daskalakis
Bruce H. Davidson
Joseph A. Deliso
Diane DiFranco
Mark A. DiTaranto
John P. Falcone
Robert P. Firriolo
Kevin G. Fitzgerald
Kevin G. Flynn
William R. Fried
Julie M. Granser
Jeff Imeri
Mark R. Irvine (Resident, Los Angeles, California Office)
Jeffery R. Kayl
Michael F. Klag
Brendan J. Malley
Roger M. Marks, Jr.
Shalem A. Massey (Resident, Los Angeles, California Office)
Dennis J. McEnery
Cathleen M. McKenna
Suzanne Naatz McNulty (Resident, Los Angeles, California Office)
James C. Miller
Wendy B. Millman
Michael E. Morley
Eugene P. Murphy
Ann L. O'Connor
Hannah M. O'Driscoll
Robert A. Parisi, Jr.
Kevin J. Philbin
Dominic M. Pisani
Margaret A. Reetz (Resident, Los Angeles, California Office)
Lawrence W. Rose
Lisa T. Simon
Estie R. Stoll (Resident, Los Angeles, California Office)
John A. Sullivan
Christine J. Testaverde
Ty S. Vanderford (Resident, Los Angeles, California Office)
Arjang Victory
Dean J. Vigliano
Mark S. Zemcik

For full biographical listings, see the Martindale-Hubbell Law Directory

MILBANK, TWEED, HADLEY & MCCLOY (AV)

1 Chase Manhattan Plaza, 10005
Telephone: 212-530-5000
Cable Address: "Miltweed NYK"
Fax: 212-530-5219
MCI Mail: MilbankTweed ABA/net Milbank NY
Midtown Office: 50 Rockefeller Plaza, 10020.
Telephone: 212-530-5800.
Fax: 212-530-0158.
Los Angeles, California Office: 601 South Figueroa Street, 30th Floor, 90017.
Telephone: 213-892-4000.
Fax: 213-629-5063.
Telex: 678754. ABA/net: Milbank LA.
Washington, D.C. Office: International Square Building, Suite 1100, 1825 Eye Street, N.W., 20006.
Telephone: 202-835-7500.
Cable Address: "Miltweed Wsh". ITT 440667.
Fax: 202-835-7586. ABA/net: Milbank DC.
Tokyo, Japan Office: Nippon Press Center Building, 2-1, Uchisaiwai-cho 2-chome, Chiyoda-ku, Tokyo 100, Japan.
Telephone: 011-81-3-3504-1050.
Fax: 011-81-3-3595-2790, 011-81-3-3502-5192.
London, England Office: Ropemaker Place, 25 Ropemaker Street, EC2Y 9AS.
Telephone: 011-44-171-374-0423.
Cable Address: "Miltuk G."
Fax: 011-44-171-374-0912.
Hong Kong Office: 3007 Alexandra House, 16 Chater Road.
Telephone: 011-852-2526-5281.
Fax: 011-852-2840-0792; 011-852-2845-9046. ABA/net: Milbank HK.
Singapore Office: 14-02 Caltex House, 30 Raffles Place, 0104.
Telephone: 011-65-534-1700.
Fax: 011-65-534-2733. ABA/net: EDNANG.
Moscow, Russia Office: 24/27 Sadovaya-Samotyochnya, Moscow, 103051.
Telephone: 011-7-502-258-5015.
Fax: 011-7-502-258-5014.

(See Next Column)

MEMBERS OF FIRM

Charles G. Berry
George Ian Brandon
Russell E. Brooks
Joseph S. Genova
Toni C. Lichstein
Richard C. Tufaro (Resident Partner, Washington, D.C. Office)

CONSULTING PARTNER

William E. Jackson

OF COUNSEL

Adlai S. Hardin, Jr.

SENIOR ATTORNEYS

Eugene F. Farabaugh
Charles W. Westland

ASSOCIATES

David R. Gelfand
Jane L. Hanson
Anne M. Ronan
Caleb A. Schwartz
Susanne M. Toes

For Complete List of Firm Personnel, See General Section

For full biographical listings, see the Martindale-Hubbell Law Directory

MILBERG WEISS BERSHAD HYNES & LERACH (AV)

One Pennsylvania Plaza, 10119
Telephone: 212-594-5300
San Diego, California Office: 600 West Broadway, 1800 One America Plaza.
Telephone: 619-231-1058.
San Francisco, California Office: 222 Kearny Street, 10th Floor.
Telephone: 415-288-4545.
Fax: 415-288-4534.

MEMBERS OF FIRM

Melvyn I. Weiss
Lawrence Milberg (1913-1989)
David J. Bershad
Jared Specthrie
William S. Lerach (Resident at San Diego Office)
Sol Schreiber
Jerome M. Congress
Richard M. Meyer
Patricia M. Hynes
Keith F. Park (Resident at San Diego Office)
Sharon Levine Mirsky
Robert P. Sugarman
John E. Grasberger (Resident at San Francisco Office)
Leonard B. Simon (Resident at San Diego Office)
Arnold N. Bressler
Alan Schulman (Resident at San Diego Office)
Jan Mark Adler (Resident at San Diego Office)
Michael C. Spencer
Anita Meley Laing (Resident at San Diego Office)
Blake M. Harper (Resident at San Diego Office)
Steven G. Schulman
Robert A. Wallner
Sanford P. Dumain
Patrick Coughlin (Resident at San Diego Office)
George A. Bauer III
Kevin P. Roddy (Resident at San Diego Office)
Dennis Stewart (Resident at San Diego Office)
Barry A. Weprin
Richard H. Weiss
Helen J. Hodges (Resident at San Diego Office)
Eric A. Isaacson (Resident at San Diego Office)
Alan M. Mansfield (Resident at San Diego Office)
Lee S. Shalov
John J. Stoia, Jr. (Resident at San Francisco Office)

ASSOCIATES

Jeffrey S. Abraham
Helen B. Alley (Not admitted in NY)
Joy A. Bull (Resident at San Diego Office)
James A. Caputo (Resident at San Diego Office)
Deborah Clark-Weintraub
George H. Cohen
Lori G. Feldman
Keith M. Fleischman
Susan Gonick (Resident at San Diego Office)
Mary M. Hurley (Resident at San Diego Office)
John W. Jeffrey (Resident at San Diego Office)
Edith M. Kallas
Jay Kenneth Kupietzky
Pamela M. Parker (Resident at San Diego Office)
Steven W. Pepich (Resident at San Diego Office)
Theodore J. Pintar (Resident at San Diego Office)
Janine L. Pollack
Henry Rosen (Resident at San Diego Office)
Ralph M. Stone
Alison M. Tattersall (Resident at San Francisco Office)
Joshua H. Vinik
Erin C. Ward (Resident at San Diego Office)
Jeff S. Westerman (Resident at San Diego Office)

OF COUNSEL

Charles S. Crandall (Resident at San Diego Office)

For full biographical listings, see the Martindale-Hubbell Law Directory

MOUND, COTTON & WOLLAN (AV)

One Battery Park Plaza, 10004
Telephone: 212-804-4200
Cable Address: "Moundlaw"
Telex: 64-9063
Telecopier: 212-344-8066
San Francisco, California Office: Suite 1650, 44 Montgomery Street.
Telephone: 415-249-4919.
Telecopier: 415-391-9076.
London, England Office: Longbow House, 14-20 Chiswell Street.
Telephone: 071-638-3688.

(See Next Column)

MOUND, COTTON & WOLLAN—*Continued*

East Hanover, New Jersey Office: 72 Eagle Rock Avenue, Building Two, P.O. Box 78.
Telephone: 201-503-9669.
Telecopier: 201-503-9494.

MEMBERS OF FIRM

Arthur N. Brook
Mitchell S. Cohen
Stuart Cotton
Leonard S. Dome
Wayne R. Glaubinger
Michael H. Goldstein
Lawrence S. Greengrass
Andrew C. Jacobson
Michael R. Koblenz
Daniel Markewich
John C. Mezzacappa
Frederic R. Mindlin
Philip C. Silverberg
Costantino P. Suriano
James D. Veach

COUNSEL

Eugene A. Leiman
Eugene Wollan

OF COUNSEL
SAN FRANCISCO, CALIFORNIA OFFICE

Alexander S. Keenan

MANAGING RESIDENT ATTORNEY
EAST HANOVER, NEW JERSEY OFFICE

Deanne Wilson

ASSOCIATES

Emilie L. Bakal
Brian F. Boardingham
Diane L. Bodenstein
Rebecca A. Buder
Mary L. Cain
Karen M. Cooke
Jeffrey C. Crawford
Guy P. Dauerty
Elisa T. Gilbert
Jeffrey B. Gold
Diana E. Goldberg
Lloyd A. Gura
Bruce R. Kaliner
Myra E. Lobel
Nancy B. London
Renee M. Plessner
Lisa S. Post
Jon Quint
Ronnie A. Rifkin
David I. Schonbrun
David A. Silva
Diane P. Simon
Sarah D. Strum
Ronald J. Theleen
Keith J. Wagner
Mark J. Weber
Jeffrey S. Weinstein
William D. Wilson
Simy C. Wolf
Rachel J. Yosevitz
Andrew L. Zalasin

For full biographical listings, see the Martindale-Hubbell Law Directory

MUDGE ROSE GUTHRIE ALEXANDER & FERDON (AV)

(Mudge, Stern, Baldwin & Todd)
(Caldwell, Trimble & Mitchell)
180 Maiden Lane, 10038
Telephone: 212-510-7000
Cable Address: "Baltuchins, New York"
Telex: 127889 & 703729
Telecopier: 212-248-2655/57
Los Angeles, California Office: 21st Floor, 333 South Grand Avenue, 90071.
Telephone: 213-613-1112.
Telecopier: 213-680-1358.
Washington, D.C. Office: 2121 K Street, N.W., 20037.
Telephone: 202-429-9355.
Telecopier: 202-429-9367.
Telex: MRGA 440264.
Cable Address: "Baltuchins, Washington, DC"
West Palm Beach, Florida Office: Suite 900, 515 North Flagler Drive, 33401.
Telephone: 407-650-8100.
Telecopier: 407-833-1722.
Telex: 514847 MRWPB.
Parsippany, New Jersey Office: Morris Corporate Center Two, Building D, One Upper Pond Road, 07054-1075.
Telephone: 201-335-0004.
Telecopier: 201-402-1593.
European Office: 12, Rue de la Paix, 75002 Paris, France.
Telephone: 42.61.57.71.
Telecopier: 42.61.79.21.
Cable Address: "Baltuchins, Paris".
Tokyo, Japan Office: Infini Akasaka, 8-7-15 Akasaka, Minato-Ku, Tokyo 107, Japan.
Telephone: (03) 3423-3970.
Fax: (03) 3423-3971.

MEMBERS OF FIRM

Paul G. Burns
Susan Millington Campbell
Kenneth Conboy
Terrence J. Connolly
Francis K. Decker, Jr.
Thomas G. Gallatin, Jr.
Robert J. Gunther, Jr.
James V. Kearney
John J. Kirby, Jr.
Harold G. Levison (Resident Partner, Parsippany, New Jersey Office)
Robert A. Longman
Walter P. Loughlin (Not admitted in NY)
Shelley B. O'Neill
Malcolm R. Schade
Stuart D. Sender
Laurence V. Senn, Jr.
Robert Sidorsky
Donald J. Zoeller

(See Next Column)

COUNSEL

Thomas W. Evans
Douglas M. Parker

ASSOCIATES

Mark D. Beckett
James S. Blank
Kenneth M. Breen
John T. Brennan
Patrick J. Carty
Phyllis Harris Clements
James O. Copley
Edward T. DeSilva
Anthony M. D'Iorio
Lisa K. Eastwood
Wendy K. Gelfand-Chaite
Jeffrey M. Goodman
Elisabeth L. Goot
Patricia A. Griffin
Elizabeth I. Hook
Thomas N. Kendris
Judith A. Lockhart (Not admitted in NY)
Gail A. Matthews
Kathleen E. McKay
Nicole S. Polley
Marc S. Reisler
Regina Lynn Scinta
Mark A. Simko
Nancy I. Solomon
Joyce J. Sun
Marc H. Supcoff
Jack V. Valinoti
Mark Vasco
Jeffrey T. Wald
Dennis M. Walsh
James Whelan

For Complete List of Firm Personnel, See General Section

For full biographical listings, see the Martindale-Hubbell Law Directory

NEWMAN SCHLAU FITCH & LANE, P.C. (AV)

305 Broadway, 10007-1198
Telephone: 212-619-4350
Fax: 212-619-3622
Glen Rock, New Jersey Office: Newman Schlau Fitch & Lane, 55 Harristown Road.
Telephone: 201-670-7040.
Fax: 201-670-4977.
Scarsdale, New York Office: 73 Greenacres Avenue.
Telephone: 914-472-0950.
Fax: 212-619-3622.

Philip Schlau
Robert A. Fitch
John C. Lane (Resident Partner, Glen Rock, New Jersey Office)
Abraham S. Altheim
Jan Kevin Myers
Jay L. Katz
Charles W. Kreines
Floyd G. Cottrell (Resident Partner, Glen Rock, New Jersey Office)
Andrew J. Cook
Olivia M. Gross

COUNSEL

William E. Bell
Howard A. Fried
Peter T. Shapiro

Ian F. Harris
Frank P. Luberti, Jr.
Kevin J. Donnelly
James K. Stern
Steven A. Carlotto
George A. Smith
Maria Sestito
Carolyn M. Green (Not admitted in NY)
Michael J. White
Ondine C. Slone
Peter C. Bobchin
Joseph P. Mooney
Ben Niderberg
Hillary P. Kahan
Ian R. Grodman (Resident, Glen Rock, New Jersey Office)
Denise Campbell
Daniel M. Schiavetta, Jr.
Debra A. Miller
Emily S. Barnett
Sim R. Shapiro
Paul A. Barkan
Andrew M. Tilem

Reference: Chase Bank, New York.

For full biographical listings, see the Martindale-Hubbell Law Directory

OHRENSTEIN & BROWN (AV)

230 Park Avenue, 10169
Telephone: 212-682-4500
Telecopier: 212-557-0910
Garden City, New York Office: 1205 Franklin Avenue.
Telephone: 516-333-1245.
Telecopier: 516-248-1947.

MEMBERS OF FIRM

Manfred Ohrenstein
Michael D. Brown
Mark J. Bunim
Terence P. Cummings
Steven D. Dreyer
John Paul Fulco, P.C.
Warren R. Graham
Abraham E. Havkins
Geoffrey W. Heineman
Christopher B. Hitchcock
Steven H. Rosenfeld

COUNSEL

Peter J. Kiernan
Stanley M. Kolber

ASSOCIATES

Peter J. Biging
Michele D. Breslow
Gerard J. Costello
Annmarie D'Amour
Joseph Francis Fields
Andrea Beth Jacobson
Bennett R. Katz
Andrew L. Margulis
Abe M. Rychik
John R. Sachs, Jr.
Robert J. Segall
Evan Shapiro
Philip Touitou

For full biographical listings, see the Martindale-Hubbell Law Directory

New York—Continued

ORANS, ELSEN & LUPERT (AV)

33rd Floor, One Rockefeller Plaza, 10020
Telephone: 212-586-2211
Cable Address: "ORELSLU"
Telecopier: 212-765-3662

MEMBERS OF FIRM

Sheldon H. Elsen
Gary H. Greenberg
Leslie A. Lupert
Lawrence Solan
Robert L. Plotz

ASSOCIATES

Melissa A. Cohen
Amelia Anne Nickles
Jonathan J. Englander

For full biographical listings, see the Martindale-Hubbell Law Directory

OTTERBOURG, STEINDLER, HOUSTON & ROSEN, P.C. (AV)

230 Park Avenue, 10169
Telephone: 212-661-9100
Cable Address: "Otlerton";
Telecopier: 212-682-6104
Telex: 960916

Kurt J. Wolff
Bernard Beitel
Donald N. Gellert
Daniel Wallen
William M. Silverman
Richard J. Rubin
Morton L. Gitter
Anthony M. Piccione
Peter H. Stolzar
Stanley L. Lane, Jr.
Peter L. Feldman

Diane B. Kaplan
Richard G. Haddad
Lloyd M. Green
Howard M. Sendrovitz

For Complete List of Firm Personnel, See General Section

For full biographical listings, see the Martindale-Hubbell Law Directory

PARKER CHAPIN FLATTAU & KLIMPL, L.L.P. (AV)

1211 Avenue of the Americas, 10036
Telephone: 212-704-6000
Telecopier: 212-704-6288
Cable Address: "Lawpark"
Telex: 640347
Great Neck, New York Office: 175 Great Neck Road.
Telephone: 516-482-4422.
Telecopier: 516-482-4469.

MEMBERS OF FIRM

Mark Abramowitz
Karen F. Lederer
Barry J. Brett
Joel Lewittes
Aurora Cassirer
Peter M. Panken
Elliot Cohen
Will Burt Sandler
Michael D. Friedman
Alvin M. Stein
Charles P. Greenman
Lee W. Stremba
Stephen F. Harmon
Joel M. Wolosky

OF COUNSEL

Daniel S. Greenfeld

For Complete List of Firm Personnel, See General Section

For full biographical listings, see the Martindale-Hubbell Law Directory

PATTERSON, BELKNAP, WEBB & TYLER, LLP (AV)

1133 Avenue of the Americas, 10036-6710
Telephone: 212-336-2000
Fax: 212-336-2222
Moscow, Russia Office: Konushkovskaya 26 Moscow 123242, Russian Federation.
Telephone: 011-7095-253-9607. Telephone/
Fax: 011-7502-221-1857; 011-7095-564-8063.

MEMBERS OF FIRM

William F. Cavanaugh, Jr.
Thomas C. Morrison
Gregory L. Diskant
Thomas W. Pippert
David F. Dobbins
Andrew D. Schau
Philip R. Forlenza
Karl E. Seib, Jr.
Eugene M. Gelernter
Theodore B. Van Itallie, Jr.
Robert P. LoBue
John Winter
Ellen M. Martin
Stephen P. Younger

OF COUNSEL

Harold R. Tyler, Jr.

COUNSEL

Blair Axel
Christine H. Miller
Frederick B. Campbell
Saul B. Shapiro
Robert D. Wilson, Jr.

(See Next Column)

ASSOCIATES

Lisa C. Cohen
Gordon L. DeMario
Philip L. Hirschhorn

For Complete List of Firm Personnel, See General Section

For full biographical listings, see the Martindale-Hubbell Law Directory

PILIERO GOLDSTEIN JENKINS & HALL (AV)

292 Madison Avenue, 10017
Telephone: 212-213-8200
Fax: 212-685-2028
Carlstadt, New Jersey Office: One Palmer Terrace.
Telephone: 201-507-5157.
FAX: 201-507-5221.
Washington, D.C. Office: 888 17th Street, N.W., Suite 1100.
Telephone: 202-467-6991.
FAX: 202-467-6703.

MEMBERS OF FIRM

Edward J. Goldstein
Jon Mark Jenkins
Christopher P. Hall
Robert D. Piliero

ASSOCIATES

John William LaRocca
Elaine B. Michetti (Not admitted in NY)
Juliana M. Moday

OF COUNSEL

Ricardo J. Davila

For full biographical listings, see the Martindale-Hubbell Law Directory

PLUNKETT & JAFFE, P.C. (AV)

230 Park Avenue, 10169
Telephone: 212-922-1800
White Plains, New York Office: 1 North Broadway.
Telephone: 914-948-7722.
Albany, New York Office: 132 State Street.
Telephone: 518-462-1800.

William F. Plunkett, Jr.
Michael J. McDermott
Phyllis S. Jaffe
Richard S. Altman
Kevin J. Plunkett
John S. Harris
John F. Burkhardt
Lynda G. Sartorio
John P. Cahill
Ellen B. Portman
Arthur J. Semetis
Amy Scatenato
Richard J. Lambert
Elizabeth Stebbins Torkelsen
Jonathan A. Ballan
Patrick E. Brown

OF COUNSEL

John C. Marbach
George L. Ryan
Andrew S. Roffe
Howard G. Seitz
Gregory J. Raphael

For full biographical listings, see the Martindale-Hubbell Law Directory

QUELLER & FISHER (AV)

A Law Partnership including Professional Corporations
110 Wall Street, 10005-3851
Telephone: 212-422-3600
Cable Address: "Quelfish, New York"
Facsimile: 212-422-2828

MEMBERS OF FIRM

Fred Queller (P.C.)
Bertram D. Fisher (P.C.)
Walter F. Benson

ASSOCIATES

Ira Bartfield
Dorothy S. Morrill
Marshall Schmeizer
David P. Horowitz
Kevin S. McDonald
Glenn Verchick
Phillip P. Nikolis
Ira Fogelgaren
Edmund L. Rothschild
Frances I. Beaupierre (Not admitted in NY)

For full biographical listings, see the Martindale-Hubbell Law Directory

REAVES & YATES (AV)

545 Madison Avenue, 10022
Telephone: 212-308-4600
Fax: 212-308-4851

James A. Reaves

OF COUNSEL

Joan Goodwin Zooper

For full biographical listings, see the Martindale-Hubbell Law Directory

New York—Continued

ROGERS & WELLS (AV)

Two Hundred Park Avenue, 10166-0153
Telephone: 212-878-8000
Facsimile: 212-878-8375
Telex: 234493 RKWUR
Washington, D.C. Office: 607 Fourteenth Street, N.W., Washington, D.C. 20005-2011.
Telephone: 202-434-0700.
Facsimile: 202-434-0800.
Los Angeles, California Office: 444 South Flower Street, Los Angeles, California 90071-2901.
Telephone: 213-689-2900.
Facsimile: 213-689-2999.
Paris, France Offices: 47, Avenue Hoche, 75008-Paris, France.
Telephone: 33-1-44-09-46-00.
Facsimile: 33-1-42-67-50-81.
Telex: 651617 EURLAW.
London, England Office: 58 Coleman Street, London EC2R 5BE, England.
Telephone: 44-71-628-0101.
Facsimile: 44-71-638-2008.
Telex: 884964 USLAW G.
Frankfurt, Germany Office: Lindenstrasse 37, 60325 Frankfurt/Main, Federal Republic of Germany. Telephone 49-69-97-57-11-0.
Facsimile: 49-69-97-57-11-33.

EXECUTIVE COMMITTEE

James N. Benedict
James B. Weidner

PARTNERS

Kevin J. Arquit
Leora Ben-Ami
James N. Benedict
Nancy A. Brown
Richard A. Cirillo
Nicholas L. Coch
John E. Daniel
Dennis J. Drebsky
Joseph Ferraro
George P. Hoare, Jr.
John E. Kidd
Donald F. Luke
James W. Paul
John M. Quitmeyer
James M. Ringer
David A. Schulz
John J. Sheehy
Louise Sommers
Margaret Blair Soyster
Joseph H. Spain
Craig M. Walker
James B. Weidner
Richard N. Winfield

SENIOR COUNSEL

James V. Ryan

WASHINGTON, D.C. OFFICE
PARTNERS

Roger A. Clark
Steven A. Newborn

LOS ANGELES, CALIFORNIA OFFICE
PARTNERS

Michael D. Berk
Allan E. Ceran
G. Howden Fraser
John A. Karaczynski
Terry O. Kelly
I. Bruce Speiser

For Complete List of Firm Personnel, See General Section

For full biographical listings, see the Martindale-Hubbell Law Directory

SACKS MONTGOMERY, P.C. (AV)

800 Third Avenue, 10022
Telephone: 212-355-4660
Telecopier: 212-593-7257
Stamford, Connecticut Office: Sacks, Montgomery, Pastore & Levine, P.C., 970 Summer Street.
Telephone: 203-325-3800.

Harry P. Sacks
David E. Montgomery
William J. Pastore (Resident at Stamford, Connecticut Office)
Stuart M. Levine
Jeffrey A. Aronson
Frederick R. Rohn
Scott D. St. Marie

Laura H. Markson
Stephen A. Stallings
Paul M. Schindler
Jocelyn D. Margolin

OF COUNSEL

Steven J. Brill

For full biographical listings, see the Martindale-Hubbell Law Directory

SCHNEIDER, KLEINICK, WEITZ, DAMASHEK, GODOSKY & GENTILE (AV)

233 Broadway, Fifth Floor, 10279-0003
Telephone: 212-553-9000
Fax: 212-804-0820

Ivan S. Schneider
Arnold L. Kleinick
Harvey Weitz
Philip M. Damashek
Richard Godosky
Anthony P. Gentile
Gregory J. Cannata
Robert B. Jackson
Brian J. Shoot

(See Next Column)

Richard B. Ancowitz
Jeffrey R. Brecker
Scott A. Buxbaum
Dawn S. DeWeil
Steven M. Fink
Steven Gold
Keith H. Gross
Wilma Guzman
Leslie Debra Kelmachter
Keith A. Kleinick
Matthew R. Kreinces
Ruth Frances Leve
Gerard Anthony Lucciola
Grace Carreras McCallen
Charles J. Nolet, Jr.
Harlan Platz
Lloyd M. Roberts
Paul Bryan Schneider
Perry D. Silver
Clifford J. Stern
Paul B. Weitz

For full biographical listings, see the Martindale-Hubbell Law Directory

SCHULTE ROTH & ZABEL (AV)

900 Third Avenue, 10022
Telephone: 212-758-0404; 800-346-9644
Cable Address: "Olympus NewYork"
Telex: 426775
West Palm Beach, Florida Office: 777 South Flagler Drive.
Cable Address: "P. B. Olympus."
Telephone: 407-659-9800.

MEMBERS OF FIRM

Robert M. Abrahams
David M. Brodsky
Michael S. Feldberg
Alan R. Glickman
Howard O. Godnick
Daniel J. Kramer
Martin L. Perschetz
Catherine Samuels
Frederick P. Schaffer
Chaye Zuckerman Shapot (Partner in Charge of Professional Development)
Irwin J. Sugarman

ASSOCIATES

Hollis Anne Bart
Glenn Eric Butash
Linda J. Cahn
Marcy Ressler Harris
Mark E. Kaplan
David J. Murray
John P. Stigi III
William Zeena, Jr. (Resident, West Palm Beach, Florida Office)

For Complete List of Firm Personnel, See General Section

For full biographical listings, see the Martindale-Hubbell Law Directory

SIMONSON HESS & LEIBOWITZ, P.C. (AV)

15 Maiden Lane, 10038
Telephone: 212-233-5000

Paul Simonson
Alan B. Leibowitz
Steven L. Hess

Nancy S. Stuzin
Kathleen Marie O'Neill
Jennifer Levine

For full biographical listings, see the Martindale-Hubbell Law Directory

SMITH MAZURE DIRECTOR WILKINS YOUNG YAGERMAN & TARALLO, P.C. (AV)

111 John Street, 10038
Telephone: 212-964-6061
Fax: 212-374-1935 (Not for Legal Service)

Gerald Director
David E. Mazure
Stanley Wilkins
Nicholas Tarallo
Jacob J. Young
Mark S. Yagerman

Lewis I. Wolf
Seymour Dicker
Marc H. Pillinger
Irwin D. Miller
Herbert Minster
Harvey Ginsberg
Michael K. Berman
John Kevin Reilly

Eugene Staub
Jeanne L. Ramasso
Irwin Bloom
Michael S. Livow
Robert P. Siegel
Mark A. Solomon
Elayna Cindy Kaplan
Jeffrey T. Miller
John Colucci
Steven P. Cahn
Beth Matus Barnett
Daniel O. Dietchweiler
Corey A. Tavel
Cary Maynard
Haydn J. Brill
Michael L. Tawil
Richard Steigman
Douglas E. Hoffer
Clara M. Villarreal-Fanizzi
Steven I. Brizel

OF COUNSEL

Robert R. MacDonnell

For full biographical listings, see the Martindale-Hubbell Law Directory

New York—Continued

SULLIVAN & CROMWELL (AV)

125 Broad Street, 10004-2498
Telephone: 212-558-4000
Cable Address: "Ladycourt, New York"
Telex: 62694 (International); 12-7816 (Domestic)
Telecopier: 212-558-3588
Midtown Office: 250 Park Avenue, 10177-0021.
Telecopier: 212-558-3792.
Washington, D.C. Office: 1701 Pennsylvania Avenue, N.W., 20006-5805.
Telephone: 202-956-7500.
Telex: 89625.
Telecopier: 202-293-6330.
Los Angeles, California Office: 444 South Flower Street, 90071-2901.
Telephone: 213-955-8000.
Telecopier: 213-683-0457.
Paris Office: 8, Place Vendôme, Paris 75001, France.
Telephone: (011)(331)4450-6000.
Telex: 240654.
Telecopier: (011)(331)4450-6060.
London Office: St. Olave's House, 9a Ironmonger Lane, London EC2V 8EY, England.
Telephone: (011)(44171)710-6500.
Telecopier: (011)(44171)710-6565.
Melbourne, Australia Office: 101 Collins Street, Melbourne, Victoria 3000.
Telephone: (011)(613)654-1500.
Telecopier: (011)(613)654-2422.
Tokyo Office: Gaikokuho Jimu Bengoshi Office of Robert G. DeLaMater, a member of the firm of Sullivan & Cromwell, Tokio Kaijo Building Shinkan, 2-1, Marunouchi, 1-chome Chiyoda-ku, Tokyo 100, Japan.
Telephone: (011)(813)3213-6140.
Telecopier: (011)(813)3213-6470.
Hong Kong Office: 28th Floor, Nine Queen's Road, Central, Hong Kong.
Telephone: (011)(852)826-8688.
Telecopier: (011)(852)522-2280.

MEMBERS OF FIRM

John W. Dickey (London Office)
Michael A. Cooper
John F. Cannon
Richard E. Carlton
John L. Warden
William R. Norfolk
Robert M. Osgood (London Office)
James H. Carter, Jr.
Philip L. Graham, Jr.
Bruce E. Clark
Richard J. Urowsky
William M. Dallas, Jr.
Margaret K. Pfeiffer * (Washington, D.C. Office)
David B. Tulchin
D. Stuart Meiklejohn
Yvonne S. Quinn
Gandolfo V. DiBlasi
Robinson B. Lacy
Garrard Russ Beeney
Richard H. Klapper
Theodore O. Rogers, Jr. *
John L. Hardiman
Robert A. Sacks ** (Los Angeles Office)
Theodore Edelman
Steven L. Holley
Joseph E. Neuhaus *
William J. Snipes
David H. Braff
Mark F. Rosenberg
Daryl A. Libow (Washington, D.C. Office)
Samuel W. Seymour
Michael H. Steinberg ** (Not admitted in NY; Los Angeles Office)

OF COUNSEL

Douglas Mark McCall * (Washington, D.C. Office)

SPECIAL COUNSEL

William L. Farris
Jeffrey W. Jacobs * (Not admitted in NY; Washington, D.C. Office)

RETIRED MEMBERS OF FIRM

Edward W. Keane
Robert MacCrate *
Marvin Schwartz *
William E. Willis

ASSOCIATES

Leta L. Applegate
Michael J. Bowe
Ellen Bresler
Hugh L. Burns
Patricia M. Clarke
John T. Corcoran
Diane D'Arcangelo **
Lisamichelle Davis
Robert A. de By
Marc De Leeuw
James C. Dugan
Tamar Feder
Robin D. Fessel
Brian T. Frawley
Edward R. Gallion
David Gaukrodger
Robert J. Giuffra, Jr. *
Deborah S. Gordon
Edward A. Harris *
Michael E. Hatchett
Jessica Hausknecht
Georgina Elspeth Hayden
Kenneth P. Held
Timothy J. Helwick
Fraser L. Hunter, Jr.
Howard J. Kaplan
Ann T. Kenny
John E. Kirklin
Nicole A. LaBarbera
Michael Lacovara
Eric K. Laumann
Scott L. Lessing
Steven R. Lowson
Michael B. Miller (London Office)
Alexandre A. Montagu
Tariq Mundiya
Elizabeth A. O'Connor
Richard C. Pepperman, II
Jay L. Pomerantz
John B. Reid-Dodick
William E. Schroeder
Penny Shane
Lori S. Sherman
Sara Kathryn Stadler
John C. Stellabotte
Michael E. Swartz
Michael T. Tomaino, Jr.
Holly Hexter Weiss
Noah M. Weissman

(See Next Column)

ASSOCIATES (Continued)

Stephanie G. Wheeler
Karen Doeblin Whetzle
E. Marcellus Williamson
Paul C. Wilson (Not admitted in NY)
Anna Yang

David Liebov (Managing Clerk)

*Attorneys also admitted to the District of Columbia Bar
**Attorneys also admitted to the California Bar

For Complete List of Firm Personnel, See General Section

For full biographical listings, see the Martindale-Hubbell Law Directory

RICHARD N. TANNENBAUM (AV)

Suite 2700, 225 Broadway, 10007
Telephone: 212-693-1963
Fax: 212-406-6890
Great Neck, N.Y. Office: Suite 301, 10 Cutter Mill Road.
Telephone: 466-2227.

References: National Westminister Bank; Bank of New York.

For full biographical listings, see the Martindale-Hubbell Law Directory

THACHER PROFFITT & WOOD (AV)

Two World Trade Center, 10048
Telephone: 212-912-7400
Cable Address: "Wallaces, New York"
Telex: 226733TPCW; 669578TPW
Facsimile: 212-912-7751; 912-7752
Washington, D.C. Office: 1500 K Street, N.W.
Telephone: 202-347-8400.
Facsimile: 202-347-6238.
White Plains, New York Office: 50 Main Street.
Telephone: 914-421-4100.
Facsimile: 914-421-4150/4151.

MEMBERS OF FIRM

Robert F. Brodegaard
Jean E. Burke
Christopher F. Graham
Joel B. Harris
John M. Woods

COUNSEL

Raymond S. Jackson, Jr.
Edward C. Kalaidjian

ASSOCIATE

Joseph G. Grasso

For Complete List of Firm Personnel, See General Section

For full biographical listings, see the Martindale-Hubbell Law Directory

TOWNLEY & UPDIKE (AV)

A Partnership including a Professional Corporation
Chrysler Building, 405 Lexington Avenue, 10174
Telephone: 212-973-6191
Telecopier: (212) 370-1348
Paramus, New Jersey Office: East 80 and Route 4.
Telephone: 201-712-0991.
Fax: 201-712-9444.
Garden City, New York Office: Garden City Center, Suite 506, 100 Quentin Roosevelt Boulevard.
Telephone: 516-227-3737.
Fax: 516-227-3746.

MEMBERS OF FIRM

John D. Canoni
Carl J. Chiappa
Jerome P. Coleman
Mario Diaz-Cruz, III
Sandra Edelman
Perez C. Ehrich
Douglas C. Fairhurst
Mark D. Geraghty
Michael F. Griffin
Jon H. I. Grouf
William O'C. Harnisch
Jonathan M. Herman
Richard Koo
Jayne M. Kurzman
Harry A. LeBien
Evelyn J. Lehman
Matthew L. Lifflander
Richard R. Lutz
Robert C. Miller
James P. O'Neill
Philip D. Pakula
Robert E. Peduzzi
Robert Lloyd Raskopf
John Paul Reiner
Danforth W. Rogers
Barbara M. Roth
Richard L. Russell
Ralph K. Smith, Jr.
James B. Swire

OF COUNSEL

Elliot Paskoff

SPECIAL COUNSEL

Frederick A. Nicoll (Resident, Paramus, New Jersey Office)

For Complete List of Firm Personnel, See General Section

For full biographical listings, see the Martindale-Hubbell Law Directory

New York—Continued

Varet & Fink P.C. (AV)

(Formerly Milgrim Thomajan & Lee P.C.)
53 Wall Street, 10005-2899
Telephone: 212-858-5300
Cable Address: "Milatom NYK"
Telex: WUI 662124
Telecopier: 212-858-5301
Washington, D.C. Office: 1110 Vermont Avenue, N.W., Suite 600.
Telephone: 202-628-6200.
Fax: 202-628-2288.

Andrew L. Deutsch
Robert F. Fink
Leo G. Kailas
James D. Kleiner
David P. Langlois
Stanley McDermott, III
Robert A. Meister

COUNSEL

Christopher J. Clay (Resident, Washington, D.C. Office)
Mitchell E. Radin

Peter M. Corrigan
Carol M. Fischer
Michael R. Hepworth
David A. McManus
Diane S. Wolfson

For Complete List of Firm Personnel, See General Section

For full biographical listings, see the Martindale-Hubbell Law Directory

White & Case (AV)

1155 Avenue of the Americas, 10036-2787
Telephone: 212-819-8200
Telex: 233188 WHCA UR
Facsimile: 212-354-8113
Washington, D.C.:
Telephone: 202-872-0013.
Facsimile: 202-872-0210.
Los Angeles, California:
Telephone: 213-620-7700.
Facsimile: 213-687-0758; 213-617-2205.
Miami, Florida:
Telephone: 305-371-2700.
Facsimile: 305-358-5744.
Mexico City, Mexico:
Telephone: (52-5) 207-9717.
Facsimile: (52-5) 208-3628.
Tokyo, Japan:
Telephone: (81-3) 3239-4300.
Facsimile: (81-3) 3239-4330.
Hong Kong:
Telephone: (852) 2822-8700.
Facsimile: (852) 2845-9070; Grice & Co., Solicitors,
Telephone: (852) 2826-0333.
Facsimile: (852) 2526-7166.
Singapore, Republic of Singapore:
Telephone: (65) 225-6000.
Facsimile: (65) 225-6009.
Bangkok, Thailand: Pacific Legal Group Ltd., In Association With White & Case,
Telephone: (662) 236-6154/7.
Facsimile: (662) 237-6771.
Hanoi, Viet Nam: Representative Office,
Telephone: (84-4) 227-575/6/7.
Facsimile: (84-4) 227-297.
Bombay, India:
Telephone: (91-22) 282-6300.
Facsimile: (91-22) 282-6305.
London, England:
Telephone: (44-171) 726-6361.
Facsimile: (44-171) 726-4314; (44-171) 726-8558.
Paris, France:
Telephone: (33-1) 42-60-34-05.
Facsimile: (33-1) 42-60-82-46.
Brussels, Belgium:
Telephone: (32-2) 647-05-89.
Facsimile: (32-2) 647-16-75.
Stockholm, Sweden:
Telephone: (46-8) 679-80-30.
Facsimile: (46-8) 611-21-22.
Helsinki, Finland:
Telephone: (358-0) 631-100.
Facsimile: (358-0) 179-477.
Moscow, Russia:
Telephone: (7-095) 201-9292/3/4/5.
Facsimile: (7-095) 201-9284.
Budapest, Hungary:
Telephone: (36-1) 269-0550; (36-1) 131-0933.
Facsimile: (36-1) 269-1199.
Prague, Czech Republic:
Telephone: (42-2) 2481-1796.
Facsimile: (42-2) 232-5522.

(See Next Column)

Warsaw, Poland: Telephone/
Facsimile: (48-22) 26-80-53; (48-22) 27-84-86. International Telephone/
Facsimile: (48-39) 12-19-06.
Istanbul, Turkey:
Telephone: (90-212) 275-68-98; (90-212) 275-75-33.
Facsimile: (90-212) 275-75-43.
Ankara, Turkey:
Telephone: (90-312) 446-2180.
Facsimile: (90-312) 437-9677.
Jeddah, Saudi Arabia: Law Office of Hassan Mahassni,
Telephone: (966-2) 651-3535.
Facsimile: (966-2) 651-3636.
Riyadh, Saudi Arabia: Law Office of Hassan Mahassni,
Telephone: (966-1) 476-7099.
Facsimile: (966-1) 479-0110.
Almaty, Kazakhstan:
Telephone: (7-3272) 50-7491/2.
Facsimile: (7-3272) 61-0842.

MEMBERS OF FIRM

Aldo A. Badini
Jeffrey Barist
Charles N. Brower (Washington, D.C. Office)
Paul J. Bschorr
Stephen M. Corse (Miami, Florida Office)
Ronald W. Davis
Edward V. Filardi
C. Randolph Fishburn (Los Angeles, California Office)
Vincent R. FitzPatrick, Jr.
Anthony Giustini
Allan L. Gropper
Rayner M. Hamilton
Laura B. Hoguet
Richard J. Holwell
Richard A. Horsch
David S. Klafter
Charles C. Kline (Miami, Florida Office)
I. Fred Koenigsberg
Carolyn B. Lamm (Washington, D.C. Office)
Nels T. Lippert
Francis J. MacLaughlin (Los Angeles, California Office)
Donald T. MacNaughton
John J. McAvoy (Washington, D.C. Office)
Thomas McGanney
Harry G. Melkonian (Los Angeles, California Office)
Janis M. Meyer
Thomas J. O'Sullivan
Owen C. Pell
Richard W. Reinthaler
Philip H. Schaeffer
John A. Sturgeon (Los Angeles, California Office)
Richard B. Sypher
Travers D. Wood (Los Angeles, California Office)

RETIRED PARTNERS

Haliburton Fales, 2d
Macdonald Flinn
John M. Johnston
Thomas Kiernan
Edward Wolfe

OF COUNSEL

Robert B. Smith

COUNSEL

Dwight A. Healy

RESIDENT PARTNERS, PARIS OFFICE

Christopher R. Seppala

For Complete List of Firm Personnel, See General Section

For full biographical listings, see the Martindale-Hubbell Law Directory

Willkie Farr & Gallagher (AV)

One Citicorp Center, 153 East 53rd Street, 10022-4669
Telephone: 212-821-8000
Fax: 212-821-8111
Telex: RCA 233780-WFGUR; RCA 238805-WFGUR
Washington, D.C. Office: Three Lafayette Centre, 1155 21st Street, N.W., 6th Floor, 20036-3384.
Telephone: 202-328-8000.
Fax: 202-887-8979; 202-331-8187.
Telex: RCA 229800-WFGIG; WU 89-2762.
Paris, France Office: 6, Avenue Velasquez 75008.
Telephone: 011-33-1-44-35-44-35.
Fax: 011-331-42-89-87-01.
Telex: 652740-WFG Paris.
London, England Office: 3rd Floor, 35 Wilson Street, EC2M 25J.
Telephone: 011-44-71-696-9060.
Fax: 011-44-71-417-9191.

MEMBERS OF FIRM

Mitchell J. Auslander
Joseph T. Baio
Kevin B. Clark (Resident Partner, Washington, D.C. Office)
Louis A. Craco
David L. Foster
Stephen W. Greiner
Lawrence O. Kamin
Gerald Kerner
Robert J. Kheel
Richard L. Klein
Jeanne M. Luboja
Richard Mancino
Francis J. Menton, Jr.
David P. Murray (Resident Partner, Washington, D.C. Office)
Roger D. Netzer
Brian E. O'Connor
John R. Oller
Anthony F. Phillips
Richard L. Posen
Steven H. Reisberg
Benito Romano
William H. Rooney
Philippe M. Salomon
Elizabeth S. Stong

(See Next Column)

WILLKIE FARR & GALLAGHER, *New York—Continued*

MEMBERS OF FIRM (Continued)

Chester J. Straub
Theodore C. Whitehouse (Resident Partner, Washington, D.C. Office)
Michael R. Young

ASSOCIATES

Sean Anderson
James H. Bicks
William J. Borner
Gregory M. Cooke
Jacqueline A. Grundei
John J. Halloran, Jr.
Gregory L. Harris
Kelly M. Hnatt
Martin B. Klotz
J. Kevin McCarthy
Steven M. Monroe
Mitchel Ochs
Carlisle E. Perkins (Washington, D.C. Office)
Mary Anne Richmond
Richard C. Rosen
Jennifer L. Stevens (Washington, D.C. Office)
Carl L. Stine

For Complete List of Firm Personnel, See General Section
For full biographical listings, see the Martindale-Hubbell Law Directory

WILSON, ELSER, MOSKOWITZ, EDELMAN & DICKER (AV)

150 East 42nd Street, 10017-5639
Telephone: 212-490-3000
Telex: 177679
Facsimile: 212-490-3038; 212-557-7810
Los Angeles, California Office: Suite 2700, 1055 West Seventh Street, 90017.
Telephone: 213-624-3044.
Telex: 17-0722.
Facsimile: 213-624-8060.
San Francisco, California Office: 555 Montgomery Street, 94111.
Telephone: 415-433-0990.
Telex: 16-0768.
Facsimile: 415-434-1370.
Washington, D.C. Office: The Colorado Building, Fifth Floor, 1341 "G" Street, N.W., 20005.
Telephone: 202-626-7660.
Telex: 89453.
Facsimile: 202-628-3606.
Newark, New Jersey Office: One Gateway Center, 07102.
Telephone: 201-624-0800.
Telex: 6853589.
Facsimile: 201-624-0808.
Philadelphia, Pennsylvania Office: The Curtis Center, Independence Square West, 10604.
Telephone: 215-627-6900.
Telex: 6711203.
Facsimile: 215-627-2665.
Baltimore, Maryland Office: 250 West Pratt Street, 21201.
Telephone: 410-539-1800.
Telex: 19-8280.
Facsimile: 410-539-1820.
Miami, Florida Office: International Place, 100 Southeast Second Street, 33131.
Telephone: 305-374-1811.
Telex: 810845940.
Facsimile: 305-579-0261.
Chicago, Illinois Office: 120 N. La Salle Street, 26th Floor, 60602.
Telephone: 312-704-0550.
Telex: 1561590.
Facsimile: 312-704-1522.
White Plains, New York Office: 925 Westchester Avenue, 10604.
Telephone: 914-946-7200.
Facsimile: 914-946-7897.
Dallas, Texas Office: 5000 Renaissance Tower, 1201 Elm Street, 75270.
Telephone: 214-698-8000.
Facsimile: 214-698-1101.
Albany, New York Office: One Steuben Place, 12207.
Telephone: 518-449-8893.
Fax: 518-449-8927.
London, England Office: 141 Fenchurch Street, EC3M 6BL.
Telephone: 01-623-6723.
Telex: 885741.
Facsimile: 01-626-9774.
Tokyo, Japan Office: AIU Building, 1-3 Marunouchi 1-chome, Chiyoda-Ku, 100.
Telephone: 011-813-216-6551.
Telex: 781-2227216.
Facsimile: 011-813-216-6965.
Paris, France Office: Honig Buffat Mettetal. 21 Rue Clément Marot, 75008.
Telephone: 33 (1) 44.43.88.88.
Fax: 33 (1) 44.43.88.77.

MEMBERS OF FIRM

Thomas W. Wilson
John T. Elser
Harold J. Moskowitz
Max Edelman (1906-1989)
Herbert Dicker
Michael D. Glatt
Martin M. Ween
Marshal S. Endick
Milton Edelman
Richard S. Klein
Stephen A. Postelnek

(See Next Column)

MEMBERS OF FIRM (Continued)

Walter J. Smith, Jr. * (Resident Partner in Charge, Washington, D.C. Office)
Thomas W. Hyland
Vincent R. Fontana
Patrick M. Kelly * (Resident Partner in Charge, Los Angeles Office)
James P. Donovan
James Crawford Orr (Resident Partner in Charge, Newark Office)
Kenneth Scott (Resident Partner in Charge, Philadelphia Office)
Richard K. Traub
Stephen M. Marcellino
Perry I. Kreidman
Jerome N. Lerch * (Resident Partner in Charge, San Francisco Office)
Ralph W. Robinson * (Resident, San Francisco Office)
Philip J. Walsh
Edward J. Boyle
Anthony J. Mercorella
Jonathon F. Sher * (Resident, Los Angeles Office)
Robert M. Young, Jr. * (Resident, Los Angeles Office)
Jeffrey D. Robertson
Robert M. Weber
Paul J. Bottari
Michael N. Stevens
Mark K. Anesh
Daniel S. Schwartz * (Resident Partner in Charge, Miami Office)
Jerry L. McDowell * (Resident Partner in Charge, Chicago Office)
L. Victor Bilger, Jr. * (Resident, Los Angeles Office)
Steven Kent
Harry P. Brett
Glenn J. Fuerth
Phillip A. Tumbarello
Thomas M. Gambardella
Thomas W. Tobin
Eileen B. Eglin
Robert F. Roarke
Andrew S. Kaufman
Glen S. Feinberg
Jonathan C. Thau
David Florin * (Resident, Washington, D.C. Office)
Steven R. Parminter * (Resident, Los Angeles Office)
Keith G. Von Glahn (Resident, Newark Office)
Robert B. Wallace * (Resident, Washington, D.C. Office)
Louis H. Castoria * (Resident, San Francisco Office)
Martin W. Johnson * (Resident, San Francisco Office)
Jonathan Dryer * (Resident, Philadelphia Office)
Keith E. Johnston * (Resident, Philadelphia Office)
Otis D. Wright, II * (Resident, Los Angeles Office)
Arnold Kideckel
Gerald D. Freed * (Resident, Baltimore Office)
James W. Bartlett, III * (Resident, Baltimore Office)
Francis P. Manchisi
James M. Kaplan (Resident, Miami Office)
H. Michael O'Brien
Vincent P. D'Angelo * (Resident, Los Angeles, California Office)
Robert J. Kelly (Resident, Newark Office)
Bruce J. Chasan * (Resident, Philadelphia Office)
Adrian J. Gordon * (Resident, Philadelphia Office)
John Gary Luboja
Wayne I. Rabinowitz (Resident, White Plains, N.Y. Office)
Steven L. Young
Meryl R. Lieberman (Resident, White Plains, N. Y. Office)
Richard H. Rubenstein
Thomas A. Leghorn
Ricki Roer
E. Paul Dougherty, Jr. (Resident, Tokyo Office)
Wayne E. Borgeest
Thomas R. Manisero
Louis J. Isaacsohn * (Resident, Philadelphia Office)
John P. McGahey * (Resident, Chicago Office)
Thomas R. Cherry (Resident, London Office)
Jerry B. Black
Richard S. Oelsner
James A. Stankowski (Resident, Los Angeles Office)
Carl J. Pernicone
Kathleen D. Wilkinson * (Resident, Philadelphia Office)
Debra Steel Sturmer (Resident, San Francisco Office)
Carolyn Karp Schwartz
Martin K. Deniston (Resident, Los Angeles Office)
Rochelle M. Fedullo (Resident, Philadelphia Office)
Roland L. Coleman, Jr. (Resident, Los Angeles Office)
William J. Riina (Resident, Newark Office)
Robin Taylor Symons (Resident, Miami Office)
Jerold R. Ruderman (Resident, White Plains, Office)
David L. Tillem (Resident, White Plains Office)
Lee Eric Berger
Jeffrey E. Bigman
Alan Kaminsky
Robert W. Littleton
Milagros A. Matos Hunter
John Renzulli
Julianna Ryan
Edward A. Taylor
Rosario M. Vignali
David L. Wong
Bernd G. Heinze * (Resident, Philadelphia Office)
Jack A. Janov * (Resident, Los Angeles Office)
Thomas F. Quinn * (Resident, Newark Office)
Ricardo J. Cata * (Resident, Miami Office)
Edward P. Garson * (Resident, San Francisco Office)
Mark Housman
J. Marks Moore, III * (Resident, Baltimore Office)
James C. Ughetta
E. Stratton Horres, Jr. * (Resident, Dallas Office)
Jay A. Brandt * (Resident, Dallas Office)
R. Douglas Noah, Jr. * (Resident, Dallas Office)
Barry J. Gainey
Robert L. Joyce
Scott R. Schaffer
Timothy J. Sheehan
John D. Morio
Yongjin Park
Philip Quaranta
David S. Rutherford

OF COUNSEL

Leonard H. Minches (Resident, Miami Office)
George H. Kolb * (Resident, Dallas Office)

(See Next Column)

WILSON, ELSER, MOSKOWITZ, EDELMAN & DICKER—*Continued*

NEW YORK CITY ASSOCIATES

Don Abraham
Bonnie Greene Ackerman
Robert T. Adams
David K. Bergman
Helmut Beron
Adam Ross Bialek
Michael L. Boulhosa
Dean A. Cambourakis
Nina Cangiano
Brian T. Del Gatto
Debra A. Demarchena
Douglas Emanuel
Julie R. Evans
Joan M. Gilbride
David S. Hebbeler
Ramon D. Held
Richard M. Hunter
Maurya Crawford Keating
Colleen A. Kirchoff
Molly Klapper
Fred Knopf
Loretta A. Krez
Allison Lambert
Richard E. Lerner
Lawrence H. Lum
Edward A. Magro
Loretta T. Menkes
Richard T. Mermelstein
James Francis O'Brien
Edward J. O'Gorman
Susan M. Petrilli
Raymi Victoria Ramseur
Rolon A. Reed, III (Not admitted in NY)
Frederick W. Reif
Angelo Rios
Michael Rosenberg
Eric J. Sauter
John J. Schwab
James K. Schwartz
Michael Schwartzberg
David S. Sheiffer
Carl L. Steccato
Stephen D. Straus
Debra Tama
Lena A. Uljanov
Steven Verveniotis
David N. Wechsler
Alexander H. Whiteaker

*(Not admitted in New York)

For full biographical listings, see the Martindale-Hubbell Law Directory

WINTHROP, STIMSON, PUTNAM & ROBERTS (AV)

One Battery Park Plaza, 10004-1490
Telephone: 212-858-1000
Telex: 62854 WINSTIM
Telefax: 212-858-1500
Stamford, Connecticut Office: Financial Centre, 695 East Main Street, P.O. Box 6760, 06904-6760.
Telephone: 203-348-2300.
Washington, D.C. Office: 1133 Connecticut Avenue, N.W., 20036.
Telephone: 202-775-9800.
Palm Beach, Florida Office: 125 Worth Avenue, 33480.
Telephone: 407-655-7297.
London Office: 2 Throgmorton Avenue, London EC2N 2AP, England.
Telephone: 011-4471-628-4931.
Brussels Office: Rue Du Taciturne 42, B-1040 Brussels, Belgium.
Telephone: 011-322-230-1392.
Tokyo, Japan Office: 608 Atagoyama Bengoshi Building 6-7, Atago 1-chome, Minato-ku, Tokyo 105 Japan.
Telephone: 011-813-3437-9740.
Hong Kong Office: 2505 Asia Pacific Finance Tower, Citibank Plaza, 3 Garden Road, Central.
Telephone: 011-852-530-3400.

MEMBERS OF FIRM

Francis Carling
Thomas F. Clauss, Jr.
Leo T. Crowley
Philip Le B. Douglas
A. Edward Grashof
Sutton Keany
David G. Keyko
Susan J. Kohlmann
David M. Lindley
John F. Pritchard
Stephen A. Weiner
Edwin J. Wesely

COUNSEL

Mark R. Hellerer

SENIOR COUNSEL

Peter H. Kaminer
Merrell E. Clark, Jr.
William W. Karatz

CONNECTICUT OFFICE
MEMBER OF FIRM

Thomas F. Clauss, Jr.

COUNSEL

Thomas R. Trowbridge, III

FLORIDA OFFICE
COUNSEL

John C. Dotterrer

WASHINGTON, D.C. OFFICE
MEMBERS OF FIRM

Donald A. Carr

WASHINGTON, D.C.
COUNSEL

Aileen Meyer

For Complete List of Firm Personnel, See General Section

For full biographical listings, see the Martindale-Hubbell Law Directory

ZUCKERMAN, SPAEDER, GOLDSTEIN, TAYLOR & KOLKER (AV)

Grace Building, 45th Floor, 1114 Avenue of the Americas, 10036
Telephone: 212-479-6500
Fax: 212-479-6512
Washington, D.C. Office: 1201 Connecticut Avenue, N.W.
Telephone: 201-778-1800.
Fax: 202-822-8106.
Miami, Florida Office: Zuckerman, Spaeder, Taylor & Evans. Suite 900, Miami Center, 201 South Biscayne Boulevard.
Telephones: 305-358-5000; 305-579-0110; Broward County: 305-523-0277.
Fax: 305-579-9749.
Ft. Lauderdale, Florida Office: Zuckerman, Spaeder, Taylor & Evans. One East Broward Boulevard, Suite 700.
Telephone: 305-356-0463.
Fax: 305-356-0406.
Baltimore, Maryland Office: Zuckerman, Spaeder, Goldstein, Taylor & Better. Suite 2440, 100 East Pratt Street.
Telephone: 410-332-0444.
Fax: 410-659-0436.
Tampa, Florida Office: Zuckerman, Spaeder, Taylor & Evans. 101 East Kennedy Boulevard, Suite 3140.
Telephone: 813-221-1010.
Fax: 813-223-7961.

MEMBER OF FIRM

Edward J. M. Little

ASSOCIATES

Lisa A. Cahill
Alan H. Scheiner (Not admitted in NY)

For full biographical listings, see the Martindale-Hubbell Law Directory

*POUGHKEEPSIE,** Dutchess Co.

CORBALLY, GARTLAND AND RAPPLEYEA (AV)

35 Market Street, 12601
Telephone: 914-454-1110
FAX: 914-454-4857
Millbrook, New York Office: Bank of Millbrook Building, Franklin Avenue.
Telephone: 914-677-5539.
Clearwater, Florida Office: Citizens Bank Building, Suite 250, 1130 Cleveland Street.
Telephone: 813-461-3144.

MEMBERS OF FIRM

John Hackett (Died 1916)
James L. Williams (Died 1908)
Charles J. Corbally (1888-1966)
John J. Gartland, Jr.
Allan E. Rappleyea
Daniel F. Curtin
Fred W. Schaeffer
Michael G. Gartland
Jon H. Adams
Vincent L. DeBiase
Paul O. Sullivan
William F. Bogle, Jr.

ASSOCIATES

Rena Muckenhoupt O'Connor
Allan B. Rappleyea, Jr.

OF COUNSEL

Joseph F. Hawkins (1916-1986)
Milton M. Haven
Edward J. Murtaugh

Representative Clients: Hudson Valley Farm Credit, A.C.A.; St. Francis Hospital; Marist College; Merritt-Meridian Construction Corp.
Counsel for: Poughkeepsie Savings Bank, F.S.B.; Bank of New York; Farm Credit Bank of Springfield; Equitable Life Assurance Society of the United States; McCann Foundation, Inc.
Reference: Bank of New York.

For full biographical listings, see the Martindale-Hubbell Law Directory

*RIVERHEAD,** Suffolk Co.

BENJAMIN E. CARTER (AV)

220 Roanoke Avenue, P.O. Box 118, 11901
Telephone: 516-727-1666
FAX: 516-727-1710

For full biographical listings, see the Martindale-Hubbell Law Directory

CURTIS, ZAKLUKIEWICZ, VASILE, DEVINE & MCELHENNY (AV)

Griffing Building, 80 West Main Street, 11901
Telephone: 516-727-1111
Merrick, New York Office: 2174 Hewlett Avenue.
Telephone: 516-623-1111.

Francis E. Zaklukiewicz

Representative Clients: General Accident Group; Kemper Insurance Cos.; The Royal Insurance Cos.; Commercial Union Insurance Cos.; Safeco Insurance Cos.; American International Group; Exxon Corp. U.S.A.; Hertz Corp.; Metropolitan Suburban Bus Authority; Long Island Railroad.

For full biographical listings, see the Martindale-Hubbell Law Directory

*ROCHESTER,** Monroe Co.

LAW OFFICES OF A. VINCENT BUZARD (AV)

The Granite Building, Suite 420, 130 East Main Street, 14604
Telephone: 716-454-3984
Fax: 716-454-2177

ASSOCIATES

Gail A. Donofrio
Adele M. Fine
Albert L. Parisi

Reference: Central Trust Co.

For full biographical listings, see the Martindale-Hubbell Law Directory

CHAMBERLAIN, D'AMANDA, OPPENHEIMER & GREENFIELD (AV)

1600 Crossroads Office Building, Two State Street, 14614
Telephone: 716-232-3730
Telecopier: 716-232-3882

MEMBERS OF FIRM

Louis D'Amanda
Sheldon W. Boyce
Henry R. Ippolito
Douglas Jones
Roy Z. Rotenberg

ASSOCIATES

James L. Bradley
Susan R. L. Bernis
Eileen M. Potash

For Complete List of Firm Personnel, See General Section

For full biographical listings, see the Martindale-Hubbell Law Directory

GEIGER AND ROTHENBERG (AV)

800 Times Square Building, 45 Exchange Street, 14614
Telephone: 716-232-1946
FAX: 716-232-4746

Alexander Geiger
David Rothenberg

Reference: First National Bank of Rochester.

For full biographical listings, see the Martindale-Hubbell Law Directory

HARTER, SECREST & EMERY (AV)

700 Midtown Tower, 14604-2070
Telephone: 716-232-6500
Telecopier: 716-232-2152
Naples, Florida Office: Suite 400, 800 Laurel Oak Drive.
Telephone: 813-598-4444.
Telecopier: 813-598-2781.
Albany, New York Office: One Steuben Place.
Telephone: 518-434-4377.
Telecopier: 518-449-4025.
Syracuse, New York Office: 431 East Fayette Street.
Telephone: 315-474-4000.
Telecopier: 315-474-7789.

MEMBERS OF FIRM

Peter M. Blauvelt
Thomas B. Garlick (Resident Partner, Naples, Florida Office)
James C. Moore
Kenneth A. Payment
James P. Burns, 3rd (Resident Partner, Syracuse Office)
William H. Helferich, III
H. Robert Herman
Thomas G. Smith
Fred G. Aten, Jr.
Margaret Artale Catillaz
John C. Herbert
Timothy R. Parry (Not admitted in NY; Resident Partner, Naples, Florida Office)
Maureen T. Alston
Edward F. Premo II
Richard E. Alexander

OF COUNSEL

John F. Mahon
Bruce E. Hansen

COUNSEL

A. Paul Britton, Jr.

ASSOCIATES

Brian V. McAvoy
Carol O'Keefe
Peter H. Abdella
Peter T. Wlasuk (Resident Associate, Naples, Florida Office)
Jeffrey P. Stone
Jane A. Conrad
Susan A. Roberts
Amy Hartman Nichols
Kathleen M. Beckman
Michelle R. Dennison
Jon D. Parrish (Resident Associate, Naples, Florida Office)
Robert L. Cholette
Jacqueline A. Phipps

For Complete List of Firm Personnel, See General Section

For full biographical listings, see the Martindale-Hubbell Law Directory

UNDERBERG & KESSLER (AV)

1800 Chase Square, 14604
Telephone: 716-258-2800
Fax: 716-258-2821

(See Next Column)

MEMBERS OF FIRM

Alan J. Underberg
Irving L. Kessler
Michael J. Beyma
Frank T. Crego
Robert W. Croessmann
John W. Crowe
Michael C. Dwyer
Bernard A. Frank
Steven R. Gersz
John L. Goldman
Lawrence P. Keller
Gordon J. Lipson
Robert F. Mechur
Paul V. Nunes
Terry M. Richman
Sharon P. Stiller
Stephen H. Waite
Russell I. Zuckerman

OF COUNSEL

Richard G. Crawford
Andrew M. Greenstein

SENIOR ATTORNEY

Thomas P. Young

ASSOCIATES

Patrick L. Cusato
Katherine Howk Karl
Sean E. Gleason
Suzanne D. Nott
Linda Prestegaard

For full biographical listings, see the Martindale-Hubbell Law Directory

SMITHTOWN, Suffolk Co.

GRESHIN, ZIEGLER & PRUZANSKY (AV)

199 East Main Street, P.O. Box 829, 11787
Telephone: 516-265-2550
Telecopier: 516-265-2832

Benjamin Greshin
Joel J. Ziegler
Joshua M. Pruzansky

ASSOCIATE

Joanne Skiadas

For full biographical listings, see the Martindale-Hubbell Law Directory

STANFORDVILLE, Dutchess Co.

WILLIAM E. STANTON (AV)

Village Centre, Route 82, P.O. Box 370, 12581
Telephone: 914-868-7514
FAX: 914-868-7761

Representative Clients: Dupont de Nemours & Co.; Millbrook School; Hanover Insurance Co.; New York Telephone Co.
Reference: Fishkill National Bank.

For full biographical listings, see the Martindale-Hubbell Law Directory

*STATEN ISLAND,** Richmond Co.

SIMONSON & COHEN, P.C. (AV)

4060 Amboy Road, 10308
Telephone: 718-948-2100
Telecopier: 718-356-2379

Sidney O. Simonson (1911-1986)
Daniel Cohen
Robert M. Cohen
James R. Cohen

Michael Adler
Lawrence J. Lorczak

For full biographical listings, see the Martindale-Hubbell Law Directory

STONY POINT, Rockland Co.

HURLEY, FOX, SELIG & KELLEHER (AV)

Liberty Building, Route 9 W, 10980
Telephone: 914-942-2222
Fax: 914-942-0378
New City, New York Office: 60 Pine Street.
Telephone: 914-634-2050.

MEMBERS OF FIRM

Benjamin E. Selig
Glenn W. Kelleher

ASSOCIATES

Jeanne Marie Hurley
Paul Anthony Hurley

LEGAL SUPPORT PERSONNEL

Eileen M. Kehnle

Representative Clients: Bradlees, Inc.; Amerisure Insurance Co.; Continental Insurance Cos.; Wausau Insurance Co.; Federal Insurance Co.; Chubb & Son; Commercial Union Group of Insurance Cos.; Empire Insurance Co.; Universal Underwriters Insurance Co.

For full biographical listings, see the Martindale-Hubbell Law Directory

*SYRACUSE,** Onondaga Co.

IRWIN BIRNBAUM (AV)

One Lincoln Center, Suite 760, 13202
Telephone: 315-422-0246
FAX: 315-476-7526

(See Next Column)

IRWIN BIRNBAUM—*Continued*

ASSOCIATE

Jane G. Kuppermann

For full biographical listings, see the Martindale-Hubbell Law Directory

BOND, SCHOENECK & KING (AV)

18th Floor One Lincoln Center, 13202-1355
Telephone: 315-422-0121
Fax: 315-422-3598
Albany, New York Office: 111 Washington Avenue.
Telephone: 518-462-7421.
Fax: 518-462-7441.
Boca Raton, Florida Office: 5355 Town Center Road, Suite 1002.
Telephone: 407-368-1212.
Fax: 407-338-9955.
Naples, Florida Office: 1167 Third Street South.
Telephone: 813-262-6812.
Fax: 813-262-6908.
Oswego, New York Office: 130 East Second Street.
Telephone: 315-343-9116.
Fax: 315-343-1231.
Overland Park, Kansas Office: 7500 College Boulevard, Suite 910.
Telephone: 913-345-8001.
Fax: 913-345-9017.

MEMBERS OF FIRM

John M. Freyer (Resident, Albany Office)
Charles T. Major, Jr.
Francis E. Maloney, Jr.
S. Paul Battaglia
George H. Lowe
John D. Allen
Thomas E. Myers
Carl Rosenbloom (Resident, Albany Office)
Thomas R. Smith
Robert C. Zundel, Jr. (Resident, Boca Raton, Florida Office)
David L. Dawson (Resident, Naples, Florida Office)
David R. Sheridan (Resident, Albany Office)
Thomas D. Keleher
Edward R. Conan
John H. Callahan
John G. McGowan
Richard A. Reed (Resident, Albany Office)
Deborah H. Karalunas
Jonathan B. Fellows
Arthur J. Siegel (Resident, Albany Office)

ASSOCIATES

Edward A. Mervine (Resident, Oswego Office)
Robert H. Kirchner

General Counsel for: Syracuse University; Unity Mutual Life Insurance Co.; Manufacturers Association of Central New York.
Regional or Special Counsel for: Newhouse Broadcasting Corp. (WSYR, AM-FM); Syracuse Herald-Post Standard Newspapers.; Miller Brewing Co.; Allied Corp.; General Electric Co.; National Grange.

For Complete List of Firm Personnel, See General Section

For full biographical listings, see the Martindale-Hubbell Law Directory

COSTELLO COONEY & FEARON (AV)

Salina Place, 205 South Salina Street, 13202
Telephone: 315-422-1152
Fax: 315-422-1139

MEMBERS OF FIRM

Vincent A. O'Neil
Robert J. Smith
James J. Gascon

ASSOCIATES

Paul G. Ferrara
Maureen G. Fatcheric

General Counsel: Auburn Memorial Hospital; Crouse-Irving Memorial Hospital.
Local Counsel: Caterpillar, Inc.; Otis Elevator; Deere & Co.; New York Telephone Co.; Crum & Forster Insurance Co.; General Motors Acceptance Corp.; American District Telegraph (A&T); Pyramid Brokerage Co.

For Complete List of Firm Personnel, See General Section

For full biographical listings, see the Martindale-Hubbell Law Directory

GROSSMAN KINNEY DWYER & HARRIGAN, P.C. (AV)

5720 Commons Park, 13057
Telephone: 315-449-2131
Telecopier: 315-449-2905

Richard D. Grossman
John P. Kinney
James F. Dwyer
C. Frank Harrigan
Robert E. Hornik, Jr.
Harris N. Lindenfeld

Ruth Moors D'Eredita
Edward P. Dunn
Joseph G. Shields

Representative Clients: County of Onondaga; County of Tompkins; Therm, Incorporated, Ithaca, New York; Village of Marcellus; Smith Barney Shearson; The Mitsubishi Bank, Limited (New York Branch); C&S Engineers, Inc.; Town of Harrietstown, New York.

For full biographical listings, see the Martindale-Hubbell Law Directory

NOTTINGHAM, ENGEL, GORDON & KERR (AV)

Eighth Floor, One Lincoln Center, 13202
Telephone: 315-474-6046
Fax: 315-474-6065

MEMBERS OF FIRM

Richard L. Engel
Richard E. Gordon
J. Craig Kerr

For full biographical listings, see the Martindale-Hubbell Law Directory

*TROY,** Rensselaer Co.

E. STEWART JONES (AV)

28 Second Street, 12181
Telephone: 518-274-5820
Fax: 518-274-5875

E. Stewart Jones, Jr.
W. Farley Jones
Jeffrey K. Anderson
David J. Taffany
Peter J. Moschetti, Jr.

OF COUNSEL

E. Stewart Jones
Arthur L. Rosen
Abbott H. Jones (1873-1939)
Charles W. Marshall (1882-1945)

References: Key Bank and On Bank; Troy Savings Bank.

For full biographical listings, see the Martindale-Hubbell Law Directory

UNIONDALE, Nassau Co.

FARRELL, FRITZ, CAEMMERER, CLEARY, BARNOSKY & ARMENTANO, PROFESSIONAL CORPORATION (AV)

EAB Plaza, 11556-0120
Telephone: 516-227-0700
Facsimile: 516-227-0777

John M. Armentano
John J. Barnosky
Igor Bilewich
John P. Cleary
John F. Coffey
George J. Farrell, Jr.
Dolores Fredrich
Robert V. Guido
Thomas J. Killeen
John R. Morken
Andrew J. Simons
Charles M. Strain
William D. Wall

For Complete List of Firm Personnel, See General Section

For full biographical listings, see the Martindale-Hubbell Law Directory

RIVKIN, RADLER & KREMER (AV)

A Partnership including Professional Corporations
EAB Plaza (Long Island), 11556-0111
Telephone: 516-357-3000
Cable Address: "Atlaw"
Telex: 645-074
Telecopier: 516-357-3333
Chicago, Illinois Office: Suite 4300, 30 North LaSalle Street.
Telephone: 312-782-5680.
Telecopier: 312-782-3112.
New York, New York Office: 275 Madison Avenue.
Telephone: 212-455-9555.
Telecopier: 212-687-9044.
Santa Rosa, California Office: 100 B Street, Suite 300, P.O. Box 14609.
Telephone: 707-576-8033.
Telecopier: 707-576-7955.
Pasadena, California Office: 123 South Marengo Avenue, Suite 400.
Telephone: 818-795-1800.
Fax: 818-795-2255.
Newark, New Jersey Office: One Gateway Center, Suite 1226.
Telephone: 201-622-0900.
Fax: 201-622-7878.

MEMBERS OF FIRM

Arthur J. Kremer
Bruce D. Drucker (P.C.)
William M. Savino (P.C.)
Donald T. McMillan (Resident, Santa Rosa, California Office)
James P. Nunemaker, Jr.
Joseph J. Ortego
John L. Rivkin
Stephen J. Smirti, Jr., (P.C.)
Peter L. Curry
Richard S. Feldman
Barry R. Shapiro
Gary D. Centola
Anthony R. Gambardella
Peter C. Contino
Erica B. Garay
Daniel A. Bartoldus
Charlotte Biblow
Steven Brock
Kenneth L. Brown
William J. Candee, III
George K. DeHaven
M. Paul Gorfinkel
Steven R. Merican (Resident, Chicago Office)
Howard J. Newman
Charles H. Reinhardt, Jr.

OF COUNSEL

Stanley Pierce

Representative Clients: Allstate Insurance Co.; Chase Manhattan Bank, N.A.; Chemical Bank; The DOW Chemical Co.; Government Employees Insurance Co.; Liquidation Bureau; New York Insurance Dept.; Prudential Property & Casualty Insurance Co.; The Dime Savings Bank of New York.

(See Next Column)

RIVKIN, RADLER & KREMER, *Uniondale—Continued*

For Complete List of Firm Personnel, See General Section

For full biographical listings, see the Martindale-Hubbell Law Directory

WESTBURY, Nassau Co.

PRYOR & MANDELUP, P.C. (AV)

675 Old Country Road, 11590
Telephone: 516-997-0999
Facsimile: 516-333-7333

Robert L. Pryor
A. Scott Mandelup
Randolph E. White

David J. Weiss
Eric J. Snyder
Jeanne Farnan
Adam H. Friedman
Gerard M. Bambrick

For full biographical listings, see the Martindale-Hubbell Law Directory

*WHITE PLAINS,** Westchester Co.

BLEAKLEY PLATT & SCHMIDT (AV)

One North Lexington Avenue, 10601-1700
Telephone: 914-949-2700
Telecopier: 914-683-6956
Somers, New York Office: 272 Route 202.
Telephone: 914-277-3924.
Telecopier: 914-277-7133.
Greenwich, Connecticut Office: Sixty-Six Field Point Road.
Telephone: 203-661-5222.
Telecopier: 203-661-1197.

MEMBERS OF FIRM

Frederick J. Martin
William F. Harrington
Joseph B. Glatthaar
John J. Ferguson (Resident, Greenwich, Connecticut Office)
Donald J. Sullivan
Robert D. Meade
Hugh D. Fyfe, Jr.
Raymond M. Planell
William Hughes Mulligan, Jr.
James J. Sullivan
Janice H. Eiseman
Lester Berkelhamer
John E. Meerbergen (Resident, Greenwich, Connecticut Office)
William P. Harrington
Mary Ellen Manley
Brian E. Lorenz
Timothy P. Coon

COUNSEL

Henry R. Barrett, III
Joseph A. Izzillo (Resident, Greenwich, Connecticut Office)
Peter T. Gahagan
Joseph De Giuseppe, Jr.
Kimberlea Shaw Rea
J. Lincoln Hallowell (Resident, Greenwich, Connecticut Office)
Mary E. Quaranta Morrissey

James W. Glatthaar
Frank J. Ingrassia
Vincent W. Crowe
Veronica C. Staplefield (Resident, Greenwich, Connecticut Office)
Sheila T. Murphy
John F. Martin
Mark K. Malone

Representative Clients: American Telephone & Telegraph Co.; The Bank of New York-County Trust Region; General Foods Corp.; The Guardian Life Insurance Co.; Mobil Oil Corp.; New York American Water Company, Inc-.(a subsidiary of American Water Works Co., Inc.); St. Joseph's Hospital, Yonkers; The Singer Co.; Yonkers Racing Corp.

For Complete List of Firm Personnel, See General Section

For full biographical listings, see the Martindale-Hubbell Law Directory

ANTHONY J. CAPUTO, P.C. (AV)

175 Main Street, 10601
Telephone: 914-948-5151

Anthony J. Caputo

OF COUNSEL

Bruce F. Caputo

Representative Clients: Aetna Life & Casualty Co.; Liberty Mutual Insurance Co.
References: Chemical Bank; Citicorp.

For full biographical listings, see the Martindale-Hubbell Law Directory

CERUSSI & SPRING, A PROFESSIONAL CORPORATION (AV)

One North Lexington Avenue, 10601-1700
Telephone: 914-948-1200
Cable Address: Cerspringlaw Whiteplainsnewyork
Facsimile: 914-948-1579
Greenwich, Connecticut Office: 66 Field Point Road.
Telephone: 203-661-4000.
Facsimile: 203-661-1197.

(See Next Column)

Michael A. Cerussi, Jr.
Ronald G. Crispi
Joseph A. D'Avanzo
Arthur J. Spring

Thomas F. Cerussi
Denise M. Cossu
Kathleen A. DePalma
Mark C. Dillon
Michael P. Fitzgerald
Matthew K. Flanagan
Thomas A. Hayes, Jr.
Anne E. Kershaw
Steven R. Lau
John J.A.M. Loveless
Curt D. Marshall
Maria J. Morreale
Owen S. Mudge, Jr.
Jeffrey C. Nagle (Not admitted in NY)
William J. Rizzo
Mary E. Toop
Gina M. Von Oehsen

For full biographical listings, see the Martindale-Hubbell Law Directory

CLARK, GAGLIARDI & MILLER, P.C. (AV)

Inns of Court Building, 99 Court Street, 10601
Telephone: 914-946-8900
Telecopier: 914-946-8960
New York, New York Office: Suite 2525, 230 Park Avenue.
Telephone: 914-926-8900.

Robert Y. Clark (1881-1961)
Frank M. Gagliardi (1886-1980)
Joseph F. Gagliardi (1911-1992)
Henry G. Miller
Lawrence T. D'Aloise, Jr.
Lucille A. Fontana
Robert J. Frisenda

Angela Morcone Giannini
Padraic D. Lee
Denise Liotta DeMarzo

OF COUNSEL

Morton B. Silberman

For full biographical listings, see the Martindale-Hubbell Law Directory

GREENE & ZINNER, P.C. (AV)

202 Mamaroneck Avenue, 10601
Telephone: 914-948-4800
FAX: 914-948-4936

Andrew Greene
Stanley S. Zinner

Jeffrey P. Rogan
Robert J. Bellinson
Daniel E. Schnapp (Not admitted in NY)

For full biographical listings, see the Martindale-Hubbell Law Directory

GREENSPAN & GREENSPAN (AV)

34 South Broadway, 6th Floor, 10601
Telephone: 914-946-2500
Cable Address: "Gadlex"
Telecopier: 914-946-1432

MEMBERS OF FIRM

Leon J. Greenspan
Michael E. Greenspan

For full biographical listings, see the Martindale-Hubbell Law Directory

KENT, HAZZARD, JAEGER, GREER, WILSON & FAY (AV)

50 Main Street, 10606
Telephone: 914-948-4700
Telecopier: 914-948-4721

MEMBERS OF FIRM

Ralph S. Kent (1878-1949)
Lawrence S. Hazzard (1900-1958)
William J. Greer (1920-1994)
Mizell Wilson, Jr.
Lawrence F. Fay
Robert D. Hazzard
Gregory C. Freeman
Robert G. O'Donnell
Katharine Wilson Conroy
John R. Dinin

OF COUNSEL

Malcolm Wilson
Edward J. Freeman
Otto C. Jaeger
George Beisheim, Jr.
Peter F. Blasi

Representative Clients: The Bank of New York.
References: Bank of New York; Peoples Westchester Savings Bank.

For full biographical listings, see the Martindale-Hubbell Law Directory

WINDHAM, Greene Co.

BROWN, KELLEHER, ZWICKEL & WILHELM (AV)

Main Street, 12496
Telephone: 518-734-3800
Fax: 518-734-4226
Catskill, New York Office: 370 Main Street 12414.
Telephone: 518-943-1111.
Fax: 518-943-4549.

MEMBERS OF FIRM

Charles J. Brown
Kevin M. Kelleher
Charles Zwickel
Terry J. Wilhelm

(See Next Column)

BROWN, KELLEHER, ZWICKEL & WILHELM—*Continued*

ASSOCIATE

Carol D. Stevens

For full biographical listings, see the Martindale-Hubbell Law Directory

NORTH CAROLINA

*ASHEVILLE,** Buncombe Co.

ELMORE & ELMORE, P.A. (AV)

53 North Market Street, 28801
Telephone: 704-253-1492
Fax: 704-253-9648

Bruce A. Elmore
Bruce A. Elmore, Jr.

Reed G. Williams

For full biographical listings, see the Martindale-Hubbell Law Directory

LONG, PARKER & PAYNE, P.A. (AV)

Suite 600, 14 Pack Square, P.O. Box 7216, 28801
Telephone: 704-258-2296
Fax: 704-253-1073

Robert B. Long, Jr.
William A. Parker
Ronald K. Payne

Joseph E. Herrin
W. Scott Jones

For full biographical listings, see the Martindale-Hubbell Law Directory

MCGUIRE, WOOD & BISSETTE, P.A. (AV)

Suite 705 First Union National Bank Building, 82 Patton Avenue, P.O. Box 3180, 28802
Telephone: 704-254-8806
Fax: 704-252-2438

Walter R. McGuire
Richard A. Wood, Jr.
W. Louis Bissette, Jr.
Douglas O. Thigpen
Joseph P. McGuire
Doris Phillips Loomis
M. Charles Cloninger
Thomas C. Grella
Grant B. Osborne
Richard A. Kort

OF COUNSEL

Frank M. Parker

Representative Clients: Asheville Citizen-Times Publishing Co.; Dave Steel Co., Inc. (Steel Fabricating); WLOS-TV; The Givens Estates, Inc. (Retirement Community); Hayes & Lunsford Electrical Contractors, Inc.; Wellco Enterprises, Inc.; BASF Corp.; First Union National Bank; St. Joseph's Hospital; Revco Scientific, Inc.

For full biographical listings, see the Martindale-Hubbell Law Directory

REYNOLDS & MCARTHUR (AV Ⓣ)

A Partnership including a Professional Corporation
The Jackson Building, 22 South Pack Square Suite 1200, 28801
Telephone: 704-254-8523
Fax: 704-254-3038
Macon, Georgia Office: 850 Walnut Street.
Telephone: 912-741-6000.
Fax: 912-742-0750.
Atlanta, Georgia Office: Suite 1080, One Buckhead Plaza, 3060 Peachtree Road, N.W.
Telephone: 404-240-0265.
Fax: 404-262-3557.

MEMBERS OF FIRM

W. Carl Reynolds (P.C.) (Not admitted in NC)
Katherine L. McArthur
Charles M. Cork, III (Not admitted in NC)
O. Wendell Horne, III (Not admitted in NC)
Bradley J. Survant (Not admitted in NC)
Steve Ray Warren

For full biographical listings, see the Martindale-Hubbell Law Directory

*BEAUFORT,** Carteret Co.

DAVIS, MURRELLE & LUMSDEN, P.A. (AV)

Beaufort Professional Center, 412 Front Street, P.O. Box 819, 28516
Telephone: 919-728-4080
FAX: 919-728-3235

Edward L. Murrelle
Treve B. Lumsden

Janet M. Lyles

(See Next Column)

OF COUNSEL

Warren J. Davis

Representative Clients: NationsBank; Cooperative Bank for Savings; Zapata Haynie Corp.; Roman Catholic Diocese of Raleigh for Carteret County; International Longshoreman's Association Local 1807; Town of Cedar Point; John Yancey Corp.; Morehead City Export Terminal, Inc.; Morehead City Docking Masters Assoc., Inc.; Crow Hill Farms, Inc.

For full biographical listings, see the Martindale-Hubbell Law Directory

WHEATLY, WHEATLY, NOBLES & WEEKS, P.A. (AV)

410 Front Street, P.O. Drawer 360, 28516
Telephone: 919-728-3158
FAX: 919-728-5282

Claud R. Wheatly, Jr.
Claud R. Wheatly, III
John E. Nobles, Jr.
Stevenson L. Weeks
J. Christy Maroules
Stephen M. Valentine

Reference: First Citizens Bank.

For full biographical listings, see the Martindale-Hubbell Law Directory

*BOONE,** Watauga Co.

CHARLES E. CLEMENT (AV)

756 West King Street, P.O. Drawer 32, 28607
Telephone: 704-264-6411
FAX: 704-264-5424

Representative Clients: First Union National Bank.
Approved Attorney for: Lawyers Title Insurance Corp.; Chicago Title Insurance Co.

For full biographical listings, see the Martindale-Hubbell Law Directory

CHAPEL HILL, Orange Co.

BERNHOLZ & HERMAN (AV)

Suite 300, The Center, 1506 East Franklin Street, 27514
Telephone: 919-929-7151
Fax: 919-929-3892

MEMBERS OF FIRM

Steven A. Bernholz
Roger B. Bernholz
G. Nicholas Herman

OF COUNSEL

J. Austin Lybrand, IV

For full biographical listings, see the Martindale-Hubbell Law Directory

LONG & LONG (AV)

116 Mallette Street, 27516
Telephone: 919-929-0408
Fax: 919-929-6819

MEMBERS OF FIRM

Lunsford Long
Florence J. Long

For full biographical listings, see the Martindale-Hubbell Law Directory

NORTHEN, BLUE, ROOKS, THIBAUT, ANDERSON & WOODS, L.L.P. (AV)

Suite 550, 100 Europa Center, P.O. Box 2208, 27515-2208
Telephone: 919-968-4441
Facsimile: 919-942-6603

MEMBERS OF FIRM

John A. Northen
J. William Blue, Jr.
David M. Rooks, III
Charles H. Thibaut
Charles T. L. Anderson
Jo Ann Ragazzo Woods
Carol J. Holcomb

ASSOCIATES

James C. Stanford
Gregory Herman-Giddens
Cheryl Y. Capron

References: Central Carolina Bank; The Village Bank; Investors Title Insurance Co.; First Union National Bank; Centura Bank; United Carolina Bank; BB&T; Balbirer & Coleman, CPA's.

For full biographical listings, see the Martindale-Hubbell Law Directory

BARRY T. WINSTON (AV)

The Center, Suite 300, 1506 East Franklin Street, 27514
Telephone: 919-967-8553
FAX: 919-968-4698

Reference: First Citizens Bank & Trust Co.

For full biographical listings, see the Martindale-Hubbell Law Directory

*CHARLOTTE,** Mecklenburg Co.

BAILEY, PATTERSON, CADDELL, HART & BAILEY, P.A. (AV)
Suite 502, Cameron Brown Building, 301 South McDowell Street, 28204
Telephone: 704-333-8612
FAX: 704-333-5279

Allen A. Bailey
Michael A. Bailey
William J. Patterson
H. Morris Caddell, Jr.
Walter L. Hart, IV

Richard A. Culler
Emery E. Milliken
David C. Cordes
Martha L. Ramsay
Thomas D. Thompson

For full biographical listings, see the Martindale-Hubbell Law Directory

BLAKENEY & ALEXANDER (AV)
3700 NationsBank Plaza, 101 South Tryon Street, 28280
Telephone: 704-372-3680
Facsimile: 704-332-2611

MEMBERS OF FIRM

Whiteford S. Blakeney (1906-1991)
J. W. Alexander, Jr. (1919-1990)
John O. Pollard
W. T. Cranfill, Jr.
Richard F. Kane
David L. Terry
Michael V. Matthews

ASSOCIATES

Jay L. Grytdahl
Robert B. Meyer
Kevin V. Parsons

Counsel for: Overnite Transportation Company; Old Dominion Freight Line, Inc.; Freightliner Corporation; U.S. Air; Trinity Industries; NationsBank Corporation; Vaughan Furniture Cos.; The Lane Company, Inc.; Ingles Markets, Inc.; Lance, Inc.

For full biographical listings, see the Martindale-Hubbell Law Directory

CAUDLE & SPEARS, P.A. (AV)
2600 Interstate Tower, 121 West Trade Street, 28202
Telephone: 704-377-1200
Telecopier: 704-338-5858

Lloyd C. Caudle
Harold C. Spears
Thad A. Throneburg
Patrick Jenkins
L. Cameron Caudle, Jr.
Nancy E. Walker
Timothy T. Leach
John A. Folmar
Sean M. Phelan
Jeffrey L. Helms

Counsel for: Bituminous Casualty Corp.; Baumann Springs A.G.; The A. G. Boone Co.; Consolidated Freightways; Employers Mutual Casualty Co.; Metromont Materials; Otis Elevator Co.; N.C. Farm Bureau Mutual Insurance Co.; Toyoda Textile Machinery, Inc.; U. S. Bottlers Machinery Co.

For full biographical listings, see the Martindale-Hubbell Law Directory

GOLDING, MEEKINS, HOLDEN, COSPER & STILES (AV)
Suite 1200, Cameron Brown Building, 301 South McDowell Street, 28204
Telephone: 704-374-1600
Fax: 704-374-1103

MEMBERS OF FIRM

John G. Golding
Frederick C. Meekins (Retired)
C. Byron Holden
Harvey L. Cosper, Jr.
Ned A. Stiles
Henry C. Byrum, Jr.
James W. Pope
Andrew W. Lax
Terry D. Horne
Elaine C. Miller

ASSOCIATES

Lawrence M. Baker
Lawrence W. Jones
Deborah G. Casey
D. Lane Matthews
Carl Spencer Alridge, II
Mark O. Crowther
Harold D. Holmes, Jr.
Paul R. Dickinson, Jr.
Scott A. Beckey
Christine E. Alaimo
Betsy J. Jones

Representative Clients: Carolina Freight Carriers Corp.; PPG Industries; Wal-Mart Stores, Inc.; State Farm Insurance Companies; St. Paul Insurance Companies.

For full biographical listings, see the Martindale-Hubbell Law Directory

MITCHELL & RALLINGS (AV)
1800 Carillon, 227 West Trade Street, 28202
Telephone: 704-376-6574
FAX: 704-342-1531

MEMBERS OF FIRM

Richard M. Mitchell
Thomas B. Rallings, Jr.

ASSOCIATES

James L. Fretwell
Joseph N. Tissue
James Dagoberto Concepcion
John W. Taylor

(See Next Column)

COUNSEL

Alvin A. London

Representative Clients: Bonitz Contracting Co.; Captain D's. Inc.; Chemical Financial Services Corp.; Dorfio, Inc.; Dyke Industries, Inc.; Edgcomb Metals; Titan Building Products, Inc.; Fairfinish Corp.
References: Republic Bank & Trust Co.; N.C.N.B.

For full biographical listings, see the Martindale-Hubbell Law Directory

RAYBURN, MOON & SMITH, P.A. (AV)
The Carillon, 227 West Trade Street, Suite 1200, 28202
Telephone: 704-334-0891
FAX: 704-377-1897; 704-358-8866

Albert F. Durham
Travis W. Moon
C. Richard Rayburn, Jr.
James C. Smith
W. Scott Cooper
Matthew R. Joyner
James L. Bagwell
Cynthia D. Lewis
Patricia B. Edmondson
Paul R. Baynard
Laura D. Fennell
G. Kirkland Hardymon

For full biographical listings, see the Martindale-Hubbell Law Directory

RUFF, BOND, COBB, WADE & MCNAIR, L.L.P. (AV)
2100 Two First Union Center, 301 South Tryon Street, 28282-8283
Telephone: 704-377-1634
FAX: 704-342-3308

MEMBERS OF FIRM

Thomas C. Ruff
Lyn Bond, Jr.
James O. Cobb
Hamlin L. Wade
William H. McNair
Marvin A. Bethune
Moses Luski
Francis W. Sturges
Robert S. Adden, Jr.
James H. Pickard

ASSOCIATES

George R. Jurch, III
Stephen D. Koehler

For full biographical listings, see the Martindale-Hubbell Law Directory

WOMBLE CARLYLE SANDRIDGE & RICE (AV)
A Professional Limited Liability Company
3300 One First Union Center, 301 S. College Street, 28202-6025
Telephone: 704-331-4900
Telecopy: 704-331-4955
Telex: 853609
Winston-Salem, North Carolina Office: 1600 Southern National Financial Center.
Telephone: 919-721-3600.
Telecopy: 919-721-3660.
Telex: 806498.
Raleigh, North Carolina Office: 2100 First Union Capitol Center, 150 Fayetteville Street Mall, P.O. Box 831.
Telephone: 919-755-2100.
Telecopy: 919-755-2150.
Telex: 806498.
Atlanta, Georgia Office: One Ninety One Peachtree Tower, 191 Peachtree Street N.E., Suite 3250.
Telephone: 404-614-2580.
Fax: 404-614-2595.

MEMBERS OF FIRM

Timothy G. Barber
Jim D. Cooley
Debbie Weston Harden
William C. Raper
F. Lane Williamson

RESIDENT ASSOCIATES

Steven D. Gardner
Mark P. Henriques

Representative Clients: Childress Klein Properties, Inc.; Food Lion, Inc.; Fieldcrest Cannon, Inc.; J.A. Jones Construction Company; Parkdale Mills, Inc.; Duke Power Company; Bowles Hollowell Conner & Company; ALLTEL Carolina, Inc.; Belk Store Services, Inc.; Philip Holzmann A.G.

For Complete List of Firm Personnel, See General Section

For full biographical listings, see the Martindale-Hubbell Law Directory

WYATT & CUNNINGHAM (AV)
435 East Morehead Street, 28202-2609
Telephone: 704-331-0767
Fax: 704-331-0773

James F. Wyatt, III
John R. Cunningham, III

For full biographical listings, see the Martindale-Hubbell Law Directory

*DURHAM,** Durham Co.

GLENN, MILLS & FISHER, P.A. (AV)
Suite 709, South Bank Building, 400 West Main Street, P.O. Drawer 3865, 27702-3865
Telephone: 919-683-2135
FAX: 919-688-9339

(See Next Column)

GLENN, MILLS & FISHER P.A.—*Continued*

Robert B. Glenn, Jr.
William S. Mills
Stewart W. Fisher

For full biographical listings, see the Martindale-Hubbell Law Directory

MOORE & VAN ALLEN, PLLC (AV)

Suite 800, 2200 West Main Street, 27705
Telephone: 919-286-8000
Fax: 919-286-8199
Charlotte, North Carolina Office: NationsBank Corporate Center, 100 North Tryon Street, Floor 47.
Telephone: 704-331-1000.
Fax: 704-331-1159.
Raleigh, North Carolina Office: One Hannover Square, Suite 1700, P.O. Box 26507.
Telephone: 919-828-4481.
Fax: 919-828-4254.

Edward L. Embree, III
William E. Freeman
Charles R. Holton
Laura Bernstein Luger
E. K. Powe

For Complete List of Firm Personnel, See General Section

For full biographical listings, see the Martindale-Hubbell Law Directory

NEWSOM, GRAHAM, HEDRICK & KENNON, P.A. (AV)

Suite 1200 University Tower, 3100 Tower Boulevard, P.O. Box 51579, 27717-1579
Telephone: 919-490-0500
Telecopier: 919-490-0873

James T. Hedrick
A. William Kennon
John L. Crill
John E. Markham, Jr.
Katherine McKee Holeman
William P. Daniell
Robert O. Belo
Joel M. Craig
John R. Long
David S. Kennett
G. Rhodes Craver

Dieter Mauch
Linda Imboden Ellington
Vedia Jones-Richardson
Henry A. Mitchell, III
Amy B. Quillen
Michelle Buerkle Beischer

OF COUNSEL

James L. Newsom
Alexander H. Graham, Jr.
Lynne Townsend Albert
Donald M. Etheridge, Jr.

Representative Clients: Wachovia Bank & Trust Co.; Duke Power Co.; Liggett Group, Inc.; General Telephone Company of the South; Exxon Corp.; Kemper Group of Insurance Cos.; Liberty Mutual Group.

For full biographical listings, see the Martindale-Hubbell Law Directory

*ELIZABETH CITY,** Pasquotank Co.

HORNTHAL, RILEY, ELLIS & MALAND, L.L.P. (AV)

301 E. Main Street, P.O. Box 220, 27909
Telephone: 919-335-0871
Fax: 919-335-4223
Nags Head, North Carolina Office: 2502 South Croatan Highway, P.O. Box 310, 27959-0310.
Telephone: 919-441-0871.
Telefax: 919-441-8822.

L. P. Hornthal, Jr.
J. Fred Riley
M. H. Hood Ellis
Mark M. Maland
Donald C. Prentiss
Robert B. Hobbs, Jr. (Resident, Nags Head Office)
John D. Leidy

ASSOCIATES

Michael P. Sanders
Lee L. Leidy
Phillip K. Woods

Representative Clients: Elizabeth City-Pasquotank County Board of Education; Kemper Insurance Group; State Farm Mutual; Travelers Insurance Co.; Wachovia Bank of North Carolina, N.A.; Great American Insurance Co.; Horace Mann Insurance Companies.

For full biographical listings, see the Martindale-Hubbell Law Directory

WHITE, HALL & DIXON (AV)

501 East Main Street, P.O. Box 304, 27907-0304
Telephone: 919-338-3906
Telecopier: 919-335-2456

MEMBERS OF FIRM

Gerald F. White
John H. Hall, Jr.
Samuel B. Dixon

Representative Clients: Shelby Mutual Insurance Co.; Lumbermen's Mutual Casualty Co.; Utica Mutual Insurance Co.; Kemper Insurance Group; Maryland Casualty Co.; Security Insurance Group; United States Automobile Assn.; Pennsylvania Manufacturers' Association Insurance Co.; Gates County Board of Education; Pasquotank County.

For full biographical listings, see the Martindale-Hubbell Law Directory

*GASTONIA,** Gaston Co.

WHITESIDES, ROBINSON, BLUE, WILSON & SMITH (AV)

246 West Main Avenue, P.O. Box 1115, 28053
Telephone: 704-864-5728
FAX: 704-864-6706
Belmont, North Carolina Office: Third Floor, Wachovia Building, Main Street, P.O. Box 901.
Telephone: 704-825-1079.
FAX: 704-825-7921.

MEMBERS OF FIRM

Henry M. Whitesides
Theodore Lamar Robinson, Jr.
Arthur C. Blue, III
Parks H. Wilson, Jr. (Resident, Belmont Office)
David W. Smith, III
Terry Albright Kenny

For full biographical listings, see the Martindale-Hubbell Law Directory

*GREENSBORO,** Guilford Co.

ADAMS KLEEMEIER HAGAN HANNAH & FOUTS (AV)

North Carolina Trust Center, 301 N. Elm Street, P.O. Box 3463, 27402
Telephone: 910-373-1600
Fax: 910-273-5357

MEMBERS OF FIRM

John A. Kleemeier, Jr. (1911-1973)
William J. Adams, Jr. (1908-1993)
Walter L. Hannah
Daniel W. Fouts
Robert G. Baynes
Joseph W. Moss
Clinton Eudy, Jr.
M. Jay DeVaney
Michael H. Godwin
W. Winburne King III
F. Cooper Brantley
Bruce H. Connors
Charles T. Hagan III
Larry I. Moore III
Elizabeth Dunn White
W. B. Rodman Davis
Thomas W. Brawner
Margaret Shea Burnham
Peter G. Pappas
William M. Wilcox IV
Katherine Bonan McDiarmid
David A. Senter
J. Alexander S. Barrett
Christine L. Myatt

OF COUNSEL

Charles T. Hagan, Jr.
Horace R. Kornegay

ASSOCIATES

Trudy A. Ennis
A. Scott Jackson
Amiel J. Rossabi
James W. Bryan
Betty Pincus Balcomb
Edward L. Bleynat, Jr.
Stephen A. Mayo
Louise Anderson Maultsby
R. Harper Heckman
Dena Beth Langley
David S. Pokela

Representative Clients: NationsBank of North Carolina, N.A.; Hafele America Co.; Duke Power Co.; U.S. Fidelity & Guaranty Co.; Dillard Paper Co.; Carolina Steel Corp.; Electrical South Inc.

For full biographical listings, see the Martindale-Hubbell Law Directory

BROOKS, PIERCE, McLENDON, HUMPHREY & LEONARD, L.L.P. (AV)

2000 Renaissance Plaza, 230 North Elm Street, P.O. Box 26000, 27420-6000
Telephone: 910-373-8850
Telex: 574301
Facsimile: 910-378-1001
Raleigh, North Carolina Office: 1600 First Union Capitol Center, 150 Fayetteville Street Mall, P.O. Box 1800.
Telephone: 919-839-0300.
Facsimile: 919-839-0304.

MEMBERS OF FIRM

Aubrey L. Brooks (1872-1958)
William H. Holderness (1904-1965)
Lennox P. McLendon (1890-1968)
Kenneth M. Brim (1898-1974)
C. Theodore Leonard, Jr. (1929-1983)
Claude C. Pierce (1913-1988)
Thornton H. Brooks (1912-1988)
G. Neil Daniels (Of Counsel, 1973--)
Lennox P. McLendon, Jr.
Hubert Humphrey
Edgar B. Fisher, Jr.
W. Erwin Fuller, Jr.
James T. Williams, Jr.
Wade H. Hargrove
M. Daniel McGinn
Michael D. Meeker
William G. McNairy
Edward C. Winslow, III
Howard L. Williams
George W. House
William P. H. Cary
Reid L. Phillips
Robert A. Singer
John H. Small
Randall A. Underwood
S. Leigh Rodenbough, IV
William G. Ross, Jr.
Jill R. Wilson
Marc D. Bishop
Jim W. Phillips, Jr.
Mack Sperling
Jeffrey E. Oleynik
Mark Davidson
Melissa H. Weaver
James R. Saintsing
John W. Ormand, III
James H. Jeffries, IV
Robert J. King, III
V. Randall Tinsley
John R. Archambault
S. Kyle Woosley
Catherine Thomas McGee
William C. Scott
Mark J. Prak
William A. Davis, II
Marcus W. Trathen

(See Next Column)

BROOKS, PIERCE, MCLENDON, HUMPHREY & LEONARD L.L.P., *Greensboro—Continued*

ASSOCIATES

Anne C. Brennan
Daniel M. Sroka
Forrest W. Campbell, Jr.
Ellen P. Hamrick
Allison M. Grimm
Jean C. Brooks
James C. Adams, II
Elizabeth S. Brewington
John K. Eason
Wayne A. Logan
H. Arthur Bolick, II
Natasha Rath Marcus

General Counsel for: N.C. Alliance of Community Financial Institutions; W.H. Weaver Construction Co.
Division Counsel for: Norfolk Southern Railway Co.
Attorneys for: Burlington Industries, Inc.; Masco Corp.; Wachovia Bank of North Carolina, N.A.; Provident Life & Accident Insurance Co.; Pennsylvania & Southern Gas Co.; AMP Inc.
Labor Counsel for: Lorillard Tobacco Co.

For full biographical listings, see the Martindale-Hubbell Law Directory

CARRUTHERS & ROTH, P.A. (AV)

235 North Edgeworth Street, P.O. Box 540, 27402
Telephone: 910-379-8651
Telecopier: 910-273-7885

Joseph T. Carruthers, Jr. (1906-1992)
Charles E. Roth (1917-1992)
Walter Rand
Seldon E. Patty
Thomas E. Wagg, III
Kenneth M. Greene
Richard L. Vanore
William L. Tankersley, III
Kenneth R. Keller
L. Worth Holleman, Jr.
Arthur A. Vreeland
Thomas W. Sinks
Howard L. Borum
J. Scott Dillon
J. Stanley Atwell
Kenneth L. Jones
June L. Basden
Desmond G. Sheridan
Michael J. Allen

Pamela Sarsfield Fox
Barbara L Curry
Gregory S. Williams
Keith A. Wood
John M. Flynn
Robert R. Niccolini

Representative Clients: AC Corporation; The Bank of New York; Barclays Commercial Corp.; Chrysler Financial Corp.; First Union Commercial Corp.; Kay Chemical Company; Kemper Insurance Group; Marine Midland Business Loans, Inc.; Metropolitan Life Insurance Co.; Thompson-Arthur Paving Co.

For full biographical listings, see the Martindale-Hubbell Law Directory

CLARK WHARTON & BERRY (AV)

600 Dixie Building, 125 South Elm Street, P.O. Box 1349, 27402
Telephone: 910-275-7275
Fax: 910-275-0672

David M. Clark
Richard L. Wharton
Frederick L. Berry

Representative Clients: The Prudential Insurance Company of America (litigation); Johnson Controls, Inc.
Approved Attorneys for: Jefferson-Pilot Insurance Co.

For Complete List of Firm Personnel, See General Section

For full biographical listings, see the Martindale-Hubbell Law Directory

GREESON, GRIFFIN & ASSOCIATES (AV)

400 West Market Street, Suite 300, P.O. Box 2460, 27402
Telephone: 910-370-4800
Fax: 910-370-0305

Harold F. Greeson
Mark F. Griffin

Christopher C. Kessler
George Podgorny, Jr.

For full biographical listings, see the Martindale-Hubbell Law Directory

HENSON HENSON BAYLISS & SUE (AV)

1610 First Union Tower, P.O. Box 3525, 27402
Telephone: 910-275-0587
Facsimile: 910-273-2585

MEMBERS OF FIRM

Perry C. Henson
Perry C. Henson, Jr.
Jack B. Bayliss, Jr.
Gary K. Sue
Walter K. Burton

ASSOCIATES

Daniel L. Deuterman
Brian A. Buchanan
Miriam S. Forbis
David K. Williams, Jr.

Representative Clients: Allstate Insurance Co.; The Home Indemnity Company; Kmart Corporation; Nationwide Mutual Insurance Co.; N.C. Farm Bureau Mutual Ins. Co.; Old Dominion Freight Line; Wausau Insurance Company.

For full biographical listings, see the Martindale-Hubbell Law Directory

NICHOLS, CAFFREY, HILL & EVANS, L.L.P. (AV)

1400 Renaissance Plaza, 230 North Elm Street, P.O. Box 989, 27402
Telephone: 910-379-1390
Fax: 910-379-1198

MEMBERS OF FIRM

Welch Jordan (1912-1976)
William D. Caffrey (1928-1991)
Karl N. Hill, Jr.
G. Marlin Evans
Thomas C. Duncan
William Welch Jordan
Lindsay Reeves Davis, Jr.
Joseph R. Beatty
Ronald P. Johnson
Fred T. Hamlet
R. Thompson Wright
Everett B. Saslow, Jr.
Dolores D. Follin
Richard J. Votta
Martha Taylor Peddrick
Douglas E. Wright

ASSOCIATES

Polly D. Sizemore
ToNola D. Brown
Gregory A. Stakias
Patricia P. Ridenhour
Michele G. Smith
Charles W. Coltrane

OF COUNSEL

Charles E. Nichols

Representative Clients: Ford Motor Credit Co.; Georgia-Pacific Corp.; Gilbarco, Inc.; Jefferson-Pilot Corp.; Nationwide Mutual Insurance Cos.; Rheem Manufacturing Company; Overnight Transportation Co.; Southern National Bank; The St. Paul Insurance Cos.

For Complete List of Firm Personnel, See General Section

For full biographical listings, see the Martindale-Hubbell Law Directory

HIGH POINT, Guilford Co.

WYATT, EARLY, HARRIS, WHEELER & HAUSER, L.L.P. (AV)

Old Courthouse Building, 258 South Main Street, P.O. Drawer 2086, 27261
Telephone: 910-884-4444
FAX: 910-889-5232

MEMBERS OF FIRM

Frank Burkhead Wyatt
William P. Harris
A. Doyle Early, Jr.
William E. Wheeler
David B. Ashcraft
Kim W. Gallimore
Kim R. Bauman
Calvin B. Bryant
R. Bruce Laney
Charles A. Alt
Frederick G. Sawyer
James R. Hundley
Charles L. Cain
Thomas E. Terrell, Jr.
Lee M. Cecil
Kevin L. Rochford
Ann E. Hanks
John David Bryson

Representative Clients: Allstate Insurance Co.; Davis Furniture Industries; First Union National Bank; United States Fidelity and Guaranty Co.; Dar-Ran Furniture Industries; First Citizens Bank & Trust Co.; Ohio Casualty Insurance Co.; Mid-State Petroleum; Rite Industries; Branch Bank & Trust Co.

For full biographical listings, see the Martindale-Hubbell Law Directory

*HILLSBOROUGH,** Orange Co.

COLEMAN, GLEDHILL & HARGRAVE, P.C. (AV)

129 East Tryon Street, P.O. Drawer 1529, 27278
Telephone: 919-732-2196
FAX: 919-732-7997

Alonzo B. Coleman, Jr.
Geoffrey E. Gledhill
Douglas Hargrave

Kim K. Steffan
Janet B. Dutton
Douglas P. Thoren

For full biographical listings, see the Martindale-Hubbell Law Directory

*KINSTON,** Lenoir Co.

WHITE & ALLEN, P.A. (AV)

106 South McLewean Street, P.O. Box 3169, 28501
Telephone: 919-527-8000
Telecopier: 919-527-8128

Thomas J. White (1903-1991)
William A. Allen, Jr.
John R. Hooten
John C. Archie
C. Gray Johnsey
Joseph Sidney Bower
David J. Fillippeli, Jr.
James B. Stephenson II
John P. Marshall
Jonathon L. Sargeant
Dale S. Davidson

Special Counsel for: Southern Railway Co.
Representative Clients: Lenoir Memorial Hospital; Carolina Power & Light Co.; First American Savings Bank; Kinston Housing Authority; First Citizens Bank & Trust Co.; Wachovia Bank of North Carolina, N.A.; NationsBank, N.A.; Kemper National Group; Hampton Industries, Inc.

For full biographical listings, see the Martindale-Hubbell Law Directory

MOREHEAD CITY, Carteret Co.

BENNETT, MCCONKEY, THOMPSON & MARQUARDT, P.A. (AV)

1007 Shepard Street, P.O. Drawer 189, 28557
Telephone: 919-726-4114
FAX: 919-726-7975

Thomas S. Bennett
James W. Thompson, III
Samuel A. McConkey, Jr.
Dennis M. Marquardt

Approved Attorneys For: Lawyers Title Insurance Corp.
Reference: First Citizens Bank & Trust Co.

For full biographical listings, see the Martindale-Hubbell Law Directory

*NEW BERN,** Craven Co.

HARRIS, SHIELDS AND CREECH, P.A. (AV)

325 Pollock Street, P.O. Drawer 1168, 28563-1168
Telephone: 919-638-6666
Facsimile: 919-638-3542

Thomas E. Harris
C. David Creech
Robert S. Shields, Jr.
R. Brittain Blackerby
Charles Everett Simpson, Jr.

For full biographical listings, see the Martindale-Hubbell Law Directory

WARD, WARD, WILLEY AND WARD (AV)

409 Pollock Street, P.O. Drawer 1428, 28560
Telephone: 919-633-1103
FAX: 919-633-9400
Other New Bern Office: Raleigh Federal Savings Building, 513 Pollock Street.
Fax: 919-633-5578.

MEMBERS OF FIRM

Alfred Decatur Ward
Joshua W. Willey, Jr.
Alfred Decatur Ward, Jr.
Thomas M. Ward

J. Michael Mills

Representative Clients: City of New Bern; Wachovia Bank & Trust Company; Raleigh Federal Savings Bank; Trent Olds-Cadillac-Buick, Inc.; Turner-Tolson, Inc.; R.A. Precision, Inc.; NationsBank; Case Equipment Co.; Chemical Residential Mortgage Corp.; AMRESCO Institutional, Inc.
Approved Attorneys for: Stewart Title Insurance Co.

For full biographical listings, see the Martindale-Hubbell Law Directory

*RALEIGH,** Wake Co.

* indicates certain Bar Register subscribers whose principal office is located elsewhere in the state and who have arranged for representation as a part of the state capital listings that follow

BAILEY & DIXON (AV)

2500 Two Hannover Square, 434 Fayetteville Street Mall, P.O. Box 1351, 27602
Telephone: 919-828-0731
Facsimile: 919-828-6592

MEMBERS OF FIRM

Ralph McDonald
Alan J. Miles
Gary S. Parsons
Patricia P. Kerner
Carson Carmichael, III
Cathleen M. Plaut
Dorothy V. Kibler
David S. Coats

OF COUNSEL

J. Ruffin Bailey
James H. Walker (1920-1994)
Wright T. Dixon, Jr.
David M. Britt

ASSOCIATES

Marcus B. Liles, III
Kenyann G. Brown
Renee C. Riggsbee
Christopher L. Mewborn
Denise Stanford Haskell
Sylvia Stanley Wood

Representative Clients: Nationwide Insurance Co.; Lawyers Mutual Liability Insurance Company of North Carolina; Aetna Life and Casualty Insurance Company; Santee Carriers; Abbott Laboratories Inc.; GAB Business Services, Inc.

For full biographical listings, see the Martindale-Hubbell Law Directory

BLANCHARD, TWIGGS, ABRAMS & STRICKLAND, P.A. (AV)

First Union Capitol Center, 150 Fayetteville Street Mall, 11th Floor, P.O. Drawer 30, 27602
Telephone: 919-828-4357
FAX: 919-833-7924

Howard F. Twiggs
Donald R. Strickland
Douglas B. Abrams
Jerome P. Trehy, Jr.

Margaret Smith Abrams
Robert O. Jenkins
Karen M. Rabenau

(See Next Column)

OF COUNSEL

Charles F. Blanchard
Donald H. Beskind

For full biographical listings, see the Martindale-Hubbell Law Directory

EVERETT, GASKINS, HANCOCK & STEVENS (AV)

The Professional Building, Suite 600, 127 West Hargett Street, P.O. Box 911, 27602
Telephone: 919-755-0025
Fax: 919-755-0009
Durham, North Carolina Office: Suite 300, 301 West Main Street, P.O. Box 586.
Telephone: 919-682-5691.
Fax: 919-682-5469.

MEMBERS OF FIRM

Eura DuVal (Ed) Gaskins, Jr.
Hugh Stevens

ASSOCIATES

Jeffrey B. Parsons
Robert (Bob) H. Gourley, Jr.

LEGAL SUPPORT PERSONNEL

Allyson S. McNeill
Alison R. Weigold

Representative Clients: AON Corporation; Chase Federal Bank; Convenience Food Suppliers, Inc.; Fleet National Bank; Honda North America, Inc.; Johnson Controls, Inc.; Lawrence Realty Co.; Tri-Fast Food Ventures, Inc.; United Carolina Bank; Welding Services, Inc.

For Complete List of Firm Personnel, See General Section

For full biographical listings, see the Martindale-Hubbell Law Directory

GULLEY KUHN & TAYLOR, L.L.P. (AV)

4601 Six Forks Road, 27609
Telephone: 919-782-6811
Facsimile: 919-782-7220

Jack P. Gulley
David J. Kuhn
Patricia Potter Taylor

OF COUNSEL

William O. Kuhn

For full biographical listings, see the Martindale-Hubbell Law Directory

MANNING, FULTON & SKINNER, P.A. (AV)

UCB Plaza, 3605 Glenwood Avenue, P.O. Box 20389, 27619-0389
Telephone: 919-787-8880
Telecopier: 919-787-8902

Howard E. Manning
David D. Dahl
Charles L. Fulton
Charles E. Nichols, Jr.
William P. Skinner, Jr.
Barry D. Mann
John B. McMillan
Linda K. Wood
W. Gerald Thornton
John C. Dorsey
Howard E. Manning, Jr.
David J. Witheft
Charles B. Morris, Jr.
William C. Smith, Jr.
Michael T. Medford
Deborah Lowder Hildebran
Samuel T. Oliver, Jr.
Stephen T. Byrd
John I. Mabe, Jr.
H. Forest Horne, Jr.
Michael S. Harrell

Alison R. Cayton
David T. Pryzwansky
Samuel W. Whitt
Cary Elizabeth Close
Kristen Gardner Lingo

Counsel for: Raleigh Merchants Bureau; Carolantic Realty, Inc.; Research Tri-Center Associates; Bright Belt Warehouse Assn., Inc.; Troxler Electronic Laboratories, Inc.; General Parts, Inc.
Representative Clients: International Business Machines Corp.; Siemens-Allis, Inc.; Mallinckrodt, Inc.; Employer Reinsurance Corp.

For full biographical listings, see the Martindale-Hubbell Law Directory

MILLBERG & GORDON (AV)

1030 Washington Street, 27605
Telephone: 919-836-0090
Fax: 919-836-8027

John C. Millberg
Frank J. Gordon

For full biographical listings, see the Martindale-Hubbell Law Directory

RAGSDALE, LIGGETT & FOLEY (AV)

Suite 400, Crosspointe Plaza, 2840 Plaza Place, P.O. Box 31507, 27622-1507
Telephone: 919-787-5200
Fax: 919-783-8991; 881-2045

MEMBERS OF FIRM

George R. Ragsdale
Frank R. Liggett III
Peter M. Foley

OF COUNSEL

Joseph E. Johnson
W. Thomas Boyd, Jr.

(See Next Column)

RAGSDALE, LIGGETT & FOLEY, *Raleigh—Continued*

ASSOCIATES

Stephanie Hutchins Autry
Dorothy Bass
Kristin Eldridge
Kathleen Pepi Southern
Martin M. Brennan, Jr.
Cristina I. Flores

For full biographical listings, see the Martindale-Hubbell Law Directory

SMITH DEBNAM HIBBERT & PAHL (AV)

Hedingham Oaks, 4700 New Bern Avenue, P.O. Box 26268, 27611-6268
Telephone: 919-250-2000
Facsimile: 919-250-2100

MEMBERS OF FIRM

Fred J. Smith, Jr.
W. Thurston Debnam, Jr.
Carl W. Hibbert
J. Larkin Pahl
John W. Narron
Bettie Kelley Sousa
Terri L. Gardner
Jerry T. Myers
Laura K. Howell
Elizabeth B. Godfrey
Rose H. Stout
Byron L. Saintsing
R. Jonathan Charleston
Franklin Drake

ASSOCIATES

Scott N. Johnson
Gerald H. Groon, Jr.
William G. Berggren
Terry M. Kilbride
R. Andrew Patty, II
Melanie J. Hogg
Caren Davis Enloe
Santiago M. Estrada
Jay P. Tobin
Clayton D. Morgan
Shannon Lowry Nagle
Michael D. Zetts, III
Martha L. Sewell
Philip R. Isley
Jeff D. Rogers
James Alan Flynt

For full biographical listings, see the Martindale-Hubbell Law Directory

THARRINGTON, SMITH & HARGROVE (AV)

209 Fayetteville Street Mall, P.O. Box 1151, 27602
Telephone: 919-821-4711
Telecopier: 919-829-1583

MEMBERS OF FIRM

Carlisle W. Higgins (1887-1980)
J. Harold Tharrington
Roger W. Smith
Wade M. Smith
George T. Rogister, Jr.
Carlyn G. Poole
Douglas E. Kingsbery
Randall M. Roden
Michael Crowell
Ann L. Majestic
C. Allison Brown Schafer

ASSOCIATES

Melissa Hill
Daniel W. Clark
Jonathan A. Blumberg
Debra R. Nickels
Rod Malone
E. Hardy Lewis
Jaye Powell Meyer

LEGAL SUPPORT PERSONNEL

Michael M. Cogswell

Representative Clients: The Prudential Insurance Co.; General Instruments Corp.; The Trane Co.; Adams Products; Crown Central Petroleum Corp.

For full biographical listings, see the Martindale-Hubbell Law Directory

*** WOMBLE CARLYLE SANDRIDGE & RICE (AV)**

A Professional Limited Liability Company
2100 First Union Capitol Center, 150 Fayetteville Street Mall, P.O. Box 831, 27602
Telephone: 919-755-2100
Telecopy: 919-755-2150
Telex: 806498
Charlotte, North Carolina Office: 3300 One First Union Center, 301 South College Street.
Telephone: 704-331-4900.
Telecopy: 704-331-4955.
Telex: 853609.
Winston-Salem, North Carolina Office: 1600 Southern National Financial Center.
Telephone: 919-721-3600.
Telecopy: 919-721-3660.
Telex: 806498.
Atlanta, Georgia Office: One Ninety One Peachtree Tower, 191 Peachtree Street N.E., Suite 3250.
Telephone: 404-614-2580.
Fax: 404-614-2595.

RESIDENT PARTNERS

Gordon Eugene Boyce
Robert E. Fields, III
Johnny M. Loper

RESIDENT ASSOCIATES

Mark Allen Davis
Christopher T. Graebe
Elizabeth Janeway Hallyburton
Elizabeth LeVan Riley

Representative Clients: Aetna Casualty and Surety Co., Inc.; ALSCO/AmeriMark Building Products, Inc.; Aoki Corporation America, Inc.; Empire of Carolina, Inc.; Hackney Brothers, Inc.; Lawyers Mutual Liability Insurance Company of North Carolina; Meredith College; Monk-Austin, Inc.; Regency Park Corporation; Wachovia Bank of North Carolina, N.A.

(See Next Column)

For Complete List of Firm Personnel, See General Section

For full biographical listings, see the Martindale-Hubbell Law Directory

YOUNG, MOORE, HENDERSON & ALVIS, P.A. (AV)

3201 Glenwood Avenue, P.O. Box 31627, 27622
Telephone: 919-782-6860
Telecopier: 919-782-6753

B. T. Henderson, II
Jerry S. Alvis
John N. Fountain
R. Michael Strickland
Joseph C. Moore, III
John A. Michaels
Robert C. Paschal
Walter E. Brock, Jr.
Evelyn M. Coman
Joseph W. Williford
David P. Sousa
J. Aldean Webster, III
Marvin M. Spivey, Jr.
M. Lee Cheney
David M. Duke
Ralph W. Meekins

OF COUNSEL

Charles H. Young

E. Knox Proctor, V
J. D. Prather
Brian E. Clemmons
Joe E. Austin, Jr.
Dana H. Davis
R. Christopher Dillon
Carolyn S. Knaut
Glenn C. Raynor
Fred M. Wood, Jr.
J. Mark Langdon

Counsel for: Bridgestone/Firestone, Inc.; CNA Insurance Co.; Duke University; Durham Life Insurance Co.; International Paper Co.; Lawyers Mutual Liability Insurance Group; Medical Mutual Insurance Co.; N.C. Farm Bureau Mutual Insurance Co.; N.C. Rate Bureau; Westinghouse Corp.

For Complete List of Firm Personnel, See General Section

For full biographical listings, see the Martindale-Hubbell Law Directory

*WILMINGTON,** New Hanover Co.

CLARK, NEWTON, HINSON & MCLEAN, L.L.P. (AV)

509 Princess Street, 28401
Telephone: 910-762-8743
Facsimile: 910-762-6206

George T. Clark, Jr.
John Richard Newton
Reid G. Hinson
J. Dickson McLean

Representative Clients: North Carolina Natural Gas; North Carolina Shipping Assn. P&I CLUBS: The Britannia Club; Liverpool & London P&I Club; London Steamship Mutual P&I; Standard Steamship P&I; Steamship Mutual P&I Club; The Swedish Club; The Gard; United Kingdom Club; West of England Shipowners Mutual Insurance Assn.

For full biographical listings, see the Martindale-Hubbell Law Directory

HOGUE, HILL, JONES, NASH AND LYNCH (AV)

101 S. Third Street, P.O. Drawer 2178, 28402
Telephone: 910-763-4565
Telecopier: 910-762-6687

OF COUNSEL

Cyrus D. Hogue, Jr.

MEMBERS OF FIRM

Cyrus D. Hogue (1888-1960)
William L. Hill, II
W. Talmage Jones
David A. Nash
William O. J. Lynch
James B. Snow, III
Wayne A. Bullard
Patricia Cramer Jenkins

Representative Clients: NationsBank of North Carolina, N.A.; Cooperative Bank for Savings; St. Paul Insurance Cos.; New Hanover County Board of Education; Lower Cape Fear Water and Sewer Authority; Cape Fear Memorial Hospital, Inc.; Royal Globe Insurance Co.; Kaiser Aluminum & Chemical Corp.; Wilmington Shipping Co.; Brunswick Hospital; International Paper Co.

For full biographical listings, see the Martindale-Hubbell Law Directory

MARSHALL, WILLIAMS & GORHAM, L.L.P. (AV)

14 South Fifth Street, P.O. Drawer 2088, 28402-2088
Telephone: 910-763-9891
Telecopier: 910-343-8604

MEMBERS OF FIRM

Alan A. Marshall (1908-1979)
Lonnie B. Williams
A. Dumay Gorham, Jr.
Jerry C. Woodell
William Robert Cherry, Jr.
Ronald H. Woodruff
Lonnie B. Williams, Jr.
John Dearman Martin
Charles D. Meier
John L. Coble

Representative Clients: Miller Building Corp.; Kemper Insurance Cos.; State Farm Insurance; K-Mart, Inc.; CNA Insurance Cos.; North Carolina Hospital; Reciprocal Insurance Exchange; New Hanover Regional Medical Center; Aetna Casualty & Surety Co.; Bituminous Insurance Company; Government Employers Insurance Co.

For full biographical listings, see the Martindale-Hubbell Law Directory

Wilmington—Continued

MURCHISON, TAYLOR, KENDRICK, GIBSON & DAVENPORT, L.L.P. (AV)

16 North Fifth Avenue, 28401-4593
Telephone: 910-763-2426
FAX: 910-763-6561

MEMBERS OF FIRM

Vaiden P. Kendrick
Michael Murchison

ASSOCIATE

Alan D. McInnes

Representative Clients: Branch Banking & Trust Co.; Southern National Bank; General Electric Co.; Landfall Assn.; Landmark Organization, Inc.; Nationwide Insurance Co.; Southern Bell; Telechron, Inc.; Trustees, Employers-ILA Pension, Welfare and Vacation Fund; Worsley Cos., Inc.

For Complete List of Firm Personnel, See General Section

For full biographical listings, see the Martindale-Hubbell Law Directory

ROUNTREE & SEAGLE, L.L.P. (AV)

2419 Market Street, P.O. Box 1409, 28402-1409
Telephone: 910-763-3404
Telecopier: 910-763-0320

MEMBERS OF FIRM

George Rountree, Jr. (1904-1979)
George Rountree, III
J. Harold Seagle
Charles M. Lineberry, Jr.

Representative Clients: American International Marine Agency; Fireman's Fund Insurance Cos.; The Japan Shipowners' Mutual Protection & Indemnity Assn., Ltd.
Approved Attorneys for: Chicago Title Insurance Co.; Commonwealth Land Insurance Co.; Investors Title Insurance Co.; Lawyers Title Insurance Corp.
References: Centura Bank; First Union National Bank of North Carolina; NationsBank of North Carolina, N.A.

For Complete List of Firm Personnel, See General Section

For full biographical listings, see the Martindale-Hubbell Law Directory

*WINSTON-SALEM,** Forsyth Co.

HUTCHINS, TYNDALL, DOUGHTON & MOORE (AV)

115 West Third Street, P.O. Drawer 20039, 27120-0039
Telephone: 910-725-8385
Telecopier: 910-723-8838

Fred S. Hutchins, Sr. (1893-1977)
John M. Minor (1917-1974)
Roy L. Deal (1889-1982)

MEMBERS OF FIRM

Fred S. Hutchins, Jr.
George E. Doughton, Jr.
Thomas W. Moore, Jr.
Richard Tyndall
Richmond W. Rucker
H. Lee Davis, Jr.
Kent L. Hamrick
Laurie Hutchins
Claude M. Hamrick

ASSOCIATES

Thomas J. Doughton
David L. Hall

General Counsel for: Wachovia Oil Co.; Crown Drugs of North Carolina, Inc.; W.R. Vernon Produce Co.
Local Counsel for: Travelers Insurance Co.; Maryland Casualty Co.; State Farm Insurance Co.; Liberty Mutual Insurance Co.; Shelby Mutual Insurance Co.; Transport Insurance Co.

For full biographical listings, see the Martindale-Hubbell Law Directory

JOHN R. SURRATT, P.A. (AV)

Suite 700, NationsBank Plaza, 102 West Third Street, 27101
Telephone: 910-725-8323
Facsimile: 910-722-5218

John R. Surratt

Anita M. Conrad
Andrew J. Gerber

For full biographical listings, see the Martindale-Hubbell Law Directory

WOMBLE CARLYLE SANDRIDGE & RICE (AV)

A Professional Limited Liability Company
1600 Southern National Financial Center, P.O. Drawer 84, 27102
Telephone: 910-721-3600
Telecopy: 910-721-3660
Telex: 806498
Charlotte, North Carolina Office: 3300 One First Union Center, 301 South College Street.
Telephone: 704-331-4900.
Telecopy: 704-331-4955.
Telex: 853609.

(See Next Column)

Raleigh, North Carolina Office: 2100 First Union Capitol Center, 150 Fayetteville Street Mall, P.O. Box 831.
Telephone: 919-755-2100.
Telecopy: 919-755-2150.
Telex: 806498.
Atlanta, Georgia Office: One Ninety One Peachtree Tower, 191 Peachtree Street, N.E., Suite 3250.
Telephone: 404-614-2580.
Fax: 404-614-2595.

MEMBERS OF FIRM

Reid C. Adams, Jr.
Conrad C. Baldwin, Jr.
Henry Grady Barnhill, Jr.
Jimmy Hamilton Barnhill
Samuel Fraley Bost
Keith Ashford Clinard
Ellis B. Drew, III
Hada de Varona Haulsee
Gary W. Jackson
R. Michael Leonard
Alexander S. Nicholas
Erna A. Patrick
Michael E. Ray
Thomas D. Schroeder
Calder W. Womble
William F. Womble, Jr.

ASSOCIATES

Charles A. Burke
Lawrence P. Egerton
Dawn Jordan
Jonathan B. Mason
Kurt C. Stakeman
J. Keith Tart

Representative Clients: Brad Ragan, Inc.; Brenner Companies; Food Lion, Inc.; Hanes Companies, Inc.; North Carolina Baptist Hospitals, Inc.; R.J. Reynolds Tobacco Company; Summit Communications Group, Inc.; Thomasville Furniture Industries, Inc.; Wachovia Corporation; Wake Forest University.

For Complete List of Firm Personnel, See General Section

For full biographical listings, see the Martindale-Hubbell Law Directory

NORTH DAKOTA

*BISMARCK,** Burleigh Co.

FLECK, MATHER & STRUTZ, LTD. (AV)

Sixth Floor, Norwest Bank Building, 400 East Broadway, P.O. Box 2798, 58502
Telephone: 701-223-6585
Telecopier: 701-222-4853

Ernest R. Fleck
Russell R. Mather
William A. Strutz
Gary R. Wolberg
Paul W. Summers
Steven A. Storslee
Brian R. Bjella
John W. Morrison, Jr.
Robert J. Udland
Curtis L. Wike
Charles S. Miller, Jr.
Craig Cordell Smith
DeeNelle Louise Ruud

Representative Clients: Norwest Bank, N.A.; ITT Hartford; CNA; American International Group; W.R. Grace; Firemen's Fund; Crum and Forster; Union Oil Company of California; Shell Oil Co.; Chevron U.S.A.

For full biographical listings, see the Martindale-Hubbell Law Directory

PEARCE AND DURICK (AV)

314 East Thayer Avenue, P.O. Box 400, 58502
Telephone: 701-223-2890
Fax: 701-223-7865

MEMBERS OF FIRM

Patrick W. Durick
B. Timothy Durick
Christine A. Hogan
Joel W. Gilbertson
Jerome C. Kettleson
Larry L. Boschee
Lawrence Bender

ASSOCIATES

Michael F. McMahon
Stephen D. Easton

Representative Clients: American Insurance Assn.; Cigna-INA Insurance Co.; Deere & Co.; F.D.I.C.; Ford Motor Co.; General Motors Corp.; MDU Resources Group, Inc.; Northwest Airlines; Royal Insurance Co.; Travelers Insurance Co.

For Complete List of Firm Personnel, See General Section

For full biographical listings, see the Martindale-Hubbell Law Directory

PETERSON, SCHMITZ, MOENCH & SCHMIDT, A PROFESSIONAL CORPORATION (AV)

Second Floor, Suite 200, 116 North Fourth Street, P.O. Box 2076, 58502-2076
Telephone: 701-224-0400
Fax: 701-224-0399

David L. Peterson
Orell D. Schmitz
Dale W. Moench
William D. Schmidt

OF COUNSEL

Gerald Glaser

(See Next Column)

PETERSON, SCHMITZ, MOENCH & SCHMIDT A PROFESSIONAL CORPORATION, *Bismarck—Continued*

LEGAL SUPPORT PERSONNEL

Vicki J. Kunz
Traci L. Albers

For full biographical listings, see the Martindale-Hubbell Law Directory

TSCHIDER & SMITH (AV)

A Partnership including Professional Corporations
Professional Building - Suite 200, 418 East Rosser Avenue, 58501
Telephone: 701-258-4000
Fax: 701-258-4001

MEMBERS OF FIRM

Morris A. Tschider (P.C.)
Sean O. Smith (P.C.)
David A. Tschider

Representative Clients: Agri Bank, FCB; Farm Credit Services of Mandan, FLCA; Farm Credit Services of Mandan, P.C.A.; Twin City Implement, Inc.; First Bank Bismarck; N.D. Independent Insurance Agents; Western Steel & Plumbing; Froelich Oil Co.; Bismarck Eagles.

For full biographical listings, see the Martindale-Hubbell Law Directory

ZUGER KIRMIS & SMITH (AV)

A Partnership including Professional Corporations
United Services Life Building, 316 North Fifth Street, P.O. Box 1695, 58502-1695
Telephone: 701-223-2711
Fax: 701-223-7387

John A. Zuger, P.C.
Lyle W. Kirmis
Thomas O. Smith, P.C.
Murray G. Sagsveen, P.C.
Lance D. Schreiner, P.C.
James S. Hill, P.C.
Patrick J. Ward
Rebecca S. Thiem, P.C.
Charles T. Edin, P.C.
Daniel S. Kuntz, P.C.
Brenda L. Blazer, P.C.
Jerry W. Evenson, P.C.

ASSOCIATES

Brent J. Edison
Patricia E. Garrity
Lawrence E. King

Representative Clients: American Family Insurance Co.; Burlington Northern Railroad Co.; Continental National Bank & Trust Company of Chicago; First Bank, Bismarck; Melroe Company; North Dakota Medical Association; St. Paul Cos.; State Farm Insurance Co.; Sun Oil & Exploration Co.; Williston Basin Interstate Pipeline Company, a wholly-owned subsidiary of Montana Dakota Utilities Resources Group, Inc.

For full biographical listings, see the Martindale-Hubbell Law Directory

*FARGO,** Cass Co.

CONMY, FESTE, BOSSART, HUBBARD & CORWIN, LTD. (AV)

400 Norwest Center, Fourth Street and Main Avenue, 58126
Telephone: 701-293-9911
Fax: 701-293-3133

Charles A. Feste
David R. Bossart
Paul M. Hubbard
Wickham Corwin
Kim E. Brust
Lauris N. Molbert
Michael M. Thomas
Robert J. Schultz
Nancy J. Morris
Jiming Zhu

OF COUNSEL

E. T. Conmy, Jr.

State Counsel for: Metropolitan Life Insurance Company.
Representative Clients: Ford Motor Credit Co.; Norwest Corporation Region VII Banks (North Dakota & Minnesota West); U.S. Gypsum Co.
Insurance: American Hardware Insurance Group; Great American Insurance Companies; The Maryland.

For full biographical listings, see the Martindale-Hubbell Law Directory

JEFFRIES, OLSON, FLOM, OPPEGARD & HOGAN, P.A. (AV)

1325 23rd Street S.W., 58103
Telephone: 701-280-2300
Moorhead, Minnesota Office: 403 Center Avenue, P.O. Box 9, 56561-0001.
Telephone: 218-233-3222.
Fax: 218-233-7065.

Richard N. Jeffries
Thomas R. Olson
Joel A. Flom
Paul R. Oppegard
Barry P. Hogan

James R. Bullis
Ronald James Knoll

Representative Clients: American International Adjustment Co.; American States/Western Insurance Co.; Farmers Insurance Group; Federated Mutual Insurance Co.; Fireman's Fund Insurance Co.; Hartford Insurance Co.; Midwest Medical Insurance Co.; St. Paul Fire & Marine Insurance Co.

For full biographical listings, see the Martindale-Hubbell Law Directory

NILLES, HANSEN & DAVIES, LTD. (AV)

1800 Radisson Tower, P.O. Box 2626, 58108
Telephone: 701-237-5544

Donald R. Hansen
Timothy Q. Davies
Duane H. Ilvedson
E. Thomas Conmy, III
Stephen W. Plambeck
Leo F. J. Wilking
Richard Henderson
Daniel J. Crothers
William P. Harrie
Mark R. Hanson
Harry M. Pippin
Thomas A. Jacobson
Douglas W. Gigler
Adele Hedley Page

Representative Clients: Burlington Northern; First Bank of North Dakota (NA); Blue Cross/Blue Shield; John Deere Company; Nash Finch Company; National Railroad Passenger Corp. (Amtrak); Metropolitan Federal Bank (fsb); Northern States Power; Lutheran Health Systems.

For Complete List of Firm Personnel, See General Section

For full biographical listings, see the Martindale-Hubbell Law Directory

VOGEL, BRANTNER, KELLY, KNUTSON, WEIR & BYE, LTD. (AV)

502 First Avenue North, P.O. Box 1389, 58107
Telephone: 701-237-6983
Facsimile: 701-237-0847

Jerry O. Brantner
John D. Kelly
David F. Knutson
H. Patrick Weir
Kermit Edward Bye
Carlton J. Hunke
C. Nicholas Vogel
Maurice G. McCormick
Mart Daniel Vogel
William A. Schlossman, Jr.
Douglas R. Herman
Jane C. Voglewede
Jon R. Brakke
Harlan G. Fuglesten
Pamela J. Hermes
W. Todd Haggart
Lori J. Beck
Frank G. Gokey
Steven A. Johnson
Bruce Douglas Quick
Wayne W. Carlson
Charles Alan Stock

Representative Clients: Associated General Contractors of North Dakota; Clark Equipment Co.; Forum Communications Company; Merit Care Medical Group; Northern Improvement Co.; Dakota Clinic; West Acres Development Company; Fargo Glass & Paint Company; Northern Bottling Company.
Insurance Companies: American Family Insurance Group; Home Insurance Company; St. Paul Insurance Companies.

For Complete List of Firm Personnel, See General Section

For full biographical listings, see the Martindale-Hubbell Law Directory

*MANDAN,** Morton Co.

BAIR, KAUTZMANN & BAIR (AV)

210 First Avenue, N.W., P.O. Box 100, 58554-0100
Telephone: 701-663-6568
Fax: 701-663-6951

MEMBERS OF FIRM

Bruce B. Bair
Dwight C. H. Kautzmann
Thomas B. Bair

Representative Clients: Diocese of Bismarck; First Southwest Bank-Mandan; University of Mary-Bismarck; KEM Rural Electric Cooperative, Inc.; Mandan Public School District #1; North Dakota Milk Stabilization Board.

For full biographical listings, see the Martindale-Hubbell Law Directory

OHIO

*AKRON,** Summit Co.

NUKES, PERANTINIDES & NOLAN CO., L.P.A. (AV)

300 Courtyard Square, 80 South Summit Street, 44308-1719
Telephone: 216-253-5454
Telecopier: 216-253-6524

S. Samuel Nukes
Paul G. Perantinides
Chris T. Nolan

James J. Gutbrod
Christopher L. Parker
Peter P. Janos

References: First National Bank of Akron; National City Bank, Akron; Society Bank; Charter One Bank.

For full biographical listings, see the Martindale-Hubbell Law Directory

RODERICK, MYERS & LINTON (AV)

One Cascade Plaza, 15th Floor, 44308
Telephone: 216-434-3000
Telecopier: 216-434-9220

(See Next Column)

RODERICK, MYERS & LINTON—*Continued*

MEMBERS OF FIRM

George T. Roderick (1909-1994) Kurt R. Weitendorf
Robert F. Linton Timothy J. Truby
Howard C. Walker, Jr. Lawrence R. Bach
Robert F. Orth Paul E. Weimer
Frederick S. Corns James E. Davis
Michael A. Malyuk Matthew W. Oby

ASSOCIATES

Stephen J. Pruneski John K. Riemenschneider

Representative Clients: National City Bank, Akron; Ohio Edison Co.; Westfield Cos.; The Prudential Insurance Co. of America; Maryland Casualty Co.; The Cincinnati Insurance Co.; PICO; Motorists Insurance Cos.

For Complete List of Firm Personnel, See General Section

For full biographical listings, see the Martindale-Hubbell Law Directory

SCANLON & GEARINGER CO., L.P.A. (AV)

1100 First National Tower, 106 South Main Street, 44308-1463
Telephone: 216-376-4558
Telecopier: 216-376-3550

Timothy F. Scanlon Michael J. Del Medico
Bradford M. Gearinger Mark Hilkert
James A. Rudgers Patrick J. Hart
Robert A. Royer

Suzanne C. Porter John F. Hill
Kevin P. Hardman Gregory M. Scanlon
Maura E. Scanlon Tamara A. O'Brien

For full biographical listings, see the Martindale-Hubbell Law Directory

A. RUSSELL SMITH (AV)

503 Society Building, 159 South Main Street, 44308
Telephone: 216-434-7167
FAX: 216-434-7195

A. Russell Smith

R. Bryan Nace

For full biographical listings, see the Martindale-Hubbell Law Directory

THOMPSON, HINE AND FLORY (AV)

50 S. Main Street, Suite 502, 44308-1828
Telephone: 216-376-8090
Fax: 216-376-8386
Cincinnati, Ohio Office: 312 Walnut Street, 14th Floor, 45202-4029.
Telephone: 513-352-6700.
Fax: 513-241-4771.
Telex: 938003.
Cleveland, Ohio Office: 1100 National City Bank Building, 629 Euclid Avenue, 44114-3070.
Telephone: 216-566-5500.
Fax: 216-556-5583.
Telex: 980217.
Cable Address: "Thomflor".
Columbus, Ohio Office: One Columbus, 10 West Broad Street, 43215-3435.
Telephone: 614-469-3200.
Fax: 614-469-3361.
Dayton, Ohio Office: 2000 Courthouse Plaza, 45402-1706.
Telephone: 513-443-6600.
Fax: 513-443-6637; 443-6635.
Palm Beach, Florida Office: 125 Worth Avenue, 33480-4466.
Telephone: 407-833-5900.
Fax: 407-833-5951.
Washington, D.C. Office: 1920 N Street, N.W., 20036-1601.
Telephone: 202-331-8800.
Fax: 202-331-8330.
Telex: 904173.
Cable Address: "Caglaw".
Brussels, Belgium Office: Rue des Chevaliers / Ridderstraat 14 - B.10, B - 1050.
Telephone: 011(32-2) 511-9326.
Fax: 011(32-2) 513-9206.

MEMBER OF FIRM

Richard E. Guster (Partner-in-Charge in Akron)

For Complete List of Firm Personnel, See General Section

For full biographical listings, see the Martindale-Hubbell Law Directory

A. WILLIAM ZAVARELLO CO., L.P.A. (AV)

313 South High Street, Corner South High and Buchtel, 44308-1532
Telephone: 216-762-9700
Fax: 216-762-1680

(See Next Column)

A. William Zavarello Rhonda G. Davis

References: First National Bank of Ohio; National City Bank, Akron.

For full biographical listings, see the Martindale-Hubbell Law Directory

*CANTON,** Stark Co.

BAKER, MEEKISON & DUBLIKAR (AV)

205 Mellett Building, 115 DeWalt Avenue, N.W., 44702
Telephone: 216-453-4999
Telecopier: 216-455-0333

MEMBERS OF FIRM

Jack R. Baker Donald P. Wiley
Ralph F. Dublikar Stephen P. Griffin
Gregory A. Beck James F. Mathews

OF COUNSEL

David F. Meekison

ASSOCIATES

Carol Ann Costa Thomas P. Mannion
Mel L. Lute, Jr. Frederic R. Scott

For full biographical listings, see the Martindale-Hubbell Law Directory

LESH, CASNER & MILLER A LEGAL PROFESSIONAL ASSOCIATION (AV)

606 Belden-Whipple Building, 4150 Belden Village Street, N.W., 44718
Telephone: 216-493-0040
Fax: 216-493-4108

Kenneth L. Lesh (1913-1991) Thomas J. Lombardi
James W. Casner Dennis J. Fox
Rex W. Miller John S. McCall, Jr.
Jacob F. Hess, Jr. Timothy W. Watkins
John R. Frank

OF COUNSEL

Ronald G. Figler

For full biographical listings, see the Martindale-Hubbell Law Directory

*CINCINNATI,** Hamilton Co.

ALTMAN & CALARDO CO. A LEGAL PROFESSIONAL ASSOCIATION (AV)

Suite 1006, 414 Walnut Street, 45202
Telephone: 513-721-2180
Fax: 513-721-2299

D. David Altman Stephen P. Calardo

Amy J. Leonard Kevin P. Braig

For full biographical listings, see the Martindale-Hubbell Law Directory

BROWN, CUMMINS & BROWN CO., L.P.A. (AV)

3500 Carew Tower, 441 Vine Street, 45202
Telephone: 513-381-2121
Fax: 513-381-2125

J. W. Brown (Retired) Amy G. Applegate
Robert S Brown Kathryn Knue Przywara
James R. Cummins Melanie S. Corwin
Lynne Skilken Jeffrey R. Teeters

Reference: Star Bank of Cincinnati.

For full biographical listings, see the Martindale-Hubbell Law Directory

DINSMORE & SHOHL (AV)

1900 Chemed Center, 255 East Fifth Street, 45202-3172
Telephone: 513-977-8200
FAX: 513-977-8141
Florence, Kentucky Office: Turfway Ridge Office Park, 7300 Turfway Road, Suite 430 41042-1355.
Telephone: 606-283-0515.
FAX: 606-283-6017.
Dayton, Ohio Office: 500 Courthouse Plaza, S.W., 10 N. Ludlow Street, 45402-1834.
Telephone: 513-228-8012.
FAX: 513-461-2543.
Columbus, Ohio Office: NBD Bank Building, Suite 330, 175 South Third Street, 43215-5134.
Telephone: 614-224-7887.
FAX: 614-224-7882.

MEMBERS OF FIRM

Thomas S. Calder Gordon C. Greene
Lawrence A. Kane, Jr. Harry L. Riggs, Jr. (Resident, Florence, Kentucky Office)
John W. Beatty Mark L. Silbersack
Lawrence R. Elleman Gerald V. Weigle, Jr.
John M. Kunst, Jr. Mark A. Vander Laan
Vincent B. Stamp
Frank C. Woodside, III

(See Next Column)

DINSMORE & SHOHL, *Cincinnati—Continued*

MEMBERS OF FIRM (Continued)

Gary L. Herfel (Resident, Florence, Kentucky Office)
John E. Schlosser
Nancy A. Lawson
Michael D. Eagen
David H. Beaver
Patrick D. Lane
Carl J. Stich, Jr. (On Leave of Absence)
Joseph E. Conley, Jr. (Resident, Florence, Kentucky Office)
John D. Luken
Deborah R. Lydon
Lynda E. Roesch
George B. Wilkinson
John E. Jevicky
Jerry S. Sallee
Nancy J. Gill
Stephen K. Shaw
Lawrence A. Flemer
Mark C. Bissinger
Joel S. Taylor (Resident, Columbus, Ohio Office)
Robert R. Furnier
Gary E. Becker
Neal D. Baker
K. C. Green
Philip J. Schworer
M. Gabrielle Hils
Stephen G. Schweller
June Smith Tyler
Gregory A. Harrison

ASSOCIATES

Andrew C. Osterbrock
David W. Gerbus
Charles H. Brown, III
Frederick M. Erny
James A. Comodeca
Beverly Hayes Pace
Susan J. Luken
Stephen M. Rosenberger
Rita A. Miller Altimari
Joan M. Verchot
Patricia B. Hogan
Charles R. Dyas, Jr.
Brian S. Sullivan
Mark S. Booher
Robert Heuck II
Randel S. Springer
David K. Mullen
John J. Hoffmann (Resident, Dayton, Ohio Office)
Christopher A. Benintendi
Richard J. Mitchell, Jr.
Sara Simrall Rorer
Michael L. Squillace (Resident, Columbus, Ohio Office)
Marlene M. Evans
Melissa A. Fetters
John A. Finley
Linda A. Cooper
Louis D. Proietti
Laurie H. Schwab
Mary-Jo Middelhoff
Robert A. Williams
Frances L. Figetakis
Thomas A. Prewitt (Resident, Florence, Kentucky Office)
M. Christine Hice
David S. Rosenthal
Debra Page Coleman
William A. Sherman, II
Kim Wilson Burke
William M. Mattes (Resident, Columbus, Ohio Office)
Scott R. Thomas
Frederick N. Hamilton
James C. Venizelos
Ernamarie Messenger
Michael J. Suffern
Theodore J. Schneider
Wilton E. Blake, II
Michael H. Strong
Robert F. Benintendi
Patrick E. Beck
Jeffrey L. Stec
Nancy Korb Griffiths
Ann Collins Hindman
Michael E. Finucane
William A. Dickhaut
Christopher L. Riegler (Resident, Dayton, Ohio Office)
Dianne Goss Paynter (Resident, Columbus, Ohio Office)
Gregory S. Lampert
Jeffrey R. Schaefer
Reuel D. Ash
Alan H. Abes
Gina M. Saelinger
Donna R. Purifoy
Robert J. Reid
Thomas M. Dixon
Jerry L. Maynard, II
Clyde Bennett, II
Letitia E. Carvey

For Complete List of Firm Personnel, See General Section

For full biographical listings, see the Martindale-Hubbell Law Directory

DREW, WARD, GRAF, COOGAN & GOEDDEL A LEGAL PROFESSIONAL ASSOCIATION (AV)

24th Floor, Central Trust Tower, 4th and Vine Streets, 45202
Telephone: 513-621-8210
Telecopier: 513-621-5444

Richard H. Ward
William R. Graf
James H. Coogan
Frederic L. Goeddel
E. Beth Farrell
Michael D. McNeil

Representative Clients: AAA Cincinnati; Deaconess Hospital; Stevenson Photo Color Co.
Reference: Star Bank, N.A.

For full biographical listings, see the Martindale-Hubbell Law Directory

FAULKNER & TEPE (AV)

2200 Central Trust Tower, 5 West Fourth Street, 45202
Telephone: 513-421-7500
FAX: 513-421-7502

MEMBERS OF FIRM

R. Edward Tepe
John C. Scott
Christopher L. Moore
Anthony W. Brock

SENIOR COUNSEL

David P. Faulkner

OF COUNSEL

A. Norman Aubin

Reference: Fifth Third Bank.

For full biographical listings, see the Martindale-Hubbell Law Directory

FROST & JACOBS (AV)

2500 PNC Center, 201 East Fifth Street, P.O. Box 5715, 45201-5715
Telephone: 513-651-6800
Cable Address: "Frostjac"
Telex: 21-4396 F & J CIN
Telecopier: 513-651-6981
Columbus, Ohio Office: One Columbus, 10 West Broad Street.
Telephone: 614-464-1211.
Telecopier: 614-464-1737.
Lexington, Kentucky Office: 1100 Vine Center Tower, 333 West Vine Street.
Telephone: 606-254-1100.
Telecopier: 606-253-2990.
Middletown, Ohio Office: 400 First National Bank Building, 2 North Main Street.
Telephone: 513-422-2001.
Telecopier: 513-422-3010.
Naples, Florida Office: 4001 Tamiami Trail North, Suite 220.
Telephone: 813-261-0582.
Telecopier: 813-261-2083.

MEMBERS OF FIRM

James R. Adams
Pierce E. Cunningham
Frederick J. McGavran
Michael F. Haverkamp
Todd H. Bailey
David C. Horn
William H. Hawkins, II
Walter E. Haggerty
Richard M. Goehler
Beth A. Myers
Grant S. Cowan
Claudia L. Schaefer
Vincent E. Mauer
Beth Schneider Naylor

COLUMBUS, OHIO OFFICE
MEMBER OF FIRM

Michael K. Yarbrough

LEXINGTON, KENTUCKY OFFICE
MEMBER OF FIRM

Richard A. Getty

Representative Clients: Armco Inc.; Arthur Andersen & Co.; Cincinnati Bell Inc.; Cincinnati Milacron Inc.; Federated Department Stores Inc.; Mercy Health Systems; PNC Bank, Onio, National Association; U.S. Shoe Corp.; Sencorp.; Champion International.

For Complete List of Firm Personnel, See General Section

For full biographical listings, see the Martindale-Hubbell Law Directory

HERMANIES, MAJOR, CASTELLI & GOODMAN (AV)

Suite 740-Cincinnati Club Building, 30 Garfield Place, 45202-4396
Telephone: 513-621-2345
Fax: 513-621-2519

MEMBERS OF FIRM

John H. Hermanies
Ronald D. Major
Anthony D. Castelli
Richard Lanahan Goodman
Mark Allen Ferestad

References: Southern Ohio Bank; First National Bank of Cincinnati; The PNC Bank.

For full biographical listings, see the Martindale-Hubbell Law Directory

KATZ, GREENBERGER & NORTON (AV)

105 East Fourth Street, 9th Floor, 45202-4011
Telephone: 513-721-5151
FAX: 513-621-9285

Leonard H. Freiberg (1885-1954)
Alfred B. Katz
Mark Alan Greenberger
Louis H. Katz
Richard L. Norton
Steven M. Rothstein
Robert Gray Edmiston
Ellen Essig

ASSOCIATES

Scott P. Kadish
Stephen E. Imm
Stephen L. Robison
Jeffrey J. Greenberger

OF COUNSEL

Charles Weiner

For full biographical listings, see the Martindale-Hubbell Law Directory

KATZ, TELLER, BRANT & HILD A LEGAL PROFESSIONAL ASSOCIATION (AV)

2400 Chemed Center, 255 East Fifth Street, 45202-4724
Telephone: 513-721-4532
Telecopier: 513-721-7120

Reuven J. Katz
Jerome S. Teller
Joseph A. Brant
Guy M. Hild
Robert A. Pitcairn, Jr.
Robert E. Brant
Ronald J. Goret
Stephen C. Kisling
Andrew R. Berger
Mark J. Jahnke
William F. Russo
John R. Gierl
Bruce A. Hunter
Gregory E. Land
Bradley G. Haas
Daniel P. Utt
Brent G. Houk
Cynthia Loren Gibson
Suzanne Prieur Land
Tedd H. Friedman

(See Next Column)

KATZ, TELLER, BRANT & HILD A LEGAL PROFESSIONAL ASSOCIATION—*Continued*

Representative Clients: Eagle Picher Industries, Inc.; F & C International, Inc.; Jewish Hospitals of Cincinnati; Johnny Bench; Texo Corporation; University of Cincinnati Medical Associates, Inc.

For full biographical listings, see the Martindale-Hubbell Law Directory

KEATING, MUETHING & KLEKAMP (AV)

1800 Provident Tower, One East Fourth Street, 45202
Telephone: 513-579-6400
Facsimile: 513-579-6457

MEMBERS OF FIRM

Louis F. Gilligan
Joseph L. Trauth, Jr.
Robert W. Maxwell II
Richard L. Creighton, Jr.
Jerome C. Randolph
James E. Burke
Kevin E. Irwin
William A. Posey
Gregory M. Utter
Patrick F. Fischer
Robert A. Klingler
David K. Montgomery
James R. Matthews

ASSOCIATES

Donald A. Lane
Robert G. Sanker
W. Keith Noel
Pamela Morgan Hodge
Daniel E. Izenson
Gail King
Mary R. True
Daniel J. Donnellon
Joseph M. Callow Jr.

Representative Clients: American Financial Corporation; BP America Inc.; Chiquita Brands International, Inc.; The Cincinnati Enquirer; Cintas Corporation; Comair Holdings, Inc.; Duke Associates; LSI Industries Inc.; Mosler Inc.; Provident Bankcorp, Inc.

For Complete List of Firm Personnel, See General Section

For full biographical listings, see the Martindale-Hubbell Law Directory

KEPLEY, MACCONNELL & EYRICH A LEGAL PROFESSIONAL ASSOCIATION (AV)

Formerly Clark & Eyrich
2200 Ameritrust Center, 525 Vine Street, 45202
Telephone: 513-241-5540; 621-1045
FAX: 513-241-8111; 621-0038

Stephen T. MacConnell
Augustine Giglio
Wm. Eric Minamyer
Paul D. Rattermann
Francis X. Lee
Christine Y. Jones

Representative Clients and References furnished upon request.

For full biographical listings, see the Martindale-Hubbell Law Directory

MICHAEL G. KOHN (AV)

2690 Madison Road, P.O. Box 8157, 45208
Telephone: 513-631-6159
Fax: 513-631-8498

For full biographical listings, see the Martindale-Hubbell Law Directory

LINDHORST & DREIDAME CO., L.P.A. (AV)

312 Walnut Street, Suite 2300, 45202-4091
Telephone: 513-421-6630
Telecopier: 513-421-0212

Robert F. Dreidame (1914-1978)
Leo J. Breslin
James L. O'Connell
William M. Cussen
Charles J. Kelly
John A. Goldberg
William N. Kirkham
James M. Moore
James H. Smith, III
Jay R. Langenbahn
Thomas E. Martin
James F. Brockman
Michael F. Lyon
Edward S. Dorsey
Harold L. Anness
Dale A. Stalf
Gary F. Franke

Peter C. Newberry

SENIOR COUNSEL

Ambrose H. Lindhorst
William J. Walsh
John A. Spain

Representative Clients: CNA; CSX Corp.; Fireman's Fund-American Group; Medical Protective Co.; Norfolk Southern Corp.; Roadway Express, Inc.; Sibcy Cline, Inc.; Jewish Hospital; T.W. Smith Aircraft, Inc.; U.S.F.&G.

For Complete List of Firm Personnel, See General Section

For full biographical listings, see the Martindale-Hubbell Law Directory

LLOYD & WEISSENBERGER (AV)

119 East Court Street, 45202-1203
Telephone: 513-632-5334
Fax: 513-721-5824

MEMBERS OF FIRM

John A. Lloyd, Jr.
Glen Weissenberger

(See Next Column)

OF COUNSEL

Jeanette H. Rost
John W. Hancock

For full biographical listings, see the Martindale-Hubbell Law Directory

REISENFELD & STATMAN (AV)

Auburn Barrister House, 2355 Auburn Avenue, 45219
Telephone: 513-381-6810
FAX: 513-381-0255

Sylvan P. Reisenfeld
Alan J. Statman

John L. Day, Jr.
Melisa J. Richter
Bradley A. Reisenfeld
Rosemary E. Scollard
John Schmidt

For full biographical listings, see the Martindale-Hubbell Law Directory

RENDIGS, FRY, KIELY & DENNIS (AV)

900 Central Trust Tower, 45202
Telephone: 513-381-9200
FAX: 513-381-9206
Courtesy Office: Kentucky National Bank Tower, Suite 1610, 50 East Rivercenter Boulevard, Covington, Kentucky.

MEMBERS OF FIRM

William H. Hutcherson, Jr.
Ralph F. Mitchell
W. Roger Fry
Thomas S. Shore, Jr.
David Winchester Peck
J. Kenneth Meagher
D. Michael Poast
Edward R. Goldman
Joseph W. Gelwicks
Leonard A. Weakley, Jr.
Carolyn A. Taggart
Donald C. Adams, Jr.
Wilson G. Weisenfelder, Jr.
Steven D. Hengehold
Thomas M. Evans
Felix J. Gora

OF COUNSEL

Robert L. McLaurin
John P. Kiely

ASSOCIATES

Jill T. O'Shea
Peter L. Ney
Terrence M. Garrigan
John M. Hands

Local Counsel for: Associated Aviation Underwriters; Commercial Union Assurance Co.; Continental National American Group; The Medical Protective Co.; St. Paul Insurance Co.; Sherwin-Williams; State Automobile Mutual Insurance Co.; U.S. Aviation Underwriters; Zurich Insurance Co.

For Complete List of Firm Personnel, See General Section

For full biographical listings, see the Martindale-Hubbell Law Directory

GATES T. RICHARDS (AV)

3807 Carew Tower, 441 Vine Street, 45202
Telephone: 513-621-1991

Reference: First National Bank, Cincinnati, Ohio.

For full biographical listings, see the Martindale-Hubbell Law Directory

SANTEN & HUGHES A LEGAL PROFESSIONAL ASSOCIATION (AV)

Suite 3100, 312 Walnut Street, 45202
Telephone: 513-721-4450
FAX: 513-721-7644; 721-0109

William E. Santen
Charles M. Meyer
Charles E. Reynolds
John D. Holschuh, Jr.
William E. Santen, Jr.
David M. Kothman
Edward E. Santen
Charles J. Kubicki, Jr.

LEGAL SUPPORT PERSONNEL

Karen W. Crane (Corporate Paralegal)
Deborah M. McKinney (Trust/Estate Paralegal)
Karen L. Jansen (Litigation Paralegal)
Bobbie S. Ebbers (Paralegal)

For Complete List of Firm Personnel, See General Section

For full biographical listings, see the Martindale-Hubbell Law Directory

LAW OFFICES OF JOSEPH W. SHEA III (AV)

36 East 7th Street, Suite 2650, 45202-4459
Telephone: 513-621-8333
Telecopier: 513-651-3272

ASSOCIATE

Shirley A. Coffey

LEGAL SUPPORT PERSONNEL

NURSE - LEGAL ASSISTANT

Marianne E. Alf

For full biographical listings, see the Martindale-Hubbell Law Directory

Cincinnati—Continued

SIRKIN PINALES MEZIBOV & SCHWARTZ (AV)

920 Fourth & Race Tower, 105 West Fourth Street, 45202-2776
Telephone: 513-721-4876
Telecopier: 513-721-0876

MEMBERS OF FIRM

H. Louis Sirkin
Martin S. Pinales
Marc D. Mezibov
Howard M. Schwartz

ASSOCIATES

Edmund J. McKenna
Matthew Brownfield
Martha K. Landesberg

References: The Central Trust Co.; The Huntington National Bank.

For full biographical listings, see the Martindale-Hubbell Law Directory

STRAUSS & TROY A LEGAL PROFESSIONAL ASSOCIATION (AV)

2100 PNC Center, 201 East Fifth Street, 45202-4186
Telephone: 513-621-2120
Telecopier: 513-241-8259
Northern Kentucky Office: Suite 1400, 50 East Rivercenter Boulevard, Covington, Kentucky, 41011.
Telephone: 513-621-8900; 513-621-2120.
Telecopier: 513-629-9444.

Charles G. Atkins
Mitchell B. Goldberg
William S. Abernethy, Jr.
William R. Jacobs
Stuart C. Brinn
R. Guy Taft
Richard S. Wayne
Paul B. Calico
Larry A. Temin
Timothy B. Theissen (Resident, Covington, Kentucky Office)
William K. Flynn

Eric H. Kearney
Thomas L. Stachler

OF COUNSEL

Douglas G. Cole
Richard D. Heiser
George H. Palmer
Leon L. Wolf

Representative Clients: BP Oil Company; PNC Bank, N.A.; Corporex Companies, Inc.; Star Bank, N.A. (Ohio and Kentucky); Steinberg's, Inc.

For Complete List of Firm Personnel, See General Section

For full biographical listings, see the Martindale-Hubbell Law Directory

THOMAS M. TEPE (AV)

22 West Ninth Street, 45202
Telephone: 513-721-7500
Fax: 513-721-1178

OF COUNSEL

Steven E. Martin
Ann M. Morgan

For full biographical listings, see the Martindale-Hubbell Law Directory

THOMPSON, HINE AND FLORY (AV)

312 Walnut Street, 14th Floor, 45202-4029
Telephone: 513-352-6700
Fax: 513-241-4771;
Telex: 938003
Akron, Ohio Office: 50 S. Main Street, Suite 502, 44308-1828.
Telephone: 216-376-8090.
Fax: 216-376-8386.
Cleveland, Ohio Office: 1100 National City Bank Building, 629 Euclid Avenue, 44114-3070.
Telephone: 216-566-5500.
Fax: 216-556-5583.
Telex: 980217.
Cable Address: "Thomflor".
Columbus, Ohio Office: One Columbus, 10 West Broad Street, 43215-3435.
Telephone: 614-469-3200.
Fax: 614-469-3361.
Dayton, Ohio Office: 2000 Courthouse Plaza, N.E., 45402-1706.
Telephone: 513-443-6600.
Fax: 513-443-6637; 443-6635.
Palm Beach, Florida Office: 125 Worth Avenue, 33480-4466.
Telephone: 407-833-5900.
Fax: 407-833-5951.
Washington, D.C. Office: 1920 N Street, N.W., 20036-1601.
Telephone: 202-331-8800.
Fax: 202-331-8330.
Telex: 904173.
Cable Address: "Caglaw".
Brussels, Belgium Office: Rue des Chevaliers / Ridderstraat 14 - B.10, B - 1050.
Telephone: 011(32-2) 511-9326.
Fax: 011(-32-2) 513-9206.

(See Next Column)

MEMBERS OF FIRM

Christopher M. Bechhold
Stephen J. Butler
Ethna Bennert Cooper
Deborah DeLong
Jack F. Fuchs
Jane E. Garfinkel
Earle Jay Maiman
Ted T. Martin
Jeffrey F. Peck
Gerald W. Simmons
Jacob K. Stein
Jill A. Weller

ASSOCIATES

John H. Beasley
Vicki Christian
Renee S. Filiatraut
Robert P. Johnson
Sandra P. Kaltman
Jeffrey A. Lydenberg

For Complete List of Firm Personnel, See General Section

For full biographical listings, see the Martindale-Hubbell Law Directory

WAITE, SCHNEIDER, BAYLESS & CHESLEY CO., L.P.A. (AV)

1513 Central Trust Tower, Fourth and Vine Streets, 45202
Telephone: 513-621-0267
Fax: 513-381-2375; 621-0262

Stanley M. Chesley

Thomas F. Rehme
Fay E. Stilz
Louise M. Roselle
D. Arthur Rabourn
Jerome L. Skinner
Janet G. Abaray
Paul M. De Marco
Terrence L. Goodman
Sherrill P. Hondorf
Colleen M. Hegge
Dianna Pendleton
Randy F. Fox
Glenn D. Feagan
Theresa L. Groh
Theodore N. Berry
Jane H. Walker
Renée Infante
Allen P. Grunes

For full biographical listings, see the Martindale-Hubbell Law Directory

WOOD & LAMPING (AV)

2500 Cincinnati Commerce Center, 600 Vine Street, 45202-2409
Telephone: 513-852-6000
Fax: 513-852-6087
Ft. Mitchell, Kentucky Office: Kentucky Executive Building, 2055 Dixie Highway, Suites 248-252.
Telephone: 606-344-4052; 344-4052.
Fax: 606-344-9631.

MEMBERS OF FIRM

Harold G. Korbee
David A. Caldwell
Eric C. Holzapfel
William R. Ellis
Thomas C. Korbee
Jane A. McTaggart
Gerald G. Salmen

ASSOCIATES

Carl J. Schmidt, III
Amy L. Tolnitch
Geraldine M. Johnson
William C. Price

Representative Clients: Armco, Inc.; Atlantic Richfield Company; Ashland Oil Company; Consolidated Grain and Barge Co.; Exxon Company; Reichhold Chemicals, Inc.; Sun Refining and Minerals Co.; Underwriters Laboratories; Union Oil Company of California; Volvo North America.

For Complete List of Firm Personnel, See General Section

For full biographical listings, see the Martindale-Hubbell Law Directory

*CLEVELAND,** Cuyahoga Co.

BAKER & HOSTETLER (AV)

3200 National City Center, 1900 East Ninth Street, 44114-3485
Telephone: 216-621-0200
Telecopier: 216-696-0740
TWX: 810 421 8375
RCA Telex: 215032
In Columbus, Ohio: Capitol Square, Suite 2100, 65 East State Street.
Telephone: 614-228-1541.
In Denver, Colorado: 303 East 17th Avenue, Suite 1100.
Telephone: 303-861-0600.
In Houston, Texas: 1000 Louisiana, Suite 2000.
Telephone: 713-751-1600.
In Long Beach, California: 300 Oceangate, Suite 620.
Telephone: 310-432-2827.
In Los Angeles, California: 600 Wilshire Boulevard.
Telephone: 213-624-2400.
In Orlando, Florida: SunBank Center, Suite 2300, 200 South Orange Avenue.
Telephone: 407-649-4000.
In Washington, D. C.: Washington Square, Suite 1100, 1050 Connecticut Avenue, N.W.
Telephone: 202-861-1500.
In College Park, Maryland: 9658 Baltimore Boulevard, Suite 206.
Telephone: 301-441-2781.
In Alexandria, Virginia: 437 North Lee Street.
Telephone: 703-549-1294.
In San Francisco, California: One Sansome Street, Suite 2000.
Telephone: 415-951-4705.

(See Next Column)

BAKER & HOSTETLER—*Continued*

PARTNERS

Diane P. Chapman
Wayne C. Dabb, Jr.
José C. Feliciano
Charles E. Jarrett
Patrick J. Jordan
Albert J. Knopp
Karen B. Newborn
Thomas H. Shunk
Randall L. Solomon
Douglas P. Whipple

RETIRED PARTNER

H. Stephen Madsen

For Complete List of Firm Personnel, See General Section

For full biographical listings, see the Martindale-Hubbell Law Directory

BENESCH, FRIEDLANDER, COPLAN & ARONOFF (AV)

2300 BP America Building, 200 Public Square, 44114-2378
Telephone: 216-363-4500
Telecopier: 216-363-4588
Columbus, Ohio Office: 88 East Broad Street, 43215-3506.
Telephone: 614-223-9300.
Telecopier: 614-223-9330.
Cincinnati, Ohio Office: 2800 Cincinnati Commerce Center, 600 Vine Street, 45202-2409.
Telephone: 713-762-6200.
Telecopier: 513-762-6245.

MEMBERS OF FIRM

Jeremy Gilman
Edward Kancler
David R. Mayo
David W. Mellott
Wayne D. Porter, Jr.
Harry T. Quick
Charles M. Rosenberg
Stephen David Williger

ASSOCIATES

Dona L. Arnold
Stephen V. Cheatham
Walter C. Danison, Jr.
Jennifer A. Lesny
David W. Neel
Daniel F. Petticord
Mark A. Phillips
Barbara Friedman Yaksic
Eric L. Zalud

COLUMBUS, OHIO
RESIDENT MEMBERS

Orla Ellis Collier, III
James F. DeLeone

COLUMBUS, OHIO
RESIDENT ASSOCIATES

Ronald L. House
Rex A. Littrell
Roger L. Schantz
John F. Stock
Mark D. Tucker

CINCINNATI, OHIO
RESIDENT MEMBERS

Donald J. Mooney, Jr.
Frederic X. Shadley

CINCINNATI, OHIO
RESIDENT ASSOCIATE

Joseph P. Thomas

For Complete List of Firm Personnel, See General Section

For full biographical listings, see the Martindale-Hubbell Law Directory

BERKMAN, GORDON, MURRAY, PALDA & DEVAN (AV)

2121 The Illuminating Building, 55 Public Square, 44113-1949
Telephone: 216-781-5245
FAX: 216-781-8207

MEMBERS OF FIRM

Larry S. Gordon
J. Michael Murray
George W. Palda
Mark R. DeVan
Lorraine R. Baumgardner
Jeremy A. Rosenbaum

ASSOCIATES

Steven D. Shafron
Brooke F. Kocab

Reference: First National Bank of Ohio.

For full biographical listings, see the Martindale-Hubbell Law Directory

BUCKLEY KING & BLUSO A LEGAL PROFESSIONAL ASSOCIATION (AV)

1400 Bank One Center, 44114
Telephone: 216-363-1400;
National Watts Line: 800-255-2825
Cable Address: "Buckinglaw"
Telecopier: 216-579 -7156
ABA/NET: ABA 2978
Columbus, Ohio Office: 2700 LeVeque Tower.
Telephone: 614-461-5600.
Fax: 614-461-5630.
Akron, Ohio Office: Tenth Floor, National City Bank Building, 1 Cascade Plaza.
Telephone: 216-376-4111.

(See Next Column)

Brent M. Buckley
Woods King III
Linda L. Bluso
Rosemary Grdina Gold
William E. Armstrong
Richard J. Disantis
Harry W. Greenfield
Timothy D. Wood
Thomas I. Blackburn
(Resident, Columbus Office)
Richard D. Brown
(Resident, Columbus Office)
Ray P. Drexel
(Resident, Columbus Office)
Robert F. Deacon

Randal G. Ammons
Barbara Lee Armstrong
Gary A. Gillett
(Resident, Columbus Office)
Michele Raia Hoffart
Nancy Howe
Andrew R. Kasle
Harold R. Rauzi
Rosemary Sweeney
Jeffrey C. Toole
Robert B. Trattner
(Resident, Columbus Office)

OF COUNSEL

John A. Hallbauer
Peter R. Harwood
Hylas A. Hilliard
(Resident, Columbus Office)
Michael T. Honohan
I. Monica Olszewski
Eugene B. Schwartz

For full biographical listings, see the Martindale-Hubbell Law Directory

CHATTMAN, SUTULA, FRIEDLANDER & PAUL A LEGAL PROFESSIONAL ASSOCIATION (AV)

6200 Rockside Road, 44131
Telephone: 216-328-8000
Telecopier: 216-328-8018
Red Bank, New Jersey Office: 241 Maple Street. 07701.
Telephone: 908-219-9000.
Facsimile: 908-219-9020.

Harold M. Chattman
(1911-1978)
Gerald B. Chattman
John J. Sutula
Lawrence Friedlander
Douglas J. Paul
Robert A. Poklar
Ronald F. Wayne
Paul B. Madow
Richard G. Ross
Raymond E. Theiss
Fred N. Carmen
Marc I. Strauss
James L. Reed
Gary H. Levine
Sanjay K. Varma
Loreen M. Robinson
Carolyn K. Matheson
Bonnie G. Kraus
Susan P. St. Onge

OF COUNSEL

Albert Krill
Kathryn T. Mengel
Daniel C. Buser

For full biographical listings, see the Martindale-Hubbell Law Directory

DUVIN, CAHN & BARNARD A LEGAL PROFESSIONAL ASSOCIATION (AV)

Erieview Tower, 20th Floor, 1301 East Ninth Street, 44114
Telephone: 216-696-7600
Telecopier: 216-696-2038

Robert P. Duvin
Stephen J. Cahn
Thomas H. Barnard
Gerald A. Messerman
Marc J. Bloch
Andrew C. Meyer
Lee J. Hutton
Martin S. List
Craig M. Brown
Frank W. Buck
Gale S. Messerman
Neal B. Wainblat
Kenneth B. Stark
Martin T. Wymer
Barton A. Bixenstine
Robert M. Wolff
Jane P. Wilson

Richard C. Hubbard, III
Lisa Froimson Mann
Philip S. Kushner
Stephen J. Sferra
Linda E. Tawil
Steven K. Aronoff
Kenneth Michael Haneline
Kevin M. Norchi
Paul A. Monahan
Jon M. Dileno
David A. Posner
Scott A. Moorman
Vincent T. Norwillo
Marc A. Duvin
Suellen Oswald
Stephen C. Sutton
Michele H. Schmidt
William Joseph Evans
Carole O. Heyward

Representative Clients: Cleveland-Akron-Canton Supermarket Industry; The Scott Fetzer Co.; Cole National Corp.; Regional Transit Authority; B.P. America.

For full biographical listings, see the Martindale-Hubbell Law Directory

GOODMAN WEISS MILLER FREEDMAN (AV)

100 Erieview Plaza, 27th Floor, 44114-1824
Telephone: 216-696-3366
Telecopier: 216-363-5835

MEMBERS OF FIRM

Robert A. Goodman
Ronald I. Weiss
John F. Ballard
Steven J. Miller
Glenn S. Hansen
Richard S. Mitchell

(See Next Column)

GOODMAN WEISS MILLER FREEDMAN, *Cleveland—Continued*

Daniel D. Domozick
Jay Faeges
James E. Goodrich
Wendy N. Weigand

OF COUNSEL

Howard J. Freedman
Roger J. Weiss
Michael D. Goler

For full biographical listings, see the Martindale-Hubbell Law Directory

HERMANN, CAHN & SCHNEIDER (AV)

Suite 500, 1301 East Ninth Street, 44114
Telephone: 216-781-5515
Facsimile: 216-781-1030

MEMBERS OF FIRM

Gary D. Hermann
James S. Cahn
Kent B. Schneider
Anthony J. Hartman
Kerry S. Volsky
Peter J. Krembs
Timothy P. McCormick

ASSOCIATES

Thomas P. Marotta
Romney B. Cullers
Forrest A. Norman, III

Representative Clients: First Nationwide Bank; Prudential Bache Securities; Allen-Bradley Co.; TRW, Inc.; Ingersoll-Rand Corp.; Fleetwood Enterprises, Inc.; Skyline Corporation; Van Dorn Company; Pfizer, Inc.; Central Transport, Inc.

For full biographical listings, see the Martindale-Hubbell Law Directory

JANIK & DUNN (AV)

400 Park Plaza Building, 1111 Chester Avenue, 44114
Telephone: 216-781-9700
Fax: 216-781-1250
Brea, California Office: 2601 Saturn Street, Suite 300.
Telephone: 714-572-1101.
Fax: 714-572-1103.

MEMBERS OF FIRM

Steven G. Janik
Theodore M. Dunn, Jr.

ASSOCIATES

Myra Staresina
David L. Mast

For full biographical listings, see the Martindale-Hubbell Law Directory

JONES, DAY, REAVIS & POGUE (AV)

North Point, 901 Lakeside Avenue, 44114
Telephone: 216-586-3939
Cable Address: "Attorneys Cleveland"
Telex: 980389
Telecopier: 216-579-0212
In Columbus, Ohio: 1900 Huntington Center.
Telephone: 614-469-3939.
Cable Address: "Attorneys Columbus."
Telecopier: 614-461-4198.
In Atlanta, Georgia: 3500 One Peachtree Center, 303 Peachtree Street, N.E.
Telephone: 404-521-3939.
Cable Address: "Attorneys Atlanta".
Telex: 54-2711.
Telecopier: 404-581-8330.
In Brussels, Belgium: Avenue Louise 480, 7th Floor. B-1050 Brussels.
Telephone: 011-32-2-645-14-11.
Telecopier: 011-32-2-645-14-45.
In Chicago, Illinois: 77 West Wacker.
Telephone: 312-782-3939.
Telecopier: 312-782-8585.
In Dallas, Texas: 2300 Trammell Crow Center, 2001 Ross Avenue.
Telephone: 214-220-3939.
Cable Address: "Attorneys Dallas."
Telex: 730852.
Telecopier: 214-969-5100.
In Frankfurt, Germany: Triton Haus, Bockenheimer Landstrasse 42, 60323 Frankfurt am Main.
Telephone: 49-69-9726-3939.
Telecopier: 49-69-9726-3993.
In Geneva, Switzerland: 20, rue de Candolle.
Telephone: 011-41-22-320-2339.
Telecopier: 011-41-22-320-1232.
In Hong Kong: 1501 One Exchange Square, 8 Connaught Place.
Telephone: 011-852-2526-6895.
Telecopier: 011-852-2810-5787.
In Irvine, California: 2603 Main Street, Suite 900.
Telephone: 714-851-3939.
Telex: 194911 Lawyers LSA.
Telecopier: 714-553-7539.
In London, England: One Mount Street.
Telephone: 011-44-71-493-9361.
Cable Address: "Surgoe London WI."
Telecopier: 011-44-71-493-9666.

(See Next Column)

In Los Angeles, California: 555 West Fifth Street, Suite 4600.
Telephone: 213-489-3939.
Telex: 181439 UD.
Telecopier: 213-243-2539.
In New York, New York: 599 Lexington Avenue.
Telephone: 212-326-3939.
Cable Address: "JONESDAY NEWYORK."
Telex: 237013 JDRP UR.
Telecopier: 212-755-7306.
In Paris, France: 62, rue du Faubourg Saint-Honore.
Telephone: 011-33-1-44-71-3939.
Cable Address: "Surgoe Paris."
Telex: 290156 Surgoe.
Telecopier: 011-33-1-49-24-0471.
In Pittsburgh, Pennsylvania: 500 Grant Street, 31st Floor.
Telephone: 412-391-3939.
Cable Address: "Attorneys Pittsburgh".
Telecopier: 412-394-7959.
In Riyadh, Saudi Arabia: Law Offices of Saud M.A. Shawwaf, P.O. Box 2700.
Telephones: 011 (966-1) 465-6543, 011 (966-1) 464-8534 or 011 (966-1) 464-8540.
Telex: 401831 SAUCON SJ.
Telecopier: (966-1) 464-8480.
In Taipei, Taiwan: 8th Floor, Tun Hwa South Road, Section 2.
Telephone: 011 (886-2) 704-6808.
Telecopier: 011 (886-2) 704-6791.
In Tokyo, Japan: Toranomon MT Building, 4th Floor, 10-3, Toranomon 3-Chome, Minato-Ku, Tokyo 105, Japan.
Telephone: 011-81-3-3433-3939.
Telecopier: 011-81-3-5401-2725.
In Washington, D.C.: Metropolitan Square, 1450 G Street, N.W.
Telephone: 202-879-3939.
Cable Address: "Attorneys Washington."
Telex: 89-2410 ATTORNEYS WASH.
Telecopier: 202-737-2832.

MEMBERS OF FIRM

Patrick F. McCartan
George J. Moscarino
John L. Strauch
Barbara B. Kacir
Dennis M. Kelly
Brian F. Toohey
John M. Newman, Jr.
John W. Edwards II
Hugh R. Whiting
Steven E. Sigalow
Robert C. Weber

For Complete List of Firm Personnel, See General Section

For full biographical listings, see the Martindale-Hubbell Law Directory

KAUFMAN & CUMBERLAND CO., L.P.A. (AV)

Third Floor, 1404 East 9th Street, 44114-1779
Telephone: 216-861-0707
Telefax: 216-694-6883
TDD: 216-694-6891
Columbus, Ohio Office: 300 South Second Street, 43215.
Telephone: 614-224-0717.
Telefax: 614-229-4111.

Steven S. Kaufman
Frank J. Cumberland, Jr.
Frank R. DeSantis
Gail E. Sindell
William W. Jacobs
Mitchell Ehrenberg

Susan L. Belman
Edda Sara Post
David P. Lodwick
Thomas L. Feher
Laura Hauser Pfahl (Resident, Columbus, Ohio Office)
David B. Webster
Christine Sommer Riley
Mary E. Darcy

OF COUNSEL

Jack G. Day
James A. Scott

Representative Clients: CertainTeed Corp.; International Insurance Co.; International Surplus Lines Insurance Co.; Morgan's Foods, Inc.; Teledyne, Inc.

For Complete List of Firm Personnel, See General Section

For full biographical listings, see the Martindale-Hubbell Law Directory

KELLER AND CURTIN CO., L.P.A. (AV)

Suite 330 The Hanna Building, 44115-1901
Telephone: 216-566-7100
Telecopier: 216-566-5430
Akron, Ohio Office: 2304 First National Tower, 44308-1419.
Telephone: 216-376-7245.
Telecopier: 216-376-8128.

Stanley S. Keller
G. Michael Curtin
Walter H. Krohngold
James M. Johnson

Joseph G. Ritzler
Phillip A. Kuri

Reference: Bank One, Cleveland.

For full biographical listings, see the Martindale-Hubbell Law Directory

Cleveland—Continued

KELLEY, McCANN & LIVINGSTONE (AV)

35th Floor, BP America Building, 200 Public Square, 44114-2302
Telephone: 216-241-3141
FAX: 216-241-3707

MEMBERS OF FIRM

Stephen M. O'Bryan
John D. Brown
Joel A. Makee
Michael D. Schenker
Mark J. Valponi
Thomas J. Lee
Carl A. Murway
Steven A. Goldfarb
David H. Wallace

OF COUNSEL

Walter C. Kelley

ASSOCIATES

Kurt D. Weaver
Robert A. Brindza, II
Sylvester Summers, Jr.
Peter M. Poulos

For Complete List of Firm Personnel, See General Section

For full biographical listings, see the Martindale-Hubbell Law Directory

KITCHEN, DEERY & BARNHOUSE (AV)

1100 Illuminating Building, 55 Public Square, 44113
Telephone: 216-241-5614
Fax: 216-241-5255

MEMBERS OF FIRM

Karl K. Kitchen (1899-1949)
Fred A. Messner (1901-1986)
George W. Leyshon (1913-1972)
James V. Suhr (1899-1983)
Ronald J. Deery (1942-1992)
Charles W. Kitchen
James W. Barnhouse
Paul S. Klug
Vincent A. Feudo
Johanna M. Sfiscko
Timothy X. McGrail
Eugene B. Meador

ASSOCIATES

William F. Schmitz
Patti Jo Mooney
Kathleen Donovan Onders

Representative Clients: Buckeye Union Insurance Co.; Continental Insurance Co.; Grange Mutual Casualty Co.; Erie Insurance Group; Home Insurance Cos.; Motorists Mutual Insurance Cos.; St. Paul Insurance Cos.; U.S. Aviation Underwriters; Ohio Medical Professional Liability Underwriting Assn. (J.U.A.).
Reference: National City Bank.

For full biographical listings, see the Martindale-Hubbell Law Directory

MARTINDALE & BRZYTWA (AV)

900 Skylight Office Tower, 1660 West Second Street, 44113
Telephone: 216-664-6900

MEMBERS OF FIRM

John E. Martindale
E. John Brzytwa
Jeffery A. Key
Margaret Mary Meko
Kevin M. Young
Jonathan R. Cooper

For full biographical listings, see the Martindale-Hubbell Law Directory

MEYERS, HENTEMANN, SCHNEIDER & REA CO., L.P.A. (AV)

21st Floor, Superior Building, 815 Superior Avenue, N.E., 44114
Telephone: 216-241-3435
Telecopier: 216-241-6568
Elyria, Ohio Office: 301 Fifth Street, 44035.
Telephone: 216-323-6920.

Kent H. Meyers (1902-1970)
Richard F. Stevens (1915-1981)
David S. Meyers (1928-1983)
Eugene J. Gilroy (1926-1984)
John S. Rea
Joseph G. Schneider
Henry A. Hentemann
Richard C. Talbert
Thomas L. Brunn
Gerald L. Jeppe
Don P. Brown
Lynn A. Lazzaro
Joseph H. Wantz
Kirk E. Roman

James C. Cochran
Kathleen Carrabine Hopkins
J. Michael Creagan
Sean P. Allan
Keith David Thomas
John Peter O'Donnell

Representative Clients: State Farm Mutual Insurance Co.; Travelers Insurance Co.; J.C. Penney Insurance, formerly Educator & Executive Insurance Co.; Lloyds Underwriters, London, England; Preferred Risk Mutual Insurance Co.; American Suzuki Motor Corp.; Detroit Automobile Inter-Insurance Exchange; Electrical Mutual; Automation Plastics, Inc.; Environmental Structures, Inc.

For full biographical listings, see the Martindale-Hubbell Law Directory

NURENBERG, PLEVIN, HELLER & McCARTHY CO., L.P.A. (AV)

1370 Ontario Street First Floor, 44113-1792
Telephone: 216-621-2300
FAX: 216-771-2242

(See Next Column)

A. H. Dudnik (1905-1963)
S. F. Komito (1902-1984)
Marshall I. Nurenberg
Leon M. Plevin
Maurice L. Heller
John J. McCarthy
Thomas Mester
Harlan M. Gordon
Andrew P. Krembs
Anne L. Kilbane
David M. Paris
Richard C. Alkire
Richard L. Demsey
Joel Levin
Jamie R. Lebovitz
William S. Jacobson

Dean C. Nieding
Jeffrey A. Leikin
Robin J. Peterson
Robert S. Zeller
James T. Schumacher
Ellen M. McCarthy
J. Charles Ruiz-Bueno
Sandra J. Rosenthal
Kathleen St. John
Jessica F. Kahn

Reference: Society Key Corp.

For full biographical listings, see the Martindale-Hubbell Law Directory

QUANDT, GIFFELS & BUCK CO., L.P.A. (AV)

800 Leader Building, 526 Superior Avenue, N.E., 44114-1460
Telephone: 216-241-2025
Telecopier: 216-241-2080

Robert G. Quandt
Walter R. Matchinga
Joseph R. Tira
Beth A. Sebaugh
Laurence F. Buzzelli
Larry C. Greathouse

OF COUNSEL

Stephen D. Richman

Hunter S. Havens
Timothy G. Sweeney
Jeffrey A. Schenk
Timothy L. Kerwin
Nita Kay Smith
Edward J. Stoll, Jr.
Ernest C. Pisanelli

Representative Clients: Physicians Insurance Company of Ohio; Royal Insurance Company; Continental Insurance Company; Heritage Insurance Company; Reliance Insurance Co.; Safeco Insurance Co.; Fireman's Fund Insurance Company.

For full biographical listings, see the Martindale-Hubbell Law Directory

RAY, ROBINSON, CARLE, DAVIES & SNYDER (AV)

1650 The East Ohio Building, 1717 East 9th Street, 44114-2898
Telephone: 216-861-4533
Telex: 810-421-8402
Cable Address: Lakelaw-Cleveland
Facsimile: 216-861-4568
Chicago, Illinois Office: 850 West Jackson Blvd, Suite 310.
Telephone: 312-421-3110.
Cable Address: Lakelaw-Chicago.
Facsimile: 312-421-2808.

MEMBERS OF FIRM

William D. Carle, III
David G. Davies
Michael A. Snyder, Ltd. (Resident at Chicago, Illinois Office)
Douglas R. Denny
Gene B. George
Julia R. Brouhard

ASSOCIATES

Robert T. Coniam
Sandra Maurer Kelly
Richard F. Schultz
Richard A. Forster (Resident at Chicago, Illinois Office)
William P. Ryan (Resident at Chicago, Illinois Office)
Charles A. Rozhon (Resident at Chicago, Illinois Office)
Shanshan Zhou (Resident at Chicago, Illinois Office)
Thomas More Wynne

OF COUNSEL

Lucian Y. Ray (1903-1987)
Theodore C. Robinson (Resident at Chicago, Illinois Office)

Representative Clients: The Cleveland-Cliffs Iron Co.; U.S.S., Great Lakes Fleet, Inc.; Bethlehem Steel Corp., Great Lakes Steamship Division; Canada Steamship Lines, Ltd.; The M.A. Hanna Co.; Canadian Shipowners Assn.; Interlake Steamship Co.; Inland Steel Co.; Amoco Oil Co.; Steamship Mutual Underwriting Assn., Ltd.

For full biographical listings, see the Martindale-Hubbell Law Directory

RUBENSTEIN, NOVAK, EINBUND, PAVLIK & CELEBREZZE (AV)

Suite 270, Skylight Office Tower Tower City Center, 44113-1498
Telephone: 216-781-8700
Telecopier: 216-781-9227

MEMBERS OF FIRM

Ronald M. Rubenstein
William J. Novak
Lewis Einbund
Thomas C. Pavlik
Frank D. Celebrezze

ASSOCIATES

Nancy J. Fleming
Christine A. Murphy
Scott H. Scharf
Peter Cummings Tucker

(See Next Column)

RUBENSTEIN, NOVAK, EINBUND, PAVLIK & CELEBREZZE, *Cleveland—Continued*

OF COUNSEL

Beverly Schneider
James Reed Foos, Jr.

For full biographical listings, see the Martindale-Hubbell Law Directory

SEELEY, SAVIDGE AND AUSSEM A LEGAL PROFESSIONAL ASSOCIATION (AV)

800 Bank One Center, 600 Superior Avenue, East, 44114-2655
Telephone: 216-566-8200
Cable Address: "See Sau"
Fax-Telecopier: 216-566-0213
Elyria, Ohio Office: 538 Broad Street.
Telephone: 216-236-8158.

Glenn J. Seeley
Keith A. Savidge
Jane T. Seelie

Carter R. Dodge
Robert C. White

References: Society National Bank; AmeriTrust.

For Complete List of Firm Personnel, See General Section

For full biographical listings, see the Martindale-Hubbell Law Directory

SELKER & FURBER (AV)

1111 Ohio Savings Plaza, 1801 East Ninth Street, 44114
Telephone: 216-781-8686
FAX: 216-781-8688

MEMBERS OF FIRM

Eugene I. Selker
Philip C. Furber
Harlan Daniel Karp

For full biographical listings, see the Martindale-Hubbell Law Directory

TIMOTHY A. SHIMKO & ASSOCIATES A LEGAL PROFESSIONAL ASSOCIATION (AV)

2010 Huntington Building, 925 Euclid Avenue, 44115
Telephone: 216-241-8300
Fax: 216-241-2702

Timothy A. Shimko

Janet I. Stich
Ronald K. Starkey
Theresa A. Tarchinski
Frank E. Piscitelli, Jr.

OF COUNSEL

Frank B. Mazzone

Reference: National City Bank, Cleveland.

For full biographical listings, see the Martindale-Hubbell Law Directory

SKULINA & HILL (AV)

24803 Detroit Road (Westlake), 44145
Telephone: 216-899-1911
FAX: 216-899-1625

MEMBERS OF FIRM

Thomas R. Skulina
Robert W. Hill

Reference: National City Bank.

For full biographical listings, see the Martindale-Hubbell Law Directory

SMITH, MARSHALL AND WEAVER (AV)

500 National City East Sixth Building, 1965 East Sixth Street, 44114
Telephone: 216-781-4994
Telecopier: 216-781-9448

MEMBERS OF FIRM

Richard C. Green (1910-1967)
Melvin M. Roberts (1911-1971)
John M. Cronquist (1931-1993)
Jack F. Smith (Retired)
Wentworth J. Marshall, Jr.
Philip J. Weaver, Jr.
Frederick P. Vergon, Jr.
T. Charles Cooper

ASSOCIATES

Stephen C. Merriam
David E. Ledman
Mary B. Percifull
Benjamin L. Moltman, III

Representative Clients: American States Insurance Co.; Fireman's Fund Insurance Co.; Hartford Insurance Group; State Automobile Mutual Insurance Co.

For full biographical listings, see the Martindale-Hubbell Law Directory

SPIETH, BELL, MCCURDY & NEWELL CO., L.P.A. (AV)

2000 Huntington Building, 925 Euclid Avenue, 44115-1496
Telephone: 216-696-4700
Telecopier: 216-696-6569; 216-696-2706; 216-696-1052

(See Next Column)

Ron Tonidandel
Bruce G. Hearey
Dianne Foley Hearey
Kevin L. Starrett
Wade M. Fricke

Representative Clients: Cleveland Cavaliers; Nationwide Advertising Services, Inc.; Independent Steel Co.; Baldwin Wallace College; The Tool-Die Engineering Company.
Representative Labor Relations Clients (Management Only): Parker Hannifin Corp.; Reliance Electric Co.; Brush Wellman Co.

For Complete List of Firm Personnel, See General Section

For full biographical listings, see the Martindale-Hubbell Law Directory

THOMPSON, HINE AND FLORY (AV)

1100 National City Bank Building, 629 Euclid Avenue, 44114-3070
Telephone: 216-566-5500
Fax: 216-566-5583
Telex: 980217
Cable Address: "Thomflor"
Akron, Ohio Office: 50 S. Main Street, Suite 502, 44308-1828.
Telephone: 216-376-8090.
Fax: 216-376-8386.
Cincinnati, Ohio Office: 312 Walnut Street, 14th Floor, 45202-4029.
Telephone: 513-352-6700.
Fax: 513-241-4771.
Telex: 938003.
Columbus, Ohio Office: One Columbus, 10 West Broad Street, 43215-3435.
Telephone: 614-469-3200.
Fax: 614-469-3361.
Dayton, Ohio Office: 2000 Courthouse Plaza, N.E., 45402-1706.
Telephone: 513-443-6600.
Fax: 513-443-6637; 443-6635.
Palm Beach, Florida Office: 125 Worth Avenue, Suite 117, 33480-4466.
Telephone: 407-833-5900.
Fax: 407-833-5951.
Washington, D.C. Office: 1920 N Street, N.W., 20036-1601.
Telephone: 202-331-8800.
Fax: 202-331-8330.
Telex: 904173.
Cable Address: "Caglaw".
Brussels, Belgium Office: Rue des Chevaliers, Ridderstraat 14 - B.10, B - 1050.
Telephone: 011(32-2) 511-9326.
Fax: 011(32-2) 513-9206.

MEMBERS OF FIRM

Jeffrey R. Appelbaum
Barbara J. Arison
Brett K. Bacon
Douglas N. Barr
Richard C. Binzley
Virginia S. Brown
Keith L. Carson
Timothy J. Coughlin
Michael A. Cyphert
Stephen H. Daniels
S. Stuart Eilers
Stephen F. Gladstone
R. Benton Gray
Daniel W. Hammer
Harry A. Hanna
Michael L. Hardy
Thomas A. Heffernan
Harold W. Henderson
David J. Hooker
George F. Karch, Jr.
William B. Leahy
Robert D. Monnin
David E. Nash
David L. Parham
James D. Robenalt
Daniel R. Warren
Elizabeth B. Wright

ASSOCIATES

Luke L. Dauchot
Richard A. DiLisi
David M. Dumas
Mark A. Gamin
Gary M. Glass (In Cincinnati, Ohio)
Patrick F. Haggerty
Dena M. Kobasic
Ellen B. Krist
Brian J. Lamb
Walt A. Linscott
H. Kevin McNeelege
Andrew J. Natale
Shawn R. Pearson
Karen E. Rubin
Donald P. Screen
Michael E. Smith
Melisa D. Stone (In Columbus, Ohio)

OF COUNSEL

William D. Ginn

STAFF ATTORNEYS

Byron J. Horn
Pamela Zarlingo

For Complete List of Firm Personnel, See General Section

For full biographical listings, see the Martindale-Hubbell Law Directory

ULMER & BERNE (AV)

Ninth Floor, Bond Court Building, 1300 East Ninth Street, 44114-1583
Telephone: 216-621-8400
Telex: 201999 UBLAW
Telecopier: 216-621-7488
Columbus, Ohio Office: 88 East Broad Street, Suite 1980.
Telephone: 614-228-8400.
Telecopier: 614-228-8561.

(See Next Column)

ULMER & BERNE—*Continued*

MEMBERS OF FIRM

Marvin L. Karp
Alan S. Sims
Richard E. Rubinstein
Ronald H. Isroff (Chairman, Commercial Litigation Group)
Murray K. Lenson
Harold H. Reader, III
Bruce P. Mandel
Stephen A. Markus
Richard D. Sweebe
Jeffrey W. Van Wagner
Steven D. Bell
Stephanie E. Trudeau
F. Thomas Vickers
Michael N. Ungar

ATTORNEYS IN COLUMBUS, OHIO OFFICE (SEE LISTING)

Alexander M. Andrews
Thomas L. Rosenberg

For Complete List of Firm Personnel, See General Section

For full biographical listings, see the Martindale-Hubbell Law Directory

WESTON HURD FALLON PAISLEY & HOWLEY (AV)

2500 Terminal Tower, 50 Public Square, 44113-2241
Telephone: 216-241-6602;
Ohio Toll Free: 800-336-4952
FAX: 216-621-8369

Joseph Philip Sullivan (1916-1974)
Lee C. Howley (1910-1983)
Harold Fallon (1910-1989)
Frank Seth Hurd (1913-1990)
Lloyd O. Brown (1928-1993)

MEMBERS OF FIRM

S. Burns Weston (Retired)
Louis Paisley
Mark O'Neill
John W. Jeffers
John M. Baker
Ronald A. Rispo
James Lincoln McCrystal, Jr.
David Arnold
Carolyn M. Cappel
Donald H. Switzer
Hilary Sheldon Taylor
Kenneth A. Torgerson
John S. Kluznik
Jeffrey D. Fincun
William H. Baughman, Jr.
John Winthrop Ours
Stephen D. Walters
Gary W. Johnson
Deirdre G. Henry
Harry Sigmier
Warren Rosman
Connie M. Horrigan
Timothy D. Johnson
William R. Fanos
Jerome W. Cook
Kathryn M. Murray
Dana A. Rose
Hernan N. Visani

OF COUNSEL

Norbert F. Werner
Andrew J. McLandrich

ASSOCIATES

John G. Farnan
Cecil Marlowe
Scott C. Smith
Raymond S. Ling
David C. Lamb
Patrick M. Dukes
Lisa G. McComas
Katherine Vierkorn
Gregory E. O'Brien
Todd G. Jackson
Ronald K. Lembright
Glenn D. Southworth
Maria A. Kortau

For Complete List of Firm Personnel, See General Section

For full biographical listings, see the Martindale-Hubbell Law Directory

ZIEGLER, METZGER & MILLER (AV)

2020 Huntington Building, 44115-1407
Telephone: 216-781-5470
FAX: 216-781-0714

MEMBERS OF FIRM

Stephen M. Darlington
Timothy M. Bittel
Mary Beth Ballard
Richard T. Spotz, Jr.

ASSOCIATES

Stephen M. Bales
John E. Redeker
Christopher W. Siemen
Jeffrey L. Koberg

For Complete List of Firm Personnel, See General Section

For full biographical listings, see the Martindale-Hubbell Law Directory

*COLUMBUS,** Franklin Co.

***** indicates certain Bar Register subscribers whose principal office is located elsewhere in the state and who have arranged for representation as a part of the state capital listings that follow

*** BAKER & HOSTETLER (AV)**

Capitol Square, Suite 2100, 65 East State Street, 43215-4260
Telephone: 614-228-1541
Telecopier: 614-462-2616
In Cleveland, Ohio: 3200 National City Center, 1900 East Ninth Street.
Telephone: 216-621-0200.
In Denver, Colorado: 303 East 17th Avenue, Suite 1100.
Telephone: 202-861-1500.
In Houston, Texas: 1000 Louisiana, Suite 2000.
Telephone: 713-751-1600.
In Long Beach, California: 300 Oceangate, Suite 620.
Telephone: 310-432-2827.

(See Next Column)

In Los Angeles, California: 600 Wilshire.
Telephone: 213-624-2400.
In Orlando, Florida: SunBank Center, Suite 2300, 200 South Orange Avenue.
Telephone: 407-649-4000.
In Washington, D. C.: Washington Square, Suite 1100, 1050 Connecticut Avenue, N.W.
Telephone: 202-861-1500.
In College Park, Maryland: 9658 Baltimore Boulevard, Suite 301.
Telephone: 301-441-2781.
In Alexandria, Virginia: 437 North Lee Street.
Telephone: 703-549-1294.
In San Francisco, California: One Sansome Street, Suite 2000.
Telephone: 415-951-4705.

MEMBER OF FIRM IN COLUMBUS, OHIO

George W. Hairston (Managing Partner-Columbus Office)

PARTNERS

John H. Burtch
Bradley Hummel
Mark A. Johnson
Robert M. Kincaid, Jr.
Sherri Blank Lazear
Thomas L. Long
Robert B. McAlister
Randall S. Rabe
John F. Winkler

ASSOCIATES

Michael D. Dortch
David C. Levine
Janine M. Marks
Karen E. Sheffer
Jerri H. Stewart
Jeffrey T. Williams

For Complete List of Firm Personnel, See General Section

For full biographical listings, see the Martindale-Hubbell Law Directory

*** BENESCH, FRIEDLANDER, COPLAN & ARONOFF (AV)**

88 East Broad Street, 43215-3506
Telephone: 614-223-9300
Telecopier: 614-223-9330
Cleveland, Ohio Office: 2300 BP American Building, 200 Public Square, 44114-2378.
Telephone: 216-363-4500.
Telecopier: 216-363-4588.
Cincinnati, Ohio Office: 2800 Cincinnati Commerce Center, 600 Vine Street, 45202-2409.
Telephone: 513-762-6200.
Telecopier: 513-762-6245.

MEMBERS OF FIRM

Orla Ellis Collier, III
James F. DeLeone

ASSOCIATES

Ronald L. House
Rex A. Littrell
Roger L. Schantz
John F. Stock
Mark D. Tucker

For Complete List of Firm Personnel, See General Section

For full biographical listings, see the Martindale-Hubbell Law Directory

BERRY & SHOEMAKER (AV)

42 East Gay Street, Suite 1515, 43215
Telephone: 614-464-0100
Portsmouth Telephone: 614-354-4838
Fax: 614-464-4033
Portsmouth, Ohio Office: 703 National City Bank Building, 45662.
Telephone: 614-354-4838.
Chillicothe, Ohio Office: 63 N. Paint Street, 45601.
Telephone: 614-775-8941.

MEMBERS OF FIRM

John F. Berry
Kevin L. Shoemaker
D. Lewis Clark, Jr.

OF COUNSEL

Brenda S. Shoemaker

For full biographical listings, see the Martindale-Hubbell Law Directory

BRICKER & ECKLER (AV)

100 South Third Street, 43215-4291
Telephone: 614-227-2300
Telecopy: 614-227-2390
Cleveland, Ohio Office: 600 Superior Avenue East, Suite 800.
Telephone: 216-771-0720. Fax 216-771-7702.

James S. Monahan
Richard D. Rogovin
Edward A. Matto
John F. Birath, Jr.
Michael J. Renner
Randolph C. Wiseman
Charles H. Walker
Richard S. Lovering, III
Percy Squire
Charles D. Smith
Anne Marie Sferra

Quintin F. Lindsmith
James J. Hughes, III
Joyce B. Link
Jack R. Rosati
Wendi R. Huntley
Drew H. Campbell
Michael D. Smith

(See Next Column)

BRICKER & ECKLER, *Columbus—Continued*

Representative Clients: Manville Personal Injury Settlement Trust; American Telephone & Telegraph Co.; Consolidated Rail Corp.; Miller Brewing Co.; Riverside Methodist Hospital; Cellular One of Ohio; Browning Ferris Industries; Argonaut Insurance Co.; Waste Technologies Industries; Abbott Foods, Inc.

For Complete List of Firm Personnel, See General Section

For full biographical listings, see the Martindale-Hubbell Law Directory

BUTLER, CINCIONE, DICUCCIO & DRITZ (AV)

Suite 700 LeVeque Lincoln Tower, 50 West Broad Street, 43215
Telephone: 614-221-3151
Fax: 614-221-8196

MEMBERS OF FIRM

Robert A. Butler
Alphonse P. Cincione
N. Gerald DiCuccio
Stanley B. Dritz
David B. Barnhart

Matthew P. Cincione
Gail M. Zalimeni

References: National City Bank, Columbus, Ohio; Bank One, Columbus, Ohio.

For full biographical listings, see the Martindale-Hubbell Law Directory

CHESTER, WILLCOX AND SAXBE (AV)

17 South High Street, Suite 900, 43215-3413
Telephone: 614-221-4000
Fax: 614-221-4012

MEMBERS OF FIRM

John J. Chester
Charles Rockwell Saxbe
John W. Bentine
Donald C. Brey
Eugene B. Lewis
Richard A. Talda

Representative Clients: American Municipal Power-Ohio, Inc.; The Limited; Scioto Downs, Inc.; Tee Jaye's Country Place Restaurants.

For Complete List of Firm Personnel, See General Section

For full biographical listings, see the Martindale-Hubbell Law Directory

CLARK, PERDUE, ROBERTS & SCOTT CO., L.P.A. (AV)

471 East Broad Street Suite 1400, 43215
Telephone: 614-469-1400
Fax: 614-469-0900

Dale K. Perdue
Paul O. Scott
Douglas S. Roberts
Edward L. Clark
Glen R. Pritchard
Robert W. Kerpsack, Jr.
D. Andrew List
Brian W. Palmer

For full biographical listings, see the Martindale-Hubbell Law Directory

CLOPPERT, PORTMAN, SAUTER, LATANICK & FOLEY (AV)

225 East Broad Street, 43215-3709
Telephone: 614-461-4455
Fax: 614-461-0072
Portsmouth, Ohio Office: 812 6th Street.
Telephone: 614-354-2553.
Fax: 614-353-5293.

MEMBERS OF FIRM

Mark A. Foley
Frederick G. Cloppert, Jr.
Frederic A. Portman
David G. Latanick
Robert W. Sauter
Robert L. Washburn, Jr.
Walter J. Gerhardstein
Michael J. Hunter
Russell E. Carnahan
Grant D. Shoub
Susan Hayest Kozlowski
Charles J. Smith

William J. Steele
Nancy E. Leech
Debra D. Paxson

LEGAL SUPPORT PERSONNEL

Victoria L. Wythe

Reference: Bank One of Columbus, N.A.

For full biographical listings, see the Martindale-Hubbell Law Directory

MICHAEL F. COLLEY CO., L.P.A. (AV)

Hoster & High Building, 536 South High Street, 43215-5674
Telephone: 614-228-6453
Fax: 614-228-7122

Michael F. Colley

David I. Shroyer
Daniel N. Abraham
Elizabeth Schorpp Burkett
Jennifer K. Thivener
Thomas F. Martello, Jr.

(See Next Column)

OF COUNSEL

Marvin Sloin
David K. Frank

Reference: Bank One of Columbus, NA.

For full biographical listings, see the Martindale-Hubbell Law Directory

CRABBE, BROWN, JONES, POTTS & SCHMIDT (AV)

500 South Front Street, Suite 1200, 43215
Telephone: 614-228-5511
Telecopier: 614-229-4559
Cincinnati, Ohio Office: 30 Garfield Place, Suite 940, 45202.
Telephone: 513-784-1525.
Telecopier: 513-784-1250.

MEMBERS OF FIRM

J. Roth Crabbe (1906-1989)
Robert C. Potts (1913-1994)
William T. McCracken (1929-1993)
Charles E. Brown
Theodore D. Sawyer
William H. Jones
Vincent J. Lodico
Steven B. Ayers
Keith H. Jung
Jeffrey M. Brown
Larry H. James
Brian E. Hurley (Resident, Cincinnati Office)
Gilbert J. Gradisar
Robert J. Behal
Jeffrey M. Lewis
Richard D. Wetzel, Jr.
Jerry A. Eichenberger
James D. Gilbert
Karen A. Seawall
Luis M. Alcalde
John C. Albert
George R. McCue, III
Gregory J. Dunn

ASSOCIATES

Michael R. Henry
Robert C. Buchbinder
John A. Van Sickle
Francesca M. Tosi
Stephen L. McIntosh
Lynne K. Schoenling
Kathleen McGarvey Hidy (Resident, Cincinnati Office)
Steven A. Davis
David J. Demers
Nicholas C. York
Todd William Collis
James P. Dinsmore
Michael C. Mentel
Kristen H. Smith

OF COUNSEL

John P. Kennedy
Wilbur W. Jones
William L. Schmidt
William Page Lewis

Representative Clients: Allstate Insurance Co.; American States Insurance Co.; General Electric.

For full biographical listings, see the Martindale-Hubbell Law Directory

DENMEAD & MALONEY (AV)

37 West Broad Street, Suite 1150, 43215-4189
Telephone: 614-228-5271
Telecopier: 614-228-7624

Craig Denmead
Kevin M. Maloney
Deborah A. Bonarrigo

OF COUNSEL

Mark A. Hutson

Representative Clients: Bode-Finn Co.; Century Surety Co.; COP, Inc.; Emco Maier Corp.; Inland Products, Inc.; National Head Injury Foundation, Inc., of Washington D.C.; Ohio Head Injury Assn.; Stonhard, Inc.; Sammons Corporate Services, Inc.

For full biographical listings, see the Martindale-Hubbell Law Directory

EMENS, KEGLER, BROWN, HILL & RITTER (AV)

Capitol Square Suite 1800, 65 East State Street, 43215-4294
Telephone: 614-462-5400
Telecopier: 614-464-2634
Cable Address: "Law EKBHR"
Telex: 246671

Donald A. Antrim
John P. Brody
William J. Brown
Lawrence F. Feheley
Thomas W. Hill
Robin Smith Hoke
Gene W. Holliker
R. Kevin Kerns
Ronald L. Mason
Larry J. McClatchey
O. Judson Scheaf, III
Theodore Scott, Jr.
S. Martijn Steger
Roger P. Sugarman
Melvin D. Weinstein

COUNSEL

John C. Deal
S. Noel Melvin

Robert Garrett Cohen
David M. Johnson
Gregory D. May
Thomas M. L. Metzger
Todd F. Palmer
Karl W. Schedler
Richard W. Schuermann, Jr.
Robert G. Schuler
Timothy T. Tullis
Christopher J. Weber

Representative Clients: BancOhio National Bank; Borden, Inc.; Columbus Metropolitan Housing Authority; Farmers Insurance Group; National Ground Water Association; The Ohio State University; Owens-Corning Fiberglas Corp.; Patrick Petroleum Co.; State Savings Bank.

(See Next Column)

EMENS, KEGLER, BROWN, HILL & RITTER—*Continued*

For Complete List of Firm Personnel, See General Section

For full biographical listings, see the Martindale-Hubbell Law Directory

GAMBLE HARTSHORN ALDEN (AV)

One Livingston Avenue, 43215-5700
Telephone: 614-221-0922
FAX: 614-365-9741

MEMBERS OF FIRM

Michael W. Hartshorn
Kenneth A. Gamble
Bryan B. Johnson

Craig A. Smith
Theodore F. Claypoole

For full biographical listings, see the Martindale-Hubbell Law Directory

GERTNER & GERTNER (AV)

Suite 1435, 88 East Broad Street, 43215
Telephone: 614-463-9393

MEMBERS OF FIRM

Abraham Gertner (Retired)
Michael H. Gertner

For full biographical listings, see the Martindale-Hubbell Law Directory

HADDEN CO., L.P.A. (AV)

150 East Wilson Bridge Road, 43085-2328
Telephone: 614-431-2000
Fax: 614-436-4500

E. Bruce Hadden

LEGAL SUPPORT PERSONNEL

Isabel M. Hadden

References: Huntington National Bank, Columbus, Ohio.

For full biographical listings, see the Martindale-Hubbell Law Directory

HARRIS, CARTER & MAHOTA (AV)

500 South Front Street, Suite 1010, 43215
Telephone: 614-221-2112
Fax: 614-221-2217
Washington, D.C. Office: 1747 Pennsylvania Avenue, N.W., Suite 704.
Telephone: 202-223-4723.

MEMBERS OF FIRM

Kenneth E. Harris
James M. Carter (Not admitted in OH; Resident, Washington D.C. Office)
John M. Mahota

ASSOCIATES

Robin L. Canowitz
Thomas G. St. Pierre

For full biographical listings, see the Martindale-Hubbell Law Directory

LAMKIN, VAN EMAN, TRIMBLE, BEALS & ROURKE (AV)

Suite 200, 500 South Front Street, 43215-5671
Telephone: 614-224-8187
Fax: 614-224-4943

MEMBERS OF FIRM

William W. Lamkin
Timothy L. Van Eman
Thomas W. Trimble
David A. Beals
Michael J. Rourke

ASSOCIATE

Kathy A. Dougherty

Reference: Huntington National Bank.

For full biographical listings, see the Martindale-Hubbell Law Directory

MCCARTHY, PALMER, VOLKEMA, BOYD & THOMAS A LEGAL PROFESSIONAL ASSOCIATION (AV)

140 East Town Street, Suite 1100, 43215
Telephone: Telephone: 614-221-4400
Telecopier: 614-221-6010

Dennis M. McCarthy
Robert Gray Palmer
Daniel R. Volkema
Jeffrey D. Boyd
Warner M. Thomas, Jr.

Craig P. Scott

COUNSEL

Russell H. Volkema
Stanton G. Darling, II

Reference: Huntington National Bank.

For full biographical listings, see the Martindale-Hubbell Law Directory

MCSHANE, BREITFELLER & WITTEN (AV)

600 South High Street, 43215
Telephone: 614-221-1919
Telecopier: 614-221-2881

MEMBERS OF FIRM

Eugene F. McShane
Ralph E. Breitfeller
Alan C. Witten

Reference: Bank One of Columbus, N.A.

For full biographical listings, see the Martindale-Hubbell Law Directory

JOHN C. NEMETH & ASSOCIATES (AV)

21 East Frankfort Street, 43206-1069
Telephone: 614-443-4866
Fax: 614-443-4860

ASSOCIATES

David A. Caborn
Joseph A. Butauski
David A. Herd

Representative Clients: Anheuser-Busch, Inc.; Central Ohio Transit Authority; Crawford & Co.; Erie Insurance Group; Home Insurance Co.; Safeco Insurance Co.; Mount Carmel Hospital; The Hartford Group; Citizens Insurance Co.; State Farm Insurance Co.

For full biographical listings, see the Martindale-Hubbell Law Directory

PORTER, WRIGHT, MORRIS & ARTHUR (AV)

41 South High Street, 43215-6194
Telephone: 614-227-2000; (800-533-2794)
Telex: 6503213584 MCI
Fax: 614-227-2100
Dayton, Ohio Office: One Dayton Centre, One South Main Street, 45402.
Telephones: 513-228-2411; (800-533-4434).
Fax: 513-449-6820.
Cincinnati, Ohio Office: 250 E. Fifth Street, 45202-4166.
Telephones: 513-381-4700; (800-582-5813).
Fax: 513-421-0991.
Cleveland, Ohio Office: 925 Euclid Avenue, 44115-1483.
Telephones: 216-443-9000; (800-824-1980).
Fax: 216-443-9011.
Washington, D.C. Office: 1233 20th Street, N.W., 20036-2395.
Telephones: 202-778-3000; (800-456-7962).
Fax: 202-778-3063.
Naples, Florida Office: 4501 Tamiami Trail North, 33940-3060.
Telephones: 813-263-8898;(800-876-7962).
Fax: 813-436-2990.

MEMBERS OF FIRM
COLUMBUS, OHIO OFFICE

Kenneth S. Blumenthal
Marjorie Crowder Briggs
Daniel A. Brown
Brian L. Buzby
Daniel W. Costello
James D. Curphey
Joyce D. Edelman
Joseph F. Elliott
Mason Evans, IV
Randall W. Knutti
Charles J. Kurtz, III
Mark K. Merkle, Jr.
Terrance M. Miller
Denise M. Mirman
Scott E. North
James S. Oliphant
James E. Pohlman
Joseph W. Ryan, Jr.
Darrell R. Shepard
Patrick J. Smith
Kathleen McManus Trafford
Robert W. Trafford
Thomas A. Young

OF COUNSEL
COLUMBUS, OHIO OFFICE

John M. Adams

DAYTON, OHIO OFFICE
RESIDENT MEMBERS

Gary W. Gottschlich
Jonathan Hollingsworth
Thomas H. Pyper
Walter Reynolds

CINCINNATI, OHIO OFFICE
RESIDENT MEMBERS

John J. Cruze
Mark E. Elsener
Jerome J. Metz, Jr.

CLEVELAND, OHIO OFFICE
RESIDENT MEMBERS

James P. Conroy
Daniel F. Gourash
Richard M. Markus
Hugh E. McKay
Ralph Streza

CLEVELAND, OHIO OFFICE
RESIDENT OF COUNSEL

James J. Schiller

Representative Clients: American Electric Power Service Corporation; AT&T; Battelle Memorial Institute; Columbus/Southern Power Co.; Ford Motor Co.; General Electric Company; Huntington Bancshares Inc.; Physicians Insurance Company of Ohio; Technical Rubber Co.

For Complete List of Firm Personnel, See General Section

For full biographical listings, see the Martindale-Hubbell Law Directory

Columbus—Continued

Walter W. Reckless (AV)

Suite 702, 33 North High Street, 43215-7315
Telephone: 614-221-4740
Fax: Available
References: Huntington National Bank; BancOhio National Bank.

For full biographical listings, see the Martindale-Hubbell Law Directory

Scherner & Hanson (AV)

130 Northwoods Boulevard, 43235-4725
Telephone: 614-431-7200
Fax: 614-431-7262
Delaware, Ohio Office: 5300 David Road.
Telephone: 614-595-3366.

Hans Scherner
Robert E. Hanson

For full biographical listings, see the Martindale-Hubbell Law Directory

*** Thompson, Hine and Flory** (AV)

One Columbus, 10 West Broad Street, 43215-3435
Telephone: 614-469-3200
Fax: 614-469-3361
Akron, Ohio Office: 50 S. Main Street, Suite 502, 44308-1828.
Telephone: 216-376-8090.
Fax: 216-376-8386.
Cincinnati, Ohio Office: 312 Walnut Street, 14th Floor, 45202-4029.
Telephone: 513-352-6700.
Fax: 513-241-4771.
Telex: 938003.
Cleveland, Ohio Office: 1100 National City Bank Building, 629 Euclid Avenue, 44114-3070.
Telephone: 216-566-5500.
Fax: 216-556-5583.
Telex: 980217.
Cable Address: "Thomflor".
Dayton, Ohio Office: 2000 Courthouse Plaza, N.E., 45402-1706.
Telephone: 513-443-6600.
Fax: 513-443-6637; 443-6635.
Palm Beach, Florida Office: 125 Worth Avenue, 33480-4466.
Telephone: 407-833-5900.
Fax: 407-833-5951.
Washington, D.C. Office: 1920 N Street, N.W., 20036-1601.
Telephone: 202-331-8800.
Fax: 202-331-8330.
Telex: 904173.
Cable Address: "Caglaw".
Brussels, Belgium Office: Rue des Chevaliers / Ridderstraat 14 - B.10, B - 1050.
Telephone: 011(32-2) 511-9326.
Fax: 011(32-2) 513-9206.

MEMBERS OF FIRM

William R. Case
Gerald L. Draper
Ben L. Pfefferle, III
John T. Sunderland
William C. Wilkinson

ASSOCIATES

Margaret R. Carmany
Christopher Jones
Michael A. Renne
Melisa D. Stone

For Complete List of Firm Personnel, See General Section

For full biographical listings, see the Martindale-Hubbell Law Directory

*DAYTON,** Montgomery Co.

Bieser, Greer & Landis (AV)

400 Gem Plaza, Third and Main Streets, 45402
Telephone: 513-223-3277
FAX: 513-223-6339

MEMBERS OF FIRM

David C. Greer
Leo F. Krebs
Howard Penn Krisher, II
Michael W. Krumholtz
Gregory P. Dunsky
John F. Haviland, Jr.
David P. Williamson

Representative Clients: Medical Protective Company; St. Paul Insurance Company; Mead Corporation; Nationwide Insurance Company; Aetna Life & Casualty Company; Continental Loss Adjusting Services; Motorists Insurance Company; Travelers Insurance Company; Kettering Medical Center; Miami Valley Regional Transit Authority.

For Complete List of Firm Personnel, See General Section

For full biographical listings, see the Martindale-Hubbell Law Directory

Bogin, Patterson & Bohman (AV)

1200 Talbott Tower, 131 North Ludlow Street, 45402
Telephone: 513-226-1200
FAX: 513-226-1625

(See Next Column)

MEMBERS OF FIRM

Dennis L. Patterson
Jerome B. Bohman
James C. Ellis
Curtis F. Slaton
Randall L. Stump

OF COUNSEL

Asher Bogin

For full biographical listings, see the Martindale-Hubbell Law Directory

Crew, Buchanan & Lowe (AV)

Formerly Cowden, Pfarrer, Crew & Becker
2580 Kettering Tower, 45423-2580
Telephone: 513-223-6211
Facsimile: 513-223-7631

MEMBERS OF FIRM

Charles A. Craighead (1857-1926)
Robert E. Cowden (1886-1954)
Robert E. Cowden, Jr. (1910-1968)
Charles P. Pfarrer (1905-1984)
Philip Rohrer Becker (1905-1989)
Joseph P. Buchanan
Charles D. Lowe
Jeffrey A. Swillinger
Robert J. Davidek

ASSOCIATES

R. Anne Shale
Dana K. Cole
James R. Crump
James G. Neary

Representative Clients: Chrysler Corporation; General Motors Corporation; Grandview/Southview Hospitals; Hilton Hotels Corporation; James River Corporation; Metropolitan Life Insurance Co.

For Complete List of Firm Personnel, See General Section

For full biographical listings, see the Martindale-Hubbell Law Directory

Faruki Gilliam & Ireland (AV)

600 Courthouse Plaza, S.W., 10 North Ludlow Street, 45402
Telephone: 513-227-3700
Fax: 513-227-3717

MEMBERS OF FIRM

Charles J. Faruki
Armistead W. Gilliam, Jr.
D. Jeffrey Ireland
Paul L. Horstman
Ann Wightman
David A. Shough

Donald E. Burton
Jeffrey T. Cox
Shaun A. Roberts
Mary L. Wiseman

For full biographical listings, see the Martindale-Hubbell Law Directory

Freund, Freeze & Arnold A Legal Professional Association (AV)

Suite 1800 One Dayton Centre, One South Main Street, 45402-2017
Telephone: 513-222-2424
Telecopier: 513-222-5369
Cincinnati, Ohio Office: Suite 2110 Carew Tower, 441 Vine Street, 45202-4157.
Telephone: 513-287-8400.
FAX: 513-287-8403.

Neil F. Freund
Stephen V. Freeze
Gordon D. Arnold
Patrick J. Janis
Jane M. Lynch
Francis S. McDaniel
Stephen C. Findley
Robert N. Snyder
Christopher W. Carrigg
Scott F. McDaniel
Lisa A. Hesse
Gregory J. Berberich
Mary E. Lentz
Thomas B. Bruns
Shawn M. Blatt
Matthew K. Fox
Fredric L. Young
Philip D. Mervis
Thomas P. Glass
Lori S. Kibby
August T. Janszen

Local Counsel for: Auto-Owners Insurance Co.; CNA Insurance Co.; Crum and Foster Underwriters; Employers Reinsurance Corp.; Farmers Insurance Group; Lloyds of London; Medical Protective; Midwestern Group; State Farm Mutual Automobile Insurance Co.; The Travelers Insurance Co.
Special Trial Counsel for: City of Dayton.

For full biographical listings, see the Martindale-Hubbell Law Directory

E. S. Gallon & Associates (AV)

1100 Miami Valley Tower, 40 West Fourth Street, 45402
Telephone: 513-461-3694
Fax: 513-461-7840
Cincinnati, Ohio Office: The Kroger Building, 1014 Vine Street, Suite 1925.
Telephone: 513-721-1139.
Fax: 513-621-2768.

MEMBERS OF FIRM

David M. Deutsch
Jack A. Cervay
Patrick W. Allen
David A. Saphire
Joseph R. Ebenger
Joan B. Brenner
James D. Dennis
James R. Piercy
Richard M. Malone

(See Next Column)

E. S. GALLON & ASSOCIATES—*Continued*

ASSOCIATES

Roger A. Lee
Kyle D. Martin
Natalie J. Tackett
David R. Salyer
Roselyn G. Lovett
Gregory J. Claycomb

For full biographical listings, see the Martindale-Hubbell Law Directory

JENKS, SURDYK & COWDREY CO., L.P.A. (AV)

205 East First Street, 45402
Telephone: 513-222-2333
Fax: 513-222-1970
Cincinnati, Ohio Office: 1500 Chiquita Center, 250 East Fifth Street.
Telephone: 513-762-7622.
Fax: 513-721-4628.

Thomas E. Jenks
Robert J. Surdyk
Robert F. Cowdrey
Christopher F. Johnson
Susan Blasik-Miller
Edward J. Dowd
Nicholas E. Subashi
Scott G. Oxley
Arden Lynn Achenberg
W. Benjamin Hood, II

Representative Clients: Beta Industries, Inc.; Cessna Aircraft Co.; Miami Valley Risk Management Association, Inc.; P H Electronics, Inc.;
Local Counsel For: American States Insurance Co.; Chubb & Son, Inc.; Westfield Companies American International Group; Shelby Mutual Insurance Co.; Meridian Mutual Insurance Co.

For full biographical listings, see the Martindale-Hubbell Law Directory

SEBALY, SHILLITO & DYER (AV)

1300 Courthouse Plaza, NE, P.O. Box 220, 45402-0220
Telephone: 513-222-2500
Telefax: 513-222-6554; 222-8279
Springfield, Ohio Office: National City Bank Building, 4 West Main Street, Suite 530, P.O. Box 1346, 45501-1346.
Telephone: 513-325-7878.
Telefax: 513-325-6151.

MEMBERS OF FIRM

James A. Dyer
Gale S. Finley
William W. Lambert
Michael P. Moloney
Mary Lynn Readey
Jon M. Sebaly
Beverly F. Shillito
Jeffrey B. Shulman
Karl R. Ulrich
Robert A. Vaughn (Resident, Springfield Office)

Martin A. Beyer
Daniel A. Brown
Anne L. Rhoades
Orly R. Rumberg
Juliana M. Spaeth
Kendra F. Thompson

For full biographical listings, see the Martindale-Hubbell Law Directory

THOMPSON, HINE AND FLORY (AV)

2000 Courthouse Plaza, N.E., 45402-1706
Telephone: 513-443-6600
Fax: 513-443-6637; 443-6635
Akron, Ohio Office: 50 S. Main Street, Suite 502, 44308-1828.
Telephone: 216-376-8090.
Fax: 216-376-8386.
Cincinnati, Ohio Office: 312 Walnut Street, 14th Floor, 45202-4029.
Telephone: 513-352-6700.
Fax: 513-241-4771.
Telex: 938003.
Cleveland, Ohio Office: 1100 National City Bank Building, 629 Euclid Avenue, 44114-3070.
Telephone: 216-566-5500.
Fax: 216-556-5583.
Telex: 980217.
Cable Address: "Thomflor".
Columbus, Ohio Office: One Columbus, 10 West Broad Street, 43215-3435.
Telephone: 614-469-3200.
Fax: 614-469-3361.
Palm Beach, Florida Office: 125 Worth Avenue, 33480-4466.
Telephone: 407-833-5900.
Fax: 407-833-5951.
Washington, D.C. Office: 1920 N Street, N.W., 20036-1601.
Telephone: 202-331-8800.
Fax: 202-331-8330.
Telex: 904173.
Cable Address: "Caglaw".
Brussels, Belgium Office: Rue des Chevaliers / Ridderstraat 14 - B.10, B - 1050.
Telephone: 011(32-2) 511-9326.
Fax: 011(32-2) 513-9206.

MEMBERS OF FIRM

Bruce M. Allman
J. Wray Blattner
Thomas A. Knoth
David M. Rickert

(See Next Column)

ASSOCIATES

Deborah D. Hunt
Scott A. King

For Complete List of Firm Personnel, See General Section

For full biographical listings, see the Martindale-Hubbell Law Directory

YOUNG & ALEXANDER CO., L.P.A. (AV)

Suite 100, 367 West Second Street, 45402
Telephone: 513-224-9291
Telecopier: 513-224-9679
Cincinnati, Ohio Office: 110 Boggs Lane, Suite 350.
Telephone: 513-326-5555.
FAX: 513-326-5550.

Robert F. Young (1905-1978)
Robert C. Alexander (1912-1982)
James M. Brennan
Anthony R. Kidd
Mark R. Chilson
John A. Smalley
A. Mark Segreti, Jr.
Margaret R. Young
Steven O. Dean

James K. Hemenway

Counsel for: The Children's Medical Center, Dayton, Ohio; The Colonial Stair & Woodwork Co.; The Greater Dayton Area Hospital Assn.; Mike-Sell's Potato Chip Co.; Moorman Pontiac, Inc.
Local Counsel for: Colonial Penn Insurance Co.; John Hancock Mutual Life Insurance Co.; Hertz Corp.; State Farm Insurance Co.

For Complete List of Firm Personnel, See General Section

For full biographical listings, see the Martindale-Hubbell Law Directory

*EATON,** Preble Co.

BENNETT & BENNETT (AV)

Bennett Law Building, 200 West Main Street, 45320
Telephone: 513-456-4100
Fax: 513-456-5100

MEMBERS OF FIRM

Lloyd B. Bennett (1909-1983)
Herd L. Bennett
Gray W. Bennett

Representative Clients: The National Hummel Foundation and Museum; Star Bank of Preble County, Ohio; Eaton National Bank & Trust Co.; First National Bank of Southwestern Ohio; Brookville National Bank; Farm Credit Services of Mid-America; Miller's Super Markets, Inc.; Northedge Shopping Center, Inc.; Herman M. Brubaker Registered Holstein Cattle; The Eaton Foundation.

For Complete List of Firm Personnel, See General Section

For full biographical listings, see the Martindale-Hubbell Law Directory

*ELYRIA,** Lorain Co.

SPIKE & MECKLER (AV)

1551 West River Street North, 44035
Telephone: 216-324-5353
Fax: 216-324-6529

MEMBERS OF FIRM

Allen S. Spike
Stephen G. Meckler
Douglas M. Brill

For full biographical listings, see the Martindale-Hubbell Law Directory

ERIC H. ZAGRANS (AV)

474 Overbrook Road, 44035-3623
Telephone: 216-365-5400
Facsimile: 216-365-5100

For full biographical listings, see the Martindale-Hubbell Law Directory

HUDSON, Summit Co.

WILLIAMS & SENNETT CO., L.P.A. (AV)

126 West Streetsboro Street, Suite 4, 44236
Telephone: 216-656-4229
Fax: 216-656-4013

Roger H. Williams
James A. Sennett

Representative Clients: Allstate Insurance Co.; The Edward J. DeBartolo Corp.; Goodyear Tire & Rubber Co.; Milwaukee Insurance Co.; Nationwide Mutual Insurance Co.; Riser Foods; Safeco Insurance Co.; State Farm Insurance Cos.; Toys "R" Us.

For full biographical listings, see the Martindale-Hubbell Law Directory

*LANCASTER,** Fairfield Co.

STEBELTON, ARANDA & SNIDER A LEGAL PROFESSIONAL ASSOCIATION (AV)

One North Broad Street, P.O. Box 130, 43130
Telephone: 614-654-4141;
Columbus Direct Line: 614-837-1212;
1-800-543-Laws
Fax: 614-654-2521

Gerald L. Stebelton
Rick L. Snider
James C. Aranda
John M. Snider

Sandra W. Davis
Jason A. Price

LEGAL SUPPORT PERSONNEL

Sandra J. Steinhauser
Sandra K. Hillyard
Rose M. Sels
Michelle K. Garlinger

For full biographical listings, see the Martindale-Hubbell Law Directory

*LIMA,** Allen Co.

GOODING, HUFFMAN, KELLEY & BECKER (AV)

127-129 North Pierce Street, P.O. Box 546, 45802
Telephone: 419-227-3423
Fax: 419-228-1937

Lawrence S. Huffman

ASSOCIATES

C. Bradford Kelley
Matthew C. Huffman
Lawrence A. Huffman
Marie A. Von der Embse
Stephen L. Becker
John C. Huffman
T. Blain Brock, II

LEGAL SUPPORT PERSONNEL

Carol L. Swem (Probate Paralegal)

Representative Clients: The Medical Protective Company; Physicians Insurance Company of Ohio; United States Fidelity and Guaranty Co.; Hamilton Mutual Insurance Company; Bank One, Lima, Ohio; Joe Ivison Chevrolet-Jeep Eagle, Inc.; Lima Contracting Company; Otis Wright & Sons Trucking, Inc.
Approved Attorneys for: Lawyers Title Insurance Corp., Richmond, Virginia.

For full biographical listings, see the Martindale-Hubbell Law Directory

SIFERD & SIFERD (AV)

210 Colonial Building, 45801
Telephone: 419-222-5045
Fax: 419-222-0473

Willis S. Siferd
Richard E. Siferd

ASSOCIATE

Jeffrey Lee Reed

Reference: Bank One, Lima.

For full biographical listings, see the Martindale-Hubbell Law Directory

*MARYSVILLE,** Union Co.

CANNIZZARO, FRASER & BRIDGES (AV)

302 South Main Street, 43040
Telephone: 513-644-9125

MEMBERS OF FIRM

John F. Cannizzaro
Don W. Fraser
Robert L. Bridges

*POMEROY,** Meigs Co.

CROW AND CROW (AV)

110 West Second Street, P.O. Box 668, 45769
Telephone: 614-992-6059; 992-5132 (non-dedicated facsimile lines)

MEMBERS OF FIRM

Fred W. Crow, Sr. (1879-1957)
Fred W. Crow, Jr.
I. Carson Crow

Representative Clients: Midwest Steel; Auto Owners Insurance Co.; State Automobile Insurance Co.; The Farmers Bank & Savings Co.; General Telephone Co.; Orkin Exterminating Company Inc.; Beneficial Ohio Inc.; City Loan Financial Services, Inc.
Approved Attorneys for: Louisville Land Title Insurance Co.; Ohio Bar Title Insurance Co. (agent); Village Solicition Syracuse, Ohio.

*TOLEDO,** Lucas Co.

ROBERT M. ANSPACH ASSOCIATES (AV)

Suite 2100, 405 Madison Avenue, 43604-1236
Telephone: 419-246-5757
FAX: 419-321-6979

(See Next Column)

Robert M. Anspach
Mark D. Meeks
Stephen R. Serraino
J. Roy Nunn
Catherine G. Hoolahan
Paul F. Burtis

ASSOCIATES

Barry Y. Freeman
L. Nathalie Hiemstra

For full biographical listings, see the Martindale-Hubbell Law Directory

BUNDA STUTZ & DEWITT (AV)

One SeaGate, Suite 650, 43604
Telephone: 419-247-2777
Telecopier: 419-247-2727

MEMBERS OF FIRM

Robert A. Bunda
Barbara J. Stutz
Theresa R. DeWitt

ASSOCIATES

Anne Y. Koester
Richard A. Papurt
John C. Stewart
Yvonne D. Powell

Representative Clients: AC and S, Inc.; Acme Steel Co.; B.F. Goodrich Co.; Conoco, Inc.; Ethyl Corp.; Gustafson, Inc.

For full biographical listings, see the Martindale-Hubbell Law Directory

FRITZ BYERS (AV)

Suite 824 The Spitzer Building, 43604
Telephone: 419-241-8013
Telecopier: 419-241-4215

General Counsel for: Blade Communications, Inc.; Toledo Blade Co.; Buckeye Cablevision, Inc.; Pittsburgh Post Gazette.
Reference: Capital Bank N.A.

For full biographical listings, see the Martindale-Hubbell Law Directory

CONNELLY, SOUTAR & JACKSON (AV)

405 Madison Avenue Suite 1600, 43604
Telephone: 419-243-2100
Fax: 419-243-7119

MEMBERS OF FIRM

David M. Soutar (1937-1981)
Steven P. Collier
William M. Connelly
Kevin E. Joyce
Reginald S. Jackson, Jr.
Anthony P. Georgetti
Steven R. Smith
Michael A. Bonfiglio

ASSOCIATES

Thomas G. Mackin
Janine T. Avila
Beverly J. Cox
Sarah Steele Riordan (Not admitted in OH)

OF COUNSEL

Gerald P. Openlander

Representative Clients: The Danberry Co.; Lucas Metropolitan Housing Authority; National City Bank, Northwest; Rudolph/Libbe Inc.; Owens-Corning Fiberglas Corporation; Society National Bank.
Special Counsel: Ohio Attorney General.

For full biographical listings, see the Martindale-Hubbell Law Directory

DOYLE, LEWIS & WARNER (AV)

202 North Erie Street, P.O. Box 2168, 43603
Telephone: 419-248-1500
Fax: 419-248-2002

MEMBERS OF FIRM

Steven Timonere
Michael E. Hyrne
Richard F. Ellenberger
John A. Borell
Michael A. Bruno

ASSOCIATE

Kevin A. Pituch

OF COUNSEL

John R. Wanick

Counsel for: Consolidated Rail Corp.; Lakefront Dock & Terminal Co.; Greyhound Lines; Prudential Insurance Company of America; Equitable Life Assurance Society of U.S.; Metropolitan Life Insurance Co.; Northwestern Mutual Life Insurance Co.; John Hancock Life Insurance Co.

For Complete List of Firm Personnel, See General Section

For full biographical listings, see the Martindale-Hubbell Law Directory

EASTMAN & SMITH (AV)

One Seagate, Twenty-Fourth Floor, 43604
Telephone: 419-241-6000
Telecopier: 419-247-1777
Columbus, Ohio Office: 65 East State Street, Suite 1000, 43215.
Telephone: 614-460-3556.
Telecopier: 614-228-5371.

(See Next Column)

EASTMAN & SMITH—*Continued*

MEMBERS OF FIRM

Richard E. Antonini
M. Donald Carmin
James F. Nooney
David M. Jones
Henry N. Heuerman
John T. Landwehr
Kenneth C. Baker
Robert J. Gilmer, Jr.
Peter R. Casey, III
David F. Cooper
Rudolph A. Peckinpaugh, Jr.
Thomas A. Dixon
Barry W. Fissel
John D. Willey, Jr.
Joseph A. Gregg
Roger Paul Klee
Stuart J. Goldberg
Thomas J. Gibney

ASSOCIATES

James L. Rogers
David W. Nunn
Timothy C. Kuhlman
Beth J. Olson
Albin Bauer, II
Michael W. Regnier
Michael J. Niedzielski

OF COUNSEL

John R. Eastman
Jamille G. Jamra
Frank E. Kane
Ralph S. Boggs

Representative Clients: Chrysler Corp.; Allstate Insurance Co.; The Medical Protective Co.; Riverside Hospital; Roadway Express, Inc.; Fireman's Fund Insurance Co.; The Travelers Group; Continental Insurance; The Buckeye Union Insurance Company; Physicians Insurance Company of Ohio.

For Complete List of Firm Personnel, See General Section

For full biographical listings, see the Martindale-Hubbell Law Directory

FREDERICKSON & HEINTSCHEL, CO., L.P.A. (AV)

1313 Fifth Third Center, 608 Madison Avenue, 43604
Telephone: 419-242-5100
FAX: 419-242-5556

Craig F. Frederickson
Thomas W. Heintschel

Douglas W. King

For full biographical listings, see the Martindale-Hubbell Law Directory

FULLER & HENRY (AV)

One Seagate Suite 1700, P.O. Box 2088, 43603-2088
Telephone: 419-247-2500
Telecopier: 419-247-2665
Port Clinton, Ohio Office: 125 Jefferson.
Telephone: 419-734-2153.
Telecopier: 419-732-8246.
Columbus, Ohio Office: 2210 Huntington Center, 41 South High Street.
Telephone: 614-228-6611.
Telecopier: 614-228-6623.

MEMBERS OF FIRM

Thomas L. Dalrymple
Ray A. Farris
Stephen B. Mosier
Thomas S. Zaremba
John J. Siciliano
Martin J. Witherell
Mary Ann Whipple
Sue A. Sikkema
Martin D. Carrigan
Dennis A. Lyle
Daniel T. Ellis

COUNSEL

Warren D. Wolfe

ASSOCIATES

Andrew K. Ranazzi
Lance Michael Keiffer
Margaret G. Beck
Mark Shaw
John Christian Everhardus

Counsel for: B. F. Goodrich; Chrysler Credit Corp.; Chubb Group of Insurance Cos.; Connaught Laboratories; Ford Motor Credit Co.; General Motors; Goodyear; Libby-Owens-Ford Co.; Owens-Illinois, Inc.; The Toledo Edison Company.

For Complete List of Firm Personnel, See General Section

For full biographical listings, see the Martindale-Hubbell Law Directory

JONES & BAHRET CO., L.P.A. (AV)

2735 N. Holland-Sylvania Road, Suite A-3, 43615-1844
Telephone: 419-536-5588
Fax: 419-536-2662

Willis P. Jones, Jr.
Robert J. Bahret

Keith J. Watkins
Peter C. Munger
Julie M. Pavelko

LEGAL SUPPORT PERSONNEL

Denise M. Conrad
Evelyn Dee Evans

Representative Clients: Auto-Owners Insurance Co.; Liberty Mutual Ins. Co.; Motorists Ins. Companies; National Casualty Ins. Co.; Podiatry Ins. Co.; Progressive Ins. Co.; State Farm Ins. Co.; Sylvania Township; Western Reserve Mutual Casualty Co.; Westfield Ins. Companies.

For full biographical listings, see the Martindale-Hubbell Law Directory

RITTER, ROBINSON, MCCREADY & JAMES (AV)

1850 National City Bank Building, 405 Madison Avenue, 43624
Telephone: 419-241-3213
Detroit, Michigan: 313-422-1610
FAX: 419-241-4925

MEMBERS OF FIRM

Ellis F. Robinson (Retired)
William S. McCready
Timothy C. James

OF COUNSEL

Milton C. Boesel, Jr.

Representative Clients: Ohio Casualty Insurance Co.; National Mutual Insurance Co.; Celina Mutual Insurance Co.; Westfield Insurance Co.; Northwestern National Insurance Co.; Midwestern Insurance Co.; United Ohio Insurance Co.

For Complete List of Firm Personnel, See General Section

For full biographical listings, see the Martindale-Hubbell Law Directory

SCHNORF & SCHNORF CO., L.P.A. A PROFESSIONAL CORPORATION (AV)

1400 National City Bank Building, 405 Madison Avenue, 43604
Telephone: 419-248-2646
Facsimile: 419-248-2889

David M. Schnorf
Christopher F. Parker
Johna M. Bella
Barry F. Hudgin

Local Counsel for: Universal Underwriters Group; Cincinnati Insurance Company; Blue Cross and Blue Shield Mutual of Ohio; Bankers Multiple Line Insurance Company; Charter One Bank.
Representative Clients: American Federation of Teachers, AFL-CIO; Ohio Federation of Teachers, AFL-CIO; Toledo Federation of Teachers, AFL-CIO; Thomas R. Hart Associates, Inc.

For Complete List of Firm Personnel, See General Section

For full biographical listings, see the Martindale-Hubbell Law Directory

SPENGLER NATHANSON (AV)

608 Madison Avenue, Suite 1000, 43604-1169
Telephone: 419-241-2201
FAX: 419-241-8599

MEMBERS OF FIRM

Frank T. Pizza
James R. Jeffery
B. Gary McBride
David G. Wise
Louis J. Hattner
Theodore M. Rowen
James D. Jensen
Truman A. Greenwood
Cheryl F. Wolff
Byron S. Choka
Susan B. Nelson
Lisa E. Pizza
Joan C. Szuberla
Michael S. Katz
Teresa L. Grigsby

ASSOCIATE

Renisa A. Dorner

Counsel for: Fifth-Third Bank of Northwestern Ohio, N.A.; Huntington Bank of Toledo; Society Bank & Trust; Capital Bank N.A.; Seaway Food Town, Inc.; The University of Toledo; U.S. Fidelity & Guaranty Co.; AP Parts; Toledo Lucas County Port Authority; Toledo Board of Education.

For Complete List of Firm Personnel, See General Section

For full biographical listings, see the Martindale-Hubbell Law Directory

WATKINS, BATES & CAREY (AV)

1200 Fifth Third Center, 608 Madison Avenue, 43604-1157
Telephone: 419-241-2100
Telecopier: 419-241-1960

MEMBERS OF FIRM

William F. Bates
John M. Carey
Gary O. Sommer
Thomas C. Gess

ASSOCIATES

Gabrielle Davis
Jennifer L. Morrison

Counsel for: Heidtman Steel Products, Inc.; National City Bank.

For Complete List of Firm Personnel, See General Section

For full biographical listings, see the Martindale-Hubbell Law Directory

*TROY,** Miami Co.

SHIPMAN, UTRECHT & DIXON CO., L.P.A. (AV)

215 West Water Street, P.O. Box 310, 45373
Telephone: 513-339-1500
Fax: 513-339-1519

William M. Dixon
W. McGregor Dixon, Jr.
James D. Utrecht
Gary A. Nasal
Gary E. Zuhl

(See Next Column)

SHIPMAN, UTRECHT & DIXON CO. L.P.A., *Troy—Continued*

General Counsel for: Star Bank, N.A.; Milton Federal Savings and Loan Assn.; Troy Daily News Inc.; City of Troy and Troy Board of Education. *Local Counsel for:* CSX Transportation, Inc.; The Dayton Power & Light Co.; Travelers Insurance Co.; Celina Group; Westfield Companies; Lawyers Title Insurance Corp.

For Complete List of Firm Personnel, See General Section

For full biographical listings, see the Martindale-Hubbell Law Directory

*WOOSTER,** Wayne Co.

KENNEDY, CICCONETTI & RICKETT, A L.P.A. (AV)

558 North Market Street, 44691-3406
Telephone: 216-262-7555
Telecopier: 216-264-5739

Charles A. Kennedy
William G. Rickett
Frank Cicconetti
David C. Knowlton

Reference: Wayne County National Bank.

For full biographical listings, see the Martindale-Hubbell Law Directory

*ZANESVILLE,** Muskingum Co.

MICHELI, BALDWIN, BOPELEY & NORTHRUP (AV)

2806 Bell Street, P.O. Box 2687, 43702
Telephone: 614-454-2545
Fax: 614-454-6372

MEMBERS OF FIRM

Frank J. Micheli
Steven R. Baldwin
Michael J. Micheli
Thomas R. Bopeley
James C. Micheli (1956-1992)
Michael A. Northrup

Representative Clients: Bank One Cambridge, N.A.; Consolidated Rail Corp.; The Chessie System; Medical Protective Co.; Nationwide Insurance Cos.; Continental Insurance Cos.; State Farm Mutual Insurance Co.; Motorists Mutual Insurance Co.; St. Paul Insurance Co.
Reference: Mutual Federal Savings Bank

For full biographical listings, see the Martindale-Hubbell Law Directory

OKLAHOMA

*ALTUS,** Jackson Co.

HAL L. GRIDER (AV)

216 West Commerce, 73521
Telephone: 405-482-3355

Representative Clients: State Farm Mutual Insurance Co.; Altus Nursing Homes, Inc.; Altus Investment Co.; Southwestern Acceptance Corp.; *General Counsel for:* Mountain Park Conservancy District.

For full biographical listings, see the Martindale-Hubbell Law Directory

*CHANDLER,** Lincoln Co.

R. PATRICK GILMORE (AV)

P.O. Box 9, 74834
Telephone: 405-258-4262
Fax: 405-258-4520
(Also Of Counsel to James, Gilmore & Hodgens, P.A., Stroud, Oklahoma)

For full biographical listings, see the Martindale-Hubbell Law Directory

*ENID,** Garfield Co.

JONES & WYATT (AV)

Suite 1100 Broadway Tower, 114 East Broadway, P.O. Box 472, 73702
Telephone: 405-242-5500
Fax: 405-242-4556

MEMBERS OF FIRM

Stephen Jones
Michael David Roberts
Robert L. Wyatt, IV
James L. Hankins
Jeremy Booth Lowrey
Julia Sims Allen

Representative Clients: Western Union; Mesa Limited Partnership; Wells Fargo; City of Enid; Sears & Roebuck Company; St. Paul Property and Liability; International Oil, Chemical and Atomic Workers Union; Associated Aviation Underwriters; Independent Petroleum Association of America; Halliburton Industries.

For full biographical listings, see the Martindale-Hubbell Law Directory

LAVERNE, Harper Co.

G. W. ARMOR (AV)

103 West Main Street, P.O. Box 267, 73848
Telephone: 405-921-3335
FAX: 405-921-5720

*MUSKOGEE,** Muskogee Co.

ROBINSON, LOCKE, GAGE, FITE & WILLIAMS (AV)

530 Court Street, P.O. Box 87, 74401
Telephone: 918-687-5424
Fax: 918-687-0761

MEMBERS OF FIRM

A. Carl Robinson
Edwin L. Gage
Robert L. Locke, Jr.
Julian K. Fite
Betty Outhier Williams

Edith M. Gregory
Douglas S. Pewitt

Representative Clients: First National Bank & Trust Co. of Muskogee; United States Fidelity & Guaranty Co.; Bacone College; Utica Mutual Insurance Co.; Yaffe Iron & Metal Co., Inc.; Cimmaron Insurance Co.; Nationwide Insurance Co.; OML Municipal Assurance Group.

For full biographical listings, see the Martindale-Hubbell Law Directory

*OKLAHOMA CITY,** Oklahoma Co.

ABEL, MUSSER, SOKOLOSKY, MARES, HAUBRICH, BURCH & KOURI (AV)

Suite 600, One Leadership Square, 211 North Robinson, 73102
Telephone: 405-239-7046
Fax: 405-272-1090

Ed Abel
Lynn B. Mares
Sidney A. Musser, Jr.
Greg Haubrich
Jerry D. Sokolosky
Derek K. Burch
Harry J. (Trey) Kouri, III

ASSOCIATES

Kenneth G. Cole
Kelly S. Bishop
Daniel Pines Markoff
Kelly A. George
Melvin R. Singleterry
Gregory J. Ryan

OF COUNSEL

Arthur R. Angel
Warner E. Lovell, Jr.
James A. Ikard
Leo H. Whinery

For full biographical listings, see the Martindale-Hubbell Law Directory

ABOWITZ, WELCH AND RHODES (AV)

Tenth Floor 15 North Robinson, P.O. Box 1937, 73101
Telephone: 405-236-4645
Telecopier: 405-239-2843

MEMBERS OF FIRM

Murray E. Abowitz
Mort G. Welch
Sarah Jackson Rhodes

Lisa Luschen Gilbert
Norman Lemonik
Denis P. Rischard
Janice M. Dansby

Representative Clients: Admiral Insurance Co.; Keene Corp.; Liberty Mutual Insurance Co.; May Department Stores Co.; Mazda Distributors, Inc. (Gulf); Oklahoma Bar Professional Liability Insurance Co.; Oklahoma Farmers Union Mutual Insurance Co.; Skaggs Alpha Beta, Inc.; Time Insurance Co.; United States Fire Insurance Co.

For full biographical listings, see the Martindale-Hubbell Law Directory

ANDREWS DAVIS LEGG BIXLER MILSTEN & PRICE, A PROFESSIONAL CORPORATION (AV)

500 West Main, 73102
Telephone: 405-272-9241
FAX: 405-235-8786

J. Edward Barth
Mona S. Lambird
John J. Breathwit
Robert D. Nelon
Gary S. Chilton
Babette Patton
James F. Davis
Joseph G. Shannonhouse, IV
John F. Fischer, II
R. Brown Wallace
Don G. Holladay
William D. Watts
William H. Whitehill, Jr.

Timothy D. DeGiusti
Michelle Johnson
Lynn O. Holloman
Shelia Darling Tims

OF COUNSEL

Joseph A. Buckles, II
Carolyn Gregg Hill

Representative Clients: ANR Pipeline Co.; Browning-Ferris Industries.; The Chase Manhattan Bank, N.A.; Dow Jones & Co.; Marathon Oil Co.; Griffin Television, Inc. (KWTV, CBS Affiliate); Maryland Casualty Co.; Palmer

(See Next Column)

Andrews Davis Legg Bixler Milsten & Price A Professional Corporation—*Continued*

Communications, Inc. (KFOR-TV, NBC Affiliate); United Bank Services; CB Commercial, Inc.

For Complete List of Firm Personnel, See General Section

For full biographical listings, see the Martindale-Hubbell Law Directory

Britton and Adcock (AV)

Suite 670, 101 Park Avenue, 73102
Telephone: 405-239-2393
Fax: 405-232-5135

James E. Britton

For full biographical listings, see the Martindale-Hubbell Law Directory

Gary L. Brooks (AV)

6303 Waterford Boulevard, Suite 220, 73118-1122
Telephone: 405-840-1066
Fax: 405-843-8446
Dayton, Ohio Office: First National Plaza, Suite 1700, 45402.
Telephone: 513-224-3400.
Fax: 513-228-0331.

ASSOCIATE

Ann Jarrard

For full biographical listings, see the Martindale-Hubbell Law Directory

Conner & Winters, A Professional Corporation (AV)

204 North Robinson, Suite 950, 73102
Telephone: 405-232-7711
Facsimile: 405-232-2695
Tulsa, Oklahoma Office: 15 East 5th Street, Suite 2400, 74103.
Telephone: 918-586-5711.
Facsimile: 918-586-8982.

Peter B. Bradford
Raymond E. Tompkins
Timothy J. Bomhoff

For full biographical listings, see the Martindale-Hubbell Law Directory

Corbyn & Hampton (AV)

Suite 790 Robinson Renaissance, 119 North Robinson, 73102
Telephone: 405-239-7055
Telefax: 405-239-2436

George S. Corbyn, Jr.
Joe M. Hampton

For full biographical listings, see the Martindale-Hubbell Law Directory

Crowe & Dunlevy, A Professional Corporation (AV)

1800 Mid-America Tower, 20 North Broadway, 73102-8273
Telephone: 405-235-7700
Fax: 405-239-6651
Tulsa, Oklahoma Office: Crowe & Dunlevy, 500 Kennedy Building, 321 South Boston.
Telephone: 918-592-9800.
Fax: 918-592-9801.
Norman, Oklahoma Office: Crowe & Dunlevy, Luttrell, Pendarvis & Rawlinson, 104 East Eufaula Street.
Telephone: 405-321-7317.
Fax: 405-360-4002.

Vincil Penny Crowe (1897-1974)
Gary W. Davis
L. E. Stringer
Andrew M. Coats
D. Kent Meyers
Clyde A. Muchmore
Arlen E. Fielden
Harry A. Woods, Jr.
Jimmy Goodman
Richard C. Ford
John J. Griffin, Jr.
Brooke Smith Murphy
Leonard Court
Judy Hamilton Morse
Kelley C. Callahan
Mark D. Christiansen
Arthur F. Hoge III
Mack J. Morgan III
Anton J. Rupert
Wesley C. Fredenburg
Marie Weston Evans
Harvey D. Ellis, Jr.
Gayle L. Barrett
L. Mark Walker
Stephen L. DeGiusti
Mark S. Grossman
Kevin D. Gordon
Todd Taylor
Robert E. Bacharach
Randal A. Sengel

Mark D. Spencer
LeAnne Burnett
Peggy L. Clay
Paul D. Trimble
Dana M. Tacker
Timila S. Rother
David Nunn
Mark B. McDaniel
Joel S. Allen
Randy D. Gordon
Tamela R. Hughlett
Joseph J. Ferretti
Rustin J. Strubhar

(See Next Column)

OF COUNSEL

Lawrence E. Walsh
Val R. Miller

For Complete List of Firm Personnel, See General Section

For full biographical listings, see the Martindale-Hubbell Law Directory

Daugherty, Fowler & Peregrin, A Professional Corporation (AV)

204 North Robinson 900 City Place, 73102-6800
Telephone: 405-232-0003
Facsimile: 405-232-0865

Daniel J. Fowler
Robert M. Peregrin
Susan H. Utecht

OF COUNSEL

Phil E. Daugherty

For full biographical listings, see the Martindale-Hubbell Law Directory

Day, Edwards, Federman, Propester & Christensen, P.C. (AV)

Suite 2900 First Oklahoma Tower, 210 Park Avenue, 73102-5605
Telephone: 405-239-2121
Telecopier: 405-236-1012

Bruce W. Day
Joe E. Edwards
William B. Federman
Richard P. Propester
D. Wade Christensen
J. Clay Christensen
Kent A. Gilliland
Rodney J. Heggy
Ricki Valerie Sonders
Thomas Pitchlynn Howell, IV
John C. Platt

David R. Widdoes
Lori R. Roberts
Carolyn A. Romberg

OF COUNSEL

Herbert F. (Jack) Hewett
Jeanette Cook Timmons
Joel Warren Harmon
Jane S. Eulberg
Mark A. Cohen

Representative Clients: Aetna Life Insurance Co.; Boatmen's First National Bank of Oklahoma; Borg-Warner Chemicals, Inc.; City Bank & Trust; Federal Deposit Insurance Corp.; Bank One, Oklahoma City; Haskell Lemon Construction Co.; Merrill Lynch, Pierce, Fenner & Smith, Inc.; Prudential Securities, Inc.

For full biographical listings, see the Martindale-Hubbell Law Directory

Foliart, Huff, Ottaway & Caldwell, A Professional Corporation (AV)

20th Floor, First National Center, 120 North Robinson, 73102
Telephone: 405-232-4633
FAX: 405-232-3462

James D. Foliart
Glen D. Huff
Larry D. Ottaway
M. Dan Caldwell
Monty B. Bottom
Michael C. Felty

Susan A. Short
David A. Branscum
Timothy M. Melton
Darrell W. Downs
David K. McPhail
Kevin E. McCarty
Michael T. Maloan
Jeffrey R. Atkins

For full biographical listings, see the Martindale-Hubbell Law Directory

Hartzog Conger & Cason, A Professional Corporation (AV)

1600 Bank of Oklahoma Plaza, 73102
Telephone: 405-235-7000
Facsimile: 405-235-7329

Larry D. Hartzog
J. William Conger
Len Cason
James C. Prince
Alan Newman
Steven C. Davis
Valerie K. Couch
Mark D. Dickey
Joseph P. Hogsett
John D. Robertson
Kurt M. Rupert
Laura Haag McConnell

Susan B. Shields
Ryan S. Wilson
Melanie J. Jester
Armand Paliotta
Julia Watson
J. Leslie LaReau

OF COUNSEL

Kent F. Frates

For full biographical listings, see the Martindale-Hubbell Law Directory

Oklahoma City—Continued

HOLLOWAY, DOBSON, HUDSON, BACHMAN, ALDEN, JENNINGS, ROBERTSON & HOLLOWAY, A PROFESSIONAL CORPORATION (AV)

Suite 900 One Leadership Square 211 North Robinson, 73102-7102
Telephone: 405-235-8593
Fax: 405-235-1707

Page Dobson
Ronald R. Hudson
Charles F. Alden, III
James A. Jennings, III
Dan L. Holloway
Don M. Vaught
John R. Denneny
Rodney L. Cook
J. William Archibald
James R. Baker

Lu Ann Stout
Stephen D. Bachman
Elizabeth J. Bradford

Representing: Associated Aviation Underwriters; Chubb Group of Insurance Cos.; Continental Insurance Cos; General Motors Corp.

For full biographical listings, see the Martindale-Hubbell Law Directory

HUCKABY, FLEMING, FRAILEY, CHAFFIN, CORDELL, GREENWOOD & PERRYMAN (AV)

1215 Classen Drive, P.O. Box 60130, 73146
Telephone: 405-235-6648
FAX: 405-235-1533
Chickasha, Oklahoma Office: 201 N. 4th. P.O. Box 533.
Telephone: 405-224-0237.
FAX: 405-222-2319.

MEMBERS OF FIRM

Owen Vaughn (1900-1981)
Clarence McElroy (1903-1970)
Steve Stack (1946-1979)
Richard A. Procter (1932-1980)
Robert L. Huckaby
Kent Fleming
Tom A. Frailey
Michael R. Chaffin
F. Thomas Cordell, Jr.
William D. Greenwood
David L. Perryman

ASSOCIATES

Deborah A. Sterkel
Brently C. Olsson
Stephen R. McCalla
David K. Ratcliff
Barry G. Burkhart
Ron R. Mason
Christopher A. Arledge

Representative Clients: Aetna Casualty & Surety Company; Aetna Life & Casualty Co.; Hartford Insurance Co.; Mid-Continent Casualty Company; Employers Insurance of Wausau; Chubb/Pacific Indemnity Company; Home Insurance Company; Scottsdale Insurance Company; Scottsdale Insurance Company; National Casualty Insurance Company.

For full biographical listings, see the Martindale-Hubbell Law Directory

HUGHES, WHITE, ADAMS & GRANT (AV)

The Paragon, 5801 North Broadway Extension, Suite 302, 73118-7438
Telephone: 405-848-0111
FAX: 405-848-3507

Carl D. Hughes
Joe E. White, Jr.
Richard S. Adams
Michael E. Grant

For Complete List of Firm Personnel, See General Section

For full biographical listings, see the Martindale-Hubbell Law Directory

KERR, IRVINE, RHODES & ABLES, A PROFESSIONAL CORPORATION (AV)

600 Bank of Oklahoma Plaza, 73102-4267
Telephone: 405-272-9221
Fax: 405-236-3121

Horace G. Rhodes

For Complete List of Firm Personnel, See General Section

For full biographical listings, see the Martindale-Hubbell Law Directory

KING, ROBERTS & BEELER (AV)

Suite 600, 15 N. Robinson, 73102
Telephone: 405-239-6143
Fax: 405-236-3934

MEMBERS OF FIRM

Tom L. King
K. David Roberts
Jeff R. Beeler

ASSOCIATES

Teresa Thomas Cauthorn
Tracy L. Pierce
Richard M. Glasgow
Linda Prine Brown
Phillip P. Owens II

References: Liberty Bank & Trust; City Bank & Trust.

For full biographical listings, see the Martindale-Hubbell Law Directory

LOONEY, NICHOLS, JOHNSON & HAYES (AV)

528 Northwest 12th, P.O. Box 468, 73103
Telephone: 405-235-7641
Fax: 405-239-2050; 239-2052

Ned Looney (1886-1965)
Clyde J. Watts (1907-1975)
Willard R. Bergstrasser (1922-1993)
Robert Dudley Looney
Henry W. Nichols, Jr.
Burton J. Johnson
John B. Hayes
Edwin F. Garrison
Robert D. Looney, Jr.
Charles J. Watts
Tenal S. Cooley, III
Timothy L. Martin
Robert L. Magrini

Brigid F. Kennedy
H. Grady Parker, Jr.
Katresa Jo Riffel
Evan Blake Gatewood
John McPherson Hayes
Bradley K. Donnell

Representative Clients: Kansas City Southern Railway Co.; United States Fidelity & Guaranty Co.; Hartford Insurance Group; Atena Casualty and Surety Co.; U.S. Aviation Insurance Underwriters; CNA Insurance Company; The Goodyear Tire & Rubber Co.; Travelers Insurance Group; Home Insurance Co.; Fireman's Fund Group.

For full biographical listings, see the Martindale-Hubbell Law Directory

LYTLE SOULÉ & CURLEE (AV)

1200 Robinson Renaissance, 119 North Robinson, 73102
Telephone: 405-235-7471
Telecopy: 405-232-3852

MEMBERS OF FIRM

Roy Cobb Lytle (1902-1982)
Edward E. Soulé (1924-1984)
William D. Curlee (1929-1992)
James C. Chandler
Peter T. Van Dyke
David E. Nichols
Donald K. Funnell
Gary C. Pierson
G. David Ross
Michael D. Carter
Tony G. Puckett

ASSOCIATES

Samuel R. Fulkerson
Nathan L. Whatley
Rochelle L. Huddleston
Deborah S. Block

OF COUNSEL

John W. Mee, Jr.
Gordon D. Ryan

Representative Clients: Twentieth Century-Fox Film Corp.; Firestone Tire & Rubber Co.; Scrivner, Inc.; NCR Corporation; Northrop Worldwide Aircraft Services, Inc.; Sears Savings Bank; The Travelers Indemnity Company; Farmers Insurance Group of Companies; Great Plains Coca-Cola Bottling Company.

For full biographical listings, see the Martindale-Hubbell Law Directory

MCCAFFREY & TAWWATER (AV)

Bank of Oklahoma Plaza, Suite 1100 201 Robert S. Kerr Avenue, 73102
Telephone: 405-235-2900
Fax: 405-235-4932
Other Oklahoma City, Oklahoma Offices: Suite 1950, One Leadership Square, 211 North Robinson.

MEMBERS OF FIRM

George J. McCaffrey
Larry A. Tawwater

ASSOCIATES

Robert M. Behlen
Charles L. Cashion
Jo Lynn Slama
Gloria E. Trout
Loren F. Gibson
David Little
Steven R. Davis
Piper E. Mills

For full biographical listings, see the Martindale-Hubbell Law Directory

MILLS & WHITTEN, A PROFESSIONAL CORPORATION (AV)

Suite 500, One Leadership Square 211 North Robinson, 73102
Telephone: 405-239-2500
Fax: 405-235-4655

Earl D. Mills
Reggie N. Whitten
Robert B. Mills
W. Wayne Mills
Bill M. Roberts

Steve L. Lawson
Barbara K. Buratti
Kathryn D. Mansell
Glynis C. Edgar
Kent R. McGuire
Donald R. Martin, Jr.
Kay L. Hargrave
Brian E. Dittrich
Douglas A. Terry

Representative Clients: Biomet, Inc.; Crum & Forster Commercial Ins. Co.; Mid-Continent Casualty Co.; Oklahoma Farm Bureau Mutual Ins. Co.; The St. Paul Insurance Companies; OML Municipal Assurance Group; Great West Casualty; Houston General Ins. Co.; National American Ins. Co.; Progressive Casualty; Tital Indemnity.

For full biographical listings, see the Martindale-Hubbell Law Directory

Oklahoma City—Continued

MOCK, SCHWABE, WALDO, ELDER, REEVES & BRYANT, A PROFESSIONAL CORPORATION (AV)

Fifteenth Floor, One Leadership Square, 211 North Robinson Avenue, 73102
Telephone: 405-235-5500
Telecopy: 405-235-2875

G. Blaine Schwabe, III
James R. Waldo
Gary A. Bryant
Steven L. Barghols
Mary S. Robertson
Richard C. Labarthe
Kevin M. Coffey
Rob F. Robertson
Jack Cameron Moore

Representative Clients: Amoco Production Co.; Atlantic Richfield Co.; Farm Credit Bank of Wichita; Federal Deposit Insurance Corporation; Massachusetts Mutual Life Insurance Co.; Metropolitan Life Insurance Co.; Sun Exploration and Production Co.; Texaco, Inc.; Liberty Bank & Trust Company of Oklahoma City.

For Complete List of Firm Personnel, See General Section

For full biographical listings, see the Martindale-Hubbell Law Directory

MONNET, HAYES, BULLIS, THOMPSON & EDWARDS (AV)

Suite 1719 First National Center, West, 73102
Telephone: 405-232-5481
Fax: 405-235-9159

MEMBERS OF FIRM

John T. Edwards
James M. Peters
Randall A. Breshears
Robert C. Smith, Jr.
Steven K. McKinney

Representative Clients: Natural Gas Pipeline Company of America; Grace Petroleum Corp.; Chevron USA, Inc.; Mid ConCorp; Deminex USA Oil Inc.; Fireman's Fund Insurance Co.; Lexington Insurance Co.; Wausau Insurance Co.; National Chiropractic Insurance Co.; First National Bank of Beaver.

For Complete List of Firm Personnel, See General Section

For full biographical listings, see the Martindale-Hubbell Law Directory

SELF, GIDDENS & LEES, INC. (AV)

2725 Oklahoma Tower, 210 Park Avenue, 73102-5604
Telephone: 405-232-3001
Telecopier: 405-232-5553

Jared D. Giddens
C. Ray Lees
Shannon T. Self

Thomas J. Blalock
Christopher R. Graves
W. Shane Smithton
Bryan J. Wells

For full biographical listings, see the Martindale-Hubbell Law Directory

*PURCELL,** McClain Co.

JOHN MANTOOTH (AV)

Suite E Professional Building, 310 West Washington Street, P.O. Box 667, 73080
Telephone: 405-527-2137; 527-6517
Fax: 405-527-3440

Representative Client: First American Bank and Trust Co., Purcell, Oklahoma.
References: McClain County National Bank, Purcell, Oklahoma; First American Bank and Trust Co., Purcell, Oklahoma.

For full biographical listings, see the Martindale-Hubbell Law Directory

SEMINOLE, Seminole Co.

ELSENER & CADENHEAD (AV)

300 East Seminole, P.O. Box 2067, 74818-2067
Telephone: 405-382-6341; 257-2773
Fax: 405-382-5513

MEMBERS OF FIRM

G. Dale Elsener
Ed Cadenhead

References furnished upon request.

For full biographical listings, see the Martindale-Hubbell Law Directory

*TULSA,** Tulsa Co.

ATKINSON, HASKINS, NELLIS, BOUDREAUX, HOLEMAN, PHIPPS & BRITTINGHAM (AV)

A Partnership including Professional Corporations
1500 ParkCentre, 525 South Main Street, 74103
Telephone: 918-582-8877
Fax: 918-585-8096

(See Next Column)

PARTNERS

Michael P. Atkinson, P.C.
Walter D. Haskins, P.C.
Gregory D. Nellis, P.C.
Paul T. Boudreaux, P.C.
Daniel E. Holeman, P.C.
K. Clark Phipps
Galen Lee Brittingham, P.C.
John S. Gladd

ASSOCIATES

Martha J. Phillips
Marthanda J. Beckworth
Ann E. Allison
William A. Fiasco
Owen T. Evans
Mark W. Maguire
Jon D. Starr
Michael R. Annis
James N. Edmonds
David A. Russell
Kirsten E. Pace

OF COUNSEL

Joseph F. Glass

Representative Clients: Allstate Insurance Co.; Crum & Forester Insurance Co.; Hartford Insurance Company; National American Insurance Co.; Federated Insurance Co.; Guaranty National Insurance Co.; Liberty Mutual Insurance Co.; Physicians Liability Insurance Co.; State Farm Mutual Automobile Insurance Co.; United States Aviation Underwriters.

For full biographical listings, see the Martindale-Hubbell Law Directory

BEST, SHARP, HOLDEN, SHERIDAN, BEST & SULLIVAN, A PROFESSIONAL CORPORATION (AV)

Oneok Plaza, 100 W. 5th, Suite 808, 74103-4225
Telephone: 918-582-1234
Fax: 918-585-9447

Joseph M. Best
Joseph A. Sharp
Steven E. Holden
John H. T. Sheridan
Timothy G. Best
Daniel S. Sullivan
Steven K. Bunting
Amy Kempfert

Karen M. Grundy
Timothy E. Tipton
Philip M. Best
Malinda S. Matlock
Catherine L. Campbell
Terry S. O'Donnell
Mark Thomas Steele
Jennifer Ellen Mustain
Douglas E. Stall
Malcom D. Smith, Jr.
Bobby L. Latham, Jr.

OF COUNSEL

William E. Patten

For full biographical listings, see the Martindale-Hubbell Law Directory

CONNER & WINTERS, A PROFESSIONAL CORPORATION (AV)

15 East 5th Street, Suite 2400, 74103-4391
Telephone: 918-586-5711
Fax: 918-586-8982
Oklahoma City, Oklahoma Office: 204 North Robinson, Suite 950, 73102.
Telephone: 405-232-7711.
Facsimile: 405-232-2695.

John T. Schmidt
D. Richard Funk
Randolph L. Jones, Jr. (Not admitted in OK)
J. David Jorgenson
Andrew R. Turner
Deirdre O'Neil E. Dexter
Tony W. Haynie
Bruce W. Freeman
David R. Cordell
G. W. Turner, III

Rebecca Sellers Woodward
C. Kevin Morrison
P. Scott Hathaway
John A. Bugg
Sean H. McKee
R. Richard Love, III

For Complete List of Firm Personnel, See General Section

For full biographical listings, see the Martindale-Hubbell Law Directory

CRAWFORD, CROWE & BAINBRIDGE, P.A. (AV)

1714 First National Building, 74103
Telephone: 918-587-1128
Fax: 918-587-3975

B. Hayden Crawford
Harry M. Crowe, Jr.
Robert L. Bainbridge
Kyle B. Haskins
Eric B. Bolusky

Representative Clients: CNA Insurance Co.; American Home Insurance Co.; Chubb Group of Insurance Companies; KCI, Inc.; Judge Royce H. Savage.

For full biographical listings, see the Martindale-Hubbell Law Directory

DOYLE & HARRIS, A PROFESSIONAL CORPORATION (AV)

Southern Hills Tower, 2431 East 61st Street, Suite 260, P.O. Box 1679, 74101-1679
Telephone: 918-743-1276
Fax: 918-748-8215

Stan P. Doyle
Steven M. Harris

(See Next Column)

DOYLE & HARRIS A PROFESSIONAL CORPORATION, *Tulsa—Continued*

Michael D. Davis
Douglas R. Haughey
Randall T. Duncan

Reference: Peoples State Bank.

For full biographical listings, see the Martindale-Hubbell Law Directory

FELDMAN, HALL, FRANDEN, WOODARD & FARRIS (AV)

1400 Park Centre, 525 South Main, 74103-4409
Telephone: 918-583-7129
Telecopier: 918-584-3814

MEMBERS OF FIRM

W. E. Green (1889-1977)
William S. Hall (1930-1991)
Raymond G. Feldman
Robert A. Franden
John R. Woodard, III
Joseph R. Farris
Larry G. Taylor
Victor R. Seagle
Tony M. Graham

ASSOCIATES

Jacqueline O'Neil Haglund
Jody Nathan
R. Jack Freeman
J. David Mustain
Margaret E. Dunn
Ellen Caslavka Edwards
Douglass R. Elliott
Cathy G. Stricker
R. Daniel Scroggins

Representative Clients: CIGNA; The Equitable Life Assurance Society of the United States; Browning-Ferris Industries, Inc.; American Cyanamid Co.; American Home Assurance Co.; Oklahoma Bar Professional Liability Insurance Co.; American Motors Corp.; Sunbeam Corp.; Aviation Underwriters Inc.; Progressive Casualty Insurance Co.

For full biographical listings, see the Martindale-Hubbell Law Directory

GABLE & GOTWALS (AV)

2000 Bank IV Center, 15 West Sixth Street, 74119-5447
Telephone: 918-582-9201
Facsimile: 918-586-8383

Teresa B. Adwan
Pamela S. Anderson
John R. Barker
David L. Bryant
Gene C. Buzzard
Dennis Clarke Cameron
Timothy A. Carney
Renee DeMoss
Elsie C. Draper
Sidney G. Dunagan
Theodore Q. Eliot
Richard W. Gable
Jeffrey Don Hassell
Patricia Ledvina Himes
Oliver S. Howard
Richard D. Koljack, Jr.
J. Daniel Morgan
Joseph W. Morris
Elizabeth R. Muratet
Richard B. Noulles
Ronald N. Ricketts
John Henry Rule
M. Benjamin Singletary
James M. Sturdivant
Patrick O. Waddel
Michael D. Hall
David Edward Keglovits
Stephen W. Lake
Kari S. McKee
Terry D. Ragsdale
Jeffrey C. Rambach

OF COUNSEL

G. Ellis Gable
Charles P. Gotwals, Jr.

For full biographical listings, see the Martindale-Hubbell Law Directory

JOYCE AND POLLARD (AV)

Suite 300, 515 South Main Mall, 74103
Telephone: 918-585-2751
Fax: 918-582-9308

MEMBERS OF FIRM

J. C. Joyce
Dwayne C. Pollard

Ted J. Nelson
Sheila M. Bradley
John C. Joyce

A list of Representative Clients furnished upon request.

For full biographical listings, see the Martindale-Hubbell Law Directory

LIPE, GREEN, PASCHAL, TRUMP & BRAGG, A PROFESSIONAL CORPORATION (AV)

3700 First National Tower, 15 East Fifth Street, Suite 3700, 74103-4344
Telephone: 918-599-9400
Fax: 918-599-9404

Larry B. Lipe
James E. Green, Jr.
Richard A. Paschal
Timothy T. Trump
Patricia Dunmire Bragg

Melodie Freeman-Burney
Mark E. Dreyer
Constance L. Young
Leah Lowder Mills

Representative Clients: The AEtna Casualty and Surety Co.; AVTAX, Inc.; Dollar Rent A Car Systems, Inc.; Heritage Propane, Corp.; Pentastar Transportation Group, Inc.; Stifel, Nicolaus & Co.; Thrifty Rent-A-Car System, Inc.; Snappy Car Rental, Inc.; Underwriters at Lloyds, London; The Williams Companies, Inc.

(See Next Column)

For full biographical listings, see the Martindale-Hubbell Law Directory

PINKERTON & ASSOCIATES (AV)

907 Philtower Building, 74103-4114
Telephone: 918-587-1800
Facsimile: 918-582-2900

Laurence L. Pinkerton

Judith A. Finn

For full biographical listings, see the Martindale-Hubbell Law Directory

PRAY, WALKER, JACKMAN, WILLIAMSON & MARLAR, A PROFESSIONAL CORPORATION (AV)

900 ONEOK Plaza, 100 West 5th Street, 74103-4218
Telephone: 918-581-5500
Fax: 918-581-5599
Oklahoma City, Oklahoma Office: One Leadership Square, 211 North Robinson.
Telephone: 405-236-8911.
Fax: 405-236-0011.

J. Warren Jackman
W. Bland Williamson, Jr.
Donald F. Marlar
Thomas G. Noulles
William D. Toney
Terry R. Doverspike
John F. McCormick, Jr.
S. Erickson Grimshaw
Jean Walpole Coulter
John L. Randolph, Jr.
William L. Eagleton, IV
Wm. Gregory James
Kevin M. Abel
Donald S. Smith
Randall G. Vaughan
Charles Bretton Crane
Rita J. Gassaway
Kevin Pierce Doyle
William A. Caldwell
Thomas M. Askew
Dee E. Dismukes
Michael W. Pierce
Mallie Marlene Lawrence
Terri S. Roberts

OF COUNSEL

Donald E. Pray
Floyd L. Walker
Charles A. Kothe

For Complete List of Firm Personnel, See General Section

For full biographical listings, see the Martindale-Hubbell Law Directory

RHODES, HIERONYMUS, JONES, TUCKER & GABLE (AV)

Bank IV Center 15 West 6th Street, Suite 2800, 74119-5430
Telephone: 918-582-1173
Fax: 918-592-3390

MEMBERS OF FIRM

Chris L. Rhodes (1902-1966)
E. D. Hieronymus (1908 -1994)
Chris L. Rhodes, III
Bert M. Jones
John H. Tucker
Robert P. Redemann
Richard M. Eldridge
Thomas E. Steichen
Jo Anne Deaton
William D. Perrine
Kevin D. Berry
Mary Quinn-Cooper
William S. Leach
Michael W. McGivern

Jim Filosa
Jill Nelson Thomas
Wilson T. White
Catherine C. Taylor
Benton T. Wheatley
David P. Reid

OF COUNSEL

Larry J. Fulton
George W. Gable
Harold C. Zuckerman

Representative Clients: Aetna Life & Casualty Group; American International Group; Chubb Group of Insurance Companies; General Motors Corporation; HCM Claims Management; Liberty Mutual Group; Nissan Motor Corporation in U.S.A.; Sheffield Steel Company; U.S. Steel Co.; Volkswagen of America, Volkswagen, A.G.

For full biographical listings, see the Martindale-Hubbell Law Directory

RICHARDS, PAUL, RICHARDS & SIEGEL (AV)

Suite 400, Reunion Center, 9 East 4th Street, 74103
Telephone: 918-584-2583
Telefax: 918-587-8521

MEMBERS OF FIRM

John R. Richards (Deceased)
John R. Paul
Phil R. Richards
Nancy Jane Siegel

ASSOCIATES

Richard E. Warzynski
Richard L. Blanchard
John G. Barnhart
Suzanne Hale Costin

OF COUNSEL

John R. Caslavka

Representative Clients: St. Paul Insurance Company; The Travelers Insurance Company; Physicians Liability Insurance Company; Hospital Casualty Company; Property & Casualty Guaranty Association; CNA Insurance Company; Oklahoma Farm Bureau; INAPRO; Employers Reinsurance Corporation; Cigna Companies.

For full biographical listings, see the Martindale-Hubbell Law Directory

Tulsa—Continued

SHIPLEY, INHOFE & STRECKER (AV)

Suite 3600 First National Tower, 15 East Fifth Street, 74103-4307
Telephone: 918-582-1720
FAX: 918-584-7681

MEMBERS OF FIRM

Charles W. Shipley
Douglas L. Inhofe
David E. Strecker
Mark B. Jennings
Blake K. Champlin

ASSOCIATES

Leslie C. Rinn
Jamie Taylor Boyd
Connie L. Kirkland
Mark Alston Waller

Reference: Western National Bank, Tulsa.

For full biographical listings, see the Martindale-Hubbell Law Directory

SNEED, LANG, ADAMS & BARNETT, A PROFESSIONAL CORPORATION (AV)

2300 Williams Center Tower II, Two West Second Street, 74103
Telephone: 918-583-3145
Telecopier: 918-582-0410

James C. Lang
D. Faith Orlowski
Brian S. Gaskill
G. Steven Stidham
Stephen R. McNamara
Thomas E. Black, Jr.
Robbie Emery Burke
C. Raymond Patton, Jr.
Frederick K. Slicker
Richard D. Black
John D. Russell
Jeffrey S. Swyers

OF COUNSEL

James L. Sneed
O. Edwin Adams
Howard G. Barnett, Jr.

Representative Clients: Amoco Production Company; Continental Bank; Deloitte & Touche; Enron Corporation; Halliburton Energy Services; Helmerich & Payne, Inc.; Lehman Brothers, Inc.; Shell Oil Company; Smith Barney, Inc.; State Farm Mutual Automobile Insurance Company.

For full biographical listings, see the Martindale-Hubbell Law Directory

YUKON, Canadian Co.

GEORGE H. RAMEY (AV)

3 South Fifth Street, 73099
Telephone: 405-354-1987
Telecopier: 405-354-1992

ASSOCIATE

William D. Tharp

Representative Clients: Northwest Bank of Oklahoma City; Canadian State Bank of Yukon, OK; Adair State Bank of Adair, OK; Bank of Chelsea, Chelsea OK; Jackie Cooper Oldsmobile, Inc.; Jackie Cooper Ford, Inc.; Jackie Cooper Lincoln-Mercury of Oklahoma City; Title Insurance Company of Minnesota; Jackie Cooper Buick-Mazda-Suzucki of Norman.

For full biographical listings, see the Martindale-Hubbell Law Directory

OREGON

*EUGENE,** Lane Co.

JAQUA & WHEATLEY, P.C. (AV)

825 East Park, 97401
Telephone: 503-686-8485
Fax: 503-343-0701

John E. Jaqua (Inactive)
William G. Wheatley
Lloyd W. Helikson
Kathryn S. Chase
Mike Ellickson
James C. Chaney
Maureen A. DeFrank
Constance E. Sullivan

Representative Insurance Clients: Fireman's Fund Insurance Cos.; Industrial Indemnity Co.; Kemper Insurance Co.; Safeco Insurance Cos.; State Farm Insurance Cos.; Zurich-American Insurance Co.; United States Fidelity & Guaranty Co.
Representative Corporate Clients: Ford Motor Corp.; General Motors Corp.; Michelin Tire Corp.

For full biographical listings, see the Martindale-Hubbell Law Directory

*OREGON CITY,** Clackamas Co.

DONALD B. BOWERMAN (AV)

1001 Molalla Avenue, Suite 208, P.O. Box 88, 97045
Telephone: 503-650-0700
FAX: 503-650-0053

ASSOCIATE

Jonathan N. Neff

(See Next Column)

OF COUNSEL

Roderick A. Boutin

For full biographical listings, see the Martindale-Hubbell Law Directory

*PORTLAND,** Multnomah Co.

BENNETT & HARTMAN (AV)

851 S.W. Sixth, Suite 1600, 97204-1376
Telephone: 503-227-4600
FAX: 503-248-6800

Robert A. Bennett
Gregory A. Hartman
JoAnn B. Reynolds
Ralph E. Wiser, III
Kathryn T. Whalen
Mark S. Toledo
Henry J. Kaplan
Elizabeth A. McKanna
John S. Bishop, II
Michael D. Levelle
Barbara J. Aaby
Lory J. Kraut

OF COUNSEL

Michael J. Morris

For full biographical listings, see the Martindale-Hubbell Law Directory

BLACK HELTERLINE (AV)

1200 The Bank of California Tower, 707 S.W. Washington Street, 97205
Telephone: 503-224-5560
Telecopier: 503-224-6148

MEMBERS OF FIRM

Ronald T. Adams
Albert J. Bannon
Michael O. Moran
Thomas K. O'Shaughnessy
Susan Jane Widder

ASSOCIATES

James M. Baumgartner
Paul R. Rundle

Representative Clients: The Bank of California, N.A.; Carr Chevrolet, Inc.; Emergency Medicine Associates, P.S.; McKinstry Co.; Goodyear Rubber and Supply Co.; James River Corp.; Lamonts Apparel, Inc.; NACCO Materials Handling Group, Inc.; Wachovia Bank and Trust Co.; Western Council of Industrial Workers--TOC Trust Funds.

For Complete List of Firm Personnel, See General Section

For full biographical listings, see the Martindale-Hubbell Law Directory

BODYFELT, MOUNT, STROUP & CHAMBERLAIN (AV)

300 Powers Building, 65 S.W. Yamhill Street, 97204
Telephone: 503-243-1022
Fax: 503-243-2019

MEMBERS OF FIRM

Barry M. Mount
Roger K. Stroup
Peter R. Chamberlain
Richard A. Lee

Simeon D. Rapoport
Jane Paulson

OF COUNSEL

E. Richard Bodyfelt

Representative Clients: American International Group; Chrysler Corp.; CIGNA; Freightliner Corp.; Georgia Pacific; Hartford Insurance Co.; Lederle Laboratories; Safeway Stores, Inc.; Texaco, Inc.

For full biographical listings, see the Martindale-Hubbell Law Directory

COONEY & CREW, P.C. (AV)

Pioneer Tower, Suite 890, 888 S.W. Fifth Avenue, 97204
Telephone: 503-224-7600
FAX: 503-224-6740

Paul A. Cooney
Thomas E. Cooney
Thomas M. Cooney
Brent M. Crew
Michael D. Crew
Kelly T. Hagan
Raymond F. Mensing, Jr.
Robert S. Perkins

LEGAL SUPPORT PERSONNEL

Alma Weber (Paralegal)

For full biographical listings, see the Martindale-Hubbell Law Directory

GRENLEY, ROTENBERG EVANS & BRAGG, P.C. (AV)

30th Floor, Pacwest Center, 1211 S.W. Fifth Avenue, 97204
Telephone: 503-241-0570
Facsimile: 503-241-0914

Gary I. Grenley
Stan N. Rotenberg
Lawrence Evans
Michael J. Bragg
Steven D. Adler
Michael S. Evans
Michael C. Zusman
Jeffrey C. Bodie

OF COUNSEL

Sol Siegel
Robert C. Laskowski
Norman A. Rickles

(See Next Column)

GRENLEY, ROTENBERG EVANS & BRAGG P.C., *Portland—Continued*

Ann M. Lane

Reference: Key Bank of Oregon.

For full biographical listings, see the Martindale-Hubbell Law Directory

LABARRE & ASSOCIATES, P.C. (AV)

Suite 1212, 900 S.W. Fifth Avenue, 97204-1268
Telephone: 503-228-3511
FAX: 503-273-8658

Jerome E. LaBarre

Dayna Ellen Peck

OF COUNSEL

Robert A. Russell

For full biographical listings, see the Martindale-Hubbell Law Directory

O'DONNELL, RAMIS, CREW, CORRIGAN & BACHRACH (AV)

Ballow & Wright Building, 1727 N.W. Hoyt Street, 97209
Telephone: 503-222-4402
FAX: 503-243-2944
Clackamas County Office: Suite 202, 181 N. Grant, Canby.
Telephone: 503-266-1149.

MEMBERS OF FIRM

Mark P. O'Donnell
Stephen F. Crew
Timothy V. Ramis
Charles E. Corrigan
Jeff H. Bachrach

SPECIAL COUNSEL

James M. Coleman

ASSOCIATES

Pamela J. Beery
G. Frank Hammond
Mark L. Busch
William A. Monahan
Gary Firestone
William J. Stalnaker
Ty K. Wyman

LEGAL SUPPORT PERSONNEL

Margaret M. Daly
G. William Selzer
Mary C. Meyers
Dawna S. Shattuck
Laurel L. Ramsey
(Legal Assistant)

For full biographical listings, see the Martindale-Hubbell Law Directory

*ROSEBURG,** Douglas Co.

DOLE, COALWELL, CLARK & WELLS, P.C. (AV)

810 S.E. Douglas Avenue, P.O. Box 1205, 97470
Telephone: 503-673-5541
Fax: 503-673-1156
ABA/net !ddole

George W. Neuner (1914-1985)
Dan W. Clark
Donald A. Dole
Inge Dortmund Wells
Bruce R. Coalwell
Stephen Mountainspring
Jeffrey A. Mornarich

Representative Clients: Douglas County Title Co.; C & D Lumber Co.; Herbert Lumber Co.; South Umpqua State Bank.

For full biographical listings, see the Martindale-Hubbell Law Directory

PENNSYLVANIA

*ALLENTOWN,** Lehigh Co.

GROSS, MCGINLEY, LABARRE & EATON (AV)

33 South Seventh Street, P.O. Box 4060, 18105-4060
Telephone: (610)-820-5450
Fax: (610)-820-6006

MEMBERS OF FIRM

Malcolm J. Gross
J. Jackson Eaton, III
Paul A. McGinley
Michael A. Henry
Donald L. LaBarre, Jr.
Patrick J. Reilly
William J. Fries

ASSOCIATES

Anne K. Manley
John D. Lychak

For full biographical listings, see the Martindale-Hubbell Law Directory

RICHARD J. MAKOUL (AV)

461 Linden Street, 18102
Telephone: 610-433-4233
FAX: 610-776-7221

For full biographical listings, see the Martindale-Hubbell Law Directory

TALLMAN, HUDDERS & SORRENTINO, P.C. (AV)

Suite 301 The Paragon Centre, 1611 Pond Road, 18104
Telephone: 610-391-1800
Fax: 610-391-1805

Robert G. Tallman
Oldrich Foucek, III
John R. Hudders
Matthew R. Sorrentino
William H. Fitzgerald
Timothy J. Siegfried
Thomas C. Sadler, Jr.
Dolores A. Laputka
Scott B. Allinson

Sherri L. Palopoli
Mary C. Crocker
David Andrew Williams
Scott R. Lipson
Theodore J. Zeller, III

OF COUNSEL

Harold Caplan
Paul J. Schoff

For full biographical listings, see the Martindale-Hubbell Law Directory

BALA CYNWYD, Montgomery Co.

RICHARD MAX BOCKOL (AV)

Suite 253 BalaPointe Centre, 111 Presidential Boulevard, 19004
Telephone: 610-667-2546
Fax: 610-667-4153
Internet Address: RBOCKOL@DELPHI.COM

For full biographical listings, see the Martindale-Hubbell Law Directory

FURMAN & HALPERN, P.C. (AV)

Suite 612, 401 City Avenue, 19004
Telephone: 610-668-5454
Fax: 610-668-5455
Cherry Hill, New Jersey Office: Suite 245, 411 Route 70 East, 08034.
Telephone: 609-795-4440.
Fax: 609-428-5485.

Barry A. Furman
Georgeann R. Fusco
Mark S. Halpern
Lisanne L. Mikula
Robert S. Levy
Caryn M. DePiano

For full biographical listings, see the Martindale-Hubbell Law Directory

KANIA, LINDNER, LASAK AND FEENEY (AV)

Suite 525, Two Bala Plaza, 19004
Telephone: 610-667-3240
Fax: 610-668-9676

Arthur J. Kania
John Lasak
Albert A. Lindner
Thomas J. Feeney, III
Robert A. Griffiths

ASSOCIATE

Michael F. Merlie

A list of Representative Clients for which the firm serves as General Counsel or Local Counsel will be supplied upon request.

For full biographical listings, see the Martindale-Hubbell Law Directory

*BELLEFONTE,** Centre Co.

MILLER, KISTLER & CAMPBELL, INC. (AV)

124 North Allegheny Street, 16823
Telephone: 814-355-5474
Fax: 814-355-5340
State College, Pennsylvania Office: 1500 South Atherton Street.
Telephone: 814-234-1500.
Fax: 814-234-1549.

R. Paul Campbell (1908-1988)
John R. Miller, III
Lewis Orvis Harvey (1912-1990)
Terry James Williams
John R. Miller, Jr.
Thomas King Kistler
Richard L. Campbell
Tracey G. Benson
Lillian G. Raycroft
James Lowell Green

OF COUNSEL

Robert K. Kistler

General Counsel for: Peoples National Bank of Central Pennsylvania; Cannon Instrument Co.; Hanover Brands.
Local Counsel for: National Gypsum Co.; Aetna Insurance Co.; Travelers Insurance Co.; The Medical Protective Co.; Corning Glass Works.
Solicitors: Borough of State College.

For full biographical listings, see the Martindale-Hubbell Law Directory

BETHLEHEM, Northampton Co.

O'HARE & HEITZMAN (AV)

18 East Market Street, P.O. Box 1446, 18018
Telephone: 610-691-5500
FAX: 610-691-7866

(See Next Column)

O'Hare & Heitczman—*Continued*

MEMBERS OF FIRM

Bernard V. O'Hare, Jr. (1923-1990)
George A. Heitczman

References: First Valley Bank; Meridan Bank.

For full biographical listings, see the Martindale-Hubbell Law Directory

BLUE BELL, Montgomery Co.

Lesser & Kaplin, Professional Corporation (AV)

350 Sentry Parkway, Bldg. 640, 19422-0757
Telephone: 610-828-2900; Telecopier: 610-828-1555
Marlton, New Jersey Office: Three Greentree Centre, Suite 104, Route 73, 08053-3215.
Telephone: 609-596-2400.
Telecopier: 609-596-8185.

Louis J. Sinatra
Harold G. Cohen (Resident, Marlton, New Jersey Office)
David N. Bressler
Michael P. Coughlin

John L. Laskey (Resident, Marlton, New Jersey Office)
Patricia L. Talcott (Resident, Marlton, New Jersey Office)
Rhonda M. Fulginiti

For full biographical listings, see the Martindale-Hubbell Law Directory

BRISTOL, Bucks Co.

Begley, Carlin & Mandio (AV)

120 Mill Street, 19007
Telephone: 215-750-0110
Langhorne, Pennsylvania Office: 680 Middletown Boulevard, P.O. Box 308.
Telephone: 215-750-0110.

MEMBERS OF FIRM

William J. Carlin
Anthony A. Mandio
S. Richard Klinges, III
Thomas J. Profy, III
Richard M. Snyder
Charles F. Sampsel
John P. Koopman
Jeffrey P. Garton
Thomas R. Hecker
James A. Downey, III
Joseph S. Britton
Douglas C. Maloney

ASSOCIATES

Thomas J. Profy, IV
William L. Weiner
Karen L. Saraco

Representative Clients: Borough of Bristol; Bristol Borough School Board; Fidelity Savings & Loan Association of Bucks County; Lower Makefield Township; Philadelphia National Bank; Waste Management, Inc.

For full biographical listings, see the Martindale-Hubbell Law Directory

*CARLISLE,** Cumberland Co.

Douglas, Douglas & Douglas (AV)

27 West High Street, 17013-0261
Telephone: 717-243-1790
Fax: 717-243-8955

MEMBERS OF FIRM

George F. Douglas, Jr.
William P. Douglas
George F. Douglas, III

Representative Client: State Farm Insurance Cos.

For full biographical listings, see the Martindale-Hubbell Law Directory

CLARKS SUMMIT, Lackawanna Co.

Beemer & Beemer (AV)

114-116 North Abington Road, P.O. Box M, 18411
Telephone: 717-587-0188

MEMBERS OF FIRM

John Barry Beemer
Diane F. Beemer

Reference: Penn Security Bank.

For full biographical listings, see the Martindale-Hubbell Law Directory

*DOYLESTOWN,** Bucks Co.

Power, Bowen & Valimont (AV)

102 North Main Street, 18901-0818
Telephone: 215-345-7500
Fax: 215-345-7507
Sellersville, Pennsylvania Office: 64 North Main Street.
Telephone: 215-257-3661.

MEMBERS OF FIRM

William B. Moyer
Samuel G. Moyer (Resident, Sellersville Office)
Gordon G. Erdenberger
John J. Hart
William T. Renz
Michael S. Valimont
William H. Fuss (Resident, Sellersville Office)

(See Next Column)

Randal S. White

Representative Clients: General Accident Group; U.S. Gauge Division of AMETEK; Nockamixon-Bucks Commercial and Industrial Development Assn.; First Savings Bank.

For Complete List of Firm Personnel, See General Section

For full biographical listings, see the Martindale-Hubbell Law Directory

ELKINS PARK, Montgomery Co.

Monaghan & Gold, P.C. (AV)

7837 Old York Road, 19027
Telephone: 215-782-1800
Fax: 215-782-1010

John F. X. Monaghan, Jr.
Alan Steven Gold

Brian E. Appel
Murray R. Glickman
Barbara Malett Weitz
Tanya M. Sweet

FORT WASHINGTON, Montgomery Co.

Daller Greenberg & Dietrich (AV)

Valley Green Corporate Center, 7111 Valley Green Road, 19034
Telephone: 215-836-1100
Facsimile: 215-836-2845
Haddon Heights, New Jersey Office: 2 White Horse Pike.
Telephone: 609-547-9068.
Telecopier: 609-547-2391.

Morton F. Daller
Edward A. Greenberg
Gerhard P. Dietrich
Charles E. Pugh
Eileen M. Johnson
Dennis R. Callahan
Nancy P. Horn
A. M. Laszlo
Tracy Canuso Nugent (Resident, Haddon Heights, New Jersey Office)
Catherine N. Walto

For full biographical listings, see the Martindale-Hubbell Law Directory

*GREENSBURG,** Westmoreland Co.

David J. Millstein (AV)

218 South Maple Avenue, 15601
Telephone: 412-837-3333
Fax: 412-837-8344

For full biographical listings, see the Martindale-Hubbell Law Directory

Walthour and Garland (AV)

Park Building, 121 North Main Street, 15601
Telephone: 412-834-4900

MEMBERS OF FIRM

Christ. C. Walthour, Jr.
Robert Wm. Garland
Holly G. Garland

Representative Clients: Peoples National Gas Co.; Baltimore & Ohio Railroad; Old Guard Insurance Company; Manor National Bank.
References: Manor National Bank; Southwest National Bank of Pennsylvania.

For full biographical listings, see the Martindale-Hubbell Law Directory

*HARRISBURG,** Dauphin Co.

Angino & Rovner, P.C. (AV)

4503 North Front Street, 17110-1799
Telephone: 717-238-6791
Fax: 717-238-5610

Richard C. Angino
Neil J. Rovner

Joseph M. Melillo
Terry S. Hyman
David L. Lutz
Michael E. Kosik
Pamela G. Shuman
Catherine M. Mahady-Smith
Richard A. Sadlock
David S. Wisneski
Nijole C. Olson
Michael J. Navitsky
Robin J. Marzella
Lawrence F. Barone
Dawn L. Jennings
Stephen R. Pedersen

References: Harrisburg Credit Exchange; Hamilton Bank.

For full biographical listings, see the Martindale-Hubbell Law Directory

Boswell, Snyder, Tintner & Piccola (AV)

315 North Front Street, P.O. Box 741, 17108-0741
Telephone: 717-236-9377
Telecopier: 717-236-9316

MEMBERS OF FIRM

William D. Boswell
Donn L. Snyder
Leonard Tintner
Jeffrey E. Piccola
Jeffrey R. Boswell
Brigid Q. Alford
Mark R. Parthemer
Charles J. Hartwell

(See Next Column)

BOSWELL, SNYDER, TINTNER & PICCOLA, *Harrisburg—Continued*

OF COUNSEL

Richard B. Wickersham

Representative Clients: Cigna Cos.; Coregis; Nationwide Insurance Co.; Pennsylvania Financial Responsibility Assigned Claims Plan; Pennsylvania Medical Society Liability Insurance Co. (PMSLIC); PHICO Insurance Co.; Travelers Insurance; Statesman Insurance Co.; Trans America Insurance Group.

For full biographical listings, see the Martindale-Hubbell Law Directory

BUCHANAN INGERSOLL, PROFESSIONAL CORPORATION (AV)

Vartan Parc, 30 North Third Street, 17101
Telephone: 717-237-4800
Telecopier: 717-233-0852
Pittsburgh, Pennsylvania Office: 5800 USX Tower, 600 Grant Street.
Telephone: 412-562-8800.
Philadelphia, Pennsylvania Office: Two Logan Square, Twelfth Floor, 18th & Arch Streets.
Telephone: 215-665-8700.
Tampa, Florida Office: 101 East Kennedy Boulevard, Suite 1030.
Telephone: 813-222-8180.
North Miami Beach, Florida Office: 19495 Biscayne Boulevard.
Telephone: 305-933-5600.
Lexington, Kentucky Office: 1210 Vine Center Office Tower, 333 West Vine Street.
Telephone: 606-225-5333.
Princeton, New Jersey Office: Buchanan Ingersoll, A Partnership, College Centre, 500 College Road East.
Telephone: 609-452-2666.

Andrew S. Gordon

SENIOR ATTORNEYS

Richard H. Friedman — Kathryn Speaker MacNett

Sarah M. Bricknell — John B. Consevage
Samuel M. First

For Complete List of Firm Personnel, See General Section

For full biographical listings, see the Martindale-Hubbell Law Directory

CALDWELL & KEARNS, A PROFESSIONAL CORPORATION (AV)

3631 North Front Street, 17110-1533
Telephone: 717-232-7661
Fax: 717-232-2766

Thomas D. Caldwell, Jr. — Timothy I. Mark
Richard L. Kearns — James G. Nealon, III
James R. Clippinger — Matthew R. Gover
James L. Goldsmith — Deborah A. Cavacini

Representative Clients: Allstate Insurance Co.; Erie Insurance Exchange; Government Employees Insurance Co.; United States Fidelity & Guaranty Insurance; Pennsylvania National Insurance Co.; St. Paul Fire & Marine Insurance Co.; The Home Insurance Co.

For full biographical listings, see the Martindale-Hubbell Law Directory

GOLDBERG, KATZMAN & SHIPMAN, P.C. (AV)

320 Market Street - Strawberry Square, P.O. Box 1268, 17108-1268
Telephone: 717-234-4161
Telecopier: 717-234-6808; 717-234-6810

Ronald M. Katzman — Michael A. Finio
F. Lee Shipman — John A. Statler
Jesse Jay Cooper — April L. Strang-Kutay
Thomas E. Brenner — Guy H. Brooks
James M. Sheehan — Jefferson J. Shipman

Karen S. Feuchtenberger

Representative Clients: Cincinnati Insurance Co.; Pennsylvania National Insurance Co.; Atlantic Mutual Cos.; Erie Insurance Co.; Merchants & Businessman's Mutual Insurance Co.; State Auto Mutual Insurance Co.; Crawford & Co.; Foremost Insurance Co.; Virginia Mutual Insurance Co.
Reference: Fulton Bank.

For Complete List of Firm Personnel, See General Section

For full biographical listings, see the Martindale-Hubbell Law Directory

HEPFORD, SWARTZ & MORGAN (AV)

111 North Front Street, P.O. Box 889, 17108-0889
Telephone: 717-234-4121
Fax: 717-232-6802
Lewistown, Pennsylvania Office: 12 South Main Street, P.O. Box 867.
Telephone: 717-248-3913.

MEMBERS OF FIRM

H. Joseph Hepford — Sandra L. Meilton
Lee C. Swartz — Stephen M. Greecher, Jr.
James G. Morgan, Jr. — Dennis R. Sheaffer

(See Next Column)

COUNSEL

Stanley H. Siegel (Resident, Lewistown Office)

ASSOCIATES

Richard A. Estacio — Michael H. Park
Andrew K. Stutzman

For full biographical listings, see the Martindale-Hubbell Law Directory

KEEFER, WOOD, ALLEN & RAHAL (AV)

210 Walnut Street, P.O. Box 11963, 17108-1963
Telephone: 717-255-8000
Telecopier: 717-255-8050

MEMBERS OF FIRM

William E. Miller, Jr. — Gary E. French
Charles W. Rubendall II — Donna S. Weldon
Eugene E. Pepinsky, Jr. — Bradford Dorrance
Thomas E. Wood — Stephen L. Grose

ASSOCIATES

Jeffrey F. Smith — Donald M. Lewis, III
Gretchen C. Hanrahan

Representative Clients: Chrysler Corp.; Ford Motor Co.; Freightliner Corp.; John Hancock Mutual Life Insurance Co.; PACCAR, Inc.; Pennsylvania Blue Shield; Rockwell International Corp.; Texas Eastern Transmission Corp.; TRW, Inc.

For Complete List of Firm Personnel, See General Section

For full biographical listings, see the Martindale-Hubbell Law Directory

KILLIAN & GEPHART (AV)

218 Pine Street, P.O. Box 886, 17108
Telephone: 717-232-1851
Telecopier: 717-238-0592

MEMBERS OF FIRM

John D. Killian — Terrence J. McGowan
Paula J. McDermott

Reference: Dauphin Deposit Bank & Trust Co.

For full biographical listings, see the Martindale-Hubbell Law Directory

JOSEPH A. KLEIN A PROFESSIONAL CORPORATION (AV)

100 Chestnut Street, Suite 210, P.O. Box 1152, 17108
Telephone: 717-233-0132
Fax: 717-233-2516

Joseph A. Klein — Mark S. Silver

For full biographical listings, see the Martindale-Hubbell Law Directory

MANCKE, WAGNER, HERSHEY AND TULLY (AV)

2233 North Front Street, 17110
Telephone: 717-234-7051
Fax: 717-234-7080

MEMBERS OF FIRM

John B. Mancke — David E. Hershey
P. Richard Wagner — William T. Tully

ASSOCIATE

David R. Breschi

For full biographical listings, see the Martindale-Hubbell Law Directory

MCNEES, WALLACE & NURICK (AV)

100 Pine Street, P.O. Box 1166, 17108
Telephone: 717-232-8000
Fax: 717-237-5300

MEMBERS OF FIRM

Alan R. Boynton, Jr. — David E. Lehman
Elizabeth A. Dougherty — Clyde W. McIntyre
Harvey Freedenberg — Stephen A. Moore
Delano M. Lantz — Diane M. Tokarsky
Lawrence R. Wieder

ASSOCIATES

James W. Kutz — Patrick J. Murphy
Jonathan H. Rudd

For Complete List of Firm Personnel, See General Section

For full biographical listings, see the Martindale-Hubbell Law Directory

METTE, EVANS & WOODSIDE, A PROFESSIONAL CORPORATION (AV)

3401 North Front Street, P.O. Box 5950, 17110-0950
Telephone: 717-232-5000
Telecopier: 717-236-1816

(See Next Column)

METTE, EVANS & WOODSIDE A PROFESSIONAL CORPORATION—*Continued*

James W. Evans | Steven D. Snyder
Lloyd R. Persun | Christopher C. Conner
Craig A. Stone | Andrew H. Dowling
Daniel L. Sullivan | Michael D. Reed

David A. Fitzsimons | Jayson R. Wolfgang
Michael D. Pipa | Scott D. Moore
Andrew J. Ostrowski

Representative Clients: Capital Blue Cross: Commerce Bank; Nortek, Inc.; Pennsylvania Hospital Insurance Co.; PNI; Polaris Industries; St. Paul Insurance Co.; USF & G; Woolrich Woolen Mills, Inc.

For Complete List of Firm Personnel, See General Section

For full biographical listings, see the Martindale-Hubbell Law Directory

METZGER, WICKERSHAM, KNAUSS & ERB (AV)

Mellon Bank Building, 111 Market Street, P.O. Box 93, 17108-0093
Telephone: 717-238-8187
Telefax: 717-234-9478
Other Harrisburg, Pennsylvania Office: 4813 Jonestown Road, P.O. Box 93, 17108.
Telephone: 717-652-7020.

MEMBERS OF FIRM

Maurice R. Metzger (1918-1980) | Robert E. Yetter
F. Brewster Wickersham (1918-1974) | James F. Carl
Robert P. Reed
Edward E. Knauss, III (Retired) | Edward E. Knauss, IV
Christian S. Erb, Jr. | Jered L. Hock
Karl R. Hildabrand

ASSOCIATES

Richard B. Druby | Steven P. Miner
Clark DeVere

Representative Clients: Allstate Insurance Co.; Chubb Group of Insurance Companies; Fireman's Fund American Insurance Group; Liberty Mutual Insurance Co.; Continental Insurance Co.; Crum & Forster.

For full biographical listings, see the Martindale-Hubbell Law Directory

NAUMAN, SMITH, SHISSLER & HALL (AV)

Eighteenth Floor, 200 North Third Street, P.O. Box 840, 17108-0840
Telephone: 717-236-3010
Telefax: 717-234-1925

MEMBERS OF FIRM

David C. Eaton | John C. Sullivan
Spencer G. Nauman, Jr. | J. Stephen Feinour
Craig J. Staudenmaier

ASSOCIATES

Benjamin Charles Dunlap, Jr. | Stephen J. Keene

OF COUNSEL

Ralph W. Boyles, Jr.

Representative Clients: Consolidated Rail Corp.; The W.O. Hickok Mfg. Co.; Delta Dental of Pennsylvania; Mellon Bank, N.A.; PNC Bank, N.A.; General Motors Acceptance Corp.; Enders Insurance Associates; Patriot-News Co.; Chrysler Credit Corp.; Capital Area Tax Collection Bureau.

For full biographical listings, see the Martindale-Hubbell Law Directory

RHOADS & SINON (AV)

One South Market Square, 12th Floor, P.O. Box 1146, 17108-1146
Telephone: 717-233-5731
Fax: 717-232-1459
Boca Raton, Florida Affiliated Office: Suite 301, 299 West Camino Gardens Boulevard.
Telephone: 407-395-5595.
Fax: 407-395-9497.
Lancaster, Pennsylvania Office: 15 North Lime Street.
Telephone: 717-397-5127.
Fax: 717-397-5267.

OF COUNSEL

John C. Dowling

MEMBERS OF FIRM

Jan P. Paden | Thomas A. French
R. Stephen Shibla | Donna M. J. Clark
David B. Dowling | Charles E. Gutshall

ASSOCIATES

Jesse Raymond Ruhl | Virginia P. Henschel

Representative Clients: Aetna Surety & Casualty Co.; The Coca-Cola Company; Dauphin Deposit Bank & Trust Company; General Motors Corp.; H. J. Heinz Co.; Home Insurance Company; Insurance Company of North America; Weis Markets, Inc.

For Complete List of Firm Personnel, See General Section

For full biographical listings, see the Martindale-Hubbell Law Directory

THOMAS, THOMAS & HAFER (AV)

305 North Front Street, 6th Floor, P.O. Box 999, 17108
Telephone: 717-237-7100
Fax: 717-237-7105
Verify: 717-255-7642

MEMBERS OF FIRM

Joseph P. Hafer | C. Kent Price
James K. Thomas, II | Randall G. Gale
Jeffrey B. Rettig | David L. Schwalm
Peter J. Curry | Kevin E. Osborne
R. Burke McLemore, Jr. | Douglas B. Marcello
Edward H. Jordan, Jr. | Peter J. Speaker
Paul J. Dellasega

OF COUNSEL

James K. Thomas

Daniel J. Gallagher | Stephen E. Geduldig
Robert A. Taylor | Paula Gayle Sanders
Sarah W. Arosell | Karen S. Coates
Eugene N. McHugh | Ann F. DePaulis
Richard C. Seneca | Margaret A. Scheaffer
Todd R. Narvol

Representative Clients: Aetna Casualty & Surety Co.; Bethlehem Steel Corp.; Commercial Union Insurance Companies; Geisinger Medical Center; Hartford Insurance Group; Liberty Mutual Insurance Co.; Pennsylvania Hospital Insurance Co.; Pennsylvania Medical Society Liability Insurance Co.; UGI Corp.; Weis Markets, Inc.

For full biographical listings, see the Martindale-Hubbell Law Directory

KING OF PRUSSIA, Montgomery Co.

POWELL, TRACHTMAN, LOGAN, CARRLE & BOWMAN, A PROFESSIONAL CORPORATION (AV)

367 South Gulph Road, 19406
Telephone: 610-354-9700
Fax: 610-354-9760
Cherry Hill, New Jersey Office: 811 Church Road, Suite 126, 08002.
Telephone: 609-663-0021.
Fax: 609-663-1590.
Harrisburg, Pennsylvania Office: 114 North Second Street, 17101.
Telephone: 717-238-9300.
Fax: 717-238-9325.

Michael G. Trachtman | Richard B. Ashenfelter Jr.
Paul A. Logan | Mark F. Brancato
Gunther O. Carrle | Jonathan K. Hollin
C. Grainger Bowman | Joel P. Perilstein

OF COUNSEL

Ralph B. Powell, Jr. | Patrick W. Liddle

Mark S. McKain | David W. Francis
Ethan N. Halberstadt | Eileen M. Coyne
David T. Bolger | Andrew P. Goode
Steven G. Bardsley

For full biographical listings, see the Martindale-Hubbell Law Directory

*LANCASTER,** Lancaster Co.

JOSEPH F. RODA, P.C. (AV)

301 Cipher Building, 36 East King Street, 17602
Telephone: 717-397-1700
Fax: 717-397-3669

Joseph F. Roda

Ronald C. Messmann | Gail A. Weber
Robin A. Jabour

For full biographical listings, see the Martindale-Hubbell Law Directory

ZIMMERMAN, PFANNEBECKER & NUFFORT (AV)

22 South Duke Street, 17602
Telephone: 717-299-0711
FAX: 717-299-1092
Columbia, Pennsylvania Office: 342 Walnut Street.
Telephone: 717-684-2665.
Fax: 717-299-1092.
Lititz, Pennsylvania Office: 10 South Broad Street.
Telephone: 717-626-2088.
Quarryville, Pennsylvania Office: 100 East State Street.
Telephone: 717-786-8335.

MEMBERS OF FIRM

S. R. Zimmerman, III | Richard P. Nuffort
Robert L. Pfannebecker | Patricia L. Kotchek
Neil L. Albert

References: Hamilton Bank, Fulton Bank, Farmers First Bank, all of Lancaster, Pennsylvania.

For full biographical listings, see the Martindale-Hubbell Law Directory

LANGHORNE, Bucks Co.

BEGLEY, CARLIN & MANDIO (AV)

680 Middletown Boulevard, P.O. Box 308, 19047
Telephone: 215-750-0110
Fax: 215-750-0954
Bristol, Pennsylvania Office: 120 Mill Street.
Telephone: 215-750-0110.

MEMBERS OF FIRM

William J. Carlin
Anthony A. Mandio
S. Richard Klinges, III
Thomas J. Profy, III
Richard M. Snyder
Charles F. Sampsel
John P. Koopman
Jeffrey P. Garton
Thomas R. Hecker
James A. Downey, III
Joseph S. Britton
Douglas C. Maloney

ASSOCIATES

Thomas J. Profy, IV
William L. Weiner
Karen L. Saraco
Michael G. Fitzpatrick

Representative Clients: Borough of Bristol; Bristol Borough School Board; Fidelity Savings & Loan Association of Bucks County; Lower Makefield Township; Philadelphia National Bank; Waste Management, Inc.

For full biographical listings, see the Martindale-Hubbell Law Directory

LANSDALE, Montgomery Co.

PEARLSTINE/SALKIN ASSOCIATES (AV)

1250 South Broad Street Suite 1000, P.O. Box 431, 19446
Telephone: 215-699-6000
Fax: 215-699-0231

MEMBERS OF FIRM

Philip Salkin
Ronald E. Robinson
Barry Cooperberg
Frederick C. Horn
Marc B. Davis
William R. Wanger
F. Craig La Rocca
Jeffrey T. Sultanik
Neal R. Pearlstine
Wendy G. Rothstein
Alan L. Eisen
Glenn D. Fox

Wilhelm L. Gruszecki
Brian E. Subers
Mark S. Cappuccio
James R. Hall
Michael S. Paul
David J. Draganosky
Lawrence P. Kempner

For full biographical listings, see the Martindale-Hubbell Law Directory

*LEBANON,** Lebanon Co.

HENRY & BEAVER (AV)

937 Willow Street, P.O. Box 1140, 17042-1140
Telephone: 717-274-3644
Facsimile: 717-274-6782

MEMBERS OF FIRM

Charles V. Henry, III
R. Hart Beaver
Frederick S. Wolf
Thomas P. Harlan
Wiley P. Parker
John H. Whitmoyer
Christopher J. Coyle
Kevin M. Richards

ASSOCIATE

Marc A. Hess

Representative Clients: Lebanon Valley National Bank; Cornwall Manor; Medical Protective Company of Fort Wayne; Nationwide Insurance Co.; Liberty Mutual Insurance Co.; Utica Mutual Insurance Co.; CIGNA Insurance Co.; The Pennsylvania Sports Hall of Fame; North Lebanon Township; United Way of Lebanon County, Inc.

For full biographical listings, see the Martindale-Hubbell Law Directory

*MEDIA,** Delaware Co.

MICHAEL G. DEFINO (AV)

Rose Tree Corporate Center II, 1400 North Providence Road, Suite 103, 19063
Telephone: 610-566-3131
Fax: 610-566-3232

For full biographical listings, see the Martindale-Hubbell Law Directory

DIORIO & FALZONE (AV)

Front and Plum Streets, P.O. Box 1789, 19063
Telephone: 610-565-5700
FAX: 610-891-0652

MEMBERS OF FIRM

Robert M. DiOrio
Raymond J. Falzone, Jr.

ASSOCIATE

Christopher R. Mattox

For full biographical listings, see the Martindale-Hubbell Law Directory

MARCH, HURWITZ, DEMARCO & MITCHELL (AV)

17 West Third Street, P.O. Box 108, 19063
Telephone: 610-565-3950
Fax: 610-892-0875
Cherry Hill, New Jersey Office: 411 Route 70, Suite 215.
Telephone: 609-661-8150.

MEMBERS OF FIRM

William D. March
Gary A. Hurwitz
Joseph M. DeMarco
Richard A. Mitchell

ASSOCIATES

Lee A. Stivale
Rosemary Reger Schnall
Ronald Aaron Katcher

For full biographical listings, see the Martindale-Hubbell Law Directory

*NORRISTOWN,** Montgomery Co.

LINDLEY M. COWPERTHWAIT, JR., P.C. (AV)

17 East Airy Street, 19401
Telephone: 610-277-6622
Fax: 610-277-6601
Cherry Hill, New Jersey Office: 1040 North Kings Highway, Suite 600, 08034.
Telephone: 609-482-8600.

Lindley M. Cowperthwait, Jr.
Adam D. Zucker

For full biographical listings, see the Martindale-Hubbell Law Directory

GERBER & GERBER (AV)

Suite 500, One Montgomery Plaza, 19401
Telephone: 610-279-6700
Fax: 610-279-7126

MEMBERS OF FIRM

Morris Gerber
A. Richard Gerber

ASSOCIATE

Parke H. Ulrich

For full biographical listings, see the Martindale-Hubbell Law Directory

MANNING, KINKEAD, BROOKS & BRADBURY, A PROFESSIONAL CORPORATION (AV)

412 DeKalb Street, 19404-0231
Telephone: 610-279-1800
Fax: 610-279-8682

Franklin L. Wright (1880-1965)
William Perry Manning, Jr.
William H. Kinkead, III
William H. Bradbury, III

Cheri D. Andrews

Counsel for: The Philadelphia National Bank; John Deere Co.; The Rouse Co.; Consolidated Rail Corp.; Bethlehem Steel Co.; Royal Globe Insurance Co.; Nationwide Mutual Insurance Co.

For full biographical listings, see the Martindale-Hubbell Law Directory

MURPHY & OLIVER, P.C. (AV)

43 East Marshall Street, 19401-4869
Telephone: 610-272-4222; 643-5900
Fax: 610-272-2549
Mount Laurel, New Jersey Office: 1288 State Highway 73, Suite 120, 08054.
Telephone: 609-234-1495.

James J. Oliver
Frank P. Murphy

Joseph M. Hoeffel III
Carla E. Connor
Barbara A. Barnes
Paul C. Cipriano, Jr.

For full biographical listings, see the Martindale-Hubbell Law Directory

PAOLI, Chester Co.

RUBIN & ASSOCIATES (AV)

MCS Building, 10 South Leopard Road, 19301
Telephone: 610-408-2000
Fax: 610-408-9000

Gregory S. Rubin

Representative Clients: Merrill Lynch, Pierce, Fenner & Smith, Inc.; Wheat First Securities, Inc.; Quick & Reilly, Inc.; McLaughlin, Piven, Vogel Securities, Inc.

For full biographical listings, see the Martindale-Hubbell Law Directory

*PHILADELPHIA,** Philadelphia Co.

ABRAMSON, FREEDMAN & THALL (AV)

2128 Locust Street, 19103
Telephone: 215-545-2400
Telecopier: 215-545-8537
Haddonfield, New Jersey Office: 20 Kings Highway West.
Telephone: 609-795-5363.
Fax: 609-354-0020.

MEMBERS OF FIRM

Gilbert B. Abramson
Jeffrey M. Freedman
Bruce L. Thall

ASSOCIATES

Michael J. Troiani
Michael B. Tolcott
Stanley B. Cheiken (Resident, Haddonfield, New Jersey Office)

For full biographical listings, see the Martindale-Hubbell Law Directory

ANAPOL, SCHWARTZ, WEISS AND COHAN, A PROFESSIONAL CORPORATION (AV)

1900 Delancey Place, 19103
Telephone: 215-735-1130
Fax: 215-735-2024
Bristol, Pennsylvania Office: 1811 Farragut Avenue.
Telephone: 215-785-3400.
Cherry Hill, New Jersey Office: 402 Park Boulevard.
Telephone: 1-609-427-9229.

Alan Schwartz
Paul R. Anapol
Richard B. Schwartz
Sol H. Weiss
Stanton Dubin
Lawrence R. Cohan
Joel D. Feldman
Howard J. Levin
Bernard W. Smalley
Margaret A. Barry
Stephen J. Pokiniewski, Jr.
Nancy L. Goldstein
Sidney M. Grobman

Colleen M. Hickey
Nathaniel E.P. Ehrlich
Nelson Levin
Thomas R. Anapol
Lisa R. Schwartz
Paul A. Czech

LEGAL SUPPORT PERSONNEL

Joanne N. Borders (Legal Assistant)

Reference: Meridian Bank, Philadelphia, Pennsylvania.

For full biographical listings, see the Martindale-Hubbell Law Directory

BALLARD SPAHR ANDREWS & INGERSOLL (AV)

1735 Market Street, 51st Floor, 19103-7599
Telephone: 215-665-8500
Fax: 215-864-8999
Denver, Colorado Office: Seventeenth Street Plaza Building, Suite 2300, 1225 17th Street.
Telephone: 303-292-2400.
Fax: 303-296-3956.
Kaunas, Lithuania Office: Donelaicio g., 71-2, Kaunas 3000.
Telephone: (370-7) 20 56 66.
Fax: (370-7) 20 56 91.
Salt Lake City, Utah Office: One Utah Center, Suite 1200, 201 South Main Street.
Telephone: 801-531-3000.
Fax: 801-531-3001.
Washington, D.C. Office: Suite 900 East, 555 13th Street, N.W.
Telephone: 202-383-8800.
Fax: 202-383-8877; 383-8893.
Baltimore, Maryland Office: 300 East Lombard Street. 19th Floor.
Telephone: 410-528-5600.
Fax: 410-528-5650.
Camden, New Jersey Office: 800 Hudson Square, 5th Floor.
Telephone: 609-541-5577.
Fax: 609-541-8272.

Creed C. Black, Jr.
James D. Coleman
Geoffrey A. Kahn
Darryl J. May
Carl G. Roberts
Robert McLaurin Boote
Alan J. Davis
Arthur Makadon
David H. Pittinsky
Mark S. Stewart
Matthew M. Strickler

Gilpin W. Bartels
Walter M. Einhorn, Jr.
Leslie E. John
Martin C. Bryce, Jr.
Anjali Jesseramsing
Alison D. Keel
Leslie H. Smith

For Complete List of Firm Personnel, See General Section
For full biographical listings, see the Martindale-Hubbell Law Directory

MARVIN I. BARISH LAW OFFICES A PROFESSIONAL CORPORATION (AV)

625 Walnut Street, Suite 801, 19106-3308
Telephone: 215-923-8900; 800-233-7101
Cable Address: "Marsbar-Philadelphia"
Fax: 215-351-0593

Marvin I. Barish

Robert J. Meyers
Stacey E. Barish
Timothy Garvey

For full biographical listings, see the Martindale-Hubbell Law Directory

HARRY P. BEGIER, JR., LTD. (AV)

1700 Sansom Street, 10th Floor, 19103-5208
Telephone: 215-994-1515
Fax: 215-994-1516

Harry P. Begier, Jr.
Arthur S. Alexion
Alan H. Casper

For full biographical listings, see the Martindale-Hubbell Law Directory

JACK M. BERNARD (AV)

Land Title Building Suite 2121, 100 South Broad Street, 19110
Telephone: 215-665-0666
FAX: 215-665-0206
Reference: Royal Bank.

For full biographical listings, see the Martindale-Hubbell Law Directory

BRUCE G. CASSIDY & ASSOCIATES, P.A. (AV)

Suite 1040, 21 South 12th Street, 19107
Telephone: 215-568-6700
Fax: 215-568-4077
Collingswood, New Jersey Office: 915 Haddon Avenue, 08108.
Telephone: 609-869-3535.

Bruce G. Cassidy

OF COUNSEL

Dr. Peter H. Feuerstein (Not admitted United States)
James A. Dunleavy

For full biographical listings, see the Martindale-Hubbell Law Directory

CLIFFORD B. COHN (AV)

1919 Walnut Street, 19103
Telephone: 215-665-1800
Fax: 215-665-8434

For full biographical listings, see the Martindale-Hubbell Law Directory

CORSON, GETSON & SCHATZ (AV)

Suite 300 The Carlton Business Center, 1819 John F. Kennedy Boulevard, 19103
Telephone: 215-564-3030; 568-2525
Fax: 215-564-5477

MEMBERS OF FIRM

Lawrence Corson
Allan Getson
Robert B. B. Schatz

For full biographical listings, see the Martindale-Hubbell Law Directory

COZEN AND O'CONNOR, A PROFESSIONAL CORPORATION (AV)

1900 Market Street, 19103
Telephone: 215-665-2000
800-523-2900
Telecopier: 215-665-2013
Charlotte, North Carolina Office: One First Union Plaza, 28202.
Telephones: 704-376-3400; 800-762-3575.
Telecopier: 704-334-3351.
Columbia, South Carolina Office: Suite 200 The Palmetto Center, 1426 Main Street.
Telephones: 803-799-3900; 800-338-1117.
Telecopier: 803-254-7233.
Dallas, Texas Office: Suite 4100, NationsBank Plaza, 901 Main Street.
Telephones: 214-761-6700; 800-448-1207.
Telecopier: 214-761-6788.
New York, N.Y. Office: 45 Broadway Atrium.
Telephones: 212-509-9400; 800-437-9400.
Telecopier: 212-509-9492.
San Diego, California Office: Suite 1610, 501 West Broadway.
Telephones: 619-234-1700; 800-782-3366.
Telecopier: 619-234-7831.
Seattle, Washington Office: Suite 5200, Washington Mutual Tower, 1201 Third Avenue.
Telephones: 206-340-1000; 800-423-1950.
Telecopier: 206-621-8783.

(See Next Column)

COZEN AND O'CONNOR A PROFESSIONAL CORPORATION, *Philadelphia—Continued*

Westmont, New Jersey Office: 316 Haddon Avenue.
Telephones: 609-854-4900; 800-523-2900.
Telecopier: 609-854-1782.

Sydney C. Orlofsky (1936-1968)
Charles A. Fisher, III (1947-1990)

FIRM MEMBERS IN PHILADELPHIA

Stephen A. Cozen
Patrick J. O'Connor
Joseph A. Gerber
Richard C. Glazer
Michael J. Izzo, Jr.
Robert R. Reeder
Christopher C. Fallon, Jr.
Miles A. Jellinek
David R. Strawbridge
A. Richard Bailey
Ronald B. Hamilton
Gerard F. Belz, Jr.
Gerald J. Dugan
Michael F. Henry
John F. Brown, Jr.
David J. Groth
Joshua Wall
Thomas M. Regan
Elliott R. Feldman
John T. Thorn
Thomas C. Zielinski
Robert W. Hayes
Eugene J. Maginnis, Jr.
Anita B. Weinstein
John D. Brinkmann
Richard M. Mackowsky
Vincent R. McGuinness, Jr.
William H. Howard
Daniel Q. Harrington
Elaine M. Rinaldi
John T. Salvucci
Richard C. Bennett
Robert E. Meyer
Douglas B. Fox
Douglas B. Lang
Mark T. Mullen
Daniel C. Theveny
Laurence M. Levin
Denise Brinker Bense
Robert H. Hawn, Jr.
Deborah Melamut Minkoff
Jeffrey L. Nash
Joseph H. Riches
Lewis A. Grafman
Huey P. Cotton
Albert G. Dugan, Jr.
Ann Thornton Field
James H. Heller
Peter G. Rossi
Brian L. Lincicome
Paul R. Bartolacci
Eric D. Freed
Steven V. Turner
Jennifer Gallagher
Mitchell S. Goldberg
William G. Flint
Kevin J. Hughes
Mark E. Opalisky
Steven L. Smith
John Dwyer
Michael R. McCarty
Cecilia M. O'Connor
Kathie D. King
Marcy C. Panzer
Arnold C. Joseph (Resident, New York, N.Y. Office)
Gregg F. Carpene
Josh M. Greenbaum
Dexter R. Hamilton
Robert A. Stutman

FIRM ASSOCIATES IN PHILADELPHIA

Kevin M. Apollo
Drew R. Barth
Joseph J. Bellew
Barbara E. Brockman
James E. Brown
Frances K. Davis
James D. Dendinger
Martin P. Duffey
Joseph P. Fenlin
Jim H. Fields, Jr.
Lori Fox
Thomas F. Gallagher
Stephen M. Halbeisen
Denise H. Houghton
Michael J. McCarrie
Stephen M. Rymal
William F. Stewart
Jeffrey R. Stoner

Representative Clients: Available upon request.

For Complete List of Firm Personnel, See General Section

For full biographical listings, see the Martindale-Hubbell Law Directory

---

KATHLEEN L. DAERR-BANNON (AV)

Suite 300, 1211 Chestnut Street, 19107-4113
Telephone: 215-563-9300
Fax: 215-563-3337

Reference: Provident National Bank.

For full biographical listings, see the Martindale-Hubbell Law Directory

---

D'ANGELO AND EURELL (AV)

Twenty-Second Floor, Land Title Building, 19110
Telephone: 215-564-5022
Fax: 215-557-7651

MEMBERS OF FIRM

George A. D'Angelo
John B. Eurell
David S. D'Angelo

For full biographical listings, see the Martindale-Hubbell Law Directory

---

DESTEFANO & WARREN, P.C. (AV)

Suite 1006, Lafayette Building, 437 Chestnut Street, 19106-2426
Telephone: 215-625-5000
FAX: 215-625-9934
Cherry Hill, New Jersey Office: 601 Longwood Avenue.
Telephone: 609-665-2552.
FAX: 609-665-7524.

William A. DeStefano
Christopher D. Warren
Philip H. Marcus

Susan Gibson Durant

(See Next Column)

LEGAL SUPPORT PERSONNEL

Joseph Silvestro

For full biographical listings, see the Martindale-Hubbell Law Directory

---

DURANT & DURANT (AV)

12th Floor, 400 Market Street, 19106
Telephone: 215-592-1818
Fax: 215-592-9994

MEMBERS OF FIRM

Marc Durant
Rita M. Durant

COUNSEL

Robin Blumenfeld Shore

ASSOCIATE

Adele Breen-Franklin

For full biographical listings, see the Martindale-Hubbell Law Directory

---

FELLHEIMER EICHEN BRAVERMAN & KASKEY, A PROFESSIONAL CORPORATION (AV)

21st Floor, One Liberty Place, 19103-7334
Telephone: 215-575-3800
FAX: 215-575-3801
Camden, New Jersey Office: 519 Federal Street, Suite 503 Parkade Building, 08103-1147.
Telephone: 609-541-5323.
Fax: 609-541-5370.

Alan S. Fellheimer
David L. Braverman
Judith Eichen Fellheimer
John E. Kaskey
Kenneth S. Goodkind
Anna Hom
Peter E. Meltzer

Barbara Anisko
Maia R. Caplan
Jeffrey L. Eichen
Michael N. Feder
Jolie G. Kahn
George F. Newton
David B. Spitofsky
W. Thomas Tither, Jr.

For Complete List of Firm Personnel, See General Section

For full biographical listings, see the Martindale-Hubbell Law Directory

---

FINEMAN & BACH, P.C. (AV)

19th Floor, 1608 Walnut Street, 19103
Telephone: 215-893-9300
Fax: 215-893-8719
Cherry Hill, New Jersey Office: 905 North Kings Highway.
Telephone: 609-795-1118.

Norman S. Berson
Robert J. Klein
S. David Fineman
Bonnie Brigance Leadbetter
Mitchell L. Bach
Tyler E. Wren
Richard A. Rubin
J. Randolph Lawlace
Jay Barry Harris
Richard J. Tanker (Resident, Cherry Hill, New Jersey Office)

Lee Applebaum
Diane C. Bernoff
Scott H. Brandt
June J. Essis
John C. Falls
Illene G. Greenberg
Julie Pearlman Meyers
Stefanie Newman Rabinowitz
Michael S. Saltzman
Alan J. Tauber
Alexander B. Zolfaghari

For full biographical listings, see the Martindale-Hubbell Law Directory

---

F. EMMETT FITZPATRICK, P.C. (AV)

926 Public Ledger Building, 19106
Telephone: 215-925-5200
Fax: 215-925-5991

F. Emmett Fitzpatrick
F. Emmett Fitzpatrick, III

For full biographical listings, see the Martindale-Hubbell Law Directory

---

GALLAGHER, REILLY AND LACHAT, P.C. (AV)

Suite 1300, 2000 Market Street, 19103
Telephone: 215-299-3000
FAX: 215-299-3010
Pennsauken, New Jersey Office: Kevon Office Center, Suite 130, 2500 McClellan Boulevard, 08109.
Telephone: 609-663-8200.

Stanley S. Frazee, Jr.
Paul F. X. Gallagher
Thomas F. Reilly
Frederick T. Lachat, Jr.
Richard K. Hohn
James Emerson Egbert
Stephen A. Scheuerle
Elizabeth F. Walker

(See Next Column)

GALLAGHER, REILLY AND LACHAT P.C.—*Continued*

David Scott Morgan
Wilfred T. Mills, Jr.
Maureen Rowan
Charles L. McNabb
Thomas O'Neill
Laurence I. Gross
Sean F. Kennedy
Milica Novakovic
John A. Livingood, Jr.

SPECIAL COUNSEL

Dolores Rocco Kulp

For full biographical listings, see the Martindale-Hubbell Law Directory

GERMAN, GALLAGHER & MURTAGH, A PROFESSIONAL CORPORATION (AV)

Fifth Floor, The Bellevue, 200 South Broad Street, 19102
Telephone: 215-545-7700
Telecopier: 215-732-4182
Cherry Hill, New Jersey Office: Suite 643, 1040 North Kings Highway.
Telephone: 609-667-7676.
Lancaster, Pennsylvania Office: 40 East Grant Street.
Telephone: 717-293-8070.

Edward C. German
Michael D. Gallagher
Dean F. Murtagh
Philip A. Ryan
Robert P. Corbin
David P. Rovner
Kathryn A. Dux
Gary R. Gremminger
Kim Plouffe
Jeffrey N. German
John P. Shusted

Kathleen M. Carson
Kevin R. McNulty
Linda Porr Sweeney
Gary H. Hunter
Frank A. Gerolamo, III
Milan K. Mrkobrad
Thomas M. Going
Vincent J. Di Stefano, Jr.
Jack T. Ribble, Jr.
Kimberly J. Keiser
Bernard E. Jude Quinn
Gerald C. Montella
Lisa Beth Zucker
Shelby L. Mattioli
Daniel J. Divis
D. Selaine Belver
Christine L. Davis
Daniel L. Grill
Marta I. Sierra-Epperson
Paul G. Kirk
Aileen R. Thompson
Otis V. Maynard
Gregory S. Capps

For full biographical listings, see the Martindale-Hubbell Law Directory

GILLIGAN & PEPPELMAN (AV)

2000 Market Street, Suite 2904, 19103
Telephone: 215-751-9400
Fax: 215-751-9616

Philip M. Gilligan
Raymond J. Peppelman, Jr.

For full biographical listings, see the Martindale-Hubbell Law Directory

GOLDFEIN & JOSEPH, A PROFESSIONAL CORPORATION (AV)

17th Floor, Packard Building, 111 South 15th Street, 19102-2695
Telephone: 215-977-9800
Fax: 215-988-0062
Princeton, New Jersey Office: Princeton Metro Center, Suite 115, 5 Vaughn Drive.
Telephone: 609-520-0400.
Fax: 609-520-1450.
Wilmington, Delaware Office: PNC Bank Center, Suite 1212, P.O. Box 2206, 222 Delaware Avenue.
Telephone: 302-656-3301.
Fax: 302-656-0643.

Edward B. Joseph
Fredric L. Goldfein
E. Chandler Hosmer, III
Ellen Brown Furman
Leslie Anne Miller
David C. Weinberg
James Patrick Hadden
Bernard L. Levinthal
Gary H. Kaplan (Resident, Wilmington, Delaware Office)
Roseann Lynn Brenner
Elissa J. Kahn

John A. Turlik
Susan Burton Stadtmauer
David M. Katzenstein (Resident, Princeton, New Jersey Office)
Scott I. Fegley
William J. Weiss
Michael A. Billotti (Not admitted in PA; Resident, Princeton, New Jersey Office)
Lawrence E. Currier
Robert P. Coleman
Robert T. Connor
Ann B. Cairns
Frederick A. Kiegel
Janet E. Golup
Ted Martin Berg (Resident, Wilmington, Delaware Office)

OF COUNSEL

Charles B. Burr, II

For full biographical listings, see the Martindale-Hubbell Law Directory

HARKINS CUNNINGHAM (AV)

1800 One Commerce Square, 2005 Market Street, 19103-7042
Telephone: 215-851-6700
Facsimile: 215-851-6710
Washington, D.C. Office: Suite 600, 1300 Nineteenth Street Northwest, 20036-1609.
Telephone: 202-973-7600.
Facsimile: 202-973-7610.

MEMBERS OF FIRM

John G. Harkins, Jr.
Paul A. Cunningham (Not admitted in PA)

Charles Bramham
Patricia L. Freeland
Richard B. Herzog (Not admitted in PA)
David A. Hirsh (Not admitted in PA)
Eleanor Morris Illoway
Robert M. Jenkins, III (Not admitted in PA)
A. Carl Kaseman, III
Gerald P. Norton (Not admitted in PA)
James G. Rafferty (Not admitted in PA)
Lloyd R. Ziff

ASSOCIATES

Elizabeth M. Chachis
Karin Engstrom Davis
Stuart L. Fullerton
James M. Guinivan (Not admitted in PA)
Neill C. Kling
Melissa E. Kraras
Joseph L. Lakshmanan (Not admitted in PA)
Joel A. Rabinovitz (Not admitted in PA)
Steven A. Reed
Melinda P. Rudolph
Gay Parks Rainville

OF COUNSEL

Margaret W. Wiener

For full biographical listings, see the Martindale-Hubbell Law Directory

HOYLE, MORRIS & KERR (AV)

Suite 4900, One Liberty Place, 1650 Market Street, 19103
Telephone: 215-981-5700
Telecopier: 851-0436

MEMBERS OF FIRM

Lawrence T. Hoyle, Jr.
Alexander Kerr
Susan K. Herschel
Arlene Fickler
Stephen J. Mathes
Charles B. Blakinger
Ralph A. Jacobs
Richard M. Bernstein
Jill A. Douthett
R. Nicholas Gimbel
Eric B. Henson
Wayne W. Suojanen
Bebe H. Kivitz
Debra G. Staples
William R. Herman
David E. Landau
Denise D. Colliers
Sean P. Wajert
Elizabeth W. Fox

OF COUNSEL

Samuel W. Morris, Jr.
Arthur R. Littleton

SENIOR ATTORNEYS

Lisa M. Salazar
Lloyd A. Gelwan

ASSOCIATES

Ellen M. Briggs
Mark H. Fisher
Marisa P. Marcin
Joseph A. Eagan, Jr.
Peter Konolige
Laurie Gottlieb
Robert J. Dougher
Michael T. Starczewski
Thomas M. Glavin
Jan Fink Call
Mary K. Miluski
Nancy Stuart
Shelly L. Urban
Barbara Jane Subkow
Andrew S. Abramson
Mark F. Bernstein
Patricia A. Brooks
Barbara Shelley Magers
Joann M. Lytle
George Stephen Bobnak

For Complete List of Firm Personnel, See General Section

For full biographical listings, see the Martindale-Hubbell Law Directory

KAUFMAN, COREN, RESS & WEIDMAN (AV)

1525 Locust Street, 16th Floor, 19102
Telephone: 215-735-8700
FAX: 215-735-5170

MEMBERS OF FIRM

Howard J. Kaufman
Steven M. Coren
Douglas Evan Ress
Peter J. Weidman

OF COUNSEL

Judith J. Jamison

Doris A. Pechkurow
Mary Jane Barrett
Peter J. Leyh
Edmund B. Luce
David Dormont

For full biographical listings, see the Martindale-Hubbell Law Directory

Philadelphia—Continued

KELLEY, JASONS, MCGUIRE & SPINELLI (AV)

Suite 1300, 1234 Market Street, 19107-3713
Telephone: 215-854-0658
Fax: 215-854-8434
Cherry Hill, New Jersey Office: 1230 Brace Road, 08034.
Telephone: 609-429-8956.
Wilmington, Delaware Office: 1220 Market Building, P.O. Box 194, 19899.
Telephone: 302-652-8560.
Fax: 302-652-8405.

MEMBERS OF FIRM

John Patrick Kelley
Catherine N. Jasons
Joseph W. McGuire
Armand J. Della Porta, Jr.
Christopher N. Santoro
Robert N. Spinelli
Thomas P. Hanna
Thomas J. Johanson
Michael L. Turner

ASSOCIATES

Kelly J. Sasso (Resident, Wilmington, Delaware Office)
Richard L. Walker, II
Bernard E. Kueny, III
Timothy McGowan
Neal C. Glenn

OF COUNSEL

Joseph P. Green
Matthew D. Blum, M.D.

For full biographical listings, see the Martindale-Hubbell Law Directory

KITTREDGE, DONLEY, ELSON, FULLEM & EMBICK (AV)

Fifth Floor, The Bank Building, 421 Chestnut Street, 19106
Telephone: 215-829-9900
Fax: 215-829-9888

MEMBERS OF FIRM

Patrick W. Kittredge
Joseph M. Donley
Barry R. Elson
Joseph W. Fullem, Jr.
John R. Embick

ASSOCIATES

Regina M. Harbaugh
Glenn E. Davis
Betsy F. Sternthal
Michael S. Soulé
Gary M. Marek
Patricia Powers
Daniel J. Maher
Susanne L. Longenhagen
Michael K. Smith
Richard J. Sestak

For full biographical listings, see the Martindale-Hubbell Law Directory

KLOVSKY, KUBY AND HARRIS (AV)

Klovsky, Kuby & Harris Building, 431 Chestnut Street, 19106
Telephone: 215-592-0300
Fax Copier: 215-592-7713

MEMBERS OF FIRM

Sidney B. Klovsky
Benjamin Kuby
William D. Harris
Paul N. Minkoff

ASSOCIATE

Wade F. Suthard

Reference: Provident National Bank.

For full biographical listings, see the Martindale-Hubbell Law Directory

KOLSBY, GORDON, ROBIN, SHORE & ROTHWEILER, A PROFESSIONAL CORPORATION (AV)

One Liberty Place, 22nd Floor, 1650 Market Street, 19103
Telephone: 215-851-9700
Fax: 215-851-9701

Herbert F. Kolsby
Allan H. Gordon
F. Philip Robin
Mitchell J. Shore
Kenneth Michael Rothweiler
Nadeem A. Bezar
Daniel Jeck

For full biographical listings, see the Martindale-Hubbell Law Directory

LAVIN, COLEMAN, FINARELLI & GRAY (AV)

12th Floor Penn Mutual Tower, 510 Walnut Street, 19106
Telephone: 215-627-0303
Fax: 215-627-2551
Mount Laurel, New Jersey Office: 10000 Midlantic Drive, Suite 300 West.
Telephone: 609-778-5544.
Fax: 609-778-3383.
New York, New York Office: 780 Third Avenue, Suite 1401.
Telephone: 212-319-6898.
Fax: 212-319-6932.

George J. Lavin, Jr.
Thomas Finarelli
William V. Coleman
Francis F. Quinn
Joseph E. O'Neil
Francis P. Burns, III
William J. Ricci
Edward A. Gray
Basil A. DiSipio
Wayne A. Graver
James Weiner
Frederick W. Rom
Gerard Cedrone
Robert Szwajkos

(See Next Column)

Mary Grace Maley
Christine O. Boyd
Michael D. Brophy
Joseph A. McGinley
Polly N. Phillippi

John J. Bateman
Stephen M. Beaudoin
Ronald W. Boak
Denise L. Carroll
Henry Michael Clinton
John J. Coughlin, IV
John Kieran Daly (Not admitted in PA)
Michael T. Droogan, Jr.
Joseph F. Dunne (Not admitted in PA)
B. Lynn Enderby
Louis Giansante
Francis J. Grey, Jr.
Mitchell Gruner
Robert J. Hafner
Eugene Hamill
Sandra Hourahan
Ernest H. Hutchinson, III
Regina A. Jones
Bridget A. Kelleher
Michael P. Kinkopf
Steven R. Kramer (Not admitted in PA)
Ellen Hatch Kueny
George J. Lavin, III
Peter W. Lee
Robert J. Martin
Karen Howard Matthews
William C. Mead, Jr.
Stephen E. Moore
Jane Elizabeth Nagle
Peter M. Newman
John J. O'Donnell
LeaNora J. Patterson
Jo E. Peifer
Michael J. Quinn
Mary D. Rafferty
Susan Ellyn Satkowski
William E. Staas, III
Fiona J. Van Dych
Thomas J. Wagner
Anne E. Walters
Maribeth Bohs Wechsler
Richard B. Wickersham, Jr.

For full biographical listings, see the Martindale-Hubbell Law Directory

LEVIN, FISHBEIN, SEDRAN & BERMAN (AV)

Suite 600, 320 Walnut Street, 19106
Telephone: 215-592-1500
Fax: 215-592-4663

MEMBERS OF FIRM

Arnold Levin
Michael D. Fishbein
Howard J. Sedran
Laurence S. Berman
Frederick S. Longer

Robert M. Unterberger
Craig D. Ginsburg
Jonathan Shub
Cheryl R. Brown Hill
Roberta Shaner

For full biographical listings, see the Martindale-Hubbell Law Directory

MANNINO GRIFFITH P.C. (AV)

2400 One Commerce Square, 19103
Telephone: 215-851-6300
Fax: 215-851-6315
Camden, New Jersey Office: 411 Cooper Street, Suite 3A, 08102.
Telephone: 609-964-3661.
Fax: 609-964-3626

James Lewis Griffith
Edward F. Mannino
Michael C. Hemsley
Virginia Lynn Hogben

OF COUNSEL

Richard T. Nassberg

Jack J. Bernstein
Charlotte E. Thomas
Amy L. Currier
Deborah Susan Baird-Diamond
Susan J. French
Peter A. Garcia
Johanna Smith
Martin J. Beck
Brett L. Messinger
David L. Comerford
Deirdre M. Richards
Michelle A. Fioravanti
William Christopher Duerr

For full biographical listings, see the Martindale-Hubbell Law Directory

MANTA AND WELGE (AV)

A Partnership of Professional Corporations
One Commerce Square, 37th Floor, 2005 Market Street, 19103
Telephone: 215-851-6600
Telecopy: 215-851-6644
Allentown, Pennsylvania Office: Suite 115 Commerce Plaza, 5050 Tilghman Street.
Telephone: 215-395-7499.
Fax: 215-398-7878.
Princeton, New Jersey Office: 101 Carnegie Center, Suite 215. P.O. Box 5306.
Telephone: 609-452-8833.
Fax: 609-452-9109.
Cherry Hill, New Jersey Office: Suite 600, 1040 North King Highway.
Telephone: 609-795-7611.
Fax: 609-795-7612.

(See Next Column)

MANTA AND WELGE—*Continued*

MEMBERS OF FIRM

Joseph G. Manta
Mark A. Welge
William R. Hourican
Albert L. Piccerilli
John C. Sullivan
Joel Schneider
Joseph M. Cincotta
James V. Bielunas
Richard S. Mannella
Joanne M. Walker
Francis McGill Hadden
Walter A. Stewart

OF COUNSEL

Albert J. Bartosic

Peter F. Rosenthal
Susan Simpson-Brown
Gregory S. Thomas
Andrea L. Smith
Anton G. Marzano
Margaret E. Wenke
Wendy F. Tucker
Jacqueline Borock
David G. C. Arnold
Karen C. Buck
Laurie A. Carroll
Mark J. Manta
David S. Florig
Stephen F. Brock
Geoffrey J. Alexander
Wendy R. S. O'Connor
Kathleen K. Kerns
Fernando Santiago
Peter L. Frattarelli
Holly C. Dobrosky

For full biographical listings, see the Martindale-Hubbell Law Directory

MARGOLIS, EDELSTEIN & SCHERLIS (AV)

The Curtis Center, Fourth Floor, One Independence Square West, 19106-3304
Telephone: 215-922-1100
FAX: 215-922-1772
Telex: 62021004
Associated Law Firm: Slimm & Goldberg, 216 Haddon Avenue, Suite 750, Westmont, New Jersey, 08108-2886.
Telephone: 609-858-7200.
FAX: 609-858-1017.

MEMBERS OF FIRM

Alan Wm. Margolis
Edward L. Edelstein
Edwin L. Scherlis
Joseph S. Bekelja
Joseph Goldberg
John L. Slimm (Not admitted in PA)
Leonard S. Lipson
Michael P. McKenna
Mitchell S. Pinsly
Carl Anthony Maio
Gordon Gelfond
Donald M. Davis
Melvin R. Shuster
Christopher J. Pakuris
Marshall A. Haislup, III
Bruce E. Barrett (Resident, Westmont, New Jersey Office)
J. Vincent Roche
Gary B. Cutler
Michael D. Eiss
Mark N. Cohen
Robert M. Kaplan (Not admitted in PA)
Andrew J. Gallogly
Marc B. Zingarini
William B. Hildebrand
Richard J. Margolis
Glenn A. Ricketti
Michael J. Cawley
Anne E. Pedersen
Kenneth J. Sylvester (Resident, Westmont, New Jersey Office)
Colleen M. Ready (Resident, Westmont, New Jersey Office)
Richard T. Smith (Resident, Westmont, New Jersey Office)
H. Marc Tepper
James B. Dougherty, Jr.
Carol Ann Murphy
Janis L. Wilson

Nancy H. Resnick
Eric J. Daniel (Resident, Westmont, New Jersey Office)
R. Barry Strosnider (Resident, Westmont, New Jersey Office)
Elit R. Felix, II
James M. Prahler
Michael G. Conroy
David F. Luvara (Resident, Westmont, New Jersey Office)
James F. Wiley, III
Lawrence J. Bunis
Kevin R. Dochney (Resident, Westmont, New Jersey Office)
Peter D. Bludman
Lisa B. Flickstein
Barbara A. Thomas
Hiliary L. Remick
Mary C. Cunnane
Deborah L. Doyle
Sandra R. Craig
Debra S. Goodman
Timothy J. McCuen
Marilyn A. Della Badia
Dawn Dezii (Resident, Westmont, New Jersey Office)
John C. Farrell
Lila Wynne Williams (Resident, Westmont, New Jersey Office)
Emily H. Armstrong (Not admitted in PA; Resident, Westmont, New Jersey Office)
Donald Caruthers III (Resident, Westmont, New Jersey Office)
Jean M. Hadley
Mark A. Minicozzi
Robert D. MacMahon
Hilary Suzanne Cornell
Marie Sambor Reilly
Jill Innamorato
Michael L. Simonini (Resident, Westmont, New Jersey Office)
Peter S. Cuddihy (Resident, Westmont, New Jersey Office)
Elizabeth Horneff
Robert D. Shapiro
Sandhya M. Feltes
Kevin S. Riechelson
Jennifer A. Mullen (Resident, Westmont, New Jersey Office)
Tracy A. Tefankjian
Frank A. LaSalvia (Resident, Westmont, New Jersey Office)
James A. Tamburro (Resident, Westmont, New Jersey Office)
Laurie Harrold Rizzo (Resident, Westmont, New Jersey Office)
Stuart L. Berman
John D. Pallante
Timothy E. Games
Frank A. DiGiacomo (Resident, Westmont, New Jersey Office)
Frederic Roller
Vincent A. Vietti
Jill A. Maslynsky
Johanna E. Markind
James P. Paoli (Resident, Westmont, New Jersey Office)

(*See Next Column*)

Diana Brilliant
Thomas P. Donnelly
Andrea M. Jenkins
Karen E. Model
Dawn S. Osman
Scott I. Feldman
Stephen P. Yuhas (Resident, Westmont, New Jersey Office)

COUNSEL TO THE FIRM

Nathan L. Edelstein

OF COUNSEL

Michael A. Orlando (Not admitted in PA; Resident, Westmont, New Jersey Office)

For full biographical listings, see the Martindale-Hubbell Law Directory

ALFRED MARROLETTI AND ASSOCIATES (AV)

The Graham Building-Suite 1504, One Penn Square West 30 S. 15th Street, 19102
Telephone: 215-563-0400

ASSOCIATES

Jacob N. Snyder
Joseph A. Marroletti

For full biographical listings, see the Martindale-Hubbell Law Directory

MARSHALL, DENNEHEY, WARNER, COLEMAN AND GOGGIN (AV)

1845 Walnut Street, 19103-4717
Telephone: 215-575-2600
Cable Address: "Marshall"
Telecopier: 215-575-0856; 575-0857; 575-0858; 575-0859; 575-0860; 575-0861
Allentown Pennsylvania Office: 640 Hamilton Mall.
Telephone: 215-776-7500.
Telecopier: 215-776-7994.
Doylestown, Pennsylvania Office: Suite 300, 20 East Court Street.
Telephone: 215-348-1611.
Telecopier: 215-348-5439.
Harrisburg, Pennsylvania Office: 100 Pine Street, Suite 400.
Telephone: 717-232-1022.
Telecopier: 717-232-1849.
Lancaster, Pennsylvania Office: Cipher Building, Second Floor, 36 East King Street.
Telephone: 717-399-1845.
Telecopier: 717-399-1853.
Media, Pennsylvania Office: 200 East State Street.
Telephone: 215-892-8700.
Telecopier: 215-892-8730.
Norristown, Pennsylvania Office: Suite 1002, One Montgomery Plaza.
Telephone: 215-292-4440.
Telecopier: 215-292-0410.
Pittsburgh, Pennsylvania Office: 600 Grant Street, USX Tower, Suite 2900.
Telephone: 412-394-4090.
Telecopier: 412-394-4095.
Scranton, Pennsylvania Office: Scranton Electric Building, 507 Linden Street, Suite 800.
Telephone: 717-342-1999.
Telecopier: 717-342-4999.
West Chester, Pennsylvania Office: The Atrium Building, 17 West Gay Street.
Telephone: 215-431-4100.
Telecopier: 215-431-4522.
Williamsport, Pennsylvania Office: One Executive Plaza, 330 Pine Street.
Telephone: 717-326-5507.
Fax: 717-326-5507.
Marlton, New Jersey Office: Suite 304, Three Greentree Centre.
Telephone: 609-985-3900.
Telecopier: 609-985-3934.
Roseland, New Jersey Office: 5 Becker Farm Road, 280 Corporate Center.
Telephone: 201-994-0303.
Telecopier: 201994-1965.

MEMBERS OF FIRM
LISTED ALPHABETICALLY

Paul A. Bechtel, Jr.
Ralph P. Bocchino
Thomas R. Bond
Wendy Johnston Bracaglia
Paul R. Brady, III
Thomas A. Brophy (Resident, Norristown Office)
Edward R. Carpenter, Jr.
John J. Coffey
Robert J. Coleman
Charles W. Craven
Michael P. Creedon
Joseph W. Cunningham (Resident, Doylestown Office)
Barbara A. DeAntonio (Resident, Allentown Office)
Thomas C. DeLorenzo
Lisa D. Eldridge
Thomas K. Ellixson (Resident, Norristown Office)
Joseph L. Feliciani (Resident, Allentown Office)
Dominick Fiorello (Resident, Marlton, New Jersey Office)
William L. Foley, Jr. (Resident, West Chester Office)
M. Scott Gemberling (Resident, Media and West Chester Offices)
Robert St. Leger Goggin
Mitchell I. Golding
Richard L. Goldstein (Resident, Marlton, New Jersey Office)
Hiliary H. Holloway
Niki T. Ingram
Audrey L. Jacobsen
John D. Kearney
Richard A. Kraemer
Kathleen M. Kramer
Michael J. McCadden
Ralph A. Michetti (Resident, Doylestown Office)
Peter S. Miller
R. Bruce Morrison

(*See Next Column*)

MARSHALL, DENNEHEY, WARNER, COLEMAN AND GOGGIN, *Philadelphia—Continued*

MEMBERS OF FIRM
LISTED ALPHABETICALLY (Continued)

John P. Penders
James E. Pocius (Resident, Scranton Office)
Vincent P. Reilly
John R. Riddell (Resident, Media Office)
Daniel J. Ryan, Jr.
Joseph J. Santarone, Jr. (Resident, Norristown Office)
Daniel J. Sherry
Paul A. Snyder (Resident, Marlton, New Jersey Office)
Paul V. Tatlow
Steven C. Tolliver
Philip B. Toran
John S. Tucci, Jr.
Joseph McCabe Walker (Resident, Doylestown Office)
John R. Warner (Resident, Norristown Office)
Kimberley J. Woodie

ASSOCIATES
LISTED ALPHABETICALLY

Laura Lubow Altman
William Lance Banton, Jr.
Thomas B. Bate, Jr. (Resident, Marlton, New Jersey Office)
Lawrence B. Berg (Not admitted in PA; Resident, Marlton, New Jersey Office)
Marcia E. Berry (Resident, Norristown Office)
Sean Robert Blake (Resident, Norristown Office)
Christine Mooney Brenner
Jacqueline H. Canter
Joseph M. Caputo (Resident, Scranton Office)
Jeffrey J. Chomko (Resident, Doylestown Office)
Maureen E. Cleary
Cathy Marie Cosgrove
Brian C. Darreff (Resident, Marlton, New Jersey Office)
Barbara J. Davis (Resident, Marlton, New Jersey Office)
Andrew W. Davitt
Daniel V. DiLoretto
Christopher E. Dougherty (Resident, Norristown Office)
Howard P. Dwoskin
Joseph A. Dych (Resident, Media Office)
Mary T. Fox
Elizabeth M. Gallagher (Resident, Marlton, New Jersey Office)
James F. Graham
Daniel A. Griffith (Resident, Marlton, New Jersey Office)
Suzanne H. Gross
Mark John Gulasarian (Resident, West Chester Office)
John N. Hernick
Michelle Tiger Heyman
Walter J. Klekotka (Resident, Marlton, New Jersey Office)
Mary Bernadette Lipinski
Howard Mankoff (Not admitted in PA; Resident, Roseland, New Jersey Office)
Joseph A. Manning (Resident, Roseland, New Jersey Office)
Victoria S. Maranzini
Deborah A. Mattei (Resident, Allentown Office)
Kathleen S. McGrath (Resident, Norristown Office)
Michelle Leigh Morgan (Resident, Norristown Office)
Lynne Nina Nahmani (Resident, Norristown Office)
Demetrius J. Parrish, Jr.
James F. Pearn, Jr.
Juliana Marie Petito
Michele R. Punturi
Conrad J. J. Radcliffe
Bradley D. Remick
Mark T. Riley (Resident, Media Office)
Robin M. Romano
Jay S. Rothman
Joseph D. Sams (Resident, Marlton, New Jersey Office)
Kathleen A. Smith
L. Rostaing Tharaud
Joseph L. Vender (Resident, Scranton Office)
Louise Ann Watson (Resident, Marlton, New Jersey Office)
Francis X. Wickersham (Resident, Norristown Office)
Stacy L. Wilson (Resident, Lancaster Office)
Michael Blaine Wolfe (Resident, Harrisburg Office)

RETIRED PARTNERS
LISTED ALPHABETICALLY

Gerald A. Dennehey
Francis E. Marshall

Representative Clients: American Mutual Insurance Co.; Chubb & Sons; Crum & Foster; Guaranty National Insurance Co.; Harris Corp.; Honda Corp.; of America; Manville Corp.; Marriot Corp.; 3-M Co.; St. Paul Insurance Co.

For Complete List of Firm Personnel, See General Section

For full biographical listings, see the Martindale-Hubbell Law Directory

MATTIONI, MATTIONI & MATTIONI, LTD. (AV)

399 Market Street, 2nd Floor, 19106
Telephone: 215-629-1600
Cable Address: "Mattioni"
TWX: 710-670-1373
Fax: 215-923-2 227
Westmont, New Jersey Office: Suite 502 Sentry Office Plaza, 216 Haddon Avenue, 08108.
Telephone: 609-772-0098.

Dante Mattioni
Faustino Mattioni
John Mattioni
Blasco Mattioni *
Eugene Mattioni
Kenneth M. Giannantonio
Francis X. Kelly
George R. Zacharkow
Andrew H. Quinn
Eva Helena Bleich
Robert W. Weidner, Jr.
Scott J. Schwarz
Stephen M. Martin
Robert R. Hyde
Bruce A. O'Neill
John J. Sellinger
Stephen J. Galati
Anthony Granato
Kristi L. Treadway
Philip J. Ford

(See Next Column)

Joseph F. Bouvier
Michael Mattioni
John E. Minihan
Alan Mattioni
Louis J. Apoldo
Joseph P. Corcoran III
Scott William Barton
Heather A. Cicalese
Frank Carano *

LEGAL SUPPORT PERSONNEL
PARALEGALS

Rosaria Tesauro
Carmela Valeno
Tracey L. Smith
Andrea L. D'Alessandro
Linda A. Morris
Karen L. Knauss

*Counsel to the Firm

For full biographical listings, see the Martindale-Hubbell Law Directory

MCKISSOCK & HOFFMAN, P.C. (AV)

1700 Market Street, Suite 3000, 19103
Telephone: 215-246-2100
Fax: 215-246-2144
Mount Holly, New Jersey Office: 211 High Street.
Telephone: 609-267-1006.
Doylestown, Pennsylvania Office: 77 North Broad Street, Second Floor.
Telephone: 215-345-4501.
Harrisburg, Pennsylvania Office: 127 State Street.
Telephone: 717-234-0103.

J. Bruce McKissock
Peter J. Hoffman
Richard L. McMonigle
Jill Baratz Clarke
Marybeth Stanton Christiansen
Catherine Hill Kunda
Bryant Craig Black (Resident, Harrisburg, Office)
John M. Willis
John J. McGrath
Debra Schwaderer Dunne
Donald J. Brooks, Jr.
William J. Mundy
Elizabeth E. Davies
Christopher Thomson
Kathleen M. Kenna
K. Reed Haywood
Sara J. Thomson
Maureen P. Fitzgerald
Veronica E. Noonan
Kathleen M. Sholette
Patricia D. Shippee

For full biographical listings, see the Martindale-Hubbell Law Directory

MCWILLIAMS AND MINTZER, P.C. (AV)

Eight Penn Center, 20th Floor, 1628 John F. Kennedy Boulevard, 19103-2708
Telephone: 215-981-1060
Fax: 215-981-0133

Edward C. Mintzer, Jr.
Anthony F. Zabicki, Jr.
Kenneth D. Powell, Jr.

OF COUNSEL

Daniel T. McWilliams

Patrick S. Mintzer
John Michael Skrocki
Patricia A. Powell
Regina Spause McGraw

LEGAL SUPPORT PERSONNEL

Frances Kelly McCaffery

Representative Clients: Pennsylvania Hospital Insurance Co.; Frankford Hospital & Health Care Systems; Thomas Jefferson University Hospital; Princeton Insurance Co.; Pawtucket Insurance Co.; Medical Inter-Insurance Exchange; Medical Protective Co.; ITT Hartford; Common of Pennsylvania Medical Professional Liability Catastrophe Loss Fund.

For full biographical listings, see the Martindale-Hubbell Law Directory

C. GEORGE MILNER, ESQ. A PROFESSIONAL CORPORATION (AV)

The Atrium, Fourth Floor, 1900 Market Street, 19103
Telephone: 215-557-7944
Fax: 215-665-2013

C. George Milner

For full biographical listings, see the Martindale-Hubbell Law Directory

MYLOTTE, DAVID & FITZPATRICK (AV)

7 Penn Center, 1635 Market Street, 13th Floor, 19103
Telephone: 215-751-9450
Facsimile: 215-751-9918
Westmont, New Jersey Office: 216 Haddon Avenue, Suite 523.
Telephone: 609-858-3322.
Wilkes-Barre, Pennsylvania Office: Bicentennial Building, Suite 200, 15 Public Square.
Telephone: 717-824-7739.
Hazleton, Pennsylvania Office: 67 North Church Street.
Telephone: 717-454-5575.

MEMBERS OF FIRM

Joseph P. Mylotte (1939-1991)
Edward J. David
Charles A. Fitzpatrick, III
John A. Fitzpatrick
Grahame P. Richards, Jr.
Robert J. Gillespie, Jr. (Resident, Wilkes-Barre Office)
John C. Janos

(See Next Column)

MYLOTTE, DAVID & FITZPATRICK—*Continued*

MEMBERS OF FIRM (Continued)

Joseph R. Ferdinand (Resident, Hazleton Office)
Daniel A. Miscavige (Resident, Hazleton Office)
William C. McGovern
Harry T. Mondoil
Bruce K. Anders (Resident, Wilkes-Barre Office)
Martin G. Malloy
Fredrick C. Hanselmann
Christine F. McCafferty
Joseph R. Baranko, Jr. (Resident, Hazleton Office)
Patrice S. O'Brien
Arthur B. Keppel
M. Susan Riley
Edward J. McCarthy
Brian J. Durkin
Kathleen Daily Mock
Peter P. O'Donnell (Resident, Wilkes-Berre Office)
Eric T. Bielawski
Edward J. Devine
James Larosa
Cynthia M. Funaro
Joseph Zola (Resident, Wilkes-Barre Office)
Martin N. Chitjian

Representative Clients: Aetna Casualty and Surety Co.; Alexis; Clover Stores; PENJERDEL Stores Mutual Assn.; Strawbridge & Clothier; Travelers Insurance Co.

For full biographical listings, see the Martindale-Hubbell Law Directory

NEMEROFF, ROBERTS & SAFFREN, A PROFESSIONAL CORPORATION (AV)

260 South Broad Street, 19102
Telephone: 215-790-9750
Elkins Park, Pennsylvania Office: Suite 104, 7848 Old York Road.
Telephone: 215-635-8980.

Milton A. Nemeroff
Lawrence J. Roberts
Kenneth S. Saffren

For full biographical listings, see the Martindale-Hubbell Law Directory

OMINSKY, WELSH & STEINBERG, P.C. (AV)

1760 Market Street, 10th Floor, 19103-4129
Telephone: 215-568-4500
Fax: 215-751-9005
Bridgeport, Pennsylvania Office: 408 East Fourth Street.
Telephone: 215-270-9600.
FAX: 215-270-9990.

Albert Ominsky
Barney B. Welsh
Lennard B. Steinberg
David M. Giles
Joseph L. Messa, Jr.
Mark W. Tanner
Glenn F. Gilman

OF COUNSEL

Jack A. Meyerson
Joel I. Fishbein
Thomas W. Sheridan

PALMER BIEZUP & HENDERSON (AV)

Suite 956 Public Ledger Building, 620 Chestnut Street Independence Mall West, 19106-3409
Telephone: 215-625-9900
Cable Address: "Palmbee" Phila
Telex: ITT: 476-1102
FAX: 215-625-0185
New York, New York Office: 53 Wall Street, 10005.
Telephone: 212-406-1855.
Fax: 215-625-0185.
Telex: ITT 476-1102.
Wilmington, Delaware Office: 1223 Foulk Road, 19803.
Telephone: 302-594-0895.
Fax: 215-625-0185.
Telex: ITT 476-1102.
Camden, New Jersey Office: 211 North 5th Street. 08102-1203.
Telephone: 609-428-7717.
Fax: 215-625-0185.
Telex: ITT 476-1102.

MEMBERS OF FIRM

Richard W. Palmer
J. Welles Henderson
Raul Betancourt
Alfred J. Kuffler
Michael B. McCauley
Stephen M. Calder
Richard Q. Whelan
Timothy J. Abeel
Frank P. De Giulio
Kevin G. O'Donovan

David P. Thompson
Gary Francis Seitz
Richard C. Mason
Richard S. Tweedie
Peter J. Williams
Betsy A. Stone
Jon Michael Dumont
Lawrence D. Jackson
James J. Musial
Kevin Haney
Thomas P. Mundy
Paul D. Rowe, Jr.

COUNSEL

Raymond T. Letulle
H. Coleman Switkay

For full biographical listings, see the Martindale-Hubbell Law Directory

POST & SCHELL, P.C. (AV)

19th Floor, 1800 J. F. K. Boulevard, 19103
Telephone: 215-587-1000
Fax: 215-587-1444
Allentown, Pennsylvania Office: 801 Hamilton Mall, 4th Floor.
Telephone: 215-433-0193.
Lancaster, Pennsylvania Office: 237 North Prince Street.
Telephone: 717-291-4532.
Harrisburg, Pennsylvania Office: 101 North Front Street.
Telephone: 717-232-5931.
Voorhees, New Jersey Office: Law Firm of Stanley P. Stahl, Adams Place, Suite 3, 701 White Horse Road.
Telephone: 609-627-8900.

Robert M. Britton
Arthur M. Toensmeier
Adrian R. King
David E. Faust
William F. Sutton (Managing Partner)
F. Evan Black (Resident, Harrisburg, Pennsylvania Office)
Stanley P. Stahl
Kenneth F. DeMarco
Israel N. Eisenberg
Brian M. Peters
Kenwyn M. Dougherty (Managing Partner)
John R. Sparks, Jr.
Alfred J. Johnston
Allan C. Molotsky
Sharon M. Reiss
Colin M. Vroome
Patrice A. Toland
George M. Nace, III (Resident, Allentown, Pennsylvania Office)
John W. Potkai
Joseph F. McNulty, Jr.
C. Andre Washington
Nancy A. Nolan
Stephen T. Potako
Donald N. Camhi
Kathleen M. Chancler
Barbara S. Magen
Beth A. Wright (Resident, Voorhees, New Jersey Office)
Patrick T. Cusick (Resident, Lancaster, Pennsylvania Office)
Dominic A. DeLaurentis, Jr. (Resident, Voorhees, New Jersey Office)
Benjamin A. Post
Peter M. Harrison
Sarah E. Reese
Daniel S. Altschuler
Paul W. Grego (Resident, Harrisburg, Pennsylvania Office)

Barbara Ann Dalvano
Robin W. Fisher
Lois M. Shenk
Abbie R. Newman
Barbara L. Young
Deborah L. Hartwell
Susan Ellis Wild (Resident, Allentown, Pennsylvania Office)
Alexander J. Palutis (Resident, Harrisburg, Pennsylvania Office)
David P. Brigham
Jonathan B. Sprague
Sharon K. Galpern (Resident, Voorhees, New Jersey Office)
Joseph G. Zack
J. Michael Doyle
John Gilbert
Joseph R. Fowler
David L. Gordon
Joseph G. Muzic (Resident, Lancaster, Pennsylvania Office)
Maureen A. Mirabella
Michael A. Vanasse (Resident, Lancaster, Pennsylvania Office)
John E. Marquis
Marcia Stander Freedman (Resident, Voorhees, New Jersey Office)
Francis P. Fitzsimmons (Resident, Lancaster, Pennsylvania Office)
Carolyn B. Sollecito
Kathleen D. Foley
Sidney R. Steinberg
Charles F. McElwee (Resident, Harrisburg Office)
Mark L. Mattioli
Audrey King Beach (Resident, Allentown, Pennsylvania Office)
Celeste R. Pisano
Joseph J. McAlee
Sandra K. Sacks
Patrick K. McCoyd
Cynthia Silas Evans (Resident, Allentown, Pennsylvania Office)
Andrew J. Connolly
Barbara A. Berry
William A. Kovalcik (Resident, Lancaster, Pennsylvania Office)
David R. Kunz
Theresa Knight N'Jai
Timothy Braden Kiser
Geoffrey D. Lawrence
Geoffrey William Dlin (Resident, Allentown, Pennsylvania Office)
Robert D. Brown (Resident, Voorhees, New Jersey Office)
Robert P. Di Domenicis
Richard N. Held
Michael R. Nelson
Kristen L. Beech (Resident, Harrisburg, Pennsylvania Office)
Samuel J. Thomas
Carol M. Cowhey
Douglas A. Brockman
Sheila A. Haren
Joseph McAleer
Amy E. Mays (Resident, Lancaster, Pennsylvania Office)
Howard J. Burk
Ann M. Hassenfratz
Thomas A. Berman
D. Holbrook Duer (Resident, Lancaster, Pennsylvania Office)
Martin S. Coleman
Timothy F. Coffey
Ann Marie Burke (Resident, Lancaster, Pennsylvania Office)
James J. Dodd-o (Resident, Allentown, Pennsylvania Office)
Patrick C. Askin
Christopher G. Piersza
Kathleen M. Granahan
Adrian R. King, Jr.
Leah B. Perry
Perry D. Merlo (Resident, Harrisburg, Pennsylvania Office)
John C. Devine (Resident, Harrisburg, Pennsylvania Office)
Gail P. Steinberg

(See Next Column)

POST & SCHELL P.C., *Philadelphia—Continued*

Carolyn Reinhard Sleeper (Resident, Voorhees, New Jersey Office)
Kimberly A. Cummings
Mary K. McCabe
Christopher P. Seerveld
Colin Kelly Lydon (Resident, Harrisburg, Pennsylvania Office)
Paula S. Silverstein
Mindy Levin Feldstein
Kenneth T. Levine
Gillian T. Bozik (Resident, Allentown, Pennsylvania Office)
Rebecca L. Dillon (Resident, Lancaster, Pennsylvania Office)
Katherine Layman
Joseph C. Bedwick
David J. Urban
Margret MacGaffey Hagar

OF COUNSEL

Nathan Hershey
Albert J. Schell, Jr.
Barton L. Post
Wendy Cherner Maneval

For full biographical listings, see the Martindale-Hubbell Law Directory

LAWRENCE S. ROSENWALD, P.C. (AV)

Suite 3901, Mellon Bank Center, 1735 Market Street, 19103-7501
Telephone: 215-994-1401
Fax: 215-994-1410

Lawrence S. Rosenwald

OF COUNSEL

Peter A. Galante
Gary M. Friedland

LEGAL SUPPORT PERSONNEL

Gretchen A. Anderson

Representative Clients: Hobart Corp.; Simkar Manufacturing; Magnetek General Neon Equipment Co.; Siemens Corp.; Philadelphia Redevelopment Authority; State Workmen's Compensation Insurance; LVI Environmental; LCOR.

For full biographical listings, see the Martindale-Hubbell Law Directory

THOMAS B. RUTTER, LTD. (AV)

Suite 750 The Curtis Center, Independence Square West, 19106
Telephone: 215-925-9200
Fax: 215-928-1669

Thomas B. Rutter

Joseph D. Cronin
Lori E. Zeid

For full biographical listings, see the Martindale-Hubbell Law Directory

SAMUEL AND BALLARD, A PROFESSIONAL CORPORATION (AV)

225 South 15th Street, Suite 1700, 19102
Telephone: 215-893-9990

Ralph David Samuel
Alice W. Ballard

OF COUNSEL

Babette Josephs

Shari Reed
Lynn Malmgren

For full biographical listings, see the Martindale-Hubbell Law Directory

SAVETT FRUTKIN PODELL & RYAN, P.C. (AV)

Suite 508, 320 Walnut Street, 19106
Telephone: 215-923-5400
FAX: 923-9353

Stuart H. Savett
Robert P. Frutkin
Barbara Anne Podell
Katharine M. Ryan

For full biographical listings, see the Martindale-Hubbell Law Directory

SCHWARTZ & BLACKMAN (AV)

Washington West Building, 235 South 8th Street, 19106-3593
Telephone: 215-925-5800
Fax: 215-925-1590
Cherry Hill, New Jersey Office: Suite 304, 1101 King Highway North.
Telephone: 609-482-1112.

Stacey L. Schwartz
Philip L. Blackman

Representative Clients: A.B. Dick Co.; Health Business Systems; Shotz, Miller & Glusman; American Mortgage Investment Corp./Suburban Financial Services; Phoenix Technologies, Inc.

For full biographical listings, see the Martindale-Hubbell Law Directory

JAMES C. SCHWARTZMAN & ASSOCIATES (AV)

The Widener Building, 1337 Chestnut Street, Seventeenth Floor, 19107
Telephone: 215-563-2233
Fax: 215-563-2134

Francine D. Wilensky

For full biographical listings, see the Martindale-Hubbell Law Directory

SHINGLES & CAPPELLI (AV)

Suite 785, The Philadelphia Bourse, 21 South Fifth Street, 19106
Telephone: 215-238-9305
Fax: 215-625-9292

MEMBERS OF FIRM

Stanley M. Shingles
Joseph J. Cappelli

For full biographical listings, see the Martindale-Hubbell Law Directory

SPECTOR GADON & ROSEN, ATTORNEYS AT LAW, P.C. (AV)

29th Floor, 1700 Market Street, 19103-3913
Telephone: 215-241-8888
Fax: 215-241-8844
Moorestown, New Jersey Office: Spector, Gadon & Rosen, P.C. 307 Fellowship Road. P.O. Box 550.
Telephone: 609-778-8100.
Fax: 609-722-5344.

Paul R. Rosen
Steven F. Gadon
Samuel L. Hirshland
Edward G. Fitzgerald, Jr.
Albert E. Janke, Jr.
Lary I. Zucker
James B. Kozloff
Niels Korup
Daniel J. Dugan
Alan H. Wallen

OF COUNSEL

Sanders D. Newman
Sidney Margulies

Leslie Beth Baskin
Jill M. Bellak
Debra Malone Berger
Christopher P. Flannery (Not admitted in PA)
Shona K. Gibson
Amy B. Goldstein
Jeffrey M. Goldstein
Robert L. Grundlock, Jr.
Jane E. Herman (Not admitted in PA)
Stanley Peter Jaskiewicz
Kenneth J. LaFiandra
Marilou Lombardi
Brooke Caroline Madonna
P. Dara Marcozzi
Bruce S. Marks
Ann Miller
Frank J. Perch, III
Steven J. Polansky
George M. Vinci, Jr.

For full biographical listings, see the Martindale-Hubbell Law Directory

SARAH M. THOMPSON (AV)

1710 Spruce Street, 19103
Telephone: 215-790-4568
Fax: 215-735-2211

For full biographical listings, see the Martindale-Hubbell Law Directory

TURNER & MCDONALD, P.C. (AV)

1708 Locust Street, 19103
Telephone: 215-546-9700
Facsimile: 215-546-9712
Haverford, Pennsylvania Office: 355 Lancaster Avenue.
Telephone: 610-649-9600.
Haddonfield, New Jersey Office: 209 Haddon Avenue.
Telephone: 609-429-6022.
Fax: 609-429-0074.

Alan A. Turner
H. Graham McDonald

OF COUNSEL

Thomas B. Rutter
Steven R. Kanes

For full biographical listings, see the Martindale-Hubbell Law Directory

ZARWIN, BAUM, DEVITO, KAPLAN & O'DONNELL, P.C. (AV)

Suite 700 Four Penn Center Plaza, 1616 John F. Kennedy Boulevard, 19103-2588
Telephone: 215-569-2800
Fax: 215-569-1606
Audubon, New Jersey Office: 510 White Horse Pike.
Telephone: 609-547-7555.

Norman P. Zarwin
E. Harris Baum
John R. O'Donnell
Mitchell S. Kaplan
Gary A. DeVito
Theodore M. Schaer
Lionel A. Prince

Lisa B. Wershaw
Gary Alan Zlotnick
Joseph M. Toddy
Kenneth J. Fleisher
Jane Griffin Malaspina
Edward J. McKenna
Adam M. Soll
Ronald N. Lebovits
Robert H. Prince

For full biographical listings, see the Martindale-Hubbell Law Directory

*PITTSBURGH,** Allegheny Co.

ADERSON, FRANK & STEINER, A PROFESSIONAL CORPORATION (AV)

2320 Grant Building, 15219
Telephone: 412-263-0500
Fax: 412-263-0565

Sanford M. Aderson
Mark S. Frank
Bruce F. Rudoy
Richard H. Malmstrom

For full biographical listings, see the Martindale-Hubbell Law Directory

ANSTANDIG, LEVICOFF & McDYER, A PROFESSIONAL CORPORATION (AV)

600 Gulf Tower, 15219
Telephone: 412-765-3700
Fax: 412-765-3730
Beckley, West Virgina Office: Brown, Levicoff & McDyer. 311 Prince Street. P.O. Drawer M.
Telephone: 304-253-3700.

Louis Anstandig
Avrum Levicoff
Daniel P. McDyer
Timothy J. Burdette
Edward A. Yurcon
James Michael Brown (Resident, Beckley, West Virginia Office)
Alan T. Silko

Paul G. Mayer, Jr.
Philip M.P. Buttenfield
Stephen J. Poljak
Eileen Anstandig Ziemke
William M. Adams
Elizabeth E. Deemer
Bryan J. Smith
Tracey A. Jordan
Jane E. Harkins (Resident, Beckley, West Virginia Office)
Mark A. Serge
James D. Stacy (Resident, Beckley, West Virginia Office)
R. Bruce Carlson

For full biographical listings, see the Martindale-Hubbell Law Directory

BALZARINI, CAREY & WATSON (AV)

3303 Grant Building, 15219
Telephone: 412-471-1200
Fax: 412-471-8326

MEMBERS OF FIRM

Edward J. Balzarini
Francis J. Carey
Edward J. Balzarini, Jr.
David J. Watson
Michael Balzarini
Joseph S. Bielecki

For full biographical listings, see the Martindale-Hubbell Law Directory

BRENNAN, ROBINS & DALEY (AV)

Fort Pitt Commons, Suite 500, 445 Fort Pitt Boulevard, 15219-1322
Telephone: 412-281-0776
Fax: 412-281-2180

PARTNERS

John Daley
Arnold M. Epstein

ASSOCIATES

Michael T. Collis
Catherine L. Waggle
John Daley, Jr.

For full biographical listings, see the Martindale-Hubbell Law Directory

BUCHANAN INGERSOLL, PROFESSIONAL CORPORATION (AV)

5800 USX Tower, 600 Grant Street, 15219
Telephone: 412-562-8800
Telecopier: 412-562-1041
Philadelphia, Pennsylvania Office: Two Logan Square, Twelfth Floor, 18th & Arch Streets.
Telephone: 215-665-8700.
Harrisburg, Pennsylvania Office: Vartan Parc, 30 North Third Street.
Telephone: 717-237-4800.
Tampa, Florida Office: 101 East Kennedy Boulevard, Suite 1030.
Telephone: 813-222-8180.
North Miami Beach, Florida Office: 19495 Biscayne Boulevard.
Telephone: 305-933-5600.
Lexington, Kentucky Office: 1210 Vine Center Office Tower, 333 West Vine Street.
Telephone: 606-225-5333.
Princeton, New Jersey Office: Buchanan Ingersoll, A Partnership, College Centre, 500 College Road East.
Telephone: 609-452-2666.

Richard J. Antonelli
George P. Baier
Samuel W. Braver
Ronald W. Crouch
Melanie DiPietro, S.C.
David B. Fawcett III
Mark Raymond Hornak
Paul D. Kruper
Deborah A. Little
Leonard J. Marsico
Pamela A. McCallum
John J. McLean, Jr.
James D. Morton
Wendelynne J. Newton
P. Jerome Richey
Arthur J. Schwab

(See Next Column)

Thomas L. VanKirk
Jacques M. Wood
Stanley Yorsz
R. Dell Ziegler

SENIOR ATTORNEY

Karen Shichman Crawford

Jeffrey J. Bresch
John M. Cerilli
Paul J. Corrado
George H. Crompton
Virginia A. DeMarco
Daniel H. Glasser
Anthony James Guida Jr.
Susan Kircher
Stanley Joel Parker
Mark T. Phillis
Lisa G. Silverman
Joseph S. Sisca
Patricia L. Wozniak

OF COUNSEL

Alexander Black

For Complete List of Firm Personnel, See General Section

For full biographical listings, see the Martindale-Hubbell Law Directory

ROBERT A. COHEN (AV)

819 Frick Building, 15219
Telephone: 412-261-9700

For full biographical listings, see the Martindale-Hubbell Law Directory

JOSEPH WM. CONWAY (AV)

2350 One PPG Place, 15222
Telephone: 412-471-8300
Fax: 412-263-6730
Reference: Integra Bank/North.

For full biographical listings, see the Martindale-Hubbell Law Directory

DAVIES McFARLAND & CARROLL, P.C. (AV)

One Gateway Center, Tenth Floor, 15222
Telephone: 412-281-0737

Ralph A. Davies
Gregg P. Otto
Edward A. McFarland
Daniel P. Carroll
William D. Geiger
Francis Garger
Lynn E. Bell
David S. Smith
James M. Poerio

C. Robert Keenan, III
David E. Lamm
Donna M. Lowman
Christopher Pierson
William S. Evans
Keith M. Hoffman
Lisa M. Montarti
Robert P. Walter

Representative Clients: The BOC Group; Continental Insurance Co.; The Goodyear Tire & Rubber Co.; Hobart Brothers Company; LTV Steel Co.; Medical Protective Co.; Motorists Insurance Cos.; Teledyne, Inc.; The Travelers Insurance Co.

For full biographical listings, see the Martindale-Hubbell Law Directory

DeFOREST & KOSCELNIK (AV)

3000 Koppers Building, 436 Seventh Avenue, 15219
Telephone: 412-227-3100
Fax: 412-227-3130

Walter P. DeForest, III
Jacqueline A. Koscelnik

Representative Clients: Carnegie Mellon University; Blue Cross of Western Pennsylvania; Ohio Valley Medical Center; Cox Enterprises, Inc.; Shamrock Broadcasting, Inc.; General Electric Co.

For full biographical listings, see the Martindale-Hubbell Law Directory

DICKIE, McCAMEY & CHILCOTE, A PROFESSIONAL CORPORATION (AV)

Suite 400, Two PPG Place, 15222-5402
Telephone: 412-281-7272
Fax: 412-392-5367
Wheeling, West Virginia Office: Suite 2002, 1233 Main Street, 26003-2839.
Telephone: 304-233-1022.
Facsimile: 304-233-1026.

David B. Fawcett
David J. Armstrong
Richard D. Klaber
Theodore O. Struk
Wilbur McCoy Otto
Clayton A. Sweeney
Herbert Bennett Conner
Richard S. Dorfzaun
Daniel P. Stefko
M. Richard Dunlap
Eugene F. Scanlon, Jr.
Charles W. Kenrick
John Edward Wall
James R. Miller
Paul W. Roman, Jr.
Joseph S. D. Christof, II
Stewart M. Flam
Thomas P. Lutz
J. Lawson Johnston
Stephen R. Mlinac
David M. Neuhart
George Edward McGrann
Robert W. Hastings
Robert J. Marino
Stephen M. Houghton
Larry A. Silverman
Arthur L. Schwarzwaelder
Frank M. Gianola
Leonard A. Costa, Jr.
Kenneth S. Mroz

(See Next Column)

DICKIE, MCCAMEY & CHILCOTE A PROFESSIONAL CORPORATION, *Pittsburgh—Continued*

Steven B. Larchuk
James D. Strader
Ingrid Medzius Lundberg
Frederick W. Bode, III
Jeffrey T. Wiley
Richard C. Polley
Christine A. Ward
Stephen C. Kifer
Thomas M. Fallert
Gloria N. Fuehrer
William D. Clifford
Robert G. Del Greco, Jr.
Judith Ference Olson
Edmund L. Olszewski, Jr.
Dorothy A. Davis
Richard J. Federowicz
John C. Conti
L. John Argento
David J. Obermeier
Leland P. Schermer
Peter T. Stinson
Thomas H. May
Ray F. Middleman
George Monroe Schumann

Jean McCree Simmonds
Eugene G. Berry
Anthony J. Williott
George P. Kachulis
John T. Pion
Hunter A. McGeary, Jr.
William M. Conwell
Gregory A. Gross
Joseph L. Luvara
Andrew G. Kimball
W. Alan Torrance, Jr.
Howard A. Chajson
Marcelle M. Theis
Brian T. Must
David S. Bloom
M. Suzanne McCartney
Alyson J. Kirleis
S. Jane Anderson
W. Scott Campbell
Paul S. Mazeski
Anthony J. Rash
Peter A. Santos
Eugene A. Giotto
Vincent Scaglione, Jr.
James M. Girman
Pamela Lee Leyden
Maureen Kowalski
Richard E. Lafferty
Michael F. Nerone
Christopher A. Brodman
Craig M. Lee
Christopher T. Lee
Ann Michailenko Wilson
Steven W. Zoffer
Rodger L. Puz
Edward A. Miller
Nathan D. Bailey

For Complete List of Firm Personnel, See General Section

For full biographical listings, see the Martindale-Hubbell Law Directory

FECZKO AND SEYMOUR (AV)
520 Grant Building, 15219
Telephone: 412-261-4970
Fax: Available upon Request
Bethel Park, Pennsylvania Office: 3400 South Park Road.
Telephone: 412-833-5554.

MEMBERS OF FIRM

Albert G. Feczko, Jr.
Michael J. Seymour

ASSOCIATES

Mark F. Bennett
Michael D. Seymour

Reference: Pittsburgh National Bank.

For full biographical listings, see the Martindale-Hubbell Law Directory

FELDSTEIN GRINBERG STEIN & MCKEE, A PROFESSIONAL CORPORATION (AV)
428 Boulevard of the Allies, 15219
Telephone: 412-471-0677
Fax: 412-263-6129
Elizabeth, Pennsylvania Office: 400 Second Street.
Telephone: 412-384-6111.
Wexford, Pennsylvania Office: 12300 Perry Highway.
Telephone: 412-935-5540.

Jay H. Feldstein
Stanley M. Stein
Gary M. Lang
James R. Hankle

Jeffrey B. Balicki
Craig L. Fishman
Jeffrey R. Lalama
Thomas P. McDermott
Francis C. Rapp, Jr.
Jeffrey B. Yao
Michelle S. Katz
Carol Jean Gatewood

For full biographical listings, see the Martindale-Hubbell Law Directory

GACA, MATIS & HAMILTON, A PROFESSIONAL CORPORATION (AV)
300 Four PPG Place, 15222-5404
Telephone: 412-338-4750
Fax: 412-338-4742

Giles J. Gaca
Thomas A. Matis
Mark R. Hamilton
John W. Jordan, IV
Alan S. Baum
Thomas P. McGinnis
Bernard R. Rizza
Jeffrey A. Ramaley
Stephen J. Dalesio
John Timothy Hinton, Jr.
Shawn Lynne Reed

LEGAL SUPPORT PERSONNEL

PARALEGALS

Tina M. Shanafelt
Jill M. Peterson

For full biographical listings, see the Martindale-Hubbell Law Directory

GAITENS, TUCCERI & NICHOLAS, A PROFESSIONAL CORPORATION (AV)
519 Court Place, 15219
Telephone: 412-391-6920
Fax: 412-391-1189

Larry P. Gaitens
Vincent A. Tucceri
Romel L. Nicholas

Reference: Pittsburgh National Bank.

For Complete List of Firm Personnel, See General Section

For full biographical listings, see the Martindale-Hubbell Law Directory

GILARDI & COOPER, P.A. (AV)
808 Grant Building, 15219
Telephone: 412-391-9770
Fax: 412-391-9780

Richard D. Gilardi
Thomas L. Cooper
Kevin R. Lomupo

Bruce J. Phillips
Marsha L. Cooper
Richard P. Gilardi

OF COUNSEL

Marianne Oliver

For full biographical listings, see the Martindale-Hubbell Law Directory

HAROLD GONDELMAN (AV)
The 38th Floor, One Oxford Centre, 15219
Telephone: 412-263-1833
(Also Counsel to Pietragallo, Bosick & Gordon)

For full biographical listings, see the Martindale-Hubbell Law Directory

STANLEY GREENFIELD & ASSOCIATES (AV)
Greenfield Court, 1035-37 Fifth Avenue, 15219
Telephone: 412-261-4466
Fax: 412-261-4408

Stanley W. Greenfield

Graydon R. Brewer
Martha E. Bailor
Paul G. Kay

For full biographical listings, see the Martindale-Hubbell Law Directory

WILLIAM W. GUTHRIE & ASSOCIATES A PROFESSIONAL CORPORATION (AV)
416 Frick Building, 437 Grant Street, 15219
Telephone: 412-562-0556
Fax: 412-562-5920

William W. Guthrie

Reference: Pittsburgh National Bank (Potter Office).

For full biographical listings, see the Martindale-Hubbell Law Directory

HEINTZMAN, WARREN & WISE (AV)
The 35th Floor, Gulf Tower, 707 Grant Street, 15219
Telephone: 412-394-7810
Fax: 412-263-5222

MEMBERS OF FIRM

Michael D. Heintzman
Charles S. Warren
Roger L. Wise

ASSOCIATES

Jeanine L. Fonner
Joseph R. Schaper
Kenneth F. Klanica
Diane K. Wohlfarth

For full biographical listings, see the Martindale-Hubbell Law Directory

KATARINCIC & SALMON (AV)
2600 CNG Tower, 625 Liberty Avenue, 15222
Telephone: 412-338-2900
Facsimile: 412-261-2212
Houston, Texas Office: First Interstate Bank Plaza, Suite 3170, 1000 Louisiana, 77002.
Telephone: 713-752-0010.
Fax: 713-752-0050.

Joseph A. Katarincic
Kenneth L. Salmon
Robert J. Ridge
Joseph Decker

Richard M. Smith
David N. Wecht
Michael Magee
Theodore N. Black
Kim M. Watterson
Ellen G. McGlone
Kimberly S. Kirk
Matthew H. Meade
Emily I. Miller

For full biographical listings, see the Martindale-Hubbell Law Directory

KIGER MESSER & ALPERN (AV)

1404 Grant Building, 15219
Telephone: 412-281-7200
Fax: 412-765-0440

MEMBERS OF FIRM

Jerome W. Kiger
Howard F. Messer
Charles H. Alpern

ASSOCIATE

Alice Warner Shumlas

For Complete List of Firm Personnel, See General Section

For full biographical listings, see the Martindale-Hubbell Law Directory

LITMAN LITMAN HARRIS & BROWN, P.C. (AV)

3600 One Oxford Centre, 15219
Telephone: 412-456-2000
Fax: 412-456-2020

S. David Litman, P.C.
Roslyn M. Litman
Stephen J. Harris
David R. Brown
Martha S. Helmreich
Lester G. Nauhaus
Daniel L. Chunko
Mark F. Flaherty
Joseph Leibowicz
Robert J. O'Hara, III

For full biographical listings, see the Martindale-Hubbell Law Directory

MARCUS & SHAPIRA (AV)

35th Floor, One Oxford Centre, 301 Grant Street, 15219-6401
Telephone: 412-471-3490
Telecopier: 412-391-8758

MEMBERS OF FIRM

Bernard D. Marcus
Daniel H. Shapira
George P. Slesinger
Robert L. Allman, II
Estelle F. Comay
Susan Gromis Flynn
Darlene M. Nowak
Glenn M. Olcerst
Elly Heller-Toig
Sylvester A. Beozzo

OF COUNSEL

John M. Burkoff

SPECIAL COUNSEL

Jane Campbell Moriarty

ASSOCIATES

Scott D. Livingston
Robert M. Barnes
Stephen S. Zubrow
David B. Rodes
Lori E. McMaster
Melody A. Pollock
James F. Rosenberg
Amy M. Gottlieb

For full biographical listings, see the Martindale-Hubbell Law Directory

MARKEL, SCHAFER P.C. (AV)

1120 Grant Building, 15219
Telephone: 412-281-6488
Fax: 412-281-3226

Seymour J. Schafer
Harvey I. Goldstein
Kenneth A. Eisner
Steven D. Irwin
Jacob A. Markel (1896-1976)
Myron B. Markel (1934-1988)
Gertrude F. Markel (Retired)

OF COUNSEL

Nathan Hershey

Reference: Pittsburgh National Bank.

For full biographical listings, see the Martindale-Hubbell Law Directory

FRANK MAST & ASSOCIATES (AV)

Chatham Tower Professional Suite 1-R, 15219
Telephone: 412-281-1819
Fax: 412-281-6170

For full biographical listings, see the Martindale-Hubbell Law Directory

MCCANN, GARLAND, RIDALL & BURKE (AV)

Suite 4000, 309 Smithfield Street, 15222
Telephone: 412-566-1818
Fax: 412-566-1817

MEMBERS OF FIRM

G. Gray Garland, Jr.
Edmund W. Ridall, Jr.
Edward C. Wachter, Jr.
Stephen J. Jurman
Michael J. Woodring

For Complete List of Firm Personnel, See General Section

For full biographical listings, see the Martindale-Hubbell Law Directory

RICHARD J. MILLS & ASSOCIATES (AV)

200 Benedum Trees Building, 223 Fourth Avenue, 15222-1713
Telephone: 412-471-2442
Fax: 412-471-2456

Richard J. Mills

Austin P. Henry
Dale S. Douglas

For full biographical listings, see the Martindale-Hubbell Law Directory

PIETRAGALLO, BOSICK & GORDON (AV)

The Thirty-Eighth Floor, One Oxford Centre, 15219
Telephone: 412-263-2000
Facsimile: 412-261-5295

MEMBERS OF FIRM

William Pietragallo, II
Joseph J. Bosick
Mark Gordon
John E. Hall
Spencer D. Hirshberg
Robert J. Behling
Lawrence J. Baldasare
William S. Smith
Francis E. Pipak, Jr.
LuAnn Haley
Paul K. Vey
Nora Barry Fischer
Thomas J. Sweeney, Jr.
Daniel D. Harshman
Robert E. Dapper, Jr.
David H. Dille

ASSOCIATES

Robert H. Gustine
Harry J. Klucher
Robert R. Leight
Christopher L. Wildfire
Heather S. Heidelbaugh
Eric K. Falk
James G. Orie
Stacey F. Vernallis
Mark F. Haak
Pamela G. Cochenour
William W. Schrimpf, Sr.
Michael P. Sosso
Vincent A Coppola
Clem C. Trischler, Jr.
Anthony G. Sanchez
Kenneth T. Newman
C. Peter Hitson
Raymond G. McLaughlin
David Paul Franklin
Brian S. Kane
Linda M. Gillen
Robert J. Colville
Brian K. Parker
Sean B. Epstein
Lisa P. McQuarrie

COUNSEL

Harold Gondelman
Alfred S. Pelaez

For full biographical listings, see the Martindale-Hubbell Law Directory

PLOWMAN, SPIEGEL & LEWIS, P.C. (AV)

Grant Building, Suite 925, 15219-2201
Telephone: 412-471-8521
Fax: 412-471-4481

Jack W. Plowman
John L. Spiegel
Frank J. Kernan
Clifford L. Tuttle, Jr.
Kenneth W. Lee

Marshall J. Conn
David Raves

Reference: Pittsburgh National Bank.

For Complete List of Firm Personnel, See General Section

For full biographical listings, see the Martindale-Hubbell Law Directory

RILEY, MCNULTY & HEWITT, P.C. (AV)

460 Cochran Road, 15228
Telephone: 412-341-9300
Fax: 412-341-9177

Patrick R. Riley
Sibyl S. McNulty
Patrick A. Hewitt

David E. Sweitzer

For full biographical listings, see the Martindale-Hubbell Law Directory

ROSE, SCHMIDT, HASLEY & DISALLE, P.C. (AV)

900 Oliver Building, 15222-2310
Telephone: 412-434-8600
Fax: 412-263-2829
Washington, Pennsylvania Office: 7th Floor, Millcraft Center.
Telephone: 412-228-8883.

Richard DiSalle
Edmund M. Carney
Brian W. Ashbaugh
Gail L. Gratton
Susan Hileman Malone
Carl Andrew McGhee
Keithley D. Mulvihill
Steven M. Petrikis
Kim D. Eaton
R. Stanley Mitchel

Mary J. Lynch

COUNSEL

Raymond G. Hasley

For Complete List of Firm Personnel, See General Section

For full biographical listings, see the Martindale-Hubbell Law Directory

Pittsburgh—Continued

ROTHMAN GORDON FOREMAN & GROUDINE, P.C. (AV)

Third Floor-Grant Building, 15219
Telephone: 412-338-1100
Telefax: 412-281-7304
Washington, D.C. Office: 1120 Connecticut Avenue, N.W. Suite 440.
Telephone: 202-338-3248.

James R. Farley
Ronald G. Backer
Carl E. Harvison

For Complete List of Firm Personnel, See General Section

For full biographical listings, see the Martindale-Hubbell Law Directory

SABLE, MAKOROFF & GUSKY, P.C. (AV)

7th Floor, Frick Building, 15219-6002
Telephone: 412-471-4996
Fax: 412-281-2859

Robert G. Sable
Stanley G. Makoroff
Henry Gusky
Stephen J. Laidhold
David W. Lampl
Gregg M. Rosen
F. Scott Gray
Robert J. Blumling
Amy S. Cunningham
Alan B. Gordon
David P. Pusateri
Jeffrey T. Morris
Michael McGreal
M. Scott Zegeer
Jeffrey J. Ludwikowski
Mark S. Seewald
Michael Kaminski
K. Bradley Mellor
Thomas M. Ferguson
James C. Heneghan
David A. Levine
Alan K. Sable
Maureen E. Sweeney

OF COUNSEL

Jerome M. Libenson

For full biographical listings, see the Martindale-Hubbell Law Directory

STONECIPHER, CUNNINGHAM, BEARD & SCHMITT (AV)

125 First Avenue, 15222
Telephone: 412-391-8510
Telecopier: 412-391-8522

MEMBERS OF FIRM

Charles L. Cunningham (1889-1961)
C. W. Cunningham (1916-1962)
Philip E. Beard
Joseph E. Schmitt
Roger S. Cunningham
Norman E. Gilkey

ASSOCIATES

Paul R. Rennie
George T. Snyder
Philip E. Beard, II
Nathaniel Beaumont Beard

Reference: Integra Bank of Pittsburgh

For full biographical listings, see the Martindale-Hubbell Law Directory

SWENSEN PERER & JOHNSON (AV)

Two PNC Plaza, Suite 2710, 15222
Telephone: 412-281-1970
Fax: 412-281-2808
Erie, Pennsylvania Office: 209 Court House Commons.
Telephone: 814-456-0489.

MEMBERS OF FIRM

Jan C. Swensen
Alan H. Perer
J. Alan Johnson
Peter B. Skeel
David M. Landay
John W. McCandless (Resident Partner, Erie, Pennsylvania Office)

ASSOCIATES

John Carl Bogut, Jr.
David A. Schroeder (Resident Associate, Erie, Pennsylvania Office)
John J. Edson, V
Anthony J. Sciarrino
George M. Kontos

For full biographical listings, see the Martindale-Hubbell Law Directory

TARASI & JOHNSON, P.C. (AV)

510 Third Avenue, 15219
Telephone: 412-391-7135
Fax: 412-471-2673

Louis M. Tarasi, Jr.
David E. Johnson

John A. Adamczyk
Elizabeth Tarasi Stevenson
Jean A. Kell
Matthew A. Hartley

For full biographical listings, see the Martindale-Hubbell Law Directory

THOMSON, RHODES & COWIE, P.C. (AV)

Tenth Floor, Two Chatham Center, 15219
Telephone: 412-232-3400
Fax: 412-232-3498

(See Next Column)

John David Rhodes
Norman J. Cowie
Richard E. Rush
James R. Hartline
Linton L. Moyer
John K. Heisey
David R. Johnson
Jerry R. Hogenmiller
David M. McQuiston
William James Rogers
Glenn H. Gillette

William M. Bernhart
G. Jay Habas
Mark William Furry

For Complete List of Firm Personnel, See General Section

For full biographical listings, see the Martindale-Hubbell Law Directory

THORP, REED & ARMSTRONG (AV)

One Riverfront Center, 15222
Telephone: 412-394-7711
Fax: 412-394-2555

MEMBERS OF FIRM

Kevin C. Abbott
John H. Bingler, Jr.
Michael R. Bucci, Jr.
G. Daniel Carney
Thomas W. Corbett, Jr.
John W. Eichleay, Jr.
George P. Faines
Craig E. Frischman
Scott E. Henderson
Clifford B. Levine
Thomas E. Lippard
Julie A. Maloney
Kurt A. Miller
Mark F. Nowak
Deborah P. Powell
David G. Ries
Ralph F. Scalera
Robert H. Shoop, Jr.
Randolph T. Struk
Richard I. Thomas
William M. Wycoff
C. James Zeszutek

ASSOCIATES

Paul D. Bangor, Jr.
Kimberly A. Brown
Chad A. Cicconi
Stacey L. Jarrell
Maureen P. Kelly
Elizabeth L. Rabenold
David E. White

OF COUNSEL

Charles Weiss

For Complete List of Firm Personnel, See General Section

For full biographical listings, see the Martindale-Hubbell Law Directory

TUCKER ARENSBERG, P.C. (AV)

1500 One PPG Place, 15222
Telephone: 412-566-1212
Telex: 902914
Fax: 412-594-5619
Harrisburg, Pennsylvania Office: 116 Pine Street.
Telephone: 717-238-2007.
Fax: 717-238-2242.
Pittsburgh Airport Area Office: Airport Professional Office Center, 1150 Thorn Run Road Ext., Moon Township, Pennsylvania, 15108.
Telephone: 412-262-3730.
Fax: 412-262-2576.

Linda A. Acheson
W. Theodore Brooks
Matthew J. Carl
Richard W. Cramer
J. Kent Culley
Donald P. Eriksen
Paul F. Fagan
Gary J. Gushard
William T. Harvey
Joel M. Helmrich
Gary P. Hunt
Raymond M. Komichak
Jeffrey J. Leech
Beverly Weiss Manne
Garland H. McAdoo, Jr.
Robert L. McTiernan
John B. Montgomery
Stanley V. Ostrow
William A. Penrod
Daniel J. Perry
Henry S. Pool
Richard B. Tucker, III
Bradley S. Tupi
Charles J. Vater
Gary E. Wieczorek
G. Ashley Woolridge

Robin K. Capozzi
Diane Hernon Chavis
Toni L. DiGiacobbe
Mark L. Heleen
David P. Hvizdos
Joni L. Landy
Jonathan S. McAnney
G. Ross Rhodes
Eric M. Schumann
Steven B. Silverman
Homer L. Walton

HARRISBURG OFFICE

J. Kent Culley

SPECIAL COUNSEL

Elliott W. Finkel
John P. Papuga
William J. Staley
Richard B. Tucker, Jr.

For Complete List of Firm Personnel, See General Section

For full biographical listings, see the Martindale-Hubbell Law Directory

VOLLMER RULONG & ASSOCIATES, P.C. (AV)

Suite 1212, Grant Building, 15219
Telephone: 412-391-2121
Telecopier: 412-391-3578

Charles J. Vollmer

(See Next Column)

VOLLMER RULONG & ASSOCIATES P.C.—*Continued*

John R. Keating
Roger G. Rulong, Jr.

For full biographical listings, see the Martindale-Hubbell Law Directory

VUONO, LAVELLE & GRAY (AV)

2310 Grant Building, 15219
Telephone: 412-471-1800
Fax: 412-471-4477

MEMBERS OF FIRM

John A. Vuono
William J. Lavelle
William A. Gray
Mark T. Vuono
Richard R. Wilson

ASSOCIATES

Dennis J. Kusturiss
Christine M. Dolfi
Peter J. Scanlon

Reference: Pittsburgh National Bank.

For full biographical listings, see the Martindale-Hubbell Law Directory

WEISMAN BOWEN & GROSS (AV)

310 Grant Street, Suite 420, 15219
Telephone: 412-566-2520
Fax: 412-566-1088

James L. Weisman
Alden Earl Bowen
Sanford P. Gross
Bradley S. Gelder
Barry J. Lipson
Christopher J. Klein
Laurel B. Diznoff
Robert L. Monks
Elliott I. Levenson

Reference: Pittsburgh National Bank.

For full biographical listings, see the Martindale-Hubbell Law Directory

WICK, STREIFF, MEYER, METZ & O'BOYLE, P.C. (AV)

1450 Two Chatham Center, 15219
Telephone: 412-765-1600
Telecopier: 412-261-3783

Henry M. Wick, Jr.
Charles J. Streiff
Carl F. Meyer
LeRoy L. Metz, II
David M. O'Boyle
Vincent P. Szeligo
Patricia J. Liptak-McGrail

Lucille N. Wick
Ronald Joseph Rademacher
Roger A. Isla
Donna Lynn Miller

Reference: PNC Bank.

For full biographical listings, see the Martindale-Hubbell Law Directory

WIMER LAW OFFICES, P.C. (AV)

Two Fox Chapel Place, 1326 Freeport Road, 15238
Telephone: 412-967-9111
Fax: 412-967-0178

Matthew R. Wimer

YUKEVICH, BLUME & ZANGRILLI (AV)

Sixth Floor, One Gateway Center, 15222
Telephone: 412-261-6777
Fax: 412-261-6789

MEMBERS OF FIRM

Michael Yukevich, Jr.
Peter K. Blume
Albert J. Zangrilli, Jr.

Mark Fischer

For full biographical listings, see the Martindale-Hubbell Law Directory

ZIMMER KUNZ, PROFESSIONAL CORPORATION (AV)

3300 USX Tower, 600 Grant Street, 15219
Telephone: 412-281-8000
Fax: 412-281-1765

Harry J. Zimmer
Thomas A. Lazaroff
John E. Kunz
Andrew J. Banyas, III
Raymond H. Conaway
Fred C. Trenor, II
George N. Stewart
Joni M. Mangino
Joseph W. Selep
Raymond J. Conlon
Edward K. Dixon

OF COUNSEL

John W. Thomas

(See Next Column)

Nancy DeCarlo Fabi
Dara A. DeCourcy
Alexander P. Bicket
John W. Zotter
Daniel E. Krauth
George R. Farneth, II
Anthony Carone

For Complete List of Firm Personnel, See General Section

For full biographical listings, see the Martindale-Hubbell Law Directory

PUNXSUTAWNEY, Jefferson Co.

LORENZO & KULAKOWSKI, P.C. (AV)

410 West Mahoning Street, 15767
Telephone: 814-938-6390

Nicholas F. Lorenzo, Jr.
George D. Kulakowski

Nicholas A. Gianvito

For full biographical listings, see the Martindale-Hubbell Law Directory

*READING,** Berks Co.

BINGAMAN, HESS, COBLENTZ & BELL, A PROFESSIONAL CORPORATION (AV)

660 Penn Square Center, 601 Penn Street, P.O. Box 61, 19603-0061
Telephone: 610-374-8377
Fax: 610-376-3105
Bernville, Pennsylvania Office: 331 Main Street.
Telephone: 610-488-0656.
Camden, New Jersey Office: 411 Cooper Street.
Telephone: 609-966-0117.
Fax: 609-965-0796.

James F. Bell (1921-1988)

OF COUNSEL

Llewellyn R. Bingaman
Raymond K. Hess
J. Wendell Coblentz
Ralph J. Althouse, Jr.
Gerald P. Sigal

David E. Turner
Clemson North Page, Jr.
Mark G. Yoder
Carl D. Cronrath, Jr.
Kurt Althouse
Harry D. McMunigal
Karen Feryo Longenecker
Shawn J. Lau

Lynne K. Beust
Elizabethanne D. McMunigal
Patrick T. Barrett
Susan N. Denaro
Daniel J. Poruban
Jill M. Scheidt

LEGAL SUPPORT PERSONNEL

Eric A. Barr (Office Administrator)

PARALEGALS

JoAnn Ruchlewicz
Laura I. Lehane
Louise E. Miller
Ruth Ann Sunderland
Kristine L. Krammes
Peter L. Torres

General Counsel for: Meridian Bank; Berks Products Corp.; Leighton Industries, Inc.; Utilities Employees Credit Union.
Local Counsel for: Erie Insurance Exchange; Liberty Mutual Insurance Co.; Old Guard Mutual Insurance Co.

For full biographical listings, see the Martindale-Hubbell Law Directory

RYAN, RUSSELL, OGDEN & SELTZER (AV)

1100 Berkshire Boulevard, P.O. Box 6219, 19610-0219
Telephone: 610-372-4761
Fax: 610-372-4177

Samuel B. Russell
W. Edwin Ogden
Alan Michael Seltzer
Harold J. Ryan (1896-1972)
John S. McConaghy (1907-1981)

ASSOCIATES

Jeffrey A. Franklin
Janet E. Arnold

For full biographical listings, see the Martindale-Hubbell Law Directory

*SCRANTON,** Lackawanna Co.

CHARITON & KEISER

(See Wilkes-Barre)

FOLEY, MCLANE, NEALON, FOLEY & MCDONALD (AV)

Linden Plaza, 600 Linden Street, P.O. Box 1108, 18501-1108
Telephone: 717-342-8194
Fax: 717-342-4658
Stroudsburg, Pennsylvania Office: 26 North Sixth Street.
Telephone: 717-424-1757.
Fax: 717-424-2764.

(See Next Column)

FOLEY, MCLANE, NEALON, FOLEY & MCDONALD, *Scranton—Continued*

Thomas J. Foley, Jr.
John T. McLane
Terrence R. Nealon
Michael J. Foley
Michael J. McDonald
Thomas J. Foley, III (Resident, Stroudsburg Office)
Kevin P. Foley
Malcolm L. MacGregor
M. Colleen Foley Canovas

For full biographical listings, see the Martindale-Hubbell Law Directory

KREDER, BROOKS, HAILSTONE & LUDWIG (AV)

Suite 200, 220 Penn Avenue, 18503
Telephone: 717-346-7922
Telecopier: 717-346-3715

Cody H. Brooks
Andrew Hailstone
Lawrence M. Ludwig
Lucille Marsh
Michael J. Donohue
James J. Wilson
Stephen William Saunders

ASSOCIATE

Barbara Sardella

Counsel for: Consolidated Rail Corp.; PNC Bank; U.S. Fidelity & Guaranty Co.; Nationwide Insurance Co.; Liberty Mutual Insurance Co.; Citizens Savings Assn.; NEP Supershooters, Inc.

For Complete List of Firm Personnel, See General Section

For full biographical listings, see the Martindale-Hubbell Law Directory

LENAHAN & DEMPSEY, A PROFESSIONAL CORPORATION (AV)

116 North Washington Avenue, 18503-0234
Telephone: 717-346-2097
Fax: 717-346-1174
Mailing Address: P.O. Box 234, Scranton, Pennsylvania, 18501-0234

John R. Lenahan, Sr.
William J. Dempsey
John R. Lenahan, Jr.
Joseph P. Lenahan
Kathleen A. Lenahan
David E. Heisler
Timothy G. Lenahan
Matthew D. Dempsey

Marianne J. Gilmartin
Alan P. Schoen
Brian J. Lenahan
Diane Hepford Lenahan
George E. Mehalchick
Brian Yeager
Thomas R. Daniels
Myles P. McAliney
Terrence E. Dempsey
Carmina M. Rinkunas
Thomas R. Chesnick
William M. Blaum
Christine S. Mayernick
Patricia Corbett

Representative Insurance Clients: Allstate Insurance Co.; America Security Insurance Co.; Metropolitan Casualty Insurance Co.; Statesman Insurance Group; Foremost Insurance Co.; Aetna Insurance Co.; Pennsylvania National Insurance Group; Kemper Insurance Group; American Mutual Insurance Cos.; American States Insurance, Co.

For full biographical listings, see the Martindale-Hubbell Law Directory

MUNLEY, MATTISE, KELLY & CARTWRIGHT (AV)

205 Madison Avenue, P.O. Box 1066, 18503
Telephone: 717-346-7401
Fax: 717-346-3452

MEMBERS OF FIRM

Robert W. Munley
Nicholas S. Mattise
P. Timothy Kelly
Marion Munley
Matthew A. Cartwright
J. Christopher Munley

Reference: First National Bank of Jermyn.

For full biographical listings, see the Martindale-Hubbell Law Directory

O'MALLEY & HARRIS, P.C. (AV)

345 Wyoming Avenue, 18503
Telephone: 717-348-3711
Fax: 717-348-4092
Stroudsburg, Pennsylvania Office: 111 North Seventh Street.
Telephone: 717-421-2252.
Wilkes-Barre, Pennsylvania Office: Courthouse Square Towers, North River Street.
Telephone: 717-829-3232.
FAX: 717-829-4418.
Williamsport, Pennsylvania Office: 321 Pine Street, Suite 308.
Telephone: 717-323-4380.

Eugene Nogi (1905-1975)
Henry Nogi (1900-1976)
Russell O. O'Malley, Sr. (1904-1993)
William H. Amesbury (Resident, Wilkes-Barre Office)
Paul A. Barrett
J. Scott Brady
Bruce L. Coyer
John Q. Durkin
Gerald J. Hanchulak
Norman Harris
Richard K. Hodges
Timothy J. Holland (Resident, Wilkes-Barre Office)
Daniel Morgan
Michael Perry
Joseph R. Rydzewski
Jane M. Carlonas
James M. Tressler
Matthew P. Barrett

(See Next Column)

Representative Clients: Robert Packer Hospital; GSGS & B Architects & Engineers; Aetna Casualty & Surety Co.; Pennsylvania Hospital Insurance Co.; United States Fidelity & Guaranty Insurance Co.; Selective Insurance Co.; Maryland Casualty Insurance Co.; Robert Packer Hospital; United Gilsonite Laboratories; Electric Mutual Insurance Co.

For full biographical listings, see the Martindale-Hubbell Law Directory

SCANLON, HOWLEY, SCANLON & DOHERTY (AV)

321 Spruce Street, 10th Floor, 18503
Telephone: 717-346-7651

MEMBERS OF FIRM

James M. Howley
James M. Scanlon
James A. Doherty, Jr.
Thomas R. Nealon
Thomas B. Helbig
Patrick R. Casey

OF COUNSEL

James W. Scanlon

Counsel for: CNA Insurance Company; Selective Insurance Company of America; The Medical Protective Co.; Harleysville Insurance Co.; Mutual Benefit Insurance Co.; The Procter & Gamble Co.; Prudential-Bach Securities, Inc.; Zurich-American Insurance Co.; The Coca-Cola Bottling Co.; The Home Insurance Co.

For full biographical listings, see the Martindale-Hubbell Law Directory

SCHNEIDER, GELB, GOFFER & HICKEY, P.C. (AV)

Mellon Bank Building, 400 Spruce Street, Suite 500, 18503-1814
Telephone: 717-341-3150
Fax: 717-341-3155

Irwin Schneider
Johanna L. Gelb
Michael R. Goffer
Eugene F. Hickey, II
Kathleen A. Walsh

For full biographical listings, see the Martindale-Hubbell Law Directory

WELLES & MCGRATH (AV)

Room 1000, 321 Spruce Street, 18503
Telephone: 717-346-7651
FAX: 717-344-1542

MEMBERS OF FIRM

Charles H. Welles, Jr. (1876-1962)
Matthew D. Mackie (1897-1965)
Charles H. Welles (Retired)
Henry C. McGrath
Charles H. Welles, IV

Counsel for: PNC Bank; Prudential Insurance Co.; Moore Products Co.; Gann-Dawson, Inc.; Massachusetts Mutual Life Insurance Co.; Metropolitan Life Insurance Co.; Bethlehem Steel Co.

For full biographical listings, see the Martindale-Hubbell Law Directory

SELLERSVILLE, Bucks Co.

POWER, BOWEN & VALIMONT (AV)

64 North Main Street, 18960-0580
Telephone: 215-257-3661
Doylestown, Pennsylvania Office: 102 North Main Street.
Telephone: 215-345-7500.

RESIDENT PARTNERS

Samuel G. Moyer (Resident)
William H. Fuss

Representative Clients: Nationwide Insurance Cos.; General Accident Group; Royal Insurance Group; U.S. Gauge Division of AMETEK; Upper Bucks County Technical School; Pennridge School District; 1st Federal Savings & Loan of Perkasie.

For full biographical listings, see the Martindale-Hubbell Law Directory

SHAMOKIN, Northumberland Co.

JACK C. YOUNKIN (AV)

One West Sunbury Street, 17872
Telephone: 717-648-6821
Fax: 717-648-4732

LEGAL SUPPORT PERSONNEL

Patricia Janovich

For full biographical listings, see the Martindale-Hubbell Law Directory

SOUTHAMPTON, Bucks Co.

MOORE & BERKOWITZ (AV)

A Partnership of Professional Corporations
Suite A-110, 928 Jaymor Road, 18966
Telephone: 215-322-4200
Fax: 215-322-4318

(See Next Column)

MOORE & BERKOWITZ—*Continued*

Richard I. Moore (P.C.) Steven H. Berkowitz (P.C.)

For full biographical listings, see the Martindale-Hubbell Law Directory

STATE COLLEGE, Centre Co.

MILLER, KISTLER & CAMPBELL, INC. (AV)

1500 South Atherton Street, 16801
Telephone: 814-234-1500
Fax: 814-234-1549
Bellefonte, Pennsylvania Office: 124 North Allegheny Street.
Telephone: 814-355-5474.
Fax: 814-355-5340.

R. Paul Campbell (1908-1988)
Lewis Orvis Harvey (1912-1990)
John R. Miller, Jr.
Richard L. Campbell
Lillian G. Raycroft
John R. Miller, III
Terry James Williams
Thomas King Kistler
Tracey G. Benson
James Lowell Green

OF COUNSEL

Robert K. Kistler

General Counsel for: Peoples National Bank of Central Pennsylvania; Canon Instrument Co.; Hanover Brands.
Local Counsel for: National Gypsum Co.; Aetna Insurance Co.; Traveler Insurance Co.; The Medical Protective Co.; Corning Glass Works.
Solicitors: Borough of State College.

For full biographical listings, see the Martindale-Hubbell Law Directory

SWARTHMORE, Delaware Co.

ROBERT A. DETWEILER (AV)

11 Amherst Avenue, 19081
Telephone: 610-328-9900; 328-9901

Representative Clients: State Farm Insurance Cos.; Westinghouse Electric Corp.
Reference: Meridian Bank.

*TUNKHANNOCK,** Wyoming Co.

FARR, DAVIS & FITZE (AV)

7 Marion Street, P.O. Box H, 18657
Telephone: 717-836-3185
Facsimile: 717-836-4991

MEMBERS OF FIRM

John B. Farr
James E. Davis
Judd B. Fitze

Representative Clients: First National Bank of Nicholson; Proctor & Gamble Paper Products Company; Pennsylvania Electric Company.
Title Agents for: Commonwealth Land Title Insurance Co.
References: Mellon Bank, Tunkhannock, PA Office; Fidelity Bank N.A. (Tunkhannock, PA Office); Community Bank and Trust Co.; Grange National Bank of Wyoming County.

For full biographical listings, see the Martindale-Hubbell Law Directory

*WASHINGTON,** Washington Co.

PEACOCK, KELLER, YOHE, DAY & ECKER (AV)

East Beau Building, 70 East Beau Street, 15301
Telephone: 412-222-4520
Telefax: 412-222-3318 ABA/NET ABA 34517
Waynesburg, Pennsylvania Office: 102 East High Street.
Telephone: 412-627-8331.
Telefax: 412-627-8025.

MEMBERS OF FIRM

Charles C. Keller
Reed B. Day
Roger J. Ecker
Robert T. Crothers
Mary Drake Korsmeyer
Douglas R. Nolin
Mary K. Pruss

ASSOCIATE

Timothy P. Stranko

Representative Clients: Consolidation Coal Co.; Washington School District; Monongahela Valley Hospital, Inc.; Nationwide Insurance Co.; Family Health Council, Inc.; Cal-Ed Federal Credit Union; Marianna & Scenery Hill Telephone Co.; Maternal & Family Health Services, Inc.; Pennsylvania Hospital Insurance Company.

For Complete List of Firm Personnel, See General Section

For full biographical listings, see the Martindale-Hubbell Law Directory

*WELLSBORO,** Tioga Co.

SPENCER, GLEASON, HEBE & RAGUE (AV)

17 Central Avenue, P.O. Box 507, 16901
Telephone: 717-724-1832
FAX: 717-724-7610

(See Next Column)

MEMBERS OF FIRM

Warren H. Spencer (1921-1991)
Gary M. Gleason
William A. Hebe
James T. Rague

ASSOCIATE

Jeffrey S. Loomis

References: Citizens & Northern Bank; Commonwealth Bank & Trust Co.

For full biographical listings, see the Martindale-Hubbell Law Directory

*WEST CHESTER,** Chester Co.

CRAWFORD, WILSON, RYAN & AGULNICK, P.C. (AV)

220 West Gay Street, 19380
Telephone: 610-431-4500
Fax: 610-430-8718
Radnor, Pennsylvania Office: 252 Radnor-Chester Road, P. O. Box 8333, 19087.
Telephone: 215-688-1205.
Fax: 215-688-7802.

Ronald M. Agulnick
Fronefield Crawford, Jr.
Thomas R. Wilson
Kevin J. Ryan

John J. Mahoney
Kim Denise Morton
Steven L. Mutart
Rita Kathryn Borzillo
Patricia T. Brennan
Richard H. Morton
Patricia J. Kelly
Charles W. Tucker

Reference: First National Bank of West Chester.

For full biographical listings, see the Martindale-Hubbell Law Directory

GOLDBERG, EVANS, MALCOLM, HERALD, DONATONI & ROHLFS (AV)

135 West Market Street, 19382
Telephone: 610-436-6220
Fax: 610-436-0628

Lawrence A. Goldberg
Eugene H. Evans
Thomas O. Malcolm
Bruce A. Herald
Robert J. Donatoni
Walter M. Rohlfs

For full biographical listings, see the Martindale-Hubbell Law Directory

LAMB, WINDLE & MCERLANE, P.C. (AV)

24 East Market Street, P.O. Box 565, 19381-0565
Telephone: 610-430-8000
Telecopier: 610-692-0877

COUNSEL

Theodore O. Rogers

William H. Lamb
Susan Windle Rogers
James E. McErlane
E. Craig Kalemjian
James C. Sargent, Jr.
John D. Snyder
William P. Mahon
Guy A. Donatelli
Vincent M. Pompo
James J. McEntee III

Tracy Blake DeVlieger
P. Andrew Schaum
Lawrence J. Persick
Thomas K. Schindler
Daniel A. Loewenstern
Thomas F. Oeste
John W. Pauciulo
Andrea B. Pettine
John J. Cunningham

Representative Clients: Chester County; First Financial Savings Bank, PaSA; Bank of Chester County; Jefferson Bank; Downingtown Area and Great Valley School Districts; Philadelphia Electric Company; Central and Western Chester County Industrial Development Authority; Valley Forge Sewer Authority; Manito Title Insurance Company.

For full biographical listings, see the Martindale-Hubbell Law Directory

MACELREE, HARVEY, GALLAGHER, FEATHERMAN & SEBASTIAN, LTD. (AV)

17 West Miner Street, P.O. Box 660, 19381-0660
Telephone: 610-436-0100
Fax: 610-430-7885
Kennett Square, Pennsylvania Office: 211 E. State Street, P. O. Box 363.
Telephone 215-444-3180.
Fax: 215-444-3270.
Spring City, Pennsylvania Office: 3694 Schuylkill Road.
Telephone: 215-948-5700.

Lawrence E. MacElree
Dominic T. Marrone
William J. Gallagher
John A. Featherman, III
Randy L. Sebastian
Terry W. Knox
Michael G. Louis
Randall C. Schauer
Stacey W. McConnell
Frederick P. Kramer, II
John F. McKenna
C. Douglas Parvin
Harry J. DiDonato
Lance J. Nelson

(See Next Column)

MACELREE, HARVEY, GALLAGHER, FEATHERMAN & SEBASTIAN LTD., *West Chester—Continued*

Bernadette M. Walsh
Linda C. Tice
Joseph F. Harvey (1921-1985)
J. Barton Rettew, Jr. (1901-1981)
Richard Reifsnyder (1928-1974)

For full biographical listings, see the Martindale-Hubbell Law Directory

*WILKES-BARRE,** Luzerne Co.

CHARITON & KEISER (AV)

138 South Main Street, P.O. Box 220, 18703-0220
Telephone: 717-822-2929
Fax: 717-824-3580

Louis Shaffer (1904-1984)
Jerry B. Chariton
Larry S. Keiser

David E. Schwager
Keith Schweppenheiser

For full biographical listings, see the Martindale-Hubbell Law Directory

GALLAGHER, BRENNAN & GILL (AV)

220 Pierce Street, 18701-4641
Telephone: 717-288-8255
Telecopier: 717-288-7005

MEMBERS OF FIRM

Joseph F. Gallagher (1912-1989)
Thomas P. Brennan
John J. Gill, Jr.
Christine E. McLaughlin

OF COUNSEL

Cecilia Meighan

Approved Attorneys for: Commonwealth Land Title Insurance Co.
Representative Clients: PNC Bank, National Association; Mercy Hospital, Wilkes Barre, Pennsylvania; Guaranty Bank.

For full biographical listings, see the Martindale-Hubbell Law Directory

MEYER AND SWATKOSKI ASSOCIATES, A PROFESSIONAL CORPORATION (AV)

405 Third Avenue, 18704
Telephone: 717-288-8482
Fax: 717-288-1003

Martin J. Meyer
John G. Swatkoski

Janet A. Conser

For full biographical listings, see the Martindale-Hubbell Law Directory

*WILLIAMSPORT,** Lycoming Co.

MCCORMICK, REEDER, NICHOLS, BAHL, KNECHT & PERSON (AV)

(Formerly McCormick, Herdic & Furst).
835 West Fourth Street, 17701
Telephone: 717-326-5131
Fax: 717-326-5529

OF COUNSEL

Henry Clay McCormick

MEMBERS OF FIRM

S. Dale Furst, Jr. (1904-1969)
Robert J. Sarno (1941-1982)
Paul W. Reeder
William E. Nichols
David R. Bahl
William L. Knecht
John E. Person, III
J. David Smith
Robert A. Eckenrode
Cynthia Ranck Person

ASSOCIATES

Joanne C. Ludwikowski
R. Matthew Patch
Sean P. Roman
Kenneth B. Young

General Counsel for: Northern Central Bank; Jersey Shore Steel Co.
Representative Clients: Pennsylvania Power & Light Co.; Consolidated Rail Corp.; Royal Insurance Co.; State Automobile Insurance Association.

For full biographical listings, see the Martindale-Hubbell Law Directory

MCNERNEY, PAGE, VANDERLIN & HALL (AV)

433 Market Street, 17701
Telephone: 717-326-6555
Fax: 717-326-3170
Muncy, Pennsylvania Office: R.D. #6, Box 260-1.
Telephone: 717-546-5111.

MEMBERS OF FIRM

Joseph M. McNerney (1909-1967)
Allen P. Page, Jr. (1923-1975)
O. William Vanderlin
T. Max Hall
George V. Cohen
Charles J. McKelvey
E. Eugene Yaw
Michael H. Collins
Ann Pepperman
Brett O. Feese
Thomas A. Marino

(See Next Column)

ASSOCIATES

Robin A. Read
Thomas C. Marshall
Peter G. Facey
Joy Reynolds McCoy

Approved Agent for: American Title Insurance.
Representative Clients: Williamsport National Bank; Textron Lycoming; Underwriters Adjustment Co.; Continental Insurance Co.; Little League Baseball, Inc.; The West Co.; Shop Vac Corp.; Divine Providence Hospital; Pennsylvania College of Technology.

For full biographical listings, see the Martindale-Hubbell Law Directory

MITCHELL, MITCHELL, GRAY & GALLAGHER, A PROFESSIONAL CORPORATION (AV)

10 West Third Street, 17701
Telephone: 717-323-8404
Fax: 717-323-8585

C. Edward S. Mitchell
Richard A. Gray
Robert A. Gallagher
Gary L. Weber

Bret J. Southard
Eric R. Linhardt

OF COUNSEL

Jacob Neafie Mitchell

For full biographical listings, see the Martindale-Hubbell Law Directory

RIEDERS, TRAVIS, MUSSINA, HUMPHREY & HARRIS (AV)

161 West Third Street, P.O. Box 215, 17703-0215
Telephone: 717-323-8711
1-800-326-9259
Fax: 717-323-4192

MEMBERS OF FIRM

Gary T. Harris
John M. Humphrey
Malcolm S. Mussina
Clifford A. Rieders
Ronald C. Travis
Thomas Waffenschmidt
C. Scott Waters

ASSOCIATES

Robert H. Vesely
Jeffrey C. Dohrmann
James Michael Wiley

LEGAL SUPPORT PERSONNEL

Kimberly A. Paulhamus

Representative Clients: Jersey Shore State Bank; Gamble Twp.; Crown American Corp.; Fowler Motors, Inc.; Twin Hills oldsmobile, Inc.; Brady Twp.; Cascade Twp.; Cogan House Twp.; Susquehana Twp.; Upper Fairfield Twp.; Borough of Picture Rocks.

For full biographical listings, see the Martindale-Hubbell Law Directory

*YORK,** York Co.

STOCK AND LEADER (AV)

35 South Duke Street, P.O. Box 5167, 17401-5167
Telephone: 717-846-9800
Fax: 717-843-6134
Hallam, Pennsylvania Office: 450 West Market Street.
Telephone: 717-840-4491.
Stewartstown, Pennsylvania Office: 5 South Main Street.
Telephone: 717-993-2845.
Shrewsbury, Pennsylvania Office: 28 Northbrook Drive, Suite 2F.
Telephone: 717-235-3608.

MEMBERS OF FIRM

McClean Stock (1881-1962)
Henry B. Leader
Raymond L. Hovis
William H. Neff, Jr.
D. Reed Anderson
William C. Gierasch, Jr.
W. Bruce Wallace
Byron H. LeCates
Michael W. King
Timothy P. Ruth
Richard A. Bramhall, Jr.
Marietta Harte Barbour
Emily J. Leader
Jane H. Schussler

ASSOCIATES

Robert R. Lloyd, Jr.
Steven M. Hovis
Craig T. Trebilcock
Amy L. Nelson
Jody N. Anderson

General Counsel: The Drovers & Mechanics Bank; Paradise Mutual Insurance Co.; Yorktowne Paper Mills, Inc.; York Electrical Supply Co.; Eisenhart Wallcoverings Co.; York Suburban School District; York Township; Central York School District.

For Complete List of Firm Personnel, See General Section

For full biographical listings, see the Martindale-Hubbell Law Directory

RHODE ISLAND

JAMESTOWN, Newport Co.

MORNEAU & MURPHY (AV)

77 Narragansett Avenue, 02835
Telephone: 401-423-0400
Telecopier: 401-423-7059
Providence, Rhode Island Office: 38 N. Court Street. 02903
Telephone: 401-453-0500.
Telecopier: 401-453-0505.

MEMBERS OF FIRM

John Austin Murphy
John B. Murphy (Resident at Providence Office)
Richard N. Morneau
Gloria C. Dahl

ASSOCIATES

Sheila M. Cooley
Stephen T. Morrissey
Anne Maxwell Livingston
Virginia Spaziano
Scott H. Moskol (Resident, Providence Office)

OF COUNSEL

Neale D. Murphy

For full biographical listings, see the Martindale-Hubbell Law Directory

MIDDLETOWN, Newport Co.

JOSEPH R. PALUMBO, JR. (AV)

294 Valley Road, 02842
Telephone: 401-846-5200
Telecopier: 401-848-0984

For full biographical listings, see the Martindale-Hubbell Law Directory

*PROVIDENCE,** Providence Co.

BLISH & CAVANAGH (AV)

Commerce Center, 30 Exchange Terrace, 02903
Telephone: 401-831-8900
Telecopier: 401-751-7542

MEMBERS OF FIRM

John H. Blish
Joseph V. Cavanagh, Jr.
William R. Landry
Michael DiBiase
Stephen J. Reid, Jr.

Karen A. Pelczarski
Raymond A. Marcaccio
Scott P. Tierney

Representative Clients: Providence Journal Co.; Fleet Financial Group; Rhode Island Hospital Trust National Bank; Allstate Insurance Co.; U-Haul International, Inc.; Delta Dental of Rhode Island; Gilbane Building Co.; Colony Communications; Providence Housing Authority.

For full biographical listings, see the Martindale-Hubbell Law Directory

BOYER, REYNOLDS & DEMARCO, LTD. (AV)

Suite 200, 170 Westminster Street, 02903
Telephone: 401-861-5522
Telecopier: 401-331-4861

Francis V. Reynolds (1905-1981)
Bernard W. Boyer
Paul V. Reynolds
Anthony F. DeMarco
John G. Rallis
John M. Boland
Gregory L. Boyer
Mark T. Reynolds

Representative Clients: Lumbermens Mutual Casualty Co.; American Motorists Insurance Co.; Federal Mutual Fire Insurance Co.; B. F. Goodrich Co.; Andover Group; Insurance Company of North America; Nationwide Mutual Insurance Co.; Worcester Co.; Amica Mutual Insurance Co.

For full biographical listings, see the Martindale-Hubbell Law Directory

CARROLL, KELLY & MURPHY (AV)

The Packet Building, 155 South Main Street, 02903
Telephone: 401-331-7272
Telecopier: 401-331-4404

MEMBERS OF FIRM

Joseph A. Kelly
C. Russell Bengtson
Ruth DiMeglio
William H. Jestings

ASSOCIATES

Robert E. Hardman
Keith B. Kyle
Shannon Gilheeney
Michael T. Sullivan

Representative Clients: Hartford Accident and Indemnity Co.; Greater New York Insurance Co.; St. Paul's Insurance Co.; Joint Underwriter's Association; Premiere Alliance Insurance Co.; Professional Risk Management Services, Inc.; General Accident Insurance Company of America; Guaranty Fund Management Services; First State Insurance Co.
Reference: Fleet National Bank.

(See Next Column)

For Complete List of Firm Personnel, See General Section

For full biographical listings, see the Martindale-Hubbell Law Directory

CHISHOLM AND FELDMAN (AV)

1410 Hospital Trust Tower, 02903
Telephone: 401-331-6300
Telecopier: 401-421-3185

MEMBERS OF FIRM

Vincent J. Chisholm
Howard L. Feldman

ASSOCIATES

Nancy M. Feldman
Denise Aiken-Salandria
Robert V. Chisholm

For full biographical listings, see the Martindale-Hubbell Law Directory

MARTIN K. DONOVAN (AV)

Second Floor, One Park Row, 02903
Telephone: 401-831-2500
Facsimile: 401-751-7830

Reference: Fleet National Bank.

For full biographical listings, see the Martindale-Hubbell Law Directory

EDWARDS & ANGELL (AV)

2700 Hospital Trust Tower, 02903
Telephone: 401-274-9200
Telecopier: 401-276-6611
Cable Address: "Edwangle Providence"
Telex: 952001 "E A PVD"
Boston, Massachusetts Office: 101 Federal Street, 02110.
Telephone: 617-439-444.
Telecopier: 617-439-4170.
New York, New York Office: 750 Lexington Avenue, 10022.
Telephone: 212-308-4411.
Telecopier: 212-308-4844.
Palm Beach, Florida Office: 250 Royal Palm Way, 33480.
Telephone: 407-833-7700.
Telecopier: 407-655-8719.
Newark, New Jersey Office: Gateway three, 07120.
Telephone: 201-623-7717.
Telecopier: 201-623-7717.
Hartford, Connecticut Office: 750 Main Street, 14th Floor, 06103.
Telephone: 203-525-5065.
Telecopier: 203-527-4198.
Newport, Rhode Island Office: 130 Bellevue Avenue, 02840.
Telephone: 401-849-7800.
Telecopier: 401-849-7887.

MEMBERS OF FIRM

Richard M. Borod
Deming E. Sherman
S. Michael Levin
Ira G. Greenberg (Resident, New York, New York Office)
William P. Robinson III
Susan S. Egan (Not admitted in RI; Resident New York, New York Office)
Philip D. O'Neill, Jr. (Resident Boston, Massachusetts Office)
Patricia A. Sullivan Zesk
John A. Houlihan (Resident Boston, Massachusetts Office; Partner-in-Charge, Boston, Massachusetts Office)
Alfred R. Paliani (Not admitted in RI; New York, New York and Newark, New Jersey Offices)
Gary A. Woodfield (Not admitted in RI; Resident, Palm Beach, Florida Office)
Mark A. Pogue
Stephen M. Prignano

COUNSEL

Rosemary Healey

ASSOCIATES

Matthew T. Oliverio
Susan Stanton Rotman (Not admitted in RI; Resident Boston, Massachusetts Office)
Mark W. Freel
Joseph S. Larisa, Jr.

OF COUNSEL

Edward F. Hindle
Stephen A. Fanning (Retired)

For Complete List of Firm Personnel, See General Section

For full biographical listings, see the Martindale-Hubbell Law Directory

FLANDERS + MEDEIROS INC. (AV)

One Turks Head Place, Suite 700, 02903
Telephone: 401-831-0700
Telecopier: 401-274-2752

Matthew F. Medeiros
Robert G. Flanders, Jr.
Robert Karmen

Neal J. McNamara
Fausto C. Anguilla
Amelia E. Edwards
Stacey P. Nakasian

For full biographical listings, see the Martindale-Hubbell Law Directory

Providence—Continued

GOLDENBERG & MURI (AV)

15 Westminster Street, 02903
Telephone: 401-421-7300
Telecopier: 401-421-7352

MEMBERS OF FIRM

Michael R. Goldenberg
Anthony F. Muri
Barbara S. Cohen

ASSOCIATES

Douglas J. Emanuel
Susan M. Pepin

For full biographical listings, see the Martindale-Hubbell Law Directory

HANSON, CURRAN, PARKS & WHITMAN (AV)

146 Westminster Street, 02903-2218
Telephone: 401-421-2154
Telecopier: 401-521-7040

Kirk Hanson (1948-1991)

MEMBERS OF FIRM

A. Lauriston Parks
David P. Whitman
Michael T. F. Wallor
Robert D. Parrillo
Dennis J. McCarten
James T. Murphy
Seth E. Bowerman
Thomas R. Bender

ASSOCIATES

Amy Beretta
Mark W. Dana
Richard H. Burrows
Daniel P. McKiernan

OF COUNSEL

William A. Curran

General Counsel for: Medical Malpractice Joint Underwriting Association of Rhode Island.
Rhode Island Counsel for: Amica Mutual Insurance Co.; CIGNA; St. Paul Insurance Cos.; Occidental Life Insurance Co.; Exchange Mutual Insurance Co.; Aetna Casualty & Surety Co.

For full biographical listings, see the Martindale-Hubbell Law Directory

HIGGINS, CAVANAGH & COONEY (AV)

The Hay Building, Fourth Floor, 123 Dyer Street, 02903
Telephone: 401-272-3500; 800-274-5299
Telecopier: 401-273-8780

James H. Higgins, Jr. (1952-1975)
Joseph V. Cavanagh (1952-1985)
John P. Cooney, Jr. (1960-1981)
Kenneth P. Borden
Gerald C. DeMaria
John T. Walsh, Jr.
Charles A. Hambly, Jr.
Stephen B. Lang
Lawrence P. McCarthy, III
James A. Ruggieri
Madeline Quirk
Michael D. Lynch

ASSOCIATES

James T. Hornstein
John J. Hogan
John F. Kelleher
Rajaram Suryanarayan
Vivian B. Dogan
Patrick B. Landers
Paul S. Callaghan
Jodie Raccio Small
Brenda A. Doyle

For full biographical listings, see the Martindale-Hubbell Law Directory

HODOSH, SPINELLA & ANGELONE (AV)

128 Dorrance Street, Shakespeare Hall, Suite 450, P.O. Box 1516, 02901-1516
Telephone: 401-274-0200
Fax: 401-274-7538

Thomas C. Angelone
Hugh L. Moore, Jr.
Kevin M. Cain

Reference: Fleet National Bank.

For Complete List of Firm Personnel, See General Section

For full biographical listings, see the Martindale-Hubbell Law Directory

KIERNAN, PLUNKETT & REDIHAN (AV)

The Remington Building, 91 Friendship Street, 02903
Telephone: 401-831-2900
Fax: 401-331-7123

MEMBERS OF FIRM

Leonard A. Kiernan, Jr.
Thomas C. Plunkett
Charles N. Redihan, Jr.
Bernard P. Healy

ASSOCIATES

Brian T. Burns
Patricia L. Sylvester
Michael R. Calise
Christopher J. O'Connor

For full biographical listings, see the Martindale-Hubbell Law Directory

LICHT & SEMONOFF (AV)

Fourth Floor, Historic Wayland Building, One Park Row, 02903
Telephone: 401-421-8030
Telecopier: 401-272-9408

MEMBERS OF FIRM

Frank Licht (1916-1987)
Ralph P. Semonoff (1918-1992)
Jeremiah J. Gorin
Melvin L. Zurier
Bruce R. Ruttenberg
Norman G. Orodenker
Nathan W. Chace
George E. Lieberman
Richard A. Licht
Robert N. Huseby, Sr.
Joseph De Angelis
Richard A. Boren
Robert B. Berkelhammer
Carl I. Freedman
Robert D. Fine
Susan Leach De Blasio
Susann G. Mark
Drew P. Kaplan
Patrick A. Guida
Anthony J. Bucci, Jr.
Casby Harrison, III

ASSOCIATES

Susan M. Huntley
Glenn R. Friedemann
Paul J. Adler
Maureen L. Mallon
Jerry H. Elmer
Michael Prescott
Steven C. Sidel

OF COUNSEL

Daniel J. Murray

For Complete List of Firm Personnel, See General Section

For full biographical listings, see the Martindale-Hubbell Law Directory

VINCENT D. MORGERA (AV)

One Old Stone Square, 02903-7104
Telephone: 401-456-0300
Telecopier: 401-456-0303

For full biographical listings, see the Martindale-Hubbell Law Directory

WILLIAM T. MURPHY (AV)

The Calart Tower, 400 Reservoir Avenue, Suite 3L, 02907
Telephone: 401-461-7740
Telecopier: 401-461-7753

ASSOCIATE

Sean P. Lardner

Reference: Fleet National Bank.

For full biographical listings, see the Martindale-Hubbell Law Directory

VETTER & WHITE, INCORPORATED (AV)

20 Washington Place, 02903
Telephone: 401-421-3060
Telecopier: 401-272-6803

George Vetter
Benjamin V. White, III
Gordon P. Cleary
Thomas W. Lyons, III
Howard A. Merten, Jr.

OF COUNSEL

David D. McKenney

Brooks R. Magratten
Michael W. Carroll
Kimberly A. Simpson
Christopher C. Roche

LEGAL SUPPORT PERSONNEL

Michael W. Long

For full biographical listings, see the Martindale-Hubbell Law Directory

WARWICK, Kent Co.

KIRSHENBAUM LAW ASSOCIATES (AV)

67 Jefferson Boulevard, 02888-1053
Telephone: 401-467-5300
Fax: 401-461-4464

MEMBERS OF FIRM

Allen M. Kirshenbaum
Carolyn R. Barone

Lauri S. Medwin
Evan M. Kirshenbaum

For full biographical listings, see the Martindale-Hubbell Law Directory

SOUTH CAROLINA

*AIKEN,** Aiken Co.

BODENHEIMER, BUSBEE, HUNTER & GRIFFITH (AV)

147 Newberry Street, N.W., P.O. Drawer 2009, 29802
Telephone: 803-648-3255
Telefax: 803-648-3278

(See Next Column)

BODENHEIMER, BUSBEE, HUNTER & GRIFFITH—*Continued*

MEMBERS OF FIRM

John T. Bodenheimer
O. Dantzler Busbee, II
John M. Hunter, Jr.
M. Anderson Griffith

For full biographical listings, see the Martindale-Hubbell Law Directory

HENDERSON & SALLEY (AV)

111 Park Avenue, Southwest, P.O. Box 517, 29802-0517
Telephone: 803-648-4213
Fax: 803-648-2601

MEMBERS OF FIRM

Julian B. Salley, Jr.
Michael K. Farmer
William H. Tucker
James D. Nance

ASSOCIATE

Amy Patterson Shumpert

Attorneys for: NationsBank South Carolina (N.A.); South Carolina Electric & Gas Co.; The Graniteville Co.; Maryland Casualty Co.; Southern Bell Telephone & Telegraph Co.; Owens Corning Fiberglass Corp.; City of Aiken; United Merchants & Manufacturers, Inc.; Allstate Insurance Co.

For full biographical listings, see the Martindale-Hubbell Law Directory

JOHNSON, JOHNSON, WHITTLE, SNELGROVE & WEEKS, P.A. (AV)

117 Pendleton Street, N.W., P.O. Box 2619, 29802-2619
Telephone: 803-649-5338
FAX: 803-641-4517

B. Henderson Johnson, Jr.
Barry H. Johnson
James E. Whittle, Jr.
Vicki Johnson Snelgrove
John W. (Bill) Weeks
Paige Weeks Johnson
Todd J. Johnson

For full biographical listings, see the Martindale-Hubbell Law Directory

*BEAUFORT,** Beaufort Co.

DOWLING LAW FIRM, P.A. (AV)

1509 King Street, P.O. Drawer 1507, 29901-1507
Telephone: 803-521-8000
Fax: 803-521-8003

Joab M. Dowling (1917-1992)

References: South Carolina National Bank; South Carolina Federal Savings Bank; Nations Bank, Community Bank; Citizens and Southern National Bank.

For Complete List of Firm Personnel, See General Section

For full biographical listings, see the Martindale-Hubbell Law Directory

SAMS AND SAMS (AV)

811 Craven Street, P.O. Box 849, 29901-0849
Telephone: 803-524-4189

MEMBERS OF FIRM

Talbird Reeve Sams
W. Toland Sams

Representative Clients: Government Employees Insurance Co.; Aetna Casualty & Surety Co.; Allstate Insurance Co.; United States Fidelity and Guaranty Co.; Grand Union Co.; National Food Processors Assn.; Auto-Owners Insurance Co.; American Southern Insurance Co.; Atlantic Mutual Fire Insurance Co.; Alexis Inc.

For full biographical listings, see the Martindale-Hubbell Law Directory

*CAMDEN,** Kershaw Co.

SAVAGE, ROYALL AND SHEHEEN (AV)

1111 Church Street, P.O. Drawer 10, 29020
Telephone: 803-432-4391
Telefax: 803-425-4816

MEMBERS OF FIRM

Edward M. Royall
Robert J. Sheheen
Moultrie B. Burns, Jr.
Dana A. Morris
John W. Rabb, Jr.
William F. Nettles IV

Representative Clients: Nations Bank NBSC; First Palmetto Bank; Farmers Bureau Insurance Cos.; Georgia Pacific Corp.; Carolina Power & Light Co.; Cassatt Water Co.; Bowaters Southern Paper Corp.; Kershaw County Memorial Hospital.
Approved Attorneys for: Stewart Title Insurance; Ticor Title Insurance,

For Complete List of Firm Personnel, See General Section

For full biographical listings, see the Martindale-Hubbell Law Directory

*CHARLESTON,** Charleston Co.

BARNWELL WHALEY PATTERSON & HELMS (AV)

134 Meeting Street, Suite 300, P.O. Drawer H, 29402
Telephone: 803-577-7700
Telecopier: 803-577-7708

MEMBERS OF FIRM

Robert A. Patterson
William C. Helms, III
Thomas J. Wills
M. Dawes Cooke, Jr.
Bruce E. Miller
B. C. Killough
Matthew H. Henrikson

ASSOCIATES

Aubrey R. Alvey
Eleanor D. Washburn
Warren William Ariail
Robert P. Gritton
Lori S. Dandridge
Thomas B. Pritchard
Heather K. Coleman
James E. Reeves

Representative Clients: General Motors; The Citadel; Carolina Shipping Co.; Design Professionals Ins. Co.; Travelers Insurance Co.; Liberty Mutual Insurance Co.; Bon Secours Xavier St. Francis Hospital; Royal Insurance Co.; General Accident Insurance Co.; U.S. Mineral Products Co.; Continental Insurance Co.; United Aviation Underwriters.

For Complete List of Firm Personnel, See General Section

For full biographical listings, see the Martindale-Hubbell Law Directory

BARR, BARR AND McINTOSH (AV)

11 Broad Street, P.O. Box 1037, 29402
Telephone: 803-577-5083
Fax: 803-723-9039

MEMBERS OF FIRM

Capers G. Barr, III
William S. Barr
H. Thomas McIntosh, Jr.
Capers G. Barr, IV

Approved Attorneys for: Lawyers Title Insurance Corp.; Title Insurance Co. of Pennsylvania.
References: NationsBank; Bank of South Carolina.

For full biographical listings, see the Martindale-Hubbell Law Directory

BERNSTEIN & BERNSTEIN, P.A. (AV)

Maritime Building, 215 East Bay Street, Suite 203, P.O. Box 7, 29402-0007
Telephone: 803-723-3502
FAX: 803-723-3534

Charles S. Bernstein

Robert Alan Bernstein

For full biographical listings, see the Martindale-Hubbell Law Directory

BUIST, MOORE, SMYTHE & McGEE, P.A. (AV)

Successors to Buist, Buist, Smythe and Smythe and Moore, Mouzon and McGee.
Five Exchange Street, P.O. Box 999, 29402
Telephone: 803-722-3400
Cable Address: "Conferees"
Telex: 57-6488
Telecopier: 803-723-7398
North Charleston, South Carolina Office: Atrium Northwood Office Building, 7301 Rivers Avenue, Suite 288. Zip: 29406-2859.
Telephone: 803-797-3000.
Telecopier: 803-863-5500.

Henry B. Smythe
Benj. Allston Moore, Jr.
Joseph H. McGee
Gordon D. Schreck
Henry B. Smythe, Jr.
Susan M. Smythe
W. Foster Gaillard
David B. McCormack
C. Allen Gibson, Jr.
Morris A. Ellison
Charles P. Summerall, IV
James L. Parris

David M. Collins
Robert A. Kerr, Jr.
James D. Myrick
Douglas M. Muller
Elizabeth H. Warner
Jeffrey A. Winkler
David S. Yandle
Patricia L. Quentel
John Marshall Allen
Robert H. Mozingo
Roger Edward George
Julius H. Hines

OF COUNSEL

David H. Crawford

Counsel for: CSX Transportation; NationsBank; Metropolitan Life Insurance Co.; E. I. du Pont de Nemours & Co.; AIG Aviation, Inc.; Lamorte, Burns & Co., Inc.; Allstate Insurance Co.; General Dynamics Corp.; Independent Life & Accident Insurance Co.; Georgia-Pacific Corp.

For Complete List of Firm Personnel, See General Section

For full biographical listings, see the Martindale-Hubbell Law Directory

Charleston—Continued

CLAWSON & STAUBES (AV)

304 Meeting Street, 29401-1544
Telephone: 803-577-2026
Fax: 803-722-2867

MEMBERS OF FIRM

Robert G. Clawson, Jr.
Christopher B. Staubes, Jr.
Samuel R. Clawson
Albert A. Lacour, III
James A. Atkins
John L. McDonald, Jr.
J. Ronald Jones, Jr.

ASSOCIATES

Ronnie F. Craig
Matthew J. Story
Timothy A. Domin
Thomas H. Milligan
Katherine W. Simons

Representative Clients: Allstate Insurance Co.; City of Charleston; Blue Cross Blue Shield of South Carolina; NationsBank; Southern National Bank; United Carolina Bank; Nationwide Mutual Insurance Company; State Farm Mutual Insurance Companies; CNA Insurance Company; Maryland Casualty Company.

For full biographical listings, see the Martindale-Hubbell Law Directory

GRIMBALL & CABANISS (AV)

The Franke Building, 171 Church Street, Suite 120, P.O. Box 816, 29402-0816
Telephone: 803-722-0311
Fax: 803-722-1374

MEMBERS OF FIRM

William H. Grimball
Joseph W. Cabaniss
Henry E. Grimball
Frank E. Grimball
Max G. Mahaffee
Eugene Patrick Corrigan, III
E. Warren Moise
Michael J. Ferri

ASSOCIATES

Kathryn S. Craven
Julie L. Weinheimer
E. Charles Grose, Jr.
Henry H. Cabaniss

Representative Clients: Chubb Group; CIGNA; CNA Insurance Cos.; Nationwide Mutual Insurance Co.; Prudential Insurance Co.; State Farm Insurance Cos.
Local Counsel for: Exxon Corp.; The Greyhound Corp.; Norfolk-Southern Corp.; Baker Hospital.

For full biographical listings, see the Martindale-Hubbell Law Directory

HALIO & HALIO (AV)

13 North Adgers Wharf, P.O. Box 747, 29402-0747
Telephone: 803-577-5200
Fax: 803-577-7468

MEMBERS OF FIRM

Elliott T. Halio
Andrew S. Halio

Approved Attorneys for: Lawyers Title Insurance Corp.; Chicago Title Insurance Co.

For full biographical listings, see the Martindale-Hubbell Law Directory

HAYNSWORTH, MARION, MCKAY & GUÉRARD, L.L.P (AV)

#2 Prioleau Street, P.O. Box 1119, 29402
Telephone: 803-722-7606
Telecopier: 803-723-5263
Columbia, South Carolina Office: Suite 2400 AT&T Building, 1201 Main Street, P.O. Drawer 7157, 29202.
Telephone: 803-765-1818.
Telecopier: 803-765-2399.
Greenville, South Carolina Office: Two Insignia Financial Plaza, 75 Beattie Place, P.O. Box 2048, 29602.
Telephone: 803-240-3200.
Telecopier: 803-240-3300.

MEMBERS OF FIRM

William C. Cleveland
James J. Hinchey, Jr. (Resident)

ASSOCIATES

James E. Lady
Coleman Miller Legerton
J. Walker Coleman, IV
Meredith Grier Buyck

Counsel for: Bank of South Carolina; Baker Hospital; Healthsources of South Carolina; Allstate Insurance Co.; CSX Corporation; Lloyd's Underwriters; Coward-Hund Construction Co.; South Carolina Public Service Authority; South Carolina Jobs - Economic Development Authority; City of Hanahan.

For Complete List of Firm Personnel, See General Section

For full biographical listings, see the Martindale-Hubbell Law Directory

HOOD LAW FIRM (AV)

172 Meeting Street, P.O. Box 1508, 29402
Telephone: 803-577-4435
FAX: 803-722-1630

(See Next Column)

MEMBERS OF FIRM

Robert H. Hood
Louis P. Herns
G. Mark Phillips
Carl Everette Pierce, II
John K. Blincow, Jr.

James G. Kennedy
James Dowell Gandy, III
William R. Hearn, Jr.
Joseph C. Wilson, IV
Dixon F. Pearce, III
Margaret Allison Snead
Barbara Wynne Showers
Christine L. Companion
Hugh Willcox Buyck
Jerry A. Smith
Allan Poe Sloan, III
Todd W. Smyth

For full biographical listings, see the Martindale-Hubbell Law Directory

GEDNEY M. HOWE, III, P.A. (AV)

8 Chalmers Street, P.O. Box 1034, 29402
Telephone: 803-722-8048
FAX: 803-722-2140

Gedney M. Howe, Jr. (1914-1981)
Gedney M. Howe, III
Alvin J. Hammer
Donald H. Howe
Robert J. Wyndham

For full biographical listings, see the Martindale-Hubbell Law Directory

OBERMAN & OBERMAN (AV)

38 Broad Street, 29401
Telephone: 803-577-7010
Fax: 803-722-7359

MEMBERS OF FIRM

Marvin I. Oberman
Harold A. Oberman

For full biographical listings, see the Martindale-Hubbell Law Directory

ROSEN, ROSEN & HAGOOD, P.A. (AV)

134 Meeting Street, Suite 200, P.O. Box 893, 29402
Telephone: 803-577-6726

Morris D. Rosen
Robert N. Rosen
Richard S. Rosen
H. Brewton Hagood
Alice F. Paylor
Susan Corner Rosen
Donald B. Clark

Randy Horner
Peter Brandt Shelbourne
Alexander B. Cash
Daniel F. Blanchard, III

Reference: NationsBank of South Carolina, N.A.

For Complete List of Firm Personnel, See General Section

For full biographical listings, see the Martindale-Hubbell Law Directory

SINKLER & BOYD, P.A. (AV)

160 East Bay Street, P.O. Box 340, 29402-0340
Telephone: 803-722-3366
FAX: 803-722-2266
Columbia, South Carolina Office: Suite 1200 The Palmetto Center, 1426 Main Street, P.O. Box 11889.
Telephone: 803-779-3080.
FAX: 803-765-1243.
Greenville, South Carolina Office: 15 South Main Street, Suite 500, Wachovia Building, P.O. Box 275.
Telephone: 803-467-1100.
FAX: 803-467-1521.

H. Simmons Tate, Jr. (Resident, Columbia Office)
William C. Boyd (Resident, Columbia Office)
Francis P. Mood (Resident, Columbia Office)
Bachman S. Smith III
Manton M. Grier (Resident, Columbia Office)
Thomas R. Gottshall (Resident, Columbia Office)
Hamilton Osborne, Jr. (Resident, Columbia Office)
Stephen E. Darling
John P. Linton
Harold E. Trask
Marvin D. Infinger
Palmer Freeman, Jr. (Resident, Columbia Office)
Daryl L. Williams (Resident, Columbia Office)
John C. Bruton, Jr. (Resident, Columbia Office)
Elizabeth A. Carpentier (Resident, Columbia Office)
Sue C. Erwin (Resident, Columbia Office)
Clarke W. DuBose (Resident, Columbia Office)
Terri Morrill Lynch
Robert Y. Knowlton (Resident, Columbia Office)
Thomas C. Hildebrand, Jr.
Robert W. Buffington (Resident, Columbia Office)
Bert Glenn Utsey III
Charles H. Gibbs, Jr.
John H. Tiller
Roy A. Howell III
Virginia L. Vroegop (Resident Columbia Office)

Edward K. Pritchard III
David W. Whittington
Mark E. Rostick
John F. Emerson (Resident, Columbia Office)
Perrin Q. Dargan, III
Joseph D. Thompson, III

(See Next Column)

SINKLER & BOYD P.A.—*Continued*

Representative Clients: The South Carolina National Bank; South Carolina Electric & Gas Co.; AT&T; Westvaco Corp.; Hartford Insurance Co.; Pennsylvania National Mutual Casualty Insurance Co.; USF & G; Ohio Casualty Group; Kemper Group; Liberty Mutual Insurance Co.

For Complete List of Firm Personnel, See General Section

For full biographical listings, see the Martindale-Hubbell Law Directory

SLOTCHIVER & SLOTCHIVER (AV)

44 State Street, 29401
Telephone: 803-577-6531
Facsimile: 803-577-0261

MEMBERS OF FIRM

Irvin J. Slotchiver
Daniel S. Slotchiver
Stephen M. Slotchiver

For full biographical listings, see the Martindale-Hubbell Law Directory

SOLOMON, KAHN, BUDMAN & STRICKER (AV)

39 Broad Street, P.O. Drawer P, 29402
Telephone: 803-577-7182
Telecopier: 803-722-0485

A. Bernard Solomon
Ellis I. Kahn
Donald J. Budman
Michael A. Stricker

ASSOCIATE

Justin S. Kahn

Local Counsel for: Lawyers Title Insurance Corp.

For full biographical listings, see the Martindale-Hubbell Law Directory

MARK C. TANENBAUM, P.A. (AV)

241-243 East Bay Street, P.O. Box 20757, 29413
Telephone: 803-577-5100
Telecopy: 803-722-4688

Mark C. Tanenbaum

Stephen A. Butaitis

For full biographical listings, see the Martindale-Hubbell Law Directory

YOUNG, CLEMENT, RIVERS & TISDALE (AV)

28 Broad Street, P.O. Box 993, 29402
Telephone: 803-577-4000
Fax: 803-724-6600
Columbia, South Carolina Office: 1901 Assembly Street, Suite 300, P.O. Box 8476.
Telephone: 803-799-4000.
Fax: 803-799-7083.
North Charleston , South Carolina Office: 2170 Ashley Phosphate Road, Suite 700, P.O. Box 61509.
Telephone: 803-720-5400.
Fax: 803-724-7796.

MEMBERS OF FIRM

Thomas S. Tisdale, Jr.
William J. Bates
J. Rutledge Young, Jr.
Wallace G. Holland
Bradish J. Waring
W. Jefferson Leath, Jr.
John C. Von Lehe, Jr.
Timothy W. Bouch
William Bobo, Jr.
H. Michael Bowers
Carol Brittain Ervin
Joseph E. DaPore
Michael A. Molony
C. Michael Branham
Randell C. Stoney, Jr.
Stephen P. Groves
Shawn Daughtridge Wallace
John Hamilton Smith
Lawrence W. Johnson, Jr.

ASSOCIATES

Shawn M. Flanagan
Robert W. Pearce, Jr.
Sally H. Rhoad
E. Courtney Gruber

OF COUNSEL

Robert L. Clement, Jr.
G. L. Buist Rivers, Jr.

RETIRED

Joseph R. Young

Counsel for: Bell South; Budd Company; Kimberly-Clark Corporation; Manitow oc Company, Inc.; Praxair, Inc.; Westinghouse Electric Corporation.

For Complete List of Firm Personnel, See General Section

For full biographical listings, see the Martindale-Hubbell Law Directory

*COLUMBIA,** Richland Co.

* indicates certain Bar Register subscribers whose principal office is located elsewhere in the state and who have arranged for representation as a part of the state capital listings that follow

ADAMS, QUACKENBUSH, HERRING & STUART, P.A. (AV)

NationsBank Plaza, 1901 Main Street, Suite 1400, P.O. Box 394, 29202
Telephone: 803-779-2650
Facsimile: 803-252-8964

James H. Quackenbush, Jr.
Hardwick Stuart, Jr.
D. Christian Goodall
Theodore von Keller
Melissa Ann Jones

Reference: Citizens and Southern National Bank.

For full biographical listings, see the Martindale-Hubbell Law Directory

BOWERS ORR & ROBERTSON (AV)

Suite 1100, 1401 Main Street, P.O. Box 7307, 29202
Telephone: 803-252-0494
Telefax: 803-252-1068

MEMBERS OF FIRM

Glenn Bowers
James W. Orr
William Dixon Robertson III
Thomas F. Dougall

ASSOCIATE

W. Jones Andrews, Jr.

Representative Clients: Bondex International, Inc.; Hamilton Materials, Inc.; Manville Personal Injury Settlement Trust; Medtronic, Inc; Proko Industries, Inc.; Republic Powdered Metals, Inc.; South Carolina Electric & Gas Company; Teledyne Continental Motors; United Piece Dye Works; Waite-Hill Services, Inc.

For full biographical listings, see the Martindale-Hubbell Law Directory

JOSEPH C. COLEMAN (AV)

1338 Main Street, Suite 500, 29201
Telephone: 803-256-8516
Fax: 803-256-1132

For full biographical listings, see the Martindale-Hubbell Law Directory

COLLINS & LACY (AV)

1330 Lady Street, Suite 601, P.O. Box 12487, 29211
Telephone: 803-256-2660
Telefax: 803-771-4484

Joel W. Collins, Jr.
Stanford E. Lacy
Yolanda Coker Courie
Gray Thomas Culbreath
Arthur K. Aiken

Ellen A. Mercer
Eric G. Fosmire
Rebecca M. Monroy

LEGAL SUPPORT PERSONNEL

LEGAL ASSISTANTS

Jane A. Lo Cicero
Kelly L. Rabel
Jeanne S. Volin
Annette L. Horton
Susan S. Hornung

For full biographical listings, see the Martindale-Hubbell Law Directory

FINKEL, GOLDBERG, SHEFTMAN & ALTMAN, P.A. (AV)

Suite 1800, 1201 Main Street, P.O. Box 1799, 29202
Telephone: 803-765-2935
Fax: 803-252-0786
Charleston, South Carolina Office: 12 Exchange Street, P.O. Box 225.
Telephone: 803-577-5460.
Fax: 803-577-5135.

Gerald M. Finkel
Harry L. Goldberg
Howard S. Sheftman

Representative Clients: Hewitt-Robins; 1st Union National Bank; Banc One Mortgage Co.; Motorola Communications & Electronics Corp.

For full biographical listings, see the Martindale-Hubbell Law Directory

FURR AND HENSHAW (AV)

A Partnership of Professional Corporations
1534 Blanding Street, 29201
Telephone: 803-252-4050
Fax: 803-254-7513
Myrtle Beach, South Carolina Office: 1900 Oak Street, P.O. Box 2909.
Telephone: 803-626-7621.
FAX: 803-448-6445.

O. Fayrell Furr, Jr. (P.C.)
Charles L. Henshaw, Jr. (P.C.)

(See Next Column)

FURR AND HENSHAW, *Columbia—Continued*

Karolan Furr Ohanesian (Resident, Myrtle Beach Office)

Reference: Anchor Bank, Myrtle Beach, S.C.

For full biographical listings, see the Martindale-Hubbell Law Directory

GLENN, IRVIN, MURPHY, GRAY & STEPP (AV)

Southern National Bank Building, Suite 390, 1901 Assembly Street, P.O. Box 1550, 29202-1550
Telephone: 803-765-1100
Telecopy: 803-765-0755

MEMBERS OF FIRM

Wilmot B. Irvin
Peter L. Murphy
Elizabeth Van Doren Gray
Robert E. Stepp
Elizabeth G. Howard

Blaney A. Coskrey, III
Robert A. Culpepper

Reference: Southern National.

For Complete List of Firm Personnel, See General Section

For full biographical listings, see the Martindale-Hubbell Law Directory

GOLDEN, TAYLOR & POTTERFIELD (AV)

A Law Partnership between a Professional Association & Attorneys
1712-1714 Main Street, 29201
Telephone: 803-779-3700
Telefax: 803-779-3422

Harvey L. Golden, P.A.
J. Michael Taylor
Ashlin Blanchard Potterfield

For full biographical listings, see the Martindale-Hubbell Law Directory

*** HAYNSWORTH, MARION, MCKAY & GUÉRARD, L.L.P. (AV)**

Suite 2400 A T & T Building, 1201 Main Street, P.O. Drawer 7157, 29202
Telephone: 803-765-1818
Telecopier: 803-765-2399
Greenville, South Carolina Office: Two Insignia Financial Plaza, 75 Beattie Place, P.O. Box 2048, 29602.
Telephone: 803-240-3200.
Telecopier: 803-240-3300.
Charleston, South Carolina Office: #2 Prioleau Street, P.O. Box 1119, 29402.
Telephone: 803-722-7606.
Telecopier: 803-723-5263.

OF COUNSEL

Julius W. McKay

MEMBERS OF FIRM

William P. Simpson
Henry P. Wall
Steven Todd Moon

ASSOCIATES

Stephen F. McKinney
Boyd B. Nicholson, Jr.
Jill R. Quattlebaum
Edward Wade Mullins, III

Counsel for: St. Paul Insurance Group; Allstate Insurance Co.; Fluor-Daniel Corp.; South Carolina Jobs - Economic Development Authority; Anheuser Busch Company; CSX Transportation; Ernst & Young, LLP; Willis Corroon of South Carolina, Inc.; Westinghouse Savannah River Co.; Wachovia Bank of South Carolina, N.A.

For Complete List of Firm Personnel, See General Section

For full biographical listings, see the Martindale-Hubbell Law Directory

KING & VERNON, P.A. (AV)

1426 Richland Street, P.O. Box 7667, 29202
Telephone: 803-779-3090
Fax: 803-779-3396

Kermit S. King
W. Thomas Vernon

For Complete List of Firm Personnel, See General Section

For full biographical listings, see the Martindale-Hubbell Law Directory

MCCUTCHEN, BLANTON, RHODES & JOHNSON (AV)

1414 Lady Street, P.O. Drawer 11209, 29211
Telephone: 803-799-9791
Telecopier: 803-253-6084
Winnsboro, South Carolina Office: Courthouse Square, 29180.
Telephone: 803-635-6884.

(See Next Column)

MEMBERS OF FIRM

Thomas E. McCutchen
Hoover C. Blanton
Jeter E. Rhodes, Jr.
T. English McCutchen, III
Pope D. Johnson, III
William R. Taylor
Evans Taylor Barnette
G. D. Morgan, Jr.
John C. Bradley, Jr.

ASSOCIATES

Creighton B. Coleman
William E. Hopkins, Jr.

Representative Clients: Liberty Mutual Insurance Co.; Sears; Firemen's Fund; Consolidated Systems, Inc.; State Farm Fire and Casualty Co.; Thurston Motor Lines; Southeastern Freight Lines; Joint Underwriters Assoc.; Allstate; National Indemnity Co.

For full biographical listings, see the Martindale-Hubbell Law Directory

MCKAY, MCKAY, HENRY & FOSTER, P.A. (AV)

1325 Laurel Street, P.O. Box 7217, 29202
Telephone: 803-256-4645
FAX: 803-765-1839

Douglas McKay, Jr.
Julius W. McKay, II
Angela L. Henry
Ruskin C. Foster

Representative Clients: Americlaim Adjustment Corp.; Amoco Oil Company; Blue Cross & Blue Shield of South Carolina; Britanco Underwriters, Inc.; Browning-Ferris Industries, Inc.; Haverty's Furniture Company; Homestead Insurance Co.; Lincoln National Life Insurance Co.; Pennsylvania Manufacturers' Association Insurance Co. (PMA); Schneider National Carriers.

For Complete List of Firm Personnel, See General Section

For full biographical listings, see the Martindale-Hubbell Law Directory

ERNEST J. NAUFUL, JR., P.C. (AV)

1330 Lady Street Suite 615, P.O. Box 5907, 29250
Telephone: 803-256-4045
Facsimile: 803-254-0776

Ernest J. Nauful, Jr.

For full biographical listings, see the Martindale-Hubbell Law Directory

NELSON MULLINS RILEY & SCARBOROUGH L.L.P. (AV)

A Registered Limited Liability Partnership including Professional Corporations
Third Floor, Keenan Building, 1330 Lady Street, P.O. Box 11070, 29211
Telephone: 803-799-2000
Telecopy: 803-256-7500; 733-9499
Atlanta, Georgia Office: 1201 Peachtree Street, N.E., P.O. Box 77707.
Telephone: 404-817-6000.
Telecopy: 404-817-6050.
Charleston, South Carolina Office: Suite 500, 151 Meeting Street, P.O. Box 1806.
Telephone: 803-853-5200.
Telecopy: 803-722-8700.
Florence, South Carolina Office: 600 W. Palmetto Street, Suite 200, P.O. Box 5955.
Telephone: 803-662-0019.
Telecopy: 803-662-0491.
Greenville, South Carolina Office: Twenty-Fourth Floor, BB&T Building, 301 North Main Street, P.O. Box 10084.
Telephone: 803-250-2300.
Telecopy: 803-232-2925.
Lexington, South Carolina Office: 334 Old Chapin Road, P.O. Box 729.
Telephone: 803-733-9494; 803-799-200.
Telecopy: 803-957-8226.
Myrtle Beach, South Carolina Office: 2411 N. Oak Street, Founders Centre, Suite 301. P.O. Box 3939.
Telephone: 803-448-3500.
Telecopy: 803-448-3437.

MEMBERS OF FIRM

Edward W. Mullins, Jr.
R. Bruce Shaw
John U. Bell, III
William S. Davies, Jr.
Stephen G. Morrison
Thornwell F. Sowell
Richard B. Watson (Resident, Charleston, SC Office)
William C. Hubbard
George B. Cauthen
Henry S. Knight, Jr.
James C. Gray, Jr.
Nina Nelson Smith
Charles R. Norris (Resident, Charleston, SC Office)
David G. Traylor, Jr.
Monteith P. Todd
Robert W. Foster, Jr. (Resident, Atlanta, GA Office)
Rebecca Laffitte
David E. Dukes
L. Walter Tollison, III
Stuart M. Andrews, Jr.
Karen Aldridge Crawford
Christopher J. Daniels
Jane Thompson Davis (Resident, Charleston, SC Office)
Lisa C. Heydinger (Resident, Charleston, SC Office)
W. Thomas Causby
John E. Schmidt, III

Representative Clients: Nassau Recycle Company; Delta Airlines; E.I. du Pont de Nemours & Co.; General Motors Corp.; American Honda Motor Co.; Owens-Illinois, Inc.; Union Camp Corp.; Weyerhaeuser Co.; Mount Vernon Mills; Policy Management Systems, Inc.

(See Next Column)

NELSON MULLINS RILEY & SCARBOROUGH L.L.P.—*Continued*

For Complete List of Firm Personnel, See General Section

For full biographical listings, see the Martindale-Hubbell Law Directory

POPE & RODGERS (AV)

Suite 615, 1330 Lady Street, P.O. Box 5907, 29250
Telephone: 803-254-0700
Fax: 803-254-0776

MEMBERS OF FIRM

William L. Pope
Paul B. Rodgers, III
Knox L. Haynsworth, III
Roy F. Laney

For full biographical listings, see the Martindale-Hubbell Law Directory

QUINN, PATTERSON & WILLARD (AV)

2019 Park Street, P.O. Box 73, 29202
Telephone: 803-779-6365
Telefax: 803-779-6372

MEMBERS OF FIRM

Michael H. Quinn
Grady L. Patterson, III
Theodore DuBose Willard, Jr.

ASSOCIATE

Heidi Brown

Approved Attorneys for: Lawyers Title Insurance Corp.

For full biographical listings, see the Martindale-Hubbell Law Directory

RICHARDSON, PLOWDEN, GRIER AND HOWSER, P.A. (AV)

1600 Marion Street, P.O. Drawer 7788, 29202
Telephone: 803-771-4400
Telecopy: 803-779-0016
Myrtle Beach, South Carolina Office: Southern National Bank Building, Suite 202, 601 21st Avenue North, P.O. Box 3646, 29578.
Telephone: 803-448-1008.
FAX: 803-448-1533.

Donald V. Richardson, III
Charles N. Plowden, Jr.
F. Barron Grier, III
R. Davis Howser
Charles E. Carpenter, Jr.
Frank E. Robinson, II
Michael A. Pulliam
George C. Beighley
William H. Hensel
Frederick A. Crawford
Francis M. Mack
Samuel F. Crews, III
Franklin Jennings Smith, Jr.
Leslie A. Cotter, Jr.
James P. Newman, Jr.

Nina Reid Mack
Deborah Harrison Sheffield
Douglas C. Baxter
William G. Besley
S. Nelson Weston Jr.
Mary L. Sowell League
Benjamin D. McCoy
Jimmy Denning, Jr.
Anne Macon Flynn
Phillip Florence, Jr.
Williams Scalise Marian

Representative Clients: Insurance: CNA Insurance Co.; The Hartford; Kemper Insurance Co.; Pennsylvania National Mutual Casualty Insurance Co.; Wausau Insurance Cos. Banking: National Bank of South Carolina. Construction: S.C. Department of Public Transportation; DPCI Companies; Northlake Construction Co.; Osmose Wood Preserving Inc.

For Complete List of Firm Personnel, See General Section

For full biographical listings, see the Martindale-Hubbell Law Directory

ROBINSON, McFADDEN & MOORE, P.C. (AV)

Fifteen Hundred NationsBank Plaza, 1901 Main Street, P.O. Box 944, 29202
Telephone: 803-779-8900
Telecopier: 803-252-0724

David W. Robinson, Sr. (1869-1935)
R. Hoke Robinson (1916-1977)
J. Means McFadden (1901-1990)
David W. Robinson (1899-1989)
David W. Robinson, II
D. Reece Williams, III
John S. Taylor, Jr.
James M. Brailsford, III
Daniel T. Brailsford
Frank R. Ellerbe, III
Thomas W. Bunch, II
J. Kershaw Spong
D. Clay Robinson
Jacquelyn Lee Bartley
E. Meredith Manning
R. William Metzger, Jr.
Kevin K. Bell
Annemarie B. Mathews

OF COUNSEL

Thomas T. Moore

Representative Clients: NationsBank; Chemical Financial Corp.; Transcontinental Gas Pipe Line Corp.; The Equitable Life Insurance Society of the U.S.; Metropolitan Life Insurance Co.; Firestone Tire & Rubber Co.; Mutual Life Insurance Company of New York.; South Carolina Insurance Reserve Fund; South Carolina Insurance Co.

For full biographical listings, see the Martindale-Hubbell Law Directory

SINKLER & BOYD, P.A. (AV)

Suite 1200 The Palmetto Center, 1426 Main Street, P.O. Box 11889, 29211-1889
Telephone: 803-779-3080
FAX: 803-765-1243
Charleston, South Carolina Office: 160 East Bay Street, P.O. Box 340.
Telephone: 803-722-3366.
FAX: 803-722-2266.
Greenville, South Carolina Office: 15 South Main Street, Suite 500, Wachovia Building, P.O. Box 275.
Telephone: 803-467-1100.
FAX: 803-467-1521.

Charles H. Gibbs (1915-1993)
H. Simmons Tate, Jr.
William C. Boyd
Francis P. Mood
Bachman S. Smith III (Resident, Charleston Office)
Manton M. Grier
Thomas R. Gottshall
Hamilton Osborne, Jr.
Stephen E. Darling (Resident, Charleston Office)
John P. Linton (Resident, Charleston Office)
Harold E. Trask (Resident, Charleston Office)
Marvin D. Infinger (Resident, Charleston Office)
Palmer Freeman, Jr.
Daryl L. Williams
John C. Bruton, Jr.
Elizabeth A. Carpentier
Sue C. Erwin
Clarke W. DuBose
Terri Morrill Lynch (Resident, Charleston Office)
Robert Y. Knowlton
Thomas C. Hildebrand, Jr. (Resident, Charleston Office)
Robert W. Buffington
Bert Glenn Utsey III (Resident, Charleston Office)
Charles H. Gibbs, Jr. (Resident, Charleston Office)
John H. Tiller (Resident, Charleston Office)
Roy A. Howell III (Resident, Charleston Office)
Virginia L. Vroegop

Edward K. Pritchard, III (Resident, Charleston Office)
David W. Whittington (Resident, Charleston Office)
Mark E. Rostick (Resident, Charleston Office)
John F. Emerson
Perrin Q. Dargan, III (Resident, Charleston Office)
Joseph D. Thompson, III (Resident, Charleston Office)

Representative Clients: The South Carolina National Bank; South Carolina Electric & Gas Co.; The Upjohn Co.; Chrysler Corp.; Exxon; Prudential Bache Securities, Inc.; AT&T; Westvaco Corp.; Palmetto Shipping and Stevedoring Co.; Hartford Insurance Co.

For Complete List of Firm Personnel, See General Section

For full biographical listings, see the Martindale-Hubbell Law Directory

TOMPKINS AND McMASTER (AV)

Palmetto Building, Fourth Floor, 1400 Main Street, P.O. Box 7337, 29202
Telephone: 803-799-4499
Telefax: 803-252-2240

MEMBERS OF FIRM

Frank G. Tompkins (1874-1956)
Frank G. Tompkins, Jr. (1908-1973)
Elizabeth Eldridge (1895-1976)
John Gregg McMaster
Henry Dargan McMaster
Frank Barnwell McMaster
Joseph Dargan McMaster

OF COUNSEL

George Hunter McMaster

For full biographical listings, see the Martindale-Hubbell Law Directory

TURNER, PADGET, GRAHAM & LANEY, P.A. (AV)

Seventeenth Floor, 1901 Main Street, P.O. Box 1473, 29202
Telephone: 803-254-2200
Telecopy: 803-799-3957
Florence, South Carolina Office: Fourth Floor, 1831 West Evans Street, P.O. Box 5478, 29501.
Telephone: 803-662-9008.
Telecopy: 803-667-0828.

Nathaniel A. Turner (1897-1959)
Edward W. Laney, III (1930-1980)
Harrell M. Graham (Retired)
George E. Lewis
Ronald E. Boston
Edwin P. Martin
Carl B. Epps, III
W. Duvall Spruill
Charles E. Hill
Thomas C. Salane
Danny C. Crowe
R. Wayne Byrd (Resident, Florence, SC, Office)
W. Hugh McAngus
John S. Wilkerson, III (Resident, Florence, SC, Office)
Steven W. Ouzts
Michael S. Church
Timothy D. St. Clair
Laura Callaway Hart
John E. Cuttino
Arthur E. Justice, Jr. (Resident, Florence, SC, Office)
Edward W. Laney, IV
Elbert S. Dorn
J. Russell Goudelock, II

OF COUNSEL

Henry Fletcher Padget, Jr.
Hugh M. Claytor (Resident, Florence, SC, Office)
James R. Courie

(See Next Column)

TURNER, PADGET, GRAHAM & LANEY P.A., *Columbia—Continued*

J. Kenneth Carter, Jr.

Representative Clients: Independent Life & Accident Insurance Co.; Ford Motor Co.; Insurance Company of North America; Navistar International Corp.; Winn-Dixie Stores, Inc.; Allstate Insurance Co.; Continental Insurance Co.; Atlantic Soft Drink Co.; National Council on Compensation Insurance.

For Complete List of Firm Personnel, See General Section

For full biographical listings, see the Martindale-Hubbell Law Directory

WOODWARD, LEVENTIS, UNGER, DAVES, HERNDON AND COTHRAN (AV)

(Formerly Woodward, Leventis, Unger, Herndon and Cothran)
1300 Sumter, P.O. Box 12399, 29211
Telephone: 803-799-9772
Fax: 803-779-3256

MEMBERS OF FIRM

James C. Leventis
Gary R. Daves
Richard M. Unger
Warren R. Herndon, Jr.
Darra Williamson Cothran

ASSOCIATE

Frances G. Smith

OF COUNSEL

Edward M. Woodward, Sr.
Gwendelyn Geidel
James S. Guignard

General Counsel for: The Columbia College.

For full biographical listings, see the Martindale-Hubbell Law Directory

*GREENVILLE,** Greenville Co.

FEW & FEW, P.A. (AV)

850 Wade Hampton Boulevard, P.O. Box 10085, Fed. Station, 29603
Telephone: 803-232-6456
Fax: 803-370-0671

J. Kendall Few
John C. Few

For full biographical listings, see the Martindale-Hubbell Law Directory

FOSTER & SULLIVAN (AV)

117 Manly Street, P.O. Box 2146, 29602
Telephone: 803-232-5662
Fax: 803-370-1436

Richard J. Foster
Mark D. Sullivan, III
Sam L. Stephenson

For full biographical listings, see the Martindale-Hubbell Law Directory

JAMES R. GILREATH, P.A. (AV)

110 Lavinia Avenue, P.O. Box 2147, 29602
Telephone: 803-242-4727
Telecopier: 803-232-4395

James R. Gilreath

Stephen G. Potts

For full biographical listings, see the Martindale-Hubbell Law Directory

GRANT, LEATHERWOOD & STERN, P.A. (AV)

306 East North Street, Suite 2, P.O. Box 10367, 29603-0367
Telephone: 803-242-2300
Telecopier: 803-242-2280

William M. Grant, Jr.
Judith A. Leatherwood
T. S. Stern, Jr.

Steven A. Snyder
Thomas E. Dudley, III
J. Antonio DelCampo

For full biographical listings, see the Martindale-Hubbell Law Directory

HAYNSWORTH, MARION, MCKAY & GUÉRARD, L.L.P. (AV)

Two Insignia Financial Plaza, 75 Beattie Place, P.O. Box 2048, 29602
Telephone: 803-240-3200
Telecopier: 803-240-3300
Columbia, South Carolina Office: Suite 2400 A T & T Building, 1201 Main Street, P.O. Drawer 7157, 29202
Telephone: 803-765-1818.
Telecopier: 803-765-2399.
Charleston, South Carolina Office: #2 Prioleau Street, P.O. Box 1119, 29402.
Telephone: 803-722-7606.
Telecopier: 803-723-5263.

(See Next Column)

MEMBERS OF FIRM

O. G. Calhoun, Jr.
Ellis M. Johnston, II
Donald L. Ferguson
Thomas H. Coker, Jr.
G. Dewey Oxner, Jr.
W. Francis Marion, Jr.
Jesse C. Belcher, Jr.
John B. McLeod
H. Donald Sellers
Edwin Brown Parkinson, Jr.
Floyd Matlock Elliott

ASSOCIATES

Amy Miller Snyder
Karen Bruning Hipp
Eric Keith Englebardt
Julie Kaye Hackworth
Sarah S. (Sally) McMillan
Matthew P. Utecht
William David Conner

Representative Clients: Wausau Insurance Co.; Prudential Property & Casualty.

For Complete List of Firm Personnel, See General Section

For full biographical listings, see the Martindale-Hubbell Law Directory

LEATHERWOOD WALKER TODD & MANN, P.C. (AV)

100 East Coffee Street, P.O. Box 87, 29602
Telephone: 803-242-6440
FAX: 803-233-8461
Spartanburg, South Carolina Office: 1451 East Main Street, P.O. Box 3188.
Telephone: 803-582-4365.
Telefax: 803-583-8961.

James H. Watson
F. Marion Hughes
J. Brantley Phillips, Jr.
Michael J. Giese
John E. Johnston
Bradford Neal Martin
Harvey G. Sanders, Jr.
Natalma M. McKnew
O. Doyle Martin
Steven E. Farrar
Joseph E. Major
Nancy Hyder Robinson
Duke K. McCall, Jr.
Samuel Wright Outten
J. Richard Kelly
Eugene C. McCall, Jr.
Jack H. Tedards, Jr.
James L. Rogers, Jr.

Tara H. Snyder

COUNSEL

Fletcher C. Mann

Counsel for: John D. Hollingsworth on Wheels, Inc.; Platt Saco Lowell Corporation; Canal Insurance Co.; Suitt Construction Co.
Representative Clients: NationsBank; Springs Industries, Inc.; American Federal Bank, F.S.B.; United States Fidelity & Guaranty Co.; Allstate Insurance Co.; Stevens Aviation Inc.

For Complete List of Firm Personnel, See General Section

For full biographical listings, see the Martindale-Hubbell Law Directory

LOVE, THORNTON, ARNOLD & THOMASON, P.A. (AV)

410 East Washington Street, P.O. Box 10045, 29603
Telephone: 803-242-6360
Telefax: 803-271-7972

Belton O. Thomason, Jr. (1926-1993)
Jack D. Griffeth
William A. Coates
William M. Hagood, III
David L. Moore, Jr.
Theron G. Cochran
James H. Cassidy
Mason A. Goldsmith
V. Clark Price
Carroll H. Roe, Jr.
John Robert Devlin, Jr.
Jennings L. Graves, Jr.
Larry Lee Plumblee

James A. Blair, III

OF COUNSEL

W. Harold Arnold

Counsel for: Aetna Life & Casualty Insurance Co.; Kemper Insurance Group; Continental Insurance Companies Group; Government Employees Insurance Co.; Owens-Corning Fiberglas; First Citizens Bank &Trust Co.; American Federal Bank, F.S.B.; Chrysler Corp.; K-Mart Corp.; Ford Motor Co.

For Complete List of Firm Personnel, See General Section

For full biographical listings, see the Martindale-Hubbell Law Directory

NELSON MULLINS RILEY & SCARBOROUGH L.L.P. (AV)

A Registered Limited Liability Partnership including Professional Corporations
Twenty-Fourth Floor, BB&T Building, 301 North Main Street, P.O. Box 10084, 29603
Telephone: 803-250-2300
Telecopy: 803-232-2925
Atlanta, Georgia Office: 1201 Peachtree Street, N.E., P.O. Box 77707.
Telephone: 404-817-6000.
Telecopy: 404-817-6050.
Charleston, South Carolina Office: Suite 500, 151 Meeting Street, P.O. Box 1806.
Telephone: 803-853-5200.
Telecopy: 803-722-8700.

(See Next Column)

NELSON MULLINS RILEY & SCARBOROUGH L.L.P.—*Continued*

Columbia, South Carolina Office: Third Floor, Keenan Building. 1300 Lady Street. P.O. Box 11070.
Telephone: 803-799-2000.
Telecopy: 803-256-7500; 803-733-9499.
Florence, South Carolina Office: 600 W. Palmetto Street, Suite 200, P.O. Box 5955.
Telephone: 803-662-0019.
Telecopy: 803-662-0491.
Lexington, South Carolina Office: 334 Old Chapin Road, P.O. Box 729.
Telephone: 803-733-9494; 803-799-200.
Telecopy: 803-957-8226.
Myrtle Beach, South Carolina Office: 2411 N. Oak Street, Founders Centre, Suite 301. P.O. Box 3939.
Telephone: 803-448-3500.
Telecopy: 803-448-3437.

MEMBERS OF FIRM

Kenneth E. Young
George K. Lyall
Erroll Anne Yarbrough Hodges

ASSOCIATE

A. Marvin Quattlebaum

Representative Clients: Bi-Lo, Inc.; Mount Vernon Mills, Inc.; Willamette Industries, Inc.; Hoescht Celanese, Inc.; Robert Bosch Corp.; Citizens and Southern National Bank of South Carolina; Westinghouse Electric Corp., Wometco, Inc.; General Motors Corp.; Navistar International Transportation Corp.

For Complete List of Firm Personnel, See General Section

For full biographical listings, see the Martindale-Hubbell Law Directory

PARHAM & SMITH (AV)
Suite 200 Falls Place, 531 South Main, 29601
Telephone: 803-235-5692; 242-9008

MEMBERS OF FIRM

Michael Parham
Barney O. Smith, Jr.

For full biographical listings, see the Martindale-Hubbell Law Directory

WYCHE, BURGESS, FREEMAN & PARHAM, PROFESSIONAL ASSOCIATION (AV)
44 East Camperdown Way, P.O. Box 728, 29602-0728
Telephone: 803-242-8200
Telecopier: 803-235-8900

C. Thomas Wyche
David L. Freeman
James C. Parham, Jr.
James M. Shoemaker, Jr.
William W. Kehl
Charles W. Wofford
Larry D. Estridge
D. Allen Grumbine
Cary H. Hall, Jr.
Carl F. Muller
Henry L. Parr, Jr.
Bradford W. Wyche
Eric B. Amstutz
Marshall Winn
Wallace K. Lightsey
Lesley R. Moore
William D. Herlong
Jo Watson Hackl
William P. Crawford, Jr.
J. Theodore Gentry
Gregory J. English

Counsel for: Multimedia, Inc.; Delta Woodside Industries, Inc.; Milliken & Company; Ryan's Family Steak Houses, Inc.; St. Francis Hospital; Span-America Medical Systems, Inc.; Carolina First Bank; KEMET Electronics Corp.; Builder Marts of America, Inc.; One Price Clothing, Inc.

For Complete List of Firm Personnel, See General Section

For full biographical listings, see the Martindale-Hubbell Law Directory

HILTON HEAD ISLAND, Beaufort Co.

JOHN J. MCKAY, JR., P.A. (AV)
Suite 203 WatersEdge at Shelter Cove, 29928
Telephone: 803-785-7648
Telefax: 803-842-2481 ABA NET ID: !MCKAYJ

John J. McKay, Jr.

For full biographical listings, see the Martindale-Hubbell Law Directory

RUTH & MACNEILLE, PROFESSIONAL ASSOCIATION (AV)
The Anchor Bank Building, 11 Pope Avenue, 29938
Telephone: 803-785-4251
Telex: 988944
Telecopier: 803-686-5404

William A. Ruth
Douglas W. MacNeille
Michael G. Olivetti
Keri A. Jordan

Michael K. Knudsen

References: NationsBank of South Carolina, N.A.; Anchor Bank; South Carolina National Bank; Chicago Title Insurance Corp.; First American Title Insurance Co.

For full biographical listings, see the Martindale-Hubbell Law Directory

MYRTLE BEACH, Horry Co.

BELLAMY, RUTENBERG, COPELAND, EPPS, GRAVELY & BOWERS, P.A. (AV)
1000 29th Avenue North, P.O. Box 357, 29578
Telephone: 803-448-2400
Telecopier: 803-448-3022

Howell V. Bellamy, Jr.
John K. Rutenberg
John E. Copeland
Claude M. Epps, Jr.
David R. Gravely
Edward B. Bowers, Jr.
Bradley D. King
Henrietta U. Golding
R. Michael Munden
M. Edwin Hinds, Jr.
Jill F. Griffith
Kathryn M. Cook
David B. Miller
Deirdre M. Whisenant-Edmonds
Daniel J. MacDonald
C. Winfield Johnson, III
Janet L. Carter

Representative Clients: Dargan Construction Co.; Coastal Federal Savings Bank; Sands Investments; Wachovia Bank of South Carolina; AVX Corp.; NationsBank of South Carolina, N.A.; Parthenon Insurance Co.; Burroughs & Chapin Co.; International Paper Co.; Hospital Corporation of America.

For full biographical listings, see the Martindale-Hubbell Law Directory

NELSON MULLINS RILEY & SCARBOROUGH L.L.P. (AV)

A Registered Limited Liability Partnership including Professional Corporations
Founders Centre, 2411 N. Oak Street, Suite 301, P.O. Box 3939, 29578-3939
Telephone: 803-448-3500
Telecopy: 803-448-3437
Atlanta, Georgia Office: 400 Colony Square, 1201 Peachtree Street, N.E., P.O. Box 77707.
Telephone: 404-817-6000.
Telecopy: 404-817-6050.
Charleston, South Carolina Office: 151 Meeting Street, Suite 400, P.O. Box 1806.
Telephone: 803-853-5200.
Telecopy: 803-722-8700.
Columbia, South Carolina Office: Third Floor, Keenan Building. 1330 Lady Street. P.O. Box 11070.
Telephone: 803-799-2000.
Telecopy: 803-256-7500; 733-9499.
Florence, South Carolina Office: 600 W. Palmetto Street, Suite 200, P.O. Box 5955.
Telephone: 803-662-0019.
Telecopy: 803-662-0491.
Greenville, South Carolina Office: Twenty-Fourth Floor, BB&T Building, 301 North Main Street.
Telephone: 803-250-2300.
Telecopy: 803-232-2925.
Lexington, South Carolina Office: 334 Old Chapin Road.
Telephone: 803-733-9494; 799-2000.
Telecopy: 803-957-8226

MEMBERS OF FIRM

Susan Pardue MacDonald
Thomas F. Moran

ASSOCIATE

Phillip Luke Hughes

Representative Clients: Federated Insurance Co.; Cincinnati Insurance Co.; American Honda Motor Co.; Chicago Title; Chubb Insurance Co.; Colonial Penn Life Insurance Co.; South Carolina National Bank; Crum & Forster Managers Corp.; Diamond Mortgage Co.

For Complete List of Firm Personnel, See General Section

For full biographical listings, see the Martindale-Hubbell Law Directory

STEVENS, STEVENS & THOMAS, P.C. (AV)
1215 48th Avenue North, 29577-2468
Telephone: 803-449-9675
Fax: 803-497-2262
Loris, South Carolina Office: 3341 Broad Street.
Telephone: 803-756-7652.
Fax: 803-756-3785.

James P. Stevens, Jr. (Resident, Loris Office)
J. Jackson Thomas

Angela T. Jordan (Resident Loris Office)

OF COUNSEL

James P. Stevens

For full biographical listings, see the Martindale-Hubbell Law Directory

*SPARTANBURG,** Spartanburg Co.

HARRISON & HAYES (AV)
200 Library Street, Second Floor, P.O. Box 5367, 29304
Telephone: 803-542-2990
Fax: 803-542-2994

(See Next Column)

HARRISON & HAYES, *Spartanburg—Continued*

Benjamin C. Harrison J. Mark Hayes, II

For full biographical listings, see the Martindale-Hubbell Law Directory

HOLCOMBE, BOMAR, COTHRAN AND GUNN, P.A. (AV)

Flagstar Plaza, 203 East Main Street, P.O. Drawer 1897, 29304
Telephone: 803-585-4273
Telecopier: 803-585-3844

William U. Gunn Reginald L. Foster
James C. Cothran, Jr. Perry D. Boulier

William B. Darwin, Jr. S. Sterling Laney, III

Representative Clients: Canteen Corp.; Denny's, Inc.; Wofford College; Community Cash Stores; Liberty Mutual Insurance Cos.; Kemper Insurance Group; Reliance Insurance Cos.; Mary Black Memorial Hospital, Inc.

For Complete List of Firm Personnel, See General Section

For full biographical listings, see the Martindale-Hubbell Law Directory

LEATHERWOOD WALKER TODD & MANN, P.C. (AV)

1451 East Main Street, P.O. Box 3188, 29304-3188
Telephone: 803-582-4365
Telefax: 803-585-8961
Greenville, South Carolina Office: 100 East Coffee Street, P.O. Box 87.
Telephone: 803-242-6440.
FAX: 803-233-8461.

H. Spencer King Russell D. Ghent

Susan A. Fretwell

For Complete List of Firm Personnel, See General Section

For full biographical listings, see the Martindale-Hubbell Law Directory

*SUMTER,** Sumter Co.

LEE, WILSON & ERTER (AV)

126 North Main Street, P.O. Drawer 580, 29150
Telephone: 803-778-2471
Telecopier: 803-778-1643

MEMBERS OF FIRM

Jack W. Erter, Jr. Harry C. Wilson, Jr.

Representative Clients: South Carolina National Bank; Carolina Power and Light Co.; Peoples Natural Gas Company of South Carolina; First Federal Savings & Loan Assn.; Allstate Insurance Co.; American Surety Co.; Prudential Insurance Company of America; General Telephone; Korn Industries, Inc.; V-B William Furniture Company, Inc.

For Complete List of Firm Personnel, See General Section

For full biographical listings, see the Martindale-Hubbell Law Directory

*WALHALLA,** Oconee Co.

LARRY C. BRANDT, P.A. (AV)

205 West Main Street, P.O. Drawer 738, 29691
Telephone: 803-638-5406
803-638-7873

Larry C. Brandt

D. Bradley Jordan J. Bruce Schumpert

LEGAL SUPPORT PERSONNEL

Debra C. Miller

For full biographical listings, see the Martindale-Hubbell Law Directory

SOUTH DAKOTA

*BELLE FOURCHE,** Butte Co.

QUINN, EIESLAND, DAY & BARKER (AV)

117 Fifth Avenue, P.O. Box 370, 57717-0370
Telephone: 605-892-2743
Fax: 605-892-4273
Rapid City, South Dakota Office: 4200 Beach Drive, P.O. Box 9335.
Telephone: 605-343-6400.
Telecopier: 605-343-4841.

Terence R. Quinn Michael W. Day
Gregory A. Eiesland (Resident, Rapid City Office) Kenneth E. Barker

(See Next Column)

ASSOCIATES

Robert L. Morris, II Michael P. Reynolds (Resident, Rapid City)
Bradley A. Schreiber
Michael A. Wilson (Resident, Rapid City Office)

OF COUNSEL

R. E. Brandenburg

Representative Clients: Pioneer Bank & Trust, Belle Fourche, Spearfish and Rapid City Offices; Belle Fourche Irrigation District; Butte-Meade Sanitary Water District; Igloo-Provo Water User Project; Strawberry Hill Mining Co.; American Family Insurance Group.

For full biographical listings, see the Martindale-Hubbell Law Directory

*BROOKINGS,** Brookings Co.

LEWAYNE M. ERICKSON, P.C. (AV)

517 Sixth Street, 57006-1436
Telephone: 605-692-6158
Fax: 605-692-7734

Lewayne M. Erickson

For full biographical listings, see the Martindale-Hubbell Law Directory

*RAPID CITY,** Pennington Co.

BANGS, MCCULLEN, BUTLER, FOYE & SIMMONS (AV)

818 St. Joseph Street, P.O. Box 2670, 57709
Telephone: 605-343-1040
Telecopier: 605-343-1503

MEMBERS OF FIRM

Joseph M. Butler Michael M. Hickey
Thomas E. Simmons Mark F. Marshall
Allen G. Nelson Terry L. Hofer
James P. Hurley Patrick Duffy

ASSOCIATES

Rodney W. Schlauger Jeffrey G. Hurd
Daniel F. Duffy Veronica L. Bowen

Representative Clients: Norwest Bank South Dakota, N.A., Rapid City, S.D.; Pete Lien & Sons; The Travelers Insurance Co.; Rapid City Regional Hospital; Dakota Steel & Supply Co.; Great American Insurance Co.; Fireman's Fund Insurance; United States Automobile Association; Moyle Petroleum; Rapid City Area School District 51-4.

For Complete List of Firm Personnel, See General Section

For full biographical listings, see the Martindale-Hubbell Law Directory

COSTELLO, PORTER, HILL, HEISTERKAMP & BUSHNELL (AV)

200 Security Building, 704 St. Joseph Street, P.O. Box 290, 57709
Telephone: 605-343-2410
Telecopier: 605-343-4262

RETIRED

John M. Costello William G. Porter

MEMBERS OF FIRM

Dennis H. Hill Thomas W. Stanton
Kenneth L. Heisterkamp Robert L. Lewis
Gene R. Bushnell Lonnie R. Braun
Richard O. Sharpe David M. Dillon
Edward C. Carpenter Gregory G. Strommen
Thomas H. Barnes Patricia A. Meyers
Donald A. Porter William A. May

ASSOCIATE

Stephen C. Hoffman

Representative Clients: St. Paul Cos.; Home Insurance Cos.; Black Hills Medical Center; Midwest Coast Transport, Inc.; Southeastern Aviation Underwriters; Pioneer Bank & Trust Co.; Burlington Northern, Inc.; Ford Motor Company; Farmers Insurance Group; Lutheran Hospital and Homes Society.

For Complete List of Firm Personnel, See General Section

For full biographical listings, see the Martindale-Hubbell Law Directory

GUNDERSON, PALMER, GOODSELL & NELSON (AV)

440 Mount Rushmore Road, 4th Floor, P.O. Box 8045, 57709-8045
Telephone: 605-342-1078
Fax: 605-342-9503

MEMBERS OF FIRM

Wynn A. Gunderson Donald P. Knudsen
J. Crisman Palmer Patrick G. Goetzinger
G. Verne Goodsell Talbot J. Wieczorek
James S. Nelson Paul S. Swedlund
Daniel E. Ashmore Mark J. Connot

Representative Clients: Norwest Bank South Dakota, N.A.; Sodak Gaming, Inc.; Bally Gaming, Inc.; SEGA of America; United States Fidelity & Guaranty Co.; Aetna Life and Casualty Co.; Homestake Mining Company; Wal-

(See Next Column)

GUNDERSON, PALMER, GOODSELL & NELSON—*Continued*

Mart Stores, Inc.; Dain Bosworth, Inc.; Underwriters Counsel/Norwest Investment Services.

For full biographical listings, see the Martindale-Hubbell Law Directory

LYNN, JACKSON, SHULTZ & LEBRUN, P.C. (AV)

Eighth Floor, Metropolitan Federal Bank Plaza, P.O. Box 8250, 57709
Telephone: 605-342-2592
Telecopier: 605-342-5185
Sioux Falls, South Dakota Office: First Bank Building, Sixth Floor, P.O. Box 1920.
Telephone: 605-332-5999.
Telecopier: 605-332-4249.

Kelton S. Lynn (1916-1974)
Horace R. Jackson (1907-1987)
Donald R. Shultz
William F. Day, Jr. (Resident, Sioux Falls Office)
Gene N. Lebrun
Thomas G. Fritz
Haven L. Stuck
Gary D. Jensen
Steven C. Beardsley
Lee A. Magnuson (Resident, Sioux Falls Office)
Steven J. Helmers
Jay C. Shultz
Larry M. VonWald
Jane Wipf Pfeifle
Jon C. Sogn (Resident, Sioux Falls Office)
Kurt E. Solay
R. Alan Peterson (Resident, Sioux Falls Office)
Leah J. Fjerstad
Craig A. Pfeifle
Steven J. Oberg
David L. Nadolski (Resident, Sioux Falls Office)

Representative Clients: First Bank of South Dakota; Employers Mutual of Wausau; South Dakota School Mines & Technology; CIGNA Insurance Co.; E.D. Jones & Co.; Prairie States Life Insurance Co.
General Counsel for: Rushmore Electric Power Cooperative; Black Hills Regional Eye Institute; Douglas School District.

For Complete List of Firm Personnel, See General Section

For full biographical listings, see the Martindale-Hubbell Law Directory

QUINN, EIESLAND, DAY & BARKER (AV)

4200 Beach Drive, P.O. Box 9335, 57709-9335
Telephone: 605-343-6400
Fax: 605-343-4841
Belle Fourche, South Dakota Office: 117 Fifth Avenue, P.O. Box 370.
Telephone: 605-892-2743.
Fax: 605-892-4273.

Terence R. Quinn
Gregory A. Eiesland (Resident)
Michael W. Day
Kenneth E. Barker

ASSOCIATES

Robert L. Morris, II
Bradley A. Schreiber
Michael A. Wilson (Resident)
Michael P. Reynolds (Resident)

OF COUNSEL

R. E. Brandenburg

Representative Clients: Pioneer Bank & Trust, Belle Fource, Spearfish and Rapid City Offices; Belle Fourche Irrigation District; Butte-Meade Sanitary Water District; Igloo-Provo Water User Project; Strawberry Hill Mining Co.; American Family Insurance Group; State Farm Insurance Companies; Twin City Testing Corp.; Eli Lilly & Co.

For full biographical listings, see the Martindale-Hubbell Law Directory

WALLAHAN, BANKS & EICHER, P.C. (AV)

Rushmore Professional Building, 731 St. Joseph Street, P.O. Box 328, 57709-0328
Telephone: 605-348-0456
Fax: 605-348-0458

Franklin J. Wallahan (1935-1994)
Ronald W. Banks
Benjamin J. Eicher
Samuel D. Kerr

Representative Clients: All Nations Insurance Company; Colonial Insurance Company of California; Dairyland Insurance Company; The Maryland Sentry Insurance Company; Union Insurance Company; U.S. Insurance Group.

For full biographical listings, see the Martindale-Hubbell Law Directory

*SIOUX FALLS,** Minnehaha Co.

DANFORTH, MEIERHENRY & MEIERHENRY (AV)

315 South Phillips, 57102
Telephone: 605-336-3075
Fax: 605-336-2593

George J. Danforth (1875-1952)
George J. Danforth, Jr. (1909-1991)
Mark V. Meierhenry
Todd V. Meierhenry
Sabrina Meierhenry

ASSOCIATE

David K. Mickelberg

For full biographical listings, see the Martindale-Hubbell Law Directory

DAVENPORT, EVANS, HURWITZ & SMITH (AV)

513 South Main Avenue, P.O. Box 1030, 57101-1030
Telephone: 605-336-2880
Telecopier: 605-335-3639

OF COUNSEL

Deming Smith

MEMBERS OF FIRM

Edwin E. Evans
Michael L. Luce
Michael J. Schaffer
Thomas M. Frankman
Rick W. Orr
Timothy M. Gebhart
Susan Jansa Brunick
Roberto A. Lange

ASSOCIATES

Michael A. Hauck
Marie Elizabeth Hovland
Cheryle M. Wiedmeier
Lori Purcell Fossen
Sandra K. Hoglund
Mark W. Haigh

Counsel for: American Society of Composers, Authors and Publishers (A.S.C.A.P.); Burlington Northern, Inc.; Continental Insurance Cos.; The First National Bank in Sioux Falls; Ford Motor Credit Co.; General Motors Corp.; The St. Paul Cos.; The Travelers.

For Complete List of Firm Personnel, See General Section

For full biographical listings, see the Martindale-Hubbell Law Directory

HOY & HOY (AV)

401 South 2nd Avenue, 57102-1004
Telephone: 605-336-2600
Fax: 605-336-8564

MEMBERS OF FIRM

Carleton R. Hoy
James L. Hoy

Representative Clients: St. Paul Cos.; Phico Insurance Co.; Minnesota Medical Insurance Exchange; IMT Insurance Co.; The Travelers; National Chiropractic Mutual Insurance Co.; The Doctors' Company; Catholic Health Corporation; Continental Western Insurance Co.; Podiatry Insurance Company of America.

For full biographical listings, see the Martindale-Hubbell Law Directory

TENNESSEE

*ATHENS,** McMinn Co.

CARTER, HARROD & CUNNINGHAM (AV)

One Madison Avenue, P.O. Box 885, 37371-0885
Telephone: 615-745-7447
FAX: 615-745-6114

MEMBERS OF FIRM

Allen H. Carter (1938-1987)
David F. Harrod
Jeffrey L. Cunningham

Counsel for: Citizens National Bank; Athens Federal Savings & Loan Assn.; Athens Utilities Board; Bowaters Incorporated.
Representative Clients: Liberty Mutual Insurance Co.; Nationwide Insurance Cos.; State Farm Mutual Automobile Insurance Co.; United States Fidelity & Guaranty Insurance Co.

For Complete List of Firm Personnel, See General Section

For full biographical listings, see the Martindale-Hubbell Law Directory

*CHATTANOOGA,** Hamilton Co.

CAMPBELL & CAMPBELL (AV)

1200 James Building, 37402
Telephone: 615-266-1108
Fax: 615-266-8222

MEMBERS OF FIRM

Paul Campbell (1885-1974)
Paul Campbell, Jr.
Michael Ross Campbell
Paul Campbell, III
Douglas M. Campbell

ASSOCIATE

Odile M. Farrell

OF COUNSEL

James C. Lee (P.C.)

Representative Clients: Tennessee Farmers Mutual Insurance Co.; Pennsylvania National Mutual Casualty Insurance Co.; Amerisure Cos.; National Grange Mutual Insurance Co.

For full biographical listings, see the Martindale-Hubbell Law Directory

CHAMBLISS & BAHNER (AV)

1000 Tallan Building, Two Union Square, 37402-2500
Telephone: 615-756-3000
Fax: 615-265-9574

(See Next Column)

CHAMBLISS & BAHNER, *Chattanooga—Continued*

MEMBERS OF FIRM

T. Maxfield Bahner
William H. Pickering
Gary D. Lander
Bruce C. Bailey
Donald J. Aho

ASSOCIATES

K. Scott Graham
Benjamin Younger Pitts
C. Caldwell H. Huckabay
Collette R. Jones
Anthony A. Jackson
Timothy M. Gibbons
Joseph A. San Filippo

General Counsel for: McKee Foods Corporation; Porter Warner Inds., Inc.; SCT Yarns, Inc.; Stein Construction Co., Inc.
Representative Clients: First American National Bank; Ernst & Young; Provident Life & Accident Insurance Company; BancBoston Financial Company; Liberty Mutual Insurance Company.

For Complete List of Firm Personnel, See General Section

For full biographical listings, see the Martindale-Hubbell Law Directory

FLEISSNER, COOPER, MARCUS & QUINN (AV)

800 Vine Street, 37403
Telephone: 615-756-3595
Telecopier: 615-266-5455

Phillip A. Fleissner
Gary A. Cooper
H. Richard Marcus
J. Bartlett Quinn
Robert L. Widerkehr, Jr.

ASSOCIATE

Cynthia D. Hall

For full biographical listings, see the Martindale-Hubbell Law Directory

FOSTER, FOSTER, ALLEN & DURRENCE (AV)

Formerly Hall, Haynes & Foster
Suite 515 Pioneer Bank Building, 37402
Telephone: 615-266-1141
Telecopier: 615-266-4618

MEMBERS OF FIRM

George Lane Foster
William M. Foster
Craig R. Allen
Phillip M. Durrence, Jr.

ASSOCIATES

David J. Ward
Clayton M. Whittaker
John M. Hull

LEGAL SUPPORT PERSONNEL

Peggy Sue Bates

Division Counsel for: Alabama Great Southern Railroad Co.; C.N.O. & T.P. Railway Co.
Attorneys for: CNA/Insurance; U.S.P. & G. Co.; The Firestone Tire & Rubber Co.; Exxon, Corp.; Murphy Oil Corp.; Chicago Title Insurance Co.; City of East Ridge; Jim Walter Homes; Raymond James & Associates; Morgan Keegan & Co.

For full biographical listings, see the Martindale-Hubbell Law Directory

GEARHISER, PETERS & HORTON (AV)

320 McCallie Avenue, 37402-2007
Telephone: 615-756-5171
Fax: 615-266-1605

MEMBERS OF FIRM

Charles J. Gearhiser
R. Wayne Peters
William H. Horton
Roy C. Maddox, Jr.
Robert L. Lockaby, Jr.
Ralph E. Tallant, Jr.
Terry Atkin Cavett
Sam D. Elliott
Lane C. Avery
Michael A. Anderson
Wade K. Cannon

ASSOCIATE

Robin L. Miller

References: First Tennessee Bank; Pioneer Bank.

For full biographical listings, see the Martindale-Hubbell Law Directory

SHUMACKER & THOMPSON (AV)

Suite 500, First Tennessee Building, 701 Market Street, 37402-4800
Telephone: 615-265-2214
Telecopier: 615-266-1842
Branch Office: Suite 103, One Park Place, 6148 Lee Highway, Chattanooga, Tennessee, 37421-2900.
Telephone: 615-855-1814.
Telecopier: 615-899-1278.

MEMBERS OF FIRM

Albert W. Secor
W. Neil Thomas, III
William Given Colvin
Harold L. North, Jr.
Everett L. Hixson, Jr.
Phillip E. Fleenor

For Complete List of Firm Personnel, See General Section

For full biographical listings, see the Martindale-Hubbell Law Directory

SPEARS, MOORE, REBMAN & WILLIAMS (AV)

8th Floor Blue Cross Building, 801 Pine Street, 37402
Telephone: 615-756-7000
Facsimile: 615-756-4801

MEMBERS OF FIRM

Alvin O'B. Moore
Silas Williams, Jr.
Edward Blake Moore
Thomas S. Kale
Joseph C. Wilson, III
W. Ferber Tracy
Fred Henry Moore
Lynnwood Hale Hamilton
Robert J. Boehm
L. Marie Williams
F. Scott LeRoy
Harry L. Dadds, II
Joseph R. White
David E. Fowler

ASSOCIATES

Barry A. Steelman
Robert G. Norred Jr.
Rodney L. Umberger, Jr.
Howell Dean Clements
John B. Bennett
E. Brent Hill (Not admitted in TN)
Angela A. Ripper

OF COUNSEL

Buckner S. Morris
Micheline Kelly Johnson

Representative Clients: State Farm Mutual Automobile Insurance Cos.; St. Paul Insurance Cos.; State Volunteer Mutual Insurance Co.; Chattanooga-Hamilton County Hospital Authority (Erlanger Medical Center); Blue Cross and Blue Shield of Tennessee; Chattanooga Gas Co.; Pioneer Bank; Tennessee Consolidated Coal Co.; USAA; The Virginia Insurance Reciprocal.

For Complete List of Firm Personnel, See General Section

For full biographical listings, see the Martindale-Hubbell Law Directory

STOPHEL & STOPHEL, P.C. (AV)

500 Tallan Building, Two Union Square, 37402-2571
Telephone: 615-756-2333
Fax: 615-266-5032

Richard W. Bethea, Jr.
W. Lee Maddux
W. Jeffrey Hollingsworth
Arthur P. Brock

Ronald D. Gorsline
Stephen S. Duggins
William R. Dearing
Lisa A. Yacuzzo
Allison A. Cardwell
John W. Rose

Representative Clients: Astec Industries, Inc.; Georgia-Pacific Corp.; State Volunteer Mutual Insurance Company; Graco Children's Products, Inc.; Browning-Ferris Industries, Inc.; Soloff Construction Company, Inc.; Police Benevolence Association, Inc.; Banker's Multiple Line Insurance Company; Roadtec, Inc.; Telsmith, Inc.

For Complete List of Firm Personnel, See General Section

For full biographical listings, see the Martindale-Hubbell Law Directory

SUMMERS, MCCREA & WYATT, P.C. (AV)

500 Lindsay Street, 37402
Telephone: 615-265-2385
Fax: 615-266-5211

Jerry H. Summers
Sandra K. McCrea
Thomas L. Wyatt
Jeffrey W. Rufolo

Representative Clients: Glass, Molders, Pottery, Plastics and Allied Workers, International; Plumbers & Steamfitters, Local 43; International Brotherhood of Boilermakers, #656; United Steelworkers, District 35; International Association of Machinists and Aerospace Workers, Local 56; Graphics Communication International Union, Local 394; International Brotherhood of Electrical Workers, Local 175; Chattanooga Building and Construction Trades Council; Carpenters Local 74; Ironworkers Local 704; Ironworkers District Council.

For full biographical listings, see the Martindale-Hubbell Law Directory

WEILL & WEILL (AV)

Eleventh Floor, Chubb Life Building, 37402
Telephone: 615-756-5900
Telecopier: 615-756-5909

MEMBERS OF FIRM

Harry Weill
Flossie Weill
James S. Dreaden
Wilfred Shawn Clelland

ASSOCIATES

James Rayburn Kennamer
Brian Kopet

For full biographical listings, see the Martindale-Hubbell Law Directory

WITT, GAITHER & WHITAKER, P.C. (AV)

1100 American National Bank Building, 37402-2608
Telephone: 615-265-8881
Telefax: 615-266-4138; 615-756-5612

(See Next Column)

WITT, GAITHER & WHITAKER P.C.—*Continued*

John P. Gaither (1915-1994)
William P. Hutcheson (1923-1991)
Philip B. Whitaker
John W. Murrey, III
Hugh J. Moore, Jr.
Frank P. Pinchak
John F. Henry, Jr.
Harold Alan Schwartz, Jr.
K. Stephen Powers
Carter J. Lynch, III
Geoffrey G. Young
Ralph M. Killebrew, Jr.
Rosemarie Luise Bryan
Douglas E. Peck
Jonathan M. Minnen

OF COUNSEL

Raymond Buckner Witt, Jr.
Shields Wilson
Gary M. Disheroon
Frank M. Groves, Jr.

Representative Clients: American National Bank & Trust Company; Chattanooga Cetropolitan Airport Authority; Chrysler Insurance Co.; Coca-Cola Bottling Co. Consolidated; Dean Witter Reynolds, Inc.; Dixie Yarns, Inc.; E.I. du Pont de Nemours & Company; Signal Apparel Company, Inc.; Southwest Motor Freight, Inc.; University of Chattanooga Foundation, Inc.

For Complete List of Firm Personnel, See General Section

For full biographical listings, see the Martindale-Hubbell Law Directory

*CLEVELAND,** Bradley Co.

BELL AND ASSOCIATES, P.C. (AV)

140 Ocoee Street, N.E., P.O. Box 1169, 37364-1169
Telephone: 615-476-8541
Facsimile: 615-339-3510

Michael E. Callaway
John F. Kimball
Marcia M. McMurray

Barrett T. Painter

Representative Clients: Tennessee Farmers Mutual Ins. Co.; State Volunteer Mutual Insurance Co.; Duracell, USA; Nationwide; Bradley Memorial Hospital; American National Bank and Trust Company of Chattanooga; South Central Bell.

For Complete List of Firm Personnel, See General Section

For full biographical listings, see the Martindale-Hubbell Law Directory

JENNE, SCOTT & BRYANT (AV)

260 Ocoee Street, P.O. Box 161, 37364-0161
Telephone: 615-476-5506
Fax: 615-476-5058

MEMBERS OF FIRM

Roger E. Jenne
D. Mitchell Bryant

For Complete List of Firm Personnel, See General Section

For full biographical listings, see the Martindale-Hubbell Law Directory

DENNY E. MOBBS (AV)

55 1/2 First Street, N.E., P.O. Box 192, 37364-0192
Telephone: 615-472-7181

Representative Clients: Liberty Mutual Ins. Co.; Shelby Mutual Insurance Co.; Carolina Casualty Co.; Maytag Corp. (Magic Chef, Inc.-Hardwick Stove Company); Industrial Development Board of Polk County; Polk County News-Citizen Advance; Ocoee Inn & Marina.

For full biographical listings, see the Martindale-Hubbell Law Directory

*COOKEVILLE,** Putnam Co.

MADEWELL & JARED (AV)

Suite One, Fourth Floor, First Tennessee Bank Building, P.O. Box 721, 38503-0721
Telephone: 615-526-6101
FAX: 615-528-1909

MEMBERS OF FIRM

Eugene Jared
James D. Madewell
William E. Halfacre, III

Representative Clients: State of Tennessee; Trial Counsel as Special Assistant to Attorney General; Bank of Putnam County; First Tennessee Bank, N.A. at Cookeville; The Maryland; Transamerica Ins. Group; Home Insurance Co.; Auto Owners Ins. Co.; Insurance Company of North America; Fireman's Fund Insurance Co.

For Complete List of Firm Personnel, See General Section

For full biographical listings, see the Martindale-Hubbell Law Directory

MOORE, RADER, CLIFT AND FITZPATRICK, P.C. (AV)

46 North Jefferson Avenue, P.O. Box 3347, 38501
Telephone: 615-526-3311
Fax: 615-526-3092

(See Next Column)

L. Dean Moore
Daniel H. Rader, III
Michael E. Clift
Walter S. Fitzpatrick, III

General Counsel for: First Tennessee Bank.
Local Counsel for: Heritage Ford-Lincoln-Mercury, Inc.
Representative Clients: Continental Insurance Co.; Kemper Group; U.S.F.&G.; Auto Owners Insurance Co.; Wausau Insurance Cos.

For full biographical listings, see the Martindale-Hubbell Law Directory

*DYERSBURG,** Dyer Co.

ASHLEY, ASHLEY & ARNOLD (AV)

322 Church Avenue, P.O. Box H, 38024
Telephone: 901-285-5074
Telecopier: 901-285-5089

MEMBERS OF FIRM

Barret Ashley
Randolph A. Ashley, Jr.
S. Leo Arnold
Stephen D. Scofield
Marianna Williams
Carol Anne Austin
Anthony Lee Winchester

OF COUNSEL

Joree G. Brownlow

Representative Clients: Illinois Central Gulf Railroad; Bekeart Steel Wire Corp.; Fidelity and Deposit Company of Maryland; St. Paul Fire and Marine Insurance Company.
Construction Company Clients: Folk Construction Co.; Ford Construction Company; Luhr Brothers, Inc.; Pine Bluff Sand & Gravel; Valley Construction Co.

For full biographical listings, see the Martindale-Hubbell Law Directory

*ELIZABETHTON,** Carter Co.

ALLEN, NELSON & BOWERS (AV)

Bowers Building, 619 East Elk Avenue, 37643-3329
Telephone: 615-542-4154

MEMBERS OF FIRM

W. R. Allen (1863-1947)
Roy C. Nelson (1904-1977)
John L. Bowers, Jr.
John L. Bowers, III
Gregory H. Bowers

General Counsel for: Elizabethton Federal Savings Bank; Elizabethon Newspaper, Inc.
Local Counsel for: North American Rayon Corp.; State Farm Mutual Automobile Insurance Co.; Home Indemnity Co.; U. S. F. & G. Co.; State Automobile Mutual Insurance Co. of Ohio; Federated Implement and Hardware Insurance Co.
Approved Attorneys for: Lawyers Title Insurance Corp.

For full biographical listings, see the Martindale-Hubbell Law Directory

*GALLATIN,** Sumner Co.

McCLELLAN, POWERS, EHMLING & DIX, P.C. (AV)

McClellan Building, 116 Public Square, 37066-2887
Telephone: 615-452-5872
FAX: 615-452-0054
Murfreesboro, Tennessee Office: Suite 201, Court Square Building, 201 West Main Street.
Telephone: 615-895-2529.
FAX: 615-896-7254.

Arthur E. McClellan
Dennis Wade Powers
M. Allen Ehmling

Kevin Carr

Representative Clients: First Independent Bank; Tennessee Farmers Mutual Insurance Co.; Travelers Insurance Co.; Blue Cross and Blue Shield of Tennessee; Aetna Casualty & Surety Co.

For full biographical listings, see the Martindale-Hubbell Law Directory

*GREENEVILLE,** Greene Co.

ROGERS, LAUGHLIN, NUNNALLY, HOOD & CRUM (AV)

100 South Main Street Corner of Main & Depot Streets, 37743
Telephone: 615-639-5183
FAX: 615-639-6154

MEMBERS OF FIRM

John T. Milburn Rogers
Jerry W. Laughlin
William S. Nunnally
Kenneth C. Hood
Edward Grant Crum

OF COUNSEL

Thomas W. Overall

Representative Clients: First Tennessee Bank; Andrew Johnson Bank; Marsh Petroleum Co.; Greeneville Insurance Agency, Inc.; Pet Credit Union; Bewley Motor Company & Olds-Subaru; Southern Packaging and Storage Co., Inc.
General Counsel for: Greene County Bank; Allen Petroleum Co., (Exxon); The Austin Co.

(See Next Column)

ROGERS, LAUGHLIN, NUNNALLY, HOOD & CRUM, *Greeneville—Continued*

For Complete List of Firm Personnel, See General Section

For full biographical listings, see the Martindale-Hubbell Law Directory

*JACKSON,** Madison Co.

MOSS, BENTON, WALLIS & PETTIGREW (AV)

325 North Parkway, P.O. Box 2103, 38302
Telephone: 901-668-5500
Telecopier: 901-664-2840

MEMBERS OF FIRM

William P. Moss (1897-1985)
George O. Benton
John R. Moss
Edwin E. Wallis, Jr.
Charles R. Pettigrew
W. Stanworth Harris

ASSOCIATE

Jon Mark Patey

OF COUNSEL

William P. Moss, Jr.

Attorneys for: First American National Bank of Jackson; South Central Bell Telephone & Telegraph Co.; CSX Transportation, Inc.; The Equitable Life Assurance Society of the United States; Jackson Utility Division; Metropolitan Life Insurance Co.; United Services Automobile Assn.; Association of Tennessee Cola-Cola Bottlers; Central Distributors, Inc.; Combined Insurance Company of America.

For Complete List of Firm Personnel, See General Section

For full biographical listings, see the Martindale-Hubbell Law Directory

RAINEY, KIZER, BUTLER, REVIERE & BELL (AV)

105 Highland Avenue South, P.O. Box 1147, 38302-1147
Telephone: 901-423-2414
Telecopier: 901-423-1386

MEMBERS OF FIRM

Thomas H. Rainey
Jerry D. Kizer, Jr.
Clinton V. Butler, Jr.
Russell E. Reviere
William C. Bell, Jr.
John D. Burleson
Gregory D. Jordan
Laura A. Williams
Clayton R. Sanders, Jr.
Robert O. Binkley, Jr.

ASSOCIATES

R. Dale Thomas
Deana C. Seymour
Mitchell Glenn Tollison
Charles C. Exum
Marty R. Phillips
Stephen P. Miller
Clay M. McCormack
Milton D. Conder, Jr.

Representative Clients: First Tennessee Bank, Jackson, Tennessee; CIGNA Insurance Co.; State Farm Mutual Automobile Insurance Co.; Auto-Owners Insurance Co.; USF&G; CNA Group; Royal Insurance Co.; Great American Insurance Co.; ITT-Hartford; Union Planters National Bank.

For full biographical listings, see the Martindale-Hubbell Law Directory

JOHNSON CITY, Washington Co.

HERRIN & HERRIN (AV)

515 East Unaka Avenue, 37601
Telephone: 615-929-7113

MEMBERS OF FIRM

Kent Herrin
Erick Herrin

References: Home Federal Savings and Loan Association; Tri City Bank and Trust Co.

For full biographical listings, see the Martindale-Hubbell Law Directory

RICHARD W. PECTOL, P.C. & ASSOCIATES (AV)

202 East Unaka Avenue, 37601
Telephone: 615-928-6106
Fax: 615-928-8802

Richard W. Pectol

Vincent A. Sikora

For full biographical listings, see the Martindale-Hubbell Law Directory

WELLER, MILLER, CARRIER, MILLER & HICKIE (AV)

160 West Springbrook Drive, P.O. Box 3217 Carroll Reece Station, 37601
Telephone: 615-282-1821
FAX: 615-283-4173

MEMBERS OF FIRM

Samuel B. Miller
Jack R. Carrier
Samuel B. Miller, II
Michael J. Hickie

Representative Clients: CNA Insurance Cos.; Coca-Cola Bottling Works; Columbus Electric Mfg. Co.; East Tennessee Natural Gas Co. (Pipeline); Hamilton Bank of Upper East Tennessee; Nationwide Insurance Co.; Pennsylvania National Mutual Insurance Cos.; TPI Corp.; USF & G Co.; Utica Mutual Insurance Co.

For full biographical listings, see the Martindale-Hubbell Law Directory

KINGSPORT, Sullivan Co.

HUNTER, SMITH & DAVIS (AV)

1212 North Eastman Road, P.O. Box 3740, 37664
Telephone: 615-378-8800;
Johnson City: 615-282-4186;
Bristol: 615-968-7604
Telecopier: 615-378-8801
Johnson City, Tennessee Office: Suite 500 First American Center, 208 Sunset Drive, 37604.
Telephone: 615-283-6300.
Telecopier: 615-283-6301.

MEMBERS OF FIRM

Edwin L. Treadway
S. Morris Hadden
William C. Bovender
William T. Wray, Jr.
Douglas S. Tweed
Jimmie Carpenter Miller
Gregory K. Haden
Michael L. Forrester
T. Martin Browder, Jr.

ASSOCIATES

Edward Jennings Webb, Jr.
James N. L. Humphreys
K. Jeff Luethke
Julie Poe Bennett

Representative Clients: State Farm Insurance Cos.; AFG Industries, Inc.; Nationwide Insurance Cos.; Arcata Graphics; Home Insurance Cos.; The Mead Corp.; United Telephone System-Southeast Group; Chubb Insurance Cos.; Bristol Regional Medical Center; First American National Bank.

For Complete List of Firm Personnel, See General Section

For full biographical listings, see the Martindale-Hubbell Law Directory

MOORE, STOUT, WADDELL & LEDFORD (AV)

238 Broad Street, P.O. Box 1345, 37662
Telephone: 615-246-2344
Fax: 615-246-2210

MEMBERS OF FIRM

J. Patrick Ledford
Robert Lane Arrington

ASSOCIATES

Angela R. Kelley
Annette M. Konikiewicz

Representative Clients: Arcata Graphics Co.; Armstrong Construction Co., Inc.; Donihe Graphics, Inc.; First Tennessee Bank National Association; First Union National Bank of Tennessee; Kingsport Foundry & Manufacturing Corp.; Kingsport Housing Authority; Scottsdale Insurance Co.; State Farm Mutual Automobile Insurance Co.; The United States Fidelity & Guaranty Co.

For Complete List of Firm Personnel, See General Section

For full biographical listings, see the Martindale-Hubbell Law Directory

WEST & ROSE (AV)

537 East Center Street, P.O. Box 1404, 37660
Telephone: 615-246-8176
Fax: 615-246-4028

MEMBERS OF FIRM

M. Lacy West
Steven C. Rose

ASSOCIATE

Julia C. West

For full biographical listings, see the Martindale-Hubbell Law Directory

WILSON, WORLEY, GAMBLE & WARD, P.C. (AV)

Fourth Floor Heritage Federal Building, 110 East Center Street, P.O. Box 1007, 37662-1007
Telephone: 615-246-8181
FAX: 615-246-2831

William T. Gamble
Richard M. Currie, Jr.
Frank A. Johnstone
Katherine W. Singleton
Russell W. Adkins
Cherie S. King

Assistant Division Counsel for: CSX Transportation, Inc.
Local Counsel for: Eastman Chemical Co.; General Motors Corp.; Holston Valley Hospital and Medical Center; United States Fidelity & Guaranty Co.; Eastman Credit Union; Heritage Federal Bank FSB; Vulcan Materials Co.; AFG Industries, Inc.; K mart Corporation.

For Complete List of Firm Personnel, See General Section

For full biographical listings, see the Martindale-Hubbell Law Directory

*KNOXVILLE,** Knox Co.

ARNETT, DRAPER & HAGOOD (AV)

Suite 2300 Plaza Tower, 37929-2300
Telephone: 615-546-7000
Telecopier: 615-546-0423

(See Next Column)

ARNETT, DRAPER & HAGOOD—*Continued*

MEMBERS OF FIRM

Foster D. Arnett
Jack B. Draper
Lewis R. Hagood
Thomas S. Scott, Jr.
William A. Simms
F. Michael Fitzpatrick
Rick L. Powers
Dan D. Rhea
Steven L. Hurdle
Thomas M. Cole
Johanna J. McGlothlin
Robert N. Townsend
R. Kim Burnette
John Steven Collins
Samuel C. Doak
Jeffrey L. Ingram
David Edward Long
W. Allen McDonald

Insurance Clients: Associated Aviation Underwriters; Crum & Forster Group; United States Aviation Underwriters; United States Fidelity & Guaranty Co.; General Accident Group.
Representative Clients: Blue Diamond Coal Co.; Fort Sanders Regional Medical Center; General Motors Corp.; Nissan Corp.; Phillips Petroleum Co.

For full biographical listings, see the Martindale-Hubbell Law Directory

BAKER, DONELSON, BEARMAN & CALDWELL (AV)

2200 Riverview Tower, 900 Gay Street, 37901
Telephone: 615-549-7000
Telecopier: 615-525-8569
Memphis, Tennessee Office: 20th Floor, First Tennessee Building, 165 Madison, 38103.
Telephone: 901-526-2000.
Telecopier: 901-577-2303.
Nashville, Tennessee Office: 1700 Nashville City Center, 511 Union Street, 37219.
Telephone: 615-726-5600.
Telecopier: 615-726-0464.
Chattanooga, Tennessee Office: 1800 Republic Centre, 633 Chestnut Street, 37450-1800.
Telephone: 615-752-4400.
Telecopier: 615-752-4410.
Huntsville, Tennessee Office: 3 Courthouse Square, 37756.
Telephone: 615-663-2321.
Telecopier: 615-663-2111.
Johnson City, Tennessee Office: Hamilton Bank Building, 207 Mockingbird Lane, 37604.
Telephone: 615-928-0181.
Telecopier: 615-928-5694; 615-928-3654; Kingsport: 615-246-6191.
Washington, D.C. Office: Market Square, 801 Pennsylvania Avenue, N.W., 20004.
Telephone: 202-508-3400.
Telecopier: 202-508-3402.

PARTNERS

Don C. Stansberry, Jr.
Nicholas A. Della Volpe
James A. McIntosh

For Complete List of Firm Personnel, See General Section

For full biographical listings, see the Martindale-Hubbell Law Directory

BAKER, MCREYNOLDS, BYRNE, BRACKETT, O'KANE & SHEA (AV)

11th Floor, 607 Market Street, P.O. Box 1708, 37901-1708
Telephone: 615-637-5600
Fax: 615-637-5608

MEMBERS OF FIRM

Harry T. Poore (1889-1956)
Taylor H. Cox (1903-1962)
J. W. Baker (1915-1991)
John W. Baker, Jr.
John A. McReynolds, Jr.
Arthur D. Byrne
Deke W. Brackett
James G. O'Kane, Jr.
James T. Shea, IV
Weldon E. Patterson
Elizabeth A. Townsend
Elizabeth M. Roy
Gerald L. Gulley, Jr.
Michael T. McClamroch

Representative Clients: CSX Transportation (Seaboard System Railroad); E.I. du Pont de Nemours & Co.; General Motors Corp.; Liberty Mutual Insurance Co.; Nationwide Mutual Insurance Co.; Amerisure Insurance Cos.; State Volunteer Insurance Co.; Kemper Insurance Group; Farmers Insurance Group; North American Van Lines.

For full biographical listings, see the Martindale-Hubbell Law Directory

BERNSTEIN, STAIR & MCADAMS (AV)

Suite 600, 530 South Gay Street, 37902
Telephone: 615-546-8030
Telecopier: 615-522-8879

MEMBERS OF FIRM

Bernard E. Bernstein
L. Caesar Stair III
Doris C. Allen
J. Thomas Jones

ASSOCIATES

Celeste H. Herbert
Elizabeth K. Bacon Meadows
Kenneth M. Brown

Representative Clients: Proffitt's Department Stores; Barclays American Corporation; Capitol Credit Plan of Tennessee, Inc.; Clayton Homes, Inc.; Whittle Communications L.P.; Plasti-Line, Inc.; ABB Flakt, Inc.; Modern Supply Co.; Union Planters National Bank.

(See Next Column)

For Complete List of Firm Personnel, See General Section

For full biographical listings, see the Martindale-Hubbell Law Directory

BUTLER, VINES AND BABB (AV)

Suite 810, First American Center, P.O. Box 2649, 37901-2649
Telephone: 615-637-3531
Fax: 615-637-3385

MEMBERS OF FIRM

Warren Butler
William D. Vines, III
Dennis L. Babb
Martin L. Ellis
Ronald C. Koksal
James C. Wright
Bruce A. Anderson
Gregory Kevin Hardin
Steven Boyd Johnson
Edward U. Babb

ASSOCIATES

John W. Butler
Vonda M. Laughlin
Gregory F. Vines
Scarlett May

LEGAL SUPPORT PERSONNEL

PARALEGALS

Virginia H. Carver
Susie DeLozier
Dena K. Martin

Reference: First American Bank.

For full biographical listings, see the Martindale-Hubbell Law Directory

EGERTON, MCAFEE, ARMISTEAD & DAVIS, P.C. (AV)

500 First American National Bank Center, P.O. Box 2047, 37901
Telephone: 615-546-0500
Fax: 615-525-5293

Lewis C. Foster, Jr.
William W. Davis, Jr.
Barry K. Maxwell
Stephen A. McSween

Wesley L. Hatmaker

Representative Clients: First American National Bank of Knoxville; Home Federal Bank of Tennessee, F.S.B.; Bush Bros. & Co.; Johnson & Galyon Contractors; Baptist Hospital of East Tennessee; Revco D.S., Inc.; White Realty Corp.; Dick Broadcasting, Inc.

For Complete List of Firm Personnel, See General Section

For full biographical listings, see the Martindale-Hubbell Law Directory

FRANTZ, MCCONNELL & SEYMOUR (AV)

Suite 500, 550 Main Avenue, 37902
Telephone: 615-546-9321
FAX: 615-637-5249

MEMBERS OF FIRM

John H. Frantz (1869-1933)
Charles M. Seymour (1882-1958)
Thomas G. McConnell (1883-1962)
Robert M. McConnell (1890-1971)
Harris M. Harton, Jr. (1906-1978)
John William Mills (1927-1977)
E. Bruce Foster (1910-1988)
Arthur G. Seymour
Fred H. Cagle, Jr.
Arthur G. Seymour, Jr.
Robert M. Bailey
Francis A. Cain
Robert L. Kahn
Reggie E. Keaton
Donald D. Howell
Charles M. Finn
Debra L. Fulton
Michael W. Ewell
Imogene Anderson King
John M. Lawhorn

ASSOCIATES

Jay E. Kohlbusch
N. David Roberts, Jr.
Lucy Dunn Hooper
James E. Wagner
Terrill L. Adkins

Counsel for: The Travelers Insurance Cos.; The Equitable Life Assurance Society of the United States; South Central Bell Telephone Co.; Palm Beach Co.; USX Corp.; ASARCO Incorporated; Coca Cola Bottlers Association; Texaco, Inc.; Aztex Energy Co.; Community Tectonics, Inc.; Norfolk Southern Corporation.

For full biographical listings, see the Martindale-Hubbell Law Directory

HODGES, DOUGHTY AND CARSON (AV)

617 Main Street, P.O. Box 869, 37901-0869
Telephone: 615-546-9611
Telecopier: 615-544-2014

MEMBERS OF FIRM

J. H. Hodges (1896-1983)
J. H. Doughty (1903-1987)
Richard L. Carson (1912-1980)
John P. Davis, Jr. (1923-1977)
Robert R. Campbell
David E. Smith
John W. Wheeler
Dalton L. Townsend
Douglas L. Dutton
William F. Alley, Jr.
Roy L. Aaron
Dean B. Farmer
David Wedekind
Julia Saunders Howard
Albert J. Harb
Edward G. White, II
Thomas H. Dickenson
J. William Coley
J. Michael Haynes
T. Kenan Smith
Wayne A. Kline

(See Next Column)

HODGES, DOUGHTY AND CARSON, *Knoxville—Continued*

ASSOCIATES

James M. Cornelius, Jr.
W. Tyler Chastain

OF COUNSEL

Jonathan H. Burnett

Counsel for: General Motors Corp.; Ernst & Young; Navistar International; Martin Marietta Energy Systems; Union Carbide Corp.; NationsBank of Tennessee; K-Mart Corporation; Aetna Life and Casualty Group; Fireman's Fund American Insurance Company; Safeco Insurance Group.

For full biographical listings, see the Martindale-Hubbell Law Directory

KENNERLY, MONTGOMERY & FINLEY, P.C. (AV)

Fourth Floor, NationsBank Center, 550 Main Avenue, P.O. Box 442, 37901-0442
Telephone: 615-546-7311
Fax: 615-524-1773

OF COUNSEL

Warren W. Kennerly

George D. Montgomery (1917-1985)
Robert A. Finley (1936-1990)
L. Anderson Galyon, III
Alexander M. Taylor
Jack M. Tallent, II
G. Wendell Thomas, Jr.
Ray J. Campbell, Jr. (1949-1986)
Steven E. Schmidt
Patti Jane Lay
Brian H. Trammell
C. Coulter Gilbert
Robert H. Green
William S. Lockett, Jr.
Rebecca Brake Murray
Robert Michael Shelor
James N. Gore, Jr.

SPECIAL COUNSEL

Jay Arthur Garrison

R. Hunter Cagle
Melody J. Bock
Rex A. Dale
Natasha K. Metcalf
Kenneth W. Ward
David Draper
James H. Price

Representative Clients: Knoxville Utilities Board; Aetna Casualty & Surety Co.; Allstate Insurance Co.; CNA Insurance Group; CIGNA Insurance; Nationwide Mutual Insurance Co.; Dow Chemical; Union Carbide; Westinghouse Electric Corp.; Mitsubishi International Corp.

For full biographical listings, see the Martindale-Hubbell Law Directory

LEWIS, KING, KRIEG & WALDROP, P.C. (AV)

One Centre Square, 5th Floor, 620 Market Street, 37902
Telephone: 615-546-4646
Fax: 615-523-6529
Nashville, Tennessee Office: Third National Financial Center, 424 Church Street, Ninth Floor.
Telephone: 615-259-1366.
Fax: 615-259-1389.

Charles B. Lewis
John K. King
Richard W. Krieg
R. Loy Waldrop, Jr.
Ellis A. Sharp
Samuel W. Rutherford
Linda Jean Hamilton Mowles
Deborah C. Stevens
R. Dale Bay (Resident, Nashville Office)
M. Edward Owens, Jr.
H. Dennis Jarvis, Jr.
Harry P. Ogden
Reba Brown (Resident, Nashville Office)
Michael J. Mollenhour
Alan M. Parker
David L. Beck
Mary Jo Mann
Michael S. Pemberton
Leonard F. Pogue, III (Resident, Nashville Office)
David Nelson Garst

SPECIAL COUNSEL

Aaron Wyckoff (Resident, Nashville Office)

OF COUNSEL

Mary M. Farmer

Elma Elizabeth Rodgers
Patty K. Wheeler
R. Neal Mynatt (Resident, Nashville Office)
John R. Tarpley (Resident, Nashville Office)
Edwin H. Batts, III
Rodney A. Fields
David W. Tipton
Joseph Brent Nolan

Representative Clients: The American Home Group; Central Mutual Insurance Co.; Cincinnati Insurance Co.; The Kemper Group; Kentucky Central Insurance Co.; The Transamerica Group; Travelers Insurance Co.; Wausau Insurance Co.; Continental National American Group; Pennsylvania National Mutual Casualty Insurance Co.

For Complete List of Firm Personnel, See General Section

For full biographical listings, see the Martindale-Hubbell Law Directory

MCCAMPBELL & YOUNG, A PROFESSIONAL CORPORATION (AV)

2021 Plaza Tower, P.O. Box 550, 37901-0550
Telephone: 615-637-1440
Telecopier: 615-546-9731

Herbert H. McCampbell, Jr. (1905-1974)
F. Graham Bartlett (1920-1982)
Robert S. Young
Lindsay Young
Robert S. Marquis
Robert S. Stone
J. Christopher Kirk
Mark K. Williams

Janie C. Porter
Gregory E. Erickson
R. Scott Elmore
Tammy Kaousias
Benét S. Theiss
Allen W. Blevins

Representative Clients: First National Bank of Knoxville; Robertshaw Controls Company; The White Lily Foods Company; Becromal of America, Inc.; Knoxville College.

For full biographical listings, see the Martindale-Hubbell Law Directory

PRYOR, FLYNN, PRIEST & HARBER (AV)

Suite 600 Two Centre Square, 625 Gay Street, P.O. Box 870, 37901
Telephone: 615-522-4191
Telecopier: 615-522-0910

Robert E. Pryor
Frank L. Flynn, Jr.
Timothy A. Priest
John K. Harber

ASSOCIATES

Mark E. Floyd
Donald R. Coffey
M. Christopher Coffey

References: Third National Bank; First National Bank.

For full biographical listings, see the Martindale-Hubbell Law Directory

WAGNER, MYERS & SANGER, A PROFESSIONAL CORPORATION (AV)

1801 Plaza Tower, P.O. Box 1308, 37929
Telephone: 615-525-4600
Fax: 615-524-5731

Sam F. Fowler, Jr.
Herbert S. Sanger, Jr.
John R. Seymour
Charles W. Van Beke
Charles A. Wagner III
William C. Myers, Jr.
M. Douglas Campbell, Jr.

Joseph N. Clarke, Jr.
Ronald D. Garland
Robert E. Hyde
Barbara D. Boulton

Representative Clients: Carolina Power & Light Co.; Cullman Electric Cooperative; Diversified Energy, Inc.; Fort Sanders Health Systems; Gatliff Coal Company, Inc.; Martin Marietta Energy Systems, Inc.; North American Rayon Corp.; Regal Cinemas, Inc.; Roddy Vending Co.; Skyline Coal Company.

For full biographical listings, see the Martindale-Hubbell Law Directory

WATSON, HOLLOW & REEVES (AV)

1700 Plaza Tower, P.O. Box 131, 37901
Telephone: 615-522-3803
Telecopier: 615-525-2514

MEMBERS OF FIRM

Robert Harmon Watson, Jr.
Richard L. Hollow
Pamela L. Reeves
Jon G. Roach
John C. Duffy
John T. Batson, Jr.
Earl Jerome Melson

ASSOCIATES

Arthur Franklin Knight, III
Robert W. Willingham

For full biographical listings, see the Martindale-Hubbell Law Directory

*MCMINNVILLE,** Warren Co.

GALLIGAN & NEWMAN (AV)

308 West Main Street, P.O. Box 289, 37110
Telephone: 615-473-8405
Fax: 615-473-1888

MEMBERS OF FIRM

Michael D. Galligan
Robert W. Newman

Reference: City Bank & Trust Co.

For full biographical listings, see the Martindale-Hubbell Law Directory

*MEMPHIS,** Shelby Co.

ARMSTRONG ALLEN PREWITT GENTRY JOHNSTON & HOLMES (AV)

80 Monroe Avenue Suite 700, 38103
Telephone: 901-523-8211
Telecopier: 901-524-4936
Jackson, Missipi Office: 1350 One Jackson Place, 188 East Capitol Street.
Telephone: 601-948-8020.
Telecopier: 601-948-8389.

MEMBERS OF FIRM

Newton P. Allen
Thomas R. Prewitt
Gavin M. Gentry
Thomas F. Johnston
Carl H. Langschmidt, Jr.
Thomas R. Prewitt, Jr.
Prince C. Chambliss, Jr.
S. Russell Headrick
Randall D. Noel
Mark S. Norris
Teresa J. Sigmon
Stephen P. Hale
Lucian T. Pera
Nathaniel L. Prosser

COUNSEL

Walter P. Armstrong, Jr.

Theodore E. Mackall, Jr.
Robertson M. Leatherman, Jr.
Cannon F. Allen
Steven W. Likens

For Complete List of Firm Personnel, See General Section

For full biographical listings, see the Martindale-Hubbell Law Directory

BAKER, DONELSON, BEARMAN & CALDWELL (AV)

20th Floor, First Tennessee Building, 165 Madison, 38103
Telephone: 901-526-2000
Telecopier: 901-577-2303
Nashville, Tennessee Office: 1700 Nashville City Center, 511 Union Street, 37219.
Telephone: 615-726-5600.
Telecopier: 615-726-0464.
Knoxville, Tennessee Office: 2200 Riverview Tower, 900 Gay Street, 37901.
Telephone: 615-549-7000.
Telecopier: 615-525-8569.
Chattanooga, Tennessee Office: 1800 Republic Centre, 633 Chestnut Street, 37450-1800.
Telephone: 615-752-4400.
Telecopier: 615-752-4410.
Huntsville, Tennessee Office: 3 Courthouse Square, 37756.
Telephone: 615-663-2321.
Telecopier: 615-663-2111.
Johnson City, Tennessee Office: Hamilton Bank Building, 207 Mockingbird Lane, 37604.
Telephone: 615-928-0181.
Telecopier: 615-928-5694; 615-928-3654; Kingsport: 615-246-6191.
Washington, D.C. Office: Market Square, 801 Pennsylvania Avenue, N.W., 20004.
Telephone: 202-508-3400.
Telecopier: 202-508-3402.

PARTNERS

Leo Bearman, Jr.
Maurice Wexler
Stephen H. Biller
Michael F. Pleasants
John C. Speer
W. Michael Richards
Samuel H. Mays, Jr.
Larry E. Killebrew
Jerry Stauffer
Gregory G. Fletcher
Stephen D. Wakefield
Charles C. Harrell
Stephen D. Goodwin
Charles G. Walker
Robert Mark Glover
George T. Lewis, III
Eugene J. Podesta, Jr.
Sam B. Blair, Jr.
John R. Branson
Jill M. Steinberg
Michael C. Patton

OF COUNSEL

Frierson M. Graves, Jr.

ASSOCIATES

Janis M. Wild
Stephen William Ragland
Monique A. Nassar
Bradley E. Trammell
Elizabeth Einstman Chance
Charles F. Morrow
Edward M. Bearman
R. Alan Pritchard, Jr.
Robbin T. Sarrazin
Paul V. Rost
Anthony B. Norris
Thad M. Barnes
Carrie Goldsby Tolbert
James W. Curry, Jr.

For Complete List of Firm Personnel, See General Section

For full biographical listings, see the Martindale-Hubbell Law Directory

THE BOGATIN LAW FIRM (AV)

A Partnership including Professional Corporations
(Formerly Bogatin Lawson & Chiapella)
860 Ridge Lake Boulevard, Suite 360, 38120
Telephone: 901-767-1234
Telecopier: 901-767-2803 & 901-767-4010

(See Next Column)

MEMBERS OF FIRM

G. Patrick Arnoult
Irvin Bogatin (P.C.)
H. Stephen Brown
Susan Callison (P.C.)
Tillman C. Carroll
Matthew P. Cavitch
John André Chiapella (P.C.)
David J. Cocke
Russell J. Hensley
Arlie C. Hooper
Charles M. Key
William H. Lawson, Jr., (P.C.)
David C. Porteous
Arthur E. Quinn
Thaddeus S. Rodda, Jr., (P.C.)

ASSOCIATES

Robert F. Beckmann
James Q. Carr, II
C. William Denton, Jr.
Thomas M. Federico (Not admitted in TN)
James S. King
John F. Murrah

For full biographical listings, see the Martindale-Hubbell Law Directory

BOROD & KRAMER, P.C. (AV)

Brinkley Plaza, 80 Monroe Avenue, 5th Floor, P.O. Box 3504, 38173-0504
Telephone: 901-524-0200
Telecopier: 901-524-0242

Marx J. Borod
Bruce S. Kramer

Sharon Lee Petty
Jeffery D. Parrish

For full biographical listings, see the Martindale-Hubbell Law Directory

BOURLAND, HEFLIN, ALVAREZ, HOLLEY & MINOR (AV)

Suite 100, 5400 Poplar Avenue, 38119
Telephone: 901-683-3526
Telecopier: 901-763-1037

MEMBERS OF FIRM

John J. Heflin, III
R. Layne Holley

ASSOCIATE

Alex C. Elder

For Complete List of Firm Personnel, See General Section

For full biographical listings, see the Martindale-Hubbell Law Directory

JAMES S. COX & ASSOCIATES (AV)

60 North Third Street, 38103
Telephone: 901-575-2040
Telecopier: 901-575-2077

ASSOCIATES

Gary K. Morrell
Russell Fowler
David A.E. Lumb
Todd B. Murrah
Sherry S. Fernandez

For full biographical listings, see the Martindale-Hubbell Law Directory

FARRIS, HANCOCK, GILMAN, BRANAN & HELLEN (AV)

50 North Front Street, Suite 1400, 38103
Telephone: 901-576-8200
Fax: 901-576-8250
East Memphis, Tennessee Office: Suite 400 United American Bank Building, 5384 Poplar Avenue.
Telephone: 901-763-4000.
Fax: 901-763-4095.

MEMBERS OF FIRM

William W. Farris
Ronald Lee Gilman
Homer B. Branan, III
Tim Wade Hellen
Edwin Dean White, III
Charles B. Welch, Jr.
G. Ray Bratton
John M. Farris
O. Douglas Shipman, III
D. Edward Harvey
Rebecca P. Tuttle
Eugene Stone Forrester, Jr.

ASSOCIATES

G. Coble Caperton
Dedrick Brittenum, Jr.
Richard Stanfill Copeland
Barry F. White
Paul E. Perry
Bryan K. Smith
Gregory W. O'Neal
Steven Caines Brammer

For Complete List of Firm Personnel, See General Section

For full biographical listings, see the Martindale-Hubbell Law Directory

EVERETT B. GIBSON LAW FIRM (AV)

950 Morgan Keegan Tower, 50 North Front Street, 38103
Telephone: 901-576-8211
Telecopier: 901-576-8149

Everett B. Gibson

Ralph T. Gibson
Danton Asher Berube

For full biographical listings, see the Martindale-Hubbell Law Directory

Memphis—Continued

GLASSMAN, JETER, EDWARDS & WADE, P.C. (AV)

26 North Second Street Building, 38103
Telephone: 901-527-4673
Telecopier: 901-521-0940
Lexington, Tennessee Office: 85 East Church.
Telephone: 901-968-2561.

Richard Glassman
William M. Jeter
Tim Edwards
B. J. Wade
John Barry Burgess
Carl K. Wyatt, Jr.
Nicholas E. Bragorgos
Ben W. Keesee
Lucinda S. Murray
Robert A. Cox
Lori J. Keen
James F. Horner, Jr.

For full biographical listings, see the Martindale-Hubbell Law Directory

HANOVER, WALSH, JALENAK & BLAIR (AV)

Fifth Floor - Falls Building, 22 North Front Street, 38103-2109
Telephone: 901-526-0621
Telecopier: 901-521-9759

MEMBERS OF FIRM

Joseph Hanover (1888-1984)
David Hanover (1899-1963)
Jay Alan Hanover
William M. Walsh
James B. Jalenak
Allen S. Blair
Michael E. Goldstein
Edward J. McKenney, Jr.
James R. Newsom, III
John Kevin Walsh
James A. Johnson, Jr.
Donald S. Holm III
Barbara B. Lapides

Jennifer A. Sevier
Christina von Cannon Burdette
Jeffrey S. Rosenblum

OF COUNSEL

Helyn L. Keith

For full biographical listings, see the Martindale-Hubbell Law Directory

MARTIN, TATE, MORROW & MARSTON, P.C. (AV)

The Falls Building, Suite 1100, 22 North Front Street, 38103-1182
Telephone: 901-522-9000
Telecopier: 901-527-3746

Lee L. Piovarcy
David Wade
William Joseph Landers, II
Shepherd D. Tate
Clare Shields
Richard M. Carter
Ron W. McAfee

C. Lee Cagle
Scott Thomas Beall
John Anthony Williamson
Christopher G. Lazarini

For Complete List of Firm Personnel, See General Section

For full biographical listings, see the Martindale-Hubbell Law Directory

THOMASON, HENDRIX, HARVEY, JOHNSON & MITCHELL (AV)

Twenty-Ninth Floor, One Commerce Square, 38103
Telephone: 901-525-8721
Telecopier: 901-525-6722

MEMBER OF FIRM

Buckner Potts Wellford

For Complete List of Firm Personnel, See General Section

For full biographical listings, see the Martindale-Hubbell Law Directory

WARING COX (AV)

Morgan Keegan Tower, 50 North Front Street, Suite 1300, 38103-1190
Telephone: 901-543-8000
Telecopy: 901-543-8030

MEMBERS OF FIRM

Louis F. Allen
Saul C. Belz
William E. Frulla
Ellen Bronaugh Vergos
Louis J. Miller
Charles W. Hill
Earle J. Schwarz
David J. Sneed

ASSOCIATES

Laurie M. Maddox
Cynthia G. Bennett
Robert B.C. Hale
Michael B. Chance
Thomas L. Parker
Jennifer W. Sammons
Frank L. Watson, III

OF COUNSEL

Roane Waring, Jr.

Representative Clients: Federal Express Corp.; South Central Bell Telephone Co.; Cook International, Inc.; Express Airlines I, Inc.; Flavorite Laboratories, Inc.; MobileComm; Osceola Foods, Inc.; Vining-Sparks IBG; United Refrigerated Services, Inc.; Perkins Family Restaurants.

For Complete List of Firm Personnel, See General Section

For full biographical listings, see the Martindale-Hubbell Law Directory

*MURFREESBORO,** Rutherford Co.

WILLIAM KENNERLY BURGER (AV)

301 North Spring Street, 37133
Telephone: 615-896-4154

For full biographical listings, see the Martindale-Hubbell Law Directory

*NASHVILLE,** Davidson Co.

BAKER, DONELSON, BEARMAN & CALDWELL (AV)

1700 Nashville City Center, 511 Union Street, 37219
Telephone: 615-726-5600
Telecopier: 615-726-0464
Memphis, Tennessee Office: 20th Floor, First Tennessee Building, 165 Madison, 38103.
Telephone: 901-526-2000.
Telecopier: 901-577-2303.
Knoxville, Tennessee Office: 2200 Riverview Tower, 900 Gay Street, 37901.
Telephone: 615-549-7000.
Telecopier: 615-525-8569.
Chattanooga, Tennessee Office: 1800 Republic Centre, 633 Chestnut Street, 37450-1800.
Telephone: 615-752-4400.
Telecopier: 615-752-4410.
Huntsville, Tennessee Office: 3 Courthouse Square, 37756.
Telephone: 615-663-2321.
Telecopier: 615-663-2111.
Johnson City, Tennessee Office: Hamilton Bank Building, 207 Mockingbird Lane, 37604.
Telephone: 615-928-0181.
Telecopier: 615-928-5694; 615-928-3654; Kingsport: 615-246-6191.
Washington, D.C. Office: Market Square, 801 Pennsylvania Avenue, N.W., 20004.
Telephone: 202-508-3400.
Telecopier: 202-508-3402.

PARTNERS

Maclin P. Davis, Jr.
William Hume Barr
Rodger B. Kesley
Ed E. Williams, III
James A. DeLanis
John Randolph Bibb, Jr.
H. Buckley Cole
Anthony M. Iannacio

OF COUNSEL

John S. Hicks

ASSOCIATES

Susan Duvier Bass
Kelly R. Duggan
Barbara A. Rose
Fred Russell Harwell
Clisby Hall Barrow
Darwin A. Hindman III

For Complete List of Firm Personnel, See General Section

For full biographical listings, see the Martindale-Hubbell Law Directory

CORNELIUS & COLLINS (AV)

Suite 2700 Nashville City Center, P.O. Box 190695, 37219-0695
Telephone: 615-244-1440
Facsimile: 615-254-9477

Charles L. Cornelius (1888-1968)
Charles L. Cornelius, Jr.
William Ovid Collins, Jr.
Charles Hampton White
Thomas I. Carlton, Jr.
Charles G. Cornelius
Noel F. Stahl
C. Bennett Harrison, Jr.
David L. Steed
Richard L. Colbert
David A. King
Blakeley D. Matthews
Joseph R. Wheeler
Kurtis J. Winstead
Rebecca Wells-Demaree
Daniel P. Berexa
Jay Nelson Chamness
Dana Davis Ballinger
Andrew Donelson Dunn

Representative Clients: General Motors Corp.; Tennessee Medical Assn; Tennessee Education Association; United Parcel Service; Hartford Insurance Group; State Volunteer Mutual Insurance Co.; Corroon & Black, Inc.; Better-Bilt Aluminum Products, Inc.; Johnson & Johnson Products, Inc.; Mercedes Benz of North American, Inc.

For full biographical listings, see the Martindale-Hubbell Law Directory

DORAMUS & TRAUGER (AV)

Southern Turf Building, 222 Fourth Avenue North, 37219
Telephone: 615-256-8585
Fax: 615-256-7444

MEMBERS OF FIRM

Byron R. Trauger
James V. Doramus
Paul C. Ney, Jr.

ASSOCIATES

David L. Kleinfelter
Gregory Mitchell
Jane H. Allen
Todd J. Campbell

For full biographical listings, see the Martindale-Hubbell Law Directory

Nashville—Continued

HOLLINS, WAGSTER & YARBROUGH, P.C. (AV)

22nd Floor Third National Financial Center, 424 Church Street, 37219
Telephone: 615-256-6666
Telecopier: 615-254-4254

John J. Hollins
John W. Wagster
Edward M. Yarbrough
John L. Norris
David L. Raybin
James L. Weatherly, Jr.
John J. Hollins, Jr.

Patrick T. McNally

References: First American National Bank; Third National Bank.

For full biographical listings, see the Martindale-Hubbell Law Directory

KING & BALLOW (AV)

1200 Noel Place, 200 Fourth Avenue, North, 37219
Telephone: 615-259-3456
Fax: 615-254-7907
San Diego, California Office: 2700 Symphony Towers, 750 B Street, 92101.
Telephone: 619-236-9401.
Fax: 619-236-9437.
San Francisco, California Office: 100 First Street, Suite 2700, 94105.
Telephone: 415-541-7803.
Fax: 415-541-7805.

MEMBERS OF FIRM

Frank S. King, Jr.
Robert L. Ballow
Richard C. Lowe
R. Eddie Wayland
Larry D. Crabtree
Alan L. Marx
Paul H. Duvall (Resident, San Diego, California Office)
Steven C. Douse
Douglas R. Pierce
James P. Thompson
Howard M. Kastrinsky
Kenneth E. Douthat
Mark E. Hunt
Charles J. Mataya
Lynn Siegel (Resident, San Diego, California Office)
Nora T. Cannon
John J. Matchulat
M. Kim Vance

ASSOCIATES

Katheryn M. Millwee
Patrick M. Thomas
R. Brent Ballow
Elizabeth B. Marney
Michael D. Oesterle
Paul H. Derrick
Richard S. Busch
Mary M. Collier

Representative Clients: American Airlines, Nashville, Tennessee; Capital Cities/ABC, Inc., New York, New York; Denver Post, Denver, Colorado; Dollar General Corp.; Houston Post, Houston, Texas; Ingram, Industries, Inc., Nashville, Tennessee; Kansas City Star Co., Kansas City, Missouri; Kroger Co., Cincinnati, Ohio; Northern Telecom, Inc.; Opryland USA, Inc.

For Complete List of Firm Personnel, See General Section

For full biographical listings, see the Martindale-Hubbell Law Directory

LEWIS, KING, KRIEG & WALDROP, P.C. (AV)

Third National Financial Center, 424 Church Street, Ninth Floor, 37219
Telephone: 615-259-1366
FAX: 615-259-1389
Knoxville, Tennessee Office: One Centre Square, 5th Floor, 620 Market Street.
Telephone: 615-546-4646.

John K. King
R. Dale Bay (Resident)
Reba Brown (Resident)

SPECIAL COUNSEL

Aaron Wyckoff (Resident)

Leonard F. Pogue, III (Resident)
R. Neal Mynatt (Resident)
John R. Tarpley (Resident)

Representative Clients: The American Home Group; Central Mutual Insurance Co.; Cincinnati Insurance Co.; The Kemper Group; The Transamerica Group; Travelers Insurance Co.; Wausau Insurance Co.; CNA Ins. Co.; Pennsylvania National Mutual Casualty Insurance Co.

For Complete List of Firm Personnel, See General Section

For full biographical listings, see the Martindale-Hubbell Law Directory

NEAL & HARWELL (AV)

Suite 2000, First Union Tower, 150 Fourth Avenue North, 37219
Telephone: 615-244-1713
Telecopier-FAX: 615-726-0573

MEMBERS OF FIRM

James F. Neal
Aubrey B. Harwell, Jr.
Jon D. Ross
James F. Sanders
Thomas H. Dundon
Robert L. Sullivan
Ronald G. Harris
Albert F. Moore
Philip N. Elbert
James G. Thomas
William T. Ramsey
Delta Anne Davis

(See Next Column)

Philip D. Irwin
George H. Cate, III
Edmund L. Carey, Jr.
John A. Coates
Pamela King
John C. Beiter
David P. Bohman
A. Scott Ross

Representative Clients: Channel 5 Television (WTVF); General Motors Corp.; Ingram Industries; Nissan Motor Corporation in U.S.A.; Tokio Marine & Fire Ins. Co.; United Technology Corp. (Sikorsky Helicopter); Westinghouse Electric Corp.; Yamaha Motor Corp.

For Complete List of Firm Personnel, See General Section

For full biographical listings, see the Martindale-Hubbell Law Directory

PARKER, LAWRENCE, CANTRELL & DEAN (AV)

Fifth Floor, 200 Fourth Avenue North, 37219
Telephone: 615-255-7500
Telecopy: 615-242-1515

MEMBERS OF FIRM

Robert E. Parker
Thomas W. Lawrence, Jr.
Rose Park Cantrell
George A. Dean
Richard K. Smith
Louis Marshall Albritton
M. Bradley Gilmore

ASSOCIATES

Michael K. Bassham
Garrett E. Asher

Representative Clients: Regions Bank; Sams Stores, Inc.; State Volunteer Mutual Ins. Co.; Harpeth Valley Utility District; Steinhouse Supply Co.

For full biographical listings, see the Martindale-Hubbell Law Directory

GAIL P. PIGG (AV)

219 Second Avenue North, 37201
Telephone: 615-244-0001
FAX: 615-244-0003

References: Sovran Bank; First American Bank.

For full biographical listings, see the Martindale-Hubbell Law Directory

WHITE & REASOR (AV)

3305 West End Avenue, 37203
Telephone: 615-383-3345
Facsimile: 615-383-5534; 615-383-9390

MEMBERS OF FIRM

David J. White, Jr.
Charles B. Reasor, Jr.
Barrett B. Sutton, Jr.
John M. Baird
Dudley M. West
Van P. East, III
Steven L. West

For full biographical listings, see the Martindale-Hubbell Law Directory

WILLIS & KNIGHT (AV)

215 Second Avenue, North, 37201
Telephone: 615-259-9600
FAX: 615-259-3490

MEMBERS OF FIRM

William R. Willis, Jr.
Alfred H. Knight
Frank Grace, Jr.
Marian F. Harrison

ASSOCIATES

Alan D. Johnson
A. Russell Willis
Jeffrey G. Rappuhn
Gregory D. Smith
W. Reese Willis, III

Representative Client: Nashville Memorial Hospital, Inc.

For full biographical listings, see the Martindale-Hubbell Law Directory

*SAVANNAH,** Hardin Co.

HOPPER & PLUNK, P.C. (AV)

404 West Main Street, P.O. Box 220, 38372
Telephone: 901-925-8076

James A. Hopper
Dennis W. Plunk

Representative Clients: United States Fidelity & Guaranty Co.; Tennessee Farmers Mutual Insurance Company; Kemper Insurance Co.; Savannah Electric; Tennessee Municipal Pool; Tennessee River Pulp & Paper Co.; Cigna Insurance Company.
References: Boatman's Bank, Savannah; The Hardin County Bank.

For Complete List of Firm Personnel, See General Section

For full biographical listings, see the Martindale-Hubbell Law Directory

TEXAS

*ABILENE,** Taylor Co.

NORVELL & ASSOCIATES, A PROFESSIONAL CORPORATION (AV)

744 Hickory Street, 79601
Telephone: 915-676-1617
Fax: 915-676-4421

James D. Norvell

Thomas G. McIlhany

LEGAL SUPPORT PERSONNEL

Margaret Roberts
David A. LeBleu
Debora Sanger
Thomas L. Brewster, Jr.

Reference: Security State Bank.

For full biographical listings, see the Martindale-Hubbell Law Directory

*AMARILLO,** Potter Co.

CONANT WHITTENBURG WHITTENBURG & SCHACHTER, P.C. (AV)

1010 South Harrison, P.O. Box 31718, 79120
Telephone: 806-372-5700
Facsimile: 806-372-5757
Dallas, Texas Office: 2300 Plaza of the Americas, 600 North Pearl, LB 133,
Telephone: 214-999-5700.
Facsimile: 214-999-5747.

A. B. Conant, Jr.
George Whittenburg
Mack Whittenburg
Cary Ira Schachter
Susan Lynn Burnette
William B. Chaney
Charles G. White
Vikram K. D. Chandhok
J. Michael McBride

OF COUNSEL

Linda A. Hale

Karl L. Baumgardner
Raymond P. Harris, Jr.
Lewis Coppedge
Francis Hangarter, Jr.
Nanneska N. Magee
Stuart J. Ford
Shawn W. Phelan
Paul M. Saraceni

For full biographical listings, see the Martindale-Hubbell Law Directory

GARNER, LOVELL & STEIN, P.C. (AV)

Amarillo National Plaza Two, 500 South Taylor, Suite 1200, 79101-2442
Telephone: 806-379-7111
Telecopier: 806-379-7176

Robert E. Garner
John H. Lovell
Joe L. Lovell
Samuel Lee Stein
Brian T. Cartwright
Tim D. Newsom

Representative Clients: Panhandle Capitol Corporation; Friona Industries, Inc.; Amarillo National Bank; Caviness Packing Co.

For full biographical listings, see the Martindale-Hubbell Law Directory

HINKLE, COX, EATON, COFFIELD & HENSLEY (AV)

1700 Bank One Center, P.O. Box 9238, 79105-9238
Telephone: 806-372-5569
FAX: 806-372-9761
Roswell, New Mexico Office: 700 United Bank Plaza, P. O. Box 10, 88202.
Telephone: 505-622-6510.
FAX: 505-623-9332.
Midland, Texas Office: 6 Desta Drive, Suite 2800, P.O. Box 3580, 79702.
Telephone: 915-683-4691.
FAX: 915-683-6518.
Santa Fe, New Mexico Office: 218 Montezuma, P.O. Box 2068, 87504.
Telephone: 505-982-4554.
FAX: 505-982-8623.
Albuquerque, New Mexico Office: Suite 800, 500 Marquette, N.W., P.O. Box 2043, 87102.
Telephone: 505-768-1500.
FAX: 505-768-1529.
Austin, Texas Office: 401 West 15th Street, Suite 800, 78701.
Telephone: 512-476-7137.
FAX: 512-476-5431.
Associated Office: Hoffman & Stephens, P.C., 401 West 15th Street, Suite 800, 78701.
Telephone: 512-476-5434. Fax; 512-476-5431.

RESIDENT PARTNERS

Maston C. Courtney
Richard R. Wilfong
Jerry F. Shackelford
John C. Chambers
Russell J. Bailey
Charles R. Watson, Jr.
Wyatt L. Brooks
David M. Russell
Kirt E. Moelling

(See Next Column)

Representative Clients: Amoco Production Company; Federated Mutual Insurance Company; Mitchell Energy Corporation; Natural Gas Pipeline Company; POGO Producing Company; Pennzoil Exploration and Production company; R.B. Operating Company; Southwestern Public Service Company; Viking Insurance.

For full biographical listings, see the Martindale-Hubbell Law Directory

*AUSTIN,** Travis Co.

* indicates certain Bar Register subscribers whose principal office is located elsewhere in the state and who have arranged for representation as a part of the state capital listings that follow

BAKER & BOTTS, L.L.P. (AV)

1600 San Jacinto Center, 98 San Jacinto Boulevard, 78701
Telephone: 512-322-2500
Fax: 512-322-2501
Houston, Texas Office: One Shell Plaza, 910 Louisiana.
Telephone: 713-229-1234.
Dallas, Texas Office: 2001 Ross Avenue.
Telephone: 214-953-6500.
Washington, D.C. Office: The Warner, 1299 Pennsylvania Avenue, N.W.
Telephone: 202-639-7700.
New York, New York Office: 885 Third Avenue, Suite 2000.
Telephone: 212-705-5000.
Moscow, Russian Federation Office: 10 ul. Pushkinskaya, 103031.
Telephone: 7095/921-5300 (Local); 7501/929-7070 (International).

MEMBERS OF FIRM

Robert I. Howell
Robert T. Stewart
Robb L. Voyles
Larry F. York

OF COUNSEL

Joe R. Greenhill
Bob E. Shannon
Robert D. Simpson

ASSOCIATES

Susan Denmon Gusky
Patrick O. Keel
Joseph R. Knight
Francesca Ortiz
Mark R. Robeck
Kevin M. Sadler
R. Walton Shelton

For Complete List of Firm Personnel, See General Section

For full biographical listings, see the Martindale-Hubbell Law Directory

WILL BARBER (AV)

1520 Austin Centre 701 Brazos, 78701
Telephone: 512-469-0360
Fax: 512-469-0967

Will G. Barber

For full biographical listings, see the Martindale-Hubbell Law Directory

CLARK, THOMAS & WINTERS, A PROFESSIONAL CORPORATION (AV)

12th Floor, Texas Commerce Bank Building, 700 Lavaca Street, P.O. Box 1148, 78767
Telephone: 512-472-8800
Fax: 512-474-1129
San Antonio, Texas Office: One Riverwalk Place, 700 North St. Mary's Street, Suite 600.
Telephone: 512-227-2691.

Edward A. Clark (1906-1992)
Donald S. Thomas
J. Sam Winters
Conrad P. Werkenthin
Mary Joe Carroll
Mike Cotten
Barry K. Bishop
Donald S. Thomas, Jr.
Rhonda H. Brink
Burgain G. Hayes
Walter Demond
Larry McNeill
James E. Mann
David C. Duggins
Kenneth J. Ferguson
Daniel R. Renner
L. G. Skip Smith
Michael R. Klatt
Jay A. Thompson
Leslie A. Benitez
Casey Wren
S. Meade Bauer
Rick Akin
Joanne Summerhays
Dan Ballard
Ted Mishtal
Chris A. Pearson
David H. Gilliland
Will Guerrant

A. Boone Almanza
Louis D. Bonder
Susan P. Burton
L. French Cadenhead
David Lill
Kerry McGrath
Christine M. Mullen
Paul S. Ruiz
Roy Spezia
Valerie L. Wenger
John F. Williams

For Complete List of Firm Personnel, See General Section

For full biographical listings, see the Martindale-Hubbell Law Directory

Austin—Continued

DAVIS & WILKERSON, P.C. (AV)

200 One American Center, Six Hundred Congress Avenue, P.O. Box 2283, 78768-2283
Telephone: 512-482-0614
Fax: 512-482-0342
Alpine, Texas Office: 1110 East Holland. P.O. Box 777. 79831-0777.
Telephone: 915-837-5547.

David M. Davis
Steven R. Welch
Jeff D. Otto
Glen Wilkerson
David A. Wright
Leonard W. Woods
Kevin A. Reed
J. Mark Holbrook
Brian E. Riewe

Fletcher H. Brown
Deborah G. Clark
Frances W. Hamermesh
Kelly Ann McDonald
Brian McElroy
Michael Wilson
Stephen G. Wohleb
Stephen A. Wood

OF COUNSEL

Pete P. Gallego
Regina C. Williams

For full biographical listings, see the Martindale-Hubbell Law Directory

DEITCH & HAMILTON, A PROFESSIONAL CORPORATION (AV)

301 Congress Avenue, Suite 1050, P.O. Box 1398, 78767
Telephone: 512-474-1554
Telecopy: 512-474-1579

Michael E. Deitch
Kendall D. Hamilton
Brian A. Turner

For full biographical listings, see the Martindale-Hubbell Law Directory

FRANKLIN W. DENIUS (AV)

700 Texas Commerce Bank Building, 700 Lavaca, 78701-3102
Telephone: 512-472-9840
Fax: 512-472-9870

Reference: Texas Commerce Bank, Austin.

For full biographical listings, see the Martindale-Hubbell Law Directory

GARY F. DESHAZO & ASSOCIATES (AV)

The Norwood Tower, 114 West Seventh Street, Suite 1200, 78701
Telephone: 512-476-3800
Fax: 512-476-0435

Jerome J. Schelfelbein (Not admitted in TX)
Jon Michael Smith

OF COUNSEL

Steven D. Peterson

For full biographical listings, see the Martindale-Hubbell Law Directory

FORD & FERRARO, L.L.P. (AV)

A Registered Limited Liability Partnership
98 San Jacinto Boulevard, Suite 2000, 78701-4286
Telephone: 512-476-2020
Telecopy: 512-477-5267

Joseph M. Ford (P.C.)
Peter E. Ferraro (P.C.)
Thomas D. Fritz
Daniel H. Byrne (P.C.)
William S. Rhea, IV
Lisa C. Fancher
Clint Hackney (P.C.)
John D. Head
Robert O. Renbarger

ASSOCIATES

Patricia A. Becker
Linda Cangelosi
Bruce Perkins
James A. Rodman
James V. Sylvester
Cari S. Young

SPECIAL COUNSEL

Clark Watts

OF COUNSEL

Salvatore F. Fiscina (Not admitted in TX)
Lawrence H. Brenner (Not admitted in TX)

For full biographical listings, see the Martindale-Hubbell Law Directory

GIBBINS, WINCKLER & HARVEY, L.L.P. (AV)

500 West 13th Street, P.O. Box 1452, 78767
Telephone: 512-474-2441

Bob Gibbins
Jay L. Winckler
Jay Harvey

ASSOCIATES

Steven Gibbins
Susan P. Russell
Wayne Prosperi
Neil M. Bonavita

Reference: Nationsbank, Austin.

For full biographical listings, see the Martindale-Hubbell Law Directory

HOHMANN, WERNER & TAUBE, L.L.P. (AV)

100 Congress Avenue, Suite 1600, 78701-4042
Telephone: 512-472-5997
Fax: 512-472-5248
Houston, Texas Office: 1300 Post Oak Boulevard, Suite 700.
Telephone: 713-961-3541.
Fax: 713-961-3542.

Guy M. Hohmann
Eric J. Taube
Paul Dobry Keeper

Nicholas S. Bressi
T. Wade Jefferies
Camille Johnson Mauldin
Sandra McFarland
Mitchell D. Savrick
Gary N. Schumann
Rachel J. Stroud

For full biographical listings, see the Martindale-Hubbell Law Directory

KAUFMAN, REIBACH & RICHIE, INC. (AV)

2150 One American Center, 600 Congress Avenue, 78701
Telephone: 512-320-7220
Fax: 512-320-7230
San Antonio, Texas Office: 300 Convent Street, Suite 900.
Telephone: 210-227-2000.
Telecopier: 210-229-1307.

Sheldon E. Richie

Katherine J. Walters

For full biographical listings, see the Martindale-Hubbell Law Directory

LONG, BURNER, PARKS & SEALY, A PROFESSIONAL CORPORATION (AV)

301 Congress, Suite 800, P.O. Box 2212, 78768-2212
Telephone: 512-474-1587
Fax: 512-322-0301

Tom Long (1922-1989)
Clay Cotten (1916-1991)
Burnie Burner
Larry Parks
Earl W. (Rusty) Sealy
Jane G. Noble
Wendy Kendall Schaefer
Elisabeth (Betty) DeLargy
James W. (Woody) Butler
Christopher A. McClellan
Paula A. Jones
M. Scott Holter

For full biographical listings, see the Martindale-Hubbell Law Directory

LUDLUM & LUDLUM (AV)

Second Floor The Enterprise Plaza, 13915 Burnet Road at Wells Branch Parkway, 78728
Telephone: 512-255-4000
Cable Address: "Ludlum"
Telecopier: 512-244-7000

FIRM FOUNDER

James N. Ludlum (Retired 1987)

MEMBERS OF FIRM

James Ludlum, Jr.
Catherine L. Kyle
Anthony G. Brocato, Jr
M. Winfield Atkins, IV

Representative Clients: American Hardware Insurance Group; American International Group; American International Underwriters, Inc.; Go Pro Underwriters, Inc.; National Casualty Company; New Hampshire Insurance Group; North American Specialty Insurance Group; United National Insurance Group.

For full biographical listings, see the Martindale-Hubbell Law Directory

MARONEY, CROWLEY & BANKSTON, L.L.P. (AV)

701 Brazos, Suite 1500, 78701
Telephone: 512-499-8855
Fax: 512-499-8886

Jack D. Maroney
Michael J. Crowley
Milton L. Bankston
Michael S. Hull
James M. Richardson
Robert L. Grove, Jr.

Jerald W. Epps
Susan Henricks
Jeffrey S. Davis
Ross H. Ehlinger
Andrew F. MacRae

OF COUNSEL

Howard N. Richards

Griffis, Motl & Junell, P.C., San Angelo, Texas
Robert A. Junell

Representative Clients: Blue Cross and Blue Shield of Texas, Inc.; Browning-Ferris Industries, Inc.; CIGNA; Coca-Cola Enterprises; EMC Underwriters, Ltd.; Employers Mutual Cos.; Northwestern National Insurance Group; Philip Morris, Inc.; Signal Aviation Underwriters, Inc.; St. Paul Insurance Co. of Texas.

(See Next Column)

MARONEY, CROWLEY & BANKSTON L.L.P., *Austin—Continued*

For full biographical listings, see the Martindale-Hubbell Law Directory

MCGINNIS, LOCHRIDGE & KILGORE, L.L.P. (AV)

1300 Capitol Center, 919 Congress Avenue, 78701
Telephone: 512-495-6000
Houston, Texas Office: 3200 One Houston Center, 1221 McKinney Street.
Telephone: 713-615-8500.

OF COUNSEL

Jack Ratliff

MEMBERS OF FIRM

Lloyd Lochridge
Shannon H. Ratliff
Barry L. Wertz
John W. Stayton, Jr.
Jeffrey A. Davis (Resident, Houston Office)
Marc O. Kniseley
Patton G. Lochridge
S. Jack Balagia, Jr.
James R. Raup
Scott Moore
Paul J. Wataha

For Complete List of Firm Personnel, See General Section

For full biographical listings, see the Martindale-Hubbell Law Directory

MINTON, BURTON, FOSTER & COLLINS, A PROFESSIONAL CORPORATION (AV)

1100 Guadalupe Street, 78701-2198
Telephone: 512-476-4873
Fax: 512-479-8315

Perry L. Jones (1908-1969)
J. Travis Blakeslee (1919-1990)
Roy Q. Minton
Charles R. Burton
John L. Foster
Warren L. (Rip) Collins, Jr.
Randy T. Leavitt
Martha S. Dickie
Scott A. Young
John C. Carsey
David F. Minton
Jennifer Ramsey

OF COUNSEL

Paul T. Holt

Representative Clients: Crum & Forster Commercial Insurance Company; The Texas Department of Commerce; Exxon; Freeport-McMoRan, Inc.; HealthTrust, Inc.; Houston Lighting & Power; Living Centers of America, Inc.; The Office of the Governor of Texas; Service Life Insurance Company; Texas Utilities Electric Company.

For full biographical listings, see the Martindale-Hubbell Law Directory

MITHOFF & JACKS, L.L.P. (AV)

Suite 1010, Franklin Plaza, 111 Congress Avenue, 78701
Telephone: 512-478-4422
Telecopier: 512-478-5015
Houston, Texas Office: Penthouse, 3450, One Allen Center.
Telephone: 713-654-1122.

Tommy Jacks
Richard Warren Mithoff
James L. Wright

Mark George Einfalt

For full biographical listings, see the Martindale-Hubbell Law Directory

MULLEN, MACINNES & REDDING (AV)

812 San Antonio, 6th Floor, 78701
Telephone: 512-477-6813
Fax: 512-477-7573
San Antonio, Texas Office: 434 South Main Street, Suite 208.
Telephone: 210-271-3791.
Fax: 210-271-7718.

MEMBERS OF FIRM

Pat Mullen
Robert A. MacInnes
James E. "Buck" Redding (1938-1992)
Jerri L. Ward
Gregory A. Whigham
Sam Lively

ASSOCIATES

Mark H. Siefken
Alicia A. Wilde
Karl Tiger Hanner
V. Jay Youngblood
Robert D. Wilkes
Elena N. Cablao
Connie Lynn Hawkins
Bradley P. Bengtson

For full biographical listings, see the Martindale-Hubbell Law Directory

JACK N. PRICE, P.C. (AV)

410 Congress Avenue, 78701
Telephone: 512-474-1563
Fax: 512-474-4727

Jack N. Price

Earl Landers (Lanny) Vickery

Reference: First City Austin.

For full biographical listings, see the Martindale-Hubbell Law Directory

SAEGERT, ANGENEND & AUGUSTINE, P.C. (AV)

1145 West Fifth Street, Suite 300, 78703
Telephone: 512-474-6521
Fax: 512-477-4512

Jerry C. Saegert
Paul D. Angenend
John C. Augustine
Mark D. Swanson
John R. Whisenhunt (1949-1994)
Harrell Glenn Hall, Jr.
Wendall Corrigan
Rebecca K. Knapik
Walter C. Guebert
Paul Vincent Mouer

For full biographical listings, see the Martindale-Hubbell Law Directory

SCOTT, DOUGLASS, LUTON & MCCONNICO, L.L.P. (AV)

A Limited Liability Partnership including a Professional Corporation
One American Center, 600 Congress Avenue, 15th Floor, 78701-3234
Telephone: 512-495-6300
Fax: 512-474-0731
Houston, Texas Office: 40th Floor, NationsBank Center, 700 Louisiana Street.
Telephone: 713-225-8400.
Dallas, Texas Office: NationsBank Plaza, 901 Main Street, Suite 2800.
Telephone: 214-651-5300.

MEMBERS OF FIRM

Wallace H. Scott, Jr.
Frank P. Youngblood
H. Philip Whitworth, Jr.
John G. Soule
Stephen E. McConnico
James N. Cowden
Richard P. Marshall, Jr.
Carroll Greer Martin
Steve Selby
Elizabeth N. Miller
John W. Camp
Daniel W. Bishop, II
Ray H. Langenberg
Thomas A. Albright
Douglas J. Dashiell
Ray N. Donley
Phyllis M. Pollard
Christopher Fuller
Casey L. Dobson
Jennifer Knauth Lipinski
Daniel C. Bitting
Sam Johnson
Robert A. Summers
Mark W. Eidman
Julie Ann Springer

OF COUNSEL

Bob Bullock
Martin L. Allday

ASSOCIATES

Jeffrey G. Henry
James P. Ray
Jane M. N. Webre
Steven J. Wingard
Elizabeth B. Pearsall
Anna M. Norris
James D. Clayton
Rebecca M. Hudson

For full biographical listings, see the Martindale-Hubbell Law Directory

SPIVEY, GRIGG, KELLY & KNISELY, P.C. (AV)

48 East Avenue, Suite 100, 78701-4320
Telephone: 512-474-6061
Fax: 512-474-1605

Broadus A. Spivey
Dicky Grigg
Patrick Michael Kelly
Paul E. Knisely

Tom P. Prehoditch
Rick Leeper

Reference: Texas Commerce Bank.

For full biographical listings, see the Martindale-Hubbell Law Directory

*** THOMPSON & KNIGHT, A PROFESSIONAL CORPORATION** (AV)

(Attorneys and Counselors)
1200 San Jacinto Center, 98 San Jacinto Boulevard, 78701
Telephone: 512-469-6100
Telecopy: 512-469-6180
Dallas, Texas Office: 1700 Pacific Avenue, Suite 3300, 75201.
Telephone: 214-969-1700.
Telecopy: 512-969-1751.
Cable Address: "Tomtex."
Telex: 732298.
Fort Worth, Texas Office: 801 Cherry Street, Suite 1600, 76102.
Telephone: 817-347-1700.
Telecopy: 817-347-1799.
Houston, Texas Office: 1700 Texas Commerce Tower, 600 Travis, 77002.
Telephone: 713-217-2800.
Telecopy: 713-217-2828; 713-217-2882.
Monterrey, Mexico Office: Edificio Losoles PD-4, Av. Lázaro Cárdenas No. 2400 Pte., San Pedro Garza Garcia, Nuevo Léon C.P. 66220.
Telephone: (52-8) 363-0096.
Telecopy: (52-8) 363-3067.

SHAREHOLDERS

Eugene W. Brees, II
James E. Cousar IV
Frank L. Hill
Debora Beck McWilliams

(See Next Column)

THOMPSON & KNIGHT A PROFESSIONAL CORPORATION—*Continued*

ASSOCIATES

Jeffrey S. Boyd
Jane E. Fields
Caroline M. LeGette

For Complete List of Firm Personnel, See General Section

For full biographical listings, see the Martindale-Hubbell Law Directory

*** VINSON & ELKINS L.L.P. (AV)**

One American Center, 600 Congress Avenue, 78701-3200
Telephone: 512-495-8400
Fax: 512-495-8612
Houston, Texas Office: 1001 Fannin, Suite 2300.
Telephone: 713-758-2222.
Fax: 713-758-2346. International
Telex: 6868314.
Cable Address: Vinelkins.
Dallas, Texas Office: 3700 Trammell Crow Center, 2001 Ross Avenue.
Telephone: 214-220-7700.
Fax: 214-220-7716.
Washington, D.C. Office: The Willard Office Building, 1455 Pennsylvania Avenue, N.W.
Telephone: 202-639-6500.
Fax: 202-639-6604.
Cable Address: Vinelkins.
London, England Office: 47 Charles Street, Berkeley Square, London W1X 7PB, England.
Telephone: 011 (44-171) 491-7236.
Fax: 011 (44-171) 499-5320.
Cable Address: Vinelkins LondonW.1.
Moscow, Russian Federation Office: 16 Alezey Tolstoy Street, Second Floor, Moscow, 103001 Russian Federation.
Telephone: 011 (70-95) 956-1995.
Telecopy: 011 (70-95) 956-1996.
Mexico City, Mexico Office: Arisóteles 77, 5°Piso, Colonia Chapultepec Polanco, 11560 Mexico, D.F.
Telephone: (52-5) 280-7828.
Fax: (52-5) 280-9223.
Singapore Office: 50 Raffles Place, #19-05 Shell Tower, 0104. U.S. Voice Mailbox: 713-758-3500.
Telephone: (65) 536-8300.
Fax: (65) 536-8311.

RESIDENT PARTNERS

Kim Edward Brightwell
Harley R. Clark, Jr.
Susan G. Conway
Richard D. Milvenan

RESIDENT ASSOCIATES

J. David Bickham, Jr.
Barry D. Burgdorf
Daniel R. Castro
Eva C. Ramos
Beverly G. Reeves

For Complete List of Firm Personnel, See General Section

For full biographical listings, see the Martindale-Hubbell Law Directory

WALSH, ANDERSON, UNDERWOOD, SCHULZE & ALDRIDGE, P.C. (AV)

La Costa Centre, 6300 La Calma, Suite 200, P.O. Box 2156, 78768
Telephone: 512-454-6864
Fax: 512-467-9318
San Antonio, Texas Office: Renaissance Plaza, Suite 800, 70 N.E. Loop 410. P.O. Box 460606.
Telephone: 210-979-6633.
Fax: 210-979-7024.

Jim Walsh
Denise Howell Anderson
Judy Underwood
Eric W. Schulze
John S. Aldridge
Chris Garza Elizalde
Paul William Hunn
Elena M. Gallegos
Nan Porett Seidenfeld

Melissa Wiginton
Oscar G. Treviño
Dorcas A. Green
Jim Hollis
Bridget R. Robinson
Robert Russo (Resident, San Antonio Office)

For full biographical listings, see the Martindale-Hubbell Law Directory

LAW OFFICES OF JOSEPH P. WEBBER (AV)

Frost Bank Plaza, Suite 1130, 816 Congress Avenue, P.O. Box 222, 78767
Telephone: 512-472-1131
Telecopier: 512-479-8977

Joseph R. Little

For full biographical listings, see the Martindale-Hubbell Law Directory

*BEAUMONT,** Jefferson Co.

LAW OFFICES OF GILBERT T. ADAMS A PROFESSIONAL CORPORATION (AV)

1855 Calder Avenue, P.O. Box 3688, 77704-3688
Telephone: 409-835-3000
Telecopier: 409-832-6162

Gilbert T. Adams (1905-1984)
Gilbert T. Adams, Jr.

Curtis L. Soileau
Earl B. Stover, III
Jesse L. English, III
Theme Sue Linh
Cheryl A. Schultz
Gilbert Timbrell Adams, III

For full biographical listings, see the Martindale-Hubbell Law Directory

BENCKENSTEIN & OXFORD, L.L.P. (AV)

First Interstate Bank Building, P.O. Box 150, 77704
Telephone: 409-833-9182
Cable Address: "Bmor"
Telex: 779485
Telefax: 409-833-8819
Austin, Texas Office: Suite 810, 400 West 15th Street, 78701.
Telephone: 512-474-8586.
Telefax: 512-478-3064.

MEMBERS OF FIRM

L. J. Benckenstein (1894-1966)
F. L. Benckenstein (1918-1987)
Hubert Oxford, III
Alan G. Sampson
Frank D. Calvert
Dana Timaeus
Mary Ellen Blade
William H. Yoes
William M. Tolin, III
Kip Kevin Lamb
Frances Blair Bethea
Robert J. Rose, Sr.

ASSOCIATES

Susan J. Oliver
F. Blair Clarke
Keith A. Pardue (Resident, Austin, Texas Office)
Josiah Wheat, Jr.
Steve Johnson
Michael Keith Eaves
Nikki L. Redden

Representative Clients: Marine Office of American Corporation (MOAC); Moran Towing and Transportation Co., Inc.

For Complete List of Firm Personnel, See General Section

For full biographical listings, see the Martindale-Hubbell Law Directory

LAW OFFICES OF ANTHONY G. BROCATO (AV)

1112 Petroleum Building, 550 Fannin Street, 77701
Telephone: 409-833-9800
Telecopier: 409-833-9213

Walter C. Brocato

Reference: Texas Commerce Bank of Beaumont, N.A.

For full biographical listings, see the Martindale-Hubbell Law Directory

MEHAFFY & WEBER, A PROFESSIONAL CORPORATION (AV)

2615 Calder Avenue, P.O. Box 16, 77704
Telephone: 409-835-5011
Fax: 409-835-5729; 835-5177
Orange, Texas Office: 1006 Green Avenue, P.O. Drawer 189.
Telephone: 409-886-7766.
Houston, Texas Office: One Allen Center, 500 Dallas, Suite 1200.
Telephone: 713-655-1200.

James W. Mehaffy (1914-1985)
Dewey J. Gonsoulin
Daniel V. Flatten
Roger S. McCabe
Jim I. Graves
John Cash Smith
Thomas L. Hanna
John J. Durkay
Arthur R. Almquist
Louis M. Scofield
Patricia Chamblin
Gene M. Williams
David B. Gaultney
Robert A. Black
Sandra F. Clark
M. C. Carrington
Kurt M. Andreason
Deborah A. Newman
Barbara J. Barron
Elizabeth Brandes Pratt
Joseph E. Broussard
John E. Haught

Elizabeth C. Lazenby
Keith W. Foley
Vickie R. Thompson
Cimron Campbell
Josephine Tennant-Hillegeist
Greg J. German
Ernest W. Boyd
Stephen H. Forman
Michele Y. Smith
Lynn M. Bencowitz
Charles S. Perry
James C. (Clay) Crawford
David W. Schultz
Deanne F. Rienstra
Paul R. Heyburn
Maria Artime
Douglas C. Monsour
Barrett F. Watson
David L. Red
Cecile E. Crabtree

(See Next Column)

MEHAFFY & WEBER A PROFESSIONAL CORPORATION, *Beaumont—Continued*

OF COUNSEL

Otto J. Weber, Jr.

Representative Clients: E.I. du Pont de Nemours and Company; Bethlehem Steel Corp.; The Kansas City Southern Railway Co.; FMC Corp.; Eli Lilly & Company; Merrell Dow; Jefferson County Tax Appraisal District.
Approved Attorneys for: Stewart Title Guaranty Co.

For full biographical listings, see the Martindale-Hubbell Law Directory

*CORPUS CHRISTI,** Nueces Co.

BRIN & BRIN, P.C. (AV)

1202 Third Street, 78404
Telephone: 512-881-9643
Fax: 512-883-0506
San Antonio, Texas Office: 8200 IH Ten West, Suite 610.
Telephone: 210-341-9711.
Fax: 512-341-1854.
Edinburg, Texas Office: 118 East Cano.
Telephone: 210-381-6602.
Fax: 210-381-0725.
Brownsville, Texas Office: 1205 North Expressway 83.
Telephone: 210-544-7110
Fax: 210-544-0607.

Ronald B. Brin
George G. Brin (Resident, San Antonio Office)
Richard W. Crews, Jr.
Douglas M. Kennedy
John R. Lyde (Resident, Edinburg Office)
Paul Swacina
Gerald D. McFarlen (Resident, San Antonio Office)
Tom F. Nye
Sandra C. Zamora (Resident, San Antonio Office)

Representative Clients: St. Paul Insurance Co.; Travelers Insurance Co.; Maryland Casualty Company; Coca Cola Bottlers Assn.; CIGNA Companies; Fireman's Fund; Texas Medical Liability Trust; Kemper Insurance Co.; National Union Insurance Co.; Medical Protective Co. (JUA).

For full biographical listings, see the Martindale-Hubbell Law Directory

EDWARDS, TERRY, BAIAMONTE & EDWARDS (AV)

802 North Carancahua, Suite 1400 (78470), P.O. Drawer 480, 78403-0480
Telephone: 512-883-0971
Toll Free: 1-800-475-0971
Fax: 512-883-7221

MEMBERS OF FIRM

William R. Edwards
Michael G. Terry
Terry Edwards Baiamonte
William R. Edwards, III
Angelina Beltran

For full biographical listings, see the Martindale-Hubbell Law Directory

FRANCIS I. GANDY, JR. (AV)

148 American Bank Plaza, P.O. Box 1316, 78475-1197
Telephone: 512-883-6333
FAX: 512-883-0148

For full biographical listings, see the Martindale-Hubbell Law Directory

HARRIS & THOMAS (AV)

1700 Mercantile Bank Tower, P.O. Drawer 1901, 78403
Telephone: 512-883-1946
Fax: 512-882-2900

James R. Harris
J. Norman Thomas

ASSOCIATES

Andrew M. Greenwell
Debra M. Rodriguez (Not admitted in TX)

For full biographical listings, see the Martindale-Hubbell Law Directory

HUNT, HERMANSEN, MCKIBBEN & ENGLISH, L.L.P. (AV)

1100 First City Tower II, 555 North Carancahua, 78478
Telephone: 512-882-6611
Telecopier: 512-883-8353

MEMBERS OF FIRM

Tom Hermansen
James F. McKibben, Jr.
Monte J. English
Ken Fields
Carlos A. Villarreal
Richard C. Woolsey

ASSOCIATES

Matthew B. Cano
Lamar G. Clemons
Jeanie D. Coltrin-Brink
Donald B. Dailey, Jr.
David W. Green
Tana S. Schlimmer
Thomas A. Silver

(See Next Column)

OF COUNSEL

Lev Hunt

Representative Clients: Reliance Insurance Co.; United States Insurance Group; Phillip Morris; St. Paul; Medical Protective.

For full biographical listings, see the Martindale-Hubbell Law Directory

MATTHEWS & BRANSCOMB, A PROFESSIONAL CORPORATION (AV)

802 North Carancahua, Suite 1900, 78470-0700
Telephone: 512-888-9261
Facsimile: 512-888-8504
Austin, Texas Office: 301 Congress Avenue, Suite 2050.
Telephone: 512-305-4400.
Facsimile: 512-305-4413.
San Antonio, Texas Office: One Alamo Center, 106 S. St. Mary's Street, Suite 800.
Telephone: 210-226-4211.
Facsimile: 210-226-0521.
Telex: 51060009283. Cable Code: MBLAW.
Eagle Pass, Texas Office: 675 Main Street.
Telephone: 210-773-6700.
Facsimile: 210-757-4045.
Uvalde, Texas Office: 200 E. Nopal #208.
Telephone: 210-278-4597.
Facsimile: 210-278-4806.
(Associated with Hall, Quintanilla & Alarcon, L.C., Laredo, Texas, under the name of Hall, Quintanilla, Alarcon, Matthews & Branscomb, P.L.L.C.).

James H. Robichaux
W. Roger Durden

For Complete List of Firm Personnel, See General Section

For full biographical listings, see the Martindale-Hubbell Law Directory

RANGEL & CHRISS (AV)

719 South Shoreline Boulevard, Suite 500, P.O. Box 880, 78403
Telephone: 512-883-8555
Facsimile: 512-883-9187

MEMBERS OF FIRM

Jorge C. Rangel
William J. Chriss

ASSOCIATE

Augustin Rivera, Jr.

For full biographical listings, see the Martindale-Hubbell Law Directory

REDFORD, WRAY, WOOLSEY & ANTHONY, L.L.P. (AV)

1000 North Tower, 500 North Water Street, 78471-0002
Telephone: 512-886-3200
Telecopier: 512-886-3299

Cecil D. Redford (1907-1990)
James W. Wray, Jr.
William N. Woolsey
James L. Anthony
Thomas M. Furlow
Scott D. Schmidt

OF COUNSEL

Ralph B. Weston

Representative Clients: Central and Southwest Corp.; United States Fidelity & Guaranty Company; Republic Insurance Company; National Indemnity Company; FMC Corporation; Great West Casualty Company; General Accident Insurance Company; United States Aviation Underwriters, Inc.

For full biographical listings, see the Martindale-Hubbell Law Directory

WHITE, HUSEMAN, PLETCHER & POWERS (AV)

600 Leopard Street, Suite 2100, P.O. Box 2707, 78403-2707
Telephone: 512-883-3563
Fax: 512-883-0210

David Yancey White
F. Van Huseman
Anthony E. Pletcher
Bryan Powers
Paul Dodson

ASSOCIATE

John O. Miller, III

Reference: First City Bank, Corpus Christi, Texas.

For full biographical listings, see the Martindale-Hubbell Law Directory

*DALLAS,** Dallas Co.

JOE B. ABBEY (AV)

1717 Main Street, Suite 2220, 75201
Telephone: 214-748-0423
Fax: 214-748-0426

For full biographical listings, see the Martindale-Hubbell Law Directory

ARANSON & ASSOCIATES (AV)

Legal Arts Center, 600 Jackson Street, 75202
Telephone: 214-748-5100
Fax: 214-741-4540

(See Next Column)

ARANSON & ASSOCIATES—*Continued*

Mike Aranson
Garry Philip Cantrell

For full biographical listings, see the Martindale-Hubbell Law Directory

BAKER & BOTTS, L.L.P. (AV)

2001 Ross Avenue, 75201
Telephone: 214-953-6500
Fax: 214-953-6503
Houston, Texas Office: One Shell Plaza, 910 Louisiana.
Telephone: 713-229-1234.
Washington, D.C. Office: The Warner, 1299 Pennsylvania Avenue, N.W.
Telephone: 202-639-7700.
Austin, Texas Office: 1600 San Jacinto Center, 98 San Jacinto Boulevard.
Telephone: 512-322-2500.
New York, New York Office: 885 Third Avenue, Suite 2000.
Telephone: 212-705-5000.
Moscow, Russian Federation Office: 10 ul. Pushkinskaya, 103031.
Telephone: 7095/921-5300 (Local); 7095/929-7070.

MEMBERS OF FIRM

Ronald L. Palmer
Rod Phelan
Robert W. Jordan
Larry D. Carlson
George C. Lamb III
Bryant C. Boren, Jr.
Robert W. Kantner
Earl B. Austin
Sarah R. Saldana
Peter A. Moir
Catharina J. H. D. Haynes

ASSOCIATES

Van H. Beckwith
Amy E. Castle
Jeffrey Joseph Cox
Timothy S. Durst
Harold Harvey Hunter
Samara Lackman Kline
Margaret N. McGann
Paul E. McGreal
Eric Donovan Pearson
James Kemp Sawers
Mary L. Scott
Lynn S. Switzer
Jeffrey M. Tillotson
Kenneth B. Tomlinson
Eric N. Whitney
David Gerald Wille

For Complete List of Firm Personnel, See General Section

For full biographical listings, see the Martindale-Hubbell Law Directory

BARRETT BURKE WILSON CASTLE DAFFIN & FRAPPIER, L.L.P. (AV)

A Limited Liability Partnership including Professional Corporations
6750 Hillcrest Plaza Drive, Suite 313, 75230
Telephone: 214-386-5040
Fax: 214-386-7673
Houston, Texas Office: 24 Greenway Plaza, Suite 2001.
Telephone: 713-621-8673.
Denver, Colorado Affiliated Office: Burke & Castle, P.C. 1099 Eighteenth Street, Suite 2200.
Telephone: 303-299-1800.
Fax: 303-299-1808.
Little Rock, Arkansas Affiliated Office: Wilson & Associates, P.A. 425 West Capitol Avenue, Suite 1500.
Telephone: 501-375-1820.
San Antonio, Texas Office: 1100 Northwest Loop 410, Suite 700. 78213.
Telephone: 512-366-8793.
Fax: 512-366-0198.

Michael C. Barrett

For full biographical listings, see the Martindale-Hubbell Law Directory

LAW OFFICES OF FRANK L. BRANSON, P.C. (AV)

18th Floor, Highland Park Place, 4514 Cole Avenue, 75205
Telephone: 214-522-0200;
Metro: 817-263-7452
Fax: 214-521-5485

Frank L. Branson
Debbie D. Branson
George A. Quesada, Jr.
Jerry M. White
J. Stephen King
Christopher A. Payne
Michael L. Parham
Joel M. Fineberg

OF COUNSEL

Ted Z. Robertson
J. Hadley Edgar, Jr.

For full biographical listings, see the Martindale-Hubbell Law Directory

THE BRICE-RIDDLE GROUP, P.C. (AV)

9400 North Central Expressway Suite 1000, 75231
Telephone: 214-265-6600
Fax: 214-373-5850

ATTORNEYS

Bill E. Brice
Max A. Wernick
Lance J. Vander Linden
Janna L. Countryman

OF COUNSEL

Michael Lee Riddle
W. S. Barron, Jr.

(See Next Column)

LEGAL SUPPORT PERSONNEL

Katherine Bandy

For full biographical listings, see the Martindale-Hubbell Law Directory

CALHOUN & STACY (AV)

5700 NationsBank Plaza, 901 Main Street, 75202-3747
Telephone: 214-748-5000
Telecopier: 214-748-1421
Telex: 211358 CALGUMP UR

Mark Alan Calhoun
David W. Elrod
Steven D. Goldston
Parker Nelson
Roy L. Stacy

ASSOCIATES

Shannon S. Barclay
Robert A. Bragalone
Dennis D. Conder
Jane Elizabeth Diseker
Lawrence I. Fleishman
Thomas C. Jones
Katherine Johnson Knight
V. Paige Pace
Veronika Willard
Michael C. Wright

LEGAL CONSULTANT

Rees T. Bowen, III

For full biographical listings, see the Martindale-Hubbell Law Directory

COCKRELL & WEED (AV)

3811 Turtle Creek, Suite 200, 75219-4421
Telephone: 214-522-5300
Fax: 214-526-1120

M. W. (Mel) Cockrell, Jr.
Allen Ray Weed

For full biographical listings, see the Martindale-Hubbell Law Directory

CONANT WHITTENBURG WHITTENBURG & SCHACHTER, P.C. (AV)

2300 Plaza of the Americas, 600 North Pearl, LB 133, 75201
Telephone: 214-999-5700
Facsimile: 214-999-5747
Amarillo, Texas Office: 1010 South Harrison.
Telephone: 806-372-5700.
Facsimile: 806-372-5757.

A. B. Conant, Jr.
George Whittenburg
Mack Whittenburg
Cary Ira Schachter
Susan Lynn Burnette
William B. Chaney
Charles G. White
Vikram K. D. Chandhok
J. Michael McBride

OF COUNSEL

Linda A. Hale

Karl L. Baumgardner
Raymond P. Harris, Jr.
Lewis Coppedge
Francis Hangarter, Jr.
Nanneska N. Magee
Stuart J. Ford
Shawn W. Phelan
Paul M. Saraceni

For full biographical listings, see the Martindale-Hubbell Law Directory

FIGARI & DAVENPORT (AV)

A Registered Limited Liability Partnership including Professional Corporations
4800 NationsBank Plaza, 901 Main Street, 75202
Telephone: 214-939-2000

MEMBERS OF FIRM

Ernest E. Figari, Jr., (P.C.)
Mark T. Davenport
Thomas A. Graves
Alan S. Loewinsohn
A. Erin Dwyer
William J. Albright
Doug K. Butler
Donald Colleluori
Gary D. Eisenstat
Andrew G. Jubinsky
Parker D. Young

ASSOCIATES

Jill D. Bohannon
Michael G. Brown
Timothy A. Daniels
Bill E. Davidoff
Debi L. Davis
Jennifer Haltom Doan
Stephen D. Howen
Monica L. Luebker
Julie H. Roberson
Craig F. Simon
Keith R. Verges
Andrew C. Whitaker

For full biographical listings, see the Martindale-Hubbell Law Directory

FORD & DOYLE, L.L.P. (AV)

Plaza of the Americas - South Tower, 600 North Pearl Street Suite 360, L.B. 167, 75201
Telephone: 214-871-0970
FAX: 214-871-0974

MEMBERS OF FIRM

Bryan Kent Ford
Rachel J. Doyle

For full biographical listings, see the Martindale-Hubbell Law Directory

Dallas—Continued

S. Stewart Frazer (AV)

2600 Lincoln Plaza, 500 North Akard, 75201
Telephone: 214-750-2666
Fax: 214-740-2601

For full biographical listings, see the Martindale-Hubbell Law Directory

Godwin & Carlton, A Professional Corporation (AV)

Suite 3300, 901 Main Street, 75202-3714
Telephone: 214-939-4400
Telecopier: 214-760-7332
Monterrey, Mexico Correspondent: Quintero y Quintero Abogodos. Martin De Zalva 840-3 Sur Esquinna Con Hidalgo.
Telephone: 44-07-74, 44-07-80, 44-06-56, 44-06-28.
Fax: 83-40-34-54.

Donald E. Godwin
David J. White
John L. Hubble
David L. Patterson
Frank P. Skipper, Jr.
Harvey M. Shapan
Danny C. Garner
Thomas S. Hoekstra

Robert R. Kincaid
Steven T. Polino

Kathleen Weidinger Foster
John M. Frick
Michael K. Hurst
Harvey Goldwater Joseph
Jeffrey M. Kershaw
Robert S. Luttrull

For Complete List of Firm Personnel, See General Section

For full biographical listings, see the Martindale-Hubbell Law Directory

Hughes & Luce, L.L.P. (AV)

A Registered Limited Liability Partnership including Professional Corporations
1717 Main Street, Suite 2800, 75201
Telephone: 214-939-5500
Fax: 214-939-6100
Telex: 730836
Austin, Texas Office: 111 Congress, Suite 900.
Telephone: 512-482-6800.
Fax: 512-482-6859.
Houston, Texas Office: Three Allen Center, 333 Clay Street, Suite 3800.
Telephone: 713-754-5200.
Fax: 713-754-5206.
Fort Worth, Texas Office: 2421 Westport Parkway, Suite 500A.
Telephone: 817-439-3000.
Fax: 817-439-4222.

MEMBERS OF FIRM

Kim Juanita Askew
R. Doak Bishop
Eric R. Cromartie
Allan B. Diamond
David C. Godbey
Clifton T. Hutchinson
Maryann Joerres
Darrell E. Jordan
David C. Kent
Paul M. Koning
James D. McCarthy
R. Matthew Molash
Robert H. Mow, Jr. (P.C.)
Bobby M. Rubarts
Mark K. Sales
J. Gregory Taylor

ASSOCIATES

Thomas A. Bramlett
Joseph M. Cox
Kimberly A. Elkjer
Holly A. Schymik
Theodore Stevenson, III

For Complete List of Firm Personnel, See General Section

For full biographical listings, see the Martindale-Hubbell Law Directory

Jackson & Walker, L.L.P. (AV)

901 Main Street, Suite 6000, 75202-3797
Telephone: 214-953-6000
Fax: 214-953-5822
Fort Worth, Texas Office: 777 Main Street, Suite 1800.
Telephone: 817-334-7200.
Fax: 817-334-7290.
Houston, Texas Office: 1100 Louisiana, Suite 4200.
Telephone: 713-752-4200.
Fax: 713-752-4221.
San Antonio, Texas Office: 112 E. Pecan Street, Suite 2100.
Telephone: 210-978-7700.
Fax: 210-978-7790.

MEMBERS OF FIRM

Susan S. Andrews
Charles L. Babcock
H. Dudley Chambers
Bryan C. Collins
Gerald C. Conley
D. Paul Dalton
Robert F. Henderson
Mark T. Josephs
Michael L. Knapek
John B. Kyle
John L. Lancaster, III
Robert P. Latham
Dena L. Mathis
Retta A. Miller
David T. Moran
David C. Myers
Jack Pew, Jr.
Robert F. Ruckman

(See Next Column)

MEMBERS OF FIRM (Continued)

Dennis Neil Ryan
Gordon M. Shapiro
Jonathan L. Snare
Frank C. Vecella
Robert B. Weathersby
Stephen Cass Weiland
Troy Michael Wilson

OF COUNSEL

Ralph E. Hartman
Laura E. Hlavach
Mary Emma Ackels Karam
Harold M. Slaughter

ASSOCIATES

Carl C. Butzer
Colin P. Cahoon
E. Leon Carter
Sarah E. Clark
Jennifer E. Dorn
Alan N. Greenspan
Kimberly Lynn Hilliard
William R. Jenkins, Jr.
Patricia A. Logsdon
Bernard H. Masters
James M. McCown
Billy R. McGill
Earl S. Nesbitt
Barbara K. Salyers
James D. Struble
Timothy E. Taylor
Kimberly O'Dawn Thompson
David S. Vassar
Sylvia Dalton Wells
Elizabeth L. Yingling

Representative Clients Furnished Upon Request.

For Complete List of Firm Personnel, See General Section

For full biographical listings, see the Martindale-Hubbell Law Directory

Johnston & Budner, A Professional Corporation (AV)

3700 First Interstate Bank Tower, 1445 Ross Avenue, 75202
Telephone: 214-855-6260
Fax: 214-855-6248

Bruce A. Budner
Coyt Randal Johnston
Stephanie L. Spardone
Robert L. Tobey

For full biographical listings, see the Martindale-Hubbell Law Directory

Kilgore & Kilgore, A Professional Corporation (AV)

700 McKinney Place, 3131 McKinney Avenue - LB 103, 75204-2471
Telephone: 214-969-9099
Fax: 214-953-0133; 214-953-0242

Wilmer D. Masterson, III
W. Stephen Swayze
Robert M. Thornton
Roger F. Claxton
Theodore C. Anderson, III

For Complete List of Firm Personnel, See General Section

For full biographical listings, see the Martindale-Hubbell Law Directory

Middleberg, Riddle & Gianna (AV)

2323 Bryan Street, Suite 1600, 75201
Telephone: 214-220-6300
Telecopier: 214-220-2785
New Orleans, Louisiana Office: 31st Floor, Place St. Charles, 201 St. Charles Avenue,
Telephone: 504-525-7200.
Telecopier: 504-581-5983.
Austin, Texas Office: 901 South Mopac Expressway.
Telephone: 512-329-3012.

Ira Joel Middleberg (Not admitted in TX)
Michael Lee Riddle
Dominic J. Gianna (Not admitted in TX)

Robert M. Duval
Craig A. Eggleston
John L. Genung
Jim Jordan
Kay A. King
Kenneth J. Lambert
Marigny A. Lanier
William Andrew Messer
Carol J. Riddle
Alexandra Smith
Sheryl Weisberg
Marsha L. Williams

OF COUNSEL

Richard S. Wilensky

For full biographical listings, see the Martindale-Hubbell Law Directory

Misko, Howie & Sweeney (AV)

Turtle Creek Centre, Suite 1900, 3811 Turtle Creek Boulevard, 75219
Telephone: 214-443-8000
Fax: 214-443-8000

Fred Misko, Jr.
John R. Howie
Paula Sweeney

ASSOCIATES

Charles S. Siegel
James L. Mitchell, Jr.
Raymond A. Williams, III
Christopher D. Jones
Bryan D. Pope

For full biographical listings, see the Martindale-Hubbell Law Directory

Dallas—Continued

Novakov, Davidson & Flynn, A Professional Corporation (AV)

2000 St. Paul Place, 750 North St. Paul, 75201-3286
Telephone: 214-922-9221
Telecopy: 214-969-7557

Ronald R. Davis
James Kevin Flynn
Thomas M. Whelan

For Complete List of Firm Personnel, See General Section

For full biographical listings, see the Martindale-Hubbell Law Directory

Olson, Gibbons, Sartain, Nicoud, Birne & Sussman, L.L.P. (AV)

2600 Lincoln Plaza, 500 North Akard, 75201-3320
Telephone: 214-740-2600
Fax: 214-740-2601

Dennis O. Olson
Mark L. Gibbons
Charles W. Sartain
Robert M. Nicoud, Jr.
Robert E. Birne
Ronald L. Sussman

For full biographical listings, see the Martindale-Hubbell Law Directory

Payne & Blanchard, L.L.P. (AV)

Plaza of the Americas, 600 North Pearl Street 2500 South Tower, 75201
Telephone: 214-953-1313
Telecopier: 214-220-0439

MEMBERS OF FIRM

Arthur Blanchard (Retired)
James C. Allums, Jr.
John William Payne
Frank J. Betancourt
Charles A. Girand
Bobby D. Dyess
Kevin J. Cook
Gary W. Maxfield
James S. Wright
Jonathan A. Manning
Harold R. McKeever, Jr.

ASSOCIATES

Brian S. Hellberg
Mark B. Greenberg

Representative Clients: American Home Products; Liberty Mutual Insurance Co.; Merrill Lynch, Pierce, Fenner & Smith, Inc.; Mutual and United of Omaha Insurance Co.; State Farm Fire & Casualty Companies; Texas Association of Counties.

For full biographical listings, see the Martindale-Hubbell Law Directory

The Law Firm of C.L. Mike Schmidt, P.C. (AV)

3102 Oak Lawn, Suite 730, LB 158, 75219
Telephone: 214-521-4898
Toll Free No. 1-800-677-4898
Fax: 214-521-9995

C. L. Mike Schmidt

Ronald D. Wren
Michael E. Schmidt

For full biographical listings, see the Martindale-Hubbell Law Directory

Harry P. Stuth (AV)

University Tower, 6440 North Central Expressway, Suite 402, 75206
Telephone: 214-363-0555
Fax: 214-369-3590

Harry P. Stuth, Jr.

For full biographical listings, see the Martindale-Hubbell Law Directory

Thompson, Coe, Cousins & Irons, L.L.P. (AV)

200 Crescent Court, Eleventh Floor, 75201-1840
Telephone: 214-871-8200 (Dallas)
512-480-8770 (Austin)
FAX: 214-871-8209

MEMBERS OF FIRM

David M. Taylor
Robert B. Wellenberger
Peter A. T. Sartin
Rhonda Johnson Byrd
Roger D. Higgins
Richard M. Mosher

ASSOCIATES

John B. Kronenberger
James D. Cartier
James Richard Harmon
James L. Sowder

Representative Clients: Bridgestone/Firestone; Marion Merrell Dow, Inc.; Frontier Financial Services Corp.; Capital Technologies (B.V.I.).

For Complete List of Firm Personnel, See General Section

For full biographical listings, see the Martindale-Hubbell Law Directory

Thompson & Knight, A Professional Corporation (AV)

(Attorneys and Counselors)
1700 Pacific Avenue Suite 3300, 75201
Telephone: 214-969-1700
Telecopy: 214-969-1751
Cable Address: "Tomtex"
Telex: 732298
Austin, Texas Office: 1200 San Jacinto Center, 98 San Jacinto Boulevard, 78701.
Telephone: 512-469-6100.
Telecopy: 512-469-6180.
Fort Worth, Texas Office: 801 Cherry Street, Suite 1600, 76102.
Telephone: 817-347-1700.
Telecopy: 817-347-1799.
Houston, Texas Office: 1700 Texas Commerce Tower, 600 Travis, 77002.
Telephone: 713-217-2800.
Telecopy: 713-217-2828.
Monterrey, Mexico Office: Edificio Losoles PD-4, Av. Lázaro Cárdenas No. 2400 Pte., San Pedro Garza Garcia, Nuevo Léon C.P. 66220.
Telephone: (52-8) 363-0096.
Telecopy: (52-8) 363-3067.

SHAREHOLDERS

G. Luke Ashley
P. Jefferson Ballew
William L. Banowsky
Michael R. Berry
Jane Politz Brandt
George C. Chapman
Cheryl E. Diaz
Frank Finn
Rachelle H. Glazer
Gerald H. Grissom
Deborah G. Hankinson
William T. Hankinson
Craig A. Haynes
Gregory S. C. Huffman
Jerry P. Jones
Stephen S. Livingston
John A. Mackintosh, Jr.
Schuyler B. Marshall, IV
John H. Martin
Timothy R. McCormick
Maureen Murry
Judy C. Norris
Joseph S. Pevsner
Stephen C. Rasch
Stephen C. Schoettmer
Bruce S. Sostek
Molly Steele
Peter J. Thoma
James M. Underwood

ASSOCIATES

Steven R. Baggett
L. James Berglund, II
Beverly Ray Burlingame
Pamela Corrigan
Greg W. Curry
Lori L. Dalton
D'Lesli M. Davis
F. Barrett Davis
Katherine Romeo Gregory
Michael G. Guajardo
Craig Naveen Kakarla
Karen L. Kendrick
Jacob B. Marshall
Leasa G. McCorkle
Mindy L. McNew
Allison Roseman
Michael E. Schonberg
Lisa A. Schumacher
Pamela J. Smith
Robert V. Vitanza
David S. White
Amy K. Witherite

STAFF ATTORNEYS

Renee H. Tobias
Dawn Marie Wright

OF COUNSEL

David S. Kidder
Malia A. Litman

For Complete List of Firm Personnel, See General Section

For full biographical listings, see the Martindale-Hubbell Law Directory

Vinson & Elkins L.L.P. (AV)

3700 Trammell Crow Center, 2001 Ross Avenue, 75201-2975
Telephone: 214-220-7700
Fax: 214-220-7716
Houston, Texas Office: 1001 Fannin, Suite 2300.
Telephone: 713-758-2222.
Fax: 713-758-2346. International
Telex: 6868314.
Cable Address: Vinelkins.
Austin, Texas Office: One American Center, 600 Congress Avenue.
Telephone: 512-495-8400.
Fax: 512-495-8612.
Washington, D.C. Office: The Willard Office Building, 1455 Pennsylvania Avenue, N.W.
Telephone: 202-639-6500.
Fax: 202-639-6604.
Cable Address: Vinelkins.
London, England Office: 47 Charles Street, Berkeley Square, London, W1X 7PB, England.
Telephone: 011 (44-71) 491-7236.
Fax: 011 (44-71) 499-5320.
Cable Address: Vinelkins LondonW.1.
Moscow, Russian Federation Office: 16 Alexey Tolstoy Street, Second Floor, Moscow, 103001 Russian Federation.
Telephone: 011 (70-95) 956-1995.
Telecopy: 011 (70-95) 956-1996.
Mexico City, Mexico Office: Aristóteles 77, 5°Piso, Colonia Chapultepec Polanco, 11560 Mexico City, Mexico, D.F.
Telephone: (52-5) 280-7828.
Fax: (52-5) 280-9223

(See Next Column)

VINSON & ELKINS L.L.P., *Dallas—Continued*

Singapore Office: 50 Raffles Place, #19-05 Shell Tower, 0104. U.S. Vocie Mailbox: 713-758-3500.
Telephone: (65) 536-8300.
Fax: (65) 536-8311.

RESIDENT PARTNERS

David P. Blanke
Orrin L. Harrison, III
Kenneth E. Johns, Jr.
Thomas S. Leatherbury
Dale Gene Markland
William D. Sims, Jr.
J. Michael Sutherland
Robert C. Walters

OF COUNSEL

V. Craig Cantrell
Sheryl L. Hopkins

RESIDENT ASSOCIATES

Steven T. Baron
William H. Church, Jr.
Scott L. Cole
Mark A. Cover
Samuel Poage Dalton
Z. Melissa Lawrence
W. David Lee
Heidi Mahon Cook
Steven C. Malin
Theodore D. Matula
Michael L. Raiff
Russell L. Reid, Jr.
Tara Hanley Reynolds
Steven L. Russell
Stacy Deanne Siegel
Cynthia A. Stephens
John C. Wander
Russell Yager

For Complete List of Firm Personnel, See General Section

For full biographical listings, see the Martindale-Hubbell Law Directory

DENISON, Grayson Co.

MICHAEL THOMPSON AND ASSOCIATES, L.L.P. (AV)

230 West Main Street, 75020
Telephone: 903-465-3455

Michael Thompson

ASSOCIATES

Carrie M. Philcox
Jim E. Walker

For full biographical listings, see the Martindale-Hubbell Law Directory

*DENTON,** Denton Co.

WOOD, SPRINGER & LYLE, A PROFESSIONAL CORPORATION (AV)

513 West Oak, 76201
Telephone: 817-387-0404
Fax: 817-566-6673

R. William Wood
J. Jeffrey Springer
Frank G. Lyle
C. Jane La Rue
Grace A. Weatherly

For full biographical listings, see the Martindale-Hubbell Law Directory

*EL PASO,** El Paso Co.

GUEVARA, REBE, BAUMANN, COLDWELL & GARAY (AV)

Suite A-201, 4171 North Mesa, P.O. Box 2009, 79950
Telephone: 915-544-6646, 544-6647
Fax: 915-544-8305

MEMBERS OF FIRM

Andrew R. Guevara
Sal Rebe
James E. Baumann
Colbert N. Coldwell
Juan Carlos Garay
Lane C. Reedman

Representative Clients: Mutual Building and Loan Association, Las Cruces, New Mexico; Beneficial Texas, Inc.; Dean Witter Reynolds, Inc.; Meca Homes, Inc.; Romney Implement, Inc.; Sam Corp. (Construction); Truck Enterprises, Inc.; Farm Fresh Product, Inc.; Truck Cab Fabrication, Inc.

For full biographical listings, see the Martindale-Hubbell Law Directory

GEORGE A. MCALMON (AV)

1501 Arizona Avenue Building 3, Suite A, 79902
Telephone: 915-544-3344
FAX: 915-532-6712

For full biographical listings, see the Martindale-Hubbell Law Directory

*FORT WORTH,** Tarrant Co.

BISHOP, PAYNE, WILLIAMS & WERLEY, L.L.P. (AV)

Eighteenth Floor NationsBank Building, 500 West Seventh Street, 76102
Telephone: 817-335-4911
Telecopier: 817-870-2631

Philip R. Bishop
Hershel R. Payne
Thomas J. Williams
S. Gary Werley
Timothy J. Harvard
Michael D. Kaitcer
James Lee Anderson

Sandra W. Gould
Daniel L. Tatum
C. Russell Riddle
Andrew S. Jones
Mark C. Roberts, II
Kristin Marie Jenkins

(See Next Column)

OF COUNSEL

Michael B. Hunter
Richard L. Brown

For full biographical listings, see the Martindale-Hubbell Law Directory

CHAPPELL & MCGARTLAND, L.L.P. (AV)

1800 City Center Tower II, 301 Commerce Street, 76102-4118
Telephone: 817-332-1800
Telecopy: 817-332-1956

David F. Chappell
Michael P. McGartland
Robert A. Parmelee

Robert S. (Bob) Johnson
James L. Williams, Jr.
Mark Allan Anderson
Jason C.N. Smith

OF COUNSEL

R. David Jones
Cathy Csaky Hirt (Not admitted in TX)

For full biographical listings, see the Martindale-Hubbell Law Directory

RUSSELL, TURNER, LAIRD & JONES, L.L.P. (AV)

One Colonial Place, 2400 Scott Avenue, 76103-2200
Telephone: 817-531-3000; 1-800-448-2889
Fax: 817-535-3046
Dallas, Texas Office: Williams Square, Central Tower, Suite 700, 5215 North O'Connor Boulevard, Las Colinas Urban Center.
Telephone: 214-444-0444; 1-800-448-2889.

Wm. Greg Russell
Randall E. Turner
Steven C. Laird
Gregory G. Jones

For full biographical listings, see the Martindale-Hubbell Law Directory

THOMPSON & KNIGHT, A PROFESSIONAL CORPORATION (AV)

(Attorneys and Counselors)
801 Cherry Street, Suite 1600, 76102
Telephone: 817-347-1700
Telecopy: 817-347-1799
Dallas, Texas Office: 1700 Pacific Avenue, Suite 3300, 75201.
Telephone: 214-969-1700.
Telecopy: 214-969-1751.
Cable Address: "Tomtex."
Telex: 732298.
Austin, Texas Office: 1200 San Jacinto Center, 98 San Jacinto Boulevard, 78701.
Telephone: 512-469-6100.
Telecopy: 512-469-6180.
Houston, Texas Office: 1700 Texas Commerce Tower, 600 Travis, 77002.
Telephone: 713-217-2800.
Telecopy: 713-217-2828; 713-2882.
Monterrey, Mexico Office: Edificio Losoles PD-4, Av. Lázaro Cárdenas No. 2400 Pte., San Pedro Garza Garcia, Nuevo Léon C.P. 66220.
Telephone: (52-8) 363-0096.
Telecopy: (52-8) 363-3067.

SHAREHOLDERS

E. Michael Sheehan

ASSOCIATE

Jennifer Pettijohn Henry

For Complete List of Firm Personnel, See General Section

For full biographical listings, see the Martindale-Hubbell Law Directory

FRISCO, Collin & Denton Cos.

WINIKATES & WINIKATES (AV)

Prosper State Bank Building, P.O. Box 249, 75034-0249
Telephone: 214-335-1122
Fax: 214-335-1125

MEMBERS OF FIRM

Charles J. Winikates
Charles J. Winikates, Jr.
Regina W. Mentesana

OF COUNSEL

Frances A. Fazio

For full biographical listings, see the Martindale-Hubbell Law Directory

HARLINGEN, Cameron Co.

FLEURIET & SCHELL (AV)

621 East Tyler, 78550
Telephone: 210-428-3030
Fax: 210-421-4339

MEMBERS OF FIRM

Edwin Randolph Fleuriet
Richard D. Schell
R. Bruce Phillips

For full biographical listings, see the Martindale-Hubbell Law Directory

*HOUSTON,** Harris Co.

ALEXANDER & MCEVILY (AV)

5 Post Oak Park at San Felipe 24th Floor, 77027
Telephone: 713-439-0000; 800-955-2539
Telecopy: 713-963-8478

Tom Alexander
Kevin J. McEvily
Richard L. Flowers, Jr.
Linda Geisler Marshall
Dan McEvily (Not admitted in TX)
Vicki L. Pinak
Kelly Deann Wilson

OF COUNSEL

John V. Singleton, Jr.

References: American Bank; Chasewood Bank.

For full biographical listings, see the Martindale-Hubbell Law Directory

ALSUP BEVIS & PETTY (AV)

333 Clay Suite 4930, 77098
Telephone: 713-739-1313
Fax: 713-739-7095

Richard C. Alsup
Randall F. Bevis
Andrew H. Petty

ASSOCIATE

Michael J. Short

For full biographical listings, see the Martindale-Hubbell Law Directory

BAKER & BOTTS, L.L.P. (AV)

One Shell Plaza, 910 Louisiana, 77002
Telephone: 713-229-1234
Cable Address: "Boterlove"
Fax: 713-229-1522
Washington, D.C. Office: The Warner, 1299 Pennsylvania Avenue, N.W.
Telephone: 202-639-7700.
New York, New York Office: 885 Third Avenue, Suite 2000.
Telephone: 212-705-5000.
Austin, Texas Office: 1600 San Jacinto Center, 98 San Jacinto Boulevard.
Telephone: 512-322-2500.
Dallas, Texas Office: 2001 Ross Avenue.
Telephone: 214-953-6500.
Moscow, Russian Federation Office: 10 ul. Pushkinskaya, 103031.
Telephone: 7095/921-5300 (Local); 7095/929-7070 (International).

MEMBERS OF FIRM

Robert J. Malinak
Joseph D. Cheavens
F. Walter Conrad, Jr.
Larry B. Feldcamp
Philip J. John, Jr.
Richard R. Brann
L. Chapman Smith
William C. Slusser
Richard L. Josephson
Rufus W. Oliver, III
G. Irvin Terrell
Michael Paul Graham
Louis Lee Bagwell
Scott F. Partridge
Stephen Gillham Tipps
James Edward Maloney
Allister M. Waldrop, Jr.
J. Michael Baldwin
Lee Landa Kaplan
Tony P. Rosenstein
Thomas H. Adolph
Claudia W. Frost
Michael S. Goldberg
David R. Poage
George T. Shipley
R. Paul Yetter
Ronald C. Lewis
Mitchell D. Lukin
David D. Sterling
Paul L. Mitchell
Karen Kay Maston

ASSOCIATES

Thomas R. Ajamie
Marc A. Antonetti
Nancy K. Archer-Yanochik
Andres M. Arismendi, Jr.
Cesar Enrique Arreaza
Richard A. Bales
Parker Bond Binion
Jane Nenninger Bland
Dorothy Fong Blefeld
Maria Wyckoff Boyce
Michael Lamar Brem
William C. Bullard
Charles Tynan Buthod
Michael L. Calhoon
Bill Brannen Caraway
Ross E. Cockburn
Stephanie K. Copp
Cynthia Crawford
Robin Elizabeth Curtis
Sashe D. Dimitroff
Phillip L. Douglass
Matthew P. Eastus
Paul R. Elliott
Jason D. Firth
Kevin S. Fiur
James M. Grace, Jr.
J. Timothy Headley
Pamela Lunn Hohensee
David Charles Hricik
Linda K. Jackson
Laura Friedl Jones
M. Lamont Jones
Myriam R. Klein
William Karl Kroger
Michael P. Lennon, Jr.
Danita J. M. Maseles
J. Bruce McDonald
Scott Joseph Miller
Elise Bauman Neal
David G. Patent
Robert H. Pemberton
Kay M. Peterson
Sandra J. Pomerantz
John K. Rentz
Jayme Partridge Roden
Travis James Sales
Michael J. Schofield
Tim T. Shen
Richard S. Siluk
Brian A. E. Smith
Jennifer M. Smith
Michael H. Smith
Carolyn Brostad Southerland
Howard L. Speight

(See Next Column)

ASSOCIATES (Continued)

Suzanne H. Stenson
Rebecca S. Stierna
Lori D. Stiffler
M. Virginia Stockbridge
J. David Tate
C. Patrick Turley
Teresa Slowen Valderrama
Kathryn S. Vaughn
Cynthia D. Vreeland
Mark L. Walters
Michael E. Wilson
Shira R. Yoshor

For Complete List of Firm Personnel, See General Section

For full biographical listings, see the Martindale-Hubbell Law Directory

BAKER & HOSTETLER (AV)

1000 Louisiana, Suite 2000, 77002-5008
Telephone: 713-751-1600
FAX: 713-751-1717
In Cleveland, Ohio: 3200 National City Center, 1900 East Ninth Street.
Telephone: 216-621-0200.
In Columbus, Ohio: Capitol Square, Suite 2100, 65 East State Street.
Telephone: 614-228-1541.
In Denver, Colorado: 303 East 17th Avenue, Suite 1100.
Telephone: 303-861-0600.
In Long Beach, California: 300 Oceangate, Suite 620.
Telephone: 310-432-2827.
In Los Angeles, California: 600 Wilshire Boulevard.
Telephone: 213-624-2400.
In Orlando, Florida: SunBank Center, Suite 2300, 200 South Orange Avenue.
Telephone: 407-649-4000.
In Washington, D.C.: Washington Square, Suite 1100, 1050 Connecticut Avenue, N. W.
Telephone: 202-861-1500.
In College Park, Maryland: 9658 Baltimore Boulevard, Suite 206.
Telephone: 301-441-2781.
In Alexandria, Virginia: 437 North Lee Street.
Telephone: 703-549-1294.
In San Francisco, California: One Sansome Street, Suite 2000.
Telephone: 415-951-4705.

PARTNERS

Scott G. Camp
Lisa H. Pennington
Kenneth R. Valka (Partner in Charge-Houston Office)

ASSOCIATES

Claudia D. Christin
Hurlie H. Collier
Ricki J. Shoss
Lilly E. Thrower
Sandy H. Wotiz

OF COUNSEL

Jon David Ivey

For Complete List of Firm Personnel, See General Section

For full biographical listings, see the Martindale-Hubbell Law Directory

BAYLESS & STOKES (AV)

2931 Ferndale Street, P.O. Box 22678, 77227-2678
Telephone: 713-522-2224
Fax: 713-522-2218

Bobbie G. Bayless
Dalia Browning Stokes

For full biographical listings, see the Martindale-Hubbell Law Directory

BEIRNE, MAYNARD & PARSONS, L.L.P. (AV)

First Interstate Tower 24th Floor, 1300 Post Oak Boulevard, 77056-3000
Telephone: 713-623-0887
Fax: 713-960-1527

MEMBERS OF FIRM

Martin D. Beirne
William L. Maynard
Jeffrey R. Parsons
Sawnie A. McEntire
Suzanne B. Baker
Gerald J. Brown
Jay W. Brown
Kay L. Burkhalter
Robert B. Dillon
David S. Gamble
Craig B. Glidden
J. Michael Jordan
Roger L. McCleary
John W. Odam
David A. Pluchinsky
James E. Smith
David K. Williams

OF COUNSEL

Cindy Ann Lopez Garcia
Robert E. Jones
Clarence E. Kendall, Jr.
Wallace T. Ward, III

PARTICIPATING ASSOCIATES

David A. Clark
Kyle L. Jennings
Philip A. Lionberger
Michael J. Stanley
Linda P. Wills

ASSOCIATES

Denise A. Acebo
Tamara L. Annalora
Mary Maydelle Bambace
Remsen H. Beitel, III
Danya W. Blair
John E. Carlson
Shelley Clarke
Kevin M. Feeney
Ron E. Frank
Jennifer A. Giaimo
Richard B. Graves, III
Gregory L. Griffith

(See Next Column)

BEIRNE, MAYNARD & PARSONS L.L.P., *Houston—Continued*

ASSOCIATES (Continued)

Timothy J. Hill
Maria C. Jorik
Jeffrey A. Kaplan
Jeffrey B. Lucas
Scott D. Marrs
David T. McDowell
Mark W. Moran
Petula P. Palmer
Tracy A. Phillips
Lenora D. Post
Keith A. Rowley
Donald W. Towe
Gregory R. Travis
Patricia H. Webb
Jared R. Woodfill, V

For full biographical listings, see the Martindale-Hubbell Law Directory

BENNETT, BROOCKS, BAKER & LANGE, L.L.P. (AV)

1700 Neils Esperson Building, 808 Travis, 77002
Telephone: 713-222-1434

Robert S. Bennett
Ben C. Broocks
Reese W. Baker
B. John Lange, III
H. Victor Thomas

Patrick O. Chukelu
Robert A. Kramer
Stephen R. Reeves

OF COUNSEL

Philip H. Hilder
James M. Lober

For full biographical listings, see the Martindale-Hubbell Law Directory

JOHN GORDON BOCK (AV)

First Interstate Bank Plaza, 1000 Louisiana, Suite 1090, 77002
Telephone: 713-739-0902
Fax: 713-650-3816

For full biographical listings, see the Martindale-Hubbell Law Directory

BOSWELL & HALLMARK, A PROFESSIONAL CORPORATION (AV)

1100 Louisiana Street, Suite 2100, 77002
Telephone: 713-650-1600
Facsimile: 713-650-1211

John H. Boswell
Jim C. Ezer
Terry M. Womac
John T. Valentine
David E. Brothers, Jr.
Gene F. Creely, II
Donald R. Hallmark (1934-1990)

Gary D. Peak
Paul C. Leggett
Lydia S. Zinkhan
Janis G. Harlan
George Andrew (Drew) Coats

LEGAL SUPPORT PERSONNEL

Dennis L. Gane (Administrator)

For full biographical listings, see the Martindale-Hubbell Law Directory

CRUSE, SCOTT, HENDERSON & ALLEN, L.L.P. (AV)

Two Houston Center, Suite 1850, 909 Fannin Street, 77010-1007
Telephone: 713-650-6600
Fax: 713-650-1720

Sam W. Cruse, Jr.
John P. Scott
Jay H. Henderson
T. Scott Allen, Jr.
Samuel A. Houston
George W. (Billy) Shepherd, III
John R. Strawn, Jr.

ASSOCIATES

Stephen R. Bailey
Michael F. Hord, Jr.
Jana F. Lohse
Debra Lynn Sales
Louis B. Sullivan, III
John D. Vogel

For full biographical listings, see the Martindale-Hubbell Law Directory

C. CHARLES DIPPEL (AV)

55 Waugh Drive, Suite 603, 77007-5836
Telephone: 713-862-4445
Fax: 713-862-4665

For full biographical listings, see the Martindale-Hubbell Law Directory

DUNN, KACAL, ADAMS, PAPPAS & LAW, A PROFESSIONAL CORPORATION (AV)

2600 America Tower, 2929 Allen Parkway at Waugh, 77019-2151
Telephone: 713-529-3992
Telefax: 713-529-8161

Charles R. Dunn
Jerry Kacal
Robert L. Adams
Christopher C. Pappas
Richard M. Law
Gordon M. Carver, III
Michael C. Feehan
Daniel D. King

(See Next Column)

Karen M. Alvarado
Kenneth D. Rhodes
Willard M. Tinsley
Frances Moore
Nancy Bolin Vassallo
Darrell R. Greer
Steven D. Strickland
A.M. "Andy" Landry, III
Sarajane Milligan
Bruce B. Kemp
James D. Smith
Leslie Dean Pickett
Marguerite M. O'Connell
Mary Abbott Martin
Robert Scherrer

For full biographical listings, see the Martindale-Hubbell Law Directory

FLOYD, TAYLOR & RILEY, L.L.P. (AV)

Suite 3440, Three Houston Center, 1301 McKinney, 77010
Telephone: 713-646-1000
Fax: 713-646-1036

MEMBERS OF FIRM

Robert C. Floyd
Warren R. Taylor
Timothy D. Riley
Diana Kay Ball
Britton B. Harris

Terri S. Harris
Ralph E. Burnham
Gary Martin Jewell
Patrick W. O'Briant

For full biographical listings, see the Martindale-Hubbell Law Directory

WAYNE C. FOX (AV)

700 Louisiana, Suite 3990, 77002
Telephone: 713-224-0123
Fax: 713-224-7112

For full biographical listings, see the Martindale-Hubbell Law Directory

FUNDERBURK & FUNDERBURK, L.L.P. (AV)

1080 Riviana Building, 2777 Allen Parkway, 77019
Telephone: 713-526-1801

MEMBERS OF FIRM

Weldon W. Funderburk
Larry B. Funderburk
Don Karotkin
Howard R. King
H. Dwayne Newton
John P. Cahill, Jr.
James A. Newsom
Ryan A. Beason
Cynthia L. Jones

ASSOCIATES

Thomas L. Cougill
Mark J. Courtois
J. Gregory Guy Funderburk
John L. Engvall, Jr.
David W. Funderburk
Brittian A. Featherston
Jeffrey Pierce Fultz

Representative Client: American States Insurance Co.; Citgo Petroleum Corporation; CNA Insurance; Texas Medical Liability Insurance Underwriting Association (JUA); Kemper National; Lawyers Surety Corporation; Maryland Insurance; The Medical Protective Company; The Mundy Companies; Waste Management, Inc.

For full biographical listings, see the Martindale-Hubbell Law Directory

GIBBS & BRUNS, L.L.P. (AV)

1100 Louisiana, Suite 3400, 77002
Telephone: 713-650-8805
Fax: 713-750-0903

PARTNERS

Robin C. Gibbs
Phillip T. Bruns
J. Christopher Reynolds
Russell B. Starbird
Paul J. Dobrowski
Kathy D. Patrick
Jeffrey C. Alexander
Robert R. Burford

ASSOCIATES

Jennifer R. Tillison
Jean C. Frizzell
Grant Harvey
Michael Napoli
Barrett H. Reasoner
Robert J. Madden
Jeffry J. Cotner
Amanda B. Nathan
Jennifer Horan Greer

OF COUNSEL

Debora D. Ratliff (Retired)

For full biographical listings, see the Martindale-Hubbell Law Directory

GILPIN, PAXSON & BERSCH (AV)

A Registered Limited Liability Partnership
1900 West Loop South, Suite 2000, 77027-3259
Telephone: 713-623-8800
Telecopier: 713-993-8451

(See Next Column)

GILPIN, PAXSON & BERSCH—*Continued*

MEMBERS OF FIRM

Gary M. Alletag
Timothy R. Bersch
Deborah J. Bullion
James L. Cornell, Jr.
George R. Diaz-Arrastia
Frank W. Gerold
John D. Gilpin
William T. Little
Darryl W. Malone
Michael W. McCoy
Michael J. Pappert
Stephen Paxson
Lionel M. Schooler
Mary E. Wilson
Kevin F. Risley

ASSOCIATES

Russell T. Abney
N. Terry Adams, Jr.
John W. Burchfield
Evan N. Kramer
Dale R. Mellencamp
P. Wayne Pickering
Susan M. Schwager

OF COUNSEL

Harless R. Benthul
Thomas F. Aubry

Representative Clients: Ingersoll-Rand Company; Mid-America Pipeline Company; Pulte Home Corporation; Seminole Pipeline Company; Toyota Motor Sales, USA; Uniroyal Goodrich Tire Company; Volkswagen of America, Inc.; Volvo North America Corporation.

For full biographical listings, see the Martindale-Hubbell Law Directory

GREGG & MIESZKUC, P.C. (AV)

17044 El Camino Real (Clear Lake City), 77058-2686
Telephone: 713-488-8680
Facsimile: 713-488-8531

Dick H. Gregg, Jr.
Marilyn Mieszkuc
Polly P. Lewis
Charles A. Daughtry

Elizabeth E. Scott
Dick H. Gregg, III

For full biographical listings, see the Martindale-Hubbell Law Directory

HARDY & JOHNS (AV)

500 Two Houston Center, 909 Fannin at McKinney, 77010
Telephone: 713-222-0381
Fax: 713-759-9650
Bay City, Texas Office: 2042 Avenue F.
Telephone: 409-245-3797.
Texas City, Texas Office: 3020 Palmer Highway.
Telephone: 409-945-0606.

G. P. Hardy, Jr. (1913-1988)
G. P. Hardy, III
Gail Johns

ASSOCIATES

Timothy M. Purcell
Mark G. Cypert
Gwen E. Richard
Patricia Haylon
Melissa Wolin

OF COUNSEL

Billie Pirner Garde

Reference: Bay City Bank & Trust.

For full biographical listings, see the Martindale-Hubbell Law Directory

HAYS, MCCONN, RICE & PICKERING (AV)

400 Two Allen Center, 1200 Smith Street, 77002
Telephone: 713-654-1111
Telecopier: 713-650-0027

MEMBERS OF FIRM

Michael S. Hays
James J. McConn, Jr.
B. Stephen Rice
Michael R. Pickering
Sharon Stagg
Frank Holcomb H.
Mark A. Padon
Bruce Clifford Gaible
Susan Crowley Stevenson
Allen Royce Till
Craig S. Wolcott
Don F. Russell
Rudy Cano
Naomi S. Ostfeld
Diana V. H. Shelby
Margaret Twomey Brenner
W. Michael Scott

ASSOCIATES

Jeffery Allen Addicks
Kevin Crawford
Steven M. Duble
Reid G. Gettys
J. Philip Griffis
Debra Donaldson Hovnatanian
Alan Scott Kidd
George A. Kurisky, Jr.
Michael W. Magee
Robert E. Purgatorio
Kathleen Reilly Richards
Brian Tew
Lance K. Thomas
Troy A. Williams

For full biographical listings, see the Martindale-Hubbell Law Directory

HILL, PARKER & JOHNSON, A PROFESSIONAL CORPORATION (AV)

Suite 700, 5300 Memorial, 77007
Telephone: 713-868-5581
Telefax: 713-868-1275

(See Next Column)

John Graham Hill
Charles R. Parker
Brian P. Johnson
John Roberson
Layne A. Thompson
Ann Pate Watson
Scott G. Burdine

Julie C. Anderson
Judy Kyrish Bryan
Brian Q. Carmichael
Tamara M. Bresee

Representative Clients: Burroughs Wellcome Co.; Houston Sports Association, Inc.; St. Luke's Episcopal Hospital; St. Paul Insurance Co.; Texas Children's Hospital; Texas Lawyers Insurance Exchange; Texas Medical Liability Trust.
Reference: Texas Commerce Bank, N.A.

For full biographical listings, see the Martindale-Hubbell Law Directory

HINTON & COX (AV)

An Association including a Professional Corporation
440 Louisiana Street, Suite 1450, 77002
Telephone: 713-223-4000
713-225-1948

Robert N. Hinton
Ted A. Cox (P.C.)

For full biographical listings, see the Martindale-Hubbell Law Directory

HOHMANN, WERNER & TAUBE, L.L.P. (AV)

1300 Post Oak Boulevard, Suite 700, 77056
Telephone: 713-961-3541
Fax: 713-961-3542
Austin, Texas Office: 100 Congress, Suite 1600.
Telephone: 512-472-5997.
Fax: 512-472-5248.

Philip A. Werner
Joseph M. Heard
Mary C. Thompson

Robert W. Craft, Jr.
Leigh Whelan

For full biographical listings, see the Martindale-Hubbell Law Directory

KRIST, GUNN, WELLER, NEUMANN & MORRISON, L.L.P. (AV)

17555 El Camino Real (Clear Lake City), 77058
Telephone: 713-283-8500
Fax: 713-488-3489

MEMBERS OF FIRM

Ronald D. Krist
Jerry W. Gunn
Harvill E. Weller, Jr.
William G. Neumann, Jr.
Richard R. Morrison, III
David A. Slaughter
Kevin D. Krist
Perry O. Barber Jr. (1938-1992)

Scott C. Krist
Todd C. Benson

Reference: Nations Bank, Houston, Texas.

For full biographical listings, see the Martindale-Hubbell Law Directory

LORANCE & THOMPSON, A PROFESSIONAL CORPORATION (AV)

303 Jackson Hill, 77007
Telephone: 713-868-5560
Fax: 713-864-4671; 868-1605
Phoenix, Arizona Office: 2525 East Camelback Road, Suite 230, 85016.
Telephone: 602-224-4000.
Fax: 602-224-4098.
San Diego, California Office: 555 West Beech Street, Suite 222, 92101.
Telephone: 800-899-1844.

Larry D. Thompson
Wayne Adams
Frank B. Stahl, Jr.
William K. Luyties
Clifford A. Lawrence, Jr.
Walter F. (Trey) Williams, III
David O. Cluck
Phillip C. Summers
David F. Webb
Richard H. Martin
Vicki F. Brann
Ronald E. Hood
Gwen W. Dobrowski
Mark D. Flanagan
F. Barham Lewis

David W. Prasifka
Gregory D. Solcher
John A. Culberson
George Eric Van Noy
James E. Simmons
John H. Thomisee, Jr.
Tracey R. Burridge
Douglas A. Haldane
Geoffrey C. Guill
Diane M. Guariglia
Kelly B. Lea
Tracey Landrum Foster
Ronnie B. Arnold
Teresa A. Carver
Terrance D. Dill, Jr.
J. Wayne Little
William T. Sebesta
Richard N. Moore
Matthew R. Pearson

OF COUNSEL

John Holman Barr
Shannon P. Davis
Alexis J. Gomez

Representative Clients: Allstate Insurance Co.; The Hartford Insurance Group.

For full biographical listings, see the Martindale-Hubbell Law Directory

McFall, Sherwood & Sheehy, A Professional Corporation (AV)

2500 Two Houston Center, 909 Fannin Street, 77010-1003
Telephone: 713-951-1000
Telecopier: 713-951-1199

Donald B. McFall
Thomas P. Sartwelle
William A. Sherwood
Richard A. Sheehy
Kent C. Sullivan
David B. Weinstein
D. Wayne Clawater
John S. Serpe
Kenneth R. Breitbeil
Shelley Rogers
Joseph A. Garnett
R. Edward Perkins
Raymond A. Neuer

Caroline E. Baker
Lauren Beck
David Brill
John M. Davidson
Robert R. Debes, Jr.
Eugene R. Egdorf
John H. Ferguson IV
Jeffrey R. Gilbert
M. Randall Jones
Christopher J. Lowman
James J. Maher
David J. McTaggart
David W. Medack
Catherine A. Mezick
Matthew G. Pletcher
Martin S. Schexnayder
David R. Tippetts
James W. K. Wilde

OF COUNSEL

Gay C. Brinson, Jr.
Edward S. Hubbard
Paul B. Radelat

Representative Clients: Dresser Industries, Inc.; The Procter & Gamble Co.; Channel Two Television; St. Paul Fire & Marine Insurance Co.; Texas Lawyers' Insurance Exchange; U.S. Aviation Underwriters; Dow Corning Corp.; Columbia Hospital Corp.; Farm & Home Savings Association.

For Complete List of Firm Personnel, See General Section

For full biographical listings, see the Martindale-Hubbell Law Directory

Mehaffy & Weber, A Professional Corporation (AV)

One Allen Center, 500 Dallas, Suite 1200, 77002
Telephone: 713-655-1200
Fax: 713-655-0222
Beaumont, Texas Office: 2615 Calder Avenue, P.O. Box 16.
Telephone: 409-835-5011.
Orange, Texas Office: 1006 Green Avenue, P.O. Drawer 189.
Telephone: 409-886-7766.

Jim I. Graves
Arthur R. Almquist
Deborah A. Newman

Josephine Tennant-Hillegeist
Charles S. Perry
James C. (Clay) Crawford
Deanne F. Rienstra
Maria Artime

Representative Client: Union Pacific Railroad Co.

For full biographical listings, see the Martindale-Hubbell Law Directory

Plummer & Farmer (AV)

Formerly: Bradshaw & Plummer, 1979-1990
Brown, Bradshaw & Plummer, 1974-1979
Brown & Bradshaw, 1963-1974
3000 Smith, 77006
Telephone: 713-524-2400
FAX: 713-524-6371

MEMBERS OF FIRM

Hugh J. Plummer
Michael D. Farmer

ASSOCIATE

Arthur A. Moure

OF COUNSEL

Herbert N. Lackshin

For full biographical listings, see the Martindale-Hubbell Law Directory

Reynolds & Sydow, L.L.P. (AV)

One Riverway, Suite 1950, 77056
Telephone: 713-840-9600
Fax: 713-840-9605

Michael D. Sydow
Kelli McDonald Sydow
Paula S. Elliott
Kay K. Morgan

OF COUNSEL

Joe H. Reynolds

For full biographical listings, see the Martindale-Hubbell Law Directory

Schwartz & Campbell, L.L.P. (AV)

1221 McKinney, Suite 1000, 77010
Telephone: 713-752-0017
Telecopier: 713-752-0327

Richard A. Schwartz
Marshall S. Campbell

Monica F. Oathout
Stephen A. Mendel
Samuel E. Dunn
Harold W. Hargis
Phillip W. Bechter
Laura M. Taylor
Michael D. Hudgins

LEGAL SUPPORT PERSONNEL

PARALEGALS

Nannette Koger
Bettye Vaughan Johnson
Lenore Chomout
Maria Pinillos

For full biographical listings, see the Martindale-Hubbell Law Directory

Taylor & Cire (AV)

An Assumed Name of a Professional Corporation
One Allen Center, 3400 Penthouse, 77002
Telephone: 713-654-7799
Galveston, Texas Office: 1721 Broadway, 77550.
Telephone: 409-762-8914.

Robert G. Taylor II

George E. (Buck) Cire, Jr.
Martha K. Adams
Robert G. Taylor, III (Resident, Galveston Office)
J. Robert Davis, Jr.

For full biographical listings, see the Martindale-Hubbell Law Directory

Thompson & Knight, A Professional Corporation (AV)

(Attorneys and Counselors)
1700 Texas Commerce Tower, 600 Travis, 77002
Telephone: 713-217-2800
Telecopy: 713-217-2828; 713-217-2882
Dallas, Texas Office: 1700 Pacific Avenue, Suite 3300, 75201.
Telephone: 214-969-1700.
Telecopy: 214-969-1751.
Cable Address: "Tomtex."
Telex: 732298.
Austin, Texas Office: 1200 San Jacinto Center, 98 San Jacinto Boulevard, 78701.
Telephone: 512-469-6100.
Telecopy: 512-469-6180.
Fort Worth, Texas Office: 801 Cherry Street, Suite 1600, 76102.
Telephone: 817-347-1700.
Telecopy: 817-347-1799.
Monterrey, Mexico Office: Edificio Losoles PD-4, Av. Lázaro Cárdenas No. 2400 PTE., San Pedro Garza Garcia, Nuevo Léon C.P. 66220.
Telephone: (52-8) 363-0096.
Telecopy: (52-8) 363-3067.

SHAREHOLDERS

David R. Noteware

ASSOCIATES

Anne Marie Finch
Patricia A. Nolan

For Complete List of Firm Personnel, See General Section

For full biographical listings, see the Martindale-Hubbell Law Directory

Ulrich and Ulrich, A Professional Corporation (AV)

4600 First City Tower, 1001 Fannin, 77002
Telephone: 713-227-4600
Telecopier: 713-227-4606

Stephen E. Ulrich (1951-1989)
Diana Dowd Ulrich

Reference: NCNB Texas National Bank.

For full biographical listings, see the Martindale-Hubbell Law Directory

Vinson & Elkins L.L.P. (AV)

2300 First City Tower, 1001 Fannin, 77002-6760
Telephone: 713-758-2222
Fax: 713-758-2346
International Telex: 6868314
Cable Address: Vinelkins
Austin, Texas Office: One American Center, 600 Congress Avenue.
Telephone: 512-495-8400.
Fax: 512-495-8612.
Dallas, Texas Office: 3700 Trammell Crow Center, 2001 Ross Avenue.
Telephone: 214-220-7700.
Fax: 214-220-7716.
Washington, D.C. Office: The Willard Office Building, 1455 Pennsylvania Avenue, N.W.
Telephone: 202-639-6500.
Fax: 202-639-6604.
Cable Address: Vinelkins.

(See Next Column)

VINSON & ELKINS L.L.P.—*Continued*

London, England Office: 47 Charles Street, Berkeley Square, London, W1X 7PB, England.
Telephone: 011 (44-171) 491-7236.
Fax: 011 (44-71) 499-5320.
Cable Address: Vinelkins London W.1.
Moscow, Russian Federation Office: 16 Alexey Tolstoy Street, Second Floor, Moscow, 103001 Russian Federation.
Telephone: 011 (70-95) 956-1995.
Telecopy: 011 (70-95) 956-1996.
Mexico City, Mexico Office: Aristóteles 77, 5°Piso, Colonia Chapultepec Polanco, 11560 Mexico, D.F.
Telephone: (52-5) 280-7828.
Fax: (52-5) 280-9223.
Singapore Office: 50 Raffles Place, #19-05 Shell Tower, 0104. U.S. Voice Mailbox: 713-758-3500.
Telephone: (65) 536-8300.
Fax: (65) 536-8311.

Walker W. Beavers
David H. Brown
Morgan Lee Copeland, Jr.
Thad T. Dameris
Elena-Faye DiIorio
Sarah A. Duckers
Phillip B. Dye, Jr.
Billy Coe Dyer
Harrell Feldt
John B. Holstead
Daniel A. Hyde
Guy S. Lipe
Louis E. McCarter
James W. McCartney
Andrew McCollam III
Jarrel D. McDaniel
D. Ferguson McNiel, III
Michael W. Mengis
H. Dixon Montague
Penelope E. Nicholson
D. Bobbitt Noel, Jr.
Knox D. Nunnally
Barbara A. Radnofsky
Robert M. Schick
Adam P. Schiffer
Russell B. Serafin
Ben H. Sheppard, Jr.
L. Boyd Smith, Jr.
Craig Smyser
Paul E. Stallings
Mary Lou Strange
Kaaran E. Thomas
James D. Thompson III
Raybourne Thompson, Jr.
Larry R. Veselka
D. Gibson Walton
H. Ronald Welsh
Margaret A. Wilson
Marie R. Yeates

HOUSTON OF COUNSEL

Frank L. Heard, Jr.
Hollis A. Hubenak
John H. Kyles

ASSOCIATES

Fields Alexander
Paul I. Aronowitz
Ann Ashton
Sherie Potts Beckman
Michael Lance Burnett
Sharon L. Burrell
Stephanie Crain
Sabrina L. DiMichele
Kathleen A. Gallagher
Roland Garcia, Jr.
Patricia Ann Gardner
Sandra R. Garza
Don C. Griffin, Jr.
Lynn G. Haufrect
Jon Scott Hollyfield
Scott A. Hooper
Tracy L. Howard
Wade T. Howard
Lisa Lynne Lepow
Deborah E. Lewis
Barbara Popper Lipshultz
Robert R. Luke
James M. McGee
Patrick W. Mizell
Michael J. Mucchetti
George Robertson Murphy, III
Joseph John Naples, III
Harold A. Odom III
Matthew S. Okin
Richard H. Page
Paige C. Patton
James E. Payne
Clayton A. Platt
Patrick Ragan Richard
R. Glen Rigby
Gwen J. Samora
Thomas Sheffield
Daniel B. Shilliday
Catherine Bukowski Smith
Paul W. Smith
Carlos Soltero
Scott Statham
Ann E. Webb
Paul S. Wells
John E. West
Michael J. Yanochik

For Complete List of Firm Personnel, See General Section

For full biographical listings, see the Martindale-Hubbell Law Directory

WILSHIRE SCOTT & DYER, A PROFESSIONAL CORPORATION (AV)

4450 First City Tower, 1001 Fannin, 77002
Telephone: 713-651-1221
Telefax: 713-651-0020

Eugene B. Wilshire, Jr.
Jacalyn D. Scott
Patrick J. Dyer
Thomas E. Bilek
Kelly Cox Thornton

For full biographical listings, see the Martindale-Hubbell Law Directory

JACKSONVILLE, Cherokee Co.

JOHN S. AMENT, III (AV)

318 Neches Street, P.O. Drawer 751, 75766
Telephone: 903-586-3561
Fax: 903-586-7338

LEGAL SUPPORT PERSONNEL

Beverly A. Miliara (Paralegal and Legal Assistant)

For full biographical listings, see the Martindale-Hubbell Law Directory

NORMAN, THRALL, ANGLE & GUY (AV)

215 East Commerce Street, P.O. Drawer 1870, 75766
Telephone: 903-586-2595
Fax: 903-586-0524
Rusk, Texas Office: 106 East Fifth Street, P.O. Box 350.
Telephone: 903-683-2226.
FAX: 903-683-5911.

MEMBERS OF FIRM

Wyatt T. Norman (1877-1945)
Summers A. Norman (1905-1986)
Steven R. Guy (Rusk Office)
Gordon F. Thrall
Marvin J. Angle

ASSOCIATES

Forrest K. Phifer (Rusk Office)
R. Christopher Day

For full biographical listings, see the Martindale-Hubbell Law Directory

*LAMESA,** Dawson Co.

JOHN SALEH (AV)

502 North First Street, 79331
Telephone: 806-872-2171; 872-2172
Fax: 806-872-2002

For full biographical listings, see the Martindale-Hubbell Law Directory

MCALLEN, Hidalgo Co.

DALE & KLEIN, L.L.P. (AV)

A Partnership including Professional Corporations
6301 North Tenth Street, 78504
Telephone: 210-687-8700
FAX: 210-687-2416
Brownsville, Texas Office: 815 Ridgewood, 78520.
Telephone: 210-546-5100.

Roy S. Dale (P.C.)
Katie Pearson Klein (P.C.)
Martin E. Morris

William D. Mount, Jr.
William L. Hubbard
Kathryn M. Flagg
Gil Peralez
Joseph A. Esparza

For full biographical listings, see the Martindale-Hubbell Law Directory

LAW OFFICE OF JOHN ROBERT KING (AV)

3409 North 10th, Suite 100, 78501
Telephone: 210-687-6294

ASSOCIATES

Robin C. Crow
Michael S. (Steve) Deck

Representative Clients: McAllen Board of Realtors; Stewart Title of Hidalgo County.

LEWIS, SKAGGS & REYNA, L.L.P. (AV)

710 Laurel, P.O. Box 2285, 78502-2285
Telephone: 210-687-8203
Fax: 210-630-6570

MEMBERS OF FIRM

John E. Lewis
John B. Skaggs
Rose Marie Guerra Reyna

Representative Clients: Farmers Insurance Group; Burlington Insurance Company; Horace Mann Insurance Company; Insurance Company of North America; The Travelers Insurance Co.; Texas Farm Bureau Insurance Cos.; Floyd West & Co.; The Home Insurance Co.; Aetna Casualty & Surety Co.; Firemen's Fund.

For full biographical listings, see the Martindale-Hubbell Law Directory

*MIDLAND,** Midland Co.

HINKLE, COX, EATON, COFFIELD & HENSLEY (AV)

6 Desta Drive, Suite 2800, P.O. Box 3580, 79702
Telephone: 915-683-4691
FAX: 915-683-6518
Roswell, New Mexico Office: 700 United Bank Plaza, P.O. Box 10.
Telephone: 505-622-6510.
FAX: 505-623-9332.
Amarillo, Texas Office: 1700 Bank One Center, P.O. Box 9238.
Telephone: 806-372-5569.
FAX: 806-372-9761.
Santa Fe, New Mexico Office: 218 Montezuma, P.O. Box 2068.
Telephone: 505-982-4554.
FAX: 505-982-8623.
Albuquerque, New Mexico Office: Suite 800, 500 Marquette, N.W., P.O. Box 2043.
Telephone: 505-768-1500.
FAX: 505-768-1529.

(See Next Column)

HINKLE, COX, EATON, COFFIELD & HENSLEY, *Midland—Continued*

Austin, Texas Office: 401 West 15th Street, Suite 800, 78701.
Telephone: 512-476-7137.
FAX: 512-476-5431.
Associated Office: Hoffman & Stephens, P.C., 401 West 15th Street, Suite 800, 78701.
Telephone: 512-476-5434.
FAX: 512-476-5431.

RESIDENT PARTNERS

William B. Burford — James M. Hudson

For full biographical listings, see the Martindale-Hubbell Law Directory

LESLIE G. MCLAUGHLIN (AV)

1209 West Texas Avenue, 79701
Telephone: 915-687-1331
Fax: 915-687-1336

For full biographical listings, see the Martindale-Hubbell Law Directory

*ORANGE,** Orange Co.

MEHAFFY & WEBER, A PROFESSIONAL CORPORATION (AV)

1006 Green Avenue, P.O. Drawer 189, 77630
Telephone: 409-886-7766
Fax: 409-886-7790
Beaumont, Texas Office: 2615 Calder Avenue, P.O. Box 16.
Telephone: 409-835-5011.
Houston Office: One Allen Center, 500 Dallas, Suite 1200.
Telephone: 713-655-1200.

John Cash Smith

Cimron Campbell

Representative Clients: Sabine River Authority of Texas; Orange Housing Authority; Orange Ship Building, Inc.; Equitable Bag Co., Southern Division; Farmers Insurance Group; Texas Farm Bureau; City of Orange.

For full biographical listings, see the Martindale-Hubbell Law Directory

*PARIS,** Lamar Co.

LYLE H. JEANES, II, P.C. (AV)

805 Lamar Avenue, 75460
Telephone: 903-737-9100
Fax: 903-784-2651

Lyle H. Jeanes, II

For full biographical listings, see the Martindale-Hubbell Law Directory

*PERRYTON,** Ochiltree Co.

LEMON, SHEARER, EHRLICH, PHILLIPS & GOOD, A PROFESSIONAL CORPORATION (AV)

311 South Main Street, P.O. Box 1066, 79070
Telephone: 806-435-6544
FAX: 806-435-4377
Booker, Texas Office: 122 South Main Street, P.O. Box 348.
Telephone: 806-658-4545.
FAX: 806-658-4524.

Robert D. Lemon — Mitchell Ehrlich
Otis C. Shearer — Randall M. Phillips
F. Keith Good

Representative Clients: The Perryton National Bank; The Perryton Equity Exchange; The North Plains Ground Water Conservation District; Natural Gas Anadarko Company; Courson Oil & Gas, Inc.; The City of Perryton; The Booker Equity Exchange; The Follett National Bank; Lyco Energy Corporation; Unit Petroleum Company.

For full biographical listings, see the Martindale-Hubbell Law Directory

*RICHMOND,** Ft. Bend Co.

TATE & ASSOCIATES (AV)

206 South 2nd Street, 77469
Telephone: 713-341-0077
Fax: 713-341-1003

Richard L. Tate — Kirkland A. Fulk
Lisa Ann Lee — Ginger R. Devine

Representative Client: Air Liquide America Corporation; Highlands Insurance Company; Houston Lighting & Power Company.

For full biographical listings, see the Martindale-Hubbell Law Directory

*RUSK,** Cherokee Co.

NORMAN, THRALL, ANGLE & GUY (AV)

106 East Fifth Street, P.O. Box 350, 75785
Telephone: 903-683-2226
FAX: 903-683-5911
Jacksonville, Texas Office: 215 East Commerce Street, P.O. Drawer 1870.
Telephone: 903-586-2595.
FAX: 903-586-0524.

MEMBERS OF FIRM

Wyatt T. Norman (1877-1945) — Marvin J. Angle (Jacksonville Office)
Summers A. Norman (1905-1986) — Steven R. Guy
Gordon F. Thrall (Jacksonville Office)

ASSOCIATES

Forrest K. Phifer — R. Christopher Day (Jacksonville Office)

For full biographical listings, see the Martindale-Hubbell Law Directory

*SAN ANTONIO,** Bexar Co.

COX & SMITH INCORPORATED (AV)

112 East Pecan Street, Suite 1800, 78205
Telephone: 210-554-5500
Telecopier: 210-226-8395

John J. Cox (1905-1971) — John T. Reynolds
J. Burleson Smith — Gardner S. Kendrick
Keith E. Kaiser — Patrick L. Huffstickler
Diann M. Bartek — Margaret Pedrick Sullivan
A. Michael Ferrill — Stephen R. Pilcher
Deborah D. Williamson — Tobin E. Olson
David B. West — Erika S. Carter
Donna K. McElroy — Britannia Hobbs Hardee
J. Daniel Harkins — David D. Jones
Charles A. Japhet

OF COUNSEL

Stephen M. Marceau

Representative Clients: Abraxas Petroleum Corporation; Eastman Kodak Company; Finmeccanica S.p.A.; Kraft General Foods, Inc.; Merrill Lynch, Pierce, Fenner & Smith, Inc.; Miller Brewing Company; NationsBank of Texas, N.A.; Phillip Morris, Inc. Rauscher, Pierce, Refsnes, Inc.; San Antonio Federal Credit Union.

For Complete List of Firm Personnel, See General Section

For full biographical listings, see the Martindale-Hubbell Law Directory

JONES KURTH & TREAT, P.C. (AV)

10100 Reunion Place, Suite 600, 78216
Telephone: 210-344-3900
Telecopier: 210-366-4301

David V. Jones — David L. Treat
Laurence S. Kurth — Daniel C. Andrews
Mark A. Lindow

Mark A. Giltner — Ray R. Ortiz
Danita J. Jarreau — Mary M. Devine
Carolyn D. Walker — Michael B. Angelovich

OF COUNSEL

Carol A. Jenson — John M. Sudyka

For full biographical listings, see the Martindale-Hubbell Law Directory

KAUFMAN, REIBACH & RICHIE, INC. (AV)

300 Convent Street, Suite 900, 78205-3791
Telephone: 210-227-2000
Fax: 210-229-1307
Austin, Texas Office: 2150 One American Center, 600 Congress Avenue.
Telephone: 512-320-7220.
Fax: 512-320-7320.

William T. Kaufman — Jack H. Kaufman
Robert E. Reibach — James H. Barrow
Robert S. Glass

Gay Gueringer — Holly H. Fuller
Nancy H. Reyes

For full biographical listings, see the Martindale-Hubbell Law Directory

JACK PAUL LEON (AV)

500 Lexington, 78215
Telephone: 210-223-4254
Fax: 210-227-7721

ASSOCIATE

Jon Christian Amberson

(See Next Column)

JACK PAUL LEON—*Continued*

OF COUNSEL

Gilbert Lang Mathews

For full biographical listings, see the Martindale-Hubbell Law Directory

MATTHEWS & BRANSCOMB, A PROFESSIONAL CORPORATION (AV)

One Alamo Center, 106 S. St. Mary's Street, Suite 800, 78205
Telephone: 210-226-4211
Facsimile: 210-226-0521
Telex: 5106009283
Cable Code: MBLAW
Austin, Texas Office: 301 Congress Avenue, Suite 2050.
Telephone: 512-305-4400.
Facsimile: 512-305-4413.
Corpus Christi, Texas Office: 802 N. Carancahua, Suite 1900.
Telephone: 512-888-9261.
Facsimile: 512-888-8504.
Eagle Pass, Texas Office: 675 Main Street.
Telephone: 210-773-6700.
Facsimile: 210-757-4045.
Uvalde, Texas Office: 200 E. Nopal #208.
Telephone: 210-278-4597.
Facsimile: 210-278-4806.
(Associated with Hall, Quintanilla & Alarcon, L.C., Laredo, Texas, under the name of Hall, Quintanilla, Alarcon, Matthews & Branscomb, P.L.L.C.)

Howard P. Newton
John McPherson Pinckney, III
Richard C. Danysh
Charles J. Fitzpatrick
Judith R. Blakeway
Annalyn G. Smith
Merritt M. Clements
Timothy H. Bannwolf
Victoria M. García
Steven J. Pugh

OF COUNSEL

Francis W. Baker

Representative Clients: Coca Cola Bottling Company of the Southwest; Concord Oil Co.; Ellison Enterprises, Inc.; H. E. Butt Grocery Co.; Frank B. Hall & Co., Inc.; The Hearst Corp., San Antonio Light Division; San Antonio Gas & Electric Utilities (City Board); Southern Pacific Transportation Co.; Southwest Texas Methodist Hospital.

For Complete List of Firm Personnel, See General Section

For full biographical listings, see the Martindale-Hubbell Law Directory

PLUNKETT, GIBSON & ALLEN, INC. (AV)

6243 IH - 10 West, Suite 600, P.O. Box BH002, 78201
Telephone: 210-734-7092
Fax: 210-734-0379

Jerry A. Gibson
Robert A. Allen
Mark R. Stein
Daniel Diaz, Jr.
Ronald Hornberger
Joseph C. Elliott
Tim T. Griesenbeck, Jr.
Keith B. O'Connell
William L. Powers
Harry S. Bates
Jennifer Gibbins Durbin
Richard N. Francis, Jr.
Ernest F. Avery
A. Dale Hicks
Richard W. Hunnicutt, III

Margaret Netemeyer
Jeffrey C. Manske
David P. Benjamin
Cathy J. Sheehan
Richard B. Copeland
John C. Howell
P. Brian Berryman
Isidro O. Castanon
Nina E. Henderson
Dan Vana
D. Ann Comerio
David L. Downs
Nancy L. Farrer
Deborah L. Klein
William J. Baine
Paul J. Janik
Tom L. Newton, Jr.
Donald L. Crook
Peter B. Gostomski
William J. Maiberger, Jr.

Representative Clients: Traveler's Insurance Co.; CIGNA; State Farm Mutual Automobile Insurance Co.; University of Texas Health Science Center at San Antonio; Commercial Union Insurance Cos.; Galen Health Care, Inc.; Ford Motor Co.; Allstate Insurance; Zurich American Insurance Group; Santa Rosa Medical Center.

For Complete List of Firm Personnel, See General Section

For full biographical listings, see the Martindale-Hubbell Law Directory

TINSMAN & HOUSER, INC. (AV)

One Riverwalk Place, 14th Floor, 700 North St. Mary's Street, 78205
Telephone: 210-225-3121
Texas Wats: 1-800-292-9999
Fax: 210-225-6235

(See Next Column)

Richard Tinsman
Franklin D. Houser
Margaret M. Maisel
David G. Jayne
Robert C. Scott
Daniel J. T. Sciano
Rey Perez
Bernard Wm. Fischman
Sharon L. Cook
Christopher Pettit
Ronald J. Salazar
Sue Dodson

For full biographical listings, see the Martindale-Hubbell Law Directory

SEALY, Austin Co.

CONNER, CANTEY & CLOVER (AV)

An Association of Attorneys including Professional Corporations
330 Main Street, P.O. Box 570, 77474
Telephone: 409-885-3533;
Houston: 713-391-0308
Fax: 409-885-4988
Brenham, Texas Office: 206 W. Vulcan 77833.
Telephone: 409-830-1279.
FAX: 409-830-8638.

Carl E. Clover, Jr., (P.C.)
Warren Wesley Conner (P.C.)

Deborah L Stolarski
Gary W. Chaney

Counsel for: Citizens State Bank, Sealy, Texas; Sealy Independent School District, Sealy, Texas; New Ulm State Bank, New Ulm, Texas.

For full biographical listings, see the Martindale-Hubbell Law Directory

TEXARKANA, Bowie Co.

ATCHLEY, RUSSELL, WALDROP & HLAVINKA, L.L.P. (AV)

1710 Moores Lane, P.O. Box 5517, 75505-5517
Telephone: 903-792-8246
Fax: 903-792-5801

MEMBERS OF FIRM

Otto H. Atchley (1904-1989)
Norman C. Russell
Howard Waldrop
Charles J. Hlavinka
Victor F. Hlavinka
Stephen Oden
J. Dennis Chambers
Robert W. Weber
Alan D. Harrel
Josh R. Morriss, III
John R. Mercy
J. Michael Smith
Jeffrey C. Elliott
Kenneth Dale Edwards (1940-1976)
Robert W. Littrell (1953-1983)
William Howard Mowery
Louise E. Tausch

ASSOCIATES

Jeffery C. Lewis
Christy P. Paddock

Representative Clients: United States Fidelity & Guaranty Co.; Employer's Casualty Co.; Liberty Mutual Insurance Co.; The Home Co.; Missouri-Pacific Railway Co.; St. Louis Southwestern Railway Co.; State First National Bank in Texas; State Bank of DeKalb; St. Paul Insurance Co.; First-Bank.

For full biographical listings, see the Martindale-Hubbell Law Directory

GOODING & DODSON (AV)

A Partnership including a Professional Corporation
300 Texarkana National Bank Building, P.O. Box 1877, 75504
Telephone: 903-794-3121
FAX: 903-793-4801

William C. Gooding (P.C.)
Robert E. Dodson
Robert S. McGinnis, Jr.
Monty G. Murry
Franklin A. Poff, Jr.
Michael F. Jones
John L. Tidwell
Glen C. Hudspeth
Mark C. Burgess

Representative Clients: Aetna Life and Casualty; American General Insurance Co.; Kansas City Southern Railway Co.; Louisiana and Arkansas Railway Co.; Maryland Casualty Co.; North Texas Production Credit Assn.

For full biographical listings, see the Martindale-Hubbell Law Directory

PATTON, HALTOM, ROBERTS, MCWILLIAMS & GREER, L.L.P. (AV)

A Registered Limited Liability Partnership including Professional Corporations
700 Texarkana National Bank Building, P.O. Box 1928, 75504-1928
Telephone: 903-794-3341
Fax: 903-792-6542; 903-792-0448

James N. Haltom (P.C.)
George L. McWilliams (P.C.)
John B. Greer, III, (P.C.)
William G. Bullock

ASSOCIATES

Kristi Ingold McCasland
Caroline Malone
Ralph K. Burgess
Johanna Elizabeth Haltom Salter (1960-1993)

Representative Clients: Allstate Insurance Co.; Aetna Casualty & Surety Co.; Royal Insurance Group; Continental Insurance Group; Ranger/Pan American Insurance Cos.; The Hanover Insurance Group; American Mutual Lia-

(See Next Column)

PATTON, HALTOM, ROBERTS, MCWILLIAMS & GREER L.L.P., *Texarkana—Continued*

bility Insurance Co.; American Hardware Mutual Insurance Co.; Kemper Insurance Co.; Texarkana National Bancshares, Inc.

For Complete List of Firm Personnel, See General Section

For full biographical listings, see the Martindale-Hubbell Law Directory

THE WOODLANDS, Montgomery Co.

GARY T. CORNWELL (AV Ⓣ)

11 Pleasure Cove, 77381
Telephone: 713-367-8392
Fax: 713-367-3065

For full biographical listings, see the Martindale-Hubbell Law Directory

*TYLER,** Smith Co.

IRELAND, CARROLL & KELLEY, P.C. (AV)

6101 South Broadway, Suite 500, P.O. Box 7879, 75711
Telephone: 903-561-1600
Fax: 903-581-1071

Donald Carroll (1929-1992)
H. Kelly Ireland
Otis W. Carroll
Patrick Kelley
Marcus Carroll
Michael G. Carroll
Bill Parker

Reference: First National Bank of Winnsboro, Tyler, Texas.

For full biographical listings, see the Martindale-Hubbell Law Directory

*VICTORIA,** Victoria Co.

HARTMAN, LAPHAM & SMITH, L.L.P. (AV)

Limited Liability Partnership including a Professional Corporation
201 South Main Street, P.O. Drawer D, 77902-1079
Telephone: 512-578-0271
Fax: 512-578-1402

MEMBERS OF FIRM

Arthur L. Lapham
David Atmar Smith (P.C.)
Joyce Zarosky Heller
Scott Kimball, III
Boniface S. Gbalazeh

OF COUNSEL

Wayne L. Hartman

For full biographical listings, see the Martindale-Hubbell Law Directory

LAW OFFICE OF O. F. JONES, III (AV)

109 West Santa Rosa Street, P.O. Drawer E, 77902
Telephone: 512-573-6381

Michael D. Seale

For full biographical listings, see the Martindale-Hubbell Law Directory

*WACO,** McLennan Co.

DUNNAM & DUNNAM, L.L.P. (AV)

4125 West Waco Drive, P.O. Box 8418, 76714-8418
Telephone: 817-753-6437
Fax: 817-753-7434

MEMBERS OF FIRM

W. V. Dunnam (1891-1974)
W. V. Dunnam, Jr.
Vance Dunnam
Vance Dunnam, Jr.
Damon L. Reed
James R. Dunnam

ASSOCIATES

Cathy Dunnam
Alan Stucky

For full biographical listings, see the Martindale-Hubbell Law Directory

JIM MEYER & ASSOCIATES, P.C. (AV)

4734 West Waco Drive, P.O. Box 21957, 76710
Telephone: 817-772-9255
Fax: 817-776-9110

Jim Meyer

Matthew E. Johnson

For full biographical listings, see the Martindale-Hubbell Law Directory

WILLIAMS, PATTILLO & SQUIRES, L.L.P. (AV)

3501 West Waco Drive, 76710
Telephone: 817-752-9966
Fax: 817-752-9972

Dale D. Williams
R. D. (Spike) Pattillo, III
Rod S. Squires

(See Next Column)

ASSOCIATES

Fadra LeBlanc Day
John H. McLeod

For full biographical listings, see the Martindale-Hubbell Law Directory

*WICHITA FALLS,** Wichita Co.

BANNER, BRILEY & WHITE, L.L.P. (AV)

900 Eighth Street, Suite 1200, 76301-6899
Telephone: 817-723-6644
Fax: 817-322-1960

Jack G. Banner
Steve Briley
Harold White

OF COUNSEL

Ed McIntosh

Reference: American National Bank.

For full biographical listings, see the Martindale-Hubbell Law Directory

MORRISON & SHELTON, A PROFESSIONAL CORPORATION (AV)

City National Building, 807 Eighth Street, Suite 1010, 76301-3319
Telephone: 817-322-2929
Telecopier: 817-322-7463

Lonny D. Morrison
Stephen R. Shelton

For full biographical listings, see the Martindale-Hubbell Law Directory

UTAH

*PROVO,** Utah Co.

HOWARD, LEWIS & PETERSEN, P.C. (AV)

Delphi Building, 120 East 300 North Street, P.O. Box 778, 84603
Telephone: 801-373-6345
Fax: 801-377-4991

Jackson Howard
Don R. Petersen
Craig M. Snyder
John L. Valentine
D. David Lambert
Fred D. Howard
Leslie W. Slaugh

Richard W. Daynes
Phillip E. Lowry
Kenneth Parkinson

OF COUNSEL

S. Rex Lewis

LEGAL SUPPORT PERSONNEL

Mary Jackson
John O. Sump
Ray Winger

For full biographical listings, see the Martindale-Hubbell Law Directory

JEFFS AND JEFFS, P.C. (AV)

90 North 100 East, P.O. Box 888, 84603
Telephone: 801-373-8848
Fax: 801-373-8878

M. Dayle Jeffs
A. Dean Jeffs
David D. Jeffs
Robert L. Jeffs
William M. Jeffs

Lorie D. Fowlke

Representative Clients: Farmers Insurance Group; American Service Life Insurance Co.; Central Reserve Life Insurance Co.; R.B.& G. Engineers, Inc.; Horrocks Engineers, Inc.; Duchesne County Upper Country Water Improvement District; Provo Postal Credit Union; Interwest Safety Supply, Inc.
References: Zion First National Bank; Bank of American Fork.

For full biographical listings, see the Martindale-Hubbell Law Directory

*SALT LAKE CITY,** Salt Lake Co.

JOEL M. ALLRED, P.C. (AV)

McIntyre Building, 68 South Main Street, 84101
Telephone: 801-531-8300
Fax: 801-363-2420

Joel M. Allred

For full biographical listings, see the Martindale-Hubbell Law Directory

BERMAN, GAUFIN & TOMSIC, A PROFESSIONAL CORPORATION (AV)

Suite 1250, 50 South Main Street, 84144
Telephone: 801-328-2200
Fax: 801-531-9926

(See Next Column)

BERMAN, GAUFIN & TOMSIC A PROFESSIONAL CORPORATION—*Continued*

Daniel L. Berman
Samuel O. Gaufin
Peggy A. Tomsic
Daniel S. Day
Ronald J. Chleboski, Jr.
Christopher A. King
Veda M. Travis

OF COUNSEL

Edward J. McDonough
D. Frank Wilkins

For full biographical listings, see the Martindale-Hubbell Law Directory

BURBIDGE AND MITCHELL (AV)

Suite 2001, 139 East South Temple, 84111
Telephone: 801-355-6677
Fax: 801-355-2341

Richard D. Burbidge
Stephen B. Mitchell

ASSOCIATES

Douglas H. Holbrook
Gary R. Johnson

Representative Clients: ARCO; Revere National Corp.; SmithKline/Beecham Corp.; Hydro Flame Corp.; Guardian State Bank; Guardian Title Company.

For full biographical listings, see the Martindale-Hubbell Law Directory

CALLISTER, NEBEKER & MCCULLOUGH, A PROFESSIONAL CORPORATION (AV)

800 Kennecott Building, 84133
Telephone: 801-530-7300
Telecopier: 801-364-9127

Louis H. Callister
Gary R. Howe
John A. Beckstead
James R. Holbrook
Charles M. Bennett
James R. Black
H. Russell Hettinger
Randall D Benson
R. Willis Orton
Mark L. Callister
P. Bryan Fishburn
Jan M. Bergeson

Representative Clients: Zions First National Bank; Chrysler Credit Corp.; Citicorp; General Host Corporation; Associates Commercial Corp.; Western Farm Credit Bank; Sinclair Oil (Little America); Utah Resources International; Workers Compensation Fund of Utah.

For Complete List of Firm Personnel, See General Section

For full biographical listings, see the Martindale-Hubbell Law Directory

CAMPBELL MAACK & SESSIONS, A PROFESSIONAL CORPORATION (AV)

One Utah Center Thirteenth Floor, 201 South Main Street, 84111-2115
Telephone: 801-537-5555
Telecopier: 801-537-5199

Robert S. Campbell, Jr.
Robert D. Maack
Clark W. Sessions
E. Barney Gesas
Kevin Egan Anderson
Martin R. Denney
Tracy H. Fowler
Mark A. Larsen

Stephen R. Cochell
Joann Shields
William H. Christensen

Representative Clients: American Honda Motor Co., Inc.; American Suzuki Motor Corp.; Amoco U.S.A., Inc.; Connaught Laboratories; Kenworth-/Peterbilt Paccar, Inc.; The Procter & Gamble Co.; Westinghouse Electric Co.

For Complete List of Firm Personnel, See General Section

For full biographical listings, see the Martindale-Hubbell Law Directory

DURHAM, EVANS, JONES & PINEGAR (AV)

Key Bank Tower 50 South Main, Suite 850, 84144
Telephone: 801-538-2424
Fax: 801-363-1835
Telluride, Colorado Office: 126 West Colorado Avenue, Suite 102-C, P.O. Box 3153, 81435.
Telephone: 303-728-5775.
Fax: 303-728-5898.

Jeffrey M. Jones
Paul M. Durham
G. Richard Hill
J. Mark Gibb
Pamela B. Slater (Resident, Telluride, Colorado Office)

For full biographical listings, see the Martindale-Hubbell Law Directory

JAY D. GURMANKIN (AV)

1010 Boston Building, 9 Exchange Place, 84111
Telephone: 801-359-3545
Fax: 801-534-0187

For full biographical listings, see the Martindale-Hubbell Law Directory

JONES, WALDO, HOLBROOK & MCDONOUGH, A PROFESSIONAL CORPORATION (AV)

1500 First Interstate Plaza, 170 South Main Street, 84101
Telephone: 801-521-3200
Telecopier: 801-328-0537
Mailing Address: P.O. Box 45444, 84145-0444
St. George, Utah Office: The Tabernacle Tower Building, 249 East Tabernacle.
Telephone: 801-628-1627.
Telecopier: 801-628-5225.
Washington, D.C. Office: Suite 900, 2300 M Street, N.W.
Telephone: 202-296-5950.
Telecopier: 202-293-2509.

Donald B. Holbrook
James S. Lowrie
Christopher L. Burton
D. Miles Holman
Craig R. Mariger
Randall N. Skanchy
George W. Pratt III
Timothy C. Houpt

Representative Clients: Utah Power and Light; Kearns Tribune Corp.; Gold Standard, Inc.; First Interstate Bank of Utah, N.A.; Design Professional Insurance Co.; Newspaper Agency Corp.

For Complete List of Firm Personnel, See General Section

For full biographical listings, see the Martindale-Hubbell Law Directory

KIMBALL, PARR, WADDOUPS, BROWN & GEE, A PROFESSIONAL CORPORATION (AV)

Suite 1300, 185 South State Street, P.O. Box 11019, 84147
Telephone: 801-532-7840
Fax: 801-532-7750

Dale A. Kimball
Clark Waddoups
Patricia W. Christensen
Robert G. Holt
James C. Swindler
Robert B. Lochhead
Gary A. Dodge
Robert S. Clark
Michael M. Later
Carolyn B. McHugh
Scott F. Young
Ronald G. Russell
Mark E. Wilkey
Matthew B. Durrant
Jill Niederhauser Parrish
Brian J. Romriell
Gregory D. Phillips
Heidi E. C. Leithead
Daniel A. Jensen
Mark F. James
Scott R. Ryther
Gregory M. Hess

OF COUNSEL

Bruce A. Maak

For Complete List of Firm Personnel, See General Section

For full biographical listings, see the Martindale-Hubbell Law Directory

KIPP AND CHRISTIAN, P.C. (AV)

175 East 400 South 330 City Centre I, 84111
Telephone: 801-521-3773
Fax: 801-359-9004

Carman E. Kipp
D. Gary Christian
J. Anthony Eyre
William W. Barrett
Gregory J. Sanders
Heinz J. Mahler
Michael F. Skolnick
Shawn McGarry
Kirk G. Gibbs
Sandra L. Steinvoort

Representative Clients: United States Fidelity & Guaranty Co.; Capital City Bank/BankOne; E & O Professionals; Edelweiss Haus, A Condominium Project; Home Insurance Company; Montgomery Elevator; National Farmers Union Ins. Co.; Utah Medical Insurance Association (UMIA); Utah State Bar; Crum & Forster.

For Complete List of Firm Personnel, See General Section

For full biographical listings, see the Martindale-Hubbell Law Directory

KIRTON & MCCONKIE, A PROFESSIONAL CORPORATION (AV)

1800 Eagle Gate Tower, 60 East South Temple, 84111
Telephone: 801-328-3600
Telecopier: 801-321-4893

Wilford W. Kirton, Jr.
Oscar W. McConkie, Jr.
Raymond W. Gee
Anthony I. Bentley, Jr.
J. Douglas Mitchell
Richard R. Neslen
Myron L. Sorensen
Robert W. Edwards
B. Lloyd Poelman
Raeburn G. Kennard
Jerry W. Dearinger
R. Bruce Findlay
Charles W. Dahlquist, II
M. Karlynn Hinman
Robert P. Lunt
Brinton R. Burbidge
Gregory S. Bell
Lee Ford Hunter
Larry R. White
William H. Wingo
David M. McConkie
Read R. Hellewell
Rolf H. Berger
Oscar W. McConkie, III
Marc Nick Mascaro
Lorin C. Barker
David M. Wahlquist
Robert S. Prince
Wallace O. Felsted
Merrill F. Nelson
Paul H. Matthews
Fred D. Essig
Clark B. Fetzer
Samuel D. McVey

(See Next Column)

KIRTON & MCCONKIE A PROFESSIONAL CORPORATION, *Salt Lake City—Continued*

Blake T. Ostler
Daniel Bay Gibbons
Gregory M. Simonsen
Von G. Keetch
Patrick Hendrickson
Stuart F. Weed
Thomas D. Walk
James E. Ellsworth
Daniel V. Goodsell
David J. Hardy
Randy T. Austin

For Complete List of Firm Personnel, See General Section

For full biographical listings, see the Martindale-Hubbell Law Directory

MORGAN & HANSEN (AV)

Kearns Building, Eighth Floor, 136 South Main Street, 84101
Telephone: 801-531-7888
Telefax: 801-531-9732

MEMBERS OF FIRM

Stephen G. Morgan
Darwin C. Hansen
John C. Hansen
Cynthia K.C. Meyer
Mitchel T. Rice
Joseph E. Minnock
Eric C. Singleton

OF COUNSEL

Dennis R. James

Representative Clients: Albertson's, Inc.; Smith Food and Drug Centers, Inc.; Colorado Casualty; Farmers Insurance Group; SLC Airport Authority; St. Paul Fire and Marine Insurance Co.; State Farm Fire and Casualty; State Farm Mutual Automobile Insurance Co.; Utah Farm Bureau Insurance Co.; Utah Local Government's Insurance Trust.

For full biographical listings, see the Martindale-Hubbell Law Directory

PARRY MURRAY WARD & MOXLEY, A PROFESSIONAL CORPORATION (AV)

1270 Eagle Gate Tower, 60 East South Temple, 84111
Telephone: 801-521-3434
Fax: 801-521-3484

Douglas J. Parry
Brent D. Ward
Paul T. Moxley

David M. McGrath
James K. Tracy
Bret F. Randall
Brad W. Merrill

Representative Clients: Trammell Crow Co.; Monroc; Salt Lake County Water Conservancy District; Western Petroleum.

For Complete List of Firm Personnel, See General Section

For full biographical listings, see the Martindale-Hubbell Law Directory

PARSONS BEHLE & LATIMER, A PROFESSIONAL CORPORATION (AV)

One Utah Center, 201 South Main Street, Suite 1800, P.O. Box 45898, 84145-0898
Telephone: 801-532-1234
Telecopy: 801-536-6111

Keith E. Taylor
James B. Lee
Gordon L. Roberts
Lawrence E. Stevens
Daniel M. Allred
Roy G. Haslam
Barbara K. Polich
Randy L. Dryer
Charles H. Thronson
Raymond J. Etcheverry
Francis M. Wikstrom
Chris Wangsgard
Val R. Antczak
Spencer E. Austin
John B. Wilson
David A. Anderson
Kent C. Dugmore
Kent O. Roche
Paul D. Veasy
Daniel W. Hindert
Lois A. Baar
Michael L. Larsen
David G. Mangum
Derek Langton
W. Mark Gavre
Mark S. Webber
J. Michael Bailey
J. Thomas Beckett
Elizabeth S. Conley
Elizabeth S. Whitney

Representative Clients: American Barrick Resources Corporation; Coastal States Energy Company; DYNO NOBEL INC.; Energy Fuels Nuclear Inc.; Hercules, Inc.; Kennecott Corporation; NERCO, Inc.; Questar Corporation; Rio Algom Mining Corporation.

For full biographical listings, see the Martindale-Hubbell Law Directory

RAY, QUINNEY & NEBEKER, A PROFESSIONAL CORPORATION (AV)

Suite 400 Deseret Building, 79 South Main Street, P.O. Box 45385, 84145-0385
Telephone: 801-532-1500
Telecopier: 801-532-7543
Provo, Utah Office: 210 First Security Bank Building, 92 North University Avenue.
Telephone: 801-226-7210.
Telecopier: 801-375-8379.

(See Next Column)

Stephen B. Nebeker
James L. Wilde (Resident at Provo)
Paul S. Felt
Jonathan A. Dibble
Steven H. Gunn
James S. Jardine
Janet Hugie Smith
A. Robert Thorup
John P. Harrington
John A. Adams
Craig Carlile (Resident at Provo)
Dee R. Chambers
Steven J. Aeschbacher
Keith A. Kelly
Mark M. Bettilyon
Rick L. Rose
Rick B. Hoggard
Lisa A. Yerkovich
Brent D. Wride
Michael E. Blue
Scott A. Hagen
Steven W. Call

Cameron M. Hancock
Elaine A. Monson
George S. Adondakis
David A. Cutt

Representative Clients: First Security Bank of Utah, N.A.; Borden, Inc.; Southern Pacific Transportation; Utah Power & Light Co.; Travelers Insurance Co.; Greyhound Leasing & Financial; Holy Cross Hospital and Health System; Amoco Production Co.

For Complete List of Firm Personnel, See General Section

For full biographical listings, see the Martindale-Hubbell Law Directory

STIRBA & HATHAWAY, A PROFESSIONAL CORPORATION (AV)

215 South State Street, Suite 1150, 84111
Telephone: 801-364-8300
Facsimile: 801-364-8355

Peter Stirba
Benson L. Hathaway, Jr.

Margaret H. Olson
R. Craig Schneider

VAN COTT, BAGLEY, CORNWALL & MCCARTHY, A PROFESSIONAL CORPORATION (AV)

Suite 1600, 50 South Main Street, P.O. Box 45340, 84145
Telephone: 801-532-3333
Telex: 453149
Telecopier: 801-534-0058
Ogden, Utah Office: Suite 900, 2404 Washington Boulevard.
Telephone: 801-394-5783.
Park City, Utah Office: 314 Main Street, Suite 205.
Telephone: 801-649-3889.
Reno, Nevada Office: Jeppson & Lee, 100 West Liberty, Suite 990.
Telephone: 702-333-6800.

E. Scott Savage
Kenneth W. Yeates
John A. Snow
David A. Greenwood
Alan L. Sullivan
John T. Nielsen
Michael F. Richman
Jeffrey E. Nelson
Patricia M. Leith
R. Stephen Marshall
Eric C. Olson
Patrick J. O'Hara
John A. Anderson
Scott M. Hadley (Resident, Ogden, Utah Office)
Donald L. Dalton
David L. Arrington
Casey K. McGarvey
Kathryn Holmes Snedaker
Phyllis J. Vetter
Jeremy M. Hoffman
Bryon J. Benevento

OF COUNSEL

Clifford L. Ashton
James P. Cowley

Robert W. Payne
James D. Gilson
Elizabeth D. Winter
Jon E. Waddoups
Melyssa D. Davidson
Craig W. Dallon
Michele Ballantyne
Michael T. Roberts (Resident, Ogden, Utah Office)

For Complete List of Firm Personnel, See General Section

For full biographical listings, see the Martindale-Hubbell Law Directory

WATKISS DUNNING & WATKISS, A PROFESSIONAL CORPORATION (AV)

Broadway Centre, Suite 800, 111 East Broadway, 84111-2304
Telephone: 801-530-1500
Telecopier: 801-530-1520

David K. Watkiss
Elizabeth T. Dunning
David B. Watkiss

Carolyn Cox
Mary J. Woodhead

OF COUNSEL

Karen Campbell Jenson

Representative Clients: Pennzoil Exploration & Production Co.; Piper Aircraft Corp.; Borden, Inc.; E.I. duPont de Nemours; Procter & Gamble; United Park City Mines Co.; Beech Aircraft Corp.; Weyerhaeuser Co.

For full biographical listings, see the Martindale-Hubbell Law Directory

Salt Lake City—Continued

LOREN E. WEISS (AV)

1000 Boston Building, 9 Exchange Place, 84111
Telephone: 801-531-6686
Fax: 801-531-6690

For full biographical listings, see the Martindale-Hubbell Law Directory

VERMONT

BRATTLEBORO, Windham Co.

CRISPE & CRISPE (AV)

114 Main Street, P.O. Box 556, 05302
Telephone: 802-254-4441
Fax: 802-254-4482

A. Luke Crispe (1911-1992) Lawrin P. Crispe

ASSOCIATE

Kristen Swartwout

Representative Clients: Mutual of New York; The Stratton Corp.; Liberty Mutual Insurance Co.; DeWitt Beverage Co.

For full biographical listings, see the Martindale-Hubbell Law Directory

WEBER, PERRA & WILSON, P.C. (AV)

16 Linden Street, P.O. Box 558, 05302
Telephone: 802-257-7161
Fax: 802-257-0572

E. Bruce Weber Richard H. Munzing

For Complete List of Firm Personnel, See General Section

For full biographical listings, see the Martindale-Hubbell Law Directory

*BURLINGTON,** Chittenden Co.

GRAVEL AND SHEA, A PROFESSIONAL CORPORATION (AV)

Corporate Plaza, 76 St. Paul Street, P.O. Box 369, 05402-0369
Telephone: 802-658-0220
Fax: 802-658-1456

Stephen R. Crampton
Robert B. Hemley
Craig Weatherly
Dennis R. Pearson
Robert F. O'Neill

Lucy T. Brown
Karin J. Immergut (Not admitted in VT)

OF COUNSEL

Clarke A. Gravel

SPECIAL COUNSEL

Norman Williams

For Complete List of Firm Personnel, See General Section

For full biographical listings, see the Martindale-Hubbell Law Directory

MANCHESTER LAW OFFICES, PROFESSIONAL CORPORATION (AV)

One Lawson Lane, P.O. Box 1459, 05402-1459
Telephone: 802-658-7444
Fax: 802-658-2078

Robert E. Manchester Patricia S. Orr

LEGAL SUPPORT PERSONNEL

LEGAL NURSE CONSULTANTS

Tina L Mulvey
Rosemeryl S. Harple
Maureen P. Tremblay

For full biographical listings, see the Martindale-Hubbell Law Directory

MILLER, EGGLESTON & ROSENBERG, LTD. (AV)

150 South Champlain Street, P.O. Box 1489, 05402-1489
Telephone: 802-864-0880
Telecopier: 802-864-0328

Martin K. Miller
Jon R. Eggleston
Michael B. Rosenberg
Anne E. Cramer
Kathleen M. Boe

Mark A. Saunders
Victoria J. Brown
Peter F. Young
Frederick S. Lane III

OF COUNSEL

Catherine Kronk

For full biographical listings, see the Martindale-Hubbell Law Directory

SHEEHEY BRUE GRAY & FURLONG, PROFESSIONAL CORPORATION (AV)

119 South Winooski Avenue, P.O. Box 66, 05402
Telephone: 802-864-9891
Facsimile: 802-864-6815

William B. Gray (1942-1994)
David T. Austin
R. Jeffrey Behm
Nordahl L. Brue
Michael G. Furlong
Ralphine Newlin O'Rourke
Donald J. Rendall, Jr.
Christina Schulz
Paul D. Sheehey
Peter H. Zamore

Rebecca L. Owen

Representative Client: Green Mountain Power Corp.

For full biographical listings, see the Martindale-Hubbell Law Directory

SYLVESTER & MALEY, INC. (AV)

78 Pine Street, P.O. Box 1053, 05402-1053
Telephone: 802-864-5722
Fax: 802-658-6124

Alan F. Sylvester
John P. Maley
Michael S. Brow

Geoffrey M. Fitzgerald Amy E. Sylvester

For full biographical listings, see the Martindale-Hubbell Law Directory

*MIDDLEBURY,** Addison Co.

CONLEY & FOOTE (AV)

11 South Pleasant Street, P.O. Drawer 391, 05753
Telephone: 802-388-4061
Fax: 802-388-0210

MEMBERS OF FIRM

John T. Conley (1900-1971)
Ralph A. Foote
Charity A. Downs
D. Michael Mathes
Richard P. Foote
Janet P. Shaw

For full biographical listings, see the Martindale-Hubbell Law Directory

*RUTLAND,** Rutland Co.

DAVID L. CLEARY ASSOCIATES A PROFESSIONAL CORPORATION (AV)

110 Merchants Row, P.O. Box 6740, 05702-6740
Telephone: 802-775-8800
Telefax: 802-775-8809

David L. Cleary

Kaveh S. Shahi
George A. Holoch, Jr.
Ellen J. Abbott
Thomas P. Aicher
Karen S. Heald

For full biographical listings, see the Martindale-Hubbell Law Directory

MILLER & FAIGNANT, A PROFESSIONAL CORPORATION (AV)

36 Merchants Row, P.O. Box 6688, 05702-6688
Telephone: 802-775-2521
Fax: 802-775-8274

Lawrence Miller John Paul Faignant

Barbara R. Blackman Christopher J. Whelton

LEGAL SUPPORT PERSONNEL

Cynthia L. Bonvouloir Marie T. Fabian

Representative Clients: Travelers Insurance Co.; Government Employees Insurance Co.; Utica Mutual Insurance Co.; Universal Underwriters Insurance Co.
Reference: Travelers Insurance Co.

For full biographical listings, see the Martindale-Hubbell Law Directory

VIRGINIA

*ABINGDON,** Washington Co.

VINYARD AND MOISE, ATTORNEYS AT LAW, P.C. (AV)

116 East Valley Street, P.O. Box 1127, 24210-1127
Telephone: 703-628-7187

Robert Austin Vinyard Lawrence L. Moise

References: Central Fidelity Bank, Abingdon, Virginia; Dominion Bank, Abingdon, Virginia; NationsBank, N.A., Abingdon, Virginia.

For full biographical listings, see the Martindale-Hubbell Law Directory

*ACCOMAC,** Accomack Co.

Jon C. Poulson (AV)

23349 Cross Street, P.O. Box 478, 23301-0478
Telephone: 804-787-2620
Facsimile: 804-787-2749

For full biographical listings, see the Martindale-Hubbell Law Directory

ALEXANDRIA, (Independent City)

Grad, Logan & Klewans, P.C. (AV)

112 North Columbus Street, P.O. Box 1417-A44, 22313
Telephone: 703-548-8400
Facsimile: 703-836-6289

John D. Grad — Michael P. Logan
Samuel N. Klewans

Sean C. E. McDonough — Claire R. Pettrone
David A. Damiani

OF COUNSEL

Jeanne F. Franklin

For full biographical listings, see the Martindale-Hubbell Law Directory

Murray, Jacobs & Abel (AV)

601 King Street Suite 400, 22314
Telephone: 703-739-1340
Telecopier: 703-836-6842

Richard Murray — Christian D. Abel
Carmen A. Jacobs, Jr. — (Not admitted in VA)

OF COUNSEL

Jacob B. Pompan — Alfred Lawrence Toombs (Not admitted in VA)

For full biographical listings, see the Martindale-Hubbell Law Directory

*ARLINGTON,** Arlington Co.

Arthur, Pearson & Martin, Ltd. (AV)

5549 Lee Highway, 22207
Telephone: 703-241-7171
Facsimile: 703-532-8660

Robert J. Arthur — John L. Martin
Paul R. Pearson — Beverley A. Ramsey

Representative Clients: Aetna Life & Casualty Co.; Carolina Casualty Co.; Harford Mutual Insurance Co.; Baker Protective Services, Inc.; SMS Data Products, Inc.; Diamond Shamrock Corp.; Fermenta Inc.

For full biographical listings, see the Martindale-Hubbell Law Directory

Cohen, Gettings, Dunham & Harrison, P.C. (AV)

2200 Wilson Boulevard, Suite 800, 22201
Telephone: 703-525-2260
Fax: 703-525-2489; 703-358-9624
Washington, D.C. Office: 1225 19th Street, N.W., 7th Floor.
Alexandria, Virginia Office: 424 North Washington Street.
Telephone: 703-549-5730.
Silver Spring, Maryland Office: Suite 700, 8701 Georgia Avenue.
Telephone: 301-589-6072.

Harvey B. Cohen — John Edwards Harrison
Brian P. Gettings — R. Scott Caulkins
Frank W. Dunham, Jr. — David D. Masterman

Joseph A. Fisher, III — Manuel A. Capsalis
Carole H. Capsalis — M. Lee Anne Washington
John C. Pasierb — John E. Gagliano
Stewart T. Leeth

References: First Virginia Bank; Virginia Commerce Bank.

For full biographical listings, see the Martindale-Hubbell Law Directory

Schwartz and Ellis, Ltd. (AV)

6950 North Fairfax Drive, 22213
Telephone: 703-532-9300
Telex: 892320
Facsimile: 703-534-0329

Philip Schwartz — John P. Ellis

OF COUNSEL

William B. Moore

John S. Petrillo

References: First Virginia Bank; Signet Bank; First Union National Bank.

For full biographical listings, see the Martindale-Hubbell Law Directory

Walsh, Colucci, Stackhouse, Emrich & Lubeley, P.C. (AV)

Courthouse Plaza, Thirteenth Floor, 2200 Clarendon Boulevard, 22201
Telephone: 703-528-4700
Facsimile: 703-525-3197
Woodbridge, Virginia Office: Village Square, 13663 Office Place, Suite 201.
Telephones: 703-680-4664; 690-4647.
Facsimile: 703-690-2412.

Peter K. Stackhouse — John E. Rinaldi
Jerry K. Emrich — (Resident, Woodbridge Office)
William A. Fogarty — Sean P. McMullen

For full biographical listings, see the Martindale-Hubbell Law Directory

BIG STONE GAP, Wise Co.

Keuling-Stout, P.C. (AV)

123 Wood Avenue East, P.O. Box 400, 24219
Telephone: 703-523-1676
FAX: 703-523-1608

Henry S. Keuling-Stout

For full biographical listings, see the Martindale-Hubbell Law Directory

BRISTOL, (Independent City)

Elliott Lawson & Pomrenke (AV)

Sixth Floor, First Union Bank Building, P.O. Box 8400, 24203-8400
Telephone: 703-466-8400
Fax: 703-466-8161

James Wm. Elliott, Jr. — Steven R. Minor
Mark M. Lawson — Kyle P. Macione
Kurt J. Pomrenke — Lisa King Crockett

For full biographical listings, see the Martindale-Hubbell Law Directory

Woodward, Miles & Flannagan, P.C. (AV)

Suite 200, Executive Plaza, 510 Cumberland Street, P.O. Box 789, 24203-0789
Telephone: 703-669-0161
Telecopier: 703-669-7376

S. Bruce Jones (1892-1966) — Francis W. Flannagan
Jno. W. Flannagan, Jr. (1885-1955) — John E. Kieffer
Waldo G. Miles (1911-1973) — Larry B. Kirksey
Wm. H. Woodward (1907-1992) — Elizabeth Smith Jones
Christen W. Burkholder
Beth Osborne Skinner

Representative Clients: CNA Companies; Cooper Tire and Rubber; Hanover Insurance Companies; Lawyers Title Insurance Company; Nationwide Mutual Co.; United Telephone-Southeast, Inc.; Universal Underwriters Group; USAA; Worldwide Insurance Group.

For full biographical listings, see the Martindale-Hubbell Law Directory

*CHARLOTTESVILLE,** (Ind. City; Seat of Albemarle Co.)

Haugh & Haugh, P.C. (AV)

435 Park Street, 22901
Telephone: 804-296-0185
Fax: 804-296-1146

Charles R. Haugh — Lair Dayton Haugh

For full biographical listings, see the Martindale-Hubbell Law Directory

Richmond and Fishburne (AV)

Queen Charlotte Square, 214 East High Street, P.O. Box 559, 22902
Telephone: 804-977-8590
Telefax: 804-296-9861

MEMBER OF FIRM

Matthew B. Murray

Representative Clients: Albemarle Home Mutual Fire Insurance Co.; Fireman's Fund; Horace Mann Insurance Co.; Nationwide Insurance Co.; Norfolk-Southern Corp.; State Farm Insurance Co.; USAA; Virginia Farm Bureau Insurance Service; The Windsor Group.

For Complete List of Firm Personnel, See General Section

For full biographical listings, see the Martindale-Hubbell Law Directory

Slaughter & Redinger, P.C. (AV)

Lewis and Clark Square, 250 West Main Street, Suite 300, P.O. Box 2964, 22902
Telephone: 804-295-8300
FAX: 804-295-3390

Edward R. Slaughter, Jr. — David Z. Izakowitz
Craig T. Redinger — Jane C. Clarke
Caroline Nunley Barber

(See Next Column)

SLAUGHTER & REDINGER P.C.—*Continued*

Patrick J. Nettesheim (Not admitted in VA)

OF COUNSEL

Neill H. Alford, Jr.

For full biographical listings, see the Martindale-Hubbell Law Directory

TAYLOR, ZUNKA, MILNOR & CARTER, LTD. (AV)

414 Park Street, P.O. Box 1567, 22902
Telephone: 804-977-0191
FAX: 804-977-0198

Robert Edward Taylor (Retired)
John W. Zunka
Richard H. Milnor
Richard E. Carter

Representative Clients: Crestar Bank; State Farm Mutual Insurance Cos.; Allstate Insurance Co.; Southern Insurance Company of Virginia; Insurance Corporation of America; Phillips Building Supply, Inc.; Blue Cross and Blue Shield of Virginia; Commercial Union Insurance Company.
Reference: Crestar Bank.

For Complete List of Firm Personnel, See General Section

For full biographical listings, see the Martindale-Hubbell Law Directory

TREMBLAY & SMITH (AV)

105-109 East High Street, P.O. Box 1585, 22902
Telephone: 804-977-4455
Fax: 804-979-1221

MEMBERS OF FIRM

John K. Taggart, III
Melvin E. Gibson, Jr.
Thomas E. Albro
Christine Thomson
Patricia D. McGraw

ASSOCIATES

R. Lee Livingston
Christopher L. McLean

Representative Clients: Commonwealth of Virginia, Department of Transportation; First Virginia Bank—Central; Sieg Distributing Co. (Anheuser-Busch Distributors); Kloeckner Pentaplast of America, Inc.; Virginia Broadcasting Corp.; Farmington Country Club; Management Services Corporation of Charlottesville; Intertrans Carrier Co.; Sprint Cellular Company.

For Complete List of Firm Personnel, See General Section

For full biographical listings, see the Martindale-Hubbell Law Directory

DANVILLE, (Independent City)

CARTER, CRAIG, BASS, BLAIR & KUSHNER, P.C. (AV)

126 South Union Street, P.O. Box 601, 24543
Telephone: 804-792-9311
Fax: 804-792-4373

OF COUNSEL

Charles E. Carter

Stuart L. Craig
Stephen G. Bass
D. Thomas Blair
Samuel A. Kushner, Jr.

Reference: Signet Bank (Danville).

For full biographical listings, see the Martindale-Hubbell Law Directory

LAW OFFICES OF MICHAEL P. REGAN, P.C. (AV)

703 Patton Street, 24541
Telephone: 804-793-9670; 793-1622
Telecopier: 804-793-6647

Michael P. Regan

LEGAL SUPPORT PERSONNEL

Janet E. Armstrong (Legal Assistant)

References: Sovran Bank, N.A.; Signet Bank.

For full biographical listings, see the Martindale-Hubbell Law Directory

*FAIRFAX,** (Ind. City; Seat of Fairfax Co.)

BRAULT, PALMER, GROVE, ZIMMERMAN, WHITE & MIMS (AV)

10533 Main Street, P.O. Box 1010, 22030-1010
Telephone: 703-273-6400
Fax: 703-273-3514
Manassas, Virginia Office: 8567-D Sudley Road. P.O. Box 534.
Telephone: 703-369-7500; 631-9727.
Fax: 703-369-2285.

MEMBERS OF FIRM

Adelard L. Brault (Emeritus)
Thomas C. Palmer, Jr. (Resident, Manassas Office)
Edward H. Grove, III
Michael L. Zimmerman
Bruce D. White
Gary B. Mims
August W. Steinhilber, III

(See Next Column)

ASSOCIATES

Nancy J. Goodiel
Andrew M. Adams (Resident, Manassas Office)
Jack A. Robbins, Jr. (Resident, Manassas Office)
Benjamin M. Smith, III
Lisa Kent Duley

Representative Clients: CIGNA Cos.; CNA Insurance Cos.; Commerical Union Insurance Co.; Erie Insurance Group; Harleysville Insurance Co.; Home Insurance Co.; Kemper Insurance Group; Selective Insurance Co.; State Farm Insurance Cos.; U.S.F. & G.

For full biographical listings, see the Martindale-Hubbell Law Directory

LEWIS, TRICHILO, BANCROFT, MCGAVIN & HORVATH, P.C. (AV)

Fairfax Bank & Trust Building, Suite 400, 4117 Chain Bridge Road, P.O. Box 22, 22030-0022
Telephone: 703-385-1000
Telecopier: 703-385-1555

Benjamin J. Trichilo
Steven W. Bancroft
John D. McGavin
Stephen A. Horvath
Julia Bougie Judkins

Elaina Holmes
Alicia M. Lehnes
Melissa S. Hogue
Dawn E. Boyce
William M. Dupray

OF COUNSEL

Richard H. Lewis

Representative Clients: Continental Insurance Co.; Virginia Farm Bureau Insurance Cos.; Amoco Oil Co.; Cigna Insurance Cos.; Erie Insurance Exchange; Hartford Insurance Co.; State Farm Insurance Cos.; Harford Mutual Insurance Co.; Ohio Casualty Group; Chubb Group of Insurance Companies; Atlantic Mutual Insurance Co.; USSA; Allstate Insurance Co.

For full biographical listings, see the Martindale-Hubbell Law Directory

ODIN, FELDMAN & PITTLEMAN, P.C. (AV)

9302 Lee Highway, Suite 1100, 22031
Telephone: 703-218-2100
Facsimile: 703-218-2160

Dexter S. Odin
Robert K. Richardson
Nelson Blitz
Donald F. King
Sally Ann Hostetler
F. Douglas Ross
Bruce M. Blanchard
Frances P. Dwornik
Robert G. Nath
Edward W. Cameron
Lawrence A. Schultis

OF COUNSEL

Stephen J. O'Brien (Not admitted in VA)

Representative Clients: Upper Occoquan Sewage Authority; National Wildlife Federation; The Hair Cuttery; The Bank of the Potomac; Stewart Title and Escrow, Inc.; Software A.G. of North America, Inc.; Recovermat Technologies, Inc.; Seaward International, Inc.

For Complete List of Firm Personnel, See General Section

For full biographical listings, see the Martindale-Hubbell Law Directory

RUST, RUST & SILVER, A PROFESSIONAL CORPORATION (AV)

4103 Chain Bridge Road Fourth Floor, P.O. Box 460, 22030
Telephone: 703-591-7000
Telecopier: 703-591-7336

John H. Rust, Jr.
Glenn H. Silver
C. Thomas Brown

James E. Kane
Paulo E. Franco, Jr.
Andrew W. White

RETIRED, EMERITUS

John H. Rust, Sr. (Retired)

Representative Clients: Crestar Bank; Commonwealth Land Title Insurance Co.; Patriot National Bank; Century Graphics Corp.

For full biographical listings, see the Martindale-Hubbell Law Directory

FALLS CHURCH, (Independent City)

GARNIER & GARNIER, P.C. (AV)

109 Rowell Court, 22046
Telephone: 703-237-2010
Fax: 703-237-9738

Jean-Pierre Garnier
Michael J. Garnier

Robert L. Garnier

Representative Clients: The Schering-Plough Corp. (Regional Coordinator); Key Pharmaceutical, Inc.; Park, Davis & Co.; Warner-Lambert Co.; Burroughs Wellcome Co.; Ciba-Geigy Corp.; Otis Elevator Co.; Montgomery Elevator Co.; Hertz Equipment Rental Corp.; Welcome Corporation (Thrifty Car Rental)

For full biographical listings, see the Martindale-Hubbell Law Directory

FREDERICKSBURG, (Independent City)

ROBERTS, SOKOL, ASHBY & JONES (AV)

(Member of the Commonwealth Law Group, Ltd.)
701 Kenmore Avenue, 22404-7166
Telephone: 703-373-3500
Telex: 151274389
Telecopier: 703-899-6394
Mailing Address: P.O. Box 7166, 22404-7166

MEMBERS OF FIRM

William M. Sokol
Russell H. Roberts
Kevin S. Jones
James Ashby, III
William E. Glover
Jeannie P. Dahnk

ASSOCIATES

Jennifer Lee Parrish
Tracy A. Houck

OF COUNSEL

Kenneth T. Whitescarver

General Counsel for: Mary Washington Hospital; The Free Lance-Star; Massaponax Building Components, Inc.; Pohanka Datsun Cadillac Oldsmobile; First Virginia Bank (Trust).

For full biographical listings, see the Martindale-Hubbell Law Directory

WOODBRIDGE & REAMY (AV)

108 Charlotte Street, P.O. Box 965, 22404
Telephone: 703-373-5300
Fax: 703-899-9110

MEMBERS OF FIRM

Benjamin H. Woodbridge, Jr.
M. R.(Chip) Reamy

For full biographical listings, see the Martindale-Hubbell Law Directory

*HALIFAX,** Halifax Co.

JAMES E. EDMUNDS (AV)

Court Square, P.O. Box 157, 24558
Telephone: 804-476-6202; 476-6578

References: First Federal Savings & Loan Assn., South Boston; Crestar Bank, South Boston.

For full biographical listings, see the Martindale-Hubbell Law Directory

HARRY L. MAPP, JR. (AV)

Courthouse Square, P.O. Box 1146, 24558
Telephone: 804-476-2161
FAX: 804-476-2162

References: South Boston Bank; Crestar Bank, South Boston, Va.

For full biographical listings, see the Martindale-Hubbell Law Directory

*LEESBURG,** Loudoun Co.

HALL, MONAHAN, ENGLE, MAHAN & MITCHELL (AV)

3 East Market Street, P.O. Box 390, 22075
Telephone: 703-777-1050
Fax: 703-771-4113
Winchester, Virginia Office: 9 East Boscawen Street. P.O. Box 848.
Telephone: 703-662-3200.
Fax: 703-662-4304.

MEMBERS OF FIRM

Wilbur C. Hall (1892-1972)
Thomas V. Monahan
Samuel D. Engle
O. Leland Mahan

Local Counsel: Prudential Insurance Co.; Harleysville Insurance Co.; United States Fidelity & Guaranty Co.; Hartford Accident & Indemnity Co.; Fidelity and Casualty Co. of New York; Loudoun Mutual Insurance Co.; Washington Gas Light Co.; Catoctin Stud, Inc.; IBM; Sovran Bank.
Counsel For: Sovran Bank, Leesburg Branch.

For full biographical listings, see the Martindale-Hubbell Law Directory

LYNCHBURG, (Independent City)

JOSEPH R. JOHNSON, JR. & ASSOCIATES (AV)

9th Floor, Allied Arts Building, 725 Church Street, P.O. Box 717, 24505
Telephone: 804-845-4541
Fax: 804-845-4134

Travis Harry Witt
P. Scott De Bruin

For full biographical listings, see the Martindale-Hubbell Law Directory

*MARTINSVILLE,** (Ind. City; Seat of Henry Co.)

DOUGLAS K. FRITH & ASSOCIATES, P.C. (AV)

(Member, Commonwealth Law Group, Ltd.)
58 West Church Street, P.O. Box 591, 24114
Telephone: 703-632-7137
FAX: 703-632-3988

Douglas K. Frith

General Counsel for: Frith Construction Co., Inc./Frith Equipment Corporation; Koger/Air Corp.; Prillaman & Pace, Inc.; Radio Station WHEE; Fuller & Gray Tire Co., Inc.; Millard's Machinery, Inc.
Representative Client: Hartford Accident & Indemnity.

For full biographical listings, see the Martindale-Hubbell Law Directory

MCLEAN, Fairfax Co.

GAMMON & GRANGE, P.C. (AV Ⓣ)

8280 Greensboro Drive, 7th Floor, 22102-3807
Telephone: 703-761-5000
Facsimile: 703-761-5023

A. Wray Fitch III
H. Robert Showers, Jr.
Michael J. Woodruff

Peter F. Rathbun
J. Matthew Szymanski
Scott J. Ward

For full biographical listings, see the Martindale-Hubbell Law Directory

PLEDGER & SANTONI (AV)

Suite 204, 1489 Chain Bridge Road, 22101
Telephone: 703-821-1250
Fax: 703-790-7250

R. Harrison Pledger, Jr.
Cynthia Vancil Santoni

Bernard G. Feord, Jr.
Cherie Kay Dibbell Durand

For full biographical listings, see the Martindale-Hubbell Law Directory

VENABLE, BAETJER AND HOWARD (AV)

A Partnership including Professional Corporations
Suite 400, 2010 Corporate Ridge, 22102
Telephone: 703-760-1600
FAX: 703-821-8949
Baltimore, Maryland Office: 1800 Mercantile Bank & Trust Building, 2 Hopkins Plaza.
Telephone: 410-244-7400.
Washington, D.C. Office: Venable, Baetjer, Howard & Civiletti, Suite 1000, 1201 New York Avenue, N.W.
Telephone: 202-962-4800.
Rockville, Maryland Office: Suite 500, One Church Street, P.O. Box 1906.
Telephone: 301-217-5600.
Towson, Maryland Office: 210 Allegheny Avenue, P. O. Box 5517.
Telephone: 410-494-6200.

MEMBERS OF FIRM

David T. Stitt
Kenneth C. Bass, III (Also at Washington, D.C. Office)
Bruce E. Titus
William D. Dolan, III (P.C.)
David G. Lane
Herbert G. Smith, II

OF COUNSEL

Mary T. Flynn

ASSOCIATES

Julian Sylvester Brown
David R. Hodnett
J. Scott Hommer, III
Jon M. Lippard
Christine M. McAnney
Michael W. Robinson

For Complete List of Firm Personnel, See General Section

For full biographical listings, see the Martindale-Hubbell Law Directory

WATT, TIEDER & HOFFAR (AV)

7929 Westpark Drive, Suite 400, 22102
Telephone: 703-749-1000
Telecopier: 703-893-8029
Washington, D.C. Office: 601 Pennsylvania Ave, N.W., Suite 900.
Telephone: 202-462-4697.
Irvine California Office: 3 Park Plaza, Suite 1530.
Telephone: 714-852-6700.

MEMBERS OF FIRM

John B. Tieder, Jr.
Robert G. Watt
Julian F. Hoffar
Robert M. Fitzgerald
Robert K. Cox
William R. Chambers
David C. Romm
Charles E. Raley (Not admitted in VA)
Francis X. McCullough
Barbara G. Werther (Not admitted in VA)
Garry R. Boehlert
Thomas B. Newell

(See Next Column)

WATT, TIEDER & HOFFAR—*Continued*

MEMBERS OF FIRM (Continued)

Lewis J. Baker
Benjamin T. Riddles, II
Timothy F. Brown
Richard G. Mann, Jr.
David C. Mancini
David C. Haas
Henry D. Danforth
Carter B. Reid
Donna S. McCaffrey
Mark J. Groff (Not admitted in VA)
Mark A. Sgarlata
Daniel E. Cohen
Michael G. Long (Resident, Irvine, California Office)

OF COUNSEL

Avv. Roberto Tassi
Clyde Harold Slease (Not admitted in VA)

ASSOCIATES

Thomas J. Powell
Douglas C. Proxmire
Tara L. Vautin
Edward Parrott
Steven G. Schassler
Joseph H. Bucci
Steven J. Weber
Paul A. Varela
Vivian Katsantonis
Charlie Lee
Kathleen A. Olden
Christopher P. Pappas (Resident, Irvine, California Office)
Shelly L. Ewald
Christopher J. Brasco
Jean V. Misterek
Charles W. Durant
Susan Latham Timoner
Fred A. Mendicino
Susan G. Sisskind
Robert G. Barbour
Keith C. Phillips
Marybeth Zientek Gaul
Timothy E. Heffernan (Not admitted in VA)
William Drew Mallender
James Moore Donahue
Heidi Brown Hering
Kerrin Maureen McCormick (Not admitted in VA)
Gretal J. Toker

For full biographical listings, see the Martindale-Hubbell Law Directory

NEWPORT NEWS, (Independent City)

PHILLIPS M. DOWDING (AV)

12335 Warwick Boulevard, 23606
Telephone: 804-595-0338
FAX: 804-595-3979

Representative Clients: The Aetna Casualty & Surety Co.; The Hartford Insurance Group; Security Group; Utica Mutual Insurance Co.; Riverside Hospital; PENTRAN; CIGNA Insurance Group; Selective Insurance Group; Commercial Union; Moore Group, Inc.

For full biographical listings, see the Martindale-Hubbell Law Directory

HALL, FOX, ATLEE AND ROBINSON, P.C. (AV)

Crestar Bank Building, 11817 Canon Boulevard, Suite 604, 23606
Telephone: 804-873-1855
Fax: 804-873-0616

Roy B. Fox, Jr. (1920-1985)
Isabel Hall Atlee
Richard Y. Atlee
Willard M. Robinson, Jr.

LeeAnn Norris Barnes

OF COUNSEL

Lewis H. Hall, Jr. (Retired)

Representative Clients: State Farm Mutual Automobile Insurance Co.; Government Employees Insurance Company; Pennsylvania National Mutual Casualty Insurance Co.; The American Insurance Group; T.H. Mastin & Co.; Liberty Mutual Insurance Co.; Harleysville Insurance Co.; USAA; Erie Insurance Co.; Chrysler Insurance Co.

For full biographical listings, see the Martindale-Hubbell Law Directory

WILLIAM V. HOYLE, JR. (AV)

10401 Warwick Boulevard, 23601
Telephone: 804-596-1850
Fax: 804-596-1925

NORFOLK, (Independent City)

CRENSHAW, WARE AND MARTIN, P.L.C. (AV)

Suite 1200 NationsBank Center, One Commercial Place, 23510-2111
Telephone: 804-623-3000
FAX: 804-623-5735

Francis N. Crenshaw
Guilford D. Ware
Howard W. Martin, Jr.
Timothy A. Coyle
Ann K. Sullivan
James L. Chapman, IV
John T. Midgett
Martha M. Poindexter

Melanie Fix
David H. Sump
Donald C. Schultz
Kristen L. Hodeen

Representative Clients: American International Group; Chubb-Group of Insurance Companies; The Connecticut Mutual Life Insurance Co.; Exxon Co., U.S.A.; Gulf Life Insurance Co.; Lakeford Sysco Food Services, Inc.; Norfolk Dredging Co.; Norfolk Redevelopment and Housing Authority; Norfolk Warehouse Distribution Centers, Inc.; Southern States Cooperative.

For full biographical listings, see the Martindale-Hubbell Law Directory

THOMAS J. HARLAN, JR., P.C. (AV)

1200 Dominion Tower, 999 Waterside Drive, 23510
Telephone: 804-625-8300
FAX: 804-625-3714

Thomas J. Harlan, Jr.

John M. Flora
Kevin M. Thompson (Not admitted in VA)

LEGAL SUPPORT PERSONNEL

Mary Hayse Grant Wareing (Paralegal)
Barry Wade Vanderhoof (Paralegal)

Reference: Commerce Bank.

For full biographical listings, see the Martindale-Hubbell Law Directory

HEILIG, MCKENRY, FRAIM & LOLLAR, A PROFESSIONAL CORPORATION (AV)

700 Newtown Road, 23502
Telephone: 804-461-2500
Fax: 804-461-2341

George H. Heilig, Jr.
James R. McKenry
John A. Heilig
Paul D. Fraim
George J. Dancigers
Charles M. Lollar
Carolyn P. Oast
Teresa R. Warner
Peter S. Lake
Thomas C. Dawson, Jr.
Stewart Penney Oast
Debra L. Mosley
Todd M. Fiorella
Robert E. Moreland
Philip R. Trapani
A. William Charters
Tena Touzos Canavos

Jason Evans Dodd
Lisa L. Howlett
Colleen Treacy Dickerson
Lynn E. Watson

Representative Clients: American International Insurance Group; Blue Cross of Virginia; Blue Shield of Virginia; The Home Insurance Company; Horace Mann Mutual Insurance Co.; Nationwide Mutual Insurance Co.; TranSouth Financial Corp.

For full biographical listings, see the Martindale-Hubbell Law Directory

PAYNE, GATES, FARTHING & RADD, P.C. (AV)

15th Floor, Dominion Tower, 23510
Telephone: 804-640-1500

Charles E. Payne
Ronald M. Gates
Philip R. Farthing
Anthony F. Radd
Reid H. Ervin
Mark R. Skolrood
Craig L. Mytelka
Todd Joseph Preti

For full biographical listings, see the Martindale-Hubbell Law Directory

RABINOWITZ, RAFAL, SWARTZ, TALIAFERRO & GILBERT, P.C. (AV)

Wainwright Building, Suite 700, 229 West Bute Street, P.O. Box 3332, 23514
Telephone: 804-622-3931; 623-6674
FAX: 804-626-1003

Ralph Rabinowitz
Edwin J. Rafal
Oscar L. Gilbert
Robert S. Brewbaker, Jr.

For full biographical listings, see the Martindale-Hubbell Law Directory

SACKS, SACKS & IMPREVENTO (AV)

Suite 501 Town Point Center, 150 Boush Street, P.O. Box 3874, 23514
Telephone: 804-623-2753
FAX: 804-640-7170

Herman A. Sacks (1886-1983)
Stanley E. Sacks
Andrew M. Sacks
Michael F. Imprevento

For full biographical listings, see the Martindale-Hubbell Law Directory

STACKHOUSE, SMITH & NEXSEN (AV)

1600 First Virginia Tower, 555 Main Street, P.O. Box 3640, 23514
Telephone: 804-623-3555
FAX: 804-624-9245

MEMBERS OF FIRM

Robert C. Stackhouse
Peter W. Smith, IV
William W. Nexsen
R. Clinton Stackhouse, Jr.
Janice McPherson Doxey

(See Next Column)

STACKHOUSE, SMITH & NEXSEN, *Norfolk—Continued*

ASSOCIATES

Mary Painter Opitz
Timothy P. Murphy
Carl J. Khalil

Representative Clients: Heritage Bank & Trust; The Atlantic Group, Inc.; Roughton Pontiac Corp; Federal National Mortgage Association; Kemper National Insurance Cos.; Shearson/American Express Mortgage Corp.; Harleysville Mutual Insurance Co.; Heritage Bankshares, Inc.; Presbyterian League of the Presbytery of Eastern Virginia, Inc.; Oakwood Acceptance Corp.

For full biographical listings, see the Martindale-Hubbell Law Directory

VANDEVENTER, BLACK, MEREDITH & MARTIN (AV)

500 World Trade Center, 23510
Telephone: 804-446-8600
Cable Address: "Hughsvan"
Telex: 823-671
Telecopier: 446-8670
North Carolina, Kitty Hawk Office: 6 Juniper Trail.
Telephone: 919-261-5055.
Fax: 919-261-8444.
London, England Office: Suite 692, Level 6, Lloyd's, 1 Lime Street.
Telephone: (071) 623-2081.
Facsimile: (071) 929-0043.
Telex: 987321.

MEMBERS OF FIRM

Walter B. Martin, Jr.
Charles F. Tucker
Morton H. Clark
John M. Ryan
Robert L. O'Donnell

For Complete List of Firm Personnel, See General Section

For full biographical listings, see the Martindale-Hubbell Law Directory

*ORANGE,** Orange Co.

SHACKELFORD, HONENBERGER, THOMAS & WILLIS, P.L.C. (AV)

One Perry Plaza, P.O. Box 871, 22960
Telephone: 703-672-2711
Fax: 703-672-2714
Culpeper, Virginia Office: 147 West Davis Street, P.O. Box 1002.
Telephone: 703-825-0305.

OF COUNSEL

Virginius R. Shackelford, Jr.
Virginius R. Shackelford, III
Christopher J. Honenberger
Frank A. Thomas, III
Jere M. H. Willis, III (Resident, Culpeper, Virginia Office)
Sarah Collins Honenberger

Sean D. Gregg

Counsel for: Woodberry Forest School; County of Madison; Rapidan Service Authority.
Assistant Division Counsel for: Norfolk Southern Corp.
Approved Attorneys for: Lawyers Title Insurance Corp.; Southern Title Insurance Co.; Chicago Title Insurance Co.; Federal Land Bank of Baltimore; Farmers Home Administration.

For full biographical listings, see the Martindale-Hubbell Law Directory

PORTSMOUTH, (Independent City)

MOODY, STROPLE & KLOEPPEL, LTD. (AV)

300 Commerce Bank Building, 500 Crawford Street, P.O. Box 1138, 23705-1138
Telephone: 804-393-4093
FAX: 804-397-7257

Willard J. Moody, Sr.
Raymond H. Strople
Byron P. Kloeppel
Willard J. Moody, Jr.
Robert A. Small
John C. Bittrick
John E. Basilone
Stephen E. Heretick
Joseph J. Perez
Thomas F. Burris, III
Kevin P. Bilms
Richard Wright West
Joseph T. McFadden, Jr.
Stan Murphy
Fred D. Smith, Jr.

Reference: Commerce Bank.

For full biographical listings, see the Martindale-Hubbell Law Directory

*PULASKI,** Pulaski Co.

GILMER, SADLER, INGRAM, SUTHERLAND & HUTTON (AV)

Midtown Professional Building, 65 East Main Street, P.O. Box 878, 24301
Telephone: 703-980-1360; 703-639-0027
Telecopier: 703-980-5264
Blacksburg (Montgomery County), Virginia Office: 201 West Roanoke Street, P.O. Box 908.
Telephone: 703-552-1061.
Telecopier: 703-552-8227.

(See Next Column)

MEMBERS OF FIRM

Howard C. Gilmer, Jr. (1906-1975)
Roby K. Sutherland (1909-1975)
Philip M. Sadler (1915-1994)
Robert J. Ingram
James L. Hutton (Resident, Blacksburg Office)
Thomas J. McCarthy, Jr.
John J. Gill
Gary C. Hancock
Jackson M. Bruce
Michael J. Barbour
Deborah Wood Dobbins
Todd G. Patrick (Resident, Blacksburg Office)
Debra Fitzgerald-O'Connell
Scott A. Rose
Timothy Edmond Kirtner

OF COUNSEL

James R. Montgomery

Representative Clients: Appalachian Power Co.; Chevron; Liberty Mutual Insurance Co.; Norfolk Southern Railway Co.; Pulaski Furniture Corp.; NationsBank; Travelers Insurance Group; Renfro, Inc.; Magnox, Inc.; Corning Glass Works.

For full biographical listings, see the Martindale-Hubbell Law Directory

RADFORD, (Independent City)

SPIERS AND SPIERS (AV)

Spiers Building, 1206 Norwood Street, P.O. Box 1052, 24141-0052
Telephone: 703-639-1601
Telecopier: 703-639-6802

John B. Spiers (1897-1956)
John B. Spiers, Jr.

For full biographical listings, see the Martindale-Hubbell Law Directory

STONE, HARRISON, TURK & SHOWALTER, P.C. (AV)

Tyler Office Plaza, 1902 Downey Street, P.O. Box 2968, 24143-2968
Telephone: 703-639-9056
Telecopier: 703-731-4665

Edwin C. Stone
Clifford L. Harrison
James C. Turk, Jr.
Josiah T. Showalter, Jr.
Margaret E. Stone

Representative Clients: St. Albans Psychiatric Hospital; Radford Community Hospital; Inland Motor Corp.; The K-C Corp.; Meadowgold Dairies; Lynchburg Foundry; Hartford Accident and Indemnity Co.; Cigna Insurance Cos.; Hercules, Inc.; Norfolk Southern Corp.

For full biographical listings, see the Martindale-Hubbell Law Directory

*RICHMOND,** (Ind. City; Seat of Henrico Co.)

COWAN & OWEN, P.C. (AV)

1930 Huguenot Road, P.O. Box 35655, 23235-0655
Telephone: 804-320-8918
Fax: 804-330-3140

Frank N. Cowan
John H. O'Brion, Jr.
W. Joseph Owen, III
Deborah S. O'Toole
David H. Gates
Frank F. Rennie, IV
Michael C. Hall
F. Neil Cowan, Jr.

Derrick Thomas
Mary Burkey Owens

References: Crestar Bank; Central Fidelity Bank.

For full biographical listings, see the Martindale-Hubbell Law Directory

DUANE AND SHANNON, P.C. (AV)

10 East Franklin Street, 23219
Telephone: 804-644-7400
Fax: 804-649-8329

Harley W. Duane, III
James C. Shannon
B. Craig Dunkum
David L. Hauck
Arnold B. Snukals
William V. Riggenbach
Carl R. Schwertz

Martha P. Smith

For full biographical listings, see the Martindale-Hubbell Law Directory

FLORANCE, GORDON AND BROWN, A PROFESSIONAL CORPORATION (AV)

800 Mutual Building, 909 East Main Street, 23219
Telephone: 804-697-5100
Facsimile: 804-697-5159

Richard Florance (1902-1980)
Walker Florance (1909-1983)
James W. Gordon, Jr. (Retired)
Delmar L. Brown
Fred J. Bernhardt, Jr.
William H. Hoofnagle, III
Hamill D. "Skip" Jones, Jr.
Cary A. Ralston
Robert J. Kloeti
Conard B. Mattox, III
Kathleen N. Scott

Christopher S. Dillon
Kimberlee Harris Ramsey
Farhad Aghdami
Bryan W. Horn
Roger Gallup Bowers

(See Next Column)

Florance, Gordon and Brown A Professional Corporation—*Continued*

Reference: Crestar Bank.

For full biographical listings, see the Martindale-Hubbell Law Directory

Levit & Mann (AV)

419 North Boulevard, 23220
Telephone: 804-355-7766
Fax: 804-358-4018

MEMBERS OF FIRM

Jay J. Levit
John B. Mann

For full biographical listings, see the Martindale-Hubbell Law Directory

Morris and Morris, A Professional Corporation (AV)

1200 Ross Building, 801 East Main Street, 23201-0030
Telephone: 804-344-8300
FAX: 804-344-8359

James W. Morris, III
Philip B. Morris
Thomas D. Stokes, III
Ann Adams Webster
Lynne Jones Blain
Kirk D. McQuiddy
Michelle Preston Wiltshire
John P. Driscoll
James W. Walker
Lori Morris Whitten
William B. Tiller

For Complete List of Firm Personnel, See General Section

For full biographical listings, see the Martindale-Hubbell Law Directory

Thompson, Smithers, Newman & Wade (AV)

5911 West Broad Street, P.O. Box 6357, 23230
Telephone: 804-288-4007
Telecopier: 804-282-5379

MEMBERS OF FIRM

Harry L. Thompson
William S. Smithers, Jr.
Nathaniel S. Newman
Winfrey T. Wade
R. Paul Childress, Jr.
Kimberly Smithers Wright
R. Ferrell Newman
Anton J. Stelly
Robert S. Carter

ASSOCIATES

James C. Bodie
Paul D. Georgiadis
Suzanne Elizabeth Wade
Glenn S. Phelps

Approved Attorneys for: Lawyers Title Insurance Corp.

For full biographical listings, see the Martindale-Hubbell Law Directory

Williams, Mullen, Christian & Dobbins, A Professional Corporation (AV)

Two James Center, 1021 East Cary Street, P.O. Box 1320, 23210-1320
Telephone: 804-643-1991
Fax: 804-783-6456
Glen Allen, Virginia Office: 4401 Waterfront Drive, Suite 140.
Telephone: 804-965-9168.
Fax: 804-965-0955.
Washington, D.C. Office: 1575 Eye Street, N.W.
Telephone: 202-289-6200.
Fax: 202-289-4126.

Stephen E. Baril
William D. Bayliss
A. Peter Brodell
James J. Burns
Howard W. Dobbins
Robert E. Eicher
Siran S. Faulders
Samuel W. Hixon, III
William R. Mauck, Jr.
Dana D. McDaniel
James V. Meath
Robert D. Perrow
Andrea Rowse Stiles
W. Scott Street, III
Sandy T. Tucker

David C. Burton
Theodore J. Edlich, IV
Calvin W. Fowler, Jr.
Curtis M. Hairston, Jr.
Kelly Harrington Johnson
Glen Andrew Lea
George W. Marget, III
Robert Temple Mayo
Tara A. McGee
Charles B. Scher
John L. Walker, III

For Complete List of Firm Personnel, See General Section

For full biographical listings, see the Martindale-Hubbell Law Directory

ROANOKE, (Independent City)

Johnson, Ayers & Matthews (AV)

Southwest Virginia Savings Bank Building Second Floor, 302 Second Street, S.W., P.O. Box 2200, 24009
Telephone: 703-982-3666
Fax: 703-982-1552

(See Next Column)

MEMBERS OF FIRM

James F. Johnson
Ronald M. Ayers
Joseph A. Matthews, Jr.
John D. Eure
William P. Wallace, Jr.
Kenneth J. Ries
Jonnie L. Speight
David B. Carson

ASSOCIATES

Robert S. Ballou
Philip O. Garland
L. Johnson Sarber, III

Representative Clients: Bell Atlantic-Virginia, Inc.; Blue Cross and Blue Shield of Virginia (Trigon); Federated Mutual Insurance Co.; General Motors Corp.; Nationwide Mutual Insurance Company; Norfolk and Western Railway Co.; Progressive Insurance Cos.; Royal Insurance Co.; State Farm Insurance Cos.; The Travelers Cos.

For full biographical listings, see the Martindale-Hubbell Law Directory

*RUSTBURG,** Campbell Co.

Overbey, Hawkins & Selz (AV)

Court House Square, P.O. Box 38, 24588
Telephone: 804-332-5155
FAX: 804-332-5143

W. Hutchings Overbey (1906-1991)
W. Hutchings Overbey, Jr.
A. David Hawkins
Bryan K. Selz

Local Counsel for: First Virginia Bank, Piedmont; Central Fidelity Bank; WESTVACO; Truck Body Corp.; Falwell Aviation, Inc.; Federal Land Bank of Baltimore; Campbell County School Board; Industrial Development Authority of the County of Campbell; Virginia State Department of Highways and Transportation.

For full biographical listings, see the Martindale-Hubbell Law Directory

SPRINGFIELD, Fairfax Co.

Madigan & Scott, Inc. (AV)

7880 Backlick Road, 22150-2288
Telephone: 703-455-1800; 451-2080
Fax: 703-451-4121
Manassas, Virginia Office: 9100 Church Street, Suite 107.
Telephone: 703-361-0185. Metro: 631-9193.
Fax: 703-631-9633.

Robert J. Madigan
Paul A. Scott
Scott H. Donovan (Resident, Manassas Office)
Mitchell Komaroff

Richard G. Hornig (1958-1994)

For full biographical listings, see the Martindale-Hubbell Law Directory

SUFFOLK, (Independent City)

Glasscock, Gardy and Savage (AV)

4th Floor National Bank Building, P.O. Box 1876, 23434
Telephone: 804-539-3474
FAX: 804-925-1419

MEMBERS OF FIRM

J. Samuel Glasscock
Jeffrey L. Gardy
William R. Savage, III

Representative Clients: Seaboard Railway System; Planters Peanuts (Division of Nabisco); Norfolk Southern Railway Co.; Nationwide Mutual Insurance Co.; State Farm Mutual Automobile Insurance Co.; Virginia Power Co.; Virginia Farm Bureau Mutual Insurance Co.; Suffolk Redevelopment and Housing Authority.
Approved Attorneys for: Lawyers Title Insurance Corp.

*TAZEWELL,** Tazewell Co.

Galumbeck Simmons and Reasor (AV)

104 West Main Street, P.O. Box 561, 24651
Telephone: 703-988-9436; 988-6561
Telecopier: 703-988-2921

MEMBERS OF FIRM

Robert M. Galumbeck
Deanis L. Simmons
Jackson E. Reasor, Jr.

References: Lawyers Title Insurance; Bank of Tazwell County.

For full biographical listings, see the Martindale-Hubbell Law Directory

VIENNA, Fairfax Co.

Boring, Parrott & Pilger, P.C. (AV)

307 Maple Avenue West, Suite D, 22180-4368
Telephone: 703-281-2161
FAX: 703-281-9464

(See Next Column)

BORING, PARROTT & PILGER P.C., *Vienna—Continued*

Karl W. Pilger
Brian V. Ebert

Representative Clients: Balmar, Inc.; Hewlett-Packard Co.; Toshiba America Information Systems, Inc.; King Wholesale, Inc.; FSM Leasing, Inc.; KDI Sylvan Pools, Inc.; Brobst International, Inc.; Telematics, Inc.; Northern Virginia Surgical Associates, P.C.; Rainbow Industries, Inc.

For full biographical listings, see the Martindale-Hubbell Law Directory

HAIGHT, TRAMONTE, SICILIANO & FLASK, P.C. (AV)

8221 Old Courthouse Road, Suite 300, 22182
Telephone: 703-734-4800
Facsimile: 703-442-9526

Gregory D. Haight
Vincent A. Tramonte, II
John A. Siciliano
Jon T. Flask
William J. Gorman
Sara Towery O'Hara
Steven M. Frei
Ronald K. Jaicks
David C. Hannah
Donald S. Culkin

Representative Clients: Pulte Home Corp.; Kettler Forlines, Inc.; Joe Theismann's Restaurants; McDonald's Corp.; The Business Bank.
Approved Attorneys for: Lawyers Title Insurance Co.; First American Title Insurance Co.

For full biographical listings, see the Martindale-Hubbell Law Directory

PETERSON & BASHA, P.C. (AV)

Tysons Square Office Park, 8214-C Old Courthouse Road, 22182-3855
Telephone: 703-442-3890
Fax: 703-448-1834

Gary G. Peterson
Leigh-Alexandra Basha

Alison K. Markell
Cynthia L. Gausvik
Ki Jun Sung

OF COUNSEL

Daniel J. O'Connell

For full biographical listings, see the Martindale-Hubbell Law Directory

STAUFFER & ABRAHAM (AV)

Suite 1000, Tycon Tower, 8000 Towers Crescent Drive, 22182-2700
Telephone: 703-893-4670
Telecopier: 703-827-0545

MEMBERS OF FIRM

Mark S. Abraham
R. Grant Decker
T. Patrick Dulany
Thomas E. Helf
Ronald I. Hyatt (Not admitted in VA)
Kurt C. Rommel
William L. Stauffer, Jr.

Lora A. Brzezynski
Robert A. Harris, IV
Jeffrey M. Mervis

For full biographical listings, see the Martindale-Hubbell Law Directory

VIRGINIA BEACH, (Independent City)

BRYDGES & MAHAN (AV)

Professional Building, 1369 Laskin Road, 23451
Telephone: 804-428-6021
FAX: 804-491-7634

MEMBERS OF FIRM

Richard G. Brydges
Stephen C. Mahan

Reference: Sovran Bank.
Approved Mediator/Arbitrator For: United States Arbitration and Mediation, Inc.; Arbitration Associates, Inc.

For full biographical listings, see the Martindale-Hubbell Law Directory

CLARK & STANT, P.C. (AV)

One Columbus Center, 23462
Telephone: 804-499-8800
Telecopier: 804-473-0395
Internet: Info @ CLRKNSTNT, COM

Donald H. Clark
Robert L. Samuel, Jr.
Thomas E. Snyder
Frederick T. Stant, III
Stephen C. Swain
Stephen G. Test
Abram W. VanderMeer, Jr.

OF COUNSEL

Frederick T. Stant, Jr.

Michael J. Gardner
S. Geoffrey Glick
James T. Lloyd, Jr.
Charles E. Malone
Frances W. Russell

Counsel For: Tidewater Regional Transit; Virginia Beach General Hospital; Portsmouth General Hospital.

(See Next Column)

Representative Clients: Central Fidelity Bank; Hillenbrand Industries, Inc.; Abbott Laboratories; Miller Oil Company, Inc.; Pet, Inc.; Denny's/TW Services, Inc.; Scottsdale Insurance Co.

For Complete List of Firm Personnel, See General Section
For full biographical listings, see the Martindale-Hubbell Law Directory

FINE, FINE, LEGUM & FINE, PROFESSIONAL ASSOCIATION (AV)

Pavilion Center, 2101 Parks Avenue, Suite 601, 23451
Telephone: 804-422-1678
Fax: 804-422-0865
Other Virginia Beach Office: 1446 Kempsville Road, Suite 201, 23464.

Louis B. Fine
Morris H. Fine
Howard I. Legum (1922-1993)
Andrew S. Fine
Lewis Allen
John R. Lomax
William B. Smith

Steven P. Letourneau
M. Michelle P. McCracken

Representative Clients: Commerce Bank; Taste Unlimited; Superior Services, Inc.; Busch, Inc.; Busch Manufacturing Co.; American Sheet Metal, Inc.; The Runnymede Corp.; Checkered Flag Motor Car Co.; United States Sales Corp.; Valjar, Inc.

For full biographical listings, see the Martindale-Hubbell Law Directory

SHUTTLEWORTH RULOFF GIORDANO AND KAHLE, P.C. (AV)

4425 Corporation Lane, Suite 300, 23462
Telephone: 804-671-6000
Fax: 804-671-6004
Newport News, Virginia Office: 603 Pilot House Drive, Suite 250.
Telephone: 804-873-9999.
Telecopier: 804-873-9758.

Judith M. Cofield
Gregory A. Giordano
Robert J. Haddad
Douglas L. Hornsby
Robert G. Morecock
R. J. Nutter, II
Thomas B. Shuttleworth, II
Lisa Palmer O'Donnell

OF COUNSEL

Richard D. Guy
Paul S. Trible, Jr.

Representative Clients: R.G. Moore Building Corp.; Brown & Root, Inc.; Camelia Food Stores Cooperative, Inc.; Elizabeth River Terminals, Inc.; N.V. Homes; Ryland Homes; Chicago Title Insurance Co.; Sovran Bank, N.A.; Cox Cable Hampton Roads, Inc.

For full biographical listings, see the Martindale-Hubbell Law Directory

WASHINGTON

POULSBO, Kitsap Co.

TOLMAN • KIRK (AV)

18925 Front N.E., P.O. Box 851, 98370
Telephone: 206-779-5561
FAX: 206-779-2516

MEMBERS OF FIRM

Jeffrey L. Tolman
Michael A. Kirk

For full biographical listings, see the Martindale-Hubbell Law Directory

PUYALLUP, Pierce Co.

CAMPBELL, DILLE AND BARNETT (AV)

A Partnership including Professional Corporations
317 South Meridian Street, 98371
Telephone: 206-848-3513
Fax: 206-845-4941

MEMBERS OF FIRM

Robert D. Campbell
Bryce H. Dille (P.S.)
Hollis H. Barnett (P.S.)
Daniel W. Smith

Patricia J. Barnett
Boyd S. Wiley
Gilbert J. Price
Charles W. Dent
Doris J. Combs

Representative Clients: Fors Farms, Inc.; Puyallup School District No. 3; Puyallup Valley Bank; Town of Eatonville; McMullen Electric Company; Larson Glass Company; Girard Wood Products; Uniland, Inc.; Cornforth-Campbell Motors, Inc. (Buick - Pontiac); Good Samaratin Community Health Care.

For full biographical listings, see the Martindale-Hubbell Law Directory

*SEATTLE,** King Co.

Betts, Patterson & Mines, P.S. (AV)

800 Financial Center, 1215 Fourth Avenue, 98161-1090
Telephone: 206-292-9988
Fax: 206-343-7053

Frederick V. Betts
Kenneth S. McEwan
Michael Mines
Steven Goldstein
William P. Fite
James D. Nelson
Paul D. Carey
David L. Hennings
Bruce H. Hurst
Lori L. Guzzo
Christopher W. Tompkins
S. Karen Bamberger
Susan C. Hacker

OF COUNSEL

Mark M. Miller
Martin T. Collier

Ronald D. Allen
Samual S. Chapin
Kimberly A. Quach
Jack A. Friedman
Robert F. Lopez
Kristen Pugsley Onsager
Deborah A. Crabbe
Glenn S. Draper

Representative Clients: Associated Grocers; Cape Fox Corporation; Chrysler Corporation; Great Lakes Chemical Corp.; Key Bank of Washington; Minnesota Mining and Manufacturing Company; Pfizer, Inc.; State Farm Fire & Casualty Co.; Supermarket Development Corp.

For full biographical listings, see the Martindale-Hubbell Law Directory

Gaitán & Cusack (AV)

30th Floor Two Union Square, 601 Union Street, 98101-2324
Telephone: 206-521-3000
Facsimile: 206-386-5259
Anchorage, Alaska Office: 425 G Street, Suite 760.
Telephone: 907-278-3001.
Facsimile: 907-278-6068.
San Francisco, California Office: 275 Battery Street, 20th Floor.
Telephone: 415-398-5562.
Fax: 415-398-4033.
Washington, D.C. Office: 2000 L Street, Suite 200.
Telephone: 202-296-4637.
Fax: 202-296-4650.

MEMBERS OF FIRM

José E. Gaitán
William F. Knowles
Kenneth J. Cusack (Resident, Anchorage, Alaska Office)
Ronald L. Bozarth

OF COUNSEL

Howard K. Todd
Christopher A. Byrne
Gary D. Gayton
Patricia D. Ryan
Michel P. Stern (Also practicing alone, Bellevue, Washington)

ASSOCIATES

Mary F. O'Boyle
Robert T. Mimbu
Bruce H. Williams
Cristina C. Kapela
David J. Onsager
Camilla M. Hedberg
Diana T. Jimenez
John E. Lenker
Kathleen C. Healy

Representative Clients: The Chubb Group of Insurance Companies; CNA Insurance Companies; Transamerica Insurance Companies; CIGNA Insurance Companies; Central National Insurance Company of Omaha; Zurich-American Insurance Companies; Raymark Industries, Inc.; Hartford Insurance Company; Allstate Insurance Companies.

For full biographical listings, see the Martindale-Hubbell Law Directory

Keller Rohrback (AV)

1201 Third Avenue, Suite 3200, 98101-3052
Telephone: 206-623-1900
FAX: 206-623-3384
Bremerton, Washington Office: 400 Warren Avenue.
Telephone: 360-479-5151.
Fax: 360-479-7403.

MEMBERS OF FIRM

Robert K. Keller (1916-1992)
Irene M. Hecht
Pinckney M. Rohrback (1923-1994)
Kirk S. Portmann
Kathleen Kim Coghlan
Fred R. Butterworth
David R. Major
Harold Fardal
Benson D. Wong
Glen P. Garrison
Nikki L. Anderson (Ms.)
Laurence Ross Weatherly
John T. Mellen
Lynn Lincoln Sarko (Mr.)
Karen E. Boxx
John H. Bright
Thomas A. Heller
William C. Smart
Stephen J. Henderson
Lawrence B. Linville
Michael Woerner

(See Next Column)

ASSOCIATES

T. David Copley
Paulette Peterson
Rob J. Crichton
Stella L. Pitts
Juli E. Farris
Roberta N. Riley
Mark A. Griffin
Britt L. Tinglum
William A. Linton
John H. Wiegenstein

OF COUNSEL

Burton C. Waldo
Melvin F. Buol

Attorneys For: Allstate Insurance Company; American Honda Motor Co., Inc.; American States Insurance Co.; American Suzuki Motor Corp.; Bell Helmets, Inc.; Pend Oreille Bank; Ohio Casualty Group; Pacific Northwest Bank; Ticor Title; United Services Automobile Association.

For Complete List of Firm Personnel, See General Section

For full biographical listings, see the Martindale-Hubbell Law Directory

Lane Powell Spears Lubersky (AV)

A Partnership including Professional Corporations
1420 Fifth Avenue, Suite 4100, 98101-2338
Telephone: 206-223-7000
Cable Address: "Embe"
Telex: 32-8808
Telecopier: 206-223-7107
Other Offices at: Mount Vernon and Olympia, Washington; Los Angeles and San Francisco, California; Anchorage, Alaska; Portland, Oregon; London, England.

MEMBERS OF FIRM

Dale E. Kremer
Rudy A. Englund
Richard C. Siefert
H. Peter Sorg, Jr.
James L. Robart
Kenneth B. Kaplan
Christopher B. Wells
Randall P. Beighle
Larry S. Gangnes (P.S.)
Gail E. Mautner (P.S.)
Christian N. Oldham

Representative Clients: Dean Witter Reynolds; First Interstate Bank of Washington; Fred Hutchinson Cancer Research Center; The Hillhaven Corp.; Litton Industries; Mitsui & Co., Ltd.; Nordstrom, Inc.; Prudential Securities; Simpson Investment Co. and Affiliates; Texaco, Inc.

For Complete List of Firm Personnel, See General Section

For full biographical listings, see the Martindale-Hubbell Law Directory

John W. Lundin, P.S. (AV)

710 Cherry, 98104
Telephone: 206-623-8346
Fax: 206-623-5951

John W. Lundin

Reference: Key Bank (Main Branch).

For full biographical listings, see the Martindale-Hubbell Law Directory

Smith, Smart, Hancock, Tabler & Schwensen (AV)

3800 Columbia Seafirst Center, 701 Fifth Avenue, 98104
Telephone: 206-624-7272
Telecopier: 206-624-5581

MEMBERS OF FIRM

J. Dimmitt Smith
Walter S. Tabler
Douglas J. Smart
Joyce S. Schwensen
David G. Hancock
Karen A. Willie

ASSOCIATES

Anne B. Tiura
Oskar E. Rey
Paul J. Battaglia
Craig A. Fielden

Reference: Seattle-First National Bank; Bank of America; Chemical Bank; Clise Properties, Inc.; Gentra Capital Corporation; Puget Sound Pilots; Aid Association for Lutherans; Citicorp Mortgage, Inc.; Lutheran Brotherhood; City of Tacoma.

For full biographical listings, see the Martindale-Hubbell Law Directory

Tousley Brain (AV)

A Partnership
56th Floor, AT&T Gateway Tower, 700 Fifth Avenue, 98104-5056
Telephone: 206-682-5600
Facsimile: 206-682-2992

Christopher I. Brain
Rebecca A. McIntyre
Kim D. Stephens (Mr.)
Susan A. Shyne
Stephan E. Todd
Stephan O. Fjelstad
Deborah A. Knapp

Kimberly J. Kernan

Representative Clients: Chicago Title Insurance Company; Healthcare International; Intrawest Companies; Koll Management Services, Inc.; Lone Star Northwest; Murray Franklyn Companies; Port of Seattle; Security Properties Companies; Trammell Crow Company; University Savings Bank.

(See Next Column)

TOUSLEY BRAIN, *Seattle—Continued*

For Complete List of Firm Personnel, See General Section

For full biographical listings, see the Martindale-Hubbell Law Directory

*WENATCHEE,** Chelan Co.

FOREMAN & ARCH, P.S. (AV)

701 N. Chelan Street, P.O. Box 3125, 98807
Telephone: 509-662-9602
Telecopier: 509-662-9606
Moses Lake, Washington Office: 821 W. Broadway, Suite 202, 98837.
Telephone: 509-766-9053.
Okanogan, Washington Office: 116 South Second.
Telephone: 509-826-4903.
Fax: 509-826-2530.
Associated Firm: Appel & Glueck, P.C., 2500 Seattle Tower, 1218 Third Avenue, Seattle, Washington.
Telephone: 206-625-0650.
Telecopier: 206-625-1807.
Associated Firm: Coufal Abogados, Montevideo 2695, Colonia Providencia 44630, Guadalajara, Jalisco, Mexico.
Telephones: 5236-41-18-34, 41-25-59, 41-17-91.
Telecopier: 41-00-26.

Dale M. Foreman
Michael A. Arch
Robert G. Dodge
Thomas E. Janisch
Ronaldo P. Delgado (Resident, Moses Lake Office)
Scott A. Volyn
Vivian L. White-Orso
Lonny D. Bauscher
James R. B. Salter (Resident, Okanogan Office)

For full biographical listings, see the Martindale-Hubbell Law Directory

WEST VIRGINIA

*BECKLEY,** Raleigh Co.

LYNCH, MANN, SMITH & MANN (AV)

108 1/2 South Heber Street, P.O. Box 1600, 25802-1600
Telephone: 304-253-3349

MEMBERS OF FIRM

Jack A. Mann
Clyde A. Smith, Jr.
Kimberly G. Mann

Representative Clients: State Farm Insurance Companies; Horace Mann Insurance Co.; Erie Insurance Company; Sears, Roebuck and Co.; Dairyland Insurance Company; Allstate Insurance Co.; U.S.F.&G. Insurance Company; American States Insurance Company; Atlantic Mutual Insurance Company; Transamerica Corporation.

For full biographical listings, see the Martindale-Hubbell Law Directory

*BUCKHANNON,** Upshur Co.

HYMES AND COONTS (AV)

Hymco Building, 23 West Main Street, P.O. Box 310, 26201-0310
Telephone: 304-472-1565
Fax: 304-472-1615

MEMBERS OF FIRM

Myron B. Hymes (1897-1988)
Gilbert Gray Coonts
Terry D. Reed

ASSOCIATE

Kelley Haught Wilmoth

For full biographical listings, see the Martindale-Hubbell Law Directory

*CHARLESTON,** Kanawha Co.

BOWLES RICE MCDAVID GRAFF & LOVE (AV)

16th Floor Commerce Square, P.O. Box 1386, 25325-1386
Telephone: 304-347-1100
Fax: 304-343-2867
Martinsburg, West Virginia Office: (Serves Berkeley Springs and Charles Town, West Virginia). 105 West Burke Street, P.O. Drawer 1419.
Telephone: 304-263-0836.
Fax: 304-267-3822.
Morgantown, West Virginia Office: 206 Spruce Street.
Telephone: 304-296-2500.
Fax: 304-296-2513.
Parkersburg, West Virginia Office: 601 Avery Street, P.O. Box 48.
Telephone: 304-485-8500.
Fax: 304-485-7973.
Lexington, Kentucky Office: Bowles Rice McDavid Graff Love & Getty, 12th Floor Vine Center Tower, 333 West Vine Street.
Telephone: 606-225-8700.
Fax: 606-225-8418.

(See Next Column)

MEMBERS OF FIRM

Paul N. Bowles (1921-1986)
F. Thomas Graff, Jr. (Firm Managing Partner)
Charles M. Love, III
P. Michael Pleska
Gary G. Markham
David C. Hardesty, Jr.
Carl D. Andrews
Edward D. McDevitt
Ricklin Brown
J. Thomas Lane
Gerard R. Stowers
P. Nathan Bowles, Jr.
Thomas B. Bennett
Sarah E. Smith
Richard M. Francis
George A. Patterson, III
Roger D. Hunter
Thomas E. Scarr
Phyllis M. Potterfield
Deborah A. Sink
Gordon C. Lane
John W. Woods, III
Thomas A. Heywood
Camden P. Siegrist
Benjamin L. Bailey
Sandra M. Murphy
Julia A. Chincheck
Anthony P. Tokarz
Leonard Knee
Marc A. Monteleone
Lesley Hiscoe Russo
Ellen Maxwell-Hoffman

ASSOCIATES

Lynn Photiadis
Fazal A. Shere
Charles B. Dollison
Kenneth E. Webb, Jr.
Michael J. Schessler
Robert G. Lilly
John R. Teare, Jr.
Elizabeth D. Harter
Douglas L. Davis
Robert V. Leydon
Elizabeth Benston Elmore
Gina E. Mazzei
Ronda L. Harvey
Stuart A. McMillan
Betsy Ennis Dulin

EXECUTIVE DIRECTOR

James N. Rogers

SPECIAL COUNSEL

Giles D. H. Snyder

OF COUNSEL

William R. McDavid

For full biographical listings, see the Martindale-Hubbell Law Directory

CICCARELLO, DEL GIUDICE & LAFON (AV)

Suite 100, 1219 Virginia Street, East, 25301
Telephone: 304-343-4440
Telecopier: 304-343-4464

MEMBERS OF FIRM

Arthur T. Ciccarello
Michael J. Del Giudice
Timothy J. LaFon

For full biographical listings, see the Martindale-Hubbell Law Directory

GOODWIN & GOODWIN (AV)

1500 One Valley Square, 25301
Telephone: 304-346-7000
Fax: 304-344-9692
Ripley, West Virginia Office: 500 Church Street, P.O. Box 349.
Telephone: 304-372-2651.
Parkersburg, West Virginia Office: 201 Third Street, Town Square.
Telephone: 304-485-2345.
Fax: 304-485-3459.

Robert B. Goodwin (1909-1955)

OF COUNSEL

C. E. Goodwin

MEMBERS OF FIRM

Thomas R. Goodwin
Joseph R. Goodwin
Stephen P. Goodwin
Michael I. Spiker
Richard E. Rowe
Robert Q. Sayre, Jr.
Susan C. Wittemeier
Robert W. Full (Resident at Parkersburg Office)
Richard D. Owen

ASSOCIATES

Suzanne Jett Trowbridge
Debra C. Price

Representative Clients: Bucyrus-Erie Co.; CSX Corp.; Eastern American Energy Corp.; The Eureka Pipe Line Company.

For Complete List of Firm Personnel, See General Section

For full biographical listings, see the Martindale-Hubbell Law Directory

HUNT, LEES, FARRELL & KESSLER (AV)

7 Players Club Drive, P.O. Box 2506, 25329-2506
Telephone: 304-344-9651
Telecopier: 304-343-1916
Huntington, West Virginia Office: Prichard Building, 601 Ninth Street, P.O. Box 2191, 25722.
Telephone: 304-529-1999.
Martinsburg, West Virginia Office: 1012 B Winchester Avenue. P.O. Box 579. 25401.
Telephone: 304-267-3100.

MEMBERS OF FIRM

James B. Lees, Jr.
Joseph M. Farrell, Jr. (Resident, Huntington Office)
John A. Kessler

(See Next Column)

HUNT, LEES, FARRELL & KESSLER—*Continued*

ASSOCIATES

James A. McKowen
Jeffrey T. Jones
Marion Eugene Ray
Mark Jenkinson (Resident, Martinsburg Office)
Meikka A. Cutlip (Resident, Huntington Office)
Sharon M. Fedorochko

OF COUNSEL

L. Alvin Hunt

For full biographical listings, see the Martindale-Hubbell Law Directory

JACKSON & KELLY (AV)

1600 Laidley Tower, P.O. Box 553, 25322
Telephone: 304-340-1000
Fax: 304-340-1130
Martinsburg, West Virginia Office: 300 Foxcroft Avenue, P.O. Box 1068.
Telephone: 304-263-8800.
Morgantown, West Virginia Office: 6000 Hampton Center, P.O. Box 619.
Telephone: 304-599-3000.
New Martinsville, West Virginia Office: 256 Russell Avenue, P.O. Box 68.
Telephone: 304-455-1751.
Charles Town, West Virginia Office: 700 East Washington Street, P.O. Box 983.
Telephone: 304-728-6088.
Clarksburg, West Virginia Office: 203 Main Street, P.O. Box 1587.
Telephone: 304-623-3002.
Lexington, Kentucky Office: 175 East Main Street, Suite 500, P.O. Box 2150.
Telephone: 606-255-9500.
Washington, D. C. Office: 2401 Pennsylvania Avenue, N.W., Suite 400.
Telephone: 202-973-0200.
Denver, Colorado Office: Suite 2710, 1660 Lincoln Street.
Telephone: 303-837-0003.

MEMBERS OF FIRM

Winfield T. Shaffer
Edward W. Rugeley, Jr.
George R. Farmer, Jr. (Resident, Morgantown, West Virginia Office)
John M. Slack, III
Stephen R. Crislip
Wm. Richard McCune, Jr. (Martinsburg and Charles Town, West Virginia Offices)
Alvin L. Emch
William A. Hoskins, III (Resident, Lexington, Kentucky Office)
Dennis C. Sauter
Larry W. Blalock (Administrative Manager, New Martinsville, West Virginia Office)
Thomas J. Hurney, Jr.
Lynn Oliver Frye
Stephen M. LaCagnin (Resident, Morgantown, West Virginia Office)
G. Lindsay Simmons (Resident, Washington, D.C. Office)
William J. Powell

ASSOCIATES

Stanton L. Cave (Resident, Lexington, Kentucky Office)
J. Rudy Martin
William Prentice Young (Martinsburg and Charles Town, West Virginia Offices)
Jeffery L. Robinette (Resident, Morgantown, West Virginia Office)
Pamela Wray Blackshire
Julia M. Chico (Resident, Morgantown, West Virginia Office)
Katherine Shand Larkin (Resident, Denver, Colorado Office)

Representative Clients: E.I. du Pont de Nemours & Co.; Rhone-Poulenc, Inc.; TRW Inc.; Island Creek Corp.; Caterpillar Inc.; Gravely International; Joy Technologies Inc.; Union Carbide Corp.; Pittston Coal Co.; General Motors Crop.

For Complete List of Firm Personnel, See General Section

For full biographical listings, see the Martindale-Hubbell Law Directory

KAY, CASTO, CHANEY, LOVE & WISE (AV)

1600 Bank One Center, P.O. Box 2031, 25327
Telephone: 304-345-8900
Telefax: 304-345-8909; 304-343-9833
Morgantown, West Virginia Office: Suite C, 3000 Hampton Center.
Telephone: 304-599-8900.
Telefax: 304-599-8901.
Abingdon, Virginia Office: 329 West Main Street.
Telephone: 703-628-9211.
Telefax: 703-628-9334.

OF COUNSEL

Vincent V. Chaney
John O. Kizer
Robert E. Magnuson

MEMBERS OF FIRM

Robert L. Brandfass
Michael T. Chaney
Ralph C. Dusic, Jr.
Barney W. Frazier, Jr.
George W. S. Grove, Jr.
Ann L. Haight
John S. Haight
Steven C. Hanley
Elliot G. Hicks
John R. Hoblitzell
John R. McGhee, Jr.
Dina M. Mohler
W. Michael Moore
Kevin A. Nelson

(See Next Column)

MEMBERS OF FIRM (Continued)

Harry M. Rubenstein (Morgantown, West Virginia Office)
Howard G. Salisbury, Jr. (Abingdon, Virginia Office)
Mark A. Swartz (Abingdon, Virginia Office)

ASSOCIATES

Bethann Regina Lloyd
Patricia Jo Loehr
F. Thomas Rubenstein (Morgantown, West Virginia Office)
Joseph E. Starkey, Jr.
Crystal S. Stump

Attorneys for: Ford Motor Co.; Bank One, West Virginia; Chrysler Corp.; Aetna Insurance Co.; Wausau Insurance Cos,; West Virginia Contractors Bargaining Assn.; Charleston Area Medical Center, Inc.

For Complete List of Firm Personnel, See General Section

For full biographical listings, see the Martindale-Hubbell Law Directory

KING, ALLEN & ARNOLD (AV)

1300 Bank One Center, P.O. Box 3394, 25333
Telephone: 304-345-7250
Telecopier: 304-345-9941

Robert B. King
George G. Guthrie
Robert B. Allen
James S. Arnold
R. Terrance Rodgers
Robert A. Goldberg
Stephen B. Farmer
John J. Polak
Robert D. Cline, Jr.
S. Benjamin Bryant
Raymond Keener, III
Wm. Scott Wickline
Robert A. Campbell
W. Mark Burnette
J. Miles Morgan
Pamela Lynn Kandzari
Michelle M. Price
Kimberly S. Fenwick

For full biographical listings, see the Martindale-Hubbell Law Directory

PAYNE, LOEB & RAY (AV)

1210 One Valley Square, 25301
Telephone: 304-342-1141
Fax: 304-342-0691

MEMBERS OF FIRM

John V. Ray (1893-1974)
Walter C. Price, Jr. (1910-1976)
Charles W. Loeb
John L. Ray
Christopher J. Winton
William H. Scharf

ASSOCIATE

Mark W. Kelley

Counsel for: One Valley Bank, N.A.; Outdoor Advertising Association of West Virginia; Trojan Steel Co.; Thomas, Field & Co.; Kanawha Village Apartments, Inc.; Guyan Machinery Co.

For full biographical listings, see the Martindale-Hubbell Law Directory

STEPTOE & JOHNSON (AV)

Seventh Floor, Bank One Center, P.O. Box 1588, 25326-1588
Telephone: 304-353-8000
Fax: 304-353-8180
Clarksburg, West Virginia Office: Bank One Center, P.O. Box 2190, 26302-2190.
Telephone: 304-624-8000.
Fax: 304-624-8183.
Morgantown, West Virginia Office: 1000 Hampton Center, P.O. Box 1616, 26507-1616.
Telephone: 304-598-8000.
Fax: 304-598-8116.
Martinsburg, West Virginia Office: 126 East Burke Street, P.O. Box 2629, 25401-5429.
Telephone: 304-263-6991.
Fax: 304-263-4785.
Charles Town, West Virginia Office: 104 West Congress Street, P.O. Box 100, 25414-0100.
Telephone: 304-725-1414.
Fax: 304-725-1913.
Hagerstown, Maryland Office: The Bryan Centre, 82 West Washington Street, Fourth Floor, P.O. Box 570, 21740-0570.
Telephone: 301-739-8600.
Fax: 301-739-8742.
Wheeling, West Virginia Office: The Riley Building, Suite 400, 14th & Chapline Streets, P.O. Box 150, 26008-0020.
Telephone: 304-233-0000.
Fax: 304-233-0014.

MEMBERS OF FIRM

Otis L. O'Connor
James R. Watson
Daniel R. Schuda
Harry P. Waddell
Steven P. McGowan
Bryan R. Cokeley
W. Randolph Fife
Martin R. Smith, Jr.
George E. Carenbauer
Arthur M. Standish
Patrick D. Kelly

(See Next Column)

STEPTOE & JOHNSON, *Charleston—Continued*

ASSOCIATES

Cynthia R. Cokeley
Susan Osenton Phillips
Luci R. Wellborn
Susan L. Basile
Janet N. Kawash
Jeffrey K. Phillips
Richard J. Wolf
Wendy D. Young
Michael J. Funk
Marc B. Lazenby
Jan L. Fox

Representative Clients: Ameribank; ARCO Chemical Co.; City National Bank of Charleston; Federal Kemper Insurance Co.; Goodyear Tire & Rubber Co.; The Hartford Group; Hope Gas, Inc.; Olin Corp.; South Charleston Stamping & Manufacturing Co.; State Farm Insurance Cos.

For Complete List of Firm Personnel, See General Section

For full biographical listings, see the Martindale-Hubbell Law Directory

*CLARKSBURG,** Harrison Co.

JOHNSON, SIMMERMAN & BROUGHTON, L.C. (AV)

Suite 210, Goff Building, P.O. Box 150, 26301
Telephone: 304-624-6555
Telecopier: 304-623-4933

Charles G. Johnson
Frank E. Simmerman, Jr.
Marcia Allen Broughton

For full biographical listings, see the Martindale-Hubbell Law Directory

MCNEER, HIGHLAND & MCMUNN (AV)

Empire Building, P.O. Drawer 2040, 26301
Telephone: 304-623-6636
Facsimile: 304-623-3035
Morgantown Office: McNeer, Highland & McMunn, Baker & Armistead, 168 Chancery Row. P.O. Box 1615.
Telephone: 304-292-8473.
Fax: 304-292-1528.
Martinsburg, Office: 1446-1 Edwin Miller Boulevard. P.O. Box 2509.
Telephone: 304-264-4621.
Fax: 304-264-8623.

MEMBERS OF FIRM

C. David McMunn
J. Cecil Jarvis
James A. Varner
George B. Armistead (Resident, Morgantown Office)
Catherine D. Munster
Robert W. Trumble (Resident, Martinsburg Office)
Dennis M. Shreve
Geraldine S. Roberts
Harold M. Sklar
Jeffrey S. Bolyard
Steven R. Bratke
Michael J. Novotny (Resident, Martinsburg Office)

OF COUNSEL

James E. McNeer
Cecil B. Highland, Jr.
William L. Fury

Representative Clients: Nationwide Insurance Group; State Automobile Insurance Co.; Insurance Company of North America (CIGNA); Home Insurance Co.; Westfield Insurance Co.; St. Paul Insurance Co.; West Virginia Fire and Casualty; United Hospital Center; One Valley Bank; Clarksburg Publishing Co.

For Complete List of Firm Personnel, See General Section

For full biographical listings, see the Martindale-Hubbell Law Directory

STEPTOE & JOHNSON (AV)

Bank One Center, P.O. Box 2190, 26302-2190
Telephone: 304-624-8000
Fax: 304-624-8183
Mailing Address: P.O. Box 2190, 26302-2190
Charleston, West Virginia Office: Seventh Floor, Bank One Center, P.O. Box 1588, 25326-1588.
Telephone: 304-353-8000
Fax: 304-353-8180.
Morgantown, West Virginia Office: 1000 Hampton Center, P.O. Box 1616, 26507-1616.
Telephone: 304-598-8000.
Fax: 304-598-8116.
Martinsburg, West Virginia Office: 126 East Burke Street, P.O. Box 2629, 25401-5429.
Telephone: 304-263-6991.
Fax: 304-263-4785.
Charles Town, West Virginia Office: 104 West Congress Street, P.O. Box 100, 25414-0100.
Telephone: 304-725-1414.
Fax: 304-725-1913.
Hagerstown, Maryland Office: The Bryan Centre, 82 West Washington Street, Fourth Floor, P.O. Box 570, 21740-0570.
Telephone: 301-739-8600.
Fax: 301-739-8742.
Wheeling, West Virginia Office: The Riley Building, Suite 400, 14th & Chapline Streets, P.O. Box 150, 26003-0020.
Telephone: 304-233-0000.
Fax: 304-233-0014.

(See Next Column)

MEMBERS OF FIRM

Herbert G. Underwood
Robert G. Steele
James M. Wilson
Patrick D. Deem
Robert M. Steptoe, Jr.
James D. Gray
Vincent A. Collins
William T. Belcher
J. Greg Goodykoontz
Evans L. King, Jr.
Walter L. Williams
Ronald H. Hanlan
C. David Morrison
Clement D. Carter, III
W. Henry Lawrence IV
Gordon H. Copland
Randall C. Light
Richard M. Yurko, Jr.
Gary W. Nickerson
Louis E. Enderle, Jr.

OF COUNSEL

Jackson L. Anderson
Anne R. Williams

ASSOCIATES

Francesca Tan
Matthew J. Mullaney
Michael Kozakewich, Jr.
Carolyn A. Wade
Daniel C. Cooper
Douglas G. Lee
Sherri S. Johns
Timothy R. Miley
Jacqueline A. Wilson
Nancy W. Brown

Representative Clients: Consolidated Gas Transmission Corp.; Consolidated Coal Co.; CNA; E.I. DuPont de Nemours & Co.; Equitable Resources, Inc.; The Hartford Group; Peabody Coal Co.; PPG Industries; Bank One, N.A.; Ogden Newspapers, Inc.

For Complete List of Firm Personnel, See General Section

For full biographical listings, see the Martindale-Hubbell Law Directory

WATERS, WARNER & HARRIS (AV)

Formerly Stathers & Cantrall
701 Goff Building, P.O. Box 1716, 26301
Telephone: 304-624-5571
Fax: 304-624-7228

Birk S. Stathers (1884-1945)
W. G. Stathers (1889-1970)
Arch M. Cantrall (1896-1967)
Stuart R. Waters
Boyd L. Warner
James A. Harris
Scott E. Wilson
James C. Turner
Francis L. Warder, Jr.
G. Thomas Smith
Thomas G. Dyer

ASSOCIATES

Michael J. Folio
Katherine M. Carpenter
Ernest Glen Hentschel, II
Katrina L. Gallagher

Representative Clients: United States Fidelity and Guaranty Co.; State Farm Insurance Companies; The Shelby Mutual Insurance Co.; Westfield Insurance Company; Bethlehem Steel Corp.; Brooklyn Union Gas Co.; The Cafaro Co.

For full biographical listings, see the Martindale-Hubbell Law Directory

WEST & JONES (AV)

360 Washington Avenue, P.O. Box 2348, 26302
Telephone: 304-624-5501
FAX: 304-624-4454

MEMBERS OF FIRM

James C. West, Jr.
Jerald E. Jones
John S. Kaull
Lewis A. Clark

ASSOCIATES

Kathryn K. Allen
Norman T. Farley

Reference: The Union National Bank of West Virginia.

For Complete List of Firm Personnel, See General Section

For full biographical listings, see the Martindale-Hubbell Law Directory

*ELKINS,** Randolph Co.

BUSCH & TALBOTT, L.C. (AV)

Court and High Streets, P.O. Box 1397, 26241
Telephone: 304-636-3560
Fax: 304-636-2290

John E. Busch
Richard H. Talbott, Jr.

Cynthia Santoro Gustke
Peter G. Zurbuch
David Thompson
Bridgette Rhoden Wilson

Representative Clients: Monongahela Power Co.; Davis Trust Co.; Community Bank & Trust Company of Randolph County; Coastal Lumber Co.; USF&G; Nationwide Insurance Co.; State Farm Insurance Companies; Nissan Motor Corporation in USA; Chrysler Corp.; General Motors.

For Complete List of Firm Personnel, See General Section

For full biographical listings, see the Martindale-Hubbell Law Directory

*HUNTINGTON,** Cabell & Wayne Cos.

JENKINS, FENSTERMAKER, KRIEGER, KAYES, FARRELL & AGEE (AV)

Eleventh Floor Coal Exchange Building, P.O. Drawer 2688, 25726
Telephone: 304-523-2100
Charleston, WV 304-345-3100
Facsimile: 304-523-2347; 304-523-9279

MEMBERS OF FIRM

John E. Jenkins (1897-1961) | Michael J. Farrell
P. Thomas Krieger | Wesley F. Agee
Henry M. Kayes | Barry M. Taylor

ASSOCIATES

Suzanne McGinnis Oxley | William J. McGee, Jr.
Charlotte A. Hoffman | Anne Maxwell McGee
Robert H. Sweeney, Jr. | Tamela J. White
Patricia A. Jennings | Lee Murray Hall
Stephen J. Golder | Thomas J. Obrokta

OF COUNSEL

John E. Jenkins, Jr. | Susan B. Saxe

For full biographical listings, see the Martindale-Hubbell Law Directory

*MADISON,** Boone Co.

SHAFFER AND SHAFFER (AV)

330 State Street, P.O. Box 38, 25130
Telephone: 304-369-0511
Fax: 304-369-5431
Charleston, West Virginia Office: 1710 Bank One Center, P.O. Box 3973.
Telephone: 304-344-8716.
Fax: 304-342-1105.

MEMBERS OF FIRM

James J. MacCallum | Harry G. Shaffer, III (Resident, Charleston Office)
George D. Blizzard, II | Anthony J. Cicconi (Resident, Charleston Office)
Charles S. Piccirillo

ASSOCIATE

Edward L. Bullman

Representative Clients: Bank One, West Virginia, N.A., Boone; Armco Inc.; Westmoreland Coal Co.; State Farm Mutual Insurance Cos.; Nationwide Insurance Co.

For Complete List of Firm Personnel, See General Section

For full biographical listings, see the Martindale-Hubbell Law Directory

*MARTINSBURG,** Berkeley Co.

BOWLES RICE MCDAVID GRAFF & LOVE (AV)

(Formerly Rice, Douglas & Shingleton)
105 West Burke Street, P.O. Drawer 1419, 25401
Telephone: 304-263-0836
Fax: 304-267-3822
Charleston, West Virginia Office: 16th Floor Commerce Square, P.O. Box 1386.
Telephone: 304-347-1100.
Fax: 304-343-2867.
Morgantown, West Virginia Office: 206 Spruce Street.
Telephone: 304-296-2500.
Fax: 304-296-2513.
Parkersburg, West Virginia Office: 601 Avery Street, P.O. Box 48.
Telephone: 304-485-7973.
Lexington, Kentucky Office: Bowles Rice McDavid Graff Love & Getty, 12th Floor Vine Center Tower, 333 West Vine Street.
Telephone: 606-225-8700.
Fax: 606-225-8418.

MEMBERS OF FIRM

Lacy I. Rice (1901-1974) | Michael E. Caryl
Lacy I. Rice, Jr. | Charles F. Printz, Jr.
Richard L. Douglas | Michael D. Lorensen
Hoy G. Shingleton, Jr. | Joan L. Casale
J. Oakley Seibert | M. Shannon Brown
Michael B. Keller | Norwood Bentley

ASSOCIATES

Stephen McDowell Mathias | David A. DeJarnett
Claudia W. Bentley | Amy R. Lamp

For full biographical listings, see the Martindale-Hubbell Law Directory

MCNEER, HIGHLAND & MCMUNN (AV)

1446-1 Edwin Miller Boulevard, P.O. Box 2509, 25401-2509
Telephone: 304-264-4621
Facsimile: 304-264-8623
Morgantown Office: McNeer, Highland & McMunn, Baker & Armistead, 168 Chancery Row. P.O. Box 1615.
Telephone: 304-292-8473.
Fax: 304-292-1528.

(See Next Column)

Clarksburg Office: Empire Building. P.O. Drawer 2040.
Telephone: 304-623-6636.
Facsimile: 304-623-3035.

Robert W. Trumble

Representative Clients: Nationwide Insurance Group; State Automobile Insurance Co.; Insurance Company of North America (CIGNA); Home Insurance Co.; Westfield Insurance Co.; St. Paul Insurance Co.; West Virginia Fire and Casualty; United Hospital Center; Empire National Bank; Clarksburg Publishing Co.

For Complete List of Firm Personnel, See General Section

For full biographical listings, see the Martindale-Hubbell Law Directory

STEPTOE & JOHNSON (AV)

126 East Burke Street, P.O. Box 2629, 25401-5429
Telephone: 304-263-6991
Fax: 304-263-4785
Clarksburg, West Virginia Office: Bank One Center, P.O. Box 2190, 26302-2190.
Telephone: 304-624-8000.
Fax: 304-624-8183.
Charleston, West Virginia Office: Seventh Floor, Bank One Center, P.O. Box 1588, 25326-1588.
Telephone: 304-353-8000.
Fax: 304-353-8180.
Morgantown, West Virginia Office: 1000 Hampton Center, P.O. Box 1616, 26507-1616.
Telephone: 304-598-8000.
Fax: 304-598-8116.
Charles Town, West Virginia Office: 104 West Congress Street, P.O. Box 100, 25414-0100.
Telephone: 304-725-1414.
Fax: 304-725-1913.
Hagerstown, Maryland Office: The Bryan Centre, 82 West Washington Street, Fourth Floor, P.O. Box 570, 21740-0570.
Telephone: 301-739-8600.
Fax: 301-739-8742.
Wheeling, West Virginia Office: The Riley Building, Suite 400, 14th & Chapline Streets, P.O. Box 150, 26003-0020.
Telephone: 304-233-0000.
Fax: 304-233-0014.

MEMBERS OF FIRM

J. Lee Van Metre, Jr. | James D. Steptoe
Lucien G. Lewin | Curtis G. Power III
Kathy M. McCarty

Representative Clients: Active Industries, Inc.; Blue Ridge Acres; Farmer and Mechanics Mutual Fire Insurance Co. of West Virginia; Great American Insurance Cos.; Insurance Corporation of America; Keyes Ferry Acres; Nationwide Mutual Insurance Cos.; One Valley Bank of Martinsburg; Peoples National Bank of Martinsburg; State Farm Mutual Insurance Cos.

For Complete List of Firm Personnel, See General Section

For full biographical listings, see the Martindale-Hubbell Law Directory

*MORGANTOWN,** Monongalia Co.

BOWLES RICE MCDAVID GRAFF & LOVE (AV)

206 Spruce Street, 26505
Telephone: 304-296-2500
Fax: 304-296-2513
Charleston, West Virginia Office: 16th Floor Commerce Square, P.O. Box 1386.
Telephone: 304-347-1100.
Fax: 304-343-2867.
Martinsburg, West Virginia Office: (Serves Berkeley Springs and Charles Town, West Virginia). 105 West Burke Street, P.O. Drawer 1419.
Telephone: 304-263-0836.
Fax: 304-267-3822.
Parkersburg, West Virginia Office: 601 Avery Street, P.O. Box 48.
Telephone: 304-485-8500.
Fax: 304-485-7973.
Lexington, Kentucky Office: Bowles Rice McDavid Graff Love & Getty, 12th Floor Vine Center Tower, 333 West Vine Street.
Telephone: 606-225-8700.
Fax: 606-225-8418.

MEMBERS OF FIRM

Robert W. Dinsmore | Paul E. Frampton

ASSOCIATES

Charles C. Wise, III | Beth Kraus Haley
Kimberly S. Croyle

For full biographical listings, see the Martindale-Hubbell Law Directory

FUSCO & NEWBRAUGH (AV)

2400 Cranberry Square, 26505-9209
Telephone: 304-594-1000
Telecopier: 304-594-1181

(See Next Column)

FUSCO & NEWBRAUGH, *Morgantown—Continued*

Andrew G. Fusco Thomas H. Newbraugh

ASSOCIATES

Margaret A. Droppleman Jeffrey A. Ray
Steven M. Prunty Debra A. Bowers

OF COUNSEL

Vincent P. Cardi

Representative Clients: Mylan Pharmaceuticals, Inc.
Reference: One Valley Bank.

For full biographical listings, see the Martindale-Hubbell Law Directory

MCNEER, HIGHLAND & MCMUNN, BAKER & ARMISTEAD (AV)

168 Chancery Row, P.O. Box 1615, 26507-1615
Telephone: 304-292-8473
Fax: 304-292-1528
Clarksburg Office: McNeer, Highland & McMunn, Empire Building, P.O. Drawer 2040.
Telephone: 304-623-6636.
Facsimile: 304-623-3035.
Martinsburg Office: McNeer, Highland & McMunn, 1446-1 Edwin Miller Boulevard, P.O. Box 2509.
Telephone: 304-264-4621.
Facsimile: 304-264-8623.

OF COUNSEL

Charles S. Armistead

Representative Clients: The Chesapeake and Potomac Telephone Company of West Virginia; Federal Kemper Insurance Co.; Home Insurance Co.

For Complete List of Firm Personnel, See General Section

For full biographical listings, see the Martindale-Hubbell Law Directory

STEPTOE & JOHNSON (AV)

1000 Hampton Center, P.O. Box 1616, 26507-1616
Telephone: 304-598-8000
Fax: 304-598-8116
Clarksburg, West Virginia Office: Bank One Center, P.O. Box 2190, 26302-2190.
Telephone: 304-624-8000.
Fax: 304-624-8183.
Charleston, West Virginia Office: Seventh Floor, Bank One Center, P.O. Box 1588, 25326-1588.
Telephone: 304-353-8000.
Fax: 304-353-8180.
Martinsburg, West Virginia Office: 126 East Burke Street, P.O. Box 2629, 25401-5429.
Telephone: 304-263-6991.
Fax: 304-263-4785.
Charles Town, West Virginia Office: 104 West Congress Street, P.O. Box 100, 25414-0100.
Telephone: 304-725-1414.
Fax: 304-725-1913.
Hagerstown, Maryland Office: The Bryan Centre, 82 West Washington Street, Fourth Floor, P.O. Box 570, 21740-0570.
Telephone: 301-739-8600.
Fax: 301-739-8742.
Wheeling, West Virginia Office: The Riley Building, Suite 400, 14th & Chapline Streets, P.O. Box 150, 26003-0020.
Telephone: 304-233-0000.
Fax: 304-233-0014.

MEMBERS OF FIRM

James A. Russell Susan Slenker Brewer
William E. Galeota

ASSOCIATES

Laurie L. Crytser David E. Dick

Representative Clients: American Electric Power; Consolidaton Coal Co.; Ford Motor Co.; The Hartford Group; State Farm Mutual; WVU Hospitals, Inc.; West Virginia Medical Corp.; W.Va. Publishing Co.

For Complete List of Firm Personnel, See General Section

For full biographical listings, see the Martindale-Hubbell Law Directory

*PARKERSBURG,** Wood Co.

BOWLES RICE MCDAVID GRAFF & LOVE (AV)

(Formerly Davis, Bailey, Pfalzgraf & Hall)
601 Avery Street, P.O. Box 48, 26102-0048
Telephone: 304-485-8500
Fax: 304-485-7973
Charleston, West Virginia Office: 16th Floor Commerce Square, P.O. Box 1386.
Telephone: 304-347-1100.
Fax: 304-343-2867.
Martinsburg, West Virginia Office (Serves Berkeley Springs and Charles Town, West Virginia): 105 West Burke Street, P.O. Drawer 1419.
Telephone: 304-263-0836.
Fax: 304-267-3822.

(See Next Column)

Morgantown, West Virginia Office: 206 Spruce Street.
Telephone: 304-296-2500.
Fax: 304-296-2513.
Lexington, Kentucky Office: Bowles Rice McDavid Graff Love & Getty, 12th Floor Vine Center Tower, 333 West Vine Street.
Telephone: 606-225-8700.
Fax: 606-225-8418.

MEMBERS OF FIRM

John S. Bailey, Jr. Robert J. Kent
Howard E. Seufer, Jr. Steven R. Hardman
Robert L. Bays

ASSOCIATES

Spencer D. Conard Ellen T. Medaglio

For full biographical listings, see the Martindale-Hubbell Law Directory

*PRINCETON,** Mercer Co.

GIBSON & ASSOCIATES (AV)

1345 Mercer Street, 24740
Telephone: 304-425-8276
800-742-3545

MEMBER OF FIRM

Michael F. Gibson

ASSOCIATES

Derrick Ward Lefler Bill Huffman
Kelly R. Charnock

LEGAL SUPPORT PERSONNEL

SOCIAL SECURITY PARALEGALS

Nancy Belcher

PERSONAL INJURY PARALEGALS

Kathy Richards

WORKERS COMPENSATION PARALEGAL

Carol Hylton

MEDICAL NEGLIGENCE PARALEGAL

Deborah Fye

For full biographical listings, see the Martindale-Hubbell Law Directory

SANDERS, AUSTIN, SWOPE & FLANIGAN (AV)

Hunter Park, 320 Courthouse Road, 24740
Telephone: 304-425-8125
FAX: 304-425-4155

MEMBERS OF FIRM

Hartley Sanders (1879-1952) William H. Sanders, III
Lane O. Austin William B. Flanigan
Derek C. Swope Gregory S. Prudich

ASSOCIATES

S. Paige Burress Omar J. Aboulhosn

OF COUNSEL

William H. Sanders, II

References: First Community Bank-Princeton; One Valley Bank-Princeton.

For full biographical listings, see the Martindale-Hubbell Law Directory

WHITES LAW OFFICES (AV)

1426 Main Street, 24740
Telephone: 304-425-8781

MEMBERS OF FIRM

Ben B. White, Jr. Ben B. White, III

ASSOCIATES

Edward K. Rotenberry Dwayne E. Cyrus

References: Mercer County Bank; Princeton Bank & Trust Co.

For full biographical listings, see the Martindale-Hubbell Law Directory

*WHEELING,** Ohio Co.

GOMPERS, BUCH, MCCARTHY & MCCLURE (AV)

Suite 302, Board of Trade Building, 26003
Telephone: 304-233-2450
Fax: 304-233-3656

MEMBERS OF FIRM

William J. Gompers (1887-1957) T. Carroll McCarthy, Jr.
Joseph A. Gompers James T. McClure
Harry L. Buch John E. Gompers

For full biographical listings, see the Martindale-Hubbell Law Directory

SCHRADER, RECHT, BYRD, COMPANION & GURLEY (AV)

1000 Hawley Building, 1025 Main Street, P.O. Box 6336, 26003
Telephone: 304-233-3390
Fax: 304-233-2769
Martins Ferry, Ohio Office: 205 North Fifth Street, P.O. Box 309.
Telephone: 614-633-8976.
Fax: 614-633-0400.

(See Next Column)

SCHRADER, RECHT, BYRD, COMPANION & GURLEY—*Continued*

PARTNERS

Henry S. Schrader (Retired)
Arthur M. Recht
Ray A. Byrd
James F. Companion
Terence M. Gurley
Frank X. Duff
Teresa Rieman-Camilletti
Yolonda G. Lambert
Patrick S. Casey
Sandra M. Chapman
Daniel P. Fry (Resident, Martins Ferry, Ohio Office)
James P. Mazzone

ASSOCIATES

Sandra K. Law
D. Kevin Coleman
Denise A. Jebbia
Edythe A. Nash
Robert G. McCoid
Denise D. Klug
Thomas E. Johnston

OF COUNSEL

James A. Byrum, Jr.

General Counsel: WesBanco Bank-Elm Grove.
Representative Clients: CIGNA Property and Casualty Cos.; Columbia Gas Transmission Corp.; Commercial Union Assurance Co.; Hazlett, Burt & Watson, Inc.; Stone & Thomas Department Stores; Transamerica Commercial Finance Corp.; Wheeling-Pittsburgh Steel Corp.

For full biographical listings, see the Martindale-Hubbell Law Directory

SEIBERT, KASSERMAN, FARNSWORTH, GILLENWATER, GLAUSER, RICHARDSON & CURTIS, L.C. (AV)

1217 Chapline Street, P.O. Box 311, 26003
Telephone: 304-233-1220
Fax: 304-233-4813

Carl B. Galbraith (1903-1972)
George H. Seibert, Jr. (1913-1986)
Ronald W. Kasserman
Sue Seibert Farnsworth
James E. Seibert
Elba Gillenwater, Jr.
M. Jane Glauser
Randolf E. Richardson
Ronald William Kasserman
Linda Weatherholt Curtis
Donald A. Nickerson, Jr.

Representative Clients: Ohio Valley Medical Center, Inc.; Ohio Valley Window Co.; The Travelers Cos.
Reference: United National Bank - Wheeling, W. Va.

For full biographical listings, see the Martindale-Hubbell Law Directory

WISCONSIN

*APPLETON,** Outagamie Co.

MCCANNA, KONZ, DUDAS & ASSOCIATES, S.C. (AV)

47 Park Place, P.O. Box 1857, 54913-1857
Telephone: 414-734-2825
Fax: 414-734-9770

Michael R. McCanna
Michael P. Konz
David G. Dudas

Representative Clients: Allstate Insurance Co.; American States Insurance Co.; Auto Owners Insurance Co.; Custom Marine Engineering, Inc.; Economy Fire & Casualty Co.; General Casualty Companies; C. R. Meyer & Sons Company; Northbrook Property & Casualty Co.; State Farm Cos.; West Bend Mutual Insurance Co.

For full biographical listings, see the Martindale-Hubbell Law Directory

BROOKFIELD, Waukesha Co.

NELSON, DRIES & ZIMMERMAN, S.C. (AV)

150 North Sunnyslope Road, Suite 305, 53005
Telephone: 414-789-5880
Facsimile: 414-789-5888

Craig W. Nelson
Christine K. Nelson
James J. Dries
Jerry D. Zimmerman
Robert W. Connell
Mark S. Nelson
Mark R. Kramer
Christopher J. Conrad
Kurt R. Anderson
Sherri A. Wolske

For full biographical listings, see the Martindale-Hubbell Law Directory

*EAU CLAIRE,** Eau Claire Co.

CARROLL, POSTLEWAITE, GRAHAM & PENDERGAST, S.C. (AV)

419 South Barstow Street, P.O. Box 1207, 54702
Telephone: 715-834-7774
Fax: 715-834-1298

Thomas J. Graham, Jr.

Attorneys for: Metropolitan Life Insurance Co.; The Continental Insurance Cos.; Indemnity Insurance Company of N.A.; Travelers Insurance Co.; Sentry Insurance Co.; Rural Mutual Insurance Co.; State Farm Insurance Co.; Tower Insurance Co.; Wisconsin Reinsurance Corp.

(See Next Column)

For Complete List of Firm Personnel, See General Section

For full biographical listings, see the Martindale-Hubbell Law Directory

KELLY & RYBERG, S.C. (AV)

1620 Ohm Avenue, P.O. Box 479, 54702-0479
Telephone: 715-833-9640
Facsimile: 715-833-9711

Richard J. Kelly
J. Drew Ryberg

Michael F. O'Brien
Kristina Marie Bourget

Reference: Firstar Bank.

For full biographical listings, see the Martindale-Hubbell Law Directory

WILCOX, WILCOX, DUPLESSIE, WESTERLUND & ENRIGHT (AV)

1030 Regis Court, P.O. Box 128, 54701
Telephone: 715-832-6645
Fax: 715-832-8438

MEMBERS OF FIRM

Roy P. Wilcox (1873-1946)
Francis J. Wilcox
Roy S. Wilcox
Richard D. Duplessie
William J. Westerlund
Daniel A. Enright
John F. Wilcox

Attorneys for: St. Paul Fire & Marine Insurance; Wisconsin Health Care Liability Insurance Health Plan; Allstate Insurance; Rural Insurance Co.; Farmers Insurance; Federated Insurance.

For full biographical listings, see the Martindale-Hubbell Law Directory

*GREEN BAY,** Brown Co.

DENISSEN, KRANZUSH, MAHONEY & EWALD, S.C. (AV)

3000 Riverside Drive, P.O. Box 10597, 54307-0597
Telephone: 414-435-4391
Fax: 414-435-0730

Cletus G. Chadek (1900-1957)
Frank P. Cornelisen (1902-1967)
Charles M. Denissen (1906-1991)
Shannon D. Mahoney (1935-1993)
William J. Ewald
Mark A. Pennow
Mary Beth Callan
F. Scott Wochos
John K. Gorton
James R. Gorton
Erik J. Pless
Beth Rahmig Pless

OF COUNSEL

Eugene D. Kranzush

Representative Clients: Aetna Casualty & Surety Co.; Wausau Insurance Cos.; The Home Insurance Cos.; CIGNA/Insurance Company of North America; Maryland Casualty Co.; Firemans' Fund American Insurance Cos.; Sentry-Dairyland Claims Service; Underwriters Adjusting Co.; The Hartford.

For full biographical listings, see the Martindale-Hubbell Law Directory

SCHOBER & ULATOWSKI, S.C. (AV)

414 East Walnut Street, Suite 150, 54305-1780
Telephone: 414-432-5355
Facsimile: 414-432-5967

Thomas L. Schober

Michael J. Kirschling

For full biographical listings, see the Martindale-Hubbell Law Directory

LAKE GENEVA, Walworth Co.

BRADEN & OLSON (AV)

716 Wisconsin Street, P.O. Box 940, 53147
Telephone: 414-248-6636
Fax: 414-248-2901

Berwyn B. Braden
John O. Olson

Michael J. Rielly
Kurt T. Van Buskirk
Christine Tomas (Not admitted in WI)

For full biographical listings, see the Martindale-Hubbell Law Directory

*MADISON,** Dane Co.

AXLEY BRYNELSON (AV)

(Formerly Brynelson, Herrick, Bucaida, Dorschel & Armstrong Including the former Easton & Assoc., S.C.)
2 East Mifflin Street, P.O. Box 1767, 53701-1767
Telephone: 608-257-5661
Fax: 608-257-5444

(See Next Column)

AXLEY BRYNELSON, *Madison—Continued*

MEMBERS OF FIRM

Frank J. Bucaida
Bradley D. Armstrong
John H. Schmid, Jr.
Timothy D. Fenner
John C. Mitby
Daniel T. Hardy
John Walsh
Bruce L. Harms
David Easton
Curtis C. Swanson
Michael S. Anderson
Patricia M. Gibeault
Michael J. Westcott
Larry K. Libman
Richard E. Petershack
Steven A. Brezinski
Steven M. Streck
Joy L. O'Grosky

ASSOCIATES

Arthur E. Kurtz
Edith F. Merila
Michael J. Modl
Sabin S. Peterson
Paul Voelker
Marcia MacKenzie

OF COUNSEL

Ralph E. Axley
Floyd A. Brynelson
James C. Herrick
Griffin G. Dorschel

For Complete List of Firm Personnel, See General Section

For full biographical listings, see the Martindale-Hubbell Law Directory

BELL, METZNER, GIERHART & MOORE, S.C. (AV)

44 East Mifflin Street, P.O. Box 1807, 53701
Telephone: 608-257-3764
FAX: 608-257-3757

Carroll E. Metzner
Roger L. Gierhart
John M. Moore
Hugh H. Bell
Steven J. Caulum
Ward I. Richter
Barrett J. Corneille
John W. Markson
Stephen O. Murray
Robert J. Kasieta
Mary L. McDaniel

W. Scott McAndrew
David J. Pliner
Teresa Ann Mueller

Counsel for: American Family Mutual Insurance Group; Superior Water, Light & Power Co.; North-West Telecommunications, Inc.; Wisconsin Southern Gas Co., Inc.; St. Paul Fire and Marine Insurance Cos.; Allstate Insurance Co.; Fireman's Fund Insurance Co.

For Complete List of Firm Personnel, See General Section

For full biographical listings, see the Martindale-Hubbell Law Directory

BOARDMAN, SUHR, CURRY & FIELD (AV)

One South Pinckney Street, Suite 410, P.O. Box 927, 53701-0927
Telephone: 608-257-9521
FAX: 608-283-1709

MEMBERS OF FIRM

Henry A. Field, Jr.
Kenneth T. McCormick, Jr.
Bradway A. Liddle, Jr.
Claude J. Covelli
Paul R. Norman
Mark W. Pernitz
Michael P. May
Richard J. Delacenserie
James E. Bartzen
Steven C. Zach
Amanda J. Kaiser
Catherine M. Rottier
Mark J. Steichen
Madelyn D. Leopold

Representative Clients: Liberty Mutual Insurance Co.; Madison Newspapers, Inc.; Minnesota Mutual Life Insurance Co.; Oscar Mayer Foods Corp.; Physicians Insurance Co.; State Farm Insurance Co.; The Medical Protective Co.; Wausau Insurance Cos.; Wisconsin Health Care Liability Insurance Plan; Wisconsin Patients Compensation Fund.

For Complete List of Firm Personnel, See General Section

For full biographical listings, see the Martindale-Hubbell Law Directory

KAY & ANDERSEN, S.C. (AV)

One Point Place, Suite 201, 53719
Telephone: 608-833-0077
Fax: 608-833-3901

Robert J. Kay
Randall J. Andersen

Edith M. Petersen

OF COUNSEL

James C. Geisler

Representative Clients: Ameritech; AT&T Co.; Employers Reinsurance Corp.; Chicago Title Insurance Co.; Dean Foods; Black & Decker, Inc.

For full biographical listings, see the Martindale-Hubbell Law Directory

LAFOLLETTE & SINYKIN (AV)

One East Main, Suite 500, 53703
Telephone: 608-257-3911
Fax: 608-257-0609
Mailing Address: P.O. Box 2719, 53701-2719
Sauk City, Wisconsin Office: 603 Water Street.
Telephone: 608-643-2408.
Stoughton, Wisconsin Office: 113 East Main Street, P.O. Box 191.
Telephone: 608-873-9464.
Fax: 608-873-0781.

MEMBERS OF FIRM

Philip F. LaFollette (1897-1965)
Gordon Sinykin (1910-1991)
James E. Doyle (1915-1987)
Earl H. Munson
Christopher J. Wilcox
Howard A. Sweet
Thomas A. Hoffner
David E. McFarlane
Brady C. Williamson
Robert E. Chritton
Timothy J. Muldowney
Michael E. Skindrud
Teresa M. Elguézabal
Linda M. Clifford
Lawrence Bensky
Jonathan C. Aked
Brett A. Thompson
Richard M. Burnham
Robert J. Dreps
Jeffrey J. Kassel
Noreen J. Parrett
Eugenia G. Carter

ASSOCIATES

Timothy F. Nixon
Joanne R. Whiting

OF COUNSEL

William E. Chritton (Resident, Stoughton Office)
Daniel Sinykin
Frank M. Tuerkheimer

Reference: M&I Madison Bank.

For Complete List of Firm Personnel, See General Section

For full biographical listings, see the Martindale-Hubbell Law Directory

LAWTON & CATES, S.C. (AV)

214 West Mifflin Street, 53703-2594
Telephone: 608-256-9031
Fax: 608-256-4670

John C. Carlson
James A. Olson
James W. Gardner
Kent I. Carnell

Reference: Bank One, Madison.

For full biographical listings, see the Martindale-Hubbell Law Directory

*MILWAUKEE,** Milwaukee Co.

BIRD, MARTIN & SALOMON S.C. (AV)

735 North Water Street, Suite 1600, 53202-4104
Telephone: 414-276-7290
Facsimile: 414-276-7291

John D. Bird, Jr.
Frances H. Martin
Allen M. Salomon

References: Firstar Bank; Biltmore Investors Bank.

For full biographical listings, see the Martindale-Hubbell Law Directory

EHLINGER & KRILL, S.C. (AV)

316 North Milwaukee Street, Suite 410, 53202-5803
Telephone: 414-272-8085
Facsimile: 414-272-8290

Ralph J. Ehlinger
R. Jeffrey Krill

For full biographical listings, see the Martindale-Hubbell Law Directory

FIORENZA & HAYES, S.C. (AV)

Kildeer Court, 3900 West Brown Deer Road, 53209
Telephone: 414-355-3600
Fax: 414-355-8080

John A. Fiorenza
Clare L. Fiorenza
Richard D. Moake
Daniel J. Miske
William J. Mantyh
Lawrence G. Wickert
Jeffrey M. Leggett
Lisa A. Dziadulewicz
Timothy M. Hughes

Representative Clients: M & I Marshall & Ilsley Bank, Silver Spring Division; Valley Bank; Miller-Bradford & Risberg, Inc.; Magnetek, Inc.; Litton Industries, Inc.; Centel Communications, Inc.; FJA Christiansen Roofing Co.; North American Van Lines; Kendor Corp.; Todd Equipment, Inc.

For full biographical listings, see the Martindale-Hubbell Law Directory

GIBBS, ROPER, LOOTS & WILLIAMS, S.C. (AV)

735 North Water Street, 53202
Telephone: 414-273-7000
Fax: 414-273-7897

(See Next Column)

GIBBS, ROPER, LOOTS & WILLIAMS S.C.—*Continued*

Clay R. Williams
John W. Hein
William J. French
Terry E. Nilles
Thomas R. Streifender
Robert L. Gegios
David J. Edquist
Beth J. Kushner

Douglas S. Knott
Mark S. Diestelmeier
Glen E. Lavy
Deanna C. Kress

Representative Clients: Twin Disc, Incorporated.

For Complete List of Firm Personnel, See General Section

For full biographical listings, see the Martindale-Hubbell Law Directory

KASDORF, LEWIS & SWIETLIK, S.C. (AV)

(Formerly Kivett and Kasdorf)
1551 South 108th Street, 53214
Telephone: 414-257-1055
Facsimile: 414-257-3759
Green Bay Office: 414 East Walnut Street, Suite 260, 54301.
Telephone: 414-436-0304.

Austin W. Kivett (1898-1993)
Clifford C. Kasdorf
John M. Swietlik
James P. Reardon
Werner E. Scherr
Terrance E. Davczyk
Jeff Schmeckpeper
Gregory J. Cook
Michael J. Cieslewicz
Michael A. Mesirow
William J. Katt
Joseph J. Ferris
James J. Kriva
David L. Styer
Robert J. Lauer
Emile H. Banks, Jr.
James M. Ryan
Robert P. Ochowicz

Michael C. Frohman
Charles G. Maris
John E. Cain
Vicki L. Arrowood
Christine M. Benson
Denise M. Harron
Kevin A. Christensen
Michael S. Murray
Cecilia M. McCormack
Denise Y. Bowen
Timothy S. Trecek
Christopher D. Stombaugh
Kristin M. Cafferty

OF COUNSEL

Kenton E. Kilmer
Hugh E. Russell
Robert B. Corris
Patti J. Kurth

Representative Clients: Bic Corporation; Dresser Industries; Browning-Ferris Industries; Bucyrus-Erie, Inc.; Baker Industries; NTB, Inc.; Canon, Inc.; Eli Lilly, Inc.; Milwaukee Transport Services, Inc.; Helwig Carbon Products Co.

For full biographical listings, see the Martindale-Hubbell Law Directory

KERSTEN & MCKINNON, S.C. (AV)

231 West Wisconsin Avenue, Suite 1200, 53203
Telephone: 414-271-0054
Fax: 414-271-7131

Charles J. Kersten (1925-1972)
J. P. McKinnon (1943-1973)
Arlo McKinnon
E. Campion Kersten
George P. Kersten
Kenan J. Kersten
Dyan Evans Barbeau
Leslie Van Buskirk
Sheila M. Hanrahan

For full biographical listings, see the Martindale-Hubbell Law Directory

KOHNER, MANN & KAILAS, S.C. (AV)

1572 East Capitol Drive, P.O. Box 19982, 53211-0982
Telephone: 414-962-5110
Fax: 414-962-8725

Marvin L. Kohner (1908-1975)
Robert L. Mann
Steve Kailas
Mark R. Wolters
Jordan B. Reich
David S. Chartier

Roy Paul Roth
Gary P. Lantzy
Christopher C. Kailas
Robert E. Nailen
Matthew P. Gerdisch
Darrell R. Zall
Daniel J. Flynn
Timothy L. Zuberbier
Shawn G. Rice

Representative Clients: EcoLab, Inc.; Parker Pen Co.; Ray O Vac, Inc.

For full biographical listings, see the Martindale-Hubbell Law Directory

MURPHY, GILLICK, WICHT & PRACHTHAUSER (AV)

Suite 1200, 330 East Kilbourn Avenue, 53202
Telephone: 414-271-1011
Milwaukee: 1-800-942-2880
South Office: Edgewood Bank Building, 4811 South 76th Street.
Telephone: 414-281-5700.
North Office: Northridge Bank Building, 9001 North 76th Street.
Telephone: 414-354-5051.
Appleton, Wisconsin Office: 54 Park Place.
Telephone: 414-730-0200. Appleton: 1-800-942-2882.

(See Next Column)

Brookfield, Wisconsin Office: Brookfield Lakes Corporate Center, 300 North Corporate Drive (180th Street and Blue Mound Road).
Telephone: 414-792-0888.

MEMBERS OF FIRM

Lawrence D. Gillick (1914-1984)
James J. Murphy
Michael H. Gillick
Dennis H. Wicht
Don C. Prachthauser
Anthony W. Welhouse (Resident, Appleton Office)
George F. Graf (Resident, Brookfield Office)
Patrick J. Gillick
Melita M. Biese
Kevin J. Kukor

ASSOCIATES

Keith R. Stachowiak
John J. Laffey
Thadd J. Llaurado
Mark D. Baus

OF COUNSEL

M. Josef Zimmermann

For full biographical listings, see the Martindale-Hubbell Law Directory

QUARLES & BRADY (AV)

411 East Wisconsin Avenue, 53202-4497
Telephone: 414-277-5000
Cable Address: "Lawdock"
Fax: 414-271-3552.
TWX: 910-262-3426
Madison, Wisconsin Office: Firstar Plaza, One South Pinckney Street, P.O. Box 2113.
Telephone: 608-251-5000.
Fax: 608-251-9166.
West Palm Beach, Florida Office: 222 Lakeview Avenue, 4th Floor.
Telephone: 407-653-5000.
Fax: 407-653-5333.
Naples, Florida Office: Barnett Center, 4501 Tamiami Trail North.
Telephone: 813-262-5959.
Fax: 813-434-4999.
Phoenix, Arizona Office: One Camelback Building, One East Camelback Road, Suite 400.
Telephone: 602-230-5500.
Fax: 602-230-5598.

MEMBERS OF FIRM
(ALPHABETICALLY BY YEAR OF ADMISSION TO BAR)

Charles Q. Kamps
Thomas O. Kloehn
Richard C. Ninneman
Samuel J. Recht
James A. McSwigan (Resident, West Palm Beach, Florida Office)
Ross R. Kinney
Michael J. Spector
George K. Whyte, Jr.
Michael L. Zaleski (Resident, Madison Office)
Wayne E. Babler, Jr.
W. Stuart Parsons
Frank J. Daily
Charles W. Herf (Resident, Phoenix, Arizona Office)
David E. Jarvis
Larry J. Martin
Ronald L. Wallenfang
Michael S. Weiden (Resident, Madison Office)
John A. Casey
Peter C. Karegeannes
William M. Shattuck (Resident, Phoenix, Arizona Office)
James H. Baxter III
Quinn W. Martin
Michael J. McGovern
Ned R. Nashban (Resident, West Palm Beach, Florida Office)
Robert L. Titley
Bruce R. Bauer
O. Thomas Armstrong
Robert E. Doyle, Jr. (Resident, Naples, Florida Office)
Matthew J. Flynn
Roy L. Prange, Jr. (Resident, Madison Office)
Michael H. Schaalman
Patrick W. Schmidt
Mary Pat Ninneman
Eric J. Van Vugt
Patricia K. McDowell
Carolyn A. Gnaedinger
William D. McEachern (Resident, West Palm Beach, Florida Office)
David B. Kern
Ely A. Leichtling
Jeffrey Morris
John A. Rothstein
William H. Harbeck
Donald K. Schott (Resident, Madison Office)
Ralph V. Topinka (Resident, Madison Office)
David B. Bartel
David R. Cross
Nancy Meissner Kennedy
Daniel L. Muchow (Resident, Phoenix, Arizona Office)
Michael J. Gonring
John D. Franzini
Thomas P. McElligott
Robert H. Duffy
Mark A. Kircher
Daniel E. Conley

OF COUNSEL

Laurence C. Hammond, Jr.
William A. Stearns

ASSOCIATES

Lindy P. Funkhouser (Mr.) (Resident, Phoenix, Arizona Office)
William G. Shofstall (Resident, West Palm Beach, Florida Office)
Waltraud A. Arts (Resident, Madison Office)
Erica M. Eisinger (Resident, Madison Office)
Cynthia L. Jewett (Resident, Phoenix, Arizona Office)
James Brennan
Francis H. LoCoco
Jeffrey O. Davis
Stuart S. Mermelstein (Resident, West Palm Beach, Florida Office)
Michelle M. Thorpe (Resident, Phoenix, Arizona Office)
Sharon S. Moyer (Resident, Phoenix, Arizona Office)
Benjamin R. Norris (Resident, Phoenix, Arizona Office)

(See Next Column)

QUARLES & BRADY, *Milwaukee—Continued*

ASSOCIATES (Continued)

Nancy Berz Colman (Resident, West Palm Beach, Florida Office)
Louis D. D'Agostino (Resident, Naples, Florida Office)
Christopher H. Kallaher
Anthony A. Tomaselli (Resident, Madison Office)
Kevin A. Denti (Resident, Naples, Florida Office)
Margaret C. Kelsey
Andra J. Palmer (Resident, Madison Office)
Jeffrey K. Spoerk
Mark A. Dotson
Carmella A. Huser
Jose L. Martinez (Resident, Phoenix, Arizona Office)
Sandra L. Tarver (Resident, Madison Office)
Elizabeth A. Dougherty (Resident, West Palm Beach, Florida Office)
Mitchell S. Moser
Kevin P. Crooks
Letha Joseph
Nora M. Platt
Harold O.M. Rocha
Daniel M. Janssen
Amy O'Melia-Endres (Resident, Phoenix, Arizona Office)

For Complete List of Firm Personnel, See General Section

For full biographical listings, see the Martindale-Hubbell Law Directory

REINHART, BOERNER, VAN DEUREN, NORRIS & RIESELBACH, S.C. (AV)

1000 North Water Street, P.O. Box 92900, 53202-0900
Telephone: 414-298-1000
Facsimile: 414-298-8097
Denver, Colorado Office: One Norwest Center, 1700 Lincoln Street, Suite 3725.
Telephone: 303-831-0909.
Fax: 303-831-4805.
Madison, Wisconsin Office: 7617 Mineral Point Road, 53701-2020.
Telephone: 608-283-7900.
Fax: 608-283-7919.
Washington, D.C. Office: 601 Pennsylvania Avenue, N.W., North Building, Suite 750.
Telephone: 202-393-3636.
Fax: 202-393-0796.

Paul V. Lucke
William R. Steinmetz
Stephen T. Jacobs
Scott W. Hansen
Richard P. Carr
Anne Willis Reed
Francis W. Deisinger
Steven P. Bogart

R. Timothy Muth
Anne Morgan Hlavacka
Kathleen S. Donius
Christine L. Thierfelder
David J. Sisson
Patrick J. Hodan
Katherine McConahay Nealon
Colleen D. Ball
Dean E. Mabie
Geri Krupp-Gordon
Daniel J. La Fave
David G. Hanson

For Complete List of Firm Personnel, See General Section

For full biographical listings, see the Martindale-Hubbell Law Directory

SLATTERY, HAUSMAN & HOEFLE, LTD. (AV)

The Milwaukee Center, Suite 1800, 111 East Kilbourn Avenue, 53202
Telephone: 414-271-4555
Facsimile: 414-271-9045

Robert A. Slattery
C. Michael Hausman
Paul R. Hoefle

Alan E. Gesler
Steven J. Snedeker

For full biographical listings, see the Martindale-Hubbell Law Directory

NEW RICHMOND, St. Croix Co.

DOAR, DRILL & SKOW, S.C. (AV)

103 North Knowles Avenue, 54017
Telephone: 715-246-2211
Fax: 715-246-4405
Baldwin, Wisconsin Office: Office Park.
Telephone: 715-684-3227.

W.T. Doar (1882-1952)
James A. Drill
Thomas D. Bell

OF COUNSEL

W. T. Doar, Jr.

Lisa M. Drill
Matthew Alan Biegert
Michael J. Brose

Counsel for: Bank of New Richmond; Polk County Bank, Centuria, Wis.

For full biographical listings, see the Martindale-Hubbell Law Directory

*OSHKOSH,** Winnebago Co.

CURTIS WILDE & NEAL LAW OFFICES (AV)

1010 West 20th Avenue, P.O. Box 2845, 54903-2845
Telephone: 414-233-1010
Markesan, Wisconsin Office: 10 East Water Street.
Telephone: 414-398-2314.

George W. Curtis
William R. Wilde
John A. Neal

Scott C. Woldt

Reference: Valley Bank.

For full biographical listings, see the Martindale-Hubbell Law Directory

*RHINELANDER,** Oneida Co.

ECKERT & STINGL (AV)

158 South Anderson Street, P.O. Box 1247, 54501-1247
Telephone: 715-369-1624
FAX: 715-369-1273

MEMBERS OF FIRM

Michael L. Eckert
Michael J. Stingl
James O. Moermond, III
Timothy B. Melms

OF COUNSEL

John R. Lund

Reference: M & I Merchants Bank.

For full biographical listings, see the Martindale-Hubbell Law Directory

*STEVENS POINT,** Portage Co.

TERWILLIGER, WAKEEN, PIEHLER & CONWAY, S.C. (AV)

1045 Clark Street, P.O. Box 1060, 54481-8260
Telephone: 715-341-7855
Fax: 715-341-7255
Wausau, Wisconsin Office: 555 Scott Street, P.O. Box 8063.
Telephone: 715-845-2121.

E. John Buzza (Resident)
Mark S. Henkel (Resident)
Gary L. Dreier (Resident)
David A. Ray (Resident)

For Complete List of Firm Personnel, See General Section

For full biographical listings, see the Martindale-Hubbell Law Directory

*WAUKESHA,** Waukesha Co.

CRAMER, MULTHAUF & HAMMES (AV)

1601 East Racine Avenue, P.O. Box 558, 53187
Telephone: 414-542-4278
Telecopier: 414-542-4270

MEMBERS OF FIRM

James W. Hammes
Richard R. Kobriger
Peter J. Plaushines

ASSOCIATES

Kathryn Sawyer Gutenkunst
Timothy J. Andringa
Brian S. Miller

Representative Clients: Waukesha State Bank; Payco American Corp.
Reference: Waukesha State Bank.

For Complete List of Firm Personnel, See General Section

For full biographical listings, see the Martindale-Hubbell Law Directory

*WAUSAU,** Marathon Co.

KELLEY, WEBER, PIETZ & SLATER, S.C. (AV)

530 Jackson Street, 54403-5589
Telephone: 715-845-9211; New York Tie Line: 212-690-7830
FAX: 715-842-9317

Richard J. Weber
Colin D. Pietz
Jerry W. Slater

OF COUNSEL

John W. Kelley

Peter C. Gunther
Michael David Graveley

Representative Clients: Firstar Bank, Wausau.
Reference: Firstar Bank, Wausau.

For full biographical listings, see the Martindale-Hubbell Law Directory

Wausau—Continued

TERWILLIGER, WAKEEN, PIEHLER & CONWAY, S.C. (AV)

555 Scott Street, P.O. Box 8063, 54402-8063
Telephone: 715-845-2121
Fax: 715-845-3538
Stevens Point, Wisconsin Office: 1045 Clark Street, P.O. Box 1060.
Telephone: 715-341-7855.
Fax: 715-341-7255.

Herbert L. Terwilliger (1914-1990)
W. Thomas Terwilliger
E. John Buzza (Resident, Stevens Point Office)
Mark S. Henkel (Resident, Stevens Point Office)
Walter Gene Lew
D. G. Graff
David A. Piehler
Richard W. Zalewski
Robert D. Reid
Randall J. Sandfort
Gary L. Dreier (Resident, Stevens Point Office)
Cassandra Brown Westgate
John P. Runde
Jeffrey J. Strande
David A. Ray (Resident, Stevens Point Office)
Mark A. Klinner
Gregory J. Strasser
Kathleen E. Grant
Kelly S. Benjamin (Resident, Stevens Point Office)
Virginia L. Erdman (Resident, Stevens Point Office)

OF COUNSEL

Emil A. Wakeen
Walter H. Piehler
Neil M. Conway

Representative Clients: American Family Ins. Group; American International Group (AIG); Federated Ins. Co.; General Casualty Company of Wisconsin; Grinnell Mutual Insurance Co.; Heritage Insurance Co.; Kemper Insurance Cos.; Milwaukee Mutual Insurance Co.; Wisconsin Counties Mut. Ins. Co.

For full biographical listings, see the Martindale-Hubbell Law Directory

WYOMING

*CASPER,** Natrona Co.

BROWN & DREW (AV)

Casper Business Center, Suite 800, 123 West First Street, 82601-2486
Telephone: 307-234-1000
800-877-6755
Telefax: 307-265-8025

MEMBERS OF FIRM

Morris R. Massey
Harry B. Durham, III
W. Thomas Sullins, II
Donn J. McCall
John A. Warnick
Thomas F. Reese
Russell M. Blood
J. Kenneth Barbe
Jeffrey C. Brinkerhoff

ASSOCIATES

Jon B. Huss
Carol Warnick
P. Jaye Rippley
Courtney Robert Kepler
Drew A. Perkins

OF COUNSEL

B. J. Baker

Attorneys for: First Interstate Bank of Wyoming, N.A.; Norwest Bank Wyoming, N.A.; Aetna Casualty & Surety Co.; Commercial Union Insurance Co.; The Doctor's Co.; MEDMARC; WOTCO, Inc.; Chevron USA; Kerr-McGee Corp.; Chicago and NorthWestern Transportation Company.

For Complete List of Firm Personnel, See General Section

For full biographical listings, see the Martindale-Hubbell Law Directory

DUNCAN & KOFAKIS (AV)

Suite 325, Key Bank Building, 300 South Wolcott Street, 82601
Telephone: 307-265-0934
Fax: 307-237-0718

Hugh M. Duncan

For full biographical listings, see the Martindale-Hubbell Law Directory

JAMES RICHARD MCCARTY, P.C. (AV)

The Ormsby Mansion, 536 South Center Street, 82601-3195
Telephone: 307-237-1568
FAX: 307-237-1570

James Richard McCarty

For full biographical listings, see the Martindale-Hubbell Law Directory

SCHWARTZ, BON, WALKER & STUDER (AV)

141 South Center, Suite 505, 82601
Telephone: 307-235-6681
Fax: 307-234-5099

(See Next Column)

William T. Schwartz
William S. Bon
Cameron S. Walker
Judith A. W. Studer

ASSOCIATES

Patrick T. Holscher
Peter J. Young
Kathleen J. Doyle

Representative Clients: Key Bank of Casper; Equitable Life Assurance Society; ANR Production; Union Carbide Corp.; Hill Top Shopping Center; Exxon Co., U.S.A.; Armco Steel Corp.; USF&G; American Insurance Cos.

For full biographical listings, see the Martindale-Hubbell Law Directory

VLASTOS, BROOKS & HENLEY, P.C. (AV)

Suite 320, Key Bank Building, 300 South Wolcott, P.O. Box 10, 82602
Telephone: 307-235-6613
Fax: 307-235-6645

J. E. Vlastos
John C. Brooks
John I. Henley
David A. Drell

OF COUNSEL

Wendy S. Eberle

Representative Clients: BKP, real estate developers; St. Paul Insurance Cos.; State Farm Mutual Auto Insurance Co.; Travelers Insurance Cos.; New Mexico Physicians Mutual Liability Co.; State Farm Fire & Casualty Co.; Crum & Forster Commercial Insurance; Golden Rule Insurance Co.; Fortis Benefits Insurance Co.; The Doctors' Company.

For full biographical listings, see the Martindale-Hubbell Law Directory

WILLIAMS, PORTER, DAY & NEVILLE, P.C. (AV)

Suite 300 Durbin Center, 145 South Durbin Street, 82601
Telephone: 307-265-0700
Fax: 307-266-2306

Houston G. Williams
Richard E. Day
Frank D. Neville
Barry G. Williams
Patrick J. Murphy
Stuart R. Day
Ann M. Rochelle
Mark L. Carman
William H. Everett
Stephenson D. Emery
Scott E. Ortiz

Representative Clients: True Industries; Pacific Power & Light Co.; Amoco Oil Co.; Conoco, Inc.; Marathon Oil Co.; Mobil Exploration and Production; Phillips Petroleum Co.; Casper College; USX Corporation; Wyoming Medical Center; First American Title Insurance Company.

For Complete List of Firm Personnel, See General Section

For full biographical listings, see the Martindale-Hubbell Law Directory

*CHEYENNE,** Laramie Co.

FITZGERALD LAW OFFICES (AV)

A Partnership of Professional Corporations
2108 Warren Avenue, 82001-3740
Telephone: 307-634-4000
Telecopier: 307-635-2391
Laramie, Wyoming Office: Suite 505, First National Bank Building.
Telephone: 307-742-4000.

MEMBERS OF FIRM

James E. Fitzgerald (P.C.)
Sharon A. Fitzgerald (P.C.)

OF COUNSEL

A. G. McClintock

For full biographical listings, see the Martindale-Hubbell Law Directory

HATHAWAY, SPEIGHT & KUNZ (AV)

Suite 402, 2424 Pioneer Avenue, P.O. Box 1208, 82003-1208
Telephone: 307-634-7723
Fax: 307-634-0985

MEMBERS OF FIRM

Stanley K. Hathaway
John B. "Jack" Speight
Brent R. Kunz
Rick A. Thompson
Michael B. Rosenthal
Robert T. McCue
Dominique D.Y. Cone

Representative Clients: Pacificorp; Exxon; NERCO; Key Bank of Wyoming; Little America Refining Co.; Sinclair Oil Corp.; Wyoming Refining Company; Blue Cross Blue Shield of Wyoming; Black Hills Bentonite; Rhone Poulenc of Wyoming.

For full biographical listings, see the Martindale-Hubbell Law Directory

HICKEY, MACKEY, EVANS, WALKER & STEWART (AV)

1712 Carey Avenue, P.O. Drawer 467, 82003
Telephone: 307-634-1525
Telecopier: 307-638-7335

MEMBERS OF FIRM

Paul J. Hickey
Terry W. Mackey
David F. Evans
John M. Walker
Mark R. Stewart III
Richard D. Tim Bush

(See Next Column)

HICKEY, MACKEY, EVANS, WALKER & STEWART, *Cheyenne—Continued*

A List of Representative Clients will be furnished upon request.
Reference: Norwest Bank, Cheyenne, N.A.

For full biographical listings, see the Martindale-Hubbell Law Directory

LATHROP & RUTLEDGE, A PROFESSIONAL CORPORATION (AV)

Suite 500 City Center Building, 1920 Thomes Avenue, P.O. Box 4068, 82003-4068
Telephone: 307-632-0554
Telecopier: 307-635-4502

Carl L. Lathrop
J. Kent Rutledge
Corinne E. Rutledge
Loyd E. Smith

Roger E. Cockerille
James T. Dinneen

OF COUNSEL

Arthur Kline
Byron Hirst

General Counsel for: Cheyenne Internal Medicine and Neurology, P.C.; Laramie County School District No. 2; Cheyenne Newspapers, Inc.; Wyoming Hospital Assn.
Insurance Clients: Omaha Property Casualty Insurance Co.; National Chiropractic Insurance Co.; Underwriters at Lloyds; Omaha Property Casualty; Underwriters at Lloyds; CIGNA Insurance Group.

For full biographical listings, see the Martindale-Hubbell Law Directory

SUNDAHL, POWERS, KAPP & MARTIN (AV)

American National Bank Building, 1912 Capitol Avenue, Suite 300, P.O. Box 328, 82001
Telephone: 307-632-6421
FAX: 307-632-7216

MEMBERS OF FIRM

John Alan Sundahl
George E. Powers, Jr.
Paul Kapp
Raymond W. Martin

ASSOCIATES

John A. Coppede
Kay Lynn Bestol

A list of Representative Clients will be furnished upon request.

For full biographical listings, see the Martindale-Hubbell Law Directory

*JACKSON,** Teton Co.

KING AND KING (AV)

Suite 201 Centennial Building, 610 West Broadway, P.O. Box 40, 83001
Telephone: 307-733-2904
Fax: 307-733-1058

MEMBERS OF FIRM

Floyd R. King
Bret F. King

Reference: Key Bank, N.A., Jackson, Wyoming.

For full biographical listings, see the Martindale-Hubbell Law Directory

SPENCE, MORIARITY & SCHUSTER (AV)

15 South Jackson Street, P.O. Box 548, 83001
Telephone: 307-733-7290
Fax: 307-733-5248
Cheyenne, Wyoming Office: Suite 302 Pioneer Center, 2424 Pioneer Avenue, P.O. Box 1006.
Telephone: 307-635-1533.
Fax: 307-635-1539.

MEMBERS OF FIRM

Gerry L. Spence
Edward P. Moriarity
Robert P. Schuster
Gary L. Shockey
J. Douglas McCalla
Roy A. Jacobson, Jr.

ASSOCIATES

Glen G. Debroder
Kent W. Spence
Robert A. Krause
Heather Noble

Reference: First Interstate Bank, Casper, Wyoming.

For Complete List of Firm Personnel, See General Section

For full biographical listings, see the Martindale-Hubbell Law Directory

*LARAMIE,** Albany Co.

FITZGERALD LAW OFFICES (AV)

A Partnership of Professional Corporations
Suite 505, First National Bank Building, 82070
Telephone: 307-742-4000
Cheyenne, Wyoming Office: 2108 Warren Avenue.
Telephone: 307-634-4000.
Telecopier: 307-635-2391.

MEMBERS OF FIRM

James E. Fitzgerald (P.C.)
Sharon A. Fitzgerald (P.C.)

For full biographical listings, see the Martindale-Hubbell Law Directory

PENCE AND MACMILLAN (AV)

501 Garfield Street, P.O. Box 1285, 82070
Telephone: 307-745-3626; 745-3434
Fax: 307-745-8669

MEMBERS OF FIRM

Alfred M. Pence (1905-1980)
H.M. "Hoke" MacMillan, II
Becky N. Klemt
Paul D. Schierer

Attorneys for: Pioneer Canal-Lake Hattie Irrigation District; Allstate Insurance Co.; Albany County School District One; Albany County Hospital District.

For full biographical listings, see the Martindale-Hubbell Law Directory

RIVERTON, Fremont Co.

HOOPER LAW OFFICES, P.C. (AV)

115 North 7th East, P.O. Box 753, 82501
Telephone: 307-856-4331
Fax: 307-856-9026

David B. Hooper
Vance Countryman

Representative Clients: State Farm Insurance Cos.; Riverton State Bank; Dubois National Bank; Fremont Chemical Co.

For full biographical listings, see the Martindale-Hubbell Law Directory

ROCK SPRINGS, Sweetwater Co.

BUSSART, WEST, ROSSETTI, PIAIA & TYLER, P.C. (AV)

Suite A, 409 Broadway, P.O. Box 1020, 82902-1020
Telephone: 307-362-3300; 307-875-4080
Telecopier: 307-362-3309

Ford T. Bussart
L. Galen West
John D. Rossetti
Marvin L. Tyler
David M. Piaia
Michael J. Finn

Representative Clients: City of Green River, Wyoming; Farmers Insurance Co.; Memorial Hospital of Sweetwater County; Rock Springs-Casper Coca-Cola Bottling Co., Inc.; The Rock Springs National Bank; Sweetwater County School District No. 1; Sweetwater County School District No. 2; Western Wyoming Community College; University of Wyoming.
Reference: Rock Springs National Bank, Rock Springs, Wyoming.

For full biographical listings, see the Martindale-Hubbell Law Directory

*SHERIDAN,** Sheridan Co.

DAVIS AND CANNON (AV)

Formerly Burgess, Davis & Cannon
40 South Main Street, P.O. Box 728, 82801
Telephone: 307-672-7491
Fax: 307-672-8955
Cheyenne, Wyoming Office: 2710 Thomes Avenue, P.O. Box 43, 82003.
Telephone: 307-634-3210.
Fax: 307-778-7118.

MEMBERS OF FIRM

Henry A. Burgess (Retired)
Richard M. Davis, Jr.
Kim D. Cannon
Hayden F. Heaphy, Jr.
Anthony T. Wendtland
Kate M. Fox

Representative Clients: Consol, Inc.; Hesston Corporation; Mutual of New York; Peter Kiewit Sons, Inc.; Wichita River Oil Corporation; Phillips Petroleum; First Interstate Bank of Commerce; Merrell Dow Pharmaceuticals, Inc.; Philip Morris, Inc.; Range Telephone Cooperative.

For Complete List of Firm Personnel, See General Section

For full biographical listings, see the Martindale-Hubbell Law Directory

LONABAUGH AND RIGGS (AV)

50 East Loucks Street, P.O. Drawer 5059, 82801
Telephone: 307-672-7444
Telecopier: 307-672-2230

MEMBERS OF FIRM

E. E. Lonabaugh (1861-1938)
A. W. Lonabaugh (1896-1971)
Ellsworth E. Lonabaugh
Dan B. Riggs
Jeffrey J. Gonda
Robert G. Berger
E. Michael Weber
Robert W. Brown
Haultain E. Corbett
Thomas J. Klepperich
Harold E. Meier

ASSOCIATE

Jonathan A. Botten

Representative Clients: Allstate Insurance Co.; CNA Group; Liberty Mutual Insurance Co.; Safeco Insurance Co.; St. Paul Insurance Cos.; U.S.F. & G. Insurance Co.; Kaneb Services, Inc.; Scurlock-Permian Corp.; First Interstate Bank of Commerce.

For full biographical listings, see the Martindale-Hubbell Law Directory

Sheridan—Continued

YONKEE & TONER (AV)

319 West Dow Street, P.O. Box 6288, 82801
Telephone: 307-674-7451
Fax: 307-672-6250

MEMBERS OF FIRM

Lawrence A. Yonkee
Michael K. Davis
Tom C. Toner
John F. Araas

ASSOCIATES

Lynne Ann Collins
John G. Fenn

Representative Clients: Equitable Life Assurance Society of the United States; Travelers Insurance Co.; Hartford Accident & Indemnity Co.; Western Casualty & Surety Co.; The Employers Group; Prudential Insurance Co. of America; State Farm Insurance Co.; Metropolitan Insurance Co.; Ohio Hospital Insurance Co.; Lexington Insurance Company.

For full biographical listings, see the Martindale-Hubbell Law Directory

*TORRINGTON,** Goshen Co.

SIGLER & SMITH LAW OFFICE (AV)

2020 East D Street, 82240
Telephone: 307-532-2121
Fax: 307-532-2122

Bob C. Sigler
Jerry M. Smith

Representative Clients: Key Bank, Torrington, Wyo.; Hill Irrigation District, North Platte Valley Water Users Assn.; Badger Ranch, Inc.; Canyon View Ranch; Van Mark Farms; Gorr Land & Livestock, Inc.; Bloedorn Lumber Co.; Imperial Holly Sugar Co.

PUERTO RICO

SAN JUAN, San Juan Dist.

FIDDLER, GONZÁLEZ & RODRÍGUEZ

Chase Manhattan Bank Building (Hato Rey), P.O. Box 363507, 00936-3507
Telephone: 809-753-3113
Telecopier: 809-759-3123

MEMBERS OF FIRM

Rafael R. Vizcarrondo
Salvador Antonetti-Zequeira
Diego A. Ramos

Representative Clients: The Chase Manhattan Bank, N.A.; General Motors Corp.; Westinghouse Electric Corp.; Pfizer, Inc.; Merck & Co., Inc.; American Cyanamid Co.; Metropolitan Life Insurance Co.; Bacardi Corp.; U.S. Aviation Insurance Group.

For Complete List of Firm Personnel, See General Section

For full biographical listings, see the Martindale-Hubbell Law Directory

GOLDMAN ANTONETTI & CÓRDOVA

American International Plaza Fourteenth & Fifteenth Floors, 250 Muñoz Rivera Avenue (Hato Rey), P.O. Box 70364, 00936-0364
Telephone: 809-759-8000
Telecopiers: 809-767-9333 (Main)
809-767-9177 (Litigation Department)
809-767-8660 (Labor & Corporate Law Departments)
809-767-9325 (Tax & Environmental Law Departments)

MEMBERS OF FIRM

Edgar Cartagena-Santiago
Carlos A. Rodríguez-Vidal
Ramón E. Dapena
Jorge Segurola
Jorge L. Martinez
Edgardo Colón Arrarás
Jesús E. Cuza

ASSOCIATES

Ivonne Palerm Cruz
Marta Figueroa-Torres
Mildred Cabán
Carlos A. García-Pérez
Wilda Rodriguez Plaza
Iván R. Fernández-Vallejo
Ina M. Berlingeri Vincenty

Representative Clients: New England Mutual Life Insurance Co.; Ponce Federal Bank, F.S.B.; Central Soya Feed Co.; Bristol Myers Puerto Rico, Inc.; Xerox Corp.

For Complete List of Firm Personnel, See General Section

For full biographical listings, see the Martindale-Hubbell Law Directory

GONZALEZ & BENNAZAR

Capital Center Building South Tower - 9th Floor, Arterial Hostos Avenue (Hato Rey), 00918
Telephone: 809-754-9191
Fax: 809-754-9325

(See Next Column)

MEMBERS OF FIRM

Raul E. González Díaz
A. J. Bennazar-Zequeira

Representative Clients: American Express Travel Related Services Co., Inc.; Mars, Inc.; Federal Deposit Insurance Corp.; Resolution Trust Co.; GIGNA Insurance Group.; BWAC International; M & M Mars; G-Tech Corporation; Wyndham Hotels; Zurich-American Insurance Group; Pacific Employers Insurance Co.

For Complete List of Firm Personnel, See General Section

For full biographical listings, see the Martindale-Hubbell Law Directory

INDIANO, WILLIAMS & WEINSTEIN-BACAL

Hato Rey Tower, 21st Floor, 268 Muñoz Rivera Avenue (Hato Rey), 00918
Telephone: 809-754-2323; 763-0485
Fax: 809-766-3366
St. Thomas, Virgin Islands Office: Stuart A. Weinstein-Bacal, P.O. Box 9820, Charlotte Amalie, 00801.
Telephone: 809-776-2500.
Telecopier: 809-779-6918.

MEMBERS OF FIRM

Stuart A. Weinstein-Bacal
David C. Indiano
Jeffrey M. Williams

ASSOCIATES

Javier A. Morales Ramos
Madeline Garcia-Rodriguez

For full biographical listings, see the Martindale-Hubbell Law Directory

JORGE R. JIMENEZ

Suite 807 Bankers Finance Tower, 654 Muñoz Rivera Avenue (Hato Rey), 00918
Telephone: 809-763-0106
Fax: 809-763-0574

For full biographical listings, see the Martindale-Hubbell Law Directory

JIMÉNEZ, GRAFFAM & LAUSELL

Formerly Jiménez & Fusté
Suite 505, Midtown Building, 421 Muñoz Rivera Avenue, Hato Rey, P.O. Box 366104, 00936-6104
Telephone: 809-767-1030; 767-1000; 767-1061; 767-1064
Telefax: 809-751-4068;
Cable: "Nezte"; RCA
Telex: 325-2730

MEMBERS OF FIRM

Nicolás Jiménez
J. Ramón Rivera-Morales
William A. Graffam
José Juan Torres-Escalera
Steven C. Lausell
Raquel M. Dulzaides
Manuel San Juan

ASSOCIATES

Manolo T. Rodríguez-Bird
Carlos E. Bayrón
Patricia Garrity
Isabel J. Vélez-Serrano
Edgardo A. Vega-López

Representative Clients: Sea-Land Service, Inc.; McAllister Brothers; Crowley Maritime Corp.; Puerto Rico Sun Oil; General Motors Overseas Distribution Corp.; Bristol Myers Squibb Co.; The United Kingdom Steamship P & I Association; The Britannia Steamship Insurance Association.

For Complete List of Firm Personnel, See General Section

For full biographical listings, see the Martindale-Hubbell Law Directory

MÁRTINEZ ODELL & CALABRIA

Banco Popular Center, 16th Floor, (Hato Rey), P.O. Box 190998, 00919-0998
Telephone: 809-753-8914
Facsimile: 809-753-8402; 809-759-9075; 809-764-5664

MEMBERS OF FIRM

Jose B. Diaz Asencio
Alberto Rodríguez-Ramos
Patrick D. O'Neill
Benjamín Hernández-Nieves
Fernando A. Pérez-Colon
Anabelle Rodriguez-Rodriguez
Carlos Berreteaga

OF COUNSEL

Eugenio C. Romero

ASSOCIATES

Maria del Carmen Garriga
Jose Antonio Fernandez-Jaquete
Eric Perez Ochoa
Eileen Landrón-Guardiola
Ramón Eugenio-Meléndez
M. Georgina Carrion-Christiansen

Representative Clients: A.T. & T. Corp.; Pepsi-Cola P.R. Bottling Co.; Banco Popular de Puerto Rico; I.T.T. Financial Corp.; John H. Harland Company of Puerto Rico, Inc.; Lutron Electronics Co., Inc.; Paine Webber, Inc.; Lotus Development Corp.; Western Digital.

For Complete List of Firm Personnel, See General Section

For full biographical listings, see the Martindale-Hubbell Law Directory

San Juan—Continued

MELLADO & MELLADO-VILLARREAL

Suite 202, 165 Ponce de Leon Avenue, 00918
Telephone: 809-767-2600
Telecopier: 809-767-2645

Ramon Mellado-Gonzalez   Jairo Mellado-Villarreal

Representative Clients: Advanced Cellular Systems; Coulter Biochemical; Coulter Electronics Sales; Meyers Parking System, Inc.; Magla Products Corporation; San Juan Gas Co., Inc.; Procesadora De Granos De Puerto Rico, Inc.; First Federal Savings Bank; Banesco Internacional Bank; Progreso Internacional Bank; Caribe Federal Credit; P.E.D. Food Distributors; San Juan Realty, Inc.

For Complete List of Firm Personnel, See General Section

For full biographical listings, see the Martindale-Hubbell Law Directory

O'NEILL & BORGES

10th Floor, Chase Manhattan Bank Building (Hato Rey), 254 Muñoz Rivera Avenue, 00918-1995
Telephone: 809-764-8181
Telecopier: 809-753-8944

MEMBERS OF FIRM

Edward M. Borges
David P. Freedman
Carlos M. Maldonado-Casillas
Mario J. Pabón
Pedro J. Santa-Sánchez
Luis Edwin González-Ortiz

ASSOCIATES

Christian M. Echavarri-Junco
Alfredo F. Ramirez-MacDonald
Jacabed Rodriguez-Coss
Gilberto Maymí
David Rivé-Power

Representative Clients: Ford Motor Co.; Kmart Corporation; Mitsubishi Motor Sales of Caribbean, Inc.; Nike International Ltd.; The Procter & Gamble Commercial Co.; Schindler Elevator Corp.; Sealand Corp.; The First National Bank of Boston; Veryfine Products, Inc.; Westinghouse Electric Corp.

For Complete List of Firm Personnel, See General Section

For full biographical listings, see the Martindale-Hubbell Law Directory

VIRGIN ISLANDS

*CHRISTIANSTED, ST. CROIX,** St. Croix

JEAN-ROBERT ALFRED

46B-47 King Street, 00820
Telephone: 809-773-2156
Telecopier: 809-773-4301

COUNSEL

Jane Wells Kleeger

For full biographical listings, see the Martindale-Hubbell Law Directory

*CHARLOTTE AMALIE, ST. THOMAS,** St. Thomas

BORNN BORNN HANDY

No. 8 Norre Gade, P.O. Box 1500, 00804
Telephone: 809-774-1400
Fax: 809-774-9607

PARTNER

Veronica J. Handy

ASSOCIATE

Tregenza A. Roach

References: Bank of Nova Scotia; Banco Popular de P.R., St. Thomas, U.S. Virgin Islands.

For Complete List of Firm Personnel, See General Section

For full biographical listings, see the Martindale-Hubbell Law Directory

GRUNERT STOUT BRUCH & MOORE

24-25 Kongensgade, P.O. Box 1030, 00804
Telephone: 809-774-1320
Fax: 809-774-7839

MEMBERS OF FIRM

John E. Stout
Susan Bruch Moorehead
Treston E. Moore

ASSOCIATES

Maryleen Thomas
Richard F. Taylor
H. Kevin Mart (Not admitted in VI)

OF COUNSEL

William L. Blum

For full biographical listings, see the Martindale-Hubbell Law Directory

CANADA
ALBERTA

*CALGARY,** Calgary Jud. Dist.

BENNETT JONES VERCHERE (AV)

4500 Bankers Hall East, 855-2nd Street S.W., T2P 4K7
Telephone: (403) 298-3100
Facsimile: (403) 265-7219
Edmonton, Alberta Office: 1000, 10035-105 Street.
Telephone: (403) 421-8133.
Facsimile: (403) 421-7951.
Toronto, Ontario Office: 3400 1 First Canadian Place. P.O. Box 130.
Telephone: (416) 863-1200.
Facsimile: (416) 863-1716.
Ottawa, Ontario Office: Suite 1800. 350 Alberta Street, Box 25, K1R 1A4.
Telephone: (613) 230-4935.
Facsimile: (613) 230-3836.
Montreal, Quebec Office: Suite 1600, 1 Place Ville Marie.
Telephone: (514) 871-1200.
Facsimile: (514) 871-8115.

MEMBER OF FIRM

Donnel O. Sabey, Q.C.

For Complete List of Firm Personnel, See General Section

For full biographical listings, see the Martindale-Hubbell Law Directory

*EDMONTON,** Edmonton Jud. Dist.

EMERY JAMIESON (AV)

1700 Oxford Tower, Edmonton Centre, 10235 - 101 Street, T5J 3G1
Telephone: 403-426-5220
Telecopier: 403-420-6277

MEMBERS OF FIRM

Howard T. Emery, Q.C. (1899-1990)
Sydney A. Bercov, Q.C.
Henry B. Martin, Q.C.
W. Paul Sharek
Phyllis A. Smith, Q.C.
Gordon D. Sustrik
Michael J. Penny
Rex M. Nielsen
Susan L. Bercov
Terrence N. Kuharchuk
Murray F. Tait
John H. Jamieson, Q.C. (Retired)
L. Wayne Drewry, Q.C.
Richard B. Drewry
Robert W. Thompson
Andrew R. Hudson
Shirley A. McNeilly
G. Bruce Comba
Donna Carson Read
Bruce F. Hughson
Helen Garwasiuk
Robert D. McDonald

ASSOCIATES

Ellen S. Ticoll
Jeffrey K. Friesen
Blair E. Maxston
Frederica L. Schutz
Donald V. Tomkins
Earl J. Evaniew
Edward T. Yoo
Janet N. Alexander-Smith
Claire M. Klassen
Jennifer Kaufman-Shaw
Regina M. Corrigan

Reference: Canadian Imperial Bank of Commerce.

For full biographical listings, see the Martindale-Hubbell Law Directory

LUCAS BOWKER & WHITE (AV)

Esso Tower - Scotia Place, 1201-10060 Jasper Avenue, T5J 4E5
Telephone: 403-426-5330
Telecopier: 403-428-1066

MEMBERS OF FIRM

George E. Bowker, Q.C.
Robert B. White, Q.C.
E. James Kindrake
Norman J. Pollock
Robert C. Dunseith
Kent H. Davidson
Alan R. Gray
David J. Stam
Donald J. Wilson

ASSOCIATES

Michael Alexander Kirk
Mark E. Lesniak
Eric C. Lund

Reference: Canadian Imperial Bank of Commerce.

For Complete List of Firm Personnel, See General Section

For full biographical listings, see the Martindale-Hubbell Law Directory

McLENNAN ROSS (AV)

600 West Chambers, 12220 Stony Plain Road, P.O. Box 12040, T5J 3L2
Telephone: 403-482-9200
Telecopier: 403-482-9100; 403-482-9101; 403-482-9102
INTERNET: mross@supernet.ab.ca

(See Next Column)

McLennan Ross—*Continued*

Roderick A. McLennan, Q.C. *
David J. Ross, Q.C.
John Sterk, Q.C. *
Peter P. Taschuk, Q.C.
Philip G. Ponting, Q.C.
D. Mark Gunderson *
Havelock B. Madill, Q.C.
Darren Becker *
Brian R. Burrows, Q.C.
Frederick A. Day, Q.C. *
Johanne L. Amonson, Q.C. *
Hugh J. D. McPhail
Kevin J. Anderson *
Jonathan P. Rossall *
Douglas G. Gorman
R. Graham McLennan *
Glenn D. Tait
William S. Rosser *
Yolanda S. Van Wachem
Ronald M. Kruhlak
Michelle G. Crighton
Gerhard J. Seifner
Walter J. Pavlic
Rodney R. Neys
Donald J. McGarvey
Damon S. Bailey
Donald W. Dear
Christopher J. Lane
Scott A. Watson
Clay K. Hamdon
Stephen J. Livingstone
Sandra J. Weber
Doreen C. Mueller
Steven J. Ferner
Douglas J. Boyer
Karen J.A. Metcalfe
John K. Gormley
Katharine L. Hurlburt
Timothy C. Mavko
Lucien R. Lamoureux
Timothy F. Garvin

*Denotes Lawyer Whose Professional Corporation is a Member of the Partnership.

For Complete List of Firm Personnel, See General Section

For full biographical listings, see the Martindale-Hubbell Law Directory

Parlee McLaws (AV)

15th Floor Manulife Place, 10180 101st Street, T5J 4K1
Telephone: 403-423-8500
Telecopier: 403-423-2870
Calgary, Alberta Office: 3400, Western Canadian Place, 707 - 8th Avenue, S.W.
Telephone: 403-294-7000.
Telecopier: 403-265-8263.

MEMBERS OF FIRM

C. H. Kerr, Q.C.
R. A. Newton, Q.C.
M. D. MacDonald
T. A. Cockrall, Q.C.
K. F. Bailey, Q.C.
H. D. Montemurro
R. B. Davison, Q.C.
F. J. Niziol
F. R. Haldane
R. W. Wilson
P. E. J. Curran
I. L. MacLachlan
D. G. Finlay
R. O. Langley
J. K. McFadyen
R. G. McBean
R. C. Secord
J. T. Neilson
D. L. Kennedy
E. G. Rice
D. C. Rolf
J. F. McGinnis
D. F. Pawlowski
J. H. H. Hockin
A. A. Garber
G. W. Jaycock
R. P. James
M. J. K. Nikel
D. C. Wintermute
B. J. Curial
J. L. Cairns
S. L. May
M. S. Poretti

ASSOCIATES

C. R. Head
P. E. S. J. Kennedy
A.W. Slemko
R. Feraco
L. H. Hamdon
R.J. Billingsley
K.A. Smith
N.B.R. Thompson
K. D. Fallis-Howell
P. A. Shenher
D. S. Tam
I. C. Johnson
J.W. McClure
K.G. Koshman
F.H. Belzil
D.D. Dubrule
R.A. Renz
G. T. Lund
J.G. Paulson
W.D. Johnston
K. E. Buss
G. E. Flemming
B. L. Andriachuk
K. P. Nayyer

For full biographical listings, see the Martindale-Hubbell Law Directory

Spitz & Carr (AV)

1870 Metropolitan Place, 10303 Jasper Avenue, T5J 3N6
Telephone: 403-428-0792
Telecopier (FAX): 403-424-7130

MEMBERS OF FIRM

Derek Spitz, Q.C. *
James W. Carr *

ASSOCIATES

Michael Kraus
Quinten Anderson

*Denotes Lawyer Whose Professional Corporation is a Member of the Partnership

For full biographical listings, see the Martindale-Hubbell Law Directory

CANADA
BRITISH COLUMBIA

*VANCOUVER,** Vancouver Co.

Camp Church & Associates (AV)

4th Floor, The Randall Building, 555 West Georgia Street, V6B 1Z5
Telephone: 604-689-7555
Fax: 604-689-7554

MEMBERS OF FIRM

J.J. Camp, Q.C.
David P. Church

Giuseppe (Joe) Fiorante
Andrew J. Pearson
Sharon D. Matthews

For full biographical listings, see the Martindale-Hubbell Law Directory

Harper Grey Easton (AV)

3100 Vancouver Centre, 650 West Georgia Street, P.O. Box 11504, V6B 4P7
Telephone: 604-687-0411
Telex: 04-55448
Telecopier: 604-669-9385

MEMBERS OF FIRM

Harvey J. Grey, Q.C.
Paul T. McGivern
L. N. Matheson
Stephen P. Grey
W. J. McJannet
Peter M. Willcock
James M. Lepp
James A. Doyle
Bryan G. Baynham
Maureen L. A. Lundell
C. E. Hinkson, Q.C.
Laura B. Gerow
Gordon G. Hilliker
Barbara J. Norell
M. M. Skorah
Guy Patrick Brown
Kathryn E. Neilson, Q.C.
Bernard S. Buettner
G. Bruce Butler
Loreen M. Williams

ASSOCIATES

Kieron G. Grady
M. Lynn McBride
Juliet A. Donnici
David W. Pilley
Cheryl L. Talbot
Anu K. Khanna
William S. Clark
Bena Wendy Stock

Solicitors for: Commercial Union Assurance Company of Canada; Lumbermens Mutual Casualty Co.; State Farm Fire and Casualty Co.

For Complete List of Firm Personnel, See General Section

For full biographical listings, see the Martindale-Hubbell Law Directory

Russell & DuMoulin (AV)

2100-1075 West Georgia Street, V6E 3G2
Telephone: 604-631-3131
Fax: 604-631-3232
A Member of the national association of Borden DuMoulin Howard Gervais, comprising Russell & DuMoulin, Vancouver, British Columbia; Howard Mackie, Calgary, Alberta; Borden & Elliot, Toronto, Ontario; Mackenzie Gervais, Montreal, Quebec and Borden DuMoulin Howard Gervais, London, England.
Strategic Alliance with Perkins Coie with offices in Seattle, Spokane and Bellevue, Washington; Portland, Oregon; Anchorage, Alaska; Los Angeles, California; Washington, D.C.; Hong Kong and Taipei, Taiwan.
Represented in Hong Kong by Vincent T.K. Cheung, Yap & Co.

MEMBERS OF FIRM

W. S. Berardino, Q.C.
Douglas G. S. Rae

Representative Clients: Alcan Smelters & Chemicals Ltd.; The Bank of Nova Scotia; Canada Trust Co.; The Canada Life Assurance Co.; Forest Industrial Relations Ltd.; Honda Canada Inc.; IBM Canada Ltd.; Macmillan Bloedel Ltd.; Nissho Iwai Canada Ltd.; The Toronto-Dominion Bank.

For Complete List of Firm Personnel, See General Section

For full biographical listings, see the Martindale-Hubbell Law Directory

CANADA
MANITOBA

*WINNIPEG,** Eastern Jud. Dist.

Aikins, MacAulay & Thorvaldson (AV)

Thirtieth Floor, Commodity Exchange Tower, 360 Main Street, R3C 4G1
Telephone: 204-957-0050
Fax: 204-957-0840

MEMBERS OF FIRM

Michael J. Mercury, Q.C.
Knox B. Foster, Q.C.
Cyril G. Labman
Colin R. MacArthur, Q.C.
Rod E. Stephenson, Q.C.
Eleanor R. Dawson, Q.C.
Daryl J. Rosin
L. William Bowles

(See Next Column)

AIKINS, MACAULAY & THORVALDSON, *Winnipeg—Continued*

MEMBERS OF FIRM (Continued)

Thor J. Hansell
Helga D. Van Iderstine
D. Salín Guttormsson
Barbara S. MacDonald

Counsel for: Air Canada; Bank of Montreal; Boeing of Canada; Canada Safeway Limited; Canadian Medical Protective Association; Federal Industries Ltd.; The Great West Life Assurance Company; John Labatt Limited; Winnipeg Free Press; Winnipeg Jets.

For Complete List of Firm Personnel, See General Section

For full biographical listings, see the Martindale-Hubbell Law Directory

CANADA NEW BRUNSWICK

*FREDERICTON,** York Co.

HANSON, HASHEY (AV)

Suite 400 Phoenix Square, Queen Street, P.O. Box 310, E3B 4Y9
Telephone: 506-453-7771
Telecopier: 506-453-9600
Saint John, New Brunswick Office: One Brunswick Square, Suite 1212.
Telephone: 506-652-7771.
Telecopier: 506-632-9600.

MEMBERS OF FIRM

David T. Hashey, Q.C.
David M. Norman, Q.C.
Michael E. Bowlin
Julian A. G. Dickson
Anne D. Wooder
J. Charles Foster
Lucie Richard

ASSOCIATES

Catherine M. Bowlen
J. Marc Richard
Amanda J. Frenette
Monika M. L. Zauhar

For Complete List of Firm Personnel, See General Section

For full biographical listings, see the Martindale-Hubbell Law Directory

*SAINT JOHN,** Saint John Co.

CLARK, DRUMMIE & COMPANY (AV)

40 Wellington Row, P.O. Box 6850 Station "A", E2L 4S3
Telephone: 506-633-3800
Telecopier (Automatic): 506-633-3811

MEMBERS OF FIRM

Thomas B. Drummie, Q.C.
M. Robert Jette
Norman J. Bossé
Deno P. Pappas, Q.C.
Barry R. Morrison, Q.C.
William B. Richards

Reference: Royal Bank of Canada.

For Complete List of Firm Personnel, See General Section

For full biographical listings, see the Martindale-Hubbell Law Directory

GILBERT, MCGLOAN, GILLIS (AV)

Suite 710, Mercantile Centre, 55 Union Street P.O. Box 7174, Station "A", E2L 4S6
Telephone: 506-634-3600
Telecopier: 506-634-3612

T. Louis McGloan, Q.C. (1896-1986)
Adrian B. Gilbert, Q.C. (1895-1986)

MEMBERS OF FIRM

Donald M. Gillis, Q.C.
Thomas L. McGloan, Q.C.
A. G. Warwick Gilbert, Q.C.
Rodney J. Gillis, Q.C.
Douglas A. M. Evans, Q.C.
Brenda J. Lutz
David N. Rogers

ASSOCIATES

Paulette C. Garnett, Q.C.
Edward Veitch
Hugh J. Flemming, Q.C.
Anne F. MacNeill
Nancy E. Forbes
Marie T. Bérubé
Guy C. Spavold
Claire B.N. Porter
Michael J. Murphy
Mark A. Canty

Representative Clients: Bank of Montreal; Canada Packers Ltd.; McCain Foods Ltd.; The Sunderland Steamship Protecting & Indemnity Association; Steamship Mutual Underwriting Association (Bermuda) Limited; Royal Insurance Co.; Wawanesa Mutual Insurance Co.; Dominion of Canada General Insurance Co.; Canadian General Insurance Co.

For full biographical listings, see the Martindale-Hubbell Law Directory

CANADA NOVA SCOTIA

*HALIFAX,** Halifax Co.

GREEN PARISH (AV)

Tower II, 1401 Purdy's Wharf, P.O. Box 1134, B3J 2X1
Telephone: 902-422-3100
Fax: 902-425-2504

Peter G. Green, Q.C.
Alan V. Parish
Peter A. Doig
Cynthia J. Levy
Lisa M. Welton
William Mahody

For full biographical listings, see the Martindale-Hubbell Law Directory

MCINNES COOPER & ROBERTSON (AV)

1601 Lower Water Street, P.O. Box 730, B3J 2V1
Telephone: 902-425-6500
Fax: 902-425-6350
St. John's, Newfoundland Office: Suite 602, Scotia Centre, 235 Water Street, P.O. Box 547. A1C, 5K8.
Telephone: 709-726-9500.
Fax: 709-726-9550.

Reginald A. Cluney, Q.C.
Stewart McInnes, P.C., Q.C.
James E. Gould, Q.C.
Robert G. Belliveau, Q.C.
Christopher C. Robinson
Thomas E. Hart
Peter M. S. Bryson
Deborah K. Smith
Harry E. Wrathall, Q.C.
David B. Ritcey, Q.C.
George W. MacDonald, Q.C.
Wylie Spicer
Harvey L. Morrison
David A. Graves
Scott C. Norton
Stephen J. Kingston
Eric LeDrew

ASSOCIATES

John Kulik
J. David Connolly
Aidan J. Meade
Michelle C. Awad
Hugh Wright

Attorneys for: Bank of Nova Scotia; Imperial Oil, Limited; Frank B. Hall & Co., Inc. (New York); American Steamship Owners Protection & Indemnity Association, Inc.; Coca-Cola, Ltd.; Scott Worldwide Inc.; Hong Kong Bank of Canada.

For Complete List of Firm Personnel, See General Section

For full biographical listings, see the Martindale-Hubbell Law Directory

CANADA ONTARIO

KITCHENER, Regional Munic. of Waterloo

GIFFEN, LEE, WAGNER, MORLEY & GARBUTT (AV)

50 Queen Street North, P.O. Box 2396, N2H 6M3
Telephone: 519-578-4150
Fax: 519-578-8740

MEMBERS OF FIRM

Jeffrey J. Mansfield (1955-1991)
J. Peter Giffen, Q.C.
Bruce L. Lee
J. Scott Morley
Brian R. Wagner
Philip A. Garbutt

ASSOCIATES

Edward J. Vanderkloet
Keith C. Masterman
Daniel J. Fife
Jeffrey W. Boich

For full biographical listings, see the Martindale-Hubbell Law Directory

*ST. CATHARINES,** Regional Munic. of Niagara

GRAVES AND ASSOCIATES (AV)

Suite 702, 55 King Street, P.O. Box 1690, L2R 7K1
Telephone: 905-641-2020
FAX: 416-641-0484

Edward W. Graves, Q.C.

ASSOCIATES

William F. Elkin
David W. Black
Anna M. Reggio
Dean J. D. Moldenhauer

For full biographical listings, see the Martindale-Hubbell Law Directory

*SAULT STE. MARIE,** Algoma Dist.

Henry M. Lang, Q.C. (AV)

157 East Street, P6A 3C8
Telephone: 705-949-3300
FAX: 705-949-3312

For full biographical listings, see the Martindale-Hubbell Law Directory

*TORONTO,** Regional Munic. of York

Borden & Elliot (AV)

Barristers & Solicitors
Scotia Plaza, 40 King Street West, M5H 3Y4
Telephone: 416-367-6000
Telecopier: 416-367-6749
Internet: @ borden.com
A Member of the national association of Borden DuMoulin Howard Gervais, comprising Borden & Elliot in Toronto, Ontario, Russell & DuMoulin in Vancouver, British Columbia, Howard, Mackie in Calgary, Alberta and Mackenzie Gervais in Montréal, Québec. Borden DuMoulin Howard Gervais also operates an office in London, England.

MEMBER AND ASSOCIATES

Edward A. Ayers, Q.C.

For Complete List of Firm Personnel, See General Section

For full biographical listings, see the Martindale-Hubbell Law Directory

Kelly Affleck Greene (AV)

One First Canadian Place, Suite 840, P.O. Box 489, M5X 1E5
Telephone: 416-360-2800
FAX: 416-360-5960

MEMBERS OF FIRM

W. Anthony Kelly, Q.C.
Donald S. Affleck, Q.C.
Peter R. Greene
James H. Grout
James C. Orr
Robert I. Thornton
John L. Finnigan
Helen A. Daley

ASSOCIATES

Melissa J. Kennedy
D.J. Miller
Aida Van Wees

For full biographical listings, see the Martindale-Hubbell Law Directory

Outerbridge and Miller (AV)

Barristers and Solicitors
571 Jarvis Street, M4Y 2J1
Telephone: 416-968-2023
FAX: 416-968-7958

Ian W. Outerbridge, Q.C.
George C. Miller
Simon Schneiderman
Cynthia R. C. Sefton
C. Gordon Ross
Grace F. Kwan
R. Lee Akazaki
Joseph H. Kary
Mary-Martin Wakim

For full biographical listings, see the Martindale-Hubbell Law Directory

Stockwood, Spies, Craigen & Le Vay (AV)

Suite 2512 The Sun Life Tower, 150 King Street West, M5H 1J9
Telephone: 416-593-7200
Fax: 416-593-9345

David T. Stockwood, Q.C.
Nancy J. Spies
Ronald T. Craigen
Paul H. Le Vay
Brian J. Gover
Robert B. MacKinnon
Timothy H. Mitchell
Christopher H. Wirth
Mary L. Macaulay
Joanne E. Fox
Susan E. Caskey

For full biographical listings, see the Martindale-Hubbell Law Directory

*WINDSOR,** Essex Co.

Gignac, Sutts (AV)

600 Westcourt Place, 251 Goyeau Street, P.O. Box 670, N9A 6V4
Telephone: 519-258-9333
Detroit Michigan: 313-962-0137
Facsimile: Windsor 519-258-9527
Detroit 313-962-0139

MEMBERS OF FIRM

Achille F. Gignac, Q.C. (1902-1984)
Robert E. Barnes, Q.C.
Clifford N. Sutts, Q.C.
Harvey T. Strosberg, Q.C.
Gary V. Wortley
James K. Ball
John C. Holland
William C. Chapman
Mary M. S. Fox
Donald M. Gordon
Sharman Sharkey Bondy
Paul C. Nesseth
Heather Rumble Peterson
Patricia A. Speight
Edward W. Ducharme

(See Next Column)

MEMBERS OF FIRM (Continued)

Michelle A. Gagnon
Craig J. Allen
Werner H. Keller
Francine A. Herlehy
Paul Simard

COUNSEL FOR CRIMINAL MATTERS

Patrick J. Ducharme

For full biographical listings, see the Martindale-Hubbell Law Directory

CANADA PRINCE EDWARD ISLAND

*CHARLOTTETOWN,** Queen's Co.

Campbell, Lea, Michael, McConnell & Pigot (AV)

15 Queen Street, P.O. Box 429, C1A 7K7
Telephone: 902-566-3400
Telecopier: 902-566-9266

MEMBERS OF FIRM

William G. Lea, Q.C.
Robert A. McConnell
Paul D. Michael, Q.C.
Kenneth L. Godfrey

General Counsel in Prince Edward Island for: Canadian Imperial Bank of Commerce; Maritime Electric Co., Ltd.; Michelin Tires (Canada) Ltd.; Newsco Investments Ltd. (Dundas Farms); Queen Elizabeth Hospital Inc.; Imperial Oil Limited; General Motors of Canada; Co-op Atlantic; Liberty Mutual; Employers Reinsurance Group.

For Complete List of Firm Personnel, See General Section

For full biographical listings, see the Martindale-Hubbell Law Directory

CANADA QUEBEC

*MONTREAL,** Montreal Dist.

Byers Casgrain (AV)

A Member of McMillan Bull Casgrain
Suite 3900, 1 Place Ville-Marie, H3B 4M7
Telephone: 514-878-8800
Telecopier: 514-866-2241
Cable Address: "Magee"
Telex: 05-24195

Philippe Casgrain, Q.C.
Jean-Pierre Dépelteau
Luc Giroux
Gérard Dugré
Louis Dumont
Martin Bernard
Christian J. Brossard
Laurent Nahmiash
Stéphane Dansereau
Sophie Latraverse
Ronald Audette
Pierre Grenier
Pascale Nolin
Claude Morency
Josée Dumoulin
Stéphane Lemay
Stéphane W. Miron

OF COUNSEL

J. Arclen Blakely, Q.C.

For Complete List of Firm Personnel, See General Section

For full biographical listings, see the Martindale-Hubbell Law Directory

McMaster Meighen (AV)

A General Partnership
7th Floor, 630 René-Lévesque Boulevard West, H3B 4H7
Telephone: 514-879-1212
Telecopier: 514-878-0605
Cable Address: "Cammerall"
Telex: "Cammerall MTL" 05-268637
Affiliated with Fraser & Beatty in Toronto, North York, Ottawa and Vancouver.

MEMBERS OF FIRM

Alex K. Paterson, O.C., O.Q., Q.C.
Alexis P. Bergeron
Michel A. Pinsonnault
Marc Duchesne
Robert J. Torralbo
Yvan Houle
John G. Murphy
Valérie Beaudin
Jacques Brien
Colin K. Irving
Daniel Ayotte
Diane Quenneville
Richard R. Provost
Jacques Gauthier
Douglas C. Mitchell
Luc Bēliveau
Kurt A. Johnson
Bruce W. Johnston

For Complete List of Firm Personnel, See General Section

For full biographical listings, see the Martindale-Hubbell Law Directory

Montreal—Continued

JOHN J. PEPPER Q.C. AND ASSOCIATES (AV)

1155 Renè Lèvesque Boulevard West, Suite 2500, H3B 2K4
Telephone: 514-875-5454
Fax: 514-875-2004

For full biographical listings, see the Martindale-Hubbell Law Directory

CANADA SASKATCHEWAN

*REGINA,** Regina Jud. Centre

BALFOUR MOSS (AV)

Bank of Montreal Building, 700-2103 11th Avenue, S4P 4G1
Telephone: 306-347-8300
Fax: 306-569-2321
Saskatoon, Saskatchewan Office: 850-410 22nd Street East.
Telephone: 306-665-7844.
Fax: 306-652-1586.

PARTNERS

A. John Beke, Q.C.
Fredrick C. McBeth
Brian J. Scherman (Resident Saskatoon)
D.E. Wayne McIntyre
Jennifer L. Garvie Pritchard
Roger J.F. Lepage
Reginald A. Watson
David C. Knoll (Resident Saskatoon)
Glen S. Lekach
Rick M. Van Beselaere
George E. Nystrom
Jeff N. Grubb

COUNSEL

E. John Moss, Q.C.
Hon. R. James Balfour, Q.C.
Robert A. Milliken, Q.C.
Roy B. Laschuk, Q.C.

ASSOCIATES

Elke Churchman (Resident Saskatoon)
Gordon D. McKenzie (Resident Saskatoon)
Karen M. Bolstad (Resident Saskatoon)
James L. Nugent
Randy R. Semenchuck
Douglas R. Sanders (Resident Saskatoon)
David G. Gerecke (Resident Saskatoon)
W. Kevin Rogers
Phyllis L. Norrie
Michele Klebuc-Simes
W. Andrew Donovan
Isa Gros-Louis Ahenakew (Resident, Saskatoon)
Susan Engel
Gil A. Malfair

Representative Clients: Bank of Montreal; Saskatchewan Wheat Pool; London Life Assurance Co.

For full biographical listings, see the Martindale-Hubbell Law Directory

McDOUGALL, READY (AV)

700 Royal Bank Building, 2010-11th Avenue, S4P 0J3
Telephone: 306-757-1641
Telecopier: 306-359-0785
Saskatoon, Saskatchewan, Canada Office: 301 - 111 2nd Avenue South.
Telephone: 306-653-1641.
Telecopier: 306-665-8511.

MEMBERS OF FIRM

Gordon J. Kuski, Q.C.
R. Shawn Smith
Kenneth A. Ready
Aaron A. Fox
Philip J. Gallet
Ronald L. Miller (Resident, Saskatoon Office)
Brian M. Banilevic
Pamela J. Lothian
Susan B. Barber

Kevin A. Lang
Brent D. Barilla (Resident, Saskatoon Office)
Catherine M. Wall
Erin M.S. Kleisinger
James Nelson Korpan
Penny Overby (Resident, Saskatoon Office)

Representative Clients: Royal Insurance Co.; Reed Stenhouse Inc.; Imperial Oil Ltd.; University of Regina; Chrysler Canada, Ltd.; Ford Motor Co. of Canada, Ltd.; General Motors of Canada, Ltd.

For Complete List of Firm Personnel, See General Section

For full biographical listings, see the Martindale-Hubbell Law Directory

*SASKATOON,** Saskatoon Jud. Centre

GAULEY & CO. (AV)

701 Broadway Avenue, P.O. Box 638, S7K 3L7
Telephone: 306-653-1212
Telecopier: 306-652-1323
Regina, Saskatchewan Office: Suite 400, 2201 11th Avenue S4P 0J8.
Telephone: 306-352-1643.
Telecopier: 306-525-8499.

MEMBERS OF FIRM

David E. "Tom" Gauley, Q.C.
Peter Foley, Q.C.
Robert G. Kennedy
Gary A. Zabos
William A. Grieve

Reference: Royal Bank of Canada.

For Complete List of Firm Personnel, See General Section

For full biographical listings, see the Martindale-Hubbell Law Directory

McKERCHER, McKERCHER & WHITMORE (AV)

374 Third Avenue, South, S7K 1M5
Telephone: 306-653-2000
Fax: 306-244-7335
Regina, Saskatchewan Office: 1000 - 1783 Hamilton Street.
Telephone: 306-352-7661.
Fax: 306-781-7113.

MEMBERS OF FIRM

Robert H. McKercher, Q.C.
Neil G. Gabrielson, Q.C.
J. D. Denis Pelletier
Richard W. Elson
C.J. Glazer
Joel A. Hesje
Gregory A. Thompson

ASSOCIATES

Shaunt Parthev
David E. Thera
Deric B. Karolat
Catherine A. Sloan

For Complete List of Firm Personnel, See General Section

For full biographical listings, see the Martindale-Hubbell Law Directory

COMMERCIAL LAW

ALABAMA

*BIRMINGHAM,** Jefferson Co.

BALCH & BINGHAM (AV)

1710 Sixth Avenue North, P.O. Box 306, 35201
Telephone: 205-251-8100
Facsimile: 205-226-8798
Other Birmingham, Alabama Office: 1901 Sixth Avenue North, 35203.
Telephone: 205-251-8100.
Facsimile: 205-226-8799.
Montgomery, Alabama Office: The Winter Building, 2 Dexter Avenue, 36101.
Telephone: 205-834-6500.
Facsimile: 205-269-3115.
Huntsville, Alabama Office: Suite 810, 200 West Court Square, 35801.
Telephone: 205-551-0171.
Facsimile: 205-551-0174.
Washington, D.C. Office: Suite 800, 1101 Connecticut Avenue, N.W., 20036.
Telephone: 202-296-0387.
Facsimile: 202-452-8180.

MEMBERS OF FIRM

Carey J. Chitwood
H. Hampton Boles
Richard L. Pearson
William S. Wright
Susan B. Bevill
Clark R. Hammond

ASSOCIATE

Felton W. Smith

Counsel for: Alabama Power Co.; Blue Cross and Blue Shield of Alabama; The Boeing Company; Brasfield & Gorrie, Inc.; Compass Bancshares, Inc.; Harbert Corp.; Kimberly-Clark Corp.; Southern Company Services, Inc.; Southern Research Institute; Vesta Insurance Group, Inc.

For Complete List of Firm Personnel, See General Section

For full biographical listings, see the Martindale-Hubbell Law Directory

BRADLEY, ARANT, ROSE & WHITE (AV)

1400 Park Place Tower, 2001 Park Place, 35203
Telephone: 205-521-8000
Telex: 494-1324
Facsimile: 205-251-8611, 251-8665, 252-0264
Facsimile (Southtrust Office): 205-251-9915
Huntsville, Alabama Office: 200 Clinton Avenue West, Suite 900.
Telephone: 205-517-5100.
Facsimile: 205-533-5069.

MEMBERS OF FIRM

Laurence Duncan Vinson, Jr.
Carleta Roberts Hawley
Bobby C. Underwood
J. David Dresher
John D. Watson, III
Michael D. McKibben

ASSOCIATES

J. David Pugh
Kenneth T. Wyatt
T. Michael Brown
L. Susan Doss
J. Patrick Darby
Matthew H. Lembke

For Complete List of Firm Personnel, See General Section

For full biographical listings, see the Martindale-Hubbell Law Directory

HASKELL SLAUGHTER YOUNG & JOHNSTON, PROFESSIONAL ASSOCIATION (AV)

1200 AmSouth/Harbert Plaza, 1901 Sixth Avenue North, 35203
Telephone: 205-251-1000
Facsimile: 205-324-1133
Montgomery, Alabama Office: Haskell Slaughter Young Johnston & Gallion. Bailey Building, Suite 375, 400 South Union Street, P.O. Box 4660. 36104
Telephone: 205-265-8573.
Facsimile: 205-264-7945.

Beall D. Gary, Jr.
Thomas E. Reynolds
Gwen L. Windle

Louise Coker Wyman
R. Scott Williams

Representative Clients: The Equitable Life Assurance Society of the United States; Farm Credit Leasing Services Corporation; Federal Deposit Insurance Corporation/Resolution Trust Corporation; First Alabama Bank, Leasing Division; First National Bank of Chicago; NationsBanc Leasing Corp.; NationsBank of Georgia, N.A.

For Complete List of Firm Personnel, See General Section

For full biographical listings, see the Martindale-Hubbell Law Directory

PRITCHARD, MCCALL & JONES (AV)

800 Financial Center, 35203
Telephone: 205-328-9190

MEMBERS OF FIRM

William S. Pritchard (1890-1967)
Alexander W. Jones (1914-1988)
William S. Pritchard, Jr.
Madison W. O'Kelley, Jr.
Julian P. Hardy, Jr.
Alexander W. Jones, Jr.
F. Hilton-Green Tomlinson
James G. Henderson
William S. Pritchard, III

ASSOCIATES

Michael L. McKerley
Robert Bond Higgins
Nina Michele LaFleur
Mary W. Burge

Representative Clients: First National Bank of Columbiana; Central State Bank of Calera; Buffalo Rock-Pepsi-Cola Bottling Co.; Gillis Advertising, Inc.; Liberty Mutual Insurance Co.; Reliance Insurance Company; SouthTrust Bank, N.A.; Bromberg & Company, Inc.; Farmers Furniture Company; First Commercial Bank.

For full biographical listings, see the Martindale-Hubbell Law Directory

SIROTE & PERMUTT, P.C. (AV)

2222 Arlington Avenue, South, P.O. Box 55727, 35255
Telephone: 205-933-7111
Facsimile: 205-930-5301
Huntsville, Alabama Office: 200 Clinton Avenue, N.W., Suite 1000.
Telephone: 205-536-1711.
Facsimile: 205-534-9650.
Mobile, Alabama Office: One St. Louis Centre, Suite 1000.
Telephone: 205-432-1671.
Facsimile: 205-434-0196.
Montgomery, Alabama Office: Colonial Commerce Center, Suite 305 One Commerce Street.
Telephone: 205-261-3400.
Facsimile: 205-261-3434.
Tuscaloosa, Alabama Office: 2216 14th Street.
Telephone: 205-752-2089.

James L. Permutt
E. M. Friend, Jr.
Harold I. Apolinsky
Joseph S. Bluestein
Richard J. Cohn
J. Mason Davis
Edward M. Friend, III
Jerry E. Held
Maurice L. Shevin
David M. Wooldridge
Jack B. Levy
Steven A. Brickman
John H. Cooper
Timothy A. Bush
Greggory M. Deitsch
Joseph T. Ritchey
Kim E. Rosenfield
Lenora W. Pate (On leave of absence effective June 1, 1993).
John N. Randolph
Bradley J. Sklar
David W. Long
Nanette Sims
Lynda L. Hendrix
J. Scott Sims

Representative Clients: International Business Machines (IBM); General Motors Corp.; Colonial Bank; Bruno's, Inc.; University of Alabama Hospitals; Westinghouse Electric Corp.; First Alabama Bank; Monsanto Chemical Company; South Central Bell; Prudential Insurance Company; American Home Products, Inc.; Minnesota Mining and Manufacturing, Inc. (3M).

For Complete List of Firm Personnel, See General Section

For full biographical listings, see the Martindale-Hubbell Law Directory

SPAIN, GILLON, GROOMS, BLAN & NETTLES (AV)

The Zinszer Building, 2117 2nd Avenue North, 35203
Telephone: 205-328-4100
Telecopier: 205-324-8866

MEMBERS OF FIRM

Samuel H. Frazier
Alton B. Parker, Jr.
J. Birch Bowdre

General Counsel for: Liberty National Life Insurance Co.; United States Fidelity & Guaranty Co.; Piggly Wiggly Alabama Distributing Co.; AmSouth Mortgage Co., Inc.; Alabama Insurance Guaranty Association; Alabama Life and Disability Insurance Guaranty Association; Alabama Insurance Underwriters Association.
Counsel for: The Prudential Insurance Company of America; Government Employees Insurance Co.; Massachusetts Mutual Life Insurance Co.

For Complete List of Firm Personnel, See General Section

For full biographical listings, see the Martindale-Hubbell Law Directory

*GADSDEN,** Etowah Co.

FORD & HUNTER, P.C. (AV)

The Lancaster Building, 645 Walnut Street, Suite 5, P.O. Box 388, 35902
Telephone: 205-546-5432
Fax: 205-546-5435

(See Next Column)

FORD & HUNTER P.C., *Gadsden—Continued*

George P. Ford
J. Gullatte Hunter, III

Richard M. Blythe

References: General Motors Acceptance Corp.; AmSouth Bank, N.A.

For Complete List of Firm Personnel, See General Section

For full biographical listings, see the Martindale-Hubbell Law Directory

*HUNTSVILLE,** Madison Co.

BALCH & BINGHAM (AV)

Suite 810, 200 West Court Square, P.O. Box 18668, 35804-8668
Telephone: 205-551-0171
Facsimile: 205-551-0174
Birmingham, Alabama Offices: 1710 Sixth Avenue North, 35203.
Telephone: 205-251-8100.
Facsimile: 205-226-8798. 1901 Sixth Avenue North, 35203.
Telephone: 205-251-8100.
Facsimile: 205-226-8799.
Montgomery, Alabama Office: The Winter Building, 2 Dexter Avenue, 36101.
Telephone: 205-834-6500.
Facsimile: 205-269-3115.
Washington, D.C. Office: Suite 800, 1101 Connecticut Avenue, N.W., 20036.
Telephone: 202-296-0387.
Facsimile: 202-452-8180.

RESIDENT COUNSEL

John David Snodgrass

RESIDENT MEMBER OF FIRM

S. Revelle Gwyn

RESIDENT ASSOCIATE

Daniel M. Wilson

Counsel for: Alabama Power Co.; Blue Cross and Blue Shield of Alabama; The Boeing Company; Brasfield & Gorrie, Inc.; Compass Bancshares, Inc.; Harbert Corp.; Kimberly-Clark Corp.; Southern Company Services, Inc.; Southern Research Institute; Vesta Insurance Group, Inc.

For full biographical listings, see the Martindale-Hubbell Law Directory

SIROTE & PERMUTT, P.C. (AV)

Suite 1000, 200 Clinton Avenue, N.W., 35801
Telephone: 205-536-1711
Facsimile: 205-534-9650
Birmingham, Alabama Office: 2222 Arlington Avenue, South, P.O. Box 55727.
Telephone: 205-933-7111.
Facsimile: 205-930-5301.
Mobile, Alabama Office: One St. Louis Centre, Suite 1000.
Telephone: 205-432-1671.
Facsimile: 205-434-0196.
Montgomery, Alabama Office: Colonial Commerce Center, Suite 305, One Commerce Street.
Telephone: 205-261-3400.
Facsimile: 205-261-3434.
Tuscaloosa, Alabama Office: 2216 14th Street.
Telephone: 205-752-2089.

Joe H. Ritch
George W. Royer, Jr.
Roderic G. Steakley
Peter L. Lowe, Jr.

For Complete List of Firm Personnel, See General Section

For full biographical listings, see the Martindale-Hubbell Law Directory

*MOBILE,** Mobile Co.

FEIBELMAN, SHULMAN AND TERRY (AV)

150 North Royal Street, Suite 1000, P.O. Box 2082, 36652
Telephone: 334-433-1597
Facsimile: 334-433-1613

MEMBERS OF FIRM

Herbert P. Feibelman, Jr. (1933-1983)
William S. Shulman
Russell S. Terry
Eric J. Breithaupt

Representative Clients: AmSouth Bank; Apex Corp.; Appraisal & Consultant Group, Inc.; Citizens' Bank; Engineered Textile Products, Inc.; First Alabama Bank; First Citizens Bank of Monroe County; ITT Commercial Finance Corp.; Julius Goldstein & Son, Inc..
Reference: First Alabama Bank.

For full biographical listings, see the Martindale-Hubbell Law Directory

FINKBOHNER AND LAWLER (AV)

169 Dauphin Street Suite 300, P.O. Box 3085, 36652
Telephone: 334-438-5871
Fax: 334-432-8052

(See Next Column)

MEMBERS OF FIRM

George W. Finkbohner, Jr.
John L. Lawler
George W. Finkbohner, III
Royce A. Ray, III

For full biographical listings, see the Martindale-Hubbell Law Directory

LYONS, PIPES & COOK, P.C. (AV)

2 North Royal Street, P.O. Box 2727, 36652-2727
Telephone: 334-432-4481
Cable Address: "Lysea"
Telecopier: 334-433-1820

G. Sage Lyons
Marion A. Quina, Jr.
Thomas F. Garth
W. David Johnson, Jr.
Allen E. Graham
Michael C. Niemeyer
John C. Bell

Representative Clients: Aetna Life & Casualty Company; Alabama Insurance Guaranty Association; American Family Life Insurance Company; Carrier's Container Council, Inc.; Champion Incorporation; Chubb; Crawford & Company; Crum & Forster Commercial Insurance; Maryland Casualty Company; Massachusetts Mutual Life Insurance Co.

For Complete List of Firm Personnel, See General Section

For full biographical listings, see the Martindale-Hubbell Law Directory

SIROTE & PERMUTT, P.C. (AV)

One St. Louis Centre, Suite 1000, P.O. Drawer 2025, 36652-2025
Telephone: 334-432-1671
Facsimile: 334-434-0196
Birmingham, Alabama Office: 2222 Arlington Avenue, South, P.O. Box 55727.
Telephone: 205-933-7111.
Facsimile: 205-930-5301.
Huntsville, Alabama Office: 200 Clinton Avenue, N.W., Suite 1000.
Telephone: 205-536-1711.
Facsimile: 205-534-9650.
Montgomery, Alabama Office: Colonial Commerce Center, Suite 305, One Commerce Street.
Telephone: 205-261-3400.
Facsimile: 205-261-3434.
Tuscaloosa, Alabama Office: 2216 14th Street.
Telephone: 205-752-2089.

William H. McDermott
Stephen R. Windom
Gordon O. Tanner
T. Julian Motes

For Complete List of Firm Personnel, See General Section

For full biographical listings, see the Martindale-Hubbell Law Directory

*MONTGOMERY,** Montgomery Co.

* indicates certain Bar Register subscribers whose principal office is located elsewhere in the state and who have arranged for representation as a part of the state capital listings that follow

* BALCH & BINGHAM (AV)

The Winter Building, 2 Dexter Avenue, P.O. Box 78, 36101
Telephone: 334-834-6500
Facsimile: 334-269-3115
Birmingham, Alabama Offices: 1710 Sixth Avenue North, 35203.
Telephone: 205-251-8100.
Facsimile: 205-226-8798. 1901 Sixth Avenue North, 35203.
Telephone: 205-251-8100.
Facsimile: 205-226-8799.
Huntsville, Alabama Office: Suite 810, 200 West Court Square, 35801.
Telephone: 205-551-0171.
Facsimile: 205-551-0174.
Washington, D.C. Office: Suite 800, 1101 Connecticut Avenue, N.W., 20036.
Telephone: 202-296-0387.
Facsimile: 202-452-8180.

RESIDENT COUNSEL

M. Roland Nachman, Jr.

RESIDENT MEMBERS OF FIRM

Charles M. Crook
Malcolm N. Carmichael

RESIDENT ASSOCIATE

Lois Smith Woodward

Counsel for: Alabama Power Co.; Blue Cross and Blue Shield of Alabama; The Boeing Company; Brasfield & Gorrie, Inc.; Compass Bancshares, Inc.; Harbert Corp.; Kimberly-Clark Corp.; Southern Company Services, Inc.; Southern Research Institute; Vesta Insurance Group, Inc.

For Complete List of Firm Personnel, See General Section

For full biographical listings, see the Martindale-Hubbell Law Directory

CAPOUANO, WAMPOLD, PRESTWOOD & SANSONE, P.A. (AV)

350 Adams Avenue, P.O. Box 1910, 36102-1910
Telephone: 334-264-6401
Fax: 334-834-4954

(See Next Column)

CAPOUANO, WAMPOLD, PRESTWOOD & SANSONE P.A.—*Continued*

Leon M. Capouano
Alvin T. Prestwood
Jerome D. Smith
Ellis D. Hanan
Joseph P. Borg
Joseph W. Warren

OF COUNSEL

Charles H. Wampold, Jr.

Thomas B. Klinner
Linda Smith Webb
James M. Sizemore, Jr.

Counsel for: First Alabama Bank of Montgomery, N.A.; Union Bank and Trust Co.; Real Estate Financing, Inc.; SouthTrust Bank; AmSouth Bank; Central Bank; City Federal Savings & Loan Assoc.; Colonial Mortgage Co.; Lomas & Nettleton; First Bank of Linden.

For full biographical listings, see the Martindale-Hubbell Law Directory

ALASKA

*ANCHORAGE,** Third Judicial District

GROH, EGGERS & PRICE (AV)

A Partnership including Professional Corporations
2550 Denali Street, 17th Floor, 99503
Telephone: 907-272-6474
Fax: 907-272-4517

MEMBERS OF FIRM

Clifford J. Groh
Kenneth P. Eggers (P.C.)
Michael W. Price
Sally J. Kucko
Robert T. Price
Dennis G. Fenerty
David A. Devine (P.C.)

ASSOCIATES

Rick L. Owen
Shawn J. Holliday
Todd J. Timmermans
Susan E. Swann

Representative Clients: Alyeska Pipeline Service Co.; National Bank of Alaska; First American Title Company.

For full biographical listings, see the Martindale-Hubbell Law Directory

WOHLFORTH, ARGETSINGER, JOHNSON & BRECHT, A PROFESSIONAL CORPORATION (AV)

900 West 5th Avenue, Suite 600, 99501
Telephone: 907-276-6401
Telecopier: 907-276-5093

Peter Argetsinger
Julius J. Brecht
Robert M. Johnson
Thomas F. Klinkner
James A. Sarafin
Kenneth E. Vassar
Eric E. Wohlforth

Cynthia Lea Cartledge
Carol L. Giles
Bradley E. Meyen

For full biographical listings, see the Martindale-Hubbell Law Directory

ARIZONA

*FLAGSTAFF,** Coconino Co.

ASPEY, WATKINS & DIESEL (AV)

123 North San Francisco, 86001
Telephone: 602-774-1478
Facsimile: 602-774-1043
Sedona, Arizona Office: 120 Soldier Pass Road.
Telephone: 602-282-5955.
Facsimile: 602-282-5962.
Page, Arizona Office: 904 North Navajo.
Telephone: 602-645-9694.
Winslow, Arizona Office: 205 North Williamson.
Telephone: 602-289-5963.
Cottonwood, Arizona Office: 905 Cove Parkway, Unite 201.
Telephone: 602-639-1881.

MEMBERS OF FIRM

Frederick M. Fritz Aspey
Harold L. Watkins
Louis M. Diesel
Bruce S. Griffen
Donald H. Bayles, Jr.
Kaign N. Christy
John J. Dempsey

Zachary Markham
James E. Ledbetter
Whitney Cunningham
Holly S. Karris

(See Next Column)

LEGAL SUPPORT PERSONNEL

Deborah D. Roberts (Legal Assistant)
C. Denece Pruett (Legal Assistant)
Dominic M. Marino, Jr, (Paralegal Assistant)

Representative Clients: Farmer's Insurance Company of Arizona; Kelley-Moore Paint Co.; Pepsi-Cola Bottling Company of Northern Arizona; Bill Luke's Chrysler-Plymouth, Inc.; First American Title Insurance Company ; Transamerica Title Insurance Co.; Page Electric Utility; Comprehensive Access Health Plan, Inc.
Reference: First Interstate Bank-Arizona, N.A., Flagstaff, Arizona.

For full biographical listings, see the Martindale-Hubbell Law Directory

*NOGALES,** Santa Cruz Co.

O'CONNOR, CAVANAGH, ANDERSON, WESTOVER, KILLINGSWORTH & BESHEARS, A PROFESSIONAL ASSOCIATION (AV)

1827 North Mastick Way, 85621
Telephone: 602-761-4215
FAX: 602-761-3505
Phoenix, Arizona Office: One East Camelback Road, Suite 1100, 85012.
Telephone: 602-263-2400.
FAX: 602-263-2900.
Tucson, Arizona Office: Suite 2200, One South Church Avenue, 85701.
Telephone: 602-882-8912.
FAX: 602-624-9564.
Sun City, Arizona Office: 13250 North Del Webb Boulevard, Suite B, 85351.
Telephone: 602-263-2808.
FAX: 602-933-3100.

Hector G. Arana
Kimberly A. Howard Arana

Representative Clients: Omega Produce Co.; Frank's Distributing, Inc.; City of Nogales; Collectron of Ariz., Inc.; James K. Wilson Produce Co.; Agricola Bon, S. de R.L. de C.V.; Angel Demerutis E.; Rene Carrillo C.; Arturo Lomeli; Theojary Crisantes E.

For Complete List of Firm Personnel, See General Section

For full biographical listings, see the Martindale-Hubbell Law Directory

*PHOENIX,** Maricopa Co.

BONN, LUSCHER, PADDEN & WILKINS, CHARTERED (AV)

805 North Second Street, 85004
Telephone: 602-254-5557
Fax: 602-254-0656

Paul V. Bonn
Brian A. Luscher
Jeff C. Padden
Randall D. Wilkins
John H. Cassidy
D. Michael Hall
Samuel C. Wisotzkey

For full biographical listings, see the Martindale-Hubbell Law Directory

BROWN & BAIN, A PROFESSIONAL ASSOCIATION (AV)

2901 North Central Avenue, P.O. Box 400, 85001-0400
Telephone: 602-351-8000
Cable: TWX 910-951-0646
Telecopier: 602-351-8516
Palo Alto, California Affiliated Office: Brown & Bain, 600 Hansen Way.
Telephone: 415-856-9411.
Telecopier: 415-856-6061.
Tucson, Arizona Affiliated Office: Brown & Bain, A Professional Association. One South Church Avenue, Nineteenth Floor, P.O. Box 2265.
Telephone: 602-798-7900
Telecopier: 602-798-7945.

Michael F. Bailey
Eddward P. Ballinger, Jr.
John A. Buttrick
Richard Calvin Cooledge
C. Timothy Delaney
Jodi Knobel Feuerhelm
Douglas Gerlach (On leave)
Brent M. Gunderson
Kyle B. Hettinger
Philip R. Higdon (Resident at Tucson Office)
Joseph E. Mais
Cynthia Y. McCoy
Daniel James Quigley (Resident at Tucson Office)
Daniel P. Quigley
Charles Van Cott
George C. Wallach

Jeanean Kirk
Lane D. Oden (Resident at Tucson Office)
Jane L. Rodda (Resident at Tucson Office)

COUNSEL

Michael C. Jones
James F. McNulty, Jr. (Resident at Tucson Office)

For Complete List of Firm Personnel, See General Section

For full biographical listings, see the Martindale-Hubbell Law Directory

Phoenix—Continued

BURCH & CRACCHIOLO, P.A. (AV)

702 East Osborn Road, Suite 200, 85014
Telephone: 602-274-7611
Fax: 602-234-0341
Mailing Address: P.O. Box 16882, Phoenix, AZ, 85011

Stephen E. Silver
Jack D. Klausner
Daryl Manhart
David G. Derickson
Edwin C. Bull
Bryan F. Murphy
Donald W. Lindholm
F. Michael Carroll
Daniel R. Malinski
Edwin D. Fleming
Ralph D. Harris

Marigene Abbott-Dessaint
Paul F. Dowdell
Stephen M. Hart
Thomas A. Longfellow
Steven M. Serrano
David M. Villadolid
J. Brent Welker

Representative Clients: Bashas' Inc.; Farmers Insurance Group; U-Haul International, Inc.

For Complete List of Firm Personnel, See General Section

For full biographical listings, see the Martindale-Hubbell Law Directory

COOK, MEDA AND LANDE, A PROFESSIONAL CORPORATION (AV)

Tishman Biltmore Office Park, 2910 East Camelback Road, Suite 150, P.O. Box 32367, 85064-2367
Telephone: 602-957-2388
Fax: 602-957-2696
1-800-ROBERT M

Robert M. Cook
Alan A. Meda
Gail R. Lande

Representative Clients: Excel Country Fresh Meats, Phoenix, AZ; Gottsch Feeding Corp., Elkhorn, NE; Rufenacht Land & Cattle Co., Phoenix, AZ; Benedict Feeding Corp., Casa Grande, AZ; Norfolk Livestock Market, Norfolk, NE; Joplin Regional Stockyard, Joplin, MO; ; U.S. Airweld, Inc., Phoenix, AZ; Health Industry Business Communications Council, Phoenix, AZ; Chapter 7 Bankruptcy Trustees; Robin Yount.

For full biographical listings, see the Martindale-Hubbell Law Directory

FENNEMORE CRAIG, A PROFESSIONAL CORPORATION (AV)

Two North Central, Suite 2200, 85004
Telephone: 602-257-8700
Fax: 602-257-8527
Scottsdale, Arizona Office: 6263 North Scottsdale Road, Suite 290, 85250.
Telephone: 602-257-5400.
Fax: 602-945-4932.
Tucson, Arizona Office: One South Church Avenue, Suite 1030, 85701.
Telephone: 602-624-9312.
Fax: 602-882-7383.

Robert P. Robinson
Robert J. Hackett
Ronald L. Ballard
Stephen M. Savage
John R. Rawling
Roger T. Hargrove
William L. Kurtz
Mark A. Nesvig
James R. Huntwork
Michael V. Mulchay
William T. Burghart
Mark R. Herriot
Peter M. Gerstman
Jay S. Kramer

Darren J. McCleve
W. T. Eggleston, Jr.
Karen Rettig Rogers

Representative Clients: ASARCO Incorporated; AT&T Communications; Bridgestone/Firestone, Inc.; Catellus Development Corp.; Citibank (Arizona); First Interstate Bank of Arizona; GIANT Industries; Phelps Dodge Corporation; The Atchison, Topeka & Santa Fe Railway, Co.; US WEST Communications.

For Complete List of Firm Personnel, See General Section

For full biographical listings, see the Martindale-Hubbell Law Directory

HORNE, KAPLAN AND BISTROW, P.C. (AV)

Renaissance Two, 40 North Central, Suite 2800, 85004
Telephone: 602-253-9700
Fax: 602-258-4805

Thomas C. Horne
Martha Bachner Kaplan
Eric J. Bistrow
Michael S. Dulberg
Kimball J. Corson
Mark D. Zuckerman

For full biographical listings, see the Martindale-Hubbell Law Directory

JOHN C. HOVER, P.C. (AV)

2901 North Central Avenue, Suite 1150, 85012
Telephone: 602-230-8777
Fax: 602-230-8707

John C. Hover

(See Next Column)

LEGAL SUPPORT PERSONNEL

PARALEGAL

Diana G. Weeks

Representative Clients: First National Bank of Arizona; Bank of Hawaii; Buckeye Irrigation Co.; Linkletter-Perris Partnership.

For full biographical listings, see the Martindale-Hubbell Law Directory

JONES, SKELTON & HOCHULI (AV)

2901 North Central, Suite 800, 85012
Telephone: 602-263-1700
Telefax: 602-263-1784

MEMBERS OF FIRM

William R. Jones, Jr.
William D. Holm
Mark D. Zukowski
Michael E. Hensley

ASSOCIATES

Robert R. Berk
Scott F. Gibson
Brian W. LaCorte
James J. Osborne

OF COUNSEL

Peter G. Dunn

For full biographical listings, see the Martindale-Hubbell Law Directory

LEWIS AND ROCA (AV)

A Partnership including Professional Corporations
40 North Central Avenue, 85004-4429
Telephone: 602-262-5311
Fax: 602-262-5747
Tucson, Arizona Office: One South Church Avenue, Suite 700.
Telephone: 602-622-2090.
Fax: 602-622-3088.

MEMBERS OF FIRM

John P. Frank
Peter D. Baird
Tom Galbraith
Jordan Green
José A. Cárdenas
Edward F. Novak
Thomas H. Campbell
John N. Iurino (Resident, Tucson Office)
Thomas G. Ryan
Rob Charles (Resident, Tucson Office)
Jessica Jeanne Youle
James T. Acuff, Jr.
Robert H. Mc Kirgan
Pamela B. Petersen
Jeremy E. Butler
Douglas L. Irish
Marty Harper
Patricia K. Norris
Dale A. Danneman
Foster Robberson
Geoffrey H. Walker
Newman R. Porter
George L. Paul
Edward M. Mansfield
Karen Carter Owens
Jesse B. Simpson
Mary Ellen Simonson
Christopher J. Brelje
James J. Belanger
L. Keith Beauchamp

ASSOCIATES

Charles W. Steese
R. Neil Taylor, III
Stephen R. Winkelman
Richard A. Halloran
Deanna Salazar

Representative Clients: Associates Financial Services; Citibank; Columbia Pictures; The Dial Corp; Digital Equipment Corporation; MCI Communications Corporation; Panasonic Industrial Corporation; Prudential Securities.

For Complete List of Firm Personnel, See General Section

For full biographical listings, see the Martindale-Hubbell Law Directory

MACLEAN & JACQUES, LTD. (AV)

Suite 202, 40 East Virginia, 85004
Telephone: 602-263-5771
FAX: 602-279-5569

John H. MacLean (1932-1992)
Raoul T. Jacques

Cary T. Inabinet
Macre S. Inabinet

For full biographical listings, see the Martindale-Hubbell Law Directory

MYERS & JENKINS, A PROFESSIONAL CORPORATION (AV)

One Renaissance Square, Suite 1200, Two North Central Avenue, 85004
Telephone: 602-253-0440
Telecopier: 602-257-0527

Stephen W. Myers
William Scott Jenkins
Teresa Dawn Farrison
Richard B. Murphy

Reference: First Interstate Bank of Arizona, N.A.

For full biographical listings, see the Martindale-Hubbell Law Directory

Phoenix—Continued

O'CONNOR, CAVANAGH, ANDERSON, WESTOVER, KILLINGSWORTH & BESHEARS, A PROFESSIONAL ASSOCIATION (AV)

One East Camelback Road, Suite 1100, 85012-1656
Telephone: 602-263-2400
FAX: 602-263-2900
Sun City, Arizona Office: 13250 North Del Webb Boulevard, Suite B, 85351.
Telephone: 602-263-2808.
FAX: 602-933-3100.
Tucson, Arizona Office: Suite 2200, One South Church Avenue, 85701.
Telephone: 602-882-8912.
FAX: 602-624-9564.
Nogales, Arizona Office: 1827 North Mastick Way, 85621.
Telephone: 602-761-4215.
FAX: 602-761-3505.

Robert S. Kant
John B. Furman
Richard B. Stagg
Jeffrey D. Buchanan
Jean E. Harris
Michelle S. Monserez
Frank M. Fox

Karen L. Liepmann
D. Scott Fehrman

Jere M. Friedman (Not admitted in AZ)
Lisa R. Tsiolis

OF COUNSEL

Shoshana B. Tancer
Sara R. Ziskin

Representative Clients: Waste Management, Inc.; Rural/Metro Corporation; Three-Five Systems, Inc.; CerProbe Corporation; Main Street & Main Incorporated; American Wireless Systems, Inc.; Dowding & Mills PLC; Microchip Technology Incorporated; Maricopa County Sports Authority; Vodaui Communications.

For Complete List of Firm Personnel, See General Section

For full biographical listings, see the Martindale-Hubbell Law Directory

RIDENOUR, SWENSON, CLEERE & EVANS, P.C. (AV)

302 North First Avenue, Suite 900, 85003
Telephone: 602-254-2143
Fax: 602-254-8670

William G. Ridenour
Gerard R. Cleere
William D. Fearnow
Tamalyn E. Lewis
John T. Moshier
Joseph A. Kendhammer
Natalie P. Garth
Peter S. Spaw
Alan R. Costello

Kurt A. Peterson
David M. Reaves
Philip Simon
Jeffrey A. Bernick
Scott A. Holden
Gregory P. Gillis

Representative Clients: American Arbitration Assn.; Arizona Agricultural Credit Assn.; Biltmore Investors Bank; Citibank (Arizona); Federal Home Life Insurance Co.; First West Bank; Guarantee Mutual Life Co.; Indianapolis Life Insurance Co.; Kahler Corp.; Marriott Corp.

For full biographical listings, see the Martindale-Hubbell Law Directory

ROBBINS & GREEN, A PROFESSIONAL ASSOCIATION (AV)

1800 CitiBank Tower, 3300 North Central Avenue, 85012-9826
Telephone: 602-248-7600
Fax: 602-266-5369

Philip A. Robbins
William H. Sandweg III
Jeffrey P. Boshes
Brian Imbornoni
Janet B. Hutchison
Alfred W. Ricciardi
K. Leonard Judson
Dorothy Baran
Austin D. Potenza, II
Sarah McGiffert
Michael S. Green
Daniel L. Brown

For Complete List of Firm Personnel, See General Section

For full biographical listings, see the Martindale-Hubbell Law Directory

SHEA & WILKS, P.C. (AV)

200 First Interstate Building, 114 West Adams Street, 85003
Telephone: 602-257-1126

Philip J. Shea
Richard B. Wilks

William W. Quinn, Jr.
M.J. Mirkin

Representative Client: Salt River Pima-Maricopa Indian Community.
Reference: First Interstate Bank of Arizona.

For full biographical listings, see the Martindale-Hubbell Law Directory

SNELL & WILMER (AV)

One Arizona Center, 85004-0001
Telephone: 602-382-6000
Fax: 602-382-6070
Tucson, Arizona Office: 1500 Norwest Tower, One South Church Avenue 85701-1612.
Telephone: 602-882-1200.
Fax: 602-884-1294.
Orange County Office: 1920 Main Street, Suite 1200, P.O. Box 19601, Irvine, California, 92714.
Telephone: 714-253-2700.
Fax: 714-955-2507.
Salt Lake City, Utah Office: Broadway Centre, 111 East Broadway, Suite 900, 84111.
Telephone: 801-237-1900.
Fax: 801-237-1950.

MEMBERS OF FIRM

John J. Bouma
George H. Lyons
Donald D. Colburn
Joel P. Hoxie
Vaughn A. Crawford
David A. Sprentall
Richard W. Shapiro
Jeffrey Messing
E. Jeffrey Walsh
Heidi L. McNeil
Janet E. Barton
Kevin J. Parker
Jon S. Cohen
Daniel J. McAuliffe
Barry D. Halpern
James R. Condo
Arthur P. Greenfield
Terry Morris Roman
Katherine M. Harmeyer
James J. Sienicki
George J. Coleman, III
Timothy W. Moser
Stephen M. Hopkins
Steven S. Guy
Robert R. Kinas

SENIOR ATTORNEYS

Bruce P. White
Shirley J. Wahl
Lisa M. Coulter

ASSOCIATES

Patrick G. Byrne
William J. Donoher, Jr.
Brian J. Foster
Joseph C. Kreamer
Barbara J. Dawson
Clinton J Elliott
Patrick X. Fowler
Scott D. Sherman

Representative Clients: Arizona Public Service Co.; Bank One, Arizona, NA.; First Security Bank of Utah, N.A.; Ford Motor Co.; Chrysler Motors Corp.; Toyota Motor Sales U.S.A.; Magma Copper Co.; U.S. Home Corp.; Pinnacle West Capital Corp.; Safeway, Inc.

For Complete List of Firm Personnel, See General Section

For full biographical listings, see the Martindale-Hubbell Law Directory

STREICH LANG, A PROFESSIONAL ASSOCIATION (AV)

Renaissance One, Two N. Central Avenue, 85004-2391
Telephone: 602-229-5200
Fax: 602-229-5690
Tucson, Arizona Office: One S. Church Avenue, Suite 1700.
Telephone: 602-770-8700.
Fax: 602-623-2518.
Las Vegas, Nevada Affiliated Office: Dawson & Associates, 3800 Howard Hughes Parkway, Suite 1500.
Telephone: 702-792-2727.
Fax: 702-792-2676.
Los Angeles, California Office: 444 S. Flower Street, Suite 1530.
Telephone: 213-896-0484.

Douglas O. Guffey
Thomas J. Lang
Henry A. Perras
Kevin J. Tourek
Nancy L. White

OF COUNSEL

Matthew Mehr

Natalie A. Spencer
Michael B. Wixom (Resident, Las Vegas Office)

Representative Clients: Allied-Signal Aerospace Company; America West Airlines, Inc.; Atlantic Richfield Co.; Chicago Title; First Interstate Bank of Arizona, N.A.; Magma Copper Co.; Motorola, Inc.; Phelps Dodge Development Corp.; TRW Inc.; The Travelers Companies.

For Complete List of Firm Personnel, See General Section

For full biographical listings, see the Martindale-Hubbell Law Directory

*PRESCOTT,** Yavapai Co.

FAVOUR, MOORE, WILHELMSEN & SCHUYLER, A PROFESSIONAL ASSOCIATION (AV)

1580 Plaza West Drive, P.O. Box 1391, 86302
Telephone: 602-445-2444
Fax: 602-771-0450

John B. Schuyler, Jr.
Mark M. Moore
David K. Wilhelmsen
Lance B. Payette
Clifford G. Cozier

(See Next Column)

FAVOUR, MOORE, WILHELMSEN & SCHUYLER A PROFESSIONAL ASSOCIATION, *Prescott—Continued*

OF COUNSEL

John M. Favour — Richard G. Kleindienst

Representative Client: Yavapai Title Co.
Reference: Bank of America.

For full biographical listings, see the Martindale-Hubbell Law Directory

SCOTTSDALE, Maricopa Co.

PESKIND HYMSON & GOLDSTEIN, P.C. (AV)

14595 North Scottsdale Road, Suite 14, 85254
Telephone: 602-991-9077
Fax: 602-443-8854

E. J. Peskind — Irving Hymson
David B. Goldstein

Alexis J. Stanton — Eddie A. Pantiliat

OF COUNSEL

Marilee Miller Clarke

For full biographical listings, see the Martindale-Hubbell Law Directory

*TUCSON,** Pima Co.

COREY & FARRELL, P.C. (AV)

Suite 830, Norwest Tower, One South Church Avenue, 85701-1620
Telephone: 602-882-4994
Telefax: 602-884-7757

Barry M. Corey — Patrick J. Farrell
Barrett L. Kime

Representative Clients: Amphitheater Public School District; Civil Service Commission of the City of Tucson; La Quinta Homes, Inc.; Pima County Merit System Commission; DANKA-Uni-Copy Corp.; Introspect Health Care Corp.

For full biographical listings, see the Martindale-Hubbell Law Directory

LAW OFFICES OF GEORGE J. FEULNER, P.C. (AV)

262 N. Main, 85701-8220
Telephone: 602-622-4866
Fax: 602-624-7034

George J. Feulner

For full biographical listings, see the Martindale-Hubbell Law Directory

MUNGER AND MUNGER, P.L.C. (AV)

333 N. Wilmot, Suite 300, 85711
Telephone: 602-721-1900
Fax: 602-747-1550
Northwest Tucson Office: 6700 N. Oracle Road, Suite 411, Tucson 85704.
Telephone: 602-797-7173.
Fax: 602-797-7178.

John F. Munger — Clark W. Munger (Resident, Northwest Tucson Office)

Philip Kimble — Martin P. Janello
Karen S. Haller — Susan Gaylord Willis
Mark Edward Chadwick

Representative Clients: Richmond American Homes, Inc.; Jones Intercable; The Nature Conservancy; Property Tax Appeals, Inc.; Photon Sciences; Tucson Greyhound Park; Tucson Realty and Trust; Associated Dermatologists; Arizona State Radiology; Allied Waste Industries, Inc.

For full biographical listings, see the Martindale-Hubbell Law Directory

O'CONNOR, CAVANAGH, ANDERSON, WESTOVER, KILLINGSWORTH & BESHEARS, A PROFESSIONAL ASSOCIATION (AV)

Suite 2200 One South Church Avenue, 85701-1621
Telephone: 602-882-8912
FAX: 602-624-9564
Phoenix, Arizona Office: One East Camelback Road, Suite 1100, 85012.
Telephone: 602-263-2400.
FAX: 602-263-2900.
Sun City, Arizona Office: 13250 North Del Webb Boulevard, Suite B, 85351.
Telephone: 602-263-2808.
FAX: 602-933-3100.
Nogales, Arizona Office: 1827 North Mastick Way, 85621.
Telephone: 602-761-4215.
FAX: 602-761-3505.

Thomas M. Pace — Scott D. Gibson

J. Matthew Derstine

(See Next Column)

Chris B. Nakamura

Representative Client: Jeffco, Inc.
Reference: Citibank.

For Complete List of Firm Personnel, See General Section

For full biographical listings, see the Martindale-Hubbell Law Directory

ARKANSAS

*LITTLE ROCK,** Pulaski Co.

ARNOLD, GROBMYER & HALEY, A PROFESSIONAL ASSOCIATION (AV)

875 Union National Plaza, 124 West Capitol Avenue, P.O. Box 70, 72203
Telephone: 501-376-1171
Fax: 501-375-3548

Benjamin F. Arnold — David H. Pennington
James F. Dowden — Joe A. Polk
Mark W. Grobmyer — Richard L. Ramsay
John H. Haley — Robert R. Ross
Charles D. McDaniel — Lee S. Thalheimer
Beth Ann Long

For Complete List of Firm Personnel, See General Section

For full biographical listings, see the Martindale-Hubbell Law Directory

BARBER, MCCASKILL, AMSLER, JONES & HALE, P.A. (AV)

2700 First Commercial Building, 400 West Capitol Avenue, 72201-3414
Telephone: 501-372-6175
Telecopier: 501-375-2802

Azro L. Barber (1885-1979) — William H. Edwards, Jr.
Elbert A. Henry (1889-1966) — Richard C. Kalkbrenner
John B. Thurman (1912-1971) — G. Spence Fricke
Austin McCaskill, Sr. — M. Stephen Bingham
Guy Amsler, Jr. — Gail Ponder Gaines
Glenn W. Jones, Jr. — Michael J. Emerson
Michael E. Hale — R. Kenny McCulloch
John S. Cherry, Jr. — Tim A. Cheatham
Robert L. Henry, III — Joseph F. Kolb
Micheal L. Alexander — Scott Michael Strauss
Karen Hart McKinney

Attorneys for: Associated Aviation Underwriters; Canal Insurance Co.; Fireman's Fund Insurance Co.; General Motors Corp.; General Motors Acceptance Corp.; Hanover Insurance Co.; Home Insurance Co.; Royal Insurance; United States Fidelity & Guaranty Co.; Universal Underwriters Insurance Co.

For full biographical listings, see the Martindale-Hubbell Law Directory

HOOVER & STOREY (AV)

111 Center Street, 11th Floor, 72201-4445
Telephone: 501-376-8500
Facsimile: 501-372-3255

MEMBERS OF FIRM

Paul W. Hoover, Jr. — William P. Dougherty
O. H. Storey, III — Max C. Mehlburger
John Kooistra, III — Joyce Bradley Babin
Lawrence Joseph Brady — Herbert W. Kell, Jr.
Letty McAdams

For full biographical listings, see the Martindale-Hubbell Law Directory

IVESTER, SKINNER & CAMP, P.A. (AV)

Suite 1200, 111 Center Street, 72201
Telephone: 501-376-7788
FAX: 501-376-8536

Hermann Ivester — Laura G. Wiltshire
H. Edward Skinner — Mildred H. Hansen
Charles R. Camp — Valerie F. Boyce
Wayne B. Ball — Todd A. Lewellen
Randal B. Frazier — Stan D. Smith
Robert Keller Jackson — S. Scott Luton

For full biographical listings, see the Martindale-Hubbell Law Directory

LASER, SHARP, WILSON, BUFFORD & WATTS, P.A. (AV)

101 S. Spring Street, Suite 300, 72201-2488
Telephone: 501-376-2981
Telecopier: 501-376-2417

(See Next Column)

LASER, SHARP, WILSON, BUFFORD & WATTS P.A.—*Continued*

Richard N. Watts
J. Kendal "Ken" Cook
Alfred F. Angulo, Jr.
David M. Donovan

Representative Clients: Allstate Insurance Co.; American International Insurance Group; Continental Insurance Cos.; Farm Bureau Insurance Cos. (Casualty & Fire); Farmers Insurance Group; GAB Business Services, Inc.; St. Paul Insurance Cos.; Scottsdale Insurance Co.; State Farm Auto (Fire) Insurance Cos.

For Complete List of Firm Personnel, See General Section

For full biographical listings, see the Martindale-Hubbell Law Directory

ROSE LAW FIRM, A PROFESSIONAL ASSOCIATION (AV)

120 East Fourth Street, 72201
Telephone: 501-375-9131
Telecopy: 501-375-1309

Herbert C. Rule, III
Allen W. Bird, II
Garland J. Garrett
Thomas P. Thrash
John T. Hardin
Stephen N. Joiner
Brian Rosenthal

Representative Clients: Arkansas Capital Corp.; The Equitable Life Assurance Society of America; John Hancock Mutual Life Insurance Co.; Harvest Food, Inc.; International Paper Co.; The Prudential Insurance Company of America; Stephens Inc.; Trammell Crow Cos.; Twin City Bank; Worthen Banking Corp.

For Complete List of Firm Personnel, See General Section

For full biographical listings, see the Martindale-Hubbell Law Directory

WALKER & BLACK (AV)

1000 West Third Street, P.O. Box 591, 72203-0591
Telephone: 501-376-2382
Fax: 501-376-3352

MEMBERS OF FIRM

W. J. Walker
Kendell R. Black

Reference: First Commercial Bank.

For full biographical listings, see the Martindale-Hubbell Law Directory

WILLIAMS & ANDERSON (AV)

Twenty-Second Floor, 111 Center Street, 72201
Telephone: 501-372-0800
FAX: 501-372-6453

MEMBERS OF FIRM

Philip S. Anderson
Peter G. Kumpe
Steven W. Quattlebaum
John E. Tull, III
Timothy W. Grooms

Thomas G. Williams
G. Alan Perkins
Jeanne L. Seewald
Sarah J. Heffley

Representative Clients: Arkansas Development Finance Authority; Coregis; Dean Witter Reynolds Inc.; Entergy Power, Inc.; Little Rock Newspapers, Inc. d/b/a Arkansas Democrat-Gazette; Texaco Inc.; Roman Catholic Diocese of Little Rock; Transport Indemnity Insurance Co.; Wal-Mart Stores, Inc.

For Complete List of Firm Personnel, See General Section

For full biographical listings, see the Martindale-Hubbell Law Directory

SPRINGDALE, Washington Co.

LISLE LAW FIRM, P.C. (AV)

210 South Thompson Street, Suite 6, P.O. Box 6877, 72766-6877
Telephone: 501-750-4444
Fax: 501-751-6792

John Lisle

Joe B. Reed
Christopher James Lisle
Donnie W. Rutledge, II

For full biographical listings, see the Martindale-Hubbell Law Directory

CALIFORNIA

*BAKERSFIELD,** Kern Co.

KLEIN, WEGIS, DENATALE, GOLDNER & MUIR (AV)

A Partnership including Professional Corporations
(Formerly Di Giorgio, Davis, Klein, Wegis, Duggan & Friedman)
ARCO Tower, 4550 California Avenue, Second Floor, P.O. Box 11172, 93389-1172
Telephone: 805-395-1000
Telecopier: 805-326-0418
Santa Ana, California Office: Park Tower Building #610, 200 W. Santa Ana Boulevard, 92701.
Telephone: 714-285-0711.
Fax: 714-285-9003.

MEMBERS OF FIRM

Anthony J. Klein (Inc.)
Thomas V. DeNatale, Jr.
Barry L. Goldner
Jay L. Rosenlieb
David J. Cooper

Representative Clients: Bank of America; California Republic Bank; San Joaquin Bank.

For Complete List of Firm Personnel, See General Section

For full biographical listings, see the Martindale-Hubbell Law Directory

CARLSBAD, San Diego Co.

WEIL & WRIGHT (AV)

1921 Palomar Oaks Way, Suite 301, 92008
Telephone: 619-438-1214
Telefax: 619-438-2666

Paul M. Weil
Archie T. Wright III
James T. Reed, Jr.
David A. Ebersole

For full biographical listings, see the Martindale-Hubbell Law Directory

COSTA MESA, Orange Co.

COULOMBE KOTTKE & KING, A PROFESSIONAL CORPORATION (AV)

Comerica Bank Tower, 611 Anton Boulevard, Suite 1260, P.O. Box 2410, 92628-2410
Telephone: 714-540-1234
Fax: 714-754-0808; 714-754-0707

Ronald B. Coulombe
Jon S. Kottke
Raymond King

COUNSEL

Mary J. Swanson
Roy B. Woolsey

LEGAL SUPPORT PERSONNEL

PARALEGALS

Karen M. Carrillo
Laura A. Bieser
Vicky M. Pearson

LEGAL ADMINISTRATOR

Sheila O. Elpern

For full biographical listings, see the Martindale-Hubbell Law Directory

MENKE, FAHRNEY & CARROLL, A PROFESSIONAL CORPORATION (AV)

650 Town Center Drive, Suite 1250, 92626
Telephone: 714-556-7111
Facsimile: 714-556-6426

Dennis V. Menke
Richard L. Fahrney II
Patrick D. Carroll

Vickie Lynn Bibro
Christopher R. Clark
Oakley C. Frost

For full biographical listings, see the Martindale-Hubbell Law Directory

RUTAN & TUCKER (AV)

A Partnership including Professional Corporations
611 Anton Boulevard, Suite 1400, P.O. Box 1950, 92626
Telephone: 714-641-5100; 213-625-7586
Telecopier: 714-546-9035

MEMBERS OF FIRM

Ronald P. Arrington
Thomas G. Brockington

For Complete List of Firm Personnel, See General Section

For full biographical listings, see the Martindale-Hubbell Law Directory

*FRESNO,** Fresno Co.

DOWLING, MAGARIAN, AARON & HEYMAN, INCORPORATED (AV)

Suite 200, 6051 North Fresno Street, 93710
Telephone: 209-432-4500
Fax: 209-432-4590

Michael D. Dowling
Richard M. Aaron
Kent F. Heyman
Bruce S. Fraser
William J. Keeler, Jr.
John C. Ganahl
Sheila M. Smith
Adolfo M. Corona
Philip David Kopp

Francine Marie Kanne
John G. Kerkorian
Richard E. Heatter
Christopher A. Brown
James C. Sherwood
Mark D. Magarian

OF COUNSEL

Donald J. Magarian
Daniel K. Whitehurst
Morris M. Sherr
Blaine Pettitt

Reference: Wells Fargo Bank (Main).

For full biographical listings, see the Martindale-Hubbell Law Directory

JORY, PETERSON, WATKINS & SMITH (AV)

555 West Shaw, Suite C-1, P.O. Box 5394, 93755
Telephone: 209-225-6700
Telecopier: 209-225-3416

MEMBERS OF FIRM

Jay V. Jory
John E. Peterson
Cal B. Watkins, Jr.
Michael Jens F. Smith

ASSOCIATES

William M. Woolman
Marcia A. Ross
Mark A. Pasculli

Reference: Valliwide Bank.

For full biographical listings, see the Martindale-Hubbell Law Directory

GLENDALE, Los Angeles Co.

LASKIN & GRAHAM (AV)

Suite 840, 800 North Brand Boulevard, 91203
Telephone: 213-665-6955; 818-547-4800; 714-957-3031
Telecopier: 818-547-3100

MEMBERS OF FIRM

Arnold K. Graham
Susan L. Vaage
John S. Peterson
Michael Anthony Cisneros
Gregson M. Perry
Lynn I. Ibara
Jason L. Glovinsky

OF COUNSEL

Richard Laskin

For full biographical listings, see the Martindale-Hubbell Law Directory

IRVINE, Orange Co.

LOBEL, WINTHROP & BROKER (AV)

Suite 1100, 19800 MacArthur Boulevard, P.O. Box 19588, 92713
Telephone: 714-476-7400
Fax: 714-476-7444
Santa Ana, California Office: 201 North Broadway, Suite 201.
Telephone: 714-543-4822.
Fax: 714-476-7444.

MEMBERS OF FIRM

William N. Lobel
Marc J. Winthrop
Todd C. Ringstad
Robert E. Opera
Lorie Dewhirst Porter

ASSOCIATES

Alan J. Friedman
Paul J. Couchot
Robert W. Pitts
Pamela Z. Karger
Whitney H. Leibow
Richard H. Golubow

For full biographical listings, see the Martindale-Hubbell Law Directory

WATT, TIEDER & HOFFAR (AVⓣ)

3 Park Plaza, Suite 1530, 92714
Telephone: 714-852-6700
Telecopier: 714-261-0771
McLean Virginia Office: 7929 Westpark Drive, Suite 400,
Telephone: 703-749-1000.
Telex: 248797 WATTR.
Telecopier: 703-893-8029.
Washington, D.C. Office: 601 Pennsylvania Avenue, N.W. Suite 900,
Telephone: 202-462-4697.

MEMBERS OF FIRM

John B. Tieder, Jr. (Not admitted in CA)
Robert M. Fitzgerald (Not admitted in CA)
Michael G. Long

(See Next Column)

ASSOCIATE

Christopher P. Pappas

For full biographical listings, see the Martindale-Hubbell Law Directory

*LOS ANGELES,** Los Angeles Co.

LAW OFFICES OF DAVID B. BLOOM A PROFESSIONAL CORPORATION (AV)

3325 Wilshire Boulevard, Ninth Floor, 90010
Telephone: 213-938-5248; 384-4088
Telecopier: 213-385-2009

David B. Bloom

Stephen S. Monroe (A Professional Corporation)
Raphael A. Rosemblat
James E. Adler
Bonni S. Mantovani
Martin A. Cooper
Roy A. Levun
Cherie S. Raidy
Jonathan Udell
Susan Carole Jay
Edward Idell
Sandra Kamenir
Steven Wayne Lazarus
Andrew Edward Briseno
Harold C. Klaskin
Shelley M. Gould
B. Eric Nelson
John C. Notti
Peter O. Israel
Anthony V. Seferian

For full biographical listings, see the Martindale-Hubbell Law Directory

SANDOR T. BOXER (AV)

10920 Wilshire Boulevard, 14th Floor, 90024
Telephone: 310-208-0055
Fax: 310-208-4801

For full biographical listings, see the Martindale-Hubbell Law Directory

BUCHALTER, NEMER, FIELDS & YOUNGER, A PROFESSIONAL CORPORATION (AV)

24th Floor, 601 South Figueroa Street, 90017
Telephone: 213-891-0700
Fax: 213-896-0400
Cable Address: "Buchnem"
Telex: 68-7485
New York, New York Office: 19th Floor, 237 Park Avenue.
Telephone: 212-490-8600.
Fax: 212-490-6022.
San Francisco, California Office: 29th Floor, 333 Market Street.
Telephone: 415-227-0900.
Fax: 415-227-0770.
San Jose, California Office: 12th Floor, 50 West San Fernando Street.
Telephone: 408-298-0350.
Fax: 408-298-7683.
Newport Beach, California Office: Suite 300, 620 Newport Center Drive.
Telephone: 714-760-1121.
Fax: 714-720-0182.
Century City, California Office: Suite 2400, 1801 Century Park East.
Telephone: 213-891-0700.
Fax: 310-551-0233.

Murray M. Fields
Sol Rosenthal
Richard Jay Goldstein
Michael L. Wachtell
Harvey H. Rosen
Robert C. Colton
Arthur Chinski
Jay R. Ziegler
Michael J. Cereseto
Bernard E. Le Sage
Terence S. Nunan
Philip J. Wolman
Mark A. Bonenfant
David S. Kyman
Kevin M. Brandt
Jeffrey S. Wruble
Pamela Kohlman Webster
Matthew W. Kavanaugh
Richard S. Angel
Bryan Mashian

OF COUNSEL

Ronald E. Gordon
Stuart D. Buchalter
Holly J. Fujie

Geoffrey Forsythe Bogeaus
Raymond H. Aver
Jonathan D. Fink
Robert J. Davidson
Stephen K. Lubega
Bernard D. Bollinger, Jr.
Cheryl Croteau Orr
Kenneth W. Swenson
Paul S. Arrow
William S. Brody
Amy L. Rubinfeld
Dean Stackel
J. Karren Baker

References: City National Bank; Wells Fargo Bank; Metrobank.

For Complete List of Firm Personnel, See General Section

For full biographical listings, see the Martindale-Hubbell Law Directory

CLARK & TREVITHICK, A PROFESSIONAL CORPORATION (AV)

800 Wilshire Boulevard, 12th Floor, 90017
Telephone: 213-629-5700
Telecopier: 213-624-9441

(See Next Column)

CLARK & TREVITHICK A PROFESSIONAL CORPORATION—*Continued*

Philip W. Bartenetti
Leonard Brazil
Dolores Cordell
Leslie R. Horowitz
Vincent Tricarico
Arturo Santana Jr.
Kerry T. Ryan

OF COUNSEL

Judith Ilene Bloom

References: Wells Fargo Bank (Los Angeles Main Office); National Bank of California.

For Complete List of Firm Personnel, See General Section

For full biographical listings, see the Martindale-Hubbell Law Directory

COSKEY & BALDRIDGE (AV)

16th Floor, 1801 Century Park East, 90067-2317
Telephone: 310-277-7001
Telecopier: 310-277-9704

MEMBERS OF FIRM

Tobias Coskey (1896-1974)
Hal L. Coskey
Mary Ellen Baldridge

ASSOCIATE

Sharon Coverly Hughes

For full biographical listings, see the Martindale-Hubbell Law Directory

RONALD D. ELLIS (AV)

Suite 313, 880 West First Street, 90012
Telephone: 213-680-2533
FAX: 213-680-3832
Torrance, California Office: 4302 Mesa Street.
Telephone: 213-375-9978.
FAX: 213-375-5997.
(Also Of Counsel to Mitch Moriyasu Michino)

For full biographical listings, see the Martindale-Hubbell Law Directory

GOLDMAN, GORDON & LIPSTONE (AV)

Suite 1920, 1801 Century Park East, 90067
Telephone: 310-277-7171
FAX: 310-277-1547

MEMBERS OF FIRM

A. S. Goldman (1895-1966)
Robert P. Gordon
Leonard A. Goldman
Ronald K. Lipstone

ASSOCIATE

Jerry A. Jacobson

References: Bank of America, Fourth and Spring Branch, Los Angeles; Bank of America, Wilshire-San Vincente Branch, Beverly Hills.

For full biographical listings, see the Martindale-Hubbell Law Directory

IVERSON, YOAKUM, PAPIANO & HATCH (AV)

One Wilshire Building, 27th Floor 624 South Grand Avenue, 90017
Telephone: 213-624-7444
Telecopier: 213 629-4563

MEMBERS OF FIRM

Paul E. Iverson (1907-1975)
Neil Papiano
Frank B. Yoakum, Jr. (1906-1991)
Dennis A. Page
Patrick M. Mc Adam
R. Noel Hatch
Arnold D. Larson
John M. Garrick

ASSOCIATES

Elsa H. Jones
Mark Pearson
Douglas C. Pease
Zachary Winner
Lesley Miller Mehran
Frederick Brevard Hayes
Andrew K. Doty
Amy J. Fink
Melissa A. Immel
Johanna Lewis
Mary P. Lightfoot
Mark B. Simpkins
Barbara Lee Berkowitz
Gioia M. Fasi

Representative Clients: Lockheed Corp.; International Paper; Bridgestone/-Firestone, Inc.
Reference: Security Pacific National Bank (Los Angeles Head Office).

For full biographical listings, see the Martindale-Hubbell Law Directory

MITCHELL, SILBERBERG & KNUPP (AV)

A Partnership of Professional Corporations
11377 West Olympic Boulevard, 90064
Telephone: 310-312-2000
Cable Address: "Silmitch"
Telex: 69-1347
Telecopier: 310-312-3200

(See Next Column)

MEMBERS OF FIRM

Chester I. Lappen (A Professional Corporation)
Alan L. Pepper (A Professional Corporation)
Lessing E. Gold (A Professional Corporation)
John E. Hatherley (A Professional Corporation)
Marvin Leon (A Professional Corporation)
Anthony A. Adler (A Professional Corporation)
John M. Kuechle (A Professional Corporation)
Laura A. Loftin (A Professional Corporation)
Joseph Ciasulli (A Professional Corporation)
Andrew E. Katz (A Professional Corporation)
Kenneth H. Levin (A Professional Corporation)

ASSOCIATES

Mary E. Sullivan
Jonathan Sears
Richard E. Ackerknecht
Sonia Ransom
Susan H. Hilderley
Patricia L. Laucella

Reference: First Interstate Bank of California (Headquarters, Los Angeles, California).

For Complete List of Firm Personnel, See General Section

For full biographical listings, see the Martindale-Hubbell Law Directory

PIZER & MICHAELSON INC. (AV)

2029 Century Park East, Suite 600, 90067
Telephone: 310-843-9729
Fax: 310-843-9619
Santa Ana, California Office: 2122 North Broadway, Suite 100, 92706.
Telephone: 714-558-0535.
Telecopier: 714-550-0841.

Bradley J. Pizer

For full biographical listings, see the Martindale-Hubbell Law Directory

STUTMAN, TREISTER & GLATT, PROFESSIONAL CORPORATION (AV)

3699 Wilshire Boulevard, Suite 900, 90010
Telephone: 213-251-5100
FAX: 213-251-5288

Jack Stutman (Retired Founder)
Bruce Bennett
George M. Treister
Michael H. Goldstein
Herman L. Glatt
Lee R. Bogdanoff
Richard M. Neiter
Frank A. Merola
Robert A. Greenfield
Jeffrey H. Davidson
Charles D. Axelrod
Ronald L. Fein
Theodore B. Stolman
Mark S. Wallace
Isaac M. Pachulski
Susan R. Purcell
Kenneth N. Klee
K. John Shaffer
Alan Pedlar
Mareta C. Hamre
George C. Webster, II
Michael L. Tuchin
Stephan M. Ray
Eric D. Goldberg
Michael A. Morris
Eve H. Karasik
Jeffrey C. Krause
Thomas R. Kreller
Martin R. Barash

For full biographical listings, see the Martindale-Hubbell Law Directory

SULMEYER, KUPETZ, BAUMANN & ROTHMAN, A PROFESSIONAL CORPORATION (AV)

300 South Grand Avenue, 14th Floor, 90071
Telephone: 213-626-2311
Fax: 213-629-4520

Irving Sulmeyer
Israel Saperstein
Arnold L. Kupetz
Victor A. Sahn
Richard G. Baumann
Steven R. Wainess
Don Rothman
David S. Kupetz
Alan G. Tippie
Howard M. Ehrenberg
Kathryn Kerfes

Nathan H. Harris
Matthew Rothman
Chandler J. Coury
Wesley Avery
Suzanne L. Weakley
Katherine Windler
Susan Frances Moley
Garrick Hollander
Moira Doherty

OF COUNSEL

Marilyn S. Scheer

Representative Clients: General Electric Capital Corp.; Continental Insurance Co.; Litton Industries; North American Phillips Corp.; Ventura Port District; Northwest Financial; Heller Financial Inc.; Transamerica Occidental Life Insurance Co.; Transamerica Realty Services, Inc.; Body Glove International.

For full biographical listings, see the Martindale-Hubbell Law Directory

Los Angeles—Continued

ZIDE & O'BIECUNAS (AV)

Suite 403, 1300 West Olympic Boulevard, 90015
Telephone: 213-487-7550
Fax: 213-382-6095
Mailing Address: P.O. Box 15363, Del Valle Station,
Ventura, California Office: 101 South Victoria Avenue.
Telephone: 805-642-8426.
Fax: 805-642-8881.

Thomas Zide
Leo G. O'Biecunas, Jr.

ASSOCIATE

Creighton A. Stephens (Resident, Ventura Office)

OF COUNSEL

Douglas M. Kaye
Nathan Swedlow

For full biographical listings, see the Martindale-Hubbell Law Directory

*OAKLAND,** Alameda Co.

EDWARD L. BLUM (AV)

1999 Harrison Street, Suite 1333, 94612
Telephone: 510-452-4400
FAX: 510-874-4155
San Francisco, California Office: 235 Montgomery Street, Suite 450.
Telephone: 415-391-3900.
FAX: 415-954-0938.
(Also of Counsel, Wilson, Ryan & Campilongo, San Francisco)

ASSOCIATE

Paul D. Hunt

For full biographical listings, see the Martindale-Hubbell Law Directory

PALO ALTO, Santa Clara Co.

GRAY CARY WARE & FREIDENRICH, A PROFESSIONAL CORPORATION (AV)

Gray Cary Established in 1927
Ware & Freidenrich Established in 1969
400 Hamilton Avenue, 94301-1825
Telephone: 415-328-6561
Telex: 348-372
Telecopier: 415-327-3699
San Diego, California Office: 401 B Street, Suite 1700.
Telephone: 619-699-2700.
La Jolla, California Office: 1200 Prospect Street, Suite 575.
Telephone: 619-454-9101.
El Centro, California Office: 1224 State Street, P.O. Box 2890.
Telephone: 619-353-6140.

Cynthia B. Carlson
Jeffrey J. Lederman

Representative Clients: Automobile Club of South California; Bank of America; Brooktree Corp.; C. A. Parr (Agencies), Ltd.; IMED; Pacific Bell; McMillin Development Co.; Scripps Clinic and Research Fdtn.; SeaWorld, Inc.; Underwriters at Lloyds; Wells Fargo Bank.

For Complete List of Firm Personnel, See General Section

For full biographical listings, see the Martindale-Hubbell Law Directory

*SAN DIEGO,** San Diego Co.

BARNHORST, SCHREINER & GOONAN, A PROFESSIONAL CORPORATION (AV)

550 West C Street, Suite 1350, 92101-3532
Telephone: 619-544-0900
Fax: 619-544-0703

Howard J. Barnhorst, II
Stephen L. Schreiner
Gregory P. Goonan
Brian A. Wright
John J. Freni
Niles Rice Sharif
Brian W. DeWitt

Representative Clients: Alex. Brown Kleinwort Benson Realty Advisors; Amron International Diving Supply; Continental American Properties; James Hardie Industries (USA), Inc.; Montrose Chemical Corp. of California; The Price Company; SeaQuest, Inc.; United Pacific Insurance Company; Anne Winton & Associates; InaCom Corp.

For full biographical listings, see the Martindale-Hubbell Law Directory

CHAPIN, FLEMING & WINET, A PROFESSIONAL CORPORATION (AV)

1320 Columbia Street, 92101
Telephone: 619-232-4261
Telefax: 619-232-4840
Vista, California Office: 410 South Melrose Drive, Suite 101.
Telephone: 619-758-4261.
Telefax: 619-758-6420.
Los Angeles, California Office: 12121 Wilshire Boulevard, Suite 401.
Telephone: 310-826-4834.
Telefax: 310-207-4236.

(See Next Column)

Edward D. Chapin
George E. Fleming
Randall L. Winet (Resident, Vista Office)
Peter C. Ward
Roger L. Popeney
Lawrence W. Shea, II
Gregory S. Tavill
Aaron H. Katz
Maria C. Roberts
Shirley A. Gauvin
Kennett L. Patrick (Resident, Vista Office)
Terence L. Greene
Amy B. Vandeveld
Victor M. Barr, Jr.
Elizabeth J. Koumas
Leslie A. Greathouse
Kelli Jean Brooks
John F. Sahhar (Resident, Vista Office)
Andrew Nicholas Kohn
Frank L. Tobin
Shawn M. Robinson
Katherine M. Green
Dean G. Chandler (Resident, Vista Office)
Joseph A. Solomon
Victoria Chen
Jane Mobaldi
Dean A. Gonsonski
Daniel P. Murphy
Steven S. Richter
Gregory Kevin Hansen

OF COUNSEL

James Michael Zimmerman

For full biographical listings, see the Martindale-Hubbell Law Directory

CHRISTISON & MARTIN (AV)

402 West Broadway 23rd Floor, 92101
Telephone: 619-236-0305

Frederick Martin, Jr.
Perry T. Christison

For full biographical listings, see the Martindale-Hubbell Law Directory

FERRIS & BRITTON, A PROFESSIONAL CORPORATION (AV)

1600 First National Bank Center, 401 West A Street, 92101
Telephone: 619-233-3131
Fax: 619-232-9316

Alfred G. Ferris
Harry J. Proctor
Tamara K. Fogg
Pauline H. G. Getz
Gary T. Moyer

OF COUNSEL

William M. Winter

Representative Clients: Allstate Insurance Co.; Cox Communications, Inc.; Enterprise Rent-a-Car; Exxon; Immuno Pharmaceutics, Inc.; Invitrogen Corporation; Teleport Communications Group; Southwest Airlines; Times-Mirror Cable Television.

For Complete List of Firm Personnel, See General Section

For full biographical listings, see the Martindale-Hubbell Law Directory

HILLYER & IRWIN, A PROFESSIONAL CORPORATION (AV)

550 West C Street, 16th Floor, 92101
Telephone: 619-234-6121
Telecopier: 619-595-1313

Henry J. Klinker
James E. Drummond
Gary S. Hardke
Colin W. Wied
John C. O'Neill

For full biographical listings, see the Martindale-Hubbell Law Directory

HOVEY, KIRBY, THORNTON & HAHN, A PROFESSIONAL CORPORATION (AV)

101 West Broadway, Suite 1100, 92101-8297
Telephone: 619-685-4000
Fax: 619-685-4004

Dean T. Kirby, Jr.
M. Leslie Hovey
Geraldine A. Valdez

For full biographical listings, see the Martindale-Hubbell Law Directory

LINDLEY, LAZAR & SCALES, A PROFESSIONAL CORPORATION (AV)

One America Plaza, 600 West Broadway, Suite 1400, 92101-3302
Telephone: 619-234-9181
Fax: 619-234-8475

Luke R. Corbett
John M. Seitman
Michael H. Wexler
Richard J. Pekin, Jr.
George C. Lazar
James Henry Fox
R. Gordon Huckins

Representative Clients: Bank of Commerce; Resolution Trust Corp.; FDIC; City Chevrolet; Metro Imports; Palomar Savings & Loan Assn.; Northern Trust Bank of California, N.A.

For Complete List of Firm Personnel, See General Section

For full biographical listings, see the Martindale-Hubbell Law Directory

San Diego—Continued

RICE FOWLER BOOTH & BANNING (AV)

Emerald - Shapery Center, 402 W. Broadway, Suite 850, 92101
Telephone: 619-230-0030
Telecopier: 619-230-1350
New Orleans, Louisiana Office: 36th Floor, Place St. Charles, 201 St. Charles Avenue, 70130
Telephone: 504-523-2600.
Telecopier: 504-523-2705.
Telex: 9102507910. ELN: 62548910.
London, England Office: Suite 692, Level 6 Lloyd's, 1 Lime Street, London EC3M 7DQ England.
Telephone: 071-327-4222.
Telecopier: 071-929-0043.
San Francisco, California Office: Embarcadero Center West, 275 Battery Street, 27th Floor, 94111.
Telephone: 415-399-9191.
Telecopier: 415-399-9192.
Telex: 451981.
Beijing, China Office: Beijing International Convention Centre, Suite 7024, No. 8 Beichendong Road, Chaoyang District, 100101, P.R.C.
Telephone: (861) 493-4250.
Telecopier: (861) 493-4251.
Bogota, Colombia Office: Avenida Jimenez #4-03 Officina 10-05.
Telephone: (571) 342-1062.
Telecopier: (571) 342-1062.

PARTNERS

William L. Banning
Keith Zakarin
Robert B. Krueger, Jr.

ASSOCIATE

Juan Carlos Dominguez

For full biographical listings, see the Martindale-Hubbell Law Directory

*SAN FRANCISCO,** San Francisco Co.

LAW OFFICE OF KEVIN W. FINCK (AV)

601 Montgomery Street, Suite 1900, 94111
Telephone: 415-296-9100
Facsimile: 415-394-6446

Marla Raucher Osborn

For full biographical listings, see the Martindale-Hubbell Law Directory

FLEISCHMANN & FLEISCHMANN (AV)

650 California Street, Suite 2550, 94108-2606
Telephone: 415-981-0140
FAX: 415-788-6234

MEMBERS OF FIRM

Hartly Fleischmann
Roger Justice Fleischmann

Stella J. Kim
Mark S. Molina

OF COUNSEL

Grace C. Shohet

LEGAL SUPPORT PERSONNEL

Lissa Dirrim

For full biographical listings, see the Martindale-Hubbell Law Directory

MURPHY, PEARSON, BRADLEY & FEENEY, A PROFESSIONAL CORPORATION (AV)

88 Kearny Street, 11th Floor, 94108
Telephone: 415-788-1900
Telecopier: 415-393-8087
Sacramento, California Office: Suite 200, 3600 American River Drive, 95864.
Telephone: 916-483-6074.
Telecopier: 916-483-6088.

James A. Murphy
Arthur V. Pearson
Michael P. Bradley
John H. Feeney
Gregory A. Bastian (Resident, Sacramento Office)
Timothy J. Halloran
Karen M. Goodman (Resident, Sacramento Office)
Mark S. Perelman
Mark Ellis (Resident, Sacramento Office)
William S. Kronenberg

Peter L. Isola
Gregg Anthony Thornton
Anne F. Marchant
Antoinette Waters Farrell
Tomislav (Tom) Peraic
Douglas L. Johnson (Resident, Sacramento Office)
Michael K. Pazdernik (Resident, Sacramento Office)
Reed R. Johnson (Resident, Sacramento Office)
Alexander J. Berline
Alec Hunter Boyd
Amy Bisson Holloway (Resident, Sacramento Office)
Peter W. Thompson (Resident, Sacramento Office)
Gregory S. Maple

(See Next Column)

Rita K. Johnson
Jane L. O'Hara Gamp
Joseph E. Addiego, III
Kevin T. Burton (Resident at Sacramento, California Office)
Stacy Marie Howard (Resident, Sacramento Office)

LEGAL SUPPORT PERSONNEL

Wilfred A. Fregeau

For full biographical listings, see the Martindale-Hubbell Law Directory

RICE FOWLER BOOTH & BANNING (AV)

Embarcadero Center West, 275 Battery Street, 27th Floor, 94111
Telephone: 415-399-9191
Telecopier: 415-399-9192
Telex: 451981
New Orleans, Louisiana Office: Place St. Charles, 36th Floor, 201 St. Charles Avenue, 70130.
Telephone: 504-523-2600.
Telecopier: 504-523-2705.
Telex: 9102507910. ELN 62548910.
San Diego, California Office: Emerald-Shapery Center, 402 W. Broadway, Suite 850, 92101.
Telephone: 619-230-0030.
Telecopier: 619-230-1350.
London, England Office: Suite 692, Level 6 Lloyd's, 1 Lime Street, London EC3M 7DQ England.
Telephone: 071-327-4222.
Telecopier: 071-929-0043.
Beijing, China Office: Beijing International Convention Centre, Suite 7024, No. 8 Beichendong Road, Chaoyang District, 100101, P.R.C.
Telephone: (861) 493-4250.
Telecopier: (861) 493-4251.
Bogota, Colombia Office: Avenida Jimenez #4-03 Oficina 10-05, Bogota, Colombia.
Telephone: (571) 342-1062.
Telecopier: (571) 342-1062.

MEMBERS OF FIRM

Forrest Booth
Kurt L. Micklow
Norman J. Ronneberg, Jr.

ASSOCIATES

Cynthia L. Mitchell
Lynn Haggerty King
Edward M. Bull, III
Kim O. Dincel
Amy Jo Poor
Janice Amenta-Jones
Heidi Loken Benas

For full biographical listings, see the Martindale-Hubbell Law Directory

ROSEN, BIEN & ASARO (AV)

Eighth Floor, 155 Montgomery Street, 94104
Telephone: 415-433-6830
Fax: 415-433-7104

Sanford Jay Rosen
Michael W. Bien
Andrea G. Asaro

Stephen M. Liacouras
Hilary A. Fox
Thomas Nolan
Mary Ann Cryan (Not admitted in CA)
Donna Petrine

For full biographical listings, see the Martindale-Hubbell Law Directory

*SAN JOSE,** Santa Clara Co.

BUCHALTER, NEMER, FIELDS & YOUNGER, A PROFESSIONAL CORPORATION (AV)

12th Floor, 50 West San Fernando Street, 95113
Telephone: 408-298-0350
Fax: 408-298-7683
Los Angeles, California Office: 24th Floor, 601 South Figueroa Street.
Telephone: 213-891-0700.
Fax: 213-896-0400.
New York, New York Office: 19th Floor, 237 Park Avenue.
Telephone: 212-490-8600.
Fax: 212-490-6022.
San Francisco, California Office: 29th Floor, 333 Market Street.
Telephone: 415-227-0900.
Fax: 415-227-0770.
Newport Beach, California Office: Suite 300, 620 Newport Center Drive.
Telephone: 714-760-1121.
Fax: 714-720-0182.
Century City, California Office: Suite 2400, 1801 Century Park East.
Telephone: 213-891-0700.
Fax: 310-551-0233.

NORTHERN CALIFORNIA RESIDENTS IN CHARGE

Gary Nemer
Stephen H. Pettigrew

References: City National Bank; Wells Fargo Bank; Metrobank.

For full biographical listings, see the Martindale-Hubbell Law Directory

San Jose—Continued

CAMPEAU & THOMAS, A LAW CORPORATION (AV)

Market Post Tower, 55 South Market Street, Suite 1660, 95113
Telephone: 408-295-9555
Fax: 408-295-6606

Kenneth J. Campeau
Wayne H. Thomas
Scott L. Goodsell

Laura Basaloco-Lapo
Marcie E. Schaap
Kathryn J. Diemer

For full biographical listings, see the Martindale-Hubbell Law Directory

*SANTA ANA,** Orange Co.

PIZER & MICHAELSON INC. (AV)

2122 North Broadway, Suite 100, 92706
Telephone: 714-558-0535
Telecopier: 714-550-0841
Los Angeles, California Office: 2029 Century Park East, Suite 600, 90067.
Telephone: 310-843-9729.
Fax: 310-843-9619.

Seymour S. Pizer (1930-1992)
Barry S. Michaelson
Hugh R. Coffin
Bradley J. Pizer (Resident, Los Angeles Office)

Laura Hinrichs

For full biographical listings, see the Martindale-Hubbell Law Directory

PRENOVOST, NORMANDIN, BERGH & DAWE A PROFESSIONAL CORPORATION (AV)

2020 East First Street, Suite 500, 92705
Telephone: 714-547-2444
Fax: 714-835-2889

Thomas J. Prenovost, Jr.
Tom Roddy Normandin
Steven L. Bergh
Michael G. Dawe

Bruce T. Bauer
Kristen L. Welles Lanham
Kimberly D. Taylor
Nancy R. Tragarz

Reference: Marine National Bank.

For full biographical listings, see the Martindale-Hubbell Law Directory

SPERLING & PERGANDE (AV)

3 Hutton Centre, Suite 670, 92707
Telephone: 714-540-8500
Facsimile: 714-540-2599

MEMBERS OF FIRM

Dean P. Sperling
K. William Pergande

For full biographical listings, see the Martindale-Hubbell Law Directory

SANTA MONICA, Los Angeles Co.

HAIGHT, BROWN & BONESTEEL (AV)

A Partnership including Professional Corporations
1620 26th Street, Suite 4000 North, P.O. Box 680, 90404
Telephone: 310-449-6000
Telecopier: 310-829-5117
Telex: 705837
Santa Ana, California Office: Suite 900, 5 Hutton Centre Drive.
Telephone: 714-754-1100.
Telecopier: 714-754-0826.
Riverside, California Office: 3750 University Avenue, Suite 650.
Telephone: 909-341-8300.
Fax: 909-341-8309.
San Francisco, California Office: Suite 300, 201 Sansome Street.
Telephone: 415-986-7700.
Fax: 415-986-6945.

MEMBERS OF FIRM

Fulton Haight (A Professional Corporation)
Bruce A. Armstrong (A Professional Corporation)
Wayne E. Peterson (A Professional Corporation)
Morton Rosen
Theresa M. Marchlewski
William E. Ireland

ASSOCIATES

Jon M. Kasimov
Tamara Equals Holmes
Jennifer A. Ellis

For Complete List of Firm Personnel, See General Section

For full biographical listings, see the Martindale-Hubbell Law Directory

O'NEILL, LYSAGHT & SUN (AV)

A Partnership including Professional Corporations
100 Wilshire Boulevard, Suite 700, 90401
Telephone: 310-451-5700
Telecopier: 310-399-7201

Brian O'Neill (A Professional Corporation)
Brian C. Lysaght (A Professional Corporation)
Frederick D. Friedman
Brian A. Sun
Yolanda Orozco
John M. Moscarino

Harriet Beegun Leva
David E. Rosen
Lisa Newman Tucker
J. Andrew Coombs
Ellyn S. Garofalo
Edward A. Klein
Robert L. Meylan

OF COUNSEL

J. Joseph Connolly
Arn H. Tellem (P.C.)

Reference: Santa Monica Bank, Santa Monica.

For full biographical listings, see the Martindale-Hubbell Law Directory

*SANTA ROSA,** Sonoma Co.

BELDEN, ABBEY, WEITZENBERG & KELLY, A PROFESSIONAL CORPORATION (AV)

1105 North Dutton Avenue, P.O. Box 1566, 95402
Telephone: 707-542-5050
Telecopier: 707-542-2589

Richard W. Abbey
Timothy W. Hoffman

Peter J. Walls

Representative Clients: Exchange Bank of Santa Rosa; Westamerica Bank; North Bay Title Co.; Northwestern Title Security Co.; Geyser Peak Winery; Arrowood Vineyards & Winery; Hansel Ford; Santa Rosa City School District.

For Complete List of Firm Personnel, See General Section

For full biographical listings, see the Martindale-Hubbell Law Directory

COLORADO

*COLORADO SPRINGS,** El Paso Co.

FLYNN MCKENNA & WRIGHT, LIMITED LIABILITY COMPANY (AV)

20 Boulder Crescent, 80903
Telephone: 719-578-8444
Fax: 719-578-8836

James T. Flynn
R. Tim McKenna
Bruce M. Wright

Michael C. Potarf

Representative Clients: Western National Bank of Colorado; Tour Ice National, Inc.; Colorado Springs Savings and Loan Association; Chase Manhattan of Colorado, Inc.; Bank One Colorado Springs N.A.; First National Bank of Canon City; Colorado Bank and Trust Company of La Junta; Merrill Lynch Credit Corporation.

For full biographical listings, see the Martindale-Hubbell Law Directory

*DENVER,** Denver Co.

ALEXANDER LAW FIRM, P.C. (AV)

216 16th Street, Suite 1300, 80202
Telephone: 303-825-7307
Fax: 303-595-3202

Hugh Alexander

C. Scott Crabtree

For full biographical listings, see the Martindale-Hubbell Law Directory

BENNINGTON JOHNSON RUTTUM & REEVE, A PROFESSIONAL CORPORATION (AV)

2480 Republic Plaza, 370 17th Street, Suite 2480, 80202
Telephone: 303-629-5200
Fax: 303-629-5718

Kenneth R. Bennington
Philip E. Johnson
Paul T. Ruttum
Thomas C. Reeve

SPECIAL COUNSEL

H. Robert Walsh, Jr.

(See Next Column)

BENNINGTON JOHNSON RUTTUM & REEVE A PROFESSIONAL CORPORATION—*Continued*

Julie Murphy Seavy

For full biographical listings, see the Martindale-Hubbell Law Directory

BURG & ELDREDGE, P.C. (AV)

Suite 900 Regency Plaza One, 4643 South Ulster, 80237-2866
Telephone: 303-779-5595
Fax: 303-779-0527
Albuquerque, New Mexico Office: 20 First Plaza, Suite 508, 87102.
Telephone: 505-242-7020.
Fax: 505-242-7247.

Michael S. Burg
Peter W. Burg
Scott J. Eldredge
David P. Hersh
David M. Houliston
R. Hunter Ellington

Thomas Willard Henderson, IV
Janet R. Spies
Tom Van Buskirk
Matthew R. Giacomini
Kerry N. Jardine
Andrew M. Ominsky
Ashley Rea Kilroy
Brendan O'Rourke Powers
Jack D. Robinson
Kirstin G. Lindberg
Willie E. Shepherd, Jr.
John J. Mattey
Bradley W. Howard (Resident, Albuquerque, New Mexico Office)
Christian C. Doherty (Resident, Albuquerque, New Mexico Office)
Gillian Cooley Morrison
Christina Gratke Nason (Resident, Albuquerque, New Mexico Office)
Rosemary Orsini
Kathleen H. Bridges

OF COUNSEL

Gregory E. Bunker
Dale J. Coplan

Representative Clients: AT&T; Budget Rent a Car; Del Webb Corporation; Douglas Toyota; First Interstate Bank of Denver, N.A.; Rocky Mountain Health Care Corp.; Safeway Inc.; Sevo Miller; Toyota West.

For full biographical listings, see the Martindale-Hubbell Law Directory

CARPENTER & KLATSKIN, P.C. (AV)

1500 Denver Club Building, 518 Seventeenth Street, 80202
Telephone: 303-534-6315
Telecopier: 303-534-0514

Willis V. Carpenter
Andrew S. Klatskin

Max A. Minnig, Jr.

LEGAL SUPPORT PERSONNEL

PARALEGAL

Holly S. Hoxeng

Reference: Colorado State Bank.

For full biographical listings, see the Martindale-Hubbell Law Directory

DUCKER, DEWEY & SEAWELL, P.C. (AV)

One Civic Center Plaza, Suite 1500, 1560 Broadway, 80202
Telephone: 303-861-2828
Telecopier: 303-861-4017
Frisco, Colorado Office: 179 Willow Lane, Suite A, P.O. Box 870, 80443.
Telephone: 303-668-3776. Direct Dial from Denver: 674-1783.

Bruce Ducker
Stephen Gurko (Resident, Frisco Office)
Michael J. Kelly
Robert C. Montgomery
Thomas C. Seawell
L. Bruce Nelson
Christopher J. Walsh

OF COUNSEL

Charles F. Dewey

For full biographical listings, see the Martindale-Hubbell Law Directory

DUFFORD & BROWN, P.C. (AV)

1700 Broadway, Suite 1700, 80290-1701
Telephone: 303-861-8013
Facsimile: 303-832-3804

Thomas G. Brown
Richard L. Fanyo
Randall J. Feuerstein
S. Kirk Ingebretsen
Edward D. White

SPECIAL COUNSEL

Morris B. Hecox, Jr.
James E. Carpenter

Representative Clients: CF&I Steel, L.P.; The Colorado and Wyoming Railway Co.; GT Land Colorado Inc.; Hall and Hall Mortgage Corporation; Hewlett Packard Co.; Hill Samuel Bank Limited; Reorganized CF&I Steel Corp.

For Complete List of Firm Personnel, See General Section

For full biographical listings, see the Martindale-Hubbell Law Directory

FEDER, MORRIS, TAMBLYN & GOLDSTEIN, P.C. (AV)

150 Blake Street Building, 1441 Eighteenth Street, 80202
Telephone: 303-292-1441
FAX: 303-292-1126

Harold A. Feder
Leonard M. Goldstein
Stephen B. Schuyler

Reference: Guaranty Bank & Trust Co., Denver, Colorado.

For full biographical listings, see the Martindale-Hubbell Law Directory

KARSH AND FULTON, PROFESSIONAL CORPORATION (AV)

Suite 710, 950 South Cherry Street, 80222
Telephone: 303-759-9669
Fax: 303-782-0902

Alan E. Karsh
Larry C. Fulton
Fred Gabler
J. Terry Wiggins
Seymour Joseph

Antonio T. Ciccarelli

Representative Clients: Commonwealth Land Title Insurance Co.; Lawyers Title Insurance Co.; Transamerica Title Insurance Co.; Fidelity National Title Insurance Co.; Karsh and Hagan Advertising; Zeff Properties (Real Estate); CTL/Thompson, Inc. (Engineering); Sport-Haley, Inc. (sport clothing design and distribution); Analytical Reference Materials International, Inc. (metal standards); Old Republic National Title Insurance Company.

For full biographical listings, see the Martindale-Hubbell Law Directory

MONTGOMERY LITTLE & MCGREW, P.C. (AV)

The Quadrant, 5445 DTC Parkway, Suite 800 (Englewood), 80111
Telephone: 303-773-8100
Telecopier: 303-220-0412

James J. Soran, III
David L. Kelble, Jr.
Michael H. Smith
Thomas C. Deline
Robert J. Bruce
Rebecca B. Givens
James P. Campbell

Representative Clients: Amoco Oil Co.; Bristol-Myers Squibb; Colorado Medical Society; Chrysler Corporation; Cyprus Minerals; Dillon Cos., Inc., d/b/a King Soopers; The St. Paul Insurance Cos.; University of Colorado Health Sciences Center.

For Complete List of Firm Personnel, See General Section

For full biographical listings, see the Martindale-Hubbell Law Directory

MYER, SWANSON & ADAMS, P.C. (AV)

The Colorado State Bank Building, 1600 Broadway, Suite 1850, 80202-4918
Telephone: 303-866-9800
Facsimile: 303-866-9818

Rendle Myer
Allan B. Adams
Robert K. Swanson
Thomas J. Wolf

Kevin M. Brady

OF COUNSEL

Robert Swanson
Fred E. Neef (1910-1986)

Representative Clients: The Oppenheimer Funds; Daily Cash Accumulation Fund; The Centennial Trusts; Mile High Chapter of American Red Cross; Master Lease; Heartland Management Company; Kan-Build of Colorado, Inc.
Reference: The Colorado State Bank of Denver.

For full biographical listings, see the Martindale-Hubbell Law Directory

NETZORG & MCKEEVER, PROFESSIONAL CORPORATION (AV)

5251 DTC Parkway (Englewood) Penthouse One, 80111
Telephone: 303-770-8200
Fax: 303-770-8342

Gordon W. Netzorg
J. Nicholas McKeever, Jr.
Susan Bernhardt
Cecil E. Morris, Jr.

For full biographical listings, see the Martindale-Hubbell Law Directory

REIMAN & ASSOCIATES, P.C. (AV)

1600 Broadway, Suite 1640, 80202
Telephone: 303-860-1500
Fax: 303-839-4380

Jeffrey Reiman

Marcie K. Bayaz
James Birch

For full biographical listings, see the Martindale-Hubbell Law Directory

Denver—Continued

REINHART, BOERNER, VAN DEUREN, NORRIS & RIESELBACH, P.C. (AV)

One Norwest Center, 1700 Lincoln Street, Suite 3725, 80203
Telephone: 303-831-0909
Fax: 303-831-4805
Milwaukee, Wisconsin Office: 1000 North Water Street.
Telephone: 414-298-1000.
Facsimile: 414-298-8097.
Madison, Wisconsin Office: 7617 Mineral Point Road, 53701-2020.
Telephone: 608-283-7900.
Fax: 608-283-7919.
Washington, D.C. Office: 601 Pennsylvania Avenue, N.W., North Building, Suite 750.
Telephone: 202-393-3636.
Fax: 202-393-0796.

Mary A. Brauer
Timothy G. Atkinson
Chester P. Schwartz
Arnold R. Kaplan

David D. Pavek

Representative Clients: OnGuard Systems, Inc.; Club Sports International, Inc.

For full biographical listings, see the Martindale-Hubbell Law Directory

WELLER FRIEDRICH, LLC (AV)

One Civic Center, Suite 2000, 1560 Broadway, P.O. Box 989, 80201-0989
Telephone: 303-812-1200
FAX: 303-812-1212

Geoffrey S. Race
Mary A. Wells
David K. Kerr
James C. Tienken
Andrew J. Friedrich
Sheryl Lynn Anderson
Marc R. Brosseau
Jerome M. Joseph
Dennis J. Bartlett

OF COUNSEL

W. Robert Ward

Suanne Marie Dell
Kelly Koepp Robinson
Gregory E. Sopkin
Karen Martinson Girard
Fermin G. Montoya

Representative Clients: Abbott Laboratories; Associated Aviation Underwriters; Commercial Union Insurance Companies.
Reference: Colorado State Bank of Denver.

For full biographical listings, see the Martindale-Hubbell Law Directory

*DURANGO,** La Plata Co.

FRANK J. ANESI (AV)

Suite 220, 835 East Second Avenue, P.O. Box 2185, 81302
Telephone: 303-247-9246
Fax: 303-259-2793

References: First National Bank of Durango; Burns Bank, Durango.

For full biographical listings, see the Martindale-Hubbell Law Directory

*FORT COLLINS,** Larimer Co.

FISCHER, HOWARD & FRANCIS (AV)

Suite 900, 125 South Howes, P.O. Box 506, 80522
Telephone: 303-482-4710
Fax: 303-482-4729

MEMBERS OF FIRM

Gene E. Fischer
Stephen E. Howard
Steven G. Francis

Approved Attorneys for: Attorney's Title Guaranty Fund, Inc.
Reference: First National Bank of Fort Collins, N.A.

For full biographical listings, see the Martindale-Hubbell Law Directory

CONNECTICUT

GREENWICH, Fairfield Co.

IVEY, BARNUM & O'MARA (AV)

Meridian Building, 170 Mason Street, P.O. Box 1689, 06830
Telephone: 203-661-6000
Telecopier: 203-661-9462

(See Next Column)

MEMBERS OF FIRM

Michael J. Allen
Edward T. Krumeich, Jr.
Robert C. Barnum, Jr.
Donat C. Marchand
Edward D. Cosden, Jr.
Miles F. McDonald, Jr.
James W. Cuminale
Edwin J. O'Mara, Jr.
Wilmot L. Harris, Jr.
Remy A. Rodas
William I. Haslun, II
Gregory A. Saum
Lorraine Slavin

ASSOCIATES

Juerg A. Heim
Nicole Barrett Lecher
Melissa Townsend Klauberg
Alan S. Rubenstein

OF COUNSEL

Philip R. McKnight

For full biographical listings, see the Martindale-Hubbell Law Directory

*HARTFORD,** Hartford Co.

GORDON, MUIR AND FOLEY (AV)

Hartford Square North, Ten Columbus Boulevard, 06106-1944
Telephone: 203-525-5361
Telecopier: 203-525-4849

MEMBERS OF FIRM

William S. Gordon, Jr. (1946-1956)
Jon Stephen Berk
William J. Gallitto
George Muir (1939-1976)
Gerald R. Swirsky
Edward J. Foley (1955-1983)
Robert J. O'Brien
Peter C. Schwartz
Philip J. O'Connor
John J. Reid
Kenneth G. Williams
John H. Goodrich, Jr.
Chester J. Bukowski
R. Bradley Wolfe
Mary Ann Santacroce

ASSOCIATES

J. Lawrence Price
Patrick T. Treacy
Mary Anne Alicia Charron
Andrew J. Hern
James G. Kelly
Eileen Geel
Kevin F. Morin
Christopher L. Slack
Claudia A. Baio
Renee W. Dwyer
David B. Heintz

OF COUNSEL

Stephen M. Riley

Reference: Fleet Bank.

For full biographical listings, see the Martindale-Hubbell Law Directory

SOROKIN SOROKIN GROSS HYDE & WILLIAMS P.C. (AV)

One Corporate Center, 06103
Telephone: 203-525-6645
Fax: 203-522-1781
Simsbury, Connecticut Office: 730 Hopmeadow Street.
Telephone: 203-651-9348.
Rocky Hill, Connecticut Office: 2360 Main Street.
Telephone: 203-563-9305.
Fax: 203-529-6931.
Glastonbury, Connecticut Office: 124 Hebron Avenue.
Telephone: 203-659-8801.

Andrew C. Glassman
Paula G. Pressman
Clifford J. Grandjean
Amelia M. Rugland

Jeffery P. Apuzzo
Laura Gold Becker
Brian S. Becker
Lisa A. Magliochetti

OF COUNSEL

Joseph D. Hurwitz

For Complete List of Firm Personnel, See General Section

For full biographical listings, see the Martindale-Hubbell Law Directory

*NEW HAVEN,** New Haven Co.

BERGMAN, HOROWITZ & REYNOLDS, P.C. (AV)

157 Church Street, 19th Floor, P.O. Box 426, 06502
Telephone: 203-789-1320
FAX: 203-785-8127
New York, New York Office: 499 Park Avenue, 26th Floor.
Telephone: 212-582-3580.

Melvin Ditman

David M. Spinner
Jeremy A. Mellitz
Richard M. Porter

For Complete List of Firm Personnel, See General Section

For full biographical listings, see the Martindale-Hubbell Law Directory

GORMAN & ENRIGHT P.C. (AV)

59 Elm Street, P.O. Box 1961, 06509
Telephone: 203-865-1382
Telecopier: 203-776-7250

(See Next Column)

GORMAN & ENRIGHT P.C.—*Continued*

John R. Gorman | Brian G. Enright

Patricia King

References: Bank of Boston Connecticut; Bank of New Haven.

For full biographical listings, see the Martindale-Hubbell Law Directory

NEW LONDON, New London Co.

WALLER, SMITH & PALMER, P.C. (AV)

52 Eugene O'Neill Drive, P.O. Box 88, 06320
Telephone: 203-442-0367
Telecopier: 203-447-9915
Old Lyme, Connecticut Office: 103-A Halls Road.
Telephone: 203-434-8063.

Birdsey G. Palmer (Retired)
William W. Miner
Robert P. Anderson, Jr.
Robert W. Marrion
Hughes Griffis
Edward B. O'Connell
Frederick B. Gahagan
Linda D. Loucony
Mary E. Driscoll
William E. Wellette

Tracy M. Collins
Donna Richer Skaats
David P. Condon
Valerie Ann Votto
Charles C. Anderson

OF COUNSEL

Suzanne Donnelly Kitchings

General Counsel for: Colotone Group.
Counsel for: Union Trust Co.; Coastal Savings Bank; Cash Home Center, Inc.
Local Counsel for: Metropolitan Insurance Co.; Connecticut General Life Insurance Co.

For Complete List of Firm Personnel, See General Section

For full biographical listings, see the Martindale-Hubbell Law Directory

STAMFORD, Fairfield Co.

WOFSEY, ROSEN, KWESKIN & KURIANSKY (AV)

600 Summer Street, 06901
Telephone: 203-327-2300
FAX: 203-967-9273

MEMBERS OF FIRM

Abraham Wofsey (1915-1944)
Michael Wofsey (1927-1951)
David M. Rosen (1926-1967)
Julius B. Kuriansky (1910-1992)
Monroe Silverman
Emanuel Margolis
Howard C. Kaplan
Anthony R. Lorenzo
Edward M. Kweskin
David M. Cohen
Marshall Goldberg
Stephen A. Finn
Judith Rosenberg
Robert L. Teicher
Mark H. Henderson

Steven D. Grushkin

OF COUNSEL

Saul Kwartin | Sydney C. Kweskin (Retired)

ASSOCIATES

Brian Bandler
John J.L. Chober
Steven M. Frederick
Eric M. Higgins
James A. Lenes
Valerie E. Maze
Maurice K. Segall
Randall M. Skigen
Gregory J. Williams

Representative Clients: Benenson Realty; Cellular Information Systems, Inc.; Gateway Bank; Hartford Provision Company; Louis Dreyfus Corp.; Norwalk Federation of Teachers; Patient Care, Inc.; People's Bank; Ridgeway Shopping Center and Stamford Housing Authority.

For full biographical listings, see the Martindale-Hubbell Law Directory

WATERBURY, New Haven Co.

TINLEY, NASTRI & RENEHAN (AV)

161 North Main Street, 06702
Telephone: 203-596-9030
Fax: 203-596-9036

Jeffrey J. Tinley
Robert Nastri, Jr.
Richard P. Renehan
Mary Piscatelli Brigham
William T. Blake, Jr.

Representative Clients: Center Capital Corporation; Citizens Fidelity Bank & Trust Co.; Gar-San Corporation; General Electric Capital Commercial Automotive Finance Inc.; Mahler Financial Group Inc.; Mobil Oil Corporation; St. Mary's Hospital; Teikyo Post University.

For full biographical listings, see the Martindale-Hubbell Law Directory

WESTPORT, Fairfield Co.

TIROLA & HERRING (AV)

1221 Post Road East, P.O. Box 631, 06881
Telephone: 203-226-8926
Fax: 203-226-9500
New York, New York Office: Suite 4E, 10 Sheridan Square.
Telephone: 212-463-9642.

MEMBERS OF FIRM

Vincent S. Tirola
Charles Fredericks, Jr.
Elizabeth C. Seeley
Buddy O. H. Herring

Dan Shaban | Marc J. Grenier

OF COUNSEL

Edward Kanowitz
C. Michael Carter
Alan D. Lieberson

Reference: The Westport Bank and Trust Co.

For full biographical listings, see the Martindale-Hubbell Law Directory

DELAWARE

*WILMINGTON,** New Castle Co.

CONNOLLY, BOVE, LODGE & HUTZ (AV)

1220 Market Street, P.O. Box 2207, 19899-2207
Telephone: 302-658-9141
Telecopier: 302-658-5614
Cable Address: "Artcon"
Telex: 83-5477

James M. Mulligan, Jr.
Arthur G. Connolly, Jr.
Henry E. Gallagher, Jr.
Richard David Levin
Jeffrey B. Bove
Collins J. Seitz, Jr.
Charles J. Durante
F. L. Peter Stone
John C. Kairis
Arthur G. Connolly, III
James D. Heisman
Anne Love Barnett (Not admitted in DE)

For Complete List of Firm Personnel, See General Section

For full biographical listings, see the Martindale-Hubbell Law Directory

SMITH, KATZENSTEIN & FURLOW (AV)

1220 Market Building, P.O. Box 410, 19899
Telephone: 302-652-8400
FAX: 302-652-8405

MEMBERS OF FIRM

Craig B. Smith | Anne E. Bookout

Stephen M. Miller | Joanne M. Shalk

For Complete List of Firm Personnel, See General Section

For full biographical listings, see the Martindale-Hubbell Law Directory

DISTRICT OF COLUMBIA

WASHINGTON, D.C. Co.

*** indicates certain Bar Register subscribers, in cities of comparable size and importance, who maintain an additional office in Washington, D.C. and who have arranged for representation as a part of the Washington, D.C. listings that follow**

*** BAKER & BOTTS, L.L.P. (AV)**

A Registered Limited Liability Partnership
The Warner, 1299 Pennsylvania Avenue, N.W., 20004-2400
Telephone: 202-639-7700
Fax: 202-639-7832
Houston, Texas Office: One Shell Plaza, 910 Louisiana.
Telephone: 713-229-1234.
Austin, Texas Office: 1600 San Jacinto Center, 98 San Jacinto Boulevard.
Telephone: 512-322-2500.
Dallas, Texas Office: 2001 Ross Avenue.
Telephone: 214-953-6500.
New York, New York Office: 805 Third Avenue, Suite 2000.
Telephone: 212-705-5000.
Moscow, Russian Federation Office: 10 ul. Pushkinskaya, 103031.
Telephone: 7095/921-5300 (Local); 7501/929-7070 (International).

(See Next Column)

BAKER & BOTTS L.L.P., *Washington—Continued*

MEMBERS OF FIRM

James R. Doty
David N. Powers
Hugh Tucker

ASSOCIATES

Ruby D'andrea Ceaser
Kevin B. Dent
Leslie Anne Freiman
Michael A. Gold (Not admitted in DC)

For Complete List of Firm Personnel, See General Section

For full biographical listings, see the Martindale-Hubbell Law Directory

KENNETH R. FEINBERG & ASSOCIATES (AV)

1120 20th Street, N.W. Suite 740 South, 20036
Telephone: 202-371-1110
Fax: 202-962-9290
New York, N.Y. Office: 780 3rd Avenue, Suite 2202.
Telephone: 212-527-9600.
Fax: 212-527-9611.

ASSOCIATES

Deborah E. Greenspan
Michael K. Rozen (Not admitted in DC)
Peter H. Woodin (Not admitted in DC)

For full biographical listings, see the Martindale-Hubbell Law Directory

MARY A. MCREYNOLDS, P.C. (AV)

Suite 400, 888 Sixteenth Street, N.W., 20006
Telephone: 202-775-1996
Telecopier: 202-296-8791

Mary A. McReynolds

For full biographical listings, see the Martindale-Hubbell Law Directory

MOSER & MOSER (AV)

1000 Connecticut Avenue, N.W., 20006
Telephone: 202-857-8450
New York, N.Y. Office: 50 Broadway.
Telephone: 212-344-4200.
Telecopier: 212-635-5470.
Albany, New York Office: 126 State Street.
Telephone: 518-449-4643.
Philadelphia, Pennsylvania Office: 1822 Spring Garden Street.
Telephone: 215-564-7649.

MEMBERS OF FIRM

Alexander S. Moser (Not admitted in DC)
Joel H. Moser (Not admitted in DC)
Jonathan A. Ballan
Janet S. Kaplan (Not admitted in DC)

ASSOCIATES

Charles H. Wasser (Not admitted in DC)
Karen J. Marsico (Not admitted in DC)
Elaine H. Neumann (Not admitted in DC)

For full biographical listings, see the Martindale-Hubbell Law Directory

SHAWN, MANN & NIEDERMAYER, L.L.P. (AV)

1850 M Street, N.W., Suite 280, 20036-5803
Telephone: 202-331-7900
Fax: 202-331-0726

MEMBERS OF FIRM

William H. Shawn
Kim D. Mann
Roy I. Niedermayer
Jeffrey L. Squires
Joseph L. Steinfeld, Jr.
Robert B. Walker
Eshel Bar-Adon

For full biographical listings, see the Martindale-Hubbell Law Directory

*** THOMPSON, HINE AND FLORY** (AV)

1920 N Street, N.W., 20036-1601
Telephone: 202-331-8800
Fax: 202-331-8330
Telex: 904173
Cable Address: "Caglaw"
Akron, Ohio Office: 50 S. Main Street, Suite 502, 44308-1828.
Telephone: 216-376-8090.
Fax: 216-376-8386.
Cincinnati, Ohio Office: 312 Walnut Street, 14th Floor, 45202-4029.
Telephone: 513-352-6700.
Fax: 513-241-4771.
Telex: 938003.
Cleveland, Ohio Office: 1100 National City Bank Building, 629 Euclid Avenue, 44114.
Telephone: 216-566-5500.
Fax: 216-566-5583.
Telex: 980217. Cable Address "Thomflor".

(See Next Column)

Columbus, Ohio Office: One Columbus, 10 West Broad Street, 43215-34353.
Telephone: 614-469-3200.
Fax: 614-469-3361.
Dayton, Ohio Office: 2000 Courthouse Plaza, N.E., 45402-1706.
Telephone: 513-443-6600.
Fax: 513-443-6637, 513-443-6635.
Palm Beach, Florida Office: 125 Worth Avenue, 33480-4466.
Telephone: 407-833-5900.
Fax: 407-833-5951.
Brussels, Belgium Office: Rue Des Chevaliers, Ridderstraat 14 - B.10, B-1050.
Telephone: 011-32-2-511-9326.
Fax: 011-32-2-513-9206.

MEMBER OF FIRM

Steven D. Cundra

For Complete List of Firm Personnel, See General Section

For full biographical listings, see the Martindale-Hubbell Law Directory

*** VENABLE, BAETJER, HOWARD & CIVILETTI** (AV)

A Partnership including Professional Corporations
Suite 1000, 1201 New York Avenue, N.W., 20005
Telephone: 202-962-4800
Fax: 202-962-8300
Baltimore, Maryland Office: Venable, Baetjer and Howard, 1800 Mercantile Bank & Trust Building, 2 Hopkins Plaza.
Telephone: 410-244-7400.
McLean, Virginia Office: Venable, Baetjer and Howard, Suite 400, 2010 Corporate Ridge.
Telephone: 703-760-1600.
Rockville, Maryland Office: Venable, Baetjer and Howard, Suite 500, One Church Street, P. O. Box 1906.
Telephone: 301-217-5600.
Towson, Maryland Office: Venable, Baetjer and Howard, 210 Allegheny Avenue, P. O. Box 5517.
Telephone: 410-494-6200.

MEMBERS OF FIRM

Benjamin R. Civiletti (P.C.) (Also at Baltimore and Towson, Maryland Offices)
Neal D. Borden (Not admitted in DC; Also at Baltimore, Maryland Office)
Douglas D. Connah, Jr. (P.C.) (Also at Baltimore, Maryland Office)
Joe A. Shull
Kenneth C. Bass, III (Also at McLean, Virginia Office)
Joel Z. Silver
Edward F. Glynn, Jr.
Michael Schatzow (Also at Baltimore and Towson, Maryland Offices)
Bryson L. Cook (P.C.) (Not admitted in DC; Also at Baltimore, Maryland Office)
James K. Archibald (Also at Baltimore and Towson, Maryland Offices)
James R. Myers
Jeffrey A. Dunn (Also at Baltimore, Maryland Office)
George F. Pappas (Also at Baltimore, Maryland Office)
James L. Shea (Not admitted in DC; also at Baltimore, Maryland Office)
William D. Coston
Amy Berman Jackson
William D. Quarles (Also at Towson, Maryland Office)
James A. Dunbar (Also at Baltimore, Maryland Office)
Robert J. Bolger, Jr. (Not admitted in DC; Also at Baltimore, Maryland Office)
Bruce H. Jurist (Also at Baltimore, Maryland Office)
Paul A. Serini (Not admitted in DC; Also at Baltimore, Maryland Office)
Gary M. Hnath

OF COUNSEL

Fred W. Hathaway

ASSOCIATES

David W. Goewey
Fernand A. Lavallee
Traci H. Mundy (Not admitted in DC)

For Complete List of Firm Personnel, See General Section

For full biographical listings, see the Martindale-Hubbell Law Directory

VERNER, LIIPFERT, BERNHARD, MCPHERSON AND HAND, CHARTERED (AV)

901 15th Street, N.W., 20005-2301
Telephone: 202-371-6000
Cable Address: "Verlip"
Telex: 1561792 VERLIP UT
Fax: 202-371-6279
McLean, Virginia Office: Sixth Floor, 8280 Greensboro Drive, 22102.
Telephone: 703-749-6000.
Fax: 703-749-6027.
Houston, Texas Office: 2600 Texas Commerce Tower, 600 Travis, 77002.
Telephone: 713-237-9034.
Fax: 713-237-1216.

(See Next Column)

VERNER, LIIPFERT, BERNHARD, MCPHERSON AND HAND CHARTERED—*Continued*

Douglas Ochs Adler
Berl Bernhard
Roy G. Bowman
Hopewell H. Darneille, III
Thomas M. Davidson
Michael D. Golden
Lloyd N. Hand
William F. Roeder, Jr.
Frederick J. Tansill
Susan O'Hearn Temkin
Buel White

OF COUNSEL

Frederick J. McConville
Mikol S. B. Neilson

For Complete List of Firm Personnel, See General Section

For full biographical listings, see the Martindale-Hubbell Law Directory

WATT, TIEDER & HOFFAR (AV)

601 Pennsylvania Avenue, N.W., Suite 900, 20004
Telephone: 202-462-4697
Telecopier: 703-893-8029
McLean Virginia Office: 7929 Westpark Drive, Suite 400.
Telephone: 703-749-1000.
Telecopier: 703-893-8029.
Irvine California Office: 3 Park Plaza, Suite 1530.
Telephone: 714-852-6700.

MEMBERS OF FIRM

John B. Tieder, Jr.
Robert K. Cox
David C. Romm

For full biographical listings, see the Martindale-Hubbell Law Directory

FLORIDA

*BRADENTON,** Manatee Co.

MCGUIRE, PRATT, MASIO & FARRANCE, P.A. (AV)

Suite 600, 1001 3rd Avenue West, P.O. Box 1866, 34206
Telephone: 813-748-7076
FAX: 813-747-9774

Hugh E. McGuire, Jr.
Charles J. Pratt, Jr.
Carol A. Masio
Robert A. Farrance
Richard G. Groff

OF COUNSEL

Carter H. Parry

Reference: Barnett Bank of Manatee County.

For full biographical listings, see the Martindale-Hubbell Law Directory

*CLEARWATER,** Pinellas Co.

LARSON & BOBENHAUSEN, PROFESSIONAL ASSOCIATION (AV)

16120 U.S. Highway 19 North, Suite 210, P.O. Box 17620, 34622-0620
Telephone: 813-535-5594
Telecopier: 813-535-4266

Roger A. Larson
Gale M. Bobenhausen
Scott Torrie
Camille J. Iurillo

Representative Clients: First Union National Bank of Florida; AmSouth Bank of Florida; Barnett Bank of Pasco County; Barnett Banks, Inc.; SunBank of Tampa Bay, N.A.; Rutenberg Housing Corp.

For full biographical listings, see the Martindale-Hubbell Law Directory

*FORT LAUDERDALE,** Broward Co.

BYRD & MURPHY (AV)

Suite 200N Justice Building, 524 South Andrews Avenue, 33301
Telephone: 305-463-1423
FAX: 305-463-5428

MEMBERS OF FIRM

Thomas E. Byrd
James O. Murphy, Jr.

Approved Attorneys for: Attorneys' Title Insurance Fund.

For Complete List of Firm Personnel, See General Section

For full biographical listings, see the Martindale-Hubbell Law Directory

DOUMAR, CURTIS, CROSS, LAYSTROM & PERLOFF (AV)

A Partnership of Professional Corporations
1177 Southeast Third Avenue, 33316
Telephone: 305-525-3441
Fax: 305-525-3423
Direct Miami Line: 305-945-3172

(See Next Column)

MEMBERS OF FIRM

Raymond A. Doumar (P.C.)
Charles L. Curtis (P.C.)
William S. Cross (P.C.)
C. William Laystrom, Jr. (P.C.)
John W. Perloff (P.C.)
E. Scott Allsworth (P.C.)
John D. Voigt (P.C.)
Jeffrey S. Wachs (P.C.)

ASSOCIATE

Mark E. Allsworth

Representative Clients: Albertson's, Inc.; Robinson-Humphrey/American Express; Deutsch-Ireland Properties; Massey-Yardley Chrysler Plymouth, Inc.; Waste Management, Inc.; Planned Development Corp.; Toys-R-Us Inc.; Lumbermans Mutual Casualty Co.; Melvin Simon And Associates.

For full biographical listings, see the Martindale-Hubbell Law Directory

MOMBACH, BOYLE & HARDIN, P.A. (AV)

Suite 1950 Broward Financial Centre, 500 East Broward Boulevard, 33394-3079
Telephone: 305-467-2200
Telecopier: 305-467-2210

Geoffrey S. Mombach
Conrad J. Boyle
David C. Hardin
Gary S. Singer
Mitchell D. Adler

Dean A. Brooks
Debra L Zelman

Representative Clients: Keenan Development Group; Net Realty Holding Trust; Mycon Corp.; BankAtlantic; Citibank, F.S.B.; Shenandoah Life; National Canada Finance Corp.; NationsBank of Florida, N.A.; Key Largo Anglers Club; Cat Cay Yacht Club.

For full biographical listings, see the Martindale-Hubbell Law Directory

SIMON, MOSKOWITZ & MANDELL, P.A. (AV)

Suite 510, 800 Corporate Drive, 33334
Telephone: 305-491-2000; Boca Raton Line: 407-750-7700
FAX: 305-491-2051

Eric A. Simon
Michael W. Moskowitz
Craig J. Mandell
Kenneth A. Rubin
William G. Salim, Jr.

Greg H. Rosenthal

OF COUNSEL

Shirley D. Weisman (P.A.) (Not admitted in FL)

Representative Clients: BP Oil Co.; Broward Marine, Inc.; Florida Palm-Aire, Inc.; Fort Lauderdale Jet Center, Inc.; Health Claims, Inc.; Health Services Network, Inc.; Holland Builders, Inc.; Humana, Inc.; NFL Alumni, Inc.; UDC Homes.

For full biographical listings, see the Martindale-Hubbell Law Directory

*FORT MYERS,** Lee Co.

GOLDBERG, GOLDSTEIN & BUCKLEY, P.A. (AV)

1515 Broadway, P.O. Box 2366, 33901-2366
Telephone: 813-334-1146
Fax: 813-334-3039
Naples, Florida Office: 2150 Goodlette Road, Suite 105, Parkway Financial Center, 33940.
Telephone: 813-262-4888.
Fax: 813-262-8716.
Port Charlotte, Florida Office: Emerald Square, Suite 1, 2852 Tamiami Trail, 33952.
Telephone: 813-624-2393.
Fax: 813-624-2155.
Cape Coral, Florida Office: 2330 S.E. 16th Place.
Telephone: 813-574-5575.
Fax: 813-574-9213.
Lehigh Acres, Florida Office: 1458 Lee Boulevard, Lee Boulevard Shopping Center, 33936.
Telephone: 813-368-6101.
Fax: 813-368-2461.
South Fort Myers, Florida Office: Horizon Plaza, 16050 South Tamiami Trail, Suites 101 and 102, 33908.
Telephone: 813-433-6777.
Fax: 813-433-0578.
Bonita Springs, Florida Office: 3431 Bonita Beach Road, Suite 208, 33923.
Telephone: 813-495-0003.
Fax: 813-495-0564.

Morton A. Goldberg
Ray Goldstein
Stephen W. Buckley
Harvey B. Goldberg
John B. Cechman
J. Jeffrey Rice
Mark A. Steinberg
David R. Linn
Donna L. Schnorr
Mark P. Smith
Richard Lee Purtz
Martin G. Arnowitz
George J. Mitar
Steven P. Kushner
Michael J. Ciccarone
Terry S. Nelson

(See Next Column)

GOLDBERG, GOLDSTEIN & BUCKLEY P.A., *Fort Myers—Continued*

William L. Welker
Jay Cooper
Jonathan D. Conant
Raymond L. Racila
Luis E. Insignares

Approved Attorneys for: Attorneys' Title Insurance Fund; Chicago Title Insurance Co.; American Pioneer Title Insurance Company; Stewart Title Guaranty Co.; First American Title Insurance Company.

For Complete List of Firm Personnel, See General Section

For full biographical listings, see the Martindale-Hubbell Law Directory

*JACKSONVILLE,** Duval Co.

KIRSCHNER, MAIN, PETRIE, GRAHAM, TANNER & DEMONT, PROFESSIONAL ASSOCIATION (AV)

One Independent Drive, Suite 2000, P.O. Box 1559, 32201-1559
Telephone: 904-354-4141
Telecopier: 904-358-2199

Barry C. Averitt
Michael E. Demont
Curtis S. Fallgatter
T. Malcolm Graham
Lee Stathis Haramis
T. Geoffrey Heekin
Kenneth M. Kirschner
James L. Main
Gayle Petrie
Michael G. Tanner

Howard L. Alford
Karen Smith French
Deborah Greene
Reese J. Henderson, Jr.
Kenneth B. Jacobs
Julie Anne Luten
Charles S. McCall
Marsha Phillips Proctor
John T. Rogerson, III
Ann Krueger Vining
Alan S. Wachs

For full biographical listings, see the Martindale-Hubbell Law Directory

LILES, GAVIN & COSTANTINO (AV)

One Enterprise Center, Suite 1500, 225 Water Street, 32202
Telephone: 904-634-1100
Fax: 904-634-1234

Rutledge R. Liles
R. Kyle Gavin
R. Scott Costantino
F. Bay Neal III

For full biographical listings, see the Martindale-Hubbell Law Directory

*KISSIMMEE,** Osceola Co.

POHL & BROWN, P.A.

(See Winter Park)

*MIAMI,** Dade Co.

CLARKE & SILVERGLATE, PROFESSIONAL ASSOCIATION (AV)

100 North Biscayne Boulevard, Suite 2401, 33132
Telephone: 305-377-0700
Fax: 305-377-3001

Mercer K. Clarke
Spencer H. Silverglate
Kelly Anne Luther

For full biographical listings, see the Martindale-Hubbell Law Directory

COLSON, HICKS, EIDSON, COLSON, MATTHEWS & GAMBA (AV)

Floor 47 First Union Financial Center, 200 South Biscayne Boulevard, 33131-2351
Telephone: 305-373-5400

MEMBERS OF FIRM

Bill Colson
William M. Hicks
Mike Eidson
Dean C. Colson
Joseph M. Matthews
Tomas F. Gamba
Tony Korvick
Enid Duany Mendoza

Reference: Northern Trust Bank of Florida.

For Complete List of Firm Personnel, See General Section

For full biographical listings, see the Martindale-Hubbell Law Directory

HALL AND O'BRIEN, P.A. (AV)

Penthouse, 1428 Brickell Avenue, 33131
Telephone: 305-374-5030
Fax: 305-374-5033

Andrew C. Hall
Richard F. O'Brien, III

Leana Marie Vastine
Christopher M. David

For full biographical listings, see the Martindale-Hubbell Law Directory

KAUFMAN MILLER DICKSTEIN & GRUNSPAN, P.A. (AV)

Suite 4650 Southeast Financial Center, 200 South Biscayne Boulevard, 33131
Telephone: 305-372-5200
Telecopy: 305-374-3200

Jeffrey W. Dickstein
Alan M. Grunspan
Edward A. Kaufman
Raymond V. Miller, Jr.

David James Smith

For full biographical listings, see the Martindale-Hubbell Law Directory

MERSHON, SAWYER, JOHNSTON, DUNWODY & COLE (AV)

A Partnership including Professional Associations
Suite 4500 First Union Financial Center, 200 South Biscayne Boulevard, 33131-2387
Telephone: 305-358-5100
Cable Address: "Mercole"
Telex: 515705
Fax: 305-376-8654
Naples, Florida Office: Pelican Bay Corporate Centre, Suite 501, 5551 Ridgewood Drive.
Telephone: 813-598-1055.
Fax: 813-598-1868.
West Palm Beach, Florida Office: 777 South Flagler Drive, Suite 900.
Telephone: 407-659-5990.
Fax: 407-659-6313.
Key West, Florida Office: 3132 North Side Drive, Suite 102.
Telephone: 305-296-1774.
Fax: 305-296-1715
London, England Office: Blake Lodge, Bridge Lane, London SW11 3AD, England.
Telephone: 44-71-978-7748.
Fax: 44-71-350-0156.

MEMBERS OF FIRM

Aubrey V. Kendall (P.A.)
William J. Dunaj (P.A.)
Henry H. Raattama, Jr., (P.A.)
James M. McCann, Jr. (Resident, West Palm Beach Office)
Barry G. Craig (P.A.)
Robert T. Wright, Jr.
Dennis M. Campbell (P.A.)
Douglas F. Darbut
Timothy J. Norris (P.A.)
Harvey W. Gurland, Jr.
Jeffrey D. Fridkin (Resident, Naples Office)
Carlos M. Sires
David B. McCrea (P.A.)
Philip M. Sprinkle, II (Resident, West Palm Beach Office)
John C. Shawde
Jorge R. Gutierrez (P.A.)
Jack A. Falk, Jr
Mary Ellen Valletta

OF COUNSEL

Alexander Penelas
John S. Schwartz

ASSOCIATES

Lawrence P. Rochefort
Doreen S. Moloney
Rona F. Morrow
Nancy A. Romfh (Resident, West Palm Beach Office)
John D. Eaton
Mario David Carballo
Elizabeth Cassidy Barber
Natalie Scharf
Gregg Metzger

Representative Clients: Arvida/JMB Partners; Bankers Trust Co.; Biscayne Kennel Club, Inc.; The Chase Manhattan Bank, N.A.; Lennar Corp.; Reynolds Metals Co.; United States Sugar Corp.; University of Miami.

For Complete List of Firm Personnel, See General Section

For full biographical listings, see the Martindale-Hubbell Law Directory

NICKLAUS, VALLE, CRAIG & WICKS (AV)

15th Floor New World Tower, 100 North Biscayne Boulevard, 33132
Telephone: 305-358-2888
Facsimile: 305-358-5501
Fort Lauderdale, Florida Office: Suite 101N, Justice Building, 524 South Andrews Avenue, 33301.
Telephone: 305-523-1858.
Facsimile: 305-523-8068.

MEMBERS OF FIRM

Edward R. Nicklaus
Laurence F. Valle
Lawrance B. Craig, III
William R. Wicks, III
James W. McCready, III
Michael W. Whitaker

ASSOCIATES

Richard D. Settler
Kevin M. Fitzmaurice
Timothy Maze Hartley
Keith S. Grybowski
Patricia Blanco
Michael J. Lynott

For full biographical listings, see the Martindale-Hubbell Law Directory

SIEGFRIED, RIVERA, LERNER, DE LA TORRE & PETERSEN, P.A. (AV)

Suite 1102, 201 Alhambra Circle (Coral Gables), 33134
Telephone: 305-442-3334
Fax: 305-443-3292
Fort Lauderdale Office: One Financial Plaza, Suite 2012, 33394.
Telephone: 305-832-0766.
Fax: 305-764-1759.

(See Next Column)

SIEGFRIED, RIVERA, LERNER, DE LA TORRE & PETERSEN P.A.—*Continued*

Steven M. Siegfried
Oscar R. Rivera
Lisa A. Lerner
Helio De La Torre
Byron G. Petersen (Resident, Fort Lauderdale Office)
Peter H. Edwards

Maria Victoria Arias
Daniel Davis
James F. Harrington
Elisabeth D. Kozlow
H. Hugh Mc Connell
Alberto Nouel Moris
Samuel A. Persaud

Reference: Southeast First National Bank of Miami.

For full biographical listings, see the Martindale-Hubbell Law Directory

SPARBER, KOSNITZKY, TRUXTON, DE LA GUARDIA SPRATT & BROOKS, P.A. (AV)

1401 Brickell Avenue Suite 700, 33131
Telephone: Dade: 305-379-7200; Broward: 305-760-9133
Fax: 305-379-0800

Byron L. Sparber
Michael Kosnitzky
Gregg S. Truxton
Oscar G. de la Guardia
Marc H. Auerbach

Jorge A. Gonzalez
Diana L. Grub
Thomas O. Wells
Deborah R. Mayo

For Complete List of Firm Personnel, See General Section

For full biographical listings, see the Martindale-Hubbell Law Directory

STEARNS WEAVER MILLER WEISSLER ALHADEFF & SITTERSON, P.A. (AV)

Suite 2200 Museum Tower, 150 West Flagler Street, 33130
Telephone: 305-789-3200
FAX: 305-789-3395
Tampa, Florida Office: Suite 2200 Landmark Centre, 401 East Jackson Street.
Telephone: 813-223-4800.
Fort Lauderdale, Florida Office: 200 East Broward Boulevard, Suite 1900.
Telephone: 305-462-9500.

E. Richard Alhadeff
Louise Jacowitz Allen
Stuart D. Ames
Thomas P. Angelo (Resident, Fort Lauderdale Office)
Lawrence J. Bailin (Resident, Tampa Office)
Patrick A. Barry (Resident, Fort Lauderdale Office)
Lisa K. Bennett (Resident, Fort Lauderdale Office)
Susan Fleming Bennett (Resident, Tampa Office)
Mark J. Bernet (Resident, Tampa Office)
Claire Bailey Carraway (Resident, Tampa Office)
Seth T. Craine (Resident, Tampa Office)
Piero Luciano Desiderio (Resident, Fort Lauderdale Office)
Mark P. Dikeman
Sharon Quinn Dixon
Alan H. Fein
Owen S. Freed
Dean M. Freitag
Robert E. Gallagher, Jr.
Alice R. Huneycutt (Resident, Tampa Office)
Theodore A. Jewell
Elizabeth J. Keeler
Teddy D. Klinghoffer
Robert T. Kofman
Thomas A. Lash (Resident, Tampa Office)
Joy Spillis Lundeen
Brian J. McDonough
Francisco J. Menendez
Antonio R. Menendez
Alison W. Miller
Vicki Lynn Monroe
Harold D. Moorefield, Jr.
John N. Muratides (Resident, Tampa Office)
John K. Olson (Resident, Tampa Office)
Robert C. Owens
Patricia A. Redmond
Carl D. Roston
Steven D. Rubin
Mark A. Schneider
Curtis H. Sitterson
Mark D. Solov
Eugene E. Stearns
Bradford Swing
Dennis R. Turner
Ronald L. Weaver (Resident, Tampa Office)
Robert I. Weissler
Patricia G. Welles
Martin B. Woods (Resident, Fort Lauderdale Office)

Shawn M. Bayne (Resident, Fort Lauderdale Office)
Lisa Berg
Hans C. Beyer (Resident, Tampa Office)
Dawn A. Carapella (Resident, Tampa Office)
Christina Maria Diaz
Robert I. Finvarb
Patricia K. Green
Marilyn D. Greenblatt
Richard B. Jackson
Aimee C. Jimenez
Cheryl A. Kaplan
Michael I. Keyes
Vernon L. Lewis
Kevin Bruce Love
Adam Coatsworth Mishcon
Elizabeth G. Rice (Resident, Tampa Office)
Glenn M. Rissman
Claudia J. Saenz
Richard E. Schatz
Robert P. Shantz (Resident, Tampa Office)
Martin S. Simkovic
Ronni D. Solomon

(See Next Column)

Jo Claire Spear (Resident, Tampa Office)
Gail Marie Stage (Resident, Fort Lauderdale Office)
Annette Torres
Barbara L. Wilhite

OF COUNSEL

Stephen A. Bennett

For full biographical listings, see the Martindale-Hubbell Law Directory

STUZIN AND CAMNER, PROFESSIONAL ASSOCIATION (AV)

25th Floor, 1221 Brickell Avenue, 33131-3260
Telephone: 305-577-0600

Charles B. Stuzin
Alfred R. Camner
Stanley A. Beiley
Marsha D. Bilzin
David S. Garbett
Nina S. Gordon
Barry D. Hunter
Nikki J. Nedbor
Neale J. Poller

Lisa R. Carstarphen
Maria E. Chang
Barry P. Gruher
Gustavo D. Llerena
Sherry D. McMillan
Roger A. Preziosi

OF COUNSEL

Anne Shari Camner

References: Citizens Federal Bank; City National Bank of Miami; Barnett Bank of South Florida, N.A.

For full biographical listings, see the Martindale-Hubbell Law Directory

*NAPLES,** Collier Co.

EMERSON & EMERSON, P.A. (AV)

Suite 300, The Four Hundred Building, 400 Fifth Avenue South, 33940
Telephone: 813-261-5200
Telecopier: 813-261-5201

John W. Emerson
Ralph W. Emerson (1932-1989)

For full biographical listings, see the Martindale-Hubbell Law Directory

NORTH MIAMI BEACH, Dade Co.

BUCHANAN INGERSOLL, PROFESSIONAL CORPORATION (AV)

One Turnberry Place, 19495 Biscayne Boulevard, 33180
Telephone: 305-933-5600
Telecopier: 305-933-2350
Pittsburgh, Pennsylvania Office: 5800 USX Tower, 600 Grant Street.
Telephone: 412-562-8800.
Philadelphia, Pennsylvania Office: Two Logan Square, Twelfth Floor, 18th & Arch Streets.
Telephone: 215-665-8700.
Harrisburg, Pennsylvania Office: Vartan Parc, 30 North Third Street.
Telephone: 717-237-4800.
Tampa, Florida Office: Suite 1030, 101 East Kennedy Boulevard.
Telephone: 813-222-8180.
Princeton, New Jersey Office: Buchanan Ingersoll, A Partnership, College Centre, 500 College Road East.
Telephone: 609-452-2666.
Lexington, Kentucky Office: Suite 600, PNC Bank Plaza, 200 West Vine Street.
Telephone: 606-225-5333.

Barry A. Nelson

For Complete List of Firm Personnel, See General Section

For full biographical listings, see the Martindale-Hubbell Law Directory

*ORLANDO,** Orange Co.

BOROUGHS, GRIMM, BENNETT & MORLAN, P.A. (AV)

201 East Pine Street, Suite 500, P.O. Box 3309, 32802-3309
Telephone: 407-841-3353
Telecopier: 407-843-9587

R. Lee Bennett
Thomas Boroughs
William A. Grimm
Harold E. Morlan, II
John R. Simpson, Jr.
Douglas E. Starcher
Robert J. Stovash

Edward R. Alexander, Jr.
Kenneth P. Hazouri

OF COUNSEL

Robert W. Boyd

General Counsel for: Autonomous Technologies Corporation; Bubble Room, Inc.; The Civil Design Group, Inc.; Datamax Corporation; The Investment Counsel Company; Sawtek Inc.

For full biographical listings, see the Martindale-Hubbell Law Directory

Orlando—Continued

FRITH, STUMP & STOREY, P.A. (AV)

SunBank Center, Suite 1424, 200 South Orange Avenue, P.O. Box 3388, 32802-3388
Telephone: 407-425-2571
Telecopier: 407-425-0827
Tampa, Florida Office: NationsBank Plaza, Suite 2610, 400 Ashley Drive North, P.O. Box 1080.
Telephone: 813-273-0073,
Telecopier: 813-272-1455.

Alfred L. Frith
Philip D. Storey
John R. Stump
W. Scott Callahan

OF COUNSEL

Robert M. Coplen (Resident, Tampa, Florida Office)

Gary J. Lublin
John S. Penton
John S. Elzeer (Resident, Tampa Office)

Representative Clients: Barnett Bank; Chase Manhattan Service Corp.; Federal Deposit Insurance Corp.; First Union National Bank; Firstcard Services, Inc.; Montgomery Wards; NationsBank of North Carolina, N.A.; Resolution Trust Corp.; Sunbank, N.A.; Visa, U.S.A.

For full biographical listings, see the Martindale-Hubbell Law Directory

O'NEILL, CHAPIN, MARKS, LIEBMAN, COOPER & CARR (AV)

A Partnership including Professional Associations
865 Eola Park Center, 200 East Robinson Street, 32801
Telephone: 407-425-2751
Telex: 407-423-1192

Bernard C. O'Neill, Jr. (P.A.)
John B. Liebman (P.A.)
Bruce E. Chapin (P.A.)
Mark O. Cooper (P.A.)
Robert O. Marks (P.A.)
George E. Carr

ASSOCIATES

Lisa M. Cvetic
Rod C. Lundy

Reference: First Union National Bank.

For full biographical listings, see the Martindale-Hubbell Law Directory

POHL & BROWN, P.A.

(See Winter Park)

ROBERTSON, WILLIAMS & McDONALD, P.A. (AV)

538 East Washington Street, 32801
Telephone: 407-425-1606
Fax: 407-872-1341
Other Orlando Office: 20 North Eola Drive.

John M. Robertson
Hubert W. Williams (1937-1986)
J. Stephen McDonald

Beth S. Schick

Reference: First Union Bank.

For full biographical listings, see the Martindale-Hubbell Law Directory

*ST. AUGUSTINE,** St. Johns Co.

DOBSON, CHRISTENSEN & BROWN, P.A. (AV)

66 Cuna Street, Suite B, 32084
Telephone: 904-824-9032
Fax: 904-824-9236

Geoffrey B. Dobson
Patti A. Christensen
Ronald W Brown

For full biographical listings, see the Martindale-Hubbell Law Directory

*SARASOTA,** Sarasota Co.

DAVID S. WATSON CHARTERED (AV)

1605 Main Street, Suite 612, 34236
Telephone: 813-366-8891
FAX: 813-366-1806

David S. Watson

OF COUNSEL

Richard W. Cooney

For full biographical listings, see the Martindale-Hubbell Law Directory

*TALLAHASSEE,** Leon Co.

RADEY HINKLE THOMAS & McARTHUR (AV)

Suite 1000 Monroe-Park Tower, 101 North Monroe Street, P.O. Drawer 11307, 32302
Telephone: 904-681-7766
Telecopier: 904-681-0506

(See Next Column)

John Radey
Elizabeth Waas McArthur
Robert L. Hinkle
Ricky L. Polston
Harry O. Thomas
Jeffrey L. Frehn
Leslie G. Street

Representative Clients: Columbia/HCA Heatlthcare Corp.; Johnson & Johnson; Electronic Data Systems Corp.; Commonwealth Land Title Insurance Co.; State Mutual Life Assurance Company of America.

For full biographical listings, see the Martindale-Hubbell Law Directory

*TAMPA,** Hillsborough Co.

CAREY, O'MALLEY, WHITAKER & LINS, P.A. (AV)

Suite 1190, 100 South Ashley Drive, P.O. Box 499, 33601-0499
Telephone: 813-221-8210
Telecopier: 813-221-1430

Michael R. Carey
D. Michael Lins
Andrew M. O'Malley
Douglas P. Manson
Daniel D. Whitaker
Randall P. Mueller
Sean V. Donnelly

For full biographical listings, see the Martindale-Hubbell Law Directory

LANGFORD, HILL & TRYBUS, P.A. (AV)

Suite 800, Bayshore Place, 601 Bayshore Boulevard, 33606
Telephone: 813-251-5533
Telecopier: 813-251-1900
Wats: 1-800-277-2005

E. C. Langford
Ronald G. Hock
Edward A. Hill
Catherine M. Catlin
Ronald H. Trybus
Debra M. Kubicsek
William B. Smith

Fredrique B. Boire
Frederick T. Reeves
Muriel Desloovere
Barbara A. Sinsley
Kevin H. O'Neill
Stephens B. Woodrough (Not admitted in FL)
Vicki L. Page
Anthony G. Woodward

Representative Clients: Affiliated of Florida, Inc.; American Federation Insurance Co.; Armor Insurance; Bank of Tampa; Central Bank of Tampa; Cintas Corp.; Container Corporation of America; CU Financial Services; Farm Stores, Inc.; First Union Home Equity Bank.

For full biographical listings, see the Martindale-Hubbell Law Directory

RYDBERG, GOLDSTEIN & BOLVES, P.A. (AV)

Suite 200, 500 East Kennedy Boulevard, 33602
Telephone: 813-229-3900
Telecopier: 813-229-6101

Marsha Griffin Rydberg
Donald Alan Workman
Bruce S. Goldstein
David M. Corry
Brian A. Bolves
Leenetta Blanton
Robert E. V. Kelley, Jr.
Peter Baker
Homer Duvall, III
Jeffery R. Ward
Richard Thomas Petitt
Roy J. Ford, Jr.
John J. Dingfelder

For full biographical listings, see the Martindale-Hubbell Law Directory

WAGNER, VAUGHAN & McLAUGHLIN, P.A. (AV)

708 Jackson Street (Corner of Jefferson), and 601 Bayshore Boulevard, Suite 910, 33602
Telephone: 813-223-7421; 813-225-4000
FAX: 813-221-0254; 813-225-4010

Bill Wagner (Resident, Bayshore Boulevard Office)
Roger A. Vaughan, Jr.
John J. McLaughlin

Alan F. Wagner (Resident, Bayshore Boulevard Office)
Denise E. Vaughan
Ruth Whetstone Wagner (Resident, Bayshore Boulevard Office)
Weldon "Web" Earl Brennan (Resident, Bayshore Boulevard Office)
Bob Vaughan

For full biographical listings, see the Martindale-Hubbell Law Directory

*WEST PALM BEACH,** Palm Beach Co.

BURT & PUCILLO (AV)

Esperanté, Suite 960, 222 Lakeview Avenue, 33401
Telephone: 407-835-9400
Telecopier: 407-835-0322

MEMBERS OF FIRM

C. Oliver Burt, III
Michael J. Pucillo

ASSOCIATES

Wendy Hope Zoberman
Andrew H. Kayton

(See Next Column)

BURT & PUCILLO—*Continued*

OF COUNSEL

Carol McLean Brewer

For full biographical listings, see the Martindale-Hubbell Law Directory

SEARCY DENNEY SCAROLA BARNHART & SHIPLEY, PROFESSIONAL ASSOCIATION (AV)

2139 Palm Beach Lakes Boulevard, P.O. Drawer 3626, 33402-3626
Telephone: 407-686-6300
800-780-8607
Fax: 407-478-0754

John Scarola
F. Gregory Barnhart
C. Calvin Warriner, III
William A. Norton
David J. Sales

LEGAL SUPPORT PERSONNEL

Emilio Diamantis (Paralegal/Investigator)
John C. Hopkins (Paralegal/Investigator)
J. Peter Love (Paralegal/Investigator)
Marjorie A. Morgan (Paralegal)
Joel C. Padgett (Paralegal/Investigator)
Kelly Lynn Hopkins (Paralegal/Investigator)

For Complete List of Firm Personnel, See General Section

For full biographical listings, see the Martindale-Hubbell Law Directory

WINTER PARK, Orange Co.

POHL & BROWN, P.A. (AV)

280 West Canton Avenue, Suite 410, P.O. Box 3208, 32789
Telephone: 407-647-7645; 407-647-POHL
Telefax: 407-647-2314

Frank L. Pohl
Usher L. Brown
Houston E. Short
Dwight I. Cool
William W. Pouzar
Mary B. Van Leuven

OF COUNSEL

Frederick W. Peirsol

Representative Clients: Orange County Comptroller; Osceola County; School Board of Osceola County, Florida; Osceola Tourist Development Council; NationsBank of Florida, N.A.; SunBank, N.A.; The Bank of Winter Park; Bekins Moving and Storage Co., Inc.; Champion Boats, Inc.; KeyCom Telephone Systems, Inc.

For full biographical listings, see the Martindale-Hubbell Law Directory

GEORGIA

*AMERICUS,** Sumter Co.

OXFORD, MCKELVEY & JONES, P.C. (AV)

Old Fire Hall, 109 North Lee Street, P.O. Box J, 31709-0298
Telephone: 912-924-6108
FAX: 912-924-0935

Charles Oliver Oxford
Howard S. McKelvey, Jr.
Randolph B. Jones, Jr.

Representative Client: Reeves Construction Co.

For full biographical listings, see the Martindale-Hubbell Law Directory

*ATLANTA,** Fulton Co.

DAVID G. CROCKETT, P.C. (AV)

1000 Equitable Building, 100 Peachtree Street, N.W., 30303
Telephone: 404-522-4280
Telecopier: 404-589-9891

David G. Crockett

Approved Attorney for: Chicago Title Insurance Co.
Reference: NationsBank, N.A.

For full biographical listings, see the Martindale-Hubbell Law Directory

DREW ECKL & FARNHAM (AV)

880 West Peachtree Street, P.O. Box 7600, 30357
Telephone: 404-885-1400
Facsimile: 404-876-0992

MEMBERS OF FIRM

James M. Poe
T. Bart Gary
Paul W. Burke
J. William Haley

Representative Clients: American International Adjustment Co.; Chicago Title Insurance Co.; CIGNA; Crum & Forster Commercial Insurance; Ford Motor Co.; Frito-Lay, Inc.; General Motors; Georgia Pacific Corp.; Liberty Mutual Insurance Co.; Parthenon/Hospital Corporation of America.

(See Next Column)

For Complete List of Firm Personnel, See General Section

For full biographical listings, see the Martindale-Hubbell Law Directory

FRANKEL, HARDWICK, TANENBAUM & FINK, P.C. (AV)

359 East Paces Ferry Road, N.E., 30305
Telephone: 404-266-2930
Fax: 404-231-3362

Pearce D. Hardwick
Allan J. Tanenbaum
Pepi Friedman
Barbara A. Lincoln

Representative Clients: Commercial Bank of Georgia; First Capital Bank; Metro Bank; The Money Store Investment Corp.; SouthTrust Bank of Georgia, N.A.; Venture Construction Company.

For Complete List of Firm Personnel, See General Section

For full biographical listings, see the Martindale-Hubbell Law Directory

GOLDNER, SOMMERS, SCRUDDER & BASS (AV)

2839 Paces Ferry Road, Suite 800, 30339-3774
Telephone: 404-436-4777
Facsimile: 404-436-8777

Henry E. Scrudder, Jr.
Glenn S. Bass
C. G. Jester, Jr.
Alfred A. Quillian, Jr.

For Complete List of Firm Personnel, See General Section

For full biographical listings, see the Martindale-Hubbell Law Directory

GREENE, BUCKLEY, JONES & MCQUEEN (AV)

P.O. Box 56446, 30343
Telephone: 404-522-3541
Telecopier: 404-522-3677

Harry L. Greene (1896-1974)

MEMBERS OF FIRM

John David Jones
C. Richard McQueen
John E. Talmadge
James C. Frenzel
Harold S. White, Jr.
Daniel A. Angelo
Francis Carl Schenck
F. Taylor Putney, Jr.
Edward D. Buckley, III
Margaret L. Milroy
J. Russell Phillips

ASSOCIATES

William D. Matthews
B. Kyle Childress
H. Lee Pruett
Leslie C. Ruiter
Rose E. Goff
Henry M. Perlowski

OF COUNSEL

Ferdinand Buckley
Jack F. Williams (Not admitted in GA)

Counsel for: Graybar Electric Co.; Pennsylvania National Mutual Casualty Insurance Co.; Reliance Insurance Co.; Roadway Services, Inc.

For full biographical listings, see the Martindale-Hubbell Law Directory

PARKER, HUDSON, RAINER & DOBBS (AV)

1500 Marquis Two Tower, 285 Peachtree Center Avenue, N.E., 30303
Telephone: 404-523-5300
FAX: 404-522-8409
Tallahassee, Florida Office: The Perkins House, 118 North Gadsden Street, 32301.
Telephone: 904-681-0191.
FAX: 904-681-9493.

MEMBERS OF FIRM

C. Edward Dobbs
Mitchell M. Purvis
Robert A. Crosby
Leigh P. Vancil

For full biographical listings, see the Martindale-Hubbell Law Directory

STOKES LAZARUS & CARMICHAEL (AV)

80 Peachtree Park Drive, N.E., 30309-1320
Telephone: 404-352-1465
Fax: 404-352-8463

MEMBERS OF FIRM

Marion B. Stokes
Wayne H. Lazarus
William K. Carmichael

ASSOCIATES

Richard J. Joseph
Douglas L. Brooks
Derek W. Johanson

For full biographical listings, see the Martindale-Hubbell Law Directory

THOMAS, KENNEDY, SAMPSON & PATTERSON (AV)

1600 Bank South Building, 55 Marietta Street, N.W., 30303
Telephone: 404-688-4503
Telecopier: 404-681-2950

(See Next Column)

THOMAS, KENNEDY, SAMPSON & PATTERSON, *Atlanta—Continued*

MEMBERS OF FIRM

John Loren Kennedy (1942-1994)
Myra H. Dixon
R. David Ware
Thomas G. Sampson
Patrise M. Perkins-Hooker
P. Andrew Patterson
Jeffrey E. Tompkins

ASSOCIATES

Rosalind T. Drakeford
Melynee C. Leftridge
Regina E. McMillan
La'Sean M. Zilton

For full biographical listings, see the Martindale-Hubbell Law Directory

WALLACE & DE MAYO, P.C. (AV)

5775-C Peachtree Dunwoody Road, Suite 250, 30342
Telephone: 404-843-0277
Fax: 404-252-5460

Richard T. De Mayo

For full biographical listings, see the Martindale-Hubbell Law Directory

WEISZ & ASSOCIATES (AV)

Suite 900 Live Oak Center, 3475 Lenox Road, N.E., 30326-1232
Telephone: 404-233-7888
Facsimile: 404-261-1925

Peter R. Weisz

ASSOCIATE

Cathy Rae Nash

LEGAL SUPPORT PERSONNEL

PARALEGALS

Jo Anne Gunn

For full biographical listings, see the Martindale-Hubbell Law Directory

*AUGUSTA,** Richmond Co.

PAINE, MCELREATH & HYDER, P.C. (AV)

301 Wheeler Executive Center, 3540 Wheeler Road, 30909
Telephone: 706-738-9710
Telecopier: 706-738-9761

Travers W. Paine, III
Benjamin F. McElreath
James D. Hyder, Jr.

For full biographical listings, see the Martindale-Hubbell Law Directory

WARLICK, TRITT & STEBBINS (AV)

15th Floor, First Union Bank Building, 30901
Telephone: 706-722-7543
Fax: 706-722-1822
Columbia County Office: 119 Davis Road, Martinez, Georgia 30907.
Telephone: 706-860-7595.
Fax: 705-860-7597.

MEMBERS OF FIRM

William Byrd Warlick
E. L. Clark Speese
Roy D. Tritt (Resident, Martinez Office)
Michael W. Terry
D. Scott Broyles
Charles C. Stebbins, III
Ross S. Snellings
C. Gregory Bryan

OF COUNSEL

Richard E. Miley

For full biographical listings, see the Martindale-Hubbell Law Directory

*CARROLLTON,** Carroll Co.

TISINGER, TISINGER, VANCE & GREER, A PROFESSIONAL CORPORATION (AV)

100 Wagon Yard Plaza, P.O. Box 2069, 30117
Telephone: 404-834-4467
FAX: 404-834-5426

Richard G. Tisinger
Phillip D. Wilkins
J. Thomas Vance
Stacey L. Blackmon
C. David Mecklin, Jr.
Steven T. Minor
G. Gregory Shadrix
Edith Freeman Rooks

Representative Clients: Pinnacle Financial Group, Inc.; Richards & Malloy Manufacturing, Inc.; Southwire Company; Tanner Medical Center, Inc.

For Complete List of Firm Personnel, See General Section

For full biographical listings, see the Martindale-Hubbell Law Directory

*COLUMBUS,** Muscogee Co.

JACOB BEIL (AV)

Heritage Tower, Suite 301, 18 - 9th Street, P.O. Box 1126, 31902
Telephone: 706-596-9912
FAX: 706-596-9913

Reference: First Union National Bank of Georgia.

For full biographical listings, see the Martindale-Hubbell Law Directory

HATCHER, STUBBS, LAND, HOLLIS & ROTHSCHILD (AV)

Suite 500 The Corporate Center, 233 12th Street, P.O. Box 2707, 31902-2707
Telephone: 706-324-0201
Telecopier: 706-322-7747

MEMBERS OF FIRM

Alan F. Rothschild
George W. Mize, Jr.
J. Barrington Vaught
John M. Tanzine, III
Charles T. Staples
Alan F. Rothschild, Jr.
Joseph L. Waldrep
William C. Pound

ASSOCIATE

Mote W. Andrews III

General Counsel for: Trust Company Bank of Columbus, N.A.; TOM'S Foods Inc.; Burnham Service Corp.; Kinnett Dairies, Inc.; Georgia Crown Distributing Co.; Bill Heard Enterprises, Inc.
Assistant Division Counsel for: Norfolk Southern Corp.
Local Counsel for: First Union National Bank of Georgia; Ford Motor Credit Corp.; Chrysler Credit Corp.

For Complete List of Firm Personnel, See General Section

For full biographical listings, see the Martindale-Hubbell Law Directory

NORCROSS, Gwinnett Co.

THOMPSON & SLAGLE, P.C. (AV)

5335 Triangle Parkway Suite 550, 30092
Telephone: 404-662-5999

DeWitte Thompson
Jefferson B. Slagle
David J. Merbaum

Gady Zeewy
David Ian Matthews

For full biographical listings, see the Martindale-Hubbell Law Directory

HAWAII

*HONOLULU,** Honolulu Co.

ASHFORD & NAKAMURA (AV)

2910 Pacific Tower, 1001 Bishop Street, 96813
Telephone: 808-528-0444
Telex: 723-8158
Telecopier: (808) 533-0761
Cable Address: Justlaw

George W. Ashford, Jr.
Lee T. Nakamura

Ann C. Kemp
Francis T. O'Brien

Representative Clients: Baker Industries, Inc.; Burns International Security Services; Clark Equipment Co.; Great Lakes Chemical Corporation; California Union Insurance Co.; Fireman's Fund Insurance Companies; Great American Insurance Companies; Guaranty National Companies; Horace Mann Insurance Company; Marine Office of America Corp.

For full biographical listings, see the Martindale-Hubbell Law Directory

DWYER IMANAKA SCHRAFF KUDO MEYER & FUJIMOTO ATTORNEYS AT LAW, A LAW CORPORATION (AV)

1800 Pioneer Plaza, 900 Fort Street Mall, 96813
Telephone: 808-524-8000
Telecopier: 808-526-1419
Mailing Address: P.O. Box 2727, 96803

John R. Dwyer, Jr.
William G. Meyer, III
Mitchell A. Imanaka
Wesley M. Fujimoto
Paul A. Schraff
Ronald Van Grant
Benjamin A. Kudo (Atty. at Law, A Law Corp.)
Jon M. H. Pang
Blake W. Bushnell
Kenn N. Kojima

Adelbert Green
Tracy Timothy Woo
Richard T. Asato, Jr.
Lawrence I. Kawasaki
Scott W. Settle
Douglas H. Inouye
Darcie S. Yoshinaga
Christine A. Low

(See Next Column)

DWYER IMANAKA SCHRAFF KUDO MEYER & FUJIMOTO ATTORNEYS AT LAW, A LAW CORPORATION—*Continued*

OF COUNSEL

Randall Y. Iwase

For full biographical listings, see the Martindale-Hubbell Law Directory

FOLEY MAEHARA NIP & CHANG (AV)

2700 Grosvenor Center, 737 Bishop Street, 96813
Telephone: 808-526-3011
Telecopier: 808-523-1171, 808-526-0121, 808-533-4814

MEMBERS OF FIRM

Thomas M. Foley
Eric T. Maehara
Renton L. K. Nip
Wesley Y. S. Chang
Carl Tom
Edward R. Brooks
Arlene S. Kishi
Susan M. Ichinose
Robert F. Miller
Christian P. Porter

ASSOCIATES

Paula W. Chong
Lenore H. Lee
Leanne A. N. Nikaido
Jordan D. Wagner
Donna H. Yamamoto
Mark J. Bernardin
Jenny K. T. Wakayama

OF COUNSEL

Elizabeth A. Ivey

References: First Hawaiian Bank; Bank of Honolulu; Bank of Hawaii.

For full biographical listings, see the Martindale-Hubbell Law Directory

IDAHO

*BOISE,** Ada Co.

ELAM & BURKE, A PROFESSIONAL ASSOCIATION (AV)

Key Financial Center, 702 West Idaho Street, P.O. Box 1539, 83701
Telephone: 208-343-5454
Telecopier: 208-384-5844

M. Allyn Dingel, Jr.
David B. Lincoln
Randall A. Peterman
Peter C. K. Marshall
Jeffery J. Ventrella

Bradlee R. Frazer

Representative Clients: Morrison-Knudsen, Inc.; Texas Instruments, Inc.; Prudential Securities, Inc.; Pechiney Corp.; Dow Corning Corporation; U.S. West Communications; State Farm Insurance Cos.; Sinclair Oil Company d/b/a Sun Valley Company; Farmers Insurance Group; Hecla Mining Company.

For Complete List of Firm Personnel, See General Section

For full biographical listings, see the Martindale-Hubbell Law Directory

HALL, FARLEY, OBERRECHT & BLANTON (AV)

Key Financial Center, 702 West Idaho Street, Suite 700, P.O. Box 1271, 83701-1271
Telephone: 208-336-0404
Facsimile: 208-336-5193

Richard E. Hall
Donald J. Farley
Phillip S. Oberrecht
Raymond D. Powers
Candy Wagahoff Dale
Robert B. Luce
J. Kevin West
Bart W. Harwood

J. Charles Blanton
John J. Burke
Steven J. Hippler
Thorpe P. Orton
Ronald S. Best (Not admitted in ID)

References: Boise State University; Farm Bureau Mutual Insurance Company of Idaho; Medical Insurance Exchange of California; The St. Paul Cos.

For full biographical listings, see the Martindale-Hubbell Law Directory

ROSHOLT, ROBERTSON & TUCKER, CHARTERED (AV)

Suite 600, 1221 W. Idaho, P.O. Box 2139, 83701-2139
Telephone: 208-336-0700
Fax: 208-344-6034
Twin Falls, Idaho Office: 142 Third Avenue North, P.O. Box 1906.
Telephone: 208-734-0700.
Fax: 208-736-0041.

James C. Tucker

Jerry Jensen
Bruce Smith
Paul W. Samuelson

For full biographical listings, see the Martindale-Hubbell Law Directory

WILSON, CARNAHAN & MCCOLL, CHARTERED (AV)

420 Washington Street, P.O. Box 1544, 83701
Telephone: 208-345-9100
FAX: 208-384-0442

Jeffrey M. Wilson
Debrha Jo Carnahan
Brian F. McColl
Stephanie Jo Williams

Representative Clients: A & J Construction, Inc.; Pure-gro Company; Transamerica Commercial Finance Corp.; John H. Crowther, Inc.; Jess W. Swan Insurance Agency; Higgins and Rutledge Insurance Co., Inc.; Communication Workers of America, Local # 8103.

For full biographical listings, see the Martindale-Hubbell Law Directory

*TWIN FALLS,** Twin Falls Co.

ROSHOLT, ROBERTSON & TUCKER, CHARTERED (AV)

142 Third Avenue North, P.O. Box 1906, 83303-1906
Telephone: 208-734-0700
Fax: 208-736-0041
Boise, Idaho Office: Suite 600, 1221 W. Idaho, P.O. Box 2139.
Telephone: 208-336-0700.
Fax: 208-344-6034.

John A. Rosholt
J. Evan Robertson
Gary D. Slette

Thomas J. Ryan
Timothy J. Stover

For full biographical listings, see the Martindale-Hubbell Law Directory

ILLINOIS

CHAMPAIGN, Champaign Co.

HARRINGTON, PORTER & WINKEL (AV)

Suite 601 Huntington Towers, 201 West Springfield Avenue, P.O. Box 1550, 61824-1550
Telephone: 217-352-4167
Telecopier: 217-352-8707

MEMBERS OF FIRM

Earl C. Harrington (1895-1981)
Louis A. Busch (1886-1946)
Robert F. Busch (1914-1969)
W. Kenneth Porter
Thomas E. Harrington
Daniel G. Harrington
Richard J. Winkel, Jr.
Jeffrey W. Tock

OF COUNSEL

Kip Randolph Pope

For full biographical listings, see the Martindale-Hubbell Law Directory

*CHICAGO,** Cook Co.

FOX & GROVE, CHARTERED (AV)

311 South Wacker Drive Suite 6200, 60606
Telephone: 312-876-0500
Telecopier: 312-362-0700
St. Petersburg, Florida Office: Fox, Grove, Abbey, Adams, Reynolds, Byclick & Kiernan, Eleventh Floor, 360 Central Avenue.
Telephone: 813-821-2080.
Tampa, Florida Office: Fox, Grove, Abbey, Adams, Reynolds, Byclick & Kiernan, 500 East Kennedy Boulevard, Suite 200.
Telephone: 813-253-0745.
San Francisco, California Office: 240 Stockton Street, Suite 900.
Telephone: 415-956-1360.

Shayle P. Fox
Lawrence M. Cohen
S. Richard Pincus
Russell M. Kofoed
Jeffrey S. Goldman
Marty Denis
Steven L. Gillman
William Henry Barrett
Allison C. Blakley
Jeffrey E. Beeson

OF COUNSEL

Kalvin M. Grove
Joseph M. Kehoe, Jr.

Tamra S. Domeyer
Jill J. Gladney
Mari Rose Hatzenbuehler
Davi L. Hirsch
Joshua D. Holleb
Diane Kristen
Steven H. Kuh
Steven I. Locke
Daniel R. Madock
Robert M. Mintz
Paul A. Olsen
Michael Paull
Joel W. Rice
Peter S. Rukin
Kerry Evan Saltzman
Michael L. Sullivan
Douglas M. Werman

Labor Counsel for: Sears Roebuck and Co.; National Association of Independent Insurers; Alliance of American Insurers.
Representative Labor Client: Liberty Mutual Insurance Co.

For full biographical listings, see the Martindale-Hubbell Law Directory

Chicago—Continued

FREEMAN, FREEMAN & SALZMAN, P.C. (AV)

Suite 3200, 401 North Michigan Avenue, 60611
Telephone: 312-222-5100
Facsimile: 312-822-0870

Lee A. Freeman
Lee A. Freeman, Jr.
Jerrold E. Salzman
John F. Kinney
James T. Malysiak
Glynna W. Freeman
Phillip L. Stern
Albert F. Ettinger
Derek J. Meyer
Scott A. Browdy
Chris S. Gair
Christopher M. Kelly
(Not admitted in IL)

For full biographical listings, see the Martindale-Hubbell Law Directory

GORDON & GLICKSON, P.C. (AV)

36th Floor, 444 North Michigan Avenue, 60611-3903
Telephone: 312-321-1700
FAX: 312-321-9324
Springfield, Illinois Office: 600 South Second Street.
Telephone: 217-789-1040.
FAX: 217-789-1077.

Scott L. Glickson
Mark L. Gordon

For full biographical listings, see the Martindale-Hubbell Law Directory

McCONNELL & MENDELSON (AV)

140 South Dearborn Street, Suite 815, 60603
Telephone: 312-263-1212
Telecopier: 312-263-0402

Francis J. McConnell
Michael Sweig Mendelson
Mitchell Bryan
David O. Toolan
Richard A. Sloan
Peter S. Lubin

ASSOCIATES

Diane Hudson Andersen
Thomas G. Grace
Arthur U. Ellis

Reference: The Northern Trust Co., Chicago, Illinois.

For full biographical listings, see the Martindale-Hubbell Law Directory

STACK, FILPI & KAKACEK, CHARTERED (AV)

Suite 411, 140 South Dearborn Street, 60603-5298
Telephone: 312-782-0690; 236-5032
Telecopier: 312-782-0936
Telex: 25-3862 Counsel Cgo

Paul F. Stack
Robert A. Filpi
John J. Kakacek

OF COUNSEL

John H. Shurtleff
Michael A. McPartlin

For full biographical listings, see the Martindale-Hubbell Law Directory

WALINSKI & TRUNKETT, P.C. (AV)

25 East Washington Street, Suite 1927, 60602
Telephone: 312-704-0771
Fax: 312-704-8431

Robert J. Walinski
Kerry S. Trunkett

Lauren Newman
Michael R. Polk

Representative Clients: Edison Credit Union; Chicago Patrolmen's Federal Credit Union; Mid America National Bank; Paterno Imports, Ltd; Central Credit Union of Illinois; Trailmobile, Inc.; Bank of Indiana; Waste Management of the South Suburbs; American Construction Management, Inc.

For full biographical listings, see the Martindale-Hubbell Law Directory

*DANVILLE,** Vermilion Co.

SAIKLEY, GARRISON & COLOMBO, LTD. (AV)

208 West North Street, P.O. Box 6, 61834-0006
Telephone: 217-442-0244
FAX: 217-442-0582

Albert Saikley (1912-1987)
William L. Garrison
Gilbert H. Saikley
Kevin M. Colombo

Jeanette E. Bahnke

References: First Midwest Bank; City National Bank.

For full biographical listings, see the Martindale-Hubbell Law Directory

*JOLIET,** Will Co.

HERSCHBACH, TRACY, JOHNSON, BERTANI & WILSON (AV)

Two Rialto Square, 116 North Chicago Street, Sixth Floor, 60431
Telephone: 815-723-8500
Fax: 815-727-4846

Wayne R. Johnson
Thomas R. Wilson
Michael W. Hansen
A. Michael Wojtak
Kenneth A. Carlson

OF COUNSEL

Donald J. Tracy

General Counsel for: First National Bank of Joliet.
Representative Clients: Chicago Title Insurance Co.; Vulcan Materials Company; Dow Chemical, U.S.A.; Marathon Oil Co.; Waste Management, Inc.; General Electric Credit Corp.; The Copley Press, Inc.; Citizens Utilities Co.; Empress River Casino Corporation.

For Complete List of Firm Personnel, See General Section

For full biographical listings, see the Martindale-Hubbell Law Directory

*KANKAKEE,** Kankakee Co.

BLANKE, NORDEN, BARMANN, KRAMER & BOHLEN, P.C. (AV)

Suite 502, 200 East Court Street, P.O. Box 1787, 60901
Telephone: 815-939-1133
FAX: 815-939-0994

Armen R. Blanke (Deceased)
Paul F. Blanke (Retired)
Dennis A. Norden
Glen R. Barmann
Christopher W. Bohlen
Michael D. Kramer

For full biographical listings, see the Martindale-Hubbell Law Directory

*MOUNT VERNON,** Jefferson Co.

LAW OFFICE OF TERRY SHARP, P.C. (AV)

1115 Harrison Street, P.O. Box 906, 62864
Telephone: 618-242-0246
Fax: 618-242-1170
Benton, Illinois Office: 105 North Main Street.
Telephone: 618-435-5109.
FAX: 618-242-1170.

Terrell Lee Sharp

Marcus H. Herbert

For full biographical listings, see the Martindale-Hubbell Law Directory

INDIANA

ELKHART, Elkhart Co.

CHESTER, PFAFF & BROTHERSON (AV)

317 West Franklin Street, P.O. Box 507, 46515-0507
Telephone: 219-294-5421
Telecopier: 219-522-1476

MEMBERS OF FIRM

Robert A. Pfaff
James R. Brotherson
Glenn E. Killoren

For Complete List of Firm Personnel, See General Section

For full biographical listings, see the Martindale-Hubbell Law Directory

*EVANSVILLE,** Vanderburgh Co.

BOWERS, HARRISON, KENT & MILLER (AV)

25 N.W. Riverside Drive, P.O. Box 1287, 47706-1287
Telephone: 812-426-1231
Fax: 812-464-3676

MEMBERS OF FIRM

David V. Miller
Paul E. Black
Gary R. Case
Timothy J. Hubert
Thomas A. Massey
Greg A. Granger
Joseph H. Harrison, Jr.

Division Counsel in Indiana for: Southern Railway Co.
District Attorneys for the Southern District of Indiana: CSX Transportation, Inc.
Representative Clients: Permanent Federal Savings Bank; Citizens Realty & Insurance, Inc.

For Complete List of Firm Personnel, See General Section

For full biographical listings, see the Martindale-Hubbell Law Directory

Evansville—Continued

Statham, Johnson & McCray (AV)

215 North West Martin Luther King Jr. Boulevard, P.O. Box 3567, 47734-3567
Telephone: 812-425-5223
Facsimile: 812-421-4238

MEMBERS OF FIRM

R. Eugene Johnson
Thomas J. Kimpel
Donald J. Fuchs

ASSOCIATES

Thomas P. Norton
Keith E. Rounder

Representative Clients: Boetticher & Kellogg Co., Inc.; Brown & Hubert, Inc.; Bruckens, Inc.; Evansville Barge & Marine Services, Inc.; Evansville Distributing Company; Indiana Wholesalers, Inc.; Leed Selling Tools, Corp.; Rogers Jewelers; Ohio Valley Wireless.

For Complete List of Firm Personnel, See General Section

For full biographical listings, see the Martindale-Hubbell Law Directory

Ziemer, Stayman, Weitzel & Shoulders (AV)

(Formerly Early, Arnold & Ziemer)
1507 Old National Bank Building, P.O. Box 916, 47706
Telephone: 812-424-7575
Telecopier: 812-421-5089

MEMBERS OF FIRM

Robert F. Stayman
Marco L. DeLucio
Stephan E. Weitzel
Gregory G. Meyer

Reference: Old National Bank in Evansville.

For full biographical listings, see the Martindale-Hubbell Law Directory

*FORT WAYNE,** Allen Co.

Hunt, Suedhoff, Borror & Eilbacher (AV)

900 Courtside, 803 South Calhoun Street, 46802-2399
Telephone: 219-423-1311
Telecopier: 219-424-5396

RETIRED

Carl J. Suedhoff, Jr.

MEMBERS OF FIRM

Leigh L. Hunt (1899-1975)
William E. Borror (1932-1989)
Leonard E. Eilbacher
Robert E. Kabisch
Arthur G. Surguine, Jr.
Thomas C. Ewing
Carolyn White Spengler
Thomas W. Belleperche
Mark W. Baeverstad
Michael D. Mustard
Branch R. Lew
Carla J. Baird
James J. Shea
Scott L. Bunnell

ASSOCIATES

Dane L. Tubergen
David M. Lutz
Carolyn M. Trier
Kathleen A. Kilar
Daniel J. Palmer
Brian L. England
Craig J. Bobay

For full biographical listings, see the Martindale-Hubbell Law Directory

Shipley & Kos (AV)

130 West Main Street, Suite 25, 46802
Telephone: 219-424-0025
Fax: 219-424-2960

Grant F. Shipley
Edmund P. Kos

ASSOCIATE

Martin E. Seifert

Representative Clients: NBD Bank, N.A.; Barclays Business Credit, Inc.

For full biographical listings, see the Martindale-Hubbell Law Directory

GREENWOOD, Johnson Co.

Van Valer Williams & Hewitt (AV)

Suite 400 National City Bank Building, 300 South Madison Avenue, P.O. Box 405, 46142
Telephone: 317-888-1121
Fax: 317-887-4069

MEMBERS OF FIRM

Joe N. Van Valer
Jon E. Williams
Brian C. Hewitt

ASSOCIATES

J. Lee Robbins
William M. Waltz
John M. White
Kim Van Valer Shilts
Mark E. Need

For full biographical listings, see the Martindale-Hubbell Law Directory

HAMMOND, Lake Co.

Beckman, Kelly & Smith (AV)

5920 Hohman Avenue, 46320
Telephone: 219-933-6200
Telecopier: 219-933-6201

MEMBERS OF FIRM

Richard P. Tinkham (1902-1973)
Daniel F. Kelly (1914-1978)
J. B. Smith
Andrew J. Fetsch
Randall J. Nye
Robert F. Parker
Daniel W. Glavin

ASSOCIATES

Larry L. Chubb
Melanie Morgan Dunajeski
Scott A. Bearby
Christine Hajduch Curosh

OF COUNSEL

Eric L. Kirschner
John F. Beckman, Jr.

Representative Clients: Waste Management of North America, Inc.; The Travelers Companies; Bethlehem Steel Corp.; ITT Finance; Northwest Indiana Public Broadcasting, Inc.; Signal Capital Corporation; CIGNA Companies; Sears Roebuck and Co.

For full biographical listings, see the Martindale-Hubbell Law Directory

*INDIANAPOLIS,** Marion Co.

Backer & Backer, A Professional Corporation (AV)

101 West Ohio Street, Suite 1500, 46204
Telephone: 317-684-3000
Telecopier: 317-684-3004

Herbert J. Backer
Stephen A. Backer
David J. Backer

Reference: Bank One, Indianapolis.

For full biographical listings, see the Martindale-Hubbell Law Directory

Buschmann, Carr & Shanks, Professional Corporation (AV)

1020 Market Tower, 10 West Market Street, 46204-2963
Telephone: 317-636-5511
Fax: 317-636-3661
Franklin, Indiana Office: 160 Fairway Lakes Drive.
Telephone: 317-738-9540.
Fax: 317-738-9310.
Fishers, Indiana Office: 9093 Technology Drive, Suite 103.
Telephone: 317-577-0756.
Fax: 317-577-9910.

John R. Carr, III
Stephen R. Buschmann
Gary L. Dilk
Lisa T. Hamilton

Representative Clients: Archer-Daniels Midland Co.; Ball Corp.; Industrial Valley Title Insurance; Creative Risk Management, Inc.; Deflecto Corporation; Glenfed Mortgage Corp.; Gates McDonald; Merchants National Bank & Trust Company of Muncie; Monumental Life Insurance Co.; National Council on Compensation Insurance.

For Complete List of Firm Personnel, See General Section

For full biographical listings, see the Martindale-Hubbell Law Directory

Feiwell & Associates (AV)

251 North Illinois Street, Suite 1700, P.O. Box 44141, 46204
Telephone: 317-237-2727
Facsimile: 317-237-2722

Murray J. Feiwell

ASSOCIATES

Douglas J. Hannoy
Lisa Kay Decker

Representative Clients: Fifth Third Bank; Revel Companies, Inc.; American Credit Indemnity; Dun & Bradstreet; Browning Management, Inc.; Queens Group; Oliver Trucking; Jewelers Board of Trade; A.G. Adjustments, Ltd.; Stanley Tulchin Associates.

For full biographical listings, see the Martindale-Hubbell Law Directory

Hopper, Wenzel & Galliher, P.C. (AV)

Bank One Center/Circle, 111 Monument Circle, Suite 452, 46204-5170
Telephone: 317-635-5005
Facsimile: 317-634-2501

George W. Hopper
Mark R. Wenzel
Mark R. Galliher
Jeffrey E. Ramsey
David G. Pardo

Representative Clients: Bank One, Indianapolis, N.A.; National City Bank, Indiana; MetroBank; Mutual Guaranty Corporation; I.T.T. Financial Services, Commercial Division; ABC Supply Co., Inc.; Sholodge, Inc.; Purina Mills, Inc.

For full biographical listings, see the Martindale-Hubbell Law Directory

Indianapolis—Continued

HOSTETLER & KOWALIK, P.C. (AV)

101 West Ohio Street Suite 2100, 46204
Telephone: 317-262-1001
Fax: 317-262-1010

Gary Lynn Hostetler
James S. Kowalik
David R. Krebs
J. Bradley Schooley

For full biographical listings, see the Martindale-Hubbell Law Directory

ICE MILLER DONADIO & RYAN (AV)

One American Square Box 82001, 46282-0002
Telephone: 317-236-2100
Fax: 317-236-2219

MEMBERS OF FIRM

Donald G. Sutherland
Berkley W. Duck, III
Jack R. Snyder
Harry L. Gonso
Thomas H. Ristine
John R. Thornburgh
Richard J. Thrapp
Henry A. Efroymson

OF COUNSEL

C. Daniel Motsinger

ASSOCIATES

Peggy J. Naile
Dominic F. Polizzotto
Michael E. Schrader

Representative Clients: Amax Coal, Inc.; Bank One, Indianapolis, N.A.; Clark Equipment Co.; Federal Home Loan Bank of Indianapolis; Ford Motor Credit Co.; General Electric Supply Co.; NBD Bank; National City Bank; Navistar Financial Corp.; Westinghouse Credit Crop.

For Complete List of Firm Personnel, See General Section

For full biographical listings, see the Martindale-Hubbell Law Directory

JOHNSON, SMITH, DENSBORN, WRIGHT & HEATH (AV)

One Indiana Square Suite 1800, 46204
Telephone: 317-634-9777
Telecopier: 317-636-9061

MEMBERS OF FIRM

John F. Joyce (1948-1994)
Wayne O. Adams, III
Thomas A. Barnard
David J. Carr
Peter D. Cleveland
David R. Day
Donald K. Densborn
Thomas N. Eckerle
Mark W. Ford
G. Ronald Heath
Robert B. Hebert
John David Hoover
Andrew W. Hull
Dennis A. Johnson
Richard L. Johnson
Michael J. Kaye
John R. Kirkwood
David Williams Russell
James T. Smith
David E. Wright

ASSOCIATES

Robert C. Wolf (1949-1993)
Carolyn H. Andretti
David G. Blachly
Robert T. Buday
Jeffrey S. Cohen
Patricia L. Marshall
David D. Robinson
Ronald G. Sentman
Sally Franklin Zweig

OF COUNSEL

Paul D. Gresk
William T. Lawrence
Mark A. Palmer
Catherine A. Singleton

For Complete List of Firm Personnel, See General Section

For full biographical listings, see the Martindale-Hubbell Law Directory

KROGER, GARDIS & REGAS (AV)

111 Monument Circle, Suite 900, 46204-3059
Telephone: 317-692-9000
Telecopier: 317-264-6832

MEMBERS OF FIRM

James A. Knauer
John J. Petr
James G. Lauck
Gary A. Schiffli
Jay P. Kennedy

ASSOCIATES

Michelle Howden Laconi
Mary Elizabeth Brames

LEGAL SUPPORT PERSONNEL

PARALEGALS

Rhonda K. Peterson
Debra K. Nix

Representative Clients: NBD Leasing, Inc.; First of America Bank; Bank One; NBD Bank; Society National Bank; Liberty National Bank and Trust Co.; Mutual Hospital Services; Transamerica Commercial Finance Corp.; America Bankers Insurance.

For full biographical listings, see the Martindale-Hubbell Law Directory

PRICE & BARKER (AV)

The Hammond Block Building, 301 Massachusetts Avenue, 46204
Telephone: 317-633-8787
Telecopier: 317-633-8797

(See Next Column)

PARTNERS

Henry J. Price
Robert G. Barker
Jennifer L. Graham
Jerry A. Garau

ASSOCIATES

H. Dean Bowman
Melissa A. Clark

For full biographical listings, see the Martindale-Hubbell Law Directory

ROCAP, WITCHGER & THRELKELD (AV)

700 Union Federal Building, 45 North Pennsylvania Street, 46204
Telephone: 317-639-6281
FAX: 317-637-9056

James E. Rocap, Sr. (1881-1969)
John T. Rocap (1909-1980)
Keith C. Reese (1920-1993)

MEMBERS OF FIRM

James E. Rocap, Jr.
James D. Witchger
W. Brent Threlkeld
Richard A. Rocap
James C. Todderud
Thomas Todd Reynolds

ASSOCIATES

Robert S. O'Dell
Nancy Grannan Curless
Michael D. Ramsey
Tara L. Becsey
Bette J. Peterson
Robert A. Durham
Jeffrey V. Crabill

OF COUNSEL

Joseph F. Quill

Counsel For: Union Federal Savings Bank; Methodist Hospital FCU; Wolf and Swickard Machine Co., Inc.; Cessna Finance Corp.; Intelligent Data Systems, Inc.; Indiana Materials and Manufacturing, Inc.; Carrier Corp.

For full biographical listings, see the Martindale-Hubbell Law Directory

RUBIN & LEVIN, P.C. (AV)

500 Marott Center, 342 Massachusetts Avenue, 46204-2161
Telephone: 317-634-0300
Telecopier: 317-263-9411

George A. Rubin
Elliott D. Levin
John W. Graub, II
Sue Figert Meyer
Christopher E. Baker

Representative Clients: Aetna Casualty & Surety; Browning Investments, Inc.; Chase Manhattan Bank of New York; General Electric Credit Corp.; Indiana Association of Credit Management; Indiana Farm Bureau Co-Operative Assn., Inc.; Sears, Roebuck & Co.; Xerox.

For full biographical listings, see the Martindale-Hubbell Law Directory

SOMMER & BARNARD, ATTORNEYS AT LAW, PC (AV)

4000 Bank One Tower, 111 Monument Circle, P.O. Box 44363, 46244-0363
Telephone: 317-630-4000
FAX: 317-236-9802
North Office: 8900 Keystone Crossing, Suite 1046, Indianapolis, Indiana, 46240-2134.
Telephone: 317-630-4000.
FAX: 317-844-4780.

James K. Sommer
William C. Barnard
James E. Hughes
Edward W. Harris, III
Frederick M. King
Jerald I. Ancel
Eric R. Johnson
Gordon L. Pittenger
Lynn Brundage Jongleux
Frank J. Deveau
John E. Taylor
Michael C. Terrell
Marlene Reich
Richard C. Richmond, III
Julianne S. Lis-Milam
Steven C. Shockley
Stephen B. Cherry
Robert J. Hicks
Lawrence A. Vanore
Donald C. Biggs
Debra McVicker Lynch

Gayle A. Reindl
Ann Carr Mackey
Gregory J. Seketa
Sandra L. Gosling
Edwin J. Broecker
Thomas R. DeVoe
Mary T. Doherty
William K. Boncosky

OF COUNSEL

Jerry Williams
Glenn Scolnik
Philip L. McCool
Charles E. Valliere
Verl L. Myers

Representative Clients: Comerica Bank; Excel Industries; Federal Express; Kimball International; Monsanto; Renault Automation; Repport International; TRW, Inc.

For full biographical listings, see the Martindale-Hubbell Law Directory

YARLING, ROBINSON, HAMMEL & LAMB (AV)

151 North Delaware, Suite 1535, P.O. Box 44128, 46204
Telephone: 317-262-8800
Fax: 317-262-3046

(See Next Column)

YARLING, ROBINSON, HAMMEL & LAMB—*Continued*

MEMBERS OF FIRM

Richard W. Yarling
Charles F. Robinson, Jr.
John W. Hammel
Linda Y. Hammel
Edgar H. Lamb
Douglas E. Rogers
Mark S. Gray

Representative Clients: Allstate Insurance Co.; American Family Mutual Insurance Company; Chrysler Credit Corporation; Fleet Financenter; General Motors Acceptance Corporation; Household Finance Corporation; Monroe Guaranty Insurance Company; Northbrook Property & Casualty Company; Pafco General Insurance Company; Security Pacific Finance Corporation.

For full biographical listings, see the Martindale-Hubbell Law Directory

MERRILLVILLE, Lake Co.

BURKE, MURPHY, COSTANZA & CUPPY (AV)

Suite 600 8585 Broadway, 46410
Telephone: 219-769-1313
Telecopier: 219-769-6806
East Chicago, Indiana Office: First National Bank Building. 720 W. Chicago Avenue.
Telephone: 219-397-2401.
Telecopier: 219-397-0506.
Palm Harbor, Florida Office: Suite 280, 33920 U.S. Highway 19 North.
Telephone: 813-787-7799.
Telecopier: 813-787-7237.

MEMBERS OF FIRM

Lester F. Murphy (East Chicago, Indiana and Palm Harbor, Florida Offices)
Frederick M. Cuppy
Andrew J. Kopko
Lambert C. Genetos
David K. Ranich
Kathryn D. Schmidt
David Cerven

ASSOCIATES

Lily M. Schaefer
Craig R. Van Schouwen

Representative Clients: Federal National Mortage Association; Waterfield Mortage Co.; ITT Commercial Financial Corp.; NBD/Gainer N.A.; National City Bank/Indiana N.A.; American Trust & Savings Bank of Whiting; Bank One, N.A.; Centier Bank; Transamerica Financial Services.

For Complete List of Firm Personnel, See General Section

For full biographical listings, see the Martindale-Hubbell Law Directory

HODGES & DAVIS, P.C. (AV)

5525 Broadway, 46410
Telephone: 219-981-2557
Fax: 219-980-7090
Portage, Indiana Office: 6508 U.S. Highway 6.
Telephone: 219-762-9129.
Fax: 219-762-2826.

Clyde D. Compton
William B. Davis
Earle F. Hites
R. Lawrence Steele
Gregory A. Sobkowski
Bonnie C. Coleman
Jill M. Madajczyk
Laura B. Brown
David H. Kreider

OF COUNSEL

Edward J. Hussey

Representative Clients: Lake Mortgage Co., Inc.; Kerr-Nielsen Buick Jeep Eagle; Pine Chevrolet, Inc.; McDonald's Corporation.

For Complete List of Firm Personnel, See General Section

For full biographical listings, see the Martindale-Hubbell Law Directory

PORTAGE, Porter Co.

HODGES & DAVIS, P.C. (AV)

6508 U.S. Highway 6, 46368
Telephone: 219-762-9129
Fax: 219-762-2826
Merrillville, Indiana Office: 5525 Broadway.
Telephone: 219-981-2557.
Fax: 219-980-7090.

Clyde D. Compton
Earle F. Hites
R. Lawrence Steele
Gregory A. Sobkowski
Bonnie C. Coleman

Representative Clients: Lake Mortgage Co., Inc.; Kerr-Nielson Buick Jeep Eagle; Pine Chevrolet, Inc.; McDonald's Corporation.

For full biographical listings, see the Martindale-Hubbell Law Directory

*SOUTH BEND,** St. Joseph Co.

DORAN BLACKMOND READY HAMILTON & WILLIAMS (AV)

1700 Valley American Bank Building, 211 W. Washington Street, 46601
Telephone: 219-288-1800
Fax: 219-236-4265

(See Next Column)

MEMBERS OF FIRM

John E. Doran
Don G. Blackmond
David T. Ready
John C. Hamilton
A. Howard Williams

For full biographical listings, see the Martindale-Hubbell Law Directory

IOWA

*COUNCIL BLUFFS,** Pottawattamie Co.

SMITH PETERSON LAW FIRM (AV)

35 Main Place, Suite 300, P.O. Box 249, 51502
Telephone: 712-328-1833
Fax: 712-328-8320
Omaha, Nebraska Office: 9290 West Dodge Road, Suite 205.
Telephone: 402-397-8500.
Fax: 402-397-5519.

MEMBERS OF FIRM

Raymond A. Smith (1892-1977)
John LeRoy Peterson (1895-1969)
Harold T. Beckman
Robert J. Laubenthal
Richard A. Heininger
Lawrence J. Beckman
Gregory G. Barntsen
W. Curtis Hewett
Steven H. Krohn
Randy R. Ewing
Joseph D. Thornton

ASSOCIATES

Trent D. Reinert (Not admitted in IA)
T. J. Pattermann

Representative Clients: Aetna Life and Casualty Co.; Employers Mutual Co.; First National Bank of Council Bluffs; IMT Insurance Co.; Monsanto Co.; United Fire & Casualty Co.; U.S. Fidelity and Guaranty.

For full biographical listings, see the Martindale-Hubbell Law Directory

*DES MOINES,** Polk Co.

SHEARER, TEMPLER, PINGEL & KAPLAN, A PROFESSIONAL CORPORATION (AV)

Suite 437 3737 Woodland Avenue (West Des Moines, 50266), P.O. Box 1991, 50309
Telephone: 515-225-3737
Fax: 515-225-9510

Ronni F. Begleiter
Thomas M. Cunningham
Jeffrey L. Goodman
Ronald M. Kaplan
Lawrence L. Marcucci
Mark L. McManigal
John R. Perkins
G. Brian Pingel
Leon R. Shearer
Brenton D. Soderstrum
Jeffrey D. Stone
David G. Stork
John A. Templer, Jr.
Ann M. Ver Heul

For Complete List of Firm Personnel, See General Section

For full biographical listings, see the Martindale-Hubbell Law Directory

*WATERLOO,** Black Hawk Co.

SWISHER & COHRT (AV)

528 West Fourth Street, P.O. Box 1200, 50704
Telephone: 319-232-6555
FAX: 319-232-4835

MEMBERS OF FIRM

Benjamin F. Swisher (1878-1959)
L. J. Cohrt (1898-1974)
Charles F. Swisher (1919-1986)
Eldon R. McCann
Steven A. Weidner
Larry J. Cohrt
J. Douglas Oberman
Stephen J. Powell
Jim D. DeKoster
Jeffrey J. Greenwood
Samuel C. Anderson
Robert C. Griffin
Kevin R. Rogers

ASSOCIATES

Beth E. Hansen
Mark F. Conway
Natalie Williams Burr

Firm is Counsel for: Koehring Corp.; Clay Equipment; Chamberlain Manufacturing Co.; Waterloo Courier.
Local Counsel for: Allied Group; John Deere Insurance; Liberty Mutual Insurance Co.

For full biographical listings, see the Martindale-Hubbell Law Directory

KANSAS

*WICHITA,** Sedgwick Co.

FOULSTON & SIEFKIN (AV)

(Formerly Foulston, Siefkin, Powers & Eberhardt)
700 Fourth Financial Center, Broadway at Douglas, 67202
Telephone: 316-267-6371
Facsimile: 316-267-6345
Topeka, Kansas Office: 1515 Bank IV Tower, 534 Kansas Avenue. 66603.
Telephone: 913-233-3600.
FAX: 913-233-1610.
Member: Lex Mundi, A Global Association of Independent Firms

MEMBERS OF FIRM

Benjamin C. Langel
James D. Oliver
William R. Wood, II

For Complete List of Firm Personnel, See General Section

For full biographical listings, see the Martindale-Hubbell Law Directory

HERSHBERGER, PATTERSON, JONES & ROTH, L.C. (AV)

600 Hardage Center, 100 South Main, 67202-3779
Telephone: 316-263-7583
Fax: 316-263-7595

Jerome E. Jones
J. Michael Kennalley
Robert J. Roth
John A. Vetter
Ken W. Dannenberg

Counsel For: First National Bank in Wichita; Andarko Petroleum Corporation; Chinese Industries; Mobil Oil Corp.; CNA Insurance; Royal Exchange Group; Central National Insurance Group; Transamerica Insurance Group; Northwestern National Insurance Group.

For Complete List of Firm Personnel, See General Section

For full biographical listings, see the Martindale-Hubbell Law Directory

YOUNG, BOGLE, McCAUSLAND, WELLS & CLARK, P.A. (AV)

106 West Douglas, Suite 923, 67202
Telephone: 316-265-7841
Facsimile: 316-265-3956

Jerry D. Bogle
William A. Wells
Paul S. McCausland
Kenneth M. Clark
Patrick C. Blanchard

Mark R. Maloney

OF COUNSEL

Orlin L. Wagner

Representative Clients: Deere Credit Services, Inc.; Agricredit Acceptance Corp.; Equitable Agri-Business, Inc.; General Mills, Inc.; Straightline Mfg., Inc.

For Complete List of Firm Personnel, See General Section

For full biographical listings, see the Martindale-Hubbell Law Directory

KENTUCKY

*BOWLING GREEN,** Warren Co.

CAMPBELL, KERRICK & GRISE (AV)

1025 State Street, P.O. Box 9547, 42102-9547
Telephone: 502-782-8160
FAX: 502-782-5856

MEMBERS OF FIRM

Joe Bill Campbell
Gregory N. Stivers
Thomas N. Kerrick
H. Brent Brennenstuhl
John R. Grise
Deborah Tomes Wilkins

ASSOCIATES

H. Harris Pepper, Jr.
Lanna Martin Kilgore
Laura Hagan

Representative Clients: Dollar General Corp.; Greenview Hospital; Hospital Corporation of America; Hardin Memorial Hospital; Monarch Environmental, Inc.; Mid-South Management Group, Inc.; Western Kentucky University; Service One Credit Union; Trans Financial Bank; TKR Cable.

For full biographical listings, see the Martindale-Hubbell Law Directory

CATRON, KILGORE & BEGLEY (AV)

918 State Street, P.O. Box 280, 42102-0280
Telephone: 502-842-1050
Fax: 502-842-4720

(See Next Column)

Stephen B. Catron
J. Patrick Kilgore
Ernest Edward Begley, II

Representative Clients: Bowling Green Bank & Trust Company, N.A.; General Growth Management Corporation; Kentucky Transportation Cabinet; Resolution Trust Corporation; International Paper Company; Convention Center Authority; Bowling Green-Warren County Industrial Park Authority, Inc.; Camping World, Inc.; National Corvette Museum; Minit Mart Foods, Inc.

For full biographical listings, see the Martindale-Hubbell Law Directory

ENGLISH, LUCAS, PRIEST & OWSLEY (AV)

1101 College Street, P.O. Box 770, 42102-0770
Telephone: 502-781-6500
Telecopier: 502-782-7782

MEMBERS OF FIRM

Whayne C. Priest, Jr.
Keith M. Carwell

For Complete List of Firm Personnel, See General Section

For full biographical listings, see the Martindale-Hubbell Law Directory

COVINGTON, Kenton Co.

GREENEBAUM DOLL & McDONALD (AV)

A Partnership including Professional Service Corporations
50 East Rivercenter Boulevard, P.O. Box 2050, 41012-2050
Telephone: 606-655-4200
Telecopier: 606-655-4239
Louisville, Kentucky Office: 3300 National City Tower.
Telephone: 502-589-4200.
Fax: 502-587-3695.
Lexington, Kentucky Office: 1400 Vine Center Tower.
Telephone: 606-231-8500.
Fax: 606-255-2742.
Cincinnati, Ohio Office: 832 Main Street.
Telephone: 513-421-8087.
Fax: 513-421-8089.

MEMBERS OF FIRM

Michael M. Fleishman *
Peggy B. Lyndrup
P. Richard Anderson, Jr.
Nicholas R. Glancy
Jeffrey A. McKenzie

OF COUNSEL

Edward B. Weinberg *

Representative Clients: Aetna Life Insurance Co.; ANDALEX Resources, Inc.; Ashland Oil, Inc.; A T & T Communications, Inc.; Bethlehem Steel Corp.; Brown-Forman Corp.; Citizens Fidelity Bank & Trust Co.; Humana, Inc.; KFC National Cooperative Advertising Program, Inc.
*A Professional Service Corporation

For Complete List of Firm Personnel, See General Section

For full biographical listings, see the Martindale-Hubbell Law Directory

*DANVILLE,** Boyle Co.

SHEEHAN, BARNETT & HAYS, P.S.C. (AV)

114 South Fourth Street, P.O. Box 1517, 40422
Telephone: 606-236-2641; 606-734-7552
FAX: 606-236-1483

James G. Sheehan, Jr.
James William Barnett
Edward D. Hays

Representative Clients: Bank One; Bank of Danville and Trust Co.; Great Financial Federal; Kentucky Farm Bureau Mutual Insurance Co.; Motorist Mutual Insurance Co.; R.R. Donnelley & Sons, Inc.; State Automobile Mutual Insurance Co.; City of Danville; Shelter Insurance Co.; Trim Masters, Inc.

For full biographical listings, see the Martindale-Hubbell Law Directory

*LEXINGTON,** Fayette Co.

GREENEBAUM DOLL & McDONALD (AV)

A Partnership including Professional Service Corporations
1400 Vine Center Tower, 40508
Telephone: 606-231-8500
Telecopier: 606-255-2742
Telex: 213029
Louisville, Kentucky Office: 3300 National City Tower.
Telephone: 502-589-4200.
Fax: 502-587-3695.
Covington, Kentucky Office: 50 East River Center Boulevard, P.O. Box 2050.
Telephone: 606-655-4200.
Fax: 606-655-4239.
Cincinnati, Ohio Office: 832 Main Street.
Telephone: 513-421-8087.
Fax: 513-421-8089.

(See Next Column)

GREENEBAUM DOLL & McDONALD—*Continued*

MEMBERS OF FIRM

A. Robert Doll *
Michael M. Fleishman *
Robert C. Stilz, Jr. (Resident)
John S. Sawyer (Resident)
John V. Wharton (Resident)
Peggy B. Lyndrup
Nicholas R. Glancy
Bruce E. Cryder
Stephen W. Switzer (Resident)

ASSOCIATES

Margaret A. Miller (Resident)
Benjamin D. Crocker

OF COUNSEL

Glen M. Krebs (Resident)

Representative Clients: Aetna Life Insurance Co.; ANDALEX Resources, Inc.; Ashland Oil, Inc.; AT&T Communications, Inc.; Bethlehem Steel Corp.; Brown-Forman Corp.; Columbia Gas & Transmission Co.; Commonwealth Aluminum Corp.; Consolidation Coal Co.; Costain Coal, Inc.
*A Professional Service Corporation

For Complete List of Firm Personnel, See General Section

For full biographical listings, see the Martindale-Hubbell Law Directory

LANDRUM & SHOUSE (AV)

106 West Vine Street, P.O. Box 951, 40588-0951
Telephone: 606-255-2424
Facsimile: 606-233-0308
Louisville, Kentucky Office: 400 West Market Street, Suite 1550, 40202.
Telephone: 502-589-7616.
Facsimile: 502-589-2119.

MEMBERS OF FIRM

John H. Burrus
William C. Shouse
Mark L. Moseley
Benjamin Cowgill, Jr.
Jack E. Toliver

ASSOCIATE

Charles E. Christian

District Attorneys: CSX Transportation, Inc.
Special Trial Counsel: Ford Motor Co. and Affiliates (Eastern Kentucky); Clark Equipment Co.
Representative Clients: The Continental Insurance Cos.; U.S. Insurance Group; U.S. Fidelity & Guaranty Co.; Ohio Casualty Insurance Co.; CIGNA; Royal Insurance Cos.

For Complete List of Firm Personnel, See General Section

For full biographical listings, see the Martindale-Hubbell Law Directory

STOLL, KEENON & PARK (AV)

201 E. Main Street, Suite 1000, 40507-1380
Telephone: 606-231-3000
Telecopier: 606-253-1093; 606-253-1027
Frankfort, Kentucky Office: 326 West Main Street.
Telephone: 502-875-6000.
Telecopier: 502-875-6008.
Louisville, Kentucky Office: 400 West Market Street, Suite 2650, 40202.
Telephone: 502-568-9100.
Telecopier: 502-568-6340.

MEMBERS OF FIRM

William E. Johnson
Samuel D. Hinkle, IV
R. David Lester
Herbert A. Miller, Jr.
Harvie B. Wilkinson
Robert W. Kellerman
Dan M. Rose
Gregory D. Pavey

ASSOCIATES

Laura Day DelCotto
Lea Pauley Goff
Culver V. Halliday

For Complete List of Firm Personnel, See General Section

For full biographical listings, see the Martindale-Hubbell Law Directory

STURGILL, TURNER & TRUITT (AV)

155 East Main Street, 40507
Telephone: 606-255-8581
Fax: 606-231-0851

MEMBERS OF FIRM

Jerry D. Truitt
Stephen L. Barker
Gina S. McCann

For Complete List of Firm Personnel, See General Section

For full biographical listings, see the Martindale-Hubbell Law Directory

VIMONT & WILLS (AV)

Suite 300, 155 East Main Street, 40507-1317
Telephone: 606-252-2202
Telecopier: 606-259-2927

MEMBERS OF FIRM

Richard E. Vimont
Timothy C. Wills
Bernard F. Lovely, Jr.
Richard M. Wehrle

(See Next Column)

ASSOCIATES

Barbara Booker Wills
Kimberly D. Lemmons
J. Thomas Rawlings
J. Stan Lee

For full biographical listings, see the Martindale-Hubbell Law Directory

*LOUISVILLE,** Jefferson Co.

GREENEBAUM DOLL & McDONALD (AV)

A Partnership including Professional Service Corporations
3300 National City Tower, 40202
Telephone: 502-589-4200
Fax: 502-587-3695
Lexington, Kentucky Office: 1400 Vine Center Tower.
Telephone: 606-231-8500.
Fax: 606-255-2742.
Covington, Kentucky Office: 50 East River Center Boulevard, P.O. Box 2050.
Telephone: 606-655-4200.
Fax: 606-655-4239.
Cincinnati, Ohio Office: 832 Main Street.
Telephone: 513-421-8087.
Fax: 513-421-8089.

A. Robert Doll *
Michael G. Shaikun *
Michael M. Fleishman *
John H. Stites, III
Robert C. Stilz, Jr. (Resident at Lexington, Kentucky)
P. Richard Anderson, Jr.
Mark S. Ament *
John S. Sawyer (Resident at Lexington, Kentucky)
John V. Wharton (Resident at Lexington, Kentucky)
Peggy B. Lyndrup
Nicholas R. Glancy (Lexington and Covington, Kentucky)
Bruce E. Cryder (Lexington, Kentucky and Cincinnati, Ohio)
Carmin D. Grandinetti
Janet P. Jakubowicz
Margaret E. Keane
Tandy C. Patrick
Patrick J. Welsh
Holland N. McTyeire, V
Jeffrey A. McKenzie
Stephen W. Switzer (Resident at Lexington, Kentucky)
Daniel E. Fisher

ASSOCIATES

Margaret A. Miller (Resident at Lexington, Kentucky)
J. Mark Grundy
Daniel P. Cherry
Daniel L. Waddell
Thomas M. Williams
John P. Fendig
Benjamin D. Crocker (Resident, Lexington Office)

OF COUNSEL

Glen M. Krebs (Resident at Lexington, Kentucky)
Edward B. Weinberg *

Representative Clients: Aetna Life Insurance Co.; ANDALEX Resources, Inc.; Ashland Oil, Inc.; A T & T Communications, Inc.; Bethlehem Steel Corp.; Brown-Forman Corp.; Humana, Inc.; Kentucky Kingdom, Inc.; KFC National Cooperative Advertising Program, Inc.
*A Professional Service Corporation

For Complete List of Firm Personnel, See General Section

For full biographical listings, see the Martindale-Hubbell Law Directory

LLOYD & McDANIEL (AV)

700 Meidinger Tower, 460 South Fourth Avenue, 40202
Telephone: 502-585-1880
Fax: 502-585-3054
Lexington, Kentucky Office: Suite 102, 177 North Upper Street, 40507.
Telephone: 606-254-2102.
Jeffersonville, Indiana Office: 220 East Court Avenue, P.O. Box 934. 47131.
Telephone: 812-282-4380.

MEMBERS OF FIRM

Jeremiah A. Lloyd
James M. Lloyd
Michael V. Brodarick

ASSOCIATES

Anthony H. Ambrose
Deborah B. Simon
Julia M. Pike

OF COUNSEL

Gerald F. McDaniel

References: Liberty National Bank & Trust Co. of Kentucky; PNC Bank, Kentucky, Inc.; United Mercantile Agencies; National Association of Credit Management (NACM).

For full biographical listings, see the Martindale-Hubbell Law Directory

MULLOY, WALZ, WETTERER, FORE & SCHWARTZ (AV)

First Trust Centre, Suite 700N, 200 South Fifth Street, 40202
Telephone: 502-589-5250
Fax: 502-589-1637

MEMBERS OF FIRM

William P. Mulloy
Karl M. Walz
William S. Wetterer, Jr.
F. Larkin Fore
Dan T. Schwartz
B. Mark Mulloy
Mary Anne Wetterer Watkins
William S. Wetterer, III
Bryan J. Dillon
J. Gregory Clare
Ronda Hartlage
T. Lee Sisney

OF COUNSEL

Stephen H. Miller

Reference: American States Insurance Co.; Crawford & Company; Paragon Group, Inc.; Queens Group; Southeastern Dairies, Inc.; Ticor Title Co.; First National Bank of Louisville; Stockyards Bank; Arrow Electric Co.

For full biographical listings, see the Martindale-Hubbell Law Directory

Louisville—Continued

OGDEN NEWELL & WELCH (AV)

1200 One Riverfront Plaza, 40202-2973
Telephone: 502-582-1601
Fax: 502-581-9564

MEMBERS OF FIRM

John T. Ballantine
Joseph C. Oldham
Stephen F. Schuster
Scott T. Wendelsdorf
W. Gregory King

ASSOCIATES

Teresa C. Buchheit
Thomas E. Rutledge
Jennifer J. Hall

Counsel for: Brown & Williamson Tobacco Corp.; Brown-Forman Corp.; National City Bank of Kentucky; Industrial Air Centers; Interlock Industries, Inc.; United Medical Corp.

For Complete List of Firm Personnel, See General Section

For full biographical listings, see the Martindale-Hubbell Law Directory

STOLL, KEENON & PARK (AV)

400 West Market Street Suite 2650, 40202
Telephone: 502-568-9100
Telecopier: 502-568-6340
Frankfort, Kentucky Office: 326 West Main Street.
Telephone: 502-875-6000.
Telecopier: 502-875-6008.
Lexington, Kentucky Office: 210 E. Main Street, Suite 1000, 40507-1380.
Telephone: 606-231-3000.
Telecopier: 606-253-1093; 606-253-1380.

MEMBER OF FIRM

Samuel D. Hinkle, IV

For Complete List of Firm Personnel, See General Section

For full biographical listings, see the Martindale-Hubbell Law Directory

*OWENSBORO,** Daviess Co.

LOVETT & LAMAR (AV)

208 West Third Street, 42303-4121
Telephone: 502-926-3000
FAX: 502-685-2625

MEMBERS OF FIRM

Wells T. Lovett
Charles L. Lamar
John T. Lovett
Marty G. Jacobs

Representative Clients: Farm Credit Services of Mid-America, ACA; Galante Manufacturing Co.; Hocker Developments, Inc.; National-Southwire Aluminum; Willamette Industries, Inc.; Bel-Cheese; Sterett Construction Co.; Green River Steel, Inc.

For full biographical listings, see the Martindale-Hubbell Law Directory

LOUISIANA

*BATON ROUGE,** East Baton Rouge Parish

KANTROW, SPAHT, WEAVER & BLITZER, A PROFESSIONAL LAW CORPORATION (AV)

Suite 300, City Plaza, 445 North Boulevard, P.O. Box 2997, 70821-2997
Telephone: 504-383-4703
Fax: 504-343-0630; 343-0637

Byron R. Kantrow
Carlos G. Spaht
Geraldine B. Weaver
Sidney M. Blitzer, Jr.
Paul H. Spaht
Lee C. Kantrow
John C. Miller
Vincent P. Fornias
David S. Rubin
Diane L. Crochet
Richard F. Zimmerman, Jr.
Bob D. Tucker
Martin E. Golden
Joseph A. Schittone, Jr.

S. Layne Lee
J. Michael Robinson, Jr.
Connell L. Archey
Richard D. Moreno
Randal J. Robert

Representative Clients: CNA Insurance Cos.; Federal Deposit Insurance Corp.; Hartford Insurance Group; Air Products and Chemicals, Inc.; CF Industries, Inc.; AT&T; United Companies Financial Corp.

For full biographical listings, see the Martindale-Hubbell Law Directory

KEAN, MILLER, HAWTHORNE, D'ARMOND, MCCOWAN & JARMAN, L.L.P. (AV)

22nd Floor, One American Place, P.O. Box 3513, 70821
Telephone: 504-387-0999
Fax: 504-388-9133
New Orleans, Louisiana Office: Energy Centre, Suite 1470, 1100 Poydras Street.
Telephone: 504-585-3050.
Fax: 504-585-3051.

MEMBERS OF FIRM

Ben R. Miller, Jr.
Robert A. Hawthorne, Jr.
Carey J. Messina
Isaac M. Gregorie, Jr.
G. Blane Clark, Jr.
James R. Lackie
Todd A. Rossi

Kelly Wilkinson
Catherine A. Filhiol

Representative Clients: The Lamar Corporation, Baton Rouge, La.; Anco Industries, Inc., Baton Rouge, La.; Piccadilly Cafeterias, Inc./Ralph & Kacoo's, Baton Rouge, La.; Amec Engineering, Inc., Houston, Tx.; Stauffer Chemical, Co., Shelton, Ct.; Exxon Chemical Americas and Exxon Corporation, Baton Rouge, La.; Mobil Oil Corporation, Fairfax, Va.; Texaco, Inc., New Orleans, La.; Hancock Bank of Louisiana, Baton Rouge, La.

For Complete List of Firm Personnel, See General Section

For full biographical listings, see the Martindale-Hubbell Law Directory

SEALE, SMITH, ZUBER & BARNETTE (AV)

Two United Plaza, Suite 200, 8550 United Plaza Boulevard, 70809
Telephone: 504-924-1600
Telecopier: 504-924-6100

Armbrust Gordon Seale (1913-1989)
Robert W. Smith (1922-1989)
Donald S. Zuber
Kenneth E. Barnette
William C. Kaufman III
John W. L. Swanner
James H. Morgan III
Ronald A. Seale
Brent E. Kinchen
Charles K. Watts
Myron A. Walker, Jr.
Daniel A. Reed
Kenner O. Miller, Jr.
William C. Rowe, Jr.
Lawrence R. Anderson, Jr.

ASSOCIATES

Richard T. Reed
Barbara G. Chatelain
Anthony J. Russo, Jr.
Catherine S. Nobile

Representative Clients: Farmers Insurance Group; St. Paul Fire and Marine Insurance Company; United Services Automobile Association; General Motors Acceptance Corporation.
Reference: City National Bank, Baton Rouge, Louisiana.

For full biographical listings, see the Martindale-Hubbell Law Directory

*LAKE CHARLES,** Calcasieu Parish

LUNDY & DAVIS, L.L.P. (AV)

A Partnership including a Professional Corporation
Calcasieu Marine Tower, One Lakeshore Drive, Suite 1600, P.O. Box 3009, 70602
Telephone: 318-439-0707
FAX: 318-439-1029
Jackson, Mississippi Office: 111 East Capitol Street, Suite 250.
Telephone: 601-948-3010.
Facsimile: 601-948-2143.
Houston, Texas Office: 13101 Northwest Freeway.
Telephone: 713-690-8949.
Facsimile: 713-690-8919.
Biloxi, Mississippi Office: 999 Howard Avenue.
Telephone: 601-435-7733.
Facsimile: 601-435-7737.

MEMBERS OF FIRM

Hunter W. Lundy
Clayton A. L. Davis
Matthew E. Lundy
Jerry A. Johnson
Winfield E. Little, Jr., (A Professional Corporation)
David A. Bowers (Resident, Jackson, Mississippi Office)

ASSOCIATES

Jackey W. South
DeAnn Gibson
Samuel B. Gabb

OF COUNSEL

Edgar F. Barnett (Resident, Houston, Texas Office)
Walter L. Nixon, Jr.

For full biographical listings, see the Martindale-Hubbell Law Directory

METAIRIE, Jefferson Parish

WEIR AND WALLEY (AV)

2721 Division Street, 70002-7084
Telephone: 504-455-7264
Fax: 504-455-7266

(See Next Column)

WEIR AND WALLEY—*Continued*

MEMBERS OF FIRM

Andrew M. Weir
James M. Walley

References: the Whitney National Bank; First National Bank of Commerce.

For full biographical listings, see the Martindale-Hubbell Law Directory

*NEW ORLEANS,** Orleans Parish

DEUTSCH, KERRIGAN & STILES (AV)

A Partnership including Professional Law Corporations
755 Magazine Street, 70130-3672
Telephone: 504-581-5141
Cable Address: "Dekest"
Telex: 584358
Telecopier: 504-566-1201

MEMBERS OF FIRM

William W. Messersmith, III, (P.L.C.)
Charles K. Reasonover (P.L.C.)
David L. Campbell
Harry S. Anderson (P.L.C.)
Matt J. Farley (P.L.C.)
Daniel A. Smith
Richard B. Montgomery III
William E. Wright, Jr.
Ellis B. Murov (P.L.C.)
Joseph L. Spilman, III
Duris L. Holmes
Judy L. Burnthorn
L. Paul Hood, Jr.

OF COUNSEL

Marian Mayer Berkett
Malcolm W. Monroe

ASSOCIATES

Michael W. Boleware
Garald P. Weller

For Complete List of Firm Personnel, See General Section

For full biographical listings, see the Martindale-Hubbell Law Directory

HEBERT, MOULEDOUX & BLAND, A PROFESSIONAL LAW CORPORATION (AV)

Pan-American Life Center, Suite 1650, 601 Poydras Street, 70130
Telephone: 504-525-3333
Cable Address: "HMBL"
Telex: 588-092;
Fax: 504-523-4224

Maurice C. Hebert, Jr.
André J. Mouledoux
Alan Guy Brackett

Representative Clients: Archer-Daniels Midland Company; Bisso Marine Company, Inc.; Carline Geismar Fleet, Inc.; Cooper/T. Smith Stevedoring Company, Inc.; Delta Queen Steamboat Co.; Diamond Offshore Drilling, Inc.; LOOP INC.; Marine Equipment Management Corporation; McDermott Incorporated; Olympic Marine Company.

For Complete List of Firm Personnel, See General Section

For full biographical listings, see the Martindale-Hubbell Law Directory

LEAKE & ANDERSSON (AV)

1700 Energy Centre, 1100 Poydras Street, 70163-1701
Telephone: 504-585-7500
Telecopier: 504-585-7775

MEMBERS OF FIRM

Robert E. Leake, Jr.
W. Paul Andersson
Lawrence A. Mann
Kevin O'Bryon
George D. Fagan

ASSOCIATES

Rebecca Olivier Hand
Guy D. Perrier

Representative Clients: Trailer Train; KFC; Heller Financial, Inc.; The Kroger Co.; Amway Corporation; Safelite Glass Co.; Secor Bank; F.S.B.; Gerrard Chevrolet.

For Complete List of Firm Personnel, See General Section

For full biographical listings, see the Martindale-Hubbell Law Directory

MIDDLEBERG, RIDDLE & GIANNA (AV)

31st Floor, Place St. Charles, 201 St. Charles Avenue, 70170-3100
Telephone: 504-525-7200
Telecopier: 504-581-5983
Dallas, Texas Office: 2323 Bryan Street, Suite 1600.
Telephone: 214-220-6300;
Telecopier: 214-220-2785.
Austin, Texas Office: 901 South Mopac Expressway.
Telephone: 512-329-3012.

MEMBERS OF FIRM

Ira Joel Middleberg
Michael Lee Riddle (Resident, Dallas, Texas)
Dominic J. Gianna

(See Next Column)

Paul J. Mirabile
John D. Person
Alan Dean Weinberger
Evelyn Foley Pugh
L. Marlene Quarles
Ronald J. Vega
Edward T. Suffern, Jr.
Gary S. Brown
Tina S. Clark
E. Ralph Lupin
A.J. Herbert, III
Cynthia A. Langston
Marshall Joseph Simien, Jr.
Wade P. Webster
Brian G. Meissner
William M. Blackston
A. Elizabeth Tarver
Maria N. Rabieh

For full biographical listings, see the Martindale-Hubbell Law Directory

RICE FOWLER (AV)

Place St. Charles, 36th Floor, 201 St. Charles Avenue, 70130
Telephone: 504-523-2600
Telecopier: 504-523-2705
Telex: 9102507910
ELN 62548910
London, England Office: Suite 692, Level 6 Lloyd's, 1 Lime Street, London EC3M 7DQ England.
Telephone: 071-327-4222.
Telecopier: 071-929-0043.
San Francisco, California Office: Embarcadero Center West, 275 Battery Street, 27th Floor, 94111.
Telephone: 415-399-9191.
Telecopier: 415-399-9192.
Telex: 451981.
San Diego, California Office: Emerald-Shapery Center, 402 W. Broadway, Suite 850, 92101.
Telephone: 619-230-0030.
Telecopier: 619-230-1350.
Beijing, China Office: Beijing International Convention Centre, Suite 7024, No. 8 Beichendong Road, Chaoyang District, 100101, P.R.C.
Telephone: (861) 493-4250.
Telecopier: (861) 493-4251.
Bogota, Colombia Office: Avenida Jimenez #4-03 Oficina 10-05.
Telephone: (571) 342-1062.
Telecopier: (571) 342-1062.

MEMBERS OF FIRM

Winston Edward Rice
George J. Fowler, III
Antonio J. Rodriguez
Thomas H. Kingsmill, III
Paul N. Vance
Delos E. Flint, Jr.
Edward F. LeBreton, III
Docia L. Dalby
Mary Campbell Hubbard
Jon W. Wise
Mat M. Gray, III

OF COUNSEL

T. C. W. Ellis

ASSOCIATES

Mary E. Kerrigan
Susan Molero Vance
Samuel A. Giberga
John F. Billera
D. Roxanne Perkins
Jeffry L. Sanford
Alanson T. Chenault, IV
Cindy T. Matherne
Barry A. Brock
Walter F. Wolf, III
Robert R. Johnston
Virginia R. Quijada
William J. Sommers, Jr.

For full biographical listings, see the Martindale-Hubbell Law Directory

WAGNER, BAGOT & GLEASON (AV)

Suite 2660, Poydras Center, 650 Poydras Street, 70130-6102
Telephone: 504-525-2141
Telecopier: 504-523-1587
TWX: 5106017673
ELN: 62928850
"INCISIVE"

Thomas J. Wagner
Michael H. Bagot, Jr.
Harvey G. Gleason
Whitney L. Cole
Eric D. Suben

For full biographical listings, see the Martindale-Hubbell Law Directory

*SHREVEPORT,** Caddo Parish

BARLOW AND HARDTNER L.C. (AV)

Tenth Floor, Louisiana Tower, 401 Edwards Street, 71101-3289
Telephone: 318-227-1131
Telecopier: 318-227-1141
Mailing Address: P.O. Box 8, Shreveport, Louisiana, 71161-0008

Ray A. Barlow
Quintin T. Hardtner, III
David R. Taggart

Representative Clients: Kelley Oil Corporation; NorAm Energy Corp. (formerly Arkla, Inc.) Central and South West; Panhandle Eastern Corp.; Pennzoil Producing Co.; Johnson Controls, Inc.; Ashland Oil, Inc.; Southwestern Electric Power Company; Goodrich Oil Company; General Electric Co.

For Complete List of Firm Personnel, See General Section

For full biographical listings, see the Martindale-Hubbell Law Directory

Shreveport—Continued

BODENHEIMER, JONES, KLOTZ & SIMMONS (AV)

509 Milam Street, 71101
Telephone: 318-221-1507
Fax: 318-221-4560

MEMBERS OF FIRM

David B. Klotz
Mary Louise Coon Blackley
Norman I. Lafargue
Claude W. Bookter, Jr.

For full biographical listings, see the Martindale-Hubbell Law Directory

COOK, YANCEY, KING & GALLOWAY, A PROFESSIONAL LAW CORPORATION (AV)

1700 Commercial National Tower, 333 Texas Street, P.O. Box 22260, 71120-2260
Telephone: 318-221-6277
Telecopier: 318-227-2606

Sidney B. Galloway
Edwin L. Blewer, Jr.
James Robert Jeter
Herschel E. Richard, Jr.
Stephen R. Yancey II
Samuel W. Caverlee
J. William Fleming
F. Drake Lee, Jr.
Charles G. Tutt
Frank M. Dodson
Jerald R. Harper
Bernard S. Johnson
Glenn L. Langley
Curtis R. Shelton
Kenneth Mascagni
Leland H. Ayres
Bryce J. Denny
Lance P. Havener
William C. Kalmbach, III
Julia E. Blewer
Tracy A. Burch

A list of representative clients will be furnished upon request.

For Complete List of Firm Personnel, See General Section

For full biographical listings, see the Martindale-Hubbell Law Directory

MAINE

LEWISTON, Androscoggin Co.

PLATZ & THOMPSON, P.A. (AV)

95 Park Street, P.O. Box 960, 04243
Telephone: 207-783-8558
Telecopier: 207-783-9487

J. Peter Thompson
Philip K. Hargesheimer
Paul S. Douglass
Roger J. O'Donnell, III
Robert V. Hoy
Michael J. LaTorre
James B. Main

Representative Clients: Platz Assoc.; BayBank; Key Bank of Maine; Androscoggin Savings Bank; Maine Education Assoc.; Pioneer Plastics, Inc.; Getty Oil Co.; Conifer Industries (KFC franchises for Maine); Livermore Falls Trust; H.P. Cummings Const. Co.

For Complete List of Firm Personnel, See General Section

For full biographical listings, see the Martindale-Hubbell Law Directory

*PORTLAND,** Cumberland Co.

AMERLING & BURNS, A PROFESSIONAL ASSOCIATION (AV)

193 Middle Street, 04101
Telephone: 207-775-3581
Facsimile: 207-775-3814
Affiliated St. Croix Office: Coon & Sanford, P.O. Box 25918, Six Chandlers's Wharf, Suite 202, 00824-0918.

W. John Amerling
George F. Burns
David P. Ray
John R. Coon
Arnold C. Macdonald
Mary DeLano
Joanne F. Cole
A. Robert Ruesch

OF COUNSEL

Bruce M. Jervis

Representative Clients: H.E. Sargent, Inc. (construction); Merrill Trust; J.M. Huber, Inc.; Jackson Laboratories; Hague International (engineering); Aetna Life & Casualty Co.; The Hartford; Great American Insurance Co.; Wausau Insurance Co.

For full biographical listings, see the Martindale-Hubbell Law Directory

PIERCE, ATWOOD, SCRIBNER, ALLEN, SMITH & LANCASTER (AV)

One Monument Square, 04101
Telephone: 207-773-6411
Fax: 207-773-3419
Augusta, Maine Office: 77 Winthrop Street.
Telephone: 207-622-6311.
Camden, Maine Office: 36 Chestnut Street, P.O. Box 780.
Telephone: 207-236-4333.

(See Next Column)

MEMBERS OF FIRM

Jeremiah D. Newbury
Bruce A. Coggeshall
James B. Zimpritch
Richard P. Hackett
Christopher E. Howard
Jacob A. Manheimer
David J. Champoux
Gloria A. Pinza

ASSOCIATES

Jennie L. Clegg
Nancy V. Savage
Foster A. Stewart, Jr

For Complete List of Firm Personnel, See General Section

For full biographical listings, see the Martindale-Hubbell Law Directory

PRETI, FLAHERTY, BELIVEAU & PACHIOS (AV)

443 Congress Street, P.O. Box 11410, 04104-7410
Telephone: 207-791-3000
Telecopier: 207-791-3111
Augusta, Maine Office: 45 Memorial Circle, P.O. Box 1058, 04332-1058.
Telephone: 207-623-5300.
Telecopier: 207-623-2914.
Rumford, Maine Office: 150 Congress Street, P.O. Drawer L, 04276-2035.
Telephone: 207-364-4593.
Telecopier: 207-369-9421.

MEMBERS OF FIRM

John J. Flaherty
Harold C. Pachios
Michael J. Gentile (Augusta Office)
Richard H. Spencer, Jr.
Eric P. Stauffer
Jonathan S. Piper
Randall B. Weill
James C. Pitney, Jr. (Augusta Office)
Leonard M. Gulino
Dennis C. Sbrega
Estelle A. Lavoie
Susan E. LoGiudice
Michael Kaplan
Michael L. Sheehan

ASSOCIATES

James E. Phipps
Jeanne T. Cohn-Connor
John P. McVeigh
Marilyn E. Mistretta
Scott T. Rodgers

Representative Clients: Key Bank of Maine; Guy Gannett Publishing Co.; Peoples Heritage Savings Bank; Liberty Group Inc.; RECOLL Management Corp.; NRG Barriers, Inc.; Hussey Corp.; Northeast Air Group; The Woodlands Club; P.H. Chadbourne and Co.

For Complete List of Firm Personnel, See General Section

For full biographical listings, see the Martindale-Hubbell Law Directory

MARYLAND

*BALTIMORE,** (Independent City)

THIEBLOT, RYAN, MARTIN & FERGUSON, P.A. (AV)

4th Floor, The World Trade Center, 21202-3091
Telephone: 410-837-1140
Washington, D.C. Line: 202-628-8223
Fax: 410-837-3282

Robert J. Thieblot
Anthony W. Ryan
J. Edward Martin, Jr.
Robert L. Ferguson, Jr.
Bruce R. Miller
Robert D. Harwick, Jr.
Thomas J. Schetelich
Christopher J. Heffernan

M. Brooke Murdock
Anne M. Hrehorovich
Donna Marie Raffaele
Michael N. Russo, Jr.
Jodi K. Ebersole
Hamilton Fisk Tyler
Peter Joseph Basile

Representative Clients: Ford Motor Credit Co.; USF & G Co.; The American Road Insurance Co.; Fidelity Engineering Corp.; The North Charles Street Design Organization; Record Collections, Inc.; Toyota Motor Credit Co.

For full biographical listings, see the Martindale-Hubbell Law Directory

VENABLE, BAETJER AND HOWARD (AV)

A Partnership including Professional Corporations
1800 Mercantile Bank & Trust Building, 2 Hopkins Plaza, 21201
Telephone: 410-244-7400
Washington, D.C. Office: Venable, Baetjer, Howard & Civiletti. Suite 1000, 1201 New York Avenue, N.W.
Telephone: 202-962-4800.
McLean, Virginia Office: Suite 400, 2010 Corporate Ridge.
Telephone: 703-760-1600.
Rockville, Maryland Office: Suite 500, One Church Street, P. O. Box 1906.
Telephone: 301-217-5600.
Towson, Maryland Office: 210 Allegheny Avenue, P. O. Box 5517.
Telephone: 410-494-6200.

(See Next Column)

VENABLE, BAETJER AND HOWARD—*Continued*

MEMBERS OF FIRM

Thomas P. Perkins, III (P.C.)
Benjamin R. Civiletti (P.C.) (Also at Washington, D.C. and Towson, Maryland Offices)
John Henry Lewin, Jr. (P.C.)
Neal D. Borden (Also at Washington, D.C. Office)
Robert A. Shelton
Roger W. Titus (Resident, Rockville, Maryland Office)
Douglas D. Connah, Jr. (P.C.) (Also at Washington, D.C. Office)
James D. Wright (P.C.)
Joe A. Shull (Resident, Washington, D.C. Office)
Kenneth C. Bass, III (Not admitted in MD; Also at Washington, D.C. and McLean, Virginia Offices)
John H. Zink, III (Resident, Towson, Maryland Office)
Bruce E. Titus (Resident, McLean, Virginia Office)
Joel Z. Silver (Not admitted in MD; Resident, Washington, D.C. Office)
Paul F. Strain (P.C.)
William D. Dolan, III (P.C.) (Not admitted in MD; Resident, McLean, Virginia Office)
Paul T. Glasgow (Resident, Rockville, Maryland Office)
Joseph C. Wich, Jr. (Resident, Towson, Maryland Office)
Edward F. Glynn, Jr. (Not admitted in MD; Resident, Washington, D.C. Office)
Michael Schatzow (Also at Washington, D.C. and Towson, Maryland Offices)
Bryson L. Cook (P.C.) (Also at Washington, D.C. Office)
Nell B. Strachan
David G. Lane (Resident, McLean, Virginia Office)
L. Paige Marvel
Susan K. Gauvey (Also at Towson, Maryland Office)
James K. Archibald (Also at Washington, D.C. and Towson, Maryland Offices)
G. Stewart Webb, Jr.
James R. Myers (Not admitted in MD; Resident, Washington, D.C. Office)
F. Dudley Staples, Jr. (Also at Towson, Maryland Office)
Edward L. Wender (P.C.)
David M. Fleishman
Jeffrey A. Dunn (also at Washington, D.C. Office)
George F. Pappas (Also at Washington, D.C. Office)
Mitchell Kolkin
William D. Coston (Not admitted in MD; Resident, Washington, D.C. Office)
James L. Shea (Also at Washington, D.C. Office)
Jeffrey P. Ayres (P.C.)
Nathaniel E. Jones, Jr.
Amy Berman Jackson (Not admitted in MD; Resident, Washington, D.C. Office)
William D. Quarles (Also at Washington, D.C. and Towson, Maryland Offices)
C. Carey Deeley, Jr. (Also at Towson, Maryland Office)
Kathleen Gallogly Cox (Resident, Towson, Maryland Office)
Christopher R. Mellott
M. King Hill, III (Resident, Towson, Maryland Office)
James A. Dunbar (Also at Washington, D.C. Office)
Robert J. Bolger, Jr. (Also at Washington, D.C. Office)
David J. Heubeck
J. Michael Brennan (Resident, Towson, Maryland Office)
Bruce H. Jurist (Also at Washington, D.C. Office)
Paul A. Serini (Also at Washington, D.C. Office)
Herbert G. Smith, II (Not admitted in MD; Resident, McLean, Virginia Office)
Gary M. Hnath (Resident, Washington, D.C. Office)
Kevin L. Shepherd
Michael H. Davis (Resident, Towson, Maryland Office)

OF COUNSEL

Emried D. Cole, Jr.
Joyce K. Becker
Mary T. Flynn (Not admitted in MD; Resident, McLean, Virginia Office)
Fred W. Hathaway (Not admitted in MD; Resident, Washington, D.C. Office)

ASSOCIATES

Michael J. Baader
Elizabeth Marzo Borinsky
Julian Sylvester Brown (Not admitted in MD; Resident, McLean, Virginia Office)
Daniel William China
Wallace E. Christner (Not admitted in MD)
Christine J. Collins
Newton B. Fowler, III
Robert H. Geis, Jr.
David W. Goewey (Not admitted in MD; Resident, Washington, D.C. Office)
Maria F. Howell
Mary-Dulany James (Resident, Towson, Maryland Office)
Gregory L. Laubach (Resident, Rockville, Maryland Office)
Fernand A. Lavallee (Not admitted in MD; Resident, Washington, D. C. Office)
Jon M. Lippard (Not admitted in MD; Resident, McLean, Virginia Office)
Vicki Margolis
John A. McCauley
Timothy J. McEvoy
Mitchell Y. Mirviss
Traci H. Mundy (Not admitted in MD; Resident, Washington, D.C. Office)
Vadim A. Mzhen
John T. Prisbe
Michael W. Robinson (Not admitted in MD; Resident, McLean, Virginia Office)
Todd K. Snyder
Neal H. Strum
J. Preston Turner
Robin L. Zimelman

For Complete List of Firm Personnel, See General Section

For full biographical listings, see the Martindale-Hubbell Law Directory

ROCKVILLE, * Montgomery Co.

SHULMAN, ROGERS, GANDAL, PORDY & ECKER, P.A. (AV)

Third Floor, 11921 Rockville Pike, 20852-2743
Telephone: 301-230-5200
Telecopier: 301-230-2891
Washington, D.C. Office: 1120-19th Street, N.W., Eighth Floor.
Telephone: 202-872-0400.

Lawrence A. Shulman
Donald R. Rogers
Larry N. Gandal
Karl L. Ecker
David A. Pordy
David D. Freishtat
Martin P. Schaffer
Christopher C. Roberts
Edward M. Hanson, Jr.
David M. Kochanski
Walter A. Oleniewski
Lawrence L. Bell
James M. Kefauver
Rebecca Oshoway
Robert B. Canter
Edward F. Schiff
Philip J. McNutt
Daniel S. Krakower
Kevin P. Kennedy
Ashley Joel Gardner
Alan B. Sternstein
Nancy P. Regelin

OF COUNSEL

Martin Levine

Michael J. Froehlich
James M. Hoffman
William C. Davis, III
James A. Powers
Elizabeth N. Shomaker
Michael V. Nakamura
Paul A. Bellegarde
Gregory J. Rupert
Douglas K. Hirsch

Reference: Maryland National Bank, Montgomery County Regional Office.

For Complete List of Firm Personnel, See General Section

For full biographical listings, see the Martindale-Hubbell Law Directory

STEIN, SPERLING, BENNETT, DE JONG, DRISCOLL, GREENFEIG & METRO, P.A. (AV)

25 West Middle Lane, 20850
Telephone: 301-340-2020; 800-435-5230
Telecopier: 301-340-8217

Millard S. Bennett
Jack A. Garson
A. Howard Metro
Donald N. Sperling

Beth H. McIntosh
Kieyasien K. Moore
Jeffrey D. Goldstein

For Complete List of Firm Personnel, See General Section

For full biographical listings, see the Martindale-Hubbell Law Directory

SILVER SPRING, Montgomery Co.

ALEXANDER, GEBHARDT, APONTE & MARKS, L.L.C. (AV)

Lee Plaza-Suite 805, 8601 Georgia Avenue, 20910
Telephone: 301-589-2222
Facsimile: 301-589-2523
Washington, D.C. Office: 1314 Nineteenth Street, N.W., 20036.
Telephone: 202-835-1555.
New York, New York Office: 330 Madison Avenue, 36th Floor.
Telephone: 212-808-0008.
Fax: 212-599-1028.

Koteles Alexander (Not admitted in MD)
S. Ricardo Narvaiz (Not admitted in MD)
Glenn K. Garnes

OF COUNSEL

Eduardo Peña, Jr. (Not admitted in MD)

J. Darrell Peterson
Y. Kris Oh (Ms.) (Not admitted in MD)
Adrian Van Nelson II

Reference: Riggs National Bank of Washington, D.C.

For full biographical listings, see the Martindale-Hubbell Law Directory

TOWSON, * Baltimore Co.

VENABLE, BAETJER AND HOWARD (AV)

A Partnership including Professional Corporations
210 Allegheny Avenue, P.O. Box 5517, 21204
Telephone: 410-494-6200
FAX: 410-821-0147
Baltimore, Maryland Office: 1800 Mercantile Bank & Trust Building, 2 Hopkins Plaza.
Telephone: 410-244-7400.
Washington, D.C. Office: Venable, Baetjer, Howard & Civiletti. Suite 1000, 1201 New York Avenue, N.W.
Telephone: 202-962-4800.
McLean, Virginia Office: Suite 400, 2010 Corporate Ridge.
Telephone: 703-760-1600.

(See Next Column)

VENABLE, BAETJER AND HOWARD, *Towson—Continued*

Rockville, Maryland Office: Suite 500, One Church Street, P. O. Box 1906.
Telephone: 301-217-5600.

PARTNERS

Benjamin R. Civiletti (P.C.) (Also at Washington, D.C. and Baltimore, Maryland Offices)
John H. Zink, III
Joseph C. Wich, Jr.
Michael Schatzow (Also at Baltimore, Maryland and Washington, D.C. Offices)
Susan K. Gauvey (Also at Baltimore, Maryland Office)
James K. Archibald (Also at Baltimore, Maryland and Washington, D.C. Offices)
F. Dudley Staples, Jr. (Also at Baltimore, Maryland Office)
William D. Quarles (Also at Washington, D.C. Office)
C. Carey Deeley, Jr. (Also at Baltimore, Maryland Office)
Kathleen Gallogly Cox
M. King Hill, III
J. Michael Brennan
Michael H. Davis

ASSOCIATE

Mary-Dulany James

For Complete List of Firm Personnel, See General Section

For full biographical listings, see the Martindale-Hubbell Law Directory

MASSACHUSETTS

AMESBURY, Essex Co.

HAMEL, DESHAIES & GAGLIARDI (AV)

Five Market Square, P.O. Box 198, 01913
Telephone: 508-388-3558
Telecopier: 508-388-0441

MEMBERS OF FIRM

Richard P. Hamel
Robert J. Deshaies
Paul J. Gagliardi

ASSOCIATES

H. Scott Haskell
Peter R. Ayer, Jr.
Roger D. Turgeon
Charles E. Schissel

Representative Clients: Essex County Gas Co., Amesbury, MA; First and Ocean National Bank, Newburyport, MA; Amesbury Co-Operative Bank, Amesbury, MA.
Approved Attorneys for: Chicago Title Insurance; Old Republic Title Insurance Co.

For full biographical listings, see the Martindale-Hubbell Law Directory

*BOSTON,** Suffolk Co.

HANIFY & KING, PROFESSIONAL CORPORATION (AV)

One Federal Street, 02110-2007
Telephone: 617-423-0400
Telefax: 617-423-0498

James Coyne King
John D. Hanify
Harold B. Murphy
David Lee Evans
Daniel J. Lyne
Donald F. Farrell, Jr.
Barbara Wegener Pfirrman
Gerard P. Richer
Timothy P. O'Neill

Gordon M. Jones, III
Kara L. Thornton
Jean A. Musiker
Ann M. Chiacchieri
Melissa J. Cassedy
Kara M. Lucciola
Philip C. Silverman
Michael R. Perry
Jeffrey S. Cedrone
Charles A. Dale, III
Joseph F. Cortellini
Hiram N. Pan
Amy Conroy
Michael S. Bloom
Andrew G. Lizotte
Peter D. Lee
Martin F. Gaynor, III

For full biographical listings, see the Martindale-Hubbell Law Directory

MERRILL I. HASSENFELD (AV)

56 Commercial Wharf, 02110
Telephone: 617-367-6400
Fax: 617-367-0280

For full biographical listings, see the Martindale-Hubbell Law Directory

SHERBURNE, POWERS & NEEDHAM, P.C. (AV)

One Beacon Street, 02108
Telephone: 617-523-2700
Fax: 617-523-6850

(See Next Column)

William D. Weeks
John T. Collins
Allan J. Landau
John L. Daly
Stephen A. Hopkins
Alan I. Falk
C. Thomas Swaim
James Pollock
William V. Tripp III
Stephen S. Young
William F. Machen
W. Robert Allison
Jacob C. Diemert
Philip J. Notopoulos
Richard J. Hindlian
Paul E. Troy
Harold W. Potter, Jr.
Dale R. Johnson
Philip S. Lapatin
Pamela A. Duckworth
Mark Schonfeld
James D. Smeallie
Paul Killeen
Gordon P. Katz
Joseph B. Darby, III
Richard M Yanofsky
James E. McDermott
Robert V. Lizza
Miriam Goldstein Altman
John J. Monaghan
Margaret J. Palladino
Mark C. Michalowski
David Scott Sloan
M. Chrysa Long
Lawrence D. Bradley
Miriam J. McKendall

Cynthia A. Brown
Cynthia M. Hern
Dianne R. Phillips
Paul M. James
Theodore F. Hanselman
Joshua C. Krumholz
Ieuan G. Mahony
Kenneth L. Harvey
Christopher J. Trombetta
Edwin F. Landers, Jr.
Amy J. Mastrobattista
William Howard McCarthy, Jr.
Douglas W. Clapp
Tamara E. Goulston
Nicholas J. Psyhogeos

COUNSEL

Haig Der Manuelian
Mason M. Taber, Jr.
Karl J. Hirshman
Benjamin Volinski
Kenneth P. Brier

OF COUNSEL

John Barr Dolan

For full biographical listings, see the Martindale-Hubbell Law Directory

WITMER & THUOTTE (AV)

One Joy Street, 02108
Telephone: 617-248-0550
Telefax: 617-248-0607

Ronald A. Witmer
Robert W. Thuotte

ASSOCIATE

Lynn C. Rooney

For full biographical listings, see the Martindale-Hubbell Law Directory

*CAMBRIDGE,** Middlesex Co.

WILLIAM M. O'BRIEN (AV)

Suite 216, 186 Alewife Brook Parkway, 02138
Telephone: 617-661-2600
Fax: 617-864-0654

For full biographical listings, see the Martindale-Hubbell Law Directory

*SPRINGFIELD,** Hampden Co.

HENDEL, COLLINS & NEWTON, P.C. (AV)

101 State Street, 01103
Telephone: 413-734-6411
Fax: 413-734-8069

Philip J. Hendel
Joseph B. Collins
Carla W. Newton

Joseph H. Reinhardt
Jonathan R. Goldsmith
Henry E. Geberth, Jr.
George I. Roumeliotis

Representative Clients: Springfield Institution for Savings; Shawmut Bank, N.A.; United Cooperative Bank.
Reference: Shawmut Bank, N.A.

For full biographical listings, see the Martindale-Hubbell Law Directory

KAMBERG, BERMAN, P.C. (AV)

One Monarch Place Twelfth Floor, 01144-1009
Telephone: 413-781-1300
Facsimile: 413-732-0860
ABA/net: KAMBERGB

Abraham Kamberg (1895-1981)
Eugene B. Berman
Richard G. Lemoine
Carolyn L. Burt
Mark W. Siegars
Kerry David Strayer

References: Shawmut Bank, N.A.; Fleet Bank of Massachusetts, N.A.; Baybank.

For full biographical listings, see the Martindale-Hubbell Law Directory

MICHIGAN

BIRMINGHAM, Oakland Co.

LOUIS J. BURNETT, P.C. (AV)

555 South Woodward, Suite 755, 48009-6782
Telephone: 810-642-4345
Fax: 810-642-2005

Louis J. Burnett

Reference: Comerica, Detroit, Michigan.

For full biographical listings, see the Martindale-Hubbell Law Directory

CARSON FISCHER, P.L.C. (AV)

Third Floor, 300 East Maple Road, 48009-6317
Telephone: 810-644-4840
Facsimile: 810-644-1832

Joseph M. Fischer
Robert A. Weisberg
Sandra L. Labovitz
Stephen J. Carson

For full biographical listings, see the Martindale-Hubbell Law Directory

AUSTIN HIRSCHHORN, P.C. (AV)

251 East Merrill Street, 2nd Floor, 48009-6150
Telephone: 810-646-9944
FAX: 810-647-8596

Austin Hirschhorn

For full biographical listings, see the Martindale-Hubbell Law Directory

KELL & LYNCH, P.C. (AV)

300 East Maple Road, Suite 200, 48009
Telephone: 810-647-2333
Fax: 810-647-2781

Michael V. Kell
Margaret A. Lynch

Lissa M. Cinat
Jose L. Patino

For full biographical listings, see the Martindale-Hubbell Law Directory

SIMPSON & BERRY, P.C. (AV)

260 East Brown, Suite 300, 48009
Telephone: 810-647-0200
Telecopier: 810-647-2776

Daniel F. Berry
Clark G. Doughty
Philip J. Goodman
James A. Simpson
Katheryne L. Zelenock

LEGAL SUPPORT PERSONNEL

Dwight Noble Baker, Jr.

Representative Clients: Hall Financial Group; Little Caesar Enterprises, Inc.; IMI Plc.; Leslie Paper Company; The Eyeglass Factory, Inc.; Dupuis & Ryden, P.C., Accountants; Rock Financial Corporation; Win Schuler Foods; Innovative Medical Technologies, Inc.; Trizec Properties, Inc.

For full biographical listings, see the Martindale-Hubbell Law Directory

BLOOMFIELD HILLS, Oakland Co.

JON H. BERKEY, P.C. (AV)

1760 South Telegraph Road, Suite 300, 48302-0183
Telephone: 810-332-2100

Jon H. Berkey

Anthony A. Yezbick

For full biographical listings, see the Martindale-Hubbell Law Directory

FEENEY KELLETT & WIENNER, PROFESSIONAL CORPORATION (AV)

950 N. Hunter Boulevard, Third Floor, 48304-3927
Telephone: 810-258-1580
Fax: 810-258-0421

James P. Feeney
S. Thomas Wienner
Peter M. Kellett
Cheryl A. Bush
Linda M. Galante
Deborah F. Collins
David N. Goltz
G. Gregory Schuetz
Tracy D. Knox (Not admitted in MI)
Patrick G. Seyferth
Mark A. Fisher

For full biographical listings, see the Martindale-Hubbell Law Directory

HARDIG & PARSONS (AV)

2000 North Woodward Avenue, Suite 100, 48304
Telephone: 313-642-3500
Facsimile: 313-645-1128
Charlevoix, Michigan Office: 212 Bridge Street.
Telephone: 616-547-1200.
Facsimile: 616-547-1026.
Pawley's Island, South Carolina Office: 216 Highway 17, P.O. Box 1607, 29585.
Telephone: 803-237-9219.
Facsimile: 803-237-9530.
West Palm Beach, Florida Office: Suite 1450, 515 North Flagler.
Telephone: 407-833-1622.
Facsimile: 407-833-6933.
Charlotte Amalie, St. Thomas, Virgin Islands Office: International Plaza, 22 Dronningens Gade.
Telephone: 809-776-7650.
Facsimile: 809-774-2729.

MEMBERS OF FIRM

Joseph L. Hardig, Jr.
Donald H. Parsons
Joseph L. Hardig, III

ASSOCIATES

Bradley S. Stout
Kevin M. O'Connell

OF COUNSEL

Frederick Wm. Heath

MEMBER IN FLORIDA

Charles Ryan Hickman

MEMBER IN SOUTH CAROLINA

John C. Benso

OF COUNSEL

Preston Bennett Haines, III

MEMBER IN CHARLOTTE AMALIE, ST. THOMAS, VIRGIN ISLANDS

Arthur Pomerantz

ASSOCIATE

Marcia B. Resnick

For full biographical listings, see the Martindale-Hubbell Law Directory

MAY, SIMPSON & STROTE, A PROFESSIONAL CORPORATION (AV)

100 West Long Lake Road Suite 200, P.O. Box 541, 48303-0541
Telephone: 810-646-9500

Richard H. May
Thomas C. Simpson
Ronald P. Strote
Steven M. Raymond
John A. Forrest
David K. McDonnell

Steven F. Alexsy
Marilynn K. Arnold
Michele A. Lerner

Representative Clients: Aamco Transmission; American Annuity Life Insurance; Container Corporation of America; Citicorp Financial Center; Century 21 Real Estate Corp.; Oak Hills Mortgage Corp.; Ziebart International Corp.
Reference: NBD Bank, N.A.

For full biographical listings, see the Martindale-Hubbell Law Directory

STROBL AND MANOOGIAN, P.C. (AV)

300 East Long Lake Road, Suite 200, 48304-2376
Telephone: 810-645-0306
Facsimile: 810-645-2690

Thomas J. Strobl
Brian C. Manoogian
John Sharp
James A. Rocchio
Kieran F. Cunningham
Michael E. Thoits
James D. Wilson

James T. Dunn
Sara S. Lisznyai
Brian M. Gottry
Thomas H. Kosik
Keith S. King
Pamela S. Ritter
Robert F. Boesiger
Douglas Young

OF COUNSEL

Glenn S. Arendsen

Representative Clients: Masco Corporation; MascoTech; American Speedy Printing Centers; Bohn Aluminium Corporation; Flat Rock Metal, Inc.; Sherwood Metal Products, Inc.

For full biographical listings, see the Martindale-Hubbell Law Directory

LAW OFFICES OF THOMAS J. TRENTA, P.C. (AV)

33 Bloomfield Hills Parkway Suite 145, 48304-2945
Telephone: 810-258-9610
Fax: 810-258-5132

Thomas J. Trenta

Richard A. Joslin, Jr.

(See Next Column)

LAW OFFICES OF THOMAS J. TRENTA, P.C., *Bloomfield Hills—Continued*

OF COUNSEL

James F. Jordan

Representative Clients: American International Group (A.I.G.); National Union Fire Insurance Company; Caronia Corporation; Secura Insurance Co.; National Guardian Risk Retention Group; Hutzel Hospital; Mt. Clemens General Hospital; United States Professional Ski Tour; Beverly Enterprises Nursing Homes; Havenwyck Hospital.

For full biographical listings, see the Martindale-Hubbell Law Directory

*DETROIT,** Wayne Co.

ALLARD & FISH, A PROFESSIONAL CORPORATION (AV)

2600 Buhl Building, 535 Griswold Avenue, 48226
Telephone: 313-961-6141
Facsimile: 313-961-6142

David W. Allard
Deborah L. Fish

Ralph R. McKee
Elias Themistocles Majoros
Rodney M. Glusac
Gary A. Hansz

For full biographical listings, see the Martindale-Hubbell Law Directory

BODMAN, LONGLEY & DAHLING (AV)

34th Floor 100 Renaissance Center, 48243
Telephone: 313-259-7777
Fax: 313-393-7579
Troy, Michigan Office: Suite 2020, 755 West Big Beaver Road.
Telephone: 810-362-2110.
Ann Arbor, Michigan Office: 110 Miller, Suite 300.
Telephone: 313-761-3780.
Northern Michigan Office: 229 Court Street, P.O. Box 405, Cheboygan.
Telephone: 616-627-4351.

MEMBERS OF FIRM

Richard D. Rohr
Theodore Souris
Walter O. Koch (Troy Office)
Alfred C. Wortley, Jr.
Thomas A. Roach (Ann Arbor Office)
Kenneth R. Lango (Troy Office)
Herold McC. Deason
James R. Buschmann
George G. Kemsley
Joseph J. Kochanek
David G. Chardavoyne
Larry R. Shulman
Thomas Van Dusen (Troy Office)
Robert J. Diehl, Jr.
James C. Conboy, Jr. (Northern Michigan Office)
Martha Bedsole Goodloe (Troy Office)
Barbara Bowman Bluford
Lawrence P. Hanson (Northern Michigan Office)

COUNSEL

Lewis A. Rockwell

Representative Clients: Abitibi Price Group; Archdiocese of Detroit; Comerica Bank; The Detroit Lions, Inc.; Ford Estates; General Motors Corporation; Charles Stewart Mott Foundation; Norfolk Southern Corporation; Panhandle Eastern Corporation; State Farm Mutual Automobile Insurance Company.

For Complete List of Firm Personnel, See General Section

For full biographical listings, see the Martindale-Hubbell Law Directory

BUTZEL LONG, A PROFESSIONAL CORPORATION (AV)

Suite 900, 150 West Jefferson, 48226
Telephone: 313-225-7000
Telecopier: 313-225-7080
Birmingham, Michigan Office: Suite 200, 32270 Telegraph Road.
Telephone: 810-258-1616.
Telecopier: 810-258-1439.
Lansing, Michigan Office: 118 West Ottawa Street.
Telephone: 517-372-6622.
Telecopier: 517-372-6672.
Ann Arbor, Michigan Office: Suite 400, 121 West Washington.
Telephone: 313-995-3110.
Telecopier: 313-995-1777.
Grosse Pointe Farms, Michigan Office: Suite 260, 21 Kercheval.
Telephone: 313-886-5446.
Telecopier: 313-886-2114.

Stephen A. Bromberg (Birmingham)
Douglas G. Graham
Frank B. Vecchio
Allan Nachman (Birmingham)
C. Peter Theut
Abba I. Friedman (Birmingham)
Thomas B. Radom (Birmingham)
Dennis B. Schultz
Keefe A. Brooks
Mark R. Lezotte
Edward M. Kalinka
Richard P. Saslow
Gordon W. Didier
Jack J. Mazzara
Susan Carino Nystrom
Lawrence A. Lichtman
Brian P. Henry (Birmingham and Lansing)

COUNSEL

Oscar H. Feldman

(See Next Column)

Anthony J. Saulino, Jr. (Birmingham)
James S. Rosenfeld
Patrick A. Karbowski (Birmingham)
Kenneth H. Adamczyk
Richard T. Hewlett
Michael R. Poterala
Daniel R. W. Rustmann
Eugene H. Boyle, Jr.
Timothy M. Labadie
James J. Giszczak
Barbara L. McQuade

Representative Clients: Bridgestone/Firestone, Inc.; The Detroit News, Inc.; Detroit Diesel Corp.; Kelly Services; Kelsey Hayes Co.; Merrill Lynch & Co., Inc.; Stroh Brewery Co.; Takata Corp.; United Parcel Services of America, Inc.; The University of Michigan.

For Complete List of Firm Personnel, See General Section

For full biographical listings, see the Martindale-Hubbell Law Directory

CLARK, KLEIN & BEAUMONT (AV)

1600 First Federal Building, 1001 Woodward Avenue, 48226
Telephone: 313-965-8300
Facsimile: 313-962-4348
Bloomfield Hills Office: 1533 North Woodward Avenue, Suite 220, 48304.
Telephone: 810-258-2900.
Facsimile: 810-258-2949.

MEMBERS OF FIRM

William B. Dunn
D. Kerry Crenshaw
John F. Burns
Michael D. Mulcahy (Resident Bloomfield Hills, Michigan Office)
Robert L. Weyhing, III
David E. Nims, III
Thomas S. Nowinski
Edward C. Dawda (Resident Bloomfield Hills, Michigan Office)
Curtis J. Mann (Resident Bloomfield Hills, Michigan Office)
Duane L. Tarnacki
Michael S. Khoury
Timothy M. Koltun
John J. Hern, Jr.
Andrea M. Kanski

ASSOCIATES

Judith Greenstone Miller
Michael I. Conlon
David A. Foster
Patrice A. Villani
Todd A. Schafer (Resident, Bloomfield Hills, Michigan Office)
Georgette Borrego Dulworth

For Complete List of Firm Personnel, See General Section

For full biographical listings, see the Martindale-Hubbell Law Directory

EAMES, WILCOX, MASTEJ, BRYANT, SWIFT & RIDDELL (AV)

1400 Buhl Building, 48226-3602
Telephone: 313-963-3750
Facsimile: 313-963-8485

MEMBERS OF FIRM

Leonard A. Wilcox, Jr.
Ronald J. Mastej
John W. Bryant
Jerry R. Swift
Neill T. Riddell
Elizabeth Roberto
Kevin N. Summers

ASSOCIATE

Keith M. Aretha

OF COUNSEL

Rex Eames
Robert E. Gesell
William B. McIntyre, Jr.

Representative Clients: NationsCredit Commercial Corporation; Chrysler Credit Corp.; D&B Engineering, Inc.; Engineering Heat Treat, Inc.; Fetz Engineering Co.; I E & E Industries, Inc.; Macoit Warehouse Co.

For full biographical listings, see the Martindale-Hubbell Law Directory

HAISCH & BOYDA (AV)

100 Renaissance Center, Suite 1750, 48243
Telephone: 313-259-4370
Facsimile: 313-259-6487

Anthony A. Haisch
John M. Boyda

ASSOCIATE

Donald C. Wheaton, Jr.

Representative Clients: AT&T Corp.; AT&T Universal Card Services Corp.; Amoco Corp.; North American Philips Corp.; Empire Blue Cross & Blue Shield; Lyon Financial Services, Inc.; Schwans' Sales Enterprises; Marshalls, Inc.; Access America Inc.; Grant Industries, Inc.

For full biographical listings, see the Martindale-Hubbell Law Directory

KERR, RUSSELL AND WEBER (AV)

One Detroit Center, 500 Woodward Avenue, Suite 2500, 48226-3406
Telephone: 313-961-0200
Telecopier: 313-961-0388
Bloomfield Hills, Michigan Office: 3883 Telegraph Road.
Telephone: 810-649-5990.

(See Next Column)

KERR, RUSSELL AND WEBER—*Continued*

East Lansing, Michigan Office: 1301 North Hagadorn Road.
Telephone: 517-336-6767.

Richard D. Weber
William A. Sankbeil
Robert Royal Nix, II
Michael B. Lewis
Curtis J. DeRoo
Michael D. Gibson
James R. Case
George J. Christopoulos
Kurt R. Vilders
James R. Cambridge
Thomas R. Williams
Edward C. Cutlip, Jr.
Mark M. Cunningham
Mark J. Stasa
Robert J. Pineau
Jeffrey A. Brantley
David E. Sims
Dennis A. Martin
Patrick J. Haddad
Richard C. Buslepp
Eric I. Lark
James E. DeLine
Daniel J. Schulte
John D. Gatti

OF COUNSEL
Robert G. Russell

For Complete List of Firm Personnel, See General Section

For full biographical listings, see the Martindale-Hubbell Law Directory

MAGER, MERCER, SCOTT & ALBER, P.C. (AV)

2400 First National Building, 48226
Telephone: 313-965-1700
Facsimile: 313-965-3690
Macomb County Office: 18285 Ten Mile Road, Suite 100, Roseville, Michigan.
Telephone: 810-771-1100.

George J. Mager, Jr.
Phillip G. Alber
Lawrence M. Scott (Resident at Roseville Office)
George D. Mercer
Raymond C. McVeigh
Michael R. Alberty
Bruce H. Hoffman
Jeffrey M. Frank
Michael A. Schwartz

Representative Clients: ABB Flakt, Inc.; American States Insurance Co.; CEI Industries; Central Venture Corp.; CIGNA; Construction Management, Inc.

For full biographical listings, see the Martindale-Hubbell Law Directory

SHAHEEN, JACOBS & ROSS, P.C. (AV)

585 East Larned, Suite 200, 48226-4316
Telephone: 313-963-1301
Telecopier: 313-963-7123

Joseph Shaheen (1920-1984)
Michael A. Jacobs (1949-1992)
Steven P. Ross
Michael J. Thomas
Leslie Kujawski Carr
Margaret Conti Schmidt

OF COUNSEL
Mark A. Armitage, P.C.

For full biographical listings, see the Martindale-Hubbell Law Directory

EAST LANSING, Ingham Co.

FARHAT, STORY & KRAUS, P.C. (AV)

Beacon Place, 4572 South Hagadorn Road, Suite 3, 48823
Telephone: 517-351-3700
Fax: 517-332-4122

Leo A. Farhat
James E. Burns (1925-1979)
Monte R. Story
Richard C. Kraus
Max R. Hoffman Jr.
Chris A. Bergstrom
Kitty L. Groh
Charles R. Toy
David M. Platt

Lawrence P. Schweitzer
Jeffrey J. Short
Kathy A. Breedlove
Thomas L. Sparks

Representative Clients: Big L. Corp.; Michigan Automotive Wholesalers Association; Hartman-Febco Inc.; Lansing Electric Motors, Inc.; Mike Miller Lincoln Mercury; Edward Rose Realty, Inc.; GTE Directories Service Corp.; Squires School & Commercial Sales; Commercial Blueprint.
Reference: Capitol National Bank.

For full biographical listings, see the Martindale-Hubbell Law Directory

FARMINGTON HILLS, Oakland Co.

COUZENS, LANSKY, FEALK, ELLIS, ROEDER & LAZAR, P.C. (AV)

33533 West Twelve Mile Road, Suite 150, P.O. Box 9057, 48333-9057
Telephone: 810-489-8600
Telecopier: 810-489-4156

Sheldon A. Fealk
Jack S. Couzens, II
Jerry M. Ellis
Donald M. Lansky
Bruce J. Lazar
Alan C. Roeder
Alan J. Ferrara
Renard J. Kolasa
Kathryn Gilson Sussman
Jeffrey A. Levine
Stephen M. Feldman
Phillip L. Sternberg
Marc L. Prey
Lisa J. Walters

(See Next Column)

Michael P. Witzke
Stephen Scapelliti
Cyrus Raamin Kashef
William P. Lyshak
Gregg A. Nathanson
Aaron H. Sherbin
Mark S. Frankel

References: Comerica Bank-Southfield;
Representative Clients: Provided upon request.

For full biographical listings, see the Martindale-Hubbell Law Directory

MICHAEL H. GOLOB (AV)

30300 Northwestern Highway, Suite 300, 48334
Telephone: 810-855-2626
Fax: 810-932-4009

For full biographical listings, see the Martindale-Hubbell Law Directory

KAUFMAN AND PAYTON (AV)

200 Northwestern Financial Center, 30833 Northwestern Highway, 48334
Telephone: 810-626-5000
Telefacsimile: 810-626-2843
Grand Rapids, Michigan Office: 420 Trust Building.
Telephone: 616-459-4200.
Fax: 616-459-4929.
Traverse City, Michigan Office: 122 West State Street.
Telephone: 616-947-4050.
Fax: 616-947-7321.

Alan Jay Kaufman
Donald L. Payton
Kenneth C. Letherwood
Stephen R. Levine
Thomas L. Vitu
Ralph C. Chapa, Jr.
Raymond I. Foley, II
Jeffrey K. Van Hattum
Leo D. Neville

For full biographical listings, see the Martindale-Hubbell Law Directory

*FLINT,** Genesee Co.

WINEGARDEN, SHEDD, HALEY, LINDHOLM & ROBERTSON (AV)

501 Citizens Bank Building, 48502-1983
Telephone: 810-767-3600
Telecopier: 810-767-8776

MEMBERS OF FIRM

William C. Shedd
Dennis M. Haley
John T. Lindholm
Donald H. Robertson
L. David Lawson
John R. Tucker

ASSOCIATES

Alan F. Himelhoch
Suellen J. Parker
Damion Frasier
Peter T. Mooney

OF COUNSEL
Howard R. Grossman

Representative Clients: Citizens Commercial and Savings Bank; R. L. White Development Corporation; Interstate Traffic Consultants (Intracon), Inc.; Downtown Development Authority of Flint; Young Olds-Cadillac, Inc.; First American Title Insurance Co.; Sorensen Gross Construction Co.; Genesee County; Insight, Inc.; Flint Counsel, National Bank of Detroit.

For Complete List of Firm Personnel, See General Section

For full biographical listings, see the Martindale-Hubbell Law Directory

*GRAND RAPIDS,** Kent Co.

DAY & SAWDEY, A PROFESSIONAL CORPORATION (AV)

200 Monroe Avenue, Suite 500, 49503-2217
Telephone: 616-774-8121
Telefax: 616-774-0168

George B. Kingston (1889-1965)
John R. Porter (1915-1975)
Charles E. Day, Jr.
Robert W. Sawdey
William A. Hubble
C. Mark Stoppels
James B. Frakie
Larry A. Ver Merris
John Boyko, Jr.
Jonathan F. Thoits
John T. Piggins
Thomas A. DeMeester

John G. Grzybek
Theodore E. Czarnecki

For full biographical listings, see the Martindale-Hubbell Law Directory

DE GROOT, KELLER & VINCENT (AV)

300 Michigan Trust Building, 49503
Telephone: 616-459-6251
Fax: 616-459-6352

MEMBERS OF FIRM

Murray B. De Groot
Brian D. Vincent

For full biographical listings, see the Martindale-Hubbell Law Directory

GRUEL, MILLS, NIMS AND PYLMAN (AV)

50 Monroe Place, Suite 700 West, 49503
Telephone: 616-235-5500
Fax: 616-235-5550

(See Next Column)

GRUEL, MILLS, NIMS AND PYLMAN, *Grand Rapids—Continued*

MEMBERS OF FIRM

Grant J. Gruel
William F. Mills
J. Clarke Nims
Norman H. Pylman, II
Scott R. Melton
Brion J. Brooks
Thomas R. Behm
J. Paul Janes

Representative Clients: Aquinas College; Bell Helmet Co.; Blodgett Memorial Medical Center; Butterworth Hospital; Chem Central, Inc.; Cook Pump Co.; Grove, Inc.; NBDC; Heim Corp.

For full biographical listings, see the Martindale-Hubbell Law Directory

ROBERTS, BETZ & BLOSS, P.C. (AV)

555 Riverfront Plaza Building, 55 Campau, 49503
Telephone: 616-235-9955
Telecopier: 616-235-0404

Michael J. Roberts
Michael W. Betz
David J. Bloss
Gregory A. Block
Michael T. Small
Ralph M. Reisinger
Elena C. Cardenas
Henry S. Emrich

For full biographical listings, see the Martindale-Hubbell Law Directory

WHEELER UPHAM, A PROFESSIONAL CORPORATION (AV)

Second Floor, Trust Building, 40 Pearl Street, N.W., 49503
Telephone: 616-459-7100
Fax: 616-459-6366

Gordon B. Wheeler (1904-1986)
Buford A. Upham (Retired)
Robert H. Gillette
Geoffrey L. Gillis
John M. Roels
Gary A. Maximiuk
Timothy J. Orlebeke
Kenneth E. Tiews
Jack L. Hoffman
Janet C. Baxter
Peter Kladder, III
James M. Shade
Thomas A. Kuiper

Counsel for: Travelers Insurance Co.; Prudential Insurance Co. of America; Farmers Insurance Group; Metropolitan Life Insurance Co.; Conrail Trans.; Monsanto Co.; Firestone Tire & Rubber Co.; Navistar, Inc.; Medtronic, Inc.; Westdale Better Homes and Gardens.

For full biographical listings, see the Martindale-Hubbell Law Directory

*KALAMAZOO,** Kalamazoo Co.

DEMING, HUGHEY, LEWIS, ALLEN & CHAPMAN, P.C. (AV)

800 Old Kent Bank Building, 49007
Telephone: 616-349-6601
Fax: 616-349-3831

Ned W. Deming
Richard M. Hughey
Dean S. Lewis
W. Fred Allen, Jr.
Ross E. Chapman
Winfield J. Hollander
John A. Scott
Bruce W. Martin (Resident)
Daniel L. Conklin
William A. Redmond
Stephen M. Denenfeld
Thomas C. Richardson
Gregory G. St. Arnauld
Roger G. Allen (Retired)
Anne McGregor Fries
Amy J. Glass
Richard M. Hughey, Jr.
Richard J. Bosch
Thomas P. Lewis
Christopher T. Haenicke

LEGAL SUPPORT PERSONNEL

Dorothy B. Kelly

General Counsel for: The Old Kent Bank of Kalamazoo; Gilmore Brothers, Inc.; Root Spring Scraper Co.; Kalamazoo County Road Commission; Loftenberg Educational Scholarship Trust; Farm Credit Services of West Michigan; Irving S. Gilmore Foundation; National Meals on Wheels Foundation; Irving S. Gilmore International Keyboard Festival.

For full biographical listings, see the Martindale-Hubbell Law Directory

DIETRICH, ZODY, HOWARD & VANDERROEST, P.C. (AV)

834 King Highway, Suite 110, 49001
Telephone: 616-344-9236
Fax: 616-344-0412

G. Philip Dietrich
Richard J. Howard
James W. Smith
James E. VanderRoest
Brenda Wheeler Zody

Barbara S. Weintraub

Representative Clients: Amplimedical S.P.A.; Arvco Container Corp.; Day's Molding & Machinery, Inc.; The Deaccelerator Corp.; DeLano Foundation; Tremble Foundation; Monroe Foundation; Do-It Corp.; Engineered Stadium Systems, Inc.

For full biographical listings, see the Martindale-Hubbell Law Directory

HOWARD & HOWARD ATTORNEYS, P.C. (AV)

The Kalamazoo Building, Suite 400, 107 West Michigan Avenue, 49007-3956
Telephone: 616-382-1483
Telecopier: 616-382-1568
Bloomfield Hills, Michigan Office: The Pinehurst Office Center, Suite 101, 1400 North Woodward Avenue.
Telephone: 810-645-1483.
Telecopier: 810-645-1568.
Lansing, Michigan Office: The Phoenix Building, Suite 500, 222 Washington Square North.
Telephone: 517-485-1483.
Telecopier: 517-485-1568.
Peoria, Illinois Office: Howard & Howard, P.C., The Creve Coeur Building, Suite 200, 321 Liberty Street.
Telephone: 309-672-1483.
Telecopier: 309-672-1568.

Eric E. Breisach
Peter J. Livingston
D. Craig Martin

Representative Clients: First of America Bank Corp.; Simpson Paper Company; W.R. Grace & Co.; Stryker Corp.; Kalamazoo Valley Community College.
Local Counsel for: Chrysler Motors Corp.
International Counsel for: Sony Corp.

For Complete List of Firm Personnel, See General Section

For full biographical listings, see the Martindale-Hubbell Law Directory

KREIS, ENDERLE, CALLANDER & HUDGINS, A PROFESSIONAL CORPORATION (AV)

One Moorsbridge, 49002
Telephone: 616-324-3000
Telecopier: 616-324-3010

Alan G. Enderle
C. Reid Hudgins III
Jeffrey C. O'Brien

For Complete List of Firm Personnel, See General Section

For full biographical listings, see the Martindale-Hubbell Law Directory

MILLER, CANFIELD, PADDOCK AND STONE, P.L.C. (AV)

A Professional Limited Liability Company
Founded in 1852 by Sidney Davy Miller
444 West Michigan Avenue, 49007-3752
Telephone: 616-381-7030
Fax: 616-382-0244
Detroit, Michigan Office: 150 West Jefferson, Suite 2500, 48226-4415.
Telephone: 313-963-6420.
Fax: 313-496-7500.
Cable Address: "Stem Detroit."
Ann Arbor, Michigan Office: 101 North Main Street, 7th Floor, 48104-1400.
Telephone: 313-663-2445.
Fax: 313-747-7147.
Bloomfield Hills, Michigan Office: Suite 100, Pinehurst Office Center, 1400 North Woodward, 48303-2014.
Telephone: 313-645-5000.
Fax: 313-645-1917.
Grand Rapids, Michigan Office: 1200 Campau Square Plaza, 99 Monroe, N.W., 49503-2639.
Telephone: 616-454-8656.
Fax: 616-776-6322.
Howell, Michigan Office: 121 South Barnard Street, Suite 4, 48843-2305.
Telephone: 517-546-7600.
Telecopier: 517-546-6974.
Lansing, Michigan Office: One Michigan Avenue, Suite 900, 48933-1609.
Telephone: 517-487-2070.
Fax: 517-374-6304.
Monroe, Michigan Office: The Executive Centre, 214 East Elm Avenue, 48161-2682.
Telephone: 313-243-2000.
Fax: 313-243-0901.
Washington, D.C. Office: 1225 Nineteenth Street, N.W., Suite 400. 20036.
Telephone: 202-429-5575; 785-0600.
Fax: 202-331-1118; 785-1234.
Pensacola, Florida Office: 25 West Cedar, 32501.
Telephone: 904-469-1088.
Fax: 904-432-0677.
St. Petersburg, Florida Office: 100 Second Avenue S., Suite 7045,33701.
Telephone: 813-982-6000.
Fax: 813-892-6002.
Gdansk, Poland Office: Suite 322, Dom Technika Building, Ul. Rajska 6, 80-850.
Telephone: 011-485-831-2808.
Fax: 011-485-831-4719.
Warsaw, Poland Office: Ul. Marszalkowska 82, Suite 561, 00-517.
Telephone: 011-482-623-6457 and 6458.
Fax: 011-482-623-6459.

(See Next Column)

MILLER, CANFIELD, PADDOCK AND STONE P.L.C.—*Continued*

MEMBER OF FIRM

Eric V. Brown, Jr. (Resident)

Representative Firm Clients: Chrysler Corp.; Comerica, Inc.; City of Detroit, Mich.; Detroit Tigers, Inc.; First of Michigan; Fretter, Inc.; Ford Motor Co.; Ford Motor Credit Co.; Great Lakes Bancorp; Henry Ford Hospital.

For Complete List of Firm Personnel, See General Section

For full biographical listings, see the Martindale-Hubbell Law Directory

LANSING, Ingham Co.

HOWARD & HOWARD ATTORNEYS, P.C. (AV)

The Phoenix Building, Suite 500, 222 Washington Square, North, 48933-1817
Telephone: 517-485-1483
Telecopier: 517-485-1568
Kalamazoo, Michigan Office: The Kalamazoo Building, Suite 400, 107 West Michigan Avenue.
Telephone: 616-382-1483.
Telecopier: 616-382-1568.
Bloomfield Hills, Michigan Office: The Pinehurst Office Center, Suite 101, 1400 North Woodward Avenue.
Telephone: 810-645-1483.
Telecopier: 810-645-1568.
Peoria, Illinois Office: Howard & Howard, P.C., The Creve Coeur Building, Suite 200, 321 Liberty Street.
Telephone: 309-672-1483.
Telecopier: 309-672-1568.

Todd D. Chamberlain
D. Craig Martin

Representative Clients: For Representative Client list, see General Practice, Lansing, MI.

For Complete List of Firm Personnel, See General Section

For full biographical listings, see the Martindale-Hubbell Law Directory

ROCHESTER, Oakland Co.

SHERMETA, CHIMKO AND KILPATRICK, P.C. (AV)

445 South Livernois, Suite 221, P.O. Box 5016, 48308
Telephone: 810-652-8200
Fax: 810-652-1292
Detroit, Michigan Office: Ford Building, 48226.
Telephone: 313-961-4848.
Fax: 313-961-4365.
Grandville, Michigan Office: 4264 Turtle Bend Drive.
Telephone: 616-531-6980.
Fax: 616-531-7475.

Douglass H. Shermeta
Darryl J. Chimko
Richardo I. Kilpatrick
Barbara L. Adams
Karen E. Evangelista
Henry J. Mittelstaedt III
Thomas L. Beadle

Mariana J. Richmond
Robert D. Dzialo
Tammy L. Terry
Kelly L. Scola
Karen Lamoreaux Rice
John L. Burket
Christopher E. Mcneely
Richard L. McDonnell
Samuel D. Sweet
David R. Shook
Lisa E. Gocha
Sheryl S. Zamplas
Patrick (Casey) Coston
Krispen S. Carroll

For full biographical listings, see the Martindale-Hubbell Law Directory

ROYAL OAK, Oakland Co.

CARDELLI, SCHAEFER & MASON, P.C. (AV)

306 South Washington Avenue, Suite 500, 48067
Telephone: 810-544-1100
Telecopier: 810-544-1191

Thomas G. Cardelli
William C. Schaefer
Laura D. Mason
Cheryl A. Cardelli
Deborah A. Hebert
Mary Ann J. O'Neil
Shelly M. Lee

Representative Clients: Cigarette Service Company; Coltec Industries (Garlock Inc); Dana Corporation; Duchossois Industries, Inc.; Fruehauf Trailer Corporation; Morton International, Inc.; Otis Elevator Company; Raymond Corporation; Terex Corporation.

For full biographical listings, see the Martindale-Hubbell Law Directory

*SAGINAW,** Saginaw Co.

BRAUN KENDRICK FINKBEINER (AV)

8th Floor Second National Bank Building, 48607
Telephone: 517-753-3461
Telecopier: 517-753-3951
Bay City, Michigan Office: 201 Phoenix Building, P.O. Box 2039.
Telephone: 517-895-8505.
Telecopier: 517-895-8437.

(See Next Column)

MEMBERS OF FIRM

Morton E. Weldy
C. Patrick Kaltenbach
Michael J. Sauer
Timothy L Curtiss
Francis J. Keating

Representative Clients: APV Chemical Machinery, Inc.; Bay Health Systems; Berger & Co.; Catholic Federal Credit Union; Charter Township of Bridgeport; City of Saginaw; City of Vassar; City of Zilwaukee; Corporate Service; Cox Cable.

For Complete List of Firm Personnel, See General Section

For full biographical listings, see the Martindale-Hubbell Law Directory

SOUTHFIELD, Oakland Co.

MASON, STEINHARDT, JACOBS & PERLMAN, PROFESSIONAL CORPORATION (AV)

Suite 1500, 4000 Town Center, 48075-1415
Telephone: 810-358-2090
Fax: 810-358-3599

John E. Jacobs
Michael B. Perlman
Jerome P. Pesick
Anthony Ilardi, Jr.
Richard A. Barr
Jeannine F. Gleeson-Smith

Carolyn J. Crawford
Diane Flagg Goldstein
H. Adam Cohen

Representative Clients: Citibank, N.A.; City of Dearborn; DeMattia Development Co.; Forest City Enterprises; Michigan Wholesale Drug Assn.; Mortgage Bankers Association of Michigan; Nationwide Insurance Co.; City of Taylor; Union Labor Life Insurance Co.; Yellow Freight Systems, Inc.

For Complete List of Firm Personnel, See General Section

For full biographical listings, see the Martindale-Hubbell Law Directory

SOMMERS, SCHWARTZ, SILVER & SCHWARTZ, P.C. (AV)

2000 Town Center, Suite 900, 48075
Telephone: 810-355-0300
Telecopier: 810-746-4001
Plymouth, Michigan Office: 747 South Main Street.
Telephone: 313-455-4250.

Steven J. Schwartz
Gary A. Taback
James J. Vlasic
David M. Black
Jon J. Birnkrant
Joseph H. Bourgon
Alan B. Koenig
David B. Deutsch

OF COUNSEL

Charles S. Farmer
Sherwin M. Birnkrant

Representative Clients: Foodland Distributors; C.A. Muer Corporation; Vlasic & Company; Nederlander Corporation; Woodland Physicians; Midwest Health Centers, P.C.; Vesco Oil Corporation.
Representative Clients: Michigan National Bank; Madison National Bank; Bank Hapoalim, B.M.

For Complete List of Firm Personnel, See General Section

For full biographical listings, see the Martindale-Hubbell Law Directory

*TRAVERSE CITY,** Grand Traverse Co.

MURCHIE, CALCUTT & BOYNTON (AV)

109 East Front Street, Suite 300, 49684
Telephone: 616-947-7190
Fax: 616-947-4341

Robert B. Murchie (1894-1975)
Harry Calcutt
Jack E. Boynton
William B. Calcutt
Mark A. Burnheimer
Dawn M. Rogers

ASSOCIATES

George W. Hyde, III
Ralph J. Dilley (Not admitted in MI)

General Counsel for: Old Kent Bank-Grand Traverse; Northwestern Savings Bank & Trust; Central-State Bancorp; Traverse City Record Eagle; WPNB-7 & WTOM-4; Emergency Consultants, Inc.; National Guardian Risk Retention Group, Inc.; Farmers Mutual Insurance Co.; Environmental Solutions, Inc.
Local Counsel For: Consumers Power Co.

For full biographical listings, see the Martindale-Hubbell Law Directory

SMITH, JOHNSON & BRANDT, ATTORNEYS, P.C. (AV)

603 Bay Street, P.O. Box 705, 49684
Telephone: 616-946-0700
Fax: 616-946-1735
Lansing, Michigan Office: Suite 402, 116 West Ottawa Street.
Telephone: 517-482-5142.

Louis A. Smith
H. Wendell Johnson
Donald A. Brandt
Allen G. Anderson
Edgar Roy III

(See Next Column)

SMITH, JOHNSON & BRANDT ATTORNEYS, P.C., *Traverse City—Continued*

Barbara Ann Assendelft Thomas A. Pezzetti
Paul T. Jarboe Joseph E. Quandt

Representative Clients: Alden State Bank; Empire National Bank of Traverse City; First of America Bank-Northern Michigan; Garland; Grand Traverse Mall Limited Partnership; Green Tree Acceptance, Inc.; Lansing Automakers' Federal Credit Union; Michigan Automobile Dealers Association; Cherry Capital Oldsmobile Cadillac L.L.C.; Elmer's Crane and Dozer, Inc.

For full biographical listings, see the Martindale-Hubbell Law Directory

MINNESOTA

*MINNEAPOLIS,** Hennepin Co.

COX & GOUDY (AV)

600A Butler Square, 100 North Sixth Street, 55403-1592
Telephone: 612-338-1414
Fax: 612-338-6754

MEMBERS OF FIRM

Charles A. Cox Craig A. Goudy
Charles A. Cox, III

For full biographical listings, see the Martindale-Hubbell Law Directory

MOORE, COSTELLO & HART (AV)

Suite 1350, Craig Hallum Center, 701 Fourth Avenue South, 55415
Telephone: 612-673-0148
FAX: 612-376-1770
St. Paul, Minnesota Office: 1400 Norwest Center.
Telephone: 612-227-7683.
FAX: 612-290-1770.

MEMBERS OF FIRM

Ronald E. Martell John G. Patterson
William M. Beadie Timothy C. Cook
Leonard W. Glewwe Kathryn A. Graves

Representative Clients: Associated General Contractors of Minnesota, Inc.; Macalester College; The St. Paul Cos.; United States Fidelity & Guaranty Co.; University of St. Thomas.

For full biographical listings, see the Martindale-Hubbell Law Directory

WAGNER, FALCONER & JUDD, LTD. (AV)

2650 IDS Center, 80 South Eighth Street, 55402-2113
Telephone: 612-339-1421
Telecopier: 612-349-6691

Alan W. Falconer James K. Sander
Robert A. Judd Mark O. Anderson
Rodney A. Honkanen

Representative Clients: Alexander & Alexander, Inc.; American Standard, Inc.; Barber Electric Co.; C.H. Carpenter Lumber Company; General Electric Supply; Honeywell, Inc.; Johnson Controls, Inc.; Edward Kraemer & Sons, Inc.; J.H. Larson Electrical Co.

For Complete List of Firm Personnel, See General Section

For full biographical listings, see the Martindale-Hubbell Law Directory

*MOORHEAD,** Clay Co.

DOSLAND, NORDHOUGEN, LILLEHAUG & JOHNSON, P.A. (AV)

Suite 203 American Bank Moorhead Building, 730 Center Avenue, P.O. Box 100, 56561-0100
Telephone: 218-233-2744
Fax: 218-233-1570

C. A. Nye (1886-1910) John P. Dosland
C. G. Dosland (1898-1945) Curtis A. Nordhougen
G. L. Dosland (1927-1983) Duane A. Lillehaug
W. B. Dosland (1954-1990) Joel D. Johnson
Bruce Romanick

General Counsel For: American Crystal Sugar Co.; American Bank Moorhead, Moorhead, Minnesota.
Representative Clients: Auto Owners Insurance Co.; Wausau Insurance Cos.; Gethsemane Episcopal Cathedral; Swift-Eckrich, Inc.; Barrett Mobile Home Transport, Inc.; Moorhead Economic Development Authority; Eventide.
Reference: American Bank Moorhead, Moorhead, Minnesota.

For full biographical listings, see the Martindale-Hubbell Law Directory

*ST. CLOUD,** Stearns, Benton & Sherburne Cos.

HUGHES, MATHEWS & DIDIER, P.A. (AV)

110 South Sixth Avenue, Suite 200, P.O. Box 548, 56302-0548
Telephone: 612-251-4397
Fax: 612-251-5781

(See Next Column)

Kevin J. Hughes Jean M. Didier

Representative Clients: The First American National Bank of St. Cloud; The St. Cloud Hospital; St. John's University; College of St. Benedict; Tanner Systems, Inc.; Anderson Trucking Service, Inc.

For Complete List of Firm Personnel, See General Section

For full biographical listings, see the Martindale-Hubbell Law Directory

HUGHES, THOREEN & KNAPP, P.A. (AV)

110 South Sixth Avenue, Suite 200, P.O. Box 1718, 56302-1718
Telephone: 612-251-6175
Fax: 612-251-6857

Keith F. Hughes Thomas P. Knapp
Gerald L. Thoreen Jerry O. Relph
Bradley W. Hanson

Representative Clients: The First American Bank of St. Cloud; North American State Bank of Belgrade, Minnesota; Holiday Inn of St. Cloud, Inc.; Catholic Charities of the Diocese of St. Cloud; Central Minnesota Mental Health Center; Central Minnesota Community Foundation; D.H. Blattner & Sons, Inc.; St. John's Abbey and University; College of St. Benedict; Sisters of the Order of St. Benedict.

For full biographical listings, see the Martindale-Hubbell Law Directory

*ST. PAUL,** Ramsey Co.

MOORE, COSTELLO & HART (AV)

1400 Norwest Center, 55101
Telephone: 612-227-7683
FAX: 612-290-1770
Minneapolis, Minnesota Office: Suite 1350, Craig Hallum Center, 701 Fourth Avenue, South.
Telephone: 612-673-0148.
FAX: 612-376-1770.

MEMBERS OF FIRM

James C. Otis, Sr. (1879-1949) Larry A. Hanson
Roland J. Faricy (1898-1962) J. Patrick Plunkett
Richard A. Moore (1915-1991) John M. Harens
Harry G. Costello (Retired) Phyllis Karasov
B. Warren Hart (1923-1981) Malcolm G. McDonald
Marvin J. Pertzik Leonard W. Glewwe (Resident, Minneapolis Office)
A. Patrick Leighton
Harold R. Fotsch John G. Patterson (Resident, Minneapolis Office)
Ronald E. Martell (Resident, Minneapolis Office) Timothy C. Cook (Resident, Minneapolis Office)
William M. Beadie (Resident, Minneapolis Office) Kathryn A. Graves (Resident, Minneapolis Office)
Denis L. Stoddard

ASSOCIATES

Steven D. Snelling James E. Blaney
Tara D. Mattessich Frederick J. Putzier

OF COUNSEL

William F. Orme Fred W. Fisher

Representative Clients: Associated General Contractors of Minnesota, Inc.; Macalester College; The St. Paul Cos., Inc.; United States Fidelity & Guaranty Co.; University of St. Thomas.

For full biographical listings, see the Martindale-Hubbell Law Directory

MISSISSIPPI

*ABERDEEN,** Monroe Co.

HOLCOMB, DUNBAR, CONNELL, CHAFFIN & WILLARD, A PROFESSIONAL ASSOCIATION (AV)

109 1/2 West Commerce Street, P.O. Box 866, 39730
Telephone: 601-369-8800
Facsimile: 601-369-9404
Jackson, Mississippi Office: 111 East Capitol Street, Suite 290, P.O. Box 2990, 39207-2990.
Telephone: 601-948-0048.
Facsimile: 601-948-0050.
Clarksdale, Mississippi Office: 152 Delta Avenue, P.O. Box 368, 38614.
Telephone: 601-627-2241.
Facsimile: 601-627-9788.
Oxford, Mississippi Office: 1217 Jackson Avenue, P.O. Drawer 707, 38655.
Telephone: 601-234-8775.
Facsimile: 601-234-8638.
Southhaven, Mississippi Office: Suite 1, 8727 Northwest Drive, P.O. Box 190, 38671.
Telephone: 601-342-6806.
Facsimile: 601-342-6792.

(See Next Column)

HOLCOMB, DUNBAR, CONNELL, CHAFFIN & WILLARD A PROFESSIONAL ASSOCIATION—*Continued*

Jack F. Dunbar | Guy T. Gillespie, III
Craig M. Geno | John H. Dunbar
David C. Dunbar

OF COUNSEL

Ralph E. Pogue

Representative Clients: United Southern Bank; Sunburst Bank; National Bank of Commerce of Mississippi; Farm Credit Bank of Texas; North Delta Compress & Warehouse Co.; Vend-A-Snack, Inc.; Cooper Tire & Rubber Co.; Dunavant Enterprises, Inc.; Mississippi Business Finance Corp.; South Central Bell Telephone Co.

For Complete List of Firm Personnel, See General Section

For full biographical listings, see the Martindale-Hubbell Law Directory

BILOXI, Harrison Co.

RUSHING & GUICE (AV)

683 Water Street, P.O. Box 1925, 39533-1925
Telephone: 601-374-2313
Telecopier: 601-374-8155

MEMBERS OF FIRM

Charles L. Rushing (1881-1923) | William L. Guice (1887-1971)
William Lee Guice III

OF COUNSEL

Jacob D. Guice

ASSOCIATES

Edgar F. Maier | R. Scott Wells

LEGAL SUPPORT PERSONNEL

Antonia Strong

For full biographical listings, see the Martindale-Hubbell Law Directory

*CLARKSDALE,** Coahoma Co.

HOLCOMB, DUNBAR, CONNELL, CHAFFIN & WILLARD, A PROFESSIONAL ASSOCIATION (AV)

152 Delta Avenue, P.O. Box 368, 38614
Telephone: 601-627-2241
Facsimile: 601-627-9788
Jackson, Mississippi Office: 111 East Capitol Street, Suite 290, P.O. Box 2990, 39207-2990.
Telephone: 601-948-0048.
Facsimile: 601-948-0050.
Aberdeen, Mississippi Office: 109 1/2 West Commerce Street, P.O. Box 866, 39730.
Telephone: 601-369-8800.
Facsimile: 601-369-9404.
Oxford, Mississippi Office: 1217 Jackson Avenue, P.O. Drawer 707, 38655.
Telephone: 601-234-8775.
Facsimile: 601-234-8638.
Southaven, Mississippi Office: Suite 1, 8727 Northwest Drive, 38671.
Telephone: 601-342-6806.
Facsimile: 601-342-6792.

William M. Chaffin | William A. Baskin
David A. Burns

Representative Clients: United Southern Bank; Sunburst Bank; National Bank of Commerce of Mississippi; Farm Credit Bank of Texas; North Delta Compress & Warehouse Co.; Deposit Guaranty National Bank; Cooper Tire & Rubber Co.; Dunavant Enterprises, Inc.; Mississippi Business Finance Corp.; South Central Bell Telephone Co.

For Complete List of Firm Personnel, See General Section

For full biographical listings, see the Martindale-Hubbell Law Directory

*COLUMBIA,** Marion Co.

AULTMAN, TYNER, MCNEESE & RUFFIN, LTD., A PROFESSIONAL LAW CORPORATION (AV)

329 Church Street, P.O. Drawer 707, 39429
Telephone: 601-736-2222
Hattiesburg, Mississippi Office: 315 Hemphill Street, P.O. Drawer 750.
Telephone: 601-583-2671.
Gulfport, Mississippi Office: 1201 25th Avenue, Suite 300, P.O. Box 607.
Telephone: 601-863-6913.

Thomas D. McNeese | Richard F. Yarborough, Jr.

Lawrence E. Hahn

OF COUNSEL

Ernest Ray Duff

Representative Clients: Hercules, Inc.; United States Steel Corp.; Ford Motor Co.; International Paper Co.; Phillips Petroleum Co.; Aetna Casualty & Surety Co.; CNA Group; Liberty Mutual Insurance Co.; St. Paul Fire & Marine Insurance Co.; Fireman's Fund.

(See Next Column)

For full biographical listings, see the Martindale-Hubbell Law Directory

*GULFPORT,** Harrison Co.

AULTMAN, TYNER, MCNEESE & RUFFIN, LTD., A PROFESSIONAL LAW CORPORATION (AV)

1201 25th Avenue, Suite 300, P.O. Box 607, 39502
Telephone: 601-863-6913
Hattiesburg, Mississippi Office: 315 Hemphill Street, P.O. Drawer 750.
Telephone: 601-583-2671.
Columbia, Mississippi Office: 329 Church Street, P.O. Drawer 707.
Telephone: 601-736-2222.

Ben E. Sheely | Paul J. Delcambre, Jr.
Dorrance (Dee) Aultman, Jr.

For full biographical listings, see the Martindale-Hubbell Law Directory

DUKES, DUKES, KEATING AND FANECA, P.A. (AV)

2308 East Beach Boulevard, P.O. Drawer W, 39501
Telephone: 601-868-1111
FAX: 601-863-2886

Hugh D. Keating | William H. Pettey, Jr.

Nick B. Roberts, Jr.

For full biographical listings, see the Martindale-Hubbell Law Directory

*HATTIESBURG,** Forrest Co.

AULTMAN, TYNER, MCNEESE & RUFFIN, LTD., A PROFESSIONAL LAW CORPORATION (AV)

315 Hemphill Street, P.O. Drawer 750, 39403-0750
Telephone: 601-583-2671
Columbia, Mississippi Office: 329 Church Street, P.O. Drawer 707.
Telephone: 601-736-2222.
Gulfport, Mississippi Office: 1201 25th Avenue, Suite 300, P.O. Box 607.
Telephone: 601-863-6913.

Dorrance Aultman
Thomas W. Tyner
Thomas D. McNeese (Resident, Columbia Office)
Louie F. Ruffin
Richard F. Yarborough, Jr. (Resident, Columbia Office)
Ben E. Sheely (Resident, Gulfport Office)
Patrick H. Zachary
Paul J. Delcambre, Jr. (Resident, Gulfport Office)
Robert J. Dambrino, III
Vicki R. Leggett
R. Curtis Smith, II
Dorrance (Dee) Aultman, Jr. (Resident, Gulfport Office)
William Nelson Graham

James L. Quinn
Walter J. Eades
Lawrence E. Hahn (Resident, Columbia Office)
Carol Ann Estes
Victor A. DuBose

OF COUNSEL

Ernest Ray Duff (Resident, Columbia Office)

Representative Clients: Hercules, Inc.; U.S. Steel Corp.; Ford Motor Co.; Phillips Petroleum Co.; Aetna Casualty & Surety Co.; CNA Group; Liberty Mutual Insurance Co.; St. Paul Fire & Marine Insurance Co.; Fireman's Fund.

For full biographical listings, see the Martindale-Hubbell Law Directory

*JACKSON,** Hinds Co.

ALLRED & DONALDSON (AV)

101 West Capitol Street, Suite 300, P.O. Box 3828, 39207-3828
Telephone: 601-948-2086
Telefax: 601-948-2175

MEMBERS OF FIRM

Michael S. Allred | John I. Donaldson

ASSOCIATES

Stephen M. Maloney | Kathleen H. Eiler

For full biographical listings, see the Martindale-Hubbell Law Directory

FERRELL & HUBBARD (AV)

Ferrell & Hubbard Building, 405 Tombigbee Street, P.O. Box 24448, 39225-4448
Telephone: 601-969-4700
Telecopier: 601-354-5548

MEMBERS OF FIRM

Wayne E. Ferrell, Jr. | Dale Hubbard
Karla J. Pierce

References: Deposit Guaranty National Bank; First National Bank of Vicksburg; Trustmark National Bank.

For full biographical listings, see the Martindale-Hubbell Law Directory

Jackson—Continued

HOLCOMB, DUNBAR, CONNELL, CHAFFIN & WILLARD, A PROFESSIONAL ASSOCIATION (AV)

111 East Capitol Street, Suite 290, P.O. Box 2990, 39207-2990
Telephone: 601-948-0048
Facsimile: 601-948-0050
Clarksdale, Mississippi Office: 152 Delta Avenue, P.O. Box 368, 38614.
Telephone: 601-627-2241.
Facsimile: 601-627-9788.
Aberdeen, Mississippi Office: 109 1/2 West Commerce Street, P.O. Box 866, 39730.
Telephone: 601-369-8800.
Facsimile: 601-369-9404.
Oxford, Mississippi Office: 1217 Jackson Avenue, P.O. Drawer 707, 38655.
Telephone: 601-234-8775.
Facsimile: 601-234-8638.
Southaven, Mississippi Office: Suite 1, 8727 Northwest Drive, P.O. Box 190, 38671.
Telephone: 601-342-6806.
Facsimile: 601-342-6792.

Jack F. Dunbar
William M. Chaffin
W. Larry Harris
Craig M. Geno
Guy T. Gillespie, III
Thomas J. Suszek
John H. Dunbar
David C. Dunbar
William A. Baskin
Thomas T. Dunbar
C. Michael Pumphrey
Robert F. Wood
David A. Burns
T. Swayze Alford

OF COUNSEL

Ralph E. Pogue

Representative Clients: United Southern Bank; Sunburst Bank; National Bank of Commerce of Mississippi; Deposit Guaranty National Bank; Trustmark National Bank; Farm Credit Bank of Texas; North Delta Compress & Warehouse Co.; Vend-A-Snack, Inc.; Cooper Tire & Rubber Co.; Dunavant Enterprises, Inc.

For Complete List of Firm Personnel, See General Section

For full biographical listings, see the Martindale-Hubbell Law Directory

MCNAMARA, KELLY & WELSH (AV)

4273 I-55 North, Suite 200, 39206
Telephone: 601-362-6700
Telecopier: 601-362-4888

MEMBERS OF FIRM

J. Leray (Ray) McNamara
Ann H. Kelly
Jennifer L. Welsh

Representative Clients: Deposit Guaranty National Bank; Sears, Roebuck and Co.; Wal-Mart Stores, Inc.; Chubb and Son, Inc.; Kawasaki Motors Corp., U.S.A.; Medical Assurance Company of Mississippi; Mississippi Hospital Association.
References: Deposit Guaranty National Bank; Sunburst Bank.

For full biographical listings, see the Martindale-Hubbell Law Directory

WATKINS & EAGER (AV)

Suite 300 The Emporium Building, P.O. Box 650, 39205
Telephone: 601-948-6470
Facsimile: (601) 354-3623

MEMBERS OF FIRM

William F. Goodman, Jr.
George R. Fair
Paul H. Stephenson, III
Frank J. Hammond, III
Frank A. Wood, Jr.
William F. Ray
M. Binford Williams, Jr.

Representative Clients: The Kroger Co.; MISSCO Corporation of Jackson; Blossman Gas, Inc.; Pavco Industries, Inc.; Trustmark National Bank; Merchants & Marine Bank; Millsaps College.

For Complete List of Firm Personnel, See General Section

For full biographical listings, see the Martindale-Hubbell Law Directory

*OXFORD,** Lafayette Co.

FREELAND & FREELAND (AV)

1013 Jackson Avenue, P.O. Box 269, 38655
Telephone: 601-234-3414
Telecopier: 601-234-0604

MEMBERS OF FIRM

T. H. Freeland, III
T. H. Freeland, IV
J. Hale Freeland

ASSOCIATE

Paul W. Crutcher

Representative Clients: The Ohio Casualty Group; Crum & Forester.

For full biographical listings, see the Martindale-Hubbell Law Directory

HOLCOMB, DUNBAR, CONNELL, CHAFFIN & WILLARD, A PROFESSIONAL ASSOCIATION (AV)

1217 Jackson Avenue P.O. Drawer 707, 38655
Telephone: 601-234-8775
Facsimile: 601-234-8638
Jackson, Mississippi Office: 111 East Capitol Street, Suite 290. P.O. Box 2990, 39207-2990.
Telephone: 601-948-0048.
Facsimile: 601-948-0050.
Clarksdale, Mississippi Office: 152 Delta Avenue, P.O. Box 368, 38614.
Telephone: 601-627-2241.
Facsimile: 601-627-9788.
Aberdeen, Mississippi Office: 109 1/2 West Commerce Street, P.O. Box 866, 39730.
Telephone: 601-369-8800.
Facsimile: 601-369-9404.
Southaven, Mississippi Office: Suite 1, 8727 Northwest Drive, P.O. Box 190, 38671.
Telephone: 601-342-6806.
Facsimile: 601-342-6792.

Jack F. Dunbar
Guy T. Gillespie, III
Thomas J. Suszek
John H. Dunbar
Thomas T. Dunbar
T. Swayze Alford
Stephan L. McDavid

Representative Clients: United Southern Bank; Sunburst Bank; National Bank of Commerce of Mississippi; Farm Credit Bank of Texas; North Delta Compress & Warehouse Co.; Vend-A-Snack, Inc.; Cooper Tire & Rubber Co.; Dunavant Enterprises, Inc.; Mississippi Business Finance Corp.; South Central Bell Telephone Co.

For Complete List of Firm Personnel, See General Section

For full biographical listings, see the Martindale-Hubbell Law Directory

SOUTHAVEN, De Soto Co.

HOLCOMB, DUNBAR, CONNELL, CHAFFIN & WILLARD, A PROFESSIONAL ASSOCIATION (AV)

Suite 1, 8727 Northwest Drive, P.O. Box 190, 38671
Telephone: 601-342-6806
Facsimile: 601-342-6792
Jackson, Mississippi Office: 111 East Capitol Street, Suite 290, P.O. Box 2990, 39207-2990.
Telephone: 601-948-0048.
Facsimile: 601-948-0050.
Clarksdale, Mississippi Office: 152 Delta Avenue, P.O. Box 368, 38614.
Telephone: 601-627-2241.
Facsimile: 601-627-9788.
Aberdeen, Mississippi Office: 109 1/2 West Commerce Street, P.O. Box 866, 39730.
Telephone: 601-369-8800.
Facsimile: 601-369-9404.
Oxford, Mississippi Office: 1217 Jackson Avenue, P.O. Drawer 707, 38655.
Telephone: 601-234-8775.
Facsimile: 601-234-8638.

William M. Chaffin
Thomas J. Suszek
William A. Baskin
David A. Burns
Barry C. Blackburn

Representative Clients: United Southern Bank; Sunburst Bank; Deposit Guaranty National Bank; Trustmark National Bank; National Bank of Commerce of Mississippi; Farm Credit Bank of Texas; Dunavant Enterprises, Inc.; Cooper Tire & Rubber Co.; Mississippi Business Finance Corp.; South Central Bell Telephone.

For Complete List of Firm Personnel, See General Section

For full biographical listings, see the Martindale-Hubbell Law Directory

*TUPELO,** Lee Co.

HOLLAND, RAY & UPCHURCH, P.A. (AV)

322 Jefferson Street, P.O. Drawer 409, 38802
Telephone: 601-842-1721
Facsimile: 601-844-6413

Sam E. Lumpkin (1908-1964)
Ralph L. Holland
James Hugh Ray
Robert K. Upchurch
W. Reed Hillen, III
Thomas A. Wicker

Michael D. Tapscott

Representative Clients: The Travelers; Continental Casualty Co.; South Central Bell Telephone Co.; The Greyhound Corp.; Mississippi Valley Gas Co.; Bryan-Rogers, Inc.; The Housing Authority of the City of Tupelo; Action Industries, Inc.; American Cable Systems, Inc.; American Funeral Assurance Co.

For full biographical listings, see the Martindale-Hubbell Law Directory

MISSOURI

*CLAYTON,** St. Louis Co.

THEODORE F. SCHWARTZ (AV)

Commerce Bank Building, Suite 1100, 11 South Meramec Avenue, 63105
Telephone: 314-863-4654
Telecopier: 314-862-4357
Los Angeles, California Office: Suite 2440, 11755 Wilshire Boulevard, 90025.
Telephone: 310-445-0076.
San Francisco, California Office: One Embarcadero Center, 40th Floor, 94111.
Telephone: 415-434-8900.

Bernard Edelman
Barry S. Ginsburg

OF COUNSEL

Burton Newman

Reference: First National Bank of Clayton.

For full biographical listings, see the Martindale-Hubbell Law Directory

KANSAS CITY, Jackson, Clay & Platte Cos.

BAKER, STERCHI & COWDEN (AV)

Suite 2100 Commerce Tower, 911 Main Street, P.O. Box 13566, 64199-3566
Telephone: 816-471-2121
FAX: 816-472-0288
Overland Park, Kansas Office: 51 Corporate Woods, 9393 West 110th Street, Suite 508.
Telephone: 913-451-6752.

MEMBERS OF FIRM

Thomas O. Baker
Thomas N. Sterchi
John W. Cowden
Thomas E. Rice, Jr.
Timothy S. Frets
Evan A. Douthit
Phillip C. Rouse
R. Douglas Gentile
James T. Seigfreid, Jr.
Robert A. Babcock
Peter F. Travis
John P. Poland

ASSOCIATES

Quentin L. Brown
James R. Jarrow
James S. Kreamer
Mary C. O'Connell
Randall L. Rhodes
D. Gregory Stonebarger
Kara Trouslot Stubbs
Robert M. Carroll
Stacy L. Cook
Patricia A. Sexton
Brent David Thomas

For full biographical listings, see the Martindale-Hubbell Law Directory

SWANSON, MIDGLEY, GANGWERE, KITCHIN & MCLARNEY, L.L.C. (AV)

1500 Commerce Trust Building, 922 Walnut, 64106-1848
Telephone: 816-842-6100
Overland Park, Kansas Office: The NCAA Building, Suite 350, 6201 College Boulevard.
Telephone: 816-842-6100.

John J. Kitchin
James H. McLarney
Robert W. McKinley
C. W. Crumpecker, Jr.
John S. Black
Lawrence M. Maher
Richard N. Bien
Neil Loren Johnson

OF COUNSEL

Daniel V. Hiatt

Counsel for: General Electric Co.; Chrysler Corp.; Conoco, Inc.; Yellow Freight System, Inc.; The Prudential Insurance Co. of America; Metropolitan Life Insurance Co.; National Collegiate Athletic Assn.; Land Title Insurance Co.; Safeway Stores, Inc.; The Lee Apparel Co.

For Complete List of Firm Personnel, See General Section

For full biographical listings, see the Martindale-Hubbell Law Directory

ST. LOUIS, (Independent City)

LAW OFFICES OF THOMAS J. NOONAN P.C. (AV)

Gateway One on the Mall, 701 Market, Suite 650, 63101
Telephone: 314-241-4747
Fax: 314-241-2039

Thomas J. Noonan

Geri L. Dreiling
Laura Gartland Meyer
David A. Saadat

(See Next Column)

OF COUNSEL

John G. Schultz

Representative Clients: Aetna Casualty & Surety; Auto-Owners Insurance Co.; Capitol Indemnity Corp.; Fireman's Fund Insurance Co.; Ford Motor Credit Co.; Ford Consumer Finance Co.; Grinnell Mutual Reinsurance; Miller's Mutual Insurance Assn. of Illinois; Paragon Group, Inc.; Shelter Mutual Insurance Co.

For full biographical listings, see the Martindale-Hubbell Law Directory

MONTANA

*BILLINGS,** Yellowstone Co.

CROWLEY, HAUGHEY, HANSON, TOOLE & DIETRICH (AV)

500 Transwestern II, 490 North 31st Street, P.O. Box 2529, 59103
Telephone: 406-252-3441
Fax: 406-259-4159
Helena, Montana Office: IBM Building, 100 North Park Avenue, Suite 300, 59601.
Telephone: 406-449-4165.
Fax: 406-449-5149.

MEMBERS OF FIRM

John M. Dietrich
Gareld F. Krieg
Arthur F. Lamey, Jr.
Myles J. Thomas
David L. Johnson
Terry B. Cosgrove
Allan L. Karell
James P. Sites
Laura A. Mitchell
Daniel N. McLean
Robert G. Michelotti, Jr.
John R. Alexander
William D. Lamdin, III
Michael S. Dockery
Malcolm H. Goodrich
Mary Scrim
Eric K. Anderson
Renee L. Coppock

ASSOCIATES

John R. Lee
Scott M. Heard

Representative Clients: General Motors Acceptance Corporation; Deaconess Medical Center of Billings; Billings Clinic; John Deere Co.; First Interstate Bank of Commerce; Aetna; Montana Livestock Ag Credit, Inc.; Turner Enterprises, Inc.

For Complete List of Firm Personnel, See General Section

For full biographical listings, see the Martindale-Hubbell Law Directory

WRIGHT, TOLLIVER AND GUTHALS A PROFESSIONAL SERVICE CORPORATION (AV)

Windsor Court, 10 North 27th Street, P.O. Box 1977, 59103-1977
Telephone: 406-245-3071
Telecopier: 406-245-3074

Kenneth D. Tolliver
Joel E. Guthals
Virginia A. Bryan

Susan Fisher Stevens
J. Reuss
Jeffery A. Hunnes
Kristin L. Omvig

For full biographical listings, see the Martindale-Hubbell Law Directory

*BOZEMAN,** Gallatin Co.

KIRWAN & BARRETT, P.C. (AV)

215 West Mendenhall, P.O. Box 1348, 59771-1348
Telephone: 406-586-1553
Fax: 406-586-8971

Peter M. Kirwan
Janice K. Whetstone
Stephen M. Barrett

Tom W. Stonecipher

Representative Clients: Boyne USA, Inc.; Kenyon Noble Lumber Company; Video Lottery Technologies, Inc.; American Bank; First Citizens Bank; Big Sky Western Bank; Security Bank of Three Forks.

For full biographical listings, see the Martindale-Hubbell Law Directory

NEBRASKA

*OMAHA,** Douglas Co.

BRASHEAR & GINN (AV)

800 Metropolitan Federal Plaza, 1623 Farnam Street, 68102-2106
Telephone: 402-348-1000; 800-746-4444
Telecopier: 402-348-1111

(See Next Column)

BRASHEAR & GINN, *Omaha—Continued*

Kermit A. Brashear
Robert V. Ginn
Julia L. Gold
Mark J. Daly
Mitchell L. Pirnie

Donald J. Straka
Paul J. Halbur

Representative Clients: APX Mortgage Services, Palatine, Illinois; Central Illinois Bancorp, Inc., Champaign, Illinois; The First National Bank of Sioux Center, Sioux Center, Iowa; Green Tree Financial Corporation, Sioux Falls, South Dakota; Nissan Motor Acceptance Corporation, Dallas, Texas; TransAmerica Commercial Finance Corporation, Chicago, Illinois; Transportation Finance & Management, Inc.; Omaha, Nebraska; Whitmire Distribution Corporation, Dallas, Texas.

For Complete List of Firm Personnel, See General Section

For full biographical listings, see the Martindale-Hubbell Law Directory

FRASER, STRYKER, VAUGHN, MEUSEY, OLSON, BOYER & BLOCH, P.C. (AV)

500 Energy Plaza, 409 South 17th Street, 68102
Telephone: 402-341-6000
Telecopier: 402-341-8290

Steven Bloch
Robert L. Freeman
Robert W. Rieke
Robert M. Yates

For Complete List of Firm Personnel, See General Section

For full biographical listings, see the Martindale-Hubbell Law Directory

NEVADA

LAS VEGAS,* Clark Co.

ALBRIGHT, STODDARD, WARNICK & ALBRIGHT, A PROFESSIONAL CORPORATION (AV)

Quail Park I, Building D-4, 801 South Rancho Drive, 89106
Telephone: 702-384-7111
FAX: 702-384-0605

G. Vern Albright
William H. Stoddard
Whitney B. Warnick
G. Mark Albright

Michael W. Brimley
Gavin C. Jangard
D. Chris Albright

Representative Clients: Tokio Marine and Fire Ins. Co.; INAPRO, a CIGNA Co.; Nevada Ready Mix; North American Health Care, Inc. (Nursing Home); Royal Insurance; First Security Bank of Utah; Nevada Community Bank; Nationwide Insurance Co.; Liberty Mutual Insurance; CB Commercial.

For full biographical listings, see the Martindale-Hubbell Law Directory

ALVERSON, TAYLOR, MORTENSEN & NELSON (AV)

3821 W. Charleston Boulevard, 89102
Telephone: 702-384-7000
FAX: 702-385-7000

MEMBERS OF FIRM

J. Bruce Alverson
Eric K. Taylor
David J. Mortensen
Erven T. Nelson
LeAnn Sanders
David R. Clayson

ASSOCIATES

Milton J. Eichacker
Douglas D. Gerrard
Marie Ellerton
James H. Randall
Peter Dubowsky
Hayley B. Chambers
Michael D. Stevenson
Cookie Lea Olshein
Kenneth M. Marias
Jeffrey H. Ballin
Jeffrey W. Daly
Kenneth R. Ivory
Edward D. Boyack
Sandra Smagac
Jill M. Chase
Francis F. Lin

Representative Clients: Citibank; First Interstate Bank; General Electric; Southwest Gas Corporation; The CIT Group; Kentucky Fried Chicken; Norwest Bank; Federal Deposit Insurance Corporation (FDIC); Resolution Trust Corporation (RTC); Yellow Cab Company.

For full biographical listings, see the Martindale-Hubbell Law Directory

GOOLD, PATTERSON, DEVORE & RONDEAU (AV)

905 Bank of America Plaza, 300 South Fourth Street, 89101
Telephone: 702-386-0038
Telecopier: 702-385-2484

Barry Stephen Goold
Jeffrey D. Patterson
Thomas J. DeVore
Thomas Rondeau

(See Next Column)

ASSOCIATES

Wilbur M. Roadhouse
Bryan K. Day
Kathryn S. Wonders

Representative Clients: Gateway Development Group; Hanshaw Partnership; Jack Tarr Development; Meridian Point Properties, Inc.; NationsBank; Pacific Cellular; Plaster Development Co.; RS Development; U.S.A. Capital Land Fund.
Reference: Bank of America.

For full biographical listings, see the Martindale-Hubbell Law Directory

HALE, LANE, PEEK, DENNISON AND HOWARD (AV)

Suite 800, Nevada Financial Center, 2300 West Sahara Avenue, Box 8, 89102
Telephone: 702-362-5118
Fax: 702-365-6940
Reno, Nevada Office: Porsche Building, 100 West Liberty Street, Tenth Floor, P.O. Box 3237.
Telephone: 702-786-7900.
Telefax: 702-786-6179.

MEMBERS OF FIRM

Steve Lane
J. Stephen Peek
Karen D. Dennison
R. Craig Howard
Stephen V. Novacek
Richard L. Elmore
Lenard E. Schwartzer
Donald L. Christensen
William C. Davis, Jr.
Patricia J. Curtis

Representative Clients: Bank of America Nevada; U.S. Bank of Nevada; U.S. Bancorp; Nevada Title Company; Falcon Development Corporation; United Gaming, Inc.; United Coin Machine Co.; Midby and Associates; Chicago Title Insurance Co.; Commonwealth Land Title Insurance Co.

For Complete List of Firm Personnel, See General Section

For full biographical listings, see the Martindale-Hubbell Law Directory

JOLLEY, URGA, WIRTH & WOODBURY (AV)

Suite 800 Bank of America Plaza, 300 South Fourth Street, 89101
Telephone: 702-385-5161
Telecopier: 702-382-6814
Boulder City, Nevada Office: Suite 105, 1000 Nevada Highway.
Telephone: 702-293-3674.

MEMBERS OF FIRM

R. Gardner Jolley
William R. Urga
Roger A. Wirth
Jay Earl Smith
Mark A. James
Donald E. Brookhyser
J. Douglas Driggs, Jr.

ASSOCIATES

Allen D. Emmel
Brian E. Holthus

Representative Clients: First Interstate Bank of Nevada; Nevada State Bank; Citicorp National Services, Inc.; Continental National Bank; First Nationwide Bank; PriMerit Bank; General Motors Acceptance Corp.; Ford Motor Credit Co.; Nissan Motor Acceptance Corp.; Toyota Motor Credit Corporation.

For Complete List of Firm Personnel, See General Section

For full biographical listings, see the Martindale-Hubbell Law Directory

KUMMER KAEMPFER BONNER & RENSHAW (AV)

Seventh Floor, 3800 Howard Hughes Parkway, 89109
Telephone: 702-792-7000
Fax: 702-796-7181

MEMBERS OF FIRM

John C. Renshaw
Thomas F. Kummer
Christopher L. Kaempfer
Martha J. Ashcraft
Michael J. Bonner
John N. Brewer
Von S. Heinz
Gerald D. Waite
Elliott R. Eisner

OF COUNSEL

H. Gregory Nasky

ASSOCIATES

Shari Cassin Patterson
Georlen K. Spangler
Sherwood N. Cook
Daurean G. Sloan
Anthony A. Zmaila
John C. Jeppsen
P. Blake Allen
L. Joe Coppedge
David A. Barksdale
George J. Claseman
Dennis M. Prince
Jeffrey W. Ray
(Not admitted in NV)
Jennifer M. Settles

For full biographical listings, see the Martindale-Hubbell Law Directory

MCDONALD, CARANO, WILSON, MCCUNE, BERGIN, FRANKOVICH & HICKS (AV)

Suite 1000, 2300 West Sahara Avenue, 89102
Telephone: 702-873-4100
Telecopier: 702-873-9966
Reno, Nevada Office: 241 Ridge Street.
Telephone: 702-322-0635.
Telecopier: 702-786-9532.

(See Next Column)

McDONALD, CARANO, WILSON, McCUNE, BERGIN, FRANKOVICH & HICKS—*Continued*

MEMBERS OF FIRM

Alvin J. (Bud) Hicks
Robert E. Armstrong
George F. Ogilvie III (Resident)

ASSOCIATES

Scott A. Swain (Resident)
Andrew P. Gordon (Resident)
Bryan R. Clark

Representative Clients: Boyde Gaming Corporation; Builders Emporium; Clark & Sullivan Constructors, Inc.; Colorite Plastics; Intermountain Federal Land Bank Association; Jackpot Enterprises, Inc.; Primadonna Resorts, Inc.; Sun State Bank.

For Complete List of Firm Personnel, See General Section

For full biographical listings, see the Martindale-Hubbell Law Directory

MONSEY & ANDREWS (AV)

3900 Paradise Road, Suite 283, 89109
Telephone: 702-732-9897
Facsimile: 702-732-9667
Boulder City, Nevada Office: 402 Nevada Highway.
Telephone: 702-294-1112.
Facsimile: 294-0235.

MEMBERS OF FIRM

Earl Monsey
B. G. Andrews (Resident, Boulder City, Nevada)

Representative Clients: Chrysler Capital Corp.; Jack Matthews Realty; Mortgage Loans America; United Pacific Insurance Co.; Planet Insurance Co.; Reliance Insurance Co.; KNPR Nevada Public Radio Corporation; Agassi Enterprises; World Savings; The Walt Disney Co.

For full biographical listings, see the Martindale-Hubbell Law Directory

MORRIS BRIGNONE & PICKERING (AV)

1203 Bank of America Plaza, 300 South Fourth Street, 89101
Telephone: 702-474-9400
Facsimile: 702-474-9422
Reno, Nevada Office: Wiegand Center, 165 West Liberty, #100, 89501.
Telephone: 702-322-7777.
Facsimile: 702-322-7791.

MEMBERS OF FIRM

Steve Morris
Mary Kristina Pickering
Mary Ann Morgan

ASSOCIATES

Mark A. Hutchison
José León

For full biographical listings, see the Martindale-Hubbell Law Directory

SCHRECK, JONES, BERNHARD, WOLOSON & GODFREY, CHARTERED (AV)

600 East Charleston Boulevard, 89104
Telephone: 702-382-2101
Fax: 702-382-8135

Frank A. Schreck
Leslie Terry Jones
Peter C. Bernhard
Kenneth A. Woloson
John A. Godfrey
David D. Johnson
James R. Chamberlain
Michelle L. Morgando
Lance C. Earl
Thomas R. Canham
Sean T. McGowan
Dawn M. Cica
F. Edward Mulholland, II
Todd L. Bice
James J. Pisanelli
Ellen L. Schulhofer
John M. McManus

OF COUNSEL

Howard W. Cannon

For full biographical listings, see the Martindale-Hubbell Law Directory

WOODBURN AND WEDGE (AV)

Suite 620 Bank of America Plaza, 300 South Fourth Street, 89101
Telephone: 702-387-1000
Reno, Nevada Office: 16th Floor, First Interstate Bank Building. P.O. Box 2311.
Telephone: 702-688-3000.
Telecopier: 702-688-3088.

MEMBERS OF FIRM

Virgil H. Wedge
Charles A. Jeannes
Richard O. Kwapil, Jr.
Kirk S. Schumacher
Harry J. Schlegelmilch

ASSOCIATE

Gregg P. Barnard

Representative Clients: Atlantic Richfield Co.; Sierra Pacific Power Co.; The Union Pacific Railroad Co.; Western Union Telegraph Co.; Cyprus Minerals Corp.; The Roman Catholic Bishop of Reno, A Corporation Sole.

For full biographical listings, see the Martindale-Hubbell Law Directory

*RENO,** Washoe Co.

HALE, LANE, PEEK, DENNISON AND HOWARD (AV)

Porsche Building, 100 West Liberty Street, Tenth Floor, P.O. Box 3237, 89501
Telephone: 702-786-7900
Telefax: 702-786-6179
Las Vegas, Nevada Office: Suite 800, Nevada Financial Center, 2300 West Sahara Avenue, Box 8.
Telephone: 702-362-5118.
Fax: 702-365-6940.

MEMBERS OF FIRM

J. Stephen Peek
Karen D. Dennison
R. Craig Howard
Stephen V. Novacek
Richard L. Elmore
Marilyn L. Skender
Donald L. Christensen
William C. Davis, Jr.

ASSOCIATE

James L. Kelly

Representative Clients: Bank of America Nevada; U.S. Bank of Nevada; U.S. Bancorp.; Home Federal Bank, Savings Bank; First Interstate Bank of Nevada; Bank of the West; Capital Holding Corp.; First California Mortgage Co.; Sierra Bank of Nevada; Western Water Development Co.

For Complete List of Firm Personnel, See General Section

For full biographical listings, see the Martindale-Hubbell Law Directory

McDONALD, CARANO, WILSON, McCUNE, BERGIN, FRANKOVICH & HICKS (AV)

241 Ridge Street, 89505
Telephone: 702-322-0635
Telecopier: 702-786-9532
Las Vegas, Nevada Office: Suite 1000, 2300 West Sahara Avenue.
Telephone: 702-873-4100.
Telecopier: 702-873-9966.

MEMBERS OF FIRM

John J. McCune
Thomas R. C. Wilson, II
Leo P. Bergin, III
John J. Frankovich
Alvin J. (Bud) Hicks
Robert E. Armstrong
William A. S. Magrath, II
James W. Bradshaw

ASSOCIATES

Valerie Cooke Skau
Gerard L. Oskam
David F. Grove

Representative Clients: Associated General Contractors of America; Clark & Sullivan Constructors, Inc.; Eldorado Hotel & Casino; Hamilton Group of Companies; Jackpot Enterprises; James Hardie (USA), Inc.; Q & D Construction Company; Regional Emergency Medical Services Authority; Scolari's Warehouse Markets, Inc.; Sierra Nevada Production Credit Association.

For Complete List of Firm Personnel, See General Section

For full biographical listings, see the Martindale-Hubbell Law Directory

WOODBURN AND WEDGE (AV)

16th Floor, First Interstate Bank Building, One East First Street, P.O. Box 2311, 89505
Telephone: 702-688-3000
Telecopier: 702-688-3088
Las Vegas, Nevada Office: Suite 620 Bank of American Plaza, 300 South Court Street.
Telephone: 702-387-1000.

MEMBERS OF FIRM

Virgil H. Wedge
Charles A. Jeannes
Richard O. Kwapil, Jr.
Kirk S. Schumacher
Harry J. Schlegelmilch

ASSOCIATE

Gregg P. Barnard

Representative Clients: Atlantic Richfield Co.; Sierra Pacific Power Co.; The Union Pacific Railroad Co.; Pacific Telesis Group; The Hillhave Corp.; National Medical Enterprises; Western Union Telegraph Co.; Bank of America; Cyprus Minerals Corp.; The Roman Catholic Bishop of Reno, A Corporation Sole.

For full biographical listings, see the Martindale-Hubbell Law Directory

NEW HAMPSHIRE

*CONCORD,** Merrimack Co.

ORR & RENO, PROFESSIONAL ASSOCIATION (AV)

One Eagle Square, P.O. Box 3550, 03302-3550
Telephone: 603-224-2381
Fax: 603-224-2318

(See Next Column)

ORR & RENO PROFESSIONAL ASSOCIATION, *Concord—Continued*

Charles F. Leahy
Neil F. Castaldo
Mary Susan Leahy

Representative Clients: Beach Aircraft Corporation; Chubb Life America; Fleet Bank; Dartmouth-Hitchcock Medical Center; EnergyNorth, Inc.; National Grange Mutual Co.; New England College; New England Electric System Co.; Newspapers of New England, Inc.; St. Paul's School.

For Complete List of Firm Personnel, See General Section

For full biographical listings, see the Martindale-Hubbell Law Directory

RANSMEIER & SPELLMAN, PROFESSIONAL CORPORATION (AV)

One Capitol Street, P.O. Box 600, 03302-0600
Telephone: 603-228-0477
Telecopier: 603-224-2780

Joseph S. Ransmeier
Lawrence E. Spellman
John C. Ransmeier
Dom S. D'Ambruoso
Lawrence S. Smith
Michael Lenehan
Steven E. Hengen
Garry R. Lane
Jeffrey J. Zellers
Timothy E. Britain
Charles P. Bauer

Thomas N. Masland
Harold T. Judd
R. Stevenson Upton
R. Matthew Cairns
Lisa L. Biklen
Carol J. Holahan
John T. Alexander
Paul H. MacDonald
Kristin E. Martin
James B. Godfrey (1909-1992)

For full biographical listings, see the Martindale-Hubbell Law Directory

*LACONIA,** Belknap Co.

NORMANDIN, CHENEY & O'NEIL (AV)

Normandin Square, 213 Union Avenue, P.O. Box 575, 03247-0575
Telephone: 603-524-4380

MEMBERS OF FIRM

Paul L. Normandin
Robert A. Dietz

ASSOCIATE

Duncan J. Farmer

Counsel for: Laconia Savings Bank; Lakes Region Mental Health Center; Laconia Airport Authority; Community TV Corp.; Central New Hampshire Realty, Inc.; All Metals Industries, Inc.; Lakes Region Anesthesiology, P.A.; Cormier Corp.; Scotia Technology; Vemaline Products.

For Complete List of Firm Personnel, See General Section

For full biographical listings, see the Martindale-Hubbell Law Directory

NEW JERSEY

ATLANTIC CITY, Atlantic Co.

LEVINE, STALLER, SKLAR, CHAN & BRODSKY, P.A. (AV)

3030 Atlantic Avenue, 08401
Telephone: 609-348-1300
Telecopier: 609-345-2473

Lee A. Levine
Alan C. Staller
Arthur E. Sklar
Paul T. Chan
Lawrence A. Brodsky
Brian J. Cullen
Benjamin Zeltner

Arthur M. Brown
Scott J. Mitnick

Representative Clients: A. G. Edwards & Sons, Inc.; Atlantic Plastic Containers Inc.; The Michaels Development Co., Inc.; Nawas International Travel Services, Inc.; Trump Casino Hotels - Atlantic City, NJ; Interstate Realty Management Company.

For full biographical listings, see the Martindale-Hubbell Law Directory

CHATHAM, Morris Co.

EICHLER, FORGOSH, GOTTILLA AND RUDNICK, A PROFESSIONAL CORPORATION (AV)

97 Main Street, P.O. Box 970, 07928
Telephone: 201-701-0500
Fax: 201-701-0333

Peter A. Forgosh
Lawrence A. Rudnick
Roger R. Gottilla
Douglas A. Kent
Michael P. Turner
Linda K. Connolly

OF COUNSEL

A. Albert Eichler
Edwin N. Gross

(See Next Column)

Miriam E. Cahn
Gary D. Nissenbaum
Scott A. Zuber
Steven D. Grossman
James A. Dempsey
Craig Macauley

Representative Clients: United Jersey Banks; Midlantic National Bank; First Fidelity Bank, N.A., New Jersey; Universal Automotive Distributors; First Commercial Corporation.

For full biographical listings, see the Martindale-Hubbell Law Directory

ELMWOOD PARK, Bergen Co.

ANDORA, PALMISANO & GEANEY, A PROFESSIONAL CORPORATION (AV)

303 Molnar Drive, P.O. Box 431, 07407-0431
Telephone: 201-791-0100
Fax: 201-791-8922

Anthony D. Andora
John P. Palmisano
John F. Geaney, Jr.
Vincent A. Siano
Joseph M. Andresini
Patrick J. Spina
Melissa A. Muilenburg
Joseph A. Venti

Representative Client: Interchange State Bank, Saddle Brook, New Jersey.

For full biographical listings, see the Martindale-Hubbell Law Directory

*FLEMINGTON,** Hunterdon Co.

LARGE, SCAMMELL & DANZIGER, A PROFESSIONAL CORPORATION (AV)

117 Main Street, 08822
Telephone: 908-782-5313
Fax: 908-782-4816

Robert F. Danziger
C. Gregory Watts
Richard L. Tice
Kenneth J. Skowronek
Joseph H. Mulherin

Christine Naples Little

OF COUNSEL

Edwin K. Large, Jr.
Scott Scammell, II (1918-1984)

Representative Clients: Agway, Inc.; Algonquin Gas Transmission Co.; E. I. duPont; Flemington National Bank and Trust Company; Prestige State Bank; Summit Bank.

For full biographical listings, see the Martindale-Hubbell Law Directory

*HACKENSACK,** Bergen Co.

CONTANT, SCHERBY & ATKINS (AV)

33 Hudson Street, 07601
Telephone: 201-342-1070
Fax: 201-342-5213

MEMBERS OF THE FIRM

John M. Contant (1907-1988)
Richard J. Contant
Michael L. Scherby
Bruce L. Atkins
Daniel P. Greenstein
Matthew S. Rogers
Andrew T. Fede
Brian T. Keane

ASSOCIATES

Julie Grapin
Geraldine E. Beers
William J. Bailey
S. Y. Kim

OF COUNSEL

Michael S. Kopelman
Fenster & Weiss, New City, New York

For full biographical listings, see the Martindale-Hubbell Law Directory

CUCCIO AND CUCCIO (AV)

45 Essex Street, 07601
Telephone: 201-487-7411
Fax: 201-487-6574
Mailing Address: P.O. Box 2223, South Hackensack, New Jersey, 07606

MEMBERS OF FIRM

Frank J. Cuccio
Emil S. Cuccio

ASSOCIATE

Pamela Beth Keitz

Representative Clients: TCI of Northern New Jersey; Huffman Koos, Inc.; The Actors Fund of America; Blue Circle-Raia, Inc.; Zimpro, Inc., Division of Sterling Drug; Honig Chemical and Processing Corp.; Napp Technologies, Inc.; River Terrace Gardens Assoc.; Franklin Lakes P.B.A. Local 150.

For full biographical listings, see the Martindale-Hubbell Law Directory

DUNN, PASHMAN, SPONZILLI, SWICK & FINNERTY (AV)

411 Hackensack Avenue, 07601
Telephone: 201-489-1500; 845-4000
Fax: 201-489-1512

(See Next Column)

DUNN, PASHMAN, SPONZILLI, SWICK & FINNERTY—*Continued*

COUNSEL

Morris Pashman
Murray L. Cole
Paul D. Rosenberg

MEMBERS OF FIRM

Joseph Dunn
Edward G. Sponzilli
Louis Pashman
Daniel A. Swick
John E. Finnerty
Robert E. Rochford
Warren S. Robins

ASSOCIATES

Nicholas F. Pellitta
Jeffrey M. Shapiro
Laura S. Kirsch
Deborah L. Ustas
Danya A. Grunyk
Mark E. Lichtblau
Richard P. Jacobson
Edward B. Stevenson
Stephen F. Roth

References: United Jersey Bank; Valley National Bank.

For full biographical listings, see the Martindale-Hubbell Law Directory

FERRO LABELLA LOGERFO & ZUCKER, A PROFESSIONAL CORPORATION (AV)

The Landmark Building, 27 Warren Street, 07601
Telephone: 201-489-9110
Fax: 201-489-5653

Michael J. Ferro, Jr.
Michael F. Logerfo
Rocco J. Labella
Arthur P. Zucker

Dennis J. Kwasnik
J. Russell Bulkeley
Camille Joseph Kassar

Representative Clients: United Jersey Bank; CoreStates New Jersey National Bank; Bio Medic Corporation; Lab Products, Inc.; COSCO North America, Inc.; Thomas J. Lipton Company; Perillo Tours, Inc.

For full biographical listings, see the Martindale-Hubbell Law Directory

HEIN, SMITH, BEREZIN, MALOOF & ROGERS (AV)

Court Plaza East, 19 Main Street, 07601-7023
Telephone: 201-487-7400
Telecopier: 201-487-4228

MEMBER OF FIRM

Alan A. Davidson

OF COUNSEL

Seymour A. Smith

For Complete List of Firm Personnel, See General Section

For full biographical listings, see the Martindale-Hubbell Law Directory

KAPS & BARTO (AV)

15 Warren Street, 07601
Telephone: 201-489-5277
Telecopier: 201-489-0477

Warren J. Kaps
Raymond Barto

Concetta R. De Lucia
Brenda P. Rosenberg

Representative Clients: Continental Baking Co.; Mayflower Vapor Seal Co.; The Society of American Magicians.
Reference: United Jersey Bank.

For full biographical listings, see the Martindale-Hubbell Law Directory

STEPHEN H. ROTH (AV)

62 Summit Avenue, 07601
Telephone: 201-489-3737
Fax: 201-489-0557

ASSOCIATE

Michele M. De Santis

Reference: Citizens First National Bank.

For full biographical listings, see the Martindale-Hubbell Law Directory

SHAPIRO & SHAPIRO (AV)

Continental Plaza II, 411 Hackensack Avenue, 07601
Telephone: 201-488-3900
Fax: 201-488-9481

Robert P. Shapiro
Susan W. Shapiro (1943-1990)
John P. Di Iorio

ASSOCIATES

David O. Marcus
Robert F. Green

Reference: National Community Bank.

For full biographical listings, see the Martindale-Hubbell Law Directory

SOKOL, BEHOT AND FIORENZO (AV)

39 Hudson Street, 07601
Telephone: 201-488-1300
Fax: 201-488-6541

MEMBERS OF FIRM

Leon J. Sokol
Joseph B. Fiorenzo
Joseph F. Behot, Jr.
Jeffrey A. Zenn

ASSOCIATES

Siobhan C. Spillane
Susan I. Wegner
Jeffrey M. Kahan

COUNSEL

Arthur Bergman
Alan Prigal

For full biographical listings, see the Martindale-Hubbell Law Directory

LIBERTY CORNER, Somerset Co.

APRUZZESE, MCDERMOTT, MASTRO & MURPHY, A PROFESSIONAL CORPORATION (AV)

25 Independence Boulevard, P.O. Box 112, 07938
Telephone: 908-580-1776
Fax: 908-647-1492

Vincent J. Apruzzese
Maurice J. Nelligan, Jr.
Frank X. McDermott
Richard C. Mariani
Francis A. Mastro
Barry Marell
James F. Murphy (1938-1990)
Robert T. Clarke
Frederick T. Danser, III
Melvin L. Gelade
Jerrold J. Wohlgemuth

Sharon P. Margello
Daniel F. Crowe
Tarquin Jay Bromley
James M. Cooney
James L. Plosia, Jr.

Representative Clients: General Public Utilities Corp.; Public Service Electric & Gas Co.; Jersey Central Power & Light Co.; Smithkline; Beecham, Inc.; U. S. Metals & Refining Co.; Kelly-Springfield Tire Co.; ASEA Brown-Boveri; Foster Wheeler Corp.; Prudential Insurance Co.; General Electric; Schering Plough Corp.

For full biographical listings, see the Martindale-Hubbell Law Directory

MAPLEWOOD, Essex Co.

FOYEN & PARTNERS (AV Ⓣ)

108 Baker Street, 07040
Telephone: 201-762-5800
Telefax: 212-762-5801
New York, N.Y. Office: 800 Third Avenue, 23rd Floor, NTC.
Telephone: 212-265-2555.
Telefax: 212-838-0374.
Affiliated Offices: Oslo, Norway Office: Advokatfirmaet Foyen & Co. ANS, Oscargate 52, N-0258 Olso 2.
Telephone: 02-44 46 40.
Telefax: 02-44 89 27.
Stockholm, Sweden Office: Advokatfirman Foyen & Partners, Nybrogatan 15, S-10246 Stockholm.
Telephone: 8-663-02-90.
Telefax: 8-662-15-90.

MEMBERS OF FIRM

Steven B. Peri
Michael T. Stewart

OF COUNSEL

Stein A. Føyen (Resident, Oslo, Norway Office)
Michael P. DiRaimondo (Resident, New York Office)

For full biographical listings, see the Martindale-Hubbell Law Directory

MORRIS PLAINS, Morris Co.

VOORHEES & ACCIAVATTI (AV)

Powder Mill Plaza, 101 Gibraltar Drive, 07950
Telephone: 201-267-6677
Fax: 201-267-9152
Mailing Address: P.O. Box 1236, Morristown, New Jersey, 07962-1236
Atlantic City, New Jersey Office: 1624 Pacific Avenue, P.O. Box 1801, 08401.
Telephone: 609-348-6698.

MEMBERS OF FIRM

William Wolverton Voorhees, Jr.
Diane M. Acciavatti
Robert W. McAndrew

ASSOCIATES

Thomas C. Plucienniк
Ana Linda Day

For full biographical listings, see the Martindale-Hubbell Law Directory

*MORRISTOWN,** Morris Co.

KIERNAN & STRENK (AV)

13 Pine Street, P.O. Box 1127, 07962-1127
Telephone: 201-898-9191
Telecopy: 201-292-1413

(See Next Column)

KIERNAN & STRENK, *Morristown—Continued*

MEMBERS OF FIRM

Charles A. Strenk
Brian Kiernan
Joseph R. Fischer

OF COUNSEL

Jeffrey P. Clemente

For full biographical listings, see the Martindale-Hubbell Law Directory

MCELROY, DEUTSCH AND MULVANEY (AV)

1300 Mount Kemble Avenue, P.O. Box 2075, 07962-2075
Telephone: 201-993-8100
Fax: 201-425-0161
Denver, Colorado Office: 1099 18th Street, Suite 3120.
Telephone: 303-293-8800.
Fax: 303-293-3116.

MEMBERS OF FIRM

Lorraine M. Armenti (Resident Partner, Denver Colorado Office)
Grace C. Bertone
John P. Beyel
William C. Carey
Margaret F. Catalano
Stephen H. Cohen (1938-1992)
Kevin T. Coughlin
Edward B. Deutsch
Timothy I. Duffy
Robert J. Kelly
Joseph P. La Sala
Paul A. Lisovicz
Fred A. Manley, Jr.
Michael J. Marone
William T. McElroy
Laurence M. McHeffey
Joseph P. McNulty, Jr.
James M. Mulvaney
Moira E. O'Connell
Loren L. Pierce
Warren K. Racusin
John H. Suminski
Kevin E. Wolff

OF COUNSEL

Richard G. McCarty (Not admitted in NJ)
John F. Whitteaker

ASSOCIATES

Caroline L. Beers
Christopher Robert Carroll
Edward V. Collins
Billy J. Cooper (Resident, Denver, Colorado Office)
John Thomas Coyne
Nada Leslie Wolff Culver (Resident, Denver, Colorado Office)
John J. Cummings
Anthony J. Davis
John Paul Gilfillan
Kevin M. Haas
Gary S. Kull
Matthew J. Lodge
Tracey L. Matura
Nancy McDonald
Robert McGuire
Suzanne Cocco Midlige
Robert W. Muilenburg
Gary Potters
Kathleen M. Quinn
Vincent E. Reilly
Agnes A. Reiss
Barbara C. Zimmerman Robertson
Samuel J. Samaro
Laura A. Sanom
Thomas P. Scrivo
Dennis T. Smith
Patricia Leen Sullivan
Pamela A. Tanis
Christine L. Thieman
Catharine Acker Vaughan

Representative Clients: ADT Security Systems, Inc.; Grove Bank; Crum & Forster Insurance Co.; Eaton Corp.; Fireman's Fund Insurance Cos.; New Jersey Manufacturers Insurance Co.; The Home Indemnity Co.; Ingersol Rand Company; The Pittston Company; Security Pacific Finance Corporation.

For full biographical listings, see the Martindale-Hubbell Law Directory

PORZIO, BROMBERG & NEWMAN, A PROFESSIONAL CORPORATION (AV)

163 Madison Avenue, 07962-1997
Telephone: 201-538-4006
Facsimile: 201-538-5146
New York, New York Office: 655 Third Avenue, 10017-5617.
Telephone: 212-986-0600.
Facsimile: 212-986-6491.

Robert J. Brennan
John M. Newman
Howard J. Schwartz

Nancy Gail Minikes
Cynthia D. Richardson
Gregory J. Schwartz
Diane M. Siana
Charles J. Stoia

Representative Clients: American Cyanamid Co.; American Home Products Corp.; ASARCO Inc.; Ayerst Laboratories; Johnson & Johnson; Pfizer Inc.; Warner-Lambert Co.

For Complete List of Firm Personnel, See General Section

For full biographical listings, see the Martindale-Hubbell Law Directory

RAND, ALGEIER, TOSTI & WOODRUFF, A PROFESSIONAL CORPORATION (AV)

Courthouse Plaza, 60 Washington Street, 07960
Telephone: 201-539-2600
Telecopier: 201-984-0430

(See Next Column)

Gary C. Algeier
David B. Rand
Robert M. Tosti
Robert B. Woodruff
John F. McDonnell
John E. Croot, Jr.
Kathryn J. Kingree
Robert A. Knee
Russell J. Schumacher
Deborah A. White

OF COUNSEL

Ronald M. Pflug

For full biographical listings, see the Martindale-Hubbell Law Directory

*NEWARK,** Essex Co.

APRUZZESE, MCDERMOTT, MASTRO & MURPHY, A PROFESSIONAL CORPORATION

(See Liberty Corner)

CARPENTER, BENNETT & MORRISSEY (AV)

(Formerly Carpenter, Gilmour & Dwyer)
Three Gateway Center, 17th Floor, 100 Mulberry Street, 07102-4079
Telephone: 201-622-7711
New York City: 212-943-6530
Telex: 139405
Telecopier: 201-622-5314
EasyLink: 62827845
ABA/net: CARPENTERB

MEMBERS OF FIRM

Michael S. Waters
James G. Gardner
Rudy B. Coleman
Edward F. Day, Jr.
John D. Goldsmith
Joseph D. Rasnek
Robert J. Stickles
Jane Andrews
Scott J. Sheldon

ASSOCIATES

Hans G. Polak
Lois H. Goodman
Michelle M. Hydrusko
Jeffrey Bernstein
Matthew Q. Berge
Laura D. Castner
Marc E. Wolin

Representative Clients: General Motors Corp.; E. I. du Pont de Nemours and Company; Texaco Inc.; AT&T; Litton Industries; ITT Corp.; International Flavors & Fragrances Inc.; New Jersey Hospital Association; Prudential Insurance Company of America; United Jersey Bank.

For Complete List of Firm Personnel, See General Section

For full biographical listings, see the Martindale-Hubbell Law Directory

DEMARIA, ELLIS, HUNT, SALSBERG & FRIEDMAN (AV)

Suite 1400, 744 Broad Street, 07102
Telephone: 201-623-1699
Telecopier: 201-623-0954

MEMBERS OF FIRM

H. Reed Ellis
Ronald H. DeMaria
William J. Hunt
Richard M. Salsberg
Paul A. Friedman
Brian N. Flynn
Richard H. Bauch
Lee H. Udelsman

ASSOCIATES

Mitchell A. Schley
Joseph D. Olivieri
Joanne M. Maxwell
Robyn L. Aversa
George W. Rettig
David S. Catuogno
Debra S. Friedman
Kathryn A. Calista

For full biographical listings, see the Martindale-Hubbell Law Directory

FOX AND FOX (AV)

570 Broad Street, 07102
Telephone: 201-622-3624
Telecopier: 201-622-6220

MEMBERS OF FIRM

David I. Fox
Arthur D. Grossman
Paul I. Rosenberg
Kenneth H. Fast
Martin Kesselhaut
Dennis J. Alessi
Gabriel H. Halpern
Steven A. Holt
Nancy C. McDonald

OF COUNSEL

Jacob Fox (1898-1992)
Martin S. Fox
Robert J. Rohrberger
Robert S. Catapano-Friedman

ASSOCIATES

Robert P. Donovan
Stacey B. Rosenberg
Susan R. Fox
Virginia S. Ryan
Ronnie Ann Powell
Katherine J. Welsh
Craig S. Gumpel
Brett Alison Rosenberg
Alfred V. Acquaviva
Anthony F. Vitiello

For full biographical listings, see the Martindale-Hubbell Law Directory

Newark—Continued

GOLDSTEIN TILL & LITE (AV)

Suite 800, 744 Broad Street, 07102-3803
Telephone: 201-623-3000
FAX: 201-623-0858
Telex: 262320 USA UR

MEMBERS OF FIRM

Andrew J. Goldstein
Peter W. Till
Allyn Z. Lite
Joseph J. DePalma

Nancy Lem
Amy M. Riel
Richard T. Luzzi
Denise L. Panicucci
Robin May Messing
Michael E. Patunas
Donna Lavista Schwartz
Charles Quinn

For full biographical listings, see the Martindale-Hubbell Law Directory

GREENBERG DAUBER AND EPSTEIN, A PROFESSIONAL CORPORATION (AV)

Suite 600, One Gateway Center, 07102-5311
Telephone: 201-643-3700
Telecopier: 201-643-1218

Melvin Greenberg
Edward J. Dauber
Stanley A. Epstein
H. Glenn Tucker
Paul J. Dillon
Linda G. Harvey
Brenda J. Rediess-Hoosein
Adam W. Jacobs
Jeffrey S. Berkowitz
Kathryn Van Deusen Hatfield

For full biographical listings, see the Martindale-Hubbell Law Directory

HELLRING LINDEMAN GOLDSTEIN & SIEGAL (AV)

One Gateway Center, 07102-5386
Telephone: 201-621-9020
Telecopier: 201-621-7406

Bernard Hellring (1916-1991)
Philip Lindeman, II
Joel D. Siegal
Jonathan L. Goldstein
James A. Scarpone
Michael Edelson
Margaret Dee Hellring
Richard D. Shapiro
Charles Oransky
Richard B. Honig
Richard K. Coplon
Robert S. Raymar
Ronny Jo Greenwald Siegal
Stephen L. Dreyfuss
John A. Adler
Judah I. Elstein
Ronnie F. Liebowitz
Bruce S. Etterman
Matthew E. Moloshok
Rachel N. Davidson
Val Mandel
Sarah Jane Jelin
Eric A. Savage
David N. Narciso
Sheryl E. Koomer

For full biographical listings, see the Martindale-Hubbell Law Directory

MCCARTER & ENGLISH (AV)

Four Gateway Center, 100 Mulberry Street, P.O. Box 652, 07101-0652
Telephone: 201-622-4444
Telecopier: 201-624-7070
Cable Address: "McCarter" Newark
Cherry Hill, New Jersey Office: 1810 Chapel Avenue West.
Telephone: 609-662-8444.
Telecopier: 609-662-6203.
New York, New York Office: Suite 1519, One World Trade Center.
Telephone: 212-466-9018.
Telecopier: 212-432-6568.
Boca Raton, Florida Office: 2255 Glades Road, Suite 319-A.
Telephone: 407-994-6262.
Telecopier: 407-241-0798.
Wilmington, Delaware Office: Mellon Bank Center, 919 Market Street.
Telephone: 302-654-8010.
Telecopier: 302-654-0795.

MEMBERS OF FIRM

Alfred L. Ferguson
Andrew T. Berry
John L. McGoldrick
Richard W. Hill
William H. Horton
Bart J. Colli
Richard M. Eittreim
William T. Reilly
Hayden Smith, Jr.
Todd M. Poland
George W. C. McCarter
Roslyn S. Harrison
Gita F. Rothschild
David R. Kott
Lanny S. Kurzweil
Frank E. Ferruggia
Michael A. Tanenbaum
Richard P. O'Leary
Theodore D. Moskowitz
Myrna L. Wigod
Joseph Lubertazzi, Jr.
Peter S. Twombly
David F. Broderick

OF COUNSEL

Peter C. Aslanides

COUNSEL

Joseph F. Falgiani
Steven A. Beckelman
Jerry P. Sattin

For Complete List of Firm Personnel, See General Section

For full biographical listings, see the Martindale-Hubbell Law Directory

MEYNER AND LANDIS (AV)

One Gateway Center, Suite 2500, 07102-5311
Telephone: 201-624-2800
Fax: 201-624-0356

MEMBERS OF FIRM

Edwin C. Landis, Jr.
Jeffrey L. Reiner
John N. Malyska
William J. Fiore
Anthony F. Siliato
Francis R. Perkins
Geralyn A. Boccher
Howard O. Thompson
Robert B. Meyner (1908-1990)

ASSOCIATES

Kathryn Schatz Koles
Linda Townley Snyder
William H. Schmidt, Jr.
Scott T. McCleary
Maureen K Higgins
Richard A. Haws
Michael J. Palumbo
Theodore E. Lorenz

For full biographical listings, see the Martindale-Hubbell Law Directory

SILLS CUMMIS ZUCKERMAN RADIN TISCHMAN EPSTEIN & GROSS, A PROFESSIONAL CORPORATION (AV)

One Riverfront Plaza, 07102-5400
Telephone: 201-643-7000
Fax: 201-643-6500
Telex: 820630 Sillsbeck Nwk
Atlantic City, New Jersey Office: 17 Gordon's Alley.
Telephone: 609-344-2800.
New York, N.Y. Office: 250 Park Avenue.
Telephone: 212-643-7000.

Clive S. Cummis
Steven S. Radin
Michael B. Tischman
Morton S. Bunis
Stanley Tannenbaum
Barry M. Epstein
Steven E. Gross
Thomas J. Demski
Jeffrey Hugh Newman
Charles J. Walsh
Jeffrey J. Greenbaum
Jeffrey Barton Cahn
Noah Bronkesh (Resident at Atlantic City, N.J. Office)
Steven M. Goldman
Kenneth F. Oettle
Ira A. Rosenberg
Robert Crane
Marc S. Klein
Philip R. Sellinger
Jack M. Zackin
Thomas S. Novak
Jerry Genberg
Stuart M. Feinblatt
Margaret F. Black
Robert M. Axelrod
Brian S. Coven
Trent S. Dickey
Richard J. Schulman (Not admitted in NJ)
Bernard I. Flateman
Joseph L. Buckley
Kathleen Gengaro
David J. Rabinowitz
Stanley U. North, III
James D. Toll (Resident at Atlantic City, N.J. Office)
James M. Hirschhorn
Ronald C. Rak
Mark S. Olinsky
Victor H. Boyajian
Philip R. White
Alan J. Cohen (Resident at Atlantic City, N.J. Office)
Lori G. Singer

Noel D. Humphreys
Patricia M. Kerins
Diane M. Lavenda
Wayne B. Heicklen (Not admitted in NJ)
Glenn E. Davis
Steven B. Jackman (Not admitted in NJ)
Stuart Rosen
Steven R. Rowland
Jack Wenik
Eric D. Mann (Resident at Atlantic City, N.J. Office)
Stephen McNally
Mark E. Duckstein
Beth S. Rose
Scott N. Rubin
Kenneth L. Moskowitz
Steven Shapiro (Not admitted in NJ)
Alma Lutjen Abrams
A. Ross Pearlson (Not admitted in NJ)
Jeffrey M. Pollock
Bennet Susser
Jodi S. Brodsky
Robert W. Burke
Scott T. Gruber
Steven S. Katz
Linda Badash Katz
Ted Zangari
N. Lynne Hughes (Resident at Atlantic City Office)
Sally H. Atkins
Lester Chanin
Paul P. Josephson
Douglas R. Weider
Patricia Brown Fugee
Paul F. Doda
Lora L. Fong
Joshua D. Goodman
Helen E. Kleiner
Rhonda Sobral
Jeffrey M. Weinhaus
Adam Kaiser
Alissa Pyrich
Robert Rosenberg
Keith J. Weingold
Gayle N. Wolkenberg
Garry Rogers
Jennifer L. Borofsky
Joseph D. Glazer
Vaughn L. McKoy
Gwen L. Posner
Susanne K. Rosenzweig
Michele-Lee Berko
Lorraine M. Potenza

Representative Clients: WWOR-TV, Inc.; Midlantic National Bank; White Rose Foods, Inc.; Jersey City Medical Center; Bally's Entertainment Corp.; BMW North America; Motor Club of America; GAF Corporation; Maidenform, Inc.; Exxon Company, U.S.A.

For Complete List of Firm Personnel, See General Section

For full biographical listings, see the Martindale-Hubbell Law Directory

ORADELL, Bergen Co.

NICOLETTE & PERKINS, P.A. (AV)

555 Kinderkamack Road, P.O. Box 549, 07649
Telephone: 201-261-9300
Telecopier: 201-261-8855

David A. Nicolette, Jr.
Eric R. Perkins

Evelyn J. Marose
Jeanette A. Odynski

For full biographical listings, see the Martindale-Hubbell Law Directory

PARSIPPANY, Morris Co.

KUMMER, KNOX, NAUGHTON & HANSBURY (AV)

Lincoln Centre, 299 Cherry Hill Road, 07054
Telephone: 201-335-3900
Telecopier: 201-335-9577

MEMBERS OF FIRM

Richard E. Kummer
Stephen R. Knox
Michael J. Naughton
Stephan C. Hansbury

ASSOCIATES

Gail H. Fraser
Kurt W. Krauss
Linda M. DeVenuto

For full biographical listings, see the Martindale-Hubbell Law Directory

PRINCETON, Mercer Co.

BUCHANAN INGERSOLL (AV)

A Partnership
College Centre, 500 College Road East, 08540-6615
Telephone: 609-452-2666
Telecopier: 609-520-0360
Pittsburgh, Pennsylvania Office: Buchanan Ingersoll, Professional Corporation, 5800 USX Tower, 600 Grant Street.
Telephone: 412-562-8800.
Philadelphia, Pennsylvania Office: Buchanan Ingersoll, Professional Corporation, Two Logan Square, Twelfth Floor, 18th & Arch Streets.
Telephone: 215-665-8700.
Harrisburg, Pennsylvania Office: Buchanan Ingersoll, Professional Corporation, Vartan Parc, 30 North Third Street.
Telephone: 717-237-4800.
Tampa, Florida Office: Buchanan Ingersoll, Professional Corporation, 101 East Kennedy Boulevard, Suite 1030.
Telephone: 813-222-8180.
North Miami Beach, Florida Office: Buchanan Ingersoll, Professional Corporation, 19495 Biscayne Boulevard.
Telephone: 305-933-5600.
Lexington, Kentucky Office: Buchanan Ingersoll, Professional Corporation, 1210 Vine Center Office Tower, 333 West Vine Street.
Telephone: 606-225-5333.

David J. Sorin

SENIOR ATTORNEY

William J. Thomas

Catherine M. Verna

For Complete List of Firm Personnel, See General Section

For full biographical listings, see the Martindale-Hubbell Law Directory

PELLETTIERI, RABSTEIN AND ALTMAN (AV)

100 Nassau Park Boulevard Suite 111, 08540
Telephone: 609-520-0900
Fax: 609-452-8796
Mount Holly, New Jersey Office: Tarnsfield & Woodlane Roads.
Telephone: 609-267-3390.

MEMBERS OF FIRM

George Pellettieri (1903-1980)
Richard M. Altman
Ira C. Miller
John A. Hartmann, III
Andrew M. Rockman
Bruce P. Miller
Edward Slaughter, Jr.
Anne P. McHugh
Neal S. Solomon
Gary E. Adams
Mel Narol
E. Elizabeth Sweetser
Arthur Penn
Thomas R. Smith
George Louis Pellettieri (1961-1973)

ASSOCIATES

Christine McHugh
James Lazzaro
Jed S. Kadish
Martin S. Pappaterra
Daniel S. Sweetser
Lydia Fabbro Keephart
Kenneth W. Lozier
John K. Semler, Jr.
Nicole J. Huckerby
Elyse Genek
Mark K. Smith

OF COUNSEL

Ruth Rabstein

For full biographical listings, see the Martindale-Hubbell Law Directory

RAMSEY, Bergen Co.

FRANCIS T. GIULIANO (AV)

102 Hilltop Road, P.O. Box 340, 07446
Telephone: 201-825-7675
Fax: 201-825-2672

For full biographical listings, see the Martindale-Hubbell Law Directory

ROSELAND, Essex Co.

CLANCY, CALLAHAN & SMITH (AV)

103 Eisenhower Parkway, 07068-1090
Telephone: 201-403-8300
Fax: 201-403-8355

MEMBERS OF FIRM

John J. Clancy (1922-1979)
Edward M. Callahan, Jr.
Dennis J. Smith

ASSOCIATES

James J. Cronin
Beth A. Callahan

For full biographical listings, see the Martindale-Hubbell Law Directory

HANNOCH WEISMAN, A PROFESSIONAL CORPORATION (AV)

4 Becker Farm Road, 07068-3788
Telephone: 201-535-5300
New York: 212-732-3262
Telecopier: 201-994-7198
Mailing Address: P.O. Box 1040, Newark, New Jersey, 07101-9819
Washington, D.C. Office: Suite 600, 1150 Seventeenth Street, N.W.
Telephone: 202-296-3432.

Bernard J. D'Avella, Jr.
Nina Laserson Dunn
Jonathan M. Gross
Michael G. Keating
Ira B Marcus
Arlene Elgart Mirsky
Richard M. Slotkin

Sheri Faith London

For Complete List of Firm Personnel, See General Section

For full biographical listings, see the Martindale-Hubbell Law Directory

MARGARET L. MOSES (AV)

85 Livingston Avenue, 07068
Telephone: 201-533-0233
Telecopier: 201-535-9217
(Also Of Counsel to Connell, Foley & Geiser)

References: National Westminster Bank; Midlantic Bank.

For full biographical listings, see the Martindale-Hubbell Law Directory

ORLOFF, LOWENBACH, STIFELMAN & SIEGEL, A PROFESSIONAL CORPORATION (AV)

101 Eisenhower Parkway, 07068
Telephone: 201-622-6200
Telecopier: 201-622-3073

Ralph M. Lowenbach
Stanley Schwartz
Floyd Shapiro
Edmund A. Mikalauskas
William J. Adelson

Jonathan R. Gamza

For Complete List of Firm Personnel, See General Section

For full biographical listings, see the Martindale-Hubbell Law Directory

POST, POLAK, GOODSELL & MACNEILL, P.A. (AV)

65 Livingston Avenue, 07068
Telephone: 201-994-1100
Telecopier: 201-994-1705
New York, New York Office: Suite 1006, 575 Madison Avenue.
Telephone: 212-486-1455.

John N. Post
Frederick B. Polak
Robert A. Goodsell
Jay Scott MacNeill
Charles R. Church
Paul D. Strauchler
David L. Epstein

G. Alexander Crispo
Peter A. Bogaard
Mark H. Peckman
Robert P. Merenich

For full biographical listings, see the Martindale-Hubbell Law Directory

Roseland—Continued

CHARLES A. ROSEN (AV)

280 Corporate Center, 5 Becker Farm Road, 07068
Telephone: 201-535-2800
Telecopier: 201-535-9777
New York, New York Office: 60 East 42nd Street, Suite 1217.
Telephone: 212-921-2236.

ASSOCIATE

Cecilia M.E. Lindenfelser

Reference: United Jersey Bank.

For full biographical listings, see the Martindale-Hubbell Law Directory

SADDLE RIVER, Bergen Co.

LEWIS & MCKENNA (AV)

82 East Allendale Road, 07458
Telephone: 201-934-9800
Telecopier: 201-934-8681
New York, N.Y. Office: 230 Park Avenue, Suite 2240.
Telephone: 212-772-0943.
Tallahassee, Florida Office: 820 E East Park Avenue, P.O. Box 10475.
Telephone: 904-681-3813
Telecopier: 904-222-1732.

MEMBERS OF FIRM

Paul Z. Lewis
Michael F. McKenna
Geoffrey McC. Johnson

ASSOCIATES

Sherry L. Foley
John A. Napolitano
Mariangela Chiaravalloti
Colin M. Quinn
David B. Beal
Timothy J. Foley

OF COUNSEL

Robert J. Bennett
James W. Anderson (Not admitted in NJ; Resident, Tallahassee, Florida Office)

For full biographical listings, see the Martindale-Hubbell Law Directory

*SOMERVILLE,** Somerset Co.

OZZARD WHARTON, A PROFESSIONAL PARTNERSHIP (AV)

75-77 North Bridge Street, P.O. Box 938, 08876
Telephone: 908-526-0700
Telecopier: 908-526-2246

William E. Ozzard
William B. Savo
Edward M. Hogan
Michael V. Camerino

Kam S. Minhas
Ellen M. Gillespie
Michael G. Friedman
Suzette Nanovic Berrios
Lori E. Salowe
Denise M. Marra

OF COUNSEL

Louis A. Imfeld
Mark F. Strauss

Representative Clients: American Cyanamid; Science Management Corp; New Jersey Manufacturers Insurance Co.; Travelers Insurance Co.; Mack Development Co.; New Jersey Savings Bank.

For Complete List of Firm Personnel, See General Section

For full biographical listings, see the Martindale-Hubbell Law Directory

SCHACHTER, TROMBADORE, OFFEN, STANTON & PAVICS, A PROFESSIONAL CORPORATION (AV)

45 East High Street, P.O. Box 520, 08876-0520
Telephone: 908-722-5700
Fax: 908-722-8853

Richard J. Schachter
Stephen M. Offen

References: Summit Bank; First National Bank of Central Jersey; New Jersey Savings Bank.

For full biographical listings, see the Martindale-Hubbell Law Directory

RAYMOND R. AND ANN W. TROMBADORE A PROFESSIONAL CORPORATION (AV)

33 East High Street, 08876
Telephone: 908-722-7555
Fax: 908-722-6269

Raymond R. Trombadore

Megan C. Seel

OF COUNSEL

Ann W. Trombadore

References: Summit Bank; New Jersey Savings Bank; Somerset Savings & Loan Assn.

For full biographical listings, see the Martindale-Hubbell Law Directory

SOUTH ORANGE, Essex Co.

CHARLES B. TURNER (AV)

76 South Orange Avenue, P.O. Box 526, 07079
Telephone: 201-763-5000
Fax: 763-0568

ASSOCIATES

Marcia Klosk Graydon
Andrew R. Turner

For full biographical listings, see the Martindale-Hubbell Law Directory

SPRINGFIELD, Union Co.

APRUZZESE, MCDERMOTT, MASTRO & MURPHY, A PROFESSIONAL CORPORATION

(See Liberty Corner)

SUMMIT, Union Co.

BOURNE, NOLL & KENYON, A PROFESSIONAL CORPORATION (AV)

382 Springfield Avenue, 07901
Telephone: 908-277-2200
Telecopier: 908-277-6808

Donald Bourne (1903-1987)
Edward T. Kenyon
Cary R. Hardy
Charles R. Berman
Kenneth R. Johanson
Martin Rubashkin
David G. White
Roger Mehner
James R. Ottobre

OF COUNSEL

Robert B. Bourne
Clyde M. Noll (Retired)

Lauren K. Harris
Jaime A. O'Brien
Ellyn A. Draikiwicz
Dean T. Bennett
Craig M. Lessner
Michael O'B. Boldt
Christopher D. Boyman
Paul Ramirez
Timothy A. Kalas
Robert F. Moriarty
Mary E. Scrupski

For full biographical listings, see the Martindale-Hubbell Law Directory

*TRENTON,** Mercer Co.

NEEDELL & MCGLONE, A PROFESSIONAL CORPORATION (AV)

Quakerbridge Commons, 2681 Quakerbridge Road, 08619-1625
Telephone: 609-584-7700
Fax: 609-584-0123

Stanley H. Needell
Patricia Hart McGlone

Michael W. Krutman
Anthony P. Castellani
Barbara Brosnan
Douglas R. D'Antonio

For full biographical listings, see the Martindale-Hubbell Law Directory

STERNS & WEINROTH (AV)

50 West State Street, Suite 1400, P.O. Box 1298, 08607-1298
Telephone: 609-392-2100
Fax: 609-392-7956
Atlantic City, New Jersey Office: 2901 Atlantic Avenue, Suite 201, 08401.
Telephone: 609-340-8300.
Fax: 609-340-8722.
Washington, D.C. Office: 1150 Seventeenth Street, N.W., Suite 600, 20036.
Telephone: 202-296-3432.

William J. Bigham
Vincent J. Paluzzi
Frank J. Petrino
Jeffrey S. Posta
David M. Roskos
Mark D. Schorr
Joel H. Sterns
Richard K. Weinroth
Robert Paul Zoller

OF COUNSEL

Joseph Feldstein (Not admitted in NJ)

Brian J. Mulligan
Marshall D. Bilder
Michael S. Stein
Bernadette Fallows

For Complete List of Firm Personnel, See General Section

For full biographical listings, see the Martindale-Hubbell Law Directory

WESTFIELD, Union Co.

DWYER & CANELLIS, P.A. (AV)

150 Elm Street, 07090
Telephone: 908-233-2000
Fax: 908-233-2041

George W. Canellis

(See Next Column)

DWYER & CANELLIS P.A., *Westfield—Continued*

Brian M. Adams
Barbara Ann Canellis

OF COUNSEL

Thomas F. Dwyer

Reference: Summit Bank; Midlantic Bank.

For full biographical listings, see the Martindale-Hubbell Law Directory

LINDABURY, MCCORMICK & ESTABROOK, A PROFESSIONAL CORPORATION (AV)

53 Cardinal Drive, P.O. Box 2369, 07091
Telephone: 908-233-6800
Fax: 908-233-5078

Richard R. Width
Anthony J. LaRusso
William R. Watkins
Edward J. Frisch
Donald F. Nicolai
J. Ferd Convery III
James D. DeRose
Robert S. Burney
Jay Lavroff
Robert W. Anderson

Joseph G. Wood
Richard J. Cino
Dina G. Kugel
Colleen D. Brennan

OF COUNSEL

Kenneth L. Estabrook

Representative Clients: Alfa Romeo Distributors of N.A.; Elizabeth General Medical Center; Ferrari Financial Services, Inc.; Great American Insurance Co.; Kessler Institute for Rehabilitation; Kuehne Chemical Co., Inc.; Mechanical Contractors Association of New Jersey; New Jersey Industrial Energy Users; Summit Bank; United Jersey Bank; Western Industries, Inc.

For Complete List of Firm Personnel, See General Section

For full biographical listings, see the Martindale-Hubbell Law Directory

WOODBRIDGE, Middlesex Co.

WILENTZ, GOLDMAN & SPITZER, A PROFESSIONAL CORPORATION (AV)

90 Woodbridge Center Drive Suite 900, Box 10, 07095
Telephone: 908-636-8000
Telecopier: 908-855-6117
Eatontown, New Jersey Office: Meridian Center I, Two Industrial Way West, 07724.
Telephone: 908-493-1000.
Telecopier: 908-493-8387.
New York, New York Office: Wall Street Plaza, 88 Pine Street, 9th Floor, 10005.
Telephone: 212-267-3091.
Telecopier: 212-267-3828.

Francis V. Bonello
Stuart A. Hoberman
Sidney D. Weiss
Sheldon E. Jaffe
Norman J. Peer
Robert C. Holmes
Hal L. Baume
Charles S. Zucker
Anthony J. Pannella, Jr.
Michael F. Schaff
Louis T. DeLucia

Steven P. Marshall
David S. DeBerry
Robert C. Kautz
Douglas Watson Lubic
Peter R. Herman
Cheryl J. Oberdorf
Deborah D. Tanenbaum
Eric S. Mandelbaum
Jonathan P. Falk
Patricia S. Gardner
Lisa A. Gorab
Anita J. Dupree
Mark S. Lichtenstein

Representative Clients: Amerada Hess Corp.; Chevron, U.S.A.; Constellation Bancorp.; Cumberland Farms, Inc.; Middlesex County Utilities Co.; New Jersey Automobile Dealers Assn.; Co-Steel Raritan; The Rouse Co.

For Complete List of Firm Personnel, See General Section

For full biographical listings, see the Martindale-Hubbell Law Directory

NEW MEXICO

*ALBUQUERQUE,** Bernalillo Co.

CAMPBELL, PICA, OLSON & SEEGMILLER (AV)

6565 Americas Parkway, N.E., Suite 800, P.O. Box 35459, 87176
Telephone: 505-883-9110
Fax: 505-884-3882

MEMBERS OF FIRM

Lewis O. Campbell
Nicholas R. Pica
David C. Olson
Douglas Seegmiller

(See Next Column)

ASSOCIATES

Brad Vaughn
Roger A. Stansbury
Philip Craig Snyder
Arthur J. G. Lacerte, Jr.
Jeffrey C. Gilmore

Representative Clients: Phelps Dodge Corporation; Chino Mines Company; Large Power Users Coalition; Sara Lee Corporation; New Mexico Retail Association; Compania Minera Ojos Del Salado S.A.; General Electric Capital Corporation; Lectrosonics, Inc.

For full biographical listings, see the Martindale-Hubbell Law Directory

GALLAGHER, CASADOS & MANN, P.C. (AV)

317 Commercial N.E., 2nd Floor, 87102
Telephone: 505-243-7848
Fax: 505-764-0153

James E. Casados
Nathan H. Mann
Michael P. Watkins
Gail S. Stewart
Doris W. Eng
Dawn T. (Penni) Adrian
Jack Carmody
Robert L. Hlady

OF COUNSEL

David R. Gallagher

For full biographical listings, see the Martindale-Hubbell Law Directory

HINKLE, COX, EATON, COFFIELD & HENSLEY (AV)

Suite 800, 500 Marquette, N.W., P.O. Box 2043, 87103
Telephone: 505-768-1500
FAX: 505-768-1529
Roswell, New Mexico Office: Suite 700, United Bank Plaza, P.O. Box 10, 88202.
Telephone: 505-622-6510.
FAX: 505-623-9332.
Midland, Texas Office: 6 Desta Drive, Suite 2800, P.O. Box 3580, 79705.
Telephone: 915-683-4691.
FAX: 915-683-6518.
Amarillo, Texas Office: 1700 Bank One Center. P.O. Box 9238, 79105-9238.
Telephone: 806-372-5569.
FAX: 806-372-9761.
Santa Fe, New Mexico Office: 218 Montezuma, P.O. Box 2068, 87504.
Telephone: 505-982-4554.
FAX: 505-982-8623.
Austin, Texas Office: 401 West 15th Street, Suite 800, 78701.
Telephone: 512-476-7137.
FAX: 512-476-5431.
Associated Office: Hoffman & Stephens, P.C., 401 West 15th Street, Suite 800, 78701.
Telephone: 512-476-5434.
Fax: 512-476-5431.

Eric D. Lanphere
Marshall G. Martin
Fred W. Schwendimann
Margaret Carter Ludewig

Representative Clients: Anadarko Petroleum Corp.; Atlantic Richfield Co.; Bass Enterprises Production Co.; BHP Petroleum; Caroon & Black Management, Inc.; Chevron, USA, Inc.; CIGNA; City of Albuquerque; Coastal Oil & Gas Corp. Co.; Diagnostek.

For Complete List of Firm Personnel, See General Section

For full biographical listings, see the Martindale-Hubbell Law Directory

LAW OFFICES OF JOHN T. PORTER, P.A. (AV)

Suite 410, 20 First Plaza, N.W., 87102
Telephone: 505-243-6665
Fax: 505-764-9890

John T. Porter

Representative Clients: First Security Bank of New Mexico, N.A.

For full biographical listings, see the Martindale-Hubbell Law Directory

RODEY, DICKASON, SLOAN, AKIN & ROBB, P.A. (AV)

Albuquerque Plaza, Suite 2200, 201 Third Street, N.W., P.O. Box 1888, 87103-1888
Telephone: 505-765-5900
Fax: 505-768-7395
Santa Fe, New Mexico Office: Suite 101 Marcy Plaza, 123 East Marcy Street, P.O. Box 1357, 87504-1357.
Telephone: 505-984-0100.
Fax: 505-989-9542.

Robert M. St. John
Duane C. Gilkey
John P. Burton (Resident, Santa Fe Office)
Catherine T. Goldberg
Jo Saxton Brayer
S. I. Betzer, Jr.
David C. Davenport, Jr. (Resident, Santa Fe Office)
Debra Romero Thal
Brian H. Lematta
Mark A. Smith
Theresa W. Parrish

(See Next Column)

RODEY, DICKASON, SLOAN, AKIN & ROBB P.A.—*Continued*

Jay D. Hill | Charles J. Vigil

For Complete List of Firm Personnel, See General Section

For full biographical listings, see the Martindale-Hubbell Law Directory

SHEEHAN, SHEEHAN & STELZNER, P.A. (AV)

Suite 300, 707 Broadway, N.E., P.O. Box 271, 87103
Telephone: 505-247-0411
Fax: 505-842-8890

Craig T. Erickson
Juan L. Flores
Kim A. Griffith
Philip P. Larragoite
Susan C. Little
Maria O'Brien
Judith D. Schrandt
Timothy M. Sheehan
Luis G. Stelzner
Elizabeth Newlin Taylor
Robert P. Warburton

OF COUNSEL

Briggs F. Cheney
Charles T. DuMars
Thomas J. Horan
Pat Sheehan

Representative Clients: Albuquerque Economic Development; Analytec Corp.; Archdiocese of Santa Fe, New Mexico; Bradbury & Stamm Construction Co.; Greater Albuquerque Chamber of Commerce; Herbert M. Denish & Associates, Inc.; Jaynes Corp.; New Mexico Legislative Council Service; New Mexico Society of Certified Public Accountants; New Mexico State University; University of New Mexico.

For full biographical listings, see the Martindale-Hubbell Law Directory

*LAS CRUCES,** Dona Ana Co.

MILLER, STRATVERT, TORGERSON & SCHLENKER, P.A. (AV)

Suite 300, 277 East Amador, P.O. Drawer 1231, 88004
Telephone: 505-523-2481
Facsimile: 505-526-2215
Albuquerque, New Mexico Office: 500 Marquette Avenue, N.W., Suite 1100. P.O. Box 25687.
Telephone: 505-842-1950.
Facsimile: 505-243-4408.
Farmington, New Mexico Office: Suite 300, 300 West Arrington. P.O. Box 869.
Telephone: 505-326-4521.
Facsimile: 505-325-5474.
Santa Fe, New Mexico Office: 125 Lincoln Avenue, Suite 221. P.O. Box 1986.
Telephone: 505-989-9614.
Facsimile: 505-989-9857.

Lawrence R. White
John R. Funk
Joel T. Newton

Representative Clients: St. Paul Insurance Cos.; State Farm Mutual Automobile Insurance Co.; The Travelers; United States Fidelity & Guaranty Co.; New Mexico Physicians Mutual Liability Insurance Co.; Farmers Insurance Group; Dona Ana Savings and Loan Assn.; U.S. West Communications; Sunrise Healthcare; Citizen s Bank of Las Cruces.

For full biographical listings, see the Martindale-Hubbell Law Directory

*ROSWELL,** Chaves Co.

HINKLE, COX, EATON, COFFIELD & HENSLEY (AV)

Suite 700, United Bank Plaza, P.O. Box 10, 88202
Telephone: 505-622-6510
FAX: 505-623-9332
Midland, Texas Office: 6 Desta Drive, Suite 2800, P.O. Box 3580, 79705.
Telephone: 915-683-4691.
FAX: 915-683-6518.
Amarillo, Texas Office: 1700 Bank One Center, P.O. Box 9238, 79105-9238.
Telephone: 806-372-5569.
FAX: 806-372-9761.
Santa Fe, New Mexico Office: 218 Montezuma, P.O. Box 2068, 87504.
Telephone: 505-982-4554.
FAX: 505-982-8623.
Albuquerque, New Mexico Office: Suite 800, 500 Marquette, N.W., P.O. Box 2043, 87103.
Telephone: 505-768-1500.
FAX: 505-768-1529.
Austin, Texas Office: 401 West 15th Street, Suite 800, 78701.
Telephone: 512-476-7137.
FAX: 512-476-5431.
Associated Office: Hoffman & Stephens, P.C., 401 West 15th Street, Suite 800, 78701.
Telephone: 512-476-5434.
Fax: 512-476-5431.

RESIDENT PARTNERS

Harold L. Hensley, Jr.
Stuart D. Shanor
Richard E. Olson
Albert L. Pitts
Thomas D. Haines, Jr.
Rebecca Nichols Johnson
William Paul Johnson
Andrew J. Cloutier

(See Next Column)

Representative Clients: ARCO; BTA; The Citizens Bank of Clovis; Exxon; Natural Gas Pipeline Company of America; Pennzoil; Phillips Petroleum Co.; Southwestern Public Service Co.; Texaco; Transwestern Pipeline Co.

For full biographical listings, see the Martindale-Hubbell Law Directory

*SANTA FE,** Santa Fe Co.

CARPENTER, COMEAU, MALDEGEN, BRENNAN, NIXON & TEMPLEMAN (AV)

Coronado Building, 141 East Palace Avenue, P.O. Box 669, 87504-0669
Telephone: 505-982-4611
Telecopier: 505-988-2987

MEMBERS OF FIRM

Richard N. Carpenter
Michael R. Comeau
Larry D. Maldegen
Michael W. Brennan
Sunny J. Nixon
William P. Templeman
Jon J. Indall
Stephen J. Lauer
Paula Ann Cook
Grey Handy
Joseph E. Manges

Representative Clients: Homestake Mining Co.; First National Bank of Santa Fe; N. M. Electric Cooperatives; Plains Electric G & T Cooperative; United Nuclear Corp.; Uranium Producers of America; BHP Minerals; Great American Insurance Co.; UNIRISC; GTE Corp.

For full biographical listings, see the Martindale-Hubbell Law Directory

CATRON, CATRON & SAWTELL, A PROFESSIONAL ASSOCIATION (AV)

2006 Botulph Road, P.O. Box 788, 87504-0788
Telephone: 505-982-1947
Telecopier: 505-986-1013

Thomas B. Catron III
John S. Catron
William A. Sawtell, Jr.
Fletcher R. Catron
W. Anthony Sawtell

LEGAL SUPPORT PERSONNEL

Peggy L. Feldt (Certified Public Accountant)

Attorneys for: Santa Fe Board of Education; American Express Co.; The Santa Fe Opera; Sunwest Bank of Santa Fe; VNS Health Services, Inc.

For Complete List of Firm Personnel, See General Section

For full biographical listings, see the Martindale-Hubbell Law Directory

GALLEGOS LAW FIRM, P.C. (AV)

141 East Palace Avenue, 87501
Telephone: 505-983-6686
Telefax: 505-986-0741

J. E. Gallegos
Mary E. Walta
Michael J. Condon
David Sandoval
Glenn Theriot

Representative Clients: Doyle Hartman Oil Operator; Cuesta Production Co.; Graham Royalty, Ltd.; Windward Energy and Marketing Co.; The Northern Trust Co.; Las Campanas Ltd. Partnership; Otero Contracting, Ltd.; San Rio Oil & Gas Co.

For full biographical listings, see the Martindale-Hubbell Law Directory

HUFFAKER & BARNES, A PROFESSIONAL CORPORATION (AV)

155 Grant Avenue, P.O. Box 1868, 87504-1868
Telephone: 505-988-8921
Fax: 505-983-3927

Gregory D. Huffaker, Jr.
Julia Hosford Barnes
Bradley C. Barron
Sharon A. Higgins (Not admitted in NM)

Representative Clients: Chevron U.S.A. Products Inc.; Federal Deposit Insurance Corp.; Barker Management Co.; Alphagraphics of Santa Fe and Los Alamos; Basis International, Ltd.; San Juan Concrete Co.; Picacho Plaza Hotel; Dougherty Real Estate Co.; Sasco Electric; Hy Power, Inc.

For full biographical listings, see the Martindale-Hubbell Law Directory

WHITE, KOCH, KELLY & MCCARTHY, A PROFESSIONAL ASSOCIATION (AV)

433 Paseo De Peralta, P.O. Box 787, 87504-0787
Telephone: 505-982-4374
ABA/NET: 1154
Fax: 505-982-0350; 984-8631

William Booker Kelly
John F. McCarthy, Jr.
Benjamin J. Phillips
David F. Cunningham
Albert V. Gonzales
Janet Clow
Kevin V. Reilly
Charles W. N. Thompson, Jr.
M. Karen Kilgore
Sandra J. Brinck

SPECIAL COUNSEL

Paul L. Bloom

(See Next Column)

WHITE, KOCH, KELLY & MCCARTHY A PROFESSIONAL ASSOCIATION, *Santa Fe—Continued*

Aaron J. Wolf
Carolyn R. Glick

Representative Clients: Southern Pacific Transportation Co.; Nationwide Insurance Co.; Risk Management Division of New Mexico General Services Department; Alliance of American Insurers; Santa Fe Community College; First American Title Insurance Co.; Century Bank; Public Service Company of New Mexico; AT&SF Railway Co.; Gallager Bassett.

For full biographical listings, see the Martindale-Hubbell Law Directory

NEW YORK

*ALBANY,** Albany Co.

MOSER & MOSER (AV)

126 State Street, 12207
Telephone: 518-449-4643
New York, N.Y. Office: 50 Broadway.
Telephone: 212-344-4200.
Telecopier: 212-635-5470.
Philadelphia, Pennsylvania Office: 1822 Spring Garden Street.
Telephone: 215-564-7649.
Washington, D.C. Office: 1000 Connecticut Avenue, N.W.
Telephone: 202-857-8450.

MEMBERS OF FIRM

Alexander S. Moser
Joel H. Moser
Janet S. Kaplan

ASSOCIATES

Charles H. Wasser
Karen J. Marsico
Elaine H. Neumann

COUNSEL

Ronald B. Stafford

For full biographical listings, see the Martindale-Hubbell Law Directory

ROWLEY, FORREST, O'DONNELL & HITE, P.C. (AV)

90 State Street Suite 729, 12207-1715
Telephone: 518-434-6187
Fax: 518-434-1287

Richard R. Rowley
Thomas J. Forrest
Brian J. O'Donnell
Robert S. Hite
John H. Beaumont
Mark S. Pelersi
David C. Rowley

James J. Seaman
David P. Miranda
Kevin S. Casey
Richard W. Bader
Daniel W. Coffey
Thomas D. Spain

OF COUNSEL

Rush W. Stehlin

Reference: Norstar Bank.

For full biographical listings, see the Martindale-Hubbell Law Directory

GARDEN CITY, Nassau Co.

FISCHOFF, GELBERG & DIRECTOR (AV)

600 Old Country Road, Suite 410, 11530
Telephone: 516-228-4255
Facsimile: 516-228-4278

MEMBERS OF FIRM

Stuart P. Gelberg
Gary C. Fischoff
Michael C. Director

ASSOCIATES

Scott R. Schneider
Heath Berger

For full biographical listings, see the Martindale-Hubbell Law Directory

JASPAN, GINSBERG, SCHLESINGER, SILVERMAN & HOFFMAN (AV)

300 Garden City Plaza, 11530
Telephone: 516-746-8000
Telecopier: 516-746-0552

MEMBERS OF FIRM

Arthur W. Jaspan
Eugene S. Ginsberg
Steven R. Schlesinger
Kenneth P. Silverman
Carol M. Hoffman
Stanley A. Camhi
Eugene P. Cimini, Jr.
Holly Juster
Stephen P. Epstein
Gary F. Herbst
Allen Perlstein

(See Next Column)

For Complete List of Firm Personnel, See General Section

For full biographical listings, see the Martindale-Hubbell Law Directory

GREAT NECK, Nassau Co.

MARTIN, VAN DE WALLE, DONOHUE, MANDRACCHIA & MCGAHAN (AV)

17 Barstow Road, P.O. Box 222074, 11022
Telephone: 516-482-6100
Telecopier: 516-482-6969

MEMBERS OF FIRM

Jules Martin
Charles R. Van de Walle
Nicholas J. Donohue
Stephen P. Mandracchia
James M. McGahan

ASSOCIATE

Ted J. Feldman

Representative Clients: Fidelity National Title Insurance Company of New York; Bancker Construction Corp.; Biener Pontiac-Nissan, Inc.; Festo Corp.; First Investors Corp.; Lighting Horizons, Inc.; Prime Realty Holdings Co.; First Financial Savings Bank, S.L.A.; Chaminade High School; Oppenheimer Management Corp.

For Complete List of Firm Personnel, See General Section

For full biographical listings, see the Martindale-Hubbell Law Directory

HAUPPAUGE, Suffolk Co.

ERIC H. HOLTZMAN (AV)

330 Vanderbilt Motor Parkway, P.O. Box 11005, 11788-0903
Telephone: 516-435-8800
Fax: 516-435-8832

Richard E. Trachtenberg

Reference: European-American Bank & Trust Co.

For full biographical listings, see the Martindale-Hubbell Law Directory

HEMPSTEAD, Nassau Co.

MORITT, HOCK & HAMROFF (AV)

Hempstead Executive Plaza, 50 Clinton Street, 11550
Telephone: 516-489-7400
Fax: 516-489-0971
Garden City, New York Office: 600 Old Country Road.
Telephone: 516-489-7400.

MEMBERS OF FIRM

Neil J. Moritt
Alan S. Hock
Marc L. Hamroff
David H. Cohen

Robert S. Cohen
Robert M. Tils
Sharon I. Feder
Donna R. Ruggiero
Leslie A. Berkoff
Kenneth Paul Horowitz
Wendy Axelrod (Not admitted in NY)
David A. Loglisci

For full biographical listings, see the Martindale-Hubbell Law Directory

*MINEOLA,** Nassau Co.

KENNEDY & COMERFORD (AV)

200 Old Country Road, 11501
Telephone: 516-741-8818
Fax: 516-741-1703
New York, N.Y. Office: 805 Third Avenue.
Telephone: 212-750-1614.
Fax: 212-750-2885.

Bernard P. Kennedy
Michael J. Comerford

ASSOCIATE

Anne Marie Caradonna

OF COUNSEL

William J. Poisson
Patrick J. Hackett

For full biographical listings, see the Martindale-Hubbell Law Directory

*NEW YORK,** New York Co.

BAKER & BOTTS, L.L.P. (AV)

885 Third Avenue Suite 2000, 10022
Telephone: 212-705-5000
Fax: 212-705-5125
Washington, D.C. Office: The Warner, 1299 Pennsylvania Avenue, N.W.
Telephone: 202-639-7700.
Austin, Texas Office: 1600 San Jacinto Center, 98 San Jacinto Boulevard.
Telephone: 512-322-2500.
Dallas, Texas Office: 2001 Ross Avenue.
Telephone: 214-953-6500.
Houston, Texas Office: One Shell Plaza, 910 Louisiana.
Telephone: 713-229-1234.

(See Next Column)

BAKER & BOTTS L.L.P.—*Continued*

Moscow, Russian Federation Office: 10 ul. Pushkinskaya, 103031.
Telephone: 7095/921-5300 (Local); 7095/929-7070 (International).

MEMBERS OF FIRM

Jerome H. Kern
Karen Leslye Wolf (Not admitted in NY)
Elizabeth M. Markowski
Frederick H. McGrath
Robert W. Murray Jr.
Kenneth S. Siegel

OF COUNSEL

Marc A. Leaf
Ronald D. Sernau

ASSOCIATES

Lee D. Charles
Thomas V. D'Ambrosio
Nancy E. Field (Not admitted in NY)
Laura S. Franco
John L. Graham (Not admitted in NY)
Alice W. Turinas (Not admitted in NY)

For Complete List of Firm Personnel, See General Section

For full biographical listings, see the Martindale-Hubbell Law Directory

BEATIE, KING & ABATE (AV)

599 Lexington Avenue, Suite 1300, 10022
Telephone: 212-888-9000
Fax: 212-888-9664

Russel H. Beatie, Jr.
Kenneth J. King
Samuel J. Abate, Jr.

ASSOCIATES

Susan Kelty Law
Charna L. Gerstenhaber
Eric J. Gruber
Philip J. Miller
Peter S. Liaskos
W.H. Ramsay Lewis

For full biographical listings, see the Martindale-Hubbell Law Directory

BLUTRICH, HERMAN & MILLER, LLP. (AV)

Three Park Avenue, 10016
Telephone: 212-686-1000
Telecopier: 212-685-2536
White Plains, New York Office: 14 Mamaroneck Avenue.
Telephone: 914-681-0715.
Marlton, New Jersey Office: One Greentree Centre, Suite 201.
Telephone: 609-988-5510.

Michael D. Blutrich
Richard Bruce Herman
Robert J. Miller
Steven C. Brown

ASSOCIATES

Paul T. Vink (Resident, Marlton, New Jersey Office)
Felix N. Papadakis

OF COUNSEL

Avery B. Seavey
Phyllis Mehler Seavey
Robert W. Seavey

For full biographical listings, see the Martindale-Hubbell Law Directory

BRAUNSCHWEIG RACHLIS FISHMAN & RAYMOND, P.C. (AV)

1114 Avenue of the Americas, 10036
Telephone: 212-944-5200
Telecopier: 212-944-5210

Robert Braunschweig
Stephen P. H. Rachlis
Bernard H. Fishman
Richard C. Raymond

OF COUNSEL

Jeffrey M. Herrmann
Jeffrey H. Teitel (Not admitted in NY)
William G. Halby
Gerard C. Smetana (P.C.)
Martin W. McCormack
Jacob Dolinger (Not admitted in NY)

Bruce D. Osborne

LEGAL SUPPORT PERSONNEL

William Hershkowitz

For full biographical listings, see the Martindale-Hubbell Law Directory

GOLENBOCK, EISEMAN, ASSOR & BELL (AV)

437 Madison Avenue, 10022
Telephone: 212-907-7300
Telecopier: 212-754-0330
Telex: 291357 Answerback: GEAB UR

MEMBERS OF FIRM

Nathan E. Assor
Lawrence M. Bell
David J. Eiseman
Jeffrey T. Golenbock
Andrew C. Peskoe
Richard S. Taffet
Robert B. Goebel
Leonard Eisenberg

OF COUNSEL

Paul D. Siegfried
Charles D. Schmerler
Jeffrey S. Berger

(See Next Column)

ASSOCIATES

Andrew S. Bogen
Andrew M. Singer
Jacqueline G. Veit
Tracy J. Brosnan
Peter C. Moskowitz
Jonathan A. Adelsberg
Howard L. Meyerson
Sofia C. Hubscher
Martin S. Hyman
Lawrence R. Haut
John E. Page
Claudia M. Freeman

For full biographical listings, see the Martindale-Hubbell Law Directory

HUTTON INGRAM YUZEK GAINEN CARROLL & BERTOLOTTI (AV)

250 Park Avenue, 10177
Telephone: 212-907-9600
Facsimile: 212-907-9681

MEMBERS OF FIRM

Ernest J. Bertolotti
Daniel L. Carroll
Roger Cukras
Larry F. Gainen
G. Thompson Hutton
Samuel W. Ingram, Jr.
Paulette Kendler
Steven Mastbaum
Dean G. Yuzek
David G. Ebert
Shane O'Neill

ASSOCIATES

Warren E. Friss
Patricia Hewitt
Gail A. Buchman
Stuart A. Christie
Beth N. Green
Timish K. Hnateyko
Jeanne F. Pucci
Jane Drummey
Adam L. Sifre
Susan Ann Fennelly
Marc J. Schneider

For full biographical listings, see the Martindale-Hubbell Law Directory

KRASNER & CHEN (AV)

555 Madison Avenue, Suite 600, 10022
Telephone: 212-751-7100
Telefax: 212-371-4551

MEMBERS OF FIRM

Wesley Chen
Harvey I. Krasner

For full biographical listings, see the Martindale-Hubbell Law Directory

MCGUIRE, KEHL & NEALON (AV)

230 Park Avenue, Suite 2830, 10169
Telephone: 212-557-0040
Telecopier: 212-953-0768

MEMBERS OF FIRM

Harold F. McGuire, Jr.
Jeffrey A. Kehl
Arthur V. Nealon
Terri E. Simon

COUNSEL

Marion C. Katzive
Shelley Sanders Kehl

For full biographical listings, see the Martindale-Hubbell Law Directory

MOSER & MOSER (AV)

50 Broadway, 10004
Telephone: 212-344-4200
Telecopier: 212-635-5470
Albany, New York Office: 126 State Street.
Telephone: 518-449-4643.
Philadelphia, Pennsylvania Office: 1822 Spring Garden Street.
Telephone: 215-564-7649.
Washington, D.C. Office: 1000 Connecticut Avenue, N.W.
Telephone: 202-857-8450.

MEMBERS OF FIRM

Alexander S. Moser
Joel H. Moser
Janet S. Kaplan

ASSOCIATES

Charles H. Wasser
Karen J. Marsico
Elaine H. Neumann

For full biographical listings, see the Martindale-Hubbell Law Directory

OTTERBOURG, STEINDLER, HOUSTON & ROSEN, P.C. (AV)

230 Park Avenue, 10169
Telephone: 212-661-9100
Cable Address: "Otlerton";
Telecopier: 212-682-6104
Telex: 960916

Kurt J. Wolff
Donald N. Gellert
William M. Silverman
Morton L. Gitter
Peter H. Stolzar
Alan R. Weiskopf
Bernard Beitel
Jonathan N. Helfat
Daniel Wallen
Scott L. Hazan
Glenn B. Rice
Albert F. Reisman
Kenneth J. Miller
Richard J. Rubin
Anthony M. Piccione
Steven B. Soll
Alan Kardon
Eugene V. Kokot

(See Next Column)

OTTERBOURG, STEINDLER, HOUSTON & ROSEN P.C., *New York—Continued*

Mitchell M. Brand
Stanley L. Lane, Jr.
David W. Morse
Peter L. Feldman

COUNSEL

Lawrence B. Milling
Stephen B. Weissman

Diane B. Kaplan
Lloyd M. Green
Bruce P. Levine
Richard G. Haddad
Lauri Blum Regan
Enid Nagler Stuart
Stephen H. Alpert
Craig D. Zlotnick
Andrew M. Kramer
Jeanne-Marie Marziliano
Jenette A. Barrow
Brett H. Miller
Matthew J. Miller
John J. Kenny
Steven H. Weitzen
Richard L. Stehl
Gary G. Michael
Marc E. Schneider
Susan A. Joyce
Howard M. Sendrovitz

For full biographical listings, see the Martindale-Hubbell Law Directory

PARKER CHAPIN FLATTAU & KLIMPL, L.L.P. (AV)

1211 Avenue of the Americas, 10036
Telephone: 212-704-6000
Telecopier: 212-704-6288
Cable Address: "Lawpark"
Telex: 640347
Great Neck, New York Office: 175 Great Neck Road.
Telephone: 516-482-4422.
Telecopier: 516-482-4469.

MEMBERS OF FIRM

Mark Abramowitz
James Alterbaum
Christopher Stewart Auguste
Barry J. Brett
Aurora Cassirer
Lloyd Frank
Charles P. Greenman
Michael A. Leichtling
Edward R. Mandell
Mitchell P. Portnoy
Stephen G. Rinehart
Herbert L. Rosedale
Henry I. Rothman
Richard A. Rubin
Michael J. Shef
Gary J. Simon
Melvin Weinberg

OF COUNSEL

Raymond W. Dusch

ASSOCIATE

Katherine Cooney Ash

For Complete List of Firm Personnel, See General Section

For full biographical listings, see the Martindale-Hubbell Law Directory

PILIERO GOLDSTEIN JENKINS & HALL (AV)

292 Madison Avenue, 10017
Telephone: 212-213-8200
Fax: 212-685-2028
Carlstadt, New Jersey Office: One Palmer Terrace.
Telephone: 201-507-5157.
FAX: 201-507-5221.
Washington, D.C. Office: 888 17th Street, N.W., Suite 1100.
Telephone: 202-467-6991.
FAX: 202-467-6703.

MEMBERS OF FIRM

Edward J. Goldstein
Christopher P. Hall
Jon Mark Jenkins
Robert D. Piliero

ASSOCIATES

John William LaRocca
Juliana M. Moday
Elaine B. Michetti (Not admitted in NY)

OF COUNSEL

Ricardo J. Davila

For full biographical listings, see the Martindale-Hubbell Law Directory

SHACK & SIEGEL, P.C. (AV)

530 Fifth Avenue, 10036
Telephone: 212-782-0700
Fax: 212-730-1964

Charles F. Crames
Pamela E. Flaherty
Paul S. Goodman
Ronald S. Katz
Donald D. Shack
Jeffrey N. Siegel
Jeffrey B. Stone

Paul A. Lucido
Steven M. Lutt
Ruby S. Teich
Keith D. Wellner
Adam F. Wergeles (Not admitted in NY)

For full biographical listings, see the Martindale-Hubbell Law Directory

ARTHUR J. TEICHBERG A PROFESSIONAL CORPORATION (AV)

Suite 1812, 370 Lexington Avenue, 10017
Telephone: 212-725-8544

(See Next Column)

Arthur J. Teichberg

OF COUNSEL

Wayne Lawrence Desimone

For full biographical listings, see the Martindale-Hubbell Law Directory

*ROCHESTER,** Monroe Co.

CHAMBERLAIN, D'AMANDA, OPPENHEIMER & GREENFIELD (AV)

1600 Crossroads Office Building, Two State Street, 14614
Telephone: 716-232-3730
Telecopier: 716-232-3882

MEMBERS OF FIRM

Robert Oppenheimer
Jerry R. Greenfield
Stanley M. Friedman
Edward C. Radin, III
Richard B. Sullivan
John F. D'Amanda

ASSOCIATES

Nancy Lynne Baker
Eugene M. O'Connor
E. Adam Leyens

For Complete List of Firm Personnel, See General Section

For full biographical listings, see the Martindale-Hubbell Law Directory

FORSYTH, HOWE, O'DWYER & KALB, P.C. (AV)

Suite 1600, Midtown Tower, 14604
Telephone: 716-325-7515
FAX: 716-325-6407
Getzville, New York Office: 2350 North Forest Road, 14068.
Telephone: 716-871-0758.
Fax: 716-871-0846.
Liverpool, New York Office: Granito & Sondej, Corporate Woods #1, 1035 Seventh North Street.
Telephone: 315-451-2387.
Fax: 315-451-3981.

Charles B. Forsyth (1890-1968)
C. Benn Forsyth
Gordon A. Howe, II
Duncan W. O'Dwyer
Robert J. Kalb

Gerald N. Murphy
Cathleen W. Smith
Caren M. Cook
Christopher J. Currier

OF COUNSEL

John F. Forsyth
Allan Wolk
Hoffman Stone
Debra A. Martin
Janice M. Iati
Valerie L. Barbic
Thad F. Sondej (Resident, Liverpool Office)
V. James Granito, Jr. (Resident, Liverpool Office)

References: Chase Manhattan Bank, N.A.; Fleet Bank.

For full biographical listings, see the Martindale-Hubbell Law Directory

SUTER DOYLE KESSELRING LAWRENCE & WERNER (AV)

Formerly Burns, Suter & Doyle
700 First Federal Plaza, 14614
Telephone: 716-325-6446
Fax: 716-262-5185
Canandaigua, New York Office: 23 Sly Street, 14424.
Telephone: 716-398-3400.
Fax: 716-398-2750.

Paul J. Suter (1918-1989)

OF COUNSEL

James B. Doyle

MEMBERS OF FIRM

Leo J. Kesselring
C. Bruce Lawrence
Christopher K. Werner
Colleen A. Brown
Steven H. Swartout

ASSOCIATE

Mary Jo S. Korona

Representative Clients: Ford Motor Credit Corp.; Wegmans Food Markets, Inc.; Johnny Antonelli Tire Company, Inc.; Grey Metal Products, Inc.; Rochester Plumbing Supply Company, Inc.; Hug-Langie Fuel Oil, Inc.; Brede Tool & Supply Company, Inc.; Sawyer's Industrial Fumigators; Lilac Laundry Company, Inc.; Hadlock Paint Company, Inc.

For full biographical listings, see the Martindale-Hubbell Law Directory

ROCKVILLE CENTRE, Nassau Co.

BATZAR & WEINBERG, A PROFESSIONAL CORPORATION (AV)

184 Sunrise Highway, P.O. Box 427, 11570
Telephone: 516-766-1860
Telecopier: 516-678-7801
Hoboken, New Jersey Office: Batzar, Weinberg & Levy, 86 Hudson Street.
Telephone: 201-653-1797.
Merion, Pennsylvania Office: 405 Andrew Road.
Telephone: 215-568-1060.

(See Next Column)

BATZAR & WEINBERG A PROFESSIONAL CORPORATION—*Continued*

Haddonfield, New Jersey Office: Batzar, Weinberg & Levy, 36 Tanner Street.
Telephone: 609-795-9456.

Jules Shank (1908-1993) | Louis K. Batzar
Sanford I. Weinberg

Roger Levy (Hoboken and Haddonfield, New Jersey Offices) | Edward J. Damsky | John E. McLoughlin

OF COUNSEL

Norma R. Frank (Resident, Merion, Pennsylvania Office)

For full biographical listings, see the Martindale-Hubbell Law Directory

*WHITE PLAINS,** Westchester Co.

GREENBURG & POSNER (AV)

399 Knollwood Road, 10603
Telephone: 914-948-6620
Telecopier: 914-948-0864

MEMBERS OF FIRM

Henry A. Greenburg | Jane Y. Posner
Martin Louis Posner | Steven N. Feinman

ASSOCIATE

Jessica Bacal

References: Chemical Bank; Citibank.

For full biographical listings, see the Martindale-Hubbell Law Directory

KEANE & BEANE, P.C. (AV)

One North Broadway, 10601
Telephone: 914-946-4777
Telecopier: 914-946-6868
Rye, New York Office: 49 Purchase Street.
Telephone: 914-967-3936.

Thomas F. Keane, Jr. (1932-1991)

Edward F. Beane | Lawrence Praga
David Glasser | Joel H. Sachs
Ronald A. Longo | Steven A. Schurkman
Richard L. O'Rourke | Judson K. Siebert

Debbie G. Jacobs | Donna E. Frosco
Lance H. Klein | Nicholas M. Ward-Willis

LEGAL SUPPORT PERSONNEL

Barbara S. Durkin | Toni Ann Huff

OF COUNSEL

Eric F. Jensen | Peter A. Borrok

For full biographical listings, see the Martindale-Hubbell Law Directory

WOODBURY, Nassau Co.

STEBEL & PASELTINER, P.C. (AV)

7600 Jericho Turnpike, 11797
Telephone: 516-496-8117
Telecopier: 516-496-8112

Bernard Stebel | David E. Paseltiner

Mindy K. Smolevitz | Steven M. Gelfman

COUNSEL

Edwin H. Baker | Mitchell G. Mandell
Alan M. Pollack | Lori Samet Schwarz
Michael E. Greene | Scott A. Sommer

References: Chemical Bank; Fleet Bank.

For full biographical listings, see the Martindale-Hubbell Law Directory

NORTH CAROLINA

*BOONE,** Watauga Co.

CHARLES E. CLEMENT (AV)

756 West King Street, P.O. Drawer 32, 28607
Telephone: 704-264-6411
FAX: 704-264-5424

Representative Clients: First Union National Bank.
Approved Attorney for: Lawyers Title Insurance Corp.; Chicago Title Insurance Co.

For full biographical listings, see the Martindale-Hubbell Law Directory

*CHARLOTTE,** Mecklenburg Co.

MITCHELL & RALLINGS (AV)

1800 Carillon, 227 West Trade Street, 28202
Telephone: 704-376-6574
FAX: 704-342-1531

MEMBERS OF FIRM

Richard M. Mitchell | Thomas B. Rallings, Jr.

ASSOCIATES

James L. Fretwell | James Dagoberto Concepcion
Joseph N. Tissue | John W. Taylor

COUNSEL

Alvin A. London

Representative Clients: Bonitz Contracting Co.; Captain D's. Inc.; Chemical Financial Services Corp.; Dorfio, Inc.; Dyke Industries, Inc.; Edgcomb Metals; Titan Building Products, Inc.; Fairfinish Corp.
References: Republic Bank & Trust Co.; N.C.N.B.

For full biographical listings, see the Martindale-Hubbell Law Directory

WOMBLE CARLYLE SANDRIDGE & RICE (AV)

A Professional Limited Liability Company
3300 One First Union Center, 301 S. College Street, 28202-6025
Telephone: 704-331-4900
Telecopy: 704-331-4955
Telex: 853609
Winston-Salem, North Carolina Office: 1600 Southern National Financial Center.
Telephone: 919-721-3600.
Telecopy: 919-721-3660.
Telex: 806498.
Raleigh, North Carolina Office: 2100 First Union Capitol Center, 150 Fayetteville Street Mall, P.O. Box 831.
Telephone: 919-755-2100.
Telecopy: 919-755-2150.
Telex: 806498.
Atlanta, Georgia Office: One Ninety One Peachtree Tower, 191 Peachtree Street N.E., Suite 3250.
Telephone: 404-614-2580.
Fax: 404-614-2595.

MEMBERS OF FIRM

Garza Baldwin, III | Cyrus M. Johnson, Jr.
Joe B. Cogdell, Jr. | David E. Johnston
J. Carlton Fleming | J. Alexander Salisbury

RESIDENT ASSOCIATES

David W. Dabbs | Jane Jeffries Jones

Representative Clients: Childress Klein Properties, Inc.; Food Lion, Inc.; Fieldcrest Cannon, Inc.; J.A. Jones Construction Company; Parkdale Mills, Inc.; Duke Power Company; Bowles Hollowell Conner & Company; ALLTEL Carolina, Inc.; Belk Store Services, Inc.; Philip Holzmann A.G.

For Complete List of Firm Personnel, See General Section

For full biographical listings, see the Martindale-Hubbell Law Directory

*GREENSBORO,** Guilford Co.

VANCE BARRON, JR. (AV)

301 South Greene Street, Suite 310, 27401
Telephone: 910-274-4782
FAX: 910-379-8592
Mailing Address: P.O. Box 2370, Greensboro, NC, 27402-2370

For full biographical listings, see the Martindale-Hubbell Law Directory

ISAACSON ISAACSON & GRIMES (AV)

Suite 400 NationsBank Building, 101 West Friendly Avenue, P.O. Box 1888, 27402
Telephone: 910-275-7626
FAX: 910-273-7293

MEMBERS OF FIRM

Henry H. Isaacson | Marc L. Isaacson
L. Charles Grimes

ASSOCIATE

Thomas B. Kobrin

For full biographical listings, see the Martindale-Hubbell Law Directory

*RALEIGH,** Wake Co.

* indicates certain Bar Register subscribers whose principal office is located elsewhere in the state and who have arranged for representation as a part of the state capital listings that follow

BURNS, DAY & PRESNELL, P.A. (AV)

Suite 560, 2626 Glenwood Avenue, P.O. Box 10867, 27605
Telephone: 919-782-1441
Fax: 919-782-2311

(See Next Column)

BURNS, DAY & PRESNELL P.A., *Raleigh—Continued*

David W. Boone
James M. Day
Daniel C. Higgins
Greg L. Hinshaw
Lacy M. Presnell III
Susan F. Vick

OF COUNSEL

F. Kent Burns

For full biographical listings, see the Martindale-Hubbell Law Directory

EVERETT, GASKINS, HANCOCK & STEVENS (AV)

The Professional Building, Suite 600, 127 West Hargett Street, P.O. Box 911, 27602
Telephone: 919-755-0025
Fax: 919-755-0009
Durham, North Carolina Office: Suite 300, 301 West Main Street, P.O. Box 586.
Telephone: 919-682-5691.
Fax: 919-682-5469.

MEMBERS OF FIRM

Eura DuVal (Ed) Gaskins, Jr.
Hugh Stevens

ASSOCIATES

Jeffrey B. Parsons
Robert (Bob) H. Gourley, Jr.

LEGAL SUPPORT PERSONNEL

Allyson S. McNeill
Alison R. Weigold

For Complete List of Firm Personnel, See General Section

For full biographical listings, see the Martindale-Hubbell Law Directory

*** WOMBLE CARLYLE SANDRIDGE & RICE (AV)**

A Professional Limited Liability Company
2100 First Union Capitol Center, 150 Fayetteville Street Mall, P.O. Box 831, 27602
Telephone: 919-755-2100
Telecopy: 919-755-2150
Telex: 806498
Charlotte, North Carolina Office: 3300 One First Union Center, 301 South College Street.
Telephone: 704-331-4900.
Telecopy: 704-331-4955.
Telex: 853609.
Winston-Salem, North Carolina Office: 1600 Southern National Financial Center.
Telephone: 919-721-3600.
Telecopy: 919-721-3660.
Telex: 806498.
Atlanta, Georgia Office: One Ninety One Peachtree Tower, 191 Peachtree Street N.E., Suite 3250.
Telephone: 404-614-2580.
Fax: 404-614-2595.

RESIDENT PARTNER

Deborah Hylton Hartzog

RESIDENT ASSOCIATE

Andrea Harris Fox

Representative Clients: Aetna Casualty and Surety Co., Inc.; ALSCO/AmeriMark Building Products, Inc.; Aoki Corporation America, Inc.; Empire of Carolina, Inc.; Hackney Brothers, Inc.; Lawyers Mutual Liability Insurance Company of North Carolina; Meredith College; Monk-Austin, Inc.; Regency Park Corporation; Wachovia Bank of North Carolina, N.A.

For Complete List of Firm Personnel, See General Section

For full biographical listings, see the Martindale-Hubbell Law Directory

*WINSTON-SALEM,** Forsyth Co.

BLANCO TACKABERY COMBS & MATAMOROS, P.A. (AV)

215 Executive Park Boulevard, P.O. Drawer 25008, 27114-5008
Telephone: 910-768-1130
Facsimile: 910-765-4830

David B. Blanco
Neal E. Tackabery
Reginald F. Combs
Ronald A. Matamoros
John S. Harrison
Gene B. Tarr
Michael D. Hurst
Steven C. Garland
Peter J. Juran
Brian L. Herndon

Bowen C. Houff
George E. Hollodick
Marguerite Self
Charles D. Luckey
Barbara Fritz Tucker
John H. Hall, Jr.
David T. Watters
Julie M. Fisher
Mary Margaret Ogburn

Reference: Southern National Bank of North Carolina, Winston-Salem, North Carolina.

For full biographical listings, see the Martindale-Hubbell Law Directory

JOHN R. SURRATT, P.A. (AV)

Suite 700, NationsBank Plaza, 102 West Third Street, 27101
Telephone: 910-725-8323
Facsimile: 910-722-5218

John R. Surratt

Anita M. Conrad
Andrew J. Gerber

For full biographical listings, see the Martindale-Hubbell Law Directory

WOMBLE CARLYLE SANDRIDGE & RICE (AV)

A Professional Limited Liability Company
1600 Southern National Financial Center, P.O. Drawer 84, 27102
Telephone: 910-721-3600
Telecopy: 910-721-3660
Telex: 806498
Charlotte, North Carolina Office: 3300 One First Union Center, 301 South College Street.
Telephone: 704-331-4900.
Telecopy: 704-331-4955.
Telex: 853609.
Raleigh, North Carolina Office: 2100 First Union Capitol Center, 150 Fayetteville Street Mall, P.O. Box 831.
Telephone: 919-755-2100.
Telecopy: 919-755-2150.
Telex: 806498.
Atlanta, Georgia Office: One Ninety One Peachtree Tower, 191 Peachtree Street, N.E., Suite 3250.
Telephone: 404-614-2580.
Fax: 404-614-2595.

MEMBERS OF FIRM

Zeb E. Barnhardt, Jr.
Kenneth G. Carroll
Linwood Layfield Davis
William Allison Davis, II
John L. W. Garrou
Murray C. Greason, Jr.
Jeffrey C. Howland

ASSOCIATE

Heather A. King

Representative Clients: Brad Ragan, Inc.; Brenner Companies; Food Lion, Inc.; Hanes Companies, Inc.; North Carolina Baptist Hospitals, Inc.; R.J. Reynolds Tobacco Company; Summit Communications Group, Inc.; Thomasville Furniture Industries, Inc.; Wachovia Corporation; Wake Forest University.

For Complete List of Firm Personnel, See General Section

For full biographical listings, see the Martindale-Hubbell Law Directory

NORTH DAKOTA

*BISMARCK,** Burleigh Co.

MALCOLM H. BROWN, P.C. (AV)

209 East Broadway Avenue, P.O. Box 2692, 58502-2692
Telephone: 701-224-8825
Fax: 701-224-8820

Malcolm H. Brown

For full biographical listings, see the Martindale-Hubbell Law Directory

PEARCE AND DURICK (AV)

314 East Thayer Avenue, P.O. Box 400, 58502
Telephone: 701-223-2890
Fax: 701-223-7865

MEMBERS OF FIRM

William P. Pearce
Patrick W. Durick
Lawrence A. Dopson

Representative Clients: American Insurance Assn.; Cigna-INA Insurance Co.; Deere & Co.; Federal Deposit Insurance Corp.; Ford Motor Co.; General Motors Corp.; MDU Resources Group, Inc.; Northwest Airlines; Royal Insurance Co.; Travelers Insurance Co.

For Complete List of Firm Personnel, See General Section

For full biographical listings, see the Martindale-Hubbell Law Directory

PETERSON, SCHMITZ, MOENCH & SCHMIDT, A PROFESSIONAL CORPORATION (AV)

Second Floor, Suite 200, 116 North Fourth Street, P.O. Box 2076, 58502-2076
Telephone: 701-224-0400
Fax: 701-224-0399

David L. Peterson
Orell D. Schmitz
Dale W. Moench
William D. Schmidt

(See Next Column)

PETERSON, SCHMITZ, MOENCH & SCHMIDT A PROFESSIONAL CORPORATION—*Continued*

OF COUNSEL

Gerald Glaser

LEGAL SUPPORT PERSONNEL

Vicki J. Kunz
Traci L. Albers

For full biographical listings, see the Martindale-Hubbell Law Directory

*FARGO,** Cass Co.

NILLES, HANSEN & DAVIES, LTD. (AV)

1800 Radisson Tower, P.O. Box 2626, 58108
Telephone: 701-237-5544

Timothy Q. Davies
Gregory B. Selbo
Daniel J. Crothers
Harry M. Pippin
Thomas A. Jacobson

Representative Clients: Blue Cross/Blue Shield; First Bank of North Dakota (NA); Metropolitan Federal Bank (fsb); Burlington Northern.

For Complete List of Firm Personnel, See General Section

For full biographical listings, see the Martindale-Hubbell Law Directory

VOGEL, BRANTNER, KELLY, KNUTSON, WEIR & BYE, LTD. (AV)

502 First Avenue North, P.O. Box 1389, 58107
Telephone: 701-237-6983
Facsimile: 701-237-0847

John D. Kelly
Kermit Edward Bye
Maurice G. McCormick
William A. Schlossman, Jr.
Douglas R. Herman
Jon R. Brakke
Frank G. Gokey
Steven A. Johnson

Representative Clients: Associated General Contractors of North Dakota; Clark Equipment Co.; Dakota Hospital; Forum Communications Company; MeritCare Medical Group; Northern Improvement Co.; Dakota Clinic; Gateway Chevrolet Inc.; West Acres Development Company; Fargo Glass and Paint Company.

For Complete List of Firm Personnel, See General Section

For full biographical listings, see the Martindale-Hubbell Law Directory

*MINOT,** Ward Co.

MCGEE, HANKLA, BACKES & WHEELER, P.C. (AV)

Suite 305 Norwest Center, 15 Second Avenue Southwest, P.O. Box 998, 58702-0998
Telephone: 701-852-2544
Fax: 701-838-4724

Richard H. McGee (1918-1992)
Walfrid B. Hankla
Orlin W. Backes
Robert A. Wheeler
Donald L. Peterson
Richard H. McGee, II
Collin P. Dobrovolny
Brian W. Hankla
Robert J. Hovland
Jon W. Backes

LEGAL SUPPORT PERSONNEL

Janice M. Eslinger
Jane K. Hutchison
Ardella M. Burtman
Michelle Erdmann

For full biographical listings, see the Martindale-Hubbell Law Directory

OHIO

*AKRON,** Summit Co.

THOMPSON, HINE AND FLORY (AV)

50 S. Main Street, Suite 502, 44308-1828
Telephone: 216-376-8090
Fax: 216-376-8386
Cincinnati, Ohio Office: 312 Walnut Street, 14th Floor, 45202-4029.
Telephone: 513-352-6700.
Fax: 513-241-4771.
Telex: 938003.
Cleveland, Ohio Office: 1100 National City Bank Building, 629 Euclid Avenue, 44114-3070.
Telephone: 216-566-5500.
Fax: 216-556-5583.
Telex: 980217.
Cable Address: "Thomflor".
Columbus, Ohio Office: One Columbus, 10 West Broad Street, 43215-3435.
Telephone: 614-469-3200.
Fax: 614-469-3361.
Dayton, Ohio Office: 2000 Courthouse Plaza, 45402-1706.
Telephone: 513-443-6600.
Fax: 513-443-6637; 443-6635.

(See Next Column)

Palm Beach, Florida Office: 125 Worth Avenue, 33480-4466.
Telephone: 407-833-5900.
Fax: 407-833-5951.
Washington, D.C. Office: 1920 N Street, N.W., 20036-1601.
Telephone: 202-331-8800.
Fax: 202-331-8330.
Telex: 904173.
Cable Address: "Caglaw".
Brussels, Belgium Office: Rue des Chevaliers / Ridderstraat 14 - B.10, B - 1050.
Telephone: 011(32-2) 511-9326.
Fax: 011(32-2) 513-9206.

MEMBER OF FIRM

Richard E. Guster (Partner-in-Charge in Akron)

For Complete List of Firm Personnel, See General Section

For full biographical listings, see the Martindale-Hubbell Law Directory

*CINCINNATI,** Hamilton Co.

FROST & JACOBS (AV)

2500 PNC Center, 201 East Fifth Street, P.O. Box 5715, 45201-5715
Telephone: 513-651-6800
Cable Address: "Frostjac"
Telex: 21-4396 F & J CIN
Telecopier: 513-651-6981
Columbus, Ohio Office: One Columbus, 10 West Broad Street.
Telephone: 614-464-1211.
Telecopier: 614-464-1737.
Lexington, Kentucky Office: 1100 Vine Center Tower, 333 West Vine Street.
Telephone: 606-254-1100.
Telecopier: 606-253-2990.
Middletown, Ohio Office: 400 First National Bank Building, 2 North Main Street.
Telephone: 513-422-2001.
Telecopier: 513-422-3010.
Naples, Florida Office: 4001 Tamiami Trail North, Suite 220.
Telephone: 813-261-0582.
Telecopier: 813-261-2083.

MEMBERS OF FIRM

Edmund J. Adams
Lawrence H. Kyte, Jr.
Richard J. Erickson
Jeffery R. Rush
E. Richard Oberschmidt
Kathleen W. Carr
Joseph W. Plye
P. Reid Lemasters
Frederick W. Kindel

SENIOR ATTORNEY

Fern E. Goldman

ASSOCIATES

John C. Krug
David S. Bence
Matthew S. Massarelli
Susan Mechley Lucci
Bryan S. Blade (Not admitted in OH)
Stuart B. Frankel

OF COUNSEL

Kimberly K. Mauer

COLUMBUS, OHIO OFFICE
MEMBER OF FIRM

John I. Cadwallader

LEXINGTON, KENTUCKY OFFICE
MEMBER OF FIRM

Greg E. Mitchell

MIDDLETOWN OFFICE
MEMBERS OF FIRM

Thomas A. Swope
Donald L. Crain

SENIOR ATTORNEY

Daniel J. Picard

NAPLES, FLORIDA OFFICE
PARTNER

Roi E. Baugher, II

Representative Clients: Bank One, Cincinnati, N.A.; Cincinnati Bell, Inc.; Cincinnati Milacron, Inc.; Federated Department Stores; First National Bank of Southwestern Ohio; PNC Bank, Ohio, National Association; Society National Bank; Turner Construction Co.; The United States Shoe Corp.; University of Cincinnati.

For Complete List of Firm Personnel, See General Section

For full biographical listings, see the Martindale-Hubbell Law Directory

LERNER, SAMPSON & ROTHFUSS A LEGAL PROFESSIONAL ASSOCIATION (AV)

120 East Fourth Street, Suite 800, 45202
Telephone: 513-241-3100
FAX: 513-241-4094

(See Next Column)

LERNER, SAMPSON & ROTHFUSS A LEGAL PROFESSIONAL ASSOCIATION, *Cincinnati—Continued*

Donald M. Lerner
Richard M. Rothfuss
Kirk Sampson
J. Michael Debbeler

Representative Clients: Lomas Mortgage USA, Inc.; Chemical Mortgage Co.; PNC Mortgage Co.
Reference: Star Bank NA of Cincinnati.

For full biographical listings, see the Martindale-Hubbell Law Directory

REISENFELD & STATMAN (AV)

Auburn Barrister House, 2355 Auburn Avenue, 45219
Telephone: 513-381-6810
FAX: 513-381-0255

Sylvan P. Reisenfeld
Alan J. Statman

John L. Day, Jr.
Bradley A. Reisenfeld
Melisa J. Richter
Rosemary E. Scollard
John Schmidt

For full biographical listings, see the Martindale-Hubbell Law Directory

SANTEN & HUGHES A LEGAL PROFESSIONAL ASSOCIATION (AV)

Suite 3100, 312 Walnut Street, 45202
Telephone: 513-721-4450
FAX: 513-721-7644; 721-0109

Harry H. Santen
David M. Kothman
Charles M. Meyer
R. Mark Addy
Charles E. Reynolds
Edward E. Santen
Charles J. Kubicki, Jr.

LEGAL SUPPORT PERSONNEL

Karen W. Crane (Corporate Paralegal)
Karen L. Jansen (Litigation Paralegal)
Deborah M. McKinney (Trust/Estate Paralegal)
Bobbie S. Ebbers (Paralegal)

For Complete List of Firm Personnel, See General Section

For full biographical listings, see the Martindale-Hubbell Law Directory

THOMPSON, HINE AND FLORY (AV)

312 Walnut Street, 14th Floor, 45202-4029
Telephone: 513-352-6700
Fax: 513-241-4771;
Telex: 938003
Akron, Ohio Office: 50 S. Main Street, Suite 502, 44308-1828.
Telephone: 216-376-8090.
Fax: 216-376-8386.
Cleveland, Ohio Office: 1100 National City Bank Building, 629 Euclid Avenue, 44114-3070.
Telephone: 216-566-5500.
Fax: 216-556-5583.
Telex: 980217.
Cable Address: "Thomflor".
Columbus, Ohio Office: One Columbus, 10 West Broad Street, 43215-3435.
Telephone: 614-469-3200.
Fax: 614-469-3361.
Dayton, Ohio Office: 2000 Courthouse Plaza, N.E., 45402-1706.
Telephone: 513-443-6600.
Fax: 513-443-6637; 443-6635.
Palm Beach, Florida Office: 125 Worth Avenue, 33480-4466.
Telephone: 407-833-5900.
Fax: 407-833-5951.
Washington, D.C. Office: 1920 N Street, N.W., 20036-1601.
Telephone: 202-331-8800.
Fax: 202-331-8330.
Telex: 904173.
Cable Address: "Caglaw".
Brussels, Belgium Office: Rue des Chevaliers / Ridderstraat 14 - B.10, B - 1050.
Telephone: 011(32-2) 511-9326.
Fax: 011(-32-2) 513-9206.

MEMBERS OF FIRM

Stephen J. Butler
Jacqueline K. McManus
Jane E. Garfinkel
Louis F. Solimine
Earle Jay Maiman
Jacob K. Stein

ASSOCIATES

Robert P. Johnson
Jeffrey A. Lydenberg

For Complete List of Firm Personnel, See General Section

For full biographical listings, see the Martindale-Hubbell Law Directory

*CLEVELAND,** Cuyahoga Co.

SEELEY, SAVIDGE AND AUSSEM A LEGAL PROFESSIONAL ASSOCIATION (AV)

800 Bank One Center, 600 Superior Avenue, East, 44114-2655
Telephone: 216-566-8200
Cable Address: "See Sau"
Fax-Telecopier: 216-566-0213
Elyria, Ohio Office: 538 Broad Street.
Telephone: 216-236-8158.

Glenn J. Seeley
Keith A. Savidge
Gregory D. Seeley
James S. Aussem

Patrick J. McIntyre
Thomas E. Sharpe
Carter R. Dodge
Robert C. White

References: Society National Bank; AmeriTrust.

For Complete List of Firm Personnel, See General Section

For full biographical listings, see the Martindale-Hubbell Law Directory

THOMPSON, HINE AND FLORY (AV)

1100 National City Bank Building, 629 Euclid Avenue, 44114-3070
Telephone: 216-566-5500
Fax: 216-566-5583
Telex: 980217
Cable Address: "Thomflor"
Akron, Ohio Office: 50 S. Main Street, Suite 502, 44308-1828.
Telephone: 216-376-8090.
Fax: 216-376-8386.
Cincinnati, Ohio Office: 312 Walnut Street, 14th Floor, 45202-4029.
Telephone: 513-352-6700.
Fax: 513-241-4771.
Telex: 938003.
Columbus, Ohio Office: One Columbus, 10 West Broad Street, 43215-3435.
Telephone: 614-469-3200.
Fax: 614-469-3361.
Dayton, Ohio Office: 2000 Courthouse Plaza, N.E., 45402-1706.
Telephone: 513-443-6600.
Fax: 513-443-6637; 443-6635.
Palm Beach, Florida Office: 125 Worth Avenue, Suite 117, 33480-4466.
Telephone: 407-833-5900.
Fax: 407-833-5951.
Washington, D.C. Office: 1920 N Street, N.W., 20036-1601.
Telephone: 202-331-8800.
Fax: 202-331-8330.
Telex: 904173.
Cable Address: "Caglaw".
Brussels, Belgium Office: Rue des Chevaliers, Ridderstraat 14 - B.10, B - 1050.
Telephone: 011(32-2) 511-9326.
Fax: 011(32-2) 513-9206.

MEMBERS OF FIRM

Barbara J. Arison
David J. Hooker
Virginia S. Brown
Leslie W. Jacobs
Keith L. Carson
George F. Karch, Jr.
Timothy J. Coughlin
Alan R. Lepene
Stephen H. Daniels
Craig R. Martahus
John H. Gherlein (Retired)
David J. Naftzinger
Harry A. Hanna
David L. Parham
Thomas C. Stevens

ASSOCIATES

Katherine D. Brandt
Patrick F. Haggerty
Dean D. Gamin
Karen E. Rubin

For Complete List of Firm Personnel, See General Section

For full biographical listings, see the Martindale-Hubbell Law Directory

ZIEGLER, METZGER & MILLER (AV)

2020 Huntington Building, 44115-1407
Telephone: 216-781-5470
FAX: 216-781-0714

MEMBER OF FIRM

Stephen M. Darlington

ASSOCIATES

Stephen M. Bales
Christopher W. Siemen
Jeffrey L. Koberg

For Complete List of Firm Personnel, See General Section

For full biographical listings, see the Martindale-Hubbell Law Directory

*COLUMBUS,** Franklin Co.

* indicates certain Bar Register subscribers whose principal office is located elsewhere in the state and who have arranged for representation as a part of the state capital listings that follow

BRICKER & ECKLER (AV)

100 South Third Street, 43215-4291
Telephone: 614-227-2300
Telecopy: 614-227-2390
Cleveland, Ohio Office: 600 Superior Avenue East, Suite 800.
Telephone: 216-771-0720. Fax 216-771-7702.

Stephen K. Yoder
David G. Baker
John C. Rosenberger
Gordon W. Johnston
John W. Cook, III
Charles H. McCreary, III
Kenneth C. Johnson
David K. Conrad
Craig A. Haddox
L. Brent Miller
Cary W. Purcell

Mark J. Palmer
Andrew A. Folkerth
Quintin F. Lindsmith
Harry Wright, IV
Kara J. Trott

Representative Clients: Bank of America, N.T. & S.A.; Bank One; The CIT Group/Equipment Financing, Inc.; CompuServe Incorporated; Figgie Leasing Corp.; Huntington National Bank; IBM Corporation; National Century Financial Enterprises, Inc.; National City Bank; National Premier Financial Services, Inc.

For Complete List of Firm Personnel, See General Section

For full biographical listings, see the Martindale-Hubbell Law Directory

*** THOMPSON, HINE AND FLORY (AV)**

One Columbus, 10 West Broad Street, 43215-3435
Telephone: 614-469-3200
Fax: 614-469-3361
Akron, Ohio Office: 50 S. Main Street, Suite 502, 44308-1828.
Telephone: 216-376-8090.
Fax: 216-376-8386.
Cincinnati, Ohio Office: 312 Walnut Street, 14th Floor, 45202-4029.
Telephone: 513-352-6700.
Fax: 513-241-4771.
Telex: 938003.
Cleveland, Ohio Office: 1100 National City Bank Building, 629 Euclid Avenue, 44114-3070.
Telephone: 216-566-5500.
Fax: 216-556-5583.
Telex: 980217.
Cable Address: "Thomflor".
Dayton, Ohio Office: 2000 Courthouse Plaza, N.E., 45402-1706.
Telephone: 513-443-6600.
Fax: 513-443-6637; 443-6635.
Palm Beach, Florida Office: 125 Worth Avenue, 33480-4466.
Telephone: 407-833-5900.
Fax: 407-833-5951.
Washington, D.C. Office: 1920 N Street, N.W., 20036-1601.
Telephone: 202-331-8800.
Fax: 202-331-8330.
Telex: 904173.
Cable Address: "Caglaw".
Brussels, Belgium Office: Rue des Chevaliers / Ridderstraat 14 - B.10, B - 1050.
Telephone: 011(32-2) 511-9326.
Fax: 011(32-2) 513-9206.

MEMBERS OF FIRM

Thomas R. Allen
William R. Case
Thomas E. Lodge
Thomas C. Scott (Partner-in-Charge in Columbus)

ASSOCIATES

Bonnie Irvin O'Neil
Susan L. Rhiel
Richard K. Stovall

OF COUNSEL

Charles B. Mills, Jr.

For Complete List of Firm Personnel, See General Section

For full biographical listings, see the Martindale-Hubbell Law Directory

*DAYTON,** Montgomery Co.

THOMPSON, HINE AND FLORY (AV)

2000 Courthouse Plaza, N.E., 45402-1706
Telephone: 513-443-6600
Fax: 513-443-6637; 443-6635
Akron, Ohio Office: 50 S. Main Street, Suite 502, 44308-1828.
Telephone: 216-376-8090.
Fax: 216-376-8386.

(See Next Column)

Cincinnati, Ohio Office: 312 Walnut Street, 14th Floor, 45202-4029.
Telephone: 513-352-6700.
Fax: 513-241-4771.
Telex: 938003.
Cleveland, Ohio Office: 1100 National City Bank Building, 629 Euclid Avenue, 44114-3070.
Telephone: 216-566-5500.
Fax: 216-556-5583.
Telex: 980217.
Cable Address: "Thomflor".
Columbus, Ohio Office: One Columbus, 10 West Broad Street, 43215-3435.
Telephone: 614-469-3200.
Fax: 614-469-3361.
Palm Beach, Florida Office: 125 Worth Avenue, 33480-4466.
Telephone: 407-833-5900.
Fax: 407-833-5951.
Washington, D.C. Office: 1920 N Street, N.W., 20036-1601.
Telephone: 202-331-8800.
Fax: 202-331-8330.
Telex: 904173.
Cable Address: "Caglaw".
Brussels, Belgium Office: Rue des Chevaliers / Ridderstraat 14 - B.10, B - 1050.
Telephone: 011(32-2) 511-9326.
Fax: 011(32-2) 513-9206.

MEMBER OF FIRM

Bruce M. Allman

For Complete List of Firm Personnel, See General Section

For full biographical listings, see the Martindale-Hubbell Law Directory

LORAIN, Lorain Co.

COLELLA, TRIGILIO & STEPHENSON (AV)

5750 Cooper Foster Park Road, 44053
Telephone: 216-988-9000
Elyria: 216-322-3767
Telecopier: 216-988-9002

Richard Colella
Timothy S. Trigilio
Mark E. Stephenson
Richard J. Colella
Thomas A. Januzzi

References: Elyria Savings and Trust National Bank; The Lorain National Bank; First Bancorporation of Ohio.

For full biographical listings, see the Martindale-Hubbell Law Directory

*TOLEDO,** Lucas Co.

JOSEPH H. PILKINGTON & CO., L.P.A. (AV)

One SeaGate, Suite 920, 43604
Telephone: 419-247-1600
Facsimile: 419-247-1602

Joseph H. Pilkington

References: Society Bank & Trust, Toledo, Ohio; Ohio Citizens Bank.

For full biographical listings, see the Martindale-Hubbell Law Directory

WATKINS, BATES & CAREY (AV)

1200 Fifth Third Center, 608 Madison Avenue, 43604-1157
Telephone: 419-241-2100
Telecopier: 419-241-1960

MEMBERS OF FIRM

William F. Bates
John M. Carey

ASSOCIATES

Gabrielle Davis
Jennifer L. Morrison

Counsel for: National City Bank; BancOhio.

For Complete List of Firm Personnel, See General Section

For full biographical listings, see the Martindale-Hubbell Law Directory

OKLAHOMA

*OKLAHOMA CITY,** Oklahoma Co.

WILLIAM C. BOSTON & ASSOCIATES (AV)

4005 Northwest Expressway, Suite 600, 73116
Telephone: 405-848-0600
Telefax: 405-848-0655

Scott D. McCreary
William Clayton Boston, III
Eric L. Johnson
KimberLee Kimzey Osby

(See Next Column)

WILLIAM C. BOSTON & ASSOCIATES, *Oklahoma City—Continued*

OF COUNSEL

Joseph T. Brennan (Not admitted in OK)
Donna M. Schmidt (Not admitted in OK)
Willis W. Luttrell (Not admitted in OK)

For full biographical listings, see the Martindale-Hubbell Law Directory

DAUGHERTY, FOWLER & PEREGRIN, A PROFESSIONAL CORPORATION (AV)

204 North Robinson 900 City Place, 73102-6800
Telephone: 405-232-0003
Facsimile: 405-232-0865

Daniel J. Fowler
Robert M. Peregrin
Susan H. Utecht

OF COUNSEL

Phil E. Daugherty

For full biographical listings, see the Martindale-Hubbell Law Directory

DAY, EDWARDS, FEDERMAN, PROPESTER & CHRISTENSEN, P.C. (AV)

Suite 2900 First Oklahoma Tower, 210 Park Avenue, 73102-5605
Telephone: 405-239-2121
Telecopier: 405-236-1012

Bruce W. Day
Joe E. Edwards
William B. Federman
Richard P. Propester
D. Wade Christensen
J. Clay Christensen
Kent A. Gilliland
Rodney J. Heggy
Ricki Valerie Sonders
Thomas Pitchlynn Howell, IV
John C. Platt

David R. Widdoes
Lori R. Roberts
Carolyn A. Romberg

OF COUNSEL

Herbert F. (Jack) Hewett
Jeanette Cook Timmons
Joel Warren Harmon
Jane S. Eulberg
Mark A. Cohen

Representative Clients: Aetna Life Insurance Co.; Boatmen's First National Bank of Oklahoma; Borg-Warner Chemicals, Inc.; City Bank & Trust; Federal Deposit Insurance Corp.; Bank One, Oklahoma City; Haskell Lemon Construction Co.; Merrill Lynch, Pierce, Fenner & Smith, Inc.; Prudential Securities, Inc.

For full biographical listings, see the Martindale-Hubbell Law Directory

DURLAND & DURLAND (AV)

300 Bank IV Tower, 1601 Northwest Expressway, 73118
Telephone: 405-840-0060
FAX: 405-842-8547

Jack R. Durland, Jr.
Harvey L. Harmon, Jr.
Kathleen Garewal

OF COUNSEL

Jack R. Durland
Robert D. Allen

For full biographical listings, see the Martindale-Hubbell Law Directory

FULLER, TUBB & POMEROY (AV)

800 Bank of Oklahoma Plaza, 201 Robert S. Kerr Avenue, 73102-4292
Telephone: 405-235-2575
Fax: 405-232-8384

MEMBERS OF FIRM

G. M. Fuller
Jerry Tubb
L. David Pomeroy
Joe Heaton
Michael A. Bickford
Terry Stokes

OF COUNSEL

Thomas J. Kenan

LEGAL SUPPORT PERSONNEL

Sherie S. Adams (Legal Assistant)

Representative Clients: French Petroleum Corp.; Independent Insurance Agents of Oklahoma, Inc.; LTV Energy Products Co.; Northwestern National Life Insurance Co.; Purina Mills, Inc.; Sequa Corp.; Halliburton Oil Producing Co.; Chemical Bank/Chemical Financial Corporation; Pitney Bowes, Inc.; Norwest Banks.

For full biographical listings, see the Martindale-Hubbell Law Directory

HARTZOG CONGER & CASON, A PROFESSIONAL CORPORATION (AV)

1600 Bank of Oklahoma Plaza, 73102
Telephone: 405-235-7000
Facsimile: 405-235-7329

(See Next Column)

Larry D. Hartzog
J. William Conger
Len Cason
James C. Prince
Alan Newman
Steven C. Davis
Valerie K. Couch
Mark D. Dickey
Joseph P. Hogsett
John D. Robertson
Kurt M. Rupert
Laura Haag McConnell

Susan B. Shields
Ryan S. Wilson
Melanie J. Jester
Armand Paliotta
Julia Watson
J. Leslie LaReau

OF COUNSEL

Kent F. Frates

For full biographical listings, see the Martindale-Hubbell Law Directory

SELF, GIDDENS & LEES, INC. (AV)

2725 Oklahoma Tower, 210 Park Avenue, 73102-5604
Telephone: 405-232-3001
Telecopier: 405-232-5553

Jared D. Giddens
C. Ray Lees
Shannon T. Self

Thomas J. Blalock
Christopher R. Graves
W. Shane Smithton
Bryan J. Wells

For full biographical listings, see the Martindale-Hubbell Law Directory

STEPHEN A. SHERMAN & ASSOCIATES (AV)

117 Park Avenue Building, Fourth Floor, 73102
Telephone: 405-235-0707
Fax: 405-235-0712

Daniel K. Zorn

Representative Clients: Aetna Realty Investors, Inc.; CB Commercial Real Estate Management Services; Insignia Commercial Group, Inc.; Kaiser-Francis Oil Co.; Nationwide Insurance Co.; Self Insurer's Service Bureau, Inc.; Trammell Crow Co., Inc.; White Swan, Inc.

For full biographical listings, see the Martindale-Hubbell Law Directory

*TULSA,** Tulsa Co.

GABLE & GOTWALS (AV)

2000 Bank IV Center, 15 West Sixth Street, 74119-5447
Telephone: 918-582-9201
Facsimile: 918-586-8383

Teresa B. Adwan
Pamela S. Anderson
John R. Barker
David L. Bryant
Gene C. Buzzard
Dennis Clarke Cameron
Timothy A. Carney
Renee DeMoss
Elsie C. Draper
Sidney G. Dunagan
Theodore Q. Eliot
Richard W. Gable
Jeffrey Don Hassell
Patricia Ledvina Himes
Oliver S. Howard
Richard D. Koljack, Jr.
J. Daniel Morgan
Joseph W. Morris
Elizabeth R. Muratet
Richard B. Noulles
Ronald N. Ricketts
John Henry Rule
M. Benjamin Singletary
James M. Sturdivant
Patrick O. Waddel
Michael D. Hall
David Edward Keglovits
Stephen W. Lake
Kari S. McKee
Terry D. Ragsdale
Jeffrey C. Rambach

OF COUNSEL

G. Ellis Gable
Charles P. Gotwals, Jr.

For full biographical listings, see the Martindale-Hubbell Law Directory

JAMES, POTTS AND WULFERS (AV)

Suite 705, 320 South Boston Avenue, 74103-3712
Telephone: 918-584-0881
FAX: 918-584-4521

MEMBERS OF FIRM

David F. James
Thomas G. Potts
David W. Wulfers

For full biographical listings, see the Martindale-Hubbell Law Directory

JOHNSON, ALLEN, JONES & DORNBLASER (AV)

900 Petroleum Club Building, 601 South Boulder, 74119
Telephone: 918-584-6644
FAX: 918-584-6645

MEMBERS OF FIRM

Mark H. Allen
W. Thomas Coffman
Kenneth E. Dornblaser
John B. Johnson, Jr.
C. Robert Jones
Richard D. Jones
Randy R. Shorb

(See Next Column)

JOHNSON, ALLEN, JONES & DORNBLASER—*Continued*

ASSOCIATE

Frances F. Hillsman

For full biographical listings, see the Martindale-Hubbell Law Directory

LIPE, GREEN, PASCHAL, TRUMP & BRAGG, A PROFESSIONAL CORPORATION (AV)

3700 First National Tower, 15 East Fifth Street, Suite 3700, 74103-4344
Telephone: 918-599-9400
Fax: 918-599-9404

Larry B. Lipe
James E. Green, Jr.
Richard A. Paschal
Timothy T. Trump
Patricia Dunmire Bragg

Melodie Freeman-Burney
Mark E. Dreyer
Constance L. Young
Leah Lowder Mills

Representative Clients: Aegon USA Realty Advisors, Inc.; The AEtna Casualty and Surety Company; Avtax, Inc.; Collegiate Systems, Inc.; Emmons & Hartog, Certified Public Accountants; Flint Industries, Inc.; McLouth Steel Corporation; Pentastar Transportation Group, Inc.; Spradlin & Associates, Inc.; Price Bednar Certified Public Accountants; Stifel, Nicolaus & Company, Inc.; Thrifty Rent-A-Car System, Inc.; 21st Century Investment Co.; Underwriters at Lloyds, London

For full biographical listings, see the Martindale-Hubbell Law Directory

SNEED, LANG, ADAMS & BARNETT, A PROFESSIONAL CORPORATION (AV)

2300 Williams Center Tower II, Two West Second Street, 74103
Telephone: 918-583-3145
Telecopier: 918-582-0410

James C. Lang
D. Faith Orlowski
Brian S. Gaskill
G. Steven Stidham
Stephen R. McNamara
Thomas E. Black, Jr.
Robbie Emery Burke
C. Raymond Patton, Jr.
Frederick K. Slicker
Richard D. Black
John D. Russell
Jeffrey S. Swyers

OF COUNSEL

James L. Sneed
O. Edwin Adams
Howard G. Barnett, Jr.

Representative Clients: Amoco Production Company; Continental Bank; Deloitte & Touche; Enron Corporation; Halliburton Energy Services; Helmerich & Payne, Inc.; Lehman Brothers, Inc.; Shell Oil Company; Smith Barney, Inc.; State Farm Mutual Automobile Insurance Company.

For full biographical listings, see the Martindale-Hubbell Law Directory

OREGON

*PORTLAND,** Multnomah Co.

BLACK HELTERLINE (AV)

1200 The Bank of California Tower, 707 S.W. Washington Street, 97205
Telephone: 503-224-5560
Telecopier: 503-224-6148

MEMBERS OF FIRM

Ronald T. Adams
John M. McGuigan
Michael O. Moran
Richard N. Roskie
David P. Roy

ASSOCIATES

Deneen M. Hubertin
James M. Baumgartner

OF COUNSEL

Robert E. Glasgow

Representative Clients: The Bank of California, N.A.; The Bank of Tokyo, Ltd.; First Nationwide Automotive Acceptance; Mitsubishi Bank, Ltd.; NACCO Materials Handling Groups, Inc.; Royal Bank of Canada.

For Complete List of Firm Personnel, See General Section

For full biographical listings, see the Martindale-Hubbell Law Directory

HAGEN, DYE, HIRSCHY & DILORENZO, P.C. (AV)

19th Floor Benj. Franklin Plaza, One S.W. Columbia Street, 97258-2087
Telephone: 503-222-1812
FAX: 503-274-7979

Joseph T. Hagen
Jeffrey L. Dye
John A. Hirschy
John A. DiLorenzo, Jr.
Dana R. Taylor
Mark A. Golding
Kenneth A. Williams

(See Next Column)

Blanche I. Sommers
Timothy J. Wachter
Annie T. Buell
Adam S. Rittenberg
Michael E. Farnell
John D. Parsons

LEGAL SUPPORT PERSONNEL

Carol A. R. Wong
Flora L. Wade

For full biographical listings, see the Martindale-Hubbell Law Directory

LABARRE & ASSOCIATES, P.C. (AV)

Suite 1212, 900 S.W. Fifth Avenue, 97204-1268
Telephone: 503-228-3511
FAX: 503-273-8658

Jerome E. LaBarre

Dayna Ellen Peck

OF COUNSEL

Robert A. Russell

For full biographical listings, see the Martindale-Hubbell Law Directory

SUSSMAN SHANK WAPNICK CAPLAN & STILES (AV)

1000 S.W. Broadway Suite 1400, 97205
Telephone: 503-227-1111
Telecopier: 503-248-0130

MEMBERS OF FIRM

Norman Wapnick
Barry P. Caplan
William N. Stiles
John P. Davenport
Jeffrey R. Spere
Howard M. Levine
Stuart I. Teicher

ASSOCIATES

Robert L. Carlton
Gary E. Enloe
Michael G. Halligan
Thomas W. Stilley

OF COUNSEL

Jerome B. Shank

For Complete List of Firm Personnel, See General Section

For full biographical listings, see the Martindale-Hubbell Law Directory

PENNSYLVANIA

*ALLENTOWN,** Lehigh Co.

GROSS, MCGINLEY, LABARRE & EATON (AV)

33 South Seventh Street, P.O. Box 4060, 18105-4060
Telephone: (610)-820-5450
Fax: (610)-820-6006

MEMBERS OF FIRM

Malcolm J. Gross
Paul A. McGinley
Donald L. LaBarre, Jr.
J. Jackson Eaton, III
Michael A. Henry
Patrick J. Reilly
William J. Fries

ASSOCIATES

Anne K. Manley
John D. Lychak

For full biographical listings, see the Martindale-Hubbell Law Directory

BALA CYNWYD, Montgomery Co.

KANIA, LINDNER, LASAK AND FEENEY (AV)

Suite 525, Two Bala Plaza, 19004
Telephone: 610-667-3240
Fax: 610-668-9676

Arthur J. Kania
Albert A. Lindner
John Lasak
Thomas J. Feeney, III
Robert A. Griffiths

ASSOCIATE

Michael F. Merlie

A list of Representative Clients for which the firm serves as General Counsel or Local Counsel will be supplied upon request.

For full biographical listings, see the Martindale-Hubbell Law Directory

BLUE BELL, Montgomery Co.

ELLIOTT, REIHNER, SIEDZIKOWSKI, NORTH & EGAN, P.C. (AV)

Union Meeting Corporate Center V, 925 Harvest Drive, 19422
Telephone: 215-977-1000
Fax: 215-977-1099
Scranton, Pennsylvania:
Telephone: 717-346-7569.
Fax: 717-969-2890.

(See Next Column)

ELLIOTT, REIHNER, SIEDZIKOWSKI, NORTH & EGAN P.C., *Blue Bell—Continued*

Cherry Hill, New Jersey:
Telephone: 609-482-7885.
Fax: 609-482-8099.
Affiliated Office: Bryan E. Barbin, 125 State Street, Harrisburg, Pennsylvania.
Telephone: 717-232-9200.
Fax: 717-232-7810.

John M. Elliott
Thomas J. Elliott
Henry F. Siedzikowski
Katherine A. Newell
Brian S. North
Gerard P. Egan
James C. Crumlish, III
Brian P. Kenney
Mark J. Schwemler
Timothy T. Myers
Mark A. Kearney
Dionysios G. Rassias

OF COUNSEL

Kevin S. Anderson
David L. Narkiewicz
Reuben A. Guttman
Timothy S. Kerr
Dean R. Phillips

Frederick P. Santarelli
Adam B. Krafczek, Jr.
Eric J. Bronstein
Mark J. Conway
Ann McGill
Margaret S. Curran
Michael P. Walsh
Peter A. Lennon
Gerald Lawrence
Brian P. McCafferty

For full biographical listings, see the Martindale-Hubbell Law Directory

LESSER & KAPLIN, PROFESSIONAL CORPORATION (AV)

350 Sentry Parkway, Bldg. 640, 19422-0757
Telephone: 610-828-2900; Telecopier: 610-828-1555
Marlton, New Jersey Office: Three Greentree Centre, Suite 104, Route 73, 08053-3215.
Telephone: 609-596-2400.
Telecopier: 609-596-8185.

Lawrence R. Lesser
William K. Stewart, Jr.
Bruce R. Lesser
Anthony J. Krol
L. Leonard Lundy
Sara Lee Keller-Smith

Alan P. Fox (Resident, Marlton, New Jersey Office)
William J. Levant
Jordan D. Warshaw

For full biographical listings, see the Martindale-Hubbell Law Directory

*CLARION,** Clarion Co.

LAW OFFICES OF RICHARD W. KOOMAN, II (AV)

Marianne Professional Center, P.O. Box 700, 16214
Telephone: 814-226-9100
Fax: 814-226-7361

ASSOCIATE

Terry R. Heeter

Representative Clients: Pennsylvania National Mutual Casualty Insurance Co.; Erie Insurance Exchange; Sorce, Inc.; Charles Tool & Supply, Inc.; Brookville Locomotive, Inc.; G&G Contracting, Inc.; Ti-Brook, Inc.; Alpha Environmental Mining Corp.; Exley Oil & Gas Co.; Clarion County Economic Development Authority.

For full biographical listings, see the Martindale-Hubbell Law Directory

*EASTON,** Northampton Co.

HERSTER, NEWTON & MURPHY (AV)

127 North Fourth Street, P.O. Box 1087, 18042
Telephone: 610-258-6219

MEMBERS OF FIRM

Andrew L. Herster, Jr.
Henry R. Newton
William K. Murphy

General Counsel For: Valley Federal Savings & Loan Assn.; Lafayette Bank; Easton Printing Co.; Northampton Community College; Eisenhardt Mills, Inc.; Delaware Wood Products, Inc.; Panuccio Construction, Inc.
References: Merchants Bank, N.A.; Lafayette Bank; Valley Federal Savings and Loan.

ELKINS PARK, Montgomery Co.

MONAGHAN & GOLD, P.C. (AV)

7837 Old York Road, 19027
Telephone: 215-782-1800
Fax: 215-782-1010

John F. X. Monaghan, Jr.
Alan Steven Gold

(See Next Column)

Brian E. Appel
Murray R. Glickman
Barbara Malett Weitz
Tanya M. Sweet

*HARRISBURG,** Dauphin Co.

BUCHANAN INGERSOLL, PROFESSIONAL CORPORATION (AV)

Vartan Parc, 30 North Third Street, 17101
Telephone: 717-237-4800
Telecopier: 717-233-0852
Pittsburgh, Pennsylvania Office: 5800 USX Tower, 600 Grant Street.
Telephone: 412-562-8800.
Philadelphia, Pennsylvania Office: Two Logan Square, Twelfth Floor, 18th & Arch Streets.
Telephone: 215-665-8700.
Tampa, Florida Office: 101 East Kennedy Boulevard, Suite 1030.
Telephone: 813-222-8180.
North Miami Beach, Florida Office: 19495 Biscayne Boulevard.
Telephone: 305-933-5600.
Lexington, Kentucky Office: 1210 Vine Center Office Tower, 333 West Vine Street.
Telephone: 606-225-5333.
Princeton, New Jersey Office: Buchanan Ingersoll, A Partnership, College Centre, 500 College Road East.
Telephone: 609-452-2666.

Mary Hannah Leavitt
Gerald K. Morrison

SENIOR ATTORNEY

Michael L. Solomon

Arbelyn Elizabeth Wolfe

For Complete List of Firm Personnel, See General Section

For full biographical listings, see the Martindale-Hubbell Law Directory

GOLDBERG, KATZMAN & SHIPMAN, P.C. (AV)

320 Market Street - Strawberry Square, P.O. Box 1268, 17108-1268
Telephone: 717-234-4161
Telecopier: 717-234-6808; 717-234-6810

Ronald M. Katzman
Neil Hendershot
Jesse Jay Cooper
Michael A. Finio

Arnold B. Kogan

Representative Clients: Pennsylvania Supply, Inc.; Elco Concrete Products, Inc.; Hirsh Valuation Group; Lemoyne Sleeper; E.N. Dunlap, Inc.; Herre Brothers, Inc.; Memorial Eye Institute; E.I. Associates; Tressler Lutheran Services.
Reference: Fulton Bank.

For Complete List of Firm Personnel, See General Section

For full biographical listings, see the Martindale-Hubbell Law Directory

MCNEES, WALLACE & NURICK (AV)

100 Pine Street, P.O. Box 1166, 17108
Telephone: 717-232-8000
Fax: 717-237-5300

MEMBERS OF FIRM

Eric L. Brossman
David B. Disney
Michael A. Doctrow
Francis B. Haas, Jr.
W. Jeffry Jamouneau
Timothy J. Pfister
Edward W. Rothman
Gary F. Yenkowski

ASSOCIATES

Brett D. Davis
Kathleen A. Dunst
P. Nicholas Guarneschelli

For Complete List of Firm Personnel, See General Section

For full biographical listings, see the Martindale-Hubbell Law Directory

METTE, EVANS & WOODSIDE, A PROFESSIONAL CORPORATION (AV)

3401 North Front Street, P.O. Box 5950, 17110-0950
Telephone: 717-232-5000
Telecopier: 717-236-1816

Robert Moore
Charles B. Zwally
Lloyd R. Persun
James A. Ulsh
Glen R. Grell
Elyse E. Rogers

Guy P. Beneventano
Karen N. Connelly

Counsel For: Gannett Fleming Affiliates, Inc.; The B. F. Goodrich Co.; Juniata Valley Financial Corp.; MCI Telecommunications Corp.; Monongahela Power Co.; The Procter and Gamble Paper Products Co.; United States Fidelity and Guaranty Co.; Community Banks; GTE Products Corp.

For Complete List of Firm Personnel, See General Section

For full biographical listings, see the Martindale-Hubbell Law Directory

KING OF PRUSSIA, Montgomery Co.

POWELL, TRACHTMAN, LOGAN, CARRLE & BOWMAN, A PROFESSIONAL CORPORATION (AV)

367 South Gulph Road, 19406
Telephone: 610-354-9700
Fax: 610-354-9760
Cherry Hill, New Jersey Office: 811 Church Road, Suite 126, 08002.
Telephone: 609-663-0021.
Fax: 609-663-1590.
Harrisburg, Pennsylvania Office: 114 North Second Street, 17101.
Telephone: 717-238-9300.
Fax: 717-238-9325.

Michael G. Trachtman
Paul A. Logan
Gunther O. Carrle
C. Grainger Bowman
Richard B. Ashenfelter Jr.
Mark F. Brancato
Jonathan K. Hollin
Joel P. Perilstein

OF COUNSEL

Ralph B. Powell, Jr.
Patrick W. Liddle

Mark S. McKain
Ethan N. Halberstadt
David T. Bolger
David W. Francis
Eileen M. Coyne
Andrew P. Goode
Steven G. Bardsley

For full biographical listings, see the Martindale-Hubbell Law Directory

*LANCASTER,** Lancaster Co.

JOSEPH F. RODA, P.C. (AV)

301 Cipher Building, 36 East King Street, 17602
Telephone: 717-397-1700
Fax: 717-397-3669

Joseph F. Roda

Ronald C. Messmann
Gail A. Weber
Robin A. Jabour

For full biographical listings, see the Martindale-Hubbell Law Directory

*MEDIA,** Delaware Co.

CRAMP, D'IORIO, MCCONCHIE AND FORBES, P.C. (AV)

215 North Olive Street, P.O. Box 568, 19063
Telephone: 610-565-1700
Fax: 610-566-0379

Ralph B. D'Iorio
George J. McConchie
Andrew J. Forbes
Joseph W. Kauffman
David G. Blake
Gary C. Bender
Guy N. Paolino

Alexander D. DiSanti
Frances Marie Piccoli

OF COUNSEL

John F. Cramp

Local Counsel for: Bell Atlantic.
Trial Counsel for: Insurance Company of North America (CIGNA); Commercial Union Insurance Co.; State Farm Insurance Co.; Continental Casualty Co.; Fireman's Fund American Insurance Group; Pennsylvania Manufacturers Assn. (PMA); U.S. Fidelity & Guaranty Co.; United Services Automobile Association.
General Counsel for: Williamson School.

For full biographical listings, see the Martindale-Hubbell Law Directory

KASSAB ARCHBOLD JACKSON & O'BRIEN (AV)

Lawyers-Title Building, 214 North Jackson Street, P.O. Box 626, 19063
Telephone: 610-565-3800
Telecopier: 610-892-6888
Wilmington, Delaware Office: 1326 King Street.
Telephone: 302-656-3393.
Fax: 302-656-1993.
Wildwood, New Jersey Office: 5201 New Jersey Avenue.
Telephone: 609-522-6559.

MEMBERS OF FIRM

Edward Kassab
William C. Archbold, Jr.
Robert James Jackson
Joseph Patrick O'Brien
Richard A. Stanko
Roy T. J. Stegena

OF COUNSEL

Matthew J. Ryan
John W. Nilon, Jr.

ASSOCIATES

Kevin William Gibson
Cynthia Kassab Larosa
Marc S. Stein
Terrance A. Kline
George C. McFarland, Jr.
Jill E. Aversa
Pamela A. La Torre
Kenneth D. Kynett

(See Next Column)

Representative Clients furnished upon request.

For full biographical listings, see the Martindale-Hubbell Law Directory

*NORRISTOWN,** Montgomery Co.

LINDLEY M. COWPERTHWAIT, JR., P.C. (AV)

17 East Airy Street, 19401
Telephone: 610-277-6622
Fax: 610-277-6601
Cherry Hill, New Jersey Office: 1040 North Kings Highway, Suite 600, 08034.
Telephone: 609-482-8600.

Lindley M. Cowperthwait, Jr.
Adam D. Zucker

For full biographical listings, see the Martindale-Hubbell Law Directory

*PHILADELPHIA,** Philadelphia Co.

ABRAMSON, FREEDMAN & THALL (AV)

2128 Locust Street, 19103
Telephone: 215-545-2400
Telecopier: 215-545-8537
Haddonfield, New Jersey Office: 20 Kings Highway West.
Telephone: 609-795-5363.
Fax: 609-354-0020.

MEMBERS OF FIRM

Gilbert B. Abramson
Jeffrey M. Freedman
Bruce L. Thall

ASSOCIATES

Michael J. Troiani
Michael B. Tolcott
Stanley B. Cheiken (Resident, Haddonfield, New Jersey Office)

For full biographical listings, see the Martindale-Hubbell Law Directory

ANDERSON GREENFIELD & DOUGHERTY (AV)

1525 Penn Mutual Tower 510 Walnut Street, 19106-3610
Telephone: 215-627-0789
Fax: 215-627-0813
Wayne, Pennsylvania Office: First Fidelity Bank Building, 301 West Lancaster Avenue.
Telephone: 215-341-9010.

MEMBERS OF FIRM

Susan L. Anderson
Marjorie E. Greenfield
Donna Dougherty

ASSOCIATES

John Randolph Prince, III
Linda K. Hobkirk

For full biographical listings, see the Martindale-Hubbell Law Directory

BALLARD SPAHR ANDREWS & INGERSOLL (AV)

1735 Market Street, 51st Floor, 19103-7599
Telephone: 215-665-8500
Fax: 215-864-8999
Denver, Colorado Office: Seventeenth Street Plaza Building, Suite 2300, 1225 17th Street.
Telephone: 303-292-2400.
Fax: 303-296-3956.
Kaunas, Lithuania Office: Donelaicio g., 71-2, Kaunas 3000.
Telephone: (370-7) 20 56 66.
Fax: (370-7) 20 56 91.
Salt Lake City, Utah Office: One Utah Center, Suite 1200, 201 South Main Street.
Telephone: 801-531-3000.
Fax: 801-531-3001.
Washington, D.C. Office: Suite 900 East, 555 13th Street, N.W.
Telephone: 202-383-8800.
Fax: 202-383-8877; 383-8893.
Baltimore, Maryland Office: 300 East Lombard Street. 19th Floor.
Telephone: 410-528-5600.
Fax: 410-528-5650.
Camden, New Jersey Office: 800 Hudson Square, 5th Floor.
Telephone: 609-541-5577.
Fax: 609-541-8272.

John N. Ake
C. Baird Brown
Carl H. Fridy
Martha J. Hays
Justin P. Klein
William H. Rheiner
Edward D. Slevin
E. Carolan Berkley
Morris Cheston, Jr.
Robert C. Gerlach
Cathleen C. Judge
James A. Lebovitz
J. Douglas Rollow, III
Kent Walker
William Y. Webb

Susan Sudick Colton
Michael J. Konowal
Gerald J. Guarcini
Robert J. Werner
John M. Zerr

(See Next Column)

BALLARD SPAHR ANDREWS & INGERSOLL, *Philadelphia—Continued*

For Complete List of Firm Personnel, See General Section

For full biographical listings, see the Martindale-Hubbell Law Directory

BOLGER PICKER HANKIN & TANNENBAUM (AV)

12th Floor, 1800 Kennedy Boulevard, 19103
Telephone: 215-561-1000
Facsimile: 215-564-2127
Cherry Hill, New Jersey Office: One Cherry Hill, One Mall Drive, Suite 801.
Telephone: 609-482-7000.
FAX: 609-482-9410.

MEMBERS OF FIRM

Bennett G. Picker
Elliot S. Gerson
Arthur W. Hankin
Carl S. Tannenbaum
Mark S. Blaskey
Terri N. Gelberg
B. Christopher Lee
David N. Zeehandelaar
Ellen Rosen Rogoff
Julia B. Fisher
E. David Chanin

ASSOCIATES

Jonathan F. Bloom
Karen Schecter Dayno
Kurt E. Kramer
Adam M. Share
Elaine D. Solomon
Kathy E. Herman
Patricia R. Kalla
Eric J. Pritchard
Jeffrey S. Brenner (Resident, Cherry Hill, New Jersey Office)
Susan J. Khantzian
Michael J. Revness

COUNSEL

Robert V. Bolger, II

OF COUNSEL

Elwood S. Levy
Neal S. Grabell
William M. Marutani

For full biographical listings, see the Martindale-Hubbell Law Directory

BUCHANAN INGERSOLL, PROFESSIONAL CORPORATION (AV)

Two Logan Square Twelfth Floor, 18th & Arch Streets, 19103
Telephone: 215-665-8700
Telecopier: 215-569-2066
Pittsburgh, Pennsylvania Office: 5800 USX Tower, 600 Grant Street.
Telephone: 412-562-8800.
Harrisburg, Pennsylvania Office: Vartan Parc, 30 North Third Street.
Telephone: 717-237-4800.
Tampa, Florida Office: 101 East Kennedy Boulevard, Suite 1030.
Telephone: 813-222-8180.
North Miami Beach, Florida Office: 19495 Biscayne Boulevard.
Telephone: 305-933-5600.
Lexington, Kentucky Office: 1210 Vine Center Office Tower, 333 West Vine Street.
Telephone: 606-225-5333.
Princeton, New Jersey Office: Buchanan Ingersoll, A Partnership, College Centre, 500 College Road East.
Telephone: 609-452-2666.

George F. Nagle

Nancy Sabol Frantz
Robert W. Scott

For Complete List of Firm Personnel, See General Section

For full biographical listings, see the Martindale-Hubbell Law Directory

COZEN AND O'CONNOR, A PROFESSIONAL CORPORATION (AV)

1900 Market Street, 19103
Telephone: 215-665-2000
800-523-2900
Telecopier: 215-665-2013
Charlotte, North Carolina Office: One First Union Plaza, 28202.
Telephones: 704-376-3400; 800-762-3575.
Telecopier: 704-334-3351.
Columbia, South Carolina Office: Suite 200 The Palmetto Center, 1426 Main Street.
Telephones: 803-799-3900; 800-338-1117.
Telecopier: 803-254-7233.
Dallas, Texas Office: Suite 4100, NationsBank Plaza, 901 Main Street.
Telephones: 214-761-6700; 800-448-1207.
Telecopier: 214-761-6788.
New York, N.Y. Office: 45 Broadway Atrium.
Telephones: 212-509-9400; 800-437-9400.
Telecopier: 212-509-9492.
San Diego, California Office: Suite 1610, 501 West Broadway.
Telephones: 619-234-1700; 800-782-3366.
Telecopier: 619-234-7831.
Seattle, Washington Office: Suite 5200, Washington Mutual Tower, 1201 Third Avenue.
Telephones: 206-340-1000; 800-423-1950.
Telecopier: 206-621-8783.
Westmont, New Jersey Office: 316 Haddon Avenue.
Telephones: 609-854-4900; 800-523-2900.
Telecopier: 609-854-1782.

(See Next Column)

FIRM MEMBERS IN PHILADELPHIA

Stephen A. Cozen
Ronald H. Isenberg
Burton K. Stein
Thomas C. Zielinski
Robert W. Hayes
Richard C. Bennett
Douglas B. Lang
Lewis A. Grafman
Huey P. Cotton
Kathie D. King
Marcy C. Panzer
Gregg F. Carpene

FIRM ASSOCIATES IN PHILADELPHIA

Kevin M. Apollo
James E. Brown
Martin P. Duffey
Joseph P. Fenlin

Representative Clients: Available upon request.

For Complete List of Firm Personnel, See General Section

For full biographical listings, see the Martindale-Hubbell Law Directory

BERNARD G. HEINZEN, LTD. (AV)

Suite 2500, One Liberty Place, 1650 Market Street, 19103
Telephone: 215-988-0290
Telex: 834615 HQPHA
Telecopier: 215-851-1420

Bernard G. Heinzen

For full biographical listings, see the Martindale-Hubbell Law Directory

KELLEY, JASONS, MCGUIRE & SPINELLI (AV)

Suite 1300, 1234 Market Street, 19107-3713
Telephone: 215-854-0658
Fax: 215-854-8434
Cherry Hill, New Jersey Office: 1230 Brace Road, 08034.
Telephone: 609-429-8956.
Wilmington, Delaware Office: 1220 Market Building, P.O. Box 194, 19899.
Telephone: 302-652-8560.
Fax: 302-652-8405.

MEMBERS OF FIRM

John Patrick Kelley
Catherine N. Jasons
Joseph W. McGuire
Armand J. Della Porta, Jr.
Christopher N. Santoro
Robert N. Spinelli
Thomas P. Hanna
Thomas J. Johanson
Michael L. Turner

ASSOCIATES

Kelly J. Sasso (Resident, Wilmington, Delaware Office)
Richard L. Walker, II
Bernard E. Kueny, III
Timothy McGowan
Neal C. Glenn

OF COUNSEL

Joseph P. Green
Matthew D. Blum, M.D.

For full biographical listings, see the Martindale-Hubbell Law Directory

KLEHR, HARRISON, HARVEY, BRANZBURG & ELLERS (AV)

1401 Walnut Street, 19102
Telephone: 215-568-6060
Fax: 215-568-6603
Cherry Hill, New Jersey Office: Colwick-Suite 200, 51 Haddonfield Road.
Telephone: 609-486-7900.
Fax: 609-486-4875.
Allentown, Pennsylvania Office: Roma Corporate Center, Suite 501, 1605 North Cedar Crest Boulevard.
Telephone: 215-432-1803.
Fax: 215-433-4031.
Wilmington, Delaware Office: 222 Delaware Avenue, Suite 1101.
Telephone: 302-426-1189.
Fax: 302-426-9193.

MEMBERS OF FIRM

Morton R. Branzburg
William A. Harvey
Leonard M. Klehr
Joan R. Sheak (Resident, Allentown Office)
Rona J. Rosen
Rosetta B. Packer
Alan M. Rosen
Carol Ann Slocum (Resident, Cherry Hill, New Jersey Office)
William R. Thompson
Jeffrey Kurtzman
Michael K. Coran
Jill E. Jachera

ASSOCIATES

Stewart Paley
Abbe F. Fletman
John Keenan Fiorillo
Marjorie Ann Thomas
Richard M. Beck
Michael J. Cordone
Mindy Friedman
Livingstone J. Johnson
Daniel J. O'Rourke
Shahan G. Teberian

For Complete List of Firm Personnel, See General Section

For full biographical listings, see the Martindale-Hubbell Law Directory

MAGER LIEBENBERG & WHITE (AV)

Two Penn Center, Suite 415, 19102
Telephone: 215-569-6921
Telecopier: 215-569-6931

MEMBERS OF FIRM

Carol A. Mager
Roberta D. Liebenberg
Ann D. White

ASSOCIATES

Matthew D. Baxter
Brett M. L. Blyshak
Michael J. Salmanson
W. Scott Magargee
Nancy F. DuBoise

OF COUNSEL

Anna M. Durbin

For full biographical listings, see the Martindale-Hubbell Law Directory

Philadelphia—Continued

MANN, UNGAR & SPECTOR, P.A. (AV)

1709 Spruce Street, 19103
Telephone: 215-732-3120
Fax: 215-790-1366

Theodore R. Mann
Barry E. Ungar
Larry H. Spector
Janet Stern Holcombe
Marc J. Zucker
Sharon C. Weinman
Carol J. Sulcoski
John C. Ungar

For full biographical listings, see the Martindale-Hubbell Law Directory

McKISSOCK & HOFFMAN, P.C. (AV)

1700 Market Street, Suite 3000, 19103
Telephone: 215-246-2100
Fax: 215-246-2144
Mount Holly, New Jersey Office: 211 High Street.
Telephone: 609-267-1006.
Doylestown, Pennsylvania Office: 77 North Broad Street, Second Floor.
Telephone: 215-345-4501.
Harrisburg, Pennsylvania Office: 127 State Street.
Telephone: 717-234-0103.

J. Bruce McKissock
Peter J. Hoffman
Richard L. McMonigle
Jill Baratz Clarke
Marybeth Stanton Christiansen
Catherine Hill Kunda
Bryant Craig Black (Resident, Harrisburg, Office)
John M. Willis
John J. McGrath
Debra Schwaderer Dunne
Donald J. Brooks, Jr.
William J. Mundy
Elizabeth E. Davies
Christopher Thomson
Kathleen M. Kenna
K. Reed Haywood
Sara J. Thomson
Maureen P. Fitzgerald
Veronica E. Noonan
Kathleen M. Sholette
Patricia D. Shippee

For full biographical listings, see the Martindale-Hubbell Law Directory

JOHN W. MORRIS (AV)

One Penn Square West, Suite 1300, 19102
Telephone: 215-569-5154
Fax: 215-569-2862

For full biographical listings, see the Martindale-Hubbell Law Directory

MOSER & MOSER (AV Ⓣ)

1822 Spring Garden Street, 19130
Telephone: 215-564-7649
New York, N.Y. Office: 50 Broadway.
Telephone: 212-344-4200.
Telecopier: 212-635-5470.
Albany, N.Y. Office: 126 State Street.
Telephone: 518-449-4643.
Washington, D.C. Office: 1000 Connecticut Avenue, N.W.
Telephone: 202-857-8450.

MEMBERS OF FIRM

Alexander S. Moser (Not admitted in PA)
Joel H. Moser
Jonathan A. Ballan (Not admitted in PA)
Janet S. Kaplan (Not admitted in PA)

ASSOCIATES

Charles H. Wasser (Not admitted in PA)
Karen J. Marsico (Not admitted in PA)
Elaine H. Neumann (Not admitted in PA)

For full biographical listings, see the Martindale-Hubbell Law Directory

PATTERSON & WEIR (AV)

Suite 1200, Land Title Building, 100 South Broad Street, 19110
Telephone: 215-665-8181
Telefax: 215-665-8464
Westmont, New Jersey Office: 216 Haddon Avenue, Suite 704, Sentry Office Plaza, 08108.
Telephone: 609-858-6100.
Telefax: 609-858-4606.

MEMBERS OF FIRM

Walter Weir, Jr.
Paul A. Patterson
Brent S. Gorey
Daniel S. Bernheim, III
Mark E. Herrera (Resident, Westmont, New Jersey Office)

ASSOCIATES

David J. Toll
Susan Verbonitz
Robert D. Sayre
Jonathan J. Bart
Scott C. Pyfer (Resident, Westmont, New Jersey Office)
Lee Ann M. Williams, Jr
Douglas J. McGill
Harry J. Giacometti

For full biographical listings, see the Martindale-Hubbell Law Directory

LAWRENCE S. ROSENWALD, P.C. (AV)

Suite 3901, Mellon Bank Center, 1735 Market Street, 19103-7501
Telephone: 215-994-1401
Fax: 215-994-1410

Lawrence S. Rosenwald

OF COUNSEL

Peter A. Galante
Gary M. Friedland

LEGAL SUPPORT PERSONNEL

Gretchen A. Anderson

Representative Clients: Hobart Corp.; Simkar Manufacturing; Siemens Corp.; Magnetek General Neon Equipment co.; LVI Environmental; Advanced Product Development, Inc.; LCOR.

For full biographical listings, see the Martindale-Hubbell Law Directory

SAMUEL AND BALLARD, A PROFESSIONAL CORPORATION (AV)

225 South 15th Street, Suite 1700, 19102
Telephone: 215-893-9990

Ralph David Samuel
Alice W. Ballard

OF COUNSEL

Babette Josephs

Shari Reed
Lynn Malmgren

For full biographical listings, see the Martindale-Hubbell Law Directory

SPECTOR GADON & ROSEN, ATTORNEYS AT LAW, P.C. (AV)

29th Floor, 1700 Market Street, 19103-3913
Telephone: 215-241-8888
Fax: 215-241-8844
Moorestown, New Jersey Office: Spector, Gadon & Rosen, P.C. 307 Fellowship Road. P.O. Box 550.
Telephone: 609-778-8100.
Fax: 609-722-5344.

Paul R. Rosen
Steven F. Gadon
Samuel L. Hirshland
Edward G. Fitzgerald, Jr.
Albert E. Janke, Jr.
Lary I. Zucker
James B. Kozloff
Niels Korup
Daniel J. Dugan
Alan H. Wallen

OF COUNSEL

Sanders D. Newman
Sidney Margulies

Leslie Beth Baskin
Jill M. Bellak
Debra Malone Berger
Christopher P. Flannery (Not admitted in PA)
Shona K. Gibson
Amy B. Goldstein
Jeffrey M. Goldstein
Robert L. Grundlock, Jr.
Jane E. Herman (Not admitted in PA)
Stanley Peter Jaskiewicz
Kenneth J. LaFiandra
Marilou Lombardi
Brooke Caroline Madonna
P. Dara Marcozzi
Bruce S. Marks
Ann Miller
Frank J. Perch, III
Steven J. Polansky
George M. Vinci, Jr.

For full biographical listings, see the Martindale-Hubbell Law Directory

TURNER & McDONALD, P.C. (AV)

1708 Locust Street, 19103
Telephone: 215-546-9700
Facsimile: 215-546-9712
Haverford, Pennsylvania Office: 355 Lancaster Avenue.
Telephone: 610-649-9600.
Haddonfield, New Jersey Office: 209 Haddon Avenue.
Telephone: 609-429-6022.
Fax: 609-429-0074.

Alan A. Turner
H. Graham McDonald

OF COUNSEL

Thomas B. Rutter
Steven R. Kanes

For full biographical listings, see the Martindale-Hubbell Law Directory

*PITTSBURGH,** Allegheny Co.

ADERSON, FRANK & STEINER, A PROFESSIONAL CORPORATION (AV)

2320 Grant Building, 15219
Telephone: 412-263-0500
Fax: 412-263-0565

Sanford M. Aderson
Mark S. Frank
Jay A. Blechman
Bruce F. Rudoy

For full biographical listings, see the Martindale-Hubbell Law Directory

Pittsburgh—Continued

APPLE AND APPLE, A PROFESSIONAL CORPORATION (AV)

4650 Baum Boulevard, 15213
Telephone: 412-682-1466; 800-477-APPLE
Fax: 412-682-3138

Marvin J. Apple
James R. Apple

Charles F. Bennett
Joel E. Hausman
James S. Alter
Marylouise Wagner

Representative Clients: Boron Oil; N.A.C.M.; Associates Commercial Corp.; Hartford Insurance; Conrail; American Refinery; WRS Motion Picture and Video Laboratory.

For full biographical listings, see the Martindale-Hubbell Law Directory

BABST, CALLAND, CLEMENTS AND ZOMNIR, A PROFESSIONAL CORPORATION (AV)

Two Gateway Center, 15222
Telephone: 412-394-5400
Fax: 412-394-6576
Philadelphia, Pennsylvania Office: The Curtis Center, Suite 1100, Sixth and Walnut Streets.
Telephone: 215-627-3056.
Fax: 215-627-3042.

Frank J. Clements
Kenneth R. Bruce
James A. Escovitz
Ronald W. Frank
Michele M. Gutman
Robert A. King
J. Frank McKenna, III
James W. Ummer
Ted Wesolowski

Sara M. Antol
Albert Bates, Jr. IV
John W. Bruni
James V. Corbelli
Kevin K. Douglass
Christian A. Farmakis
Jan L. Fox
Edward B. Gentilcore
Laura Schleich Irwin
D. Matthew Jameson III
Bruce D. Knapp
Anne E. Mulgrave
Sandra M. Renwand
Frances Ann Ross-Ray
Jessica Lieber Smolar
Bruce E. Stanley
Timothy C. Wolfson

For full biographical listings, see the Martindale-Hubbell Law Directory

BERNSTEIN AND BERNSTEIN, A PROFESSIONAL CORPORATION (AV)

1133 Penn Avenue, 15222
Telephone: 412-456-8100
Facsimile: 412-456-8135
Harrisburg, Pennsylvania Office: 204 State Street.
Telephone: 717-233-1000.
Fax: 717-233-8290.

Joseph J. Bernstein
Robert S. Bernstein
Nicholas D. Krawec
Hollie A. Bernstein

Charles E. Bobinis
David Lingenfelter

Reference: Integra Bank.

For full biographical listings, see the Martindale-Hubbell Law Directory

BUCHANAN INGERSOLL, PROFESSIONAL CORPORATION (AV)

5800 USX Tower, 600 Grant Street, 15219
Telephone: 412-562-8800
Telecopier: 412-562-1041
Philadelphia, Pennsylvania Office: Two Logan Square, Twelfth Floor, 18th & Arch Streets.
Telephone: 215-665-8700.
Harrisburg, Pennsylvania Office: Vartan Parc, 30 North Third Street.
Telephone: 717-237-4800.
Tampa, Florida Office: 101 East Kennedy Boulevard, Suite 1030.
Telephone: 813-222-8180.
North Miami Beach, Florida Office: 19495 Biscayne Boulevard.
Telephone: 305-933-5600.
Lexington, Kentucky Office: 1210 Vine Center Office Tower, 333 West Vine Street.
Telephone: 606-225-5333.
Princeton, New Jersey Office: Buchanan Ingersoll, A Partnership, College Centre, 500 College Road East.
Telephone: 609-452-2666.

Bruce A. Americus
Ronald Basso
A. Bruce Bowden
Sheryl Atkinson Clark
Carl A. Cohen
Lewis U. Davis, Jr.
Robert G. Devlin
Michael J. Flinn
Carole C. Gori
Stephen W. Johnson
William J. McCormick
Carl E. Rothenberger, Jr.
Thomas M. Thompson
Thomas L. VanKirk

SENIOR ATTORNEY

Gary R. Walker

(See Next Column)

Thomas G. Buchanan
Frances Magovern O'Connor
Ronald W. Schuler
Mark G. Stall
Deborah B. Walrath

For Complete List of Firm Personnel, See General Section

For full biographical listings, see the Martindale-Hubbell Law Directory

CAMPBELL & LEVINE (AV)

3100 Grant Building, 15219
Telephone: 412-261-0310
Fax: 412-261-5066

MEMBERS OF FIRM

Douglas A. Campbell
Stanley E. Levine
David P. Braun
David B. Salzman

ASSOCIATES

Roger M. Bould
Philip E. Milch

For full biographical listings, see the Martindale-Hubbell Law Directory

DEFOREST & KOSCELNIK (AV)

3000 Koppers Building, 436 Seventh Avenue, 15219
Telephone: 412-227-3100
Fax: 412-227-3130

Walter P. DeForest, III
Jacqueline A. Koscelnik

Representative Clients: Carnegie Mellon University; Blue Cross of Western Pennsylvania; Ohio Valley Medical Center; Cox Enterprises, Inc.; Shamrock Broadcasting, Inc.; General Electric Co.

For full biographical listings, see the Martindale-Hubbell Law Directory

GACA, MATIS & HAMILTON, A PROFESSIONAL CORPORATION (AV)

300 Four PPG Place, 15222-5404
Telephone: 412-338-4750
Fax: 412-338-4742

Giles J. Gaca
Thomas A. Matis
Mark R. Hamilton
John W. Jordan, IV
Alan S. Baum
Thomas P. McGinnis
Bernard R. Rizza
Jeffrey A. Ramaley
Stephen J. Dalesio
John Timothy Hinton, Jr.
Shawn Lynne Reed

LEGAL SUPPORT PERSONNEL

PARALEGALS

Tina M. Shanafelt
Jill M. Peterson

For full biographical listings, see the Martindale-Hubbell Law Directory

LITMAN LITMAN HARRIS & BROWN, P.C. (AV)

3600 One Oxford Centre, 15219
Telephone: 412-456-2000
Fax: 412-456-2020

S. David Litman, P.C.
Roslyn M. Litman
Stephen J. Harris
David R. Brown
Martha S. Helmreich
Lester G. Nauhaus
Daniel L. Chunko
Mark F. Flaherty
Joseph Leibowicz
Robert J. O'Hara, III

For full biographical listings, see the Martindale-Hubbell Law Directory

MARCUS & SHAPIRA (AV)

35th Floor, One Oxford Centre, 301 Grant Street, 15219-6401
Telephone: 412-471-3490
Telecopier: 412-391-8758

MEMBERS OF FIRM

Bernard D. Marcus
Daniel H. Shapira
George P. Slesinger
Robert L. Allman, II
Estelle F. Comay
Susan Gromis Flynn
Darlene M. Nowak
Glenn M. Olcerst
Elly Heller-Toig
Sylvester A. Beozzo

OF COUNSEL

John M. Burkoff

SPECIAL COUNSEL

Jane Campbell Moriarty

ASSOCIATES

Scott D. Livingston
Robert M. Barnes
Stephen S. Zubrow
David B. Rodes
Lori E. McMaster
Melody A. Pollock
James F. Rosenberg
Amy M. Gottlieb

For full biographical listings, see the Martindale-Hubbell Law Directory

Pittsburgh—Continued

MARKEL, SCHAFER P.C. (AV)

1120 Grant Building, 15219
Telephone: 412-281-6488
Fax: 412-281-3226

Seymour J. Schafer
Harvey I. Goldstein
Kenneth A. Eisner
Steven D. Irwin
Jacob A. Markel (1896-1976)
Myron B. Markel (1934-1988)
Gertrude F. Markel (Retired)

OF COUNSEL

Nathan Hershey

Reference: Pittsburgh National Bank.

For full biographical listings, see the Martindale-Hubbell Law Directory

RILEY, MCNULTY & HEWITT, P.C. (AV)

460 Cochran Road, 15228
Telephone: 412-341-9300
Fax: 412-341-9177

Patrick R. Riley
Sibyl S. McNulty
Patrick A. Hewitt

David E. Sweitzer

For full biographical listings, see the Martindale-Hubbell Law Directory

THORP, REED & ARMSTRONG (AV)

One Riverfront Center, 15222
Telephone: 412-394-7711
Fax: 412-394-2555

MEMBERS OF FIRM

James D. Chiafullo
Edward B. Harmon
Thomas E. Lippard
Richard D. Rose
Edmund S. Ruffin, III
Ralph F. Scalera
David A. Scott
Timothy M. Slavish
Leonard F. Spagnolo
Michael J. Tomana

ASSOCIATES

Jeffrey J. Conn
Kimberly L. Wakim

SENIOR COUNSEL

William D. Sutton

OF COUNSEL

Stuart C. Gaul

For Complete List of Firm Personnel, See General Section

For full biographical listings, see the Martindale-Hubbell Law Directory

WEISMAN BOWEN & GROSS (AV)

310 Grant Street, Suite 420, 15219
Telephone: 412-566-2520
Fax: 412-566-1088

James L. Weisman
Alden Earl Bowen
Sanford P. Gross
Bradley S. Gelder
Barry J. Lipson
Christopher J. Klein
Laurel B. Diznoff
Robert L. Monks
Elliott I. Levenson

Reference: Pittsburgh National Bank.

For full biographical listings, see the Martindale-Hubbell Law Directory

WITTLIN GOLDSTON & CAPUTO, P.C. (AV)

213 Smithfield Street, Suite 200, 15222
Telephone: 412-261-4200
Telecopier: 412-261-9137

Charles E. Wittlin
Robert Simcox Adams
William L. Stang
Laurence R. Landis
John J. Franciscus

For Complete List of Firm Personnel, See General Section

For full biographical listings, see the Martindale-Hubbell Law Directory

*SCRANTON,** Lackawanna Co.

CHARITON & KEISER

(See Wilkes-Barre)

LEVY & PREATE (AV)

507 Linden Street, Suite 600, 18503
Telephone: 717-346-3816
FAX: 717-346-5370

MEMBERS OF FIRM

J. Julius Levy (1891-1978)
Ernest D. Preate
Robert A. Preate
William T. Jones

(See Next Column)

ASSOCIATE

Howard C. Terreri

OF COUNSEL

David B. Miller
David J. Tomaine
Harold M. Kane
Tullio De Luca

For full biographical listings, see the Martindale-Hubbell Law Directory

*WILKES-BARRE,** Luzerne Co.

CHARITON & KEISER (AV)

138 South Main Street, P.O. Box 220, 18703-0220
Telephone: 717-822-2929
Fax: 717-824-3580

Louis Shaffer (1904-1984)
Jerry B. Chariton
Larry S. Keiser

David E. Schwager
Keith Schweppenheiser

For full biographical listings, see the Martindale-Hubbell Law Directory

RHODE ISLAND

*PROVIDENCE,** Providence Co.

BLISH & CAVANAGH (AV)

Commerce Center, 30 Exchange Terrace, 02903
Telephone: 401-831-8900
Telecopier: 401-751-7542

MEMBERS OF FIRM

John H. Blish
Joseph V. Cavanagh, Jr.
William R. Landry
Michael DiBiase
Stephen J. Reid, Jr.

Karen A. Pelczarski
Raymond A. Marcaccio
Scott P. Tierney

Representative Clients: Providence Journal Co.; Fleet Financial Group; Rhode Island Hospital Trust National Bank; Allstate Insurance Co.; U-Haul International, Inc.; Delta Dental of Rhode Island; Gilbane Building Co.; Colony Communications; Providence Housing Authority.

For full biographical listings, see the Martindale-Hubbell Law Directory

DECOF & GRIMM, A PROFESSIONAL CORPORATION (AV)

One Smith Hill, 02903
Telephone: 401-272-1110
Facsimile: 401-351-6641
Newport, Rhode Island Office: 130 Bellevue Avenue, 02840.
Telephone: 401-848-5700.
Facsimile: 401-847-3391.

Leonard Decof
E. Paul Grimm
Mark B. Decof
John S. Foley
Vincent T. Cannon
Donna M. Di Donato
David Morowitz
Daniel J. Schatz
Howard B. Klein
Suzanne M. McGrath
Peri Ann Aptaker (Not admitted in RI)
Christine M. Renda (Not admitted in RI)

OF COUNSEL

Arthur I. Fixler

For full biographical listings, see the Martindale-Hubbell Law Directory

LISA & SOUSA, LTD. (AV)

5 Benefit Street, 02904
Telephone: 401-274-0600
Fax: 401-421-6117

Carl B. Lisa
Louis A. Sousa

OF COUNSEL

Robert G. Branca, Jr.

References: Citizens Savings Bank; Fleet National Bank; Rhode Island Hospital Trust National Bank.

For full biographical listings, see the Martindale-Hubbell Law Directory

WILLIAM T. MURPHY (AV)

The Calart Tower, 400 Reservoir Avenue, Suite 3L, 02907
Telephone: 401-461-7740
Telecopier: 401-461-7753

ASSOCIATE

Sean P. Lardner

Reference: Fleet National Bank.

For full biographical listings, see the Martindale-Hubbell Law Directory

SOUTH CAROLINA

*CHARLESTON,** Charleston Co.

BERNSTEIN & BERNSTEIN, P.A. (AV)

Maritime Building, 215 East Bay Street, Suite 203, P.O. Box 7, 29402-0007
Telephone: 803-723-3502
FAX: 803-723-3534

Charles S. Bernstein

Robert Alan Bernstein

For full biographical listings, see the Martindale-Hubbell Law Directory

BUIST, MOORE, SMYTHE & MCGEE, P.A. (AV)

Successors to Buist, Buist, Smythe and Smythe and Moore, Mouzon and McGee.
Five Exchange Street, P.O. Box 999, 29402
Telephone: 803-722-3400
Cable Address: "Conferees"
Telex: 57-6488
Telecopier: 803-723-7398
North Charleston, South Carolina Office: Atrium Northwood Office Building, 7301 Rivers Avenue, Suite 288. Zip: 29406-2859.
Telephone: 803-797-3000.
Telecopier: 803-863-5500.

Susan M. Smythe · Morris A. Ellison
W. Foster Gaillard · Charles P. Summerall, IV

Robert A. Kerr, Jr. · Patricia L. Quentel
Jeffrey A. Winkler · Robert H. Mozingo
Roger Edward George

Counsel for: CSX Transportation; NationsBank; Metropolitan Life Insurance Co.; E. I. du Pont de Nemours & Co.; AIG Aviation, Inc.; Lamorte, Burns & Co., Inc.; Allstate Insurance Co.; General Dynamics Corp.; Independent Life & Accident Insurance Co.; Georgia-Pacific Corp.

For Complete List of Firm Personnel, See General Section

For full biographical listings, see the Martindale-Hubbell Law Directory

*COLUMBIA,** Richland Co.

FINKEL, GOLDBERG, SHEFTMAN & ALTMAN, P.A. (AV)

Suite 1800, 1201 Main Street, P.O. Box 1799, 29202
Telephone: 803-765-2935
Fax: 803-252-0786
Charleston, South Carolina Office: 12 Exchange Street, P.O. Box 225.
Telephone: 803-577-5460.
Fax: 803-577-5135.

Gerald M. Finkel · Beverly J. Finkel

Representative Clients: Hewitt-Robins; 1st Union National Bank; Banc One Mortgage Co.; Motorola Communications & Electronics Corp.

For full biographical listings, see the Martindale-Hubbell Law Directory

ISAACS, ALLEY & HARVEY, L.L.P. (AV)

900 Elmwood Avenue, Suite 103, P.O. Box 8596, 29202-8596
Telephone: 803-252-6323
Telecopier: 803-779-5220

W. Joseph Isaacs

Representative Clients: NationsBank of South Carolina, N.A.; GATX Corporation; First Financial Corp.; Zurich-American Insurance Group; Wetterau Incorp.; Southland Log Homes, Inc.; Thompson Dental Co.; Dairymen Credit Union; Modern Exterminating, Inc.; Elizabeth Arden Co.; J.L. Todd Auction, Inc.; Continental Cards Co., Inc.; Norton-Senn Corporation; Eastern Flatbed Systems, Inc.; Valk Brokerage, Inc.; Snipes Electric, Inc.; The Loan Pros, Inc.; Palmetto Restorations, Inc.; Palmer & Cay/Carswell, Inc.; Plastitech Products, Inc.; Marek Brothers, Inc.; Ferillo & Associates, Inc.; Jacon Associates, Inc.; Blue Ridge Log Cabins, Inc.; Jones & Frank Corp.

For full biographical listings, see the Martindale-Hubbell Law Directory

MYRTLE BEACH, Horry Co.

STEVENS, STEVENS & THOMAS, P.C. (AV)

1215 48th Avenue North, 29577-2468
Telephone: 803-449-9675
Fax: 803-497-2262
Loris, South Carolina Office: 3341 Broad Street.
Telephone: 803-756-7652.
Fax: 803-756-3785.

(See Next Column)

James P. Stevens, Jr. (Resident, Loris Office) · J. Jackson Thomas

Angela T. Jordan (Resident Loris Office)

OF COUNSEL

James P. Stevens

For full biographical listings, see the Martindale-Hubbell Law Directory

*SPARTANBURG,** Spartanburg Co.

PERRIN, PERRIN, MANN & PATTERSON (AV)

200 Library Street, P.O. Box 1655, 29304
Telephone: 803-582-5461
Fax: 803-583-5235

L. W. Perrin (1918-1980)

OF COUNSEL

Edward P. Perrin

MEMBERS OF FIRM

Franklin M. Mann · Lawrence E. Flynn, Jr.
Dwight F. Patterson, Jr. · William O. Pressley, Jr.

General Counsel for: Carolina Cash Co.; Spartanburg Sanitary Sewer District.

For full biographical listings, see the Martindale-Hubbell Law Directory

TENNESSEE

*CHATTANOOGA,** Hamilton Co.

CHAMBLISS & BAHNER (AV)

1000 Tallan Building, Two Union Square, 37402-2500
Telephone: 615-756-3000
Fax: 615-265-9574

MEMBERS OF FIRM

William P. Aiken, Jr. · Bruce C. Bailey
William H. Pickering · Jay A. Young
David R. Evans · Donald J. Aho

ASSOCIATES

Benjamin Younger Pitts · S. Mark Turner
Anthony A. Jackson · Lori L. Smith

OF COUNSEL

Charles N. Jolly · William Crutchfield, Jr.

General Counsel for: McKee Foods Corporation; SCT Yarns, Inc.; Stein Construction Co., Inc.
Representative Clients: First American National Bank; Nations Bank of Chattanooga; Ford Motor Credit Company; General Motors Acceptance Corporation; BancBoston Financial Company; Provident National Assurance Company.

For Complete List of Firm Personnel, See General Section

For full biographical listings, see the Martindale-Hubbell Law Directory

KENNEDY, FULTON & KOONTZ (AV)

320 North Holtzclaw Avenue, 37404
Telephone: 615-622-4535
Facsimile: 615-622-4583

MEMBERS OF FIRM

Richard C. Kennedy · David J. Fulton
Jerrold D. Farinash

ASSOCIATE

James W. Clements, III

OF COUNSEL

Richard T. Klingler

For full biographical listings, see the Martindale-Hubbell Law Directory

SPEARS, MOORE, REBMAN & WILLIAMS (AV)

8th Floor Blue Cross Building, 801 Pine Street, 37402
Telephone: 615-756-7000
Facsimile: 615-756-4801

MEMBERS OF FIRM

Thomas S. Kale · F. Scott LeRoy
Fred Henry Moore · Harry L. Dadds, II

Counsel for: Pioneer Bank; Chattanooga Gas Co.; South Central Bell Telephone Co.; Tennessee-American Water Co.; Blue Cross and Blue Shield of Tennessee; State Farm Mutual Automobile Insurance Cos.; Nationwide Insurance Co.; Siskin Steel & Supply Co., Inc.; CSX Transportation, Inc.; The McCallie School; Mueller Co.

(See Next Column)

SPEARS, MOORE, REBMAN & WILLIAMS—*Continued*

For Complete List of Firm Personnel, See General Section

For full biographical listings, see the Martindale-Hubbell Law Directory

STOPHEL & STOPHEL, P.C. (AV)

500 Tallan Building, Two Union Square, 37402-2571
Telephone: 615-756-2333
Fax: 615-266-5032

Glenn C. Stophel
E. Stephen Jett
Harry B. Ray
C. Douglas Williams

Brian L. Woodward
James C. Heartfield
John W. Rose

Representative Clients: Deere Credit Services, Inc.; Browning-Ferris Industries, Inc.; The National Group, Inc.; Astec Industries, Inc.; Electric Systems, Inc.; Chattanooga Armature Works, Inc.; Richardson Electric, Inc.; BHY Concrete Finishing, Inc.; Diagnostic Imaging Consultants, Inc.; FirstAmerican National Bank.

For Complete List of Firm Personnel, See General Section

For full biographical listings, see the Martindale-Hubbell Law Directory

*KNOXVILLE,** Knox Co.

KENNERLY, MONTGOMERY & FINLEY, P.C. (AV)

Fourth Floor, NationsBank Center, 550 Main Avenue, P.O. Box 442, 37901-0442
Telephone: 615-546-7311
Fax: 615-524-1773

OF COUNSEL
Warren W. Kennerly

George D. Montgomery (1917-1985)
Robert A. Finley (1936-1990)
L. Anderson Galyon, III
Alexander M. Taylor
Jack M. Tallent, II
G. Wendell Thomas, Jr.
Ray J. Campbell, Jr. (1949-1986)
Steven E. Schmidt
Patti Jane Lay
Brian H. Trammell
C. Coulter Gilbert
Robert H. Green
William S. Lockett, Jr.
Rebecca Brake Murray
Robert Michael Shelor
James N. Gore, Jr.

SPECIAL COUNSEL
Jay Arthur Garrison

R. Hunter Cagle
Melody J. Bock
Rex A. Dale
Natasha K. Metcalf
Kenneth W. Ward
David Draper
James H. Price

Representative Clients: Knoxville Utilities Board; Aetna Casualty & Surety Co.; Allstate Insurance Co.; CNA Insurance Group; CIGNA Insurance; Nationwide Mutual Insurance Co.; Dow Chemical; Union Carbide; Westinghouse Electric Corp.; Mitsubishi International Corp.

For full biographical listings, see the Martindale-Hubbell Law Directory

MCCAMPBELL & YOUNG, A PROFESSIONAL CORPORATION (AV)

2021 Plaza Tower, P.O. Box 550, 37901-0550
Telephone: 615-637-1440
Telecopier: 615-546-9731

Herbert H. McCampbell, Jr. (1905-1974)
F. Graham Bartlett (1920-1982)
Robert S. Young
Lindsay Young
Robert S. Marquis
Robert S. Stone
J. Christopher Kirk
Mark K. Williams

Janie C. Porter
Gregory E. Erickson
R. Scott Elmore
Tammy Kaousias
Benét S. Theiss
Allen W. Blevins

Representative Clients: First National Bank of Knoxville; FNB Financial Corp.; First Tennessee Bank National Association; Third National Bank; Zellweger Uster, Inc.; Becromal of America, Inc.; Knoxville Orthopedic Clinic, P.A.; Knoxville Radiological Group Associated; Garland Coal Co.; Sun Coal Company (Sun Company).

For full biographical listings, see the Martindale-Hubbell Law Directory

*MEMPHIS,** Shelby Co.

ARMSTRONG ALLEN PREWITT GENTRY JOHNSTON & HOLMES (AV)

80 Monroe Avenue Suite 700, 38103
Telephone: 901-523-8211
Telecopier: 901-524-4936
Jackson, Missipi Office: 1350 One Jackson Place, 188 East Capitol Street.
Telephone: 601-948-8020.
Telecopier: 601-948-8389.

(See Next Column)

MEMBERS OF FIRM

Thomas W. Bell, Jr.
William A. Carson, II
James B. McLaren, Jr.
Charles R. Crawford
David A. Thornton
Nathaniel L. Prosser

H. Tucker Dewey

For Complete List of Firm Personnel, See General Section

For full biographical listings, see the Martindale-Hubbell Law Directory

*NASHVILLE,** Davidson Co.

ADAMS & WHITEAKER, P.C. (AV)

444 James Robertson Parkway, 37219
Telephone: 615-726-0900
Telecopier: 615-256-3634

Alfred T. Adams (1898-1982)
Alfred T. Adams, Jr.
R. C. Whiteaker, Jr.

Worrick G. Robinson, IV

Representative Clients: BellSouth Advertising & Publishing Corp.; Gale, Smith & Company, Inc.; BellSouth Telecommunications, Inc.; Enco Materials, Inc.
References: Sovran Bank; First American Bank, N.A.

For full biographical listings, see the Martindale-Hubbell Law Directory

MANIER, HEROD, HOLLABAUGH & SMITH, A PROFESSIONAL CORPORATION (AV)

First Union Tower 2200 One Nashville Place, 150 Fourth Avenue North, 37219-2494
Telephone: 615-244-0030
Telecopier: 615-242-4203

Will R. Manier, Jr. (1885-1953)
Larkin E. Crouch (1882-1948)
Vincent L. Fuqua, Jr. (1930-1974)
J. Olin White (1907-1982)
Miller Manier (1897-1986)
William Edward Herod (1917-1992)
Lewis B. Hollabaugh
Don L. Smith
James M. Doran, Jr.
Stephen E. Cox
J. Michael Franks
Randall C. Ferguson
Terry L. Hill
James David Leckrone
Robert C. Evans
Tommy C. Estes
B. Gail Reese
Michael E. Evans
Laurence M. Papel
John M. Gillum
Gregory L. Cashion
Sam H. Poteet, Jr.
Samuel Arthur Butts III
David J. Deming
Mark S. LeVan
Richard McCallister Smith
Mary Paty Lynn Jetton
H. Rowan Leathers III
Jefferson C. Orr
William L. Penny

Lawrence B. Hammet II
John H. Rowland
Susan C. West
John E. Quinn
John F. Floyd
Paul L. Sprader
Lela M. Hollabaugh
J. Steven Kirkham
T. Richard Travis
Stephanie M. Jennings
Jerry W. Taylor
C. Benton Patton
Kenneth A. Weber
Phillip Robert Newman
Brett A. Oeser

General Counsel for: McKinnon Bridge Co., Inc.

For full biographical listings, see the Martindale-Hubbell Law Directory

WHITE & REASOR (AV)

3305 West End Avenue, 37203
Telephone: 615-383-3345
Facsimile: 615-383-5534; 615-383-9390

MEMBERS OF FIRM

David J. White, Jr.
Charles B. Reasor, Jr.
Barrett B. Sutton, Jr.
John M. Baird
Dudley M. West
Van P. East, III
Steven L. West

For full biographical listings, see the Martindale-Hubbell Law Directory

TEXAS

*AMARILLO,** Potter Co.

GARNER, LOVELL & STEIN, P.C. (AV)

Amarillo National Plaza Two, 500 South Taylor, Suite 1200, 79101-2442
Telephone: 806-379-7111
Telecopier: 806-379-7176

(See Next Column)

GARNER, LOVELL & STEIN P.C., *Amarillo—Continued*

Robert E. Garner
John H. Lovell
Joe L. Lovell
Samuel Lee Stein
Brian T. Cartwright
Tim D. Newsom

Representative Clients: Panhandle Capitol Corporation; Friona Industries, Inc.; Amarillo National Bank; Caviness Packing Co.

For full biographical listings, see the Martindale-Hubbell Law Directory

HINKLE, COX, EATON, COFFIELD & HENSLEY (AV)

1700 Bank One Center, P.O. Box 9238, 79105-9238
Telephone: 806-372-5569
FAX: 806-372-9761
Roswell, New Mexico Office: 700 United Bank Plaza, P. O. Box 10, 88202.
Telephone: 505-622-6510.
FAX: 505-623-9332.
Midland, Texas Office: 6 Desta Drive, Suite 2800, P.O. Box 3580, 79702.
Telephone: 915-683-4691.
FAX: 915-683-6518.
Santa Fe, New Mexico Office: 218 Montezuma, P.O. Box 2068, 87504.
Telephone: 505-982-4554.
FAX: 505-982-8623.
Albuquerque, New Mexico Office: Suite 800, 500 Marquette, N.W., P.O. Box 2043, 87102.
Telephone: 505-768-1500.
FAX: 505-768-1529.
Austin, Texas Office: 401 West 15th Street, Suite 800, 78701.
Telephone: 512-476-7137.
FAX: 512-476-5431.
Associated Office: Hoffman & Stephens, P.C., 401 West 15th Street, Suite 800, 78701.
Telephone: 512-476-5434. Fax; 512-476-5431.

RESIDENT PARTNERS

Maston C. Courtney
Richard R. Wilfong
Jeffrey W. Hellberg
William F. Countiss
John C. Chambers

Representative Clients: Aerion Industries, Inc.; Amarillo Diagnostic Clinic; Amarillo Federal Credit Union; Amarillo Health Facilities Corp.; Amarillo National Bank; Chrysler Management Corp.; Conoco, Inc.; Federated Insurance; First Interstate Management Co.; Flowers Cattle Co.

For full biographical listings, see the Martindale-Hubbell Law Directory

*AUSTIN,** Travis Co.

BAKER & BOTTS, L.L.P. (AV)

1600 San Jacinto Center, 98 San Jacinto Boulevard, 78701
Telephone: 512-322-2500
Fax: 512-322-2501
Houston, Texas Office: One Shell Plaza, 910 Louisiana.
Telephone: 713-229-1234.
Dallas, Texas Office: 2001 Ross Avenue.
Telephone: 214-953-6500.
Washington, D.C. Office: The Warner, 1299 Pennsylvania Avenue, N.W.
Telephone: 202-639-7700.
New York, New York Office: 885 Third Avenue, Suite 2000.
Telephone: 212-705-5000.
Moscow, Russian Federation Office: 10 ul. Pushkinskaya, 103031.
Telephone: 7095/921-5300 (Local); 7501/929-7070 (International).

MEMBERS OF FIRM

Shelley W. Austin
William F. Stutts, Jr.

ASSOCIATE

Catherine M. Del Castillo

For Complete List of Firm Personnel, See General Section

For full biographical listings, see the Martindale-Hubbell Law Directory

DEITCH & HAMILTON, A PROFESSIONAL CORPORATION (AV)

301 Congress Avenue, Suite 1050, P.O. Box 1398, 78767
Telephone: 512-474-1554
Telecopy: 512-474-1579

Michael E. Deitch
Kendall D. Hamilton
Brian A. Turner

For full biographical listings, see the Martindale-Hubbell Law Directory

*BEAUMONT,** Jefferson Co.

REAUD, MORGAN & QUINN (AV)

801 Laurel, 77701
Telephone: 409-838-1000
Fax: 409-833-8236

MEMBERS OF FIRM

Wayne A. Reaud
Glen W. Morgan
Cris Quinn
Richard J. Clarkson
Bob Wortham

(See Next Column)

ASSOCIATES

Larry W. Thorpe
Keith F. Ellis
Suzanne Maltais

For full biographical listings, see the Martindale-Hubbell Law Directory

*DALLAS,** Dallas Co.

BAKER & BOTTS, L.L.P. (AV)

2001 Ross Avenue, 75201
Telephone: 214-953-6500
Fax: 214-953-6503
Houston, Texas Office: One Shell Plaza, 910 Louisiana.
Telephone: 713-229-1234.
Washington, D.C. Office: The Warner, 1299 Pennsylvania Avenue, N.W.
Telephone: 202-639-7700.
Austin, Texas Office: 1600 San Jacinto Center, 98 San Jacinto Boulevard.
Telephone: 512-322-2500.
New York, New York Office: 885 Third Avenue, Suite 2000.
Telephone: 212-705-5000.
Moscow, Russian Federation Office: 10 ul. Pushkinskaya, 103031.
Telephone: 7095/921-5300 (Local); 7095/929-7070.

MEMBERS OF FIRM

Richard C. Johnson
James A. Taylor
Karen Leslye Wolf
Kerry C. L. North
Andrew M. Baker
Jonathan W. Dunlay
Patricia M. Stanton
John W. Martin
Carlos A. Fierro
Geoffrey L. Newton

ASSOCIATES

Julie A. Gregory
Susan Nethery Hogan
Shelley LaGere
Tamara Gail Mattison
David G. Monk
Douglass Michael Rayburn
Brenda Levine Sutherland

For Complete List of Firm Personnel, See General Section

For full biographical listings, see the Martindale-Hubbell Law Directory

CALHOUN & STACY (AV)

5700 NationsBank Plaza, 901 Main Street, 75202-3747
Telephone: 214-748-5000
Telecopier: 214-748-1421
Telex: 211358 CALGUMP UR

Mark Alan Calhoun
David W. Elrod
Steven D. Goldston
Parker Nelson
Roy L. Stacy

ASSOCIATES

Shannon S. Barclay
Robert A. Bragalone
Dennis D. Conder
Jane Elizabeth Diseker
Lawrence I. Fleishman
Thomas C. Jones
Katherine Johnson Knight
V. Paige Pace
Veronika Willard
Michael C. Wright

LEGAL CONSULTANT

Rees T. Bowen, III

For full biographical listings, see the Martindale-Hubbell Law Directory

GODWIN & CARLTON, A PROFESSIONAL CORPORATION (AV)

Suite 3300, 901 Main Street, 75202-3714
Telephone: 214-939-4400
Telecopier: 214-760-7332
Monterrey, Mexico Correspondent: Quintero y Quintero Abogodos. Martin De Zalva 840-3 Sur Esquinna Con Hidalgo.
Telephone: 44-07-74, 44-07-80, 44-06-56, 44-06-28.
Fax: 83-40-34-54.

James G. Vetter, Jr.
David J. White
Bill R. Womble
Thomas E. Rosen
William F. Pyne
Daniel P. Callahan
Maurice J. Bates
Thomas S. Hoekstra

Rodney L. Hubbard
James L. Kissire

For Complete List of Firm Personnel, See General Section

For full biographical listings, see the Martindale-Hubbell Law Directory

HUGHES & LUCE, L.L.P. (AV)

A Registered Limited Liability Partnership including Professional Corporations
1717 Main Street, Suite 2800, 75201
Telephone: 214-939-5500
Fax: 214-939-6100
Telex: 730836
Austin, Texas Office: 111 Congress, Suite 900.
Telephone: 512-482-6800.
Fax: 512-482-6859.
Houston, Texas Office: Three Allen Center, 333 Clay Street, Suite 3800.
Telephone: 713-754-5200.
Fax: 713-754-5206.

(See Next Column)

HUGHES & LUCE L.L.P.—*Continued*

Fort Worth, Texas Office: 2421 Westport Parkway, Suite 500A.
Telephone: 817-439-3000.
Fax: 817-439-4222.

MEMBERS OF FIRM

Terrence M. Babilla
Alan J. Bogdanow
Kenneth G. Hawari
Glen J. Hettinger
David G. Luther, Jr.
William A. McCormack
Ross Clayton Mulford
Dudley W. Murrey
Charles M. Schwartz
Michael W. Tankersley

ASSOCIATES

Carol J. Biondo
Ellen J. Curnes
Ethan K. Knowlden
Jon L. Mosle III
David A. Wood

For Complete List of Firm Personnel, See General Section

For full biographical listings, see the Martindale-Hubbell Law Directory

JOHNSTON & BUDNER, A PROFESSIONAL CORPORATION (AV)

3700 First Interstate Bank Tower, 1445 Ross Avenue, 75202
Telephone: 214-855-6260
Fax: 214-855-6248

Bruce A. Budner
Coyt Randal Johnston
Stephanie L. Spardone
Robert L. Tobey

For full biographical listings, see the Martindale-Hubbell Law Directory

OLSON, GIBBONS, SARTAIN, NICOUD, BIRNE & SUSSMAN, L.L.P. (AV)

2600 Lincoln Plaza, 500 North Akard, 75201-3320
Telephone: 214-740-2600
Fax: 214-740-2601

Dennis O. Olson
Mark L. Gibbons
Charles W. Sartain
Robert M. Nicoud, Jr.
Robert E. Birne
Ronald L. Sussman

For full biographical listings, see the Martindale-Hubbell Law Directory

PALMER, ALLEN & MCTAGGART, L.L.P. (AV)

A Partnership including Professional Corporations
1900 St. Paul Place, 750 North St. Paul Street, 75201
Telephone: 214-969-0069
Telecopy: 214-720-0104
Austin, Texas Office: 6505 Lohmann's Crossing (Lago Vista).
Telephone: 512-267-1993. Mailing Address: P.O. Box 4345, Lago Vista, Texas, 78645.

Steven G. Palmer (P.C.)
Joe B. Allen III
Robert D. McTaggart (P.C.)
Guy Myrph Foote, Jr., (P.C.)
Brian G. Dicus (P.C.)

OF COUNSEL

Robert S. Leithiser (P.C.)
Dick P. Wood, Jr., (P.C.)

For full biographical listings, see the Martindale-Hubbell Law Directory

*FORT WORTH,** Tarrant Co.

RUSSELL, TURNER, LAIRD & JONES, L.L.P. (AV)

One Colonial Place, 2400 Scott Avenue, 76103-2200
Telephone: 817-531-3000; 1-800-448-2889
Fax: 817-535-3046
Dallas, Texas Office: Williams Square, Central Tower, Suite 700, 5215 North O'Connor Boulevard, Las Colinas Urban Center.
Telephone: 214-444-0444; 1-800-448-2889.

Wm. Greg Russell
Randall E. Turner
Steven C. Laird
Gregory G. Jones

For full biographical listings, see the Martindale-Hubbell Law Directory

*HOUSTON,** Harris Co.

BAKER & BOTTS, L.L.P. (AV)

One Shell Plaza, 910 Louisiana, 77002
Telephone: 713-229-1234
Cable Address: "Boterlove"
Fax: 713-229-1522
Washington, D.C. Office: The Warner, 1299 Pennsylvania Avenue, N.W.
Telephone: 202-639-7700.
New York, New York Office: 885 Third Avenue, Suite 2000.
Telephone: 212-705-5000.
Austin, Texas Office: 1600 San Jacinto Center, 98 San Jacinto Boulevard.
Telephone: 512-322-2500.
Dallas, Texas Office: 2001 Ross Avenue.
Telephone: 214-953-6500.
Moscow, Russian Federation Office: 10 ul. Pushkinskaya, 103031.
Telephone: 7095/921-5300 (Local); 7095/929-7070 (International).

(See Next Column)

MEMBERS OF FIRM

Moulton Goodrum, Jr.
Robert L. Stillwell
James D. Randall
John M. Huggins
Thad T. Hutcheson, Jr.
Michael S. Moehlman
Frank W. R. Hubert, Jr.
Lewis Proctor Thomas, III
Wade H. Whilden
James L. Leader
Roy L. Nolen
John P. Cogan, Jr.
J. Patrick Garrett
David Alan Burns
Fred H. Dunlop
Joseph A. Cialone, II
R. Joel Swanson
Rufus Cormier, Jr.
Walter J. Smith
C. Michael Watson
Stephen A. Massad
Charles Szalkowski
Robert P. Wright
Marley Lott
Joe S. Poff
Pamela B. Ewen
J. David Kirkland, Jr.
Louise A. Shearer
Paul B. Landen
Gene J. Oshman
Margo S. Scholin
David F. Asmus
Darrell W. Taylor
Kenneth S. Culotta
Joshua Davidson

ASSOCIATES

Frederick William Backus
Marian L. Brancaccio
Richard A. Brooks
Karen Skeens Caldwell
William R. Caldwell
Janet Chambers
Shane Robert DeBeer
Jennifer J. De La Rosa
Victoria Donnenberg
Katherine P. Ellis
Nicolas J. Evanoff
Brian P. Fenske
Nancy E. Field
John D. Geddes
Mary Millwood Gregory
Elizabeth M. Guffy
Sten L. Gustafson
Bill Hart, Jr.
Henry Havre
Marjorie A. Hirsch
Rosalind M. Lawton
Victoria V. Lazar
Jennifer S. McGinty
Peter M. Oxman
Theodore William Paris
James LeGrand Read
Kelly Brunetti Rose
Richard S. Roth
Carol L. St. Clair
Jeffrey Alan Schlegel
W. Lance Schuler
Nancy E. Siegal
Timothy S. Taylor
Dahl C. Thompson
Diane T. Weber
Robert M. White

For Complete List of Firm Personnel, See General Section

For full biographical listings, see the Martindale-Hubbell Law Directory

EIKENBURG & STILES (AV)

1100 First City National Bank Building, 77002
Telephone: 713-652-2144
FAX: 713-655-6990

MEMBERS OF FIRM

John J. Eikenburg
R. Charles Stiles
John F. Rhem, Jr.
John R. Jones

ASSOCIATES

Donald Michael Stull
David J. Elliott
Cheryle R. Johnston

OF COUNSEL

Neil R. Mitchell

Reference: First City National Bank.

For full biographical listings, see the Martindale-Hubbell Law Directory

FARNSWORTH & VONBERG (AV)

A Partnership of Professional Corporations
333 North Sam Houston Parkway, Suite 300, 77060
Telephone: 713-931-8902
Telecopy: 713-931-6032

T Brooke Farnsworth (P.C.)
Mary Frances vonBerg (P.C.)

ASSOCIATES

Diane B. Gould
Bennett S. Bartlett

LEGAL SUPPORT PERSONNEL

Lucille P. Poole

For full biographical listings, see the Martindale-Hubbell Law Directory

GIBBS & BRUNS, L.L.P. (AV)

1100 Louisiana, Suite 3400, 77002
Telephone: 713-650-8805
Fax: 713-750-0903

PARTNERS

Robin C. Gibbs
Phillip T. Bruns
J. Christopher Reynolds
Russell B. Starbird
Paul J. Dobrowski
Kathy D. Patrick
Jeffrey C. Alexander
Robert R. Burford

ASSOCIATES

Jennifer R. Tillison
Jean C. Frizzell
Grant Harvey
Michael Napoli
Barrett H. Reasoner
Robert J. Madden
Jeffry J. Cotner
Amanda B. Nathan
Jennifer Horan Greer

(See Next Column)

GIBBS & BRUNS L.L.P., *Houston—Continued*

OF COUNSEL

Debora D. Ratliff (Retired)

For full biographical listings, see the Martindale-Hubbell Law Directory

GILPIN, PAXSON & BERSCH (AV)

A Registered Limited Liability Partnership
1900 West Loop South, Suite 2000, 77027-3259
Telephone: 713-623-8800
Telecopier: 713-993-8451

MEMBERS OF FIRM

Gary M. Alletag
Timothy R. Bersch
Deborah J. Bullion
James L. Cornell, Jr.
George R. Diaz-Arrastia
Frank W. Gerold
John D. Gilpin
William T. Little
Darryl W. Malone
Michael W. McCoy
Michael J. Pappert
Stephen Paxson
Lionel M. Schooler
Mary E. Wilson
Kevin F. Risley

ASSOCIATES

Russell T. Abney
N. Terry Adams, Jr.
John W. Burchfield
Evan N. Kramer
Dale R. Mellencamp
P. Wayne Pickering
Susan M. Schwager

OF COUNSEL

Harless R. Benthul
Thomas F. Aubry

Representative Clients: Bank of America, N.A.; Charter Bancshares, Inc.; First Interstate Bank of Texas, N.A.; Greater Houston Builders Association; ICM Mortgage Corporation; Pulte Home Corporation; Texas Association of Builders; U.S. West, Inc.; Weekley Homes, Inc.

For full biographical listings, see the Martindale-Hubbell Law Directory

HARDY & JOHNS (AV)

500 Two Houston Center, 909 Fannin at McKinney, 77010
Telephone: 713-222-0381
Fax: 713-759-9650
Bay City, Texas Office: 2042 Avenue F.
Telephone: 409-245-3797.
Texas City, Texas Office: 3020 Palmer Highway.
Telephone: 409-945-0606.

G. P. Hardy, Jr. (1913-1988)
G. P. Hardy, III
Gail Johns

ASSOCIATES

Timothy M. Purcell
Mark G. Cypert
Gwen E. Richard
Patricia Haylon
Melissa Wolin

OF COUNSEL

Billie Pirner Garde

Reference: Bay City Bank & Trust.

For full biographical listings, see the Martindale-Hubbell Law Directory

SCHWARTZ & CAMPBELL, L.L.P. (AV)

1221 McKinney, Suite 1000, 77010
Telephone: 713-752-0017
Telecopier: 713-752-0327

Richard A. Schwartz
Marshall S. Campbell

Monica F. Oathout
Stephen A. Mendel
Samuel E. Dunn
Harold W. Hargis
Phillip W. Bechter
Laura M. Taylor
Michael D. Hudgins

LEGAL SUPPORT PERSONNEL

PARALEGALS

Nannette Koger
Bettye Vaughan Johnson
Lenore Chomout
Maria Pinillos

For full biographical listings, see the Martindale-Hubbell Law Directory

*MIDLAND,** Midland Co.

HINKLE, COX, EATON, COFFIELD & HENSLEY (AV)

6 Desta Drive, Suite 2800, P.O. Box 3580, 79702
Telephone: 915-683-4691
FAX: 915-683-6518
Roswell, New Mexico Office: 700 United Bank Plaza, P.O. Box 10.
Telephone: 505-622-6510.
FAX: 505-623-9332.
Amarillo, Texas Office: 1700 Bank One Center, P.O. Box 9238.
Telephone: 806-372-5569.
FAX: 806-372-9761.
Santa Fe, New Mexico Office: 218 Montezuma, P.O. Box 2068.
Telephone: 505-982-4554.
FAX: 505-982-8623.

(See Next Column)

Albuquerque, New Mexico Office: Suite 800, 500 Marquette, N.W., P.O. Box 2043.
Telephone: 505-768-1500.
FAX: 505-768-1529.
Austin, Texas Office: 401 West 15th Street, Suite 800, 78701.
Telephone: 512-476-7137.
FAX: 512-476-5431.
Associated Office: Hoffman & Stephens, P.C., 401 West 15th Street, Suite 800, 78701.
Telephone: 512-476-5434.
FAX: 512-476-5431.

RESIDENT PARTNERS

C. D. Martin
William B. Burford
Jeffrey D. Hewett
James M. Hudson

Representative Clients: Atlantic Richfield Co.; Bass Enterprises Production Co.; BHP Petroleum; Devon Energy Corp.; Exxon Corp.; Midland National Bank; Mitchell Energy Corp.; Mobil Exploration and Producing U.S. Inc.; NationsBank of Texas, N.A.; OXY USA, Inc.; Parker & Parsley Petroleum Co.; Texas National Bank of Midland.

For full biographical listings, see the Martindale-Hubbell Law Directory

*SAN ANTONIO,** Bexar Co.

TINSMAN & HOUSER, INC. (AV)

One Riverwalk Place, 14th Floor, 700 North St. Mary's Street, 78205
Telephone: 210-225-3121
Texas Wats: 1-800-292-9999
Fax: 210-225-6235

Richard Tinsman
Franklin D. Houser
Margaret M. Maisel
David G. Jayne
Robert C. Scott
Daniel J. T. Sciano
Rey Perez
Bernard Wm. Fischman
Sharon L. Cook
Christopher Pettit
Ronald J. Salazar
Sue Dodson

For full biographical listings, see the Martindale-Hubbell Law Directory

UTAH

*PROVO,** Utah Co.

HOWARD, LEWIS & PETERSEN, P.C. (AV)

Delphi Building, 120 East 300 North Street, P.O. Box 778, 84603
Telephone: 801-373-6345
Fax: 801-377-4991

Jackson Howard
Don R. Petersen
Craig M. Snyder
John L. Valentine
D. David Lambert
Fred D. Howard
Leslie W. Slaugh

Richard W. Daynes
Phillip E. Lowry
Kenneth Parkinson

OF COUNSEL

S. Rex Lewis

LEGAL SUPPORT PERSONNEL

Mary Jackson
John O. Sump
Ray Winger

For full biographical listings, see the Martindale-Hubbell Law Directory

*SALT LAKE CITY,** Salt Lake Co.

CALLISTER, NEBEKER & MCCULLOUGH, A PROFESSIONAL CORPORATION (AV)

800 Kennecott Building, 84133
Telephone: 801-530-7300
Telecopier: 801-364-9127

Louis H. Callister
Dorothy C. Pleshe
John A. Beckstead
Randall D Benson
George E. Harris, Jr.
John H. Rees

John B. Lindsay

Representative Clients: Zions First National Bank; Zions Credit Corporation; Chrysler Credit Corp.; Associates Commercial Corp.; Western Farm Credit Bank; Factor One Funding Resources.

For Complete List of Firm Personnel, See General Section

For full biographical listings, see the Martindale-Hubbell Law Directory

KIRTON & MCCONKIE, A PROFESSIONAL CORPORATION (AV)

1800 Eagle Gate Tower, 60 East South Temple, 84111
Telephone: 801-328-3600
Telecopier: 801-321-4893

(See Next Column)

Kirton & McConkie A Professional Corporation—*Continued*

Wilford W. Kirton, Jr.
Oscar W. McConkie, Jr.
Raymond W. Gee
Anthony I. Bentley, Jr.
J. Douglas Mitchell
Richard R. Neslen
Myron L. Sorensen
Robert W. Edwards
B. Lloyd Poelman
Raeburn G. Kennard
Jerry W. Dearinger
R. Bruce Findlay
Charles W. Dahlquist, II
M. Karlynn Hinman
Robert P. Lunt
Brinton R. Burbidge
Gregory S. Bell
Lee Ford Hunter
Larry R. White
William H. Wingo
David M. McConkie
Read R. Hellewell
Rolf H. Berger
Oscar W. McConkie, III
Marc Nick Mascaro
Lorin C. Barker
David M. Wahlquist
Robert S. Prince
Wallace O. Felsted
Merrill F. Nelson
Paul H. Matthews
Fred D. Essig
Clark B. Fetzer
Samuel D. McVey
Blake T. Ostler
Daniel Bay Gibbons
Gregory M. Simonsen
Von G. Keetch
Patrick Hendrickson
Stuart F. Weed
Thomas D. Walk
James E. Ellsworth
Daniel V. Goodsell
David J. Hardy
Randy T. Austin

For Complete List of Firm Personnel, See General Section

For full biographical listings, see the Martindale-Hubbell Law Directory

Parry Murray Ward & Moxley, A Professional Corporation (AV)

1270 Eagle Gate Tower, 60 East South Temple, 84111
Telephone: 801-521-3434
Fax: 801-521-3484

Douglas J. Parry
Kevin Reid Murray
Brent D. Ward
Paul T. Moxley

Cathleen Clark

Representative Clients: Zions First National Bank; Trammell Crow Co.; Monroc; Salt Lake County Water Conservancy District; Western Petroleum; Aloha Petroleum; Minit-Lube Franchisee Assoc.

For Complete List of Firm Personnel, See General Section

For full biographical listings, see the Martindale-Hubbell Law Directory

Ray, Quinney & Nebeker, A Professional Corporation (AV)

Suite 400 Deseret Building, 79 South Main Street, P.O. Box 45385, 84145-0385
Telephone: 801-532-1500
Telecopier: 801-532-7543
Provo, Utah Office: 210 First Security Bank Building, 92 North University Avenue.
Telephone: 801-226-7210.
Telecopier: 801-375-8379.

Don B. Allen
James L. Wilde (Resident at Provo)
Scott Hancock Clark
Allan T. Brinkerhoff
Douglas Matsumori
Richard G. Allen
Dee R. Chambers
Steven T. Waterman
Stephen C. Tingey

Cameron M. Hancock
Katie A. Eccles

Representative Clients: First Security Bank of Utah, N.A.; Borden, Inc.; Southern Pacific Transportation; Utah Power & Light Co.; Travelers Insurance Co.; Greyhound Leasing & Financial; Holy Cross Hospital and Health System; Amoco Production Co.

For Complete List of Firm Personnel, See General Section

For full biographical listings, see the Martindale-Hubbell Law Directory

Van Cott, Bagley, Cornwall & McCarthy, A Professional Corporation (AV)

Suite 1600, 50 South Main Street, P.O. Box 45340, 84145
Telephone: 801-532-3333
Telex: 453149
Telecopier: 801-534-0058
Ogden, Utah Office: Suite 900, 2404 Washington Boulevard.
Telephone: 801-394-5783.
Park City, Utah Office: 314 Main Street, Suite 205.
Telephone: 801-649-3889.
Reno, Nevada Office: Jeppson & Lee, 100 West Liberty, Suite 990.
Telephone: 702-333-6800.

(See Next Column)

David E. Salisbury
M. Scott Woodland
Stephen D. Swindle
Robert D. Merrill
William G. Fowler
Rand L. Cook
Thomas T. Billings
Thomas Berggren
Ervin R. Holmes
Guy P. Kroesche
Timothy W. Blackburn (Resident, Ogden, Utah Office)
Gerald H. Suniville
Clark K. Taylor
Keith L. Lee (Resident, Reno, Nevada Office)

OF COUNSEL

Leonard J. Lewis

Nathan W. Jones
Michele Ballantyne
Daniel P. McCarthy
Andrew S. Gabriel (Resident, Reno, Nevada Office)

For Complete List of Firm Personnel, See General Section

For full biographical listings, see the Martindale-Hubbell Law Directory

VERMONT

*BURLINGTON,** Chittenden Co.

Burak & Anderson (AV)

Executive Square, 346 Shelburne Street, P.O. Box 64700, 05406-4700
Telephone: 802-862-0500
Telecopier: 802-862-8176

MEMBERS OF FIRM

Michael L. Burak
David M. Hyman

ASSOCIATE

Brian J. Sullivan

For Complete List of Firm Personnel, See General Section

For full biographical listings, see the Martindale-Hubbell Law Directory

Gravel and Shea, A Professional Corporation (AV)

Corporate Plaza, 76 St. Paul Street, P.O. Box 369, 05402-0369
Telephone: 802-658-0220
Fax: 802-658-1456

Charles T. Shea
Stephen R. Crampton
Stewart H. McConaughy
William G. Post, Jr.
Craig Weatherly
James E. Knapp
John R. Ponsetto
Peter S. Erly
Margaret L. Montgomery

James L. Vana
Stephen P. Magowan

OF COUNSEL

Clarke A. Gravel

SPECIAL COUNSEL

Norman Williams

For Complete List of Firm Personnel, See General Section

For full biographical listings, see the Martindale-Hubbell Law Directory

Manchester Law Offices, Professional Corporation (AV)

One Lawson Lane, P.O. Box 1459, 05402-1459
Telephone: 802-658-7444
Fax: 802-658-2078

Robert E. Manchester
Patricia S. Orr

LEGAL SUPPORT PERSONNEL

LEGAL NURSE CONSULTANTS

Tina L Mulvey
Rosemeryl S. Harple
Maureen P. Tremblay

For full biographical listings, see the Martindale-Hubbell Law Directory

*ST. JOHNSBURY,** Caledonia Co.

Robert A. Gensburg (AV)

65 Railroad Street, P.O. Box 276, 05819
Telephone: 802-748-5338
Fax: 802-748-1673

For full biographical listings, see the Martindale-Hubbell Law Directory

VIRGINIA

ALEXANDRIA, (Independent City)

GRAD, LOGAN & KLEWANS, P.C. (AV)

112 North Columbus Street, P.O. Box 1417-A44, 22313
Telephone: 703-548-8400
Facsimile: 703-836-6289

John D. Grad
Michael P. Logan
Samuel N. Klewans

Sean C. E. McDonough
Claire R. Pettrone
David A. Damiani

OF COUNSEL

Jeanne F. Franklin

For full biographical listings, see the Martindale-Hubbell Law Directory

THOMAS, BALLENGER, VOGELMAN AND TURNER, P.C. (AV)

124 South Royal Street, 22314
Telephone: 703-836-3400
Fax: 703-836-3549

John M. Ballenger
Jeffrey A. Vogelman

References: First Union National Bank of Virginia; Burke & Herbert Bank & Trust Co.

For Complete List of Firm Personnel, See General Section

For full biographical listings, see the Martindale-Hubbell Law Directory

*FAIRFAX,** (Ind. City; Seat of Fairfax Co.)

ODIN, FELDMAN & PITTLEMAN, P.C. (AV)

9302 Lee Highway, Suite 1100, 22031
Telephone: 703-218-2100
Facsimile: 703-218-2160

James B. Pittleman
John S. Wisiackas
David J. Brewer
Thomas J. Shaughnessy
David A. Lawrence
Robert A. Hickey
Robert G. Nath
John P. Dedon
Lawrence A. Schultis

For Complete List of Firm Personnel, See General Section

For full biographical listings, see the Martindale-Hubbell Law Directory

RUST, RUST & SILVER, A PROFESSIONAL CORPORATION (AV)

4103 Chain Bridge Road Fourth Floor, P.O. Box 460, 22030
Telephone: 703-591-7000
Telecopier: 703-591-7336

John H. Rust, Jr.
Glenn H. Silver
C. Thomas Brown

James E. Kane
Paulo E. Franco, Jr.
Andrew W. White

RETIRED, EMERITUS

John H. Rust, Sr. (Retired)

Representative Clients: Crestar Bank; Commonwealth Land Title Insurance Co.; Patriot National Bank; Century Graphics Corp.

For full biographical listings, see the Martindale-Hubbell Law Directory

FREDERICKSBURG, (Independent City)

ROBERTS, SOKOL, ASHBY & JONES (AV)

(Member of the Commonwealth Law Group, Ltd.)
701 Kenmore Avenue, 22404-7166
Telephone: 703-373-3500
Telex: 151274389
Telecopier: 703-899-6394
Mailing Address: P.O. Box 7166, 22404-7166

MEMBERS OF FIRM

William M. Sokol
Russell H. Roberts
Kevin S. Jones
James Ashby, III
William E. Glover
Jeannie P. Dahnk

ASSOCIATES

Jennifer Lee Parrish
Tracy A. Houck

OF COUNSEL

Kenneth T. Whitescarver

General Counsel for: Mary Washington Hospital; The Free Lance-Star; Massaponax Building Components, Inc.; Pohanka Datsun Cadillac Oldsmobile; First Virginia Bank (Trust).

For full biographical listings, see the Martindale-Hubbell Law Directory

*MANASSAS,** Prince William Co.

ALLEN & HAROLD, P.L.C. (AV)

10610-A Crestwood Drive, P.O. Box 2126, 22110
Telephone: 703-361-2278
Facsimile: 703-361-0594
Washington, D.C. Office: Suite 200, 2000 L Street, N.W.
Telephone: 202-452-7872; 1-800-433-2636.
Telex: 373-0708.
Facsimile: 202-833-3843.
Shenandoah Valley Office: 5413 Main Street. Stephens City, Virginia 22655.
Telephone: 703-869-0040.
Fax: 703-869-0041.

Robert G. Allen
Douglas W. Harold, Jr.

Robert A. Harris, II

For full biographical listings, see the Martindale-Hubbell Law Directory

MCLEAN, Fairfax Co.

MICHAEL HORWATT & ASSOCIATES, P.C. (AV)

1501 Farm Credit Drive, Suite 3600, 22102
Telephone: 703-790-7790
Fax: 703-790-7796

Michael S. Horwatt

Charles F. Wright

OF COUNSEL

Frances A. Scibelli
Lawrence W. Koltun (Not admitted in VA)

For full biographical listings, see the Martindale-Hubbell Law Directory

VENABLE, BAETJER AND HOWARD (AV)

A Partnership including Professional Corporations
Suite 400, 2010 Corporate Ridge, 22102
Telephone: 703-760-1600
FAX: 703-821-8949
Baltimore, Maryland Office: 1800 Mercantile Bank & Trust Building, 2 Hopkins Plaza.
Telephone: 410-244-7400.
Washington, D.C. Office: Venable, Baetjer, Howard & Civiletti, Suite 1000, 1201 New York Avenue, N.W.
Telephone: 202-962-4800.
Rockville, Maryland Office: Suite 500, One Church Street, P.O. Box 1906.
Telephone: 301-217-5600.
Towson, Maryland Office: 210 Allegheny Avenue, P. O. Box 5517.
Telephone: 410-494-6200.

MEMBERS OF FIRM

Kenneth C. Bass, III (Also at Washington, D.C. Office)
Bruce E. Titus
William D. Dolan, III (P.C.)
David G. Lane
Herbert G. Smith, II

OF COUNSEL

Mary T. Flynn

ASSOCIATES

Julian Sylvester Brown
Jon M. Lippard
Michael W. Robinson

For Complete List of Firm Personnel, See General Section

For full biographical listings, see the Martindale-Hubbell Law Directory

WATT, TIEDER & HOFFAR (AV)

7929 Westpark Drive, Suite 400, 22102
Telephone: 703-749-1000
Telecopier: 703-893-8029
Washington, D.C. Office: 601 Pennsylvania Ave, N.W., Suite 900.
Telephone: 202-462-4697.
Irvine California Office: 3 Park Plaza, Suite 1530.
Telephone: 714-852-6700.

MEMBERS OF FIRM

John B. Tieder, Jr.
Robert G. Watt
Julian F. Hoffar
Robert M. Fitzgerald
Robert K. Cox
William R. Chambers
David C. Romm
Charles E. Raley (Not admitted in VA)
Francis X. McCullough
Barbara G. Werther (Not admitted in VA)
Garry R. Boehlert
Thomas B. Newell
Lewis J. Baker
Benjamin T. Riddles, II
Timothy F. Brown
Richard G. Mann, Jr.
David C. Mancini
David C. Haas
Henry D. Danforth
Carter B. Reid
Donna S. McCaffrey
Mark J. Groff (Not admitted in VA)
Mark A. Sgarlata
Daniel E. Cohen
Michael G. Long (Resident, Irvine, California Office)

(See Next Column)

WATT, TIEDER & HOFFAR—*Continued*

OF COUNSEL

Avv. Roberto Tassi
Clyde Harold Slease (Not admitted in VA)

ASSOCIATES

Thomas J. Powell
Douglas C. Proxmire
Tara L. Vautin
Edward Parrott
Steven G. Schassler
Joseph H. Bucci
Steven J. Weber
Paul A. Varela
Vivian Katsantonis
Charlie Lee
Kathleen A. Olden
Christopher P. Pappas (Resident, Irvine, California Office)
Shelly L. Ewald
Christopher J. Brasco
Jean V. Misterek
Charles W. Durant
Susan Latham Timoner
Fred A. Mendicino
Susan G. Sisskind
Robert G. Barbour
Keith C. Phillips
Marybeth Zientek Gaul
Timothy E. Heffernan (Not admitted in VA)
William Drew Mallender
James Moore Donahue
Heidi Brown Hering
Kerrin Maureen McCormick (Not admitted in VA)
Gretal J. Toker

For full biographical listings, see the Martindale-Hubbell Law Directory

NORFOLK, (Independent City)

GOLDBLATT, LIPKIN & COHEN, P.C. (AV)

Suite 300, 415 St. Paul's Boulevard, P.O. Box 3505, 23514
Telephone: 804-627-6225
Telefax: 804-622-3698

Paul M. Lipkin
Robert S. Cohen
Steven M. Legum
Mary G. Commander
Beril M. Abraham
Larry W. Shelton

Approved Attorneys for: Lawyers Title Insurance Corp.

For full biographical listings, see the Martindale-Hubbell Law Directory

*PULASKI,** Pulaski Co.

GILMER, SADLER, INGRAM, SUTHERLAND & HUTTON (AV)

Midtown Professional Building, 65 East Main Street, P.O. Box 878, 24301
Telephone: 703-980-1360; 703-639-0027
Telecopier: 703-980-5264
Blacksburg (Montgomery County), Virginia Office: 201 West Roanoke Street, P.O. Box 908.
Telephone: 703-552-1061.
Telecopier: 703-552-8227.

MEMBERS OF FIRM

Howard C. Gilmer, Jr. (1906-1975)
Roby K. Sutherland (1909-1975)
Philip M. Sadler (1915-1994)
Robert J. Ingram
James L. Hutton (Resident, Blacksburg Office)
Thomas J. McCarthy, Jr.
John J. Gill
Gary C. Hancock
Jackson M. Bruce
Michael J. Barbour
Deborah Wood Dobbins
Todd G. Patrick (Resident, Blacksburg Office)
Debra Fitzgerald-O'Connell
Scott A. Rose
Timothy Edmond Kirtner

OF COUNSEL

James R. Montgomery

Representative Clients: Appalachian Power Co.; Chevron; Liberty Mutual Insurance Co.; Norfolk Southern Railway Co.; Pulaski Furniture Corp.; NationsBank; Travelers Insurance Group; Renfro, Inc.; Magnox, Inc.; Corning Glass Works.

For full biographical listings, see the Martindale-Hubbell Law Directory

*RICHMOND,** (Ind. City; Seat of Henrico Co.)

WILLIAMS, MULLEN, CHRISTIAN & DOBBINS, A PROFESSIONAL CORPORATION (AV)

Two James Center, 1021 East Cary Street, P.O. Box 1320, 23210-1320
Telephone: 804-643-1991
Fax: 804-783-6456
Glen Allen, Virginia Office: 4401 Waterfront Drive, Suite 140.
Telephone: 804-965-9168.
Fax: 804-965-0955.
Washington, D.C. Office: 1575 Eye Street, N.W.
Telephone: 202-289-6200.
Fax: 202-289-4126.

Paul S. Bliley, Jr.
A. Peter Brodell
Charles L. Cabell
Howard W. Dobbins
Robert E. Eicher
A. Brooks Hock
David R. Johnson
Randolph H. Lickey
Dana D. McDaniel
Robert D. Perrow
Paul G. Saunders, II
William H. Schwarzschild, III
Andrea Rowse Stiles
W. Scott Street, III

(See Next Column)

Naila Townes Ahmed
William J. Benos
Andrew M. Condlin
David L. Dallas, Jr.
Calvin W. Fowler, Jr.
Tara A. McGee
William L. Pitman
John L. Walker, III
Charles E. Wall

For Complete List of Firm Personnel, See General Section

For full biographical listings, see the Martindale-Hubbell Law Directory

VIENNA, Fairfax Co.

BORING, PARROTT & PILGER, P.C. (AV)

307 Maple Avenue West, Suite D, 22180-4368
Telephone: 703-281-2161
FAX: 703-281-9464

W. Thomas Parrott, III
Thomas J. Sawyer

Representative Clients: Balmar, Inc.; Hewlett-Packard Co.; Toshiba America Information Systems, Inc.; King Wholesale, Inc.; FSM Leasing, Inc.; KDI Sylvan Pools, Inc.; Brobst International, Inc.; Telematics, Inc.; Northern Virginia Surgical Associates, P.C.; Rainbow Industries, Inc.

For full biographical listings, see the Martindale-Hubbell Law Directory

WASHINGTON

*SEATTLE,** King Co.

CHISM, JACOBSON & JOHNSON (AV)

3950 Washington Mutual Tower, 1201 Third Avenue, 98101-3013
Telephone: 206-689-5650
Facsimile: 206-689-5649

Anita C. Braker
J. Patrick Brown
Geoffrey P. Chism
E. John Compatore
Michael C. Hoover
Jean E. Huffington
Daniel C. Jacobson
A. Kyle Johnson
William T. McKay
LuAnne Perry
H. Troy Romero

Representative Clients: Bush, Cotton, Thompson & Scott; Lakeshore Investment Corp.; McAbee Construction Co., Inc.; Gary Merlino Construction Co., Inc.; Papillon Airways, Inc.; Phoenix Mortgage & Investment; Seven Sisters, Inc.; Sasco/Hooper Electric, Inc.; Trigon Packaging Corp.; WHC, Inc. (Washington Hills).

For full biographical listings, see the Martindale-Hubbell Law Directory

GAITÁN & CUSACK (AV)

30th Floor Two Union Square, 601 Union Street, 98101-2324
Telephone: 206-521-3000
Facsimile: 206-386-5259
Anchorage, Alaska Office: 425 G Street, Suite 760.
Telephone: 907-278-3001.
Facsimile: 907-278-6068.
San Francisco, California Office: 275 Battery Street, 20th Floor.
Telephone: 415-398-5562.
Fax: 415-398-4033.
Washington, D.C. Office: 2000 L Street, Suite 200.
Telephone: 202-296-4637.
Fax: 202-296-4650.

MEMBERS OF FIRM

José E. Gaitán
Kenneth J. Cusack (Resident, Anchorage, Alaska Office)
William F. Knowles
Ronald L. Bozarth

OF COUNSEL

Howard K. Todd
Gary D. Gayton
Michel P. Stern (Also practicing alone, Bellevue, Washington)
Christopher A. Byrne
Patricia D. Ryan

ASSOCIATES

Mary F. O'Boyle
Bruce H. Williams
David J. Onsager
Diana T. Jimenez
Robert T. Mimbu
Cristina C. Kapela
Camilla M. Hedberg
John E. Lenker
Kathleen C. Healy

Representative Clients: Cummins Great Plains Diesel; Sears, Roebuck & Company; National Insurance Professional Corporation; Nabisco; Pillsbury Company; Harvest Software; Hosho America; HFI Foods.

For full biographical listings, see the Martindale-Hubbell Law Directory

WEST VIRGINIA

*CHARLESTON,** Kanawha Co.

JACKSON & KELLY (AV)

1600 Laidley Tower, P.O. Box 553, 25322
Telephone: 304-340-1000
Fax: 304-340-1130
Martinsburg, West Virginia Office: 300 Foxcroft Avenue, P.O. Box 1068.
Telephone: 304-263-8800.
Morgantown, West Virginia Office: 6000 Hampton Center, P.O. Box 619.
Telephone: 304-599-3000.
New Martinsville, West Virginia Office: 256 Russell Avenue, P.O. Box 68.
Telephone: 304-455-1751.
Charles Town, West Virginia Office: 700 East Washington Street, P.O. Box 983.
Telephone: 304-728-6088.
Clarksburg, West Virginia Office: 203 Main Street, P.O. Box 1587.
Telephone: 304-623-3002.
Lexington, Kentucky Office: 175 East Main Street, Suite 500, P.O. Box 2150.
Telephone: 606-255-9500.
Washington, D. C. Office: 2401 Pennsylvania Avenue, N.W., Suite 400.
Telephone: 202-973-0200.
Denver, Colorado Office: Suite 2710, 1660 Lincoln Street.
Telephone: 303-837-0003.

MEMBERS OF FIRM

James Knight Brown
Thomas E. Potter
John R. Lukens
Louis S. Southworth, II
Charles Q. Gage
Michael A. Albert
William K. Bodell, II (Resident, Lexington, Kentucky Office)
William F. Dobbs, Jr.
David Allen Barnette
Mary Clare Eros (Martinsburg and Charles Town, West Virginia Offices)
Charles D. Dunbar
Thad S. Huffman (Resident, Washington, D.C. Office)
Charles W. Loeb, Jr.

ASSOCIATES

Eric H. London (Resident, Morgantown Office)
William C. Miller, II

Representative Clients: One Valley Bancorp of West Virginia, Inc. and subsidiary banks; West Virginia Housing Development Fund; Go-Mart, Inc.; Provident National Bank; Chase Manhattan Bank; Shoney's, Inc.; Park Corp.; Walter Industries, Inc.; Gabriel Brothers, Inc.; United Parcel Service.

For Complete List of Firm Personnel, See General Section

For full biographical listings, see the Martindale-Hubbell Law Directory

WISCONSIN

*APPLETON,** Outagamie Co.

MENN, NELSON, SHARRATT, TEETAERT & BEISENSTEIN, LTD. (AV)

(Formerly, Fulton, Menn & Nehs, Ltd.)
222 North Oneida Street, P.O. Box 785, 54912-0785
Telephone: 414-731-6631
FAX: 414-734-0981

Homer H. Benton (1886-1957)
Alfred C. Bosser (1890-1965)
Franklin L. Nehs (1922-1979)
David L. Fulton (1911-1985)
Glenn L. Sharratt (Retired)
John B. Menn
Peter S. Nelson
John R. Teetaert
Joseph J. Beisenstein
Mark R. Feldmann
Joseph A. Bielinski
Jonathan M. Menn
Douglas D. Hahn
Keith W. Kostecke
Robert N. Duimstra

LEGAL SUPPORT PERSONNEL

Kathy J. Krause

Representative Clients: Bank One Appleton, NA; Time Warner Entertainment Company LP.

For full biographical listings, see the Martindale-Hubbell Law Directory

*MADISON,** Dane Co.

AXLEY BRYNELSON (AV)

(Formerly Brynelson, Herrick, Bucaida, Dorschel & Armstrong Including the former Easton & Assoc., S.C.)
2 East Mifflin Street, P.O. Box 1767, 53701-1767
Telephone: 608-257-5661
Fax: 608-257-5444

(See Next Column)

MEMBERS OF FIRM

Frank J. Bucaida
Timothy D. Fenner
Bruce L. Harms
Patricia M. Gibeault
Michael J. Westcott
Larry K. Libman
Richard E. Petershack

For Complete List of Firm Personnel, See General Section

For full biographical listings, see the Martindale-Hubbell Law Directory

*MILWAUKEE,** Milwaukee Co.

BIRD, MARTIN & SALOMON S.C. (AV)

735 North Water Street, Suite 1600, 53202-4104
Telephone: 414-276-7290
Facsimile: 414-276-7291

John D. Bird, Jr.
Frances H. Martin
Allen M. Salomon

References: Firstar Bank; Biltmore Investors Bank.

For full biographical listings, see the Martindale-Hubbell Law Directory

GIBBS, ROPER, LOOTS & WILLIAMS, S.C. (AV)

735 North Water Street, 53202
Telephone: 414-273-7000
Fax: 414-273-7897

Wayne J. Roper
Robert J. Loots
Clay R. Williams
John W. Hein
William J. French
George A. Evans, Jr.
Thomas P. Guszkowski
Terry E. Nilles
Thomas R. Streifender
Robert L. Gegios
Beth J. Kushner
Catherine Mode Eastham

OF COUNSEL

Richard S. Gibbs
Thomas B. Fifield

William R. West
Douglas S. Knott
Kenneth A. Hoogstra
Mark S. Diestelmeier
Glen E. Lavy

Representative Clients: David White, Inc.; Family Health Plan Cooperative; Froedtert Memorial Lutheran Hospital, Inc.; Green Bay Packaging Inc.; Kemper Clearing Corp.; Kemper Securities, Inc.; Waupaca Foundry, Inc.

For Complete List of Firm Personnel, See General Section

For full biographical listings, see the Martindale-Hubbell Law Directory

KOHNER, MANN & KAILAS, S.C. (AV)

1572 East Capitol Drive, P.O. Box 19982, 53211-0982
Telephone: 414-962-5110
Fax: 414-962-8725

Marvin L. Kohner (1908-1975)
Robert L. Mann
Steve Kailas
Mark R. Wolters
Jordan B. Reich
David S. Chartier

Roy Paul Roth
Gary P. Lantzy
Christopher C. Kailas
Robert E. Nailen
Matthew P. Gerdisch
Darrell R. Zall
Daniel J. Flynn
Timothy L. Zuberbier
Shawn G. Rice

Representative Clients: EcoLab, Inc.; Parker Pen Co.; Ray O Vac, Inc.

For full biographical listings, see the Martindale-Hubbell Law Directory

QUARLES & BRADY (AV)

411 East Wisconsin Avenue, 53202-4497
Telephone: 414-277-5000
Cable Address: "Lawdock"
Fax: 414-271-3552.
TWX: 910-262-3426
Madison, Wisconsin Office: Firstar Plaza, One South Pinckney Street, P.O. Box 2113.
Telephone: 608-251-5000.
Fax: 608-251-9166.
West Palm Beach, Florida Office: 222 Lakeview Avenue, 4th Floor.
Telephone: 407-653-5000.
Fax: 407-653-5333.
Naples, Florida Office: Barnett Center, 4501 Tamiami Trail North.
Telephone: 813-262-5959.
Fax: 813-434-4999.
Phoenix, Arizona Office: One Camelback Building, One East Camelback Road, Suite 400.
Telephone: 602-230-5500.
Fax: 602-230-5598.

(See Next Column)

QUARLES & BRADY—*Continued*

MEMBERS OF FIRM

(ALPHABETICALLY BY YEAR OF ADMISSION TO BAR)

Arthur B. Harris
David L. Petersen (Resident, West Palm Beach, Florida Office)
Stephen E. Richman
John R. Maynard
Ned R. Nashban (Resident, West Palm Beach, Florida Office)
Robert T. Bailes (Resident, Phoenix, Arizona Office)
John W. Daniels, Jr.
Judith M. Bailey (Resident, Phoenix, Arizona Office)
Andrew M. Barnes
Matthew J. Flynn
Roger K. Spencer (Resident, Phoenix, Arizona Office)
Patrick J. Goebel
Peter A. Terry (Resident, Phoenix, Arizona Office)
Ann M. Murphy
Elizabeth A. Orelup
Leo J. Salvatori (Resident, Naples, Florida Office)
David G. Beauchamp (Resident, Phoenix, Arizona Office)
Marta S. Levine

ASSOCIATES

Robert S. Bornhoft (Resident, Phoenix, Arizona Office)
Mary Z. Horton (Not admitted in WI; Resident, Phoenix, Arizona Office)
Kenneth J. Hansen (Resident, Madison Office)
Jennifer Vogel Powers
David L. Bourne
Valerie L. Bailey-Rihn (Resident, Madison Office)
Lisa A. Lyons
Cheryl A. Johnson

For Complete List of Firm Personnel, See General Section

For full biographical listings, see the Martindale-Hubbell Law Directory

REINHART, BOERNER, VAN DEUREN, NORRIS & RIESELBACH, S.C. (AV)

1000 North Water Street, P.O. Box 92900, 53202-0900
Telephone: 414-298-1000
Facsimile: 414-298-8097
Denver, Colorado Office: One Norwest Center, 1700 Lincoln Street, Suite 3725.
Telephone: 303-831-0909.
Fax: 303-831-4805.
Madison, Wisconsin Office: 7617 Mineral Point Road, 53701-2020.
Telephone: 608-283-7900.
Fax: 608-283-7919.
Washington, D.C. Office: 601 Pennsylvania Avenue, N.W., North Building, Suite 750.
Telephone: 202-393-3636.
Fax: 202-393-0796.

Paul V. Lucke
William R. Steinmetz
Stephen T. Jacobs
Scott W. Hansen
Richard P. Carr
Anne Willis Reed
Francis W. Deisinger
Steven P. Bogart

R. Timothy Muth
Anne Morgan Hlavacka
Kathleen S. Donius
Christine L. Thierfelder
David J. Sisson
Patrick J. Hodan
Katherine McConahay Nealon
Colleen D. Ball
Dean E. Mabie
Geri Krupp-Gordon
Daniel J. La Fave
David G. Hanson

For Complete List of Firm Personnel, See General Section

For full biographical listings, see the Martindale-Hubbell Law Directory

*WAUKESHA,** Waukesha Co.

CRAMER, MULTHAUF & HAMMES (AV)

1601 East Racine Avenue, P.O. Box 558, 53187
Telephone: 414-542-4278
Telecopier: 414-542-4270

MEMBERS OF FIRM

John E. Multhauf
Richard R. Kobriger
Peter J. Plaushines
John M. Remmers

Representative Clients: Payco American Corp.; Dorner Manufacturing Corp.; Safro Motor Cars; Cousins Submarine, Inc.
Reference: Waukesha State Bank.

For Complete List of Firm Personnel, See General Section

For full biographical listings, see the Martindale-Hubbell Law Directory

WYOMING

*BUFFALO,** Johnson Co.

OMOHUNDRO, PALMERLEE AND DURRANT (AV)

An Association of Attorneys
130 South Main Street, 82834
Telephone: 307-684-2207
Telecopier: 307-684-9364
Gillette, Wyoming Office: East Entrance, Suite 700, 201 West Lakeway Road.
Telephone: 307-682-7826.

William D. Omohundro (P.C.)
David F. Palmerlee
Sean P. Durrant

Representative Clients: Atlantic Richfield Co.; Total Minerals Corporation; Norwest Agricultural Credit; First National Bank of Buffalo; First Interstate Bank of Commerce-Buffalo; Wyoming Bank and Trust Co.; Union State Bank.

For full biographical listings, see the Martindale-Hubbell Law Directory

*CASPER,** Natrona Co.

BROWN & DREW (AV)

Casper Business Center, Suite 800, 123 West First Street, 82601-2486
Telephone: 307-234-1000
800-877-6755
Telefax: 307-265-8025

MEMBERS OF FIRM

Morris R. Massey
Harry B. Durham, III
W. Thomas Sullins, II
Donn J. McCall
John A. Warnick
Thomas F. Reese
Russell M. Blood
J. Kenneth Barbe
Jeffrey C. Brinkerhoff

ASSOCIATES

Jon B. Huss
Carol Warnick
P. Jaye Rippley
Courtney Robert Kepler
Drew A. Perkins

Attorneys for: First Interstate Bank of Wyoming, N.A.; Norwest Bank Wyoming, N.A.; The CIT Group/Industrial Financing; Aetna Casualty & Surety Co.; The Doctor's Co.; MEDMARC; WOTCO, Inc.; Chevron USA; Kerr-McGee Corp.; Chicago and NorthWestern Transportation Company.

For Complete List of Firm Personnel, See General Section

For full biographical listings, see the Martindale-Hubbell Law Directory

*CHEYENNE,** Laramie Co.

HICKEY, MACKEY, EVANS, WALKER & STEWART (AV)

1712 Carey Avenue, P.O. Drawer 467, 82003
Telephone: 307-634-1525
Telecopier: 307-638-7335

MEMBERS OF FIRM

Paul J. Hickey
Terry W. Mackey
David F. Evans
John M. Walker
Mark R. Stewart III
Richard D. Tim Bush

A List of Representative Clients will be furnished upon request.
Reference: Norwest Bank, Cheyenne, N.A.

For full biographical listings, see the Martindale-Hubbell Law Directory

PUERTO RICO

SAN JUAN, San Juan Dist.

DEL TORO & SANTANA

Suite 807 Royal Bank Center (Hato Rey), 00917
Telephone: 809-754-8722
Telecopier: 809-756-6677

MEMBERS OF FIRM

Russell A. Del Toro
Roberto Santana Aparicio

For full biographical listings, see the Martindale-Hubbell Law Directory

FIDDLER, GONZÁLEZ & RODRÍGUEZ

Chase Manhattan Bank Building (Hato Rey), P.O. Box 363507, 00936-3507
Telephone: 809-753-3113
Telecopier: 809-759-3123

OF COUNSEL

Ileana Fernandez-Buitrago

(See Next Column)

FIDDLER, GONZÁLEZ & RODRÍGUEZ, *San Juan—Continued*

MEMBERS OF FIRM

Rafael Cortés-Dapena
Aurelio Emanuelli-Belaval
Antonio R. Sifre
Leopoldo J. Cabassa-Sauri

For Complete List of Firm Personnel, See General Section

For full biographical listings, see the Martindale-Hubbell Law Directory

GOLDMAN ANTONETTI & CÓRDOVA

American International Plaza Fourteenth & Fifteenth Floors, 250 Muñoz Rivera Avenue (Hato Rey), P.O. Box 70364, 00936-0364
Telephone: 809-759-8000
Telecopiers: 809-767-9333 (Main)
809-767-9177 (Litigation Department)
809-767-8660 (Labor & Corporate Law Departments)
809-767-9325 (Tax & Environmental Law Departments)

MEMBERS OF FIRM

Vicente J. Antonetti
José A. Cepeda-Rodriguez
Roberto Montalvo Carbia
Luis F. Antonetti
Jorge Souss
Luis D. Ortiz-Abreu
Gregory T. Usera
Edgar Cartagena-Santiago
Pedro Morell Losada
Ramón E. Dapena
Francis Torres-Fernández
Jorge L. Martinez
Carlos A. Rodríguez-Vidal
Raymond E. Morales
Thelma Rivera-Miranda
Jorge Segurola
Francisco J. García-García
Edgardo Colón Arrarás
Jesús E. Cuza
Howard Pravda
Braulio García Jiménez
Karín G. Díaz-Toro

OF COUNSEL

Max Goldman
Enrique Córdova Díaz
Francisco de Jesús-Schuck
Charles P. Adams

ASSOCIATES

Jorge R. Rodriguez-Micheo
José M. Lorié Velasco
Ivonne Palerm Cruz
Eli Matos-Alicea
Mildred Cabán
Wilda Rodriguez Plaza
John A. Uphoff-Figueroa
Edwin J. Seda-Fernández
Carlos E. Colón-Franceschi
Carlos Rodriguez Cintron
Marta Figueroa-Torres
Carlos A. García-Pérez
Iván R. Fernández-Vallejo
Georgiana S. Colón
Mercedes M. Barreras Soler
Migdalia Davila-Garcia
Manuel E. Lopez-Fernandez
Roberto Ariel Fernández
Josefina Cruz-Melendez
Gretchen M. Mendez-Vilella
María Patricia Lake
Orlando Cabrera-Rodriguez
Jose E. Franco
Ruben Colon-Morales
Jose J. Ledesma Rodriguez
Lora J. Espada-Medina
Aileen M. Navas-Auger
Ina M. Berlingeri Vincenty
Artemio Rivera Rivera

Representative Clients: Borden, Inc.; Crown Cork de Puerto Rico, Inc.; Maidenform, Inc.; Philip Morris, Inc.; Seven Up Flavors Mfg. Co.; Xerox Corp.

For full biographical listings, see the Martindale-Hubbell Law Directory

INDIANO, WILLIAMS & WEINSTEIN-BACAL

Hato Rey Tower, 21st Floor, 268 Muñoz Rivera Avenue (Hato Rey), 00918
Telephone: 809-754-2323; 763-0485
Fax: 809-766-3366
St. Thomas, Virgin Islands Office: Stuart A. Weinstein-Bacal, P.O. Box 9820, Charlotte Amalie, 00801.
Telephone: 809-776-2500.
Telecopier: 809-779-6918.

MEMBERS OF FIRM

Stuart A. Weinstein-Bacal
David C. Indiano
Jeffrey M. Williams

ASSOCIATES

Javier A. Morales Ramos
Madeline Garcia-Rodriguez

For full biographical listings, see the Martindale-Hubbell Law Directory

JORGE R. JIMENEZ

Suite 807 Bankers Finance Tower, 654 Muñoz Rivera Avenue (Hato Rey), 00918
Telephone: 809-763-0106
Fax: 809-763-0574

For full biographical listings, see the Martindale-Hubbell Law Directory

MÁRTINEZ ODELL & CALABRIA

Banco Popular Center, 16th Floor, (Hato Rey), P.O. Box 190998, 00919-0998
Telephone: 809-753-8914
Facsimile: 809-753-8402; 809-759-9075; 809-764-5664

MEMBERS OF FIRM

Patrick D. O'Neill
Alberto Rodríguez-Ramos
Fanny Auz-Patiño
Anabelle Rodriguez-Rodriguez

OF COUNSEL

Eugenio C. Romero

(See Next Column)

ASSOCIATES

Maria del Carmen Garriga
Eric Perez Ochoa
Jose Antonio Fernandez-Jaquete
M. Georgina Carrion-Christiansen

Representative Clients: A.T. & T. Corp.; Pepsi-Cola P.R. Bottling Co.; Banco Popular de Puerto Rico; I.T.T. Financial Corp.; John H. Harland Company of Puerto Rico, Inc.; Lutron Electronics Co., Inc.; Paine Webber, Inc.; Lotus Development Corp.; Western Digital.

For Complete List of Firm Personnel, See General Section

For full biographical listings, see the Martindale-Hubbell Law Directory

VIRGIN ISLANDS

*CHARLOTTE AMALIE, ST. THOMAS,** St. Thomas

BORNN BORNN HANDY

No. 8 Norre Gade, P.O. Box 1500, 00804
Telephone: 809-774-1400
Fax: 809-774-9607

PARTNER

David A. Bornn

OF COUNSEL

Joseph M. Erwin (Not admitted in VI)

References: Bank of Nova Scotia; Banco Popular de P.R., St. Thomas, U.S. Virgin Islands.

For Complete List of Firm Personnel, See General Section

For full biographical listings, see the Martindale-Hubbell Law Directory

GRUNERT STOUT BRUCH & MOORE

24-25 Kongensgade, P.O. Box 1030, 00804
Telephone: 809-774-1320
Fax: 809-774-7839

MEMBERS OF FIRM

John E. Stout
Susan Bruch Moorehead
Treston E. Moore

ASSOCIATES

Maryleen Thomas
Richard F. Taylor
H. Kevin Mart (Not admitted in VI)

OF COUNSEL

William L. Blum

For full biographical listings, see the Martindale-Hubbell Law Directory

CANADA
ALBERTA

*CALGARY,** Calgary Jud. Dist.

BENNETT JONES VERCHERE (AV)

4500 Bankers Hall East, 855-2nd Street S.W., T2P 4K7
Telephone: (403) 298-3100
Facsimile: (403) 265-7219
Edmonton, Alberta Office: 1000, 10035-105 Street.
Telephone: (403) 421-8133.
Facsimile: (403) 421-7951.
Toronto, Ontario Office: 3400 1 First Canadian Place. P.O. Box 130.
Telephone: (416) 863-1200.
Facsimile: (416) 863-1716.
Ottawa, Ontario Office: Suite 1800. 350 Alberta Street, Box 25, K1R 1A4.
Telephone: (613) 230-4935.
Facsimile: (613) 230-3836.
Montreal, Quebec Office: Suite 1600, 1 Place Ville Marie.
Telephone: (514) 871-1200.
Facsimile: (514) 871-8115.

MEMBER OF FIRM

Walter B. O'Donoghue, Q.C.

For Complete List of Firm Personnel, See General Section

For full biographical listings, see the Martindale-Hubbell Law Directory

*EDMONTON,** Edmonton Jud. Dist.

LUCAS BOWKER & WHITE (AV)

Esso Tower - Scotia Place, 1201-10060 Jasper Avenue, T5J 4E5
Telephone: 403-426-5330
Telecopier: 403-428-1066

(See Next Column)

LUCAS BOWKER & WHITE—*Continued*

MEMBERS OF FIRM

Gerald A. I. Lucas, Q.C. | Elizabeth A. Johnson
David J. Stratton, Q.C. | Robert C. Dunseith
Cecilia I. Johnstone, Q.C. | Douglas H. Shell
John Reginald Day, Q.C. | Robert A. Seidel
Robert P. Bruce

ASSOCIATES

Kevin J. Smith | Deborah L. Hughes
Gordon V. Garside | Annette E. Koski
Douglas A. Bodner

COUNSEL

Joan C. Copp

Reference: Canadian Imperial Bank of Commerce.

For Complete List of Firm Personnel, See General Section

For full biographical listings, see the Martindale-Hubbell Law Directory

PARLEE MCLAWS (AV)

15th Floor Manulife Place, 10180 101st Street, T5J 4K1
Telephone: 403-423-8500
Telecopier: 403-423-2870
Calgary, Alberta Office: 3400, Western Canadian Place, 707 - 8th Avenue, S.W.
Telephone: 403-294-7000.
Telecopier: 403-265-8263.

MEMBERS OF FIRM

C. H. Kerr, Q.C. | R. A. Newton, Q.C.
M. D. MacDonald | T. A. Cockrall, Q.C.
K. F. Bailey, Q.C. | H. D. Montemurro
R. B. Davison, Q.C. | F. J. Niziol
F. R. Haldane | R. W. Wilson
P. E. J. Curran | I. L. MacLachlan
D. G. Finlay | R. O. Langley
J. K. McFadyen | R. G. McBean
R. C. Secord | J. T. Neilson
D. L. Kennedy | E. G. Rice
D. C. Rolf | J. F. McGinnis
D. F. Pawlowski | J. H. H. Hockin
A. A. Garber | G. W. Jaycock
R. P. James | M. J. K. Nikel
D. C. Wintermute | B. J. Curial
J. L. Cairns | S. L. May
M. S. Poretti

ASSOCIATES

C. R. Head | P. E. S. J. Kennedy
A.W. Slemko | R. Feraco
L. H. Hamdon | R.J. Billingsley
K.A. Smith | N.B.R. Thompson
K. D. Fallis-Howell | P. A. Shenher
D. S. Tam | I. C. Johnson
J.W. McClure | K.G. Koshman
F.H. Belzil | D.D. Dubrule
R.A. Renz | G. T. Lund
J.G. Paulson | W.D. Johnston
K. E. Buss | G. E. Flemming
B. L. Andriachuk | K. P. Nayyer

For full biographical listings, see the Martindale-Hubbell Law Directory

CANADA NEW BRUNSWICK

*SAINT JOHN,** Saint John Co.

CLARK, DRUMMIE & COMPANY (AV)

40 Wellington Row, P.O. Box 6850 Station "A", E2L 4S3
Telephone: 506-633-3800
Telecopier (Automatic): 506-633-3811

MEMBERS OF FIRM

Thomas B. Drummie, Q.C. | Donald F. MacGowan, Q.C.
Terrence W. Hutchinson | John M. McNair

OF COUNSEL

Richard W. Bird, Q.C. | L. Paul Zed, M.P.

Reference: Royal Bank of Canada.

For Complete List of Firm Personnel, See General Section

For full biographical listings, see the Martindale-Hubbell Law Directory

CANADA NOVA SCOTIA

*HALIFAX,** Halifax Co.

GREEN PARISH (AV)

Tower II, 1401 Purdy's Wharf, P.O. Box 1134, B3J 2X1
Telephone: 902-422-3100
Fax: 902-425-2504

Peter G. Green, Q.C. | Cynthia J. Levy
Alan V. Parish | Lisa M. Welton
Peter A. Doig | William Mahody

For full biographical listings, see the Martindale-Hubbell Law Directory

MCINNES COOPER & ROBERTSON (AV)

1601 Lower Water Street, P.O. Box 730, B3J 2V1
Telephone: 902-425-6500
Fax: 902-425-6350
St. John's, Newfoundland Office: Suite 602, Scotia Centre, 235 Water Street, P.O. Box 547. A1C, 5K8.
Telephone: 709-726-9500.
Fax: 709-726-9550.

Stewart McInnes, P.C., Q.C. | Lawrence J. Hayes, Q.C.
Joseph A. F. Macdonald, Q.C. | George T. H. Cooper, Q.C.
David H. Reardon, Q.C. | F. V. W. Penick
Linda Lee Oland | John D. Stringer
Marcia L. Brennan | Fae J. Shaw
Karen Oldfield

ASSOCIATE

David S. Mac Dougall

COUNSEL

Hector McInnes, Q.C.

Attorneys for: Bank of Nova Scotia; Imperial Oil, Limited; Frank B. Hall & Co., Inc. (New York); American Steamship Owners Protection & Indemnity Association, Inc.; Coca-Cola, Ltd.; Scott Worldwide Inc.; Hong Kong Bank of Canada.

For Complete List of Firm Personnel, See General Section

For full biographical listings, see the Martindale-Hubbell Law Directory

CANADA ONTARIO

KITCHENER, Regional Munic. of Waterloo

GIFFEN, LEE, WAGNER, MORLEY & GARBUTT (AV)

50 Queen Street North, P.O. Box 2396, N2H 6M3
Telephone: 519-578-4150
Fax: 519-578-8740

MEMBERS OF FIRM

Jeffrey J. Mansfield (1955-1991) | J. Scott Morley
J. Peter Giffen, Q.C. | Brian R. Wagner
Bruce L. Lee | Philip A. Garbutt

ASSOCIATES

Edward J. Vanderkloet | Daniel J. Fife
Keith C. Masterman | Jeffrey W. Boich

For full biographical listings, see the Martindale-Hubbell Law Directory

*TORONTO,** Regional Munic. of York

BORDEN & ELLIOT (AV)

Barristers & Solicitors
Scotia Plaza, 40 King Street West, M5H 3Y4
Telephone: 416-367-6000
Telecopier: 416-367-6749
Internet: @ borden.com
A Member of the national association of Borden DuMoulin Howard Gervais, comprising Borden & Elliot in Toronto, Ontario, Russell & DuMoulin in Vancouver, British Columbia, Howard, Mackie in Calgary, Alberta and Mackenzie Gervais in Montréal, Québec. Borden DuMoulin Howard Gervais also operates an office in London, England.

MEMBER AND ASSOCIATES

Simon B. Scott, Q.C.

For Complete List of Firm Personnel, See General Section

For full biographical listings, see the Martindale-Hubbell Law Directory

*WINDSOR,** Essex Co.

Gignac, Sutts (AV)

600 Westcourt Place, 251 Goyeau Street, P.O. Box 670, N9A 6V4
Telephone: 519-258-9333
Detroit Michigan: 313-962-0137
Facsimile: Windsor 519-258-9527
Detroit 313-962-0139

MEMBERS OF FIRM

Achille F. Gignac, Q.C. (1902-1984)
Robert E. Barnes, Q.C.
Clifford N. Sutts, Q.C.
Harvey T. Strosberg, Q.C.
Gary V. Wortley
James K. Ball
John C. Holland
William C. Chapman
Mary M. S. Fox
Donald M. Gordon
Sharman Sharkey Bondy
Paul C. Nesseth
Heather Rumble Peterson
Patricia A. Speight
Edward W. Ducharme
Michelle A. Gagnon
Craig J. Allen
Werner H. Keller
Francine A. Herlehy
Paul Simard

COUNSEL FOR CRIMINAL MATTERS

Patrick J. Ducharme

For full biographical listings, see the Martindale-Hubbell Law Directory

McTague Law Firm (AV)

455 Pelissier Street, N9A 6Z9
Telephone: 519-255-4300
Detroit, Michigan Telephone: 313-965-1332
Fax: 519-255-4360(Corporate/Labor)
Fax: 519-255-4384 (Litigation/Real Estate)

MEMBERS OF FIRM

H. M. McTague, Miss, Q.C. (1900-1986)
Alexander R. Szalkai, Q.C.
Michael K. Coughlin
Jerry B. Udell
Josephine Stark
J. Douglas Lawson, Q.C.
Roger A. Skinner
George W. King
Peter J. Kuker
Theodore Crljenica
Gerri L. Wong
R. Paul Layfield

ASSOCIATES

John D. Leslie
Tom Serafimovski
Marilee Marcotte

For full biographical listings, see the Martindale-Hubbell Law Directory

CANADA QUEBEC

*MONTREAL,** Montreal Dist.

Lengvari Braman Barbacki Moreau, s.e.n.c. (AV)

Suite 2707, One Place Ville Marie, H3B 4G4
Telephone: 514-871-9770
Telecopier: 514-866-4773

George F. Lengvari, Jr., Q.C.
Frederick A. Braman
Richard Barbacki
Bernard Moreau
Albert Zoltowski
Pascale Houde
Daniela L. Villatora
Jean-Bertrand Giroux
Seti K. Hamalian
Nathalie Marchand

OF COUNSEL

Seymour D. Steinman
Harold Dizgun

For full biographical listings, see the Martindale-Hubbell Law Directory

McMaster Meighen (AV)

A General Partnership
7th Floor, 630 René-Lévesque Boulevard West, H3B 4H7
Telephone: 514-879-1212
Telecopier: 514-878-0605
Cable Address: "Cammerall"
Telex: "Cammerall MTL" 05-268637
Affiliated with Fraser & Beatty in Toronto, North York, Ottawa and Vancouver.

MEMBERS OF FIRM

Thomas C. Camp, Q.C.
R. Jamie Plant
Timothy R. Carsley
Brian M. Schneiderman
Elizabeth A. Mitchell
Nancy G. Cleman
Janet Casey
Francois Morin
Catherine Rakush
Richard J. Riendeau, Q.C.
Hubert Senécal
Norman A. Saibil
Richard W. Shannon
Yves A. Dubois
Charles P. Marquette
Pierre Trudeau
H. John Godber
Darren E. Graham McGuire

(See Next Column)

COUNSEL

Pierre Gattuso

For Complete List of Firm Personnel, See General Section

For full biographical listings, see the Martindale-Hubbell Law Directory

CANADA SASKATCHEWAN

*REGINA,** Regina Jud. Centre

Balfour Moss (AV)

Bank of Montreal Building, 700-2103 11th Avenue, S4P 4G1
Telephone: 306-347-8300
Fax: 306-569-2321
Saskatoon, Saskatchewan Office: 850-410 22nd Street East.
Telephone: 306-665-7844.
Fax: 306-652-1586.

PARTNERS

A. John Beke, Q.C.
Fredrick C. McBeth
Brian J. Scherman (Resident Saskatoon)
D.E. Wayne McIntyre
Jennifer L. Garvie Pritchard
Roger J.F. Lepage
Reginald A. Watson
David C. Knoll (Resident Saskatoon)
Glen S. Lekach
Rick M. Van Beselaere
George E. Nystrom
Jeff N. Grubb

COUNSEL

E. John Moss, Q.C.
Hon. R. James Balfour, Q.C.
Robert A. Milliken, Q.C.
Roy B. Laschuk, Q.C.

ASSOCIATES

Elke Churchman (Resident Saskatoon)
Gordon D. McKenzie (Resident Saskatoon)
Karen M. Bolstad (Resident Saskatoon)
James L. Nugent
Randy R. Semenchuck
Douglas R. Sanders (Resident Saskatoon)
David G. Gerecke (Resident Saskatoon)
W. Kevin Rogers
Phyllis L. Norrie
Michele Klebuc-Simes
W. Andrew Donovan
Isa Gros-Louis Ahenakew (Resident, Saskatoon)
Susan Engel
Gil A. Malfair

Representative Clients: Bank of Montreal; Saskatchewan Wheat Pool; London Life Assurance Co.

For full biographical listings, see the Martindale-Hubbell Law Directory

MacPherson Leslie & Tyerman (AV)

1500-1874 Scarth Street, S4P 4E9
Telephone: 306-347-8000
Telecopier: 306-352-5250
Saskatoon, Saskatchewan Office: 1500-410 22nd Street East, S7K 5T6.
Telephone: 306-975-7100.
Telecopier: 306-975-7145.

MEMBERS OF FIRM

Harold H. MacKay, Q.C.
Robert B. Pletch, Q.C.
R. Neil MacKay (Resident, Saskatoon Office)
James S. Kerby (Resident, Saskatoon Office)
Carl A. P. Wagner
Donald K. Wilson
Douglas A. Ballou
Danny R. Anderson (Resident, Saskatoon Office)

For Complete List of Firm Personnel, See General Section

For full biographical listings, see the Martindale-Hubbell Law Directory

McDougall, Ready (AV)

700 Royal Bank Building, 2010-11th Avenue, S4P 0J3
Telephone: 306-757-1641
Telecopier: 306-359-0785
Saskatoon, Saskatchewan, Canada Office: 301 - 111 2nd Avenue South.
Telephone: 306-653-1641.
Telecopier: 306-665-8511.

MEMBERS OF FIRM

William F. Ready, Q.C.
Robert N. Millar
Lynn A. Smith
Michael W. Milani
W. Randall Rooke (Resident, Saskatoon Office)
Wayne L. Bernakevitch

Erin M.S. Kleisinger

Representative Clients: Royal Bank of Canada.

For Complete List of Firm Personnel, See General Section

For full biographical listings, see the Martindale-Hubbell Law Directory

*SASKATOON,** Saskatoon Jud. Centre

GAULEY & CO. (AV)

701 Broadway Avenue, P.O. Box 638, S7K 3L7
Telephone: 306-653-1212
Telecopier: 306-652-1323
Regina, Saskatchewan Office: Suite 400, 2201 11th Avenue S4P 0J8.
Telephone: 306-352-1643.
Telecopier: 306-525-8499.

MEMBERS OF FIRM

J. J. (Joe) Dierker, Q.C.
David J. McKeague, Q.C.
William J. Shaw
Nancy E. Hopkins, Q.C.
James Russell
Ian Sutherland

Reference: Royal Bank of Canada.

For Complete List of Firm Personnel, See General Section

For full biographical listings, see the Martindale-Hubbell Law Directory

COMMUNICATIONS LAW

ALABAMA

*BIRMINGHAM,** Jefferson Co.

BRADLEY, ARANT, ROSE & WHITE (AV)

1400 Park Place Tower, 2001 Park Place, 35203
Telephone: 205-521-8000
Telex: 494-1324
Facsimile: 205-251-8611, 251-8665, 252-0264
Facsimile (Southtrust Office): 205-251-9915
Huntsville, Alabama Office: 200 Clinton Avenue West, Suite 900.
Telephone: 205-517-5100.
Facsimile: 205-533-5069.

MEMBERS OF FIRM

Thomas Neely Carruthers, Jr. | Carleta Roberts Hawley
John H. Morrow | Joseph S. Bird, III

Counsel for: SouthTrust Bank of Alabama, National Association; Energen, Corporation (formerly Alagasco, Inc.); Blount, Inc.; Torchmark Corp.; Russell Corp.; Coca-Cola Bottling Company United, Inc.; Ford Motor Co.; Walter Industries, Inc.; The Birmingham Post Co. (Post-Herald); The New York Times Co.

For Complete List of Firm Personnel, See General Section

For full biographical listings, see the Martindale-Hubbell Law Directory

BURR & FORMAN (AV)

3000 SouthTrust Tower, 420 North 20th Street, 35203
Telephone: 205-251-3000
Telecopier: 205-458-5100
Huntsville, Alabama Office: Suite 204, Regency Center, 400 Meridian Street.
Telephone: 205-551-0010.

MEMBERS OF FIRM

John D. Clements | John F. DeBuys, Jr.

For Complete List of Firm Personnel, See General Section

For full biographical listings, see the Martindale-Hubbell Law Directory

JOHNSTON, BARTON, PROCTOR, SWEDLAW & NAFF (AV)

2900 AmSouth/Harbert Plaza, 1901 Sixth Avenue North, 35203-2618
Telephone: 205-458-9400
Telecopier: 205-458-9500

MEMBERS OF FIRM

Harvey Deramus (1904-1970) | James C. Barton, Jr.
Alfred M. Naff (1923-1993) | Thomas E. Walker
James C. Barton | Anne P. Wheeler
G. Burns Proctor, Jr. | Raymond P. Fitzpatrick, Jr.
Sydney L. Lavender | Hollinger F. Barnard
Jerome K. Lanning | William D. Jones III
Don B. Long, Jr. | David W. Proctor
Charles L. Robinson | Oscar M. Price III
J. William Rose, Jr. | W. Hill Sewell
Gilbert E. Johnston, Jr. | Robert S. Vance, Jr.
David P. Whiteside, Jr. | Richard J. Brockman
Ralph H. Smith II | Anthony A. Joseph

OF COUNSEL

Gilbert E. Johnston | Alfred Swedlaw
Alan W. Heldman

ASSOCIATES

William K. Hancock | Haskins W. Jones
James P. Pewitt | James M. Parker, Jr.
Scott Wells Ford | Michael H. Johnson
David M. Hunt | Russell L. Irby, III
Lee M. Pope | R. Scott Clark
Helen Kathryn Downs

General Counsel for: Anderson News Co.; The Birmingham News Co. (Publishers of The Birmingham News and owner of the Huntsville Times Co.); Bookland Stores, Inc.
Counsel for: BellSouth Services, Inc.; Broadcast Music, Inc.; Times-Mirror Broadcasting (WVTM-TV, Channel 13); WAPI, Inc.; Tucker Wayne/Luckie & Co.

For full biographical listings, see the Martindale-Hubbell Law Directory

*HUNTSVILLE,** Madison Co.

BRADLEY, ARANT, ROSE & WHITE (AV)

200 Clinton Avenue West, Suite 900, 35801
Telephone: 205-517-5100
Facsimile: 205-533-5069
Birmingham, Alabama Office: 1400 Park Place Tower, 2001 Park Place.
Telephone: 205-521-8000.
Telex: 494-1324.
Facsimile: 205-251-8611, 251-8665, 252-0264. Facsimile (Southtrust Office): 205-251-9915.

RESIDENT PARTNERS

Gary C. Huckaby | E. Cutter Hughes, Jr.
G. Rick Hall

RESIDENT ASSOCIATE

H. Knox McMillan

For Complete List of Firm Personnel, See General Section

For full biographical listings, see the Martindale-Hubbell Law Directory

*MONTGOMERY,** Montgomery Co.

* indicates certain Bar Register subscribers whose principal office is located elsewhere in the state and who have arranged for representation as a part of the state capital listings that follow

*** BALCH & BINGHAM (AV)**

The Winter Building, 2 Dexter Avenue, P.O. Box 78, 36101
Telephone: 334-834-6500
Facsimile: 334-269-3115
Birmingham, Alabama Offices: 1710 Sixth Avenue North, 35203.
Telephone: 205-251-8100.
Facsimile: 205-226-8798. 1901 Sixth Avenue North, 35203.
Telephone: 205-251-8100.
Facsimile: 205-226-8799.
Huntsville, Alabama Office: Suite 810, 200 West Court Square, 35801.
Telephone: 205-551-0171.
Facsimile: 205-551-0174.
Washington, D.C. Office: Suite 800, 1101 Connecticut Avenue, N.W., 20036.
Telephone: 202-296-0387.
Facsimile: 202-452-8180.

RESIDENT COUNSEL

M. Roland Nachman, Jr.

RESIDENT MEMBERS OF FIRM

Thomas W. Thagard, Jr. | Charles M. Crook

Counsel for: Alabama Power Co.; AT&T Communications, Inc.; Associated Press; Blue Cross and Blue Shield of Alabama; Brasfield & Gorrie, Inc.; Compass Bancshares, Inc.; Harbert Corp.; Kimberly-Clark Corp.; Southern Research Institute; The Advertiser Co. (Montgomery Advertiser and Alabama Journal).

For Complete List of Firm Personnel, See General Section

For full biographical listings, see the Martindale-Hubbell Law Directory

PARKER, BRANTLEY & WILKERSON, P.C. (AV)

323 Adams Avenue, P.O. Box 4992, 36103-4992
Telephone: 334-265-1500
Fax: 334-265-0319

Edward B. Parker, II | Mark D. Wilkerson
Paul A. Brantley | Leah Snell Stephens
Darla T. Furman

Representative Clients: ALLTEL; The Birmingham News; Telephone and Data Systems, Inc.; South Alabama Cellular Communications; Premiere Page; Rochester Telephone Co., Inc.; ONCOR; One Call; U.S. Long Distance, Inc.; Technologies Management, Inc.

For full biographical listings, see the Martindale-Hubbell Law Directory

ARIZONA

*PHOENIX,** Maricopa Co.

BROWN & BAIN, A PROFESSIONAL ASSOCIATION (AV)

2901 North Central Avenue, P.O. Box 400, 85001-0400
Telephone: 602-351-8000
Cable: TWX 910-951-0646
Telecopier: 602-351-8516
Palo Alto, California Affiliated Office: Brown & Bain, 600 Hansen Way.
Telephone: 415-856-9411.
Telecopier: 415-856-6061.

(See Next Column)

BROWN & BAIN A PROFESSIONAL ASSOCIATION, *Phoenix—Continued*

Tucson, Arizona Affiliated Office: Brown & Bain, A Professional Association. One South Church Avenue, Nineteenth Floor, P.O. Box 2265.
Telephone: 602-798-7900
Telecopier: 602-798-7945.

Robert E. B. Allen
Daniel C. Barr
Alan H. Blankenheimer
Jack E. Brown
H. Michael Clyde
C. Timothy Delaney
Paul F. Eckstein
Douglas Gerlach (On leave)
Philip R. Higdon (Resident at Tucson Office)
Michael W. Patten
Charles Van Cott

Charles A. Blanchard
Kelly A. O'Connor
Lee Stein

COUNSEL

Bernard Petrie (Resident at Palo Alto Office)

For Complete List of Firm Personnel, See General Section

For full biographical listings, see the Martindale-Hubbell Law Directory

MEYER, HENDRICKS, VICTOR, OSBORN & MALEDON, A PROFESSIONAL ASSOCIATION (AV)

2929 North Central Avenue Suite 2100, 85012-2794
Telephone: 602-640-9000
Facsimile: (24 Hrs.) 602-640-9050
Mailing Address: P.O. Box 33449, 85067-3449,

Andrew D. Hurwitz
Randall C. Nelson
Donald M. Peters
Michelle M. Matiski
Diane M. Johnsen

Reference: Bank One Arizona, NA.

For Complete List of Firm Personnel, See General Section
For full biographical listings, see the Martindale-Hubbell Law Directory

ARKANSAS

*LITTLE ROCK,** Pulaski Co.

IVESTER, SKINNER & CAMP, P.A. (AV)

Suite 1200, 111 Center Street, 72201
Telephone: 501-376-7788
FAX: 501-376-8536

Hermann Ivester
H. Edward Skinner
Charles R. Camp
Valerie F. Boyce
Stan D. Smith

For Complete List of Firm Personnel, See General Section

For full biographical listings, see the Martindale-Hubbell Law Directory

ROSE LAW FIRM, A PROFESSIONAL ASSOCIATION (AV)

120 East Fourth Street, 72201
Telephone: 501-375-9131
Telecopy: 501-375-1309

Phillip Carroll
W. Wilson Jones

Counsel for: Aluminum Company of America; The Equitable Life Assurance Society of The United States; Bridgestone/Firestone Inc.; General Motors Corp.; Minnesota Mining and Manufacturing Co.; The Prudential Insurance Company of America; Tyson Foods, Inc.; WEHCO Media, Inc.; Worthen Banking Corp.

For Complete List of Firm Personnel, See General Section

For full biographical listings, see the Martindale-Hubbell Law Directory

CALIFORNIA

*LOS ANGELES,** Los Angeles Co.

STEVEN J. STANWYCK (AV)

1800 Century Park East, Suite 512, 90067-1508
Telephone: 310-557-8390
Telecopier: 310-557-8391

Reference: Western Bank.

For full biographical listings, see the Martindale-Hubbell Law Directory

*SAN DIEGO,** San Diego Co.

FERRIS & BRITTON, A PROFESSIONAL CORPORATION (AV)

1600 First National Bank Center, 401 West A Street, 92101
Telephone: 619-233-3131
Fax: 619-232-9316

Alfred G. Ferris
Christopher Q. Britton
Michael R. Weinstein

OF COUNSEL

William M. Winter

Representative Clients: Allstate Insurance Co.; Cox Communications, Inc.; Enterprise Rent-a-Car; Exxon; Immuno Pharmaceutics, Inc.; Invitrogen Corporation; Teleport Communications Group; Southwest Airlines; Times-Mirror Cable Television.

For Complete List of Firm Personnel, See General Section

For full biographical listings, see the Martindale-Hubbell Law Directory

WOODLAND HILLS, Los Angeles Co.

WALLECK, SHANE, STANARD & BLENDER (AV)

5959 Topanga Canyon Boulevard, Suite 200, 91367
Telephone: 818-346-1333
Fax: 818-702-8939

MEMBER OF FIRM

Gary N. Schwartz

Representative Clients: San Fernando Valley Board of Realtors; Keffco, Inc.; Fuller-Jeffrey Broadcasting; Lynn Simay-Key Centers, Inc.; DA/PRO Rubber, Inc.; Pinnacle Estate Properties, Inc.; Comet Electric, Inc.; Wausau Insurance Company; Western States Imports Co., Inc.; California Coast Escrow, Inc.

For full biographical listings, see the Martindale-Hubbell Law Directory

CONNECTICUT

*BRIDGEPORT,** Fairfield Co.

ELSTEIN AND ELSTEIN, P.C. (AV)

Suite 400 1087 Broad Street, 06604-4231
Telephone: 203-367-4421
Telecopier: 203-366-8615

Henry Elstein
Bruce L. Elstein

For full biographical listings, see the Martindale-Hubbell Law Directory

STAMFORD, Fairfield Co.

CHAPMAN & FENNELL (AV)

Three Landmark Square, 06901
Telephone: 203-353-8000
Telecopier: 203-353-8799
New York, New York Office: 330 Madison Avenue.
Telephone: 212-687-3600.
Washington, D.C. Office: 2000 L Street, N.W., Suite 200.
Telephone: 202-822-9351.

MEMBERS OF FIRM

John Haven Chapman
Philip M. Chiappone (Resident, New York, N.Y. Office)
Darrell K. Fennell (Resident, New York, N.Y. Office)
Peter S. Gummo
D. Seeley Hubbard
Eric S. Kamisher (Resident, New York, N.Y. Office)
Brian E. Moran
Victor L. Zimmermann, Jr.

ASSOCIATE

Barton Meyerhoff (Not admitted in CT)

OF COUNSEL

Kevin T. Hoffman
Carol E. Meltzer (Resident, New York, N.Y. Office)
Brainard S. Patton
E. Gabriel Perle (Not admitted in CT)
Victor J. Toth (Resident, Washington, D.C. Office)
Michael Winger (Resident, New York, N.Y. Office)

For full biographical listings, see the Martindale-Hubbell Law Directory

WESTPORT, Fairfield Co.

ALAN NEIGHER (AV)

1804 Post Road East, 06880
Telephone: 203-259-0599
Fax: 203-255-2570
Telex: 238198 TLXAUR

(See Next Column)

ALAN NEIGHER—*Continued*

OF COUNSEL

Judith M. Trutt

For full biographical listings, see the Martindale-Hubbell Law Directory

DISTRICT OF COLUMBIA

WASHINGTON, D.C. Co.

* indicates certain Bar Register subscribers, in cities of comparable size and importance, who maintain an additional office in Washington, D.C. and who have arranged for representation as a part of the Washington, D.C. listings that follow

BAKER & HOSTETLER (AV)

Washington Square, Suite 1100, 1050 Connecticut Avenue, N.W., 20036-5304
Telephone: 202-861-1500
In Cleveland, Ohio: 3200 National City Center, 1900 East Ninth Street.
Telephone: 216-621-0200.
In Columbus, Ohio: Capitol Square, Suite 2100, 65 East State Street.
Telephone: 614-228-1541.
In Denver, Colorado: 303 East 17th Avenue, Suite 1100.
Telephone: 303-861-0600.
In Houston, Texas: 1000 Louisiana, Suite 2000.
Telephone: 713-751-1600.
In Long Beach, California: 300 Oceangate, Suite 620.
Telephone: 310-432-2827.
In Los Angeles, California: 600 Wilshire Boulevard.
Telephone: 213-624-2400.
In Orlando, Florida: SunBank Center, Suite 2300, 200 South Orange Avenue.
Telephone: 305-841-1111.
In College Park, Maryland: 9658 Baltimore Boulevard, Suite 206.
Telephone: 301-441-2781.
In Alexandria, Virginia: 437 North Lee Street.
Telephone: 703-549-1294.
In San Francisco, California: One Sansome Street, Suite 2000.
Telephone: 415-951-4705.

PARTNERS

Kenneth C. Howard, Jr.
Donald P. Zeifang

ASSOCIATE

Michael C. Ruger

For Complete List of Firm Personnel, See General Section

For full biographical listings, see the Martindale-Hubbell Law Directory

* **BELL, BOYD & LLOYD** (AV)

1615 L Street, N.W., 20036
Telephone: 202-466-6300
FAX: 202-463-0678
Chicago, Illinois Office: Three First National Plaza, Suite 3300, 70 West Madison Street.
Telephone: 312-372-1121.
FAX: 312-372-2098.

RESIDENT PARTNERS

Raymond C. Fay
Thomas R. Gibbon

For Complete List of Firm Personnel, See General Section

For full biographical listings, see the Martindale-Hubbell Law Directory

COLE, RAYWID & BRAVERMAN, L.L.P. (AV)

1919 Pennsylvania Avenue, N.W., 20006
Telephone: 202-659-9750
Cable Address: "Crab"
Telecopier: 202-452-0067

John P. Cole, Jr.
Alan Raywid (1930-1991)
Burt A. Braverman
Robert L. James
Joseph R. Reifer
Frances J. Chetwynd
John D. Seiver
Wesley R. Heppler
Paul Glist
David M. Silverman
James F. Ireland, III
Steven Jay Horvitz
Christopher W. Savage
Ann E. Flowers
Robert G. Scott, Jr.
Susan Whelan Westfall

(See Next Column)

Theresa A. Zeterberg
Stephen L. Kabler
John Dodge
Frederick W. Giroux
Matthew P. Zinn
John Davidson Thomas
Maria T. Browne
Donna Carrie Rattley
T. Scott Thompson
Todd Hartman (Not admitted in DC)
Jennifer L. Keefe (Not admitted in DC)
Christopher T. McGowan (Not admitted in DC)

For full biographical listings, see the Martindale-Hubbell Law Directory

DOW, LOHNES & ALBERTSON (AV)

Suite 500, 1255 Twenty-Third Street, N.W., 20037-1194
Telephone: 202-857-2500
Telecopier: (202) 857-2900
Atlanta, Georgia Office: One Ravinia Drive, Suite 1600.
Telephone: 404-901-8800.
Telecopier: (404) 901-8874.

MEMBERS OF THE FIRM

Michael D. Basile
Leonard J. Baxt
Raymond G. Bender, Jr.
Peter H. Feinberg
John R. Feore, Jr.
Brenda Lee Fox
Werner K. Hartenberger
Thomas J. Hutton
Leonard Jervey Kennedy (Not admitted in DC)
John S. Logan
B. Dwight Perry
J. Christopher Redding
Kevin F. Reed
Michael S. Schooler

Jeffrey A. Brueggemann (Not admitted in DC)
Christina H. Burrow
Richard S. Denning
Peter C. Godwin
Thomas K. Gump
J.G. Harrington
Jonathan M. Levy
Elizabeth Anne McGeary
Steven F. Morris
Suzanne M. Perry
Laura Hathaway Phillips
William A. Shapard (Not admitted in DC)

OF COUNSEL

Ralph W. Hardy, Jr.
Charles J. McKerns

For Complete List of Firm Personnel, See General Section

For full biographical listings, see the Martindale-Hubbell Law Directory

FISHER WAYLAND COOPER LEADER & ZARAGOZA, L.L.P. (AV)

A Registered Limited Liability Partnership
Suite 400 2001 Pennsylvania Avenue, N.W., 20006-1851
Telephone: 202-659-3494
Facsimile: 202-296-6518

Ben S. Fisher (1890-1954)
Charles V. Wayland (1910-1980)
Ben C. Fisher
Grover C. Cooper
Martin R. Leader
Richard R. Zaragoza
Clifford M. Harrington
Joel R. Kaswell
Kathryn R. Schmeltzer
Douglas Woloshin
David D. Oxenford
Barry H. Gottfried
Ann K. Ford
Bruce D. Jacobs
Eliot J. Greenwald
Carroll John Yung
Glenn S. Richards

OF COUNSEL

John Q. Hearne

Barrie Debra Berman
Bruce F. Hoffmeister
Scott R. Flick
Francisco R. Montero
Gregory L. Masters (Not admitted in DC)
Robert C. Fisher
Lauren Ann Lynch
Sharon L. Tasman
Theresa A. Smyth
Howard C. Griboff (Not admitted in DC)
Guy T. Christiansen (Not admitted in DC)
Miles S. Mason
Kevin M. Walsh (Not admitted in DC)
Mark H. Tidman (Not admitted in DC)
Theodore Stern (Not admitted in DC)
Robert L. Galbreath (Not admitted in DC)

For full biographical listings, see the Martindale-Hubbell Law Directory

FLETCHER, HEALD & HILDRETH, P.L.C. (AV)

5335 Wisconsin Avenue, N.W., Suite 810, P.O. Box 33847, 20033-0847
Telephone: 202-828-5700
Telecopier: 202-828-5786
Arlington, Virginia Office: 11th Floor, 1300 N. 17th Street.
Telephone: 703-812-0400.
Fax: 703-812-0486.

Paul D. P. Spearman (1898-1962)
Frank Roberson (1882-1961)
Russell Rowell (1910-1994)
Robert L. Heald (1917-1994)
Edward F. Kenehan (Retired)
Frank U. Fletcher (Retired)
Richard Hildreth
Marvin Rosenberg
James P. Riley
Edward W. Hummers, Jr.
Leonard R. Raish

(See Next Column)

FLETCHER, HEALD & HILDRETH P.L.C., *Washington—Continued*

Vincent J. Curtis, Jr.
Patricia A. Mahoney
George Petrutsas
Frank R. Jazzo
Howard M. Weiss

Anne Goodwin Crump
Kathryn A. Kleiman (Not admitted in DC)
Paul J. Feldman
James A. Casey (Not admitted in DC)
Kathleen Victory
Ann Bavender
M. Veronica Pastor (Not admitted in DC)

OF COUNSEL

Edward A. Caine
Eric Fishman
Charles H. Kennedy (Not admitted in DC)

For full biographical listings, see the Martindale-Hubbell Law Directory

GURMAN, KURTIS, BLASK & FREEDMAN, CHARTERED (AV)

Suite 500, 1400 16th Street, N.W., 20036
Telephone: 202-328-8200
Fax: 202-462-1784; 462-1786

Louis Gurman
Jerome K. Blask
Michael K. Kurtis
William D. Freedman

Doane F. Kiechel, III
Jeanne M. Walsh (Not admitted in DC)
Andrea S. Miano
Nadja S. Sodos (Not admitted in DC)

For full biographical listings, see the Martindale-Hubbell Law Directory

HOGAN & HARTSON L.L.P. (AV)

Columbia Square, 555 13th Street, N.W., 20004-1109
Telephone: 202-637-5600
Telex: 89-2757
Cable Address: "Hogander Washington"
Fax: 202-637-5910
Brussels, Belgium Office: Avenue des Arts 41, 1040.
Telephone: (32.2) 505.09.11.
Fax: (32.2) 502.28.60.
London, England Office: Veritas House, 125 Finsbury Pavement, EC2A 1NQ.
Telephone: (44 171) 638.9595.
Fax: (44 171) 638.0884.
Moscow, Russia Office: 33/2 Usacheva Street, Building 3, 119048.
Telephone: (7095) 245-5190.
Fax: (7095) 245-5192.
Paris, France Office: Cabinet Wolfram: 14, rue Chauveau-Lagarde, 75008.
Telephone: (33-1) 44.71.97.00.
Fax: (33-1) 47.42.13.56.
Prague, Czech Republic Office: Opletalova 37, 110 00.
Telephone: (42-2) 2422-9009.
Fax: (42-2) 2421-5105.
Warsaw, Poland Office: Marszalkowska 6/6, 00-590.
Telephone: (48 2) 628 0201; Int'l (48) 3912 1413.
Fax: (48 2) 628 7787; Int'l (48) 3912 1511.
Baltimore, Maryland Office: 111 South Calvert Street, 16th Floor.
Telephone: 410-659-2700.
Fax: 410-539-6981.
Bethesda, Maryland Office: Two Democracy Center, Suite 720, 6903 Rockledge Drive.
Telephone: 301-493-0030.
Fax: 301-493-5169.
Colorado Springs, Colorado Office: 518 North Nevada Avenue, Suite 200.
Telephone: 719-635-5900.
Fax: 719-635-2847.
Denver, Colorado Office: One Tabor Center, Suite 1500, 1200 Seventeenth Street.
Telephone: 303-899-7300.
Fax: 303-899-7333.
McLean, Virginia Office: 8300 Greensboro Drive.
Telephone: 703-848-2600.
Fax: 703-448-7650.

MEMBERS OF FIRM

Robert L. Corn-Revere
Peter A. Rohrbach
Marvin J. Diamond
Mace J. Rosenstein
Gardner F. Gillespie
David J. Saylor
William S. Reyner, Jr.
Susan Wing
Richard S. Rodin
Joel S. Winnik

COUNSEL

Gerald E. Oberst, Jr. (Resident, Brussels, Belgium Office)
Linda L. Oliver
Marissa G. Repp

(See Next Column)

ASSOCIATES

Julie T. Barton (Not admitted in DC)
Tia Cudahy (Not admitted in DC)
Jacqueline P. Cleary
Karis A. Hastings
Michelle M. Shanahan

For Complete List of Firm Personnel, See General Section

For full biographical listings, see the Martindale-Hubbell Law Directory

MCFADDEN, EVANS & SILL (AV)

1627 Eye Street, N.W., Suite 810, 20006
Telephone: 202-293-0700
Telecopier: 202-659-5409

MEMBERS OF FIRM

Douglas B. McFadden
Donald J. Evans
William J. Sill

ASSOCIATES

Christine M. Crowe
R. Bradley Koerner
Nancy L. Killien (Not admitted in DC)
Robert M. Winteringham (Not admitted in DC)

OF COUNSEL

William M. Barnard
Thomas L. Jones

For full biographical listings, see the Martindale-Hubbell Law Directory

MIDLEN & GUILLOT, CHARTERED (AV)

3238 Prospect Street, N.W., 20007-3214
Telephone: 202-333-1500
Facsimile: 202-333-6852
Internet: MGCG@delphi.com

John H. Midlen, Jr.
Gregory H. Guillot (Not admitted in DC)

For full biographical listings, see the Martindale-Hubbell Law Directory

* O'MELVENY & MYERS (AV)

555 13th Street, N.W. Suite 500 West, 20004-1109
Telephone: 202-383-5300
Cable Address: "Moms"
Facsimile: 202-383-5414
Los Angeles, California Office: 400 South Hope Street.
Telephone: 213-669-6000.
Cable Address: "Moms."
Facsimile: 213-669-6407.
Century City Office: 1999 Avenue of the Stars, 7th Floor.
Telephone: 310-553-6700.
Facsimile: 310-246-6779.
Newport Beach, California Office: 610 Newport Center Drive, Suite 1700.
Telephone: 714-760-9600.
Cable Address: "Moms."
Facsimile: 714-669-6994.
San Francisco, California Office: Embarcadero Center West Tower, 275 Battery Street, Suite 2600.
Telephone: 415-984-8700.
Facsimile: 415-984-8701.
New York, N.Y. Office: Citicorp Center, 153 East 53rd Street, 54th Floor.
Telephone: 212-326-2000.
Facsimile: 212-326-2061.
Newark, New Jersey Office: One Gateway Center, 7th Floor.
Telephone: 201-639-8600.
Facsimile: 201-639-8630.
London, England Office: 10 Finsbury Square, London, EC2A 1LA.
Telephone: 011-44-171-256-8451
Facsimile: 011-44-171-638-8205.
Tokyo, Japan Office: Sanbancho KB-6 Building, 6 Sanbancho, Chiyoda-ku, Tokyo 102, Japan.
Telephone: 011-81-3-3239-2800.
Facsimile: 011-81-3-3239-2432.
Hong Kong Office: 1104 Lippo Tower, Lippo Centre, 89 Queensway, Central Hong Kong.
Telephone: 011-852-523-8266.
Facsimile: 011-852-522-1760.

WASHINGTON, D.C.
MEMBERS OF FIRM

John H. Beisner
Donald T. Bliss, Jr.
Ben E. Benjamin
F. Amanda DeBusk
John E. Welch

SPECIAL COUNSEL

Brian C. Anderson

RESIDENT ASSOCIATE

Nina Shafran

For Complete List of Firm Personnel, See General Section

For full biographical listings, see the Martindale-Hubbell Law Directory

Washington—Continued

Sutherland, Asbill & Brennan (AV)

1275 Pennsylvania Avenue, N.W., 20004-2404
Telephone: 202-383-0100
Cable Address: "Sutab Wash"
Telex: 89-501
Facsimile: 202-637-3593
Atlanta, Georgia Office: 999 Peachtree Street, N. E., 30309-3996.
Telephone: 404-853-8000.
New York, N.Y. Office: 1270 Avenue of the Americas, 10020-1700.
Telephone: 212-332-3000.
Austin, Texas Office: 111 Congress Avenue, 23rd Floor, 78701-4079.
Telephone: 512-469-3350.

Frank J. Martin, Jr.
Randolph J. May

COUNSEL

Timothy J. Cooney

For Complete List of Firm Personnel, See General Section

For full biographical listings, see the Martindale-Hubbell Law Directory

*** Venable, Baetjer, Howard & Civiletti (AV)**

A Partnership including Professional Corporations
Suite 1000, 1201 New York Avenue, N.W., 20005
Telephone: 202-962-4800
Fax: 202-962-8300
Baltimore, Maryland Office: Venable, Baetjer and Howard, 1800 Mercantile Bank & Trust Building, 2 Hopkins Plaza.
Telephone: 410-244-7400.
McLean, Virginia Office: Venable, Baetjer and Howard, Suite 400, 2010 Corporate Ridge.
Telephone: 703-760-1600.
Rockville, Maryland Office: Venable, Baetjer and Howard, Suite 500, One Church Street, P. O. Box 1906.
Telephone: 301-217-5600.
Towson, Maryland Office: Venable, Baetjer and Howard, 210 Allegheny Avenue, P. O. Box 5517.
Telephone: 410-494-6200.

MEMBERS OF FIRM

Ian D. Volner
Robert P. Bedell (Not admitted in DC)
Edward F. Glynn, Jr.
James R. Myers
Jeffrey D. Knowles

OF COUNSEL

Frank Horton

ASSOCIATES

James W. Hedlund (Not admitted in DC)
Barbara L. Waite

For Complete List of Firm Personnel, See General Section

For full biographical listings, see the Martindale-Hubbell Law Directory

Verner, Liipfert, Bernhard, McPherson and Hand, Chartered (AV)

901 15th Street, N.W., 20005-2301
Telephone: 202-371-6000
Cable Address: "Verlip"
Telex: 1561792 VERLIP UT
Fax: 202-371-6279
McLean, Virginia Office: Sixth Floor, 8280 Greensboro Drive, 22102.
Telephone: 703-749-6000.
Fax: 703-749-6027.
Houston, Texas Office: 2600 Texas Commerce Tower, 600 Travis, 77002.
Telephone: 713-237-9034.
Fax: 713-237-1216.

Thomas J. Keller
Erwin G. Krasnow
Lawrence R. Sidman

For Complete List of Firm Personnel, See General Section

For full biographical listings, see the Martindale-Hubbell Law Directory

Wilkinson, Barker, Knauer & Quinn (AV)

1735 New York Avenue, N.W., 20006
Telephone: 202-783-4141
Fax: 202-833-2360; 783-5851
Frankfurt am Main, Germany Office: Goethestrasse 23.
Telephone: 011-49-69-2876.
Telecopier: 011-49-69-297-8453.

MEMBERS OF FIRM

Glen A. Wilkinson (1911-1985)
Robert W. Barker (1919-1987)
Rosel H. Hyde (1900-1992)
Earl R Stanley
Paul S. Quinn
Leon T. Knauer
L. Andrew Tollin
Kenneth E. Satten
Michael Deuel Sullivan
Kathryn A. Zachem
F. Thomas Moran
Kenneth D. Patrich
Luisa L. Lancetti
Lawrence J. Movshin
Christine V. Simpson

(See Next Column)

ASSOCIATES

Kelley Ann Baione
Michael A. Mandigo
Janet Fitzpatrick
Robert G. Kirk (Not admitted in DC)
Carolyn W. Malanga (Not admitted in DC)
Craig Edward Gilmore (Not admitted in DC)
Georgina M. Lopez-Oña (Not admitted in DC)

For Complete List of Firm Personnel, See General Section

For full biographical listings, see the Martindale-Hubbell Law Directory

Wilmer, Cutler & Pickering (AV)

2445 M Street, N.W., 20037-1420
Telephone: 202-663-6000
Facsimile: 202-663-6363
Internet: Law@Wilmer.Com
European Offices:
4 Carlton Gardens, London, SW1Y 5AA, England. Telephone: 011 (4471) 839-4466.
Facsimile: 011 (4471) 839-3537.
Rue de la Loi 15 Wetstraat, B-1040 Brussels, Belgium. Telephone: 011 (322) 231-0903.
Facsimile: 011 (322) 230-4322.
Friedrichstrasse 95, D-10117 Berlin, Germany. Telephone: 011 (4930) 2643-3601.
Facsimile: 011 (4930) 2643-3630.

MEMBERS OF FIRM

Joel Rosenbloom
Robert A. Hammond, III
Daniel Marcus
Timothy N. Black
William T. Lake
A. Douglas Melamed
John H. Harwood II
William R. Richardson, Jr.
Andrea Ann Timko
W. Scott Blackmer (Resident, European Office, Brussels, Belgium)
Thomas P. Olson
Patrick J. Carome

SENIOR COUNSEL

J. Roger Wollenberg

COUNSEL

David R. Johnson

For Complete List of Firm Personnel, See General Section

For full biographical listings, see the Martindale-Hubbell Law Directory

FLORIDA

*JACKSONVILLE,** Duval Co.

Gabel & Hair (AV)

76 South Laura Street, Suite 1600, 32202-3421
Telephone: 904-353-7329
Cable Address: "Wahlgabel"
Fax: 904-358-1637

MEMBERS OF FIRM

George D. Gabel, Jr.
Mattox S. Hair
Joel B. Toomey
Robert M. Dees
Sheldon Boney Forte
Timothy J. Conner
Suzanne Meyer Schnabel

ASSOCIATES

Christine S. Mayo
Michael L. Berry, Jr.
Karen Harris Hildebrand

Scott M. Loftin (1878-1953)
Harold B. Wahl (1907-1993)

Representative Clients: Florida Publishing Co. (Florida Times-Union); Southern Bell Telephone & Telegraph Co.; American District Telegraph Co.; Employers Reinsurance Co.; WTLV Channel 12 TV; Gannett, Inc.; Capital Cities/ABC, Inc.; The New York Times Company; Jacksonville Business Journal; Media/Professional Insurance, Inc.

For full biographical listings, see the Martindale-Hubbell Law Directory

*MIAMI,** Dade Co.

Joseph Z. Fleming, P.A. (AV)

620 Ingraham Building, 25 Southeast Second Avenue, 33131
Telephone: 305-373-0791
Telecopier: 305-358-5933

Joseph Z. Fleming

For full biographical listings, see the Martindale-Hubbell Law Directory

Thomson Muraro Razook & Hart, P.A. (AV)

17th Floor, One Southeast Third Avenue, 33131
Telephone: 305-350-7200
Telecopier: 305-374-1005

(See Next Column)

THOMSON MURARO RAZOOK & HART P.A., *Miami—Continued*

Parker Davidson Thomson
Carol A. Licko

Representative Clients: The Miami Herald; Community Television of South Florida; Turner Broadcasting System; Simon & Schuster, Inc.; WPLG Channel 10.

For Complete List of Firm Personnel, See General Section

For full biographical listings, see the Martindale-Hubbell Law Directory

*TALLAHASSEE,** Leon Co.

HOPPING BOYD GREEN & SAMS (AV)

123 South Calhoun Street, P.O. Box 6526, 32314
Telephone: 904-222-7500
Fax: 904-224-8551

MEMBERS OF FIRM

Carlos Alvarez
James S. Alves
Brian H. Bibeau
Kathleen L. Blizzard
Elizabeth C. Bowman
William L. Boyd, IV
Richard S. Brightman
Peter C. Cunningham
Ralph A. DeMeo
Thomas M. DeRose
William H. Green
Wade L. Hopping
Frank E. Matthews
Richard D. Melson
David L. Powell
William D. Preston
Carolyn S. Raepple
Gary P. Sams
Robert P. Smith
Cheryl G. Stuart

ASSOCIATES

Kristin M. Conroy
Charles A. Culp, Jr.
Connie C. Durrence
Jonathan S. Fox
James Calvin Goodlett
Gary K. Hunter, Jr.
Dalana W. Johnson
Jonathan T. Johnson
Angela R. Morrison
Gary V. Perko
Karen Peterson
Michael P. Petrovich
Douglas S. Roberts
R. Scott Ruth
Julie Rome Steinmeyer

OF COUNSEL

W. Robert Fokes

Representative Clients: Amelia Island Plantation; American Cyanamid Co.; ARC America Corp.; Association of American Publishers; Association of Physical Fitness Centers; Cement Products Corp.; CF Industries; Champion Realty; Chemical Bank; Deseret Properties.

For full biographical listings, see the Martindale-Hubbell Law Directory

GEORGIA

*ATLANTA,** Fulton Co.

ALSTON & BIRD (AV)

A Partnership including Professional Corporations
One Atlantic Center, 1201 West Peachtree Street, 30309-3424
Telephone: 404-881-7000
Telecopier: 404-881-7777
Cable Address: AMGRAM GA
Telex: 54-2996
Easylink: 62985848
Washington, D.C. Office: 700 Thirteenth Street, Suite 350 20005-3960.
Telephone: 202-508-3300.
Telecopier: 202-508-3333.

MEMBERS OF FIRM

Neil Williams
Timothy S. Perry
Peter Kontio
J. Vaughan Curtis
Keith O. Cowan
H. Stephen Harris, Jr.
Robert J. Middleton, Jr.
Christopher D. Mangum
Randall L. Allen

ASSOCIATES

R. Gregory Brophy
Thomas L. West III

Representative Clients: Codecomm (Inc.); GTE Mobilnet Incorporated; GTE Personal Communications Services; National Data Corporation.

For Complete List of Firm Personnel, See General Section

For full biographical listings, see the Martindale-Hubbell Law Directory

KILPATRICK & CODY (AV)

Suite 2800, 1100 Peachtree Street, 30309-4530
Telephone: 404-815-6500
Telephone Copier: 404-815-6555
Telex: 54-2307
Washington, D.C. Office: Suite 800, 700 13th Street, N.W., 20005.
Telephone: 202-508-5800. Telephone Copier: 202-508-5858.
Brussels, Belgium Office: Avenue Louise 65, BTE 3, 1050 Brussels.
Telephone: (32) (2) 533-03-00.
Telecopier: (32) (2) 534-86-38.

(See Next Column)

London, England Office: 68 Pall Mall, London, SW1Y 5ES, England.
Telephone: (44) (71) 321 0477.
Telecopier: (44) (71) 930 9733.
Augusta, Georgia Office: Suite 1400 First Union Bank Building, P.O. Box 2043, 30903. Telephone (706) 724-2622. Telecopier (706) 722-0219.

OF COUNSEL

George B. Haley

MEMBERS OF FIRM

Harold E. Abrams
Jerre B. Swann
R. Alexander Bransford, Jr.
W. Stanley Blackburn
Frederick H. von Unwerth

Representative Clients: Southern Bell Telephone and Telegraph Co.; Bell South Mobility, Inc.; First Carolina Communications; Prestige Cable T.V., Inc.

For Complete List of Firm Personnel, See General Section

For full biographical listings, see the Martindale-Hubbell Law Directory

LONG ALDRIDGE & NORMAN (AV)

A Partnership including Professional Corporations
One Peachtree Center, Suite 5300, 303 Peachtree Street, 30308
Telephone: 404-527-4000
Telecopier: 404-527-4198
Washington, D.C. Office: Suite 950, 1615 L Street, 20036.
Telephone: 202-223-7033.
Telecopier: 202-223-7013.

MEMBERS OF FIRM

Stephen L. Camp
F. T. Davis, Jr., (P.C.)
Clay C. Long
Albert G. Norman, Jr.

ASSOCIATES

Wayne N. Bradley
Roy E. Hadley, Jr.
H. Franklin Layson
Briggs L. Tobin

OF COUNSEL

Martin R. Tilson, Jr.

For Complete List of Firm Personnel, See General Section

For full biographical listings, see the Martindale-Hubbell Law Directory

ILLINOIS

*CHICAGO,** Cook Co.

SAUNDERS & MONROE (AV)

Suite 4201, 205 North Michigan Avenue, 60601
Telephone: 312-946-9000
Facsimile: 312-946-0528

MEMBERS OF FIRM

George L. Saunders, Jr.
Lee A. Monroe
Thomas F. Bush, Jr.
Matthew E. Van Tine

Thomas A. Doyle
Christina J. Norton
Gwen A. Niedbalski

For full biographical listings, see the Martindale-Hubbell Law Directory

INDIANA

*INDIANAPOLIS,** Marion Co.

BOSE MCKINNEY & EVANS (AV)

2700 First Indiana Plaza, 135 North Pennsylvania Street, 46204
Telephone: 317-684-5000
Facsimile: 317-684-5173
Indianapolis North Office: Suite 1201, 8888 Keystone Crossing, 46240.
Telephone: 317-574-3700.
Facsimile: 317-574-3716.

MEMBERS OF FIRM

Kendall C. Crook
Ronald E. Elberger
David L. Wills
Alan W. Becker
Dwight L. Miller

Representative Clients: David Letterman Companies; Columbia Management, Inc.; Emmis Broadcasting Corp.; Apollo Communications Corporation; Rodgers Broadcasting Corporation; LeSea Broadcasting Corp.; Atlanta Magazine; Nuvo News -Weekly; Indianapolis Monthly.

For Complete List of Firm Personnel, See General Section

For full biographical listings, see the Martindale-Hubbell Law Directory

Indianapolis—Continued

ICE MILLER DONADIO & RYAN (AV)

One American Square Box 82001, 46282-0002
Telephone: 317-236-2100
Fax: 317-236-2219

MEMBERS OF FIRM

Donald G. Sutherland
Jack R. Snyder
Thomas H. Ristine

OF COUNSEL

James B. Burroughs

ASSOCIATE

Michael A. Wilkins

Representative Clients: Fairbanks Communications, Inc.; VideoIndiana, Inc.; Michiana Telecasting Corp.; National Broadcasting Co.; Wabash Valley Broadcasting Corp.; Maxtel Associates; Butler University; Taylor University; Great American Television & Radio Co.; Media Professional Insurance Co.

For Complete List of Firm Personnel, See General Section

For full biographical listings, see the Martindale-Hubbell Law Directory

KANSAS

*TOPEKA,** Shawnee Co.

GOODELL, STRATTON, EDMONDS & PALMER (AV)

515 South Kansas Avenue, 66603-3999
Telephone: 913-233-0593
Telecopier: 913-233-8870

MEMBERS OF FIRM

Gerald L. Goodell
Arthur E. Palmer
Charles R. Hay
Michael W. Merriam
John H. Stauffer, Jr.
John D. Ensley

ASSOCIATE

Curtis J. Waugh

Local Counsel for: Farm Bureau Mutual Insurance Co.; Metropolitan Life Insurance Co.; St. Paul Fire & Marine Insurance Co.
General Counsel for: American Home Life Insurance Co.; Columbian National Title Insurance Co.; The Menninger Foundation; Stauffer Communications, Inc.; Kansas Association of Realtors; Kansas Medical Society; Kansas Hospital Association.

For Complete List of Firm Personnel, See General Section

For full biographical listings, see the Martindale-Hubbell Law Directory

*WICHITA,** Sedgwick Co.

FLEESON, GOOING, COULSON & KITCH, L.L.C. (AV)

125 North Market Street, Suite 1600, P.O. Box 997, 67201-0997
Telephone: 316-267-7361
Telecopier: 316-267-1754

Gerrit H. Wormhoudt
Thomas D. Kitch
William P. Tretbar
Lyndon W. Vix

Attorneys for: Bank IV, Wichita, N.A; Intrust Bank, N.A.; Wichita Eagle and Beacon Publishing Co., Inc.; Southwest Kansas Royalty Owners Assn.; Liberty Mutual Insurance Co.; Grant Thornton; The Law Company; Vulcan Materials Co.; The Wichita State University Board of Trustees.

For Complete List of Firm Personnel, See General Section

For full biographical listings, see the Martindale-Hubbell Law Directory

KENTUCKY

*LEXINGTON,** Fayette Co.

STOLL, KEENON & PARK (AV)

201 E. Main Street, Suite 1000, 40507-1380
Telephone: 606-231-3000
Telecopier: 606-253-1093; 606-253-1027
Frankfort, Kentucky Office: 326 West Main Street.
Telephone: 502-875-6000.
Telecopier: 502-875-6008.
Louisville, Kentucky Office: 400 West Market Street, Suite 2650, 40202.
Telephone: 502-568-9100.
Telecopier: 502-568-6340.

MEMBERS OF FIRM

Michael L. Judy
Robert F. Houlihan, Jr.
Dan M. Rose

(See Next Column)

ASSOCIATE

James L. Thomerson

Representative Clients: Lexington Herald Leader Co.; Knight-Ridder; GTE Of The South, GTE Products Corp.; Bell South Mobility; Kentucky Press Assn.; Thompson Newspapers Inc.; Thoroughbred Racing Communications, Inc.; The Jockey Club.

For Complete List of Firm Personnel, See General Section

For full biographical listings, see the Martindale-Hubbell Law Directory

*LOUISVILLE,** Jefferson Co.

OGDEN NEWELL & WELCH (AV)

1200 One Riverfront Plaza, 40202-2973
Telephone: 502-582-1601
Fax: 502-581-9564

MEMBERS OF FIRM

Richard F. Newell
Kendrick R. Riggs

ASSOCIATES

John Wade Hendricks
James G. Campbell

Counsel for: World Wide Communications; USX Consultants, Inc.; Airtouch Communications; RCI Long Distance, Inc.; Telaleasing Enterprises, Inc.

For Complete List of Firm Personnel, See General Section

For full biographical listings, see the Martindale-Hubbell Law Directory

WYATT, TARRANT & COMBS (AV)

Citizens Plaza, 40202
Telephone: 502-589-5235
Telecopier: 502-589-0309
Lexington, Kentucky Office: 1700 Lexington Financial Center.
Telephone: 606-233-2012.
Telecopier: 606-259-0649.
Frankfort, Kentucky Office: The Taylor-Scott Building, 311 West Main Street.
Telephone: 502-223-2104.
Telecopier: 502-227-7681.
New Albany, Indiana Office: The Elsby Building, 117 East Spring Street,
Telephone: 812-945-3561.
Telecopier: 812-949-2524.
Nashville, Tennessee Office: 1500 Nashville City Center, 511 Union Street.
Telephone: 615-244-0020.
Telecopier: 615-256-1726.
Music Row, Nashville Office: 29 Music Square East.
Telephone: 615-255-6161.
Telecopier: 615-254-4490.
Hendersonville, Tennessee Office: 313 E. Main Street, Suite 1.
Telephone: 615-822-8822.
Telecopier: 615-824-4684.

MEMBERS OF FIRM

Edgar A. Zingman
Jon L. Fleischaker
Kimberly K. Greene
William H. Hollander

Representative Clients: Alpha Cellular Telephone Co.; BellSouth Telecommunications, Inc./South Central Bell; Data Courier, Inc.; Gannett Co., Inc./-The Courier-Journal/Louisville Times; Kentucky Press Assn.; Kentucky Cable Television Assn.; McCann-Erickson of Louisville, Inc.; Telecable of Lexington; Thomas Nelson Publishers, Inc.; WHAS and WHAS T.V.

For Complete List of Firm Personnel, See General Section

For full biographical listings, see the Martindale-Hubbell Law Directory

LOUISIANA

*SHREVEPORT,** Caddo Parish

BARLOW AND HARDTNER L.C. (AV)

Tenth Floor, Louisiana Tower, 401 Edwards Street, 71101-3289
Telephone: 318-227-1131
Telecopier: 318-227-1141
Mailing Address: P.O. Box 8, Shreveport, Louisiana, 71161-0008

Joseph L. Shea, Jr.
Jay A. Greenleaf

OF COUNSEL

Paula Hazelrig Hickman

Representative Clients: AmCom General Corporation; Kelley Oil Corporation; NorAm Energy Corp. (formerly Arkla, Inc.); Central and South West; Panhandle Eastern Corp.; Pennzoil Producing Co.; Johnson Controls, Inc.; Ashland Oil, Inc.; Southwestern Electric Power Company; Brammer Engineering, Inc

For Complete List of Firm Personnel, See General Section

For full biographical listings, see the Martindale-Hubbell Law Directory

MAINE

*PORTLAND,** Cumberland Co.

PRETI, FLAHERTY, BELIVEAU & PACHIOS (AV)

443 Congress Street, P.O. Box 11410, 04104-7410
Telephone: 207-791-3000
Telecopier: 207-791-3111
Augusta, Maine Office: 45 Memorial Circle, P.O. Box 1058, 04332-1058.
Telephone: 207-623-5300.
Telecopier: 207-623-2914.
Rumford, Maine Office: 150 Congress Street, P.O. Drawer L, 04276-2035.
Telephone: 207-364-4593.
Telecopier: 207-369-9421.

MEMBERS OF FIRM

John J. Flaherty
Severin M. Beliveau (Augusta Office)
Jonathan S. Piper
Edward R. Benjamin, Jr.

ASSOCIATES

Mark B. LeDuc (Augusta Office)
Ann R. Robinson (Augusta Office)

Representative Clients: Guy Gannett Publishing Company; Maine Association of Broadcasters; Brunswick Publishing Co.; The Maine Times; State Cable T.V. Corporation; Bee Line Cable, Inc.; Better Cable Television; Public Cable Co.; New England Cable Television Association.

For Complete List of Firm Personnel, See General Section

For full biographical listings, see the Martindale-Hubbell Law Directory

MARYLAND

*BALTIMORE,** (Independent City)

VENABLE, BAETJER AND HOWARD (AV)

A Partnership including Professional Corporations
1800 Mercantile Bank & Trust Building, 2 Hopkins Plaza, 21201
Telephone: 410-244-7400
Washington, D.C. Office: Venable, Baetjer, Howard & Civiletti. Suite 1000, 1201 New York Avenue, N.W.
Telephone: 202-962-4800.
McLean, Virginia Office: Suite 400, 2010 Corporate Ridge.
Telephone: 703-760-1600.
Rockville, Maryland Office: Suite 500, One Church Street, P. O. Box 1906.
Telephone: 301-217-5600.
Towson, Maryland Office: 210 Allegheny Avenue, P. O. Box 5517.
Telephone: 410-494-6200.

MEMBERS OF FIRM

Thomas P. Perkins, III (P.C.)
James A. Cole
Ian D. Volner (Not admitted in MD; Resident, Washington, D.C. Office)
Edward F. Glynn, Jr. (Not admitted in MD; Resident, Washington, D.C. Office)
H. Russell Frisby, Jr.
James R. Myers (Not admitted in MD; Resident, Washington, D.C. Office)
Jeffrey D. Knowles (Not admitted in MD; Resident, Washington, D.C. Office)

OF COUNSEL

Frank Horton (Not admitted in MD; Resident, Washington, D.C. Office)
Robert A. Beizer (Resident, Washington, D.C. Office)

ASSOCIATES

James W. Hedlund (Not admitted in MD; Resident, Washington, D.C. Office)
Barbara L. Waite (Not admitted in MD; Resident, Washington, D.C. Office)

For Complete List of Firm Personnel, See General Section

For full biographical listings, see the Martindale-Hubbell Law Directory

SILVER SPRING, Montgomery Co.

ALEXANDER, GEBHARDT, APONTE & MARKS, L.L.C. (AV)

Lee Plaza-Suite 805, 8601 Georgia Avenue, 20910
Telephone: 301-589-2222
Facsimile: 301-589-2523
Washington, D.C. Office: 1314 Nineteenth Street, N.W., 20036.
Telephone: 202-835-1555.
New York, New York Office: 330 Madison Avenue, 36th Floor.
Telephone: 212-808-0008.
Fax: 212-599-1028.

(See Next Column)

Koteles Alexander (Not admitted in MD)
James L. Bearden (Not admitted in MD)

Reference: Riggs National Bank of Washington, D.C.

For full biographical listings, see the Martindale-Hubbell Law Directory

MASSACHUSETTS

*BOSTON,** Suffolk Co.

MINTZ, LEVIN, COHN, FERRIS, GLOVSKY AND POPEO, P.C. (AV)

One Financial Center, 02111
Telephone: 617-542-6000
FAX: 617-542-2241
Washington, D.C. Office: 701 Pennsylvania Avenue, N.W. Suite 900.
Telephone: 202-434-7300.
Fax: 202-434-7400.

Charles D. Ferris (Resident, Washington, D.C. Office)
Frank W. Lloyd (Resident, Washington, D.C. Office)
Bruce D. Sokler (Resident, Washington, D.C. Office)

Karen W. Levy (Resident, Washington, D.C. Office)

For Complete List of Firm Personnel, See General Section

For full biographical listings, see the Martindale-Hubbell Law Directory

MICHIGAN

*DETROIT,** Wayne Co.

BODMAN, LONGLEY & DAHLING (AV)

34th Floor 100 Renaissance Center, 48243
Telephone: 313-259-7777
Fax: 313-393-7579
Troy, Michigan Office: Suite 2020, 755 West Big Beaver Road.
Telephone: 810-362-2110.
Ann Arbor, Michigan Office: 110 Miller, Suite 300.
Telephone: 313-761-3780.
Northern Michigan Office: 229 Court Street, P.O. Box 405, Cheboygan.
Telephone: 616-627-4351.

MEMBERS OF FIRM

Theodore Souris
Carson C. Grunewald
Kenneth R. Lango (Troy Office)
James A. Smith
James J. Walsh

Representative Clients: Abitibi Price Group; Archdiocese of Detroit; Comerica Bank; The Detroit Lions, Inc.; Ford Estates; General Motors Corporation; Charles Stewart Mott Foundation; Norfolk Southern Corporation; Panhandle Eastern Corporation; State Farm Mutual Automobile Insurance Company.

For Complete List of Firm Personnel, See General Section

For full biographical listings, see the Martindale-Hubbell Law Directory

BUTZEL LONG, A PROFESSIONAL CORPORATION (AV)

Suite 900, 150 West Jefferson, 48226
Telephone: 313-225-7000
Telecopier: 313-225-7080
Birmingham, Michigan Office: Suite 200, 32270 Telegraph Road.
Telephone: 810-258-1616.
Telecopier: 810-258-1439.
Lansing, Michigan Office: 118 West Ottawa Street.
Telephone: 517-372-6622.
Telecopier: 517-372-6672.
Ann Arbor, Michigan Office: Suite 400, 121 West Washington.
Telephone: 313-995-3110.
Telecopier: 313-995-1777.
Grosse Pointe Farms, Michigan Office: Suite 260, 21 Kercheval.
Telephone: 313-886-5446.
Telecopier: 313-886-2114.

Richard E. Rassel
James E. Stewart
Leonard M. Niehoff

J. Michael Huget
Eugene H. Boyle, Jr.
Robin K. Luce
Barbara L. McQuade
Laurie J. Michelson

(See Next Column)

BUTZEL LONG A PROFESSIONAL CORPORATION—*Continued*

Representative Clients: Bridgestone/Firestone, Inc.; The Detroit News, Inc.; Detroit Diesel Corp.; Kelly Services; Kelsey Hayes Co.; Merrill Lynch & Co., Inc.; Stroh Brewery Co.; Takata Corp.; United Parcel Services of America, Inc.; The University of Michigan.

For Complete List of Firm Personnel, See General Section

For full biographical listings, see the Martindale-Hubbell Law Directory

CLARK, KLEIN & BEAUMONT (AV)

1600 First Federal Building, 1001 Woodward Avenue, 48226
Telephone: 313-965-8300
Facsimile: 313-962-4348
Bloomfield Hills Office: 1533 North Woodward Avenue, Suite 220, 48304.
Telephone: 810-258-2900.
Facsimile: 810-258-2949.

MEMBER OF FIRM

David E. Nims, III

Representative Clients: Booth American Company.

For Complete List of Firm Personnel, See General Section

For full biographical listings, see the Martindale-Hubbell Law Directory

HONIGMAN MILLER SCHWARTZ AND COHN (AV)

A Partnership including Professional Corporations
2290 First National Building, 48226
Telephone: 313-256-7800
Telecopier: 313-962-0176
Telex: 235705
Lansing, Michigan Office: Phoenix Building, 222 North Washington Square, Suite 400.
Telephone: 517-484-8282.
West Palm Beach, Florida Office: Suite 800 Esperante Building, 222 Lakeview Avenue.
Telephone: 407-838-4500.
Tampa, Florida Office: 2700 Landmark Centre, 401 E. Jackson Street.
Telephone: 813-221-6600.
Orlando, Florida Office: 390 North Orange Avenue, Suite 1300.
Telephone: 407-648-0300.
Houston, Texas Office: 3100 First Interstate Bank Plaza, 1000 Louisiana.
Telephone: 713-650-2600.
Los Angeles, California Office: McNeill Plaza, Suite 820, 15260 Ventura Boulevard, 91403.
Telephone: 818-784-2900.

MEMBERS OF FIRM

Herschel P. Fink
Michael A. Gruskin
I. W. Winsten

ASSOCIATE

Daniel G. Helton

RESIDENT IN WEST PALM BEACH, FLORIDA OFFICE

MEMBER

Steven L. Schwarzberg (P.A.)

OF COUNSEL

Delmer C. Gowing, III, (P.A.)

RESIDENT IN TAMPA, FLORIDA OFFICE

MEMBER

Gregory G. Jones (P.A.)

Representative Clients: The Detroit Free Press; Knight-Ridder Inc.; Capital Cities/ABC, Inc.; Crain Communications; Heritage Media Corp. (Mellus Newspapers, Dearborn Press and Guide, and News Herald Newspapers); National Broadcasting Co,; Fox, Inc.; Times-Mirror Company; The Miami Herald; American Society of Composers, Authors and Publishers (ASCAP).

For Complete List of Firm Personnel, See General Section

For full biographical listings, see the Martindale-Hubbell Law Directory

MILLER, CANFIELD, PADDOCK AND STONE, P.L.C. (AV)

A Professional Limited Liability Company
Founded in 1852 by Sidney Davy Miller
150 West Jefferson, Suite 2500, 48226-4415
Telephone: 313-963-6420
Fax: 313-496-7500
Cable Address: "Stem Detroit"
Detroit, Michigan Office: 150 West Jefferson, Suite 2500, 48226-4415.
Telephone: 313-963-6420.
Fax: 313-496-7500.
Cable Address: "Stem Detroit."
Ann Arbor, Michigan Office: 101 North Main Street, 7th Floor, 48104-1400.
Telephone: 313-663-2445.
Fax: 313-747-7147.
Bloomfield Hills, Michigan Office: Suite 100, Pinehurst Office Center, 1400 North Woodward, 48303-2014.
Telephone: 313-645-5000.
Fax: 313-645-1917.

(See Next Column)

Grand Rapids, Michigan Office: 1200 Campau Square Plaza, 99 Monroe, N.W., 49503-2639.
Telephone: 616-454-8656.
Fax: 616-776-6322.
Howell, Michigan Office: 121 South Barnard Street, Suite 4, 48843-2305.
Telephone: 517-546-7600.
Telecopier: 517-546-6974.
Kalamazoo, Michigan Office: 444 West Michigan Avenue, 49007-3752.
Telephone: 616-381-7030.
Fax: 616-382-0244.
Lansing, Michigan Office: One Michigan Avenue, Suite 900, 48933-1609.
Telephone: 517-487-2070.
Fax: 517-374-6304.
Monroe, Michigan Office: The Executive Centre, 214 East Elm Avenue, 48161-2682.
Telephone: 313-243-2000.
Fax: 313-243-0901.
Washington, D.C. Office: 1225 Nineteenth Street, N.W., Suite 400. 20036.
Telephone: 202-429-5575; 785-0600.
Fax: 202-331-1118; 785-1234.
Pensacola, Florida Office: 25 West Cedar, 32501.
Telephone: 904-469-1088.
Fax: 904-432-0677.
St. Petersburg, Florida Office: 100 Second Avenue S., Suite 7045, 33701.
Telephone: 813-982-6000.
Fax: 813-892-6002.
Gdansk, Poland Office: Suite 322, Dom Technika Building, Ul. Rajska 6, 80-850.
Telephone: 011-485-831-2808.
Fax: 011-485-831-4719.
Warsaw, Poland Office: Ul. Marszalkowska 82, Suite 561, 00-517.
Telephone: 011-482-623-6457 and 6458.
Fax: 011-482-623-6459.

MEMBER OF FIRM

John J. Collins, Jr.

Representative Firm Clients: Chrysler Corp.; Comerica, Inc.; City of Detroit, Mich.; Detroit Tigers, Inc.; First of Michigan; Fretter, Inc.; Ford Motor Co.; Ford Motor Credit Co.; Great Lakes Bancorp; Henry Ford Hospital.

For Complete List of Firm Personnel, See General Section

For full biographical listings, see the Martindale-Hubbell Law Directory

MISSISSIPPI

*JACKSON,** Hinds Co.

ALSTON, RUTHERFORD, TARDY & VAN SLYKE (AV)

121 North State Street, P.O. Drawer 1532, 39215-1532
Telephone: 601-948-6882
Fax: 601-948-6902

MEMBERS OF FIRM

Alex A. Alston, Jr.
Leonard D. Van Slyke, Jr.
Terryl K. Rushing

Counsel for: Gannett Co., Inc. (Jackson Clarion-Ledger); TV-3, Inc. (WLBT); North Star Television of Jackson, Inc. (WAPT); Newsweek; Motion Picture Association of America, Inc.; Paramount Pictures Corp.; Memphis Publishing Co. (Commercial-Appeal); Society of Professional Journalists.

For Complete List of Firm Personnel, See General Section

For full biographical listings, see the Martindale-Hubbell Law Directory

NEVADA

*LAS VEGAS,** Clark Co.

ROGERS & ROGERS (AV)

1500 Foremaster Lane, Suite 2, 89101-1103
Telephone: 702-642-3333
Fax: 702-642-3444

MEMBERS OF FIRM

James E. Rogers, P.C.
Suzanne E. Rogers
Perry Rogers

For full biographical listings, see the Martindale-Hubbell Law Directory

NEW JERSEY

*NEWARK,** Essex Co.

McCarter & English (AV)

Four Gateway Center, 100 Mulberry Street, P.O. Box 652, 07101-0652
Telephone: 201-622-4444
Telecopier: 201-624-7070
Cable Address: "McCarter" Newark
Cherry Hill, New Jersey Office: 1810 Chapel Avenue West.
Telephone: 609-662-8444.
Telecopier: 609-662-6203.
New York, New York Office: Suite 1519, One World Trade Center.
Telephone: 212-466-9018.
Telecopier: 212-432-6568.
Boca Raton, Florida Office: 2255 Glades Road, Suite 319-A.
Telephone: 407-994-6262.
Telecopier: 407-241-0798.
Wilmington, Delaware Office: Mellon Bank Center, 919 Market Street.
Telephone: 302-654-8010.
Telecopier: 302-654-0795.

MEMBERS OF FIRM

Thomas F. Daly
Richard M. Eittreim

For Complete List of Firm Personnel, See General Section

For full biographical listings, see the Martindale-Hubbell Law Directory

Sills Cummis Zuckerman Radin Tischman Epstein & Gross, A Professional Corporation (AV)

One Riverfront Plaza, 07102-5400
Telephone: 201-643-7000
Fax: 201-643-6500
Telex: 820630 Sillsbeck Nwk
Atlantic City, New Jersey Office: 17 Gordon's Alley.
Telephone: 609-344-2800.
New York, N.Y. Office: 250 Park Avenue.
Telephone: 212-643-7000.

Steven S. Radin
Ira A. Rosenberg
Thomas S. Novak
Robert M. Axelrod
James M. Hirschhorn

Noel D. Humphreys

OF COUNSEL

Mitchel E. Ostrer

Representative Clients: GTE Sprint Communications; MCI Communications Corp.; Corporate Satellite Communications; Gannett Outdoor Company of New Jersey; Ameritelephone, Inc.; Bellcore.

For Complete List of Firm Personnel, See General Section

For full biographical listings, see the Martindale-Hubbell Law Directory

NEW MEXICO

*ALBUQUERQUE,** Bernalillo Co.

Hinkle, Cox, Eaton, Coffield & Hensley (AV)

Suite 800, 500 Marquette, N.W., P.O. Box 2043, 87103
Telephone: 505-768-1500
FAX: 505-768-1529
Roswell, New Mexico Office: Suite 700, United Bank Plaza, P.O. Box 10, 88202.
Telephone: 505-622-6510.
FAX: 505-623-9332.
Midland, Texas Office: 6 Desta Drive, Suite 2800, P.O. Box 3580, 79705.
Telephone: 915-683-4691.
FAX: 915-683-6518.
Amarillo, Texas Office: 1700 Bank One Center. P.O. Box 9238, 79105-9238.
Telephone: 806-372-5569.
FAX: 806-372-9761.
Santa Fe, New Mexico Office: 218 Montezuma, P.O. Box 2068, 87504.
Telephone: 505-982-4554.
FAX: 505-982-8623.
Austin, Texas Office: 401 West 15th Street, Suite 800, 78701.
Telephone: 512-476-7137.
FAX: 512-476-5431.
Associated Office: Hoffman & Stephens, P.C., 401 West 15th Street, Suite 800, 78701.
Telephone: 512-476-5434.
Fax: 512-476-5431.

(See Next Column)

Eric D. Lanphere

Representative Clients: Anadarko Petroleum Corp.; Atlantic Richfield Co.; Bass Enterprises Production Co.; BHP Petroleum; Caroon & Black Management, Inc.; Chevron, USA, Inc.; CIGNA; City of Albuquerque; Coastal Oil & Gas Corp. Co.; Ethicon Inc., A Johnson & Johnson, Co.; Diagnostik; Conoco; Texaco; Presbyterian Healthcare Services.

For Complete List of Firm Personnel, See General Section

For full biographical listings, see the Martindale-Hubbell Law Directory

NEW YORK

*NEW YORK,** New York Co.

Chapman & Fennell (AV)

330 Madison Avenue, 10017
Telephone: 212-687-3600
Telex: WUI 880411 (ETOSHA NY)
Telefax: 212-972-5368
Stamford, Connecticut Office: Three Landmark Square.
Telephone: 203-353-8000.
Telefax: 203-353-8799.
Washington D.C. Office: 2000 L. Street, N.W., Suite 200.
Telephone: 202-822-9351.

MEMBERS OF FIRM

Darrell K. Fennell
Philip M. Chiappone

OF COUNSEL

Michael Winger
Carol E. Meltzer
Eric S. Kamisher

For full biographical listings, see the Martindale-Hubbell Law Directory

NORTH CAROLINA

*RALEIGH,** Wake Co.

Everett, Gaskins, Hancock & Stevens (AV)

The Professional Building, Suite 600, 127 West Hargett Street, P.O. Box 911, 27602
Telephone: 919-755-0025
Fax: 919-755-0009
Durham, North Carolina Office: Suite 300, 301 West Main Street, P.O. Box 586.
Telephone: 919-682-5691.
Fax: 919-682-5469.

MEMBER OF FIRM

Hugh Stevens

ASSOCIATE

Katherine R. White

LEGAL SUPPORT PERSONNEL

Allyson S. McNeill

Representative Clients: Capital Cities/ABC, Inc.; MCI Telecommunications; Media General, Inc.; Paramount Communications; Park Communications; Post Publishing Company; The News & Observer Publishing Company, Inc.; The North Carolina Press Association; The Stanford Herald, Inc.; The Washington News Publishing Company.

For Complete List of Firm Personnel, See General Section

For full biographical listings, see the Martindale-Hubbell Law Directory

Tharrington, Smith & Hargrove (AV)

209 Fayetteville Street Mall, P.O. Box 1151, 27602
Telephone: 919-821-4711
Telecopier: 919-829-1583

MEMBERS OF FIRM

Carlisle W. Higgins (1887-1980)
J. Harold Tharrington
Roger W. Smith
Wade M. Smith
George T. Rogister, Jr.
Carlyn G. Poole
Douglas E. Kingsbery
Randall M. Roden
Michael Crowell
Ann L. Majestic
C. Allison Brown Schafer

ASSOCIATES

Melissa Hill
Daniel W. Clark
Jonathan A. Blumberg
Debra R. Nickels
Rod Malone
E. Hardy Lewis
Jaye Powell Meyer

(See Next Column)

THARRINGTON, SMITH & HARGROVE—*Continued*

LEGAL SUPPORT PERSONNEL

Michael M. Cogswell

Representative Clients: North Carolina Association of Broadcasters; AT&T Communications; ABC-TV Network Affiliates Assn.; North Carolina Cable Television Assn.; Time-Warner Communications; The Hearst Corporation; Voyager Communications.

For full biographical listings, see the Martindale-Hubbell Law Directory

*WINSTON-SALEM,** Forsyth Co.

WOMBLE CARLYLE SANDRIDGE & RICE (AV)

A Professional Limited Liability Company
1600 Southern National Financial Center, P.O. Drawer 84, 27102
Telephone: 910-721-3600
Telecopy: 910-721-3660
Telex: 806498
Charlotte, North Carolina Office: 3300 One First Union Center, 301 South College Street.
Telephone: 704-331-4900.
Telecopy: 704-331-4955.
Telex: 853609.
Raleigh, North Carolina Office: 2100 First Union Capitol Center, 150 Fayetteville Street Mall, P.O. Box 831.
Telephone: 919-755-2100.
Telecopy: 919-755-2150.
Telex: 806498.
Atlanta, Georgia Office: One Ninety One Peachtree Tower, 191 Peachtree Street, N.E., Suite 3250.
Telephone: 404-614-2580.
Fax: 404-614-2595.

MEMBER OF FIRM

John L. W. Garrou

Representative Clients: Brad Ragan, Inc.; Brenner Companies; Food Lion, Inc.; Hanes Companies, Inc.; North Carolina Baptist Hospitals, Inc.; R.J. Reynolds Tobacco Company; Summit Communications Group, Inc.; Thomasville Furniture Industries, Inc.; Wachovia Corporation; Wake Forest University.

For Complete List of Firm Personnel, See General Section

For full biographical listings, see the Martindale-Hubbell Law Directory

NORTH DAKOTA

*BISMARCK,** Burleigh Co.

PEARCE AND DURICK (AV)

314 East Thayer Avenue, P.O. Box 400, 58502
Telephone: 701-223-2890
Fax: 701-223-7865

MEMBERS OF FIRM

Patrick W. Durick
Gary R. Thune
Jerome C. Kettleson

Representative Clients: American Insurance Assn.; Cigna-INA Insurance Co.; Deere & Co.; Federal Deposit Insurance Corp.; Ford Motor Co.; General Motors Corp.; MDU Resources Group, Inc.; Northwest Airlines; Royal Insurance Co.; Meyer Broadcasting Co.

For Complete List of Firm Personnel, See General Section

For full biographical listings, see the Martindale-Hubbell Law Directory

OHIO

*CINCINNATI,** Hamilton Co.

FROST & JACOBS (AV)

2500 PNC Center, 201 East Fifth Street, P.O. Box 5715, 45201-5715
Telephone: 513-651-6800
Cable Address: "Frostjac"
Telex: 21-4396 F & J CIN
Telecopier: 513-651-6981
Columbus, Ohio Office: One Columbus, 10 West Broad Street.
Telephone: 614-464-1211.
Telecopier: 614-464-1737.
Lexington, Kentucky Office: 1100 Vine Center Tower, 333 West Vine Street.
Telephone: 606-254-1100.
Telecopier: 606-253-2990.

(See Next Column)

Middletown, Ohio Office: 400 First National Bank Building, 2 North Main Street.
Telephone: 513-422-2001.
Telecopier: 513-422-3010.
Naples, Florida Office: 4001 Tamiami Trail North, Suite 220.
Telephone: 813-261-0582.
Telecopier: 813-261-2083.

MEMBERS OF FIRM

Susan Grogan Faller
Todd H. Bailey
Richard M. Goehler

Representative Clients: Multimedia, Inc.; Multimedia Entertainment, Inc.; Reams Broadcasting; Brown Publishing Company; Cincinnati Magazine; National Underwriter Company.

For Complete List of Firm Personnel, See General Section

For full biographical listings, see the Martindale-Hubbell Law Directory

*CLEVELAND,** Cuyahoga Co.

BAKER & HOSTETLER (AV)

3200 National City Center, 1900 East Ninth Street, 44114-3485
Telephone: 216-621-0200
Telecopier: 216-696-0740
TWX: 810 421 8375
RCA Telex: 215032
In Columbus, Ohio: Capitol Square, Suite 2100, 65 East State Street.
Telephone: 614-228-1541.
In Denver, Colorado: 303 East 17th Avenue, Suite 1100.
Telephone: 303-861-0600.
In Houston, Texas: 1000 Louisiana, Suite 2000.
Telephone: 713-751-1600.
In Long Beach, California: 300 Oceangate, Suite 620.
Telephone: 310-432-2827.
In Los Angeles, California: 600 Wilshire Boulevard.
Telephone: 213-624-2400.
In Orlando, Florida: SunBank Center, Suite 2300, 200 South Orange Avenue.
Telephone: 407-649-4000.
In Washington, D. C.: Washington Square, Suite 1100, 1050 Connecticut Avenue, N.W.
Telephone: 202-861-1500.
In College Park, Maryland: 9658 Baltimore Boulevard, Suite 206.
Telephone: 301-441-2781.
In Alexandria, Virginia: 437 North Lee Street.
Telephone: 703-549-1294.
In San Francisco, California: One Sansome Street, Suite 2000.
Telephone: 415-951-4705.

PARTNERS

Louis A. Colombo
David L. Marburger

For Complete List of Firm Personnel, See General Section

For full biographical listings, see the Martindale-Hubbell Law Directory

WALTER & HAVERFIELD (AV)

1300 Terminal Tower, 44113-2253
Telephone: 216-781-1212
Telecopier: 216-575-0911
Columbus, Ohio Office: 88 East Broad Street.
Telephone: 614-221-7371.

MEMBERS OF FIRM

Michael T. McMenamin
Nancy A. Noall
Christopher L. Gibbon
Frederick W. Whatley
Kenneth A. Zirm

Representative Clients: AGA Gas, Inc.; Air Products and Chemicals, Inc.; American Crane Corp.; Andrews Moving & Storage, Inc.; Applied Medical Technology, Inc.; Aribica Cafes, Inc.; Associated Aviation Underwriters; The Associated Press; Beverly Enterprises, Inc.; Brookfield Wire Company.

For Complete List of Firm Personnel, See General Section

For full biographical listings, see the Martindale-Hubbell Law Directory

*TOLEDO,** Lucas Co.

FRITZ BYERS (AV)

Suite 824 The Spitzer Building, 43604
Telephone: 419-241-8013
Telecopier: 419-241-4215

General Counsel for: Blade Communications, Inc.; Toledo Blade Co.; Buckeye Cablevision, Inc.; Pittsburgh Post Gazette.
Reference: Capital Bank N.A.

For full biographical listings, see the Martindale-Hubbell Law Directory

OKLAHOMA

*OKLAHOMA CITY,** Oklahoma Co.

ANDREWS DAVIS LEGG BIXLER MILSTEN & PRICE, A PROFESSIONAL CORPORATION (AV)

500 West Main, 73102
Telephone: 405-272-9241
FAX: 405-235-8786

Robert D. Nelon

Michelle Johnson

Representative Clients: Griffin Television, Inc. (KWTV, CBS Affilate); Oklahoma Association of Broadcasters; Palmer Communications, Inc. (KFOR-TV, NBC Affiliate); Donrey Media Group; Time, Incorporated; Dow Jones & Co.; CBS, Inc.; Capital Cities/ABC, Inc.

For Complete List of Firm Personnel, See General Section

For full biographical listings, see the Martindale-Hubbell Law Directory

*TULSA,** Tulsa Co.

GABLE & GOTWALS (AV)

2000 Bank IV Center, 15 West Sixth Street, 74119-5447
Telephone: 918-582-9201
Facsimile: 918-586-8383

Teresa B. Adwan
Pamela S. Anderson
John R. Barker
David L. Bryant
Gene C. Buzzard
Dennis Clarke Cameron
Timothy A. Carney
Renee DeMoss
Elsie C. Draper
Sidney G. Dunagan
Theodore Q. Eliot
Richard W. Gable
Jeffrey Don Hassell
Patricia Ledvina Himes
Oliver S. Howard
Richard D. Koljack, Jr.
J. Daniel Morgan
Joseph W. Morris
Elizabeth R. Muratet
Richard B. Noulles
Ronald N. Ricketts
John Henry Rule
M. Benjamin Singletary
James M. Sturdivant
Patrick O. Waddel
Michael D. Hall
David Edward Keglovits
Stephen W. Lake
Kari S. McKee
Terry D. Ragsdale
Jeffrey C. Rambach

OF COUNSEL

G. Ellis Gable
Charles P. Gotwals, Jr.

For full biographical listings, see the Martindale-Hubbell Law Directory

PENNSYLVANIA

*ALLENTOWN,** Lehigh Co.

GROSS, MCGINLEY, LABARRE & EATON (AV)

33 South Seventh Street, P.O. Box 4060, 18105-4060
Telephone: (610)-820-5450
Fax: (610)-820-6006

MEMBERS OF FIRM

Malcolm J. Gross
Paul A. McGinley
Donald L. LaBarre, Jr.
J. Jackson Eaton, III
Michael A. Henry
Patrick J. Reilly
William J. Fries

ASSOCIATES

Anne K. Manley
John D. Lychak

For full biographical listings, see the Martindale-Hubbell Law Directory

*PHILADELPHIA,** Philadelphia Co.

SCHNADER, HARRISON, SEGAL & LEWIS (AV)

Suite 3600, 1600 Market Street, 19103
Telephone: 215-751-2000
Cable Address: "Walew"
Fax: 215-751-2205; 215-751-2313
Washington, D.C. Office: Suite 600, 1913 Eye Street, N.W.
Telephone: 202-463-2900.
Cable Address: "Dejuribus, Washington."
Fax: 202-296-8930; 202-775-8741.
New York, N.Y. Office: 330 Madison Avenue.
Telephone: 212-973-8000.
Cable Address: "Dejuribus, New York."
Fax: 212-972-8798.
Harrisburg, Pennsylvania: Suite 700, 30 North Third Street.
Telephone: 717-231-4000.
Fax: 717-231-4012.

(See Next Column)

Norristown, Pennsylvania Office: Suite 901, One Montgomery Plaza.
Telephone: 215-277-7700.
Fax: 215-277-3211.
Pittsburgh, Pennsylvania Office: Suite 2700, Fifth Avenue Place, 120 Fifth Avenue.
Telephone: 412-577-5200.
Fax: 412-765-3858.
Scranton, Pennsylvania Office: Suite 700, 108 North Washington Avenue.
Telephone: 717-342-6100.
Fax: 717-342-6147.
Washington, Pennsylvania Office: 8 East Pine Street.
Telephone: 412-222-7378.
Fax: 412-222-0771.
Cherry Hill, New Jersey Office: Suite 200, Woodland Falls Corporate Park, 220 Lake Drive East.
Telephone: 609-482-5222.
Fax: 609-482-6980.
Atlanta, Georgia Office: Suite 2550 Marquis Two Tower, 285 Peachtree Center Avenue, N.E.
Telephone: 404-215-8100.
Fax: 404-223-5164.

MEMBERS OF THE FIRM

James D. Crawford
Peter S. Greenberg
Ronald E. Karam
William L. Leonard
Alan M. Lieberman
Deena Jo Schneider
Carl A. Solano
Ira P. Tiger

COUNSEL TO THE FIRM

Arlin M. Adams
Bernard G. Segal

ASSOCIATES

Theresa E. Loscalzo
Stephen Weaver

For Complete List of Firm Personnel, See General Section

For full biographical listings, see the Martindale-Hubbell Law Directory

*PITTSBURGH,** Allegheny Co.

BUCHANAN INGERSOLL, PROFESSIONAL CORPORATION (AV)

5800 USX Tower, 600 Grant Street, 15219
Telephone: 412-562-8800
Telecopier: 412-562-1041
Philadelphia, Pennsylvania Office: Two Logan Square, Twelfth Floor, 18th & Arch Streets.
Telephone: 215-665-8700.
Harrisburg, Pennsylvania Office: Vartan Parc, 30 North Third Street.
Telephone: 717-237-4800.
Tampa, Florida Office: 101 East Kennedy Boulevard, Suite 1030.
Telephone: 813-222-8180.
North Miami Beach, Florida Office: 19495 Biscayne Boulevard.
Telephone: 305-933-5600.
Lexington, Kentucky Office: 1210 Vine Center Office Tower, 333 West Vine Street.
Telephone: 606-225-5333.
Princeton, New Jersey Office: Buchanan Ingersoll, A Partnership, College Centre, 500 College Road East.
Telephone: 609-452-2666.

Ronald Basso
Bruce I. Booken
Carl A. Cohen
Vincent C. Deluzio
Mark Raymond Hornak
Leonard J. Marsico
John R. Previs
Carl E. Rothenberger, Jr.
John M. Rumin
Hugh G. Van der Veer
Paula A. Zawadzki

SENIOR ATTORNEY

Cristopher Charles Hoel

James J. Barnes
Harrison S. Lauer
S. Bryan Lawrence III
Frances Magovern O'Connor
Pamela K. Wiles

For Complete List of Firm Personnel, See General Section

For full biographical listings, see the Martindale-Hubbell Law Directory

ROTHMAN GORDON FOREMAN & GROUDINE, P.C. (AV)

Third Floor-Grant Building, 15219
Telephone: 412-338-1100
Telefax: 412-281-7304
Washington, D.C. Office: 1120 Connecticut Avenue, N.W. Suite 440.
Telephone: 202-338-3248.

Frederick A. Polner

John R. Fielding

For Complete List of Firm Personnel, See General Section

For full biographical listings, see the Martindale-Hubbell Law Directory

RHODE ISLAND

*PROVIDENCE,** Providence Co.

EDWARDS & ANGELL (AV)

2700 Hospital Trust Tower, 02903
Telephone: 401-274-9200
Telecopier: 401-276-6611
Cable Address: "Edwangle Providence"
Telex: 952001 "E A PVD"
Boston, Massachusetts Office: 101 Federal Street, 02110.
Telephone: 617-439-444.
Telecopier: 617-439-4170.
New York, New York Office: 750 Lexington Avenue, 10022.
Telephone: 212-308-4411.
Telecopier: 212-308-4844.
Palm Beach, Florida Office: 250 Royal Palm Way, 33480.
Telephone: 407-833-7700.
Telecopier: 407-655-8719.
Newark, New Jersey Office: Gateway three, 07120.
Telephone: 201-623-7717.
Telecopier: 201-623-7717.
Hartford, Connecticut Office: 750 Main Street, 14th Floor, 06103.
Telephone: 203-525-5065.
Telecopier: 203-527-4198.
Newport, Rhode Island Office: 130 Bellevue Avenue, 02840.
Telephone: 401-849-7800.
Telecopier: 401-849-7887.

MEMBERS OF FIRM

Benjamin P. Harris III
David K. Duffell
Terrence M. Finn (Resident Boston, Massachusetts Office)
Christine M. Marx (Resident, Newark, New Jersey Office)
Walter G. D. Reed
Stephen O. Meredith (Resident Boston, Massachusetts Office)
Elizabeth H. Munnell (Not admitted in RI; Resident Boston, Massachusetts Office)
Christopher D. Graham
John G. Igoe (Resident Palm Beach, Florida Office; Partner-in Charge, Palm Beach, Florida Office)
Mary P. Heffner
Karen G. DelPonte
Susan E. Siebert (Not admitted in RI; Resident Boston, Massachusetts Office)
Leonard Q. Slap (Resident Boston, Massachusetts Office)

ASSOCIATES

Alan J. Bouffard (Not admitted in RI; Resident Boston, Massachusetts Office)
Jonathan M. Lourie (Not admitted in RI; Resident, Boston, Massachusetts Office)

OF COUNSEL

George Michaels (Not admitted in RI; Resident Boston, Massachusetts Office)

For Complete List of Firm Personnel, See General Section

For full biographical listings, see the Martindale-Hubbell Law Directory

SOUTH CAROLINA

*GREENVILLE,** Greenville Co.

WYCHE, BURGESS, FREEMAN & PARHAM, PROFESSIONAL ASSOCIATION (AV)

44 East Camperdown Way, P.O. Box 728, 29602-0728
Telephone: 803-242-8200
Telecopier: 803-235-8900

David L. Freeman
Carl F. Muller
Henry L. Parr, Jr.

Counsel for: Multimedia, Inc.; Delta Woodside Industries, Inc.; Milliken & Company; Ryan's Family Steak Houses, Inc.; St. Francis Hospital; Span-America Medical Systems, Inc.; Carolina First Bank; KEMET Electronics Corp.; Builder Marts of America, Inc.; One Price Clothing, Inc.

For Complete List of Firm Personnel, See General Section

For full biographical listings, see the Martindale-Hubbell Law Directory

TENNESSEE

*KNOXVILLE,** Knox Co.

MCCAMPBELL & YOUNG, A PROFESSIONAL CORPORATION (AV)

2021 Plaza Tower, P.O. Box 550, 37901-0550
Telephone: 615-637-1440
Telecopier: 615-546-9731

(See Next Column)

Herbert H. McCampbell, Jr. (1905-1974)
F. Graham Bartlett (1920-1982)
Robert S. Young
Lindsay Young
Robert S. Marquis
Robert S. Stone
J. Christopher Kirk
Mark K. Williams

Janie C. Porter
Gregory E. Erickson
R. Scott Elmore
Tammy Kaousias
Benét S. Theiss
Allen W. Blevins

For full biographical listings, see the Martindale-Hubbell Law Directory

WATSON, HOLLOW & REEVES (AV)

1700 Plaza Tower, P.O. Box 131, 37901
Telephone: 615-522-3803
Telecopier: 615-525-2514

MEMBERS OF FIRM

Robert Harmon Watson, Jr.
Richard L. Hollow
Pamela L. Reeves
Jon G. Roach
John C. Duffy
John T. Batson, Jr.
Earl Jerome Melson

ASSOCIATES

Arthur Franklin Knight, III
Robert W. Willingham

For full biographical listings, see the Martindale-Hubbell Law Directory

*MEMPHIS,** Shelby Co.

ARMSTRONG ALLEN PREWITT GENTRY JOHNSTON & HOLMES (AV)

80 Monroe Avenue Suite 700, 38103
Telephone: 901-523-8211
Telecopier: 901-524-4936
Jackson, Missippi Office: 1350 One Jackson Place, 188 East Capitol Street.
Telephone: 601-948-8020.
Telecopier: 601-948-8389.

MEMBERS OF FIRM

S. Russell Headrick
Paul E. Prather
Lucian T. Pera

For Complete List of Firm Personnel, See General Section

For full biographical listings, see the Martindale-Hubbell Law Directory

*NASHVILLE,** Davidson Co.

KING & BALLOW (AV)

1200 Noel Place, 200 Fourth Avenue, North, 37219
Telephone: 615-259-3456
Fax: 615-254-7907
San Diego, California Office: 2700 Symphony Towers, 750 B Street, 92101.
Telephone: 619-236-9401.
Fax: 619-236-9437.
San Francisco, California Office: 100 First Street, Suite 2700, 94105.
Telephone: 415-541-7803.
Fax: 415-541-7805.

MEMBERS OF FIRM

Frank S. King, Jr.
Robert L. Ballow
Richard C. Lowe
R. Eddie Wayland
Larry D. Crabtree
Alan L. Marx
Paul H. Duvall (Resident, San Diego, California Office)
Steven C. Douse
Douglas R. Pierce
James P. Thompson
Howard M. Kastrinsky
Kenneth E. Douthat
Mark E. Hunt
Charles J. Mataya
Lynn Siegel (Resident, San Diego, California Office)
Nora T. Cannon

ASSOCIATES

Patrick M. Thomas
R. Brent Ballow
Elizabeth B. Marney
Michael D. Oesterle

Representative Clients: Capital Cities/ABC, Inc., New York, New York; Denver Post, Denver, Colorado; The Gillet Group/Houston Post, Houston, Texas; Knight-Ridder, Inc., Miami, Florida; Opryland USA, Inc., Nashville, Tennessee; Parade Magazine, Inc.; Tribune Company, Chicago, Illinois; Union Tribune Publishing Co., San Diego, California.

For Complete List of Firm Personnel, See General Section

For full biographical listings, see the Martindale-Hubbell Law Directory

WYATT, TARRANT & COMBS (AV)

1500 Nashville City Center, 511 Union Street, 37219
Telephone: 615-244-0020
Telecopier: 615-256-1726
Cable Address: "Nashlaw"
Music Row, Office: 29 Music Square East, Nashville, 37203.
Telephone: 615-255-6161.
Telecopier: 615-254-4490.
Louisville, Kentucky Office: Citizens Plaza.
Telephone: 502-589-5235.
Telecopier: 502-589-0309.

(See Next Column)

WYATT, TARRANT & COMBS, *Nashville—Continued*

Lexington, Kentucky Office: 1700 Lexington Financial Center.
Telephone: 606-233-2012.
Telecopier: 606-259-0649.
Frankfort, Kentucky Office: The Taylor-Scott Building, 311 West Main Street.
Telephone: 502-223-2104.
Telecopier: 502-227-7681.
New Albany, Indiana Office: The Elsby Building, 117 East Spring Street,
Telephone: 812-945-3561.
Telecopier: 812-949-2524.
Hendersonville, Tennessee Office: 313 E. Main Street, Suite 1.
Telephone: 615-822-8822.
Telecopier: 615-824-4684.

MEMBERS OF FIRM

W. Michael Milom (Resident, Music Row Office)
Christian A. Horsnell (Resident, Music Row Office)

COUNSEL

Robin Mitchell Joyce (Resident, Music Row Office)

Representative Clients: Country Radio Broadcasters, Inc.; Gospel Music Assn.; Landmark Community Newspapers, Inc.; Media Services Group; Shop at Home, Inc.; Thomas Nelson, Inc.; Wireless Group, Inc.; Word, Inc.

For Complete List of Firm Personnel, See General Section

For full biographical listings, see the Martindale-Hubbell Law Directory

TEXAS

*DALLAS,** Dallas Co.

CALHOUN & STACY (AV)

5700 NationsBank Plaza, 901 Main Street, 75202-3747
Telephone: 214-748-5000
Telecopier: 214-748-1421
Telex: 211358 CALGUMP UR

Mark Alan Calhoun
David W. Elrod
Steven D. Goldston
Parker Nelson
Roy L. Stacy

ASSOCIATES

Shannon S. Barclay
Robert A. Bragalone
Dennis D. Conder
Jane Elizabeth Diseker
Lawrence I. Fleishman
Thomas C. Jones
Katherine Johnson Knight
V. Paige Pace
Veronika Willard
Michael C. Wright

LEGAL CONSULTANT

Rees T. Bowen, III

For full biographical listings, see the Martindale-Hubbell Law Directory

JACKSON & WALKER, L.L.P. (AV)

901 Main Street, Suite 6000, 75202-3797
Telephone: 214-953-6000
Fax: 214-953-5822
Fort Worth, Texas Office: 777 Main Street, Suite 1800.
Telephone: 817-334-7200.
Fax: 817-334-7290.
Houston, Texas Office: 1100 Louisiana, Suite 4200.
Telephone: 713-752-4200.
Fax: 713-752-4221.
San Antonio, Texas Office: 112 E. Pecan Street, Suite 2100.
Telephone: 210-978-7700.
Fax: 210-978-7790.

MEMBERS OF FIRM

Susan S. Andrews
Charles L. Babcock
Gerald C. Conley
Robert P. Latham
Frank C. Vecella
Troy Michael Wilson

OF COUNSEL

Laura E. Hlavach

ASSOCIATES

Jennifer E. Dorn
Alan N. Greenspan

Representative Clients Furnished Upon Request.

For Complete List of Firm Personnel, See General Section

For full biographical listings, see the Martindale-Hubbell Law Directory

*SAN ANTONIO,** Bexar Co.

MATTHEWS & BRANSCOMB, A PROFESSIONAL CORPORATION (AV)

One Alamo Center, 106 S. St. Mary's Street, Suite 800, 78205
Telephone: 210-226-4211
Facsimile: 210-226-0521
Telex: 5106009283
Cable Code: MBLAW
Austin, Texas Office: 301 Congress Avenue, Suite 2050.
Telephone: 512-305-4400.
Facsimile: 512-305-4413.
Corpus Christi, Texas Office: 802 N. Carancahua, Suite 1900.
Telephone: 512-888-9261.
Facsimile: 512-888-8504.
Eagle Pass, Texas Office: 675 Main Street.
Telephone: 210-773-6700.
Facsimile: 210-757-4045.
Uvalde, Texas Office: 200 E. Nopal #208.
Telephone: 210-278-4597.
Facsimile: 210-278-4806.
(Associated with Hall, Quintanilla & Alarcon, L.C., Laredo, Texas, under the name of Hall, Quintanilla, Alarcon, Matthews & Branscomb, P.L.L.C.)

James M. Doyle, Jr.
J. Tullos Wells
James H. Kizziar, Jr.
Frank Z. Ruttenberg

Representative Clients: Coca Cola Bottling Company of the Southwest; Concord Oil Co.; Ellison Enterprises, Inc.; H. E. Butt Grocery Co.; Frank B. Hall & Co., Inc.; The Hearst Corp., San Antonio Light Division; San Antonio Gas & Electric Utilities (City Board); Southern Pacific Transportation Co.; Southwest Texas Methodist Hospital.

For Complete List of Firm Personnel, See General Section

For full biographical listings, see the Martindale-Hubbell Law Directory

UTAH

*SALT LAKE CITY,** Salt Lake Co.

PARSONS BEHLE & LATIMER, A PROFESSIONAL CORPORATION (AV)

One Utah Center, 201 South Main Street, Suite 1800, P.O. Box 45898, 84145-0898
Telephone: 801-532-1234
Telecopy: 801-536-6111

Randy L. Dryer
Val R. Antczak
David W. Zimmerman

Representative Clients: Deseret News Publishing Company; Globe Communications; KUTV Channel 2 (NBC); MCI Communications Corporation; Thomson Newspapers; Williams Telecommunications.

For full biographical listings, see the Martindale-Hubbell Law Directory

VAN COTT, BAGLEY, CORNWALL & MCCARTHY, A PROFESSIONAL CORPORATION (AV)

Suite 1600, 50 South Main Street, P.O. Box 45340, 84145
Telephone: 801-532-3333
Telex: 453149
Telecopier: 801-534-0058
Ogden, Utah Office: Suite 900, 2404 Washington Boulevard.
Telephone: 801-394-5783.
Park City, Utah Office: 314 Main Street, Suite 205.
Telephone: 801-649-3889.
Reno, Nevada Office: Jeppson & Lee, 100 West Liberty, Suite 990.
Telephone: 702-333-6800.

Brent J. Giauque
Thomas Berggren
Kathryn Holmes Snedaker

For Complete List of Firm Personnel, See General Section

For full biographical listings, see the Martindale-Hubbell Law Directory

VIRGINIA

*ARLINGTON,** Arlington Co.

HALEY, BADER & POTTS (AV)

4350 North Fairfax Drive, Suite 900, 22203-1633
Telephone: 703-841-0606
FAX: 703-841-2345
INTERNET: haleybp@access.digex.net

(See Next Column)

HALEY, BADER & POTTS—*Continued*

MEMBERS OF FIRM

Andrew G. Haley (1904-1966)
Michael H. Bader
William J. Potts, Jr.
Henry A. Solomon
William J. Byrnes
Richard M. Riehl
John Wells King
John M. Pelkey
Lee W. Shubert
John Crigler
Theodore D. Kramer
Melodie A. Virtue
James E. Dunstan
Richard H. Strodel
Benjamin J. Lambiotte

ASSOCIATES

Amelia Logan Brown (Not admitted in VA)

COUNSEL

Kenneth A. Cox (Not admitted in VA)

For full biographical listings, see the Martindale-Hubbell Law Directory

*MANASSAS,** Prince William Co.

ALLEN & HAROLD, P.L.C. (AV)

10610-A Crestwood Drive, P.O. Box 2126, 22110
Telephone: 703-361-2278
Facsimile: 703-361-0594
Washington, D.C. Office: Suite 200, 2000 L Street, N.W.
Telephone: 202-452-7872; 1-800-433-2636.
Telex: 373-0708.
Facsimile: 202-833-3843.
Shenandoah Valley Office: 5413 Main Street. Stephens City, Virginia 22655.
Telephone: 703-869-0040.
Fax: 703-869-0041.

Robert G. Allen
Douglas W. Harold, Jr.

Robert A. Harris, II

Representative Clients: Crescomm Telecommunications Services, Inc.; Meta Comm Cellular; National Capital Christian Broadcasting, Inc.

For full biographical listings, see the Martindale-Hubbell Law Directory

MCLEAN, Fairfax Co.

GAMMON & GRANGE, P.C. (AV Ⓣ)

8280 Greensboro Drive, 7th Floor, 22102-3807
Telephone: 703-761-5000
Facsimile: 703-761-5023

Richard M. Campanelli
A. Wray Fitch III
George R. Grange II

OF COUNSEL

James A. Gammon (Not admitted in VA)

For full biographical listings, see the Martindale-Hubbell Law Directory

MANDELL, LEWIS & GOLDBERG, A PROFESSIONAL CORPORATION (AV)

Tysons Executive Plaza, Suite 1075, 2000 Corporate Ridge (Tysons Corner), 22102
Telephone: 703-734-9622
Facsimile: 703-356-0005
Washington, D.C. Office: Suite 200, 4427A Wisconsin Avenue, N.W.
Telephone: 202-296-1666.
Sterling, Virginia Office: Suite 340, Pidgeon Hill Drive.
Telephone: 703-430-0828.

Steve A. Mandell
David M. Lewis
Michael L. Goldberg

Adam P. Feinberg

OF COUNSEL

Seidman & Associates, P.C., , Washington, D.C.

For full biographical listings, see the Martindale-Hubbell Law Directory

PUTBRESE & HUNSAKER (AV)

Suite 100, McLean House, 6800 Fleetwood Road, P.O. Box 539, 22101
Telephone: 703-790-8400
Telecopier: 703-827-9538

Keith E. Putbrese
David M. Hunsaker

ASSOCIATES

John C. Trent
Denise B. Moline

For full biographical listings, see the Martindale-Hubbell Law Directory

*RICHMOND,** (Ind. City; Seat of Henrico Co.)

WILLIAMS, MULLEN, CHRISTIAN & DOBBINS, A PROFESSIONAL CORPORATION (AV)

Two James Center, 1021 East Cary Street, P.O. Box 1320, 23210-1320
Telephone: 804-643-1991
Fax: 804-783-6456
Glen Allen, Virginia Office: 4401 Waterfront Drive, Suite 140.
Telephone: 804-965-9168.
Fax: 804-965-0955.
Washington, D.C. Office: 1575 Eye Street, N.W.
Telephone: 202-289-6200.
Fax: 202-289-4126.

Reginald N. Jones

Calvin W. Fowler, Jr.

For Complete List of Firm Personnel, See General Section

For full biographical listings, see the Martindale-Hubbell Law Directory

WASHINGTON

*SEATTLE,** King Co.

GRAHAM & DUNN A PROFESSIONAL SERVICE CORPORATION (AV)

33rd Floor, 1420 Fifth Avenue, 98101-2390
Telephone: 206-624-8300
Telecopier (Panafax UF-400 AD): 206-340-9599
Tacoma, Washington Office: 1300 Tacoma Financial Center, 1145 Broadway Plaza, 98402-3517.
Telephone: 206-572-9294.

Alice F. Gustafson
Michael E. Kipling

Representative Clients: Fisher Broadcasting Inc.; Puget Sound Business Journal.

For Complete List of Firm Personnel, See General Section

For full biographical listings, see the Martindale-Hubbell Law Directory

*SPOKANE,** Spokane Co.

WITHERSPOON, KELLEY, DAVENPORT & TOOLE, P.S. (AV)

1100 U.S. Bank Building, 422 West Riverside, 99201
Telephone: 509-624-5265
Fax: 509-458-2728
Coeur d'Alene, Idaho Office: 608 Northwest Boulevard, Suite 301.
Telephone: 208-667-4000.

Robert L. Magnuson
Ned M. Barnes
William D. Symmes
Robert H. Lamp
K. Thomas Connolly
Thomas D. Cochran
Duane M. Swinton
Joseph H. Wessman
Jeffrey L. Supinger
Donald J. Lukes
Leslie R. Weatherhead
Michael D. Currin
Brian T. Rekofke
R. Max Etter, Jr.
Stanley R. Schultz
Michael F. Nienstedt
John M. Riley, III
Daniel B. DeRuyter

Daniel E Finney
Mary R. Giannini
Timothy M. Lawlor
Spencer A.W. Stromberg
Kathleen D. Jensen
Theodore S. O'Neal
William M. Symmes

OF COUNSEL

William A. Davenport
John E. Heath, Jr.
William V. Kelley
Allan H. Toole
Karl K Krogue

Representative Clients: KHQ TV; The Spokesman-Review; Unicom Broadcasting, Inc.; United Broadcasting, Inc.

For full biographical listings, see the Martindale-Hubbell Law Directory

WISCONSIN

*MILWAUKEE,** Milwaukee Co.

MEISSNER & TIERNEY, S.C. (AV)

The Milwaukee Center, 111 East Kilbourn Avenue, 19th Floor, 53202-6622
Telephone: 414-273-1300
Facsimile: 414-273-5840

(See Next Column)

MEISSNER & TIERNEY S.C., *Milwaukee—Continued*

Paul F. Meissner
Dennis L. Fisher
Michael J. Cohen

Eric J. Klumb
Kenneth A. Iwinski

For full biographical listings, see the Martindale-Hubbell Law Directory

WYOMING

*CHEYENNE,** Laramie Co.

HICKEY, MACKEY, EVANS, WALKER & STEWART (AV)

1712 Carey Avenue, P.O. Drawer 467, 82003
Telephone: 307-634-1525
Telecopier: 307-638-7335

MEMBERS OF FIRM

Paul J. Hickey
Terry W. Mackey
David F. Evans
John M. Walker
Mark R. Stewart III
Richard D. Tim Bush

A List of Representative Clients will be furnished upon request.
Reference: Norwest Bank, Cheyenne, N.A.

For full biographical listings, see the Martindale-Hubbell Law Directory

CANADA BRITISH COLUMBIA

*VANCOUVER,** Vancouver Co.

RUSSELL & DUMOULIN (AV)

2100-1075 West Georgia Street, V6E 3G2
Telephone: 604-631-3131
Fax: 604-631-3232
A Member of the national association of Borden DuMoulin Howard Gervais, comprising Russell & DuMoulin, Vancouver, British Columbia; Howard Mackie, Calgary, Alberta; Borden & Elliot, Toronto, Ontario; Mackenzie Gervais, Montreal, Quebec and Borden DuMoulin Howard Gervais, London, England.
Strategic Alliance with Perkins Coie with offices in Seattle, Spokane and Bellevue, Washington; Portland, Oregon; Anchorage, Alaska; Los Angeles, California; Washington, D.C.; Hong Kong and Taipei, Taiwan.
Represented in Hong Kong by Vincent T.K. Cheung, Yap & Co.

MEMBER OF FIRM

Allan P. Seckel

Representative Clients: Alcan Smelters & Chemicals Ltd.; The Bank of Nova Scotia; Canada Trust Co.; The Canada Life Assurance Co.; Forest Industrial Relations Ltd.; Honda Canada Inc.; IBM Canada Ltd.; Macmillan Bloedel Ltd.; Nissho Iwai Canada Ltd.; The Toronto-Dominion Bank.

For Complete List of Firm Personnel, See General Section

For full biographical listings, see the Martindale-Hubbell Law Directory

CANADA ONTARIO

*TORONTO,** Regional Munic. of York

BORDEN & ELLIOT (AV)

Barristers & Solicitors
Scotia Plaza, 40 King Street West, M5H 3Y4
Telephone: 416-367-6000
Telecopier: 416-367-6749
Internet: @ borden.com
A Member of the national association of Borden DuMoulin Howard Gervais, comprising Borden & Elliot in Toronto, Ontario, Russell & DuMoulin in Vancouver, British Columbia, Howard, Mackie in Calgary, Alberta and Mackenzie Gervais in Montréal, Québec. Borden DuMoulin Howard Gervais also operates an office in London, England.

MEMBER AND ASSOCIATES

John D. Hylton, Q.C.

For Complete List of Firm Personnel, See General Section

For full biographical listings, see the Martindale-Hubbell Law Directory

CONSTRUCTION LAW

ALABAMA

*BIRMINGHAM,** Jefferson Co.

BALCH & BINGHAM (AV)

1710 Sixth Avenue North, P.O. Box 306, 35201
Telephone: 205-251-8100
Facsimile: 205-226-8798
Other Birmingham, Alabama Office: 1901 Sixth Avenue North, 35203.
Telephone: 205-251-8100.
Facsimile: 205-226-8799.
Montgomery, Alabama Office: The Winter Building, 2 Dexter Avenue, 36101.
Telephone: 205-834-6500.
Facsimile: 205-269-3115.
Huntsville, Alabama Office: Suite 810, 200 West Court Square, 35801.
Telephone: 205-551-0171.
Facsimile: 205-551-0174.
Washington, D.C. Office: Suite 800, 1101 Connecticut Avenue, N.W., 20036.
Telephone: 202-296-0387.
Facsimile: 202-452-8180.

MEMBERS OF FIRM

Carey J. Chitwood
Edward S. Allen
James O. Spencer, Jr.
M. Stanford Blanton

Counsel for: Alabama Power Co.; Blue Cross and Blue Shield of Alabama; The Boeing Company; Brasfield & Gorrie, Inc.; Compass Bancshares, Inc.; Harbert Corp.; Kimberly-Clark Corp.; Southern Company Services, Inc.; Southern Research Institute; Vesta Insurance Group, Inc.

For Complete List of Firm Personnel, See General Section

For full biographical listings, see the Martindale-Hubbell Law Directory

BRADLEY, ARANT, ROSE & WHITE (AV)

1400 Park Place Tower, 2001 Park Place, 35203
Telephone: 205-521-8000
Telex: 494-1324
Facsimile: 205-251-8611, 251-8665, 252-0264
Facsimile (Southtrust Office): 205-251-9915
Huntsville, Alabama Office: 200 Clinton Avenue West, Suite 900.
Telephone: 205-517-5100.
Facsimile: 205-533-5069.

MEMBERS OF FIRM

A. H. Gaede, Jr.
E. Mabry Rogers
Walter H. Monroe, III
Andrew J. Noble, III
Walter J. Sears, III
W. Braxton Schell, Jr.
G. Edward Cassady, III
Axel Bolvig III

COUNSEL

Stanley D. Bynum

ASSOCIATES

John J. Park, Jr.
J. David Pugh
Susan Donovan Josey
Matthew H. Lembke
James F. Archibald, III
Douglas E. Eckert

For Complete List of Firm Personnel, See General Section

For full biographical listings, see the Martindale-Hubbell Law Directory

SCHOEL, OGLE, BENTON AND CENTENO (AV)

600 Financial Center, 505 North 20th Street, P.O. Box 1865, 35201-1865
Telephone: 205-521-7000
Telecopier: 205-521-7007

MEMBERS OF FIRM

Jerry W. Schoel
Richard F. Ogle
Lee R. Benton
Paul A. Liles
Douglas J. Centeno
Melinda Murphy Dionne
Gilbert M. Sullivan, Jr.
David O. Upshaw
Paul Avron
Lynn McCreery Shaw

Reference: National Bank of Commerce; First Alabama Bank.

For full biographical listings, see the Martindale-Hubbell Law Directory

STARNES & ATCHISON (AV)

100 Brookwood Place, P.O. Box 598512, 35259-8512
Telephone: 205-868-6000
Telecopier: 205-868-6099

(See Next Column)

MEMBERS OF FIRM

W. Stancil Starnes
W. Michael Atchison
William Anthony Davis, III
L. Graves Stiff, III
Thomas Lawson Selden

ASSOCIATES

Steven T. McMeekin
Joe L. Leak
Mark W. Macoy

Representative Clients: Harbert International; Brice Building Co., Inc.; Ellard Cont. Co., Inc.; Hallmark Builders, Inc.; Brasfield & Gorrie General Contractor, Inc.; Rives Construction Co.; Morris Shea Bridge Co.; Cowin & Company, Inc.; Daniel International.

For full biographical listings, see the Martindale-Hubbell Law Directory

*MOBILE,** Mobile Co.

JOHNSTONE, ADAMS, BAILEY, GORDON AND HARRIS (AV)

Royal St. Francis Building, 104 St. Francis Street, P.O. Box 1988, 36633
Telephone: 334-432-7682
Facsimile: 334-432-2800
Telex: 782040

MEMBERS OF FIRM

I. David Cherniak
William Alexander Gray, Jr.

ASSOCIATE

Lawrence J. Seiter

General Counsel for: First Alabama Bank, Mobile; Infirmary Health System/Mobile Infirmary Medical Center/Rotary Rehabilitation Hospital (Multi-Hospital System).
Counsel for: Oil and Gas: Exxon Corp. Business and Corporate: Bell South Telecommunications, Inc.; Aluminum Co. of America; Michelin Tire Corp.; Metropolitan Life Insurance Co.; The Travelers Insurance Cos. Marine: The West of England Ship Owners Mutual Protection and Indemnity Association (Luxembourg); The Standard Steamship Owners' Protection and Indemnity Association (Bermuda) Ltd.

For Complete List of Firm Personnel, See General Section

For full biographical listings, see the Martindale-Hubbell Law Directory

*MONTGOMERY,** Montgomery Co.

CAPELL, HOWARD, KNABE & COBBS, P.A. (AV)

57 Adams Avenue, P.O. Box 2069, 36102-2069
Telephone: 334-241-8000

Jack L. Capell
Fontaine M. Howard (1908-1985)
Walter J. Knabe (1898-1979)
Edward E. Cobbs (1909-1982)
L. Lister Hill (1936-1993)
Herman H. Hamilton, Jr.
Rufus M. King
Robert S. Richard
John B. Scott, Jr.
John F. Andrews
James M. Scott
Thomas S. Lawson, Jr.
John L. Capell, III
William D. Coleman
William K. Martin
Bruce J. Downey III
Henry C. Barnett, Jr.
Palmer Smith Lehman
Richard F. Allen
Neal H. Acker
Henry H. Hutchinson
Shapard D. Ashley
D. Kyle Johnson
J. Lister Hubbard
James N. Walter, Jr.
James H. McLemore
H. Dean Mooty, Jr.
Jim B. Grant, Jr.
Wyeth Holt Speir, III
Chad S. Wachter
Ellen M. Hastings
Debra Deames Spain
William Rufus King
C. Clay Torbert, III

OF COUNSEL

Timothy Sullivan

For full biographical listings, see the Martindale-Hubbell Law Directory

ARIZONA

*FLAGSTAFF,** Coconino Co.

ASPEY, WATKINS & DIESEL (AV)

123 North San Francisco, 86001
Telephone: 602-774-1478
Facsimile: 602-774-1043
Sedona, Arizona Office: 120 Soldier Pass Road.
Telephone: 602-282-5955.
Facsimile: 602-282-5962.
Page, Arizona Office: 904 North Navajo.
Telephone: 602-645-9694.
Winslow, Arizona Office: 205 North Williamson.
Telephone: 602-289-5963.
Cottonwood, Arizona Office: 905 Cove Parkway, Unite 201.
Telephone: 602-639-1881.

(See Next Column)

ASPEY, WATKINS & DIESEL, *Flagstaff—Continued*

MEMBERS OF FIRM

Frederick M. Fritz Aspey
Harold L. Watkins
Louis M. Diesel
Bruce S. Griffen
Donald H. Bayles, Jr.
Kaign N. Christy
John J. Dempsey

Zachary Markham
James E. Ledbetter
Whitney Cunningham
Holly S. Karris

LEGAL SUPPORT PERSONNEL

Deborah D. Roberts (Legal Assistant)
C. Denece Pruett (Legal Assistant)
Dominic M. Marino, Jr, (Paralegal Assistant)

Representative Clients: Farmer's Insurance Company of Arizona; Kelley-Moore Paint Co.; Pepsi-Cola Bottling Company of Northern Arizona; Bill Luke's Chrysler-Plymouth, Inc.; First American Title Insurance Company ; Transamerica Title Insurance Co.; Page Electric Utility; Comprehensive Access Health Plan, Inc.
Reference: First Interstate Bank-Arizona, N.A., Flagstaff, Arizona.

For full biographical listings, see the Martindale-Hubbell Law Directory

*PHOENIX,** Maricopa Co.

BONN, LUSCHER, PADDEN & WILKINS, CHARTERED (AV)

805 North Second Street, 85004
Telephone: 602-254-5557
Fax: 602-254-0656

Paul V. Bonn
Randall D. Wilkins
D. Michael Hall

For full biographical listings, see the Martindale-Hubbell Law Directory

FENNEMORE CRAIG, A PROFESSIONAL CORPORATION (AV)

Two North Central, Suite 2200, 85004
Telephone: 602-257-8700
Fax: 602-257-8527
Scottsdale, Arizona Office: 6263 North Scottsdale Road, Suite 290, 85250.
Telephone: 602-257-5400.
Fax: 602-945-4932.
Tucson, Arizona Office: One South Church Avenue, Suite 1030, 85701.
Telephone: 602-624-9312.
Fax: 602-882-7383.

Calvin H. Udall
Roger T. Hargrove
John G. Ryan
Andrew M. Federhar
John Randall Jefferies

Douglas J. Grier

Representative Clients: ASARCO Incorporated; AT&T Communications; Bridgestone/Firestone, Inc.; Catellus Development Corp.; Citibank (Arizona); First Interstate Bank of Arizona; GIANT Industries; Phelps Dodge Corporation; The Atchison, Topeka & Santa Fe Railway, Co.; US WEST Communications.

For Complete List of Firm Personnel, See General Section

For full biographical listings, see the Martindale-Hubbell Law Directory

HORNE, KAPLAN AND BISTROW, P.C. (AV)

Renaissance Two, 40 North Central, Suite 2800, 85004
Telephone: 602-253-9700
Fax: 602-258-4805

Thomas C. Horne
Martha Bachner Kaplan
Eric J. Bistrow
Michael S. Dulberg
Kimball J. Corson
Mark D. Zuckerman

For full biographical listings, see the Martindale-Hubbell Law Directory

JENNINGS & HAUG (AV)

2800 North Central Avenue Suite Eighteen Hundred, 85004-1019
Telephone: 602-234-7800
Fax: 602-277-5595
Irvine, California Office: 1920 Main Street, Suite 830.
Telephone: 714-250-7800.
Fax: 602-250-4913.

MEMBERS OF FIRM

Curtis A. Jennings
William F. Haug
Robert A. Scheffing
Robert O. Dyer
Jack R. Cunningham
Jay M. Mann
Carolyn M. Kaluzniacki
Dean Kim Lough
Chad L. Schexnayder
Mark E. Barker
James L. Csontos

(See Next Column)

ASSOCIATES

J. Daniel Shell
Jeff R. Wilhelm
Julianne C. Wheeler
Edward Rubacha
Robert J. Berens
Judy J. Shell
Russell C. Brown
Paul D. Kramer (Resident, Irvine, California Office)
Paul S. Ruderman
Laurence R. Sharlot
John G. Sinodis

For full biographical listings, see the Martindale-Hubbell Law Directory

O'CONNOR, CAVANAGH, ANDERSON, WESTOVER, KILLINGSWORTH & BESHEARS, A PROFESSIONAL ASSOCIATION (AV)

One East Camelback Road, Suite 1100, 85012-1656
Telephone: 602-263-2400
FAX: 602-263-2900
Sun City, Arizona Office: 13250 North Del Webb Boulevard, Suite B, 85351.
Telephone: 602-263-2808.
FAX: 602-933-3100.
Tucson, Arizona Office: Suite 2200, One South Church Avenue, 85701.
Telephone: 602-882-8912.
FAX: 602-624-9564.
Nogales, Arizona Office: 1827 North Mastick Way, 85621.
Telephone: 602-761-4215.
FAX: 602-761-3505.

Stephen E. Richman

Michael R. Altaffer

Representative Clients: McCarthy; Pulte Home Corporation; L.M.B. Construction; Glendale Union High School District; Gilpin's Construction; Mike Greenberg Construction; The Fishel Company; Kleven Construction, Inc.

For Complete List of Firm Personnel, See General Section

For full biographical listings, see the Martindale-Hubbell Law Directory

SNELL & WILMER (AV)

One Arizona Center, 85004-0001
Telephone: 602-382-6000
Fax: 602-382-6070
Tucson, Arizona Office: 1500 Norwest Tower, One South Church Avenue 85701-1612.
Telephone: 602-882-1200.
Fax: 602-884-1294.
Orange County Office: 1920 Main Street, Suite 1200, P.O. Box 19601, Irvine, California, 92714.
Telephone: 714-253-2700.
Fax: 714-955-2507.
Salt Lake City, Utah Office: Broadway Centre, 111 East Broadway, Suite 900, 84111.
Telephone: 801-237-1900.
Fax: 801-237-1950.

OF COUNSEL

Jarril F. Kaplan

MEMBERS OF FIRM

Richard K. Mallery
Donald D. Colburn
Gerard Morales
David A. Sprentall
Stephen M. Hopkins
Jay D. Wiley
Robert J. Deeny
James R. Condo
James J. Sienicki
Shawn M. McLeran

ASSOCIATES

Bob J. McCullough
Scott D. Sherman

Representative Clients: Arizona Public Service Co.; Bank One, Arizona, NA.; First Security Bank of Utah, N.A.; Ford Motor Co.; Chrysler Motors Corp.; Toyota Motor Sales U.S.A.; Magma Copper Co.; U.S. Home Corp.; Pinnacle West Capital Corp.; Safeway, Inc.

For Complete List of Firm Personnel, See General Section

For full biographical listings, see the Martindale-Hubbell Law Directory

SCOTTSDALE, Maricopa Co.

PESKIND HYMSON & GOLDSTEIN, P.C. (AV)

14595 North Scottsdale Road, Suite 14, 85254
Telephone: 602-991-9077
Fax: 602-443-8854

E. J. Peskind

For full biographical listings, see the Martindale-Hubbell Law Directory

*TUCSON,** Pima Co.

O'CONNOR, CAVANAGH, ANDERSON, WESTOVER, KILLINGSWORTH & BESHEARS, A PROFESSIONAL ASSOCIATION (AV)

Suite 2200 One South Church Avenue, 85701-1621
Telephone: 602-882-8912
FAX: 602-624-9564
Phoenix, Arizona Office: One East Camelback Road, Suite 1100, 85012.
Telephone: 602-263-2400.
FAX: 602-263-2900.
Sun City, Arizona Office: 13250 North Del Webb Boulevard, Suite B, 85351.
Telephone: 602-263-2808.
FAX: 602-933-3100.
Nogales, Arizona Office: 1827 North Mastick Way, 85621.
Telephone: 602-761-4215.
FAX: 602-761-3505.

J. Matthew Derstine

Representative Client: Jeffco, Inc.
Reference: Citibank.

For Complete List of Firm Personnel, See General Section

For full biographical listings, see the Martindale-Hubbell Law Directory

ARKANSAS

*LITTLE ROCK,** Pulaski Co.

HOOVER & STOREY (AV)

111 Center Street, 11th Floor, 72201-4445
Telephone: 501-376-8500
Facsimile: 501-372-3255

MEMBERS OF FIRM

Paul W. Hoover, Jr.
O. H. Storey, III
John Kooistra, III
Lawrence Joseph Brady
William P. Dougherty
Max C. Mehlburger
Joyce Bradley Babin
Herbert W. Kell, Jr.
Letty McAdams

For full biographical listings, see the Martindale-Hubbell Law Directory

CALIFORNIA

*BAKERSFIELD,** Kern Co.

KLEIN, WEGIS, DENATALE, GOLDNER & MUIR (AV)

A Partnership including Professional Corporations
(Formerly Di Giorgio, Davis, Klein, Wegis, Duggan & Friedman)
ARCO Tower, 4550 California Avenue, Second Floor, P.O. Box 11172, 93389-1172
Telephone: 805-395-1000
Telecopier: 805-326-0418
Santa Ana, California Office: Park Tower Building #610, 200 W. Santa Ana Boulevard, 92701.
Telephone: 714-285-0711.
Fax: 714-285-9003.

MEMBERS OF FIRM

Anthony J. Klein (Inc.)
Barry L. Goldner

Representative Clients: Findley Construction; Kern High School District; Renfro-Russell & Associates, Inc.

For Complete List of Firm Personnel, See General Section

For full biographical listings, see the Martindale-Hubbell Law Directory

KUHS, PARKER & STANTON (AV)

Suite 200, 1200 Truxtun Avenue, P.O. Box 2205, 93303
Telephone: 805-322-4004
FAX: 805-322-2906

William C. Kuhs
James R. Parker, Jr.
David B. Stanton

Lorraine G. Adams
John P. Doering, III
Robert G. Kuhs

Reference: First Interstate Bank (Bakersfield Main Branch).

For full biographical listings, see the Martindale-Hubbell Law Directory

BEVERLY HILLS, Los Angeles Co.

SMITH & SMITH (AV)

121 South Beverly Drive, 90212
Telephone: 310-275-5132
Los Angeles: 213-272-7807

David S. Smith
Lee S. Smith

For full biographical listings, see the Martindale-Hubbell Law Directory

COSTA MESA, Orange Co.

COULOMBE KOTTKE & KING, A PROFESSIONAL CORPORATION (AV)

Comerica Bank Tower, 611 Anton Boulevard, Suite 1260, P.O. Box 2410, 92628-2410
Telephone: 714-540-1234
Fax: 714-754-0808; 714-754-0707

Ronald B. Coulombe
Jon S. Kottke
Raymond King

COUNSEL

Mary J. Swanson
Roy B. Woolsey

LEGAL SUPPORT PERSONNEL

PARALEGALS

Karen M. Carrillo
Laura A. Bieser
Vicky M. Pearson

LEGAL ADMINISTRATOR

Sheila O. Elpern

For full biographical listings, see the Martindale-Hubbell Law Directory

MURTAUGH, MILLER, MEYER & NELSON (AV)

A Partnership including Professional Corporations
3200 Park Center Drive, 9th Floor, P.O. Box 5023, 92628-5023
Telephone: 714-513-6800
Facsimile: 714-513-6899

Michael J. Murtaugh (A Professional Corporation)
Bradford H. Miller (A Professional Corporation)
Richard E. Meyer
Michael J. Nelson
Robert T. Lemen
Mark S. Himmelstein
Harry A. Halkowich
Madelyn A. Enright
James A. Murphy, IV
Lawrence A. Treglia, Jr.

Roberta A. Evans
Debra Lynn Braasch
Thomas J. Skane
Lydia R. Bouzaglou
David C. Holt
Robin L. More
Lawrence J. DiPinto
Debra L. Reilly
Susan Westover
Lawrence D. Marks
Carrie E. Phelan
Robert A. Fisher, II
John R. Browning
Eric J. Dubin
Stacey Sarowatz
Daniel E. Roston

OF COUNSEL

Susan W. Menkes
Gary M. Pohlson

Representative Clients: Continental Insurance Cos. (Continental Loss Adjusting Services); Design Professionals Insurance Co.
Reference: Wells Fargo Bank.

For full biographical listings, see the Martindale-Hubbell Law Directory

RUTAN & TUCKER (AV)

A Partnership including Professional Corporations
611 Anton Boulevard, Suite 1400, P.O. Box 1950, 92626
Telephone: 714-641-5100; 213-625-7586
Telecopier: 714-546-9035

MEMBERS OF FIRM

Robert C. Braun
Thomas S. Salinger (P.C.)
David C. Larsen (P.C.)
Clifford E. Frieden
Steven A. Nichols
Jayne Taylor Kacer

ASSOCIATE

David H. Hochner

For Complete List of Firm Personnel, See General Section

For full biographical listings, see the Martindale-Hubbell Law Directory

*FRESNO,** Fresno Co.

LANG, RICHERT & PATCH, A PROFESSIONAL CORPORATION (AV)

Fig Garden Financial Center, 5200 North Palm Avenue, 4th Floor, P.O. Box 40012, 93755
Telephone: 209-228-6700
Fax: 209-228-6727

(See Next Column)

LANG, RICHERT & PATCH A PROFESSIONAL CORPORATION, *Fresno—Continued*

Frank H. Lang
William T. Richert (1937-1993)
Robert L. Patch, II
Val W. Saldaña
Douglas E. Noll
Michael T. Hertz
Victoria J. Salisch
Bradley A. Silva
David R. Jenkins
Charles Trudrung Taylor
Mark L. Creede
Peter N. Zeitler
Charles L. Doerksen

Randall C. Nelson
Barbara A. McAuliffe
Laurie Quigley Cardot
Douglas E. Griffin
Nabil E. Zumout

References: Wells Fargo Bank (Fresno Main Office); First Interstate Bank (Fresno Main Office).

For full biographical listings, see the Martindale-Hubbell Law Directory

GLENDALE, Los Angeles Co.

GILL AND BALDWIN (AV)

130 North Brand Boulevard Fourth Floor, 91203
Telephone: 818-500-7755; 213-245-3131
Fax: 818-242-4305

MEMBERS OF FIRM

Samuel S. Gill (1912-1965)
John M. Carmack
Joseph C. Malpasuto
Kirk S. MacDonald

ASSOCIATES

L. Frank Zankich
Alan J. Carnegie

OF COUNSEL

Ernest R. Baldwin

Representative Clients: Kasler Corp.; Bireley Foundation.
Reference: American West Bank.

For full biographical listings, see the Martindale-Hubbell Law Directory

O'ROURKE, ALLAN & FONG (AV)

3rd Floor, 104 North Belmont, P.O. Box 10220, 91209-3220
Telephone: 818-247-4303
Fax: 818-247-1451

MEMBERS OF FIRM

Denis M. O'Rourke
Joan H. Allan
Roderick D. Fong

ASSOCIATE

Robert G. Mindess

Reference: Verdugo Banking Company (Glendale, California); Community Bank (Glendale, California).

For full biographical listings, see the Martindale-Hubbell Law Directory

IRVINE, Orange Co.

ANDRADE & ASSOCIATES (AV)

Marine National Bank Building, 18401 Von Karman, Suite 350, 92715
Telephone: 714-553-1951
Telecopier: 714-553-0655

Richard B. Andrade

ASSOCIATES

Jack W. Fleming
Andrew C. Muzi
Steven S. Hanagami

OF COUNSEL

Kurt Kupferman

Representative Clients: American International Cos.; American Home Assurance; Insurance Company of North America (INA); National Union Fire Insurance of Pittsburgh, PA; Aetna Insurance Co.; Fremont Insurance Co.; Maryland Casualty; Commercial Union Insurance Co.; Superior National Insurance Co.

For full biographical listings, see the Martindale-Hubbell Law Directory

BROWN, PISTONE, HURLEY, VAN VLEAR & SELTZER, A PROFESSIONAL CORPORATION (AV)

Suite 900 AT&T Building, 8001 Irvine Center Drive, 92718
Telephone: 714-727-0559
Fax: 714-727-0656
Tempe, Arizona Office: 1501 West Fountainhead Parkway, Suite 540.
Telephone: 602-968-2427.
Fax: 602-968-2401.
San Francisco, California Office: Suite 1300, Steuart Street Tower, One Market Plaza.
Telephone: 415-281-2154.
Fax: 415-281-2194.

(See Next Column)

Ernest C. Brown
Thomas A. Pistone
Gregory F. Hurley
John E. Van Vlear
Margaret A. Seltzer (Resident, San Francisco Office)

Michael K. Wolder
Francis T. Donohue, III
Kedric L. Francis
Michael W. Foster (Resident, Tempe, Arizona Office)
Robert C. Schneider (Resident, Tempe, Arizona Office)
Sarah Namnama Saria
Sheila Patterson
Michael Ray Gandee

OF COUNSEL

Robert G. Mahan
Stephen M. Wontrobski
Brian A. Runkel (Not admitted in CA)

For full biographical listings, see the Martindale-Hubbell Law Directory

WATT, TIEDER & HOFFAR (AV Ⓣ)

3 Park Plaza, Suite 1530, 92714
Telephone: 714-852-6700
Telecopier: 714-261-0771
McLean Virginia Office: 7929 Westpark Drive, Suite 400,
Telephone: 703-749-1000.
Telex: 248797 WATTR.
Telecopier: 703-893-8029.
Washington, D.C. Office: 601 Pennsylvania Avenue, N.W. Suite 900,
Telephone: 202-462-4697.

MEMBERS OF FIRM

John B. Tieder, Jr. (Not admitted in CA)
Robert M. Fitzgerald (Not admitted in CA)
Michael G. Long

ASSOCIATE

Christopher P. Pappas

For full biographical listings, see the Martindale-Hubbell Law Directory

LA JOLLA, San Diego Co.

MAURER LAW FIRM (AV)

7825 Fay Avenue, Suite 200, 92037
Telephone: 619-456-5570
Fax: 619-551-8919

Charles D. Maurer, Jr.

For full biographical listings, see the Martindale-Hubbell Law Directory

LONG BEACH, Los Angeles Co.

MADDEN, JONES & COLE, A PROFESSIONAL CORPORATION (AV)

Suite 1300, 111 W. Ocean Boulevard, 90802
Telephone: 310-435-6565
Fax: 310-590-7909

Philip M. Madden
Steven A. Jones
Montgomery Cole
Judith A. Rasmussen
Robert R. Johnson

John Vita
Mary Gillespie Frankart
Carol Y. Adams
John K. Fitle

Counsel For: Allied Refrigeration, Inc.; Walters Wholesale Electric Co., Inc.; All City Electric Supply; Milgard Manufacturing; Twining Laboratories of Southern California; Associated Soils Engineering; Ameritone Paint Corporation.

For Complete List of Firm Personnel, See General Section

For full biographical listings, see the Martindale-Hubbell Law Directory

*LOS ANGELES,** Los Angeles Co.

LAW OFFICES OF DAVID B. BLOOM A PROFESSIONAL CORPORATION (AV)

3325 Wilshire Boulevard, Ninth Floor, 90010
Telephone: 213-938-5248; 384-4088
Telecopier: 213-385-2009

David B. Bloom

Stephen S. Monroe (A Professional Corporation)
Raphael A. Rosemblat
James E. Adler
Bonni S. Mantovani
Martin A. Cooper
Roy A. Levun
Cherie S. Raidy
Jonathan Udell
Susan Carole Jay
Edward Idell
Sandra Kamenir
Steven Wayne Lazarus
Andrew Edward Briseno
Harold C. Klaskin
Shelley M. Gould
B. Eric Nelson
John C. Notti
Peter O. Israel
Anthony V. Seferian

For full biographical listings, see the Martindale-Hubbell Law Directory

Los Angeles—Continued

DANIELS, BARATTA & FINE (AV)

A Partnership including a Professional Corporation
1801 Century Park East, 9th Floor, 90067
Telephone: 310-556-7900
Telecopier: 310-556-2807

MEMBERS OF FIRM

John P. Daniels (Inc.) | Mary Hulett
James M. Baratta | Michael B. Geibel
Paul R. Fine | James I. Montgomery, Jr.
Nathan B. Hoffman | Lance D. Orloff
Mark R. Israel

ASSOCIATES

Deborah Kaplan Galer | Scott Ashford Brooks
Ilene Wendy Nebenzahl | Craig A. Laidig
Heidi Susan Hart | Paul E. Blevins
Janet Sacks | Joan T. Lind
Michael N. Schonbuch | Rodi F. Rispone
Linda A. Schweitz | Stephanie J. Berman
Christine S. Chu | Michelle C. Hopkins
Glenn T. Rosenblatt | Robin A. Webb
Scott M. Leavitt | Ronda Lynn Crowley
Karen Ann Holloway | Scott A. Spungin
Mark A. Vega | Theodore L. Wilson
Patricio Esquivel | Daniel Joseph Kolodziej
Robert B. Gibson | Craig Momita
Brett S. Markson | Spencer A. Schneider
Michelle R. Press | Angelo A. DuPlantier, III

OF COUNSEL

Timothy J. Hughes | Drew T. Hanker

For full biographical listings, see the Martindale-Hubbell Law Directory

EZER & WILLIAMSON (AV)

(Formerly Rich & Ezer)
1888 Century Park East, Suite 2020 (Century City), 90067-1706
Telephone: 310-277-7747
Telecopier: 310-277-2576

Mitchel J. Ezer | Richard E. Williamson

OF COUNSEL

John Cramer | Kelli G. Hawley

Renee Ellen Ezer

For full biographical listings, see the Martindale-Hubbell Law Directory

KOSLOV & CADY (AV)

Suite 650 Roosevelt Building, 727 West Seventh Street, 90017
Telephone: 213-629-2647
FAX: 213-689-9628

MEMBERS OF FIRM

John Koslov | Eurus Cady

ASSOCIATES

Judy L. McKelvey | Melina J. Burns
William P. Medlen

For full biographical listings, see the Martindale-Hubbell Law Directory

LOS GATOS, Santa Clara Co.

SWEENEY, MASON & WILSON, A PROFESSIONAL LAW CORPORATION (AV)

983 University Avenue, Suite 104C, 95030
Telephone: 408-356-3000
Fax: 408-354-8839

Joseph M. Sweeney | Kurt E. Wilson
Roger M. Mason | Bradley D. Bosomworth
Allan James Manzagol

For full biographical listings, see the Martindale-Hubbell Law Directory

NEWPORT BEACH, Orange Co.

FRANK B. MYERS (AV)

Suite 720, 4400 MacArthur Boulevard, 92660
Telephone: 714-752-2001
Facsimile: 714-955-3670

For full biographical listings, see the Martindale-Hubbell Law Directory

*OAKLAND,** Alameda Co.

HAIMS, JOHNSON, MACGOWAN & MCINERNEY (AV)

490 Grand Avenue, 94610
Telephone: 510-835-0500
Facsimile: 510-835-2833

(See Next Column)

MEMBERS OF FIRM

Arnold B. Haims | Lawrence A. Baker
Gary R. Johnson | Randy M. Marmor
Clyde L. MacGowan | John K. Kirby
Thomas McInerney | Robert J. Frassetto
Caroline N. Valentino

ASSOCIATES

Joseph Y. Ahn | Anne M. Michaels
Edward D. Baldwin | Dianne D. Peebles
Kathleen B. Boehm | Michelle D. Perry
Marc P. Bouret | Edward C. Schroeder, Jr.

For full biographical listings, see the Martindale-Hubbell Law Directory

MARTIN, RYAN & ANDRADA, A PROFESSIONAL CORPORATION (AV)

Twenty-Second Floor, Ordway Building, One Kaiser Plaza, 94612
Telephone: 510-763-6510
Fax: 510-763-3921

Gerald P. Martin, Jr. | Michael J. Daley
Joseph D. Ryan, Jr. | Charles E. Kallgren
J. Randall Andrada | Rhonda D. Shelton
Jill J. Lifter | Betty J. Jones
Jolie Krakauer | Lora N. Vail
Glenn Gould | Vikki L. Barron-Jennings

Representative Clients: Alameda Contra Costa County Transit District; Continental Insurance Cos.; Commercial Union Insurance Group; Liberty Mutual Insurance Co.; Safeway Stores, Inc.

For full biographical listings, see the Martindale-Hubbell Law Directory

ORANGE, Orange Co.

WALSWORTH, FRANKLIN & BEVINS (AV)

1 City Boulevard West, Suite 308, 92668
Telephone: 714-634-2522
LAW-FAX: 714-634-0686
San Francisco, California Office: 580 California Street, Suite 1335.
Telephone: 415-781-7072.
Fax: 415-391-6258.

Jeffrey P. Walsworth | David W. Epps (Resident, San Francisco Office)
Ferdie F. Franklin | Richard M. Hills (Resident, San Francisco Office)
Ronald H. Bevins, Jr. | Sandra G. Kennedy
Michael T. McCall | Randall J. Lee (Resident, San Francisco Office)
Noel Edlin (Resident, San Francisco Office) | Kimberly K. Mays
Lawrence E. Duffy, Jr. | Bruce A. Nelson (Resident, San Francisco Office)
Sheldon J. Fleming | Kevin Pegan
J. Wayne Allen | Allan W. Ruggles
James A. Anton | Jonathan M. Slipp
Ingrid K. Campagne (Resident, San Francisco Office) | Cyrian B. Tabuena (Resident, San Francisco Office)
Robert M. Channel (Resident, San Francisco Office) | John L. Trunko
Nicholas A. Cipiti | Houston M. Watson, II
Sharon L. Clisham (Resident, San Francisco Office) |
Mary A. Watson

For full biographical listings, see the Martindale-Hubbell Law Directory

PASADENA, Los Angeles Co.

COLLINS, COLLINS, MUIR & TRAVER (AV)

Successor to Collins & Collins
Suite 300, 265 North Euclid, 91101
Telephone: 818-793-1163
Los Angeles: 213-681-2773
FAX: 818-793-5982

MEMBERS OF FIRM

James E. Collins (1910-1987) | Samuel J. Muir
John J. Collins | Robert J. Traver

ASSOCIATES

John B. Foss | Robert H. Stellwagen, Jr.
Frank J. D'Oro | Tomas A. Guterres
Paul L. Rupard | Karen B. Sharp
Brian K. Stewart | Amina R. Merritt
Christine E. Drage

For full biographical listings, see the Martindale-Hubbell Law Directory

KEVIN MEENAN (AV)

790 East Colorado Boulevard Ninth Floor Penthouse, 91101-2105
Telephone: 818-398-0000
FAX: 818-585-0999

For full biographical listings, see the Martindale-Hubbell Law Directory

*SACRAMENTO,** Sacramento Co.

CAULFIELD, DAVIES & DONAHUE (AV)

3500 American River Drive, 1st Floor, 95864
Telephone: 916-487-7700
Fairfield, California Office: Fairfield West Plaza, 1455 Oliver Road, Suite 130.
Telephone: 707-426-0223.

MEMBERS OF FIRM

Richard Hyland Caulfield
Robert E. Davies
James R. Donahue
Bruce E. Leonard
Michael M. McKone
Douglas L. Smith

ASSOCIATES

David N. Tedesco
Matthew Paul Donahue
Brian C. Haydon
Paul R. Ramsey

For full biographical listings, see the Martindale-Hubbell Law Directory

HARMATA LAW OFFICES (AV)

2201 Q Street, 95816
Telephone: 916-442-2842
Fax: 916-442-2015

Donald D. Harmata

LEGAL SUPPORT PERSONNEL
PARALEGAL

Debra D. Morrow

Representative Clients: Control Data Corporation; Deloitte & Touche; General Electric Company; Myers Electric, Inc.; Syblon-Reid Co.; Systemhouse Inc.; TRW, Inc.

For full biographical listings, see the Martindale-Hubbell Law Directory

HERRIG & VOGT (AV)

Park Plaza Center, 2150 River Plaza Drive Suite 155, 95814
Telephone: 916-649-8138
Telecopier: 916-649-2864
Kennewick, Washington Office: 3104 West Kennewick, Suite 16.
Telephone: 509-943-6691.
Fax: 509-783-6477.

John R. Herrig

RESIDENT PARTNER

George F. Vogt, Jr.

RESIDENT ASSOCIATE

C. Patrick Stoll

For full biographical listings, see the Martindale-Hubbell Law Directory

WILKE, FLEURY, HOFFELT, GOULD & BIRNEY (AV)

A Partnership including Professional Corporations
400 Capitol Mall, Suite 2200, 95814-4408
Telephone: 916-441-2430
Telefax: 916-442-6664
Mailing Address: P.O. Box 15559, 95852-0559

MEMBERS OF FIRM

Richard H. Hoffelt (Inc.)
William A. Gould, Jr., (Inc.)
Philip R. Birney (Inc.)
Thomas G. Redmon (Inc.)
Scott L. Gassaway
Donald Rex Heckman II (Inc.)
Alan G. Perkins
Bradley N. Webb
Ernest James Krtil
Robert R. Mirkin
Matthew W. Powell
Mark L. Andrews
Stephen K. Marmaduke
David A. Frenznick
John R. Valencia
Angus M. MacLeod

ASSOCIATES

Paul A. Dorris
Kelli M. Kennaday
Tracy S. Hendrickson
Joseph G. De Angelis
Jennifer L. Kennedy
Anthony J. DeCristoforo
Rachel N. Kook
Alicia F. From
Michael Polis
Matthew J. Smith
Wayne L. Ordos

OF COUNSEL

Sherman C. Wilke
Anita Seipp Marmaduke
Benjamin G. Davidian

Representative Clients: NOR-CAL Mutual Insurance Co.; California Optometric Assn.; KPMG Peat Marwick; Glaxo, Inc.

For full biographical listings, see the Martindale-Hubbell Law Directory

*SAN BERNARDINO,** San Bernardino Co.

MAC LACHLAN, BURFORD & ARIAS, A LAW CORPORATION (AV)

560 East Hospitality Lane, Fourth Floor, 92408
Telephone: 909-885-4491
Fax: 909-888-6866
Rancho Cucamonga, California Office: 8280 Utica Avenue, Suite 200. 909-989-4481.

(See Next Column)

Palm Springs, California Office: 255 North El Cielo Road, Suite 470. 619-320-5761.
Victorville, California Office: 14011 Park Avenue, Suite 410. 619-243-7933.

Bruce D. Mac Lachlan
Ronald A. Burford
Joseph Arias
Michael W. Mugg
Dennis G. Popka
Leigh O. Harper (Resident, Palm Springs Office)
Clifford R. Cunningham (Resident, Rancho Cucamonga Office)
Dennis R. Stout
Sharon K. Burchett (Resident, Rancho Cucamonga Office)
Christopher D. Lockwood
Vernon C. Lauridsen (Resident, Rancho Cucamonga Office)
John G. Evans (Resident, Palm Springs Office)
Richard R. Hegner (Resident, Victorville Office)
Dennis J. Mahoney
Kathleen M. Keefe
Toni R. Fullerton
Mark R. Harris
Diana J. Carloni (Resident, Victorville Office)
Jean M. Landry
Frank M. Loo

Representative Clients: Aetna Life & Casualty; Automobile Club of Southern California; California State Automobile Association; City of San Bernardino; Reliance Insurance; Republic Insurance; Southern Pacific Transportation Co.; State Farm Fire and Casualty Co.; State Farm Mutual Automobile Insurance Co.; County of San Bernardino.

For full biographical listings, see the Martindale-Hubbell Law Directory

*SAN DIEGO,** San Diego Co.

DETISCH, CHRISTENSEN & WOOD (AV)

444 West C Street, Suite 200, 92101
Telephone: 619-236-9343
Fax: 619-236-8307

MEMBERS OF FIRM

Charles B. Christensen
Donald W. Detisch
John W. Wood

ASSOCIATE

Lydia L. Brashear

For full biographical listings, see the Martindale-Hubbell Law Directory

DUKE, GERSTEL, SHEARER & BREGANTE (AV)

A Limited Partnership including Professional Corporations
Sixth Floor Wells Fargo Bank Building, 101 West Broadway, P.O. Box 85470, 92186-5470
Telephone: 619-232-0816
800-405-0816
Fax: 619-232-4661

MEMBERS OF FIRM

Clifford L. Duke, Jr. (1921-1989)
Bryan R. Gerstel (A Professional Corporation)
William K. Shearer (A Professional Corporation)
Richard D. Bregante (A Professional Corporation)
Stephen V. Rupp (A Professional Corporation)
John S. Huiskamp (A Professional Corporation)
J. Michael Reed (A Professional Corporation)
Andrew F. Lloyd (A Professional Corporation)
David T. Pursiano (A Professional Corporation)
Daniel J. Perwich (A Professional Corporation)
Alan R. Johnston (A Professional Corporation)
Joyce J. Kapsal
Anne M. Braudis
Robert K. Goff (A Professional Corporation)
Michael S. Woodlock
Bryan R. Snyder

ASSOCIATES

Dawn R. Brennan
Carolyn J. Kaye
Paul A. Zumberge
Eric W. Sachrison
Steven L. Weisenberg

OF COUNSEL

Andrew A. Kurz
Jeffrey A. Barnett

Reference: Bank of Commerce.

For full biographical listings, see the Martindale-Hubbell Law Directory

HAASIS, POPE & CORRELL, A PROFESSIONAL CORPORATION (AV)

550 West "C" Street, 9th Floor, 92101-3509
Telephone: 619-236-9933
Fax: 619-236-8961
Voice Mail: 619-236-8955

A. Mark Pope
Harvey C. Berger
Denis Long

Michelle M. Clark
A. David Mongan
Wayne D. Thomas
David A. McMahon, Jr.

Representative Clients: American States Insurance Co.; Great American; Chubb-Pacific; Scottsdale Insurance Co.

For full biographical listings, see the Martindale-Hubbell Law Directory

San Diego—Continued

HILLYER & IRWIN, A PROFESSIONAL CORPORATION (AV)

550 West C Street, 16th Floor, 92101
Telephone: 619-234-6121
Telecopier: 619-595-1313

Norman R. Allenby
James G. Ehlers
James E. Drummond
Peter J. Ippolito
Steven M. Hill
Mark G. Budwig
Lesa Christenson

For full biographical listings, see the Martindale-Hubbell Law Directory

HOVEY, KIRBY, THORNTON & HAHN, A PROFESSIONAL CORPORATION (AV)

101 West Broadway, Suite 1100, 92101-8297
Telephone: 619-685-4000
Fax: 619-685-4004

Gregg B. Hovey
Cynthia K. Thornton
M. Leslie Hovey
Jane Hahn

For full biographical listings, see the Martindale-Hubbell Law Directory

LINDLEY, LAZAR & SCALES, A PROFESSIONAL CORPORATION (AV)

One America Plaza, 600 West Broadway, Suite 1400, 92101-3302
Telephone: 619-234-9181
Fax: 619-234-8475

Luke R. Corbett
Robert M. McLeod
Richard J. Pekin, Jr.

Representative Clients: Southern California Soil & Testing, Inc.; Westana Builders-Developers; Ham Bros. Construction; Shapell Industries, Inc.; George Wimpey, Inc.

For Complete List of Firm Personnel, See General Section

For full biographical listings, see the Martindale-Hubbell Law Directory

*SAN FRANCISCO,** San Francisco Co.

BREON, O'DONNELL, MILLER, BROWN & DANNIS (AV)

19th Floor, Stevenson Place, 71 Stevenson Street, 94105
Telephone: 415-543-4111
Fax: 415-543-4384
Palos Verdes Estates, California Office: Suite 3A, 2550 Via Tejon, 90274.
Telephone: 310-373-6857.
FAX: 310-373-6808.
Salinas, California Office: Suite H120, 17842 Moro Road, Suite F120, 93907.
Telephone: 408-663-0470.

MEMBERS OF FIRM

Keith V. Breon
Margaret E. O'Donnell
David G. Miller (Resident, Palos Verdes Estates Office)
Priscilla Brown
Gregory J. Dannis
Emi R. Uyehara
Bridget A. Flanagan
Nancy B. Bourne

Kathryn Luhe
Laurie S. Juengert
Marilyn J. Cleveland
Joan Birdt (Resident, Palos Verdes Estates Office)
David A. Wolf
Brant T. Lee
Claudia L. Madrigal
Randall O. Parent
Peter W. Sturges
Laurie E. Reynolds
Guy A. Bryant
Jane E. Mitchell

SPECIAL COUNSEL

Martha Buell Scott

Representative Clients: Monterey Peninsula Unified School Dist.; Mt. Diablo Unified School Dist.; Palo Alto Unified School Dist.; Santa Cruz City Schools.

For full biographical listings, see the Martindale-Hubbell Law Directory

FELDMAN, WALDMAN & KLINE, A PROFESSIONAL CORPORATION (AV)

2700 Russ Building, 235 Montgomery Street, 94104
Telephone: 415-981-1300
Telex: 650-223-3204
Fax: 415-394-0121
Stockton, California Office: Sperry Building, 146-148 West Weber Avenue.
Telephone: 209-943-2004.
Fax: 209-943-0905.

Murry J. Waldman
Leland R. Selna, Jr.
Michael L. Korbholz
Howard M. Wexler
Patricia S. Mar
Kenneth W. Jones
Paul J. Dion
Vern S. Bothwell
L. J. Chris Martiniak
Kenneth A. Freed
Martha Jeanne Shaver (Resident, Stockton Office)

(See Next Column)

Robert Cedric Goodman
Steven K. Denebeim
Laura Grad
William F. Adams
William M. Smith
Elizabeth A. Thompson
Julie A. Jones
David L. Kanel

Abram S. Feuerstein
John R. Capron
Ted S. Storey
A. Todd Berman
Laura J. Dawson

OF COUNSEL

Richard L. Jaeger
Malcolm Leader-Picone
Gerald A. Sherwin (Resident, Stockton Office)

For full biographical listings, see the Martindale-Hubbell Law Directory

LEACH, MCGREEVY, BAUTISTA & BRASS (AV)

1735 Pacific Avenue, 94109
Telephone: 415-775-4455
Telefax: 415-775-7435
Southern California Office: 13643 Fifth Street, Chino, 91710.
Telephone: 909-590-2224.

Theodore Tamba (1900-1973)
John T. Harmon (1928-1993)
David G. Leach
Richard E. McGreevy
M. Francis Brass

A. Marquez Bautista
Teresa A. Cunningham
J. Curtis Cox
Paul David Katerndahl

OF COUNSEL

Roger G. Eliassen
Lloyd F. Postel
Robert W. Shinnick

For full biographical listings, see the Martindale-Hubbell Law Directory

DEAN W. MCPHEE (AV)

100 Pine Street, 21st Floor, 94111
Telephone: 415-398-8220
Telecopier: 415-421-0320

For full biographical listings, see the Martindale-Hubbell Law Directory

STUBBS, HITTIG & LEONE, A PROFESSIONAL CORPORATION (AV)

Suite 818, Fox Plaza, 1390 Market Street, 94102-5399
Telephone: 415-861-8200
Telecopier: 415-861-6700

Gregory E. Stubbs
H. Christopher Hittig
Louis A. Leone

For full biographical listings, see the Martindale-Hubbell Law Directory

*SAN JOSE,** Santa Clara Co.

MAHL TULLY, A PROFESSIONAL CORPORATION (AV)

10 Almaden Boulevard, Suite 1440, 95113
Telephone: 408-494-0900
Fax: 408-494-0909

Susan J. Mahl
Deanne M. Tully
Raymond P. Bolanos
Michael T. Parsons

For full biographical listings, see the Martindale-Hubbell Law Directory

MCPHARLIN & SPRINKLES (AV)

Fairmont Plaza, 50 West San Fernando, Suite 810, 95113
Telephone: 408-293-1900
Fax: 408-293-1999

MEMBERS OF FIRM

Linda Hendrix McPharlin
Catherine C. Sprinkles

ASSOCIATES

Timothy B. McCormick
Mary Lee Malysz

For full biographical listings, see the Martindale-Hubbell Law Directory

*SANTA ANA,** Orange Co.

FIELDS AND CREASON (AV)

4 Hutton Centre Drive, Suite 300, 92707
Telephone: 714-755-7777
Facsimile: 714-755-7898
Riverside, California Office: 3993 Market Street, 92501.
Telephone: 714-788-0977.
Facsimile: 714-788-6303.

MEMBERS OF FIRM

Gary D. Fields
James A. Creason

(See Next Column)

FIELDS AND CREASON, *Santa Ana—Continued*

ASSOCIATES

Steven A. Rosenthal
Lauren L. McNerney
Michael C. Duggan
Timothy A. Hill (Resident, Riverside Office)
William S. Loomis (Resident, Riverside Office)
Maria K. Aarvig (Resident, Riverside Office)
Anthony R. Milani
Gerard V. Heckler
G. Andrew Nagle
Steven J. Talcott
Ira P. Kerker
MaryAnn Nioroux
Gary Jay Greener
Edward E. Dollar
Mark Skapik
Dirk Bruinsma
Michelle McWhorter
Sheila B. Rubinstein

For full biographical listings, see the Martindale-Hubbell Law Directory

SANTA MONICA, Los Angeles Co.

DICKSON, CARLSON & CAMPILLO (AV)

120 Broadway, Suite 300, P.O. Box 2122, 90407-2122
Telephone: 310-451-2273
Telecopier: 310-451-9071

Roxanne M. Wilson
Mark S. Geraghty

For Complete List of Firm Personnel, See General Section

For full biographical listings, see the Martindale-Hubbell Law Directory

STOKES & MURPHY (AV)

520 Broadway, Suite 300, 90401
Telephone: 310-451-3337
Atlanta, Georgia Office: Waterstone Suite 350, 4751 Best Road.
Telephone: 404-766-0076,
Fax: 404-766-8823.

Robert L. Murphy

RESIDENT ASSOCIATES

Tricia D. Mading
Coleen P. Hennig

For full biographical listings, see the Martindale-Hubbell Law Directory

*SANTA ROSA,** Sonoma Co.

BELDEN, ABBEY, WEITZENBERG & KELLY, A PROFESSIONAL CORPORATION (AV)

1105 North Dutton Avenue, P.O. Box 1566, 95402
Telephone: 707-542-5050
Telecopier: 707-542-2589

Thomas P. Kelly, Jr.
W. Barton Weitzenberg

Representative Clients: Exchange Bank of Santa Rosa; Westamerica Bank; North Bay Title Co.; Northwestern Title Security Co.; Geyser Peak Winery; Arrowood Vineyards & Winery; Hansel Ford; Santa Rosa City School District.

For Complete List of Firm Personnel, See General Section

For full biographical listings, see the Martindale-Hubbell Law Directory

WALNUT CREEK, Contra Costa Co.

FIELD, BAKER & RICHARDSON (AV)

Peri Executive Centre, 2033 North Main Street, Suite 900, 94596-3729
Telephone: 510-934-7700
Telecopier: 510-934-6090

MEMBERS

Robert C. Field
R. Gordon Baker, Jr.
Robert W. Richardson
Alan J. Wilhelmy

ASSOCIATE

Emelyn Jewett Carothers

Reference: Civic Bank of Commerce (Walnut Creek Regional Office).

For full biographical listings, see the Martindale-Hubbell Law Directory

JACKL & KATZEN (AV)

2033 North Main Street, Suite 700, 94596
Telephone: 510-932-8500
Fax: 510-932-1961

MEMBERS OF FIRM

V. James Jackl
Linda R. Katzen

Christopher J. Joy
David W. Walters
James M. Sitkin
Andrew N. Contopoulos
David A. Schuricht

For full biographical listings, see the Martindale-Hubbell Law Directory

WEST COVINA, Los Angeles Co.

CRAWFORD, BACON, BANGS & BRIESEMEISTER, A PROFESSIONAL CORPORATION (AV)

California State Bank Building 11th Floor, 100 North Barranca Street, 91791
Telephone: 818-915-1641
Telecopier: 818-332-5604

Robert L. Bacon
William J. Crawford
Shaaron A. Bangs
Wilfred E. Briesemeister
Theodore E. Bacon
Daniel Colner

E. Scott Holbrook, Jr.
Theresa Crawford Tate
James W. Colfer
Garrison H. Davidson, III
Howard S. Hou
Carl Andrew Botterud

For full biographical listings, see the Martindale-Hubbell Law Directory

COLORADO

*DENVER,** Denver Co.

ROBERT L. BARTHOLIC (AV)

Suite 600, 1600 Broadway, 80202
Telephone: 303-830-0500
Fax: 303-860-7855
(Also Of Counsel to Clarence L. Bartholic, Englewood, Colorado and Special Counsel to Hamilton and Faatz, A Professional Corporation, Denver, Colorado)

OF COUNSEL

Clarence L. Bartholic

Approved Attorney for: Mid-South Title Insurance Corp; Lawyers Title Insurance Co.
Representative Clients: Anschutz Corp.; Denver and Rio Grande Western Railroad Co.; Johnson Anderson Mortgage Co.; Arco Environmental Affairs; Burlington Northern Railroad Co. and Subsidiaries; American Association of Private Railroad Car Owners, Inc.
References: Colorado National Bank; Colorado State Bank.

For full biographical listings, see the Martindale-Hubbell Law Directory

DAVIS & WEINSTEIN (AV)

Suite 2600, 1600 Broadway, 80202
Telephone: 303-861-4166
Fax: 303-861-2976

MEMBER OF FIRM

Jo Ann Weinstein

Reference: The Women's Bank, N.A., Denver, Colo.

For full biographical listings, see the Martindale-Hubbell Law Directory

FEDER, MORRIS, TAMBLYN & GOLDSTEIN, P.C. (AV)

150 Blake Street Building, 1441 Eighteenth Street, 80202
Telephone: 303-292-1441
FAX: 303-292-1126

Harold A. Feder
Stephen B. Schuyler
Mark D. Thompson

Reference: Guaranty Bank & Trust Co., Denver, Colorado.

For full biographical listings, see the Martindale-Hubbell Law Directory

REIMAN & ASSOCIATES, P.C. (AV)

1600 Broadway, Suite 1640, 80202
Telephone: 303-860-1500
Fax: 303-839-4380

Jeffrey Reiman

Marcie K. Bayaz
James Birch

For full biographical listings, see the Martindale-Hubbell Law Directory

WELLER FRIEDRICH, LLC (AV)

One Civic Center, Suite 2000, 1560 Broadway, P.O. Box 989, 80201-0989
Telephone: 303-812-1200
FAX: 303-812-1212

David K. Kerr
Andrew J. Friedrich
Jerome M. Joseph
Dennis J. Bartlett

OF COUNSEL

W. Robert Ward
Martin J. Andrew

(See Next Column)

WELLER FRIEDRICH LLC—*Continued*

Suanne Marie Dell
Gregory E. Sopkin

Representative Clients: Abbott Laboratories; Associated Aviation Underwriters; Commercial Union Insurance Companies.
Reference: Colorado State Bank of Denver.

For full biographical listings, see the Martindale-Hubbell Law Directory

CONNECTICUT

GREENWICH, Fairfield Co.

ALBERT, WARD & JOHNSON, P.C. (AV)

125 Mason Street, P.O. Box 1668, 06836
Telephone: 203-661-8600
Telecopier: 203-661-8051

OF COUNSEL

David Albert

Tom S. Ward, Jr.
Scott R. Johnson
Jane D. Hogeman
Howard R. Wolfe

Christopher A. Kristoff

For full biographical listings, see the Martindale-Hubbell Law Directory

*HARTFORD,** Hartford Co.

GORDON, MUIR AND FOLEY (AV)

Hartford Square North, Ten Columbus Boulevard, 06106-1944
Telephone: 203-525-5361
Telecopier: 203-525-4849

MEMBERS OF FIRM

William S. Gordon, Jr. (1946-1956)
George Muir (1939-1976)
Edward J. Foley (1955-1983)
Peter C. Schwartz
John J. Reid
John H. Goodrich, Jr.
R. Bradley Wolfe
Jon Stephen Berk
William J. Gallitto
Gerald R. Swirsky
Robert J. O'Brien
Philip J. O'Connor
Kenneth G. Williams
Chester J. Bukowski
Mary Ann Santacroce

ASSOCIATES

J. Lawrence Price
Mary Anne Alicia Charron
James G. Kelly
Kevin F. Morin
Claudia A. Baio
Patrick T. Treacy
Andrew J. Hern
Eileen Geel
Christopher L. Slack
Renee W. Dwyer
David B. Heintz

OF COUNSEL

Stephen M. Riley

Reference: Fleet Bank.

For full biographical listings, see the Martindale-Hubbell Law Directory

SOROKIN SOROKIN GROSS HYDE & WILLIAMS P.C. (AV)

One Corporate Center, 06103
Telephone: 203-525-6645
Fax: 203-522-1781
Simsbury, Connecticut Office: 730 Hopmeadow Street.
Telephone: 203-651-9348.
Rocky Hill, Connecticut Office: 2360 Main Street.
Telephone: 203-563-9305.
Fax: 203-529-6931.
Glastonbury, Connecticut Office: 124 Hebron Avenue.
Telephone: 203-659-8801.

Clifford J. Grandjean
Richard C. Robinson

For Complete List of Firm Personnel, See General Section

For full biographical listings, see the Martindale-Hubbell Law Directory

DISTRICT OF COLUMBIA

WASHINGTON, D.C. Co.

* indicates certain Bar Register subscribers, in cities of comparable size and importance, who maintain an additional office in Washington, D.C. and who have arranged for representation as a part of the Washington, D.C. listings that follow

*** BELL, BOYD & LLOYD** (AV)

1615 L Street, N.W., 20036
Telephone: 202-466-6300
FAX: 202-463-0678
Chicago, Illinois Office: Three First National Plaza, Suite 3300, 70 West Madison Street.
Telephone: 312-372-1121.
FAX: 312-372-2098.

RESIDENT PARTNERS

Francis J. Pelland
Joel S. Rubinstein
Robert J. Sciaroni

OF COUNSEL

Marvin P. Sadur

RESIDENT ASSOCIATES

Brian Cohen (Not admitted in DC)
Andrew N. Cook

For Complete List of Firm Personnel, See General Section

For full biographical listings, see the Martindale-Hubbell Law Directory

BRAUDE & MARGULIES, P.C. (AV)

Suite 200, 1025 Connecticut Avenue, N.W., 20036
Telephone: 202-293-2993
Fax: 202-331-7916
Baltimore, Maryland Office: 1206 St. Paul Street.
Telephone: 410-234-0202.
Fax: 410-625-2872.
San Francisco, California Office: William R. Delaney, Citicorp Center, One Sansome Street, Suite 2000.
Telephone: 415-951-4709.
Fax: 415-951-4754.
Riyadh, Saudi Arabia Office: Mohammed A. Al-Abdullah, P.O. Box 59446, Nuzha Building, Sixth Floor, 11525.
Telephone: 966-1-405-1291.
Fax: 966-1-405-1291.
Abu Dhabi, United Arab Emirates Office: P.O. Box 43908.
Telephone: (971-2) 787222.
Fax: (971-2) 784001.

Herman M. Braude
William M. Huddles (Resident, Baltimore, Maryland Office)
Roger C. Jones (Not admitted in DC; Resident, Baltimore, Maryland Office)
Howard A. Pollack (Resident, Baltimore, Maryland Office)

Samuel M. Morrison, Jr.
Robert D. Windus
John P. McGowan, Jr. (Not admitted in DC; Resident, Abu Dhabi, U.A.E. Office)
Chuncheng Lian
Kenneth Knut Sorteberg (Resident, Baltimore, Maryland Office)

OF COUNSEL

J. Richard Margulies
William R. Delaney (Resident, San Francisco, California Office)

For full biographical listings, see the Martindale-Hubbell Law Directory

KENNETH R. FEINBERG & ASSOCIATES (AV)

1120 20th Street, N.W. Suite 740 South, 20036
Telephone: 202-371-1110
Fax: 202-962-9290
New York, N.Y. Office: 780 3rd Avenue, Suite 2202.
Telephone: 212-527-9600.
Fax: 212-527-9611.

ASSOCIATES

Deborah E. Greenspan
Michael K. Rozen (Not admitted in DC)
Peter H. Woodin (Not admitted in DC)

For full biographical listings, see the Martindale-Hubbell Law Directory

SELTZER AND ROSEN, P.C. (AV)

One Franklin Square, Suite 310 East 1301 K Street, N.W., 20005-3307
Telephone: 202-682-4585
Telecopier: 202-682-4599

(See Next Column)

SELTZER AND ROSEN P.C., *Washington—Continued*

E. Manning Seltzer Harold I. Rosen
Mark E. Davis

OF COUNSEL

Gary B. Cohen

LEGAL SUPPORT PERSONNEL

ENGINEER ADVISOR

John W. Morris

For full biographical listings, see the Martindale-Hubbell Law Directory

*** VENABLE, BAETJER, HOWARD & CIVILETTI (AV)**

A Partnership including Professional Corporations
Suite 1000, 1201 New York Avenue, N.W., 20005
Telephone: 202-962-4800
Fax: 202-962-8300
Baltimore, Maryland Office: Venable, Baetjer and Howard, 1800 Mercantile Bank & Trust Building, 2 Hopkins Plaza.
Telephone: 410-244-7400.
McLean, Virginia Office: Venable, Baetjer and Howard, Suite 400, 2010 Corporate Ridge.
Telephone: 703-760-1600.
Rockville, Maryland Office: Venable, Baetjer and Howard, Suite 500, One Church Street, P. O. Box 1906.
Telephone: 301-217-5600.
Towson, Maryland Office: Venable, Baetjer and Howard, 210 Allegheny Avenue, P. O. Box 5517.
Telephone: 410-494-6200.

MEMBERS OF FIRM

Benjamin R. Civiletti (P.C.) (Also at Baltimore and Towson, Maryland Offices)
Thomas J. Kenney, Jr. (P.C.) (Not admitted in DC)
James K. Archibald (Also at Baltimore and Towson, Maryland Offices)
Jeffrey A. Dunn (Also at Baltimore, Maryland Office)
George F. Pappas (Also at Baltimore, Maryland Office)
James L. Shea (Not admitted in DC; also at Baltimore, Maryland Office)
Maurice Baskin

For Complete List of Firm Personnel, See General Section

For full biographical listings, see the Martindale-Hubbell Law Directory

WATT, TIEDER & HOFFAR (AV)

601 Pennsylvania Avenue, N.W., Suite 900, 20004
Telephone: 202-462-4697
Telecopier: 703-893-8029
McLean Virginia Office: 7929 Westpark Drive, Suite 400,
Telephone: 703-749-1000.
Telecopier: 703-893-8029.
Irvine California Office: 3 Park Plaza, Suite 1530.
Telephone: 714-852-6700.

MEMBERS OF FIRM

John B. Tieder, Jr. Robert K. Cox
David C. Romm

For full biographical listings, see the Martindale-Hubbell Law Directory

FLORIDA

*FORT MYERS,** Lee Co.

GOLDBERG, GOLDSTEIN & BUCKLEY, P.A. (AV)

1515 Broadway, P.O. Box 2366, 33901-2366
Telephone: 813-334-1146
Fax: 813-334-3039
Naples, Florida Office: 2150 Goodlette Road, Suite 105, Parkway Financial Center, 33940.
Telephone: 813-262-4888.
Fax: 813-262-8716.
Port Charlotte, Florida Office: Emerald Square, Suite 1, 2852 Tamiami Trail, 33952.
Telephone: 813-624-2393.
Fax: 813-624-2155.
Cape Coral, Florida Office: 2330 S.E. 16th Place.
Telephone: 813-574-5575.
Fax: 813-574-9213.
Lehigh Acres, Florida Office: 1458 Lee Boulevard, Lee Boulevard Shopping Center, 33936.
Telephone: 813-368-6101.
Fax: 813-368-2461.
South Fort Myers, Florida Office: Horizon Plaza, 16050 South Tamiami Trail, Suites 101 and 102, 33908.
Telephone: 813-433-6777.
Fax: 813-433-0578.

(See Next Column)

Bonita Springs, Florida Office: 3431 Bonita Beach Road, Suite 208, 33923.
Telephone: 813-495-0003.
Fax: 813-495-0564.

Morton A. Goldberg
Ray Goldstein
Stephen W. Buckley
Harvey B. Goldberg
John B. Cechman
J. Jeffrey Rice
Mark A. Steinberg
David R. Linn
Donna L. Schnorr
Mark P. Smith
Richard Lee Purtz
Martin G. Arnowitz
George J. Mitar
Steven P. Kushner
Michael J. Ciccarone
Terry S. Nelson
William L. Welker
Jay Cooper
Jonathan D. Conant
Raymond L. Racila
Luis E. Insignares

Approved Attorneys for: Attorneys' Title Insurance Fund; Chicago Title Insurance Co.; American Pioneer Title Insurance Company; Stewart Title Guaranty Co.; First American Title Insurance Company.

For Complete List of Firm Personnel, See General Section

For full biographical listings, see the Martindale-Hubbell Law Directory

*KISSIMMEE,** Osceola Co.

POHL & BROWN, P.A.

(See Winter Park)

*MIAMI,** Dade Co.

DANIELS, KASHTAN & FORNARIS, P.A. (AV)

Two Alhambra Plaza, Suite 810 (Coral Gables), 33134
Telephone: 305-448-7988
Telecopier: 305-448-7978

Richard G. Daniels Michael F. Kashtan
Martha D. Fornaris

Jannea S. Rogers Kathleen A. Flynn
Angel Garcia John E. Oramas
Ana M. Latour

Reference: Barnett Bank.

For full biographical listings, see the Martindale-Hubbell Law Directory

SIEGFRIED, RIVERA, LERNER, DE LA TORRE & PETERSEN, P.A. (AV)

Suite 1102, 201 Alhambra Circle (Coral Gables), 33134
Telephone: 305-442-3334
Fax: 305-443-3292
Fort Lauderdale Office: One Financial Plaza, Suite 2012, 33394.
Telephone: 305-832-0766.
Fax: 305-764-1759.

Steven M. Siegfried
Oscar R. Rivera
Lisa A. Lerner
Helio De La Torre
Byron G. Petersen (Resident, Fort Lauderdale Office)
Peter H. Edwards

Maria Victoria Arias
Daniel Davis
James F. Harrington
Elisabeth D. Kozlow
H. Hugh Mc Connell
Alberto Nouel Moris
Samuel A. Persaud

Reference: Southeast First National Bank of Miami.

For full biographical listings, see the Martindale-Hubbell Law Directory

WELBAUM, ZOOK & JONES (AV)

Penthouse Suite, 901 Ponce de Leon Boulevard (Coral Gables), 33134-3009
Telephone: 305-441-8900
Fax: 305-441-2255

MEMBERS OF FIRM

D. Lloyd Zook (1922-1990)
R. Earl Welbaum
Peter C. Jones
Dan B. Guernsey
Robert A. Hingston
W. Frank Greenleaf
John H. Gregory

ASSOCIATES

Kenn W. Goff Michael Yates
Mark D. Greenwell

OF COUNSEL

René Sacasas

For full biographical listings, see the Martindale-Hubbell Law Directory

NORTH MIAMI BEACH, Dade Co.

BUCHANAN INGERSOLL, PROFESSIONAL CORPORATION (AV)

One Turnberry Place, 19495 Biscayne Boulevard, 33180
Telephone: 305-933-5600
Telecopier: 305-933-2350
Pittsburgh, Pennsylvania Office: 5800 USX Tower, 600 Grant Street.
Telephone: 412-562-8800.
Philadelphia, Pennsylvania Office: Two Logan Square, Twelfth Floor, 18th & Arch Streets.
Telephone: 215-665-8700.
Harrisburg, Pennsylvania Office: Vartan Parc, 30 North Third Street.
Telephone: 717-237-4800.
Tampa, Florida Office: Suite 1030, 101 East Kennedy Boulevard.
Telephone: 813-222-8180.
Princeton, New Jersey Office: Buchanan Ingersoll, A Partnership, College Centre, 500 College Road East.
Telephone: 609-452-2666.
Lexington, Kentucky Office: Suite 600, PNC Bank Plaza, 200 West Vine Street.
Telephone: 606-225-5333.

Gary S. Phillips

For Complete List of Firm Personnel, See General Section

For full biographical listings, see the Martindale-Hubbell Law Directory

*ORLANDO,** Orange Co.

BAKER & HOSTETLER (AV)

SunBank Center, Suite 2300, 200 South Orange Avenue, 32802-3432
Telephone: 407-649-4000
In Cleveland, Ohio: 3200 National City Center, 1900 East Ninth Street.
Telephone: 216-621-0200.
In Columbus, Ohio: Capitol Square, Suite 2100, 65 East State Street.
Telephone: 614-228-1541.
In Denver, Colorado: 303 East 17th Avenue, Suite 1100.
Telephone: 303-861-0600.
In Houston, Texas: 1000 Louisiana, Suite 2000.
Telephone: 713-751-1600.
In Long Beach, California: 300 Oceangate, Suite 620.
Telephone: 310-432-2827.
In Los Angeles, California: 600 Wilshire Boulevard.
Telephone: 213-624-2400.
In Washington, D.C.: Washington Square, Suite 1100, 1050 Connecticut Avenue, N.W., Suite 1100.
Telephone: 202-861-1500.
In College Park, Maryland: 9658 Baltimore Boulevard, Suite 206.
Telephone: 301-441-2781.
In Alexandria, Virginia: 437 North Lee Street.
Telephone: 703-549-1294.
In San Francisco, California: One Sansome Street, Suite 2000.
Telephone: 415-951-4705.

PARTNER

John W. Foster, Sr.

For Complete List of Firm Personnel, See General Section

For full biographical listings, see the Martindale-Hubbell Law Directory

DEMPSEY & ASSOCIATES, P.A. (AV)

605 East Robinson Street, P.O. Box 1980, 32802-1980
Telephone: 407-422-5166
Mailing Address: 1031 West Morse Boulevard, Suite 200, Winter Park, Florida, 32789
Winter Park, Florida Office: 1031 West Morse Boulevard, Suite 200, 32789.
Telephone: 407-740-7778.
Telecopier: 407-740-0911.

Bernard H. Dempsey, Jr. Michael C. Sasso

M. Susan Sacco
William P. Weatherford, Jr.
Daniel N. Brodersen
Lori R. Benton
Barbara B. Smithers

OF COUNSEL

Gary S. Salzman

Reference: First Union National Bank of Florida.

For full biographical listings, see the Martindale-Hubbell Law Directory

POHL & BROWN, P.A.

(See Winter Park)

RUSSELL & HULL, P.A. (AV)

537 North Magnolia Avenue, P.O. Box 2751, 32802
Telephone: 407-422-1234

(See Next Column)

Rodney Laird Russell Norman L. Hull

Reference: First Union National Bank, N.A.

For full biographical listings, see the Martindale-Hubbell Law Directory

*TAMPA,** Hillsborough Co.

MICHAEL C. ADDISON (AV)

Suite 2175, 100 North Tampa Street, 33602-5145
Telephone: 813-223-2000
Facsimile: 813-228-6000
Mailing Address: P.O. Box 2175, Tampa, Florida, 33601-2175

For full biographical listings, see the Martindale-Hubbell Law Directory

ADKINS & KISE, P.A. (AV)

2175 Barnett Plaza, 101 East Kennedy Boulevard, 33602
Telephone: 813-221-2200
Fax: 813-221-8850

Edward C. Adkins Christopher M. Kise

For full biographical listings, see the Martindale-Hubbell Law Directory

CAREY, O'MALLEY, WHITAKER & LINS, P.A. (AV)

Suite 1190, 100 South Ashley Drive, P.O. Box 499, 33601-0499
Telephone: 813-221-8210
Telecopier: 813-221-1430

Michael R. Carey
Andrew M. O'Malley
Daniel D. Whitaker
D. Michael Lins
Douglas P. Manson
Randall P. Mueller
Sean V. Donnelly

For full biographical listings, see the Martindale-Hubbell Law Directory

EDNA ELLIOTT, J.D., P.A. (AV)

111 South Boulevard, 33606
Telephone: 813-254-5051
Fax: 813-254-5471

Edna Elliott

For full biographical listings, see the Martindale-Hubbell Law Directory

WINTER PARK, Orange Co.

POHL & BROWN, P.A. (AV)

280 West Canton Avenue, Suite 410, P.O. Box 3208, 32789
Telephone: 407-647-7645; 407-647-POHL
Telefax: 407-647-2314

Frank L. Pohl
Usher L. Brown
Houston E. Short
Dwight I. Cool
William W. Pouzar
Mary B. Van Leuven

OF COUNSEL

Frederick W. Peirsol

Representative Clients: Orange County Comptroller; Osceola County; School Board of Osceola County, Florida; Osceola Tourist Development Council; NationsBank of Florida, N.A.; SunBank, N.A.; The Bank of Winter Park; Bekins Moving and Storage Co., Inc.; Champion Boats, Inc.; KeyCom Telephone Systems, Inc.

For full biographical listings, see the Martindale-Hubbell Law Directory

GEORGIA

*ATLANTA,** Fulton Co.

BOVIS, KYLE & BURCH (AV)

A Partnership including Professional Corporations
Third Floor, 53 Perimeter Center East, 30346
Telephone: 404-391-9100
Telecopier: 404-668-0878
Alpharetta, Georgia Office: 41 Milton Avenue.
Telephone: 404-391-9100.
Telecopier: 404-668-0878.

MEMBERS OF FIRM

John V. Burch (P.C.) C. Sam Thomas (P.C.)
Gregory R. Veal

ASSOCIATES

Timothy J. Burson Wade H. Purcell

For full biographical listings, see the Martindale-Hubbell Law Directory

Atlanta—Continued

FRANKEL, HARDWICK, TANENBAUM & FINK, P.C. (AV)

359 East Paces Ferry Road, N.E., 30305
Telephone: 404-266-2930
Fax: 404-231-3362

Samuel N. Frankel
James J. Brissette

Representative Clients: America's Favorite Chicken Co. (Church's and Popeye's); Softlab, Inc.; Basic, Inc.; Buffalo's Franchise Concepts, Inc.; Combustion Engineering, Inc.; Commerical Bank of Georgia; Patients Pharmacies; Hank Aaron Enterprises, Inc.; Nursecare (Nursing Homes); Sundance Products, Inc.; Venture Construction Company; Sobstad Corp.

For Complete List of Firm Personnel, See General Section

For full biographical listings, see the Martindale-Hubbell Law Directory

GRIFFIN COCHRANE & MARSHALL, A PROFESSIONAL CORPORATION (AV)

191 Peachtree Street, N.E. Suite 2000, 30303
Telephone: 404-523-2000
Fax: 404-523-9655

Harry L. Griffin, Jr.
Robert D. Marshall
Curtis W. Martin
Lee C. Davis
Jennifer Wheatley Fletcher
W. Henry Parkman
John Dean Marshall, Jr.
Michael C. Castellon
Robert Thomas Tifverman
Melissa S. Harben
Craig Alan Courville

OF COUNSEL

Luther P. Cochrane
John F. Elger

For full biographical listings, see the Martindale-Hubbell Law Directory

HENDRICK, PHILLIPS, SCHEMM & SALZMAN, A PROFESSIONAL CORPORATION (AV)

1800 Peachtree Center Tower, 230 Peachtree Street, N.W., 30303
Telephone: 404-522-1410
FAX: 404-522-9545

David R. Hendrick
Stephen M. Phillips
Neil C. Schemm
Martin R. Salzman

Victoria H. Tobin
Jeffrey J. Nix
William D. Flatt
Kamyar Molavi
Jennifer R. Levy

Reference: First Union National Bank.

For full biographical listings, see the Martindale-Hubbell Law Directory

MCREYNOLDS & WELCH, P.C. (AV)

The Lenox Building, Suite 950, 3399 Peachtree Road, N.E., 30326
Telephone: 404-233-8500
Fax: 404-231-3579

Larry S. McReynolds
Michael Welch

For full biographical listings, see the Martindale-Hubbell Law Directory

JAMES B. RITCHIE A PROFESSIONAL CORPORATION (AV)

Suite 201, West Wieuca Square, 90 West Wieuca Road, N.E., 30342-3200
Telephone: 404-255-8900
Fax: 404-255-9267

James B. Ritchie

LEGAL SUPPORT PERSONNEL

Deborah M. Clague

Representative Clients: Britton and Associates, Inc.; Douglas & Associates, Architects, Inc.; Henry Electric Co., Inc.; J & A Pipeline Co., Inc.; Kennedy Electrical, Inc.; Lewis Construction & Consulting, Inc.; McClure Electrical Constructors, Inc.; Sunbelt Structures, Inc.; Willow Construction, Inc.; W. L. Carey, General Contractor, Inc.

For full biographical listings, see the Martindale-Hubbell Law Directory

SCHREEDER, WHEELER & FLINT (AV)

1600 Candler Building, 127 Peachtree Street, N.E., 30303-1845
Telephone: 404-681-3450
Telecopy: 404-681-1046

MEMBERS OF FIRM

Charles L. Schreeder, III
Warren O. Wheeler
David H. Flint
Lawrence S. Burnat
Samuel F. Boyte
John A. Christy
Mark W. Forsling
Edward H. Brown
Leo Rose III
Timothy C. Batten

ASSOCIATES

Clifford A. Barshay
Laura R. Champion
J. Christopher Desmond
Scott W. Peters
Alexander J. Simmons, Jr.
Lynn C. Stewart
Debra A. Wilson

(See Next Column)

Reference: Fidelity National Bank; Wachovia Bank of Georgia, NA.

For full biographical listings, see the Martindale-Hubbell Law Directory

SHAPIRO, FUSSELL, WEDGE, SMOTHERMAN & MARTIN (AV)

One Midtown Plaza, Suite 1200, 1360 Peachtree Street, 30309
Telephone: 404-870-2200
Facsimile: 404-870-2222

MEMBERS OF FIRM

J. Ben Shapiro, Jr.
Ira J. Smotherman, Jr.
Herman L. Fussell
Robert B. Wedge
Ronald J. Garber
Charles F. Williams
Nicholas S. Papleacos
Seth Price
Michael P. Davis
Cyrell E. Lynch
David L. Tank

ASSOCIATES

Connie H. Buffington
Daniel M. Jennings
Scott I. Zucker

For full biographical listings, see the Martindale-Hubbell Law Directory

SMITH, CURRIE & HANCOCK (AV)

2600 Harris Tower-Peachtree Center, 233 Peachtree Street, N.E., 30303-1530
Telephone: 404-521-3800
Telecopier: 404-688-0671

MEMBERS OF FIRM

G. Maynard Smith (1907-1992).
Overton A. Currie
E. Reginald Hancock (Retired)
Luther P. House, Jr.
Glower W. Jones
Robert B. Ansley, Jr.
George K. McPherson, Jr.
Bert R. Oastler
James Allan Smith
John G. Skinner
J. Thomas Kilpatrick
Aubrey L. Coleman, Jr.
Larry E. Forrester
Thomas E. Abernathy, IV
Philip L. Fortune
John C. Stout, Jr.
Daniel M. Shea
Thomas J. Kelleher, Jr.
Frank E. Riggs, Jr.
Ronald G. Robey
Dan T. Carter
William E. Dorris
Brian G. Corgan
Charles W. Surasky
Robert N. Godfrey
John T. Flynn
James F. Butler, III
Joseph C. Staak
Hubert J. Bell, Jr.
Philip E. Beck
Neal J. Sweeney
Frederick L. Wright
James K. Bidgood, Jr.
Randall F. Hafer
S. Gregory Joy
Fredric W. Stearns
Robert C. Chambers
Karl Dix, Jr.
George Q. Sewell

OF COUNSEL

James E. Stephenson
Frank O. Hendrick III

ASSOCIATES

D. Lee Roberts, Jr.
William R. Poplin, Jr.
Ivor J. Longo
Joseph Paul Henner
John E. Menechino, Jr.
Marty N. Martenson
Edward A. Arnold
Charles A. Bledsoe, Jr.
Daniel F. DuPré
Catherine M. Hobart
George Papaioanou
M. Craig Hall
Christine M. MacIver
Craig P. Siegenthaler
Suzanne Jones
R. Randy Edwards

Labor Relations Clients: Atlanta Symphony Orchestra; Babcock & Wilcox Co.; Diversified Products Corp.; Echlin, Inc.; Genuine Parts Co. (NAPA); Proctor & Gamble Co.; Oxford Industries; Sears Roebuck and Co.
Construction Clients: Seaboard Surety Co.; Travelers Indemnity Co.

For full biographical listings, see the Martindale-Hubbell Law Directory

STOKES & MURPHY (AV)

Waterstone, Suite 350, 4751 Best Road, 30337
Telephone: 404-766-0076
Fax: 404-766-8823
Santa Monica, California Office: 520 Broadway, Suite 300.
Telephone: 310-451-3337.

Arch Y. Stokes
McNeill Stokes
Robert L. Murphy (Resident, Santa Monica Office)
John R. Hunt
Margaret Mead Stokes
Karl M. Terrell

ASSOCIATES

Cassandra Kirk
Debra Gordon
Michael Pepperman (Not admitted in GA)
Anne-Marie Mizel (Not admitted in GA)
Annette Sanford Werner (Not admitted in GA)

For full biographical listings, see the Martindale-Hubbell Law Directory

SUMNER & HEWES (AV)

Suite 700, The Hurt Building, 50 Hurt Plaza, 30303
Telephone: 404-588-9000

(See Next Column)

SUMNER & HEWES—*Continued*

PARTNERS

William E. Sumner
Nancy Becker Hewes
Stephen J. Anderson
David A. Webster

ASSOCIATES

Rosemary Smith
Andrew A. Davenport
Marguerite Patrick Bryan
Michelle Harris Jordan
Edith M. Shine

For full biographical listings, see the Martindale-Hubbell Law Directory

SUTHERLAND, ASBILL & BRENNAN (AV)

999 Peachtree Street, N.E., 30309-3996
Telephone: 404-853-8000
Facsimile: 404-853-8806
Washington, D.C. Office: 1275 Pennsylvania Avenue, N.W., 20004-2404.
Telephone: 202-383-0100.
New York, N.Y. Office: 1270 Avenue of the Americas, 10020-1700.
Telephone: 212-332-3000.
Austin, Texas Office: 111 Congress Avenue, 23rd Floor, 78701-4079.
Telephone: 512-469-3350.

James P. Groton
Charles T. Lester, Jr.
Alfred A. Lindseth
George Anthony Smith

For Complete List of Firm Personnel, See General Section

For full biographical listings, see the Martindale-Hubbell Law Directory

WEISZ & ASSOCIATES (AV)

Suite 900 Live Oak Center, 3475 Lenox Road, N.E., 30326-1232
Telephone: 404-233-7888
Facsimile: 404-261-1925

Peter R. Weisz

ASSOCIATE

Cathy Rae Nash

LEGAL SUPPORT PERSONNEL

PARALEGALS

Jo Anne Gunn

For full biographical listings, see the Martindale-Hubbell Law Directory

*NEWNAN,** Coweta Co.

GLOVER & DAVIS, P.A. (AV)

10 Brown Street, P.O. Box 1038, 30264
Telephone: 404-253-4330;
Atlanta: 404-463-1100
Fax: 404-251-7152
Peachtree City, Georgia Office: Suite 130, 200 Westpark Drive.
Telephone: 404-487-5834.
Fax: 404-487-3492.

J. Littleton Glover, Jr.
Delia T. Crouch

Representative Clients: Newnan Savings Bank; Batson-Cook Company, General Corporate and Construction Divisions; Coweta County, Georgia.
Local Counsel for: International Latex Corp.; First Union National Bank of Georgia; West Georgia Farm Credit, ACA.

For Complete List of Firm Personnel, See General Section

For full biographical listings, see the Martindale-Hubbell Law Directory

HAWAII

*HONOLULU,** Honolulu Co.

AYABE, CHONG, NISHIMOTO, SIA & NAKAMURA (AV)

A Partnership including a Professional Corporation
3000 Grosvenor Center, 737 Bishop Street, 96813
Telephone: 808-537-6119
Telecopier: 808-526-3491

MEMBER OF FIRM

Sidney K. Ayabe (P.C.)

Ann H. Aratani

Representative Clients: Travelers Insurance Co.; St. Paul Fire and Marine Insurance Co.; The Employers Group of Insurance Companies; TIG Insurance Co.; Pacific Insurance Co.; Hartford Accident and Indemnity Co.; Continental Casualty Co.; First Insurance Company of Hawaii, Ltd.

For Complete List of Firm Personnel, See General Section

For full biographical listings, see the Martindale-Hubbell Law Directory

DWYER IMANAKA SCHRAFF KUDO MEYER & FUJIMOTO ATTORNEYS AT LAW, A LAW CORPORATION (AV)

1800 Pioneer Plaza, 900 Fort Street Mall, 96813
Telephone: 808-524-8000
Telecopier: 808-526-1419
Mailing Address: P.O. Box 2727, 96803

John R. Dwyer, Jr.
Mitchell A. Imanaka
Paul A. Schraff
Benjamin A. Kudo (Atty. at Law, A Law Corp.)
William G. Meyer, III
Wesley M. Fujimoto
Ronald Van Grant
Jon M. H. Pang
Blake W. Bushnell
Kenn N. Kojima

Adelbert Green
Richard T. Asato, Jr.
Scott W. Settle
Darcie S. Yoshinaga
Tracy Timothy Woo
Lawrence I. Kawasaki
Douglas H. Inouye
Christine A. Low

OF COUNSEL

Randall Y. Iwase

For full biographical listings, see the Martindale-Hubbell Law Directory

LAW OFFICE OF KENNETH S. ROBBINS ATTORNEY AT LAW, A LAW CORPORATION (AV)

Suite 2220 Davies Pacific Center, 841 Bishop Street, 96813
Telephone: 808-524-2355
Fax: 808-526-0290

Kenneth S. Robbins

Vincent A. Rhodes
Shinken Naitoh

For full biographical listings, see the Martindale-Hubbell Law Directory

IDAHO

*BOISE,** Ada Co.

HALL, FARLEY, OBERRECHT & BLANTON (AV)

Key Financial Center, 702 West Idaho Street, Suite 700, P.O. Box 1271, 83701-1271
Telephone: 208-336-0404
Facsimile: 208-336-5193

Richard E. Hall
Donald J. Farley
Phillip S. Oberrecht
Raymond D. Powers
Candy Wagahoff Dale
Robert B. Luce
J. Kevin West
Bart W. Harwood

J. Charles Blanton
John J. Burke
Steven J. Hippler
Thorpe P. Orton
Ronald S. Best (Not admitted in ID)

References: Boise State University; Farm Bureau Mutual Insurance Company of Idaho; Medical Insurance Exchange of California; The St. Paul Cos.

For full biographical listings, see the Martindale-Hubbell Law Directory

ILLINOIS

*CHICAGO,** Cook Co.

EPSTEIN, ZAIDEMAN & ESRIG, P.C. (AV)

120 South Riverside Plaza, Suite 1150, 60606
Telephone: 312-207-0005
Fax: 312-207-1332

James R. Epstein
Robert J. Zaideman
Jerry A. Esrig

Jeffrey L. Whitcomb
Elizabeth A. Kaveny
David R. Nordwall

OF COUNSEL

Donald W. Aaronson

For full biographical listings, see the Martindale-Hubbell Law Directory

LAWRENCE, KAMIN, SAUNDERS & UHLENHOP (AV)

208 South La Salle Street, Suite 1750, 60604
Telephone: 312-372-1947
Telecopier: 312-372-2389

(See Next Column)

LAWRENCE, KAMIN, SAUNDERS & UHLENHOP, *Chicago—Continued*

MEMBERS OF FIRM

Howard P. Kamin
Kent Lawrence
David E. Muschler
Lawrence A. Rosen
Randall B. Gold

ASSOCIATE

David L. Reich

Representative Clients: Blount, Inc.; Pepper Construction Co.; Corrigan Construction Co.; O'Neil Construction Co.; United States Fidelity and Guaranty; Lyons Electric Co.; St. Paul Financial Marine Insurance Co.; Seaboard Surety Co; Mellon Stuart Co.

For full biographical listings, see the Martindale-Hubbell Law Directory

O'BRIEN, O'ROURKE & HOGAN (AV)

135 South La Salle Street, 60603
Telephone: 312-372-1462
Fax: 312-372-8029
Orlando, Florida Office: Moye, O'Brien, O'Rourke, Hogan & Pickert, 201 East Pine Street, Suite 710.
Telephone: 407-843-3341.

MEMBERS OF FIRM

James Elton Moye (Resident at Orlando, Florida Office)
Donald V. O'Brien
John C. O'Rourke, Jr.
Stephen W. Pickert (Resident at Orlando, Florida Office)

For full biographical listings, see the Martindale-Hubbell Law Directory

INDIANA

*EVANSVILLE,** Vanderburgh Co.

ZIEMER, STAYMAN, WEITZEL & SHOULDERS (AV)

(Formerly Early, Arnold & Ziemer)
1507 Old National Bank Building, P.O. Box 916, 47706
Telephone: 812-424-7575
Telecopier: 812-421-5089

MEMBER OF FIRM

Robert F. Stayman

Reference: Old National Bank in Evansville.

For full biographical listings, see the Martindale-Hubbell Law Directory

*INDIANAPOLIS,** Marion Co.

BACKER & BACKER, A PROFESSIONAL CORPORATION (AV)

101 West Ohio Street, Suite 1500, 46204
Telephone: 317-684-3000
Telecopier: 317-684-3004

Herbert J. Backer
Stephen A. Backer
David J. Backer

Reference: Bank One, Indianapolis.

For full biographical listings, see the Martindale-Hubbell Law Directory

DUTTON OVERMAN GOLDSTEIN PINKUS, A PROFESSIONAL CORPORATION (AV)

710 Century Building, 36 South Pennsylvania Street, 46204
Telephone: 317-633-4000
Telecopier: 317-633-1494

C. B. Dutton
Alan H. Goldstein
Susan Rogers Brooke

Donna J. Bays

Representative Clients: Huber, Hunt & Nichols, Inc.; The Hunt Paving Co., Inc.; Hinshaw Roofing & Sheet Metal Co., Inc.; Fink, Roberts & Petrie, Inc.; Roosevelt Building Products Company, Inc.

For full biographical listings, see the Martindale-Hubbell Law Directory

ICE MILLER DONADIO & RYAN (AV)

One American Square Box 82001, 46282-0002
Telephone: 317-236-2100
Fax: 317-236-2219

MEMBERS OF FIRM

Alan H. Lobley
Arthur P. Kalleres
Michael H. Boldt
Gary J. Dankert
Phillip L. Bayt
Fred R. Biesecker
Zeff A. Weiss

(See Next Column)

ASSOCIATES

Kristin L. Altice
Michael R. Kerr
Stephanie Alden Smithey
Curtis W. McCauley

Representative Clients: Howard Needles Tammen & Bergendoff; Geupel DeMars, Inc.; Browning Day Mullins Dierdorf, Inc.; F.A. Wilhelm Construction Company, Inc.; CSO Architects, Inc.; Ratio Architects, Inc.; Shiel-Sexton Co., Inc.

For Complete List of Firm Personnel, See General Section

For full biographical listings, see the Martindale-Hubbell Law Directory

LOCKE REYNOLDS BOYD & WEISELL (AV)

1000 Capital Center South, 201 North Illinois Street, 46204
Telephone: 317-237-3800
Telecopier: 317-237-3900

Hugh E. Reynolds, Jr.
Steven J. Strawbridge
Julia M. Blackwell
Terrence L. Brookie
James Dimos

Charles S. Eberhardt, II

Representative Clients: American States Insurance Co.; Badger Engineers; CNA Insurance; DeMars Haka Development Corp.; Fidelity & Deposit Co. of Maryland; Hagerman Construction; MSE Corp.; Miller Pipeline Corporation; PSI Energy; United States Fidelity & Guaranty Co.

For Complete List of Firm Personnel, See General Section

For full biographical listings, see the Martindale-Hubbell Law Directory

IOWA

*DES MOINES,** Polk Co.

SHEARER, TEMPLER, PINGEL & KAPLAN, A PROFESSIONAL CORPORATION (AV)

Suite 437 3737 Woodland Avenue (West Des Moines, 50266), P.O. Box 1991, 50309
Telephone: 515-225-3737
Fax: 515-225-9510

Jeffrey L. Goodman
Ronald M. Kaplan
Leon R. Shearer
Brenton D. Soderstrum
John A. Templer, Jr.

For Complete List of Firm Personnel, See General Section

For full biographical listings, see the Martindale-Hubbell Law Directory

KANSAS

*WICHITA,** Sedgwick Co.

FOULSTON & SIEFKIN (AV)

(Formerly Foulston, Siefkin, Powers & Eberhardt)
700 Fourth Financial Center, Broadway at Douglas, 67202
Telephone: 316-267-6371
Facsimile: 316-267-6345
Topeka, Kansas Office: 1515 Bank IV Tower, 534 Kansas Avenue. 66603.
Telephone: 913-233-3600.
FAX: 913-233-1610.
Member: Lex Mundi, A Global Association of Independent Firms

MEMBERS OF FIRM

Robert L. Howard
Mikel L. Stout
Charles P. Efflandt
Wyatt A. Hoch

For Complete List of Firm Personnel, See General Section

For full biographical listings, see the Martindale-Hubbell Law Directory

KENTUCKY

*BOWLING GREEN,** Warren Co.

HARLIN & PARKER, P.S.C. (AV)

519 East Tenth Street, P.O. Box 390, 42102-0390
Telephone: 502-842-5611
Telefax: 502-842-2607
Smiths Grove, Kentucky Office: Old Farmers Bank Building.
Telephone: 502-563-4701.

(See Next Column)

HARLIN & PARKER P.S.C.—*Continued*

William Jerry Parker
Jerry A. Burns
Scott Charles Marks

Insurance Clients: Allstate Insurance Co.; CNA Insurance Companies; Maryland Casualty Co.
Railroad and Utilities Clients: District Attorneys for South Central Bell Telephone Co.; CSX Transportation, Inc.
Representative Clients: Jim Walter Homes, Inc.; Morrison & Knuteson.
Local Counsel for: General Motors Corp.; News Publishing Co.

For Complete List of Firm Personnel, See General Section

For full biographical listings, see the Martindale-Hubbell Law Directory

*LEXINGTON,** Fayette Co.

THOMAS H. GLOVER (AV)

167 West Main Street, Suite 1204, 40507-1709
Telephone: 606-231-1231
Fax: 606-231-1232

For full biographical listings, see the Martindale-Hubbell Law Directory

GREENEBAUM DOLL & MCDONALD (AV)

A Partnership including Professional Service Corporations
1400 Vine Center Tower, 40508
Telephone: 606-231-8500
Telecopier: 606-255-2742
Telex: 213029
Louisville, Kentucky Office: 3300 National City Tower.
Telephone: 502-589-4200.
Fax: 502-587-3695.
Covington, Kentucky Office: 50 East River Center Boulevard, P.O. Box 2050.
Telephone: 606-655-4200.
Fax: 606-655-4239.
Cincinnati, Ohio Office: 832 Main Street.
Telephone: 513-421-8087.
Fax: 513-421-8089.

MEMBERS OF FIRM

Eric L. Ison
Job D. Turner, III (Resident)
John V. Wharton (Resident)

Representative Clients: Aetna Life Insurance Co.; ANDALEX Resources, Inc.; Ashland Oil, Inc.; AT&T Communications, Inc.; Bethlehem Steel Corp.; Brown-Forman Corp.; Columbia Gas & Transmission Co.; Commonwealth Aluminum Corp.; Consolidation Coal Co.; Costain Coal, Inc.

For Complete List of Firm Personnel, See General Section

For full biographical listings, see the Martindale-Hubbell Law Directory

STURGILL, TURNER & TRUITT (AV)

155 East Main Street, 40507
Telephone: 606-255-8581
Fax: 606-231-0851

MEMBERS OF FIRM

Gardner L. Turner
Phillip M. Moloney

For Complete List of Firm Personnel, See General Section

For full biographical listings, see the Martindale-Hubbell Law Directory

VIMONT & WILLS (AV)

Suite 300, 155 East Main Street, 40507-1317
Telephone: 606-252-2202
Telecopier: 606-259-2927

MEMBERS OF FIRM

Richard E. Vimont
Bernard F. Lovely, Jr.

ASSOCIATES

Barbara Booker Wills
J. Thomas Rawlings

For Complete List of Firm Personnel, See General Section

For full biographical listings, see the Martindale-Hubbell Law Directory

*LOUISVILLE,** Jefferson Co.

GREENEBAUM DOLL & MCDONALD (AV)

A Partnership including Professional Service Corporations
3300 National City Tower, 40202
Telephone: 502-589-4200
Fax: 502-587-3695
Lexington, Kentucky Office: 1400 Vine Center Tower.
Telephone: 606-231-8500.
Fax: 606-255-2742.
Covington, Kentucky Office: 50 East River Center Boulevard, P.O. Box 2050.
Telephone: 606-655-4200.
Fax: 606-655-4239.

(See Next Column)

Cincinnati, Ohio Office: 832 Main Street.
Telephone: 513-421-8087.
Fax: 513-421-8089.

Eric L. Ison
John V. Wharton (Resident at Lexington, Kentucky)
Job D. Turner, III (Resident at Lexington, Kentucky)
Mark S. Riddle
Jeffrey A. McKenzie

ASSOCIATES

Thomas M. Williams
Jerrold R. Perchik

Representative Clients: Aetna Life Insurance Co.; ANDALEX Resources, Inc.; Ashland Oil, Inc.; A T & T Communications, Inc.; Bethlehem Steel Corp.; Brown-Forman Corp.; Humana, Inc.; Kentucky Kingdom, Inc.; KFC National Cooperative Advertising Program, Inc.

For Complete List of Firm Personnel, See General Section

For full biographical listings, see the Martindale-Hubbell Law Directory

LOUISIANA

*BATON ROUGE,** East Baton Rouge Parish

JAMES S. HOLLIDAY, JR. (AV)

5236 Corporate Boulevard, P.O. Box 80739, 70898
Telephone: 504-926-5899
Fax: 504-926-6698

ASSOCIATE

Susan Wall Griffin

For full biographical listings, see the Martindale-Hubbell Law Directory

BERT K. ROBINSON (AV)

10357 Old Hammond Highway, 70816-8261
Telephone: 504-924-0296
Fax: 504-924-5288

ASSOCIATE

Johanna R. Landreneau

OF COUNSEL

Charles C. Holbrook

For full biographical listings, see the Martindale-Hubbell Law Directory

WRAY & KRACHT (AV)

5643 Corporate Boulevard, P.O. Box 80239, 70898
Telephone: 504-928-3200
Telecopier: 504-928-3266

MEMBERS OF FIRM

W. P. Wray, Jr.
Eric A. Kracht
Russel W. Wray

ASSOCIATES

Christopher P. Pierce
Randall C. Gregory
E. Allen Graves, Jr.
S. Brett Davis

OF COUNSEL

Charles Wm. Roberts
M. J. Bodenhamer

LEGAL SUPPORT PERSONNEL

James W. Cox (Construction Claims Consultant)
Kim Bergeron Perkins (Paralegal)

Representative Clients: The Louisiana Associated General Contractors, Inc.; Coastal Contractors, Inc.; T. L. James & Company, Inc.; Clearly Canadian Beverage Corporation (Canada).
Reference: City National Bank.

For full biographical listings, see the Martindale-Hubbell Law Directory

*NEW ORLEANS,** Orleans Parish

DEUTSCH, KERRIGAN & STILES (AV)

A Partnership including Professional Law Corporations
755 Magazine Street, 70130-3672
Telephone: 504-581-5141
Cable Address: "Dekest"
Telex: 584358
Telecopier: 504-566-1201

MEMBERS OF FIRM

Frederick R. Bott (P.L.C.)
Howard L. Murphy
Charles F. Seemann, Jr., (P.L.C.)
William E. Wright, Jr.
Victor E. Stilwell, Jr., (P.L.C.)
Joseph L. McReynolds
Matt J. Farley (P.L.C.)
William Lee Kohler
Terrence L. Brennan
Theodore L. White

OF COUNSEL

Ralph L. Kaskell, Jr.

(See Next Column)

DEUTSCH, KERRIGAN & STILES, *New Orleans—Continued*

ASSOCIATE

Herman J. Gesser, III

For Complete List of Firm Personnel, See General Section

For full biographical listings, see the Martindale-Hubbell Law Directory

LEAKE & ANDERSSON (AV)

1700 Energy Centre, 1100 Poydras Street, 70163-1701
Telephone: 504-585-7500
Telecopier: 504-585-7775

MEMBERS OF FIRM

Robert E. Leake, Jr.
W. Paul Andersson
Marta-Ann Schnabel O'Bryon
Donald E. McKay, Jr.

ASSOCIATE

Stanton E. Shuler, Jr.

Representative Clients: L.B. Hebert & Co.; Montgomery Elevator Co.; Solvation Services, Inc.; Professional Construction Services, Inc.; R.F. Varley Co., Inc.

For Complete List of Firm Personnel, See General Section

For full biographical listings, see the Martindale-Hubbell Law Directory

NESSER, KING & LEBLANC (AV)

Suite 3800 Place St. Charles, 201 St. Charles Avenue, 70170
Telephone: 504-582-3800
Telecopier: 504-582-1233

John T. Nesser, III
Henry A. King
Joseph E. LeBlanc, Jr.
David S. Bland
Patricia Ann Krebs
Robert J. Burvant
Eric Earl Jarrell
Liane K. Hinrichs

Jeffrey M. Burmaster
Jeffrey A. Mitchell
Margaret M. Sledge
Josh M. Kantrow
Elton A. Foster
Elizabeth S. Wheeler
Robert J. Bergeron
Timothy S. Madden
Elizabeth A. Meek

OF COUNSEL

Clare P. Hunter
George B. Jurgens, III
J. Grant Coleman
Len R. Brignac
George Farber, Jr.

For full biographical listings, see the Martindale-Hubbell Law Directory

PREAUS, RODDY & KREBS (AV)

Suite 1650, 650 Poydras Street, 70130
Telephone: 504-523-2111
Telecopier: 504-523-2223

MEMBERS OF FIRM

Eugene R. Preaus
Virginia N. Roddy
David J. Krebs
Maura Zivalich Pelleteri

ASSOCIATES

Teresa Rose Young
Diane Lloyd Matthews
Krystil Borrouso Cook
Edward J. Parr, Jr.

Counsel for: American Society of Composers, Authors and Publishers; Fidelity and Deposit Company of Maryland; Metropolitan Life Insurance Co.; New York Life Insurance Co.; Reliance Insurance Co.; U.S. Home Corp.; Western Sizzlin, Inc.

For full biographical listings, see the Martindale-Hubbell Law Directory

*SHREVEPORT,** Caddo Parish

BARLOW AND HARDTNER L.C. (AV)

Tenth Floor, Louisiana Tower, 401 Edwards Street, 71101-3289
Telephone: 318-227-1131
Telecopier: 318-227-1141
Mailing Address: P.O. Box 8, Shreveport, Louisiana, 71161-0008

Malcolm S. Murchison
Joseph L. Shea, Jr.
David R. Taggart
Clair F. White
Philip E. Downer, III
Michael B. Donald
Jay A. Greenleaf

Representative Clients: The Brinkman Corporation; T.L. James & Company, Inc.; Kelley Oil Corporation; NorAm Energy Corp. (formerly Arkla, Inc.) Central and South West; Panhandle Eastern Corp.; Pennzoil Producing Co.; Johnson Controls , Inc.; Ashland Oil, Inc.; Southwestern Electric Power Company.

For Complete List of Firm Personnel, See General Section

For full biographical listings, see the Martindale-Hubbell Law Directory

WEEMS, WRIGHT, SCHIMPF, HAYTER & CARMOUCHE, A PROFESSIONAL LAW CORPORATION (AV)

912 Kings Highway, 71104
Telephone: 318-222-2100
Telecopier: 318-227-0136

John O. Hayter, III
Mark W. Odom

Representative Clients: Hand Construction Co., Inc.; Max Foote Construction Co., Inc.; Red River Supply Company.

For full biographical listings, see the Martindale-Hubbell Law Directory

MAINE

*PORTLAND,** Cumberland Co.

AMERLING & BURNS, A PROFESSIONAL ASSOCIATION (AV)

193 Middle Street, 04101
Telephone: 207-775-3581
Facsimile: 207-775-3814
Affiliated St. Croix Office: Coon & Sanford, P.O. Box 25918, Six Chandlers's Wharf, Suite 202, 00824-0918.

W. John Amerling
George F. Burns
David P. Ray
John R. Coon
Arnold C. Macdonald
Mary DeLano
Joanne F. Cole
A. Robert Ruesch

OF COUNSEL

Bruce M. Jervis

Representative Clients: H.E. Sargent, Inc. (construction); Merrill Trust; J.M. Huber, Inc.; Jackson Laboratories; Hague International (engineering); Aetna Life & Casualty Co.; The Hartford; Great American Insurance Co.; Wausau Insurance Co.

For full biographical listings, see the Martindale-Hubbell Law Directory

THOMPSON & BOWIE (AV)

Three Canal Plaza, P.O. Box 4630, 04112
Telephone: 207-774-2500
Telecopier: 207-774-3591

MEMBERS OF FIRM

Roy E. Thompson, Jr.
James M. Bowie
Daniel R. Mawhinney
Rebecca H. Farnum
Glenn H. Robinson
Frank W. DeLong, III
Michael E. Saucier
Mark V. Franco

ASSOCIATES

Elizabeth G. Knox
Cathy S. Roberts
Paul C. Catsos

For full biographical listings, see the Martindale-Hubbell Law Directory

MARYLAND

*BALTIMORE,** (Independent City)

BRAUDE & MARGULIES, P.C. (AV)

1206 St. Paul Street, 21202-2706
Telephone: 410-234-0202
Fax: 410-625-2872
Washington, D.C. Office: Suite 200, 1025 Connecticut Ave., N.W.
Telephone: 202-293-2993.
Fax: 202-331-7916.
San Francisco, California Office: William R. Delaney, Citicorp Center, One Sansome Street, Suite 2000.
Telephone: 415-951-4709.
Fax: 415-951-4754.
Riyadh, Saudi Arabia Office: Mohammed A. Al-Abdullah, P.O. Box 59446, Nuzha Building, Sixth Floor, 11525.
Telephone: 966-1-405-1291.
Fax: 966-1-405-1291.
Abu Dhabi, United Arab Emirates Office: P.O. Box 43908.
Telephone: (971-2) 787222.
Fax: (971-2) 784001.

Herman M. Braude
William M. Huddles (Resident)
Roger C. Jones (Not admitted in MD; Resident, District of Columbia Office)
Howard A. Pollack (Resident)

Kenneth Knut Sorteberg (Resident)

For full biographical listings, see the Martindale-Hubbell Law Directory

Baltimore—Continued

THIEBLOT, RYAN, MARTIN & FERGUSON, P.A. (AV)

4th Floor, The World Trade Center, 21202-3091
Telephone: 410-837-1140
Washington, D.C. Line: 202-628-8223
Fax: 410-837-3282

Robert J. Thieblot
Anthony W. Ryan
J. Edward Martin, Jr.
Robert L. Ferguson, Jr.
Bruce R. Miller
Robert D. Harwick, Jr.
Thomas J. Schetelich
Christopher J. Heffernan

M. Brooke Murdock
Anne M. Hrehorovich
Donna Marie Raffaele
Michael N. Russo, Jr.
Jodi K. Ebersole
Hamilton Fisk Tyler
Peter Joseph Basile

Representative Clients: Ford Motor Credit Co.; USF & G Co.; The American Road Insurance Co.; Fidelity Engineering Corp.; The North Charles Street Design Organization; Record Collections, Inc.; Toyota Motor Credit Co.

For full biographical listings, see the Martindale-Hubbell Law Directory

VENABLE, BAETJER AND HOWARD (AV)

A Partnership including Professional Corporations
1800 Mercantile Bank & Trust Building, 2 Hopkins Plaza, 21201
Telephone: 410-244-7400
Washington, D.C. Office: Venable, Baetjer, Howard & Civiletti. Suite 1000, 1201 New York Avenue, N.W.
Telephone: 202-962-4800.
McLean, Virginia Office: Suite 400, 2010 Corporate Ridge.
Telephone: 703-760-1600.
Rockville, Maryland Office: Suite 500, One Church Street, P. O. Box 1906.
Telephone: 301-217-5600.
Towson, Maryland Office: 210 Allegheny Avenue, P. O. Box 5517.
Telephone: 410-494-6200.

MEMBERS OF FIRM

James A. Cole
Benjamin R. Civiletti (P.C.) (Also at Washington, D.C. and Towson, Maryland Offices)
John Henry Lewin, Jr. (P.C.)
Thomas J. Kenney, Jr. (P.C.) (Also at Washington, D.C. Office)
Roger W. Titus (Resident, Rockville, Maryland Office)
Daniel O'C. Tracy, Jr. (Also at Rockville, Maryland Office)
John H. Zink, III (Resident, Towson, Maryland Office)
Bruce E. Titus (Resident, McLean, Virginia Office)
Paul T. Glasgow (Resident, Rockville, Maryland Office)
Joseph C. Wich, Jr. (Resident, Towson, Maryland Office)
David G. Lane (Resident, McLean, Virginia Office)
Susan K. Gauvey (Also at Towson, Maryland Office)
James K. Archibald (Also at Washington, D.C. and Towson, Maryland Offices)
G. Stewart Webb, Jr.
F. Dudley Staples, Jr. (Also at Towson, Maryland Office)
Jeffrey A. Dunn (also at Washington, D.C. Office)
George F. Pappas (Also at Washington, D.C. Office)
Peter P. Parvis
James L. Shea (Also at Washington, D.C. Office)
Maurice Baskin (Resident, Washington, D.C. Office)
C. Carey Deeley, Jr. (Also at Towson, Maryland Office)
Christopher R. Mellott
Cynthia M. Hahn (Resident, Towson, Maryland Office)
M. King Hill, III (Resident, Towson, Maryland Office)
J. Michael Brennan (Resident, Towson, Maryland Office)
Herbert G. Smith, II (Not admitted in MD; Resident, McLean, Virginia Office)
Michael H. Davis (Resident, Towson, Maryland Office)

OF COUNSEL

Mary T. Flynn (Not admitted in MD; Resident, McLean, Virginia Office)

ASSOCIATES

Paul D. Barker, Jr.
Julian Sylvester Brown (Not admitted in MD; Resident, McLean, Virginia Office)
Daniel William China
J. Van L. Dorsey (Resident, Towson, Maryland Office)
David R. Hodnett (Not admitted in MD; Resident, McLean, Virginia Office)
Todd J. Horn
Mary-Dulany James (Resident, Towson, Maryland Office)
Jon M. Lippard (Not admitted in MD; Resident, McLean, Virginia Office)
Patricia A. Malone (Resident, Towson, Maryland Office)
Christine M. McAnney (Not admitted in MD; Resident, McLean, Virginia Office)
Timothy J. McEvoy
Michael W. Robinson (Not admitted in MD; Resident, McLean, Virginia Office)

For Complete List of Firm Personnel, See General Section

For full biographical listings, see the Martindale-Hubbell Law Directory

*ROCKVILLE,** Montgomery Co.

STEIN, SPERLING, BENNETT, DE JONG, DRISCOLL, GREENFEIG & METRO, P.A. (AV)

25 West Middle Lane, 20850
Telephone: 301-340-2020; 800-435-5230
Telecopier: 301-340-8217

Millard S. Bennett
David C. Driscoll, Jr.

For Complete List of Firm Personnel, See General Section

For full biographical listings, see the Martindale-Hubbell Law Directory

*TOWSON,** Baltimore Co.

VENABLE, BAETJER AND HOWARD (AV)

A Partnership including Professional Corporations
210 Allegheny Avenue, P.O. Box 5517, 21204
Telephone: 410-494-6200
FAX: 410-821-0147
Baltimore, Maryland Office: 1800 Mercantile Bank & Trust Building, 2 Hopkins Plaza.
Telephone: 410-244-7400.
Washington, D.C. Office: Venable, Baetjer, Howard & Civiletti. Suite 1000, 1201 New York Avenue, N.W.
Telephone: 202-962-4800.
McLean, Virginia Office: Suite 400, 2010 Corporate Ridge.
Telephone: 703-760-1600.
Rockville, Maryland Office: Suite 500, One Church Street, P. O. Box 1906.
Telephone: 301-217-5600.

PARTNERS

Benjamin R. Civiletti (P.C.) (Also at Washington, D.C. and Baltimore, Maryland Offices)
John H. Zink, III
Joseph C. Wich, Jr.
Susan K. Gauvey (Also at Baltimore, Maryland Office)
James K. Archibald (Also at Baltimore, Maryland and Washington, D.C. Offices)
F. Dudley Staples, Jr. (Also at Baltimore, Maryland Office)
C. Carey Deeley, Jr. (Also at Baltimore, Maryland Office)
Cynthia M. Hahn
M. King Hill, III
J. Michael Brennan
Michael H. Davis

ASSOCIATES

J. Van L. Dorsey
Mary-Dulany James

For Complete List of Firm Personnel, See General Section

For full biographical listings, see the Martindale-Hubbell Law Directory

MASSACHUSETTS

*BOSTON,** Suffolk Co.

PALMER & DODGE (AV)

(Storey Thorndike Palmer & Dodge)
One Beacon Street, 02108
Telephone: 617-573-0100
Telecopier: 617-227-4420
Telex: 951104
Cable Address: "Storeydike," Boston

MEMBERS OF FIRM

Michael J. Lacek
David R. Rodgers
Craig E. Stewart
Peter S. Terris

For Complete List of Firm Personnel, See General Section

For full biographical listings, see the Martindale-Hubbell Law Directory

SHERBURNE, POWERS & NEEDHAM, P.C. (AV)

One Beacon Street, 02108
Telephone: 617-523-2700
Fax: 617-523-6850

William D. Weeks
John T. Collins
Allan J. Landau
John L. Daly
Stephen A. Hopkins
Alan I. Falk
C. Thomas Swaim
James Pollock
William V. Tripp III
Stephen S. Young
William F. Machen
W. Robert Allison
Jacob C. Diemert
Philip J. Notopoulos
Richard J. Hindlian
Paul E. Troy
Harold W. Potter, Jr.
Dale R. Johnson
Philip S. Lapatin
Pamela A. Duckworth
Mark Schonfeld
James D. Smeallie
Paul Killeen
Gordon P. Katz
Joseph B. Darby, III
Richard M Yanofsky

(See Next Column)

SHERBURNE, POWERS & NEEDHAM P.C., *Boston—Continued*

James E. McDermott
Robert V. Lizza
Miriam Goldstein Altman
John J. Monaghan
Margaret J. Palladino
Mark C. Michalowski
David Scott Sloan
M. Chrysa Long
Lawrence D. Bradley
Miriam J. McKendall

Cynthia A. Brown
Cynthia M. Hern
Dianne R. Phillips
Paul M. James
Theodore F. Hanselman
Joshua C. Krumholz
Ieuan G. Mahony
Kenneth L. Harvey
Christopher J. Trombetta
Edwin F. Landers, Jr.
Amy J. Mastrobattista
William Howard McCarthy, Jr.
Douglas W. Clapp
Tamara E. Goulston
Nicholas J. Psyhogeos

COUNSEL

Haig Der Manuelian
Mason M. Taber, Jr.
Karl J. Hirshman
Benjamin Volinski
Kenneth P. Brier

OF COUNSEL

John Barr Dolan

For full biographical listings, see the Martindale-Hubbell Law Directory

*SPRINGFIELD,** Hampden Co.

ANNINO, DRAPER & MOORE, P.C. (AV)

Suite 1818 BayBank Tower, 1500 Main Street, P.O. Box 15428, 01115
Telephone: 413-732-6400
Fax: 413-732-3339
Westfield, Massachusetts Office: 52 Court Street.
Telephone: 413-562-9829.

Calvin W. Annino, Jr.
Mark E. Draper
Louis S. Moore
Michael R. Siddall

For full biographical listings, see the Martindale-Hubbell Law Directory

MICHIGAN

*ANN ARBOR,** Washtenaw Co.

HURBIS, CMEJREK & CLINTON (AV)

Fifth Floor, City Center Building, 48104
Telephone: 313-761-8358
Fax: 313-761-3134

Charles J. Hurbis
James R. Cmejrek
Mary F. Clinton

Robert Lipnik

Representative Clients: General Motors Corp.; ITT Hartford; Insurance Company of North America; The University of Michigan; North Oakland Medical Center; City of Pontiac; Sears Roebuck and Co.; Montgomery Ward and Co., Inc.; Sedjwick-James, Inc.; Michigan State Accident Fund.

For full biographical listings, see the Martindale-Hubbell Law Directory

BIRMINGHAM, Oakland Co.

CARSON FISCHER, P.L.C. (AV)

Third Floor, 300 East Maple Road, 48009-6317
Telephone: 810-644-4840
Facsimile: 810-644-1832

Peter L. Wanger

For full biographical listings, see the Martindale-Hubbell Law Directory

SIMPSON & BERRY, P.C. (AV)

260 East Brown, Suite 300, 48009
Telephone: 810-647-0200
Telecopier: 810-647-2776

Daniel F. Berry
Clark G. Doughty
Philip J. Goodman
James A. Simpson
Katheryne L. Zelenock

LEGAL SUPPORT PERSONNEL

Dwight Noble Baker, Jr.

Representative Clients: Anthony S. Brown Development Co. Inc.; Chenoweth Construction Co.; Premier Construction Co.; Edw. C. Levy Company; Trizec Properties, Inc.

For full biographical listings, see the Martindale-Hubbell Law Directory

BLOOMFIELD HILLS, Oakland Co.

MAY, SIMPSON & STROTE, A PROFESSIONAL CORPORATION (AV)

100 West Long Lake Road Suite 200, P.O. Box 541, 48303-0541
Telephone: 810-646-9500

Richard H. May
Thomas C. Simpson
Ronald P. Strote
Steven M. Raymond
John A. Forrest
David K. McDonnell

Steven F. Alexsy
Marilynn K. Arnold
Michele A. Lerner

Representative Clients: Aamco Transmission; American Annuity Life Insurance; Container Corporation of America; Citicorp Financial Center; Century 21 Real Estate Corp.; Oak Hills Mortgage Corp.; Ziebart International Corp.
Reference: NBD Bank, N.A.

For full biographical listings, see the Martindale-Hubbell Law Directory

*DETROIT,** Wayne Co.

BODMAN, LONGLEY & DAHLING (AV)

34th Floor 100 Renaissance Center, 48243
Telephone: 313-259-7777
Fax: 313-393-7579
Troy, Michigan Office: Suite 2020, 755 West Big Beaver Road.
Telephone: 810-362-2110.
Ann Arbor, Michigan Office: 110 Miller, Suite 300.
Telephone: 313-761-3780.
Northern Michigan Office: 229 Court Street, P.O. Box 405, Cheboygan.
Telephone: 616-627-4351.

MEMBERS OF FIRM

Walter O. Koch (Troy Office)
Thomas A. Roach (Ann Arbor Office)
James R. Buschmann
Robert J. Diehl, Jr.
John C. Cashen (Troy Office)

Representative Clients: Abitibi Price Group; Archdiocese of Detroit; Comerica Bank; The Detroit Lions, Inc.; Ford Estates; General Motors Corporation; Charles Steward Mott Foundation; Norfolk Southern Corporation; Panhandle Eastern Corporation; State Farm Mutual Automobile Insurance Company.

For Complete List of Firm Personnel, See General Section

For full biographical listings, see the Martindale-Hubbell Law Directory

BUTZEL LONG, A PROFESSIONAL CORPORATION (AV)

Suite 900, 150 West Jefferson, 48226
Telephone: 313-225-7000
Telecopier: 313-225-7080
Birmingham, Michigan Office: Suite 200, 32270 Telegraph Road.
Telephone: 810-258-1616.
Telecopier: 810-258-1439.
Lansing, Michigan Office: 118 West Ottawa Street.
Telephone: 517-372-6622.
Telecopier: 517-372-6672.
Ann Arbor, Michigan Office: Suite 400, 121 West Washington.
Telephone: 313-995-3110.
Telecopier: 313-995-1777.
Grosse Pointe Farms, Michigan Office: Suite 260, 21 Kercheval.
Telephone: 313-886-5446.
Telecopier: 313-886-2114.

Abba I. Friedman (Birmingham)
Michael M. Jacob (Birmingham)
Dennis B. Schultz
Michael J. Lavoie
Susan Carino Nystrom
Eric J. Flessland (Birmingham)
Brian P. Henry (Birmingham and Lansing)

David K. Tillman
Ronald E. Reynolds
Kenneth H. Adamczyk
Richard T. Hewlett
Michael R. Poterala
James J. Urban (Lansing)
Daniel R. W. Rustmann

Representative Clients: Bridgestone/Firestone, Inc.; The Detroit News, Inc.; Detroit Diesel Corp.; Kelly Services; Kelsey Hayes Co.; Merrill Lynch & Co., Inc.; Stroh Brewery Co.; Takata Corp.; United Parcel Services of America, Inc.; The University of Michigan.

For Complete List of Firm Personnel, See General Section

For full biographical listings, see the Martindale-Hubbell Law Directory

CLARK, KLEIN & BEAUMONT (AV)

1600 First Federal Building, 1001 Woodward Avenue, 48226
Telephone: 313-965-8300
Facsimile: 313-962-4348
Bloomfield Hills Office: 1533 North Woodward Avenue, Suite 220, 48304.
Telephone: 810-258-2900.
Facsimile: 810-258-2949.

(See Next Column)

CLARK, KLEIN & BEAUMONT—*Continued*

MEMBERS OF FIRM

Patrick J. Keating
Laurence M. Scoville, Jr.
J. Walker Henry
David M. Hayes
James E. Baiers
Mark L. McAlpine
Timothy M. Koltun
Tyler D. Tennent (Resident, Bloomfield Hills, Michigan Office)
John E. Berg

ASSOCIATES

Thomas M. Dixon
Thomas D. Dyze
Edward J. Hood
David A. Breuch

Representative Clients: Perini Corporation; The Robert Carter Corporation; The Christman Co.; Bechtel Group, Inc.; Centex Bateson Construction Co. Inc.; Centel Corporation; Blount, Inc.; Smith, Hinchman & Grylls; Trammel Crow Company; Commercial Contracting Corp.; Fidelity & Deposit Co. Maryland.

For Complete List of Firm Personnel, See General Section

For full biographical listings, see the Martindale-Hubbell Law Directory

KERR, RUSSELL AND WEBER (AV)

One Detroit Center, 500 Woodward Avenue, Suite 2500, 48226-3406
Telephone: 313-961-0200
Telecopier: 313-961-0388
Bloomfield Hills, Michigan Office: 3883 Telegraph Road.
Telephone: 810-649-5990.
East Lansing, Michigan Office: 1301 North Hagadorn Road.
Telephone: 517-336-6767.

Richard D. Weber
Robert Royal Nix, II
Michael B. Lewis
Michael D. Gibson
James R. Case
George J. Christopoulos
Kurt R. Vilders
James R. Cambridge
Mark M. Cunningham
Robert J. Pineau
David E. Sims
Dennis A. Martin
Richard C. Buslepp
Eric I. Lark
James E. DeLine
Daniel J. Schulte

OF COUNSEL

Robert G. Russell

For Complete List of Firm Personnel, See General Section

For full biographical listings, see the Martindale-Hubbell Law Directory

MAGER, MERCER, SCOTT & ALBER, P.C. (AV)

2400 First National Building, 48226
Telephone: 313-965-1700
Facsimile: 313-965-3690
Macomb County Office: 18285 Ten Mile Road, Suite 100, Roseville, Michigan.
Telephone: 810-771-1100.

George J. Mager, Jr.
Phillip G. Alber
Lawrence M. Scott (Resident at Roseville Office)
George D. Mercer
Raymond C. McVeigh
Michael R. Alberty
Bruce H. Hoffman
Jeffrey M. Frank
Michael A. Schwartz

Representative Clients: ABB Flakt, Inc.; American States Insurance Co.; CEI Industries; Central Venture Corp.; CIGNA; Construction Management, Inc.

For full biographical listings, see the Martindale-Hubbell Law Directory

ROSEN & LOVELL, P.C. (AV)

Penobscot Building, 645 Griswold Street, Suite 3080, 48226-4224
Telephone: 313-961-7510
Fax: 313-961-2905

Paul A. Rosen
Joan Lovell

For full biographical listings, see the Martindale-Hubbell Law Directory

*FLINT,** Genesee Co.

WINEGARDEN, SHEDD, HALEY, LINDHOLM & ROBERTSON (AV)

501 Citizens Bank Building, 48502-1983
Telephone: 810-767-3600
Telecopier: 810-767-8776

MEMBERS OF FIRM

William C. Shedd
Dennis M. Haley
John T. Lindholm
Donald H. Robertson
L. David Lawson
John R. Tucker

ASSOCIATES

Alan F. Himelhoch
Suellen J. Parker
Damion Frasier
Peter T. Mooney

OF COUNSEL

Howard R. Grossman

Representative Clients: Citizens Commercial and Savings Bank; R. L. White Development Corporation; Interstate Traffic Consultants (Intracon) Inc.; Downtown Development Authority of Flint; Young Olds-Cadillac, Inc.;

(See Next Column)

First American Title Insurance Co.; Sorensen Gross Construction Co.; Genesee County; Insight, Inc.; Modern Industries, Inc.

For Complete List of Firm Personnel, See General Section

For full biographical listings, see the Martindale-Hubbell Law Directory

*GRAND RAPIDS,** Kent Co.

DAY & SAWDEY, A PROFESSIONAL CORPORATION (AV)

200 Monroe Avenue, Suite 500, 49503-2217
Telephone: 616-774-8121
Telefax: 616-774-0168

George B. Kingston (1889-1965)
John R. Porter (1915-1975)
Charles E. Day, Jr.
Robert W. Sawdey
William A. Hubble
C. Mark Stoppels
James B. Frakie
Larry A. Ver Merris
John Boyko, Jr.
Jonathan F. Thoits
John T. Piggins
Thomas A. DeMeester

John G. Grzybek
Theodore E. Czarnecki

For full biographical listings, see the Martindale-Hubbell Law Directory

ROBERTS, BETZ & BLOSS, P.C. (AV)

555 Riverfront Plaza Building, 55 Campau, 49503
Telephone: 616-235-9955
Telecopier: 616-235-0404

Michael J. Roberts
Michael W. Betz
David J. Bloss
Gregory A. Block
Michael T. Small
Ralph M. Reisinger
Elena C. Cardenas
Henry S. Emrich

For full biographical listings, see the Martindale-Hubbell Law Directory

HANCOCK, Houghton Co.

WISTI & JAASKELAINEN, P.C. (AV)

101 Quincy Street, 49930
Telephone: 906-482-5220
Iron Mountain, Michigan Office: 623 Stephenson Avenue.
Telephone: 906-779-1280.
Marquette, Michigan Office: 117 South Front Street.
Telephone: 906-228-8204.

Andrew H. Wisti
Mark Wisti
Daniel J. Wisti

David M. Gemignani

OF COUNSEL

Gordon J. Jaaskelainen

References: Superior National Bank & Trust Company of Hancock, Michigan; Houghton National Bank, Houghton, Michigan.

For full biographical listings, see the Martindale-Hubbell Law Directory

*KALAMAZOO,** Kalamazoo Co.

KREIS, ENDERLE, CALLANDER & HUDGINS, A PROFESSIONAL CORPORATION (AV)

One Moorsbridge, 49002
Telephone: 616-324-3000
Telecopier: 616-324-3010

Alan G. Enderle
Jeffrey C. O'Brien
Stephen J. Hessen

For Complete List of Firm Personnel, See General Section

For full biographical listings, see the Martindale-Hubbell Law Directory

SOUTHFIELD, Oakland Co.

DE VINE & KOHN (AV)

29800 Telegraph Road, 48034
Telephone: 810-353-6500

Clifford J. De Vine
Sheldon B. Kohn

For full biographical listings, see the Martindale-Hubbell Law Directory

TROY, Oakland Co.

POLING, MCGAW & POLING, P.C. (AV)

Suite 275, 5435 Corporate Drive, 48098
Telephone: 810-641-0500
Telecopier: 810-641-0506

Benson T. Buck (1926-1989)
Richard B. Poling
D. Douglas McGaw
Richard B. Poling, Jr.
David W. Moore
Gregory C. Hamilton
Veronica B. Winter
James R. Parker

(See Next Column)

POLING, MCGAW & POLING P.C., *Troy—Continued*

OF COUNSEL

Ralph S. Moore

Representative Clients: County of Oakland; City of Troy; United States Fidelity & Guaranty Co.; Sentry Insurance Co.; Admiral Insurance; DeMaria Construction Co.; Leo Corporation; Aetna Casualty and Surety Co.; Concord Design; Pneumo-Abex.

For full biographical listings, see the Martindale-Hubbell Law Directory

MINNESOTA

*MINNEAPOLIS,** Hennepin Co.

MOORE, COSTELLO & HART (AV)

Suite 1350, Craig Hallum Center, 701 Fourth Avenue South, 55415
Telephone: 612-673-0148
FAX: 612-376-1770
St. Paul, Minnesota Office: 1400 Norwest Center.
Telephone: 612-227-7683.
FAX: 612-290-1770.

MEMBERS OF FIRM

Ronald E. Martell
William M. Beadie
Leonard W. Glewwe
John G. Patterson
Timothy C. Cook
Kathryn A. Graves

Representative Clients: Associated General Contractors of Minnesota, Inc.; Macalester College; The St. Paul Cos.; United States Fidelity & Guaranty Co.; University of St. Thomas.

For full biographical listings, see the Martindale-Hubbell Law Directory

WAGNER, FALCONER & JUDD, LTD. (AV)

2650 IDS Center, 80 South Eighth Street, 55402-2113
Telephone: 612-339-1421
Telecopier: 612-349-6691

Alan W. Falconer
Robert A. Judd
James K. Sander
Mark O. Anderson
Michael J. DuPont

Representative Clients: Alexander & Alexander, Inc.; American Standard, Inc.; Barber Electric Co.; C.H. Carpenter Lumber Company; General Electric Supply; Honeywell, Inc.; Johnson Controls, Inc.; Edward Kraemer & Sons, Inc.; J.H. Larson Electrical Co.

For Complete List of Firm Personnel, See General Section

For full biographical listings, see the Martindale-Hubbell Law Directory

*ST. PAUL,** Ramsey Co.

GERAGHTY, O'LOUGHLIN & KENNEY, PROFESSIONAL ASSOCIATION (AV)

One Capital Centre Plaza, Suite 1400, 55102-1308
Telephone: 612-291-1177
Fax: 612-297-6901

Terence J. O'Loughlin
James R. Gowling
Robert M. Mahoney
David C. Hutchinson
Timothy R. Murphy
William H. Leary, III
Richard J. Thomas
Patrick H. O'Neill, Jr
Mary H. Alcorn
Patricia Rosvold
Daniel R. Fritz
Matthew J. Hanzel
Ann D. Bray
Jean B. Rudolph
Bryon Ascheman

OF COUNSEL

James H. Geraghty
James W. Kenney (Retired)

Representative Clients: St. Paul Fire & Marine Insurance Cos.; Midwest Medical Insurance Co.; Minnesota Lawyers Mutual Insurance Co.; University of Minnesota Hospitals; American National Bank and Trust Co.; Continental National American Group; Commercial State Bank; MMI Co.; Hammel Green Abrahamson, Inc.; Lunda Construction Co.

For full biographical listings, see the Martindale-Hubbell Law Directory

MOORE, COSTELLO & HART (AV)

1400 Norwest Center, 55101
Telephone: 612-227-7683
FAX: 612-290-1770
Minneapolis, Minnesota Office: Suite 1350, Craig Hallum Center, 701 Fourth Avenue, South.
Telephone: 612-673-0148.
FAX: 612-376-1770.

MEMBERS OF FIRM

James C. Otis, Sr. (1879-1949)
Roland J. Faricy (1898-1962)
Richard A. Moore (1915-1991)
Harry G. Costello (Retired)
B. Warren Hart (1923-1981)
Marvin J. Pertzik
A. Patrick Leighton
Harold R. Fotsch

(See Next Column)

MEMBERS OF FIRM (Continued)

Ronald E. Martell (Resident, Minneapolis Office)
William M. Beadie (Resident, Minneapolis Office)
Denis L. Stoddard
Larry A. Hanson
J. Patrick Plunkett
John M. Harens
Phyllis Karasov
Malcolm G. McDonald
Leonard W. Glewwe (Resident, Minneapolis Office)
John G. Patterson (Resident, Minneapolis Office)
Timothy C. Cook (Resident, Minneapolis Office)
Kathryn A. Graves (Resident, Minneapolis Office)

ASSOCIATES

Steven D. Snelling
Tara D. Mattessich
James E. Blaney
Frederick J. Putzier

OF COUNSEL

William F. Orme
Fred W. Fisher

Representative Clients: Associated General Contractors of Minnesota, Inc.; Macalester College; The St. Paul Cos., Inc.; United States Fidelity & Guaranty Co.; University of St. Thomas.

For full biographical listings, see the Martindale-Hubbell Law Directory

MISSISSIPPI

*GULFPORT,** Harrison Co.

DUKES, DUKES, KEATING AND FANECA, P.A. (AV)

2308 East Beach Boulevard, P.O. Drawer W, 39501
Telephone: 601-868-1111
FAX: 601-863-2886

Hugh D. Keating
Cy Faneca
William H. Pettey, Jr.

Nick B. Roberts, Jr.

For full biographical listings, see the Martindale-Hubbell Law Directory

WAVELAND, Hancock Co.

LUCIEN M. GEX, JR. (AV)

229 Coleman Avenue, Drawer 47, 39576-0047
Telephone: 601-467-5426
Telefax: 601-467-3258

Representative Clients: City of Waveland; Waveland Housing Authority; Merchants Bank and Trust Co.; Charles H. Johnson, Inc.; Universal Warehouses, Inc.; Bay St. Louis Housing Authority; Bay St. Louis-Waveland Municipal School District; Island Utilities Inc.; Bay Waveland Yacht Club; Waveland Regional Wastewater Management District.

For full biographical listings, see the Martindale-Hubbell Law Directory

MISSOURI

KANSAS CITY, Jackson, Clay & Platte Cos.

BAKER, STERCHI & COWDEN (AV)

Suite 2100 Commerce Tower, 911 Main Street, P.O. Box 13566, 64199-3566
Telephone: 816-471-2121
FAX: 816-472-0288
Overland Park, Kansas Office: 51 Corporate Woods, 9393 West 110th Street, Suite 508.
Telephone: 913-451-6752.

MEMBERS OF FIRM

Thomas O. Baker
Thomas N. Sterchi
John W. Cowden
Thomas E. Rice, Jr.
Timothy S. Frets
Evan A. Douthit
Phillip C. Rouse
R. Douglas Gentile
James T. Seigfreid, Jr.
Robert A. Babcock
Peter F. Travis
John P. Poland

ASSOCIATES

Quentin L. Brown
James R. Jarrow
James S. Kreamer
Mary C. O'Connell
Randall L. Rhodes
D. Gregory Stonebarger
Kara Trouslot Stubbs
Robert M. Carroll
Stacy L. Cook
Patricia A. Sexton
Brent David Thomas

For full biographical listings, see the Martindale-Hubbell Law Directory

LAKE OZARK, Miller & Camden Cos.

THOMAS E. LORAINE, P.C. (AV)

2840 Bagnell Dam Boulevard, 65049
Telephone: 314-365-3035
Fax: 314-365-3044

Thomas E. Loraine
Dale M. Weppner

For full biographical listings, see the Martindale-Hubbell Law Directory

MONTANA

*BOZEMAN,** Gallatin Co.

KIRWAN & BARRETT, P.C. (AV)

215 West Mendenhall, P.O. Box 1348, 59771-1348
Telephone: 406-586-1553
Fax: 406-586-8971

Peter M. Kirwan
Stephen M. Barrett

Tom W. Stonecipher

Representative Clients: Kenyon Noble Lumber Company; McLees Incorporated; Concrete Specialties, Inc.

For full biographical listings, see the Martindale-Hubbell Law Directory

NEVADA

*LAS VEGAS,** Clark Co.

ALBRIGHT, STODDARD, WARNICK & ALBRIGHT, A PROFESSIONAL CORPORATION (AV)

Quail Park I, Building D-4, 801 South Rancho Drive, 89106
Telephone: 702-384-7111
FAX: 702-384-0605

G. Vern Albright
William H. Stoddard
Whitney B. Warnick
G. Mark Albright

Michael W. Brimley
Gavin C. Jangard
D. Chris Albright

Representative Clients: Tokio Marine and Fire Ins. Co.; INAPRO, a CIGNA Co.; Nevada Ready Mix; North American Health Care, Inc. (Nursing Home); Royal Insurance; First Security Bank of Utah; Nevada Community Bank; Nationwide Insurance Co.; Liberty Mutual Insurance; CB Commercial.

For full biographical listings, see the Martindale-Hubbell Law Directory

ALVERSON, TAYLOR, MORTENSEN & NELSON (AV)

3821 W. Charleston Boulevard, 89102
Telephone: 702-384-7000
FAX: 702-385-7000

MEMBERS OF FIRM

J. Bruce Alverson
Eric K. Taylor
David J. Mortensen
Erven T. Nelson
LeAnn Sanders
David R. Clayson

ASSOCIATES

Milton J. Eichacker
Douglas D. Gerrard
Marie Ellerton
James H. Randall
Peter Dubowsky
Hayley B. Chambers
Michael D. Stevenson
Cookie Lea Olshein
Kenneth M. Marias
Jeffrey H. Ballin
Jeffrey W. Daly
Kenneth R. Ivory
Edward D. Boyack
Sandra Smagac
Jill M. Chase
Francis F. Lin

LEGAL SUPPORT PERSONNEL

PARALEGALS

Marsha Diaz
Mary Anne Murray
Linda Rosepiler
Julie A. Tolman

Representative Clients: Falcon Development Corporation; Trophy Homes; FFC Consulting Engineers; Petacore Engineering, Inc.; The Machinery Center, Inc.; Frontier Bonding and Surety Group; Citibank Corporation; First Interstate Bank; RMJ Development, Inc.

For full biographical listings, see the Martindale-Hubbell Law Directory

JOLLEY, URGA, WIRTH & WOODBURY (AV)

Suite 800 Bank of America Plaza, 300 South Fourth Street, 89101
Telephone: 702-385-5161
Telecopier: 702-382-6814
Boulder City, Nevada Office: Suite 105, 1000 Nevada Highway.
Telephone: 702-293-3674.

MEMBERS OF FIRM

Roger A. Wirth
Donald E. Brookhyser

Representative Clients: Melvin Simon & Associates, Inc.; Owens-Corning Fiberglas Corp.; Champion Home Builders Co.; Carl's Air Conditioning; Dean Roofing Co.; Dynaelectric Company of Nevada, Inc.; Emerson Electric Co.; Western Pipeline Construction Corp.

For Complete List of Firm Personnel, See General Section

For full biographical listings, see the Martindale-Hubbell Law Directory

LEAVITT, SULLY & RIVERS (AV)

An Association of Professional Corporations
601 East Bridger Avenue, 89101
Telephone: 702-382-5111
Telecopier: 702-382-2892

K. Michael Leavitt (Chartered)
W. Leslie Sully, Jr. (Chartered)
David J. Rivers, II (Chartered)

For full biographical listings, see the Martindale-Hubbell Law Directory

*RENO,** Washoe Co.

ERICKSON, THORPE & SWAINSTON, LTD. (AV)

601 S. Arlington Avenue, P.O. Box 3559, 89505
Telephone: 702-786-3930
Fax: 702-786-4160

Roger L. Erickson
Donald A. Thorpe
George W. Swainston
William G. Cobb
James L. Lundemo
Gary A. Cardinal
Thomas Peter Beko
John A. Aberasturi

Representative Clients: Albertson's, Inc.; Allstate Insurance Co.; Avis Rent-A-Car System; Chrysler Corp.; Airport Authority of Washoe County; Dow Corning; Reno-Sparks Convention and Visitors Authority; Nevada Public Agency Insurance Pool; Airport Authority of Washoe County; Bank of America Nevada.

For full biographical listings, see the Martindale-Hubbell Law Directory

McDONALD, CARANO, WILSON, McCUNE, BERGIN, FRANKOVICH & HICKS (AV)

241 Ridge Street, 89505
Telephone: 702-322-0635
Telecopier: 702-786-9532
Las Vegas, Nevada Office: Suite 1000, 2300 West Sahara Avenue.
Telephone: 702-873-4100.
Telecopier: 702-873-9966.

MEMBER OF FIRM

John J. McCune

ASSOCIATES

Matthew C. Addison
Paul J. Georgeson

Representative Clients: Associated General Contractors of America; Clark & Sullivan Constructors, Inc.; Harker & Harker, Inc.; Monterrey Mechanical, Inc.; Shaver Construction; Sierra Nevada Buildings, Inc.; Q & D Construction, Inc.

For Complete List of Firm Personnel, See General Section

For full biographical listings, see the Martindale-Hubbell Law Directory

NEW JERSEY

*MORRISTOWN,** Morris Co.

McELROY, DEUTSCH AND MULVANEY (AV)

1300 Mount Kemble Avenue, P.O. Box 2075, 07962-2075
Telephone: 201-993-8100
Fax: 201-425-0161
Denver, Colorado Office: 1099 18th Street, Suite 3120.
Telephone: 303-293-8800.
Fax: 303-293-3116.

MEMBERS OF FIRM

Lorraine M. Armenti (Resident Partner, Denver Colorado Office)
Grace C. Bertone
John P. Beyel
William C. Carey
Margaret F. Catalano
Stephen H. Cohen (1938-1992)
Kevin T. Coughlin
Edward B. Deutsch
Timothy I. Duffy
Robert J. Kelly
Joseph P. La Sala
Paul A. Lisovicz

(See Next Column)

McElroy, Deutsch and Mulvaney, *Morristown—Continued*

MEMBERS OF FIRM (Continued)

Fred A. Manley, Jr.
Michael J. Marone
William T. McElroy
Laurence M. McHeffey
Joseph P. McNulty, Jr.
James M. Mulvaney
Moira E. O'Connell
Loren L. Pierce
Warren K. Racusin
John H. Suminski
Kevin E. Wolff

OF COUNSEL

Richard G. McCarty (Not admitted in NJ)
John F. Whitteaker

ASSOCIATES

Caroline L. Beers
Christopher Robert Carroll
Edward V. Collins
Billy J. Cooper (Resident, Denver, Colorado Office)
John Thomas Coyne
Nada Leslie Wolff Culver (Resident, Denver, Colorado Office)
John J. Cummings
Anthony J. Davis
John Paul Gilfillan
Kevin M. Haas
Gary S. Kull
Matthew J. Lodge
Tracey L. Matura
Nancy McDonald
Robert McGuire
Suzanne Cocco Midlige
Robert W. Muilenburg
Gary Potters
Kathleen M. Quinn
Vincent E. Reilly
Agnes A. Reiss
Barbara C. Zimmerman Robertson
Samuel J. Samaro
Laura A. Sanom
Thomas P. Scrivo
Dennis T. Smith
Patricia Leen Sullivan
Pamela A. Tanis
Christine L. Thieman
Catharine Acker Vaughan

Representative Clients: ADT Security Systems, Inc.; Chubb Insurance Cos.; Crum & Forster Insurance Co.; Eaton Corp.; Fireman's Fund Insurance Cos.; New Jersey Manufacturers Insurance Co.; The Home Indemnity Co.; Ingersoll-Rand Company; The Pittston Company; Security Pacific Finance Corporation.

For full biographical listings, see the Martindale-Hubbell Law Directory

*NEWARK,** Essex Co.

Sills Cummis Zuckerman Radin Tischman Epstein & Gross, A Professional Corporation (AV)

One Riverfront Plaza, 07102-5400
Telephone: 201-643-7000
Fax: 201-643-6500
Telex: 820630 Sillsbeck Nwk
Atlantic City, New Jersey Office: 17 Gordon's Alley.
Telephone: 609-344-2800.
New York, N.Y. Office: 250 Park Avenue.
Telephone: 212-643-7000.

Morton S. Bunis
Thomas J. Demski
Philip R. White

Mark E. Duckstein
Paul F. Doda
Lora L. Fong

Representative Clients: Horizon House; The International Group; O'Brien Environmental Energy, Inc.; International Fidelity Insurance Company; Bally's Park Place, Inc.; City of Woodbridge.

For Complete List of Firm Personnel, See General Section
For full biographical listings, see the Martindale-Hubbell Law Directory

ROSELAND, Essex Co.

Clancy, Callahan & Smith (AV)

103 Eisenhower Parkway, 07068-1090
Telephone: 201-403-8300
Fax: 201-403-8355

MEMBERS OF FIRM

John J. Clancy (1922-1979)
Edward M. Callahan, Jr.
Dennis J. Smith

ASSOCIATES

James J. Cronin
Beth A. Callahan

For full biographical listings, see the Martindale-Hubbell Law Directory

*TRENTON,** Mercer Co.

Needell & McGlone, A Professional Corporation (AV)

Quakerbridge Commons, 2681 Quakerbridge Road, 08619-1625
Telephone: 609-584-7700
Fax: 609-584-0123

Stanley H. Needell
Patricia Hart McGlone

Michael W. Krutman
Anthony P. Castellani
Barbara Brosnan
Douglas R. D'Antonio

For full biographical listings, see the Martindale-Hubbell Law Directory

WAYNE, Passaic Co.

Feldman & Fiorello (AV)

Suite 301, 57 Willowbrook Boulevard, 07470
Telephone: 201-890-9222
Fax: 201-890-7068

William A. Feldman
John Fiorello

OF COUNSEL

Avram S. Eule

ASSOCIATES

Linda Couso Puccio
Jacqueline I. Heath
Melissa A. Feldman

Reference: First Fidelity Bank, N.A.; Valley National Bank (Willowbrook Branch).

For full biographical listings, see the Martindale-Hubbell Law Directory

WESTFIELD, Union Co.

Lindabury, McCormick & Estabrook, A Professional Corporation (AV)

53 Cardinal Drive, P.O. Box 2369, 07091
Telephone: 908-233-6800
Fax: 908-233-5078

Richard R. Width
Edward J. Frisch
Donald F. Nicolai
Bruce P. Ogden
Barry J. Donohue

Dina G. Kugel

OF COUNSEL

Kenneth L. Estabrook

Representative Clients: Air Con, Inc.; Clinton Township Board of Education; DPIC Companies; Donald C. Rodner, Inc.; Elling Brothers; Great American Insurance Companies; Mechanical Contractors Association of America, Inc.; Mechanical Contractors Association of New Jersey; New Jersey Subcontractors Association.

For Complete List of Firm Personnel, See General Section
For full biographical listings, see the Martindale-Hubbell Law Directory

NEW MEXICO

*ALBUQUERQUE,** Bernalillo Co.

Rodey, Dickason, Sloan, Akin & Robb, P.A. (AV)

Albuquerque Plaza, Suite 2200, 201 Third Street, N.W., P.O. Box 1888, 87103-1888
Telephone: 505-765-5900
Fax: 505-768-7395
Santa Fe, New Mexico Office: Suite 101 Marcy Plaza, 123 East Marcy Street, P.O. Box 1357, 87504-1357.
Telephone: 505-984-0100.
Fax: 505-989-9542.

Jonathan W. Hewes

David W. Bunting

For Complete List of Firm Personnel, See General Section
For full biographical listings, see the Martindale-Hubbell Law Directory

Sheehan, Sheehan & Stelzner, P.A. (AV)

Suite 300, 707 Broadway, N.E., P.O. Box 271, 87103
Telephone: 505-247-0411
Fax: 505-842-8890

Craig T. Erickson
Juan L. Flores
Kim A. Griffith
Philip P. Larragoite
Susan C. Little
Maria O'Brien
Judith D. Schrandt
Timothy M. Sheehan
Luis G. Stelzner
Elizabeth Newlin Taylor
Robert P. Warburton

OF COUNSEL

Briggs F. Cheney
Charles T. DuMars
Thomas J. Horan
Pat Sheehan

Representative Clients: Bradbury & Stamm Construction Co.; Herbert M. Denish & Associates; Jaynes Corp.; Midcon, Inc.; New Mexico Legislative Council Service; Rocky Mountain Roofing Co.

For full biographical listings, see the Martindale-Hubbell Law Directory

NEW YORK

*ALBANY,** Albany Co.

DONOHUE, SABO, VARLEY & ARMSTRONG, P.C. (AV)

18 Computer Drive East, P.O. Box 15056, 12212-5056
Telephone: 518-458-8922
Telecopier: 518-438-4349

Paul F. Donohue, Sr. (Retired)
Alvin O. Sabo
Kenneth Varley, Jr.
Robert J. Armstrong
Fred J. Hutchison
Bruce S. Huttner
Kathleen L. Werther

Christine M. D'Addio
Walter M.B. Spiro

Representative Clients: CNA Insurance Cos.; Continental Loss Adjusting Services; Electric Insurance Co.; Electric Mutual Insurance Co.; General Accident Assurance Co.; General Electric Co.; NY Central Mutual Fire Insurance Co.; Preferred Mutual Insurance Co.; State Insurance Fund; Zurich-American Insurance Co.

For full biographical listings, see the Martindale-Hubbell Law Directory

ISEMAN, CUNNINGHAM, RIESTER & HYDE (AV)

9 Thurlow Terrace, 12203
Telephone: 518-462-3000
Telecopier: 518-462-4199

MEMBERS OF FIRM

Frederick C. Riester
Michael J. Cunningham
Robert Hall Iseman
Carol Ann Hyde
Michael J. McNeil

Brian M. Culnan
Linda J. Clark

For full biographical listings, see the Martindale-Hubbell Law Directory

ROCHE CORRIGAN McCOY & BUSH (AV)

The Wilem Van Zandt Building, 36 South Pearl Street, 12207
Telephone: 518-436-9370

MEMBERS OF FIRM

Robert P. Roche
Peter J. Corrigan
Joseph M. McCoy
Scott W. Bush

Reference: 1st American Bank, Albany.

For full biographical listings, see the Martindale-Hubbell Law Directory

*BINGHAMTON,** Broome Co.

O'CONNOR, GACIOCH & POPE (AV)

One Marine Midland Plaza, East Tower-Seventh Floor, P.O. Box 1964, 13902
Telephone: 607-772-9262
Fax: 607-724-6002

Thomas F. O'Connor
James C. Gacioch
Alan J. Pope
Lori Grumet Schapiro
Jeffrey A. Tait
Hugh B. Leonard
Robert N. Nielsen, Jr.
Martha Keeler Macinski
Stephen B. Atkinson
Kurt D. Schrader
Richard M. Hill
Patricia A. Cummings
Mark D. Goris
Susan E. Decker

OF COUNSEL

Walter T. Gorman

For full biographical listings, see the Martindale-Hubbell Law Directory

*BUFFALO,** Erie Co.

BROWN & KELLY (AV)

1500 Liberty Building, 14202
Telephone: 716-854-2620
Telecopier: 716-854-0082

MEMBERS OF FIRM

Mark N. Turner (1897-1985)
Thomas J. Kelly
James T. Duggan
Frederick D. Turner
Paul Michael Hassett
Peter E. Klaasesz
Donald B. Eppers
Andrew D. Merrick
Gordon D. Tresch
William E. Nitterauer
William P. Wiles
William D. Harrington
Rodney O. Personius
Paula L. Feroleto
Daniel J. Marren
Lisa T. Sofferin

COUNSEL

Ogden R. Brown
Charles F. Harrington
William E. Nowakowski
Roland R. Benzow

OF COUNSEL

Philip B. Abramowitz

(See Next Column)

ASSOCIATES

Raymond C. Stilwell
Carlton K. Brownell, III
David S. Zygaj
Kathleen F. Smith
Karen L. Cook
Colleen P. Doyle
Aileen M. Mcnamara

Representative Clients: Aetna Life & Casualty Co.; Fidelity & Deposit Company of Maryland; Maryland Casualty Co.; Herbert F. Darling, Inc.; Northeast Caissons, Inc.; F.J. Leydecker, Inc.

For full biographical listings, see the Martindale-Hubbell Law Directory

*GOSHEN,** Orange Co.

NORTON & CHRISTENSEN (AV)

Goshen Executive Building, 60 Erie Street, P.O. Box 308, 10924
Telephone: 914-294-7949
Telecopier: 914-294-7791
Rochelle Park, New Jersey Office: 151 West Passaic Street, 07662.
Telephone: 201-909-3735.
Fax: 201-368-2102.

MEMBERS OF FIRM

Stanley J. Norton
Henry N. Christensen, Jr.
Harold M. Pressberg

OF COUNSEL

John T. Mayo

For full biographical listings, see the Martindale-Hubbell Law Directory

LAKE SUCCESS, Nassau Co.

IVONE, DEVINE & JENSEN (AV)

2001 Marcus Avenue-Suite N100, 11042
Telephone: 516-326-2400
Telecopier: 516-352-4952

MEMBERS OF FIRM

Michael T. Ivone
Robert Devine
Richard C. Jensen
Brian E. Lee
Michael Ferguson

ASSOCIATES

James C. Brady
Amy S. Barash
Ann-Marie Fassl Hartline
Debora G. Nobel
Charles Costas

For full biographical listings, see the Martindale-Hubbell Law Directory

NEW ROCHELLE, Westchester Co.

COOPER & COOPER (AV)

175 Memorial Highway, 10801
Telephone: 914-636-5100
Telecopier: 914-636-6553

MEMBERS OF FIRM

Burton S. Cooper
Douglas A. Cooper

Burton J. Lasky
Joseph R. Harbeson
Deborah R. Beckmann

For full biographical listings, see the Martindale-Hubbell Law Directory

*NEW YORK,** New York Co.

BERMAN, PALEY, GOLDSTEIN & KANNRY (AV)

500 Fifth Avenue, 10110
Telephone: 212-354-9600
Fax: 212-354-9873

Murray Tim Berman (1901-1991)

MEMBERS OF FIRM

Tony Berman
David R. Paley
Alvin Goldstein
Jack S. Kannry
Robert G. Benisch
Roger S. Markowitz

COUNSEL

Joan Lawton Paley

ASSOCIATES

Howard Burger
Lawrence N. Berwitz
Judith F. Herman
Todd A. Bakal

For full biographical listings, see the Martindale-Hubbell Law Directory

GOETZ, FITZPATRICK & FLYNN (AV)

One Pennsylvania Plaza, 10119-0196
Telephone: 212-695-7455
Telecopier: 212-629-4013

MEMBERS OF FIRM

Gerard E. Fitzpatrick (1929-1985)
Peter Goetz
William B. Flynn
Thomas S. Finegan
Donald J. Carbone
Neal M. Eiseman
Thomas F. Cohen
Robert A. Sesti

(See Next Column)

GOETZ, FITZPATRICK & FLYNN, *New York—Continued*

ASSOCIATES

Lynn T. Daly
Jane Goetz
Robert M. McCartin
Alan Winkler

OF COUNSEL

Frank Muller
Charles H. Rosenberg
Harvey A. Wechsler

For full biographical listings, see the Martindale-Hubbell Law Directory

MAX E. GREENBERG, TRAGER, TOPLITZ & HERBST (AV)

100 Church Street, 10007
Telephone: 212-267-5700
Telecopier: 212-267-5814
West Orange, New Jersey Office: 200 Executive Drive West.
Telephone: 201-641-3110.
Fax: 201-731-0163.
Staten Island, New York Office: 1688 Victory Boulevard.
Telephone: 718-981-6335.
Fax: 718-981-6386.

Max E. Greenberg (1894-1980)
Murray B. Trayman (1903-1988)

MEMBERS OF FIRM

David A. Trager
George N. Toplitz
Leonard Shabasson
Todd L. Herbst
Kalvin Kamien
Mark A. Rosen
John M. Cilmi

ASSOCIATES

Regina C. Saat
Ira C. Wellen
Robert H. Schlosser
Allison Essner
Joseph G. Portela

For full biographical listings, see the Martindale-Hubbell Law Directory

HUTTON INGRAM YUZEK GAINEN CARROLL & BERTOLOTTI (AV)

250 Park Avenue, 10177
Telephone: 212-907-9600
Facsimile: 212-907-9681

MEMBERS OF FIRM

Ernest J. Bertolotti
Daniel L. Carroll
Roger Cukras
Larry F. Gainen
G. Thompson Hutton
Samuel W. Ingram, Jr.
Paulette Kendler
Steven Mastbaum
Dean G. Yuzek
David G. Ebert
Shane O'Neill

ASSOCIATES

Warren E. Friss
Patricia Hewitt
Gail A. Buchman
Stuart A. Christie
Beth N. Green
Timish K. Hnateyko
Jeanne F. Pucci
Jane Drummey
Adam L. Sifre
Susan Ann Fennelly
Marc J. Schneider

For full biographical listings, see the Martindale-Hubbell Law Directory

LONDON FISCHER (AV)

375 Park Avenue, 10152
Telephone: 212-888-3636
Facsimile: 212-888-3974

MEMBERS OF FIRM

Bernard London
James L. Fischer
John W. Manning
Daniel Zemann, Jr.
John E. Sparling

ASSOCIATES

Richard S. Endres
Nicholas Kalfa
Evan D. Lieberman
Amy M. Kramer
Robert S. Sunshine
Robert M. Vecchione
John P. Bruen
Christina M. Ambrosio
William C. Nanis
Michael P. Mezzacappa
Douglas W. Hammond
Michael S. Leavy
Robert L. Honig

For full biographical listings, see the Martindale-Hubbell Law Directory

OTTERBOURG, STEINDLER, HOUSTON & ROSEN, P.C. (AV)

230 Park Avenue, 10169
Telephone: 212-661-9100
Cable Address: "Otlerton";
Telecopier: 212-682-6104
Telex: 960916

Kurt J. Wolff
Donald N. Gellert
Daniel Wallen
Anthony M. Piccione

COUNSEL

Stephen B. Weissman

(See Next Column)

Lloyd M. Green
Richard G. Haddad

For Complete List of Firm Personnel, See General Section

For full biographical listings, see the Martindale-Hubbell Law Directory

QUELLER & FISHER (AV)

A Law Partnership including Professional Corporations
110 Wall Street, 10005-3851
Telephone: 212-422-3600
Cable Address: "Quelfish, New York"
Facsimile: 212-422-2828

MEMBERS OF FIRM

Fred Queller (P.C.)
Bertram D. Fisher (P.C.)
Walter F. Benson

ASSOCIATES

Ira Bartfield
Marshall Schmeizer
Kevin S. McDonald
Phillip P. Nikolis
Edmund L. Rothschild
Dorothy S. Morrill
David P. Horowitz
Glenn Verchick
Ira Fogelgaren
Frances I. Beaupierre (Not admitted in NY)

For full biographical listings, see the Martindale-Hubbell Law Directory

SACKS MONTGOMERY, P.C. (AV)

800 Third Avenue, 10022
Telephone: 212-355-4660
Telecopier: 212-593-7257
Stamford, Connecticut Office: Sacks, Montgomery, Pastore & Levine, P.C., 970 Summer Street.
Telephone: 203-325-3800.

Harry P. Sacks
David E. Montgomery
William J. Pastore (Resident at Stamford, Connecticut Office)
Stuart M. Levine
Jeffrey A. Aronson
Frederick R. Rohn
Scott D. St. Marie

Laura H. Markson
Stephen A. Stallings
Paul M. Schindler
Jocelyn D. Margolin

OF COUNSEL

Steven J. Brill

For full biographical listings, see the Martindale-Hubbell Law Directory

NORTH CAROLINA

*CHARLOTTE,** Mecklenburg Co.

WOMBLE CARLYLE SANDRIDGE & RICE (AV)

A Professional Limited Liability Company
3300 One First Union Center, 301 S. College Street, 28202-6025
Telephone: 704-331-4900
Telecopy: 704-331-4955
Telex: 853609
Winston-Salem, North Carolina Office: 1600 Southern National Financial Center.
Telephone: 919-721-3600.
Telecopy: 919-721-3660.
Telex: 806498.
Raleigh, North Carolina Office: 2100 First Union Capitol Center, 150 Fayetteville Street Mall, P.O. Box 831.
Telephone: 919-755-2100.
Telecopy: 919-755-2150.
Telex: 806498.
Atlanta, Georgia Office: One Ninety One Peachtree Tower, 191 Peachtree Street N.E., Suite 3250.
Telephone: 404-614-2580.
Fax: 404-614-2595.

MEMBERS OF FIRM

Timothy G. Barber
Jim D. Cooley
J. Carlton Fleming

Representative Clients: Childress Klein Properties, Inc.; Food Lion, Inc.; Fieldcrest Cannon, Inc.; J.A. Jones Construction Company; Parkdale Mills, Inc.; Duke Power Company; Bowles Hollowell Conner & Company; ALLTEL Carolina, Inc.; Belk Store Services, Inc.; Philip Holzmann A.G.

For Complete List of Firm Personnel, See General Section

For full biographical listings, see the Martindale-Hubbell Law Directory

*DURHAM,** Durham Co.

DAILEY J. DERR, P.A. (AV)

3518 Westgate Drive, Suite 350, P.O. Box 51266, 27717
Telephone: 919-493-5500
Fax: 919-489-5137

Dailey J. Derr

Representative Clients: Archon, Inc.; Brown Brothers Plumbing and Heating Co., Inc.; Century Guild (The), Inc.; Duane K. Stewart & Associates, Inc.; Ellerbe Becket, Inc.; Outdoor Lighting, Inc.; Residential Warranty Corp.; Right-Way Construction Co., Inc.; Tar II001 Inspection Services, Inc.; Tops Petroleum Corp.

For full biographical listings, see the Martindale-Hubbell Law Directory

*RALEIGH,** Wake Co.

* indicates certain Bar Register subscribers whose principal office is located elsewhere in the state and who have arranged for representation as a part of the state capital listings that follow

*** WOMBLE CARLYLE SANDRIDGE & RICE (AV)**

A Professional Limited Liability Company
2100 First Union Capitol Center, 150 Fayetteville Street Mall, P.O. Box 831, 27602
Telephone: 919-755-2100
Telecopy: 919-755-2150
Telex: 806498
Charlotte, North Carolina Office: 3300 One First Union Center, 301 South College Street.
Telephone: 704-331-4900.
Telecopy: 704-331-4955.
Telex: 853609.
Winston-Salem, North Carolina Office: 1600 Southern National Financial Center.
Telephone: 919-721-3600.
Telecopy: 919-721-3660.
Telex: 806498.
Atlanta, Georgia Office: One Ninety One Peachtree Tower, 191 Peachtree Street N.E., Suite 3250.
Telephone: 404-614-2580.
Fax: 404-614-2595.

RESIDENT PARTNERS

Donald A. Donadio
Robert Harrison Sasser, III

Representative Clients: Aetna Casualty and Surety Co., Inc.; AL-SCO/AmeriMark Building Products, Inc.; Aoki Corporation America, Inc.; Empire of Carolina, Inc.; Hackney Brothers, Inc.; Lawyers Mutual Liability Insurance Company of North Carolina; Meredith College; Monk-Austin, Inc.; Regency Park Corporation; Wachovia Bank of North Carolina, N.A.

For Complete List of Firm Personnel, See General Section

For full biographical listings, see the Martindale-Hubbell Law Directory

*WINSTON-SALEM,** Forsyth Co.

WOMBLE CARLYLE SANDRIDGE & RICE (AV)

A Professional Limited Liability Company
1600 Southern National Financial Center, P.O. Drawer 84, 27102
Telephone: 910-721-3600
Telecopy: 910-721-3660
Telex: 806498
Charlotte, North Carolina Office: 3300 One First Union Center, 301 South College Street.
Telephone: 704-331-4900.
Telecopy: 704-331-4955.
Telex: 853609.
Raleigh, North Carolina Office: 2100 First Union Capitol Center, 150 Fayetteville Street Mall, P.O. Box 831.
Telephone: 919-755-2100.
Telecopy: 919-755-2150.
Telex: 806498.
Atlanta, Georgia Office: One Ninety One Peachtree Tower, 191 Peachtree Street, N.E., Suite 3250.
Telephone: 404-614-2580.
Fax: 404-614-2595.

MEMBERS OF FIRM

Conrad C. Baldwin, Jr.
Karen Estelle Carey
Keith Ashford Clinard

Representative Clients: Brad Ragan, Inc.; Brenner Companies; Food Lion, Inc.; Hanes Companies, Inc.; North Carolina Baptist Hospitals, Inc.; R.J. Reynolds Tobacco Company; Summit Communications Group, Inc.; Thomasville Furniture Industries, Inc.; Wachovia Corporation; Wake Forest University.

For Complete List of Firm Personnel, See General Section

For full biographical listings, see the Martindale-Hubbell Law Directory

OHIO

*CINCINNATI,** Hamilton Co.

BENJAMIN, YOCUM & HEATHER (AV)

1500 Central Trust Tower, 5 West 4th Street, 45202-3681
Telephone: 513-721-5672
FAX: 513-721-5910

MEMBERS OF FIRM

John A. Benjamin
Thomas R. Yocum
Timothy P. Heather
Michael J. Bergmann
Anthony J. Iaciofano

ASSOCIATES

Lisa Marie Bitter
Jeffrey Paul McSherry

For full biographical listings, see the Martindale-Hubbell Law Directory

DINSMORE & SHOHL (AV)

1900 Chemed Center, 255 East Fifth Street, 45202-3172
Telephone: 513-977-8200
FAX: 513-977-8141
Florence, Kentucky Office: Turfway Ridge Office Park, 7300 Turfway Road, Suite 430 41042-1355.
Telephone: 606-283-0515.
FAX: 606-283-6017.
Dayton, Ohio Office: 500 Courthouse Plaza, S.W., 10 N. Ludlow Street, 45402-1834.
Telephone: 513-228-8012.
FAX: 513-461-2543.
Columbus, Ohio Office: NBD Bank Building, Suite 330, 175 South Third Street, 43215-5134.
Telephone: 614-224-7887.
FAX: 614-224-7882.

MEMBERS OF FIRM

Gary L. Herfel (Resident, Florence, Kentucky Office)
Mark C. Bissinger

ASSOCIATES

G. Franklin Miller
Christine L. McBroom
Lynn Marmer
Dianne Goss Paynter (Resident, Columbus, Ohio Office)

For Complete List of Firm Personnel, See General Section

For full biographical listings, see the Martindale-Hubbell Law Directory

THOMPSON, HINE AND FLORY (AV)

312 Walnut Street, 14th Floor, 45202-4029
Telephone: 513-352-6700
Fax: 513-241-4771;
Telex: 938003
Akron, Ohio Office: 50 S. Main Street, Suite 502, 44308-1828.
Telephone: 216-376-8090.
Fax: 216-376-8386.
Cleveland, Ohio Office: 1100 National City Bank Building, 629 Euclid Avenue, 44114-3070.
Telephone: 216-566-5500.
Fax: 216-556-5583.
Telex: 980217.
Cable Address: "Thomflor".
Columbus, Ohio Office: One Columbus, 10 West Broad Street, 43215-3435.
Telephone: 614-469-3200.
Fax: 614-469-3361.
Dayton, Ohio Office: 2000 Courthouse Plaza, N.E., 45402-1706.
Telephone: 513-443-6600.
Fax: 513-443-6637; 443-6635.
Palm Beach, Florida Office: 125 Worth Avenue, 33480-4466.
Telephone: 407-833-5900.
Fax: 407-833-5951.
Washington, D.C. Office: 1920 N Street, N.W., 20036-1601.
Telephone: 202-331-8800.
Fax: 202-331-8330.
Telex: 904173.
Cable Address: "Caglaw".
Brussels, Belgium Office: Rue des Chevaliers / Ridderstraat 14 - B.10, B - 1050.
Telephone: 011(32-2) 511-9326.
Fax: 011(-32-2) 513-9206.

MEMBER OF FIRM

Christopher M. Bechhold

For Complete List of Firm Personnel, See General Section

For full biographical listings, see the Martindale-Hubbell Law Directory

WAITE, SCHNEIDER, BAYLESS & CHESLEY CO., L.P.A. (AV)

1513 Central Trust Tower, Fourth and Vine Streets, 45202
Telephone: 513-621-0267
Fax: 513-381-2375; 621-0262

(See Next Column)

WAITE, SCHNEIDER, BAYLESS & CHESLEY CO. L.P.A., *Cincinnati—Continued*

Stanley M. Chesley

Thomas F. Rehme	Sherrill P. Hondorf
Fay E. Stilz	Colleen M. Hegge
Louise M. Roselle	Dianna Pendleton
Dwight Tillery	Randy F. Fox
D. Arthur Rabourn	Glenn D. Feagan
Jerome L. Skinner	Theresa L. Groh
Janet G. Abaray	Theodore N. Berry
Paul M. De Marco	Jane H. Walker
Terrence L. Goodman	Renée Infante

Allen P. Grunes

OF COUNSEL

Jos. E. Rosen	James F. Keller

For full biographical listings, see the Martindale-Hubbell Law Directory

*CLEVELAND,** Cuyahoga Co.

BAKER & HOSTETLER (AV)

3200 National City Center, 1900 East Ninth Street, 44114-3485
Telephone: 216-621-0200
Telecopier: 216-696-0740
TWX: 810 421 8375
RCA Telex: 215032
In Columbus, Ohio: Capitol Square, Suite 2100, 65 East State Street.
Telephone: 614-228-1541.
In Denver, Colorado: 303 East 17th Avenue, Suite 1100.
Telephone: 303-861-0600.
In Houston, Texas: 1000 Louisiana, Suite 2000.
Telephone: 713-751-1600.
In Long Beach, California: 300 Oceangate, Suite 620.
Telephone: 310-432-2827.
In Los Angeles, California: 600 Wilshire Boulevard.
Telephone: 213-624-2400.
In Orlando, Florida: SunBank Center, Suite 2300, 200 South Orange Avenue.
Telephone: 407-649-4000.
In Washington, D. C.: Washington Square, Suite 1100, 1050 Connecticut Avenue, N.W.
Telephone: 202-861-1500.
In College Park, Maryland: 9658 Baltimore Boulevard, Suite 206.
Telephone: 301-441-2781.
In Alexandria, Virginia: 437 North Lee Street.
Telephone: 703-549-1294.
In San Francisco, California: One Sansome Street, Suite 2000.
Telephone: 415-951-4705.

PARTNERS

Elliot Stephen Azoff	Lawrence V. Lindberg
Diane P. Chapman	Thomas R. Lucchesi
José C. Feliciano	Thomas H. Shunk
Albert J. Knopp	Randall L. Solomon

For Complete List of Firm Personnel, See General Section

For full biographical listings, see the Martindale-Hubbell Law Directory

JANIK & DUNN (AV)

400 Park Plaza Building, 1111 Chester Avenue, 44114
Telephone: 216-781-9700
Fax: 216-781-1250
Brea, California Office: 2601 Saturn Street, Suite 300.
Telephone: 714-572-1101.
Fax: 714-572-1103.

MEMBERS OF FIRM

Steven G. Janik	Theodore M. Dunn, Jr.

ASSOCIATES

Myra Staresina	David L. Mast

For full biographical listings, see the Martindale-Hubbell Law Directory

THOMPSON, HINE AND FLORY (AV)

1100 National City Bank Building, 629 Euclid Avenue, 44114-3070
Telephone: 216-566-5500
Fax: 216-566-5583
Telex: 980217
Cable Address: "Thomflor"
Akron, Ohio Office: 50 S. Main Street, Suite 502, 44308-1828.
Telephone: 216-376-8090.
Fax: 216-376-8386.
Cincinnati, Ohio Office: 312 Walnut Street, 14th Floor, 45202-4029.
Telephone: 513-352-6700.
Fax: 513-241-4771.
Telex: 938003.
Columbus, Ohio Office: One Columbus, 10 West Broad Street, 43215-3435.
Telephone: 614-469-3200.
Fax: 614-469-3361.

(See Next Column)

Dayton, Ohio Office: 2000 Courthouse Plaza, N.E., 45402-1706.
Telephone: 513-443-6600.
Fax: 513-443-6637; 443-6635.
Palm Beach, Florida Office: 125 Worth Avenue, Suite 117, 33480-4466.
Telephone: 407-833-5900.
Fax: 407-833-5951.
Washington, D.C. Office: 1920 N Street, N.W., 20036-1601.
Telephone: 202-331-8800.
Fax: 202-331-8330.
Telex: 904173.
Cable Address: "Caglaw".
Brussels, Belgium Office: Rue des Chevaliers, Ridderstraat 14 - B.10, B - 1050.
Telephone: 011(32-2) 511-9326.
Fax: 011(32-2) 513-9206.

MEMBERS OF FIRM

Jeffrey R. Appelbaum	David J. Hooker
Virginia S. Brown	William B. Leahy

James D. Robenalt

ASSOCIATES

Patrick F. Haggerty	Andrew J. Natale

OF COUNSEL

William D. Ginn

For Complete List of Firm Personnel, See General Section

For full biographical listings, see the Martindale-Hubbell Law Directory

*COLUMBUS,** Franklin Co.

* indicates certain Bar Register subscribers whose principal office is located elsewhere in the state and who have arranged for representation as a part of the state capital listings that follow

EMENS, KEGLER, BROWN, HILL & RITTER (AV)

Capitol Square Suite 1800, 65 East State Street, 43215-4294
Telephone: 614-462-5400
Telecopier: 614-464-2634
Cable Address: "Law EKBHR"
Telex: 246671

Stephen E. Chappelear	O. Judson Scheaf, III
Lawrence F. Feheley	Theodore Scott, Jr.
Gene W. Holliker	Melvin D. Weinstein

James M. Groner

Representative Clients: American Subcontractors Association; Dannis Industries, Inc.; Jay-Car Construction Co.; Lincoln Construction, Inc.; Presidential Construction, Inc.; S.G. Loewendick & Sons, Inc.; Trammel Crow Residential Contractors; Holdridge Mechanical, Inc.

For Complete List of Firm Personnel, See General Section

For full biographical listings, see the Martindale-Hubbell Law Directory

* THOMPSON, HINE AND FLORY (AV)

One Columbus, 10 West Broad Street, 43215-3435
Telephone: 614-469-3200
Fax: 614-469-3361
Akron, Ohio Office: 50 S. Main Street, Suite 502, 44308-1828.
Telephone: 216-376-8090.
Fax: 216-376-8386.
Cincinnati, Ohio Office: 312 Walnut Street, 14th Floor, 45202-4029.
Telephone: 513-352-6700.
Fax: 513-241-4771.
Telex: 938003.
Cleveland, Ohio Office: 1100 National City Bank Building, 629 Euclid Avenue, 44114-3070.
Telephone: 216-566-5500.
Fax: 216-556-5583.
Telex: 980217.
Cable Address: "Thomflor".
Dayton, Ohio Office: 2000 Courthouse Plaza, N.E., 45402-1706.
Telephone: 513-443-6600.
Fax: 513-443-6637; 443-6635.
Palm Beach, Florida Office: 125 Worth Avenue, 33480-4466.
Telephone: 407-833-5900.
Fax: 407-833-5951.
Washington, D.C. Office: 1920 N Street, N.W., 20036-1601.
Telephone: 202-331-8800.
Fax: 202-331-8330.
Telex: 904173.
Cable Address: "Caglaw".
Brussels, Belgium Office: Rue des Chevaliers / Ridderstraat 14 - B.10, B - 1050.
Telephone: 011(32-2) 511-9326.
Fax: 011(32-2) 513-9206.

(See Next Column)

THOMPSON, HINE AND FLORY—*Continued*

MEMBER OF FIRM

Michael T. Shannon

For Complete List of Firm Personnel, See General Section

For full biographical listings, see the Martindale-Hubbell Law Directory

*DAYTON,** Montgomery Co.

FREUND, FREEZE & ARNOLD A LEGAL PROFESSIONAL ASSOCIATION (AV)

Suite 1800 One Dayton Centre, One South Main Street, 45402-2017
Telephone: 513-222-2424
Telecopier: 513-222-5369
Cincinnati, Ohio Office: Suite 2110 Carew Tower, 441 Vine Street, 45202-4157.
Telephone: 513-287-8400.
FAX: 513-287-8403.

Neil F. Freund
Stephen V. Freeze
Gordon D. Arnold
Patrick J. Janis
Jane M. Lynch
Francis S. McDaniel
Stephen C. Findley
Christopher W. Carrigg
Scott F. McDaniel
Gregory J. Berberich
Thomas B. Bruns
Shawn M. Blatt
Matthew K. Fox
Fredric L. Young
Philip D. Mervis
Thomas P. Glass
Lori S. Kibby
August T. Janszen

Local Counsel for: Auto-Owners Insurance Co.; CNA Insurance Co.; Crum and Foster Underwriters; Employers Reinsurance Corp.; Farmers Insurance Group; Lloyds of London; Medical Protective; Midwestern Group; State Farm Mutual Automobile Insurance Co.; The Travelers Insurance Co.
Special Trial Counsel for: City of Dayton.

For full biographical listings, see the Martindale-Hubbell Law Directory

THOMPSON, HINE AND FLORY (AV)

2000 Courthouse Plaza, N.E., 45402-1706
Telephone: 513-443-6600
Fax: 513-443-6637; 443-6635
Akron, Ohio Office: 50 S. Main Street, Suite 502, 44308-1828.
Telephone: 216-376-8090.
Fax: 216-376-8386.
Cincinnati, Ohio Office: 312 Walnut Street, 14th Floor, 45202-4029.
Telephone: 513-352-6700.
Fax: 513-241-4771.
Telex: 938003.
Cleveland, Ohio Office: 1100 National City Bank Building, 629 Euclid Avenue, 44114-3070.
Telephone: 216-566-5500.
Fax: 216-556-5583.
Telex: 980217.
Cable Address: "Thomflor".
Columbus, Ohio Office: One Columbus, 10 West Broad Street, 43215-3435.
Telephone: 614-469-3200.
Fax: 614-469-3361.
Palm Beach, Florida Office: 125 Worth Avenue, 33480-4466.
Telephone: 407-833-5900.
Fax: 407-833-5951.
Washington, D.C. Office: 1920 N Street, N.W., 20036-1601.
Telephone: 202-331-8800.
Fax: 202-331-8330.
Telex: 904173.
Cable Address: "Caglaw".
Brussels, Belgium Office: Rue des Chevaliers / Ridderstraat 14 - B.10, B - 1050.
Telephone: 011(32-2) 511-9326.
Fax: 011(32-2) 513-9206.

MEMBER OF FIRM

Bruce M. Allman

For Complete List of Firm Personnel, See General Section

For full biographical listings, see the Martindale-Hubbell Law Directory

OKLAHOMA

*OKLAHOMA CITY,** Oklahoma Co.

DAY, EDWARDS, FEDERMAN, PROPESTER & CHRISTENSEN, P.C. (AV)

Suite 2900 First Oklahoma Tower, 210 Park Avenue, 73102-5605
Telephone: 405-239-2121
Telecopier: 405-236-1012

(See Next Column)

Bruce W. Day
Joe E. Edwards
William B. Federman
Richard P. Propester
D. Wade Christensen
J. Clay Christensen
Kent A. Gilliland
Rodney J. Heggy
Ricki Valerie Sonders
Thomas Pitchlynn Howell, IV
John C. Platt

David R. Widdoes
Lori R. Roberts
Carolyn A. Romberg

OF COUNSEL

Herbert F. (Jack) Hewett
Jeanette Cook Timmons
Joel Warren Harmon
Jane S. Eulberg
Mark A. Cohen

Representative Clients: Aetna Life Insurance Co.; Boatmen's First National Bank of Oklahoma; Borg-Warner Chemicals, Inc.; City Bank & Trust; Federal Deposit Insurance Corp.; Bank One, Oklahoma City; Haskell Lemon Construction Co.; Merrill Lynch, Pierce, Fenner & Smith, Inc.; Prudential Securities, Inc.

For full biographical listings, see the Martindale-Hubbell Law Directory

MANCHESTER & PIGNATO, P.C. (AV)

Third Floor Colcord Building, 15 North Robinson, 73102
Telephone: 405-235-2222
Fax: 405-235-2204

Robert Edward Manchester
Gerard F. Pignato

Stacey L. Haws
Shannon K. Emmons
Susan Ann Knight

Representative Clients: CMI Corporation; Electric Mutual Liability Insurance Company; Otis Elevator Company; Budget Rent-A-Car Systems, Inc.; Essex Insurance Company; American Bankers Insurance Company of Florida; Motors Insurance Company; Lexington Insurance Company; City of Oklahoma City.

For full biographical listings, see the Martindale-Hubbell Law Directory

OREGON

*PORTLAND,** Multnomah Co.

ALLEN, YAZBECK & O'HALLORAN, P.C. (AV)

1001 S.W. Fifth Avenue, Suite 1650, 97204
Telephone: 503-227-2242
Fax: 503-227-2669

F. Gordon Allen, III
Joseph A. Yazbeck, Jr.
Robert L. O'Halloran
Jeffrey K. Hanson
Tamara H. Lesh

OF COUNSEL

Lynnia K. Woods

For full biographical listings, see the Martindale-Hubbell Law Directory

SUSSMAN SHANK WAPNICK CAPLAN & STILES (AV)

1000 S.W. Broadway Suite 1400, 97205
Telephone: 503-227-1111
Telecopier: 503-248-0130

MEMBERS OF FIRM

Norman Wapnick
William N. Stiles
John P. Davenport
Jeffrey R. Spere

ASSOCIATES

Gary E. Enloe
Michael G. Halligan

For Complete List of Firm Personnel, See General Section

For full biographical listings, see the Martindale-Hubbell Law Directory

PENNSYLVANIA

CAMP HILL, Cumberland Co.

REAGER & ADLER, P.C. (AV)

2331 Market Street, 17011
Telephone: 717-763-1383
Fax: 717-730-7366
Harrisburg, Pennsylvania Address: P.O. Box 797 17108-0797.

Theodore A. Adler
David W. Reager

(See Next Column)

REAGER & ADLER P.C., *Camp Hill—Continued*

Thomas O. Williams

Representative Clients: Homebuilders Association of Metropolitan Harrisburg; Pennsylvania Builders Association; The Homestead Group, Inc.

For full biographical listings, see the Martindale-Hubbell Law Directory

*HARRISBURG,** Dauphin Co.

BECKLEY & MADDEN (AV)

Cranberry Court, 212 North Third Street, P.O. Box 11998, 17108
Telephone: 717-233-7691
FAX: 717-233-3740

MEMBERS OF FIRM

Thomas A. Beckley
John G. Milakovic

For full biographical listings, see the Martindale-Hubbell Law Directory

BUCHANAN INGERSOLL, PROFESSIONAL CORPORATION (AV)

Vartan Parc, 30 North Third Street, 17101
Telephone: 717-237-4800
Telecopier: 717-233-0852
Pittsburgh, Pennsylvania Office: 5800 USX Tower, 600 Grant Street.
Telephone: 412-562-8800.
Philadelphia, Pennsylvania Office: Two Logan Square, Twelfth Floor, 18th & Arch Streets.
Telephone: 215-665-8700.
Tampa, Florida Office: 101 East Kennedy Boulevard, Suite 1030.
Telephone: 813-222-8180.
North Miami Beach, Florida Office: 19495 Biscayne Boulevard.
Telephone: 305-933-5600.
Lexington, Kentucky Office: 1210 Vine Center Office Tower, 333 West Vine Street.
Telephone: 606-225-5333.
Princeton, New Jersey Office: Buchanan Ingersoll, A Partnership, College Centre, 500 College Road East.
Telephone: 609-452-2666.

Andrew S. Gordon

For Complete List of Firm Personnel, See General Section

For full biographical listings, see the Martindale-Hubbell Law Directory

MCNEES, WALLACE & NURICK (AV)

100 Pine Street, P.O. Box 1166, 17108
Telephone: 717-232-8000
Fax: 717-237-5300

MEMBERS OF FIRM

Stephen A. Moore
S. Berne Smith
Diane M. Tokarsky

ASSOCIATES

James W. Kutz
Jonathan H. Rudd

For Complete List of Firm Personnel, See General Section

For full biographical listings, see the Martindale-Hubbell Law Directory

METTE, EVANS & WOODSIDE, A PROFESSIONAL CORPORATION (AV)

3401 North Front Street, P.O. Box 5950, 17110-0950
Telephone: 717-232-5000
Telecopier: 717-236-1816

Craig A. Stone
Daniel L. Sullivan
Christopher C. Conner
Michael D. Reed

David A. Fitzsimons

Counsel for: The B. F. Goodrich Co.; Juniata Valley Financial Corp.; MCI Telecommunications Corp.; Monongahela Power Co.; The Procter and Gamble Paper Products Co.; United States Fidelity and Guaranty Co.; Community Banks; GTE Products Corp.; Commerce Bank.

For Complete List of Firm Personnel, See General Section

For full biographical listings, see the Martindale-Hubbell Law Directory

KING OF PRUSSIA, Montgomery Co.

POWELL, TRACHTMAN, LOGAN, CARRLE & BOWMAN, A PROFESSIONAL CORPORATION (AV)

367 South Gulph Road, 19406
Telephone: 610-354-9700
Fax: 610-354-9760
Cherry Hill, New Jersey Office: 811 Church Road, Suite 126, 08002.
Telephone: 609-663-0021.
Fax: 609-663-1590.
Harrisburg, Pennsylvania Office: 114 North Second Street, 17101.
Telephone: 717-238-9300.
Fax: 717-238-9325.

(See Next Column)

Michael G. Trachtman
Paul A. Logan
Gunther O. Carrle
C. Grainger Bowman
Richard B. Ashenfelter Jr.
Mark F. Brancato
Jonathan K. Hollin
Joel P. Perilstein

OF COUNSEL

Ralph B. Powell, Jr.
Patrick W. Liddle

Mark S. McKain
Ethan N. Halberstadt
David T. Bolger
David W. Francis
Eileen M. Coyne
Andrew P. Goode
Steven G. Bardsley

For full biographical listings, see the Martindale-Hubbell Law Directory

LATROBE, Westmoreland Co.

ROBERT P. LIGHTCAP (AV)

757 Lloyd Avenue Extension, P.O. Box 364, 15650
Telephone: 412-539-3007
Fax: 412-537-7562

For full biographical listings, see the Martindale-Hubbell Law Directory

*PHILADELPHIA,** Philadelphia Co.

BUCHANAN INGERSOLL, PROFESSIONAL CORPORATION (AV)

Two Logan Square Twelfth Floor, 18th & Arch Streets, 19103
Telephone: 215-665-8700
Telecopier: 215-569-2066
Pittsburgh, Pennsylvania Office: 5800 USX Tower, 600 Grant Street.
Telephone: 412-562-8800.
Harrisburg, Pennsylvania Office: Vartan Parc, 30 North Third Street.
Telephone: 717-237-4800.
Tampa, Florida Office: 101 East Kennedy Boulevard, Suite 1030.
Telephone: 813-222-8180.
North Miami Beach, Florida Office: 19495 Biscayne Boulevard.
Telephone: 305-933-5600.
Lexington, Kentucky Office: 1210 Vine Center Office Tower, 333 West Vine Street.
Telephone: 606-225-5333.
Princeton, New Jersey Office: Buchanan Ingersoll, A Partnership, College Centre, 500 College Road East.
Telephone: 609-452-2666.

Alan C. Kessler

For Complete List of Firm Personnel, See General Section

For full biographical listings, see the Martindale-Hubbell Law Directory

*PITTSBURGH,** Allegheny Co.

BABST, CALLAND, CLEMENTS AND ZOMNIR, A PROFESSIONAL CORPORATION (AV)

Two Gateway Center, 15222
Telephone: 412-394-5400
Fax: 412-394-6576
Philadelphia, Pennsylvania Office: The Curtis Center, Suite 1100, Sixth and Walnut Streets.
Telephone: 215-627-3056.
Fax: 215-627-3042.

Frank J. Clements
Kenneth R. Bruce
James A. Escovitz
Robert A. King
J. Frank McKenna, III
Mark D. Shepard
Ted Wesolowski

Tarek F. Abdalla
Sara M. Antol
Albert Bates, Jr. IV
John W. Bruni
Julie A. Coletti
James V. Corbelli
Jan L. Fox
Edward B. Gentilcore
D. Matthew Jameson III
Jessica Lieber Smolar
Bruce E. Stanley
Timothy C. Wolfson

For full biographical listings, see the Martindale-Hubbell Law Directory

BUCHANAN INGERSOLL, PROFESSIONAL CORPORATION (AV)

5800 USX Tower, 600 Grant Street, 15219
Telephone: 412-562-8800
Telecopier: 412-562-1041
Philadelphia, Pennsylvania Office: Two Logan Square, Twelfth Floor, 18th & Arch Streets.
Telephone: 215-665-8700.
Harrisburg, Pennsylvania Office: Vartan Parc, 30 North Third Street.
Telephone: 717-237-4800.
Tampa, Florida Office: 101 East Kennedy Boulevard, Suite 1030.
Telephone: 813-222-8180.
North Miami Beach, Florida Office: 19495 Biscayne Boulevard.
Telephone: 305-933-5600.
Lexington, Kentucky Office: 1210 Vine Center Office Tower, 333 West Vine Street.
Telephone: 606-225-5333.

(See Next Column)

BUCHANAN INGERSOLL PROFESSIONAL CORPORATION—*Continued*

Princeton, New Jersey Office: Buchanan Ingersoll, A Partnership, College Centre, 500 College Road East.
Telephone: 609-452-2666.

Samuel W. Braver
Ronald W. Crouch
Thomas L. VanKirk
R. Dell Ziegler

Anthony James Guida Jr.

For Complete List of Firm Personnel, See General Section

For full biographical listings, see the Martindale-Hubbell Law Directory

GACA, MATIS & HAMILTON, A PROFESSIONAL CORPORATION (AV)

300 Four PPG Place, 15222-5404
Telephone: 412-338-4750
Fax: 412-338-4742

Giles J. Gaca
Thomas A. Matis
Mark R. Hamilton
John W. Jordan, IV
Alan S. Baum
Thomas P. McGinnis
Bernard R. Rizza
Jeffrey A. Ramaley
Stephen J. Dalesio
John Timothy Hinton, Jr.

Shawn Lynne Reed

LEGAL SUPPORT PERSONNEL

PARALEGALS

Tina M. Shanafelt
Jill M. Peterson

For full biographical listings, see the Martindale-Hubbell Law Directory

MOLLICA, MURRAY & HOGUE (AV)

3400 Gulf Tower, 15219
Telephone: 412-263-5200
Fax: 412-263-5220

MEMBERS OF FIRM

James A. Mollica, Jr.
Dr. John E. Murray, Jr.
Jon Geoffrey Hogue
Blaine A. Lucas
Cathy Ann Chromulak
Timothy Murray
Sandra L. Lannis
William J. Moorhead, Jr.
Jeannine A. Schuster
Steven M. Nolan

Benjamin J. Viloski

For full biographical listings, see the Martindale-Hubbell Law Directory

PLOWMAN, SPIEGEL & LEWIS, P.C. (AV)

Grant Building, Suite 925, 15219-2201
Telephone: 412-471-8521
Fax: 412-471-4481

Jack W. Plowman
John L. Spiegel
Frank J. Kernan
Clifford L. Tuttle, Jr.

Kenneth W. Lee

Marshall J. Conn
David Raves

Reference: Pittsburgh National Bank.

For Complete List of Firm Personnel, See General Section

For full biographical listings, see the Martindale-Hubbell Law Directory

THORP, REED & ARMSTRONG (AV)

One Riverfront Center, 15222
Telephone: 412-394-7711
Fax: 412-394-2555

MEMBERS OF FIRM

John W. Eichleay, Jr.
Douglas E. Gilbert
Clifford B. Levine
Mark F. Nowak

Deborah P. Powell

ASSOCIATE

David E. White

For Complete List of Firm Personnel, See General Section

For full biographical listings, see the Martindale-Hubbell Law Directory

RHODE ISLAND

*PROVIDENCE,** Providence Co.

BLISH & CAVANAGH (AV)

Commerce Center, 30 Exchange Terrace, 02903
Telephone: 401-831-8900
Telecopier: 401-751-7542

(See Next Column)

MEMBERS OF FIRM

John H. Blish
Joseph V. Cavanagh, Jr.
William R. Landry
Michael DiBiase

Stephen J. Reid, Jr.

Karen A. Pelczarski
Raymond A. Marcaccio

Scott P. Tierney

Representative Clients: Providence Journal Co.; Fleet Financial Group; Rhode Island Hospital Trust National Bank; Allstate Insurance Co.; U-Haul International, Inc.; Delta Dental of Rhode Island; Gilbane Building Co.; Colony Communications; Providence Housing Authority.

For full biographical listings, see the Martindale-Hubbell Law Directory

SOUTH CAROLINA

*CHARLESTON,** Charleston Co.

BARNWELL WHALEY PATTERSON & HELMS (AV)

134 Meeting Street, Suite 300, P.O. Drawer H, 29402
Telephone: 803-577-7700
Telecopier: 803-577-7708

MEMBERS OF FIRM

William C. Helms, III
Thomas J. Wills

Bruce E. Miller

ASSOCIATES

Aubrey R. Alvey
Warren William Ariail
Robert P. Gritton
Thomas B. Pritchard

James E. Reeves

Representative Clients: Brown & Root, Inc.; The Cannon Corp.; Design Professionals Ins. Co.; Nielson Construction, Inc.; Reliance Ins. Co.; Ryland Group, Inc.

For Complete List of Firm Personnel, See General Section

For full biographical listings, see the Martindale-Hubbell Law Directory

HAYNSWORTH, MARION, MCKAY & GUÉRARD, L.L.P (AV)

#2 Prioleau Street, P.O. Box 1119, 29402
Telephone: 803-722-7606
Telecopier: 803-723-5263
Columbia, South Carolina Office: Suite 2400 AT&T Building, 1201 Main Street, P.O. Drawer 7157, 29202.
Telephone: 803-765-1818.
Telecopier: 803-765-2399.
Greenville, South Carolina Office: Two Insignia Financial Plaza, 75 Beattie Place, P.O. Box 2048, 29602.
Telephone: 803-240-3200.
Telecopier: 803-240-3300.

MEMBERS OF FIRM

W. E. Applegate, III
James J. Hinchey, Jr. (Resident)

ASSOCIATE

James E. Lady

Counsel for: Fluor Daniel; Odell Associates, Inc.; Piedmont Olsen Hensley, Inc.; Vercon Construction, Inc.; REA Construction Company; Yeargin Enterprises; American Equipment Company, Inc.; Westinghouse Savannah River Company; Potter Shackelford Construction Company; Coward-Hund Construction Co.

For Complete List of Firm Personnel, See General Section

For full biographical listings, see the Martindale-Hubbell Law Directory

ROBERTSON & SEEKINGS (AV)

First Union Center, 177 Meeting Street, Suite 300, 29401
Telephone: 803-723-6470
FAX: 803-853-9045

MEMBERS OF FIRM

Claron A. Robertson, III
Michael S. Seekings

ASSOCIATES

Dunn D. Hollingsworth
R. Patrick Flynn

For full biographical listings, see the Martindale-Hubbell Law Directory

ROSEN, ROSEN & HAGOOD, P.A. (AV)

134 Meeting Street, Suite 200, P.O. Box 893, 29402
Telephone: 803-577-6726

Morris D. Rosen
Richard S. Rosen
H. Brewton Hagood
Donald B. Clark

Randy Horner

Reference: NationsBank of South Carolina, N.A.

(See Next Column)

ROSEN, ROSEN & HAGOOD P.A., *Charleston—Continued*

For Complete List of Firm Personnel, See General Section

For full biographical listings, see the Martindale-Hubbell Law Directory

*COLUMBIA,** Richland Co.

* indicates certain Bar Register subscribers whose principal office is located elsewhere in the state and who have arranged for representation as a part of the state capital listings that follow

BOWERS ORR & ROBERTSON (AV)

Suite 1100, 1401 Main Street, P.O. Box 7307, 29202
Telephone: 803-252-0494
Telefax: 803-252-1068

MEMBERS OF FIRM

Glenn Bowers
William Dixon Robertson III
James W. Orr
Thomas F. Dougall

ASSOCIATE

W. Jones Andrews, Jr.

Representative Clients: The Carlson Corporation Southeast; Fireman's Fund Insurance Co.; Mashburn Construction Co., Inc.; Montague Systems, Inc.; SAE America Group, Inc.; Serv-Tech, Inc.; Stevens & Wilkinson, Inc.

For full biographical listings, see the Martindale-Hubbell Law Directory

* **HAYNSWORTH, MARION, MCKAY & GUÉRARD, L.L.P.** (AV)

Suite 2400 A T & T Building, 1201 Main Street, P.O. Drawer 7157, 29202
Telephone: 803-765-1818
Telecopier: 803-765-2399
Greenville, South Carolina Office: Two Insignia Financial Plaza, 75 Beattie Place, P.O. Box 2048, 29602.
Telephone: 803-240-3200.
Telecopier: 803-240-3300.
Charleston, South Carolina Office: #2 Prioleau Street, P.O. Box 1119, 29402.
Telephone: 803-722-7606.
Telecopier: 803-723-5263.

MEMBERS OF FIRM

William P. Simpson
Henry P. Wall

ASSOCIATES

Boyd B. Nicholson, Jr.
Jill R. Quattlebaum
Edward Wade Mullins, III

Counsel for: Fluor Daniel; Odell Associates, Inc.; Piedmont Olsen Hensley, Inc.; Vercon Construction, Inc.; REA Construction Company; yeargin Enterprises; American Equipment Company, Inc.; Westinghouse Savannah River Company; Potter Shackelford Construction Company; Tyger Construction Company; Coward-Hund Construction Co.

For Complete List of Firm Personnel, See General Section

For full biographical listings, see the Martindale-Hubbell Law Directory

RICHARDSON, PLOWDEN, GRIER AND HOWSER, P.A. (AV)

1600 Marion Street, P.O. Drawer 7788, 29202
Telephone: 803-771-4400
Telecopy: 803-779-0016
Myrtle Beach, South Carolina Office: Southern National Bank Building, Suite 202, 601 21st Avenue North, P.O. Box 3646, 29578.
Telephone: 803-448-1008.
FAX: 803-448-1533.

Donald V. Richardson, III
Francis M. Mack
Michael A. Pulliam
Franklin Jennings Smith, Jr.

Douglas C. Baxter
Jimmy Denning, Jr.

Representative Clients: S.C. Department of Public Transportation; Richland County School District No.1; DPCI Insurance Companies; Northlake Construction Co., Inc.; Boozer Lumber Co.; Osmose Wood Preserving Inc.; Ralph Whitehead & Assoc.

For Complete List of Firm Personnel, See General Section

For full biographical listings, see the Martindale-Hubbell Law Directory

*GREENVILLE,** Greenville Co.

HAYNSWORTH, MARION, MCKAY & GUÉRARD, L.L.P. (AV)

Two Insignia Financial Plaza, 75 Beattie Place, P.O. Box 2048, 29602
Telephone: 803-240-3200
Telecopier: 803-240-3300
Columbia, South Carolina Office: Suite 2400 A T & T Building, 1201 Main Street, P.O. Drawer 7157, 29202
Telephone: 803-765-1818.
Telecopier: 803-765-2399.
Charleston, South Carolina Office: #2 Prioleau Street, P.O. Box 1119, 29402.
Telephone: 803-722-7606.
Telecopier: 803-723-5263.

(See Next Column)

MEMBERS OF FIRM

Maye R. Johnson, Jr.
Thomas H. Coker, Jr.
H. Donald Sellers
Bryan Francis Hickey
Donald A. Harper
Moffatt Grier McDonald

ASSOCIATES

Norman Ward Lambert
Cynthia Buck Brown

Representative Clients: Fluor Daniel, Inc.; Yeargin Enterprises, Inc.; Suitt Construction Co., Inc.; American Equipment Co., Inc.; Piedmont Olsen Hensley, Inc.

For Complete List of Firm Personnel, See General Section

For full biographical listings, see the Martindale-Hubbell Law Directory

MYRTLE BEACH, Horry Co.

STEVENS, STEVENS & THOMAS, P.C. (AV)

1215 48th Avenue North, 29577-2468
Telephone: 803-449-9675
Fax: 803-497-2262
Loris, South Carolina Office: 3341 Broad Street.
Telephone: 803-756-7652.
Fax: 803-756-3785.

James P. Stevens, Jr. (Resident, Loris Office)
J. Jackson Thomas

Angela T. Jordan (Resident Loris Office)

OF COUNSEL

James P. Stevens

For full biographical listings, see the Martindale-Hubbell Law Directory

SOUTH DAKOTA

*ABERDEEN,** Brown Co.

MALONEY & MALONEY (AV)

Twelve Second Avenue, Southwest, P.O. Box 755, 57402-0755
Telephone: 605-229-2752
Fax: 605-226-0276

MEMBERS OF FIRM

Dennis Maloney
Marilyn Marshall Maloney

For full biographical listings, see the Martindale-Hubbell Law Directory

TENNESSEE

*CHATTANOOGA,** Hamilton Co.

FOSTER, FOSTER, ALLEN & DURRENCE (AV)

Formerly Hall, Haynes & Foster
Suite 515 Pioneer Bank Building, 37402
Telephone: 615-266-1141
Telecopier: 615-266-4618

MEMBERS OF FIRM

George Lane Foster
Craig R. Allen
William M. Foster
Phillip M. Durrence, Jr.

ASSOCIATES

David J. Ward
Clayton M. Whittaker
John M. Hull

LEGAL SUPPORT PERSONNEL

Peggy Sue Bates

Division Counsel for: Alabama Great Southern Railroad Co.; C.N.O. & T.P. Railway Co.
Attorneys for: CNA/Insurance; U.S.P. & G. Co.; The Firestone Tire & Rubber Co.; Exxon, Corp.; Murphy Oil Corp.; Chicago Title Insurance Co.; City of East Ridge; Jim Walter Homes; Raymond James & Associates; Morgan Keegan & Co.

For full biographical listings, see the Martindale-Hubbell Law Directory

STOPHEL & STOPHEL, P.C. (AV)

500 Tallan Building, Two Union Square, 37402-2571
Telephone: 615-756-2333
Fax: 615-266-5032

E. Stephen Jett
W. Jeffrey Hollingsworth

Representative Clients: Soloff Construction Company, Inc.; F.M. Russell Company; Steam & Control Systems, Inc.

(See Next Column)

STOPHEL & STOPHEL P.C.—*Continued*

For Complete List of Firm Personnel, See General Section

For full biographical listings, see the Martindale-Hubbell Law Directory

*MEMPHIS,** Shelby Co.

GLASSMAN, JETER, EDWARDS & WADE, P.C. (AV)

26 North Second Street Building, 38103
Telephone: 901-527-4673
Telecopier: 901-521-0940
Lexington, Tennessee Office: 85 East Church.
Telephone: 901-968-2561.

William M. Jeter

For full biographical listings, see the Martindale-Hubbell Law Directory

LESS, GETZ & LIPMAN (AV)

Suite 950 Brinkley Plaza, 80 Monroe Avenue, 38103
Telephone: 901-525-8700
Telecopier: 901-525-3569

MEMBERS OF FIRM

Michael I. Less
Joseph Thaddeus Getz
Clifton M. Lipman
Ted M. Hayden

Scott A. Frick
Stephen F. Libby
Adam Michael Nahmias
Susan E. Culbreath

For full biographical listings, see the Martindale-Hubbell Law Directory

TEXAS

*DALLAS,** Dallas Co.

CALHOUN & STACY (AV)

5700 NationsBank Plaza, 901 Main Street, 75202-3747
Telephone: 214-748-5000
Telecopier: 214-748-1421
Telex: 211358 CALGUMP UR

Mark Alan Calhoun
David W. Elrod
Steven D. Goldston
Parker Nelson
Roy L. Stacy

ASSOCIATES

Shannon S. Barclay
Robert A. Bragalone
Dennis D. Conder
Jane Elizabeth Diseker
Lawrence I. Fleishman
Thomas C. Jones
Katherine Johnson Knight
V. Paige Pace
Veronika Willard
Michael C. Wright

LEGAL CONSULTANT

Rees T. Bowen, III

For full biographical listings, see the Martindale-Hubbell Law Directory

CANTERBURY, STUBER, PRATT, ELDER & GOOCH, A PROFESSIONAL CORPORATION (AV)

One Lincoln Centre, 5400 LBJ Freeway, Suite 1300, 75240
Telephone: 214-239-7493
Telefax: 214-490-7739
San Antonio, Texas Office: Centre Plaza, 45 N.E. Loop 410, Suite 600.
Telephone: 210-366-3850.

Joseph F. Canterbury, Jr.
Charles W. Stuber
Donald O. Pratt
Robert C. Elder, Jr.
W. Kyle Gooch
Stanley W. Curry, Jr. (Resident, San Antonio Office)
Frederic Gover
David G. Surratt
Steve Kennedy

Paul H. Sanderford
Jeffrey A. Brannen

For full biographical listings, see the Martindale-Hubbell Law Directory

THOMAS, FELDMAN & WILSHUSEN, L.L.P. (AV)

900 Glen Lakes Tower, 9400 North Central Expressway, 75231
Telephone: 214-369-3008
Facsimile: 214-369-8393

MEMBERS OF FIRM

Richard Gary Thomas
Robert L. Feldman
Fred D. Wilshusen

ASSOCIATES

Regan Gayle O'Steen
Eric M. Cohen

(See Next Column)

OF COUNSEL

Joseph M. Stuhl

Representative Clients: American Subcontractors Association of Texas, Inc.; Case Power and Equipment; Gardner Zemke Co.; Porvene Roll-A-Door, Inc.; Potter Concrete, Inc.; Regional Electrical Systems; SAE/Spaw-Glass Constructors, Inc.; Structural Metals, Inc.; TD Mechanical Co.; Travis Industrial Painting Contractors, Inc.; United Mechanical.

For full biographical listings, see the Martindale-Hubbell Law Directory

THOMPSON & KNIGHT, A PROFESSIONAL CORPORATION (AV)

(Attorneys and Counselors)
1700 Pacific Avenue Suite 3300, 75201
Telephone: 214-969-1700
Telecopy: 214-969-1751
Cable Address: "Tomtex"
Telex: 732298
Austin, Texas Office: 1200 San Jacinto Center, 98 San Jacinto Boulevard, 78701.
Telephone: 512-469-6100.
Telecopy: 512-469-6180.
Fort Worth, Texas Office: 801 Cherry Street, Suite 1600, 76102.
Telephone: 817-347-1700.
Telecopy: 817-347-1799.
Houston, Texas Office: 1700 Texas Commerce Tower, 600 Travis, 77002.
Telephone: 713-217-2800.
Telecopy: 713-217-2828.
Monterrey, Mexico Office: Edificio Losoles PD-4, Av. Lázaro Cárdenas No. 2400 Pte., San Pedro Garza Garcia, Nuevo Léon C.P. 66220.
Telephone: (52-8) 363-0096.
Telecopy: (52-8) 363-3067.

SHAREHOLDERS

P. Jefferson Ballew
Hugh T. Blevins, Jr.
Gregg C. Davis
Jerry P. Jones
Geoffrey D. Osborn
Joseph S. Pevsner
Stephen C. Schoettmer
Clint Shouse
William R. Van Wagner

ASSOCIATES

Greg W. Curry
Shelly A. Youree

For Complete List of Firm Personnel, See General Section

For full biographical listings, see the Martindale-Hubbell Law Directory

*HOUSTON,** Harris Co.

SCHWARTZ & CAMPBELL, L.L.P. (AV)

1221 McKinney, Suite 1000, 77010
Telephone: 713-752-0017
Telecopier: 713-752-0327

Richard A. Schwartz
Marshall S. Campbell

Monica F. Oathout
Stephen A. Mendel
Samuel E. Dunn
Harold W. Hargis
Phillip W. Bechter
Laura M. Taylor
Michael D. Hudgins

LEGAL SUPPORT PERSONNEL

PARALEGALS

Nannette Koger
Bettye Vaughan Johnson
Lenore Chomout
Maria Pinillos

For full biographical listings, see the Martindale-Hubbell Law Directory

*SAN ANTONIO,** Bexar Co.

GARDNER & FERGUSON, INC., A PROFESSIONAL CORPORATION (AV)

745 East Mulberry, Suite 100, 78212
Telephone: 210-733-8191
Fax: 210-733-5538

Holmes T. Bennett
Wm. Richard Davis
Donald O. Ferguson
William W. Sommers
Carl Payne 'Chip' Tobey, Jr.
Thomas J. Walthall, Jr.

Mark M. Ferguson

Representative Clients: Litho-Press, Inc.; Morrisen Knudsen.

For full biographical listings, see the Martindale-Hubbell Law Directory

WHEATLEY, CAMPAGNOLO & SESSIONS, L.L.P. (AV)

100 West Houston, Suite 1200, 78205
Telephone: 210-227-5000
Fax: 210-225-1555

Seagal V. Wheatley
Theodore Campagnolo
William Lewis Sessions
John Frank Onion, III
Donald R. Philbin, Jr.

(See Next Column)

WHEATLEY, CAMPAGNOLO & SESSIONS L.L.P., *San Antonio—Continued*

ASSOCIATES

Bradley S. Wilder
Katrina J. Carden
Julia W. Mann

For full biographical listings, see the Martindale-Hubbell Law Directory

UTAH

*SALT LAKE CITY,** Salt Lake Co.

LYNN B. LARSEN (AV)

(associated with McKay, Burton and Thurman)
600 Kennecott Building, 10 East South Temple, 84133
Telephone: 801-521-4135
Fax: 801-521-4252

Lynn B. Larsen (Mr.)

For full biographical listings, see the Martindale-Hubbell Law Directory

PARSONS BEHLE & LATIMER, A PROFESSIONAL CORPORATION (AV)

One Utah Center, 201 South Main Street, Suite 1800, P.O. Box 45898, 84145-0898
Telephone: 801-532-1234
Telecopy: 801-536-6111

Gordon L. Roberts
Charles H. Thronson
Francis M. Wikstrom
John B. Wilson
Michael L. Larsen
Elizabeth S. Whitney

Representative Clients: Barrick Goldstrike Mines Inc.; Capitol Indemnity Corporation; Eaton-Kenway, Inc.; Kennecott Corporation; U.S. Construction, Inc.; U.S. Pollution Control, Inc.

For full biographical listings, see the Martindale-Hubbell Law Directory

VAN COTT, BAGLEY, CORNWALL & MCCARTHY, A PROFESSIONAL CORPORATION (AV)

Suite 1600, 50 South Main Street, P.O. Box 45340, 84145
Telephone: 801-532-3333
Telex: 453149
Telecopier: 801-534-0058
Ogden, Utah Office: Suite 900, 2404 Washington Boulevard.
Telephone: 801-394-5783.
Park City, Utah Office: 314 Main Street, Suite 205.
Telephone: 801-649-3889.
Reno, Nevada Office: Jeppson & Lee, 100 West Liberty, Suite 990.
Telephone: 702-333-6800.

John A. Snow
David A. Greenwood
Patricia M. Leith
R. Stephen Marshall
Eric C. Olson
Donald L. Dalton

For Complete List of Firm Personnel, See General Section

For full biographical listings, see the Martindale-Hubbell Law Directory

WATKISS DUNNING & WATKISS, A PROFESSIONAL CORPORATION (AV)

Broadway Centre, Suite 800, 111 East Broadway, 84111-2304
Telephone: 801-530-1500
Telecopier: 801-530-1520

David K. Watkiss
Elizabeth T. Dunning
David B. Watkiss

Carolyn Cox
Mary J. Woodhead

OF COUNSEL

Karen Campbell Jenson

For full biographical listings, see the Martindale-Hubbell Law Directory

VIRGINIA

BRISTOL, (Independent City)

ELLIOTT LAWSON & POMRENKE (AV)

Sixth Floor, First Union Bank Building, P.O. Box 8400, 24203-8400
Telephone: 703-466-8400
Fax: 703-466-8161

(See Next Column)

James Wm. Elliott, Jr.
Mark M. Lawson
Kurt J. Pomrenke
Steven R. Minor
Kyle P. Macione
Lisa King Crockett

For full biographical listings, see the Martindale-Hubbell Law Directory

*FAIRFAX,** (Ind. City; Seat of Fairfax Co.)

DIXON, SMITH & STAHL (AV)

4122 Leonard Drive, 22030
Telephone: 703-691-0770

MEMBERS OF FIRM

Richard E. Dixon
Donald G. Smith
Richard J. Stahl
Mark E. Sharp
Robert G. Culin, Jr.
James R. Hart
James E. Autry

ASSOCIATES

John L. Daugherty
Julie Hottle Day
Erica D.B. Glembocki

Reference: Sovran Bank, N.A.

For full biographical listings, see the Martindale-Hubbell Law Directory

MCLEAN, Fairfax Co.

VENABLE, BAETJER AND HOWARD (AV)

A Partnership including Professional Corporations
Suite 400, 2010 Corporate Ridge, 22102
Telephone: 703-760-1600
FAX: 703-821-8949
Baltimore, Maryland Office: 1800 Mercantile Bank & Trust Building, 2 Hopkins Plaza.
Telephone: 410-244-7400.
Washington, D.C. Office: Venable, Baetjer, Howard & Civiletti, Suite 1000, 1201 New York Avenue, N.W.
Telephone: 202-962-4800.
Rockville, Maryland Office: Suite 500, One Church Street, P.O. Box 1906.
Telephone: 301-217-5600.
Towson, Maryland Office: 210 Allegheny Avenue, P. O. Box 5517.
Telephone: 410-494-6200.

MEMBERS OF FIRM

Bruce E. Titus
David G. Lane
Herbert G. Smith, II

OF COUNSEL

Mary T. Flynn

ASSOCIATES

Julian Sylvester Brown
David R. Hodnett
Jon M. Lippard
Christine M. McAnney
Michael W. Robinson

For Complete List of Firm Personnel, See General Section

For full biographical listings, see the Martindale-Hubbell Law Directory

WATT, TIEDER & HOFFAR (AV)

7929 Westpark Drive, Suite 400, 22102
Telephone: 703-749-1000
Telecopier: 703-893-8029
Washington, D.C. Office: 601 Pennsylvania Ave, N.W., Suite 900.
Telephone: 202-462-4697.
Irvine California Office: 3 Park Plaza, Suite 1530.
Telephone: 714-852-6700.

MEMBERS OF FIRM

John B. Tieder, Jr.
Robert G. Watt
Julian F. Hoffar
Robert M. Fitzgerald
Robert K. Cox
William R. Chambers
David C. Romm
Charles E. Raley (Not admitted in VA)
Francis X. McCullough
Barbara G. Werther (Not admitted in VA)
Garry R. Boehlert
Thomas B. Newell
Lewis J. Baker
Benjamin T. Riddles, II
Timothy F. Brown
Richard G. Mann, Jr.
David C. Mancini
David C. Haas
Henry D. Danforth
Carter B. Reid
Donna S. McCaffrey
Mark J. Groff (Not admitted in VA)
Mark A. Sgarlata
Daniel E. Cohen
Michael G. Long (Resident, Irvine, California Office)

OF COUNSEL

Avv. Roberto Tassi
Clyde Harold Slease (Not admitted in VA)

ASSOCIATES

Thomas J. Powell
Douglas C. Proxmire
Tara L. Vautin
Edward Parrott
Steven G. Schassler
Joseph H. Bucci
Steven J. Weber
Paul A. Varela
Vivian Katsantonis
Charlie Lee

(See Next Column)

WATT, TIEDER & HOFFAR—*Continued*

ASSOCIATES (Continued)

Kathleen A. Olden
Christopher P. Pappas (Resident, Irvine, California Office)
Shelly L. Ewald
Christopher J. Brasco
Jean V. Misterek
Charles W. Durant
Susan Latham Timoner
Fred A. Mendicino
Susan G. Sisskind
Robert G. Barbour
Keith C. Phillips
Marybeth Zientek Gaul
Timothy E. Heffernan (Not admitted in VA)
William Drew Mallender
James Moore Donahue
Heidi Brown Hering
Kerrin Maureen McCormick (Not admitted in VA)
Gretal J. Toker

For full biographical listings, see the Martindale-Hubbell Law Directory

*RICHMOND,** (Ind. City; Seat of Henrico Co.)

WILLIAMS, MULLEN, CHRISTIAN & DOBBINS, A PROFESSIONAL CORPORATION (AV)

Two James Center, 1021 East Cary Street, P.O. Box 1320, 23210-1320
Telephone: 804-643-1991
Fax: 804-783-6456
Glen Allen, Virginia Office: 4401 Waterfront Drive, Suite 140.
Telephone: 804-965-9168.
Fax: 804-965-0955.
Washington, D.C. Office: 1575 Eye Street, N.W.
Telephone: 202-289-6200.
Fax: 202-289-4126.

William D. Bayliss
Charles L. Cabell
Robert E. Eicher
Samuel W. Hixon, III
A. Brooks Hock
William R. Mauck, Jr.
Walter H. Ryland
Andrea Rowse Stiles

Andrew M. Condlin
Glen Andrew Lea
George W. Marget, III

For Complete List of Firm Personnel, See General Section

For full biographical listings, see the Martindale-Hubbell Law Directory

WASHINGTON

KENNEWICK, Benton Co.

HERRIG & VOGT (AV)

3104 West Kennewick Avenue, Suite D, 99336
Telephone: 509-943-6691
Fax: 509-783-6477
Sacramento, California Office: 2150 River Plaza Drive, Suite 155, 95833.
Telephone: 916-649-8138.
Telecopier: 916-649-2864.

MEMBERS OF FIRM

John R. Herrig
George F. Vogt, Jr. (Not admitted in WA)
David D. Hilton

For full biographical listings, see the Martindale-Hubbell Law Directory

*SEATTLE,** King Co.

CHISM, JACOBSON & JOHNSON (AV)

3950 Washington Mutual Tower, 1201 Third Avenue, 98101-3013
Telephone: 206-689-5650
Facsimile: 206-689-5649

Anita C. Braker
J. Patrick Brown
Geoffrey P. Chism
E. John Compatore
Michael C. Hoover
Jean E. Huffington
Daniel C. Jacobson
A. Kyle Johnson
William T. McKay
LuAnne Perry
H. Troy Romero

Representative Clients: Atcon Construction; Construction & Rigging, Inc.; Ledcor Industries; Longview Plumbing & Heading; McAbee Construction Co.; Sacotte Construction; Seven Sisters, Inc.; Tri-State Construction, Inc.; Valley General Hospital; Osborne Construction Co.

For full biographical listings, see the Martindale-Hubbell Law Directory

GAITÁN & CUSACK (AV)

30th Floor Two Union Square, 601 Union Street, 98101-2324
Telephone: 206-521-3000
Facsimile: 206-386-5259
Anchorage, Alaska Office: 425 G Street, Suite 760.
Telephone: 907-278-3001.
Facsimile: 907-278-6068.

(See Next Column)

San Francisco, California Office: 275 Battery Street, 20th Floor.
Telephone: 415-398-5562.
Fax: 415-398-4033.
Washington, D.C. Office: 2000 L Street, Suite 200.
Telephone: 202-296-4637.
Fax: 202-296-4650.

MEMBERS OF FIRM

José E. Gaitán
Kenneth J. Cusack (Resident, Anchorage, Alaska Office)
William F. Knowles
Ronald L. Bozarth

OF COUNSEL

Howard K. Todd
Gary D. Gayton
Michel P. Stern (Also practicing alone, Bellevue, Washington)
Christopher A. Byrne
Patricia D. Ryan

ASSOCIATES

Mary F. O'Boyle
Bruce H. Williams
David J. Onsager
Diana T. Jimenez
Robert T. Mimbu
Cristina C. Kapela
Camilla M. Hedberg
John E. Lenker
Kathleen C. Healy

Representative Clients: Vertecs, Inc.; Texcel International; Specialty Excavating; The Erectron Company; McGill Construction; The Chubb Group of Insurance Companies; Commercial Union Insurance Company; Transamerica Insurance Companies; CNA Insurance Companies.

For full biographical listings, see the Martindale-Hubbell Law Directory

J. RICHARD MANNING (AV)

925 Logan Building, 98101
Telephone: 206-623-6302
Fax: 206-624-3865

Reference: West One Bank, Ranier Square, Seattle, Washington.

For full biographical listings, see the Martindale-Hubbell Law Directory

OLES, MORRISON & RINKER (AV)

3300 Columbia Center, 701 Fifth Avenue, 98104-7082
Telephone: 206-623-3427
Telecopier: 206-682-6234

MEMBERS OF FIRM

Seth W. Morrison
David C. Stewart
Sam E. Baker, Jr.
Arthur D. McGarry
B. Michael Schestopol
Theodore L. Preg
Robert J. Burke
David H. Karlen
Bradley L. Powell
Douglas S. Oles
Peter N. Ralston
Mark F. O'Donnell
John Lukjanowicz
James F. Nagle
Glenn R. Nelson
J. Craig Rusk
T. Daniel Heffernan
Harlan M. Hatfield
Robert W. Sargeant

ASSOCIATES

Todd M. Nelson
Traeger Machetanz
Richard T. Black
Evalyn K. Hodges
William D Garcia (Not admitted in WA)
George T. Schroth

OF COUNSEL

Stuart G. Oles

For full biographical listings, see the Martindale-Hubbell Law Directory

SHORT CRESSMAN & BURGESS (AV)

A Partnership including Professional Service Corporations
3000 First Interstate Center, 999 Third Avenue, 98104-4088
Telephone: 206-682-3333
Fax: 206-340-8856

MEMBERS OF FIRM

Paul R. Cressman, Sr. (P.S.)
John O. Burgess
James A. Oliver
David R. Koopmans
Kenneth L. Myer
Paul R. Cressman, Jr.
Andrew W. Maron
Christopher J. Soelling
Bryan P. Coluccio
Christopher R. Osborn
Claudia L. Crawford
Walter H. Olsen, Jr.

Representative Clients: Lakeside Industries; D.W. Close Co.; Cochran Electric Co., Inc.; ; Collins Electric; Hos Brothers Construction; Fruhling Construction; Morse Construction Group; Tri-State Construction, Inc.; Drury Construction Co., Inc.; Dyad Construction.

For Complete List of Firm Personnel, See General Section

For full biographical listings, see the Martindale-Hubbell Law Directory

TOUSLEY BRAIN (AV)

A Partnership
56th Floor, AT&T Gateway Tower, 700 Fifth Avenue, 98104-5056
Telephone: 206-682-5600
Facsimile: 206-682-2992

(See Next Column)

TOUSLEY BRAIN, *Seattle—Continued*

Russell F. Tousley
Kim D. Stephens (Mr.)
Vincent B. DePillis
Rebecca A. McIntyre
Brian P. Ward

Representative Clients: Allied Construction & Supply; Associated General Contractors of Washington; Cochrane Electric; Electrical Energy Contractors, Inc.; Evergreen State Construction, Inc.; Lamb Longo, Inc.; Obayashi; Olympic Associates, Inc.; Pirie Construction Co.

For Complete List of Firm Personnel, See General Section

For full biographical listings, see the Martindale-Hubbell Law Directory

*SPOKANE,** Spokane Co.

WINSTON & CASHATT, LAWYERS A PROFESSIONAL SERVICE CORPORATION (AV)

1900 Seafirst Financial Center, 99201-0695
Telephone: 509-838-6131
Facsimile: 509-838-1416
Coeur d'Alene, Idaho Office: 250 Northwest Boulevard, Suite 107A.
Telephone: 208-667-2103.
Facsimile: 208-765-2121.

Patrick A. Sullivan
Lynden O. Rasmussen
Lawrence H. Vance, Jr.
C. Matthew Andersen
Carl E. Hueber
Beverly L. Anderson

Representative Clients: Associated General Contractors, Inland Empire Chapter; Aztech Electric, Inc.; Harza Engineering Company; Johnson Controls, Inc.; Lydig Construction, Inc.; Max J. Kuney Co.; Performance Contracting, Inc.; Power City Electric, Inc.; Superior Air Handling Corporation; W.A. Botting Co.

For Complete List of Firm Personnel, See General Section

For full biographical listings, see the Martindale-Hubbell Law Directory

WEST VIRGINIA

*CHARLESTON,** Kanawha Co.

JACKSON & KELLY (AV)

1600 Laidley Tower, P.O. Box 553, 25322
Telephone: 304-340-1000
Fax: 304-340-1130
Martinsburg, West Virginia Office: 300 Foxcroft Avenue, P.O. Box 1068.
Telephone: 304-263-8800.
Morgantown, West Virginia Office: 6000 Hampton Center, P.O. Box 619.
Telephone: 304-599-3000.
New Martinsville, West Virginia Office: 256 Russell Avenue, P.O. Box 68.
Telephone: 304-455-1751.
Charles Town, West Virginia Office: 700 East Washington Street, P.O. Box 983.
Telephone: 304-728-6088.
Clarksburg, West Virginia Office: 203 Main Street, P.O. Box 1587.
Telephone: 304-623-3002.
Lexington, Kentucky Office: 175 East Main Street, Suite 500, P.O. Box 2150.
Telephone: 606-255-9500.
Washington, D. C. Office: 2401 Pennsylvania Avenue, N.W., Suite 400.
Telephone: 202-973-0200.
Denver, Colorado Office: Suite 2710, 1660 Lincoln Street.
Telephone: 303-837-0003.

MEMBERS OF FIRM

Thomas E. Potter
John R. Lukens
Stephen R. Crislip
Barry S. Settles (Resident Lexington, Kentucky Office)
James R. Snyder
Mary Clare Eros (Martinsburg and Charles Town, West Virginia Offices)
John Philip Melick

ASSOCIATES

Robert L. Johns
William Prentice Young (Martinsburg and Charles Town, West Virginia Offices)

For Complete List of Firm Personnel, See General Section

For full biographical listings, see the Martindale-Hubbell Law Directory

*CLARKSBURG,** Harrison Co.

JOHNSON, SIMMERMAN & BROUGHTON, L.C. (AV)

Suite 210, Goff Building, P.O. Box 150, 26301
Telephone: 304-624-6555
Telecopier: 304-623-4933

(See Next Column)

Charles G. Johnson
Frank E. Simmerman, Jr.
Marcia Allen Broughton

For full biographical listings, see the Martindale-Hubbell Law Directory

WISCONSIN

*MADISON,** Dane Co.

KAY & ANDERSEN, S.C. (AV)

One Point Place, Suite 201, 53719
Telephone: 608-833-0077
Fax: 608-833-3901

Robert J. Kay
Randall J. Andersen

Edith M. Petersen

OF COUNSEL

James C. Geisler

Representative Clients: Flad Architects; Hooper Construction Corp.; Van Ert Electric Company, Inc.; Shambaugh & Son, Inc.; Magaw Electric Construction, Inc.; Gilbert Construction, Co.; Pieper Power of Milwaukee, Wisconsin, Bay West, Inc.

For full biographical listings, see the Martindale-Hubbell Law Directory

LAWTON & CATES, S.C. (AV)

214 West Mifflin Street, 53703-2594
Telephone: 608-256-9031
Fax: 608-256-4670

John C. Carlson
Kent I. Carnell

Reference: Bank One, Madison.

For full biographical listings, see the Martindale-Hubbell Law Directory

*MILWAUKEE,** Milwaukee Co.

DECKER & GUNTA, S.C. (AV)

219 North Milwaukee Street, 53202
Telephone: 414-291-7979
Facsimile: 414-291-7960

John R. Decker
Gregg J. Gunta

Kevin P. Reak
Jennifer S. Walther
Ann C. Wirth

OF COUNSEL

John A. Decker

For full biographical listings, see the Martindale-Hubbell Law Directory

KOHNER, MANN & KAILAS, S.C. (AV)

1572 East Capitol Drive, P.O. Box 19982, 53211-0982
Telephone: 414-962-5110
Fax: 414-962-8725

Marvin L. Kohner (1908-1975)
Robert L. Mann
Steve Kailas
Mark R. Wolters
Jordan B. Reich
David S. Chartier

Roy Paul Roth
Gary P. Lantzy
Christopher C. Kailas
Robert E. Nailen
Matthew P. Gerdisch
Darrell R. Zall
Daniel J. Flynn
Timothy L. Zuberbier
Shawn G. Rice

Representative Clients: EcoLab, Inc.; Parker Pen Co.; Ray O Vac, Inc.

For full biographical listings, see the Martindale-Hubbell Law Directory

QUARLES & BRADY (AV)

411 East Wisconsin Avenue, 53202-4497
Telephone: 414-277-5000
Cable Address: "Lawdock"
Fax: 414-271-3552.
TWX: 910-262-3426
Madison, Wisconsin Office: Firstar Plaza, One South Pinckney Street, P.O. Box 2113.
Telephone: 608-251-5000.
Fax: 608-251-9166.
West Palm Beach, Florida Office: 222 Lakeview Avenue, 4th Floor.
Telephone: 407-653-5000.
Fax: 407-653-5333.
Naples, Florida Office: Barnett Center, 4501 Tamiami Trail North.
Telephone: 813-262-5959.
Fax: 813-434-4999.

(See Next Column)

QUARLES & BRADY—*Continued*

Phoenix, Arizona Office: One Camelback Building, One East Camelback Road, Suite 400.
Telephone: 602-230-5500.
Fax: 602-230-5598.

MEMBERS OF FIRM
(ALPHABETICALLY BY YEAR OF ADMISSION TO BAR)

Ronald L. Wallenfang
Robert E. Doyle, Jr. (Resident, Naples, Florida Office)

ASSOCIATES

William G. Shofstall (Resident, West Palm Beach, Florida Office)
Kevin A. Delorey (Resident, Madison Office)

For Complete List of Firm Personnel, See General Section

For full biographical listings, see the Martindale-Hubbell Law Directory

WYOMING

*CASPER,** Natrona Co.

BROWN & DREW (AV)

Casper Business Center, Suite 800, 123 West First Street, 82601-2486
Telephone: 307-234-1000
800-877-6755
Telefax: 307-265-8025

MEMBERS OF FIRM

Morris R. Massey
Harry B. Durham, III
Donn J. McCall
Thomas F. Reese

ASSOCIATES

Jon B. Huss
Courtney Robert Kepler
Drew A. Perkins

OF COUNSEL

B. J. Baker

Attorneys for: First Interstate Bank of Wyoming, N.A.; Norwest Bank Wyoming, N.A.; The CIT Group/Industrial Financing; Aetna Casualty & Surety Co.; The Doctor's Co.; MEDMARC; WOTCO, Inc.; Chevron USA; Kerr-McGee Corp.; Chicago and NorthWestern Transportation Company.

For Complete List of Firm Personnel, See General Section

For full biographical listings, see the Martindale-Hubbell Law Directory

PUERTO RICO

SAN JUAN, San Juan Dist.

INDIANO, WILLIAMS & WEINSTEIN-BACAL

Hato Rey Tower, 21st Floor, 268 Muñoz Rivera Avenue (Hato Rey), 00918
Telephone: 809-754-2323; 763-0485
Fax: 809-766-3366
St. Thomas, Virgin Islands Office: Stuart A. Weinstein-Bacal, P.O. Box 9820, Charlotte Amalie, 00801.
Telephone: 809-776-2500.
Telecopier: 809-779-6918.

MEMBERS OF FIRM

Stuart A. Weinstein-Bacal
David C. Indiano
Jeffrey M. Williams

ASSOCIATES

Javier A. Morales Ramos
Madeline Garcia-Rodriguez

For full biographical listings, see the Martindale-Hubbell Law Directory

CANADA
ALBERTA

*EDMONTON,** Edmonton Jud. Dist.

PARLEE MCLAWS (AV)

15th Floor Manulife Place, 10180 101st Street, T5J 4K1
Telephone: 403-423-8500
Telecopier: 403-423-2870
Calgary, Alberta Office: 3400, Western Canadian Place, 707 - 8th Avenue, S.W.
Telephone: 403-294-7000.
Telecopier: 403-265-8263.

(See Next Column)

MEMBERS OF FIRM

C. H. Kerr, Q.C.
M. D. MacDonald
K. F. Bailey, Q.C.
R. B. Davison, Q.C.
F. R. Haldane
P. E. J. Curran
D. G. Finlay
J. K. McFadyen
R. C. Secord
D. L. Kennedy
D. C. Rolf
D. F. Pawlowski
A. A. Garber
R. P. James
R. A. Newton, Q.C.
T. A. Cockrall, Q.C.
H. D. Montemurro
F. J. Niziol
R. W. Wilson
I. L. MacLachlan
R. O. Langley
R. G. McBean
J. T. Neilson
E. G. Rice
J. F. McGinnis
J. H. H. Hockin
G. W. Jaycock
M. J. K. Nikel

MEMBERS OF FIRM (Continued)

D. C. Wintermute
J. L. Cairns
B. J. Curial
S. L. May
M. S. Poretti

ASSOCIATES

C. R. Head
A.W. Slemko
L. H. Hamdon
K.A. Smith
K. D. Fallis-Howell
D. S. Tam
J.W. McClure
F.H. Belzil
R.A. Renz
J.G. Paulson
K. E. Buss
B. L. Andriachuk
P. E. S. J. Kennedy
R. Feraco
R.J. Billingsley
N.B.R. Thompson
P. A. Shenher
I. C. Johnson
K.G. Koshman
D.D. Dubrule
G. T. Lund
W.D. Johnston
G. E. Flemming
K. P. Nayyer

For full biographical listings, see the Martindale-Hubbell Law Directory

CANADA
BRITISH COLUMBIA

*VANCOUVER,** Vancouver Co.

RUSSELL & DUMOULIN (AV)

2100-1075 West Georgia Street, V6E 3G2
Telephone: 604-631-3131
Fax: 604-631-3232
A Member of the national association of Borden DuMoulin Howard Gervais, comprising Russell & DuMoulin, Vancouver, British Columbia; Howard Mackie, Calgary, Alberta; Borden & Elliot, Toronto, Ontario; Mackenzie Gervais, Montreal, Quebec and Borden DuMoulin Howard Gervais, London, England.
Strategic Alliance with Perkins Coie with offices in Seattle, Spokane and Bellevue, Washington; Portland, Oregon; Anchorage, Alaska; Los Angeles, California; Washington, D.C.; Hong Kong and Taipei, Taiwan.
Represented in Hong Kong by Vincent T.K. Cheung, Yap & Co.

MEMBERS OF FIRM

Helmut K. Johannsen
Marina A. Pratchett

Representative Clients: Alcan Smelters & Chemicals Ltd.; The Bank of Nova Scotia; Canada Trust Co.; The Canada Life Assurance Co.; Forest Industrial Relations Ltd.; Honda Canada Inc.; IBM Canada Ltd.; Macmillan Bloedel Ltd.; Nissho Iwai Canada Ltd.; The Toronto-Dominion Bank.

For Complete List of Firm Personnel, See General Section

For full biographical listings, see the Martindale-Hubbell Law Directory

SINGLETON URQUHART MACDONALD (AV)

1200 - 1125 Howe Street, V6Z 2K8
Telephone: 604-682-7474
Fax: 604-682-1283
Calgary, Alberta Office: 203 - 200 Barclay Parade, S.W., T2P 0J1.
Telephone: 403-261-9043.
Fax: 403-265-4632.

Glenn A. Urquhart
A. Webster Macdonald, Jr., Q.C. (Resident, Calgary Office)
John R. Singleton
Derek A. Brindle

Representative Clients: Agra Industries Ltd.; Bechtel Inc.; B.C. Hydro & Power Authority; Committee of Canadian Architectural Councils; Encon Insurance Managers, Inc.; Kilborn Engineering Ltd.; Monenco Limited; H.A. Simons Ltd.; GAN Canada.

For Complete List of Firm Personnel, See General Section

For full biographical listings, see the Martindale-Hubbell Law Directory

CANADA
NOVA SCOTIA

*HALIFAX,** Halifax Co.

McInnes Cooper & Robertson (AV)

1601 Lower Water Street, P.O. Box 730, B3J 2V1
Telephone: 902-425-6500
Fax: 902-425-6350
St. John's, Newfoundland Office: Suite 602, Scotia Centre, 235 Water Street, P.O. Box 547. A1C, 5K8.
Telephone: 709-726-9500.
Fax: 709-726-9550.

Stewart McInnes, P.C., Q.C.
Christopher C. Robinson
Thomas E. Hart
Scott C. Norton
Eric LeDrew
George W. MacDonald, Q.C.
Harvey L. Morrison
David A. Graves
Stephen J. Kingston
Malcolm D. Boyle

ASSOCIATES

John Kulik
J. David Connolly
Aidan J. Meade
Michelle C. Awad

Attorneys for: Bank of Nova Scotia; Imperial Oil, Limited; Frank B. Hall & Co., Inc. (New York); American Steamship Owners Protection & Indemnity Association, Inc.; Coca-Cola, Ltd.; Scott Worldwide Inc.; Hong Kong Bank of Canada.

For Complete List of Firm Personnel, See General Section

For full biographical listings, see the Martindale-Hubbell Law Directory

CANADA
ONTARIO

*TORONTO,** Regional Munic. of York

Borden & Elliot (AV)

Barristers & Solicitors
Scotia Plaza, 40 King Street West, M5H 3Y4
Telephone: 416-367-6000
Telecopier: 416-367-6749
Internet: @ borden.com
A Member of the national association of Borden DuMoulin Howard Gervais, comprising Borden & Elliot in Toronto, Ontario, Russell & DuMoulin in Vancouver, British Columbia, Howard, Mackie in Calgary, Alberta and Mackenzie Gervais in Montréal, Québec. Borden DuMoulin Howard Gervais also operates an office in London, England.

MEMBER AND ASSOCIATES

Kenneth W. Scott, Q.C.

For Complete List of Firm Personnel, See General Section

For full biographical listings, see the Martindale-Hubbell Law Directory

CANADA
SASKATCHEWAN

*REGINA,** Regina Jud. Centre

MacPherson Leslie & Tyerman (AV)

1500-1874 Scarth Street, S4P 4E9
Telephone: 306-347-8000
Telecopier: 306-352-5250
Saskatoon, Saskatchewan Office: 1500-410 22nd Street East, S7K 5T6.
Telephone: 306-975-7100.
Telecopier: 306-975-7145.

MEMBER OF FIRM

Robert B. Pletch, Q.C.

For Complete List of Firm Personnel, See General Section

For full biographical listings, see the Martindale-Hubbell Law Directory

CRIMINAL TRIAL PRACTICE

ALABAMA

*BIRMINGHAM,** Jefferson Co.

Baxley, Dillard, Dauphin & McKnight (AV)
2000 Sixteenth Avenue South, 35205
Telephone: 205-939-0995
Telecopier: 205-939-5025

MEMBERS OF FIRM

William J. Baxley
Joel E. Dillard
Charles A. Dauphin
Stewart D. McKnight, III

ASSOCIATE

Donald R. James, Jr

For full biographical listings, see the Martindale-Hubbell Law Directory

Richard S. Jaffe, P.C. (AV)
1905 Fourteenth Avenue South, 35205
Telephone: 205-930-9800
Telecopier: 205-930-9809

Richard S. Jaffe

Stephen A. Strickland
Dennis Wayne Jacobs

For full biographical listings, see the Martindale-Hubbell Law Directory

Redden, Mills & Clark (AV)
940 First Alabama Bank Building, 35203
Telephone: 205-322-0457
Fax: 205-322-8481

MEMBERS OF FIRM

L. Drew Redden
William H. Mills
William N. Clark
Gerald L. Miller
Stephen W. Shaw

ASSOCIATES

Maxwell H. Pulliam, Jr.
Joseph H. Hilley

References: SouthTrust Bank; First Alabama Bank.

For full biographical listings, see the Martindale-Hubbell Law Directory

*CHATOM,** Washington Co.

Turner, Onderdonk, Kimbrough & Howell, P.A. (AV)
100 Central Avenue, P.O. Drawer 1389, 36518
Telephone: 334-847-2237
Fax: 334-847-3115
Mobile, Alabama Office: 1359 Dauphin Street, P.O. Box 2821.
Telephone: 205-432-2855.
Fax: 205-432-2863.

Edward P. Turner, Jr.
A. Michael Onderdonk
William A. Kimbrough, Jr. (Resident, Mobile Office)
Gordon K. Howell
Marc E. Bradley (Resident, Mobile Office)

Halron W. Turner
Frank Woodson (Resident, Mobile Office)
David M. Huggins (Resident, Mobile Office)
E. Tatum Turner

For full biographical listings, see the Martindale-Hubbell Law Directory

*GADSDEN,** Etowah Co.

Floyd, Keener, Cusimano & Roberts, P.C. (AV)
816 Chestnut Street, P.O. Box 49, 35902
Telephone: 205-547-6328
Fax: 205-546-8173

Jack Floyd
Larry H. Keener

Mary Ann Ross Stackhouse
John D. Floyd

For Complete List of Firm Personnel, See General Section

For full biographical listings, see the Martindale-Hubbell Law Directory

*MOBILE,** Mobile Co.

Briskman & Binion, P.C. (AV)
205 Church Street, P.O. Box 43, 36601
Telephone: 334-433-7600
Fax: 334-433-4485

Donald M. Briskman
Mack B. Binion

Donna Ward Black
Alex F. Lankford, IV
Christ N. Coumanis

A List of Representative Clients will be furnished upon request.
References: First Alabama Bank; AmSouth Bank, N.A.; Southtrust Bank of Mobile.

For full biographical listings, see the Martindale-Hubbell Law Directory

Thomas M. Haas (AV)
258 State Street, 36603
Telephone: 334-432-0457

ASSOCIATE

N. Ruth Haas

ALASKA

*ANCHORAGE,** Third Judicial District

Dan E. Dennis (AV)
Suite 301 CBA Building, 3003 Minnesota Drive, 99503
Telephone: 907-272-5471
Telefax: 907-272-4474

Reference: National Bank of Alaska.

For full biographical listings, see the Martindale-Hubbell Law Directory

Young, Sanders & Feldman, Inc. (AV)
Suite 400, 500 L Street, 99501
Telephone: 907-272-3538
Telecopier: 907-274-0819

Jeffrey M. Feldman

Reference: Key Bank of Alaska.

For full biographical listings, see the Martindale-Hubbell Law Directory

ARIZONA

*FLAGSTAFF,** Coconino Co.

Aspey, Watkins & Diesel (AV)
123 North San Francisco, 86001
Telephone: 602-774-1478
Facsimile: 602-774-1043
Sedona, Arizona Office: 120 Soldier Pass Road.
Telephone: 602-282-5955.
Facsimile: 602-282-5962.
Page, Arizona Office: 904 North Navajo.
Telephone: 602-645-9694.
Winslow, Arizona Office: 205 North Williamson.
Telephone: 602-289-5963.
Cottonwood, Arizona Office: 905 Cove Parkway, Unite 201.
Telephone: 602-639-1881.

MEMBERS OF FIRM

Frederick M. Fritz Aspey
Harold L. Watkins
Louis M. Diesel
Bruce S. Griffen
Donald H. Bayles, Jr.
Kaign N. Christy
John J. Dempsey

Zachary Markham
James E. Ledbetter
Whitney Cunningham
Holly S. Karris

LEGAL SUPPORT PERSONNEL

Deborah D. Roberts (Legal Assistant)
C. Denece Pruett (Legal Assistant)
Dominic M. Marino, Jr, (Paralegal Assistant)

Representative Clients: Farmer's Insurance Company of Arizona; Kelley-Moore Paint Co.; Pepsi-Cola Bottling Company of Northern Arizona; Bill Luke's Chrysler-Plymouth, Inc.; First American Title Insurance Company ; Transamerica Title Insurance Co.; Page Electric Utility; Comprehensive Access Health Plan, Inc.

(See Next Column)

ASPEY, WATKINS & DIESEL, *Flagstaff—Continued*

Reference: First Interstate Bank-Arizona, N.A., Flagstaff, Arizona.

For full biographical listings, see the Martindale-Hubbell Law Directory

*PHOENIX,** Maricopa Co.

BLACK & GOTTLIEB (AV)

3101 North Central Avenue, Suite 530, 85012
Telephone: 602-265-7200
Fax: 602-265-2431

Michael V. Black — Stacey F. Gottlieb

For full biographical listings, see the Martindale-Hubbell Law Directory

BURCH & CRACCHIOLO, P.A. (AV)

702 East Osborn Road, Suite 200, 85014
Telephone: 602-274-7611
Fax: 602-234-0341
Mailing Address: P.O. Box 16882, Phoenix, AZ, 85011

Stephen E. Silver — David G. Derickson
Jess A. Lorona

Josephine Cuccurullo — Stephen M. Hart

Representative Clients: Bashas' Inc.; Farmers Insurance Group; U-Haul International, Inc.

For Complete List of Firm Personnel, See General Section

For full biographical listings, see the Martindale-Hubbell Law Directory

CROWE & SCOTT, A PROFESSIONAL ASSOCIATION (AV)

1100 East Washington Suite 200, 85034
Telephone: 602-252-2570
Fax: 602-252-1939

Thomas N. Crowe — Michael B. Scott

For full biographical listings, see the Martindale-Hubbell Law Directory

DEBUS & KAZAN, LTD. (AV)

335 East Palm Lane, 85004
Telephone: 602-257-8900
Fax: 602-257-0723

Larry L. Debus — Lawrence Ian Kazan

Tracey Westerhausen

References: Firstar Metropolitan Bank; Citibank, Arizona.

For full biographical listings, see the Martindale-Hubbell Law Directory

FRIEDL, RICHTER & BURI (AV)

Suite 200, 1440 East Washington Street, 85034
Telephone: 602-495-1000
Fax: 602-271-4733

MEMBERS OF FIRM

William J. Friedl — Charles E. Buri
William E. Moore

For full biographical listings, see the Martindale-Hubbell Law Directory

GOLDSTEIN, KINGSLEY & MCGRODER, LTD. A PROFESSIONAL CORPORATION (AV)

Professional Arts Building, 1110 East McDowell Road, 85006-2678
Telephone: 602-254-5581
Fax: 602-258-7390
Other Phoenix Office: 2200 East Camelback Road, Suite 221, 85016-3456.
Telephone: 602-957-1500.
Telecopier: 602-956-9294.

Philip T. Goldstein — Kathleen Delarosa
Pamela L. Kingsley — Suzanne P. Clarke
Patrick J. McGroder, III (East Camelback Road Office)

For full biographical listings, see the Martindale-Hubbell Law Directory

RICHARD J. HERTZBERG (AV)

16 Luhrs Arcade 11 West Jefferson, 85003
Telephone: 602-253-1781
Fax: 602-253-0928

For full biographical listings, see the Martindale-Hubbell Law Directory

KIMERER, LAVELLE, HAY & HOOD, P.L.C. (AV)

2715 North Third Street, 85004
Telephone: 602-279-5900
FAX: 602-264-5566

(See Next Column)

COUNSEL

Clark L. Derrick

Michael D. Kimerer

For Complete List of Firm Personnel, See General Section

For full biographical listings, see the Martindale-Hubbell Law Directory

LEWIS AND ROCA (AV)

A Partnership including Professional Corporations
40 North Central Avenue, 85004-4429
Telephone: 602-262-5311
Fax: 602-262-5747
Tucson, Arizona Office: One South Church Avenue, Suite 700.
Telephone: 602-622-2090.
Fax: 602-622-3088.

MEMBERS OF FIRM

Jordan Green — Edward F. Novak

ASSOCIATE

Charles W. Steese

For Complete List of Firm Personnel, See General Section

For full biographical listings, see the Martindale-Hubbell Law Directory

CRAIG MEHRENS, P.A. (AV)

1005 North Second Street, 85004
Telephone: 602-258-5151
FAX: 602-257-8316

Craig Mehrens — Amy Wilemon

Reference: Firstar Metropolitan Bank & Trust.

For full biographical listings, see the Martindale-Hubbell Law Directory

MEYER, HENDRICKS, VICTOR, OSBORN & MALEDON, A PROFESSIONAL ASSOCIATION (AV)

2929 North Central Avenue Suite 2100, 85012-2794
Telephone: 602-640-9000
Facsimile: (24 Hrs.) 602-640-9050
Mailing Address: P.O. Box 33449, 85067-3449,

William J. Maledon — W. Scott Bales
Larry A. Hammond — Sigmund G. Popko

Evan Haglund — Jamie McAlister

OF COUNSEL

Michael A. Berch

Reference: Bank One Arizona, NA.

For Complete List of Firm Personnel, See General Section

For full biographical listings, see the Martindale-Hubbell Law Directory

MILLER & MILLER, LTD. (AV)

Suite 2250, 3200 North Central Avenue, 85012
Telephone: 602-266-8440
Fax: 602-266-8453

Murray Miller — Robert M. Miller
Richard K. Miller — Marcus Westervelt

For full biographical listings, see the Martindale-Hubbell Law Directory

SNELL & WILMER (AV)

One Arizona Center, 85004-0001
Telephone: 602-382-6000
Fax: 602-382-6070
Tucson, Arizona Office: 1500 Norwest Tower, One South Church Avenue 85701-1612.
Telephone: 602-882-1200.
Fax: 602-884-1294.
Orange County Office: 1920 Main Street, Suite 1200, P.O. Box 19601, Irvine, California, 92714.
Telephone: 714-253-2700.
Fax: 714-955-2507.
Salt Lake City, Utah Office: Broadway Centre, 111 East Broadway, Suite 900, 84111.
Telephone: 801-237-1900.
Fax: 801-237-1950.

OF COUNSEL

Mark Wilmer — Frank L. Snell
Edward Jacobson — Jarril F. Kaplan
James D. Bruner — John A. Greene

(See Next Column)

SNELL & WILMER—*Continued*

MEMBERS OF FIRM

Frederick K. Steiner, Jr.
John J. Bouma
Richard K. Mallery
Robert C. Bates
Jon S. Cohen
Warren E. Platt
Jay D. Wiley
William A. Hicks, III
George H. Lyons
Peter J. Rathwell
Daniel J. McAuliffe
Steven M. Wheeler
Donald D. Colburn
Douglas W. Seitz
Robert J. Deeny
Joseph T. Melczer, III
William R. Hayden
Gerard Morales
Robert B. Hoffman
Barry D. Halpern
Joel P. Hoxie
James R. Condo
Lonnie J. Williams, Jr.
Richard W. Sheffield
Vaughn A. Crawford
Arthur P. Greenfield
Thomas R. Hoecker
David A. Sprentall
Peter G. Santin
Charles A. Pulaski, Jr.
Suzanne McCann
Terry Morris Roman
Donald L. Gaffney
Matthew P. Feeney
Arthur T. Anderson
Patrick E. Hoog
Joyce Kline Wright
Quinn Williams
Richard W. Shapiro
Rebecca A. Winterscheidt
Craig K. Williams
Martha E. Gibbs
Katherine M. Harmeyer
Jeffrey Messing
James J. Sienicki
Jody Kathleen Pokorski
E. Jeffrey Walsh
George J. Coleman, III
Timothy G. O'Neill
Heidi L. McNeil
G. Van Velsor Wolf, Jr.
Timothy W. Moser
Janet E. Barton
Stephen M. Hopkins
Kevin J. Parker
Donald H. Smith
Peter M. Wittekind
Charles E. James, Jr.
Alex B. Marconi
Steven S. Guy
Christopher H. Bayley
David E. Weiss, Jr.
Nicholas J. Wood
Richard D. Blau
Robert R. Kinas
Samuel C. Cowley
Shawn M. McLeran
Sherman O. Parrett
Steven D. Pidgeon
Michael K. Kelly
Donald J. Lenkszus

SENIOR ATTORNEYS

Bruce P. White
Shirley J. Wahl
Lisa M. Coulter
Cheryl A. Ikegami
William P. Allen

ASSOCIATES

Benjamin D. Aguilera
Sondri Allison
Timothy D. Brown
Terri N.A. Buccino
Patrick G. Byrne
Brian J. Campbell
Nancy Kay Campbell
Timothy J. Casey
Jeffrey Webb Crockett
Roger D. Curley
Barbara J. Dawson
Michael M. Donahey
Elisabeth B. Donnovin
William J. Donoher, Jr.
Michael C. Douglass
Clinton J Elliott
Brigitte Finley
Brian J. Foster
Patrick X. Fowler
Stacy Gabriel
Charles F. Hauff, Jr.
Charles P. Keller
Joseph C. Kreamer
Joseph E. Lambert
Jeffery W. Lantz
Christopher J. Littlefield
Christine Broghammer Long
Jeffrey W. Martin
Bob J. McCullough
Andrew G. Miller
Thomas L. Mumaw
Jon S. Musial
Maria Nutile (Not admitted in AZ)
Eugene F. O'Connor II
Jon M. Paladini
Christopher D. Payne
Loren A. Piel
David E. Rauch
Sandra J. Rogers
Carlos D. Ronstadt
GinaMarie Rossano
Philip Randolph Rudd
Sandra L. Seamans
Scott D. Sherman
Thea Foglietta Silverstein
Prithviraj S. Sivananthan
Barrie E. Stachel
Victoria M. Stevens
Marvin S. Swift, Jr.
Ptolemy H. Taylor
Renée Eileen Tetreault
Steve C. Thornton
Randall C. Urbom
Robert C. Venberg
Jonathan F. Weisbard
Robert R. Yoder

For full biographical listings, see the Martindale-Hubbell Law Directory

LAW OFFICES OF RICHARD L. STROHM, P.C. (AV)

2901 North Central Avenue Suite 200, 85012
Telephone: 602-285-5097
Telecopier: 602-285-5198

Richard L. Strohm

Representative Clients: State of Arizona; University of Arizona Medical Center; Ryder Truck Rental; The Trammell Crow Companies; Producer's Network; Sean Young.

For full biographical listings, see the Martindale-Hubbell Law Directory

THOMAS A. THINNES, P.A. (AV)

1005 North Second Street, 85004
Telephone: 602-257-8408
Fax: 602-257-8316

(See Next Column)

Thomas A. Thinnes
Cynthia E. Gonzales

Reference: Firstar Metropolitan Bank & Trust.

For full biographical listings, see the Martindale-Hubbell Law Directory

TOLES & ASSOCIATES, P.C. (AV)

1010 East Jefferson Street, 85034
Telephone: 602-253-1010

M. Jeremy Toles

Richard M. Gerry
Karyn E. Klausner
Rosann K. Johnson
M. L. (Les) Weatherly, Jr.

OF COUNSEL

Barbara A. Jarvis

For full biographical listings, see the Martindale-Hubbell Law Directory

*TUCSON,** Pima Co.

EDWARD P. BOLDING (AV)

110 South Church Avenue, Suite 9300, 85701
Telephone: 602-884-9221
Fax: 602-629-0197

For full biographical listings, see the Martindale-Hubbell Law Directory

DONAU & BOLT (AV)

Suite 501, 3505 North Campbell Avenue, 85719-2033
Telephone: 602-795-8710
Fax: 602-795-0308

MEMBER OF FIRM

Alfred S. Donau III

ASSOCIATE

Sharon M. Wolfkeil

For full biographical listings, see the Martindale-Hubbell Law Directory

HIRSH, DAVIS, WALKER & PICCARRETA, P.C. (AV)

145 South Sixth Avenue, 85701-2007
Telephone: 602-622-6900
Fax: 602-622-0521

For full biographical listings, see the Martindale-Hubbell Law Directory

THE LAW OFFICE OF ROBERT HOOKER (AV)

2525 East Broadway Boulevard, Suite 102, 85716-5303
Telephone: 602-881-2333
800-280-2333
Telecopier: 602-325-0150

For full biographical listings, see the Martindale-Hubbell Law Directory

LAW OFFICES OF NASH & JONES, P.C. (AV)

Suite 4297, Guadalajara Building, La Placita, P.O. Box 2310, 85702-2310
Telephone: 602-792-1613
Fax: 602-628-1079

Walter B. Nash III
Richard B. Jones

LEGAL SUPPORT PERSONNEL

Vicki L. Covey (Legal Assistant)

Reference: Bank One.

For full biographical listings, see the Martindale-Hubbell Law Directory

ARKANSAS

*LITTLE ROCK,** Pulaski Co.

THE PERRONI LAW FIRM, P.A. (AV)

Stewart Building, 801 West Third Street, 72201
Telephone: 501-372-6555
Fax: 501-372-6333

Samuel A. Perroni
Rita S. Looney
Mona J. McNutt

LEGAL SUPPORT PERSONNEL

Sherry Joyce

References: First Commercial Bank, Little Rock, Ark.; Bank of Little Rock, Ark.

For full biographical listings, see the Martindale-Hubbell Law Directory

Little Rock—Continued

WILSON, ENGSTROM, CORUM, DUDLEY & COULTER (AV)

809 West Third Street, P.O. Box 71, 72203
Telephone: 501-375-6453
FAX: 501-375-5914

MEMBERS OF FIRM

Roxanne Wilson (1947-1992)
Stephen Engstrom
Gary D. Corum
Timothy O. Dudley
Nate Coulter

For full biographical listings, see the Martindale-Hubbell Law Directory

CALIFORNIA

BEVERLY HILLS, Los Angeles Co.

DALE S. GRIBOW A PROFESSIONAL CORPORATION (AV)

9777 Wilshire Boulevard, Suite 918, 90212
Telephone: 310-275-4525
Southern California: 1-800-ATORNEY
Fax: 310-275-1016
Palm Desert, California Office: 184 Kiva Drive. 92260.
Telephone: 619-341-4411.
Fax: 619-773-3636.

Dale S. Gribow

Harold R. Freudenheim
Wendy Rossi
Dennis H. Boothe

For full biographical listings, see the Martindale-Hubbell Law Directory

HOCHMAN, SALKIN AND DEROY, A PROFESSIONAL CORPORATION (AV)

9150 Wilshire Boulevard Suite 300, 90212-3414
Telephone: 310-281-3200; 273-1181
Fax: 310-859-1430

Bruce I. Hochman
Avram Salkin
Charles Rettig
Dennis Perez
Steven R. Toscher

OF COUNSEL

George DeRoy
James V. Looby

Michael W. Popoff
Joanna J. Tulio

Reference: Bank of California.

For full biographical listings, see the Martindale-Hubbell Law Directory

MARKS & BROOKLIER (AV)

8383 Wilshire Boulevard, Suite 750, 90211-2406
Telephone: 310-273-7166
Fax: 213-658-8126

MEMBERS OF FIRM

Donald B. Marks
Anthony P. Brooklier

ASSOCIATE

Lawrence C. Ecoff

For full biographical listings, see the Martindale-Hubbell Law Directory

COSTA MESA, Orange Co.

SCHULMAN & MCMILLAN, INCORPORATED (AV)

3200 Park Center Drive, Suite 600, 92626-7148
Telephone: 714-434-9596
Telecopier: 714-434-1823

Marshall M. Schulman

Lynne M. Patterson

For full biographical listings, see the Martindale-Hubbell Law Directory

GLENDALE, Los Angeles Co.

FLANAGAN, BOOTH, UNGER & MOSES (AV)

1156 North Brand Boulevard, 91202-2582
Telephone: 818-244-8694
Fax: 818-244-1852
Santa Ana, California Office: 1851 East First Street, Suite 805. 92705.
Telephone: 714-835-2607.
Fax: 714-835-4825.

MEMBERS OF FIRM

J. Michael Flanagan
Douglas M. Booth
Charles J. Unger
J. Barry Moses

(See Next Column)

ASSOCIATES

Michael T. Danis
James A. Grover

For full biographical listings, see the Martindale-Hubbell Law Directory

IRVINE, Orange Co.

EARLEY & KELLER (AV)

19100 Von Karman Avenue, Suite 950, 92715
Telephone: 714-476-8900
Fax: 714-476-0900

Jack M. Earley
Jennifer L. Keller

For full biographical listings, see the Martindale-Hubbell Law Directory

LONG BEACH, Los Angeles Co.

EDWARD P. GEORGE, JR., INC. A PROFESSIONAL CORPORATION (AV)

Suite 430, 5000 East Spring Street, 90815
Telephone: 310-497-2900
Facsimile: 310-497-2904

Edward P. George, Jr.
Timothy L. O'Reilly

OF COUNSEL

Albert C. S. Ramsey

Reference: Harbor Bank, Long Beach.

For full biographical listings, see the Martindale-Hubbell Law Directory

*LOS ANGELES,** Los Angeles Co.

COLEMAN & MARCUS, A PROFESSIONAL CORPORATION (AV)

Suite 810, 1801 Avenue of the Stars (Century City), 90067
Telephone: 310-277-2700

Richard M. Coleman
Michael D. Marcus
Laurie J. Richards

For full biographical listings, see the Martindale-Hubbell Law Directory

LAW OFFICES OF ROBERT L. CORBIN, P.C. (AV)

601 South Figueroa Street, Suite 3715, 90017-5742
Telephone: 213-680-8220
Facsimile: 213-614-8666

Robert L. Corbin

James Bird
Kevin F. Ruf

For full biographical listings, see the Martindale-Hubbell Law Directory

JOSÉ Y. LAUCHENGCO, JR. (AV)

3545 Wilshire Boulevard, Suite 247, 90010
Telephone: 213-380-9897

For full biographical listings, see the Martindale-Hubbell Law Directory

TALCOTT, LIGHTFOOT, VANDEVELDE, WOEHRLE & SADOWSKY (AV)

Thirteenth Floor 655 South Hope Street, 90017
Telephone: 213-622-4750
Fax: 213-622-2690

MEMBERS OF FIRM

Robert M. Talcott
Michael J. Lightfoot
John D. Vandevelde
Carla M. Woehrle
Stephen B. Sadowsky
John S. Crouchley
John P. Martin

OF COUNSEL

Quin Denvir

ASSOCIATES

Melissa N. Widdifield
James H. Locklin
Patricia Lea Peckham

Reference: Sterling Bank, Los Angeles, California.

For full biographical listings, see the Martindale-Hubbell Law Directory

LAW OFFICES OF BARRY TARLOW A PROFESSIONAL CORPORATION (AV)

9119 Sunset Boulevard, 90069
Telephone: 310-278-2111
Cable Address: "Habeas"
Fax: 310-550-7055

Barry Tarlow

(See Next Column)

LAW OFFICES OF BARRY TARLOW A PROFESSIONAL CORPORATION—*Continued*

Mark O. Heaney | Evan A. Jenness
A. Blair Bernholz | Paul J. Loh

For full biographical listings, see the Martindale-Hubbell Law Directory

NEWPORT BEACH, Orange Co.

RICHARD W. BONNER A PROFESSIONAL CORPORATION (AV)

(Formerly Crosby, Gary & Bonner)
Suite 200, 1300 Dove Street, 92660
Telephone: 714-727-7400
Fax: 714-851-1617

Richard W. Bonner

Reference: Bank of America, Newport Beach.

For full biographical listings, see the Martindale-Hubbell Law Directory

PALO ALTO, Santa Clara Co.

NOLAN & ARMSTRONG (AV)

600 University Avenue, 94301
Telephone: 415-326-2980
Fax: 415-326-9704

MEMBERS OF FIRM

Thomas J. Nolan | Michael W. Armstrong

ASSOCIATE

Daniel L. Barton

LEGAL SUPPORT PERSONNEL

LEGAL ASSISTANTS

Lynn M. Memolo, PLS, CCLS | Terry Gray

For full biographical listings, see the Martindale-Hubbell Law Directory

*RIVERSIDE,** Riverside Co.

STEVEN L. HARMON (AV)

The Loring Building, 3685 Main Street, Suite 250, 92501
Telephone: 909-787-6800
Fax: 909-787-6700

For full biographical listings, see the Martindale-Hubbell Law Directory

*SACRAMENTO,** Sacramento Co.

BLACKMON & DROZD (AV)

U.S. Bank Plaza, 980 9th Street, Suite 2080, 95814
Telephone: 916-441-0824
Fax: 916-441-0970

MEMBERS OF FIRM

Clyde M. Blackmon | Dale A. Drozd

ASSOCIATE

Hill C. Snellings

For full biographical listings, see the Martindale-Hubbell Law Directory

ROTHSCHILD & WISHEK (AV)

901 "F" Street, Suite 200, 95814
Telephone: 916-444-9845

MEMBERS OF FIRM

Michael Rothschild | M. Bradley Wishek

ASSOCIATE

Michael G. Barth

For full biographical listings, see the Martindale-Hubbell Law Directory

*SAN BERNARDINO,** San Bernardino Co.

KASSEL & KASSEL (AV)

A Group of Independent Law Offices
Suite 207, Wells Fargo Bank Building, 334 West Third Street, 92401
Telephone: 909-884-6455
Fax: 909-884-8032

Philip Kassel | Gregory H. Kassel

References: Wells Fargo Bank; Bank of America; Bank of San Bernardino.

For full biographical listings, see the Martindale-Hubbell Law Directory

*SAN DIEGO,** San Diego Co.

DOUGLAS C. BROWN (AV)

501 West Broadway, Suite 800, 92101-3547
Telephone: 619-230-7254
Fax: 619-231-9754

For full biographical listings, see the Martindale-Hubbell Law Directory

JOHN G. COTSIRILOS (AV)

2442 Fourth Avenue, 92101
Telephone: 619-232-6022
Fax: 619-232-6052

For full biographical listings, see the Martindale-Hubbell Law Directory

COUGHLAN, SEMMER & LIPMAN (AV)

A Partnership including Professional Corporations
501 West Broadway, Suite 400, 92101
Telephone: 619-232-0800
Fax: 619-232-0107

MEMBERS OF FIRM

R. J. (Jerry) Coughlan, Jr. (A P.C.) | Robert F. Semmer (A P.C.)
Michael L. Lipman

ASSOCIATES

Cathleen Gilliland Fitch | Duane Tyler
Sheryl S. King | Carol A. Ensalaco
Angela L. Baxter

OF COUNSEL

Alexandra M. Kwoka

Representative Clients: Ernst & Young; U.S. Air; Wells Fargo Bank; Lawyers Mutual Insurance Co.; Prudential-Bache Securities, Inc.; CAMICO; Shell Oil; IBP, Inc.; UST Inc.; San Diego National Bank.

For full biographical listings, see the Martindale-Hubbell Law Directory

FRANK & MILCHEN (AV)

136 Redwood Street, 92103-5690
Telephone: 619-574-1888
Fax: 619-574-0649

Howard B. Frank | Joseph Milchen

Stephen E. Hoffman

For full biographical listings, see the Martindale-Hubbell Law Directory

GOLDBERG & HALL (AV)

Symphony Towers, 750 B Street, Suite 1930, 92101
Telephone: 619-297-1111
Fax: 619-297-1150

MEMBERS OF FIRM

Charles L. Goldberg | Patrick Q. Hall

ASSOCIATES

Judi M. Sanzo | William B. Sullivan

For full biographical listings, see the Martindale-Hubbell Law Directory

GRIMES & WARWICK (AV)

2664 Fourth Avenue, 92103
Telephone: 619-232-2014
Fax: 619-232-8857

MEMBERS OF FIRM

Robert L. Grimes | Thomas J. Warwick, Jr.

ASSOCIATES

Linda K. Grimes | Anthony J. Solare

For full biographical listings, see the Martindale-Hubbell Law Directory

PETER J. HUGHES A PROFESSIONAL CORPORATION (AV)

1010 Second Avenue, Suite 1917, 92101
Telephone: 619-234-6695
Fax: 619-696-0155

Peter J. Hughes

For full biographical listings, see the Martindale-Hubbell Law Directory

*SAN FRANCISCO,** San Francisco Co.

JUDD C. IVERSEN A PROFESSIONAL CORPORATION (AV)

Penthouse, 1231 Market Street, 94103-1488
Telephone: 415-552-6500
Fax: 415-552-1806
Burlingame, California Office: 500 Airport Boulevard, Suite 230.

Judd C. Iversen

Daniel S. Frankston

OF COUNSEL

George F. Camerlengo (Resident at Burlingame, California Office) | C. Judith Johnson (Resident at Burlingame, California Office)

For full biographical listings, see the Martindale-Hubbell Law Directory

San Francisco—Continued

LADAR & KNAPP (AV)
Suite 310, 507 Polk Street, 94102
Telephone: 415-928-2333

Jerrold M. Ladar
Joyce B. Ladar
Bernard L. Knapp

For full biographical listings, see the Martindale-Hubbell Law Directory

LAW OFFICES OF EPHRAIM MARGOLIN (AV)
Suite 300, 240 Stockton Street, 94108
Telephone: 415-421-4347
Fax: 415-397-9801

ASSOCIATES

Bradford L. Battson
Barry Helft

For full biographical listings, see the Martindale-Hubbell Law Directory

HARRIET ROSS (AV)
One Sansome Street, Suite 2000, 94104
Telephone: 415-956-7655
Fax: 415-673-8172

For full biographical listings, see the Martindale-Hubbell Law Directory

JOHN M. RUNFOLA (AV)
451 Jackson Street, 94111
Telephone: 415-391-4243
Reference: First Interstate Bank.

For full biographical listings, see the Martindale-Hubbell Law Directory

M. GERALD SCHWARTZBACH (AV)
901 Market Street, Suite 230, 94103
Telephone: 415-777-3828
Fax: 415-777-3584

For full biographical listings, see the Martindale-Hubbell Law Directory

GEORGE G. WALKER, INC. (AV)
Suite 635, 633 Battery Street, 94111
Telephone: 415-421-6911
Fax: 415-788-6787

George G. Walker

For full biographical listings, see the Martindale-Hubbell Law Directory

*SAN JOSE,** Santa Clara Co.

CRAIG M. BROWN, INC. (AV)
Suite 618 Pacific Valley Building, 333 West Santa Clara Street, 95113
Telephone: 408-286-8844
Fax: 408-286-6699

Craig M. Brown

For full biographical listings, see the Martindale-Hubbell Law Directory

GUYTON N. JINKERSON (AV)
50 West San Fernando Street Suite 400, 95113
Telephone: 408-297-8555
Fax: 408-295-6375

For full biographical listings, see the Martindale-Hubbell Law Directory

MANCHESTER & WILLIAMS (AV)
An Association of Attorneys including Professional Corporations
100 Park Center Plaza, Suite 525, 95113
Telephone: 408-287-6193
Fax: 408-287-1554

Steven R. Manchester (Inc.)
John L. Williams (Inc.)
Kurt J. Seibert

LEGAL SUPPORT PERSONNEL

L. Toni Wilson (Office Manager)

For full biographical listings, see the Martindale-Hubbell Law Directory

THOMAS F. MUELLER A PROFESSIONAL CORPORATION (AV)
255 North Market Street, Suite 190, 95110
Telephone: 408-292-2434
Fax: 408-292-1264

Thomas F. Mueller

For full biographical listings, see the Martindale-Hubbell Law Directory

TYNDALL & CAHNERS (AV)
An Association of Attorneys including a Professional Corporation
96 North Third Street, Suite 580, 95112
Telephone: 408-297-3700
Fax: 408-297-3721

John G. Tyndall, III (P.C.)
John D. Cahners

Michael Francis Brown

For full biographical listings, see the Martindale-Hubbell Law Directory

SAN MATEO, San Mateo Co.

ANDERLINI, GUHEEN, FINKELSTEIN, EMERICK & MCSWEENEY, A PROFESSIONAL CORPORATION (AV)
400 South El Camino Real, Suite 700, 94402
Telephone: 415-348-0102
Fax: 415-348-0962

P. Terry Anderlini
John J. Guheen
David G. Finkelstein
Merrill G. Emerick
Brian J. McSweeney

A. James Scholz
John P. Antonakos
Paul J. Smoot
Jennifer Gustafson

OF COUNSEL

Daniel J. Monaco (Inc.)

A list of Representative Clients will be furnished upon request.

For full biographical listings, see the Martindale-Hubbell Law Directory

*SANTA ANA,** Orange Co.

STOKKE & RIDDET, A PROFESSIONAL CORPORATION (AV)
2677 North Main Street, Suite 100, 92701-1230
Telephone: 714-543-2700
Fax: 714-543-3674

Allan H. Stokke
James D. Riddet

Robison D. Harley, Jr.
Correen Wiley Ferrentino

Reference: Corporate Bank.

For full biographical listings, see the Martindale-Hubbell Law Directory

*SANTA BARBARA,** Santa Barbara Co.

ESKIN & JACKSON (AV)
101 East Victoria Street, 93101
Telephone: 805-965-8550
Fax: 805-564-2170
Ventura, California Office: 830 East Santa Clara Street.
Telephone: 805-641-5888.
Fax: 805-641-5877.

George C. Eskin

For full biographical listings, see the Martindale-Hubbell Law Directory

SANTA MONICA, Los Angeles Co.

CHALEFF, ENGLISH AND CATALANO (AV)
Garden Suite, 1337 Ocean Avenue, 90401
Telephone: 310-458-1691
Fax: 310-393-6937

MEMBERS OF FIRM

Gerald L. Chaleff
Charles R. English
Paul A. Catalano
Audrey Winograde

For Complete List of Firm Personnel, See General Section
For full biographical listings, see the Martindale-Hubbell Law Directory

CRANE & MCCANN (AV)
530 Wilshire Boulevard, Suite 400, 90401-1423
Telephone: 310-917-9277
Fax: 310-393-7338

MEMBERS OF FIRM

Richard P. Crane, Jr.
Joseph J. McCann, Jr.

ASSOCIATES

Lawrence J. Lennemann
John Benedict
Brian D. McMahon
Daniel P. Ayala

For full biographical listings, see the Martindale-Hubbell Law Directory

Santa Monica—Continued

NASATIR, HIRSCH & PODBERESKY (AV)

2115 Main Street, 90405
Telephone: 310-399-3259
Fax: 310-392-9029

Michael D. Nasatir
Richard G. Hirsch
Vicki I. Podberesky

For full biographical listings, see the Martindale-Hubbell Law Directory

O'NEILL, LYSAGHT & SUN (AV)

A Partnership including Professional Corporations
100 Wilshire Boulevard, Suite 700, 90401
Telephone: 310-451-5700
Telecopier: 310-399-7201

Brian O'Neill (A Professional Corporation)
Brian C. Lysaght (A Professional Corporation)
Frederick D. Friedman
Brian A. Sun
Yolanda Orozco
John M. Moscarino

Harriet Beegun Leva
David E. Rosen
Lisa Newman Tucker
J. Andrew Coombs
Ellyn S. Garofalo
Edward A. Klein
Robert L. Meylan

OF COUNSEL

J. Joseph Connolly
Arn H. Tellem (P.C.)

Reference: Santa Monica Bank, Santa Monica.

For full biographical listings, see the Martindale-Hubbell Law Directory

*VENTURA,** Ventura Co.

ESKIN & JACKSON (AV)

830 East Santa Clara Street, 93001
Telephone: 805-641-5888
Fax: 805-641-5877
Santa Barbara, California Office: 101 East Victoria Street.
Telephone: 805-965-8550.
Fax: 805-564-2170.

MEMBER OF FIRM

George C. Eskin

For full biographical listings, see the Martindale-Hubbell Law Directory

COLORADO

ARVADA, Jefferson Co.

THE ELLIOTT LAW OFFICES (AV)

7884 Ralston Road, 80002
Telephone: 303-424-5319
Fax: 303-424-6130

James E. Elliott, Jr.
Mark D. Elliott

LEGAL SUPPORT PERSONNEL

James R. Elliott

Reference: Vectra Bank of Lakewood, N.A.

For full biographical listings, see the Martindale-Hubbell Law Directory

*BOULDER,** Boulder Co.

HOWARD BITTMAN (AV)

1406 Pearl Street, Suite 200, 80302
Telephone: 303-443-2281
Fax: 303-443-2862

For full biographical listings, see the Martindale-Hubbell Law Directory

LAW OFFICES OF MICHAEL R. ENWALL (AV)

720 Pearl Street, 80302
Telephone: 303-449-3891
FAX: 303-449-3992

ASSOCIATE

Barbara K. Grant

For full biographical listings, see the Martindale-Hubbell Law Directory

MCCORMICK AND CHRISTOPH (AV)

1406 Pearl Street, Suite 200, 80302
Telephone: 303-443-2281
Fax: 303-443-2862

(See Next Column)

MEMBERS OF FIRM

G. Paul McCormick
James R. Christoph

For full biographical listings, see the Martindale-Hubbell Law Directory

MILLER, HALE AND HARRISON (AV)

2305 Broadway, 80304
Telephone: 303-449-2830
Fax: 303-449-2198

MEMBERS OF FIRM

Robert Bruce Miller
Daniel C. Hale
David B. Harrison

ASSOCIATE

Joan Clifford

Reference: Norwest Bank.

For full biographical listings, see the Martindale-Hubbell Law Directory

*COLORADO SPRINGS,** El Paso Co.

ELVIN L. GENTRY, P.C. (AV)

Suite 201, 405 South Cascade, 80903
Telephone: 719-632-4647

Elvin L. Gentry

For full biographical listings, see the Martindale-Hubbell Law Directory

DENNIS W. HARTLEY, P.C. PROFESSIONAL CORPORATION (AV)

Suite 103, 620 South Cascade, 80903
Telephone: 719-635-5521
FAX: 719-635-5760

Dennis W. Hartley

Reference: First American Bank.

For full biographical listings, see the Martindale-Hubbell Law Directory

TEGTMEIER CISNEROS, P.C. (AV)

90 South Cascade Avenue, Suite 970, 80903
Telephone: 719-473-5757
Telefax: 719-473-6767

Richard L. Tegtmeier
Theresa M. Cisneros

Andrea E. Head

Reference: Norwest Bank of Colorado Springs and State Bank & Trust.

For full biographical listings, see the Martindale-Hubbell Law Directory

*DENVER,** Denver Co.

MICHAEL L. BENDER, P.C. (AV)

Suite 1160, 1660 Wynkoop Street, 80202-1146
Telephone: 303-893-8000
Fax: 303-893-8055

Michael L. Bender

For full biographical listings, see the Martindale-Hubbell Law Directory

BREGA & WINTERS, P.C. (AV)

One Norwest Center, 1700 Lincoln Street, Suite 2222, 80203
Telephone: 303-866-9400
FAX: 303-861-9109
Greeley, Colorado Office: 1100 Tenth Street, Suite 402, 80631.
Telephone: 303-352-4805.
Fax: 303-352-6547.

James W. Bain
Thomas D. Birge
Charles F. Brega
Robert R. Dormer
Robert C. Kaufman
Ronald S. Loser
Brian A. Magoon
Loren L. Mall
Pamela A. Shaddock (Resident, Greeley Office)
Jay John Schnell
Jerry D. Winters (Resident, Greeley Office)

Mark J. Appleton
Wesley B. Howard, Jr.
Jennifer G. Krolik
Bradley D. Laue (Resident, Greeley Office)
Cathryn B. Mayers
Carla B. Minckley
Nathan D. Simmons
Scott L. Terrell

OF COUNSEL

Mark Spitalnik

For full biographical listings, see the Martindale-Hubbell Law Directory

Denver—Continued

PATRICK J. BURKE (AV)

1660 Wynkoop, Suite 1160, 80202
Telephone: 303-893-8000
Telecopier: 303-893-8055

For full biographical listings, see the Martindale-Hubbell Law Directory

CANGES, IWASHKO & BETHKE, A PROFESSIONAL CORPORATION (AV)

303 East 17th Avenue Suite 400, 80203-1261
Telephone: 303-860-1900
Fax: 303-860-1665

E. Michael Canges
Nina A. Iwashko
Erich L. Bethke

Stephen R. Fatzinger
James S. Bailey

Reference: Norwest Bank Denver.

For full biographical listings, see the Martindale-Hubbell Law Directory

LOWERY AND LOWERY, P.C. (AV)

1999 Broadway, Suite 3800, 80202
Telephone: 303-296-1456
Telefax: 303-296-8538
Tempe, Arizona Office: 1707 E. Southern Avenue, Suite B, 85282.
Telephone: 602-831-1550.
Telefax: 602-838-5005.

Philip E. Lowery
Philip Scott Lowery

Marcella T. Clark
Terri B. Cohen
Spero A. Leon
Maria J. Murray
David L. Michael

References: Colorado State Bank; Bank of Denver; Jefferson Bank & Trust.

For full biographical listings, see the Martindale-Hubbell Law Directory

JERALYN E. MERRITT (AV)

303 East Seventeenth Avenue, Suite 400, 80203
Telephone: 303-837-1837
Fax: 303-860-1665

For full biographical listings, see the Martindale-Hubbell Law Directory

DAVID A. OGILVIE, P.C. (AV)

Suite 3901, One Norwest Center, 1700 Lincoln Street, 80203
Telephone: 303-837-9991
Fax: 303-832-5010

David A. Ogilvie

Representative Clients: Dwight Deere Carter Trust; Charles W. Swanson Trust.
Reference: Norwest Bank Denver, N.A.

For full biographical listings, see the Martindale-Hubbell Law Directory

POZNER HUTT KAPLAN, P.C. (AV)

1890 Gaylord Street, 80206-1211
Telephone: 303-333-1890
Fax: 303-333-1041

Larry S. Pozner
Abraham V. Hutt
David S. Kaplan

Reference: Guaranty Bank.

For full biographical listings, see the Martindale-Hubbell Law Directory

JOHN M. RICHILANO P.C. (AV)

1660 Wynkoop Suite 1160, 80202
Telephone: 303-893-8000
Telecopier: 303-893-8055

John M. Richilano

For full biographical listings, see the Martindale-Hubbell Law Directory

ARTHUR M. SCHWARTZ, P.C. (AV)

Dominion Plaza, Suite 2250 South Tower 600 Seventeenth Street, 80202
Telephone: 303-893-2500
Fax: 303-893-3349

Arthur M. Schwartz

Bradley J. Reich
Michael W. Gross
Cindy D. Schwartz

Reference: First Interstate Bank of Denver.

For full biographical listings, see the Martindale-Hubbell Law Directory

DANIEL T. SMITH (AV)

Suite 200, 430 East 7th Avenue, 80203
Telephone: 303-860-8100
Fax: 303-860-8018

For full biographical listings, see the Martindale-Hubbell Law Directory

SPRINGER & STEINBERG, A PROFESSIONAL CORPORATION (AV)

Suite 1500, 1600 Broadway, 80202
Telephone: 303-861-2800
Fax: 303-832-7116

Jeffrey A. Springer
Harvey A. Steinberg

Reference: Norwest Bank of Denver.

For full biographical listings, see the Martindale-Hubbell Law Directory

CRAIG L. TRUMAN, P.C. (AV)

Suite 205, 1444 Wazee Street, 80202
Telephone: 303-595-8008
Fax: 303-595-9505

Craig L. Truman

For full biographical listings, see the Martindale-Hubbell Law Directory

LAKEWOOD, Jefferson Co.

BUSCH AND COHEN, P.C. (AV)

Suite A-130, 12600 West Colfax Avenue, 80215
Telephone: 303-232-0362
Fax: 303-232-1125

Robert G. Busch
Michael A. Cohen

For full biographical listings, see the Martindale-Hubbell Law Directory

*MONTROSE,** Montrose Co.

EDWARD D. DURHAM (AV)

524 South First Street, P.O. Box 1721, 81402
Telephone: 303-249-2274
Fax: 303-249-6482

Reference: Norwest Bank of Montrose.

For full biographical listings, see the Martindale-Hubbell Law Directory

CONNECTICUT

*BRIDGEPORT,** Fairfield Co.

MEEHAN & MEEHAN (AV)

76 Lyon Terrace, 06604
Telephone: 203-333-1888
Fax: 203-331-0107

Richard T. Meehan, Sr.
Richard T. Meehan, Jr.
Edward J. Gavin

For full biographical listings, see the Martindale-Hubbell Law Directory

*HARTFORD,** Hartford Co.

BROWN, PAINDIRIS & ZARELLA (AV)

100 Pearl Street, 06103
Telephone: 203-522-3343
Telecopier: 203-522-2490

MEMBERS OF FIRM

Richard R. Brown
Nicholas Paindiris
Peter T. Zarella
Ronald T. Scott
John D. Maxwell
Steven W. Varney

ASSOCIATES

Christopher J. McCarthy
Sean M. Peoples

OF COUNSEL

David J. D. Evans

For full biographical listings, see the Martindale-Hubbell Law Directory

*NEW HAVEN,** New Haven Co.

LAW OFFICES OF JOHN R. WILLIAMS (AV)

51 Elm Street, 06510
Telephone: 203-562-9931
Fax: 203-776-9494

(See Next Column)

LAW OFFICES OF JOHN R. WILLIAMS—*Continued*

ASSOCIATES

Diane Polan
Katrena Engstrom
Norman A. Pattis
Denise A. Bailey-Garris

Reference: Founders Bank.

For full biographical listings, see the Martindale-Hubbell Law Directory

STAMFORD, Fairfield Co.

SILVER, GOLUB & TEITELL (AV)

184 Atlantic Street, P.O. Box 389, 06904
Telephone: 203-325-4491
FAX: 203-325-3769

MEMBERS OF FIRM

David S. Golub
Ernest F. Teitell

For Complete List of Firm Personnel, See General Section

For full biographical listings, see the Martindale-Hubbell Law Directory

WALLINGFORD, New Haven Co.

GERALD E. FARRELL, P.C. (AV)

375 Center Street, P.O. Box 369, 06492
Telephone: 203-269-7756
Fax: 203-269-1927

Gerald E. Farrell

Gerald E. Farrell, Jr.
Ann Farrell Leslie
Brian J. Leslie

References: Dime Savings Bank of Wallingford; Shawmut Bank (Wallingford Office).

For full biographical listings, see the Martindale-Hubbell Law Directory

WESTPORT, Fairfield Co.

ANDREW B. BOWMAN (AV)

1804 Post Road East, 06880
Telephone: 203-259-0599
Fax: 203-255-2570

Reference: Peoples Bank.

For full biographical listings, see the Martindale-Hubbell Law Directory

STUART A. MCKEEVER (AV)

155 Post Road, East, 06880
Telephone: 203-227-4756
Fax: 203-454-2031

Reference: Fleet Bank.

For full biographical listings, see the Martindale-Hubbell Law Directory

DELAWARE

*WILMINGTON,** New Castle Co.

BIGGS AND BATTAGLIA (AV)

1800 Mellon Bank Center, P.O. Box 1489, 19899-1489
Telephone: 302-655-9677

MEMBERS OF FIRM

Victor F. Battaglia
Robert D. Goldberg
Philip B. Bartoshesky
Victor F. Battaglia, Jr.
Christopher J. Battaglia

For Complete List of Firm Personnel, See General Section

For full biographical listings, see the Martindale-Hubbell Law Directory

JOSEPH A. HURLEY, P.A. (AV)

1215 King Street, 19801
Telephone: 302-658-8980

Joseph A. Hurley

For full biographical listings, see the Martindale-Hubbell Law Directory

EUGENE J. MAURER, JR., P.A. (AV)

1201-A King Street, 19801
Telephone: 302-652-7900
Fax: 302-652-2173

Eugene J. Maurer, Jr.
Marilou A. Szymanski

For full biographical listings, see the Martindale-Hubbell Law Directory

DISTRICT OF COLUMBIA

WASHINGTON, D.C. Co.

* indicates certain Bar Register subscribers, in cities of comparable size and importance, who maintain an additional office in Washington, D.C. and who have arranged for representation as a part of the Washington, D.C. listings that follow

ASBILL, JUNKIN & MYERS, CHTD. (AV)

1615 New Hampshire Avenue, N.W., 20009
Telephone: 202-234-9000
Facsimile: 202-332-6480
Alexandria, Virginia Office: 317 South Patrick Street.
Telephone: 703-684-7900.
Rockville, Maryland Office: Suite 315, 200-A Monroe Street.
Telephone: 301-294-0460.

Henry W. Asbill
Timothy deForest Junkin
Lenard B. Boss
Terrance G. Reed

Lauren Clingan

For Complete List of Firm Personnel, See General Section

For full biographical listings, see the Martindale-Hubbell Law Directory

CACHERIS & TREANOR (AV)

Suite 730, 1100 Connecticut Avenue, North West, 20036
Telephone: 202-775-8700
Fax: 202-775-8702; 202-775-8722
Alexandria, Virginia Office: 705 Prince Street.
Telephone: 703-549-8181.

Plato Cacheris
Gerard Treanor
Philip T. Inglima

ASSOCIATES

Judith L. Wheat
Karl A. Racine
John F. Hundley (Not admitted in DC)

OF COUNSEL

Philip T. White

For full biographical listings, see the Martindale-Hubbell Law Directory

CAPLIN & DRYSDALE, CHARTERED (AV)

One Thomas Circle, N.W., 20005
Telephone: 202-862-5000
Cable Address: "Capdale"
Telex: 904001 CAPL UR WSH
Fax: 202-429-3301
New York, N.Y. Office: 399 Park Avenue.
Telephone: 212-319-7125.
Fax: 212-644-6755.

Mortimer M. Caplin
Robert A. Klayman
Ralph A. Muoio
Elihu Inselbuch (Resident, New York Office)
Ronald B. Lewis
Richard W. Skillman
Patricia G. Lewis
Bernard S. Bailor
Stafford Smiley
Sally A. Regal
Julie W. Davis
Carl S. Kravitz
Robert A. Boisture
Charles T. Plambeck
Beth Shapiro Kaufman
Craig A. Sharon
James E. Salles
Paul G. Cellupica
Michael Doran (Not admitted in DC)
Dorothy L. Foley
Matthew W. Frank
Elizabeth M. Sellers (Not admitted in DC)
Douglas D. Drysdale
Thomas A. Troyer
David N. Webster
H. David Rosenbloom
Peter Van N. Lockwood
Cono R. Namorato
Daniel B. Rosenbaum
Richard E. Timbie
Graeme W. Bush
Albert G. Lauber, Jr.
Scott D. Michel
Kent A. Mason
Trevor W. Swett III
James Sottile, IV
Harry J. Hicks, III
C. Sanders McNew (Resident, New York Office)
Ann C. McMillan
Catherine E. Livingston
Christian R. Pastore (Resident, New York Office)
Nathan D. Finch
Jessica L. Goldstein

OF COUNSEL

Robert H. Elliott, Jr.
Milton Cerny
Myron C. Baum
Vivian L. Cavalieri

For full biographical listings, see the Martindale-Hubbell Law Directory

Washington—Continued

JOHN A. MCCAHILL

(See Alexandria, Virginia)

MILLER, CASSIDY, LARROCA & LEWIN (AV)

2555 M Street, N.W., 20037
Telephone: 202-293-6400
Telecopier: 202-293-1827

MEMBERS OF FIRM

Herbert J. Miller, Jr.
John J. Cassidy
Raymond G. Larroca
Nathan Lewin
Martin D. Minsker
William H. Jeffress, Jr.
R. Stan Mortenson
Thomas B. Carr
James E. Rocap, III
Randall J. Turk
Stephen L. Braga
Joe R. Caldwell, Jr.
Scott L. Nelson
Julia Evans Guttman
Niki Kuckes
Jay L. Alexander
Cynthia Thomas Calvert
Paul F. Enzinna

ASSOCIATES

Cathy J. Burdette
Douglas F. Curtis
Michael J. Barta
Stuart A. Levey
David S. Cohen
David R. Fontaine
James B. Bennett
Ellen Fels Berkman
Hugh P. Quinn
Nancy E. Friedman
Barry J. Pollack
James R. Heavner, Jr.
Mathew S. Nosanchuk (Not admitted in DC)
Kirsten D. Levingston
John T. Bentivoglio (Not admitted in DC)
Katherine L. Pringle (Not admitted in DC)
Robert J. McGahan (Not admitted in DC)

OF COUNSEL

Courtney A. Evans
William W. Greenhalgh (1927-1994)

For full biographical listings, see the Martindale-Hubbell Law Directory

THE ROBINSON LAW FIRM (AV)

Market Square, 717 D Street, N.W., 4th Floor, 20004
Telephone: 202-347-6100
Fax: 202-347-0081

MEMBERS OF FIRM

Kenneth Michael Robinson
Nicholas H. Hantzes
Lars H. Liebeler
Paul S. Thaler
Daniel E. Ellenbogen

ASSOCIATE

Randall W. Roy (Not admitted in DC)

OF COUNSEL

Dennis M. Hart

For full biographical listings, see the Martindale-Hubbell Law Directory

*** VENABLE, BAETJER, HOWARD & CIVILETTI (AV)**

A Partnership including Professional Corporations
Suite 1000, 1201 New York Avenue, N.W., 20005
Telephone: 202-962-4800
Fax: 202-962-8300
Baltimore, Maryland Office: Venable, Baetjer and Howard, 1800 Mercantile Bank & Trust Building, 2 Hopkins Plaza.
Telephone: 410-244-7400.
McLean, Virginia Office: Venable, Baetjer and Howard, Suite 400, 2010 Corporate Ridge.
Telephone: 703-760-1600.
Rockville, Maryland Office: Venable, Baetjer and Howard, Suite 500, One Church Street, P. O. Box 1906.
Telephone: 301-217-5600.
Towson, Maryland Office: Venable, Baetjer and Howard, 210 Allegheny Avenue, P. O. Box 5517.
Telephone: 410-494-6200.

MEMBERS OF FIRM

Benjamin R. Civiletti (P.C.) (Also at Baltimore and Towson, Maryland Offices)
Joseph G. Block
Michael Schatzow (Also at Baltimore and Towson, Maryland Offices)
Judson W. Starr (Also at Baltimore and Towson, Maryland Offices)
William D. Coston
Amy Berman Jackson
William D. Quarles (Also at Towson, Maryland Office)
Mary E. Pivec (Not admitted in DC; Also at Baltimore, Maryland Office)
Thomas J. Kelly, Jr.
Gary M. Hnath

OF COUNSEL

Geoffrey R. Garinther (Not admitted in DC; Also at Baltimore, Maryland Office)

(See Next Column)

ASSOCIATES

David W. Goewey
Samuel T. Morison

For Complete List of Firm Personnel, See General Section

For full biographical listings, see the Martindale-Hubbell Law Directory

WILLIAMS & CONNOLLY (AV)

725 Twelfth Street, N.W., 20005
Telephone: 202-434-5000

MEMBERS OF FIRM

Vincent J. Fuller
Raymond W. Bergan
Jeremiah C. Collins
Robert L. Weinberg
David Povich
Steven M. Umin
John W. Vardaman
Paul Martin Wolff
J. Alan Galbraith
John G. Kester
William E. McDaniels
Brendan V. Sullivan, Jr.
Aubrey M. Daniel, III
Richard M. Cooper
Gerald A. Feffer
Robert P. Watkins
Jerry L. Shulman
Lawrence Lucchino
Lewis H. Ferguson, III
Robert B. Barnett
David E. Kendall
Gregory B. Craig
John J. Buckley, Jr.
Douglas R. Marvin
John K. Villa
Barry S. Simon
Kevin T. Baine
Stephen L. Urbanczyk
Philip J. Ward
Frederick Whitten Peters
Peter J. Kahn
Lon S. Babby
Michael S. Sundermeyer
James T. Fuller, III
David D. Aufhauser
Bruce R. Genderson
Carolyn H. Williams
Frank Lane Heard III
Steven R. Kuney
Gerson A. Zweifach
Paul Mogin
Howard W. Gutman
Nancy F. Lesser
Richard S. Hoffman
Paula Michele Ellison
Steven A. Steinbach
Mark S. Levinstein
Mary Greer Clark
Daniel F. Katz
Nicole K. Seligman
Robert M. Krasne
Kathleen L. Beggs
Sven Erik Holmes
William R. Murray, Jr.
Eva Petko Esber
Stephen D. Raber
John D. Cline

David C. Kiernan
Nancy A. Bard
Lon E. Musslewhite
Robin E. Jacobsohn
Charles A. Sweet
Elizabeth D. Collery
Glenn J. Pfadenhauer
George A. Borden
Robert J. Shaughnessy
Jonathan P. Graham
Allen P. Waxman
William M. Wiltshire
J. Roger Williams, Jr.
Eric M. Braun
David S. Blatt
Betsy K. Wanger
Ari S. Zymelman
Joseph D. Piorkowski, Jr.
Philip B. Busch
H. Douglas Owens
Laurence Shore
Dane H. Butswinkas
Laurie S. Fulton

OF COUNSEL

Lyman G. Friedman

For Complete List of Firm Personnel, See General Section

For full biographical listings, see the Martindale-Hubbell Law Directory

WILMER, CUTLER & PICKERING (AV)

2445 M Street, N.W., 20037-1420
Telephone: 202-663-6000
Facsimile: 202-663-6363
Internet: Law@Wilmer.Com
European Offices:
4 Carlton Gardens, London, SW1Y 5AA, England. Telephone: 011 (4471) 839-4466.
Facsimile: 011 (4471) 839-3537.
Rue de la Loi 15 Wetstraat, B-1040 Brussels, Belgium. Telephone: 011 (322) 231-0903.
Facsimile: 011 (322) 230-4322.
Friedrichstrasse 95, D-10117 Berlin, Germany. Telephone: 011 (4930) 2643-3601.
Facsimile: 011 (4930) 2643-3630.

MEMBERS OF FIRM

Max O. Truitt, Jr.
Howard P. Willens
Daniel K. Mayers
Stephen H. Sachs
Arthur F. Mathews
James Robertson
Louis R. Cohen
Michael R. Klein
Paul J. Mode, Jr.
Stephen F. Black
Gary D. Wilson
James A. Rogers
Michael L. Burack
Robert B. McCaw
William J. Kolasky, Jr.
A. Stephen Hut, Jr.
John Rounsaville, Jr.
Roger M. Witten
David M. Becker
Andrew B. Weissman
Lynn Bregman
James E. Coleman, Jr.
Bruce E. Coolidge
Juanita A. Crowley
John Payton
Bruce M. Berman
Thomas F. Connell
Charles E. Davidow
Philip D. Anker
Joseph K. Brenner
Carol Clayton
Thomas P. Olson

(See Next Column)

WILMER, CUTLER & PICKERING—*Continued*

MEMBERS OF FIRM (Continued)

Patrick J. Carome
Jane C. Sherburne
David P. Donovan
Stephen M. Cutler
Roger W. Yoerges

For Complete List of Firm Personnel, See General Section

For full biographical listings, see the Martindale-Hubbell Law Directory

ZUCKERMAN, SPAEDER, GOLDSTEIN, TAYLOR & KOLKER (AV)
1201 Connecticut Avenue, N.W., 20036
Telephone: 202-778-1800
Fax: 202-822-8106
Miami, Florida Office: Zuckerman, Spaeder, Taylor & Evans. Suite 900, Miami Center, 201 South Biscayne Boulevard.
Telephones: 305-358-5000; 305-579-0110; Broward County: 305-523-0277.
Fax: 305-579-9749.
Ft. Lauderdale, Florida Office: Zuckerman, Spaeder, Taylor & Evans. One East Broward Boulevard, Suite 700.
Telephone: 305-356-0463.
Fax: 305-356-0406.
Baltimore, Maryland Office: Zuckerman, Spaeder, Goldstein, Taylor & Better. Suite 2440, 100 East Pratt Street.
Telephone: 410-332-0444.
Fax: 410-659-0436.
Tampa, Florida Office: Zuckerman, Spaeder, Taylor & Evans. 101 East Kennedy Boulevard, Suite 3140.
Telephone: 813-221-1010.
Fax: 813-223-7961.
New York, N.Y. Office: 1114 Avenue of the Americas, 45th Floor, Grace Building.
Telephone: 212-479-6500.
Fax: 212-479-6512.

MEMBERS OF FIRM

Roger E. Zuckerman
Roger C. Spaeder
William W. Taylor, III
Stephen H. Glickman
Michael R. Smith
Herbert Better (Resident, Baltimore, Maryland Office)
Michael S. Pasano (Miami and Ft. Lauderdale, Florida Offices)
Steven M. Salky
Morris Weinberg, Jr. (Resident, Tampa, Florida Office)
Blair G. Brown
Martin S. Himeles, Jr. (Resident, Baltimore, Maryland Office)
Sharon L. Kegerreis (Resident, Miami, Florida Office)
Edward J. M. Little (Resident, New York, N.Y. Office)
Thomas B. Mason

Reference: Sovran Bank/DC National.

For full biographical listings, see the Martindale-Hubbell Law Directory

FLORIDA

*BARTOW,** Polk Co.

BOSWELL, STIDHAM, PURCELL, CONNER, WILSON & BREWER, P.A. (AV)
150 East Davidson Street, P.O. Box 1578, 33830-1578
Telephone: 813-533-0866
Telecopier: 813-533-7255

Jonathan Stidham
Claude M. Harden, III

For full biographical listings, see the Martindale-Hubbell Law Directory

RICHARD D. MARS, P.A. (AV)
343 West Davidson Street, Suite 103, P.O. Box 1276, 33830
Telephone: 813-533-0855
Telecopier: 813-534-3500

Richard D. Mars

For full biographical listings, see the Martindale-Hubbell Law Directory

JOHN C. (JACK) WILKINS, III (AV)
770 East Main Street, P.O. Box 428, 33830
Telephone: 813-533-7143
Reference: Citrus & Chemical Bank of Bartow.

For full biographical listings, see the Martindale-Hubbell Law Directory

*CLEARWATER,** Pinellas Co.

MICHAEL C. CHEEK (AV)
814 Chestnut Street, 34616
Telephone: 813-443-7659

For full biographical listings, see the Martindale-Hubbell Law Directory

RONNIE G. CRIDER, P.A. (AV)
Newport Square, 4625 East Bay Drive - Suite 225, 34624
Telephone: 813-531-8070
FAX: 813-536-9644

Ronnie G. Crider

Karen Lasker McHugh

For full biographical listings, see the Martindale-Hubbell Law Directory

LEE FUGATE (AV)
Suite 108 Icot Center, 13630 58th Street North, 34620
Telephone: 813-539-6536
Tampa: 813-855-9115

For full biographical listings, see the Martindale-Hubbell Law Directory

GROSS AND KWALL, P.A. (AV)
133 North Fort Harrison Avenue, 34615
Telephone: 813-441-4947
Telecopier: 813-447-3158

Raymond O. Gross
Louis Kwall

Gregory K. Showers

For full biographical listings, see the Martindale-Hubbell Law Directory

GEORGE E. TRAGOS (AV)
600 Cleveland Street Suite 700, 34615
Telephone: 813-441-9030; Tampa: 813-223-6405
Fax: 813-441-9254

For full biographical listings, see the Martindale-Hubbell Law Directory

*DADE CITY,** Pasco Co.

GREENFELDER, MANDER, HANSON, MURPHY & DWYER (AV)
14217 Third Street, 33525
Telephone: 904-567-0411
Fax: 904-567-7758

MEMBERS OF FIRM

Albert R. Mander, III
T. Philip Hanson, Jr.

For full biographical listings, see the Martindale-Hubbell Law Directory

*FORT LAUDERDALE,** Broward Co.

BOGENSCHUTZ & DUTKO, P.A. (AV)
600 South Andrews Avenue, Suite 500, 33301
Telephone: 305-764-2500
Fax: 305-764-5040

J. David Bogenschutz
Michael E. Dutko
Mary H. McCleary

David L. Kennedy

For full biographical listings, see the Martindale-Hubbell Law Directory

EDWARD M. KAY, P.A. (AV)
Suite 4F Trial Lawyers Building, 633 Southeast Third Avenue, 33301
Telephone: 305-764-0033
Fax: 305-764-2590

Edward M. Kay
Kevin J. Kulik

For full biographical listings, see the Martindale-Hubbell Law Directory

*FORT MYERS,** Lee Co.

ALDERMAN & AHLBRAND, P.A. (AV)
Suite 200, The Historic Edison Theater Building, 1533 Hendry Street, P.O. Box 1530, 33902
Telephone: 813-334-7899
FAX: 813-334-0770

Frank C. Alderman, III
Mark W. Ahlbrand

For full biographical listings, see the Martindale-Hubbell Law Directory

*FORT PIERCE,** St. Lucie Co.

FEE, BRYAN & KOBLEGARD, P.A. (AV)
401 A South Indian River Drive, P.O. Box 1000, 34950
Telephone: 407-461-5020
FAX: 407-468-8461

Rupert N. Koblegard, III

General Counsel: Harbor Federal Savings; North St. Lucie River Water Control District; Fort Pierce Farms Water Control District; Fort Pierce Utilities Authority; Capron Trail Community Development District.

(See Next Column)

FEE, BRYAN & KOBLEGARD P.A., *Fort Pierce—Continued*

Representative Clients: Adams Ranch, Inc.; Callaway Land & Cattle Co., Inc., McArthur Farms, Inc.
Approved Attorneys for: Equitable Life Assurance Society of the United States; Equitable Agri-Business, Inc.

For Complete List of Firm Personnel, See General Section

For full biographical listings, see the Martindale-Hubbell Law Directory

*JACKSONVILLE,** Duval Co.

SHEPPARD & WHITE, P.A. (AV)

215 Washington Street, 32202
Telephone: 904-356-9661
Facsimile: 904-356-9667

Wm. J. Sheppard
Elizabeth L. White

D. Gray Thomas
Richard W. Smith
Adam Benjamin Allen

For full biographical listings, see the Martindale-Hubbell Law Directory

*MIAMI,** Dade Co.

JOSEPH BEELER, P.A. (AV)

Suite 300, 3050 Biscayne Boulevard, 33137
Telephone: 305-576-3050

Joseph Beeler

For full biographical listings, see the Martindale-Hubbell Law Directory

BIERMAN, SHOHAT, LOEWY & PERRY, PROFESSIONAL ASSOCIATION (AV)

Penthouse Two, 800 Brickell Avenue, 33131-2944
Telephone: 305-358-7000
Facsimile: 305-358-4010

Donald I. Bierman
Edward R. Shohat
Ira N. Loewy
Pamela I. Perry
Maria C. Beguiristain

Reference: United National Bank of Miami.

For full biographical listings, see the Martindale-Hubbell Law Directory

JOSEPH MARTIN DOBKIN (AV)

Marcus Centre, 9990 S.W. 77th Avenue Penthouse Three, 33156-2699
Telephone: 305-661-7000
Cable Address: "Dobkinlaw"
Fax: 305-274-0220
Associated Office: Miranda & Miranda, Ltda., Carrera 7A, No. 32-33 OF. 803 Santa Fe De Bogota, Colombia, S.A..
Telephone: 57-1 341-3855.
Facsimile: 57-1 285-9094.

For full biographical listings, see the Martindale-Hubbell Law Directory

ESSEN & ESSEN, P.A. (AV)

18305 Biscayne Boulevard, Suite 400 (North Miami Beach), 33160
Telephone: 305-935-6680
Fax: 305-935-2314
West Palm Beach, Florida Office: Commerce Centre, 324 Datura Street, Suite 145.
Telephone: 407-833-0626.

Ben Essen (Retired)
Richard Essen

Carlos A. Canet
Douglas J. Glaid
James Peter Greenfield
Alan T. Lipson
Rebecca A. Nachlas
Fredrick R. Susaneck (Resident, West Palm Beach Office)
Nancy Cayford Wear

For full biographical listings, see the Martindale-Hubbell Law Directory

FERRELL & FERTEL, P.A. (AV)

Suite 1920 Miami Center, 201 South Biscayne Boulevard, 33131-2305
Telephone: 305-371-8585
Telecopier: 305-371-5732

Milton M. Ferrell, Jr.
Alan K. Fertel

Reference: City National Bank of Florida.

For full biographical listings, see the Martindale-Hubbell Law Directory

ALBERT J. KRIEGER, P.A. (AV)

1899 South Bayshore Drive, 33133
Telephone: 305-854-0050
Fax: 305-285-1761

Albert J. Krieger
Susan W. Van Dusen

(See Next Column)

OF COUNSEL
Scott A. Srebnick

For full biographical listings, see the Martindale-Hubbell Law Directory

THOMAS W. MCALILEY, P.A. (AV)

3260 Miami Center, 201 South Biscayne Boulevard, 33131
Telephone: 305-373-6551
Telecopier: 305-358-3404

Thomas W. McAliley

For full biographical listings, see the Martindale-Hubbell Law Directory

PODHURST, ORSECK, JOSEFSBERG, EATON, MEADOW, OLIN & PERWIN, P.A. (AV)

Suite 800 City National Bank Building, 25 West Flagler Street, 33130-1780
Telephone: 305-358-2800; Fort Lauderdale: 305-463-4346
Fax: 305-358-2382

Robert C. Josefsberg

Reference: City National Bank of Miami; United National Bank of Miami.

For Complete List of Firm Personnel, See General Section

For full biographical listings, see the Martindale-Hubbell Law Directory

RICHEY, MUNROE, RODRIGUEZ & DIAZ, P.A. (AV)

3100 First Union Financial Center, 200 South Biscayne Boulevard, 33131-2327
Telephone: 305-372-8808
Telefax: 305-372-3669; 374-4652
Telex: 4932891 RAMPA

Kirk W. Munroe
William L. Richey
Juan J. Rodriguez
Michael Diaz, Jr.

Tamara R. Piety

For full biographical listings, see the Martindale-Hubbell Law Directory

ROBBINS, TUNKEY, ROSS, AMSEL, RABEN & WAXMAN, P.A. (AV)

2250 Southwest Third Avenue, 33129
Telephone: Dade County 305-858-9550; Broward County 305-522-6244 (All Telephones Open 24 Hours)

Frederick S. Robbins
William R. Tunkey
Alan S. Ross
Robert G. Amsel
David Raben

Benjamin S. Waxman
Sylvia A. Thompson
Marco A. Vazquez

Reference: United National Bank, Miami, Florida.

For full biographical listings, see the Martindale-Hubbell Law Directory

NEAL R. SONNETT, P.A. (AV)

Twenty Sixth Floor, One Biscayne Tower, Two South Biscayne Boulevard, 33131-1802
Telephone: 305-358-2000
Fax: 305-358-1233

Neal R. Sonnett
Miguel M. de la O

OF COUNSEL
Teofilo Chapa

For full biographical listings, see the Martindale-Hubbell Law Directory

THORNTON, ROTHMAN & EMAS, P.A. (AV)

200 South Biscayne Boulevard, Suite 3420 First Union Financial Center, 33131
Telephone: 305-358-9000
Fax: 305-374-5747

John W. Thornton, Jr.
David B. Rothman
Kevin M. Emas

For full biographical listings, see the Martindale-Hubbell Law Directory

JEFFREY S. WEINER, P.A. (AV)

Two Datran Center, Suite 1910, 9130 South Dadeland Boulevard, 33156-7858
Telephone: 305-670-9919
Fax: 305-670-9299
Boca Raton, Florida Office: Mizner Park. 327 Plaza Real, Suite 215, 33432.

Jeffrey S. Weiner

(See Next Column)

JEFFREY S. WEINER, P.A.—*Continued*

Molly Ebelhare
Mycki L. Ratzan
Brent A. Rose
Jeffrey R. Sullivan

LEGAL SUPPORT PERSONNEL

Duchess Weiner
Bernice Lopez

For full biographical listings, see the Martindale-Hubbell Law Directory

ZUCKERMAN, SPAEDER, TAYLOR & EVANS (AV)

Miami Center, 201 South Biscayne Boulevard, Suite 900, 33131
Telephone: 305-358-5000; 305-579-0110
Broward County: 305-523-0277
Fax: 305-579-9749
Tampa, Florida Office: 101 East Kennedy Boulevard, Suite 3140.
Telephone: 813-221-1010.
Fax: 813-223-7961.
Ft. Lauderdale, Florida Office: One East Broward Boulevard, Suite 700.
Telephone: 305-356-0463.
Fax: 305-356-0406.
Washington, D.C. Office: Zuckerman, Spaeder, Goldstein, Taylor & Kolker, 1201 Connecticut Avenue, N.W.
Telephone: 202-778-1800.
Fax: 202-822-8106.
Baltimore, Maryland Office: Zuckerman, Spaeder, Goldstein, Taylor & Better, Suite 2440, 100 East Pratt Street.
Telephone: 410-332-0444.
Fax: 410-659-0436.
New York, N.Y. Office: Zuckerman, Spaeder, Goldstein, Taylor & Kolker, 1114 Avenue of the Americas, 45th Floor, Grace Building.
Telephone: 212-479-6500.
Fax: 212-479-6512.

MEMBERS OF FIRM

Ronald B. Ravikoff (Resident)
Michael S. Pasano
Morris Weinberg, Jr. (Resident, Tampa, Florida Office)
Humberto J. Peña
Sharon L. Kegerreis

ASSOCIATES

Guy A. Rasco
Bryan R. Cleveland
Jennifer Rae Coberly
Laura L. Vaughan (Resident, Tampa, Florida Office)
Teresa Halligan (Resident, Tampa Florida Office)

For full biographical listings, see the Martindale-Hubbell Law Directory

*NAPLES,** Collier Co.

VEGA, BROWN, STANLEY, MARTIN & ZELMAN, P.A. (AV)

2660 Airport Road, South, 33962
Telephone: 813-774-3333
Fax: 813-774-6420

Lawrence D. Martin

Paula J. Rhoads

General Counsel for: Lely Estates; Naples Community Hospital.
Local Counsel: Fleischmann Trust; Quail Creek Developments.

For Complete List of Firm Personnel, See General Section

For full biographical listings, see the Martindale-Hubbell Law Directory

*OCALA,** Marion Co.

CHARLES R. HOLLOMAN, P.A. (AV)

1515 East Silver Springs Boulevard, Suite 120 East, 34470
Telephone: 904-867-0766
Fax: 904-351-9217

Charles R. Holloman, Jr.

For full biographical listings, see the Martindale-Hubbell Law Directory

ORANGE PARK, Clay Co.

HEAD, SMITH, METCALF, AGUILAR, MOSS & SIERON, P.A. (AV)

1329A Kingsley Avenue, P.O. Box 855, 32073
Telephone: 904-264-6000
Fax: 904-264-9223

Robert J. Head, Jr.
Larry Smith
Frank B. Metcalf
Robert Aguilar
John B. Moss
Mark A. Sieron

Holly Fulton Perritt

For full biographical listings, see the Martindale-Hubbell Law Directory

*ORLANDO,** Orange Co.

ROBERT J. BUONAURO, P.A. (AV)

390 North Orange Avenue, Suite 1630, 32801
Telephone: 407-841-1940
Fax: 407-649-1936

Robert J. Buonauro

Reference: Southern Bank; Security National Bank.

For full biographical listings, see the Martindale-Hubbell Law Directory

DEMPSEY & ASSOCIATES, P.A. (AV)

605 East Robinson Street, P.O. Box 1980, 32802-1980
Telephone: 407-422-5166
Mailing Address: 1031 West Morse Boulevard, Suite 200, Winter Park, Florida, 32789
Winter Park, Florida Office: 1031 West Morse Boulevard, Suite 200, 32789.
Telephone: 407-740-7778.
Telecopier: 407-740-0911.

Bernard H. Dempsey, Jr.
Michael C. Sasso

M. Susan Sacco
William P. Weatherford, Jr.
Daniel N. Brodersen
Lori R. Benton
Barbara B. Smithers

OF COUNSEL

Gary S. Salzman

Reference: First Union National Bank of Florida.

For full biographical listings, see the Martindale-Hubbell Law Directory

J. CHENEY MASON, P.A. (AV)

Barnett Bank Center, 390 North Orange Avenue, Suite 2100, 32801
Telephone: 407-843-5785
Fax: 407-422-6858

J. Cheney Mason

For full biographical listings, see the Martindale-Hubbell Law Directory

LAW OFFICES OF JAMES M. RUSS, P.A. (AV)

Tinker Building, 18 West Pine Street, 32801
Telephone: 407-849-6050
Fax: 407-849-6059

James M. Russ

Reference: First Union National Bank of Orlando.

For full biographical listings, see the Martindale-Hubbell Law Directory

*PANAMA CITY,** Bay Co.

DANIEL & KOMAREK, CHARTERED (AV)

315 East Fourth Street, P.O. Box 2547, 32402
Telephone: 904-763-6565
Fax: 904-769-8177

John F. Daniel
Paul G. Komarek

For full biographical listings, see the Martindale-Hubbell Law Directory

*SARASOTA,** Sarasota Co.

JOHN M. FITZGIBBONS (AV)

SouthTrust Bank Plaza, Suite 775, 1800 Second Street, 34236
Telephone: 813-953-5697
Tampa, Florida Office: 707 North Franklin Street, Suite 700.
Telephone: 813-221-8800.
Fax: Available upon request.

OF COUNSEL

B. Kay Neiss

*STUART,** Martin Co.

LEWIS, BERGER & FERRARO (AV)

A Partnership of Professional Associations
3601 East Ocean Boulevard, Suite 201 (Sewall's Point), 34996
Telephone: 407-221-0600
FAX: 407-220-0640
Other Stuart, Florida Office: 1115 East Ocean Boulevard. Telephone 407-286-7861. Fax 407-288-2013.
Port St. Lucie, Florida Office: 1531 S.E. Port St. Lucie Boulevard.
Telephone: 407-335-1996.
FAX: 407-335-1998.

Bruce D. Berger (P.A.)
Russell J. Ferraro, Jr. (P.A.)
J. D. Lewis, III (P.A.)

(See Next Column)

LEWIS, BERGER & FERRARO, *Stuart—Continued*

Danie V. La Guerre (P.A.)
Michael J. Mortell (P.A.)
Sharon E. Lever

LEGAL SUPPORT PERSONNEL

Dorthea M. Duncan

For full biographical listings, see the Martindale-Hubbell Law Directory

*TALLAHASSEE,** Leon Co.

WADSWORTH & DAVIS (AV)

Suite 1, 203 North Gadsden Street, P.O. Box 10529, 32302-2529
Telephone: 904-224-9037
FAX: 904-561-6119

MEMBERS OF FIRM

Murray M. Wadsworth
William H. Davis

ASSOCIATE

James J. Dean

Reference: Capital City First National Bank.

For full biographical listings, see the Martindale-Hubbell Law Directory

*TAMPA,** Hillsborough Co.

RONALD K. CACCIATORE, P.A. (AV)

100 North Tampa Street, Suite 2835, 33602
Telephone: 813-223-4831
Facsimile: 813-223-2737

Ronald K. Cacciatore

Reference: The Bank of Tampa.

For full biographical listings, see the Martindale-Hubbell Law Directory

THE LAW FIRM OF BARRY A. COHEN, P.A. (AV)

201 East Kennedy Boulevard Suite 1700, P.O. Box 172538, 33672
Telephone: 813-225-1655
FAX: 813-225-1921

Barry A. Cohen

Tracy Sheehan
Christopher P. Jayson
Todd Foster

For full biographical listings, see the Martindale-Hubbell Law Directory

JOHN M. FITZGIBBONS (AV)

707 North Franklin Street, Suite 700, 33602-4441
Telephone: 813-221-8800
Fax: Available upon request
Sarasota, Florida Office: SouthTrust Bank Plaza, Suite 775, 1800 Second Street.
Telephone: 813-953-5697.

OF COUNSEL

B. Kay Neiss

For full biographical listings, see the Martindale-Hubbell Law Directory

ANTHONY J. LASPADA, P.A. (AV)

1802 North Morgan Street, 33602
Telephone: 813-223-6048
Pinellas Line: 813-894-1788
Fax: 813-228-9471
Mailing Address: 1802 North Morgan Street, Tampa, Florida, 33602

Anthony J. LaSpada

Joseph A. Eustace, Jr.

For full biographical listings, see the Martindale-Hubbell Law Directory

MANEY, DAMSKER, HARRIS & JONES, P.A. (AV)

606 Madison Street, P.O. Box 172009, 33672-0009
Telephone: 813-228-7371
Fax: 813-223-4846

David A. Maney

For full biographical listings, see the Martindale-Hubbell Law Directory

PIPPINGER, TROPP & MATASSINI, P.A. (AV)

101 East Kennedy Boulevard, Suite 3305, 33602
Telephone: 813-225-1611

Richard G. Pippinger
Robert A. Tropp
Nicholas M. Matassini

For full biographical listings, see the Martindale-Hubbell Law Directory

ROBERT P. POLLI (AV)

Barnett Bank Plaza, 101 East Kennedy Boulevard, Suite 3130, 33602
Telephone: 813-222-8350
Fax: Available Upon Request

For full biographical listings, see the Martindale-Hubbell Law Directory

ZUCKERMAN, SPAEDER, TAYLOR & EVANS (AV)

101 East Kennedy Boulevard, Suite 3140, 33602
Telephone: 813-221-1010
Fax: 813-223-7961
Miami, Florida Office: Suite 900, Miami Center, 201 South Biscayne Boulevard.
Telephones: 305-358-5000; 305-579-0110; Broward County: 305-523-0277.
Fax: 305-579-9749.
Ft. Lauderdale, Florida Office: One East Broward Boulevard, Suite 700.
Telephone: 305-356-0463.
Fax: 305-356-0406.
Washington, D.C. Office: Zuckerman, Spaeder, Goldstein, Taylor & Kolker, 1201 Connecticut Avenue, N.W.
Telephone: 202-778-1800.
Fax: 202-822-8106.
Baltimore, Maryland Office: Zuckerman, Spaeder, Goldstein, Taylor & Better, Suite 2440, 100 East Pratt Street.
Telephone: 410-332-0444.
Fax: 410-659-0436.
New York, N.Y. Office: Zuckerman, Spaeder, Goldstein, Taylor & Kolker, 1114 Avenue of the Americas, 45th Floor, Grace Building.
Telephone: 212-479-6500.
Fax: 212-479-6512.

MEMBERS OF FIRM

Morris Weinberg, Jr.
Ronald B. Ravikoff (Resident, Miami, Florida Office)
Michael S. Pasano (Miami, Florida and Ft. Lauderdale, Florida Offices)
Humberto J. Peña (Resident, Miami, Florida Office)
Sharon L. Kegerreis (Resident, Miami, Florida Office)

ASSOCIATES

Laura L. Vaughan
Teresa Halligan
Guy A. Rasco (Resident, Miami, Florida Office)
Bryan R. Cleveland (Resident, Miami, Florida Office)
Jennifer Rae Coberly (Resident, Miami, Florida Office)

For full biographical listings, see the Martindale-Hubbell Law Directory

*WEST PALM BEACH,** Palm Beach Co.

LUBIN AND GANO, P.A. (AV)

Second Floor, Flagler Plaza, 1217 South Flagler Drive, 33401
Telephone: 407-655-2040
FAX: 407-655-2182

Richard G. Lubin
Nancy H. Hamill (1938-1980)
Thomas C. Gano

Jonathan R. Kaplan

For full biographical listings, see the Martindale-Hubbell Law Directory

ROTH, DUNCAN & LABARGA, P.A. (AV)

Northbridge Centre, Suite 325, 515 North Flagler Drive, 33401
Telephone: 407-655-5529
Telecopier: 407-655-7818
Mailing Address: P.O. Box 770, 33402

David Roth
Douglas Duncan
Jorge Labarga

For full biographical listings, see the Martindale-Hubbell Law Directory

GEORGIA

*ATHENS,** Clarke Co.

COOK, NOELL, TOLLEY & WIGGINS (AV)

304 East Washington Street, P.O. Box 1927, 30603
Telephone: 706-549-6111
Fax: 706-548-0956

MEMBERS OF FIRM

J. Vincent Cook
John S. Noell, Jr.
Edward D. Tolley
Morton M. Wiggins, III
Robert B. Bates
M. Kim Michael

For full biographical listings, see the Martindale-Hubbell Law Directory

*ATLANTA,** Fulton Co.

C. MICHAEL ABBOTT, P.C. (AV)

IBM Tower, Suite 3410, 1201 West Peachtree Street, 30309-3400
Telephone: 404-885-1994
Fax: 404-885-1677

Michael Abbott

For full biographical listings, see the Martindale-Hubbell Law Directory

JAKE ARBES (AV)

2300 Harris Tower, 233 Peachtree Street, N.E., 30303
Telephone: 404-522-1980
FAX: 404-588-0648

For full biographical listings, see the Martindale-Hubbell Law Directory

BEDFORD, KIRSCHNER AND VENKER, P.C. (AV)

Suite 450, 600 West Peachtree Street, N.W., 30308
Telephone: 404-872-6646

T. Jackson Bedford, Jr.

For full biographical listings, see the Martindale-Hubbell Law Directory

BONDURANT, MIXSON & ELMORE (AV)

1201 W. Peachtree Street Suite 3900, 30309
Telephone: 404-881-4100
FAX: 404-881-4111

MEMBERS OF FIRM

Emmet J. Bondurant II
H. Lamar Mixson
M. Jerome Elmore
Edward B. Krugman
James C. Morton
Jeffrey O. Bramlett
Dirk G. Christensen
Jane E. Fahey
Jeffrey D. Horst
John E. Floyd
Carolyn R. Gorwitz
Michael A. Sullivan

ASSOCIATES

Mary Jo Bradbury
P. Richard Game
Robin M. Hutchinson
J. Scott McClain
Keenan Rance Sephus Nix
Jill A. Pryor
Michael B. Terry
Joshua F. Thorpe

Representative Clients: The Aetna Casualty and Surety Company; Bottlers of Coca-Cola, U.S.A.; Brinks Home Security Systems, Inc.; Delta Air Lines, Inc.; Fina Oil and Chemical Company; JMB Realty Corp.; The Paradies Shops, Inc.; Sanifill, Inc.; Trammell Crow Co.

For Complete List of Firm Personnel, See General Section

For full biographical listings, see the Martindale-Hubbell Law Directory

R. DAVID BOTTS (AV)

152 Nassau Street, N.W., 30303
Telephone: 404-688-5500
FAX: 404-688-6463

For full biographical listings, see the Martindale-Hubbell Law Directory

CHILIVIS & GRINDLER (AV)

3127 Maple Drive, N.E., 30305
Telephone: 404-233-4171
Facsimile: 404-261-2842

Nickolas P. Chilivis
Gary G. Grindler
Anthony L. Cochran
John K. Larkins, Jr.
Thomas D. Bever
Daniel P. Griffin
Carol M. Kayser
Merrilee Aynes Gober
John D. Dalbey
Pamela B. Adams

For full biographical listings, see the Martindale-Hubbell Law Directory

ENGLAND & MCKNIGHT (AV)

Suite 410 River Ridge, 9040 Roswell Road, 30350
Telephone: 404-641-6010
FAX: 404-641-6003

MEMBERS OF FIRM

J. Melvin England
Robert H. McKnight, Jr.

Reference: Bank South, N.A.

For full biographical listings, see the Martindale-Hubbell Law Directory

GARLAND, SAMUEL & LOEB, P.C. (AV)

3151 Maple Drive, N.E., 30305
Telephone: 404-262-2225
FAX: 404-365-5041

(See Next Column)

Edward T. M. Garland
Donald F. Samuel
Robin N. Loeb
Patrick J. Geheren

For full biographical listings, see the Martindale-Hubbell Law Directory

KIRWAN, GOGER, CHESIN & PARKS, P.C. (AV)

2600 The Grand, 75 Fourteenth Street, 30309
Telephone: 404-873-8000
Facsimile: 404-873-8050

P. Bruce Kirwan

Representative Client: Anheuser Busch Cos., Inc.
Reference: Trust Company Bank.

For full biographical listings, see the Martindale-Hubbell Law Directory

MALOY & JENKINS (AV)

Suite 3410 One Atlantic Center, 1201 West Peachtree Street, 30309
Telephone: 404-875-2700
Fax: 404-875-8757

MEMBERS OF FIRM

James K. Jenkins
Bruce Maloy
Lisa A. Curia

For full biographical listings, see the Martindale-Hubbell Law Directory

*AUGUSTA,** Richmond Co.

RICHARD E. ALLEN (AV)

440 Greene Street, 30901
Telephone: 706-724-4466

For full biographical listings, see the Martindale-Hubbell Law Directory

*DECATUR,** De Kalb Co.

WILLIAM G. QUINN, III (AV)

Suite 480 One Decatur Town Center, 150 East Ponce De Leon Avenue, 30030
Telephone: 404-377-9254
Fax: 404-377-5776

For full biographical listings, see the Martindale-Hubbell Law Directory

*OCILLA,** Irwin Co.

WALTERS, DAVIS, MEEKS & PUJADAS, P.C. (AV)

South Cherry Street, P.O. Box 247, 31774
Telephone: 912-468-7472; 468-9433
Fax: 912-468-9022

W. Emory Walters
J. Harvey Davis
W. Edward Meeks, Jr.
Thomas E. Pujadas
C. Vinson Walters, II

Attorneys for: Irwin County Board of Education; First State Bank of Ocilla; Irwin County; Wilcox County.
Local Counsel for: Georgia Farm Bureau Mutual Insurance Co.
Approved Attorneys for: Kaiser Aluminum & Chemical Sales, Inc.; Lawyers Title Insurance Corp.; Ticor Title Insurance Co.; Farmers Home Administration; Federal Land Bank of Columbia.

For Complete List of Firm Personnel, See General Section

For full biographical listings, see the Martindale-Hubbell Law Directory

*SAVANNAH,** Chatham Co.

ZIPPERER & LORBERBAUM, P.C. (AV)

200 E. St. Julian Street, P.O. Box 9147, 31412
Telephone: 912-232-3770
FAX: 912-232-0643

Alex L. Zipperer
Ralph R. Lorberbaum
Janet Shedd Foerster
Steven L. Beauvais

For full biographical listings, see the Martindale-Hubbell Law Directory

*SUMMERVILLE,** Chattooga Co.

COOK & PALMOUR (AV)

128 South Commerce Street, P.O. Box 370, 30747
Telephone: 706-857-3421
Fax: 706-857-1520

MEMBERS OF FIRM

Bobby Lee Cook
A. Cecil Palmour (1913-1980)
L. Branch S. Connelly
Todd Johnson

For full biographical listings, see the Martindale-Hubbell Law Directory

*VALDOSTA,** Lowndes Co.

DODD & TURNER, P.C. (AV)

613 N. Patterson Street, P.O. Box 1066, 31603-1066
Telephone: 912-242-4470
Telecopier: 912-245-7731

Roger J. Dodd — L. Warren Turner, Jr.

James A. Kiger

Reference: First Union Bank.

For full biographical listings, see the Martindale-Hubbell Law Directory

HAWAII

*HONOLULU,** Honolulu Co.

BENJAMIN B. CASSIDAY, III (AV)

2440 Mauka Tower, Grosvenor Center, 737 Bishop Street, 96813-3215
Telephone: 808-523-9007
Fax: 808-531-8898

For full biographical listings, see the Martindale-Hubbell Law Directory

DAVID W. HALL ATTORNEY AT LAW, A LAW CORPORATION (AV)

735 Bishop Street Dillingham Transportation Building, Suite 237, 96813
Telephone: 808-526-0402
FAX: 808-526-0404

David W. Hall

For full biographical listings, see the Martindale-Hubbell Law Directory

HART & WOLFF ATTORNEYS AT LAW, A LAW CORPORATION (AV)

Suite 610 Melim Building, 333 Queen Street, 96813
Telephone: 808-526-0811
FAX: 808-531-2677

Brook Hart — Peter C. Wolff, Jr.

Anthony K. Bartholomew

For full biographical listings, see the Martindale-Hubbell Law Directory

MICHAEL A. WEIGHT ATTORNEY AT LAW, A LAW CORPORATION (AV)

Suite 430 Dillingham Transportation Building, 735 Bishop Street, 96813
Telephone: 808-528-3255
Fax: 808-521-5346

Michael A. Weight

Reference: City Bank.

For full biographical listings, see the Martindale-Hubbell Law Directory

ILLINOIS

*BELLEVILLE,** St. Clair Co.

KUEHN, TRENTMAN & O'GARA (AV)

2027 West Main Street, 62223
Telephone: 618-277-6646; 398-6648
Fax: 618-277-6649

MEMBERS OF FIRM

Clyde L. Kuehn — Brian K. Trentman
John J. O'Gara, Jr.

Reference: Bank of Belleville, Belleville, Illinois.

For full biographical listings, see the Martindale-Hubbell Law Directory

*CHICAGO,** Cook Co.

SUSAN BOGART (AV)

Twenty North Clark Street, Suite 808, 60602
Telephone: 312-726-9060
Fax: 312-726-9248
(Also Of Counsel to Sulzer & Shopiro)

For full biographical listings, see the Martindale-Hubbell Law Directory

EPSTEIN, ZAIDEMAN & ESRIG, P.C. (AV)

120 South Riverside Plaza, Suite 1150, 60606
Telephone: 312-207-0005
Fax: 312-207-1332

James R. Epstein

Elizabeth A. Kaveny

For full biographical listings, see the Martindale-Hubbell Law Directory

LAW OFFICES KOMIE AND ASSOCIATES (AV)

Suite 3500 Avondale Centre, 20 North Clark Street, 60602-5002
Telephone: 312-263-4383
Fax: 312-263-2803

Stephen M. Komie — Michael T. van der Veen

OF COUNSEL

Douglas W. Godfrey

LEGAL SUPPORT PERSONNEL

Paul J. Ciolino

For full biographical listings, see the Martindale-Hubbell Law Directory

MARTIN, BROWN & SULLIVAN, LTD. (AV)

321 South Plymouth Court 10th Floor, 60604
Telephone: 312-360-5000
Fax: 312-360-5026

Royal B. Martin — William G. Sullivan
Steven S. Brown — Leigh D. Roadman

Daniel T. Hartnett — Michael D. Cotton
Robert S. Grabemann

For full biographical listings, see the Martindale-Hubbell Law Directory

*HARRISBURG,** Saline Co.

JELLIFFE, FERRELL & MORRIS (AV)

108 East Walnut Street, 62946
Telephone: 618-253-7153; 253-7647
Telecopier: 618-252-1843

OF COUNSEL

Charles R. Jelliffe

MEMBERS OF FIRM

DeWitt Twente (1904-1976) — Donald V. Ferrell
Walden E. Morris

ASSOCIATES

Michal Doerge — Thomas J. Foster
Timothy L. Fornes

Representative Clients: Auto-Owners Insurance; Country Cos; Metropolitan Life Insurance; Ohio Casualty Group; Standard Mutual Insurance Co.; State Farm Cos.; Redland Insurance Co.; Aetna Casualty & Surety Co.; Kerr-McGee Coal Corp.; Sahara Coal Co.

For full biographical listings, see the Martindale-Hubbell Law Directory

*MARION,** Williamson Co.

HARRIS, LAMBERT, HOWERTON & DORRIS (AV)

300 West Main Street, P.O. Box 1005, 62959
Telephone: 618-993-2616
Fax: 618-997-1845

MEMBERS OF FIRM

Ralph W. Harris (1904-1982) — Robert H. Howerton
Richard Gordon Lambert — Douglas N. Dorris

ASSOCIATE

Eric Kirkpatrick

For full biographical listings, see the Martindale-Hubbell Law Directory

MATTOON, Coles Co.

RYAN, BENNETT & RADLOFF (AV)

300 Richmond East, P.O. Box 629, 61938-0629
Telephone: 217-234-2000
Fax: 217-234-2001

MEMBERS OF FIRM

James A. Bennett — Michael K. Radloff
Stephen R. Ryan — Christopher A. Koester
Michael D. Ryan — Brien J. O'Brien

Counsel For: State Farm Insurance Cos.; American States Insurance Co.; Auto-Owners Insurance Co.; Country Cos.; Economy Fire and Casualty Co.; Bituminous Insurance Cos.; Farmland Insurance; Millers Mutual Insurance; Horace Mann Insurance Co.
Reference: First Mid-Illinois Bank & Trust, Mattoon, Ill.

(See Next Column)

RYAN, BENNETT & RADLOFF—*Continued*

For Complete List of Firm Personnel, See General Section

For full biographical listings, see the Martindale-Hubbell Law Directory

OAK BROOK, Du Page Co.

BOTTI, MARINACCIO & TAMELING, LTD. (AV)
720 Enterprise Drive, 60521
Telephone: 708-573-8585
Fax: 708-573-8586
Wheaton, Illinois Office: Suite 401 The Ticor Title Building, 330 Naperville Road.
Telephone: 708-653-2100.

Aldo E. Botti
Stephen R. Botti
Andrew Y. Acker
Carlo F. Cavallaro
Peter M. DeLongis
Terry W. Huebner
Lee A. Marinaccio
Ronald D. Menna
Mark W. Salkeld
Eva W. Tameling
Peter M. Tumminaro
Frank J. Wesolowski

For full biographical listings, see the Martindale-Hubbell Law Directory

*SPRINGFIELD,** Sangamon Co.

METNICK, WISE, CHERRY & FRAZIER (AV)
Fourth Floor, Myers Building, 1 West Old State Capitol Plaza, P.O. Box 12140, 62791
Telephone: 217-753-4242
Telefax: 217-753-4642

MEMBERS OF FIRM

Michael B. Metnick
D. Peter Wise
Diana N. Cherry
Richard D. Frazier

For full biographical listings, see the Martindale-Hubbell Law Directory

INDIANA

CARMEL, Hamilton Co.

KNOWLES & ASSOCIATES (AV)
811 South Range Line Road, 46032
Telephone: 317-848-4360
Telecopier: 317-848-4363

William W. Knowles

Pamela Y. Rhine
D. Brandon Johnston

For full biographical listings, see the Martindale-Hubbell Law Directory

*EVANSVILLE,** Vanderburgh Co.

BERGER AND BERGER (AV)
313 Main Street, 47708-1485
Telephone: 812-425-8101;
Indiana Only: 800-622-3604;
Outside Indiana: 800-327-0182
Fax: 812-421-5909

MEMBERS OF FIRM

Sydney L. Berger (1917-1988)
Charles L. Berger
Sheila M. Corcoran
Mark W. Rietman
Robert J. Pigman

References: Citizens National Bank of Evansville; Old National Bank in Evansville.

For full biographical listings, see the Martindale-Hubbell Law Directory

*INDIANAPOLIS,** Marion Co.

McCLURE, McCLURE & KAMMEN (AV)
235 North Delaware, 46204
Telephone: 317-236-0400
Telecopier: 317-236-0404

MEMBERS OF FIRM

Richard Kammen
Nancy L. Broyles
Susan W. Brooks
James T. Flanigan
Susan D. Rayl

Reference: Indiana National Bank.

For full biographical listings, see the Martindale-Hubbell Law Directory

LAW OFFICES OF LINDA L. PENCE (AV)
2300 First Indiana Plaza, 135 North Pennsylvania Street, 46204
Telephone: 317-264-5555
Fax: 317-264-5564

(See Next Column)

ASSOCIATES

David J. Hensel
Anthony J. Rose
Jane Ann Himsel

LEGAL SUPPORT PERSONNEL

Penny S. Bloemker
Teresa L. Zembrycki
Rachel I. Lamb

For full biographical listings, see the Martindale-Hubbell Law Directory

*VALPARAISO,** Porter Co.

LAW OFFICES OF JAMES V. TSOUTSOURIS (AV)
Five Lincolnway, 46383
Telephone: 219-462-4148
Fax: 219-477-4932

ASSOCIATES

Joann Tsoutsouris
G. Anthony Bertig
John Edward Martin
Lori L. Ferngren

A list of Representative Clients and References will be furnished upon request.

For full biographical listings, see the Martindale-Hubbell Law Directory

IOWA

*DES MOINES,** Polk Co.

NICHOLAS CRITELLI ASSOCIATES, P.C. (AV)
Suite 500, 317 Sixth Avenue, 50309-4128
Telephone: 515-243-3122
Telecopier: (FAX) 515-243-3121
London, England Office: 11 Stone Buildings, Lincoln's Inn.
Telephone: 011-44-71-404-5055.
FAX: 011-44-71-405-1551.

Nick Critelli, Jr.
Lylea Dodson Critelli
Connie L. Diekema
Joseph B. Saluri

References: Boatmen's Bank of Des Moines, N.A.; Iowa State Bar Association.

For full biographical listings, see the Martindale-Hubbell Law Directory

THE ROSENBERG LAW FIRM (AV)
1010 Insurance Exchange Building, 505 Fifth Avenue, 50309
Telephone: 515-243-7600

MEMBERS OF FIRM

Raymond Rosenberg
Paul H. Rosenberg

ASSOCIATES

Dean A. Stowers
Brent D. Rosenberg

Reference: Firstar Bank, Des Moines, Iowa.

For full biographical listings, see the Martindale-Hubbell Law Directory

KANSAS

*TOPEKA,** Shawnee Co.

BENNETT & DILLON (AV)
1605 Southwest 37th Street, 66611
Telephone: 913-267-5063
Fax: 913-267-2652

MEMBERS OF FIRM

Mark L. Bennett, Jr.
Wilburn Dillon, Jr.

References: Silver Lake State Bank; Columbian National Bank and Trust.

For Complete List of Firm Personnel, See General Section

For full biographical listings, see the Martindale-Hubbell Law Directory

PORTER, FAIRCHILD, WACHTER & HANEY, P.A. (AV)
Suite 1000, Bank IV Tower, 534 South Kansas Avenue, P.O. Box 1833, 66601-1833
Telephone: 913-235-2200
Facsimile: 913-235-8950

James W. Porter
Ronald W. Fairchild
John H. Wachter
Thomas D. Haney

Douglas F. Martin
Sheldon J. Moss

For full biographical listings, see the Martindale-Hubbell Law Directory

KENTUCKY

*BOWLING GREEN,** Warren Co.

ENGLISH, LUCAS, PRIEST & OWSLEY (AV)

1101 College Street, P.O. Box 770, 42102-0770
Telephone: 502-781-6500
Telecopier: 502-782-7782

MEMBERS OF FIRM

Charles E. English Charles E. English, Jr.

ASSOCIATE

Robert A. Young

For Complete List of Firm Personnel, See General Section

For full biographical listings, see the Martindale-Hubbell Law Directory

MILLIKEN LAW FIRM (AV)

426 East Main Street, P.O. Box 1640, 42102-1640
Telephone: 502-843-0800
Fax: 502-842-1237

W. Currie Milliken Morris Lowe

Reference: Trans Financial Bank, Bowling Green, Kentucky.

For full biographical listings, see the Martindale-Hubbell Law Directory

COVINGTON, Kenton Co.

ROBERT E. SANDERS AND ASSOCIATES, P.S.C. (AV)

The Charles H. Fisk House, 1017 Russell Street, 41011
Telephone: 606-491-3000
FAX: 606-655-4642

Robert E. Sanders

Julie Lippert Duncan

LEGAL SUPPORT PERSONNEL

Shirley L. Sanders Harry E. Holtkamp
Sandra A. Head Joseph E. Schmiade, Sr.

For full biographical listings, see the Martindale-Hubbell Law Directory

*LEXINGTON,** Fayette Co.

ROBERTS & SMITH (AV)

167 West Main Street Suite 200, 40507
Telephone: 606-233-1104

MEMBERS OF FIRM

Larry S. Roberts Kenneth W. Smith

For full biographical listings, see the Martindale-Hubbell Law Directory

STOLL, KEENON & PARK (AV)

201 E. Main Street, Suite 1000, 40507-1380
Telephone: 606-231-3000
Telecopier: 606-253-1093; 606-253-1027
Frankfort, Kentucky Office: 326 West Main Street.
Telephone: 502-875-6000.
Telecopier: 502-875-6008.
Louisville, Kentucky Office: 400 West Market Street, Suite 2650, 40202.
Telephone: 502-568-9100.
Telecopier: 502-568-6340.

MEMBERS OF FIRM

Robert F. Houlihan Michael L. Judy
William E. Johnson Anita M. Britton
Spencer D. Noe J. Guthrie True
Richard M. Guarnieri

For Complete List of Firm Personnel, See General Section

For full biographical listings, see the Martindale-Hubbell Law Directory

*LOUISVILLE,** Jefferson Co.

FRANK E. HADDAD, JR. (AV)

Kentucky Home Life Building, 239 South Fifth Street, Fifth Floor, 40202
Telephone: 502-583-4881
Fax: 502-589-1058

Reference: Citizens Fidelity Bank & Trust Co.

For full biographical listings, see the Martindale-Hubbell Law Directory

FRANK MASCAGNI, III (AV)

Suite 200, Second Floor, Morrissey Building, 304 West Liberty Street, 40202-3012
Telephone: 502-583-2831
Fax: 502-583-3701

Reference: PNC Bank, Ky.

For full biographical listings, see the Martindale-Hubbell Law Directory

OGDEN NEWELL & WELCH (AV)

1200 One Riverfront Plaza, 40202-2973
Telephone: 502-582-1601
Fax: 502-581-9564

MEMBERS OF FIRM

John T. Ballantine Scott T. Wendelsdorf
W. Gregory King

For Complete List of Firm Personnel, See General Section

For full biographical listings, see the Martindale-Hubbell Law Directory

SEILLER & HANDMAKER (AV)

2200 Meidinger Tower, 40202
Telephone: 502-584-7400
Telecopier: 502-583-2100
Paris, Kentucky Office: Seiller, Handmaker & Blevins, P.S.C., 1431 South Main Street.
Telephone: 606-987-3980.
Telecopier: 606-987-3982.
New Albany, Indiana Office: 204 Pearl Street, Suite 200.
Telephone: 812-948-8307.
Telecopier: 812-948-8383.

Edward F. Seiller (1897-1990)

MEMBERS OF FIRM

Stuart Allen Handmaker Neil C. Bordy
Bill V. Seiller Kyle Anne Citrynell
David M. Cantor Maury D. Kommor
Cynthia Compton Stone

ASSOCIATES

Glenn A. Cohen Michael C. Bratcher
Pamela M. Greenwell John E. Brengle
Tomi Anne Blevins Pulliam (Resident, Paris Office) Patrick R. Holland, II
Edwin Jon Wolfe
Linda Scholle Cowan Donna F. Townsend
Mary Zeller Wing Ceridan William C. Robinson

OF COUNSEL

Robert S. Frey

For full biographical listings, see the Martindale-Hubbell Law Directory

*MOUNT VERNON,** Rockcastle Co.

CLONTZ & COX (AV)

Courthouse, 205 Main Street, P.O. Box 1350, 40456
Telephone: 606-256-5111
Fax: 606-256-2036

MEMBERS OF FIRM

Carl R. Clontz Jerry J. Cox
John E. Clontz

Representative Clients: The Bank of Mt. Vernon; Citizens Bank, Brodhead, Kentucky; Kentucky Farm Bureau Mutual Insurance Co.; Louisville Title Division of Commonwealth Land Title Insurance Co.
Reference: The Bank of Mt. Vernon, Mt. Vernon, Kentucky.

For full biographical listings, see the Martindale-Hubbell Law Directory

*OWENSBORO,** Daviess Co.

RUMMAGE, KAMUF, YEWELL, PACE & CONDON (AV)

Great Financial Federal Building, 322 Frederica Street, 42301
Telephone: 502-685-3901
FAX: 502-926-2005

MEMBERS OF FIRM

Charles J. Kamuf David L. Yewell

Representative Clients: Owensboro Municipal Utilities Commission; Lincoln Service Corp.; Hancock County Planning Commission; Daviess County Board of Education; Barmet Aluminum Corp.; Owensboro Sewer Commission; TICOR Title Insurance Co.; Chicago Title Insurance Co.; Owensboro Riverport Authority; Housing Authority of Owensboro.

For Complete List of Firm Personnel, See General Section

For full biographical listings, see the Martindale-Hubbell Law Directory

*PADUCAH,** McCracken Co.

LEN W. OGDEN, JR. (AV)

The Sinnott House, 228 North 9th Street, 42001-1850
Telephone: 502-444-0232
Fax: 502-444-0239

For full biographical listings, see the Martindale-Hubbell Law Directory

LOUISIANA

*ALEXANDRIA,** Rapides Parish

LAW OFFICE OF J. MICHAEL SMALL (AV)

1412 Centre Court Drive, Suite 201, P.O. Box 1470, 71309
Telephone: 318-487-8963
Fax: 318-442-3062

ASSOCIATES

Jesse B. Hearin, III
Phyllis E. Mann (Not admitted in LA)

For full biographical listings, see the Martindale-Hubbell Law Directory

*MONROE,** Ouachita Parish

DAVENPORT, FILES & KELLY (AV)

1509 Lamy Lane, P.O. Box 4787, 71211-4787
Telephone: 318-387-6453
FAX: 318-323-6533

MEMBERS OF FIRM

Thos. W. Davenport (1909-1962)
Wm. G. Kelly, Jr.
Thomas W. Davenport, Jr.
Jack B. Files
Mike C. Sanders
Ramsey L. Ogg
Michael J. Fontenot

ASSOCIATE

M. Shane Craighead

STAFF ATTORNEY

Stacy L. Guice

Representative Clients: American International Group (AIG); Burlington Motor Carriers; Chubb Group; Crum & Forster Group; Delta Airlines, Inc.; GAINSCO; GEICO; Highlands Ins. Co.; Trinity Universal Ins. Co.; Zurich-American Insurance Companies.

For full biographical listings, see the Martindale-Hubbell Law Directory

MCLEOD, VERLANDER, EADE & VERLANDER (AV)

A Partnership including Professional Law Corporations
1900 North 18th Street, Suite 610, P.O. Box 2270, 71207-2270
Telephone: 318-325-7000
Telecopier: 318-324-0580

MEMBERS OF FIRM

Robert P. McLeod (P.L.C.)
David E. Verlander, III (P.L.C.)
Ellen R. Eade
Paul J. Verlander
Rick W. Duplissey
Pamela G. Nathan

For full biographical listings, see the Martindale-Hubbell Law Directory

*NEW ORLEANS,** Orleans Parish

CAPITELLI & WICKER (AV)

2950 Energy Centre, 1100 Poydras Street, 70163-2950
Telephone: 504-582-2425
FAX: 504-582-2422

Ralph Capitelli
T. Carey Wicker, III
Paul Michael Elvir, Jr.

OF COUNSEL

Terry Q. Alarcon

For full biographical listings, see the Martindale-Hubbell Law Directory

GAINSBURGH, BENJAMIN, FALLON, DAVID & ATES (AV)

A Partnership including Professional Law Corporations
2800 Energy Centre, 1100 Poydras, 70163-2800
Telephone: 504-522-2304
Telecopier: 504-528-9973

OF COUNSEL

Samuel C. Gainsburgh (P.L.C.)

MEMBERS OF FIRM

Jack C. Benjamin (P.L.C.)
Eldon E. Fallon (P.L.C.)
Robert J. David
George S. Meyer (1939-1977)
J. Robert Ates (P.L.C.)
Gerald E. Meunier
Nick F. Noriea, Jr.
Irving J. Warshauer
Stevan C. Dittman
Madeleine M. Landrieu

(See Next Column)

ASSOCIATES

Darryl M. Phillips
Andrew A. Lemmon
Michael G. Calogero

For full biographical listings, see the Martindale-Hubbell Law Directory

HABANS, BOLOGNA & CARRIERE, A PROFESSIONAL LAW CORPORATION (AV)

Suite 2323, 1515 Poydras Street, 70112
Telephone: 504-524-2323
Telex: 151514 HABA M UT
Telecopier: 504-522-7224
Cable Address: HABOL

Robert N. Habans, Jr.
William F. Bologna
James D. Carriere
John C. McNeese
Aimée Carriere
Dwight L. Acomb
Julien F. Jurgens

For full biographical listings, see the Martindale-Hubbell Law Directory

MAINE

*AUGUSTA,** Kennebec Co.

* indicates certain Bar Register subscribers whose principal office is located elsewhere in the state and who have arranged for representation as a part of the state capital listings that follow

*** PIERCE, ATWOOD, SCRIBNER, ALLEN, SMITH & LANCASTER** (AV)

77 Winthrop Street, 04330
Telephone: 207-622-6311
Fax: 207-623-9367
Portland, Maine Office: One Monument Square.
Telephone: 207-773-6411.
Camden, Maine Office: 36 Chestnut Street, P.O. Box 780.
Telephone: 207-236-4333.

MEMBER OF FIRM

Malcolm L. Lyons

For Complete List of Firm Personnel, See General Section

For full biographical listings, see the Martindale-Hubbell Law Directory

*BANGOR,** Penobscot Co.

GROSS, MINSKY, MOGUL & SINGAL, P.A. (AV)

Key Plaza, 23 Water Street, P.O. Box 917, 04402-0917
Telephone: 207-942-4644
Telecopier: 207-942-3699
Ellsworth, Maine Office: 26 State Street.
Telephone: 207-667-4611.
Telecopier: 207-667-6206.

Jules L. Mogul (1930-1994)
Norman Minsky
George Z. Singal
Louis H. Kornreich
George C. Schelling
Edward W. Gould
Steven J. Mogul
James R. Wholly

Wayne P. Libhart (Resident, Ellsworth, Maine Office)
Daniel A. Pileggi
Philip K. Clarke
Christopher R. Largay (Resident, Ellsworth Office)
Hans G. Huessy
William B. Entwisle
Sandra L. Rothera

OF COUNSEL

Edward I. Gross

Representative Clients: Dahl Chase Pathology Associates; Superior Paper Products.
Local Counsel for: The St. Paul Insurance Cos.; Aetna Life & Casualty Co.; Imperial Casualty & Indemnity Co.

For full biographical listings, see the Martindale-Hubbell Law Directory

RICHARDSON, TROUBH & BADGER, A PROFESSIONAL CORPORATION (AV)

82 Columbia Street, P.O. Box 2429, 04402-2429
Telephone: 207-945-5900
Telecopier: 207-945-0758
Portland, Maine Office: Richardson & Troubh, A Professional Corporation, 465 Congress Street. P.O. Box, 9732.
Telephone: 207-774-5821.
Telecopier: 207-761-2056.

Frederick J. Badger, Jr. (Resident)
Ann M. Murray (Resident)

(See Next Column)

RICHARDSON, TROUBH & BADGER A PROFESSIONAL CORPORATION, *Bangor—Continued*

Frederick F. Costlow (Resident) John B. Lucy (Resident)

Representative Clients: Royal Globe Insurance; Travelers Insurance; Peerless Insurance; CIGNA; General Motors Corp.; Hanover Insurance; Liberty Mutual Insurance;
Local Counsel for: General Motors Corp.; Beloit Corp./Harnischfeger; Winnebago Industries.

For full biographical listings, see the Martindale-Hubbell Law Directory

VAFIADES, BROUNTAS & KOMINSKY (AV)

Key Plaza, 23 Water Street, P.O. Box 919, 04402-0919
Telephone: 207-947-6915
Telecopier: 207-941-0863

MEMBERS OF FIRM

Nicholas P. Brountas Marvin H. Glazier
Eugene C. Coughlin, III

ASSOCIATE

Amy L. Faircloth

OF COUNSEL

Lewis V. Vafiades

For Complete List of Firm Personnel, See General Section

For full biographical listings, see the Martindale-Hubbell Law Directory

BRIDGTON, Cumberland Co.

BERMAN & SIMMONS, P.A. (AV)

Route 302, Portland Street, 04009
Telephone: 207-647-3125
Fax: 207-647-3134
Lewiston, Maine Office: 129 Lisbon Street, P.O. Box 961, 04243-0961.
Telephone: 207-784-3576.
Fax: 207-784-7699.
Portland, Maine Office: 178 Middle Street.
Telephone: 207-774-5277.
Fax: 207-774-0166.
South Paris, Maine Office: 4 Western Avenue.
Telephone: 207-743- 8775.
Fax: 207-743-8559.

C. Martin Berman Julian L. Sweet
David W. Grund

For full biographical listings, see the Martindale-Hubbell Law Directory

LEWISTON, Androscoggin Co.

BERMAN & SIMMONS, P.A. (AV)

129 Lisbon Street, P.O. Box 961, 04243-0961
Telephone: 207-784-3576
Fax: 207-784-7699
Portland, Maine Office: 178 Middle Street.
Telephone: 207-774-5277.
Fax: 207-774-0166.
South Paris, Maine Office: 4 Western Avenue.
Telephone: 207-743- 8775.
Fax: 207-743-8559.
Bridgton, Maine Office: Route 302, Portland Street.
Telephone: 207-647-3125.
Fax: 207-647-3134.

C. Martin Berman
Jack H. Simmons
John E. Sedgewick
William D. Robitzek
Julian L. Sweet
Jeffrey Rosenblatt
Paul F. Macri
Jeffrey A. Thaler
Steven D. Silin
Valerie Stanfill
Tyler N. Kolle
Glenn S. Eddy
David J. Van Dyke
David W. Grund
Daniel G. Kagan
Joy C. Cantrell
Ivy L. Frignoca

For full biographical listings, see the Martindale-Hubbell Law Directory

*PORTLAND,** Cumberland Co.

BERMAN & SIMMONS, P.A. (AV)

178 Middle Street, 04101
Telephone: 207-774-5277
Fax: 207-774-0166
Lewiston, Maine Office: 129 Lisbon Street.
Telephone: 207-784-3576.
Fax: 207-784-7699.
South Paris, Maine Office: 4 Western Avenue.
Telephone: 207-743-8775.
Fax: 207-743-8559.
Bridgton, Maine Office: Route 302, Portland Street.
Telephone: 207-647-3125.
Fax: 207-647-3134.

(See Next Column)

William D. Robitzek

For full biographical listings, see the Martindale-Hubbell Law Directory

DANIEL G. LILLEY, P.A. (AV)

39 Portland Pier, P.O. Box 4803, 04112
Telephone: 207-774-6206
Telecopier: 207-774-2257

Daniel G. Lilley

John A. McArdle III Mark L. Randall
Mary Davis

OF COUNSEL

William A. Fogel

For full biographical listings, see the Martindale-Hubbell Law Directory

PIERCE, ATWOOD, SCRIBNER, ALLEN, SMITH & LANCASTER (AV)

One Monument Square, 04101
Telephone: 207-773-6411
Fax: 207-773-3419
Augusta, Maine Office: 77 Winthrop Street.
Telephone: 207-622-6311.
Camden, Maine Office: 36 Chestnut Street, P.O. Box 780.
Telephone: 207-236-4333.

MEMBERS OF FIRM

Ralph I. Lancaster, Jr.
Malcolm L. Lyons (Resident, Augusta Office)
Peter W. Culley
James R. Erwin, II
Kevin F. Gordon

ASSOCIATE

Stephen G. Grygiel

For Complete List of Firm Personnel, See General Section

For full biographical listings, see the Martindale-Hubbell Law Directory

PRESQUE ISLE, Aroostook Co.

STEVENS, ENGELS, BISHOP & SPRAGUE (AV)

428 Main Street, P.O. Box 311, 04769
Telephone: 207-768-5481
Telefax: 207-764-1663

MEMBERS OF FIRM

Albert M. Stevens
Richard C. Engels
Frank H. Bishop, Sr.
Jonathan W. Sprague
Michael L. Dubois

Representative Clients: Commercial Union Cos.; Travelers Insurance Co.; Aetna Insurance Co.; Firemans Fund Group; Hartford Insurance Group; Home Indemnity Co.; Maine Bonding and Casualty Co.; New Hampshire Group; Liberty Mutual Insurance Co.; Peoples Heritage Bank.

For full biographical listings, see the Martindale-Hubbell Law Directory

SACO, York Co.

SMITH ELLIOTT SMITH & GARMEY, P.A. (AV)

199 Main Street, P.O. Box 1179, 04072
Telephone: 207-282-1527
Telefax: 207-283-4412
Sanford Telephone: 207-324-1560
Portland Telephone: 207-774-3199
Wells Telephone: 207-646-0970
Kennebunk, Maine Office: Route One South, P.O. Box 980.
Telephone: 207-985-4464.
Telefax: 207-985-3946.
Portland, Maine Office: 100 Commercial Street, Suite 304.
Telephone: 207-774-3199.
Telefax: 207-774-2235.

Charles W. Smith, Jr. John H. O'Neil, Jr.
Harry B. Center, II

Robert M. Nadeau Michael J. Waxman

References: Casco Northern Bank, N.A. (Saco Branch); Saco & Biddeford Savings Institution.

For Complete List of Firm Personnel, See General Section

For full biographical listings, see the Martindale-Hubbell Law Directory

*SKOWHEGAN,** Somerset Co.

WRIGHT & MILLS, P.A. (AV)

218 Water Street, P.O. Box 9, 04976
Telephone: 207-474-3324
Telefax: 207-474-3609

(See Next Column)

WRIGHT & MILLS P.A.—*Continued*

Carl R. Wright
S. Peter Mills, III
Paul P. Sumberg
Kenneth A. Lexier
Dale F. Thistle

Representative Clients: Design Professionals Insurance Company, New Jersey; Solon Manufacturing Company, Solon, Maine; Kleinschmidt Associates-Engineers, Pittsfield, Maine; Acheron Engineering, Newport, Maine; E.W. Littlefield-Contractors, Hartland, Maine; WBRC-Architects, Bangor, Maine.

For full biographical listings, see the Martindale-Hubbell Law Directory

*SOUTH PARIS,** Oxford Co.

BERMAN & SIMMONS, P.A. (AV)

4 Western Avenue, 04281
Telephone: 207-743-8775
Fax: 207-743-8559
Lewiston, Maine Office: 129 Lisbon Street, P.O. Box 961.
Telephone: 207-284-3576.
Fax: 207-784-7699.
Portland, Maine Office: 178 Middle Street.
Telephone: 207-774-5277.
Fax: 207-774-0166.
Bridgton, Maine Office: Route 302, Portland Street.
Telephone: 207-647-3125.
Fax: 207-647-3134.

Jack H. Simmons
Glenn S. Eddy

For full biographical listings, see the Martindale-Hubbell Law Directory

MARYLAND

*BALTIMORE,** (Independent City)

FREISHTAT & SANDLER (AV)

Suite 1500, One Calvert Plaza, 201 E. Baltimore Street, 21202
Telephone: 410-727-7740
FAX: 410-727-7356

MEMBERS OF FIRM

David Freishtat
Paul Mark Sandler
Raymond Daniel Burke
William M. Mullen

Lloyd J. Snow
Lynn Weinberg
Stacie F. Dubnow
T. Allen Mott

For full biographical listings, see the Martindale-Hubbell Law Directory

PAUL R. KRAMER, P.A. (AV)

231 St. Paul Place, 21202-2003
Telephone: 410-727-5531
FAX: 410-727-2186

Paul R. Kramer

For full biographical listings, see the Martindale-Hubbell Law Directory

THIEBLOT, RYAN, MARTIN & FERGUSON, P.A. (AV)

4th Floor, The World Trade Center, 21202-3091
Telephone: 410-837-1140
Washington, D.C. Line: 202-628-8223
Fax: 410-837-3282

Robert J. Thieblot
Anthony W. Ryan
J. Edward Martin, Jr.
Robert L. Ferguson, Jr.
Bruce R. Miller
Robert D. Harwick, Jr.
Thomas J. Schetelich
Christopher J. Heffernan

M. Brooke Murdock
Anne M. Hrehorovich
Donna Marie Raffaele
Michael N. Russo, Jr.
Jodi K. Ebersole
Hamilton Fisk Tyler
Peter Joseph Basile

Representative Clients: Ford Motor Credit Co.; USF & G Co.; The American Road Insurance Co.; Fidelity Engineering Corp.; The North Charles Street Design Organization; Record Collections, Inc.; Toyota Motor Credit Co.

For full biographical listings, see the Martindale-Hubbell Law Directory

VENABLE, BAETJER AND HOWARD (AV)

A Partnership including Professional Corporations
1800 Mercantile Bank & Trust Building, 2 Hopkins Plaza, 21201
Telephone: 410-244-7400
Washington, D.C. Office: Venable, Baetjer, Howard & Civiletti. Suite 1000, 1201 New York Avenue, N.W.
Telephone: 202-962-4800.

(See Next Column)

McLean, Virginia Office: Suite 400, 2010 Corporate Ridge.
Telephone: 703-760-1600.
Rockville, Maryland Office: Suite 500, One Church Street, P. O. Box 1906.
Telephone: 301-217-5600.
Towson, Maryland Office: 210 Allegheny Avenue, P. O. Box 5517.
Telephone: 410-494-6200.

MEMBERS OF FIRM

Benjamin R. Civiletti (P.C.) (Also at Washington, D.C. and Towson, Maryland Offices)
John Henry Lewin, Jr. (P.C.)
Bruce E. Titus (Resident, McLean, Virginia Office)
Joseph G. Block (Not admitted in MD; Resident, Washington, D.C. Office)
Michael Schatzow (Also at Washington, D.C. and Towson, Maryland Offices)
L. Paige Marvel
Judson W. Starr (Not admitted in MD; Also at Washington, D.C. and Towson, Maryland Offices)
William D. Coston (Not admitted in MD; Resident, Washington, D.C. Office)
Amy Berman Jackson (Not admitted in MD; Resident, Washington, D.C. Office)
William D. Quarles (Also at Washington, D.C. and Towson, Maryland Offices)
Kathleen Gallogly Cox (Resident, Towson, Maryland Office)
Mary E. Pivec (Also at Washington, D.C. Office)
Thomas J. Kelly, Jr. (Not admitted in MD; Resident, Washington, D. C. Office)
Gary M. Hnath (Resident, Washington, D.C. Office)

OF COUNSEL

Joyce K. Becker
Geoffrey R. Garinther (Also at Washington, D.C. Office)

ASSOCIATES

Paul D. Barker, Jr.
David W. Goewey (Not admitted in MD; Resident, Washington, D.C. Office)
David R. Hodnett (Not admitted in MD; Resident, McLean, Virginia Office)
Paula Titus Laboy (Resident, Rockville, Maryland Office)
Timothy J. McEvoy
Mitchell Y. Mirviss
Samuel T. Morison (Not admitted in MD; Resident, Washington, D.C. Office)
Catherine L. Schuster
Terri L. Turner

For Complete List of Firm Personnel, See General Section

For full biographical listings, see the Martindale-Hubbell Law Directory

ZUCKERMAN, SPAEDER, GOLDSTEIN, TAYLOR & BETTER (AV)

Suite 2440, 100 East Pratt Street, 21202
Telephone: 410-332-0444
Fax: 410-659-0436
Washington, D.C. Office: Zuckerman, Spaeder, Goldstein, Taylor & Kolker. 1201 Connecticut Avenue, N.W.
Telephone: 202-778-1800.
Fax: 202-822-8106.
Miami, Florida Office: Zuckerman, Spaeder, Taylor & Evans. Suite 900, Miami Center, 201 South Biscayne Boulevard.
Telephones: 305-358-5000; 305-579-0110; Broward County: 305-523-0277.
Fax: 305-579-9749.
Ft. Lauderdale, Florida Office: Zuckerman, Spaeder, Taylor & Evans. One East Broward Boulevard, Suite 700.
Telephone: 305-356-0463.
Fax: 305-356-0406.
Tampa, Florida Office: Zuckerman, Spaeder, Taylor & Evans. 101 East Kennedy Boulevard, Suite 3140.
Telephone: 813-221-1010.
Fax: 813-223-7961.
New York, N.Y. Office: Zuckerman, Spaeder, Goldstein, Taylor & Kolker, 1114 Avenue of the Americas, 45th Floor, Grace Building.
Telephone: 212-479-6500.
Fax: 212-479-6512.

RESIDENT MEMBERS

Herbert Better
Donald J. McCartney

RESIDENT ASSOCIATE

Cyril V. Smith

For full biographical listings, see the Martindale-Hubbell Law Directory

*LA PLATA,** Charles Co.

DAVID NEWMAN & ASSOCIATES, P.C. (AV)

Centennial Square, P.O. Box 2728, 20646-2728
Telephone: 301-934-6100; 202-842-8400
Facsimile: 301-934-5782

David B. Newman, Jr.

Suzin C. Bailey

LEGAL SUPPORT PERSONNEL

TECHNICAL ADVISORS

Dr. Christopher J. Newman
Dr. Amy Hauck Newman

For full biographical listings, see the Martindale-Hubbell Law Directory

OCEAN CITY, Worcester Co.

Courtland K. Townsend, Jr. Chartered (AV)

The Executive Building, Suite 101, 7200 Coastal Highway, 21842
Telephone: 410-524-4300
FAX: 410-524-4953

Courtland K. Townsend, Jr.

For full biographical listings, see the Martindale-Hubbell Law Directory

*ROCKVILLE,** Montgomery Co.

Armstrong, Donohue & Ceppos, Chartered (AV)

Suite 101, 204 Monroe Street, 20850
Telephone: 301-251-0440
Telecopier: 301-279-5929

Larry A. Ceppos
Benjamin S. Vaughan
John C. Monahan

For full biographical listings, see the Martindale-Hubbell Law Directory

Catterton & Kemp (AV)

Suite 315, 200 A Monroe Street, 20850
Telephone: 301-294-0460
FAX: 301-294-6406

MEMBERS OF FIRM

Judith R. Catterton
Paul F. Kemp

ASSOCIATE

Sara M. Donohue

OF COUNSEL

Jane Macht

For full biographical listings, see the Martindale-Hubbell Law Directory

Stein, Sperling, Bennett, De Jong, Driscoll, Greenfeig & Metro, P.A. (AV)

25 West Middle Lane, 20850
Telephone: 301-340-2020; 800-435-5230
Telecopier: 301-340-8217

David C. Driscoll, Jr.
Paul T. Stein

For Complete List of Firm Personnel, See General Section

For full biographical listings, see the Martindale-Hubbell Law Directory

*TOWSON,** Baltimore Co.

Nolan, Plumhoff & Williams, Chartered (AV)

Suite 700 Court Towers, 210 West Pennsylvania Avenue, 21204
Telephone: 410-823-7800
Fax: 410-296-2765

Stephen M. Schenning

For Complete List of Firm Personnel, See General Section

For full biographical listings, see the Martindale-Hubbell Law Directory

MASSACHUSETTS

*BOSTON,** Suffolk Co.

Mintz, Levin, Cohn, Ferris, Glovsky and Popeo, P.C. (AV)

One Financial Center, 02111
Telephone: 617-542-6000
FAX: 617-542-2241
Washington, D.C. Office: 701 Pennsylvania Avenue, N.W. Suite 900.
Telephone: 202-434-7300.
Fax: 202-434-7400.

R. Robert Popeo
Thomas R. Murtagh
John K. Markey
Michael S. Gardener

For Complete List of Firm Personnel, See General Section

For full biographical listings, see the Martindale-Hubbell Law Directory

Oteri, Weinberg & Lawson (AV)

The Statler Building, 20 Park Plaza, Suite 905, 02116
Telephone: 617-227-3700
Fax: 617-338-9538

(See Next Column)

Joseph S. Oteri
Martin G. Weinberg
James W. Lawson

James H. Budreau

Sherburne, Powers & Needham, P.C. (AV)

One Beacon Street, 02108
Telephone: 617-523-2700
Fax: 617-523-6850

William D. Weeks
John T. Collins
Allan J. Landau
John L. Daly
Stephen A. Hopkins
Alan I. Falk
C. Thomas Swaim
James Pollock
William V. Tripp III
Stephen S. Young
William F. Machen
W. Robert Allison
Jacob C. Diemert
Philip J. Notopoulos
Richard J. Hindlian
Paul E. Troy
Harold W. Potter, Jr.
Dale R. Johnson
Philip S. Lapatin
Pamela A. Duckworth
Mark Schonfeld
James D. Smeallie
Paul Killeen
Gordon P. Katz
Joseph B. Darby, III
Richard M Yanofsky
James E. McDermott
Robert V. Lizza
Miriam Goldstein Altman
John J. Monaghan
Margaret J. Palladino
Mark C. Michalowski
David Scott Sloan
M. Chrysa Long
Lawrence D. Bradley
Miriam J. McKendall

Cynthia A. Brown
Cynthia M. Hern
Dianne R. Phillips
Paul M. James
Theodore F. Hanselman
Joshua C. Krumholz
Ieuan G. Mahony
Kenneth L. Harvey
Christopher J. Trombetta
Edwin F. Landers, Jr.
Amy J. Mastrobattista
William Howard McCarthy, Jr.
Douglas W. Clapp
Tamara E. Goulston
Nicholas J. Psyhogeos

COUNSEL

Haig Der Manuelian
Mason M. Taber, Jr.
Karl J. Hirshman
Benjamin Volinski
Kenneth P. Brier

OF COUNSEL

John Barr Dolan

For full biographical listings, see the Martindale-Hubbell Law Directory

Zalkind, Rodriguez, Lunt & Duncan (AV)

65A Atlantic Avenue, 02110
Telephone: 617-742-6020

MEMBERS OF FIRM

Norman S. Zalkind
Elizabeth A. Lunt
David Duncan
Janet L. Sanders

ASSOCIATE

Clifford A. Truesdell

OF COUNSEL

Barbara Equen Rodriguez
John Ward

For full biographical listings, see the Martindale-Hubbell Law Directory

*CAMBRIDGE,** Middlesex Co.

George F. Gormley, P.C. (AV)

One Main Street, P.O. Box 965, 02142-0090
Telephone: 617-349-3750
Fax: 617-661-2576

George F. Gormley

Jackie L. Segel
John D. Colucci

For full biographical listings, see the Martindale-Hubbell Law Directory

WELLESLEY, Norfolk Co.

Nicholas B. Soutter (AV)

One Washington Street, Suite 208, 02181
Telephone: 617-237-6300
Fax: 617-237-6143

ASSOCIATE

Paul S. McGovern

For full biographical listings, see the Martindale-Hubbell Law Directory

*WORCESTER,** Worcester Co.

McGuire & McGuire, P.C. (AV)

340 Main Street, Suite 910, 01608
Telephone: 508-754-3291
Fax: 508-752-0553

(See Next Column)

McGuire & McGuire P.C.—*Continued*

John K. McGuire (1952-1985)
Joseph E. McGuire
John K. McGuire, Jr.

Penelope A. Kathiwala
Paul Durkee
Christine Griggs Narcisse
Teresa Brooks

For full biographical listings, see the Martindale-Hubbell Law Directory

Reardon & Reardon (AV)

One Exchange Place, 01608
Telephone: 508-754-1111
Fax: 508-797-6176
Boston, Massachusetts Office: 69 Beacon Street.
Telephone: 617-248-6998.

MEMBERS OF FIRM

James G. Reardon
Edward P. Reardon
Frank S. Puccio, Jr.

ASSOCIATES

Austin M. Joyce
James G. Reardon, Jr.
James G. Haddad
Julie E. Reardon
Margaret Reardon Suuberg
Michael J. Akerson
Francis J. Duggan

References: Mechanics National Bank; Shawmut Worcester County Bank N.A.; Bank of New England, Worcester.

For full biographical listings, see the Martindale-Hubbell Law Directory

MICHIGAN

*ANN ARBOR,** Washtenaw Co.

Hooper, Hathaway, Price, Beuche & Wallace (AV)

126 South Main Street, 48104
Telephone: 313-662-4426
Fax: 313-662-9559

Joseph C. Hooper (1899-1980)
Gregory A. Spaly
Alan E. Price
Robert W. Southard
James R. Beuche
William J. Stapleton
Bruce T. Wallace
Bruce C. Conybeare, Jr.
Charles W. Borgsdorf
Anthony P. Patti
Mark R. Daane
Marcia J. Major

OF COUNSEL

James A. Evashevski
Roderick K. Daane

Representative Clients: Chem-Trend, Inc.; Dundee Cement Co.; Ervin Industries, Inc.; First Martin Corp.; Group 243 Design, Inc.; Honeywell; Microwave Sensors, Inc.; Shearson Lehman Hutton; O'Neal Construction Co.; Pittsfield Products, Inc.

For Complete List of Firm Personnel, See General Section

For full biographical listings, see the Martindale-Hubbell Law Directory

O'Brien and O'Brien (AV)

300 North Fifth Avenue, 48104
Telephone: 313-996-0550
Fax: 313-996-5555

MEMBERS OF FIRM

Thomas C. O'Brien
Darlene A. O'Brien

OF COUNSEL

Francis L. O'Brien (1907-1991)

Reference: Society Bank.

For full biographical listings, see the Martindale-Hubbell Law Directory

BLOOMFIELD HILLS, Oakland Co.

Baum & Associates (AV)

200 East Long Lake Road Suite 180, 48304
Telephone: 810-647-6890

Martin S. Baum

ASSOCIATE

Margo S. Horwitz

For full biographical listings, see the Martindale-Hubbell Law Directory

*DETROIT,** Wayne Co.

Baum & Associates

(See Bloomfield Hills)

Dise & Gurewitz, P.C. (AV)

3600 Cadillac Tower, 48226
Telephone: 313-963-8155
Telefax: 313-963-8438

John H. Dise, Jr.
Harold Gurewitz

Gina Ursula Puzzuoli
G. Gus Morris
Margaret Sind Raben
Elizabeth M. Malone

OF COUNSEL

Timothy Downs
Gene A. Farber

For full biographical listings, see the Martindale-Hubbell Law Directory

David F. DuMouchel, P.C. (AV)

150 West Jefferson, Suite 900, 48226-4430
Telephone: 313-225-7004

David F. DuMouchel

For full biographical listings, see the Martindale-Hubbell Law Directory

David Griem (AV)

One Woodward Avenue, Suite 2400, 48226
Telephone: 313-961-8380
Mount Clemens, Michigan Office: 14 First Street.
Telephone: 313-465-4900.

For full biographical listings, see the Martindale-Hubbell Law Directory

Honigman Miller Schwartz and Cohn (AV)

A Partnership including Professional Corporations
2290 First National Building, 48226
Telephone: 313-256-7800
Telecopier: 313-962-0176
Telex: 235705
Lansing, Michigan Office: Phoenix Building, 222 North Washington Square, Suite 400.
Telephone: 517-484-8282.
West Palm Beach, Florida Office: Suite 800 Esperante Building, 222 Lakeview Avenue.
Telephone: 407-838-4500.
Tampa, Florida Office: 2700 Landmark Centre, 401 E. Jackson Street.
Telephone: 813-221-6600.
Orlando, Florida Office: 390 North Orange Avenue, Suite 1300.
Telephone: 407-648-0300.
Houston, Texas Office: 3100 First Interstate Bank Plaza, 1000 Louisiana.
Telephone: 713-650-2600.
Los Angeles, California Office: McNeill Plaza, Suite 820, 15260 Ventura Boulevard, 91403.
Telephone: 818-784-2900.

MEMBERS OF FIRM

Jay E. Brant
Mark R. Werder
Richard E. Zuckerman

For Complete List of Firm Personnel, See General Section

For full biographical listings, see the Martindale-Hubbell Law Directory

Kenneth M. Mogill (AV)

Suite 1930, One Kennedy Square, 48226
Telephone: 313-962-7210

For full biographical listings, see the Martindale-Hubbell Law Directory

Pritchard & Thomas, Professional Corporation (AV)

918 Buhl Building, 48226
Telephone: 313-964-0030

Clyde B. Pritchard
Edith S. Thomas

LEGAL SUPPORT PERSONNEL

Morris R. Culver

For full biographical listings, see the Martindale-Hubbell Law Directory

Stringari, Fritz, Kreger, Ahearn & Crandall, P.C. (AV)

650 First National Building, 48226-3538
Telephone: 313-961-6474
Fax: 313-961-5688

Martin E. Crandall
Kenneth S. Wilson

John C. Dickinson

For full biographical listings, see the Martindale-Hubbell Law Directory

EAST LANSING, Ingham Co.

Farhat, Story & Kraus, P.C. (AV)
Beacon Place, 4572 South Hagadorn Road, Suite 3, 48823
Telephone: 517-351-3700
Fax: 517-332-4122

Leo A. Farhat
James E. Burns (1925-1979)
Monte R. Story
Richard C. Kraus
Max R. Hoffman Jr.
Chris A. Bergstrom
Kitty L. Groh
Charles R. Toy
David M. Platt

Lawrence P. Schweitzer
Jeffrey J. Short
Kathy A. Breedlove
Thomas L. Sparks

Reference: Capitol National Bank.

For full biographical listings, see the Martindale-Hubbell Law Directory

*FLINT,** Genesee Co.

O'Rourke & Joseph, P.C. (AV)
727 South Grand Traverse Street, 48502
Telephone: 810-239-3165
Fax: 810-239-5965

Edward P. Joseph (1927-1987)
Jerome F. O'Rourke

Reference: Citizens Commercial and Savings Bank.

For full biographical listings, see the Martindale-Hubbell Law Directory

*GRAND RAPIDS,** Kent Co.

David A. Dodge, P.C. (AV)
200 North Division Avenue, 49503
Telephone: 616-459-3850
FAX: 616-459-4909

David A. Dodge
Mary E. Farrell

For full biographical listings, see the Martindale-Hubbell Law Directory

HANCOCK, Houghton Co.

Wisti & Jaaskelainen, P.C. (AV)
101 Quincy Street, 49930
Telephone: 906-482-5220
Iron Mountain, Michigan Office: 623 Stephenson Avenue.
Telephone: 906-779-1280.
Marquette, Michigan Office: 117 South Front Street.
Telephone: 906-228-8204.

Andrew H. Wisti
Mark Wisti
Daniel J. Wisti

David M. Gemignani

OF COUNSEL

Gordon J. Jaaskelainen

References: Superior National Bank & Trust Company of Hancock, Michigan; Houghton National Bank, Houghton, Michigan.

For full biographical listings, see the Martindale-Hubbell Law Directory

LANSING, Ingham Co.

Dunnings & Frawley, P.C. (AV)
Duncan Building, 530 South Pine Street, 48933-2299
Telephone: 517-487-8222
Fax: 517-487-2026

Stuart J. Dunnings, Jr.
John J. Frawley

Stuart J. Dunnings, III
Steven D. Dunnings

For full biographical listings, see the Martindale-Hubbell Law Directory

*MOUNT CLEMENS,** Macomb Co.

David Griem (AV)
14 First Street, 48043
Telephone: 810-465-4900
Detroit, Michigan Office: One Woodward Avenue, Suite 2400, 48226.
Telephone: 313-961-8380.

For full biographical listings, see the Martindale-Hubbell Law Directory

*MUSKEGON,** Muskegon Co.

Parmenter O'Toole (AV)
175 West Apple Street, P.O. Box 786, 49443-0786
Telephone: 616-722-1621
Telecopier: 616-728-2206; 722-7866

(See Next Column)

MEMBERS OF FIRM

W. Brad Groom
Timothy G. Hicks

ASSOCIATE

Shawn P. Davis

General Counsel for: FMB Lumberman's Bank; AmeriBank Federal Savings Bank; City of Muskegon; Quality Tool & Stamping Co., Inc.; Radiology Muskegon, P.C.
Local Counsel for: General Electric Capital Corp.; Paine-Webber; Teledyne Industries, Inc. (Continental Motors Division); Westinghouse Electric Corporation (Knoll Group).

For Complete List of Firm Personnel, See General Section

For full biographical listings, see the Martindale-Hubbell Law Directory

*PONTIAC,** Oakland Co.

Sterling, Schilling & Thorburn, P.C. (AV)
1400 NBD Building, 48342
Telephone: 810-334-4544
Fax: 810-334-1021

Ronald F. Schilling
Bruce J. Thorburn

For full biographical listings, see the Martindale-Hubbell Law Directory

SOUTHFIELD, Oakland Co.

Fieger, Fieger & Schwartz, A Professional Corporation (AV)
19390 West Ten Mile Road, 48075-2463
Telephone: 810-355-5555
FAX: 810-355-5148

Bernard J. Fieger (1922-1988)
Geoffrey N. Fieger
Michael Alan Schwartz
Dennis Fuller
Pamela A. Hamway
Dean W. Amburn
Ronald S. Glaser
Gary S. Fields
Todd J. Weglarz

OF COUNSEL

Barry Fayne
Stephen L. Witenoff
Beverly Hires Brode

For full biographical listings, see the Martindale-Hubbell Law Directory

Sommers, Schwartz, Silver & Schwartz, P.C. (AV)
2000 Town Center, Suite 900, 48075
Telephone: 810-355-0300
Telecopier: 810-746-4001
Plymouth, Michigan Office: 747 South Main Street.
Telephone: 313-455-4250.

Lawrence Warren
Justin C. Ravitz
David M. Black
Matthew G. Curtis
Frank T. Aiello

General Counsel for: City of Taylor; Township of VanBuren.
Representative Clients: City of Pontiac.

For Complete List of Firm Personnel, See General Section

For full biographical listings, see the Martindale-Hubbell Law Directory

MINNESOTA

*AUSTIN,** Mower Co.

Hoversten, Strom, Johnson & Rysavy (AV)
807 West Oakland Avenue, 55912
Telephone: 507-433-3483
Fax: 507-433-7889

MEMBERS OF FIRM

Kermit F. Hoversten
Craig W. Johnson
Donald E. Rysavy
David V. Hoversten
John S. Beckmann
Fred W. Wellmann
Steven J Hovey

ASSOCIATE

Mary Carroll Leahy

OF COUNSEL

Kenneth M. Strom

Representative Clients: Hartford Insurance Co.; Allied Insurance Group; Travelers Insurance; American States Insurance; Royal Milbank Insurance; Prudential Insurance Co.; Independent School District 756; St. Olaf Hospital; Austin Medical Clinic; Norwest Bank, Austin.

For Complete List of Firm Personnel, See General Section

For full biographical listings, see the Martindale-Hubbell Law Directory

EDEN VALLEY, Meeker Co.

John H. Bradshaw (AV)

P.O. Box 559, 55329
Telephone: 612-453-6645
FAX: 612-453-6649

ASSOCIATE
Michael A. Bryant

For full biographical listings, see the Martindale-Hubbell Law Directory

*MANKATO,** Blue Earth Co.

Blethen, Gage & Krause (AV)

127 South Second Street, P.O. Box 3049, 56001
Telephone: 507-345-1166
Fax: 507-345-8003

MEMBER OF FIRM
Bailey W. Blethen

General Counsel For: Mankato Citizens Telephone Co.; Norwest Bank Minnesota South Central, N.A.: Waseca Mutual Insurance Co.; Hickory Tech Corporation; Winco, Inc.
Local Counsel For: American States Insurance Co.; ConAgra Fertilizer Co.; Northern Natural Gas Co., a division of Enron Corp.; General Motors Corp.; Millers Mutual Insurance Co.

For Complete List of Firm Personnel, See General Section

For full biographical listings, see the Martindale-Hubbell Law Directory

Manahan & Bluth Law Office Chartered (AV)

416 South Front Street, P.O. Box 287, 56002-0287
Telephone: 507-387-5661
Fax: 507-387-2111
CompuServe ID#73530,2374

James H. Manahan Joseph P. Bluth

Reference: Security State Bank of Mankato.

For full biographical listings, see the Martindale-Hubbell Law Directory

*MINNEAPOLIS,** Hennepin Co.

Frederic Bruno & Associates (AV)

The Colonnade, 5500 Wayzata Boulevard, Suite 730, 55416
Telephone: 612-545-7900
Fax: 612-545-0834

ASSOCIATE
Timothy R. Anderson

For full biographical listings, see the Martindale-Hubbell Law Directory

Joseph S. Friedberg Chartered (AV)

Suite 205, Commerce At The Crossings, 250 Second Avenue, South, 55401
Telephone: 612-339-8626

Joseph S. Friedberg

For full biographical listings, see the Martindale-Hubbell Law Directory

Bruce H. Hanley, P.A. (AV)

Suite 700, 701 Fourth Avenue South, 55415
Telephone: 612-339-1290
Fax: 612-339-9545

Bruce H. Hanley

Lisa D. Dejoras

For full biographical listings, see the Martindale-Hubbell Law Directory

Mauzy Law Firm (AV)

2885 Norwest Center, 90 S. 7th Street, 55402-3930
Telephone: 612-340-9108
Fax: 612-340-1628

William J. Mauzy

Douglas H. Olson Jarett B. Decker

For full biographical listings, see the Martindale-Hubbell Law Directory

Meshbesher & Spence, Ltd. (AV)

1616 Park Avenue, 55404
Telephone: 612-339-9121
Fax: 612-339-9188
St. Paul, Minnesota Office: World Trade Center.
Telephone: 612-227-0799.

(See Next Column)

St. Cloud, Minnesota Office: 400 Zapp Bank Plaza.
Telephone: 612-656-0484.

Kenneth Meshbesher Jack Nordby
Ronald I. Meshbesher John P. Sheehy

For Complete List of Firm Personnel, See General Section

For full biographical listings, see the Martindale-Hubbell Law Directory

Kevin J. Short (AV)

2890 Metropolitan Centre, 333 South Seventh Street, 55402
Telephone: 612-333-9006
Fax: 612-333-5015

For full biographical listings, see the Martindale-Hubbell Law Directory

*ST. PAUL,** Ramsey Co.

Douglas W. Thomson, Ltd. (AV)

332 Minnesota Street, Room W1260, 55101-1305
Telephone: 612-227-0856

Douglas W. Thomson

For full biographical listings, see the Martindale-Hubbell Law Directory

MISSISSIPPI

*ASHLAND,** Benton Co.

Farese, Farese & Farese, P.A. (AV)

122 Church Street, P.O. Box 98, 38603
Telephone: 601-224-6211
Fax: 601-224-3229

John B. Farese Anthony L. Farese
John Booth Farese Linda S. Laher
Steven E. Farese Robert Q. Whitwell
C. Collier Carlton, Jr. David Reid Wamble

For full biographical listings, see the Martindale-Hubbell Law Directory

*GULFPORT,** Harrison Co.

Boyce Holleman A Professional Corporation (AV)

1913 15th Street, P.O. Drawer 1030, 39502
Telephone: 601-863-3142
Telecopier: 601-863-9829

Boyce Holleman

Michael B. Holleman Leslie Dean Holleman
Timothy C. Holleman David J. White

References: Hancock Bank, Gulfport; Merchants Bank & Trust Co., Gulfport; Bank of Wiggins, Wiggins, Mississippi.

For full biographical listings, see the Martindale-Hubbell Law Directory

*JACKSON,** Hinds Co.

Royals & Hartung (AV)

Eastover Bank Building, 120 North Congress Street, Suite 1100, P.O. Box 22909, 39225-2909
Telephone: 601-948-7777
Telecopier: 601-948-7780

MEMBERS OF FIRM
Thomas E. Royals Michael Hartung

ASSOCIATE
Cynthia A. Stewart

For full biographical listings, see the Martindale-Hubbell Law Directory

*NATCHEZ,** Adams Co.

Mulhearn & Mulhearn (AV)

202 South Wall Street, P.O. Box 967, 39120
Telephone: 601-442-4808
Fax: 601-446-6224

MEMBERS OF FIRM
John E. Mulhearn (1910-1981) John E. Mulhearn, Jr.

LEGAL SUPPORT PERSONNEL
Eva Ruth Seale Norma Joyce Beasley

Representative Client: Natchez Electric & Supply Co., Inc.
Approved Attorneys for: Mississippi Valley Title Insurance Co.; American Title Insurance Co.

For full biographical listings, see the Martindale-Hubbell Law Directory

SOUTHAVEN, De Soto Co.

Taylor, Jones, Alexander, Sorrell & McFall, Ltd. (AV)

961 State Line Road, West, P.O. Box 188, 38671
Telephone: 601-342-1300
Telecopier: 601-342-1312

(See Next Column)

TAYLOR, JONES, ALEXANDER, SORRELL & MCFALL LTD., *Southaven—Continued*

Ronald L. Taylor
Jack R. Jones, III
Keith M. Alexander
Mark K. Sorrell
George McFall

Approved Attorneys for: Mississippi Valley Title Insurance Co.; First American Title, Insurance.
Reference: Sunburst Bank, Southaven, Miss.

For full biographical listings, see the Martindale-Hubbell Law Directory

MISSOURI

*CLAYTON,** St. Louis Co.

DONALD L. WOLFF (AV)

8019 Forsyth (St. Louis), 63105
Telephone: 314-725-8019
Fax: 314-725-8443

ASSOCIATES

Susan Kister
Paul J. D'Agrosa

For full biographical listings, see the Martindale-Hubbell Law Directory

KANSAS CITY, Jackson, Clay & Platte Cos.

SIMON AND SIMON (AV)

600 Gumbel Building, 801 Walnut Street, 64106
Telephone: 816-471-3430
Fax: 816-471-0408

MEMBERS OF FIRM

Kenneth K. Simon (1916-1977)
Bruce W. Simon

Reference: Mercantile Bank & Trust, Kansas City.

For full biographical listings, see the Martindale-Hubbell Law Directory

JAMES F. SPECK (AV)

1125 Grand Avenue, Suite 1500, 64106
Telephone: 816-471-4141
Fax: 816-842-9704

For full biographical listings, see the Martindale-Hubbell Law Directory

WYRSCH ATWELL MIRAKIAN LEE & HOBBS, P.C. (AV)

1300 Mercantile Tower 1101 Walnut, 64106-2122
Telephone: 816-221-0080
Fax: 816-221-3280

James R. Wyrsch
Stephen G. Mirakian
Ronald D. Lee
Charles E. Atwell
James R. Hobbs
Keith E. Drill
Michael P. Joyce
Marilyn B. Keller
Cheryl A. Pilate
W. Brian Gaddy

LEGAL SUPPORT PERSONNEL

Phillip A. Thompson (Investigative and Paralegal)
Darlene Wyrsch (Paralegal)
Dru A. Colhour (Paralegal)
Al Tolentino (Paralegal and Videographer/Photographer)
Kathy Vetsch (Paralegal)

For full biographical listings, see the Martindale-Hubbell Law Directory

ST. LOUIS, (Independent City)

GREENBERG & PLEBAN (AV)

100 South Fourth Street, Suite 600, 63102
Telephone: 314-241-4141
Telecopier: 314-241-1038

Burton M. Greenberg
C. John Pleban

ASSOCIATES

Karen A. Greenberg
George A. Kiser
Michael J. Schaller

OF COUNSEL

Sarah Shelledy Pleban

Reference: Boatmen's National Bank.

For full biographical listings, see the Martindale-Hubbell Law Directory

MOLINE & SHOSTAK (AV)

The Berkley Building, 8015 Forsyth Boulevard, 63105
Telephone: 314-725-3200
Fax: 314-725-3275

(See Next Column)

Harry O. Moline
Burton H. Shostak
Sherri Cranmore Strand
Donald J. Mehan, Jr.
Deborah J. Westling
Michael S. Ghidina

For full biographical listings, see the Martindale-Hubbell Law Directory

SINDEL & SINDEL, P.C. (AV)

Suite 301, 8008 Carondelet, 63105
Telephone: 314-721-6040
Telecopier: 314-721-8545

Richard H. Sindel

Adam J. Sipple

For full biographical listings, see the Martindale-Hubbell Law Directory

WITTNER, POGER, ROSENBLUM & SPEWAK, P.C. (AV)

Suite 400, 7700 Bonhomme Avenue, 63105
Telephone: 314-862-3535
Fax: 314-862-5741

Gerald M. Poger
Howard A. Wittner
N. Scott Rosenblum
Steven B. Spewak
David S. Spewak
Jean H. Maylack

Ramona L. Marten
Jane M. Carriker
Gary M. Siegel
Barbara Greenberg
Vanessa C. Antoniou
Joseph L. Green

For full biographical listings, see the Martindale-Hubbell Law Directory

MONTANA

*BILLINGS,** Yellowstone Co.

CROWLEY, HAUGHEY, HANSON, TOOLE & DIETRICH (AV)

500 Transwestern II, 490 North 31st Street, P.O. Box 2529, 59103
Telephone: 406-252-3441
Fax: 406-259-4159
Helena, Montana Office: IBM Building, 100 North Park Avenue, Suite 300, 59601.
Telephone: 406-449-4165.
Fax: 406-449-5149.

MEMBER OF FIRM

Donald L. Harris

ASSOCIATE

Steven Robert Milch

Representative Clients: Montana Power Co.; First Interstate Bank of Commerce; MDU Resources Group, Inc.; Chevron U.S.A., Inc.; Noranda Minerals Corp.; United Parcel Service.
Insurance Clients: Farmers Insurance Group; New York Life Insurance Co.

For Complete List of Firm Personnel, See General Section
For full biographical listings, see the Martindale-Hubbell Law Directory

NEBRASKA

*LINCOLN,** Lancaster Co.

JOHN STEVENS BERRY, P.C. (AV)

2650 North 48th Street, P.O. Box 4554, 68504
Telephone: 402-466-8444
Fax: 402-466-1793

John Stevens Berry

For full biographical listings, see the Martindale-Hubbell Law Directory

NEVADA

*LAS VEGAS,** Clark Co.

THOMAS D. BEATTY (AV)

601 East Bridger Avenue, 89101
Telephone: 702-382-5111
Telecopier: 702-382-2892

(See Next Column)

THOMAS D. BEATTY—*Continued*

ASSOCIATES

Geoffrey A. Potts
Rena G. Benefield

Reference: First Interstate Bank of Nevada.

For full biographical listings, see the Martindale-Hubbell Law Directory

BELL, DAVIDSON & MYERS (AV)

601 East Bridger Avenue, 89101
Telephone: 702-382-5111

MEMBERS OF FIRM

Stewart L. Bell
Michael D. Davidson
Andrew S. Myers

Representative Client: Jack Kent Cooke.

For full biographical listings, see the Martindale-Hubbell Law Directory

DONALD J. CAMPBELL & ASSOCIATES (AV)

1409 Bank of America Plaza, 300 South Fourth Street, 89101
Telephone: 702-382-5222
Facsimile: 702-382-0540

ASSOCIATE

J. Colby Williams

For full biographical listings, see the Martindale-Hubbell Law Directory

FRANK J. CREMEN (AV)

Suite 1004, 302 East Carson, 89101
Telephone: 702-385-7475
FAX: 702-385-9703

Reference: First Interstate Bank of Nevada, N.A.

For full biographical listings, see the Martindale-Hubbell Law Directory

CROCKETT & MYERS, LTD. A PROFESSIONAL CORPORATION (AV)

700 South Third Street, 89101
Telephone: 702-382-6711
Fax: 702-384-8102

J. R. Crockett, Jr.
Richard W. Myers
James V. Lavelle III
Eleissa C. Lavelle
Michael P. Villani

Laura E. Wunsch Stubberud

Reference: Sun State Bank.

For full biographical listings, see the Martindale-Hubbell Law Directory

GOODMAN & CHESNOFF, A PROFESSIONAL CORPORATION (AV)

520 South Fourth Street, 89101-6593
Telephone: 702-384-5563
Fax: 702-598-1425

Oscar B. Goodman
David Z. Chesnoff
Eckley M. Keach

OF COUNSEL

Stephen Stein

For full biographical listings, see the Martindale-Hubbell Law Directory

STEPHEN STEIN CHARTERED (AV)

520 South Fourth Street, 89101-6593
Telephone: 702-384-5563
Fax: 702-598-1425

Stephen Stein

For full biographical listings, see the Martindale-Hubbell Law Directory

WRIGHT, JUDD & WINCKLER (AV)

Third Floor, First Interstate Bank Building, 302 East Carson Avenue, 89101
Telephone: 702-382-4004
FAX: 702-382-4800

MEMBERS OF FIRM

Richard A. Wright
Bruce M. Judd
Karen C. Winckler

For full biographical listings, see the Martindale-Hubbell Law Directory

*RENO,** Washoe Co.

CALVIN R. X. DUNLAP (AV)

537 Ralston Street, P.O. Box 3689, 89505
Telephone: 702-323-7790
FAX: 702-323-5454

Reference: Valley Bank (Wells Ave. Branch).

For full biographical listings, see the Martindale-Hubbell Law Directory

RICHARD W. YOUNG A PROFESSIONAL CORPORATION (AV)

327 Marsh Avenue, 89509
Telephone: 702-322-9477
Facsimile: 702-322-3758

Richard W. Young

Reference: First Interstate Bank of Nevada (Reno Main Branch).

For full biographical listings, see the Martindale-Hubbell Law Directory

NEW JERSEY

CHATHAM, Morris Co.

ARSENEAULT, DONOHUE, SORRENTINO & FASSETT (AV)

560 Main Street, 07928-2119
Telephone: 201-635-3366
FAX: 201-635-0855

MEMBERS OF FIRM

Jack Arseneault
Timothy M. Donohue
Joan Sorrentino
David W. Fassett
Frank P. Arleo

ASSOCIATES

David G. Tomeo
William Strazza

For full biographical listings, see the Martindale-Hubbell Law Directory

*HACKENSACK,** Bergen Co.

BRESLIN AND BRESLIN, P.A. (AV)

41 Main Street, 07601
Telephone: 201-342-4014; 342-4015
Fax: 201-342-0068; 201-342-3077

Charles Rodgers
E. Carter Corriston
Donald A. Caminiti

Michael T. Fitzpatrick
Angelo A. Bello
Terrence J. Corriston
Kevin C. Corriston
Karen Boe Gatlin
Lawrence Farber
E. Carter Corriston, Jr.

Representative Clients: Bergen County Housing Authority; Phillips Fuel Co.; Prudential Insurance Co.; Rent Leveling Board of Township of North Bergen; Housing Authority of Passaic.
Reference: United Jersey Bank.

For Complete List of Firm Personnel, See General Section

For full biographical listings, see the Martindale-Hubbell Law Directory

CUCCIO AND CUCCIO (AV)

45 Essex Street, 07601
Telephone: 201-487-7411
Fax: 201-487-6574
Mailing Address: P.O. Box 2223, South Hackensack, New Jersey, 07606

MEMBERS OF FIRM

Frank J. Cuccio
Emil S. Cuccio

ASSOCIATE

Pamela Beth Keitz

Representative Clients: TCI of Northern New Jersey; Huffman Koos, Inc.; The Actors Fund of America; Blue Circle-Raia, Inc.; Zimpro, Inc., Division of Sterling Drug; Honig Chemical and Processing Corp.; Napp Technologies, Inc.; River Terrace Gardens Assoc.; Franklin Lakes P.B.A. Local 150.

For full biographical listings, see the Martindale-Hubbell Law Directory

LAW OFFICES OF DONALD HOROWITZ (AV)

24 Bergen Street, 07601
Telephone: 201-343-0100
FAX: 201-343-3321
New York, New York Office: 2 Park Avenue, Suite 2100.
Telephone: 212-349-1150.

For full biographical listings, see the Martindale-Hubbell Law Directory

Hackensack—Continued

BRIAN J. NEARY (AV)

190 Moore Street, 07601
Telephone: 201-488-0544
Fax: 201-488-0240
New York, N.Y. Office: 475 Park Avenue, South, Suite 3300.
Telephone: 212-683-8000.

Yung-Mi Lee

For full biographical listings, see the Martindale-Hubbell Law Directory

MILLBURN, Essex Co.

KUTTNER LAW OFFICES (AV)

24 Lackawanna Plaza, P.O. Box 745, 07041-0745
Telephone: 201-467-8300
Fax: 201-467-4333

Bernard A. Kuttner
Robert D. Kuttner

Reference: Summit Bank, Millburn, New Jersey.

For full biographical listings, see the Martindale-Hubbell Law Directory

MONTVALE, Bergen Co.

BEATTIE PADOVANO (AV)

50 Chestnut Ridge Road, P.O. Box 244, 07645-0244
Telephone: 201-573-1810
Fax: (DEX) 201-573-9736

MEMBERS OF FIRM

James R. Beattie
Ralph J. Padovano
Roger W. Breslin, Jr.
Thomas W. Dunn
Martin W. Kafafian
Adolph A. Romei
Brian R. Martinotti

ASSOCIATES

Emery C. Duell
Brenda J. McAdoo
Kathleen Smyth Cook
Francis B. Sheehan
Susan Calabrese
Antimo A. Del Vecchio
Dean J. Obeidallah
Jeffrey L. Love
Steven A. Weisfeld
S. Joseph Oey
Edward S. Kiel
Christopher Heyer
JoAnne C. Gerber
Robert A. Blass

OF COUNSEL

John J. Lamb

Reference: United Jersey Bank.

For full biographical listings, see the Martindale-Hubbell Law Directory

*MORRISTOWN,** Morris Co.

MASKALERIS & ASSOCIATES (AV)

30 Court Street, 07960
Telephone: 201-267-0222
Newark, New Jersey Office: Federal Square Station, P.O. Box 20207.
Telephone: 201-622-4300.
Far Hills, New Jersey Office: Route 202 Station Plaza.
Telephone: 201-234-0600.
New York, New York Office: 123 Bank Street.
Telephone: 212-724-8669.
Athens, Greece Office: Stadio 28, Fourth Floor.
Telephone: 322-6790.

Stephen N. Maskaleris

ASSOCIATES

Peter C. Ioannou
Christopher P. Luongo

For full biographical listings, see the Martindale-Hubbell Law Directory

STEPHEN S. WEINSTEIN A PROFESSIONAL CORPORATION (AV)

20 Park Place, Suite 301, 07960
Telephone: 201-267-5200
FAX: 201-538-1779

Stephen S. Weinstein

Gail S. Boertzel
Peter N. Gilbreth
William A. Johnson
Melissa H. Luce

For full biographical listings, see the Martindale-Hubbell Law Directory

*NEWARK,** Essex Co.

BARRY & MCMORAN, A PROFESSIONAL CORPORATION (AV)

One Newark Center, 07102
Telephone: 201-624-6500
Telecopier: 201-624-4052

(See Next Column)

John J. Barry
Bruce P. McMoran
Salvatore T. Alfano
Mark Falk
John A. Avery
John P. Flanagan

Mark F. Kluger
Madeline E. Cox
Joann K. Dobransky
Adam N. Saravay
Thomas F. Doherty
Judson L. Hand
Carmen J. Di Maria

For full biographical listings, see the Martindale-Hubbell Law Directory

BROWN & BROWN, P.C. (AV)

One Gateway Center, Fifth Floor, 07102
Telephone: 201-622-1846
Fax: 201-622-2223
Jersey City, New Jersey Office:
Telephone: 201-656-2381.

Raymond A. Brown
Raymond M. Brown

Reference: National Westminster Bank, NJ.

For full biographical listings, see the Martindale-Hubbell Law Directory

GOLDSTEIN TILL & LITE (AV)

Suite 800, 744 Broad Street, 07102-3803
Telephone: 201-623-3000
FAX: 201-623-0858
Telex: 262320 USA UR

MEMBERS OF FIRM

Andrew J. Goldstein
Peter W. Till
Allyn Z. Lite
Joseph J. DePalma

Amy M. Riel
Richard T. Luzzi
Denise L. Panicucci
Robin May Messing

For full biographical listings, see the Martindale-Hubbell Law Directory

GREENBERG DAUBER AND EPSTEIN, A PROFESSIONAL CORPORATION (AV)

Suite 600, One Gateway Center, 07102-5311
Telephone: 201-643-3700
Telecopier: 201-643-1218

Melvin Greenberg
Edward J. Dauber

For Complete List of Firm Personnel, See General Section

For full biographical listings, see the Martindale-Hubbell Law Directory

HELLRING LINDEMAN GOLDSTEIN & SIEGAL (AV)

One Gateway Center, 07102-5386
Telephone: 201-621-9020
Telecopier: 201-621-7406

Joel D. Siegal
Jonathan L. Goldstein
Richard D. Shapiro
Ronny Jo Greenwald Siegal
Stephen L. Dreyfuss
Rachel N. Davidson

For Complete List of Firm Personnel, See General Section

For full biographical listings, see the Martindale-Hubbell Law Directory

ROBINSON, ST. JOHN & WAYNE (AV)

Two Penn Plaza East, 07105-2249
Telephone: 201-491-3300
Fax: 201-491-3333
Rochester, New York Office: Robinson, St. John & Curtin. First Federal Plaza.
Telephone: 716-262-6780.
Fax: 716-262-6755.
New York, New York Office: 245 Park Avenue.
Telephone: 212-953-0700.
Fax: 212-880-6555.

MEMBERS OF FIRM

W. Hunt Dumont
Mark F. Hughes, Jr.
Kevin H. Marino
Donald A. Robinson

For Complete List of Firm Personnel, See General Section

For full biographical listings, see the Martindale-Hubbell Law Directory

SAIBER SCHLESINGER SATZ & GOLDSTEIN (AV)

One Gateway Center, 13th Floor, 07102-5311
Telephone: 201-622-3333
Telecopier: 201-622-3349

MEMBERS OF FIRM

David M. Satz, Jr.
Bruce I. Goldstein
William F. Maderer
David J. D'Aloia
James H. Aibel
Sean R. Kelly
John L. Conover
Lawrence B. Mink
Michael L. Allen
Michael L. Messer

(See Next Column)

SAIBER SCHLESINGER SATZ & GOLDSTEIN—*Continued*

MEMBERS OF FIRM (Continued)

Jeffrey W. Lorell
Jeffrey M. Schwartz
David J. Satz
Joan M. Schwab
Jennine DiSomma
James H. Forte
Vincent F. Papalia

OF COUNSEL

Samuel S. Saiber
Norman E. Schlesinger

COUNSEL

Andrew Alcorn
Robin B. Horn
Randi Schillinger

ASSOCIATES

Audrey M. Weinstein
Robert B. Nussbaum
Michael J. Geraghty
Jonathan S. Davis
Paul S. DeGiulio
Diana L. Sussman
Deanna M. Beacham
Robert W. Geiger
William S. Gyves
Barry P. Kramer
Susan Rozman
Michelle Viola

LEGAL SUPPORT PERSONNEL

DIRECTOR OF FINANCE AND ADMINISTRATION

Ronald Henry

For full biographical listings, see the Martindale-Hubbell Law Directory

SILLS CUMMIS ZUCKERMAN RADIN TISCHMAN EPSTEIN & GROSS, A PROFESSIONAL CORPORATION (AV)

One Riverfront Plaza, 07102-5400
Telephone: 201-643-7000
Fax: 201-643-6500
Telex: 820630 Sillsbeck Nwk
Atlantic City, New Jersey Office: 17 Gordon's Alley.
Telephone: 609-344-2800.
New York, N.Y. Office: 250 Park Avenue.
Telephone: 212-643-7000.

Herbert L. Zuckerman
Barry M. Epstein
Lawrence S. Horn
Charles J. Walsh
Robert J. Alter
Philip R. Sellinger
Mark S. Olinsky
Richard J. Sapinski

Jack Wenik
Kenneth L. Moskowitz
A. Ross Pearlson (Not admitted in NJ)

For Complete List of Firm Personnel, See General Section

For full biographical listings, see the Martindale-Hubbell Law Directory

TOMPKINS, MCGUIRE & WACHENFELD (AV)

A Partnership including a Professional Corporation
Four Gateway Center, 100 Mulberry Street, 07102-4070
Telephone: 201-622-3000
Telecopier: 201-623-7780

MEMBERS OF FIRM

James F. Flanagan, III
Patrick M. Callahan

Representative Clients: Corbo Jewelers, Inc.; General Electric Co.; Hartford Insurance Group; Marriott Corp.; Underwriters at Lloyd's, London.

For Complete List of Firm Personnel, See General Section

For full biographical listings, see the Martindale-Hubbell Law Directory

NORTH BRUNSWICK, Middlesex Co.

BORRUS, GOLDIN, FOLEY, VIGNUOLO, HYMAN & STAHL, A PROFESSIONAL CORPORATION (AV)

2875 U.S. Highway 1, Route 1 & Finnigans Lane, P.O. Box 1963, 08902
Telephone: 908-422-1000
Fax: 908-422-1016

Jack Borrus
Martin S. Goldin
David M. Foley
Anthony B. Vignuolo
Jeffrey M. Hyman
James E. Stahl
James F. Clarkin III
Anthony M. Campisano
Aphrodite C. Koscelansky
Robert C. Nisenson
Michael L. Marcus
Eileen Mary Foley
Rosalind Westlake

OF COUNSEL

Gerald T. Foley (1903-1976)

Representative Clients: United Jersey Bank/Franklin State; R. J. Reynolds Tobacco Co.; N.J. Aluminum Co.; K. Hovnanian Enterprises, Inc.; Chicago Title Insurance Co.; Transamerica Title Insurance Co.

For full biographical listings, see the Martindale-Hubbell Law Directory

ROSELAND, Essex Co.

HANNOCH WEISMAN, A PROFESSIONAL CORPORATION (AV)

4 Becker Farm Road, 07068-3788
Telephone: 201-535-5300
New York: 212-732-3262
Telecopier: 201-994-7198
Mailing Address: P.O. Box 1040, Newark, New Jersey, 07101-9819
Washington, D.C. Office: Suite 600, 1150 Seventeenth Street, N.W.
Telephone: 202-296-3432.

Albert G. Besser
Eric R. Breslin
Sheldon M. Finkelstein
Theodore Margolis
William W. Robertson
Ronald M. Sturtz

SPECIAL COUNSEL

David P. Wadyka

James P. Flynn

For Complete List of Firm Personnel, See General Section

For full biographical listings, see the Martindale-Hubbell Law Directory

LOWENSTEIN, SANDLER, KOHL, FISHER & BOYLAN, A PROFESSIONAL CORPORATION (AV)

65 Livingston Avenue, 07068
Telephone: 201-992-8700
Telefax: 201-992-5820
Somerville, New Jersey Office: 600 First Avenue. P.O. Box 1113.
Telephone: 201-526-3300.

Matthew P. Boylan
Theodore V. Wells, Jr.
Gerald Krovatin
David L. Harris
Terry E. Thornton

OF COUNSEL

Robert L. Krakower

John M. Nolan (Resident at Somerville Office)
John B. McCusker
Bruce S. Rosen
Paul F. Carvelli
Rosemary E. Ramsay
Lawrence M. Rolnick
Karim G. Kaspar
Robert M. Lapinsky
Henry M. Price
Andrew E. Anselmi
Alex Moreau

For Complete List of Firm Personnel, See General Section

For full biographical listings, see the Martindale-Hubbell Law Directory

WALDER, SONDAK & BROGAN, A PROFESSIONAL CORPORATION (AV)

5 Becker Farm Road, 07068
Telephone: 201-992-5300
Telecopier: 201-992-1505; 992-1006

Justin P. Walder
John A. Brogan
Barry A. Kozyra
James A. Plaisted

For full biographical listings, see the Martindale-Hubbell Law Directory

*SOMERVILLE,** Somerset Co.

SCHACHTER, TROMBADORE, OFFEN, STANTON & PAVICS, A PROFESSIONAL CORPORATION (AV)

45 East High Street, P.O. Box 520, 08876-0520
Telephone: 908-722-5700
Fax: 908-722-8853

Thomas A. Pavics

LEGAL SUPPORT PERSONNEL

Joan V. Shaw (Office Manager)

References: Summit Bank; First National Bank of Central Jersey; New Jersey Savings Bank.

For full biographical listings, see the Martindale-Hubbell Law Directory

RAYMOND R. AND ANN W. TROMBADORE A PROFESSIONAL CORPORATION (AV)

33 East High Street, 08876
Telephone: 908-722-7555
Fax: 908-722-6269

Raymond R. Trombadore

Megan C. Seel

OF COUNSEL

Ann W. Trombadore

References: Summit Bank; New Jersey Savings Bank; Somerset Savings & Loan Assn.

For full biographical listings, see the Martindale-Hubbell Law Directory

SPRINGFIELD, Union Co.

McDonough, Korn & Eichhorn, A Professional Corporation (AV)

Park Place Legal Center, 959 South Springfield Avenue, P.O. Box 712, 07081-0712
Telephone: 201-912-9099
Fax: 201-912-8604

Peter L. Korn | James R. Korn
R. Scott Eichhorn | William S. Mezzomo

Timothy J. Jaeger | Wilfred P. Coronato
Dona Feeney | Gail R. Arkin
Karen M. Lerner | Nancy Crosta Landale
Christopher K. Costa

OF COUNSEL

Robert P. McDonough

Reference: United Counties Trust Company.

For full biographical listings, see the Martindale-Hubbell Law Directory

SUMMIT, Union Co.

Haggerty, Donohue & Monaghan, A Professional Association (AV)

One Springfield Avenue, 07901
Telephone: 908-277-2600
Fax: 908-273-1641

James C. Haggerty | George J. Donohue
Walter E. Monaghan

Rose Ann Haggerty | William A. Wenzel
Thomas J. Haggerty | Mahlon H. Ortman
Alfred F. Carolonza, Jr. | Michael A. Conway
James C. Haggerty, Jr.

OF COUNSEL

Joseph D. Haggerty

Representative Clients: American International Group; Chubb/Pacific Indemnity Co.; Crawford & Co.; Crum & Forster; Hertz Corp.; Jefferson Insurance Group; Material Damage Adjustment Corp.; New Jersey Manufacturers; New Jersey Property Liability Guaranty Association; Royal Insurance Co.

For Complete List of Firm Personnel, See General Section

For full biographical listings, see the Martindale-Hubbell Law Directory

*TOMS RIVER,** Ocean Co.

Novins, York & Pentony, A Professional Corporation (AV)

202 Main Street, 08753
Telephone: 908-349-7100

Robert F. Novins | S. Karl Mohel

Counsel for: Allstate Insurance Co.; Motor Club of America.

For Complete List of Firm Personnel, See General Section

For full biographical listings, see the Martindale-Hubbell Law Directory

VINELAND, Cumberland Co.

Joseph D. O'Neill A Professional Corporation (AV)

30 West Chestnut Avenue, P.O. Box 847, 08360
Telephone: 609-692-2400
Telecopier: 609-696-9036

Joseph D. O'Neill

Charles I. Coant | James T. Dugan
Amber Sharp Pallante

For full biographical listings, see the Martindale-Hubbell Law Directory

WEST ORANGE, Essex Co.

Ruhnke & Barrett (AV)

20 Northfield Avenue, 07052
Telephone: 201-325-7970
Fax: 201-325-2248

David A. Ruhnke | Jean deSales Barrett

Alan L. Zegas (AV)

20 Northfield Avenue, 07052
Telephone: 201-736-1011
Fax: 201-325-2248

For full biographical listings, see the Martindale-Hubbell Law Directory

WOODBRIDGE, Middlesex Co.

Wilentz, Goldman & Spitzer, A Professional Corporation (AV)

90 Woodbridge Center Drive Suite 900, Box 10, 07095
Telephone: 908-636-8000
Telecopier: 908-855-6117
Eatontown, New Jersey Office: Meridian Center I, Two Industrial Way West, 07724.
Telephone: 908-493-1000.
Telecopier: 908-493-8387.
New York, New York Office: Wall Street Plaza, 88 Pine Street, 9th Floor, 10005.
Telephone: 212-267-3091.
Telecopier: 212-267-3828.

Warren W. Wilentz | Barry T. Albin
James E. Trabilsy

Linda Lashbrook | Eric J. Marcy
Kevin A. Calamoneri

Representative Firm Clients: Amerada Hess Corp.; Chevron, U.S.A.; Cumberland Farms, Inc.; Middlesex County Utilities Authority; New Jersey Automobile Dealers Assn.; Co-Steel Raritan; The Rouse Co.

For Complete List of Firm Personnel, See General Section

For full biographical listings, see the Martindale-Hubbell Law Directory

NEW MEXICO

*ALBUQUERQUE,** Bernalillo Co.

Freedman, Boyd, Daniels, Peifer, Hollander, Guttmann & Goldberg, P.A. (AV)

Suite 700, 20 First Plaza, 200 Third Street, N.W., 87102
Telephone: 505-842-9960
Fax: 505-842-0761

David A. Freedman | Charles W. Daniels
John W. Boyd | Nancy Hollander
Gary Wayne Nelson

For full biographical listings, see the Martindale-Hubbell Law Directory

Rodey, Dickason, Sloan, Akin & Robb, P.A. (AV)

Albuquerque Plaza, Suite 2200, 201 Third Street, N.W., P.O. Box 1888, 87103-1888
Telephone: 505-765-5900
Fax: 505-768-7395
Santa Fe, New Mexico Office: Suite 101 Marcy Plaza, 123 East Marcy Street, P.O. Box 1357, 87504-1357.
Telephone: 505-984-0100.
Fax: 505-989-9542.

William S. Dixon | Angela M. Martinez
R. Nelson Franse

For Complete List of Firm Personnel, See General Section

For full biographical listings, see the Martindale-Hubbell Law Directory

*ROSWELL,** Chaves Co.

Stout and Winterbottom (AV)

215 West 6th Street, 88201
Telephone: 505-624-1471
Fax: 505-622-1086
Albuquerque, New Mexico Office: 320 Central Avenue, S.W. Suite 30.
Telephone: 505-242-0117.
FAX: 505-242-7845.

MEMBERS OF FIRM

Michael L. Stout | Richard A. Winterbottom

For full biographical listings, see the Martindale-Hubbell Law Directory

*SANTA FE,** Santa Fe Co.

Steven G. Farber (AV)

409 Hillside Avenue, P.O. Box 2473, 87504-2473
Telephone: 505-988-9725

For full biographical listings, see the Martindale-Hubbell Law Directory

Santa Fe—Continued

ROTHSTEIN, DONATELLI, HUGHES, DAHLSTROM, CRON & SCHOENBURG (AV)

Sanbusco Center, 500 Montezuma Avenue, Suite 101, P.O. Box 8180, 87504-8180
Telephone: 505-988-8004
Fax: 505-982-0307
Albuquerque, New Mexico Office: 320 Central S.W., Suite 30, 87102.
Telephone: 505-243-1443.
Fax: 505-242-7845.
Phoenix, Arizona Office: 234 North Central, Suite 722, 85004.
Telephone: 602-252-3226.
Fax: 602-253-3088.

MEMBERS OF FIRM

Robert R. Rothstein
Mark H. Donatelli
Richard W. Hughes
Eric N. Dahlstrom (Not admitted in NM; Resident, Phoenix, Arizona Office)
Dan Cron
Peter Schoenburg (Resident, Albuquerque, New Mexico Office)

ASSOCIATES

Michael C. Shiel (Not admitted in NM; Resident, Phoenix, Arizona Office)
Tina S. Boradiansky
Lisa Chau

For full biographical listings, see the Martindale-Hubbell Law Directory

WHITE, KOCH, KELLY & McCARTHY, A PROFESSIONAL ASSOCIATION (AV)

433 Paseo De Peralta, P.O. Box 787, 87504-0787
Telephone: 505-982-4374
ABA/NET: 1154
Fax: 505-982-0350; 984-8631

William Booker Kelly
John F. McCarthy, Jr.
Benjamin J. Phillips
David F. Cunningham
Albert V. Gonzales
Janet Clow
Kevin V. Reilly
Charles W. N. Thompson, Jr.
M. Karen Kilgore
Sandra J. Brinck

SPECIAL COUNSEL

Paul L. Bloom

Aaron J. Wolf
Carolyn R. Glick

Representative Clients: Southern Pacific Transportation Co.; Nationwide Insurance Co.; Risk Management Division of New Mexico General Services Department; Alliance of American Insurers; Santa Fe Community College; First American Title Insurance Co.; Century Bank; Public Service Company of New Mexico; AT&SF Railway Co.; Gallager Bassett.

For full biographical listings, see the Martindale-Hubbell Law Directory

NEW YORK

*ALBANY,** Albany Co.

DREYER, BOYAJIAN & TUTTLE (AV)

75 Columbia Street, 12210
Telephone: 518-463-7784
Telecopier: 518-463-4039

William J. Dreyer
Donald W. Boyajian
James B. Tuttle
Daniel J. Stewart
Brian W. Devane
Christopher M. Scaringe
Damon J. Stewart
Jill A. Dunn

For full biographical listings, see the Martindale-Hubbell Law Directory

O'CONNELL AND ARONOWITZ, P.C. (AV)

100 State Street, 12207-1885
Telephone: 518-462-5601
Telecopier: 518-462-2670
Plattsburgh, New York Office: Grand Plaza Building, Suite 204, 159 Margaret Street.
Telephone: 518-562-0600.
Fax: 518-562-0657.
Saratoga Springs, New York Office: Suite 202, 358 Broadway.
Telephone: 518-587-0425.
Fax: 518-587-0565.

Stephen R. Coffey

For Complete List of Firm Personnel, See General Section

For full biographical listings, see the Martindale-Hubbell Law Directory

*BUFFALO,** Erie Co.

CONNORS & VILARDO (AV)

1020 Liberty Building, 420 Main Street, 14202
Telephone: 716-852-5533
Fax: 716-852-5649
Dunkirk, New York Office: 401 Central Avenue, P.O. Box 706.
Telephone: 716-366-0606.

MEMBERS OF FIRM

Terrence M. Connors
Lawrence J. Vilardo
Kevin A. Ricotta

ASSOCIATES

Randall D. White
John T. Loss
Vincent E. Doyle III
Nancy M. Langer
Michael J. Roach

For full biographical listings, see the Martindale-Hubbell Law Directory

GARDEN CITY, Nassau Co.

KASE & DRUKER (AV)

Suite 225, 1325 Franklin Avenue, 11530
Telephone: 516-746-4300
Telecopier: 516-742-9416
Mamaroneck, New York Office: 136 Palmer Avenue.
Telephone: 914-834-4600.
Telecopier: 914-698-3807.

MEMBERS OF FIRM

John L. Kase
James O. Druker

OF COUNSEL

Philip J. Luongo

LEGAL SUPPORT PERSONNEL

Marie T. DeBonis

For full biographical listings, see the Martindale-Hubbell Law Directory

HEMPSTEAD, Nassau Co.

JOSEPH R. MADDALONE, JR. (AV)

230 Hilton Avenue, 11550
Telephone: 516-486-3577
Telecopier: 516-486-3934

For full biographical listings, see the Martindale-Hubbell Law Directory

JACKSON HEIGHTS, Queens Co.

LAWRENCE M. HERRMANN (AV)

37-51 76th Street, 11372-6533
Telephone: 718-779-6630
Fax: 718-565-7278
(Also Of Counsel to Winnick Ruben Block Hawkins and Arons, New Haven, Connecticut and Slotnick and Baker, New York, N.Y.)

OF COUNSEL

Mariangela Trujillo

LEGAL SUPPORT PERSONNEL

Beatriz Restrepo

For full biographical listings, see the Martindale-Hubbell Law Directory

*NEW YORK,** New York Co.

ARKIN SCHAFFER & SUPINO (AV)

1370 Avenue of the Americas, 10019
Telephone: 212-333-0200
Fax: 212-333-2350
Los Angeles, California Office: 10940 Wilshire Blvd., Suite 700. 90024-3902.
Telephone: 310-443-7689.
Fax: 310-443-7599.

Stanley S. Arkin
Hyman L. Schaffer
Anthony M. Supino

OF COUNSEL

Jeffrey M. Kaplan

ASSOCIATES

Katherine E. Hargrove
Joseph Lee Matalon
Barry S. Pollack (Resident, Los Angeles, California Office)
Harry B. Feder
Marc S. Ullman

For full biographical listings, see the Martindale-Hubbell Law Directory

BELDOCK LEVINE & HOFFMAN (AV)

99 Park Avenue, 10016-1502
Telephone: 212-490-0400
Cable Address: "Telhofflaw, N.Y."
Telecopier: 212-557-0565

(See Next Column)

BELDOCK LEVINE & HOFFMAN, *New York—Continued*

MEMBERS OF FIRM

Myron Beldock
Brian E. Maas

For full biographical listings, see the Martindale-Hubbell Law Directory

BRAFMAN GILBERT & ROSS, P.C. (AV)

26th Floor, 767 Third Avenue, 10017
Telephone: 212-750-7800
Telecopier: 212-750-3906

Benjamin Brafman
Brett D. Gilbert
Charles A. Ross

Katherine Renee Schimkat
Mindy Leifer

OF COUNSEL

Mark M. Baker

For full biographical listings, see the Martindale-Hubbell Law Directory

CAPLIN & DRYSDALE, CHARTERED (AV)

399 Park Avenue, 10022
Telephone: 212-319-7125
Fax: 212-644-6755
Washington, D.C. Office: One Thomas Circle, N.W.
Telephone: 202-862-5000.
Fax: 202-429-3301.

Elihu Inselbuch
C. Sanders McNew
Christian R. Pastore

For full biographical listings, see the Martindale-Hubbell Law Directory

CURTIS, MALLET-PREVOST, COLT & MOSLE (AV)

101 Park Avenue, 10178
Telephone: 212-696-6000
Telecopier: 212-697-1559
Cable Address: "Migniar d New York"
Telex: 12-6811 Migniard; ITT 422127 MGND
Washington, D.C. Office: Suite 1205 L, 1801 K Street, N.W.
Telephone: 202-452-7373.
Telecopier: 202-452-7333.
Telex: ITT 440379 CMPUI.
Newark, New Jersey Office: One Gateway Center, Suite 403.
Telephone: 201-622-0605.
Telecopier: 201-622-5646.
Houston, Texas Office: 2 Houston Center, 909 Fannin Street, Suite 3725.
Telephone: 713-759-9555.
Telecopier: 713-759-0712.
Mexico City, D.F., Mexico Office: Torre Chapultepec, Ruben Dario 281, Col. Bosques de Chapultepec, 11530 Mexico, D.F.
Telephone: 525-282-0444.
Telecopier: 525-282-0637.
Paris, France Office: 8 Avenue Victor Hugo.
Telephone: 45-00-99-68.
Telecopier: 45-00-84-06.
London, England Office: Two Throgmorton Avenue, EC2N 2DL.
Telephone: 71-638-7957.
Telecopier: 71-638-5512.
Frankfurt am Main 1 Office: Staufenstrasse 42.
Telephone: 069-971-4420.
Telecopier: 69-17 33 99.

MEMBERS OF FIRM

Peter E. Fleming, Jr.
Eliot Lauer

For Complete List of Firm Personnel, See General Section

For full biographical listings, see the Martindale-Hubbell Law Directory

DUKER & BARRETT (AV)

1585 Broadway, 10036
Telephone: 212-969-5600
Telecopy: 212-969-5650
Albany, New York Office: 100 State Street.
Telephone: 518-434-0600.
Telecopy: 518-434-0665.

David A. Barrett
William F. Duker
Richard L. Crisona
Rodney L. Stenlake
George F. Carpinello
Nicholas A. Gravante, Jr.

OF COUNSEL

Gary K. Harris (Not admitted in NY)
Robert B. Silver
Michael Straus
Jack G. Stern
Karen Caudill Dyer (Not admitted in NY)
Tracey Lynn Altman

(See Next Column)

Christopher Allegaert
Cynthia Goldman
Kenneth G. Alberstadt
Richard S. Laudor
David A. Berger
Laura A. Hastings
Richard A. Schwartz
Janine Marie Gargiulo
Michael S. Vogel
Scott W. Dales
Rebecca L. Fine

For full biographical listings, see the Martindale-Hubbell Law Directory

FISCHETTI & RUSSO (AV)

950 Third Avenue, 10022-2705
Telephone: 212-593-7100

MEMBERS OF FIRM

Ronald P. Fischetti
Ronald G. Russo

For full biographical listings, see the Martindale-Hubbell Law Directory

SANDOR FRANKEL, P.C. (AV)

230 Park Avenue, 10169
Telephone: 212-661-5000
Fax: 212-661-5007

Sandor Frankel
Stuart E. Abrams
Al J. Daniel, Jr.

For full biographical listings, see the Martindale-Hubbell Law Directory

GOLDBERGER AND DUBIN, P.C. (AV)

401 Broadway, 10013
Telephone: 212-431-9380

Paul A. Goldberger
Lawrence Dubin

Robert A. Horne

For full biographical listings, see the Martindale-Hubbell Law Directory

GOLDMAN & HAFETZ (AV)

500 Fifth Avenue 29th Floor, 10110
Telephone: 212-997-7400
Fax: 212-997-7597

MEMBERS OF FIRM

Lawrence S. Goldman
Frederick P. Hafetz
Susan R. Necheles

ASSOCIATES

Candace S. Reid
Elizabeth M. Johnson
Gwen M. Schoenfeld
Anastasia G. Margaris

For full biographical listings, see the Martindale-Hubbell Law Directory

KOSTELANETZ & FINK (AV)

230 Park Avenue, Suite 1140, 10169
Telephone: 212-808-8100
Fax: 212-808-8108

OF COUNSEL

Boris Kostelanetz

MEMBERS OF FIRM

Robert S. Fink
Kevin M. Flynn
Kathryn Keneally
Nora Elizabeth Plesent
Bryan C. Skarlatos
Linda Donahue

For full biographical listings, see the Martindale-Hubbell Law Directory

LA ROSSA, MITCHELL & ROSS (AV)

41 Madison Avenue, 10010
Telephone: 212-696-9700

MEMBERS OF FIRM

James M. La Rossa
John W. Mitchell
Michael S. Ross

ASSOCIATES

Andrew J. Weinstein
Susan G. LaRossa
Evan Glassman
Wendy Z. Brenner
Kenneth Michaels

For full biographical listings, see the Martindale-Hubbell Law Directory

ANDREW M. LAWLER, P.C. (AV)

220 East 42nd Street, 10017
Telephone: 212-687-8850
Telecopier: 212-972-6387

Andrew M. Lawler
Sharon D. Feldman

OF COUNSEL

Maurice M. McDermott

For full biographical listings, see the Martindale-Hubbell Law Directory

New York—Continued

LEVENTHAL SLADE & KRANTZ (AV)

777 Third Avenue, 10017
Telephone: 212-935-0800
Fax: 212-207-8256

MEMBERS OF FIRM

Melvyn R. Leventhal
Jeffrey C. Slade
Larry H. Krantz

ASSOCIATES

Laura F. Dukess
Maryanne Yen
Marjorie E. Berman
Thomas Bartlett Wilinsky

For full biographical listings, see the Martindale-Hubbell Law Directory

LITMAN, ASCHE, LUPKIN, GIOIELLA & BASSIN (AV)

45 Broadway Atrium, 10006
Telephone: 212-809-4500
Telecopier: GP II, III (212) 509-8403

MEMBERS OF FIRM

Richard M. Asche
Stanley N. Lupkin
Jack T. Litman
Russell M. Gioiella
Steven Jay Bassin

ASSOCIATES

Mary Lou Chatterton
Frederick L. Sosinsky

OF COUNSEL

Alan C. Rothfeld
Ronald S. Pohl

For full biographical listings, see the Martindale-Hubbell Law Directory

MORVILLO, ABRAMOWITZ, GRAND, IASON & SILBERBERG, P.C. (AV)

565 Fifth Avenue, 10017
Telephone: 212-856-9600
Fax: 212-856-9494
Cable Address: "Litigator, New York"

Robert G. Morvillo
Richard D. Weinberg
Elkan Abramowitz
Barry A. Bohrer
Paul R. Grand
Lawrence S. Bader
Lawrence Iason
Robert J. Anello
Michael C. Silberberg
Diana D. Parker
Catherine M. Foti

OF COUNSEL

Michael W. Mitchell

Stephen L. Ascher
Christopher J. Gunther
Michael F. Buchanan
Jill K. Israeloff
Elizabeth Jahncke Carroll
Jamie L. Kogan
Nicole L. Felton
Monique LaPointe
Jodi M. Peikin

For Complete List of Firm Personnel, See General Section

For full biographical listings, see the Martindale-Hubbell Law Directory

MUDGE ROSE GUTHRIE ALEXANDER & FERDON (AV)

(Mudge, Stern, Baldwin & Todd)
(Caldwell, Trimble & Mitchell)
180 Maiden Lane, 10038
Telephone: 212-510-7000
Cable Address: "Baltuchins, New York"
Telex: 127889 & 703729
Telecopier: 212-248-2655/57
Los Angeles, California Office: 21st Floor, 333 South Grand Avenue, 90071.
Telephone: 213-613-1112.
Telecopier: 213-680-1358.
Washington, D.C. Office: 2121 K Street, N.W., 20037.
Telephone: 202-429-9355.
Telecopier: 202-429-9367.
Telex: MRGA 440264.
Cable Address: "Baltuchins, Washington, DC"
West Palm Beach, Florida Office: Suite 900, 515 North Flagler Drive, 33401.
Telephone: 407-650-8100.
Telecopier: 407-833-1722.
Telex: 514847 MRWPB.
Parsippany, New Jersey Office: Morris Corporate Center Two, Building D, One Upper Pond Road, 07054-1075.
Telephone: 201-335-0004.
Telecopier: 201-402-1593.
European Office: 12, Rue de la Paix, 75002 Paris, France.
Telephone: 42.61.57.71.
Telecopier: 42.61.79.21.
Cable Address: "Baltuchins, Paris".
Tokyo, Japan Office: Infini Akasaka, 8-7-15 Akasaka, Minato-Ku, Tokyo 107, Japan.
Telephone: (03) 3423-3970.
Fax: (03) 3423-3971.

(See Next Column)

MEMBERS OF FIRM

Paul G. Burns
Robert A. Longman
Susan Millington Campbell
Walter P. Loughlin (Not admitted in NY)
Terrence J. Connolly
Francis K. Decker, Jr.
Shelley B. O'Neill
Thomas G. Gallatin, Jr.
Malcolm R. Schade
Robert J. Gunther, Jr.
Laurence V. Senn, Jr.
James V. Kearney
Robert Sidorsky
John J. Kirby, Jr.
Donald J. Zoeller
Harold G. Levison (Resident Partner, Parsippany, New Jersey Office)

COUNSEL

Thomas W. Evans
Douglas M. Parker

ASSOCIATES

Mark D. Beckett
Judith A. Lockhart (Not admitted in NY)
Patricia A. Griffin
Thomas N. Kendris
Dennis M. Walsh

For Complete List of Firm Personnel, See General Section

For full biographical listings, see the Martindale-Hubbell Law Directory

NEWMAN & SCHWARTZ (AV)

950 Third Avenue, 10022
Telephone: 212-308-7900
Telecopier: (212) 826-3273

MEMBERS OF FIRM

Gustave H. Newman
Robert Hill Schwartz
Richard A. Greenberg

William Shields
Andrew J. Frisch
John R. Cuti

For full biographical listings, see the Martindale-Hubbell Law Directory

ORANS, ELSEN & LUPERT (AV)

33rd Floor, One Rockefeller Plaza, 10020
Telephone: 212-586-2211
Cable Address: "ORELSLU"
Telecopier: 212-765-3662

MEMBERS OF FIRM

Sheldon H. Elsen
Gary H. Greenberg
Leslie A. Lupert
Lawrence Solan
Robert L. Plotz

ASSOCIATES

Melissa A. Cohen
Amelia Anne Nickles
Jonathan J. Englander

For full biographical listings, see the Martindale-Hubbell Law Directory

SCHULTE ROTH & ZABEL (AV)

900 Third Avenue, 10022
Telephone: 212-758-0404; 800-346-9644
Cable Address: "Olympus NewYork"
Telex: 426775
West Palm Beach, Florida Office: 777 South Flagler Drive.
Cable Address: "P. B. Olympus."
Telephone: 407-659-9800.

MEMBERS OF FIRM

David M. Brodsky
Daniel J. Kramer
Michael S. Feldberg
Martin L. Perschetz
Howard O. Godnick
Frederick P. Schaffer

ASSOCIATES

Hollis Anne Bart
Mark E. Kaplan
David J. Murray

For Complete List of Firm Personnel, See General Section

For full biographical listings, see the Martindale-Hubbell Law Directory

SKADDEN, ARPS, SLATE, MEAGHER & FLOM (AV)

919 Third Avenue, 10022
Telephone: 212-735-3000
Telex: 645899 SKARSLAW
Fax: 212-735-2000; 212-735-2001
Boston, Massachusetts Office: One Beacon Street, 02108.
Telephone: 617-573-4800.
Fax: 617-573-4822.
Washington, D.C. Office: 1440 New York Avenue, N.W., 20005.
Telephone: 202-371-7000.
Fax: 202-393-5760.
Wilmington, Delaware Office: One Rodney Square, 19899.
Telephone: 302-651-3000.
Fax: 302-651-3001.
Los Angeles, California Office: 300 South Grand Avenue, 90071.
Telephone: 213-687-5000.
Fax: 213-687-5600.

(See Next Column)

SKADDEN, ARPS, SLATE, MEAGHER & FLOM, *New York—Continued*

Chicago, Illinois Office: 333 West Wacker Drive, 60606.
Telephone: 312-407-0700.
Fax: 312-407-0411.
San Francisco, California Office: Four Embarcadero Center, 94111.
Telephone: 415-984-6400.
Fax: 415-984-2698.
Houston, Texas Office: 1600 Smith Street, Suite 4460, 77002.
Telephone: 713-655-5100.
Fax: 713-655-5181.
Newark, New Jersey Office: One Riverfront Plaza, 07102.
Telephone: 201-596-4440.
Fax: 201-596-4444.
Tokyo, Japan Office: 12th Floor, The Fukoku Seimei Building, 2-2-2, Uchisaiwaicho, Chiyoda-ku, 100.
Telephone: 011-81-3-3595-3850.
Fax: 011-81-3-3504-2780.
London, England Office: 25 Bucklersbury EC4N 8DA.
Telephone: 011-44-71-248-9929.
Fax: 011-44-71-489-8533.
Hong Kong Office: 30/F Peregrine Tower, Lippo Centre, 89 Queensway, Central.
Telephone: 011-852-820-0700.
Fax: 011-852-820-0727.
Sydney, New South Wales, Australia Office: Level 26-State Bank Centre, 52 Martin Place, 2000.
Telephone: 011-61-2-224-6000.
Fax: 011-61-2-224-6044.
Toronto, Ontario Office: Suite 1820, North Tower, P.O. Box 189, Royal Bank Plaza, M5J 2J4.
Telephone: 416-777-4700.
Fax: 416-777-4747.
Paris, France Office: 105 rue du Faubourg Saint-Honoré, 75008.
Telephone: 011-33-1-40-75-44-44.
Fax: 011-33-1-49-53-09-99.
Brussels, Belgium Office: 523 avenue Louise, Box 30, 1050.
Telephone: 011-32-2-648-7666.
Fax: 011-32-2-640-3032.
Frankfurt, Germany Office: MesseTurm, 27th Floor, 60308.
Telephone: 011-49-69-9757-3000.
Fax: 011-49-69-9757-3050.
Beijing, China Office: 1605 Capital Mansion Tower, No. 6 Xin Yuan Nan Road, Chao Yang District, 100004.
Telephone: 011-86-1-466-8800.
Fax: 011-86-1-466-8822.
Budapest, Hungary Office: Mahart Building, H-1052 Apáczai Csere János u.11, Vl.em.
Telephone: 011-36-1-266-2145.
Fax: 011-36-1-266-4033.
Prague, Czech Republic Office: Revolucni 16, 110 00.
Telephone: 011-42-2-231-75-18.
Fax: 011-42-2-231-47-33.
Moscow, Russia Office: Pleteshkovsky Pereulok 1, 107005.
Telephone: 011-7-501-940-2304.
Fax: 011-7-501-940-2511.

MEMBERS OF FIRM

Jeffrey Glekel — David M. Zornow

WASHINGTON, D.C. OFFICE

PARTNERS

Robert S. Bennett — Carl S. Rauh
Alan Kriegel

SPECIAL COUNSEL

Edward D. Ross, Jr.

WILMINGTON, DELAWARE OFFICE

PARTNER

Marc B. Tucker

NEW YORK, N.Y. OFFICE

ASSOCIATE

Thomas M. Obermaier

WASHINGTON, D.C. OFFICE

ASSOCIATES

Bonnie J. Austin — Benjamin B. Klubes
Gregory C. C. Burton — Saul M. Pilchen
Leo J. Kane — Abigail J. Raphael

For Complete List of Firm Personnel, See General Section

For full biographical listings, see the Martindale-Hubbell Law Directory

STANLEY A. TEITLER, P.C. (AV)

321 Broadway, Penthouse, 10007
Telephone: 212-233-8031
Fax: 212-233-8864

Stanley A. Teitler — Charles R. Rondeau

For full biographical listings, see the Martindale-Hubbell Law Directory

WHITE & CASE (AV)

1155 Avenue of the Americas, 10036-2787
Telephone: 212-819-8200
Telex: 233188 WHCA UR
Facsimile: 212-354-8113
Washington, D.C.:
Telephone: 202-872-0013.
Facsimile: 202-872-0210.
Los Angeles, California:
Telephone: 213-620-7700.
Facsimile: 213-687-0758; 213-617-2205.
Miami, Florida:
Telephone: 305-371-2700.
Facsimile: 305-358-5744.
Mexico City, Mexico:
Telephone: (52-5) 207-9717.
Facsimile: (52-5) 208-3628.
Tokyo, Japan:
Telephone: (81-3) 3239-4300.
Facsimile: (81-3) 3239-4330.
Hong Kong:
Telephone: (852) 2822-8700.
Facsimile: (852) 2845-9070; Grice & Co., Solicitors,
Telephone: (852) 2826-0333.
Facsimile: (852) 2526-7166.
Singapore, Republic of Singapore:
Telephone: (65) 225-6000.
Facsimile: (65) 225-6009.
Bangkok, Thailand: Pacific Legal Group Ltd., In Association With White & Case,
Telephone: (662) 236-6154/7.
Facsimile: (662) 237-6771.
Hanoi, Viet Nam: Representative Office,
Telephone: (84-4) 227-575/6/7.
Facsimile: (84-4) 227-297.
Bombay, India:
Telephone: (91-22) 282-6300.
Facsimile: (91-22) 282-6305.
London, England:
Telephone: (44-171) 726-6361.
Facsimile: (44-171) 726-4314; (44-171) 726-8558.
Paris, France:
Telephone: (33-1) 42-60-34-05.
Facsimile: (33-1) 42-60-82-46.
Brussels, Belgium:
Telephone: (32-2) 647-05-89.
Facsimile: (32-2) 647-16-75.
Stockholm, Sweden:
Telephone: (46-8) 679-80-30.
Facsimile: (46-8) 611-21-22.
Helsinki, Finland:
Telephone: (358-0) 631-100.
Facsimile: (358-0) 179-477.
Moscow, Russia:
Telephone: (7-095) 201-9292/3/4/5.
Facsimile: (7-095) 201-9284.
Budapest, Hungary:
Telephone: (36-1) 269-0550; (36-1) 131-0933.
Facsimile: (36-1) 269-1199.
Prague, Czech Republic:
Telephone: (42-2) 2481-1796.
Facsimile: (42-2) 232-5522.
Warsaw, Poland: Telephone/
Facsimile: (48-22) 26-80-53; (48-22) 27-84-86. International Telephone/
Facsimile: (48-39) 12-19-06.
Istanbul, Turkey:
Telephone: (90-212) 275-68-98; (90-212) 275-75-33.
Facsimile: (90-212) 275-75-43.
Ankara, Turkey:
Telephone: (90-312) 446-2180.
Facsimile: (90-312) 437-9677.
Jeddah, Saudi Arabia: Law Office of Hassan Mahassni,
Telephone: (966-2) 651-3535.
Facsimile: (966-2) 651-3636.
Riyadh, Saudi Arabia: Law Office of Hassan Mahassni,
Telephone: (966-1) 476-7099.
Facsimile: (966-1) 479-0110.
Almaty, Kazakhstan:
Telephone: (7-3272) 50-7491/2.
Facsimile: (7-3272) 61-0842.

ASSOCIATE

G. William Currier

For Complete List of Firm Personnel, See General Section

For full biographical listings, see the Martindale-Hubbell Law Directory

New York—Continued

ZUCKERMAN, SPAEDER, GOLDSTEIN, TAYLOR & KOLKER (AV)

Grace Building, 45th Floor, 1114 Avenue of the Americas, 10036
Telephone: 212-479-6500
Fax: 212-479-6512
Washington, D.C. Office: 1201 Connecticut Avenue, N.W.
Telephone: 201-778-1800.
Fax: 202-822-8106.
Miami, Florida Office: Zuckerman, Spaeder, Taylor & Evans. Suite 900, Miami Center, 201 South Biscayne Boulevard.
Telephones: 305-358-5000; 305-579-0110; Broward County: 305-523-0277.
Fax: 305-579-9749.
Ft. Lauderdale, Florida Office: Zuckerman, Spaeder, Taylor & Evans. One East Broward Boulevard, Suite 700.
Telephone: 305-356-0463.
Fax: 305-356-0406.
Baltimore, Maryland Office: Zuckerman, Spaeder, Goldstein, Taylor & Better. Suite 2440, 100 East Pratt Street.
Telephone: 410-332-0444.
Fax: 410-659-0436.
Tampa, Florida Office: Zuckerman, Spaeder, Taylor & Evans. 101 East Kennedy Boulevard, Suite 3140.
Telephone: 813-221-1010.
Fax: 813-223-7961.

MEMBER OF FIRM

Edward J. M. Little

ASSOCIATES

Lisa A. Cahill
Alan H. Scheiner (Not admitted in NY)

For full biographical listings, see the Martindale-Hubbell Law Directory

STANFORDVILLE, Dutchess Co.

WILLIAM E. STANTON (AV)

Village Centre, Route 82, P.O. Box 370, 12581
Telephone: 914-868-7514
FAX: 914-868-7761

Representative Clients: Dupont de Nemours & Co.; Millbrook School; Hanover Insurance Co.; New York Telephone Co.
Reference: Fishkill National Bank.

For full biographical listings, see the Martindale-Hubbell Law Directory

*SYRACUSE,** Onondaga Co.

GROSSMAN KINNEY DWYER & HARRIGAN, P.C. (AV)

5720 Commons Park, 13057
Telephone: 315-449-2131
Telecopier: 315-449-2905

Richard D. Grossman
John P. Kinney
James F. Dwyer
C. Frank Harrigan
Robert E. Hornik, Jr.
Harris N. Lindenfeld

Ruth Moors D'Eredita
Edward P. Dunn
Joseph G. Shields

Representative Clients: County of Onondaga; County of Tompkins; Therm, Incorporated, Ithaca, New York; Village of Marcellus; Smith Barney Shearson; The Mitsubishi Bank, Limited (New York Branch); C&S Engineers, Inc.; Town of Harrietstown, New York.

For full biographical listings, see the Martindale-Hubbell Law Directory

*TROY,** Rensselaer Co.

E. STEWART JONES (AV)

28 Second Street, 12181
Telephone: 518-274-5820
Fax: 518-274-5875

E. Stewart Jones, Jr.
W. Farley Jones
Jeffrey K. Anderson
David J. Taffany
Peter J. Moschetti, Jr.

OF COUNSEL

E. Stewart Jones
Arthur L. Rosen
Abbott H. Jones (1873-1939)
Charles W. Marshall (1882-1945)

References: Key Bank and On Bank; Troy Savings Bank.

For full biographical listings, see the Martindale-Hubbell Law Directory

*WHITE PLAINS,** Westchester Co.

GREENSPAN & GREENSPAN (AV)

34 South Broadway, 6th Floor, 10601
Telephone: 914-946-2500
Cable Address: "Gadlex"
Telecopier: 914-946-1432

(See Next Column)

MEMBERS OF FIRM

Leon J. Greenspan
Michael E. Greenspan

For full biographical listings, see the Martindale-Hubbell Law Directory

B. ANTHONY MOROSCO (AV)

175 Main Street, 10601
Telephone: 914-997-9606
Fax: 914-997-1917

For full biographical listings, see the Martindale-Hubbell Law Directory

NORTH CAROLINA

*ASHEVILLE,** Buncombe Co.

ELMORE & ELMORE, P.A. (AV)

53 North Market Street, 28801
Telephone: 704-253-1492
Fax: 704-253-9648

Bruce A. Elmore
Bruce A. Elmore, Jr.

Reed G. Williams

For full biographical listings, see the Martindale-Hubbell Law Directory

LONG, PARKER & PAYNE, P.A. (AV)

Suite 600, 14 Pack Square, P.O. Box 7216, 28801
Telephone: 704-258-2296
Fax: 704-253-1073

Robert B. Long, Jr.
William A. Parker
Ronald K. Payne

Joseph E. Herrin
W. Scott Jones

For full biographical listings, see the Martindale-Hubbell Law Directory

*BEAUFORT,** Carteret Co.

WHEATLY, WHEATLY, NOBLES & WEEKS, P.A. (AV)

410 Front Street, P.O. Drawer 360, 28516
Telephone: 919-728-3158
FAX: 919-728-5282

Claud R. Wheatly, Jr.
Claud R. Wheatly, III
John E. Nobles, Jr.
Stevenson L. Weeks
J. Christy Maroules
Stephen M. Valentine

Reference: First Citizens Bank.

For full biographical listings, see the Martindale-Hubbell Law Directory

CHAPEL HILL, Orange Co.

BERNHOLZ & HERMAN (AV)

Suite 300, The Center, 1506 East Franklin Street, 27514
Telephone: 919-929-7151
Fax: 919-929-3892

MEMBERS OF FIRM

Steven A. Bernholz
Roger B. Bernholz
G. Nicholas Herman

OF COUNSEL

J. Austin Lybrand, IV

For full biographical listings, see the Martindale-Hubbell Law Directory

LONG & LONG (AV)

116 Mallette Street, 27516
Telephone: 919-929-0408
Fax: 919-929-6819

MEMBERS OF FIRM

Lunsford Long
Florence J. Long

For full biographical listings, see the Martindale-Hubbell Law Directory

RUDOLF & MAHER, P.A. (AV)

312 West Franklin Street, 27516
Telephone: 919-967-4900
Fax: 919-967-4953

David S. Rudolf
Thomas K. Maher

For full biographical listings, see the Martindale-Hubbell Law Directory

Chapel Hill—Continued

BARRY T. WINSTON (AV)

The Center, Suite 300, 1506 East Franklin Street, 27514
Telephone: 919-967-8553
FAX: 919-968-4698

Reference: First Citizens Bank & Trust Co.

For full biographical listings, see the Martindale-Hubbell Law Directory

*CHARLOTTE,** Mecklenburg Co.

FERGUSON, STEIN, WALLAS, ADKINS, GRESHAM & SUMTER, P.A. (AV)

Suite 730, 700 East Stonewall Street, 28202
Telephone: 704-375-8461
Fax: 704-334-5654
Chapel Hill, North Carolina Office: Suite 2, 312 West Franklin Street.
Telephone: 919-933-5300.
Fax: 919-967-4953.

James E. Ferguson, II
Adam Stein (Resident at Chapel Hill Office)
Jonathan Wallas
Karl Adkins
John W. Gresham
Geraldine Sumter
Thomas M. Stern (Resident at Chapel Hill Office)
C. Margaret Errington
Anita S. Hodgkiss

Stephen Luke Largess

For full biographical listings, see the Martindale-Hubbell Law Directory

RAWLS, DICKINSON AND LEDFORD, P.A. (AV)

The Carillon Building, 227 West Trade Street Suite 2140, 28202
Telephone: 704-376-3200
Facsimile: 704-332-2716

Eben T. Rawls III
Thomas W. Dickinson
Joseph L. Ledford

References: NationsBank of North Carolina; First Union National Bank of North Carolina.

For full biographical listings, see the Martindale-Hubbell Law Directory

LAW OFFICES OF MICHAEL S. SCOFIELD (AV)

Suite 980 United Carolina Bank Building, 212 South Tryon Street, 28281
Telephone: 704-331-9348
Fax: 704-336-6902

ASSOCIATE

Mary V. Carrigan

For full biographical listings, see the Martindale-Hubbell Law Directory

SMITH HELMS MULLISS & MOORE, L.L.P. (AV)

227 North Tryon Street, P.O. Box 31247, 28231
Telephone: 704-343-2000
Telecopier: 704-334-8467
Telex: 572460
Greensboro, North Carolina Office: Smith Helms Mulliss & Moore, Suite 1400 First Union Tower, 300 North Greene Street, P.O. Box 21927.
Telephone: 910-378-5200.
Telecopier: 910-379-9558.
Raleigh, North Carolina Office: 316 West Edenton Street, P.O. Box 27525.
Telephone: 919-755-8700.
Telecopier: 919-828-7938.

MEMBERS OF FIRM

E. Osborne Ayscue, Jr.
Robert B. Cordle
James G. Middlebrooks

ASSOCIATE

Maurice O. Green

For Complete List of Firm Personnel, See General Section

For full biographical listings, see the Martindale-Hubbell Law Directory

WYATT & CUNNINGHAM (AV)

435 East Morehead Street, 28202-2609
Telephone: 704-331-0767
Fax: 704-331-0773

James F. Wyatt, III
John R. Cunningham, III

For full biographical listings, see the Martindale-Hubbell Law Directory

*ELIZABETH CITY,** Pasquotank Co.

HORNTHAL, RILEY, ELLIS & MALAND, L.L.P. (AV)

301 E. Main Street, P.O. Box 220, 27909
Telephone: 919-335-0871
Fax: 919-335-4223
Nags Head, North Carolina Office: 2502 South Croatan Highway, P.O. Box 310, 27959-0310.
Telephone: 919-441-0871.
Telefax: 919-441-8822.

L. P. Hornthal, Jr.
J. Fred Riley
M. H. Hood Ellis
Mark M. Maland
Donald C. Prentiss
Robert B. Hobbs, Jr. (Resident, Nags Head Office)
John D. Leidy

ASSOCIATES

Michael P. Sanders
Lee L. Leidy
Phillip K. Woods

For full biographical listings, see the Martindale-Hubbell Law Directory

*GREENSBORO,** Guilford Co.

MCNAIRY, CLIFFORD & CLENDENIN (AV)

127 North Greene Street, Suite 300, 27401
Telephone: 910-378-1212
FAX: 910-333-9820

MEMBERS OF FIRM

Locke T. Clifford
Robert O'Hale

For full biographical listings, see the Martindale-Hubbell Law Directory

SMITH HELMS MULLISS & MOORE, L.L.P. (AV)

Suite 1400 First Union Tower, 300 North Greene Street, P.O. Box 21927, 27420
Telephone: 910-378-5200
Telecopier: 910-379-9558
Charlotte, North Carolina Office: Smith Helms Mulliss & Moore, L.L.P., 227 North Tryon Street, P.O. Box 31247.
Telephone: 704-343-2000.
Telecopier: 704-334-8467.
Telex: 572460.
Raleigh, North Carolina Office: Smith Helms Mulliss & Moore, L.L.P., 316 West Edenton Street, P.O. Box 27525.
Telephone: 919-755-8700.
Telecopier: 919-828-7938.

MEMBER OF FIRM

James A. Medford

For Complete List of Firm Personnel, See General Section

For full biographical listings, see the Martindale-Hubbell Law Directory

*HILLSBOROUGH,** Orange Co.

COLEMAN, GLEDHILL & HARGRAVE, P.C. (AV)

129 East Tryon Street, P.O. Drawer 1529, 27278
Telephone: 919-732-2196
FAX: 919-732-7997

Alonzo B. Coleman, Jr.
Geoffrey E. Gledhill
Douglas Hargrave

Kim K. Steffan
Janet B. Dutton
Douglas P. Thoren

For full biographical listings, see the Martindale-Hubbell Law Directory

*JACKSONVILLE,** Onslow Co.

TAYLOR & HORBALY (AV)

Attorneys at Military Law
Suite 117, 825 Gum Branch Road, 28540
Telephone: 910-455-6300
Facsimile: 910-455-3012

MEMBERS OF FIRM

Vaughan E. Taylor
Jan Horbaly (Not admitted in NC)

ASSOCIATE

Elizabeth Anne Haughton

For full biographical listings, see the Martindale-Hubbell Law Directory

*RALEIGH,** Wake Co.

* indicates certain Bar Register subscribers whose principal office is located elsewhere in the state and who have arranged for representation as a part of the state capital listings that follow

JOHNNY S. GASKINS (AV)

150 Fayetteville Street Suite 2700, 27601
Telephone: 919-831-8717
Facsimile: 919-831-4755

For full biographical listings, see the Martindale-Hubbell Law Directory

PHILIP O. REDWINE, P.A. (AV)

Capital Club Building, 16 West Martin Street, Suite 700, P.O. Box 1030, 27601
Telephone: 919-831-1312
Telecopier: 919-831-1327

Philip O. Redwine

For full biographical listings, see the Martindale-Hubbell Law Directory

*** SMITH HELMS MULLISS & MOORE, L.L.P.** (AV)

316 West Edenton Street, P.O. Box 27525, 27611-7525
Telephone: 919-755-8700
Telecopier: 919-828-7938
Charlotte, North Carolina Office: 227 North Tryon Street, P.O. Box 31247.
Telephone: 704-343-2000.
Telecopier: 704-334-8467.
Telex: 572460.
Greensboro, North Carolina Office: Smith Helms Mulliss & Moore, Suite 1400 First Union Tower, 300 North Greene Street, P.O. Box 21927.
Telephone: 910-378-5200.
Telecopier: 910-379-9558.

ASSOCIATES

R. L. Adams
Paul K. Sun, Jr.
Matthew W. Sawchak

For Complete List of Firm Personnel, See General Section

For full biographical listings, see the Martindale-Hubbell Law Directory

THARRINGTON, SMITH & HARGROVE (AV)

209 Fayetteville Street Mall, P.O. Box 1151, 27602
Telephone: 919-821-4711
Telecopier: 919-829-1583

MEMBERS OF FIRM

Carlisle W. Higgins (1887-1980)
J. Harold Tharrington
Roger W. Smith
Wade M. Smith
George T. Rogister, Jr.
Carlyn G. Poole
Douglas E. Kingsbery
Randall M. Roden
Michael Crowell
Ann L. Majestic
C. Allison Brown Schafer

ASSOCIATES

Melissa Hill
Daniel W. Clark
Jonathan A. Blumberg
Debra R. Nickels
Rod Malone
E. Hardy Lewis
Jaye Powell Meyer

LEGAL SUPPORT PERSONNEL

Michael M. Cogswell

Representative Clients: North Carolina Association of Broadcasters; AT&T Communications; ABC-TV Network Affiliates Assn.; North Carolina Cable Television Assn.; Time-Warner Communications; Virginia Association of Broadcasters; Pulitzer Broadcasting; The Hearst Corporation.

For full biographical listings, see the Martindale-Hubbell Law Directory

*WILMINGTON,** New Hanover Co.

HEWLETT, COLLINS AND ALLARD (AV)

515 Princess Street, P.O. Box 121, 28402
Telephone: 910-763-0156

MEMBERS OF FIRM

Addison Hewlett, Jr. (1912-1989)
John C. Collins
James L. Allard, Jr.

References: Centura Bank; North Carolina Troopers Association Inc.; North Carolina Police Benevolent Association Inc.

For full biographical listings, see the Martindale-Hubbell Law Directory

JOHNSON & LAMBETH (AV)

232 Princess Street, P.O. Box 660, 28402
Telephone: 910-763-0481
FAX: 910-251-1276

MEMBERS OF FIRM

Robert White Johnson
Carter Tate Lambeth

(See Next Column)

ASSOCIATES

Frances Youngblood Trask
Maynard M. Brown
Beth M. Bryant
John Gregory Tillery, III

References: United Carolina Bank; NCNB National Bank of North Carolina.

For full biographical listings, see the Martindale-Hubbell Law Directory

YOW, CULBRETH & FOX (AV)

102 North Fifth Avenue, P.O. Drawer 479, 28401
Telephone: 910-762-2421
FAX: 910-251-9247

MEMBERS OF FIRM

Edgar L. Yow (1902-1983)
Cicero P. Yow (1914-1990)
Lionel L. Yow
Stephen E. Culbreth
Douglas A. Fox
Jerry A. Mannen, Jr.

OF COUNSEL

William Allen Cobb

Representative Client: General Motors Acceptance Corp.
References: Central Carolina Bank; First Union National Bank; NCNB National Bank of North Carolina; Southern National Bank; United Carolina Bank.

For full biographical listings, see the Martindale-Hubbell Law Directory

ZIMMER AND ZIMMER, L.L.P. (AV)

111 Princess Street, P.O. Box 2628, 28402
Telephone: 910-763-4669
Telecopier: 910-762-1999

MEMBERS OF FIRM

Herbert J. Zimmer
Jeffrey Lee Zimmer
Melinda Haynie Crouch
Maura A. McCaughey

Reference: Centura Bank; Wachovia Bank of North Carolina, N.A.

For full biographical listings, see the Martindale-Hubbell Law Directory

*WINSTON-SALEM,** Forsyth Co.

WILLIAM L. COFER, P.A. (AV)

NationsBank Building, Suite 550, 380 Knollwood Street, 27103
Telephone: 910-722-2323

William L. Cofer

References: Wachovia Bank & Trust Co., N.A.; First Citizens Bank and Trust Company.

For full biographical listings, see the Martindale-Hubbell Law Directory

EDDIE C. MITCHELL, P.A. (AV)

Suite 550, NationsBank Building, 380 Knollwood Street, 27103
Telephone: 910-725-9597

Eddie C. Mitchell

References: Wachovia Bank & Trust Co., N.A.; First Citizens Bank and Trust Company.

For full biographical listings, see the Martindale-Hubbell Law Directory

WHITE AND CRUMPLER (AV)

11 West Fourth Street, 27101
Telephone: 910-725-1304
FAX: 910-761-8845

MEMBERS OF FIRM

James G. White (1924-1974)
Fred G. Crumpler, Jr.
G. Edgar Parker
David B. Freedman
Dudley A. Witt

ASSOCIATES

Joan E. Brodish
Teresa Hier

OF COUNSEL

Frank M. Armstrong (1900-1979)
Barbara C. Westmoreland
Clyde C. Randolph, Jr.

Reference: Wachovia Bank and Trust Co., N.A., Winston-Salem, North Carolina.

For full biographical listings, see the Martindale-Hubbell Law Directory

NORTH DAKOTA

*BISMARCK,** Burleigh Co.

PETERSON, SCHMITZ, MOENCH & SCHMIDT, A PROFESSIONAL CORPORATION (AV)

Second Floor, Suite 200, 116 North Fourth Street, P.O. Box 2076, 58502-2076
Telephone: 701-224-0400
Fax: 701-224-0399

David L. Peterson
Dale W. Moench
Orell D. Schmitz
William D. Schmidt

OF COUNSEL

Gerald Glaser

LEGAL SUPPORT PERSONNEL

Vicki J. Kunz
Traci L. Albers

For full biographical listings, see the Martindale-Hubbell Law Directory

*FARGO,** Cass Co.

VOGEL, BRANTNER, KELLY, KNUTSON, WEIR & BYE, LTD. (AV)

502 First Avenue North, P.O. Box 1389, 58107
Telephone: 701-237-6983
Facsimile: 701-237-0847

Mart Daniel Vogel
Bruce Douglas Quick
Charles Alan Stock

For Complete List of Firm Personnel, See General Section

For full biographical listings, see the Martindale-Hubbell Law Directory

WEST FARGO, Cass Co.

OHNSTAD TWICHELL, P.C. (AV)

901 13th Avenue East, P.O. Box 458, 58078-0458
Telephone: 701-282-3249
FAX: 701-282-0825
Hillsboro, North Dakota Office: West Caledonia Avenue, P.O. Box 220.
Telephone: 701-436-5700.
FAX: 701-436-4025.
Mayville, North Dakota Office: 12 Third Street, S.E., P.O. Box 547.
Telephone: 701-786-3251.
FAX: 701-786-4243.
Fargo, North Dakota Office: 15 Broadway, Suite 202.
Telephone: 701-280-5801.
Fax: 701-280-5803.

Robert E. Rosenvold
Robert G. Hoy

Representative Clients: First National Bank North Dakota; Quality Boneless Beef; City of West Fargo; Bond Counsel for Cities of Fargo, Jamestown, West Fargo and Valley City; Insurance Company of North America; Reliance Insurance Co.; The Continental Insurance Cos.; Underwriters Adjusting Co.; Industrial Indemnity Co.; Integrity Insurance Co.

For Complete List of Firm Personnel, See General Section

For full biographical listings, see the Martindale-Hubbell Law Directory

OHIO

*CINCINNATI,** Hamilton Co.

DINSMORE & SHOHL (AV)

1900 Chemed Center, 255 East Fifth Street, 45202-3172
Telephone: 513-977-8200
FAX: 513-977-8141
Florence, Kentucky Office: Turfway Ridge Office Park, 7300 Turfway Road, Suite 430 41042-1355.
Telephone: 606-283-0515.
FAX: 606-283-6017.
Dayton, Ohio Office: 500 Courthouse Plaza, S.W., 10 N. Ludlow Street, 45402-1834.
Telephone: 513-228-8012.
FAX: 513-461-2543.
Columbus, Ohio Office: NBD Bank Building, Suite 330, 175 South Third Street, 43215-5134.
Telephone: 614-224-7887.
FAX: 614-224-7882.

MEMBERS OF FIRM

Lawrence A. Kane, Jr.
Lawrence R. Elleman
Mark A. Vander Laan
Carl J. Stich, Jr. (On Leave of Absence)
Joseph E. Conley, Jr. (Resident, Florence, Kentucky Office)
Joel S. Taylor (Resident, Columbus, Ohio Office)

(See Next Column)

For Complete List of Firm Personnel, See General Section

For full biographical listings, see the Martindale-Hubbell Law Directory

THOMAS W. MILLER (AV)

Suite 2602 One West Fourth Street, 45202
Telephone: 513-241-3050
Fax: 513-241-6379

W. Kelly Johnson

For full biographical listings, see the Martindale-Hubbell Law Directory

SIRKIN PINALES MEZIBOV & SCHWARTZ (AV)

920 Fourth & Race Tower, 105 West Fourth Street, 45202-2776
Telephone: 513-721-4876
Telecopier: 513-721-0876

MEMBERS OF FIRM

H. Louis Sirkin
Marc D. Mezibov
Martin S. Pinales
Howard M. Schwartz

ASSOCIATES

Edmund J. McKenna
Matthew Brownfield
Martha K. Landesberg

References: The Central Trust Co.; The Huntington National Bank.

For full biographical listings, see the Martindale-Hubbell Law Directory

*CLEVELAND,** Cuyahoga Co.

BERKMAN, GORDON, MURRAY, PALDA & DEVAN (AV)

2121 The Illuminating Building, 55 Public Square, 44113-1949
Telephone: 216-781-5245
FAX: 216-781-8207

MEMBERS OF FIRM

Larry S. Gordon
Mark R. DeVan
J. Michael Murray
Lorraine R. Baumgardner
George W. Palda
Jeremy A. Rosenbaum

ASSOCIATES

Steven D. Shafron
Brooke F. Kocab

Reference: First National Bank of Ohio.

For full biographical listings, see the Martindale-Hubbell Law Directory

DUVIN, CAHN & BARNARD A LEGAL PROFESSIONAL ASSOCIATION (AV)

Erieview Tower, 20th Floor, 1301 East Ninth Street, 44114
Telephone: 216-696-7600
Telecopier: 216-696-2038

Robert P. Duvin
Stephen J. Cahn
Thomas H. Barnard
Gerald A. Messerman
Marc J. Bloch
Andrew C. Meyer
Lee J. Hutton
Martin S. List
Craig M. Brown
Frank W. Buck
Gale S. Messerman
Neal B. Wainblat
Kenneth B. Stark
Martin T. Wymer
Barton A. Bixenstine
Robert M. Wolff
Jane P. Wilson

Richard C. Hubbard, III
Lisa Froimson Mann
Philip S. Kushner
Stephen J. Sferra
Linda E. Tawil
Steven K. Aronoff
Kenneth Michael Haneline
Kevin M. Norchi
Paul A. Monahan
Jon M. Dileno
David A. Posner
Scott A. Moorman
Vincent T. Norwillo
Marc A. Duvin
Suellen Oswald
Stephen C. Sutton
Michele H. Schmidt
William Joseph Evans
Carole O. Heyward

Representative Clients: Cleveland-Akron-Canton Supermarket Industry; The Scott Fetzer Co.; Cole National Corp.; Regional Transit Authority; B.P. America.

For full biographical listings, see the Martindale-Hubbell Law Directory

GOLD, ROTATORI & SCHWARTZ, L.P.A. (AV)

1500 Leader Building, 44114
Telephone: 216-696-6122
FAX: 216-696-3214

Gerald S. Gold
John S. Pyle
Robert J. Rotatori
Susan L. Gragel
Niki Z. Schwartz
Robert A. Ranallo

Orville E. Stifel, II
Richard L. Stoper, Jr.
Brian P. Downey

Reference: Society National Bank of Cleveland.

For full biographical listings, see the Martindale-Hubbell Law Directory

Cleveland—Continued

KITCHEN, DEERY & BARNHOUSE (AV)

1100 Illuminating Building, 55 Public Square, 44113
Telephone: 216-241-5614
Fax: 216-241-5255

MEMBERS OF FIRM

Karl K. Kitchen (1899-1949)
Fred A. Messner (1901-1986)
George W. Leyshon (1913-1972)
James V. Suhr (1899-1983)
Ronald J. Deery (1942-1992)
Charles W. Kitchen
James W. Barnhouse
Paul S. Klug
Vincent A. Feudo
Johanna M. Sfiscko
Timothy X. McGrail
Eugene B. Meador

ASSOCIATES

William F. Schmitz
Patti Jo Mooney
Kathleen Donovan Onders

Representative Clients: Buckeye Union Insurance Co.; Continental Insurance Co.; Grange Mutual Casualty Co.; Erie Insurance Group; Home Insurance Cos.; Motorists Mutual Insurance Cos.; St. Paul Insurance Cos.; U.S. Aviation Underwriters; Ohio Medical Professional Liability Underwriting Assn. (J.U.A.).
Reference: National City Bank.

For full biographical listings, see the Martindale-Hubbell Law Directory

THOMPSON, HINE AND FLORY (AV)

1100 National City Bank Building, 629 Euclid Avenue, 44114-3070
Telephone: 216-566-5500
Fax: 216-566-5583
Telex: 980217
Cable Address: "Thomflor"
Akron, Ohio Office: 50 S. Main Street, Suite 502, 44308-1828.
Telephone: 216-376-8090.
Fax: 216-376-8386.
Cincinnati, Ohio Office: 312 Walnut Street, 14th Floor, 45202-4029.
Telephone: 513-352-6700.
Fax: 513-241-4771.
Telex: 938003.
Columbus, Ohio Office: One Columbus, 10 West Broad Street, 43215-3435.
Telephone: 614-469-3200.
Fax: 614-469-3361.
Dayton, Ohio Office: 2000 Courthouse Plaza, N.E., 45402-1706.
Telephone: 513-443-6600.
Fax: 513-443-6637; 443-6635.
Palm Beach, Florida Office: 125 Worth Avenue, Suite 117, 33480-4466.
Telephone: 407-833-5900.
Fax: 407-833-5951.
Washington, D.C. Office: 1920 N Street, N.W., 20036-1601.
Telephone: 202-331-8800.
Fax: 202-331-8330.
Telex: 904173.
Cable Address: "Caglaw".
Brussels, Belgium Office: Rue des Chevaliers, Ridderstraat 14 - B.10, B - 1050.
Telephone: 011(32-2) 511-9326.
Fax: 011(32-2) 513-9206.

MEMBERS OF FIRM

Leslie W. Jacobs
John F. McClatchey (Retired)
Daniel R. Warren

For Complete List of Firm Personnel, See General Section

For full biographical listings, see the Martindale-Hubbell Law Directory

*COLUMBUS,** Franklin Co.

KETCHAM & KETCHAM (AV)

Suite 1416, 50 West Broad Street, 43215
Telephone: 614-224-2176

MEMBERS OF FIRM

Victor A. Ketcham
Richard S. Ketcham

Reference: Society Bank.

For full biographical listings, see the Martindale-Hubbell Law Directory

TYACK, BLACKMORE & LISTON CO., L.P.A. (AV)

536 South High Street, 43215
Telephone: 614-221-1341
Fax: 614-228-0253

Thomas M. Tyack
Margaret L. Blackmore
Jefferson E. Liston

Angela F. Albert

References: Huntington National Bank; Bank One of Columbus, NA.

For full biographical listings, see the Martindale-Hubbell Law Directory

SAM B. WEINER (AV)

743 South Front Street, 43206
Telephone: 614-443-6581
References: BancOhio National Bank; Huntington National Bank.

For full biographical listings, see the Martindale-Hubbell Law Directory

DAVID C. WINTERS (AV)

30 West Hoster Street, 43215
Telephone: 614-228-0068
FAX: 614-469-0198
Reference: BancOhio National Bank.

For full biographical listings, see the Martindale-Hubbell Law Directory

*DAYTON,** Montgomery Co.

FARUKI GILLIAM & IRELAND (AV)

600 Courthouse Plaza, S.W., 10 North Ludlow Street, 45402
Telephone: 513-227-3700
Fax: 513-227-3717

MEMBERS OF FIRM

Charles J. Faruki
Armistead W. Gilliam, Jr.
D. Jeffrey Ireland

For full biographical listings, see the Martindale-Hubbell Law Directory

FLANAGAN, LIEBERMAN, HOFFMAN & SWAIM (AV)

318 West Fourth Street, 45402
Telephone: 513-223-5200
Fax: 513-223-3335

MEMBERS OF FIRM

Louis I. Hoffman
Dennis A. Lieberman
Wayne P. Stephan

References: Bank One, Dayton, NA; Society Bank, N.A.; The First National Bank, Dayton Ohio.

For Complete List of Firm Personnel, See General Section

For full biographical listings, see the Martindale-Hubbell Law Directory

*EATON,** Preble Co.

BENNETT & BENNETT (AV)

Bennett Law Building, 200 West Main Street, 45320
Telephone: 513-456-4100
Fax: 513-456-5100

MEMBERS OF FIRM

Lloyd B. Bennett (1909-1983)
Herd L. Bennett
Gray W. Bennett

Representative Clients: The National Hummel Foundation and Museum; Star Bank of Preble County, Ohio; Eaton National Bank & Trust Co.; First National Bank of Southwestern Ohio; Brookville National Bank; Farm Credit Services of Mid-America; Miller's Super Markets, Inc.; Northedge Shopping Center, Inc.; Herman M. Brubaker Registered Holstein Cattle; The Eaton Foundation.

For Complete List of Firm Personnel, See General Section

For full biographical listings, see the Martindale-Hubbell Law Directory

*POMEROY,** Meigs Co.

CROW AND CROW (AV)

110 West Second Street, P.O. Box 668, 45769
Telephone: 614-992-6059; 992-5132 (non-dedicated facsimile lines)

MEMBERS OF FIRM

Fred W. Crow, Sr. (1879-1957)
Fred W. Crow, Jr.
I. Carson Crow

Representative Clients: Midwest Steel; Auto Owners Insurance Co.; State Automobile Insurance Co.; The Farmers Bank & Savings Co.; General Telephone Co.; Orkin Exterminating Company Inc.; Beneficial Ohio Inc.; City Loan Financial Services, Inc.
Approved Attorneys for: Louisville Land Title Insurance Co.; Ohio Bar Title Insurance Co. (agent); Village Solicition Syracuse, Ohio.

OKLAHOMA

*ENID,** Garfield Co.

JONES & WYATT (AV)

Suite 1100 Broadway Tower, 114 East Broadway, P.O. Box 472, 73702
Telephone: 405-242-5500
Fax: 405-242-4556

(See Next Column)

JONES & WYATT, *Enid—Continued*

MEMBERS OF FIRM

Stephen Jones
Robert L. Wyatt, IV
Jeremy Booth Lowrey
Michael David Roberts
James L. Hankins
Julia Sims Allen

Representative Clients: Western Union; Mesa Limited Partnership; Wells Fargo; City of Enid; Sears & Roebuck Company; St. Paul Property and Liability; International Oil, Chemical and Atomic Workers Union; Associated Aviation Underwriters; Independent Petroleum Association of America; Halliburton Industries.

For full biographical listings, see the Martindale-Hubbell Law Directory

*OKLAHOMA CITY,** Oklahoma Co.

HUGHES, WHITE, ADAMS & GRANT (AV)

The Paragon, 5801 North Broadway Extension, Suite 302, 73118-7438
Telephone: 405-848-0111
FAX: 405-848-3507

Carl D. Hughes
Joe E. White, Jr.
Richard S. Adams

For Complete List of Firm Personnel, See General Section

For full biographical listings, see the Martindale-Hubbell Law Directory

MARTIN LAW OFFICE (AV)

Suite 360, 119 North Robinson Avenue, 73102
Telephone: 405-236-8888
Fax: 405-236-8844

MEMBER OF FIRM

Mack K. Martin

ASSOCIATE

Laurel Susan Smith

For full biographical listings, see the Martindale-Hubbell Law Directory

*TULSA,** Tulsa Co.

SNEED, LANG, ADAMS & BARNETT, A PROFESSIONAL CORPORATION (AV)

2300 Williams Center Tower II, Two West Second Street, 74103
Telephone: 918-583-3145
Telecopier: 918-582-0410

James C. Lang
D. Faith Orlowski
Brian S. Gaskill
G. Steven Stidham
Stephen R. McNamara
Thomas E. Black, Jr.
Robbie Emery Burke
C. Raymond Patton, Jr.
Frederick K. Slicker
Richard D. Black
John D. Russell
Jeffrey S. Swyers

OF COUNSEL

James L. Sneed
O. Edwin Adams
Howard G. Barnett, Jr.

Representative Clients: Amoco Production Company; Continental Bank; Deloitte & Touche; Enron Corporation; Halliburton Energy Services; Helmerich & Payne, Inc.; Lehman Brothers, Inc.; Shell Oil Company; Smith Barney, Inc.; State Farm Mutual Automobile Insurance Company.

For full biographical listings, see the Martindale-Hubbell Law Directory

OREGON

*EUGENE,** Lane Co.

TED CARP (AV)

1852 Willamette Street, 97401
Telephone: 503-345-8751
Fax: 503-345-8753

For full biographical listings, see the Martindale-Hubbell Law Directory

PENNSYLVANIA

*ALLENTOWN,** Lehigh Co.

RICHARD J. MAKOUL (AV)

461 Linden Street, 18102
Telephone: 610-433-4233
FAX: 610-776-7221

For full biographical listings, see the Martindale-Hubbell Law Directory

BETHLEHEM, Northampton Co.

O'HARE & HEITCZMAN (AV)

18 East Market Street, P.O. Box 1446, 18018
Telephone: 610-691-5500
FAX: 610-691-7866

MEMBERS OF FIRM

Bernard V. O'Hare, Jr. (1923-1990)
George A. Heitczman

References: First Valley Bank; Meridan Bank.

For full biographical listings, see the Martindale-Hubbell Law Directory

*HARRISBURG,** Dauphin Co.

GOLDBERG, KATZMAN & SHIPMAN, P.C. (AV)

320 Market Street - Strawberry Square, P.O. Box 1268, 17108-1268
Telephone: 717-234-4161
Telecopier: 717-234-6808; 717-234-6810

Harry B. Goldberg
Paul J. Esposito
Jerry J. Russo

OF COUNSEL

Arthur L. Goldberg

Reference: Fulton Bank.

For Complete List of Firm Personnel, See General Section

For full biographical listings, see the Martindale-Hubbell Law Directory

HEPFORD, SWARTZ & MORGAN (AV)

111 North Front Street, P.O. Box 889, 17108-0889
Telephone: 717-234-4121
Fax: 717-232-6802
Lewistown, Pennsylvania Office: 12 South Main Street, P.O. Box 867. *Telephone:* 717-248-3913.

MEMBERS OF FIRM

H. Joseph Hepford
Lee C. Swartz
James G. Morgan, Jr.
Sandra L. Meilton
Stephen M. Greecher, Jr.
Dennis R. Sheaffer

COUNSEL

Stanley H. Siegel (Resident, Lewistown Office)

ASSOCIATES

Richard A. Estacio
Michael H. Park
Andrew K. Stutzman

For full biographical listings, see the Martindale-Hubbell Law Directory

KILLIAN & GEPHART (AV)

218 Pine Street, P.O. Box 886, 17108
Telephone: 717-232-1851
Telecopier: 717-238-0592

MEMBERS OF FIRM

Smith B. Gephart
Jane Penny Malatesta
Terrence J. McGowan

Reference: Dauphin Deposit Bank & Trust Co.

For full biographical listings, see the Martindale-Hubbell Law Directory

MANCKE, WAGNER, HERSHEY AND TULLY (AV)

2233 North Front Street, 17110
Telephone: 717-234-7051
Fax: 717-234-7080

MEMBERS OF FIRM

John B. Mancke
P. Richard Wagner
David E. Hershey
William T. Tully

ASSOCIATE

David R. Breschi

For full biographical listings, see the Martindale-Hubbell Law Directory

LANSDALE, Montgomery Co.

RUBIN, GLICKMAN AND STEINBERG, A PROFESSIONAL CORPORATION (AV)

2605 North Broad Street, P.O. Box 1277, 19446
Telephone: 215-822-7575; 855-5500; 800-358-9367
Facsimile: 215-822-1713

Irwin S. Rubin
Jay C. Glickman
Marc Robert Steinberg
Toby Lynn Dickman
Gregory R. Gifford
Amy S. Newman
Lewis Goodman
Kathleen M. O'Brien
Steven M. Koloski

Reference: Union National Bank and Trust Company of Souderton.

For full biographical listings, see the Martindale-Hubbell Law Directory

*MEDIA,** Delaware Co.

Harris & Smith (AV)
211 West State Street, 19063
Telephone: 610-565-5300
Fax: 610-565-7292

MEMBER OF FIRM
G. Guy Smith
ASSOCIATES
Susan E. Murray   Russell F. Daly
OF COUNSEL
Edgar Y. Harris   Theresa Hagenbach White

For full biographical listings, see the Martindale-Hubbell Law Directory

*NORRISTOWN,** Montgomery Co.

Gerber & Gerber (AV)
Suite 500, One Montgomery Plaza, 19401
Telephone: 610-279-6700
Fax: 610-279-7126

MEMBERS OF FIRM
Morris Gerber   A. Richard Gerber
ASSOCIATE
Parke H. Ulrich

For full biographical listings, see the Martindale-Hubbell Law Directory

*PHILADELPHIA,** Philadelphia Co.

Ainslie & Bronson (AV)
26th Floor, One Reading Center, 19107
Telephone: 215-574-0800
Fax: 215-574-0515

MEMBERS OF FIRM
Elizabeth K. Ainslie   Glenn B. Bronson

For full biographical listings, see the Martindale-Hubbell Law Directory

Buchanan Ingersoll, Professional Corporation (AV)
Two Logan Square Twelfth Floor, 18th & Arch Streets, 19103
Telephone: 215-665-8700
Telecopier: 215-569-2066
Pittsburgh, Pennsylvania Office: 5800 USX Tower, 600 Grant Street.
Telephone: 412-562-8800.
Harrisburg, Pennsylvania Office: Vartan Parc, 30 North Third Street.
Telephone: 717-237-4800.
Tampa, Florida Office: 101 East Kennedy Boulevard, Suite 1030.
Telephone: 813-222-8180.
North Miami Beach, Florida Office: 19495 Biscayne Boulevard.
Telephone: 305-933-5600.
Lexington, Kentucky Office: 1210 Vine Center Office Tower, 333 West Vine Street.
Telephone: 606-225-5333.
Princeton, New Jersey Office: Buchanan Ingersoll, A Partnership, College Centre, 500 College Road East.
Telephone: 609-452-2666.

Alan C. Kessler   Antoinette R. Stone
COUNSEL
Nathaniel Metz
SENIOR ATTORNEY
Mary Ellen Krober

Robert Bruce Eyre   Mark Andrew Polemeni
Raymond McGarry   Noreen M. Walsh

For Complete List of Firm Personnel, See General Section

For full biographical listings, see the Martindale-Hubbell Law Directory

William T. Cannon, P.C. (AV)
2540 PSFS Building, 12 South 12th Street, 19107
Telephone: 215-238-9505
215-238-8811

William T. Cannon

Bruce G. Cassidy & Associates, P.A. (AV)
Suite 1040, 21 South 12th Street, 19107
Telephone: 215-568-6700
Fax: 215-568-4077
Collingswood, New Jersey Office: 915 Haddon Avenue, 08108.
Telephone: 609-869-3535.

Bruce G. Cassidy

(See Next Column)

OF COUNSEL
Dr. Peter H. Feuerstein (Not admitted United States)   James A. Dunleavy

For full biographical listings, see the Martindale-Hubbell Law Directory

DeStefano & Warren, P.C. (AV)
Suite 1006, Lafayette Building, 437 Chestnut Street, 19106-2426
Telephone: 215-625-5000
FAX: 215-625-9934
Cherry Hill, New Jersey Office: 601 Longwood Avenue.
Telephone: 609-665-2552.
FAX: 609-665-7524.

William A. DeStefano   Christopher D. Warren
Philip H. Marcus

Susan Gibson Durant
LEGAL SUPPORT PERSONNEL
Joseph Silvestro

For full biographical listings, see the Martindale-Hubbell Law Directory

Durant & Durant (AV)
12th Floor, 400 Market Street, 19106
Telephone: 215-592-1818
Fax: 215-592-9994

MEMBERS OF FIRM
Marc Durant   Rita M. Durant
COUNSEL
Robin Blumenfeld Shore
ASSOCIATE
Adele Breen-Franklin

For full biographical listings, see the Martindale-Hubbell Law Directory

F. Emmett Fitzpatrick, P.C. (AV)
926 Public Ledger Building, 19106
Telephone: 215-925-5200
Fax: 215-925-5991

F. Emmett Fitzpatrick   F. Emmett Fitzpatrick, III

For full biographical listings, see the Martindale-Hubbell Law Directory

Norris E. Gelman (AV)
Suite 750 Curtis Center, Sixth and Walnut Streets, 19106
Telephone: 215-574-0513; 574-0514
Fax: 215-928-1669

ASSOCIATE
Marie-Marcelle Benjamin

For full biographical listings, see the Martindale-Hubbell Law Directory

Kirk T. Karaszkiewicz & Associates, P.C. (AV)
Suite 2230 100 South Broad Street, 19110
Telephone: 215-563-1900
Fax: 215-563-8330

Kirk T. Karaszkiewicz

For full biographical listings, see the Martindale-Hubbell Law Directory

Jack A. Meyerson (AV)
10th Floor, 1760 Market Street, 19103
Telephone: 215-972-1376
Fax: 215-972-0277
(Also Of Counsel to Ominsky, Welsh & Steinberg, P.C.)

Joel I. Fishbein   Greg Prosmushkin

For full biographical listings, see the Martindale-Hubbell Law Directory

John W. Morris (AV)
One Penn Square West, Suite 1300, 19102
Telephone: 215-569-5154
Fax: 215-569-2862

For full biographical listings, see the Martindale-Hubbell Law Directory

Nemeroff, Roberts & Saffren, A Professional Corporation (AV)
260 South Broad Street, 19102
Telephone: 215-790-9750
Elkins Park, Pennsylvania Office: Suite 104, 7848 Old York Road.
Telephone: 215-635-8980.

(See Next Column)

NEMEROFF, ROBERTS & SAFFREN A PROFESSIONAL CORPORATION, *Philadelphia—Continued*

Milton A. Nemeroff
Lawrence J. Roberts
Kenneth S. Saffren

For full biographical listings, see the Martindale-Hubbell Law Directory

DANIEL M. PREMINGER, P.C. (AV)

Suite 1050, Robinson Building, 42 South 15th Street, 19102
Telephone: 215-564-1227; 923-7963

Daniel M. Preminger

For full biographical listings, see the Martindale-Hubbell Law Directory

THOMAS B. RUTTER, LTD. (AV)

Suite 750 The Curtis Center, Independence Square West, 19106
Telephone: 215-925-9200
Fax: 215-928-1669

Thomas B. Rutter

Joseph D. Cronin
Lori E. Zeid

For full biographical listings, see the Martindale-Hubbell Law Directory

JAMES C. SCHWARTZMAN & ASSOCIATES (AV)

The Widener Building, 1337 Chestnut Street, Seventeenth Floor, 19107
Telephone: 215-563-2233
Fax: 215-563-2134

Francine D. Wilensky

For full biographical listings, see the Martindale-Hubbell Law Directory

PETER J. SCUDERI (AV)

1420 Walnut Street, Suite 1000, 19102
Telephone: 215-546-5650

For full biographical listings, see the Martindale-Hubbell Law Directory

SHINGLES & CAPPELLI (AV)

Suite 785, The Philadelphia Bourse, 21 South Fifth Street, 19106
Telephone: 215-238-9305
Fax: 215-625-9292

MEMBERS OF FIRM

Stanley M. Shingles
Joseph J. Cappelli

For full biographical listings, see the Martindale-Hubbell Law Directory

TURNER & MCDONALD, P.C. (AV)

1708 Locust Street, 19103
Telephone: 215-546-9700
Facsimile: 215-546-9712
Haverford, Pennsylvania Office: 355 Lancaster Avenue.
Telephone: 610-649-9600.
Haddonfield, New Jersey Office: 209 Haddon Avenue.
Telephone: 609-429-6022.
Fax: 609-429-0074.

Alan A. Turner
H. Graham McDonald

OF COUNSEL

Thomas B. Rutter
Steven R. Kanes

For full biographical listings, see the Martindale-Hubbell Law Directory

*PITTSBURGH,** Allegheny Co.

DICKIE, MCCAMEY & CHILCOTE, A PROFESSIONAL CORPORATION (AV)

Suite 400, Two PPG Place, 15222-5402
Telephone: 412-281-7272
Fax: 412-392-5367
Wheeling, West Virginia Office: Suite 2002, 1233 Main Street, 26003-2839.
Telephone: 304-233-1022.
Facsimile: 304-233-1026.

David J. Armstrong
Jeffrey T. Wiley
Robert G. Del Greco, Jr.

For Complete List of Firm Personnel, See General Section

For full biographical listings, see the Martindale-Hubbell Law Directory

GAITENS, TUCCERI & NICHOLAS, A PROFESSIONAL CORPORATION (AV)

519 Court Place, 15219
Telephone: 412-391-6920
Fax: 412-391-1189

(See Next Column)

Larry P. Gaitens
Vincent A. Tucceri
Romel L. Nicholas

Reference: Pittsburgh National Bank.

For Complete List of Firm Personnel, See General Section

For full biographical listings, see the Martindale-Hubbell Law Directory

HAROLD GONDELMAN (AV)

The 38th Floor, One Oxford Centre, 15219
Telephone: 412-263-1833

For full biographical listings, see the Martindale-Hubbell Law Directory

STANLEY GREENFIELD & ASSOCIATES (AV)

Greenfield Court, 1035-37 Fifth Avenue, 15219
Telephone: 412-261-4466
Fax: 412-261-4408

Stanley W. Greenfield

Graydon R. Brewer
Martha E. Bailor
Paul G. Kay

For full biographical listings, see the Martindale-Hubbell Law Directory

SCOTT, VOGRIN, RIESTER & JAMIOLKOWSKI, A PROFESSIONAL CORPORATION (AV)

1510 Frick Building, 15219
Telephone: 412-261-0905
Fax: 412-261-3090
Shaler Township, Pennsylvania Office: 1330 Evergreen Avenue, Pittsburgh, 15209.
Telephone: 412-261-0905.
Sewickley, Pennsylvania Office: Osborne Plaza, Suite 603, 1106 Ohio River Boulevard, 15143.
Telephone: 412-261-0905.

Joseph E. Vogrin, III
Kim Wm. Riester

For full biographical listings, see the Martindale-Hubbell Law Directory

THORP, REED & ARMSTRONG (AV)

One Riverfront Center, 15222
Telephone: 412-394-7711
Fax: 412-394-2555

MEMBERS OF FIRM

John H. Bingler, Jr.
Thomas W. Corbett, Jr.
Richard I. Thomas

For Complete List of Firm Personnel, See General Section

For full biographical listings, see the Martindale-Hubbell Law Directory

*WEST CHESTER,** Chester Co.

DUFFY & GREEN (AV)

10 North Church Street, Suite 307, 19380
Telephone: 610-692-0500
FAX: 610-430-6668

MEMBERS OF FIRM

John J. Duffy
Joseph P. Green, Jr.

ASSOCIATES

Richard E. Meanix
P.J. Redmond

For full biographical listings, see the Martindale-Hubbell Law Directory

RHODE ISLAND

*PROVIDENCE,** Providence Co.

MANN & MITCHELL (AV)

Suite 501 Turks Head Place, 02903
Telephone: 401-351-5770
Telecopier: 401-521-4305

MEMBERS OF FIRM

Robert B. Mann
Suzanna J. Mitchell

For full biographical listings, see the Martindale-Hubbell Law Directory

WILLIAM T. MURPHY (AV)

The Calart Tower, 400 Reservoir Avenue, Suite 3L, 02907
Telephone: 401-461-7740
Telecopier: 401-461-7753

(See Next Column)

WILLIAM T. MURPHY—*Continued*

ASSOCIATE
Sean P. Lardner

Reference: Fleet National Bank.

For full biographical listings, see the Martindale-Hubbell Law Directory

WESTERLY, Washington Co.

ADAMO & NEWMAN (AV)

42 Granite Street, 02891
Telephone: 401-596-7795
Telecopier: 401-596-9000

MEMBERS OF FIRM

John Joseph Adamo
Edward H. Newman

OF COUNSEL
George A. Comolli

LEGAL SUPPORT PERSONNEL
Susan E. Bookataub

For full biographical listings, see the Martindale-Hubbell Law Directory

SOUTH CAROLINA

*AIKEN,** Aiken Co.

JOHNSON, JOHNSON, WHITTLE, SNELGROVE & WEEKS, P.A. (AV)

117 Pendleton Street, N.W., P.O. Box 2619, 29802-2619
Telephone: 803-649-5338
FAX: 803-641-4517

B. Henderson Johnson, Jr.
Barry H. Johnson
James E. Whittle, Jr.
Vicki Johnson Snelgrove
John W. (Bill) Weeks
Paige Weeks Johnson
Todd J. Johnson

For full biographical listings, see the Martindale-Hubbell Law Directory

*CHARLESTON,** Charleston Co.

BARR, BARR AND MCINTOSH (AV)

11 Broad Street, P.O. Box 1037, 29402
Telephone: 803-577-5083
Fax: 803-723-9039

MEMBERS OF FIRM

Capers G. Barr, III
William S. Barr
H. Thomas McIntosh, Jr.
Capers G. Barr, IV

Approved Attorneys for: Lawyers Title Insurance Corp.; Title Insurance Co. of Pennsylvania.
References: NationsBank; Bank of South Carolina.

For full biographical listings, see the Martindale-Hubbell Law Directory

GEDNEY M. HOWE, III, P.A. (AV)

8 Chalmers Street, P.O. Box 1034, 29402
Telephone: 803-722-8048
FAX: 803-722-2140

Gedney M. Howe, Jr. (1914-1981)
Gedney M. Howe, III
Alvin J. Hammer
Donald H. Howe
Robert J. Wyndham

For full biographical listings, see the Martindale-Hubbell Law Directory

LIONEL S. LOFTON (AV)

174 East Bay Street, Suite 302, P.O. Box 449, 29402-0449
Telephone: 803-722-6319
FAX: 803-722-6372

ASSOCIATE
Frances L. Cain

For full biographical listings, see the Martindale-Hubbell Law Directory

*COLUMBIA,** Richland Co.

GLENN, IRVIN, MURPHY, GRAY & STEPP (AV)

Southern National Bank Building, Suite 390, 1901 Assembly Street, P.O. Box 1550, 29202-1550
Telephone: 803-765-1100
Telecopy: 803-765-0755

MEMBERS OF FIRM

Wilmot B. Irvin
Peter L. Murphy
Elizabeth Van Doren Gray
Robert E. Stepp
Elizabeth G. Howard

(See Next Column)

Blaney A. Coskrey, III
Robert A. Culpepper

Reference: Southern National.

For Complete List of Firm Personnel, See General Section

For full biographical listings, see the Martindale-Hubbell Law Directory

KING & VERNON, P.A. (AV)

1426 Richland Street, P.O. Box 7667, 29202
Telephone: 803-779-3090
Fax: 803-779-3396

Kermit S. King
W. Thomas Vernon

For Complete List of Firm Personnel, See General Section

For full biographical listings, see the Martindale-Hubbell Law Directory

JACK B. SWERLING (AV)

1720 Main Street, Suite 301, 29201
Telephone: 803-765-2626
Fax: 803-799-4059

For full biographical listings, see the Martindale-Hubbell Law Directory

TOMPKINS AND MCMASTER (AV)

Palmetto Building, Fourth Floor, 1400 Main Street, P.O. Box 7337, 29202
Telephone: 803-799-4499
Telefax: 803-252-2240

MEMBERS OF FIRM

Frank G. Tompkins (1874-1956)
Frank G. Tompkins, Jr. (1908-1973)
Elizabeth Eldridge (1895-1976)
John Gregg McMaster
Henry Dargan McMaster
Frank Barnwell McMaster
Joseph Dargan McMaster

OF COUNSEL
George Hunter McMaster

For full biographical listings, see the Martindale-Hubbell Law Directory

*GREENVILLE,** Greenville Co.

LOVE, THORNTON, ARNOLD & THOMASON, P.A. (AV)

410 East Washington Street, P.O. Box 10045, 29603
Telephone: 803-242-6360
Telefax: 803-271-7972

Belton O. Thomason, Jr. (1926-1993)
William A. Coates
V. Clark Price

For Complete List of Firm Personnel, See General Section

For full biographical listings, see the Martindale-Hubbell Law Directory

SOUTH DAKOTA

*RAPID CITY,** Pennington Co.

LYNN, JACKSON, SHULTZ & LEBRUN, P.C. (AV)

Eighth Floor, Metropolitan Federal Bank Plaza, P.O. Box 8250, 57709
Telephone: 605-342-2592
Telecopier: 605-342-5185
Sioux Falls, South Dakota Office: First Bank Building, Sixth Floor, P.O. Box 1920.
Telephone: 605-332-5999.
Telecopier: 605-332-4249.

Gary D. Jensen
Steven C. Beardsley
Larry M. VonWald

Representative Clients: First Bank of South Dakota; Employers Mutual of Wausau; South Dakota School Mines & Technology; CIGNA Insurance Co.; E.D. Jones & Co.; Prairie States Life Insurance Co.
General Counsel for: Rushmore Electric Power Cooperative; Black Hills Regional Eye Institute; Douglas School District.

For Complete List of Firm Personnel, See General Section

For full biographical listings, see the Martindale-Hubbell Law Directory

*WATERTOWN,** Codington Co.

BARTRON, WILES, RYLANCE & HOLGERSON (AV)

A Partnership including Professional Corporations
3 East Kemp Avenue, 57201-0227
Telephone: 605-886-5881
Fax: 605-886-3934

MEMBERS OF FIRM

R. Greg Bartron (P.C.)
John C. Wiles (P.C.)
Raymond D. Rylance (P.C.)
Albert H. Holgerson (P.C.)

(See Next Column)

BARTRON, WILES, RYLANCE & HOLGERSON, *Watertown—Continued*

OF COUNSEL

Donald E. Osheim (P.C.)

Representative Clients: Allied Group Insurance Co.; Brown Clinic; Farmers and Merchants Bank and Trust of Watertown; Fireman's Fund Insurance Co.; Hartford Insurance Co.; Harvest Life Insurance Co.; Home Insurance Co.; Liberty Mutual Insurance Co.; National Farmers Union Insurance Co.; First Premier Bank, Watertown.

For full biographical listings, see the Martindale-Hubbell Law Directory

TENNESSEE

*CHATTANOOGA,** Hamilton Co.

SUMMERS, MCCREA & WYATT, P.C. (AV)

500 Lindsay Street, 37402
Telephone: 615-265-2385
Fax: 615-266-5211

Jerry H. Summers
Thomas L. Wyatt
Sandra K. McCrea
Jeffrey W. Rufolo

For full biographical listings, see the Martindale-Hubbell Law Directory

*CLEVELAND,** Bradley Co.

JENNE, SCOTT & BRYANT (AV)

260 Ocoee Street, P.O. Box 161, 37364-0161
Telephone: 615-476-5506
Fax: 615-476-5058

MEMBERS OF FIRM

Roger E. Jenne
D. Mitchell Bryant

For Complete List of Firm Personnel, See General Section

For full biographical listings, see the Martindale-Hubbell Law Directory

JOHNSON CITY, Washington Co.

RICHARD W. PECTOL, P.C. & ASSOCIATES (AV)

202 East Unaka Avenue, 37601
Telephone: 615-928-6106
Fax: 615-928-8802

Richard W. Pectol

Vincent A. Sikora

For full biographical listings, see the Martindale-Hubbell Law Directory

*KNOXVILLE,** Knox Co.

PRYOR, FLYNN, PRIEST & HARBER (AV)

Suite 600 Two Centre Square, 625 Gay Street, P.O. Box 870, 37901
Telephone: 615-522-4191
Telecopier: 615-522-0910

Robert E. Pryor
Timothy A. Priest
Frank L. Flynn, Jr.
John K. Harber

ASSOCIATES

Mark E. Floyd
Donald R. Coffey
M. Christopher Coffey

References: Third National Bank; First National Bank.

For full biographical listings, see the Martindale-Hubbell Law Directory

*MEMPHIS,** Shelby Co.

THE BOGATIN LAW FIRM (AV)

A Partnership including Professional Corporations
(Formerly Bogatin Lawson & Chiapella)
860 Ridge Lake Boulevard, Suite 360, 38120
Telephone: 901-767-1234
Telecopier: 901-767-2803 & 901-767-4010

MEMBER OF FIRM

Arthur E. Quinn

For Complete List of Firm Personnel, See General Section

For full biographical listings, see the Martindale-Hubbell Law Directory

CAUSEY, CAYWOOD, TAYLOR & MCMANUS (AV)

Suite 2400, 100 North Main Building, 38103
Telephone: 901-526-0206
Telecopier: 901-525-1540

(See Next Column)

MEMBERS OF FIRM

James D. Causey
Jean E. Markowitz
David Shepherd Walker

For Complete List of Firm Personnel, See General Section

For full biographical listings, see the Martindale-Hubbell Law Directory

*NASHVILLE,** Davidson Co.

HOLLINS, WAGSTER & YARBROUGH, P.C. (AV)

22nd Floor Third National Financial Center, 424 Church Street, 37219
Telephone: 615-256-6666
Telecopier: 615-254-4254

John J. Hollins
John L. Norris
John W. Wagster
David L. Raybin
Edward M. Yarbrough
James L. Weatherly, Jr.
John J. Hollins, Jr.

Patrick T. McNally

References: First American National Bank; Third National Bank.

For full biographical listings, see the Martindale-Hubbell Law Directory

NEAL & HARWELL (AV)

Suite 2000, First Union Tower, 150 Fourth Avenue North, 37219
Telephone: 615-244-1713
Telecopier-FAX: 615-726-0573

MEMBERS OF FIRM

James F. Neal
Ronald G. Harris
Aubrey B. Harwell, Jr.
Albert F. Moore
Jon D. Ross
Philip N. Elbert
James F. Sanders
James G. Thomas
Thomas H. Dundon
William T. Ramsey
Robert L. Sullivan
Delta Anne Davis

Philip D. Irwin
Pamela King
George H. Cate, III
John C. Beiter
Edmund L. Carey, Jr.
David P. Bohman
John A. Coates
A. Scott Ross

Representative Clients: Johnny Cash; Channel Five Television Co. (WTVF); First American National Bank; General Motors Corp.; General Electric Capital Corp.; Hughes Aircraft Corp; Ingram Industries; NationsBank; Nissan Motor Corporation in U.S.A.; Tokio Marine & Fire Insurance Company, Ltd.

For Complete List of Firm Personnel, See General Section

For full biographical listings, see the Martindale-Hubbell Law Directory

*TRENTON,** Gibson Co.

HARRELL AND HARRELL (AV)

Court Square, 38382
Telephone: 901-855-1351; 855-1352
Fax: 901-855-1212

MEMBERS OF FIRM

Limmie Lee Harrell
Limmie Lee Harrell, Jr.

Representative Clients: Trenton Gin Co., Trenton, Tenn.; State Auto Mutual Insurance Co.; Gibson County Special School District, Trenton, Tenn.; Bank of Commerce, Trenton, Tenn.; PDQ Transportation Co., Humboldt, Tenn.; Special School District, Trenton, Tenn.
Reference: The Bank of Commerce, Trenton.

For full biographical listings, see the Martindale-Hubbell Law Directory

TEXAS

*AUSTIN,** Travis Co.

MINTON, BURTON, FOSTER & COLLINS, A PROFESSIONAL CORPORATION (AV)

1100 Guadalupe Street, 78701-2198
Telephone: 512-476-4873
Fax: 512-479-8315

Perry L. Jones (1908-1969)
Randy T. Leavitt
J. Travis Blakeslee (1919-1990)
Martha S. Dickie
Roy Q. Minton
Scott A. Young
Charles R. Burton
John C. Carsey
John L. Foster
David F. Minton
Warren L. (Rip) Collins, Jr.
Jennifer Ramsey

(See Next Column)

MINTON, BURTON, FOSTER & COLLINS A PROFESSIONAL CORPORATION—*Continued*

OF COUNSEL
Paul T. Holt

Representative Clients: Crum & Forster Commercial Insurance Company; The Texas Department of Commerce; Exxon; Freeport-McMoRan, Inc.; HealthTrust, Inc.; Houston Lighting & Power; Living Centers of America, Inc.; The Office of the Governor of Texas; Service Life Insurance Company; Texas Utilities Electric Company.

For full biographical listings, see the Martindale-Hubbell Law Directory

MORRIS & FLOREY, L.L.P. (AV)

704 West 9th Street, 78701
Telephone: 512-479-8600

E. Gerry Morris
Ben Florey
James T. (Tom) O'Leary

Reference: Texas Commerce Bank; NationsBank.

For full biographical listings, see the Martindale-Hubbell Law Directory

*DALLAS,** Dallas Co.

BRUCE ANTON (AV)

2522 McKinney, Suite 201, 75201
Telephone: 214-871-1125
Telecopier: 214-871-1972

For full biographical listings, see the Martindale-Hubbell Law Directory

ARANSON & ASSOCIATES (AV)

Legal Arts Center, 600 Jackson Street, 75202
Telephone: 214-748-5100
Fax: 214-741-4540

Mike Aranson
Garry Philip Cantrell

For full biographical listings, see the Martindale-Hubbell Law Directory

DAN GUTHRIE (AV)

2311 Cedar Springs Road, Suite 250, 75201
Telephone: 214-953-1000
FAX: 214-953-1888

For full biographical listings, see the Martindale-Hubbell Law Directory

MILNER, LOBEL, GORANSON, SORRELS, UDASHEN & WELLS (AV)

Chateau Plaza, Suite 1500, 2515 McKinney Avenue, 75201
Telephone: 214-651-1121
FAX: 214-953-1366

George R. Milner, Jr.
Shirley Baccus-Lobel
Ronald L. Goranson
Barry Sorrels
Robert N. Udashen
Gary A. Udashen
Ronald D. Wells
George R. Milner, III

For full biographical listings, see the Martindale-Hubbell Law Directory

VINCENT WALKER PERINI, P.C. (AV)

3301 Elm Street, 75226-1637
Telephone: 214-747-1134
FAX: 214-939-9229

Vincent Walker Perini

For full biographical listings, see the Martindale-Hubbell Law Directory

*DENTON,** Denton Co.

PHILIPS AND HOPKINS, P.C. (AV)

P.O. Box 2027, 76202-2027
Telephone: 817-566-7010
Facsimile: 817-898-0502

Gerald W. Cobb
T. Miller Davidge, Jr.
Robert N. Eames
William P. Philips, Jr.
Gray W. Shelton
Randolph W. Stout

OF COUNSEL
George Hopkins

Chris Raesz
Leigh Hilton
Barry D. Irwin

Representative Clients: North Texas Savings & Loan Assn., Denton, Texas; First State Bank of Texas, Denton, Texas; Sanger Bank, Sanger, Texas; BankOne, Texas, N.A.; Texas Bank, Denton, Texas; Dentex Title Co., Denton, Texas.

For full biographical listings, see the Martindale-Hubbell Law Directory

*FORT WORTH,** Tarrant Co.

EVANS, GANDY, DANIEL & MOORE (AV)

An Association of Attorneys, Not a Partnership
Sundance Square, 115 West Second Street, Suite 202, 76102
Telephone: 817-332-3822
Metro: 817-429-4194

Tim Evans
Donald S. Gandy
Mark G. Daniel
Tim Moore

For full biographical listings, see the Martindale-Hubbell Law Directory

JEFF KEARNEY & ASSOCIATES (AV)

Sundance Court, 120 West Third Street, Suite 300, 76102-7414
Telephone: 817-336-5600
FAX: 817-336-5610

Jeffrey A. Kearney

ASSOCIATE
Gregory B. Westfall

OF COUNSEL
Byron Matthews

For full biographical listings, see the Martindale-Hubbell Law Directory

JACK V. STRICKLAND, JR. (AV)

909 Throckmorton Street, 76102
Telephone: 817-338-1000
Telecopier: 817-338-1020

For full biographical listings, see the Martindale-Hubbell Law Directory

*HOUSTON,** Harris Co.

BENNETT, BROOCKS, BAKER & LANGE, L.L.P. (AV)

1700 Neils Esperson Building, 808 Travis, 77002
Telephone: 713-222-1434

Robert S. Bennett

Stephen R. Reeves

OF COUNSEL
Philip H. Hilder

For full biographical listings, see the Martindale-Hubbell Law Directory

BERG & ANDROPHY (AV)

A Partnership including a Professional Corporation
3704 Travis, 77002
Telephone: 713-529-5622
FAX: 713-529-3785

David H. Berg (P.C.)
Joel M. Androphy

Sandra L. Morehead
Kyle L. Dickson

For full biographical listings, see the Martindale-Hubbell Law Directory

DEGUERIN & DICKSON (AV)

Seventh Floor, The Republic Building, 1018 Preston Avenue, 77002
Telephone: 713-223-5959
Fax: 713-223-9231

MEMBERS OF FIRM
Dick DeGuerin
Lewis Dickson

ASSOCIATES
Chris Flood
Matt Hennessy

For full biographical listings, see the Martindale-Hubbell Law Directory

SCHAFFER, LAMBRIGHT, ODOM & SPARKS (AV)

1301 McKinney, Suite 3100, 77010
Telephone: 713-951-9555
FAX: 713-951-9854

Randy Schaffer
Don Lambright
Wendell A. Odom, Jr.
Kenneth W. Sparks
Randolph A. McDonald
Robert J. Fickman

ASSOCIATES
Cynthia Russell Henley
Scott E. Kerman

For full biographical listings, see the Martindale-Hubbell Law Directory

Houston—Continued

RONALD G. WOODS (AV)

5300 Memorial, Suite 1000, 77007
Telephone: 713-862-9600
Fax: 713-864-8738

For full biographical listings, see the Martindale-Hubbell Law Directory

*SAN ANTONIO,** Bexar Co.

JACK PAUL LEON (AV)

500 Lexington, 78215
Telephone: 210-223-4254
Fax: 210-227-7721

ASSOCIATE
Jon Christian Amberson
OF COUNSEL
Gilbert Lang Mathews

For full biographical listings, see the Martindale-Hubbell Law Directory

MATTHEWS & BRANSCOMB, A PROFESSIONAL CORPORATION (AV)

One Alamo Center, 106 S. St. Mary's Street, Suite 800, 78205
Telephone: 210-226-4211
Facsimile: 210-226-0521
Telex: 5106009283
Cable Code: MBLAW
Austin, Texas Office: 301 Congress Avenue, Suite 2050.
Telephone: 512-305-4400.
Facsimile: 512-305-4413.
Corpus Christi, Texas Office: 802 N. Carancahua, Suite 1900.
Telephone: 512-888-9261.
Facsimile: 512-888-8504.
Eagle Pass, Texas Office: 675 Main Street.
Telephone: 210-773-6700.
Facsimile: 210-757-4045.
Uvalde, Texas Office: 200 E. Nopal #208.
Telephone: 210-278-4597.
Facsimile: 210-278-4806.
(Associated with Hall, Quintanilla & Alarcon, L.C., Laredo, Texas, under the name of Hall, Quintanilla, Alarcon, Matthews & Branscomb, P.L.L.C.)

Charles J. Muller, III
John McPherson Pinckney, III
Farley P. Katz
Anthony E. Rebollo
Steven J. Pugh

Representative Clients: Coca Cola Bottling Company of the Southwest; Concord Oil Co.; Ellison Enterprises, Inc.; H. E. Butt Grocery Co.; Frank B. Hall & Co., Inc.; The Hearst Corp., San Antonio Light Division; San Antonio Gas & Electric Utilities (City Board); Southern Pacific Transportation Co.; Southwest Texas Methodist Hospital.

For Complete List of Firm Personnel, See General Section

For full biographical listings, see the Martindale-Hubbell Law Directory

TEXARKANA, Bowie Co.

LAW OFFICES OF DAMON YOUNG (AV)

4122 Texas Boulevard, P.O. Box 1897, 75504
Telephone: 501-774-3206; 903-794-1303
Facsimile: 903-792-5098

ASSOCIATES
Thomas H. Holcombe
Tera Futrell Kesterson

For full biographical listings, see the Martindale-Hubbell Law Directory

*TYLER,** Smith Co.

IRELAND, CARROLL & KELLEY, P.C. (AV)

6101 South Broadway, Suite 500, P.O. Box 7879, 75711
Telephone: 903-561-1600
Fax: 903-581-1071

Donald Carroll (1929-1992)
H. Kelly Ireland
Otis W. Carroll
Patrick Kelley
Marcus Carroll
Michael G. Carroll
Bill Parker

Reference: First National Bank of Winnsboro, Tyler, Texas.

For full biographical listings, see the Martindale-Hubbell Law Directory

*WACO,** McLennan Co.

DUNNAM & DUNNAM, L.L.P. (AV)

4125 West Waco Drive, P.O. Box 8418, 76714-8418
Telephone: 817-753-6437
Fax: 817-753-7434

(See Next Column)

MEMBERS OF FIRM
W. V. Dunnam (1891-1974)
W. V. Dunnam, Jr.
Vance Dunnam
Vance Dunnam, Jr.
Damon L. Reed
James R. Dunnam

ASSOCIATES
Cathy Dunnam
Alan Stucky

For full biographical listings, see the Martindale-Hubbell Law Directory

UTAH

*SALT LAKE CITY,** Salt Lake Co.

BERMAN, GAUFIN & TOMSIC, A PROFESSIONAL CORPORATION (AV)

Suite 1250, 50 South Main Street, 84144
Telephone: 801-328-2200
Fax: 801-531-9926

Daniel L. Berman
Samuel O. Gaufin
Peggy A. Tomsic
Daniel S. Day
Ronald J. Chleboski, Jr.
Christopher A. King
Veda M. Travis

OF COUNSEL
Edward J. McDonough
D. Frank Wilkins

For full biographical listings, see the Martindale-Hubbell Law Directory

MCCAUGHEY & METOS (AV)

10 West Broadway Suite 650, 84101
Telephone: 801-364-6474
Fax: 801-364-5014

Stephen R. McCaughey
G. Fred Metos

For full biographical listings, see the Martindale-Hubbell Law Directory

VAN COTT, BAGLEY, CORNWALL & MCCARTHY, A PROFESSIONAL CORPORATION (AV)

Suite 1600, 50 South Main Street, P.O. Box 45340, 84145
Telephone: 801-532-3333
Telex: 453149
Telecopier: 801-534-0058
Ogden, Utah Office: Suite 900, 2404 Washington Boulevard.
Telephone: 801-394-5783.
Park City, Utah Office: 314 Main Street, Suite 205.
Telephone: 801-649-3889.
Reno, Nevada Office: Jeppson & Lee, 100 West Liberty, Suite 990.
Telephone: 702-333-6800.

E. Scott Savage
John T. Nielsen

James D. Gilson

For Complete List of Firm Personnel, See General Section

For full biographical listings, see the Martindale-Hubbell Law Directory

LOREN E. WEISS (AV)

1000 Boston Building, 9 Exchange Place, 84111
Telephone: 801-531-6686
Fax: 801-531-6690

For full biographical listings, see the Martindale-Hubbell Law Directory

YENGICH, RICH & XAIZ (AV)

175 East 400 South, Suite 400, 84111
Telephone: 801-355-0320
Fax: 801-364-6026

MEMBERS OF FIRM
Ronald J. Yengich
Bradley P. Rich
Earl Xaiz

ASSOCIATE
Hakeem Ishola

For full biographical listings, see the Martindale-Hubbell Law Directory

VERMONT

*RUTLAND,** Rutland Co.

CARROLL, GEORGE & PRATT (AV)
64 & 66 North Main Street, P.O. Box 280, 05702-0280
Telephone: 802-775-7141
Telecopier: 802-775-6483
Woodstock, Vermont Office: The Mill - Route #4 E., P.O. Box 388, 05091.
Telephone: 802-457-1000.
Telecopier: 802-457-1874.

MEMBERS OF FIRM

Henry G. Smith (1938-1974)
James P. Carroll
Alan B. George
Robert S. Pratt
Neal C. Vreeland
Jon S. Readnour
Timothy U. Martin
Randall F. Mayhew (Resident Partner, Woodstock Office)
Richard S. Smith
Judy Godnick Barone
John J. Kennelly

ASSOCIATES

Thomas A. Zonay
Jeffrey P. White
Susan Boyle Ford (Resident, Woodstock Office)
Charles C. Humpstone

For full biographical listings, see the Martindale-Hubbell Law Directory

VIRGINIA

*ABINGDON,** Washington Co.

TATE, LOWE & ROWLETT, P.C. (AV)
205 West Main Street, 24210
Telephone: 703-628-5185
Telecopier: 703-628-5045

Mary Lynn Tate
C. Randall Lowe
Fredrick A. Rowlett

Representative Clients: Island Creek Coal Co.; Jewell Resources, Inc.; Pikeville National Bank; Charter Federal Savings Bank; Rapoca Energy Co.
Approved Attorneys for: Lawyers Title Insurance Co.; Safeco Title Insurance Co.; Nations Bank; First Virginia Bank; Bank of Marion; Central Fidelity Bank.

For Complete List of Firm Personnel, See General Section

For full biographical listings, see the Martindale-Hubbell Law Directory

VINYARD AND MOISE, ATTORNEYS AT LAW, P.C. (AV)
116 East Valley Street, P.O. Box 1127, 24210-1127
Telephone: 703-628-7187

Robert Austin Vinyard
Lawrence L. Moise

References: Central Fidelity Bank, Abingdon, Virginia; Dominion Bank, Abingdon, Virginia; NationsBank, N.A., Abingdon, Virginia.

For full biographical listings, see the Martindale-Hubbell Law Directory

YEARY & ASSOCIATES, P.C. (AV)
161 East Main Street, P.O. Box 1685, 24210
Telephone: 703-628-9107
Telecopier: 703-628-1998

Emmitt F. Yeary

W. Hobart Robinson
Kathleen Calvert Yeary

LEGAL SUPPORT PERSONNEL

Michael A. Bragg (Legal Assistant)

Representative Clients: Abingdon Nursing Homes, Inc.; D.S. Buck, Inc.; Rapoca Energy Co.; Food Country U.S.A., Inc.; East Gate Drug Stores of Abingdon, Inc.; Abingdon Printing, Inc.; ERA Anderson & Associates; Southwest Virginia Research & Development Corp.
Approved Attorneys for: Lawyers Title Insurance Co.; Chicago Title Insurance Co.

For full biographical listings, see the Martindale-Hubbell Law Directory

ALEXANDRIA, (Independent City)

CACHERIS & TREANOR (AV)
705 Prince Street, 22314
Telephone: 703-549-8181
Washington, D.C. Office: 1100 Connecticut Avenue, North West, Suite 730.
Telephone: 202-775-8700.
Fax: 202-775-8702; 202-775-8722.

(See Next Column)

Plato Cacheris
Gerard Treanor
Philip T. Inglima (Not admitted in VA)

ASSOCIATES

Judith L. Wheat
Karl A. Racine (Not admitted in VA)
John F. Hundley

OF COUNSEL

Philip T. White (Not admitted in VA)

For full biographical listings, see the Martindale-Hubbell Law Directory

JOHN A. MCCAHILL (AV Ⓣ)
Suite 423 526 King Street, 22314
Telephone: 703-836-2880
Fax: 703-549-1924
(Not admitted in VA)

For full biographical listings, see the Martindale-Hubbell Law Directory

*ARLINGTON,** Arlington Co.

GEORGE D. VAROUTSOS (AV)
6045 Wilson Boulevard Suite 300, 22205
Telephone: 703-532-6900
Fax: 703-532-6351

ASSOCIATE

Elise R. Lapidus

OF COUNSEL

Paul G. Varoutsos
Louis Koutoulakos

For full biographical listings, see the Martindale-Hubbell Law Directory

BLACKSBURG, Montgomery Co.

GILMER, SADLER, INGRAM, SUTHERLAND & HUTTON (AV)
201 West Roanoke Street, P.O. Box 908, 24063-0908
Telephone: 703-552-1061
Telecopier: 703-552-8227
Pulaski, Virginia Office: Midtown Professional Building, 65 East Main Street, P.O. Box 878.
Telephone: 703-980-1360; 703-639-0027.
Telecopier: 703-980-5264.

MEMBERS OF FIRM

James L. Hutton
Todd G. Patrick
Howard C. Gilmer, Jr. (1906-1975)
Roby K. Sutherland (1909-1975)
Philip M. Sadler (1915-1994)
Robert J. Ingram
Thomas J. McCarthy, Jr.
John J. Gill
Gary C. Hancock
Jackson M. Bruce
Michael J. Barbour
Deborah Wood Dobbins
Debra Fitzgerald-O'Connell
Scott A. Rose
Timothy Edmond Kirtner

OF COUNSEL

James R. Montgomery

Representative Clients: Appalachian Power Co.; Magnox, Inc.; Liberty Mutual Insurance Co.; Norfolk Southern Railway Co.; Pulaski Furniture Corp.; NationsBank; Travelers Insurance Co.; Charles Lunsford Sons & Associates; Corning Glass Works.

For full biographical listings, see the Martindale-Hubbell Law Directory

*CHARLOTTESVILLE,** (Ind. City; Seat of Albemarle Co.)

HAUGH & HAUGH, P.C. (AV)
435 Park Street, 22901
Telephone: 804-296-0185
Fax: 804-296-1146

Charles R. Haugh
Lair Dayton Haugh

For full biographical listings, see the Martindale-Hubbell Law Directory

FREDERICKSBURG, (Independent City)

WOODBRIDGE & REAMY (AV)
108 Charlotte Street, P.O. Box 965, 22404
Telephone: 703-373-5300
Fax: 703-899-9110

MEMBERS OF FIRM

Benjamin H. Woodbridge, Jr.
M. R.(Chip) Reamy

For full biographical listings, see the Martindale-Hubbell Law Directory

*HALIFAX,** Halifax Co.

JAMES E. EDMUNDS (AV)
Court Square, P.O. Box 157, 24558
Telephone: 804-476-6202; 476-6578

References: First Federal Savings & Loan Assn., South Boston; Crestar Bank, South Boston.

For full biographical listings, see the Martindale-Hubbell Law Directory

LYNCHBURG, (Independent City)

JOSEPH R. JOHNSON, JR. & ASSOCIATES (AV)

9th Floor, Allied Arts Building, 725 Church Street, P.O. Box 717, 24505
Telephone: 804-845-4541
Fax: 804-845-4134

Travis Harry Witt
P. Scott De Bruin

For full biographical listings, see the Martindale-Hubbell Law Directory

*MARTINSVILLE,** (Ind. City; Seat of Henry Co.)

DOUGLAS K. FRITH & ASSOCIATES, P.C. (AV)

(Member, Commonwealth Law Group, Ltd.)
58 West Church Street, P.O. Box 591, 24114
Telephone: 703-632-7137
FAX: 703-632-3988

Douglas K. Frith

General Counsel for: Frith Construction Co., Inc.; Koger/Air Corp.; Prillaman & Pace, Inc.; Radio Station WHEE; Fuller & Gray Tire Co., Inc.; Millard's Machinery, Inc.
Representative Client: Hartford Accident & Indemnity.

For full biographical listings, see the Martindale-Hubbell Law Directory

NORFOLK, (Independent City)

RABINOWITZ, RAFAL, SWARTZ, TALIAFERRO & GILBERT, P.C. (AV)

Wainwright Building, Suite 700, 229 West Bute Street, P.O. Box 3332, 23514
Telephone: 804-622-3931; 623-6674
FAX: 804-626-1003

Franklin A. Swartz
William L. Taliaferro, Jr.
Calvin R. Depew, Jr.

For full biographical listings, see the Martindale-Hubbell Law Directory

SACKS, SACKS & IMPREVENTO (AV)

Suite 501 Town Point Center, 150 Boush Street, P.O. Box 3874, 23514
Telephone: 804-623-2753
FAX: 804-640-7170

Herman A. Sacks (1886-1983)
Stanley E. Sacks
Andrew M. Sacks
Michael F. Imprevento

For full biographical listings, see the Martindale-Hubbell Law Directory

*ORANGE,** Orange Co.

SHACKELFORD, HONENBERGER, THOMAS & WILLIS, P.L.C. (AV)

One Perry Plaza, P.O. Box 871, 22960
Telephone: 703-672-2711
Fax: 703-672-2714
Culpeper, Virginia Office: 147 West Davis Street, P.O. Box 1002.
Telephone: 703-825-0305.

OF COUNSEL

Virginius R. Shackelford, Jr.
Virginius R. Shackelford, III
Christopher J. Honenberger
Frank A. Thomas, III
Jere M. H. Willis, III (Resident, Culpeper, Virginia Office)
Sarah Collins Honenberger

Sean D. Gregg

Counsel for: Woodberry Forest School; County of Madison; Rapidan Service Authority.
Assistant Division Counsel for: Norfolk Southern Corp.
Approved Attorneys for: Lawyers Title Insurance Corp.; Southern Title Insurance Co.; Chicago Title Insurance Co.; Federal Land Bank of Baltimore; Farmers Home Administration.

For full biographical listings, see the Martindale-Hubbell Law Directory

*PULASKI,** Pulaski Co.

GILMER, SADLER, INGRAM, SUTHERLAND & HUTTON (AV)

Midtown Professional Building, 65 East Main Street, P.O. Box 878, 24301
Telephone: 703-980-1360; 703-639-0027
Telecopier: 703-980-5264
Blacksburg (Montgomery County), Virginia Office: 201 West Roanoke Street, P.O. Box 908.
Telephone: 703-552-1061.
Telecopier: 703-552-8227.

(See Next Column)

MEMBERS OF FIRM

Howard C. Gilmer, Jr. (1906-1975)
Roby K. Sutherland (1909-1975)
Philip M. Sadler (1915-1994)
Robert J. Ingram
James L. Hutton (Resident, Blacksburg Office)
Thomas J. McCarthy, Jr.
John J. Gill
Gary C. Hancock
Jackson M. Bruce
Michael J. Barbour
Deborah Wood Dobbins
Todd G. Patrick (Resident, Blacksburg Office)
Debra Fitzgerald-O'Connell
Scott A. Rose
Timothy Edmond Kirtner

OF COUNSEL

James R. Montgomery

Representative Clients: Appalachian Power Co.; Chevron; Liberty Mutual Insurance Co.; Norfolk Southern Railway Co.; Pulaski Furniture Corp.; NationsBank; Travelers Insurance Group; Renfro, Inc.; Magnox, Inc.; Corning Glass Works.

For full biographical listings, see the Martindale-Hubbell Law Directory

RADFORD, (Independent City)

STONE, HARRISON, TURK & SHOWALTER, P.C. (AV)

Tyler Office Plaza, 1902 Downey Street, P.O. Box 2968, 24143-2968
Telephone: 703-639-9056
Telecopier: 703-731-4665

Edwin C. Stone
Clifford L. Harrison
James C. Turk, Jr.
Josiah T. Showalter, Jr.
Margaret E. Stone

Representative Clients: St. Albans Psychiatric Hospital; Radford Community Hospital; Inland Motor Corp.; The K-C Corp.; Meadowgold Dairies; Lynchburg Foundry; Hartford Accident and Indemnity Co.; Cigna Insurance Cos.; Hercules, Inc.; Norfolk Southern Corp.

For full biographical listings, see the Martindale-Hubbell Law Directory

*RICHMOND,** (Ind. City; Seat of Henrico Co.)

DUANE AND SHANNON, P.C. (AV)

10 East Franklin Street, 23219
Telephone: 804-644-7400
Fax: 804-649-8329

Harley W. Duane, III
James C. Shannon
B. Craig Dunkum
David L. Hauck
Arnold B. Snukals
William V. Riggenbach
Carl R. Schwertz

Martha P. Smith

For full biographical listings, see the Martindale-Hubbell Law Directory

LEVIT & MANN (AV)

419 North Boulevard, 23220
Telephone: 804-355-7766
Fax: 804-358-4018

MEMBERS OF FIRM

Jay J. Levit
John B. Mann

For full biographical listings, see the Martindale-Hubbell Law Directory

MICHAEL MORCHOWER (AV)

9 East Franklin Street, 23219
Telephone: 804-643-0147
FAX: 804-648-5514
Washington, D.C. Office: 1730 K Street, N.W., Suite 304.
Telephone: 202-293-3246.
(Also Member of Morchower, Luxton and Whaley)

For full biographical listings, see the Martindale-Hubbell Law Directory

*TAZEWELL,** Tazewell Co.

GALUMBECK SIMMONS AND REASOR (AV)

104 West Main Street, P.O. Box 561, 24651
Telephone: 703-988-9436; 988-6561
Telecopier: 703-988-2921

MEMBERS OF FIRM

Robert M. Galumbeck
Deanis L. Simmons
Jackson E. Reasor, Jr.

References: Lawyers Title Insurance; Bank of Tazwell County.

For full biographical listings, see the Martindale-Hubbell Law Directory

VIRGINIA BEACH, (Independent City)

BRYDGES & MAHAN (AV)

Professional Building, 1369 Laskin Road, 23451
Telephone: 804-428-6021
FAX: 804-491-7634

(See Next Column)

BRYDGES & MAHAN—*Continued*

MEMBERS OF FIRM

Richard G. Brydges | Stephen C. Mahan

Reference: Sovran Bank.
Approved Mediator/Arbitrator For: United States Arbitration and Mediation, Inc.; Arbitration Associates, Inc.

For full biographical listings, see the Martindale-Hubbell Law Directory

SHUTTLEWORTH RULOFF GIORDANO AND KAHLE, P.C. (AV)
4425 Corporation Lane, Suite 300, 23462
Telephone: 804-671-6000
Fax: 804-671-6004
Newport News, Virginia Office: 603 Pilot House Drive, Suite 250.
Telephone: 804-873-9999.
Telecopier: 804-873-9758.

Judith M. Cofield
Robert J. Haddad
Robert G. Morecock
Thomas B. Shuttleworth, II

OF COUNSEL

Paul S. Trible, Jr.

For full biographical listings, see the Martindale-Hubbell Law Directory

*WARRENTON,** Fauquier Co.

ROBIN C. GULICK, P.C. (AV)
70 Main Street Suite 52, P.O. Box 880, 22186
Telephone: 703-347-3022
Fax: 703-347-9711

Robin C. Gulick | William W. Carson, Jr.

General Counsel for: Jefferson Savings & Loan.
References: Fauquier National Bank; The Peoples National Bank.

For full biographical listings, see the Martindale-Hubbell Law Directory

WASHINGTON

*SEATTLE,** King Co.

JOHN W. LUNDIN, P.S. (AV)
710 Cherry, 98104
Telephone: 206-623-8346
Fax: 206-623-5951

John W. Lundin

Reference: Key Bank (Main Branch).

For full biographical listings, see the Martindale-Hubbell Law Directory

*SPOKANE,** Spokane Co.

MAXEY LAW OFFICES, P.S. (AV)
West 1835 Broadway, 99201
Telephone: 509-326-0338
Fax: 509-325-9919

Carl Maxey
William C. Maxey
Bevan J. Maxey
Dennis C. Cronin
Lora Lee Stover

Thomas J. Alexiou

For full biographical listings, see the Martindale-Hubbell Law Directory

WEST VIRGINIA

*CHARLESTON,** Kanawha Co.

HUNT, LEES, FARRELL & KESSLER (AV)
7 Players Club Drive, P.O. Box 2506, 25329-2506
Telephone: 304-344-9651
Telecopier: 304-343-1916
Huntington, West Virginia Office: Prichard Building, 601 Ninth Street, P.O. Box 2191, 25722.
Telephone: 304-529-1999.
Martinsburg, West Virginia Office: 1012 B Winchester Avenue. P.O. Box 579. 25401.
Telephone: 304-267-3100.

MEMBERS OF FIRM

James B. Lees, Jr.
Joseph M. Farrell, Jr. (Resident, Huntington Office)
John A. Kessler

(See Next Column)

ASSOCIATES

James A. McKowen
Jeffrey T. Jones
Marion Eugene Ray
Mark Jenkinson (Resident, Martinsburg Office)
Meikka A. Cutlip (Resident, Huntington Office)
Sharon M. Fedorochko

OF COUNSEL

L. Alvin Hunt

For full biographical listings, see the Martindale-Hubbell Law Directory

JACKSON & KELLY (AV)
1600 Laidley Tower, P.O. Box 553, 25322
Telephone: 304-340-1000
Fax: 304-340-1130
Martinsburg, West Virginia Office: 300 Foxcroft Avenue, P.O. Box 1068.
Telephone: 304-263-8800.
Morgantown, West Virginia Office: 6000 Hampton Center, P.O. Box 619.
Telephone: 304-599-3000.
New Martinsville, West Virginia Office: 256 Russell Avenue, P.O. Box 68.
Telephone: 304-455-1751.
Charles Town, West Virginia Office: 700 East Washington Street, P.O. Box 983.
Telephone: 304-728-6088.
Clarksburg, West Virginia Office: 203 Main Street, P.O. Box 1587.
Telephone: 304-623-3002.
Lexington, Kentucky Office: 175 East Main Street, Suite 500, P.O. Box 2150.
Telephone: 606-255-9500.
Washington, D. C. Office: 2401 Pennsylvania Avenue, N.W., Suite 400.
Telephone: 202-973-0200.
Denver, Colorado Office: Suite 2710, 1660 Lincoln Street.
Telephone: 303-837-0003.

MEMBERS OF FIRM

W. Warren Upton
Mark N. Savit (Resident, Washington, D.C. Office)
William J. Powell

ASSOCIATES

Robert L. Johns | Anthony J. Majestro

For Complete List of Firm Personnel, See General Section

For full biographical listings, see the Martindale-Hubbell Law Directory

KING, ALLEN & ARNOLD (AV)
1300 Bank One Center, P.O. Box 3394, 25333
Telephone: 304-345-7250
Telecopier: 304-345-9941

Robert B. King
George G. Guthrie
Robert B. Allen
James S. Arnold
R. Terrance Rodgers
Robert A. Goldberg
Stephen B. Farmer
John J. Polak
Robert D. Cline, Jr.
S. Benjamin Bryant
Raymond Keener, III
Wm. Scott Wickline
Robert A. Campbell
W. Mark Burnette
J. Miles Morgan
Pamela Lynn Kandzari
Michelle M. Price
Kimberly S. Fenwick

For full biographical listings, see the Martindale-Hubbell Law Directory

*ELKINS,** Randolph Co.

BUSCH & TALBOTT, L.C. (AV)
Court and High Streets, P.O. Box 1397, 26241
Telephone: 304-636-3560
Fax: 304-636-2290

John E. Busch | Richard H. Talbott, Jr.

Cynthia Santoro Gustke
Peter G. Zurbuch
David Thompson
Bridgette Rhoden Wilson

Representative Clients: Monongahela Power Co.; Davis Trust Co.; Community Bank & Trust Company of Randolph County; Coastal Lumber Co.; USF&G; Nationwide Insurance Co.; State Farm Insurance Companies; Nissan Motor Corporation in USA; Chrysler Corp.; General Motors.

For Complete List of Firm Personnel, See General Section

For full biographical listings, see the Martindale-Hubbell Law Directory

*PRINCETON,** Mercer Co.

GIBSON & ASSOCIATES (AV)
1345 Mercer Street, 24740
Telephone: 304-425-8276
800-742-3545

MEMBER OF FIRM

Michael F. Gibson

(See Next Column)

GIBSON & ASSOCIATES, *Princeton—Continued*

ASSOCIATES

Derrick Ward Lefler
Bill Huffman
Kelly R. Charnock

LEGAL SUPPORT PERSONNEL

SOCIAL SECURITY PARALEGALS

Nancy Belcher

PERSONAL INJURY PARALEGALS

Kathy Richards

WORKERS COMPENSATION PARALEGAL

Carol Hylton

MEDICAL NEGLIGENCE PARALEGAL

Deborah Fye

For full biographical listings, see the Martindale-Hubbell Law Directory

*WHEELING,** Ohio Co.

SCHRADER, RECHT, BYRD, COMPANION & GURLEY (AV)

1000 Hawley Building, 1025 Main Street, P.O. Box 6336, 26003
Telephone: 304-233-3390
Fax: 304-233-2769
Martins Ferry, Ohio Office: 205 North Fifth Street, P.O. Box 309.
Telephone: 614-633-8976.
Fax: 614-633-0400.

PARTNERS

Henry S. Schrader (Retired)
Arthur M. Recht
Ray A. Byrd
James F. Companion
Terence M. Gurley
Frank X. Duff
Teresa Rieman-Camilletti
Yolonda G. Lambert
Patrick S. Casey
Sandra M. Chapman
Daniel P. Fry (Resident, Martins Ferry, Ohio Office)
James P. Mazzone

ASSOCIATES

Sandra K. Law
D. Kevin Coleman
Denise A. Jebbia
Edythe A. Nash
Robert G. McCoid
Denise D. Klug
Thomas E. Johnston

OF COUNSEL

James A. Byrum, Jr.

General Counsel: WesBanco Bank-Elm Grove.
Representative Clients: CIGNA Property and Casualty Cos.; Columbia Gas Transmission Corp.; Commercial Union Assurance Co.; Hazlett, Burt & Watson, Inc.; Stone & Thomas Department Stores; Transamerica Commercial Finance Corp.; Wheeling-Pittsburgh Steel Corp.

For full biographical listings, see the Martindale-Hubbell Law Directory

WISCONSIN

*KENOSHA,** Kenosha Co.

ROSE & ROSE (AV)

5529 Sixth Avenue, 53140
Telephone: 414-658-8550, 657-7556

William S. Rose (1914-1994)
Terry W. Rose

For full biographical listings, see the Martindale-Hubbell Law Directory

*MADISON,** Dane Co.

LAWTON & CATES, S.C. (AV)

214 West Mifflin Street, 53703-2594
Telephone: 608-256-9031
Fax: 608-256-4670

James W. Gardner
John L. Cates
P. Scott Hassett

Reference: Bank One, Madison.

For full biographical listings, see the Martindale-Hubbell Law Directory

*MILWAUKEE,** Milwaukee Co.

SHELLOW, SHELLOW & GLYNN, S.C. (AV)

222 East Mason Street, 53202
Telephone: 414-271-8535

James M. Shellow
Gilda B. Shellow
Stephen M. Glynn
Dean A. Strang
Robert R. Henak
Carol S. Josten
Craig W. Albee

For full biographical listings, see the Martindale-Hubbell Law Directory

WYOMING

*CHEYENNE,** Laramie Co.

HICKEY, MACKEY, EVANS, WALKER & STEWART (AV)

1712 Carey Avenue, P.O. Drawer 467, 82003
Telephone: 307-634-1525
Telecopier: 307-638-7335

MEMBERS OF FIRM

Paul J. Hickey
Terry W. Mackey
David F. Evans
John M. Walker
Mark R. Stewart III
Richard D. Tim Bush

A List of Representative Clients will be furnished upon request.
Reference: Norwest Bank, Cheyenne, N.A.

For full biographical listings, see the Martindale-Hubbell Law Directory

*JACKSON,** Teton Co.

SPENCE, MORIARITY & SCHUSTER (AV)

15 South Jackson Street, P.O. Box 548, 83001
Telephone: 307-733-7290
Fax: 307-733-5248
Cheyenne, Wyoming Office: Suite 302 Pioneer Center, 2424 Pioneer Avenue, P.O. Box 1006.
Telephone: 307-635-1533.
Fax: 307-635-1539.

MEMBERS OF FIRM

Gerry L. Spence
Edward P. Moriarity
Robert P. Schuster
Gary L. Shockey
J. Douglas McCalla
Roy A. Jacobson, Jr.

ASSOCIATES

Glen G. Debroder
Kent W. Spence
Robert A. Krause
Heather Noble

Reference: First Interstate Bank, Casper, Wyoming.

For Complete List of Firm Personnel, See General Section

For full biographical listings, see the Martindale-Hubbell Law Directory

VIRGIN ISLANDS

*CHARLOTTE AMALIE, ST. THOMAS,** St. Thomas

GRUNERT STOUT BRUCH & MOORE

24-25 Kongensgade, P.O. Box 1030, 00804
Telephone: 809-774-1320
Fax: 809-774-7839

MEMBERS OF FIRM

John E. Stout
Susan Bruch Moorehead
Treston E. Moore

ASSOCIATES

Maryleen Thomas
Richard F. Taylor
H. Kevin Mart (Not admitted in VI)

OF COUNSEL

William L. Blum

For full biographical listings, see the Martindale-Hubbell Law Directory

CANADA
BRITISH COLUMBIA

*VANCOUVER,** Vancouver Co.

HARPER GREY EASTON (AV)

3100 Vancouver Centre, 650 West Georgia Street, P.O. Box 11504, V6B 4P7
Telephone: 604-687-0411
Telex: 04-55448
Telecopier: 604-669-9385

MEMBER OF FIRM

Terrence L. Robertson, Q.C.

Solicitors for: Commercial Union Assurance Company of Canada; Lumbermens Mutual Casualty Co.; State Farm Fire and Casualty Co.

For Complete List of Firm Personnel, See General Section

For full biographical listings, see the Martindale-Hubbell Law Directory

CANADA
ONTARIO

*TORONTO,** Regional Munic. of York

Borden & Elliot (AV)

Barristers & Solicitors
Scotia Plaza, 40 King Street West, M5H 3Y4
Telephone: 416-367-6000
Telecopier: 416-367-6749
Internet: @ borden.com
A Member of the national association of Borden DuMoulin Howard Gervais, comprising Borden & Elliot in Toronto, Ontario, Russell & DuMoulin in Vancouver, British Columbia, Howard, Mackie in Calgary, Alberta and Mackenzie Gervais in Montréal, Québec. Borden DuMoulin Howard Gervais also operates an office in London, England.

MEMBER AND ASSOCIATES

Todd L. Archibald

For Complete List of Firm Personnel, See General Section

For full biographical listings, see the Martindale-Hubbell Law Directory

CANADA
QUEBEC

*MONTREAL,** Montreal Dist.

Yarosky, Daviault, La Haye, Stober & Isaacs (AV)

Suite 2536, 800 RenéLévesque Boulevard West, H3B 1X9
Telephone: 514-878-3505
Fax: 514-861-3065

MEMBERS OF FIRM

Harvey W. Yarosky, Q.C.
Francois Daviault
Gerald J. La Haye
Michael Stober
Natalie Fochs Isaacs
Marc P. David

COUNSEL

Fred Kaufman, C.M., Q.C.

For full biographical listings, see the Martindale-Hubbell Law Directory

EMPLOYMENT BENEFITS LAW

ALABAMA

*BIRMINGHAM,** Jefferson Co.

BALCH & BINGHAM (AV)
1710 Sixth Avenue North, P.O. Box 306, 35201
Telephone: 205-251-8100
Facsimile: 205-226-8798
Other Birmingham, Alabama Office: 1901 Sixth Avenue North, 35203.
Telephone: 205-251-8100.
Facsimile: 205-226-8799.
Montgomery, Alabama Office: The Winter Building, 2 Dexter Avenue, 36101.
Telephone: 205-834-6500.
Facsimile: 205-269-3115.
Huntsville, Alabama Office: Suite 810, 200 West Court Square, 35801.
Telephone: 205-551-0171.
Facsimile: 205-551-0174.
Washington, D.C. Office: Suite 800, 1101 Connecticut Avenue, N.W., 20036.
Telephone: 202-296-0387.
Facsimile: 202-452-8180.

MEMBERS OF FIRM

John Richard Carrigan
William E. Shanks, Jr.
John J. Coleman, III
Cavender Crosby Kimble

SENIOR ATTORNEY

T. Dwight Sloan

Counsel for: Alabama Power Co.; Blue Cross and Blue Shield of Alabama; The Boeing Company; Brasfield & Gorrie, Inc.; Compass Bancshares, Inc.; Harbert Corp.; Kimberly-Clark Corp.; Southern Company Services, Inc.; Southern Research Institute; Vesta Insurance Group, Inc.

For Complete List of Firm Personnel, See General Section

For full biographical listings, see the Martindale-Hubbell Law Directory

BRADLEY, ARANT, ROSE & WHITE (AV)
1400 Park Place Tower, 2001 Park Place, 35203
Telephone: 205-521-8000
Telex: 494-1324
Facsimile: 205-251-8611, 251-8665, 252-0264
Facsimile (Southtrust Office): 205-251-9915
Huntsville, Alabama Office: 200 Clinton Avenue West, Suite 900.
Telephone: 205-517-5100.
Facsimile: 205-533-5069.

MEMBERS OF FIRM

John James Coleman, Jr.
Robert G. Johnson
John William Hargrove

ASSOCIATES

James S. Christie, Jr.
Kevin J. Henderson

For Complete List of Firm Personnel, See General Section

For full biographical listings, see the Martindale-Hubbell Law Directory

GORDON, SILBERMAN, WIGGINS & CHILDS, A PROFESSIONAL CORPORATION (AV)
1400 SouthTrust Tower, 420 North 20th Street, 35203
Telephone: 205-328-0640
Telecopier: 205-254-1500

Wilbur G. Silberman
Bruce L. Gordon
Robert L. Wiggins, Jr.
Robert F. Childs, Jr.
Augustus J. Beck, Jr.
Harvey L. Wachsman
Ray D. Gibbons
C. Michael Quinn
Dennis George Pantazis

Terrill W. Sanders
James Mendelsohn
Richard J. Ebbinghouse
Ann K. Norton
Paul H. Webb
Mark P. Williams
Samuel Fisher
Timothy C. Gann
Naomi Hilton Archer
Timothy D. Davis
Joseph H. Calvin, III
Linda J. Peacock
Ann C. Robertson
Elizabeth Evans Courtney
Byron R. Perkins
Jon C. Goldfarb
Gregory O. Wiggins
Lee Winston
Jon E. Lewis
Deborah A. Mattison
Amelia H. Griffith
Rocco Calamusa, Jr.

(See Next Column)

OF COUNSEL

Robert H. Loeb

For Complete List of Firm Personnel, See General Section

For full biographical listings, see the Martindale-Hubbell Law Directory

POWELL & FREDERICK (AV)
Suite 700 2100 First Avenue North, 35203
Telephone: 205-324-4996
Telecopier: 205-324-4120

MEMBERS OF FIRM

Charles A. Powell, III
Barry V. Frederick
William G. Somerville, III

ASSOCIATE

John W. Sheffield

OF COUNSEL

Paul E. Toppins

For full biographical listings, see the Martindale-Hubbell Law Directory

SIROTE & PERMUTT, P.C. (AV)
2222 Arlington Avenue, South, P.O. Box 55727, 35255
Telephone: 205-933-7111
Facsimile: 205-930-5301
Huntsville, Alabama Office: 200 Clinton Avenue, N.W., Suite 1000.
Telephone: 205-536-1711.
Facsimile: 205-534-9650.
Mobile, Alabama Office: One St. Louis Centre, Suite 1000.
Telephone: 205-432-1671.
Facsimile: 205-434-0196.
Montgomery, Alabama Office: Colonial Commerce Center, Suite 305 One Commerce Street.
Telephone: 205-261-3400.
Facsimile: 205-261-3434.
Tuscaloosa, Alabama Office: 2216 14th Street.
Telephone: 205-752-2089.

Harold I. Apolinsky
Joseph S. Bluestein
Jack B. Levy
Joseph T. Ritchey
Lynda L. Hendrix

Representative Clients: International Business Machines (IBM); General Motors Corp.; Colonial Bank; Bruno's, Inc.; University of Alabama Hospitals; Westinghouse Electric Corp.; First Alabama Bank; Monsanto Chemical Company; South Central Bell; Prudential Insurance Company; American Home Products, Inc.; Minnesota Mining and Manufacturing, Inc. (3M).

For Complete List of Firm Personnel, See General Section

For full biographical listings, see the Martindale-Hubbell Law Directory

*MOBILE,** Mobile Co.

JOHNSTONE, ADAMS, BAILEY, GORDON AND HARRIS (AV)
Royal St. Francis Building, 104 St. Francis Street, P.O. Box 1988, 36633
Telephone: 334-432-7682
Facsimile: 334-432-2800
Telex: 782040

MEMBERS OF FIRM

Brock B. Gordon
Ben H. Harris, Jr.
E. Watson Smith
Joseph M. Allen, Jr.
Wade B. Perry, Jr.
Gregory C. Buffalow
Celia J. Collins
R. Gregory Watts

General Counsel for: First Alabama Bank, Mobile; Infirmary Health System/Mobile Infirmary Medical Center/Rotary Rehabilitation Hospital (Multi-Hospital System).
Counsel for: Oil and Gas: Exxon Corp. Business and Corporate: Bell South Telecommunications, Inc.; Aluminum Co. of America; Michelin Tire Corp.; Metropolitan Life Insurance Co.; The Travelers Insurance Cos. Marine: The West of England Ship Owners Mutual Protection and Indemnity Association (Luxembourg); The Standard Steamship Owners' Protection and Indemnity Association (Bermuda) Ltd.

For Complete List of Firm Personnel, See General Section

For full biographical listings, see the Martindale-Hubbell Law Directory

ARIZONA

*PHOENIX,** Maricopa Co.

FENNEMORE CRAIG, A PROFESSIONAL CORPORATION (AV)
Two North Central, Suite 2200, 85004
Telephone: 602-257-8700
Fax: 602-257-8527
Scottsdale, Arizona Office: 6263 North Scottsdale Road, Suite 290, 85250.
Telephone: 602-257-5400.
Fax: 602-945-4932.

(See Next Column)

FENNEMORE CRAIG A PROFESSIONAL CORPORATION, *Phoenix—Continued*

Tucson, Arizona Office: One South Church Avenue, Suite 1030, 85701.
Telephone: 602-624-9312.
Fax: 602-882-7383.

John R. Rawling — Cynthia L. Shupe

Otto S. Shill, III — Karen Rettig Rogers

Representative Clients: ASARCO Incorporated; AT&T Communications; Bridgestone/Firestone, Inc.; Catellus Development Corp.; Citibank (Arizona); First Interstate Bank of Arizona; GIANT Industries; Phelps Dodge Corporation; The Atchison, Topeka & Santa Fe Railway, Co.; US WEST Communications.

For Complete List of Firm Personnel, See General Section

For full biographical listings, see the Martindale-Hubbell Law Directory

SNELL & WILMER (AV)

One Arizona Center, 85004-0001
Telephone: 602-382-6000
Fax: 602-382-6070
Tucson, Arizona Office: 1500 Norwest Tower, One South Church Avenue 85701-1612.
Telephone: 602-882-1200.
Fax: 602-884-1294.
Orange County Office: 1920 Main Street, Suite 1200, P.O. Box 19601, Irvine, California, 92714.
Telephone: 714-253-2700.
Fax: 714-955-2507.
Salt Lake City, Utah Office: Broadway Centre, 111 East Broadway, Suite 900, 84111.
Telephone: 801-237-1900.
Fax: 801-237-1950.

MEMBERS OF FIRM

Robert J. Deeny — William R. Hayden
Gerard Morales — Rebecca A. Winterscheidt

SENIOR ATTORNEY

William P. Allen

ASSOCIATES

Charles P. Keller — Joseph E. Lambert

Representative Clients: Arizona Public Service Co.; Bank One, Arizona, NA.; First Security Bank of Utah, N.A.; Ford Motor Co.; Chrysler Motors Corp.; Toyota Motor Sales U.S.A.; Magma Copper Co.; U.S. Home Corp.; Pinnacle West Capital Corp.; Safeway, Inc.

For Complete List of Firm Personnel, See General Section

For full biographical listings, see the Martindale-Hubbell Law Directory

ARKANSAS

*LITTLE ROCK,** Pulaski Co.

HOOVER & STOREY (AV)

111 Center Street, 11th Floor, 72201-4445
Telephone: 501-376-8500
Facsimile: 501-372-3255

MEMBERS OF FIRM

Paul W. Hoover, Jr. — William P. Dougherty
O. H. Storey, III — Max C. Mehlburger
John Kooistra, III — Joyce Bradley Babin
Lawrence Joseph Brady — Herbert W. Kell, Jr.
Letty McAdams

For full biographical listings, see the Martindale-Hubbell Law Directory

CALIFORNIA

*FRESNO,** Fresno Co.

DOWLING, MAGARIAN, AARON & HEYMAN, INCORPORATED (AV)

Suite 200, 6051 North Fresno Street, 93710
Telephone: 209-432-4500
Fax: 209-432-4590

Kent F. Heyman — Bruce S. Fraser

Reference: Wells Fargo Bank (Main).

For Complete List of Firm Personnel, See General Section

For full biographical listings, see the Martindale-Hubbell Law Directory

*LOS ANGELES,** Los Angeles Co.

ANTIN & TAYLOR (AV)

1875 Century Park East, Suite 700, 90067
Telephone: 310-788-2733
Fax: 310-788-0754

MEMBERS OF FIRM

Michael Antin — Michael L. Taylor

For full biographical listings, see the Martindale-Hubbell Law Directory

ALEX M. BRUCKER A LAW CORPORATION (AV)

10880 Wilshire Boulevard, Suite 2210, 90024
Telephone: 310-475-7540
Fax: 310-470-4806

Alex M. Brucker

Linda Russano Morra — Michael L. Cotter
Scott E. Hiltunen

For full biographical listings, see the Martindale-Hubbell Law Directory

SCHWARTZ, STEINSAPIR, DOHRMANN & SOMMERS (AV)

Suite 1820, 3580 Wilshire Boulevard, 90010
Telephone: 213-487-5700
Fax: 213-487-5548

MEMBERS OF FIRM

Laurence D. Steinsapir — Margo A. Feinberg
Robert M. Dohrmann — Henry M. Willis
Richard D. Sommers — Dennis J. Murphy
Stuart Libicki — D. William Heine, Jr.
Michael R. Feinberg — Claude Cazzulino
Michael D. Four — Dolly M. Gee
William T. Payne

For full biographical listings, see the Martindale-Hubbell Law Directory

*SACRAMENTO,** Sacramento Co.

MATHENY, POIDMORE & SEARS (AV)

2100 Northrop Avenue, Building 1200, P.O. Box 13711, 95853-4711
Telephone: 916-929-9271
Fax: 916-929-2458

MEMBERS OF FIRM

Henry G. Matheny (1933-1984) — James C. Damir
Anthony J. Poidmore — Michael A. Bishop
Douglas A. Sears — Ernest A. Long
Richard S. Linkert — Joann Georgallis
Kent M. Luckey

ASSOCIATES

Matthew C. Jaime — Ronald E. Enabnit
Jill P. Telfer — Cathy A. Reynolds
Robert B. Berrigan — Byron D. Damiani, Jr.
Daryl M. Thomas — Catherine Kennedy

OF COUNSEL

A. Laurel Bennett

LEGAL SUPPORT PERSONNEL

PARALEGALS

Karen D. Fisher — Lynell Rae Steed
Fran Studer — Jennifer Bachman
David Austin Boucher

For full biographical listings, see the Martindale-Hubbell Law Directory

*SAN DIEGO,** San Diego Co.

GARRISON R. ARMSTRONG LAW CORPORATION (AV)

Suite 1300, 401 West A Street, 92101-7988
Telephone: 619-232-1811

Garrison R. Armstrong

LEGAL SUPPORT PERSONNEL

Iris R. Daniel (Legal Assistant)

For full biographical listings, see the Martindale-Hubbell Law Directory

*SAN FRANCISCO,** San Francisco Co.

LUDWIG GOLDBERG & KRENZEL, A PROFESSIONAL CORPORATION (AV)

36th Floor, 50 California Street, 94111
Telephone: 415-788-7200
Fax: 415-433-6496

(See Next Column)

LUDWIG GOLDBERG & KRENZEL A PROFESSIONAL CORPORATION—*Continued*

Ronald L. Ludwig
Laurence A. Goldberg
Jeffrey F. Krenzel
Cynthia G. McCabe
Jeanine A. Mioton

For full biographical listings, see the Martindale-Hubbell Law Directory

CONNECTICUT

*HARTFORD,** Hartford Co.

SOROKIN SOROKIN GROSS HYDE & WILLIAMS P.C. (AV)

One Corporate Center, 06103
Telephone: 203-525-6645
Fax: 203-522-1781
Simsbury, Connecticut Office: 730 Hopmeadow Street.
Telephone: 203-651-9348.
Rocky Hill, Connecticut Office: 2360 Main Street.
Telephone: 203-563-9305.
Fax: 203-529-6931.
Glastonbury, Connecticut Office: 124 Hebron Avenue.
Telephone: 203-659-8801.

Barrie K. Wetstone

Sharon Kowal Freilich

For Complete List of Firm Personnel, See General Section

For full biographical listings, see the Martindale-Hubbell Law Directory

DELAWARE

*WILMINGTON,** New Castle Co.

POTTER ANDERSON & CORROON (AV)

350 Delaware Trust Building, P.O. Box 951, 19899-0951
Telephone: 302-658-6771
FAX: 658-1192; 655-1190; 655-1199

MEMBER OF FIRM

Mary E. Copper

Representative Clients: KOA Corporation of America; The Andrew Jergens Company; Delaware Trust Capital Management; Delmarva Power & Light Company; E.I. du Pont de Nemours & Co.; The Equitable Life Assurance Society of the United States; Winterthur Museum.

For Complete List of Firm Personnel, See General Section

For full biographical listings, see the Martindale-Hubbell Law Directory

DISTRICT OF COLUMBIA

WASHINGTON, D.C. Co.

* indicates certain Bar Register subscribers, in cities of comparable size and importance, who maintain an additional office in Washington, D.C. and who have arranged for representation as a part of the Washington, D.C. listings that follow

KENNETH R. FEINBERG & ASSOCIATES (AV)

1120 20th Street, N.W. Suite 740 South, 20036
Telephone: 202-371-1110
Fax: 202-962-9290
New York, N.Y. Office: 780 3rd Avenue, Suite 2202.
Telephone: 212-527-9600.
Fax: 212-527-9611.

ASSOCIATES

Deborah E. Greenspan
Michael K. Rozen (Not admitted in DC)
Peter H. Woodin (Not admitted in DC)

For full biographical listings, see the Martindale-Hubbell Law Directory

SUTHERLAND, ASBILL & BRENNAN (AV)

1275 Pennsylvania Avenue, N.W., 20004-2404
Telephone: 202-383-0100
Cable Address: "Sutab Wash"
Telex: 89-501
Facsimile: 202-637-3593
Atlanta, Georgia Office: 999 Peachtree Street, N. E., 30309-3996.
Telephone: 404-853-8000.
New York, N.Y. Office: 1270 Avenue of the Americas, 10020-1700.
Telephone: 212-332-3000.
Austin, Texas Office: 111 Congress Avenue, 23rd Floor, 78701-4079.
Telephone: 512-469-3350.

George H. Bostick
W. Mark Smith
Carol A. Weiser

For Complete List of Firm Personnel, See General Section

For full biographical listings, see the Martindale-Hubbell Law Directory

* **THOMPSON, HINE AND FLORY** (AV)

1920 N Street, N.W., 20036-1601
Telephone: 202-331-8800
Fax: 202-331-8330
Telex: 904173
Cable Address: "Caglaw"
Akron, Ohio Office: 50 S. Main Street, Suite 502, 44308-1828.
Telephone: 216-376-8090.
Fax: 216-376-8386.
Cincinnati, Ohio Office: 312 Walnut Street, 14th Floor, 45202-4029.
Telephone: 513-352-6700.
Fax: 513-241-4771.
Telex: 938003.
Cleveland, Ohio Office: 1100 National City Bank Building, 629 Euclid Avenue, 44114.
Telephone: 216-566-5500.
Fax: 216-566-5583.
Telex: 980217. Cable Address "Thomflor".
Columbus, Ohio Office: One Columbus, 10 West Broad Street, 43215-34353.
Telephone: 614-469-3200.
Fax: 614-469-3361.
Dayton, Ohio Office: 2000 Courthouse Plaza, N.E., 45402-1706.
Telephone: 513-443-6600.
Fax: 513-443-6637, 513-443-6635.
Palm Beach, Florida Office: 125 Worth Avenue, 33480-4466.
Telephone: 407-833-5900.
Fax: 407-833-5951.
Brussels, Belgium Office: Rue Des Chevaliers, Ridderstraat 14 - B.10, B-1050.
Telephone: 011-32-2-511-9326.
Fax: 011-32-2-513-9206.

MEMBER OF FIRM

Frederick B. Gibbon

SENIOR ATTORNEY

Amy G. Davies

For Complete List of Firm Personnel, See General Section

For full biographical listings, see the Martindale-Hubbell Law Directory

* **VENABLE, BAETJER, HOWARD & CIVILETTI** (AV)

A Partnership including Professional Corporations
Suite 1000, 1201 New York Avenue, N.W., 20005
Telephone: 202-962-4800
Fax: 202-962-8300
Baltimore, Maryland Office: Venable, Baetjer and Howard, 1800 Mercantile Bank & Trust Building, 2 Hopkins Plaza.
Telephone: 410-244-7400.
McLean, Virginia Office: Venable, Baetjer and Howard, Suite 400, 2010 Corporate Ridge.
Telephone: 703-760-1600.
Rockville, Maryland Office: Venable, Baetjer and Howard, Suite 500, One Church Street, P. O. Box 1906.
Telephone: 301-217-5600.
Towson, Maryland Office: Venable, Baetjer and Howard, 210 Allegheny Avenue, P. O. Box 5517.
Telephone: 410-494-6200.

MEMBERS OF FIRM

Douglas D. Connah, Jr. (P.C.) (Also at Baltimore, Maryland Office)
George F. Pappas (Also at Baltimore, Maryland Office)
Maurice Baskin
James A. Dunbar (Also at Baltimore, Maryland Office)

For Complete List of Firm Personnel, See General Section

For full biographical listings, see the Martindale-Hubbell Law Directory

FLORIDA

*TAMPA,** Hillsborough Co.

KALISH & WARD, PROFESSIONAL ASSOCIATION (AV)
4100 Barnett Plaza, 101 East Kennedy Boulevard, P.O. Box 71, 33601-0071
Telephone: 813-222-8700
Facsimile: 813-222-8701

William Kalish
Alton C. Ward
Richard A. Schlosser
Roger J. Rovell
Michael A. Bedke
William T. Harrison, III
Thomas P. McNamara
Robert Reid Haney
Charles H. Carver
Kelley A. Bosecker

For full biographical listings, see the Martindale-Hubbell Law Directory

GEORGIA

*ATLANTA,** Fulton Co.

ALTMAN, KRITZER & LEVICK, P.C. (AV)
Powers Ferry Landing, Suite 224, 6400 Powers Ferry Road, N.W., 30339
Telephone: 404-955-3555
Telecopier: 404-952-7821, 955-2866, 955-0038, 955-3697
Schaumburg, Illinois Affiliate: Altman, Kritzer & Levick, Ltd., Suite 400, 1101 Perimeter Drive, 60173.
Telephone: 708-240-0340.
FAX: 708-240-0344.

Allen D. Altman
Craig H. Kritzer
Mark J. Levick
D. Charles Houk
Charles L. Wood
Ephraim Spielman
Emily Sanford Bair
Benno G. Rothschild, Jr.
Elizabeth H. Hutchins
Theodore H. Sandler
Frank Slover
Kenneth A. Shapiro
Linda L. West
Steven A. Pepper
George A. Mattingly
W. Daniel Hicks, Jr.

COUNSEL

Richard P. Rubenoff
Martin N. Goldsmith
Susan E. Stoffer
Robert D. Simons
Peter M. Hartman
William R. Ham

Duane D. Sitar
Debra L. Thompson
Lori E. Kilberg
Richard W. Probert
Gregory A. Jacobs
Andrew R. Bauman
Lawrence H. Freiman
Ian L. Levin

LEGAL SUPPORT PERSONNEL

Cynthia A. Groszkiewicz
Rebecca G. Middleton

Representative Clients: Atlantic Southeast Airlines, Inc.; Ingles Markets, Inc.; The Home Depot, Inc.; Pacesetter Steel Service, Inc.; Homart Development Co.

For full biographical listings, see the Martindale-Hubbell Law Directory

CLARK, PAUL, HOOVER & MALLARD (AV)
One Midtown Plaza, Suite 900, 1360 Peachtree Street, N.E., 30309-3214
Telephone: 404-874-7500
FAX: 404-874-0001

MEMBERS OF FIRM

William B. Paul
James C. Hoover
David C. Hagaman
Norman A. Quandt
Bennet D. Alsher
Peter F. Munger
Jon M. Gumbel
Robert E. Rigrish

ASSOCIATES

Paul T. Ryan
Patricia Greene Butler
Steven J. Lewengrub
J. Stephen O'Donnell (Not admitted in GA)

OF COUNSEL

Wade V. Mallard, Jr.
Fletcher L. Hudson (Not admitted in GA)
Frederick J. Lewis (Not admitted in GA)

Representative Clients: BTR; Georgia-Pacific Corp.; Johnson Controls; Melville Corp.; Miami Children's Hospital; Mississippi Power Co.; Motorola, Inc.; Nestle USA, Inc.; Pratt & Whitney, Division of United Technologies Corp.; Reliance Electric Co.

For full biographical listings, see the Martindale-Hubbell Law Directory

ELARBEE, THOMPSON & TRAPNELL (AV)
800 Peachtree-Cain Tower, 229 Peachtree Street, N.E., 30303
Telephone: 404-659-6700
Fax: 404-222-9718

(See Next Column)

MEMBERS OF FIRM

Fred W. Elarbee, Jr. (1925-1986)
Robert L. Thompson
John R. Trapnell
David M. Vaughan
John Lewis Sapp
William M. Earnest
Charles K. Howard, Jr.
Walter O. Lambeth, Jr.
Robert J. Martin, Jr.
Joseph M. Freeman
Stanford G. Wilson
Brent L. Wilson
Victor A. Cavanaugh
Nancy F. Reynolds

ASSOCIATES

Sharon Parker Morgan
Mark D. Halverson
R. Read Gignilliat
Douglas H. Duerr
Victor J. Maya
Jan M. Harrison
William Drummond Deveney
Patrick L. Lail
Bernard L. McNamee, II
Kelly Michael Hundley
Kenneth N. Winkler
Frederick L. Douglas (Not admitted in GA)

Representative Clients: Cox Communications, Inc.; Dunlop Tire Corp.; National Service Industries; Atlanta Gas Light Co.; Brown & Williamson Tobacco Corp.; Engelhard Corp.; Louisiana-Pacific Corp.; MCI Communications Corp.; Florida Power and Light Co.; Southwire Co.

For full biographical listings, see the Martindale-Hubbell Law Directory

FISHER & PHILLIPS (AV)

A Partnership including Professional Corporations and Associations
1500 Resurgens Plaza, 945 East Paces Ferry Road, N.E., 30326
Telephone: 404-231-1400
Telecopier: 404-240-4249;
Telex: 54-2331
Fort Lauderdale, Florida Office: Suite 2310 NationsBank Tower, One Financial Plaza, 33394.
Telephone: 305-525-4800.
Telecopier: 305-525-8739.
Redwood City, California Office: Suite 345, Three Lagoon Drive, 94065.
Telephone: 415-592-6160.
Telecopier: 415-592-6385.
Newport Beach, California Office: 4675 MacArthur Court, Suite 550, 92660.
Telephone: 714-851-2424.
Telecopier: 714-851-0152.
New Orleans, Louisiana Office: 3710 Place St. Charles, 201 St. Charles Avenue, 70170.
Telephone: 504-522-3303.
Telecopier: 504-522-3850.

MEMBERS OF FIRM

Robert C. Christenson
Sandra Mills Feingerts (Resident, New Orleans, Louisiana Office)

ASSOCIATES

Daniel R. Kopti
Lynne M. Murphy (Resident, New Orleans, Louisiana Office)

Representative Clients: Arvida/JMB Partners; Atlantic Gulf Communities Corp.; Eastern Asiatic Corp.; The Flagler System, Inc.; Hyatt Corp.; Johnstown America Corp.; Pneumo Abex Corp.

For full biographical listings, see the Martindale-Hubbell Law Directory

FRANKEL, HARDWICK, TANENBAUM & FINK, P.C. (AV)
359 East Paces Ferry Road, N.E., 30305
Telephone: 404-266-2930
Fax: 404-231-3362

Allan J. Tanenbaum

Representative Clients: America's Favorite Chicken Co. (Church's and Popeye's); Softlab, Inc.; Basic, Inc.; Buffalo's Franchise Concepts, Inc.; Combustion Engineering, Inc.; Commerical Bank of Georgia; Patients Pharmacies; Hank Aaron Enterprises, Inc.; Nursecare (Nursing Homes); Sundance Products, Inc.; Venture Construction Company.

For Complete List of Firm Personnel, See General Section

For full biographical listings, see the Martindale-Hubbell Law Directory

LONG ALDRIDGE & NORMAN (AV)

A Partnership including Professional Corporations
One Peachtree Center, Suite 5300, 303 Peachtree Street, 30308
Telephone: 404-527-4000
Telecopier: 404-527-4198
Washington, D.C. Office: Suite 950, 1615 L Street, 20036.
Telephone: 202-223-7033.
Telecopier: 202-223-7013.

MEMBERS OF FIRM

Phillip A. Bradley
Patricia E. Tate

(See Next Column)

LONG ALDRIDGE & NORMAN—*Continued*

OF COUNSEL

Bruce H. Wynn

For Complete List of Firm Personnel, See General Section

For full biographical listings, see the Martindale-Hubbell Law Directory

SUTHERLAND, ASBILL & BRENNAN (AV)

999 Peachtree Street, N.E., 30309-3996
Telephone: 404-853-8000
Facsimile: 404-853-8806
Washington, D.C. Office: 1275 Pennsylvania Avenue, N.W., 20004-2404.
Telephone: 202-383-0100.
New York, N.Y. Office: 1270 Avenue of the Americas, 10020-1700.
Telephone: 212-332-3000.
Austin, Texas Office: 111 Congress Avenue, 23rd Floor, 78701-4079.
Telephone: 512-469-3350.

William M. Hames
Walter H. Wingfield

For Complete List of Firm Personnel, See General Section

For full biographical listings, see the Martindale-Hubbell Law Directory

*COLUMBUS,** Muscogee Co.

HATCHER, STUBBS, LAND, HOLLIS & ROTHSCHILD (AV)

Suite 500 The Corporate Center, 233 12th Street, P.O. Box 2707, 31902-2707
Telephone: 706-324-0201
Telecopier: 706-322-7747

MEMBERS OF FIRM

Morton A. Harris
Charles T. Staples
James E. Humes, II
Alan F. Rothschild, Jr.

General Counsel for: Trust Company Bank of Columbus, N.A.; TOM'S Foods Inc.; Muscogee County Board of Education; Burnham Service Corp.; Kinnett Dairies, Inc.; St. Francis Hospital, Inc.; Georgia Crown Distributing Co.
Local Counsel for: First Union National Bank of Georgia.
Special Counsel For: Columbus Bank and Trust Company, Employee Benefit Division.

For Complete List of Firm Personnel, See General Section

For full biographical listings, see the Martindale-Hubbell Law Directory

IDAHO

*BOISE,** Ada Co.

HALL, FARLEY, OBERRECHT & BLANTON (AV)

Key Financial Center, 702 West Idaho Street, Suite 700, P.O. Box 1271, 83701-1271
Telephone: 208-336-0404
Facsimile: 208-336-5193

Richard E. Hall
Donald J. Farley
Phillip S. Oberrecht
Raymond D. Powers
Candy Wagahoff Dale
Robert B. Luce
J. Kevin West
Bart W. Harwood

J. Charles Blanton
John J. Burke
Steven J. Hippler
Thorpe P. Orton
Ronald S. Best (Not admitted in ID)

References: Boise State University; Farm Bureau Mutual Insurance Company of Idaho; Medical Insurance Exchange of California; The St. Paul Cos.

For full biographical listings, see the Martindale-Hubbell Law Directory

ILLINOIS

*CHICAGO,** Cook Co.

PAUL M. GLICK, CHARTERED (AV)

20 North Clark Street, Suite 1000, 60602
Telephone: 312-357-0320
Fax: 312-357-0323

Paul M. Glick

LANER, MUCHIN, DOMBROW, BECKER, LEVIN AND TOMINBERG, LTD. (AV)

515 North State Street, Suite 2800, 60610
Telephone: 312-467-9800
Fax: 312-467-9479

Richard W. Laner
Lawrence F. Doppelt (1935-1979)
Arthur B. Muchin
Anthony E. Dombrow
William L. Becker
Alan M. Levin
Carl S. Tominberg
Mark L. Juster
Gary Alan Wincek
Robert M. Klein
Michael Klupchak
Joseph H. Yastrow
Joseph M. Gagliardo
Robert H. Brown
James J. Convery
Robert S. Letchinger
Violet M. Clark
James F. Vanek

Thomas Bradley
Beth A. Clukey
Maureen A. Gorman
Jill P. O'Brien
Clifford R. Perry, III
Dawn E. Sellstrom
Jane E. Shaffer
Thomas Vasiljevich

OF COUNSEL

Isaiah S. Dorfman
Herman J. De Koven
Seymour Cohen

References: NBD Bank Chicago; Illinois; La Salle National Bank & Trust Co.

For full biographical listings, see the Martindale-Hubbell Law Directory

MCBRIDE BAKER & COLES (AV)

500 West Madison Street 40th Floor, 60661
Telephone: 312-715-5700
Cable Address: "Chilaw"
Telex: 270258
Telecopier: 312-993-9350

MEMBERS OF FIRM

David Ackerman
Martin J. Campanella
William J. Cooney
Kenneth A. Jenero
Thomas J. Kinasz
Anne Hamblin Schiave

ASSOCIATES

Steven R. Lifson
Jonathan E. Strouse

For Complete List of Firm Personnel, See General Section

For full biographical listings, see the Martindale-Hubbell Law Directory

MURPHY, SMITH & POLK, A PROFESSIONAL CORPORATION (AV)

Twenty-Fifth Floor, Two First National Plaza 20 South Clark Street, 60603-1891
Telephone: 312-558-1220
Telecopier: 807-3619

Charles E. Murphy
Arthur B. Smith, Jr.
Lee T. Polk
Robert P. Casey
Michael T. Roumell
Peter M. Kelly, II
Richard L. Samson
Carol A. Poplawski
Daniel J. Ashley
James M. O'Brien

Dwight D. Pancottine
Tracey L. Truesdale
Julia A. Donnelly
Caran L. Joseph
Richard P. McArdle
Peter A. Steinmeyer
Charles R. Marcordes

OF COUNSEL

Karl W. Grabemann

For full biographical listings, see the Martindale-Hubbell Law Directory

SCARIANO, KULA, ELLCH AND HIMES, CHARTERED (AV)

Two Prudential Plaza 180 North Stetson Suite 3100, 60601-6224
Telephone: 312-565-3100
Facsimile: 312-565-0000
Chicago Heights, Illinois Office: 1450 Aberdeen.
Telephone: 708-755-1900.
Facsimile: 708-755-0000.

Anthony G. Scariano
David P. Kula
Robert H. Ellch
Alan T. Sraga
A. Lynn Himes
Justino D. Petrarca
Lawrence Jay Weiner
Kathleen Field Orr
John M. Izzo
Raymond A. Hauser

OF COUNSEL

Max A. Bailey
G. Robb Cooper
Teri E. Engler
John B. Kralovec

(See Next Column)

SCARIANO, KULA, ELLCH AND HIMES CHARTERED, *Chicago—Continued*

Daniel M. Boyle
Patrick J. Broncato
Sarah R. Carlin
Diane S. Cohen
Jon G. Crawford
Douglas D. Danielson
Anthony Ficarelli
Kelly A. Hayden
Todd K. Hayden
David A. Hemenway
Kathleen Roche Hirsman
Jonathan A. Pearl
Lisa Ann Rapacz
Shelia C. Riley
Joanne W. Schochat

For full biographical listings, see the Martindale-Hubbell Law Directory

INDIANA

*INDIANAPOLIS,** Marion Co.

DUTTON OVERMAN GOLDSTEIN PINKUS, A PROFESSIONAL CORPORATION (AV)

710 Century Building, 36 South Pennsylvania Street, 46204
Telephone: 317-633-4000
Telecopier: 317-633-1494

Carl D. Overman

Diane Hubbard Kennedy

Representative Clients: Central Supply Co, Inc.; Huber, Hunt & Nichols, Inc.; The Hunt Paving Co, Inc.; Laughner Brothers, Inc.; The Howard E. Nyhart Co., Inc.; Sarkes Tarzian, Inc.; The Dalton Foundries, Inc.; Central Indiana Hardware Co, Inc.; MCM Enterprises, Inc.; Fink, Roberts & Petrie, Inc.

For full biographical listings, see the Martindale-Hubbell Law Directory

ICE MILLER DONADIO & RYAN (AV)

One American Square Box 82001, 46282-0002
Telephone: 317-236-2100
Fax: 317-236-2219

MEMBERS OF FIRM

James D. Kemper
Terry A. M. Mumford
Gary J. Dankert
E. Van Olson
Marc W. Sciscoe
Mary Beth Braitman
Melissa Proffitt Reese

ASSOCIATES

Catherine R. Beck
Brian G. Steinkamp
Timothy A. Brooks
Terrence J. Keusch
Stephanie Alden Smithey
Kathleen Weyher Kiefer

For Complete List of Firm Personnel, See General Section

For full biographical listings, see the Martindale-Hubbell Law Directory

OWEN SHOUP & KINZIE (AV)

Suite 3680 Bank One Tower, 111 Monument Circle, 46204-5136
Telephone: 317-267-3595
Fax: 317-267-3597
Fremont, Michigan Office: 3918 Skyline Drive.
Telephone: 616-924-7045.
Seattle, Washington Office: 4118 Greenwood Avenue.
Telephone: 206-633-4363.
Cedar Mountain, North Carolina Office: 54 Robin Hood Road.
Telephone: 704-862-3548.

MEMBERS OF FIRM

Michael W. Owen
Steven V. Shoup
Jan J. Kinzie

OF COUNSEL

F. Pen Cosby
Charles V. Traylor
Warren D. Krebs
Amanda A. Owen (Not admitted in IN; Resident, Seattle, Washington Office)

Reference: Bank One Indianapolis.

For full biographical listings, see the Martindale-Hubbell Law Directory

MUNSTER, Lake Co.

PINKERTON AND FRIEDMAN, PROFESSIONAL CORPORATION (AV)

The Fairmont, 9245 Calumet Avenue Suite 201, 46321
Telephone: 219-836-3050
Fax: 219-836-2955

Kirk A. Pinkerton
Stuart J. Friedman
Jeffrey F. Gunning
Gail Oosterhof

Reference: Calumet National Bank of Hammond.

For full biographical listings, see the Martindale-Hubbell Law Directory

KANSAS

*TOPEKA,** Shawnee Co.

FOULSTON & SIEFKIN (AV)

(Formerly Foulston, Siefkin, Powers & Eberhardt)
1515 Bank IV Tower, 534 Kansas Avenue, 66603
Telephone: 913-233-3600
FAX: 913-233-1610
Wichita, Kansas Office: 700 Fourth Financial Center, Broadway at Douglas. 67202.
Telephone: 316-267-6371.
Facsimile: 316-267-6345.
Member: Lex Mundi, A Global Association of Independent Firms

MEMBERS OF FIRM

James P. Rankin
Douglas L. Hanisch (Resident, Wichita Office)
Kevin J. Arnel (Resident, Wichita Office)

For full biographical listings, see the Martindale-Hubbell Law Directory

*WICHITA,** Sedgwick Co.

FOULSTON & SIEFKIN (AV)

(Formerly Foulston, Siefkin, Powers & Eberhardt)
700 Fourth Financial Center, Broadway at Douglas, 67202
Telephone: 316-267-6371
Facsimile: 316-267-6345
Topeka, Kansas Office: 1515 Bank IV Tower, 534 Kansas Avenue. 66603.
Telephone: 913-233-3600.
FAX: 913-233-1610.
Member: Lex Mundi, A Global Association of Independent Firms

MEMBERS OF FIRM

James P. Rankin (Resident, Topeka Office)
Douglas L. Hanisch
Kevin J. Arnel

For Complete List of Firm Personnel, See General Section

For full biographical listings, see the Martindale-Hubbell Law Directory

KENTUCKY

*LEXINGTON,** Fayette Co.

STOLL, KEENON & PARK (AV)

201 E. Main Street, Suite 1000, 40507-1380
Telephone: 606-231-3000
Telecopier: 606-253-1093; 606-253-1027
Frankfort, Kentucky Office: 326 West Main Street.
Telephone: 502-875-6000.
Telecopier: 502-875-6008.
Louisville, Kentucky Office: 400 West Market Street, Suite 2650, 40202.
Telephone: 502-568-9100.
Telecopier: 502-568-6340.

MEMBERS OF FIRM

Richard C. Stephenson
Eileen M. O'Brien
C. Joseph Beavin

Representative Clients: Bank One, Lexington, NA; Farmers Capital Bank Corp.; The Tokai Bank Ltd.; Link Belt Construction Equipment Co.; General Motors Corp.; International Business Machines Corp.; Ohbayashi Corp.; R. J. Reynolds Tobacco Co.; Rockwell International Corp.; Square D Co.

For Complete List of Firm Personnel, See General Section

For full biographical listings, see the Martindale-Hubbell Law Directory

*LOUISVILLE,** Jefferson Co.

GREENEBAUM DOLL & MCDONALD (AV)

A Partnership including Professional Service Corporations
3300 National City Tower, 40202
Telephone: 502-589-4200
Fax: 502-587-3695
Lexington, Kentucky Office: 1400 Vine Center Tower.
Telephone: 606-231-8500.
Fax: 606-255-2742.
Covington, Kentucky Office: 50 East River Center Boulevard, P.O. Box 2050.
Telephone: 606-655-4200.
Fax: 606-655-4239.
Cincinnati, Ohio Office: 832 Main Street.
Telephone: 513-421-8087.
Fax: 513-421-8089.

(See Next Column)

GREENEBAUM DOLL & McDONALD—*Continued*

Edwin H. Perry
Mary G. Eaves
Deborah H. Tudor (Resident at Lexington, Kentucky)

OF COUNSEL

Martin S. Weinberg

Representative Clients: Aetna Life Insurance Co.; ANDALEX Resources, Inc.; Ashland Oil, Inc.; A T & T Communications, Inc.; Bethlehem Steel Corp.; Brown-Forman Corp.; Humana, Inc.; Kentucky Kingdom, Inc.; KFC National Cooperative Advertising Program, Inc.
*A Professional Service Corporation

For Complete List of Firm Personnel, See General Section

For full biographical listings, see the Martindale-Hubbell Law Directory

OGDEN NEWELL & WELCH (AV)

1200 One Riverfront Plaza, 40202-2973
Telephone: 502-582-1601
Fax: 502-581-9564

MEMBERS OF FIRM

Joseph C. Oldham
James B. Martin, Jr.

ASSOCIATE

Sharon A. Mattingly

Counsel for: KU Energy Corp.; Kentucky Utilities Co.; Brown-Forman Corp.; B. F. Goodrich Co.; Brown & Williamson Tobacco Corp.; J.J.B. Hilliard, W.L. Lyons, Inc.; Interlock Industries, Inc.; Akzo Coatings, Inc.; United Medical Corp.; Bank of Louisville.

For Complete List of Firm Personnel, See General Section

For full biographical listings, see the Martindale-Hubbell Law Directory

LOUISIANA

*BATON ROUGE,** East Baton Rouge Parish

SCHMIDT & KUEHNE, A PROFESSIONAL LAW CORPORATION (AV)

10935 Perkins Road, P.O. Box 80317, 70898
Telephone: 504-767-7093
Telecopier: 504-767-7096

Robert C. Schmidt
G. Bruce Kuehne

For full biographical listings, see the Martindale-Hubbell Law Directory

*NEW ORLEANS,** Orleans Parish

THE GODFREY FIRM A PROFESSIONAL LAW CORPORATION (AV)

2500 Energy Centre, 1100 Poydras Street, 70163-2500
Telephone: 504-585-7538
Fax: 504-585-7535

Jarrell E. Godfrey, Jr.
Jacob S. Capraro
Glenn J. Reames
Paul F. Guarisco

For full biographical listings, see the Martindale-Hubbell Law Directory

MAINE

*PORTLAND,** Cumberland Co.

PIERCE, ATWOOD, SCRIBNER, ALLEN, SMITH & LANCASTER (AV)

One Monument Square, 04101
Telephone: 207-773-6411
Fax: 207-773-3419
Augusta, Maine Office: 77 Winthrop Street.
Telephone: 207-622-6311.
Camden, Maine Office: 36 Chestnut Street, P.O. Box 780.
Telephone: 207-236-4333.

MEMBER OF FIRM

William H. Nichols

ASSOCIATE

Eric D. Altholz

For Complete List of Firm Personnel, See General Section

For full biographical listings, see the Martindale-Hubbell Law Directory

MARYLAND

*BALTIMORE,** (Independent City)

E. FREMONT MAGEE, P.A. (AV)

The Legg Mason Tower, 111 South Calvert Street, Suite 2700, 21202
Telephone: 410-385-5295; 410-625-7540
FAX: 410-385-5201

E. Fremont Magee

Lynn K. Edwards

For full biographical listings, see the Martindale-Hubbell Law Directory

VENABLE, BAETJER AND HOWARD (AV)

A Partnership including Professional Corporations
1800 Mercantile Bank & Trust Building, 2 Hopkins Plaza, 21201
Telephone: 410-244-7400
Washington, D.C. Office: Venable, Baetjer, Howard & Civiletti. Suite 1000, 1201 New York Avenue, N.W.
Telephone: 202-962-4800.
McLean, Virginia Office: Suite 400, 2010 Corporate Ridge.
Telephone: 703-760-1600.
Rockville, Maryland Office: Suite 500, One Church Street, P. O. Box 1906.
Telephone: 301-217-5600.
Towson, Maryland Office: 210 Allegheny Avenue, P. O. Box 5517.
Telephone: 410-494-6200.

MEMBERS OF FIRM

N. Peter Lareau (P.C.)
Douglas D. Connah, Jr. (P.C.) (Also at Washington, D.C. Office)
Barbara E. Schlaff
Susan K. Gauvey (Also at Towson, Maryland Office)
G. Stewart Webb, Jr.
Jana Howard Carey (P.C.)
George F. Pappas (Also at Washington, D.C. Office)
Jeffrey P. Ayres (P.C.)
Maurice Baskin (Resident, Washington, D.C. Office)
James A. Dunbar (Also at Washington, D.C. Office)
Robert L. Waldman

OF COUNSEL

A. Samuel Cook (P.C.) (Resident, Towson, Maryland Office)

ASSOCIATES

Todd J. Horn
John A. McCauley
Michael W. Robinson (Not admitted in MD; Resident, McLean, Virginia Office)
Nathan E. Siegel
Linda Marotta Thomas

For Complete List of Firm Personnel, See General Section

For full biographical listings, see the Martindale-Hubbell Law Directory

SILVER SPRING, Montgomery Co.

ALEXANDER, GEBHARDT, APONTE & MARKS, L.L.C. (AV)

Lee Plaza-Suite 805, 8601 Georgia Avenue, 20910
Telephone: 301-589-2222
Facsimile: 301-589-2523
Washington, D.C. Office: 1314 Nineteenth Street, N.W., 20036.
Telephone: 202-835-1555.
New York, New York Office: 330 Madison Avenue, 36th Floor.
Telephone: 212-808-0008.
Fax: 212-599-1028.

Koteles Alexander (Not admitted in MD)

Suelyn Smith
Suzette Wynn Blackwell

Reference: Riggs National Bank of Washington, D.C.

For full biographical listings, see the Martindale-Hubbell Law Directory

MASSACHUSETTS

*BOSTON,** Suffolk Co.

PALMER & DODGE (AV)

(Storey Thorndike Palmer & Dodge)
One Beacon Street, 02108
Telephone: 617-573-0100
Telecopier: 617-227-4420
Telex: 951104
Cable Address: "Storeydike," Boston

(See Next Column)

PALMER & DODGE, *Boston—Continued*

MEMBERS OF FIRM

Ralph C. Derbyshire | Malcolm E. Hindin

For Complete List of Firm Personnel, See General Section

For full biographical listings, see the Martindale-Hubbell Law Directory

MERVIN M. WILF, LTD. (AV)

300 Commonwealth Avenue, 02115
Telephone: 617-437-7981
Philadelphia, Pennsylvania Office: 3200 Mellon Bank Center. 1735 Market Street.
Telephone: 215-575-7650. 568-4842.
Facsimile: 215-575-7652.

Mervin M. Wilf

A list of Representative Clients and References will be furnished upon request.

For full biographical listings, see the Martindale-Hubbell Law Directory

*SPRINGFIELD,** Hampden Co.

ELY & KING (AV)

One Financial Plaza, 1350 Main Street, 01103
Telephone: 413-781-1920
Telecopier: 413-733-3360

MEMBERS OF FIRM

Joseph Buell Ely (1905-1956)
Raymond T. King (1919-1971)
Frederick M. Kingsbury (1924-1968)
Hugh J. Corcoran (1938-1992)
Richard S. Milstein
Donald A. Beaudry
Richard F. Faille
Leland B. Seabury
Gregory A. Schmidt
Pamela Manson
Anthony T. Rice
Russell J. Mawdsley

ASSOCIATE

Donna M. Brown

Representative Clients: Hartford Accident & Indemnity Co.; Albert Steiger Cos.; Shawmut Bank N.A.; Springfield Institution for Savings; St. Paul Fire & Marine Insurance Co.; The Rouse Co.; Tighe & Bond, Inc.; Northeast Utilities.

For full biographical listings, see the Martindale-Hubbell Law Directory

GABERMAN & PARISH, P.C. (AV)

32 Hampden Street, 01103
Telephone: 413-781-5066
Fax: 413-732-5439

Richard M. Gaberman | Ronda G. Parish

Richard D. Keough

OF COUNSEL

Leonard Judelson

For full biographical listings, see the Martindale-Hubbell Law Directory

MICHIGAN

*ANN ARBOR,** Washtenaw Co.

FERGUSON & WIDMAYER, P.C. (AV)

505 East Huron Street, Suite 202, 48104
Telephone: 313-662-0222
Fax: 313-662-8884

Larry J. Ferguson | Warren J. Widmayer

For full biographical listings, see the Martindale-Hubbell Law Directory

BIRMINGHAM, Oakland Co.

MACDONALD AND GOREN, P.C. (AV)

Suite 200, 260 East Brown Street, 48009
Telephone: 810-645-5940
Fax: 810-645-2490

Harold C. MacDonald
Kalman G. Goren
Cindy Rhodes Victor
Amy L. Glenn
David D. Marsh
Glenn G. Ross
Miriam Blanks-Smart
John T. Klees

Representative Clients: Bay Corrugated Container, Inc.; Miles Fox Company; Orlandi Gear Company, Inc.; Bing Steel, Inc.; Superb Manufacturing, Inc.; Spring Engineering, Inc.; Adrian Steel Company; Southfield Radiology Associates, P.C.; Blockbuster Entertainment Corporation; E.N.U.F. Internationale, Inc.

For full biographical listings, see the Martindale-Hubbell Law Directory

*DETROIT,** Wayne Co.

ABBOTT, NICHOLSON, QUILTER, ESSHAKI & YOUNGBLOOD, P.C. (AV)

19th Floor, One Woodward Avenue, 48226
Telephone: 313-963-2500
Telecopier: 313-963-7882

C. Richard Abbott
John R. Nicholson
Thomas R. Quilter III
Gene J. Esshaki
John F. Youngblood
Donald E. Conley
James B. Perry
Carl F. Jarboe
Jay A. Kennedy
Timothy A. Stoepker
Timothy J. Kramer
Norbert T. Madison, Jr.
William D. Gilbride, Jr.

Mary P. Nelson
Michael R. Blum
Thomas Ferguson Hatch
Anne D. Warren Bagno
Mark E. Mueller
Eric J. Girdler

OF COUNSEL

Thomas C. Shumaker | Roy R. Hunsinger

For full biographical listings, see the Martindale-Hubbell Law Directory

BUTZEL LONG, A PROFESSIONAL CORPORATION (AV)

Suite 900, 150 West Jefferson, 48226
Telephone: 313-225-7000
Telecopier: 313-225-7080
Birmingham, Michigan Office: Suite 200, 32270 Telegraph Road.
Telephone: 810-258-1616.
Telecopier: 810-258-1439.
Lansing, Michigan Office: 118 West Ottawa Street.
Telephone: 517-372-6622.
Telecopier: 517-372-6672.
Ann Arbor, Michigan Office: Suite 400, 121 West Washington.
Telephone: 313-995-3110.
Telecopier: 313-995-1777.
Grosse Pointe Farms, Michigan Office: Suite 260, 21 Kercheval.
Telephone: 313-886-5446.
Telecopier: 313-886-2114.

Paul L. Triemstra (Birmingham)
Michael D. Guzick
Barbara S. Kendzierski
Diane M. Soubly

Jordan S. Schreier | Nicholas J. Stasevich

Representative Clients: Bridgestone/Firestone, Inc.; The Detroit News, Inc.; Detroit Diesel Corp.; Kelly Services; Kelsey Hayes Co.; Merrill Lynch & Co., Inc.; Stroh Brewery Co.; Takata Corp.; United Parcel Services of America, Inc.; The University of Michigan.

For Complete List of Firm Personnel, See General Section

For full biographical listings, see the Martindale-Hubbell Law Directory

CLARK, KLEIN & BEAUMONT (AV)

1600 First Federal Building, 1001 Woodward Avenue, 48226
Telephone: 313-965-8300
Facsimile: 313-962-4348
Bloomfield Hills Office: 1533 North Woodward Avenue, Suite 220, 48304.
Telephone: 810-258-2900.
Facsimile: 810-258-2949.

MEMBERS OF FIRM

Robert G. Buydens | Edward C. Hammond

ASSOCIATES

Maureen A. Darmanin | Robin D. Ferriby

Representative Clients: American Automobile Manufacturers Association; Booth American Company; Canteen Corporation; Detroit-Macomb Hospital Corporation; Detroit Symphony Orchestra Hall, Inc.; First Federal of Michigan; Fletcher Paper Corporation; La-Z-Boy Chair Company; Lectron Products, Inc.; United Community Services of Metropolitan Detroit.

For Complete List of Firm Personnel, See General Section

For full biographical listings, see the Martindale-Hubbell Law Directory

JAFFE, RAITT, HEUER & WEISS, PROFESSIONAL CORPORATION (AV)

One Woodward Avenue, Suite 2400, 48226
Telephone: 313-961-8380
Telecopier: 313-961-8358
Cable Address: "Jafsni"
Southfield,Michigan Office: Travelers Tower, Suite 1520.
Telephone: 313-961-8380.
Monroe, Michigan Office: 212 East Front Street, Suite 3.
Telephone: 313-241-6470.
Telefacsimile: 313-241-3849.

(See Next Column)

JAFFE, RAITT, HEUER & WEISS PROFESSIONAL CORPORATION—*Continued*

Alexander B. Bragdon	Arthur A. Weiss
Michael A. Rajt	Thomas H. Williams
Joseph J. Shannon	Janet G. Witkowski

See General Practice Section for List of Representative Clients.

For Complete List of Firm Personnel, See General Section

For full biographical listings, see the Martindale-Hubbell Law Directory

KELLER, THOMA, SCHWARZE, SCHWARZE, DUBAY & KATZ, P.C. (AV)

440 E. Congress, 5th Floor, 48226
Telephone: 313-965-7610
Bloomfield Hills, Michigan Office: Suite 122, 100 West Long Lake Road.
Telephone: 313-647-3114.

Anthony J. Heckemeyer

Counsel for: Livonia Public Schools; Ludington News Co., Inc.
Representative Clients: Borg-Warner Corp.; E & L Transport Co.; The Kroger Co.; Holnam, Inc.
Public Employer Clients: City of Farmington Hills; City of Flint; City of Grosse Pointe Woods; Saginaw Public Schools.

For Complete List of Firm Personnel, See General Section

For full biographical listings, see the Martindale-Hubbell Law Directory

KERR, RUSSELL AND WEBER (AV)

One Detroit Center, 500 Woodward Avenue, Suite 2500, 48226-3406
Telephone: 313-961-0200
Telecopier: 313-961-0388
Bloomfield Hills, Michigan Office: 3883 Telegraph Road.
Telephone: 810-649-5990.
East Lansing, Michigan Office: 1301 North Hagadorn Road.
Telephone: 517-336-6767.

Richard D. Weber	Thomas R. Williams
Patrick McLain	Edward C. Cutlip, Jr.
Michael B. Lewis	Mark J. Stasa
Curtis J. DeRoo	Jeffrey A. Brantley
Michael D. Gibson	David E. Sims
Daniel G. Beyer	Christopher A. Cornwall
James R. Case	Patrick J. Haddad
George J. Christopoulos	Richard C. Buslepp
Paul M. Shirilla	Eric I. Lark
Kurt R. Vilders	James E. DeLine
James R. Cambridge	Daniel J. Schulte

For Complete List of Firm Personnel, See General Section

For full biographical listings, see the Martindale-Hubbell Law Directory

STRINGARI, FRITZ, KREGER, AHEARN & CRANDALL, P.C. (AV)

650 First National Building, 48226-3538
Telephone: 313-961-6474
Fax: 313-961-5688

Richard J. Fritz	Brian S. Ahearn
Conrad W. Kreger	Martin E. Crandall

Kenneth S. Wilson

Dallas G. Moon	John C. Dickinson

OF COUNSEL

Karl R. Bennett, Jr.	Matt W. Zeigler

For full biographical listings, see the Martindale-Hubbell Law Directory

FARMINGTON HILLS, Oakland Co.

DAGUANNO AND ACCETTURA (AV)

Arboretum Office Park, 34705 West Twelve Mile Road, Suite 311, 48331
Telephone: 810-489-1444
Fax: 810-489-1453

MEMBERS OF FIRM

Richard Daguanno	P. Mark Accettura

ASSOCIATES

Robert J. Constan	Harry P. Bugeja

OF COUNSEL

John A. Zick	Robert E. Miller

References: Comerica Bank; Michigan Chamber of Commerce.

For full biographical listings, see the Martindale-Hubbell Law Directory

*GRAND RAPIDS,** Kent Co.

WARNER, NORCROSS & JUDD (AV)

900 Old Kent Building, 111 Lyon Street, N.W., 49503-2489
Telephone: 616-752-2000
Fax: 616-752-2500
Muskegon, Michigan Office: 400 Terrace Plaza, P.O. Box 900.
Telephone: 616-727-2600.
Fax: 616-727-2699.
Holland, Michigan Office: Curtis Center, Suite 300, 170 College Avenue.
Telephone: 616-396-9800.
Fax: 616-396-3656.

MEMBERS OF FIRM

Jack B. Combs	Sue O. Conway
John H. McKendry, Jr. (Resident at Muskegon Office)	

For Complete List of Firm Personnel, See General Section

For full biographical listings, see the Martindale-Hubbell Law Directory

WHEELER UPHAM, A PROFESSIONAL CORPORATION (AV)

Second Floor, Trust Building, 40 Pearl Street, N.W., 49503
Telephone: 616-459-7100
Fax: 616-459-6366

Gordon B. Wheeler (1904-1986)	Timothy J. Orlebeke
Buford A. Upham (Retired)	Kenneth E. Tiews
Robert H. Gillette	Jack L. Hoffman
Geoffrey L. Gillis	Janet C. Baxter
John M. Roels	Peter Kladder, III
Gary A. Maximiuk	James M. Shade

Thomas A. Kuiper

Counsel for: Travelers Insurance Co.; Prudential Insurance Co. of America; Farmers Insurance Group; Metropolitan Life Insurance Co.; Conrail Trans.; Monsanto Co.; Firestone Tire & Rubber Co.; Navistar, Inc.; Medtronic, Inc.; Westdale Better Homes and Gardens.

For full biographical listings, see the Martindale-Hubbell Law Directory

*KALAMAZOO,** Kalamazoo Co.

LILLY & LILLY, P.C. (AV)

505 South Park Street, 49007
Telephone: 616-381-7763
Fax: 616-344-6880

Charles M. Lilly (1990-1903)	Terrence J. Lilly

For full biographical listings, see the Martindale-Hubbell Law Directory

LANSING, Ingham Co.

FOSTER, SWIFT, COLLINS & SMITH, P.C. (AV)

313 South Washington Square, 48933-2193
Telephone: 517-371-8100
Telecopier: 517-371-8200
Farmington Hills, Michigan Office: 32300 Northwestern Highway, Suite 230.
Telephone: 810-851-7500.
Fax: 810-851-7504.

Stephen I. Jurmu	Patricia A. Calore
Sherry A. Stein	Eric E. Doster
Stephen J. Lowney	Matt G. Hrebec

LEGAL SUPPORT PERSONNEL

LEGAL ASSISTANTS

Jaxine L. Wintjen

Representative Clients: Edward W. Sparrow Hospital; Michigan Milk Producers Assn.; Industrial Metal Products Co. (IMPCO); Spartan Motors; Community First Bank; Physicians Insurance Company of Michigan.

For Complete List of Firm Personnel, See General Section

For full biographical listings, see the Martindale-Hubbell Law Directory

FRASER TREBILCOCK DAVIS & FOSTER, P.C. (AV)

1000 Michigan National Tower, 48933
Telephone: 517-482-5800
Fax: 517-482-0887
Okemos, Michigan Office: 2188 Commons Parkway.
Telephone: 517-349-1300.
Fax: 517-349-0922.

Michael E. Cavanaugh	Darrell A. Lindman
C. Mark Hoover	David D. Waddell

Counsel for: Michigan Capital Medical Center; Michigan Catholic Conference; Michigan Farm Bureau; Weyco, Inc.; Michigan State University; Physicians Health Plan of Mid-Michigan, Inc.

For Complete List of Firm Personnel, See General Section

For full biographical listings, see the Martindale-Hubbell Law Directory

TROY, Oakland Co.

POLING, MCGAW & POLING, P.C. (AV)

Suite 275, 5435 Corporate Drive, 48098
Telephone: 810-641-0500
Telecopier: 810-641-0506

Benson T. Buck (1926-1989)
Richard B. Poling
D. Douglas McGaw
Richard B. Poling, Jr.
David W. Moore
Gregory C. Hamilton
Veronica B. Winter
James R. Parker

OF COUNSEL

Ralph S. Moore

Representative Clients: County of Oakland; City of Troy; United States Fidelity & Guaranty Co.; Sentry Insurance Co.; Admiral Insurance; DeMaria Construction Co.; Leo Corporation; Aetna Casualty and Surety Co.; Concord Design; Pneumo-Abex.

For full biographical listings, see the Martindale-Hubbell Law Directory

MINNESOTA

*DULUTH,** St. Louis Co.

FRYBERGER, BUCHANAN, SMITH & FREDERICK, P.A. (AV)

700 Lonsdale Building, 302 West Superior Street, 55802
Telephone: 218-722-0861
Fax: 218-722-9568
St. Paul Office: Capitol Center, 386 N. Wabasha.
Telephone: 612-221-1044.

Bruce Buchanan
Nick Smith
Harold A. Frederick
Dexter A. Larsen
James H. Stewart
Robert E. Toftey
Michael K. Donovan
Neal J. Hessen
Joseph J. Mihalek
Shawn M. Dunlevy
Anne Lewis
David R. Oberstar
Abbot G. Apter
Michael Cowles
Martha M. Markusen

Daniel D. Maddy
Stephanie A. Ball
Paul B. Kilgore
Mary Frances Skala
Rolf A. Lindberg (Resident, St. Paul Office)
Kevin T. Walli (Resident, St. Paul Office)
Kevin J. Dunlevy (Resident, St. Paul Office)
Teresa M. O'Toole
Dean R. Borgh
James F. Voegeli (Resident, St. Paul Office)
James A. Lund
Mark D. Britton (Resident, St. Paul Office)
Judith A. Zollar

OF COUNSEL

Herschel B. Fryberger, Jr.

Representative Clients: North Shore Bank of Commerce; General Motors Acceptance Corp.; Western Lake Superior Sanitary District; City of Duluth; First Bank Minnesota (N.A.); Norwest Bank Minnesota North N.A.; Airport State Bank; Park State Bank; M & I First National Bank of Superior; St. Lukes Hospital Duluth.

For full biographical listings, see the Martindale-Hubbell Law Directory

MISSOURI

ST. LOUIS, (Independent City)

WEINHAUS AND DOBSON (AV)

Suite 900, 906 Olive Street, 63101
Telephone: 314-621-8363
Telecopier: 314-621-8366

MEMBERS OF FIRM

S. Sheldon Weinhaus
Jerome J. Dobson

ASSOCIATES

Michael Craig Goldberg
Jonathan Charles Berns

OF COUNSEL

Mark E. Moreland

Reference: The Boatmen's National Bank of St. Louis.

For full biographical listings, see the Martindale-Hubbell Law Directory

MONTANA

*BILLINGS,** Yellowstone Co.

CROWLEY, HAUGHEY, HANSON, TOOLE & DIETRICH (AV)

500 Transwestern II, 490 North 31st Street, P.O. Box 2529, 59103
Telephone: 406-252-3441
Fax: 406-259-4159
Helena, Montana Office: IBM Building, 100 North Park Avenue, Suite 300, 59601.
Telephone: 406-449-4165.
Fax: 406-449-5149.

MEMBERS OF FIRM

Gareld F. Krieg
Terry B. Cosgrove
Steven J. Lehman
Laura A. Mitchell
John R. Alexander
William J. Mattix
Joe C. Maynard, Jr.

Representative Clients: Xerox Corporation; Valley Motor Supply; Montana Power Company; Armstrong World Industries; Peabody Coal Co.; United Parcel Service; Billings Clinic; Yellowstone County; MDU Resources Group, Inc.; General Electric Co.

For Complete List of Firm Personnel, See General Section

For full biographical listings, see the Martindale-Hubbell Law Directory

NEVADA

*RENO,** Washoe Co.

MCDONALD, CARANO, WILSON, MCCUNE, BERGIN, FRANKOVICH & HICKS (AV)

241 Ridge Street, 89505
Telephone: 702-322-0635
Telecopier: 702-786-9532
Las Vegas, Nevada Office: Suite 1000, 2300 West Sahara Avenue.
Telephone: 702-873-4100.
Telecopier: 702-873-9966.

MEMBERS OF FIRM

John J. McCune
John J. Frankovich
Timothy E. Rowe
Lenard T. Ormsby

ASSOCIATES

Pat Lundvall
James P. Stefflre

Representative Clients: CDS of Nevada, Inc.; Eldorado Hotel & Casino; Jackpot Enterprises, Inc.; Q & D Construction Company; Scolari's Warehouse Markets, Inc.; Sierra nevada Production Credit Association; The Gibbons Company.

For Complete List of Firm Personnel, See General Section

For full biographical listings, see the Martindale-Hubbell Law Directory

NEW JERSEY

*HACKENSACK,** Bergen Co.

HEIN, SMITH, BEREZIN, MALOOF & ROGERS (AV)

Court Plaza East, 19 Main Street, 07601-7023
Telephone: 201-487-7400
Telecopier: 201-487-4228

MEMBER OF FIRM

Alan A. Davidson

OF COUNSEL

Seymour A. Smith

For Complete List of Firm Personnel, See General Section

For full biographical listings, see the Martindale-Hubbell Law Directory

NEW MEXICO

*ALBUQUERQUE,** Bernalillo Co.

HINKLE, COX, EATON, COFFIELD & HENSLEY (AV)

Suite 800, 500 Marquette, N.W., P.O. Box 2043, 87103
Telephone: 505-768-1500
FAX: 505-768-1529
Roswell, New Mexico Office: Suite 700, United Bank Plaza, P.O. Box 10, 88202.
Telephone: 505-622-6510.
FAX: 505-623-9332.
Midland, Texas Office: 6 Desta Drive, Suite 2800, P.O. Box 3580, 79705.
Telephone: 915-683-4691.
FAX: 915-683-6518.
Amarillo, Texas Office: 1700 Bank One Center. P.O. Box 9238, 79105-9238.
Telephone: 806-372-5569.
FAX: 806-372-9761.
Santa Fe, New Mexico Office: 218 Montezuma, P.O. Box 2068, 87504.
Telephone: 505-982-4554.
FAX: 505-982-8623.
Austin, Texas Office: 401 West 15th Street, Suite 800, 78701.
Telephone: 512-476-7137.
FAX: 512-476-5431.
Associated Office: Hoffman & Stephens, P.C., 401 West 15th Street, Suite 800, 78701.
Telephone: 512-476-5434.
Fax: 512-476-5431.

Fred W. Schwendimann
Julie P. Neerken

Representative Clients: Anadarko Petroleum Corp.; Atlantic Richfield Co.; Bass Enterprises Production Co.; BHP Petroleum; Caroon & Black Management, Inc.; Chevron, USA, Inc.; CIGNA; City of Albuquerque; Coastal Oil & Gas Corp. Co.; Ethicon Inc., A Johnson & Johnson, Co.; Diagnostik; Conoco; Texaco; Presbyterian Healthcare Services.

For Complete List of Firm Personnel, See General Section

For full biographical listings, see the Martindale-Hubbell Law Directory

SHEEHAN, SHEEHAN & STELZNER, P.A. (AV)

Suite 300, 707 Broadway, N.E., P.O. Box 271, 87103
Telephone: 505-247-0411
Fax: 505-842-8890

Craig T. Erickson
Juan L. Flores
Kim A. Griffith
Philip P. Larragoite
Susan C. Little
Maria O'Brien
Judith D. Schrandt
Timothy M. Sheehan
Luis G. Stelzner
Elizabeth Newlin Taylor
Robert P. Warburton

OF COUNSEL

Briggs F. Cheney
Charles T. DuMars
Thomas J. Horan
Pat Sheehan

Representative Clients: Albuquerque Family Health Center; Archdiocese of Santa Fe; CVI Laser Corp.; Charter Services, Inc.; Jaynes Corp.; Los Alamos Credit Union; Molzen Corbin & Associates, Inc.; University of New Mexico; Wright Mains Koester, Inc.

For full biographical listings, see the Martindale-Hubbell Law Directory

NEW YORK

*ALBANY,** Albany Co.

ROWLEY, FORREST, O'DONNELL & HITE, P.C. (AV)

90 State Street Suite 729, 12207-1715
Telephone: 518-434-6187
Fax: 518-434-1287

Richard R. Rowley
Thomas J. Forrest
Brian J. O'Donnell
Robert S. Hite
John H. Beaumont
Mark S. Pelersi
David C. Rowley

James J. Seaman
David P. Miranda
Kevin S. Casey
Richard W. Bader
Daniel W. Coffey
Thomas D. Spain

OF COUNSEL

Rush W. Stehlin

Reference: Norstar Bank.

For full biographical listings, see the Martindale-Hubbell Law Directory

*BUFFALO,** Erie Co.

ALBRECHT, MAGUIRE, HEFFERN & GREGG, P.C. (AV)

2100 Main Place Tower, 14202
Telephone: 716-853-1521
Fax: 716-852-2609

Raymond H. Barr
Gary J. Gleba

For Complete List of Firm Personnel, See General Section

For full biographical listings, see the Martindale-Hubbell Law Directory

GARDEN CITY, Nassau Co.

GALLAGHER GOSSEEN & FALLER (AV)

1010 Franklin Avenue, Suite 400, 11530-2927
Telephone: 516-742-2500
Fax: 516-742-2516
Cable: COMPROAIR
New York, New York Office: 350 Fifth Avenue.
Telephone: 212-947-5800.
FAX: 212-967-4965.

MEMBER OF FIRM

Robert I. Gosseen (Resident, New York City Office)

ASSOCIATE

Robert A. Sparer (Resident, New York City Office)

For Complete List of Firm Personnel, See General Section

For full biographical listings, see the Martindale-Hubbell Law Directory

*NEW CITY,** Rockland Co.

GRANIK SILVERMAN SANDBERG CAMPBELL NOWICKI RESNIK HEKKER (AV)

254 South Main Street, 10956
Telephone: 914-634-8822; 800-822-1238

MEMBERS OF FIRM

Joseph F. X. Nowicki (1922-1976)
Robert R. Granik (1922-1994)
David W. Silverman
Martin L. Sandberg
Patrick M. Campbell
Kenneth H. Resnik
John M. Hekker
Ricki Hollis Berger

ASSOCIATE

Catherine T. O'Toole Lauritano

OF COUNSEL

Morrie Slifkin

For full biographical listings, see the Martindale-Hubbell Law Directory

*NEW YORK,** New York Co.

GANZ, HOLLINGER & TOWE (AV)

1394 Third Avenue, 10021
Telephone: 212-517-5500; 838-9600
Cable Address: "Ganzlaw New York"
Telex: 852970 GANZLAW NYK
FAX: 212-772-2720; 772-2216

David L. Ganz
Jerrietta R. Hollinger
Teri Noel Towe

ASSOCIATE

Nancy A. Torres (Not admitted in NY)

For full biographical listings, see the Martindale-Hubbell Law Directory

OTTERBOURG, STEINDLER, HOUSTON & ROSEN, P.C. (AV)

230 Park Avenue, 10169
Telephone: 212-661-9100
Cable Address: "Otlerton";
Telecopier: 212-682-6104
Telex: 960916

Donald N. Gellert
Eugene V. Kokot

Diane B. Kaplan
Lloyd M. Green

For Complete List of Firm Personnel, See General Section

For full biographical listings, see the Martindale-Hubbell Law Directory

VLADECK, WALDMAN, ELIAS & ENGELHARD, P.C. (AV)

1501 Broadway, Suite 800, 10036
Telephone: 212-403-7300
FAX: 212-221-3172

(See Next Column)

VLADECK, WALDMAN, ELIAS & ENGELHARD P.C., *New York—Continued*

Stephen C. Vladeck (1920-1979)	Laura S. Schnell
Judith P. Vladeck	Linda E. Rodd
Seymour M. Waldman	Debra L. Raskin
Sylvan H. Elias	Julian R. Birnbaum
Sheldon Engelhard	Larry Cary
Irwin Bluestein	James I. Wasserman
Daniel Engelstein	Owen M. Rumelt
Patricia McConnell	Hanan B. Kolko (Not admitted in NY)
Anne C. Vladeck	Jay P. Levy-Warren
Karen Honeycutt	

Ivan D. Smith

John A. Beranbaum	Mary Josephine E. Provenzano
Anne L. Clark	James D. Esseks
Maureen Maria Stampp	(Not admitted in NY)

Suja A. Thomas

OF COUNSEL

Burton M. Epstein

LEGAL SUPPORT PERSONNEL

Patricia Francisco	Robert G. Ridenour
Karen Sais-Metzger	Edward Heldman
John Stauder	Christopher Antilla

For full biographical listings, see the Martindale-Hubbell Law Directory

*ROCHESTER,** Monroe Co.

HARTER, SECREST & EMERY (AV)

700 Midtown Tower, 14604-2070
Telephone: 716-232-6500
Telecopier: 716-232-2152
Naples, Florida Office: Suite 400, 800 Laurel Oak Drive.
Telephone: 813-598-4444.
Telecopier: 813-598-2781.
Albany, New York Office: One Steuben Place.
Telephone: 518-434-4377.
Telecopier: 518-449-4025.
Syracuse, New York Office: 431 East Fayette Street.
Telephone: 315-474-4000.
Telecopier: 315-474-7789.

MEMBERS OF FIRM

Ronald J. Mendrick	Maureen T. Alston

COUNSEL

Bonnie A. Blenis

SENIOR ATTORNEY

Paul M. Hetland

ASSOCIATE

Paul W. Holloway

For Complete List of Firm Personnel, See General Section

For full biographical listings, see the Martindale-Hubbell Law Directory

NORTH CAROLINA

*CHARLOTTE,** Mecklenburg Co.

WOMBLE CARLYLE SANDRIDGE & RICE (AV)

A Professional Limited Liability Company
3300 One First Union Center, 301 S. College Street, 28202-6025
Telephone: 704-331-4900
Telecopy: 704-331-4955
Telex: 853609
Winston-Salem, North Carolina Office: 1600 Southern National Financial Center.
Telephone: 919-721-3600.
Telecopy: 919-721-3660.
Telex: 806498.
Raleigh, North Carolina Office: 2100 First Union Capitol Center, 150 Fayetteville Street Mall, P.O. Box 831.
Telephone: 919-755-2100.
Telecopy: 919-755-2150.
Telex: 806498.
Atlanta, Georgia Office: One Ninety One Peachtree Tower, 191 Peachtree Street N.E., Suite 3250.
Telephone: 404-614-2580.
Fax: 404-614-2595.

MEMBER OF FIRM

James E. Daniel

Representative Clients: Childress Klein Properties, Inc.; Food Lion, Inc.; Fieldcrest Cannon, Inc.; J.A. Jones Construction Company; Parkdale Mills, Inc.; Duke Power Company; Bowles Hollowell Conner & Company; ALLTEL Carolina, Inc.; Belk Store Services, Inc.; Philip Holzmann A.G.

(See Next Column)

For Complete List of Firm Personnel, See General Section

For full biographical listings, see the Martindale-Hubbell Law Directory

*RALEIGH,** Wake Co.

* indicates certain Bar Register subscribers whose principal office is located elsewhere in the state and who have arranged for representation as a part of the state capital listings that follow

* **WOMBLE CARLYLE SANDRIDGE & RICE** (AV)

A Professional Limited Liability Company
2100 First Union Capitol Center, 150 Fayetteville Street Mall, P.O. Box 831, 27602
Telephone: 919-755-2100
Telecopy: 919-755-2150
Telex: 806498
Charlotte, North Carolina Office: 3300 One First Union Center, 301 South College Street.
Telephone: 704-331-4900.
Telecopy: 704-331-4955.
Telex: 853609.
Winston-Salem, North Carolina Office: 1600 Southern National Financial Center.
Telephone: 919-721-3600.
Telecopy: 919-721-3660.
Telex: 806498.
Atlanta, Georgia Office: One Ninety One Peachtree Tower, 191 Peachtree Street N.E., Suite 3250.
Telephone: 404-614-2580.
Fax: 404-614-2595.

RESIDENT PARTNER

Charles A. Edwards

RESIDENT ASSOCIATE

Simmons I. Patrick, Jr.

Representative Clients: Aetna Casualty and Surety Co., Inc.; ALSCO/AmeriMark Building Products, Inc.; Aoki Corporation America, Inc.; Empire of Carolina, Inc.; Hackney Brothers, Inc.; Lawyers Mutual Liability Insurance Company of North Carolina; Meredith College; Monk-Austin, Inc.; Regency Park Corporation; Wachovia Bank of North Carolina, N.A.

For Complete List of Firm Personnel, See General Section

For full biographical listings, see the Martindale-Hubbell Law Directory

*WINSTON-SALEM,** Forsyth Co.

WOMBLE CARLYLE SANDRIDGE & RICE (AV)

A Professional Limited Liability Company
1600 Southern National Financial Center, P.O. Drawer 84, 27102
Telephone: 910-721-3600
Telecopy: 910-721-3660
Telex: 806498
Charlotte, North Carolina Office: 3300 One First Union Center, 301 South College Street.
Telephone: 704-331-4900.
Telecopy: 704-331-4955.
Telex: 853609.
Raleigh, North Carolina Office: 2100 First Union Capitol Center, 150 Fayetteville Street Mall, P.O. Box 831.
Telephone: 919-755-2100.
Telecopy: 919-755-2150.
Telex: 806498.
Atlanta, Georgia Office: One Ninety One Peachtree Tower, 191 Peachtree Street, N.E., Suite 3250.
Telephone: 404-614-2580.
Fax: 404-614-2595.

MEMBERS OF FIRM

Janice C. Baldwin	Michael D. Gunter

William Robert Whitehurst

Representative Clients: Brad Ragan, Inc.; Brenner Companies; Food Lion, Inc.; Hanes Companies, Inc.; North Carolina Baptist Hospitals, Inc.; R.J. Reynolds Tobacco Company; Summit Communications Group, Inc.; Thomasville Furniture Industries, Inc.; Wachovia Corporation; Wake Forest University.

For Complete List of Firm Personnel, See General Section

For full biographical listings, see the Martindale-Hubbell Law Directory

OHIO

*CINCINNATI,** Hamilton Co.

DINSMORE & SHOHL (AV)

1900 Chemed Center, 255 East Fifth Street, 45202-3172
Telephone: 513-977-8200
FAX: 513-977-8141
Florence, Kentucky Office: Turfway Ridge Office Park, 7300 Turfway Road, Suite 430 41042-1355.
Telephone: 606-283-0515.
FAX: 606-283-6017.
Dayton, Ohio Office: 500 Courthouse Plaza, S.W., 10 N. Ludlow Street, 45402-1834.
Telephone: 513-228-8012.
FAX: 513-461-2543.
Columbus, Ohio Office: NBD Bank Building, Suite 330, 175 South Third Street, 43215-5134.
Telephone: 614-224-7887.
FAX: 614-224-7882.

MEMBERS OF FIRM

John M. Kunst, Jr.
William M. Freedman
Edward J. Buechel (Resident, Florence, Kentucky Office)

ASSOCIATES

Deborah Price Rambo
John H. Wendeln
John F. Meisenhelder

For Complete List of Firm Personnel, See General Section

For full biographical listings, see the Martindale-Hubbell Law Directory

KATZ, TELLER, BRANT & HILD A LEGAL PROFESSIONAL ASSOCIATION (AV)

2400 Chemed Center, 255 East Fifth Street, 45202-4724
Telephone: 513-721-4532
Telecopier: 513-721-7120

Reuven J. Katz
Jerome S. Teller
Joseph A. Brant
Guy M. Hild
Robert A. Pitcairn, Jr.
Robert E. Brant
Ronald J. Goret
Stephen C. Kisling
Andrew R. Berger
Mark J. Jahnke
William F. Russo
John R. Gierl
Bruce A. Hunter
Gregory E. Land
Bradley G. Haas
Daniel P. Utt
Brent G. Houk
Cynthia Loren Gibson
Suzanne Prieur Land
Tedd H. Friedman

Representative Clients: Eagle Picher Industries, Inc.; F & C International, Inc.; Jewish Hospitals of Cincinnati; Johnny Bench; Texo Corporation; University of Cincinnati Medical Associates, Inc.

For full biographical listings, see the Martindale-Hubbell Law Directory

KLAINE, WILEY, HOFFMANN & MEURER A LEGAL PROFESSIONAL ASSOCIATION (AV)

Suite 1850, 105 East Fourth Street, 45202-4080
Telephone: 513-241-0202
Fax: 513-241-9322

Donald L. Wiley
James P. Minutolo

For Complete List of Firm Personnel, See General Section

For full biographical listings, see the Martindale-Hubbell Law Directory

STRAUSS & TROY A LEGAL PROFESSIONAL ASSOCIATION (AV)

2100 PNC Center, 201 East Fifth Street, 45202-4186
Telephone: 513-621-2120
Telecopier: 513-241-8259
Northern Kentucky Office: Suite 1400, 50 East Rivercenter Boulevard, Covington, Kentucky, 41011.
Telephone: 513-621-8900; 513-621-2120.
Telecopier: 513-629-9444.

Larry A. Neuman
Claudia G. Allen

Representative Clients: PNC Bank, N.A. (Ohio and Kentucky); Corporex Companies, Inc.; Mercantile Stores Company, Inc.; Star Bank, N.A. (Ohio and Kentucky).

For Complete List of Firm Personnel, See General Section

For full biographical listings, see the Martindale-Hubbell Law Directory

THOMPSON, HINE AND FLORY (AV)

312 Walnut Street, 14th Floor, 45202-4029
Telephone: 513-352-6700
Fax: 513-241-4771;
Telex: 938003
Akron, Ohio Office: 50 S. Main Street, Suite 502, 44308-1828.
Telephone: 216-376-8090.
Fax: 216-376-8386.

(See Next Column)

Cleveland, Ohio Office: 1100 National City Bank Building, 629 Euclid Avenue, 44114-3070.
Telephone: 216-566-5500.
Fax: 216-556-5583.
Telex: 980217.
Cable Address: "Thomflor".
Columbus, Ohio Office: One Columbus, 10 West Broad Street, 43215-3435.
Telephone: 614-469-3200.
Fax: 614-469-3361.
Dayton, Ohio Office: 2000 Courthouse Plaza, N.E., 45402-1706.
Telephone: 513-443-6600.
Fax: 513-443-6637; 443-6635.
Palm Beach, Florida Office: 125 Worth Avenue, 33480-4466.
Telephone: 407-833-5900.
Fax: 407-833-5951.
Washington, D.C. Office: 1920 N Street, N.W., 20036-1601.
Telephone: 202-331-8800.
Fax: 202-331-8330.
Telex: 904173.
Cable Address: "Caglaw".
Brussels, Belgium Office: Rue des Chevaliers / Ridderstraat 14 - B.10, B - 1050.
Telephone: 011(32-2) 511-9326.
Fax: 011(-32-2) 513-9206.

MEMBER OF FIRM

Scott B. Crooks

ASSOCIATE

Timothy R. Brown

For Complete List of Firm Personnel, See General Section

For full biographical listings, see the Martindale-Hubbell Law Directory

*CLEVELAND,** Cuyahoga Co.

BAKER & HOSTETLER (AV)

3200 National City Center, 1900 East Ninth Street, 44114-3485
Telephone: 216-621-0200
Telecopier: 216-696-0740
TWX: 810 421 8375
RCA Telex: 215032
In Columbus, Ohio: Capitol Square, Suite 2100, 65 East State Street.
Telephone: 614-228-1541.
In Denver, Colorado: 303 East 17th Avenue, Suite 1100.
Telephone: 303-861-0600.
In Houston, Texas: 1000 Louisiana, Suite 2000.
Telephone: 713-751-1600.
In Long Beach, California: 300 Oceangate, Suite 620.
Telephone: 310-432-2827.
In Los Angeles, California: 600 Wilshire Boulevard.
Telephone: 213-624-2400.
In Orlando, Florida: SunBank Center, Suite 2300, 200 South Orange Avenue.
Telephone: 407-649-4000.
In Washington, D. C.: Washington Square, Suite 1100, 1050 Connecticut Avenue, N.W.
Telephone: 202-861-1500.
In College Park, Maryland: 9658 Baltimore Boulevard, Suite 206.
Telephone: 301-441-2781.
In Alexandria, Virginia: 437 North Lee Street.
Telephone: 703-549-1294.
In San Francisco, California: One Sansome Street, Suite 2000.
Telephone: 415-951-4705.

PARTNERS

Richard H. Bamberger
Raymond M. Malone
John J. McGowan, Jr.
W. James Ollinger
R. Byron Wallace

For Complete List of Firm Personnel, See General Section

For full biographical listings, see the Martindale-Hubbell Law Directory

DUVIN, CAHN & BARNARD A LEGAL PROFESSIONAL ASSOCIATION (AV)

Erieview Tower, 20th Floor, 1301 East Ninth Street, 44114
Telephone: 216-696-7600
Telecopier: 216-696-2038

Robert P. Duvin
Stephen J. Cahn
Thomas H. Barnard
Gerald A. Messerman
Marc J. Bloch
Andrew C. Meyer
Lee J. Hutton
Martin S. List
Craig M. Brown
Frank W. Buck
Gale S. Messerman
Neal B. Wainblat
Kenneth B. Stark
Martin T. Wymer
Barton A. Bixenstine
Robert M. Wolff
Jane P. Wilson

Richard C. Hubbard, III
Lisa Froimson Mann
Philip S. Kushner
Stephen J. Sferra
Linda E. Tawil
Steven K. Aronoff
Kenneth Michael Haneline
Kevin M. Norchi
Paul A. Monahan
Jon M. Dileno

(See Next Column)

DUVIN, CAHN & BARNARD A LEGAL PROFESSIONAL ASSOCIATION, *Cleveland—Continued*

David A. Posner
Scott A. Moorman
Vincent T. Norwillo
Marc A. Duvin
Suellen Oswald
Stephen C. Sutton
Michele H. Schmidt
William Joseph Evans
Carole O. Heyward

Representative Clients: Cleveland-Akron-Canton Supermarket Industry; The Scott Fetzer Co.; Cole National Corp.; Regional Transit Authority; B.P. America.

For full biographical listings, see the Martindale-Hubbell Law Directory

KADISH & BENDER A LEGAL PROFESSIONAL ASSOCIATION (AV)

2112 East Ohio Building, 44114
Telephone: 216-696-3030
Telecopier: 216-696-3492

Stephen L. Kadish
J. Timothy Bender
Kevin M. Hinkel
David G. Weibel

Aaron H. Bulloff
Joseph P. Alexander
David G. Lambert
William A. Duncan
Mary Beth Duffy
James H. Rownd

For full biographical listings, see the Martindale-Hubbell Law Directory

MILLISOR & NOBIL A LEGAL PROFESSIONAL ASSOCIATION (AV)

9150 South Hills Boulevard, 44147-3599
Telephone: 216-838-8800 Cleveland
216-253-5500 Akron
Telefax: 216-838-8805
Columbus, Ohio Office: 41 South High Street, 3737 Huntington Center, 43215-6101.
Telephone: 614-224-1010.
Telefax: 614-365-9411.

Kenneth R. Millisor
Steven M. Nobil
Thomas D. Rooney
Harley M. Kastner
David E. Schreiner
David P. Hiller
Preston J. Garvin
James P. Wilkins
Michael J. Ranallo
Paul H. Malesick
Keith L. Pryatel
John J. Krimm, Jr.
Michael J. Hickey
Maribeth Gavin
Douglas B. Brown
Linda S. Wilkins
Jodi L. Wood
Kelly E. Drushel
Mark M. McCarthy
Christine C. Covey
Richard A. Millisor
Lisa A. Kainec
Jeffrey B. Keiper (Not admitted in OH)
Bruce H. Fahey

LEGAL SUPPORT PERSONNEL
DIRECTORS

James M. Kitchin
Christine Belz
Bruce W. Baylor
Bryan D. Richert

PARALEGALS

Vicki Barnette
Angela M. Bertka
Robert C. Dowd
Rita M. Filer
Irene G. Frye
Barbara L. Micale
Yvonne M. Shaw
Laurie L. Tolbert
Shelia Wenger

Labor Counsel for: Bridgestone/Firestone, Inc.; BFGoodrich Co.; Uniroyal-Goodrich Tire Co.; Cooper Industries; May Department Stores, Co. (Kaufmann's and Payless Shoe Source); Federated Department Stores (Lazarus); Union Metal Corp.; Ohio Automobile Dealers Assn.; Children's Hospital; Kent State University.

For full biographical listings, see the Martindale-Hubbell Law Directory

THOMPSON, HINE AND FLORY (AV)

1100 National City Bank Building, 629 Euclid Avenue, 44114-3070
Telephone: 216-566-5500
Fax: 216-566-5583
Telex: 980217
Cable Address: "Thomflor"
Akron, Ohio Office: 50 S. Main Street, Suite 502, 44308-1828.
Telephone: 216-376-8090.
Fax: 216-376-8386.
Cincinnati, Ohio Office: 312 Walnut Street, 14th Floor, 45202-4029.
Telephone: 513-352-6700.
Fax: 513-241-4771.
Telex: 938003.
Columbus, Ohio Office: One Columbus, 10 West Broad Street, 43215-3435.
Telephone: 614-469-3200.
Fax: 614-469-3361.
Dayton, Ohio Office: 2000 Courthouse Plaza, N.E., 45402-1706.
Telephone: 513-443-6600.
Fax: 513-443-6637; 443-6635.
Palm Beach, Florida Office: 125 Worth Avenue, Suite 117, 33480-4466.
Telephone: 407-833-5900.
Fax: 407-833-5951.

(See Next Column)

Washington, D.C. Office: 1920 N Street, N.W., 20036-1601.
Telephone: 202-331-8800.
Fax: 202-331-8330.
Telex: 904173.
Cable Address: "Caglaw".
Brussels, Belgium Office: Rue des Chevaliers, Ridderstraat 14 - B.10, B - 1050.
Telephone: 011(32-2) 511-9326.
Fax: 011(32-2) 513-9206.

MEMBERS OF FIRM

Hugh D. Brown
Betsey Brewster Case
Donald L. Korb (In Washington, D.C. and Cleveland, Ohio)
Karen Daykin Youngstrom

ASSOCIATE

Petra J. Bradbury

For Complete List of Firm Personnel, See General Section

For full biographical listings, see the Martindale-Hubbell Law Directory

WALTER & HAVERFIELD (AV)

1300 Terminal Tower, 44113-2253
Telephone: 216-781-1212
Telecopier: 216-575-0911
Columbus, Ohio Office: 88 East Broad Street.
Telephone: 614-221-7371.

MEMBERS OF FIRM

Russell C. Shaw
Ricky Lee Bertram

OF COUNSEL

Sheldon M. Young

Representative Clients: AGA Gas, Inc.; Air Products and Chemicals, Inc.; American Crane Corp.; Andrews Moving & Storage, Inc.; Applied Medical Technology, Inc.; Aribica Cafes, Inc.; Associated Aviation Underwriters; The Associated Press; Beverly Enterprises, Inc.; Brookfield Wire Company.

For Complete List of Firm Personnel, See General Section

For full biographical listings, see the Martindale-Hubbell Law Directory

*COLUMBUS,** Franklin Co.

* indicates certain Bar Register subscribers whose principal office is located elsewhere in the state and who have arranged for representation as a part of the state capital listings that follow

*** BAKER & HOSTETLER (AV)**

Capitol Square, Suite 2100, 65 East State Street, 43215-4260
Telephone: 614-228-1541
Telecopier: 614-462-2616
In Cleveland, Ohio: 3200 National City Center, 1900 East Ninth Street.
Telephone: 216-621-0200.
In Denver, Colorado: 303 East 17th Avenue, Suite 1100.
Telephone: 202-861-1500.
In Houston, Texas: 1000 Louisiana, Suite 2000.
Telephone: 713-751-1600.
In Long Beach, California: 300 Oceangate, Suite 620.
Telephone: 310-432-2827.
In Los Angeles, California: 600 Wilshire.
Telephone: 213-624-2400.
In Orlando, Florida: SunBank Center, Suite 2300, 200 South Orange Avenue.
Telephone: 407-649-4000.
In Washington, D. C.: Washington Square, Suite 1100, 1050 Connecticut Avenue, N.W.
Telephone: 202-861-1500.
In College Park, Maryland: 9658 Baltimore Boulevard, Suite 301.
Telephone: 301-441-2781.
In Alexandria, Virginia: 437 North Lee Street.
Telephone: 703-549-1294.
In San Francisco, California: One Sansome Street, Suite 2000.
Telephone: 415-951-4705.

PARTNER

Georgeann G. Peters

For Complete List of Firm Personnel, See General Section

For full biographical listings, see the Martindale-Hubbell Law Directory

EMENS, KEGLER, BROWN, HILL & RITTER (AV)

Capitol Square Suite 1800, 65 East State Street, 43215-4294
Telephone: 614-462-5400
Telecopier: 614-464-2634
Cable Address: "Law EKBHR"
Telex: 246671

Paul D. Ritter, Jr.

Representative Clients: The Benatty Corp.; Diocese of Columbus; Drug Emporium, Inc.; Patrick Petroleum Co.; Robinson J & B Cartage Co.

(See Next Column)

EMENS, KEGLER, BROWN, HILL & RITTER—*Continued*

For Complete List of Firm Personnel, See General Section

For full biographical listings, see the Martindale-Hubbell Law Directory

MILLISOR & NOBIL A LEGAL PROFESSIONAL ASSOCIATION (AV)

41 South High Street, 3737 Huntington Center, 43215-6101
Telephone: 614-224-1010
Telefax: 614-365-9411
Cleveland, Ohio Office: 9150 South Hills Boulevard, 44147-3599.
Telephone: 216-838-8800.
Telefax: 216-838-8805.

David P. Hiller
Preston J. Garvin
John J. Krimm, Jr.
Michael J. Hickey
Mark M. McCarthy

Labor Counsel for: Bridgestone/Firestone, Inc.; BF Goodrich Co.; Uniroyal-Goodrich Tire Co.; Cooper Industries; May Department Stores, Co. (Kaufmann's and Payless Shoe Source); Federated Department Stores (Lazarus); Union Metal Corp.; Ohio Automobile Dealers Assn.; Children's Hospital; Kent State University.

For full biographical listings, see the Martindale-Hubbell Law Directory

*** THOMPSON, HINE AND FLORY (AV)**

One Columbus, 10 West Broad Street, 43215-3435
Telephone: 614-469-3200
Fax: 614-469-3361
Akron, Ohio Office: 50 S. Main Street, Suite 502, 44308-1828.
Telephone: 216-376-8090.
Fax: 216-376-8386.
Cincinnati, Ohio Office: 312 Walnut Street, 14th Floor, 45202-4029.
Telephone: 513-352-6700.
Fax: 513-241-4771.
Telex: 938003.
Cleveland, Ohio Office: 1100 National City Bank Building, 629 Euclid Avenue, 44114-3070.
Telephone: 216-566-5500.
Fax: 216-556-5583.
Telex: 980217.
Cable Address: "Thomflor".
Dayton, Ohio Office: 2000 Courthouse Plaza, N.E., 45402-1706.
Telephone: 513-443-6600.
Fax: 513-443-6637; 443-6635.
Palm Beach, Florida Office: 125 Worth Avenue, 33480-4466.
Telephone: 407-833-5900.
Fax: 407-833-5951.
Washington, D.C. Office: 1920 N Street, N.W., 20036-1601.
Telephone: 202-331-8800.
Fax: 202-331-8330.
Telex: 904173.
Cable Address: "Caglaw".
Brussels, Belgium Office: Rue des Chevaliers / Ridderstraat 14 - B.10, B - 1050.
Telephone: 011(32-2) 511-9326.
Fax: 011(32-2) 513-9206.

MEMBERS OF FIRM

Michael A. Poe
Jerry Vande Werken

For Complete List of Firm Personnel, See General Section

For full biographical listings, see the Martindale-Hubbell Law Directory

*DAYTON,** Montgomery Co.

THOMPSON, HINE AND FLORY (AV)

2000 Courthouse Plaza, N.E., 45402-1706
Telephone: 513-443-6600
Fax: 513-443-6637; 443-6635
Akron, Ohio Office: 50 S. Main Street, Suite 502, 44308-1828.
Telephone: 216-376-8090.
Fax: 216-376-8386.
Cincinnati, Ohio Office: 312 Walnut Street, 14th Floor, 45202-4029.
Telephone: 513-352-6700.
Fax: 513-241-4771.
Telex: 938003.
Cleveland, Ohio Office: 1100 National City Bank Building, 629 Euclid Avenue, 44114-3070.
Telephone: 216-566-5500.
Fax: 216-556-5583.
Telex: 980217.
Cable Address: "Thomflor".
Columbus, Ohio Office: One Columbus, 10 West Broad Street, 43215-3435.
Telephone: 614-469-3200.
Fax: 614-469-3361.
Palm Beach, Florida Office: 125 Worth Avenue, 33480-4466.
Telephone: 407-833-5900.
Fax: 407-833-5951.

(See Next Column)

Washington, D.C. Office: 1920 N Street, N.W., 20036-1601.
Telephone: 202-331-8800.
Fax: 202-331-8330.
Telex: 904173.
Cable Address: "Caglaw".
Brussels, Belgium Office: Rue des Chevaliers / Ridderstraat 14 - B.10, B - 1050.
Telephone: 011(32-2) 511-9326.
Fax: 011(32-2) 513-9206.

MEMBER OF FIRM

Allen R. Norris

ASSOCIATE

Joyce Z. Anderson

For Complete List of Firm Personnel, See General Section

For full biographical listings, see the Martindale-Hubbell Law Directory

OKLAHOMA

*OKLAHOMA CITY,** Oklahoma Co.

ANDREWS DAVIS LEGG BIXLER MILSTEN & PRICE, A PROFESSIONAL CORPORATION (AV)

500 West Main, 73102
Telephone: 405-272-9241
FAX: 405-235-8786

Mark H. Price

OF COUNSEL

Keith T. Childers

For Complete List of Firm Personnel, See General Section

For full biographical listings, see the Martindale-Hubbell Law Directory

*TULSA,** Tulsa Co.

BOONE, SMITH, DAVIS, HURST & DICKMAN, A PROFESSIONAL CORPORATION (AV)

500 Oneok Plaza, 100 West 5th Street, 74103
Telephone: 918-587-0000
Fax: 918-599-9317

Byron V. Boone (1908-1988)
Royce H. Savage (1904-1993)
L. K. Smith
Reuben Davis
J. Jerry Dickman
Frederic N. (Nick) Schneider III
William C. Kellough
J Schaad Titus
John A. Burkhardt
Paul E. Swain III
Carol A. Grissom
Kimberly Lambert Love
Teresa Meinders Burkett
Paul J. Cleary

R. Tom Hillis
Barry G. Reynolds
Laura L. Gonsalves
Scott R. Rowland
Shane Egan
Nancy Lynn Davis

OF COUNSEL

Edwin S. Hurst
Lloyd G. Minter

Representative Clients: American Airlines; Chevron U.S.A., Inc.; The F & M Bank & Trust Co.; Hillcrest Medical Center; Boatmen's First National Bank of Oklahoma; Phillips Petroleum Co.; Rockwell International; Sears, Roebuck & Co.; Thrifty Rent-A-Car Systems, Inc.; World Publishing Co.

For full biographical listings, see the Martindale-Hubbell Law Directory

GABLE & GOTWALS (AV)

2000 Bank IV Center, 15 West Sixth Street, 74119-5447
Telephone: 918-582-9201
Facsimile: 918-586-8383

Teresa B. Adwan
Pamela S. Anderson
John R. Barker
David L. Bryant
Gene C. Buzzard
Dennis Clarke Cameron
Timothy A. Carney
Renee DeMoss
Elsie C. Draper
Sidney G. Dunagan
Theodore Q. Eliot
Richard W. Gable
Jeffrey Don Hassell
Patricia Ledvina Himes
Oliver S. Howard
Richard D. Koljack, Jr.
J. Daniel Morgan
Joseph W. Morris
Elizabeth R. Muratet
Richard B. Noulles
Ronald N. Ricketts
John Henry Rule
M. Benjamin Singletary
James M. Sturdivant
Patrick O. Waddel
Michael D. Hall
David Edward Keglovits
Stephen W. Lake
Kari S. McKee
Terry D. Ragsdale
Jeffrey C. Rambach

(See Next Column)

GABLE & GOTWALS, *Tulsa—Continued*

OF COUNSEL

G. Ellis Gable
Charles P. Gotwals, Jr.

For full biographical listings, see the Martindale-Hubbell Law Directory

OREGON

*PORTLAND,** Multnomah Co.

ZALUTSKY & KLARQUIST, P.C. (AV)

215 S.W. Washington Street, 3rd Floor, 97204
Telephone: 503-248-0300
FAX: 503-274-8302

Morton H. Zalutsky
Kenneth S. Klarquist, Jr.

References: First Interstate Bank of Oregon (Trust Department); The Bank of California (Trust Department).

For full biographical listings, see the Martindale-Hubbell Law Directory

PENNSYLVANIA

*HARRISBURG,** Dauphin Co.

MCNEES, WALLACE & NURICK (AV)

100 Pine Street, P.O. Box 1166, 17108
Telephone: 717-232-8000
Fax: 717-237-5300

MEMBERS OF FIRM

Alan R. Boynton, Jr.
Michael G. Jarman
Robert D. Stets
David M. Watts, Jr.
Norman I. White

ASSOCIATE

Catherine E. Walters

For Complete List of Firm Personnel, See General Section

For full biographical listings, see the Martindale-Hubbell Law Directory

*PHILADELPHIA,** Philadelphia Co.

BALLARD SPAHR ANDREWS & INGERSOLL (AV)

1735 Market Street, 51st Floor, 19103-7599
Telephone: 215-665-8500
Fax: 215-864-8999
Denver, Colorado Office: Seventeenth Street Plaza Building, Suite 2300, 1225 17th Street.
Telephone: 303-292-2400.
Fax: 303-296-3956.
Kaunas, Lithuania Office: Donelaicio g., 71-2, Kaunas 3000.
Telephone: (370-7) 20 56 66.
Fax: (370-7) 20 56 91.
Salt Lake City, Utah Office: One Utah Center, Suite 1200, 201 South Main Street.
Telephone: 801-531-3000.
Fax: 801-531-3001.
Washington, D.C. Office: Suite 900 East, 555 13th Street, N.W.
Telephone: 202-383-8800.
Fax: 202-383-8877; 383-8893.
Baltimore, Maryland Office: 300 East Lombard Street. 19th Floor.
Telephone: 410-528-5600.
Fax: 410-528-5650.
Camden, New Jersey Office: 800 Hudson Square, 5th Floor.
Telephone: 609-541-5577.
Fax: 609-541-8272.

John Marley Bernard
Joel E. Horowitz
Rhonda Resnick Cohen
Andrew J. Rudolph

COUNSEL

Edward Ira Leeds

Lori D. Kettering
Kathleen M. Ranalli
Barry L. Klein
Esther L. von Laue

For Complete List of Firm Personnel, See General Section

For full biographical listings, see the Martindale-Hubbell Law Directory

FREEDMAN & ASSOCIATES (AV)

The Widener Building, Seventeenth Floor, One South Penn Square, 19107
Telephone: 215-563-1663
Fax: 215-563-1663

Barbara W. Freedman

(See Next Column)

ASSOCIATES

Laura J. Lifsey
Susan Bahme Blumenfeld
Donna Hill Prescott

For full biographical listings, see the Martindale-Hubbell Law Directory

MARC M. SILBERT (AV)

37th Floor, Bell Atlantic Tower, 1717 Arch Street, 19103
Telephone: 215-994-5108
Fax: 215-994-2222

For full biographical listings, see the Martindale-Hubbell Law Directory

MERVIN M. WILF, LTD. (AV)

3200 Mellon Bank Center, 1735 Market Street, 19103
Telephone: 215-575-7650; 568-4842
Facsimile: 215-575-7652
Boston, Massachusetts Office: 300 Commonwealth Avenue, 02115.
Telephone: 617-437-7981.

Mervin M. Wilf

A list of Representative Clients and References will be furnished upon request.

For full biographical listings, see the Martindale-Hubbell Law Directory

*PITTSBURGH,** Allegheny Co.

BUCHANAN INGERSOLL, PROFESSIONAL CORPORATION (AV)

5800 USX Tower, 600 Grant Street, 15219
Telephone: 412-562-8800
Telecopier: 412-562-1041
Philadelphia, Pennsylvania Office: Two Logan Square, Twelfth Floor, 18th & Arch Streets.
Telephone: 215-665-8700.
Harrisburg, Pennsylvania Office: Vartan Parc, 30 North Third Street.
Telephone: 717-237-4800.
Tampa, Florida Office: 101 East Kennedy Boulevard, Suite 1030.
Telephone: 813-222-8180.
North Miami Beach, Florida Office: 19495 Biscayne Boulevard.
Telephone: 305-933-5600.
Lexington, Kentucky Office: 1210 Vine Center Office Tower, 333 West Vine Street.
Telephone: 606-225-5333.
Princeton, New Jersey Office: Buchanan Ingersoll, A Partnership, College Centre, 500 College Road East.
Telephone: 609-452-2666.

Richard J. Antonelli
Ronald Basso
Mark Raymond Hornak
Robert A. Johnson
James D. Obermanns
P. Jerome Richey
Sidney Zonn

SENIOR ATTORNEYS

S. Howard Kline
Philip J. Weis

James J. Barnes

For Complete List of Firm Personnel, See General Section

For full biographical listings, see the Martindale-Hubbell Law Directory

FELDSTEIN GRINBERG STEIN & MCKEE, A PROFESSIONAL CORPORATION (AV)

428 Boulevard of the Allies, 15219
Telephone: 412-471-0677
Fax: 412-263-6129
Elizabeth, Pennsylvania Office: 400 Second Street.
Telephone: 412-384-6111.
Wexford, Pennsylvania Office: 12300 Perry Highway.
Telephone: 412-935-5540.

Edwin I. Grinberg
Stanley M. Stein
Robert E. McKee, Jr.
Joan Singh

For full biographical listings, see the Martindale-Hubbell Law Directory

GABLER & ASSOCIATES, P.C. (AV)

1000 Oliver Building, 535 Smithfield Street, P.O. Box 62160, 15241
Telephone: 412-854-3838
Fax: 412-854-3842
Upper St. Clair, Pennsylvania Office: Summerfield Commons, Suite 432, 2589 Washington Road, 15241.
Telephone: 412-854-3838.
Fax: 412-854-3842.

Bruce G. Gabler

Gregory R. Ray

For full biographical listings, see the Martindale-Hubbell Law Directory

Pittsburgh—Continued

THORP, REED & ARMSTRONG (AV)

One Riverfront Center, 15222
Telephone: 412-394-7711
Fax: 412-394-2555

MEMBER OF FIRM
James K. Goldberg
ASSOCIATE
Charles G. Cochenour

For Complete List of Firm Personnel, See General Section

For full biographical listings, see the Martindale-Hubbell Law Directory

SOUTH CAROLINA

*CHARLESTON,** Charleston Co.

HAYNSWORTH, MARION, MCKAY & GUÉRARD, L.L.P (AV)

#2 Prioleau Street, P.O. Box 1119, 29402
Telephone: 803-722-7606
Telecopier: 803-723-5263
Columbia, South Carolina Office: Suite 2400 AT&T Building, 1201 Main Street, P.O. Drawer 7157, 29202.
Telephone: 803-765-1818.
Telecopier: 803-765-2399.
Greenville, South Carolina Office: Two Insignia Financial Plaza, 75 Beattie Place, P.O. Box 2048, 29602.
Telephone: 803-240-3200.
Telecopier: 803-240-3300.

MEMBERS OF FIRM
James J. Hinchey, Jr. (Resident) Samuel W. Howell, IV

Counsel for: Bank of South Carolina; Baker Hospital; Healthsources of South Carolina; Allstate Insurance Co.; CSX Corporation; Lloyd's Underwriters; Coward-Hund Construction Co.; South Carolina Public Service Authority; South Carolina Jobs - Economic Development Authority; City of Hanahan.

For Complete List of Firm Personnel, See General Section

For full biographical listings, see the Martindale-Hubbell Law Directory

*GREENVILLE,** Greenville Co.

HAYNSWORTH, MARION, MCKAY & GUÉRARD, L.L.P. (AV)

Two Insignia Financial Plaza, 75 Beattie Place, P.O. Box 2048, 29602
Telephone: 803-240-3200
Telecopier: 803-240-3300
Columbia, South Carolina Office: Suite 2400 A T & T Building, 1201 Main Street, P.O. Drawer 7157, 29202
Telephone: 803-765-1818.
Telecopier: 803-765-2399.
Charleston, South Carolina Office: #2 Prioleau Street, P.O. Box 1119, 29402.
Telephone: 803-722-7606.
Telecopier: 803-723-5263.

MEMBERS OF FIRM
Jesse C. Belcher, Jr. John B. McLeod
David L. McMurray
ASSOCIATE
Arthur Frazier McLean, III

Counsel for: Duke Power Co.; Liberty Mutual Insurance Co.; Equitable Life Assurance Society of the United States; St. Paul Insurance Group; Allstate Insurance Co.; Fluor-Daniel Corp.; Snyalloy Corporation; Greenville Hospital System.

For Complete List of Firm Personnel, See General Section

For full biographical listings, see the Martindale-Hubbell Law Directory

WYCHE, BURGESS, FREEMAN & PARHAM, PROFESSIONAL ASSOCIATION (AV)

44 East Camperdown Way, P.O. Box 728, 29602-0728
Telephone: 803-242-8200
Telecopier: 803-235-8900

D. Allen Grumbine Cary H. Hall, Jr.

Counsel for: Multimedia, Inc.; Delta Woodside Industries, Inc.; Milliken & Company; Ryan's Family Steak Houses, Inc.; St. Francis Hospital; Span-America Medical Systems, Inc.; Carolina First Bank; KEMET Electronics Corp.; Builder Marts of America, Inc.; One Price Clothing, Inc.

For Complete List of Firm Personnel, See General Section

For full biographical listings, see the Martindale-Hubbell Law Directory

SOUTH DAKOTA

*ABERDEEN,** Brown Co.

MALONEY & MALONEY (AV)

Twelve Second Avenue, Southwest, P.O. Box 755, 57402-0755
Telephone: 605-229-2752
Fax: 605-226-0276

MEMBERS OF FIRM
Dennis Maloney Marilyn Marshall Maloney

For full biographical listings, see the Martindale-Hubbell Law Directory

*RAPID CITY,** Pennington Co.

LYNN, JACKSON, SHULTZ & LEBRUN, P.C. (AV)

Eighth Floor, Metropolitan Federal Bank Plaza, P.O. Box 8250, 57709
Telephone: 605-342-2592
Telecopier: 605-342-5185
Sioux Falls, South Dakota Office: First Bank Building, Sixth Floor, P.O. Box 1920.
Telephone: 605-332-5999.
Telecopier: 605-332-4249.

Steven J. Helmers Jane Wipf Pfeifle

Representative Clients: First Bank of South Dakota; Employers Mutual of Wausau; South Dakota School Mines & Technology; CIGNA Insurance Co.; E.D. Jones & Co.; Prairie States Life Insurance Co.
General Counsel for: Rushmore Electric Power Cooperative; Black Hills Regional Eye Institute; Douglas School District.

For Complete List of Firm Personnel, See General Section

For full biographical listings, see the Martindale-Hubbell Law Directory

TENNESSEE

*CHATTANOOGA,** Hamilton Co.

SPEARS, MOORE, REBMAN & WILLIAMS (AV)

8th Floor Blue Cross Building, 801 Pine Street, 37402
Telephone: 615-756-7000
Facsimile: 615-756-4801

MEMBERS OF FIRM
William L. Taylor, Jr. Randy Chennault

Counsel for: Pioneer Bank; Chattanooga Gas Co.; South Central Bell Telephone Co.; Tennessee-American Water Co.; Blue Cross and Blue Shield of Tennessee; State Farm Mutual Automobile Insurance Cos.; Nationwide Insurance Co.; Siskin Steel & Supply Co., Inc.; CSX Transportation, Inc.; The McCallie School; Mueller Co.

For Complete List of Firm Personnel, See General Section

For full biographical listings, see the Martindale-Hubbell Law Directory

*MEMPHIS,** Shelby Co.

YOUNG & PERL, P.C. (AV)

Suite 2380, One Commerce Square, 38103
Telephone: 901-525-2761
FAX: 901-526-2702

Edward R. Young
Arnold E. Perl
Jay W. Kiesewetter
Jonathan E. Kaplan
Cary Schwimmer
W. Stephen Gardner

Karen W. Grochau (Resident)
James C. Holland
Leigh A. Hollingsworth
John Marshall Jones
Shawn R. Lillie
Todd L. Sarver (Not admitted in TN)
James M. Simpson
Mark Theodore (Not admitted in TN)

LEGAL SUPPORT PERSONNEL
Patrick T. Fleming (Labor Relations Specialist)

For full biographical listings, see the Martindale-Hubbell Law Directory

TEXAS

*DALLAS,** Dallas Co.

THOMPSON & KNIGHT, A PROFESSIONAL CORPORATION (AV)

(Attorneys and Counselors)
1700 Pacific Avenue Suite 3300, 75201
Telephone: 214-969-1700
Telecopy: 214-969-1751
Cable Address: "Tomtex"
Telex: 732298
Austin, Texas Office: 1200 San Jacinto Center, 98 San Jacinto Boulevard, 78701.
Telephone: 512-469-6100.
Telecopy: 512-469-6180.
Fort Worth, Texas Office: 801 Cherry Street, Suite 1600, 76102.
Telephone: 817-347-1700.
Telecopy: 817-347-1799.
Houston, Texas Office: 1700 Texas Commerce Tower, 600 Travis, 77002.
Telephone: 713-217-2800.
Telecopy: 713-217-2828.
Monterrey, Mexico Office: Edificio Losoles PD-4, Av. Lázaro Cárdenas No. 2400 Pte., San Pedro Garza Garcia, Nuevo Léon C.P. 66220.
Telephone: (52-8) 363-0096.
Telecopy: (52-8) 363-3067.

SHAREHOLDERS

Sharon M. Fountain
Russell G. Gully
John Michael Holt

For Complete List of Firm Personnel, See General Section

For full biographical listings, see the Martindale-Hubbell Law Directory

*SAN ANTONIO,** Bexar Co.

SCHOENBAUM, CURPHY & SCANLAN, P.C. (AV)

NationsBank Plaza, Suite 1775, 300 Convent Street, 78205-3744
Telephone: 210-224-4491
Fax: 210-224-7983

Stanley Schoenbaum
R. James Curphy
William Scanlan, Jr.
Alfred G. Holcomb
Banks M. Smith
R. Bradley Oxford
Darin N. Digby

Patricia Flora Sitchler
Emily Harrison Liljenwall
Susan L. Saeger

For full biographical listings, see the Martindale-Hubbell Law Directory

UTAH

*SALT LAKE CITY,** Salt Lake Co.

CALLISTER, NEBEKER & MCCULLOUGH, A PROFESSIONAL CORPORATION (AV)

800 Kennecott Building, 84133
Telephone: 801-530-7300
Telecopier: 801-364-9127

Leland S. McCullough
Jeffrey N. Clayton
W. Waldan Lloyd
Lynda Cook

Representative Clients: Zions Bancorporation; Intermountain Health Care; WordPerfect Corporation; Novell, Inc.; Sinclair Oil (Little America); American Stores; Flying J Inc.; Nu Skin International, Inc.

For Complete List of Firm Personnel, See General Section

For full biographical listings, see the Martindale-Hubbell Law Directory

PARSONS BEHLE & LATIMER, A PROFESSIONAL CORPORATION (AV)

One Utah Center, 201 South Main Street, Suite 1800, P.O. Box 45898, 84145-0898
Telephone: 801-532-1234
Telecopy: 801-536-6111

Chris Wangsgard
David A. Anderson
Randy M. Grimshaw
Lawrence R. Barusch
Maxwell A. Miller
Richard M. Marsh
W. Mark Gavre
David W. Zimmerman

Representative Clients: Barrick Resources (USA) Inc.; Kennecott Corporation; USX Corporation.

For full biographical listings, see the Martindale-Hubbell Law Directory

VAN COTT, BAGLEY, CORNWALL & MCCARTHY, A PROFESSIONAL CORPORATION (AV)

Suite 1600, 50 South Main Street, P.O. Box 45340, 84145
Telephone: 801-532-3333
Telex: 453149
Telecopier: 801-534-0058
Ogden, Utah Office: Suite 900, 2404 Washington Boulevard.
Telephone: 801-394-5783.
Park City, Utah Office: 314 Main Street, Suite 205.
Telephone: 801-649-3889.
Reno, Nevada Office: Jeppson & Lee, 100 West Liberty, Suite 990.
Telephone: 702-333-6800.

Alan F. Mecham
Steven D. Woodland

For Complete List of Firm Personnel, See General Section

For full biographical listings, see the Martindale-Hubbell Law Directory

WATKISS DUNNING & WATKISS, A PROFESSIONAL CORPORATION (AV)

Broadway Centre, Suite 800, 111 East Broadway, 84111-2304
Telephone: 801-530-1500
Telecopier: 801-530-1520

David K. Watkiss
Elizabeth T. Dunning
David B. Watkiss

Carolyn Cox
Mary J. Woodhead

OF COUNSEL

Karen Campbell Jenson

Representative Clients: West One Bank; Ryder System, Inc.; Salt Lake City Library; Shriner's Hospital.

For full biographical listings, see the Martindale-Hubbell Law Directory

VIRGINIA

*RICHMOND,** (Ind. City; Seat of Henrico Co.)

WILLIAMS, MULLEN, CHRISTIAN & DOBBINS, A PROFESSIONAL CORPORATION (AV)

Two James Center, 1021 East Cary Street, P.O. Box 1320, 23210-1320
Telephone: 804-643-1991
Fax: 804-783-6456
Glen Allen, Virginia Office: 4401 Waterfront Drive, Suite 140.
Telephone: 804-965-9168.
Fax: 804-965-0955.
Washington, D.C. Office: 1575 Eye Street, N.W.
Telephone: 202-289-6200.
Fax: 202-289-4126.

David George Ball (Resident, Washington, D.C. Office)
C. Richard Davis
Lynn F. Jacob
Robert L. Musick, Jr.
B. Randolph Wellford, Jr.

Calvin W. Fowler, Jr.

For Complete List of Firm Personnel, See General Section

For full biographical listings, see the Martindale-Hubbell Law Directory

ROANOKE, (Independent City)

BERSCH & RHODES, P.C. (AV)

640 Crestar Plaza, P.O. Box 1529, 24007
Telephone: 703-345-7400
Facsimile: 703-345-7353

Robert S. Bersch
Harry S. Rhodes

William C. Leach
Scott A. Butler

For full biographical listings, see the Martindale-Hubbell Law Directory

VIENNA, Fairfax Co.

BORING, PARROTT & PILGER, P.C. (AV)

307 Maple Avenue West, Suite D, 22180-4368
Telephone: 703-281-2161
FAX: 703-281-9464

James L. Boring
Thomas J. Sawyer

Representative Clients: Balmar, Inc.; Hewlett-Packard Co.; Toshiba America Information Systems, Inc.; King Wholesale, Inc.; FSM Leasing, Inc.; KDI Sylvan Pools, Inc.; Brobst International, Inc.; Telematics, Inc.; Northern Virginia Surgical Associates, P.C.; Rainbow Industries, Inc.

For full biographical listings, see the Martindale-Hubbell Law Directory

WASHINGTON

*SEATTLE,** King Co.

EKMAN & BOHRER, P.S. (AV)

220 West Mercer Street, Suite 400, 98119
Telephone: 206-282-8221
Fax: 206-285-4587

Richard A. Ekman — Robert A. Bohrer

Mary L. Stoll — Melvin R. Kang
Charles H. Thulin

Representative Clients: National Roofing Industry Pension Plan; Northwest Laborers-Employers Trust Funds; Northwest Ironworkers Trust Funds; Northwest Roofers and Employers Trust Funds; Hotel Employees Restaurant Employees Health and Pension Plans; Carpenters Trusts of Western Washington; Western Washington Painters Trusts; Local 76 IBEW Trust Funds; Alaska Forest Assn., Inc.; Plasterers and Cement Masons Trust Funds.

For full biographical listings, see the Martindale-Hubbell Law Directory

WEST VIRGINIA

*CHARLESTON,** Kanawha Co.

JACKSON & KELLY (AV)

1600 Laidley Tower, P.O. Box 553, 25322
Telephone: 304-340-1000
Fax: 304-340-1130
Martinsburg, West Virginia Office: 300 Foxcroft Avenue, P.O. Box 1068.
Telephone: 304-263-8800.
Morgantown, West Virginia Office: 6000 Hampton Center, P.O. Box 619.
Telephone: 304-599-3000.
New Martinsville, West Virginia Office: 256 Russell Avenue, P.O. Box 68.
Telephone: 304-455-1751.
Charles Town, West Virginia Office: 700 East Washington Street, P.O. Box 983.
Telephone: 304-728-6088.
Clarksburg, West Virginia Office: 203 Main Street, P.O. Box 1587.
Telephone: 304-623-3002.
Lexington, Kentucky Office: 175 East Main Street, Suite 500, P.O. Box 2150.
Telephone: 606-255-9500.
Washington, D. C. Office: 2401 Pennsylvania Avenue, N.W., Suite 400.
Telephone: 202-973-0200.
Denver, Colorado Office: Suite 2710, 1660 Lincoln Street.
Telephone: 303-837-0003.

MEMBERS OF FIRM

Louis S. Southworth, II — Michael D. Foster

Representative Clients: CamCare, Inc.; West Virginia Bankers Association Group Health Insurance Trust; West Virginia Bankers Association Retirement Plan for Employees of Member Banks; Shawnee Hills Community Mental Health Assn.; United Bankshares, Inc.; Huntington National Bank, West Virginia; Go-Mart, Inc.; Associated Radiologists, Inc.; Consol Inc.; Ashland Coal, Inc.

For Complete List of Firm Personnel, See General Section

For full biographical listings, see the Martindale-Hubbell Law Directory

*WHEELING,** Ohio Co.

SCHRADER, RECHT, BYRD, COMPANION & GURLEY (AV)

1000 Hawley Building, 1025 Main Street, P.O. Box 6336, 26003
Telephone: 304-233-3390
Fax: 304-233-2769
Martins Ferry, Ohio Office: 205 North Fifth Street, P.O. Box 309.
Telephone: 614-633-8976.
Fax: 614-633-0400.

PARTNERS

Henry S. Schrader (Retired)
Arthur M. Recht
Ray A. Byrd
James F. Companion
Terence M. Gurley
Frank X. Duff
Teresa Rieman-Camilletti
Yolonda G. Lambert
Patrick S. Casey
Sandra M. Chapman
Daniel P. Fry (Resident, Martins Ferry, Ohio Office)
James P. Mazzone

ASSOCIATES

Sandra K. Law
D. Kevin Coleman
Denise A. Jebbia
Edythe A. Nash
Robert G. McCoid
Denise D. Klug
Thomas E. Johnston

(See Next Column)

OF COUNSEL

James A. Byrum, Jr.

General Counsel: WesBanco Bank-Elm Grove.
Representative Clients: CIGNA Property and Casualty Cos.; Columbia Gas Transmission Corp.; Commercial Union Assurance Co.; Hazlett, Burt & Watson, Inc.; Stone & Thomas Department Stores; Transamerica Commercial Finance Corp.; Wheeling-Pittsburgh Steel Corp.

For full biographical listings, see the Martindale-Hubbell Law Directory

WISCONSIN

*MILWAUKEE,** Milwaukee Co.

MEISSNER & TIERNEY, S.C. (AV)

The Milwaukee Center, 111 East Kilbourn Avenue, 19th Floor, 53202-6622
Telephone: 414-273-1300
Facsimile: 414-273-5840

Joseph E. Tierney III — Dennis L. Fisher
Thomas J. Nichols

Catherine M. Priebe Hertzberg

For full biographical listings, see the Martindale-Hubbell Law Directory

QUARLES & BRADY (AV)

411 East Wisconsin Avenue, 53202-4497
Telephone: 414-277-5000
Cable Address: "Lawdock"
Fax: 414-271-3552.
TWX: 910-262-3426
Madison, Wisconsin Office: Firstar Plaza, One South Pinckney Street, P.O. Box 2113.
Telephone: 608-251-5000.
Fax: 608-251-9166.
West Palm Beach, Florida Office: 222 Lakeview Avenue, 4th Floor.
Telephone: 407-653-5000.
Fax: 407-653-5333.
Naples, Florida Office: Barnett Center, 4501 Tamiami Trail North.
Telephone: 813-262-5959.
Fax: 813-434-4999.
Phoenix, Arizona Office: One Camelback Building, One East Camelback Road, Suite 400.
Telephone: 602-230-5500.
Fax: 602-230-5598.

MEMBERS OF FIRM
(ALPHABETICALLY BY YEAR OF ADMISSION TO BAR)

Robert J. Kalupa
Arthur B. Harris
J. Paul Jacobson
Darryl S. Bell
John T. Bannen
Michael D. Zeka
David P. Olson

ASSOCIATE

Dana L. O'Brien

For Complete List of Firm Personnel, See General Section

For full biographical listings, see the Martindale-Hubbell Law Directory

CANADA
ALBERTA

*CALGARY,** Calgary Jud. Dist.

BENNETT JONES VERCHERE (AV)

4500 Bankers Hall East, 855-2nd Street S.W., T2P 4K7
Telephone: (403) 298-3100
Facsimile: (403) 265-7219
Edmonton, Alberta Office: 1000, 10035-105 Street.
Telephone: (403) 421-8133.
Facsimile: (403) 421-7951.
Toronto, Ontario Office: 3400 1 First Canadian Place. P.O. Box 130.
Telephone: (416) 863-1200.
Facsimile: (416) 863-1716.
Ottawa, Ontario Office: Suite 1800. 350 Alberta Street, Box 25, K1R 1A4.
Telephone: (613) 230-4935.
Facsimile: (613) 230-3836.
Montreal, Quebec Office: Suite 1600, 1 Place Ville Marie.
Telephone: (514) 871-1200.
Facsimile: (514) 871-8115.

(See Next Column)

BENNETT JONES VERCHERE, *Calgary—Continued*

MEMBER OF FIRM

Douglas A. Ast

For Complete List of Firm Personnel, See General Section

For full biographical listings, see the Martindale-Hubbell Law Directory

*EDMONTON,** Edmonton Jud. Dist.

PARLEE MCLAWS (AV)

15th Floor Manulife Place, 10180 101st Street, T5J 4K1
Telephone: 403-423-8500
Telecopier: 403-423-2870
Calgary, Alberta Office: 3400, Western Canadian Place, 707 - 8th Avenue, S.W.
Telephone: 403-294-7000.
Telecopier: 403-265-8263.

MEMBERS OF FIRM

C. H. Kerr, Q.C.
M. D. MacDonald
K. F. Bailey, Q.C.
R. B. Davison, Q.C.
F. R. Haldane
P. E. J. Curran
D. G. Finlay
J. K. McFadyen
R. C. Secord
D. L. Kennedy
D. C. Rolf
D. F. Pawlowski
A. A. Garber
R. P. James
D. C. Wintermute
J. L. Cairns
R. A. Newton, Q.C.
T. A. Cockrall, Q.C.
H. D. Montemurro
F. J. Niziol
R. W. Wilson
I. L. MacLachlan
R. O. Langley
R. G. McBean
J. T. Neilson
E. G. Rice
J. F. McGinnis
J. H. H. Hockin
G. W. Jaycock
M. J. K. Nikel
B. J. Curial
S. L. May
M. S. Poretti

ASSOCIATES

C. R. Head
A.W. Slemko
L. H. Hamdon
K.A. Smith
K. D. Fallis-Howell
D. S. Tam
J.W. McClure
F.H. Belzil
R.A. Renz
J.G. Paulson
K. E. Buss
B. L. Andriachuk
P. E. S. J. Kennedy
R. Feraco
R.J. Billingsley
N.B.R. Thompson
P. A. Shenher
I. C. Johnson
K.G. Koshman
D.D. Dubrule
G. T. Lund
W.D. Johnston
G. E. Flemming
K. P. Nayyer

For full biographical listings, see the Martindale-Hubbell Law Directory

CANADA
NOVA SCOTIA

*HALIFAX,** Halifax Co.

MCINNES COOPER & ROBERTSON (AV)

1601 Lower Water Street, P.O. Box 730, B3J 2V1
Telephone: 902-425-6500
Fax: 902-425-6350
St. John's, Newfoundland Office: Suite 602, Scotia Centre, 235 Water Street, P.O. Box 547. A1C, 5K8.
Telephone: 709-726-9500.
Fax: 709-726-9550.

Peter McLellan, Q.C.
Maureen E. Reid

Attorneys for: Bank of Nova Scotia; Imperial Oil, Limited; Frank B. Hall & Co., Inc. (New York); American Steamship Owners Protection & Indemnity Association, Inc.; Coca-Cola, Ltd.; Scott Worldwide Inc.; Hong Kong Bank of Canada.

For Complete List of Firm Personnel, See General Section

For full biographical listings, see the Martindale-Hubbell Law Directory

CANADA
ONTARIO

KITCHENER, Regional Munic. of Waterloo

GIFFEN, LEE, WAGNER, MORLEY & GARBUTT (AV)

50 Queen Street North, P.O. Box 2396, N2H 6M3
Telephone: 519-578-4150
Fax: 519-578-8740

MEMBERS OF FIRM

Jeffrey J. Mansfield (1955-1991)
J. Peter Giffen, Q.C.
Bruce L. Lee
J. Scott Morley
Brian R. Wagner
Philip A. Garbutt

ASSOCIATES

Edward J. Vanderkloet
Keith C. Masterman
Daniel J. Fife
Jeffrey W. Boich

For full biographical listings, see the Martindale-Hubbell Law Directory

*TORONTO,** Regional Munic. of York

BORDEN & ELLIOT (AV)

Barristers & Solicitors
Scotia Plaza, 40 King Street West, M5H 3Y4
Telephone: 416-367-6000
Telecopier: 416-367-6749
Internet: @ borden.com
A Member of the national association of Borden DuMoulin Howard Gervais, comprising Borden & Elliot in Toronto, Ontario, Russell & DuMoulin in Vancouver, British Columbia, Howard, Mackie in Calgary, Alberta and Mackenzie Gervais in Montréal, Québec. Borden DuMoulin Howard Gervais also operates an office in London, England.

MEMBER AND ASSOCIATES

Barry W. Earle, Q.C.

For Complete List of Firm Personnel, See General Section

For full biographical listings, see the Martindale-Hubbell Law Directory

ENVIRONMENTAL LAW

ALABAMA

*BIRMINGHAM,** Jefferson Co.

BALCH & BINGHAM (AV)
1710 Sixth Avenue North, P.O. Box 306, 35201
Telephone: 205-251-8100
Facsimile: 205-226-8798
Other Birmingham, Alabama Office: 1901 Sixth Avenue North, 35203.
Telephone: 205-251-8100.
Facsimile: 205-226-8799.
Montgomery, Alabama Office: The Winter Building, 2 Dexter Avenue, 36101.
Telephone: 205-834-6500.
Facsimile: 205-269-3115.
Huntsville, Alabama Office: Suite 810, 200 West Court Square, 35801.
Telephone: 205-551-0171.
Facsimile: 205-551-0174.
Washington, D.C. Office: Suite 800, 1101 Connecticut Avenue, N.W., 20036.
Telephone: 202-296-0387.
Facsimile: 202-452-8180.

MEMBERS OF FIRM

Marshall Timberlake | William H. Satterfield
Steven G. McKinney

ASSOCIATES

David B. Champlin | Matthew W. Bowden
Glenn G. Waddell | C. Grady Moore III

Counsel for: Alabama Power Co.; Alabama River Pulp Co., Inc.; Blue Cross and Blue Shield of Alabama; Brasfield & Gorrie, Inc.; Compass Bancshares, Inc.; Harbert Corp.; Kimberly-Clark Corp.; National Energy Partners; Southern Company Services, Inc.; Southern Research Institute.

For Complete List of Firm Personnel, See General Section

For full biographical listings, see the Martindale-Hubbell Law Directory

BRADLEY, ARANT, ROSE & WHITE (AV)
1400 Park Place Tower, 2001 Park Place, 35203
Telephone: 205-521-8000
Telex: 494-1324
Facsimile: 205-251-8611, 251-8665, 252-0264
Facsimile (Southtrust Office): 205-251-9915
Huntsville, Alabama Office: 200 Clinton Avenue West, Suite 900.
Telephone: 205-517-5100.
Facsimile: 205-533-5069.

MEMBERS OF FIRM

Macbeth Wagnon, Jr. | Bobby C. Underwood
Andrew Robert Greene | Joseph S. Bird, III
Walter H. Monroe, III | John E. Hagefstration, Jr.

For Complete List of Firm Personnel, See General Section

For full biographical listings, see the Martindale-Hubbell Law Directory

BURR & FORMAN (AV)
3000 SouthTrust Tower, 420 North 20th Street, 35203
Telephone: 205-251-3000
Telecopier: 205-458-5100
Huntsville, Alabama Office: Suite 204, Regency Center, 400 Meridian Street.
Telephone: 205-551-0010.

MEMBERS OF FIRM

John F. DeBuys, Jr. | D. Frank Davis
James Ross Forman, III | Mark McCarroll Lawson

ASSOCIATE

Harri J. Haikala

For Complete List of Firm Personnel, See General Section

For full biographical listings, see the Martindale-Hubbell Law Directory

COOPER, MITCH, CRAWFORD, KUYKENDALL & WHATLEY (AV)
1100 Financial Center, 505 20th Street North, 35203-2605
Telephone: 205-328-9576
Telecopier: 205-328-9669

(See Next Column)

MEMBERS OF FIRM

Jerome A. Cooper | John D. Saxon
William E. Mitch | Glen M. Connor
Thomas N. Crawford, Jr. | Patricia Guthrie Fraley
Frederick T. Kuykendall, III | Jay Smith
Joe R. Whatley, Jr. | (On Leave of Absence)

ASSOCIATES

Candis A. McGowan | G. Patterson Keahey
Andrew C. Allen | Maureen Kane Berg
William Z. Cullen | Gerald B. Taylor, Jr.
Samuel H. Heldman | Rebecca Higgins Hunt
Hilary E. Ball-Walker | Marcel L. Debruge
Patrick F. Clark | Peter H. Burke

Counsel for: United Steelworkers of America, AFL-CIO; United Mine Workers of America, District 20; Birmingham Plumbers & Steamfitters Local Union No. 91 Pension Fund.
Reference: AMSouth Bank of Birmingham.

For full biographical listings, see the Martindale-Hubbell Law Directory

HOGAN, SMITH, ALSPAUGH, SAMPLES & PRATT, P.C. (AV)
2323 Second Avenue, North, 35203
Telephone: 205-324-5635
Telecopier: 205-324-5637

William W. Smith | James P. Rea
M. Clay Alspaugh | Robert D. Word, III
R. Benjamin Hogan, III | Richard D. Stratton

OF COUNSEL

Roscoe B. Hogan

Reference: First Alabama Bank.

For Complete List of Firm Personnel, See General Section

For full biographical listings, see the Martindale-Hubbell Law Directory

LIGHTFOOT, FRANKLIN, WHITE & LUCAS (AV)
300 Financial Center, 505 20th Street North, 35203-2706
Telephone: 205-581-0700
Facsimile: 205-581-0799

MEMBERS OF FIRM

John M. Johnson | Adam K. Peck

ASSOCIATES

William S. Cox, III | Sarah Bruce Jackson
Sabrina A. Simon | Kim A. Craddock

Counsel for: AT&T; Ford Motor Co.; Emerson Electric Co.; Monsanto Co.; Chrysler Corp.; Unocal Corp.; The Upjohn Co.; Bristol-Myers Squibb Co.; Kimberly-Clark Corp.; Chevron Chemical Co.

For full biographical listings, see the Martindale-Hubbell Law Directory

SIROTE & PERMUTT, P.C. (AV)
2222 Arlington Avenue, South, P.O. Box 55727, 35255
Telephone: 205-933-7111
Facsimile: 205-930-5301
Huntsville, Alabama Office: 200 Clinton Avenue, N.W., Suite 1000.
Telephone: 205-536-1711.
Facsimile: 205-534-9650.
Mobile, Alabama Office: One St. Louis Centre, Suite 1000.
Telephone: 205-432-1671.
Facsimile: 205-434-0196.
Montgomery, Alabama Office: Colonial Commerce Center, Suite 305 One Commerce Street.
Telephone: 205-261-3400.
Facsimile: 205-261-3434.
Tuscaloosa, Alabama Office: 2216 14th Street.
Telephone: 205-752-2089.

Jerry E. Held | Kaye Houser Turberville
Charles R. Driggars | Nanette Sims

Representative Clients: International Business Machines (IBM); General Motors Corp.; Colonial Bank; Bruno's, Inc.; University of Alabama Hospitals; Westinghouse Electric Corp.; First Alabama Bank; Monsanto Chemical Company; South Central Bell; Prudential Insurance Company; American Home Products, Inc.; Minnesota Mining and Manufacturing, Inc. (3M).

For Complete List of Firm Personnel, See General Section

For full biographical listings, see the Martindale-Hubbell Law Directory

SPAIN, GILLON, GROOMS, BLAN & NETTLES (AV)
The Zinszer Building, 2117 2nd Avenue North, 35203
Telephone: 205-328-4100
Telecopier: 205-324-8866

(See Next Column)

SPAIN, GILLON, GROOMS, BLAN & NETTLES, *Birmingham—Continued*

MEMBERS OF FIRM

Bert S. Nettles — Samuel H. Frazier
Alton B. Parker, Jr.

General Counsel for: Liberty National Life Insurance Co.; United States Fidelity & Guaranty Co.; Piggly Wiggly Alabama Distributing Co.; AmSouth Mortgage Co., Inc.; Alabama Insurance Guaranty Association; Alabama Life and Disability Insurance Guaranty Association; Alabama Insurance Underwriters Association.
Counsel for: The Prudential Insurance Company of America; Government Employees Insurance Co.; Massachusetts Mutual Life Insurance Co.

For Complete List of Firm Personnel, See General Section

For full biographical listings, see the Martindale-Hubbell Law Directory

STARNES & ATCHISON (AV)

100 Brookwood Place, P.O. Box 598512, 35259-8512
Telephone: 205-868-6000
Telecopier: 205-868-6099

MEMBERS OF FIRM

W. Stancil Starnes — L. Graves Stiff, III
W. Michael Atchison — Robert P. Mackenzie, III
William Anthony Davis, III — Jeffrey E. Friedman
Thomas Lawson Selden

ASSOCIATES

Steven T. McMeekin — Joe L. Leak
Mark W. Macoy

Representative Clients: Ciba-Geigy Corp.; Wyerhaeuser, Inc.; Browning-Ferris Industries, Inc.; Nobel Insurance Co.; Drummond Co., Inc.; Mobile Infirmary Medical Center; Hoffman-La Roche, Inc.

For full biographical listings, see the Martindale-Hubbell Law Directory

*HUNTSVILLE,** Madison Co.

BRADLEY, ARANT, ROSE & WHITE (AV)

200 Clinton Avenue West, Suite 900, 35801
Telephone: 205-517-5100
Facsimile: 205-533-5069
Birmingham, Alabama Office: 1400 Park Place Tower, 2001 Park Place.
Telephone: 205-521-8000.
Telex: 494-1324.
Facsimile: 205-251-8611, 251-8665, 252-0264. Facsimile (Southtrust Office): 205-251-9915.

RESIDENT PARTNER

Patrick H. Graves, Jr.

For Complete List of Firm Personnel, See General Section

For full biographical listings, see the Martindale-Hubbell Law Directory

SIROTE & PERMUTT, P.C. (AV)

Suite 1000, 200 Clinton Avenue, N.W., 35801
Telephone: 205-536-1711
Facsimile: 205-534-9650
Birmingham, Alabama Office: 2222 Arlington Avenue, South, P.O. Box 55727.
Telephone: 205-933-7111.
Facsimile: 205-930-5301.
Mobile, Alabama Office: One St. Louis Centre, Suite 1000.
Telephone: 205-432-1671.
Facsimile: 205-434-0196.
Montgomery, Alabama Office: Colonial Commerce Center, Suite 305, One Commerce Street.
Telephone: 205-261-3400.
Facsimile: 205-261-3434.
Tuscaloosa, Alabama Office: 2216 14th Street.
Telephone: 205-752-2089.

Julian D. Butler — Roderic G. Steakley
Robert W. Ruth

For Complete List of Firm Personnel, See General Section

For full biographical listings, see the Martindale-Hubbell Law Directory

*MOBILE,** Mobile Co.

HAND, ARENDALL, BEDSOLE, GREAVES & JOHNSTON (AV)

3000 First National Bank Building, P.O. Box 123, Drawer C, 36601
Telephone: 334-432-5511
Fax: 334-694-6375
Washington, D.C. Office: 410 First Street, S.E., Suite 300. 20003.
Telephone: 202-863-0053.
Fax: 202-863-0096.

(See Next Column)

MEMBERS OF FIRM

William Alexander Moseley — Neil C. Johnston
T. Bruce McGowin

General Counsel for: The Bank of Mobile; Delchamps, Inc.; The Mobile Press Register, Inc.; Mobile Asphalt Company; Gulf Telephone Company; Folmar & Associates; Mobile Community Foundation; Gulf Lumber Company; Scotch Lumber Company; Mobile Pulley & Machine Works, Inc.; Pennsylvania Shipbuilding Co.

For Complete List of Firm Personnel, See General Section

For full biographical listings, see the Martindale-Hubbell Law Directory

JOHNSTONE, ADAMS, BAILEY, GORDON AND HARRIS (AV)

Royal St. Francis Building, 104 St. Francis Street, P.O. Box 1988, 36633
Telephone: 334-432-7682
Facsimile: 334-432-2800
Telex: 782040

MEMBERS OF FIRM

Brock B. Gordon — Ben H. Harris, Jr.
Alan C. Christian

General Counsel for: First Alabama Bank, Mobile; Infirmary Health System/Mobile Infirmary Medical Center/Rotary Rehabilitation Hospital (Multi-Hospital System).
Counsel for: Oil and Gas: Exxon Corp. Business and Corporate: Bell South Telecommunications, Inc.; Aluminum Co. of America; Michelin Tire Corp.; Metropolitan Life Insurance Co.; The Travelers Insurance Cos. Marine: The West of England Ship Owners Mutual Protection and Indemnity Association (Luxembourg); The Standard Steamship Owners' Protection and Indemnity Association (Bermuda) Ltd.

For Complete List of Firm Personnel, See General Section

For full biographical listings, see the Martindale-Hubbell Law Directory

LYONS, PIPES & COOK, P.C. (AV)

2 North Royal Street, P.O. Box 2727, 36652-2727
Telephone: 334-432-4481
Cable Address: "Lysea"
Telecopier: 334-433-1820

G. Sage Lyons — Walter M. Cook, Jr.
Wesley Pipes — John Patrick Courtney, III
Norton W. Brooker, Jr. — W. David Johnson, Jr.

Representative Clients: Esenjay Petroleum Corporation; Shell Oil Company; Spectacor Management Group.

For Complete List of Firm Personnel, See General Section

For full biographical listings, see the Martindale-Hubbell Law Directory

SIROTE & PERMUTT, P.C. (AV)

One St. Louis Centre, Suite 1000, P.O. Drawer 2025, 36652-2025
Telephone: 334-432-1671
Facsimile: 334-434-0196
Birmingham, Alabama Office: 2222 Arlington Avenue, South, P.O. Box 55727.
Telephone: 205-933-7111.
Facsimile: 205-930-5301.
Huntsville, Alabama Office: 200 Clinton Avenue, N.W., Suite 1000.
Telephone: 205-536-1711.
Facsimile: 205-534-9650.
Montgomery, Alabama Office: Colonial Commerce Center, Suite 305, One Commerce Street.
Telephone: 205-261-3400.
Facsimile: 205-261-3434.
Tuscaloosa, Alabama Office: 2216 14th Street.
Telephone: 205-752-2089.

Joseph P. Jones, Jr.

For Complete List of Firm Personnel, See General Section

For full biographical listings, see the Martindale-Hubbell Law Directory

VICKERS, RIIS, MURRAY AND CURRAN (AV)

8th Floor, First Alabama Bank Building, P.O. Box 2568, 36652
Telephone: 334-432-9772
Fax: 334-432-9781

MEMBERS OF FIRM

Edwin J. Curran, Jr. — Thomas E. Sharp, III
J. Marshall Gardner

Representative Clients: Dravo Natural Resources Co.; Midstream Fuel Services; John E. Graham & Sons; McPhillips Manufacturing Co.; Spring Hill College; Steiner Shipyard, Inc.; Homeowners Marketing Services, Inc.; Marine Office of America Corp.; Cummins Alabama, Inc.; Ben M. Radcliff Contractor, Inc.

For Complete List of Firm Personnel, See General Section

For full biographical listings, see the Martindale-Hubbell Law Directory

*MONTGOMERY,** Montgomery Co.

* indicates certain Bar Register subscribers whose principal office is located elsewhere in the state and who have arranged for representation as a part of the state capital listings that follow

*** BALCH & BINGHAM (AV)**

The Winter Building, 2 Dexter Avenue, P.O. Box 78, 36101
Telephone: 334-834-6500
Facsimile: 334-269-3115
Birmingham, Alabama Offices: 1710 Sixth Avenue North, 35203.
Telephone: 205-251-8100.
Facsimile: 205-226-8798. 1901 Sixth Avenue North, 35203.
Telephone: 205-251-8100.
Facsimile: 205-226-8799.
Huntsville, Alabama Office: Suite 810, 200 West Court Square, 35801.
Telephone: 205-551-0171.
Facsimile: 205-551-0174.
Washington, D.C. Office: Suite 800, 1101 Connecticut Avenue, N.W., 20036.
Telephone: 202-296-0387.
Facsimile: 202-452-8180.

RESIDENT MEMBERS OF FIRM

Maury D. Smith
James A. Byram, Jr.
Dorman Walker

Counsel for: Alabama Power Co.; Alabama River Pulp Co., Inc.; Blue Cross and Blue Shield of Alabama; Brasfield & Gorrie, Inc.; Compass Bancshares, Inc.; Harbert Corp.; Kimberly-Clark Corp.; National Energy Partners; Southern Company Services, Inc.; Southern Research Institute.

For Complete List of Firm Personnel, See General Section

For full biographical listings, see the Martindale-Hubbell Law Directory

NIX, HOLTSFORD & VERCELLI, P.C. (AV)

A Water Street, Suite 300, P.O. Box 4128, 36103
Telephone: 334-262-2006
Fax: 334-834-3616

H. E. Nix, Jr.

Floyd R. Gilliland

Representative Clients: Alabama Chemical Association; Alabama League of Municipalities; Coastal Chemical Co.; Dupont Chemical Co.; Gay & Taylor; Tennessee Farmers Cooperative; Terra International; Ranger Insurance Co.; United States Fidelity & Guaranty Co.

For full biographical listings, see the Martindale-Hubbell Law Directory

ARIZONA

*PHOENIX,** Maricopa Co.

BESS & DYSART, P.C. (AV)

7210 North 16th Street, 82020-5201
Telephone: 602-331-4600
Telecopier: 602-331-8600

Robert L. Dysart
William M. Demlong

For full biographical listings, see the Martindale-Hubbell Law Directory

BROWN & BAIN, A PROFESSIONAL ASSOCIATION (AV)

2901 North Central Avenue, P.O. Box 400, 85001-0400
Telephone: 602-351-8000
Cable: TWX 910-951-0646
Telecopier: 602-351-8516
Palo Alto, California Affiliated Office: Brown & Bain, 600 Hansen Way.
Telephone: 415-856-9411.
Telecopier: 415-856-6061.
Tucson, Arizona Affiliated Office: Brown & Bain, A Professional Association. One South Church Avenue, Nineteenth Floor, P.O. Box 2265.
Telephone: 602-798-7900
Telecopier: 602-798-7945.

Paul F. Eckstein
Christopher R. Ottenweller
(Resident at Palo Alto Office)
Stephen A. Owens
Michael W. Patten
Lawrence G. D. Scarborough
Kim E. Williamson

For Complete List of Firm Personnel, See General Section

For full biographical listings, see the Martindale-Hubbell Law Directory

BURCH & CRACCHIOLO, P.A. (AV)

702 East Osborn Road, Suite 200, 85014
Telephone: 602-274-7611
Fax: 602-234-0341
Mailing Address: P.O. Box 16882, Phoenix, AZ, 85011

Daniel Cracchiolo
Edwin D. Fleming
Ralph D. Harris

Josephine Cuccurullo

Representative Clients: Bashas' Inc.; Farmers Insurance Group; U-Haul International, Inc.

For Complete List of Firm Personnel, See General Section

For full biographical listings, see the Martindale-Hubbell Law Directory

DAUGHTON, HAWKINS, BROCKELMAN, GUINAN & PATTERSON (AV)

40 North Central Avenue, Suite 2500, 85004
Telephone: 602-271-4400
Fax: 602-271-4300

Donald Daughton
Michael D. Hawkins
Kent Brockelman
Michael D. Guinan
Bart J. Patterson
Leslie Kyman Cooper

For Complete List of Firm Personnel, See General Section

For full biographical listings, see the Martindale-Hubbell Law Directory

FENNEMORE CRAIG, A PROFESSIONAL CORPORATION (AV)

Two North Central, Suite 2200, 85004
Telephone: 602-257-8700
Fax: 602-257-8527
Scottsdale, Arizona Office: 6263 North Scottsdale Road, Suite 290, 85250.
Telephone: 602-257-5400.
Fax: 602-945-4932.
Tucson, Arizona Office: One South Church Avenue, Suite 1030, 85701.
Telephone: 602-624-9312.
Fax: 602-882-7383.

C. Webb Crockett
John D. Everroad
James W. Johnson
Phillip F. Fargotstein
Douglas E. McAllister
Christopher L. Callahan
Robert D. Anderson

Scott H. Thomas
Douglas C. Northup
Richard A. Bark
Marc H. Lamber

Representative Clients: ASARCO Incorporated; AT&T Communications; Bridgestone/Firestone, Inc.; Catellus Development Corp.; Citibank (Arizona); First Interstate Bank of Arizona; GIANT Industries; Phelps Dodge Corporation; The Atchison, Topeka & Santa Fe Railway, Co.; US WEST Communications.

For Complete List of Firm Personnel, See General Section

For full biographical listings, see the Martindale-Hubbell Law Directory

JENNINGS, STROUSS AND SALMON, P.L.C. (AV)

A Professional Limited Liability Company
One Renaissance Square, Two North Central, 85004-2393
Telephone: 602-262-5911
Fax: 602-253-3255

M. Byron Lewis
James D. Vieregg
Richard N. Morrison
Joseph A. Drazek
Stephen E. Crofton
George Esahak-Gage
Lisa M. McKnight

Mark A. McGinnis

For Complete List of Firm Personnel, See General Section

For full biographical listings, see the Martindale-Hubbell Law Directory

KIMBALL & CURRY, P.C. (AV)

2600 North Central Avenue Suite 1600, 85004
Telephone: 602-222-5920
Fax: 602-222-5929

David P. Kimball, III
J. Stanton Curry
Dalva L. Moellenberg
Laura W. Janzik
David L. Wallis
Todd W. Rallison
John C. Giles
D. Lee Decker
Cameron T. Chandler
Walter E. Rusinek
Lisa A. Schuh
(Not admitted in AZ)
Karilee S. Ramaley
Mara G. Linder

Representative Clients: Phelps Dodge Corp.; Talley Industries, Inc.; Arizona Public Service Co.; Motorola, Inc.; Reynolds Metals Co.; Kaibab Industries; U-Haul International, Inc.; Cyprus Amax Minerals Co.; United Industrial Corp.; Southern Pacific Transportation Co.

(See Next Column)

KIMBALL & CURRY P.C., *Phoenix—Continued*

For full biographical listings, see the Martindale-Hubbell Law Directory

LEWIS AND ROCA (AV)

A Partnership including Professional Corporations
40 North Central Avenue, 85004-4429
Telephone: 602-262-5311
Fax: 602-262-5747
Tucson, Arizona Office: One South Church Avenue, Suite 700.
Telephone: 602-622-2090.
Fax: 602-622-3088.

MEMBERS OF FIRM

Edward F. Novak
Newman R. Porter
Amy R. Porter
John N. Iurino (Resident, Tucson Office)
James K. Kloss
Steven J. Burr

ASSOCIATES

Charles W. Steese
Deanna Salazar
Lynn Robbins Wagner
Noël Moran Vickers
Joni M. Wallace (Resident, Tucson Office)

Representative Clients: Arizona Hospital Association; ASARCO Incorporated; Cyprus Minerals Company; Digital Equipment; Intel Corporation; Lockheed Aeromod Center, Inc.; Woodstuff Manufacturing.

For Complete List of Firm Personnel, See General Section

For full biographical listings, see the Martindale-Hubbell Law Directory

MEYER, HENDRICKS, VICTOR, OSBORN & MALEDON, A PROFESSIONAL ASSOCIATION (AV)

2929 North Central Avenue Suite 2100, 85012-2794
Telephone: 602-640-9000
Facsimile: (24 Hrs.) 602-640-9050
Mailing Address: P.O. Box 33449, 85067-3449,

Larry A. Hammond
Robert L. Palmer
Jay I. Moyes
David G. Campbell
James G. Derouin
Jeffrey C. Zimmerman
W. Scott Bales
Shane R. Swindle
David K. Duncan
Sigmund G. Popko
Lee Herold Storey

Trevor A. Brown
Joan S. Burke

Reference: Bank One Arizona, NA.

For Complete List of Firm Personnel, See General Section

For full biographical listings, see the Martindale-Hubbell Law Directory

O'CONNOR, CAVANAGH, ANDERSON, WESTOVER, KILLINGSWORTH & BESHEARS, A PROFESSIONAL ASSOCIATION (AV)

One East Camelback Road, Suite 1100, 85012-1656
Telephone: 602-263-2400
FAX: 602-263-2900
Sun City, Arizona Office: 13250 North Del Webb Boulevard, Suite B, 85351.
Telephone: 602-263-2808.
FAX: 602-933-3100.
Tucson, Arizona Office: Suite 2200, One South Church Avenue, 85701.
Telephone: 602-882-8912.
FAX: 602-624-9564.
Nogales, Arizona Office: 1827 North Mastick Way, 85621.
Telephone: 602-761-4215.
FAX: 602-761-3505.

Richard J. Woods
Scott A. Salmon

Lucas J. Narducci

Troy B. Froderman
Carla A. Wortley
Eric A. Mark

Representative Clients: ITT Cannon; W.P.P., Inc.; Chemical Waste Management, Inc.; Granite Construction Company; City of Nogales; Continental Waste; Sentry Insurance and Great American Insurance Co.; Home Insurance Co.; Citation Insurance Co.

For Complete List of Firm Personnel, See General Section

For full biographical listings, see the Martindale-Hubbell Law Directory

SNELL & WILMER (AV)

One Arizona Center, 85004-0001
Telephone: 602-382-6000
Fax: 602-382-6070
Tucson, Arizona Office: 1500 Norwest Tower, One South Church Avenue 85701-1612.
Telephone: 602-882-1200.
Fax: 602-884-1294.
Orange County Office: 1920 Main Street, Suite 1200, P.O. Box 19601, Irvine, California, 92714.
Telephone: 714-253-2700.
Fax: 714-955-2507.
Salt Lake City, Utah Office: Broadway Centre, 111 East Broadway, Suite 900, 84111.
Telephone: 801-237-1900.
Fax: 801-237-1950.

MEMBERS OF FIRM

Steven M. Wheeler
Martha E. Gibbs
Richard W. Shapiro
E. Jeffrey Walsh

ASSOCIATES

Jeffrey Webb Crockett
Thomas L. Mumaw
Clinton J Elliott
Carlos D. Ronstadt
Steve C. Thornton

Representative Clients: Arizona Public Service Co.; Bank One, Arizona, NA.; First Security Bank of Utah, N.A.; Ford Motor Co.; Chrysler Motors Corp.; Toyota Motor Sales U.S.A.; Magma Copper Co.; U.S. Home Corp.; Pinnacle West Capital Corp.; Safeway, Inc.

For Complete List of Firm Personnel, See General Section

For full biographical listings, see the Martindale-Hubbell Law Directory

STREICH LANG, A PROFESSIONAL ASSOCIATION (AV)

Renaissance One, Two N. Central Avenue, 85004-2391
Telephone: 602-229-5200
Fax: 602-229-5690
Tucson, Arizona Office: One S. Church Avenue, Suite 1700.
Telephone: 602-770-8700.
Fax: 602-623-2518.
Las Vegas, Nevada Affiliated Office: Dawson & Associates, 3800 Howard Hughes Parkway, Suite 1500.
Telephone: 702-792-2727.
Fax: 702-792-2676.
Los Angeles, California Office: 444 S. Flower Street, Suite 1530.
Telephone: 213-896-0484.

Steven A. Betts
Roger K. Ferland

OF COUNSEL

Randall S. Theisen

Lance L. Shea
Dana Stagg Belknap

Representative Clients: Allied-Signal Aerospace Company; America West Airlines, Inc.; Atlantic Richfield Co.; Chicago Title; First Interstate Bank of Arizona, N.A.; Magma Copper Co.; Motorola, Inc.; Phelps Dodge Development Corp.; TRW Inc.; The Travelers Companies.

For Complete List of Firm Personnel, See General Section

For full biographical listings, see the Martindale-Hubbell Law Directory

SCOTTSDALE, Maricopa Co.

SPARKS & SILER, P.C. (AV)

7503 First Street, 85251-4573
Telephone: 602-949-1339
Fax: 602-949-7587

Joe P. Sparks

Kevin T. Tehan
John H. Ryley

References: Bank One, Arizona, Trust Department; Northern Trust Bank of Arizona, N.A.; First Interstate Bank of Arizona; Bank of America, Arizona, Trust Department.

For full biographical listings, see the Martindale-Hubbell Law Directory

*TUCSON,** Pima Co.

O'CONNOR, CAVANAGH, ANDERSON, WESTOVER, KILLINGSWORTH & BESHEARS, A PROFESSIONAL ASSOCIATION (AV)

Suite 2200 One South Church Avenue, 85701-1621
Telephone: 602-882-8912
FAX: 602-624-9564
Phoenix, Arizona Office: One East Camelback Road, Suite 1100, 85012.
Telephone: 602-263-2400.
FAX: 602-263-2900.
Sun City, Arizona Office: 13250 North Del Webb Boulevard, Suite B, 85351.
Telephone: 602-263-2808.
FAX: 602-933-3100.

(See Next Column)

O'CONNOR, CAVANAGH, ANDERSON, WESTOVER, KILLINGSWORTH & BESHEARS A PROFESSIONAL ASSOCIATION—*Continued*

Nogales, Arizona Office: 1827 North Mastick Way, 85621.
Telephone: 602-761-4215.
FAX: 602-761-3505.

Bruce R. Heurlin

Gregory E. Good

Representative Clients: Jeffco, Inc.; Hughes Aircraft.
Reference: Citibank.

For Complete List of Firm Personnel, See General Section

For full biographical listings, see the Martindale-Hubbell Law Directory

CALIFORNIA

APTOS, Santa Cruz Co.

DENNIS J. KEHOE A LAW CORPORATION (AV)

311 Bonita Drive, 95003
Telephone: 408-662-8444
Fax: 408-662-0227

Dennis J. Kehoe

For full biographical listings, see the Martindale-Hubbell Law Directory

*BAKERSFIELD,** Kern Co.

KLEIN, WEGIS, DENATALE, GOLDNER & MUIR (AV)

A Partnership including Professional Corporations
(Formerly Di Giorgio, Davis, Klein, Wegis, Duggan & Friedman)
ARCO Tower, 4550 California Avenue, Second Floor, P.O. Box 11172, 93389-1172
Telephone: 805-395-1000
Telecopier: 805-326-0418
Santa Ana, California Office: Park Tower Building #610, 200 W. Santa Ana Boulevard, 92701.
Telephone: 714-285-0711.
Fax: 714-285-9003.

MEMBERS OF FIRM

Anthony J. Klein (Inc.) David J. Cooper

ASSOCIATES

Manning W. Puette Christopher P. Burger
Melvin L. Ehrlich

Representative Clients: JACO Oil Company; City of Visalia; City of Farmersville; Destec, Inc.; Sandyland Nursery; Boggiato Produce, Inc.

For Complete List of Firm Personnel, See General Section

For full biographical listings, see the Martindale-Hubbell Law Directory

CARLSBAD, San Diego Co.

GATZKE, MISPAGEL & DILLON (AV)

A Partnership including a Professional Law Corporation
Suite 200, 1921 Palomar Oaks Way, P.O. Box 1636, 92009
Telephone: 619-431-9501
Fax: 619-431-9512

MEMBERS OF FIRM

Michael Scott Gatzke (A Professional Law Corporation) Mark F. Mispagel
Mark J. Dillon
Lori D. Ballance

ASSOCIATES

David P. Hubbard Kristin Beth White

For full biographical listings, see the Martindale-Hubbell Law Directory

COSTA MESA, Orange Co.

MCCORMICK, KIDMAN & BEHRENS (AV)

A Partnership of Professional Corporations
Imperial Bank Building, 695 Town Center Drive Suite 1400, 92626-1924
Telephone: 714-755-3100
Fax: 714-755-3110

MEMBERS OF FIRM

Homer L. (Mike) McCormick, Jr., (P.C.) Suzanne M. Tague (P.C.)
Arthur G. Kidman (P.C.) Michael D. Michaels (P.C.)
Russell G. Behrens (P.C.) Janet R. Morningstar (P.C.)
Douglas J. Evertz (P.C.)

(See Next Column)

ASSOCIATES

Keith E. McCullough Allison C. Hargrave
Frank W. Battaile

For full biographical listings, see the Martindale-Hubbell Law Directory

RUTAN & TUCKER (AV)

A Partnership including Professional Corporations
611 Anton Boulevard, Suite 1400, P.O. Box 1950, 92626
Telephone: 714-641-5100; 213-625-7586
Telecopier: 714-546-9035

MEMBERS OF FIRM

Michael D. Rubin Elizabeth L. (Hanna) Dixon
Richard Montevideo Kim D. Thompson

For Complete List of Firm Personnel, See General Section

For full biographical listings, see the Martindale-Hubbell Law Directory

*FRESNO,** Fresno Co.

DOWLING, MAGARIAN, AARON & HEYMAN, INCORPORATED (AV)

Suite 200, 6051 North Fresno Street, 93710
Telephone: 209-432-4500
Fax: 209-432-4590

Philip David Kopp

Francine Marie Kanne Christopher A. Brown

Reference: Wells Fargo Bank (Main).

For Complete List of Firm Personnel, See General Section

For full biographical listings, see the Martindale-Hubbell Law Directory

KIMBLE, MACMICHAEL & UPTON, A PROFESSIONAL CORPORATION (AV)

Fig Garden Financial Center, 5260 North Palm Avenue, Suite 221, P.O. Box 9489, 93792-9489
Telephone: 209-435-5500
Telecopier: 209-435-1500

Joseph C. Kimble (1910-1972)
Thomas A. MacMichael (1920-1990)
Jon Wallace Upton
Robert E. Bergin
Jeffrey G. Boswell
Steven D. McGee
Robert E. Ward
John P. Eleazarian
Robert H. Scribner
Michael E. Moss
David D. Doyle
Mark D. Miller
Michael F. Tatham
W. Richard Lee
D. Tyler Tharpe
Sylvia Halkousis Coyle

Michael J. Jurkovich
S. Brett Sutton
Douglas V. Thornton
Robert William Branch
Brian N. Folland
Christopher L. Wanger
Elise M. Krause
Donald J. Pool
Susan King Hatmaker

For full biographical listings, see the Martindale-Hubbell Law Directory

LANG, RICHERT & PATCH, A PROFESSIONAL CORPORATION (AV)

Fig Garden Financial Center, 5200 North Palm Avenue, 4th Floor, P.O. Box 40012, 93755
Telephone: 209-228-6700
Fax: 209-228-6727

Frank H. Lang
William T. Richert (1937-1993)
Robert L. Patch, II
Val W. Saldaña
Douglas E. Noll
Michael T. Hertz
Victoria J. Salisch
Bradley A. Silva
David R. Jenkins
Charles Trudrung Taylor
Mark L. Creede
Peter N. Zeitler
Charles L. Doerksen

Randall C. Nelson
Barbara A. McAuliffe
Laurie Quigley Cardot
Douglas E. Griffin
Nabil E. Zumout

References: Wells Fargo Bank (Fresno Main Office); First Interstate Bank (Fresno Main Office).

For full biographical listings, see the Martindale-Hubbell Law Directory

GLENDALE, Los Angeles Co.

BRIGHT AND BROWN (AV)

550 North Brand Boulevard, Suite 2100, 91203
Telephone: 818-243-2121; 213-489-1414
Facsimile: 818-243-3225

(See Next Column)

BRIGHT AND BROWN, *Glendale—Continued*

James S. Bright
Gregory C. Brown
Maureen J. Bright
John Quirk
Brian L. Becker
Anthony S. Brill
Simon Liversidge

For full biographical listings, see the Martindale-Hubbell Law Directory

IRVINE, Orange Co.

BROWN, PISTONE, HURLEY, VAN VLEAR & SELTZER, A PROFESSIONAL CORPORATION (AV)

Suite 900 AT&T Building, 8001 Irvine Center Drive, 92718
Telephone: 714-727-0559
Fax: 714-727-0656
Tempe, Arizona Office: 1501 West Fountainhead Parkway, Suite 540.
Telephone: 602-968-2427.
Fax: 602-968-2401.
San Francisco, California Office: Suite 1300, Steuart Street Tower, One Market Plaza.
Telephone: 415-281-2154.
Fax: 415-281-2194.

Ernest C. Brown
Thomas A. Pistone
Gregory F. Hurley
John E. Van Vlear
Margaret A. Seltzer (Resident, San Francisco Office)

Michael K. Wolder
Francis T. Donohue, III
Kedric L. Francis
Michael W. Foster (Resident, Tempe, Arizona Office)
Robert C. Schneider (Resident, Tempe, Arizona Office)
Sarah Namnama Saria
Sheila Patterson
Michael Ray Gandee

OF COUNSEL

Robert G. Mahan
Stephen M. Wontrobski
Brian A. Runkel (Not admitted in CA)

For full biographical listings, see the Martindale-Hubbell Law Directory

CALLAHAN & GAUNTLETT (AV)

A Partnership including a Professional Corporation
Suite 800, 18500 Von Karman, 92715
Telephone: 714-553-1155
Fax: 714-553-0784

Daniel J. Callahan (A Professional Corporation)
David A. Gauntlett

ASSOCIATES

Stephen E. Blaine
David A. Stall
J. Craig Williams
Jim P. Mahacek
Leo E. Lundberg, Jr.
Michael J. Sachs
Michael Danton Richardson
Craig E. Lindberg
Edward Susolik
Carol L. Meedon
Andrew A. Smits

OF COUNSEL

Gary L. Hinman
Walt D. Mahaffa
Jose Zorrilla, Jr.
H. Thomas Hicks

For full biographical listings, see the Martindale-Hubbell Law Directory

LAW OFFICES OF SUSAN M. TRAGER A PROFESSIONAL CORPORATION (AV)

The Landmark Building, Suite 104, 2100 S. E. Main Street, 92714
Telephone: 714-752-8971
Telefax: 714-863-9804

Susan M. Trager

Robert C. Hawkins
Michele A. Staples
Larry B. McKenney

Representative Client: San Luis Rey Municipal Water District.
Reference: Sanwa Bank California.

For full biographical listings, see the Martindale-Hubbell Law Directory

WATT, TIEDER & HOFFAR (AV⑦)

3 Park Plaza, Suite 1530, 92714
Telephone: 714-852-6700
Telecopier: 714-261-0771
McLean Virginia Office: 7929 Westpark Drive, Suite 400,
Telephone: 703-749-1000.
Telex: 248797 WATTR.
Telecopier: 703-893-8029.
Washington, D.C. Office: 601 Pennsylvania Avenue, N.W. Suite 900,
Telephone: 202-462-4697.

MEMBERS OF FIRM

John B. Tieder, Jr. (Not admitted in CA)
Robert M. Fitzgerald (Not admitted in CA)
Michael G. Long

(See Next Column)

ASSOCIATE

Christopher P. Pappas

For full biographical listings, see the Martindale-Hubbell Law Directory

LONG BEACH, Los Angeles Co.

FISHER & PORTER, A LAW CORPORATION (AV)

110 Pine Avenue, 11th Floor, P.O. Box 22686, 90801-5686
Telephone: 310-435-5626
Telex: 284549 FPKLAW UR
Fax: 310-432-5399

Gerald M. Fisher
David S. Porter
Therese G. Groff
Michael W. Lodwick
Frank C. Brucculeri

George P. Hassapis
Stephen Chace Bass
Robert M. White, Jr.
Paul J. Rubino
Steven Y. Otera
Jay Russell Sever
Vicki L. Hassman
Linda A. Mancini

OF COUNSEL

Stephen C. Klausen

For full biographical listings, see the Martindale-Hubbell Law Directory

TAUBMAN, SIMPSON, YOUNG & SULENTOR (AV)

Suite 700 Home Savings Building, 249 East Ocean Boulevard, P.O. Box 22670, 90801
Telephone: 310-436-9201
FAX: 310-590-9695

E. C. Denio (1864-1952)
Geo. A. Hart (1881-1967)
Geo. P. Taubman, Jr. (1897-1970)
Matthew C. Simpson (1900-1988)
Richard G. Wilson (1928-1993)
Roger W. Young
William J. Sulentor
Peter M. Williams
Scott R. Magee
Valerie K. de Martino
Maria M. Rohaidy

Attorneys for: Bixby Land Co.; Renick Cadillac, Inc.; Oil Operators Incorporated.
Local Counsel: Crown Cork & Seal Co., Inc.

For full biographical listings, see the Martindale-Hubbell Law Directory

*LOS ANGELES,** Los Angeles Co.

BAKER & HOSTETLER (AV)

600 Wilshire Boulevard, 90017-3212
Telephone: 213-624-2400
FAX: 213-975-1740
In Cleveland, Ohio, 3200 National City Center, 1900 East Ninth Street. Telephone: 216-621-0200.
In Columbus, Ohio, Capitol Square, Suite 2100, 65 East State Street. Telephone: 614-228-1541.
In Denver, Colorado, 303 East 17th Avenue, Suite 1100. Telephone: 303-861-0600.
In Houston, Texas, 1000 Louisiana, Suite 2000. Telephone: 713-236-0020.
In Long Beach, California: 300 Oceangate, Suite 620.
Telephone: 310-432-2827.
In Orlando, Florida, SunBank Center, Suite 2300, 200 South Orange Avenue. Telephone: 407-649-4000.
In Washington, D. C., Washington Square, Suite 1100, 1050 Connecticut Avenue, N. W. Telephone: 202-861-1500.
In College Park, Maryland, 9658 Baltimore Boulevard, Suite 206. Telephone: 301-441-2781.
In Alexandria, Virginia, 437 North Lee Street. Telephone: 703-549-1294.
In San Francisco, California: One Sansome Street, Suite 2000.
Telephone: 415-951-4705.

PARTNERS

Donna R. Black
John C. Mueller

ASSOCIATES

Bradley R. Hogin
Marc I. Seltzer
Gregory D. Trimarche

For Complete List of Firm Personnel, See General Section

For full biographical listings, see the Martindale-Hubbell Law Directory

CLARK & TREVITHICK, A PROFESSIONAL CORPORATION (AV)

800 Wilshire Boulevard, 12th Floor, 90017
Telephone: 213-629-5700
Telecopier: 213-624-9441

Philip W. Bartenetti
Dolores Cordell
Vincent Tricarico
Leonard Brazil
Arturo Santana Jr.
Kerry T. Ryan

References: Wells Fargo Bank (Los Angeles Main Office); National Bank of California.

For Complete List of Firm Personnel, See General Section

For full biographical listings, see the Martindale-Hubbell Law Directory

Los Angeles—Continued

DEMETRIOU, DEL GUERCIO, SPRINGER & MOYER (AV)

801 South Grand Avenue, 10th Floor, 90017
Telephone: 213-624-8407
Telecopy: 213-624-0174

MEMBERS OF FIRM

Ronald J. Del Guercio
Craig A. Moyer
Michael A. Francis
Regina Liudzius Cobb
Jennifer M. Burman
Kermit D. Marsh
Priscilla Fritz Adler
Leslie M. Smario
Kelly A. Sakir

Reference: Bank of America, L.A. Main Office, Los Angeles, Calif.

For full biographical listings, see the Martindale-Hubbell Law Directory

HANNA AND MORTON (AV)

A Partnership including Professional Corporations
Seventeenth Floor, Wilshire-Grand Building, 600 Wilshire Boulevard, 90017
Telephone: 213-628-7131

MEMBERS OF FIRM

Edward S. Renwick (A Professional Corporation)
James P. Lower
David A. Ossentjuk

OF COUNSEL

Bela G. Lugosi (A Professional Corporation)

ASSOCIATES

Stephen G. Mason
Robert J. Roche
Allison L. Malin

Representative Clients: Atlantic Richfield Co.; Air Liquide America Corp.; Carrier Corp.; Conservation Committee of California Oil & Gas Producers; Mobil Oil Corp.; Occidental Petroleum Corp.; Shell Oil Corp.; Texaco, Inc.; Union Pacific Resources Co.; Unocal.

For Complete List of Firm Personnel, See General Section

For full biographical listings, see the Martindale-Hubbell Law Directory

HORNBERGER & CRISWELL (AV)

444 South Flower, 31st Floor, 90071
Telephone: 213-488-1655
Facsimile: 213-488-1255

MEMBERS OF FIRM

Nicholas W. Hornberger
Leslie E. Criswell
Carla J. Feldman
Ann M. Ghazarians
Michael A. Brewer

ASSOCIATES

Scott Alan Freedman
Marlin E. Howes
Christopher T. Olsen
Scott B. Cloud
Celeste S. Makuta
John Shaffery
Charles I. Karlin
K. Christopher Branch
David F. Berry
James M. Slominski
Gina T. Sponzilli

For full biographical listings, see the Martindale-Hubbell Law Directory

HUFSTEDLER & KAUS (AV)

A Partnership including Professional Corporations
Thirty-Ninth Floor, 355 South Grand Avenue, 90071-3101
Telephone: 213-617-7070
Fax: 213-617-6170

MEMBERS OF FIRM

Seth M. Hufstedler (Professional Corporation)
Shirley M. Hufstedler (Professional Corporation)
Otto M. Kaus
John Sobieski
Burton J. Gindler
Thomas J. Ready (Professional Corporation)
Patricia Dominis Phillips
John P. Olson
Margot A. Metzner
Leonard L. Gumport
Dan Marmalefsky
Gary Plessman
Michael V. Toumanoff
Susan I. Schutzbank Montgomery
Mark R. McDonald

ASSOCIATES

John W. (Jack) Alden Jr.
David K. Barrett
Eliot F. Krieger

Reference: First Interstate Bank, 707 Wilshire.

For Complete List of Firm Personnel, See General Section

For full biographical listings, see the Martindale-Hubbell Law Directory

LOEB AND LOEB (AV)

A Partnership including Professional Corporations
Suite 1800, 1000 Wilshire Boulevard, 90017-2475
Telephone: 213-688-3400
Telecopier: 213-688-3460; 688-3461; 688-3462
Century City, California Office: Suite 2200, 10100 Santa Monica Boulevard, Los Angeles, 90067-4164.
Telephone: 310-282-2000.
Telecopier: 310-282-2191; 282-2192.
New York, N.Y. Office: 345 Park Avenue, 10154-0037.
Telephone: 212-407-4000.
Facsimile: 212-407-4990.
Nashville, Tennessee Office: 45 Music Square West, 37203-3205.
Telephone: 615-749-8300;
Facsimile: 615-749-8308.
Rome, Italy Office: Piazza Digione 1, 00197.
Telephone: 011-396-808-8456.
Telecopier: 011-396-674-8223.

MEMBERS OF FIRM

Malissa Hathaway McKeith
Raymond W. Thomas (Century City Office)

ASSOCIATE

Nina B. Luban

For Complete List of Firm Personnel, See General Section

For full biographical listings, see the Martindale-Hubbell Law Directory

MITCHELL, SILBERBERG & KNUPP (AV)

A Partnership of Professional Corporations
11377 West Olympic Boulevard, 90064
Telephone: 310-312-2000
Cable Address: "Silmitch"
Telex: 69-1347
Telecopier: 310-312-3200

MEMBERS OF FIRM

Marvin Leon (A Professional Corporation)
Arthur Fine (A Professional Corporation)
John E. Hatherley (A Professional Corporation)

OF COUNSEL

Douglas W. Bordewieck

Reference: First Interstate Bank of California (Headquarters, Los Angeles, California).

For Complete List of Firm Personnel, See General Section

For full biographical listings, see the Martindale-Hubbell Law Directory

REZNIK & REZNIK, A LAW CORPORATION (AV)

15456 Ventura Boulevard, Fifth Floor (Sherman Oaks), 91403-3023
Telephone: 818-907-9898; 213-872-2900
Telecopier: 818-907-8465

Benjamin M. Reznik
Janice M. Kamenir-Reznik
Penny Grosz-Salomon
Alan J. Kheel
Fred N. Gaines

John M. Bowman
Kenneth A. Ehrlich
Barak S. Platt
Jeffrey S. Raskin
William M. Samoska
Mary Lansberg Watkins

LEGAL SUPPORT PERSONNEL

PARALEGALS

Theresa Saunders
Christine R. Langteau
Serena A. Burnett

Representative Clients: MCA Development Company (subsidiary of MCA); Citicorp Real Estate, Inc. (subsidiary of Citicorp); Service Corporation International, New York Stock Exchange; BET Plant Services; Tokai Credit Corporation (subsidiary of Tokai Bank); Weyerhaeuser; RTC (Resolution Trust Corporation).

For full biographical listings, see the Martindale-Hubbell Law Directory

NEWPORT BEACH, Orange Co.

DAVIS, PUNELLI, KEATHLEY & WILLARD (AV)

610 Newport Center Drive, Suite 1000, P.O. Box 7920, 92658-7920
Telephone: 714-640-0700
Telecopier: 714-640-0714
San Diego, California Office: 4370 La Jolla Village Drive, Suite 300.
Telephone: 619-558-2581.

MEMBERS OF FIRM

Robert E. Willard
S. Eric Davis
Frank Punelli, Jr.
H. James Keathley
Leonard R. Sager
Eric G. Anderson
Katherine D. O'Brian

(See Next Column)

DAVIS, PUNELLI, KEATHLEY & WILLARD, *Newport Beach—Continued*

OF COUNSEL

Lewis K. Uhler

For full biographical listings, see the Martindale-Hubbell Law Directory

*OAKLAND,** Alameda Co.

HAIMS, JOHNSON, MACGOWAN & MCINERNEY (AV)

490 Grand Avenue, 94610
Telephone: 510-835-0500
Facsimile: 510-835-2833

MEMBERS OF FIRM

Arnold B. Haims
Gary R. Johnson
Clyde L. MacGowan
Thomas McInerney
Lawrence A. Baker
Randy M. Marmor
John K. Kirby
Robert J. Frassetto
Caroline N. Valentino

ASSOCIATES

Joseph Y. Ahn
Edward D. Baldwin
Kathleen B. Boehm
Marc P. Bouret
Anne M. Michaels
Dianne D. Peebles
Michelle D. Perry
Edward C. Schroeder, Jr.

For full biographical listings, see the Martindale-Hubbell Law Directory

HARDIN, COOK, LOPER, ENGEL & BERGEZ (AV)

1999 Harrison Street, 18th Floor, 94612-3541
Telephone: 510-444-3131
Telecopier: 510-839-7940

MEMBERS OF FIRM

Raymond J. Bergez
Willard L. Alloway
Gennaro A. Filice, III
Stephen McKae
Bruce E. McLeod
Eugene Brown, Jr.
Matthew S. Conant
Chris P. Lavdiotis
Robert D. Eassa

Amber L. Kelly
Owen T. Rooney
John A. De Pasquale
Nicholas D. Kayhan
William H. Curtis
Elsa M. Baldwin
Rodney Ian Headington
Marshall A. Johnson
Diane R. Stanton
Jennifer M. Walker
Margaret L. Kotzebue
Amee A. Mikacich
Peter A. Strotz
Timothy J. McCaffery
Stephen J. Valen
Troy D. McMahan
Lisa L. Hillegas
Richard V. Normington III

Representative Clients: Firemans Fund Insurance Cos.; City of Piedmont; The Dow Chemical Co.; Nissan Motor Corp.; Subaru of America; Weyerhauser Co.; Bay Area Rapid Transit District; Diamond Shamrock; Home Indemnity Co.; Rhone-Poulenc.

For Complete List of Firm Personnel, See General Section

For full biographical listings, see the Martindale-Hubbell Law Directory

ORANGE, Orange Co.

WALSWORTH, FRANKLIN & BEVINS (AV)

1 City Boulevard West, Suite 308, 92668
Telephone: 714-634-2522
LAW-FAX: 714-634-0686
San Francisco, California Office: 580 California Street, Suite 1335.
Telephone: 415-781-7072.
Fax: 415-391-6258.

Jeffrey P. Walsworth
Ferdie F. Franklin
Ronald H. Bevins, Jr.
Michael T. McCall
Noel Edlin (Resident, San Francisco Office)
Lawrence E. Duffy, Jr.
Sheldon J. Fleming
J. Wayne Allen
James A. Anton
Ingrid K. Campagne (Resident, San Francisco Office)
Robert M. Channel (Resident, San Francisco Office)
Nicholas A. Cipiti
Sharon L. Clisham (Resident, San Francisco Office)
David W. Epps (Resident, San Francisco Office)
Richard M. Hills (Resident, San Francisco Office)
Sandra G. Kennedy
Randall J. Lee (Resident, San Francisco Office)
Kimberly K. Mays
Bruce A. Nelson (Resident, San Francisco Office)
Kevin Pegan
Allan W. Ruggles
Jonathan M. Slipp
Cyrian B. Tabuena (Resident, San Francisco Office)
John L. Trunko
Houston M. Watson, II
Mary A. Watson

For full biographical listings, see the Martindale-Hubbell Law Directory

PASADENA, Los Angeles Co.

FREEBURG, JUDY, MACCHIAGODENA & NETTELS (AV)

600 South Lake Avenue, 91106
Telephone: 818-585-4150
FAX: 818-585-0718
Santa Ana, California Office: Xerox Centre. 1851 East First Street, Suite 120. 92705-4017.
Telephone: 714-569-0950.
Facsimile: 714-569-0955.

Steven J. Freeburg
J. Lawrence Judy
Marina A. Macchiagodena
Charles F. Nettels

ASSOCIATES

Ingall W. Bull, Jr.
Richard B. Castle
Cynthia B. Schaldenbrand (Resident, Santa Ana Office)
Robert S. Brody
Sheral A. Hyde
Holly A. McNulty
Karen S. Freeburg
Jennifer D. Helsel
James P. Habel
Marianne L. Offermans

For full biographical listings, see the Martindale-Hubbell Law Directory

LAGERLOF, SENECAL, BRADLEY & SWIFT (AV)

301 North Lake Avenue, 10th Floor, 91101-4107
Telephone: 818-793-9400
FAX: 818-793-5900

MEMBERS OF FIRM

Joseph J. Burris (1913-1980)
Stanley C. Lagerlof
H. Melvin Swift, Jr.
H. Jess Senecal
Jack T. Swafford
John F. Bradley
Timothy J. Gosney
William F. Kruse
Thomas S. Bunn, III
Andrew D. Turner
Rebecca J. Thyne

ASSOCIATES

Paul M. Norman
John F. Machtinger
James D. Ciampa
Ellen M. Burkhart

LEGAL SUPPORT PERSONNEL

Ronald E. Hagler

Representative Clients: Anchor Glass Container Corporation; Bethlehem Steel Corp.; Orthopaedic Hospital; Palmdale Water District; Public Water Agencies Group; Walnut Valley Water District.
Special Counsel: City of Redondo Beach, Calif.; Ventura Port Dist., Calif.

For full biographical listings, see the Martindale-Hubbell Law Directory

*SACRAMENTO,** Sacramento Co.

DIEPENBROCK & COSTA (AV)

455 University Avenue, Suite 300, 95825
Telephone: 916-565-6222
Fax: 916-565-6220

MEMBERS OF FIRM

Anthony C. Diepenbrock
Daniel P. Costa
John D. Broghammer
Maria R. Vail
Karen L. Kovalsky

Representative Clients: Union Pacific Railroad Systems; ARCO; Montgomery Ward & Co., Incorporated; Clements National Co.; Con Agra; Sacramento Municipal Utility District; South Placer Municipal Utility District; Union Pacific Realty.

For full biographical listings, see the Martindale-Hubbell Law Directory

DOWNEY, BRAND, SEYMOUR & ROHWER (AV)

Suite 1050, 555 Capitol Mall, 95814
Telephone: 916-441-0131
FAX: 916-441-4021

MEMBERS OF FIRM

Stephen J. Meyer
Steven H. Goldberg
Katharine E. Wagner

ASSOCIATES

David R.E. Aladjem
Craig C. Allison
Ronald Liebert
Kathryn T. Papalia

Counsel for: Roseburg Forest Products Co.; California Department of Conservation; Sunsweet Growers, Inc.; Cargill, Inc.; Diamond Lands; Procter & Gamble Co.; Raley's; Sacramento-Yolo Port District; The Hertz Corp.

For Complete List of Firm Personnel, See General Section

For full biographical listings, see the Martindale-Hubbell Law Directory

KRONICK, MOSKOVITZ, TIEDEMANN & GIRARD, A PROFESSIONAL CORPORATION (AV)

27th Floor, 400 Capitol Mall, 95814
Telephone: 916-321-4500
Fax: 916-321-4555

(See Next Column)

KRONICK, MOSKOVITZ, TIEDEMANN & GIRARD A PROFESSIONAL CORPORATION—*Continued*

Adolph Moskovitz
Edward J. Tiedemann
Clifford W. Schulz
Robert E. Murphy
Janet K. Goldsmith
Robin Leslie Stewart
Ruthann G. Ziegler
Thomas C. Hughes, III
Thomas W. Birmingham

Ann M. Siprelle
Anthony B. Manzanetti
Jeffrey M. Starsky
Jeffrey A. Mitchell
Andrew B. Pollak
Paul F. Kelly

Representative Clients: Placer County Water Agency; Kern County Water Agency; City of Los Angeles Department of Water and Power; Sonora Mining Corp.; Westlands Water District; City of Woodland; City of West Sacramento; Association of California Water Agencies, JPIA; Century Buick Pontiac; Knittel Development.

For Complete List of Firm Personnel, See General Section

For full biographical listings, see the Martindale-Hubbell Law Directory

WILKE, FLEURY, HOFFELT, GOULD & BIRNEY (AV)

A Partnership including Professional Corporations
400 Capitol Mall, Suite 2200, 95814-4408
Telephone: 916-441-2430
Telefax: 916-442-6664
Mailing Address: P.O. Box 15559, 95852-0559

MEMBERS OF FIRM

Richard H. Hoffelt (Inc.)
William A. Gould, Jr., (Inc.)
Philip R. Birney (Inc.)
Thomas G. Redmon (Inc.)
Scott L. Gassaway
Donald Rex Heckman II (Inc.)
Alan G. Perkins
Bradley N. Webb
Ernest James Krtil
Robert R. Mirkin
Matthew W. Powell
Mark L. Andrews
Stephen K. Marmaduke
David A. Frenznick
John R. Valencia
Angus M. MacLeod

ASSOCIATES

Paul A. Dorris
Kelli M. Kennaday
Tracy S. Hendrickson
Joseph G. De Angelis
Jennifer L. Kennedy
Anthony J. DeCristoforo
Rachel N. Kook
Alicia F. From
Michael Polis
Matthew J. Smith
Wayne L. Ordos

OF COUNSEL

Sherman C. Wilke
Anita Seipp Marmaduke
Benjamin G. Davidian

Representative Clients: NOR-CAL Mutual Insurance Co.; California Optometric Assn.; KPMG Peat Marwick; Glaxo, Inc.

For full biographical listings, see the Martindale-Hubbell Law Directory

*SAN BERNARDINO,** San Bernardino Co.

GRESHAM, VARNER, SAVAGE, NOLAN & TILDEN (AV)

Suite 300, 600 North Arrowhead Avenue, 92401
Telephone: 909-884-2171
Fax: 909-888-2120
Victorville, California Office: 14011 Park Avenue, Suite 140.
Telephone: 619-243-2889.
Fax: 619-243-3057.
Riverside, California Office: 3737 Main Street, Suite 420.
Telephone: 714-274-7777.
Fax: 714-274-7770.

MEMBER OF FIRM

James E. Good

ASSOCIATE

Saul Jaffe

Representative Clients: Kaiser Resources, Inc.; Viceroy Gold Corp.; Amax Gold, Inc.; California Portland Cement Corp.; Sunwest Materials; RHEOX, Inc.; CalMat Co.; Wal-Mart Stores, Inc.; Pfizer, Inc.

For Complete List of Firm Personnel, See General Section

For full biographical listings, see the Martindale-Hubbell Law Directory

*SAN DIEGO,** San Diego Co.

FRANCO BRADLEY & MARTORELLA (AV)

A Partnership of Professional Corporations
8880 Rio San Diego Drive, Suite 800, 92108
Telephone: 619-688-0080
Fax: 619-688-0081
Oakland, California Office: Suite 600, 1300 Clay Street.
Telephone: 510-466-6310.

MEMBERS OF THE FIRM

Elizabeth Franco Bradley (APC)
Daniel A. Martorella (APC)

OF COUNSEL

Charles A. Viviano (APC)

(See Next Column)

ASSOCIATES

Kerry Don Alexander
Elizabeth Leigh Bradley (Resident, Oakland, California)
Kathryn S. Clenney
Madeline Moriyama Clogston
Zoë G. Gruber
Kim Karels Resnick
Kenneth D. Richard
Daniel L. Rodriguez
Mary Crenshaw Tyler

For full biographical listings, see the Martindale-Hubbell Law Directory

GRAY CARY WARE & FREIDENRICH, A PROFESSIONAL CORPORATION (AV)

Gray Cary Established in 1927
Ware & Freidenrich Established in 1969
401 "B" Street, Suite 1700, 92101
Telephone: 619-699-2700
Telecopier: 619-236-1048
Palo Alto, California Office: 400 Hamilton Avenue.
Telephone: 415-328-6561.
La Jolla, California Office: Suite 575, 1200 Prospect Street.
Telephone: 619-454-9101.
El Centro, California Office: 1224 State Street, P.O. Box 2890.
Telephone: 619-353-6140.

Jan Shirley Driscoll
Jay W. Jeffcoat
William N. Kammer
John J. Lormon
Michael S. Tracy

Robert W. Brownlie
Robert C. Longstreth
Jonathan B. Sokol

Representative Clients: General Dynamics; McMillin Development; Midwest T.V.; Point Loma College; Scripps Clinic and Research Foundation.

For Complete List of Firm Personnel, See General Section

For full biographical listings, see the Martindale-Hubbell Law Directory

HAASIS, POPE & CORRELL, A PROFESSIONAL CORPORATION (AV)

550 West "C" Street, 9th Floor, 92101-3509
Telephone: 619-236-9933
Fax: 619-236-8961
Voice Mail: 619-236-8955

Thomas M. Correll
Kenneth E. Goates
William A. Calders
Robert V. Closson

Janelle Fike Garchie
Susan J. Gill
Nelson J. Goodin
Joan Creigh. Little
Steven B. Bitter

Representative Clients: Aetna Life & Casualty; American States; Chubb Group; Oregon Mutual; Great American West; Maryland Casualty; Ohio Casualty; Scottsdale Insurance; St. Paul; State Farm.

For full biographical listings, see the Martindale-Hubbell Law Directory

HILLYER & IRWIN, A PROFESSIONAL CORPORATION (AV)

550 West C Street, 16th Floor, 92101
Telephone: 619-234-6121
Telecopier: 619-595-1313

Robert J. Hanna
David B. Hopkins
Michael F. Millerick
Mark D. Martin

For full biographical listings, see the Martindale-Hubbell Law Directory

HOVEY, KIRBY, THORNTON & HAHN, A PROFESSIONAL CORPORATION (AV)

101 West Broadway, Suite 1100, 92101-8297
Telephone: 619-685-4000
Fax: 619-685-4004

Gregg B. Hovey
Cynthia K. Thornton
M. Leslie Hovey
Jane Hahn
Patrick R. Kitchin

For full biographical listings, see the Martindale-Hubbell Law Directory

LUCE, FORWARD, HAMILTON & SCRIPPS (AV)

A Partnership including Professional Corporations
600 West Broadway, Suite 2600, 92101
Telephone: 619-236-1414
Fax: 619-232-8311
La Jolla, California Office: 4275 Executive Square, Suite 800, 92037.
Telephone: 619-535-2639.
Fax: 619-453-2812.
Los Angeles, California Office: 777 South Figueroa, 36th Floor, 90017.
Telephone: 213-892-4992.
Fax: 213-892-7731.

(See Next Column)

LUCE, FORWARD, HAMILTON & SCRIPPS, *San Diego—Continued*

San Francisco, California Office: 100 Bush Street, 20th Floor, 94104.
Telephone: 415-395-7900.
Fax: 415-395-7949.
New York, N.Y. Office: Citicorp Center, 153 East 53rd Street, 26th Floor, 10022.
Telephone: 212-754-1414.
Fax: 212-644-9727.

MEMBERS OF FIRM

Robert E. McGinnis
Steven P. McDonald
John W. Leslie
Christopher J. Healey
Stephen L. Marsh
Jon K. Wactor (Resident, San Francisco Office)

ASSOCIATES

Cordon T. Baesel
James G. Waian

For Complete List of Firm Personnel, See General Section

For full biographical listings, see the Martindale-Hubbell Law Directory

*SAN FRANCISCO,** San Francisco Co.

ADAMS, DUQUE & HAZELTINE (AV)

A Partnership including Professional Corporations
500 Washington Street, 94111
Telephone: 415-982-1240
FAX: 415-982-0130
Los Angeles, California Office: 777 South Figueroa Street, Tenth Floor.
Telephone: 213-620-1240.
FAX: 213-896-5500.

ASSOCIATES

Ann Sparkman
Marilyn A. Rogers

For Complete List of Firm Personnel, See General Section

For full biographical listings, see the Martindale-Hubbell Law Directory

EWELL & LEVY (AV)

351 California Street, 94104-2501
Telephone: 415-788-6600
Fax: 415-433-7311

Arthur D. Levy
Gary Ewell

OF COUNSEL

Scott H. Miller
Theresa R. Owens

For full biographical listings, see the Martindale-Hubbell Law Directory

LEACH, MCGREEVY, BAUTISTA & BRASS (AV)

1735 Pacific Avenue, 94109
Telephone: 415-775-4455
Telefax: 415-775-7435
Southern California Office: 13643 Fifth Street, Chino, 91710.
Telephone: 909-590-2224.

Theodore Tamba (1900-1973)
John T. Harmon (1928-1993)
David G. Leach
Richard E. McGreevy
M. Francis Brass

A. Marquez Bautista
Teresa A. Cunningham
J. Curtis Cox
Paul David Katerndahl

OF COUNSEL

Roger G. Eliassen
Lloyd F. Postel
Robert W. Shinnick

For full biographical listings, see the Martindale-Hubbell Law Directory

LIEFF, CABRASER & HEIMANN (AV)

Embarcadero Center West, 30th Floor, 275 Battery Street, 94111
Telephone: 415-956-1000
Telecopier: 415-956-1008

Robert L. Lieff
Elizabeth J. Cabraser
Richard M. Heimann
William Bernstein
William B. Hirsch
James M. Finberg
Karen E. Karpen
Michael F. Ram
William M. Audet
Joseph R. Saveri
Steven E. Fineman
Donald C. Arbitblit
Robert J. Nelson

Kristine E. Bailey
Suzanne A. Barr
Kelly M. Dermody
Deborah A. Kemp
Anthony K. Lee
Jacqueline E. Mottek
Kimberly W. Pate
Melanie M. Piech
Morris A. Ratner
Rhonda L. Woo

For full biographical listings, see the Martindale-Hubbell Law Directory

VOGL & MEREDITH (AV)

456 Montgomery Street, 20th Floor, 94104
Telephone: 415-398-0200
Facsimile: 415-398-2820

Samuel E. Meredith
David R. Vogl
Bryan A. Marmesh
John P. Walovich
Jean N. Yeh
Janet Brayer
Thomas S. Clifton (Resident)

George C. Leal

For full biographical listings, see the Martindale-Hubbell Law Directory

*SAN JOSE,** Santa Clara Co.

THE ALEXANDER LAW FIRM (AV)

55 South Market Street, Suite 1080, 95113
Telephone: 408-289-1776
Fax: 408-287-1776
Cincinnati, Ohio Office: 1300 Mercantile Library Building, 414 Walnut Street.
Telephone: 513-723-1776.
Fax: 513-421-1776.

Richard Alexander

ASSOCIATES

Mark P. Rapazzini
Jeffrey W. Rickard
Michael T. Alexander (Resident, Cincinnati, Ohio Office)
M. Elizabeth Graham
Jotham S. Stein

For full biographical listings, see the Martindale-Hubbell Law Directory

FERRARI, ALVAREZ, OLSEN & OTTOBONI, A PROFESSIONAL CORPORATION (AV)

333 West Santa Clara Street, Suite 700, 95113
Telephone: 408-280-0535
Fax: 408-280-0151
Palo Alto, California Office: 550 Hamilton Avenue.
Telephone: 415-327-3233.

Clarence J. Ferrari, Jr.
Kent E. Olsen
John M. Ottoboni
Richard S. Bebb
James J. Eller
Robert C. Danneskiold
Terence M. Kane
Emma Peña Madrid
John P. Thurau
Roger D. Wintle
Christopher E. Cobey

Michael D. Brayton
Lisa Intrieri Caputo
Jil Dalesandro
Gregory R. Dietrich
J. Timothy Maximoff
Joseph W. Mell, Jr.
George P. Mulcaire
Eleanor C. Schuermann
Melva M. Vollersen

OF COUNSEL

Edward M. Alvarez

For full biographical listings, see the Martindale-Hubbell Law Directory

MAHL TULLY, A PROFESSIONAL CORPORATION (AV)

10 Almaden Boulevard, Suite 1440, 95113
Telephone: 408-494-0900
Fax: 408-494-0909

Susan J. Mahl
Deanne M. Tully
Raymond P. Bolanos
Michael T. Parsons

For full biographical listings, see the Martindale-Hubbell Law Directory

TYNDALL & CAHNERS (AV)

An Association of Attorneys including a Professional Corporation
96 North Third Street, Suite 580, 95112
Telephone: 408-297-3700
Fax: 408-297-3721

John G. Tyndall, III (P.C.)
John D. Cahners

Michael Francis Brown

For full biographical listings, see the Martindale-Hubbell Law Directory

SANTA MONICA, Los Angeles Co.

HAIGHT, BROWN & BONESTEEL (AV)

A Partnership including Professional Corporations
1620 26th Street, Suite 4000 North, P.O. Box 680, 90404
Telephone: 310-449-6000
Telecopier: 310-829-5117
Telex: 705837
Santa Ana, California Office: Suite 900, 5 Hutton Centre Drive.
Telephone: 714-754-1100.
Telecopier: 714-754-0826.

(See Next Column)

HAIGHT, BROWN & BONESTEEL—*Continued*

Riverside, California Office: 3750 University Avenue, Suite 650.
Telephone: 909-341-8300.
Fax: 909-341-8309.
San Francisco, California Office: Suite 300, 201 Sansome Street.
Telephone: 415-986-7700.
Fax: 415-986-6945.

MEMBERS OF FIRM

Steven L. Hoch (A Professional Corporation)
William J. Sayers
Lisa L. Oberg (Resident, San Francisco Office)

ASSOCIATE

Farah Sohaili Nicol

For Complete List of Firm Personnel, See General Section

For full biographical listings, see the Martindale-Hubbell Law Directory

TORRANCE, Los Angeles Co.

FINER, KIM & STEARNS (AV)

An Association of Professional Corporations
City National Bank Building, 3424 Carson Street, Suite 500, 90503
Telephone: 310-214-1477
Telecopier: 310-214-0764

W. A. Finer (A Professional Corporation)

Robert David Ciaccio
Robert B. Parsons
Mark Andrew Hooper

OF COUNSEL

Bennett A. Rheingold
Ryan E. Stearns

For Complete List of Firm Personnel, See General Section

For full biographical listings, see the Martindale-Hubbell Law Directory

*VENTURA,** Ventura Co.

TAYLOR MCCORD, A LAW CORPORATION (AV)

721 East Main Street, P.O. Box 1477, 93002
Telephone: 805-648-4700
Fax: 805-653-6124

Richard L. Taylor
Robert L. McCord, Jr.
Ellen G. Conroy
David L. Praver

Patrick Cherry
Susan D. Siple

For full biographical listings, see the Martindale-Hubbell Law Directory

COLORADO

*ASPEN,** Pitkin Co.

AUSTIN, PEIRCE & SMITH, P.C. (AV)

Suite 205, 600 East Hopkins Avenue, 81611
Telephone: 303-925-2600
FAX: 303-925-4720

Ronald D. Austin
Frederick F. Peirce
Thomas Fenton Smith

Rhonda J. Bazil

Counsel for: Clark's Market; Coates, Reid & Waldron Realtors; Crystal Palace Corp.; Snowmass Shopping Center; Coldwell Banker; William Poss & Assoc., Architects; Snowmass Resort Association; Real Estate Affiliates, Inc.; Raleigh Enterprises.

For full biographical listings, see the Martindale-Hubbell Law Directory

KEVIN L. PATRICK, P.C. (AV)

Suite 300, 205 South Mill Street, 81611
Telephone: 303-920-1028
FAX: 303-925-6847

Kevin L. Patrick

Brian L. Stowell
Kelly Elizabeth Archer

For full biographical listings, see the Martindale-Hubbell Law Directory

*BOULDER,** Boulder Co.

VRANESH AND RAISCH, L.L.C. (AV)

1720 14th Street, P.O. Box 871, 80306
Telephone: 303-443-6151
Telecopier: 303-443-9586

(See Next Column)

MEMBERS OF FIRM

Jerry W. Raisch
John R. Henderson
Michael D. Shimmin
Eugene J. Riordan
Paul J. Zilis
Douglas A. Goulding
George Vranesh (Retired)

Thomas Morris

Representative Clients: Cyprus Climax Metals Co.; City of Fort Collins; Colorado Association of Commerce and Industry; County of Arapahoe; Eastman Kodak Company; Hendricks Mining Company; Horizon Gold Corporation, Inc.; Metro Wastewater Reclamation District; Phillips Petroleum Company; Waste Management of North America.

For full biographical listings, see the Martindale-Hubbell Law Directory

*DENVER,** Denver Co.

BAKER & HOSTETLER (AV)

303 East 17th Avenue, Suite 1100, 80203-1264
Telephone: 303-861-0600
FAX: 303-861-7805
In Cleveland, Ohio: 3200 National City Center, 1900 East Ninth Street.
Telephone: 216-621-0200.
In Columbus, Ohio: Capitol Square, Suite 2100, 65 East State Street.
Telephone: 614-228-1541.
In Houston, Texas: 1000 Louisiana, Suite 2000.
Telephone: 713-751-1600.
In Long Beach, California: 300 Oceangate, Suite 620.
Telephone: 310-432-2827.
In Los Angeles, California: 600 Wilshire Boulevard. Telephone 213-624-2400.
In Orlando, Florida: SunBank Center, Suite 2300, 200 South Orange Avenue,
Telephone: 305-841-1111.
In Washington, D. C.: Washington Square, Suite 1100, 1050 Connecticut Avenue, N.W.
Telephone: 202-861-1500.
In College Park, Maryland: 9658 Baltimore Boulevard, Suite 206.
Telephone: 301-441-2781.
In Alexandria, Virginia: 437 North Lee Street.
Telephone: 703-549-1294.
In San Francisco, California: One Sansome Street, Suite 2000.
Telephone: 415-951-4705.

PARTNER

Kenneth J. Burke

For Complete List of Firm Personnel, See General Section

For full biographical listings, see the Martindale-Hubbell Law Directory

BROWNSTEIN HYATT FARBER & STRICKLAND, P.C. (AV)

Twenty-Second Floor, 410 Seventeenth Street, 80202-4437
Telephone: 303-534-6335
Telecopier: 303-623-1956

Thomas L. Strickland
Andrew W. Loewi
Charles B. White
Stanley L. Garnett
Wayne F. Forman
Hubert A. Farbes, Jr.

Carrie A. Mineart
Mark J. Mathews
Gregory A. Vallin

Representative Clients: Lake Catamount Joint Venture; Louisiana-Pacific Corporation; Mid-American Waste Systems, Inc.; The Prudential Insurance Co. of America; Trammell Crow Company.

For Complete List of Firm Personnel, See General Section

For full biographical listings, see the Martindale-Hubbell Law Directory

CARLSON, HAMMOND & PADDOCK (AV)

1700 Lincoln Street, Suite 3900, 80203
Telephone: 303-861-9000
Telefax: 303-861-9026

MEMBERS OF FIRM

John Undem Carlson (1940-1992)
Mary Mead Hammond
William A. Paddock

Melanie Kopperud Backes
Lee Heinrick Johnson
Peter C. Fleming
K. Gwen Beacham

Representative Clients: Atlantic Richfield Co.; Board of Water Works of Pueblo Colorado; D.C. Burns Realty & Trust Company; City of Colorado Springs; Colorado Water Resources & Power Development Authority; Forbes Inc.; OXY USA, Inc.; Rio Grande Water Users Assn.; San Luis Valley Water Conservancy District; City of Westminster.

For full biographical listings, see the Martindale-Hubbell Law Directory

Denver—Continued

DUFFORD & BROWN, P.C. (AV)
1700 Broadway, Suite 1700, 80290-1701
Telephone: 303-861-8013
Facsimile: 303-832-3804

William C. Robb — Eugene F. Megyesy, Jr.
Richard L. Fanyo — Craig B. Shaffer

Roman C. Pibl

SPECIAL COUNSEL

Deborah L. Freeman

Representative Clients: A. O. Smith Corp.; CF&I Steel, L.P.; Chemical Waste Management, Inc.; Chevron Shale Oil Company; Coors Brewing Company; Echo Bay-Sunnyside Gold; Energy Fuels Corp.; Homestake Mining Company; Kerr Coal Company; Trapper Mining Inc.

For Complete List of Firm Personnel, See General Section

For full biographical listings, see the Martindale-Hubbell Law Directory

HOLLAND & HART (AV)
Suite 2900, 555 Seventeenth Street, P.O. Box 8749, 80201
Telephone: 303-295-8000
Cable Address: "Holhart Denver"
Telecopier: 303-295-8261
TWX: 910-931-0568
Denver Tech Center, Colorado Office: Suite 1050, 4601 DTC Boulevard.
Telephone: 303-290-1600.
Telecopier: 303-290-1606.
Aspen, Colorado Office: 600 East Main Street.
Telephone: 303-925-3476.
Telecopier: 303-925-9367.
Boulder, Colorado Office: Suite 500, 1050 Walnut.
Telephone: 303-473-2700.
Telecopier: 303-473-2720.
Colorado Springs, Colorado Office: Suite 1000, 90 S. Cascade Avenue.
Telephone: 719-475-7730.
Telex: 82077 SHHTLX.
Telecopier: 719-634-2461.
Washington, D.C. Office: Suite 310, 1001 Pennsylvania Avenue, N.W.
Telephone: 202-638-5500.
Telecopier: 202-737-8998.
Boise, Idaho Office: Suite 1400, West One Plaza, 101 South Capitol Boulevard, P.O. Box 2527.
Telephone: 208-342-5000.
Telecopier: 208-343-8869.
Billings, Montana Office: Suite 1500, First Interstate Center, 401 North 31st Street, P.O. Box 639.
Telephone: 406-252-2166.
Telecopier: 406-252-1669.
Salt Lake City, Utah Office: Suite 880, 111 East Broadway.
Telephone: 801-578-6000.
FAX: 801-578-6010.
Cheyenne, Wyoming Office: Holland & Hart, A Partnership including Professional Corporations, Suite 500, 2020 Carey Avenue, P.O. Box 1347.
Telephone: 307-778-4200.
Telecopier: 307-778-8175.
Jackson, Wyoming Office: Holland & Hart, A Partnership including Professional Corporations, Suite 2, 175 South King Street, P.O. Box 68.
Telephone: 307-739-9741.
Telecopier: 307-739-9744.

MEMBERS OF FIRM

William E. Murane — Paul D. Phillips
Stephen H. Foster (Not admitted in CO) — John F. Shepherd
Robert T. Connery — Anne J. Castle
Brian R. Hanson
Denise W. Kennedy

OF COUNSEL

Lawrence E. Volmert

ASSOCIATES

Douglas L. Abbott — Marily Nixon
Margaret Althoff — David D. Powell, Jr.
Steven W. Black — Cynthia K. Simons
Jane Lowell Montgomery — Camille T. Ventrell (Not admitted in CO)

DENVER TECH CENTER, COLORADO RESIDENT PARTNER

Robert M. Pomeroy, Jr.

ASPEN, COLORADO RESIDENT PARTNER

Arthur B. Ferguson, Jr.

COLORADO SPRINGS, COLORADO PARTNER

Edward H. Flitton (Resident)

WASHINGTON, D.C. RESIDENT PARTNERS

J. Peter Luedtke — Michael J. Brennan
William F. Demarest, Jr. — Steven G. Barringer

WASHINGTON, D.C. RESIDENT ASSOCIATE

Kelly Anne Johnson

(See Next Column)

BOISE, IDAHO RESIDENT OF COUNSEL

Brian J. King

BOISE, IDAHO RESIDENT ASSOCIATES

Murray D. Feldman — Dana Lieberman Hofstetter
Linda B. Jones

BILLINGS, MONTANA PARTNER

Donald W. Quander

BILLINGS, MONTANA SPECIAL COUNSEL

Robert A. Lorenz

BILLINGS, MONTANA RESIDENT ASSOCIATE

W. Scott Mitchell

CHEYENNE, WYOMING PARTNERS

Jack D. Palma, II (P.C.) — Edward W. Harris
Donald I. Schultz (P.C.) — Lawrence J. Wolfe (P.C.)

CHEYENNE, WYOMING RESIDENT ASSOCIATE

Lynnette J. Boomgaarden

JACKSON, WYOMING RESIDENT PARTNERS

John L. Gallinger (P.C.) — Marilyn S. Kite (P.C.)

SALT LAKE CITY UTAH RESIDENT PARTNER

Lawrence J. Jensen

For Complete List of Firm Personnel, See General Section

For full biographical listings, see the Martindale-Hubbell Law Directory

HOLME ROBERTS & OWEN LLC (AV)
Suite 4100, 1700 Lincoln, 80203
Telephone: 303-861-7000
Telex: 45-4460
Telecopier: 303-866-0200
Boulder, Colorado Office: Suite 400, 1401 Pearl Street.
Telephone: 303-444-5955.
Telecopier: 303-444-1063.
Colorado Springs, Colorado Office: Suite 1300, 90 South Cascade Avenue.
Telephone: 719-473-3800.
Telecopier: 719-633-1518.
Salt Lake City, Utah Office: Suite 1100, 111 East Broadway.
Telephone: 801-521-5800.
Telecopier: 801-521-9639.
London, England Office: 4th Floor, Mellier House, 26a Albemarle Street.
Telephone: 44-171-499-8776.
Telecopier: 44-171-499-7769.
Moscow, Russia Office: 14 Krivokolenny Pr., Suite 30, 101000.
Telephone: 095-925-7816.
Telecopier: 095-923-2726.

MEMBERS OF FIRM

Edward J. McGrath — Henry W. Ipsen
Brent V. Manning (Salt Lake City Office) — Daniel J. Dunn
Raymond L. Petros
Phillip R. Clark — Linnea Brown
Thomas F. Cope — John Leonard Watson
Nick Nimmo — Robert Tuchman
Charlotte Louise Neitzel — John D. McCarthy
James W. Spensley

OF COUNSEL

A. Edgar Benton

SPECIAL COUNSEL

Richard A. Oertli (Not admitted in CO)

ASSOCIATES

Loretta (Laurie) A. Cahill — Matthew J. Lepore
Katherine Taylor Eubank — Kenneth W. Lund
Colin G. Harris — Laurence Pendleton
Edward E. Stevenson

For Complete List of Firm Personnel, See General Section

For full biographical listings, see the Martindale-Hubbell Law Directory

MYERS, HOPPIN, BRADLEY AND DEVITT, P.C. (AV)
Suite 420, 4704 Harlan Street, 80212
Telephone: 303-433-8527
Fax: 303-433-8219

Frederick J. Myers — Jon T. Bradley
Charles T. Hoppin — Jerald J. Devitt

Gregg W. Fraser

OF COUNSEL

Kent E. Hanson

Reference: Bank One Lakeside Banking Center.

For full biographical listings, see the Martindale-Hubbell Law Directory

REES & ASSOCIATES, P.C. (AV)
1675 Broadway, Suite 1400, 80202
Telephone: 303-592-5392
Fax: 303-892-3882

(See Next Column)

REES & ASSOCIATES P.C.—*Continued*

David K. Rees

For full biographical listings, see the Martindale-Hubbell Law Directory

TREECE, ALFREY & MUSAT, P.C. (AV)

Denver Place, 999 18th Street, Suite 1600, 80202
Telephone: 303-292-2700
Facsimile: 303-295-0414

Robert S. Treece

Alison F. Kyles

For full biographical listings, see the Martindale-Hubbell Law Directory

WELBORN SULLIVAN MECK & TOOLEY, P.C. (AV)

Mellon Financial Center, 1775 Sherman Street, Suite 1800, 80203
Telephone: 303-830-2500
Facsimile: 303-832-2366

John F. Welborn — Molly Sommerville

Scott L. Sells

SPECIAL COUNSEL

John S. Cowan

For Complete List of Firm Personnel, See General Section

For full biographical listings, see the Martindale-Hubbell Law Directory

WELLER FRIEDRICH, LLC (AV)

One Civic Center, Suite 2000, 1560 Broadway, P.O. Box 989, 80201-0989
Telephone: 303-812-1200
FAX: 303-812-1212

Geoffrey S. Race — Mary A. Wells
Dennis J. Bartlett

OF COUNSEL

Martin J. Andrew

Representative Clients: Abbott Laboratories; Associated Aviation Underwriters; Commercial Union Insurance Companies.
Reference: Colorado State Bank of Denver.

For full biographical listings, see the Martindale-Hubbell Law Directory

CONNECTICUT

*HARTFORD,** Hartford Co.

AUSTIN CAREY, JR., P.C. (AV)

43 Woodland Street Suite 200, 06105
Telephone: 203-724-0012
Fax: 203-724-1211

Austin Carey, Jr. — Margaret Rausch Appicelli

LEGAL SUPPORT PERSONNEL

Laura E. O'Donnell

For full biographical listings, see the Martindale-Hubbell Law Directory

KENNY, BRIMMER, MELLEY & MAHONEY (AV)

5 Grand Street, 06106
Telephone: 203-527-4226
FAX: 203-527-0214

Joseph P. Kenny (1920-1993)

MEMBERS OF FIRM

Leslie R. Brimmer — William J. Melley, III
Richard C. Mahoney

ASSOCIATES

Anita M. Varunes — Maurice M. O'Shea
Dennis F. McCarthy — Beverly Johns

For full biographical listings, see the Martindale-Hubbell Law Directory

SHIPMAN & GOODWIN (AV)

One American Row, 06103
Telephone: 203-251-5000
Telecopier: 203-251-5099
Lakeville, Connecticut Office: Porter Street.
Telephone: 203-435-2539.
Stamford, Connecticut Office: Three Landmark Square.
Telephone: 203-359-4544.

(See Next Column)

MEMBERS OF FIRM

Coleman H. Casey — John E. Wertam
Charles L. Howard — Timothy S. Hollister

ASSOCIATES

Timothy J. Covello — John J. Moroney
Timothy Patrick Brady — R. Webb Steadman

Representative Clients: Hartford Hospital; Lego Systems; Shawmut Bank, Connecticut, N.A.; The Napier Co.

For Complete List of Firm Personnel, See General Section

For full biographical listings, see the Martindale-Hubbell Law Directory

SOUTHPORT, Fairfield Co.

SHUMWAY & MERLE (AV)

200 Pequot Avenue, P.O. Box 550, 06490
Telephone: 203-255-7444
Facsimile: 203-255-0365

MEMBERS OF FIRM

Paul J. Merle — William C. Spencer
Susan H. Shumway — Pamela I. S. Missal

Representative Clients: Uniroyal Chemical Company, Inc.; Chesebrough-Pond's USA.

For full biographical listings, see the Martindale-Hubbell Law Directory

DELAWARE

*DOVER,** Kent Co.

PARKOWSKI, NOBLE & GUERKE, PROFESSIONAL ASSOCIATION (AV)

116 West Water Street, P.O. Box 598, 19903
Telephone: 302-678-3262
Telecopier: 302-678-9415

F. Michael Parkowski — Jeremy W. Homer
John W. Noble — John C. Andrade
I. Barry Guerke — Jonathan Eisenberg
Clay T. Jester — Donald R. Kinsley

Dana J. Schaefer

OF COUNSEL

George F. Gardner, III

Representative Clients: Delaware Solid Waste Authority; Cabe Associates (Consulting Engineers).
Approved Attorneys for: Ticor Title Insurance Co.
Reference: First National Bank of Wyoming.

For full biographical listings, see the Martindale-Hubbell Law Directory

*WILMINGTON,** New Castle Co.

BURT & BURT (AV)

Suite 1700 Mellon Bank Center, 919 Market Street, 19801
Telephone: 302-429-9430
Fax: 302-429-9427

Warren B. Burt — David H. Burt

Richard D. Abrams — Michael F. Duggan

For full biographical listings, see the Martindale-Hubbell Law Directory

POTTER ANDERSON & CORROON (AV)

350 Delaware Trust Building, P.O. Box 951, 19899-0951
Telephone: 302-658-6771
FAX: 658-1192; 655-1190; 655-1199

MEMBER OF FIRM

W. Harding Drane, Jr.

ASSOCIATES

Harold I. Salmons, III — David L. Baumberger

Representative Clients: Delmarva Power & Light Co.; U.S. Generating Co.; International Petroleum Corporation; KAO Infosystems Company; The Andrew Jergens Company; High Point Chemical Corporation; Rodel, Inc.; Hercules, Incorporated; Conrail; Amtrak.

For Complete List of Firm Personnel, See General Section

For full biographical listings, see the Martindale-Hubbell Law Directory

DISTRICT OF COLUMBIA

WASHINGTON, D.C. Co.

* indicates certain Bar Register subscribers, in cities of comparable size and importance, who maintain an additional office in Washington, D.C. and who have arranged for representation as a part of the Washington, D.C. listings that follow

* BAKER & BOTTS, L.L.P. (AV)

A Registered Limited Liability Partnership
The Warner, 1299 Pennsylvania Avenue, N.W., 20004-2400
Telephone: 202-639-7700
Fax: 202-639-7832
Houston, Texas Office: One Shell Plaza, 910 Louisiana.
Telephone: 713-229-1234.
Austin, Texas Office: 1600 San Jacinto Center, 98 San Jacinto Boulevard.
Telephone: 512-322-2500.
Dallas, Texas Office: 2001 Ross Avenue.
Telephone: 214-953-6500.
New York, New York Office: 805 Third Avenue, Suite 2000.
Telephone: 212-705-5000.
Moscow, Russian Federation Office: 10 ul. Pushkinskaya, 103031.
Telephone: 7095/921-5300 (Local); 7501/929-7070 (International).

MEMBERS OF FIRM

Bruce F. Kiely
Charles M. Darling, IV
Randolph Quaile McManus
J. Patrick Berry
Thomas J. Eastment
Steven R. Hunsicker
John B. Veach, III

ASSOCIATES

Debra Raggio Bolton
Drew J. Fossum
Jennifer S. Leete (Not admitted in DC)
Mark K. Lewis

For Complete List of Firm Personnel, See General Section

For full biographical listings, see the Martindale-Hubbell Law Directory

BAKER & HOSTETLER (AV)

Washington Square, Suite 1100, 1050 Connecticut Avenue, N.W., 20036-5304
Telephone: 202-861-1500
In Cleveland, Ohio: 3200 National City Center, 1900 East Ninth Street.
Telephone: 216-621-0200.
In Columbus, Ohio: Capitol Square, Suite 2100, 65 East State Street.
Telephone: 614-228-1541.
In Denver, Colorado: 303 East 17th Avenue, Suite 1100.
Telephone: 303-861-0600.
In Houston, Texas: 1000 Louisiana, Suite 2000.
Telephone: 713-751-1600.
In Long Beach, California: 300 Oceangate, Suite 620.
Telephone: 310-432-2827.
In Los Angeles, California: 600 Wilshire Boulevard.
Telephone: 213-624-2400.
In Orlando, Florida: SunBank Center, Suite 2300, 200 South Orange Avenue.
Telephone: 305-841-1111.
In College Park, Maryland: 9658 Baltimore Boulevard, Suite 206.
Telephone: 301-441-2781.
In Alexandria, Virginia: 437 North Lee Street.
Telephone: 703-549-1294.
In San Francisco, California: One Sansome Street, Suite 2000.
Telephone: 415-951-4705.

PARTNERS

Richard J. Leon
Marshall Lee Miller

ASSOCIATE

Kenneth D. Woodrow (Not admitted in DC)

For Complete List of Firm Personnel, See General Section

For full biographical listings, see the Martindale-Hubbell Law Directory

BALCH & BINGHAM (AV)

1101 Connecticut Avenue, N.W., Suite 800, 20036
Telephone: 202-296-0387
Facsimile: 202-452-8180
Birmingham, Alabama Offices: 1710 Sixth Avenue North, 35203.
Telephone: 205-251-8100.
Facsimile: 205-226-8798. 1901 Sixth Avenue North, 35203.
Telephone: 205-251-8100.
Facsimile: 205-226-8799.
Montgomery, Alabama Office: The Winter Building, 2 Dexter Avenue, 36101.
Telephone: 205-834-6500.
Facsimile: 205-269-3115.
Huntsville, Alabama Office: Suite 810, 200 West Court Square, 35801.
Telephone: 205-551-0171.
Facsimile: 205-551-0174.

(See Next Column)

RESIDENT MEMBERS OF FIRM

Karl R. Moor (Not admitted in DC)

Counsel for: Alabama Power Co.; Alabama River Pulp Co., Inc.; Blue Cross and Blue Shield of Alabama; Brasfield & Gorrie, Inc.; Compass Bancshares, Inc.; Harbert Corp.; Kimberly-Clark Corp.; National Energy Partners; Southern Company Services, Inc.; Southern Research Institute.

For Complete List of Firm Personnel, See General Section

For full biographical listings, see the Martindale-Hubbell Law Directory

* BELL, BOYD & LLOYD (AV)

1615 L Street, N.W., 20036
Telephone: 202-466-6300
FAX: 202-463-0678
Chicago, Illinois Office: Three First National Plaza, Suite 3300, 70 West Madison Street.
Telephone: 312-372-1121.
FAX: 312-372-2098.

RESIDENT PARTNER

Michael L. Italiano

For Complete List of Firm Personnel, See General Section

For full biographical listings, see the Martindale-Hubbell Law Directory

CARR, GOODSON & LEE, P.C. (AV)

1301 K Street, N.W., Suite 400, East Tower, 20005-3300
Telephone: 202-310-5500
Telecopier: 202-310-5555
Fairfax, Virginia Office: 3923 Old Lee Highway, Suite 62-B, 22030 .
Telephone: 703-691-8818.
Baltimore, Maryland Office: Suite 2700, 111 South Calvert Street, 21202.
Telephone: 410-752-1570.
Rockville, Maryland Office: 31 Wood Lane, 20850.
Telephone: 301-424-7024.

Lawrence E. Carr, Jr.
William J. Carter
Kyle A. Kane
Margaret H. Warner

M. Miller Baker (Not admitted in DC)
Ann Terrell Dorsett (Not admitted in DC)
Gregory A. Krauss
Bridget L. Kyle (Not admitted in DC)
Charles E. Leasure, III
Michelle L. Melin
Karen A. Rosenthal (Not admitted in DC)
Patricia Ann Smith
Brian M. Tauscher (Not admitted in DC)
Peter K. Tompa
Karen E. Torrent
Bruce K. Trauben

For Complete List of Firm Personnel, See General Section

For full biographical listings, see the Martindale-Hubbell Law Directory

CUTLER & STANFIELD (AV)

700 Fourteenth Street, N.W., 20005-2010
Telephone: 202-624-8400
Fax: 202-624-8410
Denver, Colorado Office: 1625 Broadway.
Telephone: 303-592-4200.
FAX: 303-592-4205.

MEMBERS OF FIRM

Eliot R. Cutler
Jeffrey L. Stanfield
Sheila D. Jones
Paige E. Reffe
Perry M. Rosen
James H. Holt
Peter J. Kirsch

OF COUNSEL

Byron Keith Huffman, Jr.
Robert Goodwin (Not admitted in DC)

ASSOCIATES

Katherine Boonin Andrus
Françoise M. Carrier
Barry Conaty
William G. Malley
Dana C. Nifosi
Michelle Benedict Nowlin
Barbara Paley
Thomas D. Roth

For full biographical listings, see the Martindale-Hubbell Law Directory

FREEDMAN, LEVY, KROLL & SIMONDS (AV)

Suite 825, 1050 Connecticut Avenue, N.W., 20036-5366
Telephone: 202-457-5100
Cable Address: "Attorneys"
Telecopier: 202-457-5151

MEMBERS OF FIRM

Richard G. Stoll
Karen M. Wardzinski

OF COUNSEL

David P. Novello

(See Next Column)

FREEDMAN, LEVY, KROLL & SIMONDS—*Continued*

ASSOCIATE
Serena P. Wiltshire

For Complete List of Firm Personnel, See General Section

For full biographical listings, see the Martindale-Hubbell Law Directory

FRANK W. FRISK, JR., P.C. (AV)

Suite 125, Canal Square, 1054 Thirty-First Street, N.W., 20007
Telephone: 202-333-8433
Fax: 202-333-8431

Frank W. Frisk, Jr.

For full biographical listings, see the Martindale-Hubbell Law Directory

*** LEWIS, WHITE & CLAY, A PROFESSIONAL CORPORATION (AV)**

1250 K Street, N.W., Suite 630, 20005
Telephone: 202-408-5419
Fax: 202-408-5456
Detroit, Michigan Office: 1300 First National Building, 660 Woodward Avenue.
Telephone: 313-961-2550.

Kathleen Miles (Resident)
Karen Kendrick Brown (Resident)
Werten F. W. Bellamy, Jr. (Not admitted in DC; Resident)

OF COUNSEL
Inez Smith Reid (Resident)

For full biographical listings, see the Martindale-Hubbell Law Directory

SELTZER AND ROSEN, P.C. (AV)

One Franklin Square, Suite 310 East 1301 K Street, N.W., 20005-3307
Telephone: 202-682-4585
Telecopier: 202-682-4599

E. Manning Seltzer
Harold I. Rosen
Mark E. Davis

OF COUNSEL
Gary B. Cohen

LEGAL SUPPORT PERSONNEL
ENGINEER ADVISOR
John W. Morris

For full biographical listings, see the Martindale-Hubbell Law Directory

SUTHERLAND, ASBILL & BRENNAN (AV)

1275 Pennsylvania Avenue, N.W., 20004-2404
Telephone: 202-383-0100
Cable Address: "Sutab Wash"
Telex: 89-501
Facsimile: 202-637-3593
Atlanta, Georgia Office: 999 Peachtree Street, N. E., 30309-3996.
Telephone: 404-853-8000.
New York, N.Y. Office: 1270 Avenue of the Americas, 10020-1700.
Telephone: 212-332-3000.
Austin, Texas Office: 111 Congress Avenue, 23rd Floor, 78701-4079.
Telephone: 512-469-3350.

Jacob Dweck
Gordon O. Pehrson, Jr.
Peter H. Rodgers
Beverly J. Rudy

For Complete List of Firm Personnel, See General Section

For full biographical listings, see the Martindale-Hubbell Law Directory

DANIEL R. THOMPSON, P.C. (AV)

Suite 925, 1620 I Street, N.W., 20006
Telephone: 202-293-5800
Facsimile: 202-463-8998

Daniel R. Thompson
Gregory E. Thompson
John B. Hallagan

Reference: NationsBank, Washington, D.C.

For full biographical listings, see the Martindale-Hubbell Law Directory

*** VENABLE, BAETJER, HOWARD & CIVILETTI (AV)**

A Partnership including Professional Corporations
Suite 1000, 1201 New York Avenue, N.W., 20005
Telephone: 202-962-4800
Fax: 202-962-8300
Baltimore, Maryland Office: Venable, Baetjer and Howard, 1800 Mercantile Bank & Trust Building, 2 Hopkins Plaza.
Telephone: 410-244-7400.

(See Next Column)

McLean, Virginia Office: Venable, Baetjer and Howard, Suite 400, 2010 Corporate Ridge.
Telephone: 703-760-1600.
Rockville, Maryland Office: Venable, Baetjer and Howard, Suite 500, One Church Street, P. O. Box 1906.
Telephone: 301-217-5600.
Towson, Maryland Office: Venable, Baetjer and Howard, 210 Allegheny Avenue, P. O. Box 5517.
Telephone: 410-494-6200.

MEMBERS OF FIRM

Benjamin R. Civiletti (P.C.) (Also at Baltimore and Towson, Maryland Offices)
Anthony M. Carey (Not admitted in DC; Also at Baltimore, Maryland Office)
Dennis J. Whittlesey
John G. Milliken (Also at McLean, Virginia Office)
Max Stul Oppenheimer (P.C.) (Also at Baltimore and Towson, Maryland Offices)
Joseph G. Block
Michael Schatzow (Also at Baltimore and Towson, Maryland Offices)
John F. Cooney
James K. Archibald (Also at Baltimore and Towson, Maryland Offices)
Judson W. Starr (Also at Baltimore and Towson, Maryland Offices)
Jeffrey A. Dunn (Also at Baltimore, Maryland Office)
James L. Shea (Not admitted in DC; also at Baltimore, Maryland Office)
John J. Pavlick, Jr.
James A. Dunbar (Also at Baltimore, Maryland Office)
Thomas J. Kelly, Jr.

OF COUNSEL
Richard H. Mays (Not admitted in DC; Also at Baltimore, Maryland and McLean, Virginia Offices)

ASSOCIATES
Gregory S. Braker (Not admitted in DC)
Andrew R. Herrup
Valerie K. Mann

For Complete List of Firm Personnel, See General Section

For full biographical listings, see the Martindale-Hubbell Law Directory

VERNER, LIIPFERT, BERNHARD, MCPHERSON AND HAND, CHARTERED (AV)

901 15th Street, N.W., 20005-2301
Telephone: 202-371-6000
Cable Address: "Verlip"
Telex: 1561792 VERLIP UT
Fax: 202-371-6279
McLean, Virginia Office: Sixth Floor, 8280 Greensboro Drive, 22102.
Telephone: 703-749-6000.
Fax: 703-749-6027.
Houston, Texas Office: 2600 Texas Commerce Tower, 600 Travis, 77002.
Telephone: 713-237-9034.
Fax: 713-237-1216.

Roy G. Bowman
R. Stuart Broom
Gary J. Klein
Neil T. Proto
Sherry A. Quirk
Clinton A. Vince

OF COUNSEL
James K. Jackson

For Complete List of Firm Personnel, See General Section

For full biographical listings, see the Martindale-Hubbell Law Directory

WATT, TIEDER & HOFFAR (AV)

601 Pennsylvania Avenue, N.W., Suite 900, 20004
Telephone: 202-462-4697
Telecopier: 703-893-8029
McLean Virginia Office: 7929 Westpark Drive, Suite 400,
Telephone: 703-749-1000.
Telecopier: 703-893-8029.
Irvine California Office: 3 Park Plaza, Suite 1530.
Telephone: 714-852-6700.

MEMBERS OF FIRM
John B. Tieder, Jr.
Robert K. Cox
David C. Romm

For full biographical listings, see the Martindale-Hubbell Law Directory

WILMER, CUTLER & PICKERING (AV)

2445 M Street, N.W., 20037-1420
Telephone: 202-663-6000
Facsimile: 202-663-6363
Internet: Law@Wilmer.Com
European Offices:
4 Carlton Gardens, London, SW1Y 5AA, England. Telephone: 011 (4471) 839-4466.
Facsimile: 011 (4471) 839-3537.
Rue de la Loi 15 Wetstraat, B-1040 Brussels, Belgium. Telephone: 011 (322) 231-0903.
Facsimile: 011 (322) 230-4322.
Friedrichstrasse 95, D-10117 Berlin, Germany. Telephone: 011 (4930) 2643-3601.
Facsimile: 011 (4930) 2643-3630.

(See Next Column)

WILMER, CUTLER & PICKERING, *Washington—Continued*

MEMBERS OF FIRM

C. Boyden Gray
James A. Rogers
Neil J. King
Daniel H. Squire
Carol Clayton
Laura B. Ahearn

For Complete List of Firm Personnel, See General Section

For full biographical listings, see the Martindale-Hubbell Law Directory

FLORIDA

*BRADENTON,** Manatee Co.

GRIMES, GOEBEL, GRIMES & HAWKINS, P.A. (AV)

The Professional Building, 1023 Manatee Avenue West, P.O. Box 1550, 34206
Telephone: 813-748-0151
Fax: 813-748-0158

William C. Grimes
Caleb J. Grimes
Leslie Horton Gladfelter

William S. Galvano

Counsel for: First Commercial Bank of Manatee County; First Federal Savings & Loan Association of Florida; Schroeder-Manatee, Inc.
Approved Attorneys for: Chicago Title Insurance Co.; Attorneys' Title Insurance Fund; American Pioneer Title Insurance Co.; Lawyers Title Insurance Corporation.

For Complete List of Firm Personnel, See General Section

For full biographical listings, see the Martindale-Hubbell Law Directory

MCGUIRE, PRATT, MASIO & FARRANCE, P.A. (AV)

Suite 600, 1001 3rd Avenue West, P.O. Box 1866, 34206
Telephone: 813-748-7076
FAX: 813-747-9774

Hugh E. McGuire, Jr.
Charles J. Pratt, Jr.
Carol A. Masio
Robert A. Farrance
Richard G. Groff

OF COUNSEL

Carter H. Parry

Reference: Barnett Bank of Manatee County.

For full biographical listings, see the Martindale-Hubbell Law Directory

*KISSIMMEE,** Osceola Co.

POHL & BROWN, P.A.

(See Winter Park)

LAKELAND, Polk Co.

PETERSON, MYERS, CRAIG, CREWS, BRANDON & PUTERBAUGH, P.A. (AV)

100 East Main Street, P.O. Box 24628, 33802-4628
Telephone: 813-683-6511; 676-6934
Telecopier: 813-682-8031
Lake Wales, Florida Office: 130 East Central Avenue, P.O. Box 1079.
Telephones: 813-676-7611; 683-8942.
Winter Haven, Florida Office: Suite 300, 141 5th Street, N.W., P.O. Drawer 7608.
Telephone: 813-294-3360

Jack P. Brandon
Beach A Brooks, Jr.
J. Davis Connor
Roy A. Craig, Jr.
Jacob C. Dykxhoorn
Dennis P. Johnson
Kevin C. Knowlton
Douglas A. Lockwood, III
Corneal B. Myers
Cornelius B. Myers, III
Robert E. Puterbaugh
Abel A. Putnam
Thomas B. Putnam, Jr.
Deborah A. Ruster
Stephen R. Senn
Andrea Teves Smith
Kerry M. Wilson

General Counsel For: Barnett Bank of Polk County.
Representative Clients: Mutual Wholesale Co.; Sun Bank/Mid-Florida, N.A.; Chase Commercial Corp.; Barnett Banks, Inc.; Ben Hill Griffin, Inc.; Alcoma Association, Inc.
Approved Attorneys For: Equitable Life Assurance Society of the United States; Federal Land Bank of Columbia, S.C.; Attorneys' Title Insurance Fund.

For full biographical listings, see the Martindale-Hubbell Law Directory

LAKE WALES, Polk Co.

PETERSON, MYERS, CRAIG, CREWS, BRANDON & PUTERBAUGH, P.A. (AV)

130 East Central Avenue, P.O. Box 1079, 33853
Telephone: 813-676-7611; 683-8942
Telecopier: 813-676-0643
Lakeland, Florida Office: 100 East Main Street, P.O. Box 24628.
Telephones: 813-683-6511; 676-6934.
Winter Haven, Florida Office: Suite 300, 141 5th Street, N.W., P.O. Drawer 7608.
Telephone: 813-294-3360.

Jack P. Brandon
Beach A Brooks, Jr.
Beach A Brooks, Jr.
J. Davis Connor
Roy A. Craig, Jr.
Jacob C. Dykxhoorn
Dennis P. Johnson
Kevin C. Knowlton
Douglas A. Lockwood, III
Corneal B. Myers
Cornelius B. Myers, III
Robert E. Puterbaugh
Robert E. Puterbaugh
Abel A. Putnam
Thomas B. Putnam, Jr.
Deborah A. Ruster
Stephen R. Senn
Andrea Teves Smith
Kerry M. Wilson

General Counsel for: Barnett Bank of Polk County.
Representative Clients: Mutual Wholesale Co.; Sun Bank/Mid-Florida, N.A.; Chase Commercial Corp.; Barnett Banks, Inc.; Ben Hill Griffin, Inc.; Alcoma Association, Inc.
Approved Attorneys for: Equitable Life Assurance Society of the United States; Federal Land Bank of Columbia, S.C.; Attorneys' Title Insurance Fund.

For full biographical listings, see the Martindale-Hubbell Law Directory

*MIAMI,** Dade Co.

JOSEPH Z. FLEMING, P.A. (AV)

620 Ingraham Building, 25 Southeast Second Avenue, 33131
Telephone: 305-373-0791
Telecopier: 305-358-5933

Joseph Z. Fleming

For full biographical listings, see the Martindale-Hubbell Law Directory

MERSHON, SAWYER, JOHNSTON, DUNWODY & COLE (AV)

A Partnership including Professional Associations
Suite 4500 First Union Financial Center, 200 South Biscayne Boulevard, 33131-2387
Telephone: 305-358-5100
Cable Address: "Mercole"
Telex: 515705
Fax: 305-376-8654
Naples, Florida Office: Pelican Bay Corporate Centre, Suite 501, 5551 Ridgewood Drive.
Telephone: 813-598-1055.
Fax: 813-598-1868.
West Palm Beach, Florida Office: 777 South Flagler Drive, Suite 900.
Telephone: 407-659-5990.
Fax: 407-659-6313.
Key West, Florida Office: 3132 North Side Drive, Suite 102.
Telephone: 305-296-1774.
Fax: 305-296-1715
London, England Office: Blake Lodge, Bridge Lane, London SW11 3AD, England.
Telephone: 44-71-978-7748.
Fax: 44-71-350-0156.

MEMBERS OF FIRM

Osmond C. Howe, Jr., (P.A.)
Brian P. Tague
Richard C. Grant (P.A.) (Resident, Naples Office)
Russell T. Kamradt (Resident, West Palm Beach Office)
Jose E. Castro (P.A.)
Richard M. Bezold
Thomas E. Streit (Resident, West Palm Beach Office)
Marjie C. Nealon (P.A.)
Michael T. Lynott (P.A.)
John F. Halula

OF COUNSEL

Jeri A. Poller

ASSOCIATE

G. Helen Athan (Resident, Naples Office)

Representative Clients: Arvida/JMB Partners; Bankers Trust Co.; Biscayne Kennel Club, Inc.; The Chase Manhattan Bank, N.A.; Lennar Corp.; Reynolds Metals Co.; United States Sugar Corp.; University of Miami.

For Complete List of Firm Personnel, See General Section

For full biographical listings, see the Martindale-Hubbell Law Directory

Miami—Continued

STEARNS WEAVER MILLER WEISSLER ALHADEFF & SITTERSON, P.A. (AV)

Suite 2200 Museum Tower, 150 West Flagler Street, 33130
Telephone: 305-789-3200
FAX: 305-789-3395
Tampa, Florida Office: Suite 2200 Landmark Centre, 401 East Jackson Street.
Telephone: 813-223-4800.
Fort Lauderdale, Florida Office: 200 East Broward Boulevard, Suite 1900.
Telephone: 305-462-9500.

E. Richard Alhadeff
Louise Jacowitz Allen
Stuart D. Ames
Thomas P. Angelo (Resident, Fort Lauderdale Office)
Lawrence J. Bailin (Resident, Tampa Office)
Patrick A. Barry (Resident, Fort Lauderdale Office)
Lisa K. Bennett (Resident, Fort Lauderdale Office)
Susan Fleming Bennett (Resident, Tampa Office)
Mark J. Bernet (Resident, Tampa Office)
Claire Bailey Carraway (Resident, Tampa Office)
Seth T. Craine (Resident, Tampa Office)
Piero Luciano Desiderio (Resident, Fort Lauderdale Office)
Mark P. Dikeman
Sharon Quinn Dixon
Alan H. Fein
Owen S. Freed
Dean M. Freitag
Robert E. Gallagher, Jr.
Alice R. Huneycutt (Resident, Tampa Office)
Theodore A. Jewell
Elizabeth J. Keeler
Teddy D. Klinghoffer
Robert T. Kofman
Thomas A. Lash (Resident, Tampa Office)
Joy Spillis Lundeen
Brian J. McDonough
Francisco J. Menendez
Antonio R. Menendez
Alison W. Miller
Vicki Lynn Monroe
Harold D. Moorefield, Jr.
John N. Muratides (Resident, Tampa Office)
John K. Olson (Resident, Tampa Office)
Robert C. Owens
Patricia A. Redmond
Carl D. Roston
Steven D. Rubin
Mark A. Schneider
Curtis H. Sitterson
Mark D. Solov
Eugene E. Stearns
Bradford Swing
Dennis R. Turner
Ronald L. Weaver (Resident, Tampa Office)
Robert I. Weissler
Patricia G. Welles
Martin B. Woods (Resident, Fort Lauderdale Office)

Shawn M. Bayne (Resident, Fort Lauderdale Office)
Lisa Berg
Hans C. Beyer (Resident, Tampa Office)
Dawn A. Carapella (Resident, Tampa Office)
Christina Maria Diaz
Robert I. Finvarb
Patricia K. Green
Marilyn D. Greenblatt
Richard B. Jackson
Aimee C. Jimenez
Cheryl A. Kaplan
Michael I. Keyes
Vernon L. Lewis
Kevin Bruce Love
Adam Coatsworth Mishcon
Elizabeth G. Rice (Resident, Tampa Office)
Glenn M. Rissman
Claudia J. Saenz
Richard E. Schatz
Robert P. Shantz (Resident, Tampa Office)
Martin S. Simkovic
Ronni D. Solomon
Jo Claire Spear (Resident, Tampa Office)
Gail Marie Stage (Resident, Fort Lauderdale Office)
Annette Torres
Barbara L. Wilhite

OF COUNSEL

Stephen A. Bennett

For full biographical listings, see the Martindale-Hubbell Law Directory

---

*ORLANDO,** Orange Co.

POHL & BROWN, P.A.

(See Winter Park)

IRBY G. PUGH (AV)

218 Annie Street, 32806
Telephone: 407-843-5840

Reference: Schofield Corporation; Kingsland Investments.

For full biographical listings, see the Martindale-Hubbell Law Directory

---

ROBERTSON, WILLIAMS & McDONALD, P.A. (AV)

538 East Washington Street, 32801
Telephone: 407-425-1606
Fax: 407-872-1341
Other Orlando Office: 20 North Eola Drive.

John M. Robertson
Hubert W. Williams (1937-1986)
J. Stephen McDonald

(See Next Column)

Beth S. Schick

Reference: First Union Bank.

For full biographical listings, see the Martindale-Hubbell Law Directory

---

PALM BEACH GARDENS, Palm Beach Co.

SCOTT, ROYCE, HARRIS, BRYAN, BARRA & JORGENSEN, PROFESSIONAL ASSOCIATION (AV)

4400 PGA Boulevard, Suite 900, 33410
Telephone: 407-624-3900
Fax: 407-524-3533

Raymond W. Royce

Representative Clients: Channing Development; John D. & Catherine T. MacArthur Foundation; First Union National Bank of Florida, N.A.; North Palm Beach Board of Realtors, Inc.; Lost Tree Village; Jupiter Hills, Pappalardo Contractors, Inc.; Art Moran Pontiac, Inc.; John D. and Catherine T. MacArthur Foundation; Wal-Mart Stores, Inc.; Whitworth Farms.

For Complete List of Firm Personnel, See General Section

For full biographical listings, see the Martindale-Hubbell Law Directory

---

*SARASOTA,** Sarasota Co.

ABEL, BAND, RUSSELL, COLLIER, PITCHFORD & GORDON, CHARTERED (AV)

Barnett Bank Center, 240 South Pineapple Avenue, P.O. Box 49948, 34230-6948
Telephone: 813-366-6660
FAX: 813-366-3999
Fort Myers, Florida Office: The Tidewater Building, 1375 Jackson Street, Suite 201, 33901.
Telephone: 813-337-0062.
FAX: 813-337-0406.
Venice, Florida Office: Suite 199, 333 South Tamiami Trail, 34285.
Telephone: 813-485-8200.
Fax: 813-488-9436.

David S. Band
Jeffrey S. Russell
Ronald L. Collier
Malcolm J. Pitchford
Cheryl Lasris Gordon
Anthony J. Abate
Steven J. Chase
Kathryn Angell Carr
Michael S. Taaffe
Mark W. McFall
Jan Walters Pitchford

OF COUNSEL

Harvey J. Abel
Johnson S. Savary

Saralyn Abel
Douglas M. Bales
Gregory S. Band
John A. Garner
Mark D. Hildreth
Jane M. Kennedy
Christine Edwards Lamia
Bradley D. Magee
George H. Mazzarantani
Philip C. Zimmerman

References: Barnett Bank of Southwest Florida; Sun Bank/Gulf Coast.

For full biographical listings, see the Martindale-Hubbell Law Directory

---

*TALLAHASSEE,** Leon Co.

HOPPING BOYD GREEN & SAMS (AV)

123 South Calhoun Street, P.O. Box 6526, 32314
Telephone: 904-222-7500
Fax: 904-224-8551

MEMBERS OF FIRM

Carlos Alvarez
James S. Alves
Brian H. Bibeau
Kathleen L. Blizzard
Elizabeth C. Bowman
William L. Boyd, IV
Richard S. Brightman
Peter C. Cunningham
Ralph A. DeMeo
Thomas M. DeRose
William H. Green
Wade L. Hopping
Frank E. Matthews
Richard D. Melson
David L. Powell
William D. Preston
Carolyn S. Raepple
Gary P. Sams
Robert P. Smith
Cheryl G. Stuart

ASSOCIATES

Kristin M. Conroy
Charles A. Culp, Jr.
Connie C. Durrence
Jonathan S. Fox
James Calvin Goodlett
Gary K. Hunter, Jr.
Dalana W. Johnson
Jonathan T. Johnson
Angela R. Morrison
Gary V. Perko
Karen Peterson
Michael P. Petrovich
Douglas S. Roberts
R. Scott Ruth
Julie Rome Steinmeyer

OF COUNSEL

W. Robert Fokes

Representative Clients: Amelia Island Plantation; American Cyanamid Co.; ARC America Corp.; Association of American Publishers; Association of Physical Fitness Centers; Cement Products Corp.; CF Industries; Champion Realty; Chemical Bank; Deseret Properties.

(See Next Column)

HOPPING BOYD GREEN & SAMS, *Tallahassee—Continued*

For full biographical listings, see the Martindale-Hubbell Law Directory

RADEY HINKLE THOMAS & MCARTHUR (AV)

Suite 1000 Monroe-Park Tower, 101 North Monroe Street, P.O. Drawer 11307, 32302
Telephone: 904-681-7766
Telecopier: 904-681-0506

John Radey
Elizabeth Waas McArthur
Jeffrey L. Frehn

Representative Clients: Lee County Mosquito Control District.

For Complete List of Firm Personnel, See General Section

For full biographical listings, see the Martindale-Hubbell Law Directory

ROSE, SUNDSTROM & BENTLEY (AV)

A Partnership including Professional Associations
2548 Blairstone Pines Drive, P.O. Box 1567, 32302-1567
Telephone: 904-877-6555
Telecopier: 904-656-4029

MEMBERS OF FIRM

Chris H. Bentley (P.A.)
John R. Jenkins
Martin S. Friedman (P.A.)
William E. Sundstrom (P.A.)
Diane D. Tremor (P.A.)

ASSOCIATE

Robert A. Antista

Representative Clients: Aloha Utilities, Inc.; Autry Petroleum Company; Bonita Springs Utility, Inc; Destec Energy; East Central Florida Services, Inc.; Hydratech Utilities, Inc.; Orange-Osceola Utilities, Inc.; Utility Board of Key West; Clay County Water and Sewer Authority.
Reference: Barnett Bank, Tallahassee.

For full biographical listings, see the Martindale-Hubbell Law Directory

*TAMPA,** Hillsborough Co.

DE LA PARTE, GILBERT & BALES, PROFESSIONAL ASSOCIATION (AV)

One Tampa City Center, Suite 2300, P.O. Box 2350, 33601-2350
Telephone: 813-229-2775
FAX: 813-229-2712

Louis A. de la Parte
John Calhoun Bales
Richard A. Gilbert
L. David de la Parte
Edward P. de la Parte, Jr.
Patrick J. McNamara
Michael A. Skelton

David M. Caldevilla
John R. Thomas
Ted R. Tamargo
David Dallas Dickey

For full biographical listings, see the Martindale-Hubbell Law Directory

HONIGMAN MILLER SCHWARTZ AND COHN (AV)

A Partnership including Professional Corporations
2700 Landmark Centre, 401 E. Jackson Street, 33602
Telephone: 813-221-6600
Telecopier: 813-223-4410
West Palm Beach, Florida Office: Suite 800 Esperante Building, 222 Lakeview Avenue.
Telephone: 407-838-4500.
Orlando, Florida Office: 390 North Orange Avenue, Suite 1300.
Telephone: 407-648-0300.
Detroit, Michigan Office: 2290 First National Building.
Telephone: 313-256-7800.
Lansing, Michigan Office: 222 North Washington Square, Suite 400.
Telephone: 517-484-8282.
Houston, Texas Office: 3100 First Interstate Bank Plaza, 1000 Louisiana.
Telephone: 713-650-2600.
Los Angeles, California Office: Watt Plaza, Suite 2200, 1875 Century Park East.
Telephone: 310-789-3800.
Fax: 310-789-3814.

MEMBER

Michael G. Cooke (P.A.)

ASSOCIATE

Susan M. Salvatore

For Complete List of Firm Personnel, See General Section

For full biographical listings, see the Martindale-Hubbell Law Directory

LANGFORD, HILL & TRYBUS, P.A. (AV)

Suite 800, Bayshore Place, 601 Bayshore Boulevard, 33606
Telephone: 813-251-5533
Telecopier: 813-251-1900
Wats: 1-800-277-2005

(See Next Column)

E. C. Langford
Ronald G. Hock
Edward A. Hill
Catherine M. Catlin
Ronald H. Trybus
Debra M. Kubicsek
William B. Smith

Fredrique B. Boire
Frederick T. Reeves
Muriel Desloovere
Barbara A. Sinsley
Kevin H. O'Neill
Stephens B. Woodrough (Not admitted in FL)
Vicki L. Page
Anthony G. Woodward

Representative Clients: Affiliated of Florida, Inc.; American Federation Insurance Co.; Armor Insurance; Bank of Tampa; Central Bank of Tampa; Cintas Corp.; Container Corporation of America; CU Financial Services; Farm Stores, Inc.; First Union Home Equity Bank.

For full biographical listings, see the Martindale-Hubbell Law Directory

RYDBERG, GOLDSTEIN & BOLVES, P.A. (AV)

Suite 200, 500 East Kennedy Boulevard, 33602
Telephone: 813-229-3900
Telecopier: 813-229-6101

Marsha Griffin Rydberg
Donald Alan Workman
Bruce S. Goldstein
David M. Corry
Brian A. Bolves
Leenetta Blanton
Robert E. V. Kelley, Jr.
Peter Baker
Homer Duvall, III
Jeffery R. Ward
Richard Thomas Petitt
Roy J. Ford, Jr.
John J. Dingfelder

For full biographical listings, see the Martindale-Hubbell Law Directory

SMITH, WILLIAMS & BOWLES, P.A. (AV)

Old Hyde Park, 712 South Oregon Avenue, 33606
Telephone: 813-253-5400
Fax: 813-254-3459
Orlando, Florida Office: Smith, Williams & Humphries, P.A., Southeast Bank Building, Suite 700, 201 East Pine Street.
Telephone: 407-849-5151.
St. Cloud, Florida Office: 1700-13th Street, Suite 2, 34769.
Telephone: 407-892-5545.

David Lisle Smith
James A. Muench
Gregory L. Williams
Dale K. Bohner
Margaret E. Bowles
Neal A. Sivyer
Jana P. Andrews
Robert L. Harding (Resident, Orlando Office)
Jeffrey A. Aman
J. Gregory Humphries (Resident, Orlando Office)
Daniel William King
Rebecca H. Forest (Resident, Orlando Office)

For full biographical listings, see the Martindale-Hubbell Law Directory

*VERO BEACH,** Indian River Co.

COLLINS, BROWN & CALDWELL, CHARTERED (AV)

756 Beachland Boulevard, P.O. Box 3686, 32964
Telephone: 407-231-4343
FAX: 407-234-5213

George G. Collins, Jr.
Bruce D. Barkett
Calvin B. Brown
Bradley W. Rossway
William W. Caldwell
Michael J. Garavaglia
John E. Moore, III

Reference: First Union Bank of Indian River County, Vero Beach, Florida.

For full biographical listings, see the Martindale-Hubbell Law Directory

*WEST PALM BEACH,** Palm Beach Co.

BURT & PUCILLO (AV)

Esperanté, Suite 960, 222 Lakeview Avenue, 33401
Telephone: 407-835-9400
Telecopier: 407-835-0322

MEMBERS OF FIRM

C. Oliver Burt, III
Michael J. Pucillo

ASSOCIATES

Wendy Hope Zoberman
Andrew H. Kayton

OF COUNSEL

Carol McLean Brewer

For full biographical listings, see the Martindale-Hubbell Law Directory

HONIGMAN MILLER SCHWARTZ AND COHN (AV)

A Partnership including Professional Corporations
Suite 800 Esperante Building, 222 Lakeview Avenue, 33401-6112
Telephone: 407-838-4500
Telecopier: 407-832-3036; 832-2645
Tampa, Florida Office: 2700 Landmark Centre, 401 E. Jackson Street.
Telephone: 813-221-6600.

(See Next Column)

HONIGMAN MILLER SCHWARTZ AND COHN—*Continued*

Orlando, Florida Office: 390 North Orange Avenue, Suite 1300.
Telephone: 407-648-0300.
Detroit, Michigan Office: 2290 First National Building.
Telephone: 313-256-7800.
Lansing, Michigan Office: 222 North Washington Square, Suite 400.
Telephone: 517-484-8282.
Houston, Texas: 3100 First Interstate Bank Plaza, 1000 Louisiana.
Telephone: 713-650-2600.
Los Angeles, California Office: Watt Plaza, Suite 2200, 1875 Century Park East.
Telephone: 310-789-3800.
Fax: 310-789-3814.

MEMBERS

Carla L. Brown
Donald H. Reed, Jr.
E. Lee Worsham (P.A.)

Representative Clients: Adler Group, Inc.; Chiquita Brands, Inc.; E. Llwyd Ecclestone, Jr.; Forbes/Cohen Properties; ITT-Rayonier, Inc.; National Advertising Company; PHM Corporation (Pulte Home Corp.); Thos. J. White Development Corp.; Linpro, Inc.; Rubin Periodical Group-FEC News.

For Complete List of Firm Personnel, See General Section

For full biographical listings, see the Martindale-Hubbell Law Directory

WINTER HAVEN, Polk Co.

PETERSON, MYERS, CRAIG, CREWS, BRANDON & PUTERBAUGH, P.A. (AV)

Suite 300, 141 5th Street N.W., P.O. Drawer 7608, 33883-7608
Telephone: 813-294-3360
Lake Wales, Florida Office: 130 East Central Avenue, P.O. Box 1079.
Telephones: 813-676-7611; 683-8942.
Lakeland, Florida Office: 100 East Main Street, P.O. Box 24628.
Telephones: 813-683-6511; 676-6934.

Jack P. Brandon
Beach A Brooks, Jr.
J. Davis Connor
Michael S. Craig
Roy A. Craig, Jr.
Jacob C. Dykxhoorn
Dennis P. Johnson
Kevin C. Knowlton
Douglas A. Lockwood, III
Corneal B. Myers
Cornelius B. Myers, III
Robert E. Puterbaugh
Abel A. Putnam
Thomas B. Putnam, Jr.
Deborah A. Ruster
Stephen R. Senn
Andrea Teves Smith
Kerry M. Wilson

General Counsel for: Barnett Bank of Polk County.
Representative Clients: Mutual Wholesale Co.; Sun Bank/Mid-Florida, N.A.; Chase Commercial Corp.; Barnett Banks, Inc.; Ben Hill Griffin, Inc.; Alcoma Association, Inc.
Approved Attorneys for: Attorneys' Title Insurance Fund; Federal Land Bank, Columbia, South Carolina; Equitable Life Assurance Society of the United States.

For full biographical listings, see the Martindale-Hubbell Law Directory

WINTER PARK, Orange Co.

POHL & BROWN, P.A. (AV)

280 West Canton Avenue, Suite 410, P.O. Box 3208, 32789
Telephone: 407-647-7645; 407-647-POHL
Telefax: 407-647-2314

Frank L. Pohl
Usher L. Brown
Houston E. Short
Dwight I. Cool
William W. Pouzar
Mary B. Van Leuven

OF COUNSEL

Frederick W. Peirsol

Representative Clients: Orange County Comptroller; Osceola County; School Board of Osceola County, Florida; Osceola Tourist Development Council; NationsBank of Florida, N.A.; SunBank, N.A.; The Bank of Winter Park; Bekins Moving and Storage Co., Inc.; Champion Boats, Inc.; KeyCom Telephone Systems, Inc.

For full biographical listings, see the Martindale-Hubbell Law Directory

GEORGIA

*ATLANTA,** Fulton Co.

ALSTON & BIRD (AV)

A Partnership including Professional Corporations
One Atlantic Center, 1201 West Peachtree Street, 30309-3424
Telephone: 404-881-7000
Telecopier: 404-881-7777
Cable Address: AMGRAM GA
Telex: 54-2996
Easylink: 62985848
Washington, D.C. Office: 700 Thirteenth Street, Suite 350 20005-3960.
Telephone: 202-508-3300.
Telecopier: 202-508-3333.

MEMBERS OF FIRM

William C. Humphreys, Jr.
James S. Stokes
Lee A. DeHihns III
Nill V. Toulme
R. Wayne Thorpe
Richard T. Fulton
Elizabeth A. Gilley

COUNSEL

Sydney S. Cleland

ASSOCIATES

Douglas E. Cloud
Robert D. Mowrey
Nicole Fletcher O'Connor
Robyn Ice Sosebee

Representative Clients: Anheuser-Busch Companies; Atlantic Steel Industries, Inc.; Exxon Corporation; Georgia-Pacific Corporation; The Goodyear Tire & Rubber Co.; Vulcan Materials Co.

For Complete List of Firm Personnel, See General Section

For full biographical listings, see the Martindale-Hubbell Law Directory

BONDURANT, MIXSON & ELMORE (AV)

1201 W. Peachtree Street Suite 3900, 30309
Telephone: 404-881-4100
FAX: 404-881-4111

MEMBERS OF FIRM

Emmet J. Bondurant II
H. Lamar Mixson
M. Jerome Elmore
Edward B. Krugman
James C. Morton
Jeffrey O. Bramlett
Dirk G. Christensen
Jane E. Fahey
Jeffrey D. Horst
John E. Floyd
Carolyn R. Gorwitz
Michael A. Sullivan

ASSOCIATES

Mary Jo Bradbury
P. Richard Game
Robin M. Hutchinson
J. Scott McClain
Keenan Rance Sephus Nix
Jill A. Pryor
Michael B. Terry
Joshua F. Thorpe

Representative Clients: The Aetna Casualty and Surety Company; Bottlers of Coca-Cola, U.S.A.; Brinks Home Security Systems, Inc.; Delta Air Lines, Inc.; Fina Oil and Chemical Company; JMB Realty Corp.; The Paradies Shops, Inc.; Sanifill, Inc.; Trammell Crow Co.

For Complete List of Firm Personnel, See General Section

For full biographical listings, see the Martindale-Hubbell Law Directory

BOVIS, KYLE & BURCH (AV)

A Partnership including Professional Corporations
Third Floor, 53 Perimeter Center East, 30346
Telephone: 404-391-9100
Telecopier: 404-668-0878
Alpharetta, Georgia Office: 41 Milton Avenue.
Telephone: 404-391-9100.
Telecopier: 404-668-0878.

MEMBERS OF FIRM

John M. Bovis (P.C.)
John V. Burch (P.C.)
C. Sam Thomas (P.C.)
James E. Singer

ASSOCIATES

Charles M. Medlin
Danna Farrell McBride
William S. Allred

For full biographical listings, see the Martindale-Hubbell Law Directory

FREEMAN & HAWKINS (AV)

4000 One Peachtree Center, 303 Peachtree Street, N.E., 30308-3243
Telephone: 404-614-7400
Fax: 404-614-750
CompuServe address: 73541,1626
Internet address: 73451.1626@compuserve.com

(See Next Column)

FREEMAN & HAWKINS, *Atlanta—Continued*

MEMBERS OF FIRM

J. Bruce Welch
Albert H. Parnell
A. Timothy Jones
Alan F. Herman
H. Lane Young, II
Joseph R. Cullens
Frank C. Bedinger, III
Julia Bennett Jagger
Stephen M. Lore
William H. Major, III
Edward M. Newsom
Jack N. Sibley
Warner S. Fox
Robert U. Wright

ASSOCIATES

Ollie M. Harton
Michael E. Hutchins
Kevin J. Bahr
Joanne Beauvoir Brown
Edwin L. Hall, Jr.
Robert Rache Elarbee
Louis E. Bridges III
Dennis J. Manganiello

Representative Clients: Ashland Oil, Inc.; Georgia Pacific Corp.; Ericsson Radio Systems, Inc.; Monsanto; Commercial Union Insurance Co.; Terminix; Mobay Corp.; Apollo Industries.

For Complete List of Firm Personnel, See General Section

For full biographical listings, see the Martindale-Hubbell Law Directory

HOLT, NEY, ZATCOFF & WASSERMAN (AV)

A Partnership including Professional Corporations
100 Galleria Parkway, Suite 600, 30339
Telephone: 404-956-9600
Facsimile Number: 404-956-1490

MEMBERS OF FIRM

J. Scott Jacobson
Richard P. Vornholt

Representative Clients: Safety-Kleen Corp.; Cummins South, Inc.; Trammell Crow Residential; Fleet Finance, Inc. of Georgia; NationsBank of Georgia, N.A.

For Complete List of Firm Personnel, See General Section

For full biographical listings, see the Martindale-Hubbell Law Directory

LONG ALDRIDGE & NORMAN (AV)

A Partnership including Professional Corporations
One Peachtree Center, Suite 5300, 303 Peachtree Street, 30308
Telephone: 404-527-4000
Telecopier: 404-527-4198
Washington, D.C. Office: Suite 950, 1615 L Street, 20036.
Telephone: 202-223-7033.
Telecopier: 202-223-7013.

MEMBERS OF FIRM

Phillip A. Bradley
Gordon D. Giffin
Edward A. Kazmarek
William F. Timmons

ASSOCIATES

Carol Russell Geiger
W. Scott Laseter

For Complete List of Firm Personnel, See General Section

For full biographical listings, see the Martindale-Hubbell Law Directory

SUTHERLAND, ASBILL & BRENNAN (AV)

999 Peachtree Street, N.E., 30309-3996
Telephone: 404-853-8000
Facsimile: 404-853-8806
Washington, D.C. Office: 1275 Pennsylvania Avenue, N.W., 20004-2404.
Telephone: 202-383-0100.
New York, N.Y. Office: 1270 Avenue of the Americas, 10020-1700.
Telephone: 212-332-3000.
Austin, Texas Office: 111 Congress Avenue, 23rd Floor, 78701-4079.
Telephone: 512-469-3350.

C. Christopher Hagy

Representative Clients: Blue Circle, Inc.; Chemical Products Corp.; China Clay Producers Association, Inc.; Ellis & Everard (J.S.) Holdings, Inc.; General Motors Corporation; LWD Inc.; Martin Marietta Corporation; Mobil Land Development Corporation; Southern Mills, Inc.; ECC International, Inc.

For Complete List of Firm Personnel, See General Section

For full biographical listings, see the Martindale-Hubbell Law Directory

HAWAII

*HONOLULU,** Honolulu Co.

DWYER IMANAKA SCHRAFF KUDO MEYER & FUJIMOTO ATTORNEYS AT LAW, A LAW CORPORATION (AV)

1800 Pioneer Plaza, 900 Fort Street Mall, 96813
Telephone: 808-524-8000
Telecopier: 808-526-1419
Mailing Address: P.O. Box 2727, 96803

John R. Dwyer, Jr.
Mitchell A. Imanaka
Paul A. Schraff
Benjamin A. Kudo (Atty. at Law, A Law Corp.)
William G. Meyer, III
Wesley M. Fujimoto
Ronald Van Grant
Jon M. H. Pang
Blake W. Bushnell
Kenn N. Kojima

Adelbert Green
Richard T. Asato, Jr.
Scott W. Settle
Darcie S. Yoshinaga
Tracy Timothy Woo
Lawrence I. Kawasaki
Douglas H. Inouye
Christine A. Low

OF COUNSEL

Randall Y. Iwase

For full biographical listings, see the Martindale-Hubbell Law Directory

IDAHO

*BOISE,** Ada Co.

ELAM & BURKE, A PROFESSIONAL ASSOCIATION (AV)

Key Financial Center, 702 West Idaho Street, P.O. Box 1539, 83701
Telephone: 208-343-5454
Telecopier: 208-384-5844

Carl P. Burke
John Magel
William G. Dryden

Kristen R. Thompson
Margaret S. Schaefer
Eric L. Berliner

Representative Clients: Morrison-Knudsen, Inc.; Texas Instruments, Inc.; Prudential Securities, Inc.; Pechiney Corp.; Dow Corning Corporation; U.S. West Communications; State Farm Insurance Cos.; Sinclair Oil Company d/b/a Sun Valley Company; Farmers Insurance Group; Hecla Mining Company.

For Complete List of Firm Personnel, See General Section

For full biographical listings, see the Martindale-Hubbell Law Directory

MOFFATT, THOMAS, BARRETT, ROCK & FIELDS, CHARTERED (AV)

First Security Building, 911 West Idaho Street, Suite 300, P.O. Box 829, 83701
Telephone: 208-345-2000
FAX: 208-385-5384
Idaho Falls Office: 525 Park Avenue, Suite 2D, P.O. Box 1367, 83403.
Telephone: 208-522-6700.
FAX: 208-522-5111.
Pocatello, Idaho Office: 1110 Call Creek Drive, P.O. Box 4941, 83201.
Telephone: 208-233-2001.

Morgan W. Richards, Jr.
Jon S. Gorski
Gary T. Dance (Idaho Falls and Pocatello Offices)

Representative Clients: BMC West Corporation; Chevron, U.S.A.; First Security Bank of Idaho, N.A.; General Motors Corp.; Idaho Potato Commission; Intermountain Gas Co.; John Alden Life Insurance Co.; Micron, Inc.; Royal Insurance Cos.; St. Luke's Regional Medical Center & Mountain States Tumor Institute.

For Complete List of Firm Personnel, See General Section

For full biographical listings, see the Martindale-Hubbell Law Directory

KETCHUM, Blaine Co.

JAMES L. KENNEDY, JR. (AV)

340 Second Street East, P.O. Box 2165, 83340
Telephone: 208-726-8255
Reference: First Interstate Bank of Idaho, N.A. (Ketchum-Sun Valley Branch); First Security Bank of Idaho, N.A. (Ketchum Branch)

For full biographical listings, see the Martindale-Hubbell Law Directory

ILLINOIS

AURORA, Kane Co.

MURPHY, HUPP, FOOTE, MIELKE AND KINNALLY (AV)

North Island Center, P.O. Box 5030, 60507
Telephone: 708-844-0056
FAX: 708-844-1905

MEMBERS OF FIRM

William C. Murphy
Robert B. Hupp
Robert M. Foote
Craig S. Mielke
Patrick M. Kinnally
Paul G. Krentz
Joseph C. Loran
Gerald K. Hodge

Timothy D. O'Neil
Thomas U. Hipp

OF COUNSEL

Robert T. Olson

Representative Clients: American Telephone & Telegraph Co.; Fox Valley Park District; Lyon Metal Products; Kane County Forest Preserve District; Hollywood Casino; Employers Mutual Insurance Co.; Forty-Eight Insulations, Inc.; UNR Asbestos Disease Trust; Richards-Wilcox Co.; National Bank & Trust Company of Syracuse.

For full biographical listings, see the Martindale-Hubbell Law Directory

*CHICAGO,** Cook Co.

BELL, BOYD & LLOYD (AV)

Three First National Plaza Suite 3300, 70 West Madison Street, 60602
Telephone: 312-372-1121
FAX: 312-372-2098
Washington, D.C. Office: 1615 L Street, N.W.
Telephone: 202-466-6300.
FAX: 202-463-0678.

MEMBERS OF FIRM

Michael K. Ohm
Neal H. Weinfield

ASSOCIATE

Thomas R. Carey

For Complete List of Firm Personnel, See General Section

For full biographical listings, see the Martindale-Hubbell Law Directory

BROWN & BRYANT, P.C. (AV)

35 East Wacker Drive Suite 1356, 60601
Telephone: 312-236-1450
Fax: 312-236-1451

Johnine J. Brown
Mary C. Bryant
Maureen Martin

Ann Parisi Messer

For full biographical listings, see the Martindale-Hubbell Law Directory

JOHNSON & BELL, LTD. (AV)

Suite 2200, 222 North La Salle Street, 60601
Telephone: 312-372-0770
Facsimile: 312-372-9818
Wheaton, Illinois Office: Suite 1640, 2100 Manchester Road.
Telephone: 708-510-0880.
Facsimile: 780-510-0939.

John W. Bell
Frederick S. Mueller
Daniel C. Murray

William J. Anaya

References available upon request.

For full biographical listings, see the Martindale-Hubbell Law Directory

WILSON & MCILVAINE (AV)

500 West Madison, Suite 3700, 60661-2511
Telephone: 312-715-5000
Telecopier: 312-715-5155

PARTNERS

C. John Anderson
Richard P. Blessen
Kendall R. Meyer

For Complete List of Firm Personnel, See General Section

For full biographical listings, see the Martindale-Hubbell Law Directory

*SPRINGFIELD,** Sangamon Co.

MOHAN, ALEWELT, PRILLAMAN & ADAMI (AV)

First of America Center, Suite 325, 1 North Old Capitol Plaza, 62701-1323
Telephone: 217-528-2517
Telecopier: 217-528-2553

MEMBER

Fred C. Prillaman

ASSOCIATES

Stephen F. Hedinger
Becky S. McCray

Representative Clients: Andrews Environmental Engineering, Inc.; B & W Land Co.; Browning-Ferris Industries of Illinois, Inc.; Carlinville Area Hospital; Evans Construction Co.; Federal Deposit Insurance Corp.; McLaughlin Manufacturing Co.; Park Realty.

For Complete List of Firm Personnel, See General Section

For full biographical listings, see the Martindale-Hubbell Law Directory

INDIANA

*EVANSVILLE,** Vanderburgh Co.

FINE & HATFIELD (AV)

520 N.W. Second Street, P.O. Box 779, 47705-0779
Telephone: 812-425-3592
Telecopier: 812-421-4269

MEMBER OF FIRM

Thomas H. Bryan

For Complete List of Firm Personnel, See General Section

For full biographical listings, see the Martindale-Hubbell Law Directory

KAHN, DEES, DONOVAN & KAHN (AV)

P.O. Box 3646, 47735-3646
Telephone: 812-423-3183
Fax: 812-423-3841

MEMBERS OF FIRM

Alan N. Shovers
Brian P. Williams
G. Michael Schopmeyer
Jeffrey K. Helfrich

ASSOCIATE

Kent A. Brasseale, II

Representative Clients: Enviro Group, Inc.; National City Bancshares; D. Patrick, Inc.; Deaconess Hospital, Inc.; Faultless Caster Corp.; Geo. Koch Sons, Inc.; Red Spot Paint & Varnish Co., Inc.; Sterling Boiler & Mechanical, Inc.; Windsor Plastics, Inc.; CSX Transporation, Inc.

For Complete List of Firm Personnel, See General Section

For full biographical listings, see the Martindale-Hubbell Law Directory

*FORT WAYNE,** Allen Co.

BARRETT & MCNAGNY (AV)

215 East Berry Street, P.O. Box 2263, 46801-2263
Telephone: 219-423-9551
Telecopier: 219-423-8924
Huntington, Indiana Office: 429 Jefferson Park Mall, P.O. Box 5156.
Telephone: 219-356-7766.
Telecopier: 219-356-7782.

MEMBERS OF FIRM

Richard E. Fox
John D. Walda
James P. Fenton
Alan VerPlanck

ASSOCIATE

David R. Steiner

Representative Clients: City of New Haven; Fort Wayne National Bank; Franklin Electric Co.; Lake George Regional Sewer District; Lincoln Food Service Products, Inc.; Omni-Source Corp.

For Complete List of Firm Personnel, See General Section

For full biographical listings, see the Martindale-Hubbell Law Directory

GALLUCCI, HOPKINS & THEISEN, P.C. (AV)

229 West Berry Street, Suite 400, P.O. Box 12663, 46864-2663
Telephone: 219-424-3800
Telecopier: 219-420-1260

William T. Hopkins, Jr.
John C. Theisen
John T. Menzie
M. Scott Hall
Loren K. Allison

(See Next Column)

GALLUCCI, HOPKINS & THEISEN P.C., *Fort Wayne—Continued*

Michael A. Scheer
Thomas N. O'Malley
Mark S. Kittaka
Tonya S. Shea
Kristen L. Maly
Eric H. J. Stahlhut
Jeffrey S. Schafer
Anthony G. Genakos (Not admitted in IN)
Frank L. Gallucci

For full biographical listings, see the Martindale-Hubbell Law Directory

HAMMOND, Lake Co.

BECKMAN, KELLY & SMITH (AV)

5920 Hohman Avenue, 46320
Telephone: 219-933-6200
Telecopier: 219-933-6201

MEMBERS OF FIRM

Richard P. Tinkham (1902-1973)
Daniel F. Kelly (1914-1978)
J. B. Smith
Andrew J. Fetsch
Randall J. Nye
Robert F. Parker
Daniel W. Glavin

ASSOCIATES

Larry L. Chubb
Melanie Morgan Dunajeski
Scott A. Bearby
Christine Hajduch Curosh

OF COUNSEL

Eric L. Kirschner
John F. Beckman, Jr.

Representative Clients: Waste Management of North America, Inc.; The Travelers Companies; Bethlehem Steel Corp.; ITT Finance; Northwest Indiana Public Broadcasting, Inc.; Signal Capital Corporation; CIGNA Companies; Sears Roebuck and Co.

For full biographical listings, see the Martindale-Hubbell Law Directory

*INDIANAPOLIS,** Marion Co.

BAKER & DANIELS (AV)

300 North Meridian Street, 46204
Telephone: 317-237-0300
FAX: 317-237-1000
Fort Wayne, Indiana Office: 2400 Fort Wayne National Bank Building.
Telephone: 219-424-8000.
South Bend, Indiana Office: First Bank Building, 205 West Jefferson Boulevard.
Telephone: 219-234-4149.
Elkhart, Indiana Office: 301 South Main Street, Suite 307,
Telephone: 219-296-6000.
Washington, D.C. Office: 1701 K Street, N.W., Suite 400.
Telephone: 202-785-1565.

MEMBERS OF FIRM

Joseph B. Carney
Michael J. Huston
Lewis D. Beckwith
Anne Slaughter Andrew
James W. Clark

ASSOCIATE

Sharon A. Hilmes

Representative Clients: Associated Insurance Companies, Inc.; Bank One, Indianapolis, N.A.; Borg-Warner Corp.; City of Indianapolis; Cummins Engine Co.; Eli Lilly and Company; General Motors Corp.; Indiana Bell; Indianapolis Public Schools; United Airlines.

For Complete List of Firm Personnel, See General Section

For full biographical listings, see the Martindale-Hubbell Law Directory

BOSE MCKINNEY & EVANS (AV)

2700 First Indiana Plaza, 135 North Pennsylvania Street, 46204
Telephone: 317-684-5000
Facsimile: 317-684-5173
Indianapolis North Office: Suite 1201, 8888 Keystone Crossing, 46240.
Telephone: 317-574-3700.
Facsimile: 317-574-3716.

MEMBERS OF FIRM

Theodore J. Nowacki
James C. Carlino
C. Joseph Russell
Kathleen G. Lucas

ASSOCIATES

Lisa C. McKinney
Daniel P. McInerny

Representative Clients: Amoco Cor.; Duke Realty Investments Inc.; ; Emmis Broadcasting Corp.; First Indiana Bank; Indiana League of Savings Institutions, Inc.; Prudential Life Insurance Co.; Metropolitan Life Insurance Co.; USX Corp.; Indiana Pork Producers Association.

For Complete List of Firm Personnel, See General Section

For full biographical listings, see the Martindale-Hubbell Law Directory

CROMER, EAGLESFIELD & MAHER (AV)

1500 Market Tower, 10 West Market Street, 46204-2968
Telephone: 317-464-1500
Fax: 317-464-1506

(See Next Column)

John R. Cromer
R. Davy Eaglesfield, III
Kenneth W. Maher

For full biographical listings, see the Martindale-Hubbell Law Directory

ICE MILLER DONADIO & RYAN (AV)

One American Square Box 82001, 46282-0002
Telephone: 317-236-2100
Fax: 317-236-2219

MEMBERS OF FIRM

W. C. Blanton
Phillip R. Scaletta, III

OF COUNSEL

Deborah A. Lawrence
Diana Lynn Wann

ASSOCIATES

Terri Ann Czajka
Philippa M. Guthrie
Jodie L. Miner

Representative Clients: Amax Coal Co.; Amoco Oil Corp.; CertainTeed Corp.; Chrysler Corp.; Dana Corp.; Joseph E. Seagram & Sons, Inc.; Lehigh Portland Cement Co.; Phelps Dodge Corp.; Reilly Industries, Inc.; Texas Eastern Corp.

For Complete List of Firm Personnel, See General Section

For full biographical listings, see the Martindale-Hubbell Law Directory

JOHNSON, SMITH, DENSBORN, WRIGHT & HEATH (AV)

One Indiana Square Suite 1800, 46204
Telephone: 317-634-9777
Telecopier: 317-636-9061

MEMBERS OF FIRM

John F. Joyce (1948-1994)
Wayne O. Adams, III
Robert M. Baker, III
Thomas A. Barnard
David J. Carr
Peter D. Cleveland
David R. Day
Donald K. Densborn
Thomas N. Eckerle
Mark W. Ford
G. Ronald Heath
Robert B. Hebert
John David Hoover
Andrew W. Hull
Dennis A. Johnson
Richard L. Johnson
Michael J. Kaye
John R. Kirkwood
David Williams Russell
James T. Smith
Martha Taylor Starkey
David E. Wright

ASSOCIATES

Robert C. Wolf (1949-1993)
Carolyn H. Andretti
Maureen F. Barnard
David G. Blachly
Robert T. Buday
Sean Michael Clapp
Jeffrey S. Cohen
Charles M. Freeland
David W. Givens, Jr.
Gary P. Goodin
Patricia L. Marshall
Bradley C. Morris
Steven J. Moss
Padric K. J. O'Brien
Cathleen J. Perry
David D. Robinson
Ronald G. Sentman
David A. Tucker
Sally Franklin Zweig

OF COUNSEL

Earl Auberry (1923-1989)
Larry A. Conrad (1935-1990)
Bruce W. Claycombe
Laura S. Cohen
Paul D. Gresk
William T. Lawrence
Mark A. Palmer
Lawrence W. Schmits
Catherine A. Singleton

For full biographical listings, see the Martindale-Hubbell Law Directory

KROGER, GARDIS & REGAS (AV)

111 Monument Circle, Suite 900, 46204-3059
Telephone: 317-692-9000
Telecopier: 317-264-6832

MEMBERS OF FIRM

James A. Knauer
John J. Petr
James G. Lauck
Gary A. Schiffli
Jay P. Kennedy
Brian C. Bosma
William C. Potter, II

ASSOCIATES

Gregory P. Cafouros
Michelle Howden Laconi
Steven R. Schafer
Marcia E. Roan
William Bock, III
Mary Elizabeth Brames

Representative Clients: First of America Bank; Consulting Engineers of Indiana, Inc.; Society National Bank; Southland Corporation; Union Oil Company of California; Citgo, Inc.; Kova Fertilizer, Inc.

For full biographical listings, see the Martindale-Hubbell Law Directory

NORRIS, CHOPLIN & SCHROEDER (AV)

Ninth Floor, 101 West Ohio Street, 46204-1906
Telephone: 317-269-9330
FAX: 317-269-9338

(See Next Column)

NORRIS, CHOPLIN & SCHROEDER—*Continued*

MEMBERS OF FIRM

Richard L. Norris
John M. Choplin, II
Peter A. Schroeder
Bruce L. Kamplain
Raymond L. Faust
Mary Jo Hunter Wedding

ASSOCIATES

Ellen White Quigley
Kyle A. Jones
Peter Peck-Koh Ho
Nelson A. Nettles
Andrew C. Chapman

OF COUNSEL

James D. Matthews

Reference: The Indiana National Bank.

For full biographical listings, see the Martindale-Hubbell Law Directory

PLEWS SHADLEY RACHER & BRAUN (AV)

1346 North Delaware Street, 46202-2415
Telephone: 317-637-0700
Telecopier: 317-637-0710

MEMBERS OF FIRM

George M. Plews
Sue A. Shadley
Peter M. Racher
Christopher J. Braun

ASSOCIATES

Harinder Kaur
Leonardo D. Robinson
Frederick D. Emhardt
S. Curtis DeVoe
Jeffrey D. Claflin
John E. Klarquist
Jeffrey D. Featherstun
Amy K. Luigs
Donna C. Marron

OF COUNSEL

Craig A. Wood
Christine C. H. Plews
M. Scott Barrett

For full biographical listings, see the Martindale-Hubbell Law Directory

SOMMER & BARNARD, ATTORNEYS AT LAW, PC (AV)

4000 Bank One Tower, 111 Monument Circle, P.O. Box 44363, 46244-0363
Telephone: 317-630-4000
FAX: 317-236-9802
North Office: 8900 Keystone Crossing, Suite 1046, Indianapolis, Indiana, 46240-2134.
Telephone: 317-630-4000.
FAX: 317-844-4780.

James K. Sommer
William C. Barnard
James E. Hughes
Edward W. Harris, III
Frederick M. King
Jerald I. Ancel
Eric R. Johnson
Gordon L. Pittenger
Lynn Brundage Jongleux
Frank J. Deveau
John E. Taylor
Michael C. Terrell
Marlene Reich
Richard C. Richmond, III
Julianne S. Lis-Milam
Steven C. Shockley
Stephen B. Cherry
Robert J. Hicks
Lawrence A. Vanore
Donald C. Biggs
Debra McVicker Lynch

Gayle A. Reindl
Ann Carr Mackey
Gregory J. Seketa
Sandra L. Gosling
Edwin J. Broecker
Thomas R. DeVoe
Mary T. Doherty
William K. Boncosky

OF COUNSEL

Jerry Williams
Glenn Scolnik
Philip L. McCool
Charles E. Valliere
Verl L. Myers

Representative Clients: Comerica Bank; Excel Industries; Federal Express; Kimball International; Monsanto; Renault Automation; Repport International; TRW, Inc.

For full biographical listings, see the Martindale-Hubbell Law Directory

STARK DONINGER & SMITH (AV)

Suite 700, 50 South Meridian Street, 46204
Telephone: 317-638-2400
Fax: 317-633-6618; 633-6619

MEMBERS OF FIRM

John C. Stark
Bruce E. Smith
John W. Van Buskirk
Richard W. Dyar
Patricia Seasor Bailey
Brian J. Tuohy
Mark A. Bailey
Lewis E. Willis, Jr.

ASSOCIATES

Neil E. Lucas
Richard B. Kaufman
Patrick J. Dietrick

COUNSEL

Clarence H. Doninger
Gregory S. Fehribach
John F. Hoehner
Robert D. Maas
William K. Byrum

(See Next Column)

Representative Clients: ATEC Environmental Consultants; ATEC Associates, Inc.; American Environmental Corp.; Douglass Environmental Services, Inc.

For full biographical listings, see the Martindale-Hubbell Law Directory

MERRILLVILLE, Lake Co.

BURKE, MURPHY, COSTANZA & CUPPY (AV)

Suite 600 8585 Broadway, 46410
Telephone: 219-769-1313
Telecopier: 219-769-6806
East Chicago, Indiana Office: First National Bank Building. 720 W. Chicago Avenue.
Telephone: 219-397-2401.
Telecopier: 219-397-0506.
Palm Harbor, Florida Office: Suite 280, 33920 U.S. Highway 19 North.
Telephone: 813-787-7799.
Telecopier: 813-787-7237.

MEMBERS OF FIRM

Joseph E. Costanza
Frederick M. Cuppy

ASSOCIATE

Paula E. Neff

Representative Clients: NBD/Gainer N.A.; The Post Tribune (Knight Ridder Publications); Town of Merrillville; Whiteco Industries; Continental Machine & Engineering Co., Inc.; Gary Steel Products Corp.; Superior Construction Co., Inc.; Federal National Mortgage Association; Morrison Construction Co.; Welsh Oil, Inc.

For Complete List of Firm Personnel, See General Section

For full biographical listings, see the Martindale-Hubbell Law Directory

*SOUTH BEND,** St. Joseph Co.

DORAN BLACKMOND READY HAMILTON & WILLIAMS (AV)

1700 Valley American Bank Building, 211 W. Washington Street, 46601
Telephone: 219-288-1800
Fax: 219-236-4265

MEMBERS OF FIRM

John E. Doran
Don G. Blackmond
David T. Ready
John C. Hamilton
A. Howard Williams

For full biographical listings, see the Martindale-Hubbell Law Directory

KANSAS

OVERLAND PARK, Johnson Co.

SHAMBERG, JOHNSON, BERGMAN & MORRIS, CHARTERED (AV)

Suite 355, 4551 West 107th Street, 66207
Telephone: 913-642-0600
Fax: 913-642-9629
Kansas City, Kansas Office: Suite 860, New Brotherhood Building, 8th and State Streets.
Telephone: 913-281-1900.
Kansas City, Missouri Office: Suite 205, Scarritt Arcade Building, 819 Walnut.
Telephone: 816-556-9431.

Lynn R. Johnson
Victor A. Bergman
David R. Morris
John M. Parisi

Steven G. Brown
John E. Rogers
Steve N. Six
Anthony L. DeWitt (Not admitted in KS)
Patrick A. Hamilton

OF COUNSEL

John E. Shamberg

For full biographical listings, see the Martindale-Hubbell Law Directory

*TOPEKA,** Shawnee Co.

GOODELL, STRATTON, EDMONDS & PALMER (AV)

515 South Kansas Avenue, 66603-3999
Telephone: 913-233-0593
Telecopier: 913-233-8870

MEMBERS OF FIRM

Gerald L. Goodell
N. Larry Bork

OF COUNSEL

Samuel D. Brownback

ASSOCIATE

Curtis J. Waugh

Local Counsel for: Farm Bureau Mutual Insurance Co.; Metropolitan Life Insurance Co.; St. Paul Fire & Marine Insurance Co.

(See Next Column)

GOODELL, STRATTON, EDMONDS & PALMER, *Topeka—Continued*

General Counsel for: American Home Life Insurance Co.; Columbian National Title Insurance Co.; The Menninger Foundation; Stauffer Communications, Inc.; Kansas Association of Realtors; Kansas Medical Society; Kansas Hospital Association.

For Complete List of Firm Personnel, See General Section

For full biographical listings, see the Martindale-Hubbell Law Directory

*WICHITA,** Sedgwick Co.

DEPEW & GILLEN (AV)

151 North Main, Suite 700, 67202-1408
Telephone: 316-265-9621
Facsimile: 316-265-3819

MEMBERS OF FIRM

Spencer L. Depew — David W. Nickel
Dennis L. Gillen — Nicholas S. Daily
Jack Scott McInteer — David E. Rogers
Charles Christian Steincamp

For full biographical listings, see the Martindale-Hubbell Law Directory

FLEESON, GOOING, COULSON & KITCH, L.L.C. (AV)

125 North Market Street, Suite 1600, P.O. Box 997, 67201-0997
Telephone: 316-267-7361
Telecopier: 316-267-1754

Thomas D. Kitch — Gregory J. Stucky
Stephen M. Stark

Scott Jensen

Attorneys for: Bank IV, Wichita, N.A; Intrust Bank, N.A.; Wichita Eagle and Beacon Publishing Co., Inc.; Southwest Kansas Royalty Owners Assn.; Liberty Mutual Insurance Co.; Grant Thornton; The Law Company; Vulcan Materials Co.; The Wichita State University Board of Trustees.

For Complete List of Firm Personnel, See General Section

For full biographical listings, see the Martindale-Hubbell Law Directory

FOULSTON & SIEFKIN (AV)

(Formerly Foulston, Siefkin, Powers & Eberhardt)
700 Fourth Financial Center, Broadway at Douglas, 67202
Telephone: 316-267-6371
Facsimile: 316-267-6345
Topeka, Kansas Office: 1515 Bank IV Tower, 534 Kansas Avenue. 66603.
Telephone: 913-233-3600.
FAX: 913-233-1610.
Member: Lex Mundi, A Global Association of Independent Firms

MEMBERS OF FIRM

Charles P. Efflandt — Wyatt A. Hoch

SPECIAL COUNSEL

Nancy M. Clifton — David M. Traster

For Complete List of Firm Personnel, See General Section

For full biographical listings, see the Martindale-Hubbell Law Directory

YOUNG, BOGLE, MCCAUSLAND, WELLS & CLARK, P.A. (AV)

106 West Douglas, Suite 923, 67202
Telephone: 316-265-7841
Facsimile: 316-265-3956

Glenn D. Young, Jr. — Paul S. McCausland

Mark R. Maloney

Representative Clients: Bridgestone/Firestone Inc.; Deere & Co.; Citibank; Metropolitan Life Insurance Co.; Equitable Assurance Society of the United States; Geotechnical Services, Inc.; Greif Bros. Corp.; Geotechnical Services, Inc.

For Complete List of Firm Personnel, See General Section

For full biographical listings, see the Martindale-Hubbell Law Directory

KENTUCKY

ASHLAND, Boyd Co.

VANANTWERP, MONGE, JONES & EDWARDS (AV)

1544 Winchester Avenue Fifth Floor, P.O. Box 1111, 41105-1111
Telephone: 606-329-2929
Fax: 606-329-0490
Ironton, Ohio Office: Cooper & VanAntwerp, A Legal Professional Association, 407 Center Street.
Telephone: 614-532-4366.

(See Next Column)

MEMBERS OF FIRM

Howard VanAntwerp, III — William H. Jones, Jr.
Gregory Lee Monge — Carl D. Edwards, Jr.
Kimberly Scott McCann

ASSOCIATES

Matthew J. Wixsom — James D. Keffer
William Mitchell Hall — Stephen S. Burchett

Representative Clients: Armco; Bank of Ashland; Calgon Carbon Corp.; King's Daughters' Hospital; Allstate Insurance Co.; Kemper Insurance Group; Commercial Union Cos.; The Mayo Coal Cos.; Maryland Casualty Co.; Merck & Co.

For full biographical listings, see the Martindale-Hubbell Law Directory

*BOWLING GREEN,** Warren Co.

ENGLISH, LUCAS, PRIEST & OWSLEY (AV)

1101 College Street, P.O. Box 770, 42102-0770
Telephone: 502-781-6500
Telecopier: 502-782-7782

MEMBERS OF FIRM

Charles E. English — Keith M. Carwell

ASSOCIATE

D. Gaines Penn

For Complete List of Firm Personnel, See General Section

For full biographical listings, see the Martindale-Hubbell Law Directory

*HINDMAN,** Knott Co.

WEINBERG, CAMPBELL, SLONE & SLONE, P.S.C. (AV)

Main Street, P.O. Box 727, 41822
Telephone: 606-785-5048; 785-5049
FAX: 606-785-3021

William R. Weinberg — Jerry Wayne Slone
Randy A. Campbell — Randy G. Slone

References: Bank of Hindman; Thacker & Grigsby Telephone Co.

For full biographical listings, see the Martindale-Hubbell Law Directory

*LEXINGTON,** Fayette Co.

BUCHANAN INGERSOLL, PROFESSIONAL CORPORATION (AV)

Suite 1210, Vine Center Office Tower, 333 West Vine Street, 40507
Telephone: 606-225-5333
Telecopier: 606-225-5334
Pittsburgh, Pennsylvania Office: 5800 USX Tower, 600 Grant Street.
Telephone: 412-562-8800.
Philadelphia, Pennsylvania Office: Two Logan Square, Twelfth Floor, 18th & Arch Streets.
Telephone: 215-665-8700.
Harrisburg, Pennsylvania Office: Vartan Parc, 30 North Third Street.
Telephone: 717-237-4800.
Tampa, Florida Office: 101 East Kennedy Boulevard, Suite 1030.
Telephone: 813-222-8180.
North Miami Beach, Florida Office: 19495 Biscayne Boulevard.
Telephone: 305-933-5600.
Princeton, New Jersey Office: Buchanan Ingersoll, A Partnership, College Centre, 500 College Road East.
Telephone: 609-452-2666.

John R. Leathers

Stephen G. Allen — Sam P. Burchett

For full biographical listings, see the Martindale-Hubbell Law Directory

GREENEBAUM DOLL & MCDONALD (AV)

A Partnership including Professional Service Corporations
1400 Vine Center Tower, 40508
Telephone: 606-231-8500
Telecopier: 606-255-2742
Telex: 213029
Louisville, Kentucky Office: 3300 National City Tower.
Telephone: 502-589-4200.
Fax: 502-587-3695.
Covington, Kentucky Office: 50 East River Center Boulevard, P.O. Box 2050.
Telephone: 606-655-4200.
Fax: 606-655-4239.
Cincinnati, Ohio Office: 832 Main Street.
Telephone: 513-421-8087.
Fax: 513-421-8089.

MEMBERS OF FIRM

Wm. T. Robinson, III — Bruce E. Cryder
Lloyd R. Cress — Carolyn M. Brown (Resident)
Marcus P. McGraw (Resident) — John C. Bender (Resident)
David A. Owen (Resident)

(See Next Column)

GREENEBAUM DOLL & MCDONALD—*Continued*

ASSOCIATES

John A. Kolanz (Resident) Bryan R. Reynolds (Resident)

Representative Clients: Aetna Life Insurance Co.; ANDALEX Resources, Inc.; Ashland Oil, Inc.; AT&T Communications, Inc.; Bethlehem Steel Corp.; Brown-Forman Corp.; Columbia Gas & Transmission Co.; Commonwealth Aluminum Corp.; Consolidation Coal Co.; Costain Coal, Inc.
*A Professional Service Corporation

For Complete List of Firm Personnel, See General Section

For full biographical listings, see the Martindale-Hubbell Law Directory

LANDRUM & SHOUSE (AV)

106 West Vine Street, P.O. Box 951, 40588-0951
Telephone: 606-255-2424
Facsimile: 606-233-0308
Louisville, Kentucky Office: 400 West Market Street, Suite 1550, 40202.
Telephone: 502-589-7616.
Facsimile: 502-589-2119.

MEMBERS OF FIRM

John H. Burrus James W. Smirz
George P. Parker (Resident, Louisville Office) Benjamin Cowgill, Jr.

District Attorneys: CSX Transportation, Inc.
Special Trial Counsel: Ford Motor Co. and Affiliates (Eastern Kentucky); Clark Equipment Co.
Representative Clients: The Continental Insurance Cos.; U.S. Insurance Group; U.S. Fidelity & Guaranty Co.; Ohio Casualty Insurance Co.; CIGNA; Royal Insurance Cos.

For Complete List of Firm Personnel, See General Section

For full biographical listings, see the Martindale-Hubbell Law Directory

STOLL, KEENON & PARK (AV)

201 E. Main Street, Suite 1000, 40507-1380
Telephone: 606-231-3000
Telecopier: 606-253-1093; 606-253-1027
Frankfort, Kentucky Office: 326 West Main Street.
Telephone: 502-875-6000.
Telecopier: 502-875-6008.
Louisville, Kentucky Office: 400 West Market Street, Suite 2650, 40202.
Telephone: 502-568-9100.
Telecopier: 502-568-6340.

MEMBERS OF FIRM

Spencer D. Noe Samuel D. Hinkle, IV
Donald P. Wagner

ASSOCIATES

Lea Pauley Goff Culver V. Halliday
John Browning Park

Representative Clients: Bank One, Lexington, NA; Farmers Capital Bank Corp.; The Tokai Bank Ltd.; Link Belt Construction Equipment Co.; General Motors Corp.; International Business Machines Corp.; Ohbayashi Corp.; R. J. Reynolds Tobacco Co.; Rockwell International Corp.; Square D Co.

For Complete List of Firm Personnel, See General Section

For full biographical listings, see the Martindale-Hubbell Law Directory

STURGILL, TURNER & TRUITT (AV)

155 East Main Street, 40507
Telephone: 606-255-8581
Fax: 606-231-0851

MEMBERS OF FIRM

Jerry D. Truitt Kevin G. Henry

For Complete List of Firm Personnel, See General Section

For full biographical listings, see the Martindale-Hubbell Law Directory

*LOUISVILLE,** Jefferson Co.

MIDDLETON & REUTLINGER, P.S.C. (AV)

2500 Brown and Williamson Tower, 40202-3410
Telephone: 502-584-1135
Fax: 502-561-0442
Jeffersonville, Indiana Office: 605 Watt Street, 47130.
Telephone: 812-282-4886.

Charles G. Middleton, III Stewart L. Prather
John W. Bilby Kathiejane Oehler

For Complete List of Firm Personnel, See General Section

For full biographical listings, see the Martindale-Hubbell Law Directory

OGDEN NEWELL & WELCH (AV)

1200 One Riverfront Plaza, 40202-2973
Telephone: 502-582-1601
Fax: 502-581-9564

(See Next Column)

MEMBERS OF FIRM

Richard F. Newell Stephen F. Schuster
D. Brian Rattliff

ASSOCIATES

Teresa C. Buchheit Douglas C. Ballantine
Tracy S. Prewitt

Counsel for: KU Energy Corp.; Kentucky Utilities Co.; Brown-Forman Corp.; B.F. Goodrich Co.; Interlock Industries, Inc.; Akzo Coatings, Inc.; United Medical Corp.

For Complete List of Firm Personnel, See General Section

For full biographical listings, see the Martindale-Hubbell Law Directory

WOODWARD, HOBSON & FULTON (AV)

2500 National City Tower, 101 South Fifth Street, 40202
Telephone: 502-581-8000
Fax: 502-581-8111
Lexington, Kentucky Office: National City Plaza, 301 East Main Street, Suite 650.
Telephone: 606-244-7100.
Telecopier: 606-244-7111.

MEMBERS OF FIRM

Thomas A. Hoy Gregory L. Smith
Arthur L. Williams

OF COUNSEL

Robert C. Hobson

Representative Clients: Custom Resins; Sun Refining and Marketing; Kopper Industries, Inc.; Concord Custom Cleaners; Louisville Forge & Gear Works; Hechingers; Rail Services, Inc.; National Waste, Inc.; Graves County Landfill, Inc.

For Complete List of Firm Personnel, See General Section

For full biographical listings, see the Martindale-Hubbell Law Directory

LOUISIANA

*BATON ROUGE,** East Baton Rouge Parish

KEAN, MILLER, HAWTHORNE, D'ARMOND, MCCOWAN & JARMAN, L.L.P. (AV)

22nd Floor, One American Place, P.O. Box 3513, 70821
Telephone: 504-387-0999
Fax: 504-388-9133
New Orleans, Louisiana Office: Energy Centre, Suite 1470, 1100 Poydras Street.
Telephone: 504-585-3050.
Fax: 504-585-3051.

MEMBERS OF FIRM

Charles S. McCowan, Jr. M. Dwayne Johnson
G. William Jarman J. Carter Wilkinson
Leonard L. Kilgore III Sandra Louise Edwards
Maureen N. Harbourt Katherine W. King

Charles S. McCowan III James Randy Young
Esteban Herrera, Jr. Robert Neill Aguiluz
Susan Knight Carter (Resident, New Orleans Office)

Representative Clients: Amoco Production Company, Houston, TX; BASF Corporation, Parsippany, NJ; Exxon Company, U.S.A., Baton Rouge, LA; Georgia-Pacific Corporation, Atlanta, GA; Louisiana Chemical Association, Baton Rouge, La.; PPG Industries, Inc., Pittsburgh, PA; Rhone-Poulenc Basic Chemicals Company, Shelton, CT; Tenneco, Inc., Houston, TX; Texaco Inc., New Orleans, LA; Transcontinental Gas Pipe Line Company, Houston, TX.

For Complete List of Firm Personnel, See General Section

For full biographical listings, see the Martindale-Hubbell Law Directory

MILLING, BENSON, WOODWARD, HILLYER, PIERSON & MILLER (AV)

A Partnership including Professional Law Corporations
Suite 402, 8555 United Plaza Boulevard, 70809
Telephone: 504-928-6880
FAX: 504-928-6881
New Orleans, Louisiana Office: Suite Twenty-Three Hundred, 909 Poydras Street.
Telephone: 504-569-7000.
Cable Address: "Milling".
Telex: 58-4211.
Telecopier: 504-569-7001 ABA net: 15656 MCI Mail: "Milling".
Lafayette, Louisiana Office: 101 LaRue France, Suite 200.
Telephone: 318-232-3929.
Telecopier: 318-233-4957.

(See Next Column)

MILLING, BENSON, WOODWARD, HILLYER, PIERSON & MILLER, *Baton Rouge—Continued*

OF COUNSEL

Stephen C. Carleton

For full biographical listings, see the Martindale-Hubbell Law Directory

*LAFAYETTE,** Lafayette Parish

HILL & BEYER, A PROFESSIONAL LAW CORPORATION (AV)

101 LaRue France, Suite 502, P.O. Box 53006, 70505-3006
Telephone: 318-232-9733
Fax: 1-318-237-2566

John K. Hill, Jr.
Bret C. Beyer
David R. Rabalais
Lisa C. McCowen
Eugene P. Matherne
Robert B. Purser
Erin J. Sherburne
Harold Adam Lawrence

For full biographical listings, see the Martindale-Hubbell Law Directory

MANGHAM, DAVIS AND OGLESBEE (AV)

Suite 1400 First National Bank Towers, 600 Jefferson Street, P.O. Box 93110, 70509-3110
Telephone: 318-233-6200
Fax: 318-233-6521

Michael R. Mangham
Louis R. Davis
Michael G. Oglesbee
Herman E. Garner, Jr.

ASSOCIATES

Dawn Mayeux Fuqua
Lisa Hanchey Sevier

SPECIAL COUNSEL

Michael J. O'Shee

OF COUNSEL

George W. Hardy, III
Robert E. Rowe

Reference: The First National Bank of Lafayette, Lafayette, Louisiana.

For full biographical listings, see the Martindale-Hubbell Law Directory

*NEW ORLEANS,** Orleans Parish

BOGGS, LOEHN & RODRIGUE (AV)

A Partnership including Law Corporations
Suite 1800 Lykes Center, 300 Poydras Street, 70130-3597
Telephone: 504-523-7090
Fax: 504-581-6822

Charles A. Boggs (A Law Corporation)
Thomas E. Loehn (A Law Corporation)
Edward A. Rodrigue, Jr., (A Law Corporation)
Chester A. Fleming, III
Thomas W. Lewis
Terry B. Deffes
Robert I. Baudouin
Samuel M. Rosamond, III
Betty P. Westbrook
Ralph T Rabalais

Reference: First National Bank of Commerce, New Orleans, La.

For full biographical listings, see the Martindale-Hubbell Law Directory

DEUTSCH, KERRIGAN & STILES (AV)

A Partnership including Professional Law Corporations
755 Magazine Street, 70130-3672
Telephone: 504-581-5141
Cable Address: "Dekest"
Telex: 584358
Telecopier: 504-566-1201

MEMBERS OF FIRM

David C. Treen
Charles K. Reasonover (P.L.C.)
Charles F. Seemann, Jr., (P.L.C.)
Robert E. Kerrigan, Jr., (P.L.C.)
A. Wendel Stout, III
Nancy J. Marshall
Janet L. MacDonell
William C. Harrison, Jr.

ASSOCIATES

Gary B. Roth
Lisa C. Winter

For Complete List of Firm Personnel, See General Section

For full biographical listings, see the Martindale-Hubbell Law Directory

GAINSBURGH, BENJAMIN, FALLON, DAVID & ATES (AV)

A Partnership including Professional Law Corporations
2800 Energy Centre, 1100 Poydras, 70163-2800
Telephone: 504-522-2304
Telecopier: 504-528-9973

OF COUNSEL

Samuel C. Gainsburgh (P.L.C.)

MEMBERS OF FIRM

Jack C. Benjamin (P.L.C.)
Eldon E. Fallon (P.L.C.)
Robert J. David
George S. Meyer (1939-1977)
J. Robert Ates (P.L.C.)
Gerald E. Meunier
Nick F. Noriea, Jr.
Irving J. Warshauer
Stevan C. Dittman
Madeleine M. Landrieu

ASSOCIATES

Darryl M. Phillips
Andrew A. Lemmon
Michael G. Calogero

For full biographical listings, see the Martindale-Hubbell Law Directory

GORDON, ARATA, MCCOLLAM & DUPLANTIS, L.L.P. (AV)

A Partnership including Professional Law Corporations
Place St. Charles, Suite 4000, 201 St. Charles Avenue, 70170-4000
Telephone: 504-582-1111
Fax: 504-582-1121
Lafayette, Louisiana Office: 625 East Kaliste Saloom Road.
Telephone: 318-237-0132.
Fax: 318-237-3451.
Baton Rouge, Louisiana Office: 1710 One American Place.
Telephone: 504-381-9643.
Fax: 504-336-9763.

MEMBERS OF FIRM

John A. Gordon (A P.L.C.)
John M. McCollam (A P.L.C.)
Philip N. Asprodites
Guy E. Wall
James L. Weiss
Loulan J. Pitre, Jr.

ASSOCIATE

Elizabeth L. Gordon

LAFAYETTE OFFICE

RESIDENT MEMBER OF FIRM

William F. Bailey

RESIDENT ASSOCIATE

Denis C. Swords

Representative Clients: Amoco Production Co.; McMoran Oil & Gas Co., Inc.; First National Bank of Commerce of New Orleans; Universal Health Services, Inc.; Cox Cable Communications, Inc.; W.R. Grace & Co.; Lorillard, Inc.; First City Bancorporation; Enron Oil and Gas Co.

For Complete List of Firm Personnel, See General Section

For full biographical listings, see the Martindale-Hubbell Law Directory

HABANS, BOLOGNA & CARRIERE, A PROFESSIONAL LAW CORPORATION (AV)

Suite 2323, 1515 Poydras Street, 70112
Telephone: 504-524-2323
Telex: 151514 HABA M UT
Telecopier: 504-522-7224
Cable Address: HABOL

Robert N. Habans, Jr.
William F. Bologna
James D. Carriere
John C. McNeese
Aimée Carriere
Dwight L. Acomb
Julien F. Jurgens

For full biographical listings, see the Martindale-Hubbell Law Directory

NESSER, KING & LEBLANC (AV)

Suite 3800 Place St. Charles, 201 St. Charles Avenue, 70170
Telephone: 504-582-3800
Telecopier: 504-582-1233

John T. Nesser, III
Henry A. King
Joseph E. LeBlanc, Jr.
David S. Bland
Patricia Ann Krebs
Robert J. Burvant
Eric Earl Jarrell
Liane K. Hinrichs

Jeffrey M. Burmaster
Jeffrey A. Mitchell
Margaret M. Sledge
Josh M. Kantrow
Elton A. Foster
Elizabeth S. Wheeler
Robert J. Bergeron
Timothy S. Madden
Elizabeth A. Meek

OF COUNSEL

Clare P. Hunter
George B. Jurgens, III
J. Grant Coleman
Len R. Brignac
George Farber, Jr.

For full biographical listings, see the Martindale-Hubbell Law Directory

PHELPS DUNBAR, L.L.P. (AV)

Texaco Center, 400 Poydras Street, 70130-3245
Telephone: 504-566-1311
Telecopier: 504-568-9130, 504-568-9007
Cable Address: "Howspencer"
Telex: 584125 WU
Telex: 6821155 WUI
Baton Rouge, Louisiana Office: Suite 701, City National Bank Building, P.O. Box 4412.
Telephone: 504-346-0285.
Telecopier: 504-381-9197.
Jackson, Mississippi Office: Suite 500, Security Centré North, 200 South Lamar Street, P.O. Box 23066.
Telephone: 601-352-2300.
Telecopier: 601-360-9777.
Tupelo, Mississippi Office: Seventh Floor, One Mississippi Plaza, P.O. Box 1220.
Telephone: 601-842-7907.
Telecopier: 601-842-3873.
Houston, Texas Office: Suite 501, 4 Houston Center, 1331 Lamar Street.
Telephone: 713-659-1386.
Telecopier: 713-659-1388.

(See Next Column)

PHELPS DUNBAR L.L.P.—*Continued*

London, England Office: Suite 976, Level 9, Lloyd's, 1 Lime Street, London EC3M 7DQ England.
Telephone: 011-44-71-929-4765.
Telecopier: 011-44-71-929-0046.
Telex: 987321.

MEMBERS OF FIRM

John P. Manard, Jr.
Steven J. Levine (Resident, Baton Rouge, Louisiana Office)

ASSOCIATES

Kyle Brackin
John R. Trahan (Resident, Baton Rouge, Louisiana Office)
Sheila T. Walet

Representative Clients: Energy Development Corp.; GATX Terminals Corp.; Liquid Carbonics; Missouri Pacific Railroad Co.; Rubicon Inc.; Underwriters at Lloyd's, London; Union Tank Car Company, Inc.; Western Waste Industries, Inc.

For Complete List of Firm Personnel, See General Section

For full biographical listings, see the Martindale-Hubbell Law Directory

PULASKI, GIEGER & LABORDE, A PROFESSIONAL LAW CORPORATION (AV)

Suite 4800, One Shell Square, 701 Poydras Street, 70139
Telephone: 504-561-0400
Telecopier: 504-561-1011

Michael T. Pulaski (P.C.)
Ernest P. Gieger, Jr., (P.C.)
Kenneth H. Laborde
Robert W. Maxwell
Keith W. McDaniel
Sharon D. Smith
Gary G. Hebert
Leo R. McAloon, III
J. Jeffrey Raborn
James E. Swinnen
Gina S. Montgomery
Diana L. Tonagel
Katherine B. Hardy
Mary Beth Meyer

For full biographical listings, see the Martindale-Hubbell Law Directory

WAGNER, BAGOT & GLEASON (AV)

Suite 2660, Poydras Center, 650 Poydras Street, 70130-6102
Telephone: 504-525-2141
Telecopier: 504-523-1587
TWX: 5106017673
ELN: 62928850
"INCISIVE"

Thomas J. Wagner
Michael H. Bagot, Jr.
Harvey G. Gleason
Whitney L. Cole
Eric D. Suben

For full biographical listings, see the Martindale-Hubbell Law Directory

*SHREVEPORT,** Caddo Parish

BARLOW AND HARDTNER L.C. (AV)

Tenth Floor, Louisiana Tower, 401 Edwards Street, 71101-3289
Telephone: 318-227-1131
Telecopier: 318-227-1141
Mailing Address: P.O. Box 8, Shreveport, Louisiana, 71161-0008

Ray A. Barlow
Malcolm S. Murchison
Joseph L. Shea, Jr.
Clair F. White
Philip E. Downer, III
Michael B. Donald

Representative Clients: Ashland Oil, Inc.; Beaird Industries, Inc.; The Brinkmann Corporation; Kelley Oil Corporation; NorAm Energy Corp. (formerly Arkla, Inc.); Central and South West; Panhandle Eastern Corp.; Pennzoil Producing Co.; Johnson Controls, Inc.; Ashland Oil, Inc.

For Complete List of Firm Personnel, See General Section

For full biographical listings, see the Martindale-Hubbell Law Directory

COOK, YANCEY, KING & GALLOWAY, A PROFESSIONAL LAW CORPORATION (AV)

1700 Commercial National Tower, 333 Texas Street, P.O. Box 22260, 71120-2260
Telephone: 318-221-6277
Telecopier: 318-227-2606

J. William Fleming
Albert M. Hand, Jr.

Representative Clients: CINTAS Corporation; Specialty Oil Company; Chevron, U.S.A., Inc.; Commercial National Bank in Shreveport; Crystal Oil Company; Hunt Oil Company.

For Complete List of Firm Personnel, See General Section

For full biographical listings, see the Martindale-Hubbell Law Directory

TUCKER, JETER, JACKSON AND HICKMAN, L.L.P. (AV)

Louisiana Tower, 401 Edwards Street Suite 905, 71101-3146
Telephone: 318-425-7764 to 425-7767
Telecopier: 318-425-7792

MEMBERS OF FIRM

John H. Tucker, Jr. (1891-1984)
Horace M. Holder (1913-1989)
Robert McLean Jeter, Jr.
T. Haller Jackson, Jr.
Katherine Leslie Brash Jeter
T. Haller Jackson, III
Kenneth L. Hickman

Attorneys for: Curtis Parker Oil Co.; Gannett River States Publishing Corporation.
Local Attorneys for: South Central Bell Telephone Co.; Morton-Thiokol, Inc.

For full biographical listings, see the Martindale-Hubbell Law Directory

WILKINSON, CARMODY & GILLIAM (AV)

1700 Beck Building, 400 Travis Street, P.O. Box 1707, 71166
Telephone: 318-221-4196
Telecopier: 318-221-3705

MEMBERS OF FIRM

John D. Wilkinson (1867-1929)
William Scott Wilkinson (1895-1985)
Arthur R. Carmody, Jr.
Bobby S. Gilliam
Mark E. Gilliam
Penny D. Sellers
Brian D. Landry

Representative Clients: Farmers Insurance Group; Home Federal Savings & Loan Association of Shreveport; The Kansas City Southern Railway Co.; KTAL-TV; Lincoln National Life Insurance Co.; Mobil Oil Co.; Schumpert Medical Center; Sears, Roebuck & Co.; Southern Pacific Transportation Co.; Southwestern Electric Power Co.

For full biographical listings, see the Martindale-Hubbell Law Directory

MAINE

*BANGOR,** Penobscot Co.

EATON, PEABODY, BRADFORD & VEAGUE, P.A. (AV)

Fleet Center-Exchange Street, P.O. Box 1210, 04402-1210
Telephone: 207-947-0111
Telecopier: 207-942-3040
Augusta, Maine Office: 2 Central Plaza.
Telephone: 207-622-3747.
Telecopier: 207-622-9732.
Brunswick, Maine Office: 167 Park Row.
Telephone: 207-729-1144.
Telecopier: 207-729-1140.
Camden, Maine Office: 7-9 Washington Street.
Telephone: 207-236-3325.
Telecopier: 207-236-8611.
Dover-Foxcroft, Maine Office: 30 East Main Street.
Telephone: 207-564-8378.
Telecopier: 207-564-7059.

Edward D. Leonard, III
Martin L. Wilk (Resident, Brunswick Office)
P. Andrew Hamilton

Dorisann B. W. Wagner (Resident, Augusta Office)
Roger Lang Huber

A List of Representative Clients available upon request.

For Complete List of Firm Personnel, See General Section

For full biographical listings, see the Martindale-Hubbell Law Directory

BAR HARBOR, Hancock Co.

FENTON, CHAPMAN, FENTON, SMITH & KANE, P.A. (AV)

109 Main Street, P.O. Box B, 04609
Telephone: 207-288-3331
FAX: 207-288-9326

William Fenton
Hancock Griffin, Jr. (1912-1980)
Douglas B. Chapman
Nathaniel R. Fenton
Chadbourn H. Smith
Daniel H. Kane

Margaret A. Timothy
Eric Lindquist

OF COUNSEL

David Einhorn
Edwin R. Smith

Reference: Bar Harbor Banking and Trust Co.

For full biographical listings, see the Martindale-Hubbell Law Directory

*BATH,** Sagadahoc Co.

CONLEY, HALEY & O'NEIL (AV)

Thirty Front Street, 04530
Telephone: 207-443-5576
Telefax: 207-443-6665

Mark L. Haley
Constance P. O'Neil
Arlyn H. Weeks

Representative Clients: Bath Iron Works Corporation; Central Maine Power Company; Saco Defense, Inc.; Sugarloaf Mountain Corporation.
References: Casco Northern Bank, N.A.; First Federal Savings & Loan Association of Bath; Shawmut Bank.

For Complete List of Firm Personnel, See General Section

For full biographical listings, see the Martindale-Hubbell Law Directory

*PORTLAND,** Cumberland Co.

AMERLING & BURNS, A PROFESSIONAL ASSOCIATION (AV)

193 Middle Street, 04101
Telephone: 207-775-3581
Facsimile: 207-775-3814
Affiliated St. Croix Office: Coon & Sanford, P.O. Box 25918, Six Chandlers's Wharf, Suite 202, 00824-0918.

W. John Amerling
George F. Burns
David P. Ray
John R. Coon
Arnold C. Macdonald
Mary DeLano
Joanne F. Cole
A. Robert Ruesch

OF COUNSEL

Bruce M. Jervis

Representative Clients: H.E. Sargent, Inc. (construction); Merrill Trust; J.M. Huber, Inc.; Jackson Laboratories; Hague International (engineering); Aetna Life & Casualty Co.; The Hartford; Great American Insurance Co.; Wausau Insurance Co.

For full biographical listings, see the Martindale-Hubbell Law Directory

FRIEDMAN & BABCOCK (AV)

Suite 400, Six City Center, P.O. Box 4726, 04112-4726
Telephone: 207-761-0900
Telecopier: 207-761-0186

MEMBERS OF FIRM

Harold J. Friedman
Ernest J. Babcock
Martha C. Gaythwaite
Gregory W. Powell
Thomas A. Cox
Karen Frink Wolf
Jennifer S. Begel
Laurence H. Leavitt

ASSOCIATES

Theodore H. Irwin, Jr.
Lee H. Bals
Michelle A. Landmann
Arthur J. Lamothe
Brian L. Champion
Laurie B. Perzley
Elizabeth A. Germani
Tracey G. Burton
Jonathan Marc Dunitz
Lori A. Desjardins

For full biographical listings, see the Martindale-Hubbell Law Directory

PIERCE, ATWOOD, SCRIBNER, ALLEN, SMITH & LANCASTER (AV)

One Monument Square, 04101
Telephone: 207-773-6411
Fax: 207-773-3419
Augusta, Maine Office: 77 Winthrop Street.
Telephone: 207-622-6311.
Camden, Maine Office: 36 Chestnut Street, P.O. Box 780.
Telephone: 207-236-4333.

MEMBERS OF FIRM

Daniel E. Boxer
John O'Leary
John D. Delahanty
Thomas R. Doyle
Philip F. W. Ahrens, III
Kenneth Fairbanks Gray
Elizabeth R. Butler
William E. Taylor

ASSOCIATES

Dixon P. Pike
Kate L. Geoffroy
Matthew D. Manahan
Adam H. Steinman
David P. Littell

For Complete List of Firm Personnel, See General Section

For full biographical listings, see the Martindale-Hubbell Law Directory

PRETI, FLAHERTY, BELIVEAU & PACHIOS (AV)

443 Congress Street, P.O. Box 11410, 04104-7410
Telephone: 207-791-3000
Telecopier: 207-791-3111
Augusta, Maine Office: 45 Memorial Circle, P.O. Box 1058, 04332-1058.
Telephone: 207-623-5300.
Telecopier: 207-623-2914.

(See Next Column)

Rumford, Maine Office: 150 Congress Street, P.O. Drawer L, 04276-2035.
Telephone: 207-364-4593.
Telecopier: 207-369-9421.

MEMBERS OF FIRM

Severin M. Beliveau (Augusta Office)
Harold C. Pachios
Michael J. Gentile (Augusta Office)
Anthony W. Buxton (Augusta Office)
Virginia E. Davis (Augusta Office)
Michael Kaplan
Joseph G. Donahue (Augusta Office)
David B. Van Slyke

ASSOCIATES

Mark B. LeDuc (Augusta Office)
Jeanne T. Cohn-Connor
John P. McVeigh
Ann R. Robinson (Augusta Office)
Deirdre M. O'Callaghan (Augusta Office)

Representative Clients: Bangor Hydroelectric Co.; Maine Turnpike Authority; Guy Gannett Publishing Co.; Maine Low-Level Waste Authority; Industrial Energy Consumer Group; James River Corp.; Maine Oil Dealers Assn.; LCP Chemicals; Wheelabrator Environmental Systems; The Maine Alliance.

For Complete List of Firm Personnel, See General Section

For full biographical listings, see the Martindale-Hubbell Law Directory

YORK, York Co.

ERWIN, OTT, CLARK & CAMPBELL (AV)

16A Woodbridge Road, P.O. Box 545, 03909
Telephone: 207-363-5208
Facsimile: 207-363-5322

MEMBERS OF FIRM

Frank E. Hancock (1923-1988)
James S. Erwin
John P. Campbell
David N. Ott
Jeffery J. Clark

For full biographical listings, see the Martindale-Hubbell Law Directory

MARYLAND

*BALTIMORE,** (Independent City)

GORDON, FEINBLATT, ROTHMAN, HOFFBERGER & HOLLANDER (AV)

The Garrett Building, 233 East Redwood Street, 21202
Telephone: 410-576-4000
Telex: 908041 BAL

MEMBERS OF FIRM

Lawrence S. Greenwald
Neil J. Schechter
Elliott Cowan
Michael C. Powell

ASSOCIATE

Gregory S. Reynolds

For Complete List of Firm Personnel, See General Section

For full biographical listings, see the Martindale-Hubbell Law Directory

VENABLE, BAETJER AND HOWARD (AV)

A Partnership including Professional Corporations
1800 Mercantile Bank & Trust Building, 2 Hopkins Plaza, 21201
Telephone: 410-244-7400
Washington, D.C. Office: Venable, Baetjer, Howard & Civiletti. Suite 1000, 1201 New York Avenue, N.W.
Telephone: 202-962-4800.
McLean, Virginia Office: Suite 400, 2010 Corporate Ridge.
Telephone: 703-760-1600.
Rockville, Maryland Office: Suite 500, One Church Street, P. O. Box 1906.
Telephone: 301-217-5600.
Towson, Maryland Office: 210 Allegheny Avenue, P. O. Box 5517.
Telephone: 410-494-6200.

MEMBERS OF FIRM

Benjamin R. Civiletti (P.C.) (Also at Washington, D.C. and Towson, Maryland Offices)
Anthony M. Carey (Also at Washington, D.C. Office)
John Henry Lewin, Jr. (P.C.)
Robert P. Bedell (Not admitted in MD; Resident, Washington, D.C. Office)
Dennis J. Whittlesey (Not admitted in MD; Resident, Washington, D.C. Office)
Robert G. Smith (P.C.)
David T. Stitt (Not admitted in MD; Resident, McLean, Virginia Office)
John G. Milliken (Not admitted in MD; Also at Washington, D.C. and McLean, Virginia Offices)
Max Stul Oppenheimer (P.C.) (Also at Washington, D.C. and Towson, Maryland Offices)
Joseph C. Wich, Jr. (Resident, Towson, Maryland Office)

(See Next Column)

VENABLE, BAETJER AND HOWARD—*Continued*

MEMBERS OF FIRM (Continued)

Joseph G. Block (Not admitted in MD; Resident, Washington, D.C. Office)
Michael Schatzow (Also at Washington, D.C. and Towson, Maryland Offices)
John F. Cooney (Not admitted in MD; Resident, Washington, D.C. Office)
Susan K. Gauvey (Also at Towson, Maryland Office)
James K. Archibald (Also at Washington, D.C. and Towson, Maryland Offices)
Judson W. Starr (Not admitted in MD; Also at Washington, D.C. and Towson, Maryland Offices)
Jeffrey A. Dunn (also at Washington, D.C. Office)
James L. Shea (Also at Washington, D.C. Office)
Brigid E. Kenney
John J. Pavlick, Jr. (Not admitted in MD; Resident, Washington, D. C. Office)
Kathleen Gallogly Cox (Resident, Towson, Maryland Office)
Christopher R. Mellott
M. King Hill, III (Resident, Towson, Maryland Office)
James A. Dunbar (Also at Washington, D.C. Office)
Ronald W. Taylor
Thomas J. Kelly, Jr. (Not admitted in MD; Resident, Washington, D. C. Office)
Kevin L. Shepherd

OF COUNSEL

Richard H. Mays (Not admitted in MD; Mclean, Virginia and Washington, D.C.)
Judith A. Armold

ASSOCIATES

Gregory S. Braker (Resident, Washington, D.C. Office)
J. Van L. Dorsey (Resident, Towson, Maryland Office)
Andrew R. Herrup (Resident, Washington, D.C. Office)
Matthew L. Iwicki
Mary-Dulany James (Resident, Towson, Maryland Office)
Paula Titus Laboy (Resident, Rockville, Maryland Office)
Thomas M. Lingan
Valerie K. Mann (Not admitted in MD; Resident, Washington, D.C. Office)
Laura K. McAfee
Christine M. McAnney (Not admitted in MD; Resident, McLean, Virginia Office)
Mitchell Y. Mirviss

For Complete List of Firm Personnel, See General Section

For full biographical listings, see the Martindale-Hubbell Law Directory

SILVER SPRING, Montgomery Co.

ALEXANDER, GEBHARDT, APONTE & MARKS, L.L.C. (AV)

Lee Plaza-Suite 805, 8601 Georgia Avenue, 20910
Telephone: 301-589-2222
Facsimile: 301-589-2523
Washington, D.C. Office: 1314 Nineteenth Street, N.W., 20036.
Telephone: 202-835-1555.
New York, New York Office: 330 Madison Avenue, 36th Floor.
Telephone: 212-808-0008.
Fax: 212-599-1028.

Koteles Alexander (Not admitted in MD)

David B. Johnson
Y. Kris Oh (Ms.) (Not admitted in MD)

Reference: Riggs National Bank of Washington, D.C.

For full biographical listings, see the Martindale-Hubbell Law Directory

LIPSHULTZ AND HONE, CHARTERED (AV)

Suite 108 Montgomery Center, 8630 Fenton Street, 20910
Telephone: 301-587-8500
Fax: 301-495-9759
Washington, D.C. Office: Suite 200, 2000 L Street, N.W.
Telephone: 202-872-0909.

John Llewellyn Hone
Joseph J. Bottiglieri

For Complete List of Firm Personnel, See General Section

For full biographical listings, see the Martindale-Hubbell Law Directory

MASSACHUSETTS

*BOSTON,** Suffolk Co.

BARRON & STADFELD, P.C. (AV)

Two Center Plaza, 02108
Telephone: 617-723-9800
Telecopier: 617-523-8359
Hyannis, Massachusetts Office: 258 Winter Street.
Telephone: 617-778-6622.

(See Next Column)

Bernard A. Dwork
David P. Dwork
Mark W. Roberts

For Complete List of Firm Personnel, See General Section

For full biographical listings, see the Martindale-Hubbell Law Directory

GOODWIN, PROCTER & HOAR (AV)

A Partnership including Professional Corporations
Exchange Place, 02109-2881
Telephone: 617-570-1000
Cable Address: "Goodproct, Boston"
Telex: 94-0640
Telecopier: 617-523-1231
Washington, D.C. Office: 901 Fifteenth Street, N.W., Suite 410.
Telephone: 202-414-6160.
Telecopier: 202-789-1720.
Albany, New York Office: One Steuben Place.
Telephone: 518-472-9460.
Telecopier: 518-472-9472.

MEMBERS OF FIRM

Susan M. Cooke (P.C.)
Jeffrey C. Bates
Christopher P. Davis
Stephen H. Schroeder
Donald S. Berry (P.C.)
E. Michael Paul Thomas

For Complete List of Firm Personnel, See General Section

For full biographical listings, see the Martindale-Hubbell Law Directory

KOPELMAN AND PAIGE, P.C. (AV)

101 Arch Street, 02110
Telephone: 617-951-0007
Cable Address: "Lawkope"
Fax: 617-951-2735

Leonard Kopelman
Donald G. Paige
Elizabeth A. Lane
Joyce F. Frank
John W. Giorgio
Barbara J. Saint Andre
Joel B. Bard
Everett Joseph Marder
Patrick J. Costello

William Hewig, III
Deborah Eliason
Judith Chanoux Cutler
Anne-Marie M. Hyland
Richard Bowen
Cheryl Ann Banks
Brian W. Riley

For Complete List of Firm Personnel, See General Section

For full biographical listings, see the Martindale-Hubbell Law Directory

PALMER & DODGE (AV)

(Storey Thorndike Palmer & Dodge)
One Beacon Street, 02108
Telephone: 617-573-0100
Telecopier: 617-227-4420
Telex: 951104
Cable Address: "Storeydike," Boston

MEMBERS OF FIRM

Ralph A. Child
William L. Lahey
Scott P. Lewis
Raymond M. Murphy

COUNSEL

David J. Corrsin
Charles E. DeWitt, Jr.

For Complete List of Firm Personnel, See General Section

For full biographical listings, see the Martindale-Hubbell Law Directory

RACKEMANN, SAWYER & BREWSTER, PROFESSIONAL CORPORATION (AV)

One Financial Center, 02111
Telephone: 617-542-2300
Telecopier: 617-542-7437

William B. Tyler
George V. Anastas
Henry H. Thayer
Stephen Carr Anderson
Albert M. Fortier, Jr.
Michael F. O'Connell
Stuart T. Freeland
Raymond J. Brassard
Alan B. Rubenstein
Martin R. Healy
James R. Shea, Jr.
Brian M. Hurley
Janet M. Smith
Peter Friedenberg
Richard S. Novak
J. David Leslie
Alexander H. Spaulding
Sanford M. Matathia
Anne P. Zebrowski

OF COUNSEL

Albert B. Wolfe
August R. Meyer
Richard H. Lovell

COUNSEL

Ronald S. Duby
Ross J. Hamlin

(See Next Column)

RACKEMANN, SAWYER & BREWSTER PROFESSIONAL CORPORATION, *Boston—Continued*

Margaret L. Hayes
Daniel J. Ossoff
Mary B. Freeley
Gordon M. Orloff
Donald R. Pinto, Jr.
Lucy West Behymer
Richard J. Gallogly
Melissa Langer Ellis
James A. Wachta
Susan Dempsey Baer
Daniel J. Bailey, III
Michael S. Giaimo
Maura E. Murphy
Mary L. Gallant
Peter A. Alpert
Lauren D. Armstrong
Robert B. Foster
Elizabeth A. Gibbons

For full biographical listings, see the Martindale-Hubbell Law Directory

RICH, MAY, BILODEAU & FLAHERTY, P.C. (AV)

The Old South Building, 294 Washington Street, 02108-4675
Telephone: 617-482-1360
FAX: 617-556-3889

John F. Rich (1908-1987)
Thomas H. Bilodeau (1915-1987)
Gerald May
Harold B. Dondis
Walter L. Landergan, Jr.
Edwin J. Carr
Arthur F. Flaherty
Franklin M. Hundley
Michael F. Donlan
Joseph F. Sullivan, Jr.
Owen P. Maher
Nicolas A. Kensington
Daniel T. Clark
Gerald V. May, Jr.
Eric J. Krathwohl
Michael J. McHugh
James M. Behnke
James M. Avery
Stephen M. Kane
Mark C. O'Connor
Walter A. Wright, III
Emmett E. Lyne

Nicholas F. Kourtis
James T. Finnigan
Carol E. Kazmer
Robert P. Snell

For full biographical listings, see the Martindale-Hubbell Law Directory

SWARTZ & SWARTZ (AV)

10 Marshall Street, 02108
Telephone: 617-742-1900
Fax: 617-367-7193

Edward M. Swartz
Alan L. Cantor
Joseph A. Swartz
Victor A. Denaro
Joan E. Swartz
James A. Swartz
Robert S. Berger
Harold David Levine

OF COUNSEL

Fredric A. Swartz

For full biographical listings, see the Martindale-Hubbell Law Directory

WARNER & STACKPOLE (AV)

75 State Street, 02109
Telephone: 617-951-9000
Cable Address: "Warstack"
Telecopier: 617-951-9151
Telex: 940139

MEMBERS OF FIRM

Joseph J. Leghorn
Michael A. Leon
Ralph T. Lepore, III
Janice Kelley Rowan
James G. Ward
Paul C. Bauer

ASSOCIATES

Richard R. Loewy
Deborah E. Barnard
Peter T. Wechsler
John T. Smolak

For Complete List of Firm Personnel, See General Section

For full biographical listings, see the Martindale-Hubbell Law Directory

*SPRINGFIELD,** Hampden Co.

ANNINO, DRAPER & MOORE, P.C. (AV)

Suite 1818 BayBank Tower, 1500 Main Street, P.O. Box 15428, 01115
Telephone: 413-732-6400
Fax: 413-732-3339
Westfield, Massachusetts Office: 52 Court Street.
Telephone: 413-562-9829.

Calvin W. Annino, Jr.
Mark E. Draper
Louis S. Moore
Michael R. Siddall

For full biographical listings, see the Martindale-Hubbell Law Directory

KAMBERG, BERMAN, P.C. (AV)

One Monarch Place Twelfth Floor, 01144-1009
Telephone: 413-781-1300
Facsimile: 413-732-0860
ABA/net: KAMBERGB

(See Next Column)

Abraham Kamberg (1895-1981)
Eugene B. Berman
Richard G. Lemoine
Carolyn L. Burt
Mark W. Siegars
Kerry David Strayer

References: Shawmut Bank, N.A.; Fleet Bank of Massachusetts, N.A.; Baybank.

For full biographical listings, see the Martindale-Hubbell Law Directory

ROBINSON DONOVAN MADDEN & BARRY, P.C. (AV)

Suite 1600, Baybank Tower, 1500 Main Street, 01115
Telephone: 413-732-2301
Fax: 413-785-4658

OF COUNSEL

Milton J. Donovan
John H. Madden, Jr.
Edward J. Barry

Gordon H. Wentworth
James H. Tourtelotte
Charles K. Bergin, Jr.
Victor Rosenberg
Ronald C. Kidd
Jeffrey W. Roberts
Jeffrey L. McCormick
James M. Rabbitt
James F. Martin
Robert P. Cunningham
John C. Sikorski
Nancy Frankel Pelletier
Paul S. Weinberg
Frederica H. McCarthy
Matthew J. King

James K. Bodurtha
Douglas F. Boyd
Susan L. Cooper
Kimberly Davis Crear
Russell F. Denver
Edmund J. Gorman
Keith A. Minoff
Patricia M. Rapinchuk
Jonathan P. Rice
Neva Kaufman Rohan

Counsel for: Shawmut Bank, N.A.; The First National Bank of Boston; United Cooperative Bank; Sunshine Art Studios.
Representative Clients: American Policyholders' Insurance Co.; C.N.A.; Commercial Union Insurance Co.; Hanover Insurance Co.

For Complete List of Firm Personnel, See General Section

For full biographical listings, see the Martindale-Hubbell Law Directory

*WORCESTER,** Worcester Co.

CHRISTOPHER & LEDOUX (AV)

370 Main Street, 01608
Telephone: 508-792-2800
FAX: 508-792-6224

MEMBERS OF FIRM

William J. LeDoux
William W. Hays
David A. Wojcik
John A. Mavricos

OF COUNSEL

Christopher Christopher

Reference: Mechanics Bank.

For full biographical listings, see the Martindale-Hubbell Law Directory

MICHIGAN

*ADRIAN,** Lenawee Co.

ROHRBACHER, NICHOLSON & LIGHT, CO., L.P.A.

(See Toledo, Ohio)

*ANN ARBOR,** Washtenaw Co.

HOOPER, HATHAWAY, PRICE, BEUCHE & WALLACE (AV)

126 South Main Street, 48104
Telephone: 313-662-4426
Fax: 313-662-9559

Bruce T. Wallace
William J. Stapleton

Representative Clients: Chem-Trend, Inc.; Dundee Cement Co.; Ervin Industries, Inc.; First Martin Corp.; Group 243 Design, Inc.; Honeywell; Microwave Sensors, Inc.; Shearson Lehman Hutton; O'Neal Construction Co.; Pittsfield Products, Inc.

For Complete List of Firm Personnel, See General Section

For full biographical listings, see the Martindale-Hubbell Law Directory

Ann Arbor—Continued

MILLER, CANFIELD, PADDOCK AND STONE, P.L.C. (AV)

A Professional Limited Liability Company
Founded in 1852 by Sidney Davy Miller
101 North Main Street, Seventh Floor, 48104-1400
Telephone: 313-663-2445
Fax: 313-747-7147
Detroit, Michigan Office: 150 West Jefferson, Suite 2500, 48226-4415.
Telephone: 313-963-6420.
Fax: 313-496-7500.
Cable Address: "Stem Detroit."
Bloomfield Hills, Michigan Office: Suite 100, Pinehurst Office Center, 1400 North Woodward, 48303-2014.
Telephone: 313-645-5000.
Fax: 313-645-1917.
Grand Rapids, Michigan Office: 1200 Campau Square Plaza, 99 Monroe, N.W., 49503-2639.
Telephone: 616-454-8656.
Fax: 616-776-6322.
Howell, Michigan Office: 121 South Barnard Street, Suite 4, 48843-2305.
Telephone: 517-546-7600.
Telecopier: 517-546-6974.
Kalamazoo, Michigan Office: 444 West Michigan Avenue, 49007-3752.
Telephone: 616-381-7030.
Fax: 616-382-0244.
Lansing, Michigan Office: One Michigan Avenue, Suite 900, 48933-1609.
Telephone: 517-487-2070.
Fax: 517-374-6304.
Monroe, Michigan Office: The Executive Centre, 214 East Elm Avenue, 48161-2682.
Telephone: 313-243-2000.
Fax: 313-243-0901.
Washington, D.C. Office: 1225 Nineteenth Street, N.W., Suite 400. 20036.
Telephone: 202-429-5575; 785-0600.
Fax: 202-331-1118; 785-1234.
Pensacola, Florida Office: 25 West Cedar, 32501.
Telephone: 904-469-1088.
Fax: 904-432-0677.
St. Petersburg, Florida Office: 100 Second Avenue S., Suite 7045, 33701.
Telephone: 813-982-6000.
Fax: 813-892-6002.
Gdansk, Poland Office: Suite 322, Dom Technika Building, Ul. Rajska 6, 80-850.
Telephone: 011-485-831-2808.
Fax: 011-485-831-4719.
Warsaw, Poland Office: Ul. Marszalkowska 82, Suite 561, 00-517.
Telephone: 011-482-623-6457 and 6458.
Fax: 011-482-623-6459.

RESIDENT PARTNER

Robert E. Gilbert

Representative Firm Clients: Chrysler Corp.; Comerica, Inc.; City of Detroit, Mich.; Detroit Tigers, Inc.; First of Michigan; Fretter, Inc.; Ford Motor Co.; Ford Motor Credit Co.; Great Lakes Bancorp; Henry Ford Hospital.

For Complete List of Firm Personnel, See General Section

For full biographical listings, see the Martindale-Hubbell Law Directory

*BAY CITY,** Bay Co.

BRAUN KENDRICK FINKBEINER (AV)

201 Phoenix Building, P.O. Box 2039, 48708
Telephone: 517-895-8505
Telecopier: 517-895-8437
Saginaw, Michigan Office: 8th Floor Second National Bank Building.
Telephone: 517-753-3461.
Telecopier: 517-753-3951.

MEMBERS OF FIRM

Ralph J. Isackson
Patrick D. Neering
George F. Gronewold, Jr.
Frank M. Quinn
Gregory E. Meter
Daniel S. Opperman
Gregory T. Demers

Representative Clients: APV Chemical Machinery, Inc.; Bay Health Systems; Berger and Co.; Catholic Federal Credit Union; Charter Township of Bridgeport; City of Saginaw; City of Vassar; City of Zilwaukee; Corporate Service; Cox Cable.

For Complete List of Firm Personnel, See General Section

For full biographical listings, see the Martindale-Hubbell Law Directory

BIRMINGHAM, Oakland Co.

CARSON FISCHER, P.L.C. (AV)

Third Floor, 300 East Maple Road, 48009-6317
Telephone: 810-644-4840
Facsimile: 810-644-1832

Peter L. Wanger

For full biographical listings, see the Martindale-Hubbell Law Directory

SIMPSON & BERRY, P.C. (AV)

260 East Brown, Suite 300, 48009
Telephone: 810-647-0200
Telecopier: 810-647-2776

Daniel F. Berry
Clark G. Doughty
Philip J. Goodman
James A. Simpson
Katheryne L. Zelenock

LEGAL SUPPORT PERSONNEL

Dwight Noble Baker, Jr.

Representative Clients: Trizec Properties, Inc.; Wayne County; Detroit Public Schools; Ferndale School District; Hall Financial Group; Premier Construction Co.; NBD Bancorp, Inc.

For full biographical listings, see the Martindale-Hubbell Law Directory

WILLIAMS, SCHAEFER, RUBY & WILLIAMS, PROFESSIONAL CORPORATION (AV)

Suite 300, 380 North Woodward Avenue, 48009
Telephone: 810-642-0333
Telecopy: 810-642-0856

Thomas G. Plunkett
Richard D. Rattner

Representative Clients: Beachum & Roeser Development Corporation; Clare County; Deerfield Township; Groveland Township; Huron Township; KinderCare Learning Centers; Lapeer County; Mundy Township; Sanilac County; Western Development Company.

For full biographical listings, see the Martindale-Hubbell Law Directory

BLOOMFIELD HILLS, Oakland Co.

CLARK, KLEIN & BEAUMONT (AV)

1533 North Woodward Avenue, Suite 220, 48304
Telephone: 810-258-2900
Facsmile: 810-258-2949
Detroit, Michigan Office: 1600 First Federal Building. 1001 Woodward Avenue.
Telephone: 313-965-8300.
Facsimile: 313-962-4348.

MEMBERS OF FIRM

Susan J. Sadler
Tyler D. Tennent
Sherwin E. Zamler

ASSOCIATES

Amy Bateson
Joseph K. Hart, Jr.

Representative Clients: Sherwin-Williams Company; BASF Corporation; The Budd Company.

For Complete List of Firm Personnel, See General Section

For full biographical listings, see the Martindale-Hubbell Law Directory

HOWARD & HOWARD ATTORNEYS, P.C. (AV)

The Pinehurst Office Center, Suite 101, 1400 North Woodward Avenue, 48304-2856
Telephone: 810-645-1483
Telecopier: 810-645-1568
Kalamazoo, Michigan Office: The Kalamazoo Building, Suite 400, 107 West Michigan Avenue.
Telephone: 616-382-1483.
Telecopier: 616-382-1568.
Lansing, Michigan Office: The Phoenix Building, Suite 500, 222 Washington Square, North.
Telephone: 517-485-1483.
Telecopier: 517-485-1568.
Peoria, Illinois Office: Howard & Howard, P.C., The Creve Coeur Building, Suite 200, 321 Liberty Street.
Telephone: 309-672-1483.
Telecopier: 309-672-1568.

Antoinette Beuche
Tammy L. Brown
Carolyn M. Claerhout
Chris T. Danikolas
John Gerald Gleeson
Steven C. Kohl
Susan E. Padley
Gary A. Peters
Brian J. Renaud
Blake K. Ringsmuth
Michael V. Sucaet
Laura A. Talt

Representative Clients: For Representative Client list, see General Practice, Bloomfield Hills, MI.

For Complete List of Firm Personnel, See General Section

For full biographical listings, see the Martindale-Hubbell Law Directory

*DETROIT,** Wayne Co.

BODMAN, LONGLEY & DAHLING (AV)

34th Floor 100 Renaissance Center, 48243
Telephone: 313-259-7777
Fax: 313-393-7579
Troy, Michigan Office: Suite 2020, 755 West Big Beaver Road.
Telephone: 810-362-2110.

(See Next Column)

BODMAN, LONGLEY & DAHLING, *Detroit—Continued*

Ann Arbor, Michigan Office: 110 Miller, Suite 300.
Telephone: 313-761-3780.
Northern Michigan Office: 229 Court Street, P.O. Box 405, Cheboygan.
Telephone: 616-627-4351.

MEMBERS OF FIRM

James A. Smith
Fredrick J. Dindoffer
Michael A. Stack (Northern Michigan Office)
R. Craig Hupp
Henry N. Carnaby (Troy Office)

Representative Clients: Abitibi Price Group; Archdiocese of Detroit; Comerica Bank; The Detroit Lions, Inc.; Ford Estates; General Motors Corporation; Charles Stewart Mott Foundation; Norfolk Southern Corporation; Panhandle Eastern Corporation; State Farm Mutual Automobile Insurance Company.

For Complete List of Firm Personnel, See General Section

For full biographical listings, see the Martindale-Hubbell Law Directory

BUTZEL LONG, A PROFESSIONAL CORPORATION (AV)

Suite 900, 150 West Jefferson, 48226
Telephone: 313-225-7000
Telecopier: 313-225-7080
Birmingham, Michigan Office: Suite 200, 32270 Telegraph Road.
Telephone: 810-258-1616.
Telecopier: 810-258-1439.
Lansing, Michigan Office: 118 West Ottawa Street.
Telephone: 517-372-6622.
Telecopier: 517-372-6672.
Ann Arbor, Michigan Office: Suite 400, 121 West Washington.
Telephone: 313-995-3110.
Telecopier: 313-995-1777.
Grosse Pointe Farms, Michigan Office: Suite 260, 21 Kercheval.
Telephone: 313-886-5446.
Telecopier: 313-886-2114.

Frank B. Vecchio
John P. Williams
John Henry Dudley, Jr.
Jack D. Shumate
Leonard F. Charla
James E. Wynne
Michael J. Lavoie
Edward M. Kalinka
Peter D. Holmes
Susan Carino Nystrom
Darlene M. Domanik

Paul S. Lewandowski
Elizabeth A. Dumouchelle

For Complete List of Firm Personnel, See General Section

For full biographical listings, see the Martindale-Hubbell Law Directory

CLARK, KLEIN & BEAUMONT (AV)

1600 First Federal Building, 1001 Woodward Avenue, 48226
Telephone: 313-965-8300
Facsimile: 313-962-4348
Bloomfield Hills Office: 1533 North Woodward Avenue, Suite 220, 48304.
Telephone: 810-258-2900.
Facsimile: 810-258-2949.

MEMBERS OF FIRM

Susan J. Sadler (Resident Bloomfield Hills, Michigan Office)
Tyler D. Tennent (Resident, Bloomfield Hills, Michigan Office)
Sherwin E. Zamler (Resident Bloomfield Hills, Michigan Office)

ASSOCIATES

Thomas M. Dixon
Amy Bateson (Resident Bloomfield Hills, Michigan Office)
Joseph K. Hart, Jr. (Resident, Bloomfield Hills, Michigan Office)

Representative Clients: Sherwin-Williams Company; BASF Corporation; The Budd Company.

For Complete List of Firm Personnel, See General Section

For full biographical listings, see the Martindale-Hubbell Law Directory

DICKINSON, WRIGHT, MOON, VAN DUSEN & FREEMAN (AV)

500 Woodward Avenue, Suite 4000, 48226-3425
Telephone: 313-223-3500
Facsimile: 313-223-3598
Bloomfield Hills, Michigan Office: 525 North Woodward Avenue, Suite 2000.
Telephone: 810-433-7200.
Facsimile: 810-433-7274.
Grand Rapids, Michigan Office: 200 Ottawa Avenue, N.W., Suite 900.
Telephone: 616-458-1300.
Facsimile: 616-458-6753.
Lansing, Michigan Office: Suite 200, 215 South Washington Square.
Telephone: 517-371-1730.
Facsimile: 517-487-4700.

(See Next Column)

Washington, D.C. Office: Suite 800, 1901 L Street, N.W.
Telephone: 202-457-0160.
Facsimile: 202-659-1559.
Chicago, Illinois Office: 225 West Washington, Suite 400.
Telephone: 312-220-0300.
Facsimile: 312-220-0021.
Warsaw, Poland Office: 46 Wilcza Street, 4th Floor, 00-679.
Telephone: (48-22) 299-241.
Facsimile: (48-2) 628-4107. Komertel Satellite Phone: (48-39) 121-510.

MEMBERS OF FIRM

Herbert G. Sparrow, III
Steven C. Nadeau
David R. Bruegel (Bloomfield Hills Office)
Margaret A. Coughlin
Keith J. Lerminiaux
Claudia Rast
Linda V. Parker
Dustin P. Ordway (Grand Rapids Office)
Thea D. Dunmire (Chicago, Illinois Office)

ASSOCIATES

Kyle M. H. Jones
Elizabeth Virginia Main
Linda S. McAlpine
Richard R. McGill, Jr. (Chicago, Illinois Office)
Sharon R. Newlon
James Gavan O'Connor (Grand Rapids Office)
John T. Panourgias (Bloomfield Hills Office)
Gregory J. Parry (Bloomfield Hills Office)
John L. Teeples (Grand Rapids Office)

For Complete List of Firm Personnel, See General Section

For full biographical listings, see the Martindale-Hubbell Law Directory

DYKEMA GOSSETT (AV)

400 Renaissance Center, 48243-1668
Telephone: 313-568-6800
Cable Address: "Dyke-Detroit"
Telex: 23-0121
Fax: 313-568-6594
Ann Arbor, Michigan Office: 315 East Eisenhower Parkway, Suite 100, 48108-3306.
Telephone: 313-747-7660.
Fax: 313-747-7696.
Bloomfield Hills, Michigan Office: 1577 North Woodward Avenue, Suite 300, 48304-2820.
Telephone: 810-540-0700.
Fax: 810-540-0763.
Grand Rapids, Michigan Office: 200 Oldtown Riverfront Building, 248 Louis Campau Promenade, N.W., 49503-2668.
Telephone: 616-776-7500.
Fax: 616-776-7573.
Lansing, Michigan Office: 800 Michigan National Tower, 48933-1707.
Telephone: 517-374-9100.
Fax: 517-374-9191.
Washington, D.C. Office: Franklin Square, Suite 300 West Tower, 1300 I Street, N.W., 20005-3306.
Telephone: 202-522-8600.
Fax: 202-522-8669.
Chicago, Illinois Office: Three First National Plaza, Suite 1400, 70 W. Madison, 60602-4270.
Telephone: 312-214-3380.
Fax: 312-214-3441.

MEMBERS OF FIRM

James W. Collier
David L. Tripp

ASSOCIATES

Paul Francis Bohn
Scott D. Broekstra (Resident at Grand Rapids Office)
Grant P. Gilezan
Mark D. Jacobs
Jerome I. Maynard (Resident at Chicago, Illinois Office)
Gregory S. Narsh
Steven J. Rollins (Resident at Chicago, Illinois Office)
Troy R. Taylor
Nicholas G. Zotos

For Complete List of Firm Personnel, See General Section

For full biographical listings, see the Martindale-Hubbell Law Directory

GROSS, NEMETH & SILVERMAN, P.L.C. (AV)

444 Penobscot Building, 48226
Telephone: 313-963-8200
Fax: 313-964-6577

Steven G. Silverman

For full biographical listings, see the Martindale-Hubbell Law Directory

HONIGMAN MILLER SCHWARTZ AND COHN (AV)

A Partnership including Professional Corporations
2290 First National Building, 48226
Telephone: 313-256-7800
Telecopier: 313-962-0176
Telex: 235705
Lansing, Michigan Office: Phoenix Building, 222 North Washington Square, Suite 400.
Telephone: 517-484-8282.

(See Next Column)

HONIGMAN MILLER SCHWARTZ AND COHN—*Continued*

West Palm Beach, Florida Office: Suite 800 Esperante Building, 222 Lakeview Avenue.
Telephone: 407-838-4500.
Tampa, Florida Office: 2700 Landmark Centre, 401 E. Jackson Street.
Telephone: 813-221-6600.
Orlando, Florida Office: 390 North Orange Avenue, Suite 1300.
Telephone: 407-648-0300.
Houston, Texas Office: 3100 First Interstate Bank Plaza, 1000 Louisiana.
Telephone: 713-650-2600.
Los Angeles, California Office: McNeill Plaza, Suite 820, 15260 Ventura Boulevard, 91403.
Telephone: 818-784-2900.

MEMBERS OF FIRM

Christopher J. Dunsky
Kenneth C. Gold
Philip A. Grashoff, Jr.
Robert A. Hykan
Norman Hyman
Brian Negele
John D. Pirich (Lansing, Michigan Office)
Joseph M. Polito
Paul Revere, III
Gary A. Trepod (Lansing, Michigan Office)
Grant R. Trigger
John W. Voelpel
William A. Wichers II
Ruth E. Zimmerman (Lansing, Michigan Office)

ASSOCIATES

Sally J. Churchill
S. Lee Johnson
Walter J. Kramarz
Jeffrey L. Woolstrum

RESIDENT IN WEST PALM BEACH, FLORIDA OFFICE

MEMBER

E. Lee Worsham (P.A.)

RESIDENT IN TAMPA, FLORIDA OFFICE

MEMBER

Michael G. Cooke (P.A.)

RESIDENT IN ORLANDO, FLORIDA OFFICE

MEMBER

J.A. Jurgens (P.A.)

ASSOCIATE

Jan A. Albanese

Representative Clients: Consumers Power Co.; The Detroit Edison Co.; Ford Motor Co.; General Motors Corp.; Edw. C. Levy Co.; Hughes Aircraft Company; Masco Corporation/MascoTech, Inc.; Auto Alliance International Inc. (formerly Mazda Motor Mfg. (USA) Corp.).; McLouth Steel Products Corp.; Morton Internationa, FWC; Weyerhaeuser Company.

For Complete List of Firm Personnel, See General Section

For full biographical listings, see the Martindale-Hubbell Law Directory

JAFFE, RAITT, HEUER & WEISS, PROFESSIONAL CORPORATION (AV)

One Woodward Avenue, Suite 2400, 48226
Telephone: 313-961-8380
Telecopier: 313-961-8358
Cable Address: "Jafsni"
Southfield,Michigan Office: Travelers Tower, Suite 1520.
Telephone: 313-961-8380.
Monroe, Michigan Office: 212 East Front Street, Suite 3.
Telephone: 313-241-6470.
Telefacsimile: 313-241-3849.

Jeffrey G. Heuer
Eric A. Linden
Arthur H. Siegal

See General Practice Section of List of Representative Clients.

For Complete List of Firm Personnel, See General Section

For full biographical listings, see the Martindale-Hubbell Law Directory

KERR, RUSSELL AND WEBER (AV)

One Detroit Center, 500 Woodward Avenue, Suite 2500, 48226-3406
Telephone: 313-961-0200
Telecopier: 313-961-0388
Bloomfield Hills, Michigan Office: 3883 Telegraph Road.
Telephone: 810-649-5990.
East Lansing, Michigan Office: 1301 North Hagadorn Road.
Telephone: 517-336-6767.

William A. Sankbeil
James R. Case
Kurt R. Vilders
Edward C. Cutlip, Jr.
Joanne Geha Swanson
Catherine Bonczak Edwards
Eric I. Lark

For Complete List of Firm Personnel, See General Section

For full biographical listings, see the Martindale-Hubbell Law Directory

KITCH, DRUTCHAS, WAGNER & KENNEY, P.C. (AV)

One Woodward, Tenth Floor, 48226-3412
Telephone: 313-965-7900
Fax: 313-965-7403
Lansing, Michigan Office: 120 Washington Square, North, Suite 805, One Michigan Avenue, 48933-1609.
Telephone: 517-372-6430.
Fax: 517-372-0441.
Macomb County Office: Towne Square Development, 10 South Main Street, Suite 301, Mount Clemens, 48043-7903.
Telephone: 810-463-9770.
Fax: 810-463-8994.
Toledo, Ohio Office: 405 Madison Avenue, Suite 1500, 43604-1235.
Telephone: 419-243-4006.
Fax: 419-243-7333.
Troy, Michigan Office: 3001 West Big Beaver Road, Suite 200, 48084-3103.
Telephone: 810-637-3500.
Fax: 810-637-6630.
Ann Arbor, Michigan Office: 303 Detroit Street, Suite 400, P.O. Box 8610, 48107-8610.
Telephone: 313-994-7600.
Fax: 313-994-7626.

Ronald E. Wagner
Mark D. Willmarth (Principal)
Richard S. Baron
Robert J. Bradfield III
Arthur F. Brandt
Christopher J. Valeriote

For Complete List of Firm Personnel, See General Section

For full biographical listings, see the Martindale-Hubbell Law Directory

LEWIS, WHITE & CLAY, A PROFESSIONAL CORPORATION (AV)

1300 First National Building, 660 Woodward Avenue, 48226-3531
Telephone: 313-961-2550
Washington, D.C. Office: 1250 Connecticut Avenue, N.W., Suite 630, 20036.
Telephone: 202-835-0616.
Fax: 202-833-3316.

David Baker Lewis
Richard Thomas White
Eric Lee Clay
Reuben A. Munday
Ulysses Whittaker Boykin
S. Allen Early, III
Carl F. Stafford
Helen Francine Strong
Derrick P. Mayes
Frank E. Barbee
Camille Stearns Miller
Melvin J. Hollowell, Jr.
Michael T. Raymond
Jacqueline H. Sellers
Thomas R. Paxton
Kathleen Miles (Resident, Washington, D.C. Office)
David N. Zacks

Karen Kendrick Brown (Resident, Washington, D.C. Office)
J. Taylor Teasdale
Wade Harper McCree
Tyrone A. Powell
Blair A. Person
Susan D. Hoffman
Stephon E. Johnson
John J. Walsh
Andrea L. Powell
Teresa N. Gueyser
Hans J. Massaquoi, Jr.
Werten F. W. Bellamy, Jr. (Resident, Washington, D.C. Office)
Akin O. Akindele
Regina P. Freelon-Solomon
Calita L. Elston
Nancy C. Borland
Terrence Randall Haugabook
Lynn R. Westfall
Lance W. Mason

OF COUNSEL

Otis M. Smith (1922-1994)
Inez Smith Reid (Resident, Washington, D.C. Office)

Representative Clients: Omnicare Health Plan; Aetna Life & Casualty Co.; Chrysler Motors Corp.; Chrysler Financial Corp.; MCI Communications Corp.; City of Detroit; City of Detroit Building Authority; City of Detroit Downtown Development Authority; Consolidated Rail Corp. (Conrail); Equitable Life Assurance Society of the United States.

For full biographical listings, see the Martindale-Hubbell Law Directory

MILLER, CANFIELD, PADDOCK AND STONE, P.L.C. (AV)

A Professional Limited Liability Company
Founded in 1852 by Sidney Davy Miller
150 West Jefferson, Suite 2500, 48226-4415
Telephone: 313-963-6420
Fax: 313-496-7500
Cable Address: "Stem Detroit"
Detroit, Michigan Office: 150 West Jefferson, Suite 2500, 48226-4415.
Telephone: 313-963-6420.
Fax: 313-496-7500.
Cable Address: "Stem Detroit."
Ann Arbor, Michigan Office: 101 North Main Street, 7th Floor, 48104-1400.
Telephone: 313-663-2445.
Fax: 313-747-7147.
Bloomfield Hills, Michigan Office: Suite 100, Pinehurst Office Center, 1400 North Woodward, 48303-2014.
Telephone: 313-645-5000.
Fax: 313-645-1917.

(See Next Column)

MILLER, CANFIELD, PADDOCK AND STONE P.L.C., *Detroit—Continued*

Grand Rapids, Michigan Office: 1200 Campau Square Plaza, 99 Monroe, N.W., 49503-2639.
Telephone: 616-454-8656.
Fax: 616-776-6322.
Howell, Michigan Office: 121 South Barnard Street, Suite 4, 48843-2305.
Telephone: 517-546-7600.
Telecopier: 517-546-6974.
Kalamazoo, Michigan Office: 444 West Michigan Avenue, 49007-3752.
Telephone: 616-381-7030.
Fax: 616-382-0244.
Lansing, Michigan Office: One Michigan Avenue, Suite 900, 48933-1609.
Telephone: 517-487-2070.
Fax: 517-374-6304.
Monroe, Michigan Office: The Executive Centre, 214 East Elm Avenue, 48161-2682.
Telephone: 313-243-2000.
Fax: 313-243-0901.
Washington, D.C. Office: 1225 Nineteenth Street, N.W., Suite 400. 20036.
Telephone: 202-429-5575; 785-0600.
Fax: 202-331-1118; 785-1234.
Pensacola, Florida Office: 25 West Cedar, 32501.
Telephone: 904-469-1088.
Fax: 904-432-0677.
St. Petersburg, Florida Office: 100 Second Avenue S., Suite 7045, 33701.
Telephone: 813-982-6000.
Fax: 813-892-6002.
Gdansk, Poland Office: Suite 322, Dom Technika Building, Ul. Rajska 6, 80-850.
Telephone: 011-485-831-2808.
Fax: 011-485-831-4719.
Warsaw, Poland Office: Ul. Marszalkowska 82, Suite 561, 00-517.
Telephone: 011-482-623-6457 and 6458.
Fax: 011-482-623-6459.

MEMBERS OF FIRM

Frank L. Andrews (Detroit and Bloomfield Hills Offices)
Thomas C. Phillips (Grand Rapids and Lansing Offices)
Steven D. Weyhing (Lansing Office)

ASSOCIATE

Anna M. Maiuri (Bloomfield Hills Office)

Representative Firm Clients: Chrysler Corp.; Comerica, Inc.; City of Detroit, Mich.; Detroit Tigers, Inc.; First of Michigan; Fretter, Inc.; Ford Motor Co.; Ford Motor Credit Co.; Great Lakes Bancorp; Henry Ford Hospital.

For Complete List of Firm Personnel, See General Section

For full biographical listings, see the Martindale-Hubbell Law Directory

TIMMIS & INMAN (AV)

300 Talon Centre, 48207
Telephone: 313-396-4200
Telecopier: 313-396-4228

MEMBERS OF FIRM

Wayne C. Inman
Robert E. Graziani
Mark W. Peyser

ASSOCIATES

Bradley J. Knickerbocker
Amy Lynn Ryntz
Mark Robert Adams

Representative Clients: Continental Insurance; Transamerica Insurance.

For Complete List of Firm Personnel, See General Section

For full biographical listings, see the Martindale-Hubbell Law Directory

VANDEVEER GARZIA, PROFESSIONAL CORPORATION (AV)

Suite 1600, 333 West Fort Street, 48226
Telephone: 313-961-4880
Fax: 313-961-3822
Oakland County Office: 220 Park Street, Suite 300, Birmingham, Michigan.
Telephone: 810-645-0100.
Fax: 810-645-2430.
Macomb County Office: 50 Crocker Boulevard, Mount Clemens, Michigan.
Telephone: 810-468-4880.
Fax: 810-465-7159.
Kent County Office: 510 Grand Plaza Place, 220 Lyon Square, Grand Rapids, Michigan.
Telephone: 616-366-8600.
Fax: 616-786-9095.
Holland, Michigan Office: 1121 Ottawa Beach Road, Suite 140.
Telephone: 616-399-8600.
Fax: 616-786-9095.

James A. Sullivan
John J. Lynch, III (Resident, Oakland County Office)
William J. Heaphy (Kent County and Holland Offices)
Leonard A. Krzyzaniak, Jr.

(See Next Column)

Lauren Elizabeth Meyer

Representative Clients: Aetna Casualty and Surety Co.; Bic Corp.; CNA Insurance Group; Travelers Insurance Co.; United States Aviation Underwriters; Goodyear Tire & Rubber Co.

For Complete List of Firm Personnel, See General Section

For full biographical listings, see the Martindale-Hubbell Law Directory

EAST LANSING, Ingham Co.

FARHAT, STORY & KRAUS, P.C. (AV)

Beacon Place, 4572 South Hagadorn Road, Suite 3, 48823
Telephone: 517-351-3700
Fax: 517-332-4122

Leo A. Farhat
James E. Burns (1925-1979)
Monte R. Story
Richard C. Kraus
Max R. Hoffman Jr.
Chris A. Bergstrom
Kitty L. Groh
Charles R. Toy
David M. Platt

Lawrence P. Schweitzer
Jeffrey J. Short
Kathy A. Breedlove
Thomas L. Sparks

Representative Clients: Big L. Corp.; Michigan Automotive Wholesalers Association; Hartman-Fabco, Inc.; Lansing Electric Motors, Inc.; Mike Miller Lincoln Mercury; Michigan Coalition of Radioactive Material Users, Inc.; Environmental Quality Co.; Michigan Aquatic Managers Association.
Reference: Capitol National Bank.

For full biographical listings, see the Martindale-Hubbell Law Directory

FARMINGTON HILLS, Oakland Co.

COOPER, FINK & ZAUSMER, P.C. (AV)

31700 Middlebelt Road, Suite 150, 48334
Telephone: 810-851-4111
Telefax: 810-851-0100
Detroit, Michigan Office: 1917 Penobscot Building.
Telephone: 313-963-3873.
Telefax: 313-961-6879.
Lansing, Michigan Office: One Michigan Avenue, Suite 1050.
Telephone: 517-372-2020.
Telefax: 517-371-3207.

David H. Fink
Avery K. Williams
Sarah D. Lile

Michael L. Caldwell
Alan D. Wasserman

For full biographical listings, see the Martindale-Hubbell Law Directory

KAUFMAN AND PAYTON (AV)

200 Northwestern Financial Center, 30833 Northwestern Highway, 48334
Telephone: 810-626-5000
Telefacsimile: 810-626-2843
Grand Rapids, Michigan Office: 420 Trust Building.
Telephone: 616-459-4200.
Fax: 616-459-4929.
Traverse City, Michigan Office: 122 West State Street.
Telephone: 616-947-4050.
Fax: 616-947-7321.

Alan Jay Kaufman
Donald L. Payton
Kenneth C. Letherwood
Stephen R. Levine
Thomas L. Vitu
Ralph C. Chapa, Jr.
Raymond I. Foley, II
Jeffrey K. Van Hattum
Leo D. Neville

For full biographical listings, see the Martindale-Hubbell Law Directory

*FLINT,** Genesee Co.

WINEGARDEN, SHEDD, HALEY, LINDHOLM & ROBERTSON (AV)

501 Citizens Bank Building, 48502-1983
Telephone: 810-767-3600
Telecopier: 810-767-8776

MEMBERS OF FIRM

William C. Shedd
Dennis M. Haley
John T. Lindholm
Donald H. Robertson
L. David Lawson
John R. Tucker

ASSOCIATES

Alan F. Himelhoch
Suellen J. Parker
Damion Frasier
Peter T. Mooney

OF COUNSEL

Howard R. Grossman

Representative Clients: Citizens Commercial and Savings Bank; R. L. White Development Corporation; Interstate Traffic Consultants (Intracon) Inc.; Downtown Development Authority of Flint; Young Olds-Cadillac, Inc.; First American Title Insurance Co.; Sorensen Gross Construction Co.; Genesee County; Insight, Inc.; Modern Industries, Inc.

(See Next Column)

WINEGARDEN, SHEDD, HALEY, LINDHOLM & ROBERTSON—*Continued*

For Complete List of Firm Personnel, See General Section

For full biographical listings, see the Martindale-Hubbell Law Directory

*GRAND RAPIDS,** Kent Co.

CLARY, NANTZ, WOOD, HOFFIUS, RANKIN & COOPER (AV)

500 Calder Plaza, 250 Monroe Avenue, N.W., 49503-2244
Telephone: 616-459-9487
Telecopier: 616-459-5121

MEMBERS OF FIRM

Leonard M. Hoffius
Scott G. Smith

OF COUNSEL

Richard J. Rankin, Jr.

Representative Clients: United Bank of Michigan; FMB First Michigan Bank-Grand Rapids; Goodrich Theatres & Radio, Inc.; S. Abraham & Sons, Inc.; Garb-Ko, Inc., d/b/a 7-Eleven; Weather Shield Manufacturing Co.; JET Electronics & Technology, Inc.; Westinghouse Credit Corp.

For Complete List of Firm Personnel, See General Section

For full biographical listings, see the Martindale-Hubbell Law Directory

DAY & SAWDEY, A PROFESSIONAL CORPORATION (AV)

200 Monroe Avenue, Suite 500, 49503-2217
Telephone: 616-774-8121
Telefax: 616-774-0168

George B. Kingston (1889-1965)
John R. Porter (1915-1975)
Charles E. Day, Jr.
Robert W. Sawdey
William A. Hubble
C. Mark Stoppels
John G. Grzybek
James B. Frakie
Larry A. Ver Merris
John Boyko, Jr.
Jonathan F. Thoits
John T. Piggins
Thomas A. DeMeester
Theodore E. Czarnecki

For full biographical listings, see the Martindale-Hubbell Law Directory

GRUEL, MILLS, NIMS AND PYLMAN (AV)

50 Monroe Place, Suite 700 West, 49503
Telephone: 616-235-5500
Fax: 616-235-5550

MEMBERS OF FIRM

Grant J. Gruel
William F. Mills
J. Clarke Nims
Norman H. Pylman, II
Scott R. Melton
Brion J. Brooks
Thomas R. Behm
J. Paul Janes

Representative Clients: Aquinas College; Bell Helmet Co.; Blodgett Memorial Medical Center; Butterworth Hospital; Chem Central, Inc.; Cook Pump Co.; Grove, Inc.; NBDC; Heim Corp.

For full biographical listings, see the Martindale-Hubbell Law Directory

ROBERTS, BETZ & BLOSS, P.C. (AV)

555 Riverfront Plaza Building, 55 Campau, 49503
Telephone: 616-235-9955
Telecopier: 616-235-0404

Michael W. Betz
David J. Bloss
Michael T. Small
Ralph M. Reisinger
Elena C. Cardenas

For full biographical listings, see the Martindale-Hubbell Law Directory

VARNUM, RIDDERING, SCHMIDT & HOWLETT (AV)

Bridgewater Place, P.O. Box 352, 49501-0352
Telephone: 616-336-6000
800-262-0011
Facsimile: 616-336-7000
Telex: 1561593 VARN
Lansing, Michigan Office: The Victor Center, Suite 810, 210 North Washington Square, 48933.
Telephone: 517-482-6237.
Facsimile: 517-482-6937.
Kalamazoo, Michigan Office: 350 East Michigan Avenue, 49007.
Telephone: 616-382-2300.
Facsimile: 616-382-2382.
Grand Haven, Michigan Office: 321 Washington Street, P.O. Box 288, 49417.
Telephone: 616-846-7100.
Facsimile: 616-846-7101.
Battle Creek, Michigan Office: 4950 West Dickman Road, Suite B-1, 49015.
Telephone: 616-962-7144.
Detroit, Michigan Office: 440 East Congress, Fourth Floor, 48226.
Telephone: 313-961-1600.
Facsimile: 313-961-1636.

(See Next Column)

MEMBERS OF FIRM

Jon F. DeWitt
Peter A. Smit
Mark C. Hanisch
Bruce Goodman
Teresa S. Decker
Richard W. Butler, Jr.
Matthew D. Zimmerman
Charles M. Denton II
Mark S. Allard
George B. Davis
David E. Preston

ASSOCIATES

Michael F. Kelly
Andrew J. Kok
Michael X. Hidalgo
Edward J. McNeely

Counsel for: CMI International; Donnelly Corporation; FKI Industries; Great Lakes Casting Corporation; HM Holdings, Inc.; Harrow Industries; Kent County; Leon Plastics, Inc.; NBD Bank, NA; Outboard Marine Corporation; Safety-Kleen; Sparton Corporation.

For Complete List of Firm Personnel, See General Section

For full biographical listings, see the Martindale-Hubbell Law Directory

WARNER, NORCROSS & JUDD (AV)

900 Old Kent Building, 111 Lyon Street, N.W., 49503-2489
Telephone: 616-752-2000
Fax: 616-752-2500
Muskegon, Michigan Office: 400 Terrace Plaza, P.O. Box 900.
Telephone: 616-727-2600.
Fax: 616-727-2699.
Holland, Michigan Office: Curtis Center, Suite 300, 170 College Avenue.
Telephone: 616-396-9800.
Fax: 616-396-3656.

MEMBERS OF FIRM

John D. Tully
Peter L. Gustafson
Michael L. Robinson
Eugene E. Smary
Paul T. Sorensen
John D. Dunn
John V. Byl
Tracy T. Larsen

For Complete List of Firm Personnel, See General Section

For full biographical listings, see the Martindale-Hubbell Law Directory

WHEELER UPHAM, A PROFESSIONAL CORPORATION (AV)

Second Floor, Trust Building, 40 Pearl Street, N.W., 49503
Telephone: 616-459-7100
Fax: 616-459-6366

Gordon B. Wheeler (1904-1986)
Buford A. Upham (Retired)
Robert H. Gillette
Geoffrey L. Gillis
John M. Roels
Gary A. Maximiuk
Timothy J. Orlebeke
Kenneth E. Tiews
Jack L. Hoffman
Janet C. Baxter
Peter Kladder, III
James M. Shade
Thomas A. Kuiper

Counsel for: Travelers Insurance Co.; Prudential Insurance Co. of America; Farmers Insurance Group; Metropolitan Life Insurance Co.; Conrail Trans.; Monsanto Co.; Firestone Tire & Rubber Co.; Navistar, Inc.; Medtronic, Inc.; Westdale Better Homes and Gardens.

For full biographical listings, see the Martindale-Hubbell Law Directory

*KALAMAZOO,** Kalamazoo Co.

DEMING, HUGHEY, LEWIS, ALLEN & CHAPMAN, P.C. (AV)

800 Old Kent Bank Building, 49007
Telephone: 616-349-6601
Fax: 616-349-3831

Ned W. Deming
Richard M. Hughey
Dean S. Lewis
W. Fred Allen, Jr.
Ross E. Chapman
Winfield J. Hollander
John A. Scott
Bruce W. Martin (Resident)
Daniel L. Conklin
William A. Redmond
Stephen M. Denenfeld
Thomas C. Richardson
Gregory G. St. Arnauld
Roger G. Allen (Retired)
Anne McGregor Fries
Amy J. Glass
Richard M. Hughey, Jr.
Richard J. Bosch
Thomas P. Lewis
Christopher T. Haenicke

LEGAL SUPPORT PERSONNEL

Dorothy B. Kelly

General Counsel for: The Old Kent Bank of Kalamazoo; Gilmore Brothers, Inc.; Root Spring Scraper Co.; Kalamazoo County Road Commission; Loftenberg Educational Scholarship Trust; Farm Credit Services of West Michigan; Irving S. Gilmore Foundation; National Meals on Wheels Foundation; Irving S. Gilmore International Keyboard Festival.

For full biographical listings, see the Martindale-Hubbell Law Directory

Kalamazoo—Continued

HOWARD & HOWARD ATTORNEYS, P.C. (AV)

The Kalamazoo Building, Suite 400, 107 West Michigan Avenue, 49007-3956
Telephone: 616-382-1483
Telecopier: 616-382-1568
Bloomfield Hills, Michigan Office: The Pinehurst Office Center, Suite 101, 1400 North Woodward Avenue.
Telephone: 810-645-1483.
Telecopier: 810-645-1568.
Lansing, Michigan Office: The Phoenix Building, Suite 500, 222 Washington Square North.
Telephone: 517-485-1483.
Telecopier: 517-485-1568.
Peoria, Illinois Office: Howard & Howard, P.C., The Creve Coeur Building, Suite 200, 321 Liberty Street.
Telephone: 309-672-1483.
Telecopier: 309-672-1568.

John W. Allen
Gerry Bartlett-McMahon
Robert C. Beck
Eric E. Breisach
Jeffrey P. Chalmers
Michael L. Chojnowski
William A. Dornbos
Richard D. Fries
James H. Geary
Edgar G. Gordon
Bruce R. Grubb
Richard L. Halpert
Joseph B. Hemker
David L. Holmes
John C. Howard
J. Michael Kemp
James H. Koning
Peter J. Livingston
D. Craig Martin
Lawrence J. Murphy
Charles C.S. Park
David E. Riggs
Bonnie Y. Sawusch
Shamra M. Van Wagoner
Steven H. Weston
Myra L. Willis
Thomas J. Wuori

Representative Clients: For Representative Client list, see General Practice, Kalamazoo, MI.

For full biographical listings, see the Martindale-Hubbell Law Directory

KREIS, ENDERLE, CALLANDER & HUDGINS, A PROFESSIONAL CORPORATION (AV)

One Moorsbridge, 49002
Telephone: 616-324-3000
Telecopier: 616-324-3010

Alan G. Enderle
Jeffrey D. Swenarton

For Complete List of Firm Personnel, See General Section

For full biographical listings, see the Martindale-Hubbell Law Directory

MILLER, CANFIELD, PADDOCK AND STONE, P.L.C. (AV)

A Professional Limited Liability Company
Founded in 1852 by Sidney Davy Miller
444 West Michigan Avenue, 49007-3752
Telephone: 616-381-7030
Fax: 616-382-0244
Detroit, Michigan Office: 150 West Jefferson, Suite 2500, 48226-4415.
Telephone: 313-963-6420.
Fax: 313-496-7500.
Cable Address: "Stem Detroit."
Ann Arbor, Michigan Office: 101 North Main Street, 7th Floor, 48104-1400.
Telephone: 313-663-2445.
Fax: 313-747-7147.
Bloomfield Hills, Michigan Office: Suite 100, Pinehurst Office Center, 1400 North Woodward, 48303-2014.
Telephone: 313-645-5000.
Fax: 313-645-1917.
Grand Rapids, Michigan Office: 1200 Campau Square Plaza, 99 Monroe, N.W., 49503-2639.
Telephone: 616-454-8656.
Fax: 616-776-6322.
Howell, Michigan Office: 121 South Barnard Street, Suite 4, 48843-2305.
Telephone: 517-546-7600.
Telecopier: 517-546-6974.
Lansing, Michigan Office: One Michigan Avenue, Suite 900, 48933-1609.
Telephone: 517-487-2070.
Fax: 517-374-6304.
Monroe, Michigan Office: The Executive Centre, 214 East Elm Avenue, 48161-2682.
Telephone: 313-243-2000.
Fax: 313-243-0901.
Washington, D.C. Office: 1225 Nineteenth Street, N.W., Suite 400. 20036.
Telephone: 202-429-5575; 785-0600.
Fax: 202-331-1118; 785-1234.
Pensacola, Florida Office: 25 West Cedar, 32501.
Telephone: 904-469-1088.
Fax: 904-432-0677.
St. Petersburg, Florida Office: 100 Second Avenue S., Suite 7045,33701.
Telephone: 813-982-6000.
Fax: 813-892-6002.

(See Next Column)

Gdansk, Poland Office: Suite 322, Dom Technika Building, Ul. Rajska 6, 80-850.
Telephone: 011-485-831-2808.
Fax: 011-485-831-4719.
Warsaw, Poland Office: Ul. Marszalkowska 82, Suite 561, 00-517.
Telephone: 011-482-623-6457 and 6458.
Fax: 011-482-623-6459.

MEMBER OF FIRM

Eric V. Brown, Jr. (Resident)

Representative Firm Clients: Chrysler Corp.; Comerica, Inc.; City of Detroit, Mich.; Detroit Tigers, Inc.; First of Michigan; Fretter, Inc.; Ford Motor Co.; Ford Motor Credit Co.; Great Lakes Bancorp; Henry Ford Hospital.

For Complete List of Firm Personnel, See General Section

For full biographical listings, see the Martindale-Hubbell Law Directory

LANSING, Ingham Co.

*** indicates certain Bar Register subscribers whose principal office is located elsewhere in the state and who have arranged for representation as a part of the state capital listings that follow**

FOSTER, SWIFT, COLLINS & SMITH, P.C. (AV)

313 South Washington Square, 48933-2193
Telephone: 517-371-8100
Telecopier: 517-371-8200
Farmington Hills, Michigan Office: 32300 Northwestern Highway, Suite 230.
Telephone: 810-851-7500.
Fax: 810-851-7504.

Webb A. Smith
Stephen O. Schultz
Charles E. Barbieri
James B. Jensen, Jr.
James B. Croom
Brent A. Titus

General Counsel for: First American Bank-Central; Story, Inc.; Michigan Milk Producers Assn.; Edward W. Sparrow Hospital; St. Lawrence Hospital; Demmer Corp.; Michigan Financial Corp.
Local Counsel for: Shell Oil Co.; Michigan-Mutual Insurance Co.; Century Cellunet.

For Complete List of Firm Personnel, See General Section

For full biographical listings, see the Martindale-Hubbell Law Directory

FRASER TREBILCOCK DAVIS & FOSTER, P.C. (AV)

1000 Michigan National Tower, 48933
Telephone: 517-482-5800
Fax: 517-482-0887
Okemos, Michigan Office: 2188 Commons Parkway.
Telephone: 517-349-1300.
Fax: 517-349-0922.

Donald A. Hines
Douglas J. Austin
Stephen L. Burlingame
Michael H. Perry
Thomas J. Waters

Counsel for: Texaco, Federated Insurance Co.; Snell Environmental Group; Mason Family Enterprises; STRATA Environmental Services; RCO Engineering, Inc.; Livingston County.

For Complete List of Firm Personnel, See General Section

For full biographical listings, see the Martindale-Hubbell Law Directory

*** HONIGMAN MILLER SCHWARTZ AND COHN (AV)**

A Partnership including Professional Corporations
222 North Washington Square, Suite 400, 48933
Telephone: 517-484-8282
Telecopier: 517-484-8286
Detroit, Michigan Office: 2290 First National Building.
Telephone: 313-256-7800.
West Palm Beach, Florida Office: Suite 800 Esperante Building, 222 Lakeview Avenue.
Telephone: 407-838-4500.
Tampa, Florida Office: Suite 350 One Harbour Place, 777 South Harbour Island Boulevard.
Telephone: 813-221-6600.
Orlando, Florida Office: 390 North Orange Avenue, Suite 1300.
Telephone: 407-648-0300.
Houston, Texas Office: 3100 First Interstate Bank Plaza, 1000 Louisiana.
Telephone: 713-650-2600.
Los Angeles, California Office: McNeill Plaza, Suite 820, 15260 Ventura Boulevard, 91403.
Telephone: 818-784-2900.

MEMBERS

Mark Morton
John D. Pirich
Gary A. Trepod

General Counsel for: Dart Container Corp; Forbes-Cohen Properties (The Lansing Mall); Granger Land Development Co.; Michigan Hospital Association.

(See Next Column)

HONIGMAN MILLER SCHWARTZ AND COHN—*Continued*

Legal or Special Counsel for: Champion International; Greater Detroit Resource Recovery Authority; First American Title Insurance Company of the Midwest; Indiana Michigan Power Co.

For Complete List of Firm Personnel, See General Section

For full biographical listings, see the Martindale-Hubbell Law Directory

HOWARD & HOWARD ATTORNEYS, P.C. (AV)

The Phoenix Building, Suite 500, 222 Washington Square, North, 48933-1817
Telephone: 517-485-1483
Telecopier: 517-485-1568
Kalamazoo, Michigan Office: The Kalamazoo Building, Suite 400, 107 West Michigan Avenue.
Telephone: 616-382-1483.
Telecopier: 616-382-1568.
Bloomfield Hills, Michigan Office: The Pinehurst Office Center, Suite 101, 1400 North Woodward Avenue.
Telephone: 810-645-1483.
Telecopier: 810-645-1568.
Peoria, Illinois Office: Howard & Howard, P.C., The Creve Coeur Building, Suite 200, 321 Liberty Street.
Telephone: 309-672-1483.
Telecopier: 309-672-1568.

Todd D. Chamberlain
Chistopher C. Cinnamon
David C. Coey
Matthew J. Coffey
Thomas L. Cooper
Michele LaForest Halloran
Patrick D. Hanes
Ellen M. Harvath
J. Michael Kemp
James E. Lozier
D. Craig Martin
C. Douglas Moran
Donald F. Tucker
Patrick R. Van Tiflin

Representative Clients: For Representative Client list, see General Practice, Lansing, MI.

For full biographical listings, see the Martindale-Hubbell Law Directory

*MONROE,** Monroe Co.

ROHRBACHER, NICHOLSON & LIGHT, CO., L.P.A.

(See Toledo, Ohio)

*PORT HURON,** St. Clair Co.

NICHOLSON, FLETCHER & DEGROW (AV)

522 Michigan Street, 48060-3893
Telephone: 810-987-8444
Facsimile: 810-987-8149

MEMBERS OF FIRM

David C. Nicholson
Gary A. Fletcher
Dan L. DeGrow

ASSOCIATES

Mark G. Clark
John D. Tomlinson

Representative Clients: Fremont Mutual Insurance Co.; Westfield Insurance Co.; Michigan Municipal Risk Management Authority; City of Port Huron; City of Marysville; Port Huron Area School District; Marysville Public Schools; Wirtz Manufacturing Co.; Raymond Excavating; Relleum Real Estate Development Co.

For Complete List of Firm Personnel, See General Section

For full biographical listings, see the Martindale-Hubbell Law Directory

*SAGINAW,** Saginaw Co.

BRAUN KENDRICK FINKBEINER (AV)

8th Floor Second National Bank Building, 48607
Telephone: 517-753-3461
Telecopier: 517-753-3951
Bay City, Michigan Office: 201 Phoenix Building, P.O. Box 2039.
Telephone: 517-895-8505.
Telecopier: 517-895-8437.

MEMBERS OF FIRM

J. Richard Kendrick
James V. Finkbeiner
Thomas R. Luplow
John A. Decker
Barry M. Levine

ASSOCIATES

Brian S. Makaric
Glenn L. Fitkin

Representative Clients: The Dow Chemical Co.; General Motors Corp.; Lobdell Emery Manufacturing Co.; Merrill, Lynch, Inc.; Saginaw General Hospital; Saginaw News; The Wickes Foundation.

For Complete List of Firm Personnel, See General Section

For full biographical listings, see the Martindale-Hubbell Law Directory

SOUTHFIELD, Oakland Co.

MASON, STEINHARDT, JACOBS & PERLMAN, PROFESSIONAL CORPORATION (AV)

Suite 1500, 4000 Town Center, 48075-1415
Telephone: 810-358-2090
Fax: 810-358-3599

John E. Jacobs
Michael B. Perlman
Richard A. Barr

Representative Clients: Citibank, N.A.; City of Dearborn; DeMattia Development Co.; Forest City Enterprises; Michigan Wholesale Drug Assn.; Mortgage Bankers Association of Michigan; Nationwide Insurance Co.; City of Taylor; Union Labor Life Insurance Co.; Yellow Freight Systems, Inc.

For Complete List of Firm Personnel, See General Section

For full biographical listings, see the Martindale-Hubbell Law Directory

SOMMERS, SCHWARTZ, SILVER & SCHWARTZ, P.C. (AV)

2000 Town Center, Suite 900, 48075
Telephone: 810-355-0300
Telecopier: 810-746-4001
Plymouth, Michigan Office: 747 South Main Street.
Telephone: 313-455-4250.

James J. Vlasic
David M. Black
Saulius K. Mikalonis

General Counsel for: City of Taylor; Foodland Distributors; C.A. Muer Corporation; Vlasic & Company; Nederlander Corporation; Woodland Physicians; Midwest Health Centers, P.C.
Representative Clients: Crum & Forster Insurance Company; City of Pontiac; Michigan National Bank; Perry Drugs.

For Complete List of Firm Personnel, See General Section

For full biographical listings, see the Martindale-Hubbell Law Directory

TROY, Oakland Co.

HAINER & DEMOREST, P.C. (AV)

100 West Big Beaver, Suite 665, 48084-5283
Telephone: 810-680-8866
Fax: 810-680-0313

Michael J. Hainer
Mark S. Demorest

James D. Zazakis
Paul S. Miller
Leonard K. Berman
Bradley D. Gorman

OF COUNSEL

John P. Charters
Michael A. Heck
Michael A. Kus
Douglas W. Mires

Representative Clients: American Empire Surplus Lines Insurance Co.; Central Distributors of Beer, Inc.; Century 21 Premier Real Estate; City Management Corp.; Clarklift of Detroit, Inc.; Federal Reserve Bank of Chicago; Mid-West Instrument, Inc.; Rockwell International Corp.; Zurich Insurance Co.; Hotel Investment Services, Inc.

For full biographical listings, see the Martindale-Hubbell Law Directory

MINNESOTA

*MINNEAPOLIS,** Hennepin Co.

ARTHUR, CHAPMAN, MCDONOUGH, KETTERING & SMETAK, P.A. (AV)

500 Young Quinlan Building, 81 South Ninth Street, 55402
Telephone: 612-339-3500
Fax: 612-339-7655

Thomas A. Pearson

Representative Clients: American International Group; American States; Bristol Myers-Squibb, Inc.; Continental Insurance Co.; General Casualty; Home Insurance Co.; Metropolitan Property & Liability Insurance Co.; Navistar International; Safeco Insurance Co.; USAA.

For Complete List of Firm Personnel, See General Section

For full biographical listings, see the Martindale-Hubbell Law Directory

BASSFORD, LOCKHART, TRUESDELL & BRIGGS, P.A. (AV)

(Formerly Richards, Montgomery, Cobb & Bassford, P.A.)
3550 Multifoods Tower, 55402-3787
Telephone: 612-333-3000
Telecopier: 612-333-8829

(See Next Column)

BASSFORD, LOCKHART, TRUESDELL & BRIGGS P.A., *Minneapolis—Continued*

Fred B. Snyder (1859-1951)
Edward C. Gale (1862-1943)
Frank A. Janes (1908-1959)
Nathan A. Cobb, Sr. (1905-1976)
Bergmann Richards (1888-1978)
Edmund T. Montgomery (1904-1987)
Charles A. Bassford (1914-1990)
Greer E. Lockhart
Lynn G. Truesdell
Jerome C. Briggs
Frederick E. Finch
John M. Degnan
Lewis A. Remele, Jr.
Kevin P. Keenan
James O. Redman
Rebecca Egge Moos
John M. Anderson
Charles E. Lundberg
Gregory P. Bulinski
Donna J. Blazevic
Mary E. Steenson
Mark P. Hodkinson
Thomas J. Niemiec
Andrew L. Marshall
Michael A. Klutho
Kathryn H. Davis
Gregory W. Deckert

Kevin P. Hickey
John P. Buckley
Bradley J. Betlach
Mark Whitmore
Christopher R. Morris
Kelly Christensen

Representative Clients: Chubb/Pacific Indemnity Group; Greyhound Lines, Inc.; John Hancock Mutual Life Insurance Co.; The Travelers Insurance Cos.; Commercial Union Insurance Co.

For full biographical listings, see the Martindale-Hubbell Law Directory

HENSON & EFRON, P.A. (AV)

1200 Title Insurance Building, 400 Second Avenue South, 55401
Telephone: 612-339-2500
FAX: 612-339-6364

Joseph T. Dixon, Jr.
William F. Forsyth
Stuart T. Williams

Representative Clients: H.B. Fuller Co.; Hawkins Chemical, Inc.; Pentair, Inc.

For Complete List of Firm Personnel, See General Section

For full biographical listings, see the Martindale-Hubbell Law Directory

*ST. CLOUD,** Stearns, Benton & Sherburne Cos.

RAJKOWSKI HANSMEIER LTD. (AV)

Daniel Building, 11 Seventh Avenue North, P.O. Box 1433, 56302-1433
Telephone: 612-251-1055
Toll Free: 800-445-9617
Fax: 612-251-5896

Frank J. Rajkowski
Gordon H. Hansmeier
Frederick L. Grunke
Thomas G. Jovanovich
John H. Scherer
Paul A. Rajkowski
Kevin F. Gray
William J. Cashman
David T. Shay
Richard W. Sobalvarro
Michael C. Rajkowski

LEGAL SUPPORT PERSONNEL

James H. Kelly, M.D. (Forensic Medical Consultant)

Representative Clients: Independent School District No. 742 (St. Cloud, Minn.); Jim W. Miller Construction Co.; City of Waite Park; The Travelers Ins. Co.; American Family Insurance Co.; Allstate Insurance Co.; Milbank/-State Auto Insurance Companies; Safeco Insurance Co.; Employers Mutual Co.; The Agricultural Group of Monsanto Company.

For full biographical listings, see the Martindale-Hubbell Law Directory

*ST. PAUL,** Ramsey Co.

BRIGGS AND MORGAN, PROFESSIONAL ASSOCIATION (AV)

2200 First National Bank Building, 55101
Telephone: 612-223-6600
Telecopier: 612-223-6450
Minneapolis, Minnesota Office: 2400 IDS Center, 80 South Eighth Street.
Telephone: 612-334-8400.
Telecopier: 612-334-8650.

RESIDENT PERSONNEL

David C. McDonald
Douglas L. Skor
John B. Van de North, Jr.

MINNEAPOLIS OFFICE

Thomas A. Larson
Charles B. Rogers
Timothy R. Thornton

For Complete List of Firm Personnel, See General Section

For full biographical listings, see the Martindale-Hubbell Law Directory

MISSISSIPPI

*ABERDEEN,** Monroe Co.

HOLCOMB, DUNBAR, CONNELL, CHAFFIN & WILLARD, A PROFESSIONAL ASSOCIATION (AV)

109 1/2 West Commerce Street, P.O. Box 866, 39730
Telephone: 601-369-8800
Facsimile: 601-369-9404
Jackson, Mississippi Office: 111 East Capitol Street, Suite 290, P.O. Box 2990, 39207-2990.
Telephone: 601-948-0048.
Facsimile: 601-948-0050.
Clarksdale, Mississippi Office: 152 Delta Avenue, P.O. Box 368, 38614.
Telephone: 601-627-2241.
Facsimile: 601-627-9788.
Oxford, Mississippi Office: 1217 Jackson Avenue, P.O. Drawer 707, 38655.
Telephone: 601-234-8775.
Facsimile: 601-234-8638.
Southhaven, Mississippi Office: Suite 1, 8727 Northwest Drive, P.O. Box 190, 38671.
Telephone: 601-342-6806.
Facsimile: 601-342-6792.

Jack F. Dunbar
James T. McCafferty, III

Representative Clients: Mississippi State Department of Environmental Quality.

For Complete List of Firm Personnel, See General Section

For full biographical listings, see the Martindale-Hubbell Law Directory

BILOXI, Harrison Co.

BROWN & WATT, P.A. (AV)

115 Main Street, P.O. Box 1377, 39533-1377
Telephone: 601-374-2999
Telecopier: 601-435-7090
Pascagoula, Mississippi Office: 3112 Canty Street, P.O. Box 2220.
Telephone: 601-762-0035.
Fax: 601-762-0299.

Raymond L. Brown
W. Lee Watt
Patrick R. Buchanan
William M. Edwards
A. Kelly Sessoms, III
R. Bradley Prewitt
Alan K. Sudduth

General Counsel For: Mississippi Export Railroad Co.; Pascagoula Municipal Separate School District.
Representative Clients: United States Fidelity & Guaranty Co.; The Travelers Companies; The Home Insurance Co.; CSX Transportation, Inc.; Blue Cross-Blue Shield of Mississippi; Burlington Insurance Co.; Continental Insurance; Deere & Company.

For full biographical listings, see the Martindale-Hubbell Law Directory

*CLARKSDALE,** Coahoma Co.

HOLCOMB, DUNBAR, CONNELL, CHAFFIN & WILLARD, A PROFESSIONAL ASSOCIATION (AV)

152 Delta Avenue, P.O. Box 368, 38614
Telephone: 601-627-2241
Facsimile: 601-627-9788
Jackson, Mississippi Office: 111 East Capitol Street, Suite 290, P.O. Box 2990, 39207-2990.
Telephone: 601-948-0048.
Facsimile: 601-948-0050.
Aberdeen, Mississippi Office: 109 1/2 West Commerce Street, P.O. Box 866, 39730.
Telephone: 601-369-8800.
Facsimile: 601-369-9404.
Oxford, Mississippi Office: 1217 Jackson Avenue, P.O. Drawer 707, 38655.
Telephone: 601-234-8775.
Facsimile: 601-234-8638.
Southaven, Mississippi Office: Suite 1, 8727 Northwest Drive, 38671.
Telephone: 601-342-6806.
Facsimile: 601-342-6792.

William M. Chaffin
William A. Baskin

Representative Clients: Mississippi State Department of Environmental Quality.

For Complete List of Firm Personnel, See General Section

For full biographical listings, see the Martindale-Hubbell Law Directory

*COLUMBIA,** Marion Co.

AULTMAN, TYNER, MCNEESE & RUFFIN, LTD., A PROFESSIONAL LAW CORPORATION (AV)

329 Church Street, P.O. Drawer 707, 39429
Telephone: 601-736-2222
Hattiesburg, Mississippi Office: 315 Hemphill Street, P.O. Drawer 750.
Telephone: 601-583-2671.
Gulfport, Mississippi Office: 1201 25th Avenue, Suite 300, P.O. Box 607.
Telephone: 601-863-6913.

Thomas D. McNeese
Richard F. Yarborough, Jr.

Lawrence E. Hahn

OF COUNSEL

Ernest Ray Duff

Representative Clients: Hercules, Inc.; United States Steel Corp.; Ford Motor Co.; International Paper Co.; Phillips Petroleum Co.; Aetna Casualty & Surety Co.; CNA Group; Liberty Mutual Insurance Co.; St. Paul Fire & Marine Insurance Co.; Fireman's Fund.

For full biographical listings, see the Martindale-Hubbell Law Directory

*GREENWOOD,** Leflore Co.

UPSHAW, WILLIAMS, BIGGERS, PAGE & KRUGER (AV)

309 Fulton Street, P.O. Drawer 8230, 38930
Telephone: 601-455-1613
Facsimile: 601-453-9245
Jackson, Mississippi Office: One Jackson Place, 188 East Capitol Street, Suite 600. P.O. Drawer 1163, 39215.
Telephone: 601-944-0005.
Facsimile: 601-355-4269.

MEMBERS OF FIRM

James E. Upshaw
Tommie G. Williams
Marc A. Biggers
Thomas Y. Page (Resident, Jackson Office)
Stephen P. Kruger (Resident, Jackson Office)
Glenn F. Beckham
James D. Holland (Resident, Jackson Office)
F. Ewin Henson, III
Lonnie D. Bailey
Robert S. Upshaw
Clinton M. Guenther
Roger C. Riddick (Resident, Jackson Office)
Edley H. Jones, III (Resident, Jackson Office)
C. Richard Benz, Jr.
Richard C. Williams, Jr.
Wes Peters (Resident, Jackson Office)

ASSOCIATES

Brent E. Southern (Resident, Jackson Office)
R.H. Burress, III
Kathleen S. Gordon (Resident, Jackson Office)
W. Hugh Gillon, IV (Resident, Jackson Office)
William C. Helm (Resident, Jackson Office)
Bryan H. Callaway
Mark C. Carroll (Resident, Jackson Office)
Paul L. Goodman
Walter C. Morrison, IV (Resident, Jackson Office)
Patrick C. Malouf (Resident, Jackson Office)
David C. Meadors
Stuart B. Harmon (Resident, Jackson Office)

OF COUNSEL

B. L. Riddick (Resident, Jackson Office)
John R. Countiss, III (Resident, Jackson Office)

Representative Clients: U.S.F. & G. Co.; State Farm Mutual Automobile Ins. Co.; ; Continental Insurance Co.; St. Paul Fire & Marine Insurance Co.; Aetna Casualty & Surety Co.; Kemper Insurance Co.; Zurich-American Ins. Group; Home Ins. Co.; Illinois Central Railroad Co.; Allstate Insurance Co.

For full biographical listings, see the Martindale-Hubbell Law Directory

*GULFPORT,** Harrison Co.

AULTMAN, TYNER, MCNEESE & RUFFIN, LTD., A PROFESSIONAL LAW CORPORATION (AV)

1201 25th Avenue, Suite 300, P.O. Box 607, 39502
Telephone: 601-863-6913
Hattiesburg, Mississippi Office: 315 Hemphill Street, P.O. Drawer 750.
Telephone: 601-583-2671.
Columbia, Mississippi Office: 329 Church Street, P.O. Drawer 707.
Telephone: 601-736-2222.

Ben E. Sheely
Paul J. Delcambre, Jr.
Dorrance (Dee) Aultman, Jr.

For full biographical listings, see the Martindale-Hubbell Law Directory

DUKES, DUKES, KEATING AND FANECA, P.A. (AV)

2308 East Beach Boulevard, P.O. Drawer W, 39501
Telephone: 601-868-1111
FAX: 601-863-2886

Walter W. Dukes
Hugh D. Keating

For full biographical listings, see the Martindale-Hubbell Law Directory

HOPKINS, DODSON, CRAWLEY, BAGWELL, UPSHAW & PERSONS (AV)

2701 24th Avenue, P.O. Box 1510, 39502-1510
Telephone: 601-864-2200
Mississippi & USA Wats: 1-800-421-3629
Fax: 601-868-9358; 601-863-4227

MEMBERS OF FIRM

Alben N. Hopkins
Lisa P. Dodson
Timothy D. Crawley
Douglas Bagwell
Jessica Sibley Upshaw
James B. Persons

ASSOCIATES

Perre M. Cabell
Christopher Anthony Davis
James Robert Reeves, Jr.
Ottis B. Crocker, III
Kaye Johnson Persons (Not admitted in MS)
Matthew G. Mestayer
Regina A. Lightsey
Mary Benton-Shaw (Not admitted in MS)
K. Douglas Lee (Not admitted in MS)
Thomas A. Waller
M. Amanda Baucum (Not admitted in MS)

LEGAL SUPPORT PERSONNEL

PARALEGALS

Cherri Nickoles
Penny W. West
Jennifer Susan Regan
Justina M. Tillman
Jayme L. Evans
Tracey L. Owen
Marcia P. Henry
Anne B. Parks

Representative Clients: Avondale Shipyards; Employers Insurance of Wausau; Fireman's Fund Insurance Company; General Cable Company; Hartford Insurance Company and Its Affiliates; Insurance Company of North America; Libery Mutual Group; Reliance Insurance; USX Corporation.

For full biographical listings, see the Martindale-Hubbell Law Directory

*HATTIESBURG,** Forrest Co.

AULTMAN, TYNER, MCNEESE & RUFFIN, LTD., A PROFESSIONAL LAW CORPORATION (AV)

315 Hemphill Street, P.O. Drawer 750, 39403-0750
Telephone: 601-583-2671
Columbia, Mississippi Office: 329 Church Street, P.O. Drawer 707.
Telephone: 601-736-2222.
Gulfport, Mississippi Office: 1201 25th Avenue, Suite 300, P.O. Box 607.
Telephone: 601-863-6913.

Dorrance Aultman
Thomas W. Tyner
Thomas D. McNeese (Resident, Columbia Office)
Louie F. Ruffin
Richard F. Yarborough, Jr. (Resident, Columbia Office)
Ben E. Sheely (Resident, Gulfport Office)
Patrick H. Zachary
Paul J. Delcambre, Jr. (Resident, Gulfport Office)
Robert J. Dambrino, III
Vicki R. Leggett
R. Curtis Smith, II
Dorrance (Dee) Aultman, Jr. (Resident, Gulfport Office)
William Nelson Graham

James L. Quinn
Walter J. Eades
Lawrence E. Hahn (Resident, Columbia Office)
Carol Ann Estes
Victor A. DuBose

OF COUNSEL

Ernest Ray Duff (Resident, Columbia Office)

Representative Clients: Hercules, Inc.; U.S. Steel Corp.; Ford Motor Co.; Phillips Petroleum Co.; Aetna Casualty & Surety Co.; CNA Group; Liberty Mutual Insurance Co.; St. Paul Fire & Marine Insurance Co.; Fireman's Fund.

For full biographical listings, see the Martindale-Hubbell Law Directory

MONTAGUE, PITTMAN & VARNADO, A PROFESSIONAL ASSOCIATION (AV)

525 Main Street, P.O. Drawer 1975, 39403-1975
Telephone: 601-544-1234
Telecopier: 601-544-1276

Reginald A. Gray, Jr. (1919-1979)
Frank D. Montague, Jr.
James C. Pittman, Jr.
F. Douglas Montague, III
Carey R. Varnado

Brian A. Montague
Bob W. Pittman, Jr.
William R. Newman
Stacy S. Ruffin

General Counsel for: Hattiesburg American (Gannett); Wesley Health System (Methodist Hospital).
Representative Clients: Georgia Pacific Corp.; South Central Bell; General Motors Acceptance Corp.; The Home Insurance Cos.; Fidelity & Deposit Company of Maryland; Canal Ins. Co.; Deposit Guaranty N.B.; Laurel Regional Corporate Association.

For full biographical listings, see the Martindale-Hubbell Law Directory

*JACKSON,** Hinds Co.

ALLRED & DONALDSON (AV)

101 West Capitol Street, Suite 300, P.O. Box 3828, 39207-3828
Telephone: 601-948-2086
Telefax: 601-948-2175

MEMBERS OF FIRM

Michael S. Allred John I. Donaldson

ASSOCIATES

Stephen M. Maloney Kathleen H. Eiler

For full biographical listings, see the Martindale-Hubbell Law Directory

FERRELL & HUBBARD (AV)

Ferrell & Hubbard Building, 405 Tombigbee Street, P.O. Box 24448, 39225-4448
Telephone: 601-969-4700
Telecopier: 601-354-5548

MEMBERS OF FIRM

Wayne E. Ferrell, Jr. Dale Hubbard
Karla J. Pierce

References: Deposit Guaranty National Bank; First National Bank of Vicksburg; Trustmark National Bank.

For full biographical listings, see the Martindale-Hubbell Law Directory

HOLCOMB, DUNBAR, CONNELL, CHAFFIN & WILLARD, A PROFESSIONAL ASSOCIATION (AV)

111 East Capitol Street, Suite 290, P.O. Box 2990, 39207-2990
Telephone: 601-948-0048
Facsimile: 601-948-0050
Clarksdale, Mississippi Office: 152 Delta Avenue, P.O. Box 368, 38614.
Telephone: 601-627-2241.
Facsimile: 601-627-9788.
Aberdeen, Mississippi Office: 109 1/2 West Commerce Street, P.O. Box 866, 39730.
Telephone: 601-369-8800.
Facsimile: 601-369-9404.
Oxford, Mississippi Office: 1217 Jackson Avenue, P.O. Drawer 707, 38655.
Telephone: 601-234-8775.
Facsimile: 601-234-8638.
Southaven, Mississippi Office: Suite 1, 8727 Northwest Drive, P.O. Box 190, 38671.
Telephone: 601-342-6806.
Facsimile: 601-342-6792.

Jack F. Dunbar W. Larry Harris
William M. Chaffin William A. Baskin
James T. McCafferty, III

Representative Clients: Mississippi State Department of Environmental Quality.

For Complete List of Firm Personnel, See General Section

For full biographical listings, see the Martindale-Hubbell Law Directory

MARKOW, WALKER, REEVES & ANDERSON, P.A. (AV)

Atrium North Building, 805 South Wheatley, Suite 400, P.O. Box 13669, 39236-3669
Telephone: 601-956-8500
Telecopier: 601-956-8423

Peter J. Markow, Jr. Terry B. Germany
Christopher J. Walker Michael T. Estep
William C. Reeves Richard C. Coker
James M. Anderson Gilson Davis (Dave) Peterson
Alfonso Nuzzo

Joseph W. McDowell L. Pepper Cossar
Richard M. Edmonson, Jr. Delia Y. Robinson
Hubert Wesley Williams, III. T.G. Bolen, Jr.
Alan C. Goodman

Reference: The Sunburst Bank, Jackson, Miss.

For full biographical listings, see the Martindale-Hubbell Law Directory

WATKINS & EAGER (AV)

Suite 300 The Emporium Building, P.O. Box 650, 39205
Telephone: 601-948-6470
Facsimile: (601) 354-3623

MEMBERS OF FIRM

P. Nicholas Harkins, III William F. Goodman, III
John G. Corlew Virginia T. Munford

Representative Clients: Ashland Oil, Inc.; Chevron U.S.A. Inc.; International Paper Co.; Shell Oil Co.; Trustmark National Bank.

For Complete List of Firm Personnel, See General Section

For full biographical listings, see the Martindale-Hubbell Law Directory

*OXFORD,** Lafayette Co.

HOLCOMB, DUNBAR, CONNELL, CHAFFIN & WILLARD, A PROFESSIONAL ASSOCIATION (AV)

1217 Jackson Avenue P.O. Drawer 707, 38655
Telephone: 601-234-8775
Facsimile: 601-234-8638
Jackson, Mississippi Office: 111 East Capitol Street, Suite 290. P.O. Box 2990, 39207-2990.
Telephone: 601-948-0048.
Facsimile: 601-948-0050.
Clarksdale, Mississippi Office: 152 Delta Avenue, P.O. Box 368, 38614.
Telephone: 601-627-2241.
Facsimile: 601-627-9788.
Aberdeen, Mississippi Office: 109 1/2 West Commerce Street, P.O. Box 866, 39730.
Telephone: 601-369-8800.
Facsimile: 601-369-9404.
Southaven, Mississippi Office: Suite 1, 8727 Northwest Drive, P.O. Box 190, 38671.
Telephone: 601-342-6806.
Facsimile: 601-342-6792.

Jack F. Dunbar

Representative Client: Mississippi State Department of Environmental Quality.

For Complete List of Firm Personnel, See General Section

For full biographical listings, see the Martindale-Hubbell Law Directory

*PASCAGOULA,** Jackson Co.

BROWN & WATT, P.A. (AV)

3112 Canty Street, P.O. Box 2220, 39569-2220
Telephone: 601-762-0035
Telecopier: 601-762-0299
Biloxi, Mississippi Office: 115 Main Street, P.O. Box 1377.
Telephone: 601-374-2999.
Fax: 601-435-7090.

Raymond L. Brown William M. Edwards
W. Lee Watt A. Kelly Sessoms, III
Patrick R. Buchanan R. Bradley Prewitt
Alan K. Sudduth

General Counsel For: Mississippi Export Railroad Co.; Pascagoula Municipal Separate School District.
Representative Clients: United States Fidelity & Guaranty Co.; The Travelers Companies; The Home Insurance Co.; CSX Transportation, Inc.; Blue Cross-Blue Shield of Mississippi; Burlington Insurance Co.; Continental Insurance; Deere & Company.

For full biographical listings, see the Martindale-Hubbell Law Directory

COLINGO, WILLIAMS, HEIDELBERG, STEINBERGER & MCELHANEY, P.A. (AV)

711 Delmas Avenue, P.O. Box 1407, 39568-0240
Telephone: 601-762-8021
FAX: 601-762-7589

Joe R. Colingo Michael J. McElhaney, Jr.
Roy C. Williams James H. Colmer, Jr.
James H. Heidelberg Robert W. Wilkinson
Karl R. Steinberger Brett K. Williams

Carol S. Noblitt Stephen Walker Burrow
Karen N. Haarala Scott D. Smith
Gina L. Bardwell

LEGAL SUPPORT PERSONNEL

Harry H. Carpenter

Representative Clients: International Paper Co.; R.J. Reynolds; Westinghouse Corp.; St. Paul Fire & Marine Ins. Co.; Kemper Group; Singing River Hospital System.

For full biographical listings, see the Martindale-Hubbell Law Directory

MISSOURI

KANSAS CITY, Jackson, Clay & Platte Cos.

BAKER, STERCHI & COWDEN (AV)

Suite 2100 Commerce Tower, 911 Main Street, P.O. Box 13566, 64199-3566
Telephone: 816-471-2121
FAX: 816-472-0288
Overland Park, Kansas Office: 51 Corporate Woods, 9393 West 110th Street, Suite 508.
Telephone: 913-451-6752.

(See Next Column)

BAKER, STERCHI & COWDEN—*Continued*

MEMBERS OF FIRM

Thomas O. Baker
Thomas N. Sterchi
John W. Cowden
Thomas E. Rice, Jr.
Timothy S. Frets
Evan A. Douthit
Phillip C. Rouse
R. Douglas Gentile
James T. Seigfreid, Jr.
Robert A. Babcock
Peter F. Travis
John P. Poland

ASSOCIATES

Quentin L. Brown
James R. Jarrow
James S. Kreamer
Mary C. O'Connell
Randall L. Rhodes
D. Gregory Stonebarger
Kara Trouslot Stubbs
Robert M. Carroll
Stacy L. Cook
Patricia A. Sexton
Brent David Thomas

For full biographical listings, see the Martindale-Hubbell Law Directory

SPENCER FANE BRITT & BROWNE (AV)

1400 Commerce Bank Building, 1000 Walnut Street, 64106-2140
Telephone: 816-474-8100
Overland Park, Kansas Office: Suite 500, 40 Corporate Woods, 9401 Indian Creek Parkway.
Telephone: 913-345-8100.
Washington, D.C. Office: 1133 Connecticut Avenue, N.W., Suite 1000.
Telephone: 202-775-2376.

MEMBERS OF FIRM

James H. Andreasen
Bruce E. Cavitt
Paul D. Cowing
Carl H. Helmstetter
Michael D. Hockley
Elaine Drodge Koch
James T. Price
Terry W. Schackmann
Sandra L. Schermerhorn
Lowell L. Smithson
Mark A. Thornhill
Jerome T. Wolf

ASSOCIATES

J. Bradley Leitch
Thomas J. Wilcox

Representative Clients: AT&T, Inc.; North American Philips Co.; W. R. Grace Co.; Kansas City Power and Light Co.; Sequa Corporation; Sandia National Laboratories; Schuylkill Metals Corp.; Witco Corporation.

For Complete List of Firm Personnel, See General Section

For full biographical listings, see the Martindale-Hubbell Law Directory

SWANSON, MIDGLEY, GANGWERE, KITCHIN & MCLARNEY, L.L.C. (AV)

1500 Commerce Trust Building, 922 Walnut, 64106-1848
Telephone: 816-842-6100
Overland Park, Kansas Office: The NCAA Building, Suite 350, 6201 College Boulevard.
Telephone: 816-842-6100.

Robert W. McKinley

Craig T. Kenworthy

Counsel for: General Electric Co.; Chrysler Corp.; Conoco, Inc.; Yellow Freight System, Inc.; The Prudential Insurance Co. of America; Metropolitan Life Insurance Co.; National Collegiate Athletic Assn.; Land Title Insurance Co.; Safeway Stores, Inc.; The Lee Apparel Co.

For Complete List of Firm Personnel, See General Section

For full biographical listings, see the Martindale-Hubbell Law Directory

LAKE OZARK, Miller & Camden Cos.

THOMAS E. LORAINE, P.C. (AV)

2840 Bagnell Dam Boulevard, 65049
Telephone: 314-365-3035
Fax: 314-365-3044

Thomas E. Loraine
Dale M. Weppner

For full biographical listings, see the Martindale-Hubbell Law Directory

ST. LOUIS, (Independent City)

ARMSTRONG, TEASDALE, SCHLAFLY & DAVIS (AV)

A Partnership including Professional Corporations
One Metropolitan Square, 63102-2740
Telephone: 314-621-5070
Facsimile: 314-621-5065
Twx: 910 761-2246
Cable: ATKV LAW
Kansas City, Missouri Office: 1700 City Center Square. 1100 Main Street, 64105.
Telephone: 816-221-3420.
Facsimile: 816-221-0786.
Belleville, Illinois Office: 23 South First Street, 62220.
Telephone: 618-397-4411.
Olathe, Kansas Office: 100 East Park, 66061.
Telephone: 913-345-0706.

(See Next Column)

MEMBERS OF FIRM

John R. Barsanti, Jr., (P.C.)
Edwin L. Noel (P.C.)
Thomas B. Weaver (P.C.)
John F. Cowling
George M. von Stamwitz
Richard L. Waters

ASSOCIATES

Norella V. Huggins
Thomas L. Orris
Susan B. Knowles
Douglas R. Sprong

Representative Clients: Anheuser-Busch Companies, Inc.; Southwestern Bell Corporation; Anschutz Corporation; Owens-Corning Fiberglas Corporation; Shell Pipeline Corporation; Syntex Corporation and its Subsidiary Syntex Agribusiness, Inc.; Union Electric Corporation; DeSoto, Inc.; Haynes International, Inc.; GSX Corporation; ATT Paradyne Corp.

For Complete List of Firm Personnel, See General Section

For full biographical listings, see the Martindale-Hubbell Law Directory

PEPER, MARTIN, JENSEN, MAICHEL AND HETLAGE (AV)

720 Olive Street, Twenty-Fourth Floor, 63101
Telephone: 314-421-3850
Fax: 314-621-4834
Fort Myers, Florida Office: 2080 McGregor Boulevard, Third Floor.
Telephone: 813-337-3850.
Fax: 813-337-0970.
Punta Gorda, Florida Office: 1625 West Marion Avenue, Suite 2.
Telephone: 813-637-1955.
Fax: 813-637-8485.
Naples, Florida Office: 850 Park Shore Drive, Suite 202.
Telephone: 813-261-6525.
Fax: 813-649-1805.
Belleville, Illinois Office: 720 West Main Street, Suite 140.
Telephone: 618-234-9574.
Fax: 618-234-9846.

MEMBER OF FIRM

Bradley S. Hiles

ASSOCIATES

Cathleen S. Bumb
Alphonse McMahon

For Complete List of Firm Personnel, See General Section

For full biographical listings, see the Martindale-Hubbell Law Directory

THOMPSON & MITCHELL (AV)

One Mercantile Center, Suite 3300, 63101
Telephone: 314-231-7676
Telecopier: 314-342-1717
Belleville, Illinois Office: 525 West Main Street.
Telephone: 618-277-4700; 314-271-1800.
Telecopier: 618-236-3434.
St. Charles, Missouri Office: 200 North Third Street.
Telephone: 314-946-7717.
Telecopier: 314-946-4938.
Washington, D.C. Office: 700 14th Street, N.W., Suite 900.
Telephone: 202-508-1000.
Telecopier: 202-508-1010.

MEMBERS OF FIRM

Gordon L. Ankney
Donald B. Dorwart
James W. Erwin
Peter S. Strassner

ASSOCIATES

Stephen G. Jeffery
Crystal M. Kennedy
Tomea C. Mayer
David A. Stratmann

Representative Clients: Chrysler Corp.; ISP Minerals, Inc.; Magna Banks; Mercantile Bancorporation, Inc.; Midland Development Group; Norfolk Southern Corporation; Peabody Coal Co.; The Pillsbury Company, Inc.; Shell Oil Co.; Union Pacific Railroad Company.

For Complete List of Firm Personnel, See General Section

For full biographical listings, see the Martindale-Hubbell Law Directory

*SPRINGFIELD,** Greene Co.

WOOLSEY, FISHER, WHITEAKER & MCDONALD, A PROFESSIONAL CORPORATION (AV)

300 S. Jefferson, Suite 600, P.O. Box 1245, 65801
Telephone: 417-869-0581
Telecopier: 417-831-7852

William H. McDonald
John E. Price
Thomas Y. Auner
Joseph Dow Sheppard, III

OF COUNSEL

Don G. Busch
Connie L. Wible

Representative Clients: AT&T/Paradyne/MRAC, Inc.; Bass Pro Shops/-Tracker Marine, Inc.; Emerson Electric Companies; Enron Liquid Fuels; Unisys; American States Insurance Company; Kemper Insurance Group; Wausau Insurance Group; Zurich-American Insurance Company.

For Complete List of Firm Personnel, See General Section

For full biographical listings, see the Martindale-Hubbell Law Directory

MONTANA

*BILLINGS,** Yellowstone Co.

CROWLEY, HAUGHEY, HANSON, TOOLE & DIETRICH (AV)

500 Transwestern II, 490 North 31st Street, P.O. Box 2529, 59103
Telephone: 406-252-3441
Fax: 406-259-4159
Helena, Montana Office: IBM Building, 100 North Park Avenue, Suite 300, 59601.
Telephone: 406-449-4165.
Fax: 406-449-5149.

OF COUNSEL

Bruce R. Toole

MEMBERS OF FIRM

Arthur F. Lamey, Jr.
Steven P. Ruffatto
Allan L. Karell
Carolyn S. Ostby
Mary Scrim
Jon T. Dyre
Renee L. Coppock
Janice L. Rehberg

ASSOCIATE

John R. Lee

Representative Clients: The Western Sugar Company; Natural Gas Processing; Peabody Coal; Grace Petroleum Corporation; Federated Insurance Company; Conoco; Inter-City Gas Corporation; First Interstate Bank of Commerce.

For Complete List of Firm Personnel, See General Section

For full biographical listings, see the Martindale-Hubbell Law Directory

*HELENA,** Lewis and Clark Co.

BROWNING, KALECZYC, BERRY & HOVEN, P.C. (AV)

139 North Last Chance Gulch, P.O. Box 1697, 59624
Telephone: 406-449-6220
Telefax: 406-443-0700

R. Stephen Browning
Stanley T. Kaleczyc
Leo Berry
J. Daniel Hoven

Catherine A. Laughner
Mark D. Etchart

Reference: First Bank Helena, Helena, Montana.

For Complete List of Firm Personnel, See General Section

For full biographical listings, see the Martindale-Hubbell Law Directory

NEBRASKA

*OMAHA,** Douglas Co.

FRASER, STRYKER, VAUGHN, MEUSEY, OLSON, BOYER & BLOCH, P.C. (AV)

500 Energy Plaza, 409 South 17th Street, 68102
Telephone: 402-341-6000
Telecopier: 402-341-8290

Joseph K. Meusey
Wayne J. Mark
Robert W. Rieke
Stephen M. Bruckner
Rex A. Rezac

Lon A. Licata

Representative Clients: Omaha Public Power District; ASARCO; Arcadian Corp.; Gould, Inc.; Ashgrove Cement Co.

For Complete List of Firm Personnel, See General Section

For full biographical listings, see the Martindale-Hubbell Law Directory

NEVADA

*LAS VEGAS,** Clark Co.

JOLLEY, URGA, WIRTH & WOODBURY (AV)

Suite 800 Bank of America Plaza, 300 South Fourth Street, 89101
Telephone: 702-385-5161
Telecopier: 702-382-6814
Boulder City, Nevada Office: Suite 105, 1000 Nevada Highway.
Telephone: 702-293-3674.

(See Next Column)

MEMBERS OF FIRM

R. Gardner Jolley
Mark A. James

ASSOCIATES

Allen D. Emmel
Gregory J. Walch

Representative Clients: First Interstate Bank of Nevada; Nevada State Bank; Melvin Simon & Associates, Inc.; Nevada Mobilehome Park Owners Association; Continental National Bank; First Nationwide Bank; PriMerit Bank; Wells Cargo, Inc.; Dean Roofing Co.; Lincoln Property Co.

For Complete List of Firm Personnel, See General Section

For full biographical listings, see the Martindale-Hubbell Law Directory

MILES & TIERNEY (AV)

3170 West Sahara Avenue Suite D-11, 89102
Telephone: 702-252-7120
FAX: 702-252-0916

MEMBERS OF FIRM

Charles H. Miles, Jr.
Keith J. Tierney

For full biographical listings, see the Martindale-Hubbell Law Directory

*RENO,** Washoe Co.

HALE, LANE, PEEK, DENNISON AND HOWARD (AV)

Porsche Building, 100 West Liberty Street, Tenth Floor, P.O. Box 3237, 89501
Telephone: 702-786-7900
Telefax: 702-786-6179
Las Vegas, Nevada Office: Suite 800, Nevada Financial Center, 2300 West Sahara Avenue, Box 8.
Telephone: 702-362-5118.
Fax: 702-365-6940.

MEMBERS OF FIRM

R. Craig Howard
Alex J. Flangas

Representative Clients: Western Water Development Co.; Washoe County; Northern Nevada Water Resources, Limited Partnership.

For Complete List of Firm Personnel, See General Section

For full biographical listings, see the Martindale-Hubbell Law Directory

McDONALD, CARANO, WILSON, McCUNE, BERGIN, FRANKOVICH & HICKS (AV)

241 Ridge Street, 89505
Telephone: 702-322-0635
Telecopier: 702-786-9532
Las Vegas, Nevada Office: Suite 1000, 2300 West Sahara Avenue.
Telephone: 702-873-4100.
Telecopier: 702-873-9966.

MEMBER OF FIRM

Sylvia L. Harrison

ASSOCIATE

Miranda Mai Du (Resident, Las Vegas Office)

Representative Clients: Horizon Resources, Inc.; Scolari's Warehouse Market's, Inc.; Shaver Construction; Time Oil Company (Nevada Counsel).

For Complete List of Firm Personnel, See General Section

For full biographical listings, see the Martindale-Hubbell Law Directory

NEW HAMPSHIRE

*CONCORD,** Merrimack Co.

ORR & RENO, PROFESSIONAL ASSOCIATION (AV)

One Eagle Square, P.O. Box 3550, 03302-3550
Telephone: 603-224-2381
Fax: 603-224-2318

Richard B. Couser

Representative Clients: Beach Aircraft Corporation; Chubb Life America; Fleet Bank; Dartmouth-Hitchcock Medical Center; EnergyNorth, Inc.; National Grange Mutual Co.; New England College; New England Electric System Co.; Newspapers of New England, Inc.; St. Paul's School.

For Complete List of Firm Personnel, See General Section

For full biographical listings, see the Martindale-Hubbell Law Directory

NEW JERSEY

BAYONNE, Hudson Co.

FITZPATRICK & WATERMAN (AV)

90 West 40th Street, P.O. Box 1227, 07002
Telephone: 201-339-4000
1-800 BOND LAW
Secaucus, New Jersey Office: 400 Plaza Drive, 07096-3159.
Telephone: 201-865-9100.
Facsimile: 201-865-4805.

Harold F. Fitzpatrick

For full biographical listings, see the Martindale-Hubbell Law Directory

CHERRY HILL, Camden Co.

GARRIGLE & PALM (AV)

Suite 204, 1415 State Highway 70 East, 08034
Telephone: 609-427-9300
Fax: 609-427-9590

MEMBERS OF FIRM

William A. Garrigle
John M. Palm

ASSOCIATES

Harold H. Thomasson
Paul F Kulinski
James J. Law
Eleanore A. Rogalski

Representative Clients: Crum & Forster Group; Kemper Insurance Group; Atlantic Mutual Group; American Hardware Mutual; National General Insurance Co.; Transamerica Group; State Farm Fire Insurance Co.; Progressive Insurance Co.; United Southern Insurance Co.; New Jersey Market Transition Facility and Joint Underwriting Association.

For full biographical listings, see the Martindale-Hubbell Law Directory

FLORHAM PARK, Morris Co.

CARLIN, MADDOCK, FAY & CERBONE, P.C. (AV)

25 Vreeland Road, P.O. Box 751, 07932
Telephone: 201-377-3350
Fax: 201-377-5626

John J. Carlin, Jr.
Laurence R. Maddock
Donald J. Fay
Richard R. Cerbone

Arthur G. Warden, III
Paul F. Liebman

For full biographical listings, see the Martindale-Hubbell Law Directory

HACK, PIRO, O'DAY, MERKLINGER, WALLACE & MCKENNA, P.A. (AV)

30 Columbia Turnpike, P.O. Box 941, 07932-0941
Telephone: 201-301-6500
Fax: 201-301-0094

M. Richard Merklinger

Robert G. Alencewicz

Representative Clients: The H.B. Smith Company, Inc.; The Johansen Company; Tishman Realty & Construction Co., Inc.; Plasco Safety Products; American Biltrite, Inc.; Hawley Industrial Supplies, Inc.; Unisul, Inc.; The Travelers Insurance Company; Special Liability Group.

For Complete List of Firm Personnel, See General Section

For full biographical listings, see the Martindale-Hubbell Law Directory

*HACKENSACK,** Bergen Co.

KAPS & BARTO (AV)

15 Warren Street, 07601
Telephone: 201-489-5277
Telecopier: 201-489-0477

Warren J. Kaps
Raymond Barto

Concetta R. De Lucia
Brenda P. Rosenberg

Representative Clients: Continental Baking Co.; Mayflower Vapor Seal Co.; The Society of American Magicians.
Reference: United Jersey Bank.

For full biographical listings, see the Martindale-Hubbell Law Directory

SOKOL, BEHOT AND FIORENZO (AV)

39 Hudson Street, 07601
Telephone: 201-488-1300
Fax: 201-488-6541

(See Next Column)

MEMBERS OF FIRM

Leon J. Sokol
Joseph F. Behot, Jr.
Joseph B. Fiorenzo
Jeffrey A. Zenn

ASSOCIATES

Siobhan C. Spillane
Susan I. Wegner
Jeffrey M. Kahan

COUNSEL

Arthur Bergman
Alan Prigal

For full biographical listings, see the Martindale-Hubbell Law Directory

LIVINGSTON, Essex Co.

GENOVA, BURNS, TRIMBOLI & VERNOIA (AV)

Eisenhower Plaza II, 354 Eisenhower Parkway, 07039
Telephone: 201-533-0777
Facsimile: 201-533-1112
Trenton, New Jersey Office: Suite One, 160 West State Street.
Telephone: 609-393-1131.

MEMBERS OF FIRM

Angelo J. Genova
James M. Burns
Stephen E. Trimboli
Francis J. Vernoia

ASSOCIATES

Meryl G. Nadler
John C. Petrella
James J. McGovern, III
Kathleen M. Connelly
Joseph Licata
Elaine M. Reyes
Lynn S. Degen
James J. Gillespie
T. Sean Jackson

For full biographical listings, see the Martindale-Hubbell Law Directory

MONTVILLE, Morris Co.

EDWARD J. BUZAK (AV)

Montville Office Park, 150 River Road, Suite N-4, 07045
Telephone: 201-335-0600
Fax: 201-335-1145

ASSOCIATES

Jacquelin P. Gioioso
Robert B. Campbell
Jeanne Ann McManus
Laura C. Tharney

For full biographical listings, see the Martindale-Hubbell Law Directory

*MORRISTOWN,** Morris Co.

MCELROY, DEUTSCH AND MULVANEY (AV)

1300 Mount Kemble Avenue, P.O. Box 2075, 07962-2075
Telephone: 201-993-8100
Fax: 201-425-0161
Denver, Colorado Office: 1099 18th Street, Suite 3120.
Telephone: 303-293-8800.
Fax: 303-293-3116.

MEMBERS OF FIRM

Lorraine M. Armenti (Resident Partner, Denver Colorado Office)
Grace C. Bertone
John P. Beyel
William C. Carey
Margaret F. Catalano
Stephen H. Cohen (1938-1992)
Kevin T. Coughlin
Edward B. Deutsch
Timothy I. Duffy
Robert J. Kelly
Joseph P. La Sala
Paul A. Lisovicz
Fred A. Manley, Jr.
Michael J. Marone
William T. McElroy
Laurence M. McHeffey
Joseph P. McNulty, Jr.
James M. Mulvaney
Moira E. O'Connell
Loren L. Pierce
Warren K. Racusin
John H. Suminski
Kevin E. Wolff

OF COUNSEL

Richard G. McCarty (Not admitted in NJ)
John F. Whitteaker

ASSOCIATES

Caroline L. Beers
Christopher Robert Carroll
Edward V. Collins
Billy J. Cooper (Resident, Denver, Colorado Office)
John Thomas Coyne
Nada Leslie Wolff Culver (Resident, Denver, Colorado Office)
John J. Cummings
Anthony J. Davis
John Paul Gilfillan
Kevin M. Haas
Gary S. Kull
Matthew J. Lodge
Tracey L. Matura
Nancy McDonald
Robert McGuire
Suzanne Cocco Midlige
Robert W. Muilenburg
Gary Potters
Kathleen M. Quinn
Vincent E. Reilly
Agnes A. Reiss
Barbara C. Zimmerman Robertson
Samuel J. Samaro
Laura A. Sanom
Thomas P. Scrivo
Dennis T. Smith
Patricia Leen Sullivan
Pamela A. Tanis
Christine L. Thieman
Catharine Acker Vaughan

Representative Clients: ADT Security Systems, Inc.; Admiral Insurance Company; Crum & Forster Insurance Co.; Eaton Corp.; Fireman's Fund Insurance Cos.; New Jersey Manufacturers Insurance Co.; The Home Indemnity

(See Next Column)

MCELROY, DEUTSCH AND MULVANEY, *Morristown—Continued*

Co.; Ingersol l-Rand Company; The Pittston Company; Security Pacific Finance Corporation.

For full biographical listings, see the Martindale-Hubbell Law Directory

PITNEY, HARDIN, KIPP & SZUCH (AV)

Park Avenue at Morris County, P.O. Box 1945, 07962-1945
Telephone: 201-966-6300
New York City: 212-926-0331
Telex: 642014
Telecopier: 201-966-1550

MEMBERS OF FIRM

William H. Hyatt, Jr.
Gail H. Allyn
Robert G. Rose
Donald W. Kiel
Peter J. Herzberg
Harriett Jane Olson

COUNSEL

David W. Payne

ASSOCIATES

Kathy Dutton Helmer
Brian S. Montag
John B. Rutherford
Frances B. Stella
Colleen R. Donovan
Bruce D. Taterka
John McGahren
Alan S. Golub
David L. Isabel

Representative Clients: AlliedSignal Inc.; AT&T; Base Ten Systems, Inc.; Exxon Corp.; Ford Motor Co.; Midlantic National Bank; Sony Electronics, Inc.; Union Carbide Corp.; United Parcel Services, Inc.; Warner-Lambert Co.

For Complete List of Firm Personnel, See General Section

For full biographical listings, see the Martindale-Hubbell Law Directory

PORZIO, BROMBERG & NEWMAN, A PROFESSIONAL CORPORATION (AV)

163 Madison Avenue, 07962-1997
Telephone: 201-538-4006
Facsimile: 201-538-5146
New York, New York Office: 655 Third Avenue, 10017-5617.
Telephone: 212-986-0600.
Facsimile: 212-986-6491.

Lisa Murtha Bromberg
Myron J. Bromberg
Edward A. Hogan

COUNSEL

Thomas Spiesman

Maura E. Blau
Howard P. Davis
Stephen L. Willis

Representative Clients: American Cyanamid Co.; American Home Products Corp.; ASARCO Inc.; Ayerst Laboratories; Johnson & Johnson; Pfizer Inc.; Warner-Lambert Co.

For Complete List of Firm Personnel, See General Section

For full biographical listings, see the Martindale-Hubbell Law Directory

SHANLEY & FISHER, A PROFESSIONAL CORPORATION (AV)

131 Madison Avenue, 07962-1979
Telephone: 201-285-1000
Telecopier: 1-201-285-1098
Telex: 475-4255 (I.T.T.)
Cable Address: "Shanley"
New York, N.Y. Office: 89th Floor, One World Trade Center.
Telephone: 212-321-1812.
Telecopier: 1-212-466-0569.

I. Leo Motiuk
Nan Bernardo
Richard A. Levao
Michael O. Adelman

Sean Monaghan
Harry M. Baumgartner
Clare Maria Begley
John M. O'Reilly
Joan E. Pearson
Jayne A. Pritchard
James A. Kozachek

For Complete List of Firm Personnel, See General Section

For full biographical listings, see the Martindale-Hubbell Law Directory

*NEWARK,** Essex Co.

CRUMMY, DEL DEO, DOLAN, GRIFFINGER & VECCHIONE, A PROFESSIONAL CORPORATION (AV)

One Riverfront Plaza, 07102
Telephone: 201-596-4500
Telecopier: 201-596-0545
Cable-Telex: 138154
Brussels, Belgium Office: Crummy, Del Deo, Dolan, Griffinger & Vecchione. Avenue Louise 475, BTE. 8, B-1050.
Telephone: 011-322-646-0019.
Telecopier: 011-322-646-0152.

Michael D. Loprete
John H. Klock
Susanne Peticolas

Gemma M. Lury
Jacqueline N. Lumley
Mary B. Holovacs

Representative Clients: Avon Products; Ball In-Con; Hoffmann-La Roche, Inc.; Seton Co.; The Sherwin-Williams Co.

For Complete List of Firm Personnel, See General Section

For full biographical listings, see the Martindale-Hubbell Law Directory

DEMARIA, ELLIS, HUNT, SALSBERG & FRIEDMAN (AV)

Suite 1400, 744 Broad Street, 07102
Telephone: 201-623-1699
Telecopier: 201-623-0954

MEMBERS OF FIRM

H. Reed Ellis
Paul A. Friedman
Ronald H. DeMaria
Brian N. Flynn
William J. Hunt
Richard H. Bauch
Richard M. Salsberg
Lee H. Udelsman

ASSOCIATES

Mitchell A. Schley
George W. Rettig
Joseph D. Olivieri
David S. Catuogno
Joanne M. Maxwell
Debra S. Friedman
Robyn L. Aversa
Kathryn A. Calista

For full biographical listings, see the Martindale-Hubbell Law Directory

HELLRING LINDEMAN GOLDSTEIN & SIEGAL (AV)

One Gateway Center, 07102-5386
Telephone: 201-621-9020
Telecopier: 201-621-7406

Philip Lindeman, II
Charles Oransky
Jonathan L. Goldstein
Robert S. Raymar
Richard D. Shapiro
John A. Adler
Ronnie F. Liebowitz

For Complete List of Firm Personnel, See General Section

For full biographical listings, see the Martindale-Hubbell Law Directory

MCMANIMON & SCOTLAND (AV)

One Gateway Center, 18th Floor, 07102-5311
Telephone: 201-622-1800
Fax: 201-622-7333; 201-622-3744
Atlantic City, New Jersey Office: 26 South Pennsylvania Avenue.
Telephone: 609-347-0040.
Fax: 609-347-0866.
Trenton, New Jersey Office: 172 West State Street.
Telephone: 609-278-1800.
Fax: 609-278-9222.
Washington, D.C. Office: 1275 Pennsylvania Avenue, N.W.
Telephone: 202-638-3100.
Fax: 202-638-4222.

MEMBERS OF FIRM

Joseph P. Baumann, Jr.
Ronald J. Ianoale
Carla J. Brundage
Andrea L. Kahn
John V. Cavaliere
Jeffrey G. Kramer
Edward F. Clark
Michael A. Lampert
Christopher H. Falcon
Joseph J. Maraziti, Jr.
Felicia L. Garland
Edward J. McManimon, III
James R. Gregory
Steven P. Natko
John B. Hall
Martin C. Rothfelder
Thomas A. Hart, Jr. (Resident, Washington, D.C. Office)
Steven Schaars (Resident, Washington, D.C. Office)
Leah C. Healey
Glenn F. Scotland
Michael A. Walker

ASSOCIATES

Carl E. Ailara, Jr.
Sheryl L. Newman
Diane Alexander-McCabe
Steven J. Reed
Leslie G. London
Erik F. Remmler
Cheryl A. Maier
David J. Ruitenberg
Daniel E. McManus
Bradford M. Stern

(See Next Column)

McManimon & Scotland—*Continued*

OF COUNSEL

John R. Armstrong
Carl H. Fogler (Not admitted in NJ)

LEGAL SUPPORT PERSONNEL

Helen Lysaght

PARALEGALS

Jane Folmer
Zulmira Donahue

References: First Fidelity Bank, N.A., New Jersey; Midlantic National Bank.

For full biographical listings, see the Martindale-Hubbell Law Directory

Sills Cummis Zuckerman Radin Tischman Epstein & Gross, A Professional Corporation (AV)

One Riverfront Plaza, 07102-5400
Telephone: 201-643-7000
Fax: 201-643-6500
Telex: 820630 Sillsbeck Nwk
Atlantic City, New Jersey Office: 17 Gordon's Alley.
Telephone: 609-344-2800.
New York, N.Y. Office: 250 Park Avenue.
Telephone: 212-643-7000.

Barry M. Epstein
Charles J. Walsh
Philip R. Sellinger
Margaret F. Black
Lori G. Singer

Jeffrey M. Pollock
Douglas R. Weider
Helen E. Kleiner

Representative Clients: Sterling Winthrop Inc.; Becton Dickinson & Company, Inc.; O'Brien Environmental Energy, Inc.; Schering AG Berlex Laboratories; Spartech Corp.; Six Flags; Bally's Park Place Hotel & Casino; Werner & Pfleiderer Corporation; Solid Waste Transfer & Recycling.

For Complete List of Firm Personnel, See General Section

For full biographical listings, see the Martindale-Hubbell Law Directory

NORTHFIELD, Atlantic Co.

Tomar, Simonoff, Adourian & O'Brien, A Professional Corporation (AV)

The Executive Plaza, Suite 202, 2111 New Road, 08225
Telephone: 609-485-0800
Telecopier: 609-484-9388
Camden, New Jersey Office: 501 Cooper Street.
Telephone: 609-338-0553.
Telecopier: 609-338-0321.
Haddonfield, New Jersey Office: 41 South Haddon Avenue.
Telephone: 609-429-1100.
Telecopier: 609-429-8164.
Atlantic City, New Jersey Office: Commerce Building, Suite 220, 1200 Atlantic Avenue.
Telephone: 609-348-5900.
Wilmington, Delaware Office: Tomar, Simonoff, Adourian & O'Brien, The Mellon Bank Center, Suite 1701, 919 Market Street.
Telephone: 302-655-0500.
Telecopier: 302-428-0963.
Media, Pennsylvania Office: 115 North Jackson Street.
Telephone: 215-574-0635.

William Tomar

For full biographical listings, see the Martindale-Hubbell Law Directory

PARSIPPANY, Morris Co.

Kummer, Knox, Naughton & Hansbury (AV)

Lincoln Centre, 299 Cherry Hill Road, 07054
Telephone: 201-335-3900
Telecopier: 201-335-9577

MEMBERS OF FIRM

Richard E. Kummer
Stephen R. Knox
Michael J. Naughton
Stephan C. Hansbury

ASSOCIATES

Gail H. Fraser
Kurt W. Krauss
Linda M. DeVenuto

For full biographical listings, see the Martindale-Hubbell Law Directory

ROSELAND, Essex Co.

Hannoch Weisman, A Professional Corporation (AV)

4 Becker Farm Road, 07068-3788
Telephone: 201-535-5300
New York: 212-732-3262
Telecopier: 201-994-7198
Mailing Address: P.O. Box 1040, Newark, New Jersey, 07101-9819
Washington, D.C. Office: Suite 600, 1150 Seventeenth Street, N.W.
Telephone: 202-296-3432.

(See Next Column)

Kevin J. Bruno
Sanders M. Chattman
Jeffrey A. Cohen
Richard J. Conway, Jr.
Lawrence W. Diamond
Irvin M. Freilich
Lee Henig-Elona

Lesley Anne Broomall
Ritaelena Marie Casavechia
Suzanne Quinn Chamberlin
Jane Dobson
Michael J. Geiger
Suzanne Stahl Heyer
Julie A. Parker
David J. Paulin

For Complete List of Firm Personnel, See General Section

For full biographical listings, see the Martindale-Hubbell Law Directory

Lowenstein, Sandler, Kohl, Fisher & Boylan, A Professional Corporation (AV)

65 Livingston Avenue, 07068
Telephone: 201-992-8700
Telefax: 201-992-5820
Somerville, New Jersey Office: 600 First Avenue. P.O. Box 1113.
Telephone: 201-526-3300.

Michael L. Rodburg
Michael Dore
James Stewart
Robert D. Chesler
Richard F. Ricci

OF COUNSEL

Norman W. Spindel
Diane K.G. Weeks

Jeffrey B. Gracer
Neale R. Bedrock
David A. Thomas
Peter E. Nahmias
Nancy Lake Martin
Thomas E. Mesevage
Michael D. Lichtenstein
Brian Weeks

For Complete List of Firm Personnel, See General Section

For full biographical listings, see the Martindale-Hubbell Law Directory

Post, Polak, Goodsell & MacNeill, P.A. (AV)

65 Livingston Avenue, 07068
Telephone: 201-994-1100
Telecopier: 201-994-1705
New York, New York Office: Suite 1006, 575 Madison Avenue.
Telephone: 212-486-1455.

Frederick B. Polak
Robert A. Goodsell

Mark H. Peckman
Robert P. Merenich

For full biographical listings, see the Martindale-Hubbell Law Directory

Walder, Sondak & Brogan, A Professional Corporation (AV)

5 Becker Farm Road, 07068
Telephone: 201-992-5300
Telecopier: 201-992-1505; 992-1006

Justin P. Walder
John A. Brogan
Barry A. Kozyra
James A. Plaisted
Jeffrey A. Walder

Representative Client: Attwoods plc.

For full biographical listings, see the Martindale-Hubbell Law Directory

Wolff & Samson, P.A. (AV)

280 Corporate Center, 5 Becker Farm Road, 07068
Telephone: 201-740-0500
Fax: 201-740-1407

David Samson
Martin L. Wiener
Gage Andretta
Daniel A. Schwartz
Dennis M. Toft

Representative Clients: International Fidelity Insurance Co.; Celentano Brothers, Inc.; Chicago Title Insurance Co.; Hartz Mountain Industries; The Hillier Group; Foster Wheeler Corp.

For Complete List of Firm Personnel, See General Section

For full biographical listings, see the Martindale-Hubbell Law Directory

SECAUCUS, Hudson Co.

Fitzpatrick & Waterman (AV)

400 Plaza Drive, P.O. Box 3159, 07096-3159
Telephone: 201-865-9100
1-800 BOND LAW
Facsimile: 201-865-4805
Bayonne, New Jersey Office: 90 West 40th Street. 07002,
Telephone: 201339-4000; 1-800 BOND LAW.

Harold F. Fitzpatrick
Stephen P. Waterman

(See Next Column)

FITZPATRICK & WATERMAN, *Secaucus—Continued*

ASSOCIATES

James F. McDonough
Glenn C. Merritt
Jeanette M. Samra

OF COUNSEL

Andre Shramenko

For full biographical listings, see the Martindale-Hubbell Law Directory

*SOMERVILLE,** Somerset Co.

OZZARD WHARTON, A PROFESSIONAL PARTNERSHIP (AV)

75-77 North Bridge Street, P.O. Box 938, 08876
Telephone: 908-526-0700
Telecopier: 908-526-2246

William E. Ozzard
Michael V. Camerino

Arthur D. Fialk
Suzette Nanovic Berrios
Michael G. Friedman
Lori E. Salowe

Representative Clients: American Cyanamid; Science Management Corp.; New Jersey Manufacturers Insurance Co.; Travelers Insurance Co.; Somerset Raritan Valley Sewerage Authority, Betham Corp.

For Complete List of Firm Personnel, See General Section

For full biographical listings, see the Martindale-Hubbell Law Directory

SUMMIT, Union Co.

COOPER ROSE & ENGLISH (AV)

480 Morris Avenue, 07901-1527
Telephone: 908-273-1212
Fax: 908-273-8922
Rumson, New Jersey Office: 20 Bingham Avenue. 07760.
Telephone: 908-741-7777.
Fax: 908-758-1879.

MEMBERS OF FIRM

John W. Cooper
Arthur H. Garvin, III
Frederick W. Rose
Peter M. Burke
Jerry Fitzgerald English
Gary F. Danis
Joseph E. Imbriaco
John J. DeLaney, Jr.
Roger S. Clapp
David G. Hardin

OF COUNSEL

Harrison F. Durand
Russell T. Kerby, Jr.
Ronald J. Tell

ASSOCIATES

Fredi L. Pearlmutter
J. Andrew Kinsey
Kristi Bragg
Jonathan S. Chester
Stephen R. Geller
Daniel Jon Kleinman
Peter W. Ulicny
Holly English
Thomas J. Sateary
Margaret R. Kalas
Gianfranco A. Pietrafesa
Mary T. Zdanowicz
Donna M. Russo
Robert A. Meyers
Richard F. Iglar

Counsel for: Ciba-Geigy Corp.; Witco Corp.; New Jersey American Water Co.; Mikropul Corp.; AT&T Bell Laboratories; Aircast.

For full biographical listings, see the Martindale-Hubbell Law Directory

*TRENTON,** Mercer Co.

NEEDELL & MCGLONE, A PROFESSIONAL CORPORATION (AV)

Quakerbridge Commons, 2681 Quakerbridge Road, 08619-1625
Telephone: 609-584-7700
Fax: 609-584-0123

Stanley H. Needell
Patricia Hart McGlone

Michael W. Krutman
Barbara Brosnan
Anthony P. Castellani
Douglas R. D'Antonio

For full biographical listings, see the Martindale-Hubbell Law Directory

PICCO MACK HERBERT, A PROFESSIONAL CORPORATION (AV)

One State Street Square, 50 West State Street, Suite 1000, 08608
Telephone: 609-393-2400
Telecopier: 609-393-2475

Steven J. Picco
Linda Mack
Kenneth H. Mack
Mary Lou Delahanty
Michael J. Herbert
David Himelman
Patrick D. Kennedy
Michael T. Hartsough
Burton J. Jaffe
David J. Kenny
Neil Yoskin
Joseph D. Priory

(See Next Column)

Susan C. Gieser
Stacy Weinstein
Maeve E. Cannon
Steven P. Goodell
James P. Manahan
Diane A. Davis
M. Paige Berry
Michael William Herbert
Susanne Culliton
Gregory J. Sullivan
Karen L. Cayci
James E. McGuire
Demery J. Roberts

OF COUNSEL

Stanley C. Van Ness

LEGAL SUPPORT PERSONNEL

PARALEGAL

Sherry Dudas
W. Keith Griesinger
Suellen Adezio

For full biographical listings, see the Martindale-Hubbell Law Directory

WAYNE, Passaic Co.

DEYOE, HEISSENBUTTEL & MATTIA (AV)

401 Hamburg Turnpike, P.O. Box 2449, 07474-2449
Telephone: 201-595-6300
Fax: 201-595-0146; 201-595-9262

MEMBERS OF FIRM

Charles P. DeYoe (1923-1973)
Philip F. Mattia
Wood M. DeYoe
Gary R. Matano
Frederick C. Heissenbuttel
Scott B. Piekarsky

ASSOCIATES

Anne Hutton
Frank A. Campana
Glenn Z. Poosikian
John E. Clarke
Jo Ann G. Durr
Jason T. Shafron
Frank D. Samperi
Maura Waters Brady

LEGAL SUPPORT PERSONNEL

Marilyn Moore (Office Manager)

Representative Clients: INA/Aetna Insurance Co. (Cigna); Medical Inter-Insurance Companies; Hanover-Amgro, Inc.; Maryland Casualty Co.; Ohio Casualty Insurance Co.; Motor Club of America; Selected Insurance Co.

For full biographical listings, see the Martindale-Hubbell Law Directory

WEST PATERSON, Passaic Co.

EVANS HAND (AV)

One Garret Mountain Plaza, Interstate 80 at Squirrelwood Road, 07424-3396
Telephone: 201-881-1100
Fax: 201-881-1369

MEMBERS OF FIRM

Thomas F. Craig, II
Roy J. Evans

ASSOCIATES

William M. Sheehy
Brian T. Higgins

Representative Clients: Midlantic National Bank; The Bank of New York/National Community Division; The Prudential Insurance Co. of America; Connecticut General Life Insurance Co.; Travelers Insurance Co.; New Jersey Manufacturers Insurance Co.; Bell Atlantic; Algonquin Gas Transmission Co.; Tenneco, Inc.; Corning Glass Works.

For Complete List of Firm Personnel, See General Section

For full biographical listings, see the Martindale-Hubbell Law Directory

WOODBRIDGE, Middlesex Co.

WILENTZ, GOLDMAN & SPITZER, A PROFESSIONAL CORPORATION (AV)

90 Woodbridge Center Drive Suite 900, Box 10, 07095
Telephone: 908-636-8000
Telecopier: 908-855-6117
Eatontown, New Jersey Office: Meridian Center I, Two Industrial Way West, 07724.
Telephone: 908-493-1000.
Telecopier: 908-493-8387.
New York, New York Office: Wall Street Plaza, 88 Pine Street, 9th Floor, 10005.
Telephone: 212-267-3091.
Telecopier: 212-267-3828.

Matthias D. Dileo
Steven J. Tripp
Stephen E. Barcan
Leslie Jeddis Lang
Brian J. Molloy
Francis X. Journick, Jr.

Richard A. Catalina, Jr.
Peter J. Tober

Representative Clients: Amerada Hess Corporation; Chevron, U.S.A., Inc.; Waken Food Corp.; Supermarkets General Corp.

For Complete List of Firm Personnel, See General Section

For full biographical listings, see the Martindale-Hubbell Law Directory

NEW MEXICO

*ALBUQUERQUE,** Bernalillo Co.

EAVES, BARDACKE & BAUGH, P.A. (AV)

6400 Uptown Boulevard N.E., Suite 110-W, P.O. Box 35670, 87176
Telephone: 505-888-4300
Facsimile: 505-883-4406

John M. Eaves
Paul Bardacke
John G. Baugh
Kerry Kiernan
Peter S. Kierst
David V. Halliburton
David A. Garcia
Lisabeth L. Occhialino

OF COUNSEL

Marianne Woodard
Jennifer J. Pruett
Susan C. Kery

For full biographical listings, see the Martindale-Hubbell Law Directory

*SANTA FE,** Santa Fe Co.

CAMPBELL, CARR, BERGE & SHERIDAN, P.A. (AV)

110 North Guadalupe, P.O. Box 2208, 87504-2208
Telephone: 505-988-4421
Telecopier: 505-983-6043

Michael B. Campbell
William F. Carr
Bradford C. Berge
Mark F. Sheridan

Michael H. Feldewert
Tanya M. Trujillo
Nancy A. Rath

For Complete List of Firm Personnel, See General Section

For full biographical listings, see the Martindale-Hubbell Law Directory

HINKLE, COX, EATON, COFFIELD & HENSLEY (AV)

218 Montezuma, P.O. Box 2068, 87504
Telephone: 505-982-4554
FAX: 505-982-8623
Roswell, New Mexico Office: Suite 700 United Bank Plaza, P.O. Box 10, 88202.
Telephone: 505-622-6510.
FAX: 505-623-9332.
Midland, Texas Office: 6 Desta Drive, Suite 2800, P.O. Box 3580, 79705.
Telephone: 915-683-4691.
FAX: 915-683-6518.
Amarillo, Texas Office: 1700 Bank One Center, P.O. Box 9238, 79105-9238.
Telephone: 806-372-5569.
FAX: 806-372-9761.
Albuquerque, New Mexico Office: Suite 800, 500 Marquette, N.W., P.O. Box 2043, 87103.
Telephone: 505-768-1500.
FAX: 505-768-1529.
Austin, Texas Office: 401 West 15th Street, Suite 800, 78701.
Telephone: 512-476-7137.
FAX: 512-476-5431.
Associated Office: Hoffman & Stephens, P.C., 401 West 15th Street, Suite 800, 78701.
Telephone: 512-476-5434.
Fax: 512-476-5431.

RESIDENT PARTNERS

Jeffrey L. Fornaciari
Thomas M. Hnasko
Ellen S. Casey

Representative Clients: Atlantic Richfield Co.; Delaware Natural Gas Co., Inc.; El Paso Natural Gas; Federated Insurance Service; Horn Distributing Co., Inc.

For full biographical listings, see the Martindale-Hubbell Law Directory

HUFFAKER & BARNES, A PROFESSIONAL CORPORATION (AV)

155 Grant Avenue, P.O. Box 1868, 87504-1868
Telephone: 505-988-8921
Fax: 505-983-3927

Gregory D. Huffaker, Jr.
Julia Hosford Barnes
Bradley C. Barron
Sharon A. Higgins
(Not admitted in NM)

Representative Clients: Chevron U.S.A. Products Inc.; Federal Deposit Insurance Corp.; Resolution Trust Corporation; Basis International, Ltd.; San Juan Concrete Co.; Picacho Plaza Hotel.

For full biographical listings, see the Martindale-Hubbell Law Directory

MONTGOMERY & ANDREWS, PROFESSIONAL ASSOCIATION (AV)

325 Paseo de Peralta, P.O. Box 2307, 87504-2307
Telephone: 505-982-3873
Albuquerque, New Mexico Office: Suite 1300 Albuquerque Plaza, 201 Third Street, N.W., P.O. Box 26927.
Telephone: 505-242-9677.
FAX: 505-243-2542.

Edmund H. Kendrick
Louis W. Rose
R. Bruce Frederick

Representative Clients: Meridian Oil, Inc.; El Paso Natural Gas Co.; McKinley Paper Co.; INTEL Corporation; LAC Minerals (USA) Inc.; St. Vincent Hospital; US WEST Communications; Giant Industries Arizona, Inc.; GPM Gas Corporation; Rexene Corporation.

For Complete List of Firm Personnel, See General Section

For full biographical listings, see the Martindale-Hubbell Law Directory

SCHEUER, YOST & PATTERSON, A PROFESSIONAL CORPORATION (AV)

125 Lincoln Avenue, Suite 223, P.O. Drawer 9570, 87504
Telephone: 505-982-9911
Fax: 505-982-1621

Ralph H. Scheuer
Mel E. Yost
John N. Patterson
Holly A. Hart
Roger L. Prucino
Elizabeth A. Jaffe
Tracy Erin Conner
Ruth M. Fuess

OF COUNSEL

Melvin T. Yost

Representative Clients: Cyprus-AMAX, Inc.; Century Bank, FSB; Chicago Insurance Co.; St. John's College; Santa Fe Housing Authority; Sun Loan Companies; Taos Development & Holding Co.; Territorial Abstract & Title Co.; Tosco Corporation.

For full biographical listings, see the Martindale-Hubbell Law Directory

NEW YORK

*ALBANY,** Albany Co.

ROWLEY, FORREST, O'DONNELL & HITE, P.C. (AV)

90 State Street Suite 729, 12207-1715
Telephone: 518-434-6187
Fax: 518-434-1287

Richard R. Rowley
Thomas J. Forrest
Brian J. O'Donnell
Robert S. Hite
John H. Beaumont
Mark S. Pelersi
David C. Rowley

James J. Seaman
David P. Miranda
Kevin S. Casey
Richard W. Bader
Daniel W. Coffey
Thomas D. Spain

OF COUNSEL

Rush W. Stehlin

Reference: Norstar Bank.

For full biographical listings, see the Martindale-Hubbell Law Directory

SHANLEY, SWEENEY & REILLY, P.C. (AV)

The Castle at Ten Thurlow Terrace, 12203
Telephone: 518-463-1415
Saratoga Springs, New York Office: 480 Broadway.
Telephone: 518-583-0777.
Fax: 518-583-1184.

Michael P. Shanley, Jr.
Robert L. Sweeney
J. Stephen Reilly (Resident, Saratoga Springs Office)
John L. Allen
Frank P. Milano
Gregory D. Faucher
J. Michael Naughton
Mark R. Marcantano
Patricia Hart Nessler
Lisa M. Peraza
Bonnie J. Riggi
Scott P. Olson

For full biographical listings, see the Martindale-Hubbell Law Directory

THORN AND GERSHON (AV)

5 Wembley Court, New Karner Road, P.O. Box 15054, 12212
Telephone: 518-464-6770
Fax: 518-464-6778

MEMBERS OF FIRM

Richard M. Gershon
Arthur H. Thorn
Jeffrey J. Tymann
Maureen Sullivan Bonanni
Robin Bartlett Phelan

(See Next Column)

THORN AND GERSHON, *Albany—Continued*

ASSOCIATES

Murry S. Brower
Noreen J. Eaton
Paul J. Catone
Nancy Nicholson Bogan
Sheila Toborg
John C. Garvey
Paul D. Jureller
Mario D. Cometti
Robert S. Bruschini

OF COUNSEL

Robert F. Doran

For full biographical listings, see the Martindale-Hubbell Law Directory

WHITEMAN OSTERMAN & HANNA (AV)

One Commerce Plaza, 12260
Telephone: 518-487-7600
Telecopier: 518-487-7777
Cable Address: "Advocate Albany"
Buffalo, New York Office: 1700 Liberty Building.
Telephone: 716-854-4420.
Telecopier: 716-854-4428.

MEMBERS OF FIRM

Michael Whiteman
Melvin H. Osterman
John Hanna, Jr.
Joel L. Hodes
Philip H. Gitlen
Scott N. Fein
Alice J. Kryzan (Resident, Buffalo Office)
Daniel A. Ruzow
Philip H. Dixon
Günter Dully
James W. Lytle
Richard E. Leckerling
Margaret J. Gillis
Jonathan P. Nye
Heather D. Diddel
Neil L. Levine
Mary Jane Bendon Couch
John T. Kolaga (Resident, Buffalo Office)

SENIOR COUNSEL

Howard T. Sprow

COUNSEL

John R. Dunne
Thomas H. Lynch

OF COUNSEL

Leslie K. Thiele

ASSOCIATES

Kenneth S. Ritzenberg
Jean F. Gerbini
Jeffrey S. Baker
Terresa M. Bakner
Elizabeth M. Morss
Carla E. Hogan
Paul C. Rapp
D. Scott Bassinson
Alan J. Goldberg (Not admitted in NY)
James H. Hoeksema, Jr.
Mary Walsh Snyder
Maria E. Villa
Beth A. Bourassa
Boty McDonald
Martin J. Ricciardi
Alicia C. Rood (Resident, Buffalo Office)
Sonya Kumari Del Peral
Carolyn Dick
David R. Everett
Michael G. Sterthous
John J. Henry
Lisa S. Kwong
Ellen M. Bach
Molly M.A. Brown
Judith Gaies Kahn
Ana-Maria Galeano
Alexandra J. Streznewski
Wayne Barr, Jr.

For full biographical listings, see the Martindale-Hubbell Law Directory

*BINGHAMTON,** Broome Co.

O'CONNOR, GACIOCH & POPE (AV)

One Marine Midland Plaza, East Tower-Seventh Floor, P.O. Box 1964, 13902
Telephone: 607-772-9262
Fax: 607-724-6002

Thomas F. O'Connor
James C. Gacioch
Alan J. Pope
Lori Grumet Schapiro
Jeffrey A. Tait
Hugh B. Leonard
Robert N. Nielsen, Jr.
Martha Keeler Macinski
Stephen B. Atkinson
Kurt D. Schrader
Richard M. Hill
Patricia A. Cummings
Mark D. Goris
Susan E. Decker

OF COUNSEL

Walter T. Gorman

For full biographical listings, see the Martindale-Hubbell Law Directory

GARDEN CITY, Nassau Co.

JASPAN, GINSBERG, SCHLESINGER, SILVERMAN & HOFFMAN (AV)

300 Garden City Plaza, 11530
Telephone: 516-746-8000
Telecopier: 516-746-0552

(See Next Column)

MEMBERS OF FIRM

Arthur W. Jaspan
Eugene S. Ginsberg
Steven R. Schlesinger
Kenneth P. Silverman
Carol M. Hoffman
Stanley A. Camhi
Eugene P. Cimini, Jr.
Holly Juster
Stephen P. Epstein
Gary M. Schwartz (1945-1985)
Gary F. Herbst
Allen Perlstein
Janet F. Brunell

Alice J. Hollmuller
Laurel Row Kretzing
Leonard M. Fischer
Marci S. Zinn
Salvatore LaMonica
Lawrence J. Tenenbaum
Michael G. McAuliffe
Suzanne Stadler
Randi-Sue Weinberg
Andrew S. Muller
Carol A. Melnick
John O. Fronce

OF COUNSEL

Leo L. Hoffman
Joseph Jaspan
Harold D. Berger
Michael E. White
Horace Z. Kramer (1918-1988)
Harry J. Winick (1899-1988)
Theodore W. Firetog

For full biographical listings, see the Martindale-Hubbell Law Directory

MONTFORT, HEALY, MCGUIRE & SALLEY (AV)

1140 Franklin Avenue, 11530
Telephone: 516-747-4082
Telecopier: 516-746-0748

MEMBERS OF FIRM

E. Richard Rimmels, Jr.
Frank J. Cafaro
Philip J. Catapano
Fredric C. Montfort
Donald S. Neumann, Jr.
James J. Keefe, Jr.
Michael A. Baranowicz
James Michael Murphy

OF COUNSEL

Fredric H. Montfort
Edward M. Salley, Jr.
David J. Fleming

ASSOCIATES

Raymond J. Geoghegan
Robert J. Mettalia
Henry J. Wheller
Claudia C. Glacken
Marcie K. Glasser
Bruce A. Cook
Jeffrey D. Present
Joan E. Resnik
Susan H. Dempsey
Camille L. Hansen
Joseph F. Ferrette
Pui C. Cheng
Kathleen Dumont
Christopher T. Cafaro
Edward R. Rimmels
Jeffrey B. Siler

For full biographical listings, see the Martindale-Hubbell Law Directory

*GOSHEN,** Orange Co.

NORTON & CHRISTENSEN (AV)

Goshen Executive Building, 60 Erie Street, P.O. Box 308, 10924
Telephone: 914-294-7949
Telecopier: 914-294-7791
Rochelle Park, New Jersey Office: 151 West Passaic Street, 07662.
Telephone: 201-909-3735.
Fax: 201-368-2102.

MEMBERS OF FIRM

Stanley J. Norton
Henry N. Christensen, Jr.
Harold M. Pressberg

OF COUNSEL

John T. Mayo

For full biographical listings, see the Martindale-Hubbell Law Directory

HAMBURG, Erie Co.

HARRIS BEACH & WILCOX (AV)

One Grimsby Drive, 14075
Telephone: 716-646-5050
Fax: 716-648-8201
Washington, DC Office: 1200 18th Street, Suite 210.
Telephone: 202-861-0001.
Fax: 202-861-0011.
Ithaca, New York Office: 119 East Seneca Street, P.O. Box 580.
Telephone: 607-273-6444.
Albany, New York Office: 20 Corporate Woods Boulevard.
Telephone: 518-427-9700.
Fax: 518-427-0235.
Syracuse, New York Office: Suite 300, Fleet Bank Building, One Clinton Square.
Telephone: 315-426-4520.
Fax: 315-426-4529.
Other Syracuse, New York Office: The Hills Building, 7th Floor, 217 Montgomery Street.
Telephone: 315-422-7383.
Fax: 315-422-9331.

MEMBERS OF FIRM

Henry W. Killeen, III
Maureen R. L. Mussenden
Raymond J. Stapell
Bradlee Wright Townsend
A. Timothy Webster

(See Next Column)

HARRIS BEACH & WILCOX—*Continued*

ASSOCIATES

Louis C. Fessard
Nelson Perel
Karin L. Stamy

For full biographical listings, see the Martindale-Hubbell Law Directory

*NEW YORK,** New York Co.

BEATIE, KING & ABATE (AV)

599 Lexington Avenue, Suite 1300, 10022
Telephone: 212-888-9000
Fax: 212-888-9664

Russel H. Beatie, Jr.
Kenneth J. King
Samuel J. Abate, Jr.

ASSOCIATES

Susan Kelty Law
Charna L. Gerstenhaber
Eric J. Gruber
Philip J. Miller
Peter S. Liaskos
W.H. Ramsay Lewis

For full biographical listings, see the Martindale-Hubbell Law Directory

CHALOS & BROWN, P.C. (AV)

300 East 42nd Street, 10017-5982
Telephone: 212-661-5440
Telecopier: 212-697-8999
Telex: 238470 (RCA)
Clifton, New Jersey Office: 1118 Clifton Avenue.
Telephone: 201-779-1116.

Michael G. Chalos
Robert J. Brown
Harry A. Gavalas
Stephan Skoufalos
Thomas M. Russo
Martin F. Casey
Robert J. Seminara

Edward P. Flood
Timothy G. Hourican
Fred G. Wexler
Steven G. Friedberg
George J. Tsimis
Martin F. Marvet
Laurence Curran

References: Citibank, N.A.; Chase Manhattan Bank.

For full biographical listings, see the Martindale-Hubbell Law Directory

JOHNSTON & MCSHANE, P.C. (AV)

Graybar Building, 420 Lexington Avenue, 10170
Telephone: 212-972-5252
Facsimilie: 212-697-2737

William R. Johnston
Bruce W. McShane
Peter F. Breheny

Dennis W. Grogan
Arthur J. Smith
Kenneth E. Moffett, Jr.
Andrew Ross
Robert D. Donahue
James M. Carman

OF COUNSEL

Charles A. Miller, II (Not admitted in NY)

For full biographical listings, see the Martindale-Hubbell Law Directory

SHEFT & SHEFT (AV)

909 Third Avenue, 10022
Telephone: 212-688-7788
Telecopier: 212-355-7373
Jersey City, New Jersey Office: Harborside Financial Center, Suite 704 Plaza Three.
Telephone: 201-332-2233.
Telecopier: 201-435-9177.

Leonard A. Sheft
Peter I. Sheft
Norman J. Golub (Resident, Jersey City, New Jersey Office)
Marjorie Heyman Mintzer
Marian S. Hertz
Leonard G. Kamlet

COUNSEL

Gerald A. Greenberger (Resident, Jersey City, New Jersey Office)

David Holmes (Resident, Jersey City, New Jersey Office)
Phillip C. Landrigan
Thomas J. Leonard
Myra Needleman
Howard K. Fishman
Mary C. Bennett
Jeffrey S. Leonard (Resident, Jersey City, New Jersey Office)
Stacy B. Parker
Edward Hayum
Daniel H. Hecht
Jerrald J. Hochman
James M. Dennis
Frank V. Kelly
Ellen G. Margolis
Guy J. Levasseur
Joseph F. Arkins
Jordan Sklar

(See Next Column)

Herbert L. Lazar
Maria E. Cannon (Resident, Jersey City, New Jersey Office)

For full biographical listings, see the Martindale-Hubbell Law Directory

WHITE, FLEISCHNER & FINO (AV)

195 Broadway, 10007
Telephone: 212-227-6292
Telex: 645255
Telecopier: 212-227-7812
Westfield, New Jersey Office: 215 North Avenue, West.
Telephone: 908-654-6266.
Telecopier: 908-654-3686.
London, England Office: Plantation House. 31/35 Fenchurch S. EC3M 3DX.
Telephone: 071-375-2037.
Telecopier: 071-375-2039.

MEMBERS OF FIRM

Allan P. White
Benjamin A. Fleischner
Paul A. Fino, Jr.
Robert G. Schenker
Marcia J. Lynn
Marisa Goetz

ASSOCIATES

Patti F. Potash
Mitchell R. Friedman
Mitchell L. Shadowitz
Debra E. Ruderman
David I. Blee
Sandra L. Bonder
Michael J. Asta
Stephanie M. Holzback
Mark R. Osherow
Virginia L. McGrane
Beth A. Goldklang
Sean Upton
Wendy K. Carrano
Nancy D. Lyness
Randy Scott Faust
Elizabeth C. Mirisola
Sheri E. Holland

LEGAL SUPPORT PERSONNEL

Darien Anderson (Paralegal)
Helen Wasey (Claims Consultant)

For full biographical listings, see the Martindale-Hubbell Law Directory

*RIVERHEAD,** Suffolk Co.

TWOMEY, LATHAM, SHEA & KELLEY (AV)

33 West Second Street, P.O. Box 398, 11901
Telephone: 516-727-2180
Telecopier: 516-727-1767
East Hampton, New York Office: 20 Main Street.
Telephone: 516-324-1200.
Hauppauge, New York Office: 400 Townline Road.
Telephone: 516-265-1414.

MEMBERS OF FIRM

Thomas A. Twomey, Jr.
Stephen B. Latham
John F. Shea, III
Christopher D. Kelley
Lawrence M. Storm
Maureen T. Liccione
David M. Dubin
P. Edward Reale
Peter M. Mott
Joan C. Hatfield

ASSOCIATES

Mary C. Cronin
J. Lee Snead
Suzanne V. Shane

OF COUNSEL

Amy B. Turner

References: Suffolk County National Bank; Bridgehampton National Bank.

For full biographical listings, see the Martindale-Hubbell Law Directory

*ROCHESTER,** Monroe Co.

CHAMBERLAIN, D'AMANDA, OPPENHEIMER & GREENFIELD (AV)

1600 Crossroads Office Building, Two State Street, 14614
Telephone: 716-232-3730
Telecopier: 716-232-3882

MEMBERS OF FIRM

Henry R. Ippolito
Douglas Jones
Steven J. Tranelli

ASSOCIATE

E. Adam Leyens

OF COUNSEL

Robert H. Antell

For Complete List of Firm Personnel, See General Section

For full biographical listings, see the Martindale-Hubbell Law Directory

HARRIS & CHESWORTH (AV)

1820 East Avenue, 14607
Telephone: 716-242-2400
Fax: 716-242-2424

MEMBERS OF FIRM

Wayne M. Harris
Donald O. Chesworth
Edward M. O'Brien

(See Next Column)

HARRIS & CHESWORTH, *Rochester—Continued*

ASSOCIATES

David J. Gutmann
Michael A. Damia
David Mayer
Timothy P. Blodgett

SPECIAL COUNSEL

Melvin Bressler

For full biographical listings, see the Martindale-Hubbell Law Directory

UNDERBERG & KESSLER (AV)

1800 Chase Square, 14604
Telephone: 716-258-2800
Fax: 716-258-2821

MEMBERS OF FIRM

Alan J. Underberg
Irving L. Kessler
Michael J. Beyma
Frank T. Crego
Robert W. Croessmann
John W. Crowe
Michael C. Dwyer
Bernard A. Frank
Steven R. Gersz
John L. Goldman
Lawrence P. Keller
Gordon J. Lipson
Robert F. Mechur
Paul V. Nunes
Terry M. Richman
Sharon P. Stiller
Stephen H. Waite
Russell I. Zuckerman

OF COUNSEL

Richard G. Crawford
Andrew M. Greenstein

SENIOR ATTORNEY

Thomas P. Young

ASSOCIATES

Patrick L. Cusato
Sean E. Gleason
Katherine Howk Karl
Suzanne D. Nott
Linda Prestegaard

For full biographical listings, see the Martindale-Hubbell Law Directory

*SYRACUSE,** Onondaga Co.

BOND, SCHOENECK & KING (AV)

18th Floor One Lincoln Center, 13202-1355
Telephone: 315-422-0121
Fax: 315-422-3598
Albany, New York Office: 111 Washington Avenue.
Telephone: 518-462-7421.
Fax: 518-462-7441.
Boca Raton, Florida Office: 5355 Town Center Road, Suite 1002.
Telephone: 407-368-1212.
Fax: 407-338-9955.
Naples, Florida Office: 1167 Third Street South.
Telephone: 813-262-6812.
Fax: 813-262-6908.
Oswego, New York Office: 130 East Second Street.
Telephone: 315-343-9116.
Fax: 315-343-1231.
Overland Park, Kansas Office: 7500 College Boulevard, Suite 910.
Telephone: 913-345-8001.
Fax: 913-345-9017.

MEMBERS OF FIRM

John M. Freyer (Resident, Albany Office)
John S. Ferguson
Anthony R. Pittarelli
H. Dean Heberlig, Jr.
George H. Lowe
John D. Allen
Barry R. Kogut
Thomas R. Smith
David R. Sheridan (Resident, Albany Office)
Edward R. Conan
John G. McGowan
Susan Phillips Read (Resident, Albany Office)
Louis A. Alexander (Resident, Albany Office)
Robert S. McLaughlin

ASSOCIATES

Virginia C. Robbins
Kevin M. Bernstein
William M. Buchan
Michael J. Grygiel (Resident, Albany Office)
Robert R. Tyson

General Counsel for: Syracuse University; Unity Mutual Life Insurance Co.; Manufacturers Association of Central New York.
Regional or Special Counsel for: Newhouse Broadcasting Corp. (WSYR, AM-FM); Syracuse Herald-Post Standard Newspapers.; Miller Brewing Co.; Allied Corp.; General Electric Co.; National Grange.

For Complete List of Firm Personnel, See General Section

For full biographical listings, see the Martindale-Hubbell Law Directory

*UTICA,** Oneida Co.

PETRONE & PETRONE, P.C. (AV)

1624 Genesee Street, 13502
Telephone: 315-735-7566
FAX: 315-735-5368
Rochester, New York Office: 929 Times Square Building, 45 Exchange Street.
Telephone: 716-232-7730.
FAX: 716-232-7788.

(See Next Column)

Syracuse, New York Office: 308 Plum Court, 528 Plum Street.
Telephone: 1-800-521-1260.
Fax: 315-474-9422.

Louis S. Petrone
John R. Petrone, II
Lori E. Petrone

Marcus M. Curry
Merle M. Troeger (Resident, Rochester Office)
Mark J. Halpin
James P. Godemann

For full biographical listings, see the Martindale-Hubbell Law Directory

*WHITE PLAINS,** Westchester Co.

GREENBURG & POSNER (AV)

399 Knollwood Road, 10603
Telephone: 914-948-6620
Telecopier: 914-948-0864

MEMBERS OF FIRM

Henry A. Greenburg
Martin Louis Posner
Jane Y. Posner
Steven N. Feinman

ASSOCIATE

Jessica Bacal

References: Chemical Bank; Citibank.

For full biographical listings, see the Martindale-Hubbell Law Directory

KEANE & BEANE, P.C. (AV)

One North Broadway, 10601
Telephone: 914-946-4777
Telecopier: 914-946-6868
Rye, New York Office: 49 Purchase Street.
Telephone: 914-967-3936.

Thomas F. Keane, Jr. (1932-1991)

Edward F. Beane
David Glasser
Ronald A. Longo
Richard L. O'Rourke
Lawrence Praga
Joel H. Sachs
Steven A. Schurkman
Judson K. Siebert

Debbie G. Jacobs
Lance H. Klein
Donna E. Frosco
Nicholas M. Ward-Willis

LEGAL SUPPORT PERSONNEL

Barbara S. Durkin
Toni Ann Huff

OF COUNSEL

Eric F. Jensen
Peter A. Borrok

For full biographical listings, see the Martindale-Hubbell Law Directory

NORTH CAROLINA

*CHARLOTTE,** Mecklenburg Co.

GRIER AND GRIER, P.A. (AV)

Suite 1240 One Independence Center, 101 North Tryon Street, 28246
Telephone: 704-375-3720
FAX: 704-332-0215

Joseph W. Grier, Jr.
Joseph W. Grier, III
Richard C. Belthoff, Jr.
Richard L. Robertson
Leigh A. Hobgood

J. Cameron Furr, Jr.
James L. Kiser
K. Lane Klotzberger

Representative Clients: Kem Wove, Inc.; Misbet Oil Co.

For full biographical listings, see the Martindale-Hubbell Law Directory

SMITH HELMS MULLISS & MOORE, L.L.P. (AV)

227 North Tryon Street, P.O. Box 31247, 28231
Telephone: 704-343-2000
Telecopier: 704-334-8467
Telex: 572460
Greensboro, North Carolina Office: Smith Helms Mulliss & Moore, Suite 1400 First Union Tower, 300 North Greene Street, P.O. Box 21927.
Telephone: 910-378-5200.
Telecopier: 910-379-9558.
Raleigh, North Carolina Office: 316 West Edenton Street, P.O. Box 27525.
Telephone: 919-755-8700.
Telecopier: 919-828-7938.

MEMBERS OF FIRM

Robert B. Cordle
Benne C. Hutson

(See Next Column)

SMITH HELMS MULLISS & MOORE L.L.P.—*Continued*

ASSOCIATE

Gregory S. Hilderbran

For Complete List of Firm Personnel, See General Section

For full biographical listings, see the Martindale-Hubbell Law Directory

WOMBLE CARLYLE SANDRIDGE & RICE (AV)

A Professional Limited Liability Company
3300 One First Union Center, 301 S. College Street, 28202-6025
Telephone: 704-331-4900
Telecopy: 704-331-4955
Telex: 853609
Winston-Salem, North Carolina Office: 1600 Southern National Financial Center.
Telephone: 919-721-3600.
Telecopy: 919-721-3660.
Telex: 806498.
Raleigh, North Carolina Office: 2100 First Union Capitol Center, 150 Fayetteville Street Mall, P.O. Box 831.
Telephone: 919-755-2100.
Telecopy: 919-755-2150.
Telex: 806498.
Atlanta, Georgia Office: One Ninety One Peachtree Tower, 191 Peachtree Street N.E., Suite 3250.
Telephone: 404-614-2580.
Fax: 404-614-2595.

OF COUNSEL

Bradford A. DeVore

Representative Clients: Childress Klein Properties, Inc.; Food Lion, Inc.; Fieldcrest Cannon, Inc.; J.A. Jones Construction Company; Parkdale Mills, Inc.; Duke Power Company; Bowles Hollowell Conner & Company; ALLTEL Carolina, Inc.; Belk Store Services, Inc.; Philip Holzmann A.G.

For Complete List of Firm Personnel, See General Section

For full biographical listings, see the Martindale-Hubbell Law Directory

*GREENSBORO,** Guilford Co.

SMITH HELMS MULLISS & MOORE, L.L.P. (AV)

Suite 1400 First Union Tower, 300 North Greene Street, P.O. Box 21927, 27420
Telephone: 910-378-5200
Telecopier: 910-379-9558
Charlotte, North Carolina Office: Smith Helms Mulliss & Moore, L.L.P., 227 North Tryon Street, P.O. Box 31247.
Telephone: 704-343-2000.
Telecopier: 704-334-8467.
Telex: 572460.
Raleigh, North Carolina Office: Smith Helms Mulliss & Moore, L.L.P., 316 West Edenton Street, P.O. Box 27525.
Telephone: 919-755-8700.
Telecopier: 919-828-7938.

MEMBERS OF FIRM

Harold N. Bynum
David M. Moore, II
Stephen W. Earp
Ramona O. O'Bryant

ASSOCIATES

William E. Burton, III
D. Marsh Prause

For Complete List of Firm Personnel, See General Section

For full biographical listings, see the Martindale-Hubbell Law Directory

*GREENVILLE,** Pitt Co.

MARVIN K. BLOUNT, JR. (AV)

400 West First Street, P.O. Drawer 58, 27835-0058
Telephone: 919-752-6000
FAX: 919-752-2174

ASSOCIATES

Joseph T. Edwards
James F. Hopf
Sharron R. Edwards

Reference: Branch Banking & Trust Co., Greenville, N.C.

For full biographical listings, see the Martindale-Hubbell Law Directory

*RALEIGH,** Wake Co.

* indicates certain Bar Register subscribers whose principal office is located elsewhere in the state and who have arranged for representation as a part of the state capital listings that follow

*** SMITH HELMS MULLISS & MOORE, L.L.P. (AV)**

316 West Edenton Street, P.O. Box 27525, 27611-7525
Telephone: 919-755-8700
Telecopier: 919-828-7938
Charlotte, North Carolina Office: 227 North Tryon Street, P.O. Box 31247.
Telephone: 704-343-2000.
Telecopier: 704-334-8467.
Telex: 572460.
Greensboro, North Carolina Office: Smith Helms Mulliss & Moore, Suite 1400 First Union Tower, 300 North Greene Street, P.O. Box 21927.
Telephone: 910-378-5200.
Telecopier: 910-379-9558.

MEMBERS OF FIRM

Richard W. Ellis
James L. Gale
Elizabeth M. Powell

ASSOCIATE

Gary R. Govert

For Complete List of Firm Personnel, See General Section

For full biographical listings, see the Martindale-Hubbell Law Directory

*** WOMBLE CARLYLE SANDRIDGE & RICE (AV)**

A Professional Limited Liability Company
2100 First Union Capitol Center, 150 Fayetteville Street Mall, P.O. Box 831, 27602
Telephone: 919-755-2100
Telecopy: 919-755-2150
Telex: 806498
Charlotte, North Carolina Office: 3300 One First Union Center, 301 South College Street.
Telephone: 704-331-4900.
Telecopy: 704-331-4955.
Telex: 853609.
Winston-Salem, North Carolina Office: 1600 Southern National Financial Center.
Telephone: 919-721-3600.
Telecopy: 919-721-3660.
Telex: 806498.
Atlanta, Georgia Office: One Ninety One Peachtree Tower, 191 Peachtree Street N.E., Suite 3250.
Telephone: 404-614-2580.
Fax: 404-614-2595.

RESIDENT ASSOCIATE

Yvonne C. Bailey

Representative Clients: Aetna Casualty and Surety Co., Inc.; ALSCO/AmeriMark Building Products, Inc.; Aoki Corporation America, Inc.; Empire of Carolina, Inc.; Hackney Brothers, Inc.; Lawyers Mutual Liability Insurance Company of North Carolina; Meredith College; Monk-Austin, Inc.; Regency Park Corporation; Wachovia Bank of North Carolina, N.A.

For Complete List of Firm Personnel, See General Section

For full biographical listings, see the Martindale-Hubbell Law Directory

*WINSTON-SALEM,** Forsyth Co.

WOMBLE CARLYLE SANDRIDGE & RICE (AV)

A Professional Limited Liability Company
1600 Southern National Financial Center, P.O. Drawer 84, 27102
Telephone: 910-721-3600
Telecopy: 910-721-3660
Telex: 806498
Charlotte, North Carolina Office: 3300 One First Union Center, 301 South College Street.
Telephone: 704-331-4900.
Telecopy: 704-331-4955.
Telex: 853609.
Raleigh, North Carolina Office: 2100 First Union Capitol Center, 150 Fayetteville Street Mall, P.O. Box 831.
Telephone: 919-755-2100.
Telecopy: 919-755-2150.
Telex: 806498.
Atlanta, Georgia Office: One Ninety One Peachtree Tower, 191 Peachtree Street, N.E., Suite 3250.
Telephone: 404-614-2580.
Fax: 404-614-2595.

MEMBERS OF FIRM

Karen Estelle Carey
R. Howard Grubbs
Keith W. Vaughan
G. Criston Windham

(See Next Column)

WOMBLE CARLYLE SANDRIDGE & RICE, *Winston-Salem—Continued*

ASSOCIATES

Jeffrey L. Furr
Lori Privette Hinnant
Celeste Elizabeth O'Keeffe

Representative Clients: Brad Ragan, Inc.; Brenner Companies; Food Lion, Inc.; Hanes Companies, Inc.; North Carolina Baptist Hospitals, Inc.; R.J. Reynolds Tobacco Company; Summit Communications Group, Inc.; Thomasville Furniture Industries, Inc.; Wachovia Corporation; Wake Forest University.

For Complete List of Firm Personnel, See General Section

For full biographical listings, see the Martindale-Hubbell Law Directory

NORTH DAKOTA

*BISMARCK,** Burleigh Co.

FLECK, MATHER & STRUTZ, LTD. (AV)

Sixth Floor, Norwest Bank Building, 400 East Broadway, P.O. Box 2798, 58502
Telephone: 701-223-6585
Telecopier: 701-222-4853

Ernest R. Fleck
Russell R. Mather
Gary R. Wolberg
Paul W. Summers
Brian R. Bjella
John W. Morrison, Jr.
Craig Cordell Smith
DeeNelle Louise Ruud

Representative Clients: Exxon Company U.S.A.; The North American Coal Corp.; Amerada Hess Corporation; W.R. Grace; Farmers Union Property and Casualty Company.

For Complete List of Firm Personnel, See General Section

For full biographical listings, see the Martindale-Hubbell Law Directory

OHIO

*CINCINNATI,** Hamilton Co.

ALTMAN & CALARDO CO. A LEGAL PROFESSIONAL ASSOCIATION (AV)

Suite 1006, 414 Walnut Street, 45202
Telephone: 513-721-2180
Fax: 513-721-2299

D. David Altman
Stephen P. Calardo
Amy J. Leonard
Kevin P. Braig

For full biographical listings, see the Martindale-Hubbell Law Directory

DINSMORE & SHOHL (AV)

1900 Chemed Center, 255 East Fifth Street, 45202-3172
Telephone: 513-977-8200
FAX: 513-977-8141
Florence, Kentucky Office: Turfway Ridge Office Park, 7300 Turfway Road, Suite 430 41042-1355.
Telephone: 606-283-0515.
FAX: 606-283-6017.
Dayton, Ohio Office: 500 Courthouse Plaza, S.W., 10 N. Ludlow Street, 45402-1834.
Telephone: 513-228-8012.
FAX: 513-461-2543.
Columbus, Ohio Office: NBD Bank Building, Suite 330, 175 South Third Street, 43215-5134.
Telephone: 614-224-7887.
FAX: 614-224-7882.

MEMBERS OF FIRM

John W. Beatty
Vincent B. Stamp
Joel S. Taylor (Resident, Columbus, Ohio Office)
Philip J. Schworer

ASSOCIATES

Charles R. Dyas, Jr.
Randel S. Springer
Robert A. Williams
Frances L. Figetakis
Theodore J. Schneider

For Complete List of Firm Personnel, See General Section

For full biographical listings, see the Martindale-Hubbell Law Directory

FROST & JACOBS (AV)

2500 PNC Center, 201 East Fifth Street, P.O. Box 5715, 45201-5715
Telephone: 513-651-6800
Cable Address: "Frostjac"
Telex: 21-4396 F & J CIN
Telecopier: 513-651-6981
Columbus, Ohio Office: One Columbus, 10 West Broad Street.
Telephone: 614-464-1211.
Telecopier: 614-464-1737.
Lexington, Kentucky Office: 1100 Vine Center Tower, 333 West Vine Street.
Telephone: 606-254-1100.
Telecopier: 606-253-2990.
Middletown, Ohio Office: 400 First National Bank Building, 2 North Main Street.
Telephone: 513-422-2001.
Telecopier: 513-422-3010.
Naples, Florida Office: 4001 Tamiami Trail North, Suite 220.
Telephone: 813-261-0582.
Telecopier: 813-261-2083.

MEMBERS OF FIRM

William H. Hawkins, II
Paul W. Casper, Jr.
Douglas E. Hart
Stephen N. Haughey

ASSOCIATES

Kevin N. McMurray
John C. Cummings
Jonathan A. Conte
Michele M. Bradley

COLUMBUS, OHIO OFFICE
MEMBER OF FIRM

Michael K. Yarbrough

Representative Clients: Armco, Inc.; Chevron U.S.A., Inc.; Cincinnati Milacron; Federated Department Stores, Inc.; Mercy Health Systems; NLO, Inc.; PNC Bank, Ohio, National Association; The Penn Central Corp.; Stone Container Corp.; U.S. Shoe Corp.

For Complete List of Firm Personnel, See General Section

For full biographical listings, see the Martindale-Hubbell Law Directory

THOMPSON, HINE AND FLORY (AV)

312 Walnut Street, 14th Floor, 45202-4029
Telephone: 513-352-6700
Fax: 513-241-4771;
Telex: 938003
Akron, Ohio Office: 50 S. Main Street, Suite 502, 44308-1828.
Telephone: 216-376-8090.
Fax: 216-376-8386.
Cleveland, Ohio Office: 1100 National City Bank Building, 629 Euclid Avenue, 44114-3070.
Telephone: 216-566-5500.
Fax: 216-556-5583.
Telex: 980217.
Cable Address: "Thomflor".
Columbus, Ohio Office: One Columbus, 10 West Broad Street, 43215-3435.
Telephone: 614-469-3200.
Fax: 614-469-3361.
Dayton, Ohio Office: 2000 Courthouse Plaza, N.E., 45402-1706.
Telephone: 513-443-6600.
Fax: 513-443-6637; 443-6635.
Palm Beach, Florida Office: 125 Worth Avenue, 33480-4466.
Telephone: 407-833-5900.
Fax: 407-833-5951.
Washington, D.C. Office: 1920 N Street, N.W., 20036-1601.
Telephone: 202-331-8800.
Fax: 202-331-8330.
Telex: 904173.
Cable Address: "Caglaw".
Brussels, Belgium Office: Rue des Chevaliers / Ridderstraat 14 - B.10, B - 1050.
Telephone: 011(32-2) 511-9326.
Fax: 011(-32-2) 513-9206.

MEMBERS OF FIRM

Jeffrey F. Peck
Jill A. Weller

ASSOCIATE

John H. Beasley

For Complete List of Firm Personnel, See General Section

For full biographical listings, see the Martindale-Hubbell Law Directory

*CLEVELAND,** Cuyahoga Co.

BAKER & HOSTETLER (AV)

3200 National City Center, 1900 East Ninth Street, 44114-3485
Telephone: 216-621-0200
Telecopier: 216-696-0740
TWX: 810 421 8375
RCA Telex: 215032
In Columbus, Ohio: Capitol Square, Suite 2100, 65 East State Street.
Telephone: 614-228-1541.
In Denver, Colorado: 303 East 17th Avenue, Suite 1100.
Telephone: 303-861-0600.

(See Next Column)

BAKER & HOSTETLER—*Continued*

In Houston, Texas: 1000 Louisiana, Suite 2000.
Telephone: 713-751-1600.
In Long Beach, California: 300 Oceangate, Suite 620.
Telephone: 310-432-2827.
In Los Angeles, California: 600 Wilshire Boulevard.
Telephone: 213-624-2400.
In Orlando, Florida: SunBank Center, Suite 2300, 200 South Orange Avenue.
Telephone: 407-649-4000.
In Washington, D. C.: Washington Square, Suite 1100, 1050 Connecticut Avenue, N.W.
Telephone: 202-861-1500.
In College Park, Maryland: 9658 Baltimore Boulevard, Suite 206.
Telephone: 301-441-2781.
In Alexandria, Virginia: 437 North Lee Street.
Telephone: 703-549-1294.
In San Francisco, California: One Sansome Street, Suite 2000.
Telephone: 415-951-4705.

PARTNERS

Mary M. Bittence — George Downing
Maureen A. Brennan — William W. Falsgraf
John E. Sullivan

For Complete List of Firm Personnel, See General Section

For full biographical listings, see the Martindale-Hubbell Law Directory

JANIK & DUNN (AV)

400 Park Plaza Building, 1111 Chester Avenue, 44114
Telephone: 216-781-9700
Fax: 216-781-1250
Brea, California Office: 2601 Saturn Street, Suite 300.
Telephone: 714-572-1101.
Fax: 714-572-1103.

MEMBERS OF FIRM

Steven G. Janik — Theodore M. Dunn, Jr.

ASSOCIATES

Myra Staresina — David L. Mast

For full biographical listings, see the Martindale-Hubbell Law Directory

KAUFMAN & CUMBERLAND CO., L.P.A. (AV)

Third Floor, 1404 East 9th Street, 44114-1779
Telephone: 216-861-0707
Telefax: 216-694-6883
TDD: 216-694-6891
Columbus, Ohio Office: 300 South Second Street, 43215.
Telephone: 614-224-0717.
Telefax: 614-229-4111.

Steven S. Kaufman — Frank J. Cumberland, Jr.

Edda Sara Post — Laura Hauser Pfahl (Resident, Columbus, Ohio Office)
David P. Lodwick

Representative Clients: International Insurance Co.; International Surplus Lines Insurance Co.; TransTec Environmental, Inc.; Ullman Oil, Inc.

For Complete List of Firm Personnel, See General Section

For full biographical listings, see the Martindale-Hubbell Law Directory

KELLER AND CURTIN CO., L.P.A. (AV)

Suite 330 The Hanna Building, 44115-1901
Telephone: 216-566-7100
Telecopier: 216-566-5430
Akron, Ohio Office: 2304 First National Tower, 44308-1419.
Telephone: 216-376-7245.
Telecopier: 216-376-8128.

Stanley S. Keller — Walter H. Krohngold
G. Michael Curtin — James M. Johnson

Joseph G. Ritzler — Phillip A. Kuri

Reference: Bank One, Cleveland.

For full biographical listings, see the Martindale-Hubbell Law Directory

KELLEY, MCCANN & LIVINGSTONE (AV)

35th Floor, BP America Building, 200 Public Square, 44114-2302
Telephone: 216-241-3141
FAX: 216-241-3707

MEMBERS OF FIRM

Stephen M. O'Bryan — James P. Oliver
John D. Brown — Bruce L. Waterhouse, Jr.
David H. Wallace

(See Next Column)

ASSOCIATE

Robert A. Brindza, II

For Complete List of Firm Personnel, See General Section

For full biographical listings, see the Martindale-Hubbell Law Directory

SEELEY, SAVIDGE AND AUSSEM A LEGAL PROFESSIONAL ASSOCIATION (AV)

800 Bank One Center, 600 Superior Avenue, East, 44114-2655
Telephone: 216-566-8200
Cable Address: "See Sau"
Fax-Telecopier: 216-566-0213
Elyria, Ohio Office: 538 Broad Street.
Telephone: 216-236-8158.

Keith A. Savidge

Patrick J. McIntyre

References: Society National Bank; AmeriTrust.

For Complete List of Firm Personnel, See General Section

For full biographical listings, see the Martindale-Hubbell Law Directory

THOMPSON, HINE AND FLORY (AV)

1100 National City Bank Building, 629 Euclid Avenue, 44114-3070
Telephone: 216-566-5500
Fax: 216-566-5583
Telex: 980217
Cable Address: "Thomflor"
Akron, Ohio Office: 50 S. Main Street, Suite 502, 44308-1828.
Telephone: 216-376-8090.
Fax: 216-376-8386.
Cincinnati, Ohio Office: 312 Walnut Street, 14th Floor, 45202-4029.
Telephone: 513-352-6700.
Fax: 513-241-4771.
Telex: 938003.
Columbus, Ohio Office: One Columbus, 10 West Broad Street, 43215-3435.
Telephone: 614-469-3200.
Fax: 614-469-3361.
Dayton, Ohio Office: 2000 Courthouse Plaza, N.E., 45402-1706.
Telephone: 513-443-6600.
Fax: 513-443-6637; 443-6635.
Palm Beach, Florida Office: 125 Worth Avenue, Suite 117, 33480-4466.
Telephone: 407-833-5900.
Fax: 407-833-5951.
Washington, D.C. Office: 1920 N Street, N.W., 20036-1601.
Telephone: 202-331-8800.
Fax: 202-331-8330.
Telex: 904173.
Cable Address: "Caglaw".
Brussels, Belgium Office: Rue des Chevaliers, Ridderstraat 14 - B.10, B - 1050.
Telephone: 011(32-2) 511-9326.
Fax: 011(32-2) 513-9206.

MEMBERS OF FIRM

Michael A. Cyphert — Michael L. Hardy
David E. Nash

ASSOCIATES

David M. Dumas — Walt A. Linscott

For Complete List of Firm Personnel, See General Section

For full biographical listings, see the Martindale-Hubbell Law Directory

WALTER & HAVERFIELD (AV)

1300 Terminal Tower, 44113-2253
Telephone: 216-781-1212
Telecopier: 216-575-0911
Columbus, Ohio Office: 88 East Broad Street.
Telephone: 614-221-7371.

MEMBER OF FIRM

Ralph E. Cascarilla

ASSOCIATE

Debora S. Lasch

Representative Clients: AGA Gas, Inc.; Air Products and Chemicals, Inc.; American Crane Corp.; Andrews Moving & Storage, Inc.; Applied Medical Technology, Inc.; Aribica Cafes, Inc.; Associated Aviation Underwriters; The Associated Press; Beverly Enterprises, Inc.; Brookfield Wire Company.

For Complete List of Firm Personnel, See General Section

For full biographical listings, see the Martindale-Hubbell Law Directory

WESTON HURD FALLON PAISLEY & HOWLEY (AV)

2500 Terminal Tower, 50 Public Square, 44113-2241
Telephone: 216-241-6602;
Ohio Toll Free: 800-336-4952
FAX: 216-621-8369

(See Next Column)

WESTON HURD FALLON PAISLEY & HOWLEY, *Cleveland—Continued*

MEMBERS OF FIRM

Ronald A. Rispo
James Lincoln McCrystal, Jr.
Carolyn M. Cappel
John Winthrop Ours
Deirdre G. Henry
Dana A. Rose

For Complete List of Firm Personnel, See General Section

For full biographical listings, see the Martindale-Hubbell Law Directory

*COLUMBUS,** Franklin Co.

* indicates certain Bar Register subscribers whose principal office is located elsewhere in the state and who have arranged for representation as a part of the state capital listings that follow

BRICKER & ECKLER (AV)

100 South Third Street, 43215-4291
Telephone: 614-227-2300
Telecopy: 614-227-2390
Cleveland, Ohio Office: 600 Superior Avenue East, Suite 800.
Telephone: 216-771-0720. Fax 216-771-7702.

Charles H. Waterman III

Frank L. Merrill
James J. Hughes, III
Martha E. Horvitz

Representative Clients: Browning-Ferris Industries, Inc.; Air Products, Inc.; PPG Industries, Inc.; Uniroyal Technology Corporation; Waste Technologies Industries; Southdown Corp.; Von Roll America, Inc.; CECOS International, Inc.; City of Columbus, Ohio; Ohio Air Quality Development Authority.

For Complete List of Firm Personnel, See General Section

For full biographical listings, see the Martindale-Hubbell Law Directory

EMENS, KEGLER, BROWN, HILL & RITTER (AV)

Capitol Square Suite 1800, 65 East State Street, 43215-4294
Telephone: 614-462-5400
Telecopier: 614-464-2634
Cable Address: "Law EKBHR"
Telex: 246671

William J. Brown
Thomas W. Hill
O. Judson Scheaf, III
Kevin L. Sykes
Michael E. Zatezalo

Representative Clients: Aluminum Company of America; The Benatty Corp.; Chambers Development Co., Inc.; Mid-American Waste Systems, Inc.; Nalco Chemical Co.; National Ground Water Association; Ohio Gas Co.; Ohio Oil and Gas Assn.; Owens-Corning Fiberglass Corp.; Patrick Petroleum Co.

For Complete List of Firm Personnel, See General Section

For full biographical listings, see the Martindale-Hubbell Law Directory

KAUFMAN & CUMBERLAND CO., L.P.A. (AV)

300 South Second Street, 43215
Telephone: 614-224-0717
Telefax: 614-229-4111
Cleveland, Ohio Office: Third Floor, 1404 East 9th Street, 44114-1779.
Telephone: 216-861-0707.
Telefax: 216-694-6883. TDD: 216-694-6891.

Steven S. Kaufman

Laura Hauser Pfahl

Representative Clients: CertainTeed Corp.; Teledyne Inc.

For full biographical listings, see the Martindale-Hubbell Law Directory

PORTER, WRIGHT, MORRIS & ARTHUR (AV)

41 South High Street, 43215-6194
Telephone: 614-227-2000; (800-533-2794)
Telex: 6503213584 MCI
Fax: 614-227-2100
Dayton, Ohio Office: One Dayton Centre, One South Main Street, 45402.
Telephones: 513-228-2411; (800-533-4434).
Fax: 513-449-6820.
Cincinnati, Ohio Office: 250 E. Fifth Street, 45202-4166.
Telephones: 513-381-4700; (800-582-5813).
Fax: 513-421-0991.
Cleveland, Ohio Office: 925 Euclid Avenue, 44115-1483.
Telephones: 216-443-9000; (800-824-1980).
Fax: 216-443-9011.
Washington, D.C. Office: 1233 20th Street, N.W., 20036-2395.
Telephones: 202-778-3000; (800-456-7962).
Fax: 202-778-3063.
Naples, Florida Office: 4501 Tamiami Trail North, 33940-3060.
Telephones: 813-263-8898;(800-876-7962).
Fax: 813-436-2990.

(See Next Column)

MEMBERS OF FIRM
COLUMBUS, OHIO OFFICE

Robert L. Brubaker
Anthony J. Celebrezze, Jr.
Daniel R. Conway
Janet J. Henry
J. Jeffrey McNealey
Samuel H. Porter
Christopher R. Schraff
Martin S. Seltzer

ASSOCIATE
COLUMBUS, OHIO OFFICE

Alaine Y. Miller

Representative Clients: American Electric Power Service Corporation; Aristech Chemical Corporation; Armco, Inc.; Champion International Corporation; The Cincinnati Gas & Electric Company; Ford Motor Co.; Ohio Chemical Council; The Ohio Edison Company; Printing Industries of Ohio.

For Complete List of Firm Personnel, See General Section

For full biographical listings, see the Martindale-Hubbell Law Directory

* **THOMPSON, HINE AND FLORY** (AV)

One Columbus, 10 West Broad Street, 43215-3435
Telephone: 614-469-3200
Fax: 614-469-3361
Akron, Ohio Office: 50 S. Main Street, Suite 502, 44308-1828.
Telephone: 216-376-8090.
Fax: 216-376-8386.
Cincinnati, Ohio Office: 312 Walnut Street, 14th Floor, 45202-4029.
Telephone: 513-352-6700.
Fax: 513-241-4771.
Telex: 938003.
Cleveland, Ohio Office: 1100 National City Bank Building, 629 Euclid Avenue, 44114-3070.
Telephone: 216-566-5500.
Fax: 216-556-5583.
Telex: 980217.
Cable Address: "Thomflor".
Dayton, Ohio Office: 2000 Courthouse Plaza, N.E., 45402-1706.
Telephone: 513-443-6600.
Fax: 513-443-6637; 443-6635.
Palm Beach, Florida Office: 125 Worth Avenue, 33480-4466.
Telephone: 407-833-5900.
Fax: 407-833-5951.
Washington, D.C. Office: 1920 N Street, N.W., 20036-1601.
Telephone: 202-331-8800.
Fax: 202-331-8330.
Telex: 904173.
Cable Address: "Caglaw".
Brussels, Belgium Office: Rue des Chevaliers / Ridderstraat 14 - B.10, B - 1050.
Telephone: 011(32-2) 511-9326.
Fax: 011(32-2) 513-9206.

MEMBER OF FIRM

Ben L. Pfefferle, III

ASSOCIATE

Christopher Jones

For Complete List of Firm Personnel, See General Section

For full biographical listings, see the Martindale-Hubbell Law Directory

*DAYTON,** Montgomery Co.

FARUKI GILLIAM & IRELAND (AV)

600 Courthouse Plaza, S.W., 10 North Ludlow Street, 45402
Telephone: 513-227-3700
Fax: 513-227-3717

MEMBERS OF FIRM

Charles J. Faruki
Armistead W. Gilliam, Jr.
D. Jeffrey Ireland
Ann Wightman

Jeffrey T. Cox
Mary L. Wiseman

For full biographical listings, see the Martindale-Hubbell Law Directory

SEBALY, SHILLITO & DYER (AV)

1300 Courthouse Plaza, NE, P.O. Box 220, 45402-0220
Telephone: 513-222-2500
Telefax: 513-222-6554; 222-8279
Springfield, Ohio Office: National City Bank Building, 4 West Main Street, Suite 530, P.O. Box 1346, 45501-1346.
Telephone: 513-325-7878.
Telefax: 513-325-6151.

MEMBERS OF FIRM

James A. Dyer
Gale S. Finley
William W. Lambert
Michael P. Moloney
Mary Lynn Readey
Jon M. Sebaly
Beverly F. Shillito
Jeffrey B. Shulman
Karl R. Ulrich
Robert A. Vaughn
(Resident, Springfield Office)

(See Next Column)

SEBALY, SHILLITO & DYER—*Continued*

Martin A. Beyer
Daniel A. Brown
Anne L. Rhoades
Orly R. Rumberg
Juliana M. Spaeth
Kendra F. Thompson

For full biographical listings, see the Martindale-Hubbell Law Directory

THOMPSON, HINE AND FLORY (AV)

2000 Courthouse Plaza, N.E., 45402-1706
Telephone: 513-443-6600
Fax: 513-443-6637; 443-6635
Akron, Ohio Office: 50 S. Main Street, Suite 502, 44308-1828.
Telephone: 216-376-8090.
Fax: 216-376-8386.
Cincinnati, Ohio Office: 312 Walnut Street, 14th Floor, 45202-4029.
Telephone: 513-352-6700.
Fax: 513-241-4771.
Telex: 938003.
Cleveland, Ohio Office: 1100 National City Bank Building, 629 Euclid Avenue, 44114-3070.
Telephone: 216-566-5500.
Fax: 216-556-5583.
Telex: 980217.
Cable Address: "Thomflor".
Columbus, Ohio Office: One Columbus, 10 West Broad Street, 43215-3435.
Telephone: 614-469-3200.
Fax: 614-469-3361.
Palm Beach, Florida Office: 125 Worth Avenue, 33480-4466.
Telephone: 407-833-5900.
Fax: 407-833-5951.
Washington, D.C. Office: 1920 N Street, N.W., 20036-1601.
Telephone: 202-331-8800.
Fax: 202-331-8330.
Telex: 904173.
Cable Address: "Caglaw".
Brussels, Belgium Office: Rue des Chevaliers / Ridderstraat 14 - B.10, B - 1050.
Telephone: 011(32-2) 511-9326.
Fax: 011(32-2) 513-9206.

MEMBER OF FIRM

J. Wray Blattner

For Complete List of Firm Personnel, See General Section

For full biographical listings, see the Martindale-Hubbell Law Directory

YOUNG & ALEXANDER CO., L.P.A. (AV)

Suite 100, 367 West Second Street, 45402
Telephone: 513-224-9291
Telecopier: 513-224-9679
Cincinnati, Ohio Office: 110 Boggs Lane, Suite 350.
Telephone: 513-326-5555.
FAX: 513-326-5550.

James M. Brennan
A. Mark Segreti, Jr.

Counsel for: The Children's Medical Center, Dayton, Ohio; The Colonial Stair & Woodwork Co.; The Greater Dayton Area Hospital Assn.; Mike-Sell's Potato Chip Co.; Moorman Pontiac, Inc.
Local Counsel for: Colonial Penn Insurance Co.; John Hancock Mutual Life Insurance Co.; Hertz Corp.; State Farm Insurance Co.

For Complete List of Firm Personnel, See General Section

For full biographical listings, see the Martindale-Hubbell Law Directory

*TOLEDO,** Lucas Co.

EASTMAN & SMITH (AV)

One Seagate, Twenty-Fourth Floor, 43604
Telephone: 419-241-6000
Telecopier: 419-247-1777
Columbus, Ohio Office: 65 East State Street, Suite 1000, 43215.
Telephone: 614-460-3556.
Telecopier: 614-228-5371.

MEMBERS OF FIRM

Richard T. Sargeant
Robert J. Gilmer, Jr.
Joseph A. Gregg
Dirk P. Plessner

ASSOCIATES

David W. Nunn
Beth J. Olson
Albin Bauer, II

Representative Clients: Envirosafe Services of Ohio, Inc.; 21 International Holdings, Inc.; United Technologies Corporation; Toledo-Lucas County Port Authority; Kelsey-Hayes Company; BEC Laboratories; Marathon Oil Company; OmniSource Corporation; Ameritech Services, Inc.; Master Chemical.

For Complete List of Firm Personnel, See General Section

For full biographical listings, see the Martindale-Hubbell Law Directory

FULLER & HENRY (AV)

One Seagate Suite 1700, P.O. Box 2088, 43603-2088
Telephone: 419-247-2500
Telecopier: 419-247-2665
Port Clinton, Ohio Office: 125 Jefferson.
Telephone: 419-734-2153.
Telecopier: 419-732-8246.
Columbus, Ohio Office: 2210 Huntington Center, 41 South High Street.
Telephone: 614-228-6611.
Telecopier: 614-228-6623.

MEMBERS OF FIRM

Louis E. Tosi
William L. Patberg
Douglas G. Haynam
Michael E. Born

COUNSEL

Nirav D. Parikh

ASSOCIATES

Michael J. O'Callaghan
Craig A. Sturtz
Linda S. Woggon

Representative Clients: General Motors Corp.; Ohio Electric Utility Institute Environmental Committee; The Toledo Edison Company; Centerior Energy Corp.; The Goodyear Tire & Rubber Company; The BF Goodrich Company; Owens-Illinois, Inc.; Libbey-Owens-Ford Co.; GSX Chemical Services of Ohio; BP America.

For Complete List of Firm Personnel, See General Section

For full biographical listings, see the Martindale-Hubbell Law Directory

OKLAHOMA

LAVERNE, Harper Co.

G. W. ARMOR (AV)

103 West Main Street, P.O. Box 267, 73848
Telephone: 405-921-3335
FAX: 405-921-5720

*OKLAHOMA CITY,** Oklahoma Co.

ANDREWS DAVIS LEGG BIXLER MILSTEN & PRICE, A PROFESSIONAL CORPORATION (AV)

500 West Main, 73102
Telephone: 405-272-9241
FAX: 405-235-8786

J. Edward Barth
C. Temple Bixler
John J. Breathwit
Charles C. Callaway, Jr.
James F. Davis
William J. Legg
Babette Patton
R. Brown Wallace
William D. Watts

Lynn O. Holloman
Shelia Darling Tims

Representative Clients: Browning-Ferris Industries, Inc.; Marathon Oil Co.; Oklahoma Dental Assn.; Oklahoma City Municipal Improvement Authority; The City of Oklahoma City.

For Complete List of Firm Personnel, See General Section

For full biographical listings, see the Martindale-Hubbell Law Directory

DAY, EDWARDS, FEDERMAN, PROPESTER & CHRISTENSEN, P.C. (AV)

Suite 2900 First Oklahoma Tower, 210 Park Avenue, 73102-5605
Telephone: 405-239-2121
Telecopier: 405-236-1012

Bruce W. Day
Joe E. Edwards
William B. Federman
Richard P. Propester
D. Wade Christensen
J. Clay Christensen
Kent A. Gilliland
Rodney J. Heggy
Ricki Valerie Sonders
Thomas Pitchlynn Howell, IV
John C. Platt

David R. Widdoes
Lori R. Roberts
Carolyn A. Romberg

OF COUNSEL

Herbert F. (Jack) Hewett
Jeanette Cook Timmons
Joel Warren Harmon
Jane S. Eulberg
Mark A. Cohen

Representative Clients: Aetna Life Insurance Co.; Boatmen's First National Bank of Oklahoma; Borg-Warner Chemicals, Inc.; City Bank & Trust; Federal Deposit Insurance Corp.; Bank One, Oklahoma City; Haskell Lemon Construction Co.; Merrill Lynch, Pierce, Fenner & Smith, Inc.; Prudential Securities, Inc.

For full biographical listings, see the Martindale-Hubbell Law Directory

Oklahoma City—Continued

Holloway, Dobson, Hudson, Bachman, Alden, Jennings, Robertson & Holloway, A Professional Corporation (AV)

Suite 900 One Leadership Square 211 North Robinson, 73102-7102
Telephone: 405-235-8593
Fax: 405-235-1707

Ronald R. Hudson Gary C. Bachman

Representing: Associated Aviation Underwriters; Chubb Group of Insurance Cos.; Continental Insurance Cos; General Motors Corp.

For full biographical listings, see the Martindale-Hubbell Law Directory

Kerr, Irvine, Rhodes & Ables, A Professional Corporation (AV)

600 Bank of Oklahoma Plaza, 73102-4267
Telephone: 405-272-9221
Fax: 405-236-3121

Horace G. Rhodes F. Andrew Fugitt

James R. Barnett R. Thomas Lay

For Complete List of Firm Personnel, See General Section

For full biographical listings, see the Martindale-Hubbell Law Directory

Manchester & Pignato, P.C. (AV)

Third Floor Colcord Building, 15 North Robinson, 73102
Telephone: 405-235-2222
Fax: 405-235-2204

Robert Edward Manchester Gerard F. Pignato

Stacey L. Haws Shannon K. Emmons
Susan Ann Knight

Representative Clients: CMI Corporation; Electric Mutual Liability Insurance Company; Otis Elevator Company; Budget Rent-A-Car Systems, Inc.; Essex Insurance Company; American Bankers Insurance Company of Florida; Motors Insurance Company; Lexington Insurance Company; City of Oklahoma City.

For full biographical listings, see the Martindale-Hubbell Law Directory

*TULSA,** Tulsa Co.

Gable & Gotwals (AV)

2000 Bank IV Center, 15 West Sixth Street, 74119-5447
Telephone: 918-582-9201
Facsimile: 918-586-8383

Teresa B. Adwan
Pamela S. Anderson
John R. Barker
David L. Bryant
Gene C. Buzzard
Dennis Clarke Cameron
Timothy A. Carney
Renee DeMoss
Elsie C. Draper
Sidney G. Dunagan
Theodore Q. Eliot
Richard W. Gable
Jeffrey Don Hassell
Patricia Ledvina Himes
Oliver S. Howard
Richard D. Koljack, Jr.
J. Daniel Morgan
Joseph W. Morris
Elizabeth R. Muratet
Richard B. Noulles
Ronald N. Ricketts
John Henry Rule
M. Benjamin Singletary
James M. Sturdivant
Patrick O. Waddel
Michael D. Hall
David Edward Keglovits
Stephen W. Lake
Kari S. McKee
Terry D. Ragsdale
Jeffrey C. Rambach

OF COUNSEL

G. Ellis Gable Charles P. Gotwals, Jr.

For full biographical listings, see the Martindale-Hubbell Law Directory

Shipley, Inhofe & Strecker (AV)

Suite 3600 First National Tower, 15 East Fifth Street, 74103-4307
Telephone: 918-582-1720
FAX: 918-584-7681

MEMBERS OF FIRM

Charles W. Shipley David E. Strecker
Douglas L. Inhofe Mark B. Jennings
Blake K. Champlin

ASSOCIATES

Leslie C. Rinn Connie L. Kirkland
Jamie Taylor Boyd Mark Alston Waller

Reference: Western National Bank, Tulsa.

For full biographical listings, see the Martindale-Hubbell Law Directory

OREGON

*PORTLAND,** Multnomah Co.

Black Helterline (AV)

1200 The Bank of California Tower, 707 S.W. Washington Street, 97205
Telephone: 503-224-5560
Telecopier: 503-224-6148

MEMBERS OF FIRM

Ronald T. Adams Paul R. Hribernick
Steven R. Schell

ASSOCIATE

Stark Ackerman

Representative Clients: Catellus Development Corporation; Columbia Corridor Association; ESCO Corp.; K-4, Inc.; MCI Communications Corporation; NAACO Materials Handling Group, Inc.; Rivergreen Construction, Inc.; The Sivers Companies; Sunshine Dairy Foods, Inc.; Thomas Industries, Inc.

For Complete List of Firm Personnel, See General Section

For full biographical listings, see the Martindale-Hubbell Law Directory

Josselson, Potter & Roberts (AV)

53 S.W. Yamhill Street, 97204
Telephone: 503-228-1455
Facsimile: 503-228-0171

MEMBERS OF FIRM

Frank Josselson Irving W. Potter
Leslie M. Roberts

OF COUNSEL

Lawrence R. Derr

For full biographical listings, see the Martindale-Hubbell Law Directory

O'Donnell, Ramis, Crew, Corrigan & Bachrach (AV)

Ballow & Wright Building, 1727 N.W. Hoyt Street, 97209
Telephone: 503-222-4402
FAX: 503-243-2944
Clackamas County Office: Suite 202, 181 N. Grant, Canby.
Telephone: 503-266-1149.

MEMBERS OF FIRM

Timothy V. Ramis Stephen F. Crew

For full biographical listings, see the Martindale-Hubbell Law Directory

Sussman Shank Wapnick Caplan & Stiles (AV)

1000 S.W. Broadway Suite 1400, 97205
Telephone: 503-227-1111
Telecopier: 503-248-0130

MEMBERS OF FIRM

John P. Davenport Jeffrey R. Spere

ASSOCIATE

Gary E. Enloe

For Complete List of Firm Personnel, See General Section

For full biographical listings, see the Martindale-Hubbell Law Directory

PENNSYLVANIA

BALA CYNWYD, Montgomery Co.

Manko, Gold & Katcher (AV)

401 City Avenue, 19004
Telephone: 610-660-5700
Fax: 610-660-5711
Marlton, New Jersey Office: 1 Eves Drive, Suite 111, 08053.
Telephone: 609-596-4062.
Fax: 609-596-7299.

MEMBERS OF FIRM

Joseph M. Manko
Marc E. Gold
Bruce S. Katcher
Kenneth J. Warren
Kermit Rader
Neil S. Witkes
Michael M. Meloy
Robert D. Fox
Steven T. Miano

(See Next Column)

MANKO, GOLD & KATCHER—*Continued*

ASSOCIATES

Deane H. Bartlett
Pamela H. Woldow
Jill M. Hyman
Jonathan E. Rinde
Randi S. Garnick
John F. Gullace
Marc LaPalombara Frohman
Bart Cassidy
Jonathan H. Spergel
Madeleine H. Cozine
Brenda Hustis Gotanda (Not admitted in PA)

LEGAL SUPPORT PERSONNEL

Darryl D. Borrelli

For full biographical listings, see the Martindale-Hubbell Law Directory

*HARRISBURG,** Dauphin Co.

BUCHANAN INGERSOLL, PROFESSIONAL CORPORATION (AV)

Vartan Parc, 30 North Third Street, 17101
Telephone: 717-237-4800
Telecopier: 717-233-0852
Pittsburgh, Pennsylvania Office: 5800 USX Tower, 600 Grant Street.
Telephone: 412-562-8800.
Philadelphia, Pennsylvania Office: Two Logan Square, Twelfth Floor, 18th & Arch Streets.
Telephone: 215-665-8700.
Tampa, Florida Office: 101 East Kennedy Boulevard, Suite 1030.
Telephone: 813-222-8180.
North Miami Beach, Florida Office: 19495 Biscayne Boulevard.
Telephone: 305-933-5600.
Lexington, Kentucky Office: 1210 Vine Center Office Tower, 333 West Vine Street.
Telephone: 606-225-5333.
Princeton, New Jersey Office: Buchanan Ingersoll, A Partnership, College Centre, 500 College Road East.
Telephone: 609-452-2666.

Michael T. McCarthy

SENIOR ATTORNEY

Richard H. Friedman

For Complete List of Firm Personnel, See General Section

For full biographical listings, see the Martindale-Hubbell Law Directory

KILLIAN & GEPHART (AV)

218 Pine Street, P.O. Box 886, 17108
Telephone: 717-232-1851
Telecopier: 717-238-0592

MEMBERS OF FIRM

John D. Killian
Smith B. Gephart
Thomas W. Scott
Jane Penny Malatesta
Terrence J. McGowan
Ronda K. Kiser
Paula J. McDermott

ASSOCIATES

Shaun E. O'Toole
J. Paul Helvy

Reference: Dauphin Deposit Bank & Trust Co.

For full biographical listings, see the Martindale-Hubbell Law Directory

MCNEES, WALLACE & NURICK (AV)

100 Pine Street, P.O. Box 1166, 17108
Telephone: 717-232-8000
Fax: 717-237-5300

MEMBERS OF FIRM

Terry R. Bossert
Elizabeth A. Dougherty
Bernard A. Labuskes, Jr.

ASSOCIATES

Scott A. Gould
Derrick P. Williamson

For Complete List of Firm Personnel, See General Section

For full biographical listings, see the Martindale-Hubbell Law Directory

METTE, EVANS & WOODSIDE, A PROFESSIONAL CORPORATION (AV)

3401 North Front Street, P.O. Box 5950, 17110-0950
Telephone: 717-232-5000
Telecopier: 717-236-1816

James W. Evans
Charles B. Zwally
Daniel L. Sullivan
Michael D. Reed
Robert P. Haynes III
Paula J. Leicht

Guy P. Beneventano
Michael D. Pipa
Robyn J. Katzman

Counsel for: The B. F. Goodrich Co.; Juniata Valley Financial Corp.; MCI Telecommunications Corp.; Monongahela Power Co.; The Procter and Gamble Paper Products Co.; United States Fidelity and Guaranty Co.; Community Banks; GTE Products Corp.; Commerce Bank.

(See Next Column)

For Complete List of Firm Personnel, See General Section

For full biographical listings, see the Martindale-Hubbell Law Directory

NAUMAN, SMITH, SHISSLER & HALL (AV)

Eighteenth Floor, 200 North Third Street, P.O. Box 840, 17108-0840
Telephone: 717-236-3010
Telefax: 717-234-1925

MEMBERS OF FIRM

David C. Eaton
Spencer G. Nauman, Jr.
John C. Sullivan
J. Stephen Feinour
Craig J. Staudenmaier

ASSOCIATES

Benjamin Charles Dunlap, Jr.
Stephen J. Keene

OF COUNSEL

Ralph W. Boyles, Jr.

Representative Clients: Consolidated Rail Corp.; The W.O. Hickok Mfg. Co.; Delta Dental of Pennsylvania; Mellon Bank, N.A.; PNC Bank, N.A.; General Motors Acceptance Corp.; Chrysler Credit Corp.

For full biographical listings, see the Martindale-Hubbell Law Directory

RHOADS & SINON (AV)

One South Market Square, 12th Floor, P.O. Box 1146, 17108-1146
Telephone: 717-233-5731
Fax: 717-232-1459
Boca Raton, Florida Affiliated Office: Suite 301, 299 West Camino Gardens Boulevard.
Telephone: 407-395-5595.
Fax: 407-395-9497.
Lancaster, Pennsylvania Office: 15 North Lime Street.
Telephone: 717-397-5127.
Fax: 717-397-5267.

MEMBERS OF FIRM

Sherill T. Moyer
Jan P. Paden
R. Stephen Shibla
Charles E. Gutshall

ASSOCIATES

Shawn D. Lochinger
Susan E. Schwab

For Complete List of Firm Personnel, See General Section

For full biographical listings, see the Martindale-Hubbell Law Directory

*INDIANA,** Indiana Co.

BONYA AND DOUGLASS (AV)

134 South Sixth Street, 15701
Telephone: 412-465-5535
Fax: 412-465-9685

MEMBERS OF FIRM

John A. Bonya
Stanley P. DeGory
Robert D. Douglass
Beverly A. Gazza
Nicholas J. Mikesic
David M. Zimmerman

Reference: S & T Bank, of Indiana, Pennsylvania.

For full biographical listings, see the Martindale-Hubbell Law Directory

LANSDALE, Montgomery Co.

PEARLSTINE/SALKIN ASSOCIATES (AV)

1250 South Broad Street Suite 1000, P.O. Box 431, 19446
Telephone: 215-699-6000
Fax: 215-699-0231

MEMBERS OF FIRM

Philip Salkin
Ronald E. Robinson
Barry Cooperberg
Frederick C. Horn
Marc B. Davis
William R. Wanger
F. Craig La Rocca
Jeffrey T. Sultanik
Neal R. Pearlstine
Wendy G. Rothstein
Alan L. Eisen
Glenn D. Fox

Wilhelm L. Gruszecki
Brian E. Subers
Mark S. Cappuccio
James R. Hall
Michael S. Paul
David J. Draganosky
Lawrence P. Kempner

For full biographical listings, see the Martindale-Hubbell Law Directory

*MEDIA,** Delaware Co.

KASSAB ARCHBOLD JACKSON & O'BRIEN (AV)

Lawyers-Title Building, 214 North Jackson Street, P.O. Box 626, 19063
Telephone: 610-565-3800
Telecopier: 610-892-6888
Wilmington, Delaware Office: 1326 King Street.
Telephone: 302-656-3393.
Fax: 302-656-1993.
Wildwood, New Jersey Office: 5201 New Jersey Avenue.
Telephone: 609-522-6559.

(See Next Column)

KASSAB ARCHBOLD JACKSON & O'BRIEN, *Media—Continued*

MEMBERS OF FIRM

Edward Kassab
William C. Archbold, Jr.
Robert James Jackson
Joseph Patrick O'Brien
Richard A. Stanko
Roy T. J. Stegena

OF COUNSEL

Matthew J. Ryan
John W. Nilon, Jr.

ASSOCIATES

Kevin William Gibson
Cynthia Kassab Larosa
Marc S. Stein
Terrance A. Kline
George C. McFarland, Jr.
Jill E. Aversa
Pamela A. La Torre
Kenneth D. Kynett

Representative Clients furnished upon request.

For full biographical listings, see the Martindale-Hubbell Law Directory

*PHILADELPHIA,** Philadelphia Co.

BALLARD SPAHR ANDREWS & INGERSOLL (AV)

1735 Market Street, 51st Floor, 19103-7599
Telephone: 215-665-8500
Fax: 215-864-8999
Denver, Colorado Office: Seventeenth Street Plaza Building, Suite 2300, 1225 17th Street.
Telephone: 303-292-2400.
Fax: 303-296-3956.
Kaunas, Lithuania Office: Donelaicio g., 71-2, Kaunas 3000.
Telephone: (370-7) 20 56 66.
Fax: (370-7) 20 56 91.
Salt Lake City, Utah Office: One Utah Center, Suite 1200, 201 South Main Street.
Telephone: 801-531-3000.
Fax: 801-531-3001.
Washington, D.C. Office: Suite 900 East, 555 13th Street, N.W.
Telephone: 202-383-8800.
Fax: 202-383-8877; 383-8893.
Baltimore, Maryland Office: 300 East Lombard Street. 19th Floor.
Telephone: 410-528-5600.
Fax: 410-528-5650.
Camden, New Jersey Office: 800 Hudson Square, 5th Floor.
Telephone: 609-541-5577.
Fax: 609-541-8272.

David G. Mandelbaum
Robert B. McKinstry, Jr.
Glenn L. Unterberger

Brendan K. Collins
Michael F. Reilly
Jeanne J. Dworetzky
Harry R. Weiss

For Complete List of Firm Personnel, See General Section

For full biographical listings, see the Martindale-Hubbell Law Directory

BUCHANAN INGERSOLL, PROFESSIONAL CORPORATION (AV)

Two Logan Square Twelfth Floor, 18th & Arch Streets, 19103
Telephone: 215-665-8700
Telecopier: 215-569-2066
Pittsburgh, Pennsylvania Office: 5800 USX Tower, 600 Grant Street.
Telephone: 412-562-8800.
Harrisburg, Pennsylvania Office: Vartan Parc, 30 North Third Street.
Telephone: 717-237-4800.
Tampa, Florida Office: 101 East Kennedy Boulevard, Suite 1030.
Telephone: 813-222-8180.
North Miami Beach, Florida Office: 19495 Biscayne Boulevard.
Telephone: 305-933-5600.
Lexington, Kentucky Office: 1210 Vine Center Office Tower, 333 West Vine Street.
Telephone: 606-225-5333.
Princeton, New Jersey Office: Buchanan Ingersoll, A Partnership, College Centre, 500 College Road East.
Telephone: 609-452-2666.

Stephen C. Braverman
Antoinette R. Stone

Fern L. McGovern

For Complete List of Firm Personnel, See General Section

For full biographical listings, see the Martindale-Hubbell Law Directory

JOHN GERARD DEVLIN & ASSOCIATES, P.C. (AV)

2100 Fidelity Building, P.O. Box 58908, 19109
Telephone: 215-545-4190
Telefax: 215-564-6732
Allentown, Pennsylvania Office: The Sovereign Building, Executive Suite 103, 609 Hamilton Mall.
Telephone: 215-820-6422.
Westmont, New Jersey Office: 216 Haddon Avenue, Suite 103, 08108.
Telephone: 609-858-1690.
FAX: 609-858-8998.

(See Next Column)

East Brunswick, New Jersey Office: 190 Route 18, Suite 3000, 08816.
Telephone: 908-214-2621.
Fax: 908-246-2917.

John Gerard Devlin
James B. Corrigan, Jr.
Joseph T. Murphy, Jr.
Louis J. Mairone, Jr.
J. Brian Durkin
Thomas Paschos
Joseph A. Whip, Jr.
Michael Malarick (East Brunswick, N.J. and Westmont, N.J. Offices)
Dora R. Garcia

Representative Clients: Lloyds of London; Commercial Union; John Hancock Property and Casualty Insurance Co.; Sentry Insurance Co.; Wausau Insurance Co.; State Farms Insurance Co.; Hanseco Insurance Co.; American Family Insurance Co.; Liberty Mutual Insurance Co.; Linberg Adjustment Co.

For full biographical listings, see the Martindale-Hubbell Law Directory

DUANE, MORRIS & HECKSCHER (AV)

Suite 4200 One Liberty Place, 19103-7396
Telephone: 215-979-1000
FAX: 215-979-1020
Harrisburg, Pennsylvania Office: 305 North Front Street, 5th Floor, P.O. Box 1003.
Telephone: 717-237-5500.
Fax: 717-232-4015.
Wilmington, Delaware Office: Suite 1500, 1201 Market Street.
Telephone: 302-571-5550.
Fax: 302-571-5560.
New York, N.Y. Office: 112 E. 42nd Street, Suite 2125.
Telephone: 212-499-0410.
Fax: 212-499-0420.
Wayne, Pennsylvania Office 735 Chesterbrook Boulevard, Suite 300.
Telephone: 610-647-3555.
Allentown, Pennsylvania Office: 968 Postal Road, Suite 200.
Telephone: 610-266-3650.
Fax: 610-640-2619.
Cherry Hill, New Jersey Office: 51 Haddonfield Road, Suite 340.
Telephone: 609-488-7300.
Fax: 609-488-7021.

MEMBERS OF FIRM

David C. Toomey
David E. Loder
Robert L. Pratter
Amy E. Wilkinson
Seth v.d.H. Cooley

ASSOCIATES

Larry D. Silver
Nancy Conrad
E. Lynne Hirsch
Lisa W. Clark
Deborah Tate Pecci
Paula Terese Ryan

*Hasday & Margulis, A Professional Corporation

For Complete List of Firm Personnel, See General Section

For full biographical listings, see the Martindale-Hubbell Law Directory

GERMAN, GALLAGHER & MURTAGH, A PROFESSIONAL CORPORATION (AV)

Fifth Floor, The Bellevue, 200 South Broad Street, 19102
Telephone: 215-545-7700
Telecopier: 215-732-4182
Cherry Hill, New Jersey Office: Suite 643, 1040 North Kings Highway.
Telephone: 609-667-7676.
Lancaster, Pennsylvania Office: 40 East Grant Street.
Telephone: 717-293-8070.

Edward C. German
Michael D. Gallagher
Dean F. Murtagh
Philip A. Ryan
Robert P. Corbin
David P. Rovner
Kathryn A. Dux
Gary R. Gremminger
Kim Plouffe
Jeffrey N. German
John P. Shusted

Kathleen M. Carson
Kevin R. McNulty
Linda Porr Sweeney
Gary H. Hunter
Frank A. Gerolamo, III
Milan K. Mrkobrad
Thomas M. Going
Vincent J. Di Stefano, Jr.
Jack T. Ribble, Jr.
Kimberly J. Keiser
Bernard E. Jude Quinn
Gerald C. Montella
Lisa Beth Zucker
Shelby L. Mattioli
Daniel J. Divis
D. Selaine Belver
Christine L. Davis
Daniel L. Grill
Marta I. Sierra-Epperson
Paul G. Kirk
Aileen R. Thompson
Otis V. Maynard
Gregory S. Capps

For full biographical listings, see the Martindale-Hubbell Law Directory

Philadelphia—Continued

KENT & MCBRIDE, P.C. (AV)

Two Logan Square, Suite 600 18th and Arch Streets, 19103
Telephone: 215-568-1800
Fax: 215-568-1830
Audubon, New Jersey Office: 201 South Whitehorse Pike.
Telephone: 609-547-4474.
Fax: 609-547-0741.

John F. Kent
Denis P. McBride

Martin A. Durkin, Jr.
Kevin G. Dronson
Anne Manero
Jay D. Branderbit
Joseph Andrew Sellitti
John P. Shea
Laura R. Shmerler
Kimberly S. Gannon

For full biographical listings, see the Martindale-Hubbell Law Directory

KITTREDGE, DONLEY, ELSON, FULLEM & EMBICK (AV)

Fifth Floor, The Bank Building, 421 Chestnut Street, 19106
Telephone: 215-829-9900
Fax: 215-829-9888

MEMBERS OF FIRM

Patrick W. Kittredge
Joseph M. Donley
Barry R. Elson
Joseph W. Fullem, Jr.
John R. Embick

ASSOCIATES

Regina M. Harbaugh
Glenn E. Davis
Betsy F. Sternthal
Michael S. Soulé
Gary M. Marek
Patricia Powers
Daniel J. Maher
Susanne L. Longenhagen
Michael K. Smith
Richard J. Sestak

For full biographical listings, see the Martindale-Hubbell Law Directory

LEVIN, FISHBEIN, SEDRAN & BERMAN (AV)

Suite 600, 320 Walnut Street, 19106
Telephone: 215-592-1500
Fax: 215-592-4663

MEMBERS OF FIRM

Arnold Levin
Michael D. Fishbein
Howard J. Sedran
Laurence S. Berman
Frederick S. Longer

Robert M. Unterberger
Craig D. Ginsburg
Jonathan Shub
Cheryl R. Brown Hill
Roberta Shaner

For full biographical listings, see the Martindale-Hubbell Law Directory

MANTA AND WELGE (AV)

A Partnership of Professional Corporations
One Commerce Square, 37th Floor, 2005 Market Street, 19103
Telephone: 215-851-6600
Telecopy: 215-851-6644
Allentown, Pennsylvania Office: Suite 115 Commerce Plaza, 5050 Tilghman Street.
Telephone: 215-395-7499.
Fax: 215-398-7878.
Princeton, New Jersey Office: 101 Carnegie Center, Suite 215. P.O. Box 5306.
Telephone: 609-452-8833.
Fax: 609-452-9109.
Cherry Hill, New Jersey Office: Suite 600, 1040 North King Highway.
Telephone: 609-795-7611.
Fax: 609-795-7612.

MEMBERS OF FIRM

Joseph G. Manta
Mark A. Welge
William R. Hourican
Albert L. Piccerilli
John C. Sullivan
Joel Schneider
Joseph M. Cincotta
James V. Bielunas
Richard S. Mannella
Joanne M. Walker
Francis McGill Hadden
Walter A. Stewart

OF COUNSEL

Albert J. Bartosic

Peter F. Rosenthal
Susan Simpson-Brown
Gregory S. Thomas
Andrea L. Smith
Anton G. Marzano
Margaret E. Wenke
Wendy F. Tucker
Jacqueline Borock
David G. C. Arnold
Karen C. Buck
Laurie A. Carroll
Mark J. Manta
David S. Florig
Stephen F. Brock
Geoffrey J. Alexander
Wendy R. S. O'Connor
Kathleen K. Kerns
Fernando Santiago
Peter L. Frattarelli
Holly C. Dobrosky

For full biographical listings, see the Martindale-Hubbell Law Directory

MARGOLIS, EDELSTEIN & SCHERLIS (AV)

The Curtis Center, Fourth Floor, One Independence Square West, 19106-3304
Telephone: 215-922-1100
FAX: 215-922-1772
Telex: 62021004
Associated Law Firm: Slimm & Goldberg, 216 Haddon Avenue, Suite 750, Westmont, New Jersey, 08108-2886.
Telephone: 609-858-7200.
FAX: 609-858-1017.

MEMBERS OF FIRM

Alan Wm. Margolis
Edward L. Edelstein
Edwin L. Scherlis
Joseph S. Bekelja
Joseph Goldberg
John L. Slimm (Not admitted in PA)
Leonard S. Lipson
Michael P. McKenna
Mitchell S. Pinsly
Carl Anthony Maio
Gordon Gelfond
Donald M. Davis
Melvin R. Shuster
Christopher J. Pakuris
Marshall A. Haislup, III
Bruce E. Barrett (Resident, Westmont, New Jersey Office)
J. Vincent Roche
Gary B. Cutler
Michael D. Eiss
Mark N. Cohen
Robert M. Kaplan (Not admitted in PA)
Andrew J. Gallogly
Marc B. Zingarini
William B. Hildebrand
Richard J. Margolis
Glenn A. Ricketti
Michael J. Cawley
Anne E. Pedersen
Kenneth J. Sylvester (Resident, Westmont, New Jersey Office)
Colleen M. Ready (Resident, Westmont, New Jersey Office)
Richard T. Smith (Resident, Westmont, New Jersey Office)
H. Marc Tepper
James B. Dougherty, Jr.
Carol Ann Murphy
Janis L. Wilson

Nancy H. Resnick
Eric J. Daniel (Resident, Westmont, New Jersey Office)
R. Barry Strosnider (Resident, Westmont, New Jersey Office)
Elit R. Felix, II
James M. Prahler
Michael G. Conroy
David F. Luvara (Resident, Westmont, New Jersey Office)
James F. Wiley, III
Lawrence J. Bunis
Kevin R. Dochney (Resident, Westmont, New Jersey Office)
Peter D. Bludman
Lisa B. Flickstein
Barbara A. Thomas
Hiliary L. Remick
Mary C. Cunnane
Deborah L. Doyle
Sandra R. Craig
Debra S. Goodman
Timothy J. McCuen
Marilyn A. Della Badia
Dawn Dezii (Resident, Westmont, New Jersey Office)
John C. Farrell
Lila Wynne Williams (Resident, Westmont, New Jersey Office)
Emily H. Armstrong (Not admitted in PA; Resident, Westmont, New Jersey Office)
Donald Caruthers III (Resident, Westmont, New Jersey Office)
Jean M. Hadley
Mark A. Minicozzi
Robert D. MacMahon
Hilary Suzanne Cornell
Marie Sambor Reilly
Jill Innamorato
Michael L. Simonini (Resident, Westmont, New Jersey Office)
Peter S. Cuddihy (Resident, Westmont, New Jersey Office)
Elizabeth Horneff
Robert D. Shapiro
Sandhya M. Feltes
Kevin S. Riechelson
Jennifer A. Mullen (Resident, Westmont, New Jersey Office)
Tracy A. Tefankjian
Frank A. LaSalvia (Resident, Westmont, New Jersey Office)
James A. Tamburro (Resident, Westmont, New Jersey Office)
Laurie Harrold Rizzo (Resident, Westmont, New Jersey Office)
Stuart L. Berman
John D. Pallante
Timothy E. Games
Frank A. DiGiacomo (Resident, Westmont, New Jersey Office)
Frederic Roller
Vincent A. Vietti
Jill A. Maslynsky
Johanna E. Markind
James P. Paoli (Resident, Westmont, New Jersey Office)
Diana Brilliant
Thomas P. Donnelly
Andrea M. Jenkins
Karen E. Model
Dawn S. Osman
Scott I. Feldman
Stephen P. Yuhas (Resident, Westmont, New Jersey Office)

COUNSEL TO THE FIRM

Nathan L. Edelstein

OF COUNSEL

Michael A. Orlando (Not admitted in PA; Resident, Westmont, New Jersey Office)

For full biographical listings, see the Martindale-Hubbell Law Directory

MARKS, O'NEILL, REILLY & O'BRIEN, P.C. (AV)

1880 John F. Kennedy Boulevard Suite 1200, 19103
Telephone: 215-564-6688
Fax: 215-564-2526
Norristown, Pennsylvania Office: 411 Cherry Street.
Telephone: 215-277-7601.
Westmont, New Jersey Office: 216 Haddon Avenue, Suite 403.
Telephone: 609-858-6110.
Fax: 609-858-3687.

(See Next Column)

MARKS, O'NEILL, REILLY & O'BRIEN P.C., *Philadelphia—Continued*

Wilmington, Delaware Office: 1326 King Street.
Telephone: 302-652-0800.
Fax: 302-656-1993.

Jerome E. Marks
Joseph M. O'Neill
Vincent F. Reilly
Kevin J. O'Brien (Resident, Westmont, New Jersey Office)
Dawn R. Courtney
Maureen Murray-O'Toole
Lisa M. Bellino
Sean Xavier Kelly
Christine G. Boyle
William A. Fynes, III
Johanna C. Pauciulo
Arnold A. Foley
Dennis P. Herbert (Resident, Westmont, New Jersey Office)
William J. Smith
Thomas D. Smith
Gino P. Mecoli
Eva M. Candeloro (Resident, Wilmington, Delaware and Westmont, New Jersey Offices)
Jennifer Ann Lawley
Jeffrey S. Friedman
Robert E. McCann
Patrick C. Lamb
Edward F. Curtin
Richard C. Kelly
Michael J. Diamond
Steven P. Cholden
Nancy P. Brennan

For full biographical listings, see the Martindale-Hubbell Law Directory

WILBRAHAM, LAWLER & BUBA, A PROFESSIONAL CORPORATION (AV)

The Curtis Center, Suite 450, 601 Walnut Street, 19106-3304
Telephone: 215-923-0133
Fax: 215-923-0471
Haddonfield, New Jersey Office: 24 Kings Highway West. 08033-2122.
Telephone: 609-795-4422.
Fax: 609-795-4699.

Edward J. Wilbraham
Robert B. Lawler
Barbara J. Buba
Mark A. Stevens
Michael J. Block
Kim Hollaender

Mary S. Cook
Pamela B. Hinton
Garry B. Hutchinson
James W. McCartney

For full biographical listings, see the Martindale-Hubbell Law Directory

---

*PITTSBURGH,** Allegheny Co.

BABST, CALLAND, CLEMENTS AND ZOMNIR, A PROFESSIONAL CORPORATION (AV)

Two Gateway Center, 15222
Telephone: 412-394-5400
Fax: 412-394-6576
Philadelphia, Pennsylvania Office: The Curtis Center, Suite 1100, Sixth and Walnut Streets.
Telephone: 215-627-3056.
Fax: 215-627-3042.

Chester R. Babst III
Dean A. Calland
Frank J. Clements
Donald C. Bluedorn II
Kenneth R. Bruce
William V. Conley
Colleen Grace Donofrio (Resident, Philadelphia, Pennsylvania Office)
Michele M. Gutman
Steven H. Haake
Lindsay P. Howard
Kenneth K. Kilbert
Robert A. King
J. Frank McKenna, III
Joseph K. Reinhart
Mark D. Shepard
Ted Wesolowski

Christopher W. Armstrong
Steven Baicker-McKee
Albert Bates, Jr. IV
John W. Bruni
James V. Corbelli
Kevin K. Douglass
Jan L. Fox
Monica Gambino
Laura Schleich Irwin
D. Matthew Jameson III
Anne E. Mulgrave
Sandra M. Renwand
Frances Ann Ross-Ray
Jessica Lieber Smolar
Bruce E. Stanley
Gregory D. Timmons
Michael H. Winek
Timothy C. Wolfson

For full biographical listings, see the Martindale-Hubbell Law Directory

BUCHANAN INGERSOLL, PROFESSIONAL CORPORATION (AV)

5800 USX Tower, 600 Grant Street, 15219
Telephone: 412-562-8800
Telecopier: 412-562-1041
Philadelphia, Pennsylvania Office: Two Logan Square, Twelfth Floor, 18th & Arch Streets.
Telephone: 215-665-8700.
Harrisburg, Pennsylvania Office: Vartan Parc, 30 North Third Street.
Telephone: 717-237-4800.
Tampa, Florida Office: 101 East Kennedy Boulevard, Suite 1030.
Telephone: 813-222-8180.
North Miami Beach, Florida Office: 19495 Biscayne Boulevard.
Telephone: 305-933-5600.
Lexington, Kentucky Office: 1210 Vine Center Office Tower, 333 West Vine Street.
Telephone: 606-225-5333.

(See Next Column)

Princeton, New Jersey Office: Buchanan Ingersoll, A Partnership, College Centre, 500 College Road East.
Telephone: 609-452-2666.

David B. Fawcett III
Stanley R. Geary
Henry McC. Ingram
R. Henry Moore
Thomas C. Reed

Stephen C. Smith
Heather A. Wyman

For Complete List of Firm Personnel, See General Section

For full biographical listings, see the Martindale-Hubbell Law Directory

DICKIE, MCCAMEY & CHILCOTE, A PROFESSIONAL CORPORATION (AV)

Suite 400, Two PPG Place, 15222-5402
Telephone: 412-281-7272
Fax: 412-392-5367
Wheeling, West Virginia Office: Suite 2002, 1233 Main Street, 26003-2839.
Telephone: 304-233-1022.
Facsimile: 304-233-1026.

David B. Fawcett
David J. Armstrong
Theodore O. Struk
Clayton A. Sweeney
Joseph S. D. Christof, II
George Edward McGrann
Stephen M. Houghton
Frank M. Gianola
Leonard A. Costa, Jr.
Frederick W. Bode, III
Jeffrey T. Wiley
William Campbell Ries
Richard J. Federowicz
Peter T. Stinson
George Monroe Schumann

Eugene G. Berry
Pamela Lee Leyden
Steven W. Zoffer

For Complete List of Firm Personnel, See General Section

For full biographical listings, see the Martindale-Hubbell Law Directory

GACA, MATIS & HAMILTON, A PROFESSIONAL CORPORATION (AV)

300 Four PPG Place, 15222-5404
Telephone: 412-338-4750
Fax: 412-338-4742

Giles J. Gaca
Thomas A. Matis
Mark R. Hamilton
John W. Jordan, IV
Alan S. Baum
Thomas P. McGinnis
Bernard R. Rizza
Jeffrey A. Ramaley
Stephen J. Dalesio
John Timothy Hinton, Jr.
Shawn Lynne Reed

LEGAL SUPPORT PERSONNEL

PARALEGALS

Tina M. Shanafelt
Jill M. Peterson

For full biographical listings, see the Martindale-Hubbell Law Directory

PLOWMAN, SPIEGEL & LEWIS, P.C. (AV)

Grant Building, Suite 925, 15219-2201
Telephone: 412-471-8521
Fax: 412-471-4481

Jack W. Plowman
John L. Spiegel
Frank J. Kernan
Clifford L. Tuttle, Jr.
Kenneth W. Lee

Marshall J. Conn
David Raves

Reference: Pittsburgh National Bank.

For Complete List of Firm Personnel, See General Section

For full biographical listings, see the Martindale-Hubbell Law Directory

THORP, REED & ARMSTRONG (AV)

One Riverfront Center, 15222
Telephone: 412-394-7711
Fax: 412-394-2555

MEMBERS OF FIRM

Joseph R. Brendel
Thomas W. Corbett, Jr.
Mark F. Nowak
David G. Ries
Michael J. Tomana
Peter Greig Veeder

ASSOCIATE

Ronald C. Gahagan, Jr.

OF COUNSEL

Charles Weiss

For Complete List of Firm Personnel, See General Section

For full biographical listings, see the Martindale-Hubbell Law Directory

Pittsburgh—Continued

WILLMAN & ARNOLD (AV)

Suite 705-708, 700 McKnight Park Drive, 15237
Telephone: 412-366-3333
Fax: 412-366-3462

MEMBERS OF FIRM

Gene E. Arnold
R. Kenneth Willman
James W. Young, Jr.
Ruth A. Antinone
Concetta A. Silvaggio

ASSOCIATES

J. Craig Brungo
John H. Kooser, III
Glenn A. Huetter, Jr.
Jacquelyn A. Knupp
Joseph D. Silvaggio
Keith E. Whitson

For full biographical listings, see the Martindale-Hubbell Law Directory

*WEST CHESTER,** Chester Co.

LAMB, WINDLE & McERLANE, P.C. (AV)

24 East Market Street, P.O. Box 565, 19381-0565
Telephone: 610-430-8000
Telecopier: 610-692-0877

COUNSEL

Theodore O. Rogers

William H. Lamb
Susan Windle Rogers
James E. McErlane
E. Craig Kalemjian
James C. Sargent, Jr.
John D. Snyder
William P. Mahon
Guy A. Donatelli
Vincent M. Pompo
James J. McEntee III

Tracy Blake DeVlieger
P. Andrew Schaum
Lawrence J. Persick
Thomas K. Schindler
Daniel A. Loewenstern
Thomas F. Oeste
John W. Pauciulo
Andrea B. Pettine
John J. Cunningham

Representative Clients: Chester County; First Financial Savings Bank, PaSA; Bank of Chester County; Jefferson Bank; Downingtown Area and Great Valley School Districts; Philadelphia Electric Company; Central and Western Chester County Industrial Development Authority; Valley Forge Sewer Authority; Manito Title Insurance Company.

For full biographical listings, see the Martindale-Hubbell Law Directory

RHODE ISLAND

*PROVIDENCE,** Providence Co.

BLISH & CAVANAGH (AV)

Commerce Center, 30 Exchange Terrace, 02903
Telephone: 401-831-8900
Telecopier: 401-751-7542

MEMBERS OF FIRM

John H. Blish
Joseph V. Cavanagh, Jr.
William R. Landry
Michael DiBiase
Stephen J. Reid, Jr.

Karen A. Pelczarski
Raymond A. Marcaccio
Scott P. Tierney

Representative Clients: Providence Journal Co.; Fleet Financial Group; Rhode Island Hospital Trust National Bank; Allstate Insurance Co.; U-Haul International, Inc.; Delta Dental of Rhode Island; Gilbane Building Co.; Colony Communications; Providence Housing Authority.

For full biographical listings, see the Martindale-Hubbell Law Directory

EDWARDS & ANGELL (AV)

2700 Hospital Trust Tower, 02903
Telephone: 401-274-9200
Telecopier: 401-276-6611
Cable Address: "Edwangle Providence"
Telex: 952001 "E A PVD"
Boston, Massachusetts Office: 101 Federal Street, 02110.
Telephone: 617-439-444.
Telecopier: 617-439-4170.
New York, New York Office: 750 Lexington Avenue, 10022.
Telephone: 212-308-4411.
Telecopier: 212-308-4844.
Palm Beach, Florida Office: 250 Royal Palm Way, 33480.
Telephone: 407-833-7700.
Telecopier: 407-655-8719.
Newark, New Jersey Office: Gateway three, 07120.
Telephone: 201-623-7717.
Telecopier: 201-623-7717.

(See Next Column)

Hartford, Connecticut Office: 750 Main Street, 14th Floor, 06103.
Telephone: 203-525-5065.
Telecopier: 203-527-4198.
Newport, Rhode Island Office: 130 Bellevue Avenue, 02840.
Telephone: 401-849-7800.
Telecopier: 401-849-7887.

MEMBERS OF FIRM

Deming E. Sherman
Gail E. McCann
Lynn Wright (Not admitted in RI; New York, New York and Newark, New Jersey Office)
Lorne W. McDougall
Mark A. Pogue

COUNSEL

Rosemary Healey

For Complete List of Firm Personnel, See General Section

For full biographical listings, see the Martindale-Hubbell Law Directory

GOLDENBERG & MURI (AV)

15 Westminster Street, 02903
Telephone: 401-421-7300
Telecopier: 401-421-7352

MEMBERS OF FIRM

Michael R. Goldenberg
Anthony F. Muri
Barbara S. Cohen

ASSOCIATES

Douglas J. Emanuel
Susan M. Pepin

For full biographical listings, see the Martindale-Hubbell Law Directory

HANSON, CURRAN, PARKS & WHITMAN (AV)

146 Westminster Street, 02903-2218
Telephone: 401-421-2154
Telecopier: 401-521-7040

Kirk Hanson (1948-1991)

MEMBERS OF FIRM

A. Lauriston Parks
David P. Whitman
Michael T. F. Wallor
Robert D. Parrillo
Dennis J. McCarten
James T. Murphy
Seth E. Bowerman
Thomas R. Bender

ASSOCIATES

Amy Beretta
Mark W. Dana
Richard H. Burrows
Daniel P. McKiernan

OF COUNSEL

William A. Curran

General Counsel for: Medical Malpractice Joint Underwriting Association of Rhode Island.
Rhode Island Counsel for: Amica Mutual Insurance Co.; CIGNA; St. Paul Insurance Cos.; Occidental Life Insurance Co.; Exchange Mutual Insurance Co.; Aetna Casualty & Surety Co.

For full biographical listings, see the Martindale-Hubbell Law Directory

KIERNAN, PLUNKETT & REDIHAN (AV)

The Remington Building, 91 Friendship Street, 02903
Telephone: 401-831-2900
Fax: 401-331-7123

MEMBERS OF FIRM

Leonard A. Kiernan, Jr.
Thomas C. Plunkett
Charles N. Redihan, Jr.
Bernard P. Healy

ASSOCIATES

Brian T. Burns
Patricia L. Sylvester
Michael R. Calise
Christopher J. O'Connor

For full biographical listings, see the Martindale-Hubbell Law Directory

SOUTH CAROLINA

*CHARLESTON,** Charleston Co.

BUIST, MOORE, SMYTHE & McGEE, P.A. (AV)

Successors to Buist, Buist, Smythe and Smythe and Moore, Mouzon and McGee.
Five Exchange Street, P.O. Box 999, 29402
Telephone: 803-722-3400
Cable Address: "Conferees"
Telex: 57-6488
Telecopier: 803-723-7398
North Charleston, South Carolina Office: Atrium Northwood Office Building, 7301 Rivers Avenue, Suite 288. Zip: 29406-2859.
Telephone: 803-797-3000.
Telecopier: 803-863-5500.

(See Next Column)

BUIST, MOORE, SMYTHE & MCGEE P.A., *Charleston—Continued*

Henry B. Smythe, Jr. Susan M. Smythe

Elizabeth H. Warner Patricia L. Quentel

Counsel for: CSX Transportation; NationsBank; Metropolitan Life Insurance Co.; E.I. duPont de Nemours & Co.; AIG Aviation, Inc.; Lamorte, Burns & Co., Inc.; Allstate Insurance Co.; General Dynamics Corp.; Independent Life & Accident Insurance Co.; Georgia-Pacific Corp; Beazer East, Inc.

For Complete List of Firm Personnel, See General Section

For full biographical listings, see the Martindale-Hubbell Law Directory

YOUNG, CLEMENT, RIVERS & TISDALE (AV)

28 Broad Street, P.O. Box 993, 29402
Telephone: 803-577-4000
Fax: 803-724-6600
Columbia, South Carolina Office: 1901 Assembly Street, Suite 300, P.O. Box 8476.
Telephone: 803-799-4000.
Fax: 803-799-7083.
North Charleston , South Carolina Office: 2170 Ashley Phosphate Road, Suite 700, P.O. Box 61509.
Telephone: 803-720-5400.
Fax: 803-724-7796.

MEMBERS OF FIRM

W. Jefferson Leath, Jr. Timothy W. Bouch

ASSOCIATES

Jonathan L. Yates H. Bowen Woodruff

Counsel for: Albright & Wilson; Exide Corp.; INCO Ltd.; Tenneco.

For Complete List of Firm Personnel, See General Section

For full biographical listings, see the Martindale-Hubbell Law Directory

*COLUMBIA,** Richland Co.

BOWERS ORR & ROBERTSON (AV)

Suite 1100, 1401 Main Street, P.O. Box 7307, 29202
Telephone: 803-252-0494
Telefax: 803-252-1068

MEMBERS OF FIRM

Glenn Bowers William Dixon Robertson III
James W. Orr Thomas F. Dougall

ASSOCIATE

W. Jones Andrews, Jr.

Representative Clients: Bondex International, Inc.; Cheraw Dyeing & Finishing; Consolidated Systems, Inc.; Kerr McGee Chemical Corporation; Proko Industries, Inc.; Republic Powdered Metals, Inc.; South Carolina Electric & Gas Company; Syntex (U.S.A.); Transtechnology Corporation; United Piece Dye Works.

For full biographical listings, see the Martindale-Hubbell Law Directory

RICHARDSON, PLOWDEN, GRIER AND HOWSER, P.A. (AV)

1600 Marion Street, P.O. Drawer 7788, 29202
Telephone: 803-771-4400
Telecopy: 803-779-0016
Myrtle Beach, South Carolina Office: Southern National Bank Building, Suite 202, 601 21st Avenue North, P.O. Box 3646, 29578.
Telephone: 803-448-1008.
FAX: 803-448-1533.

F. Barron Grier, III Francis M. Mack
William H. Hensel Franklin Jennings Smith, Jr.
Leslie A. Cotter, Jr.

Jimmy Denning, Jr.

Representative Clients: W. R. Grace; Conwed Corp.; Ampenol; Toledo Scale, Inc.; S.C. Insurance Reserve Fund; Empire Ace Manufacturing; CIGNA; Osmose Wood Preserving Inc.

For Complete List of Firm Personnel, See General Section

For full biographical listings, see the Martindale-Hubbell Law Directory

*GREENVILLE,** Greenville Co.

FEW & FEW, P.A. (AV)

850 Wade Hampton Boulevard, P.O. Box 10085, Fed. Station, 29603
Telephone: 803-232-6456
Fax: 803-370-0671

J. Kendall Few John C. Few

For full biographical listings, see the Martindale-Hubbell Law Directory

HAYNSWORTH, MARION, MCKAY & GUÉRARD, L.L.P. (AV)

Two Insignia Financial Plaza, 75 Beattie Place, P.O. Box 2048, 29602
Telephone: 803-240-3200
Telecopier: 803-240-3300
Columbia, South Carolina Office: Suite 2400 A T & T Building, 1201 Main Street, P.O. Drawer 7157, 29202
Telephone: 803-765-1818.
Telecopier: 803-765-2399.
Charleston, South Carolina Office: #2 Prioleau Street, P.O. Box 1119, 29402.
Telephone: 803-722-7606.
Telecopier: 803-723-5263.

MEMBERS OF FIRM

James B. Pressly, Jr. John B. McLeod
Moffatt Grier McDonald

Representative Clients: Fluor Daniel, Inc.; Eagle-Picher Industries; Rockwool Manufacturing Co., Inc.; Morton International.

For Complete List of Firm Personnel, See General Section

For full biographical listings, see the Martindale-Hubbell Law Directory

LEATHERWOOD WALKER TODD & MANN, P.C. (AV)

100 East Coffee Street, P.O. Box 87, 29602
Telephone: 803-242-6440
FAX: 803-233-8461
Spartanburg, South Carolina Office: 1451 East Main Street, P.O. Box 3188.
Telephone: 803-582-4365.
Telefax: 803-583-8961.

J. Richard Kelly Steven E. Farrar
Robert A. deHoll Nancy Hyder Robinson
Eugene C. McCall, Jr.

Counsel for: NationsBank; John D. Hollingsworth on Wheels, Inc.; Canal Insurance Co.; Platt Saco Lowell Corporation .
Representative Clients: Springs Industries, Inc.; American Federal Bank, F.S.B.; General Motors Acceptance Corp.; Ashland Oil, Inc.; Suitt Construction Co.

For Complete List of Firm Personnel, See General Section

For full biographical listings, see the Martindale-Hubbell Law Directory

OGLETREE, DEAKINS, NASH, SMOAK & STEWART (AV)

The Ogletree Building, 300 North Main Street, P.O. Box 2757, 29602
Telephone: 803-271-1300
Facsimile: 803-235-8806
Atlanta, Georgia Office: 3800 One Atlantic Center, 1201 West Peachtree Street, N.W.
Telephone: 404-881-1300.
Washington, D.C. Office: Fifth Floor, 2400 N Street, N.W.
Telephone: 202-887-0855.
Charleston, South Carolina Office: First Union Building, Suite 310, 177 Meeting Street, P.O. Box 1808.
Telephone: 803-853-1300.
Columbia, South Carolina Office: Palmetto Center, Suite 1820, 1426 Main Street, P.O. Box 11206.
Telephone: 803-252-1300.
Raleigh, North Carolina Office: 4101 Lake Boone Trail, Suite 511, P.O. Box 31608.
Telephone: 919-787-9700.
Nashville, Tennessee Office: St. Cloud Corner, 500 Church Street.
Telephone: 615-254-1900.
Albany, New York Office: 4th Floor, One Steuben Place.
Telephone: 518-434-1300.

MEMBERS OF FIRM

Ralph M. Mellom Ronald E. Cardwell
Eric C. Schweitzer Phillip Lee Conner
Nancy Walker Monts

Representative Clients: General Electric Company; Ethyl Corporation; Westinghouse Electric; Hoechst Celanese Corporation; W. R. Grace; Schlumberger Limited; Virgin Islands Alumina Corporation; Ravenswood Aluminum Corporation; Shell Oil; Laidlaw Environmental Services.

For full biographical listings, see the Martindale-Hubbell Law Directory

WYCHE, BURGESS, FREEMAN & PARHAM, PROFESSIONAL ASSOCIATION (AV)

44 East Camperdown Way, P.O. Box 728, 29602-0728
Telephone: 803-242-8200
Telecopier: 803-235-8900

Bradford W. Wyche Gregory J. English

Counsel for: Multimedia, Inc.; Delta Woodside Industries, Inc.; Milliken & Company; Ryan's Family Steak Houses, Inc.; St. Francis Hospital; Span-America Medical Systems, Inc.; Carolina First Bank; KEMET Electronics Corp.; Builder Marts of America, Inc.; One Price Clothing, Inc.

For Complete List of Firm Personnel, See General Section

For full biographical listings, see the Martindale-Hubbell Law Directory

SOUTH DAKOTA

*BELLE FOURCHE,** Butte Co.

BENNETT, MAIN & FREDERICKSON, A PROFESSIONAL CORPORATION (AV)

618 State Street, 57717-1489
Telephone: 605-892-2011
Fax: 605-892-4084

Max Main
John R. Frederickson

OF COUNSEL

Donn Bennett

Representative Clients: Atlantic Richfield Co.; Chevron USA., Inc.; Exxon U.S.A., Co.; Inland Oil and Gas Co.; Royal Bank; Bank of Canada; Bank of Montreal; Security Pacific National Bank; Timberline Oil & Gas Co.; Wyoming Resources Corp.; Bald Mountain Mining Co.

For Complete List of Firm Personnel, See General Section

For full biographical listings, see the Martindale-Hubbell Law Directory

*RAPID CITY,** Pennington Co.

JOHNSON HUFFMAN A PROFESSIONAL CORPORATION OF LAWYERS (AV)

3202 West Main Street, P.O. Box 6100, 57709-6100
Telephone: 605-348-7300
FAX: 605-348-4757

Glen H. Johnson
Richard E. Huffman
Scott Sumner
Wayne F. Gilbert
Timothy J. Becker
John J. Delaney
Courtney R. Clayborne
Jay A. Alderman

LEGAL SUPPORT PERSONNEL
PARALEGALS

Cynthia J. Johnson
Renee Lehr
Dory M. Maks
Timothy Crawford

For full biographical listings, see the Martindale-Hubbell Law Directory

TENNESSEE

*CHATTANOOGA,** Hamilton Co.

FOSTER, FOSTER, ALLEN & DURRENCE (AV)

Formerly Hall, Haynes & Foster
Suite 515 Pioneer Bank Building, 37402
Telephone: 615-266-1141
Telecopier: 615-266-4618

MEMBERS OF FIRM

George Lane Foster
William M. Foster
Craig R. Allen
Phillip M. Durrence, Jr.

ASSOCIATES

David J. Ward
Clayton M. Whittaker
John M. Hull

LEGAL SUPPORT PERSONNEL

Peggy Sue Bates

Division Counsel for: Alabama Great Southern Railroad Co.; C.N.O. & T.P. Railway Co.
Attorneys for: CNA/Insurance; U.S.P. & G. Co.; The Firestone Tire & Rubber Co.; Exxon, Corp.; Murphy Oil Corp.; Chicago Title Insurance Co.; City of East Ridge; Jim Walter Homes; Raymond James & Associates; Morgan Keegan & Co.

For full biographical listings, see the Martindale-Hubbell Law Directory

SHUMACKER & THOMPSON (AV)

Suite 500, First Tennessee Building, 701 Market Street, 37402-4800
Telephone: 615-265-2214
Telecopier: 615-266-1842
Branch Office: Suite 103, One Park Place, 6148 Lee Highway, Chattanooga, Tennessee, 37421-2900.
Telephone: 615-855-1814.
Telecopier: 615-899-1278.

MEMBERS OF FIRM

Ralph Shumacker
Frank M. Thompson
W. Neil Thomas, Jr.
Albert W. Secor
W. Neil Thomas, III
Ronald I. Feldman
Alan L. Cates
Ross I. Schram III
Stephen P. Parish
William Given Colvin
Harold L. North, Jr.
John K. Culpepper

(See Next Column)

MEMBERS OF FIRM (Continued)

Jeffery V. Curry
Everett L. Hixson, Jr.
Stanley W. Hildebrand
Phillip E. Fleenor
Donna S. Spurlock
James D. Henderson

ASSOCIATE

Char-La Cain Fowler

For Complete List of Firm Personnel, See General Section

For full biographical listings, see the Martindale-Hubbell Law Directory

SPEARS, MOORE, REBMAN & WILLIAMS (AV)

8th Floor Blue Cross Building, 801 Pine Street, 37402
Telephone: 615-756-7000
Facsimile: 615-756-4801

MEMBERS OF FIRM

James W. Gentry, Jr.
Michael W. Boehm

ASSOCIATE

John B. Bennett

Counsel for: Memphis Environmental Center; Velsicol Chemical Corporation; GAF; Signal Mountain Cement Company; IPC, Inc.; Mueller Company; International Specialty Products, Inc.

For Complete List of Firm Personnel, See General Section

For full biographical listings, see the Martindale-Hubbell Law Directory

STOPHEL & STOPHEL, P.C. (AV)

500 Tallan Building, Two Union Square, 37402-2571
Telephone: 615-756-2333
Fax: 615-266-5032

Harry B. Ray
W. Lee Maddux
C. Douglas Williams

Brian L. Woodward

Representative Clients: Browning Ferris Industries, Inc.; BHY Concrete Finishing, Inc.; American Manufacturing Company; Tennessee Transformers, Inc.; Maymead, Inc.

For Complete List of Firm Personnel, See General Section

For full biographical listings, see the Martindale-Hubbell Law Directory

*DYERSBURG,** Dyer Co.

ASHLEY, ASHLEY & ARNOLD (AV)

322 Church Avenue, P.O. Box H, 38024
Telephone: 901-285-5074
Telecopier: 901-285-5089

MEMBERS OF FIRM

Barret Ashley
Randolph A. Ashley, Jr.
S. Leo Arnold
Stephen D. Scofield
Marianna Williams
Carol Anne Austin
Anthony Lee Winchester

OF COUNSEL

Joree G. Brownlow

Representative Clients: Illinois Central Gulf Railroad; Bekeart Steel Wire Corp.; Fidelity and Deposit Company of Maryland; St. Paul Fire and Marine Insurance Company.
Construction Company Clients: Folk Construction Co.; Ford Construction Company; Luhr Brothers, Inc.; Pine Bluff Sand & Gravel; Valley Construction Co.

For full biographical listings, see the Martindale-Hubbell Law Directory

KINGSPORT, Sullivan Co.

HUNTER, SMITH & DAVIS (AV)

1212 North Eastman Road, P.O. Box 3740, 37664
Telephone: 615-378-8800;
Johnson City: 615-282-4186;
Bristol: 615-968-7604
Telecopier: 615-378-8801
Johnson City, Tennessee Office: Suite 500 First American Center, 208 Sunset Drive, 37604.
Telephone: 615-283-6300.
Telecopier: 615-283-6301.

MEMBERS OF FIRM

Edwin L. Treadway
William T. Wray, Jr.
Douglas S. Tweed
William C. Argabrite
Gregory K. Haden
Michael L. Forrester

ASSOCIATE

Cynthia S. Kessler

Representative Clients: Waste Management of North America, Inc.; Chemical Waste Management; The Mead Corporation; Unisys Corporation; The Budd Company; American Greetings Corp. (Plusmark); Birmingham Steel Corporation; Spatco Inc.

(See Next Column)

HUNTER, SMITH & DAVIS, *Kingsport—Continued*

For Complete List of Firm Personnel, See General Section

For full biographical listings, see the Martindale-Hubbell Law Directory

*KNOXVILLE,** Knox Co.

BAKER, DONELSON, BEARMAN & CALDWELL (AV)

2200 Riverview Tower, 900 Gay Street, 37901
Telephone: 615-549-7000
Telecopier: 615-525-8569
Memphis, Tennessee Office: 20th Floor, First Tennessee Building, 165 Madison, 38103.
Telephone: 901-526-2000.
Telecopier: 901-577-2303.
Nashville, Tennessee Office: 1700 Nashville City Center, 511 Union Street, 37219.
Telephone: 615-726-5600.
Telecopier: 615-726-0464.
Chattanooga, Tennessee Office: 1800 Republic Centre, 633 Chestnut Street, 37450-1800.
Telephone: 615-752-4400.
Telecopier: 615-752-4410.
Huntsville, Tennessee Office: 3 Courthouse Square, 37756.
Telephone: 615-663-2321.
Telecopier: 615-663-2111.
Johnson City, Tennessee Office: Hamilton Bank Building, 207 Mockingbird Lane, 37604.
Telephone: 615-928-0181.
Telecopier: 615-928-5694; 615-928-3654; Kingsport: 615-246-6191.
Washington, D.C. Office: Market Square, 801 Pennsylvania Avenue, N.W., 20004.
Telephone: 202-508-3400.
Telecopier: 202-508-3402.

PARTNER

Howard H. Baker, Jr.

For Complete List of Firm Personnel, See General Section

For full biographical listings, see the Martindale-Hubbell Law Directory

BUTLER, VINES AND BABB (AV)

Suite 810, First American Center, P.O. Box 2649, 37901-2649
Telephone: 615-637-3531
Fax: 615-637-3385

MEMBERS OF FIRM

Warren Butler
William D. Vines, III
Dennis L. Babb
Martin L. Ellis
Ronald C. Koksal
James C. Wright
Bruce A. Anderson
Gregory Kevin Hardin
Steven Boyd Johnson
Edward U. Babb

ASSOCIATES

John W. Butler
Vonda M. Laughlin
Gregory F. Vines
Scarlett May

LEGAL SUPPORT PERSONNEL

PARALEGALS

Virginia H. Carver
Susie DeLozier
Dena K. Martin

Reference: First American Bank.

For full biographical listings, see the Martindale-Hubbell Law Directory

GILREATH & ASSOCIATES (AV)

550 Main Avenue, Suite 600, P.O. Box 1270, 37901
Telephone: 615-637-2442
FAX: 615-971-4116
Nashville, Tennessee Office: Sidney W. Gilreath, 2828 Stouffer Tower, 611 Commerce Street.
Telephone: 615-256-3388.

Sidney W. Gilreath

ASSOCIATES

Meridith C. Bond
Donna Keene Holt
Richard Baker, Jr.
Mark W. Strange
Paul Kaufman
Richard L. Duncan

LEGAL SUPPORT PERSONNEL

Janie Turpin (Paralegal)
Janet L. Tucker (Paralegal)
Pamela Smith Wise (Legal Assistant to Senior Partner)
Susan Stogner (Legal Assistant to Senior Partner)
Bryan L. Capps (Legal Administrator)

Reference: Third National Bank.
Representative Client: Transportation Communications International Union.

For full biographical listings, see the Martindale-Hubbell Law Directory

*MEMPHIS,** Shelby Co.

ARMSTRONG ALLEN PREWITT GENTRY JOHNSTON & HOLMES (AV)

80 Monroe Avenue Suite 700, 38103
Telephone: 901-523-8211
Telecopier: 901-524-4936
Jackson, Missippi Office: 1350 One Jackson Place, 188 East Capitol Street.
Telephone: 601-948-8020.
Telecopier: 601-948-8389.

MEMBERS OF FIRM

S. Russell Headrick
Randall D. Noel
Stephen P. Hale

Sidney W. Farnsworth, III

For Complete List of Firm Personnel, See General Section

For full biographical listings, see the Martindale-Hubbell Law Directory

BAKER, DONELSON, BEARMAN & CALDWELL (AV)

20th Floor, First Tennessee Building, 165 Madison, 38103
Telephone: 901-526-2000
Telecopier: 901-577-2303
Nashville, Tennessee Office: 1700 Nashville City Center, 511 Union Street, 37219.
Telephone: 615-726-5600.
Telecopier: 615-726-0464.
Knoxville, Tennessee Office: 2200 Riverview Tower, 900 Gay Street, 37901.
Telephone: 615-549-7000.
Telecopier: 615-525-8569.
Chattanooga, Tennessee Office: 1800 Republic Centre, 633 Chestnut Street, 37450-1800.
Telephone: 615-752-4400.
Telecopier: 615-752-4410.
Huntsville, Tennessee Office: 3 Courthouse Square, 37756.
Telephone: 615-663-2321.
Telecopier: 615-663-2111.
Johnson City, Tennessee Office: Hamilton Bank Building, 207 Mockingbird Lane, 37604.
Telephone: 615-928-0181.
Telecopier: 615-928-5694; 615-928-3654; Kingsport: 615-246-6191.
Washington, D.C. Office: Market Square, 801 Pennsylvania Avenue, N.W., 20004.
Telephone: 202-508-3400.
Telecopier: 202-508-3402.

PARTNERS

Jerry Stauffer
Mary Aronov

For Complete List of Firm Personnel, See General Section

For full biographical listings, see the Martindale-Hubbell Law Directory

THOMASON, HENDRIX, HARVEY, JOHNSON & MITCHELL (AV)

Twenty-Ninth Floor, One Commerce Square, 38103
Telephone: 901-525-8721
Telecopier: 901-525-6722

MEMBERS OF FIRM

Michael G. McLaren
Cheryl Rumage Estes

For Complete List of Firm Personnel, See General Section

For full biographical listings, see the Martindale-Hubbell Law Directory

*NASHVILLE,** Davidson Co.

BASS, BERRY & SIMS (AV)

2700 First American Center, 37238-2700
Telephone: 615-742-6200
Telecopy: 615-742-6293
Knoxville, Tennessee Office: 1700 Riverview Tower, 900 S. Gay Street, P.O. Box 1509, 37901-1509.
Telephone: 615-521-6200.
Telecopy: 615-521-6234.

MEMBERS OF FIRM

J. Andrew Goddard
C. Dewees Berry, IV
G. Scott Thomas
William L. McCarty
R. Douglas Mefford
Jessalyn Hershinger

Representative Clients: Arcata Graphics Co.; BASF Corp.; Bowater Inc.; Eastman Chemical Co.; General Electric Co.; Goodyear Tire & Rubber Co.; Horsehead Resource Development Co., Inc.; ITT Corporation; PACCAR, Inc.; Sara Lee Corporation

For full biographical listings, see the Martindale-Hubbell Law Directory

Nashville—Continued

MANIER, HEROD, HOLLABAUGH & SMITH, A PROFESSIONAL CORPORATION (AV)

First Union Tower 2200 One Nashville Place, 150 Fourth Avenue North, 37219-2494
Telephone: 615-244-0030
Telecopier: 615-242-4203

Will R. Manier, Jr. (1885-1953)	Robert C. Evans
Larkin E. Crouch (1882-1948)	Tommy C. Estes
Vincent L. Fuqua, Jr. (1930-1974)	B. Gail Reese
	Michael E. Evans
J. Olin White (1907-1982)	Laurence M. Papel
Miller Manier (1897-1986)	John M. Gillum
William Edward Herod (1917-1992)	Gregory L. Cashion
	Sam H. Poteet, Jr.
Lewis B. Hollabaugh	Samuel Arthur Butts III
Don L. Smith	David J. Deming
James M. Doran, Jr.	Mark S. LeVan
Stephen E. Cox	Richard McCallister Smith
J. Michael Franks	Mary Paty Lynn Jetton
Randall C. Ferguson	H. Rowan Leathers III
Terry L. Hill	Jefferson C. Orr
James David Leckrone	William L. Penny

Lawrence B. Hammet II	J. Steven Kirkham
John H. Rowland	T. Richard Travis
Susan C. West	Stephanie M. Jennings
John E. Quinn	Jerry W. Taylor
John F. Floyd	C. Benton Patton
Paul L. Spradér	Kenneth A. Weber
Lela M. Hollabaugh	Phillip Robert Newman

Brett A. Oeser

General Counsel for: McKinnon Bridge Co., Inc.

For full biographical listings, see the Martindale-Hubbell Law Directory

TEXAS

*AUSTIN,** Travis Co.

* indicates certain Bar Register subscribers whose principal office is located elsewhere in the state and who have arranged for representation as a part of the state capital listings that follow

BAKER & BOTTS, L.L.P. (AV)

1600 San Jacinto Center, 98 San Jacinto Boulevard, 78701
Telephone: 512-322-2500
Fax: 512-322-2501
Houston, Texas Office: One Shell Plaza, 910 Louisiana.
Telephone: 713-229-1234.
Dallas, Texas Office: 2001 Ross Avenue.
Telephone: 214-953-6500.
Washington, D.C. Office: The Warner, 1299 Pennsylvania Avenue, N.W.
Telephone: 202-639-7700.
New York, New York Office: 885 Third Avenue, Suite 2000.
Telephone: 212-705-5000.
Moscow, Russian Federation Office: 10 ul. Pushkinskaya, 103031.
Telephone: 7095/921-5300 (Local); 7501/929-7070 (International).

MEMBERS OF FIRM

Pamela M. Giblin	Mark J. White
Robert T. Stewart	Larry F. York

ASSOCIATES

Raman N. Dewan	Francesca Ortiz
Aileen M. Hooks	Kevin M. Sadler
Jennifer Keane	R. Walton Shelton
Derek R. McDonald	Cynthia Cooke Smiley

For Complete List of Firm Personnel, See General Section

For full biographical listings, see the Martindale-Hubbell Law Directory

LLOYD, GOSSELINK, FOWLER, BLEVINS & MATHEWS, P.C. (AV)

111 Congress Avenue, Suite 1800, 78701
Telephone: 512-322-5800
Fax: 512-472-0532
San Antonio, Texas Office: 111 Soledad, Suite 300.
Telephone: 210-212-5889.

Robert H. Lloyd	Jimmie D. Mathews
Paul G. Gosselink	Martin C. Rochelle
Robert D. Fowler	George V. Basham, III
Chesley N. Blevins	George C. Baldwin

R. Lambeth Townsend

(See Next Column)

Elizabeth V. (Ginger) Rodd	C. Joe Freeland
Richard L. Hamala	Kerry E. Russell
Paula Fisher Baldwin	Erich M. Birch
Georgia N. Crump	Michael J. Nasi

OF COUNSEL

Jackson B. Battle

LEGAL SUPPORT PERSONNEL

GOVERNMENT RELATIONS CONSULTANTS

R. Steve Stagner	Mark A. Rodriguez

For full biographical listings, see the Martindale-Hubbell Law Directory

SAEGERT, ANGENEND & AUGUSTINE, P.C. (AV)

1145 West Fifth Street, Suite 300, 78703
Telephone: 512-474-6521
Fax: 512-477-4512

Jerry C. Saegert	Harrell Glenn Hall, Jr.
Paul D. Angenend	Wendall Corrigan
John C. Augustine	Rebecca K. Knapik
Mark D. Swanson	Walter C. Guebert
John R. Whisenhunt (1949-1994)	Paul Vincent Mouer

For full biographical listings, see the Martindale-Hubbell Law Directory

* **THOMPSON & KNIGHT, A PROFESSIONAL CORPORATION** (AV)

(Attorneys and Counselors)
1200 San Jacinto Center, 98 San Jacinto Boulevard, 78701
Telephone: 512-469-6100
Telecopy: 512-469-6180
Dallas, Texas Office: 1700 Pacific Avenue, Suite 3300, 75201.
Telephone: 214-969-1700.
Telecopy: 512-969-1751.
Cable Address: "Tomtex."
Telex: 732298.
Fort Worth, Texas Office: 801 Cherry Street, Suite 1600, 76102.
Telephone: 817-347-1700.
Telecopy: 817-347-1799.
Houston, Texas Office: 1700 Texas Commerce Tower, 600 Travis, 77002.
Telephone: 713-217-2800.
Telecopy: 713-217-2828; 713-217-2882.
Monterrey, Mexico Office: Edificio Losoles PD-4, Av. Lázaro Cárdenas No. 2400 Pte., San Pedro Garza Garcia, Nuevo Léon C.P. 66220.
Telephone: (52-8) 363-0096.
Telecopy: (52-8) 363-3067.

ASSOCIATES

Becky L. Jolin	Caroline M. LeGette

SENIOR ATTORNEY

Elizabeth A. Webb

For Complete List of Firm Personnel, See General Section

For full biographical listings, see the Martindale-Hubbell Law Directory

*BEAUMONT,** Jefferson Co.

BENCKENSTEIN & OXFORD, L.L.P. (AV)

First Interstate Bank Building, P.O. Box 150, 77704
Telephone: 409-833-9182
Cable Address: "Bmor"
Telex: 779485
Telefax: 409-833-8819
Austin, Texas Office: Suite 810, 400 West 15th Street, 78701.
Telephone: 512-474-8586.
Telefax: 512-478-3064.

MEMBERS OF FIRM

L. J. Benckenstein (1894-1966)	Mary Ellen Blade
F. L. Benckenstein (1918-1987)	William H. Yoes
Hubert Oxford, III	William M. Tolin, III
Alan G. Sampson	Kip Kevin Lamb
Frank D. Calvert	Frances Blair Bethea
Dana Timaeus	Robert J. Rose, Sr.

ASSOCIATES

Susan J. Oliver	Josiah Wheat, Jr.
F. Blair Clarke	Steve Johnson
Keith A. Pardue (Resident, Austin, Texas Office)	Michael Keith Eaves
	Nikki L. Redden

Representative Clients: Marine Office of American Corporation (MOAC); Moran Towing and Transportation Co., Inc.

For Complete List of Firm Personnel, See General Section

For full biographical listings, see the Martindale-Hubbell Law Directory

Beaumont—Continued

MEHAFFY & WEBER, A PROFESSIONAL CORPORATION (AV)

2615 Calder Avenue, P.O. Box 16, 77704
Telephone: 409-835-5011
Fax: 409-835-5729; 835-5177
Orange, Texas Office: 1006 Green Avenue, P.O. Drawer 189.
Telephone: 409-886-7766.
Houston, Texas Office: One Allen Center, 500 Dallas, Suite 1200.
Telephone: 713-655-1200.

Jim I. Graves
John Cash Smith
Thomas L. Hanna
Arthur R. Almquist
Gene M. Williams
David B. Gaultney
Sandra F. Clark
M. C. Carrington
Barbara J. Barron

Vickie R. Thompson
Cimron Campbell
Stephen H. Forman
Michele Y. Smith
Charles S. Perry
James C. (Clay) Crawford
Deanne F. Rienstra
Cecile E. Crabtree

Representative Clients: E.I. du Pont de Nemours and Company; Bethlehem Steel Corp.; The Kansas City Southern Railway Co.; FMC Corp.; Eli Lilly & Company; Merrell Dow; Jefferson County Tax Appraisal District.
Approved Attorneys for: Stewart Title Guaranty Co.

For Complete List of Firm Personnel, See General Section

For full biographical listings, see the Martindale-Hubbell Law Directory

*DALLAS,** Dallas Co.

CALHOUN & STACY (AV)

5700 NationsBank Plaza, 901 Main Street, 75202-3747
Telephone: 214-748-5000
Telecopier: 214-748-1421
Telex: 211358 CALGUMP UR

Mark Alan Calhoun
David W. Elrod
Steven D. Goldston
Parker Nelson
Roy L. Stacy

ASSOCIATES

Shannon S. Barclay
Robert A. Bragalone
Dennis D. Conder
Jane Elizabeth Diseker
Lawrence I. Fleishman
Thomas C. Jones
Katherine Johnson Knight
V. Paige Pace
Veronika Willard
Michael C. Wright

LEGAL CONSULTANT

Rees T. Bowen, III

For full biographical listings, see the Martindale-Hubbell Law Directory

THOMPSON & KNIGHT, A PROFESSIONAL CORPORATION (AV)

(Attorneys and Counselors)
1700 Pacific Avenue Suite 3300, 75201
Telephone: 214-969-1700
Telecopy: 214-969-1751
Cable Address: "Tomtex"
Telex: 732298
Austin, Texas Office: 1200 San Jacinto Center, 98 San Jacinto Boulevard, 78701.
Telephone: 512-469-6100.
Telecopy: 512-469-6180.
Fort Worth, Texas Office: 801 Cherry Street, Suite 1600, 76102.
Telephone: 817-347-1700.
Telecopy: 817-347-1799.
Houston, Texas Office: 1700 Texas Commerce Tower, 600 Travis, 77002.
Telephone: 713-217-2800.
Telecopy: 713-217-2828.
Monterrey, Mexico Office: Edificio Losoles PD-4, Av. Lázaro Cárdenas No. 2400 Pte., San Pedro Garza Garcia, Nuevo Léon C.P. 66220.
Telephone: (52-8) 363-0096.
Telecopy: (52-8) 363-3067.

SHAREHOLDERS

Gregg C. Davis
Scott D. Deatherage
Howard L. Gilberg
James B. Harris
James C. Morriss III

ASSOCIATES

Lisa K. Bork
Craig Naveen Kakarla
A. Kay Roska

For Complete List of Firm Personnel, See General Section

For full biographical listings, see the Martindale-Hubbell Law Directory

*HOUSTON,** Harris Co.

BAKER & BOTTS, L.L.P. (AV)

One Shell Plaza, 910 Louisiana, 77002
Telephone: 713-229-1234
Cable Address: "Boterlove"
Fax: 713-229-1522
Washington, D.C. Office: The Warner, 1299 Pennsylvania Avenue, N.W.
Telephone: 202-639-7700.
New York, New York Office: 885 Third Avenue, Suite 2000.
Telephone: 212-705-5000.
Austin, Texas Office: 1600 San Jacinto Center, 98 San Jacinto Boulevard.
Telephone: 512-322-2500.
Dallas, Texas Office: 2001 Ross Avenue.
Telephone: 214-953-6500.
Moscow, Russian Federation Office: 10 ul. Pushkinskaya, 103031.
Telephone: 7095/921-5300 (Local); 7095/929-7070 (International).

MEMBERS OF FIRM

F. Walter Conrad, Jr.
Larry B. Feldcamp
Frank W. R. Hubert, Jr.
Stephen Gillham Tipps
Robert P. Wright
George T. Shipley
David F. Asmus
Karen Kay Maston

ASSOCIATES

Nancy K. Archer-Yanochik
Ross E. Cockburn
Scott Joseph Miller
Jayme Partridge Roden
C. Patrick Turley

For Complete List of Firm Personnel, See General Section

For full biographical listings, see the Martindale-Hubbell Law Directory

MEHAFFY & WEBER, A PROFESSIONAL CORPORATION (AV)

One Allen Center, 500 Dallas, Suite 1200, 77002
Telephone: 713-655-1200
Fax: 713-655-0222
Beaumont, Texas Office: 2615 Calder Avenue, P.O. Box 16.
Telephone: 409-835-5011.
Orange, Texas Office: 1006 Green Avenue, P.O. Drawer 189.
Telephone: 409-886-7766.

Jim I. Graves
Arthur R. Almquist

Charles S. Perry
James C. (Clay) Crawford
Deanne F. Rienstra

Representative Client: Union Pacific Railroad Co.

For full biographical listings, see the Martindale-Hubbell Law Directory

WILSHIRE SCOTT & DYER, A PROFESSIONAL CORPORATION (AV)

4450 First City Tower, 1001 Fannin, 77002
Telephone: 713-651-1221
Telefax: 713-651-0020

Eugene B. Wilshire, Jr.
Jacalyn D. Scott
Patrick J. Dyer
Thomas E. Bilek
Kelly Cox Thornton

For full biographical listings, see the Martindale-Hubbell Law Directory

*ORANGE,** Orange Co.

MEHAFFY & WEBER, A PROFESSIONAL CORPORATION (AV)

1006 Green Avenue, P.O. Drawer 189, 77630
Telephone: 409-886-7766
Fax: 409-886-7790
Beaumont, Texas Office: 2615 Calder Avenue, P.O. Box 16.
Telephone: 409-835-5011.
Houston Office: One Allen Center, 500 Dallas, Suite 1200.
Telephone: 713-655-1200.

John Cash Smith

Cimron Campbell

Representative Clients: Sabine River Authority of Texas; Orange Housing Authority; Orange Ship Building, Inc.; Equitable Bag Co., Southern Division; Farmers Insurance Group; Texas Farm Bureau; City of Orange.

For full biographical listings, see the Martindale-Hubbell Law Directory

*SAN ANTONIO,** Bexar Co.

WHEATLEY, CAMPAGNOLO & SESSIONS, L.L.P. (AV)

100 West Houston, Suite 1200, 78205
Telephone: 210-227-5000
Fax: 210-225-1555

Seagal V. Wheatley
Theodore Campagnolo
William Lewis Sessions
John Frank Onion, III
Donald R. Philbin, Jr.

(See Next Column)

WHEATLEY, CAMPAGNOLO & SESSIONS L.L.P.—*Continued*

ASSOCIATES

Bradley S. Wilder
Katrina J. Carden
Julia W. Mann

For full biographical listings, see the Martindale-Hubbell Law Directory

UTAH

*SALT LAKE CITY,** Salt Lake Co.

CALLISTER, NEBEKER & McCULLOUGH, A PROFESSIONAL CORPORATION (AV)

800 Kennecott Building, 84133
Telephone: 801-530-7300
Telecopier: 801-364-9127

Fred W. Finlinson
Brian W. Burnett
James R. Holbrook
Jan M. Bergeson

John B. Lindsay

Representative Clients: Central Valley Water Reclamation Facility Board; Washington County Conservancy District; Sinclair Oil (Little America).

For Complete List of Firm Personnel, See General Section

For full biographical listings, see the Martindale-Hubbell Law Directory

KIMBALL, PARR, WADDOUPS, BROWN & GEE, A PROFESSIONAL CORPORATION (AV)

Suite 1300, 185 South State Street, P.O. Box 11019, 84147
Telephone: 801-532-7840
Fax: 801-532-7750

Carolyn B. McHugh
Daniel A. Jensen
Steven J. Christiansen
David B. Hancock
John M. Burke
Clay W. Stucki

For Complete List of Firm Personnel, See General Section

For full biographical listings, see the Martindale-Hubbell Law Directory

PARRY MURRAY WARD & MOXLEY, A PROFESSIONAL CORPORATION (AV)

1270 Eagle Gate Tower, 60 East South Temple, 84111
Telephone: 801-521-3434
Fax: 801-521-3484

Douglas J. Parry
Kevin Reid Murray
Brent D. Ward

David M. McGrath
James K. Tracy
Bret F. Randall

Representative Clients: Trammell Crow Co.; Pacificorp; Utah Power and Light; Monroc; Salt Lake County Water Conservancy District; Western Petroleum; Minit-Lube; Franchisee Assoc.; Utah Power & Light.

For Complete List of Firm Personnel, See General Section

For full biographical listings, see the Martindale-Hubbell Law Directory

PARSONS BEHLE & LATIMER, A PROFESSIONAL CORPORATION (AV)

One Utah Center, 201 South Main Street, Suite 1800, P.O. Box 45898, 84145-0898
Telephone: 801-532-1234
Telecopy: 801-536-6111

Keith E. Taylor
James B. Lee
Gordon L. Roberts
Lawrence E. Stevens
Daniel M. Allred
Dallin W. Jensen
David R. Bird
David W. Tundermann
Neil Orloff
Lee Kapaloski
Lucy B. Jenkins
David L. Deisley
Hal J. Pos
J. Michael Bailey
M. Lindsay Ford
Jim B. Butler
Craig D. Galli
James E. Karkut
Michael J. Malmquist
Alan K. Flake Jr.
Lisa A. Kirschner
Elizabeth Kitchens Jones
Clare Russell Davis
Michael J. Tomko

Representative Clients: American Barrick Resources Corporation; Kennecott Corporation; Questar Corporation; Utah Industry Environmental Coalition.

For full biographical listings, see the Martindale-Hubbell Law Directory

SCALLEY & READING, A PROFESSIONAL CORPORATION (AV)

261 East 300 South, Suite 200, 84111
Telephone: 801-531-7870
Fax: 801-531-7968

Ford G. Scalley
Michael W. Spence
J. Bruce Reading
Marlon L. Bates
Steven K. Walkenhorst
John Edward Hansen
Scott N. Rasmussen

John E. Swallow
Wesley Hutchins
Steven B. Smith
James W. Claflin, Jr.

For full biographical listings, see the Martindale-Hubbell Law Directory

VAN COTT, BAGLEY, CORNWALL & McCARTHY, A PROFESSIONAL CORPORATION (AV)

Suite 1600, 50 South Main Street, P.O. Box 45340, 84145
Telephone: 801-532-3333
Telex: 453149
Telecopier: 801-534-0058
Ogden, Utah Office: Suite 900, 2404 Washington Boulevard.
Telephone: 801-394-5783.
Park City, Utah Office: 314 Main Street, Suite 205.
Telephone: 801-649-3889.
Reno, Nevada Office: Jeppson & Lee, 100 West Liberty, Suite 990.
Telephone: 702-333-6800.

Gregory P. Williams
H. Michael Keller
Alan L. Sullivan
Matthew F. McNulty, III
John T. Nielsen
John A. Anderson

Bradley R. Cahoon
Thomas W. Clawson
Matthew M. Durham

For Complete List of Firm Personnel, See General Section

For full biographical listings, see the Martindale-Hubbell Law Directory

VERMONT

BRATTLEBORO, Windham Co.

WEBER, PERRA & WILSON, P.C. (AV)

16 Linden Street, P.O. Box 558, 05302
Telephone: 802-257-7161
Fax: 802-257-0572

Raymond P. Perra

For Complete List of Firm Personnel, See General Section

For full biographical listings, see the Martindale-Hubbell Law Directory

*BURLINGTON,** Chittenden Co.

BURAK & ANDERSON (AV)

Executive Square, 346 Shelburne Street, P.O. Box 64700, 05406-4700
Telephone: 802-862-0500
Telecopier: 802-862-8176

MEMBERS OF FIRM

Michael L. Burak
Jon Anderson
Thomas R. Melloni

ASSOCIATE

Brian J. Sullivan

For Complete List of Firm Personnel, See General Section

For full biographical listings, see the Martindale-Hubbell Law Directory

GRAVEL AND SHEA, A PROFESSIONAL CORPORATION (AV)

Corporate Plaza, 76 St. Paul Street, P.O. Box 369, 05402-0369
Telephone: 802-658-0220
Fax: 802-658-1456

Stephen R. Crampton
John R. Ponsetto
Dennis R. Pearson

OF COUNSEL

Clarke A. Gravel

SPECIAL COUNSEL

Norman Williams

For Complete List of Firm Personnel, See General Section

For full biographical listings, see the Martindale-Hubbell Law Directory

Burlington—Continued

MANCHESTER LAW OFFICES, PROFESSIONAL CORPORATION (AV)

One Lawson Lane, P.O. Box 1459, 05402-1459
Telephone: 802-658-7444
Fax: 802-658-2078

Robert E. Manchester
Patricia S. Orr

LEGAL SUPPORT PERSONNEL
LEGAL NURSE CONSULTANTS

Tina L Mulvey
Rosemeryl S. Harple
Maureen P. Tremblay

For full biographical listings, see the Martindale-Hubbell Law Directory

SHEEHEY BRUE GRAY & FURLONG, PROFESSIONAL CORPORATION (AV)

119 South Winooski Avenue, P.O. Box 66, 05402
Telephone: 802-864-9891
Facsimile: 802-864-6815

William B. Gray (1942-1994)
David T. Austin
R. Jeffrey Behm
Nordahl L. Brue
Michael G. Furlong
Ralphine Newlin O'Rourke
Donald J. Rendall, Jr.
Christina Schulz
Paul D. Sheehey
Peter H. Zamore

Rebecca L. Owen

Representative Client: Green Mountain Power Corp.

For full biographical listings, see the Martindale-Hubbell Law Directory

*RUTLAND,** Rutland Co.

CARROLL, GEORGE & PRATT (AV)

64 & 66 North Main Street, P.O. Box 280, 05702-0280
Telephone: 802-775-7141
Telecopier: 802-775-6483
Woodstock, Vermont Office: The Mill - Route #4 E., P.O. Box 388, 05091.
Telephone: 802-457-1000.
Telecopier: 802-457-1874.

MEMBERS OF FIRM

Henry G. Smith (1938-1974)
James P. Carroll
Alan B. George
Robert S. Pratt
Neal C. Vreeland
Jon S. Readnour
Timothy U. Martin
Randall F. Mayhew (Resident Partner, Woodstock Office)
Richard S. Smith
Judy Godnick Barone
John J. Kennelly

ASSOCIATES

Thomas A. Zonay
Jeffrey P. White
Susan Boyle Ford (Resident, Woodstock Office)
Charles C. Humpstone

For full biographical listings, see the Martindale-Hubbell Law Directory

HULL, WEBBER & REIS (AV)

(Formerly Dick, Hackel & Hull)
60 North Main Street, P.O. Box 890, 05702-0890
Telephone: 802-775-2361
Fax: 802-775-0739

Donald H. Hackel (1925-1985)
John B. Webber
Robert K. Reis
John C. Holler
Lisa L. Chalidze

ASSOCIATES

Phyllis R. McCoy
Karen Abatiell Kalter

OF COUNSEL

Richard A. Hull (P.C.)
Steven D. Vogl

Representative Clients: Aetna Insurance Co.; Great American Insurance Cos.

For full biographical listings, see the Martindale-Hubbell Law Directory

*ST. JOHNSBURY,** Caledonia Co.

PRIMMER & PIPER, PROFESSIONAL CORPORATION (AV)

52 Summer Street, P.O. Box 159, 05819
Telephone: 802-748-5061
Facsimile: 802-748-3976
Montpelier, Vermont Office: 44 East State Street, 05602. Box 1309.
Telephone: 802-223-2102.
Fax: 802-223-2628.

John L. Primmer
William B. Piper
Denise J. Deschenes
Jeffrey P. Johnson
Robert W. Martin, Jr.
James E. Clemons

Trevor R. Lewis
James D. Huber

For full biographical listings, see the Martindale-Hubbell Law Directory

VIRGINIA

BRISTOL, (Independent City)

ELLIOTT LAWSON & POMRENKE (AV)

Sixth Floor, First Union Bank Building, P.O. Box 8400, 24203-8400
Telephone: 703-466-8400
Fax: 703-466-8161

James Wm. Elliott, Jr.
Mark M. Lawson
Kurt J. Pomrenke
Steven R. Minor
Kyle P. Macione
Lisa King Crockett

For full biographical listings, see the Martindale-Hubbell Law Directory

CHANTILLY, Fairfax Co.

SHUTLER AND LOW (AV)

A Partnership including a Professional Corporation
14500 Avion Parkway, Suite 300, 22021-1101
Telephone: 703-818-1320
Fax: 703-818-8813

MEMBERS OF FIRM

Norman D. Shutler (P.C.)
Matthew A. Low
Roger C. Fairchild
Robert A. Weissman

For full biographical listings, see the Martindale-Hubbell Law Directory

MCLEAN, Fairfax Co.

WATT, TIEDER & HOFFAR (AV)

7929 Westpark Drive, Suite 400, 22102
Telephone: 703-749-1000
Telecopier: 703-893-8029
Washington, D.C. Office: 601 Pennsylvania Ave, N.W., Suite 900.
Telephone: 202-462-4697.
Irvine California Office: 3 Park Plaza, Suite 1530.
Telephone: 714-852-6700.

MEMBERS OF FIRM

John B. Tieder, Jr.
Robert G. Watt
Julian F. Hoffar
Robert M. Fitzgerald
Robert K. Cox
William R. Chambers
David C. Romm
Charles E. Raley (Not admitted in VA)
Francis X. McCullough
Barbara G. Werther (Not admitted in VA)
Garry R. Boehlert
Thomas B. Newell
Lewis J. Baker
Benjamin T. Riddles, II
Timothy F. Brown
Richard G. Mann, Jr.
David C. Mancini
David C. Haas
Henry D. Danforth
Carter B. Reid
Donna S. McCaffrey
Mark J. Groff (Not admitted in VA)
Mark A. Sgarlata
Daniel E. Cohen
Michael G. Long (Resident, Irvine, California Office)

OF COUNSEL

Avv. Roberto Tassi
Clyde Harold Slease (Not admitted in VA)

ASSOCIATES

Thomas J. Powell
Douglas C. Proxmire
Tara L. Vautin
Edward Parrott
Steven G. Schassler
Joseph H. Bucci
Steven J. Weber
Paul A. Varela
Vivian Katsantonis
Charlie Lee
Kathleen A. Olden
Christopher P. Pappas (Resident, Irvine, California Office)
Shelly L. Ewald
Christopher J. Brasco
Jean V. Misterek
Charles W. Durant
Susan Latham Timoner
Fred A. Mendicino
Susan G. Sisskind
Robert G. Barbour
Keith C. Phillips
Marybeth Zientek Gaul
Timothy E. Heffernan (Not admitted in VA)
William Drew Mallender
James Moore Donahue
Heidi Brown Hering
Kerrin Maureen McCormick (Not admitted in VA)
Gretal J. Toker

For full biographical listings, see the Martindale-Hubbell Law Directory

NORFOLK, (Independent City)

VANDEVENTER, BLACK, MEREDITH & MARTIN (AV)

500 World Trade Center, 23510
Telephone: 804-446-8600
Cable Address: "Hughsvan"
Telex: 823-671
Telecopier: 446-8670
North Carolina, Kitty Hawk Office: 6 Juniper Trail.
Telephone: 919-261-5055.
Fax: 919-261-8444.

(See Next Column)

VANDEVENTER, BLACK, MEREDITH & MARTIN—*Continued*

London, England Office: Suite 692, Level 6, Lloyd's, 1 Lime Street.
Telephone: (071) 623-2081.
Facsimile: (071) 929-0043.
Telex: 987321.

MEMBERS OF FIRM

Carter T. Gunn
Michael L. Sterling

ASSOCIATE

Patrick A. Genzler

For Complete List of Firm Personnel, See General Section

For full biographical listings, see the Martindale-Hubbell Law Directory

*RICHMOND,** (Ind. City; Seat of Henrico Co.)

WILLIAMS, MULLEN, CHRISTIAN & DOBBINS, A PROFESSIONAL CORPORATION (AV)

Two James Center, 1021 East Cary Street, P.O. Box 1320, 23210-1320
Telephone: 804-643-1991
Fax: 804-783-6456
Glen Allen, Virginia Office: 4401 Waterfront Drive, Suite 140.
Telephone: 804-965-9168.
Fax: 804-965-0955.
Washington, D.C. Office: 1575 Eye Street, N.W.
Telephone: 202-289-6200.
Fax: 202-289-4126.

Stephen E. Baril
Charles L. Cabell
Timothy G. Hayes
Channing J. Martin
Clayton L. Walton

Heidi Wilson Abbott

For Complete List of Firm Personnel, See General Section

For full biographical listings, see the Martindale-Hubbell Law Directory

WASHINGTON

*SEATTLE,** King Co.

BETTS, PATTERSON & MINES, P.S. (AV)

800 Financial Center, 1215 Fourth Avenue, 98161-1090
Telephone: 206-292-9988
Fax: 206-343-7053

Christopher W. Tompkins
Steven Goldstein
David L. Hennings

OF COUNSEL

Martin T. Collier

Ronald D. Allen
Stephen A. Crandall
Glenn S. Draper

Representative Clients: Amoco Corp.; Associated Grocers; Crosby & Overton, Inc.; Chrysler Realty Corporation; Great Lakes Chemical Corp.; Interstate Insurance Group; Oregon Mutual Insurance Co.; Supermarket Development Corp.; Three Rivers Insurance Company; United Insurance Company.

For full biographical listings, see the Martindale-Hubbell Law Directory

BUCK & GORDON (AV)

902 Waterfront Place, 1011 Western Avenue, 98104-1097
Telephone: 206-382-9540
Telecopier: 206-626-0675

MEMBERS OF FIRM

William H. Block
Peter L. Buck
Brent Carson
Jay P. Derr
Joel M. Gordon
Amy L. Kosterlitz
Keith E. Moxon

ASSOCIATES

Alison D. Birmingham
Shelley E. Kneip

OF COUNSEL

Madeleine A. F. Brenner

Reference: Seafirst Bank, Seattle, Washington (Metropolitan Branch).

For full biographical listings, see the Martindale-Hubbell Law Directory

GAITÁN & CUSACK (AV)

30th Floor Two Union Square, 601 Union Street, 98101-2324
Telephone: 206-521-3000
Facsimile: 206-386-5259
Anchorage, Alaska Office: 425 G Street, Suite 760.
Telephone: 907-278-3001.
Facsimile: 907-278-6068.

(See Next Column)

San Francisco, California Office: 275 Battery Street, 20th Floor.
Telephone: 415-398-5562.
Fax: 415-398-4033.
Washington, D.C. Office: 2000 L Street, Suite 200.
Telephone: 202-296-4637.
Fax: 202-296-4650.

MEMBERS OF FIRM

José E. Gaitán
Kenneth J. Cusack (Resident, Anchorage, Alaska Office)
William F. Knowles
Ronald L. Bozarth

OF COUNSEL

Howard K. Todd
Gary D. Gayton
Michel P. Stern (Also practicing alone, Bellevue, Washington)
Christopher A. Byrne
Patricia D. Ryan

ASSOCIATES

Mary F. O'Boyle
Bruce H. Williams
David J. Onsager
Diana T. Jimenez
Robert T. Mimbu
Cristina C. Kapela
Camilla M. Hedberg
John E. Lenker
Kathleen C. Healy

Representative Clients: The Chubb Group of Insurance Companies; CNA Insurance Companies; CIGNA Insurance Companies; Central National Insurance Company of Omaha; Zurich-American Insurance Companies; Switzerland Insurance Company; Hartford Insurance Company; Raymark Industries, Inc.; Commercial Union Insurance Company.

For full biographical listings, see the Martindale-Hubbell Law Directory

LANE POWELL SPEARS LUBERSKY (AV)

A Partnership including Professional Corporations
1420 Fifth Avenue, Suite 4100, 98101-2338
Telephone: 206-223-7000
Cable Address: "Embe"
Telex: 32-8808
Telecopier: 206-223-7107
Other Offices at: Mount Vernon and Olympia, Washington; Los Angeles and San Francisco, California; Anchorage, Alaska; Portland, Oregon; London, England.

MEMBERS OF FIRM

Robert R. Davis, Jr.
James B. Stoetzer
Grant S. Degginger

Representative Clients: Alaska Pulp Corp.; Fred Hutchinson Cancer Research Center; First Interstate Bank of Washington; Georgia-Pacific Corp.; The Home Depot; James River Corp.; Northwest Pulp and Paper Assn.; Simpson Investment Co. and Affiliates; Texaco, Inc.; Zurn Industries, Inc.

For Complete List of Firm Personnel, See General Section

For full biographical listings, see the Martindale-Hubbell Law Directory

PRESTON GATES & ELLIS (AV)

5000 Columbia Seafirst Center, 701 Fifth Avenue, 98104-7011
Telephone: 206-623-7580
Telex: 4740035
Telecopy: 206-623-7022
Anchorage, Alaska Office: 4th Floor, 420 L Street, 99501-1937.
Telephone: 907-276-1969.
Telecopier: 907-276-1365.
Los Angeles, California Office: 3450 Sanwa Bank Plaza, 601 South Figueroa Street.
Telephone: 213-892-4700.
Telecopier: 213-892-4701.
Coeur d'Alene, Idaho Office: 1200 Ironwood Drive, Suite 315. 83814.
Telephone: 208-667-1839.
Telecopier: 208-667-3567.
Washington, D.C. Office: Preston Gates Ellis & Rouvelas Meeds, Suite 500, 1735 New York Avenue, N.W., 20006-4759.
Telephone: 202-628-1700.
Telecopier: 202-331-1024.
Portland, Oregon Office: 3200 US Bancorp Tower 111 S.W. Fifth Avenue, 97204-3688.
Telephone: 503-228-3200.
Telecopier: 503-248-9085.
Spokane, Washington Office: 1400 Seafirst Financial Center, W. 601 Riverside Avenue, 99201-0636.
Telephone: 509-624-2100.
Telecopier: 509-456-0146.
Tacoma, Washington Office: 1500 First Interstate Plaza, 1201 Pacific Avenue, 98402-4301.
Telephone: 206-272-1500.
Telecopier: 206-272-2913.

MEMBERS OF FIRM

Frank M. Preston (1895-1985)
George W. McBroom (1923-1986)
Richard Thorgrimson (1909-1975)
Roger L. Shidler (1900-1988)
Donald L. Holman (1927-1986)
Deborah A. Allard
Thomas G. Allison
Carol Slayden Arnold
Lawrence B. Bailey
Hugh F. Bangasser
Marc L. Barreca
Mark R. Beatty

(See Next Column)

PRESTON GATES & ELLIS, *Seattle—Continued*

MEMBERS OF FIRM (Continued)

Judith A. Bigelow
David H. Binney
John C. Bjorkman
Paula E. Boggs
William H. Burkhart
Charles R. Bush
Christopher M. Carletti
C. Kent Carlson
Larry M. Carter
William H. Chapman
Connie R. Collingsworth
Gordon G. Conger
Stephan H. Coonrod
Ronald E. Cox
Lance Christopher Dahl
Scott L. David
Martha J. Dawson
Mabry C. De Buys
James K. Doane
Richard B. Dodd
Kirk A. Dublin
James R. Ellis (Retired)
David E. Fennell
Richard D. Ford
Bart J. Freedman
Michele A. Gammer
William H. Gates
Carl P. Gilmore
Peter J. Glase
Karen E. Glover
John A. Gose
G. Scott Greenburg
Robert L. Gunter
James R. Irwin
Robert S. Jaffe
B. Gerald Johnson
Susan Delanty Jones
Alan H. Kane
Thomas E. Kelly, Jr.
Paul J. Lawrence
Ross A. Macfarlane
William E. Mantle
James Markham Marshall
Pamela A. Martin
Scott A. Milburn
Yoram Milo
Robert B. Mitchell
Donald H. Mullins
Nancy M. Neraas
Robert D. Neugebauer
James L. Phillips
Charles H. Purcell
Jay A. Reich
Douglas H. Rosenberg
John A. Seethoff
James D. Sherman
Beryl N. Simpson
Shannon J. Skinner
Martin F. Smith
Stephen A. Smith
Peter C. Spratt
Diane R. Stokke
Clyde W. Summerville
David K.Y. Tang
Fredric C. Tausend
Elizabeth Thomas
Holly K. Towle
Scott R. Vokey
Forrest W. Walls
Cynthia M. Weed
Kenneth S. Weiner
Alan Wicks
Thomas H. Wolfendale

OF COUNSEL

John N. Rupp

ASSOCIATES

Sherri M. Anderson
Thomas Eli Backer
Carol Eads Bailey
Jennifer Belk
Shawn M. Carter
J. Alan Clark
Cheri Y. Cornell
Christopher H. Cunningham
Kenneth Ray Davis, II
Elizabeth J. Deckman
Keith R. Dolliver
Ramona M. Emerson
Jesse Owen Franklin IV
John D. Fugate
Michel Gahard
Michael J. Gearin
Dean George-Falvy
Adam W. Gravley
Frederick W. Green
Thomas F. Haensly
Margaret Chieko Inouye
Lisa L. Johnsen
Madeline June Kass
Aaron Keyt
Brian K. Knox
Gary J. Kocher (Not admitted in WA)
Eric S. Laschever
Liam Burgess Lavery
Jessica Stone Levy
Marc C. Levy
Konrad J. Liegel
Kirk A. Lilley
Douglas M. Love
Knoll D. Lowney
Douglas A. Luetjen
Cestjon L. McFarland
Kathleen M. McGinnis
Mary Megan McLemore
Teresa C. McNally
Jonathan T. McPhee
Richard Archibald Montfort, Jr.
Robin L. Nielsen
Margaret A. Niles
Sarah E. Oyer
Faith L. Pettis
J. Michael Philips
Anne Diehl Rees
Floyd G. Short
John D. Sullivan
Susan Naomi Takemoto
William V. Taylor
Lori A. Terry
David O. Thompson
Ruth A. Tressel
Perry S. Weinberg
Eileen Weresch-Doornink
Herbert E. Wilgis III
Mary L. Williamson
Chapin E. Wilson, III
Roger D. Wynne
Grace Tsuang Yuan

For full biographical listings, see the Martindale-Hubbell Law Directory

WEST VIRGINIA

*CHARLESTON,** Kanawha Co.

JACKSON & KELLY (AV)

1600 Laidley Tower, P.O. Box 553, 25322
Telephone: 304-340-1000
Fax: 304-340-1130
Martinsburg, West Virginia Office: 300 Foxcroft Avenue, P.O. Box 1068.
Telephone: 304-263-8800.
Morgantown, West Virginia Office: 6000 Hampton Center, P.O. Box 619.
Telephone: 304-599-3000.

(See Next Column)

New Martinsville, West Virginia Office: 256 Russell Avenue, P.O. Box 68.
Telephone: 304-455-1751.
Charles Town, West Virginia Office: 700 East Washington Street, P.O. Box 983.
Telephone: 304-728-6088.
Clarksburg, West Virginia Office: 203 Main Street, P.O. Box 1587.
Telephone: 304-623-3002.
Lexington, Kentucky Office: 175 East Main Street, Suite 500, P.O. Box 2150.
Telephone: 606-255-9500.
Washington, D. C. Office: 2401 Pennsylvania Avenue, N.W., Suite 400.
Telephone: 202-973-0200.
Denver, Colorado Office: Suite 2710, 1660 Lincoln Street.
Telephone: 303-837-0003.

MEMBERS OF FIRM

Winfield T. Shaffer
Charles Q. Gage
Mark N. Savit (Resident, Washington, D.C. Office)
Alvin L. Emch
James R. Snyder
Barbara D. Little
Dennis C. Sauter
Robert G. McLusky
Daniel L. Stickler
Thomas J. Hurney, Jr.
Lynn Oliver Frye
Thad S. Huffman (Resident, Washington, D.C. Office)
Kevin M. McGuire (Resident, Lexington, Kentucky Office)
L. Poe Leggette (Resident, Washington, D.C. Office)
Dean K. Hunt (Resident, Lexington, Kentucky Office)

ASSOCIATES

Robert K. Parsons
Patrick W. Pearlman
James Zissler (Resident, Washington, D.C. Office)
Linden R. Evans

Representative Clients: Union Carbide Corp.; Rhone Poulenc Ag Co.; FMC Corp. ; Elkem Metals Co.; West Virginia Coal Assn.; CONSOL Inc.; Pittston Coal; Ashland Coal, Inc.; S&S Grading, Inc.; Westvaco Corp.

For Complete List of Firm Personnel, See General Section

For full biographical listings, see the Martindale-Hubbell Law Directory

STEPTOE & JOHNSON (AV)

Seventh Floor, Bank One Center, P.O. Box 1588, 25326-1588
Telephone: 304-353-8000
Fax: 304-353-8180
Clarksburg, West Virginia Office: Bank One Center, P.O. Box 2190, 26302-2190.
Telephone: 304-624-8000.
Fax: 304-624-8183.
Morgantown, West Virginia Office: 1000 Hampton Center, P.O. Box 1616, 26507-1616.
Telephone: 304-598-8000.
Fax: 304-598-8116.
Martinsburg, West Virginia Office: 126 East Burke Street, P.O. Box 2629, 25401-5429.
Telephone: 304-263-6991.
Fax: 304-263-4785.
Charles Town, West Virginia Office: 104 West Congress Street, P.O. Box 100, 25414-0100.
Telephone: 304-725-1414.
Fax: 304-725-1913.
Hagerstown, Maryland Office: The Bryan Centre, 82 West Washington Street, Fourth Floor, P.O. Box 570, 21740-0570.
Telephone: 301-739-8600.
Fax: 301-739-8742.
Wheeling, West Virginia Office: The Riley Building, Suite 400, 14th & Chapline Streets, P.O. Box 150, 26008-0020.
Telephone: 304-233-0000.
Fax: 304-233-0014.

MEMBERS OF FIRM

Otis L. O'Connor
James R. Watson
Daniel R. Schuda
Harry P. Waddell
Steven P. McGowan
Bryan R. Cokeley
W. Randolph Fife
Martin R. Smith, Jr.
George E. Carenbauer
Arthur M. Standish
Patrick D. Kelly

ASSOCIATES

Cynthia R. Cokeley
Susan Osenton Phillips
Robert D. Pollitt
Luci R. Wellborn
Susan L. Basile
Joanna I. Tabit
Janet N. Kawash
Jeffrey K. Phillips
Richard J. Wolf
Wendy D. Young
Michael J. Funk
Marc B. Lazenby
Jan L. Fox
John W. Alderman, III
John C. Stump
Sarah Lovejoy Brack
Keith A. Jones
Denese Venza
Frank W. Volk
Christopher Kroger
Kelly R. Reed

Representative Clients: Ameribank; ARCO Chemical Co.; City National Bank of Charleston; Federal Kemper Insurance Co.; Goodyear Tire & Rubber Co.; The Hartford Group; Hope Gas, Inc.; Olin Corp.; South Charleston Stamping & Manufacturing Co.; State Farm Insurance Cos.

For full biographical listings, see the Martindale-Hubbell Law Directory

*CLARKSBURG,** Harrison Co.

Johnson, Simmerman & Broughton, L.C. (AV)

Suite 210, Goff Building, P.O. Box 150, 26301
Telephone: 304-624-6555
Telecopier: 304-623-4933

Charles G. Johnson
Frank E. Simmerman, Jr.
Marcia Allen Broughton

For full biographical listings, see the Martindale-Hubbell Law Directory

Steptoe & Johnson (AV)

Bank One Center, P.O. Box 2190, 26302-2190
Telephone: 304-624-8000
Fax: 304-624-8183
Mailing Address: P.O. Box 2190, 26302-2190
Charleston, West Virginia Office: Seventh Floor, Bank One Center, P.O. Box 1588, 25326-1588.
Telephone: 304-353-8000
Fax: 304-353-8180.
Morgantown, West Virginia Office: 1000 Hampton Center, P.O. Box 1616, 26507-1616.
Telephone: 304-598-8000.
Fax: 304-598-8116.
Martinsburg, West Virginia Office: 126 East Burke Street, P.O. Box 2629, 25401-5429.
Telephone: 304-263-6991.
Fax: 304-263-4785.
Charles Town, West Virginia Office: 104 West Congress Street, P.O. Box 100, 25414-0100.
Telephone: 304-725-1414.
Fax: 304-725-1913.
Hagerstown, Maryland Office: The Bryan Centre, 82 West Washington Street, Fourth Floor, P.O. Box 570, 21740-0570.
Telephone: 301-739-8600.
Fax: 301-739-8742.
Wheeling, West Virginia Office: The Riley Building, Suite 400, 14th & Chapline Streets, P.O. Box 150, 26003-0020.
Telephone: 304-233-0000.
Fax: 304-233-0014.

MEMBER OF FIRM

W. Henry Lawrence IV

ASSOCIATE

Michael J. Florio

Representative Clients: Consolidated Gas Transmission Corp.; Consolidated Coal Co.; CNA; E.I. DuPont de Nemours & Co.; Equitable Resources, Inc.; The Hartford Group; Peabody Coal Co.; PPG Industries; Union National Bank of West Virginia; Ogden Newspapers, Inc.

For Complete List of Firm Personnel, See General Section

For full biographical listings, see the Martindale-Hubbell Law Directory

WISCONSIN

*MILWAUKEE,** Milwaukee Co.

Davis & Kuelthau, S.C. (AV)

111 East Kilbourn Avenue, Suite 1400, 53202-6613
Telephone: 414-276-0200
Facsimile: 414-276-9369
Cable Address: "Shiplaw"

William E. Callahan, Jr.
Michael P. Dunn
Perry H. Friesler
William J. Mulligan
David W. Neeb
William S. Roush, Jr.

Kathryn A. Lonsdorf

For full biographical listings, see the Martindale-Hubbell Law Directory

Meissner & Tierney, S.C. (AV)

The Milwaukee Center, 111 East Kilbourn Avenue, 19th Floor, 53202-6622
Telephone: 414-273-1300
Facsimile: 414-273-5840

Dennis L. Fisher
Michael J. Cohen

Eric J. Klumb
Kenneth A. Iwinski

For full biographical listings, see the Martindale-Hubbell Law Directory

Quarles & Brady (AV)

411 East Wisconsin Avenue, 53202-4497
Telephone: 414-277-5000
Cable Address: "Lawdock"
Fax: 414-271-3552.
TWX: 910-262-3426
Madison, Wisconsin Office: Firstar Plaza, One South Pinckney Street, P.O. Box 2113.
Telephone: 608-251-5000.
Fax: 608-251-9166.
West Palm Beach, Florida Office: 222 Lakeview Avenue, 4th Floor.
Telephone: 407-653-5000.
Fax: 407-653-5333.
Naples, Florida Office: Barnett Center, 4501 Tamiami Trail North.
Telephone: 813-262-5959.
Fax: 813-434-4999.
Phoenix, Arizona Office: One Camelback Building, One East Camelback Road, Suite 400.
Telephone: 602-230-5500.
Fax: 602-230-5598.

MEMBERS OF FIRM
(ALPHABETICALLY BY YEAR OF ADMISSION TO BAR)

Charles Q. Kamps
Anthony S. Earl (Resident, Madison Office)
Michael L. Zaleski (Resident, Madison Office)
Frank J. Daily
Anthony H. Driessen
Matthew J. Flynn
Michael S. McCauley
Arthur A. Vogel, Jr.
William H. Harbeck
Ralph V. Topinka (Resident, Madison Office)
David B. Bartel
David G. Beauchamp (Resident, Phoenix, Arizona Office)
Daniel L. Muchow (Resident, Phoenix, Arizona Office)
Thomas P. McElligott
Nancy K. Peterson

OF COUNSEL

Richard W. Cutler

ASSOCIATES

Waltraud A. Arts (Resident, Madison Office)
Jane F. Clokey
Kevin A. Delorey (Resident, Madison Office)
John D. Humphreville (Resident, Naples, Florida Office)
Christopher H. Kallaher
George J. Marek
Amy M. Hindman

For Complete List of Firm Personnel, See General Section

For full biographical listings, see the Martindale-Hubbell Law Directory

*WAUSAU,** Marathon Co.

Patterson, Richards, Hessert, Wendorff & Ellison (AV)

630 Fourth Street, P.O. Box 1144, 54402-1144
Telephone: 715-845-1151
Fax: 715-845-1167

MEMBERS OF FIRM

George A. Richards
Mark P. Wendorff

ASSOCIATE

David J. Eckert

Representative Clients: M&I First American National Bank of Wausau; Allstate Insurance Co.; American Bankers Insurance Co.; American Family Mutual Insurance Co.; American Hardware Insurance Group; Auto Owners Insurance Co.; Badger Mutual Insurance Co.; Badger State Mutual Casualty Co.; CIGNA.
Reference: M&I First American National Bank.

For Complete List of Firm Personnel, See General Section

For full biographical listings, see the Martindale-Hubbell Law Directory

WYOMING

*BUFFALO,** Johnson Co.

Omohundro, Palmerlee and Durrant (AV)

An Association of Attorneys
130 South Main Street, 82834
Telephone: 307-684-2207
Telecopier: 307-684-9364
Gillette, Wyoming Office: East Entrance, Suite 700, 201 West Lakeway Road.
Telephone: 307-682-7826.

William D. Omohundro (P.C.)
David F. Palmerlee
Sean P. Durrant

For full biographical listings, see the Martindale-Hubbell Law Directory

*CASPER,** Natrona Co.

BROWN & DREW (AV)

Casper Business Center, Suite 800, 123 West First Street, 82601-2486
Telephone: 307-234-1000
800-877-6755
Telefax: 307-265-8025

MEMBERS OF FIRM

Morris R. Massey
Donn J. McCall
Harry B. Durham, III
Thomas F. Reese
Jeffrey C. Brinkerhoff

ASSOCIATES

Jon B. Huss
Courtney Robert Kepler

Attorneys for: First Interstate Bank of Wyoming, N.A.; Norwest Bank Wyoming, N.A.; Aetna Casualty & Surety Co.; The Doctor's Co.; MEDMARC; WOTCO, Inc.; Chevron USA; Kerr-McGee Corp.; Chicago and NorthWestern Transportation Company; KN Energy, Inc. and subsidiaries.

For Complete List of Firm Personnel, See General Section

For full biographical listings, see the Martindale-Hubbell Law Directory

WILLIAMS, PORTER, DAY & NEVILLE, P.C. (AV)

Suite 300 Durbin Center, 145 South Durbin Street, 82601
Telephone: 307-265-0700
Fax: 307-266-2306

Richard E. Day
Stuart R. Day
Frank D. Neville
Ann M. Rochelle
Stephenson D. Emery

Representative Clients: Amoco Oil Co.; True Industries; Texaco, Inc.; Conoco,Inc.; Phillips Petroleum Co.; Marathon Oil Co.; Pacific Power & Light Co.; Mobil Exploration and Production; Enron Oil and Trading Co.

For Complete List of Firm Personnel, See General Section

For full biographical listings, see the Martindale-Hubbell Law Directory

PUERTO RICO

SAN JUAN, San Juan Dist.

FIDDLER, GONZÁLEZ & RODRÍGUEZ

Chase Manhattan Bank Building (Hato Rey), P.O. Box 363507, 00936-3507
Telephone: 809-753-3113
Telecopier: 809-759-3123

MEMBER OF FIRM

Eduardo M. Negrón-Navas

Representative Clients: Browning Ferris; Metcalf & Eddy; The Eastman Kodak Co.; Bacardi Corp.

For Complete List of Firm Personnel, See General Section

For full biographical listings, see the Martindale-Hubbell Law Directory

GOLDMAN ANTONETTI & CÓRDOVA

American International Plaza Fourteenth & Fifteenth Floors, 250 Muñoz Rivera Avenue (Hato Rey), P.O. Box 70364, 00936-0364
Telephone: 809-759-8000
Telecopiers: 809-767-9333 (Main)
809-767-9177 (Litigation Department)
809-767-8660 (Labor & Corporate Law Departments)
809-767-9325 (Tax & Environmental Law Departments)

MEMBERS OF FIRM

José A. Cepeda-Rodriguez
Braulio García Jiménez
Francis Torres-Fernández
Karin G. Díaz-Toro

ASSOCIATES

Eli Matos-Alicea
Carlos E. Colón-Franceschi
John A. Uphoff-Figueroa
Gretchen M. Mendez-Vilella
Orlando Cabrera-Rodriguez

Representative Clients: Baxter Health Care Corp.; Chevron U.S.A.; Conagra, Inc.; Esso Standard Oil; Owen-Illinois; Puerto Rico Manufacturers Association; Britol Myers Squibb.

For Complete List of Firm Personnel, See General Section

For full biographical listings, see the Martindale-Hubbell Law Directory

JIMÉNEZ, GRAFFAM & LAUSELL

Formerly Jiménez & Fusté
Suite 505, Midtown Building, 421 Muñoz Rivera Avenue, Hato Rey, P.O. Box 366104, 00936-6104
Telephone: 809-767-1030; 767-1000; 767-1061; 767-1064
Telefax: 809-751-4068;
Cable: "Nezte"; RCA
Telex: 325-2730

MEMBERS OF FIRM

Nicolás Jiménez
J. Ramón Rivera-Morales
William A. Graffam
José Juan Torres-Escalera
Steven C. Lausell
Raquel M. Dulzaides
Manuel San Juan

ASSOCIATES

Manolo T. Rodríguez-Bird
Isabel J. Vélez-Serrano
Patricia Garrity
Edgardo A. Vega-López
Carlos E. Bayrón
Alexandra M. Serracante-Cadilla
Luis Saldaña-Roman

Representative Clients: Crowley Environmental Services; Bristol Myers Squibb Co.; Smithkline Beecham Pharmaceuticals Co.; Monsanto Agricultural Co.; Water Quality Insurance Syndicate.

For full biographical listings, see the Martindale-Hubbell Law Directory

MÁRTINEZ ODELL & CALABRIA

Banco Popular Center, 16th Floor, (Hato Rey), P.O. Box 190998, 00919-0998
Telephone: 809-753-8914
Facsimile: 809-753-8402; 809-759-9075; 809-764-5664

MEMBERS OF FIRM

Luis Morales-Steinmann
Benjamín Hernández-Nieves

ASSOCIATES

Lucé Vela Gutiérrez
Brunilda R. Santiago-Acevedo

Representative Clients: A.T. & T. Corp.; Pepsi-Cola P.R. Bottling Co.; Banco Popular de Puerto Rico; I.T.T. Financial Corp.; John H. Harland Company of Puerto Rico, Inc.; Lutron Electronics Co., Inc.; Paine Webber, Inc.; Lotus Development Corp.; Western Digital.

For Complete List of Firm Personnel, See General Section

For full biographical listings, see the Martindale-Hubbell Law Directory

O'NEILL & BORGES

10th Floor, Chase Manhattan Bank Building (Hato Rey), 254 Muñoz Rivera Avenue, 00918-1995
Telephone: 809-764-8181
Telecopier: 809-753-8944

MEMBER OF FIRM

Irwin H. Flashman

ASSOCIATE

Carlos A. Valldejuly-Sastre

Representative Clients: Blount, Inc.; C.R. Bard, Inc.; Ford Motor Co.; Hanes Mensware, Inc.; Jefferson Smurfit, Inc.; Levitt Homes Puerto Rico Inc.; Olay Company, Inc.; Puerto Rican-American Insurance Company, Inc.; TECO Power Services, Corp.

For Complete List of Firm Personnel, See General Section

For full biographical listings, see the Martindale-Hubbell Law Directory

CANADA
ALBERTA

*CALGARY,** Calgary Jud. Dist.

BENNETT JONES VERCHERE (AV)

4500 Bankers Hall East, 855-2nd Street S.W., T2P 4K7
Telephone: (403) 298-3100
Facsimile: (403) 265-7219
Edmonton, Alberta Office: 1000, 10035-105 Street.
Telephone: (403) 421-8133.
Facsimile: (403) 421-7951.
Toronto, Ontario Office: 3400 1 First Canadian Place. P.O. Box 130.
Telephone: (416) 863-1200.
Facsimile: (416) 863-1716.
Ottawa, Ontario Office: Suite 1800. 350 Alberta Street, Box 25, K1R 1A4.
Telephone: (613) 230-4935.
Facsimile: (613) 230-3836.
Montreal, Quebec Office: Suite 1600, 1 Place Ville Marie.
Telephone: (514) 871-1200.
Facsimile: (514) 871-8115.

(See Next Column)

BENNETT JONES VERCHERE—*Continued*

MEMBER OF FIRM

W. Gordon Brown, Q.C.

For Complete List of Firm Personnel, See General Section

For full biographical listings, see the Martindale-Hubbell Law Directory

*EDMONTON,** Edmonton Jud. Dist.

LUCAS BOWKER & WHITE (AV)

Esso Tower - Scotia Place, 1201-10060 Jasper Avenue, T5J 4E5
Telephone: 403-426-5330
Telecopier: 403-428-1066

MEMBERS OF FIRM

Gerald A. I. Lucas, Q.C.
George E. Bowker, Q.C.
Robert B. White, Q.C.
David J. Stratton, Q.C.
Cecilia I. Johnstone, Q.C.
John Reginald Day, Q.C.
E. James Kindrake
Elizabeth A. Johnson
Norman J. Pollock
Robert C. Dunseith
Douglas H. Shell
Kent H. Davidson
Alan R. Gray
Robert A. Seidel
Robert P. Bruce
David J. Stam
Donald J. Wilson

ASSOCIATES

Kevin J. Smith
Gordon V. Garside
Deborah L. Hughes
Annette E. Koski
Douglas A. Bodner
Michael Alexander Kirk
Mark E. Lesniak
Eric C. Lund
Linda A. Maj
Dusten E. Stewart
Debbie E. Bryden
Kathleen Audrey Scott

COUNSEL

H. Neil Bowker
Joan C. Copp
Linda R. Flynn

Reference: Canadian Imperial Bank of Commerce.

For full biographical listings, see the Martindale-Hubbell Law Directory

PARLEE McLAWS (AV)

15th Floor Manulife Place, 10180 101st Street, T5J 4K1
Telephone: 403-423-8500
Telecopier: 403-423-2870
Calgary, Alberta Office: 3400, Western Canadian Place, 707 - 8th Avenue, S.W.
Telephone: 403-294-7000.
Telecopier: 403-265-8263.

MEMBERS OF FIRM

C. H. Kerr, Q.C.
M. D. MacDonald
K. F. Bailey, Q.C.
R. B. Davison, Q.C.
F. R. Haldane
P. E. J. Curran
D. G. Finlay
J. K. McFadyen
R. C. Secord
D. L. Kennedy
D. C. Rolf
D. F. Pawlowski
A. A. Garber
R. P. James
D. C. Wintermute
J. L. Cairns
R. A. Newton, Q.C.
T. A. Cockrall, Q.C.
H. D. Montemurro
F. J. Niziol
R. W. Wilson
I. L. MacLachlan
R. O. Langley
R. G. McBean
J. T. Neilson
E. G. Rice
J. F. McGinnis
J. H. H. Hockin
G. W. Jaycock
M. J. K. Nikel
B. J. Curial
S. L. May
M. S. Poretti

ASSOCIATES

C. R. Head
A.W. Slemko
L. H. Hamdon
K.A. Smith
K. D. Fallis-Howell
D. S. Tam
J.W. McClure
F.H. Belzil
R.A. Renz
J.G. Paulson
K. E. Buss
B. L. Andriachuk
P. E. S. J. Kennedy
R. Feraco
R.J. Billingsley
N.B.R. Thompson
P. A. Shenher
I. C. Johnson
K.G. Koshman
D.D. Dubrule
G. T. Lund
W.D. Johnston
G. E. Flemming
K. P. Nayyer

For full biographical listings, see the Martindale-Hubbell Law Directory

CANADA
BRITISH COLUMBIA

*VANCOUVER,** Vancouver Co.

RUSSELL & DuMOULIN (AV)

2100-1075 West Georgia Street, V6E 3G2
Telephone: 604-631-3131
Fax: 604-631-3232
A Member of the national association of Borden DuMoulin Howard Gervais, comprising Russell & DuMoulin, Vancouver, British Columbia; Howard Mackie, Calgary, Alberta; Borden & Elliot, Toronto, Ontario; Mackenzie Gervais, Montreal, Quebec and Borden DuMoulin Howard Gervais, London, England.
Strategic Alliance with Perkins Coie with offices in Seattle, Spokane and Bellevue, Washington; Portland, Oregon; Anchorage, Alaska; Los Angeles, California; Washington, D.C.; Hong Kong and Taipei, Taiwan.
Represented in Hong Kong by Vincent T.K. Cheung, Yap & Co.

MEMBER OF FIRM

Paul C. Wilson

Representative Clients: Alcan Smelters & Chemicals Ltd.; The Bank of Nova Scotia; Canada Trust Co.; The Canada Life Assurance Co.; Forest Industrial Relations Ltd.; Honda Canada Inc.; IBM Canada Ltd.; Macmillan Bloedel Ltd.; Nissho Iwai Canada Ltd.; The Toronto-Dominion Bank.

For Complete List of Firm Personnel, See General Section

For full biographical listings, see the Martindale-Hubbell Law Directory

CANADA
NEW BRUNSWICK

*SAINT JOHN,** Saint John Co.

CLARK, DRUMMIE & COMPANY (AV)

40 Wellington Row, P.O. Box 6850 Station "A", E2L 4S3
Telephone: 506-633-3800
Telecopier (Automatic): 506-633-3811

MEMBERS OF FIRM

Barry R. Morrison, Q.C.
Terrence W. Hutchinson
William B. Richards

Reference: Royal Bank of Canada.

For Complete List of Firm Personnel, See General Section

For full biographical listings, see the Martindale-Hubbell Law Directory

CANADA
NOVA SCOTIA

*HALIFAX,** Halifax Co.

McINNES COOPER & ROBERTSON (AV)

1601 Lower Water Street, P.O. Box 730, B3J 2V1
Telephone: 902-425-6500
Fax: 902-425-6350
St. John's, Newfoundland Office: Suite 602, Scotia Centre, 235 Water Street, P.O. Box 547. A1C, 5K8.
Telephone: 709-726-9500.
Fax: 709-726-9550.

Stewart McInnes, P.C., Q.C.
F. V. W. Penick
George T. H. Cooper, Q.C.
Harvey L. Morrison
Eric LeDrew

ASSOCIATE

Bernard F. Miller

COUNSEL

Hector McInnes, Q.C.

Attorneys for: Bank of Nova Scotia; Imperial Oil, Limited; Frank B. Hall & Co., Inc. (New York); American Steamship Owners Protection & Indemnity Association, Inc.; Coca-Cola, Ltd.; Scott Worldwide Inc.; Hong Kong Bank of Canada.

For Complete List of Firm Personnel, See General Section

For full biographical listings, see the Martindale-Hubbell Law Directory

CANADA ONTARIO

*TORONTO,** Regional Munic. of York

BORDEN & ELLIOT (AV)

Barristers & Solicitors
Scotia Plaza, 40 King Street West, M5H 3Y4
Telephone: 416-367-6000
Telecopier: 416-367-6749
Internet: @ borden.com
A Member of the national association of Borden DuMoulin Howard Gervais, comprising Borden & Elliot in Toronto, Ontario, Russell & DuMoulin in Vancouver, British Columbia, Howard, Mackie in Calgary, Alberta and Mackenzie Gervais in Montréal, Québec. Borden DuMoulin Howard Gervais also operates an office in London, England.

MEMBER AND ASSOCIATES

Stephen F. Waqué

For Complete List of Firm Personnel, See General Section

For full biographical listings, see the Martindale-Hubbell Law Directory

CANADA QUEBEC

*MONTREAL,** Montreal Dist.

BYERS CASGRAIN (AV)

A Member of McMillan Bull Casgrain
Suite 3900, 1 Place Ville-Marie, H3B 4M7
Telephone: 514-878-8800
Telecopier: 514-866-2241
Cable Address: "Magee"
Telex: 05-24195

Philippe Casgrain, Q.C.
Hon. Jean Bazin, Q.C.
Pierre Langlois
William S. Grodinsky
John Hurley
Martin Bernard
Serge Tousignant
Sébastien Grammond

For Complete List of Firm Personnel, See General Section

For full biographical listings, see the Martindale-Hubbell Law Directory

MCMASTER MEIGHEN (AV)

A General Partnership
7th Floor, 630 René-Lévesque Boulevard West, H3B 4H7
Telephone: 514-879-1212
Telecopier: 514-878-0605
Cable Address: "Cammerall"
Telex: "Cammerall MTL" 05-268637
Affiliated with Fraser & Beatty in Toronto, North York, Ottawa and Vancouver.

MEMBERS OF FIRM

Marc Duchesne
Nicholas J. Spillane
Yves A. Dubois
Darren E. Graham McGuire

For Complete List of Firm Personnel, See General Section

For full biographical listings, see the Martindale-Hubbell Law Directory

CANADA SASKATCHEWAN

*REGINA,** Regina Jud. Centre

MACPHERSON LESLIE & TYERMAN (AV)

1500-1874 Scarth Street, S4P 4E9
Telephone: 306-347-8000
Telecopier: 306-352-5250
Saskatoon, Saskatchewan Office: 1500-410 22nd Street East, S7K 5T6.
Telephone: 306-975-7100.
Telecopier: 306-975-7145.

MEMBERS OF FIRM

Harold H. MacKay, Q.C.
Larry B. LeBlanc

For Complete List of Firm Personnel, See General Section

For full biographical listings, see the Martindale-Hubbell Law Directory

FAMILY LAW

ALABAMA

*BIRMINGHAM,** Jefferson Co.

BARNETT, NOBLE, HANES, O'NEAL & DUFFEE (AV)

Suite 1600 City Federal Building, 2026 Second Avenue North, 35203
Telephone: 205-322-0471; 205-322-0484

MEMBERS OF FIRM

Robert C. Barnett
G. William Noble
Thomas B. Hanes
James P. O'Neal
Cecil G. Duffee
Frederick Mott Garfield, Jr.
Janice G. Formato

OF COUNSEL

Arthur J. Hanes

Counsel for: City of Gardendale; State of Alabama Highway Department.
Approved Attorneys for: Alabama Title Co., Inc.

For full biographical listings, see the Martindale-Hubbell Law Directory

NAJJAR DENABURG, P.C. (AV)

2125 Morris Avenue, 35203
Telephone: 205-250-8400
Telecopier: 205-326-3837

Charles L. Denaburg
Thomas C. Najjar, Jr.
L. Stephen Wright, Jr.

Terry M. Cromer
Denise J. Landreth

General Counsel: Acousti Engineering of Alabama, Inc.
Representative Client: Compass Bank.
Approved Attorneys for: Mississippi Valley Title Insurance Co.
Reference: Compass Bank.

For Complete List of Firm Personnel, See General Section

For full biographical listings, see the Martindale-Hubbell Law Directory

REDDEN, MILLS & CLARK (AV)

940 First Alabama Bank Building, 35203
Telephone: 205-322-0457
Fax: 205-322-8481

MEMBERS OF FIRM

L. Drew Redden
William H. Mills
William N. Clark
Gerald L. Miller
Stephen W. Shaw

ASSOCIATES

Maxwell H. Pulliam, Jr.
Joseph H. Hilley

References: SouthTrust Bank; First Alabama Bank.

For full biographical listings, see the Martindale-Hubbell Law Directory

SIROTE & PERMUTT, P.C. (AV)

2222 Arlington Avenue, South, P.O. Box 55727, 35255
Telephone: 205-933-7111
Facsimile: 205-930-5301
Huntsville, Alabama Office: 200 Clinton Avenue, N.W., Suite 1000.
Telephone: 205-536-1711.
Facsimile: 205-534-9650.
Mobile, Alabama Office: One St. Louis Centre, Suite 1000.
Telephone: 205-432-1671.
Facsimile: 205-434-0196.
Montgomery, Alabama Office: Colonial Commerce Center, Suite 305 One Commerce Street.
Telephone: 205-261-3400.
Facsimile: 205-261-3434.
Tuscaloosa, Alabama Office: 2216 14th Street.
Telephone: 205-752-2089.

Jerry E. Held
Maurice L. Shevin
C. Randal Johnson
David W. Long

Representative Clients: International Business Machines (IBM); General Motors Corp.; Colonial Bank; Bruno's, Inc.; University of Alabama Hospitals; Westinghouse Electric Corp.; First Alabama Bank; Monsanto Chemical Company; South Central Bell; Prudential Insurance Company; American Home Products, Inc.; Minnesota Mining and Manufacturing, Inc. (3M).

(See Next Column)

For Complete List of Firm Personnel, See General Section

For full biographical listings, see the Martindale-Hubbell Law Directory

*HUNTSVILLE,** Madison Co.

BERRY, ABLES, TATUM, LITTLE & BAXTER, P.C. (AV)

Legal Building, 315 Franklin Street, S.E., P.O. Box 165, 35804-0165
Telephone: 205-533-3740
Facsimile: 205-533-3751

William H. Blanton (1889-1973)
Joe M. Berry
L. Bruce Ables
James T. Tatum, Jr.
Loyd H. Little, Jr.
James T. Baxter, III
Thomas E. Parker, Jr.
Bill G. Hall

Representative Clients: AmSouth Bank, N.A.; First Alabama Bank; General Shale Products Co.; The Hartz Corp.; Litton Industries, Inc.; Farmers Tractor Co.; Colonial Bank; Farm Credit Bank of Texas; Resolution Trust Corp.
Reference: First Alabama Bank.

For full biographical listings, see the Martindale-Hubbell Law Directory

BLANKENSHIP AND RHODES, ATTORNEYS-AT-LAW, P.C. (AV)

229 East Side Square, Drawer 345, 35801
Telephone: 205-517-1550
Telecopier: 205-536-7493

David B. Blankenship
Dinah Petree Rhodes

References: First Alabama Bank, N.A.; Altus Bank; SouthTrust Bank.

For full biographical listings, see the Martindale-Hubbell Law Directory

SIROTE & PERMUTT, P.C. (AV)

Suite 1000, 200 Clinton Avenue, N.W., 35801
Telephone: 205-536-1711
Facsimile: 205-534-9650
Birmingham, Alabama Office: 2222 Arlington Avenue, South, P.O. Box 55727.
Telephone: 205-933-7111.
Facsimile: 205-930-5301.
Mobile, Alabama Office: One St. Louis Centre, Suite 1000.
Telephone: 205-432-1671.
Facsimile: 205-434-0196.
Montgomery, Alabama Office: Colonial Commerce Center, Suite 305, One Commerce Street.
Telephone: 205-261-3400.
Facsimile: 205-261-3434.
Tuscaloosa, Alabama Office: 2216 14th Street.
Telephone: 205-752-2089.

George W. Royer, Jr.
John P. Burbach

For Complete List of Firm Personnel, See General Section

For full biographical listings, see the Martindale-Hubbell Law Directory

STEPHENS, MILLIRONS, HARRISON & WILLIAMS, P.C. (AV)

333 Franklin Street, P.O. Box 307, 35801
Telephone: 205-533-7711
Telecopier: 205-536-9388

Arthur M. Stephens
Paul L. Millirons
James G. Harrison
Bruce E. Williams
Vicki Ann Bell

Attorneys for: Lomas Mortgage USA, Inc.; AmSouth Mortgage Co., Inc.

For full biographical listings, see the Martindale-Hubbell Law Directory

*MOBILE,** Mobile Co.

BRISKMAN & BINION, P.C. (AV)

205 Church Street, P.O. Box 43, 36601
Telephone: 334-433-7600
Fax: 334-433-4485

Donald M. Briskman
Mack B. Binion

Donna Ward Black
Alex F. Lankford, IV
Christ N. Coumanis

A List of Representative Clients will be furnished upon request.
References: First Alabama Bank; AmSouth Bank, N.A.; Southtrust Bank of Mobile.

For full biographical listings, see the Martindale-Hubbell Law Directory

SIROTE & PERMUTT, P.C. (AV)

One St. Louis Centre, Suite 1000, P.O. Drawer 2025, 36652-2025
Telephone: 334-432-1671
Facsimile: 334-434-0196
Birmingham, Alabama Office: 2222 Arlington Avenue, South, P.O. Box 55727.
Telephone: 205-933-7111.
Facsimile: 205-930-5301.

(See Next Column)

SIROTE & PERMUTT P.C., *Mobile—Continued*

Huntsville, Alabama Office: 200 Clinton Avenue, N.W., Suite 1000.
Telephone: 205-536-1711.
Facsimile: 205-534-9650.
Montgomery, Alabama Office: Colonial Commerce Center, Suite 305, One Commerce Street.
Telephone: 205-261-3400.
Facsimile: 205-261-3434.
Tuscaloosa, Alabama Office: 2216 14th Street.
Telephone: 205-752-2089.

William H. McDermott

For Complete List of Firm Personnel, See General Section

For full biographical listings, see the Martindale-Hubbell Law Directory

ARIZONA

*FLAGSTAFF,** Coconino Co.

ASPEY, WATKINS & DIESEL (AV)

123 North San Francisco, 86001
Telephone: 602-774-1478
Facsimile: 602-774-1043
Sedona, Arizona Office: 120 Soldier Pass Road.
Telephone: 602-282-5955.
Facsimile: 602-282-5962.
Page, Arizona Office: 904 North Navajo.
Telephone: 602-645-9694.
Winslow, Arizona Office: 205 North Williamson.
Telephone: 602-289-5963.
Cottonwood, Arizona Office: 905 Cove Parkway, Unite 201.
Telephone: 602-639-1881.

MEMBERS OF FIRM

Frederick M. Fritz Aspey
Harold L. Watkins
Louis M. Diesel
Bruce S. Griffen
Donald H. Bayles, Jr.
Kaign N. Christy
John J. Dempsey

Zachary Markham
James E. Ledbetter
Whitney Cunningham
Holly S. Karris

LEGAL SUPPORT PERSONNEL

Deborah D. Roberts (Legal Assistant)
C. Denece Pruett (Legal Assistant)
Dominic M. Marino, Jr, (Paralegal Assistant)

Representative Clients: Farmer's Insurance Company of Arizona; Kelley-Moore Paint Co.; Pepsi-Cola Bottling Company of Northern Arizona; Bill Luke's Chrysler-Plymouth, Inc.; First American Title Insurance Company ; Transamerica Title Insurance Co.; Page Electric Utility; Comprehensive Access Health Plan, Inc.
Reference: First Interstate Bank-Arizona, N.A., Flagstaff, Arizona.

For full biographical listings, see the Martindale-Hubbell Law Directory

*PHOENIX,** Maricopa Co.

DAVID W. ADLER (AV)

4141 West Bethany Home Road, 85019
Telephone: 602-266-6010

For full biographical listings, see the Martindale-Hubbell Law Directory

BURCH & CRACCHIOLO, P.A. (AV)

702 East Osborn Road, Suite 200, 85014
Telephone: 602-274-7611
Fax: 602-234-0341
Mailing Address: P.O. Box 16882, Phoenix, AZ, 85011

Donald W. Lindholm
Jess A. Lorona

Josephine Cuccurullo
Eve Parks

Representative Clients: Bashas' Inc.; Farmers Insurance Group; U-Haul International, Inc.

For Complete List of Firm Personnel, See General Section

For full biographical listings, see the Martindale-Hubbell Law Directory

A. JERRY BUSBY, P.C. (AV)

Suite 150, 5070 North 40th Street, 85018
Telephone: 602-957-0071
Fax: 602-957-0460

(See Next Column)

A. Jerry Busby

Representative Clients: The Circle K Corp.; Sun World Corp.
Reference: Bank of Scottsdale.

For full biographical listings, see the Martindale-Hubbell Law Directory

FRIEDL, RICHTER & BURI (AV)

Suite 200, 1440 East Washington Street, 85034
Telephone: 602-495-1000
Fax: 602-271-4733

MEMBER OF FIRM

Joseph C. Richter

Reference: First Interstate Bank of Arizona, 19th Avenue and Bell.

For full biographical listings, see the Martindale-Hubbell Law Directory

JENSEN & KELLEY, P.A. (AV)

5343 North 16th Street, Suite 140, 85016
Telephone: 602-230-1118
Fax: 602-230-9622

Robert A. Jensen
Brian E. Kelley

For full biographical listings, see the Martindale-Hubbell Law Directory

MACLEAN & JACQUES, LTD. (AV)

Suite 202, 40 East Virginia, 85004
Telephone: 602-263-5771
FAX: 602-279-5569

John H. MacLean (1932-1992)
Raoul T. Jacques

Cary T. Inabinet
Macre S. Inabinet

For full biographical listings, see the Martindale-Hubbell Law Directory

MARISCAL, WEEKS, MCINTYRE & FRIEDLANDER, P.A. (AV)

2901 North Central Avenue Suite 200, 85012
Telephone: 602-285-5000
Fax: 602-279-2128; 264-0340

Phillip Weeks
Judith M. Wolf
Mark J. Robens

References: Northern Trust, Arizona; Rio Salado Bank.

For Complete List of Firm Personnel, See General Section

For full biographical listings, see the Martindale-Hubbell Law Directory

MARK & PEARLSTEIN, P.A. (AV)

Suite 150 The Brookstone, 2025 North Third Street, 85004
Telephone: 602-257-0200

Leonard J. Mark
Lynn M. Pearlstein, Mr.

OF COUNSEL

Stephen G. Campbell

For full biographical listings, see the Martindale-Hubbell Law Directory

*PRESCOTT,** Yavapai Co.

FAVOUR, MOORE, WILHELMSEN & SCHUYLER, A PROFESSIONAL ASSOCIATION (AV)

1580 Plaza West Drive, P.O. Box 1391, 86302
Telephone: 602-445-2444
Fax: 602-771-0450

John B. Schuyler, Jr.
Mark M. Moore
David K. Wilhelmsen
Lance B. Payette
Clifford G. Cozier

OF COUNSEL

John M. Favour
Richard G. Kleindienst

Representative Client: Yavapai Title Co.
Reference: Bank of America.

For full biographical listings, see the Martindale-Hubbell Law Directory

*TUCSON,** Pima Co.

DONAU & BOLT (AV)

Suite 501, 3505 North Campbell Avenue, 85719-2033
Telephone: 602-795-8710
Fax: 602-795-0308

MEMBER OF FIRM

John R. Bolt

ASSOCIATE

Sharon M. Wolfkeil

For full biographical listings, see the Martindale-Hubbell Law Directory

Tucson—Continued

KARP & WEISS, P.C. (AV)

1800 Bank of America Plaza, 33 North Stone Avenue, 85701-1415
Telephone: 602-882-9705
Telefax: 602-798-3339

Leonard Karp

Reference: National Bank of Arizona.

For full biographical listings, see the Martindale-Hubbell Law Directory

DAVID H. LIEBERTHAL (AV)

Bank of America Building, 33 North Stone Avenue, Suite 2100, 85701
Telephone: 602-622-6793
Fax: 602-624-0816

For full biographical listings, see the Martindale-Hubbell Law Directory

STOMPOLY, STROUD, GIDDINGS & GLICKSMAN, P.C. (AV)

1820 Citibank Tower, One South Church Avenue, 85702
Telephone: 602-628-8300
Telefax: 602-628-9948
Mailing Address: P.O. Box 190, Tucson, AZ, 85702-0190

James L. Stroud

For Complete List of Firm Personnel, See General Section

For full biographical listings, see the Martindale-Hubbell Law Directory

WATERFALL, ECONOMIDIS, CALDWELL, HANSHAW & VILLAMANA, P.C. (AV)

Suite 800, Williams Centre, 5210 East Williams Circle, 85711
Telephone: 602-790-5828
Telecopier: 602-745-1279

Peter Economidis W. Patrick Traynor

Cynthia Ley Anson

For Complete List of Firm Personnel, See General Section

For full biographical listings, see the Martindale-Hubbell Law Directory

CALIFORNIA

ARCADIA, Los Angeles Co.

HELMS, HANRAHAN & MYERS (AV)

Suite 685 Towne Centre Building, 150 North Santa Anita Avenue, 91006
Telephone: 818-445-1177

Sterling E. Myers

Reference: Bank of America National Trust & Savings Assn. (Arcadia Branch).

For Complete List of Firm Personnel, See General Section

For full biographical listings, see the Martindale-Hubbell Law Directory

BEVERLY HILLS, Los Angeles Co.

ARLENE COLMAN-SCHWIMMER A PROFESSIONAL CORPORATION (AV)

Suite 810, 9595 Wilshire Boulevard, 90212
Telephone: 310-273-2818
Fax: 310-273-8549
Laguna Beach, California Office: 1400 S. Coast Highway, Penthouse, 92651.
Telephone: 714-376-1107.
Facsimile: 714-497-4934.

Arlene Colman-Schwimmer

Edie Wittick Warren Laurie R. Hazman (Not admitted in CA)

For full biographical listings, see the Martindale-Hubbell Law Directory

HARRY M. FAIN (AV)

121 South Beverly Drive, 90212
Telephone: 310-275-5132; 272-7807
FAX: 310-271-5269

Reference: City National Bank (Beverly Hills Main Office).

For full biographical listings, see the Martindale-Hubbell Law Directory

FRIEDMAN & FRIEDMAN (AV)

9454 Wilshire Boulevard, Suite 313, 90212-2904
Telephone: 310-273-2800
Fax: 310-273-3642

Ira M. Friedman Abby B. Friedman

Representative Clients: Gursey Schneider & Co.; Harvey Capital Corp.; Christensen, White, Miller, Fink & Jacobs; Jeffer, Mangels, Butler & Marmaro; Key Bank of Maine; Southern California Bank.

For full biographical listings, see the Martindale-Hubbell Law Directory

JAFFE & CLEMENS (AV)

A Partnership including Professional Corporations
Suite 1000, 433 North Camden Drive, 90210
Telephone: 310-550-7477
Telecopier: 310-271-8313

Daniel J. Jaffe (A Professional Corporation) Bruce A. Clemens (A Professional Corporation)
William S. Ryden

ASSOCIATES

Cynthia S. Monaco Judy Bogen
Lauren H. Nemiroff David M. Luboff

For full biographical listings, see the Martindale-Hubbell Law Directory

KAUFMAN & YOUNG, A PROFESSIONAL CORPORATION (AV)

121 South Beverly Drive, 90212
Telephone: 310-275-5132
Los Angeles: 272-7807
Fax: 310-275-2919

Robert S. Kaufman Kenneth M. Young
Douglas S. Segal

OF COUNSEL

Marcy L. Kenerson Lance S. Spiegel

Reference: City National Bank (Beverly Hills Main Office Branch).

For full biographical listings, see the Martindale-Hubbell Law Directory

*FAIRFIELD,** Solano Co.

WILLIAM H. MCPHERSON (AV)

825 Webster Street, 94533
Telephone: 707-422-7706
Fax: 707-425-9331

For full biographical listings, see the Martindale-Hubbell Law Directory

*FRESNO,** Fresno Co.

DOWLING, MAGARIAN, AARON & HEYMAN, INCORPORATED (AV)

Suite 200, 6051 North Fresno Street, 93710
Telephone: 209-432-4500
Fax: 209-432-4590

OF COUNSEL

Donald J. Magarian

Reference: Wells Fargo Bank (Main).

For Complete List of Firm Personnel, See General Section

For full biographical listings, see the Martindale-Hubbell Law Directory

IRVINE, Orange Co.

RAY HENDRICKSON (AV)

University Tower, Suite 700, 4199 Campus Drive, 92715
Telephone: 714-833-0101; 854-8800
Fax: 714-854-4897

References: Mitsui Manufacturers Bank, Newport Beach, California; Bank of California, Newport Beach, California; Home Fed, Irvine, California.

For full biographical listings, see the Martindale-Hubbell Law Directory

LA JOLLA, San Diego Co.

RONALD W. JOHNSON (AV)

Suite 240, 4180 La Jolla Village Drive, 92037-1497
Telephone: 619-455-5015
Fax: 619-455-7924

LOS ALTOS, Santa Clara Co.

MALOVOS & KONEVICH (AV)

Los Altos Plaza, 5150 El Camino Real, Suite A-22, 94022
Telephone: 415-988-9700
Facsimile: 415-988-9639

(See Next Column)

MALOVOS & KONEVICH, *Los Altos—Continued*

Marian Malovos Konevich Robert W. Konevich

RETIRED FOUNDING PARTNER

Kenneth R. Malovos

References: Bank of America, Mountain View, California Branch; First Interstate Bank, Mountain View and Los Altos, California Branches.

For full biographical listings, see the Martindale-Hubbell Law Directory

*LOS ANGELES,** Los Angeles Co.

DEUTSCH & RUBIN (AV)

A Partnership including a Professional Corporation
Second Floor, West Tower, 11377 West Olympic Boulevard, 90064-1683
Telephone: 310-312-3222
FAX: 310-312-3205

MEMBERS OF FIRM

Miles J. Rubin (A Professional Corporation) Wendy A. Herzog

OF COUNSEL

Warren C. Deutsch (A Professional Corporation) Linda Cukier

For full biographical listings, see the Martindale-Hubbell Law Directory

NORMAN M. DOLIN (AV)

Suite 2200, 1925 Century Park East (Century City), 90067
Telephone: 310-552-9338
Fax: 310-552-1922

ASSOCIATES

Lynn Kyman Langley Ani M. Garikian

For full biographical listings, see the Martindale-Hubbell Law Directory

GOLDMAN & KAGON, LAW CORPORATION (AV)

1801 Century Park East, Suite 2222, 90067
Telephone: 310-552-1707
Telex: 701076
Cable: GOKALAW
Telecopier: 310-552-7938

Terry Mc Niff

Jared Laskin

COUNSEL

A. David Kagon

For Complete List of Firm Personnel, See General Section

For full biographical listings, see the Martindale-Hubbell Law Directory

HUFSTEDLER & KAUS (AV)

A Partnership including Professional Corporations
Thirty-Ninth Floor, 355 South Grand Avenue, 90071-3101
Telephone: 213-617-7070
Fax: 213-617-6170

MEMBER OF FIRM

Patricia Dominis Phillips

ASSOCIATES

John W. (Jack) Alden Jr. Elayna J. Youchah

Reference: First Interstate Bank, 707 Wilshire.

For Complete List of Firm Personnel, See General Section

For full biographical listings, see the Martindale-Hubbell Law Directory

RONALD A. LITZ & ASSOCIATES (AV)

Suite 1901, 1901 Avenue of the Stars, 90067
Telephone: 310-201-0100
FAX: 310-201-0226

ASSOCIATE

Jennifer A. Litz

OF COUNSEL

Arnold W. Magasinn Vicki Fisher Magasinn
Carl R. Waldman

For full biographical listings, see the Martindale-Hubbell Law Directory

LURVEY & SHAPIRO (AV)

Fox Plaza, 2121 Avenue of the Stars, Suite 1550 (Century City), 90067
Telephone: 310-203-0711
Fax: 310-203-0610

(See Next Column)

MEMBERS OF FIRM

Ira H. Lurvey Judith Salkow Shapiro

Reference: City National Bank (Beverly Hills Main Office).

For full biographical listings, see the Martindale-Hubbell Law Directory

NACHSHIN & WESTON (AV)

A Partnership including Professional Corporations
Suite 2240, 11755 Wilshire Boulevard, 90025
Telephone: 310-478-6868
Telefax: 310-473-8112

Robert J. Nachshin (A Professional Corporation) Scott N. Weston

ASSOCIATE

Joseph A. Langlois

For full biographical listings, see the Martindale-Hubbell Law Directory

MELVIN L. SILVERMAN (AV)

1925 Century Park East, Suite 2000, 90067
Telephone: 310-277-2236
Telecopier: 310-556-5653
Cable Address: "Oyez Oyez"

For full biographical listings, see the Martindale-Hubbell Law Directory

HARVEY STRASSMAN (AV)

1875 Century Park East, 15th Floor, 90067
Telephone: 310-277-6775
Fax: 310-552-3228

For full biographical listings, see the Martindale-Hubbell Law Directory

TROPE AND TROPE (AV)

12121 Wilshire Boulevard, Suite 801, 90025
Telephone: 310-207-8228
Fax: 310-826-1122

MEMBERS OF FIRM

Sorrell Trope Mark S. Patt
Eugene L. Trope Bruce E. Cooperman
Maryanne La Guardia Mark Vincent Kaplan
Steven Knowles Suzanne Harris
Larry A. Ginsberg

ASSOCIATES

Thomas Paine Dunlap Brenda A. Beswick
Donna Beck Weaver Burton Falk
Carolyn J. Kozuch Leigh R. Strauss
Scott K. Robinson Roger B. Peikin
Laurence R. Goldman Brian D. Wynne
Anne Elizabeth Campbell Gary D. Weinhouse
Pamela Somers Leslie M. Jordon

OF COUNSEL

Roland L. Trope (Not admitted in CA)

For full biographical listings, see the Martindale-Hubbell Law Directory

WALZER & WALZER, A LAW CORPORATION (AV)

Suite 2610, 2029 Century Park East, 90067
Telephone: 310-557-0915

Stuart B. Walzer Peter M. Walzer

For full biographical listings, see the Martindale-Hubbell Law Directory

ZOLLA AND MEYER (AV)

A Partnership including a Professional Corporation
Suite 1020, 2029 Century Park East, 90067
Telephone: 310-277-0725
Facsimile: 310-277-3784

MEMBERS OF FIRM

Marshall S. Zolla (A P.C.) Lisa Helfend Meyer

ASSOCIATES

Doreen Marie Olson Stephanie Emelle Johnson

Reference: Bank of California, Beverly Hills.

For full biographical listings, see the Martindale-Hubbell Law Directory

MOUNTAIN VIEW, Santa Clara Co.

J. Norman Baker (AV)

San Antonio Center, 2570 El Camino Real West, Suite 504, 94040
Telephone: 415-941-0604
Fax: 415-941-4697

Reference: Bank of the West (Los Altos Branch).

For full biographical listings, see the Martindale-Hubbell Law Directory

NEWPORT BEACH, Orange Co.

Thomas A. Bernauer A Professional Corporation (AV)

500 Newport Center Drive, Suite 950, 92660
Telephone: 714-720-1313
Fax: 714-720-7457

Thomas A. Bernauer

For full biographical listings, see the Martindale-Hubbell Law Directory

George M. Kornievsky A Professional Corporation (AV)

4400 MacArthur Boulevard, Suite 400, 92660
Telephone: 714-724-0888
FAX: 714-752-7035

George M. Kornievsky

For full biographical listings, see the Martindale-Hubbell Law Directory

John R. Schilling A Professional Corporation (AV)

Suite 6000, West Tower, 4000 MacArthur Boulevard, 92660
Telephone: 714-833-3335
FAX: 714-752-8170

John R. Schilling

References: Union Bank (Airport Branch); City National Bank (Newport Beach).

For full biographical listings, see the Martindale-Hubbell Law Directory

*OAKLAND,** Alameda Co.

Garrett C. Dailey (AV)

519 - 17th Street, 7th Floor, 94612
Telephone: 510-465-3920
Fax: 510-465-7348

Reference: Wells Fargo Bank (Oakland City Center Office).

For full biographical listings, see the Martindale-Hubbell Law Directory

Sally J. Laidlaw (AV)

405-14th Street, Suite 710, 94612-2706
Telephone: 510-891-3969

For full biographical listings, see the Martindale-Hubbell Law Directory

Miriam Steinbock (AV)

436 14th Street, Suite 1417, 94612
Telephone: 510-763-5611
FAX: 510-763-3430

For full biographical listings, see the Martindale-Hubbell Law Directory

ORANGE, Orange Co.

James K. Batchelor A Professional Corporation (AV)

765 South The City Drive Suite 270, 92668
Telephone: 714-750-8388; 714-542-2333
Fax: 714-750-8002

James K. Batchelor

Reference: Bank of America National Trust & Savings Assn.

For full biographical listings, see the Martindale-Hubbell Law Directory

Richard M. Shack (AV)

One City Boulevard West Suite 1400, 92668
Telephone: 714-978-0325
Fax: 714-937-1923

LEGAL SUPPORT PERSONNEL

Adriene D. Fowler

For full biographical listings, see the Martindale-Hubbell Law Directory

PALM DESERT, Riverside Co.

Law Offices of Virginia S. Criste (AV)

Suite B 75-005 Country Club Drive, 92211
Telephone: 619-776-1770
Fax: 619-776-1775

For full biographical listings, see the Martindale-Hubbell Law Directory

PALM SPRINGS, Riverside Co.

Lee R. Mohr A Professional Law Corporation (AV)

Suite 121, 1111 East Tahquitz Canyon Way, 92262
Telephone: 619-325-1711
Fax: 619-322-4171

Lee R. Mohr

For full biographical listings, see the Martindale-Hubbell Law Directory

PALO ALTO, Santa Clara Co.

James T. Danaher (AV)

2600 El Camino Real, Suite 506, P.O. Box 60580, 94306
Telephone: 415-857-1700
Facsimile: 415-857-9041

For full biographical listings, see the Martindale-Hubbell Law Directory

Flicker & Kerin (AV)

Suite 460, 285 Hamilton, P.O. Box 840, 94302
Telephone: 415-321-0947
Fax: 415-326-9722

MEMBERS OF FIRM

Michael R. Flicker Anthony J. Kerin, III

ASSOCIATE

Rhesa C. Rubin

For full biographical listings, see the Martindale-Hubbell Law Directory

John E. Miller (AV)

250 Cambridge Avenue, Suite 102, 94306-1504
Telephone: 415-321-8886
Fax: 415-321-8998

ASSOCIATES

Annalisa C Wood Laura L. Reynolds

Reference: Bank of the West.

For full biographical listings, see the Martindale-Hubbell Law Directory

Lincoln A. Mitchell (AV)

Suite 300, 550 Hamilton Avenue, 94301
Telephone: 415-321-5003
Fax: 415-326-2404

For full biographical listings, see the Martindale-Hubbell Law Directory

PASADENA, Los Angeles Co.

Anderson & Salisbury, A Professional Corporation (AV)

Suite 310, 350 West Colorado Boulevard, 91105
Telephone: 818-449-4812; 213-684-0920
Telecopier: 818-449-1576

Clifford R. Anderson, Jr. Lee W. Salisbury

Michael C. Robinson

For full biographical listings, see the Martindale-Hubbell Law Directory

Taylor Kupfer Summers & Rhodes (AV)

301 East Colorado Boulevard, Suite 407, 91101
Telephone: 818-304-0953; 213-624-7877
Fax: 818-795-6375

MEMBER OF FIRM

Robert C. Summers

Reference: Citizens Bank (Pasadena).

For Complete List of Firm Personnel, See General Section

For full biographical listings, see the Martindale-Hubbell Law Directory

*SACRAMENTO,** Sacramento Co.

Bartholomew & Wasznicky (AV)

1006 Fourth Street, 8th Floor, 95814
Telephone: 916-443-2055
Fax: 916-443-8287

(See Next Column)

BARTHOLOMEW & WASZNICKY, *Sacramento—Continued*

MEMBERS OF FIRM

Hal D. Bartholomew Diane Wasznicky

ASSOCIATES

Mary C. Molinaro Sarah Berryhill Orr

For full biographical listings, see the Martindale-Hubbell Law Directory

JAMES M. MIZE (AV)

3620 American River Drive, Suite 250, 95864
Telephone: 916-485-2211
FAX: 916-485-1934

For full biographical listings, see the Martindale-Hubbell Law Directory

WOODRUFF, O'HAIR & POSNER, INC. A LAW CORPORATION (AV)

2251 Fair Oaks Boulevard, Suite 100, 95825
Telephone: 916-920-0211
Telecopier: 916-920-0241

D. Thomas Woodruff Robert J. O'Hair
Jeffrey J. Posner

For full biographical listings, see the Martindale-Hubbell Law Directory

*SAN BERNARDINO,** San Bernardino Co.

STEVEN A. BECKER A PROFESSIONAL LAW CORPORATION (AV)

315 West Sixth Street, 92401
Telephone: 909-888-2211
Fax: 909-381-0586

Steven A. Becker

For full biographical listings, see the Martindale-Hubbell Law Directory

*SAN DIEGO,** San Diego Co.

E. GREGORY ALFORD (AV)

1551 Fourth Avenue, Suite 301, 92101
Telephone: 619-232-4734
FAX: 619-239-3345

For full biographical listings, see the Martindale-Hubbell Law Directory

HUNTINGTON & HAVILAND, A PROFESSIONAL CORPORATION (AV)

1551 Fourth Avenue, Suite 700, 92101-3155
Telephone: 619-233-9500
Fax: 619-237-8003

Edward B. (Ned) Huntington Phyllis H. Scutchfield
Warren E. Haviland Marjorie A. Huntington

For full biographical listings, see the Martindale-Hubbell Law Directory

LUCE, FORWARD, HAMILTON & SCRIPPS (AV)

A Partnership including Professional Corporations
600 West Broadway, Suite 2600, 92101
Telephone: 619-236-1414
Fax: 619-232-8311
La Jolla, California Office: 4275 Executive Square, Suite 800, 92037.
Telephone: 619-535-2639.
Fax: 619-453-2812.
Los Angeles, California Office: 777 South Figueroa, 36th Floor, 90017.
Telephone: 213-892-4992.
Fax: 213-892-7731.
San Francisco, California Office: 100 Bush Street, 20th Floor, 94104.
Telephone: 415-395-7900.
Fax: 415-395-7949.
New York, N.Y. Office: Citicorp Center, 153 East 53rd Street, 26th Floor, 10022.
Telephone: 212-754-1414.
Fax: 212-644-9727.

MEMBER OF FIRM

Susanne Stanford

ASSOCIATES

Stefanie Crames Solomon Frank J. Kros

For Complete List of Firm Personnel, See General Section

For full biographical listings, see the Martindale-Hubbell Law Directory

OLINS, FOERSTER & HAYES (AV)

A Partnership including Professional Corporations
2214 Second Avenue, 92101
Telephone: 619-238-1601
Fax: 619-238-1613

(See Next Column)

MEMBERS OF FIRM

Douglas F. Olins (A P.C.) Barrett J. Foerster (A P.C.)
Dennis J. Hayes

ASSOCIATE

Julia Houchin Guroff

For full biographical listings, see the Martindale-Hubbell Law Directory

LAW OFFICES OF GARY PIKE A PROFESSIONAL CORPORATION (AV)

520 West Ash Street, Suite 200, 92101
Telephone: 619-238-1234
Telecopier: 619-238-0127

Gary E. Pike

Dana F. Weinstein Leann A. Sumner
Nicola S. Blair Adam E. Slonim

For full biographical listings, see the Martindale-Hubbell Law Directory

*SAN FRANCISCO,** San Francisco Co.

G. WILLIAM FILLEY (AV)

115 Sansome Street, Suite 1100, 94104
Telephone: 415-956-5912

For full biographical listings, see the Martindale-Hubbell Law Directory

EUGENIA MACGOWAN (AV)

Suite 400 Monadnock Building, 685 Market Street, 94105
Telephone: 415-882-4940

For full biographical listings, see the Martindale-Hubbell Law Directory

SUCHERMAN & COLLINS (AV)

Suite 1750, 88 Kearny Street, 94108
Telephone: 415-956-5554
Fax: 415-781-4367

Lowell H. Sucherman Carroll J. Collins III

ASSOCIATE

Michelene Insalaco

For full biographical listings, see the Martindale-Hubbell Law Directory

LAW OFFICES OF LAWRENCE W. THORPE (AV)

115 Sansome, Suite 1100, 94104
Telephone: 415-981-3111
Telecopier: 415-982-3181

Julia M. Tracy

LEGAL SUPPORT PERSONNEL

PARALEGAL/CONSULTANT

Jan Caldwell Thorpe, M.F.C.C.

For full biographical listings, see the Martindale-Hubbell Law Directory

*SAN JOSE,** Santa Clara Co.

HAMMER JACOBS & THROGMORTON (AV)

10 Almaden Boulevard, 10th Floor, 95113-2237
Telephone: 408-297-8400
Fax: 408-297-8488

Philip L. Hammer Jamie J. Throgmorton
Paul E. Jacobs Jane Meredith Ohringer
Natalie T. Daprile

For full biographical listings, see the Martindale-Hubbell Law Directory

SAN MATEO, San Mateo Co.

HANSON & NORRIS (AV)

777 Mariners Island Boulevard, Suite 575, 94404-1562
Telephone: 415-571-0600
Fax: 415-571-0835

MEMBERS OF FIRM

Harry A. Hanson, Jr. Lana L. Norris
Anne Marie Rossi

ASSOCIATES

Stephen J. Montalvo Audrey Braker Fox
Belinda Hanson

For full biographical listings, see the Martindale-Hubbell Law Directory

*SAN RAFAEL,** Marin Co.

RICHARD BARRY AND SHARON MAH (AV)

An Association - Not a Partnership
Courthouse Square, 1000 Fourth Street, Suite 350, P.O. Box 151257, 94915-1257
Telephone: 415-453-0360
Fax: 415-453-9193

Richard F. Barry   Sharon F. Mah

For full biographical listings, see the Martindale-Hubbell Law Directory

SAN RAMON, Contra Costa Co.

LEONARD D. WEILER A PROFESSIONAL CORPORATION (AV)

Suite 200, Two Annabel Lane, 94583
Telephone: 510-275-0855
Telecopier: 510-830-8787

Leonard D. Weiler

Thomas G. Borst

For full biographical listings, see the Martindale-Hubbell Law Directory

SANTA MONICA, Los Angeles Co.

J. MICHAEL KELLY & ASSOCIATES A PROFESSIONAL CORPORATION (AV)

201 Santa Monica Boulevard, 5th Floor, 90401
Telephone: 310-393-0236

J. Michael Kelly

For full biographical listings, see the Martindale-Hubbell Law Directory

SUNNYVALE, Santa Clara Co.

JACKSON, BROWN & EFTING (AV)

415 South Murphy Avenue, 94086-6172
Telephone: 408-732-3114
Fax: 408-732-0709

Richard A. Brown   Hugh F. Jackson
James Efting

LEGAL SUPPORT PERSONNEL

Cecilia J. O'Brien

For full biographical listings, see the Martindale-Hubbell Law Directory

TORRANCE, Los Angeles Co.

CHRISTOPHER M. MOORE & ASSOCIATES A LAW CORPORATION (AV)

Suite 490 Union Bank Tower, 21515 Hawthorne Boulevard, 90503
Telephone: 310-540-8855
Fax: 310-316-1307

Christopher M. Moore

Sharon A. Bryan   Rebecca Lee Tomlinson Schroff
Julia A. Stanton

For full biographical listings, see the Martindale-Hubbell Law Directory

TUSTIN, Orange Co.

STAPLETON & STAPLETON, A PROFESSIONAL ASSOCIATION (AV)

Suite 114, Irvine Plaza Building, 17621 Irvine Boulevard, 92680-3130
Telephone: 714-832-8003
FAX: 714-832-2007

Marlin G. Stapleton   Marlin G. Stapleton, Jr.

For full biographical listings, see the Martindale-Hubbell Law Directory

*VENTURA,** Ventura Co.

TAYLOR MCCORD, A LAW CORPORATION (AV)

721 East Main Street, P.O. Box 1477, 93002
Telephone: 805-648-4700
Fax: 805-653-6124

Richard L. Taylor   Ellen G. Conroy
Robert L. McCord, Jr.   David L. Praver

Patrick Cherry   Susan D. Siple

For full biographical listings, see the Martindale-Hubbell Law Directory

VICTORVILLE, San Bernardino Co.

LYNN E. ZUMBRUNN A LAW CORPORATION (AV)

14335 Park Avenue, Suite A, 92392-6072
Telephone: 619-245-5333
Fax: 619-245-2000

Lynn Edward Zumbrunn

James Bruce Minton   Gregory L. Zumbrunn

References: First Interstate Bank; Desert Community Bank.

For full biographical listings, see the Martindale-Hubbell Law Directory

VISTA, San Diego Co.

JAMES A. HENNENHOEFER A PROFESSIONAL CORPORATION (AV)

316 South Melrose Drive, 92083
Telephone: 619-941-2260
Facsimile: 619-945-1805

James A. Hennenhoefer

Rolf G. Steeve, Jr.

For full biographical listings, see the Martindale-Hubbell Law Directory

WALNUT CREEK, Contra Costa Co.

R. KENT BREWER (AV)

1981 North Broadway, Suite 405, 94596
Telephone: 510-934-8988
Fax: 510-943-6894

For full biographical listings, see the Martindale-Hubbell Law Directory

COLORADO

AURORA, Arapahoe & Adams Cos.

LEWIS W. DYMOND, JR. A PROFESSIONAL CORPORATION (AV)

Suite 212, 13900 East Harvard Avenue, 80014
Telephone: 303-695-8700
Fax: 303-696-0923

Lewis W. Dymond, Jr.

Reference: Norwest Bank of Aurora-City Center.

For full biographical listings, see the Martindale-Hubbell Law Directory

*BOULDER,** Boulder Co.

THORBURN, SAKOL & THRONE (AV)

255 Canyon Boulevard at Cloud Creek, Suite 100, 80302-4920
Telephone: 303-449-1873
Fax: 303-447-9840

MEMBER OF FIRM

Barre M. Sakol

Reference: Bank One of Boulder.

For full biographical listings, see the Martindale-Hubbell Law Directory

*COLORADO SPRINGS,** El Paso Co.

CROSS, GADDIS, KIN, HERD & KELLY, P.C. (AV)

118 South Wahsatch, 80903
Telephone: 719-471-3848
Fax: 719-471-0317

Thomas R. Cross   David L. Quicksall (1950-1991)
Larry R. Gaddis   Thomas J. Herd
James W. Kin   Debra L. Kelly

OF COUNSEL

James B. Turner

Reference: Norwest Bank of Colorado Springs.

For full biographical listings, see the Martindale-Hubbell Law Directory

*DENVER,** Denver Co.

CANGES, IWASHKO & BETHKE, A PROFESSIONAL CORPORATION (AV)

303 East 17th Avenue Suite 400, 80203-1261
Telephone: 303-860-1900
Fax: 303-860-1665

(See Next Column)

CANGES, IWASHKO & BETHKE A PROFESSIONAL CORPORATION, *Denver—Continued*

E. Michael Canges   Nina A. Iwashko
Erich L. Bethke

Stephen R. Fatzinger   James S. Bailey

Reference: Norwest Bank Denver.

For full biographical listings, see the Martindale-Hubbell Law Directory

DAVIS & WEINSTEIN (AV)

Suite 2600, 1600 Broadway, 80202
Telephone: 303-861-4166
Fax: 303-861-2976

MEMBER OF FIRM
Wendy W. Davis
ASSOCIATE
Erica Richardson Kemmerley

Reference: The Women's Bank, N.A., Denver, Colo.

For full biographical listings, see the Martindale-Hubbell Law Directory

FEDER, MORRIS, TAMBLYN & GOLDSTEIN, P.C. (AV)

150 Blake Street Building, 1441 Eighteenth Street, 80202
Telephone: 303-292-1441
FAX: 303-292-1126

Denise K. Mills   Barbara Salomon
Gina B. Weitzenkorn
OF COUNSEL
Katherine Tamblyn

Reference: Guaranty Bank & Trust Co., Denver, Colorado.

For full biographical listings, see the Martindale-Hubbell Law Directory

STEPHEN J. HARHAI (AV)

1928 East Eighteenth Avenue, 80206
Telephone: 303-329-8300
Fax: 303-329-8119

For full biographical listings, see the Martindale-Hubbell Law Directory

ROBERT T. HINDS, JR. AND ASSOCIATES, P.C. (AV)

600 South Cherry Street Penthouse Suite 1400, 80222-1714
Telephone: 303-320-0300
Fax: 303-321-1121

Robert T. Hinds, Jr.

Ray L. Weaver   Lucy Hojo Denson
Robert T. Hinds, III
OF COUNSEL
Dr. Howard I. Rosenberg

For full biographical listings, see the Martindale-Hubbell Law Directory

STANLEY G. LIPKIN (AV)

44 Cook Street, Suite 607, 80206
Telephone: 303-393-6700
FAX: 303-388-4646

For full biographical listings, see the Martindale-Hubbell Law Directory

MCGUANE AND MALONE, PROFESSIONAL CORPORATION (AV)

Suite 825 Ptarmigan Place, 3773 Cherry Creek North Drive, 80209
Telephone: 303-388-4500
Fax: 303-388-2029

Frank L. McGuane, Jr.   Thomas P. Malone

Judith Claire Bregman   Kathleen A. Hogan

Reference: Bank One.

For full biographical listings, see the Martindale-Hubbell Law Directory

MYERS, HOPPIN, BRADLEY AND DEVITT, P.C. (AV)

Suite 420, 4704 Harlan Street, 80212
Telephone: 303-433-8527
Fax: 303-433-8219

Frederick J. Myers   Jon T. Bradley
Charles T. Hoppin   Jerald J. Devitt

Gregg W. Fraser

(See Next Column)

OF COUNSEL
Kent E. Hanson

Reference: Bank One Lakeside Banking Center.

For full biographical listings, see the Martindale-Hubbell Law Directory

LAKEWOOD, Jefferson Co.

POLIDORI, GEROME, FRANKLIN AND JACOBSON (AV)

Suite 300, 550 South Wadsworth Boulevard, 80226
Telephone: 303-936-3300
Fax: 303-936-0125

Gary L. Polidori   Dennis J. Jacobson
Peter L. Franklin

Lesleigh S. Monahan   Barry J. Seidenfeld

For Complete List of Firm Personnel, See General Section

For full biographical listings, see the Martindale-Hubbell Law Directory

*LITTLETON,** Arapahoe Co.

COX, MUSTAIN-WOOD AND WALKER (AV)

6601 South University Boulevard, 80121
Telephone: 303-730-0067
Fax: 303-730-0344

MEMBERS OF FIRM
Mary Jane Truesdell Cox   Randall C. Mustain-Wood
ASSOCIATES
James C. Schumacher   Kimberly A. Wooldridge
OF COUNSEL
Timothy B. Walker (P.C.)
SPECIAL COUNSEL
Jordon T. Sanger (P.C.)

For full biographical listings, see the Martindale-Hubbell Law Directory

*MONTROSE,** Montrose Co.

EDWARD D. DURHAM (AV)

524 South First Street, P.O. Box 1721, 81402
Telephone: 303-249-2274
Fax: 303-249-6482

Reference: Norwest Bank of Montrose.

For full biographical listings, see the Martindale-Hubbell Law Directory

CONNECTICUT

*BRIDGEPORT,** Fairfield Co.

BELINKIE & LAX (AV)

1087 Broad Street, 06604
Telephone: 203-368-4201
FAX: 203-368-3075

MEMBERS OF FIRM
Alfred R. Belinkie   Sandra P. Lax
ASSOCIATES
David Fusco   Peter Ventre

Representative Clients furnished upon request.

For full biographical listings, see the Martindale-Hubbell Law Directory

GLADSTONE, SCHWARTZ, BLUM, WOODS, L.L.C. (AV)

1087 Broad Street, P.O. Box 1900, 06604
Telephone: 203-368-6746
Telecopier: 203-576-8847

MEMBERS OF FIRM
Lawrence B. Schwartz (1929-1993)   Louis I. Gladstone
Leonard C. Blum
Matthew B. Woods
ASSOCIATES
Arthur E. Miller   Jason P. Gladstone
Roberta S. Schwartz   Stacey M. Daves-ohlin
OF COUNSEL
Peter L. Leepson   Edward N. Lerner
Arthur A. Lunin

Counsel for: Baker Companies, Inc.; D'Addario Industries, Inc.; Connecticut Jai Alai, Inc.; McNeil Brothers, Inc.; IMG & Associates Ltd., Partnership.

For full biographical listings, see the Martindale-Hubbell Law Directory

GREENWICH, Fairfield Co.

COHEN & MARLOW (AV)

779 North Street, 06831
Telephone: 203-622-8787
Fax: 203-622-8798
New Haven Connecticut Office: 157 Church Street, P.O. Box 1800.
Telephone: 203-782-9440.

Gary I. Cohen — Lee Marlow

ASSOCIATE

Melissa J. Needle

For full biographical listings, see the Martindale-Hubbell Law Directory

*HARTFORD,** Hartford Co.

JACKSON, O'KEEFE AND PHELAN (AV)

36 Russ Street, 06106-1571
Telephone: 203-278-4040
Fax: 203-527-2500
West Hartford, Connecticut Office: 62 LaSalle Road.
Telephone: 203-521-7500.
Fax: 203-561-5399.
Bethlehem, Connecticut Office: 423 Munger Lane.
Telephone: 203-266-5255.

MEMBERS OF FIRM

Jay W. Jackson — Peter K. O'Keefe
Andrew J. O'Keefe — Philip R. Dunn, Jr.
Denise Martino Phelan — Michael J. Walsh
Matthew J. O'Keefe — Anna M. Carbonaro
Denise Rodosevich

OF COUNSEL

Maureen Sullivan Dinnan

Representative Clients: Aetna Casualty & Surety Co.; ITT Hartford; Liberty Mutual Insurance Co.; Connecticut Medical Insurance Co.

For full biographical listings, see the Martindale-Hubbell Law Directory

SOROKIN SOROKIN GROSS HYDE & WILLIAMS P.C. (AV)

One Corporate Center, 06103
Telephone: 203-525-6645
Fax: 203-522-1781
Simsbury, Connecticut Office: 730 Hopmeadow Street.
Telephone: 203-651-9348.
Rocky Hill, Connecticut Office: 2360 Main Street.
Telephone: 203-563-9305.
Fax: 203-529-6931.
Glastonbury, Connecticut Office: 124 Hebron Avenue.
Telephone: 203-659-8801.

John J. Bracken III — Richard D. Tulisano (Resident, Rocky Hill Office)
Lewis Rabinovitz

Lisa A. Magliochetti

OF COUNSEL

Ethel Silver Sorokin

For Complete List of Firm Personnel, See General Section

For full biographical listings, see the Martindale-Hubbell Law Directory

*NEW HAVEN,** New Haven Co.

COHEN & MARLOW (AV)

157 Church Street, P.O. Box 1800, 06507-1800
Telephone: 203-782-9440
Facsimile: 203-772-0583
Greenwich, Connecticut Office: 779 North Street.
Telephone: 203-622-8787.

MEMBERS OF FIRM

Gary I. Cohen — Lee Marlow

ASSOCIATE

Melissa J. Needle

For full biographical listings, see the Martindale-Hubbell Law Directory

CRANE & KAHN (AV)

A Partnership of Professional Corporations
261 Bradley Street, 06511
Telephone: 203-777-0506
Facsimile: 203-776-1107

Lansing E. Crane (P.C.) — Gerald H. Kahn (P.C.)

References: Connecticut Savings Bank; Union Trust Co.

For full biographical listings, see the Martindale-Hubbell Law Directory

GREENFIELD AND MURPHY (AV)

234 Church Street, P.O. Box 1103, 06504-1103
Telephone: 203-787-6711
Telecopier: 203-777-6442

MEMBERS OF FIRM

James R. Greenfield — Helen D. Murphy
Maureen M. Murphy

Reference: Union Trust Co.

For full biographical listings, see the Martindale-Hubbell Law Directory

JEAN L. WELTY (AV)

385 Orange Street, P.O. Box 1662, 06507
Telephone: 203-781-0877
Fax: 203-781-0899

Reference: Peoples Bank.

For full biographical listings, see the Martindale-Hubbell Law Directory

STAMFORD, Fairfield Co.

SILVER, GOLUB & TEITELL (AV)

184 Atlantic Street, P.O. Box 389, 06904
Telephone: 203-325-4491
FAX: 203-325-3769

MEMBERS OF FIRM

Richard A. Silver — Elaine T. Silver

For Complete List of Firm Personnel, See General Section

For full biographical listings, see the Martindale-Hubbell Law Directory

WOFSEY, ROSEN, KWESKIN & KURIANSKY (AV)

600 Summer Street, 06901
Telephone: 203-327-2300
FAX: 203-967-9273

MEMBERS OF FIRM

Abraham Wofsey (1915-1944) — Anthony R. Lorenzo
Michael Wofsey (1927-1951) — Edward M. Kweskin
David M. Rosen (1926-1967) — David M. Cohen
Julius B. Kuriansky (1910-1992) — Marshall Goldberg
Monroe Silverman — Stephen A. Finn
Emanuel Margolis — Judith Rosenberg
Howard C. Kaplan — Robert L. Teicher
Mark H. Henderson

Steven D. Grushkin

OF COUNSEL

Saul Kwartin — Sydney C. Kweskin (Retired)

ASSOCIATES

Brian Bandler — James A. Lenes
John J.L. Chober — Valerie E. Maze
Steven M. Frederick — Maurice K. Segall
Eric M. Higgins — Randall M. Skigen
Gregory J. Williams

Representative Clients: Benenson Realty; Cellular Information Systems, Inc.; Gateway Bank; Hartford Provision Company; Louis Dreyfus Corp.; Norwalk Federation of Teachers; Patient Care, Inc.; People's Bank; Ridgeway Shopping Center and Stamford Housing Authority.

For full biographical listings, see the Martindale-Hubbell Law Directory

MARY ELLEN WYNN (AV)

One Canterbury Green, 06901
Telephone: 203-356-1355
Fax: 203-356-9412

For full biographical listings, see the Martindale-Hubbell Law Directory

WEST HARTFORD, Hartford Co.

BERMAN, BOURNS & CURRIE (AV)

970 Farmington Avenue, P.O. Box 271837, 06127-1837
Telephone: 203-232-4471
Fax: 203-523-4605

MEMBERS OF FIRM

John A. Berman — Courtney B. Bourns
John K. Currie

ASSOCIATES

Robert B. Fawber — Mary Beth Anderson

For full biographical listings, see the Martindale-Hubbell Law Directory

WESTPORT, Fairfield Co.

LAW OFFICES OF PAUL J. PACIFICO (AV)

12 Avery Place, Second Floor, 06880
Telephone: 203-221-8066
Fax: 203-221-8076

LEGAL SUPPORT PERSONNEL

Karen L. Kosinski

For full biographical listings, see the Martindale-Hubbell Law Directory

RUTKIN AND EFFRON, P.C. (AV)

323 Riverside Avenue, P.O. Box 295, 06881
Telephone: 203-227-7301
Fax: 222-9295
New Haven, Connecticut Office: 201 Orange Street.
Telephone: 203-498-1887.
Fax: 203-772-0124.

Arnold H. Rutkin — Ellen J. Effron

Sarah S. Oldham

OF COUNSEL

Kathleen A. Hogan

For full biographical listings, see the Martindale-Hubbell Law Directory

HERMAN H. TARNOW (AV)

329 Riverside Avenue, 06880
Telephone: 203-226-1701
Facsimile: 203-454-5508
New York, New York Office: 330 Madison Avenue.
Telephone: 212-297-3307.
Fax: 212-972-6521.

For full biographical listings, see the Martindale-Hubbell Law Directory

TIROLA & HERRING (AV)

1221 Post Road East, P.O. Box 631, 06881
Telephone: 203-226-8926
Fax: 203-226-9500
New York, New York Office: Suite 4E, 10 Sheridan Square.
Telephone: 212-463-9642.

MEMBERS OF FIRM

Vincent S. Tirola — Elizabeth C. Seeley
Charles Fredericks, Jr. — Buddy O. H. Herring

Dan Shaban — Marc J. Grenier

OF COUNSEL

Edward Kanowitz — C. Michael Carter
Alan D. Lieberson

Reference: The Westport Bank and Trust Co.

For full biographical listings, see the Martindale-Hubbell Law Directory

WEISMAN & LUBELL (AV)

5 Sylvan Road South, P.O. Box 3184, 06880
Telephone: 203-226-8307
Telecopier: 203-221-7279

MEMBERS OF FIRM

Lawrence P. Weisman — Ellen B. Lubell

Andrew R. Tarshis

For full biographical listings, see the Martindale-Hubbell Law Directory

DELAWARE

*WILMINGTON,** New Castle Co.

EUGENE J. MAURER, JR., P.A. (AV)

1201-A King Street, 19801
Telephone: 302-652-7900
Fax: 302-652-2173

Eugene J. Maurer, Jr. — Marilou A. Szymanski

For full biographical listings, see the Martindale-Hubbell Law Directory

TRZUSKOWSKI, KIPP, KELLEHER & PEARCE, P.A. (AV)

1020 North Bancroft Parkway, P.O. Box 429, 19899-0429
Telephone: 302-571-1782
Fax: 302-571-1638

(See Next Column)

Daniel F. Kelleher

For Complete List of Firm Personnel, See General Section

For full biographical listings, see the Martindale-Hubbell Law Directory

DISTRICT OF COLUMBIA

WASHINGTON, D.C. Co.

DECKELBAUM OGENS & FISCHER, CHARTERED (AV)

1140 Connecticut Avenue, N.W., 20036
Telephone: 202-223-1474
Fax: 202-293-1471
Bethesda, Maryland Office: 6701 Democracy Boulevard.
Telephone: 301-564-5100.

Nelson Deckelbaum — Deborah E. Reiser
Ronald L. Ogens — John B. Raftery
Lawrence H. Fischer — Charles A. Moster
Arthur G. Kahn — Andrew J. Shedlock, III

Ronald G. Scheraga — Phyllis Lea Bean
Bryn Hope Sherman — Darryl Alan Feldman (Resident, Bethesda, Maryland Office)

References: Franklin National Bank; Century National Bank.

For full biographical listings, see the Martindale-Hubbell Law Directory

FLORIDA

BOCA RATON, Palm Beach Co.

JOEL H. FELDMAN, P.A. (AV)

Suite 207, Tower D, Sanctuary Centre, 4800 North Federal Highway, 33431
Telephone: 407-392-4400
Fax: 407-392-1521

Joel H. Feldman

For full biographical listings, see the Martindale-Hubbell Law Directory

KAUFFMAN & SCHWARTZ, P.A. (AV)

Crocker Plaza, Suite 301, 5355 Town Center Road, 33486
Telephone: 407-394-7600
Fax: 407-394-0891

Alan C. Kauffman — Thomas G. Pye
Harvey A. Nussbaum — Robert M. Schwartz

Thomas U. Graner — Seth I. Cohen
Rick S. Felberbaum (Not admitted in FL)

OF COUNSEL

David M. Beckerman

For full biographical listings, see the Martindale-Hubbell Law Directory

DONALD J. SASSER, P.A. (AV)

2200 Corporate Boulevard N.W., Suite 302, 33431
Telephone: 407-998-7725
West Palm Beach Florida Office: 1800 Australian Avenue, South, Suite 203.
Telephone: 407-689-4378.

Donald J. Sasser — Jorge M. Cestero

Reference: First Union National Bank of Florida.

WEISS & HANDLER, P.A. (AV)

Suite 218A, One Boca Place, 2255 Glades Road, 33431-7313
Telephone: 407-997-9995
Broward: 305-421-5101
Palm Beach: 407-734-8008
Telecopier: 407-997-5280

Howard I. Weiss — Carol A. Kartagener
Henry B. Handler — Bruce A. Harris
Donald Feldman — David K. Friedman
Walter M. Cooperstein — William M. Franz
Mia Lucas

(See Next Column)

WEISS & HANDLER P.A.—*Continued*

OF COUNSEL

Malcolm L. Stein (Not admitted in FL)
Raoul Lionel Felder (Not admitted in FL)

For full biographical listings, see the Martindale-Hubbell Law Directory

*CLEARWATER,** Pinellas Co.

WAYNE J. BOYER, P.A. (AV)

P.O. Box 10655, 34617-8655
Telephone: 813-733-2154
Fax: 813-734-0333

Wayne J. Boyer

John C. Knecht

LEGAL SUPPORT PERSONNEL

Linda D. Abbott (Certified Legal Assistant)
Tracy M. Boyer (Legal Assistant)

For full biographical listings, see the Martindale-Hubbell Law Directory

ANN LOUGHRIDGE KERR (AV)

425 South Garden Avenue, 34616
Telephone: 813-443-6787
Fax: 813-442-1251
Tampa, Florida Office: 601 East Twiggs Street, Suite 200.
Telephone: 813-229-7251.
Fax: 813-442-1251.

For full biographical listings, see the Martindale-Hubbell Law Directory

*FORT LAUDERDALE,** Broward Co.

MARC H. BRAWER (AV)

Suite 214, Atrium West Building, 7771 West Oakland Park Boulevard (Sunrise), 33351
Telephone: 305-749-0066
Fax: 305-572-0327

For full biographical listings, see the Martindale-Hubbell Law Directory

*FORT MYERS,** Lee Co.

SHELDON E. FINMAN, P.A. (AV)

2215 First Street, P.O. Drawer 1380, 33902-1380
Telephone: 813-332-4543

Sheldon E. Finman

For full biographical listings, see the Martindale-Hubbell Law Directory

*FORT PIERCE,** St. Lucie Co.

FEE, BRYAN & KOBLEGARD, P.A. (AV)

401 A South Indian River Drive, P.O. Box 1000, 34950
Telephone: 407-461-5020
FAX: 407-468-8461

Rupert N. Koblegard, III

General Counsel: Harbor Federal Savings; North St. Lucie River Water Control District; Fort Pierce Farms Water Control District; Fort Pierce Utilities Authority; Capron Trail Community Development District.
Representative Clients: Adams Ranch, Inc.; Callaway Land & Cattle Co., Inc., McArthur Farms, Inc.
Approved Attorneys for: Equitable Life Assurance Society of the United States; Equitable Agri-Business, Inc.

For Complete List of Firm Personnel, See General Section

For full biographical listings, see the Martindale-Hubbell Law Directory

LAKE WORTH, Palm Beach Co.

RENICK, SINGER, KAMBER & FISCHER (AV)

1530 North Federal Highway, 33460
Telephone: 407-582-6644
Fax: 407-533-7975

Kenneth H. Renick
Cathy L. Kamber

For full biographical listings, see the Martindale-Hubbell Law Directory

*MIAMI,** Dade Co.

IRA L. DUBITSKY, P.A. (AV)

Courthouse Tower, Suite 300, 44 West Flagler Street, 33130
Telephone: 305-374-8919
Telecopier: 305-375-0097

Ira L. Dubitsky, Esq.

For full biographical listings, see the Martindale-Hubbell Law Directory

ELSER, GREENE, HODOR & FABAR (AV)

2100 Courthouse Tower, 44 West Flagler Street, 33130
Telephone: 305-577-0090
Fax: 305-577-4551

MEMBERS OF FIRM

Marsha B. Elser
Judith Hodor
Cynthia L. Greene
Laura M. Fabar

ASSOCIATES

Joan E. Robinson (Helfman)
Melissa Jill Jacobs

For full biographical listings, see the Martindale-Hubbell Law Directory

PAUL G. FLETCHER, P.A. (AV)

Suite 200 Barnett Bank Building, 1500 South Dixie Highway (Coral Gables), 33146
Telephone: 305-661-6125
FAX: 305-661-6197

Paul G. Fletcher

For full biographical listings, see the Martindale-Hubbell Law Directory

MELVYN B. FRUMKES & ASSOCIATES, P.A. (AV)

New World Tower, 100 North Biscayne Boulevard, 33132-2380
Telephone: 305-371-5600
Fax: 305-371-7015
Boca Raton, Florida Office: One Park Place, Suite 240, 621 N.W. 53rd Street.
Telephone: 407-338-5052.

Melvyn B. Frumkes
Christopher A. Tiso
Mark I. Frumkes

For full biographical listings, see the Martindale-Hubbell Law Directory

HALL AND O'BRIEN, P.A. (AV)

Penthouse, 1428 Brickell Avenue, 33131
Telephone: 305-374-5030
Fax: 305-374-5033

Andrew C. Hall
Richard F. O'Brien, III

For full biographical listings, see the Martindale-Hubbell Law Directory

*NAPLES,** Collier Co.

VEGA, BROWN, STANLEY, MARTIN & ZELMAN, P.A. (AV)

2660 Airport Road, South, 33962
Telephone: 813-774-3333
Fax: 813-774-6420

George Vega, Jr.
Lawrence D. Martin

Paula J. Rhoads

General Counsel for: Lely Estates; Naples Community Hospital.
Local Counsel: Fleischmann Trust; Quail Creek Developments.

For Complete List of Firm Personnel, See General Section

For full biographical listings, see the Martindale-Hubbell Law Directory

NORTH MIAMI BEACH, Dade Co.

YOUNG, BERKMAN, BERMAN & KARPF, PROFESSIONAL ASSOCIATION (AV)

17071 West Dixie Highway, 33160
Telephone: Dade: 305-945-1851; Broward: 305-920-9793
Fax: 305-940-4616
Miami
Miami, Florida Office: New World Tower. 100 N. Biscayne Boulevard, Suite 601, 33132.
Telephone: 305-373-4655.

Burton Young
Mitchell K. Karpf
Andrew S. Berman
Jason M. Berkman

Maria C. Mitropoulos-Gonzalez
Sandra Jaggard

OF COUNSEL

Pedro V. Roig

For full biographical listings, see the Martindale-Hubbell Law Directory

ORANGE PARK, Clay Co.

HEAD, SMITH, METCALF, AGUILAR, MOSS & SIERON, P.A. (AV)

1329A Kingsley Avenue, P.O. Box 855, 32073
Telephone: 904-264-6000
Fax: 904-264-9223

(See Next Column)

HEAD, SMITH, METCALF, AGUILAR, MOSS & SIERON P.A., *Orange Park—Continued*

Robert J. Head, Jr.
Larry Smith
Frank B. Metcalf
Robert Aguilar
John B. Moss
Mark A. Sieron

Holly Fulton Perritt

For full biographical listings, see the Martindale-Hubbell Law Directory

*PENSACOLA,** Escambia Co.

JAMES D. SWEARINGEN (AV)

201 East Government Street, 32501
Telephone: 904-432-7723

For full biographical listings, see the Martindale-Hubbell Law Directory

ST. PETERSBURG, Pinellas Co.

HASTINGS AND ESTREICHER, P.A. (AV)

Courthouse Square, 600 First Avenue North, Suite 306, 33701
Telephone: 813-895-3600
Fax: 813-821-8045

Michael L. Hastings
Jane L. Estreicher

For full biographical listings, see the Martindale-Hubbell Law Directory

*STUART,** Martin Co.

LEWIS, BERGER & FERRARO (AV)

A Partnership of Professional Associations
3601 East Ocean Boulevard, Suite 201 (Sewall's Point), 34996
Telephone: 407-221-0600
FAX: 407-220-0640
Other Stuart, Florida Office: 1115 East Ocean Boulevard. Telephone 407-286-7861. Fax 407-288-2013.
Port St. Lucie, Florida Office: 1531 S.E. Port St. Lucie Boulevard. *Telephone:* 407-335-1996. *FAX:* 407-335-1998.

Bruce D. Berger (P.A.)
Russell J. Ferraro, Jr. (P.A.)
J. D. Lewis, III (P.A.)

Danie V. La Guerre (P.A.)
Michael J. Mortell (P.A.)
Sharon E. Lever

LEGAL SUPPORT PERSONNEL

Dorthea M. Duncan

For full biographical listings, see the Martindale-Hubbell Law Directory

McCARTHY, SUMMERS, BOBKO, McKEY & BONAN, P.A. (AV)

2081 East Ocean Boulevard, Suite 2-A, 34996
Telephone: 407-286-1700
FAX: 407-283-1803

Terence P. McCarthy
Robert P. Summers
Noel A. Bobko
John D. McKey, Jr.
W. Martin Bonan

Representative Clients: American Bank of Martin County; First National Bank and Trust Company of the Treasure Coast; Great Western Bank; Hydratech Utilities; Lost Lake at Hobe Sound; Taylor Creek Marina, Inc.; GBS Excavating, Inc.; Seaboard Savings Bank; The Stuart News; Gary Player Design Group.

For full biographical listings, see the Martindale-Hubbell Law Directory

*TALLAHASSEE,** Leon Co.

NOVEY & MENDELSON (AV)

851 East Park Avenue, P.O. Box 1855, 32302-1855
Telephone: 904-224-2000
FAX: 904-222-4951

Jerome M. Novey
Robert D. Mendelson
Kristin Adamson

For full biographical listings, see the Martindale-Hubbell Law Directory

*TAMPA,** Hillsborough Co.

RAYMOND A. ALLEY, JR., P.A. (AV)

805 West Azeele, 33606
Telephone: 813-251-8778
Fax: 813-254-3892

Raymond A. Alley, Jr.

LEGAL SUPPORT PERSONNEL

Linda R. Albrecht

For full biographical listings, see the Martindale-Hubbell Law Directory

EDNA ELLIOTT, J.D., P.A. (AV)

111 South Boulevard, 33606
Telephone: 813-254-5051
Fax: 813-254-5471

Edna Elliott

For full biographical listings, see the Martindale-Hubbell Law Directory

GARCIA & FIELDS, P.A. (AV)

Suite 2560 Barnett Plaza, 101 East Kennedy Boulevard, 33602
Telephone: 813-222-8500
FAX: 813-222-8520

Joseph Garcia
Robert W. Fields
Lesley J. Friedsam
Victor D. Ines
Hugo C. Edberg

Reference: Barnett Bank of Tampa.

For full biographical listings, see the Martindale-Hubbell Law Directory

LANGFORD, HILL & TRYBUS, P.A. (AV)

Suite 800, Bayshore Place, 601 Bayshore Boulevard, 33606
Telephone: 813-251-5533
Telecopier: 813-251-1900
Wats: 1-800-277-2005

E. C. Langford
Edward A. Hill
Ronald H. Trybus
Ronald G. Hock
Catherine M. Catlin
Debra M. Kubicsek
William B. Smith

Fredrique B. Boire
Muriel Desloovere
Kevin H. O'Neill
Vicki L. Page
Frederick T. Reeves
Barbara A. Sinsley
Stephens B. Woodrough (Not admitted in FL)
Anthony G. Woodward

Representative Clients: Affiliated of Florida, Inc.; American Federation Insurance Co.; Armor Insurance; Bank of Tampa; Central Bank of Tampa; Cintas Corp.; Container Corporation of America; CU Financial Services; Farm Stores, Inc.; First Union Home Equity Bank.

For full biographical listings, see the Martindale-Hubbell Law Directory

MANEY, DAMSKER, HARRIS & JONES, P.A. (AV)

606 Madison Street, P.O. Box 172009, 33672-0009
Telephone: 813-228-7371
Fax: 813-223-4846

Nancy Hutcheson Harris
David A. Maney

Lorena L. Kiely
Patricia F. Kuhlman

For full biographical listings, see the Martindale-Hubbell Law Directory

PIPPINGER, TROPP & MATASSINI, P.A. (AV)

101 East Kennedy Boulevard, Suite 3305, 33602
Telephone: 813-225-1611

Richard G. Pippinger
Robert A. Tropp
Nicholas M. Matassini

For full biographical listings, see the Martindale-Hubbell Law Directory

SESSUMS & MASON, P.A. (AV)

307 South Magnolia Avenue, P.O. Box 2409, 33601-2409
Telephone: 813-251-9200
FAX: 813-254-6841

Stephen W. Sessums
Miriam E. Mason
Caroline Kapusta Black

Mark A. Sessums

LEGAL SUPPORT PERSONNEL

Mary L. McGinnis, CLA
Susanne Bailey, CLA
Jeanne Timmerman

For full biographical listings, see the Martindale-Hubbell Law Directory

*WEST PALM BEACH,** Palm Beach Co.

LEWIS KAPNER, P.A. (AV)

Suite 1402, One Clearlake Centre, 250 Australian Avenue South, P.O. Box 1428, 33402
Telephone: 407-655-3000;
Delray/Ft. Lauderdale: 305-930-9191
Fax: 407-655-8899
Boca Raton, Florida Office: 621 Northwest 53rd Street.
Telephone: 305-930-9191.

(See Next Column)

LEWIS KAPNER, P.A.—*Continued*

Lewis Kapner | Victoria A. Calebrese

For full biographical listings, see the Martindale-Hubbell Law Directory

JAMES P. O'FLARITY, P.A. (AV)

Suite 108, 215 Fifth Street, 33401-4026
Telephone: 407-659-4666

James P. O'Flarity

For full biographical listings, see the Martindale-Hubbell Law Directory

RONALD SALES, LAWYER, P.A. (AV)

Suite 300 F, 1551 Forum Place, 33402
Telephone: 407-686-2333

Ronald Sales

Reference: Palm Beach National Bank & Trust Co., Palm Beach, Florida.

For full biographical listings, see the Martindale-Hubbell Law Directory

DONALD J. SASSER, P.A. (AV)

1800 Australian Avenue, South, Suite 203, P.O. Box 2907, 33402
Telephone: 407-689-4378
Fax: 407-689-4652
Boca Raton, Florida Office: 2200 Corporate Boulevard, N.W., Suite 302, 33431.
Telephone: 407-998-7725.

Donald J. Sasser

Jorge M. Cestero

Reference: First Union National Bank of Florida.

For full biographical listings, see the Martindale-Hubbell Law Directory

WINTER HAVEN, Polk Co.

PETERSON, MYERS, CRAIG, CREWS, BRANDON & PUTERBAUGH, P.A. (AV)

Suite 300, 141 5th Street N.W., P.O. Drawer 7608, 33883-7608
Telephone: 813-294-3360
Lake Wales, Florida Office: 130 East Central Avenue, P.O. Box 1079.
Telephones: 813-676-7611; 683-8942.
Lakeland, Florida Office: 100 East Main Street, P.O. Box 24628.
Telephones: 813-683-6511; 676-6934.

Jack P. Brandon
Beach A Brooks, Jr.
J. Davis Connor
Michael S. Craig
Roy A. Craig, Jr.
Jacob C. Dykxhoorn
Dennis P. Johnson
Kevin C. Knowlton
Douglas A. Lockwood, III
Corneal B. Myers
Cornelius B. Myers, III
Robert E. Puterbaugh
Abel A. Putnam
Thomas B. Putnam, Jr.
Deborah A. Ruster
Stephen R. Senn
Andrea Teves Smith
Kerry M. Wilson

General Counsel for: Barnett Bank of Polk County.
Representative Clients: Mutual Wholesale Co.; Sun Bank/Mid-Florida, N.A.; Chase Commercial Corp.; Barnett Banks, Inc.; Ben Hill Griffin, Inc.; Alcoma Association, Inc.
Approved Attorneys for: Attorneys' Title Insurance Fund; Federal Land Bank, Columbia, South Carolina; Equitable Life Assurance Society of the United States.

For full biographical listings, see the Martindale-Hubbell Law Directory

GEORGIA

*ATLANTA,** Fulton Co.

ALEMBIK, FINE & CALLNER, P.A. (AV)

Marquis One Tower, Fourth Floor, 245 Peachtree Center Avenue, N.E., 30303
Telephone: 404-688-8800
Telecopier: 404-420-7191

Michael D. Alembik (1936-1993)
Lowell S. Fine
Bruce W. Callner
Kathy L. Portnoy
Ronald T. Gold
G. Michael Banick
Mark E. Bergeson
Russell P. Love

Z. Ileana Martinez
Kevin S. Green
Susan M. Lieppe
T. Kevin Mooney
Bruce R. Steinfeld
Janet Lichiello Franchi

For full biographical listings, see the Martindale-Hubbell Law Directory

BIVENS, HOFFMAN & FOWLER (AV)

A Partnership of Professional Corporations
5040 Roswell Road, N.E., 30342
Telephone: 404-256-6464
FAX: 404-256-1422

MEMBER OF FIRM

L. Brown Bivens (P.C.)

For full biographical listings, see the Martindale-Hubbell Law Directory

CASHIN, MORTON & MULLINS (AV)

Two Midtown Plaza - Suite 1900, 1360 Peachtree Street, N.E., 30309-3214
Telephone: 404-870-1500
Telecopier: 404-870-1529

MEMBERS OF FIRM

Harry L. Cashin, Jr.
C. Read Morton, Jr.
A. L. Mullins, Jr.
Richard A. Fishman
William T. McKenzie
James Dean Spratt, Jr.
David W. Cranshaw
Richard Gerakitis
Robert Hunt Dunlap, Jr.
Robert O. Ball, III
Steven R. Glasscock
David Tully Hazell

ASSOCIATES

Lisa S. Street
Noel B. McDevitt, Jr.
James Marx Sherman
Kara E. Albert (Not admitted in GA)
Gibson T. Hess

Representative Clients: Alex Brown Realty, Inc.; ARA Food Services; Bank South, N.A.; Carey Paul Cos.; Central Life Insurance Company; Diversified Shelter Group, Ltd.; Dymetrol Co., Inc.; Edwards-Warren Tire Co.; First Union National Bank; Flournoy Development Co.

For full biographical listings, see the Martindale-Hubbell Law Directory

DAVIS, MATTHEWS & QUIGLEY, P.C. (AV)

Fourteenth Floor, Lenox Towers II, 3400 Peachtree Road, 30326
Telephone: 404-261-3900
Telecopier: 404-261-0159

Baxter L. Davis
Richard W. Schiffman, Jr.
Frank A. DeVincent

Deborah M. Lubin
Sylvia A. Martin

Approved Attorneys for: Lawyers Title Insurance Corp.

For Complete List of Firm Personnel, See General Section

For full biographical listings, see the Martindale-Hubbell Law Directory

FRANKEL, HARDWICK, TANENBAUM & FINK, P.C. (AV)

359 East Paces Ferry Road, N.E., 30305
Telephone: 404-266-2930
Fax: 404-231-3362

Barry B. McGough
Martha J. Kuckleburg

Kimberly C. Hodgson

Representative Clients: America's Favorite Chicken Co. (Church's and Popeye's); Softlab, Inc.; Basic, Inc.; Buffalo's Franchise Concepts, Inc.; Combustion Engineering, Inc.; Commerical Bank of Georgia; Patients Pharmacies; Hank Aaron Enterprises, Inc.; Nursecare (Nursing Homes); Sundance Products, Inc.; Venture Construction Company.

For Complete List of Firm Personnel, See General Section

For full biographical listings, see the Martindale-Hubbell Law Directory

JAMES J. MACIE (AV)

400 Colony Square, Suite 1940, 1201 Peachtree Street, 30361
Telephone: 404-478-4155
Fax: 404-471-2053
Jonesboro, Georgia Office: 2212 Emerald Drive.
Telephone: 404-478-4155.
Fax: 404-471-2053.

For full biographical listings, see the Martindale-Hubbell Law Directory

MCLAIN & MERRITT, P.C. (AV)

3340 Peachtree Road, Suite 1250, 30326-1075
Telephone: 404-266-9171
Telecopier: 404-262-7531

M. David Merritt
Christopher D. Olmstead

Charlotte K. Clark

Approved Attorneys for: Lawyers Title Insurance Corporation.

For full biographical listings, see the Martindale-Hubbell Law Directory

Atlanta—Continued

STERN & EDLIN, P.C. (AV)

225 West Wieuca Road, N.E., 30342
Telephone: 404-256-0010
FAX: 404-851-9081

George S. Stern — Shiel G. Edlin

Leslie W. Wade — Carla F. Stern
Janis Y. Dickman — Jeri L. Kagel

Reference: Bank South.

For full biographical listings, see the Martindale-Hubbell Law Directory

TURNER, TURNER & TURNER, P.C. (AV)

1445 Resurgens Plaza, 945 East Paces Ferry Road, N.E., 30326
Telephone: 404-237-0045
FAX: 404-237-4989

Russell G. Turner, Sr. (1896-1981) — Nelson Goss Turner
Anne H. Jarrett
Jack P. Turner — S. Scott Critzer

For full biographical listings, see the Martindale-Hubbell Law Directory

WARNER, MAYOUE & BATES, P.C. (AV)

100 Galleria Parkway, Suite 1300, 30339
Telephone: 404-951-2700
Telecopier: 404-951-2200

C. Wilbur Warner, Jr. — Robert D. Boyd
John C. Mayoue — J. Matthew Anthony
Edward E. Bates, Jr. — John Lind Collar, Jr.
Alvah O. Smith — Richard M. Nolen

For full biographical listings, see the Martindale-Hubbell Law Directory

*COLUMBUS,** Muscogee Co.

HARP & JOHNSON, P.C. (AV)

936 Second Avenue, P.O. Box 1172, 31902
Telephone: 706-323-2761
FAX: 706-323-0182

Beverly R. Keil (1924-1983) — Gary L. Johnson
B. Seth Harp, Jr. — Trenny L. Stovall

Reference: Trust Company Bank of Columbus.

For full biographical listings, see the Martindale-Hubbell Law Directory

HIRSCH, PARTIN & GROGAN, P.C. (AV)

1021 Third Avenue, P.O. Box 469, 31993
Telephone: 706-323-6581
Fax: 706-323-6585

Milton Hirsch — Lynn L. Grogan
John P. Partin — Lee R. Grogan, Jr.

Approved Attorneys: Lawyers Title Insurance Corp.
References: Columbus Bank & Trust Co.; Bank South; First Columbus Community Bank.

For full biographical listings, see the Martindale-Hubbell Law Directory

*DECATUR,** De Kalb Co.

SIMMONS, WARREN & SZCZECKO, PROFESSIONAL ASSOCIATION (AV)

315 West Ponce de Leon Avenue, Suite 850, 30030
Telephone: 404-378-1711
Fax: 404-377-6101

M. T. Simmons, Jr. — Joseph Szczecko

Representative Clients: David Hocker & Associates (Shopping Center Development); Julian LeCraw & Company (Real Estate); Royal Oldsmobile,; Cotter & Co.; Atlanta Neurosurgical Associates, P.A.; Villager Lodge, Inc.; Troncalli Motors, Inc.

For Complete List of Firm Personnel, See General Section

For full biographical listings, see the Martindale-Hubbell Law Directory

*JONESBORO,** Clayton Co.

JAMES J. MACIE (AV)

2212 Emerald Drive, 30236
Telephone: 404-478-4155
Fax: 404-471-2053
Atlanta, Georgia Office: 400 Colony Square, Suite 1940, 1201 Peachtree Street.
Telephone: 404-478-4155.
Fax: 404-471-2053.

For full biographical listings, see the Martindale-Hubbell Law Directory

*MACON,** Bibb Co.

STONE & CHRISTIAN, P.C. (AV)

Suite 230, 484 Mulberry Street, P.O. Box 107, 31202-0107
Telephone: 912-741-0060
FAX: 912-741-7971

Kice H. Stone, Jr. — Martha Currie Christian

Lise Kaplan — Claire C. Chapman

References: Bank South, Wachovia.

For full biographical listings, see the Martindale-Hubbell Law Directory

*MARIETTA,** Cobb Co.

BARNES, BROWNING, TANKSLEY & CASURELLA (AV)

Suite 225, 166 Anderson Street, 30060
Telephone: 404-424-1500
Fax: 404-424-1740

MEMBERS OF FIRM

Roy E. Barnes — Thomas J. Casurella (1956-1989)
Thomas J. Browning — Jerry A. Landers, Jr.
Charles B. Tanksley — Jeffrey G. Casurella
Benny C. Priest

OF COUNSEL

George T. Smith — Howard D. Rothbloom

For full biographical listings, see the Martindale-Hubbell Law Directory

CUSTER & HILL, P.C. (AV)

241 Washington Avenue, P.O. Box 1224, 30061
Telephone: 404-429-8300
Fax: 404-429-8338

Lawrence B. Custer — Douglas A. Hill

Reference: First Union National Bank.

For full biographical listings, see the Martindale-Hubbell Law Directory

W. R. ROBERTSON, III (AV)

244 Roswell Street, Suite 600, 30060-2000
Telephone: 404-422-0200
Fax: 404-424-1322

For full biographical listings, see the Martindale-Hubbell Law Directory

REX R. RUFF, P.C. (AV)

278 North Marietta Parkway, 30060
Telephone: 404-422-5970
FAX: 404-422-5913

Rex R. Ruff

Reference: Charter Bank & Trust.

For full biographical listings, see the Martindale-Hubbell Law Directory

*MCDONOUGH,** Henry Co.

SMITH, WELCH & STUDDARD (AV)

41 Keys Ferry Street, P.O. Box 31, 30253
Telephone: 404-957-3937
Fax: 404-957-9165
Stockbridge, Georgia Office: 1231-A Eagle's Landing Parkway.
Telephone: 404-389-4864.
FAX: 404-389-5157.

MEMBERS OF FIRM

Ernest M. Smith (1911-1992) — Ben W. Studdard, III
A. J. Welch, Jr. — J. Mark Brittain (Resident, Stockbridge Office)

ASSOCIATES

Patrick D. Jaugstetter — J.V. Dell, Jr. (Resident, Stockbridge Office)
E. Gilmore Maxwell

Representative Clients: Alliance Corp.; Atlanta Motor Speedway, Inc.; Bellamy-Strickland Chevrolet, Inc.; Ceramic and Metal Coatings Corp.; City of Hampton; City of Locust Grove; City of Stockbridge.

For full biographical listings, see the Martindale-Hubbell Law Directory

HAWAII

*HONOLULU,** Honolulu Co.

STIRLING & KLEINTOP (AV)

20th Floor, 1100 Alakea Street, 96813
Telephone: 808-524-5183
FAX: 808-528-0261

MEMBERS OF FIRM

Thomas L. Stirling, Jr. | Charles T. Kleintop
Sara Robbins Harvey

Carolyn E. Ogami | Patrick Naehu
Twila Y. Masison

For full biographical listings, see the Martindale-Hubbell Law Directory

MICHAEL J. Y. WONG (AV)

2222 Central Pacific Plaza, 220 South King Street, 96813
Telephone: 808-536-1855
Fax: 808-536-1857

ASSOCIATE

R. Malia Taum

For full biographical listings, see the Martindale-Hubbell Law Directory

IDAHO

*BOISE,** Ada Co.

WILSON, CARNAHAN & MCCOLL, CHARTERED (AV)

420 Washington Street, P.O. Box 1544, 83701
Telephone: 208-345-9100
FAX: 208-384-0442

Jeffrey M. Wilson | Brian F. McColl
Debrha Jo Carnahan | Stephanie Jo Williams

Representative Clients: A & J Construction, Inc.; Pure-gro Company; Transamerica Commercial Finance Corp.; John H. Crowther, Inc.; Jess W. Swan Insurance Agency; Higgins and Rutledge Insurance Co., Inc.; Communication Workers of America, Local # 8103.

For full biographical listings, see the Martindale-Hubbell Law Directory

ILLINOIS

*CHICAGO,** Cook Co.

MARSHALL J. AUERBACH & ASSOCIATES, LTD. (AV)

180 North La Salle Street, Suite 2307, 60601
Telephone: 312-853-3300
Fax: 312-853-1043

Marshall J. Auerbach

Gail S. Freeman

For full biographical listings, see the Martindale-Hubbell Law Directory

OWEN L. DOSS, P.C. (AV)

Suite 4000, Three First National Plaza, 60602
Telephone: 312-726-3060

Owen L. Doss

GRUND & STARKOPF, A PROFESSIONAL CORPORATION (AV)

28th Floor One Illinois Center, 111 East Wacker Drive, 60601-4801
Telephone: 312-616-6600
FAX: 312-616-6606

David I. Grund | Lawrence S. Starkopf

Linda Kay Schneider | Richard S. Zachary

For full biographical listings, see the Martindale-Hubbell Law Directory

SUSAN CHRISTINE HADDAD (AV)

Suite 3600, Three First National Plaza, 60602
Telephone: 312-236-2298
FAX: 312-236-0089

For full biographical listings, see the Martindale-Hubbell Law Directory

KALCHEIM, SCHATZ & BERGER (AV)

A Partnership including Professional Corporations
161 North Clark Street, 28th Floor, 60601
Telephone: 312-782-3456
FAX: 312-782-8463

MEMBERS OF FIRM

Michael W. Kalcheim (P.C.) | Michael J. Berger (P.C.)
Barry A. Schatz (P.C.) | David H. Levy (P.C.)
Michael S. Cohen

Leon I. Finkel | Jacalyn Birnbaum
Andrew D. Eichner | Tara Gordon Kochman
David M. Goldman | Cecilia A. Hynes
Corri D. Fetman

For full biographical listings, see the Martindale-Hubbell Law Directory

LAW OFFICES KOMIE AND ASSOCIATES (AV)

Suite 3500 Avondale Centre, 20 North Clark Street, 60602-5002
Telephone: 312-263-4383
Fax: 312-263-2803

Stephen M. Komie | Michael T. van der Veen

OF COUNSEL

Douglas W. Godfrey

LEGAL SUPPORT PERSONNEL

Paul J. Ciolino

For full biographical listings, see the Martindale-Hubbell Law Directory

MANDEL, LIPTON AND STEVENSON LIMITED (AV)

Suite 2900, 120 North La Salle Street, 60602
Telephone: 312-236-7080
Facsimile: 312-236-0781

Richard L. Mandel | Richard A. Lifshitz
Leonard M. Malkin | Kathleen Hogan Morrison
Kathleen Roseborough | Carolyn E. Winter

Audrey L. Gaynor

OF COUNSEL

Nicholas Stevenson

References: Northern Trust Co.; American National Bank of Chicago.

For Complete List of Firm Personnel, See General Section

For full biographical listings, see the Martindale-Hubbell Law Directory

MICHAEL HARRY MINTON A PROFESSIONAL CORPORATION (AV)

Suite 1950, 222 North La Salle Street, 60601
Telephone: 312-641-2500
Fax: 312-641-6688

Michael Harry Minton

For full biographical listings, see the Martindale-Hubbell Law Directory

NOTTAGE AND WARD (AV)

Ten North Dearborn Street, Penthouse, 60602
Telephone: 312-332-2915

Rosaire M. Nottage | Eunice Ward

ASSOCIATES

Doris Schumacher McMorrow | Richard Allen Wilson

For full biographical listings, see the Martindale-Hubbell Law Directory

RINELLA AND RINELLA, LTD. (AV)

Suite 3400, One North La Salle Street, 60602
Telephone: 312-236-5454
Fax: 312-236-6975

Samuel A. Rinella (1906-1982) | Joseph G. Phelps
Kathryn B. Rinella (1906-1991) | Walter J. Monco
Bernard B. Rinella | Steven S. Russo
Richard A. Rinella | Leslie L. Veon
Francine Malek | Steven D. Gerage

For full biographical listings, see the Martindale-Hubbell Law Directory

SCHILLER, DU CANTO AND FLECK (AV)

200 North La Salle Street, Suite 2700, 60601
Telephone: 312-641-5560
Fax: 312-641-6361
Lake Forest, Illinois Office: Suite 201, 207 East Westminster Avenue.
Telephone: 708-615-8300.
Fax: 708-615-8284.

(See Next Column)

SCHILLER, DU CANTO AND FLECK, *Chicago—Continued*

MEMBERS OF FIRM

Joseph N. Du Canto
Donald C. Schiller
Charles J. Fleck
David H. Hopkins
Arnold B. Stein
David B. Yavitz
James B. O'Brien
Burton S. Hochberg
Stephen H. Katz (Resident, Lake Forest Office)
Carlton R. Marcyan
Sarane Crowther Siewerth
Timothy M. Daw
Ilene Beth Goldstein

ASSOCIATES

Todd R. Warren (Resident, Lake Forest Office)
Anita Bolaños Ward
Andrea K. Muchin
Wilfred H. Chan (Resident, Lake Forest Office)
David A. King
Karen Pinkert-Lieb

OF COUNSEL

Sidney S. Schiller
David Linn

For full biographical listings, see the Martindale-Hubbell Law Directory

---

*GENEVA,** Kane Co.

SCHAFFNER & VAN DER SNICK, P.C. (AV)

115 Campbell Street, P.O. Box 101, 60134
Telephone: 708-232-8900
Fax: 708-232-8908

Harry Schaffner
J. Brick Van Der Snick

For full biographical listings, see the Martindale-Hubbell Law Directory

---

LAKE FOREST, Lake Co.

SCHILLER, DU CANTO AND FLECK (AV)

Suite 201, 207 East Westminster Avenue, 60045-1857
Telephone: 708-615-8300
Fax: 708-615-8284
Chicago, Illinois Office: 200 North La Salle Street, Suite 2700.
Telephone: 312-641-5560.
Fax: 312-641-6361.

RESIDENT PARTNER

Stephen H. Katz (Resident)

RESIDENT ASSOCIATES

Todd R. Warren (Resident)
Wilfred H. Chan (Resident)

For full biographical listings, see the Martindale-Hubbell Law Directory

---

OAK BROOK, Du Page Co.

BOTTI, MARINACCIO & TAMELING, LTD. (AV)

720 Enterprise Drive, 60521
Telephone: 708-573-8585
Fax: 708-573-8586
Wheaton, Illinois Office: Suite 401 The Ticor Title Building, 330 Naperville Road.
Telephone: 708-653-2100.

Aldo E. Botti
Stephen R. Botti
Andrew Y. Acker
Carlo F. Cavallaro
Peter M. DeLongis
Terry W. Huebner
Lee A. Marinaccio
Ronald D. Menna
Mark W. Salkeld
Eva W. Tameling
Peter M. Tumminaro
Frank J. Wesolowski

For full biographical listings, see the Martindale-Hubbell Law Directory

---

*PEORIA,** Peoria Co.

WINGET & KANE (AV)

807 Commerce Bank Building, 61602
Telephone: 309-674-2310
Fax: 309-674-9722

Walter W. Winget
James F. Kane

Representative Clients: National Hampshire Swine Registry; Davison-Fulton Ltd.
References: Commerce Bank; Bank One - Peoria.

For full biographical listings, see the Martindale-Hubbell Law Directory

---

*SPRINGFIELD,** Sangamon Co.

METNICK, WISE, CHERRY & FRAZIER (AV)

Fourth Floor, Myers Building, 1 West Old State Capitol Plaza, P.O. Box 12140, 62791
Telephone: 217-753-4242
Telefax: 217-753-4642

MEMBERS OF FIRM

Michael B. Metnick
Diana N. Cherry

ASSOCIATE

Kathryn Saltmarsh

For full biographical listings, see the Martindale-Hubbell Law Directory

---

*WOODSTOCK,** McHenry Co.

GITLIN & GITLIN (AV)

111 Dean Street, 60098
Telephone: 815-338-0021

MEMBERS OF FIRM

H. Joseph Gitlin
Gunnar J. Gitlin

OF COUNSEL

Michelle Patzke
Peter F. Carroll

For full biographical listings, see the Martindale-Hubbell Law Directory

---

INDIANA

CARMEL, Hamilton Co.

COOTS, HENKE & WHEELER, PROFESSIONAL CORPORATION (AV)

255 East Carmel Drive, 46032
Telephone: 317-844-4693
Fax: 317-573-5385

E. Davis Coots
Steven H. Henke
James K. Wheeler
Jeffrey O. Meunier
Sheila Ann Marshall
T. Jay Curts
James D. Crum
Jeffrey S. Zipes
James E. Zoccola
Elizabeth I. Van Tassel

For full biographical listings, see the Martindale-Hubbell Law Directory

---

*COLUMBUS,** Bartholomew Co.

SHARPNACK, BIGLEY, DAVID & RUMPLE (AV)

321 Washington Street, P.O. Box 310, 47202-0310
Telephone: 812-372-1553
Fax: 812-372-1567

MEMBERS OF FIRM

John A. Stroh
Joan Tupin Crites

Representative Clients: Irwin Union Bank and Trust Co.; PSI Energy, Inc.; State Farm Mutual Insurance Cos.; American States Insurance Co.; Home News Enterprises; Cummins Federal Credit Union; Richards Elevator, Inc.

For Complete List of Firm Personnel, See General Section

For full biographical listings, see the Martindale-Hubbell Law Directory

---

ELKHART, Elkhart Co.

THORNE, GRODNIK, RANSEL, DUNCAN, BYRON & HOSTETLER (AV)

228 West High Street, 46516-3176
Telephone: 219-294-7473
FAX: 219-294-5390
Mishawaka, Indiana Office: 310 Valley American Bank and Trust Building, 310 West McKinley Avenue. P.O. Box 1210.
Telephone: 219-256-5660.
FAX: 219-674-6835.

MEMBERS OF FIRM

William A. Thorne
Charles H. Grodnik
J. Richard Ransel
Glenn L. Duncan
James R. Byron
Steven L. Hostetler

ASSOCIATES

James H. Milstone
Michael A. Trippel

OF COUNSEL

F. Richard Kramer
Joseph C. Zakas

Counsel for: Witmer-McNease Music Co., Inc.; Valley American Bank and Trust Co., Mishawaka, Indiana.

For Complete List of Firm Personnel, See General Section

For full biographical listings, see the Martindale-Hubbell Law Directory

---

*FORT WAYNE,** Allen Co.

HAYES & HAYES (AV)

Second Floor, Courtside Building, 803 South Calhoun Street, 46802
Telephone: 219-420-1800
Facsimile: 219-420-1809

C. Byron Hayes (1891-1975)
J. Byron Hayes (1920-1986)
Cornelius B. (Neil) Hayes

For full biographical listings, see the Martindale-Hubbell Law Directory

*INDIANAPOLIS,** Marion Co.

BOBERSCHMIDT, MILLER, O'BRYAN, TURNER & ABBOTT, A PROFESSIONAL ASSOCIATION (AV)

Bank One Center/Circle, 111 Monument Circle, Suite 302, 46204-5169
Telephone: 317-632-5892
Telecopier: 317-686-3423

Jerald L. Miller

A List of Representative Clients will be furnished upon request.

For Complete List of Firm Personnel, See General Section

For full biographical listings, see the Martindale-Hubbell Law Directory

MCCLURE, MCCLURE & KAMMEN (AV)

235 North Delaware, 46204
Telephone: 317-236-0400
Telecopier: 317-236-0404

MEMBERS OF FIRM

David E. McClure
Richard Kammen

Reference: Indiana National Bank.

For full biographical listings, see the Martindale-Hubbell Law Directory

MIROFF, CROSS, RUPPERT & KLINEMAN (AV)

An Association, Not a Partnership
Suite 1000, Two Market Square Center, 251 East Ohio Street, 46204-2133
Telephone: 317-264-1040
Telecopier: 317-264-1039

Franklin I. Miroff
Nancy L. Cross
Monty K. Woolsey
Penny R. Ritenour

OF COUNSEL

Michael G. Ruppert
James M. Klineman
Stephen J. Klineman

For full biographical listings, see the Martindale-Hubbell Law Directory

PHELPS & FARA (AV)

Indiana Bar Center, 230 East Ohio, Sixth Floor, 46204-2149
Telephone: 317-637-7575

MEMBERS OF FIRM

Gale M. Phelps
Thomas A. Fara
Michael Cheerva

LEGAL SUPPORT PERSONNEL

Denise Bowlby
Lisa Clouse

For full biographical listings, see the Martindale-Hubbell Law Directory

IOWA

*SIOUX CITY,** Woodbury Co.

GILES AND GILES (AV)

322 Frances Building, 505 Fifth Street, 51101
Telephone: 712-252-4458
FAX: 712-252-3400
Crofton, Nebraska Office: P. O. Box 88.
Telephone: 402-388-4215.

MEMBERS OF FIRM

W. Jefferson Giles, III
William J. Giles, IV

Representative Clients: Security National Bank, Firstar Bank, Boatmen's Bank, all in Sioux City, Iowa; Live Stock State Bank, Yankton, SD.

For Complete List of Firm Personnel, See General Section

For full biographical listings, see the Martindale-Hubbell Law Directory

KANSAS

PRAIRIE VILLAGE, Johnson Co.

HOLMAN, MCCOLLUM & HANSEN, P.C. (AV®)

9400 Mission Road Suite 205, 66206
Telephone: 913-648-7272
Fax: 913-383-9596
Kansas City, Missouri Office: 644 West 57th Terrace.
Telephone: 816-333-8522.
Fax: 913-383-9596.

(See Next Column)

Joseph Y. Holman
Frank B. W. McCollum
Eric L. Hansen
Dana L. Parks
Nancy Merrill Wilson
Amy L. Brown
E. John Edwards III (Not admitted in KS)
Katherine E. Rich

For full biographical listings, see the Martindale-Hubbell Law Directory

KENTUCKY

*BOWLING GREEN,** Warren Co.

ENGLISH, LUCAS, PRIEST & OWSLEY (AV)

1101 College Street, P.O. Box 770, 42102-0770
Telephone: 502-781-6500
Telecopier: 502-782-7782

MEMBERS OF FIRM

Charles E. English
James H. Lucas
Whayne C. Priest, Jr.
Michael A. Owsley
Keith M. Carwell
Murry A. Raines
Kurt W. Maier
Charles E. English, Jr.
Wade T. Markham, II

ASSOCIATE

D. Gaines Penn

General Counsel for: Medical Center at Bowling Green; Warren Rural Electric Cooperative Corporation; Trans Financial Bank, N.A.; Southern Sanitation, Inc.
Representative Clients: Commercial Union Insurance Cos.; Kemper Insurance Group; St. Paul Insurance Co.; Desa International; Kentucky Finance Co.; Sumitomo Electric Wiring Systems, Inc.

For Complete List of Firm Personnel, See General Section

For full biographical listings, see the Martindale-Hubbell Law Directory

COVINGTON, Kenton Co.

O'HARA, RUBERG, TAYLOR, SLOAN AND SERGENT (AV)

Suite 209 C, Thomas More Park, P.O. Box 17411, 41017-0411
Telephone: 606-331-2000
Fax: 606-578-3365

MEMBERS OF FIRM

John J. O'Hara
Robert E. Ruberg
Arnold S. Taylor
Donald J. Ruberg
David B. Sloan
Gary J. Sergent
Michael K. Ruberg
Michael O'Hara

ASSOCIATES

Lisa Kalker
Anne Marie Mielech
Suzanne Cassidy

Representative Clients: Cincinnati Bell; American Transportation Enterprises; Union Light, Heat & Power Co.; Crum & Forster; American States Insurance Co.; Ohio Casualty Co.; Monticello Insurance Co.; United States Aviation Underwriters, Inc.
Local Counsel for: Lloyds of London.

For full biographical listings, see the Martindale-Hubbell Law Directory

SMITH, WOLNITZEK, SCHACHTER & ROWEKAMP, P.S.C. (AV)

502 Greenup Street, P.O. Box 352, 41012-0352
Telephone: 606-491-4444
Fax: 606-491-1001
Fort Mitchell, Kentucky Office: 250 Grandview Avenue., Suite 500.
Telephone: 606-578-4444.
Fax: 606-578-4440.

Thomas C. Smith
Stephen D. Wolnitzek
Paul J. Schachter
Leonard G. Rowekamp
J. David Bender
Barbara Dahlenburg Bonar

Penny Unkraut Hendy
John J. Garvey, III
Timothy B. Schenkel
David A. Shearer

Representative Clients: Hartford Insurance Co.; Nationwide Insurance Co.

For full biographical listings, see the Martindale-Hubbell Law Directory

*GLASGOW,** Barren Co.

HERBERT & HERBERT (AV)

135 North Public Square, P.O. Box 1000, 42141
Telephone: 502-651-9000
FAX: 502-651-3317

MEMBERS OF FIRM

H. Jefferson Herbert, Jr.
Betty Reece Herbert

For full biographical listings, see the Martindale-Hubbell Law Directory

*LEXINGTON,** Fayette Co.

BROCK, BROCK & BAGBY (AV)

190 Market Street, P.O. Box 1630, 40592-1630
Telephone: 606-255-7795
Fax: 606-255-6198

MEMBERS OF FIRM

Walter L. Brock, Jr. | Glen S. Bagby
Daniel N. Brock | J. Robert Lyons, Jr.
Beverly Benton Polk

ASSOCIATE

Bruce A. Rector

LEGAL SUPPORT PERSONNEL

PARALEGALS

Pamela H. Brown | Freda Greer Grubbs

For full biographical listings, see the Martindale-Hubbell Law Directory

GREENEBAUM DOLL & McDONALD (AV)

A Partnership including Professional Service Corporations
1400 Vine Center Tower, 40508
Telephone: 606-231-8500
Telecopier: 606-255-2742
Telex: 213029
Louisville, Kentucky Office: 3300 National City Tower.
Telephone: 502-589-4200.
Fax: 502-587-3695.
Covington, Kentucky Office: 50 East River Center Boulevard, P.O. Box 2050.
Telephone: 606-655-4200.
Fax: 606-655-4239.
Cincinnati, Ohio Office: 832 Main Street.
Telephone: 513-421-8087.
Fax: 513-421-8089.

MEMBERS OF FIRM

A. Robert Doll * | Wm. T. Robinson, III

Representative Clients: Aetna Life Insurance Co.; ANDALEX Resources, Inc.; Ashland Oil, Inc.; AT&T Communications, Inc.; Bethlehem Steel Corp.; Brown-Forman Corp.; Columbia Gas & Transmission Co.; Commonwealth Aluminum Corp.; Consolidation Coal Co.; Costain Coal, Inc.
*A Professional Service Corporation

For Complete List of Firm Personnel, See General Section

For full biographical listings, see the Martindale-Hubbell Law Directory

LANDRUM & SHOUSE (AV)

106 West Vine Street, P.O. Box 951, 40588-0951
Telephone: 606-255-2424
Facsimile: 606-233-0308
Louisville, Kentucky Office: 400 West Market Street, Suite 1550, 40202.
Telephone: 502-589-7616.
Facsimile: 502-589-2119.

MEMBERS OF FIRM

John H. Burrus | Sandra Mendez Dawahare
William C. Shouse | Delores Hill Pregliasco
Mark L. Moseley | (Resident, Louisville Office)

ASSOCIATES

Stephen D. Milner | Charles E. Christian
Virginia W. Gregg

OF COUNSEL

Weldon Shouse | Frank J. Dougherty, Jr. (Resident, Louisville Office)

District Attorneys: CSX Transportation, Inc.
Special Trial Counsel: Ford Motor Co. and Affiliates (Eastern Kentucky); Clark Equipment Co.
Representative Clients: The Continental Insurance Cos.; U.S. Insurance Group; U.S. Fidelity & Guaranty Co.; Ohio Casualty Insurance Co.; CIGNA; Royal Insurance Cos.

For Complete List of Firm Personnel, See General Section

For full biographical listings, see the Martindale-Hubbell Law Directory

STOLL, KEENON & PARK (AV)

201 E. Main Street, Suite 1000, 40507-1380
Telephone: 606-231-3000
Telecopier: 606-253-1093; 606-253-1027
Frankfort, Kentucky Office: 326 West Main Street.
Telephone: 502-875-6000.
Telecopier: 502-875-6008.
Louisville, Kentucky Office: 400 West Market Street, Suite 2650, 40202.
Telephone: 502-568-9100.
Telecopier: 502-568-6340.

MEMBERS OF FIRM

Michael L. Judy | Anita M. Britton

(See Next Column)

ASSOCIATE

Susan Beverly Jones

For Complete List of Firm Personnel, See General Section

For full biographical listings, see the Martindale-Hubbell Law Directory

*LOUISVILLE,** Jefferson Co.

GREENEBAUM DOLL & McDONALD (AV)

A Partnership including Professional Service Corporations
3300 National City Tower, 40202
Telephone: 502-589-4200
Fax: 502-587-3695
Lexington, Kentucky Office: 1400 Vine Center Tower.
Telephone: 606-231-8500.
Fax: 606-255-2742.
Covington, Kentucky Office: 50 East River Center Boulevard, P.O. Box 2050.
Telephone: 606-655-4200.
Fax: 606-655-4239.
Cincinnati, Ohio Office: 832 Main Street.
Telephone: 513-421-8087.
Fax: 513-421-8089.

A. Robert Doll * | Margaret E. Keane
Wm. T. Robinson, III | Roger N. Braden (Resident at Covington, Kentucky)

ASSOCIATES

Angela McCormick Bisig | Nora J. Clevenger

Representative Clients: Aetna Life Insurance Co.; ANDALEX Resources, Inc.; Ashland Oil, Inc.; A T & T Communications, Inc.; Bethlehem Steel Corp.; Brown-Forman Corp.; Humana, Inc.; Kentucky Kingdom, Inc.; KFC National Cooperative Advertising Program, Inc.
*A Professional Service Corporation

For Complete List of Firm Personnel, See General Section

For full biographical listings, see the Martindale-Hubbell Law Directory

LANDRUM & SHOUSE (AV)

400 West Market Street Suite 1550, 40202
Telephone: 502-589-7616
Facsimile: 502-589-2119
Lexington, Kentucky Office: 106 West Vine Street, P.O. Box 951.
Telephone: 606-255-2424.
Facsimile: 606-233-0308.

RESIDENT MEMBERS OF THE FIRM

George P. Parker | Michael J. O'Connell
John R. Martin, Jr. | R. Kent Westberry
Delores Hill Pregliasco | J. Denis Ogburn

RESIDENT ASSOCIATES

David G. Hazlett | G. Bruce Stigger
Thomas E. Roma, Jr. | Courtney T. Baxter
Dave Whalin | D. Sean Nilsen

OF COUNSEL

Frank J. Dougherty, Jr.

For Complete List of Firm Personnel, See General Section

For full biographical listings, see the Martindale-Hubbell Law Directory

MOSLEY, CLARE & TOWNES (AV)

Fifth Floor, Hart Block Building, 730 West Main Street, 40202
Telephone: 502-583-7400
Telecopier: 502-589-4997

MEMBER OF FIRM

W. Waverley Townes

For full biographical listings, see the Martindale-Hubbell Law Directory

OLDFATHER & MORRIS (AV)

One Mezzanine The Morrissey Building, 304 West Liberty Street, 40202
Telephone: 502-589-5500
Fax: 502-589-5338

Ann B. Oldfather

For Complete List of Firm Personnel, See General Section

For full biographical listings, see the Martindale-Hubbell Law Directory

RUBIN HAYS & FOLEY (AV)

First Trust Centre 200 South Fifth Street, 40202
Telephone: 502-569-7550
Telecopier: 502-569-7555

(See Next Column)

RUBIN HAYS & FOLEY—*Continued*

MEMBERS OF FIRM

Wm. Carl Fust
Harry Lee Meyer
David W. Gray
Irvin D. Foley
Joseph R. Gathright, Jr.
Lisa Koch Bryant
Sharon C. Hardy
Charles S. Musson
W. Randall Jones
K. Gail Russell

ASSOCIATE

Christian L. Juckett

OF COUNSEL

James E. Fahey
Newman T. Guthrie

Representative Clients: J.C. Bradford & Co., Inc.; J.J.B. Hilliard, W.L. Lyons, Inc.; Huntington National Bank; Liberty National Bank and Trust Company; National City Bank; PNC Bank; Prudential Bache & Co., Inc.; Prudential Securities, Inc.; Society Bank; Stock Yards Bank and Trust Co.

For full biographical listings, see the Martindale-Hubbell Law Directory

SEILLER & HANDMAKER (AV)

2200 Meidinger Tower, 40202
Telephone: 502-584-7400
Telecopier: 502-583-2100
Paris, Kentucky Office: Seiller, Handmaker & Blevins, P.S.C., 1431 South Main Street.
Telephone: 606-987-3980.
Telecopier: 606-987-3982.
New Albany, Indiana Office: 204 Pearl Street, Suite 200.
Telephone: 812-948-8307.
Telecopier: 812-948-8383.

Edward F. Seiller (1897-1990)

MEMBERS OF FIRM

Stuart Allen Handmaker
Bill V. Seiller
David M. Cantor
Neil C. Bordy
Kyle Anne Citrynell
Maury D. Kommor
Cynthia Compton Stone

ASSOCIATES

Glenn A. Cohen
Pamela M. Greenwell
Tomi Anne Blevins Pulliam (Resident, Paris Office)
Linda Scholle Cowan
Mary Zeller Wing Ceridan
Michael C. Bratcher
John E. Brengle
Patrick R. Holland, II
Edwin Jon Wolfe
Donna F. Townsend
William C. Robinson

OF COUNSEL

Robert S. Frey

For full biographical listings, see the Martindale-Hubbell Law Directory

*OWENSBORO,** Daviess Co.

RUMMAGE, KAMUF, YEWELL, PACE & CONDON (AV)

Great Financial Federal Building, 322 Frederica Street, 42301
Telephone: 502-685-3901
FAX: 502-926-2005

MEMBERS OF FIRM

William E. Rummage
Charles J. Kamuf
David L. Yewell
Patrick D. Pace
David C. Condon

ASSOCIATE

John M. Mischel

Representative Clients: Owensboro Municipal Utilities Commission; Lincoln Service Corp.; Hancock County Planning Commission; Daviess County Board of Education; Barmet Aluminum Corp.; Owensboro Sewer Commission; TICOR Title Insurance Co.; Chicago Title Insurance Co.; Owensboro Riverport Authority; Housing Authority of Owensboro.

For full biographical listings, see the Martindale-Hubbell Law Directory

LOUISIANA

*MONROE,** Ouachita Parish

MCLEOD, VERLANDER, EADE & VERLANDER (AV)

A Partnership including Professional Law Corporations
1900 North 18th Street, Suite 610, P.O. Box 2270, 71207-2270
Telephone: 318-325-7000
Telecopier: 318-324-0580

MEMBERS OF FIRM

Robert P. McLeod (P.L.C.)
David E. Verlander, III (P.L.C.)
Ellen R. Eade
Paul J. Verlander
Rick W. Duplissey
Pamela G. Nathan

For full biographical listings, see the Martindale-Hubbell Law Directory

MAINE

PRESQUE ISLE, Aroostook Co.

STEVENS, ENGELS, BISHOP & SPRAGUE (AV)

428 Main Street, P.O. Box 311, 04769
Telephone: 207-768-5481
Telefax: 207-764-1663

MEMBERS OF FIRM

Albert M. Stevens
Richard C. Engels
Frank H. Bishop, Sr.
Jonathan W. Sprague
Michael L. Dubois

Representative Clients: Commercial Union Cos.; Travelers Insurance Co.; Aetna Insurance Co.; Firemans Fund Group; Hartford Insurance Group; Home Indemnity Co.; Maine Bonding and Casualty Co.; New Hampshire Group; Liberty Mutual Insurance Co.; Peoples Heritage Bank.

For full biographical listings, see the Martindale-Hubbell Law Directory

MARYLAND

*BALTIMORE,** (Independent City)

ALLEN, JOHNSON, ALEXANDER & KARP, P.A. (AV)

Suite 1540, 100 East Pratt Street, 21202
Telephone: 410-727-5000
Fax: 410-727-0861
Washington, D.C. Office: 1707 L Street, N.W., Suite 1050.
Telephone: 202-828-4141.

John D. Alexander, Jr.

For Complete List of Firm Personnel, See General Section

For full biographical listings, see the Martindale-Hubbell Law Directory

VENABLE, BAETJER AND HOWARD (AV)

A Partnership including Professional Corporations
1800 Mercantile Bank & Trust Building, 2 Hopkins Plaza, 21201
Telephone: 410-244-7400
Washington, D.C. Office: Venable, Baetjer, Howard & Civiletti. Suite 1000, 1201 New York Avenue, N.W.
Telephone: 202-962-4800.
McLean, Virginia Office: Suite 400, 2010 Corporate Ridge.
Telephone: 703-760-1600.
Rockville, Maryland Office: Suite 500, One Church Street, P. O. Box 1906.
Telephone: 301-217-5600.
Towson, Maryland Office: 210 Allegheny Avenue, P. O. Box 5517.
Telephone: 410-494-6200.

MEMBERS OF FIRM

John H. Zink, III (Resident, Towson, Maryland Office)
Paul T. Glasgow (Resident, Rockville, Maryland Office)
Craig E. Smith
Michael Schatzow (Also at Washington, D.C. and Towson, Maryland Offices)
L. Paige Marvel
Christopher R. Mellott

ASSOCIATES

Carla Draluck Craft (Resident, Washington, D.C. Office)
J. Van L. Dorsey (Resident, Towson, Maryland Office)
Mary-Dulany James (Resident, Towson, Maryland Office)
Gregory L. Laubach (Resident, Rockville, Maryland Office)
Patricia A. Malone (Resident, Towson, Maryland Office)
Vicki Margolis
John A. McCauley
Timothy J. McEvoy
Mitchell Y. Mirviss
Michael W. Robinson (Not admitted in MD; Resident, McLean, Virginia Office)

For Complete List of Firm Personnel, See General Section

For full biographical listings, see the Martindale-Hubbell Law Directory

BETHESDA, Montgomery Co.

DECKELBAUM OGENS & FISCHER, CHARTERED (AV)

6701 Democracy Boulevard, 20817
Telephone: 301-564-5100
Washington D.C. Office: 1140 Connecticut Avenue, N.W.
Telephone: 202-223-1474.

Nelson Deckelbaum
Ronald L. Ogens
Lawrence H. Fischer
Arthur G. Kahn
Deborah E. Reiser

Ronald G. Scheraga

(See Next Column)

DECKELBAUM OGENS & FISCHER CHARTERED, *Bethesda—Continued*

LEGAL SUPPORT PERSONNEL

Shirley Mostow

References: First Liberty Bank; Sovran Bank, D.C.

For full biographical listings, see the Martindale-Hubbell Law Directory

GRONER AND GRONER, CHARTERED (AV)

Suite 403N, Air Rights Plaza III, 4550 Montgomery Avenue, 20814
Telephone: 301-657-2828

Beverly Anne Groner
Samuel B. Groner (On Leave of Absence)

Reference: Nation's Bank, Bethesda, Maryland Branch.

For full biographical listings, see the Martindale-Hubbell Law Directory

MOSS & STRICKLER, P.A. (AV)

Suite 700 N, 4550 Montgomery Avenue, 20814
Telephone: 301-657-8805
Facsimile: 301-657-8815

Stephen E. Moss
Scott Michael Strickler

Nancy A. Sachitano
Marni B. Schwartz
Joel Weinshank

For full biographical listings, see the Martindale-Hubbell Law Directory

*ROCKVILLE,** Montgomery Co.

KATZ, FROME AND BLEECKER, P.A. (AV)

6116 Executive Boulevard, Suite 200, 20852
Telephone: 301-230-5800
Facsimile: 301-230-5830

Steven M. Katz
Morton J. Frome
Lorin H. Bleecker
Gail B. Landau

Susan J. Rubin
Marilyn J. Brasier
Leslie Anne Sullivan
Seth B. Popkin
Richard O'Connor
Stanley A. Snyder

OF COUNSEL

Philip F. Finelli, Jr.

For full biographical listings, see the Martindale-Hubbell Law Directory

MILLER & STEINBERG (AV)

Suite 414, 414 Hungerford Drive, 20850
Telephone: 301-424-1180
FAX: 301-424-8459

MEMBERS OF FIRM

James Robert Miller
Harvey B. Steinberg
Kevin G. Hessler

Reference: NationsBank, Rockville Branch.

For full biographical listings, see the Martindale-Hubbell Law Directory

STEIN, SPERLING, BENNETT, DE JONG, DRISCOLL, GREENFEIG & METRO, P.A. (AV)

25 West Middle Lane, 20850
Telephone: 301-340-2020; 800-435-5230
Telecopier: 301-340-8217

David C. Driscoll, Jr.
Stuart S. Greenfeig
Paul T. Stein

For Complete List of Firm Personnel, See General Section

For full biographical listings, see the Martindale-Hubbell Law Directory

*TOWSON,** Baltimore Co.

TURNBULL, WASE & LYONS, P.A. (AV)

Suite 200, 555 Fairmount Avenue, 21204
Telephone: 410-583-8300
FAX: 410-583-7068

Ann McKenrick Turnbull
Joseph J. Wase
Joseph S. Lyons

Francis D. DeMuro
Mary Roby Sanders
D. Lynne Jenkins

For full biographical listings, see the Martindale-Hubbell Law Directory

MASSACHUSETTS

*BOSTON,** Suffolk Co.

ATWOOD & CHERNY (AV)

Mason House 211 Commonwealth Avenue, 02116
Telephone: 617-262-6400
Telecopier: 617-421-9482

Jacob M. Atwood
David E. Cherny
Susan G. Lillis
Pasquale DeSantis

For full biographical listings, see the Martindale-Hubbell Law Directory

CUDDY BIXBY (AV)

One Financial Center, 02111
Telephone: 617-348-3600
Telecopier: 617-348-3643
Wellesley, Massachusetts Office: 60 Walnut Street.
Telephone: 617-235-1034.

Francis X. Cuddy (Retired)
Wayne E. Hartwell
Brian D. Bixby
Anthony M. Ambriano
William E. Kelly
Paul G. Boylan
Robert A. Vigoda
Paul J. Murphy
Alexander L. Cataldo
Duncan S. Payne
Stephen T. Kunian
Arthur P. Menard
Joseph H. Walsh
Michael J. Owens
Robert J. O'Regan
Andrew R. Menard
David F. Hendren
Glenn B. Asch
Timothy E. McAllister
William R. Moriarty
Kevin P. Sweeney
Denise I. Murphy

For full biographical listings, see the Martindale-Hubbell Law Directory

GELB & GELB (AV)

20 Custom House Street, 02110
Telephone: 617-345-0010
Telecopier: 617-345-0009

MEMBER OF FIRM

Gail Kleven Gelb

For full biographical listings, see the Martindale-Hubbell Law Directory

SHERBURNE, POWERS & NEEDHAM, P.C. (AV)

One Beacon Street, 02108
Telephone: 617-523-2700
Fax: 617-523-6850

William D. Weeks
John T. Collins
Allan J. Landau
John L. Daly
Stephen A. Hopkins
Alan I. Falk
C. Thomas Swaim
James Pollock
William V. Tripp III
Stephen S. Young
William F. Machen
W. Robert Allison
Jacob C. Diemert
Philip J. Notopoulos
Richard J. Hindlian
Paul E. Troy
Harold W. Potter, Jr.
Dale R. Johnson
Philip S. Lapatin
Pamela A. Duckworth
Mark Schonfeld
James D. Smeallie
Paul Killeen
Gordon P. Katz
Joseph B. Darby, III
Richard M Yanofsky
James E. McDermott
Robert V. Lizza
Miriam Goldstein Altman
John J. Monaghan
Margaret J. Palladino
Mark C. Michalowski
David Scott Sloan
M. Chrysa Long
Lawrence D. Bradley
Miriam J. McKendall

Cynthia A. Brown
Cynthia M. Hern
Dianne R. Phillips
Paul M. James
Theodore F. Hanselman
Joshua C. Krumholz
Ieuan G. Mahony
Kenneth L. Harvey
Christopher J. Trombetta
Edwin F. Landers, Jr.
Amy J. Mastrobattista
William Howard McCarthy, Jr.
Douglas W. Clapp
Tamara E. Goulston
Nicholas J. Psyhogeos

COUNSEL

Haig Der Manuelian
Mason M. Taber, Jr.
Karl J. Hirshman
Benjamin Volinski
Kenneth P. Brier

OF COUNSEL

John Barr Dolan

For full biographical listings, see the Martindale-Hubbell Law Directory

WHITE, INKER, ARONSON, P.C. (AV)

One Washington Mall, 02108
Telephone: 617-367-7700
Telecopier: 617-523-5085

(See Next Column)

WHITE, INKER, ARONSON P.C.—*Continued*

Monroe L. Inker
Martin L. Aronson
John P. White, Jr.
Ann E. Wagner
Leilah Anne Keamy
John Newman Flanagan
Frances M. Giordano
Kim D. Vo
Robert J. Rivers, Jr.
Laura J. DiPasquale
Kevin R. Connelly
Libby G. Fulgione, II
Amy Lyn Blake
Bryna S. Klevan

OF COUNSEL

Sanford N. Katz

For full biographical listings, see the Martindale-Hubbell Law Directory

WITMER & THUOTTE (AV)

One Joy Street, 02108
Telephone: 617-248-0550
Telefax: 617-248-0607

Ronald A. Witmer
Robert W. Thuotte

ASSOCIATE

Lynn C. Rooney

For full biographical listings, see the Martindale-Hubbell Law Directory

*CAMBRIDGE,** Middlesex Co.

BENJAMIN & BENSON (AV)

Bulfinch Square, 43 Thorndike Street, 02141
Telephone: 617-577-1515

Roberta F. Benjamin
Jon Benson

ASSOCIATE

Phyllis K. Kolman

For full biographical listings, see the Martindale-Hubbell Law Directory

*PLYMOUTH,** Plymouth Co.

MILES AND MILES, A PROFESSIONAL ASSOCIATION (AV)

7 South Park Avenue, 02360
Telephone: 508-746-2660
Fax: 508-830-0395
Duxbury, Massachusetts Office: 907 Tremont Street, P.O. BOx 1686, 02331 -1686.
Telephone: 617-934-5474

Frankland W. L. Miles (1897-1974)
Frankland W. L. Miles, Jr.
John Grother Miles

For full biographical listings, see the Martindale-Hubbell Law Directory

MICHIGAN

*ANN ARBOR,** Washtenaw Co.

MILLER, CANFIELD, PADDOCK AND STONE, P.L.C. (AV)

A Professional Limited Liability Company
Founded in 1852 by Sidney Davy Miller
101 North Main Street, Seventh Floor, 48104-1400
Telephone: 313-663-2445
Fax: 313-747-7147
Detroit, Michigan Office: 150 West Jefferson, Suite 2500, 48226-4415.
Telephone: 313-963-6420.
Fax: 313-496-7500.
Cable Address: "Stem Detroit."
Bloomfield Hills, Michigan Office: Suite 100, Pinehurst Office Center, 1400 North Woodward, 48303-2014.
Telephone: 313-645-5000.
Fax: 313-645-1917.
Grand Rapids, Michigan Office: 1200 Campau Square Plaza, 99 Monroe, N.W., 49503-2639.
Telephone: 616-454-8656.
Fax: 616-776-6322.
Howell, Michigan Office: 121 South Barnard Street, Suite 4, 48843-2305.
Telephone: 517-546-7600.
Telecopier: 517-546-6974.
Kalamazoo, Michigan Office: 444 West Michigan Avenue, 49007-3752.
Telephone: 616-381-7030.
Fax: 616-382-0244.
Lansing, Michigan Office: One Michigan Avenue, Suite 900, 48933-1609.
Telephone: 517-487-2070.
Fax: 517-374-6304.
Monroe, Michigan Office: The Executive Centre, 214 East Elm Avenue, 48161-2682.
Telephone: 313-243-2000.
Fax: 313-243-0901.

(See Next Column)

Washington, D.C. Office: 1225 Nineteenth Street, N.W., Suite 400. 20036.
Telephone: 202-429-5575; 785-0600.
Fax: 202-331-1118; 785-1234.
Pensacola, Florida Office: 25 West Cedar, 32501.
Telephone: 904-469-1088.
Fax: 904-432-0677.
St. Petersburg, Florida Office: 100 Second Avenue S., Suite 7045, 33701.
Telephone: 813-982-6000.
Fax: 813-892-6002.
Gdansk, Poland Office: Suite 322, Dom Technika Building, UI. Rajska 6, 80-850.
Telephone: 011-485-831-2808.
Fax: 011-485-831-4719.
Warsaw, Poland Office: UI. Marszalkowska 82, Suite 561, 00-517.
Telephone: 011-482-623-6457 and 6458.
Fax: 011-482-623-6459.

RESIDENT PARTNER

Robert E. Gilbert

Representative Firm Clients: Chrysler Corp.; Comerica, Inc.; City of Detroit, Mich.; Detroit Tigers, Inc.; First of Michigan; Fretter, Inc.; Ford Motor Co.; Ford Motor Credit Co.; Great Lakes Bancorp; Henry Ford Hospital.

For Complete List of Firm Personnel, See General Section

For full biographical listings, see the Martindale-Hubbell Law Directory

PEAR SPERLING EGGAN & MUSKOVITZ, P.C. (AV)

Domino's Farms, 24 Frank Lloyd Wright Drive, 48105
Telephone: 313-665-4441
Fax: 313-665-8788
Ypsilanti, Michigan Offices: 5 South Washington Street.
Telephone: 313-483-3626 and 2164 Bellevue at Washtenaw.
Telephone: 313-483-7177.

Edwin L. Pear
Andrew M. Eggan
Thomas E. Daniels
Paul R. Fransway
Francyne Stacey
Helen Conklin Vick

Counsel For: Domino's Pizza, Inc.; Townsend and Bottum, Inc.; The Credit Bureau of Ypsilanti; Margolis Nursery, Inc.; Wiards Orchards; Ann Arbor Housing Commission.

For Complete List of Firm Personnel, See General Section

For full biographical listings, see the Martindale-Hubbell Law Directory

BIRMINGHAM, Oakland Co.

BUTZEL LONG, A PROFESSIONAL CORPORATION (AV)

Suite 200, 32270 Telegraph Road, 48025
Telephone: 810-258-1616
Telecopier: 810-258-1439
Detroit, Michigan Office: Suite 900, 150 West Jefferson.
Telephone: 313-225-7000.
Telecopier: 313-225-7080.
Lansing, Michigan Office: 118 West Ottawa Street.
Telephone: 517-372-6622.
Telecopier: 517-372-6672.
Ann Arbor, Michigan Office: Suite 400, 121 West Washington.
Telephone: 313-995-3110.
Telecopier: 313-995-1777.
Grosse Pointe Farms, Michigan Office: Suite 260, 21 Kercheval.
Telephone: 313-886-5446.
Telecopier: 313-886-2114.

Edward D. Gold (Resident)
Frederick G. Buesser, III (Resident)
T. Gordon Scupholm II (Resident)

For Complete List of Firm Personnel, See General Section

For full biographical listings, see the Martindale-Hubbell Law Directory

CARSON FISCHER, P.L.C. (AV)

Third Floor, 300 East Maple Road, 48009-6317
Telephone: 810-644-4840
Facsimile: 810-644-1832

Robert M. Carson
Anne Cole Pierce

For full biographical listings, see the Martindale-Hubbell Law Directory

HYMAN AND LIPPITT, P.C. (AV)

185 Oakland Avenue, Suite 300, P.O. Box 1750, 48009
Telephone: 810-646-8292
Facsimile: 810-646-8375

J. Leonard Hyman
Norman L. Lippitt
Douglas A. Hyman
Brian D. O'Keefe
H. Joel Newman
Nazli G. Sater
Kenneth F. Neuman
Terry S. Givens
Paul J. Fischer
Sanford Plotkin
John A. Sellers
Robert H. Lippitt
Roger L. Myers

(See Next Column)

HYMAN AND LIPPITT P.C., *Birmingham—Continued*

COUNSEL

Alice L. Gilbert

For full biographical listings, see the Martindale-Hubbell Law Directory

SHELDON G. LARKY (AV)

Suite 3350, 30600 Telegraph Road, 48025-4533
Telephone: 810-642-4660

For full biographical listings, see the Martindale-Hubbell Law Directory

WEINGARDEN & HAUER, P.C. (AV)

30100 Telegraph Road, Suite 221, 48025
Telephone: 810-258-0800
Telecopier: 810-258-2750

Harvey I. Hauer

Reference: Security Bank & Trust.

For full biographical listings, see the Martindale-Hubbell Law Directory

WILLIAMS, SCHAEFER, RUBY & WILLIAMS, PROFESSIONAL CORPORATION (AV)

Suite 300, 380 North Woodward Avenue, 48009
Telephone: 810-642-0333
Telecopy: 810-642-0856

John F. Schaefer
Richard D. Rattner
Thomas G. Plunkett
James P. Cunningham
James J. Williams

For full biographical listings, see the Martindale-Hubbell Law Directory

BLOOMFIELD HILLS, Oakland Co.

HARDIG & PARSONS (AV)

2000 North Woodward Avenue, Suite 100, 48304
Telephone: 313-642-3500
Facsimile: 313-645-1128
Charlevoix, Michigan Office: 212 Bridge Street.
Telephone: 616-547-1200.
Facsimile: 616-547-1026.
Pawley's Island, South Carolina Office: 216 Highway 17, P.O. Box 1607, 29585.
Telephone: 803-237-9219.
Facsimile: 803-237-9530.
West Palm Beach, Florida Office: Suite 1450, 515 North Flagler.
Telephone: 407-833-1622.
Facsimile: 407-833-6933.
Charlotte Amalie, St. Thomas, Virgin Islands Office: International Plaza, 22 Dronningens Gade.
Telephone: 809-776-7650.
Facsimile: 809-774-2729.

MEMBERS OF FIRM

Joseph L. Hardig, Jr.
Donald H. Parsons
Joseph L. Hardig, III

ASSOCIATES

Bradley S. Stout
Kevin M. O'Connell

OF COUNSEL

Frederick Wm. Heath

MEMBER IN FLORIDA

Charles Ryan Hickman

MEMBER IN SOUTH CAROLINA

John C. Benso

OF COUNSEL

Preston Bennett Haines, III

MEMBER IN CHARLOTTE AMALIE, ST. THOMAS, VIRGIN ISLANDS

Arthur Pomerantz

ASSOCIATE

Marcia B. Resnick

For full biographical listings, see the Martindale-Hubbell Law Directory

LAW OFFICES OF THOMAS J. TRENTA, P.C. (AV)

33 Bloomfield Hills Parkway Suite 145, 48304-2945
Telephone: 810-258-9610
Fax: 810-258-5132

Thomas J. Trenta

Richard A. Joslin, Jr.

OF COUNSEL

James F. Jordan

For full biographical listings, see the Martindale-Hubbell Law Directory

*DETROIT,** Wayne Co.

BEVERLY CLARK (AV)

440 E. Congress, Suite 4R, 48226-2917
Telephone: 313-961-4440

For full biographical listings, see the Martindale-Hubbell Law Directory

JAFFE, RAITT, HEUER & WEISS, PROFESSIONAL CORPORATION (AV)

One Woodward Avenue, Suite 2400, 48226
Telephone: 313-961-8380
Telecopier: 313-961-8358
Cable Address: "Jafsni"
Southfield,Michigan Office: Travelers Tower, Suite 1520.
Telephone: 313-961-8380.
Monroe, Michigan Office: 212 East Front Street, Suite 3.
Telephone: 313-241-6470.
Telefacsimile: 313-241-3849.

Joel S. Golden
Sharon J. LaDuke

Susan S. Lichterman

See General Practice Section for List of Representative Clients.

For Complete List of Firm Personnel, See General Section

For full biographical listings, see the Martindale-Hubbell Law Directory

MEYER, KIRK, SNYDER & SAFFORD (AV)

2500 Penobscot Building, 48226
Telephone: 313-961-1261
Fax: 810-647-6079
Bloomfield Hills, Michigan Office: Suite 100, 100 West Long Lake Road.
Telephone: 313-647-5111.
Telecopier: 313-647-6079.

George E. Snyder

Representative Clients: Chemical Waste Management, Inc.; Ervin Advertising; The Michigan and S.E. Michigan McDonald's Operators Assn.; The Southland Corp. (7-Eleven Food Stores); Stauffer Chemical Co.; Techpoint, Inc.

For Complete List of Firm Personnel, See General Section

For full biographical listings, see the Martindale-Hubbell Law Directory

MILLER, CANFIELD, PADDOCK AND STONE, P.L.C. (AV)

A Professional Limited Liability Company
Founded in 1852 by Sidney Davy Miller
150 West Jefferson, Suite 2500, 48226-4415
Telephone: 313-963-6420
Fax: 313-496-7500
Cable Address: "Stem Detroit"
Detroit, Michigan Office: 150 West Jefferson, Suite 2500, 48226-4415.
Telephone: 313-963-6420.
Fax: 313-496-7500.
Cable Address: "Stem Detroit."
Ann Arbor, Michigan Office: 101 North Main Street, 7th Floor, 48104-1400.
Telephone: 313-663-2445.
Fax: 313-747-7147.
Bloomfield Hills, Michigan Office: Suite 100, Pinehurst Office Center, 1400 North Woodward, 48303-2014.
Telephone: 313-645-5000.
Fax: 313-645-1917.
Grand Rapids, Michigan Office: 1200 Campau Square Plaza, 99 Monroe, N.W., 49503-2639.
Telephone: 616-454-8656.
Fax: 616-776-6322.
Howell, Michigan Office: 121 South Barnard Street, Suite 4, 48843-2305.
Telephone: 517-546-7600.
Telecopier: 517-546-6974.
Kalamazoo, Michigan Office: 444 West Michigan Avenue, 49007-3752.
Telephone: 616-381-7030.
Fax: 616-382-0244.
Lansing, Michigan Office: One Michigan Avenue, Suite 900, 48933-1609.
Telephone: 517-487-2070.
Fax: 517-374-6304.
Monroe, Michigan Office: The Executive Centre, 214 East Elm Avenue, 48161-2682.
Telephone: 313-243-2000.
Fax: 313-243-0901.
Washington, D.C. Office: 1225 Nineteenth Street, N.W., Suite 400. 20036.
Telephone: 202-429-5575; 785-0600.
Fax: 202-331-1118; 785-1234.
Pensacola, Florida Office: 25 West Cedar, 32501.
Telephone: 904-469-1088.
Fax: 904-432-0677.

(See Next Column)

MILLER, CANFIELD, PADDOCK AND STONE P.L.C.—*Continued*

St. Petersburg, Florida Office: 100 Second Avenue S., Suite 7045, 33701.
Telephone: 813-982-6000.
Fax: 813-892-6002.
Gdansk, Poland Office: Suite 322, Dom Technika Building, Ul. Rajska 6, 80-850.
Telephone: 011-485-831-2808.
Fax: 011-485-831-4719.
Warsaw, Poland Office: Ul. Marszalkowska 82, Suite 561, 00-517.
Telephone: 011-482-623-6457 and 6458.
Fax: 011-482-623-6459.

MEMBER OF FIRM

James W. Williams (Bloomfield Hills Office)

ASSOCIATE

Dawn M. Schluter (Bloomfield Hills Office)

Representative Firm Clients: Chrysler Corp.; Comerica, Inc.; City of Detroit, Mich.; Detroit Tigers, Inc.; First of Michigan; Fretter, Inc.; Ford Motor Co.; Ford Motor Credit Co.; Great Lakes Bancorp; Henry Ford Hospital.

For Complete List of Firm Personnel, See General Section

For full biographical listings, see the Martindale-Hubbell Law Directory

PRATHER & ASSOCIATES, P.C. (AV)

3800 Penobscot Building, 48226-4220
Telephone: 313-962-7722
Facsimile: 313-962-2653

Kenneth E. Prather

Jan Rewers McMillan

For full biographical listings, see the Martindale-Hubbell Law Directory

SCHUREMAN, FRAKES, GLASS & WULFMEIER (AV)

440 East Congress, Fourth Floor, 48226
Telephone: 313-961-1500
Telecopier: 313-961-1087
Harbor Springs, Michigan Office: One Spring Street Sq., 49740.
Telephone: 616-526-1145.
Telecopier: 616-526-9343.

MEMBERS OF FIRM

Jeptha W. Schureman
John C. Frakes, Jr.
Charles F. Glass
LeRoy H. Wulfmeier, III
Cheryl L. Chandler
David M. Ottenwess

ASSOCIATES

Daniel J. Dulworth
John J. Moran
Paul A. Salyers
Erane C. Washington

Reference: Comerica.

For full biographical listings, see the Martindale-Hubbell Law Directory

EAST LANSING, Ingham Co.

FARHAT, STORY & KRAUS, P.C. (AV)

Beacon Place, 4572 South Hagadorn Road, Suite 3, 48823
Telephone: 517-351-3700
Fax: 517-332-4122

Leo A. Farhat
James E. Burns (1925-1979)
Monte R. Story
Richard C. Kraus
Max R. Hoffman Jr.
Chris A. Bergstrom
Kitty L. Groh
Charles R. Toy
David M. Platt

Lawrence P. Schweitzer
Jeffrey J. Short
Kathy A. Breedlove
Thomas L. Sparks

Reference: Capitol National Bank.

For full biographical listings, see the Martindale-Hubbell Law Directory

*ESCANABA,** Delta Co.

BUTCH, QUINN, ROSEMURGY, JARDIS, BUSH, BURKHART & STROM, P.C. (AV)

816 Ludington Street, 49829
Telephone: 906-786-4422
Fax: 906-786-5128
Gladstone, Michigan Office: 201 First National Bank Building.
Telephone: 906-428-3123.
Marquette, Michigan Office: 300 South Front Street.
Telephone: 906-228-4440.
Iron Mountain, Michigan Office: 500 South Stephenson Avenue.
Telephone: 906-774-4460.
Marinette, Wisconsin Office: 2008 Ella Court.
Telephone: 715-732-4154.

(See Next Column)

Michael B. Quinn
Bonnie Lee Hoff
James E. Soderberg
JoJean A. Miller

Representative Clients: MFC First National Bank, Escanaba, Michigan; United States Fidelity & Guaranty Co.; City of Gladstone; Baybank; Bresnan Cable Communications Co.; Engineered Machined Products, Inc.; Upper Peninsula Association of Realtors.

For Complete List of Firm Personnel, See General Section

For full biographical listings, see the Martindale-Hubbell Law Directory

FARMINGTON HILLS, Oakland Co.

MICHAEL H. GOLOB (AV)

30300 Northwestern Highway, Suite 300, 48334
Telephone: 810-855-2626
Fax: 810-932-4009

For full biographical listings, see the Martindale-Hubbell Law Directory

*FLINT,** Genesee Co.

WINEGARDEN, SHEDD, HALEY, LINDHOLM & ROBERTSON (AV)

501 Citizens Bank Building, 48502-1983
Telephone: 810-767-3600
Telecopier: 810-767-8776

MEMBERS OF FIRM

William C. Shedd
Dennis M. Haley
John T. Lindholm
Donald H. Robertson
L. David Lawson
John R. Tucker

ASSOCIATES

Alan F. Himelhoch
Suellen J. Parker
Damion Frasier
Peter T. Mooney

Representative Clients: Citizens Commercial and Savings Bank; R. L. White Development Corporation; Interstate Traffic Consultants (Intracon) Inc.; Downtown Development Authority of Flint; Young Olds-Cadillac, Inc.; First American Title Insurance Co.; Sorensen Gross Construction Co.; Genesee County; Insight, Inc.; Modern Industries, Inc.

For Complete List of Firm Personnel, See General Section

For full biographical listings, see the Martindale-Hubbell Law Directory

*GRAND RAPIDS,** Kent Co.

VARNUM, RIDDERING, SCHMIDT & HOWLETT (AV)

Bridgewater Place, P.O. Box 352, 49501-0352
Telephone: 616-336-6000
800-262-0011
Facsimile: 616-336-7000
Telex: 1561593 VARN
Lansing, Michigan Office: The Victor Center, Suite 810, 210 North Washington Square, 48933.
Telephone: 517-482-6237.
Facsimile: 517-482-6937.
Kalamazoo, Michigan Office: 350 East Michigan Avenue, 49007.
Telephone: 616-382-2300.
Facsimile: 616-382-2382.
Grand Haven, Michigan Office: 321 Washington Street, P.O. Box 288, 49417.
Telephone: 616-846-7100.
Facsimile: 616-846-7101.
Battle Creek, Michigan Office: 4950 West Dickman Road, Suite B-1, 49015.
Telephone: 616-962-7144.
Detroit, Michigan Office: 440 East Congress, Fourth Floor, 48226.
Telephone: 313-961-1600.
Facsimile: 313-961-1636.

MEMBERS OF FIRM

Bruce A. Barnhart
N. Stevenson Jennette III

STAFF ATTORNEY

Robert C. Rutgers, Jr.

For Complete List of Firm Personnel, See General Section

For full biographical listings, see the Martindale-Hubbell Law Directory

ZERRENNER & ROANE (AV)

Grand Plaza Place, Suite 450, 220 Lyon Square, N.W., 49503
Telephone: 616-774-4414
Fax: 616-774-8203

James W. Zerrenner
Richard A. Roane

For full biographical listings, see the Martindale-Hubbell Law Directory

*HOWELL,** Livingston Co.

PETER B. VAN WINKLE, P.C. (AV)

105 East Grand River, 48843
Telephone: 517-546-2680

(See Next Column)

PETER B. VAN WINKLE, P.C., *Howell—Continued*

William P. Van Winkle (1858-1920)
Don W. Van Winkle (1887-1971)
Charles K. Van Winkle (Retired)
Peter B. Van Winkle

Reference: First National Bank in Howell, Howell, Mich.

For full biographical listings, see the Martindale-Hubbell Law Directory

*JACKSON,** Jackson Co.

POTTER & HAMILTON (AV)

404 South Jackson Street, P.O. Box 764, 49204
Telephone: 517-788-6290
Fax: 517-784-7188

George E. Potter
Janet L. Hamilton

ASSOCIATE

Frederick Girodat, II

Reference: City Bank & Trust Company, N.A.

For full biographical listings, see the Martindale-Hubbell Law Directory

*KALAMAZOO,** Kalamazoo Co.

KREIS, ENDERLE, CALLANDER & HUDGINS, A PROFESSIONAL CORPORATION (AV)

One Moorsbridge, 49002
Telephone: 616-324-3000
Telecopier: 616-324-3010

Russell A. Kreis
Jeffery S. Rubel
Julie A. Sullivan

For Complete List of Firm Personnel, See General Section

For full biographical listings, see the Martindale-Hubbell Law Directory

MILLER, CANFIELD, PADDOCK AND STONE, P.L.C. (AV)

A Professional Limited Liability Company
Founded in 1852 by Sidney Davy Miller
444 West Michigan Avenue, 49007-3752
Telephone: 616-381-7030
Fax: 616-382-0244
Detroit, Michigan Office: 150 West Jefferson, Suite 2500, 48226-4415.
Telephone: 313-963-6420.
Fax: 313-496-7500.
Cable Address: "Stem Detroit."
Ann Arbor, Michigan Office: 101 North Main Street, 7th Floor, 48104-1400.
Telephone: 313-663-2445.
Fax: 313-747-7147.
Bloomfield Hills, Michigan Office: Suite 100, Pinehurst Office Center, 1400 North Woodward, 48303-2014.
Telephone: 313-645-5000.
Fax: 313-645-1917.
Grand Rapids, Michigan Office: 1200 Campau Square Plaza, 99 Monroe, N.W., 49503-2639.
Telephone: 616-454-8656.
Fax: 616-776-6322.
Howell, Michigan Office: 121 South Barnard Street, Suite 4, 48843-2305.
Telephone: 517-546-7600.
Telecopier: 517-546-6974.
Lansing, Michigan Office: One Michigan Avenue, Suite 900, 48933-1609.
Telephone: 517-487-2070.
Fax: 517-374-6304.
Monroe, Michigan Office: The Executive Centre, 214 East Elm Avenue, 48161-2682.
Telephone: 313-243-2000.
Fax: 313-243-0901.
Washington, D.C. Office: 1225 Nineteenth Street, N.W., Suite 400. 20036.
Telephone: 202-429-5575; 785-0600.
Fax: 202-331-1118; 785-1234.
Pensacola, Florida Office: 25 West Cedar, 32501.
Telephone: 904-469-1088.
Fax: 904-432-0677.
St. Petersburg, Florida Office: 100 Second Avenue S., Suite 7045,33701.
Telephone: 813-982-6000.
Fax: 813-892-6002.
Gdansk, Poland Office: Suite 322, Dom Technika Building, Ul. Rajska 6, 80-850.
Telephone: 011-485-831-2808.
Fax: 011-485-831-4719.
Warsaw, Poland Office: Ul. Marszalkowska 82, Suite 561, 00-517.
Telephone: 011-482-623-6457 and 6458.
Fax: 011-482-623-6459.

MEMBER OF FIRM

Eric V. Brown, Jr. (Resident)

Representative Firm Clients: Chrysler Corp.; Comerica, Inc.; City of Detroit, Mich.; Detroit Tigers, Inc.; First of Michigan; Fretter, Inc.; Ford Motor Co.; Ford Motor Credit Co.; Great Lakes Bancorp; Henry Ford Hospital.

(See Next Column)

For Complete List of Firm Personnel, See General Section

For full biographical listings, see the Martindale-Hubbell Law Directory

LANSING, Ingham Co.

DUNNINGS & FRAWLEY, P.C. (AV)

Duncan Building, 530 South Pine Street, 48933-2299
Telephone: 517-487-8222
Fax: 517-487-2026

Stuart J. Dunnings, Jr.
John J. Frawley

Stuart J. Dunnings, III
Steven D. Dunnings

For full biographical listings, see the Martindale-Hubbell Law Directory

*MUSKEGON,** Muskegon Co.

PARMENTER O'TOOLE (AV)

175 West Apple Street, P.O. Box 786, 49443-0786
Telephone: 616-722-1621
Telecopier: 616-728-2206; 722-7866

MEMBER OF FIRM

George D. Van Epps

General Counsel for: FMB Lumberman's Bank; AmeriBank Federal Savings Bank; City of Muskegon; Quality Tool & Stamping Co., Inc.; Radiology Muskegon, P.C.
Local Counsel for: General Electric Capital Corp.; Paine-Webber; Teledyne Industries, Inc. (Continental Motors Division); Westinghouse Electric Corporation (Knoll Group).

For Complete List of Firm Personnel, See General Section

For full biographical listings, see the Martindale-Hubbell Law Directory

*PONTIAC,** Oakland Co.

STERLING, SCHILLING & THORBURN, P.C. (AV)

1400 NBD Building, 48342
Telephone: 810-334-4544
Fax: 810-334-1021

Robert P. Sauer (1906-1974)
J. Robert Sterling
Ronald F. Schilling
Bruce J. Thorburn

Reference: First of America, O.M.

For full biographical listings, see the Martindale-Hubbell Law Directory

ROYAL OAK, Oakland Co.

KATHERINE L. BARNHART, P.C. (AV)

Sixth Floor Washington Square Plaza, 48067
Telephone: 810-543-2400
Detroit, Michigan Office: 975 E. Jefferson.
Telephone: 313-567-2337.

Katherine L. Barnhart
Elaine P. Goren

For full biographical listings, see the Martindale-Hubbell Law Directory

SOUTHFIELD, Oakland Co.

SOMMERS, SCHWARTZ, SILVER & SCHWARTZ, P.C. (AV)

2000 Town Center, Suite 900, 48075
Telephone: 810-355-0300
Telecopier: 810-746-4001
Plymouth, Michigan Office: 747 South Main Street.
Telephone: 313-455-4250.

Lawrence Warren
William M. Brukoff

General Counsel for: City of Taylor; Foodland Distributors; C.A. Muer Corporation; Vlasic & Company; Nederlander Corporation; Woodland Physicians; Midwest Health Centers, P.C.
Representative Clients: Crum & Forster Insurance Company; City of Pontiac; Michigan National Bank; Perry Drugs.

For Complete List of Firm Personnel, See General Section

For full biographical listings, see the Martindale-Hubbell Law Directory

TROY, Oakland Co.

HUTSON, SAWYER, CHAPMAN & REILLY (AV)

292 Town Center Drive, 48084-1799
Telephone: 810-689-5700
Fax: 810-689-5741

MEMBERS OF FIRM

Thomas G. Sawyer
Michael W. Hutson
Ronald A. Chapman
Michael J. Reilly

References: First of America Bank; Michigan National Bank.

For full biographical listings, see the Martindale-Hubbell Law Directory

MINNESOTA

BLOOMINGTON, Hennepin Co.

JACK S. JAYCOX LAW OFFICES, LTD. (AV)
201 Southgate Office Plaza, 5001 West 80th Street, 55437
Telephone: 612-835-6300
Fax: 612-835-7870

Jack S. Jaycox

Peggy E. O'Hare Gerald O. Williams, Jr.

For full biographical listings, see the Martindale-Hubbell Law Directory

EDINA, Hennepin Co.

KISSOON AND CLUGG (AV)
3205 West 76th Street, 55435-5244
Telephone: 612-896-1099
Fax: 612-896-1132

K. Worner Kissoon Lorraine S. Clugg

Karen I. Linder Michael D. Dittberner

For full biographical listings, see the Martindale-Hubbell Law Directory

SWADEN LAW OFFICES (AV)
7301 Ohms Lane, Suite 550, 55439
Telephone: 612-832-5990
FAX: 612-832-0984

Martin L. Swaden

Tsippi Wray

For full biographical listings, see the Martindale-Hubbell Law Directory

*MANKATO,** Blue Earth Co.

JOHNSON, ANDERSON & ZELLMER (AV)
600 South Second Street, P.O. Box 637, 56001
Telephone: 507-387-4002
FAX: 507-345-5001

MEMBERS OF FIRM

C. A. (Gus) Johnson, II Randy J. Zellmer
Jerome T. Anderson Suzette E. Johnson

For full biographical listings, see the Martindale-Hubbell Law Directory

MANAHAN & BLUTH LAW OFFICE CHARTERED (AV)
416 South Front Street, P.O. Box 287, 56002-0287
Telephone: 507-387-5661
Fax: 507-387-2111
CompuServe ID#73530,2374

James H. Manahan Joseph P. Bluth

Reference: Security State Bank of Mankato.

For full biographical listings, see the Martindale-Hubbell Law Directory

*MINNEAPOLIS,** Hennepin Co.

ARNOLD & McDOWELL (AV)
5881 Cedar Lake Road, 55416-1492
Telephone: 612-545-9000
Minnesota Wats Line: 800-343-4545
Fax: 612-545-1793
Princeton, Minnesota Office: 501 South Fourth Street.
Telephone: 612-389-2214.
Hutchinson, Minnesota Office: 101 Park Place.
Telephone: 612-587-7575.

MEMBERS OF FIRM

David B. Arnold Gary D. McDowell
Laura K. Fretland

OF COUNSEL

Jane Van Valkenburg

For Complete List of Firm Personnel, See General Section

For full biographical listings, see the Martindale-Hubbell Law Directory

HENSON & EFRON, P.A. (AV)
1200 Title Insurance Building, 400 Second Avenue South, 55401
Telephone: 612-339-2500
FAX: 612-339-6364

(See Next Column)

Robert F. Henson Alan C. Eidsness
William F. Forsyth

For Complete List of Firm Personnel, See General Section

For full biographical listings, see the Martindale-Hubbell Law Directory

OLUP & ASSOCIATES (AV)
7300 Metro Boulevard (Edina), 55439
Telephone: 612-835-4070
FAX: 612-835-3107

Linda A. Olup

For full biographical listings, see the Martindale-Hubbell Law Directory

*ST. PAUL,** Ramsey Co.

COLLINS, BUCKLEY, SAUNTRY AND HAUGH (AV)
West 1100 First National Bank Building, 332 Minnesota Street, 55101
Telephone: 612-227-0611
Telecopier: 612-227-0758

MEMBERS OF FIRM

William E. Haugh, Jr. Dan C. O'Connell
Thomas R. O'Connell Christine L. Stroemer

Reference: First National Bank of St. Paul.

For Complete List of Firm Personnel, See General Section

For full biographical listings, see the Martindale-Hubbell Law Directory

GOFF, KAPLAN & WOLF, PROFESSIONAL ASSOCIATION (AV)
900 Capital Centre, 386 North Wabasha, 55102
Telephone: 612-222-6341
Fax: 612-222-6346

Richard D. Goff J. Peter Wolf

Sonja Trom Eayrs

For full biographical listings, see the Martindale-Hubbell Law Directory

MISSISSIPPI

*GULFPORT,** Harrison Co.

BOYCE HOLLEMAN A PROFESSIONAL CORPORATION (AV)
1913 15th Street, P.O. Drawer 1030, 39502
Telephone: 601-863-3142
Telecopier: 601-863-9829

Boyce Holleman

Michael B. Holleman Leslie Dean Holleman
Timothy C. Holleman David J. White

References: Hancock Bank, Gulfport; Merchants Bank & Trust Co., Gulfport; Bank of Wiggins, Wiggins, Mississippi.

For full biographical listings, see the Martindale-Hubbell Law Directory

MEADOWS, RILEY, KOENENN AND TEEL, P.A. (AV)
1720 23rd Avenue, P.O. Box 550, 39502
Telephone: 601-864-4511
Telecopier: 601-868-2178

Joseph R. Meadows Walter W. Teel
Donnie D. Riley Jerry D. Riley
Alfred R. Koenenn Karen J. Young

Representative Clients: Bubba Oustalat Lincoln Mercury, Inc.; Lee Tractor Co. of Mississippi.
Reference: Hancock Bank.

For full biographical listings, see the Martindale-Hubbell Law Directory

*JACKSON,** Hinds Co.

PRICE & ZIRULNIK (AV)
Suite 1150 Capital Towers, 125 South Congress Street, P.O. Box 3439, 39207-3439
Telephone: 601-353-3000
Telecopier: 601-353-3007

John H. Price, Jr. Barry S. Zirulnik

ASSOCIATE

William G. Cheney, Jr.

Representative Clients: Yellow Freight System, Inc.; Mississippi Dairy Products Association, Inc.; LuVel Dairy Products, Inc.; Mississippi Farm Bureau Federation; Mississippi Department of Transportation; Mississippi High

(See Next Column)

PRICE & ZIRULNIK, *Jackson—Continued*

School Activities Association, Inc.; Variety Wholesalers, Inc.; Mississippi Bankers Association; Metal Rolling, Inc.

For full biographical listings, see the Martindale-Hubbell Law Directory

SOUTHAVEN, De Soto Co.

TAYLOR, JONES, ALEXANDER, SORRELL & MCFALL, LTD. (AV)

961 State Line Road, West, P.O. Box 188, 38671
Telephone: 601-342-1300
Telecopier: 601-342-1312

Ronald L. Taylor
Jack R. Jones, III
Keith M. Alexander
Mark K. Sorrell
George McFall

Approved Attorneys for: Mississippi Valley Title Insurance Co.; First American Title, Insurance.
Reference: Sunburst Bank, Southaven, Miss.

For full biographical listings, see the Martindale-Hubbell Law Directory

MISSOURI

*INDEPENDENCE,** Jackson Co.

JAMES & BIAGIOLI, P.C. (AV)

123 West Kansas, 64050
Telephone: 816-836-5500
FAX: 816-836-2273

Jimmie D. James
John A. Biagioli

Mary Ellen Bigge
Jonathan C. Lourenco
Douglas A. Hick

OF COUNSEL

David G. Sperry

References: Noland Road Bank; Boatmen's Bank; Bank of Grain Valley.

KANSAS CITY, Jackson, Clay & Platte Cos.

LAW OFFICES OF BARTON S. BLOND, P.C. (AV)

One Ward Parkway, Suite 118, 64112
Telephone: 816-756-0080
Fax: 816-756-1121

Barton S. Blond

Jill C. Allison

For full biographical listings, see the Martindale-Hubbell Law Directory

SWANSON, MIDGLEY, GANGWERE, KITCHIN & MCLARNEY, L.L.C. (AV)

1500 Commerce Trust Building, 922 Walnut, 64106-1848
Telephone: 816-842-6100
Overland Park, Kansas Office: The NCAA Building, Suite 350, 6201 College Boulevard.
Telephone: 816-842-6100.

W. Ann Hansbrough

Craig T. Kenworthy

Counsel for: General Electric Co.; Chrysler Corp.; Conoco, Inc.; Yellow Freight System, Inc.; The Prudential Insurance Co. of America; Metropolitan Life Insurance Co.; National Collegiate Athletic Assn.; Land Title Insurance Co.; Safeway Stores, Inc.; The Lee Apparel Co.

For Complete List of Firm Personnel, See General Section

For full biographical listings, see the Martindale-Hubbell Law Directory

THAYER, BERNSTEIN, BASS & MONACO, P.C. (AV)

8900 Ward Parkway, Suite 210, 64114
Telephone: 816-444-8030
Fax: 816-523-2158

Charlotte P. Thayer
Sheldon Bernstein
Regina Keelan Bass
Ralph A. Monaco II
Anita I. Rodarte

Tamara S. Hatheway

OF COUNSEL

Daniel H. Bowers

For full biographical listings, see the Martindale-Hubbell Law Directory

MONTANA

*BILLINGS,** Yellowstone Co.

CROWLEY, HAUGHEY, HANSON, TOOLE & DIETRICH (AV)

500 Transwestern II, 490 North 31st Street, P.O. Box 2529, 59103
Telephone: 406-252-3441
Fax: 406-259-4159
Helena, Montana Office: IBM Building, 100 North Park Avenue, Suite 300, 59601.
Telephone: 406-449-4165.
Fax: 406-449-5149.

MEMBER OF FIRM

Donald L. Harris

ASSOCIATE

Michael S. Lahr

Representative Clients: Montana Power Co.; First Interstate Bank of Commerce; MDU Resources Group, Inc.; Chevron U.S.A., Inc.; Noranda Minerals Corp.; United Parcel Service.
Insurance Clients: Farmers Insurance Group; New York Life Insurance Co.

For Complete List of Firm Personnel, See General Section

For full biographical listings, see the Martindale-Hubbell Law Directory

NEBRASKA

*LINCOLN,** Lancaster Co.

BARLOW, JOHNSON, FLODMAN, SUTTER, GUENZEL & ESKE (AV)

1227 Lincoln Mall, P.O. Box 81686, 68501-1686
Telephone: 402-475-4240
Fax: 402-475-0329

MEMBER OF FIRM

Steven J. Flodman

Special Counsel: Nebraska Public Power District.
Representative Clients: Allied Group; Chubb/Pacific Indemnity Group; Citizens State Bank, Polk, Nebraska; Crum & Foster; Federated Rural Electric Insurance Corp.; Runza Drive-Inns of America; United States Fidelity & Guaranty Co.; Viking Insurance Company of Wisconsin.

For Complete List of Firm Personnel, See General Section

For full biographical listings, see the Martindale-Hubbell Law Directory

NEVADA

*LAS VEGAS,** Clark Co.

DICKERSON, DICKERSON, LIEBERMAN & CONSUL (AV)

Suite 1130, 330 South Third Street, 89101
Telephone: 702-388-8600
Fax: 702-388-0210

MEMBERS OF FIRM

George M. Dickerson
Robert P. Dickerson
Barry L. Lieberman
Vincent A. Consul
Richard J. Pocker

ASSOCIATES

Douglass A. Mitchell
Luke Puschnig
Paul J. Lal
Bryce C. Duckworth

Reference: Nevada State Bank.

For full biographical listings, see the Martindale-Hubbell Law Directory

JOLLEY, URGA, WIRTH & WOODBURY (AV)

Suite 800 Bank of America Plaza, 300 South Fourth Street, 89101
Telephone: 702-385-5161
Telecopier: 702-382-6814
Boulder City, Nevada Office: Suite 105, 1000 Nevada Highway.
Telephone: 702-293-3674.

MEMBERS OF FIRM

Roger A. Wirth
Kathryn Elizabeth Stryker

(See Next Column)

JOLLEY, URGA, WIRTH & WOODBURY—*Continued*

ASSOCIATE

Craig M. Murphy

For Complete List of Firm Personnel, See General Section

For full biographical listings, see the Martindale-Hubbell Law Directory

*RENO,** Washoe Co.

RICHARD W. YOUNG A PROFESSIONAL CORPORATION (AV)

327 Marsh Avenue, 89509
Telephone: 702-322-9477
Facsimile: 702-322-3758

Richard W. Young

Reference: First Interstate Bank of Nevada (Reno Main Branch).

For full biographical listings, see the Martindale-Hubbell Law Directory

NEW JERSEY

CHERRY HILL, Camden Co.

MICHAEL D. FIORETTI (AV Ⓣ)

1101 Kings Highway North, Suite 304, 08034
Telephone: 609-482-2488
Philadelphia, Pennsylvania Office: The Bourse Building, Suite 790, 111 South Independence Mall East, 19106.
Telephone: 215-440-7612.
Fax: 215-440-0328.

ASSOCIATE

Philip A. Charamella

FORKIN, MCSHANE & ROTZ, A PROFESSIONAL ASSOCIATION (AV)

750 Kings Highway North, 08034-1581
Telephone: 609-779-8500
Fax: 609-779-8030

Thomas S. Forkin
Joseph Patrick McShane, III
Richard B. Rotz
George W. Stevenson, III

For full biographical listings, see the Martindale-Hubbell Law Directory

*HACKENSACK,** Bergen Co.

ARONSOHN & WEINER (AV)

263 Main Street, 07601
Telephone: 201-487-4747
Telecopier: 201-487-7601

MEMBERS OF FIRM

Richard F. Aronsohn
Richard H. Weiner
Gerald R. Salerno

ASSOCIATES

Karl W. Reidel
Louis John Cirrilla
Michael J. Young

For full biographical listings, see the Martindale-Hubbell Law Directory

DUNN, PASHMAN, SPONZILLI, SWICK & FINNERTY (AV)

411 Hackensack Avenue, 07601
Telephone: 201-489-1500; 845-4000
Fax: 201-489-1512

COUNSEL

Morris Pashman
Murray L. Cole
Paul D. Rosenberg

MEMBERS OF FIRM

Joseph Dunn
Louis Pashman
John E. Finnerty
Edward G. Sponzilli
Daniel A. Swick
Robert E. Rochford
Warren S. Robins

ASSOCIATES

Nicholas F. Pellitta
Laura S. Kirsch
Danya A. Grunyk
Richard P. Jacobson
Jeffrey M. Shapiro
Deborah L. Ustas
Mark E. Lichtblau
Edward B. Stevenson
Stephen F. Roth

References: United Jersey Bank; Valley National Bank.

For full biographical listings, see the Martindale-Hubbell Law Directory

STEPHEN H. ROTH (AV)

62 Summit Avenue, 07601
Telephone: 201-489-3737
Fax: 201-489-0557

(See Next Column)

ASSOCIATE

Michele M. De Santis

Reference: Citizens First National Bank.

For full biographical listings, see the Martindale-Hubbell Law Directory

HACKETTSTOWN, Warren Co.

MULLIGAN & MULLIGAN (AV)

480 Highway 517, P.O. Box 211, 07840
Telephone: 908-852-0202
Fax: 908-852-0626

MEMBERS OF FIRM

William G. Mulligan (1906-1991)
Elinor Patterson Mulligan
Amy O'Connor

ASSOCIATE

Richard D. Fifield

For full biographical listings, see the Martindale-Hubbell Law Directory

HADDONFIELD, Camden Co.

WEINBERG, MCCORMICK AND CHATZINOFF, A PROFESSIONAL ASSOCIATION (AV)

109 Haddon Avenue, 08033
Telephone: 609-795-1600
Telecopier: 609-795-9469

Joseph M. Weinberg
Joseph A. McCormick, Jr.
Barry Chatzinoff

Edward L. Paul
Antonieta M. Paiva
Donafaye Wilson Zoll
Stephanie Onorato

Representative Clients: Mobile Field Office Co.; Landress Computers; L & L Redi Mix; Aurora Financial Group, Inc.; Case Credit Corp.
Local Counsel For: John Deere Credit Services, Inc.; John Deere Company; John Deere Industrial Equipment Co.
Solicitor For: Berlin Township Planning Board.
Reference: United Jersey Bank/South.

For full biographical listings, see the Martindale-Hubbell Law Directory

LIVINGSTON, Essex Co.

SKOLOFF & WOLFE (AV)

293 Eisenhower Parkway, 07039
Telephone: 201-992-0900
Fax: 201-992-0301
Morristown, New Jersey Office: 10 Park Place.
Telephone: 201-267-3511.

Gary N. Skoloff
Francis W. Donahue
Richard H. Singer, Jr. (Resident at Morristown Office)
Stephen P. Haller
Cary B. Cheifetz
Edward J. O'Donnell
Stephanie Frangos Hagan
Michael R. Pallarino
Phyllis S. Klein
Beatrice E. Kandell
Maryanne Fantalis

OF COUNSEL

Bertram Polow

For full biographical listings, see the Martindale-Hubbell Law Directory

JEFFREY P. WEINSTEIN A PROFESSIONAL CORPORATION (AV)

354 Eisenhower Parkway, 07039
Telephone: 201-994-4000
Fax: 201-994-2767

Jeffrey P. Weinstein
Rachel Zakarin
Lizabeth Allison Bard

OF COUNSEL

Cathy M. Abrams

For full biographical listings, see the Martindale-Hubbell Law Directory

MILLBURN, Essex Co.

GROSMAN & GROSMAN (AV)

75 Main Street Suite 304, 07041
Telephone: 201-467-9520
FAX: 201-467-0322

Charles M. Grosman (1921-1970)
Alan M. Grosman

LEGAL SUPPORT PERSONNEL

Thea R. Bachman

Reference: The Bank of New York; National Community Bank Division.

For full biographical listings, see the Martindale-Hubbell Law Directory

MONTVALE, Bergen Co.

BEATTIE PADOVANO (AV)

50 Chestnut Ridge Road, P.O. Box 244, 07645-0244
Telephone: 201-573-1810
Fax: (DEX) 201-573-9736

MEMBERS OF FIRM

James R. Beattie
Ralph J. Padovano
Roger W. Breslin, Jr.
Thomas W. Dunn
Martin W. Kafafian
Adolph A. Romei
Brian R. Martinotti

ASSOCIATES

Emery C. Duell
Brenda J. McAdoo
Kathleen Smyth Cook
Francis B. Sheehan
Susan Calabrese
Antimo A. Del Vecchio
Dean J. Obeidallah
Jeffrey L. Love
Steven A. Weisfeld
S. Joseph Oey
Edward S. Kiel
Christopher Heyer
JoAnne C. Gerber
Robert A. Blass

OF COUNSEL

John J. Lamb

Reference: United Jersey Bank.

For full biographical listings, see the Martindale-Hubbell Law Directory

*MORRISTOWN,** Morris Co.

BRODERICK, NEWMARK & GRATHER, A PROFESSIONAL CORPORATION (AV)

20 South Street, 07960
Telephone: 201-538-0084
Fax: 201-538-2509

Edward F. Broderick, Jr.
Martin A. Newmark
Francis G. Grather
Alan J. Baldwin

OF COUNSEL

Edward F. Broderick (1905-1987)
I. Ezra Newmark (1901-1979)
George F. Sweeny (P.C.)

Stephen I. Weichert

For full biographical listings, see the Martindale-Hubbell Law Directory

LAURENCE J. CUTLER (AV)

60 Washington Street, 07960
Telephone: 201-539-0075
Telecopier: 201-539-4151

For full biographical listings, see the Martindale-Hubbell Law Directory

*NEWARK,** Essex Co.

GOLDSTEIN TILL & LITE (AV)

Suite 800, 744 Broad Street, 07102-3803
Telephone: 201-623-3000
FAX: 201-623-0858
Telex: 262320 USA UR

MEMBERS OF FIRM

Andrew J. Goldstein
Peter W. Till
Allyn Z. Lite
Joseph J. DePalma

Nancy Lem
Amy M. Riel
Richard T. Luzzi
Denise L. Panicucci
Robin May Messing
Michael E. Patunas
Donna Lavista Schwartz

For full biographical listings, see the Martindale-Hubbell Law Directory

HELLRING LINDEMAN GOLDSTEIN & SIEGAL (AV)

One Gateway Center, 07102-5386
Telephone: 201-621-9020
Telecopier: 201-621-7406

Joel D. Siegal
Margaret Dee Hellring
Charles Oransky
Richard K. Coplon
Robert S. Raymar
Ronny Jo Greenwald Siegal
Ronnie F. Liebowitz
Bruce S. Etterman
Sheryl E. Koomer

For Complete List of Firm Personnel, See General Section

For full biographical listings, see the Martindale-Hubbell Law Directory

MCCARTER & ENGLISH (AV)

Four Gateway Center, 100 Mulberry Street, P.O. Box 652, 07101-0652
Telephone: 201-622-4444
Telecopier: 201-624-7070
Cable Address: "McCarter" Newark
Cherry Hill, New Jersey Office: 1810 Chapel Avenue West.
Telephone: 609-662-8444.
Telecopier: 609-662-6203.
New York, New York Office: Suite 1519, One World Trade Center.
Telephone: 212-466-9018.
Telecopier: 212-432-6568.
Boca Raton, Florida Office: 2255 Glades Road, Suite 319-A.
Telephone: 407-994-6262.
Telecopier: 407-241-0798.
Wilmington, Delaware Office: Mellon Bank Center, 919 Market Street.
Telephone: 302-654-8010.
Telecopier: 302-654-0795.

MEMBERS OF FIRM

Alfred L. Ferguson
Myrna L. Wigod

ASSOCIATE

Cynthia Spera Neff

For Complete List of Firm Personnel, See General Section

For full biographical listings, see the Martindale-Hubbell Law Directory

*NEW BRUNSWICK,** Middlesex Co.

EDWARD SCHOIFET A PROFESSIONAL CORPORATION (AV)

75 Paterson Street, 08903
Telephone: 908-545-2235
Fax: 908-545-2840

Edward Schoifet

Michelle J. Tomasso

For full biographical listings, see the Martindale-Hubbell Law Directory

NORTH BRUNSWICK, Middlesex Co.

BORRUS, GOLDIN, FOLEY, VIGNUOLO, HYMAN & STAHL, A PROFESSIONAL CORPORATION (AV)

2875 U.S. Highway 1, Route 1 & Finnigans Lane, P.O. Box 1963, 08902
Telephone: 908-422-1000
Fax: 908-422-1016

Jack Borrus
Martin S. Goldin
David M. Foley
Anthony B. Vignuolo
Jeffrey M. Hyman
James E. Stahl
James F. Clarkin III
Anthony M. Campisano
Aphrodite C. Koscelansky
Robert C. Nisenson
Michael L. Marcus
Eileen Mary Foley
Rosalind Westlake

OF COUNSEL

Gerald T. Foley (1903-1976)

Representative Clients: United Jersey Bank/Franklin State; R. J. Reynolds Tobacco Co.; N.J. Aluminum Co.; K. Hovnanian Enterprises, Inc.; Chicago Title Insurance Co.; Transamerica Title Insurance Co.

For full biographical listings, see the Martindale-Hubbell Law Directory

PARAMUS, Bergen Co.

STERN STEIGER CROLAND, A PROFESSIONAL CORPORATION (AV)

One Mack Centre Drive, Mack Centre II, 07652
Telephone: 201-262-9400
Telecopier: 201-262-6055

Howard Stern
Joel J. Steiger
Barry I. Croland
Gerald Goldman
Donald R. Sorkow (1930-1985)
Norman Tanenbaum
Barry L. Baime
Jay Rubenstein
Frank L. Brunetti
Kenneth S. Goldrich
Bruce J. Ackerman
Thomas Loikith
John J. Stern
Stuart Reiser
William J. Heimbuch
Edward P. D'Alessio
E. Drew Britcher
Meridith J. Bronson
Valerie D. Solimano

William R. Kugelman
Mindy Michaels Roth
Neil E. Kozek
Lizabeth Sarakin
Joanne T. Nowicki
Armand Leone, Jr.
Craig P. Caggiano
Jeffrey P. Gardner
David Torchin

OF COUNSEL

Harvey R. Sorkow

Representative Clients: K Mart Corp.; Meyer Brothers Department Stores.

For full biographical listings, see the Martindale-Hubbell Law Directory

PRINCETON, Mercer Co.

BERGMAN & BARRETT (AV)

9 Tamarack Circle, Montgomery Knoll, U. S. Highway 206 North, P.O. Box 1273, 08542
Telephone: 609-921-1502
Fax: 609-683-0288

Edward J. Bergman — Michael T. Barrett

For full biographical listings, see the Martindale-Hubbell Law Directory

MCCARTHY AND SCHATZMAN, P.A. (AV)

228 Alexander Street, P.O. Box 2329, 08543-2329
Telephone: 609-924-1199
Fax: 609-683-5251

John F. McCarthy, Jr. — John F. McCarthy, III
Richard Schatzman — Michael A. Spero
G. Christopher Baker — Barbara Strapp Nelson
W. Scott Stoner

James A. Endicott — Angelo J. Onofri

Representative Clients: Trustees of Princeton University; The Linpro Co.; United Jersey Bank; Chemical Bank, New Jersey, N.A.; Carnegie Center Associates; Merrill Lynch Pierce Fenner & Smith, Inc.; Prudential Insurance Co.

For full biographical listings, see the Martindale-Hubbell Law Directory

ROSELAND, Essex Co.

HANNOCH WEISMAN, A PROFESSIONAL CORPORATION (AV)

4 Becker Farm Road, 07068-3788
Telephone: 201-535-5300
New York: 212-732-3262
Telecopier: 201-994-7198
Mailing Address: P.O. Box 1040, Newark, New Jersey, 07101-9819
Washington, D.C. Office: Suite 600, 1150 Seventeenth Street, N.W.
Telephone: 202-296-3432.

Todd M. Sahner

Terri L. Freeman — Robert H. Solomon

For Complete List of Firm Personnel, See General Section

For full biographical listings, see the Martindale-Hubbell Law Directory

HOCHBERG, KRIEGER, DANZIG & GARUBO (AV)

75 Livingston Avenue, 07068
Telephone: 201-535-5700
Telecopier: 201-535-6293

MEMBERS OF FIRM

George S. Hochberg — Howard Danzig
Lewis L. Krieger — Angelo G. Garubo

OF COUNSEL

David M. Kaye

For full biographical listings, see the Martindale-Hubbell Law Directory

POST, POLAK, GOODSELL & MACNEILL, P.A. (AV)

65 Livingston Avenue, 07068
Telephone: 201-994-1100
Telecopier: 201-994-1705
New York, New York Office: Suite 1006, 575 Madison Avenue.
Telephone: 212-486-1455.

John N. Post — Mary H. Post

Allison D. B. Liebowitz — Robert P. Merenich

For full biographical listings, see the Martindale-Hubbell Law Directory

SHORT HILLS, Essex Co.

HODES & BRAUN, P.A. (AV)

11 Short Hills Avenue, 07078
Telephone: 201-467-5556
Fax: 201-467-0636

Robert D. Hodes — Neil S. Braun

For full biographical listings, see the Martindale-Hubbell Law Directory

*SOMERVILLE,** Somerset Co.

OZZARD WHARTON, A PROFESSIONAL PARTNERSHIP (AV)

75-77 North Bridge Street, P.O. Box 938, 08876
Telephone: 908-526-0700
Telecopier: 908-526-2246

(See Next Column)

Victor A. Rizzolo — George A. Mauro, Jr.

Arthur D. Fialk — Wendy L. Wiebalk

OF COUNSEL

Miles S. Winder, III

Representative Clients: American Cyanamid; Science Management Corp; New Jersey Manufacturers Insurance Co.; Travelers Insurance Co.; Mack Development Co.; New Jersey Savings Bank.

For Complete List of Firm Personnel, See General Section

For full biographical listings, see the Martindale-Hubbell Law Directory

SCHACHTER, TROMBADORE, OFFEN, STANTON & PAVICS, A PROFESSIONAL CORPORATION (AV)

45 East High Street, P.O. Box 520, 08876-0520
Telephone: 908-722-5700
Fax: 908-722-8853

John J. Trombadore — Michael J. Stanton

William D. Alden — Mary Ann Bauer

References: Summit Bank; First National Bank of Central Jersey; New Jersey Savings Bank.

For full biographical listings, see the Martindale-Hubbell Law Directory

SPRINGFIELD, Union Co.

ELLIOT H. GOURVITZ, P.A. (AV)

150 Morris Avenue, P.O. Box 476, 07081
Telephone: 201-467-3200
Fax: 201-912-0432
New Brunswick, New Jersey Office: 75 Paterson Street.
Fax: 908-545-2840.
New York, New York Office: Elliot H. Gourvitz, 295 Madison Avenue.
Telephone: 212-679-3999.
Fax: 212-370-5822.

Elliot H. Gourvitz

Richard A. Outhwaite — Stacey Z. Rodkin

For full biographical listings, see the Martindale-Hubbell Law Directory

JAMES P. YUDES A PROFESSIONAL CORPORATION (AV)

80 Morris Avenue, 07081
Telephone: 201-467-3700
Fax: 201-467-9303

James P. Yudes — Kevin M. Mazza
Charles F. Vuotto, Jr.

Reference: United Counties Trust Co.

For full biographical listings, see the Martindale-Hubbell Law Directory

SUMMIT, Union Co.

COOPER ROSE & ENGLISH (AV)

480 Morris Avenue, 07901-1527
Telephone: 908-273-1212
Fax: 908-273-8922
Rumson, New Jersey Office: 20 Bingham Avenue. 07760.
Telephone: 908-741-7777.
Fax: 908-758-1879.

MEMBERS OF FIRM

John W. Cooper — Arthur H. Garvin, III
Frederick W. Rose — Peter M. Burke
Jerry Fitzgerald English — Gary F. Danis
Joseph E. Imbriaco — John J. DeLaney, Jr.
Roger S. Clapp — David G. Hardin

OF COUNSEL

Harrison F. Durand — Russell T. Kerby, Jr.
Ronald J. Tell

ASSOCIATES

Fredi L. Pearlmutter — J. Andrew Kinsey
Kristi Bragg — Jonathan S. Chester
Stephen R. Geller — Daniel Jon Kleinman
Peter W. Ulicny — Holly English
Thomas J. Sateary — Margaret R. Kalas
Gianfranco A. Pietrafesa — Mary T. Zdanowicz
Donna M. Russo — Robert A. Meyers
Richard F. Iglar

Counsel for: Ciba-Geigy Corp.; Witco Corp.; New Jersey American Water Co.; Mikropul Corp.; AT&T Bell Laboratories; Aircast.

For full biographical listings, see the Martindale-Hubbell Law Directory

TEANECK, Bergen Co.

ROBERT D. ARENSTEIN (AV㊉)

691 Cedar Lane, 07666
Telephone: 201-836-9648
New York, N.Y. Office: Suite 1002, 295 Madison Avenue.
Telephone: 212-679-3999.
Telecopier: 212-370-5822.
(Also Of Counsel to Tendler, Goldberg, Biggins, Geltzer & Asher, Chartered, Washington, D.C. and Dranoff & Johnson, Pearl River, N.Y.)

For full biographical listings, see the Martindale-Hubbell Law Directory

WAYNE, Passaic Co.

DEYOE, HEISSENBUTTEL & MATTIA (AV)

401 Hamburg Turnpike, P.O. Box 2449, 07474-2449
Telephone: 201-595-6300
Fax: 201-595-0146; 201-595-9262

MEMBERS OF FIRM

Charles P. DeYoe (1923-1973)
Wood M. DeYoe
Frederick C. Heissenbuttel
Philip F. Mattia
Gary R. Matano
Scott B. Piekarsky

ASSOCIATES

Anne Hutton
Glenn Z. Poosikian
Jo Ann G. Durr
Frank D. Samperi
Frank A. Campana
John E. Clarke
Jason T. Shafron
Maura Waters Brady

LEGAL SUPPORT PERSONNEL

Marilyn Moore (Office Manager)

Representative Clients: INA/Aetna Insurance Co. (Cigna); Medical Inter-Insurance Companies; Hanover-Amgro, Inc.; Maryland Casualty Co.; Ohio Casualty Insurance Co.; Motor Club of America; Selected Insurance Co.

For full biographical listings, see the Martindale-Hubbell Law Directory

FELDMAN & FIORELLO (AV)

Suite 301, 57 Willowbrook Boulevard, 07470
Telephone: 201-890-9222
Fax: 201-890-7068

William A. Feldman
John Fiorello

OF COUNSEL

Avram S. Eule

ASSOCIATES

Linda Couso Puccio
Jacqueline I. Heath
Melissa A. Feldman

Reference: First Fidelity Bank, N.A.; Valley National Bank (Willowbrook Branch).

For full biographical listings, see the Martindale-Hubbell Law Directory

WOODBRIDGE, Middlesex Co.

WILENTZ, GOLDMAN & SPITZER, A PROFESSIONAL CORPORATION (AV)

90 Woodbridge Center Drive Suite 900, Box 10, 07095
Telephone: 908-636-8000
Telecopier: 908-855-6117
Eatontown, New Jersey Office: Meridian Center I, Two Industrial Way West, 07724.
Telephone: 908-493-1000.
Telecopier: 908-493-8387.
New York, New York Office: Wall Street Plaza, 88 Pine Street, 9th Floor, 10005.
Telephone: 212-267-3091.
Telecopier: 212-267-3828.

David M. Wildstein
Peter C. Paras (Resident, Eatontown Office)
Bonnie M. S. Reiss

Jean R. Campbell
Jeffrey K. Epstein
Noel S. Tonneman (Resident, Eatontown Office)
Risa A. Kleiner
Amy H. Soled

Representative Firm Clients: Amerada Hess Corp.; Chevron, U.S.A.; Cumberland Farms, Inc.; Middlesex County Utilities Authority; New Jersey Automobile Dealers Assn.; Co-Steel Raritan; The Rouse Co.

For Complete List of Firm Personnel, See General Section

For full biographical listings, see the Martindale-Hubbell Law Directory

NEW MEXICO

*ALBUQUERQUE,** Bernalillo Co.

ATKINSON & KELSEY, P.A. (AV)

6501 Americas Parkway Suite 901, P.O. Box 3070, 87190
Telephone: 505-883-3070
FAX: 505-889-3111

David H. Kelsey
Jon A. Feder
Thomas C. Montoya
Sanford H. Siegel
Stephen J. E. Sprague
Suzanne G. Lubar
Claire E. Sanderson

References: Sunwest Bank; United New Mexico Bank.

For full biographical listings, see the Martindale-Hubbell Law Directory

*LAS CRUCES,** Dona Ana Co.

WEINBRENNER, RICHARDS, PAULOWSKY & RAMIREZ, P.A. (AV)

8th Floor, First National Tower, P.O. Drawer O, 88004-1719
Telephone: 505-524-8624
Fax: 505-524-4252

Michael T. Murphy

General Counsel for: Stahmann Farms, Inc.; First National Bank of Dona Ana County.
Representative Clients: American General Cos.; Hartford Group; CNA Insurance; Fireman's Fund; United States Fidelity & Guaranty Co.; Travelers Insurance Co.; General Accident Group.

For Complete List of Firm Personnel, See General Section

For full biographical listings, see the Martindale-Hubbell Law Directory

*SANTA FE,** Santa Fe Co.

CATRON, CATRON & SAWTELL, A PROFESSIONAL ASSOCIATION (AV)

2006 Botulph Road, P.O. Box 788, 87504-0788
Telephone: 505-982-1947
Telecopier: 505-986-1013

Thomas B. Catron III
John S. Catron
Fletcher R. Catron
W. Anthony Sawtell
Kathrin M. Kinzer-Ellington

LEGAL SUPPORT PERSONNEL

Peggy L. Feldt (Certified Public Accountant)

Attorneys for: Santa Fe Board of Education; American Express Co.; The Santa Fe Opera; Sunwest Bank of Santa Fe; VNS Health Services, Inc.

For Complete List of Firm Personnel, See General Section

For full biographical listings, see the Martindale-Hubbell Law Directory

WALTHER ASSOCIATES (AV)

1640 Old Pecos Trail, Suite E, 87505
Telephone: 505-984-0097
Fax: 505-983-2467

David L. Walther
Mark A. Walther
Ann Wagner Maddox

LEGAL SUPPORT PERSONNEL

Mary A. Granger
Marjorie L. Mizerak

For full biographical listings, see the Martindale-Hubbell Law Directory

WHITE, KOCH, KELLY & McCARTHY, A PROFESSIONAL ASSOCIATION (AV)

433 Paseo De Peralta, P.O. Box 787, 87504-0787
Telephone: 505-982-4374
ABA/NET: 1154
Fax: 505-982-0350; 984-8631

William Booker Kelly
John F. McCarthy, Jr.
Benjamin J. Phillips
David F. Cunningham
Albert V. Gonzales
Janet Clow
Kevin V. Reilly
Charles W. N. Thompson, Jr.
M. Karen Kilgore
Sandra J. Brinck

SPECIAL COUNSEL

Paul L. Bloom

Aaron J. Wolf
Carolyn R. Glick

Representative Clients: Southern Pacific Transportation Co.; Nationwide Insurance Co.; Risk Management Division of New Mexico General Services Department; Alliance of American Insurers; Santa Fe Community College; First American Title Insurance Co.; Century Bank; Public Service Company of New Mexico; AT&SF Railway Co.; Gallager Bassett.

For full biographical listings, see the Martindale-Hubbell Law Directory

NEW YORK

*BROOKLYN,** Kings Co.

GOLDBERG & COHN (AV)
16 Court Street, Suite 2304, 11241
Telephone: 718-875-2400
Fax: 718-858-2101

MEMBERS OF FIRM
Richard S. Goldberg   Steven D. Cohn

ASSOCIATES
Marlene Schwarz   Aimee L. Richter

For full biographical listings, see the Martindale-Hubbell Law Directory

COMMACK, Suffolk Co.

LAW OFFICES OF LYNNE ADAIR KRAMER (AV)
6165 Jericho Turnpike, 11725
Telephone: 516-462-5850
Telecopier: 516-462-5862

ASSOCIATES
Joy E. Jorgensen   Jennifer Feingold

OF COUNSEL
Ruth Sovronsky   Carole S. Becker

For full biographical listings, see the Martindale-Hubbell Law Directory

GARDEN CITY, Nassau Co.

DASILVA & KEIDEL (AV)
585 Stewart Avenue, 11530
Telephone: 516-222-0700
Fax: 516-222-0743

Willard H. DaSilva   Richard J. Keidel

For full biographical listings, see the Martindale-Hubbell Law Directory

GASSMAN FISHER & FASS (AV)
666 Old Country Road, 11530
Telephone: 516-228-9181
Telecopier: 516-745-6712

MEMBERS OF FIRM
Stephen Gassman   Barry J. Fisher
Florence M. Fass

Lydia A. Milone   Charlotte Betts

For full biographical listings, see the Martindale-Hubbell Law Directory

SAMUELSON RIEGER & YOVINO (AV)
300 Garden City Plaza, 11530
Telephone: 516-294-6666
Telecopier: 516-294-6622

Elliot D. Samuelson   Anthony Yovino
Kieth I. Rieger   Richard L. Hause
Wendy B. Samuelson

For full biographical listings, see the Martindale-Hubbell Law Directory

SAWYER, DAVIS & HALPERN (AV)
600 Old Country Road, 11530
Telephone: 516-222-4567
Telecopier: 516-222-4585

MEMBER OF FIRM
Jay Davis

ASSOCIATE
Ralph W. Lee

For Complete List of Firm Personnel, See General Section
For full biographical listings, see the Martindale-Hubbell Law Directory

STEPHEN R. TAUB (AV)
600 Old Country Road, 11530
Telephone: 516-227-2100

For full biographical listings, see the Martindale-Hubbell Law Directory

TAYLOR, ATKINS & OSTROW (AV)
300 Garden City Plaza, 11530
Telephone: 516-877-1800
Telecopier: 516-294-0227

(See Next Column)

MEMBER OF FIRM
Michael J. Ostrow

ASSOCIATES
Barbara Brown   Mark Mensher

COUNSEL
Michael B. Atkins

For full biographical listings, see the Martindale-Hubbell Law Directory

HUNTINGTON, Suffolk Co.

GOLDSTEIN & RUBINTON, P.C. (AV)
18 West Carver Street, 11743
Telephone: 516-421-9051
Telefax: 516-421-9122

Arthur Goldstein   Ronald L. Goldstein
Peter D. Rubinton   S. Russ Di Fazio

References: Chemical Bank; New York Trust Co.; Town of Huntingdon.

For full biographical listings, see the Martindale-Hubbell Law Directory

*JAMAICA,** Queens Co.

DIKMAN AND DIKMAN (AV)
161-10 Jamaica Avenue, 11432
Telephone: 718-739-4830
Roslyn, New York Office: 98 Shrub Hollow Road.
Telephone: 516-354-2526.

MEMBERS OF FIRM
Leo Dikman   Michael Dikman

ASSOCIATE
Donna Dikman Dubinsky

Reference: Chase Manhattan Bank.

For full biographical listings, see the Martindale-Hubbell Law Directory

*NEW YORK,** New York Co.

ROBERT D. ARENSTEIN (AV)
Suite 1002, 295 Madison Avenue, 10017
Telephone: 212-679-3999
Telecopier: 212-370-5822
Teaneck, New Jersey Office: 691 Cedar Lane.
Telephone: 201-836-9648.
(Also Of Counsel to Dranoff & Johnson, Pearl River, N.Y. and Barbara Bevando Sobal, New York, N.Y.)

ASSOCIATE
Tara A. Duggan

For full biographical listings, see the Martindale-Hubbell Law Directory

BELDOCK LEVINE & HOFFMAN (AV)
99 Park Avenue, 10016-1502
Telephone: 212-490-0400
Cable Address: "Telhofflaw, N.Y."
Telecopier: 212-557-0565

MEMBER OF FIRM
Katherine G. Thompson

Jonathan K. Pollack

For full biographical listings, see the Martindale-Hubbell Law Directory

LAW OFFICE OF WILLIAM S. BESLOW (AV)
919 Third Avenue, 10022
Telephone: 212-371-7225
Fax: 212-751-2540

OF COUNSEL
Andrew Schepard

For full biographical listings, see the Martindale-Hubbell Law Directory

BRONSTEIN, VAN VEEN & BRONSTEIN, P.C. (AV)
Carnegie Hall Tower, 152 West 57th Street, 10019
Telephone: 212-956-8300
Telefax: 212-956-1452

Peter E. Bronstein

Ann Cynthia Diamond   Donna S. Levin

OF COUNSEL
Donald Lockhart Schuck   Eli H. Bronstein (1903-1979)
Henry G. Van Veen (1904-1992)

For full biographical listings, see the Martindale-Hubbell Law Directory

New York—Continued

COHEN, HENNESSEY & BIENSTOCK, P.C. (AV)

605 Third Avenue - 25th Floor, 10158-0125
Telephone: 212-843-6230
Fax: 212-949-7052

Harriet Newman Cohen
Patricia Hennessey
Peter Bienstock

Martha Cohen Stine

For full biographical listings, see the Martindale-Hubbell Law Directory

DRANOFF & JOHNSON (AV)

950 3rd Avenue
Telephone: 212-643-5351
Pearl River Office: Suite 900, One Blue Hill Plaza. P.O. Box 1629. 10965-8629.
Telephone: 914-735-6200.
Fax: 914-735-7585.
Tarrytown, New York Office: 220 White Plains Road.
Telephone: 914-631-1900.

MEMBERS OF FIRM

Sanford S. Dranoff
Sylvia Goldschmidt

Donna M. Genovese

ELLENBOGEN & GOLDSTEIN, P.C. (AV)

Metropolitan Tower, 142 West 57th Street, 10019
Telephone: 212-245-3260

Joan L. Ellenbogen
Marcia C. Goldstein
Kenneth Ludman

Joseph R. Donohue
Diane Krasnow Weinberger
Linda Loving

For full biographical listings, see the Martindale-Hubbell Law Directory

THE FIRM OF RAOUL LIONEL FELDER, P.C. (AV)

437 Madison Avenue, 10022
Telephone: 212-832-3939
Cable Address: "Lawfelder Newyork"

Raoul Lionel Felder
Myrna Felder

Richard MacKay
Kenneth B. Goldstein
Michael J. Kaper
Marisa Gardini

Reference: Citibank.

For full biographical listings, see the Martindale-Hubbell Law Directory

FINKELSTEIN BRUCKMAN WOHL MOST & ROTHMAN (AV)

575 Lexington Avenue, 10022-6102
Telephone: 212-754-3100
Telecopier: 212-371-2980
Stamford, Connecticut Office: 1 Landmark Square.
Telephone: 203-358-9200.
Telecopier: 203-969-6140.
Hackensack, New Jersey Office: 20 Court Street.
Telephone: 201-525-1800.
Telecopier: 201-489-4509.

MEMBERS OF FIRM

Allen L. Finkelstein
Bernard Rothman

OF COUNSEL

Stuart Abrams

For Complete List of Firm Personnel, See General Section

For full biographical listings, see the Martindale-Hubbell Law Directory

LIDDLE, ROBINSON & SHOEMAKER (AV)

685 Third Avenue, 10017
Telephone: 212-687-8500
Telecopier: 212-687-1505

MEMBERS OF FIRM

Samuel Finkelstein (Retired)
Jeffrey L. Liddle
Miriam M. Robinson
Paul T. Shoemaker
Laurence S. Moy
W. Dan Boone

ASSOCIATES

James A. Batson
Blaine H. Bortnick
Ethan A. Brecher
Linda A. Danovitch
Jeffrey A. Koslowsky
Douglas A. Lopp

For full biographical listings, see the Martindale-Hubbell Law Directory

ORANS, ELSEN & LUPERT (AV)

33rd Floor, One Rockefeller Plaza, 10020
Telephone: 212-586-2211
Cable Address: "ORELSLU"
Telecopier: 212-765-3662

MEMBERS OF FIRM

Sheldon H. Elsen
Leslie A. Lupert
Gary H. Greenberg
Lawrence Solan
Robert L. Plotz

ASSOCIATES

Melissa A. Cohen
Amelia Anne Nickles
Jonathan J. Englander

For full biographical listings, see the Martindale-Hubbell Law Directory

RICHARD N. TANNENBAUM (AV)

Suite 2700, 225 Broadway, 10007
Telephone: 212-693-1963
Fax: 212-406-6890
Great Neck, N.Y. Office: Suite 301, 10 Cutter Mill Road.
Telephone: 466-2227.

References: National Westminister Bank; Bank of New York.

For full biographical listings, see the Martindale-Hubbell Law Directory

HERMAN H. TARNOW (AV)

330 Madison Avenue, 10017
Telephone: 212-297-3307
Fax: 212-972-6521
Westport, Connecticut Office: 329 Riverside Avenue.
Telephone: 203-226-1701.
Facsimile: 203-454-5508.

For full biographical listings, see the Martindale-Hubbell Law Directory

PEARL RIVER, Rockland Co.

DRANOFF & JOHNSON (AV)

Suite 900, One Blue Hill Plaza, P.O. Box 1629, 10965-8629
Telephone: 914-735-6200
Fax: 914-735-7585
Tarrytown, New York Office: 220 White Plains Road.
Telephone: 914-631-1900.
New York, N.Y. Office: 950 3rd Avenue.
Telephone: 212-643-5351.

MEMBERS OF FIRM

Sanford S. Dranoff
Martin T. Johnson
Veronica A. Shea
Daniel J. Block
Sylvia Goldschmidt
Mitchell Y. Cohen

Susan G. Yellen
Donna M. Genovese
Kenneth P. Silver

For full biographical listings, see the Martindale-Hubbell Law Directory

*RIVERHEAD,** Suffolk Co.

BENJAMIN E. CARTER (AV)

220 Roanoke Avenue, P.O. Box 118, 11901
Telephone: 516-727-1666
FAX: 516-727-1710

For full biographical listings, see the Martindale-Hubbell Law Directory

*STATEN ISLAND,** Richmond Co.

SIMONSON & COHEN, P.C. (AV)

4060 Amboy Road, 10308
Telephone: 718-948-2100
Telecopier: 718-356-2379

Sidney O. Simonson (1911-1986)
Daniel Cohen
Robert M. Cohen
James R. Cohen

Michael Adler
Lawrence J. Lorczak

For full biographical listings, see the Martindale-Hubbell Law Directory

NORTH CAROLINA

*ASHEVILLE,** Buncombe Co.

ELMORE & ELMORE, P.A. (AV)

53 North Market Street, 28801
Telephone: 704-253-1492
Fax: 704-253-9648

(See Next Column)

ELMORE & ELMORE P.A.—*Continued*

Bruce A. Elmore | Bruce A. Elmore, Jr.

Reed G. Williams

For full biographical listings, see the Martindale-Hubbell Law Directory

CHAPEL HILL, Orange Co.

LONG & LONG (AV)

116 Mallette Street, 27516
Telephone: 919-929-0408
Fax: 919-929-6819

MEMBERS OF FIRM

Lunsford Long | Florence J. Long

For full biographical listings, see the Martindale-Hubbell Law Directory

NORTHEN, BLUE, ROOKS, THIBAUT, ANDERSON & WOODS, L.L.P. (AV)

Suite 550, 100 Europa Center, P.O. Box 2208, 27515-2208
Telephone: 919-968-4441
Facsimile: 919-942-6603

MEMBERS OF FIRM

John A. Northen | Charles H. Thibaut
J. William Blue, Jr. | Charles T. L. Anderson
David M. Rooks, III | Jo Ann Ragazzo Woods
Carol J. Holcomb

ASSOCIATES

James C. Stanford | Gregory Herman-Giddens
Cheryl Y. Capron

References: Central Carolina Bank; The Village Bank; Investors Title Insurance Co.; First Union National Bank; Centura Bank; United Carolina Bank; BB&T; Balbirer & Coleman, CPA's.

For full biographical listings, see the Martindale-Hubbell Law Directory

*RALEIGH,** Wake Co.

* indicates certain Bar Register subscribers whose principal office is located elsewhere in the state and who have arranged for representation as a part of the state capital listings that follow

GULLEY KUHN & TAYLOR, L.L.P. (AV)

4601 Six Forks Road, 27609
Telephone: 919-782-6811
Facsimile: 919-782-7220

Jack P. Gulley | David J. Kuhn
Patricia Potter Taylor

OF COUNSEL

William O. Kuhn

For full biographical listings, see the Martindale-Hubbell Law Directory

HOWARD, FROM, STALLINGS & HUTSON, P.A. (AV)

Suite 400, 4000 WestChase Boulevard, P.O. Box 12347, 27607
Telephone: 919-833-2983
Fax: 919-834-3481
New Bern, North Carolina Office: 405 Middle Street, P.O. Box 975.
Telephones: 919-633-3006; 800-822-4182.
FAX: 919-633-3097.

Edward Cader Howard | Catherine C. McLamb
I. Allan From | Peggy S. Vincent
Joseph H. Stallings | B. Joan Davis
John N. Hutson, Jr. | Charles H. Livaudais, Jr.
William M. Black, Jr. | Kory J. Goldsmith
Beth Ferebee Atkins (Resident, New Bern Office) | Scott A. Miskimon
| Lewis E. Lamb III

Representative Client: Branch Banking and Trust Co.

For full biographical listings, see the Martindale-Hubbell Law Directory

HOWARD & GREEN, L.L.P. (AV)

4000 Westchase Boulevard Suite 200, P.O. Box 10305, 27605
Telephone: 919-833-2422
Fax: 919-833-2430

Robert E. Howard

ASSOCIATE

Dori Casey McDarris

References: United Carolina Bank; NationsBank; First Citizens Bank & Trust, Wachovia.

For Complete List of Firm Personnel, See General Section

For full biographical listings, see the Martindale-Hubbell Law Directory

THARRINGTON, SMITH & HARGROVE (AV)

209 Fayetteville Street Mall, P.O. Box 1151, 27602
Telephone: 919-821-4711
Telecopier: 919-829-1583

MEMBERS OF FIRM

J. Harold Tharrington | Carlyn G. Poole

ASSOCIATES

Debra R. Nickels | Jaye Powell Meyer

Representative Clients: North Carolina Association of Broadcasters; AT&T Communications; ABC-TV Network Affiliates Assn.; North Carolina Cable Television Assn.; Time-Warner Communications; Virginia Association of Broadcasters; Pulitzer Broadcasting; The Hearst Corporation.

For full biographical listings, see the Martindale-Hubbell Law Directory

* WOMBLE CARLYLE SANDRIDGE & RICE (AV)

A Professional Limited Liability Company
2100 First Union Capitol Center, 150 Fayetteville Street Mall, P.O. Box 831, 27602
Telephone: 919-755-2100
Telecopy: 919-755-2150
Telex: 806498
Charlotte, North Carolina Office: 3300 One First Union Center, 301 South College Street.
Telephone: 704-331-4900.
Telecopy: 704-331-4955.
Telex: 853609.
Winston-Salem, North Carolina Office: 1600 Southern National Financial Center.
Telephone: 919-721-3600.
Telecopy: 919-721-3660.
Telex: 806498.
Atlanta, Georgia Office: One Ninety One Peachtree Tower, 191 Peachtree Street N.E., Suite 3250.
Telephone: 404-614-2580.
Fax: 404-614-2595.

RESIDENT PARTNER

Marilyn R. Forbes

RESIDENT ASSOCIATE

Susan D. Crooks

Representative Clients: Aetna Casualty and Surety Co., Inc.; ALSCO/AmeriMark Building Products, Inc.; Aoki Corporation America, Inc.; Empire of Carolina, Inc.; Hackney Brothers, Inc.; Lawyers Mutual Liability Insurance Company of North Carolina; Meredith College; Monk-Austin, Inc.; Regency Park Corporation; Wachovia Bank of North Carolina, N.A.

For Complete List of Firm Personnel, See General Section

For full biographical listings, see the Martindale-Hubbell Law Directory

*SMITHFIELD,** Johnston Co.

ARMSTRONG & ARMSTRONG, P.A. (AV)

P.O. Box 27, 27577-4352
Telephone: 919-934-1575
FAX: 919-934-1846

Marcia H. Armstrong

For full biographical listings, see the Martindale-Hubbell Law Directory

*WINSTON-SALEM,** Forsyth Co.

WHITE AND CRUMPLER (AV)

11 West Fourth Street, 27101
Telephone: 910-725-1304
FAX: 910-761-8845

MEMBERS OF FIRM

James G. White (1924-1974) | G. Edgar Parker
Fred G. Crumpler, Jr. | David B. Freedman
Dudley A. Witt

ASSOCIATES

Joan E. Brodish | Teresa Hier

OF COUNSEL

Frank M. Armstrong (1900-1979) | Barbara C. Westmoreland
| Clyde C. Randolph, Jr.

Reference: Wachovia Bank and Trust Co., N.A., Winston-Salem, North Carolina.

For full biographical listings, see the Martindale-Hubbell Law Directory

Winston-Salem—Continued

WOMBLE CARLYLE SANDRIDGE & RICE (AV)

A Professional Limited Liability Company
1600 Southern National Financial Center, P.O. Drawer 84, 27102
Telephone: 910-721-3600
Telecopy: 910-721-3660
Telex: 806498
Charlotte, North Carolina Office: 3300 One First Union Center, 301 South College Street.
Telephone: 704-331-4900.
Telecopy: 704-331-4955.
Telex: 853609.
Raleigh, North Carolina Office: 2100 First Union Capitol Center, 150 Fayetteville Street Mall, P.O. Box 831.
Telephone: 919-755-2100.
Telecopy: 919-755-2150.
Telex: 806498.
Atlanta, Georgia Office: One Ninety One Peachtree Tower, 191 Peachtree Street, N.E., Suite 3250.
Telephone: 404-614-2580.
Fax: 404-614-2595.

MEMBER OF FIRM

Jimmy Hamilton Barnhill

ASSOCIATE

Elizabeth B. McGee

Representative Clients: Brad Ragan, Inc.; Brenner Companies; Food Lion, Inc.; Hanes Companies, Inc.; North Carolina Baptist Hospitals, Inc.; R.J. Reynolds Tobacco Company; Summit Communications Group, Inc.; Thomasville Furniture Industries, Inc.; Wachovia Corporation; Wake Forest University.

For Complete List of Firm Personnel, See General Section

For full biographical listings, see the Martindale-Hubbell Law Directory

NORTH DAKOTA

*BISMARCK,** Burleigh Co.

PETERSON, SCHMITZ, MOENCH & SCHMIDT, A PROFESSIONAL CORPORATION (AV)

Second Floor, Suite 200, 116 North Fourth Street, P.O. Box 2076, 58502-2076
Telephone: 701-224-0400
Fax: 701-224-0399

David L. Peterson
Orell D. Schmitz
Dale W. Moench
William D. Schmidt

OF COUNSEL

Gerald Glaser

LEGAL SUPPORT PERSONNEL

Vicki J. Kunz
Traci L. Albers

For full biographical listings, see the Martindale-Hubbell Law Directory

OHIO

*CINCINNATI,** Hamilton Co.

PHYLLIS G. BOSSIN CO., L.P.A. (AV)

Suite 1210, 36 East Fourth Street, 45202
Telephone: 513-421-4420
Fax: 513-421-0691

Phyllis G. Bossin

J. Michael Kaufman

For full biographical listings, see the Martindale-Hubbell Law Directory

JAMES J. CHALFIE CO., L.P.A. (AV)

36 East Seventh Street, Suite 1600, 45202
Telephone: 513-381-8616
FAX: 513-381-8619

James J. Chalfie

For Complete List of Firm Personnel, See General Section

For full biographical listings, see the Martindale-Hubbell Law Directory

DREW, WARD, GRAF, COOGAN & GOEDDEL A LEGAL PROFESSIONAL ASSOCIATION (AV)

24th Floor, Central Trust Tower, 4th and Vine Streets, 45202
Telephone: 513-621-8210
Telecopier: 513-621-5444

Frederic L. Goeddel
E. Beth Farrell

Michael D. McNeil

Representative Clients: AAA Cincinnati; Deaconess Hospital; Stevenson Photo Color Co.
Reference: Star Bank, N.A.

For full biographical listings, see the Martindale-Hubbell Law Directory

KATZ, TELLER, BRANT & HILD A LEGAL PROFESSIONAL ASSOCIATION (AV)

2400 Chemed Center, 255 East Fifth Street, 45202-4724
Telephone: 513-721-4532
Telecopier: 513-721-7120

Reuven J. Katz
Jerome S. Teller
Joseph A. Brant
Guy M. Hild
Robert A. Pitcairn, Jr.
Robert E. Brant
Ronald J. Goret
Stephen C. Kisling
Andrew R. Berger
Mark J. Jahnke
William F. Russo
John R. Gierl
Bruce A. Hunter
Gregory E. Land
Bradley G. Haas
Daniel P. Utt
Brent G. Houk
Cynthia Loren Gibson
Suzanne Prieur Land
Tedd H. Friedman

Representative Clients: Eagle Picher Industries, Inc.; F & C International, Inc.; Jewish Hospitals of Cincinnati; Johnny Bench; Texo Corporation; University of Cincinnati Medical Associates, Inc.

For full biographical listings, see the Martindale-Hubbell Law Directory

REISENFELD & STATMAN (AV)

Auburn Barrister House, 2355 Auburn Avenue, 45219
Telephone: 513-381-6810
FAX: 513-381-0255

Sylvan P. Reisenfeld
Alan J. Statman

John L. Day, Jr.
Melisa J. Richter
Bradley A. Reisenfeld
Rosemary E. Scollard

John Schmidt

For full biographical listings, see the Martindale-Hubbell Law Directory

THOMPSON, HINE AND FLORY (AV)

312 Walnut Street, 14th Floor, 45202-4029
Telephone: 513-352-6700
Fax: 513-241-4771;
Telex: 938003
Akron, Ohio Office: 50 S. Main Street, Suite 502, 44308-1828.
Telephone: 216-376-8090.
Fax: 216-376-8386.
Cleveland, Ohio Office: 1100 National City Bank Building, 629 Euclid Avenue, 44114-3070.
Telephone: 216-566-5500.
Fax: 216-556-5583.
Telex: 980217.
Cable Address: "Thomflor".
Columbus, Ohio Office: One Columbus, 10 West Broad Street, 43215-3435.
Telephone: 614-469-3200.
Fax: 614-469-3361.
Dayton, Ohio Office: 2000 Courthouse Plaza, N.E., 45402-1706.
Telephone: 513-443-6600.
Fax: 513-443-6637; 443-6635.
Palm Beach, Florida Office: 125 Worth Avenue, 33480-4466.
Telephone: 407-833-5900.
Fax: 407-833-5951.
Washington, D.C. Office: 1920 N Street, N.W., 20036-1601.
Telephone: 202-331-8800.
Fax: 202-331-8330.
Telex: 904173.
Cable Address: "Caglaw".
Brussels, Belgium Office: Rue des Chevaliers / Ridderstraat 14 - B.10, B - 1050.
Telephone: 011(32-2) 511-9326.
Fax: 011(-32-2) 513-9206.

MEMBER OF FIRM

William L. Martin, Jr.

For Complete List of Firm Personnel, See General Section

For full biographical listings, see the Martindale-Hubbell Law Directory

*CLEVELAND,** Cuyahoga Co.

HERMANN, CAHN & SCHNEIDER (AV)

Suite 500, 1301 East Ninth Street, 44114
Telephone: 216-781-5515
Facsimile: 216-781-1030

MEMBER OF FIRM

James S. Cahn

For full biographical listings, see the Martindale-Hubbell Law Directory

ILANA HOROWITZ (AV)

310 Chagrin Plaza East, 23811 Chagrin Boulevard, 44122
Telephone: 216-464-2777
FAX: 216-464-4731

Ilana Horowitz Ratner

Lisa R. Kraemer

For full biographical listings, see the Martindale-Hubbell Law Directory

KELLEY, MCCANN & LIVINGSTONE (AV)

35th Floor, BP America Building, 200 Public Square, 44114-2302
Telephone: 216-241-3141
FAX: 216-241-3707

MEMBERS OF FIRM

John D. Brown
Joel A. Makee
Carl A. Murway
Steven A. Goldfarb

ASSOCIATE

Peter M. Poulos

For Complete List of Firm Personnel, See General Section

For full biographical listings, see the Martindale-Hubbell Law Directory

HERBERT PALKOVITZ (AV)

1600 Standard Building, 44113
Telephone: 216-771-3777
FAX: 216-771-1950

ASSOCIATE

LaVonne R. Dye

LEGAL SUPPORT PERSONNEL

Sherri A. Lanzilotta (Legal Assistant)

References: National City Bank; Society National Bank.

For full biographical listings, see the Martindale-Hubbell Law Directory

SEELEY, SAVIDGE AND AUSSEM A LEGAL PROFESSIONAL ASSOCIATION (AV)

800 Bank One Center, 600 Superior Avenue, East, 44114-2655
Telephone: 216-566-8200
Cable Address: "See Sau"
Fax-Telecopier: 216-566-0213
Elyria, Ohio Office: 538 Broad Street.
Telephone: 216-236-8158.

OF COUNSEL

John F. Seelie

References: Society National Bank; AmeriTrust.

For Complete List of Firm Personnel, See General Section

For full biographical listings, see the Martindale-Hubbell Law Directory

WOLF AND AKERS A LEGAL PROFESSIONAL ASSOCIATION (AV)

1515 The East Ohio Building, 1717 East Ninth Street, 44114
Telephone: 216-623-9999
FAX: 216-623-0629

Marshall J. Wolf
Deborah R. Akers

For full biographical listings, see the Martindale-Hubbell Law Directory

*COLUMBUS,** Franklin Co.

BERRY & SHOEMAKER (AV)

42 East Gay Street, Suite 1515, 43215
Telephone: 614-464-0100
Portsmouth Telephone: 614-354-4838
Fax: 614-464-4033
Portsmouth, Ohio Office: 703 National City Bank Building, 45662.
Telephone: 614-354-4838.
Chillicothe, Ohio Office: 63 N. Paint Street, 45601.
Telephone: 614-775-8941.

MEMBERS OF FIRM

John F. Berry
Kevin L. Shoemaker
D. Lewis Clark, Jr.

(See Next Column)

OF COUNSEL

Brenda S. Shoemaker

For full biographical listings, see the Martindale-Hubbell Law Directory

FRIEDMAN & BABBITT CO., L.P.A. (AV)

500 South Front Street Suite 810, 43215-5627
Telephone: 614-221-0090
Fax: 614-221-7213

William S. Friedman
Gerald J. Babbitt

Gary S. Wellbaum

For full biographical listings, see the Martindale-Hubbell Law Directory

TIMOTHY D. GERRITY (AV)

50 West Broad Street, 43215
Telephone: 614-464-2211

For full biographical listings, see the Martindale-Hubbell Law Directory

JEFFREY A. GROSSMAN CO., L.P.A. (AV)

32 West Hoster Street, 43215
Telephone: 614-221-7711

Jeffrey A. Grossman

Thomas J. Jedinak
Anthony R. Auten

For full biographical listings, see the Martindale-Hubbell Law Directory

R. CHRIS HARBOLD (AV)

32 West Hoster Street, Suite 100, 43215-5632
Telephone: 614-221-7711
Fax: 614-221-7145

Reference: Bank One.

For full biographical listings, see the Martindale-Hubbell Law Directory

LUPER, WOLINETZ, SHERIFF & NEIDENTHAL A LEGAL PROFESSIONAL ASSOCIATION (AV)

1200 LeVeque Tower, 50 West Broad Street, 43215-3374
Telephone: 614-221-7663
Telecopier: 614-464-2425

Barry H. Wolinetz

For full biographical listings, see the Martindale-Hubbell Law Directory

MOOTS, COPE & STANTON A LEGAL PROFESSIONAL ASSOCIATION (AV)

3600 Olentangy River Road, 43214-3913
Telephone: 614-459-4140
FAX: 614-459-4503

Philip R. Moots
Jon M. Cope
Elizabeth M. Stanton

Wanda L. Carter
Catherine A. Cunningham

OF COUNSEL

Benson A. Wolman

For full biographical listings, see the Martindale-Hubbell Law Directory

TYACK, BLACKMORE & LISTON CO., L.P.A. (AV)

536 South High Street, 43215
Telephone: 614-221-1341
Fax: 614-228-0253

Thomas M. Tyack
Margaret L. Blackmore
Jefferson E. Liston

Angela F. Albert

References: Huntington National Bank; Bank One of Columbus, NA.

For full biographical listings, see the Martindale-Hubbell Law Directory

EDWARD F. WHIPPS & ASSOCIATES (AV)

500 South Front Street, Suite 900, 43215
Telephone: 614-461-6006
Fax: 614-461-6010

ASSOCIATE

Susan D. Brown

OF COUNSEL

Robert N. Wistner

For full biographical listings, see the Martindale-Hubbell Law Directory

*DAYTON,** Montgomery Co.

CREW, BUCHANAN & LOWE (AV)

Formerly Cowden, Pfarrer, Crew & Becker
2580 Kettering Tower, 45423-2580
Telephone: 513-223-6211
Facsimile: 513-223-7631

MEMBERS OF FIRM

Charles A. Craighead (1857-1926)
Robert E. Cowden (1886-1954)
Robert E. Cowden, Jr. (1910-1968)
Charles P. Pfarrer (1905-1984)
Philip Rohrer Becker (1905-1989)
Charles D. Lowe

ASSOCIATES

R. Anne Shale
Dana K. Cole

For Complete List of Firm Personnel, See General Section

For full biographical listings, see the Martindale-Hubbell Law Directory

ROGERS & GREENBERG (AV)

2160 Kettering Tower, 45423
Telephone: 513-223-8171
Fax: 513-223-1649

MEMBERS OF FIRM

Stanley Z. Greenberg
Keith R. Kearney
L. Anthony Lush

For Complete List of Firm Personnel, See General Section

For full biographical listings, see the Martindale-Hubbell Law Directory

*ELYRIA,** Lorain Co.

SPIKE & MECKLER (AV)

1551 West River Street North, 44035
Telephone: 216-324-5353
Fax: 216-324-6529

MEMBERS OF FIRM

Allen S. Spike
Stephen G. Meckler
Douglas M. Brill

For full biographical listings, see the Martindale-Hubbell Law Directory

*LANCASTER,** Fairfield Co.

STEBELTON, ARANDA & SNIDER A LEGAL PROFESSIONAL ASSOCIATION (AV)

One North Broad Street, P.O. Box 130, 43130
Telephone: 614-654-4141;
Columbus Direct Line: 614-837-1212;
1-800-543-Laws
Fax: 614-654-2521

Gerald L. Stebelton
James C. Aranda
Rick L. Snider
John M. Snider

Sandra W. Davis
Jason A. Price

LEGAL SUPPORT PERSONNEL

Sandra J. Steinhauser
Rose M. Sels
Sandra K. Hillyard
Michelle K. Garlinger

For full biographical listings, see the Martindale-Hubbell Law Directory

*TOLEDO,** Lucas Co.

AUBRY, MEYER, WALSH & POMMERANZ (AV)

(An Association of Independent Attorneys)
Lawyers Building, 329-10th Street, P.O. Box 2068, 43603-2068
Telephone: 419-241-4288
FAX: 419-241-5764

Jude T. Aubry

For full biographical listings, see the Martindale-Hubbell Law Directory

LACKEY, NUSBAUM, HARRIS, RENY & TORZEWSKI A LEGAL PROFESSIONAL ASSOCIATION (AV)

Two Maritime Plaza Third Floor, 43604
Telephone: 419-243-1105
Fax: 419-243-8953

Melvin G. Nusbaum
Kenneth E. Boyd

References: Fifth Third Bank; Society Bank.

For full biographical listings, see the Martindale-Hubbell Law Directory

MORAN & MORAN (AV)

626 Madison Avenue, Suite 300, 43604
Telephone: 419-241-8171
Fax: Available Upon Request

Peter L. Moran
Mary Beth Moran

Representative Clients: The Exchange Bank; Payak Insurance Agency; Monroe Pharmacy, Inc.
References: Society Bank; The Fifth Third Bank, Toledo, Ohio.

For Complete List of Firm Personnel, See General Section

For full biographical listings, see the Martindale-Hubbell Law Directory

OKLAHOMA

*DUNCAN,** Stephens Co.

ELLIS, LEONARD & BUCKHOLTS (AV)

Patterson Building, 929 West Willow, 73533-4921
Telephone: 405-252-3240
Fax: 405-252-9596

Thomas T. Ellis
Phillip H. Leonard
E. J. Buckholts, II

Reference: Security National Bank & Trust Co., Duncan, Oklahoma.

For full biographical listings, see the Martindale-Hubbell Law Directory

*OKLAHOMA CITY,** Oklahoma Co.

JON L. HESTER, P.C. A PROFESSIONAL CORPORATION (AV)

Suite 265, 5400 N. Grand Boulevard, 73112
Telephone: 405-947-8866
Fax: 405-947-1140

Jon L. Hester

Reference: Citybank & Trust, Oklahoma City.

For full biographical listings, see the Martindale-Hubbell Law Directory

*TULSA,** Tulsa Co.

CLARK & WILLIAMS (AV)

Suite 600 Fox Plaza Office Center, 5416 South Yale Avenue, 74135
Telephone: 918-496-9200
Fax: 918-496-3851

MEMBERS OF FIRM

Wendell W. Clark
Darrell E. Williams

ASSOCIATES

Mark R. Reents
Michael DeCarlo
Kathryn A. Herwig

References: Bank of Oklahoma; Peoples State Bank.

For full biographical listings, see the Martindale-Hubbell Law Directory

CRAWFORD, CROWE & BAINBRIDGE, P.A. (AV)

1714 First National Building, 74103
Telephone: 918-587-1128
Fax: 918-587-3975

B. Hayden Crawford
Harry M. Crowe, Jr.
Robert L. Bainbridge
Kyle B. Haskins
Eric B. Bolusky

For full biographical listings, see the Martindale-Hubbell Law Directory

GABLE & GOTWALS (AV)

2000 Bank IV Center, 15 West Sixth Street, 74119-5447
Telephone: 918-582-9201
Facsimile: 918-586-8383

Teresa B. Adwan
Pamela S. Anderson
John R. Barker
David L. Bryant
Gene C. Buzzard
Dennis Clarke Cameron
Timothy A. Carney
Renee DeMoss
Elsie C. Draper
Sidney G. Dunagan
Theodore Q. Eliot
Richard W. Gable
Jeffrey Don Hassell
Patricia Ledvina Himes
Oliver S. Howard
Richard D. Koljack, Jr.
J. Daniel Morgan
Joseph W. Morris
Elizabeth R. Muratet
Richard B. Noulles
Ronald N. Ricketts
John Henry Rule
M. Benjamin Singletary
James M. Sturdivant
Patrick O. Waddel
Michael D. Hall
David Edward Keglovits
Stephen W. Lake
Kari S. McKee
Terry D. Ragsdale
Jeffrey C. Rambach

(See Next Column)

GABLE & GOTWALS—*Continued*

OF COUNSEL

G. Ellis Gable
Charles P. Gotwals, Jr.

For full biographical listings, see the Martindale-Hubbell Law Directory

HOOD, THORNBRUGH & RAYNOLDS, P.C. (AV)

1914 South Boston, 74119
Telephone: 918-583-5825
Fax: 918-583-8740

William W. Hood
P. Thomas Thornbrugh
William F. Raynolds, II

Dana L. Gish
Buckley W. Barlow

For full biographical listings, see the Martindale-Hubbell Law Directory

UNGERMAN & IOLA (AV)

Riverbridge Office Park, 1323 East 71st Street, Suite 300, P.O. Box 701917, 74170-1917
Telephone: 918-495-0550
Fax: 918-495-0561

MEMBERS OF FIRM

Irvine E. Ungerman (1908-1980)
Maynard I. Ungerman
Mark H. Iola

ASSOCIATE

Randall L. Iola

Representative Client: Northeastern Oklahoma Building and Construction Trades Council.

For full biographical listings, see the Martindale-Hubbell Law Directory

WAGNER AND GRUNDY (AV)

Suite 1100, 525 Main Mall, 74103
Telephone: 918-587-2547
Fax: 918-587-2886

MEMBERS OF FIRM

Richard A. Wagner, II
Bradley A. Grundy

For full biographical listings, see the Martindale-Hubbell Law Directory

OREGON

*GRANTS PASS,** Josephine Co.

MYRICK, SEAGRAVES, ADAMS & DAVIS (AV)

600 N.W. Fifth Street, 97526
Telephone: 503-476-6627
Fax: 503-476-7048

MEMBERS OF FIRM

Donald H. Coulter (Retired)
Charles H. Seagraves, Jr.
Lynn Michael Myrick
Richard D. Adams
John E. Davis
Holly A. Preslar

Reference: United States National Bank of Oregon.

For full biographical listings, see the Martindale-Hubbell Law Directory

*PORTLAND,** Multnomah Co.

STAHANCYK, GAZZOLA, GEARING & RACKNER, P.C. (AV)

200 Jackson Tower, 806 S.W. Broadway, 97205-3304
Telephone: 503-222-9115
Facsimile: 503-222-4037

Jody L. Stahancyk
Charles D. Gazzola
David C. Gearing
Laura Rackner Stanford

David A. White
Ronald M. Johnson
Brett N. Bender (Not admitted in OR)

For full biographical listings, see the Martindale-Hubbell Law Directory

PENNSYLVANIA

*ALLENTOWN,** Lehigh Co.

GROSS, McGINLEY, LABARRE & EATON (AV)

33 South Seventh Street, P.O. Box 4060, 18105-4060
Telephone: (610)-820-5450
Fax: (610)-820-6006

(See Next Column)

MEMBERS OF FIRM

Malcolm J. Gross
Paul A. McGinley
Donald L. LaBarre, Jr.
J. Jackson Eaton, III
Michael A. Henry
Patrick J. Reilly
William J. Fries

ASSOCIATES

Anne K. Manley
John D. Lychak

For full biographical listings, see the Martindale-Hubbell Law Directory

JOHN R. MONDSCHEIN (AV)

1809 Allen Street, 18104
Telephone: 610-437-7850
Fax: 610-437-7122

ASSOCIATES

Melissa T. Pavlack
Dawn E. Miller Medvesky

LEGAL SUPPORT PERSONNEL

Helen L. Jones (Paralegal)

For full biographical listings, see the Martindale-Hubbell Law Directory

*DOYLESTOWN,** Bucks Co.

WILLIAM L. GOLDMAN (AV)

90 East State Street, P.O. Box 1989, 18901
Telephone: 215-348-2605
Fax: 215-348-5247
Levittown, Pennsylvania Office: One Stonybrook Drive, P.O. Box 38.
Telephone: 215-945-8700.

ASSOCIATES

William L. Goldman, Jr.
John D. Conroy
Patricia Handy Cooley
Donna M. McKillop
J. Todd Savarese

Representative Clients: Sinkler, Inc., Southampton, Pennsylvania; Fraternal Order of Police Lodge #53, State Police Lodge; Bucks County Federation of Sportsmen's Club.

For full biographical listings, see the Martindale-Hubbell Law Directory

*EASTON,** Northampton Co.

HERSTER, NEWTON & MURPHY (AV)

127 North Fourth Street, P.O. Box 1087, 18042
Telephone: 610-258-6219

MEMBERS OF FIRM

Andrew L. Herster, Jr.
Henry R. Newton
William K. Murphy

General Counsel For: Valley Federal Savings & Loan Assn.; Lafayette Bank; Easton Printing Co.; Northampton Community College; Eisenhardt Mills, Inc.; Delaware Wood Products, Inc.; Panuccio Construction, Inc.
References: Merchants Bank, N.A.; Lafayette Bank; Valley Federal Savings and Loan.

*HARRISBURG,** Dauphin Co.

GOLDBERG, KATZMAN & SHIPMAN, P.C. (AV)

320 Market Street - Strawberry Square, P.O. Box 1268, 17108-1268
Telephone: 717-234-4161
Telecopier: 717-234-6808; 717-234-6810

Harry B. Goldberg
Paul J. Esposito

Jerry J. Russo

OF COUNSEL

Arthur L. Goldberg

Representative Client: Fulton Bank.

For Complete List of Firm Personnel, See General Section

For full biographical listings, see the Martindale-Hubbell Law Directory

HEPFORD, SWARTZ & MORGAN (AV)

111 North Front Street, P.O. Box 889, 17108-0889
Telephone: 717-234-4121
Fax: 717-232-6802
Lewistown, Pennsylvania Office: 12 South Main Street, P.O. Box 867.
Telephone: 717-248-3913.

MEMBERS OF FIRM

H. Joseph Hepford
Lee C. Swartz
James G. Morgan, Jr.
Sandra L. Meilton
Stephen M. Greecher, Jr.
Dennis R. Sheaffer

COUNSEL

Stanley H. Siegel (Resident, Lewistown Office)

ASSOCIATES

Richard A. Estacio
Michael H. Park
Andrew K. Stutzman

For full biographical listings, see the Martindale-Hubbell Law Directory

Harrisburg—Continued

MANCKE, WAGNER, HERSHEY AND TULLY (AV)

2233 North Front Street, 17110
Telephone: 717-234-7051
Fax: 717-234-7080

MEMBERS OF FIRM

John B. Mancke
P. Richard Wagner
David E. Hershey
William T. Tully

ASSOCIATE

David R. Breschi

For full biographical listings, see the Martindale-Hubbell Law Directory

LANSDALE, Montgomery Co.

RUBIN, GLICKMAN AND STEINBERG, A PROFESSIONAL CORPORATION (AV)

2605 North Broad Street, P.O. Box 1277, 19446
Telephone: 215-822-7575; 855-5500; 800-358-9367
Facsimile: 215-822-1713

Irwin S. Rubin
Jay C. Glickman
Marc Robert Steinberg
Toby Lynn Dickman
Gregory R. Gifford
Amy S. Newman
Lewis Goodman
Kathleen M. O'Brien
Steven M. Koloski

Reference: Union National Bank and Trust Company of Souderton.

For full biographical listings, see the Martindale-Hubbell Law Directory

*MEDIA,** Delaware Co.

KASSAB ARCHBOLD JACKSON & O'BRIEN (AV)

Lawyers-Title Building, 214 North Jackson Street, P.O. Box 626, 19063
Telephone: 610-565-3800
Telecopier: 610-892-6888
Wilmington, Delaware Office: 1326 King Street.
Telephone: 302-656-3393.
Fax: 302-656-1993.
Wildwood, New Jersey Office: 5201 New Jersey Avenue.
Telephone: 609-522-6559.

MEMBERS OF FIRM

Edward Kassab
William C. Archbold, Jr.
Robert James Jackson
Joseph Patrick O'Brien
Richard A. Stanko
Roy T. J. Stegena

OF COUNSEL

Matthew J. Ryan
John W. Nilon, Jr.

ASSOCIATES

Kevin William Gibson
Cynthia Kassab Larosa
Marc S. Stein
Terrance A. Kline
George C. McFarland, Jr.
Jill E. Aversa
Pamela A. La Torre
Kenneth D. Kynett

Representative Clients furnished upon request.

For full biographical listings, see the Martindale-Hubbell Law Directory

LAW OFFICES I.B. SINCLAIR (AV)

30 West Third Street, 19063-2824
Telephone: 610-565-2500
Fax: 610-565-2508

Harold B. Ramsey (1901-1986)

For full biographical listings, see the Martindale-Hubbell Law Directory

*NORRISTOWN,** Montgomery Co.

EMANUEL A. BERTIN, P.C. (AV)

One Meetinghouse Place, 19401
Telephone: 610-277-1500
FAX: 610-272-2242

Emanuel A. Bertin

For full biographical listings, see the Martindale-Hubbell Law Directory

MARY CUSHING DOHERTY (AV)

One Montgomery Plaza, Suite 609, 19401
Telephone: 610-279-6500
Fax: 610-275-3631
(Also Special Counsel to Abrahams, Loewenstein, Bushman & Kauffman, Philadelphia)

For full biographical listings, see the Martindale-Hubbell Law Directory

MANNING, KINKEAD, BROOKS & BRADBURY, A PROFESSIONAL CORPORATION (AV)

412 DeKalb Street, 19404-0231
Telephone: 610-279-1800
Fax: 610-279-8682

Franklin L. Wright (1880-1965)
William Perry Manning, Jr.
William H. Kinkead, III
William H. Bradbury, III

Cheri D. Andrews

Counsel for: The Philadelphia National Bank; John Deere Co.; The Rouse Co.; Consolidated Rail Corp.; Bethlehem Steel Co.; Royal Globe Insurance Co.; Nationwide Mutual Insurance Co.

For full biographical listings, see the Martindale-Hubbell Law Directory

*PHILADELPHIA,** Philadelphia Co.

ASTOR WEISS KAPLAN & ROSENBLUM (AV)

The Bellevue, 6th Floor, Broad Street at Walnut, 19102
Telephone: 215-790-0100
Fax: 215-790-0509
Bala Cynwyd, Pennsylvania Office: Suite 100, Three Bala Plaza West, P.O. Box 1665.
Telephone: 610-667-8660.
Fax: 610-667-2783.
Cherry Hill, New Jersey Office: Woodland Falls Corporate Park, 210 Lake Drive East, Suite 201.
Telephone: 609-795-1113.
Fax: 609-795-7413.

MEMBERS OF FIRM

Paul C. Astor
Alvin M. Weiss (1936-1976)
G. David Rosenblum
Arthur H. Kaplan
Barbara Oaks Silver
Richard H. Martin
Allen B. Dubroff
David S. Workman
David S. Mandel
David Gutin (Resident at Bala Cynwyd Office)
Joseph B. Finlay, Jr.
Howard K. Goldstein
Steven W. Smith
Gerald J. Schorr
Jean M. Biesecker (Resident, Bala Cynwyd Office)

ASSOCIATES

Carol L. Vassallo
Thomas J. Maiorino
John R. Poeta
Bradley J. Begelman
Andrew S. Kessler
Marc S. Zamsky
Janet G. Felgoise (Resident, Bala Cynwyd Office)
Jacqueline G. Segal (Resident, Bala Cynwyd Office)

SPECIAL COUNSEL

Neil Hurowitz (Resident, Bala Cynwyd Office)

OF COUNSEL

Erwin L. Pincus
Edward W. Silver
Lloyd Zane Remick

For full biographical listings, see the Martindale-Hubbell Law Directory

MICHAEL D. FIORETTI (AV)

The Bourse Building, Suite 790, 111 South Independence Mall East, 19106
Telephone: 215-440-7612
Fax: 215-440-0328
Cherry Hill, New Jersey Office: 1101 Kings Highway North, Suite 304.
Telephone: 609-482-2488.

ASSOCIATES

Philip A. Charamella
Lynn Bennett-Hamlin

For full biographical listings, see the Martindale-Hubbell Law Directory

ALFRED MARROLETTI AND ASSOCIATES (AV)

The Graham Building-Suite 1504, One Penn Square West 30 S. 15th Street, 19102
Telephone: 215-563-0400

ASSOCIATES

Jacob N. Snyder
Joseph A. Marroletti

For full biographical listings, see the Martindale-Hubbell Law Directory

*PITTSBURGH,** Allegheny Co.

ADERSON, FRANK & STEINER, A PROFESSIONAL CORPORATION (AV)

2320 Grant Building, 15219
Telephone: 412-263-0500
Fax: 412-263-0565

William L. Steiner
Jay A. Blechman

For full biographical listings, see the Martindale-Hubbell Law Directory

Pittsburgh—Continued

BUCHANAN INGERSOLL, PROFESSIONAL CORPORATION (AV)

5800 USX Tower, 600 Grant Street, 15219
Telephone: 412-562-8800
Telecopier: 412-562-1041
Philadelphia, Pennsylvania Office: Two Logan Square, Twelfth Floor, 18th & Arch Streets.
Telephone: 215-665-8700.
Harrisburg, Pennsylvania Office: Vartan Parc, 30 North Third Street.
Telephone: 717-237-4800.
Tampa, Florida Office: 101 East Kennedy Boulevard, Suite 1030.
Telephone: 813-222-8180.
North Miami Beach, Florida Office: 19495 Biscayne Boulevard.
Telephone: 305-933-5600.
Lexington, Kentucky Office: 1210 Vine Center Office Tower, 333 West Vine Street.
Telephone: 606-225-5333.
Princeton, New Jersey Office: Buchanan Ingersoll, A Partnership, College Centre, 500 College Road East.
Telephone: 609-452-2666.

Stewart B. Barmen
Denise W. Ford

Candice Komar Ewonce
Daniel H. Glasser

For Complete List of Firm Personnel, See General Section

For full biographical listings, see the Martindale-Hubbell Law Directory

FELDSTEIN GRINBERG STEIN & MCKEE, A PROFESSIONAL CORPORATION (AV)

428 Boulevard of the Allies, 15219
Telephone: 412-471-0677
Fax: 412-263-6129
Elizabeth, Pennsylvania Office: 400 Second Street.
Telephone: 412-384-6111.
Wexford, Pennsylvania Office: 12300 Perry Highway.
Telephone: 412-935-5540.

Jay H. Feldstein

Christine Gale
Mary Erin Cole

For full biographical listings, see the Martindale-Hubbell Law Directory

GOLDBERG, GRUENER, GENTILE, VOELKER & HOROHO, P.C. (AV)

Suite 1320 Grant Building, 15219
Telephone: 412-261-9900
Fax: 412-261-7100

Mark J. Goldberg
Harry J. Gruener
Gary G. Gentile
Charles P. Voelker
Kenneth J. Horoho, Jr.

Velma B. Hirsch
Kerri Lee Cappella
Serena M. Williams
Timothy J. Gricks

For full biographical listings, see the Martindale-Hubbell Law Directory

KING & KING (AV)

Twenty Chatham Square, 15219
Telephone: 412-391-1200
Fax: 412-391-7082

Peter J. King
Linda A. King

Approved Attorneys for: First American Title Insurance Company.

For full biographical listings, see the Martindale-Hubbell Law Directory

MARCUS & SHAPIRA (AV)

35th Floor, One Oxford Centre, 301 Grant Street, 15219-6401
Telephone: 412-471-3490
Telecopier: 412-391-8758

MEMBERS OF FIRM

Bernard D. Marcus
Daniel H. Shapira
George P. Slesinger
Robert L. Allman, II
Estelle F. Comay
Susan Gromis Flynn
Darlene M. Nowak
Glenn M. Olcerst
Elly Heller-Toig
Sylvester A. Beozzo

OF COUNSEL

John M. Burkoff

SPECIAL COUNSEL

Jane Campbell Moriarty

(See Next Column)

ASSOCIATES

Scott D. Livingston
Robert M. Barnes
Stephen S. Zubrow
David B. Rodes
Lori E. McMaster
Melody A. Pollock
James F. Rosenberg
Amy M. Gottlieb

For full biographical listings, see the Martindale-Hubbell Law Directory

PILLAR AND MULROY, P.C. (AV)

Suite 700, 312 Boulevard of Allies, 15222
Telephone: 412-471-3300
Fax: 412-471-6068

Thomas M. Mulroy

Lynn E. MacBeth

Reference: Pittsburgh National Bank.

For full biographical listings, see the Martindale-Hubbell Law Directory

ROSENBERG, KIRSHNER P.A. (AV)

1500 Grant Building, 15219-2203
Telephone: 412-281-4256
Telefax: 412-642-2380
Robinson Township, Pennsylvania Office: 5996-F Steubenville Pike, 15136.
Telephone: 412-788-0600.
Fax: 412-788-1503.
Imperial, Pennsylvania Office: 223 Main Street, 15126.
Telephone: 412-695-7888.
North Palm Beach, Florida Office: 4th Floor, 712 U.S. Highway One, 33408.
Telephone: 407-844-6206.
Telefax: 407-842-4104.

H. N. Rosenberg
Charles Kirshner
Arthur L. Bloom

Bernadette M. Staroschuck

Representative Clients: Erie Insurance Co.; Keene Corporation; Liberty Mutual Insurance Co.; Kemper Insurance; Union Carbide; McDonald's Corp.; General Electric Capital Corp.; Equitable Lomas Leasing Corp.; Hyatt Legal Services; Rite Aid Corp.

For Complete List of Firm Personnel, See General Section

For full biographical listings, see the Martindale-Hubbell Law Directory

*READING,** Berks Co.

MOGEL, SPEIDEL, BOBB & KERSHNER, A PROFESSIONAL CORPORATION (AV)

520 Walnut Street, P.O. Box 8581, 19603-8581
Telephone: 610-376-1515
Telecopier: 610-372-8710

George B. Balmer (1902-1969)
George A. Kershner (1907-1969)
Carl F. Mogel (1919-1994)
Donald K. Bobb
Edwin H. Kershner
Frederick R. Mogel
Samuel R. Fry II
Kathleen A. B. Kovach
Michael L. Mixell
George M. Lutz
Stephen H. Price
Kathryn K. Harenza

OF COUNSEL

Harry W. Speidel
Henry A. Gass

Representative Clients: Great Valley Savings Bank; Clover Farms Dairy Co.; National Penn Bank; Meridian Leasing, Inc.; Ducharme, McMillen & Associates; Edwards Business Machines, Inc.; Greater Berks Development Fund; Union Township, Berks County, Pennsylvania.

For full biographical listings, see the Martindale-Hubbell Law Directory

*WEST CHESTER,** Chester Co.

BUCKLEY, NAGLE, GENTRY, MCGUIRE & MORRIS (AV)

304 North High Street, P.O. Box 133, 19380
Telephone: 610-436-4400
Telecopier: 610-436-8305
Thorndale, Pennsylvania Office: 3532 East Lincoln Highway.
Telephone: 215-383-5666.

MEMBERS OF FIRM

C. Barry Buckley
Ronald C. Nagle
W. Richard Gentry
Stephen P. McGuire
Anthony Morris
John J. Teti, Jr.
Jeffrey R. Sommer
Isabel M. Albuquerque

OF COUNSEL

R. Curtis Schroder

For full biographical listings, see the Martindale-Hubbell Law Directory

RHODE ISLAND

WARWICK, Kent Co.

KIRSHENBAUM LAW ASSOCIATES (AV)
67 Jefferson Boulevard, 02888-1053
Telephone: 401-467-5300
Fax: 401-461-4464

MEMBERS OF FIRM
Allen M. Kirshenbaum Carolyn R. Barone

Lauri S. Medwin Evan M. Kirshenbaum

For full biographical listings, see the Martindale-Hubbell Law Directory

WESTERLY, Washington Co.

ADAMO & NEWMAN (AV)
42 Granite Street, 02891
Telephone: 401-596-7795
Telecopier: 401-596-9000

MEMBERS OF FIRM
John Joseph Adamo Edward H. Newman
OF COUNSEL
George A. Comolli
LEGAL SUPPORT PERSONNEL
Susan E. Bookataub

For full biographical listings, see the Martindale-Hubbell Law Directory

SOUTH CAROLINA

AIKEN,* Aiken Co.

JOHNSON, JOHNSON, WHITTLE, SNELGROVE & WEEKS, P.A. (AV)
117 Pendleton Street, N.W., P.O. Box 2619, 29802-2619
Telephone: 803-649-5338
FAX: 803-641-4517

B. Henderson Johnson, Jr.
Barry H. Johnson
James E. Whittle, Jr.
Vicki Johnson Snelgrove
John W. (Bill) Weeks
Paige Weeks Johnson
Todd J. Johnson

For full biographical listings, see the Martindale-Hubbell Law Directory

CHARLESTON,* Charleston Co.

OBERMAN & OBERMAN (AV)
38 Broad Street, 29401
Telephone: 803-577-7010
Fax: 803-722-7359

MEMBERS OF FIRM
Marvin I. Oberman Harold A. Oberman

For full biographical listings, see the Martindale-Hubbell Law Directory

ROSEN, ROSEN & HAGOOD, P.A. (AV)
134 Meeting Street, Suite 200, P.O. Box 893, 29402
Telephone: 803-577-6726

Morris D. Rosen Robert N. Rosen

Diane C. Current

Reference: NationsBank of South Carolina, N.A.

For Complete List of Firm Personnel, See General Section

For full biographical listings, see the Martindale-Hubbell Law Directory

SOLOMON, KAHN, BUDMAN & STRICKER (AV)
39 Broad Street, P.O. Drawer P, 29402
Telephone: 803-577-7182
Telecopier: 803-722-0485

A. Bernard Solomon
Ellis I. Kahn
Donald J. Budman
Michael A. Stricker
ASSOCIATE
Justin S. Kahn

Local Counsel for: Lawyers Title Insurance Corp.

For full biographical listings, see the Martindale-Hubbell Law Directory

COLUMBIA,* Richland Co.

GOLDEN, TAYLOR & POTTERFIELD (AV)
A Law Partnership between a Professional Association & Attorneys
1712-1714 Main Street, 29201
Telephone: 803-779-3700
Telefax: 803-779-3422

Harvey L. Golden, P.A. J. Michael Taylor
Ashlin Blanchard Potterfield

For full biographical listings, see the Martindale-Hubbell Law Directory

ISAACS, ALLEY & HARVEY, L.L.P. (AV)
900 Elmwood Avenue, Suite 103, P.O. Box 8596, 29202-8596
Telephone: 803-252-6323
Telecopier: 803-779-5220

W. Joseph Isaacs G. Robin Alley

Representative Clients: NationsBank of South Carolina, N.A.; GATX Corporation; First Financial Corp.; Zurich-American Insurance Group; Wetterau Incorp.; Southland Log Homes, Inc.; Thompson Dental Co.; Dairymen Credit Union; Modern Exterminating, Inc.; Elizabeth Arden Co.; J.L. Todd Auction, Inc.; Continental Cards Co., Inc.; Norton-Senn Corporation; Eastern Flatbed Systems, Inc.; Valk Brokerage, Inc.; Snipes Electric, Inc.; The Loan Pros, Inc.; Palmetto Restorations, Inc.; Palmer & Cay/Carswell, Inc.; Plastitech Products, Inc.; Marek Brothers, Inc.; Ferillo & Associates, Inc.; Jacon Associates, Inc.; Blue Ridge Log Cabins, Inc.; Jones & Frank Corp.

For full biographical listings, see the Martindale-Hubbell Law Directory

KING & VERNON, P.A. (AV)
1426 Richland Street, P.O. Box 7667, 29202
Telephone: 803-779-3090
Fax: 803-779-3396

Kermit S. King W. Thomas Vernon

For Complete List of Firm Personnel, See General Section

For full biographical listings, see the Martindale-Hubbell Law Directory

SHERRILL AND ROGERS, PC (AV)
1441 Main Street, 10th Floor, P.O. Box 100200, 29202-3200
Telephone: 803-771-7900
Fax: 803-254-6305

Carl L. Holloway, Jr.
Eugene F. Rogers
Robert J. Thomas
Joe W. Underwood

For Complete List of Firm Personnel, See General Section

For full biographical listings, see the Martindale-Hubbell Law Directory

SPARTANBURG,* Spartanburg Co.

HARRISON & HAYES (AV)
200 Library Street, Second Floor, P.O. Box 5367, 29304
Telephone: 803-542-2990
Fax: 803-542-2994

Benjamin C. Harrison J. Mark Hayes, II

For full biographical listings, see the Martindale-Hubbell Law Directory

TENNESSEE

CLARKSVILLE,* Montgomery Co.

RUNYON AND RUNYON (AV)
Main Street at Third, P.O. Box 1023, 37041-1023
Telephone: 615-647-3377

MEMBER OF FIRM
Frank J. Runyon

Representative Clients: Clarksville Department of Electricity; St. Paul Insurance Co.; The Trane Co.; Aetna Life & Casualty Co.
Reference: First Union Bank, Clarksville.

For full biographical listings, see the Martindale-Hubbell Law Directory

GREENEVILLE,* Greene Co.

KING & KING (AV)
124 South Main Street, 37743
Telephone: 615-639-6881

MEMBERS OF FIRM
Kyle K. King K. Kidwell King, Jr.

For full biographical listings, see the Martindale-Hubbell Law Directory

*MEMPHIS,** Shelby Co.

CAUSEY, CAYWOOD, TAYLOR & McMANUS (AV)

Suite 2400, 100 North Main Building, 38103
Telephone: 901-526-0206
Telecopier: 901-525-1540

MEMBERS OF FIRM

James D. Causey
David E. Caywood
Daniel Loyd Taylor
John E. McManus
Darrell D. Blanton
Craid B. Flood
Jean E. Markowitz
Amy R. Fulton
Marc E. Reisman
James H. Taylor III
David Shepherd Walker

For full biographical listings, see the Martindale-Hubbell Law Directory

JAMES S. COX & ASSOCIATES (AV)

60 North Third Street, 38103
Telephone: 901-575-2040
Telecopier: 901-575-2077

ASSOCIATES

Gary K. Morrell
Russell Fowler
David A.E. Lumb
Todd B. Murrah
Sherry S. Fernandez

For full biographical listings, see the Martindale-Hubbell Law Directory

TEXAS

ARLINGTON, Tarrant Co.

GOODMAN & CLARK (AV)

1600 East Lamar Boulevard, Suite 115, 76011
Telephone: 817-460-8171
Metro: 817-265-9195
Fax: 817-861-2125

MEMBERS OF FIRM

Toby R. Goodman
John A. Clark

For full biographical listings, see the Martindale-Hubbell Law Directory

*AUSTIN,** Travis Co.

THOMAS L. AUSLEY A PROFESSIONAL CORPORATION (AV)

3307 Northland Drive Mopac at Northland, Suite 420, 78731
Telephone: 512-454-8791
Fax: 512-454-9091

Thomas L. Ausley

Kristen A. Algert

LEGAL SUPPORT PERSONNEL

Charlyne Ragsdale
Ann G. Young

Reference: NationsBank of Austin.

For full biographical listings, see the Martindale-Hubbell Law Directory

FARRIS & GREEN (AV)

Suite 201, 1300 West Lynn, 78703
Telephone: 512-473-8591
Fax: 512-473-2271

MEMBERS OF FIRM

James E. Farris
Janice L. Green

Reference: First State Bank-Austin.

For full biographical listings, see the Martindale-Hubbell Law Directory

LAW OFFICES OF JO BETSY LEWALLEN (AV)

3307 Northland Drive, Suite 420, 78731
Telephone: 512-454-8791
Telefax: 512-454-9091

LEGAL SUPPORT PERSONNEL

Sherry McMillin (Legal Assistant)

For full biographical listings, see the Martindale-Hubbell Law Directory

*CORPUS CHRISTI,** Nueces Co.

NICOLAS, MORRIS & BARROW (AV)

Suite 545, The Klee Square Building, 505 South Water Street, 78401
Telephone: 512-883-6341
Fax: 512-883-3923

(See Next Column)

MEMBER OF FIRM

Pat Morris

Representative Clients: Olson-Kessler Meat Company, Inc.; Warehouse Liquors, Inc.; Maverick Markets, Inc.; Zarsky Lumber Co.; Corpus, Inc.; Nolan Steakhouses; Navy-Army Federal Credit Union; San Jacinto Title Co.; Duke Control, Inc.
Reference: First City Bank of Corpus Christi.

For Complete List of Firm Personnel, See General Section

For full biographical listings, see the Martindale-Hubbell Law Directory

*DALLAS,** Dallas Co.

ARANSON & ASSOCIATES (AV)

Legal Arts Center, 600 Jackson Street, 75202
Telephone: 214-748-5100
Fax: 214-741-4540

Mike Aranson
Garry Philip Cantrell

For full biographical listings, see the Martindale-Hubbell Law Directory

DAVID CARLOCK, P.C. (AV)

Suite 600, Preston Commons West, 8117 Preston Road, 75225-6326
Telephone: 214-373-9100
FAX: 214-373-6688

G. David Carlock

For full biographical listings, see the Martindale-Hubbell Law Directory

KOONS, FULLER & VANDEN EYKEL, A PROFESSIONAL CORPORATION (AV)

2311 Cedar Springs Road, Suite 300, 75201
Telephone: 214-871-2727
Fax: 214-871-0196

William C. Koons
Kenneth D. Fuller
Ike Vanden Eykel
Kevin R. Fuller
Michael R. DeBruin

Joseph H. Amberson, III
Karen L. Blakely

For full biographical listings, see the Martindale-Hubbell Law Directory

McCURLEY, WEBB, KINSER, McCURLEY & NELSON, L.L.P. (AV)

4242 Renaissance Tower, 1201 Elm Street, 75270
Telephone: 214-744-4620

Mike McCurley
Brian L. Webb
Katherine A. Kinser
Mary Johanna McCurley
Keith M. Nelson
Diana S. Friedman

Kim W. Foster

For full biographical listings, see the Martindale-Hubbell Law Directory

DENISON, Grayson Co.

MICHAEL THOMPSON AND ASSOCIATES, L.L.P. (AV)

230 West Main Street, 75020
Telephone: 903-465-3455

Michael Thompson

ASSOCIATES

Carrie M. Philcox
Jim E. Walker

For full biographical listings, see the Martindale-Hubbell Law Directory

*DENTON,** Denton Co.

PHILIPS AND HOPKINS, P.C. (AV)

P.O. Box 2027, 76202-2027
Telephone: 817-566-7010
Facsimile: 817-898-0502

Robert N. Eames
Randolph W. Stout

Representative Clients: North Texas Savings & Loan Assn., Denton, Texas; First State Bank of Texas, Denton, Texas; Sanger Bank, Sanger, Texas; BankOne, Texas, N.A.; Texas Bank, Denton, Texas; Dentex Title Co., Denton, Texas.

For Complete List of Firm Personnel, See General Section

For full biographical listings, see the Martindale-Hubbell Law Directory

*EL PASO,** El Paso Co.

DAVID R. MCCLURE (AV)
218 West Franklin, 79901
Telephone: 915-544-8181
Fax: 915-544-8438

For full biographical listings, see the Martindale-Hubbell Law Directory

*FORT WORTH,** Tarrant Co.

A. DAVID COURTADE ATTORNEY AND COUNSELOR AT LAW A PROFESSIONAL CORPORATION (AV)
6000 Western Place, P.O. Box 121811, 76121-1811
Telephone: 817-377-2889

A. David Courtade

For full biographical listings, see the Martindale-Hubbell Law Directory

JON MICHAEL FRANKS (AV)
111 North Houston Street, 76102
Telephone: 817-877-1841; 429-9788; Metro 817-429-9788
FAX: 817-877-1843

For full biographical listings, see the Martindale-Hubbell Law Directory

*HOUSTON,** Harris Co.

ALEXANDER & MCEVILY (AV)
5 Post Oak Park at San Felipe 24th Floor, 77027
Telephone: 713-439-0000; 800-955-2539
Telecopy: 713-963-8478

Tom Alexander
Kevin J. McEvily
Richard L. Flowers, Jr.
E. Mathew Hennessy
Linda Geisler Marshall
Dan McEvily (Not admitted in TX)
Vicki L. Pinak
Halley Wallingford
Kelly Deann Wilson

OF COUNSEL

John V. Singleton, Jr.

References: American Bank; Chasewood Bank.

For full biographical listings, see the Martindale-Hubbell Law Directory

J. D. BUCKY ALLSHOUSE A PROFESSIONAL CORPORATION (AV)
1200 Smith Street, Suite 2340, 77002
Telephone: 713-951-0002
FAX: 713-951-0778

J. D. Bucky Allshouse

For full biographical listings, see the Martindale-Hubbell Law Directory

JOHN GORDON BOCK (AV)
First Interstate Bank Plaza, 1000 Louisiana, Suite 1090, 77002
Telephone: 713-739-0902
Fax: 713-650-3816

For full biographical listings, see the Martindale-Hubbell Law Directory

BILL DE LA GARZA & ASSOCIATES, P.C. (AV)
17050 El Camino, 77058-2610
Telephone: 713-486-7007
Fax: 713-486-0229

Bill De La Garza

David M. Oualline
Finis Royal
Sondra Kaighen

For full biographical listings, see the Martindale-Hubbell Law Directory

PLUMMER & FARMER (AV)
Formerly: Bradshaw & Plummer, 1979-1990
Brown, Bradshaw & Plummer, 1974-1979
Brown & Bradshaw, 1963-1974
3000 Smith, 77006
Telephone: 713-524-2400
FAX: 713-524-6371

MEMBERS OF FIRM

Hugh J. Plummer
Michael D. Farmer

ASSOCIATE

Arthur A. Moure

OF COUNSEL

Herbert N. Lackshin

For full biographical listings, see the Martindale-Hubbell Law Directory

SHORT & JENKINS A PROFESSIONAL LEGAL CORPORATION (AV)
Phoenix Tower, 3200 Southwest Freeway, Suite 3150, 77027
Telephone: 713-626-0208
Telefax: 713-877-1658

J. Lindsey Short, Jr.
Joan F. Jenkins

Lynn Kamin

For full biographical listings, see the Martindale-Hubbell Law Directory

MCALLEN, Hidalgo Co.

LAW OFFICE OF JOHN ROBERT KING (AV)
3409 North 10th, Suite 100, 78501
Telephone: 210-687-6294

ASSOCIATES

Robin C. Crow
Michael S. (Steve) Deck

Representative Clients: McAllen Board of Realtors; Stewart Title of Hidalgo County.

*WACO,** McLennan Co.

DUNNAM & DUNNAM, L.L.P. (AV)
4125 West Waco Drive, P.O. Box 8418, 76714-8418
Telephone: 817-753-6437
Fax: 817-753-7434

MEMBERS OF FIRM

W. V. Dunnam (1891-1974)
W. V. Dunnam, Jr.
Vance Dunnam
Vance Dunnam, Jr.
Damon L. Reed
James R. Dunnam

ASSOCIATES

Cathy Dunnam
Alan Stucky

For full biographical listings, see the Martindale-Hubbell Law Directory

JIM MEYER & ASSOCIATES, P.C. (AV)
4734 West Waco Drive, P.O. Box 21957, 76710
Telephone: 817-772-9255
Fax: 817-776-9110

Jim Meyer

Matthew E. Johnson

For full biographical listings, see the Martindale-Hubbell Law Directory

UTAH

*PROVO,** Utah Co.

HOWARD, LEWIS & PETERSEN, P.C. (AV)
Delphi Building, 120 East 300 North Street, P.O. Box 778, 84603
Telephone: 801-373-6345
Fax: 801-377-4991

Jackson Howard
Don R. Petersen
Craig M. Snyder
John L. Valentine
D. David Lambert
Fred D. Howard
Leslie W. Slaugh

Richard W. Daynes
Phillip E. Lowry
Kenneth Parkinson

OF COUNSEL

S. Rex Lewis

LEGAL SUPPORT PERSONNEL

Mary Jackson
John O. Sump
Ray Winger

For full biographical listings, see the Martindale-Hubbell Law Directory

*SALT LAKE CITY,** Salt Lake Co.

JOEL M. ALLRED, P.C. (AV)
McIntyre Building, 68 South Main Street, 84101
Telephone: 801-531-8300
Fax: 801-363-2420

Joel M. Allred

For full biographical listings, see the Martindale-Hubbell Law Directory

Salt Lake City—Continued

DART, ADAMSON & DONOVAN (AV)

A Partnership of Professional Corporations
Suite 1330, 310 South Main, 84101
Telephone: 801-521-6383
Telefax: 801-355-2513

B. L. Dart (P.C.) Sharon A. Donovan (P.C.)
John D. Sheaffer, Jr. (P.C.)

ASSOCIATES

Eric P. Lee (P.C.) Shannon W. Clark

A list of References will be furnished upon request.

For full biographical listings, see the Martindale-Hubbell Law Directory

VERMONT

BRATTLEBORO, Windham Co.

WEBER, PERRA & WILSON, P.C. (AV)

16 Linden Street, P.O. Box 558, 05302
Telephone: 802-257-7161
Fax: 802-257-0572

E. Bruce Weber

For Complete List of Firm Personnel, See General Section

For full biographical listings, see the Martindale-Hubbell Law Directory

*MIDDLEBURY,** Addison Co.

CONLEY & FOOTE (AV)

11 South Pleasant Street, P.O. Drawer 391, 05753
Telephone: 802-388-4061
Fax: 802-388-0210

MEMBERS OF FIRM

John T. Conley (1900-1971)
Ralph A. Foote
Charity A. Downs
D. Michael Mathes
Richard P. Foote
Janet P. Shaw

For full biographical listings, see the Martindale-Hubbell Law Directory

*RUTLAND,** Rutland Co.

CARROLL, GEORGE & PRATT (AV)

64 & 66 North Main Street, P.O. Box 280, 05702-0280
Telephone: 802-775-7141
Telecopier: 802-775-6483
Woodstock, Vermont Office: The Mill - Route #4 E., P.O. Box 388, 05091.
Telephone: 802-457-1000.
Telecopier: 802-457-1874.

MEMBERS OF FIRM

Henry G. Smith (1938-1974)
James P. Carroll
Alan B. George
Robert S. Pratt
Neal C. Vreeland
Jon S. Readnour
Timothy U. Martin
Randall F. Mayhew (Resident Partner, Woodstock Office)
Richard S. Smith
Judy Godnick Barone
John J. Kennelly

ASSOCIATES

Thomas A. Zonay
Jeffrey P. White
Susan Boyle Ford (Resident, Woodstock Office)
Charles C. Humpstone

For full biographical listings, see the Martindale-Hubbell Law Directory

VIRGINIA

*ABINGDON,** Washington Co.

VINYARD AND MOISE, ATTORNEYS AT LAW, P.C. (AV)

116 East Valley Street, P.O. Box 1127, 24210-1127
Telephone: 703-628-7187

Robert Austin Vinyard Lawrence L. Moise

References: Central Fidelity Bank, Abingdon, Virginia; Dominion Bank, Abingdon, Virginia; NationsBank, N.A., Abingdon, Virginia.

For full biographical listings, see the Martindale-Hubbell Law Directory

ALEXANDRIA, (Independent City)

GANNON, COTTRELL & WARD, P.C. (AV)

411 North Washington Street, P.O. Box 1286, 22313
Telephone: 703-836-2770
FAX: 703-836-9086
Fairfax, Virginia Office: Suite 202, The Equity Building, 4085 Chain Bridge Road, Fairfax, Virginia, 20030.
Telephone: 703-591-7700.

Martin A. Gannon James Ray Cottrell
Michael A. Ward

David H. Fletcher Margaret W. Gannon
B. Scott Wash

General Counsel For: Virginia Military Institute, Research Laboratories.
Approved Attorneys For: Columbia Real Estate Title Insurance Co; Lawyers Title Insurance Co.; American Title Insurance Co.; Commonwealth Land Title Insurance Co.; Chicago Title Insurance Co.

For full biographical listings, see the Martindale-Hubbell Law Directory

GRENADIER, DAVIS & SIMPSON (AV)

(Ilona Ely Grenadier, P.C.)
649 South Washington Street, 22314
Telephone: 703-683-9000
Fax: 703-549-3087

MEMBERS OF FIRM

Ilona Ely Freedman Grenadier (P.C.)
Karen C. Davis
Stephen K. Simpson

Reid F. Trautz Benton S. Duffett, III

For full biographical listings, see the Martindale-Hubbell Law Directory

*ARLINGTON,** Arlington Co.

BEAN, KINNEY & KORMAN, A PROFESSIONAL CORPORATION (AV)

2000 North 14th Street, Suite 100, 22201
Telephone: 703-525-4000
Facsimile: 703-525-2207

James W. Korman
Jonathan C. Kinney
Frederick R. Taylor
Leo S. Fisher
James Bruce Davis
James R. Schroll
Carol Schrier-Polak
Joseph P. Corish

OF COUNSEL

L. Lee Bean (1916-1989)
Clifford A. Dougherty
Marilyn Tebor Shaw
David B. Kinney (Emeritus)
Barbara S. Kinosky

J. Carlton Howard, Jr.
Marbeth M. Spreyer
Charles E. Curran
Jennifer A. Brust
Karen L. Keyes
Eric H. D. Sahl
Dannon G. Williams

Counsel for: Nations Bank, N.A.
Reference: Nations Bank, N.A.

For full biographical listings, see the Martindale-Hubbell Law Directory

RICHARD E. CROUCH (AV)

2111 Wilson Boulevard, Suite 550, 22201
Telephone: 703-JA 8-6700

For full biographical listings, see the Martindale-Hubbell Law Directory

SCHWARTZ AND ELLIS, LTD. (AV)

6950 North Fairfax Drive, 22213
Telephone: 703-532-9300
Telex: 892320
Facsimile: 703-534-0329

Philip Schwartz

John S. Petrillo

References: First Virginia Bank; Signet Bank; First Union National Bank.

For full biographical listings, see the Martindale-Hubbell Law Directory

BETTY A. THOMPSON, LTD. (AV)

Suite 1001, Plaza East, 1800 North Kent Street, 22209
Telephone: 703-522-8100
FAX: 703-522-3770

Betty A. Thompson

Bruce M. Westbrook

References: Central Fidelity Bank of Northern Virginia; First American Bank of Virginia.

For full biographical listings, see the Martindale-Hubbell Law Directory

*FAIRFAX,** (Ind. City; Seat of Fairfax Co.)

GANNON, COTTRELL & WARD, P.C. (AV)

Suite 202, The Equity Building, 4085 Chain Bridge Road, 22030
Telephone: 703-591-7700
Alexandria, Virginia Office: 411 North Washington Street. 22313.
Telephone: 703-836-2770.

Martin A. Gannon
James Ray Cottrell
Michael A. Ward

David H. Fletcher
Margaret W. Gannon
B. Scott Wash

General Counsel For: Virginia Institute, Research Laboratories.
Approved Attorneys For: Columbia Real Estate Title Insurance Co; Lawyers Title Insurance Co.; American Title Insurance Co.; Commonwealth Land Title Insurance Co.; Chicago Title Insurance Co.

For full biographical listings, see the Martindale-Hubbell Law Directory

DENNIS M. HOTTELL & ASSOCIATES (AV)

10680 Main Street, Suite 200, 22030
Telephone: 703-352-5666
FAX: 703-352-5669

ASSOCIATE

Carolyn T. Hogans

OF COUNSEL

Garfinkle & Associates, Washington, D.C.

For full biographical listings, see the Martindale-Hubbell Law Directory

ODIN, FELDMAN & PITTLEMAN, P.C. (AV)

9302 Lee Highway, Suite 1100, 22031
Telephone: 703-218-2100
Facsimile: 703-218-2160

David E. Feldman
J. Patrick McConnell
Leslye S. Fenton
Elizabeth L. Salans

For Complete List of Firm Personnel, See General Section

For full biographical listings, see the Martindale-Hubbell Law Directory

SHOUN, SMITH & BACH, P.C. (AV)

12700 Fair Lakes Circle, Suite 300, 22033
Telephone: 703-222-3330
FAX: 703-222-3340

Robert E. Shoun
Dennis J. Smith
Beverly J. Bach
Melinda S. Norton
Carole A. Roop
Debra S. Shoun
Peter M. Fitzner
Edward J. Walinsky
Marc Astore (Not admitted in VA)
Julie A. Austin

LEGAL SUPPORT PERSONNEL

Joan W. Macleod

For full biographical listings, see the Martindale-Hubbell Law Directory

*LEESBURG,** Loudoun Co.

HANES, SEVILA, SAUNDERS & MCCAHILL, A PROFESSIONAL CORPORATION (AV)

30 North King Street, P.O. Box 678, 22075
Telephone: 703-777-5700
Metro: 471-9800; Fax: 703-771-4161

William B. Hanes
Robert E. Sevila
Richard R. Saunders, Jr.
Burke F. McCahill
Douglas L. Fleming, Jr.
Jon D. Huddleston
Craig E. White

For full biographical listings, see the Martindale-Hubbell Law Directory

LYNCHBURG, (Independent City)

JOSEPH R. JOHNSON, JR. & ASSOCIATES (AV)

9th Floor, Allied Arts Building, 725 Church Street, P.O. Box 717, 24505
Telephone: 804-845-4541
Fax: 804-845-4134

Travis Harry Witt
P. Scott De Bruin

For full biographical listings, see the Martindale-Hubbell Law Directory

*MARTINSVILLE,** (Ind. City; Seat of Henry Co.)

DOUGLAS K. FRITH & ASSOCIATES, P.C. (AV)

(Member, Commonwealth Law Group, Ltd.)
58 West Church Street, P.O. Box 591, 24114
Telephone: 703-632-7137
FAX: 703-632-3988

Douglas K. Frith

General Counsel for: Frith Construction Co., Inc.; Koger/Air Corp.; Prillaman & Pace, Inc.; Radio Station WHEE; Fuller & Gray Tire Co., Inc.; Millard's Machinery, Inc.
Representative Client: Hartford Accident & Indemnity.

For full biographical listings, see the Martindale-Hubbell Law Directory

NEWPORT NEWS, (Independent City)

HALL, FOX, ATLEE AND ROBINSON, P.C. (AV)

Crestar Bank Building, 11817 Canon Boulevard, Suite 604, 23606
Telephone: 804-873-1855
Fax: 804-873-0616

Roy B. Fox, Jr. (1920-1985)
Isabel Hall Atlee
Richard Y. Atlee
Willard M. Robinson, Jr.

LeeAnn Norris Barnes

OF COUNSEL

Lewis H. Hall, Jr. (Retired)

Representative Clients: State Farm Mutual Automobile Insurance Co.; Government Employees Insurance Company; Pennsylvania National Mutual Casualty Insurance Co.; The American Insurance Group; T.H. Mastin & Co.; Liberty Mutual Insurance Co.; Harleysville Insurance Co.; USAA; Erie Insurance Co.; Chrysler Insurance Co.

For full biographical listings, see the Martindale-Hubbell Law Directory

NORFOLK, (Independent City)

GOLDBLATT, LIPKIN & COHEN, P.C. (AV)

Suite 300, 415 St. Paul's Boulevard, P.O. Box 3505, 23514
Telephone: 804-627-6225
Telefax: 804-622-3698

Paul M. Lipkin
Robert S. Cohen
Steven M. Legum
Mary G. Commander
Beril M. Abraham
Larry W. Shelton

Approved Attorneys for: Lawyers Title Insurance Corp.

For full biographical listings, see the Martindale-Hubbell Law Directory

WEINBERG & STEIN, A PROFESSIONAL CORPORATION (AV)

1825 Dominion Tower, P.O. Box 3789, 23514-3789
Telephone: 804-627-1066
Telecopier: 804-622-6870

Jerrold G. Weinberg
Edward S. Stein
Debra Cooney Albiston
Cecelia A. Weschler
Michael H. Wojcik

Reference: Crestar Bank.

For full biographical listings, see the Martindale-Hubbell Law Directory

ROANOKE, (Independent City)

MUNDY, ROGERS & FRITH (AV)

Third Street and Woods Avenue, S.W., P.O. Box 2240, 24009
Telephone: 703-982-2900
FAX: 703-982-1362

MEMBERS OF FIRM

G. Marshall Mundy
Frank W. Rogers, III
T. Daniel Frith, III
Cheryl Watson Smith

Reference: First Union.

For full biographical listings, see the Martindale-Hubbell Law Directory

VIENNA, Fairfax Co.

JOSEPH A. CONDO & ASSOCIATES, P.C. (AV)

Suite 830, 1921 Gallows Road Tysons Corner, 22182
Telephone: 703-442-0888
Facsimile: 703-442-0294

Joseph A. Condo
Jeffrey P. Sprowls
Beth A. Bittel
Evelyn H. Sandground
Sean P. Kelly

For full biographical listings, see the Martindale-Hubbell Law Directory

VIRGINIA BEACH, (Independent City)

RIXEY AND RIXEY (AV)

Suite 100, 500 Birdneck Road, P.O. Box 1330, 23451-0330
Telephone: 804-425-1414
Fax: 804-425-1213

MEMBERS OF FIRM

John F. Rixey
J. Barbour Rixey

Representative Clients: Virginia Farm Bureau Mutual Insurance Co.; Colonial Insurance Company of California; Water Works Supply Co., Inc.; H.D. Oliver Funeral Apartments, Inc.; Norfolk Business Forms, Inc.

For full biographical listings, see the Martindale-Hubbell Law Directory

*WARRENTON,** Fauquier Co.

ROBIN C. GULICK, P.C. (AV)

70 Main Street Suite 52, P.O. Box 880, 22186
Telephone: 703-347-3022
Fax: 703-347-9711

Robin C. Gulick
William W. Carson, Jr.

General Counsel for: Jefferson Savings & Loan.
References: Fauquier National Bank; The Peoples National Bank.

For full biographical listings, see the Martindale-Hubbell Law Directory

WASHINGTON

MERCER ISLAND, King Co.

LAW OFFICES OF LOWELL K. HALVERSON (AV)

3035 Island Crest Way, 98040
Telephone: 206-236-9000

ASSOCIATE

Sarah L. Hunter

For full biographical listings, see the Martindale-Hubbell Law Directory

*SPOKANE,** Spokane Co.

MAXEY LAW OFFICES, P.S. (AV)

West 1835 Broadway, 99201
Telephone: 509-326-0338
Fax: 509-325-9919

Carl Maxey
Bevan J. Maxey
Dennis C. Cronin

Thomas J. Alexiou

For full biographical listings, see the Martindale-Hubbell Law Directory

WEST VIRGINIA

*WHEELING,** Ohio Co.

SCHRADER, RECHT, BYRD, COMPANION & GURLEY (AV)

1000 Hawley Building, 1025 Main Street, P.O. Box 6336, 26003
Telephone: 304-233-3390
Fax: 304-233-2769
Martins Ferry, Ohio Office: 205 North Fifth Street, P.O. Box 309.
Telephone: 614-633-8976.
Fax: 614-633-0400.

PARTNERS

Henry S. Schrader (Retired)
Arthur M. Recht
Ray A. Byrd
James F. Companion
Terence M. Gurley
Frank X. Duff
Teresa Rieman-Camilletti
Yolonda G. Lambert
Patrick S. Casey
Sandra M. Chapman
Daniel P. Fry (Resident, Martins Ferry, Ohio Office)
James P. Mazzone

ASSOCIATES

Sandra K. Law
D. Kevin Coleman
Denise A. Jebbia
Edythe A. Nash
Robert G. McCoid
Denise D. Klug
Thomas E. Johnston

(See Next Column)

OF COUNSEL

James A. Byrum, Jr.

General Counsel: WesBanco Bank-Elm Grove.
Representative Clients: CIGNA Property and Casualty Cos.; Columbia Gas Transmission Corp.; Commercial Union Assurance Co.; Hazlett, Burt & Watson, Inc.; Stone & Thomas Department Stores; Transamerica Commercial Finance Corp.; Wheeling-Pittsburgh Steel Corp.

For full biographical listings, see the Martindale-Hubbell Law Directory

WISCONSIN

*MADISON,** Dane Co.

BALISLE & ROBERSON, S.C. (AV)

217 South Hamilton, Suite 302, P.O. Box 870, 53701-0870
Telephone: 608-259-8702
Fax: 608-259-0807

Linda S. Balisle
Linda Roberson
Rachel L. L. Caplan

LEGAL SUPPORT PERSONNEL

Diana K. Fleming

For full biographical listings, see the Martindale-Hubbell Law Directory

*MILWAUKEE,** Milwaukee Co.

MARGOLIS & CASSIDY (AV)

324 East Wisconsin Avenue Suite 700, 53202-4304
Telephone: 414-272-5333
Fax: 414-271-8506

Scott M. Cassidy (1933-1989)
Marvin A. Margolis
F. Brian McElligott
Julie A. O'Halloran

Reference: First Bank (N.A.)

PODELL & PODELL (AV)

Suite 204, 250 West Coventry Court, 53217
Telephone: 414-228-5800
Fax: 414-228-5815

MEMBERS OF FIRM

James J. Podell
Peggy L. Podell
Nina M. Vitek
Carlton D. Stansbury

For full biographical listings, see the Martindale-Hubbell Law Directory

RICHARD J. PODELL & ASSOCIATES, S.C. (AV)

Suite 2800, 100 East Wisconsin Avenue, 53202
Telephone: 414-224-6060
Fax: 414-224-6067

Richard J. Podell
Linda Swagger Maris
Sheryl A. Haarmann Cahn
Barbara J. Stippich
Todd M. Podell

For full biographical listings, see the Martindale-Hubbell Law Directory

QUARLES & BRADY (AV)

411 East Wisconsin Avenue, 53202-4497
Telephone: 414-277-5000
Cable Address: "Lawdock"
Fax: 414-271-3552.
TWX: 910-262-3426
Madison, Wisconsin Office: Firstar Plaza, One South Pinckney Street, P.O. Box 2113.
Telephone: 608-251-5000.
Fax: 608-251-9166.
West Palm Beach, Florida Office: 222 Lakeview Avenue, 4th Floor.
Telephone: 407-653-5000.
Fax: 407-653-5333.
Naples, Florida Office: Barnett Center, 4501 Tamiami Trail North.
Telephone: 813-262-5959.
Fax: 813-434-4999.
Phoenix, Arizona Office: One Camelback Building, One East Camelback Road, Suite 400.
Telephone: 602-230-5500.
Fax: 602-230-5598.

MEMBERS OF FIRM
(ALPHABETICALLY BY YEAR OF ADMISSION TO BAR)

Jackson M. Bruce, Jr.
David E. Jarvis
Patricia K. McDowell
Paul J. Tilleman

(See Next Column)

QUARLES & BRADY, *Milwaukee—Continued*

ASSOCIATES

Sandra L. Tarver (Resident, Madison Office) | Mark A. Sanders

For Complete List of Firm Personnel, See General Section

For full biographical listings, see the Martindale-Hubbell Law Directory

WYOMING

*CASPER,** Natrona Co.

BROWN & DREW (AV)

Casper Business Center, Suite 800, 123 West First Street, 82601-2486
Telephone: 307-234-1000
800-877-6755
Telefax: 307-265-8025

MEMBERS OF FIRM

John A. Warnick | Russell M. Blood
J. Kenneth Barbe

ASSOCIATES

Carol Warnick | P. Jaye Rippley

For Complete List of Firm Personnel, See General Section

For full biographical listings, see the Martindale-Hubbell Law Directory

VIRGIN ISLANDS

*CHARLOTTE AMALIE, ST. THOMAS,** St. Thomas

BORNN BORNN HANDY

No. 8 Norre Gade, P.O. Box 1500, 00804
Telephone: 809-774-1400
Fax: 809-774-9607

SENIOR PARTNER
Edith L. Bornn
PARTNER
Veronica J. Handy
ASSOCIATE
Tregenza A. Roach

References: Bank of Nova Scotia; Banco Popular de P.R., St. Thomas, U.S. Virgin Islands.

For Complete List of Firm Personnel, See General Section

For full biographical listings, see the Martindale-Hubbell Law Directory

CANADA
BRITISH COLUMBIA

*VANCOUVER,** Vancouver Co.

CLARK, WILSON (AV)

Suite 800 - 885 West Georgia Street, V6C 3H1
Telephone: 604-687-5700
Telecopier: 604-687-6314
Associated with: Eiko General Law Office, Osaka, Japan.
Telephone: (06) 365-1251.
Fax: (06) 365-1252.

MEMBERS OF FIRM

David W. Buchanan, Q.C. | Diane M. E. Bell
Richard P. Hamilton | A. Anita Vergis

Representative Clients: Hongkong Bank of Canada; Shell Canada Limited.
Reference: Hongkong Bank of Canada.

For full biographical listings, see the Martindale-Hubbell Law Directory

RUSSELL & DUMOULIN (AV)

2100-1075 West Georgia Street, V6E 3G2
Telephone: 604-631-3131
Fax: 604-631-3232
A Member of the national association of Borden DuMoulin Howard Gervais, comprising Russell & DuMoulin, Vancouver, British Columbia; Howard Mackie, Calgary, Alberta; Borden & Elliot, Toronto, Ontario; Mackenzie Gervais, Montreal, Quebec and Borden DuMoulin Howard Gervais, London, England.

(See Next Column)

Strategic Alliance with Perkins Coie with offices in Seattle, Spokane and Bellevue, Washington; Portland, Oregon; Anchorage, Alaska; Los Angeles, California; Washington, D.C.; Hong Kong and Taipei, Taiwan. Represented in Hong Kong by Vincent T.K. Cheung, Yap & Co.

MEMBERS OF FIRM

Bryce A. Dyer | Lauri Ann Fenlon

Representative Clients: Alcan Smelters & Chemicals Ltd.; The Bank of Nova Scotia; Canada Trust Co.; The Canada Life Assurance Co.; Forest Industrial Relations Ltd.; Honda Canada Inc.; IBM Canada Ltd.; Macmillan Bloedel Ltd.; Nissho Iwai Canada Ltd.; The Toronto-Dominion Bank.

For Complete List of Firm Personnel, See General Section

For full biographical listings, see the Martindale-Hubbell Law Directory

CANADA
NEW BRUNSWICK

*SAINT JOHN,** Saint John Co.

CLARK, DRUMMIE & COMPANY (AV)

40 Wellington Row, P.O. Box 6850 Station "A", E2L 4S3
Telephone: 506-633-3800
Telecopier (Automatic): 506-633-3811

MEMBER OF FIRM
John C. Warner

Reference: Royal Bank of Canada.

For Complete List of Firm Personnel, See General Section

For full biographical listings, see the Martindale-Hubbell Law Directory

CANADA
NOVA SCOTIA

*HALIFAX,** Halifax Co.

MCINNES COOPER & ROBERTSON (AV)

1601 Lower Water Street, P.O. Box 730, B3J 2V1
Telephone: 902-425-6500
Fax: 902-425-6350
St. John's, Newfoundland Office: Suite 602, Scotia Centre, 235 Water Street, P.O. Box 547. A1C, 5K8.
Telephone: 709-726-9500.
Fax: 709-726-9550.

David A. Graves | Deborah K. Smith

Attorneys for: Bank of Nova Scotia; Imperial Oil, Limited; Frank B. Hall & Co., Inc. (New York); American Steamship Owners Protection & Indemnity Association, Inc.; Coca-Cola, Ltd.; Scott Worldwide Inc.; Hong Kong Bank of Canada.

For Complete List of Firm Personnel, See General Section

For full biographical listings, see the Martindale-Hubbell Law Directory

CANADA
ONTARIO

KITCHENER, Regional Munic. of Waterloo

GIFFEN, LEE, WAGNER, MORLEY & GARBUTT (AV)

50 Queen Street North, P.O. Box 2396, N2H 6M3
Telephone: 519-578-4150
Fax: 519-578-8740

MEMBERS OF FIRM

Jeffrey J. Mansfield (1955-1991) | J. Scott Morley
J. Peter Giffen, Q.C. | Brian R. Wagner
Bruce L. Lee | Philip A. Garbutt

ASSOCIATES

Edward J. Vanderkloet | Daniel J. Fife
Keith C. Masterman | Jeffrey W. Boich

For full biographical listings, see the Martindale-Hubbell Law Directory

*TORONTO,** Regional Munic. of York

Borden & Elliot (AV)

Barristers & Solicitors
Scotia Plaza, 40 King Street West, M5H 3Y4
Telephone: 416-367-6000
Telecopier: 416-367-6749
Internet: @ borden.com
A Member of the national association of Borden DuMoulin Howard Gervais, comprising Borden & Elliot in Toronto, Ontario, Russell & DuMoulin in Vancouver, British Columbia, Howard, Mackie in Calgary, Alberta and Mackenzie Gervais in Montréal, Québec. Borden DuMoulin Howard Gervais also operates an office in London, England.

MEMBER AND ASSOCIATES

W. Douglas R. Beamish

For Complete List of Firm Personnel, See General Section

For full biographical listings, see the Martindale-Hubbell Law Directory

CANADA
SASKATCHEWAN

*SASKATOON,** Saskatoon Jud. Centre

McKercher, McKercher & Whitmore (AV)

374 Third Avenue, South, S7K 1M5
Telephone: 306-653-2000
Fax: 306-244-7335
Regina, Saskatchewan Office: 1000 - 1783 Hamilton Street.
Telephone: 306-352-7661.
Fax: 306-781-7113.

MEMBERS OF FIRM

Brian W. Wilkinson C.J. Glazer

For Complete List of Firm Personnel, See General Section

For full biographical listings, see the Martindale-Hubbell Law Directory

ALABAMA

ALBERTVILLE, Marshall Co.

GULLAHORN & HARE, P.C. (AV)

310 West Main Street, P.O. Box 1669, 35950
Telephone: 205-878-1891
FAX: 205-878-1965

Charles R. Hare, Jr.
John C. Gullahorn

Representative Clients: First Bank of Boaz; The Home Bank; Bank of Albertville; Peoples Independent Bank of Boaz; AmSouth Bank; Compass Bank of the South; Albertville Industrial Development Board; Boaz Industrial Development Board; Marshall-Dekalb Electric Cooperative; Olympia Construction, Inc.

For full biographical listings, see the Martindale-Hubbell Law Directory

ANDALUSIA,* Covington Co.

W. SIDNEY FULLER (AV)

28 South Court Square, P.O. Drawer 1637, 36420
Telephone: 334-222-4196
Fax: 334-222-4197

LEGAL SUPPORT PERSONNEL

Lenora O'Neal (Legal Assistant)

Representative Clients: City of Andalusia; Covington County Board of Education; Covington County Bank.

For full biographical listings, see the Martindale-Hubbell Law Directory

POWELL, PEEK & WEAVER (AV)

102 North Cotton Street, P.O. Drawer 969, 36420
Telephone: 334-222-4103
Facsimile: 334-222-4105

MEMBERS OF FIRM

Abner R. Powell (1875-1940)
Abner R. Powell, Jr. (1916-1987)
Abner R. Powell, III
John M. Peek
Gary L. Weaver

ASSOCIATES

Abner Riley Powell, IV

Representative Clients: Southern Guaranty Co.; State Farm Insurance Group; U.S.F. & G. Co.; CNA Insurance; ALFA, Auto Owners Insurance Co.; Georgia Farm Bureau.

For full biographical listings, see the Martindale-Hubbell Law Directory

ANNISTON,* Calhoun Co.

BURNHAM, KLINEFELTER, HALSEY, JONES & CATER, P.C. (AV)

South Trust Bank Building, Suite 401, P.O. Box 1618, 36202
Telephone: 205-237-8515
Fax: 205-236-5150

Herbert D. Jones, Jr. (1945-1988)
H. R. Burnham
J. L. Klinefelter
William S. Halsey
Richard H. Cater
Patrick S. Burnham
Thomas M. Sowa
J. Thomas Corbett
C. David Stubbs
Cynthia M. Calhoun
Polly D. Enger (Not admitted in AL)

Representative Clients: Alfa Insurance Cos.; American International Insurance Group; Alabama Municipal Insurance Corp.; Fireman's Fund; SouthTrust Bank of Calhoun County, N.A.; America's First Credit Union; First South Production Credit; Calhoun County, Anniston City and City of Jacksonville Boards of Education; Calhoun County Commission; Coca-Cola Enterprises, Inc.

For full biographical listings, see the Martindale-Hubbell Law Directory

MERRILL, PORCH, DILLON & FITE, P.A. (AV)

Formerly Knox, Jones, Woolf & Merrill
5th Floor SouthTrust Bank, P.O. Box 580, 36202
Telephone: 205-237-2871
FAX: 205-237-3022

Robert C. Dillon
Arthur F. Fite, III
George A. Monk
Brenda S. Stedham
Carl E. Underwood, III

OF COUNSEL

Walter J. Merrill
Ralph D. Porch

General Counsel for: Farmers & Merchants Bank; Northeast Alabama Regional Medical Center; City of Anniston.
Assistant Division Counsel: Norfolk Southern Corp.
Attorneys for: Alabama Power Co.; Browning Ferris Industries of Alabama, Inc.; Nationwide Mutual Insurance Co.; Maryland Casualty Co.; Lawyers Title Insurance Corp.; Monsanto Co.

For full biographical listings, see the Martindale-Hubbell Law Directory

ASHLAND,* Clay Co. — (Refer to Talladega)

ATHENS,* Limestone Co.

PATTON, LATHAM, LEGGE & COLE (AV)

Professional Building, 315 West Market Street, P.O. Box 470, 35611
Telephone: 205-232-2010
Fax: 205-230-0610

MEMBERS OF FIRM

Roy B. Patton (1885-1954)
David U. Patton (Retired)
Byrd R. Latham
Winston V. Legge, Jr.
P. Michael Cole

Local Counsel for: Auto-Owners Insurance Co.; Avis; Blue Cross and Blue Shield of Alabama; CIGNA Insurance Cos.; Gold Kist, Inc.; State Farm Life Insurance Co.; State Farm Mutual Automobile Insurance Co.; Travelers Insurance Co.; United States Fidelity and Guaranty Co.; Wausau Insurance Company.

For full biographical listings, see the Martindale-Hubbell Law Directory

WOODROOF & WOODROOF (AV)

McDaniel Building, 117 West Washington Street, P.O. Box 1149, 35611
Telephone: 205-232-0120
Fax: 205-232-4109

MEMBERS OF FIRM

Thomas S. Woodroof (1900-1981)
James W. Woodroof (1924-1980)
T. Schram Woodroof
James W. Woodroof, IV

Representative Clients: Central Bank of Alabama, N.A.; C.S.X Transportation; U. S. Fidelity & Guaranty Co.; Lawyers Title Insurance Corporation of Richmond, Virginia; South Central Bell Telephone Co.

For full biographical listings, see the Martindale-Hubbell Law Directory

BESSEMER, Jefferson Co. — (Refer to Birmingham)

BIRMINGHAM,* Jefferson Co.

BAINBRIDGE, MIMS & ROGERS (AV)

The Luckie Building, Suite 415, 600 Luckie Drive, P.O. Box 530886, 35253
Telephone: 205-879-1100
Fax: 205-879-4300

MEMBERS OF FIRM

Frank Bainbridge (1895-1980)
Walter L. Mims (1910-1993)
Frank M. Bainbridge
Bruce F. Rogers

For full biographical listings, see the Martindale-Hubbell Law Directory

BALCH & BINGHAM (AV)

1710 Sixth Avenue North, P.O. Box 306, 35201
Telephone: 205-251-8100
Facsimile: 205-226-8798
Other Birmingham, Alabama Office: 1901 Sixth Avenue North, 35203.
Telephone: 205-251-8100.
Facsimile: 205-226-8799.
Montgomery, Alabama Office: The Winter Building, 2 Dexter Avenue, 36101.
Telephone: 205-834-6500.
Facsimile: 205-269-3115.
Huntsville, Alabama Office: Suite 810, 200 West Court Square, 35801.
Telephone: 205-551-0171.
Facsimile: 205-551-0174.
Washington, D.C. Office: Suite 800, 1101 Connecticut Avenue, N.W., 20036.
Telephone: 202-296-0387.
Facsimile: 202-452-8180.

William Logan Martin (1883-1959)
Schuyler A. Baker (1915-1990)

COUNSEL

S. Eason Balch
John Bingham
Joseph M. Farley
M. Roland Nachman, Jr. (Resident, Montgomery Office)
Edward M. Rogers, Jr. (Resident, Washington, D.C. Office)
John David Snodgrass (Resident, Huntsville Office)

MEMBERS OF FIRM

Maury D. Smith (Resident, Montgomery Office)
William J. Ward
Harold A. Bowron, Jr.
Carey J. Chitwood
A. Key Foster, Jr.
John S. Bowman (Resident, Montgomery Office)
Thomas W. Thagard, Jr. (Resident, Montgomery Office)
Charles M. Crook (Resident, Montgomery Office)
Sterling G. Culpepper, Jr. (Resident, Montgomery Office)
Edward S. Allen
Warren H. Goodwyn (Resident, Montgomery Office)
James O. Spencer, Jr.
H. Hampton Boles
Michael L. Edwards

(See Next Column)

BALCH & BINGHAM, *Birmingham—Continued*

MEMBERS OF FIRM (Continued)

Marshall Timberlake
Walter M. Beale, Jr.
Rodney O. Mundy
James F. Hughey, Jr.
S. Eason Balch, Jr.
John P. Scott, Jr.
S. Allen Baker, Jr.
J. Foster Clark
Stanley M. Brock
Randolph H. Lanier
John Richard Carrigan
David R. Boyd (Resident, Montgomery Office)
William E. Shanks, Jr.
S. Revelle Gwyn (Resident, Huntsville Office)
William H. Satterfield
Steven G. McKinney
Steven F. Casey
Malcolm N. Carmichael (Resident, Montgomery Office)
Richard L. Pearson
James A. Bradford
Dan H. McCrary
William P. Cobb, II (Resident, Montgomery Office)
Alan T. Rogers
James A. Byram, Jr. (Resident, Montgomery Office)
William S. Wright
Susan B. Bevill
John J. Coleman, III
John F. Mandt
M. Stanford Blanton
T. Kurt Miller
J. Thomas Francis, Jr.
Timothy J. Tracy
Clark R. Hammond
W. Joseph McCorkle, Jr. (Resident, Montgomery Office)
Karl R. Moor (Resident, Washington, D.C. Office)
Patrick J. McCormick, III (Resident, Washington, D.C. Office)
Will Hill Tankersley, Jr.
Suzanne Ashe
Mark Adam Crosswhite
Leonard Charles Tillman
Dorman Walker (Resident, Montgomery Office)
Alex B. Leath, III
Cavender Crosby Kimble

SENIOR ATTORNEYS

T. Dwight Sloan
Virginia S. Boliek

ASSOCIATES

Daniel M. Wilson (Resident, Huntsville Office)
Julia S. McIntyre
Lois Smith Woodward (Resident, Montgomery Office)
David B. Champlin
Michael D. Freeman
Patricia Anne Hamilton (Resident, Montgomery Office)
James H. Hancock, Jr.
Robin G. Laurie (Resident, Montgomery Office)
Jesse Stringer Vogtle, Jr.
Donald R. Jones, Jr. (Resident, Montgomery Office)
John S. Bowman, Jr. (Resident, Montgomery Office)
Gregory S. Curran
John Douglas Buchanan
Felton W. Smith
Glenn G. Waddell
Suzanne Alldredge
Leslie M. Allen (Resident, Montgomery Office)
James Ernest Bridges, III (Resident, Montgomery Office)
John Russell Campbell (Not admitted in AL)
Gregory Carl Cook
Lyle David Larson
Colin H. Luke
Phillip Anthony Nichols
Debra Carter White
R. Bruce Barze, Jr.
David B. Block
Matthew W. Bowden
Leigh Anne Hodge
Cynthia Anne Holland (Resident, Montgomery Office)
Larry Stephen Logsdon
Randall D. McClanahan
C. Grady Moore III
Lisa Johnson Sharp
Terri E. Wilson
Ed R. Haden
Lorrie Lizak
Teresa G. Minor
G. Scott Morris
Leeann Morgan Pounds

OF COUNSEL

Harold Williams

Counsel for: Alabama Power Co.; Blue Cross and Blue Shield of Alabama; The Boeing Company; Brasfield & Gorrie, Inc.; Compass Bancshares, Inc.; Harbert Corp.; Kimberly-Clark Corp.; Southern Company Services, Inc.; Southern Research Institute; Vesta Insurance Group, Inc.

For full biographical listings, see the Martindale-Hubbell Law Directory

BELL AND ODOM (AV)

625 South 38th Street, P.O. Box 11244, 35202-1244
Telephone: 205-322-1225
Fax: 205-664-8695
Pelham, Alabama Office: 211-B Yeager Parkway.
Telephone: 205-664-8691.
Fax: 205-664-8695.
Sylacauga, Alabama Office: 223 North Norton Avenue.
Telephone: 205-245-7486.
Fax: 205-245-7487.

James J. Odom, Jr.

For full biographical listings, see the Martindale-Hubbell Law Directory

BERKOWITZ, LEFKOVITS, ISOM & KUSHNER, A PROFESSIONAL CORPORATION (AV)

1600 SouthTrust Tower, 420 North Twentieth Street, 35203
Telephone: 205-328-0480
Telecopier: 205-322-8007

(See Next Column)

A. Berkowitz (1907-1985)
Arnold K. Lefkovits
Chervis Isom
Harold B. Kushner
Lee H. Zell
B. G. Minisman, Jr.
Henry I. Frohsin
David A. Larsen
Anne W. Mitchell
William R. Sylvester
Susan S. Wagner
D. J. Simonetti
David L. Silverstein
W. Clark Goodwin
Barry S. Marks
Steven B. Corenblum
Patricia Clotfelter
Ronald A. Levitt
Frank S. James III
Marvin T. Griff
Wesley C. Redmond
Denise W. Killebrew
Thomas O. Kolb

J. Fred Kingren
Lisa Wright Borden
Andrew J. Potts
Vincent R. Ledlow
Michael R. Silberman
Richard A. Pizitz, Jr.
Walton E. Williams III
Lisa B. Singer
Robin L. Tucker

OF COUNSEL

Kelly D. Reese

Representative Clients: AlaTenn Resources, Inc.; AlaTenn Natural Gas Co.; B.A.S.S., Inc.; Hanna Steel Co., Inc.; Liberty Trouser Co., Inc.; McDonald's Corp.; Parisian, Inc.; Southern Pipe & Supply Co., Inc.

For full biographical listings, see the Martindale-Hubbell Law Directory

BISHOP, COLVIN, JOHNSON & KENT (AV)

317-20th Street, North, P.O. Box 370404, 35237
Telephone: 205-251-2881
Fax: 205-254-3987

MEMBERS OF FIRM

Maurice F. Bishop (1913-1982)
Gerald D. Colvin, Jr.
Carl E. Johnson, Jr.
Burgin H. Kent

Representative Clients: Miller Transporters, Inc.; Osborne Carriers, Inc.; Bowman International Domestic Transportation, Inc.; C. E. Sawyer's Industrial Sheet Metal Fabricators, Inc.; The City of Trussville, Alabama; Utilities Board of the City of Trussville, Alabama; Jefferson County Board of Education; University of Montevallo; Milan Express, Inc.
Reference: AmSouth Bank, N.A.

For full biographical listings, see the Martindale-Hubbell Law Directory

BRADLEY, ARANT, ROSE & WHITE (AV)

1400 Park Place Tower, 2001 Park Place, 35203
Telephone: 205-521-8000
Telex: 494-1324
Facsimile: 205-251-8611, 251-8665, 252-0264
Facsimile (Southtrust Office): 205-251-9915
Huntsville, Alabama Office: 200 Clinton Avenue West, Suite 900.
Telephone: 205-517-5100.
Facsimile: 205-533-5069.

MEMBERS OF FIRM

Douglas Arant (1897-1987)
Wm. Alfred Rose (1900-1981)
Ellene Winn (1911-1986)
William W. Johnson, Jr. (1943-1984)
Mary Louise Ahearn (1934-1985)
Bernard A. Monaghan (1916-1987)
Wm. Allen Smyly (1954-1993)
Lee C. Bradley, Jr.
John James Coleman, Jr.
Edward M. Selfe
Robert R. Reid, Jr.
John N. Wrinkle
Thomas Neely Carruthers, Jr.
J. Robert Fleenor
John H. Morrow
Hobart A. McWhorter, Jr.
Macbeth Wagnon, Jr.
Robert Sellers Smith (Resident, Huntsville Office)
Thad Gladden Long
John P. Adams
A. H. Gaede, Jr.
William L. Hinds, Jr.
Gary C. Huckaby (Resident, Huntsville Office)
James W. Gewin
Charles Larimore Whitaker
John G. Harrell
James Patrick Alexander
Robert G. Johnson
Robert C. Walthall
Brittin Turner Coleman
E. Cutter Hughes, Jr. (Resident, Huntsville Office)
Andrew Robert Greene
P. Nicholas Greenwood
James E. Rotch
Patrick H. Graves, Jr. (Resident, Huntsville Office)
Laurence Duncan Vinson, Jr.
E. Mabry Rogers
John P. Whittington
Walter H. Monroe, III
Alan K. Zeigler
Andrew J. Noble, III
Walter J. Sears, III
Linda A. Friedman
Robert K. Spotswood
Joseph B. Mays, Jr.
W. Braxton Schell, Jr.
John K. Molen
Charles A. J. Beavers, Jr.
Scott M. Phelps
Lant B. Davis
Carleta Roberts Hawley
James Walker May
M. Williams Goodwyn, Jr.
Bobby C. Underwood
Norman Jetmundsen, Jr.
Joseph S. Bird, III
John B. Grenier
J. David Dresher
John D. Watson, III
Jay D. St. Clair
Joan Crowder Ragsdale
Patricia Trott Mandt
Ralph Howard Yeilding
Scott E. Ludwig (Resident, Huntsville Office)
G. Edward Cassady, III
Michael R. Pennington
Michael D. McKibben
David Glenn Hymer

(See Next Column)

BRADLEY, ARANT, ROSE & WHITE—*Continued*

MEMBERS OF FIRM (Continued)

John William Hargrove
G. Rick Hall (Resident, Huntsville Office)
John E. Hagefstration, Jr.
Stuart Joseph Frentz
Paul S. Ware
Virginia Calvert Patterson
Sid J. Trant
Stewart M. Cox
Axel Bolvig III

COUNSEL

Wm. Bew White, Jr.
J. Reese Murray
Romaine S. Scott, Jr.
Stanley D. Bynum

ASSOCIATES

John J. Park, Jr.
Forrest K. Covington
Philip J. Carroll III
James S. Christie, Jr.
Sherri Tucker Freeman
Stephen K. Greene
J. David Pugh
Kenneth T. Wyatt
Denson Nauls Franklin III
John E. Goodman
Frank C. Galloway, III
T. Michael Brown
J. Paul Compton, Jr.
Deane K. Corliss
Michael S. Denniston
L. Susan Doss
George Bryan Harris
Warne S. Heath (Resident, Huntsville Office)
Amy McNeer Tucker
Gregory G. Smith
Anne R. Yuengert
Susan Donovan Josey
J. Patrick Darby
Kevin J. Henderson
H. Knox McMillan (Resident, Huntsville Office)
Frank M. Caprio (Resident, Huntsville Office)
Christopher L. Howard
Paul B. Seeley (Resident, Huntsville Office)
Denise Avery Dodson
Matthew H. Lembke
Paige Maddox Davis
Richard H. Monk III
Hall B, Bryant III
Amy K. Myers
Paul D. Gilbert
Arnold W. Umbach, III
K. Wood Herren
John W. Smith T
Jennifer Byers McLeod
James W. Davis
James Tassin (Resident, Huntsville Office)
James F. Archibald, III
Jay R. Bender
Justin T. McDonald
Carolyn Reed Douglas (Resident, Huntsville Office)
Douglas E. Eckert
Kenneth M. Perry
Richard L. Sharff, Jr.

Counsel for: SouthTrust Bank of Alabama, National Association; Energen, Corporation; Blount, Inc.; Torchmark Corp.; Russell Corp.; Coca-Cola Bottling Company United, Inc.; Ford Motor Co.; Walter Industries, Inc.; The Birmingham Post Co. (Post-Herald); The New York Times Co.

For full biographical listings, see the Martindale-Hubbell Law Directory

BURR & FORMAN (AV)

3000 SouthTrust Tower, 420 North 20th Street, 35203
Telephone: 205-251-3000
Telecopier: 205-458-5100
Huntsville, Alabama Office: Suite 204, Regency Center, 400 Meridian Street.
Telephone: 205-551-0010.

Borden H. Burr (1876-1952)
James R. Forman (1880-1942)
Andrew J. Thomas (1897-1984)
Mark L. Taliaferro (1906-1981)

MEMBERS OF FIRM

C. V. Stelzenmuller
Robert G. Tate
J. Fred Powell
L. Tennent Lee, III (Resident, Huntsville, Alabama Office)
Samuel W. Oliver, Jr.
Paul O. Woodall
J. Fredric Ingram
Louis H. Anders, Jr.
Robert B. Rubin
William C. Knight, Jr.
Joseph G. Stewart
John D. Clements
John F. DeBuys, Jr.
Mark Taliaferro, Jr.
John W. Evans (Resident, Huntsville, Alabama Office)
James Ross Forman, III
D. Frank Davis
A. Brand Walton
John T. Mooresmith
William F. Murray, Jr.
Jack P. Stephenson, Jr.
Eric L. Carlton
S. Dagnal Rowe (Resident, Huntsville, Alabama Office)
James J. Robinson
Joseph W. Letzer
T. Thomas Cottingham, III
J. Patrick Logan
George M. Taylor, III
Gary M. London
Bruce A. Rawls
F. A. Flowers, III
Michael L. Hall
Michael L. Lucas
Dwight L. Mixson, Jr.
J. Hunter Phillips, III
David D. Dowd, III
Carol H. Stewart
Robert H. Rutherford, Jr.
Gene T. Price
Henry Graham Beene
Deborah P. Fisher
Richard A. Freese
Gail Livingston Mills
John C. Morrow
Victor L. Hayslip
W. Benjamin Johnson
E. Clayton Lowe, Jr.
Robert S. W. Given
Marvin Glenn Perry, Jr.
Mark McCarroll Lawson
Dent M. Morton
Sue Ann Willis

OF COUNSEL

James R. Forman, Jr.
William K. Murray
Samuel H. Burr
A. Jackson Noble, Jr.

(See Next Column)

ASSOCIATES

Jeffrey T. Baker
Paul P. Bolus
David A. Elliott
Gary W. Farris
William S. Hereford
Jill Verdeyen Deer
Nancy L. Carter (Resident, Huntsville, Alabama Office)
Harri J. Haikala
Frank Hampton McFadden, Jr.
Christopher W. Weller
Jennifer M. Busby
James A. Taylor, Jr.
Warren C. Matthews
Gerald P. Gillespy
Timothy M. Lupinacci
Edwin O. Rogers
Alan P. Judge (Resident, Huntsville, Alabama Office)
Peter A. Grammas
Patricia Powell Burke
Darin W. Collier
Eric Franz
Gregory F. Harley
Jeffrey S. Miller
Howard E. Bogard
William K. Holbrook
Pamela Morse Arenberg
D. Christopher Carson
Gary Lane Howard
Richard C. Keller
Courtnay L. Stallings

LEGAL SUPPORT PERSONNEL

J. Michael Tarpley (Director of Administration)

For full biographical listings, see the Martindale-Hubbell Law Directory

CABANISS, JOHNSTON, GARDNER, DUMAS & O'NEAL (AV)

Park Place Tower, 2001 Park Place North, Suite 700, P.O. Box 830612, 35283-0612
Telephone: 205-252-8800
Telecopier: 205-716-5389
Mobile, Alabama Office: 700 AmSouth Center, P.O. Box 2906.
Telephone: 205-433-6961.
Telecopier: 205-433-1060.

Edward H. Cabaniss (1857-1936)
Forney Johnston (1879-1965)
Lucien D. Gardner, Jr. (1903-1988)
M. Camper O'Neal (1907-1989)

MEMBERS OF FIRM

William F. Gardner
Crawford S. McGivaren, Jr.
Sydney F. Frazier, Jr.
Benjamen T. Rowe (Resident at Mobile Office)
William A. Robinson
Patrick H. Sims (Resident at Mobile Office)
Donald J. Stewart (Resident at Mobile Office)
Roy J. Crawford
William K. Thomas
F. Gerald Burnett
David S. Dunkle
David L. Kane (Resident at Mobile Office)
R. Boyd Miller (Mobile Office)
R. Carlton Smyly
Steve A. Tucker
R. Taylor Abbot, Jr.

COUNSEL

L. Murray Alley

OF COUNSEL

Joseph F. Johnston
E. T. Brown, Jr.

ASSOCIATES

Herbert H. West, Jr.
Cecil H. Macoy, Jr.
Richard Eldon Davis
Melanie Merkle Bass
Cathryn Anne Berryman
John M. Graham
Samuel D. Payne
Douglas B. Kauffman
Gary W. Fillingim

Counsel for: Alabaster Industries, Inc.; Schuler Industries, Inc.; Carraway Methodist Hospitals of Alabama; Doster Construction Co., Inc.; Liberty Mutual Insurance Co.; John Alden Life Insurance Co.; MacMillan Bloedel Inc.; Norfolk Southern Corp.; O'Neal Steel, Inc.

For full biographical listings, see the Martindale-Hubbell Law Directory

COGGIN & ASSOCIATES (AV)

Suite 710 One Independence Plaza, 35209
Telephone: 205-871-9065
Telecopier: 205-871-9069

John C. Coggin, III

References: AmSouth Bank; First Commercial Bank; SouthTrust Bank.

For full biographical listings, see the Martindale-Hubbell Law Directory

COOPER, MITCH, CRAWFORD, KUYKENDALL & WHATLEY (AV)

1100 Financial Center, 505 20th Street North, 35203-2605
Telephone: 205-328-9576
Telecopier: 205-328-9669

MEMBERS OF FIRM

Jerome A. Cooper
William E. Mitch
Thomas N. Crawford, Jr.
Frederick T. Kuykendall, III
Joe R. Whatley, Jr.
John D. Saxon
Glen M. Connor
Patricia Guthrie Fraley
Jay Smith (On Leave of Absence)

ASSOCIATES

Candis A. McGowan
Andrew C. Allen
William Z. Cullen
Samuel H. Heldman
Hilary E. Ball-Walker
Patrick F. Clark
G. Patterson Keahey
Maureen Kane Berg
Gerald B. Taylor, Jr.
Rebecca Higgins Hunt
Marcel L. Debruge
Peter H. Burke

(See Next Column)

COOPER, MITCH, CRAWFORD, KUYKENDALL & WHATLEY, *Birmingham—Continued*

Counsel for: United Steelworkers of America, AFL-CIO; United Mine Workers of America, District 20; Birmingham Plumbers & Steamfitters Local Union No. 91 Pension Fund.
Reference: AMSouth Bank of Birmingham.

For full biographical listings, see the Martindale-Hubbell Law Directory

CORLEY, MONCUS & WARD, P.C. (AV)

Suite 650, 2100 SouthBridge Parkway, 35209
Telephone: 205-879-5959
Telecopier: 205-879-5859

Dale Corley (1942-1989)
Claude McCain Moncus
James S. Ward
Gene W. Gray, Jr.
W. Lewis Garrison, Jr.
Ezra B. Perry, Jr.
Kathryn H. Sumrall

F. Page Gamble
Walter Gladstone Chavers

For full biographical listings, see the Martindale-Hubbell Law Directory

DOMINICK, FLETCHER, YEILDING, WOOD & LLOYD, P.A. (AV)

2121 Highland Avenue, 35205
Telephone: 205-939-0033

Frank Dominick
Walter Fletcher
Manly Yeilding
J. Fred Wood, Jr.
Harold L. Ferguson, Jr.
C. Fred Daniels
A. Lee Martin, Jr.
Susan Dominick Doughton
J. Terrell McElheny
Sammye Oden Kok
Brian T. Williams
C. Clark Collier
B. Boozer Downs, Jr.
Mary P. Thornton
J. Mitchell Frost, Jr.

Judy Bateman Shepura
Victoria VanValkenburgh Norris
John W. Dodson
Judy P. Hamer

OF COUNSEL

Lee B. Lloyd

Counsel for: Citizens Federal Savings Bank; St. Vincent's Hospital; Birmingham-Southern College; Castle Mortgage Corporation; Methodist Homes for the Aging; American Home Assurance Co.; New Hampshire Insurance Group; The Cigna Cos.; Amerisure Companies.

For full biographical listings, see the Martindale-Hubbell Law Directory

GORDON, SILBERMAN, WIGGINS & CHILDS, A PROFESSIONAL CORPORATION (AV)

1400 SouthTrust Tower, 420 North 20th Street, 35203
Telephone: 205-328-0640
Telecopier: 205-254-1500

Louis Silberman (1889-1976)
Robert S. Gordon (1914-1983)
Wilbur G. Silberman
Bruce L. Gordon
Robert L. Wiggins, Jr.
Robert F. Childs, Jr.
Augustus J. Beck, Jr.
Harvey L. Wachsman
Ray D. Gibbons
C. Michael Quinn
Dennis George Pantazis

Terrill W. Sanders
James Mendelsohn
Richard J. Ebbinghouse
Ann K. Norton
Paul H. Webb
Mark P. Williams
Samuel Fisher
Timothy C. Gann
Naomi Hilton Archer
Timothy D. Davis
Joseph H. Calvin, III
Linda J. Peacock
Ann C. Robertson
Elizabeth Evans Courtney
Byron R. Perkins
Jon C. Goldfarb
Gregory O. Wiggins
Lee Winston
Jon E. Lewis
Deborah A. Mattison
Amelia H. Griffith
Rocco Calamusa, Jr.
Brian M. Clark

OF COUNSEL

Robert H. Loeb

For full biographical listings, see the Martindale-Hubbell Law Directory

GORHAM, STEWART, KENDRICK, BRYANT & BATTLE, P.C. (AV)

2101 6th Avenue North, Suite 700, 35203
Telephone: 205-254-3216, 251-9166
Telecopier: 205-324-3802

Charles W. Gorham
Thomas L. Stewart
Michael G. Kendrick
William J. Bryant
LaVeeda Morgan Battle
Frank G. Alfano
Kay L. McNabb Cason
Victor Kelley

(See Next Column)

K. Mark Parnell
Mark T. Waggoner
Victoria Franklin-Sisson
Karen Brown Evans
James Hoover
Mary H. Thompson
Nancy E. Khalaf
Leslie Miller Klasing

OF COUNSEL

John T. Natter

Representative Clients: Jefferson County Personnel Board; Birmingham-Jefferson Civic Center Authority; The Water Works and Sewer Board of the City of Birmingham; City of Homewood; American Federation of Government Employees Local #1945; City of Pelham; Town of Kimberly; Alabama Tire Dealers Assn.; Southern States Body Shop Assn.

For full biographical listings, see the Martindale-Hubbell Law Directory

HASKELL SLAUGHTER YOUNG & JOHNSTON, PROFESSIONAL ASSOCIATION (AV)

1200 AmSouth/Harbert Plaza, 1901 Sixth Avenue North, 35203
Telephone: 205-251-1000
Facsimile: 205-324-1133
Montgomery, Alabama Office: Haskell Slaughter Young Johnston & Gallion. Bailey Building, Suite 375, 400 South Union Street, P.O. Box 4660. 36104
Telephone: 205-265-8573.
Facsimile: 205-264-7945.

Wyatt Rushton Haskell
William M. Slaughter
Frank M. Young, III
J. Brooke Johnston, Jr.
Benjamin B. Spratling III
Thomas T. Gallion, III (Resident, Montgomery Office)
E. Alston Ray
James C. Huckaby, Jr.
Mark Edward Ezell
Beall D. Gary, Jr.
Stephen L. Poer
Thomas E. Reynolds
Beverly P. Baker
Ross N. Cohen
Richard H. Walston
Charles A. McCallum, III
Constance A. Caldwell (Resident, Montgomery Office)
Gwen L. Windle

Robert D. Shattuck, Jr.
Michael K. K. Choy
Louise Coker Wyman
Carter H. Dukes
Paula J. Baker
R. Scott Williams
Barry D. Woodham

Representative Clients: The Bradford Group, Inc.; City of Birmingham; The Equitable Life Assurance Society of the United States; Exxon Corporation; Federal Deposit Insurance Corporation/Resolution Trust Corporation; HEALTHSOUTH Rehabilitation Corporation/HEALTHSOUTH Medical Centers; Hughes Missile Systems; Montgomery County, Alabama; Psychiatric Healthcare Corporation; USX Corporation.

For full biographical listings, see the Martindale-Hubbell Law Directory

HOGAN, SMITH, ALSPAUGH, SAMPLES & PRATT, P.C. (AV)

2323 Second Avenue, North, 35203
Telephone: 205-324-5635
Telecopier: 205-324-5637

William W. Smith
M. Clay Alspaugh
R. Benjamin Hogan, III
S. Shay Samples
James R. Pratt, III
James P. Rea
Ronald R. Crook
Robert D. Word, III
Richard D. Stratton
Pamela D. Beard

OF COUNSEL

Roscoe B. Hogan
C. W. (Dugan) Callaway, Jr.

Reference: First Alabama Bank.

For full biographical listings, see the Martindale-Hubbell Law Directory

JOHNSTON, BARTON, PROCTOR, SWEDLAW & NAFF (AV)

2900 AmSouth/Harbert Plaza, 1901 Sixth Avenue North, 35203-2618
Telephone: 205-458-9400
Telecopier: 205-458-9500

MEMBERS OF FIRM

Harvey Deramus (1904-1970)
Alfred M. Naff (1923-1993)
James C. Barton
G. Burns Proctor, Jr.
Sydney L. Lavender
Jerome K. Lanning
Don B. Long, Jr.
Charles L. Robinson
J. William Rose, Jr.
Gilbert E. Johnston, Jr.
David P. Whiteside, Jr.
Ralph H. Smith II
James C. Barton, Jr.
Thomas E. Walker
Anne P. Wheeler
Raymond P. Fitzpatrick, Jr.
Hollinger F. Barnard
William D. Jones III
David W. Proctor
Oscar M. Price III
W. Hill Sewell
Robert S. Vance, Jr.
Richard J. Brockman
Anthony A. Joseph

OF COUNSEL

Gilbert E. Johnston
Alfred Swedlaw
Alan W. Heldman

(See Next Column)

JOHNSTON, BARTON, PROCTOR, SWEDLAW & NAFF—*Continued*

ASSOCIATES

William K. Hancock
James P. Pewitt
Scott Wells Ford
David M. Hunt
Lee M. Pope
Haskins W. Jones
James M. Parker, Jr.
Michael H. Johnson
Russell L. Irby, III
R. Scott Clark
Helen Kathryn Downs

General Counsel for: The Birmingham News Co.
Counsel for: General Motors Corp.; General Electric Capital Corp.; Goldome Credit Corp.

For full biographical listings, see the Martindale-Hubbell Law Directory

LEITMAN, SIEGAL, PAYNE & CAMPBELL, P.C. (AV)

Suite 400 The Land Title Building, 600 North 20th Street, 35203
Telephone: 205-251-5900
Telecopier: 205-323-2098

F. Don Siegal
Eddie Leitman
Jackson M. Payne
Andrew P. Campbell
Lynne Stephens O'Neal
Phillip G. Stutts
Shawn Hill Crook
Virginia K. Hopper
Bradley G. Siegal
Suzanne Johnson Miceli
Kerry Phillip Luke

For full biographical listings, see the Martindale-Hubbell Law Directory

McDANIEL, HALL, CONERLY & LUSK, P.C. (AV)

1400 Financial Center, 505 North 20th Street, 35203-2626
Telephone: 205-251-8143

William J. McDaniel
Jack J. Hall
Edward O. Conerly
Donald Dewitt Lusk
W. Scott McGarrah, III
Roger C. Foster
William A. Mudd
C. Peter Bolvig
John M. Fraley
Jack J. Hall, Jr.
David L. McAlister

John F. McDaniel
Keri Donald Simms
Jack Martin Bains, Jr.
Matthew W. Veal
Teresa D. Davenport
Patrick R. Norris

Counsel for: Alabama Farm Bureau Insurance Cos.; Allstate Insurance Co.; Insurance Company of North America; Crum & Forster Insurance Co.; Canal Insurance Co.; Argonaut Insurance Co.; Chubb Pacific Indemnity Group; Commercial Union Cos.; General Accident Group.

For full biographical listings, see the Martindale-Hubbell Law Directory

NAJJAR DENABURG, P.C. (AV)

2125 Morris Avenue, 35203
Telephone: 205-250-8400
Telecopier: 205-326-3837

Charles L. Denaburg
Thomas C. Najjar, Jr.
Edward P. Meyerson
Ben L. Zarzaur
L. Stephen Wright, Jr.
Leonard Wertheimer, III
David A. (Chip) Schwartz
Douglas L. McWhorter
Richard D. Greer
Gary S. Schiff
Robert H. Adams
Marvin E. Franklin
Marvin L. Stewart, Jr.
Jesse P. Evans, III
Hub Harrington

Richard W. Theibert
Michael G. Graffeo
Keith J. Nadler
Terry M. Cromer
Walter F. McArdle
Allan L. Armstrong
Denise J. Landreth
Rachel Jackson Moore
Thomas M. Lewis
Laurie K. Boston

General Counsel: Acousti Engineering of Alabama, Inc.
Representative Client: Compass Bank.
Approved Attorneys for: Mississippi Valley Title Insurance Co.
Reference: Compass Bank.

For full biographical listings, see the Martindale-Hubbell Law Directory

PARSONS, LEE & JULIANO, P.C. (AV)

2200 AmSouth/Harbert Plaza, 1901 Sixth Avenue, North, P.O. Box 371088, 35237-1088
Telephone: 205-326-6600
Fax: 205-324-7097

Robert E. Parsons
Jasper P. Juliano
Marcus W. Lee
Marda W. Sydnor
David A. Lee
John M. Bergquist
Paul J. DeMarco
Deborah Ann Payne

OF COUNSEL

Patricia Shaw
Dorothy A. Powell

For full biographical listings, see the Martindale-Hubbell Law Directory

PORTERFIELD, HARPER & MILLS, P.A. (AV)

22 Inverness Center Parkway, Suite 600, P.O. Box 530790, 35253-0790
Telephone: 205-980-5000
Fax: 205-980-5001

Jack B. Porterfield, Jr.
Larry W. Harper
William T. Mills, II
William Dudley Motlow, Jr.
Stanley K. Smith
Philip F. Hutcheson
H. C. "Trey" Ireland, III
Keith Pflaum

Connie Shaw Granata
Michael L. Haggard
Stephen Douglas Christie
Timothy W. Knight
Mark E. King
Karen Walker Casey
Kristin Daniels Horn
Don L. Hall

Representative Clients: CIGNA; Equitable Life Assurance Society of the U.S.; Figge International; The Hanover Insurance Co.; Ingersoll-Rand Co.; New York Life Insurance Co.; The St. Paul Insurance Co.; Terex Corp.; The Travelers.

For full biographical listings, see the Martindale-Hubbell Law Directory

PRITCHARD, McCALL & JONES (AV)

800 Financial Center, 35203
Telephone: 205-328-9190

MEMBERS OF FIRM

William S. Pritchard (1890-1967)
Alexander W. Jones (1914-1988)
William S. Pritchard, Jr.
Madison W. O'Kelley, Jr.
Julian P. Hardy, Jr.
Alexander W. Jones, Jr.
F. Hilton-Green Tomlinson
James G. Henderson
William S. Pritchard, III

ASSOCIATES

Michael L. McKerley
Robert Bond Higgins
Nina Michele LaFleur
Mary W. Burge

Representative Clients: First National Bank of Columbiana; Central State Bank of Calera; Buffalo Rock-Pepsi-Cola Bottling Co.; Gillis Advertising, Inc.; Liberty Mutual Insurance Co.; Reliance Insurance Company; SouthTrust Bank, N.A.; Bromberg & Company, Inc.; Farmers Furniture Company; First Commercial Bank.

For full biographical listings, see the Martindale-Hubbell Law Directory

REDDEN, MILLS & CLARK (AV)

940 First Alabama Bank Building, 35203
Telephone: 205-322-0457
Fax: 205-322-8481

MEMBERS OF FIRM

L. Drew Redden
William H. Mills
William N. Clark
Gerald L. Miller
Stephen W. Shaw

ASSOCIATES

Maxwell H. Pulliam, Jr.
Joseph H. Hilley

References: SouthTrust Bank; First Alabama Bank.

For full biographical listings, see the Martindale-Hubbell Law Directory

SIROTE & PERMUTT, P.C. (AV)

2222 Arlington Avenue, South, P.O. Box 55727, 35255
Telephone: 205-933-7111
Facsimile: 205-930-5301
Huntsville, Alabama Office: 200 Clinton Avenue, N.W., Suite 1000.
Telephone: 205-536-1711.
Facsimile: 205-534-9650.
Mobile, Alabama Office: One St. Louis Centre, Suite 1000.
Telephone: 205-432-1671.
Facsimile: 205-434-0196.
Montgomery, Alabama Office: Colonial Commerce Center, Suite 305 One Commerce Street.
Telephone: 205-261-3400.
Facsimile: 205-261-3434.
Tuscaloosa, Alabama Office: 2216 14th Street.
Telephone: 205-752-2089.

Morris K. Sirote (1909-1994)
James L. Permutt
E. M. Friend, Jr.
Karl B. Friedman
Jerry E. Held
Harold I. Apolinsky
Joseph S. Bluestein
Richard J. Cohn
J. Mason Davis
Edward M. Friend, III
C. Lee Reeves
John C. Falkenberry
James C. Wilson, Jr.
Jerry E. Held
Maurice L. Shevin
David M. Wooldridge
Rodney A. Max
Melinda McEachern Mathews
Jack B. Levy
Steven A. Brickman
John H. Cooper
George M. (Jack) Neal, Jr.
Judith F. Todd
John R. Chiles
Dale B. Stone
Charles R. Driggars
Kaye Houser Turberville
Timothy A. Bush
Greggory M. Deitsch
Joseph T. Ritchey
Kim E. Rosenfield

(See Next Column)

SIROTE & PERMUTT P.C., *Birmingham—Continued*

Lenora W. Pate (On leave of absence effective June 1, 1993).
W. McCollum Halcomb
C. Randal Johnson
Jeffrey H. Wertheim
Donald M. Wright
Stephen B. Porterfield
Daniel J. Burnick
Donna Bowling Nathan
John N. Randolph
Candace Lee Hemphill
Rodney E. Nolen
Gail Crummie Washington
Robert R. Baugh
David W. Long
J. Rushton McClees
Nanette Sims
Thomas A. Ansley
James Sarven Williams
Frances Heidt
W. Todd Carlisle
Bradley J. Sklar
Lynda L. Hendrix
Thomas G. Tutten, Jr.
J. Scott Sims
Matthew A. Vega

OF COUNSEL

Mayer U. Newfield
Joseph W. Blackburn

Representative Clients: International Business Machines (IBM); General Motors Corp.; Colonial Bank; Bruno's, Inc.; University of Alabama Hospitals; Westinghouse Electric Corp.; First Alabama Bank; Monsanto Chemical Company; South Central Bell; Prudential Insurance Company; American Home Products, Inc.; Minnesota Mining and Manufacturing, Inc. (3M).

For full biographical listings, see the Martindale-Hubbell Law Directory

SPAIN, GILLON, GROOMS, BLAN & NETTLES (AV)

The Zinszer Building, 2117 2nd Avenue North, 35203
Telephone: 205-328-4100
Telecopier: 205-324-8866

MEMBERS OF FIRM

H. Hobart Grooms, Jr.
Elizabeth Ann McMahan
Ollie L. Blan, Jr.
J. Mark Hart
Bert S. Nettles
Glenn E. Estess, Jr.
John P. McKleroy, Jr.
J. Sanford Mullins, III
Allwin E. Horn, III
Harold H. Goings
Eugene P. Stutts
Thomas M. Eden, III
Samuel H. Frazier
James A. Kee, Jr.
Alton B. Parker, Jr.
Paul S. Leonard
Charles D. Stewart
Gary Charles Smith
J. Birch Bowdre
Paul L. Sotherland
Robert L. Williams

OF COUNSEL

Richard S. Riley
John P. Ansley
Ralph B. Tate
Ira L. Burleson
J. W. Gillon (1900-1992)

ASSOCIATES

W. Gregory Smith
Anthony C. Harlow
Steve R. Burford
Mark M. Hogewood
Earl H. Lawson, Jr.
Philip G. Piggott
Edward M. Weed
Howard K. Glick
Joey D. Duke
Damon P. Denney
Mark D. Hess
Sally A. Broatch

LEGAL SUPPORT PERSONNEL

Margaret M. Kain (Librarian)

General Counsel for: Liberty National Life Insurance Co.; United States Fidelity & Guaranty Co.; Piggly Wiggly Alabama Distributing Co.; AmSouth Mortgage Co., Inc.; Alabama Insurance Guaranty Association; Alabama Life and Disability Insurance Guaranty Association; Alabama Insurance Underwriters Association.
Counsel for: The Prudential Insurance Company of America; Government Employees Insurance Co.; Massachusetts Mutual Life Insurance Co.

For full biographical listings, see the Martindale-Hubbell Law Directory

TINGLE, MURVIN, WATSON & BATES, P.C. (AV)

Suite 900 Park Place Tower, 2001 Park Place North, 35203
Telephone: 205-324-4400
Telecopier: 205-322-1163

James M. Tingle
I. Ripon Britton, Jr.
Christopher R. Murvin
George M. Vaughn
W. Clark Watson
David A. Ryan
Roger L. Bates
Leigh Ann Dean
Brannon Donnell Anthony

References: National Bank of Commerce of Birmingham; Compass Bank.

For full biographical listings, see the Martindale-Hubbell Law Directory

WALSTON, STABLER, WELLS, ANDERSON & BAINS (AV)

Suite 500 Financial Center, 505 20th Street North, 35203
Telephone: 205-251-9600
Telecopier: 205-251-0700
Mailing Address: P.O. Box 830642, Birmingham, AL, 35283-0642

(See Next Column)

Robert H. Walston
James L. Birchall
Frank C. Galloway, Jr.
Michael C. Quillen
L. Vastine Stabler, Jr.
David B. Anderson
Charles L. Hayes
Larry B. Childs
Lawrence Dumas, III
Kay K. Bains
C. Henry Marston
Heyward C. Hosch III
Vernon L. Wells, II
Helen Currie Foster
Elizabeth Champlin Bishop

COUNSEL

Edward J. Ashton

ASSOCIATES

C. Ellis Brazeal, III
Jeffry B. Gordon (Not admitted in AL)
David B. Walston
Samuel M. Hill
Kimberly Goldfarb Gordon (Not admitted in AL)
William H. Pryor Jr.
Anne Byrne Stone
Jerry Dean Hillman
Emily Sides Bonds
Randall D. Quarles
N. Christian Glenos

For full biographical listings, see the Martindale-Hubbell Law Directory

*BREWTON,** Escambia Co.

OTTS, MOORE & JORDAN (AV)

401 Evergreen Avenue, P.O. Box 467, 36427
Telephone: 334-867-7724
Fax: 334-867-2624

MEMBERS OF FIRM

Lee M. Otts
John Thaddeus Moore
J. David Jordan

Representative Clients: Container Corporation of America; First National Bank, Brewton; Southern Pine Electric Cooperative ; Exxon Corp.; Mobil-GC Corp.; Pennzoil Exploration & Production Co.; Oryx Energy Co.; Auto-Owners Insurance Co.
Approved Attorneys for: Mississippi Valley Title Insurance Co.

THOMPSON, GARRETT & HINES (AV)

218 Belleville Avenue, P.O. Box 387, 36427-0387
Telephone: 334-867-6063
Fax: 334-867-6067
Atmore, Alabama Office: 101 3rd Avenue, P.O. Box 737.
Telephone: 205-368-4999.

MEMBERS OF FIRM

Joe B. Thompson, Jr.
Broox G. Garrett, Jr.
Edward T. Hines

Counsel for: First National Bank, Brewton, Alabama; Alabama Power Co.; St. Louis-San Francisco Railway; State Farm Insurance Co.; Royal-Liverpool Insurance Group; Southern Guaranty Insurance Cos.; Home Insurance Co.; Federated Insurance Co.; Hartford Accident & Indemnity Co.; First National Bank of Atmore.

For full biographical listings, see the Martindale-Hubbell Law Directory

*CAMDEN,** Wilcox Co. — (Refer to Selma)

*CARROLLTON,** Pickens Co. — (Refer to Tuscaloosa)

*CENTRE,** Cherokee Co.

KEENER & KEENER (AV)

150 East Main Street, P.O. Box 604, 35960
Telephone: 205-927-5518

Irby A. Keener (1900-1965)
Irby A. Keener, Jr.

*CENTREVILLE,** Bibb Co. — (Refer to Tuscaloosa)

*CLANTON,** Chilton Co. — (Refer to Montgomery)

*CLAYTON,** Barbour Co. — (Refer to Troy)

*COLUMBIANA,** Shelby Co. — (Refer to Birmingham)

*CULLMAN,** Cullman Co.

ST. JOHN & ST. JOHN (AV)

108 Third Street South East, P.O. Drawer K, 35055
Telephone: 205-734-3542; 734-3543
Fax: 205-734-3544

MEMBERS OF FIRM

F. E. St. John (1874-1943)
Juliet G. St. John
Finis E. St. John (1909-1984)
Finis E. St. John, IV
Finis E. St. John, III (1933-1984)
Gaynor L. St. John

Attorneys for: CSX Transportation, Inc.; U.S. Fidelity & Guaranty Co.; Alabama Power Co.; Golden-Rod Broilers, Inc.; Travelers Insurance Cos.; South Central Bell Telephone Co.; Liberty Mutual Insurance Cos.; ALFA Mutual Insurance Co.; First Federal Savings & Loan.

For full biographical listings, see the Martindale-Hubbell Law Directory

*DADEVILLE,** Tallapoosa Co. — (Refer to Opelika)

*DECATUR,** Morgan Co.

EYSTER, KEY, TUBB, WEAVER & ROTH (AV)

Eyster Building, 402 East Moulton Street, S.E., P.O. Box 1607, 35602
Telephone: 205-353-6761
Fax: 205-353-6767

John C. Eyster (1863-1926) Charles H. Eyster, Sr. (1888-1964)

OF COUNSEL

Wm. B. Eyster

MEMBERS OF FIRM

John S. Key
J. Glynn Tubb
Larry C. Weaver
Nicholas B. Roth
J. Witty Allen
William L. Middleton, III
James G. Adams, Jr.

ASSOCIATES

Gina M. Fichter
Jenny L. Mcleroy

General Counsel for: Alabama Farmers Cooperative.
Regional Counsel for: AmSouth Bank.
Local Counsel for: Allstate Insurance Co.; Liberty Mutual Insurance Co.; Maryland Casualty Co.; Saginaw Steering Gear Division, General Motors Corp.; State Farm Mutual Automobile Insurance Co.; The Travelers.

For full biographical listings, see the Martindale-Hubbell Law Directory

HARRIS, CADDELL & SHANKS, P.C. (AV)

214 Johnston Street, S.E., P.O. Box 2688, 35602-2688
Telephone: 205-340-8000
Telecopier: 205-340-8040

Julian Harris (Retired)
Norman W. Harris (P.C.) (Retired)
John A. Caddell (P.A.)
Philip T. Shanks (P.A.) (Retired)
Robert H. Harris
Jon H. Moores
Thomas A. Caddell
Charles L. Murphree (Retired)
William E. Shinn, Jr.
Gary A. Phillips
Dow M. Perry, Jr.
Barnes F. Lovelace, Jr.
Steven C. Sasser
Arthur W. Orr
J. Noel King
Jeffrey S. Brown

Attorneys for: First American Bank, Decatur, Alabama; SouthTrust Bank of Morgan County; Morgan County Commission; The Industrial Development Board of the City of Decatur, Alabama; Amoco Chemical Co.; South Central Bell Telephone Co.; Auto-Owners Insurance Co.; ALFA Insurance Cos.; American General Life & Accident Insurance Co.; U.S.F. & G. Co.

For full biographical listings, see the Martindale-Hubbell Law Directory

DEMOPOLIS, Marengo Co. — (Refer to Selma)

*DOTHAN,** Houston Co.

COBB & SHEALY, P.A. (AV)

206 North Lena Street, P.O. Box 6346, 36302
Telephone: 334-794-8526
Fax: 334-677-0030

Herman W. Cobb
Steadman S. Shealy, Jr.
Brad E. Mendheim
Julie Sorrells

OF COUNSEL

Joey Hornsby

Representative Clients: Travelers Insurance; Nationwide Insurance; Auto-Owners, Ins.; Employers Casualty of Texas; Safeco Insurance; Federated Insurance; Universal Underwriters; National Security Ins.; Great Central Ins.
Approved Title Attorneys for: Lawyers Title Insurance Corp.

For full biographical listings, see the Martindale-Hubbell Law Directory

LEE & McINISH (AV)

238 West Main Street, P.O. Box 1665, 36302
Telephone: 334-792-4156
Facsimile: 334-794-8342

MEMBERS OF FIRM

W. L. Lee (1873-1944)
Alto V. Lee, III (1915-1987)
William L. Lee, III
Alan C. Livingston
William C. Carn, III
Peter A. McInish
Jerry M. White

OF COUNSEL

H. Dwight McInish

Counsel for: Seaboard Coast Line Railroad Co.; Atlanta & St. Andrews Bay Railroad Co.; ALFA; U. S. F. & G. Co.; Maryland Casualty Co.; Continental Insurance Cos.; Royal-Globe Group; Slocomb National Bank; The Federal Land Bank of Jackson; GTE South.

For full biographical listings, see the Martindale-Hubbell Law Directory

*DOUBLE SPRINGS,** Winston Co. — (Refer to Decatur)

*ELBA,** Coffee Co. — (Refer to Enterprise)

ENTERPRISE, Coffee Co.

CASSADY, FULLER & MARSH (AV)

203 East Lee Avenue, P.O. Box 780, 36331
Telephone: 334-347-2626
Telecopier: 334-393-1396

MEMBERS OF FIRM

Joe C. Cassady
Kenneth T. Fuller
M. Dale Marsh
Joe C. Cassady, Jr.
Mark E. Fuller

Representative Clients: First Alabama Bank; Enterprise Hospital Board; Sessions Co., Inc.; Allstate; State Farm Mutual Insurance Co.; Coffee County Bank.
Approved Attorneys for: First American Title Insurance Co.

For full biographical listings, see the Martindale-Hubbell Law Directory

J. E. SAWYER, JR. (AV)

203 South Edwards Street, P.O. Box 720, 36331-0720
Telephone: 334-347-6447
Fax: 334-347-8217

For full biographical listings, see the Martindale-Hubbell Law Directory

EUFAULA, Barbour Co.

WILLIAM V. NEVILLE, JR. (AV)

302 East Broad Street, P.O. Box 337, 36072-0337
Telephone: 334-687-5183
Fax: 334-687-6602

For full biographical listings, see the Martindale-Hubbell Law Directory

*EUTAW,** Greene Co. — (Refer to Tuscaloosa)

*EVERGREEN,** Conecuh Co.

WILLIAM D. MELTON (AV)

Melton Building, 100 Liberty Hill, P.O. Drawer 800, 36401-0800
Telephone: 334-578-2423

Reference: Bank of Evergreen, Evergreen, Alabama.

For full biographical listings, see the Martindale-Hubbell Law Directory

*FAYETTE,** Fayette Co. — (Refer to Tuscaloosa)

*FLORENCE,** Lauderdale Co.

POTTS & YOUNG (AV)

107 East College Street, 35630
Telephone: 205-764-7142
Fax: 205-764-7717

OF COUNSEL

Doyle R. Young (Retired)
Robert L. Potts

MEMBERS OF FIRM

Frank V. Potts
Frank B. Potts

ASSOCIATES

Robert W. Beasley
Debra H. Coble
Mark A. Sanderson

Representative Clients: E. A. Nelson Co., Inc.; Nelco, Inc.; Lauderdale County Board of Education; American Abrasive Air & Service Co., Inc.; Diversified Products, Inc.; BIG DELI STORES, Inc.; Spry Funeral Homes of Russellville, Sheffield & Florence; Americans United for the Separation of Church & State; Colbert County Community Economic Development Corp.
Reference: Bank Independent.

For full biographical listings, see the Martindale-Hubbell Law Directory

*FORT PAYNE,** De Kalb Co.

KELLETT, GILLIS & KELLETT, P.A. (AV)

Black Building, P.O. Box 715, 35967
Telephone: 205-845-4541

Joseph C. Kellett
Terry D. Gillis
Patricia Kellett

Attorneys for: V.I. Prewett & Son, Inc.; AmSouth Bank, N.A.; St. Paul Insurance Cos.; Employers of Wausau Insurance Co.; DeKalb-Cherokee Counties Gas District; Williamson Oil Co.; Home Insurance Co.; Bank of Fyffe; Johnson Hosiery Mills, Inc.; Cherokee Hosiery Mills, Inc.

For full biographical listings, see the Martindale-Hubbell Law Directory

SCRUGGS, JORDAN & DODD, P.A. (AV)

207 Alabama Avenue, South, P.O. Box 1109, 35967
Telephone: 205-845-5932
Fax: 205-845-4325

(See Next Column)

SCRUGGS, JORDAN & DODD P.A., *Fort Payne—Continued*

William D. Scruggs, Jr. | David Dodd
Robert K. Jordan | E. Allen Dodd, Jr.

Representative Clients: State Farm Insurance Company; Allstate Insurance Co., Inc.; USF&G Insurance Co.; Nucor, Inc.; Ladd Engineering, Inc.; ALABAMA Band; First Federal Savings & Loan Association of Dekalb County; Fritz Structural Steel, Inc.; Williamson Oil Co., Inc.

For full biographical listings, see the Martindale-Hubbell Law Directory

*GADSDEN,** Etowah Co.

DORTCH, WRIGHT & WRIGHT (AV)

239 College Street, P.O. Box 405, 35902
Telephone: 205-546-4616

MEMBERS OF FIRM

Walter R. Dortch (1847-1926) | William B. Dortch (1892-1983)
G. C. Allen (1872-1935) | Curtis Wright
Curtis Wright, II

Attorneys for: St. Paul Insurance Cos.; Employers Insurance of Wausau; Mutual Assurance Society of Alabama; State Farm Insurance Cos.; Alabama Hospital Association Trust; Mutual Savings Life Insurance Co.; Lawyers Title Insurance Corp.; Nationwide Mutual Insurance Co.; Government Employees Insurance Co.; CSX Transportation Systems.

For full biographical listings, see the Martindale-Hubbell Law Directory

FLOYD, KEENER, CUSIMANO & ROBERTS, P.C. (AV)

816 Chestnut Street, P.O. Box 49, 35902
Telephone: 205-547-6328
Fax: 205-546-8173

Jack Floyd | Gregory S. Cusimano
Larry H. Keener | Michael L. Roberts
David A. Kimberley

Mary Ann Ross Stackhouse | Philip E. Miles
John D. Floyd | Elizabeth Ragsdole Howard

For full biographical listings, see the Martindale-Hubbell Law Directory

FORD & HUNTER, P.C. (AV)

The Lancaster Building, 645 Walnut Street, Suite 5, P.O. Box 388, 35902
Telephone: 205-546-5432
Fax: 205-546-5435

George P. Ford | J. Gullatte Hunter, III

Richard M. Blythe | H. Edgar Howard

References: General Motors Acceptance Corp.; AmSouth Bank, N.A.

For full biographical listings, see the Martindale-Hubbell Law Directory

INZER, STIVENDER, HANEY & JOHNSON, P.A. (AV)

(Inzer, Suttle, Swann & Stivender)
(Lusk, Swann, Burns & Stivender)
(Inzer, Suttle & Inzer)
Second Floor, Compass Bank Building, 601 Broad Street, P.O. Drawer 287, 35999-0287
Telephone: 205-546-1656
Telecopier: 205-546-1093

James C. Inzer (1887-1967) | James C. Inzer, Jr. (Of Counsel)
John A. Lusk, Jr. (1891-1970) | James C. Stivender
Hubert Burns (1915-1975) | W. Roscoe Johnson, III
Julius S. Swann, Sr. (1907-1989) | James C. Inzer, III
Frank J. Martin (1905-1992) | F. Michael Haney
Roger C. Suttle (Of Counsel) | Robert D. McWhorter, Jr.

James W. McGlaughn | Elizabeth Golson McGlaughn

Assistant Division Counsel for: Southern Railway System.
Attorneys for: General Motors Corp.; Goodyear Tire and Rubber Co.; Alabama Power Co.; Southern Natural Gas Co.; Allstate Insurance Co.; Travelers Insurance Co.; Central Bank of the South.

For full biographical listings, see the Martindale-Hubbell Law Directory

SIMMONS, BRUNSON, SASSER AND CALLIS, ATTORNEYS, P.A. (AV)

1411 Rainbow Drive, P.O. Box 1189, 35902
Telephone: 205-546-9206
Telecopier: 205-546-8091

Clarence Simmons, Jr. | James T. Sasser
Steve P. Brunson | Clifford Louis Callis, Jr.

(See Next Column)

Rebecca A. Walker | Jeffrey A. Brown

Attorneys for: Preferred Risk Mutual Insurance Co.; ALFA Mutual Insurance Co.; Royal Insurance Cos.
Approved Attorneys for: Lawyers Title Insurance Corp.; Mississippi Valley Title Insurance Co.

For full biographical listings, see the Martindale-Hubbell Law Directory

*GREENSBORO,** Hale Co. — (Refer to Selma)

*GREENVILLE,** Butler Co.

POOLE & POOLE (AV)

600 East Commerce Street, P.O. Box 308, 36037
Telephone: 334-382-3123
Telecopier: 334-382-2714

MEMBERS OF FIRM

Calvin Poole (1893-1990) | Elisha C. Poole
Calvin Poole, III

Counsel for: First National Bank of Greenville; Town of Fort Deposit.

For full biographical listings, see the Martindale-Hubbell Law Directory

*GUNTERSVILLE,** Marshall Co.

LUSK & LUSK (AV)

452 Gunter Avenue, P.O. Box 609, 35976
Telephone: 205-582-3248

MEMBERS OF FIRM

Marion F. Lusk (1896-1986) | Louis B. Lusk

Representative Clients: AmSouth Bank, N.A., Guntersville; United States Fidelity & Guaranty Co.; The Travelers Insurance Co.; St. Paul Cos.; ALFA Mutual Insurance Cos.; Hartford Group; Liberty Mutual Insurance Co.; Allstate Insurance Co.; Home of New York Group.

For full biographical listings, see the Martindale-Hubbell Law Directory

WRIGHT AND WRIGHT, A PROFESSIONAL CORPORATION (AV)

Worth Street, P.O. Box 70, 35976-0070
Telephone: 205-582-3721; 582-8590; 582-8411
Fax: 205-582-3733

T. Harvey Wright (1890-1972) | Harvey J. Wright
Wade K. Wright

Approved Attorneys for: Commonwealth Land Title Insurance Co.; Lawyers Title Insurance Corp.

HALEYVILLE, Winston Co.

JAMES, LOWE & MOBLEY (AV)

1210-21st Street, P.O. Box 576, 35565
Telephone: 205-486-5296
Fax: 205-486-4531

MEMBERS OF FIRM

Walter Joe James, Jr. (1923-1990) | John W. Lowe
| Jeffery A. Mobley
Robert B. Aderholt

Representative Clients: Traders & Farmers Bank; Burdick-West Memorial Hospital.
Approved Attorneys for: Lawyers Title Insurance Corp.

For full biographical listings, see the Martindale-Hubbell Law Directory

*HAMILTON,** Marion Co.

FITE, DAVIS, ATKINSON, GUYTON & BENTLEY, P.C. (AV)

Court Square, P.O. Box 157, 35570-0157
Telephone: 205-921-7878; 921-4464
Fax: 205-921-9717
Winfield, Alabama Office: Highway 43 South. P.O. Box 1080.
Telephone: 205-487-4848.
Fax: 205-487-4890.

Rankin Fite (1916-1980) | William T. Atkinson
James K. Davis | Jerry F. Guyton
William H. Atkinson | John H. Bentley

Representative Clients: First State Bank of Lamar County; City of Winfield.

For full biographical listings, see the Martindale-Hubbell Law Directory

HEADLAND, Henry Co. — (Refer to Abbeville)

*HEFLIN,** Cleburne Co. — (Refer to Anniston)

*HUNTSVILLE,** Madison Co.

BALCH & BINGHAM (AV)

Suite 810, 200 West Court Square, P.O. Box 18668, 35804-8668
Telephone: 205-551-0171
Facsimile: 205-551-0174
Birmingham, Alabama Offices: 1710 Sixth Avenue North, 35203.
Telephone: 205-251-8100.
Facsimile: 205-226-8798. 1901 Sixth Avenue North, 35203.
Telephone: 205-251-8100.
Facsimile: 205-226-8799.
Montgomery, Alabama Office: The Winter Building, 2 Dexter Avenue, 36101.
Telephone: 205-834-6500.
Facsimile: 205-269-3115.
Washington, D.C. Office: Suite 800, 1101 Connecticut Avenue, N.W., 20036.
Telephone: 202-296-0387.
Facsimile: 202-452-8180.

RESIDENT COUNSEL

John David Snodgrass

RESIDENT MEMBERS OF FIRM

S. Revelle Gwyn

RESIDENT ASSOCIATES

Daniel M. Wilson

Counsel for: Alabama Power Co.; Blue Cross and Blue Shield of Alabama; The Boeing Company; Brasfield & Gorrie, Inc.; Compass Bancshares, Inc.; Harbert Corp.; Kimberly-Clark Corp.; Southern Company Services, Inc.; Southern Research Institute; Vesta Insurance Group, Inc.

For full biographical listings, see the Martindale-Hubbell Law Directory

BERRY, ABLES, TATUM, LITTLE & BAXTER, P.C. (AV)

Legal Building, 315 Franklin Street, S.E., P.O. Box 165, 35804-0165
Telephone: 205-533-3740
Facsimile: 205-533-3751

William H. Blanton (1889-1973)
Joe M. Berry
L. Bruce Ables
James T. Tatum, Jr.
Loyd H. Little, Jr.
James T. Baxter, III
Thomas E. Parker, Jr.
Bill G. Hall

Representative Clients: AmSouth Bank, N.A.; First Alabama Bank; General Shale Products Co.; The Hartz Corp.; Litton Industries, Inc.; Farmers Tractor Co.; Colonial Bank; Farm Credit Bank of Texas; Resolution Trust Corp.
Reference: First Alabama Bank.

For full biographical listings, see the Martindale-Hubbell Law Directory

BRADLEY, ARANT, ROSE & WHITE (AV)

200 Clinton Avenue West, Suite 900, 35801
Telephone: 205-517-5100
Facsimile: 205-533-5069
Birmingham, Alabama Office: 1400 Park Place Tower, 2001 Park Place.
Telephone: 205-521-8000.
Telex: 494-1324.
Facsimile: 205-251-8611, 251-8665, 252-0264. Facsimile (Southtrust Office): 205-251-9915.

RESIDENT PARTNERS

Robert Sellers Smith
Gary C. Huckaby
E. Cutter Hughes, Jr.
Patrick H. Graves, Jr.
Scott E. Ludwig
G. Rick Hall

RESIDENT ASSOCIATES

Warne S. Heath
H. Knox McMillan
Frank M. Caprio
Paul B. Seeley
James Tassin
Carolyn Reed Douglas

Counsel for: SouthTrust Bank of Alabama, National Association; Energen, Corporation; Blount, Inc.; Torchmark Corp.; Russell Corp.; Coca-Cola Bottling Company United, Inc.; Ford Motor Co.; Walter Industries, Inc.; The Birmingham Post Co. (Post-Herald); The New York Times Co.

For full biographical listings, see the Martindale-Hubbell Law Directory

LANIER FORD SHAVER & PAYNE, P.C. (AV)

200 West Court Square, Suite 500, P.O. Box 2087, 35804
Telephone: 205-535-1100
FAX: 205-533-9322

M. H. Lanier (1878-1946)
Earle Raymond Ford (1890-1973)
Ralph H. Ford (1916-1986)
James L. Caldwell (1914-1991)
Charles E. Shaver (1907-1993)
M. H. Lanier
Joe L. Payne
William T. Galloway, Jr.
Jerry B. Ange
W. Stanley Rodgers
James E. Davis, Jr.
John M. Heacock, Jr.
Charles E. Shaver, Jr.
John R. Wynn
Thomas R. Robinson
J. R. Brooks
William Blanton Tatum
William W. Sanderson, Jr.
H. Harold Stephens
Joe W. Campbell
D. Edward Starnes, III

(See Next Column)

Donna S. Pate
Robert E. Ledyard, III
Ronald F. Suber
Elizabeth W. Abel
Y. Albert Moore, III
Claude E. Hundley, III

George E. Knox, Jr.
Jeffrey T. Kelly
Kelly M. McDonald
Apsilah G. Owens
Anita J. Kimbrell
Edward E. Wilson, Jr.
Rodney C. Lewis

OF COUNSEL

Frank McRight

Representative Clients: Aetna Life & Casualty Company; First American Federal Savings & Loan; General Motors Corp.; Huntsville Coca-Cola Bottling Co.; Huntsville Hospital; Royal Insurance; St. Paul Insurance Co.; Teledyne Industries, Inc.; The Travelers Insurance Co.; United States Fidelity & Guaranty.

For full biographical listings, see the Martindale-Hubbell Law Directory

SIROTE & PERMUTT, P.C. (AV)

Suite 1000, 200 Clinton Avenue, N.W., 35801
Telephone: 205-536-1711
Facsimile: 205-534-9650
Birmingham, Alabama Office: 2222 Arlington Avenue, South, P.O. Box 55727.
Telephone: 205-933-7111.
Facsimile: 205-930-5301.
Mobile, Alabama Office: One St. Louis Centre, Suite 1000.
Telephone: 205-432-1671.
Facsimile: 205-434-0196.
Montgomery, Alabama Office: Colonial Commerce Center, Suite 305, One Commerce Street.
Telephone: 205-261-3400.
Facsimile: 205-261-3434.
Tuscaloosa, Alabama Office: 2216 14th Street.
Telephone: 205-752-2089.

Julian D. Butler
Joe H. Ritch
George W. Royer, Jr.
Roderic G. Steakley
Wanda S. McNeil
Johnnie Frank Vann
John P. Burbach
Christine Sampson Hinson
Peter L. Lowe, Jr.
June Wang
Robert W. Ruth
Fred L. Coffey, Jr.
J. Jeffery Rich
Melissa C. Wimberley

For full biographical listings, see the Martindale-Hubbell Law Directory

WATSON, GAMMONS & FEES, P.C. (AV)

200 Clinton Avenue, N.W., Suite 800, P.O. Box 46, 35804
Telephone: 205-536-7423
Telecopier: 205-536-2689

Herman Watson, Jr.
Robert C. Gammons
Michael L. Fees
Joseph A. Jimmerson
J. Barton Warren
Charles H. Pullen
Billie B. Line, Jr.

OF COUNSEL

George K. Williams

LEGAL SUPPORT PERSONNEL

James W. Lowery, Jr. (Administrator)

For full biographical listings, see the Martindale-Hubbell Law Directory

LANETT, Chambers Co. — (Refer to Lafayette)

*LINDEN,** Marengo Co. — (Refer to Selma)

*LIVINGSTON,** Sumter Co. — (Refer to Demopolis)

*MARION,** Perry Co. — (Refer to Selma)

*MOBILE,** Mobile Co.

ARMBRECHT, JACKSON, DEMOUY, CROWE, HOLMES & REEVES (AV)

1300 AmSouth Center, P.O. Box 290, 36601
Telephone: 334-432-6751
Facsimile: 334-432-6843; 433-3821

MEMBERS OF FIRM

Wm. H. Armbrecht (1908-1991)
Theodore K. Jackson (1910-1981)
F.M. Keeling (1943-1993)
Marshall J. DeMouy
Wm. H. Armbrecht, III
Rae M. Crowe
Broox G. Holmes
W. Boyd Reeves
E. B. Peebles III
William B. Harvey
Kirk C. Shaw
Norman E. Waldrop, Jr.
Conrad P. Armbrecht
Edward G. Hawkins
Grover E. Asmus II
David A. Bagwell
Douglas L. Brown
Donald C. Radcliff
Christopher I. Gruenewald
James Donald Hughes
M. Kathleen Miller
Dabney Bragg Foshee
Edward A. Dean
David E. Hudgens
Ray Morgan Thompson
James Dale Smith
Duane A. Graham

(See Next Column)

ARMBRECHT, JACKSON, DEMOUY, CROWE, HOLMES & REEVES, *Mobile—Continued*

MEMBERS OF FIRM (Continued)

Robert J. Mullican
Wm. Steele Holman, II
Coleman F. Meador
Broox G. Holmes, Jr.

ASSOCIATES

James E. Robertson, Jr.
Scott G. Brown
Clifford C. Brady
Richard W. Franklin
Stephen Russell Copeland
Tara T. Bostick
Rodney R. Cate
James F. Watkins
P. Vincent Gaddy
Richard G. Brock

Representative Clients: AmSouth Bank N.A. (Regional Counsel); Burlington Northern Railroad Co. (District Counsel); Ryan-Walsh, Inc.; Scott Paper Co.; Travelers Insurance Co.

For full biographical listings, see the Martindale-Hubbell Law Directory

CABANISS, JOHNSTON, GARDNER, DUMAS & O'NEAL (AV)

700 AmSouth Center, P.O. Box 2906, 36652
Telephone: 334-433-6961
Telecopier: 334-433-1060
Birmingham, Alabama Office: Park Place Tower. 2001 Park Place North, Suite 700. P.O. Box 830612.
Telephone: 205-252-8800.
Telecopier: 205-716-5389.

MEMBERS OF FIRM

Benjamen T. Rowe (Resident)
William A. Robinson
Patrick H. Sims (Resident)
Donald J. Stewart (Resident)
William K. Thomas
David L. Kane (Resident)
R. Boyd Miller (Resident)

Representative Clients: American Marine Underwriters, Inc.; Liberty Mutual Insurance Co.; Union Carbide Corp.; Rohr, Inc.

For full biographical listings, see the Martindale-Hubbell Law Directory

CUNNINGHAM, BOUNDS, YANCE, CROWDER & BROWN (AV)

1601 Dauphin Street, P.O. Box 66705, 36660
Telephone: 334-471-6191
Fax: 334-479-1031

Richard Bounds
James A. Yance
John T. Crowder, Jr.
Robert T. Cunningham, Jr.
Joseph M. Brown, Jr.
Gregory B. Breedlove
Andrew T. Citrin
Michael A. Worel

David G. Wirtes, Jr.
Randolph B. Walton
Toby D. Brown
Mitchell K. Shelly

OF COUNSEL

Robert T. Cunningham
Valentino D. B. Mazzia

References: First Alabama Bank; AmSouth Bank, N.A.

For full biographical listings, see the Martindale-Hubbell Law Directory

FINKBOHNER AND LAWLER (AV)

169 Dauphin Street Suite 300, P.O. Box 3085, 36652
Telephone: 334-438-5871
Fax: 334-432-8052

MEMBERS OF FIRM

George W. Finkbohner, Jr.
John L. Lawler
George W. Finkbohner, III
Royce A. Ray, III

For full biographical listings, see the Martindale-Hubbell Law Directory

HAND, ARENDALL, BEDSOLE, GREAVES & JOHNSTON (AV)

3000 First National Bank Building, P.O. Box 123, Drawer C, 36601
Telephone: 334-432-5511
Fax: 334-694-6375
Washington, D.C. Office: 410 First Street, S.E., Suite 300. 20003.
Telephone: 202-863-0053.
Fax: 202-863-0096.

MEMBERS OF FIRM

Charles C. Hand (1890-1980)
Charles B. Arendall, Jr. (1915-1993)
Vivian G. Johnston, Jr.
Paul W. Brock
Alexander F. Lankford, III
Jack Edwards
Lyman F. Holland, Jr.
J. Thomas Hines, Jr.
Louis E. Braswell
Harold D. Parkman
G. Porter Brock, Jr.
Jerry A. McDowell
Stephen G. Crawford
Michael D. Knight
G. Hamp Uzzelle, III
Gregory L. Leatherbury, Jr.
William C. Roedder, Jr.
William C. Tidwell, III
Edward S. Sledge, III
Joseph Hodge Alves, III
Caine O'Rear, III
William Alexander Moseley
Joe E. Basenberg
Neil C. Johnston
George M. Walker
R. Preston Bolt, Jr.
M. Mallory Mantiply
T. Bruce McGowin
Orrin K. Ames, III
Douglas L. McCoy
Henry A. Callaway, III
Blane H. Crutchfield
David R. Quittmeyer

(See Next Column)

MEMBERS OF FIRM (Continued)

Forrest C. Wilson, III
Judith L. McMillin
William B. Givhan
P. Russel Myles
Brian P. McCarthy
Walter T. Gilmer, Jr.
Archibald T. Reeves, IV

OF COUNSEL

T. Massey Bedsole
Thomas G. Greaves, Jr.

COUNSEL

Kathy Dunston Jones

ASSOCIATES

J. Burruss Riis
Karen Pailette Turner
Henry T. Morrissette
Allen S. Reeves
J. Stephen Harvey
J. Michael Fincher
John P. Kavanagh, Jr
Douglas Warren Fink
Lisa Tinsley O'Hara

General Counsel for: The Bank of Mobile; Delchamps, Inc.; The Mobile Press Register, Inc.; Mobile Asphalt Company; Gulf Telephone Company; Folmar & Associates; Mobile Community Foundation; Gulf Lumber Company; Scotch Lumber Company; Mobile Pulley & Machine Works, Inc.; Pennsylvania Shipbuilding Co.

For full biographical listings, see the Martindale-Hubbell Law Directory

HELMSING, LYONS, SIMS & LEACH, P.C. (AV)

The Laclede Building, 150 Government Street, P.O. Box 2767, 36652
Telephone: 334-432-5521
Telecopy: 334-432-0633

Larry U. Sims
Champ Lyons, Jr.
Frederick G. Helmsing
John N. Leach, Jr.
Warren C. Herlong, Jr.
James B. Newman
Robert H. Rouse
Charles H. Dodson, Jr.
Sandy Grisham Robinson
Richard E. Davis
Joseph P. H. Babington
John J. Crowley, Jr.
Joseph D. Steadman

Todd S. Strohmeyer
William R. Lancaster
Robin Kilpatrick Fincher

For full biographical listings, see the Martindale-Hubbell Law Directory

INGE, TWITTY & DUFFY (AV)

1410 First Alabama Bank Building, P.O. Box 1109, 36633
Telephone: 334-433-3200
Facsimile: 334-433-3444

MEMBERS OF FIRM

James J. Duffy, Jr.
James J. Duffy, III

Francis H. Inge (1902-1959)
Thos. E. Twitty (1901-1975)
Richard H. Inge (1912-1980)

For full biographical listings, see the Martindale-Hubbell Law Directory

JOHNSTONE, ADAMS, BAILEY, GORDON AND HARRIS (AV)

Royal St. Francis Building, 104 St. Francis Street, P.O. Box 1988, 36633
Telephone: 334-432-7682
Facsimile: 334-432-2800
Telex: 782040

MEMBERS OF FIRM

Charles B. Bailey, Jr.
Brock B. Gordon
Ben H. Harris, Jr.
William H. Hardie, Jr.
E. Watson Smith
Joseph M. Allen, Jr.
I. David Cherniak
David C. Hannan
Wade B. Perry, Jr.
Thomas S. Rue
Alan C. Christian
Gregory C. Buffalow
Celia J. Collins
R. Gregory Watts
William Alexander Gray, Jr.

ASSOCIATES

Robert S. Frost
Tracy P. Turner
Lawrence J. Seiter
C. William Rasure, Jr.
W. Andrew Wing, II
E. Erich Bergdolt
E. Russell March, III

OF COUNSEL

C. A. L. Johnstone, Jr.
Robert F. Adams

General Counsel for: First Alabama Bank, Mobile; Infirmary Health System/Mobile Infirmary Medical Center/Rotary Rehabilitation Hospital (Multi-Hospital System).
Counsel for: Oil and Gas: Exxon Corp. Business and Corporate: Bell South Telecommunications, Inc.; Aluminum Co. of America; Michelin Tire Corp.; Metropolitan Life Insurance Co.; The Travelers Insurance Cos. Marine: The West of England Ship Owners Mutual Protection and Indemnity Association (Luxembourg); The Standard Steamship Owners' Protection and Indemnity Association (Bermuda) Ltd.

For full biographical listings, see the Martindale-Hubbell Law Directory

Mobile—Continued

LOVELESS, BANKS & LYONS (AV)

28 North Florida Street, 36607
Telephone: 334-476-7857
Fax: 334-476-8510

MEMBERS OF FIRM

Ralph P. Loveless
J. Donald Banks
Beth Marietta Lyons

ASSOCIATES

T. Allen Tippy

For full biographical listings, see the Martindale-Hubbell Law Directory

LYONS, PIPES & COOK, P.C. (AV)

2 North Royal Street, P.O. Box 2727, 36652-2727
Telephone: 334-432-4481
Cable Address: "Lysea"
Telecopier: 334-433-1820

Joseph H. Lyons (1874-1957)
Sam W. Pipes, III (1916-1982)
Walter M. Cook (1915-1988)
G. Sage Lyons
Wesley Pipes
Norton W. Brooker, Jr.
Cooper C. Thurber
Marion A. Quina, Jr.
Thomas F. Garth
Claude D. Boone
Walter M. Cook, Jr.
John Patrick Courtney, III
Reggie Copeland, Jr.
Charles L. Miller, Jr.
W. David Johnson, Jr.
Joseph J. Minus, Jr.
Caroline C. McCarthy
William E. Shreve, Jr.
R. Mark Kirkpatrick
Kenneth A. Nixon
Dan S. Cushing
Allen E. Graham
Michael C. Niemeyer
John C. Bell
Richard D. Morrison
M. Warren Butler
Christopher Lee George

General Counsel: Inchcape Shipping Services.
Counsel: The Hertz Corp.; McKenzie Tank Lines, Inc.; SCNO Barge Lines, Inc.; Scott Paper Co.; Shell Oil Corp.
Trial Counsel: Aetna Life & Casualty Co.; Chubb Group of Insurance Companies.

For full biographical listings, see the Martindale-Hubbell Law Directory

AUGUSTINE MEAHER, III, P.C. (AV)

Suite 2118, First National Bank Building, 36602
Telephone: 334-432-9971
FAX: 334-432-9978

Augustine Meaher, III

References: Bank of Mobile, Mobile, Alabama; AmSouth Bank, Mobile, Alabama.

For full biographical listings, see the Martindale-Hubbell Law Directory

MILLER, HAMILTON, SNIDER & ODOM, L.L.C. (AV)

254-256 State Street, P.O. Box 46, 36601
Telephone: 334-432-1414
Telecopier: 334-433-4106
Montgomery, Alabama Office: Suite 802, One Commerce Street.
Telephone: 205-834-5550.
Telecopier: 205-265-4533.
Washington, D.C. Office: Miller, Hamilton, Snider, Odom & Bridgeman, L.L.C., Suite 1150, 1747 Pennsylvania Avenue, N.W.
Telephone: 202-429-9223.
Telecopier: 202-293-2068.

MEMBERS OF FIRM

John C. H. Miller, Jr.
Ronald A. Snider
Palmer C. Hamilton
Thomas Troy Zieman, Jr.
Michael D. Waters (Resident Partner, Montgomery Office)
Bradley R. Byrne
George A. LeMaistre, Jr.
Lester M. Bridgeman
Louis T. Urbanczyk (Not admitted in AL; Washington, D.C. Office)
Jerome E. Speegle
Christopher G. Hume, III
Richard A. Wright
M. Kathryn Knight
Matthew C. McDonald
Mark J. Tenhundfeld
Joseph R. Sullivan
Thomas P. Oldweiler
Susan Russ Walker (Resident, Montgomery Office)
Anne Carson Irvine Nicolson

OF COUNSEL

George A. LeMaistre, Sr.
Lewis G. Odom, Jr.

ASSOCIATES

Robert G. Jackson, Jr.
Christopher Kern
James Rebarchak
Michael M. Shipper
M. Stephen Dampier
Anthony Michael Hoffman
Elizabeth Barry Johnson
Eric J. Dyas
Jean M. Powers

Representative Clients: The Colonial BancGroup, Inc.; Colonial Mortgage Co.; Chase Manhattan Bank, N.A.; The Mitchell Co.; Poole Truck Line, Inc.; Brittania Airways, Ltd. (U.K.); Air Europe (Italy); K-Mart Corporation; K & B Alabama Corp.; Ford Consumer Finance Company, Inc.

(See Next Column)

For full biographical listings, see the Martindale-Hubbell Law Directory

REAMS, PHILIPS, BROOKS, SCHELL, GASTON & HUDSON, P.C. (AV)

The Pillans Building, 3662 Dauphin Street, P.O. Box 8158, 36608
Telephone: 334-344-4721
Telex: 78-2025
Telecopier: 334-343-9760

Harry Pillans (1847-1940)
William Cowley (1880-1948)
Palmer Pillans (1876-1976)
W. Dewitt Reams (Retired)
John H. Tappan (Retired)
George F. Wood (Retired)
Bonnerrae H. Roberts (Retired)
Abe L. Philips, Jr.
James D. Brooks
Sidney H. Schell
Geary A. Gaston
Victor T. Hudson
C. Robert Gottlieb, Jr.
John R. Nix
Richard L. Reed
William W. Watts, III
David M. O'Brien
A. Lewis Philips, III
Kenneth A. Watson
Earle W. Long, IV

Attorneys for: Ciba-Geigy; Degussa Corp., Inc.; Getty Oil Co.; Hartford Insurance Co.; The Swedish P. & I. Club; Mobil Oil Corp.; Olin Corp.; State Farm Insurance Cos.; Texaco Inc.; The United Kingdom Mutual Steam Ship Assurance Assn. (Bermuda) Ltd.

For full biographical listings, see the Martindale-Hubbell Law Directory

SIROTE & PERMUTT, P.C. (AV)

One St. Louis Centre, Suite 1000, P.O. Drawer 2025, 36652-2025
Telephone: 334-432-1671
Facsimile: 334-434-0196
Birmingham, Alabama Office: 2222 Arlington Avenue, South, P.O. Box 55727.
Telephone: 205-933-7111.
Facsimile: 205-930-5301.
Huntsville, Alabama Office: 200 Clinton Avenue, N.W., Suite 1000.
Telephone: 205-536-1711.
Facsimile: 205-534-9650.
Montgomery, Alabama Office: Colonial Commerce Center, Suite 305, One Commerce Street.
Telephone: 205-261-3400.
Facsimile: 205-261-3434.
Tuscaloosa, Alabama Office: 2216 14th Street.
Telephone: 205-752-2089.

William H. McDermott
Stephen R. Windom
Gordon O. Tanner
Richard H. Sforzini, Jr.
Shirley Mahan Justice
Joseph P. Jones, Jr.
M. Donald Davis, Jr.
T. Julian Motes
Steven L. Nicholas
Michael A. Youngpeter

For full biographical listings, see the Martindale-Hubbell Law Directory

VICKERS, RIIS, MURRAY AND CURRAN (AV)

8th Floor, First Alabama Bank Building, P.O. Box 2568, 36652
Telephone: 334-432-9772
Fax: 334-432-9781

MEMBERS OF FIRM

Marion R. Vickers, Jr. (1935-1989)
Erling Riis, Jr.
J. Manson Murray
Edwin J. Curran, Jr.
J. W. Goodloe, Jr.
Zebulon M. P. Inge, Jr.
Thomas E. Sharp, III
Ronald P. Davis
J. Marshall Gardner
C. Richard Wilkins

Representative Clients: Dravo Natural Resources Co.; Midstream Fuel Services; John E. Graham & Sons; McPhillips Manufacturing Co.; Spring Hill College; Steiner Shipyard, Inc.; Homeowners Marketing Services, Inc.; Marine Office of America Corp.; Cummins Alabama, Inc.; Ben M. Radcliff Contractor, Inc.

For full biographical listings, see the Martindale-Hubbell Law Directory

*MONROEVILLE,** Monroe Co. — (Refer to Evergreen)

*MONTGOMERY,** Montgomery Co.

* indicates certain Bar Register subscribers whose principal office is located elsewhere in the state and who have arranged for representation as a part of the state capital listings that follow

* BALCH & BINGHAM (AV)

The Winter Building, 2 Dexter Avenue, P.O. Box 78, 36101
Telephone: 334-834-6500
Facsimile: 334-269-3115
Birmingham, Alabama Offices: 1710 Sixth Avenue North, 35203.
Telephone: 205-251-8100.
Facsimile: 205-226-8798. 1901 Sixth Avenue North, 35203.
Telephone: 205-251-8100.
Facsimile: 205-226-8799.
Huntsville, Alabama Office: Suite 810, 200 West Court Square, 35801.
Telephone: 205-551-0171.
Facsimile: 205-551-0174.

(See Next Column)

BALCH & BINGHAM, *Montgomery—Continued*

Washington, D.C. Office: Suite 800, 1101 Connecticut Avenue, N.W., 20036.
Telephone: 202-296-0387.
Facsimile: 202-452-8180.

RESIDENT COUNSEL

M. Roland Nachman, Jr.

RESIDENT MEMBERS OF FIRM

Maury D. Smith
John S. Bowman
Thomas W. Thagard, Jr.
Charles M. Crook
Sterling G. Culpepper, Jr.
Warren H. Goodwyn
David R. Boyd
Malcolm N. Carmichael
William P. Cobb, II
James A. Byram, Jr.
W. Joseph McCorkle, Jr.
Dorman Walker

RESIDENT ASSOCIATES

Lois Smith Woodward
Patricia Anne Hamilton
Robin G. Laurie
Donald R. Jones, Jr.
John S. Bowman, Jr.
Leslie M. Allen
James Ernest Bridges, III
Cynthia Anne Holland

Counsel for: Alabama Power Co.; Blue Cross and Blue Shield of Alabama; The Boeing Company; Brasfield & Gorrie, Inc.; Compass Bancshares, Inc.; Harbert Corp.; Kimberly-Clark Corp.; Southern Company Services, Inc.; Southern Research Institute; Vesta Insurance Group, Inc.

For full biographical listings, see the Martindale-Hubbell Law Directory

---

BALL, BALL, MATTHEWS & NOVAK, P.A. (AV)

1100 Union Bank Tower, P.O. Drawer 2148, 36102-2148
Telephone: 334-834-7680
Fax: 334-265-3222

Fred S. Ball (1866-1942)
Charles A. Ball (1904-1969)
Fred S. Ball, Jr. (1896-1974)
Richard A. Ball (1906-1983)
John R. Matthews, Jr.
Richard A. Ball, Jr.
Tabor R. Novak, Jr.
Clyde C. Owen, Jr.
C. Winston Sheehan, Jr.
William H. Brittain II
Joana S. Ellis
E. Hamilton Wilson, Jr.
Richard E. Broughton
T. Cowin Knowles
Gerald C. Swann, Jr.

Mark T. Davis
James A. Rives
Fred B. Matthews
Allison L. Alford

Counsel for: Bell Helicopter Co.; John Deere Co.; Government Employees Insurance Co.; Chubb & Son; Cigna Co.; Chrysler Corp.; Associated Aviation Underwriters.

For full biographical listings, see the Martindale-Hubbell Law Directory

---

CAPELL, HOWARD, KNABE & COBBS, P.A. (AV)

57 Adams Avenue, P.O. Box 2069, 36102-2069
Telephone: 334-241-8000

Jack L. Capell
Fontaine M. Howard (1908-1985)
Walter J. Knabe (1898-1979)
Edward E. Cobbs (1909-1982)
L. Lister Hill (1936-1993)
Herman H. Hamilton, Jr.
Rufus M. King
Robert S. Richard
John B. Scott, Jr.
John F. Andrews
James M. Scott
Thomas S. Lawson, Jr.
John L. Capell, III
William D. Coleman
William K. Martin
Bruce J. Downey III
Henry C. Barnett, Jr.
Palmer Smith Lehman
Richard F. Allen
Neal H. Acker
Henry H. Hutchinson
Shapard D. Ashley
D. Kyle Johnson
J. Lister Hubbard
James N. Walter, Jr.
James H. McLemore
H. Dean Mooty, Jr.
Jim B. Grant, Jr.
Wyeth Holt Speir, III
Chad S. Wachter
Ellen M. Hastings
Debra Deames Spain
William Rufus King
C. Clay Torbert, III

OF COUNSEL

Timothy Sullivan

For full biographical listings, see the Martindale-Hubbell Law Directory

---

CAPOUANO, WAMPOLD, PRESTWOOD & SANSONE, P.A. (AV)

350 Adams Avenue, P.O. Box 1910, 36102-1910
Telephone: 334-264-6401
Fax: 334-834-4954

Leon M. Capouano
Alvin T. Prestwood
Jerome D. Smith
Ellis D. Hanan
Joseph P. Borg
Joseph W. Warren

OF COUNSEL

Charles H. Wampold, Jr.

(See Next Column)

Thomas B. Klinner
Linda Smith Webb
James M. Sizemore, Jr.

Counsel for: First Alabama Bank of Montgomery, N.A.; Union Bank and Trust Co.; Real Estate Financing, Inc.; SouthTrust Bank; AmSouth Bank; Central Bank; City Federal Savings & Loan Assoc.; Colonial Mortgage Co.; Lomas & Nettleton; First Bank of Linden.

For full biographical listings, see the Martindale-Hubbell Law Directory

---

HASKELL SLAUGHTER YOUNG JOHNSTON & GALLION, PROFESSIONAL ASSOCIATION (AV)

Suite 375 Bailey Building, 400 South Union Street, P.O. Box 4660, 36104
Telephone: 334-265-8573
Facsimile: 334-264-7945
Birmingham, Alabama Office: Haskell Slaughter Young & Johnston. 1200 AmSouth/Harbert Plaza, 1901 Sixth Avenue North. 35203
Telephone: 205-251-1000.
Facsimile: 205-324-1133.

Thomas T. Gallion, III
Constance A. Caldwell

Barry D. Woodham

Representative Clients: The Bradford Group, Inc.; City of Birmingham; The Equitable Life Assurance Society of the United States; Exxon Corporation; Federal Deposit Insurance Corporation/Resolution Trust Corporation; HEALTHSOUTH Rehabilitation Corporation/HEALTHSOUTH Medical Centers; Hughes Missile Systems; Montgomery County, Alabama; Psychiatric Healthcare Corporation; USX Corporation.

For full biographical listings, see the Martindale-Hubbell Law Directory

---

HILL, HILL, CARTER, FRANCO, COLE & BLACK, P.C. (AV)

425 South Perry Street, P.O. Box 116, 36101-0116
Telephone: 334-834-7600
Fax: 334-263-5969

Thomas B. Hill, Jr. (1903-1984)
James T. Stovall (1905-1972)
James J. Carter (1913-1985)
William A. Oldacre (1932-1973)
Wm. Inge Hill
Ralph A. Franco
T. Bowen Hill, III
Harry Cole
Robert C. Black, Sr.
William I. Hill, II
John M. Milling, Jr.
William Inge Hill, Jr.
Gerald W. Hartley
Randall Morgan
Robert W. Bradford, Jr.
David E. Allred
Laura L. Crum
Charles A. Stewart, III
Mark A. Franco
Terry A. Sides
John R. Bradwell

H. Byron Carter, III
William C. McGowin
Robert C. Black, Jr.
David E. Avery, III
R. Rainer Cotter, III
Susan E. Kennedy
Pamela Pelekis Swan

Representative Clients: The Aetna Group; The State Farm Group; ALFA; General Electric Co.; General Motors Corp; Blue Cross and Blue Shield of Alabama; Allstate Insurance Co.; Winn-Dixie Stores, Inc.; Scottsdale Insurance Co.; National Casualty Co.

For full biographical listings, see the Martindale-Hubbell Law Directory

---

RUSHTON, STAKELY, JOHNSTON & GARRETT, P.A. (AV)

184 Commerce Street, P.O. Box 270, 36104
Telephone: 334-834-8480
Fax: 334-262-6277

Charles A. Stakely
Jesse M. Williams, III
Nicholas T. Braswell, III
Henry B. Hardegree
Henry C. Chappell, Jr.
J. Theodore Jackson
Thomas G. Mancuso
James W. Garrett, Jr.
Robert A. Huffaker
Thomas H. Keene
Richard B. Garrett
Jeffrey W. Blitz
Dennis R. Bailey
Ronald G. Davenport
Fred W. Tyson
Robert C. Brock
F. Chadwick Morriss
T. Kent Garrett
Frank J. Stakely
William S. Haynes
Helen Crump Wells
Jack B. Hinton, Jr.
Amy Catherine Vibbart
Paul M. James, Jr
N. Wayne Simms, Jr.
Christopher S. Simmons
D. Mitchell Henry

OF COUNSEL

William B. Moore, Jr.

General Counsel for: Automobile Dealers Association of Alabama, Inc.; Alabama Rural Electric Association Cooperative; Alabama Roadbuilders Association.
Representative General Clients: Sears Roebuck & Co.; Dow Chemical U.S.A.; The Advertiser Co.
Representative Insurance Clients: United States Fidelity and Guaranty Co.; The Travelers Insurance Co.; The Continental National American Group.

For full biographical listings, see the Martindale-Hubbell Law Directory

Montgomery—Continued

SIROTE & PERMUTT, P.C. (AV)

Colonial Commerce Center, Suite 305, One Commerce Street, 36104
Telephone: 334-261-3400
Facsimile: 334-261-3434
Birmingham, Alabama Office: 2222 Arlington Avenue, South, P.O. Box 55727.
Telephone: 205-933-7111.
Facsimile: 205-930-5301.
Huntsville, Alabama Office: 200 Clinton Avenue, N.W., Suite 1000.
Telephone: 205-536-1711.
Facsimile: 205-534-9650.
Mobile, Alabama Office: One St. Louis Centre, Suite 1000.
Telephone: 205-432-1671.
Facsimile: 205-434-0196.
Tuscaloosa, Alabama Office: 2216 14th Street.
Telephone: 205-752-2089.

Susan B. Anderson
Jeff Kohn
M. Fredrick Simpler, Jr.
Richard H. Sforzini, Jr.
Charles Middleton

For full biographical listings, see the Martindale-Hubbell Law Directory

*MOULTON,** Lawrence Co. — (Refer to Decatur)

*OPELIKA,** Lee Co.

SAMFORD, DENSON, HORSLEY, PETTEY & MARTIN (AV)

709 Avenue A, P.O. Box 2345, 36803-2345
Telephone: 334-745-3504
Fax: 334-745-3506

MEMBERS OF FIRM

N. D. Denson (1856-1927)
John V. Denson (1885-1940)
N. D. Denson, Jr. (1887-1958)
Yetta G. Samford, Jr.
John V. Denson
William F. Horsley
Robert H. Pettey, Jr.
Stanley A. Martin

Attorneys for: The Farmers National Bank; South Central Bell Telephone Co.; International Paper Co.; Liberty National Life Insurance Co.; Wehadkee Yarn Mills; The First National Bank.

For full biographical listings, see the Martindale-Hubbell Law Directory

WALKER, HILL, ADAMS, UMBACH, MEADOWS & WALTON (AV)

Walker Building, 205 South 9th Street, P.O. Box 2069, 36803
Telephone: 334-745-6466
Fax: 334-749-2800

MEMBERS OF FIRM

Jacob A. Walker (1889-1973)
Jacob Walker
Hoyt W. Hill
Phillip E. Adams, Jr.
Arnold W. Umbach, Jr.
Robert T. Meadows, III
Will O. (Trip) Walton, III
Jacob A. Walker, III
Russell K. Bush

Local Counsel for: Liberty Mutual Insurance Co.; Aetna Casualty & Surety Co. ; Fireman's Fund Insurance Group; U.S.F. & G. Co.; Bituminous Insurance Group; American Interstate Insurance Company of Georgia; Carolina Casualty Insurance Co.; Cotton States Insurance Co.; Kemper Insurance Group; The Hartford Insurance Co.

For full biographical listings, see the Martindale-Hubbell Law Directory

*OZARK,** Dale Co. — (Refer to Dothan)

PELL CITY, St. Clair Co.

BLAIR, HOLLADAY AND PARSONS (AV)

St. Clair Land Title Building, 1711 Cogswell Avenue, 35125
Telephone: 205-884-3440
Fax: 205-884-3442

MEMBERS OF FIRM

A. Dwight Blair
Hugh E. Holladay
Elizabeth S. Parsons

Representative Clients: Colonial Bank; Metro Bank; St. Clair Federal Savings Bank; State Farm Mutual Insurance Cos; ALFA Mutual Insurance Co.; Allstate Insurance Co.; St. Paul Insurance Cos.; Auto Owners Insurance Co.; Reliance Insurance Cos.; St. Clair Land Title Co., Inc.

For full biographical listings, see the Martindale-Hubbell Law Directory

*PHENIX CITY,** Russell Co. — (Refer to Opelika)

*ROCKFORD,** Coosa Co. — (Refer to Opelika)

*RUSSELLVILLE,** Franklin Co.

FINE & McDOWELL (AV)

507 North Jackson, P.O. Box 818, 35653
Telephone: 205-332-1660
Fax: 205-332-0318

(See Next Column)

Joe Fine
Daniel G. McDowell

ASSOCIATES

Eddie Beason
John F. Pilati

Representative Clients: Citizens Bank & Savings Co. of Russellville; Citigroup; City of Phil Campbell; Russellville City Board of Education; Franklin County Board of Education; Mutual Savings Life Insurance Co.; State Farm Fire & Casualty Co.; State Farm Mutual Automobile Ins. Co.; Franklin County Board of Commissioners; Marshall Durbin Co.

For full biographical listings, see the Martindale-Hubbell Law Directory

*SCOTTSBORO,** Jackson Co.

LIVINGSTON, PORTER & PAULK, P.C. (AV)

123 East Laurel Street, P.O. Box 1108, 35768
Telephone: 205-259-1919
Telecopier: 205-259-1189

Jack Livingston
John F. Porter, III
Gerald R. Paulk

Counsel for: Jackson County, Alabama; Jackson County Board of Education; Jackson County Health Care Authority; Scottsboro Electric Power Board; First National Bank of Stevenson, Alabama; Jacobs Bank.
Local Counsel for: State Farm Insurance Cos.; The Travelers Insurance Cos.; Liberty Mutual Insurance Co.; The Hartford Insurance Co.

For full biographical listings, see the Martindale-Hubbell Law Directory

*SELMA,** Dallas Co.

PITTS, PITTS & THOMPSON (AV)

Suite 201 Amsouth Bank Building, Drawer 537, 36702-0537
Telephone: 334-875-7213
Fax: 334-874-8218

MEMBERS OF FIRM

Arthur M. Pitts (1880-1955)
W. McLean Pitts (1911-1982)
Philip Henry Pitts
J. Garrison Thompson

Local Attorneys for: U. S. F. & G. Co.; St. Paul Mercury Insurance Cos.; Maryland Casualty Co.; Traveler's Insurance Co.; CSX Transportation; City of Selma.
Approved Attorneys for: Lawyers Title Insurance Corp.; Farm Credit Bank of Texas.

For full biographical listings, see the Martindale-Hubbell Law Directory

REEVES & STEWART, P.C. (AV)

First Alabama Bank Building, P.O. Box 457, 36702-0457
Telephone: 334-875-7236

Edgar A. Stewart (Retired)
Archie T. Reeves, Jr.
B. Kincey Green, Jr.
Robert E. Armstrong, III

Local Attorneys for: State Farm Mutual Automobile Insurance Cos.; St. Paul Insurance Cos.; International Paper Co.; First Alabama Bank; Alabama Power Co.; South Central Bell Telephone; Alabama Gas Corp.; HealthTrust, Inc.
Assistant Division Counsel for: Norfolk Southern Corp.

For full biographical listings, see the Martindale-Hubbell Law Directory

SYLACAUGA, Talladega Co.

BELL AND ODOM (AV)

223 North Norton Avenue, P.O. Box 101, 35150-0101
Telephone: 205-245-7486
Facsimile: 205-245-7487
Birmingham, Alabama Office: 625 South 38th Street, P.O. Box 11244,
Telephone: 205-322-1225.
Fax: 205-664-8695
Pelham, Alabama Office: 211-B Yeager Parkway.
Telephone: 205-664-8691.
Fax: 205-664-8695.

Thomas Reuben Bell

For full biographical listings, see the Martindale-Hubbell Law Directory

*TROY,** Pike Co.

CALHOUN, FAULK, WATKINS & CLOWER (AV)

78 South Court Square, P.O. Box 489, 36081
Telephone: 334-566-7200
Fax: 334-566-7584

Richard F. Calhoun
Joseph E. Faulk
William Keith Watkins
James G. Clower

General Counsel for: City of Troy; City of Brundidge; First Alabama Bank, Troy; First National Bank of Brundidge; Troy City Board of Education; Pike County Board of Education; South Alabama Electric Cooperative, Inc.; B & D Plastics, Inc.; Battery Marketing Corporation.

For full biographical listings, see the Martindale-Hubbell Law Directory

*TUSCALOOSA,** Tuscaloosa Co.

DAVIDSON, WIGGINS & CROWDER, P.C. (AV)

2625 Eighth Street, P.O. Box 1939, 35403
Telephone: 205-759-5771
Fax: 205-752-8259

M. McCoy Davidson
G. Stephen Wiggins
Courtney Crowder
David Ryan

OF COUNSEL

Hugh W. Roberts, Jr.

Attorneys for: Aetna Life & Casualty Co.; Canal Insurance Co.; Government Employees Insurance Co.; The Travelers Group; Auto-Owners Insurance Co.; Continental National American Group; Federated Insurance; Lynn Insurance Group; The Trinity Cos.; The PMA Group.

For full biographical listings, see the Martindale-Hubbell Law Directory

PHELPS, JENKINS, GIBSON & FOWLER (AV)

1201 Greensboro Avenue, P.O. Box 020848, 35402-0848
Telephone: 205-345-5100
Fax: 205-758-4394
Fax: 205-391-6658

MEMBERS OF FIRM

Sam M. Phelps
James J. Jenkins
Johnson Russell Gibson, III
Randolph M. Fowler
Michael S. Burroughs
C. Barton Adcox
Farley A. Poellnitz

ASSOCIATES

K. Scott Stapp
Karen C. Welborn
Sandra C. Guin
Kimberly B. Glass
Stephen E. Snow

Attorneys for: Aetna Insurance Co.; Allstate Insurance Co.; Carolina Casualty Insurance Co.; Continental Insurance Cos.; Fireman's Fund-American Insurance Cos.; Great American Insurance Co.; Hanover Insurance Co.

For full biographical listings, see the Martindale-Hubbell Law Directory

ZEANAH, HUST, SUMMERFORD & DAVIS, L.L.C. (AV)

Seventh Floor, AmSouth Bank Building, P.O. Box 1310, 35403
Telephone: 205-349-1383
Fax: 205-391-1319

MEMBERS OF FIRM

Olin W. Zeanah (1922-1987)
Wilbor J. Hust, Jr.
E. Clark Summerford
Kenneth D. Davis
Christopher H. Jones
Beverly A. Smith

OF COUNSEL

Marvin T. Ormond

Representative Clients: Alfa Insurance Cos.; Hartford Insurance Group; Home Insurance Co.; Nationwide Insurance Co.; Alabama Power Co.; Liberty Mutual Ins. Co.; The Uniroyal Goodrich Tire Co.

For full biographical listings, see the Martindale-Hubbell Law Directory

*UNION SPRINGS,** Bullock Co. — (Refer to Tuskegee)

*VERNON,** Lamar Co. — (Refer to Tuscaloosa)

*WETUMPKA,** Elmore Co. — (Refer to Montgomery)

ALASKA

*ANCHORAGE,** Third Judicial District

DELANEY, WILES, HAYES, REITMAN & BRUBAKER, INC. (AV)

1007 West Third Avenue, 99501
Telephone: 907-279-3581
Fax: 907-277-1331

Eugene F. Wiles (1922-1990)
John K. Brubaker (1937-1992)
Raymond E. Plummer
Daniel A. Gerety
Stephen M. Ellis
Clay A. Young
William E. Moseley
Marc D. Bond
J. D. Cellars
James B. Friderici
Andrew Guidi
Howard A. Lazar
Donald C. Thomas
Timothy J. Lamb
Donna M. Meyers
Susan C. Orlansky
Jeffrey P. Stark

OF COUNSEL

James J. Delaney
George N. Hayes
Stanley H. Reitman

Representative Clients: Liberty Mutual Insurance Company; Carr-Gottstein Foods Co.; Royal Globe Insurance Company; NORCAL Mutual Insurance Company; Medical Indemnity Exchange of California; The Doctor's Company; American Insurance Company; Royal Insurance; Alaska Insurance Guaranty Association; Seibu, Inc.

For full biographical listings, see the Martindale-Hubbell Law Directory

FAULKNER, BANFIELD, DOOGAN & HOLMES, A PROFESSIONAL CORPORATION (AV)

550 West Seventh Avenue, Suite 1000, 99501
Telephone: 907-274-0666
Telecopier: 907-277-4657
Juneau, Alaska Office: 302 Gold Street. 99501.
Telephone: 907-586-2210.
Telecopier: 970-586-8090.
Seattle, Washington Office: 999 Third Avenue, Suite 2600. 98104.
Telephone: 206-292-8008.
Telecopier: 206-340-0289.

Herbert L. Faulkner (1882-1972)
Frank M. Doogan (1923-1977)
Michael M. Holmes (Resident at the Seattle, Washington Office)
Randall J. Weddle (Resident)
William B. Rozell (Resident at the Juneau Office)
Michael A. Barcott (Resident at the Seattle, Washington Office)
Richard B. Brown (Resident)
Timothy A. McKeever (Resident)
James E. Hutchins (Resident)
Constance E. Livsey (Resident)

OF COUNSEL

Lawrence T. Feeney (Retired)
Norman C. Banfield (Retired)

Theresa M. Hennemann (Resident)
Jane E. Steiner (Resident)
Gilman Dana S. Burke (Resident)
Elizabeth D. Goudreau (Resident)
Matthew D. Regan (Resident)
Sandra J. Cole (Resident)
Suzanne H. Lombardi (Resident)

For full biographical listings, see the Martindale-Hubbell Law Directory

ROBERTSON, MONAGLE & EASTAUGH, A PROFESSIONAL CORPORATION (AV)

Suite 1200 The Enserch Center, 550 West Seventh Avenue, 99501
Telephone: 907-277-6693
Telecopy: 907-279-1959
Juneau, Alaska Office: Goldbelt Place Office Building, 801 West 10th Street, Suite 300.
Telephone: 907-586-3340.
Telecopy: 907-586-6818.
Arlington, Virginia Office: Arlington Courthouse Plaza II, 2300 Clarendon Boulevard, Suite 1010.
Telephone: 703-527-4414.
Telecopy: 703-527-0421.

Royal Arch Gunnison (1893-1918)
R. E. Robertson (1885-1961)
M. E. Monagle (1902-1985)
Frederick O. Eastaugh (1913-1992)
Michael T. Thomas (Resident at Arlington, Virginia Office)
Leroy J. Barker
James F. Clark (Resident at Juneau Office)
Paul M. Hoffman (Resident at Juneau Office)
L. G. Berry
Harold E. Snow, Jr.
D. Elizabeth Cuadra (Resident at Juneau Office)
Steven W. Silver (Resident at Arlington, Virginia Office)
Carl Winner (Resident at Arlington, Virginia Office)
Bradley D. Gilman (Resident at Arlington, Virginia Office)
Robert Blasco (Resident at Juneau Office)
Julia Barrows Bockmon
Terry L. Thurbon (Resident at Juneau Office)
Margaret Ogden Dullanty

(See Next Column)

James T. Morgan, Jr. (Not admitted in AK; Resident at Arlington, Virginia Office)
Wayne D. Hawn (Resident at Juneau Office)
Daniel J. Boone (Resident at Juneau Office)

LEGAL SUPPORT PERSONNEL

LEGAL ASSISTANTS

Chloe Clark-Berry
Deborah Sims

Representative Clients: Alaska Pulp Corp.; Alyeska Pipeline Service Co.; Associated Aviation Underwriters; Brunswick Corp.; Fireman's Fund Insurance Group; U.S. Aviation Insurance Group; U.S. Borax Chemical Corp.

For full biographical listings, see the Martindale-Hubbell Law Directory

*FAIRBANKS,** Fourth Judicial District

CALL, BARRETT & BURBANK, A PROFESSIONAL CORPORATION (AV)

711 Gaffney Road, 99701
Telephone: 907-452-2211
Fax: 907-456-1137

David H. Call
Paul A. Barrett
Winston S. Burbank
Michael P. McConahy
Gary Foster
Christopher E. Zimmerman

Reference: Denali State Bank.

For full biographical listings, see the Martindale-Hubbell Law Directory

*JUNEAU,** First Judicial District

FAULKNER, BANFIELD, DOOGAN & HOLMES, A PROFESSIONAL CORPORATION (AV)

302 Gold Street, 99801
Telephone: 907-586-2210
Telecopier: 907-586-8090
Anchorage, Alaska Office: 550 West Seventh Avenue, Suite 1000. 99501.
Telephone: 907-274-0666.
Telecopier: 907-277-4657.
Seattle, Washington Office: 999 Third Avenue, Suite 2600. 98104.
Telephone: 206-292-8008.
Telecopier: 206-340-0289.

Herbert L. Faulkner (1882-1972)
Frank M. Doogan (1923-1977)
Michael M. Holmes (Resident at the Seattle, Washington Office)
Randall J. Weddle (Resident at the Anchorage Office)
William B. Rozell (Resident)
Charles N. Drennan (Resident)
Anthony M. Sholty (Resident)
James R. Webb (Resident)
Michael A. Barcott (Resident at the Seattle, Washington Office)
Richard B. Brown (Resident at the Anchorage Office)
Timothy A. McKeever (Resident at the Anchorage Office)
Leon T. Vance (Resident)
James E. Hutchins (Resident at the Anchorage Office)
John E. Casperson (Resident at the Seattle, Washington Office)
Ann Gifford Vance (Resident)
Eric A. Kueffner (Resident)
Constance E. Livsey (Resident at the Anchorage Office)
Bethann Boudah Chapman (Resident)

OF COUNSEL

Lawrence T. Feeney (Retired)
Norman C. Banfield (Retired)

Bruce B. Weyhrauch (Resident)
William D. DeVoe (Resident at the Seattle, Washington Office)
Mala J. Reges (Resident)
Theresa M. Hennemann (Resident at the Anchorage Office)
Jane E. Steiner (Resident at the Anchorage Office)
James P. Crawford (Resident)
Gilman Dana S. Burke (Resident at the Anchorage Office)
Elizabeth D. Goudreau (Resident at the Anchorage Office)
Raymond H. Warns, Jr. (Not admitted in AK; Resident at the Seattle, Washington Office)
Dwight L. Guy (Not admitted in AK; Resident at the Seattle, Washington Office)
F. Lachicotte Zemp, Jr (Resident)
Mary H. Zemp (Resident)
Philip W. Sanford (Resident at the Seattle, Washington Office)
Matthew D. Regan (Resident at the Anchorage Office)
Sandra J. Cole (Resident at the Anchorage Office)
Michael A. Barnhill
Suzanne H. Lombardi (Resident at the Anchorage Office)
Alec W. Brindle, Jr. (Not admitted in AK; Resident at the Seattle, Washington Office)
Wendy J. Wallace (Resident)

For full biographical listings, see the Martindale-Hubbell Law Directory

KETCHIKAN, First Judicial District

ZIEGLER, CLOUDY, PETERSON, WOODELL & SEAVER (AV)

307 Bawden Street, 99901
Telephone: 907-225-9401
Fax: 907-225-5513

(See Next Column)

ZIEGLER, CLOUDY, PETERSON, WOODELL & SEAVER, *Ketchikan—Continued*

MEMBERS OF FIRM

A. H. Ziegler (1889-1972)
Robert H. Ziegler, Sr. (1921-1991)
Charles L. Cloudy
John W. Peterson
Will Woodell
Mitchell A. Seaver

LEGAL SUPPORT PERSONNEL

Christy G. Elliott

Counsel for: Ketchikan Pulp Co.

For full biographical listings, see the Martindale-Hubbell Law Directory

KODIAK, Third Judicial District

JAMIN, EBELL, BOLGER & GENTRY, A PROFESSIONAL CORPORATION (AV)

323 Carolyn Street, 99615
Telephone: 907-486-6024
Telecopier: 907-486-6112
Seattle, Washington Office: 300 Mutual Life Building, 605 First Avenue.
Telephone: 206-622-7634.
Telecopier: 206-623-7521.

Matthew D. Jamin
C. Walter Ebell
Joel H. Bolger
Dianna R. Gentry
Alan L. Schmitt

Walter W. Mason (Resident, Seattle Office)
Duncan S. Fields
Karen E. Bendler (Resident, Seattle, Washington Office)

For full biographical listings, see the Martindale-Hubbell Law Directory

ARIZONA

*BISBEE,** Cochise Co. — (Refer to Nogales)

CASA GRANDE, Pinal Co.

FITZGIBBONS LAW OFFICES (AV)

Suite E, 711 East Cottonwood Lane, P.O. Box 11208, 85230-1208
Telephone: 602-426-3824
Fax: 602-426-9355

David A. Fitzgibbons

ASSOCIATES

Robert M. Yates
David A. Fitzgibbons, III
Denis M. Fitzgibbons

OF COUNSEL

E.D. "Bud" McBryde

Representative Clients: Bank of Casa Grande Valley; Charlie Case Tire Co., Inc.; Fletcher's Cobre Tire; M&O Agencies; Maricopa Turf, Inc. a/b/a Western Sod; Vaquero Foundation; Vern Wlaton Motors; West Pinal Family Health Center; Casa Grande Regional Medical Center; Verde Grande Vineyards.

For full biographical listings, see the Martindale-Hubbell Law Directory

CHANDLER, Maricopa Co. — (Refer to Mesa)

COOLIDGE, Pinal Co. — (Refer to Casa Grande)

COTTONWOOD, Yavapai Co.

ASPEY, WATKINS & DIESEL (AV)

905 Cove Parkway, Unit 201, 86326
Telephone: 602-639-1881
Flagstaff, Arizona Office: 123 North San Francisco.
Telephone: 602-774-1478.
Facsimile: 774-1043.
Sedona, Arizona Office: 120 Soldier Pass Road.
Telephone: 602-282-5955.
Facsimile: 602-282-5962.
Winslow, Arizona Office: 205 North Williamson.
Telephone: 602-289-5963.
Page, Arizona Office: 904 North Navajo.
Telephone: 602-645-9694.

Kaign N. Christy

For full biographical listings, see the Martindale-Hubbell Law Directory

DOUGLAS, Cochise Co. — (Refer to Tucson)

*FLAGSTAFF,** Coconino Co.

ASPEY, WATKINS & DIESEL (AV)

123 North San Francisco, 86001
Telephone: 602-774-1478
Facsimile: 602-774-1043
Sedona, Arizona Office: 120 Soldier Pass Road.
Telephone: 602-282-5955.
Facsimile: 602-282-5962.
Page, Arizona Office: 904 North Navajo.
Telephone: 602-645-9694.
Winslow, Arizona Office: 205 North Williamson.
Telephone: 602-289-5963.
Cottonwood, Arizona Office: 905 Cove Parkway, Unite 201.
Telephone: 602-639-1881.

MEMBERS OF FIRM

Frederick M. Fritz Aspey
Bruce S. Griffen
Harold L. Watkins
Donald H. Bayles, Jr.
Louis M. Diesel
Kaign N. Christy
John J. Dempsey

Zachary Markham
Whitney Cunningham
James E. Ledbetter
Holly S. Karris

LEGAL SUPPORT PERSONNEL

Deborah D. Roberts (Legal Assistant)
Dominic M. Marino, Jr, (Paralegal Assistant)
C. Denece Pruett (Legal Assistant)

Representative Clients: Farmer's Insurance Company of Arizona; Kelley-Moore Paint Co.; Pepsi-Cola Bottling Company of Northern Arizona; Bill Luke's Chrysler-Plymouth, Inc.; First American Title Insurance Company ; Transamerica Title Insurance Co.; Page Electric Utility; Comprehensive Access Health Plan, Inc.
Reference: First Interstate Bank-Arizona, N.A., Flagstaff, Arizona.

For full biographical listings, see the Martindale-Hubbell Law Directory

MANGUM, WALL, STOOPS & WARDEN, P.L.L.C. (AV)

222 East Birch Avenue, P.O. Box 10, 86002
Telephone: 602-779-6951
Fax: 602-773-1312

H. Karl Mangum (1908-1993)

OF COUNSEL

Douglas J. Wall
Robert W. Warden

MEMBERS OF FIRM

Daniel J. Stoops
Stephen K. Smith
A. Dean Pickett
Melinda L. Garrahan
Jon W. Thompson

ASSOCIATES

Kathleen O'Brien
Corbin Vandemoer
David W. Rozema
Kevin S. Heinonen

Representative Clients: Northern Arizona University; Flagstaff Unified School District; Museum of Northern Arizona; City of Sedona; Arizona School Board Association.
Local Counsel for: Bank of America-Arizona; Arizona Public Service; U.S-.A.A.; State Farm Fire & Casualty Ins. Co.; Hartford Ins. Co.

For full biographical listings, see the Martindale-Hubbell Law Directory

*GLOBE,** Gila Co. — (Refer to Coolidge)

GREEN VALLEY, Pima Co.

DUFFIELD, MILLER, YOUNG, ADAMSON & ALFRED, P.C. (AV)

101-65 South La Canada, Green Valley Mall, 85614
Telephone: 602-625-4404
Tucson, Arizona Office: Suite 711, Transamerica Building, 177 North Church Avenue.
Telephone: 602-792-1181.
LaPaloma Office: LaPaloma Corporate Center, 3573 East Sunrise Drive, Suite 115, Tucson, Arizona.
Telephone: 602-577-1135.

Richard Duffield
Larry R. Adamson
Michael C. Young
K. Alexander Hobson
Eugene C. Gieseler

Representative Clients: San Xavier Rock & Materials, Inc.; Mobat-Adamson Tire Co.; Community Water Company of Green Valley.
Insurance Company Clientele: State Farm Mutual Insurance Cos.; Automobile Club Insurance Co.; Colonial Penn Insurance Co.; Crum & Forster Group; National Indemnity Insurance Co.

For full biographical listings, see the Martindale-Hubbell Law Directory

*HOLBROOK,** Navajo Co. — (Refer to Flagstaff)

*KINGMAN,** Mohave Co. — (Refer to Flagstaff)

LAKE HAVASU CITY, Mohave Co.

WACHTEL, BIEHN & MALM (AV)

Suite A, 2240 McCulloch Boulevard, 86403
Telephone: 602-855-5115
Fax: 602-855-5211

OF COUNSEL

Wing Wachtel

MEMBERS OF FIRM

Don Biehn
James B. Wyss
Denis R. Malm
Steven A. Biehn
Rex L. Martin

For full biographical listings, see the Martindale-Hubbell Law Directory

MESA, Maricopa Co.

KILLIAN, NICHOLAS, FISCHER, WIRKEN, COOK & PEW, P.L.C. (AV)

40 North Center Street, Suite 200, 85201
Telephone: 602-461-4600
Facsimile: 602-461-4763
Mailing Address: P.O. Box 1467, Mesa, Arizona, 85211-1467

Vernon L. Nicholas
Douglas K. Cook
M. Paul Fischer
W. Ralph Pew
Charles W. Wirken
Gail M. Ledward

OF COUNSEL

C. Max Killian

Elaine N. Blunck
David R. Baker
Thomas J. Griggs
Renée P. Roelants
Wilford L. Taylor
Ezra T. Clark, III

Representative Clients: Dunkin' Donuts of America; Pulte Home Corp.; Tempe Life Care Village, Inc.; Continental Homes; Bingham Equipment; Tomar Electronics; Queen Creek Irrigation District; Chandler Ginning Co.; Electrical District No. 5.

For full biographical listings, see the Martindale-Hubbell Law Directory

*NOGALES,** Santa Cruz Co.

O'CONNOR, CAVANAGH, ANDERSON, WESTOVER, KILLINGSWORTH & BESHEARS, A PROFESSIONAL ASSOCIATION (AV)

1827 North Mastick Way, 85621
Telephone: 602-761-4215
FAX: 602-761-3505
Phoenix, Arizona Office: One East Camelback Road, Suite 1100, 85012.
Telephone: 602-263-2400.
FAX: 602-263-2900.
Tucson, Arizona Office: Suite 2200, One South Church Avenue, 85701.
Telephone: 602-882-8912.
FAX: 602-624-9564.
Sun City, Arizona Office: 13250 North Del Webb Boulevard, Suite B, 85351.
Telephone: 602-263-2808.
FAX: 602-933-3100.

Hector G. Arana
Kimberly A. Howard Arana

OF COUNSEL

James D. Robinson

Representative Clients: Omega Produce Co.; Frank's Distributing, Inc.; City of Nogales; Collectron of Ariz., Inc.; James K. Wilson Produce Co.; Agricola Bon, S. de R.L. de C.V.; Angel Demerutis E.; Rene Carrillo C.; Arturo Lomeli; Theojary Crisantes E.

For full biographical listings, see the Martindale-Hubbell Law Directory

PAGE, Coconino Co.

ASPEY, WATKINS & DIESEL (AV)

904 North Navajo, 86040
Telephone: 602-645-9694
Flagstaff, Arizona Office: 123 North San Francisco.
Telephone: 602-774-1478.
Facsimile: 774-1043.
Sedona, Arizona Office: 120 Soldier Pass Road.
Telephone: 602-282-5955.
Facsimile: 602-282-5962.
Winslow, Arizona Office: 205 North Williamson.
Telephone: 602-289-5963.
Cottonwood, Arizona Office: 905 Cove Parkway, Unit 201.
Telephone: 602-639-1881.

MEMBERS OF FIRM

Bruce S. Griffen

Representative Clients: Page Electric Utility.
Reference: First Interstate Bank.

For full biographical listings, see the Martindale-Hubbell Law Directory

*PHOENIX,** Maricopa Co.

APKER, APKER, HAGGARD & KURTZ, P.C. (AV)

2111 East Highland Avenue, Suite 230, 85016
Telephone: 602-381-0085
Telecopier: 602-956-3457

Burton M. Apker
Jerry L. Haggard
David B. Apker
Gerrie Apker Kurtz

Cynthia M. Chandley
Kevin M. Moran

Representative Clients: Ancala Global Company; ASARCO Incorporated; Douglas Land Corp.; Frito-Lay, Inc.; Lawyers Title Insurance Corp.; Nevada Power Company; The North West Life Assurance Co.; Phelps Dodge Corporation; Santa Fe Pacific Gold Corporation; Western Federal Savings & Loan Assn.

For full biographical listings, see the Martindale-Hubbell Law Directory

BROWN & BAIN, A PROFESSIONAL ASSOCIATION (AV)

2901 North Central Avenue, P.O. Box 400, 85001-0400
Telephone: 602-351-8000
Cable: TWX 910-951-0646
Telecopier: 602-351-8516
Palo Alto, California Affiliated Office: Brown & Bain, 600 Hansen Way.
Telephone: 415-856-9411.
Telecopier: 415-856-6061.
Tucson, Arizona Affiliated Office: Brown & Bain, A Professional Association. One South Church Avenue, Nineteenth Floor, P.O. Box 2265.
Telephone: 602-798-7900
Telecopier: 602-798-7945.

Lois W. Abraham (Resident at Palo Alto Office)
Lynne Christensen Adams
Robert E. B. Allen
Michael F. Bailey
C. Randall Bain
Eddward P. Ballinger, Jr.
Daniel C. Barr
Philip P. Berelson (Resident at Palo Alto Office)

(See Next Column)

Alan H. Blankenheimer
Jack E. Brown
John A. Buttrick
Howard Ross Cabot
H. Michael Clyde
William S. Coats (Resident at Palo Alto Office)
Richard Calvin Cooledge
Stephen W. Craig
C. Timothy Delaney
Paul F. Eckstein
Terry E. Fenzl
Jodi Knobel Feuerhelm
Douglas Gerlach (On leave)
Amy J. Gittler
Brent M. Gunderson
Kyle B. Hettinger
Philip R. Higdon (Resident at Tucson Office)
Roy W. Kyle (Resident at Tucson Office)
Karl J. Kramer (Resident at Palo Alto Office)
Don F. Kumamoto (Resident at Palo Alto Office)
Martin L. Lagod (Resident at Palo Alto Office)
Stephen E. Lee
Joseph E. Mais
Cynthia Y. McCoy
Michael F. McNulty (Resident at Tucson Office)
Joseph W. Mott
Joel W. Nomkin
Christopher R. Ottenweller (Resident at Palo Alto Office)
Stephen A. Owens
Michael W. Patten
Frank M. Placenti
Charles S. Price
Daniel James Quigley (Resident at Tucson Office)
Daniel P. Quigley
Jeffrey G. Randall (Resident at Palo Alto Office)
Joseph P. Richardson
John W. Rogers
Lawrence G. D. Scarborough
D. Bruce Sewell (Resident at Palo Alto Office)
Sarah R. Simmons (Resident at Tucson Office)
Lex J. Smith
Craig W. Soland
Scott M. Theobald
Charles Van Cott
Antonio T. Viera
George C. Wallach
Kim E. Williamson

Craig Y. Allison (Resident at Palo Alto Office)
Sarah W. Anderson (Resident at Palo Alto Office)
David M. Barkan (Not admitted in AZ; Resident at Palo Alto Office)
Susan D. Berney-Key (Resident at Palo Alto Office)
Charles A. Blanchard
Carolyn F. Bostick (Resident at Palo Alto Office)
David P. Brooks
Chad S. Campbell
Chuck P. Ebertin (Resident at Palo Alto Office)
Timothy J. Franks
Patricia A. Hubbard
Jonathan M. James
Shirley Ann Kaufman
Todd R. Kerr
Jin Sun Kim (Not admitted in AZ)
Jeanean Kirk
C. Mark Kittredge
Grant A. Koppelman
N. Todd Leishman
Robin M. Lightner (Resident at Palo Alto Office)
Sherry (Xiao-Hong Liu) Liu
Deborah Henscheid Lyon
Diane Madenci (Resident at Tucson Office)
Anthony L. Marks
Daniel G. Martin
Jolene L. McCaleb
Kelly A. O'Connor
Lane D. Oden (Resident at Tucson Office)
Peter J. Osetek
Joel L. Poppen
Sarah Ellison Porter
Christopher J. Raboin
Jane L. Rodda (Resident at Tucson Office)
Steven R. Rodgers
Daria Roithmayr
Lee Stein
Samuel A. Thumma
Karen M. Wilkinson

COUNSEL

Roger S. Borovoy (Resident at Palo Alto Office)
Paul S. Davis (Resident at Tucson Office)
Michael C. Jones
Victoria S. Lewis
James F. McNulty, Jr. (Resident at Tucson Office)
Bernard Petrie (Resident at Palo Alto Office)
Judith K. Weiss

For full biographical listings, see the Martindale-Hubbell Law Directory

BURCH & CRACCHIOLO, P.A. (AV)

702 East Osborn Road, Suite 200, 85014
Telephone: 602-274-7611
Fax: 602-234-0341
Mailing Address: P.O. Box 16882, Phoenix, AZ, 85011

Daniel Cracchiolo
Stephen E. Silver
Brian Kaven
Jack D. Klausner
Guadalupe Iniguez
Brad S. Ostroff
Daryl Manhart
Ian Neale
David G. Derickson
Edwin C. Bull
Bryan F. Murphy
Linda A. Finnegan
Andrew Abraham
Clare H. Abel
Donald W. Lindholm
F. Michael Carroll
Daniel R. Malinski
Edwin D. Fleming
Ralph D. Harris
Jess A. Lorona

Marigene Abbott-Dessaint
Josephine Cuccurullo
Marvin Davis
Paul F. Dowdell
Stephen M. Hart
Theodore (Todd) Julian
Steven J. Lippman
Thomas A. Longfellow
Eve Parks
Martha C. Patrick
Steven M. Serrano
James M. Stipe
David M. Villadolid
J. Brent Welker

(See Next Column)

BURCH & CRACCHIOLO P.A.—*Continued*

OF COUNSEL

Frank Haze Burch
Howard C. Meyers

Representative Clients: Bashas' Inc.; Farmers Insurance Group; U-Haul International, Inc.

For full biographical listings, see the Martindale-Hubbell Law Directory

DAUGHTON, HAWKINS, BROCKELMAN, GUINAN & PATTERSON (AV)

40 North Central Avenue, Suite 2500, 85004
Telephone: 602-271-4400
Fax: 602-271-4300

Donald Daughton
Michael D. Hawkins
Kent Brockelman
Michael D. Guinan
Bart J. Patterson
Leslie Kyman Cooper
Christopher J. Berry

For full biographical listings, see the Martindale-Hubbell Law Directory

FENNEMORE CRAIG, A PROFESSIONAL CORPORATION (AV)

Two North Central, Suite 2200, 85004
Telephone: 602-257-8700
Fax: 602-257-8527
Scottsdale, Arizona Office: 6263 North Scottsdale Road, Suite 290, 85250.
Telephone: 602-257-5400.
Fax: 602-945-4932.
Tucson, Arizona Office: One South Church Avenue, Suite 1030, 85701.
Telephone: 602-624-9312.
Fax: 602-882-7383.

Calvin H. Udall
James Powers
James M. Bush
Linwood Perkins, Jr. (Retired)
Edward C. LeBeau
Arthur D. Ehrenreich
C. Webb Crockett
William T. Boutell, Jr.
Kenneth J. Sherk
Neal Kurn
Robert P. Robinson
Michael Preston Green
Philip A. Edlund
John D. Everroad
James W. Johnson
F. Pendleton Gaines, III
Robert J. Hackett
Louis F. Comus, Jr.
Donald R. Gilbert
Ronald L. Ballard
Timothy J. Burke
Ronald J. Stolkin
Stephen M. Savage
John R. Rawling
Roger T. Hargrove
William L. Kurtz
Mark A. Nesvig
James R. Huntwork
David T. Maddox (Not admitted in AZ)
George T. Cole
John G. Ryan
Lauren J. Caster
Leland M. Jones
Timothy Berg
C. Owen Paepke
William L. Thorpe
Charles M. King
David T. Cox
Cynthia L. Shupe
Michael V. Mulchay
Phillip F. Fargotstein
Paul J. Mooney
David A. Weatherwax
Graeme E. M. Hancock
Rita A. Eisenfeld
Ray K. Harris
Margaret R. Gallogly
Kaye L. McCarthy
Scott M. Finical
William T. Burghart
Mark R. Herriot
Andrew M. Federhar
Douglas E. McAllister
Cathy L. Reece
Gregg Hanks
Peter M. Gerstman
Karen Ciupak McConnell
Jay S. Kramer
Christopher L. Callahan
Robert P. Simbro
Loral Deatherage
Jim L. Wright
Bryan A. Albue
J. Barry Shelley
Lesa J. Storey
Christopher P. Staring
Janet W. Lord
John Randall Jefferies
Robert D. Anderson
John J. Balitis, Jr.

Marc L. Spitzer
James J. Trimble
Karen A. Curosh
Brenda K. Church
Theresa Dwyer
Gary H. Ashby
Paul Sala
Mark H. Brain
Debra L. Runbeck
Scott H. Thomas
Jon R. Hulburd
Janice Procter-Murphy
Otto S. Shill, III
Robert J. Kramer
Darren J. McCleve
Jean Marie Sullivan
Keith L. Hendricks
Ann-Martha Andrews
Polly S. Rapp
Howard M. Shanker (Not admitted in AZ)
Douglas J. Grier
Elizabeth M. Behnke
W. T. Eggleston, Jr.
Tamra E. Walker
Douglas C. Northup
Stephen A. Good
Richard A. Bark
Karen Rettig Rogers
Marc H. Lamber
Richard A. Kasper
Joseph P. Mikitish
Christopher W. Zaharis
Stacie K. Smith
Dewain D. Fox
Mark N. Rogers
Kendis K. Muscheid
Dean M. Fink
Michael L. Kaplan
Alan S. Hall
Scott T. Ashby
Laurel J. Davis
Mary Beth Phillips

(See Next Column)

OF COUNSEL

Philip E. von Ammon

Representative Clients: ASARCO Incorporated; AT&T Communications; Bridgestone/Firestone, Inc.; Catellus Development Corp.; Citibank (Arizona); First Interstate Bank of Arizona; GIANT Industries; Phelps Dodge Corporation; The Atchison, Topeka & Santa Fe Railway, Co.; US WEST Communications.

For full biographical listings, see the Martindale-Hubbell Law Directory

GAMMAGE & BURNHAM (AV)

One Renaissance Square, Two North Central Avenue, Suite 1800, 85004
Telephone: 602-256-0566
Fax: 602-256-4475

MEMBERS OF FIRM

Richard B. Burnham
Grady Gammage, Jr.
F. William Sheppard
Michael R. King
Richard K. Mahrle
Shawn E. Tobin
Curtis A. Ullman
Mary B. Fylstra
Michael B. Withey
Thomas J. McDonald
James A. Craft
Ellen Harris Hoff
Kevin R. Merritt
Randall S. Dalton
Corinne E. Giagnorio
Kevin J. Blakley
John R. Dacey
Jeffrey J. Miller
Cameron C. Artigue
Timothy J. Martens
Susan L. Watchman
Stephen W. Anderson
Colleen E. Grant
Margo S. Kirchner
Christopher A. Womack

For full biographical listings, see the Martindale-Hubbell Law Directory

GOODSON & MANLEY, P.C. (AV)

The Brookstone Building, 2025 North 3rd Street, Suite 200, 85004-1471
Telephone: 602-252-5110
Fax: 602-257-1883

John F. Goodson
Colleen C. Manley
Richard E. Durfee, Jr.
Joel M. Klinge

A list of Representative Clients will be furnished upon request.
Reference: Caliber (Arizona).

For full biographical listings, see the Martindale-Hubbell Law Directory

JENNINGS, STROUSS AND SALMON, P.L.C. (AV)

A Professional Limited Liability Company
One Renaissance Square, Two North Central, 85004-2393
Telephone: 602-262-5911
Fax: 602-253-3255

Irving A. Jennings (1896-1972)
Charles L. Strouss (1891-1958)
Riney B. Salmon (1902-1970)
J. A. Riggins, Jr. (1912-1986)
Rex H. Moore (1906-1971)
Charles R. Esser (1929-1972)
William T. Birmingham
John R. Christian
Gary G. Keltner
Lee E. Esch
Charles E. Jones
Richard L. Lassen
T. Patrick Flood
W. Michael Flood
I. Douglas Dunipace
Ronald H. Moore
Gary L. Stuart
M. Byron Lewis
Douglas G. Zimmerman
Michael A. Beale
K. Thomas Finke
Gerald W. Alston
David L. White
John B. Weldon, Jr.
James D. Vieregg
John G. Sestak, Jr.
Philip J. MacDonnell
Donald J. Oppenheim
Douglas L. Christian
Kenneth C. Sundlof, Jr.
Rita A. Meiser
Diane K. Geimer
Gerrit M. Steenblik
Gary L. Lassen
Richard N. Morrison
John A. Micheaels
Barry E. Lewin
Anne L. Kleindienst
Ann M. Dumenil
Jay A. Fradkin
Michael R. Palumbo
Joseph A. Drazek
Glenn J. Carter
Richard C. Onsager
H. Christian Bode
Stephen E. Crofton
James M. Ackerman
Carol A. Cluff
Preston H. Longino, Jr.
George Esahak-Gage
Robert J. Werner
Ernest Calderon
Jon D. Schneider
Frederick M. Cummings
Wendy D. Woodrow
Brian N. Spector
Michael J. O'Connor
Leo L. Miller
Robert E. Coltin
Katherine M. Cooper
John J. Egbert
Matthew D. Kleifield
Lisa M. McKnight
John R. Becker

OF COUNSEL

Nicholas Udall
Frank B. Campbell, Jr.
Earl F. Glenn, Jr.

Tracy A. Gromer
Charles D. Onofry
Carol Ann Salvati
J. Matthew Powell
Robert D. Haws
James D. Shook
Jennifer M. Bligh
Margaret A. Gillespie
K. Thomas Slack
Kim D. Steinmetz
Cody M. Hall
Elizabeth C. Painter

(See Next Column)

JENNINGS, STROUSS AND SALMON P.L.C., *Phoenix—Continued*

Mark A. McGinnis
David B. Earl
William F. Auther
Brett L Hopper
Thomas B. Dixon
Brian D. Wallace
Brian C. Silbernagel
Lisa A. Frey
Gordon Lewis
Stephanie McRae
Martin A. Tetreault

Representative Clients: Best Western International, Inc.; Chemical Waste Management, Inc.; CNA Insurance; Salt River Project; Southwest Gas Corp.; St. Joseph's Hospital and Medical Center; Karsten Manufacturing; Mutual Insurance of Arizona; Shamrick Foods Co.; Smitty's Super Valu, Inc.

For full biographical listings, see the Martindale-Hubbell Law Directory

KIMERER, LAVELLE, HAY & HOOD, P.L.C. (AV)

2715 North Third Street, 85004
Telephone: 602-279-5900
FAX: 602-264-5566

COUNSEL

Clark L. Derrick

John L. Hay
Richard B. Hood
Michael D. Kimerer
Michael J. LaVelle

Merrick B. Firestone

For full biographical listings, see the Martindale-Hubbell Law Directory

LEWIS AND ROCA (AV)

A Partnership including Professional Corporations
40 North Central Avenue, 85004-4429
Telephone: 602-262-5311
Fax: 602-262-5747
Tucson, Arizona Office: One South Church Avenue, Suite 700.
Telephone: 602-622-2090.
Fax: 602-622-3088.

MEMBERS OF FIRM

Orme Lewis (1903-1990)
Edwin Beauchamp (1916-1964)
Joseph E. McGarry
Jeremy E. Butler
Gerald K. Smith
Douglas L. Irish
Douglas R. Chandler
Marty Harper
R. Kent Klein
Jordan Green
Barry Fish
Frank S. Bangs, Jr. (Resident, Tucson Office)
Patricia K. Norris
Patrick Derdenger
Edward F. Novak
Thomas H. Campbell
Geoffrey H. Walker
Kevin L. Olson
Gabriel Beckmann (Resident, Tucson Office)
David M. Bixby
Amy R. Porter
George L. Paul
James L. Hohnbaum
Betty L. Hum
Stephen M. Bressler
Thomas Klinkel
Allen R. Clarke
Karen Carter Owens
Jesse B. Simpson
Jessica Jeanne Youle
Michael Owen Miller (Resident, Tucson Office)
Mary Ellen Simonson
Lewis D. Schorr (Resident, Tucson Office)
James T. Acuff, Jr.
Rosemarie Christofolo
Bryant D. Barber
Bret A. Maidman
Robert H. Mc Kirgan
James J. Belanger
L. Keith Beauchamp
Paul M. Roca (1911-1979)
John P. Frank
S. L. Schorr (Resident, Tucson Office)
Peter D. Baird
Merton E. Marks (P.C.)
Tom Galbraith
Richard N. Goldsmith
Richard S. Cohen
Susan M. Freeman
David E. Manch
Randolph J. Haines
Judith E. Sirkis
José A. Cárdenas
Dale A. Danneman
Foster Robberson
Michael J. Holden
Beth J. Schermer
John N. Iurino (Resident, Tucson Office)
David J. Cantelme
Newman R. Porter
Sheila Carmody
D. Randall Stokes
Thomas G. Ryan
Steven J. Labensky
Edward M. Mansfield
Barbara J. Muller
Rob Charles (Resident, Tucson Office)
Scott DeWald
James K. Kloss
Robert F. Roos
Brent C. Gardner
Andrew Daru Schorr (Resident, Tucson Office)
Cathy M. Holt
Steven J. Hulsman
Carl F. Mariano
Christopher J. Brelje
Kenneth Van Winkle, Jr.
Steven J. Burr
Pamela B. Petersen
Jane E. Reddin

ASSOCIATES

Charles W. Steese
John R. Worth
Deborah A. Nye
Barbara A. Anstey
Bradley P. Balson
David A. Kelly
R. Neil Taylor, III
J. Tyler Haahr
Noël Moran Vickers
Kim C. Stanger
Greg S. Como
Stephen R. Winkelman
Michael G. Galloway
Kevin G. Hunter

(See Next Column)

ASSOCIATES (Continued)

Christine Ann Hartland
Deanna Salazar
Juliet A. Lim
David D. Rodgers
Laura Knoll
Kathryn E. Underwood
Lynn Robbins Wagner
Dawn M. Bergin
Corey C. Watson
Randy Warner
Julia A. Kossak-Fuller
Julie M. Arvo MacKenzie
Richard A. Halloran
Michael L. Burke
Joni M. Wallace (Resident, Tucson Office)
Karl C. Eppich
Margaret R. Russell
Thel W. Casper
Mary Beth Savel (Resident, Tucson Office)
Anthony J. Blackwell
Jeff A. Shumway
Janell M. Adams-Vogl
Todd A. Rigby

OF COUNSEL

Lyman A. Manser
Steven Marc Weinberg (Not admitted in AZ)
Thomas V. Rawles
Hope Leibsohn
Craig W. Phillips

Representative Clients: Blood Systems, Inc.; CIT Corp.; City of Phoenix; The Dial Corp; E.I. du Pont de Nemours and Co.; The Frank Lloyd Wright Foundation; Litton Industries, Inc.; The Prudential Insurance Company of America; Samaritan Health System.

For full biographical listings, see the Martindale-Hubbell Law Directory

LIEBERMAN, DODGE, SENDROW & GERDING, LTD. (AV)

First Interstate Tower, Suite 1801 3550 North Central Avenue, 85012-2114
Telephone: 602-277-3000
Fax: 602-277-7478
Chicago, Illinois Office: LaSalle Bank Building, Suite 1407, 135 South La Salle Street.
Telephone: 312-541-8510.
Fax: 312-845-2902.

David D. Dodge
Paul S. Gerding
Marc R. Lieberman
Susan G. Sendrow

Mary K. Farrington-Lorch
Paul S. Gerding, Jr. (Not admitted in AZ; Resident, Chicago, Illinois Office)

OF COUNSEL

Terence D. Woolston
Karen L. Kothe
Robert G. Anderson

For full biographical listings, see the Martindale-Hubbell Law Directory

MARISCAL, WEEKS, MCINTYRE & FRIEDLANDER, P.A. (AV)

2901 North Central Avenue Suite 200, 85012
Telephone: 602-285-5000
Fax: 602-279-2128; 264-0340

Phillip Weeks
Rudolph Mariscal
Donald N. McIntyre
Richard A. Friedlander
Gerald Gaffaney
William L. Novotny
Michael S. Rubin
Gary L. Birnbaum
Robert A. Shull
Peter A. Winkler
Michael R. Scheurich
Fred C. Fathe
Michael P. West
Les S. Raatz
Andrew L. Pringle
Brian M. Mueller
Anne L. Tiffen
P. Bruce Converse
Judith M. Wolf
James T. Braselton
Leslie A. Kresin
Leonce A. Richard
Scott A. Holcomb
Terry L. Tedesco
David J. Ouimette
D. Samuel Coffman
Kathryn A. Krecke
Mark J. Robens
Michael D. Hool
Donna M. Somsky
Cindra L. White
Steven D. Wolfson
John B. Even
Scot L. Claus
Stacy Crouch
Mary Grace Blasko

References: Northern Trust, Arizona; Rio Salado Bank.

For full biographical listings, see the Martindale-Hubbell Law Directory

MCCABE, O'DONNELL & WRIGHT, A PROFESSIONAL ASSOCIATION (AV)

Suite 2000, 300 East Osborn, 85012
Telephone: 602-264-0800
Telecopier: 602-274-0146

Joseph I. McCabe
Kathleen M. O'Donnell
Michael W. Wright
Jerry W. Lawson
Jeffrey A. Ekbom

References: First Interstate Bank of Arizona, N.A., Trust Department.

For full biographical listings, see the Martindale-Hubbell Law Directory

Phoenix—Continued

MEYER, HENDRICKS, VICTOR, OSBORN & MALEDON, A PROFESSIONAL ASSOCIATION (AV)

2929 North Central Avenue Suite 2100, 85012-2794
Telephone: 602-640-9000
Facsimile: (24 Hrs.) 602-640-9050
Mailing Address: P.O. Box 33449, 85067-3449,

Paul J. Meyer
Ed Hendricks
David Victor
Jones Osborn II
William J. Maledon
Larry A. Hammond
Andrew D. Hurwitz
Robert L. Palmer
Randall C. Nelson
Jeffrey L. Sellers
R. Douglas Dalton
Don Bivens
Ron Kilgard
Jay I. Moyes
Donald M. Peters
Thomas H. Curzon
David G. Campbell
John A. LaSota, Jr.
C. Taylor Ashworth
Howard N. Singer
James G. Derouin
Gary A. Gotto
Thomas D. Proffitt
William M. Hardin
Brett L. Dunkelman
Helen Perry Grimwood
Michelle M. Matiski
Jeffrey C. Zimmerman
David B. Rosenbaum
Diane M. Johnsen
W. Scott Bales
Bruce E. Meyerson
Lucia Fakonas Howard
Robert V. Kerrick
Mark D. Samson
Shane R. Swindle
Mary E. Berkheiser
Jay S. Ruffner
Thayne Lowe
G. Murray Snow
Brent Ghelfi
David K. Duncan
Craig D. Hansen
Thomas J. Salerno
Christopher D. Johnson
Michael A. Lechter
Clark M. Porter
Mark Andrew Fuller
Debra A. Hill
Sigmund G. Popko
Catherine R. Hardwick
Lee Herold Storey

Dawn L. Dauphine
Scott W. Rodgers
Bradley S. Paulson
Christopher Graver
Laurie B. Shough
Ronald R. Gallegos
Evan Haglund
Trevor A. Brown
Geoffrey M.T. Sturr
Joan S. Burke
Susan Ann Cannata
Cynthia P. Moehring
Daniel J. Noblitt
Jamie McAlister
Douglas C. Anderson
Quentin T. Phillips
Joseph M. Udall
Laurel Finch
Christine A. Dupnik
Robin A. Goble
Michael F. Barry
Sheryl L. Andrew

OF COUNSEL

Michael A. Berch

CONSULTANTS

Myron M. Sheinfeld (Not admitted in AZ)
W. John Glancy (Not admitted in AZ)

Reference: Bank One Arizona, NA.

For full biographical listings, see the Martindale-Hubbell Law Directory

MOHR, HACKETT, PEDERSON, BLAKLEY, RANDOLPH & HAGA, P.C. (AV)

2800 North Central Avenue, Suite 1100, 85004-1043
Telephone: 602-240-3000
Fax: 602-240-6600

William C. Blakley (1946-1987)
Robert C. Hackett
Gordon A. Mohr
Arthur W. Pederson
John M. Randolph
David L. Haga, Jr.
Thomas K. Chenal
Charles I. Kelhoffer
John R. Hoopes
Peter N. Spiller
David W. Dow
Michele M. Feeney
Bridget M. Gaughan
M. Maureen Anders
Gregory W. Falls
Michael R. Perry
Azim Q. Hameed
Thomas C. Axelsen
John J. Nicgorski
Thomas M. Quigley
Grant Pearson
Daniel P. Beeks
Ronald P. Adams
Daniel W. McCarthy
Carolyn Ratti Matthews
Nathaniel B. Rose
Karen L. Karr

For full biographical listings, see the Martindale-Hubbell Law Directory

O'CONNOR, CAVANAGH, ANDERSON, WESTOVER, KILLINGSWORTH & BESHEARS, A PROFESSIONAL ASSOCIATION (AV)

One East Camelback Road, Suite 1100, 85012-1656
Telephone: 602-263-2400
FAX: 602-263-2900
Sun City, Arizona Office: 13250 North Del Webb Boulevard, Suite B, 85351.
Telephone: 602-263-2808.
FAX: 602-933-3100.

(See Next Column)

Tucson, Arizona Office: Suite 2200, One South Church Avenue, 85701.
Telephone: 602-882-8912.
FAX: 602-624-9564.
Nogales, Arizona Office: 1827 North Mastick Way, 85621.
Telephone: 602-761-4215.
FAX: 602-761-3505.

James H. O'Connor (1922-1978)
Harry J. Cavanagh
Wilbert G. Anderson (Retired)
John H. Westover
John H. Killingsworth (1922-1993)
Robert G. Beshears
Ralph E. Hunsaker
Gerald L. Jacobs
Thomas A. McGuire, Jr.
George H. Mitchell
Richard J. Woods
Richard E. Mitchell
Mayor Shanken
Jeffrey B. Smith
Jolyon Grant
Lawrence H. Lieberman
Harding B. Cure
Richard C. Smith
Steven D. Smith
Robert S. Kant
K. David Lindner
J. Victor Stoffa
Henry L. Timmerman
Michael E. Woolf
Philip C. Gerard
Franzula M. Bacher
Michael W. Carnahan
Charles L. Fine
Jeffrey H. Verbin
David W. Earl
John B. Furman
Charles F. Myers
Carol N. Cure
Scott A. Rose
Scott A. Salmon
Richard B. Stagg
Steven L. Lisker
Peter C. Guild
Paul J. Roshka, Jr.
John E. DeWulf
Glenn M. Feldman
Richard M. Lorenzen
Jeffrey D. Buchanan
Gilbert L. Rudolph
Jean E. Harris
Max K. Boyer
Daniel W. Peters
David L. Kurtz
Stephen E. Richman
David A. Van Engelhoven
Paul J. Giancola
Neil D. Biskind
Pamela M. Overton
Michelle S. Monserez
Frank M. Fox
Raymond S. Heyman
David L. Lansky
Stanley D. Mabbitt
Norman L. Miller
Michael Cafiso
Christina S. Hamilton
Lisa M. Sommer
Donald R. Greene (Not admitted in AZ)
William H. Westover
Janice H. Moore
Donald L. Cross

Michael R. Altaffer
Lucas J. Narducci
Janet E. Kornblatt
Leigh A. Kaylor
Arthur T. Carter
Robert J. Itri
Christopher Robbins
Craig J. Bolton
Karen L. Liepmann
Steven M. Rudner
Robert W. Blesch
D. Scott Fehrman

Jeffrey R. Hovik
Philip G. Mitchell
Robert H. Nagle
Robert L. Ehmann
R. Corey Hill
Steven G. Biddle
Timothy F. Bolden
Mark J. DePasquale
Troy B. Froderman
Karl A. Freeburg
Paul G. Schmidt
Mark W. Daliere
John D. Titus
John A. Felix
Ashley D. Adams
Carla A. Wortley
Carl O. Wortley, III
Janet M. Walsh
Timothy P. Stallcup
Mark D. Dillon
Frank W. Moskowitz
Darren L. Brooks
Eric A. Mark
Kent S. Berk
Jamal F. Allen
Steven J. German
Peter C. Prynkiewicz
Jere M. Friedman (Not admitted in AZ)
Lisa R. Tsiolis

OF COUNSEL

Shoshana B. Tancer
Sara R. Ziskin

Representative Clients: Three-Five Systems; Micro Chip; Main Street and Main; ITT Cannon; Bank of America; The Deal Corp.; The Hartford; Dow Corning Corp.; Charles Schwab & Co., Inc.; Playtex Family Products, Inc.

For full biographical listings, see the Martindale-Hubbell Law Directory

ROBBINS & GREEN, A PROFESSIONAL ASSOCIATION (AV)

1800 CitiBank Tower, 3300 North Central Avenue, 85012-9826
Telephone: 602-248-7600
Fax: 602-266-5369

Philip A. Robbins
Richard W. Abbuhl
Wayne A. Smith
Joe M. Romley
Edmund F. Richardson
William H. Sandweg III
Jack N. Rudel
Jeffrey P. Boshes
Brian Imbornoni
Janet B. Hutchison
Bradley J. Stevens
Ronald G. Wilson
Dwayne Ross
Alfred W. Ricciardi
K. Leonard Judson
Dorothy Baran
Austin D. Potenza, II
Sarah McGiffert
Michael S. Green
Kenneth A. Hodson
Daniel L. Brown

For full biographical listings, see the Martindale-Hubbell Law Directory

Phoenix—Continued

SACKS TIERNEY P.A. (AV)

2929 North Central Avenue, Fourteenth Floor, 85012-2742
Telephone: 602-279-4900
Fax: 602-279-2027

Seymour Sacks
Marvin S. Cohen
David C. Tierney
Stephen Aron Benson
Michael R. Rooney
Lawrence J. Rosenfeld
Robert G. Kimball
Susan H. Navran
Robert J. DuComb, Jr.
Marcia J. Busching
Scot C. Stirling
Randall S. Yavitz
Peter W. Sorensen
Sharon Brook Shively
James W. Armstrong
Robert J. Lord
Paul G. Johnson
Susan Strawn de Mars
Steven M. Goldstein

M. Joyce Geyser

Helen Rubenstein Holden
Gaye L. Gould
Sandra E. Price
Candess J. Hunter

Reference: M&I Thunderbird Bank.

For full biographical listings, see the Martindale-Hubbell Law Directory

SHIMMEL, HILL, BISHOP & GRUENDER, P.C. (AV)

3700 North 24th Street, 85016
Telephone: 602-224-9500
Telecopier: 602-955-6176

Blaine B. Shimmel (1891-1965)
Rouland W. Hill (1901-1980)
Brice I. Bishop (1918-1991)
Daniel F. Gruender
Richard B. Kelly
David N. Farren
Keith F. Overholt
Scott J. Richardson
Joseph Wm. Kruchek
Margaret L. Steiner
Michael V. Perry
Susan M. Swick
S. Gregory Jones

OF COUNSEL

Charles A. Finch

James C. Paul
James H. Hazlewood
Glenn B. Hotchkiss
C. Peter Delgado, Jr.
Judith M. Dworkin

Representative Clients: Harkins Amusement Enterprises, Inc.; Citizen Auto Stage Line; Delta Airlines; Grayline Sightseeing Association; Grinnell Mutual Reinsurance Co.; Hensel Phelps Construction Co.

For full biographical listings, see the Martindale-Hubbell Law Directory

SNELL & WILMER (AV)

One Arizona Center, 85004-0001
Telephone: 602-382-6000
Fax: 602-382-6070
Tucson, Arizona Office: 1500 Norwest Tower, One South Church Avenue 85701-1612.
Telephone: 602-882-1200.
Fax: 602-884-1294.
Orange County Office: 1920 Main Street, Suite 1200, P.O. Box 19601, Irvine, California, 92714.
Telephone: 714-253-2700.
Fax: 714-955-2507.
Salt Lake City, Utah Office: Broadway Centre, 111 East Broadway, Suite 900, 84111.
Telephone: 801-237-1900.
Fax: 801-237-1950.

OF COUNSEL

Mark Wilmer
Edward Jacobson
James D. Bruner
Frank L. Snell
Jarril F. Kaplan
John A. Greene

MEMBERS OF FIRM

Frederick K. Steiner, Jr.
Richard K. Mallery
Jon S. Cohen
Jay D. Wiley
George H. Lyons
Daniel J. McAuliffe
Donald D. Colburn
Robert J. Deeny
William R. Hayden
Robert B. Hoffman
Joel P. Hoxie
Lonnie J. Williams, Jr.
Vaughn A. Crawford
Thomas R. Hoecker
Peter G. Santin
Suzanne McCann
Donald L. Gaffney
Arthur T. Anderson
Joyce Kline Wright
John J. Bouma
Robert C. Bates
Warren E. Platt
William A. Hicks, III
Peter J. Rathwell
Steven M. Wheeler
Douglas W. Seitz
Joseph T. Melczer, III
Gerard Morales
Barry D. Halpern
James R. Condo
Richard W. Sheffield
Arthur P. Greenfield
David A. Sprentall
Charles A. Pulaski, Jr.
Terry Morris Roman
Matthew P. Feeney
Patrick E. Hoog
Quinn Williams

(See Next Column)

MEMBERS OF FIRM (Continued)

Richard W. Shapiro
Craig K. Williams
Katherine M. Harmeyer
James J. Sienicki
E. Jeffrey Walsh
Timothy G. O'Neill
G. Van Velsor Wolf, Jr.
Janet E. Barton
Kevin J. Parker
Peter M. Wittekind
Alex B. Marconi
Christopher H. Bayley
Nicholas J. Wood
Robert R. Kinas
Shawn M. McLeran
Steven D. Pidgeon
Rebecca A. Winterscheidt
Martha E. Gibbs
Jeffrey Messing
Jody Kathleen Pokorski
George J. Coleman, III
Heidi L. McNeil
Timothy W. Moser
Stephen M. Hopkins
Donald H. Smith
Charles E. James, Jr.
Steven S. Guy
David E. Weiss, Jr.
Richard D. Blau
Samuel C. Cowley
Sherman O. Parrett
Michael K. Kelly
Donald J. Lenkszus

SENIOR ATTORNEYS

Bruce P. White
Lisa M. Coulter
Shirley J. Wahl
Cheryl A. Ikegami
William P. Allen

ASSOCIATES

Benjamin D. Aguilera
Timothy D. Brown
Patrick G. Byrne
Nancy Kay Campbell
Jeffrey Webb Crockett
Barbara J. Dawson
Elisabeth B. Donnovin
Michael C. Douglass
Brigitte Finley
Patrick X. Fowler
Charles F. Hauff, Jr.
Joseph C. Kreamer
Jeffery W. Lantz
Christine Broghammer Long
Bob J. McCullough
Thomas L. Mumaw
Maria Nutile
(Not admitted in AZ)
Christopher D. Payne
David E. Rauch
Carlos D. Ronstadt
Philip Randolph Rudd
Scott D. Sherman
Prithviraj S. Sivananthan
Victoria M. Stevens
Ptolemy H. Taylor
Steve C. Thornton
Robert C. Venberg
Sondri Allison
Terri N.A. Buccino
Brian J. Campbell
Timothy J. Casey
Roger D. Curley
Michael M. Donahey
William J. Donoher, Jr.
Clinton J Elliott
Brian J. Foster
Stacy Gabriel
Charles P. Keller
Joseph E. Lambert
Christopher J. Littlefield
Jeffrey W. Martin
Andrew G. Miller
Jon S. Musial
Eugene F. O'Connor II
Jon M. Paladini
Loren A. Piel
Sandra J. Rogers
GinaMarie Rossano
Sandra L. Seamans
Thea Foglietta Silverstein
Barrie E. Stachel
Marvin S. Swift, Jr.
Renée Eileen Tetreault
Randall C. Urbom
Jonathan F. Weisbard
Robert R. Yoder

Representative Clients: Arizona Public Service Co.; Bank One, Arizona, NA.; First Security Bank of Utah, N.A.; Ford Motor Co.; Chrysler Motors Corp.; Toyota Motor Sales U.S.A.; Magma Copper Co.; U.S. Home Corp.; Pinnacle West Capital Corp.; Safeway, Inc.

For full biographical listings, see the Martindale-Hubbell Law Directory

SQUIRE, SANDERS & DEMPSEY (AV)

Two Renaissance Square, 40 North Central Avenue, Suite 2700, 85004-4441
Telephone: 602-528-4000
Fax: 602-253-8129
Cleveland, Ohio Office: 4900 Society Center, 127 Public Square, Cleveland, Ohio 44114-1304.
Telephone: 216-479-8500. Fax's: 216-479-8780, 216-479-8781, 216-479-8787, 216-479-8795, 216-479-8777, 216-479-8793, 216-479-8776, 216-479-8788.
Columbus, Ohio Offices: 1300 Huntington Center, 41 South High Street, Columbus, Ohio 43215.
Telephone: 614-365-2700.
Fax: 614-365-2499.
Jacksonville, Florida Office: One Enterprise Center, Suite 2100, 225 Water Street, Jacksonville, Florida 32202.
Telephone: 904-353-1264.
Fax: 904-356-2986.
Miami, Florida Office: 201 South Biscayne Boulevard, Suite 3000 Miami Center, Miami, Florida 33131.
Telephone: 305-577-8700.
Fax: 305-358-1425.
New York, New York Office: 520 Madison Avenue, 32nd Floor, New York, New York 10022.
Telephone: 212-715-4990.
Fax: 212-715-4915.
Washington, D.C. Office: 1201 Pennsylvania Avenue, N.W., P.O. Box 407, Washington, D.C. 20044.
Telephone: 202-626-6600.
Fax: 202-626-6780.

(See Next Column)

SQUIRE, SANDERS & DEMPSEY—*Continued*

London, England Office: 1 Gunpowder Square, Printer Street, London EC4A 3DE.
Telephone: 011-44-71-830-0055.
Fax: 011-44-71-830-0056.
Brussels, Belgium Office: Avenue Louise, 165-Box 15, 1050 Brussels, Belgium.
Telephone: 011-322-648-1717.
Fax: 011-322-648-1064.
Prague Office: Adria Palace, Jungmannova 31/36, 11000 Prague 1, Czech Republic.
Telephone: 011-42-2-231-5661.
Fax: 011-42-2-231-5482.
Bratislava Office: Mudronova 37, 81101 Bratislava, Slovak Republic.
Telephone: 011-42-7-313-362; 011-42-7-315-370.
Fax: 011-42-7-313-918.
Budapest, Hungary Office: Deak Ferenc Ut. 10, Office 304, H-1052 Budapest V., Hungary.
Telephone: 011-361-266-2024.
Fax: 011-36-1-266-2025.
Kiev, Ukraine Office: vul. Prorizna 9 KV 20, Kiev, Ukraine 25203.
Telephones: 011-7-044-244-3452, 011-7-044-244-3453, 011-7-044-228-8687.
Fax: 011-7-044-228-4938.

RESIDENT MEMBERS

James L. Adler, Jr.
Karen T. Kahler
David W. Kreutzberg
Robert L. Matia
Mark A. Nadeau
William L. Nelson
Robert H. Olson, Jr.
Richard F. Ross
Norman C. Storey
Christopher D. Thomas
Donald A. Wall

RESIDENT ASSOCIATES

Steven J. Brown
Liana C. Cocanower
Mark E. Freeze
Melinda Vest Grayson
Benjamin E. Hall
Hugh A. Madden
Linda M. Mitchell
Karen L. Peters
Cynthia A. Ricketts
Ann Thompson Uglietta
Stephen B. White
Rachel L. Yosha

For full biographical listings, see the Martindale-Hubbell Law Directory

STEPTOE & JOHNSON (AV)

Two Renaissance Square, 40 N. Central, Suite 2400, 85004
Telephone: 602-266-6610
Telecopier: 602-274-1970
Washington, D.C. Office: 1330 Connecticut Avenue, N.W.
Telephone: 202-429-3000.
Cable Address: "Stepjohn".
Telex: 89-2503.
Telecopier: 202-429-9204.
Moscow, Russia Office: 7 Maly Levshinsky, #3.
Telephone: 011-7-502-220-2220.

PARTNERS

Lawrence A. Katz
Barry J. Dale
David J. Bodney
Floyd P. Bienstock
Francis J. Burke, Jr.

OF COUNSEL

David A. Selden
Gerard E. Wimberly, Jr.

ASSOCIATES

David E. Vieweg
Bennett Evan Cooper
Monica L. Goebel
Steven M. Hoffman
Kevin M. Judiscak
Kimberly A. Fatica
Peter B. Swann
Lisa Morganstern Bickel
Julie A. Pace
Andrew J. Sweet
Tracy Lorenz
Suzanne C. Lehmer (Not admitted in AZ)
Emily R. Froimson (Not admitted in AZ)

For full biographical listings, see the Martindale-Hubbell Law Directory

STREICH LANG, A PROFESSIONAL ASSOCIATION (AV)

Renaissance One, Two N. Central Avenue, 85004-2391
Telephone: 602-229-5200
Fax: 602-229-5690
Tucson, Arizona Office: One S. Church Avenue, Suite 1700.
Telephone: 602-770-8700.
Fax: 602-623-2518.
Las Vegas, Nevada Affiliated Office: Dawson & Associates, 3800 Howard Hughes Parkway, Suite 1500.
Telephone: 702-792-2727.
Fax: 702-792-2676.
Los Angeles, California Office: 444 S. Flower Street, Suite 1530.
Telephone: 213-896-0484.

Steven A. Betts
Susan G. Boswell (At Tucson, Arizona and Las Vegas, Nevada Offices)
John R. Clemency
John J. Dawson
Dan M. Durrant
Booker T. Evans, Jr. (Resident, Las Vegas Office)
Roger K. Ferland
Douglas O. Guffey
Diane M. Haller

(See Next Column)

William Shepard Hawgood, II
Steven R. Haydon (Resident, Tucson Office)
Douglas W. Holly
R. Neil Irwin
Charles W. Jirauch
Craig H. Kaufman (Resident, Tucson Office)
Thomas J. Lang
Don P. Martin
Bruce B. May
Robert E. Miles
James F. Morrow (Resident, Tucson Office)
Deana S. Peck
Henry A. Perras
Ronold P. Platner
Karen A. Potts
Ronald E. Reinsel
Mark E. Rinehart (Not admitted in AZ)
James A. Ryan
Louis A. Stahl
Preston J. Steenhoek
Kent W. Stevens
John A. Swain
Timothy J. Thomason
Kevin J. Tourek
John C. Vryhof
Edwin Baird Wainscott
Richard K. Walker
Nancy L. White
Jeffrey Willis (Partner-in-Charge, Tucson Office)
Fred T. Witt, Jr.

OF COUNSEL

Raymond R. Cusack (Resident, Tucson Office)
Laurence J. De Respino
Matthew Mehr
Randall S. Theisen

Thomas D. Arn
Jeffrey D. Barlow
David Bray
Leigh Lani Taylor Brown
Scott B. Cohen
Thomas B. Crosbie
Robin L. De Respino
Linda B. Dubnow
Lisa Dibbern Duran
Russell O. Farr
Dawn R. Gabel
Michael R. Hall (Resident, Tucson Office)
John Anthony Harris
Robert P. Harris
Joy E. Herr-Cardillo (Resident, Tucson Office)
Elliot S. Isaac
David L. Johnson
Jay M. Johnson
Scott A. Klundt
Nancy J. March (Resident, Tucson Office)
Stephen R. Mick (Resident, Los Angeles Office)
David V. Millard (Resident, Tucson Office)
Robert J. Miller
Kevin J. Morris
Roger N. Morris
Steven Rand Owens (Resident, Tucson Office)
Lance L. Shea
Shawn Eric Shearer
Brian Sirower
Natalie A. Spencer
Dana Stagg Belknap
Debra A. Stanton
Laurel I. Wala
Michael B. Wixom (Resident, Las Vegas Office)

Representative Clients: Allied-Signal Aerospace Company; America West Airlines, Inc.; Atlantic Richfield Co.; Chicago Title; First Interstate Bank of Arizona, N.A.; Magma Copper Co.; Motorola, Inc.; Phelps Dodge Development Corp.; TRW Inc.; The Travelers Companies.

For full biographical listings, see the Martindale-Hubbell Law Directory

LAW OFFICES OF DAVID WM. WEST, P.C. (AV)

1300 E. Missouri Avenue, Suite B-200, 85014
Telephone: 602-263-7891
Fax: 602-263-5031

David Wm. West

Reference: Bank of America, Arizona.

For full biographical listings, see the Martindale-Hubbell Law Directory

*PRESCOTT,** Yavapai Co.

FAVOUR, MOORE, WILHELMSEN & SCHUYLER, A PROFESSIONAL ASSOCIATION (AV)

1580 Plaza West Drive, P.O. Box 1391, 86302
Telephone: 602-445-2444
Fax: 602-771-0450

John B. Schuyler, Jr.
Mark M. Moore
David K. Wilhelmsen
Lance B. Payette
Clifford G. Cozier

OF COUNSEL

John M. Favour
Richard G. Kleindienst

Representative Client: Yavapai Title Co.
Reference: Bank of America.

For full biographical listings, see the Martindale-Hubbell Law Directory

MURPHY, LUTEY, SCHMITT & BECK (AV)

Elks Building, 117 East Gurley Street, 86301
Telephone: 602-445-6860
Fax: 602-445-6488
Yuma, Arizona Office: Valley Professional Plaza. 1763 West Twenty-Fourth Street, Suite 200.
Telephone: 602-726-0314.
Fax: 602-341-1079.

MEMBERS OF FIRM

Thelton D. Beck
Michael R. Murphy
Selmer D. Lutey
Robert E. Schmitt

(See Next Column)

MURPHY, LUTEY, SCHMITT & BECK, *Prescott—Continued*

ASSOCIATES

Dan A. Wilson Bruce E. Rosenberg

OF COUNSEL

Keith F. Quail

Northern Arizona Counsel for: State Farm Mutual Automobile Insurance Co.; Transamerica Title Insurance Co.; Allstate Insurance Co.
Local Counsel for: Bank One Arizona, N.A.; General Motors Corp.
Representative Clients: Chino Valley Irrigation District; Prescott College; Galpin Ford, Inc.; Yavapai Medical Center, P.C.

For full biographical listings, see the Martindale-Hubbell Law Directory

*ST. JOHNS,** Apache Co. — (Refer to Flagstaff)

SCOTTSDALE, Maricopa Co.

FENNEMORE CRAIG, A PROFESSIONAL CORPORATION (AV)

6263 North Scottsdale Road, Suite 290, 85250
Telephone: 602-257-5400
Fax: 602-945-4932
TWX: 910-950-4608
Phoenix, Arizona Office: Two North Central Avenue, Suite 2200, 85004.
Telephone: 602-257-8700.
Fax: 602-257-8527.
Tucson, Arizona Office: One South Church Avenue, Suite 1030, 85701.
Telephone: 602-624-9312.
Fax: 602-882-7383.

Edward C. LeBeau Philip A. Edlund
George T. Cole

Representative Clients: ASARCO Incorporated; AT&T Communications; Bridgestone/Firestone, Inc.; Catellus Development Corp.; Cyprus Amax Mineral Co.; First Interstate Bank of Arizona; GFC Financial Corp.; GIANT Industries; PETsMART, Inc.; Phelps Dodge Corporation.

For full biographical listings, see the Martindale-Hubbell Law Directory

SEDONA, Coconino & Yavapai Cos.

ASPEY, WATKINS & DIESEL (AV)

120 Soldier Pass Road, 86336
Telephone: 602-282-5955
Facsimile: 602-282-5962
Flagstaff, Arizona Office: 123 North San Francisco.
Telephone: 602-774-1478.
Facsimile: 774-1043.
Page, Arizona Office: 904 North Navajo.
Telephone: 602-645-9694.
Winslow, Arizona Office: 205 North Williamson.
Telephone: 602-289-5963.
Cottonwood, Arizona Office: 905 Cove Parkway, Unit 201.
Telephone: 602-639-1881.

MEMBERS OF FIRM

Harold L. Watkins Kaign N. Christy
Bruce S. Griffen

Representative Clients: Sedona-Verde Valley Board of Realtors, Inc.; Sedona Physician Center; Sedona Center Development Group; The Gilomen Group; Foothills North Homeowners Association; Shadows Estates Homeowners Assn., Inc.
References: Security Pacific Bank- Arizona; First Interstate Bank.

For full biographical listings, see the Martindale-Hubbell Law Directory

SIERRA VISTA, Cochise Co.

RILEY & HOGGATT, P.C. (AV)

Suite M-12 Haymore Plaza, 500 E. Fry Boulevard, 85635
Telephone: 602-458-0130
FAX: 602-459-5181

Richard J. Riley Wallace R. Hoggatt

Laura A. Cardinal Adela Maria Flores

LEGAL SUPPORT PERSONNEL

Yvonne Morris (Paralegal)

For full biographical listings, see the Martindale-Hubbell Law Directory

SUN CITY, Maricopa Co.

O'CONNOR, CAVANAGH, ANDERSON, WESTOVER, KILLINGSWORTH & BESHEARS, A PROFESSIONAL ASSOCIATION (AV)

13250 North Del Webb Boulevard, Suite B, 85351-3053
Telephone: 602-263-2808
FAX: 602-933-3100
Phoenix, Arizona Office: One East Camelback Road, Suite 1100, 85012.
Telephone: 602-263-2400.
FAX: 602-263-2900.

(See Next Column)

Tucson, Arizona Office: Suite 2200, One South Church Avenue, 85701.
Telephone: 602-882-8912.
FAX: 602-624-9564.
Nogales, Arizona Office: 1827 North Mastick Way, 85621.
Telephone: 602-761-4215.
FAX: 602-761-3505.

William C. Wahl, Jr.

For full biographical listings, see the Martindale-Hubbell Law Directory

*TUCSON,** Pima Co.

BROWN & BAIN, A PROFESSIONAL ASSOCIATION (AV)

One South Church Avenue, Nineteenth Floor, P.O. Box 2265, 85702-2265
Telephone: 602-798-7900
Telecopier: 602-798-7945
Phoenix, Arizona Affiliated Office: Brown & Bain, A Professional Association, 2901 North Central Avenue, P.O. Box 400.
Telephone: 602-351-8000.
Telecopier: 602-351-8516.
Palo Alto, California Affiliated Office: Brown & Bain, 600 Hansen Way.
Telephone: 415-856-9411.
Telecopier: 415-856-6061.

RESIDENT PERSONNEL

Philip R. Higdon Michael F. McNulty
Roy W. Kyle Daniel James Quigley
Sarah R. Simmons

Diane Madenci Lane D. Oden
Jane L. Rodda

COUNSEL

Paul S. Davis James F. McNulty, Jr.

For full biographical listings, see the Martindale-Hubbell Law Directory

CHANDLER, TULLAR, UDALL & REDHAIR (AV)

1700 Bank of America Plaza, 33 North Stone Avenue, 85701
Telephone: 602-623-4353
Telefax: 602-792-3426

MEMBERS OF FIRM

Thomas Chandler Edwin M. Gaines, Jr.
D. B. Udall Dwight M. Whitley, Jr.
Jack Redhair E. Hardy Smith
Joe F. Tarver, Jr. John J. Brady
Steven Weatherspoon Christopher J. Smith
S. Jon Trachta Charles V. Harrington
Bruce G. MacDonald

ASSOCIATES

Margaret A. Barton Mark Fredenberg
Joel T. Ireland Mariann T. Shinoskie
Kurt Kroese

Representative Clients: Arizona Electric Power Cooperative, Inc.; Atlantic Richfield Co.; CNA Insurance; Farmers Insurance Exchange; MICA; Chubb Insurance Group; Aetna Casualty; State Farm Mutual Insurance Companies; Santa Cruz Valley Water Authority.
Reference: Arizona Bank.

For full biographical listings, see the Martindale-Hubbell Law Directory

DUFFIELD, MILLER, YOUNG, ADAMSON & ALFRED, P.C. (AV)

Suite 711, Transamerica Building, 177 North Church Avenue, 85701
Telephone: 602-792-1181
Green Valley, Arizona Office: 101-65 South La Canada, Green Valley Mall.
Telephone: 602-625-4404.
LaPaloma Office: LaPaloma Corporate Center, 3573 East Sunrise Drive, Suite 115, Tucson, Arizona.
Telephone: 602-577-1135.

Philip Hawley Smith Richard Duffield
Larry R. Adamson Eugene C. Gieseler
Samuel D. Alfred K. Alexander Hobson
Thomas R. Althaus Arthur H. Miller
Michael C. Young

LEGAL SUPPORT PERSONNEL

Cynthia Sargent Althaus Joan Shelton, CLA
Mary Jane Arnesen Christine M. Smith
Katrina Hillman Barbara L. Steimle
Elizabeth Kohl-Sturgeon Elaine Webb

Representative Clients: San Xavier Rock & Materials; Community Water Company of Green Valley.
Insurance Company Clientele: State Farm Mutual Insurance Cos.; Automobile Club Insurance Co.; Colonial Penn Insurance Co.; Metropolitan Property & Liability Insurance Co.; National Indemnity Ins. Co.

For full biographical listings, see the Martindale-Hubbell Law Directory

Tucson—Continued

Fennemore Craig, A Professional Corporation (AV)

Suite 1030, One South Church Avenue, 85701-1620
Telephone: 602-624-9312
Fax: 602-882-7383
Phoenix, Arizona Office: Two North Central Avenue, Suite 2200, 85004.
Telephone: 602-257-8700.
Fax: 602-257-8527.
Scottsdale, Arizona Office: 6263 North Scottsdale Road, Suite 290, 85250.
Telephone: 602-257-5400.
Fax: 602-945-4932.

Andrew M. Federhar
Ronald J. Stolkin
Christopher P. Staring

Representative Clients: ASARCO Incorporated; AT&T Communications; Bridgestone/Firestone, Inc.; Catellus Development Corp.; Cyprus Amax Minerals Co.; First Interstate Bank of Arizona; GFC Financial Corp.; GIANT Industries; PETsMART, Inc.; Phelps Dodge Corporation.

For full biographical listings, see the Martindale-Hubbell Law Directory

Gabroy, Rollman & Bossé, P.C. (AV)

Suite 201, 2195 E. River Road, 85718
Telephone: 602-577-1300
Telefax: 602-577-0717

Steven L. Bossé
Richard M. Rollman
John Gabroy
Ronald M. Lehman
Fred A. Farsjo
Lyle D. Aldridge

Ronna Lee Fickbohm
Richard A. Brown

For full biographical listings, see the Martindale-Hubbell Law Directory

Peter T. Gianas, P.C. (AV)

4400 East Broadway, Suite 800, 85711
Telephone: 602-795-6630
Fax: 602-327-1922

Peter T. Gianas

For full biographical listings, see the Martindale-Hubbell Law Directory

Hazlett & Wilkes (AV)

310 South Williams Boulevard, Suite 305, 85711
Telephone: 602-790-9663
Fax: 602-790-9616

MEMBERS OF FIRM

Carl E. Hazlett
James M. Wilkes

ASSOCIATE

Thomas M. Bayham

For full biographical listings, see the Martindale-Hubbell Law Directory

Kimble, Gothreau & Nelson, P.C. (AV)

5285 East Williams Circle, Suite 3500, 85711-7411
Telephone: 602-748-2440
Fax: 602-748-2469

Michael J. Gothreau (1943-1990)
Darwin J. Nelson
Daryl A. Audilett
Stephen E. Kimble
Lawrence McDonough
David F. Toone
Michael P. Morrison
Michelle T. Lopez
Negatu Molla
Carroll E. Mizelle
Michael E. Medina

OF COUNSEL

William Kimble

Representative Clients: State of Arizona; General Motors Corp.; Procter & Gamble Co.; St. Paul Fire and Marine Insurance Co.; City of Tucson; Tucson Electric Power Co.; United States Fidelity & Guaranty Co.; Industrial Indemnity Insurance Co.; Allstate Insurance Co.

For full biographical listings, see the Martindale-Hubbell Law Directory

Lesher & Williams, A Professional Corporation (AV)

3773 East Broadway, 85716
Telephone: 602-795-4800
Telefax: 602-325-7609
Douglas, Arizona Office: 1930 Eleventh Street, 85608.
Telephone: 602-364-4418.
Fax: 602-364-2606.
Phoenix, Arizona Office: 777 East Thomas Road, 85014.
Telephone: 602-265-2155.
Fax: 602-252-7465.

Robert O. Lesher
Ben F. Williams, Jr.
Stephen H. Lesher
Stefano D. Corradini
Nathan B. Hannah

(See Next Column)

Representative Clients: Arizona Public Service Co.; Associated Aviation Underwriters; CIGNA Insurance Group; Empire Fire and Marine Insurance Co.; Merck and Co., Inc.; Professional Mutual Risk Retention Group; Underwriters at Lloyd's, London; White Knight Manufacturing Co.

For full biographical listings, see the Martindale-Hubbell Law Directory

Miller, Pitt & McAnally, P.C. (AV)

111 South Church Avenue, 85701-1680
Telephone: 602-792-3836
Telecopier: 602-624-5080
Nogales, Arizona Office: 272 West View Point, 85621.
Telephone: 602-281-1361.
Correspondent Office: Lizarraga, Robles, Savinon & Tapia, S.C. Boulevard Hidalgo 64, Colonia Centenario. CP 83000 Hermosillo, Sonora, Mexico.
Telephone: (62) 17-27-28, 12-79-89, 13-47-10, 12-79-18, 13-33-25, 12-77-70.

Barry N. Akin (1939-1988)
G. Eugene Isaak
Gerald Maltz
Janice A. Wezelman
T. Patrick Griffin
Philip J. Hall
Grace McIlvain
Thomas G. Cotter
Lindsay E. Brew
Armando Rivera
Gus Aragón, Jr.
Eugene N. Goldsmith

Denneen L. Peterson
Jonathan Reich
Carole A. Summers

OF COUNSEL

Richard L. McAnally

RETIRED

Robert F. Miller
Donald Pitt

Representative Clients: Bell Atlantic Metro Mobile; Evergreen International Aviation; Farmers Investment Co.; Forest City Enterprises; Vince Granatelli Racing; KVOA Channel 4 TV; Newmont Mining Corp.; S.L. Industries, Inc.; Tucson Unified School District; University of Arizona Foundation.

For full biographical listings, see the Martindale-Hubbell Law Directory

Molloy, Jones & Donahue, P.C. (AV)

33 North Stone Avenue, Suite 2100, P.O. Box 2268, 85702
Telephone: 602-622-3531
Telecopier: 602-624-2816

Klaus T. Axen
Michael W. Baldwin
Benjamin W. Bauer
Richard T. Coolidge
Jennifer M. Dubay
David K. Gray
Jennifer C. Guerin
Russell E. Jones
George O. Krauja
D. Michael Mandig
William W. Pearson
Dale F. Regelman
Paul A. Relich

OF COUNSEL

John F. Molloy (Retired)
John L. Donahue Jr.

Representative Clients: Arizona Department of Health Services; Arizona Mail Order Company, Inc.; CTI (Transporters); General Motors Acceptance Corporation; KGUN-TV (ABC); Stewart Title & Trust of Tucson; Sundt Corp.; Trico Electric Cooperative, Inc.; University Medical Center Corp.
Reference: Bank of America Arizona.

For full biographical listings, see the Martindale-Hubbell Law Directory

Murphy, Goering, Roberts & Berkman, P.C. (AV)

Suite 302, 1840 East River Road, 85718
Telephone: 602-577-9300
FAX: 602-577-0848

James M. Murphy
Thomas M. Murphy
Scott Goering
Howard T. Roberts, Jr.
David L. Berkman
William L. Rubin
Carmine A. Brogna

Representative Client: Roman Catholic Church Diocese of Tucson.
Reference: Bank One.

For full biographical listings, see the Martindale-Hubbell Law Directory

O'Connor, Cavanagh, Anderson, Westover, Killingsworth & Beshears, A Professional Association (AV)

Suite 2200 One South Church Avenue, 85701-1621
Telephone: 602-882-8912
FAX: 602-624-9564
Phoenix, Arizona Office: One East Camelback Road, Suite 1100, 85012.
Telephone: 602-263-2400.
FAX: 602-263-2900.
Sun City, Arizona Office: 13250 North Del Webb Boulevard, Suite B, 85351.
Telephone: 602-263-2808.
FAX: 602-933-3100.
Nogales, Arizona Office: 1827 North Mastick Way, 85621.
Telephone: 602-761-4215.
FAX: 602-761-3505.

(See Next Column)

O'CONNOR, CAVANAGH, ANDERSON, WESTOVER, KILLINGSWORTH & BESHEARS A PROFESSIONAL ASSOCIATION, *Tucson—Continued*

Donald L. Cross — Bruce R. Heurlin
Thomas M. Pace — Scott D. Gibson
Ted A. Schmidt — Peter Akmajian

Jenne S. Forbes — Drue A. Morgan-Birch
J. Matthew Derstine

Chris B. Nakamura — Amy M. Samberg
Gregory E. Good — James D. Campbell

Representative Client: Three-Five Systems; Micro Chip; Main Street & Main; ITT Cannon; Bank of America; The Deal Corp; The Hartford; Dow Corning Corp.; Charles Schwab & Co., Inc.; Playtex Family Products, Inc.

For full biographical listings, see the Martindale-Hubbell Law Directory

---

RAVEN, KIRSCHNER & NORELL, P.C. (AV)

Suite 1600, One South Church Avenue, 85701-1612
Telephone: 602-628-8700
Telefax: 602-798-5200

Donald T. Awerkamp — Barry Kirschner
Benis E. Bernstein — Michael A. Lyons
Dennis J. Clancy — Andrew Oldland Norell
Bradley G.A. Cloud — Mark B. Raven
Sally M. Darcy — S. Leonard Scheff
L. Anthony Fines — Karen B. Tavolaro
Susan M. Freund — Stephen A. Thomas

LEGAL SUPPORT PERSONNEL
Elizabeth G. Epperson (Administrator)

Representative Clients: Pace American Bonding Company; Citibank (Arizona); Continental Medical Systems, Inc.; El Paso Natural Gas Co.; Norwest Bank Arizona; El Rio-Santa Cruz Neighborhood Health Center, Inc.; Resolution Trust Corp.; Sierra Vista Community Hospital; Southern Arizona Rehabilitation Hospital; Ford Motor Credit.

For full biographical listings, see the Martindale-Hubbell Law Directory

---

SLUTES, SAKRISON, EVEN, GRANT & PELANDER, P.C. (AV)

33 North Stone Avenue, Suite 1100, 85701-1489
Telephone: 602-624-6691
Fax: 602-791-9632

Tom Slutes — Christopher C. Browning
James M. Sakrison — Mark D. Rubin
John R. Even — Jerome J. Bromiel
Philip H. Grant — Alphus R. Christensen
A. John Pelander — Michael B. Smith
David E. Hill — Mary Beth Joublanc
Neil H. Ashley

Representative Clients: Allstate Insurance Co.; St. Paul Insurance Co.; Aetna Casualty and Surety Co.; Montgomery Ward & Co.; Northbrook Insurance Co.; Farmers Insurance Group; Jim Click Auto Group; Beneficial Corp.

For full biographical listings, see the Martindale-Hubbell Law Directory

---

STOMPOLY, STROUD, GIDDINGS & GLICKSMAN, P.C. (AV)

1820 Citibank Tower, One South Church Avenue, 85702
Telephone: 602-628-8300
Telefax: 602-628-9948
Mailing Address: P.O. Box 190, Tucson, AZ, 85702-0190

John G. Stompoly — Charles E. Giddings
James L. Stroud — Elliot A. Glicksman
George Erickson

For full biographical listings, see the Martindale-Hubbell Law Directory

---

STREICH LANG, A PROFESSIONAL ASSOCIATION (AV)

One S. Church Avenue, Suite 1700, 85701-1621
Telephone: 602-770-8700
Fax: 602-623-2418
Phoenix, Arizona Office: Renaissance One, Two N. Central Avenue. 85004-2391.
Telephone: 602-229-5200.
Fax: 602-229-5690.
Las Vegas, Nevada Affiliated Office: Dawson & Associates, 3800 Howard Hughes Parkway, Suite 1500. 89109.
Telephone: 702-792-2727.
Fax: 702-792-2676.
Los Angeles California Office: 444 S. Flower Street, Suite 1530.
Telephone: 213-896-0484.

Susan G. Boswell — Craig H. Kaufman
Steven R. Haydon — James F. Morrow
Jeffrey Willis (Partner-in-Charge)

OF COUNSEL
Raymond R. Cusack

(See Next Column)

Michael R. Hall — Nancy J. March
Joy E. Herr-Cardillo — David V. Millard
Steven Rand Owens

Representative Clients: Allied-Signal Aerospace Company; America West Airlines, Inc.; Atlantic Richfield Co.; Chicago Title; First Interstate Bank of Arizona, N.A.; Magma Copper Co.; Motorola, Inc.; Phelps Dodge Development Corp.; TRW Inc.; The Travelers Companies.

For full biographical listings, see the Martindale-Hubbell Law Directory

---

WATERFALL, ECONOMIDIS, CALDWELL, HANSHAW & VILLAMANA, P.C. (AV)

Suite 800, Williams Centre, 5210 East Williams Circle, 85711
Telephone: 602-790-5828
Telecopier: 602-745-1279

A. Alan Hanshaw — Steven M. Cox
Gordon G. Waterfall — James W. Stuehringer
Peter Economidis — Cary Sandman
Hugh M. Caldwell, Jr. — Jane L. Eikleberry
Robert L. Villamana — John C. Rambow
W. Patrick Traynor — John D. Kendall
Ronald J. Newman

Lisa Rice Wilmer — Robert C. Craff
Cynthia Ley Anson

Representative Clients: First Interstate Bank of Arizona, N.A.; National Bank of Arizona; Magma Copper Company; General Electric Credit; Greentree Acceptance, Inc.; Sheraton El Conquistador Resort Hotel; Viscount Suite Hotel; Chicago Title Insurance Company; Tucson Psychiatric Institute.

For full biographical listings, see the Martindale-Hubbell Law Directory

---

WINSLOW, Navajo Co.

ASPEY, WATKINS & DIESEL (AV)

205 North Williamson, 86047
Telephone: 602-289-5963
Flagstaff, Arizona Office: 123 North San Francisco.
Telephone: 602-774-1478.
Facsimile: 774-1043.
Sedona, Arizona Office: 120 Soldier Pass Road.
Telephone: 602-282-5955.
Facsimile: 602-282-5962.
Page, Arizona Office: 904 North Navajo.
Telephone: 602-645-9694.
Cottonwood, Arizona Office: 905 Cove Parkway, Unit 201.
Telephone: 602-639-1881.

Zachary Markham — James E. Ledbetter

Representative Clients: Coconino County Industrial Development Authority; Coconino Community Guidance Center; Farmer's Insurance Company of Arizona; Kelley-Moore Paint Co.; Pepsi-Cola Bottling Company of Northern Arizona; Bill Luke's Chrysler-Plymouth, Inc.
Reference: First Interstate Bank of Arizona, N.A., Flagstaff, Arizona.

For full biographical listings, see the Martindale-Hubbell Law Directory

---

*YUMA,** Yuma Co.

BYRNE & BENESCH, P.C. (AV)

230 W. Morrison Street, P.O. Box 6446, 85364
Telephone: 602-782-1805
Fax: 602-782-1808

Peter C. Byrne (1916-1994) — William S. Dieckhoff
Wayne C. Benesch — Pamela Walsma

For full biographical listings, see the Martindale-Hubbell Law Directory

ARKANSAS

*ARKADELPHIA,** Clark Co.

WRIGHT, CHANEY, BERRY & DANIEL, P.A. (AV)

303 Professional Park Drive, P.O. Drawer 947, 71923
Telephone: 501-246-6796
Telefax: 501-246-2178

William G. Wright | Travis R. Berry
Donald P. Chaney, Jr. | LeAnne Daniel
Bryan L. Chesshir

Counsel for: Elk Horn Bank and Trust Co.; Farm Bureau Mutual Insurance Company of Arkansas, Inc.; Southern Farm Bureau Casualty Insurance Co.; Underwriters Adjustment Co.; Nationwide Insurance Co.; Central Production Credit Assn.; Shelter Insurance Co.; Colonial Insurance Co.
Approved Attorneys for: Farmers Home Administration; American Title Insurance Co.

For full biographical listings, see the Martindale-Hubbell Law Directory

*ASHDOWN,** Little River Co.

BISHOP & BISHOP (AV)

171 West Main Street, P.O. Box 609, 71822
Telephone: 501-898-5058
Fax: 501-898-8110

MEMBERS OF FIRM

Eric W. Bishop | Eric T. Bishop

Representative Clients: Bank of Ashdown; First National Bank of De Queen; Citizens National Bank of Nashville; Little River County Rural Development Authority; Ashdown Clinic, Ltd.; E-Z Mart Stores, Inc.; Little River Memorial Hospital.

For full biographical listings, see the Martindale-Hubbell Law Directory

*ASH FLAT,** Sharp Co. — (Refer to Batesville)

*AUGUSTA,** Woodruff Co. — (Refer to Newport)

*BATESVILLE,** Independence Co.

BLAIR & STROUD (AV)

Suite 201, 500 East Main, P.O. Box 2135, 72501
Telephone: 501-793-8350
FAX: 501-793-3989

MEMBERS OF FIRM

H. David Blair | Robert D. Stroud
J. Scott Davidson

Counsel for: Worthen National Bank, Batesville, Ark.; Worthen National Bank, Newark, Arkansas; First National Bank of Izard County, Arkansas.

For full biographical listings, see the Martindale-Hubbell Law Directory

GREGG, HART & FARRIS (AV)

262 Boswell Street, P.O. Box 2496, 72501
Telephone: 501-793-7556
Fax: 501-793-6921
Mountain View, Arkansas Office: Peabody Avenue.
Telephone: 501-269-3716.
Fax: 501-269-8169.

MEMBERS OF FIRM

John C. Gregg | Josephine Linker Hart
Phillip B. Farris

For full biographical listings, see the Martindale-Hubbell Law Directory

WALMSLEY AND BLANKENSHIP (AV)

398 Barnett, P.O. Box 2535, 72503
Telephone: 501-793-6818
Fax: 501-793-6977

MEMBERS OF FIRM

Bill H. Walmsley | Leroy Blankenship

ASSOCIATES

Timothy M. Weaver

For full biographical listings, see the Martindale-Hubbell Law Directory

*BERRYVILLE,** Carroll Co. — (Refer to Springdale)

*BLYTHEVILLE,** Mississippi Co.

REID, BURGE, PREVALLET & COLEMAN (AV)

417 North Broadway, P.O. Box 107, 72316-0107
Telephone: 501-763-4586
Fax: 501-763-4642

(See Next Column)

MEMBERS OF FIRM

Max B. Reid (1895-1959) | Richard A. Reid
Dan M. Burge | Donald E. Prevallet
Robert Lynn Coleman

Counsel for: Farmers Bank and Trust Co.; Arkansas Power & Light Co.; Bush Canning Co.; Allstate Insurance Cos.; Farmers Insurance Group; Wausau Insurance Cos.; United States Fidelity & Guaranty Co.; State Farm Cos.; Hartford Group.

For full biographical listings, see the Martindale-Hubbell Law Directory

*BOONEVILLE,** Logan Co. — (Refer to Fort Smith)

BRINKLEY, Monroe Co. — (Refer to Clarendon)

*CAMDEN,** Ouachita Co.

BRAMBLETT & PRATT (AV)

146 Washington Street, N.W., P.O. Box 938, 71701
Telephone: 501-836-7328
Fax: 501-836-4442

MEMBERS OF FIRM

Eugene D. Bramblett | James M. Pratt, Jr.

Representative Clients: Hartford Accident and Indemnity Co.; Liberty Mutual Insurance Co.; International Paper Co.; Stephens Security Bank.

For full biographical listings, see the Martindale-Hubbell Law Directory

ALLEN P. ROBERTS, P.A. (AV)

119 Van Buren Street, NW, P.O. Box 280, 71707
Telephone: 501-836-5310
FAX: 501-836-9662

Allen P. Roberts

Representative Clients: International Paper Co.; Camden Fairview School District; The City of Camden; Byars Oil Co.; American Fuel Cell & Coated Fabrics Co.; Star City School District; Highland Resources, Inc.; Peace Flooring; Circle B Logging Co.; Atlantic Research Corp.

For full biographical listings, see the Martindale-Hubbell Law Directory

*CHARLESTON,** Franklin Co. — (Refer to Fort Smith)

*CLARENDON,** Monroe Co.

MOORE & SERIO (AV)

109 Court Street, P.O. Box 224, 72029
Telephone: 501-747-3813
Fax: 501-747-3767

Robert G. Serio

OF COUNSEL

John B. Moore, Jr.

Representative Clients: Clarendon and Townsend Divisions, Potlatch, Inc. (Lumber); Clarendon Levee District; Farmers Home Administration; Menard Title & Abstract.
Approved Attorneys For: Chicago Title Insurance Co.; Lawyers Title Insurance Corp.; Mid South Title Co.

For full biographical listings, see the Martindale-Hubbell Law Directory

*CLARKSVILLE,** Johnson Co. — (Refer to Fort Smith)

*CLINTON,** Van Buren Co. — (Refer to Conway)

*CONWAY,** Faulkner Co.

HENRY & HENRY (AV)

627 Locust Avenue, P.O. Box 1107, 72032
Telephone: 501-329-5623
Fax: 501-329-7816

J. Wendell Henry (1897-1958) | Robert W. Henry
Clifford J. Henry

General Counsel for: The First National Bank; Security Savings Bank, F.S.A.; Conway Corp. (Light & Power Co.).

For full biographical listings, see the Martindale-Hubbell Law Directory

*CORNING,** Clay Co. — (Refer to Pocahontas)

CROSSETT, Ashley Co.

GRIFFIN, RAINWATER & DRAPER, P.A. (AV)

310 Main Street, P.O. Box 948, 71635
Telephone: 501-364-2111
Fax: 501-364-3126

Richard Earl Griffin | Paul S. Rainwater
Gary M. Draper

Reference: First State Bank of Crossett, Arkansas.

For full biographical listings, see the Martindale-Hubbell Law Directory

*DANVILLE,** Yell Co. — (Refer to Russellville)

*DE QUEEN,** Sevier Co. — (Refer to Ashdown)

*DE WITT,** Arkansas Co. — (Refer to Pine Bluff)

*EL DORADO,** Union Co.

COMPTON, PREWETT, THOMAS & HICKEY, P.A. (AV)

423 North Washington Avenue, P.O. Box 1917, 71731-1917
Telephone: 501-862-3478
Fax: 501-862-7228

Walter L. Brown (1893-1972)
Robert C. Compton
William I. Prewett
Floyd M. Thomas, Jr.
Joseph Hickey
Cathleen V. Compton

OF COUNSEL

Jerry W. Watkins

LEGAL SUPPORT PERSONNEL

Jerri L. Agerton (Paralegal)

General Counsel for: National Bank of Commerce of El Dorado.
Local Counsel for: Shelter Insurance Co.; Farmers Insurance Group; Employers Mutual Companies; Murphy Oil Corp.; Beren Corp.; Figgie International, Inc.; Waite-Hill Services, Inc.
Representative Clients: Prescolite Manufacturing Co.; South Arkansas Oil Co.

For full biographical listings, see the Martindale-Hubbell Law Directory

CRUMPLER O'CONNOR & WYNNE (AV)

308 National Bank of Commerce Building, 71730
Telephone: 501-863-8118
FAX: 501-863-8110

Claude B. Crumpler (1890-1978)
John A. O'Connor, Jr. (1913-1988)

MEMBER OF FIRM

William J. Wynne

Representative Clients: Monsanto Co.; Texas Eastern Transmission Corp.; El Dorado Paper Bag and Manufacturing Co., Inc.; Gulf Central Pipeline Co.; Arkansas Oil and Gas Commission; Conoco, Inc.; Alcorn Properties, Inc.; Great Lakes Chemical Corp.; Dairyland-Sentry; Life of Georgia.

For full biographical listings, see the Martindale-Hubbell Law Directory

SHACKLEFORD, SHACKLEFORD & PHILLIPS, P.A. (AV)

100 East Church Street, P.O. Box 1718, 71731-1718
Telephone: 501-862-5523
FAX: 501-862-9443

John M. Shackleford (1896-1968)
John M. Shackleford, Jr.
Dennis L. Shackleford
Norwood Phillips
Teresa Wineland
Brian H. Ratcliff

Representative Insurance Clients: Allstate Insurance Co.; CIGNA Cos.; Commercial Union Insurance Co.; Fireman's Fund Insurance Co.; ITT Hartford Insurance Co.; Kemper Insurance Co.; Liberty Mutual Insurance Co.; Maryland-American General Insurance Co.; The St. Paul Cos.; U.S. Fidelity & Guaranty Co.

For full biographical listings, see the Martindale-Hubbell Law Directory

*EUREKA SPRINGS,** Carroll Co. — (Refer to Springdale)

*FAYETTEVILLE,** Washington Co.

BALL & MOURTON, LTD. A PROFESSIONAL CORPORATION (AV)

Suite 700, E.J. Ball Plaza, P.O. Box 1948, 72702
Telephone: 501-442-6213
Fax: 501-442-6233

E. J. Ball
Kenneth R. Mourton
Neal R. Pendergraft

Andy E. Adams
Rayburn W. Green
Ernest B. Cate
Teresa D. Bailey

Representative Clients: Arkansas Western Gas Co.; Coors of Western Arkansas, Inc.; Rebel Enterprises, Inc.; Southwestern Energy Co.; Stephens Production Co.; Ohlendorf Investment Co.; Norman Lures; Central Health Corporation; First National Bank of Huntsville; McIlroy Bank & Trust.

For full biographical listings, see the Martindale-Hubbell Law Directory

BASSETT LAW FIRM (AV)

221 North College Avenue, P.O. Box 3618, 72702-3618
Telephone: 501-521-9996
Fax: 501-521-9600

(See Next Column)

MEMBERS OF FIRM

Woodson W. Bassett, Jr.
Woodson W. Bassett, III
Tod C. Bassett
Wm. Robert Still, Jr.
Walker Dale Garrett
Curtis L. Nebben
Earl Buddy Chadick, Jr.
Angela M. Doss
Gary V. Weeks
J. David Wall
Shawn David Twing
Vincent O. Chadick
Michael W. Langley

Representative Clients: The Home Insurance Co.; Hartford Insurance Group; Tyson Foods, Inc.; Farmers Insurance Group; CIGNA; Commercial Union Insurance Co.; St. Paul Fire and Marine Insurance Co.; AIG Aviation Ins. Co.; WAUSAU; USAA.

For full biographical listings, see the Martindale-Hubbell Law Directory

DAVIS, COX & WRIGHT (AV)

19 East Mountain Street, P.O. Drawer 1688, 72702-1688
Telephone: 501-521-7600
Fax: 501-521-7661

MEMBERS OF FIRM

Sidney P. Davis, Jr.
Walter B. Cox
Tilden P. Wright, III
Constance G. Clark
William Jackson Butt, II
Kelly P. Carithers
Tim E. Howell
Don A. Taylor
Paul H. Taylor

ASSOCIATES

Laura J. Andress
John G. Trice

Representative Clients: Aetna Casualty & Surety Co.; Arkansas Farm Bureau Insurance Cos.; Fireman's Fund Insurance Group; United States Fidelity and Guaranty Co.; St. Paul Insurance Cos; Chrysler Motors Corp.; Kemper Insurance Group; Kawasaki Motors Corp.; CIGNA.

For full biographical listings, see the Martindale-Hubbell Law Directory

GREENHAW & GREENHAW (AV)

22 East Center Street, 72702
Telephone: 501-442-2562
FAX: 501-442-8479

Karl Greenhaw (1892-1967)
Leonard F. Greenhaw
William K. Greenhaw
John F. Greenhaw

Representative Clients: Southwestern Electric Power Co.; Commonwealth Theatres, Inc.; Federal Deposit Insurance Corp.; Foremost Dairies, Inc.; Pillsbury Mills, Inc.; Burlington Northern Railroad; Royal-Globe Insurance Group; St. Paul-Mercury Indemnity Co.; Government Employees Insurance Co.; General Electric Co.

For full biographical listings, see the Martindale-Hubbell Law Directory

*FORREST CITY,** St. Francis Co.

BUTLER, HICKY & LONG (AV)

2216 North Washington Street, P.O. Box 989, 72335
Telephone: 501-633-4611
FAX: 501-633-6848

Philip Hicky
Fletcher Long, Jr.

ASSOCIATES

Gary J. Mitchusson

OF COUNSEL

E. J. Butler

Representative Clients: First National Bank of Eastern Arkansas; Southern Farm Bureau Insurance Cos.; United States Aviation Underwriters Group; National Aviation Underwriters; Hartford Accident and Indemnity Co.; Peoples Implement Co.

For full biographical listings, see the Martindale-Hubbell Law Directory

*FORT SMITH,** Sebastian Co.

BETHELL, CALLAWAY, ROBERTSON, BEASLEY & COWAN (AV)

615 North "B" Street, P.O. Box 23, 72902
Telephone: 501-782-7911
FAX: 501-782-7964

MEMBERS OF FIRM

Donald P. Callaway (1935-1984)
Thomas E. Robertson, Jr.
John R. Beasley
Kenneth W. Cowan
J. Michael Fitzhugh

ASSOCIATES

Matthew J. Ketcham

OF COUNSEL

Edgar E. Bethell

Representative Clients: The Aetna Casualty & Surety Co.; James River - Dixie Cup; Arkansas-Oklahoma Gas Corp.; Beverage Products Corp. (Pepsi-Cola); The Prudential Insurance Company of America; Sentry - Dairyland Insurance Co; General Tire and Rubber; Quanex Corp.; The Fort Smith Municipal Airport Commission; Southern Steel & Wire Co.

For full biographical listings, see the Martindale-Hubbell Law Directory

Fort Smith—Continued

DAILY, WEST, CORE, COFFMAN & CANFIELD (AV)

Stephens Office Building, 623 Garrison Avenue, P.O. Box 1446, 72902
Telephone: 501-782-0361
Fax: 501-782-6160

MEMBERS OF FIRM

Ben Core
Eldon F. Coffman
Jerry L. Canfield
Thomas A. Daily
Wyman R. Wade, Jr.
Stanley A. Leasure
Douglas M. Carson
Michael C. Carter
Robert W. Bishop

OF COUNSEL

James E. West

Counsel for: Claims Management, Inc. (Wal-Mart); Arkla, Inc.; City of Fort Smith; Commercial Union Insurance Cos.; Pennzoil Exploration and Production Co.; Silvey Cos., Inc.; CIGNA; Metropolitan Life Insurance Co.; Chevron U.S.A., Inc.

For full biographical listings, see the Martindale-Hubbell Law Directory

HARDIN, JESSON, DAWSON & TERRY (AV)

Suite 500, Superior Federal Tower, 5000 Rogers Avenue, P.O. Box 10127, 72917-0127
Telephone: 501-452-2200
FAX: 501-452-9097

MEMBERS OF FIRM

G. C. Hardin (1884-1964)
P. H. Hardin
Bradley D. Jesson
Robert T. Dawson
Rex M. Terry
Robert M. Honea
J. Leslie Evitts III
James Rodney Mills
Kirkman T. Dougherty
J. Gregory Magness

Counsel for: Superior Federal Bank, FSB; The Kansas City Southern Railway Co.; KFSM-TV; Johnson & Johnson; Ortho Pharmaceutical Corp; ASARCO Inc.; Allstate Insurance Co.; Southern Farm Bureau Insurance Co.; Dodson Insurance Group.

For full biographical listings, see the Martindale-Hubbell Law Directory

HARPER, YOUNG, SMITH & MAURRAS, P.L.C. (AV)

510 North Greenwood Avenue, P.O. Box 10205, 72917
Telephone: 501-782-1001
Telefax: 501-782-1279

Thomas Harper (1908-1989)
R. A. Young, Jr. (1908-1973)
Don A. Smith
Tom Harper, Jr.
S. Walton Maurras
Robert Y. Cohen, II
Michael K. Redd

Counsel for: Arkansas Best Corp.; ABF Freight System, Inc.; Riverside Furniture Corp.; The City National Bank of Fort Smith; O.K. Industries, Inc.
Insurance Clients: Zurich Insurance Co.; Wausau Insurance Companies.

For full biographical listings, see the Martindale-Hubbell Law Directory

JONES, GILBREATH, JACKSON & MOLL (AV)

401 North Seventh Street, P.O. Box 2023, 72902
Telephone: 501-782-7203
Fax: 501-782-9460

MEMBERS OF FIRM

Robert L. Jones, Jr.
E. C. Gilbreath
Robert L. Jones, III
Randolph C. Jackson
Kendall B. Jones
Mark A. Moll

ASSOCIATES

Charles R. Garner, Jr.
Daniel W. Gilbreath
Lynn M. Flynn
Christina Dawn Ferguson

Insurance Counsel for: Argonaut Insurance Cos.; Farmers Insurance Group; Maryland-American General Insurance Cos.; Shelter Insurance Cos.; Travelers Insurance Co.; Continental Insurance Cos.
Counsel for: Merchants National Bank, Fort Smith, Ar.; Ryder Truck Rental, Inc.; Whirlpool Corp.

For full biographical listings, see the Martindale-Hubbell Law Directory

SHAW, LEDBETTER, HORNBERGER, COGBILL & ARNOLD (AV)

South Seventh and Parker, P.O. Box 185, 72902-0185
Telephone: 501-782-7294
FAX: 501-782-1493

Bruce H. Shaw (1904-1990)
Richard B. Shaw (1927-1988)

MEMBERS OF FIRM

Charles R. Ledbetter
Robert E. Hornberger
J. Michael Cogbill
James A. Arnold, II
Ronald D. Harrison

ASSOCIATES

E. Diane Graham
R. Ray Fulmer, II
Gill A. Rogers

(See Next Column)

OF COUNSEL

J. Michael Shaw

Representative Clients: General: First National Bank of Fort Smith; Bank of Mansfield; Commercial Bank at Alma; Mid-South Dredging Co.
Local Attorneys for: Liberty Mutual Insurance Co.; St Paul Insurance Cos.; General Electric.

For full biographical listings, see the Martindale-Hubbell Law Directory

WARNER AND SMITH (AV)

214 North Sixth Street, P.O. Box 1626, 72901
Telephone: 501-782-6041
Fax: 501-782-0841

MEMBERS OF FIRM

Harry Preston Warner (1885-1969)
Cecil Randolph Warner (1890-1955)
Thomas G. Graves (1939-1971)
Douglas O. Smith, Jr.
C. Wayne Harris
Gerald L. DeLung
Patrick Neill Moore
Lillard Cody Hayes
G. Alan Wooten
James Melvin Dunn
John Alan Lewis
Joel D. Johnson
Gary W. Udouj
J. Randall McGinnis
Kathryn A. Stocks

Matthew H. P. Warner

OF COUNSEL

C. R. Warner, Jr.

District Attorneys for: Burlington Northern Railroad Co.
Counsel for: Fairfield Communities, Inc.; River Valley Bank.
Local Counsel for: Planters Division, Nabisco Brands, Inc.; Gerber Products Co.; United States Fidelity & Guaranty Co.; Aetna Group; Fireman's Fund-American Insurance Cos.; Hiram Walker & Sons, Inc.; Continental National American Group.

For full biographical listings, see the Martindale-Hubbell Law Directory

*HARRISBURG,** Poinsett Co. — (Refer to Jonesboro)

*HARRISON,** Boone Co.

ADAMS, NICHOLS AND EVANS, P.A. (AV)

623 South Pine, P.O. Box 1912, 72601-1912
Telephone: 501-741-8515
Fax: 501-741-1351

Donald J. Adams
Johnny L. Nichols
Deanna S. Evans

For full biographical listings, see the Martindale-Hubbell Law Directory

*HELENA,** Phillips Co.

DAVID SOLOMON (AV)

427 Cherry Street, P.O. Box 490, 72342
Telephone: 501-338-7427

Representative Clients: 1st National Bank of Phillips County; Delta State Bank; Home Insurance Cos.; Helena Cotton Oil Co.; Silver Companies (Insurance); Royal-Globe Insurance Co.; McKnight Plywood, Inc.; Webb & Co., Inc.; Home Indemnity Co.; Helena Insurance and Real Estate Co.

For full biographical listings, see the Martindale-Hubbell Law Directory

*HOPE,** Hempstead Co.

PILKINTON, PILKINTON & YOCOM (AV)

116-118 East Second Street, P.O. Box 583, 71801
Telephone: 501-777-8871
Fax: 501-777-2781

MEMBERS OF FIRM

James H. Pilkinton
James H. Pilkinton, Jr.
Tony Lynn Yocom

Representative Clients: First National Bank of Hope; Tol-E-Tex Oil Co.; Pioneer Washington Restoration Foundation; Tex-Ark Joist Steel, Inc.; Pyramid Plastics, Inc.; Young Chevrolet Co.; Michigan Chrome & Chemical; Bank of Blevins, Ark.
Approved Attorneys for: Commonwealth Land Title Insurance Co.; Lawyers Title Insurance Corp.

For full biographical listings, see the Martindale-Hubbell Law Directory

*HOT SPRINGS NATIONAL PARK,** Garland Co.

WOOTTON & SLAGLE, P.A. (AV)

Rix Professional Center, 1401 Malvern, 71901
Telephone: 501-623-2593
FAX: 501-623-1485

Richard H. Wootton
Richard L. Slagle

Attorneys for: Worthen National Bank; American Surety Co.; Jefferson Standard Life Insurance Co.; Mountain Valley Springs Co.; Zurich American Insurance Co.; Western Surety Co; National Life & Accident Co.

(See Next Column)

WOOTTON & SLAGLE P.A., *Hot Springs National Park—Continued*

Approved Attorneys for: Lawyers Title Insurance Corp.

For full biographical listings, see the Martindale-Hubbell Law Directory

*HUNTSVILLE,** Madison Co. — (Refer to Fayetteville)

*JASPER,** Newton Co. — (Refer to Fayetteville)

*JONESBORO,** Craighead Co.

BARRETT & DEACON (AV)

Mercantile Bank Building, 300 South Church Street, P.O. Box 1700, 72403
Telephone: 501-931-1700
FAX: 501-931-1800

MEMBERS OF FIRM

Joe C. Barrett (1897-1980)
John C. Deacon
J. Barry Deacon
David W. Cahoon
Ralph W. Waddell
Paul D. Waddell

ASSOCIATES

D. Price Marshall, Jr.
James D. Bradbury (Not admitted in AR)
Kevin W. Cole

For full biographical listings, see the Martindale-Hubbell Law Directory

MOONEY LAW FIRM (AV)

214 East Washington, P.O. Box 1423, 72403-1423
Telephone: 501-935-5847
Fax: 501-935-4438

MEMBERS OF FIRM

Charles M. Mooney
Charles M (Skip) Mooney, Jr.
Tom A. Bennett

Representative Clients: Simmons First Bank of Jonesboro; The Bert Cruse Agency, Inc.; Prudential Insurance Company of America.
Approved Attorneys for: Chicago Title Co.; Chelsea Title & Guaranty Co.; Commerce Title Guaranty Co.; Lawyers Title Insurance Corp.
References: Citizens Bank of Jonesboro; The Mercantile Bank of Jonesboro.

For full biographical listings, see the Martindale-Hubbell Law Directory

PENIX, PENIX & LUSBY (AV)

401 South Main Street, P.O. Box 1306, 72403-1306
Telephone: 501-932-7449
FAX: 501-933-7281

MEMBERS OF FIRM

Roy Penix (1891-1978)
Marian F. Penix (1924-1991)
Bill Penix
Richard A. Lusby

ASSOCIATE

J. Robin Nix, II

Representative Clients: American Policyholders Ins. Co.; CIGNA Cos.; K-Mart Corp.; Liberty Mutual Insurance Co.; Sentry and Dairyland Insurance; Southwestern Bell Telephone Co.; The Jonesboro Sun.

For full biographical listings, see the Martindale-Hubbell Law Directory

SNELLGROVE, LASER, LANGLEY, LOVETT & CULPEPPER (AV)

Second Floor, 111 East Huntington, P.O. Box 1346, 72403-1346
Telephone: 501-932-8357
Fax: 501-932-5488

MEMBERS OF FIRM

G. D. Walker (1910-1989)
Frank Snellgrove, Jr.
David N. Laser
Stanley R. Langley
Glenn Lovett, Jr.
Malcolm Culpepper
D. Todd Williams
Michael E. Mullally

ASSOCIATE

P. Sanders Huckabee

Representative Clients: Mercantile Bank; First Bank of Arkansas; Travelers Insurance Co.; Aetna Insurance Co.; ITT Hartford Insurance Co.; Commercial Union Insurance Co.; CNA Insurance Group; State Farm Insurance Cos.; Columbia Mutual Insurance Co.; Bituminous Insurance Co.

For full biographical listings, see the Martindale-Hubbell Law Directory

WOMACK, LANDIS, PHELPS, MCNEILL & MCDANIEL, A PROFESSIONAL ASSOCIATION (AV)

Century Center, Washington at Madison, P.O. Box 3077, 72403
Telephone: 501-932-0900
Fax: 501-932-2553

Tom D. Womack
Carl David Landis
John V. Phelps
Paul D. McNeill
Lucinda McDaniel

(See Next Column)

Brant Perkins
Jeffrey W. Puryear
Mark Alan Mayfield

Representative Clients: Arkansas State University; Bank of Trumann; E.C. Barton & Co.; Kraft General Foods Corp.; Home Indemnity Company of N.Y.; St. Paul Insurance Cos.; Shelter Insurance Co.; United States Fidelity & Guaranty Co.

For full biographical listings, see the Martindale-Hubbell Law Directory

*LAKE VILLAGE,** Chicot Co. — (Refer to Hamburg)

*LEWISVILLE,** Lafayette Co. — (Refer to Magnolia)

*LITTLE ROCK,** Pulaski Co.

ARNOLD, GROBMYER & HALEY, A PROFESSIONAL ASSOCIATION (AV)

875 Union National Plaza, 124 West Capitol Avenue, P.O. Box 70, 72203
Telephone: 501-376-1171
Fax: 501-375-3548

Erwin M. Arnold (1906-1985)
Benjamin F. Arnold
James F. Dowden
Mark W. Grobmyer
John H. Haley
Charles D. McDaniel
David H. Pennington
Joe A. Polk
Richard L. Ramsay
Robert R. Ross
Lee S. Thalheimer
Beth Ann Long

OF COUNSEL

Robert A. Blair (P.C.) (Not admitted in AR)
G. Hite McLean, Jr. (Not admitted in AR)
Scott E. Slaughter (Not admitted in AR)
Lloyd S. Wolf (Not admitted in AR)

For full biographical listings, see the Martindale-Hubbell Law Directory

BARBER, MCCASKILL, AMSLER, JONES & HALE, P.A. (AV)

2700 First Commercial Building, 400 West Capitol Avenue, 72201-3414
Telephone: 501-372-6175
Telecopier: 501-375-2802

Azro L. Barber (1885-1979)
Elbert A. Henry (1889-1966)
John B. Thurman (1912-1971)
Austin McCaskill, Sr.
Guy Amsler, Jr.
Glenn W. Jones, Jr.
Michael E. Hale
John S. Cherry, Jr.
Robert L. Henry, III
Micheal L. Alexander
William H. Edwards, Jr.
Richard C. Kalkbrenner
G. Spence Fricke
M. Stephen Bingham
Gail Ponder Gaines
Michael J. Emerson
R. Kenny McCulloch
Tim A. Cheatham
Joseph F. Kolb
Scott Michael Strauss
Karen Hart McKinney

Attorneys for: Associated Aviation Underwriters; Canal Insurance Co.; Fireman's Fund Insurance Co.; General Motors Corp.; General Motors Acceptance Corp.; Hanover Insurance Co.; Home Insurance Co.; Royal Insurance; United States Fidelity & Guaranty Co.; Universal Underwriters Insurance Co.

For full biographical listings, see the Martindale-Hubbell Law Directory

CEARLEY LAW FIRM (AV)

Suite 350 Gans Building, 217 West Second Street, 72201
Telephone: 501-375-9451
Fax: 501-374-3463

Robert M. Cearley, Jr.

Counsel for: Arkansas Bankers Association; Greyhound Lines, Inc.

For full biographical listings, see the Martindale-Hubbell Law Directory

DAVIDSON, HORNE & HOLLINGSWORTH, A PROFESSIONAL ASSOCIATION (AV)

401 West Capitol, Suite 501, P.O. Box 3363, 72203
Telephone: 501-376-4731
FAX: 501-372-7142

Walter W. Davidson (Retired)
Allan W. Horne
Cyril Hollingsworth
Michael O. Parker
Garland W. Binns, Jr.
James P. Beachboard
Mark H. Allison
Judy P. McNeil

William S. Roach

Representative Clients: Associated Industries of Arkansas, Inc.; Arkansas Blue Cross and Blue Shield; Worthen National Bank of Arkansas; J.B. Hunt Transport, Inc.; American Insurance Association; Arkansas Kraft Corp.; Gaylord Container Corp.; American Pioneer Life Insurance Co.; Robinette-Burnett Construction Co.

For full biographical listings, see the Martindale-Hubbell Law Directory

Little Rock—Continued

DOVER & DIXON, P.A. (AV)

425 West Capitol, Suite 3700, 72201
Telephone: 501-375-9151
Telecopier: 501-375-6484

Darrell D. Dover
Philip E. Dixon
Thomas S. Stone
Steve L. Riggs
Joseph H. Purvis
Charles W. Reynolds
John B. Peace
Wm. Dean Overstreet
Gary B. Rogers
Michael R. Johns
W. Michael Reif
David A. Couch
M. Darren O'Quinn
Monte D. Estes
Patrick E. Hollingsworth
Derrick Davidson

Representative Clients: Wood Manufacturing Company, Inc. (Ranger Boats); J.B. Hunt; Affiliated Foods; St. Vincent Infirmary; First Commercial Bank; Arkansas Teacher Retirement System; Assurance Alliance, Inc.; City of Little Rock; Connecticut Mutual Life Insurance; Old Republic National Title Insurance Company.

For full biographical listings, see the Martindale-Hubbell Law Directory

EICHENBAUM, SCOTT, MILLER, LILES & HEISTER, P.A. (AV)

Union National Bank Building, 124 West Capitol Avenue, Suite 1400, 72201-3736
Telephone: 501-376-4531
Fax: 501-376-8433

E. Chas. Eichenbaum (1907-1993)
Leonard L. Scott
William S. Miller, Jr.
Gary F. Liles
Peter B. Heister
Steve Bauman
Frank S. Hamlin
Dan P. Kennett
C. Douglas McDaniel
Chris O. Parker

Daniel L. Parker
Barbara W. Webb
James H. Penick, III
Martha Jett McAlister
Douglas Jewell Stanley

COUNSEL

Edward M. Penick

Representative Clients: Arkansas Aluminum Alloys, Inc. (manufacturing); Boatmen's National Bank; Delta Life and Annuity Company; Foremost Insurance Co.; Kubota Tractor Corp.; Lawyers Title Insurance Corp; Mel Simon & Associates, Inc./McCain Mall/University Mall (Developer); Paccar Financial Corp.; Underwriters Adjusting Co.; Warmack & Co. (Developer).

For full biographical listings, see the Martindale-Hubbell Law Directory

FRIDAY, ELDREDGE & CLARK (AV)

A Partnership including Professional Associations
Formerly, Smith, Williams, Friday, Eldredge & Clark
2000 First Commercial Building, 400 West Capitol, 72201-3493
Telephone: 501-376-2011
Telecopier: 501-376-2147; 376-6369

MEMBERS OF FIRM

Robert V. Light (P.A.)
William H. Sutton (P.A.)
James W. Moore
Byron M. Eiseman, Jr., (P.A.)
Joe D. Bell (P.A.)
John C. Echols (P.A.)
James A. Buttry (P.A.)
Frederick S. Ursery (P.A.)
H. T. Larzelere, Jr., (P.A.)
Oscar E. Davis, Jr., (P.A.)
James C. Clark, Jr., (P.A.)
Thomas P. Leggett, (P.A.)
John Dewey Watson (P.A.)
Paul B. Benham, III, (P.A.)
Larry W. Burks (P.A.)
A. Wyckliff Nisbet, Jr., (P.A.)
James E. Harris (P.A.)
J. Phillip Malcom (P.A.)
James M. Simpson, Jr., (P.A.)
Meredith P. Catlett (P.A.)
James M. Saxton (P.A.)
J. Shepherd Russell, III, (P.A.)
Donald H. Bacon (P.A.)
W. Thomas Baxter (P.A.)
Walter A. Paulson, II, (P.A.)
Barry E. Coplin (P.A.)
Richard D. Taylor (P.A.)
Joseph B. Hurst, Jr., (P.A.)
Elizabeth J. Robben (P.A.)
Christopher J. Heller (P.A.)
Laura Hensley Smith (P.A.)
Robert S. Shafer (P.A.)
William Mell Griffin III, (P.A.)
Thomas N. Rose (P.A.)
Michael Scott Moore (P.A.)
Diane S. Mackey (P.A.)
Walter M. Ebel, III, (P.A.)
Kevin A. Crass (P.A.)
William A. Waddell, Jr., (P.A.)
Tab Turner (P.A.)
Calvin J. Hall (P.A.)
Jerry L. Malone (P.A.)
M. Gayle Corley (P.A.)
Robert B. Beach, Jr., (P.A.)
Scott J. Lancaster (P.A.)
J. Lee Brown (P.A.)
James C. Baker (P.A.)
H. Charles Gschwend, Jr., (P.A.)
Harry A. Light (P.A.)
Scott H. Tucker (P.A.)
John Clayton Randolph (P.A.)
Guy Alton Wade (P.A.)

ASSOCIATES

Price C. Gardner
J. Michael Pickens
Tonia P. Jones
David D. Wilson
Jeffrey H. Moore
Andrew T. Turner
John Ray White
David M. Graf
Carla G. Spainhour
John C. Fendley, Jr
Allison Graves Bazzel
Jonann C. Roosevelt

(See Next Column)

ASSOCIATES (Continued)

R. Christopher Lawson
Gregory D. Taylor
Tony L. Wilcox
Fran C. Hickman
Betty J. Demory

COUNSEL

William J. Smith
John T. Williams (1909-1988)
Herschel H. Friday (1922-1994)
William A. Eldredge, Jr., (P.A.)
B. S. Clark
William L. Terry
William L. Patton, Jr.

Counsel for: Union Pacific System; St. Paul Insurance Co.; Liberty Mutual Insurance Co.; Cigna Property & Casualty Co.; Arkansas Power & Light Co.; Dillard Department Stores, Inc.; First Commercial Corp.; Browning Arms Co.; Phillips Petroleum Co.; Aetna Casualty & Surety Co.

For full biographical listings, see the Martindale-Hubbell Law Directory

GILL LAW FIRM (AV)

3801 TCBY Tower, Capitol and Broadway, 72201
Telephone: 501-376-3800
Fax: 501-372-3359

John P. Gill
Charles C. Owen
W. W. Elrod, II
Victor A. Fleming
Heartsill Ragon, III
Joseph D. Calhoun, III

ASSOCIATES

Glenn E. Kelley
C. Tad Bohannon

OF COUNSEL

John A. Fogleman

For full biographical listings, see the Martindale-Hubbell Law Directory

HARGIS, WOOD & LOCKHART, A PROFESSIONAL ASSOCIATION (AV)

809 West 2nd Street, 72201
Telephone: 501-375-0200
FAX: 501-375-0218

David M. Hargis
David J. Wood (P.A.)
W. Kirby Lockhart

Counsel for: Arkansas Motor Carriers Assn.
References: Union National Bank of Little Rock; Union Modern Mortgage; Modern American Mortgage Assn.

For full biographical listings, see the Martindale-Hubbell Law Directory

HILBURN, CALHOON, HARPER, PRUNISKI & CALHOUN, LTD. (AV)

P.O. Box 1256, 72203-1256
Telephone: 501-372-0110
FAX: 501-372-2029
North Little Rock, Arkansas Office: Eighth Floor, The Twin City Bank Building, One Riverfront Place, P.O. Box 5551, 72119.
Telephone: 501-372-0110.
FAX: 501-372-2029.

Sam Hilburn
Ken F. Calhoon
Ernest H. Harper, Jr.
John E. Pruniski, III
John C. Calhoun, Jr.
David M. Fuqua
James M. McHaney, Jr.
Phillip W. Campbell
J. Maurice Rogers
Paula Jamell Storeygard
Scott E. Daniel
Carrold E. Ray
Scott Thomas Vaughn
Susan Gordon Gunter

Dorcy Kyle Corbin
James D. Lawson
Graham F. Sloan
Mark K. Halter
Michael E. Hartje, Jr.
Dean L. Worley
Bruce D. Eddy
Pamela A. Moseley
Randy L. Grice

Representative Clients: The Twin City Bank; Merrill Lynch Pierce Fenner & Smith, Inc.

For full biographical listings, see the Martindale-Hubbell Law Directory

HOOVER & STOREY (AV)

111 Center Street, 11th Floor, 72201-4445
Telephone: 501-376-8500
Facsimile: 501-372-3255

MEMBERS OF FIRM

Paul W. Hoover, Jr.
O. H. Storey, III
John Kooistra, III
Lawrence Joseph Brady
William P. Dougherty
Max C. Mehlburger
Joyce Bradley Babin
Herbert W. Kell, Jr.
Letty McAdams

For full biographical listings, see the Martindale-Hubbell Law Directory

Little Rock—Continued

IVESTER, SKINNER & CAMP, P.A. (AV)

Suite 1200, 111 Center Street, 72201
Telephone: 501-376-7788
FAX: 501-376-8536

Hermann Ivester
H. Edward Skinner
Charles R. Camp
Wayne B. Ball
Randal B. Frazier
Robert Keller Jackson
Laura G. Wiltshire
Mildred H. Hansen
Valerie F. Boyce
Todd A. Lewellen
Stan D. Smith
S. Scott Luton

For full biographical listings, see the Martindale-Hubbell Law Directory

LASER, SHARP, WILSON, BUFFORD & WATTS, P.A. (AV)

101 S. Spring Street, Suite 300, 72201-2488
Telephone: 501-376-2981
Telecopier: 501-376-2417

Sam Laser
Jacob Sharp, Jr.
Ralph R. Wilson
Dan F. Bufford
Richard N. Watts
J. Kendal "Ken" Cook
Kevin J. Staten
Alfred F. Angulo, Jr.
David M. Donovan
Walter A. Kendel, Jr.
Brian A. Brown
Karen J. Hughes
Gena Gregory
Keith Martin McPherson
Thomas J. Diaz
(Not admitted in AR)

Representative Clients: Allstate Insurance Co.; American International Insurance Group; Continental Insurance Cos.; Farm Bureau Insurance Cos. (Casualty & Fire); Farmers Insurance Group; GAB Business Services, Inc.; St. Paul Insurance Cos.; Scottsdale Insurance Co.; State Farm Auto (Fire) Insurance Cos.

For full biographical listings, see the Martindale-Hubbell Law Directory

MEEKS & JERNIGAN, P.A. (AV)

404 Superior Federal Building, Capitol and Broadway 500 South Broadway, P.O. Box 34193, 72203
Telephone: 501-376-4660
FAX: 501-376-3203

W. Russell Meeks, III
George O. Jernigan, Jr.

Representative Clients: Kemper Insurance Group; Lumbermen's Mutual Casualty Co.; Firemen's Fund Insurance Cos.; Arkansas Children's Hospital; First Commercial Bank, N.A.; Arkansas Association of Educational Administrators; Cleveland Chemical Company.
General Counsel for: Arkansas Health Care Association; Arkansas Pharmacist Association; Arkansas Travelers Baseball Club, Inc.

For full biographical listings, see the Martindale-Hubbell Law Directory

ROSE LAW FIRM, A PROFESSIONAL ASSOCIATION (AV)

120 East Fourth Street, 72201
Telephone: 501-375-9131
Telecopy: 501-375-1309

Phillip Carroll
W. Dane Clay
George E. Campbell
Herbert C. Rule, III
W. Wilson Jones
Allen W. Bird, II
William E. Bishop
C. Brantly Buck
Tim Boe
M. Jane Dickey
Kenneth Robert Shemin
Ronald M. Clark
Garland J. Garrett
Jerry C. Jones
Thomas P. Thrash
Charles W. Baker
David L. Williams
Jackson Farrow Jr.
Les R. Baledge
James Hunter Birch
Kevin R. Burns
Richard T. Donovan
Richard N. Massey
Gary N. Speed
John T. Hardin
Stephen N. Joiner
James M. Gary
James H. Druff
Gordon M. Wilbourn
Jess Askew, III
Amy Lee Stewart
David A. Smith
Brian Rosenthal
T. Craig Jones
J. Scott Schallhorn

COUNSEL

J. Gaston Williamson
John A. Davis, III

Steven D. Durand
Jeffrey J. Gearhart
James L. Harris
Mark Alan Peoples
Clay H. Davis
Franklin M. Faust
Bryant K. Cranford
Stephen E. Snider
Grant E. Fortson
David P. Martin
Kathryn Bennett Perkins
Randall L. Bynum
John P. Fletcher
Todd P. Guthrie
Goodloe M. Partee
Marti S. Toennies

Counsel for: Aluminum Company of America; Bridgestone/Firestone, Inc.; The Equitable Life Assurance Society of The United States; General Motors Corp.; The Prudential Insurance Company of America; Stephens Inc.; TCBY Enterprises, Inc.; Tyson Foods, Inc.; WEHCO Media, Inc.; Worthen Banking Corp.

(See Next Column)

For full biographical listings, see the Martindale-Hubbell Law Directory

WILLIAM F. SHERMAN (AV)

Suite 504, Pyramid Place, 221 West Second Street, 72201
Telephone: 501-372-3148
FAX: 501-372-2630

For full biographical listings, see the Martindale-Hubbell Law Directory

WILLIAMS & ANDERSON (AV)

Twenty-Second Floor, 111 Center Street, 72201
Telephone: 501-372-0800
FAX: 501-372-6453

MEMBERS OF FIRM

W. Jackson Williams
Philip S. Anderson
Peter G. Kumpe
David F. Menz
Steven W. Quattlebaum
James E. Hathaway III
John E. Tull, III
Rush B. Deacon
J. Leon Holmes
Timothy W. Grooms

Thomas G. Williams
J. Madison Barker
G. Alan Perkins
J. Cal McCastlain
Jeanne L. Seewald
Sarah J. Heffley

Representative Clients: Arkansas Development Finance Authority; Coregis; Dean Witter Reynolds Inc.; Entergy Power, Inc.; Little Rock Newspapers, Inc. d/b/a Arkansas Democrat-Gazette; Texaco Inc.; Roman Catholic Diocese of Little Rock; Transport Indemnity Insurance Co.; Wal-Mart Stores, Inc.

For full biographical listings, see the Martindale-Hubbell Law Directory

WRIGHT, LINDSEY & JENNINGS (AV)

2200 Worthen Bank Building, 200 West Capitol Avenue, 72201
Telephone: 501-371-0808
Fax: 501-376-9442
Fayetteville, Arkansas Office: 101 West Mountain Street, Suite 206, 72701.
Telephone: 501-575-0808.
Fax: 501-575-0999.
Russellville, Arkansas Office: Suite E, 1110 West B Street.
Telephone: 501-968-7995.

Edward L. Wright (1903-1977)
Robert S. Lindsey (1913-1991)
Ronald A. May
Isaac A. Scott, Jr.
James M. Moody
John G. Lile
Gordon S. Rather, Jr.
Terry L. Mathews
David M. Powell
Roger A. Glasgow
C. Douglas Buford, Jr.
Patrick J. Goss
Alston Jennings, Jr.
John R. Tisdale
Kathlyn Graves
M. Samuel Jones, III
John William Spivey, III
Lee J. Muldrow
Wendell L. Griffen
N. M. Norton, Jr.
Edgar J. Tyler
Charles C. Price
Charles T. Coleman
James J. Glover
Edwin L. Lowther, Jr.
Beverly Bassett Schaffer
(Resident, Fayetteville Office)
Charles L. Schlumberger
Sammye L. Taylor
Walter E. May
Anna Hirai Gibson
Gregory T. Jones
H. Keith Morrison
(Resident, Fayetteville Office)
Bettina E. Brownstein
Walter McSpadden
Roger D. Rowe
Nancy Bellhouse May
John D. Davis
Judy Simmons Henry
Kimberly Wood Tucker
Mark L. Pryor
Ray F. Cox, Jr.
Harry S. Hurst, Jr.
Troy A. Price
Patricia Sievers Lewallen
James M. Moody, Jr.
Kathryn A. Pryor
J. Mark Davis
Kevin W. Kennedy
Mark Alan Rogers
M. Todd Wood
R. Gregory Aclin
Fred M. Perkins, III
William Stuart Jackson
Michael D. Barnes
Stephen R. Lancaster
Fred A. Wood
Judy M. Robinson
Betsy Meacham

OF COUNSEL

Alston Jennings
George E. Lusk, Jr.

Representative Clients: Allstate Insurance Co.; Arkansas Electric Cooperative Corp.; CNA; Ford Motor Company; Helena Chemical Company; Hudson Foods, Inc.; J.B. Hunt Transport Services, Inc.; Stephens, Inc.; United States Aviation Underwriters; Worthen Banking Corp.

For full biographical listings, see the Martindale-Hubbell Law Directory

*MAGNOLIA,** Columbia Co.

WOODWARD & EPLEY (AV)

105 West Calhoun Street, P.O. Box 765, 71753
Telephone: 501-234-4781
FAX: 501-234-7751

Joe D. Woodward
Michael G. Epley

(See Next Column)

WOODWARD & EPLEY—*Continued*

David P. Price

Representative Clients: American Fuel Cell and Coated Fabrics Co.; The Banner News Publishing Co.; First National Bank of Lewisville; Peoples Bank, Waldo, Arkansas; Worthen National Bank of South Arkansas; Unit Structures Systems, Inc.; Prescott Land & Timber Company, Inc.; Harold Rogers Logging, Inc.; J. W. Miller Timber Co., Inc.; Miller Hardwood, Inc.

For full biographical listings, see the Martindale-Hubbell Law Directory

*MALVERN,** Hot Spring Co. — (Refer to Hot Springs National Park)

*MARIANNA,** Lee Co. — (Refer to Helena)

*MARSHALL,** Searcy Co. — (Refer to Mountain Home)

*MELBOURNE,** Izard Co. — (Refer to Batesville)

*MENA,** Polk Co. — (Refer to Ashdown)

*MONTICELLO,** Drew Co.

BALL, BARTON & HOFFMAN (AV)

North Main at Oakland, P.O. Box 507, 71655
Telephone: 501-367-6288
Fax: 501-367-7851

MEMBERS OF FIRM

Lamar Williamson (1887-1974)
Adrian Williamson (1892-1982)
William K. Ball
Walter W. Barton
David D. Hoffman

Representative Clients: Southern Division of Potlatch Corp.; Crossett Division of Georgia-Pacific Corp.; Union Bank & Trust Co.; Sea Ark Marine, Inc.; Monticello School District; Southern Farm Bureau Casualty Insurance Co.; R. A. Pickens & Son; Arkansas Land & Cattle Co.; State Auto Insurance U.S.A.A.

ROSS & ROSS (AV)

115 East Shelton Avenue, P.O. Box 209, 71655
Telephone: 501-367-5351
FAX: 501-367-2221

James A. Ross (1911-1983)
James A. Ross, Jr.

Reference: Heritage Bank, A Federal Savings Bank, Monticello, Ark.

For full biographical listings, see the Martindale-Hubbell Law Directory

*MORRILTON,** Conway Co. — (Refer to Russellville)

MOUNTAINBURG, Crawford Co. — (Refer to Fort Smith)

*MOUNTAIN HOME,** Baxter Co.

POYNTER & GEARHART, P.A. (AV)

123 East Seventh Street, P.O. Box 370, 72653
Telephone: 501-425-2196
FAX: 501-425-2198

Terry M. Poynter
Van A. Gearhart

Representative Clients: First National Bank & Trust Co.; First Ozark National Bank; United States Fidelity & Guaranty Co.
Approved Attorneys for: Farmers Home Administration; Chicago Title Insurance Co.; Mid-South Title Insurance Co.
References: First National Bank and Trust Co.; The Peoples Bank & Trust Co.; Farmers Home Administration; First Ozark National Bank.

For full biographical listings, see the Martindale-Hubbell Law Directory

*MOUNTAIN VIEW,** Stone Co. — (Refer to Batesville)

*MURFREESBORO,** Pike Co. — (Refer to Nashville)

*NASHVILLE,** Howard Co.

STEEL & STEEL (AV)

102 North Main Street, 71852
Telephone: 501-845-1870
Fax: 501-845-3355

MEMBERS OF FIRM

George E. Steel
George E. Steel, Jr.

Attorneys for: First National Bank, Nashville; Pike County Bank, Murfreesboro and Mineral Springs, Nashville; Weyerhaeuser Co.; Nashville Trucking ; R.D. Plant Contracting Co.; Bank of Amity, Amity; Southwestern Electric Power Co.; M & P Paving Company; Walmart Stores, Inc.

For full biographical listings, see the Martindale-Hubbell Law Directory

*NEWPORT,** Jackson Co.

BOYCE & BOYCE, A PROFESSIONAL ASSOCIATION (AV)

515 Second Street, P.O. Box 948, 72112
Telephone: 501-523-5242
FAX: 501-523-5196

(See Next Column)

Wayne Boyce
Edward W. Boyce, III

For full biographical listings, see the Martindale-Hubbell Law Directory

BOYCE LAW FIRM (AV)

307 Main, P.O. Box 38, 72112
Telephone: 501-523-3626; Jonesboro: 501-932-7189
Fax: 501-523-4839

Sam H. Boyce

ASSOCIATES

Henry H. Boyce

LEGAL SUPPORT PERSONNEL

Betty Butler (Paralegal)

Reference: Merchants & Planters Bank, Newport, Arkansas.

For full biographical listings, see the Martindale-Hubbell Law Directory

THAXTON, HOUT & HOWARD (AV)

600 Third Street, P.O. Box 8, 72112
Telephone: 501-523-3677
Fax: 501-523-5015

MEMBERS OF FIRM

Judson N. Hout (1911-1966)
Marvin D. Thaxton
Phillip D. Hout
Steven G. Howard

Representative Clients: The First State Bank of Newport; Farm Credit Services; Newport Municipal Water Co.; Natural Gas Pipeline Company of America, Inc.; Chicago Title Insurance Co.; Northwestern National Life Insurance Co.; Arkansas Louisiana Gas Co.; Newport Hospital & Clinic, Inc.; Travelers Insurance Co.

For full biographical listings, see the Martindale-Hubbell Law Directory

TIMOTHY F. WATSON, SR. (AV)

209 Walnut Street, P.O. Box 988, 72112
Telephone: 501-523-8420
Fax: 501-523-4639

For full biographical listings, see the Martindale-Hubbell Law Directory

*OZARK,** Franklin Co. — (Refer to Fort Smith)

*PARAGOULD,** Greene Co. — (Refer to Jonesboro)

*PARIS,** Logan Co. — (Refer to Fort Smith)

*PIGGOTT,** Clay Co. — (Refer to Jonesboro)

*PINE BLUFF,** Jefferson Co.

BRIDGES, YOUNG, MATTHEWS & DRAKE PLC (AV)

315 East Eighth Avenue, P.O. Box 7808, 71611
Telephone: 501-534-5532
Fax: 501-534-5582

F. G. Bridges (1866-1959)
Frank G. Bridges, Jr. (1906-1973)
Paul B. Young
Stephen A. Matthews
Ted N. Drake
Joseph A. Strode
Jack A. McNulty
Terry F. Wynne
James L. (Lee) Moore, III
Michael J. Dennis
David L. Sims
R. Scott Morgan

Jeffrey H. Dixon
Carrington E. (Cary) Young
Ruth Ann Wisener
James C. Moser, Jr.

Representative Clients: Corporate: Arkansas Power & Light Co.; Central Moloney, Inc.; International Paper Co.; Worthen National Bank of Pine Bluff, Arkansas. Insurance: Hartford Insurance Group; The Travelers; United States Fidelity & Guaranty Co. Other: Jefferson Regional Medical Center.

For full biographical listings, see the Martindale-Hubbell Law Directory

RAMSAY, BRIDGFORTH, HARRELSON & STARLING (AV)

11th Floor, Simmons First National Building, P.O. Drawer 8509, 71611
Telephone: 501-535-9000
FAX: 501-535-8544

MEMBERS OF FIRM

William Franklin Coleman (1870-1956)
Nicholas J. Gantt, Jr. (1879-1975)
Marion J. Starling, Jr. (1941-1990)
William C. Bridgforth
F. Daniel Harrelson
Spencer F. Robinson
Phillip A. Raley
Patrick A. Burrow
Rosalind M. Mouser

ASSOCIATES

William M. Bridgforth
David R. Bridgforth
William Jay Harrelson
John Thomas Starling

(See Next Column)

RAMSAY, BRIDGFORTH, HARRELSON & STARLING, *Pine Bluff—Continued*

OF COUNSEL

Louis L. Ramsay, Jr.

Representative Clients: Simmons First National Bank; Pine Bluff Sand & Gravel Co.; Stant, Inc.; Aetna Life & Casualty Insurance Co.; McGeorge Contracting Co., Inc.; Television Station KATV.

For full biographical listings, see the Martindale-Hubbell Law Directory

*RISON,** Cleveland Co. — (Refer to Pine Bluff)

*RUSSELLVILLE,** Pope Co.

LAWS & MURDOCH, P.A. (AV)

2nd & South Arkansas, 72801
Telephone: 501-968-1168
Fax: 501-968-5590

Ike Allen Laws, Jr.
Ike Allen Laws, III
Timothy W. Murdoch
Hugh R. Laws

Representative Clients: Delhi Gas Pipeline Corp.; Invesco, Inc.; Ozark Gas Transmission Co.; Worthen National Bank of Russellville, Arkansas; United General Title; Bibler Bros, Inc.; Pope County Levee District; Baker Refrigeration, Inc.; Dixon Poultry, Inc.
Approved Attorneys for: United General Title.

For full biographical listings, see the Martindale-Hubbell Law Directory

*SALEM,** Fulton Co. — (Refer to Batesville)

*SHERIDAN,** Grant Co. — (Refer to Little Rock)

SPRINGDALE, Washington Co.

CYPERT, CROUCH, CLARK & HARWELL (AV)

111 Holcomb Street, P.O. Box 869, 72764-1400
Telephone: 501-751-5222
Fax: 501-751-5777

Courtney C. Crouch (1912-1975)
William M. Clark, Jr.
James D. Cypert
Charles L. Harwell
James E. Crouch
Brian L. Spaulding
R. Jeffrey Reynerson

OF COUNSEL

Leslie L. Reid
Stanley W. Ludwig

General Counsel for: First National Bank of Springdale; Springdale Memorial Hospital; Springdale School District.
Representative Clients: Purina Mills, Inc.; Swift-Eckrich, Inc.
Insurance Clients: Western Casualty & Surety Co.; The John Hancock Cos.; Home Ins. Co.; Liberty Mutual; Fireman's Fund.

For full biographical listings, see the Martindale-Hubbell Law Directory

ROY & LAMBERT (AV)

2706 South Dividend Drive, P.O. Drawer 7030, 72766-7030
Telephone: 501-756-8510
Fax: 501-756-8562

MEMBERS OF FIRM

James M. Roy, Jr.
Robert J. Lambert, Jr.

ASSOCIATES

Jerry L. Lovelace
Jon P. Robinson
Brian D. Wood
James H. Bingaman

OF COUNSEL

John D. Copeland

Representative Clients: Springdale Bank & Trust; 4-State Poultry Supply, Inc.; Barnhill, Inc.
Insurance Clients: State Farm Mutual Automobile Insurance Co.; State Farm Fire and Casualty Co.; Shelter Insurance Co.; Silvey Insurance Cos.; Tri-State Insurance Co.; Columbia Mutual Insurance Co.; State Volunteer Mutual Insurance Co.

For full biographical listings, see the Martindale-Hubbell Law Directory

*STAR CITY,** Lincoln Co. — (Refer to Pine Bluff)

*STUTTGART,** Arkansas Co. — (Refer to Pine Bluff)

*TEXARKANA,** Miller Co.

LAVENDER, ROCHELLE, BARNETTE & PICKETT (AV)

507 Hickory Street, P.O. Box 1938, 75504
Telephone: 501-773-3187
Telecopier: 501-773-3181

MEMBERS OF FIRM

G. William Lavender
Charles Decker Barnette
Jerry A. Rochelle
John M. Pickett

(See Next Column)

ASSOCIATES

Shannon Tuckett

Counsel for: Southwestern Electric Power Co.; Prudential Insurance Company of America; E.I. DuPont De Nemours & Company, Inc.; John Hancock Mutual Life Insurance Co.; Federal Deposit Insurance Corp.; Farmers Insurance Group of Cos.; New York Life Insurance Co.; Commercial National Bank of Texarkana; Builders Transport, Inc., Resolution Trust Corp.

For full biographical listings, see the Martindale-Hubbell Law Directory

SMITH, STROUD, MCCLERKIN, DUNN & NUTTER (AV)

State Line Plaza, Box 8030, 75502-5945
Telephone: 501-773-5651
Telecopier: 501-772-2037

MEMBERS OF FIRM

Willis B. Smith (1926-1980)
Charles A. Morgan
John F. Stroud, Jr.
James N. Nutt (1949-1983)
Hayes C. McClerkin
Nelson V. Shaw
Charles M. Conway (1925-1976)
R. David Freeze
Winford L. Dunn, Jr.
Demaris A. Hart
R. Gary Nutter
William David Carter

ASSOCIATES

Carol Cannedy Dalby

OF COUNSEL

Alex G. Sanderson

LEGAL SUPPORT PERSONNEL

LEGAL ASSISTANTS

Myra J. Conaway
Sonja L. Oliver

Representative Clients: North American Energy Corporation (NorAm); The State First National Bank of Texarkana; Prudential Insurance Company of America; CNA Insurance Cos.; Cigna Insurance Cos.; First Federal Savings & Loan Assn.; St. Michael Hospital; Southwest Arkansas Water District; Mobil Oil Co.; Southwest Arkansas Electric Cooperative Corp.

For full biographical listings, see the Martindale-Hubbell Law Directory

*VAN BUREN,** Crawford Co. — (Refer to Fort Smith)

*WALDRON,** Scott Co. — (Refer to Fort Smith)

*WALNUT RIDGE,** Lawrence Co. — (Refer to Jonesboro)

*WARREN,** Bradley Co. — (Refer to Monticello)

WEST MEMPHIS, Crittenden Co.

HALE, FOGLEMAN & ROGERS (AV)

108 Dover Road, P.O. Box 1666, 72301
Telephone: 501-735-1900
FAX: 501-735-1662

MEMBERS OF FIRM

Julian B. Fogleman
Joe M. Rogers
James C. Hale, Jr.
John N. Fogleman

General Counsel for: Drainage Districts # 2, 3 and 8 of Crittenden County; Edmondson Hotel Service, Inc.; Heath & House Construction Co.
Local Counsel for: Arkansas Louisiana Gas Co.; Southern Farm Bureau Casualty Insurance Co.; Shelby Mutual Insurance Co.; Greyhound Lines, Inc.; Fidelity National Bank; American Justice Insurance Reciprocal.

For full biographical listings, see the Martindale-Hubbell Law Directory

RIEVES & MAYTON (AV)

304 East Broadway, P.O. Box 1359, 72303
Telephone: 501-735-3420
Telecopier: 501-735-4678

MEMBERS OF FIRM

Elton A. Rieves, Jr. (1909-1984)
Michael R. Mayton
Elton A. Rieves, III
Elton A. Rieves, IV

ASSOCIATES

Martin W. Bowen
William J. Stanley

For full biographical listings, see the Martindale-Hubbell Law Directory

SLOAN, RUBENS & PEEPLES (AV)

600 North Missouri Street, P.O. Box 768, 72303
Telephone: 501-735-5500
Telecopy: 501-735-2624

MEMBERS OF FIRM

Edward J. Rubens (1913-1977)
Kent J. Rubens
Ralph W. Sloan
David C. Peeples

ASSOCIATES

J. Michael Stephenson
James A. Davis

General Counsel for: Bank of West Memphis; Crittenden Publishing Co., Inc.; East Arkansas Family Health Center, Inc.; Mid-Continent Investments, Inc.; Federal Savings Bank; West Memphis School District.
Representative Clients: C.P.S. Chemical Co., Inc.; First Tennessee Bank, Memphis, Tenn.; Petro, Inc.; Razorback Concrete.

For full biographical listings, see the Martindale-Hubbell Law Directory

*WYNNE,** Cross Co. — (Refer to Forrest City)

*YELLVILLE,** Marion Co. — (Refer to Harrison)

CALIFORNIA

ALAMEDA, Alameda Co. — (Refer to Oakland)

ALHAMBRA, Los Angeles Co. — (Refer to Pasadena)

*ALTURAS,** Modoc Co. — (Refer to Redding)

ARCADIA, Los Angeles Co.

HELMS, HANRAHAN & MYERS (AV)

Suite 685 Towne Centre Building, 150 North Santa Anita Avenue, 91006
Telephone: 818-445-1177

James R. Helms, Jr.
James J. Hanrahan
Sterling E. Myers

LEGAL SUPPORT PERSONNEL

PARALEGALS

Michelle L. Upp
Josephine Phillips

Reference: Bank of America National Trust & Savings Assn. (Arcadia Branch).

For full biographical listings, see the Martindale-Hubbell Law Directory

*AUBURN,** Placer Co. — (Refer to Sacramento)

*BAKERSFIELD,** Kern Co.

BORTON, PETRINI & CONRON (AV)

The Borton, Petrini & Conron Building, 1600 Truxtun Avenue, P.O. Box 2026, 93303
Telephone: 805-322-3051
Cable: "Verdict"
Telex: 181-341
Fax: 805-322-4628
San Luis Obispo, California Office: 1065 Higuera Street, P.O. Box 927.
Telephone: 805-541-4340.
Fax: 805-541-4558.
Visalia, California Office: 206 South Mooney Boulevard, P.O. Box 1028.
Telephone: 209-627-5600.
Fax: 209-627-4309.
Fresno, California Office: T. W. Patterson Building, Suite 830, 2014 Tulare Street.
Telephone: 209-268-0117.
Fax: 209-237-7995.
Sacramento, California Office: Suite 350, 1545 River Park Drive.
Telephone: 916-920-2812.
Fax: 916-920-1514.
Santa Barbara, California Office: Suite D, 211 East Victoria Street.
Telephone: 805-564-2404.
Fax: 805-564-2176.
Los Angeles, California Office: One Wilshire Building, 624 South Grand Avenue, Suite 1100.
Telephone: 213-624-2869.
Fax: 213-489-3930.
San Diego, California Office: 610 West Ash Street, 9th Floor.
Telephone: 619-232-2424.
Fax: 619-531-0794.
Newport Beach, California Office: 4675 MacArthur Court, Suite 1150.
Telephone: 714-752-2333.
Fax: 714-752-2854.
Modesto, California Office: The Turner Building, 900 "H" Street, Suite D.
Telephone: 209-576-1701.
Fax: 209-527-9753.
San Francisco, California Office: Citicorp Center, One Sansome Street, Suite 1000.
Telephone: 415-981-4415.
Fax: 415-391-5538.
Redding, California Office: Suite 120, 457 Knollcrest Drive.
Telephone: 916-222-1530.
Fax: 916-222-4498.
San Bernardino, California Office: Suite 500, 290 North "D" Street.
Telephone: 909-381-0527.
Fax: 909-381-0658.
San Jose, California Office: 55 South Market Street, Suite 1212.
Telephone: 408-298-3997.
Fax: 408-298-3365.
Ventura, California Office: Suite 310, 1000 Hill Road.
Telephone: 805-650-9994.
Fax: 805-650-7125.
Santa Rosa, California: 50 Santa Rosa Avenue, 5th Floor.
Telephone: 707-527-9477.
FAX: 707-527-9488.

MEMBERS OF FIRM

Fred E. Borton (1877-1948)
James Petrini (1897-1978)
Harry M. Conron (1907-1971)
Kenneth D. Pinsent (1953-1984)
Richard E. Hitchcock
John F. Petrini
George F. Martin
Stephen M. Dake
Paul A. Lafranchise
Michael D. Worthing
Guy J. Gattuso, Jr.
Kenneth W. Scott

(See Next Column)

John J. Korbol
Steven M. Karcher
Mark Alan Jones
Victoria R. Allard
Charles R. Brehmer
Richard O. Middlebrook
Craig N. Beardsley
Randall Steven Joyce
William H. Cantrell (Resident Member, Newport Beach Office)
J. David Petrie (Resident Member, Fresno Office)
Daniel L. Ferguson (Resident Member, San Bernardino Office)
Craig R. McCollum (Resident Member, San Luis Obispo Office)
Rocky K. Copley (Resident Member, San Diego Office)
Mark S. Newman (Resident Member, Sacramento Office)
Thomas Simonian (Resident Member, Visalia Office)
James M. McKanna (Resident Member, Newport Beach Office)
Dale M. Dorfmeier (Resident Member, Fresno Office)
Larry R. Nelson (Resident Member, Los Angeles Office)
Jeffrey F. Paccassi (Resident Member, San Francisco Office)
Knut W. Barde (Resident Member, Visalia Office)
Bob H. Grove (Resident Member, Ventura Office)
Randall L. Harr (Resident Member, Redding Office)
Robert J. Gundert (Resident Member, San Luis Obispo Office)
Steven M. Shewry (Resident Member, San Diego Office)
Robert N. Ridenour (Resident Member, Los Angeles Office)
Rick D. Hardin (Resident Member, Santa Barbara Office)
George J. Hernandez, Jr. (Resident Member, Los Angeles Office)
J. Jeffrey Egan (Resident Member, San Jose Office)
Paul Kissel (Resident Member, San Diego Office)
Charles L. Carson (Resident Member, San Luis Obispo Office)
Michael F. Long (Resident Member, Newport Beach Office)
Bradley A. Post (Resident Member, Modesto Office)
Michael J. Macko (Resident Member, Modesto Office)
Calvin R. Stead (Resident Member, Santa Rosa Office)
Tracy W. Goldberg (Resident Member, San Bernardino Office)
Thomas J. Griffin (Resident Member, Los Angeles Office)
Samuel L. Phillips (Resident Member, Modesto Office)
Thomas J. Stoddard (Resident Member, San Diego Office)
Gary C. Harvey (Resident Member, Fresno Office)
Thomas A. Gifford (Resident Member, Sacramento Office)
Adam D. H. Grant (Resident Member, Los Angeles Office)

ASSOCIATES

Anthony B. Nixon (Resident Associate, Ventura Office)
Richard M. Macias (Resident Associate, Los Angeles Office)
Dennis D. Resh (Resident Associate, Los Angeles Office)
William F. Klausner (Resident Associate, San Bernardino Office)
Phillip B. Greer (Resident Associate, Newport Beach Office)
R. Stephen Kinnaird (Resident Associate, Santa Barbara Office)
Thomas F. Brooks (Resident Associate, Ventura Office)
Richard E. Korb (Resident Associate, San Francisco Office)
Paul T. McBride (Resident Associate, Newport Beach Office)
Carla J. Hartley (Resident Associate, San Francisco Office)
Brian T. McKibbin (Resident Associate, Los Angeles Office)
Sharon G. Pratt (Resident Associate, San Jose Office)
Kim Cantil-Cohen (Resident Associate, Sacramento Office)
Francis P. Aspessi (Resident Associate, San Bernardino Office)
Marc D. Yablon (Resident Associate, Sacramento Office)
Guy W. Murray (Resident Associate, San Luis Obispo Office)
David S. Cohn (Resident Associate, San Bernardino Office)
Tuvana B. Jeffrey (Resident Associate, San Francisco Office)
Christopher Der Manuelian, Jr. (Resident Associate, San Jose Office)
Lynne L. Bentley (Resident Associate, San Jose Office)
Todd R. Phillippi (Resident Associate, Los Angeles Office)
Samuel M. Besse, Jr. (Resident Associate, Ventura Office)
Michael V. Peros (Resident Associate, San Bernardino Office)
Kenneth B. Arthofer (Resident Associate, Redding Office)
Barton C. Merrill (Resident Associate, Santa Barbara Office)
Paige M. Hibbert (Resident Associate, Sacramento Office)
Daniel A. Nassie (Resident Associate, Newport Beach Office)
Darlene M. Ball (Resident Associate, Visalia Office)
Steven G. Gatley (Resident Associate, Los Angeles Office)
Kevin A. Brown (Resident Associate, Sacramento Office)
Philip F. Sinco (Resident Associate, San Luis Obispo Office)
Judith J. Propp (Resident Associate, San Luis Obispo Office)
Randall K. Walton (Resident Associate, Redding Office)
Kerre L. Baker (Resident Associate, Newport Beach Office)
Rosemarie Suazo Lewis (Resident Associate, Los Angeles Office)
Denise M. Di Mascio (Resident Associate, Fresno Office)
Richard T. Collins (Resident Associate, Los Angeles Office)
Mark T. Coffin (Resident Associate, Santa Barbara Office)
Jeffrey J. Witthun (Resident Associate, Fresno Office)

(See Next Column)

BORTON, PETRINI & CONRON—*Continued*

ASSOCIATES (Continued)

Richard A. Aharonian (Resident Associate, Visalia Office)
Kathleen M. Howington (Resident Associate, Sacramento Office)
Randall J. Billington (Resident Associate, San Bernardino Office)
Carol J. Stair (Resident Associate, Santa Rosa Office)
Armand D. Thruston (Resident Associate, San Bernardino Office)
LeNan Bradley (Resident Associate, San Francisco Office)
Michelle L. Van Dyke (Resident Associate, San Diego Office)
Barry M. Zlotowicz (Resident Associate, Los Angeles Office)
Marc C. Gessford (Resident Associate, Sacramento Office)
Archie Clarizio (Resident Associate, Ventura Office)
Brent C. Vian (Resident Associate, Newport Beach Office)
William C. Belanger (Resident Associate, Sacramento Office)
Steven J. Green (Resident Associate, Sacramento Office)
Elisabeth A. Bowman (Resident Associate, San Diego Office)
Lee M. Amidon (Resident Associate, San Bernardino Office)
Douglas B. Inman (Resident Associate, San Bernardino Office)

OF COUNSEL

Roy J. Gargano
Jere N. Sullivan, Sr.

Representative Clients: Castle and Cooke; Wells Fargo Bank; Pacific Gas & Electric.

For full biographical listings, see the Martindale-Hubbell Law Directory

BUNKER, SAGHATELIAN & GIBBS (AV)

A Law Partnership
2821 "H" Street, 93301-1913
Telephone: 805-634-1144
Telecopier: 805-327-1923

Bruce F. Bunker
Tommi R. Saghatelian
Steven G. Gibbs

ASSOCIATES

Timothy L. Kleier

For full biographical listings, see the Martindale-Hubbell Law Directory

ELDON R. HUGIE A PROFESSIONAL CORPORATION (AV)

Suite 100, 1405 Commercial Way, 93309
Telephone: 805-328-0200
Telecopier: 805-328-0204

Eldon R. Hugie

Representative Clients: Tri-Fanucchi Farms, Inc.; Aquaculture Enterprises; Kern College Land Co.
Reference: Community First Bank (Bakersfield Main Branch).

For full biographical listings, see the Martindale-Hubbell Law Directory

KLEIN, WEGIS, DENATALE, GOLDNER & MUIR (AV)

A Partnership including Professional Corporations
(Formerly Di Giorgio, Davis, Klein, Wegis, Duggan & Friedman)
ARCO Tower, 4550 California Avenue, Second Floor, P.O. Box 11172, 93389-1172
Telephone: 805-395-1000
Telecopier: 805-326-0418
Santa Ana, California Office: Park Tower Building #610, 200 W. Santa Ana Boulevard, 92701.
Telephone: 714-285-0711.
Fax: 714-285-9003.

Thomas R. Davis (1920-1990)

MEMBERS OF FIRM

Anthony J. Klein (Inc.)
Ralph B. Wegis (Inc.)
Thomas V. DeNatale, Jr.
Gregory A. Muir
Barry L. Goldner
Jay L. Rosenlieb
David J. Cooper
Claude P. Kimball
Laurence C. Hall (Resident, Santa Ana Office)

ASSOCIATES

Denise Martin
David L. Saine
William H. Slocumb
Ned E. Dunphy
Barry E. Rosenberg
Kirk S. Tracey
John M. Perisich
Manning W. Puette
Christopher P. Burger
Carol J. Kern
Kevin C. Findley
Carol J. Grogan
Michael E. Hugie
Jose Benavides
Michael S. Abril
Melvin L. Ehrlich
Krystyna L. Jamieson
Stacy Henry Bowman
Thomas J. Jamieson, Jr.
Kristin Anne Smith
Jeffrey W. Noe
William A. Bruce
Kenneth E. James

(See Next Column)

Representative Clients: Bank of America; Great Western Bank; Mojave Pipeline Co.; Transamerican Title Insurance Co.; Dean Whittier Reynolds, Inc.; California Republic Bank; San Joaquin Bank; Nahama & Weagant Energy Co.; Freymiller Trucking, Inc.; Westinghouse Electric Co.

For full biographical listings, see the Martindale-Hubbell Law Directory

KUHS, PARKER & STANTON (AV)

Suite 200, 1200 Truxtun Avenue, P.O. Box 2205, 93303
Telephone: 805-322-4004
FAX: 805-322-2906

William C. Kuhs
James R. Parker, Jr.
David B. Stanton

Lorraine G. Adams
John P. Doering, III
Robert G. Kuhs

Reference: First Interstate Bank (Bakersfield Main Branch).

For full biographical listings, see the Martindale-Hubbell Law Directory

ROBINSON, PALMER & LOGAN (AV)

Suite 150, 3434 Truxtun Avenue, 93301
Telephone: 805-323-8277
Fax: 805-323-4205

MEMBERS OF FIRM

Oliver U. Robinson
William D. Palmer
Gary L. Logan

ASSOCIATES

Luke A. Foster
Jeffrey B. Held

For full biographical listings, see the Martindale-Hubbell Law Directory

LAW OFFICES OF YOUNG WOOLDRIDGE (AV)

1800 30th Street, Fourth Floor, 93301
Telephone: 805-327-9661
Facsimile: 805-327-1087

MEMBERS OF FIRM

Joseph Wooldridge
A. Cameron Paulden (1927-1984)
Robert J. Self
G. Neil Farr
Michael R. Young
Ernest A. Conant
Steve W. Nichols
Larry R. Cox
Scott K. Kuney
Michael A. Kaia

ASSOCIATES

Russell B. Hicks
Vickie Y. Wheeler
Steven M. Torigiani
Scott D. Howry
James E. Millar
David F. Leon

OF COUNSEL

John B. Young
Edward M. Carpenter

Representative Clients: Arvin-Edison Water Storage District; Motor City Truck Sales and Service.
References: Wells Fargo Bank; First Interstate Bank; California Republic Bank.

For full biographical listings, see the Martindale-Hubbell Law Directory

BEVERLY HILLS, Los Angeles Co.

ERVIN, COHEN & JESSUP (AV)

A Partnership including Professional Corporations
9401 Wilshire Boulevard, 90212-2974
Telephone: 310-273-6333
Facsimile: 310-859-2325

MEMBERS OF FIRM

John W. Ervin (1917-1982)
W. Edgar Jessup, Jr.
Melvin S. Spears
Bertram K. Massing
Marvin H. Lewis
Harold J. Delevie (P.C.)
David P. Kassoy
Gary J. Freedman (P.C.)
Lee I. Silver
Roger J. Holt
Allan B. Cooper
David R. Eandi
Gary Q. Michel (A P.C.)
Thomas A. Kirschbaum
Joan B. Velazquez
E. A. (Stacey) Olliff III
Thomas F. R. Garvin
Robert M. Waxman
Reeve E. Chudd
J. Richard Griggs
Kenneth A. Luer
Ronald M. St. Marie
Linda A. Kirios
Philip Starr
Barry J. MacNaughton
Penelope Parmes
Steven A. Roseman
Elsa Bañuelos
Jacob D. Lee

ASSOCIATES

Sylvia D. Lautsch
Howard Z. Berman
Natalie C. Ziontz
Kelly O. Scott
Layton L. Pace
Mark T. Kawa
Garee T. Gasperian
Darcy L. Honig
Bari J. Cooper
Paul F. Lawrence
Chung Jay Won
Ellen S. Kornblum

(See Next Column)

ERVIN, COHEN & JESSUP, *Beverly Hills—Continued*

Reference: Bank of California, N.A. (Beverly Hills).

For full biographical listings, see the Martindale-Hubbell Law Directory

TURNER, GERSTENFELD, WILK, TIGERMAN & YOUNG (AV)

Formerly, Turner, Gerstenfeld & Wilk. . . est. 1972
Suite 510, 8383 Wilshire Boulevard, 90211
Telephone: 213-653-3900
Facsimile: 213-653-3021

MEMBERS OF FIRM

Rubin M. Turner
Gerald F. Gerstenfeld
Barry R. Wilk
Bert Z. Tigerman
Steven E. Young
Edward Friedman
Linda Wight Mazur

ASSOCIATES

Joan R. Isaacs
Dortha Larene Pyles
Steven A. Morris
Vicki L. Cresap

For full biographical listings, see the Martindale-Hubbell Law Directory

BURLINGAME, San Mateo Co.

CARR, McCLELLAN, INGERSOLL, THOMPSON & HORN, PROFESSIONAL CORPORATION (AV)

216 Park Road, P.O. Box 513, 94011-0513
Telephone: 415-342-9600
Telecopier: 415-342-7685
San Francisco, California Office: Suite 2220, One California Street.
Telephone: 415-362-1400.
Telecopier: 415-362-5149.

E. H. Cosgriff (1880-1947)
J. Ed McClellan (1895-1985)
Albert J. Horn
Arthur H. Bredenbeck
Norman I. Book, Jr.
Quentin L. Cook
Robert A. Nebrig
Marion L. Brown
L. Michael Telleen
Lage E. Andersen
Keith P. Bartel
Mark A. Cassanego
Laurence M. May
Michael J. McQuaid
Penelope Creasey Greenberg
James R. Cody
Jordan W. Clements
Edward J. Willig, III
Sarah J. DiBoise
W. George Wailes
Carol B. Schwartz
Lori A. Lutzker
Moira C. Walsh
Jeremy W. Katz
Lisa Hayhurst Stalteri
Elizabeth A. Franklin

SENIOR COUNSEL

Allan E. Low
Denny S. Roja

Steven D. Anderson
James F. Blood
Todd L. Burlingame
Terese M. Raddie

OF COUNSEL

Luther M. Carr (Retired)
Frank B. Ingersoll, Jr. (Retired)
Cyrus J. McMillan (Retired)
Robert R. Thompson (Retired)
David C. Carr (Retired)

For full biographical listings, see the Martindale-Hubbell Law Directory

CHICO, Butte Co.

LEONARD & LYDE (AV)

A Partnership including Professional Corporations
1600 Humboldt Road, Suite 1, 95927
Telephone: 916-345-3494
Fax: 916-345-0460
Oroville, California Office: 1453 Huntoon Street.
Telephone: 916-533-2662.
Fax: 916-533-3843.

Raymond A. Leonard (1961-1981)
C. Keith Lyde (Inc.)
George E. Washington
Dorsett Marc Lyde
Robert L. Davis (Inc.)

For full biographical listings, see the Martindale-Hubbell Law Directory

PETERS, FULLER, RUSH, FARNSWORTH & HABIB (AV)

414 Salem Street, P.O. Box 3509, 95928
Telephone: 916-342-3593
FAX: 916-342-4272

MEMBERS OF FIRM

Jerome D. Peters (1891-1953)
Jerome D. Peters, Jr.
David R. Fuller
David H. Rush
James C. Farnsworth
Mark A. Habib

ASSOCIATES

Nancy E. Hooten

Local Counsel: Pacific Gas & Electric Co.; Southern Pacific Co.; Helena Chemical Co.; California Water Service Co.

(See Next Column)

Insurance Companies: Great American Insurance Co.; Industrial Indemnity; Lloyds of London; Zurich Insurance Co.; U.S.F. & G.; Progressive Insurance Co.

For full biographical listings, see the Martindale-Hubbell Law Directory

STEWART, HUMPHERYS, BURCHETT & SANDELMAN (AV)

Suite 6, 3120 Cohasset Road, P.O. Box 720, 95927
Telephone: 916-891-6111
Telecopier: 916-894-2103

MEMBERS OF FIRM

Ronald E. Stewart
Keith S. Humpherys
Alan E. Burchett
Raymond L. Sandelman

John Mark Felder
Richard J. Molin

For full biographical listings, see the Martindale-Hubbell Law Directory

CLAREMONT, Los Angeles Co.

PAUL BRYAN GRAY (AV)

341 West First Street, 91711
Telephone: 909-624-6259
FAX: 909-624-2359

*COLUSA,** Colusa Co. — (Refer to Marysville)

CORONA, Riverside Co.

CLAYSON, MANN, AREND & YAEGER, A PROFESSIONAL LAW CORPORATION (AV)

Clayson Law Building, 601 South Main Street, P.O. Box 1447, 91718-1447
Telephone: 909-737-1910
Riverside: 909-689-7241
Fax: 909-737-4384

Walter S. Clayson (1887-1972)
E. Spurgeon Rothrock (1918-1979)
Roy H. Mann
Erling C. Arend
Derrill E. Yaeger
Evan G. Evans
Gary K. Rosenzweig
Elisabeth Sichel
Kent A. Hansen
Roland C. Bainer
David R. Saunders
Sallie Barnett
Tambra L. Raush

Counsel for: Chino Valley Bank; Lee Lake Municipal Water District; Palo Verde Irrigation District; Loma Linda University.
Local Counsel: Minnesota Mining & Manufacturing Co.; Western Waste Industries.

For full biographical listings, see the Martindale-Hubbell Law Directory

COSTA MESA, Orange Co.

BALFOUR MACDONALD TALBOT MIJUSKOVIC & OLMSTED, A PROFESSIONAL CORPORATION (AV)

Suite 720, 611 Anton Boulevard, 92626
Telephone: 714-546-2400
Fax: 714-546-5008

Ralph E. Balfour
James B. MacDonald
R. Wayne Olmsted
Ruth Mijuskovic
M. D. Talbot

For full biographical listings, see the Martindale-Hubbell Law Directory

DRUMMY KING & WHITE, A PROFESSIONAL CORPORATION (AV)

3200 Park Center Drive, Suite 1000, 92626
Telephone: 714-850-1800
Fax: 714-850-4500

Stephen C. Drummy
John P. King, Jr.
Alan I. White
Charles W. Parret
Michael G. Joerger
Leroy M. Gire
Jeffrey M. Richard
Lisa A. Stepanski
Geoffrey S. Payne
James L. Vandeberg

Mark R. Beckington
Douglas F. Rubino
Lawrence M. Burek
Kenneth W. Curtis
Alan A. Greenberg
Robert M. De Feo
Leigh Otsuka

For full biographical listings, see the Martindale-Hubbell Law Directory

McCAULEY & ASSOCIATES (AV)

Bank of the West, 611 Anton Boulevard, Suite 1240, 92626
Telephone: 714-957-3710
Fax: 714-957-3718

(See Next Column)

McCauley & Associates—*Continued*

MEMBERS OF FIRM

John J. McCauley

For full biographical listings, see the Martindale-Hubbell Law Directory

McCormick, Kidman & Behrens (AV)

A Partnership of Professional Corporations
Imperial Bank Building, 695 Town Center Drive Suite 1400, 92626-1924
Telephone: 714-755-3100
Fax: 714-755-3110

MEMBERS OF FIRM

Homer L. (Mike) McCormick, Jr., (P.C.)
Arthur G. Kidman (P.C.)
Russell G. Behrens (P.C.)
Suzanne M. Tague (P.C.)
Michael D. Michaels (P.C.)
Janet R. Morningstar (P.C.)
Douglas J. Evertz (P.C.)

ASSOCIATES

Keith E. McCullough
Allison C. Hargrave
Frank W. Battaile

For full biographical listings, see the Martindale-Hubbell Law Directory

Murtaugh, Miller, Meyer & Nelson (AV)

A Partnership including Professional Corporations
3200 Park Center Drive, 9th Floor, P.O. Box 5023, 92628-5023
Telephone: 714-513-6800
Facsimile: 714-513-6899

Michael J. Murtaugh (A Professional Corporation)
Bradford H. Miller (A Professional Corporation)
Richard E. Meyer
Michael J. Nelson
Robert T. Lemen
Mark S. Himmelstein
Harry A. Halkowich
Madelyn A. Enright
James A. Murphy, IV
Lawrence A. Treglia, Jr.

Roberta A. Evans
Debra Lynn Braasch
Thomas J. Skane
Lydia R. Bouzaglou
David C. Holt
Robin L. More
Lawrence J. DiPinto
Debra L. Reilly
Susan Westover
Lawrence D. Marks
Carrie E. Phelan
Robert A. Fisher, II
John R. Browning
Eric J. Dubin
Stacey Sarowatz
Daniel E. Roston

OF COUNSEL

Susan W. Menkes
Gary M. Pohlson

Representative Clients: Continental Insurance Cos. (Continental Loss Adjusting Services); Design Professionals Insurance Co.
Reference: Wells Fargo Bank.

For full biographical listings, see the Martindale-Hubbell Law Directory

Paul, Hastings, Janofsky & Walker (AV)

A Partnership including Professional Corporations
Firm Established in 1951; Office in 1974
Seventeenth Floor, 695 Town Center Drive, 92626-1924
Telephone: 714-668-6200
Los Angeles, California Office: Twenty-Third Floor, 555 South Flower Street.
Telephone: 213-683-6000.
Cable Address: "Paulhast."
Twx: 910-321-4065.
Washington, D.C. Office: Tenth Floor, 1299 Pennsylvania Avenue, N.W.
Telephone: 202-508-9500.
Atlanta, Georgia Office: 42nd Floor, Georgia Pacific Center, 133 Peachtree Street, N.E.
Telephone: 404-588-9900.
Santa Monica, California Office: Fifth Floor, 1299 Ocean Avenue.
Telephone: 310-319-3300.
Stamford, Connecticut Office: Ninth Floor, 1055 Washington Boulevard.
Telephone: 203-961-7400.
New York, New York Office: 31st Floor, 399 Park Avenue.
Telephone: 212-318-6000.
Tokyo, Japan Office: Toranomon Ohtori Building, 8th Floor, 4-3 Toranomon 1-Chome, Minato-Ku.
Telephone: (03) 3507-0730.

MEMBERS OF FIRM

Claudia A. Carver
Paul S. Clark
Glenn D. Dassoff
Janet Toll Davidson
Oliver F. Green, Jr.
Howard C. Hay
Matthew A. Hodel
Michael A. Hood
Donald L. Morrow
Douglas A. Schaaf
William J. Simpson
John E. Trinnaman

SENIOR COUNSEL

Robert R. Burge
James W. Hamilton

OF COUNSEL

Stephen D. Cooke
Anthony J. Rossi

(See Next Column)

ASSOCIATES

Terry Jon Allen
Robert P. Bryant
Mary L. Cornwell
Barbara R. Danz
Jeannine DePhillips
Tod A. Devine
Jessica S. Dorman-Davis
Jason O. Engel
Violet F. Fiacco
Laura A. Forbes
Lisa M. LaFourcade
Scott N. Leslie
A. Alan Manning
Sean A. O'Brien
Malinda A. Palomares
Gulwinder S. Singh
Eric C. Sohlgren
Diane Desfor Stalder
John B. Stephens
Christopher A. Whytock
Darla L. Yancey

For full biographical listings, see the Martindale-Hubbell Law Directory

Rutan & Tucker (AV)

A Partnership including Professional Corporations
611 Anton Boulevard, Suite 1400, P.O. Box 1950, 92626
Telephone: 714-641-5100; 213-625-7586
Telecopier: 714-546-9035

MEMBERS OF FIRM

James R. Moore (P.C.)
Paul Frederic Marx
William R. Biel
Richard A. Curnutt
Leonard A. Hampel, Jr.
John B. Hurlbut, Jr.
Michael W. Immell
Milford W. Dahl, Jr.
Theodore I. Wallace, Jr., (P.C.)
Ronald P. Arrington
Richard P. Sims
Robert C. Braun
Edward D. Sybesma, Jr., (P.C.)
Thomas S. Salinger (P.C.)
David C. Larsen (P.C.)
Clifford E. Frieden
Michael D. Rubin
Ira G. Rivin (P.C.)
Jeffrey M. Oderman (P.C.)
Joseph D. Carruth
Stan Wolcott (P.C.)
Robert S. Bower
David J. Aleshire
Marcia A. Forsyth
William M. Marticorena
James L. Morris
Anne Nelson Lanphar
William J. Caplan
Michael T. Hornak
Philip D. Kohn
Joel D. Kuperberg
Steven A. Nichols
Thomas G. Brockington
William W. Wynder
Evridiki (Vicki) Dallas
Randall M. Babbush
Mary M. Green
Philip M. Prince
Thomas J. Crane
Mark B. Frazier
M. Katherine Jenson
Duke Wahlquist
Richard Montevideo
Lori Sarner Smith
Ernest W. Klatte, III
Elizabeth L. (Hanna) Dixon
Kim D. Thompson
Jayne Taylor Kacer
David B. Cosgrove
Hans Van Ligten
Stephen A. Ellis
Matthew K. Ross
Jeffrey Wertheimer
Robert Owen
Adam N. Volkert
Jeffrey A. Goldfarb
F. Kevin Brazil
Layne H. Melzer
Lien Ski Harrison

ASSOCIATES

Michael K. Slattery
Debra J. Dunn
David H. Hochner
Kathleen Forbath Esfahani
Elise K. Traynum
Carol Landis Demmler
Patrick D. McCalla
Richard K. Howell
A. Patrick Muñoz
Ellen S. Bancroft
Mark A. Thompson
Paul J. Sievers
S. Daniel Harbottle
Davina F. Harden
Ina Raileanu
Douglas Brent Vanderpool
Joseph Louis Maga, III
Kraig C. Kilger
Scott R. Santagata
Sandra J. Young
Allen C. Ostergar, III
Julia L. Bond
Jennifer White-Sperling
Robert Elliot Adel, II
Matthew McQueen
Lori L. Heimeri
Barry M. Taira
Joseph Mathew Yaffe
Steven M. Coleman
Steven John Goon

OF COUNSEL

Garvin F. Shallenberger
David J. Garibaldi, III

For full biographical listings, see the Martindale-Hubbell Law Directory

EL CAJON, San Diego Co. — (Refer to San Diego)

*EL CENTRO,** Imperial Co.

Ewing & Johnson, A Professional Law Corporation (AV)

636 State Street, P.O. Box 2568, 92244
Telephone: 619-352-6371
Telecopier: 619-353-5355

William J. Ewing
Charles G. Johnson
James K. Graves

Representative Clients: Bonanza Farms, Inc.; Foster Feedyard, Inc.; Kandal Insurance Agency; Imperial Printers; Robert Hawk Farming; Foss Accountancy Corp.; Hartman & Williams; Ryerson Concrete Co.; Elmer C. Werner Medical Corp.; T. C. Worthy Cash & Carry, Inc.

For full biographical listings, see the Martindale-Hubbell Law Directory

El Centro—Continued

GRAY CARY WARE & FREIDENRICH, A PROFESSIONAL CORPORATION (AV)

Gray Cary Established in 1927
Ware & Freidenrich Established in 1969
1224 State Street, P.O. Box 2890, 92244
Telephone: 619-353-6140
Telecopier: 619-353-6228
San Diego, California Office: 401 "B" Street, Suite 1700.
Telephone: 619-699-2700.
Palo Alto, California Office: 400 Hamilton Avenue.
Telephone: 415-328-6561.
La Jolla, California Office: Suite 575, 1200 Prospect Street.
Telephone: 619-454-9101.

Jay W. Jeffcoat
Ronald E. Pettis
Merrill F. Storms, Jr.

Representative Clients: American Bankers Life; Asgrow Seed; Boise Cascade; California State Automobile Assn.; Helena Chemical Co.; Hospital Council of San Diego and Imperial Counties; Imperial Valley Press/Brawley News; Unocal; Valley Independent Bank.

For full biographical listings, see the Martindale-Hubbell Law Directory

HORTON, KNOX, CARTER & FOOTE (AV)

Suite 101 Law Building, 895 Broadway, 92243
Telephone: 619-352-2821
Telefax: 619-352-8540
Brawley, California Office: 195 South Second Street.
Telephone: 619-344-2360.
Fax: 619-344-9778.

MEMBERS OF FIRM

Harry W. Horton (1892-1966)
James H. Carter (1918-1978)
Orlando B. Foote, III
John Penn Carter, III
Frank A. Oswalt, III
Dennis H. Morita
Philip J. Krum, Jr.
Mercedes Z. Wheeler (Resident, Brawley Office)

ASSOCIATES

Thomas V. Barrington
Bradley S. Ellis
Jeffrey L. Cox
Patrick M. Pace
Ruth P. Bermudez
Sherri L. Smith
Jeffrey M. Garber

OF COUNSEL

Paul D. Engstrand

Representative Clients: Automobile Club of Southern Calif.; Imperial Irrigation District; Southern Pacific Co.; Reliance Insurance Cos.; Surplus Lines Adjusting Co.; Pioneer Memorial Hospital District; City of Imperial; San Diego Gas & Electric Co.; Chevron U.S.A.; Bixby Land Co.

For full biographical listings, see the Martindale-Hubbell Law Directory

EL TORO, Orange Co. — (Refer to Santa Ana)

ESCONDIDO, San Diego Co.

HIGGS, FLETCHER & MACK (AV)

613 West Valley Parkway, Suite 345, 92025-2552
Telephone: 619-743-1201
Telecopier: 619-743-9926
San Diego, California Office: 2000 First National Bank Building, 401 West "A" Street.
Telephone: 619-236-1551.
Telecopier: 619-696-1410.

RESIDENT MEMBERS

David W. Ferguson
Bruce D. Jaques, Jr.
Gregory Y. Lievers
Erick R. Altona
Helen H. Peak

OF COUNSEL

Kenneth H. Lounsbery

ASSOCIATES

Charles A. LePla

Representative Clients: Frazee Industries; Kawasaki Motors Corp.; Rohr Industries; HomeFed Bank; Allstate Insurance Co.; Associated Aviation Underwriters; Physicians & Surgeons Insurance Exchange; City of Vista; City of San Marcos.

For full biographical listings, see the Martindale-Hubbell Law Directory

*EUREKA,** Humboldt Co.

HUBER & GOODWIN (AV)

Huber-Goodwin Building, 550 "I" Street, P.O. Box 23, 95502-0023
Telephone: 707-443-4573
Fax: 707-443-7182

(See Next Column)

MEMBERS OF FIRM

Milton L. Huber (1914-1994)
G. Edward Goodwin (Retired)
Dayton D. Murray, Jr. (1923-1981)
Norman C. Cissna (1923-1989)
Robert D. Prior
William H. Carson, Jr.

Representative Clients: Hoff Broadcasting (radio stations); D & B Cattle Co. (livestock); Simpson Timber Co.; Miller & Rellim Redwood Cos.; The Pacific Lumber Co.; Western Self Insurance Service (Workers Compensation).

For full biographical listings, see the Martindale-Hubbell Law Directory

JANSSEN, MALLOY, MARCHI, NEEDHAM & MORRISON (AV)

730 Fifth Street, P.O. Drawer 1288, 95501
Telephone: 707-445-2071
Fax: 707-445-8305

MEMBERS OF FIRM

Clayton R. Janssen
Nicholas R. Marchi
Michael F. Malloy
Michael W. Morrison
W. Timothy Needham

ASSOCIATES

Catherine M. Koshkin

Counsel for: Ming Tree Realty, Inc.; Clinic Mutual Insurance Co.; TRW, Inc.; U.S. Bank; The Travelers Insurance Co.; General Hospital; Pacific Bell; Reichhold Chemicals, Inc.; Safeco Insurance Companies of America; Lawyers Mutual Insurance Company.

For full biographical listings, see the Martindale-Hubbell Law Directory

MITCHELL, BRISSO, DELANEY, REINHOLTSEN & VRIEZE (AV)

814 Seventh Street, P.O. Drawer 1008, 95502
Telephone: 707-443-5643
Fax: 707-444-9586

MEMBERS OF FIRM

Clifford B. Mitchell
Dale A. Reinholtsen
Nancy K. Delaney
Paul A. Brisso
John M. Vrieze

ASSOCIATES

C. Todd Endres
William F. Mitchell

RETIRED PARTNER

Robert C. Dedekam

Representative Clients: Louisiana-Pacific Corp.; City of Eureka; Housing Authority; St. Joseph Health Systems; California Automobile Assn.; K Mart; Hertz Corp.; Walmart; StairMaster Sports/Medical Products, Inc.; Montgomery Ward.

For full biographical listings, see the Martindale-Hubbell Law Directory

*FAIRFIELD,** Solano Co.

KNOX RICKSEN (AV)

Corporate Plaza, Suite 300, 1261 Travis Boulevard, 94533
Telephone: 707-426-3313
Fax: 707-426-0426
Oakland, California Office: Suite 1700, 1999 Harrison Street.
Telephone: 510-893-1000.
Fax: 510-446-1946.
San Jose, Santa Clara County, California Office: 100 Park Center Plaza, Suite 560.
Telephone: 408-295-2828.
Fax: 408-295-6868.

William C. Robbins, III
James T. Gotch

For full biographical listings, see the Martindale-Hubbell Law Directory

FREMONT, Alameda Co. — (Refer to Hayward)

*FRESNO,** Fresno Co.

BAKER, MANOCK & JENSEN, A PROFESSIONAL CORPORATION (AV)

5260 North Palm, Suite 421, 93704
Telephone: 209-432-5400

John H. Baker
Kendall L. Manock
Douglas B. Jensen
Donald R. Fischbach
Robert G. Fishman
Howard M. Zidenberg
John L. B. Smith
George L. Strasser
Joseph M. Marchini
Craig A. Houghton
Andrew R. Weiss
Mark W. Snauffer
James E. Shekoyan
Carl R. Refuerzo
John G. Michael
Christopher L. Campbell
Robert D. Wilkinson
Jeffrey A. Jaech
David M. Camenson
Lisa M. Martin
Michelle T. Tutelian
Gayle D. Hearst
Glenn J. Holder
Mark B. Canepa

(See Next Column)

BAKER, MANOCK & JENSEN A PROFESSIONAL CORPORATION—*Continued*

Raymond L. Carlson
William S. Barcus
Douglas M. Larsen
Michael W. Goldring
Randall J. Krause
Michele A. Engnath
William M. White
Kathleen A. Meehan
Gary B. Wells
Richard S. Salinas
Richard A. Ryan
Lisa F. Talley
David E. Holland
Glen F. Dorgan
Charles K. Manock
Gabrielle M. Jackson
Chrys A. Hutchings
Glenn A. Rowley
Matthew Earl Hoffman
Colleen Schulthies

OF COUNSEL

Leonard I. Meyers
James E. Ganulin

Representative Clients: Bank of America NT&SA; Challenge Dairy Products, Inc.; Fresno Metropolitan Flood Control District; Metropolitan Life Insurance Company; Norcal Mutual Insurance Company; Wells Fargo Bank, N.A.; Sun-Maid Growers of California.

For full biographical listings, see the Martindale-Hubbell Law Directory

DOWLING, MAGARIAN, AARON & HEYMAN, INCORPORATED (AV)

Suite 200, 6051 North Fresno Street, 93710
Telephone: 209-432-4500
Fax: 209-432-4590

Michael D. Dowling
Richard M. Aaron
Kent F. Heyman
Bruce S. Fraser
William J. Keeler, Jr.
John C. Ganahl
Sheila M. Smith
Adolfo M. Corona
Philip David Kopp

Francine Marie Kanne
John G. Kerkorian
Richard E. Heatter
Christopher A. Brown
James C. Sherwood
Mark D. Magarian

OF COUNSEL

Donald J. Magarian
Daniel K. Whitehurst
Morris M. Sherr
Blaine Pettitt

Reference: Wells Fargo Bank (Main).

For full biographical listings, see the Martindale-Hubbell Law Directory

LANG, RICHERT & PATCH, A PROFESSIONAL CORPORATION (AV)

Fig Garden Financial Center, 5200 North Palm Avenue, 4th Floor, P.O. Box 40012, 93755
Telephone: 209-228-6700
Fax: 209-228-6727

Frank H. Lang
William T. Richert (1937-1993)
Robert L. Patch, II
Val W. Saldaña
Douglas E. Noll
Michael T. Hertz
Victoria J. Salisch
Bradley A. Silva
David R. Jenkins
Charles Trudrung Taylor
Mark L. Creede
Peter N. Zeitler
Charles L. Doerksen

Randall C. Nelson
Barbara A. McAuliffe
Laurie Quigley Cardot
Douglas E. Griffin
Nabil E. Zumout

References: Wells Fargo Bank (Fresno Main Office); First Interstate Bank (Fresno Main Office).

For full biographical listings, see the Martindale-Hubbell Law Directory

McCORMICK, BARSTOW, SHEPPARD, WAYTE & CARRUTH (AV)

Five River Park Place East, 93720-1501
Telephone: 209-433-1300
Mailing Address: P.O. Box 28912, 93729-8912

Richard A. McCormick (1915-1981)
Stephen Barnett (1931-1988)

MEMBERS OF FIRM

Lawrence E. Wayte
Lowell T. Carruth
James H. Perkins
Stephen R. Cornwell
Andrew W. Wright
Mario Louis Beltramo, Jr.
Michael G. Woods
James P. Wagoner
Steven G. Rau
Gordon M. Park
Wade M. Hansard
W. F. Docker
Justus C. Spillner
Hilton A. Ryder
D. Greg Durbin
Marshall C. Whitney
Donald S. Black
Daniel P. Lyons
Riley C. Walter
Michael L. Wilhelm
John A. Drolshagen
Brian M. Arax
Walter W. Whelan
Michael F. Ball
Stephen E. Carroll
James H. Wilkins
Timothy Jones
Kevin D. Hansen
Philip M. Flanigan
Matthew K. Hawkins

(See Next Column)

MEMBERS OF FIRM (Continued)

Kenneth A. Baldwin
David R. McNamara
Timothy L. Thompson
Wendy S. Lloyd
Michael J. Czeshinski
John A. Leonard

ASSOCIATES

René L. Sample
Gregory S. Mason
Mart B. Oller, IV
Todd W. Baxter
Paul J. O'Rourke, Jr.
Donald L. Mariotto
Roger A. Johnson
E. Todd Crowley
Ted A. Smith
Michael J. Ryan
Kurt F. Vote
James D. Garriott
John M. Dunn
James B. Fernow
Jeffrey Y. Hamilton, Jr.
Bruce W. Kelley
Patrick M. Martucci
Blake A. Meyen
Julie A. Noble
Trevin E. Sims
L. Drew Metcalf

OF COUNSEL

James H. Barstow
Dudley W. Sheppard
Deborah A. Byron

Counsel for: Aetna Life & Casualty Co.; California State Automobile Assn.; Firemen's Fund Insurance Co.; Bank of Fresno; Kings River State Bank; Glendale Federal Bank; Hartford Accident & Indemnity Co.; Kemper Insurance Group; The Travelers Insurance Co.; United Pacific/Reliance Insurance Co.

For full biographical listings, see the Martindale-Hubbell Law Directory

McGREGOR, DAHL & KLUG (AV)

7080 North Whitney Avenue, Suite 105, 93720-0154
Telephone: 209-322-9292
FAX: 209-322-9191

John J. McGregor
William A. Dahl
Kenneth M. Klug

For full biographical listings, see the Martindale-Hubbell Law Directory

THOMAS, SNELL, JAMISON, RUSSELL AND ASPERGER, A PROFESSIONAL CORPORATION (AV)

2445 Capitol Street, P.O. Box 1461, 93716
Telephone: 209-442-0600; 800-559-9009
Telecopier: 209-442-5078

Howard B. Thomas (1912-1993)
Fenton Williamson, Jr. (1926-1993)
Roger E. Fipps
Samuel C. Palmer, III
James O. Demsey
Robert J. Tyler
Gerald D. Vinnard
E. Robert Wright
David M. Gilmore
Russell O. Wood
Scott R. Shewan
Hilary A. Chittick

OF COUNSEL

William N. Snell
T. Newton Russell
Charles E. Small
James E. LaFollette

RETIRED

Paul Asperger (Retired)
Oliver M. Jamison (Retired)

Bren K. Thomas
Olga A. Balderama
Marcus Don Magness

Representative Clients: California Table Grape Commission; Gottschalk's, Inc.; The Vendo Co.
Local Counsel for: Metropolitan Life Insurance Co.; PPG Industries.

For full biographical listings, see the Martindale-Hubbell Law Directory

GLENDALE, Los Angeles Co.

IRSFELD, IRSFELD & YOUNGER (AV)

A Partnership including Professional Corporations
Suite 900, 100 West Broadway, 91210-1296
Telephone: 818-242-6859
Fax: 818-240-7728

MEMBERS OF FIRM

James B. Irsfeld (1880-1966)
John H. Brink (P.C.)
Peter J. Irsfeld (P.C.)
James J. Waldorf (P.C.)
C. Phillip Jackson (P.C.)
Ross R. Hart (P.C.)
Norman H. Green (P.C.)
Diane L. Walker (P.C.)

ASSOCIATES

Peter C. Wright
Andrew J. Thomas
Kathryn E. Van Houten

RETIRED

James B. Irsfeld, Jr.
Kenneth C. Younger

Representative Clients: Lear Siegler, Inc.; Chrysler Credit Corp.
References: First Interstate Bank (Glendale Main Office); Bank of Hollywood.

For full biographical listings, see the Martindale-Hubbell Law Directory

HAYWARD, Alameda Co.

HALEY, PURCHIO, SAKAI & SMITH (AV)

P.O. Box 450, 22320 Foothill Boulevard, Suite 620, 94543
Telephone: 510-538-6400
Oakland: 510-351-1932

MEMBERS OF FIRM

J. Kenneth Birchfield (1920-1978)
John K. Smith
Robert Sakai
Cynthia K. Smith

OF COUNSEL

John J. Purchio
Donald A. Pearce (1898-1982)
Marlin W. Haley (1910-1993)

Representative Clients: City Center Commercial (Shopping Center); Oak Hills, Walnut Hills, Creekwood (Apartment Complexes); R. Zaballos & Sons (General Contractors); Hospital Associates; Wolf Investment Co.; Chicago Title Company of Alameda County; Sunnyside Nurseries, Inc.; Mission Valley Rock Co. (quarry); LaVista Quarry.

For full biographical listings, see the Martindale-Hubbell Law Directory

HEMET, Riverside Co.

COX & COX (AV)

805 East Florida Avenue, 92543
Telephone: 909-652-1400
Fax: 909-652-3990

MEMBERS OF FIRM

Thomas M. Cox
James A. Cox

ASSOCIATES

Julie M. Clark

For full biographical listings, see the Martindale-Hubbell Law Directory

*HOLLISTER,** San Benito Co. — (Refer to Salinas)

INDIO, Riverside Co.

THOMAS T. ANDERSON & ASSOCIATES (AV)

45-926 Oasis Street, 92201
Telephone: 619-347-3364
Fax: 619-347-5572

ASSOCIATES

Douglas P. Miller
David M. Chapman
Samuel F. Trussell

Reference: First LA Bank.

For full biographical listings, see the Martindale-Hubbell Law Directory

IRVINE, Orange Co.

ALLEN, MATKINS, LECK, GAMBLE & MALLORY (AV)

A Partnership including Professional Corporations
Fourth Floor, 18400 Von Karman, 92715
Telephone: 714-553-1313
Telecopier: 714-553-8354
Los Angeles, California Office: Eighth Floor, 515 South Figueroa Street, 90071.
Telephone: 213-622-5555.
Telecopier: 213-620-8816.
San Diego, California Office: 501 West Broadway, Suite 900, 92101.
Telephone: 619-233-1155.
Facsimile: 619-233-1158.
West Los Angeles, California Office: 1999 Avenue of the Stars, 90067.
Telephone: 310-788-2400.
Fax: 310-788-2410.

RESIDENT PARTNERS

John C. Gamble
Thomas C. Foster
R. Michael Joyce
Lawrence D. Lewis (P.C.)
Monica E. Olson
Thomas E. Gibbs
Dwight L. Armstrong
Paul D. O'Connor
S. Lee Hancock
Richard E. Stinehart
Stephen R. Thames
Anne E. Klokow
David W. Wensley
Gary S. McKitterick
Patrick J. Grady
Jeremy D. Glaser
Kenneth L. Perkins, Jr.
Robert M. Hamilton
Vincent M. Coscino

RESIDENT ASSOCIATES

Bradley N. Schweitzer
Gretchen K. Hudson
Alan J. Gordee
Pamela L. Andes
Jay M. Gabriel
Catherine M. Page
Leslie Tucker Fischer
Ralph H. Winter
Michael S. Greger
A. Kristine Floyd
Michael A. Alvarado
Mary Kay Ruck
Robert G. Bentley
Mark J. Hattam

For full biographical listings, see the Martindale-Hubbell Law Directory

CALLAHAN & GAUNTLETT (AV)

A Partnership including a Professional Corporation
Suite 800, 18500 Von Karman, 92715
Telephone: 714-553-1155
Fax: 714-553-0784

Daniel J. Callahan (A Professional Corporation)
David A. Gauntlett

ASSOCIATES

Stephen E. Blaine
David A. Stall
J. Craig Williams
Jim P. Mahacek
Leo E. Lundberg, Jr.
Michael J. Sachs
Michael Danton Richardson
Craig E. Lindberg
Edward Susolik
Carol L. Meedon
Andrew A. Smits

OF COUNSEL

Gary L. Hinman
Walt D. Mahaffa
Jose Zorrilla, Jr.
H. Thomas Hicks

For full biographical listings, see the Martindale-Hubbell Law Directory

CROWELL & MORING (AV)

2010 Main Street, Suite 1200, 92714-7217
Telephone: 714-263-8400
Fax: 714-263-8414
Washington, D.C. Office: 1001 Pennsylvania Avenue, N.W.
Telephone: 202-624-2500.
Telex: W.U.I. (International) 64344; W.U. (Domestic) 89-2448.
Cable Address: "Cromor".
Fax: (202) 628-5116.
London, England Office: Denning House, 90 Chancery Lane, WC2A 1ED.
Telephone: 011-44-71-413-0011.
Fax: 011-44-71-413-0333.

MEMBERS OF FIRM

Donald E. Sovie
Randall L. Erickson
Michael D. Newman

OF COUNSEL

John A. Burkholder
Steven A. Fink

ASSOCIATES

Cecelia A. Tripi
Donald E. Bradley
Stuart Einbinder
Diane Smith Daruty
Deborah E. Colaner

For full biographical listings, see the Martindale-Hubbell Law Directory

JONES, DAY, REAVIS & POGUE (AV)

2603 Main Street, Suite 900, 92714-6232
Telephone: 714-851-3939
Telex: 194911 Lawyers LSA
Telecopier: 714-553-7539
In Los Angeles, California: 555 West Fifth Street, Suite 4600.
Telephone: 213-489-3939.
Telex: 181439 UD.
Telecopier: 213-243-2539.
In Atlanta, Georgia: 3500 One Peachtree Center, 303 Peachtree Street, N.E.
Telephone: 404-521-3939.
Cable Address: "Attorneys Atlanta".
Telex: 54-2711.
Telecopier: 404-581-8330.
In Brussels, Belgium: Avenue Louise 480, 7th Floor, B-1050 Brussels.
Telephone: 011-32-2-645-14-11.
Telecopier: 011-32-2-645-14-45.
In Chicago, Illinois: 77 West Wacker.
Telephone: 312-782-3939.
Telecopier: 312-782-8585.
In Cleveland, Ohio: North Point, 901 Lakeside Avenue.
Telephone: 216-586-3939.
Cable Address: "Attorneys Cleveland."
Telex: 980389.
Telecopier: 216-579-0212.
In Columbus, Ohio: 1900 Huntington Center.
Telephone: 614-469-3939.
Cable Address: "Attorneys Columbus."
Telecopier: 614-461-4198.
In Dallas, Texas: 2300 Trammell Crow Center, 2001 Ross Avenue.
Telephone: 214-220-3939.
Cable Address: "Attorneys Dallas."
Telex: 730852.
Telecopier: 214-969-5100.
In Frankfurt, Germany: Triton Haus, Bockenheimer Landstrasse 42, 60323, Franfurt am Main.
Telephone: 49-69-9726-3939.
Telecopier: 49-69-9726-3993.
In Geneva, Switzerland: 20, rue de Candolle.
Telephone: 011-41-22-320-2339.
Telecopier: 011-41-22-320-1232.
In Hong Kong: 1501 One Exchange Square, 8 Connaught Place.
Telephone: 011-852-2526-6895.
Telecopier: 011-852-2810-5787.

(See Next Column)

JONES, DAY, REAVIS & POGUE—*Continued*

In London, England: One Mount Street.
Telephone: 011-44-71-493-9361.
Cable Address: "Surgoe London WI."
Telecopier: 011-44-71-493-9666.
In New York, New York: 599 Lexington Avenue.
Telephone: 212-326-3939.
Cable Address: "JONESDAY NEWYORK."
Telex: 237013 JDRP UR.
Telecopier: 212-755-7306.
In Paris, France: 62, rue du Faubourg Saint-Honore.
Telephone: 011-33-1-44-71-3939.
Cable Address: "Surgoe Paris."
Telex: 290156 Surgoe.
Telecopier: 011-33-1-49-24-0471.
In Pittsburgh, Pennsylvania: 500 Grant Street, 31st Floor.
Telephone: 412-391-3939.
Cable Address: "Attorneys Pittsburgh."
Telecopier: 412-394-7959.
In Riyadh, Saudi Arabia: Law Offices of Saud M.A. Shawwaf, P.O. Box 2700.
Telephones: 011 (966-1) 465-6543, 011 (966-1) 464-8534 or 011 (966-1) 464-8540.
Telex: 401831 SAUCON SJ.
Telecopier: (966-1) 464-8480.
In Taipei, Taiwan: 8th Floor, 2 Tun Hwa South Road, Section 2.
Telephone: 011 (886-2) 704-6808.
Telecopier: 011 (886-2) 704-6791.
In Tokyo, Japan: Toranomon MT Building, 4th Floor, 10-3, Toranomon 3-Chome, Minato-Ku, Tokyo 105, Japan.
Telephone: 011-81-3-3433-3939.
Telecopier: 011-81-3-5401-2725.
In Washington, D.C.: Metropolitan Square, 1450 G Street, N.W.
Telephone: 202-879-3939.
Cable Address: "Attorneys Washington."
Telex: 89-2410 ATTORNEYS WASH.
Telecopier: 202-737-2832.

MEMBERS OF FIRM IN IRVINE

Thomas R. Malcolm
Peter J. Tennyson
Joanne M. Frasca
John F. Della Grotta
Dulcie D. Brand (Not admitted in CA)

OF COUNSEL

Randy McDonald
David A. Robinson

ASSOCIATES

J. Scott Schoeffel
David W. Greenman
Richard J. Grabowski
Dana L. Halle
Marc K. Callahan
Jeffrey B. Kirzner
Michelle M. Nuszkiewicz
Jarret L. Johnson
Michael D. Fabiano
Vincent D. Lowder

For full biographical listings, see the Martindale-Hubbell Law Directory

KINDEL & ANDERSON (AV)

A Partnership including Professional Corporations
5 Park Plaza, Suite 1000, 92714
Telephone: 714-752-0777
Los Angeles, California Office: Twenty-Ninth Floor, 555 South Flower Street.
Telephone: 213-680-2222.
Woodland Hills, California Office: Suite 244, 5959 Topanga Canyon Boulevard.
Telephone: 818-712-0036.
San Francisco, California Office: 580 California Street, 15th Floor.
Telephone: 415-398-0110.

MEMBERS OF FIRM

Gerard C. Bastiaanse (Resident)
John E. James
James H. Kindel, Jr.
Ronald J. Kohut (Managing Partner)
Steven P. Rice (Resident)

ASSOCIATES

Ruth Claire Black (Resident)
William E. Halle (Resident)
M. Colleen Harty (Resident)
Deirdre M. Kelly (Resident)
Amy W. Larkin (Resident)
Megan L. Wagner (Resident)

For full biographical listings, see the Martindale-Hubbell Law Directory

LOBEL, WINTHROP & BROKER (AV)

Suite 1100, 19800 MacArthur Boulevard, P.O. Box 19588, 92713
Telephone: 714-476-7400
Fax: 714-476-7444
Santa Ana, California Office: 201 North Broadway, Suite 201.
Telephone: 714-543-4822.
Fax: 714-476-7444.

MEMBERS OF FIRM

William N. Lobel
Marc J. Winthrop
Todd C. Ringstad
Robert E. Opera
Lorie Dewhirst Porter

(See Next Column)

ASSOCIATES

Alan J. Friedman
Paul J. Couchot
Robert W. Pitts
Pamela Z. Karger
Whitney H. Leibow
Richard H. Golubow

For full biographical listings, see the Martindale-Hubbell Law Directory

MESERVE, MUMPER & HUGHES (AV)

A Partnership including a Professional Corporation
18500 Von Karman Avenue, Suite 600, P.O. Box 19591, 92713-9591
Telephone: 714-474-8995
Telecopier: 714-975-1065
Los Angeles, California Office: 555 South Flower Street, 18th Floor.
Telephone: 213-620-0300.
Telecopier: 213-625-1930.
San Diego, California Office: 701 "B" Street, Suite 2250.
Telephone: 619-237-0500.
Telecopier: 619-237-0073.

MEMBERS OF FIRM

Edwin A. Meserve (1863-1955)
Shirley E. Meserve (1889-1959)
Hewlings Mumper (1889-1968)
Clifford E. Hughes (1894-1981)
Bernard A. Leckie
E. Avery Crary
L. Allan Songstad, Jr.
Andrew K. Ulich
Douglas P. Smith
Timothy L. Randall
Thomas J. Bois, II, (P.C.)
David R. Eichten
Roger A. Grad

OF COUNSEL

J. Robert Meserve

ASSOCIATES

John F. Damiani
William D. Coffee
Andrew V. Leitch
Janet E. Humphrey
Joseph B. McGinley
Amy Toboco Dibb
James R. Parke
Jennifer M. Whelan
Jeffrey Dill
Jerri A. Fullmer
Christopher J. Menjou

For full biographical listings, see the Martindale-Hubbell Law Directory

PALMIERI, TYLER, WIENER, WILHELM & WALDRON (AV)

A Partnership including Professional Corporations
East Tower - Suite 1300, 2603 Main Street, P.O. Box 19712, 92714-6228
Telephone: 714-851-9400
Telecopier: 714-851-1554; 851-3844; 757-1225

MEMBERS OF FIRM

Angelo J. Palmieri (A Professional Corporation)
Robert F. Waldron (A Professional Corporation)
Alan H. Wiener (A Professional Corporation)
Robert C. Ihrke (A Professional Corporation)
James E. Wilhelm (A Professional Corporation)
Dennis G. Tyler (A Professional Corporation)
Michael J. Greene (A Professional Corporation)
Frank C. Rothrock (A Professional Corporation)
Dennis W. Ghan (A Professional Corporation)
David D. Parr (A Professional Corporation)
Charles H. Kanter (A Professional Corporation)
George J. Wall
L. Richard Rawls
Patrick A. Hennessey
Don Fisher
Gregory N. Weiler
Warren A. Williams
John R. Lister
Bruce W. Dannemeyer
Cynthia M. Wolcott
Joel P. Kew
Michelle M. Fujimoto

Elinor J. Votaw
Norman J. Rodich
Gary C. Weisberg
Michael H. Leifer
Michele D. Murphy
Scott R. Carpenter
Richard A. Salus
Douglas M. Stevens
D. Susan Wiens
Ronald M. Cole
Cynthia B. Paulsen
Sean P. O'Connor
Susan T. Sakura
Timothy S. Galusha
Robyn Dimino

For full biographical listings, see the Martindale-Hubbell Law Directory

RUS, MILIBAND, WILLIAMS & SMITH (AV)

Suite 700, 2600 Michelson Drive, 92715
Telephone: 714-752-7100
Fax: 714-252-1514

Ronald Rus
Joel S. Miliband
J. Scott Williams
Randall A. Smith

Laurel Zaeske
M. Peter Crinella
Jeffrey H. Sussman
Mark H. Smith
Cathrine M. Castaldi
David Edward Hays
Steven Joseph Kraemer
Lisa M. Farrington
Leo J. Presiado

For full biographical listings, see the Martindale-Hubbell Law Directory

Irvine—Continued

SNELL & WILMER (AV)

1920 Main Street, Suite 1200, P.O. Box 19601, 92714
Telephone: 714-253-2700
FAX: 714-955-2507
Phoenix, Arizona Office: One Arizona Center, 85004-0001.
Telephone: 602-382-6000.
Fax: 602-382-6070.
Tucson, Arizona Office: 1500 Norwest Tower, One South Church Avenue, 85701-1612.
Telephone: 602-882-1200.
Fax: 602-884-1294.
Salt Lake City, Utah Office: Broadway Centre, 111 East Broadway, Suite 900, 84111.
Telephone: 801-237-1900.
Fax: 801-237-1950.

MEMBERS OF FIRM

Robert J. Gibson (Resident)
Creighton D. Mills (Resident)
Gary A. Wolensky (Resident)
William S. O'Hare, Jr. (Resident)
Arthur P. Greenfield
Steven T. Graham (Resident)
Diane R. Smith (Resident)
Charles W. Hurst (Resident)
Gilbert N. Kruger (Resident)
David W. Evans (Resident)
Raymond J. Ikola (Resident)
Richard A. Derevan
Randolph T. Moore
Nanette D. Sanders

OF COUNSEL

Kim R. Frank

ASSOCIATES

Alison A. Brooks
Alexander L. Conti
Ellen L. Darling
Bart Greenberg
Jon J. Janecek
Christy D. Joseph
Bruce R. Keiser
Roland Labriola
Mark D. O'Connor
Debora M. Rodriguez
Gerda M. Roy
Julianne Sartain
Sean Michael Sherlock
Martin W. Taylor
Luke A. Torres

For full biographical listings, see the Martindale-Hubbell Law Directory

WATT, TIEDER & HOFFAR (AV Ⓣ)

3 Park Plaza, Suite 1530, 92714
Telephone: 714-852-6700
Telecopier: 714-261-0771
McLean Virginia Office: 7929 Westpark Drive, Suite 400,
Telephone: 703-749-1000.
Telex: 248797 WATTR.
Telecopier: 703-893-8029.
Washington, D.C. Office: 601 Pennsylvania Avenue, N.W. Suite 900,
Telephone: 202-462-4697.

MEMBERS OF FIRM

John B. Tieder, Jr. (Not admitted in CA)
Robert M. Fitzgerald (Not admitted in CA)
Michael G. Long

ASSOCIATES

Christopher P. Pappas

For full biographical listings, see the Martindale-Hubbell Law Directory

*JACKSON,** Amador Co. — (Refer to Stockton)

LA JOLLA, San Diego Co.

GRAY CARY WARE & FREIDENRICH, A PROFESSIONAL CORPORATION (AV)

Suite 575, 1200 Prospect Street, 92037
Telephone: 619-454-9101
Telecopier: 619-456-3075
San Diego, California Office: 401 "B" Street, Suite 1700.
Telephone: 619-699-2700.
Palo Alto, California Office: 400 Hamilton Avenue.
Telephone: 415-328-6561.
El Centro, California Office: 1224 State Street, P.O. Box 2890.
Telephone: 619-353-6140.

Edward V. Brennan
Theodore J. Cranston
Melitta Fleck
Karl ZoBell

Mildred Basden
Fredrica S. Maveety
Ellen H. Whelan

Representative Clients: The Copley Press, Inc.; Home Capital Corp.; Dr. Seuss Foundation; Ernest W. Hahn, Inc.; Imperial Corporation of America; La Jolla Bank & Trust Co.; La Jolla Real Estate Brokers Association; Merrill, Lynch, Pierce, Fenner & Smith; Scripps Clinic and Research Foundation; Timkin-Sturgis Foundation.

For full biographical listings, see the Martindale-Hubbell Law Directory

LUCE, FORWARD, HAMILTON & SCRIPPS (AV)

A Partnership including Professional Corporations
La Jolla Golden Triangle, 4275 Executive Square Suite 800, 92037
Telephone: 619-535-2639
Fax: 619-453-2812
San Diego, California Office: 600 West Broadway, Suite 2600, 92101.
Telephone: 619-236-1414.
Fax: 619-232-8311.
Los Angeles, California Office: 777 South Figueroa, 36th Floor, 90017.
Telephone: 213-892-4992.
Fax: 213-892-7731.
San Francisco, California Office: 100 Bush Street, 20th Floor, 94104.
Telephone: 415-395-7900.
Fax: 415-395-7949.
New York, N.Y. Office: Citicorp Center, 153 East 53rd Street, 26th Floor, 10022.
Telephone: 212-754-1414.
Fax: 212-644-9727.

MEMBERS OF FIRM

Jack G. Charney
Robert J. Durham, Jr.
Frederick R. Vandeveer
Mary F. Gillick

ASSOCIATES

Richard E. Showen
James H. Siegel
Carol K. Kao

For full biographical listings, see the Martindale-Hubbell Law Directory

LANCASTER, Los Angeles Co.

COSGROVE, MICHELIZZI, SCHWABACHER, WARD & BIANCHI, A PROFESSIONAL CORPORATION (AV)

767 West Lancaster Boulevard, 93534-3135
Telephone: 805-948-5021
Telecopier: 805-948-5395

Philip M. Schwabacher
Leonard A. Cosgrove
Frank G. Michelizzi
Thomas J. Ward
David W. Bianchi
David T. Collins

James Lillicrap
Kevin L. Von Tungeln

For full biographical listings, see the Martindale-Hubbell Law Directory

LODI, San Joaquin Co. — (Refer to Stockton)

LONG BEACH, Los Angeles Co.

LAW OFFICES OF JAMES H. ACKERMAN (AV)

Suite 1440, One World Trade Center, 90831-1440
Telephone: 310-436-9911
Cable Address: "Jimack"
Telecopier: 310-436-1897
References: Farmers and Merchants Bank (Long Beach Main Office); Sumitomo Bank of California (Long Beach Main Office).

For full biographical listings, see the Martindale-Hubbell Law Directory

BAKER & HOSTETLER (AV)

300 Oceangate, Suite 620, 90802-6807
Telephone: 310-432-2827
FAX: 310-432-6698
In Cleveland, Ohio: 3200 National City Center, 1900 East Ninth Street.
Telephone: 216-621-0200.
In Columbus, Ohio: Capitol Square, Suite 2100, 65 East State Street.
Telephone: 614-228-1541.
In Denver, Colorado: 303 East 17th Avenue, Suite 1100.
Telephone: 303-861-0600.
In Houston, Texas: 1000 Louisiana, Suite 2000.
Telephone: 713-236-0020.
In Los Angeles, California: 600 Wilshire Boulevard.
Telephone: 213-624-2400.
In Orlando, Florida: SunBank Center, Suite 2300, 200 South Orange Avenue.
Telephone: 407-649-4000.
In Washington, D. C.: Washington Square, Suite 1100, 1050 Connecticut Avenue, N. W.
Telephone: 202-861-1500.
In College Park, Maryland: 9658 Baltimore Boulevard, Suite 206.
Telephone: 301-441-2781.
In Alexandria, Virginia: 437 North Lee Street.
Telephone: 703-549-1294.
In San Francisco, California: One Sansome Street, Suite 2000.
Telephone: 415-951-4705.

MEMBERS OF FIRM IN LONG BEACH, CALIFORNIA

Sheldon A. Gebb (Managing Partner, Los Angeles and Long Beach, California and Houston, Texas Offices)

PARTNERS

Robert E. Coppola (Partner in Charge)
Kenneth E. Johnson
David A. Kettel
Christina L. Owen

(See Next Column)

BAKER & HOSTETLER—*Continued*

ASSOCIATES

Paul W. Chandler
Andrew H. Do
George M. Jones

For full biographical listings, see the Martindale-Hubbell Law Directory

BURNS, AMMIRATO, PALUMBO, MILAM & BARONIAN, A PROFESSIONAL LAW CORPORATION (AV)

One World Trade Center, Suite 1200, 90831-1200
Telephone: 310-436-8338; 714-952-1047
Fax: 310-432-6049
Pasadena, California Office: 65 North Raymond Avenue, 2nd Floor.
Telephone: 818-796-5053; 213-258-8282.
Fax: 818-792-3078.

Vincent A. Ammirato

Thomas L. Halliwell
Joseph F. O'Hara
Robert Gary Mendoza
Michael P. Vicencia
Michael E. Wenzel

For full biographical listings, see the Martindale-Hubbell Law Directory

CAMERON, MADDEN, PEARLSON, GALE & SELLARS (AV)

One World Trade Center Suite 1600, 90831-1600
Telephone: 310-436-3888
Telecopier: 310-437-1967

MEMBERS OF THE FIRM

Timothy C. Cameron
Patrick T. Madden
Charles M. Gale
Paul R. Pearlson
James D. Sellars

ASSOCIATES

Lillian D. Salinger

For full biographical listings, see the Martindale-Hubbell Law Directory

CARLSMITH BALL WICHMAN MURRAY CASE & ICHIKI (AV)

A Partnership including Law Corporations
301 East Ocean Boulevard, 7th Floor, P.O. Box 1287, 90802-4828
Telephone: 310-435-5631
Fax: 310-437-3760; 310-590-9771
Honolulu, Hawaii Office: Suite 2200, Pacific Tower, 1001 Bishop Street. P.O. Box 656.
Telephone: 808-523-2500.
Los Angeles, California Office: 555 South Flower Street, 25th Floor.
Telephone: 213-955-1200.
Washington, D.C. Office: 700 14th Street, N.W., 9th Floor.
Telephone: 202-508-1025.
Mexico City, Mexico Office: Monte Pelvious 111, Piso 1, Col. Lomas de Chapultepec, 11000 Mexico, D.F.
Telephone: (011-52-5) 520-8514.
Fax: (011-52-5) 540-1545.
Mexico, D.F. Office of Carlsmith Ball Garcia Cacho y Asociados, S.C. (Authorized to practice Mexican Law): Monte Pelvoux 111, Piso 1, Col. Lomas deChapultepec, 11000, Mexico, D.F.
Telephone: (011-52-5) 520-8514.
Fax: (011-52-5) 540-1545.
Agana, Guam Office: 4th Floor, Bank of Hawaii Building, P.O. Box BF.
Telephone: 671-472-6813.
Saipan, Commonwealth of the Northern Mariana Islands Office: Carlsmith Building, Capitol Hill, P.O. Box 5241.
Telephone: 670-322-3455.
Wailuku, Maui, Hawaii Office: One Main Plaza, Suite 400, 2200 Main Street, P.O. Box 1086.
Telephone: 808-242-4535.
Kailua-Kona, Hawaii Office: Second Floor, Bank of Hawaii Annex Building, P.O. Box 1720.
Telephone: 808-329-6464.
Hilo, Hawaii Office: 121 Waianuenue Avenue, P.O. Box 686.
Telephone: 808-935-6644.
Kapolei, Hawaii Office: Kapolei Building, Suite 318, 1001 Kamokila Boulevard.
Telephone: 808-674-0850.

Robert E. Aitken
Joseph A. Ball
Richard E. Conway
Brian C. Cuff
Harman M. Hitt
Albert Saul Israel
George T. Mooradian
Lynn E. Moyer
Joseph D. Mullender, Jr.
Anthony Murray
Allan Edward Tebbetts
Donald C. Williams

Misty L. Colwell
Peter N. Greenfeld
Sharon S. Mequet
Daniel J. Payne

OF COUNSEL

Charles E. Greenberg
George A. Hart, Jr.
Clark Heggeness
John D. Miller (A Professional Corporation)

(See Next Column)

Bank References: Bank of America, Third & Long Beach Blvd., Long Beach; Union Bank, 400 Oceangate, Long Beach.

For full biographical listings, see the Martindale-Hubbell Law Directory

CAYER, KILSTOFTE & CRATON, A PROFESSIONAL LAW CORPORATION (AV)

Suite 700, 444 West Ocean Boulevard, 90802
Telephone: 310-435-6008
Fax: 310-435-3704

John J. Cayer
Stephen R. Kilstofte
Curt R. Craton

Stephen B. Clemmer

For full biographical listings, see the Martindale-Hubbell Law Directory

FISHER & PORTER, A LAW CORPORATION (AV)

110 Pine Avenue, 11th Floor, P.O. Box 22686, 90801-5686
Telephone: 310-435-5626
Telex: 284549 FPKLAW UR
Fax: 310-432-5399

Gerald M. Fisher
Therese G. Groff
David S. Porter
Michael W. Lodwick
Frank C. Brucculeri

George P. Hassapis
Steven Y. Otera
Stephen Chace Bass
Jay Russell Sever
Robert M. White, Jr.
Vicki L. Hassman
Paul J. Rubino
Linda A. Mancini

OF COUNSEL

Stephen C. Klausen

For full biographical listings, see the Martindale-Hubbell Law Directory

FORD, WALKER, HAGGERTY & BEHAR, PROFESSIONAL LAW CORPORATION (AV)

One World Trade Center, Twenty Seventh Floor, 90831
Telephone: 310-983-2500
Telecopier: 310-983-2555

G. Richard Ford
Timothy L. Walker
William C. Haggerty
Jeffrey S. Behar
Mark Steven Hennings
Donna Rogers Kirby
Tina Ivankovic Mangarpan
Jamiel G. Dave
Susan D. Berger
Joseph A. Heath
Robert J. Chavez
J. Michael McClure

Arthur W. Schultz
Jon T. Moseley
Maxine J. Lebowitz
Timothy P. McDonald
K. Michele Williams
Kevin P. Bateman
Stephen Ward Moore
James D. Savage
Todd D. Pearl
Patrick J. Gibbs
James O. Miller
David Huchel
Sheila Anne Alexander
Heidi M. Yoshioka
Robert Reisinger
Theodore A. Clapp
Stanley L. Scarlett
Scott A. Ritsema
Michael Guy Martin
Colleen A. Strong
Kristin L. Jervis
Thomas L. Gourde
Patrick J. Stark
Shayne L. Wulterin

OF COUNSEL

Theodore P. Shield, P.L.C.

For full biographical listings, see the Martindale-Hubbell Law Directory

MADDEN, JONES & COLE, A PROFESSIONAL CORPORATION (AV)

Suite 1300, 111 W. Ocean Boulevard, 90802
Telephone: 310-435-6565
Fax: 310-590-7909

Philip M. Madden
Steven A. Jones
Montgomery Cole
Judith A. Rasmussen
Robert R. Johnson

John Vita
Mary Gillespie Frankart
Carol Y. Adams
John K. Fitle
Richard P. Wagner

Counsel for: Ameritone Paint Corporation; St. Mary Medical Center; St. Bernardine Medical Center; Farmers & Merchants Trust Co.; Wells Fargo Bank; Mack Truck, Inc.; Long Beach Public Transportation.

For full biographical listings, see the Martindale-Hubbell Law Directory

Long Beach—Continued

RUSSELL & MIRKOVICH (AV)

One World Trade Center, Suite 1450, 90831-1450
Telephone: 310-436-9911
FAX: 310-436-1897

Carlton E. Russell
Joseph N. Mirkovich

ASSOCIATES

Maria Cecilia Inawati Tjandrasuwita

For full biographical listings, see the Martindale-Hubbell Law Directory

SIMON, McKINSEY, MILLER, ZOMMICK, SANDOR & DUNDAS, A LAW CORPORATION (AV)

2750 Bellflower Boulevard, 90815
Telephone: 310-421-9354
Facsimile: 310-420-6455
Irvine, California Office: Suite 670, 4199 Campus Drive.
Telephone: 714-856-1916.
Facsimile: 714-856-3834.

Harry J. Simon (1922-1977)
Thomas W. McKinsey (1920-1990)
Arthur W. Miller (Retired)
Kenneth Zommick
David L. Sandor
Geraldine G. Sandor (Resident, Irvine Office)
David G. Dundas (Resident, Irvine Office)
Robert M. Stone

Carrie Block (Resident, Irvine Office)

For full biographical listings, see the Martindale-Hubbell Law Directory

TAUBMAN, SIMPSON, YOUNG & SULENTOR (AV)

Suite 700 Home Savings Building, 249 East Ocean Boulevard, P.O. Box 22670, 90801
Telephone: 310-436-9201
FAX: 310-590-9695

E. C. Denio (1864-1952)
Geo. A. Hart (1881-1967)
Geo. P. Taubman, Jr. (1897-1970)
Matthew C. Simpson (1900-1988)
Richard G. Wilson (1928-1993)
Roger W. Young
William J. Sulentor
Peter M. Williams
Scott R. Magee
Valerie K. de Martino
Maria M. Rohaidy

Attorneys for: Bixby Land Co.; Renick Cadillac, Inc.; Oil Operators Incorporated.
Local Counsel: Crown Cork & Seal Co., Inc.

For full biographical listings, see the Martindale-Hubbell Law Directory

WISE, WIEZOREK, TIMMONS & WISE, A PROFESSIONAL CORPORATION (AV)

3700 Santa Fe Avenue, Suite 300, 90810
Telephone: 310-834-5028
Facsimile: 310-834-8018
Mailing Address: P.O. Box 2190, 90801
Los Angeles, California Office: 888 South Figueroa Street, Suite 840.
Telephone: 213-628-3717.
Redding, California Office: 280 Hemsted Drive, Suite 115.
Telephone: 916-221-7632.

George E. Wise
Duane H. Timmons
Anthony F. Wiezorek
Susan E. Anderson Wise
Albert F. Padley, III (Resident at Los Angeles)
Michael J. Pearce
Mark C. Allen, III
Richard P. Dieffenbach
Steven C. Rice
Stephen M. Smith (Resident at Los Angeles)
Thomas J. Yocis
James M. Cox
Mathew J. Vande Wydeven (Resident at Los Angeles)
Bailey J. Farrin
William P. Bennett
Tae J. Im (Resident at Los Angeles)

OF COUNSEL

John W. Nelson
Brownell Merrell, Jr.

For full biographical listings, see the Martindale-Hubbell Law Directory

*LOS ANGELES,** Los Angeles Co.

ADAMS, DUQUE & HAZELTINE (AV)

A Partnership including Professional Corporations
777 South Figueroa Street, Tenth Floor, 90017
Telephone: 213-620-1240
FAX: 213-896-5500
San Francisco, California Office: 500 Washington Street.
Telephone: 415-982-1240.
FAX: 415-982-0130.

(See Next Column)

MEMBERS OF FIRM

Earl C. Adams (1892-1986)
Henry Duque (1904-1971)
Herbert S. Hazeltine, Jr. (1907-1993)
Waller Taylor, II (1925-1991)
James B. Isaacs (1922-1986)
James S. Cline (1927-1991)
Thomas F. Call (1919-1988)
Byron O. Smith (P.C.)
Wilson B. Copes
Bruce A. Beckman
Richard R. Terzian
Lonnie E. Woolverton (P.C.)
Dale A. Welke
Kimler G. Casteel
James R. Willcox (San Francisco Office)
Frederick A. Clark
David L. Bacon
Richard T. Davis, Jr.
C. Forrest Bannan
John A. Blue
George G. Weickhardt (San Francisco Office)
Margaret Levy
R. Stephen Doan
Charles D. Schoor
Jeffrey P. Smith
Catherine Hunt Ruddy
Joseph M. Rimac, Jr. (San Francisco Office)
Paul M. Smith
Daniel H. Slate
James J. Moak
Edward F. Pearson
John L. Viola
Jack Welch
Ward D. Smith
Lauren T. Diehl
Cristina L. Sierra
Ronald F. Frank
Lesley C. Green
William J. Kopesky
Berna Warner-Fredman
Kevin P. Farmer
David R. Shane (San Francisco Office)
Margaret Lynn Oldendorf
G. Andrew Jones
Thomas Myers
J. Timothy Scott
Marc Barrett Leh
Remy Kessler

OF COUNSEL

Sidney W. Bishop
Barrie Cowan (San Francisco Office)
John H. Welborne

ASSOCIATES

Rande Sherman Sotomayor
Cheryl A. De Bari
Peter James Bado
Gordon N. Kojima
Sara Anne Culp
Matthew S. Meza
Ann Sparkman (San Francisco Office)
Maura B. O'Connor
Marilyn A. Rogers (San Francisco Office)
Daren R. Brinkman
Carla J. Bennett
Russell G. Petti
Susan G. Spira
Stephen P. Pfahler
Thomas J. Kearney
Howard S. Fallman
Terry L. Tron
Tamarra T. Rennick
Kristin Pelletier
Anna Maria Martin (San Francisco Office)
Thomas B. Croke IV
Gregg M. Audet
Samuel A. Chuck
Gail C. Huang
Leslie A. Salem
Kathryn J. Black
Lisa B. Stein
David Z. Ribakoff
John C. Barker (San Francisco Office)
John G. Piano
Damon C. Anastasia
Sharon C. Sartorius
Robert J. Taitz (San Francisco Office)
Jay M. Miller
Allison B. Gruettner
Mitchell L. Norton
Scott C. Glovsky

For full biographical listings, see the Martindale-Hubbell Law Directory

ALLEN, MATKINS, LECK, GAMBLE & MALLORY (AV)

A Partnership including Professional Corporations
Eighth Floor, 515 South Figueroa Street, 90071
Telephone: 213-622-5555
Telecopier: 213-620-8816
Irvine, California Office: Fourth Floor, 18400 Von Karman, 92715.
Telephone: 714-553-1313.
Telecopier: 714-553-8354.
San Diego, California Office: 501 West Broadway, Suite 900, 92101.
Telephone: 619-233-1155.
Facsimile: 619-233-1158.
West Los Angeles, California Office: 1999 Avenue of the Stars, Suite 1800, 90067.
Telephone: 310-788-2400.
Fax: 310-788-2410.

PARTNERS

Frederick L. Allen
John C. Gamble (Resident, Irvine Office)
Brian C. Leck
Richard C. Mallory
Michael L. Matkins
Marvin E. Garrett
Michael E. Gleason (P.C.) (Resident, San Diego Office)
Thomas C. Foster (Resident, Irvine Office)
Robert J. Cathcart
R. Michael Joyce (Resident, Irvine Office)
Gerben Hoeksma
Thomas W. Henning
Patrick E. Breen
Lawrence D. Lewis (P.C.) (Resident, Irvine Office)
George T. McDonnell
Michael F. Sfregola
David A. B. Burton (P.C.)
Monica E. Olson (Resident, Irvine Office)
Thomas E. Gibbs (Resident, Irvine Office)
Vernon C. Gauntt (Resident, San Diego Office)
Dwight L. Armstrong (Resident, Irvine Office)
Paul D. O'Connor (Resident, Irvine Office)
S. Lee Hancock (Resident, Irvine Office)

(See Next Column)

ALLEN, MATKINS, LECK, GAMBLE & MALLORY—*Continued*

PARTNERS (Continued)

David L. Osias
William R. Harmsen
Debra Dison Hall
Anton N. Natsis
George J. Berger (Resident, San Diego Office)
Michael C. Pruter (Resident, San Diego Office)
Michael H. Cerrina
Richard E. Stinehart (Resident, Irvine Office)
Stephen R. Thames (Resident, Irvine Office)
John K. McKay
Dana I. Schiffman (Resident, San Diego Office)
Anne E. Klokow (Resident, Irvine Office)
Neil N. Gluck
David W. Wensley (Resident, Irvine Office)
Gary S. McKitterick (Resident, Irvine Office)
Patrick J. Grady (Resident, Irvine Office)
John R. Zebrowski
William J. Harris (Resident, San Diego Office)
Ray B. Gliner (Resident, San Diego Office)
Anthony S. Bouza
Charles N. Kenworthy
Anthony J. Oliva
Jeremy D. Glaser
Kenneth L. Perkins, Jr. (Resident, Irvine Office)
Robert M. Hamilton (Resident, Irvine Office)
David R. Zaro
Janet A. Winnick
Robert R. Barnes
Vincent M. Coscino

ASSOCIATES

Cheryl S. Rivers
Michael J. Murphy
Jeffrey R. Patterson (Resident, San Diego Office)
Craig D. Swanson (Resident, San Diego Office)
Dean E. Roeper (Resident, San Diego Office)
Bradley N. Schweitzer (Resident, Irvine Office)
Gretchen K. Hudson (Resident, Irvine Office)
Gregory G. Gorman
Alan J. Gordee (Resident, Irvine Office)
Mark R. Hartney
Pamela L. Andes (Resident, Irvine Office)
Rebecca L. Gundzik
John M. Tipton
Jay M. Gabriel
Adela Carrasco
Melissa K. Gerard
Martha K. Guy (Resident, San Diego Office)
George W. Kuney (Resident, San Diego Office)
Daniel L. Goodkin
Catherine M. Page (Resident, Irvine Office)
Lee Ali Shirani
Scott P. Schomer
Kelli L. Fuller (Resident, San Diego Office)
Deirdre Ann Sullivan
Scott C. Pinkner
Leslie Tucker Fischer (Resident, Irvine Office)
Michael J. Kiely
David Adam Swartz (Resident, San Diego Office)
Ralph H. Winter
Brian J. Kelly
Michael S. Greger (Resident, Irvine Office)
Stacy Lyn Faierman (Resident, West Los Angeles Office)
A. Kristine Floyd (Resident, Irvine Office)
Robert A. Lurie (Resident, West Los Angeles Office)
Susan H. Lambert
Cynthia Ann Eder
Michael A. Alvarado (Resident, Irvine Office)
Mary Kay Ruck (Resident, Irvine Office)
Hadar Gonen
Elizabeth Botsford
David T. Hathaway
Janet M. Wilson
Robert G. Bentley (Resident, Irvine Office)
Dana R. Landsdorf
Christopher G. Lund
Mark J. Hattam (Resident, Irvine Office)
Michael R. Farrell
Steve Wellington (Resident, San Diego Office)

OF COUNSEL

John G. Davies (Resident, San Diego Office)
Joe M. Davidson (Resident, San Diego Office)

Reference: Wells Fargo Bank (Los Angeles Main Office).

For full biographical listings, see the Martindale-Hubbell Law Directory

ALSCHULER, GROSSMAN & PINES (AV)

A Partnership including Professional Corporations
Twelfth Floor, 1880 Century Park East, Century City, 90067
Telephone: 310-277-1226
Fax: 310-552-6077

MEMBERS OF FIRM

Leon S. Alschuler (1910-1987)
Bruce D. Andelson
Michael J. Brill (P.C.)
Michael Cypers
Melvyn B. Fliegel (P.C.)
Andrew D. Friedman
Dale J. Goldsmith
Gail B. Greenberg
Marshall B. Grossman (P.C.)
Gerald B. Kagan (P.C.)
Frank Kaplan (P.C.)
Karen Kaplowitz (P.C.)
Dana N. Levitt (P.C.)
Katherine L. McDaniel
Burt Pines (P.C.)
Paul H. Rochmes
John A. Schwimmer
Michael A. Sherman
Sandra G. Slon
William S. Small (P.C.)
Linda Sutton
Pierre Vogelenzang (P.C.)
Bruce Warner (P.C.)
Karen Africk Wolfen
Joan A. Wolff
Henry S. Zangwill (P.C.)

(See Next Column)

ASSOCIATES

Betty Bales
Rebecca Edelson
Lisa M. Flashner
Barbara J. Harris
Johnnie A. James
Caroline S. Lee
Jonathan A. Loeb
Ann K. Penners
Gwyn Quillen
Michael A. Taitelman

LEGAL SUPPORT PERSONNEL

W. Jack Kessler (Executive Director)
Denise J. Grigst (Librarian)

For full biographical listings, see the Martindale-Hubbell Law Directory

ANDREWS & KURTH L.L.P. (AV)

Suite 4200, 601 S. Figueroa Street, 90017
Telephone: 213-896-3100
Telecopier: 213-896-3137
Houston, Texas Office: 4200 Texas Commerce Tower.
Telephone: 713-220-4200.
Telecopier: 713-220-4285.
Washington, D.C. Office: Suite 200, 1701 Pennsylvania Avenue, N.W.
Telephone: 202-662-2700.
Telecopier: 213-896-3137.
Dallas, Texas Office: 4400 Thanksgiving Tower.
Telephone: 214-979-4400.
Telecopier: 214-979-4401.
The Woodlands, Texas Office: Suite 150, 2170 Buckthorne Place, 77380.
Telephone: 713-364-9199.
Telecopier: 713-364-9538.
New York, N.Y. Office: 10th Floor, 425 Lexington Avenue.
Telephone: 212-850-2800.
Telecopier: 212-850-2929.

MEMBERS OF FIRM

Steven H. Haney
James B. Hicks
Kathy A. Jorrie
William H. Lancaster
Carl B. Phelps
Shelly Rothschild
Ralph W. Tarr
Michael T. Williams

OF COUNSEL

Marta Thoerner Kurland

ASSOCIATES

Graeme Lawrence Currie
Jon L. R. Dalberg
Christie Gaumer
Judy Ann Kim
Steve Malakassiotis
David W. Meadows
Maxine F. Miller
Rebecca O'Malley
Gale Tobin

STAFF ATTORNEYS

Diane C. Weil

For full biographical listings, see the Martindale-Hubbell Law Directory

ARTER & HADDEN (AV)

700 South Flower Street, 90017-4101
Telephone: 213-629-9300
Cable Address: "Oslaw"
Telecopier: 213-617-9255
In Cleveland, Ohio: 1100 Huntington Building, 925 Euclid Avenue.
Telephone: 216-696-1100.
In Columbus, Ohio: 21st Floor, One Columbus, 10 West Broad Street.
Telephone: 614-221-3155.
In Washington, D.C.: 1801 K Street, N.W., Suite 400K.
Telephone: 202-775-7100.
In Dallas, Texas: 1717 Main Street, Suite 4100.
Telephone: 214-761-2100.
In Irvine, California: Two Park Plaza, Suite 700, Jamboree Center.
Telephone: 714-252-7500.
In Austin, Texas: 100 Congress Avenue, Suite 1800.
Telephone: 512-479-6403.
In San Antonio, Texas: Suite 540, Harte-Hanks Tower, 7710 Jones Maltsberger Road.
Telephone: 210-805-8497.

MEMBERS OF FIRM

Charles K. Arter (1875-1957)
John A. Hadden (1886-1979)
Oscar Lawler (1875-1966)
Max Felix (1899-1954)
John M. Hall (1891-1973)
Richard N. Ellner
Richard D. DeLuce
Bruce H. Newman
Kenneth J. Murphy
Richard L. Fruin, Jr.
Jack Goldman
Roger A. Ferree
Edwin W. Duncan
Stephen T. Swanson
James S. Bryan
Jay M. Davis
James E. Durbin
William S. Davis
Curtiss L. Isler
Sheldon B. Chernove
Donald C. Erickson
Wayne S. Grajewski
John R. Tate
Jacqueline I. Valenzuela
Kim W. West
Andrea Y. Slade
Kay Rustand
J. Douglas Post
Michael C. Zellers
Robert P. Andreani
Kathleen M. K. Brahn
Arletta Shirinian
Michael S. Kogan
Bart L. Kessel

(See Next Column)

ARTER & HADDEN, *Los Angeles—Continued*

RETIRED PARTNERS

Marcus Mattson
Reed A. Stout
Robert Henigson
Richard F. Outcault, Jr.

OF COUNSEL

E. Bruce Butler (Not admitted in CA)

ASSOCIATES

Kurt M. Schmeltzer
Karen L. Stevens
James T. Ballard
Julie Dean Larsen
Robert G. Soper
Juliana Stamato
Claire Elizabeth White
Barry S. Babok
Thomas A. Buckley
Martha L. Melendez
Alexander G. Rufus-Isaacs
Victor M. Bartholetti
Helen A. Sabo
Martin L. Togni
Karen M. Stuckey
John M. Orr
Katessa M. Charles
Mary Devereaux Mackey
Daniel R. Villegas
Susan A. Bland
David B. Zolkin
Benjamin H. Anderson
Byron Cooper
Adam Gubner
Gadi Navon
Sheryl A. Tappert

Representative Clients: Chevron Corp.; American International Group; ADT, Inc.; PacTel Properties; The Bank of California, N.A.; Brunswick Corp.; Reliance Steel & Aluminum Co.; Scope Industries; National Railroad Passenger Car; Boral Industries, Inc.

For full biographical listings, see the Martindale-Hubbell Law Directory

BAKER & HOSTETLER (AV)

600 Wilshire Boulevard, 90017-3212
Telephone: 213-624-2400
FAX: 213-975-1740
In Cleveland, Ohio, 3200 National City Center, 1900 East Ninth Street. Telephone: 216-621-0200.
In Columbus, Ohio, Capitol Square, Suite 2100, 65 East State Street. Telephone: 614-228-1541.
In Denver, Colorado, 303 East 17th Avenue, Suite 1100. Telephone: 303-861-0600.
In Houston, Texas, 1000 Louisiana, Suite 2000. Telephone: 713-236-0020.
In Long Beach, California: 300 Oceangate, Suite 620. *Telephone:* 310-432-2827.
In Orlando, Florida, SunBank Center, Suite 2300, 200 South Orange Avenue. Telephone: 407-649-4000.
In Washington, D. C., Washington Square, Suite 1100, 1050 Connecticut Avenue, N. W. Telephone: 202-861-1500.
In College Park, Maryland, 9658 Baltimore Boulevard, Suite 206. Telephone: 301-441-2781.
In Alexandria, Virginia, 437 North Lee Street. Telephone: 703-549-1294.
In San Francisco, California: One Sansome Street, Suite 2000. *Telephone:* 415-951-4705.

MEMBERS OF FIRM IN LOS ANGELES, CALIFORNIA

Edward J. McCutchen (1857-1933)
G. William Shea (1911-1986)
Harold A. Black (1895-1970)
George Harnagel (1903-1962)
Sheldon A. Gebb (Managing Partner-Los Angeles and Long Beach, California and Houston, Texas Offices)

PARTNERS

David M. Agler
Donna R. Black
Penny M. Costa
G. Richard Doty
Richard C. Giller
Byron Hayes, Jr.
Dennis F. Hernandez
Peter W. James
Judd L. Jordan
Larry W. McFarland
Howard J. Privett
Thomas G. Roberts
David C. Sampson
Diane C. Stanfield
William P. Barry
Patrick J. Cain
David A. Destino
Jack D. Fudge
Richard A. Goette
Emil W. Herich
Joseph B. Hudson, Jr.
Michael M. Johnson
Anthony M. Keats
John C. Mueller
Dean G. Rallis Jr.
Jack I. Samet
Bill E. Schroeder
Teresa R. Tracy
Ralph Zarefsky

ASSOCIATES

Steve W. Ackerman
Kathleen E. Bailey
Richard A. Deeb
Keith A. Fink
John S. Grizel
David J. Kaloyanides
Rebecca Lobl
Peggy A. Propper
Brooke K. Richter
Marc I. Seltzer
Gregory D. Trimarche
Angela C. Agrusa
Barry Bookbinder
Andrew J. Durkovic
Edward T. Goines
Bradley R. Hogin
Marcia T. Law
Lynn S. Loeb
Gregg A. Rapoport
Nicholas Rockefeller (Not admitted in CA)
Cranston J. Williams
Dennis L. Wilson

(See Next Column)

OF COUNSEL

Richard Clark
Janet S. Hoffman
Richard E. Sobelle
Meri A. deKelaita
Paul R. Katz
John R. Sommer
Franklin H. Wilson

For full biographical listings, see the Martindale-Hubbell Law Directory

BARTON, KLUGMAN & OETTING (AV)

A Partnership including Professional Corporations
37th Floor, 333 South Grand Avenue, 90071-1599
Telephone: 213-621-4000
Telecopier: 213-625-1832
Newport Beach Office: Suite 700, 4400 MacArthur Boulevard, P.O. Box 2350, 92660.
Telephone: 714-752-7551.
Telecopier: 714-752-0288.

COUNSEL TO FIRM

Robert M. Barton *

MEMBERS OF FIRM

Robert H. Klugman *
Richard F. Oetting *
David F. Morgan *
William D. Herz *
Charles J. Schufreider *
Robert Louis Fisher *
Gilbert D. Jensen *
Cynthia Garrett (1951-1990)
David J. Cartano *
Craig C. Alexander * (Resident Partner at Newport Beach Office)
Dale A. Hudson * (Resident Partner at Newport Beach Office)
Richard L. Brown * (Resident Partner at Newport Beach Office)
Tod V. Beebe *
Michael H. Feldman *
Ronald R. St. John
Mark A. Newton *
Margot I. McLeay

ASSOCIATES

Barbara W. G. Crowley
Linda Guthmann Krieger (Resident Associate at Newport Beach Office)
Kristen C. Kihiczak
Reiko L. Furuta
Donald G. Furness
Jaleen Nelson
Mielissa M. Cowan (Resident Associate at Newport Beach Office)

References: The Bank of California (Southern California Headquarters); Wells Fargo Bank, N.A. (Wells Fargo Center, Los Angeles).
*Denotes a lawyer whose Professional Corporation is a member of the partnership or is Counsel to the Firm

For full biographical listings, see the Martindale-Hubbell Law Directory

BELCHER, HENZIE & BIEGENZAHN, A PROFESSIONAL CORPORATION (AV)

333 South Hope Street, Suite 3650, 90071-1479
Telephone: 213-624-8293
Telecopier: 213-895-6082

Frank B. Belcher (1891-1979)
David Bernard (1931-1978)
John S. Curtis
E. Lee Horton
William T. DelHagen
Julia Azrael

Jeffrey L. Horwith
Georgette Renata Herget
David L. Bonar
Raymond E. Hane, III
James C. Hildebrand
Robert S. Cooper
Wun-ee Chelsea Chen
John Erin McOsker
Mary E. Gram
Diane C. Bass

OF COUNSEL

George M. Henzie
Leo J. Biegenzahn
James M. Derr

Reference: Bank of America (Los Angeles Main Office).

For full biographical listings, see the Martindale-Hubbell Law Directory

BENOIT LAW CORPORATION (AV)

2551 Colorado Boulevard, 90041-1040
Telephone: 213-255-0000; 818-577-0700
Telecopier: 213-254-4538

Luc P. Benoit

For full biographical listings, see the Martindale-Hubbell Law Directory

LAW OFFICES OF DAVID B. BLOOM A PROFESSIONAL CORPORATION (AV)

3325 Wilshire Boulevard, Ninth Floor, 90010
Telephone: 213-938-5248; 384-4088
Telecopier: 213-385-2009

David B. Bloom

(See Next Column)

LAW OFFICES OF DAVID B. BLOOM A PROFESSIONAL CORPORATION—*Continued*

Stephen S. Monroe (A Professional Corporation)
Raphael A. Rosemblat
James E. Adler
Bonni S. Mantovani
Martin A. Cooper
Roy A. Levun
Cherie S. Raidy
Jonathan Udell
Susan Carole Jay
Edward Idell
Sandra Kamenir
Steven Wayne Lazarus
Andrew Edward Briseno
Harold C. Klaskin
Shelley M. Gould
B. Eric Nelson
John C. Notti
Peter O. Israel
Anthony V. Seferian

For full biographical listings, see the Martindale-Hubbell Law Directory

BODKIN, MCCARTHY, SARGENT & SMITH (AV)

Fifty-First Floor, First Interstate Bank Building, 707 Wilshire Boulevard, 90017
Telephone: 213-620-1000
Facsimile: 213-623-5224
Cable Address: "Bolindy"

MEMBERS OF FIRM

Henry G. Bodkin, Jr.
J. Thomas McCarthy
Edward B. Smith, III
Gordon F. Sausser
Michael A. Branconier
Robert H. Berkes
Donna D. Melby
Barbara S. Hodous
James F. Boyle

ASSOCIATES

Joseph T. Teglovic
William Balderrama
Richard P. Kinnan
Michael T. Ohira
Mark W. Lau
Jacqueline A. Armstrong
Judith G. Belsito
William G. Lieb
Marco P. Ferreira
Angela M. Brown
Anna Orlowski
Charise A. Fong
Thomas M. Phillips
Gayle L. Wilder
Ty Shimoguchi
Ronald L. Nelson
Thomas A. Delaney
Francine B. Logan
Daniel K. Shapiro
David S. Blau
Patrick M. Malone

Reference: First Interstate Bank (Los Angeles Main Office, Los Angeles, California).

For full biographical listings, see the Martindale-Hubbell Law Directory

BROBECK, PHLEGER & HARRISON (AV)

A Partnership including A Professional Corporation
550 South Hope Street, 90071-2604
Telephone: 213-489-4060
Facsimile: 213-745-3345
Cable Address: "Brobeck"
Telex: 181164 BPH LSA
San Francisco, California Office: Spear Street Tower, One Market.
Telephone: 415-442-0900.
Palo Alto, California Office: Two Embarcadero Place, 2200 Geng Road.
Telephone: 415-424-0160.
San Diego, California Office: 550 West C Street, Suite 1300.
Telephone: 619-234-1966.
Orange County, California Office: 4675 MacArthur Court, Suite 1000, Newport Beach.
Telephone: 714-752-7535.
Austin, Texas Office: 620 Congress Avenue, Suite 320.
Telephone: 512-477-5495.
Fax: 512-477-5813. Denver, Colorado Office: 1125 Seventeenth Street, 15th Floor.
Telephone: 303-293-0760.
Fax: 303-299-8819.
New York, N.Y. Office: 1301 Avenue of the Americas, 30th Floor.
Telephone: 212-581-1600.
Fax: 212-586-7878.
Brobeck Hale and Dorr International Offices:
London, England Office: Veritas House, 125 Finsbury Pavement, London EC2A 1NQ.
Telephone: 44 071 638 6688.
Facsimile: 44 071 638 5888.
Prague, Czech Republic Office: Brehova 1, 110 00 Praha 1.
Telephone: 422 232-8461.
Facsimile: 422 232-8444.

RESIDENT PARTNERS

Kenneth R. Bender
Linda J. Bozung
Thomas P. Burke (A Professional Corporation)
Edmond R. Davis
Mitchell L. Edwards
Gregg A. Farley
David M. Halbreich
Susan B. Hall
Jeffery D. Hermann
David M. Higgins
John Francis Hilson
Sue L. Himmelrich
Drew Jones
Albert R. Karel
George H. Link
Richard S. Odom
Todd B. Serota
V. Joseph Stubbs
William K. Swank
Jeffrey S. Turner
Daniel J. Tyukody

(See Next Column)

RESIDENT PARTNERS (Continued)

Kenneth L. Waggoner
Gerard J. Walsh
John J. Wasilczyk
Michael S. Whalen
Daniel James Woods
Michael T. Zarro

OF COUNSEL

Tom Bradley
D. Barton Doyle
Chris Steven Jacobsen
Earle Miller
John A. Payne, Jr.
Thomas H. Petrides

RESIDENT ASSOCIATES

Laurie A. Allen
Marcy Berkman
Elizabeth A. Carroll
Jordan S. Cohen
Bren C. Conner
B. Maria Dennis
Sabrina Y. T. Fang
Paul M. Gleason
Joan M. Goddard
John Hameetman
Lynne M. Hobbs
James W. Irey
Jamie L. Johnson
Brian W. Kasell
Christopher W. Kelly
Karen L. Lawlor
Bub-Joo S. Lee
Howard N. Madris
Robert C. McNitt, Jr.
Cynthia M. Patton
Raul Perez
Neil F. Radick
Douglas C. Rawles
Mitchell C. Regenstreif
Steven J. Renshaw
Lynn A. Robertson
David L. Schrader
Raymond T. Sung
Sandee Ting
Edward D. Totino
Perrie M. Weiner
Daniel Weisberg
Thomas B. Youth
Marcia R. Zylber

For full biographical listings, see the Martindale-Hubbell Law Directory

BRONSON, BRONSON & MCKINNON (AV)

A Partnership including Professional Corporations
444 South Flower Street, 24th Floor, 90071
Telephone: 213-627-2000
Fax: 213-627-2277
San Francisco, California Office: 505 Montgomery Street.
Telephone: 415-986-4200.
Santa Rosa, California Office: 100 B Street, Suite 400.
Telephone: 707-527-8110.
San Jose, California Office: 10 Almaden Boulevard, Suite 600.
Telephone: 408-293-0599.

RESIDENT PARTNERS

Edwin W. Green
Lucinda Dennis (A Professional Corporation)
L. Morris Dennis (A Professional Corporation)
William B. Creim
Charles N. Bland, Jr.
Sheldon J. Warren
John D. Boyle
Ralph S. LaMontagne, Jr.
Thomas T. Carpenter
Jane C. Fennelly
Richard C. Macias
Stuart I. Koenig
Sarah M. Sisson
Dolores M. Yarmoff-Nelson
Claudia L. Greenspoon
Stephen L. Backus
Donna P. Arlow
James H. Fox
David M. Walsh
Elizabeth A. Erskine

RESIDENT ASSOCIATES

Janet T. Andrea
Manuel Saldaña
Dani H. Rogers
M. Guadalupe Valencia
Eric A. Amador
Scott E. Blakeley
Nancy L. Tetreault
James B. Yobski
Laurie S. Julien
Raymon B. Bilbeaux, III
Thomas J. Faughnan
Timothy C. Smith
Hayley L. Sneiderman

OF COUNSEL

Robert Weber, Jr.

CONTRACT

Elizabeth A. McConville
Kathleen R. O'Laughlin
Clara Maehara Driscoll

For full biographical listings, see the Martindale-Hubbell Law Directory

BUCHALTER, NEMER, FIELDS & YOUNGER, A PROFESSIONAL CORPORATION (AV)

24th Floor, 601 South Figueroa Street, 90017
Telephone: 213-891-0700
Fax: 213-896-0400
Cable Address: "Buchnem"
Telex: 68-7485
New York, New York Office: 19th Floor, 237 Park Avenue.
Telephone: 212-490-8600.
Fax: 212-490-6022.
San Francisco, California Office: 29th Floor, 333 Market Street.
Telephone: 415-227-0900.
Fax: 415-227-0770.
San Jose, California Office: 12th Floor, 50 West San Fernando Street.
Telephone: 408-298-0350.
Fax: 408-298-7683.
Newport Beach, California Office: Suite 300, 620 Newport Center Drive.
Telephone: 714-760-1121.
Fax: 714-720-0182.
Century City, California Office: Suite 2400, 1801 Century Park East.
Telephone: 213-891-0700.
Fax: 310-551-0233.

(See Next Column)

BUCHALTER, NEMER, FIELDS & YOUNGER A PROFESSIONAL CORPORATION, *Los Angeles—Continued*

Murray M. Fields
Sol Rosenthal
Richard Jay Goldstein
Marvin D. Heileson
Michael L. Wachtell
Harvey H. Rosen
Robert C. Colton
Arthur Chinski
Jay R. Ziegler
Michael J. Cereseto
Bernard E. Le Sage
Terence S. Nunan
Philip J. Wolman
Mark A. Bonenfant
David S. Kyman
James H. Turken
Kevin M. Brandt
Jeffrey S. Wruble
Pamela Kohlman Webster
Matthew W. Kavanaugh
Richard S. Angel
Bryan Mashian

OF COUNSEL

Ronald E. Gordon
Stuart D. Buchalter
Barry A. Smith
Scott O. Smith
Holly J. Fujie
Harriet M. Welch
Randye B. Soref

Geoffrey Forsythe Bogeaus
Jerry A. Hager
Raymond H. Aver
Jonathan D. Fink
Robert J. Davidson
Stephen K. Lubega
Bernard D. Bollinger, Jr.
Cheryl Croteau Orr
Kenneth W. Swenson
Julie A. Goren
Paul S. Arrow
William S. Brody
Amy L. Rubinfeld
Dean Stackel
Abraham J. Colman
J. Karren Baker
John L. Ingersoll
Monika L. McCarthy
Mary LePique Dickson
Shirley Sheau-Lih Lu
Robert A. Willner
Adam Joel Bass
David L. Aronoff
Thomas M. Walker
David I. Sunkin
Kim Allman
William P. Fong
Brett Michael Broderick
Robert Alexander Pilmer
Patricia D. Watkins
Kirk H. Sharpe
Nicolas M. Kublicki
Jamie Rudman
Douglas L. Vining
Gary J. Vyneman
Peter T. Maloney (Not admitted in CA)
K. Todd Shollenbarger

References: City National Bank; Wells Fargo Bank; Metrobank.

For full biographical listings, see the Martindale-Hubbell Law Directory

---

CARLSMITH BALL WICHMAN MURRAY CASE & ICHIKI (AV)

A Partnership including Law Corporations
555 South Flower Street, 25th Floor, 90071
Telephone: 213-955-1200
Cable Address: CWCMI LOSANGELESCALIFORNIA
Fax: 213-623-0032; 213-624-7183
Honolulu, Hawaii Office: Suite 2200, Pacific Tower, 1001 Bishop Street. P.O. Box 656.
Telephone: 808-523-2500.
Long Beach, California Office: 301 East Ocean Boulevard, 7th Floor.
Telephone: 310-435-5631.
Washington, D.C. Office: 700 14th Street, N.W., 9th Floor.
Telephone: 202-508-1025.
Mexico City, Mexico Office: Monte Pelvous 111, Piso 1, Col. Lomas de Chapultepec 11000, Mexico, D.F.
Telephone: (011-52-5) 520-8514.
Fax: (011-52-5) 540-1545.
Mexico, D.F. Office of Carlsmith Ball Garcia Cacho y Asociados, S.C. (Authorized to practice Mexican Law): Monte Pelvoux 111, Piso 1, Col. Lomas de Chapultepec, 11000 Mexico, D.F.
Telephone: (011-52-5) 520-8514.
Fax: (011-52-5) 540-1545.
Agana, Guam Office: 4th Floor, Bank of Hawaii Building, P.O. Box BF.
Telephone: 671-472-6813.
Saipan, Commonwealth of the Northern Mariana Islands Office: Carlsmith Building, Capitol Hill, P.O. Box 5241.
Telephone: 670-322-3455.
Wailuku, Maui, Hawaii Office: One Main Plaza, Suite 400, 2200 Main Street, P.O. Box 1086.
Telephone: 808-242-4535.
Kailua-Kona, Hawaii Office: Second Floor, Bank of Hawaii Annex Building, P.O. Box 1720.
Telephone: 808-329-6464.
Hilo, Hawaii Office: 121 Waianuenue Avenue, P.O. Box 686.
Telephone: 808-935-6644.
Kapolei, Hawaii Office: Kapolei Building, Suite 318, 1001 Kamokila Boulevard.
Telephone: 808-674-0850.

MEMBERS OF FIRM

Robert A. Alsop
Roger B. Baymiller
Nancy M. Beckner
Stephen L. Bradford
Donn A. Dimichele
Albert H. Ebright
Terrence A. Everett
Jonathan R. Hodes
Robert F. Kull
John R. McDonough
Randolph G. Muhlestein
Anthony Murray
Richard R. Pace
James Polish

(See Next Column)

MEMBERS OF FIRM (Continued)

Peter Starn (A Law Corporation)
Robert R. Thornton
Donald C. Williams
Duane H. Zobrist

RESIDENT ASSOCIATES

Annie Kun Baker
David S. Olson
Jonathan L. Smoller
Ann Luotto Wolf

RESIDENT OF COUNSEL

Herbert G. Baerwitz
Douglas Dalton
Dagmar V. Halamka
Tom K. Houston
Barry R. Ogilby (Resident at Los Angeles, California Office)

For full biographical listings, see the Martindale-Hubbell Law Directory

---

CHADBOURNE & PARKE (AV Ⓣ)

601 South Figueroa Street, 90017
Telephone: 213-892-1000
Telecopier: 213-622-9865
New York, N.Y. Office: 30 Rockefeller Plaza, 10112.
Telephone: 212-408-5100.
Telecopier: 212-541-5369.
Washington, D.C. Office: Suite 900, 1101 Vermont Avenue, N.W., 20005.
Telephone: 202-289-3000.
Telecopier: 202-289-3002.
London, England Office: 86 Jermyn Street, SW1 6JD.
Telephone: 44-171-925-7400.
Telecopier: 44-171-839-3393.
Moscow, Russia Office: 38 Maxim Gorky Naberezhnaya, 113035.
Telephone: 7095-974-2424.
Telecopier: 7095-974-2025. International satellite lines via U.S.:
Telephone: 212-408-1190.
Telecopier: 212-408-1199.
Hong Kong Office: Suite 3704, Peregrine Tower, Lippo Centre, 89 Queensway.
Telephone: (852) 2842-5400.
Telecopier: (852) 2521-7527.
New Delhi, India Office: Chadbourne & Parke Associates, A16-B Anand Niketan, 110 021.
Telephone: 91-11-301-7568/7581/7582.
Telecopier: 91-11-301-7351.

RESIDENT PARTNERS

Richard J. Ney
Jonathan F. Bank
Peter R. Chaffetz
Jay R. Henneberry
Linda S. Dakin

RESIDENT COUNSEL

Kenneth J. Langan
Stuart M. de Haaff

RESIDENT ASSOCIATES

Glenn R. Bronson
Gisela Colón-Latta
Anahid Gharakhanian
Jonathan Gluck
Armen K. Hovannisian
Pamela A. Kelley
William J. Kelley, III
Marvin D. Mohn
Melinda R. Smolin

For full biographical listings, see the Martindale-Hubbell Law Directory

---

CLARK & TREVITHICK, A PROFESSIONAL CORPORATION (AV)

800 Wilshire Boulevard, 12th Floor, 90017
Telephone: 213-629-5700
Telecopier: 213-624-9441

Donald P. Clark
Alexander C. McGilvray, Jr.
Philip W. Bartenetti
Kevin P. Fiore
Dolores Cordell
Vincent Tricarico
John A. Lapinski
Leonard Brazil
Dean I. Friedman
Michael K. Wofford
Leslie R. Horowitz
Brent A. Reinke
Arturo Santana Jr.
Kerry T. Ryan
James S. Arico

OF COUNSEL

John A. Tucker, Jr.
Judith Ilene Bloom

References: Wells Fargo Bank (Los Angeles Main Office); National Bank of California.

For full biographical listings, see the Martindale-Hubbell Law Directory

---

CORINBLIT & SELTZER, A PROFESSIONAL CORPORATION (AV)

Suite 820 Wilshire Park Place, 3700 Wilshire Boulevard, 90010-3085
Telephone: 213-380-4200
Telecopier: 213-385-7503; 385-4560

Marc M. Seltzer

OF COUNSEL

Jack Corinblit
Earl P. Willens

Gretchen M. Nelson
Christina A. Snyder
George A. Shohet

Reference: Bank of America (Wilshire & Harvard Office).

For full biographical listings, see the Martindale-Hubbell Law Directory

Los Angeles—Continued

COTKIN & COLLINS, A PROFESSIONAL CORPORATION (AV)

1055 West Seventh Street, Suite 1900, 90017
Telephone: 213-688-9350
FAX: 213-688-9351
Santa Ana, California Office: 200 West Santa Ana Boulevard, Suite 800.
Telephone: 714-835-2330.
FAX: 714-835-2209.

Raphael Cotkin
James P. Collins, Jr. (Resident, Santa Ana Office)
Steven Lincoln Paine
Bradley C. Withers
William D. Naeve (Resident, Santa Ana Office)
Terry C. Leuin
Roger W. Simpson
Joan M. Dolinsky
David A. Winkle (Resident, Santa Ana Office)
Philip S. Gutierrez (Resident, Santa Ana Office)
Karen C. Freitas
Robert G. Wilson
Brian R. Hill (Resident, Santa Ana Office)
Edward M. Rubinstein (Resident, Santa Ana Office)

Lori S. Blitstien
Carrie F. Smith
Amy E. Abdo (Resident, Santa Ana Office)
Gregory A. Sargenti (Resident, Santa Ana Office)
Terry L. Kesinger (Resident, Santa Ana Office)
Richard E. A. Dwyer (Resident, Santa Ana Office)
Cynthia L.K. Steele (Resident, Santa Ana Office)
Michelle Lee Flores (Resident, Santa Ana Office)

References: American City Bank (Downtown Branch); Security Pacific Bank (7th and Grand Branch); Bank of America.

For full biographical listings, see the Martindale-Hubbell Law Directory

DAAR & NEWMAN, PROFESSIONAL CORPORATION (AV)

Suite 2500, 865 South Figueroa Street, 90017-2567
Telephone: 213-892-0999
FAX: 213-892-1066

David Daar
Michael R. Newman
Jeffery J. Daar
Marsha McLean-Utley
Michael J. White

OF COUNSEL

Rodney W. Loeb
William F. White, Jr.
Samuel T. Rees

LEGAL SUPPORT PERSONNEL

Joe A. Morton
Frank E. Raab

Representative Clients: Allianz Insurance Co.; American Income Life Insurance Co.; American Life and Casualty Insurance Co.; Balboa Insurance Co.; California Casualty Insurance Co.; National Benefit Life Insurance Co.; Capital Life Insurance Co.; Charter National Life; Columbian Mutual Life; Connecticut Mutual Life Insurance Co.

For full biographical listings, see the Martindale-Hubbell Law Directory

DEBEVOISE & PLIMPTON (AV)

601 South Figueroa Street, Suite 3700, 90017
Telephone: 213-680-8000
Telecopier: 213-680-8100
New York, N.Y. Office: 875 Third Avenue, 10022.
Telephone: 212-909-6000.
Telex: (Domestic) 148377 DEBSTEVE NYK.
Telecopier: (212) 909-6836.
Washington, D.C. Office: 555 13th Street, N.W., 20004.
Telephone: 202-383-8000.
Telex: 405586 DPDC WUUD.
Telecopier: (202) 383-8118.
Paris, France Office: 21 Avenue George V 75008.
Telephone: (33-1) 40 73 12 12.
Telecopier: (33-1) 47 20 50 82.
Telex: 648141F DPPAR.
London, England Office: 1 Creed Court, 5 Ludgate Hill, EC4M 7AA.
Telephone: (44-171) 329-0779.
Telex: 884569 DPLON G.
Telecopier: (44-171) 329-0860.
Budapest, Hungary Office: 1065 Budapest, Révay Köz 2.III/2. Telephone; (36-1) 131-0845.
Telecopier: (36-1) 132-7995.
Hong Kong Office: 13/F Entertainment Building, 30 Queen's Road Central.
Telephone: (852) 2810-7918.
Fax: (852) 2810-9828.

RESIDENT PARTNERS

Robert L. King
Bruce G. Merritt
John M. Allen, Jr.
Peter R. Schwartz (Not admitted in CA)

RESIDENT COUNSEL

Daniel G. Murphy

(See Next Column)

RESIDENT ASSOCIATES

Mark A. Conley
Nicholas A. Crincoli
David D. Klein
Jeffy Scott Koenig
Marcellus A. McRae
Michael T. O'Reilly

For full biographical listings, see the Martindale-Hubbell Law Directory

GOLDMAN & KAGON, LAW CORPORATION (AV)

1801 Century Park East, Suite 2222, 90067
Telephone: 310-552-1707
Telex: 701076
Cable: GOKALAW
Telecopier: 310-552-7938

Mark A. Goldman
Kenneth L. Goldman
Barry Felsen
Richard D. Goldman
Charles D. Meyer
Terry Mc Niff

Christopher B. Fagan
Jared Laskin
Christian E. Markey III
Phillip C. Mendelsohn

COUNSEL

A. David Kagon

For full biographical listings, see the Martindale-Hubbell Law Directory

GRAHAM & JAMES (AV)

14th Floor, 801 South Figueroa Street, 90017
Telephone: 213-624-2500
Telex: 4720414 GRJAUI
Telecopier: 213-623-4581
Other offices located in: San Francisco, Newport Beach, Palo Alto, Sacramento and Fresno, California; Washington, D.C.; New York, New York; Milan, Italy; Beijing, China; Tokyo, Japan; London, England; Dusseldorf, Germany; Taipei, Taiwan.
Associated Offices: Deacons in Association with Graham & James, Hong Kong; Sly and Weigall, Sydney, Melbourne, Brisbane, Perth and Canberra, Australia.
Affiliated Offices: Graham & James in Affiliation with Taylor Joynson Garrett, London, England; Bucharest, Romania and Brussels, Belgium; Hanafiah Soeharto Ponggawa, Jakarta, Indonesia; Deacons and Graham & James, Bangkok, Thailand; Haarmann, Hemmelrath & Partner, Berlin, Munich, Leipzig, Frankfurt and Dusseldorf, Germany; Mishare M. Al-Ghazali & Partners, Kuwait; Sly & Weigall Deacons in Association with Graham & James, Hanoi, Vietnam and Guangzhou, China; Gallastegui y Lozano, S.C., Mexico City, Mexico; Law Firm of Salah Al-Hejailan, Jeddah and Riyadh, Saudi Arabia.

John J. Allen
Hidetoshi Asakura
Vincent J. Belusko
James H. Broderick, Jr.
George A. Brumder
Susan Kay Chandler
Jeffrey A. Chester
Anthony C. Ching
Hillel T. Cohn
Henry S. David
Craig J. de Recat
Steven S. Doi
David L. Fehrman
Rodney A. Fujii
Benjamin E. Goldman
Randolph H. Gustafson
Yasuhiro Hagihara (Not admitted in CA)
David A. Hayden
David L. Henty
John C. Holberton
J. Eric Isken
William J. James
Cheryl Lee Johnson
Wolfgang M. Kau
Joon Yong Kim
Stan H. Koyanagi
Ken M. Kurosu
Christopher C. Larkin
Michael R. Lindsay
Thomas T. Liu
David A. Livdahl
Richard P. Manson
Thomas J. Masenga
Stuart L. Merkadeau
Marylin Jenkins Milner
David T. Miyamoto
John T. Nagai
Kunichika Nakano
Stephen T. Owens
Denis H. Oyakawa
Charles Paturick
Steven G. Polard
Pamela K. Prickett
Don A. Proudfoot, Jr.
Edwin B. Reeser, III
James C. Roberts
William J. Robinson
Minda R. Schechter
Brian E. Schield
Allan A. Shenoi
Arthur F. Silbergeld
Brian A. Sullivan
Derrick K. Takeuchi
Martin J. Trupiano
Les J. Weinstein
Barry Leigh Weissman
James B. Woodruff
Bertram R. Zweig

SENIOR COUNSEL

Daniel E. Champion
Patrick J. Fields
Nora Chin Hong Tay

ASSOCIATES

David B. Abel
Mark Anchor Albert
Michael B. Annis
Martha L. Applebaum (Not admitted in CA)
Matthew W. Balding
Merrill J. Baumann, Jr.
Brian M. Berliner
Kimberly A. Bomar
Mary Jo Bowman
Mitchell P. Brook (Not admitted in CA)
James M. Burgess
Johnna C. Cho
Marjorie Turk Desmond
Robert Desmond
Joseph T. FitzGerald
Evelyn Jane Fong

(See Next Column)

GRAHAM & JAMES, *Los Angeles—Continued*

ASSOCIATES (Continued)

Franklin R. Fraley, Jr.
David S. Gooder
Shivbir S. Grewal
Les Bradford Hairrell
Marc E. Hankin
Carlos D. Heredia
Jonathan E. Johnson III
Kenneth Benton Julian
Allen Choo Kim
Asher M. Leids
Kimberly E. Lewand
James H. McPhail
David J. Meyer
Larry W. Mitchell
Elizabeth C. Moeller
Don K. Mun
Hisako Muramatsu
Lisa A. Palombo
Tiffany J. Prusia
Daniel Robbins
Thomas P. Schmidt
Wayne M. Smith
Milo M. Stevanovich
Jennifer M. Tsao
Mark B. Tuvim
Brian Van Vleck
John R. Walton
John Jinshu Zhang

For full biographical listings, see the Martindale-Hubbell Law Directory

GRAY, YORK, DUFFY & RATTET (AV)

15760 Ventura Boulevard, 16th Floor (Encino), 91436
Telephone: 818-907-4000; 310-553-0445
FAX: 818-783-4551

MEMBERS OF FIRM

Gary S. Gray
James R. York
John J. Duffy
Gary S. Rattet
James C. Mavridis (Retired)
Arlene A. Colman

ASSOCIATES

Amalia L. Taylor
Kenneth A. Hearn
Gabriel H. Wainfeld
James B. Sanborn
Stephen Coopersmith
John L. Barber
Vincent F. Bennett
Miloslav Khadilkar
Michael S. Eisenbaum
Kevin S. Wattles
Frank J. Ozello, Jr.
Marc E. Carlson

Reference: Marathon National Bank, Los Angeles, California.

For full biographical listings, see the Martindale-Hubbell Law Directory

GREENBERG, GLUSKER, FIELDS, CLAMAN & MACHTINGER (AV)

20th Floor, 1900 Avenue of the Stars (Century City), 90067
Telephone: 310-553-3610
Fax: 310-553-0687

MEMBERS OF FIRM

Arthur N. Greenberg
Philip Glusker
Sidney J. Machtinger
Stephen Claman
Bertram Fields
Harvey R. Friedman
Bernard Shearer
Jon J. Gallo
Paula J. Peters
Michael K. Collins
John L. Child
C. Bruce Levine
Michael A. Greene
Joseph M. Cahn
Garrett L. Hanken
Norman H. Levine
William A. Halama
James E. Hornstein
Robert S. Chapman
Robert F. Marshall
Robert E. Bennett, Jr.
Marc S. Cohen
Charles N. Shephard
Dennis B. Ellman
Gary L. Kaplan
Robert W. Barnes
Lawrence Y. Iser
E. Barry Haldeman
Mark Stankevich
Martin H. Webster
Michael V. Bales
Henry D. Finkelstein
Diane J. Crumpacker
Jean Morris
Elizabeth Watson
Elizabeth G. Chilton
Jill A. Cossman
Lilianne G. Chaumont
Peter J. Niemiec
Roger L. Funk
Richard A. Kale
Debby R. Zurzolo
Arnold D. Kahn
Mark A. Gochman
Theodore F. Kahan
Jill Lynn Smith
Eve H. Wagner
Gerald L. Sauer
Nancy A. Bertrando
Bonnie E. Eskenazi
Glenn A. Dryfoos

ASSOCIATES

Lee A. Dresie
Jeffrey Spitz
Nancy C. Hsieh
Sandra A. Dewey
Carrie A. Levinson
Steven J. Lurie
Roberta Marlene Wolff
Brian L. Edwards
Jill E. Burtis
Kelly Ann Coleman
Nanette Lynn Klein
Glenn E. Lerman
Elizabeth M. Priestley
Elizabeth H. Pugh
David R. Mersten
Patricia A. Millett
Amy L. Dixon
Elisabeth A. Basini
Laurie B. Hiller
Jeffrey A. Krieger
Carla M. Roberts
Edward N. Sabin
Christine H. Belgrad
Laura E. Reece
Jeffrey M. Osteen
Michael W. Scholtz
Joan E. Smiles
Mark S. Weinstock
Kevin L. James
Sheri E. Porath
Michael L. Blend
Stephanie H. Gold
Trisha Lynn Farber
Matthew M. Johnson
Wendy M. Mesnick
Marc M. Stern

Reference: Wells Fargo Bank, 1800 Century Park East, Los Angeles, CA 90067.

(See Next Column)

For full biographical listings, see the Martindale-Hubbell Law Directory

HALSTEAD, BAKER & OLSON (AV)

Suite 500, 1000 Wilshire Boulevard, 90017
Telephone: 213-622-0200
Telecopier: 213-623-3836

MEMBERS OF FIRM

Harry M. Halstead
Sheldon S. Baker
Eric Olson
John J. Jacobson
Charles L. LeCroy, III
William C. Hansen
Arsen Danielian

ASSOCIATES

Michael S. Simon
Andrea L. Esterson
Donald J. Gary, Jr.

For full biographical listings, see the Martindale-Hubbell Law Directory

HANNA AND MORTON (AV)

A Partnership including Professional Corporations
Seventeenth Floor, Wilshire-Grand Building, 600 Wilshire Boulevard, 90017
Telephone: 213-628-7131

MEMBERS OF FIRM

Byron C. Hanna (1887-1951)
Harold C. Morton (1895-1978)
John H. Blake (1916-1971)
Edward S. Renwick (A Professional Corporation)
James P. Lower
Gregory R. Ryan
Glenn Lorin Krinsky
Robert M. Newell, Jr.
James P. Modisette
David A. Ossentjuk

OF COUNSEL

Bela G. Lugosi (A Professional Corporation)
William N. Greene
Milo V. Olson
David A. Thomas

ASSOCIATES

Stephen G. Mason
Thomas N. Campbell
Robert J. Roche
Michael P. Wippler
Allison L. Malin

For full biographical listings, see the Martindale-Hubbell Law Directory

HILL, FARRER & BURRILL (AV)

A Partnership including Professional Corporations
35th Floor, Union Bank Square, 445 South Figueroa Street, 90071
Telephone: 213-620-0460
Fax: 213-624-4840; 488-1593

William M. Farrer (1894-1971)
Alfred J. Hill (1881-1953)
Stanley S. Burrill (1902-1957)

MEMBERS OF FIRM

Leon S. Angvire (P.C.)
Stanley E. Tobin (P.C.)
Jack R. White (P.C.)
Kyle D. Brown (P.C.)
William M. Bitting (P.C.)
Stuart H. Young, Jr., (P.C.)
Steven W. Bacon (P.C.)
Wm. Harold Borthwick (P.C.)
Arthur B. Cook, II, (P.C.)
James G. Johnson (P.C.)
George Koide (P.C.)
Jonathan M. Brandler (P.C.)
Darlene Fischer Phillips (P.C.)
Scott L. Gilmore
Kevin H. Brogan
James A. Bowles (P.C.)
Neil D. Martin
Michael J. DiBiase
Alfred M. Clark, III
Daniel J. McCarthy
Ronald W. Novotny (P.C.)
David E. Parry
Benjamin B. Salvaty
Dean E. Dennis
Thomas F. Reed
Craig J. Whitney
R. Curtis Ballantyne
Suzanne J. Holland
William A. White
James R. Evans, Jr.
G. Cresswell Templeton III
Curtis A. Westfall

OF COUNSEL

Edwin H. Franzen (P.C.)

RETIRED

Carl M. Gould
Vincent C. Page
William C. Farrer (P.C.)

ASSOCIATES

Jennifer Cook Lewis
Michael S. Turner
Michelle A. Meghrouni
Jennifer L. Pancake
Ondrea D. Hidley
Ian M. Green
Gregory Lawrence Evans
Byron T. Ball
Dean A. Reeves
Brett B. Curlee
Paul M. Porter
Leslie G. Van Zyl
Arnold D. Woo
Samuel S. Boykin
Karen S. Seigel
Kenneth W. Muller
Lynne Marie Pregenzer

For full biographical listings, see the Martindale-Hubbell Law Directory

HOLLEY & GALEN (AV)

800 South Figueroa, Suite 1100, 90017
Telephone: 213-629-1880
Fax: 213-895-0363

(See Next Column)

HOLLEY & GALEN—*Continued*

MEMBERS OF FIRM

Clyde E. Holley (1891-1980)
Albert J. Galen (Retired)
W. Michael Johnson
Richard E. Llewellyn, II
A. Steven Brown

ASSOCIATES

Debra Burchard Coffeen
Charles A. Jordan

For full biographical listings, see the Martindale-Hubbell Law Directory

HONIGMAN MILLER SCHWARTZ AND COHN (AV)

A Partnership including Professional Corporations
Watt Plaza, Suite 2200, 1875 Century Park East, 90067-2799
Telephone: 310-789-3800
Fax: 310-789-3814
Detroit, Michigan Office: 2290 First National Building.
Telephone: 313-256-7800.
Lansing, Michigan Office: 222 North Washington Square, Suite 400.
Telephone: 517-484-8282.
West Palm Beach, Florida Office: Suite 800 Esperante Building, 222 Lakeview Avenue.
Telephone: 407-838-4500.
Tampa, Florida Office: 2700 Landmark Centre, 401 E. Jackson Street.
Telephone: 813-221-6600.
Orlando, Florida Office: 390 North Orange Avenue, Suite 1300.
Telephone: 407-648-0300.
Houston, Texas Office: 3100 First Interstate Bank Plaza, 1000 Louisiana.
Telephone: 713-650-2600.

MEMBERS OF FIRM

Robert C. Danner
Daniel E. Martyn, Jr.
George E. Schulman

ASSOCIATES

Melanie J. Bingham
Adryane R. Omens

Representative Clients: American Magnetics Corp.; Atlantic Richfield Co.; Catellus Management Corp.; Comerica Bank; General Motors Acceptance Corporation; Hughes Aircraft Co.; Hyundai Motor Finance Company; Security Pacific Automotive Financial Services Corp.; V.W. Credit, Inc.; World Omni Leasing, Inc.

For full biographical listings, see the Martindale-Hubbell Law Directory

HUFSTEDLER & KAUS (AV)

A Partnership including Professional Corporations
Thirty-Ninth Floor, 355 South Grand Avenue, 90071-3101
Telephone: 213-617-7070
Fax: 213-617-6170

MEMBERS OF FIRM

Charles E. Beardsley (1904-1975)
Samuel L. Williams (1933-1994)
Seth M. Hufstedler (Professional Corporation)
Shirley M. Hufstedler (Professional Corporation)
Otto M. Kaus
Joseph L. Wyatt, Jr.
John Sobieski
Burton J. Gindler
Fred L. Leydorf
Jerome H. Craig (Professional Corporation)
Thomas J. Ready (Professional Corporation)
Patricia Dominis Phillips
Dudley M. Lang
John P. Olson
Dennis M. Perluss
Margot A. Metzner
Leonard L. Gumport
Dan Marmalefsky
Gary Plessman
Michael V. Toumanoff
Susan I. Schutzbank Montgomery
Mark R. McDonald

ASSOCIATES

John W. (Jack) Alden Jr.
David K. Barrett
Randall Lee Clark
Eliot F. Krieger
Steven M. Haines
Ann Haberfelde
Rob Rader
Tina Wolfson
Lester I. Yano
Elayna J. Youchah

Reference: First Interstate Bank, 707 Wilshire.

For full biographical listings, see the Martindale-Hubbell Law Directory

HUGHES HUBBARD & REED (AV)

350 South Grand Avenue, Suite 3600, 90071-3442
Telephone: 213-613-2800
Telecopier: 213-613-2950
New York, New York Office: One Battery Park Plaza, 10004.
Telephone: 212-837-6000.
Cable Address: "Hughreed, New York."
Telex: 427120.
Telecopier: 212-422-4726.
Miami, Florida Office: 801 Brickell Avenue, 33131.
Telephone: 305-358-1666.
Telex: 51-8785.
Telecopier: 305-371-8759.

(See Next Column)

Paris, France Office: 47, Avenue Georges Mandel, 75116.
Telephone: 33.1.44.25.80.00.
Cable Address: "Hughreed, Paris."
Telex: 645440.
Telecopier: 33.1.45.53.15.04.
Washington, D.C. Office: 1300 I Street, N.W., Suite 900 West, 20005.
Telephone: 202-408-3600.
Telex: 89-2674.
Telecopier: 202-408-3636.
Berlin, Germany Office: Kurfürstendamm 44, D-1000 Berlin 15.
Telephone: 030-880008-0.
Telefax: 030-880008-65.
Telex: 185803 KNAPA D.

RESIDENT PARTNERS

Charles Avrith
William T. Bisset
Richard S. Friedman
George A. Furst
Rita M. Haeusler
Spencer L. Harrison
Gordon R. Kanofsky
Richard J. Kaplan
Peter M. Langenberg
Theodore H. Latty
David A. Lombardero
Michael J. Maloney
Mark R. Moskowitz

OF COUNSEL

Andrea H. Bricker

For full biographical listings, see the Martindale-Hubbell Law Directory

JONES, DAY, REAVIS & POGUE (AV)

555 West Fifth Street Suite 4600, 90013-1025
Telephone: 213-489-3939
Telex: 181439 UD
Telecopier: 213-243-2539
In Irvine, California: 2603 Main Street, Suite 900.
Telephone: 714-851-3939.
Telex: 194911 Lawyers LSA.
Telecopier: 714-553-7539.
In Atlanta, Georgia: 3500 One Peachtree Center, 303 Peachtree Street, N.E.
Telephone: 404-521-3939.
Cable Address: "Attorneys Atlanta".
Telex: 54-2711.
Telecopier: 404-581-8330.
In Brussels, Belgium: Avenue Louise 480, 7th Floor, B-1050 Brussels.
Telephone: 011-32-2-645-14-11.
Telecopier: 011-32-2-645-14-45.
In Chicago, Illinois: 77 West Wacker.
Telephone: 312-782-3939.
Telecopier: 312-782-8585.
In Cleveland, Ohio: North Point, 901 Lakeside Avenue.
Telephone: 216-586-3939.
Cable Address: "Attorneys Cleveland."
Telex: 980389.
Telecopier: 216-579-0212.
In Columbus, Ohio: 1900 Huntington Center.
Telephone: 614-469-3939.
Cable Address: "Attorneys Columbus."
Telecopier: 614-461-4198.
In Dallas, Texas: 2300 Trammell Crow Center, 2001 Ross Avenue.
Telephone: 214-220-3939.
Cable Address: "Attorneys Dallas."
Telex: 730852.
Telecopier: 214-969-5100.
In Frankfurt, Germany: Triton Haus, Bockenheimer Landstrasse 42, 60323 Frankfurt am Main.
Telephone: 49-69-9726-3939.
Telecopier: 49-69-9726-3993.
In Geneva, Switzerland: 20, rue de Candolle.
Telephone: 011-41-22-320-2339.
Telecopier: 011-41-22-320-1232.
In Hong Kong: 1501 One Exchange Square, 8 Connaught Place.
Telephone: 011-852-2526-6895.
Telecopier: 011-852-2810-5787.
In London England: One Mount Street.
Telephone: 011-44-71-493-9361.
Cable Address: "Surgoe London WI."
Telecopier: 011-44-71-493-9666.
In New York, New York: 599 Lexington Avenue.
Telephone: 212-326-3939.
Cable Address: "JONESDAY NEWYORK."
Telex: 237013 JDRP UR.
Telecopier: 212-755-7306.
In Paris, France: 62, rue du Faubourg Saint-Honore.
Telephone: 011-33-1-44-71-3939.
Cable Address: "Surgoe Paris."
Telex: 290156 Surgoe.
Telecopier: 011-33-1-49-24-0471.
In Pittsburgh, Pennsylvania: 500 Grant Street, 31st Floor.
Telephone: 412-391-3939.
Cable Address: "Attorneys Pittsburgh".
Telecopier: 412-394-7959.

(See Next Column)

JONES, DAY, REAVIS & POGUE, *Los Angeles—Continued*

In Riyadh, Saudi Arabia: Law Offices of Saud M.A. Shawwaf, P.O. Box 2700.
Telephones: 011 (966-1) 465-6543, 011 (966-1) 464-8534 or 011 (966-1) 464-8540.
Telex: 401831 SAUCON SJ.
Telecopier: (966-1) 464-8480.
In Taipei, Taiwan: 8th Floor, 2 Tun Hwa South Road, Section 2.
Telephone: 011 (886-2) 704-6808.
Telecopier: 011 (886-2) 704-6791.
In Tokyo, Japan: Toranomon MT Building, 4th Floor, 10-3, Toranomon 3-Chome, Minato-Ku, Tokyo 105, Japan.
Telephone: 011-81-3-3433-3939.
Telecopier: 011-81-3-5401-2725.
In Washington, D.C.: Metropolitan Square, 1450 G Street, N.W.
Telephone: 202-879-3939.
Cable Address: "Attorneys Washington."
Telex: 89-2410 ATTORNEYS WASH.
Telecopier: 202-737-2832.

MEMBERS OF FIRM IN LOS ANGELES

James F. Childs, Jr.
Ronald S. Rizzo
William G. Wilson
Ross E. Stromberg
Gerald W. Palmer
Victor G. Savikas
Elwood Lui
Robert Dean Avery
Donald D. Gralnek
Richard A. Shortz
James L. Baumoel (Not admitted in CA)
Frederick L. McKnight
Dean B. Allison
Christine W. Byrd
Marsha S. Croninger
David S. Boyce
Donald P. Paskewitz
Deborah Crandall Saxe
Andrew J. Demetriou
Thomas R. Mueller
Howard J. Steinberg
Scott D. Harvel (Not admitted in CA)
Thomas M. McMahon
Eric V. Rowen
Louis L. Touton
Daniel J. McLoon
Scott D. Bertzyk
Sarah Heck Griffin
Jeffrey A. LeVee
Lester O. Brown
Erich Lawson Spangenberg (Not admitted in CA)

OF COUNSEL

Ralph E. Erickson
David C. Zucker
Richard J. Frick
Jerald B. Serviss
Patricia A. Van Dyke
Daniel K. Settelmayer

SENIOR ATTORNEY

Douglas F. Landrum
Lynn Leversen Kambe

ASSOCIATES

Marsha E. Durko
Laura A. Matz
Peter G. McAllen
Thomas Botz
Clayton J. Vreeland
Craig H. Averch
Adam Siegler
Robert K. Brown, Jr.
David J. DiMeglio
Robert M. Gilchrest
Kevin A. Dorse
Catherine A. Ehrgott
Daniel D. McMillan
Chris M. Amantea
Kevin R. Lussier
Jeffrey A. Miller
Kenneth A. Remson
Bruce J. Shih
Catherine A. Cleveland
Nancy L. de Brier (Not admitted in CA)
Karl J. Lott
Jane M. Nowotny
Randa A. Osman
Steven M. Ruskin
Christine A. Samsel
Ricky L. Shackelford
Valerie A. Brown
Mary K. Hartigan
Mark M. Kassabian
Maria K. Nelson
Wendy L. Thomas
David C. Bolstad
Ann K. Bowman
Peter C. Ku (Not admitted in CA)
Gregory T. May
Kimberly S. Stenton
Miwon Yi
Matthew F. Burke
Sharon L. Faris
David B. Fischer
David B. Hoppe
James J. Kershaw, III
Alonzo B. Wickers, IV
Christopher B. Donahoe
Brian D. McAllister
Kirstin D. Poirier-Whitley
Karen R. Thorland

For full biographical listings, see the Martindale-Hubbell Law Directory

KAYE, SCHOLER, FIERMAN, HAYS & HANDLER (AV)

1999 Avenue of the Stars, Suite 1600, 90067
Telephone: 310-788-1000
Facsimile: 310-788-1200
New York, N.Y.: 425 Park Avenue, 10022.
Telephone: 212-836-8000.
Telex: 234860 KAY UR.
Facsimile: 212-836-8689.
Washington, D.C.: McPherson Building, 901 Fifteenth Street, N.W., Suite 1100, 20005.
Telephone: 202-682-3500.
Telex: 897458 KAYSCHOL WSH.
Facsimile: 202-682-3580.
Hong Kong: 9 Queen Road Centre, 18th Floor.
Telephone: 852-8458989.
Telex: 62816 KAY HX.
Facsimile: 852-8453682; 852-8452389.

(See Next Column)

Beijing (Peking), People's Republic of China: Scite Tower, Suite 708, 22 Jianguomenwai Dajie, 100004.
Telephone: 861-5124755.
Telex: 222540 KAY CN.
Facsimile: 861-5124760.

MEMBERS OF FIRM

Gary Apfel
Aton Arbisser
Gregory S. Dovel
Kenneth A. Freeling
Jeffrey S. Gordon
Channing D. Johnson
Barry H. Lawrence
Ronald L. Leibow
Pierce O'Donnell
Sanford C. Presant
Hushmand Sohaili
William E. Thomson, Jr.

SPECIAL COUNSEL

Cruz Reynoso

OF COUNSEL

Susan A. Grode
M. Kenneth Suddleson

ASSOCIATES

Robert Barnes
Lynne M. O. Brickner
Russ Alan Cashdan
Brian T. Corrigan
R. Scott Feldman
Alan L. Friel
Peter L. Haviland
Lillie Hsu
Lisa Ilona Karsai
Ronald E. Levinson
Michael A. Lloyd
Sean Aaron Luaer
Sean Aarow Luner
Ann Marie Mortimer
A. Ken Okamoto
Belynda Reck
Rex T. Reeves, Jr.
Anthony R. Salandra
John J. Shaeffer
Mitchell J. Steinberger
Bonnie Stylides
W. Casey Walls
Renee I. Wolf
Juan E. Zuniga

For full biographical listings, see the Martindale-Hubbell Law Directory

KINDEL & ANDERSON (AV)

A Partnership including Professional Corporations
Twenty-Ninth Floor, 555 South Flower Street, 90071
Telephone: 213-680-2222
Cable Address: "Kayanda"
Telex: 67-7497
FAX: 213-688-7564
Irvine, California Office: 5 Park Plaza, Suite 1000.
Telephone: 714-752-0777.
Woodland Hills, California Office: Suite 244, 5959 Topanga Canyon Boulevard.
Telephone: 818-712-0036.
San Francisco, California Office: 580 California Street, 15th Floor.
Telephone: 415-398-0110.

MEMBERS OF FIRM

Robert K. Baker
Gerard C. Bastiaanse (Irvine, CA Office)
John A. Belcher
Russell W. Bogda
Hugh M. Boss
Neal H. Brockmeyer
Joseph W. Burdett (P.C.)
Paul J. Coady
Thomas Curtiss, Jr.
Dale S. Fischer
Allan I. Grossman (P.C.)
David Gurnick (Woodland Hills, CA Office)
Christopher J. Husa (Woodland Hills, CA Office)
John E. James
Daniel G. Jordan
James H. Kindel, Jr.
Manuel S. Klausner (P.C.)
Ronald J. Kohut (Irvine, CA Office)
David Laufer (Woodland Hills, CA Office)
Michael P. Lewis (Woodland Hills, CA Office)
Gary W. Maeder
Stephen E. Newton
S. Kendall Patton (San Francisco, CA Office)
Carol A. Pfaffmann
Brian G. Prentice
Jon L. Rewinski
Steven P. Rice (Irvine, CA Office)
Bruce J. Russell (San Francisco, CA Office)
James S. Russell (San Francisco, CA Office)
Carlos Solis
William C. Staley (P.C.)
Robert H. Takeuchi (P.C.)
Elizabeth S. Trussell
Victor F. Yacullo (P.C.)
William L. Yerkes (P.C.)

ASSOCIATES

David F. Abele (San Francisco, CA Office)
Kristine T. Aoyama
Elena R. Baca
Susanne M. Bendavid-Arbiv (Woodland Hills, CA Office)
Ruth Claire Black (Irvine, CA Office)
Steven M. Friedman
William E. Halle (Irvine, CA Office)
M. Colleen Harty (Irvine, CA Office)
Deirdre M. Kelly (Irvine, CA Office)
Mark G. Kisicki
Amy W. Larkin (Irvine, CA Office)
Mark A. McLean
Maryann S. Meggelin
Paul W. Poareo
Scott Price
Mary J. Snyder
Joshua R. Steinhauer (San Francisco, CA Office)
Megan L. Wagner (Irvine, CA Office)
Richard E. Walker (San Francisco, CA Office)
Mary E. Wright

(See Next Column)

KINDEL & ANDERSON—*Continued*

OF COUNSEL

John E. Anderson
John W. Armagost (P.C.)
Paul L. Freese
Gilbert E. Haakh
Robert L. Whitmire (P.C.)

For full biographical listings, see the Martindale-Hubbell Law Directory

LAGERLOF, SENECAL, BRADLEY & SWIFT

(See Pasadena)

LOEB AND LOEB (AV)

A Partnership including Professional Corporations
Suite 1800, 1000 Wilshire Boulevard, 90017-2475
Telephone: 213-688-3400
Telecopier: 213-688-3460; 688-3461; 688-3462
Century City, California Office: Suite 2200, 10100 Santa Monica Boulevard, Los Angeles, 90067-4164.
Telephone: 310-282-2000.
Telecopier: 310-282-2191; 282-2192.
New York, N.Y. Office: 345 Park Avenue, 10154-0037.
Telephone: 212-407-4000.
Facsimile: 212-407-4990.
Nashville, Tennessee Office: 45 Music Square West, 37203-3205.
Telephone: 615-749-8300;
Facsimile: 615-749-8308.
Rome, Italy Office: Piazza Digione 1, 00197.
Telephone: 011-396-808-8456.
Telecopier: 011-396-674-8223.

MEMBERS OF FIRM

Joseph P. Loeb (1883-1974)
Edwin J. Loeb (1886-1970)
Mortimer H. Hess (1889-1968)
Phillip E. Adler (A P.C.)
Christopher K. Aidun (New York City Office)
Debra J. Albin-Riley
Kenneth B. Anderson (New York City Office)
John Arao
Roger M. Arar (Century City Office)
Donald L. B. Baraf (New York City Office)
Robert S. Barry, Jr.
Harold A. Barza
Michael D. Beck (New York City Office)
Carol Laurene Belfield
Leroy Bobbitt (Century City Office)
Stephen D. Bomes
Maribeth A. Borthwick (Century City Office)
David H. Carlin (New York City Office)
Marc A. Chamlin (New York City Office)
Andrew S. Clare (A P.C.)
Kenneth R. Costello
Terence F. Cuff
John J. Dellaverson (Century City and Rome, Italy Offices)
Lorenzo De Sanctis (Rome, Italy Office)
David B. Eizenman (New York City Office)
Roger L. Ellison
Frank E. Feder (A P.C.) (Century City and New York Offices)
Martin D. Fern
David L. Ficksman
David C. Fischer (New York City Office)
John T. Frankenheimer (A P.C.) (Century City Office)
Kenneth D. Freeman (New York City Office)
Howard I. Friedman (A P.C.)
James D. Friedman
Andrew S. Garb (A P.C.)
Fred B. Griffin (Century City Office)
Philip J. Grosz (Century City Office)
Lawrence B. Gutcho
Abraham S. Guterman (New York City Office)
Joseph P. Heffernan (A P.C.)
Irv Hepner (New York City Office)
Robert A. Holtzman (A P.C.)
James C. Hughes
Ralph Jonas
Gerald D. Kleinman (A P.C.) (Century City Office)
Richard W. Kopenhefer (Century City Office)
Mary D. Lane
John F. Lang (New York City Office)
Michael Langs
Thomas N. Lawson
Jerome L. Levine (New York City Office)
Andrew E. Lippmann (New York City Office)
Jeffrey M. Loeb
William J. Marlow (New York City Office)
Michael A. Mayerson (Century City Office)
Malissa Hathaway McKeith
Robert A. Meyer
Charles H. Miller (New York City Office)
Malcolm L. Mimms, Jr. (Nashville, Tennessee Office)
Douglas E. Mirell
Susan V. Noonoo
Alden G. Pearce (A P.C.)
Robert L. Pelz (New York City Office)
Martin R. Pollner (New York City Office)
Guendalina Ponti (Rome, Italy Office)
Shirley M. Price
Robert S. Reich (New York City Office)
Thomas E. Rohlf (A P.C.)
Adrian F. Roscher (Century City Office)
Andrew M. Ross (New York City Office)
Stanford K. Rubin (A P.C.) (Century City Office)
Fredric M. Sanders (New York City Office)
David M. Satnick (New York City Office)
David S. Schaefer (New York City Office)
P. Gregory Schwed (New York City Office)
Paul A. Sczudlo
Peter S. Selvin
David B. Shontz (New York City Office)

(*See Next Column*)

MEMBERS OF FIRM (Continued)

Clark B. Siegel (Century City Office)
Michael F. Sitzer
Myron L. Slobodien (A P.C.) (Century City Office)
Lee N. Steiner (New York City Office)
Rebel R. Steiner, Jr. (Century City Office)
Bruce M. Stiglitz (A P.C.)
Richard P. Streicher (New York City Office)
Raymond W. Thomas (Century City Office)
Robert Thorne (Century City Office)
William P. Wasserman (A P.C.)
Ronald Weinstein (A P.C.)
Debre Katz Weintraub
Bruce J. Wexler (New York City Office)
Alan W. Wilken
Susan A. Wolf
William S. Woods, II
Michael P. Zweig (New York City Office)

OF COUNSEL

Harold D. Berkowitz (A P.C.) (Century City Office)
James R. Birnberg
Harry First (New York City Office)
Marvin Greene (A P.C.)
Harold I. Kahen (New York City Office)
Jay Adams Knight
Saul N. Rittenberg (A P.C.) (Century City Office)
Alfred I. Rothman (A P.C.)
Arthur A. Segall (New York City Office)
Alan D. Shulman
Bernard M. Silbert (Century City Office)
Harvey L. Silbert (Century City Office)
Albert F. Smith (A P.C.)
John S. Warren (A P.C.)

ASSOCIATES

Sheila E. Acker (New York City Office)
Jean-Marie L. Atamian (New York City Office)
Curtis W. Bajak (Century City Office)
David J. Becker
Michele E. Beuerlein
Paula A. Bryant (Not admitted in CA)
Marguerite L. Bui
Matthew Clark Bures
Edwin A. Burgos
Charlene A. Busch
David A. Byrnes
Paula K. Colbath (New York City Office)
Jean A. Cooper
Marco D. Costales
Marita T. Covarrubias (Century City Office)
Bert C. Cozart
Kathryn Lee Crawford (New York City Office)
David P. Crochetiere
M. Katharine Davidson
Anne P. Donovan (New York City Office)
Brant H. Dveirin
Linda F. Edell (Nashville, Tennessee Office)
Lee A. Edlund
Carla Fels (New York City Office)
Jay Fenster (New York City Office)
John J. Fleming (New York City Office)
Kenneth R. Florin (New York City Office)
Margo E. Freedman
Richard Frey (Century City Office)
Daniel J. Friedman
Helen Gavaris (New York City Office)
Miriam J. Golbert (Century City Office)
James P. Goodkind (Century City Office)
Meryl Gordon (Not admitted in CA; Century City Office)
Scott L. Grossfeld
Kurtiss Lee Grossman
Nina J. Haller
Adrienne Halpern (New York City Office)
Gerard A. Hefner (New York City Office)
Karen Nielsen Higgins
Richard M. Johnson, Jr.
Joyce S. Jun (Century City Office)
Lance N. Jurich
Duane O. Kamei
Michael Bryce Kinney (New York City Office)
John W. Kittleson
Allison D. Klayman (New York City Office)
Maarten B. Kooij (New York City Office)
Robert B. Lachenauer (New York City Office)
Jonathan E. Ladd (New York City Office)
Paul J. Laurin
Nina B. Luban
Linda McCauley Mack (Century City Office)
John W. MacPete
Paola Amelia Massardi (Rome, Italy Office)
Eric W. McCormick (New York City Office)
Jill Anne Myers
Sandra Stradling Nascimento (Century City Office)
Lloyd Charles Nathan (Century City Office)
David C. Nelson
Joanne B. O'Donnell
Giovanni A. Pedde (Rome, Italy Office)
Harry S. Prawer (New York City Office)
Gregory V. Redlitz (Century City Office)
Robert B. Rosen (New York City Office)
Michael E. Ross
Jonathan P. Roth (Century City Office)
Laurie S. Ruckel (New York City Office)
Stephen L. Saltzman (Century City Office)
Roni Schneider (New York City Office)
Scott I. Schneider (New York City Office)
Terri J. Seligman (New York City Office)
Riccardo Siciliani (Rome, Italy Office)
Adam F. Streisand
James D. Taylor (New York City Office)
Robert N. Treiman
Rebecca E. White (New York City Office)

(*See Next Column*)

LOEB AND LOEB, *Los Angeles—Continued*

ASSOCIATES (Continued)

Susan Z. Williams (Century City Office)
Jan Stephen Wimpfheimer (New York City Office)
Nena W. Wong
Richard S. Zuniga (Century City Office)

For full biographical listings, see the Martindale-Hubbell Law Directory

LORD, BISSELL & BROOK (AV)

300 South Grand Avenue, 90071-3200
Telephone: 213-485-1500
Telecopy: 213-485-1200
Telex: 18-1135
Chicago, Illinois Office: Suites 2600-3600 Harris Bank Building, 115 South LaSalle Street, 60603.
Telephone: 312-443-0700.
Telecopy: 312-443-0570.
Cable Address: "Lowirco".
Telex: 25-0336.
Atlanta, Georgia Office: One Atlantic Center, 1201 West Peachtree Street, N.W., Suite 3700, 30309.
Telephone: 404-870-4600.
Telecopy: 404-872-5547.
Rockford, Illinois Office: 120 West State Street, Suite 200, 61105.
Telephone: 815-963-8050.

RESIDENT PARTNERS

Charles A. Adamek
Gail M. Baev
Charles L. Crouch, III
Jeffrey S. Kravitz
Rudolf H. Schroeter
Keith G. Wileman

RESIDENT ASSOCIATES

Brenda Adams Bissett
John D. Buchanan
C. Guerry Collins
Franklin T. Dunn
Mark Scott Fall
Cynthia M. Frey
Barbara J. Klass
Jacqueline Redin Klein
LouCinda Laughlin
Jeri Rouse Looney
Darrell D. Miller
Mitchell J. Popham
Anthony F. Witteman

For full biographical listings, see the Martindale-Hubbell Law Directory

MARKS & MURASE (AV)

The Wells Fargo Center, 333 South Grand Avenue Suite 1570, 90071-1535
Telephone: 213-620-9690
Cable Address: "Wemulaw"
Telex: 673132
FAX: 213-617-9109
New York, New York Office: 399 Park Avenue.
Telephone: 212-318-7700.
Washington, D.C. Office: Suite 750, 2001 L Street, N.W.
Telephone: 202-955-4900.

PARTNERS IN LOS ANGELES, CALIFORNIA

Shu Tokuyama
Matthew E. Digby
Dane Lee Miller
Robert A. West

ASSOCIATES IN LOS ANGELES, CALIFORNIA

Margaret C. Carroll
Tanya K. Danforth (Not admitted in CA)
John J. Del Propost
Douglas H. Morseburg
Craig L. Sheldon

For full biographical listings, see the Martindale-Hubbell Law Directory

MAYER, BROWN & PLATT (AV)

350 South Grand Avenue, 25th Floor, 90071-1503
Telephone: 213-229-9500
Pitney Bowes: 213-625-0248
Telex: 188089
Cable: LEMAYLA
Chicago, Illinois Office: 190 South LaSalle Street, 60603-3441.
Telephone: (312) 782-0600. Pitney Bowes: (312) 701-7711.
Telex: 190404.
Cable: LEMAY.
Washington, D.C. Office: 2000 Pennsylvania Avenue, N.W., 20006-1882.
Telephone: (202) 463-2000. Pitney Bowes: (202) 861-0484, Pitney Bowes: (202) 861-0473.
Telex: 892603.
Cable: LEMAYDC.
New York, New York Office: 787 Seventh Avenue, Suite 2400, 10019-6018.
Telephone: (212) 554-3000. Pitney Bowes: (212) 262-1910.
Telex: 701842.
Cable: LEMAYEN.
Houston, Texas Office: 700 Louisiana Street, Suite 3600, 77002-2730.
Telephone: (713) 221-1651. Pitney Bowes: (713) 224-6410.
Telex: 775809.
Cable: LEMAYHOU.
London, England Office: 162 Queen Victoria Street, EC4V 4DB.
Telephone: 011-44-71-248-1465.
Fax: 011-44-71-329-4465.
Telex: 8811095.
Cable: LEMAYLDN.

(See Next Column)

Tokyo, Japan Office: (Kawachi Gaikokuho Jimu Bengoshi Jimusho), Urbannet Otemachi Building 13F 2-2, Otemachi 2-chome, Chiyoda-ku, Tokyo 100.
Telephone: 011-81-3-5255-9700.
Facsimile: 011-81-3-5255-9797.
Berlin, Germany Office: Spreeufer 5, 10178.
Telephone: 011-49-30-240-7930.
Facsimile: 011-49-30-240-79344.
Brussels, Belgium Office: Square de Meeûs 19/20, Bte. 4, 1040.
Telephone: 011-32-2-512-9878.
Fax: 011-32-2-511-3305.
Telex: 20768 MBPBRU B.
Mexico City, Mexico, D.F., Mexico Correspondent: Jáuregui, Navarrete, Nader y Rojas, S.C., Abogados, Paseo de la Reforma 199, Pisos, 15 16 y 17, 06500, Mexico.
Telephone: 011-525-591-16-55.
Facsimile: 011-525-535-80-62, 011-525-703-22-47.
Cable: JANANE.

PARTNERS

Teresa A. Beaudet
Louis P. Eatman (Century City Office)
L. Bruce Fischer
Barry Gassman
Steven K. Hazen
Jeffrey A. Klopf
Kenneth E. Kohler
Alec G. Nedelman
Brian E. Newhouse
William J. Reifman
M. Ellen Robb
Kevin L. Shaw
Neil M. Soltman
Robert A. Southern (Not admitted in CA)
James R. Walther
Don L. Weaver

ASSOCIATES

Jacqueline R. Brady
Christopher D. Chen
Anthony G. Graham
Richard Greta
Jerome M.F.J. Jauffret
Adam B. Kastner
Monte M. Lemann II (Not admitted in CA)
Christopher P. Murphy
Nina E. Scholtz
William O. Stein
Carl J. Thomas

For full biographical listings, see the Martindale-Hubbell Law Directory

MCCUTCHEN, DOYLE, BROWN & ENERSEN (AV)

355 South Grand Avenue Suite 4400, 90071-1560
Telephone: 213-680-6400
Facsimile: 213-680-6499
San Francisco, California Office: Three Embarcadero Center, 94111-4066.
Telephone: 415-393-2000.
Facsimile: 415-393-2286 (G I, II, III).
Telex: 340817 MACPAG SFO.
San Jose, California Office: Market Post Tower, Suite 1500, 55 South Market Street, 95113-2327.
Telephone: 408-947-8400.
Facsimile: 408-947-4750.
Telex: 910 250 2931 MACPAG SJ.
Walnut Creek, California Office: 1331 North California Boulevard, Post Office Box V, 94596-4502.
Telephone: 510-937-8000.
Facsimile: 510-975-5390.
Menlo Park, California Office: 2740 Sand Hill Road, 94025-7020.
Telephone: 415-233-4000.
Facsimile: 415-233-4086.
Washington, D.C. Office: The Evening Star Building, Suite 800, 1101 Pennsylvania Avenue, N.W., 20004-2514.
Telephone: 202-628-4900.
Facsimile: 202-628-4912.
Taipei, Taiwan Republic of China Office: International Trade Building, Tenth Floor, 333 Keelung Road, Section 1, 110.
Telephone: 886-2-723-5000.
Facsimile: 886-2-757-6070.
Affiliated Offices In: Bangkok, Thailand; Beijing, China; Shanghai, China.

MEMBERS OF FIRM

Joseph R. Austin
Colleen P. Doyle
James J. Dragna
Cherie Erickson-Harris
William H. Freedman (Resident)
Melinda L. Hayes (Resident)
Susan L. Hoffman
Michael B. Lubic
Michael L. Miller
John C. Morrissey
James Franklin Owens
Patricia L. Shanks

COUNSEL

Peter Hsiao
Douglas R. Painter
Brian J. Lamb
Robyn A. Meinhardt

ASSOCIATES

Rajesh A. Aji
William D. Araiza
Karen A. Caffee
Victoria L. Calkins
Jill F. Cooper
Douglas C. Emhoff
Debra L. Fischer
Victoria S. Kaufman
Harry H. W. Kim
Carol A. McDermott
Jean M. Mohrbacher (Resident)
John E. Opel (Resident)
Neal A. Rubin
Sandra Hughes Waddell
Kenneth J. Yood (Resident)
Margaret A. Yowell

For full biographical listings, see the Martindale-Hubbell Law Directory

Los Angeles—Continued

McDermott, Will & Emery (AV)

A Partnership including Professional Corporations
2049 Century Park East, 90067-3208
Telephone: 310-277-4110
Facsimile: 310-277-4730
Chicago, Illinois Office: 227 West Monroe Street.
Telephone: 312-372-2000.
Telex: 253565 MILAM CGO.
Facsimile: 312-984-7700.
Boston, Massachusetts Office: 75 State Street, Suite 1700.
Telephone: 617-345-5000.
Telex: 951324 MILAM BSN.
Facsimile: 617-345-5077.
Miami, Florida Office: 201 South Biscayne Boulevard.
Telephone: 305-358-3500.
Telex: 441777 LEYES.
Facsimile: 305-347-6500.
Washington, D.C. Office: 1850 K Street, N.W.
Telephone: 202-887-8000.
Telex: 253565 MILAM CGO.
Facsimile: 202-778-8087.
Newport Beach, California Office: 1301 Dove Street, Suite 500.
Telephone: 714-851-0633.
Facsimile: 714-851-9348.
New York, N.Y. Office: 1211 Avenue of the Americas.
Telephone: 212-768-5400.
Facsimile: 212-768-5444.
St. Petersburg, Russia Office: 2/2 Tchaikovsky Street, #517, 191187 St. Petersburg, Russia.
Telephone: (7) (812) 273-9831.
Facsimile: (7) (812) 273-9831.
Vilnius, Lithuania Office: Smetonos 6, 2600 Vilnius, Lithuania.
Telephone: 370 2 61-43-08.
Facsimile: 370 2 22-79-55.
Associated (Independent) Offices:
Brussels, Belgium: Uettwiller Grelon Lippens Dekeyser, 73 avenue Vandendriessche, 1150 Brussels, Belgium.
Telephone: (32) (2) 772-87-50.
Facsimile: (32) (2) 772-87-52.
London, England: Paisner & Co, Bouverie House, 154 Fleet Street, London EC4A 2DQ, England.
Telephone: (44) (71) 353-0299.
Facsimile: (44) (71) 583-8621.
Paris, France: Uettwiller Grelon Gout Canat & Associes, 68, boulevard de Courcelles, 75017 Paris, France.
Telephone: (33) (1) 48 88 89 00.
Facsimile: (33) (1) 48 88 05 50.

MEMBERS OF FIRM

Paul A. Beck *
Joel M. Bernstein
Lee L. Blackman
Timothy P. Blanchard
Peter M. Bransten
John E. Curtis, Jr.
Kathleen L. Houston Drummy
Gary B. Gertler
Anita Rae Goff
Donald A. Goldman
Eric B. Gordon
Michael I. Gottfried
David Gould *
Margaret G. Graf
Daniel Grunfeld
Mary Ellen Hogan
Douglas A. Jaques
Ivan L. Kallick *
Stephen A. Kroft
Lewis R. Landau
Jeffrey W. Lemkin
Robert P. Mallory
Douglas M. Mancino
Mark J. Mihanovic
Robyn-Marie Lyon Monteleone
Terese A. Mosher-Beluris
David L. Oberg
Denise G. Paully
Ira J. Rappeport
J. Peter Rich
Robert H. Rosenfield
Robert H. Rotstein
Cynthia Maduro Ryan
Thomas A. Ryan
Allan L. Schare
Richard K. Simon
Steven M. Spector *
Virginia Vance Sullivan

COUNSEL

Martin J. Schnitzer
Allison Sher Arkin (Not admitted in CA)

Jane E. Boubelik
Bryan T. Castorima
David R. Gabor
Laurence L. Gottlieb
Randall Kaplan
David L. Klatsky
Nicole Lance
Rodger M. Landau
Daniel B. Lantry
J. Michael Lehmann
Jeffrey K. Sanders
Theodore R. Schneck
Steven Sevrin

*Denotes a lawyer employed by a Professional Corporation which is a member of the Firm

For full biographical listings, see the Martindale-Hubbell Law Directory

Mendes & Mount (AV)

Citicorp Plaza, 725 South Figueroa Street Nineteenth Floor, 90017
Telephone: 213-955-7700
Telecopy: 213-955-7725
Telex: 6831520
Cable Address: "MNDMT"
New York, N.Y. Office: 750 Seventh Avenue.
Telephone: 212-261-8000.
Fax: 212-261-8750.
Newark, New Jersey Office: 1 Newark Center.
Telephone: 201-639-7300.
Fax: 201-639-7350.

MEMBERS OF FIRM

William Blanc Mendes (1891-1957)
Russell Theodore Mount (1881-1962)
James M. FitzSimons
Donald K. Fitzpatrick
James W. Hunt

Charles G. Carluccio, III
Mark S. Facer
Richard R. Nelson
Robert B. Schultz

ASSOCIATES

Garth W. Aubert
John Francis Bazan
Richard D. Brisacher
Joan E. Cochran
Alan H. Collier
Thomas J. Edson
Lydia A. Hervatin
Mark R. Irvine
Abel M. Lezcano
Shalem A. Massey
Suzanne Naatz McNulty
Patrick T. Michael
Dennis Morris
Erin K. Nugent
Michael S. Patterson
Margaret A. Reetz
David A. Robinson
Estie R. Stoll
Ty S. Vanderford

For full biographical listings, see the Martindale-Hubbell Law Directory

Meserve, Mumper & Hughes (AV)

A Partnership including a Professional Corporation
555 South Flower Street, 18th Floor, 90071-2319
Telephone: 213-620-0300
Telecopier: 213-625-1930
Irvine, California Office: 18500 Von Karman Avenue, Suite 600.
Telephone: 714-474-8995.
Telecopier: 714-975-1065.
San Diego, California Office: 701 "B" Street, Suite 2250.
Telephone: 619-237-0500.
Telecopier: 619-237-0073.

MEMBERS OF FIRM

Edwin A. Meserve (1863-1955)
Shirley E. Meserve (1889-1959)
Hewlings Mumper (1889-1968)
Clifford E. Hughes (1894-1981)
Dennett F. Kouri
Bernard A. Leckie (Resident, Irvine Office)
E. Avery Crary (Resident, Irvine Office)
L. Allan Songstad, Jr. (Resident, Irvine Office)
Linda M. Lawson
Joan E. Aarestad
Andrew K. Ulich (Resident, Irvine Office)
Douglas P. Smith (Resident, Irvine Office)
William E. von Behren
Timothy L. Randall (Resident, Irvine Office)
Thomas J. Bois, II, (P.C.) (Resident, Irvine Office)
David R. Eichten (San Diego and Irvine Offices)
Roger A. Grad (Resident, Irvine Office)
Timothy A. Gravitt

OF COUNSEL

J. Robert Meserve (Resident, Irvine Office)
Thomas E. Kellett
Julian Scheiner

ASSOCIATES

John F. Damiani (Resident, Irvine Office)
Patricia A. Ellis
Brian K. Mazen
Robert F. Nunes, Jr.
Geoffrey T. Tong
William D. Coffee (Resident, Irvine Office)
Andrew V. Leitch (Resident, Irvine Office)
Janet E. Humphrey (Resident, Irvine Office)
Joseph B. McGinley (Resident, Irvine Office)
Amy Toboco Dibb (Resident, Irvine Office)
Stephanie L. Chilton
James R. Parke (Resident, Irvine Office)
Jennifer M. Whelan (Resident, Irvine Office)
Matthew T. Currie
Christopher M. Stevens
Bret Graham
Carol B. Burney
Jeffrey Dill (Resident, Irvine Office)
Kendra S. Meinert
Jerri A. Fullmer (Resident, Irvine Office)
Christopher J. Menjou (Resident, Irvine Office)
Andrew L. Satenberg

For full biographical listings, see the Martindale-Hubbell Law Directory

Los Angeles—Continued

MILBANK, TWEED, HADLEY & McCLOY (AV)

601 South Figueroa Street, 90017
Telephone: 213-892-4000
Fax: 213-629-5063
Telex: 678754 ABA/net: Milbank LA
New York, New York Office: 1 Chase Manhattan Plaza, 10005.
Telephone: 212-530-5000.
Cable Address: "Miltweed NYK" ITT: 422962; 423893.
Fax: 212- 530-5219. ABA/net: Milbank NY; MCI Mail: Milbank Tweed.
Midtown Office: 50 Rockefeller Plaza, 10020.
Telephone: 212-530-5800.
Fax: 212-530-0158.
Washington, D.C. Office: International Square Building, Suite 1100, 1825 Eye Street, N.W., 20006.
Telephone: 202-835-7500.
Cable Address: "Miltweed Wsh". ITT 440667.
Fax: 202-835-7586. ABA/net: Milbank DC.
Tokyo, Japan Office: Nippon Press Center Building, 2-1, Uchisaiwai-cho 2-chome, Chiyoda-ku, Tokyo 100.
Telephone: 011-81-3-3504-1050.
Fax: 011-81-3-3595-2790, 011-81-3-3502-5192.
London, England Office: Ropemaker Place, 25 Ropemaker Street, EC2Y 9AS.
Telephone: 011-44-171-374-0423.
Cable Address: "Miltuk G."
Fax: 011-44-171-374-0912.
Hong Kong Office: 3007 Alexandra House, 16 Charter Road.
Telephone: 011-852-2526-5281.
Fax: 011-852-2840-0792, 011-8522-845-9046. ABA/net: Milbank HK.
Singapore Office: 14-02 Caltex House, 30 Raffles Place, 0104.
Telephone: 011-65-534-1700.
Fax: 011-65-534-2733. ABA/net: EDNANG.
Moscow, Russia Office: 24/27 Sadovaya-Samotyochnya, Moscow, 103051.
Telephone: 011-7-501-258-5015.
Fax: 011-7-501-258-5014.
Jakarta, Indonesia Correspondent Office: Makarim & Taira S., 17th Floor, Summitmas Tower, Jl, Jend. Sudirman 61, Jakarta.
Telephone: 011-62-21252-1272 or 2460.
Fax: 011-62-21-252-2750 or 2751.

RESIDENT PARTNERS

Paul S. Aronzon
Edwin F. Feo
David C. L. Frauman
Cynthia Futter
C. Stephen Howard
David A. Lamb
Ted Obrzut
Eric H. Schunk
Peter P. Wallace

RESIDENT ASSOCIATES

Dino Barajas
Kenneth J. Baronsky
Devan D. Beck
J. Keith Biancamano
Michael Dayen
Jose M. Deetjan
Michael T. Fisher
Belinda Maughan Foxworth
R. Lee Garner III
David A. Godfrey
John S. Hodgkins
C. Thomas Hopkins
Elizabeth Hunt
Timothy M. Ison
David A. Jones
Valerie Longmire
Allan T. Marks
Sharon L. Meymarian
Fred Neufeld
John J. O'Connor
Eric R. Reimer
Eileen Driscoll Rubens
Joseph Schohl
Scot Tucker
Anne Wells
Susan P. Widule
John D. Wilmore
Karen B. Wong
Desiree Woo
Kym R. Wulfe

For full biographical listings, see the Martindale-Hubbell Law Directory

MITCHELL, SILBERBERG & KNUPP (AV)

A Partnership of Professional Corporations
11377 West Olympic Boulevard, 90064
Telephone: 310-312-2000
Cable Address: "Silmitch"
Telex: 69-1347
Telecopier: 310-312-3200

MEMBERS OF FIRM

Shepard Mitchell (1908-1979)
M. B. Silberberg (1908-1965)
Guy Knupp (1907-1970)
Arthur Groman (A Professional Corporation)
Chester I. Lappen (A Professional Corporation)
Harold Friedman (A Professional Corporation)
Allan E. Biblin (A Professional Corporation)
Edward M. Medvene (A Professional Corporation)
Lessing E. Gold (A Professional Corporation)
Russell J. Frackman (A Professional Corporation)
Thomas P. Lambert (A Professional Corporation)
Eugene H. Veenhuis (A Professional Corporation)
Philip Davis (A Professional Corporation)
Roy L. Shults (A Professional Corporation)
Steven M. Schneider (A Professional Corporation)
Richard R. Mainland (A Professional Corporation)
Marvin Leon (A Professional Corporation)
Patricia H. Benson (A Professional Corporation)

(See Next Column)

MEMBERS OF FIRM (Continued)

Arthur Fine (A Professional Corporation)
Gary O. Concoff (A Professional Corporation)
Hayward J. Kaiser (A Professional Corporation)
David S. Gubman (A Professional Corporation)
Deborah P. Koeffler (A Professional Corporation)
John M. Kuechle (A Professional Corporation)
William L. Cole (A Professional Corporation)
Richard S. Hessenius (A Professional Corporation)
Stephen D. Marks (A Professional Corporation)
Robert N. Block (A Professional Corporation)
Joseph Ciasulli (A Professional Corporation)
Kenneth H. Levin (A Professional Corporation)
Frida Popik Glucoft (A Professional Corporation)
Jean Pierre Nogues (A Professional Corporation)
Michael I. Adler (A Professional Corporation)
David Wheeler Newman (A Professional Corporation)
Roger Sherman (A Professional Corporation)
Seymour M. Bricker (A Professional Corporation)
Alan L. Pepper (A Professional Corporation)
John E. Hatherley (A Professional Corporation)
Lawrence A. Ginsberg (A Professional Corporation)
Daniel M. Petrocelli (A Professional Corporation)
Mark A. Wasserman (A Professional Corporation)
Allen J. Gross (A Professional Corporation)
Anthony A. Adler (A Professional Corporation)
Elia Weinbach (A Professional Corporation)
Allan B. Cutrow (A Professional Corporation)
Scott T. Brisbin (A Professional Corporation)
Laura A. Loftin (A Professional Corporation)
Peter B. Gelblum (A Professional Corporation)
David P. Schack (A Professional Corporation)
Beatrice H. Nemlaha (A Professional Corporation)
Paul R. Glassman (A Professional Corporation)
Lawrence A. Michaels (A Professional Corporation)
Bruce A. Friedman (A Professional Corporation)
Ronald A. DiNicola (A Professional Corporation)
Andrew E. Katz (A Professional Corporation)
James O. Thoma (A Professional Corporation)
Kevin Gaut (A Professional Corporation)
Jill H. Berliner (A Professional Corporation)
Danna L. Cook (A Professional Corporation)
Larry C. Drapkin (A Professional Corporation)
David Herskovitz (A Professional Corporation)
Elliot L. Shelton (A Professional Corporation)
Bernard Donnenfeld (A Professional Corporation)
Harvey W. Geller (A Professional Corporation)
Ann R. Loeb (A Professional Corporation)
Douglas R. Stone (A Professional Corporation)
Donald W. Steele (A Professional Corporation)
Lucia E. Coyoca (A Professional Corporation)

OF COUNSEL

Edward Rubin (A Professional Corporation)
Harold A. Lipton (A Professional Corporation)
Stanley I. Arenberg (A Professional Corporation)
Marvin A. Demoff (A Professional Corporation)
Jeffrey A. Dankworth (A Professional Corporation)
Christine S. Cuddy
Kenneth S. Meyers
David Comsky (A Professional Corporation)
Douglas W. Bordewieck
Douglas R. Ring (A Professional Corporation)
Jeffrey B. Wheeler
William M. Kaplan (A Professional Corporation)

ASSOCIATES

Mary E. Sullivan
Robert C. Welsh
David A. Steinberg
Richard E. Ackerknecht
Anthony J. Amendola
J. Eugene Salomon, Jr.
Christopher B. Leonard
John L. Segal
George M. Borkowski
Thomas M. Hines
Susan H. Hilderley
Scott H. Bauman
Amy L. Pucker
Nicholas Strozza
Jonathan Sears
Yvette Molinaro
Steven M. Rich
Richard B. Sheldon, Jr.
Yakub Hazzard
Mark L. Kovinsky
Marta I. Stanton
Mary M. Courtney
Jeffrey H. Frankel
Jeffrey D. Goldman
David A. Leventhal
Reynolds T. Cafferata
Ann S. Lee
Brenda S. Barton
Brian S. Arbetter
Joshua L. Rosen
Jerold B. Neuman
A. Catherine Norian
Ignacio J. Lazo
Daniel A. Lev
Sonia Ransom
Donald H. Yee
Patricia L. Laucella
Joel McKuin
Michelle L. Abend
Jeffrey L. Richardson
Matt J. Railo
Adam Levin
Robert E. Allen
Tammy C. Cain
Gary H. Green, II
David B. Miercort
Michael Tsao
Richard L. Motzkin

Reference: First Interstate Bank of California (Headquarters, Los Angeles, California).

For full biographical listings, see the Martindale-Hubbell Law Directory

Los Angeles—Continued

MONTELEONE & MCCRORY (AV)

A Partnership including Professional Corporations
10 Universal City Plaza, Suite 2500 (Universal City), 91608-7806
Telephone: 818-509-6100
FAX: 818-509-6148
Santa Ana, California Office: Suite 750, 1551 North Tustin Avenue.
Telephone: 714-565-3170.
Fax: 714-565-3184.

MEMBERS OF FIRM

Stephen Monteleone (1886-1962)
G. Robert Hale (P.C.)
Patrick J. Duffy, III (P.C.)
Michael F. Minchella (P.C.)
Thomas P. McGuire (P.C.)
William J. Ingalsbe (P.C.) (Resident, Santa Ana Office)
Philip C. Putnam (P.C.)
Joseph A. Miller (P.C.)
Diana M. Dron (Resident, Santa Ana Office)
Donald J. Shields
Douglas Yokomizo

ASSOCIATES

David C. Romyn
Barry J. Jensen (Resident, Santa Ana Office)
W. Jeffrey Burch
Gregory John Dukellis

OF COUNSEL

Darrell P. McCrory (P.C.)
Stanton P. Belland (P.C.)

For full biographical listings, see the Martindale-Hubbell Law Directory

MUNGER, TOLLES & OLSON (AV)

A Law Partnership including Professional Corporations
355 South Grand Avenue 35th Floor, 90071
Telephone: 213-683-9100
Cable Address: "Muntoll"
Telex: 677574
Telecopier: 213-687-3702
San Francisco, California Office: 33 New Montgomery Street, Suite 1900.
Telephone: 415-512-4000.
FAX: 415-512-4077.

MEMBERS OF FIRM

Richard D. Esbenshade (A Professional Corporation)
Frederick B. Warder, Jr. (1932-1972)
Peter R. Taft (A Professional Corporation)
Robert K. Johnson (A Professional Corporation)
Alan V. Friedman (A Professional Corporation)
Ronald L. Olson (A Professional Corporation)
Dennis E. Kinnaird (A Professional Corporation)
Dennis C. Brown (A Professional Corporation)
Jeffrey I. Weinberger
Melvyn H. Wald (1947-1992)
Edwin V. Woodsome, Jr., (A Professional Corporation)
Allen M. Katz
Robert L. Adler
Cary B. Lerman
William L. Cathey
Charles D. Siegal
Ronald K. Meyer
Gregory P. Stone
Vilma S. Martinez
Lucy T. Eisenberg
Brad D. Brian
Bradley S. Phillips
George M. Garvey
Rita J. Miller
D. Barclay Edmundson
William D. Temko
Steven L. Guise (A Professional Corporation)
Robert B. Knauss
R. Gregory Morgan
Stephen M. Kristovich
Carolyn B. Kuhl
John W. Spiegel
Terry E. Sanchez
Steven M. Perry
Ruth E. Fisher
Edwin G. Schuck, Jr.
Mark B. Helm
Joseph D. Lee
Michael R. Doyen
Michael E. Soloff
Gregory D. Phillips
John B. Frank
Lawrence C. Barth
Kathleen M. McDowell
Glenn D. Pomerantz
Thomas B. Walper
Ronald C. Hausmann (Resident, San Francisco Office)
Patrick J. Cafferty, Jr. (Resident, San Francisco Office)
Jay Masa Fujitani
O'Malley M. Miller
Sandra A. Seville-Jones
Mark H. Epstein
Henry Weissmann
Kevin S. Allred
Marc A. Becker
Cynthia L. Burch
Bart H. Williams
Judith T. Kitano
Kristin A. Linsley
Marc T. G. Dworsky

ASSOCIATES

Eric A. Webber
Marsha Hymanson
Garth T. Vincent
Robin N. Rogers
Stuart N. Senator
Ted Dane
Elizabeth Abrams Sellung
Ian L. Kramer
Eva Orlebeke Caldera
Stephen D. Rose
Monica Wahl Shaffer
Leonard P. Leichnitz
Debra K. Judy (Resident, San Francisco Office)
Dominic T. Holzhaus
Amalie Moses Reichblum
Steven J. Cowan
Andrew J. Thomas
Jeffrey L. Bleich (Resident, San Francisco Office)
Robert L. DellAngelo
Gregory J. Weingart
John Griffith Davies, Jr.
Martin D. Bern (Resident, San Francisco Office)
Luis Li

(See Next Column)

ASSOCIATES (Continued)

Margaret Elizabeth Deane (Resident, San Francisco Office)
Deanne L. Burnett
Susan R. Szabo
Inez D. Hope
Thomas A. Waldman
Kristin S. Escalante
Manuel A. Abascal
Jonathan E. Altman
Ayaz R. Shaikh
Gregg W. Kettles
Steven B. Weisburd
Carla N. Jones
Mary Ann Lyman
Ilana B. Rubenstein
Jeffrey A. Heintz

Reference: The Bank of California.

For full biographical listings, see the Martindale-Hubbell Law Directory

MUSICK, PEELER & GARRETT (AV)

Suite 2000, One Wilshire Boulevard, 90017-3321
Telephone: 213-629-7600
Cable Address: "Peelgar"
Facsimile: 213-624-1376
San Diego, California Office: 1900 Home Savings Tower, 225 Broadway.
Telephone: 619-231-2500.
Facsimile: 619-231-1234.
San Francisco, California Office: Suite 1300, Steuart Street Tower, One Market Plaza.
Telephone: 415-281-2000.
Facsimile: 415-281-2010.
Sacramento, California Office: Suite 100, 1121 L Street.
Telephone: 916-442-1200.
Facsimile: 916-442-8644.
Fresno, California Office: 6041 North First Street.
Telephone: 209-228-1000.
Facsimile: 209-447-4670.

MEMBERS OF FIRM

Elvon Musick (1890-1968)
Joseph D. Peeler (1895-1991)
Leroy A. Garrett (1906-1963)
James E. Ludlam
Alan R. Perry (Resident at San Diego Office)
Charles F. Forbes
J. Patrick Whaley
Willie R. Barnes
Leonard E. Castro
C. Donald McBride (Resident at San Francisco Office)
Edward A. Landry
John R. Browning
R. Joseph De Briyn
William J. Bird
Lawrence E. Stickney
Brian J. Seery
James B. Bertero (Resident at San Diego Office)
William McD. Miller, III
J. Robert Liset
Robert Y. Nagata
Robert D. Girard
Janet L. Wright (Resident at Fresno Office)
James M. Hassan
Stuart W. Rudnick
David C. Wright
M. Steven Lipton (Resident at San Francisco Office)
Gary F. Overstreet
Wayne B. Littlefield
Robert M. Stone
Steven D. Weinstein
Richard J. Simmons
James W. Miller
Michael W. Monk
Stephen A. Hansen (Resident at Fresno Office)
Richard S. Conn
Gerald M. Hinkley (Resident at San Francisco Office)
Robert M. Zeller
Marilyn B. O'Toole
Robert L. Schuchard
David L. Volk
Jon C. Cederberg
Mark H. Van Brussel (Resident at Sacramento Office)
Gerard Smolin, Jr. (Resident at San Diego Office)
Mark J. Grushkin
William L. Abalona (Resident at Sacramento Office)
Susan J. Hazard
Stephen D. Holz
Susan J. Field
Geoffrey C. Brown
Charles E. Slyngstad
Jeffrey A. Tidus
Linda S. Husar
Mary Anne Silvestri
Harry W. R. Chamberlain, II
Larry C. Hart
William R. Warhurst (Resident at San Francisco Office)
Thomas E. Hill
W. Clark Stanton (Resident at San Francisco Office)
Dennis S. Diaz
Donald P. Asperger (Resident at Fresno Office)
Martin L. Fineman (Resident at San Francisco Office)
Lynn A. O'Leary
Eric L. Troff
James B. Betts (Resident at Fresno Office)
Paul D. Hesse
Gary L. Wollberg (Resident at San Diego Office)
Douglas R. Hart
Anne Yeager Higgins
David A. Tartaglio
Alan J. Zuckerman (Resident at San Diego Office)
Cheryl L. Schreck
Craig M. Hughes (Resident at San Francisco Office)
John L. Hunter
Mary Catherine M. Bohen
David M. Lester
Philip Ewen
Mary Beth Sipos
Thomas T. Kawakami

OF COUNSEL

Mark Kiguchi
Louis S. Weller (Resident at San Francisco Office)
Orene Levenson Kearn (Resident at San Francisco Office)
John F. Feldsted

(See Next Column)

MUSICK, PEELER & GARRETT, *Los Angeles—Continued*

ASSOCIATES

Juan A. Torres
Michael J. Hickman (Resident at San Diego Office)
James E. Durkee (Resident at Fresno Office)
William A. Bossen
Caroline G. Smith (Resident at San Francisco Office)
Steven J. Elie
David A. Radovich
Robert G. Warshaw
Robert K. Yasui
Kelly L. Hensley
Lawrence A. Tabb
Gregory M. Emi
Samuel H. Stein
Marie A. LaSala (Resident at San Diego Office)
Araceli K. Cole
Jane Chotard Wheeler
William Reece Hirsch (Resident at Fresno Office)
Greg S. Labate
Lisa B. Lai (Resident at San Francisco Office)
Cindi Aronberg
A. Natasha Cortina (Resident at San Diego Office)
Michael R. Goldstein
Jacqueline H. Nguyen
Jane H. Root
S. Ellen D'Arcangelo
John T. Gilbertson
Bryan M. Bourbin
Son Young Kahng
Jeffrey S. Silvyn
Carole M. Wertheim (Resident at San Diego Office)
S. Andrew Pharies
Michelle D. Astabie (Resident at San Francisco Office)
James T. Cahalan (Resident at Sacramento Office)
Dennis M. P. Ehling
Mara T. McGeagh
Jennifer A. Woo
Robin L. Hayward
Michael G. Morgan

For full biographical listings, see the Martindale-Hubbell Law Directory

O'MELVENY & MYERS (AV)

400 South Hope Street, 90071-2899
Telephone: 213-669-6000
Cable Address: "Moms"
Facsimile: 213-669-6407
Century City, California Office: 1999 Avenue of the Stars, 7th Floor, 90067-6035.
Telephone: 310-553-6700.
Facsimile: 310-246-6779.
Newport Beach, California Office: 610 Newport Center Drive, Suite 1700, 92660.
Telephone: 714-760-9600.
Cable Address: "Moms".
Facsimile: 714-669-6994.
San Francisco, California Office: Embarcadero Center West Tower, 275 Battery Street, Suite 2600, 94111.
Telephone: 415-984-8700.
Facsimile: 415-984-8701.
New York, N.Y. Office: Citicorp Center, 153 East 53rd Street, 54th Floor, 10022-4611.
Telephone: 212-326-2000.
Facsimile: 212-326-2061.
Washington, D.C. Office: 555 13th Street, N.W., Suite 500 West, 20004-1109.
Telephone: 202-383-5300.
Cable Address: "Moms".
Facsimile: 202-383-5414.
Newark, New Jersey Office: One Gateway Center, 7th Floor, 07102.
Telephone: 201-639-8600.
Facsimile: 201-639-8630.
London, England Office: 10 Finsbury Square, London, EC2A 1LA.
Telephone: 011-44-171-256 8451.
Facsimile: 011-44-171-638-8205.
Tokyo, Japan Office: Sanbancho KB-6 Building, 6 Sanbancho, Chiyoda-ku, Tokyo 102, Japan.
Telephone: 011-81-3-3239-2800.
Facsimile: 011-81-3-3239-2432.
Hong Kong Office: 1104 Lippo Tower, Lippo Centre, 89 Queensway, Central Hong Kong.
Telephone: 011-852-523-8266.
Facsimile: 011-852-522-1760.

MEMBERS OF FIRM

Douglas W. Abendroth (Newport Beach Office)
William G. Adams (Newport Beach Office)
Wallace M. Allan
Russell G. Allen (Newport Beach Office)
Kermit W. Almstedt (Not admitted in CA; Washington, D.C. Office)
John L. Altieri, Jr. (New York, N.Y. Office)
D. Stephen Antion
Jean M. Arnwine
Seth Aronson
James R. Asperger
Richard E. Ayres (Not admitted in CA; Washington, D.C. Office)
George M. Bartlett
Thomas W. Baxter
John H. Beisner (Washington, D.C. Office)
Charles W. Bender
Ben E. Benjamin (Washington, D.C. Office)
Kendall R. Bishop (Century City Office)
Leah Margaret Bishop (Century City Office)
Robert D. Blashek, III (Century City Office)
Donald T. Bliss, Jr. (Not admitted in CA; Washington, D.C. Office)
Richard A. Boehmer
Daniel H. Bookin (San Francisco Office)
Greyson Lee Bryan

(See Next Column)

MEMBERS OF FIRM (Continued)

Francis J. Burgweger, Jr. (New York, N.Y. Office)
Joseph A. Calabrese (Century City Office)
Jerry W. Carlton (Newport Beach Office)
David W. Cartwright (Century City Office)
Dale M. Cendali (Not admitted in CA; New York, N.Y. Office)
Theresa A. Cerezola (Not admitted in CA; New York, N.Y. Office)
Howard Chao (Hong Kong Office)
Martin S. Checov (San Francisco Office)
Denise M. Clolery (Century City Office)
Alan M. Cohen (Not admitted in CA; New York, N.Y. Office)
James W. Colbert, III
William T. Coleman, Jr. (Not admitted in CA; Washington, D.C. Office)
William N. Cooney
Bertrand M. Cooper
Stephen A. Cowan (San Francisco Office)
Arthur B. Culvahouse, Jr. (Washington, D.C. Office)
Michael A. Curley (New York, N.Y. Office)
Brian S. Currey
Ralph W. Dau
John F. Daum (Washington, D.C. Office)
F. Amanda DeBusk (Not admitted in CA; Washington, D.C. Office)
James H. De Meules
Charles P. Diamond (Century City Office)
Robert S. Draper
Scott H. Dunham
Robert N. Eccles (Not admitted in CA; Washington, D.C. Office)
Steven L. Edwards (Newport Beach Office)
Michael J. Fairclough
Richard N. Fisher
Cliff H. Fonstein (New York, N.Y. Office)
Andrew J. Frackman (Not admitted in CA; New York, N.Y. Office)
Patricia Frobes (Newport Beach and Los Angeles Offices)
Marc H. Gamsin (Century City Office)
Travis C. Gibbs
Martin Glenn (New York, N.Y. Office)
Richard B. Goetz
Gregory W. Goff
David E. Gordon
Kent V. Graham (Century City Office)
Pamela C. Gray
Linda Boyd Griffey
Steven L. Grossman (New York, N.Y. Office)
Catherine Burcham Hagen (Newport Beach Office)
Christopher D. Hall (Not admitted in CA; London, England Office)
L. Jane Hamblen (Not admitted in CA; New York, N.Y. Office)
Theodore C. Hamilton (Newport Beach Office)
Marc Hanrahan (New York, N.Y. Office)
Stephen J. Harburg (Not admitted in CA; Washington, D.C. Office)
John D. Hardy, Jr.
Adam C. Harris (Not admitted in CA; New York, N. Y. Office)
Peter T. Healy (San Francisco Office)
Howard M. Heitner
Joseph J. Herron (Newport Beach Office)
Linda Shannon Heumann (Newport Beach Office)
Jack B. Hicks III
Edward W. Hieronymus
B. Boyd Hight
Bruce A. Hiler (Washington, D.C. Office)
Michael S. Hobel (Century City Office)
Gary N. Horlick (Not admitted in CA; Washington, D.C. Office)
Robert S. Insolia (Not admitted in CA; New York, N.Y. Office)
Philip D. Irwin
Wayne Jacobsen (Newport Beach Office)
Tom A. Jerman
Evan M. Jones
Richard M. Jones
Phillip R. Kaplan (Newport Beach Office)
Holly E. Kendig
David E. Killough
Joseph K. Kim
Louis B. Kimmelman (Not admitted in CA; New York, N.Y. Office)
James H. Kinney (Century City Office)
Matthew T. Kirby
F. Curt Kirschner, Jr. (San Francisco Office)
Paul R. Koepff (New York, N.Y. Office)
Jeffrey I. Kohn (Not admitted in CA; New York, N.Y. Office)
C. Douglas Kranwinkle (New York, N.Y. Office)
David A. Krinsky (Newport Beach Office)
Gordon E. Krischer
Perry A. Lerner (New York, N.Y. Office)
C. James Levin
Douglas P. Ley (San Francisco Office)
Charles C. Lifland
Ben H. Logan, III
Warren R. Loui (Century City Office)
Patrick Lynch
Joseph M. Malkin (San Francisco Office)
Lowell C. Martindale, Jr. (Newport Beach Office)
Marie L. Martineau
Cheryl White Mason
Jill H. Matichak (San Francisco Office)
Edward J. McAniff (San Francisco Office)
Thomas Michael McCoy
Kathleen G. McGuinness
Frederick B. McLane
Julie A. McMillan (San Francisco Office)
Paul G. McNamara
Mitchell B. Menzer
Scott A. Meyerhoff (Newport Beach Office)
Paul E. Mosley (Newport Beach Office)
F. Thomas Muller, Jr.
Christopher C. Murray (Century City Office)
Michael Newman
Charles F. Niemeth (Century City and New York, N.Y. Offices)
John G. Niles

(See Next Column)

O'MELVENY & MYERS—*Continued*

MEMBERS OF FIRM (Continued)

Jeffery L. Norton (New York, N.Y. Office)
Christine M. Olsen
Gregg Oppenheimer
M. Randall Oppenheimer (Century City Office)
Kenneth R. O'Rourke
Peter V. Pantaleo (Not admitted in CA; New York, N.Y. Office)
Richard G. Parker (Washington, D.C. Office)
Stephen P. Pepe
Donald V. Petroni (Century City Office)
David G. Pommerening (Not admitted in CA; Washington, D. C. Office)
John B. Power
Laurence G. Preble (New York, N.Y. Office)
Alan Rader (Century City Office)
Gilbert T. Ray
Charles C. Read
Frederick A. Richman (Century City Office)
George A. Riley (San Francisco Office)
Robert A. Rizzi (Newport Beach Office)
Jeffrey J. Rosen (Not admitted in CA; Washington, D.C. Office)
Richard R. Ross (Century City Office)
Frank L. Rugani (Newport Beach Office)
Mark A. Samuels
Kathryn A. Sanders
William H. Satchell (Washington, D.C. Office)
Stephen Scharf (Century City Office)
Carl R. Schenker, Jr. (Washington, D.C. Office)
Patricia Ann Schmiege (San Francisco Office)
Robert M. Schwartz (Century City Office)
James V. Selna (Newport Beach Office)
Ralph J. Shapira
Robert A. Siegel
Gary J. Singer (Newport Beach Office)
Linda Jane Smith
Steven L. Smith (San Francisco Office)
Masood Sohaili
John W. Stamper
Stephen J. Stern
Victoria Dagy Stratman
Drake S. Tempest (Not admitted in CA; New York, N.Y. Office)
Gregory B. Thorpe
Henry C. Thumann
Stuart P. Tobisman (Century City Office)
Ko-Yung Tung (Not admitted in CA; New York, N.Y. Office)
James R. Ukropina
Debra A. Valentine (Not admitted in CA; Washington, D.C. Office)
Robert C. Vanderet
William W. Vaughn
Framroze M. Virjee
Ulrich Wagner (New York, N.Y. Office)
Diana L. Walker
Kim McLane Wardlaw
Richard C. Warmer (San Francisco Office)
David D. Watts
David I. Weil (Century City Office)
Dean M. Weiner
Jacqueline A. Weiss (Not admitted in CA; New York, N.Y. Office)
John E. Welch (Washington, D.C. Office)
Robert J. White
Robert E. Willett
Jonathan P. Williams
Michael A. Wisnev
Charles C. Wolf
Thomas E. Wolfe (Newport Beach Office)
W. Mark Wood
Michael G. Yoder (Newport Beach Office)
Joel B. Zweibel (Not admitted in CA; New York, N. Y. Office)

OF COUNSEL

Charles G. Bakaly, Jr.
Barton Beek (Newport Beach Office)
R. Bradbury Clark
Everett B. Clary
Katherine L. Hensley
Donn B. Miller
Owen Olpin
John H. Roney
Lawrence J. Sheehan (Century City Office)
Donald R. Spuehler
Clyde E. Tritt

SPECIAL COUNSEL

Peter B. Ackerman
Brian C. Anderson (Washington, D.C. Office)
Dale M. Araki (Tokyo, Japan Office)
Madonna Shannon Baumeister
David T. Beddow (Not admitted in CA; Washington, D.C. Office)
Ira M. Belsky (New York, N.Y. Office)
Rosemary B. Boller (New York, N.Y. Office)
Paul C. Borden
Joseph E. Boury (Newark, N.J. Office)
Brian David Boyle (Washington, D.C. Office)
Thomas K. Braun
Richard W. Buckner
Cormac J. Carney (Newport Beach Office)
Thomas G. Carruthers (New York, N.Y. Office)
Joseph L. Coleman (Newport Beach Office)
Fiona M. Connell (Hong Kong Office)
Christopher M. Crain
John A. Crose, Jr.
Daniel A. Deshon, IV (San Francisco Office)
Douglas E. Dexter (San Francisco Office)
Karen K. Dreyfus (Newport Beach Office)
Suzanne F. Duff
David G. Estes (San Francisco Office)
M. Manuel Fishman (San Francisco Office)
Charles W. Fournier (New York, N.Y. Office)
Daniel M. Freedman (Not admitted in CA; New York, N.Y. Office)
Kathleen A. Gallagher (New York, N.Y. Office)
H. Douglas Galt
David R. Garcia
Joseph G. Giannola (Not admitted in CA; New York, N.Y. Office)
Lawrence M. Goldman

(See Next Column)

SPECIAL COUNSEL (Continued)

Robert A. Grauman (Not admitted in CA; New York, N.Y. Office)
Karen R. Growdon
Robert D. Haymer (Century City Office)
David A. Hollander
Daniel M. Jochnowitz (New York, N.Y. Office)
Kenneth E. Johnson
Abigail A. Jones
Christopher N. Kandel (London, England Office)
Peter C. Kelley (Century City Office)
Michael S. Lebovitz (Century City Office)
Frances Elizabeth Lossing
Michael G. McGuinness
John Charles Maddux (San Francisco Office)
Marcy Jo Mandel
Daniel M. Mansueto
Dean E. Miller
Mary Molyneux (London, England Office)
Mia E. Montpas
Gregory R. Oxford
Diane E. Pritchard
Thomas H. Reilly (Newport Beach Office)
Stephanie I. Splane (New York, N.Y. Office)
Jane Taylor (Not admitted in CA; New York, N.Y. Office)
Glenn W. Trost
Dana K. Welch (San Francisco Office)
Pamela Lynne Westhoff
Alfred M. Wurglitz (Washington, D.C. Office)

ASSOCIATES

Susan E. Akens (Century City Office)
Gregory N. Albright (Century City Office)
Paul M. Alfieri (New York, N.Y. Office)
Iman Anabtawi (Century City Office)
Mary Amilea Anderson (Washington, D.C. Office)
James D. Arbogast (New York, N.Y. Office)
Reed N. Archambault (Newport Beach Office)
Linda A. Bagley (San Francisco Office)
Kevin Ray Baker (Newport Beach Office)
W. Kirk Baker (New York, N.Y. Office)
Patrick J. Bannon (San Francisco Office)
Alec M. Barinholtz
Bernard C. Barmann, Jr.
Steven Basileo
Evelyn Becker
Kathleen L. Beiermeister (Newark, N.J. Office)
Diane Wasil Biagianti (Newport Beach Office)
Robert H. Bienstock (Not admitted in CA; New York, N.Y. Office)
Stanley Blumenfeld
Corey A. Boock
Sharon A. Borak (Century City Office)
Jennifer L. Borow (Century City Office)
Michael G. Bosko (Newport Beach Office)
John M. Bowers
Debra L. Boyd
Brandon F.R. Bradkin
Mark L. Bradshaw (San Francisco Office)
Laura C. Bremer (San Francisco Office)
Renée Turkell Brook
Avery R. Brown
Deborah J. Brown (Century City Office)
William R. Burford (San Francisco Office)
Nadia St. George Burgard (New York, N.Y. Office)
C. Bradley Call
John R. Call
Bruce L. Campbell (Newport Beach Office)
Viola I. Canales (San Francisco Office)
K. Leigh Chapman
Peter C. Choharis (Washington, D.C. Office)
Apalla U. Chopra
Cynthia Jeann Christian
Carla J. Christofferson (Century City Office)
Peggy Ann Clarke (Not admitted in CA; Washington, D.C. Office)
Christine E. Coleman (Century City Office)
Steven M. Cooper
Craig A. Corman (Century City Office)
Regina Covitt (Century City Office)
Karen D. Craig (Newport Beach Office)
Ira A. Daves, III
Teresa E. Dawson (Not admitted in CA; Washington, D.C. Office)
Elizabeth A. Delaney (Washington, D.C. Office)
George C. Demos (Newport Beach Office)
Ralph P. DeSanto (New York, N.Y. Office)
Elena Bocca Dietrich (San Francisco Office)
Marian J. Dillon
Thomas J. Di Resta (New York, N.Y. Office)
Erica K. Doran (Not admitted in CA; New York, N.Y. Office)
Paul F. Douglas
Kate W. Duchene
Mark C. Easton
David P. Enzminger
Marcia A. Fay (Washington, D.C. Office)
Benjamin D. Feder (Not admitted in CA; New York, N.Y. Office)
Marc F. Feinstein
Aaron F. Fishbein (New York, N.Y. Office)
Roger M. Freeman (Washington, D.C. Office)
Jennifer M. Friedland (Newport Beach Office)
Randy J. Funk
James H. Gianninoto (Newark, N.J. Office)
Robin L. Gohlke
Kenneth A. Goldberg (Not admitted in CA; New York, N.Y. Office)
David B. Goldman
Lisa Maree Campbell Gooden (Century City Office)
Lawrence M. Gordon
Edward Gregory
Greg Groeneveld
Karin Lyn Gustafson (Century City Office)
Lawrence M. Hadley
Edward C. Hagerott, Jr. (San Francisco Office)

(See Next Column)

O'MELVENY & MYERS, *Los Angeles—Continued*

ASSOCIATES (Continued)

Lise Hamilton
(Newport Beach Office)
Peter Hammer
Clint M. Hanni
Molly C. Hansen
Eugene P. Hanson
(New York, N.Y. Office)
Maria Snyder Hardy
(Century City Office)
Kevin M. Harr
Daniel M. Hartman
J. Michael Harty
(New York, N.Y. Office)
Hilary R. Hegener
(Washington, D.C. Office)
Harold Henderson (Not admitted in CA; Washington, D. C. Office)
Peter R. Herman (Not admitted in CA; New York, N.Y. Office)
David L. Herron
Lawrence J. Hilton
(Newport Beach Office)
Bruce R. Hirsh
(Washington, D.C. Office)
John E. Hoffman
Chris Hollinger
Richard J. Holmstrom (Not admitted in CA; New York, N.Y. Office)
John D. Hudson
(Newport Beach Office)
Vicki L. Huntwork
Sandra Segal Ikuta
Yongjin Im
Jennifer L. Isenberg
(San Francisco Office)
Bruce Gen Iwasaki
Neil Scot Jahss
Gloria Ching-hua Jan
(New York, N.Y. Office)
Lynn A. Jansen
Teresa L. Johnson
Carol A. Johnston
(Century City Office)
Jeffrey M. Judd
(San Francisco Office)
M. Flynn Justice, III
(Newport Beach Office)
Deborah L. Kanter
(Century City Office)
Thomas J. Karr (Not admitted in CA; Washington, D. C. Office)
Kevin M. Kelcourse (Not admitted in CA; Washington, D.C. Office)
Mark J. Kelson
(Century City Office)
Jeffrey W. Kilduff (Not admitted in CA; Washington, D.C. Office)
Patricia H. Kim (Not admitted in CA; New York, N.Y. Office)
Kathleen E. Kinney
(Newport Beach Office)
David S. Kitchen
Stephen V. Kovarik
(New York, N.Y. Office)
Robert F. Kramer (Not admitted in CA; New York, N.Y. Office)
Malcolm M. Kratzer (Not admitted in CA; New York, N. Y. Office)
John A. Laco
Scott L. Landsbaum
(Washington, D.C. Office)
Thomas J. Leary
Elizabeth Leckie (Not admitted in CA; New York, N. Y. Office)
Paul A. Leodori
(Newark, N.J. Office)
Sharon G. Levin (Not admitted in CA; Washington, D.C. Office)
Michael Cary Levine

Greta L. Lichtenbaum
(Washington, D.C. Office)
David G. Litt
(Tokyo, Japan Office)
John G. Littell
(Not admitted in CA)
Lisa Litwiller
(Newport Beach Office)
Monique Janelle London
(San Francisco Office)
Karen M. Lower
Michele Logan Lynch
Helen P. Mac Donald
Michael M. Maddigan
Robyn Manos
David A. Marcus
Dennis J. Martin
(New York, N.Y. Office)
Greg K. Matson
Maria Rose Mazur
(Washington, D.C. Office)
Marion K. McDonald
(Washington, D.C. Office)
Joseph G. McHugh
Craig L. McKee (Not admitted in CA; Washington, D.C. Office)
Darren S. McNally
(Newark, N.J. Office)
Susan M. McNeill
(New York, N.Y. Office)
Linda M. Mealey-Lohmann
Ann Catherine Menard
Karen M. Mendalka
(Newark, N.J. Office)
Michael A. Meyer
(Washington, D.C. Office)
Kathleen A. Mishkin
(Newark, N.J. Office)
Anthony L. Morrison (Not admitted in CA; New York, N. Y. Office)
Robert C. Murray
Thomas A. Musante
Vicki A. Nash
(Newport Beach Office)
Poh-Leng Ng
(Newport Beach Office)
Maureen O'Connor (Not admitted in CA; New York, N.Y. Office)
Geoffrey D. Oliver (Not admitted in CA; Washington, D.C. Office)
Matthew B. Pachman
(Washington, D.C. Office)
Dean Pappas
(Century City Office)
Lynn E. Parseghian (Not admitted in CA; Washington, D.C. Office)
Gregory P. Patti, Jr. (Not admitted in CA; New York, N.Y. Office)
Achilles M. Perry (Not admitted in CA; New York, N.Y. Office)
Mark D. Peterson
(Newport Beach Office)
George R. Phillips, Jr.
M. Catherine Powell
Katherine W. Pownell
Simon H. Prisk
Soraya Rashid
Claudia E. Ray
(New York, N.Y. Office)
Anthony W. Rayburn
Eric Reid
(New York, N.Y. Office)
David J. Reis
(San Francisco Office)
Eric A. S. Richards
Kenneth M. Richman
(Century City Office)
Patrick R. Rizzi (Not admitted in CA; Washington, D.C. Office)
James Gerard Rizzo
(New York, N.Y. Office)

(See Next Column)

ASSOCIATES (Continued)

Mark A. Robertson
(Century City Office)
Gregory Roer
(Newark, N.J. Office)
Stephanie R. Rosen (Not admitted in CA; New York, N.Y. Office)
Edward A. Rosic, Jr. (Not admitted in CA; Washington, D.C. Office)
Kendrick F. Royer
William M. Sage
Pamela D. Samuels
Philip C. Scheurer
(Washington, D.C. Office)
Tancred V. Schiavoni, III
(New York, N.Y. Office)
Scott Schrader
(New York Office)
Darrel M. Seife
(New York, N.Y. Office)
Mary Louise Serafine
(Century City Office)
Jeanne C. Serocke (Not admitted in CA; New York, N. Y. Office)
Nina Shafran (Not admitted in CA; Washington, D.C. Office)
Sam S. Shaulson
(New York, N.Y. Office)
Jan P. Shelburne
(New York, N.Y. Office)
James P. Sileneck (Not admitted in CA; New York, N.Y. Office)
Sheryl O. Silver (Not admitted in CA; New York, N.Y. Office)
Craig W. Smith
Gary M. Smith
(New York, N.Y. Office)
Sandra E. Smith
Darin W. Snyder
(San Francisco Office)
Albert J. Solecki, Jr. (Not admitted in CA; New York, N.Y. Office)

Anders E. Stenstedt
(San Francisco Office)
Irene E. Stewart
Michael I. Stockman
Nancy E. Sussman
(Century City Office)
Janet I. Swerdlow
Edward J. Szczepkowski
Frieda A. Taylor
Stergios Theologides
(Newport Beach Office)
Mark E. Thierfelder
(New York, N.Y. Office)
Gloria Trattles
(New York, N.Y. Office)
Scott Treanor
(San Francisco Office)
Todd R. Triller (Not admitted in CA; Washington, D. C. Office)
Kenneth J. Turnbull (Not admitted in CA; New York, N.Y. Office)
Suzzanne Uhland
Sheree S. Ung
Robin F.P. Urban
Kelby Van Patten
(Newport Beach Office)
Karen Mary Wahle
(Washington, D.C. Office)
William M. Walker
Larry A. Walraven
(Newport Beach Office)
Stephen H. Warren
Brett J. Williamson
(Newport Beach Office)
Michael A. Williamson
Dean A. Willis
David A. Wimmer
Mary Catherine Wirth
Todd R. Wulffson
(Newport Beach Office)
Scott N. Yamaguchi
Masami Yamamoto
Kenneth S. Ziman
(New York, N.Y. Office)

For full biographical listings, see the Martindale-Hubbell Law Directory

OSTROVE, KRANTZ & OSTROVE, A PROFESSIONAL CORPORATION (AV)

(Successor To: Ostrove and Lancer, A Professional Corporation; David Ostrove, A Professional Corporation)
5757 Wilshire Boulevard, Suite 535, 90036-3600
Telephone: 213-939-3400
Fax: 213-939-3500
Telex: 213-211523 OKOC UR

David Ostrove
David S. Krantz
Kenneth E. Ostrove

Reference: First Business Bank.

For full biographical listings, see the Martindale-Hubbell Law Directory

PAUL, HASTINGS, JANOFSKY & WALKER (AV)

A Partnership including Professional Corporations
Twenty-Third Floor, 555 South Flower Street, 90071-2371
Telephone: 213-683-6000
FAX: 213-627-0705
"Paulhast" TWX: 910-321-4065
Orange County, California Office: Seventeenth Floor, 695 Town Center Drive, Costa Mesa.
Telephone: 714-668-6200.
Washington, D.C. Office: Tenth Floor, 1299 Pennsylvania Avenue, N.W.
Telephone: 202-508-9500.
Atlanta, Georgia Office: 42nd Floor, Georgia Pacific Center, 133 Peachtree Street, N.E.
Telephone: 404-588-9900.
Santa Monica, California Office: Fifth Floor, 1299 Ocean Avenue.
Telephone: 310-319-3300.
Stamford, Connecticut Office: Ninth Floor, 1055 Washington Boulevard.
Telephone: 203-961-7400.
New York, New York Office: 31st Floor, 399 Park Avenue.
Telephone: 212-318-6000.
Tokyo, Japan Office: Toranomon Ohtori Building, 8th Floor, 4-3 Toranomon 1-Chome, Minato-Ku.
Telephone: (03) 3507-0730.

(See Next Column)

PAUL, HASTINGS, JANOFSKY & WALKER—*Continued*

COUNSEL

Robert Pusey Hastings
Leonard S. Janofsky (Resident Counsel, Santa Monica, California Office)
Lee G. Paul
Charles M. Walker (Resident Counsel, Santa Monica, California Office)

MEMBERS OF FIRM

Nancy L. Abell (Resident Partner, Santa Monica, California Office)
Carl T. Anderson (Resident Partner, Stamford, Connecticut Office)
Steven Reed Armstrong (Resident Partner, Stamford, Connecticut Office)
Richard M. Asbill (Resident Partner, Atlanta, Georgia Office)
R. Lawrence Ashe, Jr., (P.C.) (Resident Partner, Atlanta, Georgia Office)
Mark W. Atkinson
Jesse H. Austin, III (Resident Partner, Atlanta, Georgia Office)
E. Lawrence Barcella, Jr. (Resident Partner, Washington, D.C. Office)
Christopher A. Barreca (Resident Partner, Stamford, Connecticut Office)
Alan J. Barton
Earl M. Benjamin
Keith W. Berglund (Resident Partner, Atlanta, Georgia Office)
Daniel G. Bergstein (Resident Partner, New York, New York Office)
Stephen L. Berry
Woodson Toliver Besson (P.C.) (Resident Partner, Santa Monica, California Office)
Thomas P. Brennan (P.C.)
John H. Brinsley
Jamie Broder
Barry A. Brooks (Resident Partner, New York, New York Office)
Barbara Berish Brown (Resident Partner, Washington D.C. Office)
Daryl R. Buffenstein (Resident Partner, Atlanta, Georgia Office)
Thomas G. Burch, Jr. (Resident Partner, Atlanta, Georgia Office)
Siobhan McBreen Burke
Paul W. Cane, Jr.
Robert E. Carlson
Grace A. Carter
Claudia A. Carver (Resident Partner, Costa Mesa, California Office)
Paul S. Clark (Resident Partner, Costa Mesa, California Office)
Kevin Conboy (Resident Partner, Atlanta, Georgia Office)
Paul J. Connell (Resident Partner, Atlanta, Georgia Office)
Douglas C. Conroy (Resident Partner, Stamford, Connecticut Office)
James H. Cox (Resident Partner, Atlanta, Georgia Office)
Victoria A. Cundiff (Resident Partner, New York, New York Office)
Glenn D. Dassoff (Resident Partner, Costa Mesa, California Office)
Donald A. Daucher (P.C.)
Janet Toll Davidson (Resident Partner, Costa Mesa, California Office)
Barbra L. Davis
Nicholas DeWitt
Robert A. DeWitt (P.C.)
R. Bruce Dickson (Washington. D.C. and New York, New York Offices)
Robert M. Dudnik (Resident Partner, Santa Monica, California Office)
Norman A. Dupont
William E. Eason, Jr. (Resident Partner, Atlanta, Georgia Office)
Ralph B. Everett (Resident Partner, Washington, D.C. Office)
Zachary D. Fasman (Resident Partner, Washington, D.C. Office)
Philip N. Feder
Alfred G. Feliu (Resident Partner, New York, New York Office)
Esteban A. Ferrer, III (Resident Partner, Stamford, Connecticut Office)
Bruce W. Fraser
John C. Funk
Norman A. Futami
John J. Gallagher (Resident Partner, Washington, D.C. Office)
Michael Glazer
George L. Graff (Resident Partner, New York, New York Office)
Oliver F. Green, Jr. (Resident Partner, Costa Mesa, California Office)
Paul Grossman
William M. Hart (Resident Partner, New York, New York Office)
Lawrence J. Hass (Resident Partner, Washington, D.C. Office)
Howard C. Hay (Resident Partner, Costa Mesa, California Office)
Matthew A. Hodel (Resident Partner, Costa Mesa, California Office)
Michael A. Hood (Resident Partner, Costa Mesa, California Office)
Judith Richards Hope (Resident Partner, Washington, D.C. Office)
John P. Howitt (Resident, New York, New York Office)
Mario J. Ippolito (Resident Partner, Stamford, Connecticut Office)
Nancy L. Iredale (P.C.)
Euclid A. Irving (Resident Partner, New York, New York Office)
Weyman T. Johnson, Jr. (Resident Partner, Atlanta, Georgia Office)
Eric H. Joss (Resident Partner, Santa Monica, California Office)
Marguerite R. Kahn (Resident Partner, New York, New York Office)
James W. Kennedy (Resident Partner, New York, New York Office)
Nancy N. Kennerly
Ronald Kreismann (Resident Partner, New York, New York Office)
Thomas R. Lamia (New York, New York and Washington, D.C. Offices)
J. Al Latham, Jr.

(See Next Column)

MEMBERS OF FIRM (Continued)

Charles T. Lee (Resident Partner, Stamford, Connecticut Office)
Michael K. Lindsey
Ethan Lipsig
G. Hamilton Loeb (Resident Partner, Washington, D.C. Office)
M. Guy Maisnik
Philip J. Marzetti (Resident Partner, Atlanta, Georgia Office)
John S. McGeeney (Resident Partner, Stamford, Connecticut Office)
Keith A. Meyer
Roger M. Milgrim (Resident Partner, New York, New York Office)
Robert A. Miller, Jr.
Chris D. Molen (Resident Partner, Atlanta, Georgia Office)
Donald L. Morrow (Resident Partner, Costa Mesa, California Office)
Julian D. Nealy (Resident Partner, Atlanta, Georgia Office)
Belinda K. Orem
Brendan J. O'Rourke (Resident Partner, New York, New York Office)
Charles B. Ortner (Resident Partner, New York, New York Office)
Kevin J. O'Shea (Resident Partner, New York, New York Office)
Ronald M. Oster (P.C.)
Michael L. Owen
John G. Parker (Resident Partner, Atlanta, Georgia Office)
Charles A. Patrizia (Resident Partner, Washington, D.C. Office)
Paul L. Perito (Resident Partner, Washington, D.C. Office)
Andrew C. Peterson
John E. Porter
Patrick A. Ramsey
David M. Roberts
Samuel D. Rosen (Resident Partner, New York, New York Office)
Bruce D. Ryan (Resident Partner, Washington, D.C. Office)
Leigh P. Ryan (Resident Partner, New York, New York Office)
Douglas A. Schaaf (Resident Partner, Costa Mesa, California Office)
William A. Schmidt (Resident Partner, Washington, D.C. Office)
Carl W. Shapiro (Resident Partner, Santa Monica, California Office)
Charles T. Sharbaugh (Resident Partner, Atlanta, Georgia Office)
Patrick W. Shea (Resident Partner, Stamford, Connecticut Office)
Robert L. Sherman (Resident Partner, New York, New York Office)
Andrew M. Short (Resident Partner, New York, New York Office)
Wayne H. Shortridge (Resident Partner, Atlanta, Georgia Office)
Marc L. Silverman (Resident Partner, New York, New York Office)
William J. Simpson (Resident Partner, Costa Mesa, California Office)
David E. Snediker (Resident Partner, Stamford, Connecticut Office)
Robert S. Span (Resident Partner, Santa Monica, California Office)
John H. Steed (Resident Partner, Atlanta, Georgia Office)
Alan K. Steinbrecher
George E. Stephens, Jr., (P.C.)
Harvey A. Strickon (Resident Partner, New York, New York Office)
Kaoruhiko Suzuki
Geoffrey L. Thomas (P.C.)
Charles V. Thornton
Gary F. Torrell
John E. Trinnaman (Resident Partner, Costa Mesa, California Office)
Dennis H. Vaughn (Partner, Santa Monica, California and Washington, D.C. Offices)
William Stewart Waldo
Elizabeth W. Walker
Paul R. Walker
Robert F. Walker (Resident Partner, Santa, Monica, California Office)
Alan Wade Weakland
Lawrence I. Weinstein (Resident Partner, New York, New York Office)
C. Geoffrey Weirich (Resident Partner, Atlanta, Georgia Office)
Michael A. Wiegard (Resident Partner, Washington, D.C. Office)
Thomas S. Wisialowski
Seth M. Zachary (Resident Partner, New York, New York Office)
James A. Zapp
Harry A. Zinn (Resident Partner, Santa Monica, California Office)

SENIOR COUNSEL

Robert R. Burge (Resident Senior Counsel, Costa Mesa, California Office)
James W. Hamilton (Resident Senior Counsel, Costa Mesa, California Office)
David Bruce Harriman

OF COUNSEL

Laura J. Carroll
Anthony B. Casareale (Resident Of Counsel, Stamford, Connecticut Office)
Michael F. Cole (Resident Of Counsel, Washington, D.C. Office)
Edwin I. Colodny (Resident Of Counsel, Washington, D.C. Office)
Stephen D. Cooke (Resident Of Counsel, Costa Mesa, California Office)
William A. Crowfoot
Julian B. Decyk
William D. DeGrandis (Resident Of Counsel, Washington, D.C. Office)
Leslie A. Dent (Resident Of Counsel, Atlanta, Georgia Office)
Jane Elizabeth Eakins (Resident Of Counsel, Santa Monica, California Office)
Charles S. Farman
Jon A. Geier (Resident Of Counsel, Washington, D.C. Office)

(See Next Column)

PAUL, HASTINGS, JANOFSKY & WALKER, *Los Angeles—Continued*

OF COUNSEL (Continued)

Elliot K. Gordon (Resident Of Counsel, Santa Monica, California Office)
Randall S. Henderson
Frank Koszorus, Jr. (Resident Of Counsel, Washington, D.C. Office)
Kevin C. Logue (Resident Of Counsel, New York, New York Office)
Deborah A. Marlowe (Resident Of Counsel, Atlanta, Georgia Office)
Judith L. Meadow (Resident Of Counsel, Santa Monica, California Office)
Joseph T. Moldovan (Resident Of Counsel, New York, New York Office)
Robert C. Moot, Jr. (Resident Of Counsel, Atlanta, Georgia Office)
Craig K. Pendergrast (Resident Of Counsel, Atlanta, Georgia Office)
Robert S. Plotkin (Resident Of Counsel, Washington, D.C. Office)
Robert E. Pokusa (Resident Of Counsel, Washington, D.C. Office)
Lucy Prashker (Resident Of Counsel, New York, New York Office)
Suzanne Edgar Randolph
Anthony J. Rossi (Resident Of Counsel, Costa Mesa, California Office)
Douglas J. Rovens
John L. Sander (Resident Of Counsel, New York, New York Office)
Christine A. Scheuneman
W. Andrew Scott (Resident Of Counsel, Atlanta, Georgia Office)
Charles A. Shanor (Of Counsel, Atlanta, Georgia and Washington, D.C. Offices)
Margaret H. Spurlin (Resident Of Counsel, Washington, D.C. Office)
Richard J. Sweetnam (Resident Of Counsel, Stamford, Connecticut Office)
Julia Tachikawa (Resident Of Counsel, Santa Monica, California Office)
Neil A. Torpey (Resident Of Counsel, New York, New York Office)
Jeffrey G. Varga
William P. Wade
Michael S. Woodward
Clarisse W. J. Young

ASSOCIATES

David M. Abbey (Resident Associate, Washington, D.C. Office)
Leslie Abbott
George W. Abele
Elizabeth A. Adolff (Resident Associate, Stamford, Connecticut Office)
Terry Jon Allen (Resident Associate, Costa Mesa, California Office)
I. Barbra Allue (Resident Associate, Stamford, Connecticut Office)
Toshiyuki Arai
Kenneth T. Araki
Julie L. Arias (Resident Associate, Santa Monica, California Office)
Daron J. Arnold
Peter Aronson
Mary K. Asher (Resident Associate, Santa Monica, California Office)
Jennifer Stivers Baldocchi
Edward J. Bennett (Resident Associate, Stamford, Connecticut Office)
Donna R. Besteiro (Resident Associate, New York, New York Office)
Brent R. Bohn
David B. Booker (Resident Associate, New York, New York Office)
Janet D. Booth (Resident Associate, New York, New York Office)
Robert L. Boyd (Resident Associate, New York, New York Office)
Mark Bronson
Robert P. Bryant (Resident Associate, Costa Mesa, California Office)
David J. Burge (Resident Associate, Atlanta, Georgia Office)
Gwyneth A. Campbell
Peter S. Canelias (Resident Associate, New York, New York Office)
Jack L. Caynon, III (Resident Associate, Stamford, Connecticut Office)
Beverly A. Chaney (Resident Associate, New York, New York Office)
Alpa Patel Chernof
Justin C. Choi (Resident Associate, New York, New York Office)
Roxanne E. Christ
Eve Mary Coddon
Michelle Weisberg Cohen (Resident Associate, Washington, D.C. Office)
Ronald T. Coleman, Jr. (Resident Associate, Atlanta, Georgia Office)
Mary L. Cornwell (Resident Associate, Costa Mesa, California Office)
Sandra A. Crawshaw (Resident Associate, New York, New York Office)
Jonathan C. Curtis
Barbara R. Danz (Resident Associate, Costa Mesa, California Office)
Cindy J.K. Davis (Resident Associate, Atlanta, Georgia Office)
Daniel P. Delaney
David S. Denenberg (Resident Associate, New York, New York Office)
Jeannine DePhillips (Resident Associate, Costa Mesa, California Office)
Tod A. Devine (Resident Associate, Costa Mesa, California Office)
Alejandro J. Diaz (Resident Associate, Stamford, Connecticut Office)
Mary C. Dollarhide (Resident Associate, Stamford, Connecticut Office)
Jessica S. Dorman-Davis (Resident Associate, Costa Mesa, California Office)
Janet A. W. Dray

(See Next Column)

ASSOCIATES (Continued)

Patricia A. Driscoll (Resident Associate, Stamford, Connecticut Office)
Harold N. Eddy, Jr. (Resident Associate, Stamford, Connecticut Office)
Linda M. Edwards (Resident Associate, Santa Monica, California Office)
David B. Ehrlich
Kirsten Shirley Ellis
Jason O. Engel (Resident Associate, Costa Mesa, California Office)
William P. Ewing (Resident Associate, Atlanta, Georgia Office)
Wendell M. Faria (Resident Associate, Washington, D.C. Office)
Elizabeth A. Fealy (Resident Associate, New York, New York Office)
Alan M. Feld
Violet F. Fiacco (Resident Associate, Costa Mesa, California Office)
Regina M. Flaherty (Resident Associate, Stamford, Connecticut Office)
Scott M. Flicker (Resident Associate, Washington, D.C. Office)
Laura A. Forbes (Resident Associate, Costa Mesa, California Office)
Gerard P. Fox (Resident Associate, Santa Monica, California Office)
Robert F. Foxworth, III (Resident Associate, Stamford, Connecticut Office)
Michele Freedenthal
Intra L. Germanis (Resident Associate, Washington, D.C. Office)
Charles J. Gernazian (Resident Associate, Atlanta, Georgia Office)
Bruce C. Geyer
Lisa M. Gigliotti (Resident Associate, New York, New York Office)
Ronald K. Giller
James R. Glenister (Resident Associate, Atlanta, Georgia Office)
Joel A. Goldberg (Resident Associate, New York, New York Office)
Jill Greenwald (Resident Associate, New York, New York Office)
Karen K. Greenwalt
Lynette M. Gridiron
E. Jeffrey Grube
Delia Guevara
Maryanne Becka Haller
John W. Hamlin (Resident Associate, Stamford, Connecticut Office)
Kurt W. Hansson (Resident Associate, Stamford, Connecticut Office)
Mark W. Harrigian
James Che-Ming Hsu (Resident Associate, New York, New York Office)
Jocelyn J. Hunter (Resident Associate, Atlanta, Georgia Office)
Patricia L. Hurst (Resident Associate, Washington, D.C. Office)
Edward S. Johnson, Jr. (Resident Associate, Atlanta, Georgia Office)
Gage Randolph Johnson (Resident Associate, Washington, D.C. Office)
Steven D. Johnson (Resident Associate, New York, New York Office)
George R.A. Jones (Resident Associate, Washington, D.C. Office)
Lynn A. Kappelman (Resident Associate, Stamford, Connecticut Office)
Nancy Kardon
Roy S. Kaufman (Resident Associate, New York, New York Office)
Susan R. Keith
Michael C. Keller
A. Peter Kezirian, Jr.
Jong Han Kim
Ken Kimura (Resident Associate, New York, New York Office)
Rosemary Mahar Kirbach
Janet L. Kishbaugh (Resident Associate, Atlanta, Georgia Office)
Karen L. Kleiderman
Judith M. Kline (Resident Associate, Santa Monica, California Office)
Patricia A. Krieg (Resident Associate, New York, New York Office)
Scott J. Krowitz (Resident Associate, Stamford, Connecticut Office)
Kevin A. Kyle (Not admitted in CA)
Lisa M. LaFourcade (Resident Associate, Costa Mesa, California Office)
Douglas E. Lahammer
Steven A. Lamb
Edmund S. Latour (Resident Associate, Washington, D.C. Office)
Michelle A. Leftwich (Resident Associate, New York, New York Office)
Scott N. Leslie (Resident Associate, Costa Mesa, California Office)
Katherine B. Lipton (Resident Associate, New York, New York Office)
Robert L. Madok
A. Alan Manning (Resident Associate, Costa Mesa, California Office)
Michael S. Marx
Andrew M. Mayer (Resident Associate, New York, New York Office)
Kathleen L. McAchran
Denise Marie McGorrin
Sarah M. McWilliams (Resident Associate, Washington, D.C. Office)
Martin C. Mead
Jon Douglas Meer
Michael T. Mervis (Resident Associate, New York, New York Office)
Keith F. Millhouse
Melinda L. Moseley (Resident Associate, Atlanta, Georgia Office)
John J. Neely, III (Resident Associate, Atlanta, Georgia Office)
Nicolle Renée Nelson
Greg M. Nitzkowski
Tait O. Norton (Resident Associate, Atlanta, Georgia Office)
Sean A. O'Brien (Resident Associate, Costa Mesa, California Office)
Robert J. Odson
John C. O'Malley
Joseph P. Opich (Resident Associate, New York, New York Office)
DeAnne H. Ozaki
Dwan E. Packnett (Resident Associate, Atlanta, Georgia Office)

(See Next Column)

PAUL, HASTINGS, JANOFSKY & WALKER—*Continued*

ASSOCIATES (Continued)

Malinda A. Palomares (Resident Associate, Costa Mesa, California Office)
Philip J. Paseltiner (Resident Associate, Stamford, Connecticut Office)
Lawrence Peikes (Resident Associate, Stamford, Connecticut Office)
Suzanne Marie Pepe-Robbins (Resident Associate, New York, New York Office)
Lauren S. Peterson (Resident Associate, New York, New York Office)
David S. Phelps
Todd O. Piccus
Bonnie Pierson-Murphy (Resident Associate, Stamford, Connecticut Office)
Alexis Pinto (Resident Associate, New York, New York Office)
Leslie A. Plaskon (Resident Associate, Stamford, Connecticut Office)
Holly A. Porter
L. Lynne Pulliam (Resident Associate, Atlanta, Georgia Office)
Nancy E. Rafuse (Resident Associate, Atlanta, Georgia Office)
William Thomas Reeder, Jr. (Resident Associate, Washington, D.C. Office)
Alesia Selby Regan (Resident Associate, New York, New York Office)
Rey M. Rodriguez
Peter J. Roth
Joel H. Rothstein
Cheryl R. Saban (Resident Associate, New York, New York Office)
Howard J. Schechter (Resident Associate, Atlanta, Georgia Office)
Joseph E. Schmitz (Resident Associate, Washington, D.C. Office)
Jenny Schneider (Resident Associate, Santa Monica, California Office)
Mathew Anthony Schuh (Resident Associate, Atlanta, Georgia Office)
Alan F. Seiffert (Resident, Santa Monica, California Office)
Nancy E. Shallow (Resident Associate, Washington, D.C. Office)
Joseph C. Sharp (Resident Associate, Atlanta, Georgia Office)
Kim M. Shipley (Resident Associate, Atlanta, Georgia Office)
Glenn C. Shrader
Betty M. Shumener
Gulwinder S. Singh (Resident Associate, Costa Mesa, California Office)
Derek E. Smith
Brent C. Snyder
Eric C. Sohlgren (Resident Associate, Costa Mesa, California Office)
Nancy L. Sommer (Resident Associate, New York, New York Office)
Stephen P. Sonnenberg (Resident Associate, Santa Monica, California Office)
E. Gary Spitko (Resident Associate, Atlanta, Georgia Office)
Richard A. Spitz
Andree M. St. Martin (Resident associate, Washington, D.C. Office)
Diane Desfor Stalder (Resident Associate, Costa Mesa, California Office)
John B. Stephens (Resident Associate, Costa Mesa, California Office)
Randall M. Stone (Resident Associate, Washington, D.C. Office)
Benjamin S. Strouse (Resident Associate, New York, New York Office)
Kristen K. Swartz (Resident Associate, Atlanta, Georgia Office)
Michael D. Taxay (Resident Associate, Washington, D.C. Office)
Eric Jon Taylor (Resident Associate, Atlanta, Georgia Office)
Todd D. Thibodo (Not admitted in CA)
Katherine A. Traxler
Michael W. Traynham
Linda Trembicki (Resident Associate, New York, New York Office)
Angela Tung (Resident Associate, New York, New York Office)
David T. Van Pelt (Resident Associate, Santa Monica, California Office)
Sylvia M. Virsik (Resident Associate, Santa Monica, California Office)
Michael T. Voytek (Resident Associate, Atlanta, Georgia Office)
Stanley F. Wasowski (Resident Associate, Atlanta, Georgia Office)
Philip R. Weingold (Resident Associate, New York, New York Office)
Deborah S. Weiser (Resident Associate, Santa Monica, California Office)
Timothy J. Wellman (Resident Associate, Washington, D.C. Office)
Annita M. Whichard (Resident Associate, Washington, D.C. Office)
Christopher A. Whytock (Resident Associate, Costa Mesa, California Office)
Sandra Wilkinson (Resident Associate, Washington, D.C. Office)
Crystal L. Williams (Resident Associate, Atlanta, Georgia Office)
Kenneth M. Willner (Resident Associate, Washington, D.C. Office)
Jonathan B. Wilson (Resident Associate, Atlanta, Georgia Office)
Melinda C. Witmer (Resident Associate, New York, New York Office)
Jenny C. Wu (Resident Associate, Washington, D.C. Office)
Stephen A. Yamaguchi (Resident Associate, Tokyo, Japan Office)
Darla L. Yancey (Resident Associate, Costa Mesa, California Office)
Mark W. Yocca

(See Next Column)

ASSOCIATES (Continued)

Lori Zablow (Resident Associate, New York, New York Office)
Teresa K. Zintgraff (Resident Associate, Santa Monica, California Office)
Arthur L. Zwickel
Kimberly Zywicki (Resident Associate, Atlanta, Georgia Office)

For full biographical listings, see the Martindale-Hubbell Law Directory

PILLSBURY MADISON & SUTRO (AV)

Citicorp Plaza, 725 South Figueroa Street, Suite 1200, 90017-2513
Telephone: 213-488-7100
Fax: 213-629-1033
Costa Mesa, California Office: Plaza Tower, 600 Anton Boulevard, Suite 1100, 92626.
Telephone: 714-436-6800.
Fax: 714-662-6999.
Menlo Park, California Office: 2700 Sand Hill Road, 94025.
Telephone: 415-233-4500.
Fax: 415-233-4545.
Sacramento, California Office: 400 Capitol Mall, Suite 1700, 95814.
Telephone: 916-329-4700.
Fax: 916-441-3583.
San Diego, California Office: 101 West Broadway, Suite 1800, 92101.
Telephone: 619-234-5000.
Fax: 619-236-1995.
San Francisco, California Office: 225 Bush Street, 94104.
Telephone: 415-983-1000.
Fax: 415-398-2096.
San Jose, California Office: Ten Almaden Boulevard, 95113.
Telephone: 408-947-4000.
Fax: 408-287-8341.
Washington, D. C. Office: 1667 K Street, N.W., Suite 1100, Suite 20006.
Telephone: 202-887-0300.
Fax: 202-296-7605.
New York, New York Office: One Liberty Plaza, 165 Broadway, 51st Floor.
Telephone: 212-374-1890.
Fax: 212-374-1852.
Hong Kong Office: 6/F Asia Pacific Finance Tower, Citibank Plaza, 3 Garden Road, Central.
Telephone: 011-852-509-7100.
Fax: 011-852-509-7188.
Tokyo, Japan Office: Churchill and Shimazaki, Gaiko-Jimo-Bengoshi Jimusho, 11-12, Toranomon, 5-chome Minato-ku, Tokyo 105, Japan.
Telephone: 800-729-9830; 011-81-3-5472-6561.
Fax: 011-81-3-5472-5761.

MEMBERS OF FIRM

Marvin I. Bartel
Reid R. Briggs
Anthon S. Cannon, Jr.
James A. Churchill (Gaikokuho-Jimu-Bengoshi) (Foreign legal Consultant)
John J. Duffy
L. Gail Gordon
Terrence J. Grasmick
John Randolph Haag
Karen L. Heilman
Jeffrey W. Hill
Carolyn M. Huestis
Sidney K. Kanazawa
Steven O. Kramer
Jennie L. La Prade
Peter V. Leparulo
Eugene Y. C. Lu
Christopher J. McNevin
Catherine D. Meyer
Ruth Modisette
Robert L. Morrison
Dana P. Newman
Henry Y. Ota
Charles E. Patterson
Teresa M. Quinn
Patrick G. Rogan
Kenneth N. Russak
Faisal Shah
Walter V. Stafford
William E. Stoner
Timothy J. Sweeney
Reed S. Waddell
William S. Waller
John W. Whitaker
Douglas Woo
Lawrence D. Bradley, Jr.
John R. Cadarette, Jr.
Kenneth R. Chiate
Anthony R. Delling
William K. Dial
Blase P. Dillingham
Jerone J. English
Kent B. Goss
Robert A. Gutkin
David L. Hayutin
Donald J. Hess
Amy D. Hogue
Yuji Iwanaga
Ralph D. Kirwan
Howard A. Kroll
Thomas R. Larmore
John Y. Liu
James A. Magee
Donald W. Meaders
Michael E. Meyer
Nancy G. Morrison
J. Richard Morrissey
F. John Nyhan
Jackie K. Park
Edward A. Perron
James M. Rishwain, Jr.
Matthew R. Rogers
Karl A. Schmidt
Robert V. Slattery Jr.
Sheryl E. Stein
Mark K. Suzumoto
David B. Van Etten
Robert L. Wallan
Don R. Weigandt
John G. Wigmore
Thomas E. Workman, Jr.
Gordon K. Wright

OF COUNSEL

Charles E. Anderson
George W. Finch
Joseph S. Biderman
A. Todd Littleworth
Roland G. Simpson

SENIOR COUNSEL

Susan S. Grover
Steven M. Nakasone

(See Next Column)

PILLSBURY MADISON & SUTRO, *Los Angeles—Continued*

ASSOCIATES

Keith A. Allen-Niesen
Brett H. Bailey
Dimitrios P. Biller
J. Mark Childs
Michael J. Crowley
Peter F. Del Greco
Julie G. Duffy
Sheri F. Eisner
William B. Freeman
Michael B. Garfinkel
Tracy Birnkrant Gray
Stewart S. Harrison
Sabina A. Helton
Kensuke Inoue
Suzanne Cate Jones
Linda S. Koffman
Nicholas L. Kondoleon
Jean A. Martin
Mary T. Michelena-Monroe
J. Kelly Moffat
Jeffrey A. Rich
Bruce S. Schildkraut
Susan M. St. Denis
Jay M. Vogel
Farhad Bahar
Ian R. Barrett
J. Douglas Bishop
Barbara L. Croutch
Douglas H. Deems
Michael F. Dooner
Weston A. Edwards
Michael J. Finnegan
Jeffrey D. Frost
William T. Gillespie
Jan C. Harris
L. Keven Hayworth
David A. Hoover
Christine M. Johnson
Kelly A. Kightlinger
Hyong S. Koh
David G. Mann
Paul J. McCue
Margaret L. Milam
David S. Rauch
Timothy C. Riley
Keith A. Sipprelle
Steven A. Velkei
Marcus G. Whittle

For full biographical listings, see the Martindale-Hubbell Law Directory

---

PROSKAUER ROSE GOETZ & MENDELSOHN LLP (AV)

2121 Avenue of the Stars, Suite 2700, 90067-3003
Telephone: 310-557-2900
FAX: 310-557-2193
New York, N.Y. Office: 1585 Broadway.
Telephone: 212-969-3000.
Washington, D.C. Office: 1233 Twentieth Street, N.W., Suite 800.
Telephone: 202-416-6800.
San Francisco, California Office: 555 California Street, Suite 4604.
Telephone: 415-956-2218.
Boca Raton, Florida Office: One Boca Place, Suite 340 West, 2255 Glades Road.
Telephone: 407-241-7400.
Clifton, New Jersey Office: 1373 Broad Street, P.O. Box 4444.
Telephone: 201-779-6300.
Paris, France Office: 9 rue Le Tasse.
Telephone: (33-1) 45 27 43 01

RESIDENT PARTNERS

Howard D. Behar
Henry Ben-Zvi
Jeffrey A. Berman
Harold M. Brody
Scott P. Cooper
Thomas W. Dollinger
Steven G. Drapkin
Howard D. Fabrick
Mitchell M. Gaswirth
Bernard D. Gold
Carole E. Handler
Paul D. Rubenstein
Marvin Sears
Lois D. Thompson
Martin S. Zohn

SPECIAL COUNSEL

Walter Cochran-Bond
Kenneth Krug

RESIDENT ASSOCIATES

Aaron P. Allan
Nicholas P. Connon
Julie M. Doyle
Alan H. Finkel
Dana Hirsch Lipman
David S. Lippman
Guy A. Mason
Seth A. Miller (Not admitted in CA)
Antonia Ozeroff
Mary H. Rose
Adam J. Rosen (Not admitted in CA)
James W. Ryals
Lori E. Sambol
David R. Scheidemantle
Karen L. Stefflre (Not admitted in CA)
Leslie A. Wederich
Michael R. Wilner
Scott J. Witlin

For full biographical listings, see the Martindale-Hubbell Law Directory

---

QUINN, KULLY AND MORROW, A PROFESSIONAL LAW CORPORATION (AV)

Eighth Floor 520 South Grand Avenue, 90071
Telephone: 213-622-0300
Telecopier: 213-622-3799

John J. Quinn
Russel I. Kully
Margaret M. Morrow
Richard C. Smith
Laurence J. Hutt
Gregory C. Fant
J. David Oswalt
Lawrence A. Cox
Polly Horn
Eric L. Dobberteen
David S. Eisen
James I. Ham
Julie M. Ward

(See Next Column)

Martha Jeannette Clark
Patricia A. Libby
Michael H. Walizer
D. Jay Ritt
Kerry R. Bensinger
James D. Layden
Brian K. Condon
Claire M. Corcoran
Sharon L. Douglass
Janine M. Watkins
Tracy E. Loomis
Kelley P. Potter

OF COUNSEL

Craig N. Hentschel
Lisa S. Kantor

For full biographical listings, see the Martindale-Hubbell Law Directory

---

ROGERS & WELLS (AV)

444 South Flower Street, 90071-2901
Telephone: 213-689-2900
Facsimile: 213-689-2999
New York, N.Y. Office: Two Hundred Park Avenue, New York, N.Y. 10166-0153.
Telephone: 212-878-8000.
Facsimile: 212-878-8375.
Telex: 234493 RKWUR.
Washington, D.C. Office: 607 Fourteenth Street, N.W., Washington, D.C. 20005-2011.
Telephone: 202-434-0700.
Facsimile: 202-434-0800.
Paris, France Office: 47, Avenue Hoche, 75008-Paris, France.
Telephone: 33-1-44-09-46-00.
Facsimile: 33-1-42-67-50-81.
Telex: 651617 EURLAW.
London, England Office: 58 Coleman Street, London EC2R 5BE, England.
Telephone: 44-71-628-0101.
Facsimile: 44-71-638-2008.
Telex: 884964 USLAW G.
Frankfurt, Germany Office: Lindenstrasse 37, 60325 Frankfurt/Main, Federal Republic of Germany.
Telephone: 49-69-97-57-11-0.
Telecopier: 49-69-97-57-11-33.

PARTNERS

Jeffrey S. Allen
Michael D. Berk
Allan E. Ceran
G. Howden Fraser
John A. Karaczynski
Terry O. Kelly
Michael A. McAndrews
Carl W. Sonne
I. Bruce Speiser

COUNSEL

Randolph H. Elkins
Edward Lasker
Aaron M. Peck

ASSOCIATES

Bryan H. Baumeister
Donald R. Brown
John M. Byrne
Kathleen D. De Vaney
Kathleen Hixson Langan
Malcolm Loeb
Kristin A. Regan
Raúl F. Salinas
Andrew J. Yamamoto
Mitch C. Ziontz

For full biographical listings, see the Martindale-Hubbell Law Directory

---

ROPERS, MAJESKI, KOHN & BENTLEY, A PROFESSIONAL CORPORATION (AV)

550 South Hope Street, Suite 1900, 90071
Telephone: 213-312-2000
Fax: 213-312-2001
Redwood City, California Office: 1001 Marshall Street.
Telephone: 415-364-8200.
Fax: 415-367-0997.
San Jose, California Office: 80 North 1st Street.
Telephone: 408-287-6262.
Fax: 408-297-6819.
San Francisco, California Office: 670 Howard Street.
Telephone: 415-543-4800.
Fax: 415-512-1574.
Santa Rosa, California Office: Fountaingrove Center, 3558 Round Barn Boulevard, Suite 300.
Telephone: 707-524-4200.
Fax: 707-523-4610.
Sacramento, California Office: 1000 G. Street, Suite 400.
Telephone: 916-556-3100.
Fax: 916-442-7121.

Stephen J. Erigero
Frank T. Sabaitis (Resident)
Marta B. Arriandiaga
Kirk C. Chamberlin
Stephen P. Ellingson

Michael W. Parks
Christopher R. Wagner
Elizabeth A. Moussouros
Sean S. Varner
Ernest E. Price
Andrew D. Castricone
Daniel S. Lee
Kevin W. Alexander
Vanci Y. Fuller

For full biographical listings, see the Martindale-Hubbell Law Directory

Los Angeles—Continued

Shearman & Sterling (AV)

725 South Figueroa Street, 21st Floor, 90017-5421
Telephone: (213) 239-0300
Fax: (213) 239-0381, 614-0936
New York, N.Y. Office: 599 Lexington Avenue, New York, New York 10022-6069 and Citicorp Center, 153 East 53rd Street, New York, New York 10022-4676.
Telephone: (212) 848-4000.
Telex: 667290 Num Lau.
Fax: 599 Lexington Avenue: (212) 848-7179. Citicorp Center: (212) 848-5252.
Abu Dhabi, United Arab Emirates Office: P.O. Box 2948.
Telephone: (971-2) 324477.
Fax: (971-2) 774533.
Beijing, People's Republic of China Office: Suite #2205, Capital Mansion, No. 6, Xin Yuan Nan Road. Chao Yang District Beijing, 100004.
Telephone: (861) 465-4574.
Fax: (861) 465-4578.
Budapest, Hungary Office: Szerb utca 17-19, 1056 Budapest.
Telephone: (36-1) 266-3522.
Fax: (36-1) 266-3523.
Düsseldorf, Federal Republic of Germany Office: Königsallee 46, D-40212 Düsseldorf.
Telephone: (49-211) 13 62 80.
Telex: 8 588 294 NYLO.
Fax: (49-211) 13 33 09.
Frankfurt, Federal Republic of Germany Office: Bockenheimer Landstrasse 55, D-60325 Frankfurt am Main.
Telephone: (49-69) 97-10-70.
Fax: (49-69) 97-10-71-00.
Hong Kong, Hong Kong Office: Standard Chartered Bank Building, 4 Des Voeux Road Central, Hong Kong.
Telephone: (852) 2978-8000.
Fax: (852) 2978-8099.
London, England Office: 199Bishopsgate, London EC2M 3TY.
Telephone: (44-71) 920-9000.
Fax: (44-71) 920-9020.
Paris, France Office: 12 rue d'Astorg, 75008.
Telephone: (33-1) 44-71-17-17.
Telex: 282964 Royale.
Fax: (33-1) 44-71-01-01.
San Francisco, California Office: 555 California Street, 94104-1522.
Telephone: (415) 616-1100.
Fax: (415) 616-1199.
Taipei, Taiwan Office: 7th Floor, Hung Kuo Building, 167 Tun Hwa North Road.
Telephone: (886-2) 545-3300.
Fax: (866-2) 545-3322.
Tokyo, Japan Office: Shearman & Sterling (Thomas Wilner Gaikokuho-Jimu-Bengoshi Jimusho), Fukoku Seimei Building, 5th Fl. 2-2-2, Uchisaiwaicho, Chiyoda-ku, Tokyo 100, Japan.
Telephone: (81 3) 5251-1601.
Fax: (81 3) 5251-1602.
Toronto, Ontario, Canada Office: Commerce Court West, Suite 4405, P.O. Box 247, M5L 1E8.
Telephone: (416) 360-8484.
Fax: (416) 360-2958.
Washington, D.C. Office: 801 Pennsylvania Avenue, N.W., Suite 900, 20004-2604.
Telephone: (202) 508-8000.
Fax: (202) 508-8100.

RESIDENT PARTNERS

Reade H. Ryan, Jr. (Managing Partner)
Jaculin T. Aaron
Ronald M. Bayer
William M. Burke
Richard B. Kendall
Rebecca Foster Prentice
Darryl Snider
Brice T. Voran

ENTERTAINMENT LAW COUNSEL

Dennis Ardi

SENIOR CHINA COUNSEL

Chu Liu

For full biographical listings, see the Martindale-Hubbell Law Directory

---

Sheppard, Mullin, Richter & Hampton (AV)

A Partnership including Professional Corporations
Forty-Eighth Floor, 333 South Hope Street, 90071-1406
Telephone: 213-620-1780
Telecopier: 213-620-1398
Cable Address: "Sheplaw"
Telex: 19-4424
Orange County, California Office: Seventh Floor, 4695 MacArthur Court, Newport Beach.
Telephone: 714-752-6400.
Telecopier: 714-851-0739.
Telex: 19-4424.

(See Next Column)

San Francisco, California Office: Seventeenth Floor, Four Embarcadero Center.
Telephone: 415-434-9100.
Telecopier: 415-434-3947.
Telex: 19-4424.
San Diego, California Office: Nineteenth Floor, 501 West Broadway.
Telephone: 619-338-6500.
Telecopier: 619-234-3815.
Telex: 19-4424.

COUNSEL

Gordon F. Hampton
J. Stanley Mullin
Frank Simpson III (1926-1993)

MEMBERS OF FIRM

Charles F. Barker
John D. Berchild, Jr.
Anthony J. Bishop
Kathleen Borrero Bloch (San Francisco Office)
John R. Bonn (San Diego Office)
Barbara L. Borden (San Diego Office)
David M. Bosko (Orange County Office)
Lawrence M. Braun
Arthur Wm. Brown, Jr.
Richard W. Brunette, Jr.
James J. Carroll, III *
Michael J. Changaris (San Diego Office)
Dennis Childs (San Diego Office)
John D. Collins * (San Diego Office)
John C. Cook (San Francisco Office)
Joseph F. Coyne, Jr.
André J. Cronthall
Joseph A. Darrell (San Francisco Office)
Phillip A. Davis
Dean A. Demetre (Orange County Office)
Polly Towill Dennis
Domenic C. Drago (San Diego Office)
Juliette M. Ebert (San Francisco Office)
Frank Falzetta
Michael D. Fernhoff *
Robert B. Flaig
Merrill R. Francis *
Dale E. Fredericks (San Francisco Office)
Geraldine A. Freeman (San Francisco Office)
Richard M. Freeman * (San Diego Office)
Marsha D. Galinsky
John J. Giovannone (Orange County Office)
Randolph B. Godshall (Orange County Office)
Gerald N. Gordon
Joseph G. Gorman, Jr. *
Gordon A. Greenberg
Andrew J. Guilford (Orange County Office)
Guy N. Halgren (San Diego Office)
Harold E. Hamersmith
Don T. Hibner, Jr.
James Blythe Hodge * (San Francisco Office)
Robert Joe Hull *
John D. Hussey *
Brent R. Liljestrom (Orange County Office)
Samuel M. Livermore (San Francisco Office)
James A. Lonergan
Gregory A. Long *
Richard L. Lotts *
Charles H. MacNab, Jr. (San Francisco Office)
David A. Maddux *
Paul S. Malingagio
David J. McCarty
Charles E. McCormick
James F. McShane
James J. Mittermiller (San Diego Office)
Christopher B. Neils (San Diego Office)
Mark L. Nelson
Gary J. Nevolo (San Francisco Office)
Jon W. Newby
Wesley L Nutten, III * (1929-1993)
Kathyleen A. O'Brien
Prentice L. O'Leary *
Stephen J. O'Neil
Joel R. Ohlgren
Mark T. Okuma
T. William Opdyke
John R. Pennington
Sara Pfrommer
Robert H. Philibosian
Fred R. Puglisi
Kent R. Raygor
Nancy Baldwin Reimann
Paul M. Reitler *
Mark Riera
Susan Herbst Roos (San Francisco Office)
Jack H. Rubens
John F. Runkel, Jr. (San Francisco Office)
D. Ronald Ryland (San Francisco Office)
James L. Sanders
Myrl R. Scott *
William M. Scott IV
Pierce T. Selwood *
Thomas R. Sheppard *
John R. Simon * (Orange County Office)
James J. Slaby, Jr.
Ann Kane Smith
Dianne Baquet Smith
Richard L. Sommers
Richard L. Stone
Finley L. Taylor * (Orange County Office)
Laura S. Taylor (San Diego Office)
Stephen C. Taylor *
Timothy B. Taylor (San Diego Office)
John M. Temple
Jane L. Thomas (San Francisco Office)
Carlton A. Varner *
Victor A. Vilaplana (San Diego Office)
Edward D. Vogel (San Diego Office)
L. Kirk Wallace
Michael J. Weaver * (San Diego Office)
Daniel P. Westman (San Francisco Office)
Robert E. Williams
Darryl M. Woo (San Francisco Office)
Roy G. Wuchitech (Director, The Sheppard, Mullin Environmental Practice Group)
William R. Wyatt (San Francisco Office)

SPECIAL COUNSEL

C. W. Bergere, Jr. (San Francisco Office)
Ann Cretsinger (San Diego Office)
Frederick V. Geisler
Laurence K. Gould, Jr.
Jack Chi-Husan Liu
Scott J. Lochner

(See Next Column)

SHEPPARD, MULLIN, RICHTER & HAMPTON, *Los Angeles—Continued*

SPECIAL COUNSEL (Continued)

M. Elizabeth McDaniel (San Francisco Office)
Steven C. Nock (Orange County Office)
Allan J. Thompson (San Francisco Office)
William V. Whelan (San Diego Office)

ASSOCIATES

Robert B. Ajemian (San Francisco Office)
Fredric I. Albert (Orange County Office)
Nancy McAniff Annick
Cindy Thomas Archer (Orange County Office)
Vincent J. Axelson (San Diego Office)
Carrie Battilega (San Diego Office)
Robert S. Beall (Orange County Office)
David M. Beckwith (San Diego Office)
Barbara A. Benner (Orange County Office)
Rebecca Berg (Orange County Office)
Jason Brauser
Scott Brutocao
Ann A. Byun
Steven W. Cardoza (Orange County Office)
Justine Mary Casey (Orange County Office)
David B. Chidlaw (San Diego Office)
Gene R. Clark (Orange County Office)
Thomas A. Counts (San Francisco Office)
Katherine H. Cowan (San Francisco Office)
Angela A. Dahl (San Diego Office)
Brian M. Daucher (Orange County Office)
Susan Morton Derian
Kristina M. Diaz
Karin A. Dougan (San Diego Office)
Joelle Drucker
Dana DuFrane (San Francisco Office)
Stephen J. Duggan (San Francisco Office)
Phillip J. Eskenazi
Laura C. Fentonmiller
Teresa M. Fitzgerald
Linda Fox (San Diego Office)
Ann H. Fromholz
William Garrett
Robert S. Gerber (San Diego Office)
Anna E. Goodwin (San Francisco Office)
David T. Han
William Davis Harn
Paula A. Hobson
Donna L. Hueckel
Frank W. Iaffaldano
Karen L. Imbernino (Orange County Office)
David E. Isenberg
Kristen A. Jensen (San Francisco Office)
Beverly Johnson
Mark D. Johnson
Brian W. Jones (San Francisco Office)
Christopher J. Kearns (San Diego Office)
Sarah D. Keller
Tracey A. Kennedy
Jay T. Kinn
Kelly Kinnon
Rebecca C. Klipfel (Orange County Office)
Bridget Lanouette (San Francisco Office)
Laura A. Larks
H. Anthony Lewis (San Diego Office)
Courtney M. Lynch
Philip A. Magen (San Diego Office)
Harold S. Marenus
Alan H. Martin (Orange County Office)
Candace L. Matson
Ryan D. McCortney
Susan F. McCortney
Maureen C. McLaughlin (San Francisco Office)
Leslie J. McShane
Dani Jo Young Merryman
Lisa Goodwin Michael
Paul M. Miloknay
Elena Muravina
Randy J. Myricks
Timothy W. J. O'Brien (San Diego Office)
Cindy M. Oakes (San Francisco Office)
Patricia V. Ostiller
Jeffrey J. Parker
David A. Pursley (San Francisco Office)
Lynne M. Rasmussen
Felicia R. Reid (San Francisco Office)
Michael Reisz
James M. René
Steven A. Ross
Scott F. Roybal
Betty J. Santohigashi (San Diego Office)
Lara A. Saunders (Orange County Office)
Craig M. Schmitz
Richard C. Seavey
Erlinda G. Shrenger
Mark K. Slater (San Francisco Office)
Kay S. Solomon
Mark A. Spitzer
Michael St. Denis
Michael D. Stewart (Orange County Office)
Lisa H. Sturzenegger
Barry Sullivan
Stanley Sze
Lei K. Udell (San Diego Office)
Alan Van Derhoff (San Diego Office)
Perry Joseph Viscounty (Orange County Office)
Nellwyn Voorhies
Holly O. Whatley
Michael E. Wilbur (San Francisco Office)
Tara L. Wilcox (San Diego Office)
Margaret W. Wolfe
John A. Yacovelle (San Diego Office)
Timothy J. Yoo

*Professional Corporation

For full biographical listings, see the Martindale-Hubbell Law Directory

SIDLEY & AUSTIN (AV)

A Partnership including Professional Corporations
555 West Fifth Street, 40th Floor, 90013-1010
Telephone: 213-896-6000
Telecopier: 213-896-6600
Chicago, Illinois Office: One First National Plaza 60603.
Telephone: 312-853-7000.
Telecopier: 312-853-7036.
New York, New York Office: 875 Third Avenue 10022.
Telephone: 212-906-2022.
Telecopier: 212-906-2021.
Washington, D.C. Office: 1722 Eye Street, N.W. 20006.
Telephone: 202-736-8000.
Telecopier: 202-736-8711.
London, England Office: Broadwalk House, 5 Appold Street, EC2A 2AA.
Telephone: 011-44-71-621-1616.
Telecopier: 011-44-71-626-7937.
Tokyo, Japan Office: Taisho Seimei Hibiya Building, 7th Floor, 9-1, Yurakucho, 1 Chome, Chiyoda-ku, 100.
Telephone: 011-81-3-3218-5900.
Facsimile: 011-81-3-3218-5922.
Singapore Office: 36 Robinson Road, #18-01 City House, Singapore 0106.
Telephone: 011-65-224-5000.
Telecopier: 011-65-224-0530.

RESIDENT PARTNERS

Amy L. Applebaum
Philip M. Battaglia
David W. Burhenn
Gary J. Cohen
Stephen G. Contopulos
M. Scott Cooper
George Deukmejian
Lori Huff Dillman
James F. Donlan
Edward D. Eddy III
Bradley H. Ellis
Donald Etra
Robert Fabrikant
Howard D. Gest
Richard J. Grad
Johnny D. Griggs
Larry G. Gutterridge
Kent A. Halkett
Adam M. Handler
Thomas P. Hanrahan
James M. Harris
Richard W. Havel
Marc I. Hayutin
Stuart L. Kadison
Michael C. Kelley
Daniel G. Kelly, Jr.
Moshe J. Kupietzky
Perry L. Landsberg
Theodore N. Miller
Sally Schultz Neely
Edwin L. Norris
Peter I. Ostroff
Thomas E. Patterson
Richard T. Peters
Linda S. Peterson
Howard J. Rubinroit
Donald L. Samuels
Joel G. Samuels
Sherwin L. Samuels
J. Ronald Trost *
D. William Wagner

RETIRED PARTNERS

George W. McBurney
Robert H. Shutan *

RETIRED COUNSEL

Richard Schauer

RESIDENT ASSOCIATES

David G. Andersen
William Archer
Alan Au
Lee L. Auerbach
Randee J. Barak
Ellie Mask Bertwell
Jonathan M. Brenner
Karen L. Burrus
Linda F. Callison
Ronald C. Cohen
Russell L. Dees
Christopher G. Emch
Gordon K. Eng
Jeffrey M. Fisher
Jennifer C. Hagle
Mark J. Jenness
Robert J. Keenan
Kevin T. Lantry
Jefferson K. Logan
Thomas A. McWatters III
George M. Means
J. Kevin Mills
Deborah A. Nolan
Sharon H. Pohoryles
Judith M. Praitis
John V. Pridjian
Jay D. Rockey
Ronie M. Schmelz
John W. Scruton
Douglas P. Solomon
Sarah V. J. Spyksma
Joseph G. Swan
Shawna M. Swanson
Laurine E. Tuleja
Joyce L. Wallach
Stanley J. Wallach
Michael D. Wright

*Denotes a lawyer employed by a Professional Corporation which is a member of the Firm.

For full biographical listings, see the Martindale-Hubbell Law Directory

SONNENSCHEIN NATH & ROSENTHAL (AV)

601 South Figueroa Street, Suite 1500, 90017
Telephone: 213-623-9300
Telecopier: 213-623-9924
Chicago, Illinois Office: Suite 8000 Sears Tower, 233 South Wacker Drive.
Telephone: 312-876-8000.
Cable Address: "Sonberk".
Telex: 25-3526.
Facsimile: 312-876-7934.
New York, N.Y. Office: 1221 Avenue of the Americas, 24th Floor.
Telephone: 212-768-6700.
Facsimile: 212-391-1247.
Washington, D.C. Office: 1301 K Street, N.W., Suite 600 East Tower.
Telephone: 202-408-6400.
Fax: 202-408-6399.

(See Next Column)

SONNENSCHEIN NATH & ROSENTHAL—*Continued*

San Francisco, California Office: 685 Market Street, 10th Floor.
Telephone: 415-882-5000.
Facsimile: 415-543-5472; 882-5038.
St. Louis, Missouri Office: One Metropolitan Square, Suite 3000.
Telephone: 314-241-1800.
Facsimile: 314-259-5959.

Michael J. Bayard	Ronald D. Kent
Ernest P. Burger	Lee T. Paterson
Charles R. Campbell, Jr.	Laura R. Petroff
Martin J. Foley	Andria K. Richey
Matthew C. Fragner	Michael W. Ring
Peter J. Gurfein	Robert F. Scoular
Elliott J. Hahn	Norbert M. Seifert
Mark T. Hansen	J. A. Shafran

Susan M. Walker

ASSOCIATES

Adam Scott Bram	Kenji Kawahigashi (Not admitted in CA)
Anthony Capobianco	Paul Kuruk
Nargis Choudhry	Pauline Ng Lee
Rubin E. Cruse, Jr.	Richard J. Mathias
Stephen J. Curran	Dwayne P. McKenzie
Karin Mason Garell	Grace Ellen Mueller
Brent Matthew Giddens	Bin Xue Sang
Bryan C. Jackson	David Simantob
Scott L. Jones	T. Mark Smith
Matthew I. Kaplan (Not admitted in CA)	Diane Sovereign

Lauren M. Yu

For full biographical listings, see the Martindale-Hubbell Law Directory

---

STROOCK & STROOCK & LAVAN (AV)

Suite 1800, 2029 Century Park East, 90067-3086
Telephone: 310-556-5800
Telecopier: (310) 556-5959
Cable Address: "Plastroock, L.A."
Telex: Plastroock LSA 677190 (Domestic and International)
New York, N.Y. Office: Seven Hanover Square, 10004-2696.
Telephone: 212-806-5400.
Telecopiers: (212) 806-5919; (212) 806-6006; (212) 806-6086; (212) 425-9509; (212) 806-6176. Telexes: Stroock UT 177693 and Plastroock NYK 177077 (International).
Cable Address: "Plastroock, NYK."
New York Conference Center: 767 Third Avenue, New York, N.Y., 10017-2023.
Telephones: 212-806-5767; 5768; 5769; 5770.
Telecopier: (212) 421-6234.
Washington, D.C. Office: 1150 Seventeenth Street, N.W., Suite 600, 20036-4652.
Telephone: 202-452-9250.
Telecopier: (202) 293-2293.
Cable Address: "Plastroock-Washington." Telexes: 64238 STROOCK DC; 89401 STROOCK DC.
Miami, Florida Office: 200 South Biscayne Boulevard, Suite 3300, First Union Financial Center, 33131-2385.
Telephone: 305-358-9900.
Telecopier: (305) 789-9302.
Telex: 803133 Stroock Mia. (Domestic and International); Broward Line: 527-9900.
Budapest, Hungary Office: East-West Business Center, Rákóczi ut 1-3, H-1088.
Telephone: 001-361-266-9520 or 011-361-266-7770.
Telecopier: 011-361-266-9279.

RESIDENT PARTNERS

Barry L. Dastin	Margaret A. Nagle
David L. Gersh	Michael F. Perlis
Rick S. Kirkbride	Arnold M. Quittner (P.C.)
Joel M. Kozberg	Henry J. Silberberg
Gerald J. Mehlman	Julia B. Strickland
Schuyler M. Moore	Michael M. Umansky

Bennett J. Yankowitz

RETIRED PARTNERS

Merrill E. Jenkins	William H. Levit (P.C.)

Robert M. Shafton

Judith L. Anderson	David S. Lippes (Not admitted in CA)
Lynda Attenborough	Mary D. Manesis
Erik A. Christiansen	Karynne G. Popper
James W. Denison	Denise K. Russell
Richard S. Forman (Not admitted in CA)	Craig S. Seligman
Anna M. Graves	Lisa Simonetti
Sheri Jeffrey	Glenn D. Smith
Nicholas F. Klein	John E. Somorjai
Kevin J. Leichter	Chauncey M. Swalwell

Robin Van Es

For full biographical listings, see the Martindale-Hubbell Law Directory

SULLIVAN & CROMWELL (AV)

444 South Flower Street, 90071-2901
Telephone: 213-955-8000
Telecopier: 213-683-0457
New York City Offices: 125 Broad Street, 10004-2498; Midtown Office: 250 Park Avenue, 10177-0021.
Telephone: 212-558-4000.
Telex: 62694 (International); 12-7816 (Domestic).
Cable Address: "Ladycourt, New York".
Telecopier: 125 Broad Street 212-558-3588; 250 Park Avenue 212-558-3792.
Washington, D.C. Office: 1701 Pennsylvania Avenue, N.W., 20006-5805.
Telephone: 202-956-7500.
Telex: 89625.
Telecopier: 202-293-6330.
Paris Office: 8, Place Vendôme, Paris 75001, France.
Telephone: (011)(331)4450-6000.
Telex: 240654.
Telecopier: (011)(331)4450-6060.
London Office: St. Olave's House, 9a Ironmonger Lane, London EC2V 8EY, England.
Telephone: (011)(44171)710-6500.
Telecopier: (011)(44171)710-6565.
Melbourne, Australia Office: 101 Collins Street, Melbourne, Victoria 3000.
Telephone: (011)(613)654-1500.
Telecopier: (011)(613)654-2422.
Tokyo Office: Gaikokuho Jimu Bengoshi Office of Robert G. DeLaMater, a member of the firm of Sullivan & Cromwell, Tokio Kaijo Building Shinkan, 2-1, Marunouchi, 1-chome Chiyoda-ku, Tokyo 100, Japan.
Telephone: (011)(813)3213-6140.
Telecopier: (011)(813)3213-6470.
Hong Kong Office: 28th Floor, Nine Queen's Road, Central, Hong Kong.
Telephone: (011)(852)826-8688.
Telecopier: (011)(852)522-2280.

PARTNERS IN LOS ANGELES

Stanley F. Farrar	Robert A. Sacks
Charles F. Rechlin	Alison S. Ressler
Frank H. Golay, Jr.	Michael H. Steinberg

ASSOCIATES IN LOS ANGELES

Elizabeth S. Bluestein	Ellen C. Nachtigall (Not admitted in CA)
Andrew M. Burton	Harry A. Olivar, Jr.
Paul M. Kinsella	Michael J. O'Sullivan
Steven S. Lucas	Michael L. Preston
Cathleen E. McLaughlin (Not admitted in CA)	John L. Savva
Keith C. Nashawaty	Steven B. Stokdyk

Steven W. Thomas

For full biographical listings, see the Martindale-Hubbell Law Directory

---

SULLIVAN, WALSH & WOOD (AV)

Wells Fargo Center, 333 South Grand Avenue, 37th Floor, 90071-1599
Telephone: 213-488-9200
Telecopier: 213-488-9664

MEMBERS OF FIRM

Michael R. Sullivan	E. Eugene Walsh

ASSOCIATES

Douglas G. Carroll	Richard J. Sestak

OF COUNSEL

Scott E. Wood	Martin J. Spear

For full biographical listings, see the Martindale-Hubbell Law Directory

---

SULLIVAN, WORKMAN & DEE (AV)

A Partnership including a Professional Corporation
Twelfth Floor, 800 Figueroa Street, 90017
Telephone: 213-624-5544
Fax: 213-627-7128

PARTNERS

Roger M. Sullivan (A Professional Corporation)	Charles D. Cummings
	Charles F. Callanan
Henry K. Workman	Gary A. Kovacic
John J. Dee	Joseph S. Dzida, Jr.

John E. Mackel, III

Paul C. Epstein	Ernest E. Sanchez
Susan Mapel Kahn	Christopher K. Cooper

Emil J. Wohl

Reference: First Business Bank.

For full biographical listings, see the Martindale-Hubbell Law Directory

---

TAYLOR KUPFER SUMMERS & RHODES

(See Pasadena)

Los Angeles—Continued

TUTTLE & TAYLOR, A LAW CORPORATION (AV)

355 South Grand Avenue, 90071-3101
Telephone: 213-683-0600
Facsimile: 213-683-0225
Washington, D.C. Office: Tuttle, Taylor & Heron, 1025 Thomas Jefferson Street, N.W..
Telephone: 202-342-1300.
Facsimile: 202-342-5880.
Sacramento, California Office: Tuttle & Taylor, A Law Corporation, 980 Ninth Street.
Telephone: 916-449-9950.
Facsimile: 916-449-9953.

Edward W. Tuttle (1877-1960)
Edward E. Tuttle
Robert G. Taylor
Merlin W. Call
Frank C. Christl
Patrick L. Shreve
C. David Anderson
Richard S. Berger
John R. Liebman
Alan E. Friedman
Timi Anyon Hallem
Merrick John Bobb
Charles L. Woltmann
Douglas W. Beck
John Arthur Moe, II
Robert L. Shuler (Resident, Sacramento, California Office)
Mark A. Borenstein
Nancy E. Howard
Marc L. Brown
Michael H. Bierman
Louis E. Kempinsky
Frank E. Melton
Gordon A. Goldsmith
Gregory D. Schetina
James R. Gilson
Diann H. Kim
Marla J. Aspinwall
Robin D. Wiener
Edward A. Mendoza
Jeffrey D. Wexler
David B. Friedman

Kathleen M. Wohn
Rosario M. Sindel
Julio A. Thompson
John R. Dent
Nicolas H. Miller
Sung H. Shin
Marnie S. Carlin
Kate Schneider
Brenda R. Landau
Ralph M. Semien
Dahni K. Tsuboi
Andrea V. Ramos
Hillary A. Davidson
Peter V. Lee
Sam S. Oh
Sherry L. Appel
Malissia R. Lennox
Kathryn E. Olson
Thomas I. Dupuis
Shannon Sullivan-Martinez

OF COUNSEL

Julian B. Heron, Jr. (Resident, Washington, D.C. Office)
Jerry W. Kennedy (Resident, Washington, D.C. Office)
Pamela G. Bothwell

Reference: Union Bank, Century Boulevard Office (Los Angeles, California).

For full biographical listings, see the Martindale-Hubbell Law Directory

WITTER AND HARPOLE (AV)

270 Los Angeles World Trade Center, 350 South Figueroa Street, 90071
Telephone: 213-624-1311
FAX: 213-620-0430
Newport Beach, California Office: Suite 1050, 610 Newport Center Drive.
Telephone: 714-644-7600.
Fax: 714-759-1014.

MEMBERS OF FIRM

Myron E. Harpole
George G. Witter (1895-1978)
Eugene Harpole (1896-1987)
Debra M. Olsen (Resident, Newport Beach Office)

OF COUNSEL

James D. Harris (A Professional Corporation)

Reference: Union Bank (Newport Beach, Calif.).

For full biographical listings, see the Martindale-Hubbell Law Directory

MANHATTAN BEACH, Los Angeles Co.

RICHARD W. LYMAN, JR. (AV)

1601 North Sepulveda Boulevard Box 194, 90266-5133
Telephone: 310-546-7607
Fax: 310-546-7608

For full biographical listings, see the Martindale-Hubbell Law Directory

*MARTINEZ,** Contra Costa Co.

BERNARD F. CUMMINS (AV)

917 Las Juntas Street, P.O. Box 351, 94553
Telephone: 510-228-3001
Fax: 510-228-6825

For full biographical listings, see the Martindale-Hubbell Law Directory

*MARYSVILLE,** Yuba Co.

RICH, FUIDGE, MORRIS & SANBROOK, INC. (AV)

1129 D Street, Drawer "A", 95901
Telephone: 916-742-7371
Fax: 916-742-5982

William P. Rich (1880-1965)
Richard H. Fuidge (1906-1976)
Chester Morris
John Sanbrook
Roland K. Iverson, Jr.
David R. Lane
Brant J. Bordsen
Stephen W. Berrier
Jill Cernuda
Michael E. Hennessy

Joshua G. Harris

General Counsel: Linda Fire Protection District; City of Yuba City; County of Yuba; City of Live Oak.
Local Counsel: California State Automobile Assn.; State Farm Insurance Cos.

For full biographical listings, see the Martindale-Hubbell Law Directory

MENLO PARK, San Mateo Co.

JORGENSON, SIEGEL, MCCLURE & FLEGEL (AV)

Suite 210, 1100 Alma Street, 94025-3392
Telephone: 415-324-9300
Fax: 415-324-0227

MEMBERS OF FIRM

John D. Jorgenson
Marvin S. Siegel
William L. McClure
John L. Flegel

ASSOCIATES

Dan K. Siegel
Barbara Anne Murphy

Counsel for: City of Menlo Park.
References: University National Bank & Trust Co. (Palo Alto); Bank of America National Trust & Savings Assn.

For full biographical listings, see the Martindale-Hubbell Law Directory

*MERCED,** Merced Co.

ALLEN, POLGAR, PROIETTI & FAGALDE (AV)

A Partnership including a Professional Corporation
1640 "N" Street, Suite 200, P.O. Box 2184, 95344
Telephone: 209-723-4372
Fax: 209-723-7397
Mariposa, California Office: 5079 Highway 140. P.O. Box 1907.
Telephone: 209-966-3007.
Fax: 209-742-6353.

MEMBERS OF FIRM

Terry L. Allen (P.C.)
Gary B. Polgar
Donald J. Proietti
Michael A. Fagalde
F. Dana Walton (Resident, Mariposa Office)
Jeffrey S. Kaufman
Julie E. Furman-Stodolka
Brian L. McCabe

For full biographical listings, see the Martindale-Hubbell Law Directory

*MODESTO,** Stanislaus Co.

CRABTREE, SCHMIDT, ZEFF & JACOBS (AV)

1100 14th Street, Second Floor, P.O. Box 3307, 95353
Telephone: 209-522-5231
Fax: 209-526-0632

MEMBERS OF FIRM

Robert W. Crabtree
Walter J. Schmidt
Thomas D. Zeff
Nan Cohan Jacobs

ASSOCIATES

E. Daniel Farrar

Counsel for: Great American Insurance Co.; United Pacific/Reliance Insurance Co.; Hahn Property Management Corp.; Kemper Insurance Co.; State Farm Fire & Casualty; National Can Co.; Pacific Valley National Bank; Central Valley Production Credit Association.

For full biographical listings, see the Martindale-Hubbell Law Directory

DAMRELL, NELSON, SCHRIMP, PALLIOS & LADINE, A PROFESSIONAL CORPORATION (AV)

1601 I Street, Fifth Floor, 95354
Telephone: 209-526-3500
Fax: 209-526-3534
Sacramento, California Office: Suite 200, 1100 K Street.
Telephone: 916-447-2909.
Fax: 916-447-0552.
Oakdale, California Office: 703 West "F" Street, P.O. Drawer C.
Telephone: 209-848-3500.
Fax: 209-848-3400.

(See Next Column)

DAMRELL, NELSON, SCHRIMP, PALLIOS & LADINE A PROFESSIONAL CORPORATION—*Continued*

Frank C. Damrell (1898-1988)	Steven G. Pallios
Frank C. Damrell, Jr.	Wray F. Ladine
Duane L. Nelson	Matthew O. Pacher
Roger M. Schrimp	Susan D. Siefkin

Fred A. Silva

Craig W. Hunter	Wendelin Z. Warwick
Anthony J. Sarkis	Elizabeth T. Clayton
John K. Peltier	Christopher G. Daniel
James F. Lewis	Debra L. Klevatt
Jefferey A. Wooten	Lisa L. Gillispie

Robert F. Pomper

OF COUNSEL

Ann M. Veneman	Cressey H. Nakagawa

Representative Clients: American Honda Motor Co., Inc.; Bronco Wine Co.; E. & J. Gallo Winery; Gallo Glass Co.; The Luckey Co.; Norfolk Southern Corp.; Pep Boys of California, Inc.; W. R. Grace & Co.; National Medical Enterprises, Inc.; Ogden Corp.

For full biographical listings, see the Martindale-Hubbell Law Directory

GIANELLI & FORES, A PROFESSIONAL LAW CORPORATION (AV)

1014 16th Street, P.O. Box 3212, 95353
Telephone: 209-521-6260
Telecopier: 209-521-5971

Louis F. Gianelli	David L. Gianelli
Michael L. Gianelli	Stephen A. Critzer
Robert P. Fores	James R. McDade

Alison A. Sconyers

For full biographical listings, see the Martindale-Hubbell Law Directory

STOCKTON & SADLER (AV)

1034 Twelfth Street, P.O. Box 3153, 95353
Telephone: 209-523-6416
Fax: 209-523-2315

MEMBERS OF FIRM

Cleveland J. Stockton	James L. Sadler

ASSOCIATES

Karen Tall Sadler

Representative Clients: Dan Mellis Liquors; American Lumber Co.; Paul's Rexall Drug Stores; American Distributing Co.; Tro-Pic-Kal Mfg. Co.; Pete Pappas Broadcasting Co.; Pete Pappas Broadcasting, Inc.; Sanders Construction Co.; Goldrush Broadcasting, Inc.; Paul M. Zagaris Realtor, Inc.

For full biographical listings, see the Martindale-Hubbell Law Directory

MONROVIA, Los Angeles Co. — (Refer to Arcadia)

MONTEREY, Monterey Co.

HUDSON, MARTIN, FERRANTE & STREET (AV)

490 Calle Principal, P.O. Box 112, 93940
Telephone: 408-375-3151
Telecopier: 408-375-0131

MEMBERS OF FIRM

W. G. Hudson (1877-1954)	Carmel Martin, Jr.
Carmel Martin (1879-1965)	Peter J. Coniglio
Peter J. Ferrante (1903-1975)	Gerald B. Dalton
William L. Hudson (1907-1982)	Michael S. Sosnowski
Webster Street (1898-1984)	Michael A. Albov
John F. Martin	Peter R. Williams

Representative Clients: California-American Water Co.; Monterey County Bank; Fisherman's Wharf Property Owners Assn.; Monterey Peninsula TV Cable; Granite Construction Co., Inc.; CTB-MacMillan/McGraw-Hill; Cypress Coast Bank.
References: Bank of America National Trust & Savings Assn. (Monterey and Pacific Grove Offices); Wells Fargo Bank (Monterey Branch).

For full biographical listings, see the Martindale-Hubbell Law Directory

THOMPSON, HUBBARD & OMETER, A LAW CORPORATION (AV)

Aguajito Building, 400 Camino Aguajito, 93940
Telephone: 408-372-7571
Salinas: 408-422-6763
Fax: 408-372-1700
Fax: 408-372-9003

Ralph W. Thompson	Jo Marie Ometer
Donald G. Hubbard	Timothy J. Walsh

Alexander F. Hubbard

For full biographical listings, see the Martindale-Hubbell Law Directory

*NAPA,** Napa Co.

COOMBS & DUNLAP (AV)

1211 Division Street, 94559
Telephone: 707-252-9100
Fax: 707-252-8516
St. Helena, California Office: 1110 Adams Street.
Telephone: 707-963-5202; 944-8779.

Frank L. Coombs (1853-1934)	Nathan F. Coombs (1881-1973)

Frank L. Dunlap (1913-1984)

MEMBERS OF FIRM

Malcolm A. Mackenzie	Diane L. Dillon
C. Preston Shackelford	L. Randolph Skidmore
Diane M. Price	Charles P. Kuntz

Donald M. Davis	Rafael Rios, III

OF COUNSEL

June E. Moroney

Representative Client: Town of Yountville.

For full biographical listings, see the Martindale-Hubbell Law Directory

*NEVADA CITY,** Nevada Co. — (Refer to Marysville)

NEWPORT BEACH, Orange Co.

BARTON, KLUGMAN & OETTING (AV)

A Partnership of Professional Corporations
Suite 700, 4400 MacArthur Boulevard, P.O. Box 2350, 92660
Telephone: 714-752-7551
Telecopier: 714-752-0288
Los Angeles, California Office: 37th Floor, 333 South Grand Avenue, 90071-1599.
Telephone: 213-621-4000.
Telecopier: 213-625-1832.

COUNSEL TO FIRM

Robert M. Barton *

MEMBERS OF FIRM

Craig C. Alexander * (Resident)	Richard L. Brown * (Resident)
Dale A. Hudson * (Resident)	Cynthia Garrett (1951-1990)

ASSOCIATES

Linda Guthmann Krieger (Resident)	Mielissa M. Cowan (Resident)

*Denotes a lawyer whose Professional Corporation is a member of the partnership or is Counsel to the Firm

For full biographical listings, see the Martindale-Hubbell Law Directory

BROBECK, PHLEGER & HARRISON (AV)

A Partnership including A Professional Corporation
4675 MacArthur Court, Suite 1000, 92660
Telephone: 714-752-7535
Facsimile: 714-752-7522
San Francisco, California Office: Spear Street Tower, One Market.
Telephone: 415-442-0900.
Palo Alto, California Office: Two Embarcadero Place, 2200 Geng Road.
Telephone: 415-424-0160.
Los Angeles, California Office: 550 South Hope Street.
Telephone: 213-489-4060.
San Diego, California Office: 550 West C Street, Suite 1300.
Telephone: 619-234-1966.
Austin, Texas Office: 620 Congress Avenue, Suite 320.
Telephone: 512-477-5495.
Fax: 512-477-5813.
Denver, Colorado Office: 1125 Seventeenth Street, 15th Floor.
Telephone: 303-293-0760.
Fax: 303-299-8819.
New York, N.Y. Office: 1301 Avenue of the Americas, 30th Floor.
Telephone: 212-581-1600.
Fax: 212-586-7878.
Brobeck Hale and Dorr International Offices:
London, England Office: Veritas House, 125 Finsbury Pavement, London EC2A 1NQ.
Telephone: 44 071 638 6688.
Facsimile: 44 071 638 5888.
Prague, Czech Republic Office: Brehova 1, 110 00 Praha 1.
Telephone: 422 232-8461.
Facsimile: 422 232-8444.

RESIDENT PARTNERS

Roger M. Cohen	Gregory W. Preston
Richard A. Fink	Frederic Alport Randall, Jr.
Bruce R. Hallett	Joseph E. Thomas
Kathlene W. Lowe	Gabrielle M. Wirth

OF COUNSEL

R. Terrence Crowley

(See Next Column)

BROBECK, PHLEGER & HARRISON, *Newport Beach—Continued*

ASSOCIATES

Phillip Ashman
Richard J. Babcock
John S. Baker
James S. Brennan
Laura M. Brower
Susan N. Cayley
Kent M. Clayton
Nancy J. Dewhirst
Steven N. Holland
Lisa L. Horlick
Bernard C. Jasper
Lee J. Leslie
Robert I. Newton
Pamela M. Roberson
Lisa Anne Schechter
Ann M. Sterling
J. Russell Tyler, Jr.

For full biographical listings, see the Martindale-Hubbell Law Directory

BUCHALTER, NEMER, FIELDS & YOUNGER, A PROFESSIONAL CORPORATION (AV)

Suite 300, 620 Newport Center Drive, 92660
Telephone: 714-760-1121
Fax: 714-720-0182
Los Angeles, California Office: 24th Floor, 601 South Figueroa Street.
Telephone: 213-891-0700.
Fax: 213-896-0400.
New York, New York Office: 19th Floor, 237 Park Avenue.
Telephone: 212-490-8600.
Fax: 212-490-6022.
San Francisco, California Office: 29th Floor, 333 Market Street.
Telephone: 415-227-0900.
Fax: 415-227-0770.
San Jose, California Office: 12th Floor, 50 West San Fernando Street.
Telephone: 408-298-0350.
Fax: 408-298-7683.
Century City, California Office: Suite 2400, 1801 Century Park East.
Telephone: 213-891-0700.
Fax: 310-551-0233.

Clifford John Meyer
Theodor C. Albert
Debra Solle Healy
Kirk S. Rense

OF COUNSEL

Marcus M. Kaufman

Bruce M. Boyd
Lori S. Ross
Jeffrey I. Golden
Mark M. Scott
Jennifer Ann Golison
David Mark Hershorin
Brian A. Kumamoto
Lori Suzanne Carver
Evan D. Smiley

References: City National Bank; Wells Fargo Bank; Metrobank.

For full biographical listings, see the Martindale-Hubbell Law Directory

DAVIS, PUNELLI, KEATHLEY & WILLARD (AV)

610 Newport Center Drive, Suite 1000, P.O. Box 7920, 92658-7920
Telephone: 714-640-0700
Telecopier: 714-640-0714
San Diego, California Office: 4370 La Jolla Village Drive, Suite 300.
Telephone: 619-558-2581.

MEMBERS OF FIRM

Robert E. Willard
S. Eric Davis
Frank Punelli, Jr.
H. James Keathley
Leonard R. Sager
Eric G. Anderson
Katherine D. O'Brian

OF COUNSEL

Lewis K. Uhler

For full biographical listings, see the Martindale-Hubbell Law Directory

MCDERMOTT, WILL & EMERY (AV)

A Partnership including Professional Corporations
1301 Dove Street, Suite 500, 92660-2444
Telephone: 714-851-0633
Facsimile: 714-851-9348
Chicago, Illinois Office: 227 West Monroe Street.
Telephone: 312-372-2000.
Telex: 253565 MILAM CGO.
Facsimile: 312-984-7700.
Boston, Massachusetts Office: 75 State Street, Suite 1700.
Telephone: 617-345-5000.
Telex: 951324 MILAM BSN.
Facsimile: 617-345-5077.
Miami, Florida Office: 201 South Biscayne Boulevard.
Telephone: 305-358-3500.
Telex: 441777 LEYES.
Facsimile: 305-347-6500.
Washington, D.C. Office: 1850 K Street, N.W.
Telephone: 202-887-8000.
Telex: 253565 MILAM CGO.
Facsimile: 202-778-8087.
Los Angeles, California Office: 2049 Century Park East.
Telephone: 310-277-4110.
Facsimile: 310-277-4730.

(See Next Column)

New York, N.Y. Office: 1211 Avenue of the Americas.
Telephone: 212-768-5400.
Facsimile: 212-768-5444.
St. Petersburg, Russia Office: 2/2 Tchaikovsky Street, #517, 191187 St. Petersburg, Russia.
Telephone: (7) (812) 273-9831.
Facsimile: (7) (812) 9831.
Vilnius, Lithuania Office: Smetonos 6, 2600 Vilnius, Lithuania.
Telephone: 370 2 61-43-08.
Facsimile: 370 2 22-79-55.
Associated (Independent) Offices:
Brussels, Blegium: Uettwiller Grelon Lippens Dekeyser, 73 avenue Vandendriessche, 1150 Brussels, Belgium.
Telephone: (32) (2) 772-87-50.
Facsimile: (32) (2) 772-87-52.
London, England: Paisner & Co, Bouverie House, 154 Fleet Street, London EC4A 2DQ, England.
Telephone: (44) (71) 353-0299.
Facsimile: (44) (71) 583-8621.
Paris, France: Uettwiller Grelon Gout Canat & Associes, 68, boulevard de Courcelles, 75017 Paris, France.
Telephone: (33) (1) 48 88 89 00.
Facsimile: (33) (1) 48 88 05 50.

MEMBERS OF FIRM

Thomas K. Brown
Jill M. Draffin
Paul B. George
Peter D. Holbrook
John B. Miles
Bernard E. Schneider
Steven M. Schott
Michael Schulman
David A. Sprowl

Anne Heller Duncan
Martin P. Florman
Susan E. Graham
Maria E. Grecky
Kimberly Knill
Claudia Kihano Parker
Stuart W. Price
Renée M. Raithel
Marianne Van Riper

For full biographical listings, see the Martindale-Hubbell Law Directory

O'MELVENY & MYERS (AV)

610 Newport Center Drive, Suite 1700, 92660
Telephone: 714-760-9600
Cable Address: "Moms"
Facsimile: 714-669-6994
Los Angeles, California Office: 400 South Hope Street.
Telephone: 213-669-6000.
Cable Address: "Moms".
Facsimile: 213-669-6407.
Century City, California Office: 1999 Avenue of the Stars, 7th Floor.
Telephone: 310-553-6700.
Facsimile: 310-246-6779.
San Francisco, California Office: Embarcadero Center West Tower, 275 Battery Street, Suite 2600.
Telephone: 415-984-8700.
Facsimile: 415-984-8701.
New York, N.Y. Office: Citicorp Center, 153 East 53rd Street, 54th Floor.
Telephone: 212-326-2000.
Facsimile: 212-326-2061.
Washington, D.C. Office: 555 13th Street, N.W., Suite 500 West.
Telephone: 202-383-5300.
Cable Address: "Moms".
Facsimile: 202-383-5414.
Newark, New Jersey Office: One Gateway Center, 7th Floor, 07102.
Telephone: 201-639-8600.
Facsimile: 201-639-8630.
London, England Office: 10 Finsbury Square, London, EC2A 1LA.
Telephone: 011-44-171-256-8451.
Facsimile: 011-44-171-638-8205.
Tokyo, Japan Office: Sanbancho KB-6 Building, 6 Sanbancho, Chiyoda-ku, Tokyo 102, Japan.
Telephone: 011-81-3-3239-2800.
Facsimile: 011-81-3-3239-2432.
Hong Kong Office: 1104 Lippo Tower, Lippo Centre, 89 Queensway, Central Hong Kong.
Telephone: 011-852-523-8266.
Facsimile: 011-852-522-1760.

MEMBERS OF FIRM

Douglas W. Abendroth
William G. Adams
Russell G. Allen
Jerry W. Carlton
Steven L. Edwards
Patricia Frobes
Pamela C. Gray
Catherine Burcham Hagen
Theodore C. Hamilton
Joseph J. Herron
Linda Shannon Heumann
Wayne Jacobsen
Phillip R. Kaplan
David A. Krinsky
Lowell C. Martindale, Jr.
Scott A. Meyerhoff
Paul E. Mosley
Robert A. Rizzi
Frank L. Rugani
James V. Selna
Gary J. Singer
Thomas E. Wolfe
Michael G. Yoder

OF COUNSEL

Barton Beek

(See Next Column)

O'MELVENY & MYERS—*Continued*

RESIDENT SPECIAL COUNSEL

Cormac J. Carney
Joseph L. Coleman
Karen K. Dreyfus
Thomas H. Reilly

RESIDENT ASSOCIATES

Reed N. Archambault
Kevin Ray Baker
Diane Wasil Biagianti
Michael G. Bosko
Bruce L. Campbell
Karen D. Craig
George C. Demos
Jennifer M. Friedland
Lise Hamilton
Lawrence J. Hilton
John D. Hudson
M. Flynn Justice, III
Kathleen E. Kinney
Lisa Litwiller
Vicki A. Nash
Poh-Leng Ng
Mark D. Peterson
Stergios Theologides
Kelby Van Patten
Larry A. Walraven
Brett J. Williamson
Todd R. Wulffson

For full biographical listings, see the Martindale-Hubbell Law Directory

---

SHEPPARD, MULLIN, RICHTER & HAMPTON (AV)

A Partnership including Professional Corporations
Seventh Floor, 4695 MacArthur Court, 92660
Telephone: 714-752-6400
Telecopier: 714-851-0739
Telex: 19-4424
Los Angeles, California Office: Forty-Eighth Floor, 333 South Hope Street.
Telephone: 213-620-1780.
Telecopier: 213-620-1398.
Cable Address: "Sheplaw".
Telex: 19-4424.
San Francisco, California Office: Seventeenth Floor, Four Embarcadero Center.
Telephone: 415-434-9100.
Telecopier: 415-434-3947.
Telex: 19-4424.
San Diego, California Office: Nineteenth Floor, 501 West Broadway.
Telephone: 619-338-6500.
Telecopier: 619-234-3815.
Telex: 19-4424.

MEMBERS OF FIRM

David M. Bosko
Dean A. Demetre
John J. Giovannone
Randolph B. Godshall
Andrew J. Guilford
Brent R. Liljestrom
John R. Simon *
Finley L. Taylor *

SPECIAL COUNSEL

Steven C. Nock

ASSOCIATES

Fredric I. Albert
Cindy Thomas Archer
Robert S. Beall
Barbara A. Benner
Rebecca Berg
Steven W. Cardoza
Justine Mary Casey
Gene R. Clark
Brian M. Daucher
Karen L. Imbernino
Rebecca C. Klipfel
Alan H. Martin
Lara A. Saunders
Michael D. Stewart
Perry Joseph Viscounty

*Professional Corporation

For full biographical listings, see the Martindale-Hubbell Law Directory

---

STRADLING, YOCCA, CARLSON & RAUTH, A PROFESSIONAL CORPORATION (AV)

Suite 1600, Wells Fargo Building, 660 Newport Center Drive, 92660-6441
Telephone: 714-725-4000
Telecopier: 714-725-4100
Mailing Address: P.O. Box 7680, 92658-7680

Fritz R. Stradling
Nick E. Yocca
C. Craig Carlson
William R. Rauth III
K. C. Schaaf
Richard C. Goodman
John J. Murphy
Thomas P. Clark, Jr.
Ben A. Frydman
David R. McEwen
Paul L. Gale
Rudolph C. Shepard
Robert J. Kane
Bruce C. Stuart
E. Kurt Yeager
Robert J. Whalen
Robert E. Rich
Randall J. Sherman
Bruce W. Feuchter
Mark J. Huebsch
Karen A. Ellis
Bruce D. May
Andrew F. Puzder
Donald J. Hamman
John J. Swigart, Jr.
Celeste Stahl Brady
Christopher J. Kilpatrick
Joel H. Guth
Julie McCoy Akins
Dawn C. Honeywell
Lawrence B. Cohn
Harley L. Bjelland
Stephen T. Freeman
Michael E. Flynn
Carol L. Lew

Michael A. Zablocki
Neila R. Bernstein
Nicholas J. Yocca
Julie M. Porter
Gary A. Pemberton
Denise Harbaugh Hering
Barbara Zeid Leibold
Jon E. Goetz

(See Next Column)

John D. Ireland
David H. Mann
Christopher M. Moropoulos
Elizabeth A. Newell
Darryl S. Gibson
Jee Hi Park
Dana M. Strabic
Todd R. Thakar
Richard T. Needham
Robert Craig Wallace
John F. Cannon
Jay Rappaport
John E. Woodhead, IV
Douglas P. Feick
William J. Morley
Mark L. Skaist
Jeffrey B. Coyne
Christine L. Luketic
Sandra Wakamiya Schaal
Matthew P. Thullen
Andrea S. Levitan
John David Vaughan
Steven M. Hanle
Michael Hennessey Mulroy
Mary Anne Wagner
Scott R. Maples

OF COUNSEL

John E. Breckenridge
Rena C. Stone

For full biographical listings, see the Martindale-Hubbell Law Directory

---

*OAKLAND,** Alameda Co.

BERRY & BERRY, A PROFESSIONAL CORPORATION (AV)

1300 Clay Street, Ninth Floor, P.O. Box 70250, Station D, 94612-0250
Telephone: 510-835-8330
Fax: 510-835-5117

Samuel H. Berry (1904-1990)
Phillip S. Berry
Carolyn Collins
Leonardo J. Vacchina
Peter R. Gilbert

Lynne P. Blair
Evanthia Spanos
Gregory D. Meronek
Ellen D. Berris
Laura Przetak

Representative Clients: Parke-Davis; Warner-Lambert; St. Paul Insurance Co.; Fireman's Fund Insurance Co.; American International Underwriters; Lloyd's of London; Celina Insurance Group; American Optical; Biomet, Inc.

For full biographical listings, see the Martindale-Hubbell Law Directory

---

FITZGERALD, ABBOTT & BEARDSLEY (AV)

A Partnership including Professional Corporations
1221 Broadway, 21st Floor, 94612-1837
Telephone: 510-451-3300
Telecopy: 510-451-1527

MEMBERS OF FIRM

Robert M. Fitzgerald (1858-1934)
Carl H. Abbott (1867-1933)
Charles A. Beardsley (1882-1963)
James C. Soper (Inc.)
Philip M. Jelley (Inc.)
Gerald C. Smith
Lawrence R. Shepp
Richard T. White
Michael P. Walsh
J. Brittain Habegger
Virginia Palmer
Timothy H. Smallsreed
Stephen M. Judson
Stephen M. Williams
Jonathan W. Redding
Beth E. Aspedon

ASSOCIATES

Kristin A. Pace
Robert F. Campbell
Michael M.K. Sebree
Antonia L. More
Maria I. Lawless
Matthew P. Matiasevich
Paul B. Salvaty

Attorneys for: Peterson Tractor Co.; Sunset View Cemetery Assn.; Bigge Crane & Rigging Corp.; Gillig Corp.
Local Counsel for: Exxon Corp.; J. I. Case Co.

For full biographical listings, see the Martindale-Hubbell Law Directory

---

HARDIN, COOK, LOPER, ENGEL & BERGEZ (AV)

1999 Harrison Street, 18th Floor, 94612-3541
Telephone: 510-444-3131
Telecopier: 510-839-7940

MEMBERS OF FIRM

J. Marcus Hardin (1905-1993)
L. S. Fletcher (1905-1964)
Herman Cook (1914-1982)
John C. Loper
Barrie Engel
Raymond J. Bergez
George S. Peyton, Jr.
Ralph A. Lombardi
Sandra F. Wagner
Willard L. Alloway
Gennaro A. Filice, III
Stephen McKae
Bruce P. Loper
Bruce E. McLeod
Eugene Brown, Jr.
Linda C. Roodhouse
Matthew S. Conant
Chris P. Lavdiotis
Robert D. Eassa
Peter O. Glaessner

Amber L. Kelly
Owen T. Rooney
John A. De Pasquale
Nicholas D. Kayhan
William H. Curtis
Elsa M. Baldwin
Rodney Ian Headington
Marshall A. Johnson
Diane R. Stanton
Jennifer M. Walker
Margaret L. Kotzebue
Amee A. Mikacich
Peter A. Strotz
Timothy J. McCaffery
Stephen J. Valen
Troy D. McMahan
Lisa L. Hillegas
GayLynn Renee Kirn
Richard V. Normington III
Kevin J. Chechak

(See Next Column)

HARDIN, COOK, LOPER, ENGEL & BERGEZ, *Oakland—Continued*

David A. Levin
Lisa M. Brown
Irene R. Hoffman
Jason J. Curliano

OF COUNSEL

Ronald A. Wagner
Lydia T. Van't Rood

Representative Clients: Firemans Fund Insurance Cos.; City of Piedmont; The Dow Chemical Co.; Nissan Motor Corp.; Subaru of America; Weyerhauser Co.; Bay Area Rapid Transit District; Diamond Shamrock; Home Indemnity Co.; Rhone-Poulenc.

For full biographical listings, see the Martindale-Hubbell Law Directory

KNOX RICKSEN (AV)

Lake Merritt Plaza, Suite 1700, 1999 Harrison Street, 94612
Telephone: 510-893-1000
Fax: 510-446-1946
Fairfield, Solano County, California Office: Corporate Plaza, Suite 300, 1261 Travis Boulevard.
Telephone: 707-426-3313.
Fax: 707-426-0426.
San Jose, Santa Clara County, California Office: 100 Park Center Plaza, Suite 560.
Telephone: 408-295-2828.
Fax: 408-295-6868.

MEMBERS OF FIRM

Wallace W. Knox (1905-1982)
Marshall Ricksen (1908-1975)
John C. Ricksen
Rupert H. Ricksen
William C. Robbins, III
Stephen S. Harper
Robert G. Allen
Thomas A. Palmer
Richard G. Logan, Jr.
Jeffrey A. Harper
Thomas E. Fraysse
Frederick D. Schwarz
Kenneth G. Hecht, Jr.
Mark L. Cederborg
Gregory D. Pike
Thomas V. Bret

ASSOCIATES

Pamela H. Bennett
John S. Boat
Kenneth A. Dreyfuss
James T. Gotch (Resident, Fairfield Office)
Thomas H. LemMon
Hubert Lenczowski
Kenneth J. McCarthy
Timothy Cass McKenzie
Mark C. Skilling
R. Patrick Snook

Representative Clients: Citicorp Savings; Southern Pacific Co.; American Home Products Corp.; Warren's Turf Nursery, Inc.; Kaiser Foundation Hospitals; Devcon Corp; Markstein Beverage Co.; California State Automobile Assn.; Inter Insurance Bureau; The Greater New York Insurance Group.

For full biographical listings, see the Martindale-Hubbell Law Directory

LARSON & BURNHAM, A PROFESSIONAL CORPORATION (AV)

1901 Harrison Street, 11th Floor, P.O. Box 119, 94604
Telephone: 510-444-6800
Fax: 510-835-6666

A. Hubbard Moffitt, Jr. (1908-1969)
Howard S. Rode (1907-1973)
Arthur Jay Moore, Jr. (1918-1984)
David O. Larson
Clark J. Burnham
Gregory D. Brown
George J. Ziser
Robert J. Lyman
Eric R. Haas
Scott C. Finch
Steven M. Marden
Ralph A. Zappala
Peter Dixon
Monica Dell'Osso
Jeffrey G. Bairey
Susan Feldsted Halman
Patrick K. M. McCarthy
Gary R. Selvin
H. Wayne Goodroe
Robert A. Ford
David R. Pinelli
Michael R. Reynolds
James L. Wraith
Richard J. Finn

Christopher L. Aguilar
Cathy L. Arias
Eric Axelsen
John P. Bevan
Tara D. Bodden
Melissa A. Bruzzano
Paul D. Caleo
Christopher J. Connell
Vera C. De Martini
Jacqueline de Souza
Michelle A. DesJardins
Lynn Diringer
Thomas M. Downey
William J. Duke
John B. Ellis
Pamela Fastiff Ellman
Susan E. Firtch
Douglas S. Free
Beth S. Freedman
Jennifer B. Gieseler
Ayesha Z. Hassan
James F. Hodgkins
Michael K. Johnson
Jane E. Kelly
Kathleen Kresnak
Frank C. Liuzzi
Pelayo Antonio Llamas, Jr.
Nancy K. McDonald
Michael T. McKeeman
Steven A. Nielsen
Peña Gustavo
Andrico Q. Penick
Noreen N. Quan
Trelawney James Riechert
James J. Rosati
Stephen Q. Rowell
Walter C. Rundin, III
Mai Sharif Shiver
Catherine Squillace
Bryan K. Stainfield
Anjali Talwar
Darrell T. Thompson
Shawn A. Toliver
John J. Verber

(See Next Column)

David H. Waters
David S. Webster
Stephen C. Whitney
Bradley M. Zamczyk
Barry Zoller

OF COUNSEL

James H. Riggs

Representative Clients: The Travelers Insurance Co.; Wholesale Building Supply Co.; U.S. Fidelity & Guaranty Co.; Home Insurance Co.; County of Alameda; City of Livermore; Shell Oil Co.; Exxon; Allied-Signal Inc.; Rohm and Haas Co.

For full biographical listings, see the Martindale-Hubbell Law Directory

MILLER, STARR & REGALIA, A PROFESSIONAL LAW CORPORATION (AV)

16th Floor, Ordway Building, One Kaiser Plaza, 94612
Telephone: 510-465-3800
Walnut Creek, California Office: 1331 North California Boulevard, Suite 700.
Telephone: 510-935-9400.

Edmund L. Regalia
Marvin B. Starr (Resident, Walnut Creek Office)
Harry D. Miller
Jefferson Frazier
Wilson F. Wendt
Leslie A. Johnson
Eugene H. Miller
James Frassetto
Gary E. Rosenberg
George B. Speir (Resident, Walnut Creek Office)
Karl Erich Geier (Resident, Walnut Creek Office)
Paul D. Marienthal (Resident, Walnut Creek Office)
Richard G. Carlston (Resident, Walnut Creek Office)
Victor Harris
James A. Tiemstra
Amy Matthew
Mark A. Cameron
William R. Plapinger
Lance H. Anderson
Arthur F. Coon
Michael E. DiGeronimo
Daniel R. Miller
Laurence W. Paradis
Lewis J. Soffer
Sean B. Absher
Thomas S. McConnell
Michael J. Hassen (Resident, Walnut Creek Office)
John H. Wunsch
William A. Falik
Lynne Yerkes (Resident, Walnut Creek Office)

Rachel J. Dragolovich
Basil S. Shiber
Linda A. Chung
Donald H. Baum (Resident, Walnut Creek Office)
W. Scott Shepard
Leslie E. Orr
Audrey Irwin
Kenneth R. Styles
Heidi Timken (Resident, Walnut Creek Office)
Melissa Bauman Ward
David E. Harris
Janine C. Ogando
Andrew Sabey

Representative Clients: Bank of the West; Hewlett Packard; Prometheus Development; First American Title Insurance Co.; Weyerhaeuser Co.

For full biographical listings, see the Martindale-Hubbell Law Directory

ONTARIO, San Bernardino Co.

COVINGTON & CROWE (AV)

1131 West Sixth Street, P.O. Box 1515, 91762
Telephone: 909-983-9393
Fax: 909-391-6762

MEMBERS OF FIRM

Harold A. Bailin (1930-1988)
Samuel P. Crowe
George W. Porter
Robert E. Dougherty
Donald G. Haslam
Robert F. Schauer
Edward A. Hopson
Stephen R. Wade
Jette R. Anderson
Audrey A. Perri
Tracy L. Tibbals
Melanie Fisch
Douglas C. Frost
Robert H. Reeder
R. Doug Donesky

ASSOCIATES

Howard S. Borenstein
Tammy S. Jager
Denise Matthey
Katrina West
Richard R. Muir
Kimberly A. Rohn
Debra L. Barbin
Rakesh C. Vail
Louis Jay Dennis
Daryl J. Lander
J. Michael Kaler
Eric S. Vail
Michael L. Armstrong

For full biographical listings, see the Martindale-Hubbell Law Directory

*OROVILLE,** Butte Co.

LEONARD & LYDE (AV)

A Partnership including Professional Corporations
1453 Huntoon Street, 95965
Telephone: 916-533-2662
Fax: 916-533-3843
Chico, California Office: 1600 Humboldt Road, Suite 1.
Telephone: 916-345-3494.
Fax: 916-345-0460.

(See Next Column)

LEONARD & LYDE—*Continued*

MEMBERS OF FIRM

Raymond A. Leonard (1916-1981)
C. Keith Lyde (Inc.)
George E. Washington
Dorsett Marc Lyde
Robert L. Davis (Inc.)

For full biographical listings, see the Martindale-Hubbell Law Directory

OXNARD, Ventura Co.

ENGLAND, WHITFIELD, SCHRÖEDER & TREDWAY (AV)

6th Floor, Union Bank Tower, 300 Esplanade Drive, 93030
Telephone: 805-485-9627
Ventura: 647-8237
Southern California Toll Free: 800-255-3485
Fax: 805-983-0297
Thousand Oaks, California Office: Rolling Oaks Office Center. 351 Rolling Oaks Drive.
Telephone: Southern California Toll Free: 800-255-3485.

MEMBERS OF FIRM

Theodore J. England
Anson M. Whitfield
Robert W. Schröeder
David W. Tredway
Robert A. McSorley
Stuart A. Comis
Mitchel B. Kahn
Mark A. Nelson
Eric J. Kananen
Mary E. Schröeder
Oscar C. Gonzalez
Steven K. Perrin

ASSOCIATES

William J. Kesatie
Melissa E. Cohen
Terry R. Bailey
Andrew S. Hughes
Madison M. Christian
Kurt Edward Kananen
William W. Webb
Jeremy J. F. Gray
Melodee A. Yee
Robert David Schwartz
Linda Kathryn Ash
Carla Jean Ortega

Representative Clients: Seneca Resources Corp. (oil & gas); Cal-Sun Produce Co.; Waste Management of California, Inc; Dah Chong Hong (Honda, Toyota, Mazda, Lexus, Accura, Saturn automobile dealerships); Willamette Industries; Oxnard Harbor Association of Realtors; Port of Hueneme; Conejo Valley Association of Realtors; Power-One, Inc.

For full biographical listings, see the Martindale-Hubbell Law Directory

LOWTHORP, RICHARDS, MCMILLAN, MILLER, CONWAY & TEMPLEMAN, A PROFESSIONAL CORPORATION (AV)

300 Esplanade Drive, Suite 850, P.O. Box 5167, 93031
Telephone: 805-981-8555
FAX: 805-983-1967

Carl F. Lowthorp, Jr. (1933-1992)
Richard A. Richards
Robert C. McMillan
Paul A. Miller
Charles J. Conway, Jr.
Alan R. Templeman
Patrick T. Loughman
Glenn J. Campbell
E.P. Michael Karcis
John Q. Masteller
Gregory J. Ramirez

LEGAL SUPPORT PERSONNEL

Elizabeth T. Ladiana, CLA

Reference: Ventura County National Bank.

For full biographical listings, see the Martindale-Hubbell Law Directory

NORDMAN, CORMANY, HAIR & COMPTON (AV)

1000 Town Center Drive, Sixth Floor, P.O. Box 9100, 93031-9100
Telephone: 805-485-1000
Ventura: 805-656-3304
Telecopier: 805-988-8387
805-988-7790
Westlake Village, California Office: 890 Hampshire Road, Suite A, 91361.
Telephone: 805-497-2795.

Ben E. Nordman, Founder (1913-1985)

MEMBERS OF FIRM

William H. Hair
Robert L. Compton (Also at Westlake Village Office)
Marc L. Charney
Ronald H. Gill
Larry L. Hines
Kenneth M. High, Jr.
Michael C. O'Brien
Laura K. McAvoy
Randall H. George
Janet Anne Reese (Also at Westlake Village Office)
Paul W. Kurzeka
Anthony H. Trembley
Jonathan Fraser Light
Kent M. Kellegrew (Also at Westlake Village Office)
William E. Winfield
Gerald M. Etchingham
Chris K. Kitasaki
Scott B. Samsky
Guy C. Parvex, Jr.
Robert J. Lent (Also at Westlake Village Office)

OF COUNSEL

Ralph L. Cormany
David A. Gerber (Also at Westlake Village Office)
John A. Slezak

(See Next Column)

ASSOCIATES

Anne M. Larsen
Susan M. Seemiller
John M. Andersen (Also at Westlake Village Office)
Laurel A. McLaughlin
Mark R. Pachowicz
Patricia A. Malone
Susan Westeen Novatt
Kathleen Janetatos Smith

LEGAL SUPPORT PERSONNEL

Edward L. Barry, Jr. (Administrator)

Representative Clients: Bank of A. Levy; Real Estate Investment Trust of California; Berry Petroleum Company; Amgen; Kmart Corp.; Saticoy Lemon Association; The Procter & Gamble Paper Products Co.; Clairol, Inc.; Halliburton Services; Schlumberger.

For full biographical listings, see the Martindale-Hubbell Law Directory

PALM SPRINGS, Riverside Co.

SCHLECHT, SHEVLIN & SHOENBERGER, A LAW CORPORATION (AV)

Suite 100, 801 East Tahquitz Canyon Way, P.O. Box 2744, 92263-2744
Telephone: 619-320-7161
Facsimile: 619-323-1758; 619-325-4623

James M. Schlecht
John C. Shevlin
Jon A. Shoenberger
Daniel T. Johnson

Bonnie Garland Guss
Karen S. Helmuth
R. Brad Sevier
David Darrin
Elizabeth A. Harreus

OF COUNSEL

Donald B. McNelley
Allen O. Perrier (Retired)

Representative Clients: Outdoor Resorts of America; The Escrow Connection; Wells Fargo Bank; Canyon Country Club; Waste Management Co.

For full biographical listings, see the Martindale-Hubbell Law Directory

PALO ALTO, Santa Clara Co.

BAKER & MCKENZIE (AV)

660 Hansen Way, P.O. Box 60309, 94304-0309
Telephone: (415) 856-2400
Intn'l. Dialing: (1-415) 856-2400
Facsimile: (1-415) 856-9299
Associated Offices of Baker & McKenzie in: Almaty, Amsterdam, Bangkok, Barcelona, Beijing, Berlin, Bogotá, Brasília, Brussels, Budapest, Buenos Aires, Cairo, Caracas, Chicago, Dallas, Frankfurt, Geneva, Hanoi, Ho Chi Minh City, Hong Kong, Juárez, Kiev, London, Madrid, Manila, Melbourne, México City, Miami, Milan, Monterrey, Moscow, New York, Paris, Prague, Rio de Janeiro, Riyadh, Rome, St. Petersburg, San Diego, San Francisco, São Paulo, Singapore, Stockholm, Sydney, Taipei, Tijuana, Tokyo, Toronto, Valencia, Warsaw, Washington, D.C. and Zürich.
Correspondent Law Firm: Hadiputranto, Hadinoto & Partners, Jakarta.

MEMBERS OF FIRM

Peter M. Astiz
Maurice S. Emmer
Tod L. Gamlen
John C. Klotsche (Not admitted in CA)
Michael J. Madda
Susan H. Nycum
John M. Peterson, Jr.
J. Pat Powers
André M. Saltoun
Gary D. Sprague

LOCAL PARTNER

Kent F. Wisner

ASSOCIATES

Michael Bumbaca
Robin A. Chesler
Robin L. Filion
Brian G. Geoghegan
Richard A. Manso
Owen P. Martikan (Not admitted in CA)
Michelle J. Wachs
John F. Weinkopf

For full biographical listings, see the Martindale-Hubbell Law Directory

BLASE, VALENTINE & KLEIN, A PROFESSIONAL CORPORATION (AV)

1717 Embarcadero Road, P.O. Box 51050, 94303
Telephone: 415-857-1717
Telecopier: 415-857-1288

Lawrence A. Klein
Peter A. Whitman
George C. Fisher
Craig S. Ritchey
Ellen B. Turbow
Jean K. McCown
Martha Corcoran Luemers
Karen E. Wentzel
John G. Hursh
Terence M. Kelly
Gillian G. Hays
David A. Kays
Anne Marie Flaherty
Terrence H. Cross
Jennifer Dew De Castro

COUNSEL

C. Grant Spaeth
Guy Blase
Paul C. Valentine

For full biographical listings, see the Martindale-Hubbell Law Directory

Palo Alto—Continued

BROBECK, PHLEGER & HARRISON (AV)

A Partnership including a Professional Corporation
Two Embarcadero Place, 2200 Geng Road, 94303
Telephone: 415-424-0160
San Francisco, California Office: Spear Street Tower, One Market.
Telephone: 415-442-0900.
Los Angeles, California Office: 550 South Hope Street.
Telephone: 213-489-4060.
San Diego, California Office: 550 West C Street, Suite 1300.
Telephone: 619-234-1966.
Orange County, California Office: 4675 MacArthur Court, Suite 1000, Newport Beach.
Telephone: 714-752-7535.
Austin, Texas Office: 620 Congress Avenue, Suite 320.
Telephone: 512-477-5495.
Fax: 512-477-5813.
Denver, Colorado Office: 1125 Seventeenth Street, 15th Floor.
Telephone: 303-293-0760.
Fax: 303-299-8819.
New York, N.Y. Office: 1301 Avenue of the Americas, 30th Floor.
Telephone: 212-581-1600.
Fax: 212-586-7878.
Brobeck Hale and Dorr International Offices :
London, England Office: Veritas House, 125 Finsbury Pavement, London EC2A 1NQ.
Telephone: 44 071 638 6688.
Facsimile: 44 071 638 5888.
Prague, Czech Republic Office: Brehova 1, 110 00 Praha 1.
Telephone: 422 232-8461.
Facsimile: 422 232-8444.

RESIDENT PARTNERS

William C. Anderson
William L. Anthony, Jr.
Robert Barr
Gari L. Cheever
Robert DeBerardine
Scott C. Dettmer
S. James DiBernardo
Jonathan C. Dickey
J. Stephan Dolezalek
Noemi C. (Nicky) Espinosa
Steven R. Franklin
David M. Furbush
Joshua L. Green
Robert V. Gunderson, Jr.
Jay K. Hachigian
Thomas W. Kellerman
Warren T. Lazarow
Edward M. Leonard
Luther Kent Orton
Denis R. Salmon
Brooks Stough
Thomas F. Villeneuve
Ronald S. Wynn

OF COUNSEL

Linda B. Daley
Shawn E. Lampron

RESIDENT ASSOCIATES

Valerie L. Aks
Anthony M. Allen
Craig Y. Allison
Ralph L. (Buddy) Arnheim III (Not admitted in CA)
Charles K. Ashley II
Christina L. Baker
Andrew Baw
Brian K. Beard
Edgar B. Cale, III
Thomas H. Carlson
Michael J. Casey
Vivian K. F. Chan
Colin Daniel Chapman
Jacqueline Cowden
Brian V. Donnelly
Luciana Fato Erb
Sonya F. Erickson
William W. Ericson
Carol R. Freeman
Tamar Fruchtman
William P. Garvey
Aarti C. Gurnani
Daniel R. Hansen
Dixie K. Hieb
Jeffrey P. Higgins
Franklin P. Huang
H. Richard Hukari
Karen Ikeda
Daniel M. Kaufman
Kina Lamblin
L.C. Lau
Gregory S. Lemmer
Elaine Llewelyn
Deborah J. Ludewig
Craig Mallery
David R. Mandelbrot
Paul G. Martino
Sharon E. Meieran
Keith A. Miller
Margaret E. Nibbi
Dan O'Connor
Michael A. Plumleigh
Zaitun Poonja
Christine L. Richardson
Melinda Collins Riechert
Roger F. Ross II
John H. Sellers
Douglas T. Sheehy
Lisa Ann Sobrato
Shannon Soqui
Robert G. Specker
Karen Y. Spencer
Kara Diane Spotts
Steven M. Spurlock
Jeffrey Y. Suto
Kay Tittle
Winnie Van
Glen R. Van Ligten
Craig R. Venable
John V. Wadsworth
M. Kip Welch
David S. Welsh
Eric L. Wesenberg
Deann K. Wright
James Y. M. Wu
Bennett Lyle Yee
David Thomas Young
Maribeth Younger
Robert V. W. Zipp

For full biographical listings, see the Martindale-Hubbell Law Directory

BROWN & BAIN (AV)

600 Hansen Way, 94306
Telephone: 415-856-9411
Telecopier: 415-856-6061
Phoenix, Arizona Affiliated Office: Brown & Bain, A Professional Association, 2901 North Central Avenue, P.O. Box 400.
Telephone: 602-351-8000.
Telecopier: 602-351-8516.
Tucson, Arizona Affiliated Office: Brown & Bain, A Professional Association. One South Church Avenue, Nineteenth Floor, P.O. Box 2265.
Telephone: 602-798-7900
Telecopier: 602-798-7945.

RESIDENT PERSONNEL

Lois W. Abraham
Philip P. Berelson
William S. Coats
Karl J. Kramer
Don F. Kumamoto
Martin L. Lagod
Christopher R. Ottenweller
Jeffrey G. Randall
D. Bruce Sewell

David M. Barkan
Susan D. Berney-Key
Carolyn F. Bostick
Chuck P. Ebertin
Robin M. Lightner

COUNSEL

Roger S. Borovoy
Bernard Petrie

For full biographical listings, see the Martindale-Hubbell Law Directory

COOLEY GODWARD CASTRO HUDDLESON & TATUM (AV)

Suite 400, 5 Palo Alto Square, 94306
Telephone: 415-843-5000
Telex: 380816 COOLEY PA
Fax: 415-857-0663
San Francisco, California Office: 20th Floor, One Maritime Plaza.
Telephone: 415-693-2000.
Telex: 380815 COOLEY SFO
Fax: 415-951-3698 or 415-951-3699.
Menlo Park, California Office: 3000 Sand Hill Road, Building 3, Suite 230.
Telephone: 415-843-5000.
Telex: 380816 COOLEY PA.
Fax: 415-854-2691.
San Diego, California Office: 4365 Executive Drive, 12th Floor.
Telephone: 619-550-6000.
Fax: 619-453-3555.
Boulder, Colorado Office: 2595 Canyon Boulevard, Suite 250.
Telephone: 303-546-4000.
Fax: 303-546-4099.
Denver, Colorado Office: One Tabor Center, 1200 17th Street, Suite 2100.
Telephone: 303-546-4000.

MEMBERS OF FIRM

Frederick D. Baron
Lois K. Benes
Lee F. Benton
Christopher S. Bertics
Craig Hill Casebeer
Paul Churchill
Paul B. Cleveland
Richard E. Climan
Janet L. Cullum
Brian C. Cunningham
Lloyd R. Day, Jr.
Stephen W. Fackler
William S. Freeman
John W. Girvin, Jr.
Willis E. Higgins
Michael R. Jacobson
Ronald L. Jacobson
Daniel Johnson, Jr.
Robert L. Jones
Louis M. Lupin
David M. Madrid
Andrei M. Manoliu
Deborah A. Marshall
Alan C. Mendelson
Webb B. Morrow, III
Richard L. Neeley
B. Lynne Parshall
Timothy G. Patterson
Mark B. Pitchford
Anna B. Pope
Diane Wilkins Savage
Peter F. Stone
John F. Young

OF COUNSEL

Bradford Jeffries

SPECIAL COUNSEL

Luann Cserr
James R. Jones
Tom M. Moran
Gary H. Ritchey
Gretchen R. Stroud

ASSOCIATES

Gregg H. Alton
Kevin C. Austin
James Batchelder
Laura A. Berezin
Robert J. Brigham
Terrence J. Carroll
Theodore Chen
Elisa Clowes
Julia Loewy Davidson
Linda Demelis
Larry Downes
James P. Dugan
David T. Emerson
David J. Estrada
Tracy L. Friedman
Michelle Greer Galloway
Robert M. Galvin
Michele T. Granaada
Kathleen M. Hallinan
Matthew B. Hemington
Jeffrey N. Hyman
Madison C. Jellins
Alexis D. Johns
Dan S. Johnston
Barclay J. Kamb
Deborah J. Kanarek
Bradley M. Kancigor
Karin A. Keitel
Anthony R. Klein
Barbara A. Kosacz

(See Next Column)

COOLEY GODWARD CASTRO HUDDLESON & TATUM—*Continued*

ASSOCIATES (Continued)

Karen J. Kramer
T. Gregory Lanier
John R. Leflar
Tricia T. Lin
H. Mark Lyon
Julie C. Lythcott-Haims
Pamela J. Martinson
Barbara J. McGeoch
Gerald T. McLaughlin
Mark D. McLaughlin
John D. Mendlein
Wm. Bradford Middlekauff
Donald J. Morrissey, Jr.
Craig P. Opperman
Laura M. Owen
Vincent P. Pangrazio
Stephanie J. Parr
Anne Harris Peck
Mary-Alice Pomputius
Christopher K. Richey
Julie M. Robinson
Ricardo Rodriguez
Deborah Z. Romani
Erika F. Rottenberg
Eric Schlachter
John Peter Shearer
Gregory C. Smith
Matthew W. Sonsini
Deidre Lynn Sparks
Barbara E. Tanzillo
Andrea H. Vachss
William S. Veatch
Julie A. Vehrenkemp
Laurie A. Webb
Michael L. Weiner
Emily B. Weinstein
Marianne T. Wolf

PATENT AGENTS

Melya J. Hughes
Timothy E. Torchia, Ph.D.

LEGAL SUPPORT PERSONNEL

SENIOR LEGAL ASSISTANTS

J. Paul Armstrong
Susan P. Bermel
C. Kim Miller
Celeste M. Pierce
Linda M. Rigas
Gary A. Thunell

PALO ALTO PATENT PROSECUTION ASSISTANT

Andrew T. Serafini

For full biographical listings, see the Martindale-Hubbell Law Directory

FTHENAKIS & VOLK (AV)

540 University Avenue, Suite 300, 94301
Telephone: 415-326-1397
Telecopier: 415-326-3203

MEMBERS OF FIRM

Basil P. Fthenakis
John D. Volk

ASSOCIATES

Oliver P. Colvin

For full biographical listings, see the Martindale-Hubbell Law Directory

GRAHAM & JAMES (AV)

5 Palo Alto Square, Suite 1000, 3000 El Camino Real, 94306
Telephone: 415-856-6500
Telecopier: 415-856-3619
Other offices located in: San Francisco, Los Angeles, Palo Alto, Sacramento and Fresno, California; Washington, D.C.; New York, New York; Milan, Italy; Beijing, China; Tokyo, Japan; London, England; Dusseldorf, Germany; Taipei, Taiwan.
Associated Offices: Deacons in Association with Graham & James, Hong Kong; Sly and Weigall, Sydney, Melbourne, Brisbane, Perth and Canberra, Australia.
Affiliated Offices: Graham & James in Affiliation with Taylor Joynson Garrett, London, England, Bucharest, Romania and Brussels, Belgium; Hanafiah Soeharto Ponggawa, Jakarta, Indonesia; Deacons and Graham & James, Bangkok, Thailand; Haarmann, Hemmelrath & Partner, Berlin, Munich, Leipzig, Frankfurt and Dusseldorf, Germany; Mishare M. Al-Ghazali & Partners, Kuwait; Sly & Weigall Deacons in Association with Graham & James, Hanoi, Vietnam and Guangzhou, China; Gallastegui y Lozano, S.C., Mexico City, Mexico; Law Firm of Salah Al-Hejailan, Jeddah and Riyadh, Saudi Arabia.

MEMBERS OF FIRM

Donald R. Davis
Chris Scott Graham
Lawrence W. Granatelli
David F. Gross
Timothy T. Huber
Alan B. Kalin
Michael H. Kalkstein
Ronald S. Lemieux
Ralph M. Pais
Robert E. Patterson
Thomas R. Radcliffe
Joe C. Sorenson

RESIDENT ASSOCIATES

David S. Elkins
Brien B. Kirk
Laura A. Majerus
(Not admitted in CA)
Thomas A. M'Guinness

For full biographical listings, see the Martindale-Hubbell Law Directory

GRAY CARY WARE & FREIDENRICH, A PROFESSIONAL CORPORATION (AV)

Gray Cary Established in 1927
Ware & Freidenrich Established in 1969
400 Hamilton Avenue, 94301-1825
Telephone: 415-328-6561
Telex: 348-372
Telecopier: 415-327-3699
San Diego, California Office: 401 B Street, Suite 1700.
Telephone: 619-699-2700.

(See Next Column)

La Jolla, California Office: 1200 Prospect Street, Suite 575.
Telephone: 619-454-9101.
El Centro, California Office: 1224 State Street, P.O. Box 2890.
Telephone: 619-353-6140.

Douglas B. Aikins
Cynthia B. Carlson
John Howard Clowes
Lawrence A. Cogan
Steven G. Cohen
Ian N. Feinberg
Mark Fowler
Diane Holt Frankle
Thomas M. French
Thomas W. Furlong
Gregory M. Gallo
Penny Howe Gallo
Hugh Goodwin, Jr.
Judith V. Gordon
Robert N. Grant
Louis B. Green
John B. Hale
George H. Hohnsbeen, II
Aimée E. Jorgensen
Margaret H. Kavalaris
James M. Koshland
Eric J. Lapp
Mary LaVigne-Butler
Jeffrey J. Lederman
Patrick J. McGaraghan
Marvin Meisel
Robert H. Miller
Timothy J. Moore
Carla S. Newell
Mark F. Radcliffe
Jonathan E. Rattner
Peter M. Rehon
Douglas J. Rein
Arthur C. Rinsky
Lisa Roberts
J. Martin Robertson
Bradley J. Rock
Robert T. Russell
Bruce E. Schaeffer
John R. Shuman, Jr.
Stacy Snowman
Jay M. Spitzen
Lillian G. Stenfeldt
Dennis C. Sullivan
Craig M. Tighe
Jeffrey A. Trant
Janet R. Walworth
Richard I. Yankwich

James E. Anderson
Elizabeth M. Baum
Mary Elizabeth Berry
Paul A. Blumenstein
Larry J. Bradfish
Hope A. Case
Beth Detweiler Castleberry
Kathleen Cattani
Paula N. Chavez
Jeffrey D. Cherry
Eric H. Dorf
Russell S. Elmer
Zahra Emami
Rebecca P. Falco
Shannon Fallon
Susan Goodhue
David R. Graham
Michelle R. Harbottle
Jeanne W. Harvey
William H. Hoffman
Cheryl K. House
David Alan Hubb
Jeffrey R. Ii
Joan S. Kato
Lori A. Kish
Janie T. Kuo
(Not admitted in CA)
John W. Kuo
(Not admitted in CA)
Victoria W-Y Lee
Michael J. Madison
Martin H. Myers
Michele Milnes Nadan
Nels Raymond Nelsen
Kevin O'Neill
Denise Woodson Ofria
Darren J. Pittenger
Margaret M. Powers
MeMe Jacobs Rasmussen
Michelle M. Reichert
Dianne B. Salesin
William R. Schreiber
Daniel K. Seubert
Scott M. Stanton
Paul Startz
Matthew J. Stepovich
Marilyn N. Taketa
R. Allyn Taylor
Andrew Paul Valentine
Elizabeth H. Ward
Joyce T. Whitaker
Karen K. Williams
Heayoon J. Woo
Stephen Yu

RETIRED PARTNERS

John Freidenrich
Leonard Ware

OF COUNSEL

Albert F. Knorp
Marta L. Morando

Representative Clients: Automobile Club of South California; Bank of America; Brooktree Corp.; C. A. Parr (Agencies), Ltd.; IMED; Pacific Bell; McMillin Development Co.; Scripps Clinic and Research Fdtn.; SeaWorld, Inc.; Underwriters at Lloyds; Wells Fargo Bank.

For full biographical listings, see the Martindale-Hubbell Law Directory

HOLTZMANN, WISE & SHEPARD (AV)

3030 Hansen Way, 94304
Telephone: 415-856-1200
Telecopier: 415-856-1344
New York, N. Y. Office: 1271 Avenue of the Americas.
Telephone: 212-753-4300.
Cable Address: "Lawise." International
Telex: 422664.
Telecopier: 212-838-8279.

PARTNERS

Thomas L. Barton
Susan Blackfield Crawford
M. Scott Donahey
David W. Herbst
Philip R. Hyde
Jerrold F. Petruzzelli

ASSOCIATES

Timothy R. Curry
Amy L. Gilson
Michelle E. Lentzner
Michael G. McClory
Susan K. Meyer
Edward L. Quevedo
James M. Smith
Benjamin F. Spater
Alison E. Spong

(See Next Column)

HOLTZMANN, WISE & SHEPARD, *Palo Alto—Continued*

COUNSEL

Lorraine A. Clasquin
David N. Schachter

Representative Clients: City of San Jose: Insight Development Corp.; Pilkington Visioncare, Inc.; Sola Optical U.S.A.; Syntex Corporation; Wells Fargo Bank, N.A.; Varian Associates, Inc.; Videonics Inc.

For full biographical listings, see the Martindale-Hubbell Law Directory

WILSON, SONSINI, GOODRICH & ROSATI, PROFESSIONAL CORPORATION (AV)

650 Page Mill Road, 94304-1050
Telephone: 415-493-9300
Internet: wsgr@wsgr.com
Telex: 345500 wilson pla
Fax: 415-493-6811

Aaron J. Alter
Denise M. Amantea
Aileen L. Arrieta
Alan K. Austin
Jonathan Axelrad
Michael Barclay
Henry V. Barry
David J. Berger
Steven L. Berson
Mark A. Bertelsen
Jerome F. Birn, Jr.
Steven E. Bochner
Mark E. Bonham
Donald E. Bradley
Tor Braham
Harry B. Bremond
Andrew P. Bridges
Richard J. Char
Peter P. Chen
Kenneth A. Clark
Robert T. Clarkson
Douglas H. Collom
Charles T. C. Compton
Susan A. Creighton
Francis S. Currie
Michael J. Danaher
Thomas C. DeFilipps
Richard C. DeGolia
James A. DiBoise
Stephen C. Durant
Boris Feldman
Robert P. Feldman
Elizabeth R. Flint
Herbert P. Fockler
John A. Fore
John B. Goodrich
Dana Haviland
Ivan H. Humphreys
Robert B. Jack
Terry T. Johnson
Jared L. Kopel
Peter LaBoskey
Michael A. Ladra
Robert P. Latta
Douglas M. Laurice
Nina Locker
Page Mailliard
Henry P. Massey, Jr.
J. Casey McGlynn
Allen L. Morgan
Bradford C. O'Brien
Judith Mayer O'Brien
Michael J. O'Donnell
Mark Parnes
Donna M. Petkanics
Harry K. Plant
Gary L. Reback
John V. Roos
Mario M. Rosati
Ronald M. Roth
Jeffrey D. Saper
Steven M. Schatz
Arthur F. Schneiderman
Timothy T. Scott
David J. Segre
Ron E. Shulman
(Not admitted in CA)
Kenneth M. Siegel
Laurie B. Smilan
Larry W. Sonsini
Timothy J. Sparks
Marcia Kemp Sterling
David S. Steuer
Blair W. Stewart, Jr.
James Neilson Strawbridge
Debra S. Summers
Barry E. Taylor
Bruce G. Vanyo
Ann Yvonne Walker
Kenneth B. Wilson
Neil Jay Wolff
Howard S. Zeprun

COUNSEL

John A. Wilson

Denise L. Altman
Bryan K. Anderson
James B. Appelbaum
Jessica L. Armstrong
Colleen Bal
John S. Banas, III
Marilyn U. Bauriedel
Suzanne Y. Bell
Stephen P. Berke
Steven V. Bernard
(Not admitted in CA)
Lauren I. Boro
Susan Bower
Christopher F. Boyd
Shawn M. Britton
Carmine J. Broccole
Ivan J. Brockman
Henry A. Brown, III
Thomas G. Brown
Robert D. Brownell
Megan J. Carroll
Bernard James Cassidy
Armando Castro
Richard F. Cauley
Marta Cervantes
Carmen I-Hua Chang
Warren Chao
Trevor J. Chaplick
Michael A. Chapman
Antony E. Chiang
Sandra Chutorian
Douglas J. Clark
Mark A. Clawson
Kimberly L. Clayton
Olabisi L. Clinton
Nicole Ernsberger Cook
Gregory T. Cox
Janet M. Craycroft
Robert G. Day
Sean P. DeBruine
Patrick J. DeSouza
Pascal W. Di Fronzo
Rana B. DiOrio
Stephen G. Driggers
David C. Drummond
Cynthia A. Dy
Keith E. Eggleton
Bryn Ekroot
Nevan C. Elam
Vera M. Elson
Rebecca L. Epstein
Ronald S. Epstein
Brian C. Erb
Robert Fabela
Janice Leyrer Fall
Chris F. Fennell

(See Next Column)

Eric J. Finseth
Diane Jean Fong
Adele C. Freedman
(Not admitted in CA)
Jeff Friedman
Isabella E. Fu
Neil M. Garfinkel
(Not admitted in CA)
Carla J. Garrett
Jon E. Gavenman
Tyler J. Goldman
Sarah Ann Good
Linda S. Grais
Lawrence T. Greenberg
Irwin R. Gross
Chihoe Hahn
(Not admitted in CA)
Geoffrey B. Hale
Jason A. Hammerman
Ramsey Hanna
Sara Duval Harrington
(Not admitted in CA)
Kevin V. Haynes
Peter S. Heinecke
John H. Hemann
Jeffrey A. Herbst
Susanne Öst Hereford
Michael Hetherington
Andrew J. Hirsch
John Mathias Horan
(Not admitted in CA)
Dwayne M. Horii
Gail Clayton Husick
Meredith S. Jackson
James L. Jacobs
(Not admitted in CA)
Peeyush Jain
Ari Kahan
Steven S. Kaufhold
Adit M. Khorana
David A. Killam
Jason D. Kipnis
Catherine S. Kirkman
Kelly M. Klaus
Thomas Christopher Klein
Martin W. Korman
(Not admitted in CA)
Robert F. Kornegay
James N. Kramer
Elizabeth M. Kurr
Joan E. Lambert
Marthe LaRosiliere
David L. Larson
Joshua A. Lipp
David M. Lisi
Suzanne K. List
Paul O. Livesay
Robert W. Luckinbill
Jose F. Macias
Steven Maddox
Richard L. Marasse
Thomas J. Martin
Nancy D. Martindale
Thomas P. McLean
James K. McMurray
Janine McNally
Bruce M. McNamara
Ruth Ann McNees
Millicent S. Meroney
Noah D. Mesel
Tanya R. Meyers
Christopher D. Mitchell
Daniel R. Mitz
(Not admitted in CA)
Robert Moll
Diana M. Morrow
Michael J. Murphy
Melinda D. Myers
Andrea L. Nagin
Neil Nathanson
Marnia Nichols
Craig D. Norris
Michael Occhiolini
James C. Otteson
Christopher J. Ozburn
(Not admitted in CA)
Agnes Pak
(Not admitted in CA)
Michael J. Panepucci
(Not admitted in CA)
Felix P. Phillips
Eric G. Pinckert
Sarah Preisler
David Priebe
Gregory M. Priest
Stacey Giamalis Prochaska
Michael S. Rabson
Mark L. Reinstra
Susan Pasquinelli Reinstra
Ruth C. Reitman
Christine Riordan
Mary Anne Rodgers
Debra B. Rosler
Sandy L. Roth
Paul M. Rothstein
Alisande M. Rozynko
Frederick Neil Saal
Christopher K. Sadeghian
Ignacio E. Salceda
Elizabeth M. Saunders
Richard J. Schachtili
Patrick J. Schultheis
Joanne Renée Scully
Stephanie Sharron
Laura J. Shaw
Elizabeth A. Sheets
John T. Sheridan
Susan Jul Skaer
John M. Smelzer
Beatrice E. Solis
Susan L. Stapleton
Roger D. Stern
Timothy J. Stevens
Rodney G. Strickland, Jr.
J. Robert Suffoletta, Jr.
Romy S. Taubman
Michael G. Taylor
D. John Theodorakis
Susan Stuermer Thomas
Kathryn A. Vaclavik
Alicia J. Vasquez
Issac J. Vaughn
Jason B. Wacha
Clyde J. Wadsworth
Don S. Williams
James E. Williams
Lloyd Winawer
Christopher O. B. Wright
Eric W. Wright
Christopher J. Younger

For full biographical listings, see the Martindale-Hubbell Law Directory

PASADENA, Los Angeles Co.

BURNS, AMMIRATO, PALUMBO, MILAM & BARONIAN, A PROFESSIONAL LAW CORPORATION (AV)

65 North Raymond Avenue, 2nd Floor, 91103-3919
Telephone: 818-796-5053; 213-258-8282
Fax: 818-792-3078
Long Beach, California Office: One World Trade Center, Suite 1200.
Telephone: 310-436-8338; 714-952-1047.
Fax: 310-432-6049.

Michael A. Burns
Bruce Palumbo
Jeffrey L. Milam
Robert H. Baronian
Steven J. Banner

Normand A. Ayotte
Colleen Clark
Vincent F. De Marzo
William D. Dodson
Valerie Julien-Peto
Susan E. Luhring
Grace C. Mori

(See Next Column)

BURNS, AMMIRATO, PALUMBO, MILAM & BARONIAN A PROFESSIONAL LAW CORPORATION—*Continued*

Reference: First Los Angeles Bank.

For full biographical listings, see the Martindale-Hubbell Law Directory

FRANSCELL, STRICKLAND, ROBERTS & LAWRENCE, A PROFESSIONAL CORPORATION (AV)

Penthouse, 225 South Lake Avenue, 91101-3005
Telephone: 818-304-7830; 213-684-7830; 800-303-5503 (CA Only)
Fax: 818-795-7460
Santa Ana, California Office: Suite 800, 401 Civic Center Drive West.
Telephone: 714-543-6511.
Fax: 714-543-6711.
Riverside, California Office: Suite 670, 3801 University Avenue.
Telephone: 909-686-1000.
Fax: 909-686-2565.

George J. Franscell
Tracy Strickland (Resident, Santa Ana Office)
Barbara E. Roberts (Resident, Riverside Office)
David D. Lawrence
Carol Ann Rohr
Scott D. MacLatchie
W. Charles Bradley (Resident, Riverside Office)
S. Frank Harrell (Resident, Santa Ana Office)
Conrad R. Clark (Resident, Riverside Office)
Jeri Tabback Thompson
Olaf W. Hedberg (Resident, Santa Ana Office)
Spencer Krieger
Jack D. Hoskins

For full biographical listings, see the Martindale-Hubbell Law Directory

HAHN & HAHN (AV)

A Partnership including Professional Corporations
9th Floor, 301 East Colorado Boulevard, 91101
Telephone: 818-796-9123
Los Angeles: 213-681-6948
Orange Co.: 714-971-5590
Cable Address: "Hahnlaw"
Telecopier: 818-449-7357

MEMBERS OF FIRM

Stanley L. Hahn (P.C.)
David K. Robinson (P.C.)
Loren H. Russell (P.C.)
Leonard M. Marangi (P.C.)
William S. Johnstone, Jr., (P.C.)
George R. Baffa (P.C.)
Don Mike Anthony (P.C.)
Robert W. Anderson
William K. Henley (P.C.)
Clark R. Byam (P.C.)
Richard L. Hall (P.C.)
Susan T. House (P.C.)
Dianne H. Bukata
Gene E. Gregg, Jr. (P.C.)
R. Scott Jenkins (P.C.)
Charles J. Greaves
Dale R. Pelch
William S. Garr
Karl I. Swaidan

ASSOCIATES

Sandra K. Murphy
Laura V. Farber
Sally S. Costanzo

OF COUNSEL

George E. Zillgitt
Emrys J. Ross

Representative Clients: Becton Dickinson & Co.; California Institute of Technology; City of Glendale; City of Pasadena, City of Long Beach; Flint Ink Corp.; Pasadena Tournament of Roses Assn.; Symes Cadillac, Inc.

For full biographical listings, see the Martindale-Hubbell Law Directory

TAYLOR KUPFER SUMMERS & RHODES (AV)

301 East Colorado Boulevard, Suite 407, 91101
Telephone: 818-304-0953; 213-624-7877
Fax: 818-795-6375

MEMBERS OF FIRM

Stanley A. Barker (1920-1965)
Owen E. Kupfer (1908-1991)
Edwin W. Taylor (Retired)
John D. Taylor
Robert C. Summers
Stephen F. Peters

COUNSEL

Kenneth O. Rhodes

Reference: Citizens Bank (Pasadena).

For full biographical listings, see the Martindale-Hubbell Law Directory

THROCKMORTON, BECKSTROM, OAKES & TOMASSIAN (AV)

A Partnership including Professional Corporations
Corporate Center Pasadena, 225 South Lake Avenue, Suite 500, 91101-3005
Telephone: 818-568-2500; 213-681-2321
Fax: 818-405-0786
Newport Beach, California Office: Suite 1200, 4695 Macarthur Court.
Telephone: 714-955-2280.
Fax: 714-467-8081.

(See Next Column)

MEMBERS OF FIRM

A. Robert Throckmorton (A Professional Corporation)
Spencer S. Beckstrom (A Professional Corporation)
George A. Oakes
Serge Tomassian
Alan Stanfill
David Alan Huffaker

References Available Upon Request.

For full biographical listings, see the Martindale-Hubbell Law Directory

PETALUMA, Sonoma Co. — (Refer to Santa Rosa)

*RED BLUFF,** Tehama Co. — (Refer to Redding)

*REDDING,** Shasta Co.

BARR, SINCLAIR & HILL, A PROFESSIONAL CORPORATION (AV)

1824 Court Street, P.O. Box 994390, 96099-1648
Telephone: 916-243-8008
Fax: 916-243-1648

John D. Barr
Craig A. Sinclair
Larry L. Hill

Lauren E. Leisz
Rodney J. Key
David L. Case
Douglas Mudford
Steven H. Schultz
J. Michael Favor
Pamela H. Burgess

Representative Clients: Farmers Insurance Group; Cal Farm Insurance Co.; Safeco Insurance Co; Gibraltar Savings & Loan Assn.; The Home Insurance Co.; Aetna Casualty & Surety Co.; Lloyds of London; Insurance Company of North America; Travelers Insurance Co.; County of Tehama.

For full biographical listings, see the Martindale-Hubbell Law Directory

CARR, KENNEDY, PETERSON & FROST, A LAW CORPORATION (AV)

420 Redcliff Drive, P.O. Box 492396, 96049
Telephone: 916-222-2100
Fax: 916-222-0504

Francis Carr (1875-1944)
Lawrence J. Kennedy, Sr. (1883-1975)
Laurence J. Kennedy, Jr. (1918-1986)
Laurence W. Carr (1912-1991)
R. Russ Peterson
Daniel S. Frost
Robert M. Harding
Evan L. Delgado
Stephen H. Baker
Michael P. Ashby

Representative Clients: Chicago Title Insurance Co.; CH2M Hill California, Inc.; Fruit Growers Supply Co.; ITT Rayonier, Inc.; Louisiana-Pacific Corp.; Minnesota Mining & Manufacturing; Northbrook Insurance Co.; Roseburg Lumber Co.; Security Union Title Insurance Co.; Stewart Title Insurance Co.

For full biographical listings, see the Martindale-Hubbell Law Directory

MOSS & ENOCHIAN, A LAW CORPORATION (AV)

2701 Park Marina Drive, P.O. Drawer 994608, 96099-4608
Telephone: 916-225-8990
Fax: 916-241-5734

Steven R. Enochian
Larry B. Moss
Todd E. Slaughter
Stewart C. Altemus
John S. Kenny
Robert A. Spano

Michael R. Deems
Sandra L. Johnson
Mark D. Norcross
Eric A. Omstead
Adam M. Pressman
Darryl L. Wagner
Gustavo L. Martinez

Reference: Tri Counties Bank.

For full biographical listings, see the Martindale-Hubbell Law Directory

REDLANDS, San Bernardino Co.

DILL & SHOWLER (AV)

411 Brookside Avenue, 92373
Telephone: 909-793-2377
Fax: 909-798-6557

MEMBERS OF FIRM

Fred H. Dill
Scott Showler

ASSOCIATES

Kevin F. Gillespie

Representative Clients: Alpha Corp. of Tennessee; Homestead Supplies, Inc.; Riverside County Lumber Co.; American Buildings Co.

For full biographical listings, see the Martindale-Hubbell Law Directory

*REDWOOD CITY,** San Mateo Co.

OWEN & MELBYE, A PROFESSIONAL CORPORATION (AV)

700 Jefferson Street, 94063
Telephone: 415-364-6500
Fax: 415-365-7036
Tahoe City, California Office: P.O. Box 1524.
Telephone: 916-546-2473.

William H. Owen
Richard B. Melbye
Norman J. Roger
Edmund M. Scott
Pamela J. Helmer
John S. Posthauer
Paul R. Mangiantini

Albert P. Blake, Jr.
Dawn M. Patterson
Conor A. Meyers

Representative Clients: Aetna Cravens Dargan Co.; Avco Lycoming; Beech Aircraft Corp.; California Casualty Indemnity Exchange; K & K Claims Service; Kemper Insurance Cos.; Mutual Service Insurance Co.; State Farm Mutual Insurance Cos.; Underwriters at Lloyds; United States Aviation Insurance Group.

For full biographical listings, see the Martindale-Hubbell Law Directory

---

ROPERS, MAJESKI, KOHN & BENTLEY, A PROFESSIONAL CORPORATION (AV)

1001 Marshall Street, 94063
Telephone: 415-364-8200
Fax: 415-367-0997
San Jose, California Office: 80 North 1st Street.
Telephone: 408-287-6262.
Fax: 408-297-6819.
San Francisco, California Office: 670 Howard Street.
Telephone: 415-543-4800.
Fax: 415-512-1574.
Santa Rosa, California Office: Fountaingrove Center, 3558 Round Barn Boulevard, Suite 300.
Telephone: 707-524-4200.
Fax: 707-523-4610.
Los Angeles, California Office: 550 South Hope Street, Suite 1900.
Telephone: 213-312-2000.
Fax: 213-312-2001.
Sacramento, California Office: 1000 G Street, Suite 400. Phone: 916-556-3100.
Fax: 916-442-7121.

Harold Ropers (1905-1966)
John M. Rubens (1936-1993)
Eugene J. Majeski
John M. Bentley
James H. McKibben
Michael J. Brady
Charles G. Rigg
Frank J. Pagliaro, Jr.
John S. Simonson
Stephen A. Scott
Daniel E. Alberti
Mark G. Bonino
Richard K. Wilson
Stephen M. Hayes
Katherine S. Clark
Lawrence M. Guslani
Ted J. Hannig
Theodore C. Zayner
David J. Miclean
Pamela E. Cogan
David A. Levy
Colin R. Campbell
Brad W. Blocker
Marc D. Rosati
Thomas H. Clarke, Jr.
Robert P. Andris, II
Todd A. Roberts
Michael Ropers (Resident)
David M. McLaughlin
William R. Garrett
Raymond A. Greene III
Robert G. Ittig
V. Raymond Swope, III

OF COUNSEL

Ron W. Fields
Walter C. Kohn

Michael E. Pitts
Linda J. Dvorak
Charlene Rudio Ingersoll
Peter C. Suhr
Allison Lindley Dobbrow
Justice C. McPherson
Ralph Tortorella, III
Francois G. Laugier
Susan H. Handelman
Janet C. Noble
JoAnna R. Reichel
Kathryn C. Curry
Richard Fisher
John L. Slebir
J. Byron Fleck
John R. Meehan
Laura L. Reidenbach
Brian R. Davis
Milan C. Dimich
Kimberly A. Donovan
Edward G. Rogan
Kevin G. McCurdy
Brian A. Marty
Robert P. Soran
Kelly Franks
Jeffrey T. Stromberg
Anthony Joseph Hoglund
Hans Stephen Steinhoffer
Kevin Hunsaker
Ida Skikos (Resident)
W. Bradley Thomas
John Fitzpatrick Vannucci
Tammy M. Albertsen-Murray
Jennifer C. Coates
Bruce M. MacKay
Stacy Ann Smith (Resident)
Michael David Morehead
Mark Casper
John Fitzpatrick Vannucci

For full biographical listings, see the Martindale-Hubbell Law Directory

---

RICHMOND, Contra Costa Co. — (Refer to Walnut Creek)

*RIVERSIDE,** Riverside Co.

BEST, BEST & KRIEGER (AV)

A Partnership including Professional Corporations
400 Mission Square, 3750 University Avenue, P.O. Box 1028, 92502
Telephone: 909-686-1450
Fax: 909-686-3083; 909-682-4612
Palm Springs, California Office: Suite C, 600 East Tahquitz Canyon Way, P.O. Box 2710.
Telephone: 619-325-7264.
Fax: 619-325-0365.
Rancho Mirage, California Office: Hope Square Professional Centre, 39700 Bob Hope Drive, Suite 312, P.O. Box 1555.
Telephone: 619-568-2611.
Fax: 619-340-6698; 619-341-7039.
Ontario, California Office: 800 North Haven, Suite 120.
Telephone: 909-989-8584.
Fax: 909-944-1441.
San Diego, California Office: 550 West C Street, 16th Floor.
Telephone: 619-595-1333.
Fax: 619-233-6118.

MEMBERS OF FIRM

Raymond Best (1868-1957)
James H. Krieger (1913-1975)
Eugene Best (1893-1981)
Arthur L. Littleworth (P.C.)
Glen E. Stephens (P.C.)
William R. DeWolfe (P.C.)
Barton C. Gaut (P.C.)
Paul T. Selzer (P.C.) (Palm Springs Office)
Dallas Holmes (P.C.)
Christopher L. Carpenter (P.C.)
Richard T. Anderson (P.C.)
John D. Wahlin (P.C.)
Michael D. Harris (P.C.) (Palm Springs Office)
W. Curt Ealy (P.C.) (Palm Springs Office)
John E. Brown (P.C.)
Michael T. Riddell (P.C.)
Meredith A. Jury (P.C.) (Ontario Office)
Michael Grant (P.C.)
Francis J. Baum (P.C.)
Anne T. Thomas (P.C.)
D. Martin Nethery (P.C.) (Rancho Mirage Office)
George M. Reyes
William W. Floyd, Jr.
Gregory L. Hardke
Kendall H. MacVey
Clark H. Alsop
David J. Erwin (P.C.) (Rancho Mirage Office)
Michael J. Andelson (P.C.) (Rancho Mirage Office)
Douglas S. Phillips (P.C.) (Rancho Mirage Office)
Antonia Graphos (Palm Springs Office)
Gregory K. Wilkinson
Wynne S. Furth (Ontario Office)
Gene Tanaka
Basil T. Chapman (Rancho Mirage Office)
Timothy M. Connor (San Diego Office)
Victor L. Wolf
Daniel E. Olivier (Palm Springs Office)
Howard B. Golds
Stephen P. Deitsch (Ontario Office)
Marc E. Empey (Rancho Mirage Office)
John R. Rottschaefer
Martin A. Mueller (Palm Springs Office)
J. Michael Summerour
Victoria N. King (Ontario Office)
Scott C. Smith (San Diego Office)
Brian M. Lewis (Rancho Mirage Office)
Jack B. Clarke, Jr.
Bradley E. Neufeld
Peter M. Barmack (Ontario Office)
Matt H. Morris (Rancho Mirage Office)
Jeffrey V. Dunn
Steven C. DeBaun
Eric L. Garner
Dennis M. Cota (Ontario Office)
Patrick H.W.F. Pearce

ASSOCIATES

Jeannette A. Peterson
William D. Dahling, Jr.
Robert W. Hargreaves (Rancho Mirage Office)
Kirk W. Smith
Jason D. Dabareiner (Rancho Mirage Office)
Kyle A. Snow
Mark A. Easter
Diane L. Finley
Michelle Ouellette
David P. Phippen, Sr.
Susan C. Nauss
Bernie L. Williamson
Kevin K. Randolph (Ontario Office)
Marshall S. Rudolph (Rancho Mirage Office)
Mary E. Gilstrap (Rancho Mirage Office)
Cynthia M. Germano
Kim A. Byrens
James Gilpin (San Diego Office)
Glenn N. Sabine
Diane C. Blasdel (Palm Springs Office)
Dorothy I. Anderson
G. Henry Welles (Palm Springs Office)
James R. Harper
Dina O. Harris
Barbara R. Baron (Rancho Mirage Office)
Richard T. Egger (Ontario Office)
Patrick D. Dolan (Rancho Mirage Office)
Dean Derleth
Helene P. Dreyer (Rancho Mirage Office)
Emily P. Hemphill (Palm Springs Office)
Sonia Rubio Carvalho (Ontario Office)
John Pinkney (Rancho Mirage Office)
Dearing D. English (San Diego Office)
Theodore J. Griswold (San Diego Office)
Patricia Byars Cisneros
Juliann Anderson
Lora Halcomb Wilson
Jeffrey R. Thorpe
Mark D. Becker (Rancho Mirage Office)
D. Anthony Rodriguez
Susan E. Dumouchel
Jacqueline E. Bailey (Rancho Mirage Office)
Jennifer Olson Dolan (Rancho Mirage Office)

(See Next Column)

BEST, BEST & KRIEGER—*Continued*

ASSOCIATES (Continued)

Alexandra D. Lopez
Julie Roberts Furgerson (San Diego Office)
David Cabral (San Diego Office)
Nancy E. Davis
David J. Hancock
Michael S. Henderson
Joan M. Huckabone
Michele A. Powers (Ontario Office)
Marc T. Rasich
Philip M. Savage, IV
Christopher J. Seiber

OF COUNSEL

James B. Corison (P.C.)
C. Michael Cowett (San Diego Office)
Bruce W. Beach (San Diego Office)
Arlene Prater (San Diego Office)
John C. Tobin

For full biographical listings, see the Martindale-Hubbell Law Directory

BUTTERWICK, BRIGHT & O'LAUGHLIN, INC., A PROFESSIONAL LAW CORPORATION (AV)

4000 Tenth Street, P.O. Box 1229, 92502
Telephone: 909-686-3092
Telefax: 909-684-5743

J. D. Butterwick
Michael T. Bright
John F. O'Laughlin
Robert J. Mitchell

Reference: Riverside National Bank.

For full biographical listings, see the Martindale-Hubbell Law Directory

ROBERTS & MORGAN (AV)

Citrus Park, 1650 Iowa Avenue, Suite 200, 92507
Telephone: 909-682-2881
FAX: 909-682-2928

MEMBERS OF FIRM

Roger W. Roberts (1973-1986)
Bruce Morgan
John M. Porter
James C. Packer
Arthur K. Cunningham
Matthew J. Marnell
James L. Price
Douglas McCarthy
John F. Molay
Paula B. Tobler
Shirley Anne Mace
Fiona G. Luke

Representative Clients: Farmers Insurance Group; Ohio Casualty Insurance Group; State Farm Mutual Automobile Insurance Co.; City of Riverside; County of Riverside; City of Corona; Automobile Club of Southern California; K-Mart Corporation; Aetna Casualty & Surety Co. (Personal & Commercial Lines); Liberty Mutual Insurance Co.

For full biographical listings, see the Martindale-Hubbell Law Directory

*SACRAMENTO,** Sacramento Co.

* indicates certain Bar Register subscribers whose principal office is located elsewhere in the state and who have arranged for representation as a part of the state capital listings that follow

THE DIEPENBROCK LAW FIRM A PROFESSIONAL CORPORATION (AV)

400 Capitol Mall, Suite 1800, 95814
Telephone: 916-446-4469
Facsimile: 916-446-4535

John V. Diepenbrock
R. James Diepenbrock
Karen L. Diepenbrock
Paul F. Dauer
Keith W. McBride
John R. Haluck
Eileen M. Diepenbrock
Bradley J. Elkin
Mark D. Harrison

John W. Rakow, III
James Clarke

Representative Clients: Southern Pacific Transportation Co.; Chevron Corp.; Metropolitan Life Insurance Co.; Aerojet-General Corp.; Farmers Insurance Group; Sears, Roebuck and Co.; California Public Employees Retirement System.

For full biographical listings, see the Martindale-Hubbell Law Directory

DOWNEY, BRAND, SEYMOUR & ROHWER (AV)

Suite 1050, 555 Capitol Mall, 95814
Telephone: 916-441-0131
FAX: 916-441-4021

MEMBERS OF FIRM

Stephen W. Downey (1926-1959)
Clyde H. Brand (1926-1964)
Harry B. Seymour (1926-1977)
John F. Downey (1930-1991)
George D. Basye
Richard D. Waugh
James A. Willett
John J. Hamlyn, Jr.
Philip A. Stohr
J. Keith McKeag
Brian R. Van Camp
Henry E. Rodegerdts
D. Steven Blake
James M. Day, Jr.
Thomas N. Cooper
Stephen J. Meyer
Daniel James McVeigh
George L. O'Connell
Michael A. Kvarme
Fred A. Dawkins

(See Next Column)

MEMBERS OF FIRM (Continued)

Roberta Lee Franklin
James L. Deeringer
Keith E. Pershall
Kevin M. O'Brien
R. Dale Ginter
David E. Lindgren
Dan L. Carroll
Stephen G. Stwora-Hail
Whitney F. Washburn
Anthony A. Arostegui
Judy Holzer Hersher
Steven P. Saxton
Julie A. Carter
Lisa Lauritzen Ditora
Sharon K. Sandeen
Peter E. Glick
Steven H. Goldberg
Julia L. Jenness
Jeffrey M. Koewler
Katharine E. Wagner

COUNSEL

Barbara L. Berg
Ronald F. Lipp
Patrick G. Mitchell

ASSOCIATES

Adisa-Mari Abudu
David R.E. Aladjem
Craig C. Allison
Krista C. Breuer
Gordon B. Burns
Robert C. Bylsma
Timothy Michael Cary
Wendy M. Fisher
JanLynn R. Fleener
Carl D. Hill
Barton L. Jacka
Russell K. Jensen
James T. Jones
Kathryn L. Kempton
Spencer L. Kenner
Ronald Liebert
JudyAnne McGinley
Barbara A. Morris
Sean B. Murphy
Katherin A. Nukk-Freeman
Kathryn T. Papalia
Kim M. Peterson
Robin Raff
Silvio Reggiardo, III
Laura A. Reimche
Lisa L. Ruth
Scott L. Shapiro
Peter Keller Southworth
Robert G. Strauch
William R. Warne
Lawrence T. Woodlock

Representative Clients: Hertz Corp.; Pacific Bell; Raley's Supermarkets; Sacramento Municipal Utility District; Steelcase, Inc.

For full biographical listings, see the Martindale-Hubbell Law Directory

FRIEDMAN AND COLLARD, PROFESSIONAL CORPORATIONS (AV)

Suite 300, 7750 College Town Drive, 95826
Telephone: 916-381-9011
Telecopier: 916-381-7048

Morton L. Friedman
William H. Collard
Peter J. Stubbs
Douglas R. Thorn
C. Brooks Cutter
John Panneton
Samuel D. Hale
Eric J. Ratinoff

For full biographical listings, see the Martindale-Hubbell Law Directory

GREVE, CLIFFORD, WENGEL & PARAS (AV)

980 Ninth Street, Suite 1900, 95814-2739
Telephone: 916-443-2011
Telecopier: 916-441-7457
San Francisco, California Office: 425 California Street, Suite 2600.
Telephone: 415-274-3345.
FAX: 415-392-7349.

MEMBERS OF FIRM

Edward T. Clifford
Lawrence A. Wengel
Gary L. Vinson
Bradley R. Larson
Maureen A. Lenihan
William L. Baker
Robert L. Collins

ASSOCIATES

William J. Barcellona
Adam C. Brown
Scott E. Cofer
Amy L. Dobberteen
Bradley W. Kragel
Christine A. Roloff
Craig L. Scott

OF COUNSEL

Claire H. Greve
Irving H. Perluss

RETIRED

George E. Paras

Representative Clients: Allstate Insurance Co.; Atlantic Richfield, Corp.; Commercial Union Insurance Co.; Design Professionals Insurance Co.; E & O Professionals; Great American Insurance Cos.; Perini Corp.; State of California; Union Oil Company; United Pacific/Reliance Insurance Cos.

For full biographical listings, see the Martindale-Hubbell Law Directory

HARMATA LAW OFFICES (AV)

2201 Q Street, 95816
Telephone: 916-442-2842
Fax: 916-442-2015

Donald D. Harmata

LEGAL SUPPORT PERSONNEL

PARALEGAL

Debra D. Morrow

Representative Clients: Control Data Corporation; Deloitte & Touche; General Electric Company; Myers Electric, Inc.; Syblon-Reid Co.; Systemhouse Inc.; TRW, Inc.

(See Next Column)

HARMATA LAW OFFICES, *Sacramento—Continued*

For full biographical listings, see the Martindale-Hubbell Law Directory

KRONICK, MOSKOVITZ, TIEDEMANN & GIRARD, A PROFESSIONAL CORPORATION (AV)

27th Floor, 400 Capitol Mall, 95814
Telephone: 916-321-4500
Fax: 916-321-4555

Stanley W. Kronick
Adolph Moskovitz
Edward J. Tiedemann
Frederick G. Girard
Lloyd Hinkelman
Clifford W. Schulz
James E. Thompson
Robert E. Murphy
Robert S. Shelburne
James M. Boyd, Jr.
Janet K. Goldsmith
Robin Leslie Stewart
William A. Kershaw
Robert A. Rundstrom
Ruthann G. Ziegler
Paul W. Tozer
Donald W. Fitzgerald
Thomas C. Hughes, III
Richard H. Hart, Jr.
Michael A. Grob
P. Addison Covert
Thomas W. Birmingham
Jan K. Damesyn
Deborah J. Frick
Ann Freers Murray
Susan B. Carlsen
Philip A. Wright

James P. Wiezel
Robert A. Galgani
Dorothy S. Landsberg
Ann M. Siprelle
Michael McShane
Anthony B. Manzanetti
Janis J. Purtee
Jeffrey M. Starsky
James Scot Yarnell
Donna M. Matties
Jeffrey A. Mitchell
Lyle W. Cook
George C. Hollister
Jonathan P. Cristy
Andrew B. Pollak
William T. Chisum
Wendy Gomez Getty
Paul F. Kelly
Brenda J. Pence
Douglas H. Kraft
Emily E. Vasquez
Kristin L. Cihak
Diane E. Lockareff
Michael F. Dean
Vida L. Thomas
Steven A. Royston
Thomas H. Keeling
Susan R. Denious
Deborah M. Cooke

OF COUNSEL

Leonard M. Friedman (Retired)
Charles A. Barrett
Margaret P. Hastings-Hale

Representative Clients: Placer County Water Agency; Kern County Water Agency; Truckee-Carson Irrigation District; City of Los Angeles; Westlands Water District; City of West Sacramento; Association of California Water Agencies (JPIA).

For full biographical listings, see the Martindale-Hubbell Law Directory

*** LANDELS, RIPLEY & DIAMOND (AV)**

400 Capitol Mall, Suite 2140, 95814-4407
Telephone: 916-448-8300
Telex 2781 61 Cable Address: LARDI UR
Fax: 916-448-4923
San Francisco, California Office: Hills Plaza, 350 Steuart Street.
Telephone: 415-788-5000.
Fax: 415-788-7550.

Frederick M. Pownall
Eric R. Newman
Jonathan M. Ross

Representative Clients: California Mortgage Bankers Assn.; Chemical Waste Management, Inc.; Citicorp and Subsidiaries; American Bakers Assn.; Collagen Corp.; Federated Mutual Insurance Co.; General Electric Co. and Subsidiaries; New York Stock Exchange; Nonprescription Drug Manufacturers Assn.; WMX Technologies, Inc. and Subsidiaries.

For full biographical listings, see the Martindale-Hubbell Law Directory

MCDONOUGH, HOLLAND & ALLEN, A PROFESSIONAL CORPORATION (AV)

9th Floor, 555 Capitol Mall, 95814
Telephone: 916-444-3900
Fax: 916-444-8334
Yuba City, California Office: 422 Century Park Drive, Suite A, P.O. Box 776.
Telephone: 916-674-9761.
Fax: 916-671-0990.
Oakland, California Office: 1999 Harrison Street, Suite 1300.
Telephone: 510-444-7372.
Fax: 510-839-9104.

Martin McDonough (1915-1987)
Alfred E. Holland (Retired)
Bruce F. Allen (Retired)
Joseph E. Coomes, Jr.
David J. Spottiswood
Richard W. Nichols
Donald C. Poole
Richard W. Osen
Richard E. Brandt
G. Richard Brown
David W. Post
Susan K. Edling
David F. Beatty
Michael T. Fogarty
Harry E. Hull, Jr.

(See Next Column)

Natalie E. West (Resident, Oakland Office)
Ann H. O'Connell
Robert W. O'Connor
Jeffry R. Jones
T. Brent Hawkins
James M. Ruddick (Resident, Yuba City Office)
Richard M. Ross
Dawn H. Cole
Sharon D. Roseme
Susan L. Schoenig
James L. Leet
Mark A. Wasser
David S. Salem
Virginia A. Cahill
Harriet A. Steiner
William A. Lichtig
Edward J. Quinn, Jr.
Mark Gorton
Robert R. Rubin
Patricia D. Elliott
William C. Hilson, Jr.
Iris P. Yang
Mary Powers Antoine
Cathy Deubel Salenko
Craig Labadie (Resident, Oakland Office)
Jack D. Brown (Resident, Yuba City Office)
Thomas L. Hill (Resident, Yuba City Office)
Nancy P. Lee
Mary E. Olden
Edward J. Wright, Jr.
Michelle Marchetta Kenyon (Resident, Oakland Office)
Michele M. Clark
Stephen L. Goff
Michael K. Iwahiro
Glenn W. Peterson
David L. Krotine
Julie E. Green

Marcia L. Augsburger
Timothy P. Hayes (Resident, Yuba City Office)
Michael V. Brady
Nancy T. Templeton
David E. Macchiavelli
L. Stuart List
Kent William Silvester
Todd M. Bailey
Daniel V. Martinez (Resident, Yuba City Office)
Jan Patrick Sherry
Don F. Harris
Steven A. Lamon
Douglas A. Potts
Troy L. Ellerman
Clyde T. Ogata
C. Nicole Murphy
Madeline K. Davis
Christopher W. Ewing
Jeremy S. Millstone
Carolyn Masone
Jennifer Smith Davis
Paul C. Anderson (Resident, Oakland Office)

OF COUNSEL

V. Barlow Goff
Ann Taylor Schwing
Daniel L. Simmons
Seth P. Brunner
Richard E. Maroun

Representative Clients: A. Teichert & Son, Inc.; California Public Employees Retirement System; Sutter Health; Northern California Power Agency; Robert C. Powell Properties; Redevelopment Agency of the City of San Francisco; Honeywell, Inc.; Martin MacFarlane, Inc.; First American Title Insurance Co.

For full biographical listings, see the Martindale-Hubbell Law Directory

MOORE, MEEGAN, HANSCHU & KASSENBROCK (AV)

1545 River Park Drive, Suite 550, 95815
Telephone: 916-925-1800

MEMBERS OF FIRM

John M. Moore
David M. Meegan
James L. Hanschu
Mark R. Kassenbrock

Roberta Lindsey-Scott
Mary Clarke Ver Hoef
Peter J. Pullen

For full biographical listings, see the Martindale-Hubbell Law Directory

ROPERS, MAJESKI, KOHN & BENTLEY, A PROFESSIONAL CORPORATION (AV)

1000 G Street, Suite 400, 95814
Telephone: 916-556-3100
Fax: 916-442-7121
Redwood City, California Office: 1001 Marshall Street.
Telephone: 415-364-8200.
Fax: 415-367-0997.
San Jose, California Office: 80 North 1st Street.
Telephone: 408-287-6262.
Fax: 408-297-6819.
San Francisco, California Office: 670 Howard Street.
Telephone: 415-543-4800.
Fax: 415-512-1574.
Santa Rosa, California Office: Fountaingrove Center, 3558 Round Barn Boulevard, Suite 300.
Telephone: 707-524-4200.
Fax: 707-523-4610.
Los Angeles, California Office: 550 South Hope Street, Suite 1900.
Telephone: 213-312-2000.
Fax: 213-312-2001.

Matthew P. Guichard (Resident)
Steven H. Gurnee

Brian G. Kindsvater
James E. McFetridge (Resident)
Ellen C. Arabian

For full biographical listings, see the Martindale-Hubbell Law Directory

Sacramento—Continued

TUTTLE & TAYLOR, A LAW CORPORATION (AV)

Sixteenth Floor, 980 Ninth Street, 95814-2736
Telephone: 916-449-9950
Facsimile: 916-449-9953
Los Angeles, California Office: Tuttle & Taylor, A Law Corporation, 355 South Grand Avenue, Fortieth Floor,
Telephone: 213-683-0600.
Facsimile: 213-683-0225.
Washington, D.C. Office: Tuttle, Taylor & Heron, 1025 Thomas Jefferson Street, N.W..
Telephone: 202-342-1300.
Facsimile: 202-342-5880.

Robert L. Shuler

For full biographical listings, see the Martindale-Hubbell Law Directory

WILKE, FLEURY, HOFFELT, GOULD & BIRNEY (AV)

A Partnership including Professional Corporations
400 Capitol Mall, Suite 2200, 95814-4408
Telephone: 916-441-2430
Telefax: 916-442-6664
Mailing Address: P.O. Box 15559, 95852-0559

MEMBERS OF FIRM

Richard H. Hoffelt (Inc.)
William A. Gould, Jr., (Inc.)
Philip R. Birney (Inc.)
Thomas G. Redmon (Inc.)
Scott L. Gassaway
Donald Rex Heckman II (Inc.)
Alan G. Perkins
Bradley N. Webb
Ernest James Krtil
Robert R. Mirkin
Matthew W. Powell
Mark L. Andrews
Stephen K. Marmaduke
David A. Frenznick
John R. Valencia
Angus M. MacLeod

ASSOCIATES

Paul A. Dorris
Kelli M. Kennaday
Tracy S. Hendrickson
Joseph G. De Angelis
Jennifer L. Kennedy
Anthony J. DeCristoforo
Rachel N. Kook
Alicia F. From
Michael Polis
Matthew J. Smith
Wayne L. Ordos

OF COUNSEL

Sherman C. Wilke
Anita Seipp Marmaduke
Benjamin G. Davidian

Representative Clients: NOR-CAL Mutual Insurance Co.; California Optometric Assn.; KPMG Peat Marwick; Glaxo, Inc.

For full biographical listings, see the Martindale-Hubbell Law Directory

*SALINAS,** Monterey Co.

NOLAND, HAMERLY, ETIENNE & HOSS, A PROFESSIONAL CORPORATION (AV)

333 Salinas Street, P.O. Box 2510, 93902
Telephone: 408-424-1414; 372-7525
Fax: 408-424-1975
Monterey, California Office: Heritage Harbor, 99 Pacific Street, Building 200, Suite C.
Telephone: 408-373-4427.
Fax: 408-373-4797.

Harry L. Noland (1904-1991)
Paul M. Hamerly
Myron E. Etienne, Jr.
Peter T. Hoss
James D. Schwefel, Jr.
Martin J. May
Stephen W. Pearson
Lloyd W. Lowrey, Jr.
Anne K. Secker
Paula Robinson
Jerome F. Politzer, Jr.
Werner D. ("Randy") Meyenberg
Christine P. Gianascol
Lisa Nakata

Representative Clients: Union Carbide; McCormick Co., Inc.; First National Bank of Central California; Household Bank; First Interstate Bank; Mobil Oil; Quail Lodge; Mann Packing Co.; J.M. DeForest Trucking Co.; The Lantis Corporation; Clint Eastwood, West Cor, Inc.; Woodman Development.

For full biographical listings, see the Martindale-Hubbell Law Directory

*SAN BERNARDINO,** San Bernardino Co.

GRESHAM, VARNER, SAVAGE, NOLAN & TILDEN (AV)

Suite 300, 600 North Arrowhead Avenue, 92401
Telephone: 909-884-2171
Fax: 909-888-2120
Victorville, California Office: 14011 Park Avenue, Suite 140.
Telephone: 619-243-2889.
Fax: 619-243-3057.
Riverside, California Office: 3737 Main Street, Suite 420.
Telephone: 714-274-7777.
Fax: 714-274-7770.

(See Next Column)

MEMBERS OF FIRM

Allen B. Gresham
Bruce D. Varner
Philip M. Savage, III
John C. Nolan
M. William Tilden
James E. Good
Mark A. Ostoich
Thomas N. Jacobson
Stephan G. Saleson
Robert W. Ritter, Jr.
Robin Bramlett Cochran
Duke D. Rouse
John B. McCauley
Ernest E. Riffenburgh
Michael Duane Davis (Resident, Victorville Office)
Bart W. Brizzee
Craig O. Dobler (Resident, Riverside Office)
Richard D. Marca

ASSOCIATES

Daryl H. Carlson
Michael O. Wolf (Resident, Riverside Office)
Jay C. Egenes
Penelope Alexander-Kelley
Tara Reilly
Brendan W. Brandt
Ronald D. Getchey
Saul Jaffe
George Lasko

Representative Clients: Kaiser Resources, Inc.; Southern California Edison Co.; General Telephone Company of California; Southern California Gas Co.; General Motors Corp.; Specialty Minerals, Inc.; Sunwest Materials; TTX Company; Amax Gold, Inc.; San Bernardino Valley, Pomona Valley, Covina-San Gabriel, Azusa-Glendora Boards of Realtors.

For full biographical listings, see the Martindale-Hubbell Law Directory

KASSEL & KASSEL (AV)

A Group of Independent Law Offices
Suite 207, Wells Fargo Bank Building, 334 West Third Street, 92401
Telephone: 909-884-6455
Fax: 909-884-8032

Philip Kassel
Gregory H. Kassel

References: Wells Fargo Bank; Bank of America; Bank of San Bernardino.

For full biographical listings, see the Martindale-Hubbell Law Directory

MAC LACHLAN, BURFORD & ARIAS, A LAW CORPORATION (AV)

560 East Hospitality Lane, Fourth Floor, 92408
Telephone: 909-885-4491
Fax: 909-888-6866
Rancho Cucamonga, California Office: 8280 Utica Avenue, Suite 200. 909-989-4481.
Palm Springs, California Office: 255 North El Cielo Road, Suite 470. 619-320-5761.
Victorville, California Office: 14011 Park Avenue, Suite 410. 619-243-7933.

Bruce D. Mac Lachlan
Ronald A. Burford
Joseph Arias
Michael W. Mugg
Dennis G. Popka
Leigh O. Harper (Resident, Palm Springs Office)
Clifford R. Cunningham (Resident, Rancho Cucamonga Office)
Dennis R. Stout
Sharon K. Burchett (Resident, Rancho Cucamonga Office)
Christopher D. Lockwood
Vernon C. Lauridsen (Resident, Rancho Cucamonga Office)
John G. Evans (Resident, Palm Springs Office)
Richard R. Hegner (Resident, Victorville Office)
Dennis J. Mahoney
Kathleen M. Keefe
Toni R. Fullerton
Mark R. Harris
Diana J. Carloni (Resident, Victorville Office)
Jean M. Landry
Frank M. Loo

Representative Clients: Aetna Life & Casualty; Automobile Club of Southern California; California State Automobile Association; City of San Bernardino; Reliance Insurance; Republic Insurance; Southern Pacific Transportation Co.; State Farm Fire and Casualty Co.; State Farm Mutual Automobile Insurance Co.; County of San Bernardino.

For full biographical listings, see the Martindale-Hubbell Law Directory

WILSON, BORROR, DUNN, SCOTT & DAVIS (AV)

Suite 307, The Bank of California Building, 255 North D Street, P.O. Box 540, 92401
Telephone: 909-884-8855
Fax: 909-884-5161

MEMBERS OF FIRM

Fred A. Wilson (1886-1973)
Wm. H. Wilson (1915-1981)
Caywood J. Borror
James R. Dunn
Richard L. Scott
Thomas M. Davis
Keith D. Davis

ASSOCIATES

Timothy P. Prince
Sarah L. Overton

Representative Clients: Travelers Insurance Co.; Rockwell International; Westinghouse Air Brake Co.; Goodyear Tire and Rubber Co.; Home Insurance Co.; Cities of: Redlands, Chino, Colton, San Bernardino and Upland; The Canadian Insurance Co.

For full biographical listings, see the Martindale-Hubbell Law Directory

SAN BRUNO, San Mateo Co. — (Refer to Burlingame)

*SAN DIEGO,** San Diego Co.

ALLEN, MATKINS, LECK, GAMBLE & MALLORY (AV)

A Partnership including Professional Corporations
501 West Broadway, Suite 900, 92101
Telephone: 619-233-1155
Facsimile: 619-233-1158
Los Angeles, California Office: Eighth Floor, 515 South Figueroa Street, 90071.
Telephone: 213-622-5555.
Telecopier: 213-620-8816.
Irvine, California Office: Fourth Floor, 18400 Von Karman, 92715.
Telephone: 714-553-1313.
Telecopier: 714-553-8354.
West Los Angeles, California Office: 1999 Avenue of the Stars, 90067.
Telephone: 310-788-2400.
Fax: 310-788-2410.

RESIDENT PARTNERS

Michael E. Gleason (P.C.)
Vernon C. Gauntt
George J. Berger
Michael C. Pruter
Dana I. Schiffman
David L. Osias (Resident, San Diego and Los Angeles Offices)
William J. Harris
Ray B. Gliner
Robert R. Barnes

RESIDENT ASSOCIATES

Jeffrey R. Patterson
Craig D. Swanson
Dean E. Roeper
Martha K. Guy
George W. Kuney (Resident, San Diego Office)
Kelli L. Fuller
David Adam Swartz
Steve Wellington

OF COUNSEL

John G. Davies
Joe M. Davidson

Reference: Wells Fargo Bank (Los Angeles Main Office).

For full biographical listings, see the Martindale-Hubbell Law Directory

BAKER & MCKENZIE (AV)

The Wells Fargo Plaza Twelfth Floor, 101 West Broadway, 92101
Telephone: (619) 236-1441
Intl. Dialing: (1-619) 236-1441
Cable Address: ABOGADO SD
Telex: 9102503468
Answer Back: ABOGADO SD
Facsimile: (1-619) 236-0429
Associated Offices of Baker & McKenzie in: Almaty, Amsterdam, Bangkok, Barcelona, Beijing, Berlin, Bogotá, Brasília, Brussels, Budapest, Buenos Aires, Cairo, Caracas, Chicago, Dallas, Frankfurt, Geneva, Hanoi, Ho Chi Minh City, Hong Kong, Juárez, Kiev, London, Madrid, Manila, Melbourne, México City, Miami, Milan, Monterrey, Moscow, New York, Palo Alto, Paris, Prague, Rio de Janeiro, Riyadh, Rome, St. Petersburg, San Francisco, São Paulo, Singapore, Stockholm, Sydney, Taipei, Tijuana, Tokyo, Toronto, Valencia, Warsaw, Washington, D.C. and Zürich.
Correspondent Law Firm: Hadiputranto, Hadinoto & Partners, Jakarta.

MEMBERS OF FIRM

Gordon G. Chang
Charles H. Dick, Jr.
David C. Doyle
Thomas W. Ferrell
John J. Hentrich
Donald McGrath II
Ali M. M. Mojdehi
Thomas M. Shoesmith
Abby B. Silverman

LOCAL PARTNERS

Ian L. Kessler
Clark H. Libenson
Pamela J. Naughton
Dana M. Sabraw

OF COUNSEL

Edward T. Butler

ASSOCIATES

David M. Bassham
Randall K. Broberg
Wanda Wan-Hwa Chang
Steven E. Comer
Ernest Cordero, Jr.
Ronald F. Hoffman
Cynthia G. Iliff
Katherine S. Kruis
Laura Loberman
Michael P. McCloskey
J. Michael Roake
Eric M. Robinson
Renee S. Schor
Claire Wright

For full biographical listings, see the Martindale-Hubbell Law Directory

BROBECK, PHLEGER & HARRISON (AV)

A Partnership including a Professional Corporation
550 West C Street Suite 1300, 92101
Telephone: 619-234-1966
Telecopier: 619-236-1403 (13th Floor); 619-234-3848 (12th Floor)
San Francisco, California Office: Spear Street Tower, One Market.
Telephone: 415-442-0900.
Palo Alto, California Office: Two Embarcadero Place, 2200 Geng Road.
Telephone: 415-424-0160.
Los Angeles, California Office: 550 South Hope Street.
Telephone: 213-489-4060.

(See Next Column)

Orange County, California Office: 4675 MacArthur Court, Suite 1000, Newport Beach.
Telephone: 714-752-7535.
Austin, Texas Office: 620 Congress Avenue, Suite 320.
Telephone: 512-477-5495.
Fax: 512-477-5813.
Denver, Colorado Office: 1125 Seventeenth Street, 15th Floor.
Telephone: 303-293-0760.
Fax: 303-299-8819.
New York, N.Y. Office: 1301 Avenue of the Americas, 30th Floor.
Telephone: 212-581-1600.
Fax: 212-586-7878.
Brobeck Hale and Dorr International Offices:
London, England Office: Veritas House, 125 Finsbury Pavement, London EC2A 1NQ.
Telephone: 44 071 638 6688.
Facsimile: 44 071 638 5888.
Prague, Czech Republic Office: Brehova 1, 110 00 Praha 1.
Telephone: 422 232-8461.
Facsimile: 422 232-8444.

RESIDENT PARTNERS

Craig S. Andrews
Todd J. Anson
John A. de Groot
John A. Denniston
Theodore W. Graham
Richard L. Kintz
Daniel G. Lamb, Jr.
Richard L. Parker
Maria K. Pum
Ellen B. Spellman
William F. Sullivan
Hayden J. Trubitt
Mary L. Walker

OF COUNSEL

Robin E. Werner

ASSOCIATES

Richard J. Babcock
Michael J. Barry
William S. Biel
Marc Channick
John R. Cook
Wayne Fong
Jeffrey Garfinkle
Kristen E. Harkness
Nancy Gundermann Henderson
Ellen Kaulbach Jamason
Michael S. Kagnoff
Jennifer A. Kearns
Mary Kathryn Kelley
Chris A. Knudsen
Christopher H. McGrath
Martin Clark Nichols
Barbara Taylor Oetting
Cindy S. Pittman
Faye H. Russell
Joan I. Stafslien
Beth Weinberger

For full biographical listings, see the Martindale-Hubbell Law Directory

FERRIS & BRITTON, A PROFESSIONAL CORPORATION (AV)

1600 First National Bank Center, 401 West A Street, 92101
Telephone: 619-233-3131
Fax: 619-232-9316

Alfred G. Ferris
Christopher Q. Britton
Harry J. Proctor
Steven J. Pynes
Tamara K. Fogg
Pauline H. G. Getz
Michael R. Weinstein
Gary T. Moyer

OF COUNSEL

James J. Granby
William M. Winter
Allan J. Reniche

Representative Clients: Allstate Insurance Co.; Cox Communications, Inc.; Enterprise Rent-a-Car; Exxon; Immuno Pharmaceutics, Inc.; Invitrogen Corporation; Teleport Communications Group; Southwest Airlines; Times-Mirror Cable Television.

For full biographical listings, see the Martindale-Hubbell Law Directory

FRANK & MILCHEN (AV)

136 Redwood Street, 92103-5690
Telephone: 619-574-1888
Fax: 619-574-0649

Howard B. Frank
Joseph Milchen

Stephen E. Hoffman

For full biographical listings, see the Martindale-Hubbell Law Directory

LAW OFFICES OF LOUIS E. GOEBEL, P.C. (AV)

Suite 6000, McClintock Plaza, 1202 Kettner Boulevard, 92101
Telephone: 619-239-2611
FAX: 619-239-4269

Louis E. Goebel

For full biographical listings, see the Martindale-Hubbell Law Directory

San Diego—Continued

Gray Cary Ware & Freidenrich, A Professional Corporation (AV)

Gray Cary Established in 1927
Ware & Freidenrich Established in 1969
401 "B" Street, Suite 1700, 92101
Telephone: 619-699-2700
Telecopier: 619-236-1048
Palo Alto, California Office: 400 Hamilton Avenue.
Telephone: 415-328-6561.
La Jolla, California Office: Suite 575, 1200 Prospect Street.
Telephone: 619-454-9101.
El Centro, California Office: 1224 State Street, P.O. Box 2890.
Telephone: 619-353-6140.

John Allcock
Robert Ames
Robert W. Ayling
William E. Beamer
Robert W. Bell, Jr.
T. Knox Bell
J. Rod Betts
Charles E. Black
William S. Boggs
Edward V. Brennan
Michael D. Breslauer
Richard Alexander Burt
Robert G. Copeland
Theodore J. Cranston
Frederick P. Crowell
Guylyn R. Cummins
Jeffry A. Davis
Charles L. Deem
Joseph A. Delaney
David L. Dick
David Henry Dolkas
Jan Shirley Driscoll
L. B. Chip Edleson
Elisabeth Eisner
R. Reaves Elledge, Jr.
Melitta Fleck (Resident, La Jolla Office)
Brian L. Forbes
Brian A. Foster
David B. Geerdes
G. Eric Georgatos
William E. Grauer (Resident, Palo Alto Office)
W. Terrance Guiney
Jay D. Hanson
Michael M. Hogan
James W. Huston
Sterling Hutcheson
Jay W. Jeffcoat
William N. Kammer
Paul E. Kreutz
Peter N. Larrabee
W. Alan Lautanen
John J. Lormon
Richard F. Luther
Jeff L. Mangum
Browning E. Marean, III
Guillermo Marrero
William McCurine, Jr.
Robert A. McGregor
Edward J. McIntyre
Marcelle E. Mihaila
David E. Monahan
Josiah L. Neeper
J. Terence O'Malley
Barbara Jean Orr
Richard A. Paul
Ronald E. Pettis
Fred M. Plevin
Ralph M. Pray, III
Cameron Jay Rains
Terry D. Ross
Don G. Rushing
William B. Sailer
Dennis A. Schoville
Jeffrey M. Shohet
James K. Smith
Anthony M. Stiegler
James F. Stiven
Merrill F. Storms, Jr.
Paul R. Syrowik
Lawrence I. Tannenbaum
Michael S. Tracy
Shirli Fabbri Weiss
James C. Weseman
Mark C. Zebrowski
Karl ZoBell (Resident, La Jolla Office)

Louis G. Arnell
Neil P. Balmert
Marnie Wright Barnhorst
Mildred Basden (Resident, La Jolla Office)
Brian L. Behmer
Cathy A. Bencivengo
Christopher P. Bifone
Kevin A. Bové
Ann K. Bradley
Harris F. Brotman
Lorna Alksne Brown
Robert W. Brownlie
Eric P. Campbell
Alejandro D. Campillo
E. Joseph Connaughton
Nancy O. Dix
Terri P. Durham
Daniel E. Eaton
Rodney S. Edmonds
Janis S. Fagan
Bryan M. Garrie
Andrew M. Greene
Gail Armist Greene
Mark H. Hamer
James T. Hannink
Robert Hitchcock Hayes
Duane S. Horning
Paul E. Hurdlow
Christopher J. Hurley
Therese H. Hymer
Kathryn E. Karcher
Nancy Kawano
Matt A. Kirmayer
Selena Loh LaCroix
James E. Lauth
Diane L. Levitsky
Robert C. Longstreth
G. Scott Lutz
Jonathan D. Mack
Jeanne Malitz
Mark A. Mandio
Fredrica S. Maveety (Resident, La Jolla Office)
Lisa C. Merrill
Andrea E. Migdal
Randy Munyon
Maria E. Núñez
Tracy L. Nation
Erin E Norberg
Daniel T. Pascucci
Dayna J. Pineda
Alison L. Pivonka
Heather E. Pollock
Douglas J. Renert
K. English Robinson
Paul H. Roeder
Alexander H. Rogers
Ian N. Rose
Rebecca K. Schmitt
Jennifer A. Schuman
Jonathan B. Sokol
Chulho P. Song
Kimberly S. Stanley
Clare H. Stebbing
Donald J. Sullivan
Michael C. Sullivan
Beatrice A. Tice
Lynn E. Todd
Michael S. van Dyke
David E. Watson

(See Next Column)

Ellen H. Whelan (Resident, La Jolla Office)
Amy T. Wintersheimer
Marie A. Wright-Travis
Christopher M. Young

OF COUNSEL

H. Cushman Dow
Bruce A. Hecker (Not admitted in CA)

Representative Clients: Automobile Club of South California; Bank of America; Brooktree Corp.; C. A. Parr (Agencies), Ltd.; IMED; Pacific Bell; McMillin Development Co.; Scripps Clinic and Research Fdtn.; SeaWorld, Inc.; Underwriters at Lloyds; Wells Fargo Bank.

For full biographical listings, see the Martindale-Hubbell Law Directory

Higgs, Fletcher & Mack (AV)

2000 First National Bank Building, 401 West "A" Street, 92101
Telephone: 619-236-1551
ABA Net: 9011
Telex: 382028 HFM UD
Telecopier: 619-696-1410
North County Office: 613 West Valley Parkway, Suite 345. Escondido, California, 92025-2552.
Telephone: 619-743-1201.
Telecopier: 619-743-9926.

MEMBERS OF FIRM

Henry Pitts Mack (1909-1974)
David D. Randolph
John W. Netterblad
Gerald J. O'Neill
Joe N. Turner
Craig D. Higgs
J. Tim Konold
Harry L. Carter
Ronald E. Null
Franklin T. Lloyd
David W. Ferguson (Resident Partner, Escondido Office)
Michael F. Boyle
Steven B. Davis
Linda McKathnie Woolcott
Bruce D. Jaques, Jr. (Resident Partner, Escondido Office)
John Morris
Kurt L. Kicklighter
John L. Morrell
Steven H. Kruis
David R. Clark
Gregory Y. Lievers (Resident Partner, Escondido Office)
Jeanne S. Gallagher
M. Cory Brown
Erick R. Altona (Resident Partner, Escondido Office)
Patricia P. Hollenbeck
Thomas P. Sayer, Jr.
Helen H. Peak (Resident Partner, Escondido Office)
James M. Peterson
James A. Cunningham

OF COUNSEL

DeWitt A. Higgs
Ferdinand T. Fletcher
Vincent E. Whelan
Margaret Anne Payne
Kenneth H. Lounsbery

ASSOCIATES

Greg A. McAtee
Susan D. Moriarty
Martin A. Eliopulos
Scott S. Payzant
Phillip C. Samouris
Dolores E. Gonzales
Charles A. LePla (Resident Associate, Escondido Office)
Daniel C. Herbert
Liong Lie Gan
Christopher S. Morris

Representative Clients: Frazee Industries; Kawasaki Motors Corp.; Rohr Industries; Allstate Insurance Co.; Associated Aviation Underwriters; Physicians & Surgeons Insurance Exchange.

For full biographical listings, see the Martindale-Hubbell Law Directory

King & Ballow (AV)

2700 Symphony Towers, 750 B Street, 92101
Telephone: 619-236-9401
Fax: 619-236-9437
Nashville, Tennessee Office: 1200 Noel Place, 200 Fourth Avenue, North.
Telephone: 615-259-3456.
Fax: 615-254-7907.
San Francisco, California Office: 100 First Street Suite 2700, 94105.
Telephone: 415-541-7803.
Fax: 415-541-7805.

MEMBERS OF FIRM

Frank S. King, Jr. (Not admitted in CA)
Robert L. Ballow (Not admitted in CA)
Richard C. Lowe (Not admitted in CA)
R. Eddie Wayland (Not admitted in CA)
Paul H. Duvall (Resident)
Mark E. Hunt (Not admitted in CA)
Lynn Siegel

ASSOCIATES

Kevin M. Bagley
Leslie E. Lewis
Linda L. Stuessi

Representative Clients: City of Chula Vista, Chula Vista, California; Ingram Micro, Inc., Santa Ana, California; KNSD-TV, San Diego, California; San Diego Daily Transcript, San Diego, California; Sullivan Graphics, Inc., Brentwood, Tennessee; Union-Tribune Publishing Company, San Diego, California.

For full biographical listings, see the Martindale-Hubbell Law Directory

San Diego—Continued

LINDLEY, LAZAR & SCALES, A PROFESSIONAL CORPORATION (AV)

One America Plaza, 600 West Broadway, Suite 1400, 92101-3302
Telephone: 619-234-9181
Fax: 619-234-8475

Fred E. Lindley (1876-1971)
George A. Lazar (1909-1992)
Leon W. Scales (1908-1983)
Luke R. Corbett
John M. Seitman
Robert M. McLeod
William E. Johns
Stephen F. Treadgold
Michael H. Wexler
Richard J. Pekin, Jr.
George C. Lazar
Raymond L. Heidemann
James Henry Fox
Elise Streicher Rogerson
R. Gordon Huckins
Kenneth C. Jones

Donna C. Looper
William A. Larkin

OF COUNSEL

Maurice T. Watson
Philip P. Martin, Jr.

Representative Clients: Palomar Savings & Loan Assn.; McGraw-Hill Broadcasting Co.; Chicago Title Insurance Co.; San Diego Hospital Association.

For full biographical listings, see the Martindale-Hubbell Law Directory

LUCE, FORWARD, HAMILTON & SCRIPPS (AV)

A Partnership including Professional Corporations
600 West Broadway, Suite 2600, 92101
Telephone: 619-236-1414
Fax: 619-232-8311
La Jolla, California Office: 4275 Executive Square, Suite 800, 92037.
Telephone: 619-535-2639.
Fax: 619-453-2812.
Los Angeles, California Office: 777 South Figueroa, 36th Floor, 90017.
Telephone: 213-892-4992.
Fax: 213-892-7731.
San Francisco, California Office: 100 Bush Street, 20th Floor, 94104.
Telephone: 415-395-7900.
Fax: 415-395-7949.
New York, N.Y. Office: Citicorp Center, 153 East 53rd Street, 26th Floor, 10022.
Telephone: 212-754-1414.
Fax: 212-644-9727.

MEMBERS OF FIRM

Edgar A. Luce (1881-1958)
F. Tudor Scripps, Jr. (1908-1963)
Charles H. Forward (1886-1981)
Thomas M. Hamilton (1915-1994)
Edgar A. Luce, Jr.
Robert E. McGinnis
Robert G. Steiner
William M. McKenzie, Jr.
Gerald S. Davee
John W. Brooks
Steven S. Wall
Thomas M. Murray
Ronald W. Rouse
Charles L. Hellerich
Jack G. Charney
Charles A. Bird
Craig K. Beam
Susanne Stanford
Scott W. Sonne (Managing Partner)
Robert J. Bell
G. Edward Arledge
George S. Howard, Jr.
Steven P. McDonald
Mark L. Mann
John B. McNeece III
Michael L. Jensen
Robert J. Durham, Jr.
Mark Hagarty
Frederick R. Vandeveer
Lawrence J. Kouns
Albert T. Harutunian III
Mikel R. Bistrow
Margaret M. Mann
Darryl L. Steinhause
Craig A. Schloss
Richard R. Spirra
Vickie E. Turner
Nancy T. Scull
R. William Bowen
John W. Leslie
Robert A. Levy
Mark W. Hansen
Peter H. Klee
Christopher J. Healey
Thomas A. May
Stephen T. Toohill
Mary F. Gillick
Robert D. Buell
Daniel N. Riesenberg
Stephen L. Marsh
Marjorie J. Floyd
Valentine S. Hoy, VIII
R. Randal Crispen
Edward Patrick "Pat" Swan, Jr.
Dennis J. Doucette
Kathryn A. Bernert
Mitchell L. Lathrop (Resident, New York, N.Y. Office)
Terrence L. Bingman
Otto E. Sorensen
Robert H. Roe, Jr.
Kathy P. Waring
John L. Riedl
Jon K. Wactor (Resident, San Francisco Office)
Mary L. Russell
Rex Heeseman (Resident, Los Angeles Office)
James E. Fitzgerald (Resident, Los Angeles Office)
Andrew Jay Waxler (Resident, Los Angeles Office)
Cathy L. Croshaw (Resident, San Francisco Office)
Jeffrey L. Fillerup (Resident, San Francisco Office)
Kimball Ann Lane (Resident, New York, N.Y. Office)
Craig R. Brown (Resident, New York, N.Y. Office)
Daniel I. Simon (Resident, Los Angeles Office)
Christopher Celentino
Phillip L. Jelsma
Timothy R. Pestotnik

(See Next Column)

OF COUNSEL

Michael T. Andrew
Stephen R. Brown
E. Miles Harvey (Retired)
Gregory D. Roper
William A. Yale
William L. Hoese

SPECIAL COUNSEL

Richard T. Forsyth
Harvey T. Elam (Resident, San Francisco Office)

ASSOCIATES

Richard E. Showen
Nathan S. Arrington
James H. Siegel
Dan Lawton
Christopher K. Barnette
David M. Hymer
Jeffrey A. Chine
Roger C. Haerr
Callie A. Bjurstrom
Bruce D. Lundstrom
Robert B. Clark
Thomas B. Reeve, Jr.
Charles A. Danaher
Marc J. Feldman
William T. Earley
Edward L. Bushor
Pamela S. Ewers
Cordon T. Baesel
Michael L. Branch
Teryl S. Murabayashi
Kathryn M. S. Catherwood
Jane P. Bahnson
Carol K. Kao
Maria C. Rodriguez
Stefanie Crames Solomon
Valerie J. Tanney
Jeffrey K. Brown
John P. Cooley
Michael G. Fraunces
Terrance L. Toavs
Nancy Fuller-Jacobs
Frank J. Kros
Roger D. Brown
James G. Waian
Sonia S. Waisman
Nancy L. Beattie
Armin R. Callo
Vonnie L. Hansen
Marnin Weinreb (Resident, Los Angeles Office)
Robin D. Craig-Olson (Resident, San Francisco Office)
Roger S. Sampson (Resident, San Francisco Office)
James A. Goniea (Resident, San Francisco Office)
Patricia Dee-Bilka (Resident, New York, N.Y. Office)
Joseph F. Bermudez (Resident, New York, N.Y. Office)
Huhnsik Chung (Resident, New York, N.Y. Office)
Frances J. Phillips (Resident, New York, N.Y. Office)
Anne T. Turilli (Resident, New York, N.Y. Office)
Richard J. Fabian (Resident, New York, N.Y. Office)
Julie B. Pollack (Resident, New York, N.Y. Office)
Kerry A. Griffin (Resident, New York, N.Y. Office)
Lourdes M. Slater (Resident, New York, N.Y. Office)
Lisa J. Greene (Resident, New York, N.Y. Office)
Peter K. Hahn
Dominic S. Nesbitt
James A. Mercer III
Tami L. Johnson Penner
Kelly Capen Douglas
Bridget Klein Moorhead
Raymond J. Liddy
John T. Brooks
Lynne D. Kaelin
Laura L. Jackson (Resident, San Francisco Office)
Richard C. Turner
Christopher H. Findley

For full biographical listings, see the Martindale-Hubbell Law Directory

MULVANEY, KAHAN & BARRY, A PROFESSIONAL CORPORATION (AV)

Seventeenth Floor, First National Bank Center, 401 West "A" Street, 92101-7994
Telephone: 619-238-1010
Fax: 619-238-1981
Los Angeles, California Office: Union Bank Plaza, 445 South Figueroa Street, Suite 2600.
Telephone: 213-612-7765.
La Jolla, California Office: Glendale Federal Building, 7911 Herschel, Suite 300, P.O Box 1885.
Telephone: 619-454-0142.
Fax: 619-454-7858.
Orange, California Office: The Koll Center, 500 North State College Boulevard, Suite 440.
Telephone: 714-634-7069.
Fax: 714-939-8000.

James F. Mulvaney
Lawrence Kahan
Everett G. Barry, Jr.
Donald G. Johnson, Jr.
Robert A. Linn
Maureen E. Markey
Paula Rotenberg
Melissa A. Blackburn
Rex B. Beatty
Julie A. Jones
Maureen H. Edwards
Greta C. Botka
Mark R. Raftery
Charles F. Bethel
Carrie L. Gleeson
Diane M. Racicot
John A. Mayers
Linda P. Lucal
Steven W. Pite
Patricia A. Sieveke (Resident, Los Angeles and Orange Offices)
Michael S. Umansky

OF COUNSEL

James P. McGowan, Jr. (Resident, La Jolla Office)
Derrick W. Samuelson (Not admitted in CA)

Representative Clients: Air Products & Chemicals, Inc.; Revlon, Inc.; Rhône-Poulenc Rorer, Inc.; Union Bank; Unilab Corporation; Union Land Title Co.; Wells Fargo Bank; Esselte Pendaflex Corp.

For full biographical listings, see the Martindale-Hubbell Law Directory

San Diego—Continued

Page, Polin, Busch & Boatwright, A Professional Corporation (AV)

350 West Ash Street, Suite 900, 92101-3404
Telephone: 619-231-1822
Fax: 619-231-1877
FAX: 619-231-1875

David C. Boatwright
Michael E. Busch
Robert K. Edmunds
Kathleen A. Cashman-Kramer
Richard L. Moskitis
Richard W. Page
Kenneth D. Polin
Steven G. Rowles

OF COUNSEL

Richard Edward Ball, Jr.

Rod S. Fiori
Christina B. Gamache
Dorothy A. Johnson
Theresa McCarthy
Jolene L. Parker
Deidre L. Schneider
Sandra L. Shippey

For full biographical listings, see the Martindale-Hubbell Law Directory

Pillsbury Madison & Sutro (AV)

101 West Broadway, Suite 1800, 92101
Telephone: 619-234-5000
Telex: 559755
FAX: 619-236-1995
Costa Mesa, California Office: Plaza Tower, 600 Anton Boulevard, Suite 1100,92626.
Telephone: 714-436-6800.
Fax: 714-662-6999.
Los Angeles, California Office: Citicorp Plaza, 725 South Figueroa, Suite 1200, 90017.
Telephone: 213-488-7100.
Fax: 213-629-1033.
New York, New York Office: One Liberty Plaza, 165 Broadway, 51st Floor.
Telephone: 212-374-1890.
Fax: 212-374-1852.
Menlo Park, California Office: 2700 Sand Hill Road, 94025.
Telephone: 415-233-4500.
Fax: 415-233-4545.
Sacramento, California Office: 400 Capitol Mall, Suite 1700, 95814.
Telephone: 916-329-4700.
Fax: 916-441-3583.
San Francisco, California Office: 225 Bush Street, 94104.
Telephone: 415-983-1000.
Fax: 415-398-2096.
San Jose, California Office: Ten Almaden Boulevard, 95113.
Telephone: 408-947-4000.
Fax: 408-287-8341.
Washington, D.C. Office: Suite 1100, 1667 K Street, N.W., 20006.
Telephone: 202-887-0300.
Fax: 202-296-7605.
Hong Kong Office: 6/F Asia Pacific Finance Tower, Citibank Plaza, 3 Garden Road, Central.
Telephone: 011-852-509-7100.
Fax: 011-852-509-7188.
Tokyo, Japan Office: Churchill and Shimazaki, Gaikokuho-Jimu-Bengoshi-Jimusho, 11-12, Toranomon 5-Chome, Minato-Ku, Tokyo, 105, Japan.
Telephone: 800-729-9830; 011-81-3-5472-6561.
Fax: 011-81-3-5472-5761.

MEMBERS OF FIRM

John L. Donahue
John M. Dunn
P. Garth Gartrell
Sue J. Hodges
David E. Kleinfeld
Daniel C. Minteer
William A. Reavey, III
Patrick C. Shea
David R. Snyder
James K. Sterrett II
Jo Ann Taormina
Douglas R. Tribble
Mark R. Wicker
Angela M. Yates

OF COUNSEL

Matthew S. Walker

ASSOCIATES

Karen M. Buttemer
T. Michael Hird
Eric A. Kremer
Christopher B. Latham
Douglas M. Leigh
Laura K. Licht
David MacLennon Logan
Kimberly A. Mc Donnell
Kathryn L. Partrick
Thomas P. Redick
Richard M. Segal
Daniel S. Silverman
Ron A. Symm
John E. Timmons
Barry J. Tucker
Jan Harden Webster
Eric C. Young

For full biographical listings, see the Martindale-Hubbell Law Directory

Procopio, Cory, Hargreaves and Savitch (AV)

2100 Union Bank Building, 530 B Street, 92101
Telephone: 619-238-1900
Telecopier: 619-235-0398

(See Next Column)

A. T. Procopio (1900-1974)
Harry Hargreaves (Retired)
John H. Barrett (Retired)
Dennis H. McKee (Retired)
Gerald E. Olson (Retired)

MEMBERS OF FIRM

Alec L. Cory
Emmanuel Savitch
Paul B. Wells
Todd E. Leigh
Jeffrey Isaacs
Robert J. Berton
Frederick K. Kunzel
Robert G. Russell, Jr.
George L. Damoose
Kelly M. Edwards
Raymond G. Wright
James G. Sandler
Thomas R. Laube
Philip J. Giacinti, Jr.
Steven J. Untiedt
Steven M. Strauss
Craig P. Sapin
Robert K. Butterfield, Jr.
Michael J. Kinkelaar
Kenneth J. Rose
Eric B. Shwisberg
Gerald P. Kennedy
Lynne R. Lasry
Edward I. Silverman
Jeffrey D. Cawdrey
Thomas W. Turner, Jr.
Stephen R. Robinson

ASSOCIATES

Kenneth J. Witherspoon
William W. Eigner
Matthew W. Argue
Jeffrey M. Byer
Richard M. Valdez
Kathryn M. Otto
Martina Mende
Allison D. Cato
Gary A. Perlmutter

OF COUNSEL TO

Milch & Wolfsheimer, , San Diego, California

Representative Clients: Union Bank; Associated General Contractors of America; Daley Corp.; Dixieline Lumber Co.; Otay International Center; GEA Power Cooling Systems, Inc.; The Koll Co.; Kvaas Construction Co.; Mobil Oil Corp.; Office Club.

For full biographical listings, see the Martindale-Hubbell Law Directory

Seltzer Caplan Wilkins & McMahon, A Professional Corporation (AV)

2100 Symphony Towers, 750 B Street, 92101
Telephone: 619-685-3003
Fax: 619-685-3100

Floyd Wilkins, Jr. (Retired)
James B. Person (1947-1991)
Norman T. Seltzer
Robert Caplan
Gerald L. McMahon
Reginald A. Vitek
James B. Franklin
Stephen D. Royer
David J. Dorne
James R. Dawe
Brian T. Seltzer
Elizabeth A. Smith
Julie P. Dubick
Joyce A. McCoy
Dennis J. Wickham
Frederick J. Stocker
John H. Alspaugh
Bruce H. Fagan
Donald A. English
Michael H. Riney
James P. Delphey
Kevin A. Werner
Craig E. Courter
Karen M. ZoBell
Elinor T. Merideth
Michael G. Nardi
Thomas F. Steinke
Neal P. Panish
Janice Patrice Brown
Mark M. Gloven
Sean T. Hargaden
Vera P. Pardee
Michael J. Snider
Julie Genthner Simon
Michael R. Seyle
David S. Minton
Adrienne Jeffrey
James M. Phillipi
Daniel A. Andrist
Susan A. Verner
Richard B. Flisher
J. Scott Scheper
Marta J. Burg
David J. Zubkoff
Andrew M. Kaplan
Elisa A. Brandes
Virginia C. Pearson
Cynthia B. Chapman
Patricia Garcia
Cheryl Sueing-Jones
Gregory E. Flynn
Tamara L. Reed
Kelly Rae Waggonner
Lee E. Hejmanowski
Christy I. Yee
David P. Chiappetta
Christine M. Dabrowski

OF COUNSEL

Bonnie Nelson Reading
Elizabeth C. Eldridge

Representative Clients: Girard Savings Bank; W.R. Grace & Co--Conn.; McDonnell-Douglas Corp.; McMillin Communities; Philip Morris Incorporated; Taco Bell Corp.; Western Financial Savings Bank.

For full biographical listings, see the Martindale-Hubbell Law Directory

Sheppard, Mullin, Richter & Hampton (AV)

A Partnership including Professional Corporations
Nineteenth Floor, 501 West Broadway, 92101
Telephone: 619-338-6500
Telecopier: 619-234-3815
Telex: 19-4424
Los Angeles, California Office: Forty-Eighth Floor, 333 South Hope Street.
Telephone: 213-620-1780.
Telecopier: 213-620-1398.
Cable Address: "Sheplaw."
Telex: 19-4424.

(See Next Column)

SHEPPARD, MULLIN, RICHTER & HAMPTON, *San Diego—Continued*

Orange County, California Office: Seventh Floor, 4695 MacArthur Court, Newport Beach.
Telephone: 714-752-6400.
Telecopier: 714-851-0739.
Telex: 19-4424.
San Francisco, California Office: Seventeenth Floor, Four Embarcadero Center.
Telephone: 415-434-9100.
Telecopier: 415-434-3947.
Telex: 19-4424.

MEMBERS OF FIRM

John R. Bonn
Barbara L. Borden
Michael J. Changaris
Dennis Childs
John D. Collins *
Domenic C. Drago
Richard M. Freeman *
Guy N. Halgren
James J. Mittermiller
Christopher B. Neils
Laura S. Taylor
Timothy B. Taylor
Victor A. Vilaplana
Edward D. Vogel
Michael J. Weaver *

SPECIAL COUNSEL

William V. Whelan
Ann Cretsinger

ASSOCIATES

Vincent J. Axelson
Carrie Battilega
David M. Beckwith
David B. Chidlaw
Angela A. Dahl
Karin A. Dougan
Linda Fox
Robert S. Gerber
Christopher J. Kearns
H. Anthony Lewis
Philip A. Magen
Timothy W. J. O'Brien
Betty J. Santohigashi
Lei K. Udell
Alan Van Derhoff
Tara L. Wilcox
John A. Yacovelle

*Professional Corporation

For full biographical listings, see the Martindale-Hubbell Law Directory

THORSNES, BARTOLOTTA, MCGUIRE & PADILLA (AV)

A Partnership including Professional Corporations
Fifth Avenue Financial Center, 11th Floor, 2550 Fifth Avenue, 92103
Telephone: 619-236-9363
Fax: 619-236-9653

Michael T. Thorsnes (P.C.)
Vincent J. Bartolotta, Jr., (P.C.)
John F. McGuire (P.C.)
Michael D. Padilla (P.C.)
Kevin F. Quinn (P.C.)
C. Brant Noziska (P.C.)
Mitchell S. Golub (P.C.)
Frederic L. Gordon (P.C.)
Palma Cesar Hooper (P.C.)
Neal H. Rockwood (P.C.)
Daral B. Mazzarella (P.C.)

ASSOCIATES

R. Christian Hulburt
Jeffrey F. LaFave
Stephen D. Lipkin
Rhonda J. Holmes
Martin W. Hagan
John J. Rice
Robert E. Bright
B. James Pantone
Douglas J. Billings

For full biographical listings, see the Martindale-Hubbell Law Directory

*SAN FRANCISCO,** San Francisco Co.

ADAMS, DUQUE & HAZELTINE (AV)

A Partnership including Professional Corporations
500 Washington Street, 94111
Telephone: 415-982-1240
FAX: 415-982-0130
Los Angeles, California Office: 777 South Figueroa Street, Tenth Floor.
Telephone: 213-620-1240.
FAX: 213-896-5500.

MEMBERS OF FIRM

James R. Willcox
George G. Weickhardt
Joseph M. Rimac, Jr.
David R. Shane

OF COUNSEL

Barrie Cowan

ASSOCIATES

Ann Sparkman
Marilyn A. Rogers
Anna Maria Martin
John C. Barker
Robert J. Taitz

For full biographical listings, see the Martindale-Hubbell Law Directory

BAKER & MCKENZIE (AV)

Two Embarcadero Center 24th Floor, 94111-3909
Telephone: (415) 576-3000
Intl. Dialing: (1-415) 576-3000
Cable: ABOGADO
Telex: 278588
Answer Back: 278588 ABOG UR
Facsimiles: (1-415) 576-3099; 576-3098
Associated Offices of Baker & McKenzie in: Almaty, Amsterdam, Bangkok, Barcelona, Beijing, Berlin, Bogotá, Brasília, Brussels, Budapest, Buenos Aires, Cairo, Caracas, Chicago, Dallas, Frankfurt, Geneva, Hanoi, Ho Chi Minh City, Hong Kong, Juárez, Kiev, London, Madrid, Manila, Melbourne, México City, Miami, Milan, Monterrey, Moscow, New York, Palo Alto, Paris, Prague, Rio de Janeiro, Riyadh, Rome, St. Petersburg, San Diego, São Paulo, Singapore, Stockholm, Sydney, Taipei, Tijuana, Tokyo, Toronto, Valencia, Warsaw, Washington, D.C. and Zürich.
Correspondent Law Firm: Hadiputranto, Hadinoto & Partners, Jakarta.

MEMBERS OF FIRM

Michael E. Arruda
Russell Baker (1901-1979)
Frank S. Bayley
Edward D. Burmeister
Klaus H. Burmeister
Juan G. Collas, Jr.
Howard F. Fine
John L. Fruth
Virginia L. Gibson
Bruce H. Jackson
Dennis Keeley
Jonathan S. Kitchen
John F. McKenzie
Timothy A. Tosta
Robert T. Yahng

LOCAL PARTNERS

Judy V. Davidoff
Peter J. Engstrom

COUNSEL

Catherine J. Boggs

ASSOCIATES

Edward S. Atkinson, Jr.
Bartley B. Baer
Philip A. Boyle
Peter R. Denwood
Valerie H. Diamond
Rebecca O. Fruchtman
Kim Gelman
Amy Dickman Gray
Maurice L. Hoo
Mark J. Jarrett
Chirag V. Karia
Joel D. Lee
Charles V. Moseley
Tyrrell M. Prosser
Richard H. Rahm
Jason C. Schaffer
Kerry Shapiro
Joyce Y. Smith (Not admitted in CA)
Elena V. Speed
Helen H. Surh
A. Alyce Werdel
Edwin T. Whatley

For full biographical listings, see the Martindale-Hubbell Law Directory

BEVERIDGE & DIAMOND (AV)

One Sansome Street, Suite 3400, 94104-4438
Telephone: 415-397-0100
FAX: 415-397-4238
Washington, D.C. Office: Beveridge & Diamond, P.C. 1350 I Street, N.W., Suite 700, 20005-3311.
Telephone: 202-789-6000.
Telecopier: 202-789-6190.
New York, N.Y. Office: Beveridge & Diamond, P.C. 40th Floor, 437 Madison Avenue, 10022-7380.
Telephone: 212-702-5400.
Telecopier: 212-702-5450.
Fort Lee, New Jersey Office: Suite 400, One Bridge Plaza, 07024-7502.
Telephone: 201-585-8162.
Telecopier: 201-592-7720.

Lawrence S. Bazel
David D. Cooke
Jennifer L. Hernandez
James L. Meeder
Gary J. Smith
Robert D. Wyatt

Stuart I. Block
Susan C. Cagann
Marc E. Gottschalk
Kimberly Martin McMorrow
Scott A. Miller
Brett P. Moffatt
Eileen M. Nottoli
Daniel J. O'Hanlon
Katherine B. Steuer
Julie K. Walters

For full biographical listings, see the Martindale-Hubbell Law Directory

BROBECK, PHLEGER & HARRISON (AV)

A Partnership including a Professional Corporation
Spear Street Tower, One Market, 94105
Telephone: 415-442-0900
Cable Address: "Brobeck"
Telex: 34228 BPH SFO
Los Angeles, California Office: 550 South Hope Street.
Telephone: 213-489-4060.
Palo Alto, California Office: Two Embarcadero Place, 2200 Geng Road.
Telephone: 415-424-0160.
San Diego, California Office: 550 West C Street, Suite 1300.
Telephone: 619-234-1966.
Telecopier: 619-236-1403 (13th Floor); 619-234-3848 (12th Floor).

(See Next Column)

BROBECK, PHLEGER & HARRISON—*Continued*

Orange County, California Office: 4675 MacArthur Court, Suite 1000, Newport Beach.
Telephone: 714-752-7535.
Facsimile: 714-752-7522.
Austin, Texas Office: 620 Congress Avenue, Suite 320.
Telephone: 512-477-5495.
Fax: 512-477-5813.
Denver, Colorado Office: 1125 Seventeenth Street, 15th Floor.
Telephone: 303-293-0760.
Fax: 303-299-8819.
New York, N.Y. Office: 1301 Avenue of the Americas, 30th Floor.
Telephone: 212-581-1600.
Fax: 212-586-7878.
Brobeck Hale and Dorr International Offices:
London, England Office: Veritas House, 125 Finsbury Pavement, London EC2A 1NQ.
Telephone: 44 071 638 6688.
Facsimile: 44 071 638 5888.
Prague, Czech Republic Office: Brehova 1, 110 00 Praha 1.
Telephone: 422 232-8461.
Facsimile: 422 232-8444.

MEMBERS OF FIRM

Thomas A. Bevilacqua
Grady M. Bolding
William S. Boyd
David J. Brown
Donald W. Brown
James E. Burns, Jr.
John E. Carlson
Rollin B. Chippey, II
Roy E. Crawford, III
George A. Cumming, Jr.
Robert S. Daggett
Susan R. Diamond
Brendan G. Dolan
Preston P. DuFauchard, Jr.
Rebecca D. Eisen
G. Larry Engel
Carol S. Etherington
Gary S. Fergus
Vincent P. Finigan, Jr.
Stephen R. Finn
Kevin B. Fisher
Tom M. Freeman
Anthony O. Garvin
A. Bruce Gilmore
Franklin Brockway Gowdy
William B. Griffin
Max Gutierrez, Jr.
G. Hopkins Guy, III
Pamela K. Hagenah
George A. Hisert
Frederick D. Holden, Jr.
Susan E. Hollander
Barry W. Homer
William L. Hudson
William R. Irwin
Karen Johnson-McKewan
Eric W. Jorgensen
Jeffrey S. Kingston
John W. Larson
Scott D. Lester
F. Daniel Leventhal
William A. Levin
Robert C. Livsey
Roderick A. McLeod
Timothy A. Meltzer
James L. Miller
John B. Missing
Michael E. Molland
Ronald B. Moskovitz
Kevin P. Muck
Thomas M. Peterson
Barbara Pletcher
James H. Quirk
Laura J. Remington
Diane S. Rice
Kent M. Roger
Rony Sagy
Susan Samuels-Muck
Bradford J. Shafer
Douglas D. Smith
Tower C. Snow, Jr.
Stephen M. Snyder
John E. Sparks
Michael P. Stanley
William J. "Zak" Taylor
W. Scott Thomas
William E. Trautman
George D. Tuttle
Russell D. Uzes
Robert P. Varian
L. Christopher Vejnoska
Nicholas B. Waranoff
Cecily A. Waterman
Thomas A. Welch
Kelly C. Wooster

OF COUNSEL

Donald J. Bouey
Hamilton W. Budge
Wiebke L. Buxbaum
John J. Corrigan
George T. Cronin
Gordon E. Davis
E. Judge Elderkin
Jean C. Gaskill
Charles E. Hanger
J. Stewart Harrison
Edward E. Kallgren
Charles W. LaGrave
David N. Lillevand, Jr.
Robert N. Lowry
John Anthony Mendez
Elizabeth Meyer
Alvin J. Rockwell
Hart H. Spiegel
Sylvia Yau

ASSOCIATES

Jeffrey T. Amann
D. Cameron Baker
Paul R. Bessette
Mark H. Boxer
Caleb J. (Jeff) Brinton, IV
Sara B. Brody
Kellee Brown
John A. Burke
Andrew E. Chau
Leila Clark-Riddell
Bridget A. Clarke
Heather L. Criss
David Daniels
Sayed M. Darwish
Christine A. Deaton
David F. Dedyo
Suzanne L. Snyder Edwards
Brian L. Ferrall
Samuel J. Fleischmann
Holly M. Fridholm
John M. Fujii
Nora L. Gibson
Theodore Goldin
Lawrence J. Gornick
Jennifer S. Gorovitz
Michael B. Green
David C. Grosek
Mortimer H. Hartwell
Bernard L. Hatcher
Renata Bianca Hesse
Edith M. Hofmeister
Howard Holderness III
Otto C. Holz
Elizabeth A. Howard

(See Next Column)

ASSOCIATES (Continued)

Jeffrey A. Kaiser
Susan E. Kaye
Stephen M. Knaster
Andrew B. Koslow
Meredith Nelson Landy
Molly Moriarty Lane
Diane M. L. Lee
James A. Lico
Thomas J. Lima
Gregory L. Lippetz
Jayne Loughry
Norma Loza
Ellen Staley Lussier
Teresa Ann Maginn
Richard Marquez
Jeffrey D. McFarland
Carrie M. McIntyre
Mark E. McKeen
Andrea Syran Meghrouni-Brown
David K. Michaels (Not admitted in CA)
Lisa J. Morelli
Barbara W. Moser
Robert S. Orgel
Jonathan Palmer
Judy Lynn Paraventi
Amy M. Paul
Michael J. Penner
Jon C. Perry
Michael F. Potter
Margo N. Rabinovitz
A. Michelle Ramirez
Amy R. Ratner
Christopher D. Roberts
Robyn Diane Roberts
Jeffrey M. Rollings
John F. Scalia
Larry W. Schwartz
Regina M. Sharrow
Michelle Sicula
Erika B. Smith
Michael L. Spolan
Craig C. Stevens
Teresa L. Stricker
David W. Thill
Tracy Thompson
Steven J. Tonsfeldt
Douglas G. Van Gessel
Dana P. Veeder
Jan D. Wadsworth
David E. Weiss

For full biographical listings, see the Martindale-Hubbell Law Directory

BRONSON, BRONSON & MCKINNON (AV)

A Partnership including Professional Corporations
505 Montgomery Street, 94111-2514
Telephone: 415-986-4200
Fax: 415-982-1394
Telex: 255921 KINBR UR
Los Angeles, California Office: 444 South Flower Street, 24th Floor.
Telephone: 213-627-2000.
Santa Rosa, California Office: 100 B Street, Suite 400.
Telephone: 707-527-8110.
San Jose, California Office: 10 Almaden Boulevard, Suite 600.
Telephone: 408-293-0599.

MEMBERS OF FIRM

Roy A. Bronson (1889-1977)
E. D. Bronson (1893-1976)
Harold R. McKinnon (1894-1977)
Bernard C. Kearns (1930-1987)
Stephen C. Tausz (1946-1989)
Grant P. DuBois (1937-1990)
Jack Berman (1957-1993)
Frederick S. Fields
Edwin L. Currey, Jr.
Paul J. Sanner
Terrence V. Ponsford
Alexander L. Brainerd
Victor J. Bacigalupi
Michael H. Ahrens
Robert C. Gebhardt
William H. G. Norman
Gilmore F. Diekmann, Jr.
Richard J. Stratton
Richard A. Ardoin
Thomas H. Sloan, Jr.
William T. Manierre
Kenneth E. Keller
Robert J. Stumpf
James C. Krieg
A. John Murphy, Jr.
Robert W. Tollen
Joseph G. Mason
Julia A. Molander
Mary Eileen Reilley
Stan G. Roman
Bonnie R. Cohen
Janine S. Simerly
Keith R. Weed
Patricia H. Cullison
John G. Mackie, Jr.
Leo J. Murphy, Jr.
Charles Schug
Stephen H. Dye
Michele K. Trausch
Zela G. Claiborne
Lawrence M. Cirelli
Carlyn Clause
David Eiseman
Craig Stuppi
Maureen McQuaid
Donald P. Rubenstein
Caroline K. Hinshaw
Jay P. Sanders
Robert W. Crockett
Roxanne L. Holmes
T. Scott Tate
Robert N. Phillips
Richard P. Walker
Jeffrey D. Ebstein
William P. O'Connell, Jr.
José H. García
Heidi Kohn Hugo
Richard A. Saffir
Kathleen M. Hayes
Scott W. Pink

OF COUNSEL

Max Weingarten
Charles W. Tuckman
John H. Sears
Gary Widman
Rongjie Ma
John W. Carr
David L. Hall

ASSOCIATES

Patricia J. Porter
Kymberly E. Speer
Lynn A. Bersch
Anne M. Lawlor Goyette
Robert S. Gebhard
Evelyn G. Heilbrunn
Lawrence R. Katzin
Andrew S. Miller
Sarah Robertson McCuaig
Albert P. Bedecarre
Craig A. Livingston
Abraham S. Simmons
Keith A. Flaum
Linda B. Ross
Claudia R. Carrington
Carl R. Goldberg
Mary Bossart Halfpenny
Steven H. Winick
Julie C. Grollmus
Richard C. Darwin

(See Next Column)

BRONSON, BRONSON & MCKINNON, *San Francisco—Continued*

ASSOCIATES (Continued)

Paul R. Mohun
Jennifer R. Woods
Christopher T. Holland
Craig M. Rankin
Monica Mucchetti
Christopher J. Sundermeier
Steven S. Cherensky
Andrea L. Hackett
Erik H. Adams
Connie L. Chen
Raymond A. Chenault
Clifford J. Gleicher
Debora A. Morrison
Jason A. Doren
Traci L. Van Pelt

For full biographical listings, see the Martindale-Hubbell Law Directory

BUCHALTER, NEMER, FIELDS & YOUNGER, A PROFESSIONAL CORPORATION (AV)

29th Floor, 333 Market Street, 94105
Telephone: 415-227-0900
Fax: 415-227-0770
Los Angeles, California Office: 24th Floor, 601 South Figueroa Street.
Telephone: 213-891-0700.
Fax: 213-896-0400.
New York, New York Office: 19th Floor, 237 Park Avenue.
Telephone: 212-490-8600.
Fax: 212-490-6022.
San Jose, California Office: 12th Floor, 50 West San Fernando Street.
Telephone: 408-298-0350.
Fax: 408-298-7683.
Newport Beach, California Office: Suite 300, 620 Newport Center Drive.
Telephone: 714-760-1121.
Fax: 714-720-0182.
Century City, California Office: Suite 2400, 1801 Century Park East.
Telephone: 213-891-0700.
Fax: 310-551-0233.

NORTHERN CALIFORNIA RESIDENTS IN CHARGE

Roxani M. Gillespie
Richard de Saint Phalle (Resident)
William McC. Wright (Resident)
Gary Nemer
Robert E. Izmirian (Resident)
James B. Wright
Peter G. Bertrand
W. David Campagne
Shawn M. Christianson (Resident)

OF COUNSEL

Robert A. Zadek

Stephen W. Sommerhalter (Resident)
Jared A. Goldin
Mary P. McCurdy (Resident)
Mary E. Jameson (Resident)
Kimberly A. Fanady
Ronald S. Beacher
Dennis D. Miller
Jeffrey L. Fazio
David Sturgeon-Garcia
Aron Mark Oliner
Mark C. Goodman
Marie G. Quashnock
Barbara Mikalson
David M. Serepca

References: City National Bank; Wells Fargo Bank; Metrobank.

For full biographical listings, see the Martindale-Hubbell Law Directory

COBLENTZ, CAHEN, MCCABE & BREYER (AV)

(Formerly Jacobs, Sills & Coblentz)
222 Kearny Street, 7th Floor, 94108
Telephone: 415-391-4800
Facsimile: 415-989-1663

MEMBERS OF FIRM

Tevis Jacobs (1906-1974)
Jonathan R. Bass
Jeffry A. Bernstein
Charles Roberts Breyer
Allen E. Broussard
William K. Coblentz
Virginia A. Crisp
Pamela S. Duffy
Paul Escobosa
Philip B. Feldman
Louis J. Giraudo
Susan K. Jamison
William F. McCabe (1939-1983)
Jeffrey G. Knowles
Stephen T. Lanctot
Michael L. Meyers
Barbara A. Milanovich
James P. Mitchell
Harry C. O'Brien
William H. Orrick, III
Susan J. Passovoy
Richard R. Patch
Barry Reder
Joseph C. Spero
Jon R. Tandler

ASSOCIATES

Andrew S. Coblentz
Jacqueline Scott Corley (Not admitted in CA)
Rachelle L. DesVaux
Alan C. Gennis
Jeffrey B. Maso
Audrey R. Ogawa
Stephen N. Rosenfield
Cynthia R. Rowland
Daniel J. Stromberg
Susan L. Sullivan

OF COUNSEL

Donald M. Cahen

SPECIAL COUNSEL

Ann E. Johnston

For full biographical listings, see the Martindale-Hubbell Law Directory

COOLEY GODWARD CASTRO HUDDLESON & TATUM (AV)

20th Floor, One Maritime Plaza, 94111
Telephone: 415-693-2000
Telex: 380815 COOLEY SFO
Fax: 415-951-3698 or 415-951-3699
Palo Alto, California Office: Suite 400, 5 Palo Alto Square.
Telephone: 415-843-5000.
Telex: 380816 COOLEY PA.
Fax: 415-857-0663.
Menlo Park, California Office: 3000 Sand Hill Road, Building 3 Suite 230.
Telephone: 415-843-5000.
Telex: 380816 COOLEY PA.
Fax: 415-854-2691.
Boulder, Colorado Office: 2595 Canyon Boulevard, Suite 250.
Telephone: 303-546-4000.
Fax: 303-546-4099.
San Diego, California Office: 4365 Executive Drive, 12th Floor.
Telephone: 619-550-6000.
Fax: 619-453-3555.
Denver, Colorado Office: One Tabor Center, 1200 17th Street, Suite 2100.
Telephone: 303-546-4000.

MEMBERS OF FIRM

Arthur E. Cooley (1882-1972)
Louis V. Crowley (1887-1971)
H. Rowan Gaither, Jr. (1909-1961)
Thomas A. H. Hartwell (1927-1990)
Andrew Kopperud (1924-1973)
Kenneth J. Adelson
John A. Anzur
Gordon C. Atkinson
John L. Cardoza
Peter H. Carson
John W. Crittenden
Robert L. Eisenbach III
Howard G. Ervin, III
Daniel W. Frank
Richard H. Frank
James C. Gaither
Kenneth L. Guernsey
J. Michael Kelly
Karen J. Kubin
Paul J. Laveroni
Lance Director Nagel
Susan Cooper Philpot
Paul A. Renne
James A. Richman
Benjamin K. Riley
Joseph P. Russoniello
Joseph A. Scherer
Myron G. Sugarman
Michael Traynor
Christopher A. Westover
Vernon M. Winters
Michael C. Wood
John F. Young
Jeffrey S. Zimman

OF COUNSEL

Augustus Castro
William W. Godward
Edwin E. Huddleson, Jr.
Paul M. Little
Erving Sodos
Harley J. Spitler
Frank D. Tatum, Jr.

SPECIAL COUNSEL

Cydney S. Posner
Sandra B. Price

ASSOCIATES

Maya L. Armour
Irl S. Barefield
Jodie M. Bourdet
Thea M. Chester
Kristin K. Croft
Kimberly D. Fanning (Not admitted in CA)
Steven L. Friedlander
William G. Gaede, III
Lisa Constance Gerhauser
Yvonne Gonzalez-Rogers
Philip M. Guess
Phillip Kirk Hobbs
Kathleen A. Howard
Noel C. Johnson
Isobel Ann Jones
Tracy S. Kaplan
Marina Landau
Martin J. Lobdell
Kathleen T. McCarthy
Ann M. Mooney
Charles M. Schaible
Karyn R. Smith
Anita F. Stork
Christopher E. Stretch
John W. Vander Vort
James R. Vidano
Patrick Walravens
Kathryn M. Wheble (Not admitted in CA)

LEGAL SUPPORT PERSONNEL

SENIOR PARALEGALS

Laura D. Herrera
Alisa O. Young

For full biographical listings, see the Martindale-Hubbell Law Directory

FABRIS, BURGESS & RING, A PROFESSIONAL CORPORATION (AV)

456 Montgomery Street, Suite 1800, 94104
Telephone: 415-982-6393
Fax: 415-982-2429

Alvin J. Fabris (1912-1983)
David D. Ring
Joseph I. Burgess
Barri Kaplan Bonapart
James H. Duncan, Jr.
Deborah Daniloff
Edward F. Mitchell, III
Karen M. Porter
Russell J. Brubaker
Kevin A. Mills

LEGAL SUPPORT PERSONNEL

PARALEGALS

Susan E. R. Parker
Katherine A. O'Connell
Hampton S. Coley
Karen J. Ruocco
Leslie L. Neidleman

For full biographical listings, see the Martindale-Hubbell Law Directory

San Francisco—Continued

FELDMAN, WALDMAN & KLINE, A PROFESSIONAL CORPORATION (AV)

2700 Russ Building, 235 Montgomery Street, 94104
Telephone: 415-981-1300
Telex: 650-223-3204
Fax: 415-394-0121
Stockton, California Office: Sperry Building, 146-148 West Weber Avenue.
Telephone: 209-943-2004.
Fax: 209-943-0905.

Murry J. Waldman
Leland R. Selna, Jr.
Michael L. Korbholz
Howard M. Wexler
Patricia S. Mar
Kenneth W. Jones
Paul J. Dion
Vern S. Bothwell
L. J. Chris Martiniak
Kenneth A. Freed
Martha Jeanne Shaver (Resident, Stockton Office)
Robert Cedric Goodman
Steven K. Denebeim
Laura Grad
William F. Adams
William M. Smith
Elizabeth A. Thompson
Julie A. Jones
David L. Kanel

Abram S. Feuerstein
John R. Capron
Ted S. Storey
A. Todd Berman
Laura J. Dawson

OF COUNSEL

Richard L. Jaeger
Malcolm Leader-Picone
Gerald A. Sherwin (Resident, Stockton Office)

For full biographical listings, see the Martindale-Hubbell Law Directory

FOLGER & LEVIN (AV)

Embarcadero Center West, 275 Battery Street, 23rd Floor, 94111
Telephone: 415-986-2800
FAX: 415-986-2827
Los Angeles, California Office: 28th Floor, 1900 Avenue of the Stars.
Telephone: 310-556-3700.
FAX: 310-556-3770.

MEMBERS OF FIRM

John P. Levin
Peter M. Folger
Michael A. Kahn
Donald E. Kelley, Jr.
Thomas P. Laffey
Scott W. Bowen
Samuel R. Miller
Mary C. Castle
Richard Keenan
Roger B. Mead
Douglas W. Sullivan
Teressa K. Lippert
Margaret R. Dollbaum
James Goldberg
Lisa McCabe van Krieken
Gregory D. Call
Janice B. Lawrence
Susan W. Ansberry
Thomas F. Koegel
Katharine Livingston
Adam Sachs
Wesley D. Hurst

ASSOCIATES

Robert J. McCoy
Deborah Harrawood
Charles R. Perry
J. Daniel Sharp
Margaret E. Murray
Brian C. Bunger
Carol R. Kerr
Jonathan M. Linden
Christopher B. Conner
Jonathan K. Sobel
Christine D. Kennedy
M. Kay Martin
Julie M. Kennedy
Roland Voize-Valayre
Kenneth R. Hillier
Theresa I. McFarland
Michael F. Kelleher
Raquel L. Wilkening
John C. Baum
Theresa A. Nagle
Karen Jensen Petrulakis
Jennifer L. Wright
Kelvin T. Wyles
Katherine Lowe Olsen
Robert A. McFarlane
Beatrice B. Nguyen

For full biographical listings, see the Martindale-Hubbell Law Directory

GRAHAM & JAMES (AV)

Suite 300 Alcoa Building, One Maritime Plaza, 94111
Telephone: 415-954-0200
Cable Address: "Chalgray"
Telex: WU 340143; WUI 67565
Telecopier: 415-391-2493
Other offices located in: Los Angeles, Newport Beach, Palo Alto, Sacramento and Fresno, California; Washington, D.C.; New York, New York; Milan, Italy; Beijing, China; Tokyo, Japan; London, England; Dusseldorf, Germany; Taipei, Taiwan.
Associated Offices: Deacons in Association with Graham & James, Hong Kong; Sly and Weigall, Sydney, Melbourne, Brisbane, Perth and Canberra, Australia.
Affiliated Offices: Graham & James in Affiliation with Taylor Joynson Garrett, London, England, Bucharest, Romania and Brussels, Belgium; Hanafiah Soeharto Ponggawa, Jakarta, Indonesia; Deacons and Graham & James, Bangkok, Thailand; Haarmann, Hemmelrath & Partner, Berlin, Munich, Leipzig, Frankfurt and Dusseldorf, Germany; Mishare M. Al-Ghazali & Partners, Kuwait; Sly & Weigall Deacons in Association with Graham & James, Hanoi, Vietnam and Guangzhou, China; Gallastegui y Lozano, S.C., Mexico City, Mexico; Law Firm of Salah Al-Hejailan, Jeddah and Riyadh, Saudi Arabia.

(See Next Column)

Bruce W. Belding
David V. Biesemeyer
Hobart McK. Birmingham
Debra A. Chong
David Colker
Eric M. Danoff
Mark C. Dosker
Paul N. Dubrasich
Jill Feldman
Diane L. Gibson
Chalmers G. Graham (1895-1967)
David F. Gross
Peter W. Hanschen
Rupert P. Hansen, Jr.
Kevin Hobgood-Brown
Kent Jonas
David C. Kenny
Michael Kross
Boris H. Lakusta (1912-1992)
Nathan Lane, III
Michael D. Levin
David M. Lofholm
Nancy Lundeen
Douglas D. Mancill
David J. Marchant
Martin A. Mattes
Michael R. Moyle
James A. Murray
Andrew I. Port
Thomas F. Smegal, Jr.
Francis L. Tetreault (1920-1983)
Gilda R. Turitz
Nicholas Unkovic
Thomas H. Woofter

OF COUNSEL

Alexander D. Calhoun
F. Conger Fawcett
Leonard G. James
Thomas Y. Yasuda

ASSOCIATES

Maureen Bennett
Mark S. Burton (Not admitted in CA)
Michelle A. Cooke
Priscilla J. Cortez
Suzanne E. Curtis
Christine L. Kopitzke
Warren P. Kujawa
Raissa T. Lyvers (Not admitted in CA)
Matthew E. Marquis
Caroline H. Mead
Emily Porter Merriman
Robert M. Monti
Victor C. Murphy
David M. Niebauer
Ellen A. O'Donnell
Julianne Owens
Leo J. Peters
Angela Lauer Polk
David Rakonitz
Jennifer J. Sam
Serafina Sands
Michael E. Sobel
John M. Spilman, Jr.
Eric Stein
Vadim D. Stepanchenko
Lisa Petricone Sullivan
Theresa V. Tao
Kristen J. Thorsness
Elizabeth A. Willes
Peter J. Wulsin
Philip R. Zender

For full biographical listings, see the Martindale-Hubbell Law Directory

HANCOCK, ROTHERT & BUNSHOFT (AV)

10th Floor, Four Embarcadero Center, 94111-4168
Telephone: 415-981-5550
Telecopy: 415-955-2599
Los Angeles, California Office: 17th Floor, 515 South Figueroa Street, 90071-3334.
Telephone: 213-623-7777.
Telecopy: 213-623-5405.
Tahoe City, California Office: Lighthouse Center, 850 North Lake Boulevard, Suite 15, P.O. Box 7199, 96145-7199.
Telephone: 916-583-7767.
Telecopy: 916-581-3215.
London Office: Forum House, 15/18 Lime Street, Sixth Floor, London EC3M 7AP, England.
Telephone: 071-220-7567.
Telecopy: 071-220-7609.
Associated Office: Staiger, Schwald & Sauter. Genferstrasse 24, 8002 Zurich, Switzerland.
Telephone: 01-282-8686.
Telecopy: 01-283-8787.
Telex: 813-273-GND.

MEMBERS OF FIRM

Barry L. Bunshoft
George L. Waddell
James P. Barber
Paul D. Nelson
Aubin K. Barthold
Richard L. Seabolt
Patrick A. Cathcart (Resident, Los Angeles Office)
Patricia Shuler Schimbor
Philip R. Matthews
Ray L. Wong
David L. Suddendorf
Earl J. Imhoff, Jr. (Resident, Los Angeles Office)
Deborah Pitts (Resident, Los Angeles Office)
Paul S. Rosenlund
Robert C. Hendrickson
Ernest J. Beffel, Jr.
Andrew K. Gordon
Ronald E. Ruma
Vito C. Peraino (Resident, Los Angeles Office)
John E. Fagan (Resident, Tahoe City Office)
W. Andrew Miller
Michael L. Donovan
William J. Casey
Eric J. Sinrod
Nancy B. Ranney
Brian A. Kelly
Dominica Cortum Anderson
Paul J. Killion
Devin F. O'Brien
Lisa J. Evans
Michael A. Gevertz
Daniel J. Crawford
Yvette D. Roland (Resident, Los Angeles Office)
Peter J. Koenig
Peter J. Whalen
Marc J. Derewetzky (Resident, Los Angeles Office)

(See Next Column)

HANCOCK, ROTHERT & BUNSHOFT, *San Francisco—Continued*

ASSOCIATES

L. Savannah Lichtman
Stephanie L. Choy
William J. Baron
Robert V. Richter
Kenneth D. Ayers
Andrea J. Schoeneman
Mark D. Tokunaga (Resident, Tahoe City Office)
Michael M. Strage (Resident, Los Angeles Office)
Lisa Huettner Dolan
Douglas T. Gneiser
Julia Baughman Vining (Resident, Los Angeles Office)
Linda B. Carr (Resident, Los Angeles Office)
Mary Guilfoyle Leupold
Brian Gearinger
William K. Enger (Resident, Los Angeles Office)
Mark E. Kushner
Christopher B. Laukenmann (Resident, Los Angeles Office)
David J. Potkul
Mark A. Robbins (Resident, Los Angeles Office)
Michael S. Overing (Resident, Los Angeles Office)
Mitchell F. Ducey (Resident, Los Angeles Office)
Colleen A. Cassidy
Eileen M. Corbett
Reginald D. Davis
Heidi Honora Frenzel
Jonathan U. Lee
Kelly Lynn Quigley
Mary V. Ringwalt
Avalyn Y. Castillo
Juliana J. Keaton (Resident, Los Angeles Office)
Mary Cavins Anderson
Joan N. D'Ambrosio
Carin Duryee (Resident, Tahoe City Office)
Beth Frensilli
Katherine A. Knopoff
Suzanne Ryder Fogarty
Maximilian H. Stern
Peter J. Bowers (Resident, Los Angeles Office)
Christopher B. Wilkinson
Leslie E. Wolf
David A. Greene
Vipal J. Patel (Resident, Los Angeles Office)
Dominique R. Shelton (Resident, Los Angeles Office)
John R. Garnett
Hein Helene Kim
Joseph P. Collins (Resident, Los Angeles Office)
Arthur J. Friedman
Kevin M. Haithcox
Merton A. Howard
Elizabeth C. Krivátsy
Helena C. Pappas
Kevin M. Stineman
Sarah K. Chang
R. Christopher Rhody
John T. Clappison
David W. Jordan
Lisa Ann Mango
Monica M. Slakey
Candace Anne Younger (Resident, Los Angeles Office)
Charles E. Webb
Joi True (Resident, Los Angeles Office)
John E. Breen (Resident, Los Angeles Office)
Brian T. Hafter
Samantha Mitty
Bruce J. Rome
Stephen H. Sutro

For full biographical listings, see the Martindale-Hubbell Law Directory

HANSON, BRIDGETT, MARCUS, VLAHOS & RUDY (AV)

23rd Floor, 333 Market Street, 94105
Telephone: 415-777-3200
Facsimile: 415-541-9366
Telex: 6502628734 MCI

MEMBERS OF FIRM

Gerald D. Marcus
John J. Vlahos
Sidney Rudy
William J. Bush
Ronald C. Peterson
Richard N. Rapoport
David J. Miller
Duane B. Garrett
Laurence W. Kessenick
Ray E. McDevitt
Douglas H. Barton
Jerrold C. Schaefer
James D. Holden
Paul A. Gordon
Michael A. Duncheon
William D. Taylor
Fred B. Weil
Ted Carleton Krumland
Craig J. Cannizzo
Steven V. Schnier
Theodore A. Hellman
Kevin M. O'Donnell
Stephen L. Taber
Joan L. Cassman
Stephen B. Peck
Allan D. Jergesen
Kim T. Schoknecht
Robert L. Rusky
Bonnie Kathleen Gibson
Howard W. Ashcraft, Jr.
Joel S. Goldman
Rory J. Campbell
Jacquelyn J. Garman
David W. Baer
Madeline Chun
Lora J. Thielbar
Paul F. Goldsmith
Susan C. Barton
Peter Dmytryk
Jane Siegel Woodside
Susan G. O'Neill
Patrick M. Glenn
David C. Longinotti
Pamela S. Kaufmann
Diane Marie O'Malley
Jeffrey M. Chu
Linda E. Klamm

ASSOCIATES

Jonathan S. Storper
Michael N. Conneran
Matthew J. Dulka
Lee Ann M. La France
Steven J. Levine
Edward S. Grenville
Lynn Tracy Nerland
Peter Chadwick
Andrew G. Giacomini
Debra L. Watanuki
James A. Napoli
Marie B. Curry
Patrick T. Miyaki
Mabel Ng
Ann K. Ryles
Dana B. Wolf
Charles L. Thompson IV
Myron D. Moye
Laura L. Hauck
Jeffrey G. Angeja
Michael B. McNaughton
Moona Nandi
Lisa M. Pooley
Amy L. Brown

(See Next Column)

ASSOCIATES (Continued)

Philip E. Fagone
Meredith E. Brown
Lisa K. Puntillo
Sandra L. Rappaport
William A. Hickey

OF COUNSEL

Raymond L. Hanson
Arthur T. Bridgett
Jack P. Wong
Daniel W. Baker
Robert E. Simms
John W. Broad

Representative Clients: AC Transit; American Baptist Homes of the West; Bank of America; NT & SA; Bekins Van Lines; Blue Cross and Blue Shield Assn.; Blue Diamond Growers; California Association of Homes for the Aging; California Pear Growers; California Tomato Growers.

For full biographical listings, see the Martindale-Hubbell Law Directory

JACKSON, TUFTS, COLE & BLACK (AV)

A Partnership including Professional Corporations
650 California Street, Thirty-Second Floor, 94108
Telephone: 415-433-1950
Fax: 415-392-3494
San Jose, California Office: 60 South Market Street, 10th Floor.
Telephone: 408-998-1952.
Fax: 408-998-4889.

MEMBERS OF FIRM

Bartlett A. Jackson (A Professional Corporation)
Robert R. Tufts
George H. Cole, Jr.
J. David Black
Templeton C. Peck
Charles G. Stephenson
John S. Siamas
David T. Alexander
Carl J. Stoney, Jr.
Kenneth J. Philpot
Michael J. Baker
David Ayers Thompson
Ellen McGinty King
Peter S. Muñoz
Dennis V. Swanson
Debra S. Belaga
Emil G. Pesiri
D. D. Hughmanick
William H. Booth
Terrence P. McMahon
Twila L. Foster
Nicole A. Dillingham
Janice W. Fox
George R. Theofel
Jeffrey J. Cole
Roy M. Bartlett, Jr.
Daniel M. Elkort
Richard Scudellari
Donna M. Mezias
Gregory P. Farnham
Martin S. Schenker
Michael F. McCabe
Joseph S. Faber
Debra L. Kasper
Margaret A. Sloan
Paul H. Goldstein
Lynn Marie McLean
Carolyn A. Lown

OF COUNSEL

Toby Cozart
Wayne W. Lew
Gerald Z. Marer

ASSOCIATES

Marily Peatman Lerner
Paul S. Avilla
Thomas D. Murtha
Reneé Lanam Barton
Jane M. Hawkins
Sean A. Lincoln
Eric T. Sullivan
Lynn Acker Starr
Robert G. White
Stephen M. Debenham
Melissa A. Finocchio
Gretchen Dean Hug
Joanne Marshall Shea
Régine Shambrook
Steven N. Sherr
Maya Lakshmi Harris
Amy E. Margolin
Deborah L. Breiner
Robin E. Kelsey
Marion C. Ingersoll
Eleanor Baldwin Lacey

For full biographical listings, see the Martindale-Hubbell Law Directory

KINDEL & ANDERSON (AV)

A Partnership including Professional Corporations
580 California Street, 15th Floor, 94104
Telephone: 415-398-0110
Los Angeles, California Office: Twenty-Ninth Floor, 555 South Flower Street.
Telephone: 213-680-2222.
Irvine, California Office: 5 Park Plaza, Suite 1000.
Telephone: 714-752-0777.
Woodland Hills, California Office: Suite 244, 5959 Topanga Canyon Boulevard.
Telephone: 818-712-0036.

S. Kendall Patton (Resident)
Bruce J. Russell (Resident)
James S. Russell (Resident)

ASSOCIATES

David F. Abele (Resident)
Joshua R. Steinhauer (Resident)
Richard E. Walker (Resident)

For full biographical listings, see the Martindale-Hubbell Law Directory

LANDELS, RIPLEY & DIAMOND (AV)

Hills Plaza, 350 Steuart Street, 94105-1250
Telephone: 415-788-5000
Fax: 415-788-7550
Sacramento, California Office: 400 Capitol Mall, Suite 2140.
Telephone: 916-448-8300.
Fax: 916-448-4923.

(See Next Column)

LANDELS, RIPLEY & DIAMOND—*Continued*

MEMBERS OF FIRM

Edward D. Landels (1899-1991)
Earl M. Ripley (Retired)
Philip E. Diamond (Retired)
John H. Bickel
Bruce W. Hyman
Frederick M. Pownall
John M. Anderson
Yaroslav Sochynsky
James A. Bruen
Jon Enscoe
Stephen C. Lewis
Richard C. Coffin
Susan M. Reid
Bruce W. Laidlaw
Geoffrey M. Dugan
Thomas D. Trapp
Deborah J. Schmall
Curtis E. A. Karnow
John F. Barg
Deborah K. Miller
Paul Zieff
Scott D. Rogers
Julie Finley
Eric R. Newman
R. Christopher Locke
Eugene K. Yamamoto
Matthew J. Geyer
Peter C. Turner
Gregory L. Germain
Beth S. Jordan
Sanford Svetcov
Robert L. Hines
Brian S. Haughton
Raymond F. Lynch
Jonathan M. Ross
Deborah K. Tellier
Patrick Schlesinger
Robert J. Breakstone
Michael H. Zischke
Margaret Hart Edwards
Howard A. Simon
Beth Aboulafia
Daniel W. McGovern
Neil L. Shapiro
Stafford Matthews
Kathleen M. Meagher
R. Morgan Gilhuly
Karen Valentia Clopton

Michele S. Benson
Mary J. Decker
Margaret Reidy
Sheryl Wilkins
Kathleen M. Wardlaw
Derrick K. Watson
Carrie M. Callaway
Donald P. Margolis
Ligi Coleen Yee
Robert A. Bryan
Kevin E. Solliday
Peter S. Modlin
Barbara Cohen Stikker
John D. Fiero
Jennifer G. Redmond
Melinda L. Haag
Janet E. Shestakov
Deborah C. Brown
Mary C. Parker
Julie Hammel Brook
Mark D. Johnson
Ross D. Tillman
James H. Colopy
Francisco X. Márquez

Representative Clients: Bank of America; California Mortgage Bankers Association; Catellus Development Corp.; General Electric Co.; Metropolitan Life Insurance Co.; Occidental Petroleum Corp. and Subsidiaries; Sega of America; Union Oil Co.; WMX Technologies, Inc. and Subsidiaries; Weyerhauser Corp.

For full biographical listings, see the Martindale-Hubbell Law Directory

LELAND, PARACHINI, STEINBERG, FLINN, MATZGER & MELNICK (AV)

27th Floor, 333 Market Street, 94105
Telephone: 415-957-1800
FAX: 415-974-1520
Los Angeles, California Office: 500 South Grand Avenue, Suite 1100.
Telephone: 213-623-7505;
Fax: 213-623-7595

Herbert A. Leland (1907-1984)

PARTNERS

James M. Allen
Nick A. Boodrookas
David B. Flinn
Harvey L. Gould
Catherine M. Grundmann
Nina P. Kwan
Steven B. Mains
Paul J. Matzger
David H. Melnick
Teresa Viskovich Pahl
Donald G. Parachini
Merrill E. Steinberg
Neil E. Taxy
Kenneth R. Wachtel

ASSOCIATES

Christopher J. Donnelly
Christopher J. Hunter
Nicole S. Kamian
Craig A. Kepler
William Lee
Torrey A. Olins
Jenifer P. Schatten
Adam P. Siegman
Anna Simmons
Michael Louis Violanti

Peter K. Wolff, Jr.

OF COUNSEL

David J. Block
Emmet B. Hayes
Gayle Nin Rosenkrantz
Stephan R. Silen

For full biographical listings, see the Martindale-Hubbell Law Directory

LONG & LEVIT (AV)

A Partnership including a Professional Corporation
101 California Street, Suite 2300, 94111
Telephone: 415-397-2222
Telex: 340924 HOME OFC SFO-LONG & LEVIT
Facsimile: 415-397-6392
Los Angeles, California Office: 633 West Fifth Street, 59th Floor.
Telephone: 213-356-5900.
Facsimile: 213-613-0664.

(See Next Column)

MEMBERS OF FIRM

Percy V. Long (1870-1953)
Bert W. Levit (1903-1980)
John B. Hook
Ronald E. Mallen (Professional Corporation)
Howard M. Garfield
Joseph P. McMonigle
Donald W. Carlson
David W. Evans
Marsha Lee Morrow
Barry D. Brown
Louis A. "Michael" Boli, IV
John E. Peer (Resident, Los Angeles Office)
Russell S. Roeca
Guy D. Calladine
Robert M. Peterson
Edward F. Donohue, III
Mark S. Kannett
Don A. Lesser
Christopher T. Borgeson
Robert C. Chiles
Esther Z. Hirsh
Kevin P. Kamraczewski (Resident, Los Angeles Office)
Linda Landry Miller (Resident, Los Angeles Office)
Randall A. Miller (Resident, Los Angeles Office)
Elizabeth Colpoys
David I. Dalby
Joyce C. Wang
David C. Veis (Resident, Los Angeles Office)
J. Kevin Snyder (Resident, Los Angeles Office)
Debra Baker (Resident, Los Angeles Office)
Martin T. Lee (Resident, Los Angeles Office)
Michael A. Vasquez
Michael C. Cooper
Claire L. Cortner
Stephen J. Kaufman (Resident, Los Angeles Office)
Burton C. Allyn, IV

Gerald Gamliel Weisbach

ASSOCIATES

Louise E. Abbis (Resident, Los Angeles Office)
Reilly Atkinson, IV
Karen L. Bizzini (Resident, Los Angeles Office)
Gretchen S. Carner (Resident, Los Angeles Office)
Gerald K. Carroll
Kristina H. Chung
Sherri J. Conrad
Patricia M. De La Peña (Resident, Los Angeles Office)
Jeffrey A. Dollinger (Resident, Los Angeles Office)
J. Andrew Douglas (Resident, Los Angeles Office)
Renelde Espinosa
Michael J. Estrada
Kathleen M. Ewins
John M. Farrell, Jr.
Darío J. Frommer
Seth A. Gold (Resident, Los Angeles Office)
Ira D. Goldberg
Mark A. Gordon (Resident, Los Angeles Office)
Scott J. Hyman
Christine L. Judas (Resident, Los Angeles Office)
Christina Katris (Resident, Los Angeles Office)
Allison Lane
Debbie Ling Lee (Resident, Los Angeles Office)
Sherman C. Lee
Juliet A. Leftwich
Jeffrey D. Livingston
Cory M. Martin
Kathleen Mary McKnight
Douglas J. Melton
Jeffrey P. Miller
John R. Miller (Resident, Los Angeles Office)
Kim Morimoto (Resident, Los Angeles Office)
Edward Muramoto (Resident, Los Angeles Office)
Laura Pulido Nash (Resident, Los Angeles Office)
Mark L. Nissenbaum
Lauren O'Brien
Robert A. O'Brien
Susan A. O'Neal (Resident, Los Angeles Office)
David P. Osako
Dow W. Patten (Resident, Los Angeles Office)
JoLynn M. Pollard (Resident, Los Angeles Office)
Stephen P. Randall
Eliza M. Rodrigues
Robert J. Romero
Christine D. Ryan (Resident, Los Angeles Office)
Henry O. Schaefer
Richard J. Sciaroni
Steven M. Sharafian
Mark M. Smith
Paul K. Smith (Resident, Los Angeles Office)
Ann L. Strayer
Jennifer Wong Suzuki
Jeanette Traverso
Judith A. Tury
Chinye Uwechue-Akpati (Resident, Los Angeles Office)
Sarah Valentine
Paul E. Vallone
William E. Waddell
Allison K. West
Valerie J. Wiles (Resident, Los Angeles Office)
Mark K. Williams (Resident, Los Angeles Office)

SENIOR COUNSEL

Linda S. Votaw

OF COUNSEL

Edward D. Haas
J. Michael Higginbotham

For full biographical listings, see the Martindale-Hubbell Law Directory

MCCUTCHEN, DOYLE, BROWN & ENERSEN (AV)

Three Embarcadero Center, 94111-4066
Telephone: 415-393-2000
Facsimile: 415-393-2286 (G I, II, III)
Telex: 340817 MACPAG SFO
Los Angeles, California Office: 355 South Grand Avenue, Suite 4400, 90071-1560.
Telephone: 213-680-6400.
Facsimile: 213-680-6499.
San Jose, California Office: Market Post Tower, Suite 1500, 55 South Market Street, 95113-2327.
Telephone: 408-947-8400.
Facsimile: 408-947-4750.
Telex: 9102502931 MACPAG SJ.

(See Next Column)

McCutchen, Doyle, Brown & Enersen, *San Francisco—Continued*

Walnut Creek, California Office: 1331 North California Boulevard, Post Office Box V, 94596-4502.
Telephone: 510-937-8000.
Facsimile: 510-975-5390.
Menlo Park, California Office: 2740 Sand Hill Road, 94025-7020.
Telephone: 415-233-4000.
Facsimile: 415-233-4086.
Washington, D.C. Office: The Evening Star Building, Suite 800, 1101 Pennsylvania Avenue, N.W., 20004-2514.
Telephone: 202-628-4900.
Facsimile: 202-628-4912.
Taipei, Taiwan Republic of China Office: International Trade Building, Tenth Floor, 333 Keelung Road, Section 1, 110.
Telephone: 886-2-723-5000.
Facsimile: 886-2-757-6070.
Affiliated Offices In: Bangkok, Thailand; Beijing, China; Shanghai, China.

MEMBERS OF FIRM

David R. Andrews
William H. Armstrong (Resident, Walnut Creek Office)
Joseph R. Austin
David M. Balabanian
Dale E. Barnes, Jr.
William Bates, III
Christopher P. Berka (Resident, San Jose Office)
Gilbert C. Berkeley (Resident, Walnut Creek Office)
Susan S. Briggs
Michael A. Brown (Not admitted in CA; Resident, Washington, D.C. Office)
Ross E. Campbell (Resident, San Jose Office)
Patrick O. Cavanaugh (Not admitted in CA)
Byde W. Clawson (Resident, San Jose Office)
Cynthia A. Coe (Resident, Washington, D.C. Office)
Daniel Cooperman
Robert E. Cox (San Francisco and Taipei Offices)
Charles William Craycroft (Resident, San Jose Office)
Philip T. Cummings (Not admitted in CA; Resident, Washington, D.C. Office)
Daniel J. Curtin, Jr. (Resident, Walnut Creek Office)
Barry J. Cutler (Not admitted in CA; Resident, Washington, D.C. Office)
Bartley C. Deamer
Carol K. Dillon (at San Jose and Menlo Park Offices)
Colleen P. Doyle (Resident, Los Angeles Office)
James J. Dragna (Resident, Los Angeles Office)
Kenta K. Duffey
Michael P. Durkee (Resident, Walnut Creek Office)
Robert L. Ebe
Roger D. Ehlers (Resident, Walnut Creek Office)
James B. Ellis
Cherie Erickson-Harris (Resident, Los Angeles Office)
Henry D. Evans, Jr.
Warren P. Felger
Pecos Bill Field
James C. Fowler
John W. Fowler (Resident, San Jose Office)
William H. Freedman (Resident, Los Angeles Office)
Warren E. George
Sandra A. Golze (Resident, Walnut Creek Office)
Barry P. Goode
Michael L. Greene (Resident, Walnut Creek Office)
John N. Hauser
Melinda L. Hayes (Resident, Los Angeles Office)
David M. Heilbron
Daniel B. Higgins
Christopher B. Hockett
Susan L. Hoffman (Resident, Los Angeles Office)
Terry J. Houlihan
Donald D. Howard (Resident, San Jose Office)
James L. Hunt
John Edward Hurley, Jr.
Mark O. Kasanin
James P. Kleinberg
Stephen L. Kostka (Resident, Walnut Creek Office)
Leslie G. Landau
Gregory Paul Landis
Ronald S. Laurie
Rebecca A. Lenaburg
James Boyd Lewis
Robert A. Lewis
Jane Elizabeth Lovell
John B. Lowry
Michael B. Lubic (Resident, Los Angeles Office)
Palmer Brown Madden
Raymond Charles Marshall
Loyd W. McCormick
Edward J. McCutchen (1857-1933)
Edward S. Merrill (Resident, Walnut Creek Office)
Robert E. Merritt (Resident, Walnut Creek Office)
Randy Michelson
Michael L. Miller
Robert A. Mills
Gary H. Moore
John C. Morrissey (Resident, Los Angeles Office)
David E. Moser
G. Richard Murray
Karen J. Nardi
William J. Newell
Susan A. Ogdie
James Franklin Owens (Resident, Los Angeles Office)
Beth H. Parker
Robert P. Parker
Lynn H. Pasahow
Sara Louise Peterson
Alfred C. Pfeiffer, Jr.
Donn P. Pickett
Michael J. Plishner
Thomas G. Reddy
John R. Reese
Geoffrey L. Robinson (Resident, Walnut Creek Office)
Ulrico S. Rosales (Resident, Menlo Park Office)
Jerome C. Roth
Philip R. Rotner
Jonathan H. Sakol
James Severson
Patricia L. Shanks
Charlene Sachi Shimada
Sanford M. Skaggs (Resident, Walnut Creek Office)
Robert H. Solomon
Edward L. Strohbehn, Jr.
Daniel M. Wall
George J. Weiner (Not admitted in CA; Resident, Washington, D.C. Office)
Harlan Wendell
Gayl A. Westendorf

(See Next Column)

MEMBERS OF FIRM (Continued)

Michael C. White (Not admitted in CA; Resident, Washington, D.C. Office)
Thomas B. Worth
Gordon T. Yamate (Resident, San Jose Office)
Stephen A. Zovickian

COUNSEL

Brent M. Abel
Marilee J. Allan
Denise Savoie Blocker
Neil Boorstyn
Joan C. Y. Chen (Resident, Taipei, Taiwan Office)
Henry A. Cirillo
Edward B. Collins
Marie A. Cooper (Resident, Walnut Creek Office)
Charles S. Crompton, III
Morris M. Doyle
Sally A. Drach
John D. Edgcomb
Burnham Enersen
Margaret A. Freeston (Not admitted in CA; Resident, Washington, D.C. Office)
Susan Herald (Resident, Menlo Park Office)
Susan K. Hoerger (Resident, Menlo Park Office)
Holly A. House
Peter Hsiao (Resident, Los Angeles Office)
Mary T. Huser
Owen Jameson
David I. Katzen
William D. Kissinger
Jack G. Knebel
Brian J. Lamb (Resident, Los Angeles Office)
Robyn A. Meinhardt (Resident, Los Angeles Office)
Douglas R. Painter (Resident, Los Angeles Office)
Elizabeth A. Pierce (Resident, Washington, D.C. Office)
Norman B. Richards
Maria P. Rivera (Resident, Walnut Creek Office)
Christine E. Sherry
Jane Cosgriff Sullwold (Resident, Walnut Creek Office)
Cecily T. Talbert
Beverly A. Tiffany
Richard B. Ulmer Jr.

ASSOCIATES

Sharon J. Adams (Resident, Walnut Creek Office)
Mabell Y. Aguilar (Resident, San Jose Office)
Rajesh A. Aji (Resident, Los Angeles Office)
Janet C. Allen
Brandt Andersson (Resident, Walnut Creek Office)
William D. Araiza (Resident, Los Angeles Office)
Christine Banks
Page R. Barnes
Eric J. Baysinger
Maria Bee (Resident, Walnut Creek Office)
Michael I. Begert
Shashikala Bhat (Resident, San Jose Office)
Margaret Bielak
Barbara A. Boczar
Gregory L. Bowling
Robert A. Brundage
David C. Burke
Karen A. Caffee (Resident, Los Angeles Office)
Victoria L. Calkins (Resident, Los Angeles Office)
William Carpenter
William Wei-Li Chuang
Julie E. Cohen
Jill F. Cooper (Resident, Los Angeles Office)
Claire T. Cormier (Resident, San Jose Office)
Richard G. Costello
Molly Mitchell Danciger
Louisa M. Daniels
Anne M. Deibert
Krystal N. Denley
Megan Dixon
Rhonda L. Donato
Maureen S. Dorney
Scott A. Edelstein
Douglas C. Emhoff (Resident, Los Angeles Office)
Elizabeth Meinert Fielder
Debra L. Fischer (Resident, Los Angeles Office)
Jacqueline C. Fu (Resident, Taipei Office)
Angel A. Garganta
Laura Buchmann Gasho
David C. Getzinger (Resident, Taipei, Taiwan Office)
Laura E. Gonzales
Grant A. Guerra (Resident, Walnut Creek Office)
John P. Halfpenny
Karen A. Hall
Sue C. Hansen
Frank M. Hinman
Geoffrey M. Howard
Flora M. Hsu (Resident, Taipei, Taiwan Office)
Keating H.S. Hsu (Resident, Taipei, Taiwan Office
Victoria S. Kaufman (Resident, Los Angeles Office)
Karen L. Kennard
Harry H. W. Kim (Resident, Los Angeles Office)
Christine S. Lam (Resident, San Jose Office)
Laura F. Lee
Niall E. Lynch
Dagny Maidman
Carol L. Martin (Resident, San Jose Office)
Kirstie A. McCornock
Carol A. McDermott (Resident, Los Angeles Office)
Kathleen A. McDonald (Resident, San Jose Office)
Beth A. McGowen (Resident, San Jose Office)
Amy J. Metzler
Jean M. Mohrbacher (Resident, Los Angeles Office)
Holly Morris
Jill Neiman
Eric P. Newell
Trenton H. Norris
John E. Opel (Resident, Los Angeles Office)
J. Stuart Patterson
Michael T. Pyle
Marco Quazzo
Gregory A. Randall (Resident, Walnut Creek Office)
Carolyn L. Reid
Steven Glenn Rosen
Rick R. Rothman
Neal A. Rubin (Resident, Los Angeles Office)
Hope A. Schmeltzer
Barbara J. Schussman (Resident, Walnut Creek Office)
Julie H. Shu (Resident, Taipei, Taiwan Office)
Joseph K. Siino
Stephanie N. Simonds
Carissa M. Smith
James Grant Snell (Resident, San Jose Office)
Neal J. Stephens (Resident, San Jose Office)
Nitin Subhedar
John F. Sullivan
Duy Thai
Ashley M. Tobin

(See Next Column)

McCutchen, Doyle, Brown & Enersen—*Continued*

ASSOCIATES (Continued)

Jennifer Tsay (Resident, San Jose Office)
Christopher G. Van Gundy
Sandra Hughes Waddell
M. Russell Wofford, Jr.
Cynthia J. Woolley
Kenneth J. Yood (Resident, Los Angeles Office)
Heather A. Young
Margaret A. Yowell (Resident, Los Angeles Office)

LEGAL SUPPORT PERSONNEL

SCIENTIFIC STAFF

Michael J. Shuster

For full biographical listings, see the Martindale-Hubbell Law Directory

Morgenstein & Jubelirer (AV)

A Partnership including a Professional Corporation
One Market Plaza, Spear Street Tower, 32nd Floor, 94105
Telephone: 415-896-0666
Fax: 415-896-5592

MEMBERS OF FIRM

Marvin D. Morgenstein (P.C.)
Eliot S. Jubelirer
Lee Ann Huntington
Jean L. Bertrand
Jeffrey R. Williams
James R. Balich
Rocky N. Unruh
Laurie K. Anger
Larry C. Lowe
James L. McGinnis

Wendi J. Berkowitz
David H. Bromfield
Randi Covin
Roberta Nicol Dempster
Stephen M. Hankins
Robert B. Mullen
John J. Petry
Margaret E. Schaus
Samantha J. Smith
Bruce A. Wagman
John S. Worden

For full biographical listings, see the Martindale-Hubbell Law Directory

O'Melveny & Myers (AV)

Embarcadero Center West Tower, 275 Battery Street, Suite 2600, 94111
Telephone: 415-984-8700
Facsimile: 415-984-8701
Los Angeles, California Office: 400 South Hope Street.
Telephone: 213-669-6000.
Cable Address: "Moms".
Facsimile: 213-669-6407.
Century City, California Office: 1999 Avenue of the Stars, 7th Floor.
Telephone: 310-553-6700.
Facsimile: 310-246-6779.
Newport Beach, California Office: 610 Newport Center Drive, Suite 1700.
Telephone: 714-760-9600.
Cable Address: "Moms".
Facsimile: 714-669-6994.
New York, New York Office: Citicorp Center, 153 E. 53rd Street, 54th Floor.
Telephone: 212-326-2000.
Facsimile: 212-326-2061.
Washington, D.C. Office: 555 13th Street, N.W., Suite 500 West.
Telephone: 202-383-5300.
Cable Address: "Moms".
Facsimile: 202-383-5414.
Newark, New Jersey Office: One Gateway Center, 7th Floor, 07102.
Telephone: 201-639-8600.
Facsimile: 201-639-8630.
London, England Office: 10 Finsbury Square, London, EC2A 1LA.
Telephone: 011-44-171-256-8451.
Facsimile: 011-44-171-638-8205.
Tokyo, Japan Office: Sanbancho KB-6 Building, 6 Sanbancho, Chiyoda-ku, Tokyo 102, Japan.
Telephone: 011-81-3-3239-2800.
Facsimile: 011-81-3-3239-2432.
Hong Kong Office: 1104 Lippo Tower, Lippo Centre, 89 Queensway, Central Hong Kong.
Telephone: 011-852-523-8266.
Facsimile: 011-852-522-1760.

RESIDENT PARTNERS

Daniel H. Bookin
Martin S. Checov
Stephen A. Cowan
Peter T. Healy
F. Curt Kirschner, Jr.
Douglas P. Ley
Joseph M. Malkin
Jill H. Matichak
Edward J. McAniff
Julie A. McMillan
George A. Riley
Patricia Ann Schmiege
Steven L. Smith
Richard C. Warmer

RESIDENT SPECIAL COUNSEL

Daniel A. Deshon, IV
Douglas E. Dexter
David G. Estes
M. Manuel Fishman
John Charles Maddux
Dana K. Welch

(See Next Column)

RESIDENT ASSOCIATES

Linda A. Bagley
Patrick J. Bannon
Mark L. Bradshaw
Laura C. Bremer
William R. Burford
Viola I. Canales
Elena Bocca Dietrich
Edward C. Hagerott, Jr.
Jennifer L. Isenberg
Jeffrey M. Judd
Monique Janelle London
David J. Reis
Darin W. Snyder
Anders E. Stenstedt
Scott Treanor

For full biographical listings, see the Martindale-Hubbell Law Directory

Pettit & Martin (AV)

A Partnership including Professional Corporations
Thirty-Fifth Floor, 101 California Street, 94111
Telephone: 415-434-4000
Cable Address: "Pemlaw"
Telex: 330443
Telecopier: 415-982-4608
Washington, D.C. Office: 601 Thirteenth Street.
Telephone: 202-637-3600.
Los Angeles, California Office: 355 South Grand Avenue, 33rd Floor.
Telephone: 213-626-1717.
San Jose, California Office: 50 West San Fernando Street, Seventh Floor.
Telephone: 408-295-3210.
Newport Beach, California Office: 4695 MacArthur Court, Suite 1200.
Telephone: 714-476-7676.

ADVISORY PARTNERS

Joseph Martin, Jr.
Walter F. Pettit

PARTNERS

David V. Anthony *
Philip F. Atkins-Pattenson
Cameron Baker (A Professional Corporation)
Daniel T. Bernhard
Brian F. Berger
John L. Boos
Robert T. Burke
James T. Caleshu
Bonnie A. Glatzer
Michael C. Hallerud
Richard A. Holderness
Thomas C. Holman
William D. Hunter
D. Wayne Jeffries
Reverdy Johnson (A Professional Corporation)
Thomas F. Kostic (A Professional Corporation)
Bobby C. Lawyer
Lawrence B. Low
James M. Lowy
Robert L. Maines (A Professional Corporation) ***
Tia S. Miyamoto
Robert L. Nelson, Jr.
Sharon L. O'Grady
J. Ronald Pengilly
Theodore A. Russell (A Professional Corporation)
C. Jean Ryan
Richard M. Shapiro
Randal B. Short
Kerry C. Smith (A Professional Corporation)
Joan H. Story
Robert A. Thompson
James E. Topinka
Sheldon H. Wolfe

OF COUNSEL

John Lockwood Bradley
Al Hirshen
Stephen N. Hollman ***
Joseph E. Petrillo

ASSOCIATES

Nancy L. Asbill
Jack S. Bailey
Bernadette Davison Bantly
Saul D. Bercovitch
Janine D. Bloch
Deborah J. Broyles
Barbara A. Clark
Orna A. Edgar (Not admitted in CA)
David A. Eligator
Scott R. Ferguson
Richard M. Gaynor
D. Kirk Jamieson
Alan M. Koschik
Kathryn E. McQueen
Charles M. Miller
Christie M. Musser
Sandra A. Schutz
Michael B. Schwarz
Mary E. Shallman
Sheldon M. Siegel
Charles R. Sullivan
Robert L. Wainess
David E. Webster
Alisa Won

*In Washington, D.C.
***In San Jose, California

For full biographical listings, see the Martindale-Hubbell Law Directory

Pillsbury Madison & Sutro (AV)

225 Bush Street, 94104
Telephone: 415-983-1000
FAX: 415-398-2096
Costa Mesa, California Office: Plaza Tower, 600 Anton Boulevard, Suite 1100, Costa Mesa, California, 92626.
Telephone: 714-436-6800.
Fax: 714-662-6999.
Los Angeles, California Office: Citicorp Plaza, 725 South Figueroa Street, Suite 1200, 90017.
Telephone: 213-488-7100.
Fax: 213-629-1033.
New York, New York Office: One Liberty Plaza, 165 Broadway, 51st Floor.
Telephone: 212-374-1890.
Fax: 212-374-1852.

(See Next Column)

PILLSBURY MADISON & SUTRO, *San Francisco—Continued*

Menlo Park, California Office: 2700 Sand Hill Road, 94025.
Telephone: 415-233-4500.
FAX: 415-233-4545.
Sacramento, California Office: 400 Capitol Mall, Suite 1700, 95814.
Telephone: 916-329-4700.
Fax: 916-441-3583.
San Diego, California Office: 101 West Broadway, Suite 1800, 92101.
Telephone: 619-234-5000.
Fax: 619-236-1995.
San Jose, California Office: Ten Almaden Boulevard, 95113.
Telephone: 408-947-4000.
Fax: 408-287-8341.
Washington, D. C. Office: 1667 K Street, N.W., Suite 1100, 20006.
Telephone: 202-887-0300.
Fax: 202-296-7605.
Hong Kong Office: 6/F Asia Pacific Finance Tower, Citibank Plaza, 3 Garden Road, Central.
Telephone: 011-852-509-7100.
Fax: 011-852-509-7188.
Tokyo, Japan Office: Churchill and Shimazaki, Gaikokuho-Jimu--Bengoshi-Jimusho, 11-12, Toranomon 5-chome, Minato-ku, Tokyo 105, Japan.
Telephone: 800-729-9830; 011-81-3-5472-6561.
Fax: 011-81-3-5472-5761.

MEMBERS OF FIRM

William G. Alberti
Walter R. Allan
Fred W. Alvarez
Gary H. Anderson
Rebeca P. Anderson
Christopher R. Ball
Joseph E. Bare, Jr.
Michael R. Barr
John B. Bates
William D. Berry
Michael J. Bettinger
Ronald E. Bornstein
Gary E. Botto
Harold I. Boucher
Albert J. Brown
Anthony P. Brown
Christopher L. Byers
Terrence A. Callan
James M. Canty
Nathaniel M. Cartmell III
Mark J. Coleman
Robert W. Cosby
Mary B. Cranston
Barbara B. Creed
Richard B. Daugherty
Julie A. Divola
Bartly A. Dzivi
John L. Donahue
Noel J. Dyer
William I. Edlund
Richard M. Eigner
Bruce A. Ericson
David R. Farabee
Patrick L. Finley
William O. Fisher
Sarah G. Flanagan
Kevin M. Fong
Maurice D. L. Fuller
William Gaus
Robert B. Gex IV
Robert A. Gordon, Jr.
John M. Grenfell
Richard S. Grey
Paul R. Griffin
Kennen D. Hagen
George P. Haley
Willis D. Hannawalt
John T. Hansen
Shawn E. Hanson
John E. Hartman
Kirke M. Hasson
Thomas E. Haven
Robert L. Heimbichner
Robert C. Herr
William J. Hoehler
Lawrence L. Hoenig
John R. Hofmann, Jr.
David E. Hopmann
Harry R. Horrow
Philip Hudner
Timothy R. Jacobs
Robert A. James
Jonathan D. Joseph
Philip L. Judson
Wallace L. Kaapcke
Mary Ellen Kazimer
Terry M. Kee
Alson R. Kemp, Jr.
Francis R. Kirkham
James F. Kirkham
David L. Klott
Teresa C. Lahaderne
Carlisle B. Lane
Anne E. Libbin
Allan N. Littman
Thomas V. Loran III
Frederick K. Lowell
Richard J. MacLaury
Stanley J. Madden
Parker A. Maddux
Richard Maggio
Francis N. Marshall
Patrick C. Marshall
Stephen J. Martin
William J. Martin, Jr.
Bruce W. McDiarmid
Jason McDonell
John F. McLean
T. Neal McNamara
James Michael
William C. Miller
Frederick D. Minnes
M. David Minnick
Robert A. Mittelstaedt
George F. Montgomery II
Daniel J. Niehans
James C. Olson
Rodney R. Peck
Mark H. Penskar
Alfred L. Pepin, Jr.
Robert C. Phelps
Marcia L. Pope
Jay E. Powell
Charles F. Prael
Charles R. Purnell
Charles R. Ragan
Toni Rembe
Harlan M. Richter
Ina J. Risman
Frank H. Roberts
Walter J. Robinson III
Margaret N. Rosegay
Jerry W. Ross
Steven L. Saxe
Mark Schallert
George A. Sears
James M. Seff
Roland W. Selman III
Elisa W. Smith
Glenn Q. Snyder
Sharon M. Solomon
Thomas E. Sparks, Jr.
Emmett C. Stanton
Michael J. Steel
Reginald D. Steer
David T. Steffen
Craig E. Stewart
Charles A. Storke III
Stephen Stublarec
Robert E. Sullivan
Chinin Tana
E. Hugh Taylor
Graham R. Taylor
Robert P. Taylor

(See Next Column)

MEMBERS OF FIRM (Continued)

Roderick M. Thompson
Joseph R. Tiffany II
James O'M. Tingle
Ronald E. Van Buskirk
Jeffrey M. Vesely
Gregg F. Vignos
C. Brian Wainwright
James J. Walsh
James L. Wanvig
Philip S. Warden
Paula M. Weber
Robert M. Westberg
Blair W. White
Carole V. White
Mark N. White
Linda C. Williams
Andrea A. Wirum
Stanton D. Wong
James B. Young
Bernard Zimmerman
Benjamin C. Zuraw

OF COUNSEL

William E. Bonano
Michael Th. Bourque
Maureen E. Corcoran
C. Douglas Floyd
William J. Moran
Nancy J. Murray
Richard E. Nielsen

SENIOR COUNSEL

Mark A. Beskind
Marita M. Daly
Karen S. Frank
Keith R. Gercken
Susan R. Mendelsohn
Warren H. Nelson, Jr.
Victoria R. Nuetzel
Robert S. Rosborough
David W. Trotter
Cydney A. Tune
David S. Winton

ASSOCIATES

Terence M. Abad
Stephanie M. Alexander
Erin G. Austin
Gregor Baer
(Not admitted in CA)
Kristen M. Bamford
Marte J. Bassi
Craig A. Becker
Marta Y. Beckwith
Jessee Berg
Carol M. Birnhak
Thomas G. Blomberg, Jr.
Roger E. Booth
Sally A. Brammell
Demaris L. Brinton
Arnold E. Brown II
James F. Brown
Timothy P. Burns
Brian C. Burr
Paula F. Carney
Lisa F. Cetlin
Christopher P. Cline
Teresa M. Corbin
Matthew S. Crowley
Joanne Crowther
Jacqueline S. Dailey
Elizabeth A. Davidson
J. Daniel Davis
David A. De Groot
Margaret A. de Lisser
Maureen C. Dellinger
Karen A. Dempsey
Andrew J. Dhuey
Lucienne F. Dilworth
Patricia M. Downey
James B. Duncan
Donald M. Egeland
Ethan D. Feffer
Deborah S. Fox
Steven W. Frank
Ellyn Freed
Patricia A. Furlong
Gilbert J. Garcia-Pumento
Ruth E. Gaube
Andrea L. Gross
George A. Gucker
Laura E. Hannusch
Jeffrey B. Hays
Joseph A. Hearst III
Constance M. Hiatt
Michael J. Higgins
Curt Holbreich
John O'Hara Horsley
Victoria N. Kaempf
Jennifer M. Kawamura
Brian J. Keating
Austin D. Kim
Joelyn E. Knopf
Ed Kolto
Judith B. Kridle
Beth J. Kurz
Michael F. LaBianca
David R. Lamarre
Lindy M. Lilien
Jean I. Liu
Gabriella A. Lombardi
Patricia A. Loretz
Dale C. Lysak
Robert T. Manicke
Mehran Massih
Andrew D. Mastin
Elena E. Matsis
Ann Colter Matthews
Anita D. Mayo
David A. Messinger
David J. Miller
Caroline N. Mitchell
Theresa G. Moran
Chad D. Naylor
William J. Needle
Margaret M. Niver
Maria L. Pizzoli
Roxane Alicia Polidora
Adam D. Pressman
Richard P. Rados
Vicki L. Randall
Jesus G. Roman
Elizabeth K. Roodner
Jeffrey S. Ross
Jenny E. Ross
Mary L. Rotunno
Rona H. Sandler
David J. Saul
Melanie A. Sherk
Morgan R. Smock
Betsy G. Stauffer
Junji Tabata
Scott C. Taylor
Patrick S. Thompson
Nancy M. Vu
Lisa M. Watanabe
Joseph A. Whitecavage
Sara Hansen Wilson
Laura A. Woodman
Jennifer A. Wysong
Bruce L. Yonehiro
Ann Keller Young
Kim Zeldin
Dudley A. Zinke

For full biographical listings, see the Martindale-Hubbell Law Directory

ROGERS, JOSEPH, O'DONNELL & QUINN, A PROFESSIONAL CORPORATION (AV)

311 California Street, 94104
Telephone: 415-956-2828
Fax: 415-956-6457

(See Next Column)

ROGERS, JOSEPH, O'DONNELL & QUINN A PROFESSIONAL CORPORATION—*Continued*

Allan J. Joseph
Martin Quinn
Neil H. O'Donnell
Margot Wenger
Pamela Phillips
Anna M. Rossi
Kyra A. Subbotin
Linda R. Koenig
Connie M. Teevan
Allen Samelson
Suzanne M. Mellard
John G. Heller
David Nied
Neil H. Weinstein
Patricia A. Meagher

OF COUNSEL

Joseph W. Rogers
William Bennett Turner

Joelle Tobin
Valerie Ackerman
Merri A. Baldwin
David F. Innis

For full biographical listings, see the Martindale-Hubbell Law Directory

ROPERS, MAJESKI, KOHN & BENTLEY, A PROFESSIONAL CORPORATION (AV)

670 Howard Street, 94105
Telephone: 415-543-4800
Fax: 415-512-1574
Redwood City, California Office: 1001 Marshall Street.
Telephone: 415-364-8200.
Fax: 415-367-0997.
San Jose, California Office: 80 North 1st Street.
Telephone: 408-287-6262.
Fax: 408-297-6819.
Santa Rosa, California Office: Fountaingrove Center, 3558 Round Barn Boulevard, Suite 300.
Telephone: 707-524-4200.
Fax: 707-523-4610.
Los Angeles, California Office: 550 South Hope Street, Suite 1900.
Telephone: 213-312-2000.
Fax: 213-312-2001.
Sacramento, California Office: 1000 G Street, Suite 400.
Telephone: 916-556-3100.
Fax: 916-442-7121.

John A. Koeppel (Resident)
John A. Rowland (Resident)
Charles M. Louderback (Resident)
James A. Lassart (Resident)
Jeffrey W. Allen (Resident)
Gail Y. Norton (Resident)
Paul D. Herbert (Resident)
David C. Anderson (Resident)
Dennis D. Strazulo (Resident)
John Curran Ladd (Resident)
James M. Rockett (Resident)
Stacey L. Pratt (Resident)
Allan E. Anderson (Resident)
Lawrence O. Monin

Carol P. La Plant (Resident)
Bruce Hunter Hinze (Resident)
Mark G. Crawford (Resident)
Maurice J. Fitzgerald (Resident)
Steven J. Skikos (Resident)
Adrian G. Driscoll (Resident)
I. Paul Bae (Resident)
Stephanie H. Scherby (Resident)
Mary Ellen Gambino
Karen M. Gronowski
Gary S. Garfinkle
Anne S. Hilleary
Narendra B. Patel
Keith D. Ungles
Tiffanie Kovcacevich Kalmbach
David Gershon
Jon Giffen
Timothy Joseph Lucey

OF COUNSEL

Ronald F. Sullivan
Stephen S. Austin

For full biographical listings, see the Martindale-Hubbell Law Directory

ROBERT G. SCHUCHARDT (AV)

Four Embarcadero Center, Suite 1700, 94111
Telephone: 415-986-5000
Fax: 415-434-3947

LEGAL SUPPORT PERSONNEL

Michelle Koskella

Reference: Bank of America (Main Office).

For full biographical listings, see the Martindale-Hubbell Law Directory

SEDGWICK, DETERT, MORAN & ARNOLD (AV)

A Partnership including Professional Corporations
16th Floor, One Embarcadero Center, 94111-3765
Telephone: 415-781-7900
Cable Address: "SEDMA"
Fax: 415-781-2635
Los Angeles, California Office: 9th Floor, Wilshire Colonnade, 3701 Wilshire Boulevard.
Telephone: 213-386-2833.
Fax: 213-487-5456.
New York, New York Office: 41st Floor, 59 Maiden Lane.
Telephone: 212-422-0202.
Fax: 212-422-0925.
Telex: 141027.

(See Next Column)

Irvine, California Office: 3 Park Plaza, 17th Floor.
Telephone: 714-852-8200.
Fax: 714-852-8282.
Chicago, Illinois Office: The Rookery Building, Seventh Floor, 209 South La Salle Street.
Telephone: 312-641-9050.
Fax: 312-641-9530.
London, England Office: Lloyds Avenue House, 6 Lloyds Avenue, EC3N 3AX.
Telephone: 071-929-1829.
Fax: 071-929-1808.
Telex: 927037.
Zurich, Switzerland Office: Spluegenstrasse 3, CH-8002.
Telephone: 011-411-201-1730.
Fax: 011-411-201-4404.

Wallace E. Sedgwick (1908-1982)
Gunther R. Detert (1913-1994)
Edward T. Moran (1914-1975)

OF COUNSEL

Ernest Arnold *
James L. Gault *

MEMBERS OF FIRM

Andrew J. Collins *
Roger W. Sleight *
Douglas M. Moore, Jr. *
Stephen W. Jones *
Gregory C. Read *
W. Bruce Wold *
Warren J. Krauss
Michael B. McGeehon
Nicholas W. Heldt
Marilyn Klinger
Roger D. Rizzo
John T. Ronan III
Scott D. Mroz
David De Busschere
Stuart W. Miller
Kathleen D. Patterson
Martin J. O'Leary
Eugene V. Elsbree III
Alan H. Packer
P. Beach Kuhl *
William C. Judge *
Kevin J. Dunne *
David E. Bordon *
Mark W. Hudson *
Cynthia H. Plevin *
Berridge R. Marsh
Paul B. Lahaderne
Michael F. Healy
Rebecca A. Hull
Steven D. Roland
Steven D. Wasserman
Michael R. Davisson
Paul J. Riehle
Frederick D. Baker
Kaye Washington
Christopher A. Nedeau
Stephanie A. Sheridan
Ann L. Wilson

ASSOCIATES

Carol V. Holland
Sigrid Owczarek
James S. Brown
Kathryn H. Edwards
Micki S. Singer
Annette C. Warfield Hughes
William E. Adams
Lauren F. Weidner
Teresa Stinson
Gary A. Cerio
Sarah E. Lucas
Janet M. Alexander
Wayne A. Wolff
Alicia J. Donahue
Kathleen A. McKinley
James F. Waite
Tracy M. Preston
David P. Gardner
Melanie Grant Jones
Judith J. Loach
Roy Mosley
James V. Weixel, Jr.
Barbara H. Clement
Nadine Permutt Lauren
Ingrid E. von Kaschnitz
Karen Segar Salty
Stephen A. Schram
Holly A. Harris
Jimmy L. Hom
Anthony J. Anscombe
Charles O. Geerhart
Ann J. Reavis
Earl L. Hagström
Constance A. Leahy
Sean H. Gallagher
Kenneth C. Ryken
Charles T. Sheldon
Kris A. Cox
James P. Diwik
Judy S. Ireland
Elizabeth Yelland Lara
Robert Spagat
Thomas A. Douvan
Melinda Knupp Walker
Dennis P. Scott
Jay M. Goldman
Shannon Ball Jones
Noreen E. McDermott
Diane D. Papan
Sally J. Bertuccelli
Richard B. Curtis
Juan B. Otero
Anthony W. White
Kirk Christopher Jenkins (Not admitted in CA)
Daniel S. Harris
Ilene S. Kreitzer

Representative Clients: Aetna Casualty & Surety Co.; Bristol Meyers Squibb; Chrysler Corp.; Lockheed Missiles & Space Co.; Underwriters at Lloyd's.
*A Professional Corporation

For full biographical listings, see the Martindale-Hubbell Law Directory

SEVERSON & WERSON, A PROFESSIONAL CORPORATION (AV)

Twenty-Fifth Floor, 1 Embarcadero Center, 94111
Telephone: 415-398-3344
Telex: 278934
Telecopier: 415-956-0439

Nathan R. Berke (1912-1985)
Walter R. Severson (1903-1986)
James B. Werson
Ernest Y. Sevier
Edmund T. King, II
Robert L. Lofts
Donald J. Yellon
Dennis M. Talbott
Roger S. Mertz
Allan L. Fink
Jan T. Chilton
William T. McGivern, Jr.
Lawrence A. Callaghan
Steven W. Waldo
Michael J. Bertinetti
Donald J. Querio
Gerald J. Buchwald
John W. Bergholt

(See Next Column)

SEVERSON & WERSON A PROFESSIONAL CORPORATION, *San Francisco—Continued*

Larry W. Telford
Roberta V. Romberg
James R. Arnold
Mark Joseph Kenney
Patricia L. McClaran
William L. Stern
John B. Sullivan
Loraine P. Eber
Edward A. Giedgowd
Michael J. Steiner
Duane M. Geck
Michael B. Murphy
Scott H. McNutt
Kennedy A. Brooks

Carin W. Sinrod
Mark D. Lonergan
Jeffrey C. Selman
Gregory Nuti
David A. Ericksen
A. Mark Hom
Susun Kim
Christina G. Hong
Susan Bade Hull
Carolyn Powell
Kristine H. Kim
Michele F. Kyrouz
Bruce M. Price

OF COUNSEL

Ransom S. Cook
Robert V. Magor

For full biographical listings, see the Martindale-Hubbell Law Directory

---

SHARTSIS, FRIESE & GINSBURG (AV)

One Maritime Plaza, Eighteenth Floor, 94111
Telephone: 415-421-6500

Paul M. Ginsburg
Robert Charles Friese
Arthur J. Shartsis
Mary Jo Shartsis
Robert D. Evans
Douglas L. Hammer
Ronald Hayes Malone
Joel Zeldin
John P. Broadhurst
David H. Kremer
Charles R. Rice
Anthony B. Leuin
Douglas Mo
Robert E. Schaberg
Tracy L. Salisbury
Jeffrey A. O'Connell
Susan York Janin
Carolyn R. Klasco
Jeffrey J. Goodrich
Eric Sippel
Jonathan M. Kennedy
Adam K. Elsesser
Steven O. Gasser

Zesara C. Chan
Geoffrey W. Haynes
Seth K. Schalit
Christopher J. Rupright
Sean M. SeLegue
Carolyn S. Reiser
Ellen S. Mouchawar
Robert Charles Ward
H. Perry Taubman

OF COUNSEL

Barbara W. Staman
Rachel Wagner
Denise M. Alter

For full biographical listings, see the Martindale-Hubbell Law Directory

---

SHEARMAN & STERLING (AV)

555 California Street, 94104-1522
Telephone: (415) 616-1100
Fax: (415) 616-1199
New York, N.Y. Office: 599 Lexington Avenue, New York, New York 10022-6069 and Citicorp Center, 153 East 53rd Street, New York, New York 10022-4676.
Telephone: (212) 848-4000.
Telex: 667290 Num Lau.
Fax: 599 Lexington Avenue: (212) 848-7179. Citicorp Center: (212) 848-5252.
Abu Dhabi, United Arab Emirates Office: P.O. Box 2948.
Telephone: (971-2) 324477.
Fax: (971-2) 774533.
Beijing, People's Republic of China Office: Suite #2205, Capital Mansion, No. 6, Xin Yuan Nan Road. Chao Yang District Beijing, 100004.
Telephone: (861) 465-4574.
Fax: (861) 465-4578.
Budapest, Hungary Office: Szerb utca 17-19, 1056 Budapest.
Telephone: (36-1) 266-3522.
Fax: (36-1) 266-3523.
Düsseldorf, Federal Republic of Germany Office: Königsallee 46, D-40212 Düsseldorf.
Telephone: (49-211) 13 62 80.
Telex: 8 588 294 NYLO.
Fax: (49-211) 13 33 09.
Frankfurt, Federal Republic of Germany Office: Bockenheimer Landstrasse 55, D-60325 Frankfurt am Main.
Telephone: (49-69) 97-10-70.
Fax: (49-69) 97-10-71-00.
Hong Kong, Hong Kong Office: Standard Chartered Bank Building, 4 Des Voeux Road Central, Hong Kong.
Telephone: (852) 2978-8000.
Fax: (852) 2978-8099.
London, England Office: 199 Bishopsgate, London EC2M 3TY.
Telephone: (44-71) 920-9000.
Fax: (44-71) 920-9020.
Los Angeles, California Office: 725 South Figueroa Street, 21st Floor, 90017-5421.
Telephone: (213) 239-0300.
Fax: (213) 239-0381, 614-0936.

(See Next Column)

Paris, France Office: 12 rue d'Astorg, 75008.
Telephone: (33-1) 44-71-17-17.
Telex: 282964 Royale.
Fax: (33-1) 44-71-01-01.
Taipei, Taiwan Office: 7th Floor, Hung Kuo Building, 167 Tun Hwa North Road.
Telephone: (886-2) 545-3300.
Fax: (866-2) 545-3322.
Tokyo, Japan Office: Shearman & Sterling (Thomas Wilner Gaikokuho-Jimu-Bengoshi Jimusho), Fukoku Seimei Building, 5th Fl. 2-2-2, Uchisaiwaicho, Chiyoda-ku, Tokyo 100, Japan.
Telephone: (81 3) 5251-1601.
Fax: (81 3) 5251-1602.
Toronto, Ontario, Canada Office: Commerce Court West, Suite 4405, P.O. Box 247, M5L 1E8.
Telephone: (416) 360-8484.
Fax: (416) 360-2958.
Washington, D.C. Office: 801 Pennsylvania Avenue, N.W., Suite 900, 20004-2604.
Telephone: (202) 508-8000.
Fax: (202) 508-8100.

RESIDENT PARTNERS

Steven E. Sherman (Managing Partner)
William H. Hinman (Not admitted in CA; Managing Partner)
Jeffrey S. Facter
Alfred C. Groff
Michael J. Kennedy
Dean S. Krystowski

OF COUNSEL

William F. Baxter

For full biographical listings, see the Martindale-Hubbell Law Directory

---

SHEPPARD, MULLIN, RICHTER & HAMPTON (AV)

A Partnership including Professional Corporations
Seventeenth Floor, Four Embarcadero Center, 94111
Telephone: 415-434-9100
Telecopier: 415-434-3947
Telex: 19-4424
Los Angeles, California Office: Forty-Eighth Floor, 333 South Hope Street.
Telephone: 213-620-1780.
Telecopier: 213-620-1398.
Cable Address: "Sheplaw".
Telex: 19-4424.
Orange County, California Office: Seventh Floor, 4695 MacArthur Court, Newport Beach.
Telephone: 714-752-6400.
Telecopier: 714-851-0739.
Telex: 19-4424.
San Diego, California Office: Nineteenth Floor, 501 West Broadway.
Telephone: 619-338-6500.
Telecopier: 619-234-3815.
Telex: 19-4424.

MEMBERS OF FIRM

Kathleen Borrero Bloch
John C. Cook
Joseph A. Darrell
Juliette M. Ebert
Dale E. Fredericks
Geraldine A. Freeman
James Blythe Hodge *
Samuel M. Livermore
Charles H. MacNab, Jr.
Gary J. Nevolo
Susan Herbst Roos
John F. Runkel, Jr.
D. Ronald Ryland
Jane L. Thomas
Daniel P. Westman
Darryl M. Woo
William R. Wyatt

SPECIAL COUNSEL

C. W. Bergere, Jr.
M. Elizabeth McDaniel
Allan J. Thompson

ASSOCIATES

Robert B. Ajemian
Thomas A. Counts
Katherine H. Cowan
Dana DuFrane
Stephen J. Duggan
Anna E. Goodwin
Kristen A. Jensen
Brian W. Jones
Bridget Lanouette
Maureen C. McLaughlin
Cindy M. Oakes
David A. Pursley
Felicia R. Reid
Mark K. Slater
Michael E. Wilbur

*Professional Corporation

For full biographical listings, see the Martindale-Hubbell Law Directory

---

SKJERVEN, MORRILL, MACPHERSON, FRANKLIN & FRIEL (AV)

Suite 800, 601 California Street, 94104
Telephone: 415-986-8383
Telecopier: 415-982-7372
San Jose, California Office: Suite 700, 25 Metro Drive.
Telephone: 408-283-1222.
Telecopier: 408-283-1233.
Austin, Texas Office: Suite 1050, 100 Congress Street.
Telephone: 512-404-3600.
Telecopier: 512-404-3601.

(See Next Column)

SKJERVEN, MORRILL, MACPHERSON, FRANKLIN & FRIEL—*Continued*

MEMBERS OF FIRM

Richard H. Skjerven (At San Jose, California and Austin, Texas Offices)
Robert B. Morrill
Alan H. MacPherson (Resident, San Jose Office)
Richard K. Franklin (Resident, San Jose Office)
Thomas J. Friel, Jr.
Marc David Freed (Resident, San Jose Office)
Anthony de Alcuaz (Resident, San Jose Office)
Paul J. Winters (Resident, San Jose Office)
Justin T. Beck (Resident, San Jose Office)
Joseph A. Greco (Resident, San Jose Office)
David W. Heid (Resident, San Jose Office)
David H. Carroll (Resident, Austin, Texas Office)
Forrest Gunnison (Resident, San Jose Office)
Norman R. Klivans, Jr. (Resident, San Jose Office)
Charles D. Chalmers (Resident, San Jose Office)
Kenneth E. Leeds (Resident, San Jose Office)
Brian Ogonowsky (Resident, San Jose Office)
David E. Steuber (Resident, San Jose Office)
Laura Terlizzi (Resident, San Jose Office)
Edward V. Anderson (Resident, San Jose Office)
Edward C. Kwok (Resident, San Jose Office)
Michelle G. Breit (Resident, San Jose Office)

ASSOCIATES

Michael Shenker (Resident, San Jose Office)
Kimberly Paul Zapata (Resident, San Jose Office)
Scott R. Brown (Resident, San Jose Office)
Patrick T. Bever (Resident, San Jose Office)
James E. Parsons (Resident, San Jose Office)
T. Lester Wallace (Resident, San Jose Office)
Peter H. Kang (Resident, San Jose Office)
Alexandra J. Horne (Resident, San Jose Office)
David T. Millers (Resident, San Jose Office)
E. Eric Hoffman (Resident, San Jose Office)
Omkarmurthy K. Suryadevara (Resident, San Jose Office)
Emily M. Haliday (Resident, San Jose Office)
Elizabeth Ann Hemphill (Resident, San Jose Office)
Philip J. McKay (Resident, San Jose Office)
Lawrence E. Lycke (Resident, San Jose Office)
L. Scott Primak (Resident, San Jose Office)
H. Fredrick Zimmermann (Resident, San Jose Office)
Thomas E. Rossmeissl (Resident, San Jose Office)
Steven M. Levitan (Resident, San Jose Office)
Michael A. Gelblum (Resident, San Jose Office)
Arthur J. Behiel (Resident, San Jose Office)
Michael J. Halbert (Resident, San Jose Office)
Jennifer A. Ochs (Resident, San Jose Office)

SPECIAL COUNSEL

Guy W. Shoup (Resident, San Jose Office)

OF COUNSEL

Thomas S. MacDonald (Resident, San Jose Office)
Ronald J. Meetin (Resident, San Jose Office)

PATENT AGENT

Anthony G. Dervan (Resident, San Jose Office)

Reference: Bank of America.

For full biographical listings, see the Martindale-Hubbell Law Directory

SONNENSCHEIN NATH & ROSENTHAL (AV)

10th Floor, 685 Market Street, 94105
Telephone: 415-882-5000
Telecopier: 415-543-5472; 882-5038
Chicago, Illinois Office: Suite 8000 Sears Tower, 233 South Wacker Drive.
Telephone: 312-876-8000.
Cable Address: "Sonberk".
Telex: 25-3526.
Facsimile: 312-876-7934.
New York, N.Y. Office: 1221 Avenue of the Americas, 24th Floor.
Telephone: 212-768-6700.
Facsimile: 212-391-1247.
Washington, D.C. Office: 1301 K Street, N.W., Suite 600, East Tower.
Telephone: 202-408-6400.
Facsimile: 202-408-6399.
Los Angeles, California Office: Suite 1500, 601 South Figueroa Street.
Telephone: 213-623-9300.
Facsimile: 213-623-9924.
St. Louis, Missouri Office: One Metropolitan Square, Suite 3000.
Telephone: 314-241-1800.
Facsimile: 314-259-5959.

RESIDENT PARTNERS

Michael A. Barnes
Robin M. Edwards
Steven H. Frankel (Not admitted in CA)
Paul E. B. Glad
Thomas Holden
Oliver L. Holmes
Gayle M. Jones
H. Sinclair Kerr, Jr.
Robert H. King, Jr.
Sandra R. McCandless
Michael W. Melendez
Cynthia L. Mellema
William C. Morison-Knox

(See Next Column)

RESIDENT PARTNERS (Continued)

Philip A. O'Connell, Jr.
Arnold P. Schuster
John Leland Williams
Nicholas C. Yost

RESIDENT ASSOCIATES

Jon K. Adams
Dana L. Ballinger
Cheryl Dyer Berg
Shelley R. (Barber) De Leo
Bryce P. Goeking
Katharine A. Kates
Mary Kay Lacey
Paul A. Leboffe
Mark J. Linderman
Matthew F. Lintner
Andrew R. Livingston
Rhonda V. Magee
J. Robert Maxwell
Sean McEneaney
Lori E. Romley
Catherine A. Salton
Tamara Seyler-James
Peter A. Smalbach
Gregory L. Smith (Not admitted in CA)
Christopher P. Sonderby
Charles Spiegel
Craig A. Sterling
Pamela J. Tennison
Kelly B. Valen
William B. Van lonkhuyzen
Lisabeth Jacobs Wesselkamper
Paula M. Yost

For full biographical listings, see the Martindale-Hubbell Law Directory

STEEFEL, LEVITT & WEISS, A PROFESSIONAL CORPORATION (AV)

29th Floor, One Embarcadero Center, 94111
Telephone: 415-788-0900
Telecopier: 415-397-7802; 415-788-2019

Edward R. Steefel
Alvin T. Levitt
Lenard G. Weiss
Richard A. Kramer
Harvey S. Schochet
Michael J. Lawson
Christine A. Murphy
Janet C. Norris
Marvin B. Pearlstein
Harvey L. Leiderman
Laura R. Craft
Bruce E. Prigoff
Frank T. Pepler
Leonard R. Stein
Michael D. Early
Marc A. Lackner
Philip J. Nicholsen
Clayton B. Gantz
Craig P. Wood
Barry W. Lee
Jordan P. Rose
James F. Eastman
Stephen S. Mayne
Paul E. Manasian
Brenda Jansen
Daryl S. Landy

Richard Aiello
Andrew A. Bassak
Kenneth A. Brunetti
Jeffrey K. Compton
Brian J. Danzig
Jill S. Dodd
Diane E. Eisenberg
Joseph E. Floren
Karen L. Frasier
Mark R. Goldberg
David L. Kasper
Robin Smith King
Jonathan A. Klein
Ralph T. Kokka
Julie B. Landau
Felice P. Liang
William L. Lowery
Peter A. Mastromonaco
Trina N. Parker
Teresa A. Rice
Michael G. Schinner
Jerome Schreibstein
Lisa M.C. Sims
Richard J. Tannenbaum (Not admitted in CA)
Leonard H. Watkins

OF COUNSEL

Gary J. Shapiro

For full biographical listings, see the Martindale-Hubbell Law Directory

*SAN JOSE,** Santa Clara Co.

BERGESON, ELIOPOULOS, GRADY & GRAY (AV)

Ten Almaden Boulevard, Suite 200, 95113
Telephone: 408-291-6200
Fax: 408-297-6000

Daniel J. Bergeson
William T. Eliopoulos
Michael F. Grady
Richard J. Gray
John L. Antracoli
Mark E. Waite

ASSOCIATES

Lisa V. Heilbron

For full biographical listings, see the Martindale-Hubbell Law Directory

BUCHALTER, NEMER, FIELDS & YOUNGER, A PROFESSIONAL CORPORATION (AV)

12th Floor, 50 West San Fernando Street, 95113
Telephone: 408-298-0350
Fax: 408-298-7683
Los Angeles, California Office: 24th Floor, 601 South Figueroa Street.
Telephone: 213-891-0700.
Fax: 213-896-0400.
New York, New York Office: 19th Floor, 237 Park Avenue.
Telephone: 212-490-8600.
Fax: 212-490-6022.
San Francisco, California Office: 29th Floor, 333 Market Street.
Telephone: 415-227-0900.
Fax: 415-227-0770.
Newport Beach, California Office: Suite 300, 620 Newport Center Drive.
Telephone: 714-760-1121.
Fax: 714-720-0182.

(See Next Column)

BUCHALTER, NEMER, FIELDS & YOUNGER A PROFESSIONAL CORPORATION, *San Jose—Continued*

Century City, California Office: Suite 2400, 1801 Century Park East.
Telephone: 213-891-0700.
Fax: 310-551-0233.

NORTHERN CALIFORNIA RESIDENTS IN CHARGE

Gary Nemer
Stephen H. Pettigrew

References: City National Bank; Wells Fargo Bank; Metrobank.

For full biographical listings, see the Martindale-Hubbell Law Directory

CAMPBELL, WARBURTON, BRITTON, FITZSIMMONS & SMITH, A PROFESSIONAL CORPORATION (AV)

Suite 1200, 101 Park Center Plaza, P.O. Box 1867, 95113
Telephone: 408-295-7701
Fax: 408-295-1423

Frank Valpey Campbell (1892-1971)
Frank L. Custer (1902-1962)
Alfred B. Britton, Jr. (1919-1991)
Austen D. Warburton
Willard R. Campbell
John R. Fitzsimmons, Jr.
C. Michael Smith
Ralph E. Mendell
Nicholas Pastore
J. Michael Fitzsimmons

William R. Colucci
Carolyn M. Rose

LEGAL SUPPORT PERSONNEL

Susan Frederick

Representative Corporate Clients: Marriott Corp.; Swenson Builders; Helene Curtis, Inc.; Viking Freight Systems.
Representative Insurance Clients: California State Automobile Assn.; Farmers Insurance Group; Travelers Insurance Co.; Westfield Insurance Cos.; Michelin Tire Corp. (Self Insured).

For full biographical listings, see the Martindale-Hubbell Law Directory

LAW OFFICES OF THOMAS R. HOGAN (AV)

60 South Market Street Suite 1125, 95113-2332
Telephone: 408-292-7600
Facsimile: 408-292-7611

PARALEGAL

Leslie Holmes

For full biographical listings, see the Martindale-Hubbell Law Directory

WILLIAM HOLLEY (AV)

1871 The Alameda, Suite 190, 95126
Telephone: 408-244-8122
Fax: 408-244-8087

For full biographical listings, see the Martindale-Hubbell Law Directory

JACKSON, TUFTS, COLE & BLACK (AV)

A Partnership including Professional Corporations
60 South Market Street, 10th Floor, 95113
Telephone: 408-998-1952
Fax: 408-998-4889
San Francisco, California Office: 650 California Street, Thirty-Second Floor.
Telephone: 415-433-1950.
Fax: 415-392-3494.

MEMBERS OF FIRM

Bartlett A. Jackson (A Professional Corporation)
Robert R. Tufts
George H. Cole, Jr.
J. David Black
Templeton C. Peck
Charles G. Stephenson
John S. Siamas
David T. Alexander
Carl J. Stoney, Jr.
Kenneth J. Philpot
Michael J. Baker
David Ayers Thompson
Ellen McGinty King
Peter S. Muñoz
Dennis V. Swanson
Debra S. Belaga
Emil G. Pesiri
D. D. Hughmanick
William H. Booth
Terrence P. McMahon
Twila L. Foster
Nicole A. Dillingham
Janice W. Fox
George R. Theofel
Jeffrey J. Cole
Roy M. Bartlett, Jr.
Daniel M. Elkort
Richard Scudellari
Donna M. Mezias
Gregory P. Farnham
Martin S. Schenker
Michael F. McCabe
Joseph S. Faber
Debra L. Kasper
Margaret A. Sloan
Paul H. Goldstein
Lynn Marie McLean
Carolyn A. Lown

OF COUNSEL

Toby Cozart
Wayne W. Lew
Gerald Z. Marer

(See Next Column)

ASSOCIATES

Marily Peatman Lerner
Paul S. Avilla
Thomas D. Murtha
Reneé Lanam Barton
Jane M. Hawkins
Sean A. Lincoln
Eric T. Sullivan
Lynn Acker Starr
Robert G. White
Stephen M. Debenham
Melissa A. Finocchio
Gretchen Dean Hug
Joanne Marshall Shea
Régine Shambrook
Steven N. Sherr
Maya Lakshmi Harris
Amy E. Margolin
Deborah L. Breiner
Robin E. Kelsey
Marion C. Ingersoll
Eleanor Baldwin Lacey

For full biographical listings, see the Martindale-Hubbell Law Directory

MCCUTCHEN, DOYLE, BROWN & ENERSEN (AV)

Market Post Tower, Suite 1500, 55 South Market Street, 95113-2327
Telephone: 408-947-8400
Facsimile: 408-947-4750
Telex: 910 250 2931 MACPAG SJ
San Francisco, California Office: Three Embarcadero Center, 94111-4066.
Telephone: 415-393-2000.
Facsimile: 415-393-2286 (G I, II, III).
Telex: 340817 MACPAG SFO.
Los Angeles, California Office: 355 South Grand Avenue, Suite 4400, 90071-1560.
Telephone: 213-680-6400.
Facsimile: 213-680-6499.
Walnut Creek, California Office: 1331 North California Boulevard, Post Office Box V, 94596-4502.
Telephone: 510-937-8000.
Facsimile: 510-975-5390.
Menlo Park, California Office: 2740 Sand Hill Road, 94025-7020.
Telephone: 415-233-4000.
Facsimile: 415-233-4086.
Washington, D.C. Office: The Evening Star Building, Suite 800, 1101 Pennsylvania Avenue, N.W., 20004-2514.
Telephone: 202-628-4900.
Facsimile: 202-628-4912.
Taipei, Taiwan Republic of China Office: International Trade Building, Tenth Floor, 333 Keelung Road, Section 1, 110.
Telephone: 886-2-723-5000.
Facsimile: 886-2-757-6070.
Affiliated Offices In: Bangkok, Thailand; Beijing, China; Shanghai, China.

MEMBERS OF FIRM

Christopher P. Berka
Ross E. Campbell
Byde W. Clawson
Daniel Cooperman
Charles William Craycroft
Carol K. Dillon
John W. Fowler
Donald D. Howard
James P. Kleinberg
Ronald S. Laurie
Gordon T. Yamate

OF COUNSEL

Beverly A. Tiffany

ASSOCIATES

Mabell Y. Aguilar
Shashikala Bhat
Claire T. Cormier
Christine S. Lam
Carol L. Martin
Kathleen A. McDonald (Resident)
Beth A. McGowen
Steven G. Rosen
Carissa M. Smith
James Grant Snell
Neal J. Stephens
Jennifer Tsay

For full biographical listings, see the Martindale-Hubbell Law Directory

MILLER, MORTON, CAILLAT & NEVIS (AV)

50 West San Fernando Street, Suite 1300, 95112
Telephone: 408-292-1765
Telecopier: 408-292-4484

Richard W. Morton (1916-1975)
Charles V. Caillat (1920-1990)
Harvey C. Miller (1906-1993)

MEMBERS OF FIRM

David L. Nevis
Francis J. Hughes
Peter A. Kline
Stevan C. Adelman
Joseph A. Scanlan, Jr.
Pamela J. Silberstein
Carolyn F. Tobiason-Stuart
William K. Hurley

OF COUNSEL

Nancy F. Symons
Susan L. Sutton

ASSOCIATES

Peter V. Dessau
Eric Mogensen
Kathryn E. Barrett
Katherine S. Pak

Representative Clients: Tramwell Crow Residential; Joe Kerley Lincoln Mercury Co.; Milligan News Co.; Joseph George Distributors; Watsonville Employers Frozen Foods Assn.; New West Foods, Inc.; Norris, Beggs & Simpson; American Motors Corp.; E. A. Hathaway Co.; United Way of Santa Clara County; Berkshire Life Insurance Co.

For full biographical listings, see the Martindale-Hubbell Law Directory

San Jose—Continued

MORGAN, RUBY, SCHOFIELD, FRANICH & FREDKIN (AV)

A Partnership of Law Corporations
99 Almaden Boulevard, Suite 1000, 95113
Telephone: 408-288-8288
Fax: 408-288-8325

MEMBERS OF FIRM

Mark B. Fredkin (L.C.)
Mark Franich (L.C.)
Glen W. Schofield (L.C.)
Allen Ruby (L.C.)
Douglas J. Morgan (L.C.)
Anthony E. Marsh (L.C.)
Brian P. Preston (L.C.)
Robert E. Dunne (L.C.)

ASSOCIATES

William N. Siamas
Linda M. Bertolucci
Kathleen L. Kerr-White

For full biographical listings, see the Martindale-Hubbell Law Directory

PILLSBURY MADISON & SUTRO (AV)

Ten Almaden Boulevard, 95113
Telephone: 408-947-4000
FAX: 408-287-8341
Costa Mesa, California Office: Plaza Tower, 600 Anton Boulevard, Suite 1100, 92626.
Telephone: 714-436-6800.
Fax: 714-662-6999.
Los Angeles, California Office: Citicorp Plaza, 725 South Figueroa Street, Suite 1200, 90017.
Telephone: 213-488-7100.
Fax: 213-629-1033.
New York, New York Office: One Liberty Plaza, 165 Broadway, 51st Floor.
Telephone: 212-374-1890.
Fax: 212-374-1852.
Menlo Park, California Office: 2700 Sand Hill Road, 94025.
Telephone: 415-233-4500.
Fax: 415-233-4545.
Sacramento, California Office: 400 Capitol Mall, Suite 1700, 95814.
Telephone: 916-329-4700.
Fax: 916-441-3583.
San Diego, California Office: 101 West Broadway, Suite 1800, 92101.
Telephone: 619-234-5000.
Fax: 619-236-1995.
San Francisco, California Office: 225 Bush Street, 94104.
Telephone: 415-983-1000.
Fax: 415-398-2096.
Cable Address: "Evans"
Telex: 34743.
Washington, D.C. Office: 1667 K Street, N.W., Suite 1100, 20006.
Telephone: 202-887-0300.
Fax: 202-296-7605.
Hong Kong Office: 6/F Asia Pacific Finance Tower, Citibank Plaza, 3 Garden Road, Central.
Telephone: 011-852-509-7100.
Fax: 011-852-509-7188.
Tokyo, Japan Office: Churchill and Shimazaki, Gaikokuho-Jimo-Bengoshi Jimusho, 11-12, Toranomon 5-Chome Minato-ku, Tokyo 105, Japan.
Telephone: 800-729-9830; 011-81-3-5472-6561.
Fax: 011-81-3-5472-5761.

MEMBERS OF FIRM

Edward P. Davis, Jr.
Jorge A. del Calvo
Jacques M. Dulin
Vernon H. Granneman
F. Kinsey Haffner
Russell L. Johnson
Patricia H. McCall
Lynn L. Miller
Thomas P. O'Donnell
Megan Waters Pierson
Randolf J. Rice
Albert J. Ruffo
Frank E. Sieglitz
Georgia K. Van Zanten
Toni Pryor Wise
Debra L. Zumwalt

OF COUNSEL

Theodore J. Biagini
Robert W. Dunaway

SENIOR COUNSEL

Judy Alexander
John S. Wesolowski

ASSOCIATES

Thomas J. Angioletti III
John P. Castro
James M. Chadwick
Patricia L. Cotton
Patrick H. Dunkley
Suzanne A. Heinrich
Greg L. Johnson
Sharon S. Kirsch
Catherine L. Marken
Barbara R. Shufro
Wynne D. Spadafora
Michelle C. Trapani
Frederick J. Zustak

For full biographical listings, see the Martindale-Hubbell Law Directory

ROPERS, MAJESKI, KOHN & BENTLEY, A PROFESSIONAL CORPORATION (AV)

80 North 1st Street, 95113
Telephone: 408-287-6262
Fax: 408-297-6819
Redwood City, California Office: 1001 Marshall Street.
Telephone: 415-364-8200.
Fax: 415-367-0997.
San Francisco, California Office: 670 Howard Street.
Telephone: 415-543-4800.
Fax: 415-512-1574.
Santa Rosa, California Office: Fountaingrove Center, 3558 Round Barn Boulevard, Suite 300.
Telephone: 707-524-4200.
Fax: 707-523-4610.
Los Angeles, California Office: 550 South Hope Street, Suite 1900.
Telephone: 213-312-2000.
Fax: 213-312-2001.
Sacramento, California Office: 1000 G Street, Suite 400.
Telephone: 916-556-3100.
Fax: 916-442-7121.

Robert S. Luft (Resident)
Dennis J. Ward (Resident)
Richard M. Williams (Resident)
Michael J. Ioannou (Resident)
Stephan A. Barber (Resident)
Kevin P. Cody (Resident)
Mary H. Atwell (Resident)
George E. Clause (Resident)
Curtis R. Tingley (Resident)
Mary L. Scharrenberg (Resident)
Dean A. Pappas (Resident)
John R. Bernal (Resident)
Jo Ann DeRuvo (Resident)
James C. Hyde
David B. Draper

Matthew T. Yuen (Resident)
Michael O. Lamphere (Resident)
John I. Jeter (Resident)
Christopher J. Cox (Resident)
Daniel R. Kirwan (Resident)
Anne C. Stromberg (Resident)
Craig A. Langley (Resident)
Jon M. Thacker (Resident)
Carol Seidler Golbranson (Resident)
Robert L. Banfield, Jr.
H. Gregory Nelch
John Komar
Douglas W. Dalcielo
Crystal T. H. Bui
Martin Dioli
Eva Yablonsky

For full biographical listings, see the Martindale-Hubbell Law Directory

SKJERVEN, MORRILL, MACPHERSON, FRANKLIN & FRIEL (AV)

Suite 700, 25 Metro Drive, 95110
Telephone: 408-283-1222
Telecopier: 408-283-1233
San Francisco, California Office: Suite 800, 601 California Street.
Telephone: 415-986-8383.
Telecopier: 415-982-7372.
Austin, Texas Office: Suite 1050, 100 Congress Street.
Telephone: 512-404-3600.
Telecopier: 512-404-3601.

MEMBERS OF FIRM

Richard H. Skjerven
Robert B. Morrill (Resident, San Francisco Office)
Alan H. MacPherson
Richard K. Franklin
Thomas J. Friel, Jr. (Resident, San Francisco Office)
Marc David Freed
Anthony de Alcuaz
Paul J. Winters
Justin T. Beck
Joseph A. Greco
David W. Heid
David H. Carroll (Resident, Austin, Texas Office)
Forrest Gunnison
Norman R. Klivans, Jr.
Charles D. Chalmers (Resident, San Francisco Office)
Kenneth E. Leeds
Brian Ogonowsky
David E. Steuber
Laura Terlizzi
Edward V. Anderson
Edward C. Kwok
Michelle G. Breit

ASSOCIATES

Michael Shenker
Kimberly Paul Zapata
Scott R. Brown
Patrick T. Bever
James E. Parsons
T. Lester Wallace
Peter H. Kang
Alexandra J. Horne
David T. Millers
E. Eric Hoffman
Omkarmurthy K. Suryadevara
Emily M. Haliday
Elizabeth Ann Hemphill
Philip J. McKay
Lawrence E. Lycke
William L. Paradice III
L. Scott Primak
H. Fredrick Zimmermann
Thomas E. Rossmeissl
Steven M. Levitan
Michael A. Gelblum
Arthur J. Behiel
Michael J. Halbert
Jennifer A. Ochs

SPECIAL COUNSEL

Guy W. Shoup

OF COUNSEL

Thomas S. MacDonald
Ronald J. Meetin

PATENT AGENT

Anthony G. Dervan

Reference: Bank of America.

For full biographical listings, see the Martindale-Hubbell Law Directory

San Jose—Continued

VAN LOUCKS & HANLEY (AV)

First American Building, 160 West Santa Clara Street, Suite 1050, 95113
Telephone: 408-287-2773
Fax: 408-297-5480

Geoffrey Van Loucks
Anthony L. Hanley

Michael K. Budra
Laura Uddenberg

Reference: San Jose National Bank.

For full biographical listings, see the Martindale-Hubbell Law Directory

SAN LEANDRO, Alameda Co. — (Refer to Hayward)

SAN MATEO, San Mateo Co.

ANDERLINI, GUHEEN, FINKELSTEIN, EMERICK & MCSWEENEY, A PROFESSIONAL CORPORATION (AV)

400 South El Camino Real, Suite 700, 94402
Telephone: 415-348-0102
Fax: 415-348-0962

P. Terry Anderlini
John J. Guheen
David G. Finkelstein
Merrill G. Emerick
Brian J. McSweeney

A. James Scholz
John P. Antonakos
Paul J. Smoot
Jennifer Gustafson

OF COUNSEL

Daniel J. Monaco (Inc.)

A list of Representative Clients will be furnished upon request.

For full biographical listings, see the Martindale-Hubbell Law Directory

QUADROS & JOHNSON (AV)

1400 Fashion Island Boulevard, Suite 800, 94404
Telephone: 415-377-4300
Telecopier: 415-573-1387

Katherine M. Quadros
Benjamin A. Johnson

OF COUNSEL

Arthur L. Hillman, Jr.

Denise Trani-Morris
Leslie A. Eberhardt

LEGAL SUPPORT PERSONNEL

Coleen M. Divito (Paralegal)

Representative Clients: Liberty Mutual Insurance Co.; Wausau Insurance Cos.; Blue Cross of California; Ryder Truck Rentals, Inc.; Anning Johnson Co.; Pacific Gas & Electric Company; Browning-Ferris Industries; Yellow Freight Trucking Lines, Inc.; Sasco Electric Company.

For full biographical listings, see the Martindale-Hubbell Law Directory

*SAN RAFAEL,** Marin Co.

FREITAS, MCCARTHY, MACMAHON & KEATING (AV)

960 Fifth Avenue, 94901
Telephone: 415-456-7500
Fax: 415-456-0266
Point Reyes, California Office: Point Reyes Station.
Telephone: 415-663-1333.

MEMBERS OF FIRM

Carlos R. Freitas (1904-1979)
Bryan R. McCarthy
Jay Ross MacMahon
David P. Freitas
Thomas F. Keating, Jr.
Robert J. Turrini
Neil J. Moran
Richard P. Murray

OF COUNSEL

Richard V. Bettini

ASSOCIATES

Beverly Wood
Peter A. Kleinbrodt

Representative Clients: Westamerica Bank; Fireman's Fund American; Allstate Insurance Co.; Commerce Clearing House; Pacific Telesis; Industrial Indemnity Co.

For full biographical listings, see the Martindale-Hubbell Law Directory

NELSON, BOYD, MACDONALD, MITCHELL, MASON & HEDIN (AV)

Suite 375 Courthouse Square, 1000 Fourth Street, 94901
Telephone: 415-453-0534
Fax: 415-453-0441

MEMBERS OF FIRM

Thomas C. Nelson (1892-1975)
Thomas P. Boyd (1914-1985)
DeWitt K. MacDonald
Peter E. Mitchell
Terrel J. Mason
Todd C. Hedin

(See Next Column)

References: Bank of America National Trust & Savings Assn.; Wells Fargo Bank; Bank of California; Westamerica Bank.

For full biographical listings, see the Martindale-Hubbell Law Directory

*SANTA ANA,** Orange Co.

BEAM, BROBECK & WEST (AV)

600 West Santa Ana Boulevard, Suite 1000, 92701
Telephone: 714-558-3944
Fax: 714-568-0129

MEMBERS OF FIRM

Byron J. Beam
David J. Brobeck, Jr.
John E. West
Kirk H. Nakamura
Robert H. McMillan
Daniel R. Sullivan

ASSOCIATES

Richard M. Stoll
Betsey J. LeBeau
Charles W. Matheis, Jr.
Robert C. Hastie
Susan D. Morgenstern
Jeffrey A. Nix
Gregory L. Rippetoe
Jennifer J. Miller
Donald S. Zalewski
Geralyn L. Skapik
David R. Rosenberg

Representative Clients: Aetna Insurance Co.; American General Life Insurance Co.; American Hospital Supply; Carl Warren & Co.; Casualty Insurance Co.; City of Anaheim; City of Fullerton; City of Newport Beach; Empire Insurance Cos.; Physicians Interindemnity.

For full biographical listings, see the Martindale-Hubbell Law Directory

COTKIN & COLLINS, A PROFESSIONAL CORPORATION (AV)

200 West Santa Ana Boulevard, Suite 800, 92701
Telephone: 714-835-2330
FAX: 714-835-2209
Los Angeles, California Office: 1055 West Seventh Street, Suite 1900.
Telephone: 213-688-9350.
FAX: 213-688-9351.

James P. Collins, Jr.
William D. Naeve
David A. Winkle
Philip S. Gutierrez
Brian R. Hill
Edward M. Rubinstein

Amy E. Abdo
Gregory A. Sargenti
Terry L. Kesinger
Richard E. A. Dwyer
Cynthia L.K. Steele
Michelle Lee Flores

References: American City Bank (Downtown Branch); Security Pacific Bank (7th and Grand Branch); Bank of America.

For full biographical listings, see the Martindale-Hubbell Law Directory

HAIGHT, BROWN & BONESTEEL (AV)

A Partnership including Professional Corporations
Suite 900, 5 Hutton Centre Drive, 92707
Telephone: 714-754-1100
Telecopier: 714-754-0826
Santa Monica, California Office: 1620 26th Street, Suite 4000 North, P.O. Box 680.
Telephone: 310-449-6000.
Telecopier: 310-829-5117.
Telex: 705837.
Riverside, California Office: 3750 University Avenue, Suite 650.
Telephone: 909-341-8300.
Fax: 909-341-8309.

RESIDENT MEMBERS

Ronald C. Kline (A Professional Corporation)
Bruce L. Cleeland
Jay T. Thompson

ASSOCIATES

Paul N. Jacobs
Laura M. Knox (Resident)
Jeffrey S. Gerardo (Resident)
Jenifer L. Johnston

Counsel for: Orange County: Aetna Casualty and Surety Co.; Zurich-American Insurance Cos.; Industrial Indemnity Co.; Professional Liability Claims Managers; Maryland Casualty Insurance Co.; Royal Insurance Company of America.

For full biographical listings, see the Martindale-Hubbell Law Directory

KLEIN, WEGIS, DENATALE, GOLDNER & MUIR (AV)

Park Tower Building #610, 200 W. Santa Ana Boulevard, 92701
Telephone: 714-285-0711
Fax: 714-285-9003
Bakersfield, California Office: Arco Tower, 4550 California Avenue, Second Floor, P.O. Box 11172.
Telephone: 805-395-1000.
Telecopier: 805-326-0418.

RESIDENT PARTNER

Laurence C. Hall

For full biographical listings, see the Martindale-Hubbell Law Directory

Santa Ana—Continued

RINOS & PACKER (AV)

A Partnership including Professional Corporations
550 North Parkcenter Drive, Suite 100, 92705
Telephone: 714-834-1500
Fax: 714-834-0480
Riverside, California Office: 1770 Iowa Avenue, Suite 170.
Telephone: 909-686-3380.
Fax: 909-686-2732.

MEMBERS OF FIRM

Dimitrios C. Rinos (A Professional Corporation)
Michael R. Packer (A Professional Corporation)
Linda B. Martin
Douglas G. Dickson
Robert C. Shephard

Michael E. Huff
Caleb W. Sullivan
Sandra G. Foraker
Deborah L. Tallon
Keith A. Weaver
Robert C. Risbrough
Matthew D. Barton
John A. Dragonette
Jennifer Lynn Zager
Jill E. Siegel

For full biographical listings, see the Martindale-Hubbell Law Directory

SIKORA AND PRICE, INCORPORATED (AV)

2913 Pullman Street, Suite B, P.O. Box 15707, 92705
Telephone: 714-261-2233
Telecopier: 714-261-6935
Laguna Hills, California Office: Suite 115, 23521 Paseo de Valencia.
Telephone: 714-855-8001.

Warren Sikora
Donald R. Price
Steven C. Crooke
Bruce J. Gary

Christopher Price

For full biographical listings, see the Martindale-Hubbell Law Directory

SPERLING & PERGANDE (AV)

3 Hutton Centre, Suite 670, 92707
Telephone: 714-540-8500
Facsimile: 714-540-2599

MEMBERS OF FIRM

Dean P. Sperling
K. William Pergande

For full biographical listings, see the Martindale-Hubbell Law Directory

SANTA ANA HEIGHTS, Orange Co. — (Refer to Santa Ana)

*SANTA BARBARA,** Santa Barbara Co.

ALLEN AND KIMBELL (AV)

317 East Carrillo Street, 93101
Telephone: 805-963-8611
FAX: 805-962-1940

MEMBERS OF FIRM

W. Joe Bush
Charles D. Kimbell
Paul A. Graziano
Steven K. McGuire
John H. Parke

ASSOCIATES

Jennifer J. Tice

OF COUNSEL

George H. Allen

Reference: Santa Barbara Bank.

For full biographical listings, see the Martindale-Hubbell Law Directory

ARCHBALD & SPRAY (AV)

505 Bath Street, 93101
Telephone: 805-564-2070
Telecopier: 805-564-2081

MEMBERS OF FIRM

Joseph L. Spray (1927-1985)
Kenneth L. Moes
J. William McLafferty
Douglas B. Large
James P. Gazdecki
Karen T. Burgett
Edwin K. Loskamp
Wm. Brennan Lynch
Michael A. Colton
Ann Gormican Anderson

SENIOR ATTORNEYS

Peri Maziarz
Katherine H. Bower

ASSOCIATES

Emmet J. Hawkes

OF COUNSEL

Malcolm Archbald

Representative Clients: Caterpillar Inc.; General Motors Corp.; Lawyers Mutual; City of Lompoc; Nissan Motor Corp.; St. Paul Fire & Marine Insurance Co.; State Farm Insurance Cos.; Volkswagen of America, Inc.; Nationwide Insurance Co.; Travelers Insurance Co.

(See Next Column)

For full biographical listings, see the Martindale-Hubbell Law Directory

HOLLISTER & BRACE, A PROFESSIONAL CORPORATION (AV)

1126 Santa Barbara Street, P.O. Box 630, 93101
Telephone: 805-963-6711
FAX: 805-965-0329

William A. Brace (Retired)
J. James Hollister, III (Retired)
John S. Poucher
Richard C. Monk
George A. Rempe, III
Steven Evans Kirby
Bradford F. Ginder
John G. Busby
Susan H. McCollum
Richard G. Kravetz
Robert L. Brace
Janean Acevedo Daniels
Marcus Scott Bird

OF COUNSEL

Julie A. Turner

Attorneys for: First American Title Insurance Co.; Celite Corp.; Chevron, U.S.A., Inc.; Mission Industries; Gaviota Marine Terminal Co.; Hyatt Hotels; Occidential Petroleum Corp.; Great Universal Capital Corp; Mobil Oil Corp.; Texaco Trading & Transportation Inc.

For full biographical listings, see the Martindale-Hubbell Law Directory

MULLEN & HENZELL (AV)

A Partnership including Professional Corporations
112 East Victoria Street, Post Office Drawer 789, 93102-0789
Telephone: 805-966-1501
FAX: 805-966-9204

MEMBERS OF FIRM

Thomas M. Mullen (1915-1991)
Arthur A. Henzell (Retired)
Philip S. Wilcox
J. Robert Andrews
James W. Brown
Dennis W. Reilly
Jeffrey C. Nelson
Charles S. Bargiel
Joseph F. Green
Gary W. Robinson
Joel C. Baiocchi
Lawrence T. Sorensen
Gregory F. Faulkner
Richard G. Battles
William E. Degen

OF COUNSEL

Kim A. Harley Seefeld

ASSOCIATES

Adam Brooks Firestone
Andrew M. Polinsky
Holly S. Bander
Michael E. Cage
Catherine Perlman
Paul K. Wilcox
Maria May Foulke

Representative Clients: Goleta Sanitary District; Interinsurance Exchange of the Automobile Club of Southern California; State Farm Fire & Casualty Co.; State Farm Mutual Automobile Insurance Co.

For full biographical listings, see the Martindale-Hubbell Law Directory

SCHRAMM & RADDUE (AV)

15 West Carrillo Street, P.O. Box 1260, 93102
Telephone: 805-963-2044
Fax: 805-564-4181

MEMBERS OF FIRM

Edward W. Schramm (1913-1982)
Ralph C. Raddue (1906-1986)
Lawrence M. Parma (1911-1957)
Paul W. Hartloff, Jr.
Dale E. Hanst
Charles H. Jarvis
Douglas E. Schmidt
Kurt H. Pyle
Daniel A. Reicker
Weldon U. Howell, Jr.
Frederick W. Clough
Brian G. Gough
Richard F. Lee
Michael E. Pfau
Edward C. Thoits

ASSOCIATES

Judith E. Koper
Marjorie F. Allen
Christine M. Sontag
Diana Jessup Lee

OF COUNSEL

Howard M. Simon
Bruce W. McRoy

Representative Clients: Berkus Group Architects; Circon Corp.; LaArcada Investment Corp.; Michael Towbes Construction and Development Co.; Santa Barbara Bank & Trust; Santa Barbara Medical Foundation Clinic.

For full biographical listings, see the Martindale-Hubbell Law Directory

*SANTA CRUZ,** Santa Cruz Co.

ATCHISON, ANDERSON, HURLEY & BARISONE, A PROFESSIONAL CORPORATION (AV)

333 Church Street, 95060
Telephone: 408-423-8383
Fax: 408-423-9401
Salinas, California Office: 137 Central Avenue, Suite 6. 93901.
Telephone: 408-755-7833.
Fax: 408-753-0293.

(See Next Column)

ATCHISON, ANDERSON, HURLEY & BARISONE A PROFESSIONAL CORPORATION, *Santa Cruz—Continued*

Rodney R. Atchison
Neal R. Anderson (1947-1986)
Vincent P. Hurley
John G. Barisone

Justin B. Lighty
Mitchell A. Jackman
David Y. Imai
Anthony P. Condotti
Mary C. Logan

Counsel for: City of Santa Cruz.

For full biographical listings, see the Martindale-Hubbell Law Directory

BOSSO, WILLIAMS, LEVIN, SACHS & BOOK, A PROFESSIONAL CORPORATION (AV)

133 Mission Street, Suite 280, P.O. Box 1822, 95061-1822
Telephone: 408-426-8484
Fax: 408-458-9172; 423-2839

Robert E. Bosso
Lloyd R. Williams
Alan J. Levin
Philip M. Sachs
Dennis R. Book
Charlene B. Atack
John M. Gallagher

Catherine A. Rodoni

Representative Clients: Santa Cruz Seaside Co.; World Savings & Loan; Coast Dairies & Land Co.; Sunset Farms, Inc.; Valley Packing Service, Inc.; Soquel Creek Water District.
References: Coast Commercial Bank (Santa Cruz); Pacific Western Bank.

For full biographical listings, see the Martindale-Hubbell Law Directory

SANTA MARIA, Santa Barbara Co.

TWITCHELL AND RICE (AV)

215 North Lincoln Street, P.O. Box 520, 93456-0520
Telephone: 805-925-2611
Telecopier: 805-925-1635

MEMBERS OF FIRM

T. A. Twitchell (1902-1955)
William C. Rice (1924-1960)
Maurice F. Twitchell
Burton J. Twitchell
W. Kenneth Rice

A list of Representative Clients and References will be furnished upon request.

For full biographical listings, see the Martindale-Hubbell Law Directory

SANTA MONICA, Los Angeles Co.

CHALEFF, ENGLISH AND CATALANO (AV)

Garden Suite, 1337 Ocean Avenue, 90401
Telephone: 310-458-1691
Fax: 310-393-6937

MEMBERS OF FIRM

Gerald L. Chaleff
Charles R. English
Paul A. Catalano
Audrey Winograde

Steven Gold

For full biographical listings, see the Martindale-Hubbell Law Directory

GEORGE W. COLLINS, INC. A PROFESSIONAL CORPORATION (AV)

1240 Sixth Street, P.O. Box 2133, 90401
Telephone: 310-451-5584
Fax: 310-458-2907

George W. Collins

Camille J. Everett
Jonathan Eoyang
F. Kevin Loughran
Edward M. Lynch

General Counsel for: Santa Monica Bank, Santa Monica, California; Bowman Merritt Associates.
Reference: Santa Monica Bank, Santa Monica, California.

For full biographical listings, see the Martindale-Hubbell Law Directory

CRANE & McCANN (AV)

530 Wilshire Boulevard, Suite 400, 90401-1423
Telephone: 310-917-9277
Fax: 310-393-7338

MEMBERS OF FIRM

Richard P. Crane, Jr.
Joseph J. McCann, Jr.

(See Next Column)

ASSOCIATES

Lawrence J. Lennemann
John Benedict
Brian D. McMahon
Daniel P. Ayala

For full biographical listings, see the Martindale-Hubbell Law Directory

DICKSON, CARLSON & CAMPILLO (AV)

120 Broadway, Suite 300, P.O. Box 2122, 90407-2122
Telephone: 310-451-2273
Telecopier: 310-451-9071

Robert L. Dickson
Jeffery J. Carlson
Ralph A. Campillo
William B. Fitzgerald
Hall R. Marston
Debra E. Pole
Roxanne M. Wilson
David J. Fleming
George E. Berry
Charles R. Messer
Kathryn C. Grogman
Mark S. Geraghty
William A. Hanssen
Mario Horwitz
Frederick J. Ufkes
Aylene M. Geringer
Daniel D. Rodarte

SPECIAL COUNSEL

Nicholas J. Toghia

Karen S. Bril
Mark C. Riedel
Stephen H. Turner
Brian A. Cardoza
Pamela J. Yates
Robert C. Bohner
Wendy Tucker
Deborah A. Lee-Germain
Jean A. Hobart
Neil M. Popowitz
Thomas M. Madruga
James K. Lee
Michael P. Pizzuti
Georgia Michaels Kyriacou
Yvonne D. Arvanitis
Cori Beth Steinberg
Jane E. Ghaly
David R. Venderbush
Richard L. Daniels
David Adida
Lydia Faith Ng Ho
Gregg Zucker
Helen Glogovac Arens
Lisa J. Kanovsky
Jonathan M. Rolbin
David J. Kaminski
Mimi M. Lee
Marina Maniatis
John A. Chatowski
Robert A. Cocchia

For full biographical listings, see the Martindale-Hubbell Law Directory

HAIGHT, BROWN & BONESTEEL (AV)

A Partnership including Professional Corporations
1620 26th Street, Suite 4000 North, P.O. Box 680, 90404
Telephone: 310-449-6000
Telecopier: 310-829-5117
Telex: 705837
Santa Ana, California Office: Suite 900, 5 Hutton Centre Drive.
Telephone: 714-754-1100.
Telecopier: 714-754-0826.
Riverside, California Office: 3750 University Avenue, Suite 650.
Telephone: 909-341-8300.
Fax: 909-341-8309.
San Francisco, California Office: Suite 300, 201 Sansome Street.
Telephone: 415-986-7700.
Fax: 415-986-6945.

MEMBERS OF FIRM

Sidney A. Moss (1893-1963)
Gerald C. Dunn (1911-1980)
George C. Lyon (1906-1990)
Charles B. Smith (1908-1990)
Fulton Haight (A Professional Corporation)
Harold Hansen Brown (A Professional Corporation)
Michael J. Bonesteel (A Professional Corporation)
Gary C. Ottoson (A Professional Corporation)
Ronald C. Kline (A Professional Corporation) (Resident, Santa Ana Office)
Roy G. Weatherup
William K. Koska (A Professional Corporation)
Peter Q. Ezzell (A Professional Corporation)
Dennis K. Wheeler (A Professional Corporation)
Steven L. Hoch (A Professional Corporation)
John W. Sheller (A Professional Corporation)
William G. Baumgaertner (A Professional Corporation)
Bruce A. Armstrong (A Professional Corporation)
Wayne E. Peterson (A Professional Corporation)
Morton Rosen
Peter A. Dubrawski
Michael J. Leahy
Lori R. Behar
David F. Peterson
Robert L. Kaufman
William J. Sayers
Michael McCarthy
Barry Z. Brodsky
Gary A. Bague
Kathryn M. Forgie
J. R. Seashore
Kevin R. Crisp
Lee Marshall
Bruce L. Cleeland (Resident, Santa Ana Office)
Donald S. Ralphs
George Christensen
Steven E. Moyer
Denis J. Moriarty
Desmond J. Hinds, Jr.
Jules Solomon Zeman
Frank Kendo Berfield (Resident, San Francisco Office)
David L. Jones
Thomas N. Charchut
Neil G. McNiece
Thomas M. Moore
Rita (Sucharita) Gunasekaran
Kenneth G. Anderson
Victor Anderson III
William O. Martin, Jr.
Theresa M. Marchlewski
Jennifer K. Saunders
Mark S. Lester (Resident, Riverside Office)

(See Next Column)

HAIGHT, BROWN & BONESTEEL—*Continued*

MEMBERS OF FIRM (Continued)

Timothy B. Bradford
Amor A. Esteban
William E. Ireland
Lisa L. Oberg (Resident, San Francisco Office)
Jay T. Thompson

ASSOCIATES

Ted J. Duffy
Susan Lerner
David C. McGovern
Paul N. Jacobs (Resident, Santa Ana Office)
Kelly C. McSpadden
Cynthia A. Robins
Marsha L. Palmer
Valerie A. Moore
Birgit Sale
Jon M. Kasimov
Richard E. Wirick
Lisa K. Sepe
Alicia E. Taylor
Stephen M. Caine (Resident, San Francisco Office)
Jeffrey B. Margulies
Dorothy B. Ceccon
Laura M. Knox (Resident, Santa Ana Office)
Andrew J Marton
Nancy E. Lucas
Robin Zukin
Tammy L. Andrews
Nancy Doyle
Pamela F. Worth
Tamara Equals Holmes
Zēb F. Gleason
Margaret Johnson Wiley
Jodi L. Girten
Maureen Haight Gee
Robert D. Wilson
Frances Mary O'Meara
Kevin M. Osterberg (Resident, Riverside Office)
Holly M. Teel
Marti E. Longo
Jeffrey S. Gerardo (Resident, Santa Ana Office)
Armando M. Galvan
Christopher I. Ritter
Sean E. Judge
Lisa J. Golden
Laureen B. Grayson
Daniel J. Kelly
Ronald S. Hodges (Resident, Riverside Office)
Elizabeth A. Livesay
S. Christian Stouder
Thomas J. Roesser
Michael J. Sipos
Cary D. Glassner
Barry J. Thompson
Caroline E. Chan
Nancy W. Carman
Thomas A. Moore
Robert R. Shiri
Mary M. La Cesa
Caroline S. Craddock
Celeste Elig
Michael H. Gottschlich
Jennifer A. Ellis
Russell William Schatz, Jr.
Debra Gemgnani
Joanne Lembert Rosen
Kristine J. Westhaver
Michael S. Kelly (Resident, Riverside Office)
Michael Mark McMahon
John T. Burnite, Jr. (Resident, San Francisco Office)
Caroline Kelley Hunt
Stacey R. Konkoff
Farah Sohaili Nicol
Amy C. Weinreich
Christopher Kendrick
Eric Joseph Chaves
Eric P. Early
Erica St. Louis Krikorian
Barbara Z. Safechuck
Cynthia Weingart Venuti
Suzanne M. VanDer Meulen
Kristine E. Kwong
Douglas Alan Barker
Jenifer L. Johnston (Resident, Santa Ana Office)
Amy E. Moffett
Caroline M. Dee
Derrick F. Coleman
Michael R. Heimbold
George Joseph MacKoul
Karen A. Sinkhorn (Resident, Riverside Office)
Damon B. Bonesteel
Shanna R. Davis
Deborah L. Fink
Jack A. Halprin
Lisa Marie Schinnerer

OF COUNSEL

William M. Fitzhugh
Ira E. Bilson
Richard F. Runkle
R. Roy Finkle
Mitchell Albert
Lyn Skinner Foster
Robert B. Leck III

For full biographical listings, see the Martindale-Hubbell Law Directory

MALONEY & MULLEN, A PROFESSIONAL CORPORATION (AV)

520 Broadway, Suite 300, 90401
Telephone: 310-393-0175
Fax: 310-394-9323

J. William Maloney
Dennis M. Mullen
Jack M. Panagiotis
Charles A. Gruber, Jr.
Christine M. Arden

Reference: Santa Monica Bank.

For full biographical listings, see the Martindale-Hubbell Law Directory

PAUL, HASTINGS, JANOFSKY & WALKER (AV)

A Partnership including Professional Corporations
Firm Established in 1951; Office in 1981
Fifth Floor, 1299 Ocean Avenue, 90401-1078
Telephone: 310-319-3300
Los Angeles, California Office: Twenty-Third Floor, 555 South Flower Street.
Telephone: 213-683-6000.
Cable Address: "Paulhast."
Fax: 910-321-4065.
Orange County, California Office: Seventeenth Floor, 695 Town Center Drive, Costa Mesa.
Telephone: 714-668-6200.
Washington, D.C. Office: Tenth Floor, 1299 Pennsylvania Avenue, N.W.
Telephone: 202-508-9500.

(See Next Column)

Atlanta, Georgia Office: 42nd Floor, Georgia Pacific Center, 133 Peachtree Street, N.E.
Telephone: 404-588-9900.
Stamford, Connecticut Office: Ninth Floor, 1055 Washington Boulevard.
Telephone: 203-961-7400.
New York, New York Office: 31st Floor, 399 Park Avenue.
Telephone: 212-318-6000.
Tokyo, Japan Office: Toranomon Ohtori Building, 8th Floor, 4-3 Toranomon 1-Chome, Minato-Ku.
Telephone: (03) 3507-0730.

COUNSEL

Leonard S. Janofsky
Charles M. Walker

MEMBERS OF FIRM

Nancy L. Abell
Woodson Toliver Besson (P.C.)
Robert M. Dudnik
Eric H. Joss
Keith A. Meyer
Patrick A. Ramsey
Carl W. Shapiro
Robert S. Span
Dennis H. Vaughn
Robert F. Walker
Harry A. Zinn

OF COUNSEL

Jan Elizabeth Eakins
Elliot K. Gordon
Judith L. Meadow
Julia Tachikawa

ASSOCIATES

Julie L. Arias
Mary K. Asher
Linda M. Edwards
Gerard P. Fox
Judith M. Kline
Jenny Schneider
Alan F. Seiffert
Stephen P. Sonnenberg
David T. Van Pelt
Sylvia M. Virsik
Deborah S. Weiser
Teresa K. Zintgraff

For full biographical listings, see the Martindale-Hubbell Law Directory

SACKS & ZWEIG (AV)

A Partnership of Professional Corporations
100 Wilshire Building, Suite 1300, 100 Wilshire Boulevard, 90401
Telephone: 310-451-3113
Facsimile: 310-451-0089

Lee Sacks
Michael K. Zweig
Filomena E. Meyer

OF COUNSEL

Dennis Holahan

For full biographical listings, see the Martindale-Hubbell Law Directory

*SANTA ROSA,** Sonoma Co.

ACHOR, MILLER, CULVER & MAILLIARD (AV)

A Partnership including a Professional Corporation
100 B Street, Suite 200, P.O. Box 5257, 95402
Telephone: 707-571-8112
Fax: 707-575-9116

Christopher R. Miller (P.C.)
David C. Culver
William S. Mailliard, Jr.
Michael E. Kinney
Laura G. Drenning
R. W. Achor (P.C.) (Retired)

Representative Clients: Warrack Medical Center Hospital; WD-40 Co.
Representative Insurance Client: Farmers/Truck Insurance Exchange.

For full biographical listings, see the Martindale-Hubbell Law Directory

ANDERSON, ZEIGLER, DISHAROON, GALLAGHER & GRAY, PROFESSIONAL CORPORATION (AV)

50 Old Courthouse Square, 5th Floor, P.O. Box 1498, 95404
Telephone: 707-545-4910
Fax: 707-544-0260
Other Santa Rosa, California Office: 6641 Oakmont Drive, 95409.
Telephone: 707-539-3880.
Petaluma, California Office: 715 Southpoint Boulevard, 94952.
Telephone: 707-763-0937.

Edwin C. Anderson, Jr.
Kirt F. Zeigler
Robert Disharoon
Barbara Detrich Gallagher
Margaret M. Elliott
David G. Bjornstrom
Robert S. Rutherfurd
Christopher M. Mazzia

Tricia A. Shindledecker
Jeremy L. Olsan
Wendy D. Whitson
Daniel E. Post

OF COUNSEL

Gerald W. Gray
B. Scott Foster
John J. King, Jr.

LEGAL SUPPORT PERSONNEL

Daniel B. Flock (Director of Information)

For full biographical listings, see the Martindale-Hubbell Law Directory

Santa Rosa—Continued

BELDEN, ABBEY, WEITZENBERG & KELLY, A PROFESSIONAL CORPORATION (AV)

1105 North Dutton Avenue, P.O. Box 1566, 95402
Telephone: 707-542-5050
Telecopier: 707-542-2589

Clarendon W. Anderson (1895-1987)
Lester M. Belden (1927-1993)
Thomas P. Kelly, Jr.
Richard W. Abbey
W. Barton Weitzenberg
Candace H. Shirley
Timothy W. Hoffman

Wayne R. Wolski
Lewis R. Warren
Dennis J. Byrne
Peter J. Walls

Representative Clients: Exchange Bank of Santa Rosa; Westamerica Bank; North Bay Title Co.; Northwestern Title Security Co.; Geyser Peak Winery; Arrowood Vineyards & Winery; Hansel Ford; Santa Rosa City School District; Prestige Imports; Henry Curtis Ford Mercury.

For full biographical listings, see the Martindale-Hubbell Law Directory

BRONSON, BRONSON & MCKINNON (AV)

A Partnership including Professional Corporations
100 B Street, Suite 400, 95401
Telephone: 707-527-8110
Fax: 707-575-8143
San Francisco, California Office: 505 Montgomery Street.
Telephone: 415-986-4200.
Los Angeles, California Office: 444 South Flower Street, 24th Floor.
Telephone: 213-627-2000.
San Jose, California Office: 10 Almaden Boulevard, Suite 600.
Telephone: 408-293-0599.

RESIDENT PARTNERS

John G. Mackie, Jr.
T. Scott Tate
Delphine Szyndrowski Adams

RESIDENT OF COUNSEL

Richard W. Power
Mary M. Bush

RESIDENT ASSOCIATES

Dawn Lee Ross

CONTRACT

Kimberly Corcoran

For full biographical listings, see the Martindale-Hubbell Law Directory

JAMES, BERNHEIM & HICKS (AV)

1330 North Dutton Avenue, Suite 200, P.O. Box 12009, 95406
Telephone: 707-528-7555
Fax: 707-528-2307

MEMBERS OF FIRM

C. Kenneth James, Jr.
Lawrence Bernheim
Richard J. Hicks
Tadd C. Aiona
Ian Gordon
Roger J. Illsley

Representative Clients: Albertson's, Inc.; Home Insurance Co.; General Motors Corp.; Great American Insurance Co.; Nationwide Insurance Co.; Redwood Empire Municipal Insurance Fund; Safeco Insurance Cos.; Safeway Stores, Inc.; The Travelers Insurance Co.; Western Surety Co.

For full biographical listings, see the Martindale-Hubbell Law Directory

ROPERS, MAJESKI, KOHN & BENTLEY, A PROFESSIONAL CORPORATION (AV)

Fountaingrove Center, Suite 300, 3558 Round Barn Boulevard, 95403
Telephone: 707-524-4200
Fax: 707-523-4610
Redwood City, California Office: 1001 Marshall Street.
Telephone: 415-364-8200.
Fax: 415-367-0997.
San Jose, California Office: 80 North 1st Street.
Telephone: 408-287-6262.
Fax: 408-297-6819.
San Francisco, California Office: 670 Howard Street.
Telephone: 415-543-4800.
Fax: 415-512-1574.
Los Angeles, California Office: 550 South Hope Street, Suite 1900.
Telephone: 213-312-2000.
Fax: 213-312-2001.
Sacramento, California Office: 1000 G Street, Suite 400.
Telephone: 916-556-3100.
Fax: 916-442-7121.

Daniel J. Lanahan
Martin T. Reilley
Gigi M. Knudtson
Geza Kadar, Jr.
Robert J. Intner
Sue Carol Rokaw
Daniel F. Crowley
Cynthia Ribas Rosen
Kevin MacDougald
Debra Ann Crow

(See Next Column)

Nancie J. Mika
Kevin M. Maguire
Steven M. Goldberg
Tammy M. Alcock
Cheryl A. Hoey
Deanna J. Shirley
Patrick Kevin O'Brien
Jineen Tara Cuddy
Timothy R. Fulkerson

OF COUNSEL

Douglas H. Bosco

For full biographical listings, see the Martindale-Hubbell Law Directory

*SONORA,** Tuolumne Co. — (Refer to Modesto)

*STOCKTON,** San Joaquin Co.

BRAY, GEIGER, RUDQUIST & NUSS (AV)

400 Bank of Stockton Building, 311 East Main Street, 95202
Telephone: 209-948-0434
Fax: 209-948-9451

MEMBERS OF FIRM

Mark S. Bray
Dennis D. Geiger
John B. Rudquist
James T. C. Nuss
Alan R. Coon
Anthony S. Guerriero
Steven P. Emrick

ASSOCIATES

Laureen J. Keen
Jeffrey S. Nelson

Representative Clients: Bank of Stockton; Stockton Savings Bank, F.S.B.; Georgia-Pacific Corp.; Holly Sugar Corp.; South San Joaquin Irrigation District; Banta-Carbona Irrigation District; Stockton Newspapers Inc.; University of the Pacific.

For full biographical listings, see the Martindale-Hubbell Law Directory

DIEHL, STEINHEIMER, RIGGIO, HAYDEL & MORDAUNT, A PROFESSIONAL LAW CORPORATION (AV)

400 East Main Street, Suite 600, 95290
Telephone: 209-464-8732
Fax: 209-464-9165
Mailing Address: P.O. Box 201072, Stockton, California, 95201-3022
Sonora, California Office: 38 North Washington Street, Suite A.
Telephone: 209-532-1424.
Fax: 209-532-4233.

M. Max Steinheimer
Donald M. Riggio
Douglas A. Haydel
Michael R. Mordaunt
Peter J. Kelly
P. Gary Cassel
Scott Malm
Mark F. Ornellas
Joseph H. Fagundes
William D. Johnson
Frank J. Enright
Kate Powell Segerstrom (Resident, Sonora Office)
Kevin M. Seibert
Scott A. Ginns
Tamara M. Polley
Edward S. Maxwell
David W. Culp
Kay E. Gorman
Elizabeth R. Bogart
Darin T. Judd
Frank R. Perrott
Lance Burtis Smith
Rachelle C. Sanchez

OF COUNSEL

Joseph W. Diehl

Counsel for: Pacific Gas and Electric Co.; Kleinfelder Inc.; Turlock Irrigation District.
Insurance Clients: Allied Insurance Group; Design Professional Insurance Co.; The Doctors Co.; Kemper Insurance Co.; Norcal Mutual Insurance Co.; The Travelers.

For full biographical listings, see the Martindale-Hubbell Law Directory

KROLOFF, BELCHER, SMART, PERRY & CHRISTOPHERSON (AV)

7540 Shoreline Drive, P.O. Box 692050, 95269-2050
Telephone: 209-478-2000
Fax: 209-478-0354

FOUNDING PARTNERS

Yale S. Kroloff (1907-1987)
Richard Belcher (Retired)

MEMBERS OF FIRM

Claude H. Smart, Jr.
Thomas O. Perry
Gary Christopherson
J. Douglas Van Sant
John F. Strangman
Orlie L. Curtis
Christopher H. Engh
Elizabeth Humphreys
Lesley D. Holland
Velma K. Lim
Robert J. Harrington
Kim A. Smith

ASSOCIATES

Randy G. Lockwood
Phyllis S. Berger
Thomas V. Hinshaw
Kathleen M. Abdallah
Ron A. Northup
Michael J. Christian

Counsel for: American Savings; Moorman Manufacturing Company of California; Foster Farms.
Representative Clients: Allstate Insurance Co.; California Casualty Indemnity Exchange; CIGNA; Farmers Insurance Group; Nationwide Insurance; Transamerica Insurance; Zurich-American.

(See Next Column)

KROLOFF, BELCHER, SMART, PERRY & CHRISTOPHERSON—*Continued*

For full biographical listings, see the Martindale-Hubbell Law Directory

NEUMILLER & BEARDSLEE, A PROFESSIONAL CORPORATION (AV)

5th Floor, Waterfront Office Towers II, 509 West Weber Avenue, P.O. Box 20, 95201-3020
Telephone: 209-948-8200
Fax: 209-948-4910

Charles L. Neumiller (1873-1933)
George A. Ditz (1889-1971)
Irving L. Neumiller (1899-1970)
Thomas J. Shephard, Sr.
Duncan R. McPherson
Rudy V. Bilawski
Robert C. Morrison
James R. Dyke
James A. Askew
John W. Stovall
Steven A. Herum
Richard M. Archbold
Michael J. Dyer
Paul N. Balestracci
Steven D. Crabtree
Jeanne Marie Zolezzi
Thomas E. Jeffry, Jr.

OF COUNSEL

Robert L. Beardslee
Christopher A. Greene

Brooke K. Birkie
Daniel J. Schroeder
Thomas H. Terpstra
Carrie L. Brown
Clifford W. Stevens
Craig M. Willey
Dana R. Rivers
Daniel S. Truax
Leah S. Goldberg
Karna E. Harrigfeld
Michael D. Daudt
Dwayne C. King
Robert K. Sandman
Matthew I. Friedrich
Lynette B. Veenstra

Representative Clients: Roman Catholic Bishop of Stockton; Diamond Walnut-Sunsweet; Equitable Insurance Co.; The Grupe Cos.; Kaufman & Broad; Central Valley, Inc.; St. Joseph's Regional Health System & Medical Center; Solano County Water Agency; Stockton-East Water District; Teichert Aggregate; Thrifty Corporation.

For full biographical listings, see the Martindale-Hubbell Law Directory

TARZANA, Los Angeles Co.

WASSERMAN, COMDEN & CASSELMAN (AV)

5567 Reseda Boulevard, Suite 330, P.O. Box 7033, 91357-7033
Telephone: 818-705-6800; 213-872-0995
Fax: 818-345-0162; 818-996-8266

MEMBERS OF FIRM

Steve K. Wasserman
Leonard J. Comden
David B. Casselman
Clifford H. Pearson
Mark S. Roth
Rebecca J. Schroer
Jay N. Rosenwald
Daniel E. Lewis
Crystal A. Zarpas
Gary S. Soter

ASSOCIATES

Joel Fischman
Jeffrey K. Jayson
Catherine Stevenson Garcia
Glenn A. Brown, Jr.
Robin F. Genchel
Lloyd S. Mann
J. Christopher Bennington
Paul H. Lasky
Norman L. Pearl
Todd A. Chamberlain
Howard S. Blum
Ted G. Schwartz
Richard A. Brownstein
Albert G. Turner, Jr.
Kenneth M. Jones
Sharon Zemel
Robert T. Leonard
Stephen D. Adler
Keith Nussbaum
L. Stephen Albright
John A. Raymond
Penny L. Wheat
Caroline S. Manankichian

OF COUNSEL

Cecilia S. Wu
John P. Doyle

Representative Clients: Toplis & Harding; Appalachian Insurance; Lumbermens Mutual Insurance Co.; State Farm Fire and Casualty Co.; Factory Mutual Engineering; Cravens, Dargan & Co.; Lloyd's of London.

For full biographical listings, see the Martindale-Hubbell Law Directory

TEMPLE CITY, Los Angeles Co. — (Refer to Arcadia)

THOUSAND OAKS, Ventura Co.

ENGLAND, WHITFIELD, SCHRÖEDER & TREDWAY (AV)

Rolling Oaks Office Center, 351 Rolling Oaks Drive, 91360
Telephone: 805-485-9627; Southern California Toll Free: 800-255-3485
Oxnard, California Office: 6th Floor, Union Bank Tower, 300 Esplanade Drive.
Telephones: 805-485-9627; Ventura: 647-8237; Southern California Toll Free: 800-255-3485.
Fax: 805-983-0297.

MEMBERS OF FIRM

Robert W. Schröeder
Stuart A. Comis
Mitchel B. Kahn
Eric J. Kananen

For full biographical listings, see the Martindale-Hubbell Law Directory

TORRANCE, Los Angeles Co.

FINER, KIM & STEARNS (AV)

An Association of Professional Corporations
City National Bank Building, 3424 Carson Street, Suite 500, 90503
Telephone: 310-214-1477
Telecopier: 310-214-0764

Harry J. Kim (A Professional Corporation)
W. A. Finer (A Professional Corporation)

Robert David Ciaccio
Robert B. Parsons
Mark Andrew Hooper

OF COUNSEL

Bennett A. Rheingold
Ryan E. Stearns

LEGAL SUPPORT PERSONNEL

Marcia E. Talbert

For full biographical listings, see the Martindale-Hubbell Law Directory

*UKIAH,** Mendocino Co. — (Refer to Lakeport)

UPLAND, San Bernardino Co.

ALTHOUSE & BAMBER (AV)

Second Floor, Home Federal Savings & Loan Building, 188 North Euclid Avenue, P.O. Box 698, 91785
Telephone: 909-985-9828
Telecopier: 909-985-3282

Charles S. Althouse
James E. Bamber (1947-1989)
Sherril L. Alexander
Elizabeth A. McDonough

References: Security Pacific National Bank, Upland Branch; First National Bank & Trust Company, Upland Branch.

For full biographical listings, see the Martindale-Hubbell Law Directory

VALLEJO, Solano Co.

DUNN, ROGASKI, PREOVOLOS & WEBER (AV)

241 Georgia Street, P.O. Box 1072, 94590
Telephone: 707-553-1555

MEMBERS OF FIRM

Robert C. Dunn
Chester A. Rogaski, Jr.
Michael J. Preovolos
Howard R. Weber

ASSOCIATES

Jill Noonan
Stephen J. Liberatore
Jeffrey S. Olds

Representative Clients: Exxon, U.S.A.; Norcal Mutual Insurance Co.; Nationwide Insurance Co.; Medical Insurance Exchange of California; California Insurance Guarantee Assn.; Scottsdale Insurance Co.
Reference: Bank of America, NT & SA.

For full biographical listings, see the Martindale-Hubbell Law Directory

FAVARO, LAVEZZO, GILL, CARETTI & HEPPELL, A PROFESSIONAL CORPORATION (AV)

Suite A Courthouse Plaza, 300 Tuolumne Street, 94590
Telephone: 707-552-3630
Facsimile: 707-552-8913

Bernard J. Favaro
Albert M. Lavezzo
Thomas L. Gill
Gary K. Heppell
Louis S. Caretti
Deborah Durr Ferras

For full biographical listings, see the Martindale-Hubbell Law Directory

*VENTURA,** Ventura Co.

BENTON, ORR, DUVAL & BUCKINGHAM, A PROFESSIONAL CORPORATION (AV)

39 North California Street, P.O. Box 1178, 93002
Telephone: 805-648-5111; 656-1166
Fax: 805-648-7218

James T. Sherren
Ronald L. Colton
Robert A. Davidson
Thomas E. Olson
Dean W. Hazard
Brenda L. DeHart

Mark S. Borrell

Counsel for: American Commercial Bank; Petoseed Co., Inc.
Trial Counsel for: Southern California Edison Co.; Shell Oil Co.; Automobile Club of Southern California; Southern California Physicians Insurance Exchange.

For full biographical listings, see the Martindale-Hubbell Law Directory

Ventura—Continued

LAW OFFICES OF FREDERICK H. BYSSHE, JR. (AV)

10 South California Street, 93001
Telephone: 805-648-3224
Fax: 805-653-0267

Terence Geoghegan

For full biographical listings, see the Martindale-Hubbell Law Directory

ENGLE & BRIDE (AV)

353 San Jon Road, 93001
Telephone: 805-643-2200
Fax: 805-643-3062

MEMBERS OF FIRM

Benjamin J. Engle
Robert F. Bride

ASSOCIATES

Walter M. Leighton
Daniel J. Carobine
Gary M. Schumacher
Matthew P. Guasco

For full biographical listings, see the Martindale-Hubbell Law Directory

FERGUSON, CASE, ORR, PATERSON & CUNNINGHAM (AV)

1050 South Kimball Road, 93004
Telephone: 805-659-6800
Telecopier: 805-659-6818

Thomas R. Ferguson
Michael W. Case
John C. Orr
William E. Paterson
David L. Cunningham
Lou Carpiac
Joseph L. Strohman, Jr.
Allen F. Camp
Robert L. Gallaway
Sandra M. Robertson
William B. Smith

Annette M. Lercel
Ramon L. Guizar
Gisele Goetz
Gregory W. Herring
Douglas E. Kulper

Representative Clients: First American Title Insurance Company; Wells Fargo Bank; Lincoln Title Insurance Co.; The Hahn Company (Oaks Regional Shopping Center); Area Housing Authority of the County of Ventura; Buenaventura Medical Clinic, Inc.; H.F. Ahmanson Company; Southern Pacific Milling Company; USA Petroleum Corporation; Cellular One.

For full biographical listings, see the Martindale-Hubbell Law Directory

LASCHER & LASCHER, A PROFESSIONAL CORPORATION (AV)

605 Poli Street, P.O. Box 25540, 93002
Telephone: 805-648-3228
Fax: 805-643-7692

Edward L. Lascher (1928-1991)
Wendy Cole Lascher
Gabriele Mezger-Lashly

Reference: First National Bank of Ventura.

For full biographical listings, see the Martindale-Hubbell Law Directory

MUEGENBURG, NORMAN & DOWLER, A PROFESSIONAL LAW CORPORATION (AV)

840 County Square Drive, 93003
Telephone: 805-654-0911
Fax: 805-654-1902

Richard M. Norman
F. T. Muegenburg, Jr.
Peter C. Dowler
Robert M. Sawyer
Michael M. Israel
Diana G. Hancock
Margaret Keller
Eugenia M. Bernacchi

William J. Corbett
Michael G. Walker
Loye M. Barton

OF COUNSEL

James D. Loebl

For full biographical listings, see the Martindale-Hubbell Law Directory

*VISALIA,** Tulare Co.

KLOSTER, RUDDELL, HORNBURG, COCHRAN, STANTON & SMITH (AV)

1102 North Chinowth Road, Suite A, 93291-4113
Telephone: 209-733-5770
Fax: 209-733-4922

MEMBERS OF FIRM

Gary H. Ruddell
Richard H. Cochran
Philip T. Hornburg
Glenn A. Stanton
D. Zackary Smith

(See Next Column)

ASSOCIATES

Michael A. Gulla

RETIRED

Erling H. Kloster

Representative Clients: Dairyman's Cooperative Creamery Assn.; Kaweah Delta Water Conservation District; Wileman Brothers & Elliott, Inc.; Visalia Medical Clinic, Inc.; Visalia Community Bank.

For full biographical listings, see the Martindale-Hubbell Law Directory

WALNUT CREEK, Contra Costa Co.

MCCUTCHEN, DOYLE, BROWN & ENERSEN (AV)

1331 North California Boulevard Post Office Box V, 94596-4502
Telephone: 510-937-8000
Facsimile: 510-975-5390
San Francisco, California Office: Three Embarcadero Center, 94111-4066.
Telephone: 415-393-2000.
Facsimile: 415-393-2286 (G I, II, III).
Telex: 340817 MACPAG SFO.
Los Angeles, California Office: 355 South Grand Avenue, Suite 4400, 90071-1560.
Telephone: 213-680-6400.
Facsimile: 213-680-6499.
San Jose, California Office: Market Post Tower, Suite 1500, 55 South Market Street, 95113-2327.
Telephone: 408-947-8400.
Facsimile: 408-947-4750.
Telex: 910 250 2931 MACPAG SJ.
Menlo Park, California Office: 2740 Sand Hill Road, 94025-7020.
Telephone: 415-233-4000.
Facsimile: 415-233-4086.
Washington, D.C. Office: The Evening Star Building, Suite 800, 1101 Pennsylvania Avenue, N.W., 20004-2514.
Telephone: 202-628-4900.
Facsimile: 202-628-4912.
Taipei, Taiwan Republic of China Office: International Trade Building, Tenth Floor, 333 Keelung Road, Section 1, 110.
Telephone: 886-2-723-5000.
Facsimile: 886-2-757-6070.
Affiliated Offices In: Bangkok, Thailand; Beijing, China; Shanghai, China.

MEMBERS OF FIRM

William H. Armstrong
Gilbert C. Berkeley
Daniel J. Curtin, Jr.
Michael P. Durkee
Roger D. Ehlers
James B. Ellis
Sandra A. Golze
Michael L. Greene
Stephen L. Kostka
Palmer Brown Madden
Edward S. Merrill
Robert E. Merritt
Geoffrey L. Robinson
Sanford M. Skaggs

COUNSEL

Marie A. Cooper
David I. Katzen
Maria P. Rivera
Jane Cosgriff Sullwold

ASSOCIATES

Sharon J. Adams
Brandt Andersson
Maria Bee
Grant A. Guerra
Gregory A. Randall
Barbara J. Schussman

For full biographical listings, see the Martindale-Hubbell Law Directory

MILLER, STARR & REGALIA, A PROFESSIONAL LAW CORPORATION (AV)

1331 North California Boulevard, Suite 700, 94596
Telephone: 510-935-9400
Oakland, California Office: 16th Floor, Ordway Building, One Kaiser Plaza.
Telephone: 510-465-3800.

Marvin B. Starr (Resident)
Richard G. Carlston (Resident)
Karl Erich Geier (Resident)
Paul D. Marienthal (Resident)
George B. Speir (Resident)
Michael J. Hassen
Lynne Yerkes

Donald H. Baum
Heidi Timken

For full biographical listings, see the Martindale-Hubbell Law Directory

WHITTIER, Los Angeles Co.

BEWLEY, LASSLEBEN & MILLER (AV)

A Law Partnership including Professional Corporations
Suite 510 Whittier Square, 13215 East Penn Street, 90602
Telephone: 310-698-9771; 723-8062; 714-994-5131
Telecopier: 310-696-6357

MEMBERS OF FIRM

Thomas W. Bewley (1903-1986)
William M. Lassleben, Jr. (A Professional Corporation)
Edward L. Miller (A Professional Corporation)
J. Terrence Mooschekian
Richard A. Hayes (A Professional Corporation)
Ernie Zachary Park (A Professional Corporation)
Robert H. Dewberry (A Professional Corporation)

(See Next Column)

BEWLEY, LASSLEBEN & MILLER—*Continued*

MEMBERS OF FIRM (Continued)

Richard L. Dewberry (A Professional Corporation)
Jeffrey S. Baird
Kevin P. Duthoy
Joseph A. Vinatieri
Jason C. Demille
Suzanne R. Kramer
John P. Godsil
Peter B. Fan

Representative Clients: Quaker City Federal Savings & Loan Assn.; Whittier College; Presbyterian Intercommunity Hospital; Bank of Whittier; Circuit Systems, Inc.; Lockhart Industries, Inc.; Subdivided Land, Inc.; United Ad-Label Co., Inc.
References: Bank of America National Trust & Savings Assn. (Whittier Main Office); Southern California Bank.

For full biographical listings, see the Martindale-Hubbell Law Directory

THOMSON & NELSON, A PROFESSIONAL LAW CORPORATION (AV)

Suite 400, 15111 East Whittier Boulevard, 90603-2189
Telephone: 310-945-3536
714-680-0674
Telecopier: 310-693-2866

Alexander D. Thomson
John G. Nelson

Laura Ann Davis
Michael A. Rule

Representative Clients: Blue Hills Nursery; Copzel Properties; E. B. Manning & Son, Inc.; Great Western Hotels Corporation; ICBO Evaluation Service, Inc.; International Conference of Building Officials; Shima Pearl, Inc.; Sunset Tropicals, Inc.; Trico Trading Co.; Zelman Development Co.

For full biographical listings, see the Martindale-Hubbell Law Directory

*WILLOWS,** Glenn Co. — (Refer to Chico)

WOODLAND HILLS, Los Angeles Co.

KINDEL & ANDERSON (AV)

A Partnership including Professional Corporations
Suite 244, 5959 Topanga Canyon Boulevard, 91367
Telephone: 818-712-0036
Los Angeles, California Office: Twenty-Ninth Floor, 555 South Flower Street.
Telephone: 213-680-2222.
Irvine, California Office: 5 Park Plaza, Suite 1000.
Telephone: 714-752-0777.
San Francisco, California Office: 580 California Street, 15th Floor.
Telephone: 415-398-0110.

MEMBERS OF FIRM

David Gurnick (Resident)
Christopher J. Husa (Resident)
David Laufer (Resident Partner in Charge)
Michael P. Lewis (Resident)

ASSOCIATES

Susanne M. Bendavid-Arbiv (Resident)

For full biographical listings, see the Martindale-Hubbell Law Directory

*YUBA CITY,** Sutter Co. — (Refer to Marysville)

COLORADO

*AKRON,** Washington Co.

W.B. Paynter, P.C. (AV)

117 Main Street, P.O. Box A, 80720
Telephone: 303-345-2219
FAX: 303-345-2210

William B. Paynter, Jr.

Representative Clients: First National Bank of Akron; First National Bank of Otis; Farmers Home Administration.

For full biographical listings, see the Martindale-Hubbell Law Directory

*ALAMOSA,** Alamosa Co.

Lucero, Lester & Sigmond (AV)

311 San Juan Avenue, P.O. Box 1270, 81101-1270
Telephone: 719-589-6626
Telecopier: 719-589-5555

Carlos F. Lucero
James K. Lester
Helen Sigmond

David A. Rooney
Erich Schwiesow

OF COUNSEL

Richard A. Kadinger

For full biographical listings, see the Martindale-Hubbell Law Directory

*ASPEN,** Pitkin Co.

Austin, Peirce & Smith, P.C. (AV)

Suite 205, 600 East Hopkins Avenue, 81611
Telephone: 303-925-2600
FAX: 303-925-4720

Ronald D. Austin
Frederick F. Peirce
Thomas Fenton Smith

Rhonda J. Bazil

Counsel for: Clark's Market; Coates, Reid & Waldron Realtors; Crystal Palace Corp.; Snowmass Shopping Center; Coldwell Banker; William Poss & Assoc., Architects; Snowmass Resort Association; Real Estate Affiliates, Inc.; Raleigh Enterprises.

For full biographical listings, see the Martindale-Hubbell Law Directory

Holland & Hart (AV)

600 East Main Street, 81611
Telephone: 303-925-3476
Telecopier: 303-925-9367
Denver, Colorado Office: Suite 2900, 555 Seventeenth Street. P.O. Box 8749.
Telephone: 303-295-8000.
Cable Address: "Holhart Denver."
Telecopier: 303-295-8261.
TWX: 910-931-0568.
Denver Tech Center, Colorado Office: Suite 1050, 4601 DTC Boulevard.
Telephone: 303-290-1600.
Telecopier: 303-290-1606.
Boulder, Colorado Office: Suite 500, 1050 Walnut.
Telephone: 303-473-2700.
Telecopier: 303-473-2720.
Colorado Springs, Colorado Office: Suite 1000, 90 S. Cascade Avenue.
Telephone: 719-475-7730.
Telex: 820770 SHHTLX.
Telecopier: 719-634-2461.
Washington, D.C. Office: Suite 310, 1001 Pennsylvania Avenue, N.W.
Telephone: 202-638-5500.
Telecopier: 202-737-8998.
Boise, Idaho Office: Suite 1400, West One Plaza, 101 South Capitol Boulevard, P.O. Box 2527.
Telephone: 208-342-5000.
Telecopier: 208-343-8869.
Billings, Montana Office: Suite 1500, First Interstate Center, 401 North 31st Street, P.O. Box 639.
Telephone: 406-252-2166.
Telecopier: 406-252-1669.
Cheyenne, Wyoming Office: Holland & Hart, A Partnership including Professional Corporations, Suite 500, 2020 Carey Avenue, P.O. Box 1347.
Telephone: 307-778-4200.
Telecopier: 307-778-8175.
Jackson, Wyoming Office: Holland & Hart, A Partnership including Professional Corporations, Suite 2, 175 South King Street, P.O. Box 68.
Telephone: 307-739-9741.
Telecopier: 307-739-9744.
Salt Lake City, Utah Office: Suite 880, 111 East Broadway.
Telephone: 801-578-6000.
FAX: 801-578-6010.

(See Next Column)

RESIDENT PARTNERS

James T. Moran
Arthur C. Daily
Charles T. Brandt
Arthur B. Ferguson, Jr.

RESIDENT OF COUNSEL

James B. Boyd
Thomas J. Todd

For full biographical listings, see the Martindale-Hubbell Law Directory

J. Nicholas McGrath, P.C. (AV)

Suite 203, 600 East Hopkins Avenue, 81611
Telephone: 303-925-2612
Telecopier: 303-925-4402

J. Nicholas McGrath

Cynthia C. Tester
Susan W. Laatsch (Not admitted in CO)

Representative Clients: Alpine Surveys, Inc.; Aspen Alps Condominium Assn.; Aspen Center for Physics; Gant Condominium Assn.; Hotel Jerome Associates, Ltd. Partners; Redstone Investments, Inc. (Cleveholm Castle).

For full biographical listings, see the Martindale-Hubbell Law Directory

Oates, Hughes & Knezevich, P.C. (AV)

Aspen Plaza Building, 3rd Floor, 533 East Hopkins Avenue, 81611
Telephone: 303-920-1700
Telecopier: 303-920-1121

Leonard M. Oates
Richard A. Knezevich
Robert W. Hughes
Ted D. Gardenswartz

OF COUNSEL

John Thomas Kelly

Counsel for: Stapleton Insurance Agency; Silvertree Hotel; Pitkin County Title, Inc.

For full biographical listings, see the Martindale-Hubbell Law Directory

*BOULDER,** Boulder Co.

Howard Bittman (AV)

1406 Pearl Street, Suite 200, 80302
Telephone: 303-443-2281
Fax: 303-443-2862

For full biographical listings, see the Martindale-Hubbell Law Directory

Cook & Lee, P.C. (AV)

Canyonside Office Park, 100 Arapahoe Avenue, Suite 9, 80302-5862
Telephone: 303-444-9700
Fax: 303-444-9691
Denver, Colorado Office: Sherman Street Plaza, 1888 Sherman Street, Suite 375, 80203-1158.
Telephone: 303-831-8008.

Stephen H. Cook
Larry D. Lee

Patti L. Holt
Daniel E. Bronstein

For full biographical listings, see the Martindale-Hubbell Law Directory

Holland & Hart (AV)

Suite 500, 1050 Walnut, 80302
Telephone: 303-473-2700
Telecopier: 303-473-2720
Denver, Colorado Office: Suite 2900, 555 Seventeenth Street, P.O. Box 8749.
Telephone: 303-295-8000.
Cable Address: "Holhart Denver."
Telecopier: 303-295-8261.
TWX: 910-931-0568.
Denver Tech Center, Colorado Office: Suite 1050, 4601 DTC Boulevard.
Telephone: 303-290-1600.
Telecopier: 303-290-1606.
Aspen, Colorado Office: 600 East Main Street.
Telephone: 303-925-3476.
Telecopier: 303-925-9367.
Colorado Springs, Colorado Office: Suite 1000, 90 S. Cascade Avenue.
Telephone: 719-475-7730.
Telex: 82077 SHHTLX.
Telecopier: 719-634-2461.
Washington, D.C. Office: Suite 310, 1001 Pennsylvania Avenue, N.W.
Telephone: 202-638-5500.
Telecopier: 202-737-8998.
Boise, Idaho Office: Suite 1400, West One Plaza, 101 South Capitol Boulevard, P.O. Box 2527.
Telephone: 208-342-5000.
Telecopier: 208-343-8869.

(See Next Column)

HOLLAND & HART—*Continued*

Billings, Montana Office: Suite 1500, First Interstate Center, 401 North 31st Street, P.O. Box 639.
Telephone: 406-252-2166.
Telecopier: 406-252-1669.
Salt Lake City, Utah Office: Suite 880, 111 East Broadway.
Telephone: 801-578-6000.
FAX: 801-578-6010.
Cheyenne, Wyoming Office: Holland & Hart, A Partnership including Professional Corporations, Suite 500, 2020 Carey Avenue, P.O. Box 1347.
Telephone: 307-778-4200.
Telecopier: 307-778-8175.
Jackson, Wyoming Office: Holland & Hart, A Partnership including Professional Corporations, Suite 2, 175 South King Street, P.O. Box 68.
Telephone: 307-739-9741.
Telecopier: 307-739-9744.

PARTNERS

William J. Kubida
William E. Mooz, Jr.
Camron R. Kuelthau
Scott Havlick

OF COUNSEL

Homer L. Knearl
Earl C. Hancock
Francis A. Sirr

BOULDER, COLORADO ASSOCIATES

Jennifer L. Bales
Judith A. (Jude) Biggs

For full biographical listings, see the Martindale-Hubbell Law Directory

HOLME ROBERTS & OWEN LLC (AV)

Suite 400, 1401 Pearl Street, 80302
Telephone: 303-444-5955
Telecopier: 303-444-1063
Denver, Colorado Office: Suite 4100, 1700 Lincoln.
Telephone: 303-861-7000.
Telex: 45-4460.
Telecopier: 303-866-0200.
Colorado Springs, Colorado Office: Suite 1300, 90 South Cascade Avenue.
Telephone: 719-473-3800.
Telecopier: 719-633-1518.
Salt Lake City, Utah Office: Suite 1100, 111 East Broadway.
Telephone: 801-521-5800.
Telecopier: 801-521-9639.
London, England Office: 4th Floor, Mellier House, 26a Albemarle Street.
Telephone: 44-171-499-8776.
Telecopier: 44-171-499-7769.
Moscow, Russia Office: 14 Krivokolenny Pr., Suite 30, 101000.
Telephone: 095-925-7816.
Telecopier: 095-923-2726.

MEMBERS OF FIRM

Glenn E. Porzak (Managing Member)
Paul E. Smith
James R. Ghiselli
William R. Roberts
Richard A. Johnson
Michael F. Browning
Kay M. Small (Resident)
Jill K. Rood

ASSOCIATES

Steven J. Bushong (Resident)
David E. Tenzer (Resident)
Patrick K. Perrin (Resident)
Maureen C. Weston (Resident)

For full biographical listings, see the Martindale-Hubbell Law Directory

HURTH, YEAGER & SISK (AV)

4860 Riverbend Road, P.O. Box 17850, 80308
Telephone: 303-443-7900
Telecopier: 303-443-8733

MEMBERS OF FIRM

John M. Yeager
Christopher W. Blakemore
Charles L. Sisk
Beverly C. Nelson
Barbara J. Gifford

OF COUNSEL

Charles A. Hurth, Jr.
Edward R. Kellenberger

Representative Clients: Colorado National Bank, Boulder; Boulder Valley Bank and Trust; Bank of Louisville; Commonwealth Land Title Insurance Co.; Data Storage Marketing, Inc.; Ugland USA, Inc.
References: Colorado National Bank, Boulder; Boulder Valley National Bank.

For full biographical listings, see the Martindale-Hubbell Law Directory

PURVIS, GRAY, SCHUETZE & GORDON (AV)

The Exeter Building, Suite 501, 1050 Walnut Street, 80302
Telephone: 303-442-3366
Fax: 303-440-3688
Denver, Colorado Office: 303 East 17th Avenue, Suite 700.
Telephone: 303-860-1888.

MEMBERS OF FIRM

William R. Gray
Robert A. Schuetze
John A. Purvis
Glen F. Gordon

For full biographical listings, see the Martindale-Hubbell Law Directory

*BRECKENRIDGE,** Summit Co.

FRENCH, WEST & BROWN, P.C. (AV)

Suite 204, 100 South Ridge Street, P.O. Box 588, 80424
Telephone: 303-453-2901
Fax: 303-453-0192

Robert H. S. French
Stephen C. West
D. Wayne Brown

Lynne M. Sholler
Felice Furst Huntley
Garth Q. Ainslie

LEGAL SUPPORT PERSONNEL
LEGAL ASSISTANT

Mary Casey Michaelson

Representative Clients: McG Outlet Centers Limited Partnership; Rec Sports, Inc.; Breckenridge Brewery, Inc.; Snake River Water District; Coldwell Banker Bunchman Real Estate; Breckenridge Building Center, Inc.; Breckenville Management Corp.
Reference: The Bank, N.A., Breckenridge.

For full biographical listings, see the Martindale-Hubbell Law Directory

*BRIGHTON,** Adams Co.

DANIEL, MCCAIN, BROWN, WALLACE & BRUBAKER, LLC (AV)

Brighton Professional Building, 105 Bridge Street, 80601
Telephone: 303-659-0731
Telecopier: 303-659-0752
Fort Lupton, Colorado Office: First Security Bank Building.
Telephone: 303-857-2777.

MEMBERS OF FIRM

Orrel A. Daniel
Edward A. Brown
Leonard H. McCain
T. William Wallace
Margaret R. Brubaker

Counsel for: First Security Bank, Fort Lupton, Colo.; Valley Bank, Brighton, Colo.; City of Brighton; City of Ft. Lupton.
Approved Attorneys for: Attorneys Title Guaranty Fund, Inc.
Reference: Valley Bank, Brighton, Colo.

For full biographical listings, see the Martindale-Hubbell Law Directory

BRUSH, Morgan Co. — (Refer to Greeley)

*CANON CITY,** Fremont Co.

FREDRICKSON & JOHNSON, P.C. (AV)

3rd Floor, First National Bank Building, Suite 329, 831 Royal Gorge Boulevard, P.O. Box 889, 81215-0889
Telephone: 719-275-4161
Fax: Available upon request

Robert G. Fredrickson
Bruce Johnson
Bryan T. Fredrickson

Attorneys for: I.O.O.F. of Colorado; Fremont County Board of Realtors; Canon City Area Fire Protection District; St. Thomas More Hospital, Canon City; Royal Gorge Company of Colorado; City of Florence, Colorado.
References: The First National Bank of Canon City; Fremont National Bank.

For full biographical listings, see the Martindale-Hubbell Law Directory

*CASTLE ROCK,** Douglas Co.

FOLKESTAD, KOKISH & FAZEKAS, P.C. (AV)

316 Wilcox Street, 80104-2495
Telephone: 303-688-3045
FAX: 303-688-3189

James B. Folkestad
John Kokish
Ernest F. Fazekas, II

Susan B. Shoemaker
Douglas E. Saunders

Representative Clients: Bank of Douglas County; Johnson & Sons Construction, Inc.; B & W Construction Co.; Proto Construction & Paving, Inc.; Grimm Construction Co.; Ashcroft Homes of Denver LLC.
References: Bank of Douglas County; First National Bank of Castle Rock; First Bank of Castle Rock; Colorado National Bank.

For full biographical listings, see the Martindale-Hubbell Law Directory

*COLORADO SPRINGS,** El Paso Co.

DANIEL P. EDWARDS, P.C. (AV)

Suite 310, 128 South Tejon, 80903
Telephone: 719-634-6620
Fax: 719-634-3142

Daniel P. Edwards

Representative Clients: A.M.I. Industries, Inc.; Analytical Surveys, Inc.; A.C. Israel Enterprises, Inc.; Boddington Lumber Co., Inc.; Cardiovascular Surgeons of Colorado Springs, P.C.; Colorado Springs Radiologists, P.C.; Digi-

(See Next Column)

DANIEL P. EDWARDS, P.C., *Colorado Springs—Continued*

tal, Inc.; Music Semi-Conductors, Inc.; Schlage Lock Co.; Texas Instruments.

For full biographical listings, see the Martindale-Hubbell Law Directory

HALL & EVANS, L.L.C. (AV)

Suite 600, 102 South Tejon Street, 80903
Telephone: 719-578-5600; Toll-Free From Denver Telephone: 303-628-3400
Telecopier: 719-635-7458
Denver
Denver, Colorado Office: Suite 1700, 1200 Seventeenth Street, 80202.
Telephone: 303-628-3300.
Telecopier: 303-628-3368

COLORADO SPRINGS RESIDENT ATTORNEYS

Denis K. Lane, Jr. — Christopher Cipoletti

Jeffrey L. Bodily — Craig W. Cain
Cornelia P. Weiss

For full biographical listings, see the Martindale-Hubbell Law Directory

HECOX, TOLLEY, KEENE & BELTZ, P.C. (AV)

316 North Tejon Street, P.O. Box 316, 80901-0316
Telephone: 719-473-4444
Telecopier: 719-473-4642

Lawrence A. Hecox — Bruce N. Warren
Gerald G. Tolley — H. William Mahaffey
Kenneth P. Keene — Ann S. Irwin Vessels
W. Thomas Beltz — Gilbert G. Weiskopf
John W. Sabo, III — Mary W. Evans

Jeffrey L. Weeks — E. Jay Wells

Representative Clients: Colorado National Bank - Exchange; Merrill Lynch, Pierce, Fenner & Smith; Ford Motor Land Development Corp.; Digital Equipment Co.; Cray Research, Inc.; Liquid Air Corporation; Federal Express Corp.; Junior Achievement, Inc.

For full biographical listings, see the Martindale-Hubbell Law Directory

HOLLAND & HART (AV)

Suite 1000, 90 S. Cascade Avenue, 80903
Telephone: 719-475-7730
Telecopier: 719-634-2461
Telex: 820770 SHHTLX
Denver, Colorado Office: Suite 2900, 555 Seventeenth Street, P.O. Box 8749.
Telephone: 303-295-8000.
Cable Address: "Holhart Denver."
Telecopier: 303-295-8261.
TWX: 910-931-0568.
Denver Tech Center, Colorado Office: Suite 1050, 4601 DTC Boulevard.
Telephone: 303-290-1600.
Telecopier: 303-290-1606.
Aspen, Colorado Office: 600 Main Street.
Telephone: 303-925-3476.
Telecopier: 303-925-9367.
Boulder, Colorado Office: Suite 500, 1050 Walnut.
Telephone: 303-473-2700.
Telecopier: 303-473-2720.
Washington, D.C. Office: Suite 310, 1001 Pennsylvania Avenue, N.W.
Telephone: 202-638-5500.
Telecopier: 202-737-8998.
Boise, Idaho Office: Suite 1400, West One Plaza, 101 South Capitol Boulevard, P.O. Box 2527.
Telephone: 208-342-5000.
Telecopier: 208-343-8869.
Billings, Montana Office: Suite 1500, First Interstate Center, 401 North 31st Street, P.O. Box 639.
Telephone: 406-252-2166.
Telecopier: 406-252-1669.
Cheyenne, Wyoming Office: Holland & Hart, A Partnership including Professional Corporations, Suite 500, 2020 Carey Avenue, P.O. Box 1347.
Telephone: 307-778-4200.
Telecopier: 307-778-8175.
Jackson, Wyoming Office: Holland & Hart, A Partnership including Professional Corporations, Suite 2, 175 South King Street, P.O. Box 68.
Telephone: 307-739-9741.
Telecopier: 307-739-9744.
Salt Lake City, Utah Office: Suite 880, 111 East Broadway.
Telephone: 801-578-6000.
FAX: 801-578-6010.

PARTNERS

John T. Haney (1883-1971) — James B. Day (Retired)
William Q. Haney (1909-1977) — Jack W. Foutch (Retired)
W. Allen Spurgeon (1936-1982) — J. Donald Haney (Retired)
Robert L. Spurgeon (1904-1986) — Irving Howbert (Retired)
Byron L. Akers, Jr. (Retired) — Bruce T. Buell
William R. Aman (Retired) — Ronald M. Martin

(See Next Column)

PARTNERS (Continued)

Ronald A. Lehmann (Resident) — William K. Brown (Resident)
Randolph M. Karsh — Gary R. Burghart (Resident)
Edward H. Flitton (Resident) — William J. Kubida

RESIDENT SPECIAL COUNSEL

Elaine Holland Turner

RESIDENT ASSOCIATES

Brian T. Murphy — Wendy J. Pifher
David Scott Prince

For full biographical listings, see the Martindale-Hubbell Law Directory

HOLME ROBERTS & OWEN LLC (AV)

Suite 1300, 90 South Cascade Avenue, 80903
Telephone: 719-473-3800
Telecopier: 719-633-1518
Denver, Colorado Office: Suite 4100, 1700 Lincoln.
Telephone: 303-861-7000.
Telex: 45-4460.
Telecopier: 303-866-0200.
Boulder, Colorado Office: Suite 400, 1401 Pearl Street.
Telephone: 303-444-5955.
Telecopier: 303-444-1063.
Salt Lake City, Utah Office: Suite 1100, 111 East Broadway.
Telephone: 801-521-5800.
Telecopier: 801-521-9639.
London, England Office: 4th Floor, Mellier House, 26a Albemarle Street.
Telephone: 44-171-499-8776.
Telecopier: 44-171-499-7769.
Moscow, Russia Office: 14 Krivokolenny Pr., Suite 30, 101000.
Telephone: 095-925-7816.
Telecopier: 095-923-2726.

MEMBERS OF FIRM

Richard R. Young (Managing Member) — Michael D. Strugar
Richard L. Nagl — Susan E. Duffey Campbell
Randy G. Bobier — Brent E. Rychener
Steve L. Gaines — John R. Wylie
Thomas M. James
Sharon A. Higgins

ASSOCIATES

Robert J. Kaukol — Dominic Jude Ricotta
Timothy G. Pfeifer (Not admitted in CO) — Walter H. Sargent II
Steven B. Smith
Sharon A. Thomas

For full biographical listings, see the Martindale-Hubbell Law Directory

KANE, DONLEY & SHAFFER (AV)

90 South Cascade Avenue, Suite 1100, P.O. Box 1119, 80901
Telephone: 719-471-1650
Fax: 719-471-1663

MEMBERS OF FIRM

Jerry A. Donley — Thomas Kelly Kane
E. William Shaffer, Jr. — Mark H. Kane
Jack E. Donley

ASSOCIATES

William A. Palmer — Hayden W. Kane, II

OF COUNSEL

Hayden W. Kane

Representative Clients: American States Insurance Co.; Hawkeye-Security Insurance Co.
Reference: Norwest Bank of Colorado Springs.

For full biographical listings, see the Martindale-Hubbell Law Directory

RETHERFORD, MULLEN, JOHNSON & BRUCE (AV)

A Partnership including Professional Corporations
415 South Sahwatch, P.O. Box 1580, 80901
Telephone: 719-475-2014
Fax: 719-630-1267
Pueblo, Colorado Office: Suite 510, 201 West 8th Street, 81003.
Telephone: 719-543-7181.
Fax: 719-543-5650.

MEMBERS OF FIRM

Jerry A. Retherford — Neil C. Bruce
J. Stephen Mullen (P.C.) — Thomas J. Barton (P.C.)
Anthony A. Johnson (P.C.) — Patrick R. Salt
J. Ronald Voss

ASSOCIATES

Lori M. Moore — Chad J. Hessel
Amelia L. Klemme — M. James Zendejas

References: Norwest Banks.

For full biographical listings, see the Martindale-Hubbell Law Directory

Colorado Springs—Continued

SHERMAN & HOWARD L.L.C. (AV)

Attorneys at Law
Suite 1500, 90 South Cascade Avenue, 80903
Telephone: 719-475-2440
Telecopier: 719-635-4576
Denver, Colorado Office: 633 17th Street, Suite 3000, 80202.
Telephone: 303-297-2900.
Las Vegas, Nevada Office: Swendseid & Stern a member in Sherman & Howard L.L.C., 317 Sixth Street, 89101.
Telephone: 702-387-6073
Reno, Nevada Office: Swendseid & Stern, a member in Sherman & Howard L.L.C., 50 West Liberty Street, Suite 660, 89501.
Telephone: 702-323-1980.

Ben S. Wendelken (1899-1991)
William A. Baker (1913-1991)
Raymond M. Deeny
Durward E. Timmons, Jr.
N. Dawn Webber
Glenn H. Schlabs
Jeffrey M. Goldsmith
Bruce A. Kolbezen

Wayne W. Williams
Milton L. "Skip" Smith, III
Thomas E. O'Connor, Jr.

Representative Clients: El Pomar Foundation Co.; Ampex, Inc.; Broadmoor Hotel, Inc.; Signal Processing Technologies, Inc.; Colorado Springs Gazette-Telegraph.
References: Colorado National Bank-Exchange; First National Bank, Colorado Springs; United Bank of Colorado Springs.

For full biographical listings, see the Martindale-Hubbell Law Directory

THE WILLS LAW FIRM (AV)

Holly Sugar Building, 2 North Cascade Avenue, Suite 1000, 80903-1651
Telephone: 719-633-8500
Telecopier: 719-471-7750

MEMBERS OF FIRM

Lee R. Wills
Wm. Andrew Wills, II

For full biographical listings, see the Martindale-Hubbell Law Directory

*CORTEZ,** Montezuma Co. — (Refer to Durango)

*DEL NORTE,** Rio Grande Co. — (Refer to Alamosa)

*DENVER,** Denver Co.

BAKER & HOSTETLER (AV)

303 East 17th Avenue, Suite 1100, 80203-1264
Telephone: 303-861-0600
FAX: 303-861-7805
In Cleveland, Ohio: 3200 National City Center, 1900 East Ninth Street.
Telephone: 216-621-0200.
In Columbus, Ohio: Capitol Square, Suite 2100, 65 East State Street.
Telephone: 614-228-1541.
In Houston, Texas: 1000 Louisiana, Suite 2000.
Telephone: 713-751-1600.
In Long Beach, California: 300 Oceangate, Suite 620.
Telephone: 310-432-2827.
In Los Angeles, California: 600 Wilshire Boulevard. Telephone 213-624-2400.
In Orlando, Florida: SunBank Center, Suite 2300, 200 South Orange Avenue,
Telephone: 305-841-1111.
In Washington, D. C.: Washington Square, Suite 1100, 1050 Connecticut Avenue, N.W.
Telephone: 202-861-1500.
In College Park, Maryland: 9658 Baltimore Boulevard, Suite 206.
Telephone: 301-441-2781.
In Alexandria, Virginia: 437 North Lee Street.
Telephone: 703-549-1294.
In San Francisco, California: One Sansome Street, Suite 2000.
Telephone: 415-951-4705.

MEMBERS OF FIRM IN DENVER, COLORADO

James A. Clark (Managing Partner-Denver Office)

PARTNERS

Timothy R. Beyer
Kenneth J. Burke
Alfred C. Chidester
Kathryn A. Elzi
Marc D. Flink
Phillip S. Lorenzo
Todd L. Lundy
Richard S. Mandelson
James R. Martin
Thomas H. Maxfield
John B. Moorhead
Raymond L. Sutton, Jr.
Victor L. Wallace, II

ASSOCIATES

Mary Price Birk
Stephen D. Gurr
Gerald H. Hansen
Peter J. Korneffel, Jr.
Judith M. Krieg
Michael G. Martin
Michael J. Roche
Marjorie N. Sloan
Michelle M. St. Pierre

(See Next Column)

OF COUNSEL

Gregory S. Brown
Winchester Cooley, III
(Not admitted in CO)
Roger M. Morris
Fred M. Winner

For full biographical listings, see the Martindale-Hubbell Law Directory

BALLARD SPAHR ANDREWS & INGERSOLL (AV)

Seventeenth Street Plaza Building, Suite 2300, 1225 17th Street, 80202-5596
Telephone: 303-292-2400
Fax: 303-296-3956
Philadelphia, Pennsylvania Office: 1735 Market Street, 51st Floor.
Telephone: 215-665-8500.
Fax: 215-864-8999.
Kaunas, Lithuania Office: Donelaičio 71-2, Kaunas 3000.
Telephone: (370-7) 20 56 66.
Fax: (370-7) 20 56 91.
Salt Lake City, Utah Office: One Utah Center, 201 South Main Street, Suite 1200.
Telephone: 801-531-3000.
Fax: 801-531-3001.
Washington, D.C. Office: Suite 900 East, 555 13th Street, N.W.
Telephone: 202-383-8800.
Fax: 202-383-8877; 383-8893.
Baltimore, Maryland Office: 300 East Lombard Street, 19th Floor.
Telephone: 410-528-5600.
Fax: 410-528-5650.
Camden, New Jersey Office: 800 Hudson Square, 5th Floor.
Telephone: 609-541-5577.
Fax: 609-541-8272.

John M. Gardner
Loring E. Harkness III
M. Julia Hook
Kenneth D. Hubbard
John L. Ruppert
Donald Salcito
Paul J. Schlauch
Lyle B. Stewart
Elizabeth H. Temkin
Roger P. Thomasch
Niki Frangos Tuttle
Mark Wielga

OF COUNSEL

Thomas H. Duncan
Claire E. Holmes

David Whitney Brown
(Not admitted in CO)
Leslie A. Eaton
Barbara A. Grandjean
Adrienne G. Greene
Scott W. Hardt
Matthew J. Hogan
David B. Kelly
Jacquelyn Kilmer
Denise S. Maes
Judith I. Meyka
Matthew R. Perkins
Elizabeth A. Woodcock
(Not admitted in CO)
C. Erika Zimmer
Mary Gilliam Zuchegno

For full biographical listings, see the Martindale-Hubbell Law Directory

BERENBAUM, WEINSHIENK & EASON, P.C. (AV)

Suite 2600 Republic Plaza, 370 17th Street, 80202
Telephone: 303-825-0800
Telecopier: 303-629-7610
Durango, Colorado Office: 2815 Main.
Telephone: 303-247-1333.

Mandel Berenbaum (1914-1993)
Hubert T. Weinshienk (1931-1983)
Joseph Berenbaum
Charles A. Bewley
Joseph S. Borus
Martin D. Buckley
John E. Bush
M. Frances Cetrulo
David R. Eason
Richard L. Eason
Steven C. Hoth
James A. Jacobson
I. H. Kaiser
Kenneth S. Kramer
James L. Kurtz-Phelan
Charles P. Leder
Amy Therese Loper
H. Michael Miller
Neil B. Oberfeld
Dean G. Panos
Edwin G. Perlmutter
Barry M. Permut
Keith M. Pockross
Dan A. Sciullo
Edward L. Sperry
Eugene M. Sprague
Robert G. Wilson, Jr.
Ronald I. Zall

Patricia Bellac
Daniel S. Duggan
Heather Scheel Hagemann
A. Elizabeth Meyers
Christopher W. Payne
Mark A. Redmiles
Stephan K. Schutte

Representative Clients: Citibank, N.A.; Confederation Life Insurance Co.; First Interstate Mortgage of Illinois; O'Connell Development Co.; Olympia & York Cherry Creek Co.; Columbine Venture Fund, Ltd.; Karman Western Wear; The Registry Hotel Corp.; The Stanley Works; Yellow Cab Cooperative.

For full biographical listings, see the Martindale-Hubbell Law Directory

Denver—Continued

BREGA & WINTERS, P.C. (AV)

One Norwest Center, 1700 Lincoln Street, Suite 2222, 80203
Telephone: 303-866-9400
FAX: 303-861-9109
Greeley, Colorado Office: 1100 Tenth Street, Suite 402, 80631.
Telephone: 303-352-4805.
Fax: 303-352-6547.

James W. Bain
Thomas D. Birge
Charles F. Brega
Robert R. Dormer
Robert C. Kaufman
Ronald S. Loser
Brian A. Magoon
Loren L. Mall
Pamela A. Shaddock (Resident, Greeley Office)
Jay John Schnell
Jerry D. Winters (Resident, Greeley Office)

Mark J. Appleton
Wesley B. Howard, Jr.
Jennifer G. Krolik
Bradley D. Laue (Resident, Greeley Office)
Cathryn B. Mayers
Carla B. Minckley
Nathan D. Simmons
Scott L. Terrell

OF COUNSEL

Mark Spitalnik

For full biographical listings, see the Martindale-Hubbell Law Directory

BROWNSTEIN HYATT FARBER & STRICKLAND, P.C. (AV)

Twenty-Second Floor, 410 Seventeenth Street, 80202-4437
Telephone: 303-534-6335
Telecopier: 303-623-1956

Norman Brownstein
Steven W. Farber
Mark F. Leonard
Edward N. Barad
John R. Call
Steven M. Sommers
Thomas L. Strickland
Ronald B. Merrill
Lynda A. McNeive
Laura Jean Christman
Andrew W. Loewi
Charles B. White
Wayne H. Hykan
Stanley L. Garnett
Michael J. Sternick
Gary M. Reiff
Michael R. McGinnis
Lisa A. Hogan
Wayne F. Forman
Bruce A. James
Brian Hoffmann
Nesa E. Hassanein
Thomas J. Mancuso
P. Cole Finegan
Jeffrey M. Knetsch (Not admitted in CO)
Hubert A. Farbes, Jr.

OF COUNSEL

Jack N. Hyatt
Ann B. Riley
Susan F. Hammerman

Robert Kaufmann
Brent T. Slosky
Anne M. Murphy
Jay F. Kamlet
Terence C. Gill
Carrie A. Mineart
Robert C. Troyer
Patrick F Carrigan
Beth Morrison Klein
Ana Lazo Tenzer
Mark J. Mathews
David M. Brown
Kyle M. Hall (Not admitted in CO)
Gregory A. Vallin
Jill E. Murray
Gregory W. Berger
Marquitte C. Starkey
Howard J. Pollack (Not admitted in CO)
Peter Q. Murphy

Representative Clients: Citicorp North America, Inc.; Donaldson Lufkin & Jenrette Securities Corporation; Louisiana-Pacific Corporation; Metropolitan Life Insurance Co. of America; The Prudential Insurance Co. of America; Rose Medical Center/Rose Health Care Systems; SunAmerica, Inc.; Trammell Crow Company; Vail Associates, Inc.; Western Union.

For full biographical listings, see the Martindale-Hubbell Law Directory

BURNS WALL SMITH AND MUELLER, A PROFESSIONAL CORPORATION (AV)

Suite 800, 303 East Seventeenth Avenue, 80203-1260
Telephone: 303-830-7000
Telecopier: 303-830-6708
Telex: 650-278-8717 (MCI UW)

Peter J. Wall
Gregory J. Smith
George W. Mueller
James E. Bosik
Steven F. Mueller
Robert T. Cosgrove

James P. Rouse
Gretchen L. Aultman
Donald D. Farlow
Mark D. Masters

OF COUNSEL

Thomas M. Burns
Frank H. Houck
Darrell C. Miller
Anthony van Westrum

(See Next Column)

SPECIAL COUNSEL

John D. Amen
Robert Neece
Jack M. Merritts

Representative Clients: IBM Credit Corporation; PIPTO Holdings, Inc.; Advance Geophysical Corporation ; Snyder Oil Corporation; Colorado Chapter of the American Physical Therapy Assn; Ford Motor Company; QC Data Inc.; Meteor Industries, Inc.; In-Situ, Inc.

For full biographical listings, see the Martindale-Hubbell Law Directory

CLANAHAN, TANNER, DOWNING AND KNOWLTON, P.C. (AV)

Suite 2400, 1600 Broadway, 80202
Telephone: 303-830-9111
Telecopier: 303-830-0299

David C. Knowlton
Thomas C. McKee
Denis B. Clanahan
Michael J. Wozniak
James M. Colosky
J. David Arkell
James T. Ayers, Jr.
Janet N. Harris
Sheryl L. Howe
Jack D. Henderson
Peter T. Moore
Judith M. Matlock
C. Kevin Cahill
Gary P. LaPlante
Richard L. Shearer
David M. Rich
Langdon J. Jorgensen
Brian D. Fitzgerald
William J. Bourke

Robert J. Bricmont, Jr.
Dino A. Ross
Robert M. O'Hayre
Richard J. Gognat
Gary Younger
Kip I. Plankinton

SPECIAL COUNSEL

Joseph K. Reynolds
Leslie Abrams Pizzi

OF COUNSEL

Barkley L. Clanahan
Ira E. Tanner, Jr.
Richard Downing, Jr.

Representative Clients: Amoco Production Co.; Ampol (U.S.A.), Inc.; Apache Corporation; Celebrity Homes, Inc.; Farmers Reservoir & Irrigation Company; KN Production Company; Maxus Exploration, Inc.; Oryx Energy Company; Pace Membership Warehouse, Inc.; Snyder Oil Corporation.

For full biographical listings, see the Martindale-Hubbell Law Directory

COOK & LEE, P.C. (AV)

Sherman Street Plaza, 1888 Sherman Street, Suite 375, 80203-1158
Telephone: 303-831-8008
Fax: 303-860-1844
Boulder, Colorado Office: Canyonside Office Park, 100 Arapahoe Avenue, Suite 9, 80302-5862.
Telephone: 303-444-9700.
Fax: 303-444-9691.

Stephen H. Cook
Larry D. Lee

Patti L. Holt
Daniel E. Bronstein

For full biographical listings, see the Martindale-Hubbell Law Directory

DAVIS, GRAHAM & STUBBS, L.L.C. (AV)

A Limited Liability Company
Suite 4700, 370 Seventeenth Street, P.O. Box 185, 80201-0185
Telephone: 303-892-9400
Telecopier: (303) 893-1379
Cable Address: "Davgram, Denver"
Telex: 413726 DGS DVR UD
Washington, D.C. Office: Suite 1200, 1225 New York Avenue, N.W.
Telephone: 202-822-8660.
Telecopier: 202-293-4794.
Telex: 248260 DGSW.
Houston, Texas Office: 515 Post Oak Boulevard, Suite 870.
Telephone: 713-850-9400.
Facsimile: 713-850-0807.

MEMBERS OF FIRM

Wanda J. Abel
Howard Adler, Jr. (Not admitted in CO; Resident, Washington, D.C. Office)
Alison L. Berkes (Resident, Washington, D.C. Office)
William A. Bianco
Charles D. Calvin
Charles L. Casteel
Mark D. Colley (Not admitted in CO; Resident, Washington, D.C. Office)
James E. Culhane
Elizabeth C. Darling
Brian T. Dolan
Roger L. Freeman
L. Richard Freese, Jr.
Harold I. Freilich (Not admitted in CO; Resident, Washington, D.C. Office)
Daniel E. D. Friesen
Michael J. Gallagher
Christopher J. Hagan (Not admitted in CO; Resident, Washington, D.C. Office)
David R. Hammond
Felicity Hannay
Dale R. Harris
Paul Hilton
Richard P. Holme
Marcia Chadwick Holt
Dennett L. Hutchinson
John R. Jacus
Carole K. Jeffery

(See Next Column)

DAVIS, GRAHAM & STUBBS L.L.C.—*Continued*

MEMBERS OF FIRM (Continued)

Thomas P. Johnson
Lisa S. Kahn
Charles L. Kaiser
Glen E. Keller, Jr.
J. Hovey Kemp (Resident, Washington, D.C. Office)
Ronald R. Levine, II
Alan M. Loeb
Andrew M. Low
John L. McCabe
Joseph P. McMahon, Jr.
Steven J. Merker
Glenn W. Merrick
David P. Metzger (Not admitted in CO; Resident, Washington, D.C. Office)
Gale T. Miller
Zach C. Miller
Laurence E. Nemirow
Thomas S. Nichols
Donald J. O'Connor
Neil Peck
Kurt M. Petersen
Patricia Peterson
Donald E. Phillipson
James M. Piccone
Jeffrey R. Pilkington
Robert S. Rich
Christopher L. Richardson
John M. Roche
Anthony J. Shaheen
Beat U. Steiner
Randall Weeks
John R. Wilson
Kenneth S. Witt
Lester R. Woodward
Gail L. Wurtzler

OF COUNSEL

Richard Marden Davis (1912-1987)
Donald S. Graham
Donald S. Stubbs
Robert H. Harry
Donald W. Hoagland
George M. Hopfenbeck, Jr.
S. Neil Hosenball (Not admitted in CO; Resident, Washington, D.C. Office)
Clyde O. Martz
Quigg Newton, Jr.
Robert A. Ruyle
John M. Sayre
Lorna A. Schnase (Resident, Houston, Texas Office)
James D. Voorhees

ASSOCIATES

Barry C. Bartel
Laura A. Battle
Thomas C. Bell
Joel Benson
Geoffrey Berman
Mark D. Bingham
Charles A. Breer
Petrina M. Burnham (Not admitted in CO; Resident, Washington, D.C. Office)
Gena E. Cadieux (Not admitted in CO; Resident, Washington, D.C. Office)
Ronald K. Edquist (Not admitted in CO)
Timothy G. Ehresman
John A. Francis
Laura E. Gasser (Not admitted in CO; Resident, Washington, D.C. Office)
R. Keith Hotle
Patrick A. Jackman (Not admitted in CO)
N. Anthony Jeffries
Martin J. Katz
Paula J. Koenig
Christopher M. Leh
Joanne E. Loercher (Not admitted in CO; Resident, Washington, D.C. Office)
Horace Anthony Lowe
David A. Makarechian (Not admitted in CO)
John G. McGrath
Thomas B. McNamara
Anthony F. Medeiros
Sara A. Moon
Barbara J. Mueller
Laura J. Nagle
Peter V. O'Connor
Brian E. Onorato
Karen Lund Page
Andjali Prahasto
Nancy B. Printz
Mark Enger Saliman
Jean Justyn Sirkin
Kevin P. Stichter
Mark T. Urban
Linda K. Wackwitz
Richard A. Westfall

For full biographical listings, see the Martindale-Hubbell Law Directory

DEMUTH & KEMP (AV)

1660 Colorado State Bank Building, 1600 Broadway, 80202
Telephone: 303-861-9100
Fax: 303-861-8787

MEMBERS OF FIRM

Lael S. DeMuth
William G. Kemp
Alan C. DeMuth

ASSOCIATES

Barbara G. Chamberlain

Representative Clients: Mount Evans Co.; Jefferson Standard Life Insurance Co.; H.W. Stewart, Inc.; Colorado State Employees Credit Union; Bellco First Federal Credit Union; Fidelity Union Life Insurance Co.; Decals, Inc.; Craftsmen Construction Co.

For full biographical listings, see the Martindale-Hubbell Law Directory

DUFFORD & BROWN, P.C. (AV)

1700 Broadway, Suite 1700, 80290-1701
Telephone: 303-861-8013
Facsimile: 303-832-3804

Philip G. Dufford
Thomas G. Brown
Dale Tooley (1933-1985)
David W. Furgason
William C. Robb
Beverly J. Quail
Richard L. Fanyo
Phillip D. Barber
Gregory A. Ruegsegger
Jack F. Ross
Eugene F. Megyesy, Jr.
Randall J. Feuerstein
S. Kirk Ingebretsen
Douglas P. Ruegsegger

(See Next Column)

Edward D. White
Peggy J. Anderson
Craig B. Shaffer
Scott J. Mikulecky

Terry Jo Epstein
Thomas E. J. Hazard
Roman C. Pibl
Douglas J. Kotarek
Thomas M. Stern
Laura J. Gibson

SPECIAL COUNSEL

Morris B. Hecox, Jr.
Marc A. Chorney
Deborah L. Freeman
Claude M. Maer, Jr.
James E. Carpenter

Representative Clients: BHP-Minerals, Inc.; CF&I Steel L.P.; The Colorado and Wyoming Railway Co.; Echo Bay-Sunnyside Gold; Hall and Hall Mortgage Corporation; Hewlett-Packard Co.; Ingersoll Rand Financial Co.; Reorganized CF&I Steel Corp.; Starbucks Coffee Company; Stewart & Stevenson Services, Inc.

For full biographical listings, see the Martindale-Hubbell Law Directory

FAEGRE & BENSON (AV)

Professional Limited Liability Partnership
2500 Republic Plaza, 370 Seventeenth Street, 80202-4004
Telephone: 303-592-5900
Facsimile: 303-592-5693
Minneapolis, Minnesota Office: 2200 Norwest Center, 90 South Seventh Street, 55402-3901.
Telephone: 612-336-3000.
Facsimile: 612-336-3026.
Des Moines, Iowa Office: 400 Capital Square, 400 Locust Street, 50309-2335.
Telephone: 515-248-9000.
Facsimile: 515-248-9010.
Washington, D.C. Office: The Homer Building, Suite 450 North, 601 Thirteenth Street, N.W., 20005-3807.
Telephone: 202-783-3880.
Facsimile: 202-783-3899.
London, England Office: 10 Eastcheap, EC 3M 1ET.
Telephone: 44-71-623-6163.
Facsimile: 44-71-623-3227.
Frankfurt, Germany Office: Westendstrasse 24, 6000 Frankfurt am Main 1.
Telephone: 49-69-1743 43.
Facsimile: 49-69-1743 49.

RESIDENT MEMBERS

Joseph M. Montano
Frederic K. Conover, II
John D. Shively
Bruce W. Sattler
Dirk W. De Roos
Michael S. McCarthy
Michael J. Cook
Gerald A. Niederman
Christian Carl Onsager
Harlan S. Abrahams
Leslie A. Fields
Catherine A. Lemon
Elizabeth A. MacDonald
Daniel F. Warden
Russell O. Stewart
Diane B. Davies
Charlotte Wiessner

OF COUNSEL

Jo Frances Walsh

RESIDENT ASSOCIATES

Colin C. Deihl
Adrienne O'Connell McNamara
Steven N. Jacobs
Natalie Hanlon-Leh
Mary B. Tribby
Arthur G. Woodward
Michael J. Pankow
Michel L. Glawe
Matthew Nelson
John R. Sperber

For full biographical listings, see the Martindale-Hubbell Law Directory

FAIRFIELD AND WOODS, P.C. (AV)

One Norwest Center, Suite 2400, 1700 Lincoln Street, 80203-4524
Telephone: 303-830-2400
Telecopier: 303-830-1033

Peter F. Breitenstein
Charlton H. Carpenter
Howard Holme
Robert S. Slosky
James L. Stone
Michael M. McKinstry
Jac K. Sperling
Robert L. Loeb, Jr.
Daniel R. Frost
Stephen W. Seifert
Mary Jo Gross
Robert A. Holmes
John J. Silver
Thomas P. Kearns
Rocco A. Dodson
Mary E. Moser
Christine K. Truitt
Brent T. Johnson
Craig A. Umbaugh
Stephen H. Leonhardt
Caroline C. Fuller
John M. Frew
Gregory C. Smith
John M. Tanner
Neil T. Duggan

OF COUNSEL

George C. Keely (Retired)

Douglas J. Becker
Brent A. Waite
Thomas M. Pierce
Suzanne R. Kalutkiewicz
Philip J. Roselli
Mary Sommerville Welch
Lisa A. D'Ambrosia (Not admitted in CO)
Jacalyn W. Peter
David L. Joeris

(See Next Column)

FAIRFIELD AND WOODS P.C., *Denver—Continued*

Representative Clients: American Web, Inc.; Colorado Bankers Association; Copper Mountain, Inc.; The Denver Nuggets; Denver Metropolitan Major League Baseball Stadium District; Gates Foundation; Greater Denver Chamber of Commerce; ITT Commercial Finance Corp.; Security Title Guaranty Co.; Southeastern Colorado Water Conservancy District.

For full biographical listings, see the Martindale-Hubbell Law Directory

FULLER AND EVANS

(See Hamilton and Faatz, A Professional Corporation)

GUTHERY & RICKLES, P.C. (AV)

Cherry Creek Plaza II, 650 South Cherry Street Suite 1000, 80222
Telephone: 303-320-5889
Fax: 303-320-5890

Peter C. Guthery
Stephen P. Rickles
Kerrie A. Boese

Representative Clients: Colorado National Guard Foundation; Denver Firefighters Protective Association; Denver Health Care Group, P.C.; Denver Museum of Natural History Foundation; Eastern Star Center; Jimmie Heuga Center; Karsh & Hagan Advertising, Inc.; City of Thornton; United States Olympic Foundation; YMCA of the Rockies.

For full biographical listings, see the Martindale-Hubbell Law Directory

HALL & EVANS, L.L.C. (AV)

Suite 1700, 1200 Seventeenth Street, 80202
Telephone: 303-628-3300
Telecopier: 303-628-3368
Colorado Springs, Colorado Office: Suite 600, 102 South Tejon Street, 80903.
Telephone: 719-578-5600. Toll-Free From Denver
Telephone: 303-628-3400.
Telecopier: 719-635-7458.

Ronald V. Yegge (1905-1970)
Don R. Evans (1925-1976)
John D. Phillips, Jr.
Eugene O. Daniels
Edward H. Widmann
Richard A. Hanneman
David R. Brougham
Samuel David Cheris
Peter F. Jones
John P. Mitzner
Michael W. Jones
Bruce A. Menk
Jeffery B. Stalder
James W. Britt
Eugene R. Commander
Daniel R. Satriana, Jr.
Kevin E. O'Brien
Stuart G. Rifkin
C. Willing Browne
Chris A. Mattison
Robert M. Ferm
Alan Epstein
Paul R. Franke, III
Charles Greenhouse
Marilyn Sterrenberg-Rose
John E. Bolmer, II
Barbara A. Duff
Linda S. Comer
Kenneth H. Lyman
Clinton P. Swift
Joyce H. Nakamura
Michael R. McCurdy
Cathy Havener Greer
Thomas R. Dolven
Robert J. McCormick
Alan J. Schmitz
Dominic A. Lloyd
Matthew Y. Biscan
Thomas J. Lyons
Anthony L. Joseph

SPECIAL COUNSEL

Carol M. Welch
Patricia Jean Clisham

OF COUNSEL

Richard D. Hall
Brooke Wunnicke
G. Walter Bowman

Robert D. Baker
Robin Lee Beattie
LaDonne Bush
Kristen L. Case
Greg M. Cornell
Miles M. Dewhirst
Scott T. Erickson
Sean R. Gallagher
Scott V. Goettelman
Marlene Triggs Gresh
Steven M. Gutierrez
Kris Edwin Jukola
S. Kent Karber
Todd K. Lanting
Michael L. Luchetta
Josh A. Marks
Malcolm S. Mead
Kimberly Y. Nash
Marianne E. Pierce
Dana C. Rock
R. Scott Roswell
Joel B. Schaefer
Pamela Skelton
Christine M. Stegehuis
Susan J. Trout
Christine Van Coney
John Jos. Zodrow

Representative Clients: American Family Insurance Group; American International Group (A.I.G.); The Chubb Group of Insurance Companies; The CIGNA Companies; Diamond Shamrock Refining & Marketing Company; Ford Motor Company; Monfort, Inc.; Mortgage Guaranty Insurance Corporation; Panhandle Eastern Pipe Line Corporation; United States Aviation Underwriters, Inc.

For full biographical listings, see the Martindale-Hubbell Law Directory

HAMILTON AND FAATZ, A PROFESSIONAL CORPORATION (AV)

Suite 600 Colorado State Bank Building, 1600 Broadway, 80202-4988
Telephone: 303-830-0500
Facsimile: 303-860-7855

Pierpont Fuller (1906-1983)
John M. Evans (1911-1984)
Dwight Alan Hamilton
Clyde A. Faatz, Jr.
John T. Willson
James H. Marlow
Jan E. Montgomery
Gregory W. Smith

Robert L. Bartholic

SPECIAL COUNSEL

Michael E. Gurley

OF COUNSEL

Kenneth W. Caughey

Representative Clients: PPG Industries, Inc.; Public Employees Retirement Association of Colorado; Masonic Temple Association of Denver; Lockton Silversmith, Inc.; Muller, Sirhall and Associates, Inc.; South Denver Cardiology Associates, P.C.; Landmark Reclamation, Inc.; Stone's Farm Supply, Inc.; Heather Gardens Association; DCX, Inc.

For full biographical listings, see the Martindale-Hubbell Law Directory

HOLLAND & HART (AV)

Suite 2900, 555 Seventeenth Street, P.O. Box 8749, 80201
Telephone: 303-295-8000
Cable Address: "Holhart Denver"
Telecopier: 303-295-8261
TWX: 910-931-0568
Denver Tech Center, Colorado Office: Suite 1050, 4601 DTC Boulevard.
Telephone: 303-290-1600.
Telecopier: 303-290-1606.
Aspen, Colorado Office: 600 East Main Street.
Telephone: 303-925-3476.
Telecopier: 303-925-9367.
Boulder, Colorado Office: Suite 500, 1050 Walnut.
Telephone: 303-473-2700.
Telecopier: 303-473-2720.
Colorado Springs, Colorado Office: Suite 1000, 90 S. Cascade Avenue.
Telephone: 719-475-7730.
Telex: 82077 SHHTLX.
Telecopier: 719-634-2461.
Washington, D.C. Office: Suite 310, 1001 Pennsylvania Avenue, N.W.
Telephone: 202-638-5500.
Telecopier: 202-737-8998.
Boise, Idaho Office: Suite 1400, West One Plaza, 101 South Capitol Boulevard, P.O. Box 2527.
Telephone: 208-342-5000.
Telecopier: 208-343-8869.
Billings, Montana Office: Suite 1500, First Interstate Center, 401 North 31st Street, P.O. Box 639.
Telephone: 406-252-2166.
Telecopier: 406-252-1669.
Salt Lake City, Utah Office: Suite 880, 111 East Broadway.
Telephone: 801-578-6000.
FAX: 801-578-6010.
Cheyenne, Wyoming Office: Holland & Hart, A Partnership including Professional Corporations, Suite 500, 2020 Carey Avenue, P.O. Box 1347.
Telephone: 307-778-4200.
Telecopier: 307-778-8175.
Jackson, Wyoming Office: Holland & Hart, A Partnership including Professional Corporations, Suite 2, 175 South King Street, P.O. Box 68.
Telephone: 307-739-9741.
Telecopier: 307-739-9744.

MEMBERS OF FIRM

Charles M. Johnson (1956-1994)
Josiah G. Holland (1900-1975)
Stephen H. Hart (1908-1993)
Frank H. Morison (Retired)
Jay W. Tracey, Jr. (Retired)
Samuel P. Guyton (Retired)
Warren L. Tomlinson (Retired)
Patrick M. Westfeldt (Retired)
William C. McClearn
James E. Hegarty
David Butler
Bruce T. Buell
Harry L. Hobson
Gordon G. Greiner
William E. Murane
H. Gregory Austin
James P. Lindsay
John S. Castellano
Dennis M. Jackson
Robert E. Benson
Stephen H. Foster (Not admitted in CO)
Richard M. Koon
Robert T. Connery
Michael D. Martin
Haradon Beatty
Ralph F. Crandell
Gary M. Polumbus
Jack L. Smith
Jesse B. Heath, Jr.
Mark R. Levy
R. Brooke Jackson
Wiley E. Mayne, Jr.
Frederick G. Meyer
Gregory A. Eurich
Ronald M. Martin
Gregory Russell Piché
Randolph M. Karsh
John Arthur Ramsey
Jane Michaels
James E. Hartley
W. Harold Flowers, Jr.
Peter C. Houtsma
John R. Ley
Gregg I. Anderson
Betty Carter Arkell
Paul D. Phillips
John M. Husband
Joseph W. Halpern
John F. Shepherd
John M. Vaught
Davis O. O'Connor

(See Next Column)

HOLLAND & HART—*Continued*

MEMBERS OF FIRM (Continued)

Brian Muldoon
Jeffrey T. Johnson
Mark D. Safty
Kevin S. Crandell
Jeanine Feriancek
Elizabeth A. Sharrer
Mary Ellen Scanlan
Scott S. Barker
Anne J. Castle
Timothy M. Rastello
Brian R. Hanson
John C. Tredennick, Jr.
Maureen Reidy Witt
Elizabeth Ann Phelan
Jack M. Englert, Jr.
A. Bruce Jones
John R. Maxfield
Holly Stein Sollod
Daniel W. Patterson
Geraldine A. Brimmer
Sandra R. Goldman
Harry Shulman
Marcy G. Glenn
Denise W. Kennedy
Elaine A. Welle
William J. Kubida
Christopher H. Toll
Renée W. O'Rourke
Steven C. Choquette
David E. Crandall
Debra S. Fagan

OF COUNSEL

John L. J. Hart (1904-1986)
William Dean Embree, Jr.
Susan N.H. Dixon
Robert R. Keatinge
Charles E. Pear, Jr.
Karen Sweeney
Howard R. Tallman
Lawrence E. Volmert

SPECIAL COUNSEL

James J. Gonzales
Brian M. Mumaugh

ASSOCIATES

Douglas L. Abbott
Margaret Althoff
Stephen A. Bain
Judith A. (Jude) Biggs
Steven W. Black
Sheryl L. Bollinger
J. Kevin Bridston
Virginia L. Briggs
Carol W. Burton
Elizabeth Carney
Charles C. Cary (Not admitted in CO)
R. Dana Cephas
Steven E. Christoffersen
Lynn A. Cleveland
Elizabeth Loring Crane
Patricia Dean
Donald A. Degnan
Robert P. Detrick
Daniel C. Doherty
Lynn Bolinske Dolven
Mark D. Ebel
Fay C. Fong
Maria Theresa (Terry) Fox
Jane Oglesby Francis
Heidi S. Glance
Daniel J. Glivar
Jimmy Goh
Stephen P. Gottesfeld
Heather R. Hanneman
Charles Henson
Eric L. Hilty
Sunhee Juhon
Ian S. Karpel
Robert H. Kelly (Not admitted in CO)
Dana L. Klapper
Barry S. Korman (Not admitted in CO)
Shari R. Lefkoff
Stephen Masciocchi
Veronica J. May
Jane Lowell Montgomery
Marily Nixon
Michael Noone
Fiona W. Ong
Lee R. Osman
Stephanie Sue Padilla
John B. Phillips
David D. Powell, Jr.
Michael S. Quinn
Carlos A. Samour, Jr.
Cynthia K. Simons
Alan N. Stern
Craig E. Stewart
Rufus C. Taylor, Jr.
Jacqueline Sandoval Tahsuda
John Tahsuda
Natalie F. Bocock Turnage
Valerie W. Tyler
Camille T. Ventrell (Not admitted in CO)
Stephanie D. Welsh
Risa L. Wolf-Smith

DENVER TECH CENTER, COLORADO RESIDENT PARTNERS

Robert M. Pomeroy, Jr.
Robert Alan Poe
William W. Maywhort
Michael S. Beaver
Perry L. Glantz
Todd W. Miller

DENVER TECH CENTER RESIDENT OF COUNSEL

Mary D. Metzger

DENVER TECH CENTER, COLORADO RESIDENT ASSOCIATES

Robert E. Botts, Jr.
Rachel A. Yates

ASPEN, COLORADO RESIDENT PARTNERS

James T. Moran
Charles T. Brandt
Arthur C. Daily
Arthur B. Ferguson, Jr.

ASPEN, COLORADO OF COUNSEL

James B. Boyd
Thomas J. Todd

BOULDER, COLORADO PARTNERS

William J. Kubida
Camron R. Kuelthau
William E. Mooz, Jr.
Scott Havlick

OF COUNSEL

Homer L. Knearl
Earl C. Hancock
Francis A. Sirr

BOULDER, COLORADO ASSOCIATES

Jennifer L. Bales
Judith A. (Jude) Biggs

COLORADO SPRINGS, COLORADO PARTNERS

John T. Haney (1883-1971)
William Q. Haney (1909-1977)
W. Allen Spurgeon (1936-1982)
Robert L. Spurgeon (1904-1986)
Byron L. Akers, Jr. (Retired)
William R. Aman (Retired)
James B. Day (Retired)
Jack W. Foutch (Retired)
J. Donald Haney (Retired)
Irving Howbert (Retired)
Bruce T. Buell
Ronald M. Martin
Ronald A. Lehmann (Resident)
Randolph M. Karsh

(See Next Column)

COLORADO SPRINGS, COLORADO PARTNERS (Continued)

Edward H. Flitton (Resident)
William K. Brown (Resident)
Gary R. Burghart (Resident)
William J. Kubida

COLORADO SPRINGS, COLORADO RESIDENT SPECIAL COUNSEL

Elaine Holland Turner

COLORADO SPRINGS, COLORADO RESIDENT ASSOCIATES

Brian T. Murphy
Wendy J. Pifher
David Scott Prince

WASHINGTON, D.C. RESIDENT PARTNERS

J. Peter Luedtke
William F. Demarest, Jr.
Michael J. Brennan
Steven G. Barringer

OF COUNSEL

Thomas L. Sansonetti
Linda Arey Skladany

WASHINGTON, D.C. SPECIAL COUNSEL

Adelia Smith Borrasca

WASHINGTON, D.C. RESIDENT ASSOCIATES

Marci B. Anderson
C. William Groscup
Kelly Anne Johnson

BOISE, IDAHO RESIDENT PARTNERS

Willis E. Sullivan (1911-1992)
Edith Miller Klein (Retired)
Walter H. Bithell
J. Frederick Mack
Larry E. Prince
B. Newal Squyres, Jr.
Steven B. Andersen

BOISE, IDAHO RESIDENT OF COUNSEL

Debra K. Ellers
Brian J. King

BOISE, IDAHO RESIDENT ASSOCIATES

Sandra L. Clapp
Kim J. Dockstader
Robert A. Faucher
Murray D. Feldman
Dana Lieberman Hofstetter
Kurt D. Holzer
Linda B. Jones

BILLINGS, MONTANA PARTNERS

Stephen H. Foster
Paul D. Miller
Donald W. Quander
Jeanne Matthews Bender
James M. Ragain
David R. Chisholm

BILLINGS, MONTANA SPECIAL COUNSEL

Kyle A. Gray
Robert A. Lorenz

BILLINGS, MONTANA RESIDENT ASSOCIATES

Bruce F. Fain
W. Scott Mitchell
Patricia D. Peterman

CHEYENNE, WYOMING PARTNERS

Ronald M. Martin
Jack D. Palma, II (P.C.)
Donald I. Schultz (P.C.)
Patrick R. Day (P.C.)
Edward W. Harris
Joe M. Teig (P.C.)
Lawrence J. Wolfe (P.C.)

CHEYENNE, WYOMING OF COUNSEL

Teresa Burkett Buffington
Thomas L. Sansonetti

CHEYENNE, WYOMING RESIDENT ASSOCIATES

James R. Belcher
Lynnette J. Boomgaarden
Bradley T. Cave
William R. Dabney
Catherine W. Hansen
Susan E. Laser-Bair
Edward E. Risha
Richard Schneebeck

JACKSON, WYOMING RESIDENT PARTNERS

John L. Gallinger (P.C.)
Marilyn S. Kite (P.C.)

JACKSON RESIDENT OF COUNSEL

Stephen R. Duerr

SALT LAKE CITY UTAH RESIDENT PARTNERS

Lawrence J. Jensen
Bruce N. Lemons
David R. Rudd

RESIDENT ASSOCIATES

Linda Hamada
Brian T. Hansen

LEGAL SUPPORT PERSONNEL

Richard J. Crawford (Professional Development Coordinator)
Regis P. Malloy (Legal Assistant)
Shannon S. Davis

For full biographical listings, see the Martindale-Hubbell Law Directory

HOLME ROBERTS & OWEN LLC (AV)

Suite 4100, 1700 Lincoln, 80203
Telephone: 303-861-7000
Telex: 45-4460
Telecopier: 303-866-0200
Boulder, Colorado Office: Suite 400, 1401 Pearl Street.
Telephone: 303-444-5955.
Telecopier: 303-444-1063.
Colorado Springs, Colorado Office: Suite 1300, 90 South Cascade Avenue.
Telephone: 719-473-3800.
Telecopier: 719-633-1518.
Salt Lake City, Utah Office: Suite 1100, 111 East Broadway.
Telephone: 801-521-5800.
Telecopier: 801-521-9639.
London, England Office: 4th Floor, Mellier House, 26a Albemarle Street.
Telephone: 44-171-499-8776.
Telecopier: 44-171-499-7769.

(See Next Column)

HOLME ROBERTS & OWEN LLC, *Denver—Continued*

Moscow, Russia Office: 14 Krivokolenny Pr., Suite 30, 101000.
Telephone: 095-925-7816.
Telecopier: 095-923-2726.

MEMBERS OF FIRM

Peter H. Holme (1903-1961)
Harold Dewitt Roberts (1917-1956)
Robert E. More (1916-1963)
Peter H. Holme, Jr. (1946-1981)
J. Churchill Owen (1926-1992)
James E. Bye
James C. Owen Jr.
Richard G. Wohlgenant
Joseph W. Morrisey, Jr.
Donald K. Bain
G. Kevin Conwick
Paul D. Holleman
Robert J. Welter
Judson W. Detrick
W. Dean Salter
Lawrence L. Levin
Charles J. Kall
Edward J. McGrath
Frank Erisman
Thomas A. Richardson
William D. Watson
David T. Mitzner
Charles A. Ramunno
William S. Huff
Bruce R. Kohler (Resident Managing Member, London, England Office; Co-Director, Moscow, Russia Office)
Richard R. Young (Managing Member, Colorado Springs Office)
Donald J. Hopkins
Glenn E. Porzak (Managing Member, Boulder Office)
John R. Webb
Bruce L. Likoff
Spencer T. Denison
Stephen E. Snyder
Jeffrey A. Chase
Brent V. Manning (Salt Lake City Office)
James D. Butler
Richard L. Nagl (Colorado Springs Office)
William R. Roberts (Boulder Office)
Phillip R. Clark
Carolyn E. Daniels
Randy G. Bobier (Colorado Springs Office)
Michael F. Browning (Boulder Office)
Martha Traudt Collins
David K. Detton (Salt Lake City Office)
Thomas F. Cope
Lynn Parker Hendrix
Nick Nimmo
Charlotte Louise Neitzel
Douglas R. Wright
Francis R. Wheeler
Steve L. Gaines (Colorado Springs Office)
David S. Steefel
Henry W. Ipsen
Judith L. L. Roberts (Co-Director, Moscow Office; London Office)
Jan N. Steiert
R. Bruce Johnson (Salt Lake City Office)
Nancy J. Gegenheimer
Paul E. Smith (Boulder Office)
Marla J. Williams
Daniel J. Dunn
Douglas A. Pluss
Kevin Michael Shea
Raymond L. Petros
Linnea Brown
David D. Kleinkopf
Steven B. Richardson
Boyd N. Boland
Robert Craig Ewing
John Leonard Watson
Mark K. Buchi (Managing Member, Salt Lake City Office)
McKay Marsden (Salt Lake City Office)
LeGrand R. Curtis, Jr. (Salt Lake City Office)
Martha Dugan Rehm
Robert Tuchman
John F. Knoeckel
Kay M. Small (Boulder Office)
Anne Stark Walker
Michael D. Strugar (Colorado Springs Office)
Katherine Jean Peck
Jill K. Rood (Boulder Office)
Bruce F. Black
P. Christian Anderson (Salt Lake City Office)
Brent E. Rychener (Colorado Springs Office)
Susan E. Duffey Campbell (Colorado Springs Office)
David R. Child
John R. Wylie (Colorado Springs Office)
David Harold Little (Salt Lake City Office)
Stephanie M. Tuthill
Robert H. Bach
Richard A. Johnson (Boulder Office)
David B. Wilson
James R. Ghiselli (Boulder Office)
Alan C. Bradshaw (Salt Lake City Office)
Patricia C. Tisdale
Garth B. Jensen
John D. McCarthy
James W. Spensley
Eric E. Johnson
Mary L. Groves
Wm. Kelly Nash (Salt Lake City Office)
Wm. Robert Wright (Salt Lake City Office)
Alan W. Cathcart (Not admitted in CO)
Thomas M. James (Colorado Springs Office)
K. Preston Oade, Jr.
Duncan E. Barber
David J. Crapo (Salt Lake City Office)
Richard L. Gabriel
Sharon A. Higgins (Colorado Springs Office)
Manuel L. Martinez
Paul V. Timmins

OF COUNSEL

Ted P. Stockmar
A. Edgar Benton
Harold S. Bloomenthal
Richard L. Schrepferman
Nancy J. Severson

SPECIAL COUNSEL

David Akers Weinstein
Thomas F. Dixon
Richard A. Oertli (Not admitted in CO)
Stephanie J. Shafer
David K. Schollenberger (London, England Office)
Diane S. Barrett
Lawrence A. Leporte (London, England Office)
John P. Babb
Stephen P. Ward
Laurence B. James

(See Next Column)

SENIOR COUNSEL

Stephen C. Rench
Mary Hurley Stuart
Kathryn B. Stoker

ASSOCIATES

Kristen L. Alleman
Jensie L. Anderson (Salt Lake City Office)
Leslie C. Annand
Edwin P. Aro
William H. Auerswald, Jr.
John Adams Barrett, Jr. (On Leave of Absence)
Steven C. Bednar (Salt Lake City Office)
Jon Bernhardt
Charles B. Bruce, Jr.
Michael W. Bruzga
Steven J. Bushong (Boulder Office)
Loretta (Laurie) A. Cahill
Diane D. Card (Salt Lake City Office)
Allen R. Christy
Steven A. Cohen
James F. Cress
J. Robert Crook
Katherine Taylor Eubank
Paul V. Franke
Staunton L. T. Golding
Mary C. Gordon (Salt Lake City Office)
Colin G. Harris
Lisa A. Hawkins
Dennis J. Herman
Pamela B. Hunsaker (Salt Lake City Office)
Rhonda R. Johnson
Kelvin D. Jones III
Robert J. Kaukol (Colorado Springs Office)
Kevin H. Kelley
Susana E. Laos Konon (Not admitted in CO)
Elena Kuryatnikova (Moscow, Russia Office)
Matthew J. Lepore
Martin D. Litt
Kenneth W. Lund
Maria Mashenka Lundberg
Daniel P. Maguire
Richard E. Malmgren (Salt Lake City Office)
Margaret B. McLean (Resident Managing Lawyer, Moscow, Russia Office)
Beth Harkins Miller
Sheri Ann Mower (Salt Lake City Office)
Sandra Orihuela
Laurence Pendleton
Patrick K. Perrin (Boulder Office)
Timothy G. Pfeifer (Not admitted in CO; Colorado Springs Office)
John N. Raby
Thad W. Renaud
Dominic Jude Ricotta (Colorado Springs Office)
Matthew J. Rita
Alan Romero (Salt Lake City Office)
Michelle M. Rose-Hughes
Susanne D. Roubidoux
Walter H. Sargent II (Colorado Springs Office)
Rashid Sharipov (Resident, Moscow, Russia Office)
Erin Marie Smith
Steven B. Smith (Colorado Springs Office)
Edward E. Stevenson
David E. Tenzer (Boulder Office)
Sharon A. Thomas (Colorado Springs Office)
Paul G. Thompson
Gary R. Thorup (Salt Lake City Office)
Christopher T. Toll
Alexander Udovenko (Moscow, Russia Office)
Maureen C. Weston (Boulder Office)
R. Gary Winger (Salt Lake City Office)
Masahiro Max Yoshimura
Lawrence M. Zavadil

LEGAL SUPPORT PERSONNEL

Katherine Fadeeva (Office Administrator, Moscow, Russia Office)
John C. Hanley (Firm Administrator)
Mark E. Estes (Librarian)
Judith A. Fisk (Facilities and Services Manager)
Howard E. Jenkins (Controller)
Margaret Ann Lane (Director of Personnel)

For full biographical listings, see the Martindale-Hubbell Law Directory

---

IRELAND, STAPLETON, PRYOR & PASCOE, P.C. (AV)

Suite 2600, 1675 Broadway, 80202
Telephone: 303-623-2700
Telecopier: 303-623-2062

Clarence Ireland (1889-1992)
Benjamin F. Stapleton (1919-1993)
D. Monte Pascoe
John G. Lewis
Richard C. Linquanti
Tucker K. Trautman
William E. Tanis
Margaret L. Toal-Rossi
Michael A. Smith
Lawrence P. Terrell
Mark J. Sather
Susan L. (Jones) Oakes
Rebecca B. DeCook
Hardin Holmes
Michael Touff
Ann C. Kirwin

Scot M. Peterson
Van Aaron Hughes
Richard A. Nielson
Mitchell H. Menezes
Joseph G. Webb
Roger A. Hauptman
David A. Freilicher

OF COUNSEL

Wilbur M. Pryor

SPECIAL COUNSEL

Norton L. Steuben
Winthrop D. Johnson

Representative Clients: Bank of Denver; Mountain States Bank; Central Bank of Denver, N.A.; Freeport-McMoran, Inc,; Price Waterhouse; Shaw Construction Co.; NBI, Inc.; Western Equities Group, Inc.; AT&T Communications of the Mountain States, Inc.; Trust Company of America.

For full biographical listings, see the Martindale-Hubbell Law Directory

Denver—Continued

KUTAK ROCK (AV)

A Partnership including Professional Corporations
Suite 2900, 717 Seventeenth Street, 80202-3329
Telephone: 303-297-2400
Fax: 303-292-7799
Atlanta, Georgia Office: 4400 Georgia-Pacific Center, 133 Peachtree Street, NE, 30303-1808.
Telephone: 404-222-4600.
Facsimile: 404-222-4654.
Baton Rouge, Louisiana Office: 300 Four United Plaza, 8555 United Plaza Boulevard, 70809-2251.
Telephone: 504-929-8585.
Facsimile: 504-929-8580.
Little Rock, Arkansas Office: Suite 1770, 124 West Capitol Avenue, 72201-3719.
Telephone: 501-376-9208.
Facsimile: 501-375-3749.
Kansas City, Missouri Office: United Missouri Bank Building, Third Floor, 9201 Ward Parkway.
Telephone: 816-361-3363.
Telecopier: 816-361-8397.
Los Angeles, California Office: Suite 1330, 2049 Century Park East, 90067-3115.
Telephone: 310-785-3900.
Facsimile: 310-785-3999.
New York, New York Office: Seventh Floor, 505 Park Avenue, 10022-1155.
Telephone: 212-752-0800.
Facsimile: 212-752-2281.
Oklahoma City, Oklahoma Office: Suite 475, 6305 Waterford Boulevard, 73118-1116.
Telephone: 405-232-9827.
Facsimile: 405-232-8307.
Omaha, Nebraska Office: The Omaha Building, 1650 Farnam Street, 68102-2186.
Telephone: 402-346-6000.
Facsimile: 402-346-1148.
Phoenix, Arizona Office: 16th Floor, 3300 North Central Avenue, 85012-1984.
Telephone: 602-285-1700.
Facsimile: 602-285-1868.
Pittsburgh, Pennsylvania Office: 1214 Frick Building, 437 Grant Street, 15219-6002.
Telephone: 412-261-6720.
Facsimile: 412-261-6717.
Washington, D.C. Office: Suite 1000, 1101 Connecticut Avenue, NW, 20036-4374.
Telephone: 202-828-2400.
Facsimile: 202-828-2488.

MEMBERS OF FIRM

James D. Arundel
Paul E. Belitz
Robert D. Irvin
Michael K. Reppe
John H. Bernstein
Warren L. Troupe
Larry L. Carlile
Timothy J. Flanagan, P.C.
Robert J. Ahrenholz
Cassandra G. Sasso
Thane R. Hodson
Frederic H. Marienthal III
David A. Caprera
Michael R. Johnson
Charles L. Borgman
William C. Gorham
M. Lou Raders
Michael T. Lambert
Scott H. Beck
Diana C. Fields
Richard L. Buddin
Tana K. Simard
Brian V. Caid

SPECIAL COUNSEL

Howard Kenison
Donald R. Bieber
Peter D. Willis

ASSOCIATES

Lydia A. Mangan
Donald R. Stover
Kris A. Pestl
William S. Martin
John P. Jones
Anne M. Gish
Kent Christopher Veio
Stephen J. Ismert
Charles E. Bedford
Craig N. Johnson
Timothy M. Jones
Deborah A. Hogan (Not admitted in CO)
Michael L. Sharb
Lisa A. Martin

For full biographical listings, see the Martindale-Hubbell Law Directory

LEVENTHAL AND BOGUE, P.C. (AV)

950 South Cherry Street, Suite 600, 80222
Telephone: 303-759-9945
Fax: 303-759-9692

Jim Leventhal
Jeffrey A. Bogue
Bruce J. Kaye
Natalie Brown
Victoria J. Koury
Kelly P. Roberts

Reference: Omni Bank.

For full biographical listings, see the Martindale-Hubbell Law Directory

LONG & JAUDON, P.C. (AV)

The Bailey Mansion, 1600 Ogden Street, 80218-1414
Telephone: 303-832-1122
FAX: 303-832-1348

Lawrence A. Long (1908-1992)
Joseph C. Jaudon, Jr.
David B. Higgins
James A. Dierker
Frederick W. Long
Gary B. Blum
Michael T. McConnell
Stephen P. Hopkins
Robert M. Baldwin
Dennis Woodfin Brown
Celine Lillie
Alan D. Avery
Cecelia A. Fleischner
Walter N. Houghtaling
Ellen Rubright Ivy
Christine Anne Craigmile
Carla M. LaRosa
Sheri Lyn Hood
Thomas C. Kearns, Jr.
Michael Shaefer Drew
Margaret J. Walton
David H. Yun

OF COUNSEL

Michael T. DePinto

Representative Clients: Goodman Buick-GMC Trucks, Inc.; Keystone Resorts, Inc.; King Soopers, Inc. (Dillon Companies, Inc.); St. Joseph Hospital; Watersaver; Aetna Life & Casualty Company; The Doctors Company; Home Insurance Company; Baxter Healthcare; CNA.

For full biographical listings, see the Martindale-Hubbell Law Directory

LOWERY AND LOWERY, P.C. (AV)

1999 Broadway, Suite 3800, 80202
Telephone: 303-296-1456
Telefax: 303-296-8538
Tempe, Arizona Office: 1707 E. Southern Avenue, Suite B, 85282.
Telephone: 602-831-1550.
Telefax: 602-838-5005.

Philip E. Lowery
Philip Scott Lowery

Marcella T. Clark
Terri B. Cohen
Spero A. Leon
Maria J. Murray
David L. Michael

References: Colorado State Bank; Bank of Denver; Jefferson Bank & Trust.

For full biographical listings, see the Martindale-Hubbell Law Directory

MONTGOMERY LITTLE & MCGREW, P.C. (AV)

The Quadrant, 5445 DTC Parkway, Suite 800 (Englewood), 80111
Telephone: 303-773-8100
Telecopier: 303-220-0412

Roy E. Montgomery (1907-1986)
Robert R. Montgomery
David C. Little
Dan McGrew
James J. Soran, III
Richard L. Murray, Jr.
Kevin J. Kuhn
Brian K. Stutheit
David A. Burlage
Robert J. Beattie
David L. Kelble, Jr.
Michael H. Smith
William H. ReMine, III
Debra Piazza
William H. Knapp
Thomas C. Deline
Craig A. Adams
Robert J. Bruce
Karen B. Best
John R. Riley
Zion Avdi
Rebecca B. Givens
Theresa A. Raynor
Daniel P. Murphy
Christopher B. Little
Melinda L. Sanders
Timothy M. Schulte
Carole Salamaha
James P. Campbell
James X. Quinn

OF COUNSEL

J. Bayard Young

LEGAL SUPPORT PERSONNEL

Rodney R. Germeroth (Director of Administration and Finance)
Mary Kay Ackley (Legal Assistant)
Carmen L. Antonio (Legal Assistant)
Margaret M. Green (Legal Assistant)
Debbie L. Kirke (Legal Assistant)
Traci J. Libis (Legal Assistant)
Shannon R. Marshall (Legal Assistant)
Connie Streich (Legal Assistant)
Lynne M. Thill (Legal Assistant)
Shirley R. Chugden (Legal Assistant)
Ginny A. Leiker (Legal Assistant)
Anna M. Krigger
Allyson K. Snyder-Mueller
Kelly J. Roberge
Monica L. Sharp

Representative Clients: Amoco Oil Co.; Bristol-Myers Squibb; Colorado Medical Society; Chrysler Corporation; Cyprus Minerals; Dillon Cos., Inc., d/b/a King Soopers; The St. Paul Insurance Cos.; University of Colorado Health Sciences Center.

For full biographical listings, see the Martindale-Hubbell Law Directory

MOYE, GILES, O'KEEFE, VERMEIRE & GORRELL (AV)

A Law Partnership including Professional Corporations
29th Floor, 1225 Seventeenth Street, 80202
Telephone: 303-292-2900
Telecopier: 303-292-4510

(See Next Column)

MOYE, GILES, O'KEEFE, VERMEIRE & GORRELL, *Denver—Continued*

MEMBERS OF FIRM

John E. Moye (P.C.)
Edward M. Giles (P.C.)
Edward F. O'Keefe (P.C.)
Richard S. Vermeire (P.C.)
Teryl R. Gorrell (P.C.)
James T. Burghardt (P.C.)
Edwin A. Naylor (P.C.)
Patricia M. Nagel (P.C.)
Charles F. Luce, Jr., (P.C.)
J. William Callison (P.C.)
John R. Paddock, Jr., (P.C.)
Paul F. Lewis (P.C.)
John A. O'Brien (P.C.)
Susan M. Rogers (P.C.)
Erik K. Foster (P.C.)
Jerry N. Jones (P.C.)
Dwight K. Shellman III (P.C.)
William C. Jensen (P.C.)
Elaine G. Edinburg (P.C.)
Thomas H. Keyse
C. Jean Stewart (P.C.)
Jeffrey C. Pond

ASSOCIATES

Chesley K. "Bud" Culp III
Martha E. Cox
Patrick E. Meyers
Laura Gaudian Kastetter
Kevin E. Burr
Brent P. Karasiuk
Vincent G. Toenjes

For full biographical listings, see the Martindale-Hubbell Law Directory

MYER, SWANSON & ADAMS, P.C. (AV)

The Colorado State Bank Building, 1600 Broadway, Suite 1850, 80202-4918
Telephone: 303-866-9800
Facsimile: 303-866-9818

Rendle Myer
Allan B. Adams
Robert K. Swanson
Thomas J. Wolf

Kevin M. Brady

OF COUNSEL

Robert Swanson
Fred E. Neef (1910-1986)

Representative Clients: The Oppenheimer Funds; Daily Cash Accumulation Fund; The Centennial Trusts; Mile High Chapter of American Red Cross; Master Lease; Heartland Management Company; Kan-Build of Colorado, Inc.
Reference: The Colorado State Bank of Denver.

For full biographical listings, see the Martindale-Hubbell Law Directory

OTTEN, JOHNSON, ROBINSON, NEFF & RAGONETTI, P.C. (AV)

950 Seventeenth Street, 16th Floor, 80202
Telephone: 303-825-8400
Telecopier: 303-825-6525

Arthur E. Otten, Jr.
William F. Schoeberlein
Frank L. Robinson
Bruce B. Johnson
A. Bruce Campbell
William R. Neff
Thomas J. Ragonetti
David W. Stark
Lawrence W. Marquess
Darrell G. Waas
Robert C. Fisher, Jr.
Neil M. Goff
Blair L. Lockwood
Hugh Q. Gottschalk
J. Thomas Macdonald
John D. Sternberg
Michael Westover
Edward P. Timmins
Daniel M. Minzer
Kevin A. Gliwa
Henry I. Lowe
P. Kathleen Lower
David T. Brennan
Kathleen M. Bottagaro
Terence M. Ridley
Kenneth K. Skogg
David W. Fell
Karen L. Barsch
Brad W. Schacht
R. Michael Shomo
David P. Hutchinson
Elizabeth Savage
Michael C. Villano
Alex Iskenderian
James D. Leonard
Todd A. Fredrickson
Darin Mackender
Amy J. Griffin
Mark F. Copertino
William H. Brierly
Victoria L. Hellmer

OF COUNSEL

Kenneth M. Robins

SPECIAL COUNSEL

Marguerite L. Sadler

Representative Clients: Aetna Life Insurance Co.; The Broe Companies; Inc.; Colorado National Bank; Connecticut General Life Insurance Co.; First Nationwide Bank; Homart Development Co.; Land Title Guarantee Co.; Trizec Corporation Ltd.; U.S. West Communications, Inc.; The Western Sugar Co.

For full biographical listings, see the Martindale-Hubbell Law Directory

PRYOR, CARNEY AND JOHNSON, A PROFESSIONAL CORPORATION (AV)

Carrara Place, Suite 400, 6200 South Syracuse Way (Englewood), P.O. Box 22003, 80222-0003
Telephone: 303-771-6200
Facsimile: 303-779-0740

(See Next Column)

Peter W. Pryor
Robert W. Carney
Irving G. Johnson
W. Randolph Barnhart
Thomas L. Roberts
Rodney R. Patula
David D. Karr
Christopher N. Mammel
Edward D. Bronfin
John L. Wheeler
Scott S. Nixon
Bruce A. Montoya
Arlene V. Dykstra
JoAnne M. Zboyan
Peggy S. Ball
Marilee E. Langhoff
Michael J. McNally
Elizabeth C. Moran
C. Gregory Tiemeier
Todd E. Kastetter
Daniel M. Hubbard
Geri O'Brien Williams
Steven G. York
Nick S. Kaluk, Jr.
Teresa L. Thraikill
Gary J. Benson
Mark D. Sullivan
Kristi J. Livedalen
Kimberly Berkman Turnbow
Ricardo M. Barrera
John B. Grow, III
Harriet M. Hageman (Not admitted in CO)
Karen V. Reutzel

OF COUNSEL

Mark E. Haynes
Dorothy Huysman Dean

Representative Clients: CNA Insurance Group; Owens-Illinois, Inc.; Kaiser Foundation Health Plan of Colorado; Levitz Furniture Corp.; Newport Construction Co.; Lasalle National Bank; GLS Development, Inc.; KN Energy; Placer Dome U.S., Inc.; Big O Tire Co.

For full biographical listings, see the Martindale-Hubbell Law Directory

SHERMAN & HOWARD L.L.C. (AV)

Attorneys at Law
633 Seventeenth Street, Suite 3000, 80202
Telephone: 303-297-2900
Telecopier: 303-298-0940
Colorado Springs, Colorado Office: Suite 1500, 90 South Cascade Avenue, 80903.
Telephone: 719-475-2440.
Las Vegas, Nevada Office: Swendseid & Stern a member in Sherman & Howard L.L.C., 317 Sixth Street, 89101.
Telephone: 702-387-6073.
Reno, Nevada Office: Swendseid & Stern, a member in Sherman & Howard L.L.C., 50 West Liberty Street, Suite 660, 89501.
Telephone: 702-323-1980.

James H. Pershing (1863-1948)
Robert Graham Bosworth (1888-1954)
Lewis A. Dick (1889-1954)
Fritz A. Nagel (1891-1978)
Clyde C. Dawson (1905-1979)
Samuel S. Sherman, Jr. (1909-1988)
Winston S. Howard (Retired)
Garth C. Grissom
James E. Hautzinger
Paul E. Roberts
James L. Cunningham
Douglas M. Cain
Duane F. Wurzer
E. Lee Dale
Christopher Lane
Kurt A. Kaufmann
Hugh J. McClearn
R. Michael Sanchez
Andrew L. Blair, Jr.
Howard B. Gelt
Charles W. Newcom
Mark L. Fulford
James F. Wood
Robert P. Mitchell
Kenneth B. Siegel
David Thomas III
Cynthia C. Benson
Joseph J. Bronesky
John O. Swendseid (Las Vegas and Reno, Nevada Offices)
Charles Y. Tanabe
Robert L. Brown
Dee P. Wisor
Arlene S. Bobrow
Alan J. Gilbert
Raymond M. Deeny (Colorado Springs Office)
W.V. Bernie Siebert
Stanley M. Raine
Theodore A. Olsen
Manuel D. Savage
Richard K. Parks
Paul Curtis Daw
Ronald M. Eddy
Durward E. Timmons, Jr. (Colorado Springs Office)
Susan Hicks Walker
Rebecca Anderson Fischer
Steven D. Miller
Peggy Berning Knight
Calvin T. Hanson
B. Scott Pullara
Stephen S. Halasz
Leanne B. DeVos
Jennifer Stern (Las Vegas and Reno, Nevada Offices)
N. Dawn Webber (Colorado Springs Office)
Ann Marie (Amy) Kennedy
Richard N. Baer
Glenn H. Schlabs (Colorado Springs Office)
Elizabeth I. Kiovsky
Jeffrey M. Goldsmith (Colorado Springs Office)
Cynthia P. Delaney
Leslie A. Nichols
William T. Diss (Colorado Springs Office)
Bruce A. Kolbezen

COUNSEL

John W. Low
Raymond J. Turner
Michael D. Groshek
Gary L. Greer
William P. Cantwell
Carolyn Lubchenco
James E. McCarty
Ann Coulbourn Gail
Jane R. Levine (Not admitted in CO)

Carol Hildebrand
Amy L. Hirter
Carol V. Berger
Katherine F. Beckes
James P. Lane
Kathleen A. Odle
Joanne F. Norris
Diana M. Wendel
Doran L. Matzke
J. Mark Baird
Maria L. Prevedel
Andrew W. Volin
Wayne W. Williams (Colorado Springs Office)

(See Next Column)

SHERMAN & HOWARD L.L.C.—*Continued*

Stephanie J. Griffin
Sean C. Lindsay
Bridget K. Sullivan
James G. Fiero
Donna K. McNamara
Milton L. "Skip" Smith, III (Colorado Springs Office)
Heidi J. Kesinger
John W. Mill
Dominick Sekich
Richard T. Galanits
Leslie A. Petri
Deborah L. Land
Christopher R. Mosley
Sarah J. Kilgore
Thomas E. O'Connor, Jr. (Colorado Springs Office)
Mark D. Williamson
Christopher M. Kamper
Shannon W. Roberts
Patricia A. Templar
Daniel J. Tangeman (Las Vegas and Reno, Nevada Offices)

Representative Clients: Adolph Coors Co.; AT&T Corp.; Eastman Kodak Co.; Hathaway Corp.; Keystone Resort; Newmont Gold Corp.; The Prudential Insurance Company of America; Public Service Company of Colorado; Public Employees' Retirement Assn.; Tele-Communications, Inc.

For full biographical listings, see the Martindale-Hubbell Law Directory

WALDBAUM, CORN, KOFF AND BERGER, P.C. (AV)

303 East Seventeenth Avenue, Suite 940, 80203
Telephone: 303-861-1166
Telecopier: 303-861-0601

Leonard N. Waldbaum
Douglas B. Koff
Robert O. Corn
Michael H. Berger
Nancy L. Cohen
Maureen E. Dobel
Christopher M. Melton

Representative Clients: Bestop, Inc.; Capitol Color Imaging, Inc.; Chatfield Dean & Co.; Contact Lens Association of Ophthalmologists, Inc. (CLAO); First Winthrop Properties, Inc.; Hayashida Farms, Inc.; J.A. Balistreri Farms, Inc.; Premier Enterprises, Inc.; Sevo-Miller, Inc.; Western Optical, Inc.

For full biographical listings, see the Martindale-Hubbell Law Directory

WALTERS & JOYCE, P.C. (AV)

2015 York Street, 80205
Telephone: 303-322-1404
FAX: 303-377-5668

William E. Walters, III
Craig D. Joyce

Anne Baudino Holton

Reference: Norwest Bank of Buckingham Square.

For full biographical listings, see the Martindale-Hubbell Law Directory

WELBORN SULLIVAN MECK & TOOLEY, P.C. (AV)

Mellon Financial Center, 1775 Sherman Street, Suite 1800, 80203
Telephone: 303-830-2500
Facsimile: 303-832-2366

John F. Welborn
Stephen J. Sullivan
John F. Meck
Keith D. Tooley
Kendor P. Jones (Not admitted in CO)
Molly Sommerville
Marla E. Valdez
Karen Ostrander-Krug
Brian S. Tooley

Scott L. Sells
Tamara Barnes

OF COUNSEL

Robert F. Welborn

SPECIAL COUNSEL

John S. Cowan

For full biographical listings, see the Martindale-Hubbell Law Directory

WHITE AND STEELE, PROFESSIONAL CORPORATION (AV)

1225 17th Street, Suite 2800, 80202
Telephone: 303-296-2828
Telecopier: 303-296-3131
Cheyenne, Wyoming Office: 1912 Capital Avenue, Suite 404, 82003.
Telephone: 307-778-4160.

Lowell White (1897-1983)
Walter A. Steele
R. Eric Peterson
Stephen K. Gerdes
Michael W. Anderson
James M. Dieterich
Glendon L. Laird
John M. Lebsack
Stephen G. Sparr
John P. Craver
David J. Nowak
Sandra Spencer
John M. Palmeri
Frederick W. Klann
William F. Campbell, Jr.
Richard M. Kaudy
Peter W. Rietz
Kurt A. Horton
Stewart J. Rourke
Allan Singer
Michael J. Daugherty
Robert R. Carlson
Ted A. Krumreich

(See Next Column)

Thomas B. Quinn
Michael A. Perales
Lina C. George-Sauro
George A. Codding, III
Christopher P. Kenney
Regina Marie Walsh
June Baker
Peter H. McGuire
Robert H. D. Coate
Michelle R. Magruder
Monty L. Barnett
Joseph R. King
Frank D. Sledge
Kristi Blumhardt

OF COUNSEL

Fred L. Witsell

Colorado Tort Counsel for: Goodyear Tire and Rubber Co.; The Dow Chemical Co.; Firestone Tire and Rubber Co.
Insurance Clients: Allied Insurance Co.; CNA; Kemper Insurance Group; Massachusetts Mutual Life Insurance Co.; Underwriters at Lloyds; U.S.A.A.

For full biographical listings, see the Martindale-Hubbell Law Directory

WOOD, RIS & HAMES, PROFESSIONAL CORPORATION (AV)

1775 Sherman Street, Suite 1600, 80203-4317
Telephone: 303-863-7700
Telecopier: 303-830-8772

Edward L. Wood (1899-1974)
Stephen E. Connor
F. Michael Ludwig
Donald L. Cook
Charles E. Weaver
Clayton B. Russell
Christopher M. Brandt
Mark R. Davis
Colin C. Campbell
Christian M. Lind
Jeffrey Clay Ruebel
Clifton J. Latiolais, Jr.
Mary E. Kanan
William H. Short
Dennis A. Hanson
Jennifer L. Veiga
Michel P. Williams
Mary E. Gibbons
Barbara L. Brundin
William A. Rogers, III

OF COUNSEL

William K. Ris
Eugene S. Hames

SPECIAL COUNSEL

E. Gregory Martin
Donald B. Gentry

Counsel for: American Family Insurance Company; American International Companies; Continental Insurance Companies; Equitable Life Assurance Society of the United States; Fireman's Fund Insurance Company; Home Insurance Company; Maryland Casualty Company; Metropolitan Life Insurance Company; Prudential Insurance Co. of America; Safeco Insurance Company.

For full biographical listings, see the Martindale-Hubbell Law Directory

*DURANGO,** La Plata Co.

FRANK J. ANESI (AV)

Suite 220, 835 East Second Avenue, P.O. Box 2185, 81302
Telephone: 303-247-9246
Fax: 303-259-2793

References: First National Bank of Durango; Burns Bank, Durango.

For full biographical listings, see the Martindale-Hubbell Law Directory

DUTHIE & TATE (AV)

A Partnership of Professional Corporations
835 East Second Avenue, Suite 444, P.O. Box 219, 81302
Telephone: 303-247-4545
Fax: 303-247-2471

Alonzo M. Emigh (1915-1971)
Frederic B. Emigh (1910-1987)

MEMBERS OF FIRM

Harry G. Tate (P.C.)
Robert C. Duthie, III (P.C.)

ASSOCIATES

Paul W. Whistler

Counsel for: The First National Bank of Durango; Centennial Savings Bank, F.S.B.; Basin Properties, Inc.; Strater Hotel; Bula.
Local Counsel: State Farm Mutuals; United Fire & Casualty Co.; U.S.A.A.; Commercial Union and Hawkeye Insurance Companies.

For full biographical listings, see the Martindale-Hubbell Law Directory

MAYNES, BRADFORD, SHIPPS & SHEFTEL (AV)

West Building, Suite 123, 835 East Second Avenue, P.O. Box 2717, 81302
Telephone: 303-247-1755
Fax: 303-247-8827

MEMBERS OF FIRM

Frank E. (Sam) Maynes
Byron V. Bradford (1907-1985)
Thomas H. Shipps
Janice C. Sheftel
Sam W. Maynes
Patricia A. Hall
John Barlow Spear

ASSOCIATES

Nancy S. Grief

Counsel for: Southwestern Water Conservation District; San Miguel and La Plata Water Conservancy Districts; La Plata Electric Association, Inc. (REA); Southern Ute Indian Tribe; South Durango Water District; Dolores

(See Next Column)

MAYNES, BRADFORD, SHIPPS & SHEFTEL, *Durango—Continued*

Water Conservancy District; PacifiCorp; Animas-La Plata Water Conservancy District.

For full biographical listings, see the Martindale-Hubbell Law Directory

ENGLEWOOD, Arapahoe Co.

BANTA, HOYT, GREENE & EVERALL, P.C. (AV)

Suite 555, 6300 South Syracuse Way, 80111
Telephone: 303-220-8000
Fax: 303-220-0153

Richard L. Banta, Jr. (1912-1993)
Richard J. Banta
Stephen G. Everall
Darryl L. Farrington
Charles A. Kuechenmeister
Jane S. Brautigam

John L. Palmquist

OF COUNSEL

R. Val Hoyt
Richard D. Greene
Craig E. Wagner

Representative Clients: American Institute of Timber Construction; Cherry Creek School District No. 5; City of Greenwood Village; Colorado School District Self Insurance Pool; Intermountain Rural Electric Association; Kiewit Western Co.; Littleton Public Schools; National Union Fire Insurance Co. (local); Southgate Sanitation and Water Districts.

For full biographical listings, see the Martindale-Hubbell Law Directory

*FORT COLLINS,** Larimer Co.

ALLEN, ROGERS, METCALF AND VAHRENWALD (AV)

Eleventh Floor, Key Bank Building, 125 South Howes, P.O. Box 608, 80522
Telephone: 303-482-5058
Fax: 303-482-5175

MEMBERS OF FIRM

William H. Allen (1917-1990)
Garth W. Rogers
Thomas W. Metcalf
Jack D. Vahrenwald
Donald E. Johnson, Jr.
J. Brian McMahill
Russell B. Sanford
Allan S. Massey

ASSOCIATES

Todd W. Rogers

Representative Clients: Everitt Enterprises, Inc.; LaPorte Water and Sanitation District; Foothills Fashion Mall (shopping center); TapeWorks LLC (computer hardware).
References: First National Bank of Fort Collins, N.A.; Poudre Valley Bank, Fort Collins.

For full biographical listings, see the Martindale-Hubbell Law Directory

FISCHER, BROWN, HUDDLESON & GUNN, P.C. (AV)

Tenth Floor, First Tower, 215 West Oak Street Drawer J, 80522
Telephone: 303-482-1056
Facsimile: 303-482-3840

Ward H. Fischer
William H. Brown
Charles R. Huddleson
William C. Gunn
Steven B. Ray
David E. Dwyer
James E. Ringenberg
T. Thomas Metier
William R. Fischer
Stephen J. Jouard
Clinton L. Hubbard
Margaret A. Brown
Thomas K. Higley
Joel M. Funk
Lynette Korb

General Counsel for: First National Bank of Fort Collins, N.A.; The Water Supply and Storage Co.; Baldwin Construction Co., Inc.; Cache La Poudre Water Users Assn.
Counsel for: Anheuser-Busch Cos., Inc.; Leggett & Platt Incorporated; Allstate Insurance Co.; Platte River Power Authority; The Travelers Cos.; Stelbar Oil Corp.

For full biographical listings, see the Martindale-Hubbell Law Directory

FISCHER, HOWARD & FRANCIS (AV)

Suite 900, 125 South Howes, P.O. Box 506, 80522
Telephone: 303-482-4710
Fax: 303-482-4729

MEMBERS OF FIRM

Gene E. Fischer
Stephen E. Howard
Steven G. Francis

Approved Attorneys for: Attorney's Title Guaranty Fund, Inc.
Reference: First National Bank of Fort Collins, N.A.

For full biographical listings, see the Martindale-Hubbell Law Directory

MARCH & MYATT, P.C. (AV)

110 East Oak Street, Suite 200, P.O. Box 469, 80522
Telephone: 303-482-4322
Fax: 303-482-3038

Arthur E. March (1909-1981)
Arthur E. March, Jr.
Ramsey D. Myatt
Robert W. Brandes, Jr.
Richard Shaeffer Gast
Lucia A. Liley
J. Brad March
Linda S. Miller

William C. Beyers
Jeffrey J. Johnson

Local Counsel for: Big O Tires; Union Colony Bank (Fort Collins).
General Counsel For: Bank One, Fort Collins/Loveland, N.A.; Schrader Oil Co.; First Bank of Fort Collins; Fort Collins Downtown Development Authority; Factual Data Corp.; Connell Resources, Inc.

For full biographical listings, see the Martindale-Hubbell Law Directory

FORT LUPTON, Weld Co. — (Refer to Brighton)

*FORT MORGAN,** Morgan Co. — (Refer to Greeley)

*GLENWOOD SPRINGS,** Garfield Co.

DELANEY & BALCOMB, P.C. (AV)

818 Colorado Avenue, P.O. Drawer 790, 81602
Telephone: 303-945-6546, 945-2371
Fax: 303-945-8902

John A. Thulson
Edward Mulhall, Jr.
Scott M. Balcomb
Lawrence R. Green
Robert M. Noone
Timothy A. Thulson
Margaret O'Donnell
Lori J.M. Satterfield

OF COUNSEL

Robert Delaney
Kenneth Balcomb

General Counsel for: Ski Sunlight, Inc.
Local Counsel for: Farm Credit Services.

For full biographical listings, see the Martindale-Hubbell Law Directory

*GOLDEN,** Jefferson Co.

BRADLEY, CAMPBELL, CARNEY & MADSEN, PROFESSIONAL CORPORATION (AV)

1717 Washington Avenue, 80401-1994
Telephone: 303-278-3300
Fax: 303-278-3379

Leo N. Bradley
Tim L. Campbell
Thomas J. Carney
Earl K. Madsen
Victor F. Boog
William J. Campbell
Earle D. Bellamy, II
Thomas A. Nolan
Jim Michael Hansen
Ronald K. Reeves
Shelly M. Rowan
Russell Carparelli
Dennis L. Arfmann
Thomas E. Root
John N. Galbavy
Matthew S. McElhiney
Bryant S. Messner
Ilona L. Dotterrer
John K. Shunk
Gary W. Truman

OF COUNSEL

Laura J. Vogelgesang

Counsel for: Adolph Coors Co.; Coors Brewing Co.; Evergreen National Bank, Evergreen, Colorado; Coors Ceramics Co.; Clear Creek National Bank, Georgetown, Colorado; ASARCO, Inc.; Morrison-Knudsen; Westinghouse Electric Corp.
Local Counsel for: Public Service Company of Colorado.
Reference: Colorado National Bank, Denver, Colorado.

For full biographical listings, see the Martindale-Hubbell Law Directory

FLEMING, PATTRIDGE & RUNNERSTROM, P.C. (AV)

1200 Arapahoe Street, 80401
Telephone: 303-279-2563
Fax: 303-279-2677

Robert G. Fleming
Frederick J. Pattridge
Lars R. Runnerstrom
Michelle A. Dobbins

Counsel for: Goldenbank of Colorado, Inc.
Representative Clients: Goldenbank, N.A. (Golden); Goldenbank, N.A., Westminister; Goldenbank, N.A., Englewood; Ardourel Construction Co.; The Foss Co.; Meyer Home Center, Inc.; Mesa Meadows Land Company; Metrolist, Inc.

For full biographical listings, see the Martindale-Hubbell Law Directory

*GRAND JUNCTION,** Mesa Co.

ELDER & PHILLIPS, P.C. (AV)

562 White Avenue, 81501
Telephone: 303-243-0946
Fax: 303-243-8743

(See Next Column)

ELDER & PHILLIPS P.C.—*Continued*

Walter J. Phillips
W. Bruce Phillips
Keith Boughton
Mary Frances McCracken
Mark R. Luff

OF COUNSEL

Tom E. Elder

References: Grand Junction Board of Realtors; Royal Insurance Co.; Ranger Insurance; Farmers Insurance Group of Cos.; Bituminous Insurance Co.; McMillan Claim Service; Crawford & Co.

For full biographical listings, see the Martindale-Hubbell Law Directory

HOSKIN, FARINA, ALDRICH & KAMPF, PROFESSIONAL CORPORATION (AV)

Bank of Colorado Building, 200 Grand Avenue, Suite 400, P.O. Box 40, 81502
Telephone: 303-242-4903
FAX: 303-241-3760

William H. Nelson (1926-1992)
Gregory K. Hoskin
Terrance L. Farina
Frederick G. Aldrich
Gregg K. Kampf
Curtis G. Taylor
David M. Scanga
David A. Younger
Michael J. Russell

Susan R. Lundberg
John T. Howe
Matthew G. Weber

Attorneys for: Great American First Savings Bank, FSB; Central Bank of Grand Junction; Grand Valley National Bank; City Market, Inc.; Rangely School District RE-4; Rocky Mountain Health Maintenance Organization; Unocal Corp.; Equitable Life Assurance Society; Grand Valley Rural Power Lines, Inc.; Pepsi-Cola Bottling Group.

For full biographical listings, see the Martindale-Hubbell Law Directory

*GREELEY,** Weld Co.

HOUTCHENS, DANIEL & GREENFIELD (AV)

1007 Ninth Avenue, 80631
Telephone: 303-353-9195
Facsimile: 303-353-0151

OF COUNSEL

Barnard Houtchens

MEMBERS OF FIRM

S. Robert Houtchens (1917-1989)
Rodger I. Houtchens (1921-1988)
John B. Houtchens
Jerry C. Daniel
Kim R. Houtchens
Thomas A. Houtchens
Dallas D. Greenfield

ASSOCIATES

Julie Christine Hoskins
Mark J. Geil

Counsel for: Norwest Bank Greeley; Greeley Gas Co.; Miner and Miner, Consulting Engineers; State Farm Insurance Cos.; United States Fidelity and Guaranty Co.; Home Builders Association of Northern Colorado; Noffsinger Manufacturing Co., Inc.; Cornerstone Builders, Inc.; Farmers Insurance Cos.

For full biographical listings, see the Martindale-Hubbell Law Directory

KAROWSKY, WITWER, MILLER & OLDENBURG (AV)

Suite 760, 822 7th Street, P.O. Box 1407, 80632
Telephone: 303-352-3161
Facsimile: 303-352-3165

MEMBERS OF FIRM

Stow L. Witwer, Jr.
Walker Miller
R. Sam Oldenburg
John J. Barry
Marilyn J. David

ASSOCIATES

Jacqueline Johnson
Curtis R. Sears

OF COUNSEL

Charles A. Karowsky

Representative Clients: Bank One-Greely; Bank One-Ault; Greeley School District; Aims Junior College; John Hancock Mutual Life Insurance Co.

For full biographical listings, see the Martindale-Hubbell Law Directory

*JULESBURG,** Sedgwick Co. — (Refer to Greeley)

*LA JUNTA,** Otero Co. — (Refer to Lamar)

LAKEWOOD, Jefferson Co.

POLIDORI, GEROME, FRANKLIN AND JACOBSON (AV)

Suite 300, 550 South Wadsworth Boulevard, 80226
Telephone: 303-936-3300
Fax: 303-936-0125

(See Next Column)

Gary L. Polidori
R. Jerold Gerome
Dennis J. Jacobson
Peter L. Franklin

Lesleigh S. Monahan
Barry J. Seidenfeld

Representative Clients: Lakewood City Center; Treeforms, Inc.; Lakewood Chrysler-Plymouth, Inc.; Western Fasteners U.S.A., Inc.; Horizon Glass and Glazing Co., Inc.; Grif-Fab Corp.; Fred Schmid Appliance and TV Co., Inc.; Commercial Architectural Products, Inc.; Voyaguers International, Inc.; 1st Bank, Villa Italia.

For full biographical listings, see the Martindale-Hubbell Law Directory

*LAMAR,** Prowers Co.

SHINN LAWYERS (AV)

200 West Elm Street, P.O. Box 390, 81052
Telephone: 719-336-4313
Fax: 719-336-4315

MEMBERS OF FIRM

Carl M. Shinn
Wendy S. Shinn

ASSOCIATES

Donald L. Steerman

Counsel for: Amity Canal; Lamar Canal; Lower Arkansas Water Management Assn.; District 67 Ditch Assn.; County of Cheyenne, Colorado; County of Kiowa, Colorado; Ragsdale Farms, Inc.; Sherler Farms; Hatcher Farms, Inc.; Young Bros. Equipment Co., Inc.

For full biographical listings, see the Martindale-Hubbell Law Directory

*LITTLETON,** Arapahoe Co.

JAMES S. KIMMEL (AV)

Suite 207 Norwest Bank Building, 5601 South Broadway, 80121
Telephone: 303-794-2036
Fax: 303-794-2073

Reference: Norwest Bank Littleton, N.A.

For full biographical listings, see the Martindale-Hubbell Law Directory

LONGMONT, Boulder Co.

FLANDERS, SONNESYN & STOVER (AV)

Suite 1 First National Bank Building, 401 Main Street, 80501
Telephone: 303-776-5380; Metro Denver Fax: 303-629-0530

MEMBERS OF FIRM

David N. Sonnesyn
John C. Flanders
Thomas L. Stover

ASSOCIATES

Peter M. Reinhardt
Kathleen A. Ellis

OF COUNSEL

L. B. Flanders

Representative Clients: The First National Bank of Longmont; The Boulder & White Rock Ditch & Reservoir Co.; The Animal Hospital; The Charles L. Hover Family Foundation; Longmont Realty & Insurance Co.; Longmont United Hospital; Plasco, Inc.; Longmont Toyota, Inc.

For full biographical listings, see the Martindale-Hubbell Law Directory

GRANT, BERNARD, LYONS & GADDIS, A PROFESSIONAL CORPORATION (AV)

515 Kimbark Street, P.O. Box 978, 80502-0978
Telephone: 303-776-9900 Denver: 303-571-5506
Telecopier: 303-772-6105

Howard Grant (1906-1966)
John S. Hough (1918-1979)
Wallace H. Grant
Daniel F. Bernard
Richard N. Lyons, II
Jeffrey J. Kahn
H. William Sims, Jr.
John W. Gaddis
Bradley A. Hall

Steven P. Jeffers

Representative Clients: Fox Hill-The Longmont Country Club; Left Hand Water District; Longmont Foods; Longs Peak Water District; Mountain View Fire Protection District; St. Vrain & Left Hand Water Conservancy District; St. Vrain Valley School District RE-1J; The Water Users Association of District No. 6 (Boulder Creek);

For full biographical listings, see the Martindale-Hubbell Law Directory

LOVELAND, Larimer Co.

HAMMOND, CLARK AND WHITE (AV)

Suite 418 Bank One Building, 200 East 7th Street, 80537
Telephone: 303-667-1023
Fax: 303-669-9380

(See Next Column)

HAMMOND, CLARK AND WHITE, *Loveland—Continued*

MEMBERS OF FIRM

Lynn A. Hammond | Roger E. Clark
Gregory A. White

ASSOCIATES

Martha Phillips Allbright

Representative Clients: Hewlett-Packard Co.; Hach Co.; Bank One, Fort Collins-Loveland, N.A.; Town of Estes Park; Loveland Rural Fire Protection District; Colorado Crystal Corp.; Loveland Economic Development Council, Inc.; City of Loveland (Water Matters).
References: Bank One. Fort Collins-Loveland, N.A.

For full biographical listings, see the Martindale-Hubbell Law Directory

MONTE VISTA, Rio Grande Co. — (Refer to Alamosa)

*MONTROSE,** Montrose Co.

WOODROW, ROUSHAR & CAREY (AV)

144 South Uncompahgre Avenue, P.O. Box 327, 81401
Telephone: 303-249-4531
Fax: 303-249-3102

MEMBERS OF FIRM

Frank J. Woodrow | Victor T. Roushar
Margaret L. Carey

Representative Clients: Western Gravel, Inc.; Horace Mann Insurance Co.; Farmers Insurance Group.

For full biographical listings, see the Martindale-Hubbell Law Directory

ROCKY FORD, Otero Co. — (Refer to Lamar)

*SALIDA,** Chaffee Co.

RUSH & RUSH (AV)

124 West 2nd Street, 81201
Telephone: 719-539-6606
FAX: 719-539-6607

William S. Rush (1898-1980) | Robert P. Rush

ASSOCIATES

Paula M. Lallier

General Counsel for: Sangre De Cristo Electric Assn.; Salida Building & Loan Assn.; Salida Hospital District.

*STERLING,** Logan Co. — (Refer to Greeley)

*TRINIDAD,** Las Animas Co. — (Refer to Canon City)

VAIL, Eagle Co.

DUNN, ABPLANALP & CHRISTENSEN, P.C. (AV)

Suite 300 Vail National Bank Building, 108 South Frontage Road West, 81657-5087
Telephone: 303-476-0300
Telecopier: 303-476-4765

John W. Dunn | Allen C. Christensen
Arthur A. Abplanalp, Jr. | Diane L. Herman
Carol E. Davis

SPECIAL COUNSEL

Jerry W. Hannah

LEGAL SUPPORT PERSONNEL

Karen M. Dunn (Paralegal)

Representative Clients: Towns of Avon, Minturn and Red Cliff, Colorado.

For full biographical listings, see the Martindale-Hubbell Law Directory

OTTO, PORTERFIELD & POST (AV)

0020 Eagle Road, P.O. Box 3149, 81658-3149
Telephone: 303-949-5380
Denver Direct Line: 303-623-5926
Fax: 303-845-9135

Frederick S. Otto | Wendell B. Porterfield, Jr.
William J. Post

Reference: 1st Bank of Vail; Vail Bank.

For full biographical listings, see the Martindale-Hubbell Law Directory

*WALSENBURG,** Huerfano Co. — (Refer to Canon City)

WHEAT RIDGE, Jefferson Co. — (Refer to Golden)

CONNECTICUT

*BRIDGEPORT,** Fairfield Co.

COHEN AND WOLF, P.C. (AV)

1115 Broad Street, P.O. Box 1821, 06601
Telephone: 203-368-0211
Facsimile: 203-576-8504
Danbury, Connecticut Office: 158 Deer Hill Avenue.
Telephone: 203-792-2771.
Facsimile: 203-791-8149.
Stamford, Connecticut Office: 595 Summer Street.
Telephone: 203-964-9907.
Facsimile: 203-967-4452.

Herbert L. Cohen (1905-1983)
Austin K. Wolf
Martin F. Wolf
Robert J. Ashkins
Stuart A. Epstein (Resident at Stamford Office)
Richard L. Albrecht
Jonathan S. Bowman
Irving J. Kern
Martin J. Albert
Stewart I. Edelstein
Neil R. Marcus (Resident at Danbury Office)
Richard A. Krantz
David L. Grogins (Resident at Danbury Office)
Robert B. Adelman
Michael S. Rosten
Greta E. Solomon
Joram Hirsch
Paul B. Edelberg (Resident at Stamford Office)
Robin A. Kahn (Resident at Danbury Office)
Richard G. Kent
Richard L. Newman (Resident at Danbury Office)
Richard Slavin
Frederick S. Gold (Resident at Stamford Office)
Linda Lederman (Resident at Stamford Office)
Daniel S. Nagel
Richard J. Di Marco
David B. Zabel
Mark A. Kirsch
Christopher J. Smith
Neil W. Sutton
David M. Levine
Joseph G. Walsh (Resident at Danbury Office)
Alexander H. Schwartz
Mary Ann Connors
Robin G. Frederick (Resident at Stamford Office)
Marci J. Silverman
David A. Ball
Michael F. Ewing
Jennifer Landsman Chobor
Jocelyn B. Hurwitz
Sharon Bradley Bowler
Stuart M. Katz
Daniel F. Wolf (Resident at Danbury Office)
Steven L. Elbaum
Monte Frank
Ellen A. Jawitz
Durwin P. Jones
Jessica S. Rubin (Resident at Stamford Office)
Jeffrey S. Wildstein

LEGAL SUPPORT PERSONNEL

Sherry E. Sopin

For full biographical listings, see the Martindale-Hubbell Law Directory

GLADSTONE, SCHWARTZ, BLUM, WOODS, L.L.C. (AV)

1087 Broad Street, P.O. Box 1900, 06604
Telephone: 203-368-6746
Telecopier: 203-576-8847

MEMBERS OF FIRM

Lawrence B. Schwartz (1929-1993)
Louis I. Gladstone
Leonard C. Blum
Matthew B. Woods

ASSOCIATES

Arthur E. Miller
Roberta S. Schwartz
Jason P. Gladstone
Stacey M. Daves-ohlin

OF COUNSEL

Peter L. Leepson
Edward N. Lerner
Arthur A. Lunin

Counsel for: Baker Companies, Inc.; D'Addario Industries, Inc.; Connecticut Jai Alai, Inc.; McNeil Brothers, Inc.; IMG & Associates Ltd., Partnership.

For full biographical listings, see the Martindale-Hubbell Law Directory

GOLDSTEIN AND PECK, P.C. (AV)

955 Main Street, P.O. Box 1538, 06601
Telephone: 203-334-9421
Telecopier: 203-334-6949
Westport, Connecticut Office: 190 Main Street. P.O. Box 5031.
Telephone: 203-226-7488.
Telecopier: 203-226-6403.

David Goldstein (1898-1992)
William J. Kupinse, Jr.
George J. Markley
Walter A. Flynn, Jr.
G. Kenneth Bernhard
Eugene E. Cederbaum
John G. Dzurik
Dennis M. Laccavole
Kathleen H. Allsup
Gregory C. Hammonds
Patricia E. Curtin
Lisa Kasden Kent
John H. Kane

Representative Clients: Bee Publishing Company, Inc.; The Chase Manhattan Bank of Connecticut, N.A.; Fairfield County Medical Association; Great American Insurance Companies; Segua Corp.; Inco, Ltd.; Physicians Health Services, Inc.; Town of Westport.

(See Next Column)

For full biographical listings, see the Martindale-Hubbell Law Directory

MARSH, DAY & CALHOUN (AV)

955 Main Street, 06604
Telephone: 203-259-8993
Fax: 203-254-1772
Southport, Connecticut Office: 2507 Post Road.
Telephone: 203-259-8993.
Fax: 203-254-1772.

MEMBERS OF FIRM

Thomas F. Maxwell, Jr.

Counsel for: Citytrust; Southern Connecticut Gas Co.; Metropolitan Life Insurance Co.; General Electric Co.; Sturm Ruger & Co., Inc.; The Producto Machine Co.

For full biographical listings, see the Martindale-Hubbell Law Directory

WILLIAMS, COONEY & SHEEHY (AV)

One Lafayette Circle, 06604
Telephone: 203-331-0888
Telecopier: 203-331-0896

MEMBERS OF FIRM

Ronald D. Williams
Robert J. Cooney
Edward Maum Sheehy
Peter D. Clark
Peter J. Dauk
Dion W. Moore
Ronald D. Williams, Jr.
Francis A. Smith, Jr. (1951-1989)

Lawrence F. Reilly
Michael P. Bowler
Michael Cuff Deakin

Representative Clients: Aetna Life & Casualty Co.; Nationwide Insurance Co.; Connecticut Medical Insurance Co.; ; Zimmer Manufacturing Co.; Textron-Lycoming; The Stop & Shop Companies, Inc.; Shawmut Bank Connecticut, N.A.; Allied Van Lines, Inc.; Podiatary Insurance Company of America; Town of Easton, Conn.

For full biographical listings, see the Martindale-Hubbell Law Directory

ZELDES, NEEDLE & COOPER, A PROFESSIONAL CORPORATION (AV)

1000 Lafayette Boulevard, P.O. Box 1740, 06601-1740
Telephone: 203-333-9441
Telecopiers: 203-333-1489; 579-2933

Jacob D. Zeldes
Elaine S. Amendola
Charles M. Needle
Robert S. Cooper
L. Douglas Shrader
Alfred J. Jennings, Jr.
Stuart Bear
Frank J. Silvestri, Jr.
William C. Longa
Robert A. Harris
Paul F. Thomas
Gregory J. Cava
David P. Atkins
Maximino Medina, Jr.
Jonathan B. Orleans
Shelley R. Sadin
Dominick C. Esposito, Jr.
Edward R. Scofield
David P. Friedman
Leslie Paier Aceto

Beverly Stauffer Knapp
Bette L. Bono
Adele V. Patterson
Ann M. VanDeventer
Jennifer L. Forrence
Lisa Campisi
Patrick J. Fitzgerald
Caryn A. Lowry
Martin L. McCann
S. Dave Vatti
Marcy Tench Stovall
Brian E. Spears

Representative Clients: Circuit-Wise, Inc.; Pace Motor Lines, Inc.; Rudel Machinery Co., Inc.; C.W. Pond Electrical Service, Inc.; Jeneric/Pentron, Inc.; H.L. Hayden Co.; U.S. Surgical Corp.

For full biographical listings, see the Martindale-Hubbell Law Directory

BRISTOL, Hartford Co.

ANDERSON, ALDEN, HAYES & ZIOGAS, L.L.C. (AV)

238 Main Street, P.O. Box 1197, 06011-1197
Telephone: 203-589-4121
Fax: 203-589-4966

Frederick W. Beach (1903-1994)
George T. Calder (Retired)

MEMBERS OF FIRM

Sherwood L. Anderson, III
Richard H. Alden
Margaret M. Hayes
Mark Ziogas

Attorneys for: Eagle Federal Savings Bank; J.H. Sessions and Son; Wasley Products, Inc.; The Barnes Group; The Fletcher-Terry Co.; Bristol Shopping Plaza, Inc.; Bristol Press Publishing Co.; Bristol Savings Bank.

For full biographical listings, see the Martindale-Hubbell Law Directory

CHESHIRE, New Haven Co.

HITT, SACHNER & COLEMAN (AV)
673 South Main Street, P.O. Box 724, 06410
Telephone: 203-272-0371
FAX: 203-272-9854

MEMBERS OF FIRM
Fred A. Hitt
Stephen P. Sachner
Andrew D. Coleman

ASSOCIATES
James M. Miele
S. Peter Sachner

Representative Clients: The Aetna Casualty & Surety Division; Lafayette American Bank & Trust; Liberty Mutual Insurance Co.; National Paint Distributors, Inc.; Ravenswood Properties, Inc.; Harte Nissan, Inc.; Dowling Ford, Inc.; Shawmut Bank Connecticut, N.A.; Frank R. DiNatali Inc.; Doug Calcagni Associates, Inc.

For full biographical listings, see the Martindale-Hubbell Law Directory

DANBURY, Fairfield Co.

SECOR, CASSIDY & McPARTLAND, P.C. (AV)
301 Main Street, 06810
Telephone: 203-743-9145
Fax: 203-798-9844
Waterbury, Connecticut Office: 41 Church Street, P.O. Box 2818.
Telephone: 203-757-9261.
Fax: 203-756-5762.
Southbury, Connecticut Office: 370 Main Street South.
Telephone: 203-264-8223.
Fax: 203-264-6730.

Martin A. Rader, Jr.
Richard D. Arconti
Daniel E. Casagrande
Robin Edwards Otto
Kim E. Nolan (Resident)

For full biographical listings, see the Martindale-Hubbell Law Directory

WANDERER, HANNA & TALARICO (AV)
142 Deer Hill Avenue, 06810-7727
Telephone: 203-792-8333
Telecopier: 203-778-9570

MEMBERS OF FIRM
Herbert B. Wanderer (1902-1979)
Richard W. Hanna
Robert N. Talarico

For full biographical listings, see the Martindale-Hubbell Law Directory

DANIELSON, Windham Co.

JACKSON, HARRIS, BURLINGAME & HUBERT (AV)
245 Main Street, P.O. Box 409, 06239
Telephone: 203-774-9627
Fax: 203-774-5784

MEMBERS OF FIRM
George H. Jackson, III
John K. Harris, Jr.
Stephen J. Burlingame
David M. Hubert

Representative Client: Danielson Federal Savings & Loan Assn.

For full biographical listings, see the Martindale-Hubbell Law Directory

DARIEN, Fairfield Co.

McANERNEY & MILLAR (AV)
23 Old King's Highway South, 06820-1267
Telephone: 203-655-7931
FAX: 203-656-2055

MEMBERS OF FIRM
Robert M. McAnerney
Samuel D. B. Millar, Jr.
L. Conrad Ambrette

OF COUNSEL
Peter M. Ryan

ASSOCIATES
Patricia Moreland Gross
Carolyn C. Swiggart

For full biographical listings, see the Martindale-Hubbell Law Directory

RUCCI, GLEASON & BURNHAM (AV)
800 Post Road, P.O. Box 1107, 06820
Telephone: 203-655-7695
Facsimile: 203-655-4302

MEMBERS OF FIRM
Joseph J. Rucci, Jr.
Wilder G. Gleason
Paul H. Burnham
Kevin C. Beuttenmuller

ASSOCIATES
William Michael Carello
Colette C. Symon
Karen Kolesar Linder

(See Next Column)

OF COUNSEL
Ian R. Crawford
James C. Dempsey
George A. Reilly

For full biographical listings, see the Martindale-Hubbell Law Directory

FAIRFIELD, Fairfield Co.

MOREHOUSE, HARLOW & WELDY (AV)
1735 Post Road, P.O. Box 827, 06430-0827
Telephone: 203-255-5981
Telecopier: 203-259-0130

MEMBERS OF FIRM
Samuel G. Payne (1907-1988)
W. Bradley Morehouse
Albert L. Harlow
Thomas P. Weldy

OF COUNSEL
Gregory C. Willis
Philip Y. Reinhart

Representative Clients: The Connecticut Audubon Society; The Swan Engineering Co.; Harvey Hubbell, Inc.; People's Bank; Fairfield Board of Realtors, Inc.

For full biographical listings, see the Martindale-Hubbell Law Directory

FARMINGTON, Hartford Co. — (Refer to Hartford)

GREENWICH, Fairfield Co.

ALBERT, WARD & JOHNSON, P.C. (AV)
125 Mason Street, P.O. Box 1668, 06836
Telephone: 203-661-8600
Telecopier: 203-661-8051

OF COUNSEL
David Albert

Tom S. Ward, Jr.
Scott R. Johnson
Jane D. Hogeman
Howard R. Wolfe
Christopher A. Kristoff

For full biographical listings, see the Martindale-Hubbell Law Directory

DUEL AND HOLLAND (AV)
289 Greenwich Avenue, 06830
Telephone: 203-869-5600
Fax: 203-869-4648

Arthur B. Duel, III
Alexander J. Holland
Charles B. Kaufmann, III
Philip H. Bartels
Day R. Shields
Beth K. Hansson
Amy Kohler Wilfert (Not admitted in CT)
Harold R. Burke
Jennifer E. Clement
Lori E. Gargagliano

For full biographical listings, see the Martindale-Hubbell Law Directory

HEAGNEY, LENNON & SLANE (AV)
248 Greenwich Avenue, P.O. Box 7910, 06836
Telephone: 203-661-8400
FAX: 203-661-7496

MEMBERS OF FIRM
John G. Heagney (1925-1982)
Francis X. Lennon, Jr.
John F. Slane, Jr.
Thomas J. Heagney

For full biographical listings, see the Martindale-Hubbell Law Directory

IVEY, BARNUM & O'MARA (AV)
Meridian Building, 170 Mason Street, P.O. Box 1689, 06830
Telephone: 203-661-6000
Telecopier: 203-661-9462

MEMBERS OF FIRM
Michael J. Allen
Robert C. Barnum, Jr.
Edward D. Cosden, Jr.
James W. Cuminale
Wilmot L. Harris, Jr.
William I. Haslun, II
Edward T. Krumeich, Jr.
Donat C. Marchand
Miles F. McDonald, Jr.
Edwin J. O'Mara, Jr.
Remy A. Rodas
Gregory A. Saum
Lorraine Slavin

ASSOCIATES
Juerg A. Heim
Melissa Townsend Klauberg
Nicole Barrett Lecher
Alan S. Rubenstein

OF COUNSEL
Philip R. McKnight

For full biographical listings, see the Martindale-Hubbell Law Directory

Greenwich—Continued

WHITMAN BREED ABBOTT & MORGAN (AV)

Two Greenwich Plaza, 06830
Telephone: 203-869-3800
Telecopier: 203-869-1951
New York, N.Y. Office: 200 Park Avenue.
Telephone: 212-351-3000.
Los Angeles, California Office: 633 West Fifth Street.
Telephone: 213-896-2400.
Sacramento, California Office: Senator Hotel Building, 1121 L Street.
Telephone: 916-441-4242.
Washington, D.C. Offices: 1215 17th Street, N.W.
Telephone: 202-887-0353; 1818 N. Street, N.W.
Telephone: 202-466-1100.
Telecopier: 202-466-2745.
Newark, New Jersey Office: One Gateway Center.
Telephone: 201-621-2230.
Palm Beach, Florida Office: 220 Sunrise Avenue.
Telephone: 407-832-5458.
London, England Office: 11 Waterloo Place.
Telephone: 71-839-3226.
Telex: 917881.
Tokyo, Japan Office: Suite 450, New Otemachi Building, 2-2-1 Otemachi, Chiyoda-Ku, Tokyo 100.
Telephone: 81-3-3242-1289.
Associated with: Tyan & Associates, 22 La Sagesse Street, Beirut, Lebanon.
Telephone: 337968.
Fax: 200969.
Telex: 43928.

PARTNERS

Frank Lewis Baker, III
Mark R. Carta
Charles E. Coates, III
Bruce F. Cohen
James A. Fulton
Kenneth M. Gammill
Charles E. Janson
Richard F. Lawler
Thomas J. McKee
Robert C. O'Brien
Harry E. Peden, Jr.
Harry E. Peden, III
Leland C. Selby
Christopher A. Stack (Not admitted in CT)

RETIRED PARTNERS

Mortimer P. Barnes
William T. Cahill
Joseph Mitchell Kaye
Jacob R. Lynch
Alan M. MacCracken
Richard Joyce Smith
Clark McK. Whittemore, Jr.

COUNSEL

Jennifer N. Boyd
Everett Fisher
Brian D. Forrow
Richard L. Rose
David P. Tuttle

ASSOCIATES

Joseph V. Cuomo
Sarah O. Conrades
Joseph C. Gasparrini
Deborah S. Gordon
Elizabeth M. Grant
Maurice H. Hartigan, III
L. Page Heslin
Richard E. Mancuso
Elizabeth B. Palache
Charles W. Pieterse
James C. Riley
Douglas S. Skalka
William Bradford Smith, Jr.
Margaret Ann Triolo
Sujata Yalamanchili

For full biographical listings, see the Martindale-Hubbell Law Directory

GROTON, New London Co.

BROWN, JACOBSON, TILLINGHAST, LAHAN & KING, P.C. (AV)

4 Fort Hill Road, 06340
Telephone: 203-449-8765
Telecopier: 203-445-7634
Norwich, Connecticut Office: Uncas-Merchants National Bank Building, 22 Courthouse Square.
Telephone: 203-889-3321.
Fax: 203-886-0673.

Timothy D. Bates
Deborah J. Tedford
Robert A. Avena
Peter A. Anderson

Representative Clients: Nationwide Insurance Co.; Aetna Casualty & Surety Co.; Chelsea-Groton Savings Bank; Norwich Community Development Corp.

For full biographical listings, see the Martindale-Hubbell Law Directory

O'BRIEN, SHAFNER, STUART, KELLY & MORRIS, P.C. (AV)

475 Bridge Street, P.O. Drawer 929, 06340
Telephone: 203-445-2463
Fax: 203-445-4539
Norwich, Connecticut Office: 2 Courthouse Square.
Telephone: 203-889-3855.
Fax: 203-886-6352.

(See Next Column)

John C. O'Brien
Matthew Shafner
Peter F. Stuart
Carolyn P. Kelly
Granville R. Morris
Frank N. Eppinger
Mark E. Block (Resident at Norwich Office)
Raymond T. Trebisacci
Mark W. Oberlatz
Lloyd L. Langhammer
Susan B. Pochal
Nathan J. Shafner
Richard J. Pascal
Daniel R. Cunningham
Amy M. Stone
Thomas W. Teixeira, II
Eric M. Janney
Stephen M. Reck

For full biographical listings, see the Martindale-Hubbell Law Directory

*HARTFORD,** Hartford Co.

* indicates certain Bar Register subscribers whose principal office is located elsewhere in the state and who have arranged for representation as a part of the state capital listings that follow

BINGHAM, DANA & GOULD (AV)

100 Pearl Street, 06103
Telephone: 203-244-3770
Telefax: 203-527-5188
Boston, Massachusetts Office: 150 Federal Street.
Telephone: 617-951-8000.
Cable Address: "Blodgham Bsn".
Telex: 275147 BDGBSN UR.
Telecopy: 617-951-8736.
London, England Office: 39 Victoria Street, SWIH 0EE.
Telephone: 011-44-71-799-2646.
Telecopy: 011-44-71-799-2654.
Telex: 888179 BDGLDN G.
Cable Address: "Blodgham Ldn".
Washington, D.C. Office: 1550 M Street, N.W.
Telephone: 202-822-9320.
Telecopy: 202-833-1506.

RESIDENT PARTNERS

Jonathan K. Bernstein
Ben M. Krowicki
Neal C. Mizner
James G. Scantling
Scott M. Schooley (Not admitted in CT)
John R. Snyder
Lee A. Spielman
Judy K. Weinstein

RESIDENT OF COUNSEL

David R. Glissman
Catherine E. LaMarr

RESIDENT ASSOCIATES

Frank A. Appicelli
Robert M. Borden
Carol A. Fantozzi
Walter F. Garger
Gerald B. Goldberg
Michael P. Panagrossi (Not admitted in CT)
Daniel I. Papermaster
James Scott Rollins

For full biographical listings, see the Martindale-Hubbell Law Directory

BROWN, PAINDIRIS & ZARELLA (AV)

100 Pearl Street, 06103
Telephone: 203-522-3343
Telecopier: 203-522-2490

MEMBERS OF FIRM

Richard R. Brown
Nicholas Paindiris
Peter T. Zarella
Ronald T. Scott
John D. Maxwell
Steven W. Varney

ASSOCIATES

Christopher J. McCarthy
Sean M. Peoples

OF COUNSEL

David J. D. Evans

For full biographical listings, see the Martindale-Hubbell Law Directory

COONEY, SCULLY AND DOWLING (AV)

Hartford Square North, Ten Columbus Boulevard, 06106
Telephone: 203-527-1141
Fax: 203-247-5215

MEMBERS OF FIRM

Joseph P. Cooney (1906-1984)
John F. Scully
Vincent J. Dowling
Patrick J. Flaherty
Louis B. Blumenfeld
John W. Sitarz
Eugene A. Cooney
John T. Scully
Richard A. Ferris
Karen Jansen Casey
Jeffrey C. Pingpank
Paul T. Nowosadko
Herbert J. Shepardson
David A. Haught
Joseph A. La Bella
James T. Scully
William J. Scully

(See Next Column)

COONEY, SCULLY AND DOWLING, *Hartford—Continued*

ASSOCIATES

Lorinda S. Coon
Jeffrey V. Phelon
Elizabeth D. Fairbanks
Robert G. Clemente
Eileen Mohan Flaherty
Sharone G. Kornman
Rodd J. Mantell
Arthur J. Hudon
Anthony J. Pantuso
Robb J. Canning
Matthew J. Scott

Reference: Fleet Bank.

For full biographical listings, see the Martindale-Hubbell Law Directory

DAY, BERRY & HOWARD (AV)

Cityplace, 06103-3499
Telephone: 203-275-0100
Telecopier: 203-275-0343
Stamford, Connecticut Office: One Canterbury Green.
Telephone: 203-977-7300.
Telecopier: 203-977-7301.
Boston, Massachusetts Office: 260 Franklin Street.
Telephone: 617-345-4600.
Telex: 990686.
Telecopier: 617-345-4745.

Edward M. Day (1872-1947)
Joseph Francis Berry (1880-1953)
Lawrence Augustus Howard (1881-1960)
J. Danford Anthony, Jr.
C. Duane Blinn
Robert A. Brooks
Harold C. Buckingham, Jr.
Martin L. Budd
Dean M. Cordiano
William H. Cuddy
Rodney J. Dillman
David T. Doot
David J. Elliott
Michael W. Elsass
Steven M. Fast
Daniel L. FitzMaurice
Gerald Garfield
John C. Glezen
Raymond B. Green
Steven M. Greenspan
Thomas J. Groark, Jr.
Jeffrey G. Grody
Michael F. Halloran
J. Roger Hanlon
Thomas F. Harrison
Paula Lacey Herman
Robert P. Knickerbocker, Jr.
Charles H. Lenore
Timothy R. Lyman
Richard C. MacKenzie
Daniel S. Matos
Ernest J. Mattei
Paul F. McAlenney
James A. McGraw
Joseph A. Moniz
Francis H. Morrison, III
Scott P. Moser
John B. Nolan
Thomas Z. Reicher
Richard M. Reynolds
James H. Rotondo
Edmund M. See
James Sicilian
Robert G. Siegel
Felix J. Springer
James J. Tancredi
Allan B. Taylor
Robert M. Taylor, III
M. Louise Turilli
Lyn Gammill Walker
Philip S. Walker
Richard J. Wasserman
Thomas R. Wildman
Paul D. Williams
Martin Wolman
Albert Zakarian

ASSOCIATES

Marsha L. Anastasia
Esther R. Aronson
John B. Ashmeade
Sarah C. Baskin
Gary M. Becker
Matthew J. Becker
Paul N. Belval
Jonathan C. Black
Susan Busby-Mott
Mary Beth Cardin
Victoria Woodin Chavey
John E. Deitelbaum
Kathleen N. Dondero
Glenn W. Dowd
Peter J. Duffy
Dean A. Dulchinos
Kenneth H. Eagle
Marylou Fabbo
James L. Fischer
William J. Fiske
Charles W. Fortune
Beverly W. Garofalo
Alex C. Geisinger
Douglas W. Gillette
Ronald A. Gonzalez
Lauren R. Greenspoon
Laurie A. Hall
Joseph L. Hammer
Mitchell R. Harris
Richard D. Harris
Tricia A. Haught
Ora-Anne E. Jarvis
C. J. Karbowicz
Joseph Kershenbaum
Edward F. Krzanowski
Ruth A. Kurien
Robin S. Linker
Judy S. Loitherstein
Regina A. Long
Rosemary Maccarone
Leah A. Martin
Carolyn B. Martino
Kathleen M. McFadden
Edward F. McHugh
Shane T. Munoz
Michael K. Murray
Scott P. Myers
Robert C. Papay
Barbara A. Petitjean
Bryan K. Pollard
Louis A. Ricciuti, Jr.
David C. Robinson
Monique Rowtham-Kennedy
Rhoda L. Rudnick
Daniel L. Schwartz
Kent I. Scott-Smith
Peter M. Seka
Robin L. Smith
Margaret J. Strange
Jonathan B. Tropp
Athena R. Tsakanikas
Kathleen K. Vella
Stephanie A. Watkins
Philip S. Wellman
Jean E. Winn

OF COUNSEL

George H. Cain
Palmer S. McGee, Jr.
James R. McIntosh
A. Peter Quinn, Jr. (Not admitted in CT)
Olcott D. Smith

(See Next Column)

RESIDENT PARTNERS IN BOSTON OFFICE

James L. Ackerman
Joseph W. Ambash
Glenn E. Brace
David B. Broughel
Lewis A. Burleigh
Daniel J. Carragher
Jeffrey A. Clopeck
Nancy M. Cullen
George L. Cushing
Lisa J. Damon
Charles Donelan
Thomas D. Gill, Jr.
William A. Hunter
J. Charles Mokriski
Ross A. Pascal
William Shields
H. Lawrence Tafe, III
Kenneth E. Werner
Cynthia J. Williams

RESIDENT PARTNERS IN STAMFORD OFFICE

Jerome Berkman
Michael P. Byrne
Patricia A. Carpenter
Ronald Osburn Dederick
Thomas D. Goldberg
F. Lee Griffith, III
Michael S. Leo
Robert J. Miller
Kenneth W. Ritt
Sabino Rodriguez, III
James F. Stapleton
David A. Swerdloff
Stanley A. Twardy, Jr.
Stefan R. Underhill
Carla R. Walworth

RESIDENT COUNSEL IN BOSTON OFFICE

Richard C. Csaplar, Jr.
Kenneth A. Reich

RESIDENT COUNSEL IN STAMFORD OFFICE

John Crosskey
Ellen B. Wells

RESIDENT ASSOCIATES IN BOSTON OFFICE

Colin Hugh Buckley
David C. Camp
Bruce D. Hickey
Carol F. Liebman
Kathleen S. Moore
Kenneth B. Newton
Kathryn A. O'Leary
Nancy M. Reimer
Mark C. Rosenthal
Maura D. Sullivan
Danielle Y. Vanderzanden
James E. Venable, Jr.
Mary Ellen C. Whiteman
Mark C. Wilson
G. Perry Wu
Anne Magill Ziebarth

RESIDENT ASSOCIATES IN STAMFORD OFFICE

Jean Mills Aranha
R. Scott Beach
Joy Beane
J. Bradley Britton
Edward M. Brown
Wendy D. DiChristina
Kenneth W. Gage
Craig Goldberg
Susan E. Gorman
Gregory A. Hayes
Jeanine M. Lynch
Christopher W. Murphy
Eileen Reynolds
Samuel V. Schoonmaker, IV
Steven M. Torkelsen
Carole F. Wilder

For full biographical listings, see the Martindale-Hubbell Law Directory

GERSTEN & GERSTEN (AV)

234 Pearl Street, 06103
Telephone: 203-522-0173

MEMBERS OF FIRM

Maurice R. Gersten
Aaron L. Gersten

ASSOCIATES

Philip K. Meister
Thomas D. Jacobs
Neil A. McPhail
Karen S. Gersten

For full biographical listings, see the Martindale-Hubbell Law Directory

GORDON, MUIR AND FOLEY (AV)

Hartford Square North, Ten Columbus Boulevard, 06106-1944
Telephone: 203-525-5361
Telecopier: 203-525-4849

MEMBERS OF FIRM

William S. Gordon, Jr. (1946-1956)
George Muir (1939-1976)
Edward J. Foley (1955-1983)
Peter C. Schwartz
John J. Reid
John H. Goodrich, Jr.
R. Bradley Wolfe
Jon Stephen Berk
William J. Gallitto
Gerald R. Swirsky
Robert J. O'Brien
Philip J. O'Connor
Kenneth G. Williams
Chester J. Bukowski
Mary Ann Santacroce

ASSOCIATES

J. Lawrence Price
Mary Anne Alicia Charron
James G. Kelly
Kevin F. Morin
Claudia A. Baio
Patrick T. Treacy
Andrew J. Hern
Eileen Geel
Christopher L. Slack
Renee W. Dwyer
David B. Heintz

OF COUNSEL

Stephen M. Riley

Reference: Fleet Bank.

For full biographical listings, see the Martindale-Hubbell Law Directory

GOULD, KILLIAN & WYNNE (AV)

One Commercial Plaza, 25th Floor, 06103-3595
Telephone: 203-278-1270
Telecopier: 203-244-9290

(See Next Column)

GOULD, KILLIAN & WYNNE—*Continued*

MEMBERS OF FIRM

Samuel Gould
Robert K. Killian
Francis J. Wynne
Martin A. Gould
Mark W. Baronas
William F. Healey

ASSOCIATES

Nancy E. Gould
Robert O. Wynne

For full biographical listings, see the Martindale-Hubbell Law Directory

HALLORAN & SAGE (AV)

One Goodwin Square, 225 Asylum Street, 06103
Telephone: 203-522-6103
Fax: 203-548-0006
Middletown, Connecticut Office: 300 Plaza Middlesex.
Telephone: 203-346-8641.
Fax: 203-344-1641.

MEMBERS OF FIRM

Joseph G. Lynch
Joseph T. Sweeney
George D. Royster, Jr.
Arthur P. McGowan, Jr.
John W. Lemega
Robert C. Engstrom
Vincent M. Marino (Middletown Office)
Richard C. Tynan
William P. Borchert
Thomas J. Hagarty, Jr.
Paul V. Knopf
Brian J. Donnell
James J. Szerejko
Mark B. Seiger
William J. McGrath, Jr.
Dennis C. Cavanaugh
Christopher J. Lynch
Paul D. Meade
Joseph G. Fortner, Jr.
Stephen P. Fogerty
Peter G. Boucher
Jean M. D'Aquila (Middletown Office)
Steven H. Malitz
Michael J. Gustafson

COUNSEL

Milford F. Rhines
Irwin D. Mittelman (Middletown Office)
David B. Losee
Michael A. Pease
Elizabeth A. Curtis
Janet L. Lawler

ASSOCIATES

Deborah L. Bradley
Erin M. Kallaugher
John B. Farley
Matthew E. Karanian
Mark R. Cramer
Harris B. Appelman
Mark T. Altermatt
Michele P. Rosano
Susan O'Donnell Rotondo
Bruce H. Raymond
Kevin M. Roche
David G. Hill
Daniel P. Scapellati
James M. Sconzo
William P. Breen, Jr.
Donna-Maria Lonergan
Janet M. Helmke
Thomas P. O'Dea, Jr.
Robert M. Barrack
James E. Mack
Terrence M. O'Neill
Peter F. Carello
Heidi J. Daraskevich
Steven M. Barry
Lynda A. Barry
John W. Dietz

Representative Clients: Beech Aircraft Corp.; Catholic Relief Insurance Co.; LWP Claims Services, Inc.; Guardian Life Insurance Co.; Hertz Cos.; Keystone Insurance Co.; State Farm Insurance Cos.; Travelers Insurance; Western World Insurance Co.

For full biographical listings, see the Martindale-Hubbell Law Directory

HEBB & GITLIN, A PROFESSIONAL CORPORATION (AV)

One State Street, 06103-3178
Telephone: 203-240-2700
Telecopier: 203-278-8968

G. Eric Brunstad, Jr.
Richard F. Casher
Chester L. Fisher III
Douglas E. Fiske
Evan D. Flaschen
John J. Gillies, Jr.
Richard A. Gitlin
James Greenfield
Gary S. Hammersmith
Edwin Gordon Hebb, Jr.
Harold S. Horwich
Eric W. Johnson
William E. Kelly
Jeffery S. Kuperstock
Thomas J. Love, Jr.
George A. McKeon (Of Counsel)
M. Bree Nesbitt
Gregory W. Nye
Michael J. Reilly
R. Jeffrey Smith
Elliot N. Solomon
Lorraine Murphy Weil
Jeffrey L. Williams

Patti Lynn Boss
Claude M. Brouillard
Katherine A. Burroughs
Mark E. Chavey
Laura Gonzalez Ciabarra
Thomas H. Day
Jane M. Domboski
Scott A. Falk
Alison R. Faltersack
Christine E. Farrell
Deborah Samuels Freeman
Matthew F. Furlong
Elena M. Gervino
Jonathan A. Harris
John D. Inwood (Not admitted in CT)
Jeffrey A. Jones
James P. Juliano
James P. Maher
Theodore C. Morris
Thomas F. O'Connor
Thomas J. O'Shea
Joyce M. Resnick
Barry G. Russell
Joseph L. Scibilia
Patricia Ann Shackelford

(See Next Column)

James W. Shaughnessy
David Silber
Ronald J. Silverman
Robert C. Walsh, Jr.
Brian N. Watkins

For full biographical listings, see the Martindale-Hubbell Law Directory

JACKSON, O'KEEFE AND PHELAN (AV)

36 Russ Street, 06106-1571
Telephone: 203-278-4040
Fax: 203-527-2500
West Hartford, Connecticut Office: 62 LaSalle Road.
Telephone: 203-521-7500.
Fax: 203-561-5399.
Bethlehem, Connecticut Office: 423 Munger Lane.
Telephone: 203-266-5255.

MEMBERS OF FIRM

Jay W. Jackson
Andrew J. O'Keefe
Denise Martino Phelan
Matthew J. O'Keefe
Peter K. O'Keefe
Philip R. Dunn, Jr.
Michael J. Walsh
Anna M. Carbonaro
Denise Rodosevich

OF COUNSEL

Maureen Sullivan Dinnan

Representative Clients: Aetna Casualty & Surety Co.; ITT Hartford; Liberty Mutual Insurance Co.; Connecticut Medical Insurance Co.

For full biographical listings, see the Martindale-Hubbell Law Directory

KENNY, BRIMMER, MELLEY & MAHONEY (AV)

5 Grand Street, 06106
Telephone: 203-527-4226
FAX: 203-527-0214

Joseph P. Kenny (1920-1993)

MEMBERS OF FIRM

Leslie R. Brimmer
William J. Melley, III
Richard C. Mahoney

ASSOCIATES

Anita M. Varunes
Dennis F. McCarthy
Maurice M. O'Shea
Beverly Johns

Representative Clients: Allstate Insurance Co.; Peerless Insurance Co.; Berkshire Mutual Fire Insurance Co.; Dorchester Mutual Fire Insurance Co.; Abington Mutual Fire Insurance Co.

For full biographical listings, see the Martindale-Hubbell Law Directory

LEVIN & D'AGOSTINO (AV)

One State Street, 06103
Telephone: 203-527-0400
Telecopier: 203-249-7500

MEMBERS OF FIRM

Michael R. Levin
John B. D'Agostino
Paul W. Ford
Nancy DuBois Wright
Walter E. Paulekas
Eugene N. Axelrod

ASSOCIATES

Peter Menting
Lawrence A. Dvorin
William J. Egan
David A. Hill, Jr.
Margaret A. McCue

For full biographical listings, see the Martindale-Hubbell Law Directory

MOLLER, HORTON & SHIELDS, P.C. (AV)

90 Gillett Street, 06105
Telephone: 203-522-8338

William R. Moller
Wesley W. Horton
Robert M. Shields, Jr.
Susan M. Cormier
Kimberly A. Knox
Karen L. Murdoch

Christy Scott

For full biographical listings, see the Martindale-Hubbell Law Directory

O'BRIEN, TANSKI, TANZER & YOUNG (AV)

Cityplace, 06103-3402
Telephone: 203-525-2700

MEMBERS OF FIRM

Donald W. O'Brien
James M. Tanski
Lois B. Tanzer
Roland F. Young, III
Thomas O. Anderson
Robert E. Kiley
Nancy Phillips Maxwell

ASSOCIATES

Caroline Schnog
Robert D. Silva
Albert G. Danker, Jr.
Kathleen Morrison Grover
P. Jo Anne Burgh
Jennifer L. Cox
Mary R. Knack

(See Next Column)

O'BRIEN, TANSKI, TANZER & YOUNG, *Hartford—Continued*

References: United Bank & Trust Co.; Connecticut National Bank & Trust Co.

For full biographical listings, see the Martindale-Hubbell Law Directory

REID AND RIEGE, P.C. (AV)

One State Street, 06103
Telephone: 203-278-1150
FAX: 203-240-1002
West Hartford, Connecticut Office: 65 LaSalle Road.
Telephone: 203-232-6565.
FAX: 203-232-6066.

Clifford S. Burdge, Jr.
William R. Judy
Robert C. McNally
James C. Ervin, Jr.
Andrew J. Howat
Travers T. Auburn
Maurice T. FitzMaurice
Bruce M. Lutsk
Maynard R. Miller, Jr.
Michael L. Coyle
Suzanne S. Bocchini
John J. Jacobson
John E. D'Amico
Lawrence H. Lissitzyn
Frederick J. Mullen, Jr.
Neil P. Coughlan
Edmund A. Mikolowsky
Robert U. Sattin
John M. Horak
Edward F. Spinella
Craig L. Sylvester
Robert M. Mulé
Paul B. Sonoski, Jr.
Eileen M. Marks
Earl F. McMahon
Thomas C. Lee, Jr.
Christopher J. Sowden

Karen L. Brand
Paul H. D. Stoughton
Nancy Zytkewick McLucas
Jo-Ann Leigh Bowen
Jon P. Newton
Mark X. Ryan
Steven R. Reid
Robert C. Reichert
Seth L. Cooper
John R. Ivimey
Carolyn A. Magnan
Douglas K. Knight
Eric A. Henzy (Not admitted in CT)
Theodore A. Donahue, Jr.

OF COUNSEL

John H. Riege
Thomas C. McKone
Raymond J. Payne
Suzanne M. Batchelor

For full biographical listings, see the Martindale-Hubbell Law Directory

SCHATZ & SCHATZ, RIBICOFF & KOTKIN (AV)

90 State House Square, 06103-3902
Telephone: 203-522-3234
Telecopier: 203-246-1225
Stamford, Connecticut Office: 1 Landmark Square.
Telephone: 203-964-0027.
Telecopier: 203-357-9251.

MEMBERS OF FIRM

Irving S. Ribicoff (1915-1994)
Nathan A. Schatz (1892-1956)
Louis M. Schatz (1894-1953)
Thomas M. Armstrong
Mark A. Asmar
R. Mark Chamberlin
Scott P. Consoli
Thomas F. Cullen (Resident, Stamford Office)
Ira M. Dansky (Resident, Stamford Office)
Robert M. Dombroff
Lori A. Epstein
Ross G. Fingold
Matthew J. Forstadt (Resident, Stamford Office)
F. Mark Fucci
Steven M. Gold (Resident, Stamford Office)
Stanford N. Goldman, Jr.
Walter J. Gorski
Thomas A. Gugliotti
Donald R. Gustafson (Resident, Stamford Office)
Gregory E. Harmer (Resident, Stamford Office)
Mitchell S. Jaffe
Gary D. Jones
Andrew W. Krevolin
Peter H. Levine
Richard S. Lipman
Michael F. Maglio
Stephen Marcovich (Resident, Stamford Office)
Peter M. Nolin (Resident, Stamford Office)
Mark Oland
Stuart D. Rosen
Stuart M. Roth
Michael E. Satti
Andrew M. Schatz
Louis B. Schatz
Robert F. Schatz
Lewis G. Schwartz (Resident, Stamford Office)
Ann M. Siczewicz
Bruce C. Silvers
Steven B. Steinmetz (Resident, Stamford Office)
James E. Wakim
Michael L. Widland (Resident, Stamford Office)
Carol K. Young (Resident, Stamford Office)

ASSOCIATES

Jonathan B. Alter
Stephen W. Aronson
Laurie L. Caldarella
Susan A. Connors
Franca L. DeRosa
Marianne M. Downie
Mary C. Duffy
Douglas M. Evans
Michael L. Fantozzi
David E. Golden
Patrick E. Gonya, Jr.
Sadie Rose Gordon
Jason B. Harris
Elizabeth R. Houde
Lisa J. Kerner
Rachel L. Kittredge
Daniel W. Levin
Kevin P. Mallery (Not admitted in CT)
Julie A. Manning
Lawrence J. Marks
Jeffrey S. Nobel
Alan S. Parker
Anthony M. Pepper

(See Next Column)

ASSOCIATES (Continued)

Nathan A. Schatz
Jay Sobel
Eliot R. Streim
Steven I. Weinberger
Mark H. Zackin

OF COUNSEL

Davida S. Edelson
Jeffrey A. Fillman (Not admitted in CT)
Melvin S. Katz
David Kotkin
I. Oscar Levine
S. Michael Schatz
Walter B. Schatz
I. Milton Widem

For full biographical listings, see the Martindale-Hubbell Law Directory

SHIPMAN & GOODWIN (AV)

One American Row, 06103
Telephone: 203-251-5000
Telecopier: 203-251-5099
Lakeville, Connecticut Office: Porter Street.
Telephone: 203-435-2539.
Stamford, Connecticut Office: Three Landmark Square.
Telephone: 203-359-4544.

MEMBERS OF FIRM

H. Martyn Owen
Paul W. Orth
Robert J. Cathcart
Francis M. Dooley (Lakeville Office)
Theodore M. Space
Stuyvesant K. Bearns (Lakeville Office)
Alex Lloyd
Daniel P. Brown, Jr.
James T. Betts
Brian Clemow
Ira H. Goldman
Scott L. Murphy
Coleman H. Casey
Brenda A. Eckert
John E. Kreitler
Peter W. Benner
Thomas B. Mooney
Thomas F. Tresselt
John T. Harris
Robert L. Wyld
Frank J. Marco (Hartford and Stamford Offices)
Charles L. Howard
J. Michael Sconyers (Lakeville Office)
John H. Lawrence, Jr.
James W. Bergenn
Paul D. Sanson
Saranne P. Murray
Alan E. Lieberman
William George Rock
Donna L. Brooks
Linda L. Yoder
John E. Wertam
Richard I. Cohen
Timothy S. Hollister
Joan W. Feldman
Richard A. Mills, Jr.
Deborah Smith Frisone
Stephen J. Geissler
Jeffrey Hellman
Mark K. Ostrowski

ASSOCIATES

Paul R. Pescatello
Timothy J. Covello
Leslie L. Davenport
Stephen K. Gellman
Thomas P. Flynn
Carrie A. Brodzinski
Timothy Patrick Brady
John J. Moroney
Mary Jo Blain Andrews
John W. Mahoney
Clare E. Kindall
Patrick J. McHale
Glenn M. Cunningham
Michael J. Palmieri
Christine E. Rua
R. Webb Steadman
Susan C. Freedman
Christine S. Horrigan
Richard M. Borden
Christine L. Chinni
Donna A. Muschell
Jill J. Rendeiro
Desiree A. Ralls
Kimberly A. Mango
Sheila A. Huddleston
Sanjoy K. Goyle
Kay K. Tolbert
Carolyn A. Ikari
Maureen J. Anderson
Howard L. Pierce
Gerald P. Stergio
Stephen J. Courtney
Raymond M. Bernstein

COUNSEL

T. Mitchell Ford
Warren S. Randall
Charles B. Milliken
Robert L. Rosensweig
William H. Wood, Jr.
Robert Ewing

SPECIAL COUNSEL

Charles B. Spadoni

Representative Clients: Aetna Casualty & Surety Co.; Agri-Mark, Inc.; Blue Cross & Blue Shield of Connecticut, Inc.; City of Hartford; The Dexter Corp.; The First National Bank of Boston; Hartford Hospital; Shawmut Bank, Connecticut, N.A.; United Technologies Corp.; Yankee Energy System, Inc.

For full biographical listings, see the Martindale-Hubbell Law Directory

SKELLEY ROTTNER P.C. (AV)

P.O. Box 340890, 06134-0890
Telephone: 203-561-7077
Telecopier: 203-561-7088

Joseph F. Skelley, Jr.
Joel J. Rottner
Susan L. Miller
James G. Geanuracos
Randall M. Hayes
Elizabeth M. Cristofaro
Kirby G. Huget

OF COUNSEL

Susan E. Malliet
Barbara S. Levison

(See Next Column)

SKELLEY ROTTNER P.C.—*Continued*

Edward W. Gasser
Laura Ondrush
Matthew Dallas Gordon
Robyn Sondak
Alys Portman Smith
Brad N. Mondschein
Jonathan Kline

LEGAL SUPPORT PERSONNEL

Karen L. Sonnie

References: Connecticut National Bank & Trust Co.; Society for Savings.

For full biographical listings, see the Martindale-Hubbell Law Directory

SOROKIN SOROKIN GROSS HYDE & WILLIAMS P.C. (AV)

One Corporate Center, 06103
Telephone: 203-525-6645
Fax: 203-522-1781
Simsbury, Connecticut Office: 730 Hopmeadow Street.
Telephone: 203-651-9348.
Rocky Hill, Connecticut Office: 2360 Main Street.
Telephone: 203-563-9305.
Fax: 203-529-6931.
Glastonbury, Connecticut Office: 124 Hebron Avenue.
Telephone: 203-659-8801.

Morris W. Banks
John J. Bracken III
Richard G. Convicer
James G. Dowling, Jr.
Andrew C. Glassman
Clifford J. Grandjean
Jeffrey R. Martin
Charles R. Moore, Jr.
Paula G. Pressman
Lewis Rabinovitz
Richard C. Robinson
Richard D. Tulisano (Resident, Rocky Hill Office)
Barrie K. Wetstone
Amelia M. Rugland

Jeffery P. Apuzzo
Brian S. Becker
Laura Gold Becker
Jamie N. Cody
Sharon Kowal Freilich
Lisa A. Magliochetti

OF COUNSEL

Joseph D. Hurwitz
Ethel Silver Sorokin
Milton Sorokin

For full biographical listings, see the Martindale-Hubbell Law Directory

TYLER COOPER & ALCORN (AV)

City Place, 06103-3488
Telephone: 203-725-6200
Telecopier: 203-278-3802
New Haven, Connecticut Office: 205 Church Street.
Telephone: 203-784-8200.
Telecopier: 203-789-2133.
Stamford, Connecticut Office: One Landmark Square.
Telephone: 203-348-5555.
Telecopier: 203-348-3875.

MEMBERS OF FIRM

William S. Rogers
Ralph G. Elliot
Lewis Segal
William H. Champlin III
Robert J. Metzler II
William W. Bouton III
Mark V. Connolly
William S. Fish, Jr.
Kevin McCann
David J. Wiese
Fillis W. Stober

OF COUNSEL

Henry W. Pascarella

COUNSEL

Kurt W. Johnson

ASSOCIATES

Thomas S. Marrion
Kevin G. Ferrigno
Barry M. Winnick
William F. Cummings
Glory Martyn Lena
Jeffrey G. Tougas
Kent D. B. Sinclair

Representative Clients: Purolator Courier Corp.; American Society of Composers, Authors and Publishers (ASCAP); The Hartford Courant Co.; Sears, Roebuck & Co.; Shearson Lehman Brothers; Prudential Securities Inc.; Aetna Life and Casualty Co.; Town of Glastonbury; The Travellers Companies.

For full biographical listings, see the Martindale-Hubbell Law Directory

* WIGGIN & DANA (AV)

One City Place, 06103-3402
Telephone: 203-297-3700
Fax: 203-525-9380
New Haven, Connecticut Office: One Century Tower.
Telephone: 203-498-4400.
Telefax: 203-782-2889.
Stamford, Connecticut Office: Three Stamford Plaza, 301 Tresser Boulevard.
Telephone: 203-363-7600.
Telefax: 203-363-7676.

(See Next Column)

PARTNERS

Robert F. Cavanagh
Robert M. Langer
Peter J. Lefeber
Patrick J. Monahan, II
R. Jeffrey Sands
Valerie A. Seiling

ASSOCIATES

Alison K. Gilligan
Stephen B. Harris (Not admitted in CT)
Marcella Ann Hourihane
Bernard E. Jacques (Not admitted in CT)
Marcia Kenny Keegan
Eric P. Neff
Daniel McKendree Sessa
Thomas J. Witt

For full biographical listings, see the Martindale-Hubbell Law Directory

LAKEVILLE, Litchfield Co.

SHIPMAN & GOODWIN (AV)

Porter Street, 06039
Telephone: 203-435-2539
Telecopier: 203-435-0011
Hartford, Connecticut Office: One American Row.
Telephone: 203-251-5000.
Stamford, Connecticut Office: Three Landmark Square.
Telephone: 203-359-4544.

MEMBERS

Francis M. Dooley (Resident)
Stuyvesant K. Bearns (Resident)
J. Michael Sconyers (Resident)

Representative Clients: American Title Insurance Co.; Berkshire Construction Co.; Colonial Bank and Trust Co., Sharon; Lakeville Journal, Inc.; Lawyers Title Insurance Co.; Salisbury Bank & Trust Co., Lakeville, Conn.

For full biographical listings, see the Martindale-Hubbell Law Directory

*LITCHFIELD,** Litchfield Co.

CRAMER & ANDERSON (AV)

46 West Street, P.O. Box 278, 06759-0278
Telephone: 203-567-8718
Telecopier: 203-567-4531
New Milford, Connecticut Office: 51 Main Street, P.O. Box 330.
Telephone: 203-355-2631.
Kent, Connecticut Office: Kent Green, P.O. Box 333.
Telephone: 203-927-3568.
Washington Depot, Connecticut Office: P.O. Box 321.
Telephone: 203-868-0527.

MEMBERS OF FIRM

David Cramer (1902-1981)
Henry B. Anderson (Resident at New Milford Office)
Clayton L. Blick
Robert M. FitzGerald
Paul B. Altermatt (Resident at New Milford Office)
Maurice A. Goldstein (Resident at New Milford Office)
Grant J. Nelson (Resident at Kent Office)
Perley H. Grimes, Jr.
Robert L. Fisher, Jr.
Reginald W. H. Fairbairn (Resident at Washington Depot Office)
William C. Franklin
Arthur C. Weinshank (Resident at New Milford Office)
Katherine Vines Cook (Resident at New Milford Office)
David P. Burke (Resident at New Milford Office)
Jeffrey W. Reinen

ASSOCIATES

James D. Hirschfield
Barry S. Moller
John D. Tower
Eric A. Russman
Joseph B. White

OF COUNSEL

Stephen N. Hume (Resident at New Milford Office)

Counsel for: The First National Bank of Litchfield; New Mil BanCorp. Inc.; Town of Cornwall.
Local Counsel for: The Equitable Life Assurance Society of the United States; Colonial Bank & Trust Co.; Son & Chief Electrics, Inc.

For full biographical listings, see the Martindale-Hubbell Law Directory

GUION, STEVENS & RYBAK (AV)

93 West Street, P.O. Box 338, 06759-0338
Telephone: 203-567-0821
Telecopier: 203-567-0825

H. Gibson Guion (1908-1994)

(See Next Column)

GUION, STEVENS & RYBAK, *Litchfield—Continued*

MEMBERS OF FIRM

E. Seward Stevens | R. Christopher Blake
Michael D. Rybak | Brian M. Yard

Counsel for: Town of Thomaston.
References: Thomaston Savings Bank; The First National Bank of Litchfield; Southern New England Farm Credit, ACA, Litchfield, Connecticut.

*MIDDLETOWN,** Middlesex Co.

HALLORAN & SAGE (AV)

300 Plaza Middlesex, 06457
Telephone: 203-346-8641
Hartford, Connecticut Office: One Goodwin Square, 225 Asylum Street.
Telephone: 203-522-6103.

RESIDENT PARTNERS

Vincent M. Marino | Jean M. D'Aquila

RESIDENT COUNSEL

Irwin D. Mittelman

MILFORD, New Haven Co.

BERCHEM, MOSES & DEVLIN, A PROFESSIONAL CORPORATION (AV)

75 Broad Street, 06460
Telephone: 203-783-1200
Telecopiers: 203-878-2235; 877-8422

Robert L. Berchem | Stephen W. Studer
Marsha Belman Moses | Robert W. Blythe
Michael P. Devlin | Richard J. Buturla
Floyd J. Dugas

Winthrop S. Smith, Jr. | Lawrence B. Pellegrino
David F. Weber | Warren L. Holcomb
Brian A. Lema | Gregory B. Ladewski

OF COUNSEL

John J. Kelly | Brian M. Stone

For full biographical listings, see the Martindale-Hubbell Law Directory

HARLOW, ADAMS & FRIEDMAN, P.C. (AV)

300 Bic Drive, 06460-3508
Telephone: 203-878-0661
Fax: 203-878-9568

William D. Harlow (1921-1988) | Dana Eric Friedman
George W. Adams, III | Theodore H. Shumaker
Stephen P. Wright

Eric R. Gaynor | Joseph A. Kubic

For full biographical listings, see the Martindale-Hubbell Law Directory

HURWITZ & SAGARIN, P.C. (AV)

147 North Broad Street, P.O. Box 112, 06460
Telephone: 203-877-8000
Fax: 203-878-9800

Lewis A. Hurwitz | Elias A. Alexiades
J. Daniel Sagarin | Margaret E. Haering
Christine M. Gonillo | David Slossberg

For full biographical listings, see the Martindale-Hubbell Law Directory

NEW BRITAIN, Hartford Co.

JANUSZEWSKI, MCQUILLAN AND DENIGRIS (AV)

165 West Main Street, P.O. Box 150, 06050-0150
Telephone: 203-225-7667
Fax: 203-826-1814

MEMBERS OF FIRM

Edward Januszewski | Nicholas E. DeNigris
Paul J. McQuillan | John C. Matulis, Jr.
Steven D. Anderson

ASSOCIATES

Martin McQuillan

Representative Client: The Peoples Savings Bank of New Britain, Inc.

For full biographical listings, see the Martindale-Hubbell Law Directory

NEW CANAAN, Fairfield Co.

HAWTHORNE, ACKERLY & DORRANCE (AV)

25 South Avenue, P.O. Box 937, 06840
Telephone: 203-966-9583
Fax: 203-966-1296

(See Next Column)

MEMBERS OF FIRM

Dana C. Ackerly | Michelle R. Hubbard
Jeremiah S. Miller | Robert M. Di Scipio

ASSOCIATES

Timothy H. Throckmorton

OF COUNSEL

Samuel R. Dorrance | Louis S. Pryor
Paul L. Rathblott

Reference: Union Trust Co.

For full biographical listings, see the Martindale-Hubbell Law Directory

*NEW HAVEN,** New Haven Co.

BERGMAN, HOROWITZ & REYNOLDS, P.C. (AV)

157 Church Street, 19th Floor, P.O. Box 426, 06502
Telephone: 203-789-1320
FAX: 203-785-8127
New York, New York Office: 499 Park Avenue, 26th Floor.
Telephone: 212-582-3580.

Stanley N. Bergman | James Russell Brockway
Robert H. Horowitz | Bruce I. Judelson
David L. Reynolds | David A. Ringold
Melvin Ditman | Kathryn Harner Smith
Kenneth N. Musen | Donald S. Hendel
William C. G. Swift, Jr. | Joy M. Miyasaki
Richard J. Klein | Paul M. Roy

David M. Spinner | Frederick A. Thomas
Louis R. Piscatelli | Richard M. Porter
Jeremy A. Mellitz | Tina E. Albright
James G. Dattaro | (Not admitted in CT)
Edward A. Renn | Jay F. Krause
Anthony L. Galvagna | Isaiah D. Cooper

LEGAL SUPPORT PERSONNEL

Susan H. Ryan (Legal Administrator)

For full biographical listings, see the Martindale-Hubbell Law Directory

BRENNER, SALTZMAN & WALLMAN (AV)

A Partnership including Professional Corporations
271 Whitney Avenue, P.O. Box 1746, 06507-1746
Telephone: 203-772-2600
Facsimile: 203-562-2098

Newton D. Brenner (P.C.) | Donald W. Anderson (P.C.)
Stephen L. Saltzman (P.C.) | Carol N. Theodore (P.C.)
Marc A. Wallman (P.C.) | Samuel M. Hurwitz
David R. Schaefer (P.C.) | Wayne A. Martino, P.C.
Stuart Jay Mandel (P.C.) | M. Anne Peters
Kenneth Rosenthal

Peter K. Marsh | Brian P. Daniels
Alice Jo Mick | John R. Bashaw
George Brencher, IV

For full biographical listings, see the Martindale-Hubbell Law Directory

CARMODY & TORRANCE (AV)

195 Church Street, P.O. Box 1950, 06509
Telephone: 203-777-5501
Telecopier: 203-784-3199
Waterbury, Connecticut Office: 50 Leavenworth Street. P.O. Box 1110, 06721.
Telephone: 203-573-1200.
Telecopier: 203-575-2600.

MEMBERS OF FIRM

Anthony M. Fitzgerald (Resident) | William P. Yelenak (Resident)
Burton Z. Alter (Resident) | Susan Seidler Chambers (Resident)
Thomas R. Candrick, Jr. (Resident) | Ann Harris Rubin (Resident)
Ann Hedges Zucker (Resident)
Christopher Rooney (Resident)

OF COUNSEL

David W. Collins (Resident)

ASSOCIATES

Joseph J. Packtor (Resident) | Heena Kapadia (Resident)
Kevin C. Doyle (Resident) | Donna M. Rigg

Representative Clients: Algonquin Gas Transmission Co.; Bank of Boston Connecticut; Blue Cross & Blue Shield of Connecticut, Inc.; City of Waterbury; Northeast Utilities; T. Sendzimir, Inc.; Timex Corporation; Waterbury Hospital.
Trial Counsel for: Aetna Insurance Co.; Stop & Shop Companies; Travelers Insurance Cos.

For full biographical listings, see the Martindale-Hubbell Law Directory

New Haven—Continued

WILLIAM H. CLENDENEN, JR. A PROFESSIONAL CORPORATION (AV)

400 Orange Street, P.O. Box 301, 06502-0301
Telephone: 203-787-1183
Fax: 203-787-2847

William H. Clendenen, Jr.

James E. Clifford
Nancy L. Walker

For full biographical listings, see the Martindale-Hubbell Law Directory

GALLAGHER GALLAGHER & CALISTRO (AV)

1377 Boulevard, P.O. Box 1925, 06509
Telephone: 203-624-4165
Fax: 203-865-5598

William F. Gallagher
Elizabeth A. Gallagher
Roger B. Calistro
Cynthia C. Bott
Barbara L. Cox
Kurt D. Koehler

Approved Attorneys for: Chicago Title Insurance Co.; Security Title and Guaranty Co.; American Title Insurance Co.; Connecticut Savings Bank; Dime Savings Bank of Wallingford; New Haven Savings Bank; Essex Savings Bank; Branford Savings Bank; First Federal Savings & Loan of Madison; First Constitution Bank.

For full biographical listings, see the Martindale-Hubbell Law Directory

GREENFIELD AND MURPHY (AV)

234 Church Street, P.O. Box 1103, 06504-1103
Telephone: 203-787-6711
Telecopier: 203-777-6442

MEMBERS OF FIRM

James R. Greenfield
Helen D. Murphy
Maureen M. Murphy

Reference: Union Trust Co.

For full biographical listings, see the Martindale-Hubbell Law Directory

LYNCH, TRAUB, KEEFE AND ERRANTE, A PROFESSIONAL CORPORATION (AV)

52 Trumbull Street, P.O. Box 1612, 06506
Telephone: 203-787-0275
Fax: 203-782-0278

Stephen I. Traub
Hugh F. Keefe
Steven J. Errante
John J. Keefe, Jr.
Donn A. Swift
Charles E. Tiernan, III
Robert W. Lynch
Richard W. Lynch

Mary Beattie Schairer
John M. Walsh, Jr.
Suzanne L. McAlpine
David J. Vegliante
Christopher M. Licari
David S. Monastersky

OF COUNSEL

William C. Lynch

Local Counsel for: Transport Insurance Co., Dallas, Texas; American Trucking Associations; Roadway Express, Inc., Akron, Ohio; A.R.A. Philadelphia, Penn.; Consolidated Freightways, Menlo Park, California; Ogden Corp.
Labor Counsel: Coca-Cola, U.S.A., Atlanta, Georgia (Private Truck Operation); The Dow Chemical Co.; Cincinnati Milacron.

For full biographical listings, see the Martindale-Hubbell Law Directory

SACHS, BERMAN & SHURE, SKLARZ & GALLANT, P.C. (AV)

Granite Square 700 State Street, P.O. Box 1960, 06509-1960
Telephone: 203-782-3000
Telex: ESL 62239500
Telecopier: 203-777-3347

Louis Sachs (1916-1982)
Florence G. Brodman (1932-1990, Retired)
Arthur S. Sachs
Steven A. Berman
H. William Shure
Mark G. Sklarz
Keith Bradoc Gallant
Eric I. B. Beller
Edwin L. Doernberger
Howard D. Komisar
Richard K. Brown
Paul B. Hahn
Daniel N. Hoffnung
Paul E. Proto
Marc Wm. Vallen
Lauragene Lyons
Catherine K Lin
Lloyd S. Lowinger
Andrew C. Kruger

OF COUNSEL

Edward Gallant
Sonja Goldstein

LEGAL SUPPORT PERSONNEL

Gerald Froehlich

For full biographical listings, see the Martindale-Hubbell Law Directory

SUSMAN, DUFFY & SEGALOFF, P.C. (AV)

55 Whitney Avenue, 06510-1300
Telephone: 203-624-9830
Telecopier: 203-562-8430
Mailing Address: P.O. Box 1684, New Haven, Connecticut, 06507-1684

Allen H. Duffy (1931-1986)
Michael Susman
James H. Segaloff
David A. Reif
Joseph E. Faughnan
Susan W. Wolfson
Laura M. Sklaver
Andrew R. Lubin
James J. Perito
Matthew C. Susman
Thomas E. Katon

Charles J. Filardi, Jr.
Jennifer L. Schancupp
Donna Decker Morris
Peter G. Kruzynski
Joshua W. Cohen

OF COUNSEL

Diana C. Ballard

For full biographical listings, see the Martindale-Hubbell Law Directory

TYLER COOPER & ALCORN (AV)

205 Church Street, P.O. Box 1936, 06509-1910
Telephone: 203-784-8200
Telecopier: 203-789-2133
Hartford, Connecticut Office: CityPlace.
Telephone: 203-725-6200.
Telecopier: 203-278-3802.
Stamford, Connecticut Office: One Landmark Square.
Telephone: 203-348-5555.
Telecopier: 203-348-3875.

MEMBERS OF FIRM

William R. Murphy
Milton P. DeVane
Richard G. Bell (Managing Partner of the Firm)
William S. Rogers (Resident at Hartford Office)
Ralph G. Elliot (Resident at Hartford Office)
Michael J. Dorney
Samuel W. Bowlby
Bruce Lewellyn
Robert K. Ciulla
Joseph C. Lee
James G. Kenefick, Jr.
Lewis Segal (Resident at Hartford Office)
Barry C. Hawkins (Resident at Stamford Office)
Irving S. Schloss
Jon T. Hirschoff
William H. Champlin III (Resident at Hartford Office)
Timothy W. Bingham
David W. Schneider
Robert W. Allen
Richard W. Bowerman
George E. O'Brien, Jr.
Robert J. Metzler II (Resident at Hartford Office)
Ronald J. Cohen
Margaret P. Mason
William W. Bouton III (Resident at Hartford Office)
Veronica M. Fallon
Mark V. Connolly (Resident at Hartford Office)
William S. Fish, Jr. (Resident at Hartford Office)
Kevin McCann (Resident at Hartford Office)
Roberta L. McCaw
David J. Wiese (Resident at Hartford Office)
Alan J. Sobol
Emmett E. Brown III (Resident at Stamford Office)
Margaret A. Little
Ben A. Solnit
Jacqueline DeAndrus Bucar
Fillis W. Stober (Resident at Hartford Office)

OF COUNSEL

Henry W. Pascarella

COUNSEL

Nan Budde Chequer (Resident at Stamford Office)
Kurt W. Johnson (Resident at Hartford Office)
Kathleen A. Maher

ASSOCIATES

Christopher L. Ulrich (Resident at Stamford Office)
Charles R. Andres
Thomas S. Marrion (Resident at Hartford Office)
Shawn L. O'Sullivan
Christopher P. McCormack
Stephen G. Murphy, Jr.
Patricia M. O'Neil
Kevin G. Ferrigno (Resident at Hartford Office)
Lori B. Alexander
Greg R. Barringer
Jeffrey M. Donofrio
Emily R. Levin
John W. O'Meara (Resident at Stamford Office)
Patricia E. Reilly
Barry M. Winnick (Resident at Hartford Office)
William F. Cummings (Resident at Hartford Office)
Noble F. Allen
Douglas S. Brown (Resident at Stamford Office)
Glory Martyn Lena (Resident at Hartford Office)
Robert H. McAndrew (Resident at Hartford Office)
Ellen M. Fusco
Niclas A. Ferland
Scott B. Nabel
Jeffrey G. Tougas (Resident at Hartford Office)
Karyl Lee Hall
Kent D. B. Sinclair (Resident at Hartford Office)

Counsel for: Echlin, Inc.; Hospital of St. Raphael; The Stanley Works; The Southern Connecticut Gas Co.; Southern New England Telephone Co.; Shawmut Bank; Science Park Development Corp.; Connecticut American Water Co.; General Electric Co.; The Rouse Co.

For full biographical listings, see the Martindale-Hubbell Law Directory

New Haven—Continued

WIGGIN & DANA (AV)

One Century Tower, 06508-1832
Telephone: 203-498-4400
Telefax: 203-782-2889
Hartford, Connecticut Office: One CityPlace.
Telephone: 203-297-3700.
FAX: 203-525-9380.
Stamford, Connecticut Office: Three Stamford Plaza, 301 Tresser Boulevard.
Telephone: 203-363-7600.
Telefax: 203-363-7676.

MEMBERS OF FIRM

Frederick H. Wiggin (1882-1963)
J. Dwight Dana (1889-1951)
John Q. Tilson
Charles N. Schenck, III
John W. Barnett
William C. Baskin, Jr.
Robert F. Cavanagh
S. Robert Jelley
Charles C. Kingsley
William J. Doyle
William J. Egan
David P. Faulkner
William E. Craig
Noel E. Hanf
Shaun S. Sullivan
Jeremy G. Zimmermann
J. Michael Eisner
Norman Fineberg
Michael K. Brown
William H. Prout, Jr.
J. Drake Turrentine (Resident at Stamford)
Linda L. Randell
Paul L. Behling
D. Terence Jones
Mark R. Kravitz
Melinda A. Agsten
Edward Wood Dunham
Norman J. Fleming
Peter J. Lefeber
R. Jeffrey Sands (Resident at Hartford)
John G. Zandy
Sherry L. Dominick
Alan G. Schwartz
Penny Quinn Seaman
Valerie A. Seiling (Resident at Hartford)
Bennett J. Bernblum
Susan J. Bryson
William G. Millman, Jr.
Jeanette Carpenter Schreiber
Patrick J. Monahan, II (Resident at Hartford)
Peter H. Gruen
Anthony M. Macleod
Mary R. Norris
Maureen Weaver
Robert M. Langer (Resident at Hartford)

COUNSEL

Dale L. Carlson
Abbie Eremich
William A. Simons (Not admitted in CT)

ASSOCIATES

Joan M. Allen
Ann K. Anderson
Jennifer S. Aniskovich
Jeffrey R. Babbin
Dean W. Baker
Nancy A. Beatty
Penelope I. Bellamy
Ian E. Bjorkman
Joaquina L. Borges
John E. Buerkert, Jr. (Not admitted in CT)
Thomas L. Casagrande
Isabel E. Chenoweth
Tanya F. Clark
Karen L. Clute
John F. Conway
Michelle Wilcox DeBarge
Eleanor Stuart Devane
Alison K. Gilligan (Resident at Hartford)
Elizabeth P. Gilson
Merton G. Gollaher
Gerald Lewis Harmon
Stephen B. Harris (Not admitted in CT; Resident at Hartford)
Claudia Damsky Heyman
Marcella Ann Hourihane
Bernard E. Jacques (Not admitted in CT; Resident at Hartford)
Marcia Kenny Keegan (Resident at Hartford)
Kevin M. Kennedy
Andrea C. Kramer
Keith M. Krom
Deborah Whitlock Madden
James Thomas Maye
Eric P. Neff (Resident at Hartford)
Susan M. Neilson
Karen E. Overchuck
Christine E. Owens
Phyllis M. Pari
Bonnie Lynne Patten
Charles P. Reed
Gregory S. Rosenblatt (Not admitted in CT)
James Edward Rosenbluth (Not admitted in CT)
Sigismund L. Sapinski
Daniel McKendree Sessa (Resident at Hartford)
Kevin Christopher Shea
Eric J. Stockman
Harry M. Stokes
Littleton Waller Tazewell
Robert Tilewick
Janis Lynn Warrecker
Thomas J. Witt (Resident at Hartford)
Laura Wright Wooton (Resident at Stamford)

OF COUNSEL

David J. Harrigan
Peter B. Trumbull

For full biographical listings, see the Martindale-Hubbell Law Directory

NEW LONDON, New London Co.

GREENBERG & PARENTEAU, P.C. (AV)

130 Eugene O'Neill Drive, 06320
Telephone: 203-442-5373
Fax: 203-443-8131

Lawrence J. Greenberg
Jacques J. Parenteau
Philip M. Johnstone
Frank J. Liberty
Karen Reilly

(See Next Column)

Representative Clients: Sterling Trucking, Inc.; Stonington Community Credit Union; DiCesare Bentley Engineers; Tri County Distributors; United Builders Supply.

For full biographical listings, see the Martindale-Hubbell Law Directory

PAVETTI & FREEMAN (AV)

Court House Square Building, 83 Huntington Street, P.O. Box 829, 06320
Telephone: 203-442-9409
Telecopier: 203-443-0264

MEMBERS OF FIRM

Francis J. Pavetti
Jane W. Freeman

For full biographical listings, see the Martindale-Hubbell Law Directory

WALLER, SMITH & PALMER, P.C. (AV)

52 Eugene O'Neill Drive, P.O. Box 88, 06320
Telephone: 203-442-0367
Telecopier: 203-447-9915
Old Lyme, Connecticut Office: 103-A Halls Road.
Telephone: 203-434-8063.

Tracy Waller (1862-1947)
J. Rodney Smith (1906-1979)
Birdsey G. Palmer (Retired)
William W. Miner
Robert P. Anderson, Jr.
Robert W. Marrion
Hughes Griffis
Edward B. O'Connell
Frederick B. Gahagan
Linda D. Loucony
Mary E. Driscoll
William E. Wellette

Tracy M. Collins
Donna Richer Skaats
David P. Condon
Valerie Ann Votto
Charles C. Anderson

OF COUNSEL

Suzanne Donnelly Kitchings

General Counsel for: Colotone Group.
Counsel for: Union Trust Co.; Coastal Savings Bank; Cash Home Center, Inc.
Local Counsel for: Metropolitan Insurance Co.; Connecticut General Life Insurance Co.

For full biographical listings, see the Martindale-Hubbell Law Directory

NEW MILFORD, Litchfield Co.

CRAMER & ANDERSON (AV)

51 Main Street, P.O. Box 330, 06776-0330
Telephone: 203-355-2631
Telecopier: 203-355-9460
Litchfield, Connecticut Office: 46 West Street. P.O. Box 278.
Telephone: 203-567-8718.
Kent, Connecticut Office: Kent Green, P.O. Box 333.
Telephone: 203-927-3568.
Washington Depot, Connecticut Office: P.O. Box 321.
Telephone: 203-868-0527.

MEMBERS OF FIRM

David Cramer (1902-1981)
Henry B. Anderson (Resident)
Paul B. Altermatt (Resident)
Maurice A. Goldstein (Resident)
Arthur C. Weinshank (Resident)
Katherine Vines Cook (Resident)
David P. Burke (Resident)
Jeffrey W. Reinen

ASSOCIATES

John D. Tower
Joseph B. White

OF COUNSEL

Stephen N. Hume (Resident)

Counsel for: The First National Bank of Litchfield; New Mil BanCorp. Inc.; Town of Cornwall.
Local Counsel for: The Equitable Life Assurance Society of the United States; Kimberly-Clark Corp.; Colonial Bank & Trust Co.; Son & Chief Electrics, Inc.

For full biographical listings, see the Martindale-Hubbell Law Directory

NORWALK, Fairfield Co.

KEOGH, BURKHART & VETTER (AV)

34 Wall Street, P.O. Box 126, 06852
Telephone: 203-866-2535, 866-2536
Fax: 203-855-9016

MEMBERS OF FIRM

John Keogh (1871-1960)
John Keogh, Jr. (1910-1992)
Alfred W. Burkhart
Thomas J. Vetter
Stephen B. Keogh

Local Counsel for: Metropolitan Life Insurance Co.

For full biographical listings, see the Martindale-Hubbell Law Directory

Norwalk—Continued

Tierney, Zullo, Flaherty & Murphy, P.C. (AV)

134 East Avenue, P.O. Box 2028-Belden Station, 06852
Telephone: 203-853-7000
FAX: 203-838-4829
Other Norwalk Office: 401 Merritt 7, First Floor.
Telephone: 203-853-7000.
FAX: 203-849-1452.

Thomas Tierney
Frank N. Zullo
Thomas A. Flaherty
Frank W. Murphy
Reuben S. Midler
Gary Lorusso
Steven M. Warren
Andrew F. Kordas
Barbara Coughlan
Elizabeth A.B. Suchy

OF COUNSEL

Thomas A. Keating, Jr.

References: Union Trust Co.; Shawmut Bank.

For full biographical listings, see the Martindale-Hubbell Law Directory

*NORWICH,** New London Co.

Brown, Jacobson, Tillinghast, Lahan & King, P.C. (AV)

Uncas-Merchants National Bank Building, 22 Courthouse Square, 06360
Telephone: 203-889-3321
Fax: 203-886-0673
Groton, Connecticut Office: 4 Fort Hill Road.
Telephone: 203-449-8765.
Fax: 203-445-7634.

Allyn L. Brown, Jr.
Milton L. Jacobson
Charles W. Jewett
Vincent A. Laudone
James J. Dutton, Jr.
Wayne G. Tillinghast
P. Michael Lahan
Michael E. Driscoll
Timothy D. Bates
Deborah J. Tedford
David S. Williams
Robert A. Avena
Michael A. Blanchard
John C. Wirzbicki
Michael D. Colonese
Peter A. Anderson
Karl-Erik Sternlof
Michael P. Carey
Jeffrey R. Godley
Michael E. Kennedy
Doreen A. West
Elizabeth Conway
John F. Duggan
Gerald M. Smith, Jr.
Valerie G. Bataille-Ferry
Jeffrey F. Buebendorf

OF COUNSEL

Jackson T. King, Jr.

Representative Clients: Nationwide Insurance Co.; Aetna Casualty & Surety Co.; Chelsea-Groton Savings Bank; Norwich Community Development Corp.

For full biographical listings, see the Martindale-Hubbell Law Directory

O'Brien, Shafner, Stuart, Kelly & Morris, P.C. (AV)

2 Courthouse Square, P.O. Box 310, 06360
Telephone: 203-889-3855
Fax: 203-886-6352
Groton, Connecticut Office: 475 Bridge Street.
Telephone: 203-445-2463.
Fax: 203-445-4539.

Mark E. Block (Resident)
Lloyd L. Langhammer
Susan B. Pochal
Richard J. Pascal

For full biographical listings, see the Martindale-Hubbell Law Directory

OLD LYME, New London Co.

Waller, Smith & Palmer, P.C. (AV)

103-A Halls Road, 06371
Telephone: 203-434-8063
New London, Connecticut Office: 52 Eugene O'Neill Drive.
Telephone: 203-442-0367.
Telecopier: 203-447-9915.

Robert W. Marrion
Frederick B. Gahagan
Linda D. Loucony
William E. Wellette

Valerie Ann Votto

General Counsel for: Colotone Group.
Counsel for: Union Trust Co.; Coastal Savings Bank; Cash Home Center, Inc.
Local Counsel for: Metropolitan Insurance Co.; Connecticut General Life Insurance Co.

For full biographical listings, see the Martindale-Hubbell Law Directory

*PUTNAM,** Windham Co. — (Refer to Willimantic)

SOUTHBURY, New Haven Co.

Secor, Cassidy & McPartland, P.C. (AV)

Successors to Bronson, Lewis, Upson & Secor; Lewis, Hart, Upson & Secor; Upson, Secor, Greene & Cassidy and Upson, Secor, Cassidy & McPartland, P.C.
370 Main Street South, 06488
Telephone: 203-264-8223
Fax: 203-264-6730
Waterbury, Connecticut Office: 41 Church Street, P.O. Box 2818.
Telephone: 203-757-9261.
Fax: 203-756-5762.
Danbury, Connecticut Office: 301 Main Street.
Telephone: 203-743-9145.
Fax: 203-798-9844.

James R. Healey

Attorneys for: The Mattatuck Museum; American Republican, Inc.; The Meriden Record Co.; Hubbard-Hall, Inc.; The Siemon Co.; The Romantic Manufacturing Co.; Engineered Sinterings and Plastics, Inc.; Heminway Corp.; Boutin Industries; County Line Buick-Nissan, Inc.

For full biographical listings, see the Martindale-Hubbell Law Directory

SOUTHPORT, Fairfield Co.

Marsh, Day & Calhoun (AV)

2507 Post Road, 06490
Telephone: 203-259-8993
Fax: 203-254-1772
Bridgeport, Connecticut Office: 955 Main Street.
Telephone: 203-259-8993.
Fax: 203-254-1772.
Greenwich, Connecticut Office: 125 Mason Street, 06830. Telephone 203-861-2626.

MEMBERS OF FIRM

Peter Wilkinson
Robert J. Berta
Thomas F. Maxwell, Jr.
James E. Rice
Michael P. A. Williams
Peter T. Mott
Roy W. Moore, III
Robert L. Danaher
Thomas J. Walsh, Jr.
Christopher G. Martin
Jevera Kaye Hennessey

ASSOCIATES

Tracey C. Kammerer
John R. Mitola
Katherine E. Caulfield
Tracy Wheeler Lennon
Linda R. Pesce

SPECIAL COUNSEL

Bruce E. Dillingham
David S. Maclay
Muriel E. Zacharias

Counsel for: Citytrust; Southern Connecticut Gas Co.; Metropolitan Life Insurance Co.; General Electric Co.; Sturm Ruger & Co., Inc.; The Producto Machine Co.

For full biographical listings, see the Martindale-Hubbell Law Directory

STAMFORD, Fairfield Co.

Curtis, Brinckerhoff & Barrett, P.C. (AV)

666 Summer Street, 06901-1486
Telephone: 203-324-6777
Telecopier: 203-324-9621

T. Ward Cleary (1916-1988)
John D. Hertz
Frederick M. Tobin
Jane F. Donovan
John Wayne Fox
Ward Frank Cleary
James D'Alton Murphy
Randolph T. Lovallo

OF COUNSEL

Richard L. Brinckerhoff

Susan L. Stratton
Derek Gilman

Counsel for: The F. A. Bartlett Tree Expert Co.; Town of Darien; Miller Automobile Corporation; Bolliger, Inc.; Titan Sports; People's Bank, Bridgeport; Shawmut Bank Connecticut, N.A.; Fleet Bank; Federal Deposit Insurance Company; William Pitt Foundation.

For full biographical listings, see the Martindale-Hubbell Law Directory

Day, Berry & Howard (AV)

One Canterbury Green, 06901
Telephone: 203-977-7300
Telecopier: 203-977-7301
Hartford, Connecticut Office: CityPlace.
Telephone: 203-275-0100.
Telecopier: 203-275-0343.
Boston, Massachusetts Office: 260 Franklin Street.
Telephone: 617-345-4600.
Telex: 990686.
Telecopier: 617-439-4453.

(See Next Column)

DAY, BERRY & HOWARD, *Stamford—Continued*

MEMBERS OF FIRM IN STAMFORD

Jerome Berkman
Michael P. Byrne
Patricia A. Carpenter
Ronald Osburn Dederick
Thomas D. Goldberg
F. Lee Griffith, III
Michael S. Leo
(Not admitted in CT)
Robert J. Miller
Kenneth W. Ritt
Sabino Rodriguez, III
James F. Stapleton
David A. Swerdloff
Stanley A. Twardy, Jr.
Stefan R. Underhill
Carla R. Walworth

ASSOCIATES OF FIRM IN STAMFORD

Jean Mills Aranha
R. Scott Beach
Joy Beane
J. Bradley Britton
Edward M. Brown
Wendy D. DiChristina
Kenneth W. Gage
Craig Goldberg
Susan E. Gorman
(Not admitted in CT)
Gregory A. Hayes
Jeanine M. Lynch
(Not admitted in CT)
Christopher W. Murphy
Eileen Reynolds
Samuel V. Schoonmaker, IV
Steven M. Torkelsen
Carole F. Wilder

OF COUNSEL IN STAMFORD

John Crosskey
Ellen B. Wells

For full biographical listings, see the Martindale-Hubbell Law Directory

PAUL, HASTINGS, JANOFSKY & WALKER (AV)

A Partnership including Professional Corporations
Ninth Floor, 1055 Washington Boulevard, 06901-2217
Telephone: 203-961-7400
Los Angeles, California Office: Twenty-Third Floor, 555 South Flower Street.
Telephone: 213-683-6000.
Cable Address: "Paulhast."
Twx: 910-321-4065.
Orange County, California Office: Seventeenth Floor, 695 Town Center Drive, Costa Mesa.
Telephone: 714-668-6200.
Washington, D.C. Office: Tenth Floor, 1299 Pennsylvania Avenue, N.W.
Telephone: 202-508-9500.
Atlanta, Georgia Office: 42nd Floor, Georgia Pacific Center, 133 Peachtree Street, N.E.
Telephone: 404-588-9900.
Santa Monica, California Office: Fifth Floor, 1299 Ocean Avenue.
Telephone: 310-319-3300.
New York, New York Office: 31st Floor, 399 Park Avenue.
Telephone: 212-318-6000.
Tokyo, Japan Office: Toranomon Ohtori Building, 8th Floor, 4-3 Toranomon 1-Chome, Minato-Ku.
Telephone: (03) 3507-0730.

MEMBERS OF FIRM

Carl T. Anderson
(Not admitted in CT)
Steven Reed Armstrong
Christopher A. Barreca
Douglas C. Conroy
Esteban A. Ferrer, III
Mario J. Ippolito
(Not admitted in CT)
Charles T. Lee
John S. McGeeney
Patrick W. Shea
David E. Snediker

OF COUNSEL

Anthony B. Casareale
(Not admitted in CT)
Richard J. Sweetnam

ASSOCIATES

Elizabeth A. Adolff
I. Barbra Allue (Not admitted in the United States)
Edward J. Bennett
Jack L. Caynon, III
Alejandro J. Diaz
Mary C. Dollarhide
(Not admitted in CT)
Patricia A. Driscoll
Harold N. Eddy, Jr.
Regina M. Flaherty
Robert F. Foxworth, III
John W. Hamlin
Kurt W. Hansson
Lynn A. Kappelman
Scott J. Krowitz
Philip J. Paseltiner
Lawrence Peikes
Bonnie Pierson-Murphy
Leslie A. Plaskon
(Not admitted in CT)

For full biographical listings, see the Martindale-Hubbell Law Directory

RYAN, RYAN, JOHNSON, CLEAR & DELUCA (AV)

80 Fourth Street, P.O. Box 3057, 06905
Telephone: 203-357-9200
FAX: 203-357-7915
New York, New York Office: Park Avenue Atrium, 237 Park Avenue.
Telephone: 212-949-0722.

MEMBERS OF FIRM

Daniel E. Ryan, Jr.
W. Patrick Ryan
Jon Paul Johnson
Michael Gene Clear
Charles A. Deluca
Daniel E. Ryan, III
Michael T. Ryan
Charles M. McCaghey
John W. Mullin

(See Next Column)

ASSOCIATES

Elizabeth W. Carter
Beverly J. Hunt
Holly K. Dustin
Gary R. Khachian
Joan P. Freydberg
Laureen V. Holland
Richard P. Colbert
John F. Leydon, Jr.
Barbara J. Pulaski
Thomas J. O'Neill
Robert C.E. Laney

For full biographical listings, see the Martindale-Hubbell Law Directory

SCHATZ & SCHATZ, RIBICOFF & KOTKIN (AV)

1 Landmark Square, 06901-2676
Telephone: 203-964-0027
Telecopier: 203-357-9251
Hartford, Connecticut Office: 90 State House Square.
Telephone: 203-522-3234.
Fax: 203-246-1225

RESIDENT PARTNERS

Thomas F. Cullen
Ira M. Dansky
Matthew J. Forstadt
Steven M. Gold
Donald R. Gustafson
Gregory E. Harmer
Stephen Marcovich
Peter M. Nolin
Lewis G. Schwartz
Steven B. Steinmetz
Michael L. Widland
Carol K. Young

RESIDENT ASSOCIATES

Ellen E. Bromley
Aimee B. Davis
Jodi P. Dottori
Scott G. Grubin
Gary S. Klein
Andrea J. Levine
Beth R. Meyers
Michael Montecalvo
Karla J. Pankratz
Gerald A. Reynolds
David Rubin
Cathy S. Satz
James M. Weisbard
June D. Wolfman

For full biographical listings, see the Martindale-Hubbell Law Directory

SHIPMAN & GOODWIN (AV)

Three Landmark Square, 06901
Telephone: 203-359-4544
Telecopier: 203-327-0287
Hartford, Connecticut Office: One American Row.
Telephone: 203-251-5000.
Lakeville, Connecticut Office: Porter Street.
Telephone: 203-435-2539.

PARTNER IN CHARGE

Frank J. Marco (Stamford and Hartford Offices)

For full biographical listings, see the Martindale-Hubbell Law Directory

SILVER, GOLUB & TEITELL (AV)

184 Atlantic Street, P.O. Box 389, 06904
Telephone: 203-325-4491
FAX: 203-325-3769

MEMBERS OF FIRM

Richard A. Silver
David S. Golub
Ernest F. Teitell
Patricia M. Haugh (1942-1988)
Elaine T. Silver

John D. Josel
Mario DiNatale
Jonathan M. Levine
Marilyn J. Ramos
Jack Zaremski
(Not admitted in CT)

For full biographical listings, see the Martindale-Hubbell Law Directory

TYLER COOPER & ALCORN (AV)

One Landmark Square, 06901-2501
Telephone: 203-348-5555
Telecopier: 203-348-3875
Hartford, Connecticut Office: CityPlace.
Telephone: 203-725-6200.
Telecopier: 203-278-3802.
New Haven, Connecticut Office: 205 Church Street.
Telephone: 203-784-8200.
Telecopier: 203-789-2133.

MEMBERS OF FIRM

Barry C. Hawkins
Emmett E. Brown III

COUNSEL

Nan Budde Chequer

ASSOCIATES

Christopher L. Ulrich
John W. O'Meara
Douglas S. Brown

OF COUNSEL

Henry W. Pascarella

For full biographical listings, see the Martindale-Hubbell Law Directory

Stamford—Continued

WINTHROP, STIMSON, PUTNAM & ROBERTS (AV)

Financial Centre, 695 East Main Street, P.O. Box 6760, 06904-6760
Telephone: 203-348-2300
Telefax: 203-965-8226
New York, N.Y. Office: One Battery Park Plaza, 10004.
Telephone: 212-858-1000.
Washington, D.C. Office: 1133 Connecticut Avenue, N.W., 20036.
Telephone: 202-775-9800.
Palm Beach, Florida Office: 125 Worth Avenue, 33480.
Telephone: 407-655-7297.
London, England Office: 2 Throgmorton Avenue, London, EC2N 2AP, England.
Telephone: O11-4471-628-4931.
Brussels, Belgium Office: Rue Du Taciturne 42, B-1040 Brussels, Belgium.
Telephone: 011-322-230-1392.
Tokyo, Japan Office: 608 Atagoyama Bengoshi Building 6-7, Atago 1-chome, Minato-ku, Tokyo 105 Japan.
Telephone: 011-813-3437-9740.
Hong Kong Office: 2505 Asia Pacific Finance Tower, Citibank Plaza, 3 Garden Road, Central.
Telephone: 011-852-530-3400.

MEMBERS OF FIRM

Thomas F. Clauss, Jr.
Elizabeth H. W. Fry
Arthur W. Hooper, Jr.
Frode Jensen, III
G. William Sisley
Edward W. Wellman, Jr.

COUNSEL

Thomas R. Trowbridge, III

SENIOR COUNSEL

Endicott P. Davison
David M. Payne
Richard B. Tweedy

ASSOCIATES

Matthew S. Eisenberg
Marc R. Esterman
Eric X. Fishman
Francis W. Hogan, III
Steven Kapiloff
Kent S. Nevins
Sheila A. Ozalis
Robert J. Rawn
Paul A. Sherrington
Karen P. Wackerman

For full biographical listings, see the Martindale-Hubbell Law Directory

TORRINGTON, Litchfield Co.

WALL, WALL & FRAUENHOFER (AV)

117 Main Street, P.O. Box 57, 06790
Telephone: 203-489-3176
FAX: 203-496-9820

OF COUNSEL

Thomas F. Wall

MEMBERS OF FIRM

Thomas F. Wall, Jr.
Thomas J. Wall (1879-1948)
David J. Frauenhofer

ASSOCIATES

Christopher G. Wall

Representative Clients: Shawmut Bank Connecticut, N.A.; The Torrington Savings Bank; Winsted Savings Bank; Patterson Oil; Fernwood Rest Home; Eagle Federal Savings Bank; Intrim Health Care of Hartford, Inc.

For full biographical listings, see the Martindale-Hubbell Law Directory

*VERNON,** Tolland Co.

FLAHERTY, MEISLER & COURTNEY (AV)

30 Lafayette Square, P.O. Box 508, 06066
Telephone: 203-872-7200
Fax: 203-875-6594
Willimantic, Connecticut Office: 321 Bricktop Road, P.O. Box 4.
Telephone: 203-423-4588.

MEMBERS OF FIRM

Leo B. Flaherty Jr.
Arthur P. Meisler (Resident, Willimantic Office)
Joseph D. Courtney
Mark C. Hauslaib

References: Connecticut Bank & Trust Co. (Rockville); New England Bank & Trust Co.

For full biographical listings, see the Martindale-Hubbell Law Directory

WALLINGFORD, New Haven Co.

GERALD E. FARRELL, P.C. (AV)

375 Center Street, P.O. Box 369, 06492
Telephone: 203-269-7756
Fax: 203-269-1927

Gerald E. Farrell

(See Next Column)

Gerald E. Farrell, Jr.
Ann Farrell Leslie
Brian J. Leslie

References: Dime Savings Bank of Wallingford; Shawmut Bank (Wallingford Office).

For full biographical listings, see the Martindale-Hubbell Law Directory

CHARLES J. WOOD, JR. (AV)

Elm Professional Center, 105 South Elm Street, P.O. Box 805, 06492
Telephone: 203-284-9988
Fax: 203-294-1516

ASSOCIATES

Helen M. Doherty

Representative Clients: Carolina Freight Carriers Corp.; Central National Insurance Co.; Jefferson Insurance Company of New York/American Underwriting Managers; Lumber Insurance Cos.; National Indemnity Co.; Norfolk & Dedham Mutual Fire Insurance Co.; Transport Insurance Co.; Van Liner Insurance Co.; Olympus Construction Co.

For full biographical listings, see the Martindale-Hubbell Law Directory

WATERBURY, New Haven Co.

CARMODY & TORRANCE (AV)

50 Leavenworth Street, P.O. Box 1110, 06721
Telephone: 203-573-1200
Telecopy: 203-575-2600
New Haven, Connecticut Office: 195 Church Street, P.O. Box 1950, 06509.
Telephone: 203-777-5501.
Telecopier: 203-784-3199.

MEMBERS OF FIRM

G. Bradford Palmer
Walter F. Torrance, Jr.
Timothy R. Carmody
Joseph F. Budny
Anthony M. Fitzgerald (Resident, New Haven Office)
Norman K. Jellinghaus
Kenneth J. Pocius
Burton Z. Alter (Resident, New Haven Office)
James K. Robertson, Jr.
Thomas R. Candrick, Jr. (Resident, New Haven Office)
Trudie Ross Hamilton
James Wu
David L. Sfara
William P. Yelenak (Resident, New Haven Office)
John D. Yarbrough, Jr.
Maureen Danehy Cox
Mark J. Malaspina
Susan Seidler Chambers (Resident, New Haven Office)
D. Charles Stohler
Ann Harris Rubin (Resident, New Haven Office)
Marianne Barbino Dubuque
William I. Garfinkel
Thomas J. Sansone
Joseph A. Wellington
Joseph L. Kinsella
Ann Hedges Zucker (Resident, New Haven Office)
Kathleen Lenehan Nastri
Christopher Rooney (Resident, New Haven Office)
Joseph E. Dornfried

OF COUNSEL

David W. Collins (Resident, New Haven Office)

ASSOCIATES

Leonard M. Isaac
Jay L. Goldstein
Michael J. Reardon
Patrick J. O'Connell
Brian T. Henebry
Paul S. Tagatac
Joseph J. Packtor (Resident, New Haven Office)
Brian L. Smith
Kevin C. Doyle (Resident, New Haven Office)
Giovanna Tiberii Weller
Heena Kapadia (Resident, New Haven Office)
Susan M. LoFaso
Donna M. Rigg (Resident, New Haven Office)
Brian R. Shagan
Jennifer E. Sills
Richard L. Street
Viktoria K. Cech
George Moreira

Representative Clients: Algonquin Gas Transmission Co.; Bank of Boston Connecticut; Blue Cross & Blue Shield of Connecticut, Inc.; City of Waterbury; Northeast Utilities; T. Sendzimir, Inc.; Timex Corporation; Waterbury Hospital.
Trial Counsel for: Aetna Insurance Co.; Stop & Shop Companies; Travelers Insurance Cos.

For full biographical listings, see the Martindale-Hubbell Law Directory

GAGER & HENRY (AV)

One Exchange Place, P.O. Box 2480, 06722
Telephone: 203-597-5100
Telecopier: 203-757-7888
Danbury, Connecticut Office: Danbury Executive Tower, 30 Main Street.
Telephone: 203-743-6363.
Telecopier: 203-790-5954.
Sharon, Connecticut Office: West Main Street, P.O. Box 158.
Telephone: 203-364-5531.
Telecopier: 203-364-5805.
Southbury, Connecticut Office: 325 Main Street South.
Telephone: 203-262-6600.
Telecopier: 203-262-6780.
Litchfield, Connecticut Office: Litchfield Commons, P.O. Box 1544.
Telephone: 203-567-0828.
Fax: 203-567-5844.

(See Next Column)

GAGER & HENRY, *Waterbury—Continued*

MEMBERS OF FIRM

William W. Gager (1892-1967)
Carl A. Peterson
Curtis V. Titus
William C. Crutcher
David R. Chipman (Danbury Office)
Alan Birmingham
Thomas J. McHale
Richard A. Hoppe
Edward S. Hill
Richard L. Emerson
Augustus R. Southworth, III
Robert W. Elmore
Louise F. Brown (Sharon Office)
Francis G. Pennarola
Richard S. Land (Danbury Office)
Mary M. Ackerly (Litchfield Office)
John V. Galiette
Thomas M. Rickart
Mark W. Dost
Beth A. Barrett
Jo E. Friday (Sharon Office)
Edward M. Rosenblatt
Lisa J. Cappalli
C. Robert Zelinger
Frank J. Scinto
Edward J. Kelleher
Hilary Fisher Nelson
Randolph E. Richardson, II

ASSOCIATES

Kathy S. Bower
Ann Martindale
Richard C. Martin
Thomas A. Kaelin
George A. Chmael, II
Hillel Goldman (Danbury Office)
Linda T. Wihbey
Regina Duchin Kraus
John R. Horvack, Jr.
Kristin C. Cunningham
Alisa R. Namacher
James B. Schomburg
Barbara W. Reynolds

Counsel for: Bank of Boston Connecticut; Centerbank; Colonial Bancorp, Inc.; The Eastern Co.; Risdon Corp.; Anamet, Inc.; General DataComm Industries; Timex Corporation.
Trial Counsel for: Aetna Casualty and Surety Co.; Continental National Assurance Co.

For full biographical listings, see the Martindale-Hubbell Law Directory

SECOR, CASSIDY & MCPARTLAND, P.C. (AV)

Successors to Bronson, Lewis, Upson & Secor; Lewis, Hart, Upson & Secor; Upson, Secor, Greene & Cassidy and Upson, Secor, Cassidy & McPartland, P.C.
41 Church Street, P.O. Box 2818, 06723-2818
Telephone: 203-757-9261
Fax: 203-756-5762
Danbury, Connecticut Office: 301 Main Street.
Telephone: 203-743-9145.
Fax: 203-798-9844.
Southbury, Connecticut Office: 370 Main Street South. Telephon e: 203-264-8223.
Fax: 203-264-6730.

Nath'l R. Bronson (1860-1949)
Lawrence L. Lewis (1881-1965)
Charles E. Hart (1884-1972)
J. Warren Upson (1903-1992)
John H. Cassidy, Jr.
Donald McPartland
W. Fielding Secor
Martin A. Rader, Jr. (Resident at Danbury Office)
James R. Healey
Thomas P. Rush
Gail E. McTaggart
Richard D. Arconti
Thomas G. Parisot
Daniel E. Casagrande
Elizabeth A. Bozzuto
Patrick W. Finn
Robin Edwards Otto
Pamela D. Siemon
Kim E. Nolan (Resident at Danbury Office)
Eric R. Brown

COUNSEL

William J. Secor, Jr.
Charles E. Hart, 3rd (Not admitted in CT)
Milton A. Seymour

Attorneys For: The Mattatuck Museum; American Republican, Inc.; The Meriden Record Co.; Hubbard-Hall, Inc.; The Siemon Co.; The Romantic Manufacturing Company; Engineered Sinterings and Plastics, Inc.; Heminway Corporation; Boutin Industries; County Line Buick-Nissan, Inc.

For full biographical listings, see the Martindale-Hubbell Law Directory

WEST HARTFORD, Hartford Co.

ADINOLFI, O'BRIEN & HAYES, P.C. (AV)

Corporate Center West, 433 South Main Street, 06110-1692
Telephone: 203-561-5020
Facsimile: 203-561-0229

Joseph Adinolfi, Jr.
Joseph A. O'Brien
Valentino D. Clementino
Edward W. Case
Stephen H. Minich

Representative Clients: Aetna Casualty & Surety Co.; Olivetti Corporation of America; Viking Glass Co. (Manufacturing); Associated Construction Co. (General Contractors); Cummings Insulation Co. (Sub-Contractors); Adwst Bank; Shawmut Manufacturing Co.
Reference: Fleet Bank, N.A.

For full biographical listings, see the Martindale-Hubbell Law Directory

BERMAN, BOURNS & CURRIE (AV)

970 Farmington Avenue, P.O. Box 271837, 06127-1837
Telephone: 203-232-4471
Fax: 203-523-4605

MEMBERS OF FIRM

John A. Berman
Courtney B. Bourns
John K. Currie

ASSOCIATES

Robert B. Fawber
Mary Beth Anderson

For full biographical listings, see the Martindale-Hubbell Law Directory

WESTPORT, Fairfield Co.

BLAZZARD, GRODD & HASENAUER, P.C. (AV)

943 Post Road East, P.O. Box 5108, 06881
Telephone: 203-226-7866
Telecopier: 203-454-4855

Norse N. Blazzard
Leslie E. Grodd
Judith A. Hasenauer
William E. Hasenauer
Raymond A. O'Hara, III

Lynn Korman Stone

For full biographical listings, see the Martindale-Hubbell Law Directory

GOLDSTEIN AND PECK, P.C. (AV)

190 Main Street, P.O. Box 5031, 06881
Telephone: 203-226-7488
Telecopier: 203-226-6403
Bridgeport, Connecticut Office: 955 Main Street.
Telephone: 203-334-9421.
Telecopier: 203-334-6949.

William J. Kupinse, Jr.
Walter A. Flynn, Jr.
G. Kenneth Bernhard
Eugene E. Cederbaum
Gregory C. Hammonds

Representative Clients: Bee Publishing Company, Inc.; The Chase Manhattan Bank of Connecticut, N.A.; Fairfield County Medical Association; Great American Insurance Companies; Segua Corporation; Inco, Ltd.; Physicians Health Services, Inc.; Town of Westport.

For full biographical listings, see the Martindale-Hubbell Law Directory

LEVETT, ROCKWOOD & SANDERS, PROFESSIONAL CORPORATION (AV)

33 Riverside Avenue, P.O. Box 5116, 06881
Telephone: 203-222-0885
Telecopier: 203-226-8025

David R. Levett
William O. Rockwood, Jr.
John Sanders
Gregory Griffin
Madeleine F. Grossman
Judy A. Rabkin
Dorit Schutzengel Heimer
Sharon M. Schweitzer
Barbara A. Young
Steven M. Siegelaub
Marc J. Kurzman
Suzanne B. Albani
Alfred U. Pavlis
Peter H. Struzzi

OF COUNSEL

John W. Auchincloss, II

Ellen S. Aho
Edward B. Chansky
Margaret H DeSaussure
Cheryl L. Johnson
Ernest C. Mysogland
Robert W. Riordan
Patricia D. Weitzman

Representative Clients: Advantage Health Corporation; Business Express, Inc.; Cannondale Corporation; Caradon, Inc.; Fabrique de Fer de Charleroi (USA), Inc.; Heyman Properties; Hospital of Saint Raphael; Marketing Corporation of America; St. Vincent's Medical Center; Shawmut Bank, N.A.

For full biographical listings, see the Martindale-Hubbell Law Directory

STUART A. MCKEEVER (AV)

155 Post Road, East, 06880
Telephone: 203-227-4756
Fax: 203-454-2031

Reference: Fleet Bank.

For full biographical listings, see the Martindale-Hubbell Law Directory

TIROLA & HERRING (AV)

1221 Post Road East, P.O. Box 631, 06881
Telephone: 203-226-8926
Fax: 203-226-9500
New York, New York Office: Suite 4E, 10 Sheridan Square.
Telephone: 212-463-9642.

MEMBERS OF FIRM

Vincent S. Tirola
Charles Fredericks, Jr.
Elizabeth C. Seeley
Buddy O. H. Herring

(See Next Column)

TIROLA & HERRING—*Continued*

Dan Shaban Marc J. Grenier

OF COUNSEL

Edward Kanowitz C. Michael Carter
Alan D. Lieberson

Reference: The Westport Bank and Trust Co.

For full biographical listings, see the Martindale-Hubbell Law Directory

WAKE, SEE, DIMES & BRYNICZKA (AV)

27 Imperial Avenue, P.O. Box 777, 06881
Telephone: 203-227-9545
Telecopier: 203-226-1641

MEMBERS OF FIRM

Hereward Wake (1905-1977) Amy L. Y. Day
Edgar T. See Ira W. Bloom
Edwin K. Dimes Ernest Michael Dichele
Jacob P. Bryniczka Jonathan A. Flatow

ASSOCIATES

Douglas E. LoMonte Rosamond A. Koether

OF COUNSEL

Richard S. Gibbons

General Counsel for: L.H. Gault & Son, Inc.; M.B.I., Inc.; The Danbury Mint; Beta Shim, Co.; Easton Press; Coverbind Corp.; D.L. Ryan Companies, Ltd.;
Approved Attorneys for: Lawyers Title Insurance Corporation of Richmond, Va.; Chicago Title Insurance Co.; Old Republic National Title Insurance Co.

For full biographical listings, see the Martindale-Hubbell Law Directory

WEISMAN & LUBELL (AV)

5 Sylvan Road South, P.O. Box 3184, 06880
Telephone: 203-226-8307
Telecopier: 203-221-7279

MEMBERS OF FIRM

Lawrence P. Weisman Ellen B. Lubell

Andrew R. Tarshis

For full biographical listings, see the Martindale-Hubbell Law Directory

WILLIMANTIC, Windham Co.

LANE, ROSEN AND STARKEY, P.C. (AV)

433 Valley Street, 06226
Telephone: 203-423-7761
Fax: 203-423-7764

Herbert A. Lane (1915-1989) Jerome A. Rosen
Noah H. Starkey

Reference: Fleet Bank.

For full biographical listings, see the Martindale-Hubbell Law Directory

WILTON, Fairfield Co.

GREGORY AND ADAMS, P.C. (AV)

190 Old Ridgefield Road, P.O. Box 190, 06897
Telephone: 203-762-9000
Telefacsimile: 203-834-1628
New York, New York Office: 156 West 56th Street, 10019.
Telephone: 212-757-0434.
Telefacsimile: 212-977-9583.

Thomas T. Adams (Resident Partner, New York, N.Y. Office) Steven G. Berg
J. Casey Healy
Ralph E. Slater

SENIOR COUNSEL

Julian A. Gregory

OF COUNSEL

Anne E. Crane Mark R. Jacobs
Mark A. de Regt (Not admitted in CT)
Derrel M. Mason

Andrew H. Bernstein Susan Lacy Goldman
William A. Schofield

For full biographical listings, see the Martindale-Hubbell Law Directory

WINSTED, Litchfield Co.

HOWD, LAVIERI & FINCH (AV)

682 Main Street, P.O. Box 1080, 06098
Telephone: 203-379-2761; 203-496-0889
Fax: 203-379-5187; 203-738-4393

(See Next Column)

MEMBERS OF FIRM

Hadleigh H. Howd (1896-1971) Douglas K. O'Connell
Carmine R. Lavieri (1918-1984) Patrick E. Power, Jr.
David M. Cusick Bruce C. Schmidt
Frank H. Finch, Jr. Maureen E. Donahue

Representative Clients: Shawmut Bank, Connecticut, N.A.; Squire Hill Condominium Association; PTC Aerospace; D&M Construction Corporation; New England Bark Mulch; Winsted Savings Bank; Litchfield Bancorp.; Standard Cycle and Auto Supply Company; Town of Norfolk Planning & Zoning Commission; Winsted Memorial Hospital.

For full biographical listings, see the Martindale-Hubbell Law Directory

DELAWARE

*DOVER,** Kent Co.

*** indicates certain Bar Register subscribers whose principal office is located elsewhere in the state and who have arranged for representation as a part of the state capital listings that follow**

BROWN, SHIELS & CHASANOV (AV)

108 East Water Street, P.O. Drawer "F", 19903
Telephone: 302-734-4766
FAX: 302-674-0903
Georgetown, Delaware Office: 10 East Pine Street.
Telephones: 302-856-7361, 422-7747.
Fax: 302-856-9043.

MEMBERS OF FIRM

Herman C. Brown
Roy S. Shiels
William M. Chasanov (Resident at Georgetown)
Jackson R. Dunlap, Jr. (Resident at Georgetown)
Herman Cubbage Brown, Jr.
Merritt Burke, III (Resident at Georgetown)
André M. Beauregard
Roger D. Kelsey

Local Counsel for: Carl King Inc.; J.C. Penney National Bank, Harrington, Delaware.
Local Attorneys for: American Title Insurance Company; Industrial Valley Title Co.
Reference: JCPenney National Bank, Harrington, Delaware.

For full biographical listings, see the Martindale-Hubbell Law Directory

* MORRIS, JAMES, HITCHENS & WILLIAMS (AV)

Suite 202, 32 West Loockerman Street, 19904
Telephone: 302-678-8815
Telecopier: 302-678-9063
Wilmington, Delaware Office: 222 Delaware Avenue. P.O. Box 2306, 19899-2306.
Telephone: 302-888-6800.
Telecopier: 302-571-1750.

RESIDENT PARTNER

Glenn E. Hitchens

For full biographical listings, see the Martindale-Hubbell Law Directory

PARKOWSKI, NOBLE & GUERKE, PROFESSIONAL ASSOCIATION (AV)

116 West Water Street, P.O. Box 598, 19903
Telephone: 302-678-3262
Telecopier: 302-678-9415

F. Michael Parkowski
John W. Noble
I. Barry Guerke
Clay T. Jester
Jeremy W. Homer
John C. Andrade
Jonathan Eisenberg
Donald R. Kinsley

Dana J. Schaefer

OF COUNSEL

George F. Gardner, III

Representative Clients: Delaware Solid Waste Authority; Cabe Associates (Consulting Engineers).
Approved Attorneys for: Ticor Title Insurance Co.
Reference: First National Bank of Wyoming.

For full biographical listings, see the Martindale-Hubbell Law Directory

* PRICKETT, JONES, ELLIOTT, KRISTOL & SCHNEE (AV)

26 The Green, 19901
Telephone: 302-674-3841
Telecopier: 302-674-5864
Wilmington, Delaware Office: 1310 King Street.
Telephone: 302-888-6500.
Kennett Square, Pennsylvania Office: 217 West State Street.
Telephone: 610-444-1573.

RESIDENT MEMBERS

Gary F. Dalton
William L. Witham, Jr.
Kevin M. Howard

RESIDENT ASSOCIATES

Gary F. Traynor
Mark F. Dunkle
John W. Paradee
Rebecca D. Batson

For full biographical listings, see the Martindale-Hubbell Law Directory

SCHMITTINGER & RODRIGUEZ, PROFESSIONAL ASSOCIATION (AV)

414 South State Street, 19901
Telephone: 302-674-0140
Cable Address: "Schmittrod"
FAX: 302-674-1830
Wilmington, Delaware Office: Suite 205, 1300 North Market Street.
Telephone: 302-652-3676.
Rehoboth Beach, Delaware Office: 4602 Highway One.
Telephone: 302-227-1400.
Odessa, Delaware Office: Odessa Professional Park, P.O. Box 626.
Telephone: 302-378-1697.
Telecopier: 302-378-1659.

Harold Schmittinger
Nicholas H. Rodriguez
Paul H. Boswell
John J. Schmittinger
Bruce C. Ennis
Larry W. Fifer (Resident, Rehoboth Beach, Delaware)
Douglas B. Catts
William D. Fletcher, Jr.
William A. Denman
James T. Vaughn, Jr.
Catherine T. Hickey
William W. Pepper
Craig T. Eliassen
Mark Houghton (Resident, Wilmington, Delaware)
Crystal L. Reihm
Scott E. Chambers
Mardi F. Pyott
John J. Sullivan, Jr.
Noel E. Primos
David A. Boswell

Representative Clients: Delaware Trust Co.; Chesapeake Utilities Corp.; Travelers Insurance Co.; State Farm Mutual Automobile Insurance Co.; Dover Downs, Inc.; City of Dover.

For full biographical listings, see the Martindale-Hubbell Law Directory

*GEORGETOWN,** Sussex Co.

BROWN, SHIELS & CHASANOV (AV)

10 East Pine Street, 19947
Telephone: 302-856-7361, 422-7747
FAX: 302-856-9043
Dover, Delaware Office: 108 East Water Street, P.O. Drawer "F".
Telephone: 302-734-4766.
Fax: 302-674-0903.

RESIDENT MEMBERS

William M. Chasanov
Jackson R. Dunlap, Jr.
Merritt Burke, III

For full biographical listings, see the Martindale-Hubbell Law Directory

YOUNG, CONAWAY, STARGATT & TAYLOR (AV)

110 West Pine Street, 19947
Telephone: 302-856-3571
Telecopy: 302-856-9338
Wilmington, Delaware Office: 11th Floor, Rodney Square North, P.O. Box 391.
Telephone: 302-571-6600.
Telecopy: 302-571-1253.

MEMBERS OF FIRM

H. James Conaway, Jr. (1922-1990)
Craig A. Karsnitz (Resident)

ASSOCIATES

E. Scott Bradley

For full biographical listings, see the Martindale-Hubbell Law Directory

*WILMINGTON,** New Castle Co.

ASHBY & GEDDES (AV)

One Rodney Square, P.O. Box 1150, 19899
Telephone: 302-654-1888
FAX: 302-654-2067

MEMBERS OF FIRM

Lawrence C. Ashby
James McC. Geddes
Stephen E. Jenkins
Randall E. Robbins
Steven J. Balick

ASSOCIATES

Regina A. Iorii
William P. Bowden
Richard D. Heins
Philip Trainer, Jr.
Amy Arnott Quinlan
Steven T. Margolin
Christopher S. Sontchi
John S. Grimm

For full biographical listings, see the Martindale-Hubbell Law Directory

BIGGS AND BATTAGLIA (AV)

1800 Mellon Bank Center, P.O. Box 1489, 19899-1489
Telephone: 302-655-9677

MEMBERS OF FIRM

Victor F. Battaglia
Alan W. Behringer
Francis S. Babiarz
Robert D. Goldberg
Robert K. Beste, Jr.
Jeffrey S. Marlin
Philip B. Bartoshesky
Victor F. Battaglia, Jr.
Christopher J. Battaglia
David L. Finger
Linda F. Shopland

(See Next Column)

BIGGS AND BATTAGLIA—*Continued*

OF COUNSEL

John Biggs, III | Gerard P. Kavanaugh, Sr.
S. Bernard Ableman

For full biographical listings, see the Martindale-Hubbell Law Directory

CONNOLLY, BOVE, LODGE & HUTZ (AV)

1220 Market Street, P.O. Box 2207, 19899-2207
Telephone: 302-658-9141
Telecopier: 302-658-5614
Cable Address: "Artcon"
Telex: 83-5477

Arthur G. Connolly (Emeritus)
James M. Mulligan, Jr.
Arthur G. Connolly, Jr.
Rudolf E. Hutz
Harold Pezzner
John D. Fairchild (Not admitted in DE)
Richard M. Beck (Not admitted in DE)
Paul E. Crawford
Stanley C. Macel, III
Thomas M. Meshbesher
Henry E. Gallagher, Jr.
George Pazuniak
N. Richard Powers
Richard David Levin
John A. Clark, III
Jeffrey B. Bove
James J. Woods, Jr.
Collins J. Seitz, Jr.
Edward F. Eaton
Charles J. Durante
F. L. Peter Stone
Olha N. M. Rybakoff
Patricia Smink Rogowski
Mary W. Bourke
R. Eric Hutz
John C. Kairis
Robert G. McMorrow, Jr. (Not admitted in DE)
Arthur G. Connolly, III
James D. Heisman
Ashley I. Pezzner (Not admitted in DE)
William E. McShane (Not admitted in DE)
James T. Moore (Not admitted in DE)
Anne Love Barnett (Not admitted in DE)
Gerard M. O'Rourke

For full biographical listings, see the Martindale-Hubbell Law Directory

DUANE, MORRIS & HECKSCHER (AV)

1201 Market Street, 19801
Telephone: 302-571-5550
Fax: 302-571-5560
Philadelphia, Pennsylvania Office: Suite 4200 One Liberty Place.
Telephone: 215-979-1000.
FAX: 215-979-1020.
Harrisburg, Pennsylvania Office: The Flynn Group Building, 305 North Front Street, 5th Floor, P.O. Box 1003.
Telephone: 717-237-5500.
Fax: 717-232-4015.
New York, N.Y. Office: 112 E. 42nd Street, Suite 2125.
Telephone: 212-499-0410.
Fax: 212-499-0420.
Wayne, Pennsylvania Office: 735 Chesterbrook Boulevard, Suite 300.
Telephone: 610-647-3555.
Allentown, Pennsylvania Office: 968 Postal Road, Suite 200.
Telephone: 610-266-3650.
Fax: 610-640-2619.
Cherry Hill, New Jersey Office: 51 Haddonfield Road, Suite 340.
Telephone: 609-488-7300.
Fax: 609-488-7021.

RESIDENT PARTNERS

David S. Swayze
Thomas P. Preston
William E. Manning
Daniel F. Lindley
Judith Nichols Renzulli
James S. Green
Joseph A. Fillip, Jr.
David C. Weiss
Teresa K. D. Currier

RESIDENT ASSOCIATES

Richard A. Forsten
Michelle Shriro
Mark A. Morton
Bonnie Lynne Wolfgang
Kevin W. Goldstein
Daniel B. Rath
Mary Catherine Biondi
Richard S. Cobb
Mary F. Caloway
Teri L. Thompson
Robert J. Valihura, Jr.
Linda J.C. Jennings (Not admitted in DE)

For full biographical listings, see the Martindale-Hubbell Law Directory

MCCARTER & ENGLISH (AV)

Mellon Bank Center, 919 Market Street, 19899
Telephone: 302-654-8010
Telecopier: 302-654-0795
Newark, New Jersey Office: Four Gateway Center, 100 Mulberry Street. P.O. Box 652.
Telephone: 201-622-4444.
Telecopier: 201-624-7070.
Cable Address: "McCarter" Newark.
Cherry Hill, New Jersey Office: 1810 Chapel Avenue West.
Telephone: 609-662-8444.
Telecopier: 609-662-6203.

(See Next Column)

New York, New York Office: Suite 1519, One World Trade Center.
Telephone: 212-466-9018.
Telecopier: 212-432-6568.
Boca Raton, Florida Office: 2255 Glades Road, Suite 319-A.
Telephone: 407-994-6262.
Telecopier: 407-241-0798.

RESIDENT PARTNERS

Robert B. Anderson | Paul A. Bradley

RESIDENT ASSOCIATES

Karen S. Brehm
James J. Maron
Wayne A. Marvel
David E. Wilks

For full biographical listings, see the Martindale-Hubbell Law Directory

MORRIS, JAMES, HITCHENS & WILLIAMS (AV)

222 Delaware Avenue, P.O. Box 2306, 19899-2306
Telephone: 302-888-6800
Telecopier: 302-571-1750
Dover, Delaware Office: Suite 202, 32 West Loockerman Street, 19904.
Telephone: 302-678-8815.
Telecopier: 302-678-9063.

MEMBERS OF FIRM

Henry N. Herndon, Jr.
George C. Hering, III
Alfred M. Isaacs
Grover C. Brown
William R. Hitchens, Jr.
Richard P. Beck
Glenn E. Hitchens (Resident at Dover)
Edward M. McNally
Norris P. Wright
James W. Semple
David H. Williams
P. Clarkson Collins, Jr.
Richard Galperin
Steven R. Director
Barbara D. Crowell
Richard D. Kirk
Lewis H. Lazarus
Francis J. Jones, Jr.
Daniel P. McCollom
Barbara MacDonald
Joanne B. Wills
Kent A. Jordan
Robert L. Symonds, Jr.
John D. Demmy

ASSOCIATES

Maureen M. Blanding
Mary M. Culley
Sherry C. McReynolds
Joseph R. Slights, III
Neal C. Belgam
Norman M. Powell
Eileen K. Andersen
Gretchen S. Knight
Peter A. Pietra
Bruce Charles Doeg
Walter Hamberg, III
Janet M. Burris (Not admitted in DE)
Joseph C. Schoell
Eric D. Schwartz
John T. Meli, Jr.
Matthew J. O'Toole

OF COUNSEL

Howard L. Williams | William F. Lynch, II

For full biographical listings, see the Martindale-Hubbell Law Directory

MORRIS AND MORRIS (AV)

Suite 1600, 1105 North Market Street, P.O. Box 2166, 19899-2166
Telephone: 302-426-0400
Facsimile: 302-426-0406

Irving Morris
Karen L. Morris
Abraham Rappaport

ASSOCIATES

Patrick F. Morris
Liam G. B. Murphy
Jacqueline L. Jenkin (Not admitted in DE)
Seth D. Rigrodsky

For full biographical listings, see the Martindale-Hubbell Law Directory

MORRIS, NICHOLS, ARSHT & TUNNELL (AV)

1201 North Market Street, P.O. Box 1347, 19899-1347
Telephone: 302-658-9200
Telecopier: 302-658-3989

MEMBERS OF FIRM

Andrew B. Kirkpatrick, Jr.
Richard L. Sutton
Johannes R. Krahmer
O. Francis Biondi
Lewis S. Black, Jr.
Paul P. Welsh
William O. LaMotte, III
Douglas E. Whitney
William H. Sudell, Jr.
Martin P. Tully
Thomas Reed Hunt, Jr.
A. Gilchrist Sparks, III
Richard D. Allen
David Ley Hamilton
John F. Johnston
Walter C. Tuthill
Donald F. Parsons, Jr.
Jack B. Blumenfeld
Donald Nelson Isken
Donald E. Reid
Denison H. Hatch, Jr.
Thomas C. Grimm
Kenneth J. Nachbar
Andrew M. Johnston
Mary B. Graham
Michael Houghton
Edmond D. Johnson
Matthew B. Lehr

ASSOCIATES

John S. McDaniel
Thomas R. Pulsifer
Jon E. Abramczyk
Rachel A. Dwares (Not admitted in DE)
Alan J. Stone
Louis G. Hering
Frederick H. Alexander
R. Judson Scaggs, Jr.
William M. Lafferty

(See Next Column)

MORRIS, NICHOLS, ARSHT & TUNNELL, *Wilmington—Continued*

ASSOCIATES (Continued)

Andrea L. Rocanelli
Karen Jacobs Louden
Karen L. Pascale
David G. Thunhorst
Elaine C. Reilly
Donna L. Culver
Julia Heaney
Jonathan I. Lessner
Kurt M. Heyman
Michael L. Vild
Lisa B. Baeurle
Justin M. Miller (Not admitted in DE)
Christine M. Hansen
Jeffrey R. Wolters
Kendra S. Hill
Maryellen Noreika
David J. Teklits

COUNSEL

S. Samuel Arsht
David A. Drexler
S. Maynard Turk
Hugh M. Morris (1878-1966)
Alexander L. Nichols (1906-1985)
James M. Tunnell, Jr. (1910-1986)

Representative Clients: The Coca Cola Co.; Delaware River and Bay Authority; Ford Motor Co.; J.P. Morgan Delaware; Longwood Foundation, Inc.; Rollins, Inc.; Texaco Inc.

For full biographical listings, see the Martindale-Hubbell Law Directory

PEPPER, HAMILTON & SCHEETZ (AV)

1201 Market Street, Suite 1401, P.O. Box 1709, 19899-1709
Telephone: 302-571-6555
Telecopy: 302-656-8865
Philadelphia, Pennsylvania Office: 3000 Two Logan Square, Eighteenth and Arch Streets, 19103-2799.
Telephone: 215-981-4000.
Fax: 215-981-4750.
Washington, D.C. Office: 1300 Nineteenth Street, N.W., 20036-1685.
Telephone: 202-828-1200.
Fax: 202-828-1665.
Detroit, Michigan Office: 100 Renaissance Center, 36th Floor, 48243-1157.
Telephone: 313-259-7110.
Fax: 313-259-7926.
Harrisburg, Pennsylvania Office: 200 One Keystone Plaza, North Front and Market Streets, P.O. Box 1181, 17108-1181.
Telephone: 717-255-1155.
Fax: 717-238-0575.
Berwyn, Pennsylvania Office: 1235 Westlakes Drive, Suite 400, 19312-2401.
Telephone: 610-640-7800.
Fax: 610-640-7835.
New York, New York Office: 450 Lexington Avenue, Suite 1600, 10017-3904.
Telephone: 212-878-3800.
Fax: 212-878-3835.
Westmont, New Jersey Office: Sentry Office Plaza, Suite 321, 216 Haddon Avenue, 08108-2811.
Telephone: 609-869-9555.
Fax: 609-869-9595.
London, England Office: City Tower, 40 Basinghall Street, EC2V 5DE.
Telephone: 011-44-71-628-1122.
Fax: 011-44-71-628-6010.
Moscow, Russia Office: 19-27 Grokholsky Pereulok, 129010.
Telephone: 011-7-095-280-4493.
Fax: 011-7-095-280-5518.

PARTNERS

Alfred J. D'Angelo, Jr. (Managing Partner)
Richard P. Eckman
Carl J. Fernandes
M. Duncan Grant
David B. Stratton
James J. Sullivan, Jr.

ASSOCIATES

David M. Fournier
Kathryn A. Kelly
Christopher J. Lamb
Kenneth J. Marino
Benjamin Strauss

For full biographical listings, see the Martindale-Hubbell Law Directory

POTTER ANDERSON & CORROON (AV)

350 Delaware Trust Building, P.O. Box 951, 19899-0951
Telephone: 302-658-6771
FAX: 658-1192; 655-1190; 655-1199

MEMBERS OF FIRM

Richard L. McMahon
Charles S. Crompton, Jr.
Robert K. Payson
Leonard S. Togman
Richard E. Poole
Michael D. Goldman
James F. Burnett
David A. Anderson
Daniel F. Wolcott, Jr.
David J. Garrett
Charles S. McDowell
David B. Brown
Somers S. Price, Jr.
Donald J. Wolfe, Jr.
Gregory A. Inskip
David J. Baldwin
John E. James
W. Harding Drane, Jr.
Mary E. Copper
W. Laird Stabler, III
Richard L. Horwitz
Michael M. Ledyard
William J. Marsden, Jr.
Michael B. Tumas
Kathleen Furey McDonough
Laurie Selber Silverstein
Peter J. Walsh, Jr.
Stephen C. Norman

COUNSEL

Robert P. Barnett
W. Laird Stabler, Jr.

(See Next Column)

OF COUNSEL

William Poole
John P. Sinclair
Blaine T. Phillips
Hugh Corroon
Joseph H. Geoghegan

SENIOR ATTORNEY

Frederick H. Altergott

ASSOCIATES

Arthur L. Dent
Harold I. Salmons, III
David L. Baumberger
William R. Denny
Philip A. Rovner
Peter L. Tracey
Jennifer G. Gimler
Lewis C. Ledyard, III
Scott E. Waxman
Joanne Ceballos
Eric T. Kirschner
Gayle P. Lafferty
Walter S. Peake (Not admitted in DE)
Wendy K. Voss
Kevin R. Shannon
Linda S. Kranitz
Todd L. Goodman
Michael A. Pittinger

Counsel for: Delaware Trust Co.; ConRail; Delmarva Power & Light Co.; Diamond State Telephone Co.; Hercules Inc.; Corporation Trust Co.; General Motors Corp.; Chrysler Corp.; Citicorp.

For full biographical listings, see the Martindale-Hubbell Law Directory

PRICKETT, JONES, ELLIOTT, KRISTOL & SCHNEE (AV)

1310 King Street, P.O. Box 1328, 19899-1328
Telephone: 302-888-6500
Telecopier: 302-658-8111; 658-7257
Dover, Delaware Office: 26 The Green.
Telephone: 302-674-3841.
Kennett Square, Pennsylvania Office: 217 West State Street.
Telephone: 610-444-1573.

MEMBERS OF FIRM

William S. Prickett (1862-1926)
William Prickett (1894-1964)
William Prickett
Richard I. G. Jones
Wayne N. Elliott
Daniel M. Kristol
Carl Schnee
Walter P. McEvilly, Jr.
Mason E. Turner, Jr.
James L. Holzman
John H. Small
Richard P. S. Hannum
George H. Seitz, III
Gary F. Dalton (Resident at Dover Office)
Michael Hanrahan
David E. Brand
William L. Witham, Jr. (Resident at Dover Office)
Dennis Spivack
James P. Dalle Pazze
Timothy A. Casey
Wayne J. Carey
Paul M. Lukoff
Elizabeth M. McGeever
Wendie Cohen Stabler
Kevin M. Howard (Resident at Dover Office)
Norman L. Pernick
Ralph K. ("Dirk") Durstein, III
W. Wade W. Scott
Joseph Grey
Ellisa Opstbaum Habbart

ASSOCIATES

Gary F. Traynor (Resident at Dover Office)
Keith R. Brady
Mark F. Dunkle (Resident at Dover Office)
Chandlee Johnson Kuhn
April Caso Ishak
John W. Paradee (Resident at Dover Office)
Janet K. Stickles
Thomas C. Marconi
Michael P. Freebery
Ronald A. Brown, Jr.
Bruce E. Jameson
Gretchen Ann Bender
John E. Tracey
Jeen Kim
Curtis C. Johnston
Thomas A. Mullen
Patricia Ann Pyles
Rebecca D. Batson (Resident at Dover Office)
Daniel P. Conneen

Representative Clients: Browning-Ferris Industries; Computer Associates International; Delmarva Power & Light; Nationwide.

For full biographical listings, see the Martindale-Hubbell Law Directory

RICHARDS, LAYTON & FINGER, P.A. (AV)

One Rodney Square, P.O. Box 551, 19899
Telephone: 302-658-6541
Telecopier: 302-658-6548

Robert H. Richards, Jr. (1905-1977)
Rodney M. Layton (1921-1983)

James T. McKinstry
Max S. Bell, Jr.
Richard J. Abrams
Charles F. Richards, Jr.
Thomas P. Sweeney
Pierre S. du Pont, IV
Robert H. Richards, III
R. Franklin Balotti
Martin I. Lubaroff
Richard G. Elliott, Jr.
Wendell Fenton
Allen M. Terrell, Jr.
Glenn C. Kenton
Richard G. Bacon
Stephen E. Herrmann
Julian H. Baumann, Jr.
Daniel L. Klein
Donald A. Bussard
William J. Wade
Thomas L. Ambro
Jesse A. Finkelstein
Samuel A. Nolen
Thomas A. Beck
John A. Parkins, Jr.
Gregory P. Williams
Paul M. Altman
Gregory V. Varallo
Mark J. Gentile
Robert J. Krapf
Kevin G. Abrams

(See Next Column)

RICHARDS, LAYTON & FINGER P.A.—*Continued*

Eric A. Mazie
Robert W. Whetzel
W. Donald Sparks, II
C. Stephen Bigler
Charles Malcolm Cochran, IV
Anne C. Foster
Cynthia Deans Kaiser
Daniel A. Dreisbach
James Gerard Leyden, Jr.

David J. Anderson
Mark D. Collins
Frederick L. Cottrell, III
Doneene Keemer Damon
Daniel J. DeFranceschi
Claudia A. Delgross
Raymond J. DiCamillo
Francis DiGiovanni
John T. Dorsey
Darlene Marchesani Fasic
Michael J. Feinstein
Matthew J. Ferretti
David A. Firn
Matthew E. Fischer
Scott R. Haiber
William J. Haubert
Bernard J. Kelley
Peter S. Kirsh
Youngna Lee (Not admitted in DE)
David L. Renauld
Helen M. Richards
Todd Schiltz
Lisa A. Schmidt
Deborah E. Spivack
Robert J. Stearn, Jr.
Helen L. Winslow
William A. Yemc

General Counsel for: Wilmington Trust Company; Continental-American Life Insurance Co.
Local Counsel for: General Motors Corp.; Shell Oil Co.; Aetna Group; Dean Witter Reynolds, Inc.; Gulf & Western Industries Inc.

For full biographical listings, see the Martindale-Hubbell Law Directory

ROSENTHAL, MONHAIT, GROSS & GODDESS, P.A. (AV)

Suite 214 First Federal Plaza, P.O. Box 1070, 19899-1070
Telephone: 302-656-4433
Telecopier: 302-658-7567

Joseph A. Rosenthal
Kevin Gross
Norman M. Monhait
Jeffrey S. Goddess

Carmella Piscopo Keener

Counsel for: Delaware Incorporating Company.

For full biographical listings, see the Martindale-Hubbell Law Directory

SKADDEN, ARPS, SLATE, MEAGHER & FLOM (AV)

One Rodney Square, 19899
Telephone: 302-651-3000
Fax: 302-651-3001
New York, New York Office: 919 Third Avenue, 10022.
Telephone: 212-735-3000.
Fax: 212-735-2000; 212-735-2001.
Telex: 645899 Skarslaw.
Boston, Massachusetts Office: One Beacon Street, 02108.
Telephone: 617-573-4800.
Fax: 617-573-4822.
Washington, D.C. Office: 1440 New York Avenue, N.W., 20005.
Telephone: 202-371-7000.
Fax: 202-393-5760.
Los Angeles, California Office: 300 South Grand Avenue, 90071.
Telephone: 213-687-5000.
Fax: 213-687-5600.
Chicago, Illinois Office: 333 West Wacker Drive, 60606.
Telephone: 312-407-0700.
Fax: 312-407-0411.
San Francisco, California Office: Four Embarcadero Center, 94111.
Telephone: 415-984-6400.
Fax: 415-984-2698.
Houston, Texas Office: 1600 Smith Street, Suite 4460, 77002.
Telephone: 713-655-5100.
Fax: 713-655-5181.
Newark, New Jersey Office: One Riverfront Plaza, 07102.
Telephone: 201-596-4440.
Fax: 201-596-4444.
Tokyo, Japan Office: 12th Floor, The Fukoku Seimei Building, 2-2-2, Uchisaiwaicho, Chiyoda-ku, 100.
Telephone: 011-81-3-3595-3850.
Fax: 011-81-3-3504-2780.
London, England Office: 25 Bucklersbury EC4N 8DA.
Telephone: 011-44-71-248-9929.
Fax: 011-44-71-489-8533.
Hong Kong Office: 30/F Peregrine Tower, Lippo Centre, 89 Queensway, Central.
Telephone: 011-852-820-0700.
Fax: 011-852-820-0727.
Sydney, New South Wales, Australia Office: Level 26-State Bank Centre, 52 Martin Place, 2000.
Telephone: 011-61-2-224-6000.
Fax: 011-61-2-224-6044.
Toronto, Ontario Office: Suite 1820, North Tower, P.O. Box 189, Royal Bank Plaza, M5J 2J4.
Telephone: 416-777-4700.
Fax: 416-777-4747.

(See Next Column)

Paris, France Office: 105 rue du Faubourg Saint-Honoré, 75008.
Telephone: 011-33-1-40-75-44-44.
Fax: 011-33-1-49-53-09-99.
Brussels, Belgium Office: 523 avenue Louise, Box 30, 1050.
Telephone: 011-32-2-648-7666.
Fax: 011-32-2-640-3032.
Frankfurt, Germany Office: MesseTurm, 27th Floor, 60308.
Telephone: 011-49-69-9757-3000.
Fax: 011-49-69-9757-3050.
Beijing, China Office: 1605 Capital Mansion Tower, No. 6 Xin Yuan Nan Road, Chao Yang District, 100004.
Telephone: 011-86-1-466-8800.
Fax: 011-86-1-466-8822.
Budapest, Hungary Office: Mahart Building, H-1052 Apáczai Csere János u.11, Vl.em.
Telephone: 011-36-1-266-2145.
Fax: 011-36-1-266-4033.
Prague, Czech Republic Office: Revolucni 16, 110 00.
Telephone: 011-42-2-231-75-18.
Fax: 011-42-2-231-47-33.
Moscow, Russia Office: Pleteshkovsky, Pereulok 1, 107005.
Telephone: 011-7-501-940-2304.
Fax: 011-7-501-940-2511.

Rodman Ward, Jr.
Steven J. Rothschild
Richard L. Easton
Stephen P. Lamb
Edward P. Welch
Thomas J. Allingham II
Anthony W. Clark
Robert B. Pincus
Marc B. Tucker
Patricia Moran Chuff

OF COUNSEL

Irving S. Shapiro

SPECIAL COUNSEL

Andrew J. Turezyn
Randolph K. Herndon

ASSOCIATES

Curtis S. Alva
Allison L. Amorison
Joseph M. Asher
Clayton Asweenek, Jr. (Not admitted in DE)
Andre G. Bouchard
Kevin F. Brady
Jon A. Brilliant (Not admitted in DE)
Mark S. Chehi
Anne E. Connolly (Not admitted in DE)
John G. Day
Matthew Denn
Ronald J. Fisher (Not admitted in DE)
Joel E. Friedlander
Gregg M. Galardi
Jaya B. Gokhalé
R. Michael Lindsey
Mary M. Maloney-Huss
Kathleen H. Miller
Herbert W. Mondros (Not admitted in DE)
Jeanene F. Patterson
Cathy L. Reese
Robert S. Saunders
Cathy J. Testa

For full biographical listings, see the Martindale-Hubbell Law Directory

SMITH, KATZENSTEIN & FURLOW (AV)

1220 Market Building, P.O. Box 410, 19899
Telephone: 302-652-8400
FAX: 302-652-8405

MEMBERS OF FIRM

Craig B. Smith
Clark W. Furlow
Robert J. Katzenstein
David A. Jenkins
Anne E. Bookout
Susan L. Parker
Vicki A. Hagel
Laurence V. Cronin

Brett D. Fallon
Stephen M. Miller
Michele C. Gott
Joanne M. Shalk
Kathleen M. Miller
Patricia A. Garthwaite

For full biographical listings, see the Martindale-Hubbell Law Directory

TRZUSKOWSKI, KIPP, KELLEHER & PEARCE, P.A. (AV)

1020 North Bancroft Parkway, P.O. Box 429, 19899-0429
Telephone: 302-571-1782
Fax: 302-571-1638

Francis J. Trzuskowski
James F. Kipp
Daniel F. Kelleher
Robert K. Pearce
Edward F. Kafader
Francis J. Schanne

For full biographical listings, see the Martindale-Hubbell Law Directory

WILLIAMS, HERSHMAN & WISLER, P.A. (AV)

Suite 600, One Commerce Center, Twelfth and Orange Streets, P.O. Box 511, 19899-0511
Telephone: 302-575-0873
Telecopier: 302-575-1642

David Nicol Williams
Douglas M. Hershman
Jeffrey C. Wisler
Barbara Snapp Danberg
F. Peter Conaty, Jr.

References: Wilmington Trust Co.; PNC Bank.

For full biographical listings, see the Martindale-Hubbell Law Directory

Wilmington—Continued

YOUNG, CONAWAY, STARGATT & TAYLOR (AV)

Eleventh Floor, Rodney Square North, P.O. Box 391, 19899-0391
Telephone: 302-571-6600
Telecopy: 302-571-1253
Georgetown, Delaware Office: 110 West Pine Street.
Telephone: 302-856-3571.
Telecopy: 302-856-9338.

MEMBERS OF FIRM

H. Albert Young (1904-1982)
H. James Conaway, Jr. (1922-1990)
Bruce M. Stargatt
Richard H. May
Stuart B. Young
Ben T. Castle
Edward B. Maxwell, 2nd
Sheldon A. Weinstein
Arthur Inden
Sheldon N. Sandler
Richard A. Levine
Richard A. Zappa
Frederick William Iobst
David C. McBride
Richard H. Morse
Joseph M. Nicholson
John Vincent Alexander
Barry M. Willoughby
Josy W. Ingersoll
Anthony G. Flynn
Jerome K. Grossman
Eugene A. DiPrinzio
James L. Patton, Jr.
Robert L. Thomas
William D. Johnston
Timothy J. Snyder
Laura Davis Jones
Bruce L. Silverstein
William W. Bowser
Larry J. Tarabicos

OF COUNSEL

William F. Taylor

ASSOCIATES

Richard A. DiLiberto, Jr.
Melanie K. Sharp
Cassandra Faline Kaminski
Neilli Mullen Walsh
Teresa C. Fariss
Jan R. Jurden
David W. O'Connor
Sasson David Peress
Janet Z. Charlton
Robert S. Brady
Timothy Jay Houseal
Maureen Dunn McGlynn
Joel A. Waite
Brian R. Murphy
Bhavana Sontakay
James P. Hughes, Jr.
Omar Y. McNeill
Brendan Linehan Shannon
Martin S. Lessner
Nancy E. Whinnery
Gregory K. Wingate
Natalie S. Wolf

GEORGETOWN, DELAWARE OFFICE

RESIDENT PARTNERS

Craig A. Karsnitz

ASSOCIATES

E. Scott Bradley

For full biographical listings, see the Martindale-Hubbell Law Directory

DISTRICT OF COLUMBIA

WASHINGTON, D.C. Co.

* indicates certain Bar Register subscribers, in cities of comparable size and importance, who maintain an additional office in Washington, D.C. and who have arranged for representation as a part of the Washington, D.C. listings that follow

* Akin, Gump, Strauss, Hauer & Feld, L.L.P. (AV)

A Registered Limited Liability Partnership including Professional Corporations
1333 New Hampshire Avenue, N.W., Suite 400, 20036
Telephone: 202-887-4000
FAX: 202-887-4288
Dallas, Texas Office: 1700 Pacific Avenue, Suite 4100.
Telephone: 214-969-2800.
FAX: 214-969-4343.
Austin, Texas Office: 2100 Franklin Plaza, 111 Congress Avenue.
Telephone: 512-499-6200.
San Antonio, Texas Office: 300 Convent Street, Suite 1500.
Telephone: 210-270-0800.
Houston, Texas Office: 1900 Pennzoil Place-South Tower, 711 Louisiana Street.
Telephone: 713-220-5800.
New York, New York Office: 65 East 55th Street, 33rd Floor.
Telephone: 212-872-1000.
Fax: 212-872-1002.
Brussels, Belgium Office: Akin, Gump, Strauss, Hauer, Feld & Dassesse, 65 Avenue Louise, P.B. #7, 1050.
Telephone: 011-322-535-29-11.
Moscow, Russia Office: Bolshoi Sukharevsky Pereulok 26, Building 1.
Telephone: 011/7-095-974-2411.
Fax: 011/7-095-974-2412.

MEMBERS OF FIRM

Donald C. Alexander
David C. Allen (P.C.)
Edward John Allera (P.C.)
Richard N Appel (P.C.)
Clinton R. Batterton
Andrew G. Berg
Janet C. Boyd (P.C.)
Cheryl C. Burke (P.C.)
David P. Callet (P.C.)
Patricia A. Casey (P.C.)
James W. Cicconi
Joel M. Cohn (P.C.)
Warren E. Connelly (P.C.)
Tom W. Davidson (P.C.)
Smith W. Davis (P.C.)
Sylvia A. de Leon (P.C.)
David B. Dempsey (P.C.)
James P. Denvir, III
David A. Donohoe (P.C.)
Marilyn L. Doria (P.C.)
John M. Dowd (P.C.)
Jeffry R. Dwyer (P.C.)
David H. Eisenstat (P.C.)
Courtenay Ellis (P.C.)
Joseph P. Esposito (P.C.)
Mark P. Fitzsimmons (P.C.)
David Geanacopoulos
Avrum M. Goldberg (P.C.)
Larry S. Gondelman (P.C.)
William J. Grealis
Spencer S. Griffith
Thad Grundy Jr.
Paul E. Gutermann
Scott M. Heimberg (P.C.)
Frank H. Henneburg (P.C.)
Paul B. Hewitt (P.C.)
Laurence J. Hoffman (P.C.)
William G. Hundley
Howard B. Jacobson (P.C.)
Joel Jankowsky (P.C.)
Owen M. Johnson, Jr., (P.C.)
Ronald M. Johnson (P.C.)
Vernon E. Jordan, Jr.
Daniel Joseph (P.C.)
Sukhan Kim
Merrill L. Kramer (P.C.)
James C. Langdon, Jr., (P.C.)
Malcolm Lassman (P.C.)
Roy P. Lessy, Jr.
Lawrence D. Levien (P.C.)
Donald R. Livingston
Jorge Lopez, Jr. (P.C.)
Terence J. Lynam (P.C.)
Patrick F. J. Macrory (P.C.)
Michael J. Madigan (P.C.)
Michael S. Mandel (P.C.)
Michael S. Marcus (P.C.)
Roger J. Marzulla (P.C.)
R. Bruce McLean (P.C.)
Bruce S. Mendelsohn (P.C.)
Michael J. Mueller (P.C.)
Daniel L. Nash
L. Kirk O'Donnell
David B. Palmer (P.C.)
Russell W. Parks, Jr., (P.C.)
Duane H. Pellervo
Robert G. Pinco (P.C.)
Alexander Hartley Platt
Donald R. Pongrace
(Not admitted in DC)
Michael Quigley
Dennis M. Race (P.C.)
Franz R. Rassman (P.C.)
Richard R. Rivers (P.C.)
Jerry E. Rothrock
Edward L. Rubinoff (P.C.)
George R. Salem (P.C.)
Stanley J. Samorajczyk (P.C.)
Dianne H. Sanford
Randall L. Sarosdy
Sanford M. Saunders, Jr. (P.C.)
Earl L. Segal (P.C.)
Jeffrey K. Sherwood (P.C.)
Valerie A. Slater (P.C.)
Roxane N. Sokolove (P.C.)
Jonathan S. Spaeth
C. Fairley Spillman (P.C.)
Robert S. Strauss (P.C.)
Larry E. Tanenbaum (P.C.)
L. Kay Tatum (P.C.)
W. Randolph Teslik (P.C.)
Margaret L. Tobey (P.C.)
Charles L. Warren (P.C.)
Richard L. Wyatt, Jr. (P.C.)
Clifford J. Zatz (P.C.)
Jay D. Zeiler

ASSOCIATES

Kenneth D. Alderfer
Micha Barach
Janet Zoe Barsy
William A. Bianco
William F. Birchfield III
(Not admitted in DC)
John M. Bradham
Cindy M. Bryton
John David Carlin
Kris O. Carter
(Not admitted in DC)
Kimberly Hincken Chamberlain

(See Next Column)

ASSOCIATES (Continued)

Matthew A. Chosid
(Not admitted in DC)
Anne Clark Christman
Kelly A. Clement
(Not admitted in DC)
M. Lisbeth Coen
(Not admitted in DC)
Marlene M. Colucci
Maryellen Connor
Colleen M. Coyle
John C. Crespo
(Not admitted in DC)
Sean G. D'Arcy
Barbara J. Deakin
Hillary S. DeNigro
Alexander Drew
H. Noh Edmunds
(Not admitted in DC)
Eugene E. Elder
Benjamin Erulkar
Cheryl Adams Falvey
William J. Farah
Robin A. Fastenau
Shari L. Fleishman
Vicki Scheer Foster
Michael S. Fuchs
Edwin P. Geils
Nicholas D. Giordano
Jonathan I.J. Goldberg
(Not admitted in DC)
Alison Leigh Gray
Tracy Greer
Kelly Compton Grems
Sarah L. Harpham
(Not admitted in DC)
Gary A. Heimberg
Nick A. Henderson
Victoria A. Higman
John J. Hoffman
(Not admitted in DC)
Mark V. Holden
Cynthia C. Humphries
John R. Jacob
Charles W. Johnson, IV
(Not admitted in DC)
James L. Johnson, Jr.
Elizabeth A. Kandravy
Jonathan E. Kapp
(Not admitted in DC)
Donald Michael Kaye
Kathleen A. Kenealy
(Not admitted in DC)
Sybil R. Kisken
Alexander Kogan
Robert E. Kohn
Imtiaz T. Ladak
(Not admitted in DC)
Paul C. Lembesis
Michael T. Lempres
John C. Le Pore
(Not admitted in DC)
Naomi Joy Levan
(Not admitted in DC)
Robert G. Lian, Jr.
(Not admitted in DC)
Alan S. Macdonald
Mark J. MacDougall
Lilliam L. Machado
Kathryn D. MacKinnon
Lori A. Manca
W. David Mann
Jennifer Abbe Manner
Demetrios J. Marantis
(Not admitted in DC)
Theodore C. Marcus
Stephanie J. Markiewicz
Gayle McKenzie
(Not admitted in DC)
Melissa Heitmann McNiven
Lisa E. Meadows
(Not admitted in DC)
Luis R. Mejia
James E. Mendenhall
Andrew Miller
(Not admitted in DC)
Robert L. Miller
John N. Moore
Rebecca A. Naser
(Not admitted in DC)
Robin M. Nuschler
James C. Osborne, Jr.
J. Steven Patterson
(Not admitted in DC)
Anthony T. Pierce
Lucy W. Pliskin
Margaret L.H. Png
(Not admitted in DC)
Richard J. Rabin
(Not admitted in DC)
Georgia C. Ravitz
(Not admitted in DC)
Michael S. Ray
Sanford C. Reback
Laura M. Reifschneider
Lee H. Roberts
(Not admitted in DC)
Edward M. Rogers
Mary B. Rosenthal
Tamineh Roshanian
Paul D. Rubin
Robert Salcido
(Not admitted in DC)
Richard P. Schlegel
Fritz Schneider
Wynn H. Segall
Elizabeth Wells Skaggs
(Not admitted in DC)
Sheila Christine Stark
Henry A. Terhune
Joseph A. Turzi
T. Cy Walker
Neil J. Welch, Jr.
F. Robert Wheeler III
Jacqueline A. White
(Not admitted in DC)
Damon E. Xenopoulos
Mark M. Yacura
Christopher P. Yost

OF COUNSEL

Ronald R. Adee
Linda S. Broyhill
James E. Conway
George H. Lawrence
(Not admitted in DC)
William E. Potts, Jr.
Stark Ritchie
Steven R. Ross
Donald E. Segal
Dawn E. Starr
Rosemary Stewart
Alan N. Tawshunsky
Samuel Wolff

SENIOR COUNSEL

Richard P. Bonsignore

For full biographical listings, see the Martindale-Hubbell Law Directory

Allen, Johnson, Alexander & Karp, P.A. (AV)

1707 L Street, N.W., Suite 1050, 20036
Telephone: 202-828-4141
Fax: 202-429-8798
Baltimore, Maryland Office: Suite 1540, 100 East Pratt Street.
Telephone: 410-727-5000.

D'Ana E. Johnson

(See Next Column)

ALLEN, JOHNSON, ALEXANDER & KARP P.A., *Washington—Continued*

Anne Marie McGinley
George B. Breen
Robert G. McGinley

Representative Clients: Scottsdale Insurance Co.; Nautilus Insurance Co.; Jefferson Insurance Co.; Liberty Mutual Insurance Co.; Avis Rent-A-Car; Otis Elevator Co.; Montgomery Elevator Co.; Admiral Insurance Co.; Local Government Insurance Trust; Lancer Insurance Co.

For full biographical listings, see the Martindale-Hubbell Law Directory

*** ANDERSON KILL OLICK & OSHINSKY (AV)**

2000 Pennsylvania Avenue, N.W. Suite 7500, 20006
Telephone: 202-728-3100
Telecopier: 202-728-3199
New York, N.Y. Office: Anderson Kill Olick & Oshinsky, P.C., 1251 Avenue of the Americas.
Telephone: 212-278-1000.
Fax: 212-278-1733 and 212-953-7249.
Philadelphia, Pennsylvania Office: Anderson Kill Olick & Oshinsky, P.C. 1600 Market Street.
Telephone: 215-568-4202.
Telecopier: 215-568-4573.
Newark, New Jersey Office: Anderson Kill Olick & Oshinsky, P.C. One Gateway Center, Suite 901.
Telephone: 201-642-5858.
Telecopier: 201-621-6361.
San Francisco, California Office: Anderson Kill Olick & Oshinsky, P.C., One Sansome Street, Suite 1610.
Telephone: 415-677-1450.
Telecopier: 415-677-1475.
New Haven, Connecticut Office: Anderson Kill Olick & Oshinsky, P.C., 59 Elm Street.
Telephone: 203-777-2230.
Telecopier: 203-777-9717.
Phoenix, Arizona Office: Anderson Kill Olick & Oshinsky, P.C., One Renaissance Square, Two North Central, Suite 1250.
Telephone: 602-252-0002.
Telecopier: 602-252-0003.

Sarah Afshar (Not admitted in DC)
Alexander E. Barnett (Not admitted in DC)
Lisa Barsoomian (Not admitted in DC)
Karen L. Bush
Robert L. Carter, Jr.
Suzan F. Charlton
Dana M. Dicarlo
Neal Dittersdorf (Not admitted in DC)
David L. Elkind
Barry J. Fleishman
Lawrence M. Gleason, Jr. (Not admitted in DC)
Eric Taylor Gormsen (Not admitted in DC)
Gerald S. Hartman
Gregory W. Homer
Diane M. Horan
Kimm Hudley (Not admitted in DC)
Michelle M. Jardine
Joseph V. Jest
Leon B. Kellner (Not admitted in DC)
Mark H. Kolman
Geri Weiseman Kolesar
Lorelie S. Masters
Karen L. Meengs
John E. Menditto
Mark E. Miller (Not admitted in DC)
Michael A. Nardolilli
Rhonda D. Orin
Jerold Oshinsky
Robert W. Pommer, III (Not admitted in DC)
Andrew M. Reidy
Jennifer D. Richard (Not admitted in DC)
Dirk R. Rountree
Murray D. Sacks
Catherine J. Serafin (Not admitted in DC)
Lauren B. Sobel
Lee M. Straus
Deborah A. Swindells
Koorosh Talieh (Not admitted in DC)
Barbara Musfeldt Tapscott
Joseph D. Tydings
James R. Wagner
Stephan G. Weil
Kent T. Withycombe (Not admitted in DC)

For full biographical listings, see the Martindale-Hubbell Law Directory

ANDERSON & QUINN (AV)

1220 L Street, N.W., Suite 540, 20005
Telephone: 202-371-1245
Rockville, Maryland Office: Adams Law Center, 25 Wood Lane.
Telephone: 301-762-3303.
FAX: 301-762-3776.

MEMBERS OF FIRM

Charles C. Collins (1900-1973)
Robert E. Anderson (Retired)
Francis X. Quinn
William Ray Scanlin
Donald P. Maiberger
Robert P. Scanlon

ASSOCIATES

Richard L. Butler

Representative Clients: C & P Telephone; Commercial Union Insurance Cos.; Allstate Insurance Co.; State Farm Mutual Automobile Insurance Co.; Northbrook Insurance Cos.; Travelers Insurance Co.; National General Insurance Co.; American International Adjustment Co.; Marriott Corp.

For full biographical listings, see the Martindale-Hubbell Law Directory

*** ANDREWS & KURTH L.L.P. (AV)**

A Registered Limited Liability Partnership
Suite 200, 1701 Pennsylvania Avenue, N.W., 20006
Telephone: 202-662-2700
Telecopier: 202-662-2739
Houston, Texas Office: 4200 Texas Commerce Tower.
Telephone: 713-220-4200.
Telecopier: 713-220-4285.
Dallas, Texas Office: 4400 Thanksgiving Tower.
Telephone: 214-979-4400.
Telecopier: 214-979-4401.
The Woodlands, Texas Office: Suite 150, 2170 Buckthorne Place, 77380.
Telephone: 713-364-9199.
Telecopier: 713-364-9538.
Los Angeles, California Office: Suite 4200, 601 South Figueroa Street.
Telephone: 213-896-3100.
Telecopier: 213-896-3137.
New York, N.Y. Office: 10th Floor, 425 Lexington Avenue, 10017.
Telephone: 212-850-2800.
Telecopier: 212-850-2929.

MEMBERS OF FIRM

Rush Moody, Jr.
Richard C. Green
C. Howard Hardesty, Jr.
David G. Wilson
John W. Ebert (Not admitted in DC)
Robert N. Steinwurtzel
Michael J. Fremuth
Thomas R. Kline
Kenneth L. Wiseman
Mark F. Sundback
Mary Anne Mason
Stephen E. Roady
Jennifer M. Porter
Judy A. Johnson
Constance Collins Davis
Michael L. Kessler
Douglas V. Rigler
Gilbert P. Sperling
Joanne W. Young (Resident)
Anthony J. Ivancovich
Thomas Richard Lotterman

OF COUNSEL

David E. Short
Thomas E. Starnes
Gregory J. Marich

ASSOCIATES

Dawn M. Becker
A. Lindsey Crawford
John W. Enerson
Matthew T. Gould (Not admitted in DC)
Jeffery S. Hannapel
Maureen Z. Hurley
Christine Anne Jones (Not admitted in DC)
Kristina Ann Mack (Not admitted in DC)
Virginia T. Mc Gee (Not admitted in DC)
Kenneth M. Minesinger (Not admitted in DC)
Susan J. Panzik
Shemin V. Proctor
Scott A. Richie
Charles W. Runnete (Not admitted in DC)
Peter J. Thompson
Craig B. Young

STAFF ATTORNEY

Heatherun W. Allison (Not admitted in DC)
Mary Douglas Dick

For full biographical listings, see the Martindale-Hubbell Law Directory

ARENT FOX KINTNER PLOTKIN & KAHN (AV)

Washington Square, 1050 Connecticut Avenue, N.W., 20036-5339
Telephone: 202-857-6000
Fax: 202-857-6395
Cable: "Arfox."
Telex: WU-892672; ITT-440266
Bethesda, Maryland Office: Suite 900, 7475 Wisconsin Avenue.
Telephone: 202-857-6000.
Fax: 202-857-6395.
Vienna, Virginia Office: Suite 700, 8000 Towers Crescent Drive.
Telephone: 202-857-6000.
Fax: 202-857-6395.
N.Y.C. Office: 1675 Broadway, 25th Floor.
Telephone: 212-484-3900.
Telecopier: 212-484-3990.
Budapest Representative Office: Nagymezo utca 44, H-1065 Budapest, Hungary.
Telephones: (36-1) 269 0596; 269 0597.
Fax: (36-1) 269 0599.
Kingdom of Saudi Arabia Office: Law Offices of His Royal Highness Prince Saad Al Faisel Bin Abdul Aziz, P.O. Box 15836, Jeddah 21454, Kingdom of Saudi Arabia.
Telephone: (966-2) 651-9373.
Facsimile: (966-2) 651-9465.

MEMBERS OF FIRM

Henry J. Fox (1911-1990)
Earl W. Kintner (1912-1992)
Jerome P. Akman
Jennifer A. Albert
Mark E. Alberta
David J. Bardin
Donald M. Barnes
Joel E. Bassett
Evan R. Berlack
Richard L. Brand
Jean-François Carreras (Resident, New York, N.Y. Office)
Ronald L. Castle
William R. Charyk
Earl M. Colson
John C. Culver
Morris F. DeFeo, Jr.
David T. Dekker
Mary Joanne Dowd

(See Next Column)

ARENT FOX KINTNER PLOTKIN & KAHN—*Continued*

MEMBERS OF FIRM (Continued)

Alan S. Dubin
Michael M. Eaton
Bart S. Fisher
Marc L. Fleischaker
Stephen B. Forman
Jeremy B. Fox
Theodore D. Frank
Andre H. Friedman (Budapest, Hungary and New York, N.Y. Offices)
Joseph M. Fries
Richard N. Gale
Stephen L. Gibson
Coralyn G. Goode
William W. Goodrich, Jr.
Michael A. Gordon
James B. Halpern
C. Stephen Heard, Jr. (Resident, New York, N.Y. Office)
Lawrence F. Henneberger
Robert B. Hirsch
R. Steven Holt
James H. Hulme
John D. Hushon
Michael Evan Jaffe
Jeffrey E. Jordan
Stephen D. Kahn
Mark M. Katz
George R. Kucik
Michael J. Kurman
Michael H. Leahy
Gerard Leval
George P. Levendis
Lawrence A. Levit
John B. Madden, Jr. (Resident, New York, N.Y. Office)
Alan R. Malasky
Stewart S. Manela
Eugene A. Massey
Wayne H. Matelski
Gerald P. McCartin
John C. McCoy, Jr.
Donald C. McLean
Eugene J. Meigher
James P. Mercurio
Lawrence G. Meyer
Steven R. Miles
Donald B. Mitchell, Jr.
Gerald L. Mitchell
Henry Morris, Jr.
Jeffrey B. Newman (Resident, Budapest, Hungary Office)
Richard A. Newman
David M. Osnos
Deborah K. Owen (Not admitted in DC)
Rodney F. Page
James P. Parker
Lynn K. Pearle
William R. Pendergast
Matthew S. Perlman
Howard B. Possick
Deborah A. Randall
Marc Rauch (Resident, New York, N.Y. Office)
Peter S. Reichertz
Alan E. Reider
John R. Risher, Jr.
Salvatore A. Romano
Lewis Rose
Thomas Schattenfield
Joanne Schehl
George H. Shapiro
Allen G. Siegel
Joel N. Simon
Howard V. Sinclair
Sheryl L. Sklorman
Christopher Smith
Timothy J. Smith
Marilyn D. Sonn
Michael L. Stevens
Carter Strong
Carl A. Valenstein
Barbara S. Wahl
Robert J. Waters
Richard J. Webber
Arnold R. Westerman
Burton V. Wides
Breckinridge L. Willcox
David N. Wynn (Resident, New York, N.Y. Office)
Harvey A. Yampolsky
John J. Yurow
Lynda S. Zengerle

COUNSEL

Albert E. Arent (Retired)
William C. Basil
Samuel Efron
Ben I. Haraguchi (Resident, New York, N.Y. Office)
Edwin L. Kahn (Retired)
David L. Kelleher
Craig S. King
Leonard S. Melrod
Patrick F. O'Leary
Harry M. Plotkin (Retired)
Lipman Redman
Lucy F. Reed (Resident, New York, N.Y. Office)
Paul Jackson Rice
Charles B. Ruttenberg
Malvern J. Sheffield, Jr. (Retired)
Karen Maloy Sprecher
Angela E. Vallot
Kathleen E. Voelker
Gerald Zingone

ASSOCIATES

Nancy Susan Appel
Hallie M. Bastian
Robert A. Bauman
Laurel A. Bedig
Tracy Palmer Berns
Lawrence E. Blatnik
Margo S. Block (Not admitted in DC)
Randall J. Boe
Karen Bayley Bowen (Resident, New York, N.Y. Office)
R. Grant Brady (Resident, New York, N.Y. Office)
Jennifer Brooke-Davidson
Piero Bussani
Melissa L. Callahan (Not admitted in DC)
Hunter T. Carter
Samuel K. Charnoff
Aileen Miller Cohen
Andrew C. Cooper
Brian E. Danaher
Marilyn Tiki Dare
Kendra L. Dimond (Not admitted in DC)
D. Jeffrey Disbrow (Not admitted in DC)
Marta Erceg (Not admitted in DC)
Patricia A. Gaegler
Helen L. Gemmill
Sean W. Glynn
Hendrik Gordenker
Kimberly A. Grossman
Anne M. Hamilton (Not admitted in DC)
Kathryn Toub Harris
Rebecca S. Hartley (Not admitted in DC)
Christine L. Herrell
David A. Hyman (Not admitted in DC)
Kenneth S. Jacob
Quana C. Jew
Elizabeth Aimee Kelly (Not admitted in DC)
Trent M. Kittleman (Not admitted in DC)
Mindy L. Klasky
Noreen M. Lavan
Mitchell Lazarus
Philip L. Lee (Not admitted in DC)
Dominique M.H. Lemoine

(See Next Column)

ASSOCIATES (Continued)

Bret L. Limage
David L. London (Not admitted in DC)
Peder van Wagonen Magee (Not admitted in DC)
Susan A. Marshall
Camilla C. McKinney (Not admitted in DC)
John J. Meyer (Not admitted in DC)
John T. Mitchell
Genevieve Murphy Moore
Kimberly L. Myers
Jill R. Newman (Not admitted in DC)
Jeffrey Nimz
John J. O'Brien
Jose M. Ochoa
Paul A. O'Hop, Jr.
David A. Ontko
Deanne M. Ottaviano
Jason Scott Palmer
William E. Penn (Not admitted in DC)
Jennifer R. Pitarresi (Not admitted in DC)
Elliott I. Portnoy
Robert D. Primosch
Deborah M. Rochkind
Adam J. Ruttenberg
Andrea Kupfer Schneider
Steven F. Schroeder (Not admitted in DC)
Larri A. Short
Lynn Frendt Shotwell
Christopher J. Smart (Not admitted in DC)
Joseph R. Sollee (Not admitted in DC)
James K. Stronski (Resident, New York, N.Y. Office)
John N. Suhr, Jr.
Nada S. Sulaiman (Not admitted in DC)
Brian D. Sullivan
Kerry S. Sullivan (Resident, New York, N.Y. Office)
Peter L. Sultan
Erin M. Sweeney
Samantha R. Turian
Christopher Van Hollen, Jr. (Not admitted in DC)
Gregory J. Voell
Jeffrey Walker (Resident, New York, N.Y. Office)
Molly B.F. Walls
Nicole Marie Walthour
John E. Wood (Not admitted in DC)
Jeanine M. Worden
Howard J. Young

For full biographical listings, see the Martindale-Hubbell Law Directory

ARNOLD & PORTER (AV)

Thurman Arnold Building, 1200 New Hampshire Avenue, N.W., 20036-6885
Telephone: 202-872-6700
Cable Address: "Arfopo"
Telecopy: 202-872-6720
Los Angeles, California Office: 44th Floor, 777 Figueroa Street, 90017-2513.
Telephone: 213-243-4000.
Telecopy: 213-243-4199.
Denver, Colorado Office: 1700 Lincoln Street, 80203-4540.
Telephone: 303-863-1000.
Telecopy: 303-832-0428.
New York, New York Office: 399 Park Avenue, 10022-4690.
Telephone: 212-715-1000.
Telecopy: 212-715-1399.
Budapest, Hungary Representative Office: Retek utca 26, H-1024.
Telephone: 36-1-212-1110.
Telefax: 36-1-135-7857.
Istanbul, Turkey Representative Office: Büyükdere Caddesi No. 118/10, Esentepe 80280.
Telephone: 90-212-275-2160.
Fax: 90-212-275-2079.
Moscow, Russia Representative Office: Ozerkovskaya NA. 50, 113532.
Telephone: 7095-235-3774.
Telefax: 7095-235-5181.

WASHINGTON, D.C. OFFICE

MEMBERS OF FIRM

Thurman Arnold (1891-1969)
Paul A. Porter (1904-1975)
William L. McGovern (1913-1977)
B. Howell Hill (1922-1977)
James R. McAlee (1931-1985)
David H. Lloyd (1938-1988)
Bruce A. Adams
Carolyn E. Agger
Richard M. Alexander
David B. Apatoff
Geoffrey F. Aronow
William J. Baer
Donald O. Beers
Alexander E. Bennett
Paul S. Berger (Partner in Charge, Istanbul, Turkey Representative Office)
Blake A. Biles
Peter K. Bleakley
Brooksley Elizabeth Born
Jeffrey S. Bromme
Jeffrey A. Burt (Partner in Charge, Moscow, Russia Representative Office)
Howard Neil Cayne
Bruce M. Chadwick
Jerome I. Chapman
Lynda M. Clarizio
Charles H. Cochran
Martha L. Cochran
George E. Covucci
Patricia Ann Dean
Eli Whitney Debevoise, II
Paul T. Denis
Jacqueline R. Denning
Norman Diamond
Steven S. Diamond
James A. Dobkin
A. Patrick Doyle
Douglas A. Dworkin
Thomas R. Dwyer
David S. Eggert
Richard S. Ewing
Melanie L. Fein
Roger P. Fendrich
Richard M. Firestone
James F. Fitzpatrick
Samuel A. Flax
Milton V. Freeman
Melvin C. Garbow
Murray R. Garnick
Robert A. Garrett
David P. Gersch
Neil M. Goodman
Richard M. Graf
Patrick J. Grant
Julius M. Greisman
Peter T. Grossi, Jr.
Althea L. Harlin

(See Next Column)

ARNOLD & PORTER, *Washington—Continued*

WASHINGTON, D.C. OFFICE
MEMBERS OF FIRM (Continued)

John D. Hawke, Jr.
Vivian Lee Hobbs
Philip W. Horton
Richard L. Hubbard
Gary E. Humes
Darryl W. Jackson
Richard A. Johnson
James W. Jones
Robert J. Jones
Kenneth I. Juster
Steven Kaplan
Andrew T. Karron
Hadrian R. Katz
David R. Kentoff
Abe Krash
Werner Kronstein
Kenneth J. Krupsky
Stuart J. Land
J. Stephen Lawrence, Jr.
Michael A. Lee
Kenneth A. Letzler
Arthur N. Levine
Daniel Martin Lewis
Jack L. Lipson
Steven P. Lockman
Dennis G. Lyons
Helene B. Madonick
Robert E. Mannion
Catherine Collins McCoy
Thomas J. McGrew
Mark R. Merley
Michael B. Mierzewski
Thomas H. Milch
Reed Miller
Nancy K. Mintz
Robert S. Mintz
Bruce L. Montgomery
S. Lee Narrow
Irvin B. Nathan
G. Philip Nowak
Fern Phillips O'Brian
Robert B. Ott
L. Stevenson Parker
Donna E. Patterson
Stephanie M. Phillipps
Stephen W. Porter
Claire E. Reade
Steven G. Reade
Daniel A. Rezneck
Walter J. Rockler
William D. Rogers
Richard L. Rosen
Robert D. Rosenbaum
Stanford G. Ross
Stephen M. Sacks
James J. Sandman
Ronald A. Schechter
K. Peter Schmidt
Lawrence A. Schneider
Scott B. Schreiber
Matthew J. Seiden
Cary Howard Sherman
Michael T. Shor
Thomas E. Silfen
Norman M. Sinel
Jeffrey H. Smith
Michael N. Sohn
Lester Sotsky
Melvin Spaeth
Mark J. Spooner
Mary Gabrielle Sprague
Michael A. Stosser
Mark H. Stumpf
Rebecca E. Swenson
Bryan J. Tomasek
Causton A. Toney
G. Duane Vieth
William W. Vodra
Douglas L. Wald
Daniel Waldman
Robert N. Weiner
Richard J. Wertheimer
Joseph D. West
Leslie Wharton
Robert H. Winter
Jay Kelly Wright

OF COUNSEL

Edward E. Bintz
J. Bradway Butler
Myron P. Curzan
Glenda A. Fowler
Michael D. Goodwin
George W. Kaufman
(Not admitted in DC)
Donald P. McHugh
Robert Pitofsky
Richard P. Schifter

SPECIAL COUNSEL

March Coleman
Marcia Ann Cranberg
Lawrence E. Culleen
M. Grace Fleeman
Lisa B. Horowitz
Howard L. Hyde
Janet Lee Johnson
Mark A. Kass
Joan G. Ochs
Randal M. Shaheen

ASSOCIATES

Lisa M. Arnold
Susan G. Arnold
Paul F. Baker
Richard E. Baltz
Kathleen A. Behan
David B. Bergman
Deena R. Bernstein
Michael L. Bernstein
Theodore S. Boone
John M. Boyd, Jr.
Katherine L. Q. Britton
Neil S. Bromberg
William L. Busis
(Not admitted in DC)
Daphne E. Butler
Michael Caglioti
Margaret A. Campell
Mary E. Cassidy
Susan Booth Cassidy
Abby Strongin Cherner
Susan B. Chertkof
Linda B. Coe
Robert B. Conley
(Not admitted in DC)
William Edro Cook, Jr.
Edward N. Cooper
James L. Cooper
Michael D. Daneker
Beth S. DeSimone
Steven R. Englund
Jill T. Feeney
Deborah L. Feinstein
Holly R. Fogler
Sonia (Turcotte) Fois
Carl A. Fornaris
(Not admitted in DC)
Lesley R. Frank
David F. Freeman, Jr.
Johnathan M. Frenkel
(Not admitted in DC)
Tracey K. Friedlander
David Frohlich
Matthew Frumin
Michael R. Geske
Jonathan Gleklen
(Not admitted in DC)
Frederick W. Guinee
Drew A. Harker
Bruce A. Henoch
Eric Bradford Hermanson
(Not admitted in DC)
Laura Jean Hines
Cathy Hoffman
Roberta Lazarus Horton
J. Robert Humphries
Even Hurwitz
Aimee L. Imundo
Richard L. Jacobs
James P. Joseph
Hilde Elisabeth Kahn
Sarah Elizabeth Kahn
David L. Katz

(See Next Column)

ASSOCIATES (Continued)

Michael E. Korens
David E. Korn
Robert J. Kulperger
(Not admitted in DC)
M. Sean Laane
Brian E. J. Lam
(Not admitted in DC)
Annette M. Lang
Susan G. Lee
Franklin R. Liss
James A. Losey
Richard M. Lucas
Jennifer C. Maloney
(Not admitted in DC)
John C. Massaro
Susan K. Matlow
Rosemary Maxwell
Cindy Leigh McAfee
Raymond C. Meyer
Lawrence R. Miller
(Not admitted in DC)
Susan T. Morita
Peter G. Neiman
(Not admitted in DC)
Ruth Ann Nicastri
Donna Katherine Norman
David F. Noteware
Anthony N. O'Brien
Michelle B. O'Connor
Nancy M. Olson
(Not admitted in DC)
Annemarie O'Shea
Andrew Pace
Jennifer S. Perkins
Nancy L. Perkins
Erica Frohman Plave
Gary P. Poon
William Michael Quinn, Jr.
Sally D. Rainey
Stefanie L. Raker
Thomas W. Richardson
Bradley M. Risinger
Jonathan C. Ritter
(Not admitted in DC)
Marc A. Rockford
Melissa A. Scanlan
Charles Wylie Scarborough
Kenneth L. Schwartz
(Not admitted in DC)
Ho Sik Shin
(Not admitted in DC)
Edward H. Sisson
Michael S. Solender
Walter L. Stone
Sharon L. Taylor
Joseph G. Tirone
Asim Varma
Marilyn J. Weiss
(Not admitted in DC)
Paolo G. Wright-Carozza
Walter F. Zenner

For full biographical listings, see the Martindale-Hubbell Law Directory

* ARTER & HADDEN (AV)

1801 K Street, N.W., Suite 400K, 20006-1301
Telephone: 202-775-7100
Cable Address: "Stem Washington";
Telex: 6502156242-MCI
In Cleveland, Ohio: 1100 Huntington Building, 925 Euclid Avenue.
Telephone: 216-696-1100.
In Columbus, Ohio: 21st Floor, One Columbus, 10 West Broad Street.
Telephone: 614-221-3155.
In Dallas, Texas: 1717 Main Street, Suite 4100.
Telephone: 214-761-2100.
In Los Angeles, California: 700 South Flower Street.
Telephone: 213-629-9300.
In Irvine, California: Two Park Plaza, Suite 700, Jamboree Center.
Telephone: 714-252-7500.
In Austin, Texas: 100 Congress Avenue, Suite 1800.
Telephone: 512-479-6403.
In San Antonio, Texas: Suite 540, Harte-Hanks Tower, 7710 Jones Maltsberger Road.
Telephone: 210-805-8497.

MEMBERS OF FIRM

Charles K. Arter (1875-1957)
John A. Hadden (1886-1979)
Jerome A. Hochberg
Francis R. Snodgrass
James L. Bikoff
David I. Wilson
David L. Miller
Mark E. Solomons
William K. Dabaghi
Richard A. Dean
Philip M. Horowitz
Allan J. Weiner
Howard M. Liberman
John D. Maddox
Samuel J. Winer
Dennis E. Eckart
(Not admitted in DC)
Michael L. Cohen
(Not admitted in DC)
Paul H. Friedman
Laura Metcoff Klaus
William L. Gehrig
Laurence E. Bensignor
Michael P. Murphy
H. John Steele
Kenneth B. Winer
Peter L. Canzano
Mary Jane Saunders
Roger P. Furey
Gerald Stevens-Kittner
Lawrence H. Gesner
Douglas M. Mangel
James U. Troup
John C. Hockenbury

OF COUNSEL

N. Barr Miller
Sol Schildhause
R. Lewis Gable

ASSOCIATES

Jodi Mintzer Krame
James Grier Hoyt
Peter H. Doyle
Joseph V. Gatti
Timothy P. Trainer
William E. Berlin
Karen S. Rapaport
Michael J. Pollack
David S. Jenks
Patricia Adams McQuillen
Thomas K. Slattery
Mary M. Nordberg
Linda Shea Gieseler
Michael B. Adlin
Sharon L. Webber
Janine F. Goodman
Sirina Tsai
(Not admitted in DC)
Todd D. Snyder
Marsha M. Baumgarner
(Not admitted in DC)
Bryan A. Sims
(Not admitted in DC)

Reference: The Century Bank, Washington, D.C.

For full biographical listings, see the Martindale-Hubbell Law Directory

Washington—Continued

ASBILL, JUNKIN & MYERS, CHTD. (AV)

1615 New Hampshire Avenue, N.W., 20009
Telephone: 202-234-9000
Facsimile: 202-332-6480
Alexandria, Virginia Office: 317 South Patrick Street.
Telephone: 703-684-7900.
Rockville, Maryland Office: Suite 315, 200-A Monroe Street.
Telephone: 301-294-0460.

Henry W. Asbill
Timothy deForest Junkin
Matthew L. Myers
Lenard B. Boss
Terrance G. Reed

Lauren Clingan

For full biographical listings, see the Martindale-Hubbell Law Directory

*** BAKER & BOTTS, L.L.P. (AV)**

A Registered Limited Liability Partnership
The Warner, 1299 Pennsylvania Avenue, N.W., 20004-2400
Telephone: 202-639-7700
Fax: 202-639-7832
Houston, Texas Office: One Shell Plaza, 910 Louisiana.
Telephone: 713-229-1234.
Austin, Texas Office: 1600 San Jacinto Center, 98 San Jacinto Boulevard.
Telephone: 512-322-2500.
Dallas, Texas Office: 2001 Ross Avenue.
Telephone: 214-953-6500.
New York, New York Office: 805 Third Avenue, Suite 2000.
Telephone: 212-705-5000.
Moscow, Russian Federation Office: 10 ul. Pushkinskaya, 103031.
Telephone: 7095/921-5300 (Local); 7501/929-7070 (International).

MEMBERS OF FIRM

James Addison Baker, III (Not admitted in DC)
O. Donaldson Chapoton (Not admitted in DC)
Bruce F. Kiely
James R. Doty
William D. Kramer
Daniel J. Riley (Not admitted in DC)
Charles M. Darling, IV
Scott F. Partridge
Randolph Quaile McManus
J. Patrick Berry
Thomas J. Eastment
Rodger L. Tate
B. Donovan Picard
Steven R. Hunsicker
Kirk K. Van Tine
David N. Powers
Hugh Tucker
James A. Baker IV
John B. Veach, III
John B. McDaniel

ASSOCIATES

Jesse R. Adams, III
Claude A. Allen
James B. Arpin
Taaka K. Awori (Not admitted in DC)
Debra Raggio Bolton
Christopher C. Campbell
Ruby D'andrea Ceaser
N. Catherine Claypoole
Kevin B. Dent
Sue Ann Dilts
Andrea Fraser-Reid Farr
Drew J. Fossum
Leslie Anne Freiman
James G. Gatto
Michael A. Gold (Not admitted in DC)
Jacqueline R. Helmberger (Not admitted in DC)
Sheila Wallace Holmes
Jay B. Johnson
Jane Boland Keough
Wendy J. Lang
Jennifer S. Leete (Not admitted in DC)
Estee S. Levine (Not admitted in DC)
Mark K. Lewis
Charles B. Lobsenz
Paul T. Luther
Martin T. Lutz
David E. Maranville
Michael X. Marinelli
James Remenick
Kelly A. Riley
Martin Schaefermeier
Gregory D. Shorin
Tamar C. Snyder (Not admitted in DC)
Jeffrey A. Stonerock
David A. Super
O. Kevin Vincent (Not admitted in DC)
Samuel J. Waldon (Not admitted in DC)
Cheryl J. Walker

For full biographical listings, see the Martindale-Hubbell Law Directory

BAKER & HOSTETLER (AV)

Washington Square, Suite 1100, 1050 Connecticut Avenue, N.W., 20036-5304
Telephone: 202-861-1500
In Cleveland, Ohio: 3200 National City Center, 1900 East Ninth Street.
Telephone: 216-621-0200.
In Columbus, Ohio: Capitol Square, Suite 2100, 65 East State Street.
Telephone: 614-228-1541.
In Denver, Colorado: 303 East 17th Avenue, Suite 1100.
Telephone: 303-861-0600.
In Houston, Texas: 1000 Louisiana, Suite 2000.
Telephone: 713-751-1600.
In Long Beach, California: 300 Oceangate, Suite 620.
Telephone: 310-432-2827.
In Los Angeles, California: 600 Wilshire Boulevard.
Telephone: 213-624-2400.

(See Next Column)

In Orlando, Florida: SunBank Center, Suite 2300, 200 South Orange Avenue.
Telephone: 305-841-1111.
In College Park, Maryland: 9658 Baltimore Boulevard, Suite 206.
Telephone: 301-441-2781.
In Alexandria, Virginia: 437 North Lee Street.
Telephone: 703-549-1294.
In San Francisco, California: One Sansome Street, Suite 2000.
Telephone: 415-951-4705.

MEMBERS OF FIRM IN WASHINGTON, D.C.

William H. Schweitzer (Managing Partner, Washington, D.C. Office)

PARTNERS

Edward Jay Beckwith
Joseph M. Berl
Frederick W. Chockley, III
Gerald A. Connell
William F. Conroy
William J. Conti
Mark A. Cymrot
Lee T. Ellis, Jr.
Frederick H. Graefe
David Alistair Grant
Leonard C. Greenebaum
Brian S. Harvey
Richard A. Hauser
Webb C. Hayes, III
Henry S. Hoberman
Kenneth C. Howard, Jr.
Thomas Hylden
N. William Jarvis
Sargent Karch
E. Andrew Keeney
Kenneth J. Kies
Richard J. Leon
Marshall Lee Miller
Mario V. Mirabelli
Shelby F. Mitchell (Not admitted in DC)
Thomas R. Mounteer
Betty Southard Murphy
Robert H. Neuman
John Daniel Reaves
Bruce W. Sanford
Belinda Jayne Scrimenti
Louis R. Sernoff
Lee H. Simowitz
John Lewis Smith, III
Alan S. Ward
Donald P. Zeifang
H. Karl Zeswitz, Jr.

ASSOCIATES

Stephanie S. Abrutyn
Ralph G. Blasey, III
Jenifer M. Brown
Adam K. Derman (Not admitted in DC)
John S. Farrington (Not admitted in DC)
Paul O. Gagnier, Jr.
Eric J. Geppert
Kelly Matthews Gerber
Renee L. Giachino
David Morgan Giles (Not admitted in DC)
Margaret E. Goss
James E. Houpt
Paul F. Kirgis
Sean H. Lane
Robert D. Lystad
David L. Marshall
Kent W. McAllister (Not admitted in DC)
M. Tracy McPherson
Beth Elise Morrow
Gregory A. Paw
Dawn M. Porter
Michael C. Ruger
Jon A. Soderberg
John M. Taladay
Charles S. Verdery (Not admitted in DC)
Ronald F. Wick (Not admitted in DC)
Kenneth D. Woodrow (Not admitted in DC)
Elizabeth M. Yeonas

OF COUNSEL

William W. Beckett
E. Mark Braden
Jack Evans
Richard H. Jones
Laurence Levitan
Guy Vander Jagt (Not admitted in DC)

RETIRED PARTNERS

Samuel K. Abrams
Harlan Pomeroy

For full biographical listings, see the Martindale-Hubbell Law Directory

*** BAKER & MCKENZIE (AV)**

815 Connecticut Avenue, N.W., 20006-4078
Telephone: (202) 452-7000
Intn'l. Dialing: (1-202) 452-7000
Cable: ABOGADO
Telex: 89552
Answer Back: 89552 ABOGADO WSH
Int'l Telex: 248441
Answer Back: 248441 ABOG UR
Facsimiles: (1-202) 452-7074, 452-7073, 452-7072
Associated Offices of Baker & McKenzie in: Almaty, Amsterdam, Bangkok, Barcelona, Beijing, Berlin, Bogotá, Brasília, Brussels, Budapest, Buenos Aires, Cairo, Caracas, Chicago, Dallas, Frankfurt, Geneva, Hanoi, Ho Chi Minh City, Hong Kong, Juárez, Kiev, London, Madrid, Manila, Melbourne, México City, Miami, Milan, Monterrey, Moscow, New York, Palo Alto, Paris, Prague, Rio de Janeiro, Riyadh, Rome, St. Petersburg, San Diego, San Francisco, São Paulo, Singapore, Stockholm, Sydney, Taipei, Tijuana, Tokyo, Toronto, Valencia, Warsaw and Zürich.
Correspondent Law Firm: Hadiputranto, Hadinoto & Partners, Jakarta.

MEMBERS OF FIRM

Joseph L. Andrus
Mary C. Bennett
Bruce E. Clubb
Nicholas F. Coward
Robert H. Dilworth (Not admitted in DC)
Edward E. Dyson
Thomas J. Egan, Jr.
Daniel L. Goelzer
Bertrand M. Harding, Jr.
Lafayette G. Harter, III (Not admitted in DC)
Jack P. Janetatos
Bradford E. Kile
David R. Macdonald
Dennis I. Meyer
Philip D. Morrison
Kevin M. O'Brien
Thomas A. O'Donnell
Thomas P. Ondeck

(See Next Column)

BAKER & MCKENZIE, *Washington—Continued*

MEMBERS OF FIRM (Continued)

William D. Outman, II
B. Thomas Peele III
C. David Swenson
Leonard B. Terr
Eugene Theroux
A. Duane Webber

LOCAL PARTNERS

Paul M. Cacciatore
David A. Clanton
Marc R. Paul

OF COUNSEL

John W. Polk
John R. Reilly
Ernest T. Sanchez

RESIDENT ASSOCIATES

Daniel S. Berger (Not admitted in DC)
David N. Bowen (Not admitted in DC)
Sandra E. Chavez (Not admitted in DC)
Ruffin B. Cordell (Not admitted in DC)
J. Michael Cornett
Joseph E. Downey (Not admitted in DC)
Pascale Hélène Dubois (Not admitted in DC)
Steven F. Fabry
Marc J. Gerson (Not admitted in DC)
Teresa A. Gleason
Noël H. Gordon
Daniel M. Hess (Not admitted in DC)
Richard J. Kearns
Mark S. Kirk
David J. Laing
Edgar D. McClellan
Marie C. Milnes-Vasquez (Not admitted in DC)
Richard G. Minor
Jeffrey M. O'Donnell (Not admitted in DC)
Eleanor Pelta
Laura Foote Reiff
Diane U. Mage Roberts
Diane S. Rohleder
Martin S. Rowley (Not admitted in DC)
Richard L. Slowinski
Kimberly J. Tan Majure (Not admitted in DC)
Stuart M. Weitz
Jacob R. Wyatt (Not admitted in DC)
Hans-Jörg Ziegenhain (Not admitted in United States)
Simon Zornoza

For full biographical listings, see the Martindale-Hubbell Law Directory

BALCH & BINGHAM (AV)

1101 Connecticut Avenue, N.W., Suite 800, 20036
Telephone: 202-296-0387
Facsimile: 202-452-8180
Birmingham, Alabama Offices: 1710 Sixth Avenue North, 35203.
Telephone: 205-251-8100.
Facsimile: 205-226-8798. 1901 Sixth Avenue North, 35203.
Telephone: 205-251-8100.
Facsimile: 205-226-8799.
Montgomery, Alabama Office: The Winter Building, 2 Dexter Avenue, 36101.
Telephone: 205-834-6500.
Facsimile: 205-269-3115.
Huntsville, Alabama Office: Suite 810, 200 West Court Square, 35801.
Telephone: 205-551-0171.
Facsimile: 205-551-0174.

RESIDENT COUNSEL

Edward M. Rogers, Jr.

RESIDENT MEMBERS OF FIRM

Karl R. Moor (Not admitted in DC)
Patrick J. McCormick, III

Counsel for: Alabama Power Co.; Blue Cross and Blue Shield of Alabama; The Boeing Company; Brasfield & Gorrie, Inc.; Compass Bancshares, Inc.; Harbert Corp.; Kimberly-Clark Corp.; Southern Company Services, Inc.; Southern Research Institute; Vesta Insurance Group, Inc.

For full biographical listings, see the Martindale-Hubbell Law Directory

*** BALLARD SPAHR ANDREWS & INGERSOLL (AV)**

Suite 900 East, 555 13th Street, N.W., 20004-1112
Telephone: 202-383-8800
Fax: 202-383-8877
Philadelphia, Pennsylvania Office: 1735 Market Street, 51st Floor.
Telephone: 215-665-8500.
Fax: 215-864-8999.
Denver, Colorado Office: Seventeenth Street Plaza Building, Suite 2300, 1225 17th Street.
Telephone: 303-292-2400.
Fax: 303-296-3956.
Kaunas, Lithuania Office: Donelaičio 71-2 Kaunas 3000.
Telephone: (370-7) 20 56 66.
Fax: (370-7) 20 56 91.
Salt Lake City, Utah Office: One Utah Center, 201 South Main Street, Suite 1200.
Telephone: 801-531-3000.
Fax: 801-531-3001.
Baltimore, Maryland Office: 300 East Lombard Street, 19th Floor.
Telephone: 410-528-5600.
Fax: 410-528-5650.
Camden, New Jersey Office: 800 Hudson Square, 5th Floor.
Telephone: 609-541-5577.
Fax: 609-541-8272.

(See Next Column)

Nancy V. Alquist (Not admitted in DC)
Frederic L. Ballard, Jr.
Charles S. Henck
Justin P. Klein
F. Joseph Nealon
Howard H. Shafferman
Russell B. Stevenson, Jr.
Allan R. Winn

OF COUNSEL

Paul K. Casey
Mary Jo George (Not admitted in DC)

David Lewis Haselkorn
Ernesto A. Lanza (Not admitted in DC)
Jeffrey W. Larroca (Not admitted in DC)
Constantinos G. Panagopoulos (Not admitted in DC)
James D. Peterson
Linda B. Schakel
Kelly Mitchell Wrenn

For full biographical listings, see the Martindale-Hubbell Law Directory

*** BELL, BOYD & LLOYD (AV)**

1615 L Street, N.W., 20036
Telephone: 202-466-6300
FAX: 202-463-0678
Chicago, Illinois Office: Three First National Plaza, Suite 3300, 70 West Madison Street.
Telephone: 312-372-1121.
FAX: 312-372-2098.

RESIDENT PARTNERS

Edward A. Bloom
John C. Christie, Jr.
Raymond C. Fay
Lynn C. Fields
Thomas R. Gibbon
Michael L. Italiano
Neal A. Jackson
Christopher G. Mackaronis
Francis J. Pelland
Henry M. Polmer
Patrick J. Roach
Joel S. Rubinstein
Robert J. Sciaroni

OF COUNSEL

Andrew I. Gavil
Marvin P. Sadur

RESIDENT ASSOCIATES

Anthony M. Black
Brian Cohen (Not admitted in DC)
Andrew N. Cook
Susan J. King
Hillary L. Pettegrew
Timothy W. Seaver (Not admitted in DC)

For full biographical listings, see the Martindale-Hubbell Law Directory

BEVERIDGE & DIAMOND, P.C. (AV)

1350 I Street, N.W., Suite 700, 20005-3311
Telephone: 202-789-6000
Telecopier: 202-789-6190
New York, N.Y. Office: 40th Floor, 437 Madison Avenue, 10022-7380.
Telephone: 212-702-5400.
Telecopier: 212-702-5450.
San Francisco, California Office: Beveridge & Diamond, Suite 3400, One Sansome Street, 94104-4438.
Telephone: 415-397-0100.
Telecopier: 415-397-4238.
Fort Lee, New Jersey Office: Beveridge & Diamond, Suite 400, One Bridge Plaza, 07024-7502.
Telephone: 201-585-8162.
Telecopier: 201-592-7720.

Virginia S. Albrecht
Lawrence S. Bazel (Resident, San Francisco, CA Office)
Albert J. Beveridge, III
Karl S. Bourdeau
Robert Brager
Dean H. Cannon
David D. Cooke (Resident, San Francisco, CA Office)
Devarieste Curry
Richard S. Davis
Henry L. Diamond
David M. Friedland
Aaron H. Goldberg
Stephen L. Gordon (New York, N.Y. and Fort Lee, N.J. Offices)
John S. Guttmann, Jr.
John N. Hanson
Jennifer L. Hernandez (Resident, San Francisco, CA Office)
Harold Himmelman
Thomas C. Jackson
Steven M. Jawetz
David S. Krakoff
Cynthia Ann Lewis
Christopher W. Mahoney
Brenda Mallory
James L. Meeder (Resident, San Francisco, CA Office)
Andrew E. Mishkin
Donald J. Patterson, Jr.
Alan Charles Raul
Thomas Richichi
Harold L. Segall
Paul E. Shorb, III
Brian H. Siegel
Gary J. Smith (Resident, San Francisco, CA Office)
Kathryn E. Szmuszkovicz
Mark A. Turco
Benjamin F. Wilson
Robert D. Wyatt (Resident, San Francisco, CA Office)

OF COUNSEL

Gus Bauman
John French III (Resident, New York, N.Y. Office)

SPECIAL COUNSEL

A. James Barnes

(See Next Column)

BEVERIDGE & DIAMOND P.C.—*Continued*

Deanne L. Ayers-Howard (Not admitted in DC)
Laurie G. Ballenger (Not admitted in DC)
Margaret Lattin Bazany
Scott F. Belcher
Stuart I. Block (Resident, San Francisco, CA Office)
Susan C. Cagann (Resident, San Francisco, CA Office)
Robert W. Chamberlin (Not admitted in DC)
Susan H. Ephron
Kathryn B. Fuller (New York, N.Y. and Fort Lee, N.J. Offices)
Marc E. Gottschalk (Resident, San Francisco, CA Office)
Sy Gruza (Resident, New York, N.Y. Office)
Paul E. Hagen
Timothy J. Hagerty (Not admitted in DC)
Craig B. Kravit (New York, N.Y. and Fort Lee, N.J. Offices)
David S. Langer (New York, N.Y. and Fort Lee, N.J. Offices)
Margaret A. Lynch (Not admitted in DC)
Patricia Ross McCubbin
David A. McKay
Christopher J. McKenzie (Resident, New York, N.Y. Office)
Kimberly Martin McMorrow (Resident, San Francisco, CA Office)
Scott A. Miller (Resident, San Francisco, CA Office)
Brett P. Moffatt (Resident, San Francisco, CA Office)
Eileen M. Nottoli (Resident, San Francisco, CA Office)
Daniel J. O'Hanlon (Resident, San Francisco, CA Office)
Terry F. Quill
Christopher F. Regan
Anne Sprightley Ryan
James B. Slaughter
Adam D. Snyder
Joseph C. Stanko, Jr.
Katherine B. Steuer (Resident, San Francisco, CA Office)
Nancy D. Tammi
Caroline Tipton (Not admitted in DC)
Alec I. Ugol (Not admitted in DC)
Fred R. Wagner
John D. Walke (Not admitted in DC)
Julie K. Walters (Resident, San Francisco, CA Office)
Bernard A. Weintraub (Resident, New York, N.Y. Office)
Michelle A. Wenzel (Not admitted in DC)
Joshua S. Wyner (Not admitted in DC)
Nancy N. Young

For full biographical listings, see the Martindale-Hubbell Law Directory

* BINGHAM, DANA & GOULD (AV)

1550 M Street, N.W., 20005
Telephone: 202-822-9320
Telecopy: 202-833-1506
Boston, Massachusetts Office: 150 Federal Street.
Telephone: 617-951-8000.
Cable Address: "Blodgham Bsn".
Telex: 275147 BDGBSN UR.
Telecopy: 617-951-8736.
Hartford, Connecticut Office: 100 Pearl Street.
Telephone: 203-244-3770.
Telefax: 203-527-5188.
London, England Office: 39 Victoria Street, SWIH 0EE.
Telephone: 011-44-71-799-2646.
Telecopy: 011-44-71-799-2654.
Telex: 888179 BDGLDN G.
Cable Address: "Blodgham Ldn".

RESIDENT PARTNERS

Paul J. Lambert
Peter D. Schellie
Joseph C. Zengerle, III

RESIDENT ASSOCIATES

Teresa Burke
Carolyn M. Landever
Joseph P. Pelican

For full biographical listings, see the Martindale-Hubbell Law Directory

BRAULT, GRAHAM, SCOTT & BRAULT (AV)

1906 Sunderland Place, N.W., 20036
Telephone: 202-785-1200
Fax: 202-785-4301
Rockville, Maryland Office: 101 South Washington Street.
Telephone: 301-424-1060.
FAX: 301-424-7991.
Arlington, Virginia Office: Suite 1201, 2300 North Clarendon Boulevard, Courthouse Plaza.
Telephone: 703-522-1781.

OF COUNSEL

Laurence T. Scott

MEMBERS OF FIRM

Denver H. Graham (1922-1987)
Albert E. Brault (Retired)
Albert D. Brault (Resident, Rockville, Maryland Office)
Leo A. Roth, Jr.
James S. Wilson (Resident, Rockville, Maryland Office)
Ronald G. Guziak (Resident, Rockville, Maryland Office)
Daniel L. Shea (Resident, Rockville, Maryland Office)
Keith M. Bonner
M. Kathleen Parker (Resident, Rockville, Maryland Office)
Regina Ann Casey (Resident, Rockville, Maryland Office)
James M. Brault (Resident, Rockville, Maryland Office)

(See Next Column)

ASSOCIATES

David G. Mulquin (Not admitted in DC; Resident, Rockville, Maryland Office)
Sanford A. Friedman
Holly D. Shupert (Not admitted in DC; Resident, Rockville, Maryland Office)
Eric A. Spacek
Rhonda Ann Hurwitz (Resident at Rockville, Maryland Office)
Joan F. Brault (Resident, Rockville, Maryland Office)

Representative Clients: American Oil Co.; Crum & Forster Group; Fireman's Fund American Insurance Cos.; Kemper Group; Reliance Insurance Cos.; Safeco Group; Government Employees Insurance Co.; Medical Mutual Society of Maryland; Legal Mutual Liability Insurance Society of Maryland.

For full biographical listings, see the Martindale-Hubbell Law Directory

BROWN & TIGHE (AV)

5247 Wisconsin Avenue, N.W., Suite 4, 20015
Telephone: 202-966-9000
Telecopier: 202-966-2513

MEMBERS OF FIRM

Thomas P. Brown, III
Alfred Joseph Tighe, Jr.

For full biographical listings, see the Martindale-Hubbell Law Directory

* BROWN & WOOD (AV)

815 Connecticut Avenue, N.W., Suite 701, 20006-4004
Telephone: 202-973-0600
Telecopier: 202-223-0495
Los Angeles, California Office: 10900 Wilshire Boulevard, 90024-3959.
Telephone: 310-443-0200.
New York, New York Office: One World Trade Center, 10048-0557.
Telephone: 212-839-5300.
San Francisco, California Office: 555 California Street, 94104-1715.
Telephone: 415-772-1200.
London, England Office: Blackwell House, Guildhall Yard.
Telephone: 0171-606-1888.
Trenton, New Jersey Office: 172 West State Street, 08608-1104.
Telephone: 609-393-0303.
Tokyo, Japan Office: Shiroyama JT Mori Building, 3-1 Toranomon 4-Chome, Minato-ku.
Telephone: 011-813-5472-5360.
Hong Kong Office: Suite 2606, Asia Pacific Finance Tower, Citibank Plaza, 3 Garden Road, Central.
Telephone: 011-852-2509-7888.

RESIDENT PARTNERS

John Arnholz
James A. Blalock III
Walter T. Eccard
James E. Murray

COUNSEL

Catherine S. Gallagher

RESIDENT ASSOCIATES

James W. C. Canup
John P. Fielding (Not admitted in DC)
Edward E. Gainor
Samir A. Gandhi (Not admitted in DC)
Kevin James Kelly
Susanne M. Kogut

For full biographical listings, see the Martindale-Hubbell Law Directory

* BUTLER & BINION, L.L.P. (AV)

A Partnership including Professional Corporations
1747 Pennsylvania Avenue, N.W., 20006
Telephone: 202-466-6900
Telecopier: 202-833-1274
Houston, Texas Office: 1000 Louisiana, Suite 1600.
Telephone: 713-237-3111.
Telecopier: 713-237-3202.
Dallas, Texas Office: 750 N. St. Paul, Suite 1800.
Telephone: 214-220-3100.
Telecopiers: 214-969-7013; 214-954-4245.
San Antonio, Texas Office: 112 East Pecan, 27th Floor.
Telephone: 210-227-2200.
Telecopier: 210-223-6730.

RESIDENT MEMBERS

John K. McDonald
Richard E. Powers, Jr.

ASSOCIATES

Steven A. Adducci

For full biographical listings, see the Martindale-Hubbell Law Directory

* CAHILL GORDON & REINDEL (AV)

A Partnership including a Professional Corporation
1990 K Street, N.W., 20006
Telephone: 202-862-8900
Facsimile: 202-862-8958.
Cable Address: "Cottofrank Washington"
New York City Office: 80 Pine Street.
Telephone: 212-701-3000.
European Office: 19 rue François 1er, 75008, Paris, France.
Telephone: 33.1-47.20.10.50.

(See Next Column)

CAHILL GORDON & REINDEL, *Washington—Continued*

RESIDENT PARTNERS

Donald J. Mulvihill

COUNSEL

Corydon B. Dunham

RESIDENT ASSOCIATES

Barbara O. Brincefield
Vicki S. Haberkorn
(Not admitted in DC)
Kathy Silberthau Strom

For full biographical listings, see the Martindale-Hubbell Law Directory

CARLSMITH BALL WICHMAN MURRAY CASE & ICHIKI (AV)

A Partnership including Law Corporations
700 14th Street, N.W., 9th Floor, 20005
Telephone: 202-508-1025
Telecopier: 202-508-1026
Honolulu, Hawaii Office: Suite 2200, Pacific Tower, 1001 Bishop Street. P.O. Box 656.
Telephone: 808-523-2500.
Los Angeles, California Office: 555 South Flower Street, 25th Floor.
Telephone: 213-955-1200.
Long Beach, California Office: 301 East Ocean Boulevard, 7th Floor.
Telephone: 310-435-5631.
Mexico City, Mexico Office: Monte Pelvoux 111, Piso 1, Col. Lomas de Chapultepec, 11000 Mexico, D.F.
Telephone: (011-52-5) 520-8514.
Fax: (011-52-5) 520-1545.
Mexico, D.F. Office of Carlsmith Ball Garcia Cacho y Asociados, S.C. (Authorized to practice Mexican Law): Monte Pelvoux 111, Piso 1, Col. Lomas de Chapultepec, 11000, Mexico, D.F.
Telephone: (011-52-5) 520-8514.
Fax: (011-52-5) 540-1545.
Agana, Guam Office: 4th Floor, Bank of Hawaii Building, P.O. Box BF.
Telephone: 671-472-6813.
Saipan, Commonwealth of the Northern Mariana Islands Office: Carlsmith Building, Capitol Hill, P.O. Box 5241.
Telephone: 670-322-3455.
Wailuku, Maui, Hawaii Office: One Main Plaza, Suite 400, 2200 Main Street, P.O. Box 1086.
Telephone: 808-242-4535.
Kailua-Kona, Hawaii Office: Second Floor, Bank of Hawaii Annex Building, P.O. Box 1720.
Telephone: 808-329-6464.
Hilo, Hawaii Office: 121 Waianuenue Avenue, P.O. Box 686.
Telephone: 808-935-6644.
Kapolei, Hawaii Office: Kapolei Building, Suite 318, 1001 Kamokila Boulevard.
Telephone: 808-674-0850.

RESIDENT PARTNERS

Anne Price Fortney
Renee L. Stransky

OF COUNSEL

Aaron Schildhaus
James T. Stovall, III

For full biographical listings, see the Martindale-Hubbell Law Directory

CARR, GOODSON & LEE, P.C. (AV)

1301 K Street, N.W., Suite 400, East Tower, 20005-3300
Telephone: 202-310-5500
Telecopier: 202-310-5555
Fairfax, Virginia Office: 3923 Old Lee Highway, Suite 62-B, 22030 .
Telephone: 703-691-8818.
Baltimore, Maryland Office: Suite 2700, 111 South Calvert Street, 21202.
Telephone: 410-752-1570.
Rockville, Maryland Office: 31 Wood Lane, 20850.
Telephone: 301-424-7024.

Lawrence E. Carr, Jr.
William J. Carter
William M. Cusmano
Robert W. Goodson
Catherine A. Hanrahan
Kyle A. Kane
James F. Lee, Jr.
Paul J. Maloney
Thomas L. McCally
Kevin M. Murphy
Walter J. Murphy, Jr.
Brian H. Rhatigan
Margaret H. Warner
James A. Welch

OF COUNSEL

Edward J. Krill

M. Miller Baker
(Not admitted in DC)
Janette M. Blee
(Not admitted in DC)
Louis S. Bonanni
Hollis B. Brewer III
(Not admitted in DC)
Paul V. Butler
Matthew J. Cuccias
(Not admitted in DC)
Ann Terrell Dorsett
(Not admitted in DC)
Lawrence Eiser
Karen E. Evans
Teresa Grace Fay
Jan E. Fieldsteel
Richard S. Gordon
(Not admitted in DC)
Shadonna E. Hale
Timothy R. Hughes

(See Next Column)

Kent G. Huntington
Carla S. Jackson
David H. Jacobs
(Not admitted in DC)
Gregory A. Krauss
Bridget L. Kyle
(Not admitted in DC)
Charles E. Leasure, III
Terrence M. McShane
Michelle L. Melin
Joseph P. Morra
(Not admitted in DC)
Timothy J. Mulreany
(Not admitted in DC)
Mary C. Nevius
Kathleen A. O'Connell
Karen A. Rosenthal
(Not admitted in DC)
Alexander D. Shoaibi
Patricia Ann Smith
Samuel J. Smith, Jr.
(Not admitted in DC)
Spencer K. Stephens
Brian M. Tauscher
(Not admitted in DC)
John A. Taylor
Peter K. Tompa
Karen E. Torrent
James A. Towns
Bruce K. Trauben
Clifton B. Welch

For full biographical listings, see the Martindale-Hubbell Law Directory

* CHADBOURNE & PARKE (AV)

Suite 900, 1101 Vermont Avenue, N.W., 20005
Telephone: 202-289-3000
Telex: WU 904256
Telecopier: 202-289-3002
New York, N.Y. Office: 30 Rockefeller Plaza, 10112.
Telephone: 212-408-5100.
Telex: 645383.
Telecopier: 212-541-5369.
Los Angeles, California Office: 601 South Figueroa Street, 90017.
Telephone: 213-892-1000.
Telecopier: 213-622-9865.
London, England Office: 86 Jermyn Street, SW1 6JD.
Telephone: 44-71-925-7400.
Telecopier: 44-71-839-3393.
Moscow, Russia Office: 38 Maxim Gorky Naberezhnaya, 113035.
Telephone: (7095) 974-2424.
Telecopier: (7095) 974-2425. International Satellite Via US:
Telephone: (212) 408-1190.
Telecopier: (212) 408-1199.
Hong Kong Office: Suite 3704, Peregrine Tower, Lippo Centre, 89 Queensway.
Telephone: (852)2842-5400.
Telecopier: (852)2521-7527.
New Delhi, India Office: Chadbourne & Parke Associates, A16-B Anand Niketan, 110 021.
Telephone: 91-11-301-7568/7581/7582.
Telecopier: 91-11-301-7351.

RESIDENT PARTNERS

Edmund S. Muskie
William S. D'Amico
John B. O'Sullivan
Keith Martin
Cornelius J. Golden, Jr.
Robert F. Shapiro
Russell S. Frye
David M. Raim
Nancy M. Persechino
(Not admitted in DC)
Thomas E. Hirsch III
Peter F. Fitzgerald
(Not admitted in DC)
William K. Perry
(Not admitted in DC)
Ellen H. Woodbury
(Not admitted in DC)
Andrew A. Giaccia
Keith W. Kriebel
Kenneth R. Pierce

RESIDENT COUNSEL

Lynn N. Hargis
Leslie S. Ritts

RESIDENT OF COUNSEL

Edmund E. Harvey

RESIDENT ASSOCIATES

Stephen J. Axtell
Michele E. Beasley
(Not admitted in DC)
Roy S. Belden
Steven A. Bennett
Erin Buckley Bradley
Kerian Bunch
(Not admitted in DC)
Kathryn L. Cervon
Carey G. Child
(Not admitted in DC)
Daniel J. Cohen
(Not admitted in DC)
Kenneth J. Diamond
Timothy J. DiCintio
(Not admitted in DC)
Lisa C. Dorr
(Not admitted in DC)
Lynne E. Gedanken
Margaret M. Groarke
(Not admitted in DC)
Theresa W. Hajost
Craig J. Jones
Anat Keller
(Not admitted in DC)
Tracey W. Laws
Sheila V. Malkani
(Not admitted in DC)
Susan C. Maxson
Don J. Mros
Jonathan R. Pawlow
John W. Rauber, Jr.
(Not admitted in DC)
David K. Schumacher
John W. Scott

For full biographical listings, see the Martindale-Hubbell Law Directory

* CLEARY, GOTTLIEB, STEEN & HAMILTON (AV)

1752 N Street, N.W., 20036-2806
Telephone: 202-728-2700
Facsimile: 202-429-0946
New York, New York Office: One Liberty Plaza, New York, N.Y. 10006.
Telephone: 212-225-2000.

(See Next Column)

CLEARY, GOTTLIEB, STEEN & HAMILTON—*Continued*

Paris, France Office: 41, Avenue de Friedland, 75008 Paris, France.
Telephone: 33-1-4074-6800.
Brussels, Belgium Office: Rue de la Loi 23, Bte 5, 1040 Brussels, Belgium.
Telephone: 32-2-287-2000.
London, England Office: City Place House, 55 Basinghall Street, London EC2V 5EH England.
Telephone: 44-71-614-2200.
Hong Kong Office: 56th Floor, Bank of China Tower, One Garden Road, Hong Kong.
Telephone: 852-521-4122.
Tokyo, Japan Office: Morgan Carroll Terai Gaikokuho Jimubengoshi Jimusho, 20th Floor, Shin Kasumigaseki Building, 3-2, Kasumigaseki 3-Chome, Chiyoda-Ku, Tokyo 100, Japan.
Telephone: 81-3-3595-3911.
Frankfurt, Germany Office: Ulmenstrasse 37-39, 60325 Frankfurt am Main, Germany.
Telephone: 49-69-971-03-0.

COUNSEL

Robert C. Barnard
Fred D. Turnage

WASHINGTON, D.C. PARTNERS

J. Eugene Marans
Douglas E. Kliever
Daniel B. Silver
Kenneth L. Bachman, Jr.
Charles F. Lettow
Richard deC. Hinds
Sara D. Schotland
Mark Leddy
John C. Murphy, Jr.
Henry J. Plog, Jr.
Dana L. Trier
Eugene M. Goott
Janet L. Weller
Mitchell S. Dupler
Linda J. Soldo
Giovanni P. Prezioso
John T. Byam
John C. Palenberg
Matthew D. Slater
Steven N. Robinson
Michael R. Lazerwitz

SPECIAL COUNSEL

W. Richard Bidstrup
Scott N. Benedict
Linda S. Matlack

ASSOCIATES

Ricardo A. Anzaldúa-Montoya
William A. Baten
Barbara W. Bernstein (Not admitted in DC)
Julie B. Bloch
Matthew P. Blischak
Frank R. Borchert III
Elizabeth M. Burke
Michael J. Byrnes
Robert W. Cook (Not admitted in DC)
George R. A. Doumar
Michael G. Egge
David I. Gelfand
Brandt J. Goldstein (Not admitted in DC)
Scott R. Goodwin
Kevin A. Griffin
Katherine C. Hall
Mitchell E. Herr
Jean E. Kalicki
Karen A. Kerr
Constance B. Kiggins
John M. Kincaid
Daniel C. Kolb (Not admitted in DC)
Jennifer M. Lester
Peter S. Levitt
Kristin S. Mackert
Judith R. Margolin
Michael A. Mazzuchi (Not admitted in DC)
Joyce E. McCarty
David H. McClain (Not admitted in DC)
Robert J. Mueller
Mark W. Nelson
Jon S. Nicholas
Michael F. O'Connor (Not admitted in DC)
Ruth E. Olson
Mitchell L. Rabinowitz
Charles E. Rhodes
Michael P. Shea (Not admitted in DC)
Steven K. Shevick (Not admitted in DC)
Andra J. Shuster
Mark A. Singley
Christopher G. Smith
Michael S. Steele (Not admitted in DC)
Kristen A. Stilt (Not admitted in DC)
Michael J. Sussman
Jo Anne Swindler
Sandra E. Trimble
Kirk Van Brunt
James G. Votaw
Julie A. Waddell
Amy Deen Westbrook
Carla L. Wheeler

For full biographical listings, see the Martindale-Hubbell Law Directory

H. CLAYTON COOK, JR. (AV)

2828 Pennsylvania Avenue, N.W., 20007
Telephone: 202-338-8088
Rapifax: 202-338-1843
McLean, Virginia Office: 1011 Langley Hill Drive. 22101.
Telephone: 703-821-2468.
Rapifax: 703-821-2469.

For full biographical listings, see the Martindale-Hubbell Law Directory

* COUDERT BROTHERS (AV)

1627 I Street, N.W., 20006
Telephone: 202-775-5100
Telecopier: 202-775-1168
Cable Address: "Treduoc"
New York, New York 10036-7794: 1114 Avenue of the Americas.
San Francisco, California 94111: 4 Embarcadero Center, Suite 3300.
Los Angeles, California 90017: 1055 West Seventh Street, Twentieth Floor.
San Jose, California 95113: Suite 1250, Ten Almaden Boulevard.
Paris 75008, France: Coudert Frères, 52, Avenue des Champs-Elysées.
London EC4M 7JP England: 20 Old Bailey.
Brussels B-1050, Belgium: Tour Louise-Box 8, 149 Avenue Louise.
Beijing, People's Republic of China 100020: Suite 2708-09, Jing Guang Centre, Hu Jia Lou, Chao Yang Qu.
Shanghai, People's Republic of China 200002: c/o Suite 1804, Union Building, 100 Yanan Road East.
Hong Kong: 25th Floor, Nine Queen's Road Central.
Singapore 0104: Tung Centre, 20 Collyer Quay.
Sydney N.S.W. 2000, Australia: Suite 2202, State Bank Centre, 52 Martin Place.
Tokyo 107, Japan: 1355 West Tower, Aoyama Twin Towers, 1-1-1 Minami-Aoyama, Minato-Ku.
Moscow, U.S.S.R.: 15 Petrovka, Second Floor.
01301 Sao Paulo, SP, Brazil: Machado, Meyer, Sendacz e Opice Advogados, Rua da Consolacao, 247, 8 Andar.
Bangkok 10550, Thailand: Bubhajit Building, 20 North Sathorn Road, 10th Floor.
Ho Chi Minh City, Vietnam: c/o Saigon Business Centre, 49-57 Dong Du Street, District 1.

MEMBERS OF THE FIRM

Milo G. Coerper (Resident)
Richard N. Dean (Not admitted in DC)
Robert F. Pietrowski, Jr.
Arthur F. Sampson, III (Resident)

RESIDENT ASSOCIATES

Kay Georgi
Mary E. Hartnett
James S. Keller
Rebecca A. Matthias
Susan M. Muchmore
Nancy J. Rosenfeld

For full biographical listings, see the Martindale-Hubbell Law Directory

CROWELL & MORING (AV)

1001 Pennsylvania Avenue, N.W., 20004-2595
Telephone: 202-624-2500
Telex: W.U.I.(International) 64344; W.U.(Domestic) 89-2448
Cable Address: "Cromor"
Fax: (202) 628-5116
Irvine, California Office: 2010 Main Street, Suite 1200.
Telephone: 714-263-8400.
Fax: 714-263-8414.
London, England Office: Denning House, 90 Chancery Lane. WC2A 1ED.
Telephone: 011-44-71-413-0011.
Fax: 011-44-71-413-0333.

MEMBERS OF FIRM

Jerry W. Ryan
Philip A. Fleming
Calvin Davison
Roger N. Boyd
Frederick Moring
Brian C. Elmer
Patrick W. Lee
W. Stanfield Johnson
Peter B. Work
Victor E. Schwartz
Ridgway M. Hall, Jr.
Harold J. Heltzer
Richard L. Beizer
Donald L. Flexner
R. Bruce Keiner, Jr.
Joseph N. Onek
Steven P. Quarles
L. Graeme Bell, III
Jeffrey H. Howard
Thomas P. Humphrey
Michael M. Levy
John A. Macleod
Kent R. Morrison
Barry E. Cohen
Marc F. Efron
Joseph M. Oliver, Jr.
Timothy M. Biddle
Herbert J. Martin
Richard McMillan, Jr.
Thomas C. Watson
Dana C. Contratto
George D. Ruttinger
Richard E. Schwartz
Jean-Pierre Swennen
Howard M. Weinman
Karen Hastie Williams
Terry L. Albertson
James J. Maiwurm
Richard J. Morvillo
Nancy S. Bryson
JoAnn E. Macbeth
Peter J. Romatowski
Wm. Randolph Smith
Fred S. Souk
John I. Stewart, Jr.
Frederick W. Claybrook, Jr.
Robert T. Ebert
Thomas P. Gies
Andrew H. Marks
William P. O'Neill
James J. Regan
Jennifer N. Waters
Rosemary M. Collyer
Kenneth M. Bruntel
Robert C. Davis, Jr.
Warren J. DeVecchio
Clifford B. Hendler
Thomas C. Means
John T. Scott, III
Clifton S. Elgarten
Laurel Pyke Malson
Stuart H. Newberger
David B. Siegel
Robert M. Halperin
Raymond F. Monroe
Alan W.H. Gourley
Mark D. Plevin
David Z. Bodenheimer
M. Lisanne Crowley
Kent A. Gardiner
Eileen F. Serene
Mark E. Baker
Ellen B. Moran
Luther Zeigler
J. Michael Klise
Scott L. Winkelman

(See Next Column)

CROWELL & MORING, *Washington—Continued*

OF COUNSEL

Eldon H. Crowell
Richard J. Bednar
Paul Shnitzer
Edward M. Green
Robert P. Charrow
C. Michael Hathaway
Brian G. Donohue
Thomas J. Plotz
Rebecca W. Thomson
(Not admitted in DC)
Shauna E. Alonge
Linda S. Bruggeman
Lorraine Berman Halloway
Paula J. Desio
Anne M. ("Nancy") Wheeler
Robert L. Willmore
R. Timothy McCrum
Jeffrey M. Villet
Paul William Kalish

Thomas R. Lundquist (Special Counsel)

ASSOCIATES

Susan M. Hoffman
Daryl A. Lander
Richard J. Mannix
Kathleen Liberto Ranowsky
Joan H. Moosally
Cameron S. Hamrick
Brian E. Sweeney
William D. Wallace
Edward M. Barberic
(Not admitted in DC)
Michael E. Cain
(Not admitted in DC)
Steven P. Taub
William L. Anderson
Edward Jackson
Charles C. Hwang
Amy J. Mauser
James C. Minnis
Cary Hastings Plamondon
Curtis S. Renner
(Not admitted in DC)
Ramona E. Romero
(Not admitted in DC)
Steven C. Schnitzer
Amy Lynn Schreiber
Tina M. Singh
Michael A. Bazany, Jr.
Christopher C. Fennell
Stephen G. Harvey
Kathryn Dean Kirmayer
John E. McCarthy, Jr.
Stephanie B. N. Renzi
David M. Schnorrenberg
(Not admitted in DC)
Jeane A. Thomas
Michael J. Zoeller
Mark A. Behrens
Robert Goldberg
Alexandre de Gramont
Glenn D. Grant
Dolly Bowman Hauck
Kathleen E. Karelis
Peter J. Lipperman
(Not admitted in DC)
Paul L. Lumnitzer, II
(Not admitted in DC)
Kris David Meade
Jonathan Hale Pittman
Robert D. Rowe
Daniel Aronowitz
David Line Batty
Stephanie V. Corrao
Devon S. Engel
Caryl Lazzaro Flannery
Javier M. Guzman
(Not admitted in DC)
Kelly J. Harris
Todd Hutchen
(Not admitted in DC)
Karen M. Johnston
Alice M. Jones
Mark R. Koehn
Christopher Mcguire
Colleen Rachel Olszowy
Thomas S. Respess, III
Thomas A. Stock
Mark D. Taylor
Mark F. Tesone
(Not admitted in DC)
Katherine K. White
Matthew S. Bewig
(Not admitted in DC)
Brenda Healey Bosch
(Not admitted in DC)
Stephen M. Byers
(Not admitted in DC)
Christopher M. Farris
Lisa Taeko Greenlees
Charon J. Harris
Pamela J. Hicks
Phyllis Heather Hurwitz
Carol Iancu
(Not admitted in DC)
Douglas T. Kendall
Jennifer M. Lear
Lauren P. Liss
Elizabeth W. Newsom
(Not admitted in DC)
Howard B. Crystal
(Not admitted in DC)
Nabil W. Istafanous
(Not admitted in DC)
Gregory C. Jackson
(Not admitted in DC)
Phyllis A. Jaudes
(Not admitted in DC)
Mark C. Kalpin
Ann H. Kim
(Not admitted in DC)
Monica G. Parham
(Not admitted in DC)
Anne R. Price
(Not admitted in DC)
Lisa A. Price
(Not admitted in DC)
Heidi J. Stock
(Not admitted in DC)
Michael A. Valerio
(Not admitted in DC)
David F. White
(Not admitted in DC)
Nancy L. Anderson
(Not admitted in DC)
Nygina T. Mills
(Not admitted in DC)

For full biographical listings, see the Martindale-Hubbell Law Directory

* CURTIS, MALLET-PREVOST, COLT & MOSLE (AV)

Suite 1205L, 1801 K Street, N.W., 20006
Telephone: 202-452-7373
Telecopier: 202-452-7333
Cable Address: "Migniard Washington, D.C."
Telex: ITT 440379 CMPUI
New York, N.Y. Office: 101 Park Avenue.
Telephone: 212-696-6000.
Telecopier: 212-697-1559.
Cable Address: "Migniard New York".
Telex: 12-6811 Migniard; ITT 422127 MGND.
Newark, New Jersey Office: One Gateway Center, Suite 403.
Telephone: 201-622-0605.
Telecopier: 201-622-5646.

(See Next Column)

Houston, Texas Office: 2 Houston, Center, 909 Fannin Street, Suite 3725.
Telephone: 713-759-9555.
Telecopier: 713-759-0712.
Mexico City, D.F., Mexico Office: Torre Chapultepec, Ruben Dario 281, Col. Bosques de Chapultepec, 11530 Mexico, D.F.
Telephone: 525-282-0444.
Telecopier: 525-282-0637.
Paris, France Office: 8 Avenue Victor Hugo.
Telephone: 45-00-99-68.
Telecopier: 45-00-84-06.
London, England Office: Two Throgmorton Avenue, EC2N 2DL.
Telephone: 71-638-7957.
Telecopier: 71-638-5512.
Frankfurt am Main 1 Office: Staufenstrasse 42.
Telephone: 069-971-4420.
Telecopier: 69-17 33 99.

RESIDENT PARTNERS

Preston Brown
Samuel Rosenthal
Jeffrey I. Zuckerman

RESIDENT COUNSEL

Roger V. Barth
Keith Highet

For full biographical listings, see the Martindale-Hubbell Law Directory

DAVID & HAGNER, P.C. (AV)

1120 Nineteenth Street, N.W., 20036
Telephone: 202-467-6900
Telecopier: 202-467-6910

Richard G. David
John D. Hagner
David R. Kuney
Dennis A. Davison
Jay P. Krupin
Stanley J. Wrobel
Paul A. Kaplan
Stanley E. Majors
Bruce M. Levy
Kenneth W. Logwood
Christine M. Carstens
Desmond D. Connall, Jr.
Stuart A. Kruger
Howard N. Solodky
Pamela V. Rothenberg
Janet M. Meiburger
Jeffrey L. Tarkenton
Janis B. Schiff
Philip M. Keating
Cameron Cohick
Marc R. Engel
Steven C. Hilsee
Jonathan W. Greenbaum
Elizabeth C. Lee
Robert P. Goodridge
James J. O'Brien

Caryn G. Pass
Jerome G. Grzeca
Alice Goldman
(Not admitted in DC)
Sharon L. Terry
Erik D. Bolog
Terence F. Flynn
Timothy R. Epp
(Not admitted in DC)
Tara A. Scanlon
(Not admitted in DC)
Christine C. Zebrowski
(Not admitted in DC)
John G. Nahajzer
(Not admitted in DC)
Alison J. Smiley
(Not admitted in DC)
Theodore J. Humphrey
(Not admitted in DC)

For full biographical listings, see the Martindale-Hubbell Law Directory

* DAVIS, GRAHAM & STUBBS, L.L.C. (AV)

A Limited Liability Company
Suite 1200, 1225 New York Avenue, N.W., 20005-3919
Telephone: 202-822-8660
Telecopier: 202-293-4794
Telex: 248260 DGSW
Denver, Colorado Office: Suite 4700, 370 Seventeenth Street, P.O. Box 185.
Telephone: 303-892-9400.
Telecopier: 303-893-1379.
Cable Address: "Davgram, Denver."
Telex: 413726 DGS DVR UD.
Houston, Texas Office: 515 Post Oak Boulevard, Suite 870.
Telephone: 713-850-9400.
Facsimile: 713-850-0807.

RESIDENT MEMBERS

Howard Adler, Jr.
Alison L. Berkes
Mark D. Colley
Harold I. Freilich
Christopher J. Hagan
J. Hovey Kemp
David P. Metzger

RESIDENT COUNSEL

S. Neil Hosenball

RESIDENT ASSOCIATES

Petrina M. Burnham
Gena E. Cadieux
Laura E. Gasser
Joanne E. Loercher

For full biographical listings, see the Martindale-Hubbell Law Directory

Washington—Continued

* DAVIS POLK & WARDWELL (AV)

1300 I Street, N.W., 20005
Telephone: 202-962-7000
Telecopier: 202-962-7111
New York, N.Y. Office: 450 Lexington Avenue, 10017.
Telephone: 212-450-4000.
Cable Address: "Davispolk New York."
Telex: ITT-421341; ITT-423356.
Telecopier: 212-450-4800.
Paris, France Office: 4, Place de la Concorde, 75008.
Telephone: 011-331-40.17.36.00.
Telecopier: 011-331-42.65.22.34.
Cable Address: "Davispolk Paris."
London, England Office: 1 Frederick's Place, EC2R 8AB.
Telephone: 011-44-71-418-1300.
Telex: 888238.
Telecopier: 011-44-71-418-1400.
Tokyo, Japan Office: In Tokyo practicing as Reid Gaikokuho-Jimu-Bengoshi Jimusho. Tokio Kaijo Building Annex, 2-1, Marunouchi 1-chome, Chiyoda-ku, 100.
Telephone: 011-81-3-201-8421.
Telecopier: 011-81-3-201-8444.
Telex: 2224472 DPWTOK.
Frankfurt, Germany Office: MesseTurm, 60308 Frankfurt am Main 1, Federal Republic of Germany.
Telephone: 011-49-69-97-57-03-0.
Telecopier: 011-49-69-74-77-44.
Hong Kong Office: The Hong Kong Club Building, 3A Chater Road.
Telephone: 852 533 3300.
Fax: 852 5 33 3388.

MEMBERS OF FIRM

Milton Carr Ferguson, Jr.
Stephen H. Case (Resident)
William F. Kroener, III (Resident)
Scott W. Muller (Resident)
Gary G. Lynch
Michael P. Carroll (Resident)
Samuel Dimon
Randall D. Guynn

RESIDENT COUNSEL

Theodore A. Doremus, Jr.
Jordan Luke

SENIOR ATTORNEYS

Margaret Miles Ayres
Linda Chatman Thomsen

RESIDENT ASSOCIATES

Jeffrey D. Berman
Steven L. Chuslo
Kathleen L. Ferrell
David C. Finn
Beth Louise Golden
James Kent Lehman
Jeanine P. McGuinness (Not admitted in DC)
Catherine M. O'Neil
Michael H. Pryor
Graciela M. Rodriguez
Suzanne E. Rowe
Arnon D. Siegel (Not admitted in DC)
Amy J. St. Eve
Margaret E. Tahyar
Thomas E. Vita
Robert W. Weaver

For full biographical listings, see the Martindale-Hubbell Law Directory

* DEBEVOISE & PLIMPTON (AV)

555 13th Street N.W., 20004
Telephone: 202-383-8000
Telecopier: 202-383-8118
New York, N.Y. Office: 875 Third Avenue, 10022.
Telephone: 212-909-6000.
Telex: (Domestic) 148377 DEBSTEVE NYK.
Telecopier: (212) 909-6836.
Los Angeles, California Office: 601 South Figueroa Street, Suite 3700.
Telephone: 213-680-8000.
Telex: 401527 DPLA.
Telecopier: 213-680-8100.
Paris, France Office: 21 Avenue George V 75008.
Telephone: (33-1) 40 73 12 12.
Telecopier: (33-1) 47 20 50 82.
Telex: 648141F DPPAR.
London, England Office: 1 Creed Court, 5 Ludgate Hill, EC4M 7AA.
Telephone: (44-71) 329-0779.
Telex: 884569 DPLON G.
Telecopier: (44-71) 329-0860.
Budapest, Hungary Office: 1065 Budapest, Révay Köz 2 III.
Telephone: (36-1) 131-0845.
Telecopier: (36-1) 132-7995.
Hong Kong Office: 13/F Entertainment Building, 30 Queen's Road Central.
Telephone: 852-810-7918.
Fax: 852-810-9828.

MEMBERS OF FIRM

Judah Best
Ralph C. Ferrara
Loren Kieve
Eric D. Roiter
Marcia L. MacHarg
Jeffrey P. Cunard

COUNSEL

Thomas A. Ferrigno
Paul C. Palmer
Francis J. Sailer
John B. Reynolds, III

(See Next Column)

RETIRED PARTNER

Robert J. Geniesse

ASSOCIATES

Kevin T. Abikoff
Ann M. Ashton
Scott N. Auby (Not admitted in DC)
Bridget M. Bush
Lance Cole
William Formon
Joseph M. Furey (Not admitted in DC)
Lawrence M. Garrett
Roberta R. W. Kameda
Lothar A. Kneifel
Ariadne Dawn Makris (Not admitted in DC)
Theodore A. Mathas
Elizabeth A. Nark (Not admitted in DC)
Greg Shapiro
Herbert C. Thomas

For full biographical listings, see the Martindale-Hubbell Law Directory

* DECHERT PRICE & RHOADS (AV)

1500 K St., N. W., 20005
Telephone: 202-626-3300
Telefax: 202-626-3334
Philadelphia, Pennsylvania: 4000 Bell Atlantic Tower, 1717 Arch Street.
Telephone: 215-994-4000.
New York, N.Y.: 477 Madison Avenue.
Telephone: 212-326-3500.
Harrisburg, Pennsylvania: Thirty North Third Street.
Telephone: 717-237-2000.
Princeton, New Jersey: Princeton Pike Corporate Center, P.O. Box 5218.
Telephone: 609-520-3200.
Boston, Massachusetts: Ten Post Office Square South, 12th Floor.
Telephone: 617-728-7100.
London, England: 2 Serjeants' Inn, EC4Y 1LT.
Telephone: (0171) 583-5353. (Also see Titmuss Sainer Dechert).
Brussels, Belgium: 65 Avenue Louise, 1050.
Telephone: (02) 535-5411.

RESIDENT PARTNERS

Bettina Lawton Alexander
Sander M. Bieber
Ronald S. Cohn
Frank J. Eisenhart
Robert W. Helm
Arthur W. Leibold, Jr.
Allan S. Mostoff
Jeffrey S. Puretz
Paul F. Roye
Theodore Sonde
Jeffrey L. Steele

RESIDENT COUNSEL

David K. Diebold
Alan Rosenblat
Robert L. Roth
Donald Zarin

RESIDENT ASSOCIATES

Olivia P. Adler
Karen L. Anderberg
Anne M. Barr
Natalie S. Bej
Catherine Botticelli
Neil R. Crowley
Kimberly J. Dopkin
John S. Duessel
Brendan C. Fox
David J. Harris
Liane L. Heggy (Not admitted in DC)
Bonnie Howe
William J. Kotapish
Thomas W. MacIsaac
Stephanie J. Owen (Not admitted in DC)
Susan Keller Pascocello
Keith T. Robinson
Michelle D. Smith
Patrick W.D. Turley
Julia J. Tyler

For full biographical listings, see the Martindale-Hubbell Law Directory

* DEWEY BALLANTINE (AV)

1775 Pennsylvania Avenue, N.W., 20006-4605
Telephone: 202-862-1000; Telecopier: 202-862-1093
Cable Address: "Dewbalaw"
N.Y., N.Y., L.A., Calif., Budapest, Hungary, Prague, Czech Republic & Warsaw, Poland
New York, New York Office: 1301 Avenue of the Americas, 10019-6092.
Telephone: 212-259-8000.
Fax: 212-259-6333.
Los Angeles, California Office: 333 South Hope Street, 90071-1406.
Telephone: 213-626-3399.
Fax: 213-625-0562.
London, England Office: 150 Aldersgate Street, EC1A 4EJ.
Telephone: 011-44-71-606-6121.
Telefax: 011-44-71-600-3754.
Hong Kong Office: Asia Pacific Finance Tower, Suite 3907, Citibank Plaza, 3 Garden Road, Central, Hong Kong.
Telephone: 852-2509-7000.
Fax: 852-2509-7088.
Budapest, Hungary Office: Dewey Ballantine Theodore Goddard, Vadasz utca 31, H-1054 Budapest Hungary.
Telephone: (36-1) 111-9620.
Fax: (36-1) 112-2272.
Prague, Czech Republic Office: Dewey Ballantine Theodore Goddard, Revolucni 13, 110 00 Prague 1, Czech Republic.
Telephone: (42-2) 2481-0283.
Fax: (42-2) 231-0983.
Warsaw, Poland Office: Dewey Ballantine Theodore Goddard, ul. Klonowa 8, 00-591 Warsaw, Poland.
Telephone: 48-22-49-32-88.
Fax: 48-22-49-80-23.

(See Next Column)

DEWEY BALLANTINE, *Washington—Continued*

Kraków, Poland Office: Dewey Ballantine Theodore Goddard, Pl. Axentowicza 6. 30-034 Kraków Poland.
Telephone: 48-12-340-339.
Fax: 48-12-333-624.

RESIDENT PARTNERS

J. Goodwin Bennett
James F. Bowe, Jr.
David H. Brockway
Joseph K. Dowley
Matt E. Egger
Zori G. Ferkin
David C. Garlock
Thomas R. Howell
Gerald A. Kafka
Alicia M. Kershaw
Felix B. Laughlin
Myles V. Lynk
Kevin G. McAnaney
W. Clark McFadden II
Earle H. O'Donnell
John A. Ragosta
Howard J. Rosenstock
John J. Salmon
Michael H. Stein
Martha J. Talley
Alan Wm. Wolff

COUNSEL

Laurel W. Glassman
B. Thomas Mansbach
O. Julia Weller

OF COUNSEL

Philip W. Buchen

RESIDENT ASSOCIATES

Donna M. Attanasio
Eleanor Lorraine Bell
Joseph A. Black
Daniel M. Bricken (Not admitted in DC)
Rita A. Cavanagh
Judith A. Center
Evan Y. Chuck (Not admitted in DC)
Harry Lewis Clark
Julia Dryden English
Jewell L. Esposito (Not admitted in DC)
Benga L. Farina
James J. Ferguson, Jr. (Not admitted in DC)
Scott L. Forseth
Kathleen Foudy (Not admitted in DC)
Michael Geroe (Not admitted in DC)
Annette J. Guarisco
Anna-Liza B. Harris
John K. Hughes
Andrew W. Kentz
Joe Leiman (Not admitted in DC)
John R. Magnus
Mitchell Lane Marcus (Not admitted in DC)
Linda C. Menghetti
Glenn S. Miller (Not admitted in DC)
Jeffrey D. Neuchterlein
Joseph M. Pari
Karen Renfree
John D. Renneisen (Not admitted in DC)
Patti M. Richards (Not admitted in DC)
Paul M. Schmidt (Not admitted in DC)
Guy C. Smith
Margaret Stern-Bird (Not admitted in DC)
Ellen S. Tenenbaum
Marcy A. Toney
Bradford L. Ward
James P. West
Robin L. Wexler (Not admitted in DC)
Robert H.C. Wilkerson (Not admitted in DC)

For full biographical listings, see the Martindale-Hubbell Law Directory

* DICKINSON, WRIGHT, MOON, VAN DUSEN & FREEMAN (AV)

Suite 800, 1901 L Street, N.W., 20036-3506
Telephone: 202-457-0160
Facsimile: 202-659-1559
Detroit, Michigan Office: 500 Woodward Avenue, Suite 4000.
Telephone: 313-223-3500.
Facsimile: 313-223-3598.
Bloomfield Hills, Michigan Office: 525 North Woodward Avenue, Suite 2000.
Telephone: 810-433-7200.
Facsimile: 810-433-7274.
Grand Rapids, Michigan Office: 200 Ottawa Avenue, N.W., Suite 900.
Telephone: 616-458-1300.
Facsimile: 616-458-6753.
Lansing, Michigan Office: Suite 200, 215 South Washington Square.
Telephone: 517-371-1730.
Facsimile: 517-487-4700.
Chicago, Illinois Office: 225 West Washington, Suite 400.
Telephone: 312-220-0300.
Facsimile: 312-220-0021.
Warsaw, Poland Office: 46 Wilcza Street, 4th Floor, 00-679.
Telephone: (48-22) 299-241.
Facsimile: (48-2) 628-4107. Komertel Satellite Phone: (48-39) 121-510.

RESIDENT PARTNERS

Michael T. Platt
Jeffrey M. Petrash
Kirk Howard Betts
William E. Elwood
Samuel D. Littlepage
Conrad J. Clark

RESIDENT OF COUNSEL

Lucien N. Nedzi
Bruce A. Tassan
Marc A. Bergsman
Jill M. Barker

For full biographical listings, see the Martindale-Hubbell Law Directory

DONOVAN LEISURE NEWTON & IRVINE (AV)

1250 Twenty-Fourth Street, N.W., 20037
Telephone: 202-467-8300
Telecopier: 202-467-8484
New York, New York Office: 30 Rockefeller Plaza.
Telephone: 212-632-3000.
Cable Address: "Donlard, N.Y."
Telecopiers: 212-632-3315; 212-632-3321; 212-632-3322.
Los Angeles, California Office: 333 South Grand Avenue.
Telephone: 213-253-4000.
Cable Address: "Donlard, L.A."
Telecopier: 213-617-2368; 213-617-3246.
Paris, France Office: 130, rue du Faubourg, Saint-Honoré 75008 Paris.
Telephone: (011-33-1)42-25-47-10.
Telecopier: 011-33-1-42-56-08-06.
Palm Beach, Florida Office: 450 Royal Palm Way.
Telephone: 407-833-1040.
Telecopier: 407-835-8511.

MEMBERS OF FIRM

Mitchell Rogovin

COUNSEL

William E. Colby

RESIDENT ASSOCIATES

John R. Brautigam
John D. Worland, Jr.

For full biographical listings, see the Martindale-Hubbell Law Directory

DOW, LOHNES & ALBERTSON (AV)

Suite 500, 1255 Twenty-Third Street, N.W., 20037-1194
Telephone: 202-857-2500
Telecopier: (202) 857-2900
Atlanta, Georgia Office: One Ravinia Drive, Suite 1600.
Telephone: 404-901-8800.
Telecopier: (404) 901-8874.

MEMBERS OF THE FIRM

Marion H. Allen III (Chairman, Board of Partners) (Resident, Atlanta, Georgia Office)
Corinne M. Antley
Michael D. Basile
Leonard J. Baxt
Raymond G. Bender, Jr.
Richard L. Braunstein
Blain B. Butner
John T. Byrnes, Jr.
Peter C. Canfield (Resident, Atlanta, Georgia Office)
J. Eric Dahlgren (Resident, Atlanta, Georgia Office)
James A. Demetry (Resident, Atlanta, Georgia Office)
Peter H. Feinberg
John R. Feore, Jr.
Michael P. Fisher (Resident, Atlanta, Georgia Office)
Brenda Lee Fox
Linda A. Fritts
Michael B. Goldstein
Todd D. Gray
Joyce Trimble Gwadz
Jonathan D. Hart
Werner K. Hartenberger
Michael D. Hays
David A. Hildebrandt
Jonathan B. Hill
J. Michael Hines
Thomas J. Hutton
John C. Jost
Timothy J. Kelley
Joseph F. Kelly, Jr.
Gaylen D. Kemp (Resident, Atlanta, Georgia Office)
Leonard Jervey Kennedy (Not admitted in DC)
Paul R. Lang
John S. Logan
Bernard J. Long, Jr.
Richard D. Marks
Judith A. Mather
Richard P. McHugh
David E. Mills
Edward J. O'Connell
Timothy J. O'Rourke
B. Dwight Perry
John H. Pomeroy
J. Christopher Redding
Kevin F. Reed
Curtis A. Ritter
Kenneth D. Salomon
Michael S. Schooler
Elliot H. Shaller
Stuart A. Sheldon
Daniel W. Toohey
James A. Treanor, III
John D. Ward
Leslie H. Wiesenfelder
David Daniel Wild
Richard A. Wilhelm (Resident, Atlanta, Georgia Office)
David J. Wittenstein

John D. Allison
Pamela Arluk
James C. Armitage
Andrea R. Biller
Alan S. Bloom
Jeffrey A. Brueggemann (Not admitted in DC)
Lisa C. Bureau
Christina H. Burrow
Thomas M. Clyde (Resident, Atlanta, Georgia Office)
Kelli J. Crummer
Scott D. Dailard (Not admitted in DC)
Richard S. Denning
Lisa J. Flaxman (Not admitted in DC)
Craig A. Folds (Resident, Atlanta, Georgia Office)
Patricia A. Francis (Not admitted in DC)
Yolanda R. Gallegos
Jonathon C. Glass
Peter C. Godwin
David R. Goldberg
Sadhna Govindarajulu
Thomas K. Gump
J.G. Harrington
Michael A. Hepburn
Peter D. Horkitz
R. Dale Hughes (Resident, Atlanta, Georgia Office)
Sean D. Hughto
Karen Hunter (Not admitted in DC)
James W. Kimmell, Jr.
Michael Kovaka
Jonathan M. Levy
Ramie C. Little (Resident, Atlanta, Georgia Office)
Mark I. Lloyd
Stephanie M. Loughlin
C. David Lumsden (Resident, Atlanta, Georgia Office)

(See Next Column)

DOW, LOHNES & ALBERTSON—*Continued*

Sherry Booth Mastrostefano
Elizabeth Anne McGeary
Mary McCarron McVey (Not admitted in DC)
Margaret L. Miller
Steven F. Morris
Diane M. Morse
Steven B. Nickerson
Clint E. Odom (Not admitted in DC)
Frances A. Peale (Not admitted in DC)
Suzanne M. Perry
Thomas J. Peters IV (Resident, Atlanta, Georgia Office)
Laura Hathaway Phillips
Michael J. Pierce
Karen A. Post
Leslie S. Price (Resident, Atlanta, Georgia Office)
J. Duane Pugh Jr.
Mary K. Qualiana
Todd J. Rolapp (Not admitted in DC)
Elisa P. Rosen (Not admitted in DC)
Robin H. Sangston
William A. Shapard (Not admitted in DC)
David S. Shillman (Not admitted in DC)
Christina S. Wadyka
Seth M. Warner (Not admitted in DC)
Beth Davis Wilkinson
Rachel I. Wollitzer
H. Anthony Lehy

OF COUNSEL

Fayette B. Dow (1881-1962)
Horace L. Lohnes (1897-1954)
Fred W. Albertson
Ralph W. Hardy, Jr.
Charles J. McKerns
Thomas J. Schoenbaum (Resident, Atlanta, Georgia Office)
Stanley O. Sher

For full biographical listings, see the Martindale-Hubbell Law Directory

* DRINKER BIDDLE & REATH (AV)

901 15th Street, N.W., Suite 900, 20005
Telephone: 202-842-8800
Fax: 202-842-8465.
Cable Address: "Debemac"
Philadelphia, Pennsylvania Office: Philadelphia National Bank Building, 1345 Chestnut Street.
Telephone: 215-988-2700.
Fax: 215-988-2757.
Cable Address: "Debemac."
Princeton, New Jersey Office: Suite 400, 47 Hulfish Street.
Telephone: 609-921-6336.
Fax: 609-921-2265.
Berwyn, Pennsylvania Office: Suite 300, 1000 Westlakes Drive.
Telephone: 610-993-2200.
Fax: 610-993-8585.

RESIDENT PARTNERS

Robert M. Adler
Joe D. Edge
Michael L. Gassmann
Joseph F. Johnston, Jr.
Joaquin A. Marquez
Philip J. Mause
James A. Meyers
John W. Pettit
Richard M. Singer
Robert A. Skitol

OF COUNSEL

John P. Bankson, Jr.

RESIDENT ASSOCIATES

Richard J. Arsenault
John P. Bartholomay (Not admitted in DC)
David J. Berson
Sue W. Bladek
Keith B. Brooks (Not admitted in DC)
Mark F. Dever (Not admitted in DC)
Kevin M. Gross
Alan J. Joaquin (Not admitted in DC)
Ute A. Joas (Not admitted in DC)
Robert A. Kosik
Deborah M. Levy
Penelope M. Lister-Farano
Elizabeth A. Marshall

For full biographical listings, see the Martindale-Hubbell Law Directory

DUNCAN & ALLEN (AV)

1575 Eye Street, N.W., 20005
Telephone: 202-289-8400
Telecopier: 202-289-8450

MEMBERS OF FIRM

C. Emerson Duncan, II
Donald R. Allen
David P. Yaffe
Gregg D. Ottinger
John P. Williams
John P. Coyle

COUNSEL

Colette K. Bohatch

For full biographical listings, see the Martindale-Hubbell Law Directory

DWIGHT, ROYALL, HARRIS, KOEGEL & CASKEY

(See Rogers & Wells)

* DYKEMA GOSSETT P.L.L.C. (AV)

Franklin Square, Suite 300 West Tower, 1300 I Street, N.W., 20005-3306
Telephone: 202-522-8600
Fax: 202-522-8669
Detroit, Michigan Office: 400 Renaissance Center. 48243-1668.
Telephone: 313-568-6800.
Fax: 313-568-6594.
Ann Arbor, Michigan Office: 315 East Eisenhower Parkway, Suite 100, 48108-3306.
Telephone: 313-747-7660.
Fax: 313-747-7696.
Bloomfield Hills, Michigan Office: 1577 North Woodward Avenue, Suite 300, 48304-2820.
Telephone: 810-540-0700.
Fax: 810-540-0763.
Grand Rapids, Michigan Office: 200 Oldtown Riverfront Building, 248 Louis Campau Promenade, N.W. 49503-2667.
Telephone: 616-776-7500.
Fax: 616-776-7573.
Lansing, Michigan Office: 800 Michigan National Tower, 48933-1707.
Telephone: 517-374-9100.
Fax: 517-374-9191.
Chicago, Illinois Office: Three First National Plaza, Suite 1400, 70 W. Madison, 60602-4270.
Telephone: 312-214-3380.
Fax: 312-214-3441.

RESIDENT MEMBERS

Fred L. Woodworth
Howard E. O'Leary, Jr.
J. Timothy Hobbs
Timothy Sullivan
Teresa A. Brooks
Katherine S. Nucci
Bruce A. McDonald

RESIDENT ASSOCIATES

Judy Parker Jenkins
Martin R. Fischer
Christopher Kelly

For full biographical listings, see the Martindale-Hubbell Law Directory

* ECKERT SEAMANS CHERIN & MELLOTT (AV)

Suite 600, 2100 Pennsylvania Avenue, N.W., 20037
Telephone: 202-659-6600
Telex: 62030761
Facsimile: 202-659-6699
Pittsburgh, Pennsylvania Office: 42nd Floor, 600 Grant Street.
Telephone: 412-566-6000.
Telex: 866172.
Facsimile: 412-566-6099.
Harrisburg, Pennsylvania Office: One South Market Square Building, 213 Market Street.
Telephone: 717-237-6000.
Facsimile: 717-237-6019.
Allentown, Pennsylvania Office: Sovereign Building, 609 Hamilton Mall, 3rd Floor.
Telephone: 610-432-3000.
Facsimile: 610-432-8827.
Philadelphia, Pennsylvania Office: 1700 Market Street, Suite 3232.
Telephone: 215-575-6000.
Telex: 845226.
Facsimile: 215-575-6015.
Boston, Massachusetts Office: 18th Floor, One International Place.
Telephone: 617-342-6800.
Facsimile: 617-342-6899.
Buffalo, New York Office: 606 Liberty Building.
Telephone: 716-854-4100.
Facsimile: 716-854-4227.
Fort Lauderdale, Florida Office: First Fort Lauderdale Place, Suite 900, 100 Northeast Third Avenue.
Telephone: 305-523-0400.
Facsimile: 305-523-7002.
Boca Raton, Florida Office: Suite 902, The Plaza, 5355 Town Center Road.
Telephone: 407-394-7775.
Facsimile: 407-394-9998.
Miami, Florida Office: Barnett Tower, 18th Floor, 701 Brickell Avenue.
Telephone: 305-373-9100.
Facsimile: 305-372-9400.
Tallahassee, Florida Office: 206 South Adams Street.
Telephone: 904-222-2515.
Facsimile: 904-222-3452.

MEMBERS OF FIRM

Anthony A. Anderson
Keith L. Baker
R. Sarah Compton
Jerry W. Cox
William R. Martin (Not admitted in DC)
Jane Sutter Starke
Margaret N. Strand
George J. Wallace
G. Kent Woodman

SPECIAL COUNSEL

R. Lawrence Coughlin, Jr.

(See Next Column)

ECKERT SEAMANS CHERIN & MELLOTT, *Washington—Continued*

RESIDENT ASSOCIATES

Nancy L. Hicks
Ross A. Keene
Sean P. Morgan
Leslie Deming Schwartz

For full biographical listings, see the Martindale-Hubbell Law Directory

KENNETH R. FEINBERG & ASSOCIATES (AV)

1120 20th Street, N.W. Suite 740 South, 20036
Telephone: 202-371-1110
Fax: 202-962-9290
New York, N.Y. Office: 780 3rd Avenue, Suite 2202.
Telephone: 212-527-9600.
Fax: 212-527-9611.

ASSOCIATES

Deborah E. Greenspan
Michael K. Rozen
(Not admitted in DC)
Peter H. Woodin
(Not admitted in DC)

For full biographical listings, see the Martindale-Hubbell Law Directory

FISHER WAYLAND COOPER LEADER & ZARAGOZA, L.L.P. (AV)

A Registered Limited Liability Partnership
Suite 400 2001 Pennsylvania Avenue, N.W., 20006-1851
Telephone: 202-659-3494
Facsimile: 202-296-6518

Ben S. Fisher (1890-1954)
Charles V. Wayland (1910-1980)
Ben C. Fisher
Grover C. Cooper
Martin R. Leader
Richard R. Zaragoza
Clifford M. Harrington
Joel R. Kaswell
Kathryn R. Schmeltzer
Douglas Woloshin
David D. Oxenford
Barry H. Gottfried
Ann K. Ford
Bruce D. Jacobs
Eliot J. Greenwald
Carroll John Yung
Glenn S. Richards

OF COUNSEL

John Q. Hearne

Barrie Debra Berman
Bruce F. Hoffmeister
Scott R. Flick
Francisco R. Montero
Gregory L. Masters
(Not admitted in DC)
Robert C. Fisher
Lauren Ann Lynch
Sharon L. Tasman
Theresa A. Smyth
Howard C. Griboff
(Not admitted in DC)
Guy T. Christiansen
(Not admitted in DC)
Miles S. Mason
Kevin M. Walsh
(Not admitted in DC)
Mark H. Tidman
(Not admitted in DC)
Theodore Stern
(Not admitted in DC)
Robert L. Galbreath
(Not admitted in DC)

For full biographical listings, see the Martindale-Hubbell Law Directory

* **FOLEY, HOAG & ELIOT** (AV)

1615 L Street, N.W., 20036
Telephone: 202-775-0600
Telecopier: 202-857-0140
Boston, Massachusetts Office: One Post Office Square.
Telephone: 617-482-1390. Cable Address "Foleyhoag".
Telex: 94-0693.
Telecopier: 617-482-7347.

MEMBERS OF FIRM

Paul E. Tsongas
(Not admitted in DC)
Dennis R. Kanin
John L. Burke, Jr.
(Managing Partner)
James T. Montgomery, Jr.
(Resident)
Ellyn R. Weiss (Resident)

ASSOCIATES

Leslie Beth Bellas
Stephanie Cutler (Resident)
C. Erik Gustafson (Resident)

For full biographical listings, see the Martindale-Hubbell Law Directory

* **FOLEY & LARDNER** (AV)

Washington Harbour, Suite 500, 3000 K Street, N.W., 20007-5109
Telephone: 202-672-5300
Facsimile: 202-672-5399
Telex: 904136 (FoleyLard Wash)
Milwaukee, Wisconsin Office: Firstar Center, 777 East Wisconsin Avenue.
Telephone: 414-271-2400.
Telex: 26-819 (Foley Lard Mil).
Facsimile: 414-297-4900.
Madison, Wisconsin Office: Firstar Plaza, One South Pinckney Street, P.O. Box 1497.
Telephone: 608-257-5035.
Telex: 262051 (F L Madison).
Facsimile: 608-258-4258.

(See Next Column)

Chicago, Illinois Office: Suite 3300, One IBM Plaza, 330 N. Wabash Avenue.
Telephone: 312-755-1900.
Facsimile: 312-755-1925.
Annapolis, Maryland Office: Suite 102, 175 Admiral Cochrane Drive.
Telephone: 301-266-8077.
Telex: 899149 (Oldtownpat).
Facsimile: 301-266-8664.
Jacksonville, Florida Office: The Greenleaf Building, 200 Laura Street, P.O. Box 240.
Telephone: 904-359-2000.
Facsimile: 904-359-8700.
Orlando, Florida Office: Suite 1800, 111 North Orange Avenue, P.O. Box 2193.
Telephone: 407-423-7656.
Telex: 441781 (HQ ORL).
Facsimile: 407-648-1743.
Tallahassee, Florida Office: Suite 450, 215 South Monroe Street, P.O. Box 508.
Telephone: 904-222-6100.
Facsimile: 904-224-0496.
Tampa, Florida Office: Suite 2700, One Hundred N. Tampa Street, P.O. Box 3391.
Telephones: 813-229-2300; Pinellas County: 813-442-3296.
Facsimile: 813-221-4210. 813-446-9641.
Facsimile: 813-229-6282.
West Palm Beach, Florida Office: Suite 200, Phillips Point East Tower, 777 South Flagler Drive.
Telephone: 407-655-5050.
Facsimile: 407-655-6925.

RESIDENT PARTNERS

Stephen A. Bent
James N. Bierman
David A. Blumenthal
Robert A. Burka
Steven B. Chameides
Paul E. Cooney
John J. Feldhaus
(Not admitted in DC)
Wendy L. Fields
Howard W. Fogt, Jr.
Ilene Knable Gotts
Donald D. Jeffery
Jack L. Lahr
Peter C. Linzmeyer
Peter G. Mack
Brian J. McNamara
Sybil Meloy
(Not admitted in DC)
Paul R. Monsees
George E. Quillin
(Not admitted in DC)
David A. Sacks
Colin G. Sandercock
Jacqueline Marie Saue
Bernhard D. Saxe
(Not admitted in DC)
Richard L. Schwaab
(Not admitted in DC)
Arthur Schwartz
Charles J. Steele
Jay N. Varon
Samuel H. Weissbard
Ira C. Wolpert

RETIRED PARTNERS

Edwin Jason Dryer

OF COUNSEL

Melvin Blecher
Linda Heller Kamm
Barbara Ann McDowell
(Not admitted in DC)

SPECIAL COUNSEL

Lisa A. Smith
(Not admitted in DC)
Harold C. Wegner
(Not admitted in DC)

RESIDENT ASSOCIATES

Phillip John Articola
(Not admitted in DC)
Deborah A. Corsico
Karen Kaechele Costantino
(Not admitted in DC)
Patrick A. Doody
(Not admitted in DC)
Janell Mayo Duncan
(Not admitted in DC)
Joseph D. Edmondson, Jr.
William E. Eshelman
Lloyd N. Fantroy
Allison C. George
(Not admitted in DC)
Patricia D. Granados
John P. Isacson, Jr.
Mary Cynthia Atchley Jester
Phillip B. C. Jones
Joongi Kim
Johnny A. Kumar
Glenn Law
Eugene M. Lee
Melinda F. Levitt
Stephen B. Maebius
(Not admitted in DC)
Lisa S. Mankofsky
William D. Miller
(Not admitted in DC)
Cynthia K. Nicholson
Richard C. Peet
(Not admitted in DC)
Don J. Pelto
Gary L. Shaffer
(Not admitted in DC)
Samuel B. Sterrett, Jr.
Ann St. Laurent
John P. Veschi
(Not admitted in DC)
Scott A. Westfahl
Marcus P. Williams
David Warren Woodward
Gary M. Zinkgraf

For full biographical listings, see the Martindale-Hubbell Law Directory

FREEDMAN, LEVY, KROLL & SIMONDS (AV)

Suite 825, 1050 Connecticut Avenue, N.W., 20036-5366
Telephone: 202-457-5100
Cable Address: "Attorneys"
Telecopier: 202-457-5151

(See Next Column)

FREEDMAN, LEVY, KROLL & SIMONDS—*Continued*

MEMBERS OF FIRM

Walter Freedman
Peter E. Panarites
Gary O. Cohen
Jay W. Freedman
Arthur H. Bill
Thomas C. Lauerman
Richard G. Stoll
Marc B. Dorfman
John H. Chettle
Karen M. Wardzinski
Lawrence G. McBride
Emil Hirsch

OF COUNSEL

Arnold Levy
Milton P. Kroll
Jerome H. Simonds
David P. Novello

SPECIAL TAX COUNSEL

Norman C. Bensley (Not admitted in DC)

ASSOCIATES

Thomas L. James
Richard T. Choi
Serena P. Wiltshire
Patrick J. Kearney
Philip Lawrence DeCamara
(Not admitted in DC)

For full biographical listings, see the Martindale-Hubbell Law Directory

* FRIED, FRANK, HARRIS, SHRIVER & JACOBSON (AV)

A Partnership including Professional Corporations
Suite 800, 1001 Pennsylvania Avenue, N.W., 20004-2505
Telephone: 202-639-7000
Cable Address: "Steric Washington"
Telex: 892406
Telecopy Rapifax: 202-639-7008
Zap Mail: 202-338-0110
New York, New York Office: One New York Plaza.
Telephone: 212-859-8000.
Cable Address: "Steric New York." W.U. Int.
Telex: 620223. W.U. Int.
Telex: 662119. W.U. Domestic: 128173.
Telecopier: 212-859-4000 (Dex 6200).
Los Angeles, California Office: 725 South Figueroa Street.
Telephone: 213- 689-5800.
London, England Office: 4 Chiswell Street, London EC1Y 4UP.
Telephone: 011-44-171-972-9600.
Fax: 011-44-171-972-9602.
Paris, France Office: 7, Rue Royale, 75008.
Telephone: (+331) 40-17-04-04.
Fax: (+331) 40-17-08-30.

WASHINGTON, D.C. PARTNERS

David L. Ansell
T. J. Anthony, Jr.
John T. Boese
Diane E. Burkley
John W. Chierichella
Peter V. Z. Cobb
(Not admitted in DC)
Milton Eisenberg (P.C.)
E. Donald Elliott
Joel R. Feidelman (P.C.)
June Munford Gertig
Stephen I. Glover
Jack B. Gordon
David B. Hardison
Thomas S. Harman
Dixie Lynn Johnson
Robert E. Juceam
(Not admitted in DC)
Alan S. Kaden
Jay R. Kraemer
Kenneth S. Kramer (P.C.)
Robert H. Ledig
Daniel E. Loeb
James J. McCullough
Robert P. Mollen
Carleton K. Montgomery
Matt T. Morley
Lynda Troutman O'Sullivan
Harvey L. Pitt
Elliot E. Polebaum
Marcus A. Rowden
Richard A. Sauber
James H. Schropp
Richard A. Steinwurtzel
Joseph A. Stern
(Not admitted in DC)
William H. Taft, IV
Thomas P. Vartanian
Louis D. Victorino
Leonard A. Zax

OF COUNSEL

J. Gail Bancroft
(Not admitted in DC)
Martin D. Ginsburg (P.C.)
Max M. Kampelman
Sargent Shriver
Daniel M. Singer

ASSOCIATES

Douglas W. Baruch
Ronni S. Bianco
(Not admitted in DC)
James R. Bruner
Michael J. Burke
Bruce J. Casino
Anthony C. Cianciotti
Jonathan M. Coleman
William A. Davis
Mark J. Dorsey
Barry M. Faber
Mark J. Fajfar
David L. Fenimore
Cynthia M. Fornelli
Michele E. Foster
Lisa Ann Fuller
Janet G. Gamer
Karen T. Grisez
Karl A. Groskaufmanis
Susan White Haag
Shannon L. Haralson
Brian "D" Henretty
Lanae Holbrook
(Not admitted in DC)
Alan B. Horowitz
James A. Hutchinson
(Not admitted in DC)
Jonathan M. Jacobs
Maureen T. Kelly
James S. Kennell
Jay D. Majors
(Not admitted in DC)
Deneen J. Melander
Karen E. Miller
(Not admitted in DC)
R. Patrick Murphy
Laurie Anne Oberembt
Doron D. Patt

(See Next Column)

ASSOCIATES (Continued)

Anne B. Perry
(Not admitted in DC)
Douglas E. Perry
John D. Petro
Catherine Evans Pollack
(Not admitted in DC)
Michael J. Rivera
Pamela A. Roth
(Not admitted in DC)
Lawrence E. Ruggiero
Richard N. Seaman
M. Gilbey Strub
Jocelyn M. Sturdivant
(Not admitted in DC)
Vasiliki B. Tsaganos
Andrew P. Varney
Michael L. Waldman
James McKay Weitzel, Jr.
Robert C. Westerfeldt
(Not admitted in DC)
Richard A. Wolfe
Shari A. Wynne

For full biographical listings, see the Martindale-Hubbell Law Directory

FRIEDLANDER, MISLER, FRIEDLANDER, SLOAN & HERZ (AV)

Suite 700, 1101 Seventeenth Street, N.W., 20036
Telephone: 202-872-0800
Cable Address: "FMSHLAW"
Telex: 64273

OF COUNSEL

Jack L. Friedlander

MEMBERS OF FIRM

Stephen H. Friedlander
Leonard A. Sloan
Gerald Herz
Morris Kletzkin
Jeffrey W. Ochsman
Jerome Ostrov
Arnold S. Albert

ASSOCIATES

Jana Kay Guggenheim
Philippa T. Gasnier
James J. Gallinaro
Seth B. Shapiro
Robert J. Strayhorne
Alan Dean Sundburg
Andrew B. Schulwolf
(Not admitted in DC)
Mark D. Crawford
(Not admitted in DC)

For full biographical listings, see the Martindale-Hubbell Law Directory

GOLD & STANLEY, P.C. A PROFESSIONAL CORPORATION (AV)

Suite 300, 1155 Connecticut Avenue, N.W., 20016
Telephone: 703-836-7004
Alexandria, Virginia Office: Third Floor, 1800 Diagonal Road.
Telephone: 703-836-7004.
Telefax: 703-548-9430.
Silver Spring, Maryland Office: 1010 Wayne Avenue, Suite 1440.
Telephone: 301-589-7800.

Valerie P. Morrison

Loraine E. O'Hanlon
Howard I. Rubin

For full biographical listings, see the Martindale-Hubbell Law Directory

* GRAHAM & JAMES (AV)

Suite 700, 2000 M Street, N.W., 20036
Telephone: 202-463-0800
Telex: 90-4103 Chalgray Wsh
Telecopier: 202-463-0823
Other offices located in: San Francisco, Los Angeles, Newport Beach, Palo Alto, Sacramento and Fresno, California; New York, New York; Milan, Italy; Beijing, China; Tokyo, Japan; London, England; Dusseldorf, Germany; Taipei, Taiwan.
Associated Offices: Deacons in Association with Graham & James, Hong Kong; Sly and Weigall, Sydney, Melbourne, Brisbane, Perth and Canberra, Australia.
Affiliated Offices: Graham & James in Affiliation with Taylor Joynson Garrett, London, England, Bucharest, Romania and Brussels, Belgium; Hanafiah Soeharto Ponggawa, Jakarta, Indonesia; Deacons and Graham & James, Bangkok, Thailand; Haarmann, Hemmelrath & Partner, Berlin, Munich, Leipzig, Frankfurt and Dusseldorf, Germany; Mishare M. Al-Ghazali & Partners, Kuwait; Sly & Weigall Deacons in Association with Graham & James, Hanoi, Vietnam and Guangzhou, China; Gallastegui y Lozano, S.C., Mexico City, Mexico; Law Firm of Salah Al-Hejailan, Jeddah and Riyadh, Sauda Arabia.

MEMBERS OF FIRM

Richard K. Bank
Gregory Bartko
(Not admitted in DC)
Lawrence D. Blume
J. Michael Cavanaugh
Mary Boney Denison
Carroll E. Dubuc
Stuart S. Dye
L. Peter Farkas
Grace Parke Fremlin
Yasuhiro Hagihara
Eliot J. Halperin
Aidan D. Jones
Paul J. Kennedy
A. Wayne Lalle, Jr.
Daniel J. Manelli
Thomas F. Railsback
Yoshihiro Saito
Christopher "Kip" Schwartz
(Not admitted in DC)
Michael H. Selter
Jeffrey L. Snyder
Ernest M. Stern
Pheng Theng Tan
Ronald I. Tisch
Lawrence R. Walders
Samuel Xiangyu Zhang
(Not admitted in DC)

(See Next Column)

GRAHAM & JAMES, *Washington—Continued*

RESIDENT ASSOCIATES

Stefano Agostini (Not admitted in the United States)
Stuart H. Anolik (Not admitted in DC)
Andrea Fekkes Dynes
Christopher Eliopulos
Susan B. Gerson
Richard Karpinski
Rebekah Martin Liu
Gregory S. Menegaz (Not admitted in DC)
Julie Chasen Ross
C. Dennis Southard, IV (Not admitted in DC)
Richard S. Toikka

For full biographical listings, see the Martindale-Hubbell Law Directory

GROVE, JASKIEWICZ AND COBERT (AV)

Suite 400, 1730 M Street, N.W., 20036
Telephone: 202-296-2900
Telecopier: 202-296-1370
Baltimore, Maryland Office: The Park Plaza, 800 North Charles Street, Suite 400.
Telephone: 301-727-7010.

MEMBERS OF FIRM

William J. Grove (1914-1988)
Ronald N. Cobert
Paul H. Lamboley (Not admitted in DC)
Edward J. Kiley
Robert L. Cope
Joseph Michael Roberts
Andrew M. Danas
Andrew M. Whitman (Not admitted in DC)

OF COUNSEL

Leonard A. Jaskiewicz
James F. Flint
Lawrence E. Dubé, Jr.
James K. Jeanblanc
Edmund M. Jaskiewicz

For full biographical listings, see the Martindale-Hubbell Law Directory

* HALE AND DORR (AV)

A Partnership including Professional Corporations
1455 Pennsylvania Avenue, N.W., 20004
Telephone: 202-942-8400
Cable Address: "Hafis Wsh"
Telecopier: 202-942-8484
Boston, Massachusetts Office: 60 State Street.
Telephone: 617-526-6000.
Cable Address: "Hafis."
Telex: 94-0472.
Telecopier: Domestic 617-526-5000; 617-742-9108.
Manchester, New Hampshire Office: 1155 Elm Street.
Telephone: 603-628-7400.
Telecopier: 603-627-3880.

MEMBERS OF FIRM

James L. Quarles, III (Resident)
Allen H. Fox (Resident)
Paul G. Wallach (Resident)
Geoffrey S. Stewart (Resident)
Steven S. Snider (Resident)
David Sylvester (Resident)
Jay P. Urwitz (Resident)
Jeffrey J. Davidson (Resident)
William G. McElwain (Resident)
Gilbert B. Kaplan (Resident)
Robert S. Mueller, III (Not admitted in DC; Resident)
Kenneth H. Slade
Hollie L. Baker (Resident)
William F. Leahy (Resident)
Brent B. Siler (Resident)
Daniel Levin (Resident)
Henry N. Wixon (Resident)
Kenneth R. Meade (Resident)
Mary E. Cavanaugh
Paul W. Jameson (Resident)
David A. Wilson (Resident)

RESIDENT ASSOCIATES

Kathleen M. Weinstein
Albert P. Parker, II
Sean P. Sherman
William J. Healey
Susan McWhan Tobin
Wendy E. Anderson
Sloane Elizabeth Anders
Cris R. Revaz
Judith A. Evans (Not admitted in DC)
Wendy Rae Rodano (Not admitted in DC)
Rusty Wilson (Not admitted in DC)
Susanne M. Hopkins-Klima (Not admitted in DC)

For full biographical listings, see the Martindale-Hubbell Law Directory

HOBBS, STRAUS, DEAN & WALKER (AV)

Suite 800, 1819 H Street, N.W., 20006
Telephone: 202-783-5100
Fax: 202-296-8834
Portland, Oregon Office: Suite 10, 0225 S.W. Montgomery Street.
Telephone: 503-242-1745.
Fax: 503-242-0716.

MEMBERS OF FIRM

Charles A. Hobbs
Jerry C. Straus
S. Bobo Dean
Frances L. Horn
Carol L. Barbero
Hans Walker, Jr.
Marsha Kostura
Michael L. Roy

(See Next Column)

ASSOCIATES

Matthew S. Jaffe
Judith A. Shapiro
Sandra L. Ferguson (Not admitted in DC)
Cheryl Lynne Sanfilipo
William R. Norman, Jr. (Not admitted in DC)

OF COUNSEL

Kaighn Smith, Jr. (Not admitted in DC)
Dean B. Suagee

LEGAL SUPPORT PERSONNEL

Karen J. Funk
Cindy Darcy
Marie Osceola-Branch

For full biographical listings, see the Martindale-Hubbell Law Directory

HOGAN & HARTSON L.L.P. (AV)

Columbia Square, 555 13th Street, N.W., 20004-1109
Telephone: 202-637-5600
Telex: 89-2757
Cable Address: "Hogander Washington"
Fax: 202-637-5910
Brussels, Belgium Office: Avenue des Arts 41, 1040.
Telephone: (32.2) 505.09.11.
Fax: (32.2) 502.28.60.
London, England Office: Veritas House, 125 Finsbury Pavement, EC2A 1NQ.
Telephone: (44 171) 638.9595.
Fax: (44 171) 638.0884.
Moscow, Russia Office: 33/2 Usacheva Street, Building 3, 119048.
Telephone: (7095) 245-5190.
Fax: (7095) 245-5192.
Paris, France Office: Cabinet Wolfram: 14, rue Chauveau-Lagarde, 75008.
Telephone: (33-1) 44.71.97.00.
Fax: (33-1) 47.42.13.56.
Prague, Czech Republic Office: Opletalova 37, 110 00.
Telephone: (42-2) 2422-9009.
Fax: (42-2) 2421-5105.
Warsaw, Poland Office: Marszalkowska 6/6, 00-590.
Telephone: (48 2) 628 0201; Int'l (48) 3912 1413.
Fax: (48 2) 628 7787; Int'l (48) 3912 1511.
Baltimore, Maryland Office: 111 South Calvert Street, 16th Floor.
Telephone: 410-659-2700.
Fax: 410-539-6981.
Bethesda, Maryland Office: Two Democracy Center, Suite 720, 6903 Rockledge Drive.
Telephone: 301-493-0030.
Fax: 301-493-5169.
Colorado Springs, Colorado Office: 518 North Nevada Avenue, Suite 200.
Telephone: 719-635-5900.
Fax: 719-635-2847.
Denver, Colorado Office: One Tabor Center, Suite 1500, 1200 Seventeenth Street.
Telephone: 303-899-7300.
Fax: 303-899-7333.
McLean, Virginia Office: 8300 Greensboro Drive.
Telephone: 703-848-2600.
Fax: 703-448-7650.

MEMBERS OF FIRM

Frank J. Hogan (1877-1944)
Nelson T. Hartson (1887-1976)
Jonathan L. Abram
Gil A. Abramson (Resident, Baltimore, Maryland Office)
Charles E. Allen
Patricia Riley Ambrose
Jeanne S. Archibald
John P. Arness
Deborah Taylor Ashford
Helen Clark Atkeson (Resident, Denver, Colorado Office)
Steven E. Ballew (Resident, Warsaw, Poland Office)
Michael D. Barnes
George P. Barsness
Raymond J. Batla, Jr. (Prague, Czech and London, England Offices)
George Beall (Resident, Baltimore, Maryland Office)
Richard K.A. Becker (Resident, McLean, Virginia Office)
Joseph C. Bell (Resident, Warsaw, Poland Office)
A. Lee Bentley, III
Scott A. Blackmun (Resident, Colorado Springs, Colorado Office)
Lisa Bonanno
David W. Bonser
William J. Bowman
William A. Bradford, Jr.
Patricia A. Brannan
Rebecca B. Bronson (Resident, Moscow, Russia Office)
Stanley J. Brown (Resident, Bethesda, Maryland Office)
Thomas N. Bulleit, Jr.
David W. Burgett
George U. Carneal
Robert B. Cave
Michael L. Cheroutes (Resident, Denver, Colorado Office)
Alphonso A. Christian, II
Claudette M. Christian
Ty Cobb (Resident, Baltimore, Maryland Office)
Vincent H. Cohen
Michael D. Colglazier (Resident, Baltimore, Maryland Office)
Joseph G. Connolly, Jr.
Jonathan A. Constine
Robert L. Corn-Revere
Dean W. Crowell (Resident, Moscow, Russia Office)
Sara-Ann Determan
Marvin J. Diamond
Edward C. Dolan
Mark D. Dopp
Edward C. Duckers
Richard E. Dunne, III (Resident, Baltimore, Maryland Office)
Isabel P. Dunst
Alan L. Dye
Claud v. S. Eley (Resident, Brussels, Belgium Office)

(See Next Column)

HOGAN & HARTSON L.L.P.—*Continued*

MEMBERS OF FIRM (Continued)

E. Tazewell Ellett
Robert J. Elliott
Frank J. Fahrenkopf, Jr.
Kenneth W. Farber
Prentiss E. Feagles
P. Dustin Finney, Jr.
Howard I. Flack
Gerald E. Gilbert (Resident, McLean, Virginia Office)
Bruce W. Gilchrist
Gardner F. Gillespie
C. Michael Gilliland
J. Warren Gorrell, Jr.
David F. Grady
Kevin G. Gralley (Resident, Baltimore, Maryland Office)
Benton R. Hammond
Mary L. Harmon
Anthony S. Harrington
Joseph M. Hassett
Kenneth J. Hautman (Resident, McLean, Virginia Office)
Elizabeth Blossom Heffernan
David J. Hensler
Patrick F. Hofer
Steven P. Hollman (Resident, Bethesda, Maryland Office)
Howard M. Holstein
Janet Pitterle Holt
Craig A. Hoover
James A. Hourihan
William Mike House
Irene E. Howie
Stephen J. Immelt (Resident, Baltimore, Maryland Office)
Robert M. Jeffers
Harry T. Jones, Jr.
Jonathan S. Kahan
Robert H. Kapp
Steven M. Kaufman
John C. Keeney, Jr.
M. Langhorne Keith (Resident, McLean, Virginia Office)
J. Clinton Kelly (Resident, Baltimore, Maryland Office)
Nevin J. Kelly
Robert J. Kenney, Jr.
David A. Kikel
Andrew J. Kilcarr
Carol Weld King
David P. King (Resident, Baltimore, Maryland Office)
Duncan S. Klinedinst (Resident, McLean, Virginia Office)
Edward L. Korwek
Gary Jay Kushner
Catherine James LaCroix
M. Gary LaFever (Resident, McLean, Virginia Office)
Kevin J. Lanigan
Philip C. Larson
Stephan E. Lawton
Thomas B. Leary
Robert F. Leibenluft
Lewis E. Leibowitz
David G. Leitch
Kevin J. Lipson
Timothy A. Lloyd
Walter G. Lohr, Jr. (Resident, Baltimore, Maryland Office)
Daniel H. Maccoby (Resident, London, England Office)
David B. H. Martin, Jr.
Warren H. Maruyama
John P. Mathis
George W. Mayo, Jr.
Mark E. Mazo
Mark S. McConnell
Janet L. McDavid
James G. McMillan
George H. Mernick, III
Martin Michaelson
Kathleen M. Miko
Evan Miller
George W. Miller
H. Todd Miller
Randy E. Miller (Resident, Brussels Office)
Barbara F. Mishkin
Austin S. Mittler
Jean S. Moore
Dennis K. Moyer (Resident, McLean, Virginia Office)
Rodney R. Munsey
William L. Neff
Karol Lyn Newman
William D. Nussbaum
Maureen E. O'Bryon
Bob Glen Odle
Thomas F. O'Neil III (Resident, Baltimore, Maryland Office)
Bruce E. Parmley
Bert R. Peña
E. Barrett Prettyman, Jr.
Patrick M. Raher
Terri Steinhaus Reiskin
William S. Reyner, Jr.
John G. Roberts, Jr.
Richard S. Rodin
Paul G. Rogers
Peter A. Rohrbach
Peter J. Romeo
James J. Rosenhauer
Mace J. Rosenstein
Steven J. Routh
Edward A. Ryan
David J. Saylor
William C. Schmidt
Jeffrey G. Schneider
David J. Scott (Resident, Denver, Colorado Office)
James E. Showen
Michael J. Silver (Resident, Baltimore, Maryland Office)
Richard S. Silverman
Paul C. Skelly
Walter A. Smith, Jr.
Maree Sneed
Allen R. Snyder
Jerome N. Sonosky
Clyde H. Sorrell, Jr. (Resident, Bethesda, Maryland Office)
Timothy Charles Stanceu
John S. Stanton
Stuart G. Stein
Clifford D. Stromberg
Kimberley E. Thompson
Peter W. Tredick
Helen R. Trilling
Craig H. Ulman
Ann Morgan Vickery
Eric Von Salzen
Robert J. Waldman
Donis G. Walker (Denver and Colorado Springs, Colorado Offices)
Eric T. Washington
Richard L.A. Weiner (Resident, Brussels, Belgium Office)
T. Clark Weymouth
Michael Cunningham Williams
Susan Wing
Joel S. Winnik
Pamela G. Winthrop

COUNSEL

Lee E. Berner (Resident, McLean, Virginia Office)
Pavel Bradac (Not admitted in the United States) (Resident, Prague, Czech Republic Office)
Nancy Andreas Clodfelter (Resident, Denver, Colorado Office)
Colin W. Craik (Resident, Prague, Czech Republic Office)
Anne M. Dellinger
Kevin P. Gallagher
Jacquelyn E. Grillon
Maciej Jamka (Resident, Warsaw, Poland Office)
Susan E. Joseph
Lynn G. Kamarck
Piotr Kochanski (Adwokat) (Not admitted in the United States) (Resident, Warsaw, Poland Office)
Daniel B. Kohrman
James R. Laramie
C. Stephen Lawrence

(See Next Column)

COUNSEL (Continued)

Elizabeth J. Lentini (Resident, Denver, Colorado Office)
Colleen J. Martin
Gerald E. Oberst, Jr. (Resident, Brussels, Belgium Office)
Linda L. Oliver
Diane B. Patrick (Not admitted in DC)
Marissa G. Repp
Steven A. Robins (Resident, Bethesda, Maryland Office)
Margaret E. Roggensack
Beth L. Rubin
Patricia Brown Shrader
Howard S. Silver
David W. Stroh (Resident, McLean, Virginia Office)
Rose Ann C. Sullivan (Resident, Colorado Springs, Colorado Office)
Jan Tanzer (Not admitted in United States) (Resident, Prague, Czech republic Office)
Philippa Watson (Not admitted in United States; Resident, Brussels, Belgium Office)
Michael L. Whitener
Steven L. Wolfram (Resident, Paris, France Office)

OF COUNSEL

Dennis J. Lehr
Lee Loevinger
Sherwin J. Markman
Seymour S. Mintz
John J. Ross
Clayton K. Yeutter

ASSOCIATES

Elizabeth A. Abdoo
Amy M. Allen (Not admitted in DC)
Donna Lady Alpi
Audrey J. Anderson
Merry C. Anderson
Robert L. Asher
Rose Marie L. Audette (Not admitted in DC)
H. Christopher Bartolomucci (Not admitted in DC)
Julie T. Barton (Not admitted in DC)
Robert A. Begotka
Susan Taylor Bell (Resident, Baltimore, Maryland Office)
Suzanne M. Bonnet (Not admitted in DC)
John W. Borkowski (Also practicing individually, New Orleans, Louisiana)
Krystna Boron
Donna A. Boswell
James H. R. Brady (Not admitted in DC)
Karen-Ann Broe (Resident, Bethesda, Maryland Office)
Donald C. Brown Jr.
D. Lea Browning
Andrea M. Bruce (Not admitted in DC)
James R. Brueneman (Resident, McLean, Virginia Office)
Brooke Bumpers
Timothy J. Carlson (Resident, McLean, Virginia Office)
Adam H. Charnes
Jane M. Church (Resident, McLean, Virginia Office)
Regina V. Ciccone (Not admitted in DC)
Laurie A. Clarke
Jacqueline P. Cleary
Helene O. Cobb
Tracy M.J. Colden
N. Thomas Connally, III (Resident, McLean, Virginia Office)
Maryanne Courtney
Tia Cudahy (Not admitted in DC)
David A. Dedman
Dennis J. Dee, Jr. (Not admitted in DC)
Elizabeth Gordon Dellenbaugh (Not admitted in DC)
Edward S. Desmarais, Jr.
Kyle D. Dixon (Not admitted in DC)
Pierre M. Donahue
James H. Doyle
Alexander A. Dubitsky (Resident, Moscow, Russia Office)
Robert B. Duncan
Paul W. Durham
Stacy L. Ehrlich (Not admitted in DC)
David H. Engvall
Douglas A. Fellman
Michael A. Fitzpatrick (Not admitted in DC)
William P. Flanagan
Jody M. Foster (Not admitted in DC)
Susan L. Fox
Jonathan S. Franklin
Bonnie E. Freeman (Not admitted in DC)
Aleksander Galos (Not admitted in United States; Resident, Warsaw, Poland Office)
Gregory G. Garre
John F. Gaul
Christopher P. Gilkerson
Carol A. Groben
David S. Haddock, II (Resident, McLean, Virginia Office)
Martin J. Hahn
Shannon Thee Hanson (Resident, Baltimore, Maryland Office)
Karen M. Hardwick
Michele Sasse Harrington
Peter H. Harris (Not admitted in DC)
Karis A. Hastings
Christopher P. Healey (Not admitted in DC)
Linda A. Hildreth (Resident, McLean, Virginia Office)
Richard T. Horan, Jr. (Resident, McLean, Virginia Office)
Eve N. Howard
Jana Hrstková (Not admitted in United States) (Resident, Prague, Czech Republic Office)
Kevin D. Hughes (Not admitted in DC)
Sten A. Jensen (Not admitted in DC)
Thomas E. Joaquin (Not admitted in DC)
Melissa R. Jones
Lawrence D. Kaplan
Jordan P. Karp (Resident, Baltimore, Maryland Office)
Nancy J. Kellner (Not admitted in DC)
Amy Folsom Kett (Not admitted in DC)
Michael L. Kidney
David D. Kim (Not admitted in DC)
Bogudar Kordasiewicz (Resident, Warsaw, Poland Office)
Joan H. Krause (Not admitted in DC)
S. Gregg Kunzi (Not admitted in DC)
Mark L. Landis (Not admitted in DC)
Mark J. Larson
Wendy A. Learmont (Not admitted in DC)
Joanne L. Leasure
Scott R. Lilienthal (Not admitted in DC)

(See Next Column)

HOGAN & HARTSON L.L.P., *Washington—Continued*

ASSOCIATES (Continued)

David L. Littleton (Not admitted in DC)
Margaret C. Liu (Not admitted in DC)
Laura E. Loeb
Elizabeth J. Logsdon (Not admitted in DC)
Kathryn Webb Lovill
Milan Lovišek (Not admitted in United States; Resident, Prague, Czech Republic Office)
L. Weatherly Lowe
Martin K. Lowen
James H. Lystad
Mike Yuh-hung Ma
Barbara G. Martin (Resident, Baltimore, Maryland Office)
Thene M. Martin
Brian E. Mazurek (Not admitted in DC)
Michael O. McCarthy III
Helen P. McClure
Scott D. McClure
Katherine M. McCormack (Not admitted in DC)
Thomas L. McGovern III
James H. McGrath, IV (Resident, McLean, Virginia Office)
Mona M. Meeker (Resident, McLean, Virginia Office)
Timothy F. Mellett
Craig B. Mendelsohn (Not admitted in DC)
Jeremy B. Miller (Not admitted in DC)
Mary Beth Miller
Sheryl R. Miller (Not admitted in DC)
Paul A. Minorini
William L. Monts, III
James J. Moore
Steven A. Museles
Andrew B. Nace (Not admitted in DC)
Lech Najbauer (Not admitted in United States) (Resident, Warsaw, Poland Office)
J. Patrick Nevins (Not admitted in DC)
David Newmann (Not admitted in DC)
M. Elizabeth Peters
Douglas S. Phillips
Catherine L. Pinkerton
Janet S. Pollan (Resident, Warsaw, Poland Office)
Lisa L. Poole
Gwendolyn A. Powell
Michael A. Proett (Resident, Moscow, Russia Office)
Gerard J. Prud'homme (Not admitted in DC)
Helen E. Quick
Robert N. Rabecs
Rosemary H. Ratcliff (Not admitted in DC)
Jonathan T. Rees
Scott H. Reisch
Thomas E. Repke (Resident, McLean, Virginia Office)
Patrick J. Reynolds (Resident, Baltimore, Maryland Office)
Beth L. Roberts (Not admitted in DC)
Evan L. Rosenfeld
Christopher M. Rossomondo (Not admitted in DC)
Susan M. Rotatori
James P. Ruggeri
Richard T. Saas (Not admitted in DC)
Christopher A. Schindler (Not admitted in DC)
Timothy L. Schroer
Michelle M. Shanahan
Scott G. Silverstein (Not admitted in DC)
David W. Smail (Resident, Paris, France Office)
David V. Snyder
Joshua N. Sondheimer
Margaret U. Song (Not admitted in DC)
Robert L. Spencer
Steven A. Spencer
Eric P. Spooner (Not admitted in DC)
Robert F. Stankey
Sanford W. Stark
Krzysztof Stefanowicz (Not admitted in United States) (Resident, Warsaw, Poland Office)
Steven B. Steinborn
Lowell R. Stern
Agnieszka Suchecka-Tarnacka (Adwokat) (Not admitted in United States) (Resident, Warsaw, Poland Office)
Andrzej Sutkowski (Not admitted in United States) (Resident, Warsaw, Poland Office)
Christine M. Svinth (Resident, McLean, Virginia Office)
Cynthia G. Swann (Not admitted in DC)
Marta I. Tanenhaus
Farinaz S. Tehrani
Sonia Gustafson Thomsen
Pamela Tillinghast (Not admitted in DC)
Andrew C. Topping (Resident, Baltimore, Maryland Office)
James K. Trefil (Not admitted in DC)
Albert W. Turnbull
Emily S. Uhrig
Stephen G. Vaskov
Luigi D. Vissicchio (Not admitted in DC)
K. Michele Walters (Not admitted in DC)
Lori-Christina Webb (Not admitted in DC)
Jill E. Welna
Glenn P. Wicks
Pamela McKenzie Williams (Resident, Baltimore, Maryland Office)
Edward C. Wilson, Jr.
Ronald J. Wiltsie, II (Resident, McLean, Virginia Office)
David A. Winter (Not admitted in DC)
Kathryn M. Woodruff
Philip H. Wright (Resident, Baltimore, Maryland Office)
Wilhelmina M. Wright
Katherine Ennis Wychulis (Resident, McLean, Virginia Office)
Emily M. Yinger
Mitchell E. Zamoff
Elizabeth (Elzbieta) M. Zechenter (Not admitted in DC)
Stephen J. Zempolich

For full biographical listings, see the Martindale-Hubbell Law Directory

* HOLLAND & HART (AV)

Suite 310, 1001 Pennsylvania Avenue, N.W., 20004
Telephone: 202-638-5500
Telecopier: 202-737-8998
Denver, Colorado Office: Suite 2900, 555 Seventeenth Street. P.O. Box 8749.
Telephone: 303-295-8000.
Cable Address: "Holhart Denver."
Telecopier: 303-295-8261.
TWX: 910-931-0568.
Denver Tech Center, Colorado Office: Suite 1050, 4601 DTC Boulevard.
Telephone: 303-290-1600.
Telecopier: 303-290-1606.
Aspen, Colorado Office: 600 East Main Street.
Telephone: 303-925-3476.
Telecopier: 303-925-9367.
Boulder, Colorado Office: Suite 500, 1050 Walnut.
Telephone: 303-473-2700.
Telecopier: 303-473-2720.
Colorado Springs, Colorado Office: Suite 1000, 90 Cascade Avenue.
Telephone: 719-475-7730.
Telex: 820770 SHHTLX.
Telecopier: 719-634-2461.
Boise, Idaho Office: Suite 1400, West One Plaza, 101 South Capitol Boulevard, P.O. Box 2527.
Telephone: 208-342-5000.
Telecopier: 208-343-8869.
Billings, Montana Office: Suite 1500, First Interstate Center, 401 North 31st Street, P.O. Box 639.
Telephone: 406-252-2166.
Telecopier: 406-252-1669.
Salt Lake City, Utah Office: Suite 880, 111 East Broadway.
Telephone: 801-578-6000.
FAX: 801-578-6010.
Cheyenne, Wyoming Office: Holland & Hart, A Partnership including Professional Corporations, Suite 500, 2020 Carey Avenue, P.O. Box 1347.
Telephone: 307-778-4200.
Telecopier: 307-778-8175.
Jackson, Wyoming Office: Holland & Hart, A Partnership including Professional Corporations, Suite 2, 175 South King Street, P.O. Box 68.
Telephone: 307-739-9741.
Telecopier: 307-739-9744.

RESIDENT PARTNERS

J. Peter Luedtke
William F. Demarest, Jr.
Michael J. Brennan
Steven G. Barringer

OF COUNSEL

Thomas L. Sansonetti (Not admitted in DC)
Linda Arey Skladany

RESIDENT SPECIAL COUNSEL

Adelia Smith Borrasca

RESIDENT ASSOCIATES

Marci B. Anderson (Not admitted in DC)
C. William Groscup (Not admitted in DC)
Kelly Anne Johnson

For full biographical listings, see the Martindale-Hubbell Law Directory

HOLLAND & KNIGHT (AV)

A Partnership including Professional Corporations
2100 Pennsylvania Avenue, N.W., 20037
Telephone: 202-955-3000
Fax: 202-955-5564
Fort Lauderdale, Florida Office: One East Broward Boulevard, Suite 1300.
Telephone: 305-525-1000.
Fax: 305-463-2030.
Jacksonville, Florida Office: 50 N. Laura Street, Suite 3900.
Telephone: 904-353-2000.
Fax: 904-358-1872.
Lakeland, Florida Office: 92 Lake Wire Drive.
Telephone: 813-682-1161.
Fax: 813-688-1186.
Miami, Florida Office: 701 Brickell Avenue, 30th Floor.
Telephone: 305-374-8500.
Fax: 305-787-7799.
Orlando, Florida Office: 200 S. Orange Avenue, Suite 2600.
Telephone: 407-425-8500.
Fax: 407-244-5288.
St. Petersburg, Florida Office: 360 Central Avenue.
Telephone: 813-896-7171.
Fax: 813-822-8048.
Tallahassee, Florida Office: 315 Calhoun Street, Suite 600.
Telephone: 904-224-7000.
Fax: 904-224-8832.
Tampa, Florida Office: 400 North Ashley, Suite 2300.
Telephone: 813-227-8500.
Fax: 813-229-0134.
West Palm Beach, Florida Office: 625 N. Flagler Drive, Suite 700.
Telephone: 407-833-2000.
Fax: 407-650-8399.

(See Next Column)

HOLLAND & KNIGHT—*Continued*

Atlanta, Georgia Office: One Atlantic Center, 1201 West Peachtree Street, N.W., Suite 3100.
Telephone: 404-817-8500.
Fax: 404-881-0470.
Special Counsel: Shaw, Licitra, Parente, Esernio & Schwartz, P.C. 1010 Franklin Avenue, Garden City, N.Y., 11530 and 300 East 42nd Street, New York, N.Y., 10017.

WASHINGTON, D.C. MEMBERS AND ASSOCIATES

James E. Akers
Vicki-Ann E. Assevero
David H. Baker
Timothy J. Bloomfield
Stephen A. Bogorad
Mark E. Brodsky
Henry J. Brothers II
Harold R. Bucholtz
William B. Canfield, III
George A. Dalley
Ross W. Dembling
William J. Dempster
Steven A. Diaz (Not admitted in DC)
G. Richard Dunnells
Richard O. Duvall
Amy L. Edwards
Caleb L. Fowler
J. Edward Fowler (Not admitted in DC)
Robert E. Glenn, IV
Alvin J. Geske
Steven D. Gordon
T. Wayne Gray
John M. Himmelberg
Dennis M. Horn
David S. Kahn
Alan S. Kerxton
Paul J. Kiernan
Richard E. Lear
Jerry Levine
Michael L. Martinez
Dorn C. McGrath, III
Richard Lee Moorhouse
Alberto J. Mora
S. Scott Morrison
William J. Mutryn
Christopher A. Myers
Stephen J. Powell
Robert L. Rhodes, Jr.
John Thorpe Richards, Jr.
Christopher L. Rissetto
Michael J. Ruane
Alban Salaman
Stephen Brett Shapiro
Richard P. Sills
Judy G. Sinkin
Chesterfield Smith
Mitchell H. Stabbe
Andrew W. Stephenson
Scott Andrew Sterling
Janet R. Studley
Charles Welch Tiedemann
Robert P. Trout
Brent A. Wegner
Stephen J. Weiss

David G. Baldacci
Jennifer Crowe
Grover E. Czech
Philip Tucker Evans
Edward V. Hickey, III
Gina Schaar Howard
Abhi-Shé Jain (Not admitted in DC)
Edgar J. Jenkins
Bruce E. Kasold
George T. Magee
Joseph A. Massaro III (Not admitted in DC)
La Fonte Nesbitt
Stephen D. Niles
Suzanne Parmet
Angela T. Patrick
Henry Michael Renaud
Leslie A. Shanklin (Not admitted in DC)
Theodore S. Silva, Jr.
David C. Silver
Jennifer M. Smith
Gloria B. Solomon
Mary F. Withum

OF COUNSEL

Richard S. Weinstein (Not admitted in DC)

For full biographical listings, see the Martindale-Hubbell Law Directory

HOWREY & SIMON (AV)

1299 Pennsylvania Avenue, N.W., 20004-2402
Telephone: 202-783-0800
Fax: 202-383-6610
Los Angeles, California Office: Suite 1400, 550 South Hope Street.
Telephone: 213-892-1800.
Fax: 213-892-2300.

COUNSEL

Edward F. Howrey
William Simon
David C. Murchison
Harold F. Baker

MEMBERS OF FIRM

Robert G. Abrams
Scott Arnold
Jeffrey I. Auerbach
Gregory L. Baker
Alan I. Baron
George D. Billinson
John Bodner, Jr.
Ray S. Bolze
Gaspare J. Bono
Marguerite Smith Boyd
John DeQ. Briggs, III
Robert J. Brookhiser, Jr.
John F. Bruce
Robert M. Bruskin
William M. Bumpers
John G. Calender
Joanne E. Caruso
Michael R. Charness
Matthew J. Clark
Richard T. Colman
Basil C. Culyba
Lee P. Curtis
James F. Davis
James C. Duff
David C. Eddy
Charles J. Engel, III
Margaret H. Fitzsimmons
Scott E. Flick
Joel M. Freed
John G. Froemming
Kenneth A. Gallo
Jerrold J. Ganzfried
Sherry W. Gilbert
Cecilia H. Gonzalez
David B. Graham
Robert L. Green, Jr.
Alan M. Grimaldi
Stuart H. Harris
Philip H. Hecht
John E. Heintz
Edward P. Henneberry
Roxann E. Henry
Michael A. Hertzberg
Thomas N. Heyer
Thomas J. Horton
Robert H. Huey
Michael J. Hurley
Thomas A. Isaacson

(See Next Column)

MEMBERS OF FIRM (Continued)

Raymond A. Jacobsen, Jr.
Marcia Press Kaplan
Joel D. Kaufman
Richard H. Kjeldgaard
Roger A. Klein
John F. Kovin
Joseph P. Lavelle
Steven L. Leifer
Ezra C. Levine
Kathleen C. Little
Christopher H. Marraro
Rosemary H. McEnery
Katherine D. McManus
Peter E. Moll
Harold D. Murry, Jr.
John W. Nields, Jr.
Gary H. Nunes
William R. O'Brien
John C. Peirce
Eberhard W. Pfaller, Jr.
Paul Plaia, Jr.
Keith E. Pugh, Jr.
William A. Roberts, III
Stephen J. Rosenman
Robert F. Ruyak
Lisa J. Saks
Charles H. Samel
Ralph J. Savarese
Marc G. Schildkraut
Sheila Rae Schreiber
Claude F. Scott, Jr.
Thomas J. Scott, Jr.
Steven A. Shaw
Terrence C. Sheehy
Herbert C. Shelley
Harvey G. Sherzer
Robert H. Shulman
Richard E. Wallace, Jr.
William E. Wallace, III
Paul C. Warnke
William L. Webber
Mark D. Wegener
Judy Whalley
Edwin H. Wheeler
A. Duncan Whitaker
Lois G. Williams
Alan M. Wiseman
Alan R. Yuspeh
Carmine R. Zarlenga
Margaret M. Zwisler

OF COUNSEL

J. Eric André
Jonathan S. Feld

INTERNATIONAL TRADE COUNSEL

Alice Alexandra Kipel

GOVERNMENT CONTRACTS COUNSEL

Lucy Eliasof Gies

RESEARCH AND INFORMATION SERVICES COUNSEL

Kerry L. Adams

ASSOCIATES

Nancy E. Allin
F. Alexander Amrein
Michele Arington
Kyra C. Armstrong
Timothy K. Armstrong (Not admitted in DC)
Yvette F. Benguerel
Darren B. Bernhard
Leiv H. Blad, Jr.
John W. Bohn (Not admitted in DC)
Joanne Borsh
William M. Bosch (Not admitted in DC)
Timothy E. Boyle
R. Edward Brake (Not admitted in DC)
Daniel E. Brannen, Jr. (Not admitted in DC)
Mark D. Brazeal (Not admitted in DC)
Kenneth W. Brothers
Jeffrey D. Brown
James M. Burns
Patricia G. Butler
Celine T. Callahan
Allen Cannon III
Jerone C. Cecelic
Richard B. Clifford, Jr.
Juliana M. Cofrancesco
Michael Paul Austern Cohen
Gregory J. Commins, Jr.
Deborah L. Connor (Not admitted in DC)
Kellie A. Cosgrove (Not admitted in DC)
Michael G. Cowie
Alice M. Crook
Martin F. Cunniff
Brian A. Darst
Jeffrey S. Davis
Mindy G. Davis
Lara A. Degenhart (Not admitted in DC)
Diana L. Dietrich (Not admitted in DC)
Marlin Dohlman (Not admitted in DC)
Nicole B. Donath
Eric M. Drattell
Jon B. Dubrow
Dana A. Elfin
Elizabeth J. Faecher (Not admitted in DC)
Therese K. Francese
Jay W. Freiberg (Not admitted in DC)
Barbara A. Friedman
Ashley G. Gable
Peder A. Garske
Steven N. Gersten
Thomas E. Gilbertsen
Kathleen M. Graber (Not admitted in DC)
Charles E. Graf
Douglas S. Grandstaff
Jonathan G. Graves
Paul Greco
William J. Griffin (Not admitted in DC)
Jennifer M. Hall (Not admitted in DC)
Edward Han
Gregg A. Hand
Ronald G. Haron
Alan N. Harris
Joseph A. Hayes, III
Diane B. Heller
Maura Beth Henry (Not admitted in DC)
Gerald W. Hodgkins
John G. Horan
Julius Lloyd Horwich
William F. Hughes
Elissa L. Isaacs
Lisalyn R. Jacobs (Not admitted in DC)
Robert P. Jacobs
Karen L. James
Leo J. Jennings
Debra J. Jezouit
David R. Johnson
Stephen A. Jones
Karen E. Jorik (Not admitted in DC)
Mark L. Josephs (Not admitted in DC)
John W. Kampman
Andrew T. Kerr (Not admitted in DC)
Gilbert S. Keteltas
Anthony F. King
Carole R. Klein
James G. Kress
Lisa I. Latorre
Robert E. Leidenheimer, Jr.
Jeffrey M. Lenser

(See Next Column)

HOWREY & SIMON, *Washington—Continued*

ASSOCIATES (Continued)

Nancy C. Libin
(Not admitted in DC)
Charles A. Loughlin
(Not admitted in DC)
William E. McCabe
(Not admitted in DC)
James J. McGuire
(Not admitted in DC)
James T. McLaughlin
Scott S. Megregian
Richard S. Meyer
Helen Katherine Michael
Victor J. Miller
(Not admitted in DC)
Richard D. Milone, Jr.
Cynthia Mitchell
Harriet Mountcastle-Walsh
P. Todd Mullins
Karen L. Nicastro
Dimitri J. Nionakis
Rodney J. Nydam
Wendy S. Oatis
Patricia L. O'Beirne
Jennifer L. O'Connor
(Not admitted in DC)
Joseph A. Ostoyich
Callie Georgeann Pappas
David K. Park
(Not admitted in DC)
Hae-Chan Park
(Not admitted in DC)
Maria Tan Pedersen
(Not admitted in DC)
Dianne S. Pickersgill
(Not admitted in DC)
Michael R. Reck
H. Jonathan Redway
Kimberly D. Reed
(Not admitted in DC)
Kenneth M. Reiss
(Not admitted in DC)
Richard A. Ripley
Moira T. Roberts
(Not admitted in DC)
Jon Randall Roellke

Robin P. Rosen
(Not admitted in DC)
Howard T. Rosenblatt
John J. Rosenthal
William A. Sarraille
Scott A. Scheele
Matthew J. Schlesinger
Lisa A. Schneider
(Not admitted in DC)
Edward B. Schwartz
Craig P. Seebald
Suzanne Seftel
(Not admitted in DC)
Annelise L. Selvaggi
Andrew R. Shoemaker
Laura S. Shores
David F. Smutny
Kipp David Snider
(Not admitted in DC)
Andrew L. Snowdon
Patricia M. Steele
Marcia L. Stuart
(Not admitted in DC)
Gil M. Strobel
Anne Talbot
C. Scott Talbot
Andrew E. Thomas
Tamra L. Thompson
Thomas J. Trendl
ToQuyen T. Truong
Jill Tuennerman
James D. Villa
Ronald B. Vogt
James R. Wade
David S. Waehen
Brian D. Wallach
Adam W. Wegner
Ellen S. Winter
(Not admitted in DC)
Kirsten A. Wolfe
Richard L. Woodworth
(Not admitted in DC)
Christina S. Yu
(Not admitted in DC)
Paul N. Zolfagari

For full biographical listings, see the Martindale-Hubbell Law Directory

* HUGHES HUBBARD & REED (AV)

1300 I Street, N.W., Suite 900 West, 20005-3306
Telephone: 202-408-3600
Telex: 89-2674
Telecopier: 202-408-3636
New York, New York Office: One Battery Park Plaza, 10004.
Telephone: 212-837-6000.
Cable Address: "Hughreed, New York".
Telex: 427120.
Telecopier: 212-422-4726.
Los Angeles, California Office: 350 S. Grand Avenue, Suite 3600, 90071-3442.
Telephone: 213-613-2800.
Telecopier: 213-613-2950.
Miami, Florida Office: 801 Brickell Avenue, 33131.
Telephone: 305-358-1666.
Telex: 51-8785.
Telecopier: 305-3718759.
Paris, France Office: 47, Avenue Georges Mandel, 75116.
Telephone: 33.1.44.05.80.00.
Cable Address: "Hughreed, Paris."
Telex: 645440.
Telecopier: 33.1.45.53.15.04.
Berlin, Germany Office: Kurfürstendamm 44, W-1000 Berlin 15.
Telephone: 030-880008-0.
Telefax: 030-880008-65.
Telex: 185803 KNAPA D.

RESIDENT PARTNERS

Lawrence F. Bates
Elizabeth J. Keefer
Dennis S. Klein

Robert P. Reznick
Kathleen M. Russo
William R. Stein

John M. Townsend

SENIOR ATTORNEY

Alan G. Kashdan

OF COUNSEL

Albert P. Lindemann, Jr.

For full biographical listings, see the Martindale-Hubbell Law Directory

JACKSON & CAMPBELL, P.C. (AV)

South Tower, One Lafayette Centre, 1120-20th Street, N.W., 20036
Telephone: 202-457-1600
International Telex: 64706
Telecopier: 202-457-1678
Rockville, Maryland Office: Suite 225, 200 A Monroe Street.
Telephone: 301-340-0450.
Baltimore, Maryland Office: 111 S. Calvert Street, Suite 2700.
Telephone: 410-385-5343.
Arlington, Virginia Office: 2009 North 14th Street, Suite 408.
Telephone: 703-522-1330.

Thomas Searing Jackson
(1909-1989)
Benjamin W. Dulany
Kenneth Wells Parkinson
Peter F. Axelrad
Arthur C. Elgin, Jr.
James P. Schaller
Jo V. Morgan, Jr.
Patricia D. Gurne
Alan R. Swendiman
Nicholas S. McConnell
Donald N. Memmer
James R. Michal
M. Elizabeth Medaglia
David H. Cox
Michael J. McManus
John J. Brennan, III
Richard W. Bryan
Christopher B. Hanback
Arthur D. Burger
William F. Causey
Christine A. Nykiel
Timothy R. Dingilian
Paul S. Schleifman
Robert N. Kelly
Richard J. DeFeo, Jr.
Mary Lynn Reed
H. Kenneth Kudon
Martha Purcell Rogers
Peter E. Robey
James E. Cervenak
Nicholas P. Jellins
(Not admitted in DC)
Kathleen Kenny
(Not admitted in DC)
Richard L. Schwartz
Mary Rudolph
(Not admitted in DC)

Warren Lutz
Maureen P. Kerrigan
Kirsten Kingdon
(Not admitted in DC)
Peter A. von Mehren
John M. Vassiliades
Douglas C. McAllister
Robert Clayton Cooper
Scott Alton Mills
Robert E. Rider, Jr.
Margery J. Lexa
Kenneth E. Ryan
Richard S. Kuhl
(Not admitted in DC)
Vernon W. Johnson, III
Donald L. Uttrich
Joanna M. Pedas
Tonia Jones Powell
John A. Bonello
David M. Treese
Elizabeth Deren Breast
Louis E. Dolan, Jr.
(Not admitted in DC)
Mark A. Goodin
Paul T. Gallagher
Robert G. Honigman
Gwendolyn R. Majette
(Not admitted in DC)
Gregory H Horowitz
(Not admitted in DC)
Kent E. Lewis
(Not admitted in DC)
Adam S. Caldwell
(Not admitted in DC)
Maria A. Perugini
(Not admitted in DC)
Mary Anne Hilliard

OF COUNSEL

Edmund D. Campbell

For full biographical listings, see the Martindale-Hubbell Law Directory

JACKSON & KELLY (AV)

2401 Pennsylvania Avenue, N.W., Suite 400, 20037
Telephone: 202-973-0200
Fax: 202-973-0232
Charleston, West Virginia Office: 1600 Laidley Tower, P.O. Box 553.
Telephone: 304-340-1000.
Martinsburg, West Virginia Office: 300 Foxcroft Avenue, P. O. Box 1068.
Telephone: 304-263-8800.
Charles Town, West Virginia Office: 700 East Washington Street, P.O. Box 983.
Telephone: 304-728-6088.
Clarksburg, West Virginia Office: 203 Main Street.
Telephone: 304-623-3002.
Morgantown, West Virginia Office: 6000 Hampton Center, P.O. Box 619.
Telephone: 304-599-3000.
New Martinsville, West Virginia Office: 256 Russell Avenue, P.O. Box 68.
Telephone: 304-455-1751.
Lexington, Kentucky Office: 175 East Main Street, Suite 500, P.O. Box 2150.
Telephone: 606-255-9500.
Denver, Colorado Office: Suite 2700, 1660 Lincoln Street.
Telephone: 303-837-0003.

MEMBERS OF FIRM

Henry Chajet
Mark N. Savit

Thad S. Huffman
G. Lindsay Simmons

L. Poe Leggette

ASSOCIATES

James Zissler (Not admitted in DC)

LEGAL SUPPORT PERSONNEL

Janet R. Robin

For full biographical listings, see the Martindale-Hubbell Law Directory

Washington—Continued

*** JONES, DAY, REAVIS & POGUE (AV)**

Metropolitan Square, 1450 G Street, N.W., 20005-2088
Telephone: 202-879-3939
Cable Address: "Attorneys Washington"
Telex: W.U. (Domestic) 89-2410 ATTORNEYS WASH (International) 64363 ATTORNEYS WASH
Telecopier: 202-737-2832
In Atlanta, Georgia: 3500 One Peachtree Center, 303 Peachtree Street, N.E .
Telephone: 404-521-3939.
Cable Address: "Attorneys Atlanta".
Telex: 54-2711.
Telecopier: 404-581-8330.
In Brussels, Belgium: Avenue Louise 480, 7th Floor, B-1050 Brussels.
Telephone: 011-32-2-645-14-11.
Telecopier: 011-32-2-645-14-45.
In Chicago, Illinois: 77 West Wacker.
Telephone: 312-782-3939.
Telecopier: 312-782-8585.
In Cleveland, Ohio: North Point, 901 Lakeside Avenue.
Telephone: 216-586-3939.
Cable Address: "Attorneys Cleveland."
Telex: 980389.
Telecopier: 216-579-0212.
In Columbus, Ohio: 1900 Huntington Center.
Telephone: 614-469-3939.
Cable Address: "Attorneys Columbus."
Telecopier: 614-461-4198.
In Dallas, Texas: 2300 Trammell Crow Center, 2001 Ross Avenue.
Telephone: 214-220-3939.
Cable Address: "Attorneys Dallas."
Telex: 730852.
Telecopier: 214-969-5100.
In Frankfurt, Germany: Triton Haus, Bockenheimer Landstrasse 42, 60323 Frankfurt am Main.
Telephone: 49-69-9726-3939.
Telecopier: 49-69-9726-3993.
In Geneva, Switzerland: 20, rue de Candolle.
Telephone: 011-41-22-320-2339.
Telecopier: 011-41-22-320-1232.
In Hong Kong: 1501 One Exchange Square, 8 Connaught Place.
Telephone: 011-852-2526-6895.
Telecopier: 011-852-2810-5787.
In Irvine, California: 2603 Main Street, Suite 900 .
Telephone: 714-851-3939.
Telex: 194911 Lawyers LSA.
Telecopier: 714-553-7539.
In London, England: One Mount Street.
Telephone: 011-44-71-493-9361.
Cable Address: "Surgoe London WI."
Telecopier: 011-44-71-493-9666.
In Los Angeles, California: 555 West Fifth Street, Suite 4600.
Telephone: 213-489-3939.
Telex: 181439 UD.
Telecopier: 213-243-2539.
In New York, New York: 599 Lexington Avenue.
Telephone: 212-326-3939.
Cable Address: "JONESDAY NEWYORK."
Telex: 237013 JDRP UR.
Telecopier: 212-755-7306.
In Paris, France: 62, rue du Faubourg Saint-Honore.
Telephone: 011-33-1-44-71-3939.
Cable Address: "Surgoe Paris."
Telex: 290156 Surgoe.
Telecopier: 011-33-1-49-24-0471.
In Pittsburgh, Pennsylvania: 500 Grant Street, 31st Floor.
Telephone: 412-391-3939.
Cable Address: "Attorneys Pittsburgh".
Telecopier: 412-394-7959.
In Riyadh, Saudi Arabia: Law Offices of Saud M.A. Shawwaf, P.O. Box 2700.
Telephones: 011 (966-1) 465-6543, 011 (966-1) 464-8534 or 011 (966-1) 464-8540.
Telex: 401831 SAUCON SJ.
Telecopier: (966-1) 464-8480.
In Taipai, Taiwan: 8th Floor, 2 Tun Hwa South Road, Section 2.
Telephone: 011 (886-2) 704-6808.
Telecopier: 011 (886-2) 704-6791.
In Tokyo, Japan: Toranomon MT Building, 4th Floor, 10-3, Toranomon 3-Chome, Minato-Ku, Tokyo 105, Japan.
Telephone: 011-81-3-3433-3939.
Telecopier: 011-81-3-5401-2725.

MEMBERS OF FIRM IN WASHINGTON, D.C.

Joseph S. Iannucci
Michael Bradfield
Timothy B. Dyk
James T. O'Hara
David A. Copus
Frieda K. Wallison
J. Lawrence Manning, Jr.
Jonathan C. Rose
Sigmund T. Weiner
Robert F. McDermott, Jr.
Joe Sims
William E. Sudow
James J. Graham
Donald D. Kozusko
C. Thomas Long
Mark K. Sisitsky
Junius C. McElveen, Jr.
Paul S. Ryerson

(See Next Column)

MEMBERS OF FIRM IN WASHINGTON, D.C. (Continued)

Tom D. Smith
Joseph M. David, Jr. (Not admitted in DC)
Clark Evans Downs
Willis J. Goldsmith
Phillip A. Proger
Thomas F. Cullen, Jr.
George T. Manning
Robert S. Waters
Richard D. Avil, Jr.
Donald B. Ayer
Lawrence L. Lamade
Norman A. Pedersen
David C. Roseman
Lester W. Droller
Raymond J. Wiacek
Stephen J. Brogan
Randall E. Davis
Timothy J. Finn
Stephen C. Jones
Gregory M. Luce
Toby G. Singer
Kathryn M. Fenton
Peter F. Garvin, III
Kevin D. McDonald
Thomas F. McKim
Kenneth J. Ayres
Charles A. James
Robert H. Klonoff
Mary Ellen Powers
Steven A. Teitelbaum
Peter J. Biersteker
Susan Zywien Haller
Carolyn Y. Thompson
Christopher F. Dugan
Patricia A. Dunn
Kevin D. Cramer
Glen D. Nager
Adrian Wager-Zito
Barbara McDowell

OF COUNSEL

Herbert J. Hansell (Not admitted in DC)
William E. Swope
William J. Schilling
George Van Cleve
Peter E. Heyward
Timothy E. Flanigan

SENIOR ATTORNEYS

Robert C. Jones
Edward B. Myers
Jerome J. Zaucha
Mary Dobson McDonald
Stephen J. Goodman

ASSOCIATES

Melissa T. Scanlon
Adel B.A. Al-Ali (Not admitted in the United States)
Heidi Hughes Bumpers
Brian P. Maschler (Not admitted in DC)
Kay Albaugh Hooker
Mary L. Hale
Charles V. Stewart
Julia M. Broas
Beth Heifetz
Ismail E. Laher (Not admitted in DC)
David M. Matuszewski
Kathleen Marie McChesney
William V. O'Reilly
Richard F. Shaw
James D. Wareham
James E. Anklam
Thomas B. Burnside (Not admitted in DC)
Mary T. Borer Green
Michael P. Gurdak
Robert J. Hill
David E. Miller
Gregory M. Shumaker
Kevin J. McIntyre
Candace A. Ridgway
Karen E. Silverman
James E. Gauch (Not admitted in DC)
Keith W. Holman
Deena B. Jenab
R. Todd Johnson
Anthony P. Lalla
Steven J. Mintz
Laura A. Scruggs
Lily Diane Bellini
Gregory A. Castanias
Colleen Covell
Denise A. Fee
Edwin L. Fountain
Paul W. Moskowitz
James R. Saxenian
Kevin D. Solonsky
Karl M. Tilleman (Not admitted in DC)
Dennis D. Dillon (Not admitted in DC)
Sharon Fast Gustafson
Janet A. Hendrick
Stephen J. Jorden
Stephen D. Kiess
Martin V. Kirkwood
Darryl R. Marsch
Ronald Wesley Sharpe
Padmini Singh
Lynne A. Wurzburg (Not admitted in DC)
Geoffrey K. Beach
Thomas M. Beck
Jonathan D. Bergman
Daniel H. Bromberg (Not admitted in DC)
Alice M. Goldwire
Dianne Schaefer Gurdak
Heather A. Lowry
Philip C. Nchekwube
Andrew S. Reilly
Michael J. Robinson
David J. Schenck
Michael R. Shumaker
Peter J. Wang
Jonathan Berman (Not admitted in DC)
Richard J. Caplan (Not admitted in DC)
Karie L. Delshad-Nik (Not admitted in DC)
Gregory G. Katsas (Not admitted in DC)
William K. Kelso (Not admitted in DC)
Peter J. Love (Not admitted in DC)
Laura Musial (Not admitted in DC)
Mary-Helen Perry (Not admitted in DC)
Gary P. Zanfagna (Not admitted in DC)
Joshua A. Briggs (Not admitted in DC)
Gretchen E. Crews
Sarah B. McClure (Not admitted in DC)
Hendrik A. Bourgeois (Not admitted in DC)
Catherine M. Stavrakis (Not admitted in DC)
Kristian E. Wiggert (Not admitted in DC)
Hussein A.H. Damirji (Not admitted in DC)
Harry I. Johnson III (Not admitted in DC)
Michael L. Kolis (Not admitted in DC)
Michael J. Kresslein (Not admitted in DC)
Kevin C. Maclay (Not admitted in DC)
Stephen F. Smith (Not admitted in DC)
Debra A. Ulven (Not admitted in DC)
Mark E. Ulven (Not admitted in DC)

(See Next Column)

JONES, DAY, REAVIS & POGUE, *Washington—Continued*

SENIOR STAFF ATTORNEY

John P. McGrane, Jr.

For full biographical listings, see the Martindale-Hubbell Law Directory

* JONES, WALDO, HOLBROOK & McDONOUGH, A PROFESSIONAL CORPORATION (AV)

Suite 900, 2300 M Street, N.W., 20037
Telephone: 202-296-5950
Telecopier: 202-293-2509
Salt Lake City, Utah Office: 1500 First Interstate Plaza, 170 South Main Street.
Telephone: 801-521-3200.
Telecopier: 801-328-0537.
St. George, Utah Office: The Tabernacle Tower Building, 249 East Tabernacle.
Telephone: 801-628-1627.
Telecopier: 801-628-5225.

David B. Lee
Barry D. Wood
Kay Allan Morrell
(Not admitted in DC)

For full biographical listings, see the Martindale-Hubbell Law Directory

* KAYE, SCHOLER, FIERMAN, HAYS & HANDLER (AV)

McPherson Building, 901 Fifteenth Street, N.W., Suite 1100, 20005
Telephone: 202-682-3500
Telex: 897458 KAYSCHOL WSH.
Facsimile: 202-682-3580
New York, N.Y.: 425 Park Avenue, 10022.
Telephone: 212-836-8000.
Telex: 234860 KAY UR.
Facsimile: 212-836-8689.
Los Angeles, California: 1999 Avenue of the Stars, Suite 1600, 90067.
Telephone: 213-788-1000.
Facsimile: 213-788-1200.
Hong Kong: 9 Queen Road Centre, 18th Floor.
Telephone: 852-8458989.
Telex: 62816 KAY HX.
Facsimile: 852-8453682; 852-8452389.
Beijing (Peking), People's Republic of China: Scite Tower, Suite 708, 22 Jianguomenwai Dajie, 100004.
Telephone: 861-5124755.
Telex: 222540 KAY CN.
Facsimile: 861-5124760.

RESIDENT PARTNERS

Terrence B. Adamson
David O. Bickart
David J. Branson
Alan W. Granwell
G. Christopher Griner
Ronald K. Henry
Michael P. House
Jonathan D. Schiller
Jason L. Shrinsky
Randall L. Speck

SPECIAL COUNSEL

William D. Eberle (P.A.)
(Not admitted in DC)
Abraham A. Ribicoff

COUNSEL

Robert C. Bell, Jr.
Christopher R. Brewster
Bruce Alan Eisen
Irving Gastfreund
John W. Schryber
James M. Weitzman

RESIDENT ASSOCIATES

Tracy E. Ballard
(Not admitted in DC)
Sylvia M. Becker
John G. Bickerman
Annette M. Capretta
Peter C. Condron
Daniel J. Culhane
Jana DeSirgh
Nancy Evert
(Not admitted in DC)
Timothy J. Feighery
(Not admitted in DC)
William A. Isaacson
Farhad Jalinous
Laura E. Jehl
Nancy L. Kiefer
(Not admitted in DC)
Kenneth L. Marcus
John R. Miles
Allan Gary Moskowitz
Raymond Paretzky
R. Will Planert
Gary S. Thompson

For full biographical listings, see the Martindale-Hubbell Law Directory

* KECK, MAHIN & CATE (AV)

A Partnership including Professional Corporations
Penthouse, 1201 New York Avenue, N.W., 20005-3919
Telephone: 202-789-3400
Telecopier: 202-789-1158
Chicago, Illinois Office: 77 West Wacker Drive, Suite 4900.
Telephone: 312-634-7700.
Fax: 312-634-5000.
Peoria, Illinois Office: Suite 640, 331 Fulton Street.
Telephone: 309-673-1681.
Oakbrook Terrace, Illinois Office: Suite 1000, One Mid America Plaza.
Telephone: 708-954-2100.
Telecopier: 708-954-2112.

(See Next Column)

Schaumburg, Illinois Office: Suite 250 Schaumburg Corporate Center, 1515 East Woodfield Road.
Telephone: 708-330-1200.
Telecopier: 708-330-1220.
Houston, Texas Office: 2800 First City Main Building, 1021 Main Street.
Telephone: 713-951-0990.
Telecopier: 713-951-0987.
Los Angeles, California Office: 2029 Century Park East, Suite 2500.
Telephone: 310-284-8771.
Fax: 310-284-8359.
San Francisco, California Office: One Maritime Plaza, Golden Gateway Center, 23rd Floor.
Telephone: 415-392-7077.
Fax: 415-392-3969.
New York, N.Y. Office: 220 E. 42nd Street.
Telephone: 212-682-3060.
Fax: 212-490-3918.

MEMBERS OF FIRM

Robert F. Aldrich
David F. Bantleon
Kenneth D. Brody
Ronald D. Cohn
Martin Fleit
Gary J. Gasper
Stephen C. Glazier
Michael A. Gollin
Robert E. Greenberg
Daniel G. Grove
Robin W. Grover
Carol A. Joffe
Thomas R. Jolly
Stanley S. Jutkowitz
Albert H. Kramer
George William Lewis
(Not admitted in DC)
Charles B. Molster, III
Philip L. O'Neill
Lewis J. Paper
Cyrus E. Phillips, IV
(Not admitted in DC)
Carlos M. Recio
Susan Anne Sinclair
Norman H. Singer
Kenneth S. Slaughter
Joan F. Symansky
Steven A. Weiler

OF COUNSEL

Louis H. Diamond
Carl E. Zwisler III

ASSOCIATES

Matthew T. Bailey
Thomas P. Cassidy
John M. Craig
Richard R. Diefendorf
(Not admitted in DC)
Glenn W. D. Golding
Judith A. Hoggan
David B. Jeppsen
Dana J. Lesemann
(Not admitted in DC)
Todd E. Marlette
(Not admitted in DC)
Ruth N. Morduch
Patrick W. Reilly
Douglas E. Rosenfeld

For full biographical listings, see the Martindale-Hubbell Law Directory

* KILPATRICK & CODY (AV)

Suite 800, 700 13th Street, N.W., 20005
Telephone: 202-508-5800
Telephone Copier: 202-508-5858
Atlanta, Georgia Office: Suite 2800, 1100 Peachtree Street.
Telephone: 404-815-6500. Telephone Copier: 404-815-6555.
Telex: 54-2307.
Augusta, Georgia Office: Suite 1400, First Union Bank Building, P.O. Box 2043, 30903.
Telephone: 706-724-2622.
Telecopier: 706-722-0219.
Brussels, Belgium Office: Avenue Louise 65, BTE 3, 1050 Brussels.
Telephone: (32) (2) 533-03-00.
Telecopier: (32) (2) 534-86-38.
London, England Office: 68 Pall Mall, London SW1Y 5ES, England.
Telephone: (44) (71) 321 0477.
Telecopier: (44) (71) 930 9733.

MEMBERS OF FIRM

Elliott H. Levitas
Frederick H. von Unwerth
J. Vance Hughes
C. Randall Nuckolls
Martha Jo Wagner
Thomas K. Bick
Neil I. Levy (Resident)
Mark D. Wincek
Walter E. Spiegel (Resident)
John C. Hall (Resident)
Kurt E. Blase

COUNSEL

David P. Phippen (Resident)

ASSOCIATES

John C. Anderson
Joel D. Bush, II
Victoria A. Cochran
Diane L. Griffin
(Not admitted in DC)
Paul Vincent Lalli
(Not admitted in DC)
Christopher B. Lyman
(Not admitted in DC)
Kenneth J. Markowitz
Devon Lee Miller (Resident)
Emmett H. Miller
Ronald L. Raider (Resident)
Charles T. Simmons (Resident)

For full biographical listings, see the Martindale-Hubbell Law Directory

Washington—Continued

*** KING & SPALDING (AV)**

1730 Pennsylvania Avenue, N.W., 20006-4706
Telephone: 202-737-0500
FAX: 202-626-3737
Atlanta, Georgia Office: 191 Peachtree Street, N.E., 30303-1763.
Telephone: 404-572-4600.
FAX: 404-572-5100.
Cable: "Terminus".
Telex: 54-2917 KINSPALD ATL.
New York, N.Y. Office: 120 West 45th Street. 10036-4003.
Telephone: 212-556-2100.
Fax: 212-556-2222.
Telex: 6716353. Answerback: Compris.

RESIDENT PARTNERS

William S. McKee
Theodore M. Hester (Not admitted in DC)
Abraham N. M. Shashy, Jr. (Not admitted in DC)
Harry L. Gutman (Not admitted in DC)
Joseph W. Dorn
James D. Miller
Jackie S. Levinson
Steven R. Lainoff
Eugene M. Pfeifer
William C. Hendricks III
Mark A. Kuller (Not admitted in DC)
Jess H. Stribling
Edward M. Basile
Stanley H. Abramson
Katherine L. Rhyne
Joseph Sedwick Sollers III
Thomas F. Wessel
Martin M. McNerney
Frederick H. Degnan
Sandra W. Hallmark
R. Anthony Howard, Jr.
Michael P. Mabile
Dvorah A. Richman

RESIDENT COUNSEL

William C. Talmadge (Not admitted in DC)
Susan Jewett
Veronica G. Kayne
Harold M. Shaw
Sandra Cohen Kalter
James A. Hughes, Jr.
Paul J. Larkin, Jr.
Herbert A. Glaser
Mark S. Brown (Not admitted in DC)

RESIDENT ASSOCIATES

Deborah J. Andrews
Donald D. Ashley (Not admitted in DC)
Matthew L. Bennett (Not admitted in DC)
Daniel D. Bosis, Jr. (Not admitted in DC)
Barbara D. Carswell
Ellen J. Case (Not admitted in DC)
Stephen G. Charbonnet (Not admitted in DC)
Kerrie Covell Dent
Gregory C. Dorris
Keith E. Engel
Zachary Thomas Fardon (Not admitted in DC)
Joe Garcia, Jr. (Not admitted in DC)
Susan L. Heilbronner (Not admitted in DC)
Mona Lucille Hymel (Not admitted in DC)
Neil J. Kiely (Not admitted in DC)
Jill Swerdloff Klein
Marilyn J. Kuray
Todd Y. McArthur
Michael R. Pauze (Not admitted in DC)
Polly J. Price (Not admitted in DC)
Susan S. Quarngesser (Not admitted in DC)
Elizabeth A. Schmidtlein (Not admitted in DC)
William S. Shackelford
James C. Snyder, Jr.

For full biographical listings, see the Martindale-Hubbell Law Directory

KROOTH & ALTMAN (AV)

Suite 400, 1850 M Street, N.W., 20036-5803
Telephone: 202-293-8200
Telecopier: 202-872-0145, 202-775-5872
Columbia, Maryland Office: 5401 Twin Knolls Road, Suite 7, 21045.
Telephone: 301-596-1140.
Sterling, Virginia Office: 20 Pidgeon Hill Drive, Suite 101, 22170.
Telephone: 703-450-2755.

MEMBERS OF FIRM

David L. Krooth (1907-1978)
Norman S. Altman
Victor A. Altman
William S. Tennant
William J. Delany
Donald F. Libretta
E. Joseph Knoll
Michael E. Mazer
Daniel Randolph Cole, Jr.
Patrick J. Clancy
James F. Perna
Harrison C. Smith
Robert C. Seldon

OF COUNSEL

Michael J. Milton (Not admitted in DC)
John E. Vihstadt (Not admitted in DC)
Robert J. Siciliano

ASSOCIATES

Mario Greszes
David A. Barsky
Jon I. Opert (Not admitted in DC)
Felicia M. Groner
Bonnie Y. Hochman

For full biographical listings, see the Martindale-Hubbell Law Directory

*** KUTAK ROCK (AV)**

A Partnership including Professional Corporations
Suite 1000, 1101 Connecticut Avenue, N.W., 20036-4374
Telephone: 202-828-2400
Fax: 202-828-2488
Atlanta, Georgia Office: 4400 Georgia-Pacific Center, 133 Peachtree Street, NE, 30303-1808.
Telephone: 404-222-4600.
Facsimile: 404-222-4654.
Baton Rouge, Louisiana Office: 300 Four United Plaza, 8555 United Plaza Boulevard, 70809-2251.
Telephone: 504-929-8585.
Facsimile: 504-929-8580.
Denver, Colorado Office: Suite 2900, 717 Seventeenth Street, 80202-3329.
Telephone: 303-297-2400.
Facsimile: 303-292-7799.
Kansas City, Missouri Office: United Missouri Bank Building, Third Floor, 9201 Ward Parkway.
Telephone: 816-361-3363.
Telecopier: 816-361-8397.
Little Rock, Arkansas Office: Suite 1770, 124 West Capitol Avenue, 72201-3719.
Telephone: 501-376-9208.
Facsimile: 501-375-3749.
Los Angeles, California Office: Suite 1330, 2049 Century Park East, 90067-3115.
Telephone: 310-785-3900.
Facsimile: 310-785-3999.
New York, New York Office: Seventh Floor, 505 Park Avenue, 10022-1155.
Telephone: 212-752-0800.
Facsimile: 212-752-2281.
Oklahoma City, Oklahoma Office: Suite 475, 6305 Waterford Boulevard, 73118-1116.
Telephone: 405-232-9827.
Facsimile: 405-232-8307.
Omaha, Nebraska Office: The Omaha Building, 1650 Farnam Street, 68102-2186.
Telephone: 402-346-6000.
Facsimile: 402-346-1148.
Phoenix, Arizona Office: 16th Floor, 3300 North Central Avenue, 85012-1984.
Telephone: 602-285-1700.
Facsimile: 602-285-1868.
Pittsburgh, Pennsylvania Office: 1214 Frick Building, 437 Grant Street, 15219-6002.
Telephone: 412-261-6720.
Facsimile: 412-261-6717.

SPECIAL COUNSEL

George R. Schlossberg

OF COUNSEL

Thomas E. Plank

MEMBERS OF FIRM

Mitchell J. Bragin
W. Kimball Griffith
Thomas C. Evans
Allen S. Rugg
Joseph A. Ingrisano
Arlene Fine
Dianne Loennig Stoddard
John E. Theberge
Robert L. Magielnicki
Patricia Magee Daly
Alan D. Strasser
Margo BeVier Stern
Patrick F. Brown
Alicia A. Terry

ASSOCIATES

Ronald R. Massumi
Jill Ann Byrne
Gilbert W. Boyce
Sunita B. Lough
Jeffrey S. Ballard
James B. Hoffman
Michael D. Bopp (Not admitted in DC)
Bruce M. Serchuk (Not admitted in DC)
Pamela Schmidt Joaquin (Not admitted in DC)
Susan A. Mathews

For full biographical listings, see the Martindale-Hubbell Law Directory

LEFTWICH & DOUGLAS (AV)

Suite 1100, 1133 15th Street, N.W., 20005
Telephone: 202-872-1155
Facsimile: 202-467-4182

MEMBERS OF FIRM

Willie L. Leftwich
Frederick A. Douglas
James R. Murphy
Michael M. Hicks
Natalie O. Ludaway
Nicholas S. Penn

ASSOCIATES

Melvin L. Doxie
Brian K. Pearlstein
Thomas D. Bridenbaugh
Julie Ann Kaminski (Not admitted in DC)
Tinya L. Banks (Not admitted in DC)
Vicki Craig

For full biographical listings, see the Martindale-Hubbell Law Directory

Washington—Continued

*** LINOWES AND BLOCHER (AV)**

Suite 840, 800 K Street, N.W., 20001
Telephone: 202-408-3220
Telecopier: 202-408-1719
Silver Spring, Maryland Office: Suite 1000, 1010 Wayne Avenue.
Telephone: 301-588-8580.
Telecopier: 301-495-9044.
Greenbelt, Maryland Office: Suite 402, 6411 Ivy Lane.
Telephone: 301-982-3382.
Telecopier: 301-982-0595.
Annapolis, Maryland Office: 145 Main Street, P.O. Box 31.
Telephone: 410-268-0881.
Telecopier: 301-261-2603.
Frederick, Maryland Office: Suite 102, 228 W. Patrick Street.
Telephone: 301-695-0244.
Telecopier: 301-663-6656.
Columbia, Maryland Office: Suite B215, 10015 Old Columbia Road.
Telephone: 410-312-5457.
Fax: 410-290-5285.

MEMBERS OF FIRM

Phil T. Feola (Resident)
Cynthia A. Giordano (Resident)
Jerry A. Moore III (Resident)
John R. Orrick, Jr.

SENIOR COUNSEL

R. Robert Linowes

OF COUNSEL

Gary Altman
Myles Hannan (Not admitted in DC)

For full biographical listings, see the Martindale-Hubbell Law Directory

MARKS & MURASE (AV)

Suite 750, 2001 L Street, N.W., 20036-4910
Telephone: 202-955-4900
Telex: 248749
FAX: (202) 955-4933; 955-4932
New York, New York Office: 399 Park Avenue.
Telephone: 212-318-7700.
Los Angeles, California Office: Suite 1570, The Wells Fargo Center, 333 South Grand Avenue.
Telephone: 213-620-9690.

MEMBERS OF FIRM

Michael D. Bednarek
Paul Devinsky
Ronald P. Kananen
Richard Linn
George T. Marcou
Ramon P. Marks (Not admitted in DC)
Neil E. McDonell (Not admitted in DC)
Roger L. Selfe

OF COUNSEL

Matthew J. Marks

ASSOCIATES

George C. Beck

For full biographical listings, see the Martindale-Hubbell Law Directory

*** MAYER, BROWN & PLATT (AV)**

2000 Pennsylvania Avenue, N.W., 20006-1882
Telephone: (202) 463-2000
Pitney Bowes: (202) 861-0484, Pitney Bowes: (202) 861-0473
Telex: 892603
Cable: LEMAYDC
Chicago, Illinois Office: 190 South LaSalle Street, 60603-3441.
Telephone: (312) 782-0600. Pitney Bowes: (312) 701-7711.
Telex: 190404.
Cable: LEMAY.
New York, New York Office: 787 Seventh Avenue, Suite 2400, 10019-6018.
Telephone: (212) 554-3000. Pitney Bowes: (212) 262-1910.
Telex: 701842.
Cable: LEMAYEN.
Houston, Texas Office: 700 Louisiana Street, Suite 3600, 77002-2730.
Telephone: (713) 221-1651. Pitney Bowes: (713) 224-6410.
Telex: 775809.
Cable: LEMAYHOU.
Los Angeles, California Office: 350 South Grand Avenue, 25th Floor, 90071-1503.
Telephone: (213) 229-9500. Pitney Bowes: (213) 625-0248.
Telex: 188089.
Cable: LEMAYLA.
London, England Office: 162 Queen Victoria Street, EC4V 4DB.
Telephone: 011-44-71-248-1465.
Fax: 011-44-71-329-4465.
Telex: 8811095.
Cable: LEMAYLDN.
Tokyo, Japan Office: (Kawachi Gaikokuho Jimu Bengoshi Jimusho), Urbannet Otemachi Building 13F 2-2, Otemachi 2-chome, Chiyoda-ku, Tokyo 100.
Telephone: 011-81-3-5255-9700.
Facsimile: 011-81-3-5255-9797.

(See Next Column)

Berlin, Germany Office: Spreeufer 5, 10178.
Telephone: 011-49-30-240-7930.
Facsimile: 011-49-30-240-79344.
Brussels, Belgium Office: Square de Meeûs 19/20, Bte. 4, 1040.
Telephone: 011-32-2-512-9878.
Fax: 11-32-2-511-3305.
Telex: 20768 MBPBRU B.
Mexico City, Mexico, D.F., Mexico Correspondent: Jáuregui, Navarrete, Nader y Rojas, S.C., Abogados, Paseo de la Reforma 199, Pisos 15, 16 y 17, 06500, Mexico.
Telephone: 011-525-591-16-55.
Facsimile: 011-525-535-80-62; 011-525-703-22-47.
Cable: JANANE.

PARTNERS

Diane E. Ambler
Robert E. Bloch
David I. Bloom
Charles Chu
Robert P. Davis
Roy T. Englert, Jr.
Richard J. Favretto
Andrew L. Frey
Marc Gary
Kenneth S. Geller
Mark H. Gitenstein
Lloyd S. Guerci
Charles M. Horn
Erika Z. Jones
Simeon M. Kriesberg
Philip Allen Lacovara
Jerry L. Oppenheimer
Carolyn P. Osolinik
Stuart P. Pergament
Andrew J. Pincus
Lawrence S. Robbins
Mark W. Ryan
John P. Schmitz
Brian W. Smith
Adrian L. Steel, Jr.
Robert H. Swart
Evan M. Tager
Charles S. Triplett (Tax Counsel)

OF COUNSEL

Richard K. Matta
Amy L. Nathan
Charles Rothfeld

ASSOCIATES

Courtney D. Allison (Not admitted in DC)
Carol J. Bilzi
Paul S. Bock
Kim Marie Kozaczek Boylan
H. Thomas Byron, III (Not admitted in DC)
M. Lindsay Childress
David C. Crane (Not admitted in DC)
Thomas DiLenge (Not admitted in DC)
James Gregory Duncan (Not admitted in DC)
Kerry Lynn Edwards
Donald M. Falk
Michael I. Gilman
Myles R. Hansen (Not admitted in DC)
Molly F. James (Not admitted in DC)
Kathryn A. Kusske
Scott P. Perlman
Laurie R. Rubenstein
Adam C. Sloane (Not admitted in DC)
John J. Sullivan
Alan E. Untereiner
Gary A. Winters (Not admitted in DC)

For full biographical listings, see the Martindale-Hubbell Law Directory

*** McCUTCHEN, DOYLE, BROWN & ENERSEN (AV)**

The Evening Star Building, Suite 800, 1101 Pennsylvania Avenue, N.W., 20004-2514
Telephone: 202-628-4900
Facsimile: 202-628-4912
San Francisco, California Office: Three Embarcadero Center, 94111-4066.
Telephone: 415-393-2000.
Facsimile: 415-393-2286 (GI, II, III).
Telex: 340817 MACPAG SFO.
Los Angeles, California Office: 355 South Grand Avenue, Suite 4400, 90071-1560.
Telephone: 213-680-6400.
Facsimile: 213-680-6499.
San Jose, California Office: Market Post Tower, Suite 1500, 55 South Market Street, 95113-2327.
Telephone: 408-947-8400.
Facsimile: 408-947-4750.
Telex: 910 250 2931 MACPAG SJ.
Walnut Creek, California Office: 1331 North California Boulevard, Post Office Box V, 94596-4502.
Telephone: 510-937-8000.
Facsimile: 510-975-5390.
Menlo Park, California Office: 2740 Sand Hill Road, 94025-7020.
Telephone: 415-233-4000.
Facsimile: 415-233-4086.
Taipei, Taiwan Republic of China Office: International Trade Building, Tenth Floor, 333 Keelung Road, Section 1, 110.
Telephone: 886-2-723-5000.
Facsimile: 886-2-757-6070.
Affiliated Offices in: Bangkok, Thailand; Beijing, China; Shanghai, China.

MEMBERS OF FIRM

David R. Andrews
Michael A. Brown
Patrick O. Cavanaugh
Cynthia A. Coe
Philip T. Cummings (Not admitted in DC)
Barry J. Cutler
George J. Weiner
Michael C. White (Not admitted in DC)

(See Next Column)

McCutchen, Doyle, Brown & Enersen—*Continued*

OF COUNSEL

Margaret A. Freeston
Elizabeth A. Pierce

For full biographical listings, see the Martindale-Hubbell Law Directory

* McDermott, Will & Emery (AV)

A Partnership including Professional Corporations
1850 K Street, N.W., 20006-2296
Telephone: 202-887-8000
Telex: 253565 MILAM CGO
Facsimile: 202-778-8087
Chicago, Illinois Office: 227 West Monroe Street.
Telephone: 312-372-2000.
Telex: 253565 MILAM CGO.
Facsimile: 312-984-7700.
Boston, Massachusetts Office: 75 State Street, Suite 1700.
Telephone: 617-345-5000.
Telex: 951324 MILAM BSN.
Facsimile: 617-345-5077.
Miami, Florida Office: 201 South Biscayne Boulevard.
Telephone: 305-358-3500.
Telex: 441777 LEYES.
Facsimile: 305-347-6500.
Los Angeles, California Office: 2049 Century Park East.
Telephone: 310-277-4110.
Facsimile: 310-277-4730.
Newport Beach, California Office: 1301 Dove Street, Suite 500.
Telephone: 714-851-0633.
Facsimile: 714-851-9348.
New York, N.Y. Office: 1211 Avenue of the Americas.
Telephone: 212-768-5400.
Facsimile: 212-768-5444.
St. Petersburg, Russia Office: 2/2 Tchaikovsky Street, #517, 191187 St. Petersburg, Russia.
Telephone: (7) (812) 273-9831.
Facsimile: (7) (812) 273-9831.
Tallinn, Estonia Office: Tallinn Business Center, 6 Harju Street, EE0001 Tallinn, Estonia.
Telephone: 372 6 31-05-53.
Facsimile: 372 6 31-05-54.
Vilnius, Lithuania Office: Smetonos 6, 2600 Vilnius, Lithuania.
Telephone: 370 2 61-43-08.
Facsimile: 370 2 22-79-55.
Associated (Independent) Offices:
Brussels, Belgium: Uettwiller Grelon Lippens Dekeyser, 73 avenue Vandendriessche, 1150 Brussels, Belgium.
Telephone: (32) (2) 772-87-50.
Facsimile: (32) (2) 772-87-52.
London, England: Paisner & Co, Bouverie House, 154 Fleet Street, London EC4A 2DQ, England.
Telephone: (44) (71) 353-0299.
Facsimile: (44) (71) 583-8621.
Paris, France: Uettwiller Grelon Gout Canat & Associes, 68, boulevard de Courcelles, 75017 Paris, France.
Telephone: (33) (1) 48 88 89 00.
Facsimile: (33) (1) 48 88 05 50.

MEMBERS OF FIRM

Matthew T. Adams
William H. Barrett
James M. Boyle
Jeanne A. Carpenter
Gray C. Castle
Dale W. Church
H. Guy Collier
Karen A. Dewis (Not admitted in DC)
Mark S. Dreux, Sr.
Robert Feldgarden
Roger D. Feldman *
Charles Friedlander
Michael E. Friedlander
Jennifer Britt Giannattasio (Not admitted in DC)
Lisa J. Gilden
Nathalie F. P. Gilfoyle
Carolyn B. Gleason
Eugene I. Goldman
William L. Goldman
Robert C. Gombar
Luis L. Granados, III
Seth D. Greenstein
Paul M. Hamburger
Amy E. Hancock
Mary B. Hevener
Robert G. Hibbert
Jerry C. Hill
Thomas M. Ingoldsby
Gregory F. Jenner
Robert N. Jensen
Christopher Kliefoth
George M. Knapp
Wendy L. Krasner
Christopher M. Lahiff
James A. Lastowka
David J. Levine
E. Grey Lewis
James H. Mann
Philip A. McCarty
Donald S. McCauley, Jr.
J. Gary McDavid
Sean P. McGuinness
Evan M. Migdail
Diane S. Millman
Robert B. Nicholas
Patrick K. O'Hare
Paul J. Pantano, Jr.
Stephen Pavlick
J. Craig Potter
James A. Riedy
David E. Rogers
Michael A. Romansky
Sally A. Rosenberg
Edward M. Ruckert
Arthur G. Sapper
Robert S. Schwartz
Carl W. Schwarz
Larry E. Shapiro
Albert W. Shay
James H. Sneed
Roger D. Stark
Joel I. Suldan
Jon W. van Horne
Roger B. Wagner
Pamela D. Walther
Timothy J. Waters

(See Next Column)

MEMBERS OF FIRM (Continued)

Stephen E. Wells
Melvin White
T. Raymond Williams
Jane E. Wilson
John P. Wintrol
Charles R. Work
Stephen C. Yohay

COUNSEL

Ronald A. Bloch
Jerrold J. Hercenberg
Robert G. Kalik
Phoebe A. Mix
Ralph I. Petersberger
Bonnie S. Temple

Jana Baldwin
Eric P. Berezin (Not admitted in DC)
Harold L. Cohen
Lisa S. Derman (Not admitted in DC)
Leah J. Domitrovic
Marianna G. Dyson
Darlene M. Hampton
Martha Hausman
Donald J. Kissinger, Jr.
Cynthia Joanne Levitt
Robert C. Louthian, III
Joni Lupovitz
Marsha Dula Matthews (Not admitted in DC)
Karla L. Palmer (Not admitted in DC)
Melissa L. Peppe
J. Bryan Puterbaugh
Jeffrey L. Quillen
Pamela S. Reiman
David L. Rosen
Matthew C. Rosser
Richard S. Saver (Not admitted in DC)
Cathy Zeman Scheineson
Karen S. Sealander
Frances E. Snyder (Not admitted in DC)
Jan C. Stewart (Not admitted in DC)
Robert D. Vander Lugt

*Denotes a lawyer employed by a Professional Corporation which is a member of the Firm

For full biographical listings, see the Martindale-Hubbell Law Directory

* McGuire, Woods, Battle & Boothe (AV)

The Army and Navy Club Building, 1627 Eye Street, N.W., 20006-4007
Telephone: 202-857-1700
Fax: 202-857-1737
Alexandria, Virginia Office: Transpotomac Plaza, Suite 1000, 1199 North Fairfax Street, 22314-1437.
Telephone: 703-739-6200.
Fax: 703-739-6270.
Baltimore, Maryland Office: The Blaustein Building, One North Charles Street, 21201-3793.
Telephone: 410-659-4400.
Fax: 410-659-4599.
Charlottesville, Virginia Office: Court Square Building, P.O. Box 1288, 22902-1288.
Telephone: 804-977-2500.
Fax: 804-980-2222.
Jacksonville, Florida Office: Barnett Center, Suite 2750, 50 North Laura Street, 32202-3635.
Telephone: 904-798-3200.
Fax: 904-798-3207.
McLean, (Tysons Corner) Virginia Office: 8280 Greensboro Drive, Suite 900, Tysons Corner, 22102-3892.
Telephone: 703-712-5000.
Fax: 703-712-5050.
Norfolk, Virginia Office: World Trade Center, Suite 9000, 101 West Main Street, 23510-1655.
Telephone: 804-640-3700.
Fax: 804-640-3701.
Richmond, Virginia Office: One James Center, 901 East Cary Street, 23219-4030.
Telephone: 804-775-1000.
Fax: 804-775-1061.
Brussels, Belgium Office: 250 Avenue Louise, Bte. 64, 1050.
Telephone: (32 2) 629 42 11.
Fax: (32 2) 629 42 22.
Zürich, Switzerland Office: P.O. Box 4930, Bahnhofstrasse 3, 8022.
Telephone: (41 1) 225 20 00.
Fax: (41 1) 225 20 20.

MEMBERS OF FIRM

James E. Ballowe, Jr.
James D. Bridgeman
John L. Fugh
Larry B. Grimes
Steven D. Kittrell
Thomas J. McGonigle
Clive R. G. O'Grady (Not admitted in DC)
David H. Pankey
Stephen W. Robinson
Charlotte Rothenberg Rosen
Larry D. Sharp
Robert S. Smith (Not admitted in DC)
George J. Terwilliger III
Wallace L. Timmeny

OF COUNSEL

Mary S. Head
Clifford R. Oviatt, Jr.

ASSOCIATES

Mary Ellen Albin (Not admitted in DC)
Valerie A. Fant (Not admitted in DC)
R. Lisa Mojiri-Azad
Susan Morley Olson
Jonathan R. Tuttle (Not admitted in DC)
Ann W. Zedd

For full biographical listings, see the Martindale-Hubbell Law Directory

Washington—Continued

* Milbank, Tweed, Hadley & McCloy (AV)

Suite 1100, 1825 Eye Street, N.W., 20006
Telephone: 202-835-7500
Cable Address: "Miltweed Wsh"
ITT: 440667
Fax: 202-835-7586 ABA/net: Milbank DC
New York, New York Offices: 1 Chase Manhattan Plaza, 10005.
Telephone: 212-530-5000.
Cable Address: "Miltweed NYK" ITT: 422962; 423893.
Fax: 212-530-5219. ABA/net: Milbank NY. MCI Mail: Miolbank Tweed.
Midtown Office: 50 Rockefeller Plaza, 10020.
Telephone: 212-530-5800;
Fax: 212-530-0158.
Los Angeles, California Office: 601 South Figueroa Street, 90017.
Telephone: 213-892-4000.
Fax: 213-629-5063.
Telex: 678754. ABA/net: Milbank LA.
Tokyo, Japan Office: Nippon Press Center Building, 2-1, Uchisaiwai-cho 2-chome, Chiyoda-ku, Tokyo 100.
Telephone: 011-813-3504-1050. ITT: (781) 2222992.
Fax: 011-81-3-3595-2790, 011-81-3-3502-5192.
London, England Office: Ropemaker Place, 25 Ropemaker Street, EC2Y 9AS.
Telephone: 011-44-171-374-0423.
Cable Address: "Miltuk G."
Fax: 011-44-171-374-0912.
Hong Kong: 3007 Alexandra House, 16 Chater Road.
Telephone: 011-852-2526-5281.
Fax: 011-852-2840-0792, 011-852-2854-9046. ABA/net: Milbank HK.
Singapore Office: 14-02 Caltex House, 30 Raffles Place, 0104.
Telephone: 011-65-534-1700.
Fax: 011-65-534-2733. ABA/net: EDNANG.
Moscow, Russia Office: 28 Pokrovka Street, 1st Floor, Moscow, 103062. International
Telephone: 011-7-502-220-4776. International
Fax: 011-7-502-220-4617. Local
Telephone: 011-7-095-956-3750. Local Telephone/
Fax: 011-7-095-956-3991.
Jakarta, Indonesia Correspondent Office: Law Firm L. Gunawan SH, Jalan Alaydrus 64, Jakarta 10130.
Telephone: 011-6221-384-9870.
Fax: 011-6221-380-7950.

RESIDENT PARTNERS

Mark A. Kantor
Gregory Evers May
John E. Shockey
Richard C. Tufaro
William H. Webster
Adam Wenner

RETIRED PARTNER

Elliot L. Richardson

RESIDENT OF COUNSEL

David S. Katz
Robert F. Lawrence
Amy G. Rudnick

RESIDENT ASSOCIATES

Christos T. Antoniou
Helen F. Choi
Mary C. Ericson
Deanna Flores
James R. Gunther, Jr.
Kathryn E. Hoff-Patrinos
Michael D. Hornstein
Julie M. Jacobs
(Not admitted in DC)
Rohit H. Kirpalani
(Not admitted in DC)
Dean A. Manson
(Not admitted in DC)
Christopher C. McIsaac
Jane B. Morgan
Fred W. Reinke
Wade R. Wright

For full biographical listings, see the Martindale-Hubbell Law Directory

* Miles & Stockbridge, A Professional Corporation (AV)

1450 G. Street, N.W., Suite 445, 20005-2001
Telephone: 202-737-9600
Telecopier: 737-0097
Baltimore, Maryland Office: 10 Light Street.
Telephone: 410-727-6464.
Telecopier: 385-3700.
Towson, Maryland Office: 600 Washington Avenue, Suite 300.
Telephone: 410-821-6565.
Telecopier: 823-8123.
Easton, Maryland Office: 101 Bay Street.
Telephone: 410-822-5280.
Telecopier: 822-5450.
Cambridge, Maryland Office: 300 Academy Street.
Telephone: 410-228-4545.
Telecopier: 228-5652.
Rockville, Maryland Office: 22 West Jefferson Street.
Telephone: 301-762-1600.
Telecopier: 762-0363.
Frederick, Maryland Office: 30 West Patrick Street.
Telephone: 301-662-5155.
Telecopier: 662-3647.

(See Next Column)

Fairfax, Virginia Office: Fair Oaks Plaza, 11350 Random Hills Road.
Telephone: 703-273-2440.
Telecopier: 273-4446.

Samuel A. Bleicher
Richard S. Wasserstrom
Peter W. Segal
Olav B. Kollevoll, Jr.
Ronald S. Gart
Margaret Ann Brown
(Not admitted in DC)
Edward J. Longosz, II
Clement D. Erhardt, III

Kerry L. Iris
Adam W. Smith
Scott A. Harvey
(Not admitted in DC)
Margaret H. Everson-Fisher
(Not admitted in DC)

For full biographical listings, see the Martindale-Hubbell Law Directory

Miller & Chevalier, Chartered (AV)

655 Fifteenth Street, N.W., Suite 900, 20005-5701
Telephone: 202-626-5800
Fax: 202-628-0858

Robert Netherland Miller
(1879-1968)
Stuart Chevalier (1879-1956)
John Stephan Nolan
John Mourer Bixler
Clarence T. Kipps, Jr.
Philip S. Neal
Robert L. Moore, II
Lawrence B. Gibbs
(Not admitted in DC)
Donald B. Craven
Phillip L. Mann
A. John Gabig
Dennis P. Bedell
John Lloyd Rice
Jay L. Carlson
Mark L. Evans
Homer E. Moyer, Jr.
Leonard Bickwit, Jr.
F. Brook Voght
Frederick H. Robinson
John B. Magee
Emmett B. Lewis
Craig D. Miller
Robert K. Huffman
Alexander Zakupowsky, Jr.
Gerald Goldman
C. Frederick Oliphant III
Ronald D. Aucutt
James A. Bensfield
Stuart E. Benson
Terry Bancroft Dowd
Thomas D. Johnston
James P. Tuite
Richard C. Stark
Catherine Tift Porter
Alan C. Brown
David B. Cubeta
Thomas W. Mahoney, Jr.
Anne E. Moran
Robert E. Liles, II
Alan I. Horowitz
Lucinda A. Low
Scott E. Pickens
Patricia J. Sweeney
Grant D. Aldonas
James B. Altman
J. Bradford Anwyll
Catherine Curtiss
F. Scott Farmer
Robert A. Katcher
Catherine Veihmeyer Hughes
Mary Lou Soller
Kathryn Bucher
Hal I. Gann
Kevin C. Dwyer
Kevin L. Kenworthy
Patricia M. Lacey

COUNSEL

David W. Richmond
Numa L. Smith, Jr.
Charles T. Akre

Christopher S. Rizek
Joseph B. Kennedy
Anthony F. Shelley
William M. McGlone
Catherine L. Creech
Jean A. Pawlow
Amy L. Rothstein
Ross W. Branstetter
Helen M. Hubbard
(Not admitted in DC)
Susan G. Whitman
Bruce A. Cohen
Elizabeth P. Askey
Peter B. Miller
Claire S. Wellington
James R. Lovelace
Mandy Jones
Michael L. Schultz
(Not admitted in DC)
Angela E. Clark
Laura G. Ferguson
Suzanne M. Papiewski
S. Kelly Myers
John E. Davis
Angela Lykos
Paul R. Maguffee
Michael Diehl
Kathryn Cameron Atkinson
Jeffrey A. Green
(Not admitted in DC)
Elizabeth F. Judge
Alvaro I. Anillo
(Not admitted in DC)
Rhonda Nesmith Crichlow
(Not admitted in DC)
Michael E. Baillif
Carla McKitten Seebald
(Not admitted in DC)
Lisa T. Murphy
(Not admitted in DC)
Heidi A. Sorensen
(Not admitted in DC)
Frances B. Morgan
(Not admitted in DC)
Michael W. Wright
(Not admitted in DC)
Andrea K. Bjorklund
(Not admitted in DC)
Brooke E. Frewing
(Not admitted in DC)
Carol E. Lockwood
(Not admitted in DC)

For full biographical listings, see the Martindale-Hubbell Law Directory

Washington—Continued

* MINTZ, LEVIN, COHN, FERRIS, GLOVSKY AND POPEO, P.C. (AV)

701 Pennsylvania Avenue, N.W., Suite 900, 20004-2608
Telephone: 202-434-7300
FAX: 202-434-7400
Boston, Massachusetts Office: One Financial Center.
Telephone: 617-542-6000.
Cable Address: "Colemin."
Telex: 94-0198.

Francis X. Meaney
Charles D. Ferris
William C. Brashares
Frank W. Lloyd
Bruce D. Sokler
Alvin J. Lorman
Charles Alan Samuels
Howard J. Symons
Rebecca L. Jackson
Ann K. Friedman
Peter Kimm, Jr.
James A. Kirkland

Christopher J. Harvie (Not admitted in DC)
Cherie R. Kiser
Kecia Boney (Not admitted in DC)
Anthony E. Varona
Tara M. Corvo (Not admitted in DC)
Michael F. Kleine (Not admitted in DC)

For full biographical listings, see the Martindale-Hubbell Law Directory

MONTEDONICO, HAMILTON & ALTMAN, P.C. (AV)

Chevy Chase Plaza, Suite 400, 5301 Wisconsin Avenue, N.W., 20015
Telephone: 202-364-1434
FAX: 202-364-1544
Fairfax, Virginia Office: 10306 Eaton Place, Suite 500.
Telephone: 703-591-9700.
FAX: 703-591-0023.
Frederick, Maryland Office: 220 North Market Street.
Telephone: 301-695-7004.
FAX: 301-695-0055.
Richmond, Virginia Office: 700 East Main Street, Suite 1633.
Telephone: 804-780-2898.
Rockville, Maryland Office: Suite 201, 600 East Jefferson Street.
Telephone: 301-424-3900.
FAX: 301-217-0409.

RESIDENT PERSONNEL

Joseph Montedonico
Steven A. Hamilton
Francis X. Canale
William J. Hickey, Jr.
John J. Dillon
Alfred F. Belcuore
Melvin R. Wright
Patricia M. Tazzara
Scott D. Austin

COUNSEL

Michael B. McGovern

Vicki Jean Hunt (Resident)
Denise Adams Hill
Linwood L. Rayford, III
Timothy S. Menter
Andrew J. Spence
Thomas Ramsay Mooers
Thomas C. Mugavero
Carol A. Alexander
Karen Y. Roberts
Elisa Ann Eisenberg
Kathleen Blake Asdorian
Debra E. Posin (Not admitted in DC)

FAIRFAX, VIRGINIA PERSONNEL

Stephen L. Altman
Kenneth G. Roth
Joseph C. Veith, III
Dennis R. Carluzzo

Bruce A. Levine
Brendy B. Esmond
Kathryn A.K. Untiedt
Leah Hadad

FREDERICK, MARYLAND OFFICE PERSONNEL

David O. Godwin, Jr.

RICHMOND, VIRGINIA OFFICE PERSONNEL

Stephen L. Altman
Joseph C. Veith, III

ROCKVILLE, MARYLAND OFFICE PERSONNEL

John J. Dillon

For full biographical listings, see the Martindale-Hubbell Law Directory

TIMOTHY D. NAEGELE & ASSOCIATES (AV)

Suite 300, 1250 24th Street, N.W., 20037
Telephone: 202-466-7500
Facsimile: 202-466-3079 or 466-2888
Los Angeles, California Office: Suite 2430, 1900 Avenue of the Stars, 90067
Telephone: 310-557-2300.
Facsimile: 310-457-4014.

ASSOCIATES

Ashley Gauthier (Not admitted in DC)

LEGAL SUPPORT PERSONNEL

LAW CLERKS

Robert C. Kersey
Craig Boyd Garner

For full biographical listings, see the Martindale-Hubbell Law Directory

* O'CONNOR & HANNAN (AV)

Suite 800, 1919 Pennsylvania Avenue, N.W., 20006-3483
Telephone: 202-887-1400
Telecopy: 202-466-2198
Minneapolis, Minnesota Office: 700 Baker Building, 706 South Second Avenue.
Telephone: 612-343-1200.
Telecopy: 612-343-1256.

MEMBERS OF FIRM

William T. Hannan (1911-1985)
H. Robert Halper (1931-1988)
John J. Flynn (1925-1990)
Patrick J. O'Connor
Edward W. Brooke
Thomas H. Quinn
David R. Melincoff
Hope S. Foster
Patrick E. O'Donnell
Joseph H. Blatchford
F. Gordon Lee
George J. Mannina, Jr.
John J. McDermott
James W. Symington
Donald R. Dinan
Michael Colopy
Thomas J. Schneider
David L. Hill
Thomas J. Corcoran
Peter M. Kazon
Christina W. Fleps
Timothy W. Jenkins
Gary C. Adler
Wayne M. Zell
J. Timothy O'Neill
David L. Anderson
Audrey P. Rasmussen

Stephen C. Fogleman
Elissa Garber Kon
Craig A. Koenigs

OF COUNSEL

David C. Treen (Not admitted in DC)
E. William Crotty
Charles R. McCarthy, Jr.
William W. Nickerson
H. George Schweitzer
Joseph F. Castiello (1909-1985)

For full biographical listings, see the Martindale-Hubbell Law Directory

* O'MELVENY & MYERS (AV)

555 13th Street, N.W. Suite 500 West, 20004-1109
Telephone: 202-383-5300
Cable Address: "Moms"
Facsimile: 202-383-5414
Los Angeles, California Office: 400 South Hope Street.
Telephone: 213-669-6000.
Cable Address: "Moms."
Facsimile: 213-669-6407.
Century City Office: 1999 Avenue of the Stars, 7th Floor.
Telephone: 310-553-6700.
Facsimile: 310-246-6779.
Newport Beach, California Office: 610 Newport Center Drive, Suite 1700.
Telephone: 714-760-9600.
Cable Address: "Moms."
Facsimile: 714-669-6994.
San Francisco, California Office: Embarcadero Center West Tower, 275 Battery Street, Suite 2600.
Telephone: 415-984-8700.
Facsimile: 415-984-8701.
New York, N.Y. Office: Citicorp Center, 153 East 53rd Street, 54th Floor.
Telephone: 212-326-2000.
Facsimile: 212-326-2061.
Newark, New Jersey Office: One Gateway Center, 7th Floor.
Telephone: 201-639-8600.
Facsimile: 201-639-8630.
London, England Office: 10 Finsbury Square, London, EC2A 1LA.
Telephone: 011-44-171-256-8451
Facsimile: 011-44-171-638-8205.
Tokyo, Japan Office: Sanbancho KB-6 Building, 6 Sanbancho, Chiyoda-ku, Tokyo 102, Japan.
Telephone: 011-81-3-3239-2800.
Facsimile: 011-81-3-3239-2432.
Hong Kong Office: 1104 Lippo Tower, Lippo Centre, 89 Queensway, Central Hong Kong.
Telephone: 011-852-523-8266.
Facsimile: 011-852-522-1760.

WASHINGTON, D.C.
MEMBERS OF FIRM

Kermit W. Almstedt
Richard E. Ayres
John H. Beisner
Ben E. Benjamin
Donald T. Bliss, Jr.
William T. Coleman, Jr.
Arthur B. Culvahouse, Jr.
John F. Daum
F. Amanda DeBusk
Robert N. Eccles
Stephen J. Harburg
Bruce A. Hiler (Not admitted in DC)
Gary N. Horlick
Richard G. Parker
David G. Pommerening (Not admitted in DC)
Jeffrey J. Rosen
William H. Satchell
Carl R. Schenker, Jr.
Debra A. Valentine
John E. Welch

SPECIAL COUNSEL

Brian C. Anderson
David T. Beddow
Brian David Boyle
Alfred M. Wurglitz

(See Next Column)

O'MELVENY & MYERS, *Washington—Continued*

RESIDENT ASSOCIATES

Mary Amilea Anderson
(Not admitted in DC)
Peter C. Chboharis
(Not admitted in DC)
Peggy Ann Clarke
(Not admitted in DC)
Teresa E. Dawson
Elizabeth A. Delaney
(Not admitted in DC)
Marcia A. Fay
(Not admitted in DC)
Roger M. Freeman
(Not admitted in DC)
Hilary R. Hegener
Harold Henderson
Bruce R. Hirsh
Thomas J. Karr
Kevin M. Kelcourse
Jeffrey W. Kilduff
Scott L. Landsbaum
(Not admitted in DC)
Sharon G. Levin
(Not admitted in DC)
Greta L. Lichtenbaum
(Not admitted in DC)
Maria Rose Mazur
Marion K. McDonald
Craig L. McKee
Michael A. Meyer
(Not admitted in DC)
Geoffrey D. Oliver
Matthew B. Pachman
Lynn E. Parseghian
(Not admitted in DC)
Patrick R. Rizzi
(Not admitted in DC)
Edward A. Rosic, Jr.
Philip C. Scheurer
Nina Shafran
Todd R. Triller
(Not admitted in DC)
Karen Mary Wahle
(Not admitted in DC)

For full biographical listings, see the Martindale-Hubbell Law Directory

✻ PAUL, HASTINGS, JANOFSKY & WALKER (AV)

A Partnership including Professional Corporations
Tenth Floor, 1299 Pennsylvania Avenue, N.W., 20004
Telephone: 202-508-9500
Fax: 202-508-9700
Los Angeles, California Office: Twenty-Third Floor, 555 South Flower Street.
Telephone: 213-683-6000.
Cable Address: "Paulhast."
Twx: 910-321-4065.
Orange County, California Office: Seventeenth Floor, 695 Town Center Drive, Costa Mesa.
Telephone: 714-668-6200.
Atlanta, Georgia Office: 442nd Floor, Georgia Pacific Center, 133 Peachtree Street, N.E.
Telephone: 404-588-9900.
Santa Monica, California Office: Fifth Floor, 1299 Ocean Avenue.
Telephone: 310-319-3300.
Stamford, Connecticut Office: Ninth Floor, 1055 Washington Boulevard.
Telephone: 203-961-7400.
New York, New York Office: 31st Floor, 399 Park Avenue.
Telephone: 212-318-6000.
Tokyo, Japan Office: Toranomon Ohtori Building, 8th Floor, 4-3 Toranomon 1-Chome, Minato-Ku.
Telephone: (03) 3507-0730.

MEMBERS OF FIRM

E. Lawrence Barcella, Jr.
Barbara Berish Brown
R. Bruce Dickson
Ralph B. Everett
Zachary D. Fasman
John J. Gallagher
Lawrence J. Hass
Judith Richards Hope
Thomas R. Lamia
G. Hamilton Loeb
Charles A. Patrizia
Paul L. Perito
Bruce D. Ryan
William A. Schmidt
Dennis H. Vaughn
Michael A. Wiegard

OF COUNSEL

Michael F. Cole
(Not admitted in DC)
Edwin I. Colodny
William D. DeGrandis
Jon A. Geier
Frank Koszorus, Jr.
Robert S. Plotkin
Robert E. Pokusa
Charles A. Shanor
Margaret H. Spurlin

ASSOCIATES

David M. Abbey
Michelle Weisberg Cohen
Wendell M. Faria
(Not admitted in DC)
Scott M. Flicker
Intra L. Germanis
(Not admitted in DC)
Patricia L. Hurst
Gage Randolph Johnson
George R. A. Jones
(Not admitted in DC)
Edmund S. Latour
Sarah M. McWilliams
William Thomas Reeder, Jr.
Andrée M. St. Martin
Joseph E. Schmitz
Nancy E. Shallow
Randall M. Stone
Michael D. Taxay
(Not admitted in DC)
Timothy J. Wellman
Annita M. Whichard
(Not admitted in DC)
Sandra Wilkinson
Kenneth M. Willner
Jenny C. Wu

For full biographical listings, see the Martindale-Hubbell Law Directory

✻ PAUL, WEISS, RIFKIND, WHARTON & GARRISON (AV)

1615 L Street, N.W. Suite 1300, 20036-5694
Telephone: 202-223-7300
TDD 202-223-7490
Telex: 248237 PWA UR
Facsimile: 202-223-7420
Cable Address: "Longsight, Washington"
New York, N.Y. Office: 1285 Avenue of the Americas, 10019-6064.
Telephones: 212-373-3000, TDD 212-373-2000.
Cable Address: "Longsight, New York".
Telex: WUI 666-843.
Facsimile: 212-757-3990.
Paris, France Office: 199, Boulevard Saint Germain, 75007.
Telephone: (33-1) 45.49.33.85.
Cable Address: "Longsight, Paris".
Telex: 203178F.
Facsimile: (33-1) 42-22-64-38.
Tokyo, Japan Office: 11th Floor, Main Tower, Akasaka Twin Tower, 17-22 Akasaka 2-chome, Minato-ku, 107.
Telephone: (81-3) 3505-0291.
Facsimile: 011 (81-3) 3505-4540.
Telex: 02428120 PWRWGT.
Beijing, People's Republic of China Office: Suite 1910, Scite Tower, 22 Jianguomenwai Dajie, 100004.
Telephones: (86-1) 5123628-30, (86-1) 5122288X.1910.
Telex: 210169 PWRWG CN.
Facsimile: 011 (86-1) 5123631.
Hong Kong Office: 13th Floor, Hong Kong Club Building, 3A Chater Road, Central Hong Kong.
Telephone: (011-852) 2536-9933.
Facsimile: 011 (852) 2536-9622.

RESIDENT PARTNERS

Terence J. Fortune
Robert E. Montgomery, Jr.
Lionel H. Olmer
Warren B. Rudman
Phillip L. Spector

COUNSEL

A. Leon Higginbotham, Jr.

COMMUNICATIONS COUNSEL

Jeffrey H. Olson

INTERNATIONAL TRADE COUNSEL

Richard S. Elliott

RESIDENT ASSOCIATES

Carl W. Hampe
Norman J. Harrison
George D. Kleinfeld
Paul J. Kollmer
Soon-Yub Samuel Kwon
Robert P. Parker
Susan E. Ryan
Frank J Schuchat
Barbara A. Yellen

For full biographical listings, see the Martindale-Hubbell Law Directory

PEPPER, HAMILTON & SCHEETZ (AV)

1300 Nineteenth Street, N.W., 20036-1685
Telephone: 202-828-1200
Telecopy: 202-828-1665
Philadelphia, Pennsylvania Office: 3000 Two Logan Square, Eighteenth and Arch Streets, 19103-2799.
Telephone: 215-981-4000.
Fax: 215-981-4750.
Detroit, Michigan Office: 100 Renaissance Center, 36th Floor, 48243-1157.
Telephone: 313-259-7110.
Fax: 313-259-7926.
Harrisburg, Pennsylvania Office: 200 One Keystone Plaza, North Front and Market Streets, P.O. Box 1181, 17108-1181.
Telephone: 717-255-1155.
Fax: 717-238-0575.
Berwyn, Pennsylvania Office: 1235 Westlakes Drive, Suite 400, 19312-2401.
Telephone: 610-640-7800.
Fax: 610-640-7835.
New York, New York Office: 450 Lexington Avenue, Suite 1600, 10017-3904.
Telephone: 212-878-3800.
Fax: 212-878-3835.
Wilmington, Delaware Office: 1201 Market Street, Suite 1401, P.O. Box 1709, 19899-1709.
Telephone: 302-571-6555.
Fax: 302-656-8865.
Westmont, New Jersey Office: Sentry Office Plaza, Suite 321, 216 Haddon Avenue, 08108-2811.
Telephone: 609-869-9555.
Fax: 609-869-9595.
London, England Office: City Tower, 40 Basinghall Street, EC2V 5DE.
Telephone: 011-44-71-628-1122.
Fax: 011-44-71-628-6010.
Moscow, Russia Office: 19-27 Grokholsky Pereulok, 129010.
Telephone: 011-7-095-280-4493.
Fax: 011-7-095-280-5518.

(See Next Column)

PEPPER, HAMILTON & SCHEETZ—*Continued*

PARTNERS

Michael B. Staebler (Not admitted in DC; Managing Partner)
Donald H. Green (Deputy Managing Partner)
Arthur B. Axelson
Jonathan D. Cahn
Alfred W. Cortese, Jr.
Elliot J. Feldman
John B. Huffaker
Susan L. Launer
George A. Lehner
Edward H. Lieberman
Marc D. Machlin
Edward A. McCullough
John Will Ongman
Daniel I. Prywes
Sheldon L. Schreiberg
Gary S. Smuckler
Stephen M. Truitt
William J. Walsh
David A. Wormser

OF COUNSEL

Larisa A. Afanasyeva (Not admitted in DC)
Kathleen L. Blaner
John F. DePodesta (Not admitted in DC)
Otto J. Hetzel
Stephen B. Ives, Jr.
William B. Simons (Not admitted in DC)

ASSOCIATES

JoAnna J. Barnes
John J. Burke
Charles H. Carpenter
Gregory Scott Carter (Not admitted in DC)
David O. Chinofsky
Diane Ruth Holt
H. David Kotz
Barbara E. McDonald (Not admitted in DC)
David J. McPherson
Michelle J Morris
Richard B. Nash, Jr.

For full biographical listings, see the Martindale-Hubbell Law Directory

* PERKINS COIE (AV)

A Law Partnership including Professional Corporations
Strategic Alliance with Russell & DuMoulin
607 Fourteenth Street, N.W., 20005
Telephone: 202-628-6600
Facsimile: 202-434-1690
Telex: 44-0277 PCSO
Seattle, Washington Office: 1201 Third Avenue, 40th Floor.
Telephone: 206-583-8888.
Facsimile: 206-583-8500.
Cable Address: "Perkins Seattle."
Telex: 32-0319 PERKINS SEA.
Anchorage, Alaska Office: 1029 West Third Avenue, Suite 300.
Telephone: 907-279-8561.
Facsimile: 907-276-3108.
Telex: 32-0319 PERKINS SEA.
Los Angeles, California Office: Ninth Floor, 1999 Avenue of the Stars.
Telephone: 310-788-9900.
Telex: 32-0319 PERKINS SEA.
Facsimile: 310-788-3399.
Olympia, Washington Office: 1110 Capital Way South, Suite 405.
Telephone: 206-956-3300.
Facsimile: 206-956-1208.
Portland, Oregon Office: U.S. Bancorp Tower, Suite 2500, 111 S.W. Fifth Avenue.
Telephone: 503-295-4400.
Facsimile: 503-295-6793.
Telex: 32-0319 PERKINS SEA.
Bellevue, Washington Office: Suite 1800, One Bellevue Center, 411 - 108th Avenue N.E.
Telephone: 206-453-6980.
Facsimile: 206-453-7350.
Telex: 32-0319 PERKINS SEA.
Spokane, Washington Office: North 221 Wall Street, Suite 600.
Telephone: 509-624-2212.
Facsimile: 509-458-3399.
Telex: 32-0319 PERKINS SEA.
Taipei, Taiwan Office: 8/F, TFIT Tower, 85 Jen Ai Road, Sec. 4.
Telephone: 886-2-778-1177.
Facsimile: 886-2-777-9898.
Hong Kong Office: 23rd Floor, Asia Pacific Finance Tower, Citibank Plaza, 3 Garden Road.
Telephone: 852-878-1177.
Facsimile: 852-524-9988.
London, England Office: 36/38 Cornhill, EC3V 3ND.
Telephone: 0171-369-9966.
Facsimile: 0171-369-9968.
Canada: Strategic Alliance with Russell & Dumoulin, 1700-1075 West Georgia Street, Vancouver, B.C. V6E 3G2.
Telephone: 604-631-3131.

RESIDENT MEMBERS

Robert F. Bauer
Donald C. Baur
Judith L. Corley
Robert L. Deitz
Donald J. Friedman
Mary Rose Hughes
John P. Hume
Kerry B. Long
Guy R. Martin
M. Margaret McKeown
James R. Moore (Not admitted in DC)
Nancy W. Newkirk
Barry J. Reingold
Leonard E. Santos
Benjamin S. Sharp
Stuart G. Steingold
Thomas V. Vakerics

(See Next Column)

OF COUNSEL

Jeffrey G. Miller

RESIDENT ASSOCIATES

John M. Devaney
Karen Donovan (Not admitted in DC)
Marc E. Elias
Andrew E. Falk
J. Christopher Groobey
Lynn F. Kaufmann
Kara M. Sacilotto
B. Holly Schadler
Martin P. Willard

For full biographical listings, see the Martindale-Hubbell Law Directory

* PILLSBURY MADISON & SUTRO (AV)

1667 K Street, N.W., Suite 1100, 20006-1676
Telephone: 202-887-0300
FAX: 202-296-7605
Costa Mesa, California Office: Plaza Tower, 600 Anton Boulevard, Suite 1100, 92626.
Telephone: 714-436-6800.
Fax: 714-662-6999.
Los Angeles, California Office: Citicorp Plaza, 725 South Figueroa, Suite 1200, 90017.
Telephone: 213-488-7100.
Fax: 213-629-1033.
New York, New York Office: One Liberty Plaza, 165 Broadway, 51st Floor.
Telephone: 212-374-1890.
Fax: 212-374-1852.
Menlo Park, California Office: 3000 Sand Hill Road, Building 4, Suite 255, 94025.
Telephone: 415-233-4500.
Fax: 415-233-4545.
Sacramento, California Office: 400 Capitol Mall, Suite 1700, 95814.
Telephone: 916-329-4700.
Fax: 916-441-3583.
San Diego, California Office: 101 West Broadway, Suite 1800, 92101.
Telephone: 619-234-5000.
Fax: 619-236-1995.
San Francisco, California Office: 225 Bush Street, 94104.
Telephone: 415-983-1000.
Fax: 415-398-2096.
San Jose, California Office: Ten Almaden Boulevard, 95113.
Telephone: 408-947-4000.
Fax: 408-287-8341.
Hong Kong Office: 6/F Asia Pacific Finance Tower, Citibank Plaza, 3 Garden Road, Central.
Telephone: 011-852-509-7100.
Fax: 011-852-509-7188.
Tokyo, Japan Office: 802 Churchill and Shumazaki Gaikokuho-Jimu-Bengoshi-Jimusho, Toranomon ACT Building, 6th Floor, 11-12, Toranomon 5-chome, Minato-ku, Tokyo 105, Japan.
Telephone: 800-729-9830; 011-813-5472-6561.
Fax: 011-813-5472-5761.

MEMBERS OF FIRM

James B. Atkin
Ken M. Brown
Terry Calvani (Not admitted in DC)
Kathleen Wooley Collins
Julia B. Epley (Not admitted in DC)
Paul F. McQuade
Keith J. Mendelson
W. Jeffrey Schmidt
Jay B. Stephens (Not admitted in DC)
Thomas D. Terry (Not admitted in DC)
Benjamin M. Vandegrift

OF COUNSEL

Sally D. Garr

SPECIAL COUNSEL

Theresa Fenelon

ASSOCIATES

Holly E. Blewer
Michael A. Conley (Not admitted in DC)
Nancy K. Figg
Bradley K. Gordon (Not admitted in DC)
James A. Meade
W. Todd Miller
Juleen E. Savarese
Bert Ubamadu (Not admitted in DC)
Patricia R. Zeigler

For full biographical listings, see the Martindale-Hubbell Law Directory

* PIPER & MARBURY (AV)

1200 Nineteenth Street, N.W., 20036-2430
Telephone: 202-861-3900
FAX: 202-223-2085
Baltimore, Maryland Office: Charles Center South, 36 South Charles Street, 21201-3010.
Telephone: 410-539-2530.
FAX: 410-539-0489.
Easton, Maryland Office: 117 Bay Street, 21601-2703.
Telephone: 410-820-4460.
FAX: 410-820-4463.
Garrison, New York Office: Garrison Landing.
Telephone: 914-424-3711.
Fax: 914-424-3045.

(See Next Column)

PIPER & MARBURY, *Washington—Continued*

New York, N.Y. Office: 31 West 52nd Street, 10019-6118.
Telephone: 212-261-2000.
FAX: 212-261-2001.
Philadelphia, Pennsylvania Office: Suite 1500, 2 Penn Center Plaza, 19102-1715.
Telephone: 215-656-3300.
FAX: 215-656-3301.
London, England Office: 14 Austin Friars, EC2N 2HE.
Telephone: 071-638-3833.
FAX: 071-638-1208.

MEMBERS OF FIRM

Nathan B. Feinstein
Charles C. Abeles
Robert B. Barnhouse (Not admitted in DC)
Lewis A. Noonberg
Sheldon Krantz
Toni K. Allen
Thomas H. Truitt
William R. Weissman
Edwin M. Martin, Jr.
Geoffrey R. W. Smith
Philip L. Cohan
Steven K. Yablonski
J. Brian Molloy
Ronald L. Plesser
Mark J. Tauber
Anthony L. Young
Randall B. Lowe
Francis X. Markey
Joseph A. Fanone
Jeffrey F. Liss
George P. Stamas
Stephen R. Mysliwiec
Daniel J. Carrigan (Not admitted in DC)
Alan C. Porter
William D. Blakely
I. Scott Bass (Not admitted in DC)
Michael F. Brockmeyer (Not admitted in DC)
Stephen L. Owen
Joyce J. Gorman
Jay Gary Finkelstein
Cynthia J. Morris
David H. Bamberger
David Clarke, Jr.
Mary F. Edgar
James M. Brogan (Not admitted in DC)
Anthony H. Rickert
Douglas H. Green
Steven J. Mandell
David N. Baumann

OF COUNSEL

Daniel R. Mackesey

SENIOR ATTORNEY

Richard C. Walters

RESIDENT ASSOCIATES

James P. Rathvon
Nora E. Garrote
Emilio W. Cividanes
Cyd Beth Wolf (Not admitted in DC)
Theodore D. Segal
Michael C. Carter
James B. Reach
Carolyn M. Bamberger
Mitchell S. Marder (Not admitted in DC)
Benjamin S. Boyd
Gretchen L. Lowe
Joseph V. Gote (Not admitted in DC)
Leonard L. Gordon (Not admitted in DC)
John E. Benedict
Mary E. Gately
David A. Franchina
Leila B. Boulton
Timothy P. Branigan
Norman L. Rave, Jr.
John A. Washington, Jr. (Not admitted in DC)
Nancy A. Spangler
Kimberly E. Wolod
Marianne Mancino Thiede
Eric L. Keller (Not admitted in DC)
Judith Altenberg
Barry P. McDonald (Not admitted in DC)
Timothy M. Cramer
Carla G. Pennington-Cross
Denise Giraldez (Not admitted in DC)
Jennifer A. White
Wayne E. Tumlin (Not admitted in DC)
Mark J. O'Connor
Brian D. Henderson (Not admitted in DC)
Keara M. O'Donnell (Not admitted in DC)

For full biographical listings, see the Martindale-Hubbell Law Directory

* POPHAM, HAIK, SCHNOBRICH & KAUFMAN, LTD. (AV)

655 Fifteenth Street, N.W., Suite 800, 20005
Telephone: 202-824-8000
Denver, Colorado Office: Suite 2400, 1200 17th Street.
Telephone: 303-893-1200.
Minneapolis, Minnesota Office: 222 South 9th Street, Suite 3300.
Telephone: 612-333-4800.
Miami, Florida Office: 4000 International Place, 100 Southeast 2nd Street.
Telephone: 305-530-0050.
Affiliated Offices: Kasper, Knacke, Schauble and Wintterlin
Stuttgart, Germany Office: Schützenstrasse 13, 70182 Stuttgart.
Telephone: 0-1149-711-22363.
Fax: 011-49-711-223-6410.
Leipzig, Germany Office: Könneritzstrasse 43, 04229 Leipzig.
Telephone: 01149-341-4918429.
Fax: 01149-341-491-8215.
Beijing, China Office: Tianping Law Office, 20, Wangfujing Avenue, P.O. Code 100006.
Telephone: 861-513-5261.

Donald A. Farmer, Jr.
Michael K. Hammaker
Allen S. Melser
Nathaniel A. Humphries
Robert DeVos
Paul A. Koches
Dale Curtis Hogue, Sr.
James P. Gallatin, Jr.
Harold J. Engel
B. Parker Livingston, Jr.

(See Next Column)

David C. Gryce
Joseph Brooks
Donald H. Seifman
Brian B. Darville
Stephen P. Murphy
Mark Fox Evens
Susan A. Aaron

SPECIAL COUNSEL

Zachery M. Jones
Bassam N. Ibrahim
Brian P. O'Shaughnessy

Linda J. Shapiro
Deborah E. Bouchoux
Raymond C. Glenny
Sandra K. Scholar
Douglas V. Wolfe
Mark Brian Wychulis
Mark G. Seifert
Ludwig P. Gaines (Not admitted in DC)
Donald W. Muirhead (Not admitted in DC)
Jeanne McMullin
Juan Carlos A. Marquez
Holly M. Ford (Not admitted in DC)
Becky L. Troutman (Not admitted in DC)

OF COUNSEL

Orville L. Freeman (Not admitted in DC)

For full biographical listings, see the Martindale-Hubbell Law Directory

* PORTER, WRIGHT, MORRIS & ARTHUR (AV)

1233 20th Street, N.W., 20036-2395
Telephone: 202-778-3000; (800-456-7962)
Fax: 202-778-3063
Telex: 6503213584 MCI
Columbus, Ohio Office: 41 South High Street, 43215-6194.
Telephones: 614-227-2000; (800-533-2794).
Telex: 6503213584 MCI.
Fax: 614-227-2100.
Dayton, Ohio Office: One Dayton Centre, One South Main Street, 45402.
Telephones: 513-228-2411; (800-533-4434).
Fax: 513-449-6820.
Cincinnati, Ohio Office: 250 E. Fifth Street, 45202-4166.
Telephones: 513-381-4700; (800-582-5813).
Fax: 513-421-0991.
Cleveland, Ohio Office: 925 Euclid Avenue, 44115-1483.
Telephones: 216-443-9000; (800-824-1980).
Fax: 216-443-9011.
Naples, Florida Office: 4501 Tamiami Trail North, 33940-3060.
Telephones: 813-263-8898; (800-876-7962).
Fax: 813-436-2990.

MEMBERS OF FIRM

Anthony J. Celebrezze, Jr. (Not admitted in DC)
Michael G. Dowd
E. Jay Finkel
Leslie Alan Glick
Judd L. Kessler
Mark L. Lezell
Ronald S. Perlman
Robert E. Steinberg

RESIDENT ASSOCIATES

Matthew Steven Bergman
Richard J. Burke
Ellen F. Randel (Not admitted in DC)
Elizabeth C. Sandoval (Not admitted in DC)

RESIDENT OF COUNSEL

Hugh O'Neill
William G. Porter, Jr.
James C. Stearns
Donald P. Young
John Hardin Young

For full biographical listings, see the Martindale-Hubbell Law Directory

* POWELL, GOLDSTEIN, FRAZER & MURPHY (AV)

6th Floor, 1001 Pennsylvania Avenue, N.W., 20004
Telephone: 202-347-0066
Atlanta, Georgia Office: Sixteenth Floor, 191 Peachtree Street, N.E., 30303.
Telephone: 404-572-6600.
Telex: 542864.
Telecopier: 404-572-6999.
Cable Address: Pgfm.

RESIDENT MEMBERS

Elliott B. Adler
Richard M. Belanger
Craig J. Blakeley
Jerome A. Breed
Anne B. Camper
Michael H. Chanin
William C. Crenshaw
George L. Daves
Keith A. Dunsmore (Not admitted in DC)
Neil R. Ellis
Michael E. Fine
W. Wyche Fowler, Jr.
Anthony S. Freedman
Lawrence R. Fullerton
Larry S. Gage
John J. Knapp
Simon Lazarus, III
John K. McIlwain
Alan K. Parver
Daniel M. Price
Charles H. Roistacher
Lisa Alpert Rosen
Victoria P. Rostow
Lawrence B. Simons
Susan P. Strommer
Peter O. Suchman
Robert Torresen, Jr.
Florence A. Wood

(See Next Column)

POWELL, GOLDSTEIN, FRAZER & MURPHY—*Continued*

RESIDENT ASSOCIATES

Lee Ann Alexander (Not admitted in DC)
K. Sabrina Austin
P. Bryan Christy, III
Catherine M. Cook
T. George Davis, Jr.
William Gerald Driggers (Not admitted in DC)
Barbara D.A. Eyman (Not admitted in DC)
Robert N. Falk
Kristen M. Galles
Elizabeth Cole Hafner
David C. Hammond
Robin Heimann-McGhee
Brett G. Kappel
Sheryl Krongold
Jennifer Lewis Smith
William R. Marks
Susan M. Mathews
Niall P. Meagher
Carmen Lea Neuberger
John Derek Ratliff (Not admitted in DC)
John Reardon (Not admitted in DC)
Michael Spivey
Susan J. Thomas
William H.E. von Oehsen
Ursula Werner
Donna Christine Wood (Not admitted in DC)
David A. Zybala

OF COUNSEL

Kenneth W. Ellison
Brenda A. Jacobs (Resident)

For full biographical listings, see the Martindale-Hubbell Law Directory

* PROSKAUER ROSE GOETZ & MENDELSOHN LLP (AV)

1233 Twentieth Street, N.W. Suite 800, 20036
Telephone: 202-416-6800
FAX: 202-416-6899
New York, New York Office: 1585 Broadway.
Telephone: 212-969-3000.
Los Angeles, California Office: 2121 Avenue of the Stars, Suite 2700.
Telephone: 310-557-2900.
San Francisco, California Office: 555 California Street, Suite 4604.
Telephone: 415-956-2218.
Boca Raton, Florida Office: One Boca Place, Suite 340 West, 2255 Glades Road.
Telephone: 407-241-7400.
Clifton, New Jersey Office: 1373 Broad Street, P.O. Box 4444.
Telephone: 201-779-6300.
Paris, France Office: 9 rue Le Tasse.
Telephone: (33-1) 45 27 43 01.

MEMBERS OF FIRM

Jon A. Baumgarten
Mark J. Biros
Arnold I. Burns
Joseph E. Casson
Warren L. Dennis
Malcolm J. Harkins, III
Ian K. Portnoy
Richard H. Rowe
Christopher Wolf

WASHINGTON, D.C. SPECIAL COUNSEL

David C. Beck
Thomas H. Brock
Bradley L. Kelly
Peter B. Robb (Not admitted in DC)
Eric J. Schwartz
Duane K. Thompson
Michael K. Wyatt

WASHINGTON, D.C. ASSOCIATES

William M. Altman
Margaret J. Babb (Not admitted in DC)
Donald L. Bell, II (Not admitted in DC)
Richard S. Binstein
Robert S. Canterman
Stephen B. Fabrizio (Not admitted in DC)
James P. Holloway
Dorothy M. Ingalls
Elizabeth A. Lewis (Not admitted in DC)
Laura J. Oberbroeckling (Not admitted in DC)
Matthew J. Oppenheim (Not admitted in DC)
Cheralyn E. Schessler (Not admitted in DC)
Pamela Beth Small
Michael D. Smith (Not admitted in DC)

For full biographical listings, see the Martindale-Hubbell Law Directory

LOUIS RABIL (AV)

Suite 901, 1825 K Street, N.W., 20006
Telephone: 202-466-4944
Fax: 202-223-3260

For full biographical listings, see the Martindale-Hubbell Law Directory

* REED SMITH SHAW & McCLAY (AV)

Ring Building, 1200 18th Street, N.W., 20036-2506
Telephone: 202-457-6100
Cable Address: "Reedsmith Washington" FAX &
TWX: 202-457-6113
Pittsburgh, Pennsylvania Offices: James H. Reed Building, Mellon Square, 435 Sixth Avenue, 15219-1886.
Telephone: 412-288-3131.
FAX: 412-288-3063.
Philadelphia, Pennsylvania Office: 2500 One Liberty Place, 19103-7301.
Telephone: 215-851-8100.
FAX: 215-851-1420.

(See Next Column)

Harrisburg, Pennsylvania Office: 213 Market Street, 17101-2132.
Telephone: 717-234-5988.
FAX: 717-236-3777.
McLean, Virginia Office: Suite 1100, 8251 Greensboro Drive, 22102-3844.
Telephone: 703-734-4600.
FAX: 703-734-4699.
Princeton, New Jersey Office: 136 Main Street, 08540-5799.
Telephone: 609-987-0050.
FAX: 609-951-0824.

MEMBERS OF FIRM

Robert J. Aamoth
Kevin R. Barry
William O. Bittman
Beatrice K. Bleicher
Elizabeth B. Carder
Bernard J. Casey
George R. Clark
Robert D. Clark
Carol Colborn
Francis P. Dicello
John F. Dienelt, P.C.
Robert A. Emmett
John R. Erickson
David C. Evans
Thomas C. Fox
Virginia D. Green
Benjamin J. Griffin
Joel M. Hamme
Gordon W. Hatheway, Jr.
Brian A. Johnson
James K. Kearney
Michael C. Lynch
Kathleen H. McGuan
Donald J. Myers
Peter D. O'Connell
Sherry L. Rhodes
Joseph A. Rieser, Jr.
Marnie K. Sarver
J. Laurent Scharff
Delbert D. Smith
Douglas K. Spaulding
Frederic T. Spindel
Judith St. Ledger-Roty
Alexander P. Starr
Eugene Tillman
Mark H. Tuohey, III
John M. Wood
Erik B. Wulff (Not admitted in DC)

COUNSEL

John A. Beck
Vincent C. Burke III
James J. Freeman
William A. Geoghegan
John W. Hunter
Stefan M. Lopatkiewicz
John J. McDonnell
W. John McGuire
Phillips S. Peter (Not admitted in DC)
Gordon B. Schatz
Ann E. Schmitt
Neil A. Simon
M. Stephanie Wickouski
William H. Willcox

OF COUNSEL

Frank R. Barnako
Harold D. Cohen
William Shalom Green
Robert B. Hankins
Warren L. Miller
Jerome Powell
Edward T. Tait
William F. Wetmore, Jr.

ASSOCIATES

Jennifer S. Blank (Not admitted in DC)
A. Scott Bolden
Mary E. Buckles
Rebecca R. Burkholder
James G. Flood
Jay L. Halpern
Laura H. Jones
Christopher L. Killion
Diane Feldman Killion
Kathleen A. Kirby
Helen G. Kirsch
Janet A. Laufer (Not admitted in DC)
Richard D. Lerner
Linda J. Lewis
Ellen R. Lokker
Paul G. Madison
Robert M. Marino
Joseph W. Metro
David A. Mustone
David Ober
Jerome D. Pinn
Michael B. Richman
Annemarie C. Scanlon
Enrico C. Soriano (Not admitted in DC)
Daniel K. Steen
Jing Wang (Not admitted in United States)
Arthur G. Wyatt

For full biographical listings, see the Martindale-Hubbell Law Directory

* REID & PRIEST LLP (AV)

Market Square, 701 Pennsylvania Ave., N.W., 20004
Telephone: 202-508-4000
Telex: WASH
Facsimile: 202-508-4321
New York City Office: 40 West 57th Street.
Telephone: 212-603-2000.
Fax: 212-603-2298.

Howard A. Cooper
Raymond F. Dacek
Deborah A. DeMasi
Lee M. Goodwin
Robert T. Hall, III
Patricia M. Healy
Jeanne Simkins Hollis
David E. Jacobson
Peter M. Kirby
William A. Kirk, Jr.
Richard J. Leidl
Phillip G. Lookadoo
John D. McGrane
Tedson J. Meyers
Stephan M. Minikes
Floyd L. Norton, IV
Judith D. O'Neill
Courtney M. Price
Mark J. Riedy
John R. Schaefgen, Jr.
Bruce A. Templeton
Michael J. Zimmer

RESIDENT SENIOR COUNSEL

Richard M. Merriman

OF COUNSEL

Jeffrey G. Berman
David A. Gantz

(See Next Column)

REID & PRIEST LLP, *Washington—Continued*

RESIDENT ASSOCIATES

Dean M. Colucci (Not admitted in DC)
Laura M. D'Orsi
M. Christine Cornett Drummond (Not admitted in DC)
William M. Dudley
Gerald P. Farano (Not admitted in DC)
Kevin C. Fitzgerald (Not admitted in DC)
Tara Kalagher Giunta
Jonathan W. Gottlieb
Janet Hernandez (Not admitted in DC)
Mary Ann K. Huntington
Jennifer L. Karas (Not admitted in DC)
Alan Lescht (Not admitted in DC)
Brian J. McManus
Douglas B. Miller (Not admitted in DC)
Manuel A. Miranda (Not admitted in DC)
James K. Mitchell
Timothy M. Murphy
Gregory L. Nelson
Michelle H. Phillips
Bruce L. Richardson
Kenneth B. Weiner (Not admitted in DC)

For full biographical listings, see the Martindale-Hubbell Law Directory

LEWIS A. RIVLIN (AV)

Suite 440, 5335 Wisconsin Avenue, N.W., 20015
Telephone: 301-897-2003/202-895-1718
Fax: 301-897-2005/202-244-8257

Representative Clients: Capitol Hill Community Rehabilitation & Specialty Care Center; British-American Forfaiting; The Piscataway Conoy Confederacy and Sub-Tribes; Chinese Petroleum Supply Corporation; Hojushu Hojukai.

For full biographical listings, see the Martindale-Hubbell Law Directory

*** ROGERS & WELLS** (AV)

607 Fourteenth Street, N.W., 20005-2011
Telephone: 202-434-0700
Facsimile: 202-434-0800
New York, New York Office: 200 Park Avenue, New York, N.Y. 10166-0153.
Telephone: 212-878-8000.
Facsimile: 212-878-8375.
Telex: 234493 RKWUR.
Los Angeles, California Office: 444 South Flower Street, Los Angeles, California 90071-2901.
Telephone: 213-689-2900.
Facsimile: 213-689-2999.
Paris, France Offices: 47, Avenue Hoche, 75008-Paris, France.
Telephone: 33-1-44-09-46-00.
Facsimile: 33-1-42-67-50-81.
Telex: 651617 EURLAW.
London, England Office: 58 Coleman Street, London EC2R 5BE, England.
Telephone: 44-71-628-0101.
Facsimile: 44-71-638-2008.
Telex: 884964 USLAW G.
Frankfurt, Germany Office: Lindenstrasse 37, 60325 Frankfurt/Main, Federal Republic of Germany.
Telephone: 49-69-97-57-11-0.
Facsimile: 49-69-97-57-11-33.

SENIOR PARTNER

William P. Rogers

PARTNERS

Kevin J. Arquit
John H. C. Barron, Jr.
Robert T. Carney
Roger A. Clark
Roberto Dañino
Anthony F. Essaye
Brandon J. Fields
Ira D. Hammerman
John Paul Ketels
Steven A. Newborn (Not admitted in DC)
William Silverman
Ryan Trainer
Dale C. Turza
Charles A. Zielinski (Not admitted in DC)

SENIOR COUNSEL

Eugene T. Rossides

COUNSEL AND OF COUNSEL

Whitney Adams
James M. Lynch
William Morris
Thomas R. Petty
Stuart Rothman
Carrie A. Simon
Samuel A. Stern

CONSULTANTS

Barbara J. Covell
Rinaldo Petrignani
Virginia L. Snider

ASSOCIATES

Jorge E. Alers (Not admitted in DC)
Hollis T. Chen (Not admitted in DC)
Stephen J. Claeys
Charles M. Cole (Not admitted in DC)
David D. DiBari
Jennifer M. Drogula
Paul S. Dwyer Jr. (Not admitted in DC)
Douglas J. Heffner
Timothy P. Keller

(See Next Column)

ASSOCIATES (Continued)

Laurie M. Mathewson (Not admitted in DC)
Cristina M. Mendoza
Michael J. Metzger
Anthony J. Renzi, Jr.
E. Pepper van Noppen
Douglas D. Wetmore IV
David S. Whitescarver
Dawn A. Wilson

For full biographical listings, see the Martindale-Hubbell Law Directory

ROPES & GRAY (AV)

Suite 1200 S, 1001 Pennsylvania Avenue, N.W., 20004
Telephone: 202-626-3900
Telecopy: 202-626-3961
Boston, Massachusetts Office: One International Place.
Telephone: 617-951-7000.
Fax: 617-951-7050.
Providence, Rhode Island Office: 30 Kennedy Plaza.
Telephone: 401-455-4400.
Fax: 401-455-4401.

RESIDENT MEMBERS

Russell A. Gaudreau, Jr.
Thomas M. Susman
Martin E. Lybecker
Colburn T. Cherney
David O. Stewart
Samuel J. Buffone
J. Daniel Berry
Alan G. Priest
Peter M. Brody

COUNSEL

Daniel I. Halperin

RESIDENT ASSOCIATES

Thomas B. Smith
Margaret A. Sheehan (Not admitted in DC)
James M. Lichtman
Linda Dallas Rich (Not admitted in DC)
Maryellen M. Lundquist
Felice C. Wagner
Françoise M. Haan
Margaret C. Curtin (Not admitted in DC)

For full biographical listings, see the Martindale-Hubbell Law Directory

*** ROSENMAN & COLIN** (AV)

1300 19th Street, N.W., 20036
Telephone: 202-463-7177
Telecopier: (202) 429-0046
New York, N.Y. Office: 575 Madison Avenue, 10022.
Telephone: 212-940-8800.
Cable Address: "Rocokay New York."
Telecopiers: (212) 940-8776; (212) 935-0679.
Telex: 427571 ROSCOL (ITT); 971520 RCFLC NYK (WU).
New Jersey Office: Suite 2600, 1 Gateway Center, Newark, New Jersey 07102-5397.
Telephone: 201-645-0572.
Telecopier: 201-645-0573.

RESIDENT PARTNERS

Howard J. Braun
Richard A. Gross
Marybeth Sorady

COUNSEL

Lionel E. Pashkoff

SPECIAL COUNSEL

Theodore A. Howard
Richard A. Ifft
Jerold L. Jacobs
Robert A. Mazer
Sandra L. Spalletta

RESIDENT ASSOCIATES

Michael Dean Gaffney (Not admitted in DC)
Lisa B. Lapinski
Diane L. Mooney
Shelley Sadowsky (Not admitted in DC)
J. Mark Young

For full biographical listings, see the Martindale-Hubbell Law Directory

ROYALL, KOEGEL & WELLS

(See Rogers & Wells)

*** SCHIFF HARDIN & WAITE** (AV)

A Partnership including Professional Corporations
Founded 1864
1101 Connecticut Avenue, N.W., 20036
Telephone: 202-778-6400
Facsimile: 202-778-6460
Chicago, Illinois Office: 7200 Sears Tower.
Telephone: 312-876-1000.
Facsimile: 312-258-5600.
TWX: 910-221-2463.
New York, New York Office: 150 East 52nd Street, Suite 2900.
Telephone: 212-753-5000.
Facsimile: 212-753-5044.
Peoria, Illinois Office: 300 Hamilton Boulevard, Suite 100.
Telephone: 309-673-2800.
Facsimile: 309-673-2801.

(See Next Column)

SCHIFF HARDIN & WAITE—*Continued*

Merrillville, Indiana Office: 8585 Broadway, Suite 842.
Telephone: 219-738-3820.
Facsimile: 219-738-3826.

RESIDENT PARTNERS

Edward J. Finn
Barbara K. Heffernan
Drexel D. Journey
Andrew M. Klein
Gearold L. Knowles
Shaheda Sultan

RESIDENT OF COUNSEL

John W. Glendening, Jr.
Edwin S. Rockefeller
John S. Schmid

RESIDENT ASSOCIATES

Genaro G. Fullano
Cheryl L. Jones
Debra Ann Palmer
M. Thompson Rattray

For full biographical listings, see the Martindale-Hubbell Law Directory

* SCHNADER, HARRISON, SEGAL & LEWIS (AV)

Suite 600, 1913 Eye Street, N.W., 20006-2106
Telephone: 202-463-2900
Cable Address: "Dejuribus Washington"
Fax: 202-296-8930; 775-8741
Philadelphia, Pennsylvania Office: Suite 3600, 1600 Market Street.
Telephone: 215-751-2000.
Cable Address: "Walew."
Fax: 215-751-2205; 215-751-2313.
New York, N.Y. Office: 330 Madison Avenue.
Telephone: 212-973-8000.
Cable Address: "Dejuribus, New York."
Fax: 212-972-8798.
Harrisburg, Pennsylvania Office: Suite 700, 30 North Third Street.
Telephone: 717-231-4000.
Fax: 717-231-4012.
Norristown, Pennsylvania Office: Suite 901, One Montgomery Plaza.
Telephone: 215-277-7700.
Fax: 215-277-3211.
Pittsburgh, Pennsylvania Office: Suite 2700, Fifth Avenue Place, 120 Fifth Avenue.
Telephone: 412-577-5200.
Fax: 412-765-3858.
Scranton, Pennsylvania Office: Suite 700, 108 North Washington Avenue.
Telephone: 717-342-6100.
Fax: 717-342-6147.
Washington, Pennsylvania Office: 8 East Pine Street.
Telephone: 412-222-7378.
Fax: 412-222-0771.
Cherry Hill, New Jersey Office: Suite 200, Woodland Falls Corporate Park, 220 Lake Drive East.
Telephone: 609-482-5222.
Fax: 609-482-6980.
Atlanta, Georgia Office: Suite 2550 Marquis Two Tower, 285 Peachtree Center Avenue, N.E.
Telephone: 404-215-8100.
Fax: 404-223-5164.

MEMBERS OF THE FIRM IN WASHINGTON

Cherie Beth Artz
Alan A. D'Ambrosio
Alan H. Kent
Greggory B. Mendenhall

SENIOR COUNSEL

Paul G. Dembling

COUNSEL TO THE FIRM IN WASHINGTON

Lisa J. Savitt

RETIRED MEMBERS OF THE FIRM IN WASHINGTON

Harold F. Blasky

ASSOCIATES IN WASHINGTON

David J. Zarfes

For full biographical listings, see the Martindale-Hubbell Law Directory

SEDKY, WITTIE & LETSCHE (AV)

A Professional Limited Liability Company
1115 30th Street, N.W., Suite 150, 20007
Telephone: 202-333-5133
Fax: 202-342-2067

Cherif Sedky
Patricia Heckmann Wittie
Karla Jayne Letsche

For full biographical listings, see the Martindale-Hubbell Law Directory

* SEWARD & KISSEL (AV)

(Smith & Martin 1890)
1200 G Street, N.W. Suite 350, 20005
Telephone: 202-737-8833
Cable Address: "Sewkis New York"
Telex: 23-9046; 62-0982
Facsimile: 202-737-5184
New York, New York Office: One Battery Park Plaza.
Telephone: 212-574-1200.
Facsimile: 212-480-8421.
Budapest, Hungary Representative Office: Nádor utca 11, 1051 Budapest, Hungary.
Telephone: 361-132-7115.
Facsimile: 361-132-7940.

RESIDENT PARTNERS

Anthony C. J. Nuland
Paul T. Clark

RESIDENT ASSOCIATES

Alison M. Fuller (Not admitted in DC)
Elizabeth Warner

RESIDENT COUNSEL

Keith H. Ellis

For full biographical listings, see the Martindale-Hubbell Law Directory

SHAW, PITTMAN, POTTS & TROWBRIDGE (AV)

A Partnership including Professional Corporations
2300 N Street, N.W., 20037
Telephone: 202-663-8000
Cable Address: "Shawlaw"
Telex: 89-2693 (Shawlaw Wsh)
Telecopier: 202-663-8007
McLean, Virginia Office 1501 Farm Credit Drive. Telephone: 703-790-7900.
Telecopier: 703-821-2397.
Leesburg, Virginia Office: 201 Liberty Street, S.W.
Telephone: 703-777-0004. Metro: 478-8989. Facsmile: 703-777-9320.
Alexandria, Virginia Office: 115 South Union Street.
Telephone: 703-739-6650.
Fax: 703-739-6699.
New York, N.Y. Office: 900 Third Avenue, Suite 1800.
Telephone: 212-836-4200.
Facsimile: 212-836-4201.

MEMBERS OF FIRM

George F. Trowbridge (1919-1989)
George F. Albright, Jr. (Not admitted in DC)
Scott A. Anenberg (P.C.)
Richard I. Ansbacher
Mark Augenblick (P.C.)
Dean D. Aulick (P.C.)
Frank J. Baltz (P.C.) (Resident, McLean, Virginia Office)
Deborah Brand Baum
Thomas A. Baxter (P.C.)
Richard S. Beatty
Ernest L. Blake, Jr. (P.C.)
Phillip D. Bostwick (P.C.)
Nathaniel P. Breed, Jr. (P.C.)
Winthrop N. Brown (P.C.)
John M. Bryson, II
Jonathan T. Cain
John L. Carr, Jr.
Kenneth A. Caruso (Resident, New York, N.Y. Office)
Michael A. Carvin
Thomas J. Catliota
Deborah B. Charnoff
Gerald Charnoff (P.C.)
Craig E. Chason
Howard L. Clemons
Robert E. Cohn
Charles J. Cooper
Alan B. Croft (Resident, McLean, Virginia Office)
B. Scott Custer, Jr.
David J. Cynamon (P.C.)
Robert J. Cynkar
Craig A. de Ridder
Robert M. Di Giovanni
Mary Jane Dodson
Richard C. Donaldson (Not admitted in DC)
John Engel (P.C.)
Jay A. Epstien (P.C.)
David G. Fiske (Resident, Alexandria, Virginia Office)
Ellen A. Fredel (P.C.)
J. Mark Gidley
Harry H. Glasspiegel
Lewis S. Goodman (Not admitted in DC)
Robert M. Gordon
Ellen Canan Grady
Andrew N. Greene
James B. Hamlin (P.C.)
R. Timothy Hanlon (P.C.)
Philip J. Harvey (Resident, Alexandria, Virginia Office)
Sheila McC. Harvey
J. Patrick Hickey (P.C.)
C. Thomas Hicks III (P.C.) (Resident, McLean, Virginia Office)
Thomas C. Hill (P.C.)
Jeffrey D. Hutchings
Stephen B. Huttler (P.C.)
Jeffrey R. Keitelman
Campbell Killefer
Allen J. Klein
Frederick L. Klein (P.C.)
Martin D. Krall (P.C.)
M. David Krohn
Charles J. Landy
Weldon H. Latham
J. Thomas Lenhart (P.C.)
David R. Lewis
Fred A. Little (P.C.)
Sylvia M. Mahaffey
Louise A. Mathews
Thomas H. McCormick
Jack McKay (P.C.)
Steven L. Meltzer (P.C.)
David E. Menotti
Paul F. Mickey, Jr.
David L. Miller (P.C.)
Michael C. Moetell
Thomas D. Morton
J. E. Murdock III (Resident)
Trevor W. Nagel (Not admitted in DC)
Leslie A. Nicholson, Jr. (P.C.)
John H. O'Neill, Jr. (P.C.)
Richard J. Parrino (P.C.)
Robert D. Paul
William F. Pedersen, Jr.
Victoria J. Perkins (P.C.)
Paul S. Pilecki (P.C.)
Ira H. Raphaelson (Not admitted in DC)
John B. Rhinelander (P.C.)

(See Next Column)

SHAW, PITTMAN, POTTS & TROWBRIDGE, *Washington—Continued*

MEMBERS OF FIRM (Continued)

Robert B. Robbins (P.C.)
George M. Rogers, Jr. (P.C.)
Barbara M. Rossotti (P.C.)
David R. Sahr
John F. Seymour
Jay E. Silberg (P.C.)
Leslie K. Smith
Lynn A. Soukup (P.C.)
John L. Sullivan, III (Resident, McLean, Virginia Office)
Ralph A. Taylor, Jr. (P.C.)
Charles B. Temkin (P.C.)
Paul M. Thomas
Anthony J. Thompson
Alexander D. Tomaszczuk
Matias F. Travieso-Diaz (P.C.)
John M. Weaver (Not admitted in DC)
R. Kenly Webster (P.C.)
Robert N. Weinstock
Sheldon J. Weisel (P.C.)
Wendelin A. White
Milton B. Whitfield
Richard F. Williamson (Not admitted in DC)
Blair C. Woodside, III
Jeffery L. Yablon (P.C.)
Robert E. Zahler (P.C.)

SENIOR COUNSEL

George V. Allen, Jr.
Caryl S. Bernstein
Robert E. Conn
John F. Dealy (Not admitted in DC)
Fred Drasner
Steuart L. Pittman (P.C.)
Ramsay D. Potts (P.C.)
Roger M. Whelan

COUNSEL

Scott E. Barat (Resident, McLean, Virginia Office)
Brenda Jean Boykin
Eileen L. Brownell
Mindy Buren
Thomas E. Crocker, Jr.
Anita J. Finkelstein
Ethan J. Friedman
Paul A. Gaukler
Katharine Herber Gustafson (Not admitted in DC)
Elizabeth A. Karmin
Joseph E. Kendall
Susan C. Longstreet
Singleton B. McAllister
Paul J. McNulty (Not admitted in DC)
Joyce L. Oliner
Diane Shapiro Richer
Howard K. Shapar
Danielle R. Srour
C. Elizabeth Espin Stern
Jill Abeshouse Stern
Michael Stern
Timothy Hansen Watkins
Gino Zaccardelli

ASSOCIATES

Maureen Byrne Beahn (Resident, Alexandria, Virginia Office)
Mark H. Berman
Michelle D. Bernard
Christine R. Bianchine
David H. Brody
Lisa M. Byington
Denise R. Cade
John D. Caine (Not admitted in DC)
Cecelia A. Calaby
Jennifer P. Clasby (Not admitted in DC)
Mandy S. Cohen (Not admitted in DC)
Vincent J. Colatriano
Teresa L. Diaz
Alvin Dunn
Peter G. Emerson (Not admitted in DC)
Steven R. Escobar (Not admitted in DC)
Daniela P. Feldhausen (Not admitted in DC)
Joseph C. Figini
Arnold R. Finlayson
Alan G. Fishel
Tara M. Flynn
Michael C. Friedman (Not admitted in DC)
F. Edwin Froelich
John D. Gardiner
Jennifer A. Giblin
David C. Goldberg
Theresa V. Gorski
Mary Jo Grote
Maria E. Hallas
Elisabeth J. Harper
Robert E. Hasty
Lana K. Hawkins
M. Scott Hemphill (Not admitted in DC)
D. Bruce Hendrick
Michael L. Hentrel
Devon Elizabeth Hewitt
Sheryl R. Israel
Michael A. Jacobs
Ellen M. Jakovic
David M. Janet (Not admitted in DC)
Christopher G. Janney
John E. Jensen
Alexander W. Joel
Christine Nicolaides Kearns
Charis R. Keitelman (Resident, McLean, Virginia Office)
Michael W. Kirk
Michael E. Lavine
Warren U. Lehrenbaum (Not admitted in DC)
Todd A. Lehtonen (Not admitted in DC)
Susan M. Lennon
Michael G. Lepre
Jay L. Levine (Not admitted in DC)
Karen W. Levy (Not admitted in DC)
Robert Y. Lewis (Not admitted in DC)
Josephine S. Lo
Anne Marie Longobucco (Not admitted in DC)
Amy Hurite Macdonald
David J. Manderscheid
Darryl G. McCallum
Michael J. McCue
John M. McDonald (Not admitted in DC)
Michael P. McGowan
William L. McGrath
Thomas W. Mitchell (Resident, Alexandria, Virginia Office)
Ian Thomas Moar
Daniel W. Monks (Not admitted in DC)
Michael F. Newbold (Not admitted in DC)
Richard J. Nizzardini (Not admitted in DC)
Mitchell S. Nusbaum
Elizabeth Ann O'Brien
Thomas J. Pax
Steven W. Pearlman
Frederick S. Phillips
W. Eric Pilsk
Anne K. Planning
Patrick John Potter
Edward M. Prince, Jr. (Not admitted in DC)
Edward J. Reed
Mitchell S. Ross
Elisabeth T. Roth
Harry Rubin
Frederick R. Scarboro
Saul A. Scherl

(See Next Column)

ASSOCIATES (Continued)

Paul K. Schwartzberg
Edward C. Schweitzer, Jr.
Jackson H. Sherrill III (Resident, McLean, Virginia Office)
Hala M. Sibay (Not admitted in DC; Resident, McLean, Virginia Office)
Margery B. Silberstein
Thomas J. Simeone
Debbie Beecher Spartin
Julia A. Springer
Traci J. Stegemann
Danielle O. Stieger (Resident, McLean, Virginia Office)
Lea Ann P. Stone
Leslie A. Stout-Tabackman
Jane M. Sullivan
Lori L. Vaughn (Resident, Alexandria, Virginia Office)
James P. Veillette
Jeffrey A. Watiker
Aen W. Webster
Peter P. Weidenbruch, III (Not admitted in DC)
Gadi Weinreich
Michael J. Wendorf (Resident, Alexandria, Virginia Office)
Linda S. Wendtland
Amy Span Wergeles
Mark L. Whitaker
D. Craig Wolff
Mark T. Womack
Maryelena Zaccardelli
Constantine J. Zepos (Not admitted in DC)
Janice Helen Ziegler

For full biographical listings, see the Martindale-Hubbell Law Directory

SHEA & GARDNER (AV)

1800 Massachusetts Avenue, N.W., 20036
Telephone: 202-828-2000
Cable Address: "Sandg"
Telex: 89-2399
Telecopier: 202-828-2195

MEMBERS OF FIRM

Francis M. Shea (1905-1989)
Warner W. Gardner
Lawrence J. Latto
Richard T. Conway
Robert T. Basseches
Benjamin W. Boley
Ralph J. Moore, Jr.
Martin J. Flynn
Stephen J. Pollak
David Booth Beers
Anthony A. Lapham
Richard M. Sharp
John D. Aldock
William S. Moore
John Townsend Rich
James R. Bieke
I. Michael Greenberger
William F. Sheehan
Frederick C. Schafrick
David B. Cook
Stephen J. Hadley
Franklin D. Kramer
Wendy S. White
William R. Galeota
Patrick M. Hanlon
Nancy C. Shea
Timothy K. Shuba
James R. Bird
Michael S. Giannotto
Jeffrey C. Martin
William R. Hanlon
Elizabeth Runyan Geise
Collette C. Goodman
Julie M. Edmond
Laura S. Wertheimer
Richard M. Wyner
Thomas J. Mikula
Eugenia Langan
Nancy B. Stone
Christopher E. Palmer
Mark S. Raffman
Elizabeth Merrill Brown

OF COUNSEL

William H. Dempsey

ASSOCIATES

Eric C. Jeffrey
Elise J. Rabekoff
Joseph F. Yenouskas
Robert B. Wasserman
Bernice M. Blair
Anne R. Bowden
David A. Bono
William D. Weinreb
Kenneth F. Sparks
Lisa A. Landsman
Anthony Hong
Amanda Berlowe Jaffe
John Moustakas (Not admitted in DC)
David E. Jones
Jonathan D. Boggs
Cynthia Gurnee Pugh
Dana J. Martin
John Bradford Wiegmann
David M. Battan
Lloyd D. Collier
Michael K. Isenman
Valerie Ellen Ross (Not admitted in DC)
David B. Goodhand
Benjamin J. Vernia
David J. Katz
Celestine Richards McConville
Kim Dettelbach (Not admitted in DC)
Amy Horton
Edward J. Naughton (Not admitted in DC)
Martha Hirschfield
Martin F. Hansen (Not admitted in DC)
Susan L. Pacholski (Not admitted in DC)
James R. Bramson (Not admitted in DC)

For full biographical listings, see the Martindale-Hubbell Law Directory

SHEARMAN & STERLING (AV)

801 Pennsylvania Avenue, N.W., Suite 900, 20004-2604
Telephone: (202) 508-8000
Fax: (202) 508-8100
New York, N.Y. Office: 599 Lexington Avenue, New York, New York 10022-6069 and Citicorp Center, 153 East 53rd Street, New York, New York 10022-4676.
Telephone: (212) 848-4000.
Telex: 667290 Num Lau.
Fax: 599 Lexington Avenue: (212) 848-7179. Citicorp Center: (212) 848-5252.
Abu Dhabi, United Arab Emirates Office: P.O. Box 2948.
Telephone: (971-2) 324477.
Fax: (971-2) 774533.

(See Next Column)

SHEARMAN & STERLING—*Continued*

Beijing, People's Republic of China Office: Suite #2205, Capital Mansion, No. 6, Xin Yuan Nan Road. Chao Yang District Beijing, 100004.
Telephone: (861) 465-4574.
Fax: (861) 465-4578.
Budapest, Hungary Office: Szerb utca 17-19, 1056 Budapest.
Telephone: (36-1) 266-3522.
Fax: (36-1) 266-3523.
Düsseldorf, Federal Republic of Germany Office: Königsallee 46, D-40212 Düsseldorf.
Telephone: (49-211) 13 62 80.
Telex: 8 588 294 NYLO.
Fax: (49-211) 13 33 09.
Frankfurt, Federal Republic of Germany Office: Bockenheimer Landstrasse 55, D-60325 Frankfurt am Main.
Telephone: (49-69) 97-10-70.
Fax: (49-69) 97-10-71-00.
Hong Kong, Hong Kong Office: Standard Chartered Bank Building, 4 Des Voeux Road Central, Hong Kong.
Telephone: (852) 978-8000.
Fax: (852) 978-8099.
London, England Office: 199 Bishopsgate, London EC2M 3TY.
Telephone: (44-71) 920-9000.
Fax: (44-71) 920-9020.
Los Angeles, California Office: 725 South Figueroa Street, 21st Floor, 90017-5421.
Telephone: (213) 239-0300.
Fax: (213) 239-0381, 614-0936.
Paris, France Office: 12 rue d'Astorg, 75008.
Telephone: (33-1) 44-71-17-17.
Telex: 282964 Royale.
Fax: (33-1) 44-71-01-01.
San Francisco, California Office: 555 California Street, 94104-1522.
Telephone: (415) 616-1100.
Fax: (415) 616-1199.
Taipei, Taiwan Office: 7th Floor, Hung Kuo Building, 167 Tun Hwa North Road.
Telephone: (886-2) 545-3300.
Fax: (866-2) 545-3322.
Tokyo, Japan Office: Shearman & Sterling (Thomas Wilner Gaikokuho-Jimu-Bengoshi Jimusho), Fukoku Seimei Building, 5th Fl. 2-2-2, Uchisaiwaicho, Chiyoda-ku, Tokyo 100, Japan.
Telephone: (81 3) 5251-1601.
Fax: (81 3) 5251-1602.
Toronto, Ontario, Canada Office: Commerce Court West, Suite 4405, P.O. Box 247, M5L 1E8.
Telephone: (416) 360-8484.
Fax: (416) 360-2958.

RESIDENT PARTNERS

Thomas S. Martin (Managing Partner)
Robert E. Dineen, Jr. (Not admitted in DC)
Robert A. Bergquist
Jonathan L. Greenblatt (Not admitted in DC)
Robert E. Herzstein
Thomas B. Wilner (Also at Tokyo Office)

OF COUNSEL

Edward Bransilver

OTHER COUNSEL

Stephan E. Becker (International Trade Counsel)

For full biographical listings, see the Martindale-Hubbell Law Directory

SHERMAN, MEEHAN & CURTIN, P.C. (AV)

Suite 600, 1900 M Street, N.W., 20036-3565
Telephone: 202-331-7120
Facsimile: 202-296-1529

Peter R. Sherman
Thomas P. Meehan
Michael F. Curtin
Sanford K. Ain
Lee H. Spence
David Barmak
Thomas E. Dunigan
David Bradford Law
Randell C. Ogg
Faith D. Dornbrand
Mark S. Carlin
Mark S. Tenenbaum
Claudia Anne Pott
Sam H. Roberson

OF COUNSEL

John O. Fox

Charles B. Day
Douglas E. Fierberg
Laurence E. Salans
Lauren E. Shea
Charlotte D. Young
Nancy L. Walsh
Robert E. Sarazen
Rose Kriger Renberg
Matthew P. Maloney
Jeffrey C. Weinstock
Charles A. Zdebski (Not admitted in DC)

For full biographical listings, see the Martindale-Hubbell Law Directory

* SIDLEY & AUSTIN (AV)

A Partnership including Professional Corporations
1722 Eye Street, N.W., 20006
Telephone: 202-736-8000
Telecopier: 202-736-8711
Chicago, Illinois Office: One First National Plaza 60603.
Telephone: 312-853-7000.
Telecopier: 312-853-7036.
Los Angeles, California Office: 555 W. 5th Street, 40th Flr., 90013-1010.
Telephone: 213-896-6000.
Telecopier: 213-896-6600.
New York, New York Office: 875 Third Avenue 10022.
Telephone: 212-906-2000.
Telecopier: 212-906-2021.
London, England Office: Broadwalk House 5 Appold Street, EC2A 2AA.
Telephone: 011-44-71-621-1616.
Telecopier: 011-44-71-626-7937.
Tokyo, Japan Office: Taisho Seimei Hibiya Building, 7th Floor, 9-1, Yura Kucho, 1 Chome, Chiyoda-ku, 100.
Telephone: 011-81-3-3218-5900.
Facsimile: 011-81-3-3218-5922.
Singapore Office: UIC Building, 32nd Floor, Suite 3207, 5 Shenton Way, Singapore 0106.
Telephone: 011-65-224-5000.
Telecopier: 011-65-224-0530.

RESIDENT PARTNERS

Christopher L. Bell
Judith Hippler Bello
James F. Bendernagel, Jr.
Jeffrey S. Berlin
Frederic G. Berner, Jr.
Richard D. Bernstein
David T. Buente, Jr.
C. John Buresh
Ann E. Bushmiller
Daniel M. Davidson
Eugene R. Elrod
Lester G. Fant III
Ronald S. Flagg
Alan C. Geolot
Thomas C. Green
Joseph R. Guerra
Samuel I. Gutter
Mark E. Haddad
Kevin Hawley
Stephen S. Hill
Alan F. Holmer
Mark D. Hopson
Terence M. Hynes
George W. Jones, Jr.
Peter D. Keisler
David M. Levy
David J. Lewis
Angus Macbeth
Marc E. Manly
Lorrie M. Marcil
Robert D. McLean
David Michael Miles
Lawrence A. Miller
G. Paul Moates
Michael A. Nemeroff
Francis J. O'Toole
Carter G. Phillips
Vincent F. Prada
Imad I. Qasim
P. David Richardson, II
Melvin Rishe
Constance Arden Sadler
Gene C. Schaerr
Mark D. Schneider
Langley R. Shook
Joseph B. Tompkins, Jr.
R. Clark Wadlow
R. Merinda Wilson
Elroy H. Wolff
Robert R. Wootton (Not admitted in DC)
Thomas H. Yancey

COUNSEL

David R. Ford
Rex E. Lee
Stephen B. Lyons
Mark E. Martin
Gary P. Quigley
Richard E. Young

RESIDENT ASSOCIATES

Ann K. Adams
Bradford A. Berenson
Samuel B. Boxerman (Not admitted in DC)
Robert J. Conlan, Jr. (Not admitted in DC)
James L. Connaughton
Denise W. DeFranco
Christine L. Di Bacco (Not admitted in DC)
Christopher R. Drahozal
Thomas G. Echikson
Doris S. Finnerman
Nina B. Finston
Paula G. Friedman
Jacqueline Gerson (Not admitted in DC)
Nancy Yaeger Gorman
Jeffrey T. Green
Dennis D. Hirsch (Not admitted in DC)
Adam D. Hirsh
Kurt H. Jacobs
E. Michael Johnson
Paul E. Kalb
Susan Gomory Keisler
Richard D. Klingler
Richard L. Larach
David L. Lawson
"Jaye" Janet M. Letson
Christine A. Liverzani (Not admitted in DC)
Christopher P. Lu
Teresa L. McGhie
Molly A. Meegan
Alexandra G. Mihalas
Jonathan E. Nuechterlein
Tamara R. Parker
Joseph C. Port, Jr.
Linda S. Portasik
Jeremy O. Preiss
Tamara L. Preiss
Nathan C. Sheers
Donald H. Smith
Margaret F. Spring (Not admitted in DC)
Howard J. Stanislawski
Julia E. Sullivan
Kathryn B. Thomson
Thomas P. Van Wazer
Frank R. Volpe (Not admitted in DC)
Michael D. Warden
Mark E. Warren
John F. Wester
James P. Young (Not admitted in DC)

For full biographical listings, see the Martindale-Hubbell Law Directory

Washington—Continued

*** SKADDEN, ARPS, SLATE, MEAGHER & FLOM (AV)**

1440 New York Avenue, N.W., 20005
Telephone: 202-371-7000
Fax: 202-393-5760
New York, New York Office: 919 Third Avenue, 10022.
Telephone: 212-735-3000.
Fax: 212-735-2000; 212-735-2001.
Telex: 645899 Skarslaw.
Boston, Massachusetts Office: One Beacon Street, 02108.
Telephone: 617-573-4800.
Fax: 617-573-4822.
Wilmington, Delaware Office: One Rodney Square, 19899.
Telephone: 302-651-3000.
Fax: 302-651-3001.
Los Angeles, California Office: 300 South Grand Avenue, 90071.
Telephone: 213-687-5000.
Fax: 213-687-5600.
Chicago, Illinois Office: 333 West Wacker Drive, 60606.
Telephone: 312-407-0700.
Fax: 312-407-0411.
San Francisco, California Office: Four Embarcadero Center, 94111.
Telephone: 415-984-6400.
Fax: 415-984-2698.
Houston, Texas Office: 1600 Smith Street, Suite 4460, 77002.
Telephone: 713-655-5100.
Fax: 713-655-5181.
Newark, New Jersey Office: One Riverfront Plaza, 07102.
Telephone: 201-596-4440.
Fax: 201-596-4444.
Tokyo, Japan Office: 12th Floor, The Fukoku Seimei Building, 2-2-2, Uchisaiwaicho, Chiyoda-ku, 100.
Telephone: 011-81-3-3595-3850.
Fax: 011-81-3-3504-2780.
London, England Office: 25 Bucklersbury EC4N 8DA.
Telephone: 011-44-71-248-9929.
Fax: 011-44-71-489-8533.
Hong Kong Office: 30/F Peregrine Tower, Lippo Centre, 89 Queensway, Central.
Telephone: 011-852-820-0700.
Fax: 011-852-820-0727.
Sydney, New South Wales, Australia Office: Level 26-State Bank Centre, 52 Martin Place, 2000.
Telephone: 011-61-2-224-6000.
Fax: 011-61-2-224-6044.
Toronto, Ontario Office: Suite 1820, North Tower, P.O. Box 189, Royal Bank Plaza, M5J 2J4.
Telephone: 416-777-4700.
Fax: 416-777-4747.
Paris, France Office: 105 rue du Faubourg Saint-Honoré, 75008.
Telephone: 011-33-1-40-75-44-44.
Fax: 011-33-1-49-53-09-99.
Brussels, Belgium Office: 523 avenue Louise, Box 30, 1050.
Telephone: 011-32-2-648-7666.
Fax: 011-32-2-640-3032.
Frankfurt, Germany Office: MesseTurm, 27th Floor, 60308.
Telephone: 011-49-69-9757-3000.
Fax: 011-49-69-9757-3050.
Beijing, China Office: 1605 Capital Mansion Tower, No. 6 Xin Yuan Nan Road, Chao Yang District, 100004.
Telephone: 011-86-1-466-8800.
Fax: 011-86-1-466-8822.
Budapest, Hungary Office: Mahart Building, H-1052 Apáczai Csere János u.11, Vl.em.
Telephone: 011-36-1-266-2145.
Fax: 011-36-1-266-4033.
Prague, Czech Republic Office: Revolucni 16, 110 00.
Telephone: 011-42-2-231-75-18.
Fax: 011-42-2-231-47-33.
Moscow, Russia Office: Pleteshkovsky Pereulok 1, 107005.
Telephone: 011-7-501-940-2304.
Fax: 011-7-501-940-2511.

Neal S. McCoy
J. Phillip Adams (Not admitted in DC)
John M. Nannes
Rodney O. Thorson
Lynn R. Coleman
Leslie J. Goldman
Douglas G. Robinson
C. Benjamin Crisman, Jr.
Michael P. Rogan
Thomas R. Graham
Robert E. Lighthizer
Fred T. Goldberg, Jr.
Ronald C. Barusch
Stephen W. Hamilton
Dorothy A. Darrah
William J. Sweet, Jr.
Enid L. Veron
Erica A. Ward
Gilbert T. Schwartz
Clifford M. Naeve
Martin Klepper
Paul W. Oosterhuis
Richard L. Brusca
Marcia R. Nirenstein
Douglas E. Nordlinger
Thomas J. Casey
Robert S. Bennett
Carl S. Rauh
Alan Kriegel
Janet L. Goetz
Pamela F. Olson
Jeanine L. Matte
John J. Mangan
William S. Scherman
Antoinette Cook Bush

(See Next Column)

Albert H. Turkus
Kenneth Berlin
Mitchell S. Ettinger
Kenneth A. Gross

SPECIAL COUNSEL

Robert B. Greenbaum
Kenneth F. Kraus
Edward D. Ross, Jr.

COUNSEL

Thomas E. Weil, Jr.
Leonard M. Rawicz
June P. Broadstone
Brian C. Mohr
Mona E. Ehlenberger
Matthew W. S. Estes
Mark C. Del Bianco
David Scott Nance

OF COUNSEL

Stephen E. McGregor
Philip McBride Johnson

ASSOCIATES

James V. Alpi
John A. Amodeo
Bonnie J. Austin
Faton A. Bacaj
Nancy D. Baird
Kevin Barnette
Alicia J. Batts
Kurt W. Bilas
Jonathan Biran (Not admitted in DC)
Jay L. Birnbaum
Jessie M. Brooks
Lance T. Brasher
John Burke
William Charles Claiborne, III (Not admitted in DC)
Todd R. Coles
Paul J. Crispino (Not admitted in DC)
Roseann M. Cutrone
David A. Domansky
Henry C. Eisenberg
John N. Estes, III
James A. Frazer
Michael R. Freed (Not admitted in DC)
Don Joaquin Frost, Jr.
Barry J. Gilman
William F. Gould
Clifford R. Gross
Bernice Harleston (Not admitted in DC)
Robert L. Harris (Not admitted in DC)
J. Dean Hinderliter
Richard A. Hindman
Scot B. Hutchins
Laura Anne Ingraham
Zygmunt Jablonski
Jerry Jackson
Chad S. Johnson (Not admitted in DC)
Leo J. Kane
Benjamin B. Klubes
Andrew L. Kolesar
Ellen L. Lyons
Gary A. MacDonald
Marc Stukhart Martin (Not admitted in DC)
August J. Matteis (Not admitted in DC)
Stacie E. McGinn
Nancy J. McGlynn
John McNamara
Edward J. Meehan
Alan J. Meese
Nancy K. Oliver (Not admitted in DC)
Saul M. Pilchen
Timothy R. Robinson
Catherine Kane Ronis
Nancy G. Rubin
Peter B. Saba
Amy R. Sabrin
Andrew L. Sandler
Alan G. Schiffman
Curtis W. Schuhmacher (Not admitted in DC)
Frank C. Shaw
Kenneth K. Shiu (Not admitted in DC)
Pankaj K. Sinha
Matthew A. Stevens
Katharine R. Stollman
Alan J.J. Swirski
James L. Tanner, Jr. (Not admitted in DC)
Donald Leo Toker, Jr.
Mayling Tom
Pranav Lalit Trivedi
Carol R. Van Cleef
James D. Veltrop
David J. Waksman (Not admitted in DC)
Katherine T. Wallace
Jennifer K. Walter
Troy S. Watkinson
Rhoda L. Weeks
Roger D. Williams
Nancy A. Wodka
Lawrence T. Yanowitch

For full biographical listings, see the Martindale-Hubbell Law Directory

SONNENSCHEIN NATH & ROSENTHAL (AV)

1301 K Street, N.W. Suite 600 East Tower, 20005
Telephone: 202-408-6400
Fax: 202-408-6399
Chicago, Illinois Office: Suite 8000 Sears Tower, 233 South Wacker Drive.
Telephone: 312-876-8000.
Cable Address: "Sonberk".
Telex: 25-3526.
Facsimile: 312-876-7934.
New York, N.Y. Office: 1221 Avenue of the Americas, 24th Floor.
Telephone: 212-768-6700.
Facsimile: 212-391-1247.
San Francisco, California Office: 685 Market Street, 10th Floor.
Telephone: 415-882-5000.
Facsimile: 415-543-5472; 882-5038.
Los Angeles, California Office: 601 South Figueroa Street, Suite 1500.
Telephone: 213-623-9300.
Facsimile: 213-623-9924.
St. Louis, Missouri Office: One Metropolitan Square, Suite 3000.
Telephone: 314-241-1800.
Facsimile: 314-259-5959.

RESIDENT PARTNERS

Amy L. Bess
Todd R. Eskelsen
Elizabeth A. Ferrell
John S. Hahn
Stuart E. Hunt
Fred L. Levy
Roger W. Patrick
Caryl A. Potter, III
Douglas E. Rosenthal
Timothy C. Russell
Kirk R. Ruthenberg
Michael A. Schlanger
Ronald E. Stauffer
Jerome P. Weiss

(See Next Column)

SONNENSCHEIN NATH & ROSENTHAL—*Continued*

OF COUNSEL

Robert B. Murphy

RESIDENT ASSOCIATES

William F. Burton
John J. Calkins
(Not admitted in DC)
Maria Sileno DeLoughry
(Not admitted in DC)
Jill Gould (Not admitted in DC)
Joseph P. Hornyak
Lisa A. MacVittie
(Not admitted in DC)
Michael R. Maryn
Laura F. Peters
Kenneth J. Pfaehler
(Not admitted in DC)
Debra McGuire Piliero
Stephanie A. Rigaux
Felicia L. Silber
Pamela Grose Welty

For full biographical listings, see the Martindale-Hubbell Law Directory

SQUIRE, SANDERS & DEMPSEY (AV)

1201 Pennsylvania Avenue, N.W., P.O. Box 407, 20044
Telephone: 202-626-6600
Fax: 202-626-6780
Cleveland, Ohio Office: 4900 Society Center, 127 Public Square.
Telephone: 216-479-8500. Fax's: 216-479-8780, 216-479-8781, 216-479-8777, 216-479-8787, 216-479-8795, 216-479-8793, 216-479-8776, 216-479-8788.
Columbus, Ohio Office: 1300 Huntington Center, 41 South High Street, Columbus, Ohio 43215.
Telephone: 614-365-2700.
Fax: 614-365-2499.
Jacksonville, Florida Office: One Enterprise Center, Suite 2100, 225 Water Street.
Telephone: 904-353-1264.
Fax: 904-356-2986.
Miami, Florida Office: 201 South Biscayne Boulevard, Suite 2900 Miami Center.
Telephone: 305-577-8700.
Fax: 305-358-1425.
New York, New York Office: 520 Madison Avenue, 32nd Floor.
Telephone: 212-872-9800.
Fax: 212-872-9814.
Phoenix, Arizona Office: Two Renaissance Square, 40 North Central Avenue, Suite 2700.
Telephone: 602-528-4000.
Fax: 602-253-8129.
European Office: Avenue Louise, 165, Box 15, 1050 Brussels, Belgium.
Telephone: 011-32-2-648-1717.
TLX: 61961.
Cable: "Coxsquire".
Rapifax: 011-322-648-1064.
European Office: Adria Palace Jungmannova 31/36, 11000 Prague 1, Czech Republic.
Telephone: 011-42-2-231-5661, 011-42-2-231-5678, 011-42-2-231-5698.
Fax: 011-42-2-231-5482.
European Office: Mudronova 37, 811 01 Bratislava, Slovak Republic.
Telephone: 011-42-7-313-362; 011-42-7-315-370.
Fax: 011-42-7-313-918.
European Office: Deak Ferenc Ut. 10, Office 304, H-1052 Budapest V., Hungary.
Telephones: 011-36-1-226-2024; 011-36-1-226-5038.
Fax: 011-36-1-226-2025.
European Office: 1 Gunpowder Square, Printer Street, London EC4A 3DE.
Telephone: 011-44-71-830-0055.
Fax: 011-44-71-830-0056.
Kiev, Ukraine Office: Vul. Prorizna 9, Suite 20, Kiev 252035, Ukraine.
Telephone: 011-7-044-244-3452, 011-7-044-244-3453, 011-7-044-228-8687.
Fax: 011-7-044-228-4938.

MEMBERS OF FIRM

Stephen R. Bell
Timothy W. Bergin
Samuel H. Black
Alan L. Briggs
(Not admitted in DC)
Donald T. Bucklin
James V. Dick
Edward A. Geltman
Edward J. Hawkins
John C. Henry, Jr.
Sherman E. Katz (Resident)
Scott T. Kragie
Ann J. LaFrance
Henry W. Lavine
Joseph P. Markoski
Herbert E. Marks
Michael H. Mobbs
James P. Murphy
Robert D. Papkin
Barry A. Pupkin
Edward W. Sauer
Michael R. Silverman
Marshall Sanford Sinick
Ritchie T. Thomas
Glenn M. Young

RESIDENT OF COUNSEL

Patricia P. Bailey
James M. Cole
J. Edward Day (Retired)
Paul George Dietrich
(Not admitted in DC)
Elizabeth Glass Geltman
John Lansdale, Jr. (Retired)
Richard B. Lavine (Retired)
Vladimir Lechtman
Thomas J. Quigley (Retired)
Judith Jurin Semo
Abelardo L. Valdez
Charles A. Vanik

(See Next Column)

ASSOCIATES

Rawle Andrews, Jr.
Charles A. Bieneman
Miriam A. Bishop
Ann R. Brashear
Amy L Brown
(Not admitted in DC)
John B. Bulgozdy
Jeffrey A. Campbell
(Not admitted in DC)
Andrew W. Cohen
Colleen A. Conry
Keith E. Dobbins
(Not admitted in DC)
Charles F. Donley II
Wm. Smith Greig
(Not admitted in DC)
Lauren H. Kravetz
Joy Langford
(Not admitted in DC)
Jonathan Jacob Nadler
Charulata B. Pagar
(Not admitted in DC)
Monique V. Perez
John C. Reilly
Thomas E. Skilton
Donald J. Snyder
John P. Youle
(Not admitted in DC)

For full biographical listings, see the Martindale-Hubbell Law Directory

STEPTOE & JOHNSON (AV)

1330 Connecticut Avenue, N.W., 20036
Telephone: 202-429-3000
Cable Address: "Stepjohn"
Telex: 89-2503
Telecopier: 202-429-3902
Phoenix, Arizona Office: Two Renaissance Square, 40 N. Central Avenue, Suite 2400, 85004.
Telephone: 602-257-5200.
Moscow, Russia Office: Steptoe & Johnson International Affiliate in Moscow. 25 Tsvetnoy Boulevard, Building 3 Moscow, Russia 103051.
Telephone: 011-7-501-929-9700.
Fax: 501-929-9701.

MEMBERS

Louis A. Johnson (1891-1966)
Calvin H. Cobb, Jr.
Monroe Leigh
Richard P. Taylor
John E. Nolan, Jr.
Robert D. Wallick
N. Thompson Powers
Laurence A. Short
James P. Holden
Betty Jo Christian
Robert E. Jordan, III
Matthew J. Zinn
Robert E. McLaughlin
Sarah C. Carey
Martin D. Schneiderman
Richard O. Cunningham
David L. Roll
Shirley D. Peterson
Richard H. Porter
Sheldon E. Hochberg
Kenneth I. Jonson
Theodore E. Rhodes
J. A. Bouknight, Jr.
Ronald S. Cooper
Daniel J. Plaine
Terence P. Quinn
Roger E. Warin
John R. Labovitz
William A. Butler
F. Michael Kail
Mark J. Silverman
William Karas
John T. Collins
Steven H. Brose
Robert W. Fleishman
Howard H. Stahl
W. George Grandison
Arthur L. Bailey
Morgan D. Hodgson
Ellen d'Alelio
Mark F. Horning
Christopher T. Lutz
Samuel T. Perkins
James B. Vasile
Ellen M. McNamara
Paul J. Ondrasik, Jr.
Richard K. Willard
Reid H. Weingarten
Stewart A. Baker
Charles G. Cole
Susan H. Serling
Francis J. Burke, Jr.
William L. Martin, II
Filiberto Agusti
Thomas P. Barletta
Timothy M. Walsh
Peter L. Wellington
Olin L. Wethington
Stephen A. Fennell
Seth Goldberg
Samuel M. Sipe, Jr.
Maureen O'Keefe Ward
Barry J. Dale
Gary A. Morgans
J. William Koegel, Jr.
Steven Reed
Daniel C. Sauls
David J. Bodney
Blake D. Rubin
Walter H. White, Jr.
(Not admitted in DC)
Melanie F. Nussdorf
Philip L. Malet
Antonia B. Ianniello
Edward J. Krauland
J. Walker Johnson
Erik L. Kitchen
Floyd P. Bienstock
John D. Graubert
Scott H. Katzman
Steven J. Ross
Jane I. Ryan
Carol A. Rhees
Ellen Kohn
Jerald S. Howe Jr.
Robert T. Novick
Virginia L. White-Mahaffey
David H. Coburn
Kevin M. Keyes
Anthony J. LaRocca
Alfred M. Mamlet
Arthur Randolph Bregman
Steven K. Davidson
Harry Lee
Mark A. Moran
Douglas G. Green
David B. Raskin

PHOENIX, ARIZONA PARTNERS

Lawrence A. Katz

OF COUNSEL

Laidler B. Mackall
Richard A. Whiting
Robert J. Corber
William K. Condrell
Cecil J. Olmstead
Richard Diamond
Stanley Smilack
Kenneth D. Ludwig
Thomas M. Barba
Victoria A. Judson
Edward R. Mackiewicz
Linda S. Stein
Anita G. Fox
David A. Selden
Gerard E. Wimberly, Jr.
Philip R. West

(See Next Column)

STEPTOE & JOHNSON, *Washington—Continued*

OF COUNSEL (Continued)

Sara Beth Watson
Carol A. Mitchell
Scott A. Harman
Joseph E. Stubbs
Edward J. Twomey

ASSOCIATES

Michael Hall Abbey
F. Franklin Amanat
M. Jean Anderson
Robert C. Barber
Steven J. Barber
Benjamin R. Barnett
Mark A. Barnett
Evan T. Barr
Christian R. Bartholomew
Gracia M. Berg
David S. Biderman
Merritt R. Blakeslee
Marina T. Charles
Margaret M. Clark
Carolyn Doozan Clayton
John S. Cullina
Stefania Shamet
Karen M. Eisenhauer
Eric C. Emerson
Kenneth P. Ewing
Hania E. Farah (Not admitted in DC)
Michelle Alison Fishburne
John Flyger
Glenn G. Fuller
Caroline Gaudet (Not admitted in DC)
Gregory M. Giammittorio
Gary L. Goldsholle
Clifford E. Greenblatt
Jorge A. Guerrero (Not admitted in DC)
Dima Sami Hakura
Richard E. Harris
William T. Hassler
Sara E. Hauptfuehrer
Henry E. Hockeimer, Jr.
Frederick J. Horne
Brenda D. Horrigan
Meredith L. Jason
Jared W. Johnson (Not admitted in DC)
Barbara K. Kagan
Mindy A. Kaiden
Jennifer L. Key
Miguel S. Lawson
Faye D. Levin
Peter Lichtenbaum
John R. Lilyestrom (Not admitted in DC)
Margaret Feczko May
Kelly C. Maynard
Lynn S. McIntosh
Pantelis Michalopoulos (Not admitted in DC)
Mary Beth Murphy
Samuel Olchyk
Evan Anne O'Neill
George A. B. Peirce
Stephanie A. Philips
Helen Hiser Recinos
Jay Reiziss
Richard L. Roberts
Shelley Goldstein Robinson
Maury D. Shenk
John M. Shoreman
Barbara Sloan
Ann M. Slowinski
Clint N. Smith
Lauren Talner Spiliotes
David A. Stein
Roderick L. Thomas
Donald E. Wellington
Howard Widra
John M. Yetter
Tracy A. Zorpette
Kent D. Bressie (Not admitted in DC)
Sara P. Crovitz (Not admitted in DC)
Brian A. Davis (Not admitted in DC)
James B. Dilsheimer
Jodi H. Epstein (Not admitted in DC)
J. Patrick Kennedy (Not admitted in DC)
Patrick O'Donnell
Katherine P. Rosefsky (Not admitted in DC)
Colleen Sechrest (Not admitted in DC)
Stephanie L. Siegel (Not admitted in DC)
Pamela Strauss (Not admitted in DC)
Cynthia L. Taub (Not admitted in DC)
George C. Vitelli (Not admitted in DC)

For full biographical listings, see the Martindale-Hubbell Law Directory

---

STEWART AND STEWART (AV)

808 Seventeenth Street, N.W., 20006-3910
Telephone: 202-785-4185
Telex: 89-533
Telecopier: 202-466-1286; 466-1287; 466-1288

MEMBERS OF FIRM

Terence P. Stewart
James R. Cannon, Jr.
Wesley K. Caine
Charles A. St. Charles
William A. Fennell
Jimmie V. Reyna (Not admitted in DC)
Geert De Prest
John M. Breen

FOUNDER AND SENIOR PARTNER EMERITUS

Eugene L. Stewart

ASSOCIATES

Lane Steven Hurewitz
Patrick John McDonough (Not admitted in DC)
Amy S. Dwyer
Gary V. Litman

COUNSEL

Olufemi A. Areola (Not admitted in DC)
Bernard Spinoit (Not admitted in the United States)

For full biographical listings, see the Martindale-Hubbell Law Directory

* STROOCK & STROOCK & LAVAN (AV)

1150 Seventeenth Street, N.W. Suite 600, 20036-4652
Telephone: 202-452-9250
Telecopier: (202) 293-2293
Cable Address: "Plastroock, Washington"
Telex: 89401 STROOCK DC
New York, N.Y. Office: Seven Hanover Square, 10004-2696.
Telephone: 212-806-5400.
Telecopiers: (212) 806-5919; (212) 806-6006; (212) 806-6086; (212) 425-9509; (212) 806-6176. Telexes: Stroock UT 177693 and Plastroock NYK 177077 (International).
Cable Address: "Plastroock, NYK."
New York Conference Center: 767 Third Avenue, New York, N.Y., 10017-2023.
Telephones: 212-806-5767; 5768; 5769; 5770.
Telecopier: (212) 421-6234.
Los Angeles, California Office: Suite 1800, 2029 Century Park East, 90067-3086.
Telephone: 310-556-5800.
Telecopier: (310) 556-5959.
Cable Address: "Plastroock, L.A."
Telex: Plastroock LSA 677190. (Domestic and International).
Miami, Florida Office: 200 South Biscayne Boulevard, Suite 3300, First Union Financial Center, 33131-2385.
Telephone: 305-358-9900.
Telecopiers: (305) 789-9302; (305) 372-3727.
Telex: 803133 StroockMia (Domestic and International); Broward Line: 527-9900.
Budapest, Hungary Office: East-West Business Center, Rákóczi ut 1-3, H 1088.
Telephone: (361) 266-9520; (361) 266-7770.
Telecopier: (361) 266-9279.

RESIDENT PARTNERS

Barry J. Israel
Will E. Leonard
George G. Lorinczi
Marvin G. Pickholz
Walter Pozen
Mark N. Rae
James Taylor, Jr.

OF COUNSEL

Howard L. Hills

Panagiotis C. Bayz
Alexei J. Cowett
Matthew H. McCarthy
Linda P. Reppert

For full biographical listings, see the Martindale-Hubbell Law Directory

* SULLIVAN & CROMWELL (AV)

1701 Pennsylvania Avenue, N.W., 20006-5805
Telephone: 202-956-7500
Telex: 89625
Telecopier: 202-293-6330
New York City Offices: 125 Broad Street, 10004-2498; Midtown Office: 250 Park Avenue, 10177-0021.
Telephone: 212-558-4000.
Telex: 62694 (International);12-7816 (Domestic).
Telecopier: 125 Broad Street 212-558-3588; 250 Park Avenue 212-558-3792.
Los Angeles, California Office: 444 South Flower Street, 90071-2901.
Telephone: 213-955-8000.
Telecopier: 213-683-0457.
Paris Office: 8, Place Vendôme, 75001, Paris, France.
Telephone: (011)(331)4450-6000.
Telex: 240654.
Telecopier: (011)(331)4450-6060.
London Office: St. Olave's House, 9a Ironmonger Lane, London EC2V 8EY, England.
Telephone: (011)(44171)710-6500.
Telecopier: (011)(44171)710-6565.
Melbourne, Australia Office: 101 Collins Street, Melbourne, Victoria 3000.
Telephone: (011)(613)654-1500.
Telecopier: (011)(613)654-2422.
Tokyo Office: Gaikokuho Jimu Bengoshi Office of Robert G. DeLaMater, a member of the firm of Sullivan & Cromwell. Tokio Kaijo Building Shinkan, 2-1, Marunouchi, 1-chome Chiyoda-ku, Tokyo 100, Japan.
Telephone: (011)(813)3213-6140.
Telecopier: (011)(813)3213-6470.
Hong Kong Office: 28th Floor, Nine Queen's Road, Central, Hong Kong.
Telephone: (011)(852)826-8688.
Telecopier: (011)(852)522-2280.

PARTNERS IN WASHINGTON, D.C.

M. Bernard Aidinoff
Edwin D. Williamson
H. Rodgin Cohen (Not admitted in DC)
Robert H. Craft, Jr.
Margaret K. Pfeiffer
Daryl A. Libow (Not admitted in DC)

OF COUNSEL IN WASHINGTON, D.C.

Janet Thiele Geldzahler (Not admitted in DC)
Douglas Mark McCall

SPECIAL COUNSEL IN WASHINGTON, D.C.

Patricia Diaz Dennis
Jeffrey W. Jacobs
Dennis C. Sullivan

(See Next Column)

SULLIVAN & CROMWELL—*Continued*

ASSOCIATES IN WASHINGTON, D.C.

William J. Brown
Samantha Evans
(Not admitted in DC)
Jose Ignacio Fernandez
Alice Stevens Fisher
Ari Q. Fitzgerald
Bernard A. Joseph
(Not admitted in DC)
David S.J. Kim
Kevin J. Lavin
(Not admitted in DC)
Thomas R. Leuba
J. Michael Locke
Paul J. McElroy
Mary C. Moynihan
(Not admitted in DC)
Jack O'Kelley
Kathryn E. Rorer
(Not admitted in DC)
Richard H. Sauer
Brett G. Scharffs
(Not admitted in DC)
Timothy E. Sheil

For full biographical listings, see the Martindale-Hubbell Law Directory

SUTHERLAND, ASBILL & BRENNAN (AV)

1275 Pennsylvania Avenue, N.W., 20004-2404
Telephone: 202-383-0100
Cable Address: "Sutab Wash"
Telex: 89-501
Facsimile: 202-637-3593
Atlanta, Georgia Office: 999 Peachtree Street, N. E., 30309-3996.
Telephone: 404-853-8000.
New York, N.Y. Office: 1270 Avenue of the Americas, 10020-1700.
Telephone: 212-332-3000.
Austin, Texas Office: 111 Congress Avenue, 23rd Floor, 78701-4079.
Telephone: 512-469-3350.

MEMBERS OF THE FIRM IN WASHINGTON, D.C.

William A. Sutherland (1896-1987)
Mac Asbill, Sr. (1893-1992)
Joseph B. Brennan (1903-1991)
Mac Asbill, Jr. (1922-1992)

Waltraut Susanne Addy
Frederick R. Bellamy
Steven B. Boehm
George H. Bostick
James M. Cain
Sheila J. Carpenter
William W. Chip
Nicholas T. Christakos
Robert W. Clark
N. Jerold Cohen
William S. Corey
James L. Dahlberg
James D. Darrow
Warren N. Davis
Jacob Dweck
Philip R. Ehrenkranz
N. Beth Emery
Paul F. Forshay
Hamilton P. Fox, III
Thomas A. Gick
Francis M. Gregory, Jr. (1941-1993)
Edward J. Grenier, Jr.
Karen L. Grimm
James V. Heffernan
Mark D. Herlach
Joel E. Hoffman
Glen S. Howard
Paul W. Killian
Robert G. Levy
(Not admitted in DC)
Jerome B. Libin
Frank J. Martin, Jr.
Paul J. Mason
David A. Massey
Randolph J. May
Keith R. McCrea
Michael R. Miles
Michael T. Mishkin
Clifford E. Muller
Gordon O. Pehrson, Jr.
William H. Penniman
Lloyd Leva Plaine
G. Garner Prillaman, Jr.
Peter H. Rodgers
Stephen E. Roth
Beverly J. Rudy
Richard J. Safranek
David Schwinger
Bradley M. Seltzer
Michael J. Shea
W. Mark Smith
Kenneth G. Starling
Steuart H. Thomsen
Randolph W. Thrower
Carol A. Weiser

COUNSEL

Lovida H. Coleman, Jr.
Timothy J. Cooney
David A. Golden
Susan S. Krawczyk
Sterling H. Smith
Giovanna T. Sparagna
William J. Walderman

For full biographical listings, see the Martindale-Hubbell Law Directory

* TAFT, STETTINIUS & HOLLISTER (AV)

Suite 500, 625 Indiana Avenue, N.W., 20004-2901
Telephone: 202-628-2838
Facsimile: 202-347-3419
Cincinnati, Ohio Office: 1800 Star Bank Center, 425 Walnut Street.
Telephone: 513-381-2838.
Columbus, Ohio Office: 21 East State Street.
Telephone: 614-221-2838.
Crestview Hills, Kentucky Office: Thomas More Centre, 2670 Chancellor Drive.
Telephone: 606-331-2838; 513-381-2838.

RESIDENT MEMBERS

G. David Schiering
Toshio Nakao

RESIDENT ASSOCIATES

Andrew L. Woods

Counsel for: Cincinnati Stock Exchange; Federal Home Loan Bank; Great American Broadcasting Co.; Morton International, Inc.; Star Banc Corporation; Toyota Tsusho America, Inc.

For full biographical listings, see the Martindale-Hubbell Law Directory

* THACHER PROFFITT & WOOD (AV)

1500 K Street, N.W., 20005
Telephone: 202-347-8400
Facsimile: 202-347-6238
New York, N.Y. Office: Two World Trade Center.
Telephone: 212-912-7400.
Cable Address: "Wallaces, New York."
Telex: 226733TPCW; 669578TPW.
Facsimile: 212-912-7751; 912-7752.
White Plains, New York Office: 50 Main Street.
Telephone: 914-421-4100.
Facsimile: 914-421-4150/4151.

WASHINGTON, D.C.
MEMBERS OF FIRM

Edward R. Leahy
Donald B. Susswein

ASSOCIATES

Mary Seminara Diemer
Adam W. Gurwitz
(Not admitted in DC)
Stephen F. Ornstein

For full biographical listings, see the Martindale-Hubbell Law Directory

* THOMPSON, HINE AND FLORY (AV)

1920 N Street, N.W., 20036-1601
Telephone: 202-331-8800
Fax: 202-331-8330
Telex: 904173
Cable Address: "Caglaw"
Akron, Ohio Office: 50 S. Main Street, Suite 502, 44308-1828.
Telephone: 216-376-8090.
Fax: 216-376-8386.
Cincinnati, Ohio Office: 312 Walnut Street, 14th Floor, 45202-4029.
Telephone: 513-352-6700.
Fax: 513-241-4771.
Telex: 938003.
Cleveland, Ohio Office: 1100 National City Bank Building, 629 Euclid Avenue, 44114.
Telephone: 216-566-5500.
Fax: 216-566-5583.
Telex: 980217. Cable Address "Thomflor".
Columbus, Ohio Office: One Columbus, 10 West Broad Street, 43215-34353.
Telephone: 614-469-3200.
Fax: 614-469-3361.
Dayton, Ohio Office: 2000 Courthouse Plaza, N.E., 45402-1706.
Telephone: 513-443-6600.
Fax: 513-443-6637, 513-443-6635.
Palm Beach, Florida Office: 125 Worth Avenue, 33480-4466.
Telephone: 407-833-5900.
Fax: 407-833-5951.
Brussels, Belgium Office: Rue Des Chevaliers, Ridderstraat 14 - B.10, B-1050.
Telephone: 011-32-2-511-9326.
Fax: 011-32-2-513-9206.

MEMBERS OF FIRM

Roberta B. Aronson
Steven D. Cundra
Charles L. Freed
Frederick B. Gibbon
Alfred M. Goldberg
Peter A. Greene
(Partner-in-Charge in Washington, D.C.)
Donald L. Korb
William R. Naeher
Norman J. Philion, III
Louis Pohoryles
Michael Wm. Sacks
Mark Roy Sandstrom
Robert V. Staton
Paul R. Webber, IV

ASSOCIATES

Lisa Sullivan Franzen
Adam H. Gordon
(Not admitted in DC)
Michele D. Lynch
Andrew J. Sloniewsky
Patricia L. Taylor

SENIOR ATTORNEY

Amy G. Davies

OF COUNSEL

William E. Constable
Glenn D. Simpson

For full biographical listings, see the Martindale-Hubbell Law Directory

* THOMPSON & MITCHELL (AV)

Suite 900, 700-14th Street, N.W., 20005-2010
Telephone: 202-508-1000
Telecopier: 202-508-1010
St. Louis, Missouri Office: One Mercantile Center, Suite 3300.
Telephone: 314-231-7676.
Telecopier: 314-342-1717.
Belleville, Illinois Office: 525 West Main Street.
Telephone: 618-277-4700; 314-271-1800.
Telecopier: 618-236-3434.
St. Charles, Missouri Office: 200 North Third Street.
Telephone: 314-946-7717.
Telecopier: 314-946-4938.

(See Next Column)

THOMPSON & MITCHELL, *Washington—Continued*

MEMBERS OF FIRM

Murray J. Belman
Milton D. Andrews
Michael A. Greenspan
John V. Austin
Barbara B. Powell
Edward J. Sheppard, IV
Gerald D. Stoltz
Marjorie F. Krumholz
Richard A. Schaberg

ASSOCIATES

Catherine M. Beresovski
Halpin J. Burke
Randall K. Hulme

Representative Clients: Cold Finished Steel Bar Institute; ComericA, Inc. (Michigan); Fleet Financial Corporation (Rhode Island); Kidder Peabody & Co., Incorporated; Manildra Milling Company; Risco, Inc.; Shell Bermuda (Overseas) Limited; Tecumseh Products Co.; Union Carbide Corporation; United Jersey Banks (New Jersey).

For full biographical listings, see the Martindale-Hubbell Law Directory

TUTTLE, TAYLOR & HERON (AV)

1025 Thomas Jefferson Street, N.W., 20007
Telephone: 202-342-1300
Facsimile: 202-342-5880
Los Angeles, California Office: Tuttle & Taylor, A Law Corporation, 355 South Grand Avenue.
Telephone: 213-683-0600.
Facsimile: 213-683-0225.
Sacramento, California Office: Tuttle & Taylor, A Law Corporation, 980 Ninth Street.
Telephone: 916-449-9950.
Facsimile: 916-449-9953.

OF COUNSEL

Julian B. Heron, Jr.
Jerry W. Kennedy

For full biographical listings, see the Martindale-Hubbell Law Directory

*** VARET & FINK P.C. (AV)**

(Formerly Milgrim Thomajan & Lee P.C.)
1110 Vermont Avenue, N.W., Suite 600, 20005
Telephone: 202-628-6200
Fax: 202-628-2288
New York, N.Y. Office: 53 Wall Street.
Telephone: 212-858-5300.
Cable Address: "Milatom NYK."
Telex: WUI 662124.
Telecopier: 212-858-5301.

Robert F. Fink (Not admitted in DC)

COUNSEL

Christopher J. Clay (Resident)

John L. Moore, Jr.

For full biographical listings, see the Martindale-Hubbell Law Directory

*** VEDDER, PRICE, KAUFMAN, KAMMHOLZ & DAY (AV)**

A Partnership including Vedder, Price, Kaufman & Kammholz, P.C.
1600 M. Street, N.W., 20036
Telephone: 202-296-0500
Fax: 202-296-2339
Chicago, Illinois Office: Vedder, Price, Kaufman & Kammholz, 222 North La Salle Street.
Telephone: 312-609-7500.
Rockford, Illinois Office: Vedder, Price, Kaufman & Kammholz, 4615 East State Street, Suite 201.
Telephone: 815-226-7700.
New York, N.Y. Office: Vedder, Price, Kaufman, Kammholz & Day, 805 Third Avenue.
Telephone: 212-407-7700.

MEMBERS OF FIRM

Virgil B. Day (P.C.)
Edwin H. Seeger
Thomas L. Farmer
George J. Pantos
Thomas A. Brooks
Jane C. Luxton

For full biographical listings, see the Martindale-Hubbell Law Directory

*** VENABLE, BAETJER, HOWARD & CIVILETTI (AV)**

A Partnership including Professional Corporations
Suite 1000, 1201 New York Avenue, N.W., 20005
Telephone: 202-962-4800
Fax: 202-962-8300
Baltimore, Maryland Office: Venable, Baetjer and Howard, 1800 Mercantile Bank & Trust Building, 2 Hopkins Plaza.
Telephone: 410-244-7400.
McLean, Virginia Office: Venable, Baetjer and Howard, Suite 400, 2010 Corporate Ridge.
Telephone: 703-760-1600.

(See Next Column)

Rockville, Maryland Office: Venable, Baetjer and Howard, Suite 500, One Church Street, P. O. Box 1906.
Telephone: 301-217-5600.
Towson, Maryland Office: Venable, Baetjer and Howard, 210 Allegheny Avenue, P. O. Box 5517.
Telephone: 410-494-6200.

MEMBERS OF FIRM

Benjamin R. Civiletti (P.C.) (Also at Baltimore and Towson, Maryland Offices)
Anthony M. Carey (Not admitted in DC; Also at Baltimore, Maryland Office)
Neal D. Borden (Not admitted in DC; Also at Baltimore, Maryland Office)
Thomas J. Kenney, Jr. (P.C.) (Not admitted in DC)
Jan K. Guben (Not admitted in DC; Also at Baltimore, Maryland Office)
Ian D. Volner
Thomas J. Madden
Ronald R. Glancz
David J. Levenson
Robert P. Bedell (Not admitted in DC)
Dennis J. Whittlesey
Douglas D. Connah, Jr. (P.C.) (Also at Baltimore, Maryland Office)
Joe A. Shull
Robert E. Madden (Also at Baltimore, Maryland and McLean, Virginia Offices)
Kenneth C. Bass, III (Also at McLean, Virginia Office)
John G. Milliken (Also at McLean, Virginia Office)
Joel Z. Silver
Max Stul Oppenheimer (P.C.) (Also at Baltimore and Towson, Maryland Offices)
Joseph G. Block
Edward F. Glynn, Jr.
Robert G. Ames (Also at Baltimore, Maryland Office)
Thomas B. Hudson (Also at Baltimore, Maryland Office)
Michael Schatzow (Also at Baltimore and Towson, Maryland Offices)
John F. Cooney
Bryson L. Cook (P.C.) (Not admitted in DC; Also at Baltimore, Maryland Office)
N. Frank Wiggins
James K. Archibald (Also at Baltimore and Towson, Maryland Offices)
Judson W. Starr (Also at Baltimore and Towson, Maryland Offices)
James R. Myers
Jeffrey D. Knowles
Jeffrey A. Dunn (Also at Baltimore, Maryland Office)
George F. Pappas (Also at Baltimore, Maryland Office)
James L. Shea (Not admitted in DC; also at Baltimore, Maryland Office)
William D. Coston
Maurice Baskin
John J. Pavlick, Jr.
Amy Berman Jackson
William D. Quarles (Also at Towson, Maryland Office)
Jeffrey L. Ihnen
James A. Dunbar (Also at Baltimore, Maryland Office)
Mary E. Pivec (Not admitted in DC; Also at Baltimore, Maryland Office)
Thomas J. Kelly, Jr.
Robert J. Bolger, Jr. (Not admitted in DC; Also at Baltimore, Maryland Office)
Joel J. Goldberg (Also at McLean, Virginia Office)
James F. Worrall
Bruce H. Jurist (Also at Baltimore, Maryland Office)
Linda L. Lord
John M. Gurley
Paul A. Serini (Not admitted in DC; Also at Baltimore, Maryland Office)
Patrick J. Stewart (Also at Baltimore, Maryland Office)
Gary M. Hnath

OF COUNSEL

Frank Horton
Richard H. Mays (Not admitted in DC; Also at Baltimore, Maryland and McLean, Virginia Offices)
Robert A. Beizer
Thomas J. Cooper
Jerome S. Gabig, Jr. (Not admitted in DC)
Geoffrey R. Garinther (Not admitted in DC; Also at Baltimore, Maryland Office)
Fred W. Hathaway

ASSOCIATES

Gregory S. Braker (Not admitted in DC)
Carla Draluck Craft
Royal W. Craig (Not admitted in DC)
Donald P. Creston
David S. Darland
Fred Joseph Federici, III
David W. Goewey
D. Brent Gunsalus
James W. Hedlund (Not admitted in DC)
Andrew R. Herrup
Fernand A. Lavallee
Edward Brendan Magrab (Not admitted in DC)
Valerie K. Mann
Lindsay Beardsworth Meyer
Samuel T. Morison
Traci H. Mundy (Not admitted in DC)
Karen A. Schultz (Not admitted in DC)
Melissa Landau Steinman (Not admitted in DC)
Barbara L. Waite
Paul N. Wengert
Karen D. Woodard

For full biographical listings, see the Martindale-Hubbell Law Directory

VERNER, LIIPFERT, BERNHARD, MCPHERSON AND HAND, CHARTERED (AV)

901 15th Street, N.W., 20005-2301
Telephone: 202-371-6000
Cable Address: "Verlip"
Telex: 1561792 VERLIP UT
Fax: 202-371-6279
McLean, Virginia Office: Sixth Floor, 8280 Greensboro Drive, 22102.
Telephone: 703-749-6000.
Fax: 703-749-6027.

(See Next Column)

VERNER, LIIPFERT, BERNHARD, MCPHERSON AND HAND CHARTERED—*Continued*

Houston, Texas Office: 2600 Texas Commerce Tower, 600 Travis, 77002.
Telephone: 713-237-9034.
Fax: 713-237-1216.

Douglas Ochs Adler
Leslie M. Alden
Berl Bernhard
Graham Kerin Blair (Resident, Houston, Texas Office)
Amy Laura Bondurant
Roy G. Bowman
R. Stuart Broom
Steven A. Buxbaum (Resident, Houston, Texas Office)
John P. Campbell
Douglas J. Colton
Brendan D. Cook (Resident, Houston, Texas Office)
Hopewell H. Darneille, III
Thomas M. Davidson
Frances C. DeLaurentis
Andrew D. Eskin
William C. Evans
Anne M. Ferazzi (Resident, Houston, Texas Office)
Benjamin H. Flowe, Jr.
J. Cathy Fogel
Michael D. Golden
Andrea Jill Grant
J. Richard Hammett (Resident, Houston, Texas Office)
Lloyd N. Hand
James F. Hibey
John F. Higgins, IV (Resident, Houston, Texas Office)
Patrick L. Hughes (Resident, Houston, Texas Office)
Thomas J. Keller
Gary J. Klein
Erwin G. Krasnow
Kyung S. Lee (Resident, Houston, Texas Office)
Don Charles Lewis
Lawrence Z. Lorber
Joseph L. Manson, III
Harry McPherson
John P. Melko (Resident, Houston, Texas Office)
John A. Merrigan
Ronald B. Natalie
Paul E. Nordstrom
Clark H. Onstad
Glen L. Ortman
Lenard M. Parkins (Resident, Houston, Texas Office)
Russell E. Pommer
Neil T. Proto
Sherry A. Quirk
Barry D. Rhoads (Not admitted in DC)
Michael J. Roberts
William F. Roeder, Jr.
Lawrence R. Sidman
Keith D. Spickelmier (Resident, Houston, Texas Office)
Frederick J. Tansill
Susan O'Hearn Temkin
James M. Verner (Emeritus)
Clinton A. Vince
Buel White
Bernhardt K. Wruble
William A. Zeitler
John H. Zentay

OF COUNSEL

Dennis A. Adelson
Howell E. Begle, Jr.
Michael D. Berg
James K. Jackson
David B. Jacobsohn
Bruce A. Kimble (Resident, McLean, Virginia Office)
J. Robert Kirk
Stanley W. Legro
Frederick J. McConville
Martin Mendelsohn
James F. Miller
Mikol S. B. Neilson
Nancy A. Nord
Nell Payne
Richard H. Saltsman
Gene Schleppenbach

Gregg S. Avitabile
Matthew C. Bernstein (Not admitted in DC)
Susan G. Blumenthal
David A. Brakebill (Resident, Houston, Texas Office)
John B. Britton
Linda Eichelbaum Collier (Resident, McLean, Virginia Office)
Lawrence N. Cooper
Kathleen M. Cronin (Not admitted in DC)
Alessandra F. Via Daigneault
J. Elizabeth Dame (Resident, McLean, Virginia Office)
Sherry Lane Deaver (Resident, Houston, Texas Office)
Andrea Renee Dillman (Not admitted in DC)
Christine F. Ericson
Lisa A. Federici
Henry Flores (Resident, Houston, Texas Office)
Peter A. Gould
Marla Grossman (Not admitted in DC)
Douglas W. Hall
Lori A. Hood (Resident, Houston, Texas Office)
Lisa K. Hsiao (Not admitted in DC)
Lisa S. Jensen
Steven R. Johnson (Not admitted in DC)
Kenric D. Kattner (Resident, Houston, Texas Office)
E. John Krumholtz
MaryLou Lundin (Not admitted in DC)
Neil H. MacBride
John R. Mietus, Jr.
Brian A. Mizoguchi
Trey A. Monsour (Resident, Houston, Texas Office)
Glenn Moore (Not admitted in DC)
Guy A. Morley (Not admitted in DC)
Hedy L. Nelson
John A. Ordway, Jr.
Jane S. Patterson (Resident, Houston, Texas Office)
Robert R. Pierce (Resident, Houston, Texas Office)
Tamara Schiebel Rickman (Resident, McLean, Virginia Office)
Elizabeth J. Sadove (Not admitted in DC)
William R. Sherman
Kathy D. Smith
Deborah A. Swanstrom
Mary A. VanCleve (Not admitted in DC)
Catherine S. Weil (Resident, Houston, Texas Office)
Linda M. Weinberg
Eric T. Werner
Gretchen M. White (Not admitted in DC)
Beth Wolffe
Michael S. Wroblewski (Not admitted in DC)

(See Next Column)

LEGAL SUPPORT PERSONNEL

Suzanne D. Cartwright (Director of Legislative Affairs)
Denis J. Dwyer (Director of Legislative and Federal Affairs)
Rosemary B. Freeman (Legislative Consultant)
Nancy A. Sheliga (Legislative Consultant)
Kevin Stoltzfus (Legislative Consultant)

For full biographical listings, see the Martindale-Hubbell Law Directory

---

* VINSON & ELKINS L.L.P. (AV)

A Registered Limited Liability Partnership
The Willard Office Building, 1455 Pennsylvania Avenue, N.W., 20004-1008
Telephone: 202-639-6500
Fax: 202-639-6604
Cable Address: Vinelkins
Houston, Texas Office: 1001 Fannin, Suite 2300.
Telephone: 713-758-2222.
Fax: 713-758-2346. International
Telex: 6868314.
Cable Address: Vinelkins
Austin, Texas Office: One American Center, 600 Congress Avenue.
Telephone: 512-495-8400.
Fax: 512-495-8612.
Dallas, Texas Office: 3700 Trammell Crow Center, 2001 Ross Avenue.
Telephone: 214-220-7700.
Fax: 214-220-7716.
London Office: 47 Charles Street, Berkeley Square, London, W1X 7PB, England.
Telephone: 011 (441-71) 491-7236.
Fax: 011 (44-171) 499-5320.
Cable Address: VinelkinsLondon W.1.
Moscow, Russia Federation Office: 16 Alexey Tolstoy Street, Second Floor, Moscow, 103001 Russia Federation.
Telephone: 011 (70-95) 956-1995.
Telecopy: 011 (70-95) 956-1996.
Mexico City, Mexico Office: Aristóteles 77, 5ºPiso, Colonia Chapultepec Polanco, 11560 Mexico, D.F.
Telephone: (52-5) 280-7828.
Fax: (52-5) 280-9223.
Singapore Office: 50 Raffles Place, #19-05 Shell Tower, 0104. U.S. Voice Mailbox: 713-758-3500.
Telephone: (65) 536-8300.
Fax: (65) 536-8311.

RESIDENT PARTNERS

Charles L. Almond
David T. Andril
Robert A. Armitage
Ronald T. Astin
Alden L. Atkins
Dennis M. Barry
Gary E. Block
C. Michael Buxton
John E. Chapoton
David B. Cohen
Thomas Crichton, IV
Ky P. Ewing, Jr.
Kevin A. Gaynor
Michael J. Henke
Neil W. Imus
Theodore W. Kassinger
Gary M. Kotara (Not admitted in DC)
Cathy A. Lewis
Hugh M. McIntosh
Larry A. Oday
Mark R. Spivak
John D. Taurman
Charles D. Tetrault
Christine L. Vaughn

RESIDENT OF COUNSEL

Roderick Glen Ayers, Jr.
Thomas R. Bartman
Samuel B. Sterrett
Thomas A. Stout, Jr.

RESIDENT ASSOCIATES

Alex J. Bourelly (Not admitted in DC)
J. Barclay Collins, III (Not admitted in DC)
Robert H. Cox
Christopher L. Crosswhite (Not admitted in DC)
John S. Decker (Not admitted in DC)
Debra J. Duncan
Mary E. Edmondson
Jeffrey W. Ferguson
Tegan M. Flynn
Scott Mitchell Frederick (Not admitted in DC)
Mary H. Hirth (Not admitted in DC)
George C. Hopkins
Tara Isa Koslov (Not admitted in DC)
Bruce E. Kosub (Not admitted in DC)
Holley Thomas Lutz (Not admitted in DC)
James R. Markham
Lori E. Peterson (Not admitted in DC)
Dimitri P. Racklin
Michael A. Sanzo
Carin J. Sigel
Russell W. Sullivan
Anita Rutkowski Wilson
Jonathan M. Zeitler (Not admitted in DC)

For full biographical listings, see the Martindale-Hubbell Law Directory

Washington—Continued

*** VORYS, SATER, SEYMOUR AND PEASE (AV)**

Suite 1111, 1828 L Street, N.W., 20036-5104
Telephone: 202-467-8800
Telex: 440693
Telecopier: 202-467-8900
Columbus, Ohio Office: 52 East Gay Street, P.O. Box 1008, 43216-1008.
Telephone: 614-464-6400.
Telex: 241348.
Telecopier: 614-464-6350.
Cable Address: "Vorysater".
Cleveland, Ohio Office: 2100 One Cleveland Center, 1375 East Ninth Street, 44114-1724.
Telephone: 216-479-6100.
Telecopier: 216-479-6060.
Cincinnati, Ohio Office: Suite 2100, 221 East Fourth Street, P.O. Box 0236, 45201-0236.
Telephone: 513-723-4000.
Telecopier: 513-723-4056.

RESIDENT MEMBERS

Thomas R. Boland
Randal C. Teague
John W. Wilmer, Jr.
Ellen A. Efros
Warren W. Glick
James K. Alford
William Mack Webner
Michael A. Grow

RESIDENT ASSOCIATES

Brian C. Harrison
Stephen H. Brown (Not admitted in DC)
Barbara A. Duncombe
Timothy N. McGarey
Dale R. Harburg
Douglas R. Bush
Robert A. Hager
George W. Swenson, Jr. (Not admitted in DC)
Claire L. Wudowsky (Not admitted in DC)
Scott D. Balderston (Not admitted in DC)

For full biographical listings, see the Martindale-Hubbell Law Directory

WATT, TIEDER & HOFFAR (AV)

601 Pennsylvania Avenue, N.W., Suite 900, 20004
Telephone: 202-462-4697
Telecopier: 703-893-8029
McLean Virginia Office: 7929 Westpark Drive, Suite 400,
Telephone: 703-749-1000.
Telecopier: 703-893-8029.
Irvine California Office: 3 Park Plaza, Suite 1530.
Telephone: 714-852-6700.

MEMBERS OF FIRM

John B. Tieder, Jr.
Robert K. Cox
David C. Romm

For full biographical listings, see the Martindale-Hubbell Law Directory

WHITE & CASE (AV)

1747 Pennsylvania Avenue, NW, 20006-4604
Telephone: 202-872-0013
Telex: 650 562 4069 MCI UW
Facsimile: 202-872-0210
New York, New York:
Telephone: 212-819-8200.
Facsimile: 212-354-8113.
Los Angeles, California:
Telephone: 213-620-7700.
Facsimile: 213-687-0758; 213-617-2205.
Miami, Florida:
Telephone: 305-371-2700.
Facsimile: 305-358-5744.
Mexico City, Mexico:
Telephone: (52-5) 207-9717.
Facsimile: (52-5) 208-3628.
Tokyo, Japan:
Telephone: (81-3) 3239-4300.
Facsimile: (81-3) 3239-4330.
Hong Kong:
Telephone: (852) 2822-8700.
Facsimile: (852) 2845-9070; Grice & Co., Solicitors,
Telephone: (852) 2826-0333.
Facsimile: (852) 2526-7166.
Singapore, Republic of Singapore:
Telephone: (65) 225-6000.
Facsimile: (65) 225-6009.
Bangkok, Thailand: Pacific Legal Group Ltd., In Association With White & Case,
Telephone: (662) 236-6154/7.
Facsimile: (662) 237-6771.
Hanoi, Viet Nam: Representative Office,
Telephone: (84-4) 227-575/6/7.
Facsimile: (84-4) 227-297.
Bombay, India:
Telephone: (91-22) 282-6300.
Facsimile: (91-22) 282-6305.
London, England:
Telephone: (44-171) 726-6361.
Facsimile: (44-171) 726-4314; (44-171) 726-8558.

(See Next Column)

Paris, France:
Telephone: (33-1) 42-60-34-05.
Facsimile: (33-1) 42-60-82-46.
Brussels, Belgium:
Telephone: (32-2) 647-05-89.
Facsimile: (32-2) 647-16-75.
Stockholm, Sweden:
Telephone: (46-8) 679-80-30.
Facsimile: (46-8) 611-21-22.
Helsinki, Finland:
Telephone: (358-0) 631-100.
Facsimile: (358-0) 179-477.
Moscow, Russia:
Telephone: (7-095) 201-9292/3/4/5.
Facsimile: (7-095) 201-9284.
Budapest, Hungary:
Telephone: (36-1) 269-0550; (36-1) 131-0933.
Facsimile: (36-1) 269-1199.
Prague, Czech Republic:
Telephone: (42-2) 2481-1796.
Facsimile: (42-2) 232-5522.
Warsaw, Poland: Telephone/
Facsimile: (48-22) 26-80-53; (48-22) 27-84-86. International Telephone/
Facsimile: (48-39) 12-19-06.
Istanbul, Turkey:
Telephone: (90-212) 275-68-98; (90-212) 275-75-33.
Facsimile: (90-212) 275-75-43.
Ankara, Turkey:
Telephone: (90-312) 446-2180.
Facsimile: (90-312) 437-9677.
Jeddah, Saudi Arabia: Law Office of Hassan Mahassni,
Telephone: (966-2) 651-3535.
Facsimile: (966-2) 651-3636.
Riyadh, Saudi Arabia: Law Office of Hassan Mahassni,
Telephone: (966-1) 476-7099.
Facsimile: (966-1) 479-0110.
Almaty, Kazakhstan:
Telephone: (7-3272) 50-7491/2.
Facsimile: (7-3272) 61-0842.

PARTNERS

Charles N. Brower
William J. Clinton
Victor J. DeSantis
Alan M. Dunn
Carolyn B. Lamm
John J. McAvoy
Walter J. Spak

ASSOCIATES

David E. Bond (Not admitted in DC)
Vincent Bowen
Daniel S. Chen (Not admitted in DC)
Anna-Marie Christello-Roop
Christopher M. Curran
Charlotte J. Hart
William C. Holland (Not admitted in DC)
Lisa L. Hubbard
Joseph H. Hunt
Patricia Y. Lee
Barry N. Machlin
Rachel Mariner (Not admitted in DC)
Ellen S. Moore (Not admitted in DC)
George L. Paul (Not admitted in DC)
Harriet A. Robinson
Edmund W. Sim
Katherine Simonetti (Not admitted in DC)
Anne D. Smith
Abbey Cohen Smutny
David R. Stepp
Francis A. Vasquez

For full biographical listings, see the Martindale-Hubbell Law Directory

*** WHITEFORD, TAYLOR & PRESTON (AV)**

888 17th Street, N.W., 20006-3939
Telephone: 202-659-6800
Baltimore, Maryland Office: 7 Saint Paul Street.
Telephone: 301-347-8700.
Towson, Maryland Office: 210 West Pennsylvania Avenue.
Telephone: 410-832-2000.

RESIDENT PARTNERS

Arthur P. Rogers
Glenn R. Bonard
Kenneth J. Ingram
Joseph D. Douglass
John J. Hathway

OF COUNSEL

C. William Tayler
Jeffrey M. Glosser
Lee A. Satterfield

RESIDENT ASSOCIATES

Kristine L. Meyer
Andrew J. Terrell
Brendan P. Bunn
Julianne Erin Dymowski

For full biographical listings, see the Martindale-Hubbell Law Directory

WHITMAN BREED ABBOTT & MORGAN (AV)

1215 17th Street, N.W., 20036
Telephone: 202-887-0353
Telecopier: 202-293-8684
Other Washington, D.C. Office: 1818 N Street, N.W.
Telephone: 202-466-1100.
Telecopier: 202-466-2745.
New York, New York Office: 200 Park Avenue.
Telephone: 212-351-3000.

(See Next Column)

WHITMAN BREED ABBOTT & MORGAN—*Continued*

Los Angeles, California Office: 633 West Fifth Street.
Telephone: 213-896-2400.
Sacramento, California Office: Senator Hotel Building, 1121 L Street.
Telephone: 916-441-4242.
Greenwich, Connecticut Office: 2 Greenwich Plaza.
Telephone: 203-869-3800.
Newark, New Jersey Office: One Gateway Center.
Telephone: 201-621-2230.
Palm Beach, Florida Office: 220 Sunrise Avenue.
Telephone: 407-832-5458.
London, England Office: 11 Waterloo Place.
Telephone: 71-839-3226.
Telex: 917881.
Tokyo, Japan Office: Suite 450, New Otemachi Building, 2-2-1 Otemachi, Chiyoda-Ku, Tokyo 100.
Telephone: 81-3-3242-1289.
Associated with: Tyan & Associes, 22, La Sagesse Street, Beirut, Lebanon.
Telephone: 337968.
Fax: 200969.
Telex: 43928.

MEMBERS OF FIRM

Michael G. Carey
(Not admitted in DC)
Donald O. Clark
(Not admitted in DC)
William N. Hall
Marcia A. Wiss

ASSOCIATES

John Fehrenbach

For full biographical listings, see the Martindale-Hubbell Law Directory

WILEY, REIN & FIELDING (AV)

1776 K Street, N.W., 20006-2304
Telephone: 202-429-7000
Facsimile: 202-429-7207

MEMBERS OF FIRM

Richard E. Wiley
Bert W. Rein
Fred F. Fielding
Thomas W. Brunner
James H. Wallace, Jr.
Charles Owen Verrill, Jr.
John C. Quale
Lawrence W. Secrest, III
R. Michael Senkowski
Rand L. Allen
Andrew S. Krulwich
Bruce L. McDonald
John L. Bartlett
Richard C. Lowery
Philip V. Permut
Thomas W. Queen
Jan Witold Baran
Danny E. Adams
John B. Wyss
Stuart F. Carwile
Richard L. McConnell
James M. Johnstone
Carl R. Ramey
Richard J. Bodorff
Matthew S. Simchak
Robert L. Pettit
Michael Yourshaw
Bruce G. Joseph
Robert B. Bell
Paul C. Smith
Thomas W. Kirby
Michael E. Zacharia
Philip J. Davis
Robert J. Butler
James R. W. Bayes
Walter J. Andrews
Laura A. Foggan
Brad E. Mutschelknaus
Jeffrey S. Linder
Edwin O. Bailey
David E. Hilliard
Ida Wurczinger Draim
John A. Hodges
Hugh Latimer
Keith S. Watson
John I. Davis
Richard H. Gordin
Susan D. Sawtelle
Robert A. Smith
Donna Coleman Gregg
Diane R. Zipursky
Marilyn E. Kerst
Katherine M. Holden
William B. Baker
Jerry V. Haines
James T. Bruce, III
Dag Wilkinson
Alan H. Price
Peter D. Ross
Daniel E. Troy
Samuel D. Walker
Lon A. Berk
Thomas B. Griffith
Paul F. Khoury
Carol A. Laham
Joseph L. Ruby
Stanley R. Soya
John E. Barry
Eileen P. Bradner
Kirk J. Nahra
Michael L. Sturm
Frank Winston, Jr.
Edward A. Yorkgitis, Jr.

OF COUNSEL

Donald P. Arnavas
Howard H. Bell
(Not admitted in DC)
William H. Berman
Tyrone Brown
Russell D. Duncan

SENIOR ATTORNEYS

Kurt E. DeSoto
Carl R. Frank

ASSOCIATES

Paul C. Adair
David R. Anderson
Steven A. Augustino
Michael K. Baker
Nancy M. Barnes
(Not admitted in DC)
Connie N. Bertram
Thomas J. Bluth
Dominic T. Bodensteiner
Mary E. Borja
John M. Burgett
Lauren A. Carbaugh
Matthew A. Chavez
(Not admitted in DC)
Scott A. Coffina
Christine E. Connelly

(See Next Column)

ASSOCIATES (Continued)

Michael L. Converse
John W. Creighton, III
(Not admitted in DC)
Jason P. Cronic
Luis de la Torre
Eric W. DeSilva
David L. Douglass
(Not admitted in DC)
Alison M. Duncan
Bryan E. Earl
Elizabeth Ann Eastwood
Gregg L. Elias
Craig H. Factor
(Not admitted in DC)
Anthony Fama
Marisa G. Faunce
(Not admitted in DC)
James J. Gildea
Stephen D. Goldman
Edward J. Grass
(Not admitted in DC)
Matthew B. Greiner
(Not admitted in DC)
Rosemary C. Harold
Phillip H. Harrington
Scott S. Harris
(Not admitted in DC)
G. Michael Harvey
(Not admitted in DC)
Dale E. Hausman
Tanja E. Hens
(Not admitted in DC)
David R. Hill
Mark T. Hurt
David J. Ignall
Julie L. Jacobs
Paul E. Janaskie
(Not admitted in DC)
Wayne D. Johnsen
Craig A. Johnson
Robert E. Johnson
(Not admitted in DC)
Jacqueline A. Jones
(Not admitted in DC)
Peter S. Jordan
Valerie E. Keller
(Not admitted in DC)
Cindy Kendrick
Karen A. Kincaid
(Not admitted in DC)
Lara Levinson
(Not admitted in DC)
James M. Ludwig, III
Gregory Lyons
Kevin J. Martin
(Not admitted in DC)
Willis S. Martyn, III
Bernard A. McDonough
William A. McGrath
Sean X. McKessy
Bruce P. Mehlman
(Not admitted in DC)
William G. Miller
Paul E. Misener
(Not admitted in DC)
Carlos M. Nalda
(Not admitted in DC)
Mark H. Neblett
(Not admitted in DC)
Richard T. Pfohl
Ann M. Plaza
(Not admitted in DC)
Jennifer L. Radner
(Not admitted in DC)
David H. Robbins
(Not admitted in DC)
Stacy R. Robinson
(Not admitted in DC)
Russell J. Rogers
(Not admitted in DC)
Stephen J. Rosen
Rachel Joy Rothstein
John M. Ryan
(Not admitted in DC)
Alan K. Schneider
(Not admitted in DC)
John R. Shane
Jonathan M. Shaw
(Not admitted in DC)
Steven D. Silverman
(Not admitted in DC)
William E. Smith
Todd M. Stansbury
David L. Strickland
Jeannie Su
(Not admitted in DC)
Russell Sullivan
(Not admitted in DC)
Antoinette Marie Tease
Michael E. Toner
Bryan N. Tramont
(Not admitted in DC)
Nancy J. Victory
David A. Vogel
Ilene T. Weinreich
(Not admitted in DC)
John C. Yang
Suzanne Yelen
Christopher R. Yukins
Marieann K. Zochowski
(Not admitted in DC)

For full biographical listings, see the Martindale-Hubbell Law Directory

WILKES, ARTIS, HEDRICK & LANE, CHARTERED (AV)

Suite 1100, 1666 K Street, N.W., 20006-2897
Telephone: 202-457-7800
Cable Address: "Wilan, Washington, D.C."
Annapolis, Maryland Office: Suite 400, 47 State Circle.
Telephone: 410-263-7800.
Bethesda, Maryland Office: Suite 800, 3 Bethesda Metro Center.
Telephone: 301-654-7800.
Fairfax, Virginia Office: Suite 600, 11320 Random Hills Road.
Telephone: 703-385-8000.
Greenbelt, Maryland Office: Suite 410, 6305 Ivy Lane.
Telephone: 301-345-7700.

James C. Wilkes (1899-1968)
James E. Artis (1907-1978)
David M. Bond
Charles A. Camalier, III
Jerald S. Cohn
Christopher H. Collins
James P. Downey (Resident, Fairfax, Virginia Office)
Maureen Ellen Dwyer
John T. Epting
Jonathan L. Farmer
Nancy G. Fax (Resident, Bethesda, Maryland Office)
Stanley J. Fineman
Norman M. Glasgow
Norman M. Glasgow, Jr.
Robert L. Gorham
Robert R. Harris (Bethesda & Greenbelt, Maryland Office)
Allen Jones, Jr.
Eric S. Kassoff (Resident, Bethesda, Maryland Office)
John D. Lane
Albert L. Ledgard, Jr.
J. Carter McKaig
Robert X. Perry, Jr.
Allison Carney Prince
John E. Prominski, Jr.
Whayne S. Quin
Richard K. Reed
(Not admitted in DC)
Louis P. Robbins
Frank W. Stearns (Resident at Fairfax, Virginia Office)
Dana Brewington Stebbins
Lois J. Vermillion
Joseph B. Whitebread, Jr.
David L. Winstead
Ramsey L. Woodworth

(See Next Column)

WILKES, ARTIS, HEDRICK & LANE CHARTERED, *Washington—Continued*

Matthew G. Ahrens (Resident, Bethesda, Maryland Office)
Ilene Baxt Campbell (Resident, Fairfax, Virginia Office)
Carlos J. Deupi
Katherine Watson Downs
Timothy Dugan (Resident, Bethesda, Maryland Office)
David A. Fuss
Robert M. Gurss
Patricia Ann Harris (Resident, Bethesda, Maryland Office)
Daniel G. Lloyd (Not admitted in DC)
Gail Prentiss Miller (Resident, Fairfax, Virginia Office)
Mark S. Randall
Karin M. Ryan
David H. Saffern
Stuart A. Turow

For full biographical listings, see the Martindale-Hubbell Law Directory

WILKINSON, BARKER, KNAUER & QUINN (AV)

1735 New York Avenue, N.W., 20006
Telephone: 202-783-4141
Fax: 202-833-2360; 783-5851
Frankfurt am Main, Germany Office: Goethestrasse 23.
Telephone: 011-49-69-2876.
Telecopier: 011-49-69-297-8453.

MEMBERS OF FIRM

Glen A. Wilkinson (1911-1985)
Robert W. Barker (1919-1987)
Rosel H. Hyde (1900-1992)
Earl R Stanley
Paul S. Quinn
Leon T. Knauer
Pierre J. LaForce
Paul A. Lenzini
Joel L. Greene
L. Andrew Tollin
Kenneth E. Satten
Barbara S. Jost
Michael Deuel Sullivan
Kathryn A. Zachem
Donald H. Clarke
F. Thomas Moran
Kenneth D. Patrich
Luisa L. Lancetti
William H. Boger, III (Not admitted in DC)
Lawrence J. Movshin
Dipl. Kfm. Richard Leitermann (Resident, Frankfurt am Main, Germany Office)
Christine V. Simpson

ASSOCIATES

Kelley Ann Baione
J. Wade Lindsay
Michael A. Mandigo
Cynthia S. Thomas
Janet Fitzpatrick
Robert G. Kirk (Not admitted in DC)
Carolyn W. Malanga (Not admitted in DC)
Craig Edward Gilmore (Not admitted in DC)
Georgina M. Lopez-Oña (Not admitted in DC)
Thomas Matthew Lynch (Not admitted in DC)

For full biographical listings, see the Martindale-Hubbell Law Directory

WILLIAMS & CONNOLLY (AV)

725 Twelfth Street, N.W., 20005
Telephone: 202-434-5000

MEMBERS OF FIRM

Edward Bennett Williams (1920-1988)
Paul R. Connolly (1922-1978)
Vincent J. Fuller
Raymond W. Bergan
Jeremiah C. Collins
Robert L. Weinberg
David Povich
Steven M. Umin
John W. Vardaman
Paul Martin Wolff
J. Alan Galbraith
John G. Kester
William E. McDaniels
Brendan V. Sullivan, Jr.
Aubrey M. Daniel, III
Richard M. Cooper
Gerald A. Feffer
Robert P. Watkins
Jerry L. Shulman
Lawrence Lucchino
Lewis H. Ferguson, III
Robert B. Barnett
David E. Kendall
Gregory B. Craig
John J. Buckley, Jr.
Terrence O'Donnell
Douglas R. Marvin
John K. Villa
Barry S. Simon
Kevin T. Baine
Stephen L. Urbanczyk
Philip J. Ward
Frederick Whitten Peters
James A. Bruton, III
Peter J. Kahn
Lon S. Babby
Michael S. Sundermeyer
James T. Fuller, III
David D. Aufhauser
Bruce R. Genderson
Carolyn H. Williams
Frank Lane Heard III
Steven R. Kuney
Gerson A. Zweifach
Paul Mogin
Howard W. Gutman
Nancy F. Lesser
Richard S. Hoffman
Paula Michele Ellison
Steven A. Steinbach
Mark S. Levinstein
Mary Greer Clark
Daniel F. Katz
Nicole K. Seligman
Robert M. Krasne
Kathleen L. Beggs
Sven Erik Holmes
William R. Murray, Jr.
Eva Petko Esber
Stephen D. Raber
John D. Cline

David C. Kiernan
Nancy A. Bard
Lon E. Musslewhite
Robin E. Jacobsohn
Charles A. Sweet
Elizabeth D. Collery
Heidi K. Hubbard
Glenn J. Pfadenhauer
George A. Borden
Robert J. Shaughnessy
Jonathan P. Graham
Allen P. Waxman

(See Next Column)

William M. Wiltshire
J. Roger Williams, Jr.
Eric M. Braun
David S. Blatt
Betsy K. Wanger
Ari S. Zymelman
Joseph D. Piorkowski, Jr.
Philip B. Busch
Paul K. Dueffert
Regina G. Maloney
H. Douglas Owens
Laurence Shore
Dane H. Butswinkas
Laurie S. Fulton
Dennis M. Black
Philip Andrew Sechler
Karen L. Peck
Christopher W. Schmeisser
Richard Hackney Wiegmann
Martin C. Calhoun
Lynda Schuler
Benjamin H. Harris, III
Jacqueline E. Maitland Davies
Donald R. Carlson
Charles W. Gittins
Erik S. Jaffe
Robert M. Cary
Jonathan P. Bach
Kevin M. Hodges
Eric A. Kuhl
Thomas F. Urban, II
S. Hollis M. Greenlaw
Paul A. Murphy
Nancy E. Weiss
David M. Zinn
James P. A. Ryan
John T. Parry
Joseph G. Petrosinelli
Philip J. Deutch
Eric N. Lieberman
Eric J. Moss
James W. Shannon, Jr. (Not admitted in DC)
Steven M. Farina
Sharon L. Davis
Kevin Downey
Paul B. Gaffney
Thomas G. Hentoff
Julie L. Ferguson
Timothy S. Driscoll
Rebecca G. Haile
Stuart G. Nash (Not admitted in DC)
Lindsay Held (Not admitted in DC)
Emmet T. Flood (Not admitted in DC)
Timothy D. Zick (Not admitted in DC)
Megan E. Hills
Philip J. Goodman (Not admitted in DC)
Marcie R. Ziegler (Not admitted in DC)
Kenneth C. Smurzynski
John E. Schmidtlein
Stephen D. Sencer
Katharine Weymouth
Jonathan Banks (Not admitted in DC)
Travis M. Dodd (Not admitted in DC)
Matthew J. Herrington (Not admitted in DC)
Kathleen H. Quimby (Not admitted in DC)

OF COUNSEL

Lyman G. Friedman

For full biographical listings, see the Martindale-Hubbell Law Directory

* WILLKIE FARR & GALLAGHER (AV)

Three Lafayette Centre, 1155 21st Street, N.W., 6th Floor, 20036-3384
Telephone: 202-328-8000
Fax: 202-887-8979
Telex: RCA 229800-WFGIG; WU 89-2762
New York, N.Y. Office: One Citicorp Center, 153 East 53rd Street, 10022-4669.
Telephone: 212-821-8000.
Fax: 212-821-8111
Telex: RCA 233780-WRGUR; RCA 23880 5-WFGUR.
Paris, France Office: 6, Avenue Velasquez 75008.
Telephone: 011-33-1-44-35-44-35.
Fax: 011-33-1-42-89-87-01.
Telex: 652740 WFG Paris.
London, England Office: 3rd Floor, 35 Wilson Street, EC2M 25J.
Telephone: 011-44-71-696-9060.
Fax: 011-44-71-417-9191.

RESIDENT MEMBERS

William H. Barringer
Sue D. Blumenfeld
Kevin B. Clark
Brian Conboy
John P. Dean
Christopher A. Dunn
James P. Durling
Michael H. Hammer
Thomas F. Kaufman
David P. Murray
Steven M. Oster
Kenneth J. Pierce
Matthew R. Schneider
Susan P. Thomases (Not admitted in DC)
Philip L. Verveer
Theodore C. Whitehouse

RESIDENT COUNSEL

Noel Hemmendinger
Russell L. Smith

RESIDENT ASSOCIATES

Randy Branitsky
Francis M. Buono
Carolyn W. Conkling
Jennifer A. Donaldson
Robert H. Edwards, Jr.
Brian Finley
Nancy A. Fischer
Christopher J. Hart
Daniel R. Hunter
Thomas Jones
Bonni Fine Kaufman
David R. King
Jonathan Kopp (Not admitted in DC)
Robert L. LaFrankie
Adams Chi-Peng Lee (Not admitted in DC)
William B. Lindsey
John L. McGrew
Edgar B. Miller (Not admitted in DC)
Melissa E. Newman (Not admitted in DC)
Matthew R. Nicely
Masaaki Ogawa (Not admitted in DC)
Carlisle E. Perkins
Michele R. Pistone
Daniel L. Porter
Linda S. Rahnema
John M. Ratino
Gabriel R. Sanz-Rexach (Not admitted in DC)
Conrad J. Smucker

(See Next Column)

WILLKIE FARR & GALLAGHER—*Continued*

RESIDENT ASSOCIATES (Continued)

Jennifer L. Stevens
Christopher S. Stokes
Raymond F. Sullivan, Jr.
Susan F. Wegner (Not admitted in DC)
Jacqueline Weisman
Lois Wye

For full biographical listings, see the Martindale-Hubbell Law Directory

WILMER, CUTLER & PICKERING (AV)

2445 M Street, N.W., 20037-1420
Telephone: 202-663-6000
Facsimile: 202-663-6363
Internet: Law@Wilmer.Com
European Offices:
4 Carlton Gardens, London, SW1Y 5AA, England. Telephone: 011 (4471) 839-4466.
Facsimile: 011 (4471) 839-3537.
Rue de la Loi 15 Wetstraat, B-1040 Brussels, Belgium. Telephone: 011 (322) 231-0903.
Facsimile: 011 (322) 230-4322.
Friedrichstrasse 95, D-10117 Berlin, Germany. Telephone: 011 (4930) 2643-3601.
Facsimile: 011 (4930) 2643-3630.

Richard H. Wilmer (1892-1976)

MEMBERS OF FIRM

Robert P. Stranahan, Jr.
Max O. Truitt, Jr.
Joel Rosenbloom
Howard P. Willens
Robert A. Hammond, III
Daniel K. Mayers
Stephen H. Sachs
Arthur F. Mathews
James S. Campbell
Dennis M. Flannery
Daniel Marcus
James Robertson
Louis R. Cohen
Michael R. Klein
Timothy N. Black
F. David Lake, Jr.
Paul J. Mode, Jr.
Stephen F. Black
C. Boyden Gray
Ronald J. Greene
Gary D. Wilson
C. Loring Jetton, Jr.
William T. Lake
James A. Rogers
Michael L. Burack
Michael S. Helfer
Neil J. King
Dieter G. F. Lange (Not admitted in DC; Resident, European Office, London, England)
Charles S. Levy
Robert B. McCaw
A. Douglas Melamed
Dr. Manfred Balz (Not admitted in the United States); (Resident, European Office, Berlin, Germany)
Richard W. Cass
Kenneth W. Gideon
William J. Kolasky, Jr.
Arthur L. Marriott (Resident, European Office, London, England)
A. Stephen Hut, Jr.
John Rounsaville, Jr.
Roger M. Witten
Robert C. Cassidy, Jr.
John D. Greenwald (Not admitted in DC)
John H. Harwood II
David M. Becker
Mary Carolyn Cox
Christopher R. Lipsett
William J. Perlstein
Marianne K. Smythe
Andrew B. Weissman
Lynn Bregman
James E. Coleman, Jr.
Stephen P. Doyle
William R. Richardson, Jr.
Russell J. Bruemmer
Bruce E. Coolidge
Juanita A. Crowley
John Payton
William J. Wilkins
Andrea Ann Timko
Andrew N. Vollmer
Thomas W. White
Bruce M. Berman
Thomas F. Connell
Charles E. Davidow
Terrill A. Hyde
Duane D. Morse
James S. Venit (Not admitted in DC; Resident, European Office, Brussels, Belgium)
Daniel H. Squire
W. Scott Blackmer (Resident, European Office, Brussels, Belgium)
Gary B. Born (Resident, European Office, London, England)
Philip D. Anker
Joseph K. Brenner
Carol Clayton
Anastasia D. Kelly
Thomas P. Olson
Patrick J. Carome
Jane C. Sherburne
David P. Donovan
Paul A. von Hehn (Not admitted in DC; Resident, European Office, Brussels, Belgium)
Bryan Slone (Not admitted in DC; Resident, European Office, Berlin, Germany)
Stephen M. Cutler
Andrew K. Parnell (Resident, European Office, London, England)
Roger W. Yoerges
Laura B. Ahearn
Mark D. Cahn
Eric R. Markus
Randolph D. Moss

SENIOR COUNSEL

Lloyd N. Cutler
John H. Pickering
J. Roger Wollenberg

COUNSEL

David R. Johnson
Ezekiel G. Stoddard
Lester Nurick
Leonard M. Shambon
Dr. Andreas Weitbrecht (Not admitted in DC; Resident, European Office, Brussels, Belgium)

(See Next Column)

COUNSEL (Continued)

Jeffrey N. Shane
Murray A. Indick
Marc C. Hansen (Resident, European Office, Brussels, Belgium)
Carol H. Fishman
Roger J. Patterson
Jeremy N. Rubenstein

SPECIAL COUNSEL

John J. Kallaugher (Not admitted in DC; Resident, European Office, London, England)
R. Scott Kilgore
Joseph E. Killory, Jr.
Thomas J. Delaney (Not admitted in DC)

OF COUNSEL

Marshall Hornblower
William R. Perlik

ASSOCIATES

Margaret L. Ackerley
James E. Anderson (Not admitted in DC)
Dr. Constantin Von Alvensleben (Not admitted in DC; Resident, European Office, Brussels, Belgium)
Rebecca Arbogast
Warren O. Asher
Karen L. Barr
Angela Bedford (Not admitted in DC; Resident, European Office, London, England)
John B. Bellinger, III
Brigida Benitez (Not admitted in DC)
Gail C. Bernstein
Karan Bhatia (Not admitted in DC)
Craig M. Blackwell
Anne D. Bolling
Katherine A. Bradley (Not admitted in DC)
Tonya L. Brito
Anthony G. Brown (Not admitted in DC)
Craig J. Brown
Michael B. Bressman
Mercer E. Bullard
J. Beckwith Burr (Not admitted in DC)
W. Hardy Callcott
Gregorio B. Cater (Not admitted in DC)
David J. Charles (Not admitted in DC)
Lynn R. Charytan
Steven F. Cherry
Michelle Chua (Not admitted in DC)
Thomas M. Clark
John H. Cobb (Not admitted in DC)
Michael E. Coe
Marc R. Cohen
Patrick T. Connors
Erik H. Corwin
Susan P. Crawford
James E. Day
Peggy Delinois
David Domenici (Not admitted in DC)
William P. Donovan, Jr.
Margaret M. Dotzel
Elizabeth Stevens Duane
Paul R. Dubinsky
Steven M. Dunne
Christian L. Duvernoy (Resident, European Office, Brussels, Belgium)
Lance W. Edwards
Sara E. Emley (Not admitted in DC)
Denise Esposito (Not admitted in DC)
Jutta Von Falkenhausen (Resident, European Office, Berlin, Germany)
Patrice Alexander Ficklin
Steven P. Finizio (Not admitted in DC)
Gregory R. Firehock (Not admitted in DC)
Joshua B. Fisher (Not admitted in DC)
Timothy P. Fox
Helen Anne Gaebler (Not admitted in DC)
Katherine H. Gibson
Allison C. Giles
John M. Glazer (Not admitted in DC)
Craig Goldblatt (Not admitted in DC)
Julia R. Gordon
Stuart P. Green
Leon B. Greenfield (Not admitted in DC)
Melinda Hardy
Christopher M. Heimann
Michael E. Herde
Catherine Snyder Hill
Michael R. Holter (Not admitted in DC; Resident, European Office, London, England)
Christopher Howard
Robert F. Hoyt
Peter B. Hutt II
Edward J. Janger
Trina Jones
Elizabeth M. Kiingi
Satish M. Kini (Not admitted in DC)
Amy N. Kroll
Frank Edward Kulbaski, III
Stavros J. Lambrinidis
Thomas K. Landry (Not admitted in DC)
Brian C. Lee (Not admitted in DC)
Yoon-Young Lee
Deborah Levine
Ginger L. Levy
Alyza D. Lewin (Not admitted in DC)
Lourdes M. Lopez-Isa (Not admitted in DC)
Dr. Natalie Lübben (Resident, European Office, Berlin, Germany)
Mary C. Manemann
Nancy L. Manzer
Susan D. McAndrew
Jeffrey E. McFadden
Audrey G. McFarlane
Ronald I. Meltzer
Charles Alan Mendels
Brian J. Menkes
Henning Mennenoeh (Resident, European Office, Berlin, Germany)
Neil D. Midgley (Resident, European Office, London, England)
Linda J. Miller
Eric J. Mogilnicki (Not admitted in DC)
Thomas Mueller
Miriam R. Nemetz
Alan J. Ostfield
Michael P. Pergola
Bruce L. Plotkin
Sharon A. Pocock
Robert A. Pulver (Not admitted in DC)
Bernard T. Roberts (Not admitted in DC)
Amy Farr Robertson
Alex E. Rogers (Not admitted in DC)
Jacquelynn Ruff
Penelope W. Saltzman
David Shub (Not admitted in DC)
John Siddeek

(See Next Column)

WILMER, CUTLER & PICKERING, *Washington—Continued*

ASSOCIATES (Continued)

Richard Sigel (Not admitted in DC)
Jeffrey P. Singdahlsen
Andrés Snaider
Robert B. Stack
Laurie Michelle Stegman (Not admitted in DC)
Kenneth P. Stern
Ali M. Stoeppelwerth (Not admitted in DC)
G. Sharon Stone (Not admitted in DC)
Stephen F. Thurber
Rene L. Todd (Not admitted in DC)
David H. Topol
Robert N. Walton
Sarah Waywell (Resident, European Office, Brussels, Belgium)
Sheryl A. Weingrow
Stuart M. Weiser (Not admitted in DC)
P. Kathleen Wells (Not admitted in DC)
Amey C. Winterer
Douglas A. Winthrop
James R. Wrathall
Soo J. Yim (Not admitted in DC)
Bahram A. Zia

Robert S. McCormick (Not admitted in DC; Executive Director of the Firm)

For full biographical listings, see the Martindale-Hubbell Law Directory

* WINSTON & STRAWN (AV)

1400 L Street, N.W., 20005-3502
Telephone: 202-371-5700
Telex: 440574 INTLAW UI
Telecopier: 202-371-5950
Chicago, Illinois Office: 35 West Wacker Drive.
Telephone: 315-558-5600.
Cable Address: "Winston Chicago."
Facsimile: 312-558-5700.
New York, N.Y. Office: 175 Water Street.
Telephone: 212-269-2500.
Telecopier: 212-952-1474/5.
Cable Address: "Coledeitz, NYK."
Telex: (RCA) 232459.
Geneva, Switzerland Office: 43 Rue du Rhone, 1204.
Telephone: (4122) 7810506.
Fax: (4122) 7810361.

MEMBERS OF FIRM

Leonard W. Belter
Richard C. Browne
Thomas M. Buchanan
Deborah C. Costlow
Donald K. Dankner
Scott M. DuBoff
Edward F. Gerwin, Jr.
Peter N. Hiebert
Eric L. Hirschhorn
William K. Keane (Not admitted in DC)
John R. Keys, Jr.
Frederick J. Killion
John C. Kirtland
Joseph B. Knotts, Jr.
Michael R. Lemov
William J. Madden, Jr.
J. Michael McGarry, III
Dean L. Overman
Malcolm H. Philips, Jr.
John P. Proctor
Robert M. Rader
Nicholas S. Reynolds
Daniel F. Stenger
Mark J. Wetterhahn
John E. Williams
David A. Repka
Peter Kryn Dykema
Margaret A. Hill
John A. Waits, II
James H. Burnley IV
LaJuana S. Wilcher (Not admitted in DC)
Beryl F. Anthony, Jr. (Not admitted in DC)
Norman R. Vander Clute
M. Javade Chaudhri
Benjamin P. Fishburne, III
Barry J. Hart
Steven M. Lucas
David W. Roderer
Charles L. Kinney
James R. Curtiss
Sheldon L. Trubatch
Robert A. Mangrum
James T. Pitts
Thomas C. Power
John Albert Whittaker, IV

OF COUNSEL

Robert M. Bor
John H. More
Graham B. Purcell, Jr.
Charles R. Sharp (Not admitted in DC)
Carl J. Peckinpaugh

SENIOR ATTORNEYS

Anne W. Cottingham
William A. Horin

ASSOCIATES

John R. Ates
Michael K. Atkinson
D. Randall Benn
Robert A. Berger
Eric W. Bloom
Cathy L. Burgess
Peter W. Colby
Jeanne M. Dennis
Robert Linn Draper
F. Stanley Echols
Joan B. Tucker Fife
Marcia R. Gelman
Yusuf E. Giansiracusa
Karen L. Grubber
John F. Guyot
Mark J. Hedien
Robert E. Helfrich (Not admitted in DC)
Kathryn M. Kalowsky
Andreas H. Leskovsek
John A. MacEvoy
Jan A. MacGregor
Eric J. Marcotte (Not admitted in DC)
Donn C. Meindertsma
Francisco J. Pavia
Thomas C. Poindexter
Michael I. Raschid
Perry D. Robinson (Not admitted in DC)

(See Next Column)

ASSOCIATES (Continued)

Katherine A. Rutemiller (Not admitted in DC)
Joanne M. Scanlon
Patrick L. Schmidt
Blaise A. Scinto (Not admitted in DC)
Michael L. Sibarium
William B. Fenning Steinman
Treg T. Tremont
Daphine Trotter
Monique M. Vasilchik
Malcolm D. Woolf (Not admitted in DC)
Raymond B. Wuslich

For full biographical listings, see the Martindale-Hubbell Law Directory

* WINTHROP, STIMSON, PUTNAM & ROBERTS (AV)

1133 Connecticut Avenue, N.W., 20036
Telephone: 202-775-9800
Telex: WINSTIM DC 316229
Telefax: 202-833-8491
New York, N.Y. Office: One Battery Park Plaza, 10004.
Telephone: 212-858-1000.
Stamford, Connecticut Office: Financial Centre, 695 East Main Street, P.O. Box 6760, 06904-6760.
Telephone: 203-348-2300.
Palm Beach, Florida Office: 125 Worth Avenue, 33480.
Telephone: 407-655-7297.
London, England Office: 2 Throgmorton Avenue, London EC2N 2AP, England.
Telephone: 011-4471-628-4931.
Brussels, Belgium Office: Rue Du Taciturne 42, B-1040 Brussels, Belgium.
Telephone: 011-322-230-1392.
Tokyo, Japan Office: 608 Atagoyama Bengoshi Building 6-7, Atago 1-chome, Minato-ku, Tokyo 105 Japan.
Telephone: 011-813-3437-9740.
Hong Kong Office: 2505 Asia Pacific Finance Tower, Citibank Plaza, 3 Garden Road, Central.
Telephone: 011-852-530-3400.

RESIDENT PARTNERS

Raymond S. Calamaro
Donald A. Carr
John E. Gillick
Jeffrey M. Lang
Gerald D. Morgan, Jr.
Christopher R. Wall
Roger D. Wiegley

COUNSEL

Stuart N. Brotman (Not admitted in DC)
Robert Reed Gray
Louis H. Kurrelmeyer
Aileen Meyer
Kenneth P. Quinn (Not admitted in DC)

RESIDENT ASSOCIATES

Paul Bousquet
Laura M. Brank
David S. Christy, Jr.
David A. Crichlow
Thomas M. deButts
Taina E. M. Edlund
William H. Espinosa
Gwyneth E. Hambley (Not admitted in DC)
Katherine J. Henry
Michael J. Levitin
Margaret K. Minister (Not admitted in DC)
Mark A. Monborne
Joshua I. Romanow
Paul W. Terry
William L. Thomas

For full biographical listings, see the Martindale-Hubbell Law Directory

FLORIDA

*ARCADIA,** De Soto Co.

BROWN, WALDRON & CARLTON (AV)

A Partnership of Professional Associations
124 North Brevard Avenue, 33821
Telephone: 813-494-4323
Telecopier: 813-494-6790

Fletcher Brown
Eugene E. Waldron, Jr.
David P. Carlton
Vincent A Sica

Representative Clients: Sorrells Bros. Packing Co., Inc.; School Board of DeSoto County; First State Bank of Arcadia; DeSoto Memorial Hospital.
Approved Attorneys for: Federal Land Bank of Columbia, S.C.; Farm Credit Bank; Chicago Title Insurance Co.; Attorney's Title Insurance Fund; Commonwealth Land Title Insurance Co.
Reference: First State Bank of Arcadia.

For full biographical listings, see the Martindale-Hubbell Law Directory

*BARTOW,** Polk Co.

FROST, O'TOOLE & SAUNDERS, P.A. (AV)

395 South Central Avenue, P.O. Box 2188, 33830
Telephone: 813-533-0314; 800-533-0967
Telecopier: 813-533-8985

John W. Frost, II
Neal L. O'Toole
Thomas C. Saunders
Richard E. "Rick" Dantzler
Robert A. Carr
Robert H. Van Hart
James R. Franklin
John Marc Tamayo

Reference: Community National Bank, Bartow.

For full biographical listings, see the Martindale-Hubbell Law Directory

BOCA RATON, Palm Beach Co.

BOND, SCHOENECK & KING (AV)

5355 Town Center Road, Suite 1002, 33486
Telephone: 407-368-1212
Fax: 407-338-9955
Syracuse, New York Office: 18th Floor One Lincoln Center.
Telephone: 315-422-0121.
Fax: 315-422-3598.
Albany, New York Office: 111 Washington Avenue.
Telephone: 518-462-7421.
Fax: 518-462-7441.
Naples, Florida Office: 1167 Third Street South.
Telephone: 813-262-6812.
Fax: 813-262-6908.
Oswego, New York Office: 130 East Second Street.
Telephone: 315-343-9116.
Fax: 315-343-1231.
Overland Park, Kansas Office: 7500 College Boulevard, Suite 910.
Telephone: 913-345-8001.
Fax: 913-345-9017.

MEMBERS OF FIRM

James P. McDonald
James E. Wilber
Robert C. Zundel, Jr.

For full biographical listings, see the Martindale-Hubbell Law Directory

CARTER & CONNOLLY, P.A. (AV)

Suite 312, 1200 North Federal Highway, 33432
Telephone: 407-368-9900

John Edward Carter
Andrew James Connolly

OF COUNSEL

Robert T. Carlile

For full biographical listings, see the Martindale-Hubbell Law Directory

OSBORNE, OSBORNE & DECLAIRE, P.A. (AV)

Suite 100 Via Mizner Financial Plaza, 798 South Federal Highway, P.O. Drawer 40, 33429-9974
Telephone: 407-395-1000
Fax: 407-368-6930

Ray C. Osborne
R. Brady Osborne, Jr.
George F. deClaire

Approved Attorneys for: First Union National Bank of Florida, N.A.; SunBank/South Florida, N.A.; Northern Trust Bank of Florida; Boca Bank, a Florida Banking Corp.

For full biographical listings, see the Martindale-Hubbell Law Directory

BARNETT ROBINSON, JR., P.A. (AV)

Suite 319 Atrium - One Boca Place, 2255 Glades Road, 33431
Telephone: 407-997-2277
Fax: 407-997-5718
Coral Gables, Florida Office: 328 Minorca Avenue.
Telephone: 305-444-3555.

Barnett Robinson, Jr.

OF COUNSEL

Norma F. Echarte

For full biographical listings, see the Martindale-Hubbell Law Directory

DONALD J. SASSER, P.A. (AV)

2200 Corporate Boulevard N.W., Suite 302, 33431
Telephone: 407-998-7725
West Palm Beach Florida Office: 1800 Australian Avenue, South, Suite 203.
Telephone: 407-689-4378.

Donald J. Sasser
Jorge M. Cestero

Reference: First Union National Bank of Florida.

*BONIFAY,** Holmes Co. — (Refer to De Funiak Springs)

*BRADENTON,** Manatee Co.

GRIMES, GOEBEL, GRIMES & HAWKINS, P.A. (AV)

The Professional Building, 1023 Manatee Avenue West, P.O. Box 1550, 34206
Telephone: 813-748-0151
Fax: 813-748-0158

E. Glenn Grimes (1888-1967)
William C. Grimes
Clyde C. Goebel (1921-1991)
Caleb J. Grimes
John D. Hawkins
Leslie Horton Gladfelter

William S. Galvano
John F. Jewell

Counsel for: First Commercial Bank of Manatee County; First Federal Savings & Loan Association of Florida; Schroeder-Manatee, Inc.
Approved Attorneys for: Chicago Title Insurance Co.; Attorneys' Title Insurance Fund; American Pioneer Title Insurance Co.; Lawyers Title Insurance Corporation.

For full biographical listings, see the Martindale-Hubbell Law Directory

LANE, TROHN, CLARKE, BERTRAND, VREELAND & JACOBSEN, P.A. (AV)

233 15th Street, West, P.O. Box 551, 34206
Telephone: 813-747-1871
Telecopier: 813-745-2866
Lakeland, Florida Office: One Lake Morton Drive, P.O. Box 3.
Telephone: 813-284-2200.

Robert J. Bertrand
Lynn H. Groseclose
Patrick J. Murphy
John V. Quinlan
Gary S. Rabin
Robert L. Trohn

Gilbert A. Smith, Jr.
Andrew R. McCumber
Nancy C. Harrison

For full biographical listings, see the Martindale-Hubbell Law Directory

*BRONSON,** Levy Co. — (Refer to Gainesville)

*BROOKSVILLE,** Hernando Co. — (Refer to Dade City)

*BUSHNELL,** Sumter Co. — (Refer to Ormond Beach)

*CHIPLEY,** Washington Co. — (Refer to Panama City)

*CLEARWATER,** Pinellas Co.

* indicates certain Bar Register subscribers whose principal office is located elsewhere in the state and who have arranged for representation as a part of the state capital listings that follow

BONNER, HOGAN & COLEMAN, P.A. (AV)

613 South Myrtle Avenue, P.O. Box 1640, 34617
Telephone: 813-461-7777
Telecopier: 813-447-1517

John R. Bonner, Sr.
Elwood Hogan, Jr.
Jeffrey P. Coleman
Milton A. Galbraith, Jr.

General Counsel for: First National Bank of Florida; Countryside Bankers; Monarch Marketing, Inc.; Decorating, Inc.; Professional Site Development, Inc.; Richmond Development, Inc.; J.G. Ranch.
Local Counsel for: Pinellas County Employees Federal Credit Union; Oxford Medical, Inc.

For full biographical listings, see the Martindale-Hubbell Law Directory

Clearwater—Continued

GROSS AND KWALL, P.A. (AV)

133 North Fort Harrison Avenue, 34615
Telephone: 813-441-4947
Telecopier: 813-447-3158

Raymond O. Gross
Louis Kwall

Gregory K. Showers

For full biographical listings, see the Martindale-Hubbell Law Directory

JOHNSON, BLAKELY, POPE, BOKOR, RUPPEL & BURNS, P.A. (AV)

911 Chestnut Street, P.O. Box 1368, 34617
Telephone: 813-461-1818
Telecopier: 813-441-8617
Tampa, Florida Office: 100 N. Tampa Street, Suite 1800. P.O. Box 1100.
Telephone: 813-225-2500.
Telecopier: 813-223-7118.

E. D. Armstrong III
John T. Blakely
Bruce H. Bokor
Guy M. Burns
Michael T. Cronin
Elizabeth J. Daniels
Marion Hale
Rebecca A. Henson
Scott C. Ilgenfritz
Frank R. Jakes
Timothy A. Johnson, Jr.
John R. Lawson, Jr.
David J. Ottinger
F. Wallace Pope, Jr.
Darryl R. Richards
Dennis G. Ruppel
John A. Schaefer
Philip M. Shasteen
Charles M. Tatelbaum
Joan M. Vecchioli
Julius J. Zschau

Bruce W. Barnes (Resident at Tampa)
Alexis Pauline Brooks (Resident at Tampa)
Duane A. Daiker
Lisa B. Dodge (Resident at Tampa)
James W. Humann
Sharon E. Krick
Michael G. Little
Michael C. Markham
Charles A. Samarkos
Bethann Scharrer
Anthony P. Zinge (Resident at Tampa)

For full biographical listings, see the Martindale-Hubbell Law Directory

*** MACFARLANE AUSLEY FERGUSON & McMULLEN** (AV)

AmSouth Bank Building, Suite 800, 400 Cleveland Street, P.O. Box 1669, 34617
Telephone: 813-441-8966
FAX: 813-442-8470
Palm Harbor, Florida Office: Republic Bank Building, Suite 150, 33920 U.S. Highway 19 North, 34684.
Telephone: 813-785-4402.
Fax: 813-785-0735.
Tallahassee, Florida Office: Washington Square Building, 227 South Calhoun Street, 32301.
Telephone: 904-224-9115.
FAX: 904-222-7560.
Tampa, Florida Office: 2300 First Florida Tower, 111 Madison Street, 33602.
Telephone: 813-273-4200.
Fax: 813-273-4396.

MEMBERS OF FIRM

Harry S. Cline
Stephen O. Cole
D. Scott Douglas
R. Nathan Hightower
Emil C. Marquardt, Jr.
James A. Martin, Jr.
John Tweed McMullen
Thomas C. Nash, II
J. Paul Raymond

ASSOCIATES

Marie L. DeMarco
Joshua Magidson
John Matthew Marquardt
Nancy S. Paikoff

Representative Clients: BellSouth Telecommunications, Inc.; Capital City Bank Group, Inc.; CSX Transportation, Inc.; Lykes Bros. Inc. and Subsidiary Companies; Morton Plant Hospital; National Medical Enterprises, Inc.; Peoples Gas System, Inc.; Sprint Corp./United Telephone; Tampa Electric Co.; The Procter & Gamble Co.

For full biographical listings, see the Martindale-Hubbell Law Directory

RICHARDS, GILKEY, FITE, SLAUGHTER, PRATESI & WARD, P.A. (AV)

Richards Building, 1253 Park Street, 34616
Telephone: 813-443-3281
Fax: 813-446-3741
Port Richey, Florida Office: 8410 U.S. Highway 19, Suite 104. 34668.
Telephone: 813-841-7833.
Fax: 813-847-6742.

(See Next Column)

Ralph Richards (1893-1980)
John D. Fite
John E. Slaughter, Jr.
Emil G. Pratesi
R. Carlton Ward
Cynthia I. Rice

OF COUNSEL

William W. Gilkey
William M. MacKenzie

Representative Clients: USR Realty Development Division of USX Corp.; Pall Corp; Orange Bank; Rutland's Florida Gulf Bank; First Union National Bank of Florida; Park Group Companies of America; Donald Roebling Trusts; Calvin P. Vary Trust; Morton F. Plant Hospital Trust; Madison Savings and Loan Assn.

For full biographical listings, see the Martindale-Hubbell Law Directory

COCOA, Brevard Co.

WESTMAN & LINTZ (AV)

1970 Michigan Avenue, Building F, 32922
Telephone: 407-690-1970
Facsimile: 407-690-2349

Robert T. Westman
Lester C. Lintz

Representative Clients: Watson Paving, Inc.; Clontz Construction, Inc.; Circles of Care, Inc.; Harvey's Indian River Groves, Inc.; Goodson Paving, Inc.; BRPH Architects/Engineers, Inc.; Miorelli Engineering, Inc.; Southern Comfort Builders, Inc.; CMH Parks, Inc.

CORAL GABLES, Dade Co.

PADGETT & SHAW, P.A. (AV)

2511 Ponce de Leon Boulevard, 33134
Telephone: 305-444-7611
Fort Lauderdale, Florida Office: 8795 W. McNab Road.
Telephone: 305-722-3500.

Inman Padgett (1897-1992)
Richard L. Shaw

Richard L. Shaw, II
Andrew G. Kolondra (Resident, Fort Lauderdale Office)
Wanda Rodriguez
Peter V. Fullerton

Approved Attorneys for: Attorneys' Title Insurance Fund.

For full biographical listings, see the Martindale-Hubbell Law Directory

BARNETT ROBINSON, JR., P.A. (AV)

328 Minorca Avenue, 33134
Telephone: 305-444-3555
FAX: 305-444-1655
Boca Raton, Florida Office: Suite 319 Atrium - One Boca Place, 2255 Glades Road.
Telephone: 407-997-2277.
Fax: 407-997-5718.

Barnett Robinson, Jr.

OF COUNSEL

Norma F. Echarte

For full biographical listings, see the Martindale-Hubbell Law Directory

TAYLOR, BRION, BUKER & GREENE (AV)

2801 Ponce de Leon Boulevard, Suite 707, 33134-6994
Telephone: 305-445-7577
Telecopier: 305-446-9944
Other offices located in: Miami, Tallahassee, Key West and Fort Lauderdale, Florida.

Pierre-Tristan Bourgoignie

OF COUNSEL

Frank D. Hall

For full biographical listings, see the Martindale-Hubbell Law Directory

WALTON LANTAFF SCHROEDER & CARSON (AV)

A Partnership including Professional Associations
Suite 1101 Gables International Plaza, 2655 Le Jeune Road, 33134
Telephone: 305-379-6411
Telecopier: 305-446-9206
Miami, Florida Office: One Biscayne Tower, 25th Floor, 2 South Biscayne Boulevard.
Telephone: 305-379-6411.
Telecopier: 305-577-3875.
West Palm Beach, Florida Office: United National Bank Tower, Suite 800, 1645 Palm Beach Lakes Boulevard.
Telephone: 407-689-6700.
Telecopier: 407-689-2647.
Fort Lauderdale, Florida Office: Third Floor, Blackstone Building, 707 Southeast Third Avenue.
Telephone: 305-463-8456.
Telecopier: 305-763-6294.

(See Next Column)

WALTON LANTAFF SCHROEDER & CARSON—*Continued*

RESIDENT PARTNERS

Charles P. Sacher (P.A.) | Robert M. Donlon
Nicholas E. Christin (P.A.) | Gregory T. Martini

RESIDENT OF COUNSEL

Laurence A. Schroeder | Martin E. Segal (P.A.)

RESIDENT ASSOCIATES

Charles S. Sacher

For full biographical listings, see the Martindale-Hubbell Law Directory

CORAL SPRINGS, Broward Co.

WILLIAM E. BLYLER (AV)

1881 University Drive, Suite 206, 33071
Telephone: 305-753-2333

*DADE CITY,** Pasco Co.

SUMNER & WARREN, P.A. (AV)

14150 South Sixth Street, P.O. Drawer 1047, 33526-1047
Telephone: 904-567-5658
Telecopier: 904-567-3928

Donna Sumner Cox (1958-1990) | Robert D. Sumner
Tim H. Warren

General Counsel for: SunBank of Pasco County; First National Bank of the South, Dade City, Florida; Pasco County Property Appraiser.
Local Counsel for: The Four Score Corp.

For full biographical listings, see the Martindale-Hubbell Law Directory

DANIA, Broward Co. — (Refer to Fort Lauderdale)

DAYTONA BEACH, Volusia Co.

COBB COLE & BELL (AV)

150 Magnolia Avenue, P.O. Box 2491, 32115-2491
Telephone: 904-255-8171
Fax: 904-258-5068
Tallahassee, Florida Office: 131 North Gadsden Street.
Telephone: 904-681-3233.
Fax: 904-681-3241.
Maitland, Florida Office: 900 Winderley Place, Suite 122.
Telephone: 407-661-1123.
Fax: 407-661-5743.
Orlando, Florida Office: Suite 1428 SunBank Center, 200 South Orange Avenue.
Telephone: 407-843-3337.
Fax: 407-843-0553.
Palm Coast, Florida Office: Sun Bank Building, 1 Florida Park Drive South, Suite 350.
Telephone: 904-446-2622.
Fax: 904-446-2654.

Thomas T. Cobb
W. Warren Cole, Jr.
Samuel P. Bell, III (Tallahassee and Orlando Offices)
Jay D. Bond, Jr.
Jonathan D. Kaney Jr.
J. Lester Kaney
John J. Upchurch
James M. Barclay (Tallahassee and Orlando Offices)
C. Allen Watts
Larry D. Marsh
Kevin X. Crowley (Tallahassee and Orlando Offices)
Thomas S. Hart
Terrence M. White
Theodore E. Mack (Resident, Tallahassee Office)
Janet E. Martinez
Kenneth R. Artin
Gregory D. Snell
Scott W. Cichon
J. Joaquin Fraxedas (Resident, Maitland Office)
Michael D. Williams (Resident, Orlando Office)
Robert A. Merrell, III
Dennis K. Bayer
Carol A. Forthman (Resident, Tallahassee Office)
Norma Stanley (Resident, Palm Coast Office)
Renee K. Fehr
Gary L. Butler
William H. Hughes III (Resident, Tallahassee Office)
Bruce A. Hanna
Robert W. Lloyd
John E. Cole
John P. Ferguson
James Andrew Hagan
Godwin J. Essien
Jonathan D. Kaney III

OF COUNSEL

Philip H. Elliott, Jr.
Paul N. Upchurch
Casey J. Gluckman (Resident, Tallahassee Office)

MEDIATION COUNSEL

C. Welborn Daniel
Robert P. Miller
R. A. Green, Jr.
Michelle Jernigan Grocock (Resident, Maitland Office)
Lisa J. Long (Resident, Maitland Office)
Candace W. Watson (Resident, Tallahassee Office)
John S. Neely, Jr. (Resident, Maitland Office)

General Counsel for: Daytona Beach Racing & Recreational Facilities District; News Journal Corporation.

(See Next Column)

Local Counsel for: Canal Insurance Co.; First Union National Bank of Florida; Southern Bell Telephone & Telegraph Co.; United States Fidelity & Guaranty Co.
Approved Attorneys for: American Pioneer Title Insurance Co.; Attorneys' Title Insurance Fund.

For full biographical listings, see the Martindale-Hubbell Law Directory

FINK & SWEET (AV)

149 East International Speedway Boulevard, P.O. Box 5386, 32118
Telephone: 904-252-7653
FAX: 904-238-3604

Wesley A. Fink | Jeffrey C. Sweet

Representative Client: Sun Bank of Volusia County.
Approved Attorneys for: Attorneys' Title Insurance Fund; Title Insurance Company of Minnesota; Chicago Title Insurance Co.
Reference: Sun Bank of Volusia County.

For full biographical listings, see the Martindale-Hubbell Law Directory

LANDIS, GRAHAM, FRENCH, HUSFELD, SHERMAN & FORD, P.A. (AV)

Formerly Hull, Landis, Graham & French
543 South Ridgewood Avenue, P.O. Box 265428, 32118
Telephone: 904-252-4717
Fax: 904-253-7352
De Land, Florida Office: 145 East Rich Avenue, P.O. Box 48.
Telephone: 904-734-3451.
Deltona, Florida Office: 204 Medical Arts Center, 1555 Saxon Boulevard.
Telephone: 407-574-1461.
Fax: 407-574-0242.

John L. Graham (1905-1978) | William E. Sherman
Richard S. Graham | Sam N. Masters
Bryan D. Austin

OF COUNSEL

J. Compton French

Counsel for: Barnett Bank of Volusia County; State Farm Mutual Automobile Insurance Co.; West Volusia Hospital Authority (West Volusia Hospital; Fish Memorial Hospital; SouthWest Volusia Healthcare Corporation); Central Florida Fern Cooperative, Inc.; General Motors Corp.; South Florida Natural Gas Co.; Florida Public Utilities Co.; Volusia County Industrial Development Authority; SouthTrust Bank of Volusia County.

For full biographical listings, see the Martindale-Hubbell Law Directory

DEERFIELD BEACH, Broward Co.

PATTERSON & HARMON, P.A. (AV)

665 S.E. 10th Street, 33441
Telephone: 305-421-7700
Fax: 305-421-7956

George A. Patterson | Blake M. Harmon

Susan A. Lopez

Representative Clients: C. L. Whiteside Construction Co.; E.P. Giuliano Construction, Inc.; Foxe Chase Development Corp.; Rivertown Apartments, Inc.; Rivertown Manor Condominium Assn.; Stainless Incorporated; Vichota Corp.
Approved Attorneys for: Attorneys' Title Insurance Fund; Chicago Title Insurance Co.
Reference: Barnett Bank of Broward County, N.A.

For full biographical listings, see the Martindale-Hubbell Law Directory

*DE FUNIAK SPRINGS,** Walton Co.

ANGUS G. ANDREWS (AV)

Professional Building, 10 Baldwin Avenue, P.O. Box 112, 32433
Telephone: 904-892-2181
FAX: 904-892-5383

Representative Clients: Walton County School District; DeFuniak Springs Housing Authority; Gulf Power Co.; Coca-Cola Bottling Co.; Walton County Sheriff's Department; CSX Railroad Co.; Chautauqua Vinyards and Winery, Inc.; 4-Mile Village Property Owners Assoc.; Walton County Fair Assoc.

*DE LAND,** Volusia Co.

LANDIS, GRAHAM, FRENCH, HUSFELD, SHERMAN & FORD, P.A. (AV)

Formerly Hull, Landis, Graham & French
145 East Rich Avenue, P.O. Box 48, 32721-0048
Telephone: 904-734-3451
Fax: 904-736-1350
Daytona Beach, Florida Office: 543 South Ridgewood Avenue, P.O. Box 265428.
Telephone: 904-252-4717.

(See Next Column)

LANDIS, GRAHAM, FRENCH, HUSFELD, SHERMAN & FORD P.A., *De Land—Continued*

Deltona, Florida Office: 204 Medical Arts Center, 1555 Saxon Boulevard.
Telephone: 407-574-1461.
Fax: 407-574-0242.

Erskine W. Landis (1900-1967)
John L. Graham (1905-1978)
Thorwald J. Husfeld
William E. Sherman
Richard S. Graham (Daytona Beach Office)
William A. Ottinger (Deltona Office)
Joe G. Dykes, Jr.
Frank A. Ford, Jr.
Sam N. Masters (Daytona Beach Office)
Philip L. Partridge
Bryan D. Austin
Edwin Channing Coolidge, Jr.
Donald B. Dempsey, Jr. (Deltona Office)

OF COUNSEL

J. Compton French (Daytona Beach Office)
Frank A. Ford, Sr.

Counsel for: Barnett Bank of Volusia County; State Farm Mutual Automobile Insurance Co.; West Volusia Hospital Authority (West Volusia Hospital; Fish Memorial Hospital; SouthWest Volusia Healthcare Corporation); Central Florida Fern Cooperative, Inc.; General Motors Corp.; South Florida Natural Gas Co.; Florida Public Utilities Co.; Volusia County Industrial Development Authority; SouthTrust Bank of Volusia County.

For full biographical listings, see the Martindale-Hubbell Law Directory

DELRAY BEACH, Palm Beach Co.

SIMON & SCHMIDT (AV)

100 N.E. Fifth Avenue, P.O. Box 2020, 33447
Telephone: 407-278-2601
Fax: 407-265-0286

MEMBERS OF FIRM

Ernest G. Simon
David W. Schmidt

Reference: Sun Bank/South Florida, N.A.

For full biographical listings, see the Martindale-Hubbell Law Directory

DELTONA, Volusia Co.

LANDIS, GRAHAM, FRENCH, HUSFELD, SHERMAN & FORD, P.A. (AV)

204 Medical Arts Center, 1555 Saxon Boulevard, 32725
Telephone: 407-574-1461
Fax: 407-574-0242
Daytona Beach, Florida Office: 543 South Ridgewood Avenue. P.O. Box 265428.
Telephone: 904-252-4717.
De Land, Florida Office: 145 East Rich Avenue, P.O. Box 48.
Telephone: 904-734-3451.

John L. Graham (1905-1978)
William A. Ottinger
Donald B. Dempsey, Jr.

Counsel for: Barnett Bank of Volusia County; State Farm Mutual Automobile Insurance Co.; West Volusia Hospital Authority (West Volusia Hospital; Fish Memorial Hospital; SouthWest Volusia Healthcare Corporation); Central Florida Fern Cooperative, Inc.; General Motors Corp.; South Florida Natural Gas Co.; Florida Public Utilities Co.; Volusia County Industrial Development Authority; SouthTrust Bank of Volusia County.

For full biographical listings, see the Martindale-Hubbell Law Directory

DESTIN, Okaloosa Co.

ANCHORS, FOSTER, MCINNIS & KEEFE, P.A. (AV)

P.O. Box 308, 32541
Telephone: 904-863-4064
Telefax: 904-862-1138
Fort Walton Beach, Florida Office: 909 Mar Walt Drive, Suite 1014, 32547.
Telephone: 904-863-4064.
Fax: 904-862-1138.

C. LeDon Anchors
William Scott Foster
C. Jeffrey McInnis
Lawrence Keefe

Representative Clients: Okaloosa County School District; Destin Water Users; Sunshine Bank of Fort Walton Beach; Emerald Coast Board of Realtors; Town of Cinco Bayou; South Walton Utility Co.; Holley-Navarre Water Systems; Harbor Oaks Hospital; HCA Twin Cities Hospital.

For full biographical listings, see the Martindale-Hubbell Law Directory

J. JEROME MILLER (AV)

Suite 3, 415 Mountain Drive, 32541
Telephone: 904-837-3860
Fax: 904-837-6158

Lamar A. Conerly, Jr.

For full biographical listings, see the Martindale-Hubbell Law Directory

POWELL, JONES & REID (AV)

Suite 21 Commerce Row, 225 Main Street, 32541
Telephone: 904-837-9099
Fax: 904-678-8336
Niceville, Florida Office: 107 North Partin Drive, P.O. Box 400.
Telephone: 904-678-2118.

MEMBERS OF FIRM

Stanley Bruce Powell
Michael A. Jones
Charles W. Reid
Keith J. Kinderman

References: Destin Bank; Peoples National Bank of Niceville; Barnett Bank of Northwest Florida; Vanguard Bank and Trust Co.

For full biographical listings, see the Martindale-Hubbell Law Directory

*FERNANDINA BEACH,** Nassau Co. — (Refer to Jacksonville)

*FORT LAUDERDALE,** Broward Co.

ATLAS, PEARLMAN, TROP & BORKSON, P.A. (AV)

New River Center, Suite 1900, 200 East Las Olas Boulevard, 33301
Telephone: 305-763-1200
Miami Line: 305-940-7847
West Palm Beach Line: 407-737-2627
Telex: (US) WU 522340; (INT'L) TRT 153529
Telecopier: 305-523-1952
Boca Raton, Florida Office: 3200 North Military Trail, Suite 205.
Telephone: 407-241-7084.
Miami, Florida Office: Atlas, Pearlman, Trop & Borkson, P.A., 100 SE 2nd Street, Suite 3320.
Telephone: 305-379-8100.
Telecopier: 305-358-5917.

Jan Douglas Atlas
Stephen M. Beyer
Elliot P. Borkson
Robin Corwin Campbell
Howard N. Kahn
Charles B. Pearlman
James M. Schneider
Douglas Paul Solomon
Michael L. Trop

Roxanne K. Beilly
Gayle E. Coleman
Sandra P. Greenblatt
Eric Lee
Joel D. Mayersohn
Jonathan S. Robbins
Wayne H. Schwartz
Karen E. Shumer

OF COUNSEL

Robert A. Kasky
Benedict P. Kuehne
Andrew Dale Ledbetter (Not admitted in FL)
Philip T. Medico, Jr. (Not admitted in FL)
Jon A. Sale

Reference: Capital Bank.

For full biographical listings, see the Martindale-Hubbell Law Directory

BERRYHILL, WILLIAMS & JORDAN, P.A. (AV)

2826 East Oakland Park Boulevard, P.O. Box 24266, 33307
Telephone: 305-563-7143
FAX: 305-563-7208

Thomas O. Berryhill (1908-1978)
Martin F. Avery, Jr. (Retired)
O. Edgar Williams, Jr.
John G. Jordan

Local Counsel for: Bridgestone/Firestone, Inc.
Approved Attorneys for: Attorneys' Title Insurance Fund.
Reference: First Union National Bank of Florida.

For full biographical listings, see the Martindale-Hubbell Law Directory

BYRD & MURPHY (AV)

Suite 200N Justice Building, 524 South Andrews Avenue, 33301
Telephone: 305-463-1423
FAX: 305-463-5428

MEMBERS OF FIRM

Thomas E. Byrd
James O. Murphy, Jr.
Carmine D. Gigliotti

Approved Attorneys for: Attorneys' Title Insurance Fund.

For full biographical listings, see the Martindale-Hubbell Law Directory

CLARK & SCHOLNIK (AV)

A Partnership of Professional Associations
California Federal Tower, 2400 East Commercial Boulevard, Suite 820, 33308
Telephone: 305-776-3800
Telecopier: 305-776-3825

MEMBERS OF FIRM

Thomas M. Clark (P.A.)
Louis N. Scholnik (P.A.)

For full biographical listings, see the Martindale-Hubbell Law Directory

Fort Lauderdale—Continued

Conrad, Scherer, James & Jenne (AV)

A Partnership of Professional Associations
Eighth Floor, 633 South Federal Highway, P.O. Box 14723, 33302
Telephone: 305-462-5500
Facsimile: 305-463-9244
Miami, Florida Office: 2180 Southwest 12th Avenue, P.O. Box 450888, 33245-0888.
Telephone: 305-856-9920.
Facsimile: 305-856-4546.

MEMBERS OF FIRM

William R. Scherer, Jr., (P.A.)
Gordon James, III, (P.A.)
Kenneth C. Jenne, II (P.A.)
Gary S. Genovese (P.A.)
Valerie Shea (P.A.)
Jay D. Schwartz (P.A.)
William V. Carcioppolo (P.A.)
James M. Eckhart

OF COUNSEL

Rex Conrad

ASSOCIATES

Linda Rae Spaulding
Lynn Futch Cooney
Kimberly A. Kisslan
Reid A. Cocalis
Albert L. Frevola, Jr.
James F. Carroll
Willie Earl Hall
Walter H. Djokic
Robin L. Supler
Denise L. Schumann
Derick J. Roulhac
Cathy Jo Goodwin
Mary Wilson Monaco

Local Counsel for: American Home Assurance Group; Caterpillar Tractor Co.; Division of Risk Management, State of Florida; Florida East Coast Railway; Fort Motor Co.; Liberty Mutual Insurance Co.; Ryder Truck Lines; Unigard Insurance Group.
Approved Attorneys for: Attorneys' Title Insurance Fund.
Reference: Barnett Bank of Fort Lauderdale.

For full biographical listings, see the Martindale-Hubbell Law Directory

Deuschle and Associates, P.A. (AV)

888 Southeast Third Avenue, Suite 300, 33316
Telephone: 305-763-7200
Facsimile: 305-522-7728

Brian C. Deuschle

Christopher D. Hale

Representative Clients: Drexel Investments, Inc.; Seabulk Tankers, Ltd.; Seabulk Chemical Carriers, Inc.; Selkirk Communications, Inc.; Hvide Shipping, Inc.
Approved Attorneys for: Attorneys' Title Insurance Fund.

For full biographical listings, see the Martindale-Hubbell Law Directory

Doumar, Curtis, Cross, Laystrom & Perloff (AV)

A Partnership of Professional Corporations
1177 Southeast Third Avenue, 33316
Telephone: 305-525-3441
Fax: 305-525-3423
Direct Miami Line: 305-945-3172

MEMBERS OF FIRM

Raymond A. Doumar (P.C.)
Charles L. Curtis (P.C.)
William S. Cross (P.C.)
C. William Laystrom, Jr. (P.C.)
John W. Perloff (P.C.)
E. Scott Allsworth (P.C.)
John D. Voigt (P.C.)
Jeffrey S. Wachs (P.C.)

ASSOCIATES

Mark E. Allsworth

Representative Clients: Albertson's, Inc.; Robinson-Humphrey/American Express; Deutsch-Ireland Properties; Massey-Yardley Chrysler Plymouth, Inc.; Waste Management, Inc.; Planned Development Corp.; Toys-R-Us Inc.; Lumbermans Mutual Casualty Co.; Melvin Simon And Associates.

For full biographical listings, see the Martindale-Hubbell Law Directory

Esler Petrie & Salkin, P.A. (AV)

Suite 300 The Advocate Building, 315 S.E. Seventh Street, 33301
Telephone: 305-764-5400
FAX: 305-764-5408

Gary A. Esler
C. Daniel Petrie, Jr.
Sonya L. Salkin

Laurie S. Moss

Representative Clients: The Chubb Group of Insurance Cos.; Fireman's Fund Insurance Co.; State of Florida-Department of Risk Management; Marriott Corp.; Gregson Furniture Industries, Inc.; Loewenstein, Inc.; Richfield Hotel Management, Inc.; Mobile America Insurance Group, Inc.; Colonial Penn Insurance Co.
References: Capital Bank.

For full biographical listings, see the Martindale-Hubbell Law Directory

Law Offices Goldberg & Young, P.A. (AV)

1630 North Federal Highway, P.O. Box 23800, 33307
Telephone: 305-564-8000
Telecopier: 305-564-0015

Paul Young
Lawrence H. Goldberg
William Berger
Paul S. Gravenhorst
Gregory John Blodig
Patrick S. Scott
Jonathan S. Marcus

Kimberly Lynn Barbar
Courtney A. Callahan
R. Bradley Chapman
Susan K. Connor
Daniel A. Jacobson
David Eric Jankowitz
Edmund O. Loos III
Frank A. Utset

Approved Attorneys for: Chicago Title Insurance Co.; Attorney's Title Insurance Fund; First American Title Insurance Co.; Commonwealth Land Title Insurance Cos.; American Pioneer Title Insurance Co.

For full biographical listings, see the Martindale-Hubbell Law Directory

Gunther & Whitaker, P.A. (AV)

Fifth Floor The Legal Center, 888 Southeast Third Avenue, P.O. Box 14608, 33302
Telephone: 305-523-5885
FAX: 305-760-9531

Dieter K. Gunther
Alan B. Whitaker, Jr.
Robert Hunt Schwartz
Jack T. Frost
Scott C. Burgess

Representative Clients: State Farm Mutual Automobile Insurance Co.; United States Fidelity Guaranty Co.; Home Insurance Co.; Cincinnati Insurance Companies; City of Fort Lauderdale; City of Plantation; City of Pompano Beach; Government Employees Insurance Company.

For full biographical listings, see the Martindale-Hubbell Law Directory

Heinrich Gordon Batchelder Hargrove & Weihe (AV)

A Partnership including Professional Associations
500 East Broward Boulevard, Suite 1000, 33394-3092
Telephone: 305-527-2800
Telecopier: 305-524-9481

MEMBERS OF FIRM

Drake M. Batchelder
Mark R. Boyd
Richard G. Gordon (P.A.)
John R. Hargrove (P.A.)
Eugene L. Heinrich (P.A.)
Jeffrey A. O'Keefe
Bruce A. Weihe (P.A.)

ASSOCIATES

William Kent Brown
Kandice L. Kilkelly
Melissa A. Notice
Christine M. Peirano
Paula Revene
Jodi R. Stone
Kenneth W. Waterway
Eric M. Zivitz

OF COUNSEL

Gerald M. Morris
Gilbert E. Theissen
Rodney Earl Walton
Jeffrey D. Welsh
(Not admitted in FL)

Representative Clients: Allstate Insurance Company; The BellSouth Companies; Federal Express; First Union National Bank of Florida; Phillips Petroleum Company; Schindler Elevator Corporation; Sears, Roebuck and Co.; U.S. Trust Company of Florida; W.R. Grace & Co.; Westinghouse Electric Corporation.

For full biographical listings, see the Martindale-Hubbell Law Directory

Holland & Knight (AV)

A Partnership including Professional Corporations
One East Broward Boulevard, Suite 1300, 33301-4811
Telephone: 305-525-1000
Fax: 305-463-2030
Mailing Address: P.O. Box 14070, 33302-4070,
Jacksonville, Florida Office: 50 N. Laura Street, Suite 3900.
Telephone: 904-353-2000.
Fax: 904-358-1872.
Lakeland, Florida Office: 92 Lake Wire Drive.
Telephone: 813-682-1161.
Fax: 813-688-1186.
Miami, Florida Office: 701 Brickell Avenue, 30th Floor.
Telephone: 305-374-8500.
Fax: 305-787-7799.
Orlando, Florida Office: 200 S. Orange Avenue, Suite 2600.
Telephone: 407-425-8500.
Fax: 407-244-5288.
St. Petersburg, Florida Office: 360 Central Avenue.
Telephone: 813-896-7171.
Fax: 813-822-8048.
Tallahassee, Florida Office: 315 Calhoun Street, Suite 600.
Telephone: 904-224-7000.
Fax: 904-224-8832.

(See Next Column)

HOLLAND & KNIGHT, *Fort Lauderdale—Continued*

Tampa, Florida Office: 400 North Ashley, Suite 2300.
Telephone: 813-227-8500.
Fax: 813-229-0134.
West Palm Beach, Florida Office: 625 N. Flagler Drive, Suite 700.
Telephone: 407-833-2000.
Fax: 407-650-8399.
Washington, D.C. Office: 2100 Pennsylvania Avenue, N.W.
Telephone: 202-955-3000.
Fax: 202-955-5564.
Atlanta, Georgia Office: 1201 West Peachtree Street, N.W., Suite 3100.
Telephone: 404-817-8500.
Fax: 404-881-0470.
Special Counsel: Shaw, Licitra, Parente, Esernio & Schwartz, P.C., 1010 Franklin Avenue, Garden City, N.Y., 11530, 300 East 42nd Street, New York, N.Y., 10017.

FORT LAUDERDALE MEMBERS AND ASSOCIATES

Martin J. Alexander
Kathryn Klein Anderson
Curtis R. Cowan
Susan F. Delegal
Diane A. DePoy
Irwin J. Fayne
Lori R. Hartglass
Thomas L. Kautz (Not admitted in FL)
Judith Epstein Kreitzer
Marie Lefere
Peter J. Manso (Not admitted in FL)
Theresa Wright McLaughlin
Stephen B. Moss
James M. Norman
Gary L. Rudolf
Donald S. Showalter (Not admitted in FL)
Steven Sonberg
Roma W. Theus, II

Robert J. Capko
Michael Heller
Adam J. Hodkin
Brian K. Hole
Heather C. Keith
Robbin Newman
Janna D. Peters
Jon K. Stage
Carlos O. Torano
Philip E. Ward
Arnold M. Zipper (Not admitted in FL)

For full biographical listings, see the Martindale-Hubbell Law Directory

---

KRUPNICK CAMPBELL MALONE ROSELLI BUSER & SLAMA, P.A. (AV)

700 Southeast 3rd Avenue, 33316
Telephone: 305-763-8181
FAX: 305-763-8292

Jon E. Krupnick
Walter G. Campbell, Jr.
Kevin A. Malone
Richard J. Roselli
Thomas E. Buser
Joseph J. Slama
Kelly D. Hancock
Lisa A. McNelis

Kelley Badger Gelb
Elaine P. Krupnick
Scott S. Liberman
Robert J. McKee
Adria E. Quintela

Reference: Citizens and Southern Bank.

For full biographical listings, see the Martindale-Hubbell Law Directory

---

KUBICKI DRAPER (AV)

One East Broward Boulevard Suite 1600, 33301
Telephone: 305-768-0011
Fax: 305-768-0514
Miami, Florida Office: Penthouse City National Bank Building, 25 West Flagler Street, 33130.
Telephone: 305-374-1212.
Fax: 305-374-7846.
West Palm Beach, Florida Office: 1100 United National Bank Tower, Suite 1100, 1675 Palm Beach Lakes Boulevard, 33401.
Telephone: 407-640-0303.
Fax: 407-640-0524.

Robert J. Cousins
Kenneth M. Oliver
Jane Carlene Rankin
Robert N. Sechen

William J. Bosch, III
Earleen H. Cote
Lisa Schloss McMillan
Nicholas G. Milano
Jorge A. Peña
Collen R. Rosenblum
Harold A. Saul
Peter J. Van Dyke (Resident)

For full biographical listings, see the Martindale-Hubbell Law Directory

---

LEONARD & MORRISON (AV)

Tenth Floor, 4875 North Federal Highway, P.O. Box 11025, 33339
Telephone: 305-776-3600
Fax: 305-776-3609

MEMBERS OF FIRM

William F. Leonard
Richard W. Morrison
C. Glenn Leonard
Tina L. Pratt

(See Next Column)

OF COUNSEL

William Robert Leonard

General Counsel for: Coral Ridge Golf Course, Inc.; Gill Hotels Co.; Sheraton Yankee Clipper Hotel; Haines Food Services, Inc.; Sunrise Bay Harbour, Inc.; Royal Petroleum, Inc.
Representative Client: Plimpton Trusts.
Reference: Intercontinental Bank.

For full biographical listings, see the Martindale-Hubbell Law Directory

---

KENNETH R. MIKOS, P.A. (AV)

2780 East Oakland Park Boulevard, 33306
Telephone: 305-566-7200
Facsimile: 305-566-1568

Kenneth R. Mikos

Douglas F. Hoffman

Special Counsel to: Fort Lauderdale Civil Service Board.

For full biographical listings, see the Martindale-Hubbell Law Directory

---

MORGAN, CARRATT AND O'CONNOR, P.A. (AV)

Suite 500, 2601 East Oakland Park Boulevard, 33306
Telephone: 305-565-0501

Charles R. Morgan (Retired)
Harry G. Carratt
Francis D. O'Connor
Terrence P. O'Connor
Michael E. O'Connor
Gus H. Carratt

Approved Attorneys for: Attorneys' Title Insurance Fund.
Reference: First Union National Bank of Florida, Fort Lauderdale Branch.

For full biographical listings, see the Martindale-Hubbell Law Directory

---

PETERS, ROBERTSON, LAX, PARSONS & WELCHER (AV)

Suite 600, 600 South Andrews Avenue, 34945
Telephone: 305-761-8999
Fax: 305-761-8990
Miami, Florida Office: Suite 600, Ingraham Building, 25 Southeast 2nd Avenue.
Telephone: 305-374-3103.
Fax: 305-377-9805.
Fort Myers, Florida Office: Key West Professional Centre, 1342 Colonial Boulevard, Suite 7.
Telephone: 813-936-1129.
Fax: 813-936-4036.
West Palm Beach, Florida Office: 515 North Flagler Drive, Suite 300, Pavilion Northbridge Centre.
Telephone: Palm Beach: 407-832-9698; Broward: 305-771-7493.
Facsimile: 407-832-5654.

Geralyn M. Passaro (Resident)

Representative Clients: Auto-Owners Insurance Co.; Dade County School Board; Employers Reinsurance Group; Gallagher Bassett Insurance Service; Maryland Casualty Co.

For full biographical listings, see the Martindale-Hubbell Law Directory

---

LAW OFFICES PRINCE, GLICK & MCFARLANE, P.A. (AV)

1112 Southeast 3rd Avenue, 33316
Telephone: Broward: 305-525-1112
Dade: 305-940-6414
FAX: 305-462-1243

Charles M. Prince
Joseph Glick
William J. McFarlane, III

For full biographical listings, see the Martindale-Hubbell Law Directory

---

PYSZKA, KESSLER, MASSEY, WELDON, CATRI, HOLTON & DOUBERLEY, P.A. (AV)

110 Tower, Twentieth Floor, 110 Southeast Sixth Street, 33301
Telephone: 305-463-8593
Miami, Florida Office: Fifth Floor, Grand Bay Plaza, 2665 South Bayshore Drive.
Telephone: 305-858-6614.

Gerard E. Pyszka
Charles T. Kessler (Resident)
Albert P. Massey, III (Resident)
Wesley L. Catri (Resident)
Raymond O. Holton, Jr. (Resident)
Paula C. Kessler (Resident)
Gregory G. Coican (Resident)
Andrea L. Kessler (Resident)
Kenneth A. Cutler (Resident)
Edward D. Schuster (Resident)

J. Michael Magee (Resident)
Jason T. Selwood (Resident)
Gerard A. Tuzzio (Resident)
Brenda F. Pagliaro
Ivan F. Cabrera (Resident)

For full biographical listings, see the Martindale-Hubbell Law Directory

Fort Lauderdale—Continued

TAYLOR, BRION, BUKER & GREENE (AV)

Barnett Bank Plaza, 12th Floor, One East Broward Boulevard, 33301-1806
Telephone: 305-522-6700
Telecopier: 305-522-6711
Miami, Florida Office: Fourteenth Floor, 801 Brickell Avenue.
Telephone: 305-377-6700.
Telex: 153653 Taybri.
Telecopier: 305-371-4578; 371-4579.
Tallahassee, Florida Office: Suite 250, 225 South Adams Street.
Telephone: 904-222-7717.
Telecopier: 904-222-3494.
Key West, Florida Office: 500 Fleming Street.
Telephone: 305-292-1776.
Telecopier: 305-292-1982.
Coral Gables, Florida Office: 2801 Ponce De Leon Boulevard, Suite 707.
Telephone: 305-445-7577.
Telecopier: 305-446-9944.

Leila D. Anderson
John S. Andrews
David S. Bowman

For full biographical listings, see the Martindale-Hubbell Law Directory

WALTON LANTAFF SCHROEDER & CARSON (AV)

A Partnership including Professional Associations
Blackstone Building, Third Floor, 707 Southeast Third Avenue, P.O. Box 14309, 33302
Telephone: 305-463-8456
Telecopier: 305-763-6294
Miami, Florida Office: One Biscayne Tower, 25th Floor, 2 South Biscayne Boulevard.
Telephone: 305-379-6411.
Telecopier: 305-577-3875.
West Palm Beach, Florida Office: United National Bank Tower, Suite 800, 1645 Palm Beach Lakes Boulevard.
Telephone: 407-689-6700.
Telecopier: 407-689-2647.
Coral Gables, Florida Office: Suite 1101, Gables International Plaza, 2655 Le Jeune Road.
Telephone: 305-379-6411.
Telecopier: 305-446-9206.

RESIDENT PARTNERS

Stephen W. Bazinsky
Jonathan J. Davis
Deborah Poore Knight

RESIDENT ASSOCIATES

Harvey D. Ginsburg
Michael W. Baker

OF COUNSEL

Carl E. Jenkins (P.A.)

For full biographical listings, see the Martindale-Hubbell Law Directory

*FORT MYERS,** Lee Co.

ALDERMAN & AHLBRAND, P.A. (AV)

Suite 200, The Historic Edison Theater Building, 1533 Hendry Street, P.O. Box 1530, 33902
Telephone: 813-334-7899
FAX: 813-334-0770

Frank C. Alderman, III
Mark W. Ahlbrand

For full biographical listings, see the Martindale-Hubbell Law Directory

GOLDBERG, GOLDSTEIN & BUCKLEY, P.A. (AV)

1515 Broadway, P.O. Box 2366, 33901-2366
Telephone: 813-334-1146
Fax: 813-334-3039
Naples, Florida Office: 2150 Goodlette Road, Suite 105, Parkway Financial Center, 33940.
Telephone: 813-262-4888.
Fax: 813-262-8716.
Port Charlotte, Florida Office: Emerald Square, Suite 1, 2852 Tamiami Trail, 33952.
Telephone: 813-624-2393.
Fax: 813-624-2155.
Cape Coral, Florida Office: 2330 S.E. 16th Place.
Telephone: 813-574-5575.
Fax: 813-574-9213.
Lehigh Acres, Florida Office: 1458 Lee Boulevard, Lee Boulevard Shopping Center, 33936.
Telephone: 813-368-6101.
Fax: 813-368-2461.
South Fort Myers, Florida Office: Horizon Plaza, 16050 South Tamiami Trail, Suites 101 and 102, 33908.
Telephone: 813-433-6777.
Fax: 813-433-0578.
Bonita Springs, Florida Office: 3431 Bonita Beach Road, Suite 208, 33923.
Telephone: 813-495-0003.
Fax: 813-495-0564.

(See Next Column)

Morton A. Goldberg
Ray Goldstein
Stephen W. Buckley
Harvey B. Goldberg
John B. Cechman
J. Jeffrey Rice
Mark A. Steinberg
David R. Linn
Donna L. Schnorr
Mark P. Smith
Richard Lee Purtz
Martin G. Arnowitz
George J. Mitar
Steven P. Kushner
Michael J. Ciccarone
Terry S. Nelson
William L. Welker
Jay Cooper
Jonathan D. Conant
Raymond L. Racila
Luis E. Insignares

OF COUNSEL

Dudley Burton

Approved Attorneys for: Attorneys' Title Insurance Fund; Chicago Title Insurance Co.; American Pioneer Title Insurance Company; Stewart Title Guaranty Co.; First American Title Insurance Company.

For full biographical listings, see the Martindale-Hubbell Law Directory

HENDERSON, FRANKLIN, STARNES & HOLT, PROFESSIONAL ASSOCIATION (AV)

1715 Monroe Street, P.O. Box 280, 33902-0280
Telephone: 813-334-4121
Telecopier: 813-332-4494

Albert M. Frierson
Ernest H. Hatch, Jr.
Stephen L. Helgemo
Ronald W. Smalley
John A. Noland
William N. Horowitz
Gerald W. Pierce
J. Terrence Porter
Michael J. Corso
Vicki L. Sproat
Denis H. Noah
John W. Lewis
Craig Ferrante
James L. Nulman
Harold N. Hume, Jr.
Bruce M. Stanley
Daniel W. Sheppard
Russell P. Schropp
Chad J. Motes
Guy E. Whitesman
Jack E. Lundy
Steven G. Koeppel
Douglas B. Szabo
Charles J. Basinait
Randal H. Thomas
Thomas H. Gunderson
Andrew L. Ringers, Jr.
John F. Potanovic, Jr.
James E. Kane
David K. Fowler
Robert C. Shearman
Paula F. Kelley
Joseph R. North
Timothy J. Jesaitis
Kevin D. Cooper
Jeffrey D. Kottkamp
J. Eric Stiffler
Gregory D. Whitworth

Representative Clients: Aetna Life & Casualty Group; CIGNA Group; CSX Transportation, Inc.; Fireman's Fund Insurance Cos.; Barnett Bank of Lee County, N.A.; Northern Trust Bank of Florida, N.A.; The Hartford Insurance Group; Travelers Group; United Telephone Company of Florida.

For full biographical listings, see the Martindale-Hubbell Law Directory

LAW OFFICES OF LLOYD G. HENDRY, P.A. (AV)

Society First Federal Center, 2201 Second Street, Suite 502, P.O. Box 1509, 33902
Telephone: 813-332-7123
Fax: 813-332-5147

Lloyd G. Hendry
Mary Hendry Sonne
Harry O. Hendry

For full biographical listings, see the Martindale-Hubbell Law Directory

PETERS, ROBERTSON, LAX, PARSONS & WELCHER (AV)

Key West Professional Centre, 1342 Colonial Boulevard, Suite 7, 33907
Telephone: 813-936-1129
Fax: 813-936-4036
Miami, Florida Office: Suite 600, Ingraham Building, 25 Southeast 2nd Avenue.
Telephone: 305-374-3103.
Fax: 305-377-9805.
Fort Lauderdale, Florida Office: Suite 600, 600 South Andrews Avenue.
Telephone: 305-761-8999.
Fax: 305-761-8990.
West Palm Beach, Florida Office: 515 North Flagler Drive, Suite 300-Pavilion Northbridge Centre.
Telephone: Palm Beach: 407-832-9698; Broward: 305-771-7493.
Facsimile: 407-832-5654.

ASSOCIATES

Steven B. Sundook (Resident)
Paul A. Poland

Representative Clients: Auto-Owners Insurance Co.; Dade County School Board; Employers Reinsurance Group; Gallagher Bassett Insurance Service; Maryland Casualty Co.

For full biographical listings, see the Martindale-Hubbell Law Directory

SHEPPARD, BRETT & STEWART, P.A. (AV)

(Formerly Sheppard & Woolslair)
2121 West First Street, P.O. Drawer 400, 33902
Telephone: 813-334-1141
Fax: 813-334-3965

(See Next Column)

SHEPPARD, BRETT & STEWART P.A., *Fort Myers—Continued*

W. A. Sheppard (1898-1971)
John K. Woolslair (1908-1968)
Jay Andrew Brett
John F. Stewart

OF COUNSEL

John Woolslair Sheppard

Craig R. Hersch
D. Hugh Kinsey, Jr.

Approved Attorneys for: Attorneys' Title Insurance Fund; Chicago Title Insurance Co.

For full biographical listings, see the Martindale-Hubbell Law Directory

SMOOT ADAMS EDWARDS & GREEN, P.A. (AV)

One University Park Suite 600, 12800 University Drive, P.O. Box 60259, 33906-6259
Telephone: 813-489-1776
(800) 226-1777 (in Florida)
Fax: 813-489-2444

J. Tom Smoot, Jr.
Hal Adams
Franklyn A. (Chip) Johnson (1947-1991)
Charles B. Edwards
Bruce D. Green
Steven I. Winer
Mark R. Komray
Thomas P. Clark

Lynne E. Denneler
Clayton W. Crevasse
M. Brian Cheffer
Robert S. Forman
Thomas M. Howell
Scott B. Albee
Plutarco M. Villalobos
Kathleen W. McBride
Lowell Schoenfeld
C. Berk Edwards, Jr.

For full biographical listings, see the Martindale-Hubbell Law Directory

*FORT PIERCE,** St. Lucie Co.

BRENNAN, HAYSKAR, JEFFERSON, GORMAN, WALKER & SCHWERER, PROFESSIONAL ASSOCIATION (AV)

515 and 519 South Indian River Drive, P.O. Box 3779, 34948-3779
Telephone: 407-461-2310
FAX: 407-468-6580

John T. Brennan
Thad H. Carlton (1906-1965)
Robert J. Gorman
Stephen G. Hayskar
Bradford L. Jefferson
Robert V. Schwerer
James T. Walker

William F. Gallese
Garrison M. Dundas

Representative Clients: Allstate Insurance Co.; Auto Owners Insurance Co.; Canal Insurance Co.; City of Fort Pierce; City of Stuart; First Union National Bank; First National Bank & Trust Co. of the Treasure Coast; Florida Farm Bureau Insurance Group; Kemper Insurance Group.

For full biographical listings, see the Martindale-Hubbell Law Directory

FEE, BRYAN & KOBLEGARD, P.A. (AV)

401 A South Indian River Drive, P.O. Box 1000, 34950
Telephone: 407-461-5020
FAX: 407-468-8461

Frank Fee (1913-1983)
Frank H. Fee, III
Benjamin L. Bryan, Jr.
Rupert N. Koblegard, III

Robert E. Maloney, Jr.
J. Curtis Boyd

General Counsel: Harbor Federal Savings; North St. Lucie River Water Control District; Fort Pierce Farms Water Control District; Fort Pierce Utilities Authority; Capron Trail Community Development District.
Representative Clients: Adams Ranch, Inc.; Callaway Land & Cattle Co., Inc., McArthur Farms, Inc.
Approved Attorneys for: Equitable Life Assurance Society of the United States; Equitable Agri-Business, Inc.

For full biographical listings, see the Martindale-Hubbell Law Directory

FORT WALTON BEACH, Okaloosa Co.

ANCHORS, FOSTER, MCINNIS & KEEFE, P.A. (AV)

Suite 1014, 909 Mar Walt Drive, 32547
Telephone: 904-863-4064
FAX: 904-862-1138
Destin, Florida Office: P.O. Box 308, 32541.
Telephone: 904-863-4064.
Telefax: 904-862-1138.

C. LeDon Anchors
William Scott Foster
C. Jeffrey McInnis
Lawrence Keefe

Representative Clients: Okaloosa County School District; Destin Water Users; Sunshine Bank of Fort Walton Beach; Emerald Coast Board of Realtors; Town of Cinco Bayou; South Walton Utility Co.; Holley-Navarre Water Systems; Harbor Oaks Hospital; HCA Twin Cities Hospital.

(See Next Column)

For full biographical listings, see the Martindale-Hubbell Law Directory

JOHNNY FORTUNE, P.A. (AV)

92 Eglin Parkway N.E., P.O. Drawer 2167, 32549
Telephone: 904-243-7184
FAX: 904-244-2148

Johnny A. Fortune

Representative Client: Trust Department, Vanguard Bank & Trust Co.
Approved Attorney for: Chicago Title Insurance Co.; Attorney's Title Insurance Fund, Inc.

For full biographical listings, see the Martindale-Hubbell Law Directory

SMITH, GRIMSLEY, BAUMAN, PINKERTON, PETERMANN, SAXER & WELLS (AV)

A Partnership of Professional Associations
25 Walter Martin Avenue, 32549
Telephone: 904-243-8194
Telecopier: 904-664-5728

MEMBERS OF FIRM

Walter J. Smith (P.A.)
James W. Grimsley (P.A.)
Steven B. Bauman (P.A.)
Drew S. Pinkerton (P.A.)
Richard P. Petermann (P.A.)
Christopher P. Saxer (P.A.)
Kelvin Clyde Wells (P.A.)

Representative Clients: First City Bank of Fort Walton; Moore Oil of Florida, Inc.; Regions Bank; First Alabama Bank; Vanguard Bank; Eglin BMW-Mazda; Preston Hood Chevrolet; ITT Financial Services, Inc.

For full biographical listings, see the Martindale-Hubbell Law Directory

*GAINESVILLE,** Alachua Co.

HENRY L. GRAY, JR., P.A. (AV)

211 N.E. First Street, P.O. Box 23879, 32602
Telephone: 904-376-5226
Fax: 904-372-8858

Henry L. Gray, Jr.

Reference: Sun Bank.

For full biographical listings, see the Martindale-Hubbell Law Directory

*GREEN COVE SPRINGS,** Clay Co. — (Refer to Jacksonville)

HOLLYWOOD, Broward Co.

ELLIS, SPENCER AND BUTLER (AV)

Emerald Hills Executive Plaza I, 4601 Sheridan Street, Suite 505, 33021
Telephone: Broward: 305-986-2291
Dade Line: 305-947-0620
Facsimile: 305-986-2778

MEMBERS OF FIRM

Robert B. Butler
W. Tinsley Ellis
William S. Spencer
Mark F. Butler
Robert Paul Keeley
Jonathan E. Brody
Chapman L. Smith, Jr.

OF COUNSEL

Sherwood Spencer (Retired)
E. Paige Drummond Brody

General Counsel for: American Bank of Hollywood.
Representative Clients: American Bank of Hollywood; Bank of North America; State Farm Fire & Casualty Company; Banaszak Concrete Corp.; Peakload, Inc. of America; Doby Building Supply, Inc.; Michael Swerdlow Companies; Construction Management Services, Inc.; Raintree Golf Club.

For full biographical listings, see the Martindale-Hubbell Law Directory

MILLER, SCHWARTZ AND MILLER, P.A. (AV)

4040 Sheridan Street, 33021
Telephone: Hollywood: 305-962-2000
Miami: 625-3630
Telefax: 305-961-2124
305-962-3963

Joseph L. Schwartz
James Fox Miller
A. Matthew Miller
Robert M. Schwartz
Charles Fox Miller

Approved Attorneys for: Attorneys' Title Insurance Fund.
Reference: First Union National Bank of Florida, Hollywood, Florida.

For full biographical listings, see the Martindale-Hubbell Law Directory

*JACKSONVILLE,** Duval Co.

ALLEN, BRINTON & SIMMONS, P.A. (AV)

One Independent Drive, Suite 3200, 32202
Telephone: 904-353-8800
Fax: 904-353-8770

(See Next Column)

ALLEN, BRINTON & SIMMONS P.A.—*Continued*

A. Graham Allen
William D. Brinton
Sidney S. Simmons, II

Edward McCarthy, III
Lisa Lloyd Pickert
Joelle J. Dillard

For full biographical listings, see the Martindale-Hubbell Law Directory

CORBIN, DICKINSON, DUVALL & MARGULIES (AV)

121 West Forsyth Street, Suite 1000, P.O. Box 41566, 32203
Telephone: 904-356-8073
Telecopier: 904-358-2319

MEMBERS OF FIRM

Peter Reed Corbin
John F. Dickinson
John E. Duvall
Richard N. Margulies

ASSOCIATES

Frank Damon Kitchen

For full biographical listings, see the Martindale-Hubbell Law Directory

FANNIN, TYLER & HAMILTON, P.A. (AV)

Park Pointe, Suite D, 4741 Atlantic Boulevard, 32207-2127
Telephone: 904-398-9999
Facsimile: 904-398-0806

John F. Fannin
H. Tyrone Tyler
J. Clark Hamilton, Jr.
Jay C. Floyd

For full biographical listings, see the Martindale-Hubbell Law Directory

FOLEY & LARDNER (AV)

The Greenleaf Building, 200 Laura Street, P.O. Box 240, 32201-0240
Telephone: 904-359-2000
Facsimile: 904-359-8700
Milwaukee, Wisconsin Office: Firstar Center, 777 East Wisconsin Avenue.
Telephone: 414-271-2400.
Telex: 26-819 (Foley Lard Mil).
Facsimile: 414-297-4900.
Madison, Wisconsin Office: Firstar Plaza, One South Pinckney Street, P.O. Box 1497.
Telephone: 608-257-5035.
Telex: 262051 (F L Madison).
Facsimile: 608-258-4258.
Chicago, Illinois Office: Suite 3300, One IBM Plaza, 330 N. Wabash Avenue.
Telephone: 312-755-1900.
Facsimile: 312-755-1925.
Washington, D.C. Office: Washington Harbour, Suite 500, 3000 K Street, N.W.
Telephone: 202-672-5300.
Telex: 904136 (Foley Lard Wsh).
Facsimile: 202-672-5399.
Annapolis, Maryland Office: Suite 102, 175 Admiral Cochrane Drive.
Telephone: 301-266-8077.
Telex: 899149 (Oldtownpat).
Facsimile: 301-266-8664.
Orlando, Florida Office: Suite 1800, 111 North Orange Avenue, P.O. Box 2193.
Telephone: 407-423-7656.
Telex: 441781 (HQ ORL).
Facsimile: 407-648-1743.
Tallahassee, Florida Office: Suite 450, 215 South Monroe Street, P.O. Box 508.
Telephone: 904-222-6100.
Facsimile: 904-224-0496.
Tampa, Florida Office: Suite 2700, One Hundred N. Tampa Street, P.O. Box 3391.
Telephones: 813-229-2300; Pinellas County: 813-442-3296.
Facsimile: 813-221-4210. Pinellas County: 813-446-9641.
Facsimile: 813-229-6282.
West Palm Beach, Florida Office: Suite 200, Phillips Point East Tower, 777 South Flagler Drive.
Telephone: 407-655-5050.
Facsimile: 407-655-6925.

PARTNERS

Charles E. Commander, III
Gardner F. Davis
Guy O. Farmer, II
Charles V. Hedrick
Linda Yayoi Kelso
William D. King
Mitchell W. Legler
Chauncey W. Lever, Jr.
Emerson M. Lotzia
Jean M. Mangu
E. Robert Meek
Sybil Meloy
Luther F. Sadler, Jr.
John T. Sefton
John M. Welch, Jr.
Steven A. Werber

OF COUNSEL

Jack H. Chambers
Christopher H. Smith (Not admitted in FL)
Paul C. Vance (Not admitted in FL)

(See Next Column)

RETIRED PARTNERS

Thomas B. Slade, III

RESIDENT ASSOCIATES

Laura Henry Allen
Robert S. Bernstein
Adam J. Buss
Tracy S. Carlin
David C. Cook
Richard W. Hawthorne
Chanley T. Howell
Kevin E. Hyde
Kevin P. Leasure
Charles C. Lemley
Amy Wright Littrell
J. Hugh Middlebrooks

For full biographical listings, see the Martindale-Hubbell Law Directory

GABEL & HAIR (AV)

76 South Laura Street, Suite 1600, 32202-3421
Telephone: 904-353-7329
Cable Address: "Wahlgabel"
Fax: 904-358-1637

MEMBERS OF FIRM

George D. Gabel, Jr.
Mattox S. Hair
Joel B. Toomey
Robert M. Dees
Sheldon Boney Forte
Timothy J. Conner
Suzanne Meyer Schnabel

ASSOCIATES

Christine S. Mayo
Michael L. Berry, Jr.
Karen Harris Hildebrand

Scott M. Loftin (1878-1953)
Harold B. Wahl (1907-1993)

Representative Clients: Florida Publishing Co. (Florida Times-Union); Florida Hotel-Motel Self Insurers Fund; Southern Bell Telephone & Telegraph Co.; Florida East Coast Railway Co.; WTLV Channel 12 TV; The Steamship Mutual Underwriting Association, Ltd.; The Standard Steamship Owners Protection & Indemnity Association, Ltd.; The Japan Ship Owners Mutual Protection & Indemnity Association; Liverpool & London Steamship Protection & Indemnity Association; Exxon Corp.

For full biographical listings, see the Martindale-Hubbell Law Directory

HOLLAND & KNIGHT (AV)

A Partnership including Professional Corporations
50 N. Laura Street, Suite 3900, 32202
Telephone: 904-353-2000
Fax: 904-358-1872
Mailing Address: P.O. Box 52687, 32201
Fort Lauderdale, Florida Office: One East Broward Boulevard, Suite 1300.
Telephone: 305-525-1000.
Fax: 305-463-2030.
Lakeland, Florida Office: 92 Lake Wire Drive.
Telephone: 813-682-1161.
Fax: 813-688-1186.
Miami, Florida Office: 701 Brickell Avenue, 30th Floor.
Telephone: 305-374-8500.
Fax: 305-787-7799.
Orlando, Florida Office: 200 S. Orange Avenue, Suite 2600.
Telephone: 407-425-8500.
Fax: 407-244-5288.
St. Petersburg, Florida Office: 360 Central Avenue.
Telephone: 813-896-7171.
Fax: 813-822-8048.
Tallahassee, Florida Office: 315 Calhoun Street, Suite 600.
Telephone: 904-224-7000.
Fax: 904-224-8832.
Tampa, Florida Office: 400 North Ashley, Suite 2300.
Telephone: 813-227-8500.
Fax: 813-229-0134.
West Palm Beach Office: 625 N. Flagler Drive, Suite 700.
Telephone: 407-833-2000.
Fax: 407-650-8399.
Washington, D.C. Office: 2100 Pennsylvania Avenue, N.W.
Telephone: 202-955-3000.
Fax: 202-955-5564.
Atlanta, Georgia Office: 1201 West Peachtree Street, N.W., Suite 3100.
Telephone: 404-817-8500.
Fax: 404-881-0470.
Special Counsel: Shaw, Licitra, Parente, Esernio & Schwartz, P.C., 1010 Franklin Avenue, Garden City, N.Y., 11530, 300 East 42nd Street, New York, N.Y., 10017.

JACKSONVILLE MEMBERS AND ASSOCIATES

Mark G. Alexander
Charles W. Arnold, Jr.
L. Kinder Cannon, III
Valerie C. Chritton
Hume F. Coleman
Raymond Ehrlich
Robert R. Feagin, III
Charlene Francis
Daniel J. Gallagher
William S. Graessle
Christopher J. Greene
Lawrence J. Hamilton II
Linda Connor Kane
Sharon Strayer Learch
Frederick J. Lotterhos, III
Dominic C. MacKenzie
John J. Mikals
Richard Nichols
George E. Schulz, Jr.
Leonard A. Selber
Donald W. Wallis
Alan M. Weiss
Martha McMahon Wirtz

(See Next Column)

HOLLAND & KNIGHT, *Jacksonville—Continued*

Crystal J. Adkins
Michele Griffith Dulsky
Gwen Hutcheson Griggs
Celeste R. Holland
Paul Pei-Chang Huang
Todd C. Johnson
Adam J. Kohl
Frank A. Lonegro
Scott D. Makar
Andrew H. Nachman
Rosel Rodriguez Pine
Jennifer Lee Stoner
Margaret A. Widman

COUNSEL

J. Shepard Bryan, Jr.
Philip Selber

For full biographical listings, see the Martindale-Hubbell Law Directory

MARKS, GRAY, CONROY & GIBBS, P.A. (AV)

Suite 800, 1200 Riverplace Boulevard, 32207
Telephone: 904-398-0900
Telecopier: 904-399-8440
Mailing Address: P.O. Box 447, 32201

Richard P. Marks (1876-1942)
Francis Michael Holt (1884-1946)
James A. Yates (1885-1960)
Sam R. Marks (1885-1973)
Harry T. Gray (1890-1975)
Francis P. Conroy (1912-1991)
Delbridge L. Gibbs (1917-1992)
James C. Rinaman, Jr.
H. Franklin Perritt, Jr.
Victor M. Halbach, Jr.
Gerald W. Weedon
William Lewis Thompson, Jr.
Nicholas V. Pulignano, Jr.
William M. Corley
Jeptha F. Barbour
Stephen C. Bullock
Karen Cappock Hoffman
Linda Cobb Ingham
Susan Smith Erdelyi
Robert E. Broach
Alan K. Ragan
Christopher D. Gray
Gary S. Stere
Daniel A. Nicholas
Stephen B. Gallagher
Milo Scott Thomas
Gregory A. Lawrence

OF COUNSEL

Randal C. Fairbanks

Representative Clients: Barnett Banks, Inc.; Baxter Healthcare Corp.; First Union Nat'l Bank of Florida; Government Employees Insurance Cos.; General Motors; Scottsdale Ins. Co.; Sears, Roebuck & Co.; Shearson, Lehman Bros., Inc.; Owens-Corning Fiberglas Corp.; The Travelers Insurance Cos.

For full biographical listings, see the Martindale-Hubbell Law Directory

MARTIN, ADE, BIRCHFIELD & MICKLER, P.A. (AV)

One Independent Square Suite 3000, Post Office Box 59, 32201
Telephone: 904-354-2050
Fax: 904-354-5842

James L. Ade
Lynda R. Aycock
W. O. Birchfield
Timothy A. Burleigh
Charles L. Cranford
Stephen H. Durant
T. William Glocker
Stephen D. Halker
Koko Head
Sharon Roberts Henderson
Barbara Christie Johnston
Ralph H. Martin
Robert O. Mickler
John D. Milton, Jr.
George T. Morrison
Daniel B. Nunn, Jr.
Scott G. Schildberg
Gary Wilkinson

Michael E. Goodbread, Jr.
Myra Loughran

Representative Clients: BancBoston Mortgage Corp.; Continental Cablevision, Inc. (CATV); General Waterworks Corp.; Mercedes-Benz of North America, Inc.; United Artists Communications, Inc.; Westinghouse Electric Corp.; Wilma South Corp.; First Union National Bank of Florida; Mac Papers, Inc.; Tree of Life, Inc.

For full biographical listings, see the Martindale-Hubbell Law Directory

MCGUIRE, WOODS, BATTLE & BOOTHE (AV)

Barnett Center, Suite 2750, 50 North Laura Street, 32202-3635
Telephone: 904-798-3200
Fax: 904-798-3207
Alexandria, Virginia Office: Transpotomac Plaza, Suite 1000, 1199 North Fairfax Street, 22314-1437.
Telephone: 703-739-6200.
Fax: 703-739-6270.
Baltimore, Maryland Office: The Blaustein Building, One North Charles Street, 21201-3793.
Telephone: 410-659-4400.
Fax: 410-659-4599.
Charlottesville, Virginia Office: Court Square Building, P.O. Box 1288, 22902-1288.
Telephone: 804-977-2500.
Fax: 804-980-2222.
McLean, (Tysons Corner) Virginia Office: 8280 Greensboro Drive, Suite 900, Tysons Corner, 22102-3892.
Telephone: 703-712-5000.
Fax: 703-712-5050.

(See Next Column)

Norfolk, Virginia Office: World Trade Center, Suite 9000, 101 West Main Street, 23510-1655.
Telephone: 804-640-3700.
Fax: 804-640-3701.
Richmond, Virginia Office: One James Center, 901 East Cary Street, 23219-4030.
Telephone: 804-775-1000.
Fax: 804-775-1061.
Washington, D.C. Office: The Army and Navy Club Building, 1627 Eye Street, N.W., 20006-4007.
Telephone: 202-857-1700.
Fax: 202-857-1737.
Brussels, Belgium Office: 250 Avenue Louise, Bte. 64, 1050.
Telephone: (32 2) 629 42 11.
Fax: (32 2) 629 42 22.
Zürich, Switzerland Office: P.O. Box 4930, Bahnhofstrasse 3, 8022.
Telephone: (41 1) 225 20 00.
Fax: (41 1) 225 20 20.

MEMBERS OF FIRM

Scott S. Cairns
Michael F. Dawes
Nathan D. Goldman
Gresham R. Stoneburner

ASSOCIATES

Marcia Morales Howard
Keith D. Munson

For full biographical listings, see the Martindale-Hubbell Law Directory

ROGERS, TOWERS, BAILEY, JONES & GAY, P.A. (AV)

1301 Riverplace Boulevard, Suite 1500, 32207
Telephone: 904-398-3911
Facsimile: 904-396-0663
Tallahassee, Florida Office: 106 South Monroe Street.
Telephone: 904-222-7200.

William Harlow Rogers (1884-1967)
Charles Daughtry Towers (1894-1969)
Cecil Cabaniss Bailey (1901-1992)
Taylor Jones (1911-1982)
J. Edwin Gay (Retired)
Charles D. Towers, Jr.
James M. McLean
Fred M. Ringel
David M. Foster
C. William Reiney
Clyde A. Reese, Jr.
Allan T. Geiger
Samuel L. LePrell
G. Kenneth Norrie
Douglas A. Ward
Paul P. Sanford
Irvin M. Weinstein
Robert T. Hyde, Jr.
H. Joseph O'Shields
Donald C. Wright
Joseph O. Stroud, Jr.
Richard B. Schwalbe
William H. Schroder, Jr.
Michael A. Wodrich
Cecile Evans Bass
E. Allen Hieb, Jr.
J. Kirby Chritton
Theodore R. Hainline, Jr.
Jeffrey C. Regan
Christopher C. Hazelip
Susan C. McDonald
Betsy Cox Mahin
Anthony A. Anderson
Fred D. Franklin, Jr.
Marcia Penman Parker
Anne K. Buzby

Andrew Keith Daw
Leonardo J. Maiman
Kurt H. Dunkle
Richard L. Maguire
Mark M. Arnold
James M. Riley
C. Davis Ely
Rick Monte Reznicsek
Kathy J. Tayon
Emily G. Pierce
Gregory F. Lunny
William A. O'Leary
Clinton Allen Wright, III
A. Barry Grosse
John Rodger Ibach
Barbara A. Puestow
Cheryl L. Worman
Regina L. Alberini

OF COUNSEL

Howard I. Korman

RESIDENT TALLAHASSEE OFFICE

Frank L. Jones

LEGAL SUPPORT PERSONNEL

Marvin Arrington

General Counsel for: Gate Petroleum Co.; Sun Bank/North Florida.
Representative Clients: Amerada Hess Corp.; CSX Corp.; First Union National Bank of Florida; Fruehauf Corp. (Jacksonville Shipyards); Grumann St. Augustine; Mayo Clinic Jacksonville; Metropolitan Life Insurance Company; Stone Container.

For full biographical listings, see the Martindale-Hubbell Law Directory

SMITH HULSEY & BUSEY (AV)

1800 First Union National Bank Tower, 225 Water Street, P.O. Box 53315, 32201-3315
Telephone: 904-359-7700
Facsimile: 904-359-7708; 353-9908

Lloyd Smith (1915-1987)

MEMBERS OF FIRM

Dennis L. Blackburn
Charles Guy Bond
Stephen D. Busey
Douglas D. Chunn
Jeanne E. Helton
Mark Hulsey
Cynthia C. Jackson
G. Preston Keyes
William E. Kuntz
M. Richard Lewis, Jr.

(See Next Column)

SMITH HULSEY & BUSEY—*Continued*

MEMBERS OF FIRM (Continued)

John F. MacLennan
Raymond R. Magley
E. Owen McCuller, Jr.
James H. Post
Bryan L. Putnal
E. Lanny Russell
Joel Settembrini, Jr.
Tim E. Sleeth
John R. Smith, Jr.
Timothy W. Volpe
Waddell A. Wallace, III
Harry M. Wilson, III

Michael M. Bajalia
James A. Bolling, Jr.
David Rodney Brown
C. William Curtis, III
E. Lanier Drew
Bruce J. Fletcher
Earl E. Googe, Jr.
Denise M. Hochberg
Lee G. Kellison
Eric S. Kolar
Marianne Lloyd
Marjorie Conner Makar
Bradley R. Markey
Tracy L. Markham (Not admitted in FL)
Mary E. McManus
Lauren Parsons
Kimberly Nall Rhodes
John A. Sapora
Howard J. Smith
Steven G. Spears
Richard A. Staggard
Melissa Smith Turra
Herschel T. Vinyard, Jr
Leslie A. Wickes
Karl A. Zillgitt

OF COUNSEL

John E. Thrasher

Representative Clients: Baptist Medical Center; Browning-Ferris Industries, Inc.; Champion Realty Corp. (Florida); First Union National Bank of Florida; Florida Rock Industries, Inc.; PGA Tour, Inc.; KPMG Peat Marwick; The Regency Group, Inc.; The Ritz-Carlton Hotel Company; University of Florida.

For full biographical listings, see the Martindale-Hubbell Law Directory

SQUIRE, SANDERS & DEMPSEY (AV)

One Enterprise Center Suite 2100, 225 Water Street, 32202-4424
Telephone: 904-353-1264
Fax: 904-356-2986
Cleveland, Ohio Office: 4900 Society Center, 127 Public Square, Cleveland, Ohio 44114-1304.
Telephone: 216-479-8500. Fax's: 216-479-8780, 216-479-8781, 216-479-8787, 216-479-8795, 216-479-8793, 216-479-8776, 216-479-4877.
Columbus, Ohio Offices: 1300 Huntington Center, 41 South High Street, Columbus, Ohio 43215.
Telephone: 614-365-2700.
Fax: 614-365-2499.
Miami, Florida Office: 201 South Biscayne Boulevard, Suite 2900 Miami Center, Miami, Florida 33131.
Telephone: 305-577-8700.
Fax: 305-358-1425.
New York, New York Office: 520 Madison Avenue, 32nd Floor, New York, New York 10022.
Telephone: 212-872-9800.
Fax: 212-872-9814.
Phoenix, Arizona Office: Two Renaissance Square, 40 North Central Avenue, Suite 2700, Phoenix, Arizona 85004-4441.
Telephone: 602-528-4000.
Fax: 602-253-8129.
Washington, D.C. Office: 1201 Pennsylvania Avenue, N.W., P.O. Box 407, Washington, D.C. 20044.
Telephone: 202-626-6600.
Fax: 202-626-6780.
London, England Office: 1 Gunpowder Square, Printer Street, London EC4A 3DE.
Telephone: 011-44-71-830-0055.
Fax: 011-44-71-830-0056.
Brussels, Belgium Office: Avenue Louise, 165-Box 15, 1050 Brussels, Belgium.
Telephone: 011-32-2-648-1717.
Fax: 011-32-2-648-1064.
Prague Office: Adria Palace, Jungmannova 31/36, 11000 Prague 1, Czech Republic.
Telephone: 011-42-2-231-5661.
Fax: 011-42-2-231-5482.
Bratislava Office: Mudronova 37, 811 01 Bratislava, Slovak Republic.
Telephone: 011-42-7-313-362; 011-42-7-315-370.
Fax: 011-42-7-313-918.
Budapest, Hungary Office: Deak Ferenc Ut. 10, Office 304, H-1052 Budapest V., Hungary.
Telephones: 011-361-226-2024; 011-361-226-5038.
Fax: 011-361-226-2025.
Kiev, Ukraine Office: vul. Prorizna 9, Suite 20, Kiev 252035, Ukraine.
Telephones: 011-7-044-244-3452, 011-7-044-244-3453, 011-7-044-228-8687.
Fax: 011-7-044-228-4938.

RESIDENT MEMBERS

Peter L. Dame
Judson Freeman, Jr.
Robert O. Freeman
John L. McWilliams, III

RESIDENT ASSOCIATES

Alexandra M. MacLennan

For full biographical listings, see the Martindale-Hubbell Law Directory

TAYLOR, MOSELEY & JOYNER, P.A. (AV)

501 West Bay Street, 32202
Telephone: 904-356-1306
Cable Address: "Ragland"
Telex: 5-6374
Telecopier: 904-354-0194

Reuben Ragland (1882-1954)
Louis Kurz (1891-1965)
E. Dale Joyner (1943-1993)
Neil C. Taylor
James F. Moseley
Robert E. Warren
Joseph W. Prichard, Jr.
Robert B. Parrish
Andrew J. Knight II
Richard K. Jones
James F. Moseley, Jr.
Phillip A. Buhler
Melanie E. Shepherd
Victor J. Zambetti
Mathew G. Nasrallah

Stanley M. Weston

OF COUNSEL

James E. Williams

Counsel for: CSX Transportation; Britannia Steam Ship Insurance Assn., Ltd.; The West of England Protection & Indemnity Assn. (Luxembourg); Crowley American Transport Services, Inc.; Howard Johnson Co.; United Kingdom Mutal Steamship Assurance Assn., Ltd. (Bermuda); General Food Corp.; The London Steam-Ship Owners' Mutual Insurance Assn., Ltd.

For full biographical listings, see the Martindale-Hubbell Law Directory

*JASPER,** Hamilton Co. — (Refer to Madison)

JUPITER, Palm Beach Co.

LEE, SCHULTE, EATON & BARRON (AV)

Suite 504, 1001 North U.S. Highway One, 33477
Telephone: 407-746-8600
Fax: 407-575-5934
Miami, Florida Office: 5th Floor, Concord Building, 66 West Flagler St.
Telephone: 305-358-9346.
FAX: 305-372-3987.

Thomas E. Lee, Jr.
Thomas J. Schulte
William E. Eaton, Jr.
Carol Dunn Barron

Representative Clients: Peerless Insurance Co.; Firemens' Fund Insurance Co.; Liberty Mutual Insurance, Co.; CIGNA; United Liquors Corp.; Professional Risk Management Services, Inc.; Florida Out-Patient Self Insurance Co.; Florida Physicians Insurance Trust; Investors Insurance Group.

For full biographical listings, see the Martindale-Hubbell Law Directory

*KEY WEST,** Monroe Co.

TAYLOR, BRION, BUKER & GREENE (AV)

500 Fleming Street, 33040-1900
Telephone: 305-292-1776
Telecopier: 305-292-1982
Miami, Florida Office: Fourteenth Floor, 801 Brickell Avenue.
Telephone: 305-377-6700.
Telex: 153653 Taybri.
Telecopier: 305-371-4578; 371-4579.
Tallahassee, Florida Office: Suite 250, 225 South Adams Street.
Telephone: 904-222-7717.
Telecopier: 904-222-3494.
Fort Lauderdale, Florida Office: Barnett Bank Plaza, 12th Floor, One East Broward Boulevard.
Telephone: 305-522-6700.
Telecopier: 305-522-6711.
Coral Gables, Florida Office: 2801 Ponce De Leon Boulevard, Suite 707.
Telephone: 305-445-7577.
Telecopier: 305-446-9944.

R. Bruce Wallace

OF COUNSEL

Robert A. Spottswood

For full biographical listings, see the Martindale-Hubbell Law Directory

*KISSIMMEE,** Osceola Co.

OVERSTREET RITCH & THACKER (AV)

100 Church Street, P.O. Box 420760, 34742
Telephone: 407-847-5151
FAX: 407-847-3353

MEMBERS OF FIRM

Murray Overstreet
John B. Ritch
Jo Overstreet Thacker

Representative Clients: Osceola County Tax Collector; Kissimmee Live Stock Market; Security National Bank of Osceola.
Approved Attorneys for: Attorneys' Title Insurance Fund; Commonwealth Land Title Insurance Co.; Chicago Title Insurance Co.

For full biographical listings, see the Martindale-Hubbell Law Directory

Kissimmee—Continued

TROUTMAN, WILLIAMS, IRVIN, GREEN & HELMS, PROFESSIONAL ASSOCIATION (AV)

Suite 206, 120 Broadway, 34741
Telephone: 407-933-8834
FAX: 407-933-8253
Winter Park, Florida Office: 311 West Fairbanks Avenue.
Telephone: 407-647-2277.
FAX: 407-628-2986.

Russell Troutman
Jack E. Bowen

For full biographical listings, see the Martindale-Hubbell Law Directory

*LAKE CITY,** Columbia Co.

BRANNON, BROWN, HALEY, ROBINSON & COLE, P.A. (AV)

10 North Columbia Street, P.O. Box 1029, 32056
Telephone: 904-752-3213

W. Brantley Brannon (1907-1985)
Clarence E. Brown
William J. Haley
Thomas W. Brown
Bruce W. Robinson
Ronald H. Cole
Donna Houghton Thames
Robert E. Case, Jr.

Counsel for: Aero Corporation; Barnett Bank of North Central Florida; Florida Farm Bureau Insurance Co.; Florida Power & Light Co.; Home Insurance Co.; Maryland Casualty Co.; Suwannee River Water Management District; Travelers Insurance Co.; Packaging Corporation of America.

For full biographical listings, see the Martindale-Hubbell Law Directory

DARBY, PEELE, BOWDOIN & PAYNE (AV)

A Partnership including Professional Associations
327 North Hernando Street, P.O. Drawer 1707, 32056
Telephone: 904-752-4120
Fax: 904-755-4569

Herbert F. Darby (P.A.)
S. Austin Peele (P.A.)
W. Roderick Bowdoin (P.A.)
M. Blair Payne
Thomas J. Kennon, III
Teresa Byrd Morgan

Representative Clients: City of Lake City; Cigna Insurance Cos.; Barnett Bank of North Central Florida; General Motors Acceptance Corp.; NationsBank of Florida; State Farm Insurance Cos.; Town of Fort White; Farmers and Dealers Bank.

For full biographical listings, see the Martindale-Hubbell Law Directory

LAKELAND, Polk Co.

HAHN, McCLURG, WATSON, GRIFFITH & BUSH, P.A. (AV)

101 South Florida Avenue, P.O. Box 38, 33802
Telephone: 813-688-7747
Telecopier: 813-683-4582

James P. Hahn
E.V. McClurg
Stephen C. Watson
John R. Griffith
Philip H. Bush

OF COUNSEL

J. Tom Watson

Special Counsel: Peoples Bank of Lakeland; First Federal of Florida; Publix Super Markets, Inc.
Approved Attorneys For: Attorneys' Title Insurance Fund; American Title Insurance Co.; Title & Trust Company of Florida; Federal Land Bank of Columbia, Columbia, S.C.
Reference: Peoples Bank of Lakeland.

For full biographical listings, see the Martindale-Hubbell Law Directory

HARRIS, MIDYETTE & GEARY, P.A. (AV)

2012 South Florida Avenue, P.O. Box 2451, 33806-2451
Telephone: 813-683-7567
FAX: 813-688-8099

Christy F. Harris (Mr.)
William M. Midyette, III
Joseph A. Geary

Eduardo F. Morrell
Ben H. Darby, Jr.
Louise D. Wilkinson

Approved Attorneys for: Attorneys' Title Insurance Fund.
Reference: Barnett Bank of Polk County.

For full biographical listings, see the Martindale-Hubbell Law Directory

HOLLAND & KNIGHT (AV)

A Partnership including Professional Corporations
92 Lake Wire Drive, 33801
Telephone: 813-682-1161
Fax: 813-688-1186
Mailing Address: P.O. Box 32092, 33802
Fort Lauderdale, Florida Office: One East Broward Boulevard, Suite 1300.
Telephone: 305-525-1000.
Fax: 305-463-2030.
Jacksonville, Florida Office: 50 N. Laura Street, Suite 3900.
Telephone: 904-353-2000.
Fax: 904-358-1872.
Miami, Florida Office: 701 Brickell Avenue, 30th Floor.
Telephone: 305-374-8500.
Fax: 305-787-7799.
Orlando, Florida Office: 200 S. Orange Avenue, Suite 600.
Telephone: 407-425-8500.
Fax: 407-244-5288.
St. Petersburg, Florida Office: 360 Central Avenue.
Telephone: 813-896-7171.
Fax: 813-822-8048.
Tallahassee, Florida Office: 315 Calhoun Street, Suite 600.
Telephone: 904-224-7000.
Fax: 904-224-8832.
Tampa, Florida Office: 400 North Ashley, Suite 2300.
Telephone: 813-227-8500.
Fax: 813-229-0134.
West Palm Beach, Florida Office: 625 N. Flagler Drive, Suite 700.
Telephone: 407-833-2000.
Fax: 407-650-8399.
Washington, D.C. Office: 2100 Pennsylvania Avenue, N.W.
Telephone: 202-955-3000.
Fax: 202-955-5564.
Atlanta, Georgia Office: 1201 West Peachtree Street, N.W., Suite 3100.
Telephone: 404-817-8500.
Fax: 404-881-0470.
Special Counsel: Shaw, Licitra, Parente, Esernio & Schwartz, P.D., 1010 Franklin Avenue, Garden City, N.Y., 11530, 300 East 42nd Street, New York, NY., 10017.

LAKELAND MEMBERS AND ASSOCIATES

Thomas R. Bayless
Charles E. Bentley
Randall C. Clement
William S. Dufoe
William O. E. Henry
Monique R. Johnson
D. Burke Kibler, III
Henry M. Kittleson
Edward F. Koren
C. Parkhill Mays, Jr.
Henry M. Morgan, Jr.
Robert P. Murray
Michael P. Sampson
Harry M. Sawyer, Jr.
Richard B. Stephens, Jr.
Richard L. Stockton
Edward W. Vogel, III

Jeffrey E. Appel
Laura Barber Belflower
Michael L. Davis
Walter E. Engle, III
Curt L. Harbsmeier
Gregory J. Johansen
Thomas O. McGimpsey
Sandra Graham Sheets
Barbara A. Willman

For full biographical listings, see the Martindale-Hubbell Law Directory

LANE, TROHN, CLARKE, BERTRAND, VREELAND & JACOBSEN, P.A. (AV)

One Lake Morton Drive, P.O. Box 3, 33802-0003
Telephone: 813-284-2200
Telecopier: 813-688-0310
Bradenton, Florida Office: 233 15th Street, West, P.O. Box 551.
Telephone: 813-747-1871.

A. H. Lane (Retired)
Robert L. Trohn
Thomas L. Clarke, Jr.
Robert J. Bertrand
John K. Vreeland
Donald G. Jacobsen
Christopher M. Fear
Gary S. Rabin
Lynn H. Groseclose
Robert M. Brush
Kingswood Sprott, Jr.
John V. Quinlan
John A. Attaway, Jr.
Hank B. Campbell
Judith J. Flanders
Patrick J. Murphy
Mitchell D. Franks
Janet Messervey Stuart
Robert G. Stokes
Mark N. Miller

Jonathan B. Trohn
Edwin A. Scales, III
Andrew R. McCumber
Nancy C. Harrison
Mia L. McKown
Deborah Laux Slowik
Gilbert A. Smith, Jr.
Christine M. Casingal
Jonathan M. Crowder

Counsel for: Ewell Industries, Inc.
Local Counsel for: Auto Owners Insurance Co.; Liberty Mutual Insurance Co.; St. Paul Fire & Marine Insurance Cos.; U.S. Fidelity & Guaranty Co.; State Farm Insurance Cos.
Approved Attorneys for: Attorneys' Title Insurance Fund; Chicago Title Insurance Co.

For full biographical listings, see the Martindale-Hubbell Law Directory

Lakeland—Continued

MARTIN & MARTIN, P.A. (AV)

200 Lake Morton Drive, 33801
Telephone: 813-688-7611
Telefax: 813-688-7329

E. Snow Martin
E. Snow Martin, Jr.
Michael D. Martin

For full biographical listings, see the Martindale-Hubbell Law Directory

M. CRAIG MASSEY (AV)

1701 South Florida Avenue, P.O. Box 2787, 33806
Telephone: 813-682-1178
Telecopier: 813-683-2849

General Counsel: State of Florida, Department of Citrus (Florida Citrus Commission).
References: Citrus Chemical Bank; Peoples Bank of Lakeland.

For full biographical listings, see the Martindale-Hubbell Law Directory

PETERSON, MYERS, CRAIG, CREWS, BRANDON & PUTERBAUGH, P.A. (AV)

100 East Main Street, P.O. Box 24628, 33802-4628
Telephone: 813-683-6511; 676-6934
Telecopier: 813-682-8031
Lake Wales, Florida Office: 130 East Central Avenue, P.O. Box 1079.
Telephones: 813-676-7611; 683-8942.
Winter Haven, Florida Office: Suite 300, 141 5th Street, N.W., P.O. Drawer 7608.
Telephone: 813-294-3360

Jack P. Brandon
Beach A Brooks, Jr.
J. Davis Connor
Roy A. Craig, Jr.
Jacob C. Dykxhoorn
Dennis P. Johnson
Kevin C. Knowlton
Douglas A. Lockwood, III
Corneal B. Myers
Cornelius B. Myers, III
Robert E. Puterbaugh
Abel A. Putnam
Thomas B. Putnam, Jr.
Deborah A. Ruster
Stephen R. Senn
Andrea Teves Smith
Kerry M. Wilson

General Counsel for: Barnett Bank of Polk County.
Representative Clients: Mutual Wholesale Co.; Sun Bank/Mid-Florida, N.A.; Chase Commercial Corp.; Barnett Banks, Inc.; Ben Hill Griffin, Inc.; Alcoma Association, Inc.
Approved Attorneys for: Equitable Life Assurance Society of the United States; Federal Land Bank of Columbia, S.C.; Attorneys' Title Insurance Fund.

For full biographical listings, see the Martindale-Hubbell Law Directory

LAKE MARY, Seminole Co. — (Refer to Longwood)

LAKE PLACID, Highlands Co.

SWAINE AND HARRIS, P.A. (AV)

212 Interlake Boulevard, P.O. Box 548, 33852
Telephone: 813-465-2811
Fax: 813-465-6999
Sebring, Florida Office: 425 South Commerce Avenue.
Telephone: 813-385-1549.
Fax: 813-471-0008.

J. Michael Swaine
Bert J. Harris, III
John K. McClure

Alison B. Copley
William J. Nielander

Representative Clients: Barnett Bank of Highlands County; Lykes Bros.,Inc; City of Sebring; City of Lake Placid; Lakeshore Mall.
Approved Attorneys for: Attorneys' Title Insurance Corp.

For full biographical listings, see the Martindale-Hubbell Law Directory

LAKE WALES, Polk Co.

PETERSON, MYERS, CRAIG, CREWS, BRANDON & PUTERBAUGH, P.A. (AV)

130 East Central Avenue, P.O. Box 1079, 33853
Telephone: 813-676-7611; 683-8942
Telecopier: 813-676-0643
Lakeland, Florida Office: 100 East Main Street, P.O. Box 24628.
Telephones: 813-683-6511; 676-6934.
Winter Haven, Florida Office: Suite 300, 141 5th Street, N.W., P.O. Drawer 7608.
Telephone: 813-294-3360.

Jack P. Brandon
Beach A Brooks, Jr.
Beach A Brooks, Jr.
J. Davis Connor
Roy A. Craig, Jr.
Jacob C. Dykxhoorn
Dennis P. Johnson
Kevin C. Knowlton
Douglas A. Lockwood, III
Corneal B. Myers

(See Next Column)

Cornelius B. Myers, III
Robert E. Puterbaugh
Robert E. Puterbaugh
Abel A. Putnam
Thomas B. Putnam, Jr.
Deborah A. Ruster
Stephen R. Senn
Andrea Teves Smith
Kerry M. Wilson

General Counsel for: Barnett Bank of Polk County.
Representative Clients: Mutual Wholesale Co.; Sun Bank/Mid-Florida N.A.; Chase Commercial Corp.; Barnett Banks, Inc.; Ben Hill Griffin, Inc.; Alcoma Association, Inc.
Approved Attorneys for: Equitable Life Assurance Society of the United States; Federal Land Bank of Columbia, S.C.; Attorneys' Title Insurance Fund.

For full biographical listings, see the Martindale-Hubbell Law Directory

LEESBURG, Lake Co.

AUSTIN & PEPPERMAN (AV)

Suite C 1321 West Citizens Boulevard, P.O. Drawer 490200, 34749-0200
Telephone: 904-728-1020
FAX: 904-728-0595

Robert E. Austin, Jr.
Carla R. Pepperman

ASSOCIATES

Robin L. Hoyle

Representative Clients: Allstate Insurance Co.; American Excess Insurance Co.; American Re-Insurance Co.; Florida Rock Industries, Inc.; Goodyear Tire & Rubber Co.; Great American Insurance Co.

For full biographical listings, see the Martindale-Hubbell Law Directory

*LIVE OAK,** Suwannee Co. — (Refer to Lake City)

*MADISON,** Madison Co.

DAVIS, BROWNING & SCHNITKER (AV)

901 West Base Street, P.O. Drawer 652, 32340
Telephone: 904-973-4186
Fax: 904-973-8564

MEMBERS OF FIRM

W. T. Davis (1901-1988)
Edwin B. Browning, Jr.
Clay A. Schnitker

ASSOCIATES

George T. Reeves

General Counsel for: Bank of Madison County; First Federal Bank; City of Madison; County of Madison; Town of Greenville.
Representative Clients: District School Board for Madison County; District School Board for Lafayette County; Quitman Federal Savings & Loan Association of Quitman, Georgia; First Union National Bank.

For full biographical listings, see the Martindale-Hubbell Law Directory

*MARIANNA,** Jackson Co. — (Refer to Panama City)

MELBOURNE, Brevard Co.

KRASNY AND DETTMER (AV)

A Partnership of Professional Associations
780 South Apollo Boulevard, P.O. Box 428, 32902-0428
Telephone: 407-723-5646
Telecopier: 407-768-1147

Myron S. (Mike) Krasny (P.A.)
Dale A. Dettmer (P.A.)

Scott Krasny

Representative Client: Security National Bank.

For full biographical listings, see the Martindale-Hubbell Law Directory

NANCE, CACCIATORE, SISSERSON, DURYEA AND HAMILTON (AV)

525 North Harbor City Boulevard, 32935
Telephone: 407-254-8416
Fax: 407-259-8243

MEMBERS OF FIRM

James H. Nance
Sammy Cacciatore
James A. Sisserson
Ronald G. Duryea
John N. Hamilton
Charles G. Barger, Jr.

Reference: Reliance Bank, Melbourne.

For full biographical listings, see the Martindale-Hubbell Law Directory

*MIAMI,** Dade Co.

ADAMS & ADAMS (AV)

5th Floor, Concord Building, 66 West Flagler Street, 33130
Telephone: 305-371-3333
Broward: 305-728-8770
Telecopier: 305-372-3987

(See Next Column)

ADAMS & ADAMS, *Miami—Continued*

Richard B. Adams (1926-1983)
Richard B. Adams, Jr.
R. Wade Adams

ASSOCIATES

Mai-Ling E. Castillo
Anthony P. Strasius

For full biographical listings, see the Martindale-Hubbell Law Directory

ANGONES, HUNTER, MCCLURE, LYNCH & WILLIAMS, P.A. (AV)

Ninth Floor-Concord Building, 66 West Flagler Street, 33130
Telephone: 305-371-5000
Fort Lauderdale: 305-728-9112
FAX: 305-371-3948

Frank R. Angones
Steven Kent Hunter
John McClure
Christopher J. Lynch
Stewart D. Williams
B. Scott Hunter

Leopoldo Garcia, Jr.
Thomas W. Paradise
Donna Joy Hunter
Lourdes Alfonsin Ruiz
Matthew K. Mitchell
Kara D. Phinney
C. David Durkee

Insurance Clients: Allstate Insurance Co.; Prudential Property & Casualty Insurance Company; State Farm Fire & Casualty Insurance Company; Rollins Hudig Hall Healthcare Risk, Inc.

For full biographical listings, see the Martindale-Hubbell Law Directory

BAKER & MCKENZIE (AV)

Barnett Tower, Suite 1600 701 Brickell Avenue, 33131-2827
Telephone: (305) 789-8900
Intn'l. Dialing: (1-305) 789-8900
Facsimile: (1-305) 789-8953
Associated Offices of Baker & McKenzie in: Almaty, Amsterdam, Bangkok, Barcelona, Beijing, Berlin, Bogotá, Brasília, Brussels, Budapest, Buenos Aires, Cairo, Caracas, Chicago, Dallas, Frankfurt, Geneva, Hanoi, Ho Chi Minh City, Hong Kong, Juárez, Kiev, London, Madrid, Manila, Melbourne, México City, Milan, Monterrey, Moscow, New York, Palo Alto, Paris, Prague, Rio de Janeiro, Riyadh, Rome, St. Petersburg, San Diego, San Francisco, São Paulo, Singapore, Stockholm, Sydney, Taipei, Tijuana, Tokyo, Toronto, Valencia, Warsaw, Washington, D.C. and Zürich.
Correspondent Law Firm: Hadiputranto, Hadinoto & Partners, Jakarta.

MEMBERS OF FIRM

Robert F. Hudson, Jr.
Sergio A. Leiseca, Jr. (Not admitted in FL)
Noel H. Nation
Richard J. Ovelmen
Eugene Alan Rostov
Edward Soto

LOCAL PARTNERS

James H. Barrett
Laura A. Gangemi
Lisa A. Giles-Klein
Seth P. Joseph

OF COUNSEL

Martin I. Kalish

COUNSEL

Landon K. Clayman
Anthony J. O'Donnell, Jr.

ASSOCIATES

C. Coleman G. Edmunds
W. Eugene Gandy, Jr.
Stephen E. Mander
Paulo C. Miranda (Not admitted in the United States)
R. Allen Naudé
Claudio Riedi
Mary K. Wiedmeier

For full biographical listings, see the Martindale-Hubbell Law Directory

BIERMAN, SHOHAT, LOEWY & PERRY, PROFESSIONAL ASSOCIATION (AV)

Penthouse Two, 800 Brickell Avenue, 33131-2944
Telephone: 305-358-7000
Facsimile: 305-358-4010

Donald I. Bierman
Edward R. Shohat
Ira N. Loewy
Pamela I. Perry
Maria C. Beguiristain

Reference: United National Bank of Miami.

For full biographical listings, see the Martindale-Hubbell Law Directory

BLACKWELL & WALKER ATTORNEYS AT LAW A PROFESSIONAL ASSOCIATION (AV)

Suite 2500, One Southeast Third Avenue, 33131
Telephone: 305-358-8880
Cable Address: "Blackwalk"
Telecopier: 305-372-1468
Dadeland Office: 9200 South Dadeland Boulevard, Suite 500, Miami, 33156.
Telephone: 306-670-5080.

(See Next Column)

Fort Lauderdale, Florida Office: Barnett Bank Building, One East Broward Boulevard, Suite 910.
Telephone: 305-728-9000.
West Palm Beach, Florida Office: Suite 100, 5 Harvard Circle.
Telephone: 407-686-4800.

Thomas Joseph Blackwell (1896-1964)
William L. Gray, Jr. (1902-1976)
Samuel J. Powers, Jr. (1917-1991)
W. H. Walker (1907-1992)
Paul R. Larkin, Jr.,
James E. Tribble
R. Layton Mank
Rodd R. Buell
Charles E. Sammons
Charles P. Flick
Charles D. Robbins
John C. Seipp, Jr.
Patrick C. Barthet
David S. Wood
Robert D. Brown
Bradley K. Hanafourde
William N. Charouhis

Arthur M. Simon
Laurie Schack Cohen
Martin E. Doyle
A. Blackwell Stieglitz
Bruce G. Hermelee (Resident, Fort Lauderdale Office)
William L. Bromagen
Nan Blumenfeld Bolz (Resident, West Palm Beach Office)
Steven W. Hyatt
Daniel J. Kissane
Joanne Garone
Bonnie S. Crouch
David A. Cornell
Catherine B. Parks
Lori Jean Johnson
David F. Higgs
Christine L. Welstead
Carlos J. Reyes, Jr. (Resident, Ft. Lauderdale Office)
Marilyn Blanco-Reyes
Stephen G. York
Thomas F.X. Carr
Thomas J. Hess
Monica A. Rey-Moran
Rafael Cruz-Alvarez
James M. Walker
Margaret C. Simonetti

OF COUNSEL

John R. Hoehl
Robert Asti
John B. Kelley
Martin J. Kurzer
Willis H. Flick (P.A.) (Inactive)

Representative Clients: Allied-Signal, Inc.; Bristol-Myers Squibb Company; Citibank F.S.B.; Equitable Life Assurance; Ford Motor Company; Honda North America, Inc.; Maryland Casualty Company; Post, Buckley, Schuh & Jernigan, Inc.; Showa Denko KK; Westbrooke Communities.

For full biographical listings, see the Martindale-Hubbell Law Directory

COLSON, HICKS, EIDSON, COLSON, MATTHEWS & GAMBA (AV)

Floor 47 First Union Financial Center, 200 South Biscayne Boulevard, 33131-2351
Telephone: 305-373-5400

MEMBERS OF FIRM

Bill Colson
William M. Hicks
Mike Eidson
Dean C. Colson
Joseph M. Matthews
Tomas F. Gamba
Tony Korvick
Enid Duany Mendoza
Newton P. Porter
Julie Braman

Reference: Northern Trust Bank of Florida.

For full biographical listings, see the Martindale-Hubbell Law Directory

THOMAS L. DAVID, P.A. (AV)

8th Floor, 1428 Brickell Avenue, 33131
Telephone: 305-371-6600
FAX: 305-371-5511

Thomas L. David

Reference: Citibank (Florida) N.A.

For full biographical listings, see the Martindale-Hubbell Law Directory

LAW OFFICES OF DUBÉ AND WRIGHT, P.A. (AV)

Suite 2608 New World Tower, 100 North Biscayne Boulevard, 33132
Telephone: 305-374-7472
Fax: 305-374-3219

Robert L. Dubé
Wilkinson D. Wright, III

OF COUNSEL

Richard M. Gale

For full biographical listings, see the Martindale-Hubbell Law Directory

FLOYD PEARSON RICHMAN GREER WEIL BRUMBAUGH & RUSSOMANNO, P.A. (AV)

Miami Center, Tenth Floor, 201 South Biscayne Boulevard, 33131
Telephone: 305-373-4000
Fax: 305-373-4099

Robert L. Floyd
Ray H. Pearson
Gerald F. Richman
Alan G. Greer
Kenneth J. Weil
John M. Brumbaugh
Herman J. Russomanno
Andrew J. Mirabito
Bruce A. Christensen
Scott D. Sheftall
Charles H. Johnson
Gary S. Betensky

(See Next Column)

FLOYD PEARSON RICHMAN GREER WEIL BRUMBAUGH & RUSSOMANNO P.A.—*Continued*

Diane Wagner Katzen
Robert C. Levine
Robert J. Fiore
Robert J. Borrello
Manuel A. Garcia-Linares
Carroll J. Kelly
Mark Anthony Romance
Richard C. Alvarez
Steven M Brady

OF COUNSEL

Paul M. Bunge
James W. Middleton

Representative Clients: AT&T Information Systems, Inc.; Shriners Hospitals for Crippled Children; Motorola, Inc.; Minnesota Mining and Manufacturing Co.; South Florida Hotel and Motel Assn.; The Lubrizol Corp.; Republic of Panama; Hallmark.

For full biographical listings, see the Martindale-Hubbell Law Directory

FOWLER, WHITE, BURNETT, HURLEY, BANICK & STRICKROOT, A PROFESSIONAL ASSOCIATION (AV)

International Place, Seventeenth Floor, 100 S.E. Second Street, 33131
Telephone: 305-358-6550
Cable Address: "Fowhite"
Telex: 6811696

Cody Fowler (1892-1978)
Morris E. White (1892-1988)
James L. Hurley (1920-1989)
Henry Burnett
Richard S. Banick
John C. Strickroot
Stuart H. Altman
John R. Kelso
A. Rodger Traynor, Jr.
Allan R. Kelley
Jonathan H. Warner
Charles G. DeLeo
William R. Clayton
Ronald D. Shindler
Daniel F. Beasley
Sara Soto
Steven E. Stark
Christopher E. Knight
Kimberly A. Cook
John H. Friedhoff
Valerie Fernandez Settles
Cromwell A. Anderson
Donald E. Kubit
Curtis J. Mase
Fred R. Ober
James P. Murray
Michael B. Buckley
Brian Elias
Michael N. Kreitzer
Morton P. Brown
Norman I. Weil
Elizabeth Pryor Johnson

OF COUNSEL

Daryl L. Jones

Peter J. Delahunty
Richard E. Douglas
Beverly D. Eisenstadt
J. Wesley Holston
Robbie Dale Lake
Darren R. Latham
Alix C. Michel
Richard A. Morgan
Patricia I. Murray
Kyle Lewis Weigel
James D. Gassenheimer
Heather B. Brock
J. Michael Pennekamp
Alix J. M. Apollon
Dorothy F. Easley

Representative Clients: Bahamasair; Cunard Line Ltd.; International Business Machines Corp. (IBM); North American Philips Corp.; Prudential Securities, Inc.; Royal Caribbean Cruise Line.
Reference: City National Bank of Florida.

For full biographical listings, see the Martindale-Hubbell Law Directory

HADDAD, JOSEPHS, JACK, GAEBE & MARKARIAN (AV)

1493 Sunset Drive (Coral Gables), P.O. Box 345118, 33114
Telephone: Dade County: 305-666-6006
Broward County: 305-463-6699
Telecopier: 305-662-9931

MEMBERS OF FIRM

Gil Haddad
Michael R. Josephs
Lewis N. Jack, Jr.
John S. Gaebe
David K. Markarian

ASSOCIATES

Amarillys E. Garcia-Perez
Elisabeth M. McClosky

For full biographical listings, see the Martindale-Hubbell Law Directory

HARDY, BISSETT & LIPTON, P.A. (AV)

501 Northeast First Avenue, 33132
Telephone: 305-358-6200
Broward: 305-462-6377
Fax: 305-577-8230
Boca Raton, Florida Office: 2201 Corporate Boulevard, N.W., Suite 205.
Telephone: 407-998-9202.
Telecopier: 407-998-9693.

G. Jack Hardy
G. William Bissett
Stephen N. Lipton (Resident, Boca Raton Office)

Howard K. Cherna
Lee Philip Teichner
Matthew Kennedy
H. Dane Mottlau

Representative Clients: International Paper Co.; Masonite Corp.; Bridgestone/Firestone Inc.; American International Underwriters; American International Group, Inc.; Pennsylvania National Insurance Cos.; Crown Equipment Corp.; The Coleman Co., Inc.; Interamerican Car Rental, Inc.; York International Corp.

For full biographical listings, see the Martindale-Hubbell Law Directory

HICKS, ANDERSON & BLUM, P.A. (AV)

Twenty Fourth Floor, 100 North Biscayne Boulevard, 33132
Telephone: 305-374-8171
Fax: 305-372-8038

Mark Hicks
Ralph O. Anderson
Bambi G. Blum

Jean Anne Kneale
Gary A. Magnarini
Alyssa M. Campbell
Elizabeth M. Moya-Fernandez
Gina E. Caruso
Cindy L. Ebenfeld
Matthew S. Nelles

For full biographical listings, see the Martindale-Hubbell Law Directory

HIGH, STACK, LAZENBY, PALAHACH & DEL AMO (AV)

A Partnership including Professional Associations
3929 Ponce de Leon Boulevard (Coral Gables), 33134
Telephone: 305-443-3329
Fax: 305-443-0850
Melbourne, Florida Office: High, Stack, Lazenby, Palahach, Maxwell & Morgan, 525 Strawbridge Avenue.
Telephone: 407-725-5525.
FAX: 407-984-2411.
Fort Pierce, Florida Office: High, Stack, Lazenby, Palahach, Maxwell & Morgan, 115 South 2nd Street.
Telephone: 407-461-6161.

MEMBERS OF FIRM

Robert King High (1924-1967)
Charles R. Stack (P.A.)
Robert A. Lazenby (P.A.)
Michael Palahach, III, (P.A.)
Carlos C. del Amo
George W. Maxwell, III (Resident at Melbourne Office)
Clay D. Morgan (Resident at Melbourne Office)

ASSOCIATES

Jack L. Platt
George A. Sarduy

OF COUNSEL

Alvin S. Cawn
Fernando M. Palacios
Reed C. Cary

For full biographical listings, see the Martindale-Hubbell Law Directory

HOLLAND & KNIGHT (AV)

A Partnership including Professional Corporations
701 Brickell Avenue, 30th Floor, 33131
Telephone: 305-374-8500
Fax: 305-789-7799
Mailing Address: P.O. Box 015441, 33101
Fort Lauderdale, Florida Office: One East Broward Boulevard, Suite 1300.
Telephone: 305-525-1000.
Fax: 305-463-2030.
Jacksonville, Florida Office: 50 N. Laura Street, Suite 3900.
Telephone: 904-353-2000.
Fax: 904-358-1872.
Lakeland, Florida Office: 92 Lake Wire Drive.
Telephone: 813-682-1161.
Fax: 813-688-1186.
Orlando, Florida Office: 200 S. Orange Avenue, Suite 2600.
Telephone: 407-425-8500.
Fax: 407-244-5288.
St. Petersburg, Florida Office: 360 Central Avenue.
Telephone: 813-896-7171.
Fax: 813-822-8048.
Tallahassee, Florida Office: 315 Calhoun Street, Suite 600.
Telephone: 904-224-7000.
Fax: 904-224-8832.
Tampa, Florida Office: 400 North Ashley, Suite 2300.
Telephone: 813-227-8500.
Fax: 813-229-0134.
West Palm Beach, Florida Office: 625 N. Flagler Drive, Suite 700.
Telephone: 407-833-2000.
Fax: 407-650-8399.
Washington, D.C. Office: 2100 Pennsylvania Avenue, N.W.
Telephone: 202-955-3000.
Fax: 202-955-5564.
Atlanta, Georgia Office: 1201 West Peachtree Street, N.W., Suite 3100.
Telephone: 404-817-8500.
Fax: 404-881-0470.
Special Counsel: Shaw, Licitra, Parente, Esernio & Schwartz, P.C., 1010 Franklin Avenue, Garden City, N.Y., 11530, 300 East 42nd Street, New York, N.Y., 10017.

MIAMI MEMBERS AND ASSOCIATES

Kathryn Klein Anderson
Susan H. Aprill
Alcides I. Avila
Gregory A. Baldwin
Christopher Noel Bellows
Rachel Blechman
William R. Bloom
Sanford L. Bohrer

(See Next Column)

HOLLAND & KNIGHT, *Miami—Continued*

MIAMI MEMBERS AND ASSOCIATES (Continued)

John Campbell
Mirta (Mikki) Canton
Matthew P. Coglianese
Bruce Jay Colan
J. Thomas Cookson
J. Raul Cosio
Donald K. Duffy
Juan C. Enjamio
R. Thomas Farrar
Dante B. Fascell
Martin Fine
Robert J. Friedman
Daniel Gelber
W. Reeder Glass
James S. Groh
Steven H. Hagen
William F. Hamilton
Jorge L. Hernandez-Toraño
Stuart K. Hoffman
Marilyn J. Holifield
Bernard Jacobson
Judith M. Korchin
Barbara Ehrich Locke
Amelia Rea Maguire
George Mencio, Jr.
Michael T. Moore
Tracy Nichols
James M. Porter
Craig V. Rasile
Constance M. Ridder
Wilfredo A. Rodriguez
José E. Sirvén
Chesterfield Smith
Robert H. Smith
Marty Steinberg
Leon O. Stock
Bruce Stone
Lynn C. Washington
Andrew H. Weinstein
Linda Ann Wells
James D. Wing

Ronald Albert, Jr.
Louise McAlpin Brais
Jose A. Casal
L. Frank Cordero
George Crimarco
Samuel A. Danon
Julio C. Esquivel
Kelly-Ann Gibbs
Alex M. Gonzalez
Robert C. Griffin
Michelle A. Hanna
D. Bruce Hoffman
Lucinda A. Hofmann
Daniel Jacobson
Adolfo E. Jimenez
Thomas H. Loffredo
Walfrido J. Martinez
Roland Sanchez-Medina, Jr.
Duccio Mortillaro
Claude R. Moulton
Helen Bergman Moure
Peter E. Salomon
Lenore C. Smith
Stephen S. Stallings
Maggie Barreto Tercilla
Laurie A. Thompson
Jeffrey A. Weissman
D. Farrington Yates

COUNSEL

Daniel S. Pearson
Roderick N. Petrey

For full biographical listings, see the Martindale-Hubbell Law Directory

---

HOWARD, BRAWNER & STONE (AV)

Suite 210 Grove Professional Building, 2950 S.W. 27th Avenue, 33133
Telephone: 305-448-2131
Telefax: 305-448-3184

MEMBERS OF FIRM

Philip L. Brawner
Richard J. Stone

ASSOCIATES

Kevin I. Schwartz

Reference: Coconut Grove Bank.

For full biographical listings, see the Martindale-Hubbell Law Directory

---

HUGHES HUBBARD & REED (AV)

Suite 1100, 801 Brickell Avenue, 33131
Telephone: 305-358-1666
Telecopier: 305-371-8759
Telex: 51-8785
New York, New York Office: One Battery Park Plaza, 10004. Telephone 212-837-6000.
Cable Address: "Hughreed, New York."
Telex: 427120.
Telecopier: 212-422-4726.
Los Angeles, California Office: 350 S. Grand Street, Suite 3600, 90071-3442.
Telephone: 213-613-2800.
Telecopier: 213-613-2950.
Washington, D.C. Office: 1300 I Street, N.W., Suite 900 West, 20005.
Telephone: 202-408-3600.
Telex: 89-2674.
Telecopier: 202-408-3636.
Paris, France Office: 47, Avenue Georges Mandel, 75116.
Telephone: 33144058000.
Cable Address: "Hughreed, Paris."
Telex: 611986.
Telecopier: 33-1-45-53-1504.
Berlin, Germany Office: Kurfürstendamm 44, W-1000 Berlin 15.
Telephone: 030-880008-0.
Telefax: 030-880008-65.
Telex: 185803 KNAPA D.

RESIDENT PARTNERS

Robert Goldfarb
John E. Pearson
Herschel E. Sparks, Jr.
William A. Weber

OF COUNSEL

John H. Young (Not admitted in FL)
Antonio R. Zamora

(See Next Column)

SPECIAL COUNSEL

Jeffrey H. Lapidus

For full biographical listings, see the Martindale-Hubbell Law Directory

---

KEITH, MACK, LEWIS, COHEN & LUMPKIN (AV)

First Union Financial Center, Twentieth Floor, 200 South Biscayne Boulevard, 33131-2310
Telephone: 305-358-7605
Fax: 305-358-4755

MEMBERS OF FIRM

Edgar Lewis
Robert A. Cohen
R. Hugh Lumpkin
Gregg S. Ahrens
Loren S. Granoff
Keith T. Grumer
Carlos D. Lerman
Jack S. Lewis
Alan Rosenthal
Norman S. Segall
Jeffrey P. Shapiro
Barry S. Yarchin

ASSOCIATES

Melanie Anne Dernis
Michele S. Primeau
Cynthia Perez
Dawn Marshall
Michael J. Hogsten
Henry J. Eichler
Charles D. Nostra
Sarah Clasby

OF COUNSEL

Seymour D. Keith
James L. Mack
Robert L. Roth
Bernard Dane Stein

Representative Clients: CitiBank, F.S.B.; Attorneys Title Insurance Fund, Inc.; Barnett Bank, N.A.
Approved Counsel: First American Title Insurance Co.; Attorneys Title Insurance Fund, Inc.; Commonwealth Title Insurance Co.
Reference: CitiBank, F.S.B.

For full biographical listings, see the Martindale-Hubbell Law Directory

---

KELLY, BLACK, BLACK, BYRNE & BEASLEY, PROFESSIONAL ASSOCIATION (AV)

1400 Alfred I. du Pont Building, 169 East Flagler Street, 33131
Telephone: 305-358-5700

Hugo L. Black, Jr.
Robert Carleton Byrne
Joseph W. Beasley
Bonnie J. Losak-Jimenez
Eric L. Lundt

Representative Clients: Credit Suisse; Multi-Media Entertainment, Inc.; Japan Development Company; Israel Discount Bank; Bank of North America; EquityLine Securities, Inc.; Bacardi Imports, Inc.; Safecard Services, Inc.
Reference: United National Bank.

For full biographical listings, see the Martindale-Hubbell Law Directory

---

KENNY NACHWALTER SEYMOUR ARNOLD CRITCHLOW & SPECTOR, PROFESSIONAL ASSOCIATION (AV)

1100 Miami Center, 201 South Biscayne Boulevard, 33131-4327
Telephone: 305-373-1000
Facsimile: 305-372-1861
ABA/net: 18338
Rogersville, Tennessee Office: 107 East Main Street, Suite 301, 37857-3347.
Telephone: 615-272-5300.
Facsimile: 615-272-4961.

James J. Kenny
Michael Nachwalter
Thomas H. Seymour
Richard Alan Arnold
Richard H. Critchlow
Brian F. Spector
Kevin J. Murray
William J. Blechman
Harry R. Schafer
Deborah A. Sampieri
David H. Lichter
Scott E. Perwin
Jeffrey T. Foreman
Lauren C. Ravkind
Katherine Clark Silverglate
Amanda M. McGovern
Paul C. Huck, Jr.
Tara M. Higgins

Representative Clients: Albertson's, Inc.; American Bankers; Cartier, Inc.; Ethan Allen; Federated Department Stores, Inc.; The Florida Bar; General Telephone Company of Florida; GTE Directories Corp.; Health Trust, Inc.; Hospital Corporation of America.

For full biographical listings, see the Martindale-Hubbell Law Directory

---

KIMBRELL & HAMANN, PROFESSIONAL ASSOCIATION (AV)

Suite 900 Brickell Centre, 799 Brickell Plaza, 33131
Telephone: 305-358-8181
FAX: 305-374-1563
Telex: 51-9516

John G. McKay (1886-1951)
H. Reid DeJarnette (1897-1964)
John G. McKay, Jr. (1916-1980)
A. Lee Bradford (1906-1992)
James F. Crowder, Jr.
Thomas C. Woods
Bradford A. Thomas
John E. Phelan
James F. Asher
Gerard M. Kouri, Jr.

OF COUNSEL

Arthur H. Toothman
Charles A. Kimbrell
Warren D. Hamann
Carl K. Hoffmann

(See Next Column)

KIMBRELL & HAMANN PROFESSIONAL ASSOCIATION—*Continued*

Edward Etcheverry
Guy W. Harrison
Russell A. Yagel
L. Robert Elias, III
Kelley H. Armitage
Anne M. Sylvester

Representative Clients: General Motors Corp.; Ford Motor Co.; Westinghouse Electric Corp.; Coca Cola; Eastern Airlines; The Ryder System.
Insurance Clients: Lloyds Underwriters, Inc.; Kemper Insurance Croup; Fidelity & Deposit Company of Maryland; Massachusetts Mutual Life Insurance Co.

For full biographical listings, see the Martindale-Hubbell Law Directory

KUBICKI DRAPER (AV)

Penthouse City National Bank Building, 25 West Flagler Street, 33130
Telephone: 305-374-1212
Fax: 305-374-7846
West Palm Beach, Florida Office: Suite 1100 United National Bank Tower, 1675 Palm Beach Lakes Boulevard, 33401.
Telephone: 407-640-0303.
Fax: 407-640-0524.
Fort Lauderdale, Florida Office: Suite 1600, One East Broward Boulevard, 33301.
Telephone: 305-768-0011.
Fax: 305-768-0514.

Gene Kubicki
Daniel Draper, Jr.
Robert F. Bouchard
Robert Baldwin Brown, III
Angela C. Flowers
Virginia Easley Johnson
Joseph J. Kalbac, Jr.
Elwood T. Lippincott, Jr.
Peter H. Murphy
Robert N. Sechen

James T. Armstrong
Michael Paul Bennett
J. Bowen Brown
Roland A. Diaz
Suzanne A. Dockerty
Donald J. Fann (Resident)
Betsy Ellwanger Gallagher
Brad J. McCormick
Manuel A. Mesa
Dennis J. Murphy
Charles Mustell
David B. Pakula
Anthony L. Pietrofesa
Antonio J. Rodriguez
Elizabeth M. Rodriguez
Michael J. Rotundo
Jeffrey A. Rubinton
Carol A. Scott
Martin Van Haasteren
Charles Handel Watkins
Harold West

OF COUNSEL

Aubrey L. Talburt

For full biographical listings, see the Martindale-Hubbell Law Directory

KUTNER, RUBINOFF & BUSH (AV)

501 N.E. 1st Avenue, 33132
Telephone: 305-358-6200; Broward: 305-462-6377

Arno Kutner
Edward G. Rubinoff
Kenneth J. Bush

ASSOCIATES

Susan Scrivani Lerner

For full biographical listings, see the Martindale-Hubbell Law Directory

LEE, SCHULTE, EATON & BARRON (AV)

5th Floor, Concord Building, 66 West Flagler Street, 33130
Telephone: 305-358-9346
Fax: 305-372-3987
Jupiter, Florida Office: Suite 504, 1001 North U.S. Highway One.
Telephone: 407-746-8600.
Fax: 407-575-5934.

Thomas E. Lee, Jr.
Thomas J. Schulte
William E. Eaton, Jr.
Carol Dunn Barron

Representative Clients: Peerless Insurance Co.; Firemen's Fund Insurance Co.; Liberty Mutual Insurance Co.; CIGNA; United Liquors Corp.; Professional Risk Management Services, Inc.; Florida Out-Patient Self Insurance Trust; Florida Physicians Insurance Trust; Investors Insurance Group.

For full biographical listings, see the Martindale-Hubbell Law Directory

LEESFIELD, LEIGHTON, RUBIO & HILLENCAMP, P.A. (AV)

2350 South Dixie Highway, 33133
Telephone: 305-854-4900/1-800-836-6400 (toll free)
Fax: 305-854-8266
Key West, Florida Office: 615 1/2 Whitehead Street.
Telephone: 305-296-1342.
Fax: 305-294-1793.

(See Next Column)

Ira H. Leesfield
John Elliott Leighton
Maria L. Rubio
Ibis J. Hillencamp
Robert S. Glazier
Alex Alvarez
Sally Gross-Farina

For full biographical listings, see the Martindale-Hubbell Law Directory

LIVINGSTON & KALETA (AV)

Third Floor, 150 S.E. Second Avenue, 33131
Telephone: 305-373-5766
FAX: 305-374-4194

MEMBERS OF FIRM

Robert E. Livingston
Charles J. Kaleta, Jr.

Representative Clients: Banque Paribas; City of Coral Gables; The Kern Company; L.D. Pankey Dental Foundation; Metropolitan Life Insurance Company; Nichols Partnership, Inc.

For full biographical listings, see the Martindale-Hubbell Law Directory

JOHN CYRIL MALLOY (AV)

Suite 1480 701 Buckell Avenue, 33131
Telephone: 305-374-1003

For full biographical listings, see the Martindale-Hubbell Law Directory

McDERMOTT, WILL & EMERY (AV)

A Partnership including Professional Corporations
201 South Biscayne Boulevard, 33131-4336
Telephone: 305-358-3500
Telex: 441777 LEYES
Facsimile: 305-347-6500
Chicago, Illinois Office: 227 West Monroe Street.
Telephone: 312-372-2000.
Telex: 253565 MILAM CGO.
Facsimile: 312-984-7700.
Boston, Massachusetts Office: 75 State Street, Suite 1700.
Telephone: 617-345-5000.
Telex: 951324 MILAM BSN.
Facsimile: 617-345-5077.
Washington, D.C. Office: 1850 K Street, N.W.
Telephone: 202-887-8000.
Telex: 904261 MILAM CGO.
Facsimile: 202-778-8087.
Los Angeles, California Office: 2049 Century Park East.
Telephone: 310-277-4110.
Facsimile: 310-277-4730.
Newport Beach, California Office: 1301 Dove Street, Suite 500.
Telephone: 714-851-0633.
Facsimile: 714-851-9348.
New York, N.Y. Office: 1211 Avenue of the Americas.
Telephone: 212-768-5400.
Facsimile: 212-768-5444.
St. Petersburg, Russia Office: 2/2 Tchaikovsky Street, #517, 191187 St. Petersburg, Russia.
Telephone: (7) (812) 273-9831.
Facsimile: (7) (812) 273-9831.
Tallinn, Estonia Office: Tallinn Business Center, 6 Harju Street, EE0001 Tallinn, Estonia.
Telephone: 372 6 31-05-53.
Facsimile: 372 6 31-05-54.
Vilnius, Lithuania Office: Smetonos 6, 2600 Vilnius, Lithuania.
Telephone: 370 2 61-43-08.
Facsimile: 370 2 22-79-55.
Associated (Independent) Offices:
Brussels, Belgium: Uettwiller Grelon Lippens Dekeyser, 73 avenue Vandendriessche, 1150 Brussels, Belgium.
Telephone: (32) (2) 772-87-50.
Facsimile: (32) (2) 772-87-52.
London, England: Paisner & Co, Bouverie House, 154 Fleet Street, London EC4A 2DQ, England.
Telephone: (44) (71) 353-0299.
Facsimile: (44) (71) 583-8621.
Paris, France: Uettwiller Grelon Gout Canat & Associes, 68, boulevard de Courcelles, 75017 Paris, France.
Telephone: (33) (1) 48 88 89 00.
Facsimile: (33) (1) 48 88 05 50.

MEMBERS OF FIRM

Mark Bonacquisti
Ira J. Coleman
Jeffrey D. Feldman
Gregg H. Fierman
Lawrence P. Lataif
(Not admitted in FL)
David M. Levine
Byron B. Mathews, Jr.
James E. McDonald
Paul W. Radensky
Thomas G. Schultz
Steven E. Siff
Norman J. Silber
James D. Silver

OF COUNSEL

David P. Wood, Jr.

COUNSEL

James A. Gale
Forrest G. McSurdy
Valerie A. Stott

(See Next Column)

McDermott, Will & Emery, *Miami—Continued*

Lisa R. Daugherty
Lisa R. Hecht-Cronstedt
Jennifer A. Huffman
Lisa Moran
Philip N. Nicholas, III
Sergio Eduardo Pagliery
Michael J. Weber

For full biographical listings, see the Martindale-Hubbell Law Directory

Mershon, Sawyer, Johnston, Dunwody & Cole (AV)

A Partnership including Professional Associations
Suite 4500 First Union Financial Center, 200 South Biscayne Boulevard, 33131-2387
Telephone: 305-358-5100
Cable Address: "Mercole"
Telex: 515705
Fax: 305-376-8654
Naples, Florida Office: Pelican Bay Corporate Centre, Suite 501, 5551 Ridgewood Drive.
Telephone: 813-598-1055.
Fax: 813-598-1868.
West Palm Beach, Florida Office: 777 South Flagler Drive, Suite 900.
Telephone: 407-659-5990.
Fax: 407-659-6313.
Key West, Florida Office: 3132 North Side Drive, Suite 102.
Telephone: 305-296-1774.
Fax: 305-296-1715
London, England Office: Blake Lodge, Bridge Lane, London SW11 3AD, England.
Telephone: 44-71-978-7748.
Fax: 44-71-350-0156.

MEMBERS OF FIRM

W. I. Evans (1893-1938)
O. B. Simmons, Jr. (1900-1962)
M. L. Mershon (1891-1968)
Herbert S. Sawyer (1889-1978)
Aubrey V. Kendall (P.A.)
Osmond C. Howe, Jr., (P.A.)
William J. Dunaj (P.A.)
Henry H. Raattama, Jr., (P.A.)
Brian P. Tague
Richard C. Grant (P.A.) (Resident, Naples Office)
Robert D. W. Landon, II, (P.A.)
James M. McCann, Jr. (Resident, West Palm Beach Office)
Barry G. Craig (P.A.)
Robert T. Wright, Jr.
Russell T. Kamradt (Resident, West Palm Beach Office)
Dennis M. Campbell (P.A.)
Douglas F. Darbut
Timothy J. Norris (P.A.)
Harvey W. Gurland, Jr.
Jeffrey D. Fridkin (Resident, Naples Office)
Jose E. Castro (P.A.)
Carlos M. Sires
David F. Parish
Richard M. Bezold
David B. McCrea (P.A.)
Philip M. Sprinkle, II (Resident, West Palm Beach Office)
Thomas E. Streit (Resident, West Palm Beach Office)
John C. Shawde
Jorge R. Gutierrez (P.A.)
Ronald L. Fick (P.A.) (Resident, West Palm Beach Office)
Marjie C. Nealon (P.A.)
Michael T. Lynott (P.A.)
William M. Pearson (P.A.)
Jack A. Falk, Jr
John F. Halula
John J. Grundhauser
Neil R. Chrystal
Mary Ellen Valletta

OF COUNSEL

Atwood Dunwody
Robert B. Cole
Robert A. White (P.A.)
Alexander Penelas
Jeri A. Poller
Ron Saunders
John S. Schwartz
Jose R. Cuervo
William T. Muir
Charles L. Brackbill, Jr. (Not admitted in FL)
Griffith F. Pitcher
A. Patrick Giles (Resident, London, England Office)
James P. Reeder (1896-1985)
W. E. Dunwody, Jr. (1910-1988)
Claude Pepper (1900-1989)
Thos. McE. Johnston (1897-1989)
John D. Armstrong (1918-1992)

ASSOCIATES

Lawrence P. Rochefort
Mitchell E. Silverstein
G. Helen Athan (Resident, Naples Office)
Jonna Stukel Brown
Doreen S. Moloney
Rona F. Morrow
Nancy A. Romfh (Resident, West Palm Beach Office)
John D. Eaton
Mario David Carballo
Elizabeth Cassidy Barber
Natalie Scharf
Gregg Metzger
Martha de Zayas
Phillip T. Ridolfo, Jr. (Resident, West Palm Beach Office)
Floyd Brantley Chapman (Resident, West Palm Beach Office)
Kurt E. Lee (Resident, Naples Office)
Michael A. Feldman (Resident, Naples Office)
Robin C. Thomes (Resident, Naples Office)
Brenda Ozaki (Resident, West Palm Beach Office)
G. Michael Deacon

Representative Clients: Arvida/JMB Partners; Bankers Trust Co.; Biscayne Kennel Club, Inc.; The Chase Manhattan Bank, N.A.; Lennar Corp.; Reynolds Metals Co.; United States Sugar Corp.; University of Miami.

For full biographical listings, see the Martindale-Hubbell Law Directory

Murai, Wald, Biondo & Moreno, P.A. (AV)

9th Floor Ingraham Building, 25 Southeast 2nd Avenue, 33131
Telephone: 305-358-5900
Fax: 305-358-9490

Rene V. Murai
Gerald B. Wald
Gerald J. Biondo
M. Cristina Moreno
William E. Davis

Cristina Echarte Brochin
Ana Maria Escagedo
Manuel Kadre
Lynette Ebeoglu McGuinness
Mary Leslie Smith

Reference: Republic National Bank of Miami.

For full biographical listings, see the Martindale-Hubbell Law Directory

Patterson, Claussen, Santos & Hume (AV)

A Partnership of Professional Associations
18th Floor, Courthouse Tower, 44 West Flagler Street, 33130-1808
Telephone: 305-350-9000
Fax: 305-372-3940

John H. Patterson (P.A.)
Kenneth F. Claussen (P.A.)
Jose A. Santos, Jr. (P.A.)
John H. Patterson, Jr. (P.A.)
Charles Lea Hume (P.A.)

ASSOCIATES

Lawrence D.W. Graves (Not admitted in FL)

OF COUNSEL

James H. Sweeny, III (P.A.)
Maria Isabel Hoelle

For full biographical listings, see the Martindale-Hubbell Law Directory

Peters, Robertson, Lax, Parsons & Welcher (AV)

Suite 600, Ingraham Building, 25 Southeast 2nd Avenue, 33131-1691
Telephone: 305-374-3103 Broward: 305-522-5997
Fax: 305-377-9805
Fort Lauderdale, Fort Myers & West Palm Beach
Fort Lauderdale, Florida Office: Suite 600, 600 South Andrews Avenue.
Telephone: 305-761-8999.
Fax: 305-761-8990.
Fort Myers, Florida Office: Key West Professional Centre, 1342 Colonial Boulevard, Suite 7.
Telephone: 813-936-1129.
Fax: 813-936-4036.
West Palm Beach, Florida Office: 515 North Flagler Drive, Suite 300, Pavilion Northbridge Centre.
Telephone: Palm Beach: 407-832-9698; Broward: 305-771-7493.
Facsimile: 407-832-5654.

MEMBERS OF FIRM

Michael H. Lax
Neil P. Robertson
John R. W. Parsons
Roger G. Welcher
Jeffrey A. Mowers
Geralyn M. Passaro (Resident at Fort Lauderdale Office)
Joan I. Valdes

OF COUNSEL

Jackson L. Peters

ASSOCIATES

Lawrence E. Margolis
Steven B. Sundook (Resident at Fort Myers Office)
Jeanette G. Edwards
Timothy J. Moffatt
Esther B. Nickas
Maria A. Nieto
Steven Charles Simon (Resident at West Palm Beach Office)
Paul A. Poland
Gracian Celaya

Representative Clients: Auto-Owners Insurance Co.; Dade County School Board; Employers Reinsurance Group; Gallagher Bassett Insurance Service; Maryland Casualty Co.

For full biographical listings, see the Martindale-Hubbell Law Directory

Podhurst, Orseck, Josefsberg, Eaton, Meadow, Olin & Perwin, P.A. (AV)

Suite 800 City National Bank Building, 25 West Flagler Street, 33130-1780
Telephone: 305-358-2800; Fort Lauderdale: 305-463-4346
Fax: 305-358-2382

Aaron Podhurst
Robert Orseck (1934-1978)
Robert C. Josefsberg
Joel D. Eaton
Barry L. Meadow
Michael S. Olin
Joel S. Perwin
Steven C. Marks
Victor M. Diaz, Jr.
Katherine W. Ezell

Karen B. Podhurst

OF COUNSEL

Walter H. Beckham, Jr.

Reference: City National Bank of Miami; United National Bank of Miami.

For full biographical listings, see the Martindale-Hubbell Law Directory

Miami—Continued

PROENZA, WHITE & ROBERTS, P.A. (AV)

Grove Plaza, 2900 Middle Street, 33133
Telephone: 305-442-1700
Telecopier: 305-442-2559

Morris C. Proenza
David J. White
H. Clay Roberts
H. Mark Vieth
Robert C. Tilghman

Ana C. Souto

For full biographical listings, see the Martindale-Hubbell Law Directory

PYSZKA, KESSLER, MASSEY, WELDON, CATRI, HOLTON & DOUBERLEY, P.A. (AV)

Fifth Floor, Grand Bay Plaza, 2665 South Bayshore Drive, 33133
Telephone: 305-858-6614
Fort Lauderdale, Florida Office: 110 Tower, Twentieth Floor, 110 Southeast Sixth Street.
Telephone: 305-463-8593.

Gerard E. Pyszka
Charles T. Kessler (Resident at Fort Lauderdale)
Albert P. Massey, III (Resident at Fort Lauderdale)
Malcolm W. "Mac" Weldon
Wesley L. Catri (Resident at Fort Lauderdale)
Raymond O. Holton, Jr. (Resident at Fort Lauderdale)
William M. Douberley
Phillip D. Blackmon, Jr.
Benjamin D. Levy
Paula C. Kessler (Resident at Fort Lauderdale)
Gregory G. Coican (Resident at Fort Lauderdale)
Andrea L. Kessler (Resident at Fort Lauderdale)
L.H. Steven Savola
Kenneth A. Cutler (Resident at Fort Lauderdale)
Edward D. Schuster (Resident at Fort Lauderdale)
Jordan J. Lewis

J. Michael Magee (Resident at Fort Lauderdale)
Jason T. Selwood (Resident at Fort Lauderdale)
Gerard A. Tuzzio (Resident at Fort Lauderdale)
Lisa Marie Connor
Brenda F. Pagliaro (Resident, Fort Lauderdale)
Michael Morris
Cindy J. Mishcon
James P.E. Roen
Robert F. Lasky
Ivan F. Cabrera (Resident at Fort Lauderdale)

OF COUNSEL

Donald E. Stone

For full biographical listings, see the Martindale-Hubbell Law Directory

SAMS, MARTIN & LISTER, P.A. (AV)

The Atrium, Suite 200, 1500 San Remo Avenue (Coral Gables), 33146
Telephone: 305-666-3181
Fax: 305-666-5867
Fort Lauderdale, Florida Office: Sams, Spier, Hoffman and Hastings, P.A., 500 Southeast Sixth Street, Suite 101, 33301.
Telephone: 305-467-3181.
Fax: 305-523-5462.
Jacksonville, Florida Office: Sams, Spier, Hoffman and Hastings, P.A., 1301 Gulf Life Drive, Suite 2010, 32207.
Telephone: 904-399-5546.
Fax: 904-354-0182.

Murray Sams, Jr.
Timothy M. Martin
David P. Lister

Julianne K. Lara

For full biographical listings, see the Martindale-Hubbell Law Directory

SCHANTZ, SCHATZMAN, AARONSON & CAHAN, P.A. (AV)

Suite 3650 First Union Financial Center, 200 South Biscayne Boulevard, 33131
Telephone: 305-371-3100
Fax: 305-371-2024

Lawrence M. Schantz
Robert A. Schatzman
Geoffrey S. Aaronson
Richard J. Alan Cahan
Carmen A. Accordino
Alan Dagen

Allison R. Day
Alan J. Perlman
Ivan J. Reich
Joshua N. Bennett

For full biographical listings, see the Martindale-Hubbell Law Directory

SHAPO, FREEDMAN & FLETCHER, P.A. (AV)

First Union Financial Center, 47th Floor, 200 South Biscayne Boulevard, 33131
Telephone: 305-358-4440
Telefax: 305-358-0521

(See Next Column)

Ronald A. Shapo
David A. Freedman
Patricia Kimball Fletcher

Howard Allen Cohen
Luis E. Rojas
Richard Daniel Friess
Geoffrey T. Kirk

For full biographical listings, see the Martindale-Hubbell Law Directory

SHEEHE & VENDITTELLI, P.A. (AV)

Miami Center, Suite 1800, 201 South Biscayne Boulevard, 33131
Telephone: 305-379-3515
Telecopier: 305-379-5404

Phillip J. Sheehe
Louis V. Vendittelli
Henry E. Mendia

Reference: First Union Bank of Florida; Northern Trust Bank of Florida, N.A.

For full biographical listings, see the Martindale-Hubbell Law Directory

SHUTTS & BOWEN (AV)

A Partnership including Professional Associations
1500 Miami Center, 201 South Biscayne Boulevard, 33131
Telephone: 305-358-6300
Cable Address: "Shuttsbo"
Telefax: 305-381-9982
Key Largo, Florida Office: Suite A206, 31 Ocean Reef Drive.
Telephone: 305-367-2881.
Orlando, Florida Office: 20 North Orange Avenue, Suite 1000.
Telephone: 407-423-3200.
Fax: 407-425-8316.
West Palm Beach, Florida Office: One Clearlake Centre, 250 Australian Avenue South, Suite 500.
Telephone: 407-835-8500.
Fax: 407-650-8530.
Amsterdam, The Netherlands Office: Shutts & Bowen, B.V., Europa Boulevard 59, 1083 AD, Amsterdam.
Telephone: (31 20) 661-0969.
Fax: (31 20) 642-1475.
London, England Office: 48 Mount Street, London W1Y 5RE.
Telephone: 4471493-4840.
Telefax: 4471493-4299.

MEMBERS OF FIRM

Frank B. Shutts (1870-1947)
Crate D. Bowen (1871-1959)
Gary M. Bagliebter
Arnold L. Berman (Resident at West Palm Beach Office)
Joseph D. Bolton
Bowman Brown (P.A.)
Andrew M. Brumby (Resident at Orlando Office)
Judith A. Burke
Sheila M. Cesarano
Jonathan Cohen
Kevin D. Cowan
Luis A. de Armas
Jean-Charles Dibbs
James F. Durham, II
Charles Robinson Fawsett (P.A.)
Esteban A. Ferrer
Robert G. Fracasso, Jr.
Robert A. Freyer (Resident at Orlando Office)
Roger Friedbauer
Andrew L. Gordon
Michael L. Gore (Resident at Orlando Office)
Robert E. Gunn (P.A.) (Resident at West Palm Beach Office)
John K. Harris, Jr.
Edmund T. Henry, III
William N. Jacobs
Marvin A. Kirsner (Resident at West Palm Beach Office)
John Thomas Kolinski
Richard M. Leslie (P.A.)
Maxine Master Long
Don A. Lynn (P.A.)
Lee D. Mackson
Antonio Martinez, Jr., (P.A.)
Joseph F. McSorley (Resident at West Palm Beach Office)
John E. Meagher
Arthur J. Menor (Resident at West Palm Beach Office)
Robert D. Miller (Resident at West Palm Beach Office)
Alan I. Mishael
C. Richard Morgan
Timothy J. Murphy
Phillip G. Newcomm (P.A.)
Louis Nostro
Harold E. Patricoff Jr.
Stephen L. Perrone (P.A.)
Geoffrey Randall
Sally M. Richardson
Margaret A. Rolando
Allan M. Rubin
Raul J. Salas
Robert A. Savill (Resident at Orlando Office)
Rosemarie N. Sanderson Schade (P.A.) (Resident at Amsterdam, The Netherlands)
Alfred G. Smith, II
William F. Smith
Robert C. Sommerville (P.A.) (Resident; West Palm Beach Office)
Kimarie R. Stratos
Xavier L. Suarez
Robert E. Venney
Barbara E. Vicevich (P.A.)
Robert A. Wainger
Joseph Donald Wasil
John B. White (P.A.)
James G. Willard (Resident at Orlando Office)
Scott G. Williams (Resident at West Palm Beach Office)
Kenneth W. Wright (Resident at Orlando Office)

ASSOCIATES

Katrina D. Baker
Mark J. Boulris
Christopher W. Boyett
Thomas P. Callan (Resident at Orlando Office)
Steven L. Chudnow
Gregory L. Denes
Kathleen L. Deutsch
Terry B. Fein
Robert B. Goldman (Resident at West Palm Beach Office)
Joseph M. Goldstein

(See Next Column)

SHUTTS & BOWEN, *Miami—Continued*

ASSOCIATES (Continued)

Mary Ruth Houston (Resident at Orlando Office)
Jeffrey M. Landau
Lourdes B. Martinez-Esquivel
William G. Mc Cullough
Patrick M. Muldowney (Resident at Orlando Office)
Lisa R. Pearson (Resident, Orlando Office)
Andrew P. Tetzeli
Geoffrey L. Travis
Daniel J. Weidmann (Resident in Orlando)
Robert Wexler (Resident at West Palm Beach Office)

OF COUNSEL

Jordan Bittel (P.A.)
John S. Chowning (P.A.)
John R. Day (P.A.)
Stephen J. Gray (Resident, London, England Office)
Rod Jones (Resident at Orlando Office)
Marshall J. Langer (P.A.) (Resident, London, England Office)
Preston L. Prevatt

CONSULTING ATTORNEY

Patrick L. Murray (Not admitted in the United States)

Representative Clients: Southern Bell Telephone Co.; General Electric Co.; Equitable Life Assurance Society of the U.S.; New England Mutual Life Insurance Co.; New York Life Insurance Co.

For full biographical listings, see the Martindale-Hubbell Law Directory

SPARBER, KOSNITZKY, TRUXTON, DE LA GUARDIA SPRATT & BROOKS, P.A. (AV)

1401 Brickell Avenue Suite 700, 33131
Telephone: Dade: 305-379-7200; Broward: 305-760-9133
Fax: 305-379-0800

Byron L. Sparber
Michael Kosnitzky
Gregg S. Truxton
Oscar G. de la Guardia
William J. Spratt, Jr.
Gary S. Brooks
Marc H. Auerbach
Louise T. Jeroslow
Mitchell W. Mandler

Jorge A. Gonzalez
Diana L. Grub
Thomas O. Wells
Ralph Shalom
Alan G. Geffin
Komal J. Bhojwani
Deborah R. Mayo
Martin B. Kofsky

For full biographical listings, see the Martindale-Hubbell Law Directory

SPENCER AND KLEIN, PROFESSIONAL ASSOCIATION (AV)

Suite 1901, 801 Brickell Avenue, 33131
Telephone: 305-374-7700
Telecopier: 305-374-4890

Thomas R. Spencer, Jr.
Brent D. Klein

Samuel B. Reiner, II
Steven W. Simon
Alberto Rodriguez
Jose M. Companioni
Stephen L. Vinson, Jr.
Gregory A. Wald

OF COUNSEL

Linda L. Carroll

Representative Clients: America Publishing Group; Amerivend Corp.; Buen Hogar Magazine; Editorial America; Gold Star Medical Management, Inc.; Grupo Anaya, S.A.; Independent Living Care, Inc.; Lourdes Health Services, Inc.; Managed Care of America, Inc.

For full biographical listings, see the Martindale-Hubbell Law Directory

SQUIRE, SANDERS & DEMPSEY (AV)

201 South Biscayne Boulevard, Suite 2900 Miami Center, 33131-4330
Telephone: 305-577-8700
Fax: 305-358-1425
Cleveland, Ohio Office: 4900 Society Center, 127 Public Square, Cleveland, Ohio 44114-1304.
Telephone: 216-479-8500. Fax's: 216-479-8780, 216-479-8781, 216-479-8787, 216-479-8795, 216-479-8793, 216-479-8776, 216-479-8788.
Columbus, Ohio Offices: 1300 Huntington Center, 41 South High Street, Columbus, Ohio 43215.
Telephone: 614-365-2700.
Fax: 614-365-2499.
Jacksonville, Florida Office: One Enterprise Center, Suite 2100, 225 Water Street, Jacksonville, Florida 32202.
Telephone: 904-353-1264.
Fax: 904-356-2986.
New York, New York Office: 520 Madison Avenue, 32nd Floor, New York, New York 10022.
Telephone: 212-872-9800.
Fax: 212-872-9814.
Phoenix, Arizona Office: Two Renaissance Square, 40 North Central Avenue, Suite 2700, Phoenix, Arizona 85004-4441.
Telephone: 602-528-4000.
Fax: 602-253-8129.

(See Next Column)

Washington, D.C. Office: 1201 Pennsylvania Avenue, N.W., P.O. Box 407, Washington, D.C. 20044.
Telephone: 202-626-6600.
Fax: 202-626-6780.
London, England Office: 1 Gunpowder Square, Printer Street, London EC4A 3DE.
Telephone: 011-44-71-830-0055.
Fax: 011-44-71-830-0056.
Brussels, Belgium Office: Avenue Louise, 165-Box 15, 1050 Brussels, Belgium.
Telephone: 011-32-2-648-1717.
Fax: 011-32-2-648-1064.
Prague Office: Adria Palace, Jungmannova 31/36, 11000 Prague 1, Czech Republic.
Telephone: 011-42-2-231-5661.
Fax: 011-42-2-231-5482.
Bratislava Office: Mudronova 37, 811-01 Bratislava, Slovak Republic.
Telephone: 011-42-7-313-362; 011-42-7-315-370.
Fax: 011-42-7-313-918.
Budapest, Hungary Office: Deak Ferenc Ut. 10, Office 304, H-1052 Budapest V., Hungary.
Telephones: 011-36-1-226-2024; 011-36-1-226-5038.
Fax: 011-361-226-2025.
Kiev, Ukraine Office: vul. Prorizna 9, Suite 20, Kiev 252035, Ukraine.
Telephones: 011-7-044-244-3452, 011-7-044-244-3453, 011-7-044-228-8687.
Fax: 011-7-044-228-4938.

RESIDENT MEMBERS

Albert A. del Castillo
Kenneth M. Myers
Luis Reiter

For full biographical listings, see the Martindale-Hubbell Law Directory

STROOCK & STROOCK & LAVAN (AV)

200 South Biscayne Boulevard Suite 3300, First Union Financial Center, 33131-2385
Telephone: 305-358-9900
Telecopier: (305) 789-9302
Telex: 803133 Stroock Mia (Domestic and International)
Broward Line: 527-9900
New York, N.Y. Office: Seven Hanover Square, 10004-2696.
Telephone: 212-806-5400.
Telecopiers: (212) 806-5919; (212) 806-6006; (212) 806-6086; (212) 425-9509; (212) 806-6176. Telexes: Stroock UT 177693 and Plastroock NYK 177077 (International).
Cable Address: "Plastroock, NYK."
New York Conference Center: 767 Third Avenue, New York, N.Y., 10017-2023.
Telephones: 212-806-5767; 5768; 5769; 5770.
Telecopier: (212) 421-6234.
Washington, D.C. Office: 1150 Seventeenth Street, N.W., Suite 600, 20036-4652.
Telephone: 202-452-9250.
Telecopier: (202) 293-2293.
Cable Address: "Plastroock, Washington." Telexes: 64238 STROOCK DC; 89401 STROOCK DC.
Los Angeles, California Office: Suite 1800, 2029 Century Park East, 90067-3086.
Telephone: 310-556-5800.
Telecopier: (310) 556-5959.
Cable Address: "Plastroock, L.A."
Telex: 677190 (Domestic and International).
Budapest, Hungary Office: East-West Business Center, Rákóczi ut 1-3, H-1088.
Telephone: 011-361-266-7770.
Telecopier: 011-361-266-9279.

RESIDENT PARTNERS

Scott L. Baena
Michael Basile
Jeffrey Bercow
Robert K. Jordan
Daniel Lampert
David C. Pollack
Arnold D. Shevin
Robert L. Shevin
Paul Steven Singerman
Robert W. Turken

RETIRED PARTNER

Charles R. Taine

COUNSEL

Richard S. Savitt

SPECIAL COUNSEL

Mindy A. Mora
Robert M. Siegel
Carey A. Stiss

Ben J. Fernandez
Manuel A. Fernandez
Brent A. Friedman
Ilyse Wrubel Homer
Judith A. Jarvis
John M. Kuhn
Nee Marie Laurita
Jana K. McDonald
Jorge J. Perez
Susan Johnson Pontigas
Michael E. Radell
Jeff C. Schneider
Richard B. Simring
Jerry Jay Sokol
Steven J. Solomon
Steven M. Stoll

For full biographical listings, see the Martindale-Hubbell Law Directory

Miami—Continued

Stuzin and Camner, Professional Association (AV)

25th Floor, 1221 Brickell Avenue, 33131-3260
Telephone: 305-577-0600

Charles B. Stuzin
Alfred R. Camner
Stanley A. Beiley
Marsha D. Bilzin
David S. Garbett
Nina S. Gordon
Barry D. Hunter
Nikki J. Nedbor
Neale J. Poller

Lisa R. Carstarphen
Maria E. Chang
Barry P. Gruher
Gustavo D. Llerena
Sherry D. McMillan
Roger A. Preziosi

OF COUNSEL

Anne Shari Camner

References: Citizens Federal Bank; City National Bank of Miami; Barnett Bank of South Florida, N.A.

For full biographical listings, see the Martindale-Hubbell Law Directory

Taylor, Brion, Buker & Greene (AV)

Fourteenth Floor, 801 Brickell Avenue, 33131-2900
Telephone: 305-377-6700
Telex: 153653 Taybri
Telecopier: 305-371-4578; 371-4579
Tallahassee, Florida Office: Suite 250, 225 South Adams Street.
Telephone: 904-222-7717.
Telecopier: 904-222-3494.
Key West, Florida Office: 500 Fleming Street.
Telephone: 305-292-1776.
Telecopier: 305-292-1982.
Fort Lauderdale, Florida Office: Barnett Bank Plaza, 12th Floor, One East Broward Boulevard.
Telephone: 305-522-6700.
Telecopier: 305-522-6711.
Coral Gables, Florida Office: 2801 Ponce De Leon Boulevard, Suite 707.
Telephone: 305-445-7577.
Telecopier: 305-446-9944.

H. H. Taylor (1882-1961)
John D. Brion (Retired, 1990)
George F. Allen, Jr.
Leila D. Anderson (Fort Lauderdale)
John S. Andrews (Fort Lauderdale)
Peter C. Bianchi, Jr.
Kenneth M. Bloom
Pierre-Tristan Bourgoignie (Coral Gables)
David S. Bowman (Fort Lauderdale)
Wilbur E. Brewton (Tallahassee)
Murray H. Dubbin
Carlos Eduardo Goncalves (Not admitted in United States)
Harold L. Greene
Michael E. Hill
Joel N. Minsker (P.A.)
W. Douglas Moody, Jr. (Tallahassee)
Gerald W. Moore
James W. Moore
Thomas J. Palmieri
I. Ed Pantaleon (Tallahassee)
Robert J. Paterno
Kelly Brewton Plante (Tallahassee)
Anthony F. Sanchez
Karl J. Schumer
Robert S. Singer
Thomas J. Skola
Henry H. Taylor, Jr.
Arnaldo Velez
R. Bruce Wallace

OF COUNSEL

Frank D. Hall (Coral Gables)
Burton Harrison
A. Stephen Kotler
Robert A. Spottswood

For full biographical listings, see the Martindale-Hubbell Law Directory

Thomson Muraro Razook & Hart, P.A. (AV)

17th Floor, One Southeast Third Avenue, 33131
Telephone: 305-350-7200
Telecopier: 305-374-1005

Parker Davidson Thomson
Robert E. Muraro
Richard J. Razook
Brian A. Hart
Jeffrey Watkin
Carol A. Licko
Steven W. Davis
Sarah L. Schweitzer

PRACTICE ADVISOR

Elliott Manning

Jennifer R. Guilford
Joseph H. Izhakoff
Todd A. Bancroft

Representative Clients: Bacardi; The Brandon Company; Community Television Foundation of South Florida, Inc.; Florida Jai-Alai; The Miami Herald Publishing Company; State of Florida; United States Sugar Corporation; Miami Columbus, Inc.; The Exotic Gardens, Inc.; Bank Audi.

For full biographical listings, see the Martindale-Hubbell Law Directory

Thornton, Davis & Murray, P.A. (AV)

World Trade Center, 80 Southwest 8th Street Suite 2900, 33130
Telephone: 305-446-2646
Fax: 305-441-2374

(See Next Column)

John M. Murray
Barry L. Davis
J. Thompson Thornton
Gregory P. Sreenan

Lori B. Brody
Patricia E. Bruce
John E. Calles
Frederick J. Fein
Holly S. Harvey
David P. Herman
Ana Maria Marin
Kathleen M. O'Connor
Jeffrey B. Shalek
Rebecca B. Watford

For full biographical listings, see the Martindale-Hubbell Law Directory

Tralins and Associates, P.A. (AV)

Suite 3310 2 South Biscayne Boulevard, 33131
Telephone: 305-374-3300
Telefax: 305-374-4933
New York, N.Y. Office: 521 Fifth Avenue, 28th Floor.
Telephone: 212-661-2386.

Myles J. Tralins

Carmen L. Leon

COUNSEL

Jonathan L. Rosner (Not admitted in FL)

For full biographical listings, see the Martindale-Hubbell Law Directory

Walton Lantaff Schroeder & Carson (AV)

A Partnership including Professional Associations
One Biscayne Tower, 25th Floor, 2 South Biscayne Boulevard, 33131
Telephone: 305-379-6411
Telecopier: 305-577-3875
West Palm Beach, Florida Office: United National Bank Tower, Suite 800, 1645 Palm Beach Lakes Boulevard.
Telephone: 407-689-6700.
Telecopier: 407-689-2647.
Fort Lauderdale, Florida Office: Blackstone Building, Third Floor, 707 Southeast Third Avenue.
Telephone: 305-463-8456.
Telecopier: 305-763-6294.
Coral Gables, Florida Office: Suite 1101, Gables International Plaza, 2655 Le Jeune Road.
Telephone: 305-379-6411.
Telecopier: 305-446-9206.

MEMBERS OF FIRM

Miller Walton (1901-1987)
William C. Lantaff (1913-1970)
Charles P. Sacher (P.A.) (Coral Gables Office)
Michael R. Jenks (P.A.)
David K. Tharp
Wayne T. Gill (P.A.) (West Palm Beach Office)
Nicholas E. Christin (P.A.) (Coral Gables Office)
Richard P. Cole (P.A.)
Stephen W. Bazinsky (Ft. Lauderdale Office)
Charles Brown Mirman (P.A.)
Jonathan J. Davis (Ft. Lauderdale Office)
Bernard I. Probst
Lawrence D. Smith, Jr.
John P. Joy
John W. McLuskey
Gregory J. Willis
Beth J. Leahy
Robert J. Strunin
Deborah Poore Knight (Ft. Lauderdale Office)
Marla A. Mudano (West Palm Beach Office)
Richard G. Rosenblum
Roberta J. Karp (West Palm Beach Office)
John G. White, III (West Palm Beach Office)
G. Bartram Billbrough, Jr.
Henry Suarez
David M. McDonald
Michael W. Baker (Ft. Lauderdale Office)
Robert M. Donlon (Coral Gables Office)
Gregory T. Martini (Coral Gables Office)
Robert L. Teitler

OF COUNSEL

Laurence A. Schroeder (Coral Gables Office)
Samuel O. Carson
William J. Gray (P.A.)
Carl E. Jenkins (P.A.) (Ft. Lauderdale Office)
Martin E. Segal (P.A.) (Coral Gables Office)

ASSOCIATES

Anthony A. Balasso (Ft. Lauderdale Office)
Harvey D. Ginsburg (Ft. Lauderdale Office)
Geoffrey B. Marks
Allison B. Chittem
Juliean Lynn Rice
Patrick J. Toomey, Jr.
Paul S. Martin
Amy L. Smith (West Palm Beach Office)
Frank J Taddeo
Gene P. Kissane
Gregory William Coleman (West Palm Beach Office)
Scott Allan Cole
William G. Hersman
Lawrence D. King
Laura Mackle Castillo
Charles S. Sacher (Coral Gables Office)
George W. Bush, Jr. (West Palm Beach Office)
Kurt A. Wyland (West Palm Beach Office)
Susan R. Kent
Lisa M. Torron-Bautista
Nancy C. Valcarce
Kip O. Lassner
Joseph P. Cinney
David S. Tadros (West Palm Beach Office)
Rhett P. Dove, III
Walton Lantaff

(See Next Column)

WALTON LANTAFF SCHROEDER & CARSON, *Miami—Continued*

ASSOCIATES (Continued)

Russell A. Dohan
Kenneth L. Valentini
Steven E. Foor (West Palm Beach Office)

For full biographical listings, see the Martindale-Hubbell Law Directory

WELBAUM, ZOOK & JONES (AV)

Penthouse Suite, 901 Ponce de Leon Boulevard (Coral Gables), 33134-3009
Telephone: 305-441-8900
Fax: 305-441-2255

MEMBERS OF FIRM

D. Lloyd Zook (1922-1990)
R. Earl Welbaum
Peter C. Jones
Dan B. Guernsey
Robert A. Hingston
W. Frank Greenleaf
John H. Gregory

ASSOCIATES

Kenn W. Goff
Michael Yates
Mark D. Greenwell

OF COUNSEL

René Sacasas

For full biographical listings, see the Martindale-Hubbell Law Directory

MIAMI BEACH, Dade Co.

THERREL BAISDEN & MEYER WEISS (AV)

Suite 500 Sun Bank/Miami, 1111 Lincoln Road Mall, 33139
Telephone: 305-672-1921
Telecopier: 305-674-0807

MEMBERS OF FIRM

Catchings Therrel (1890-1971)
Fred R. Baisden (1903-1971)
Baron De Hirsch Meyer (1899-1974)
Milton Weiss (1913-1980)
L. Jules Arkin
Nicholas M. Daniels
Ellen Rose
Leo Rose, Jr.
Fred R. Stanton
Richard A. Wood

ASSOCIATES

Jonathan Feuerman
Joseph B. Ryan, III (Resident, Miami, Florida Office)
Peter M. Lopez

OF COUNSEL

David Darlow
Bruce E. Lazar
Mark E. Pollack

General Counsel: Chase Federal Bank; Miami Postal Service Credit Union; Jefferson National Bank Trust Department; American Equity Site Developers.
Counsel for: City Planned Communities Corp.; Anthony Abraham Chevrolet.

For full biographical listings, see the Martindale-Hubbell Law Directory

*MILTON,** Santa Rosa Co.

JOHNSON, GREEN & LOCKLIN, P.A. (AV)

6850 Highway 90, P.O. Box 605, 32572-0605
Telephone: 904-623-3841
Fax: 904-623-3555

T. Sol Johnson
Paul R. Green
Jack Locklin, Jr.
Johnny L. Miller, Jr.

Michael Gibson
Julie L. Jones

Representative Clients: Pace Water System; School Board of Santa Rosa County; Civil Service Board, City of Milton; First National Bank of Santa Rosa; Nationwide Santa Rosa Milton Housing Authority.

For full biographical listings, see the Martindale-Hubbell Law Directory

*MONTICELLO,** Jefferson Co. — (Refer to Tallahassee)

*NAPLES,** Collier Co.

BOND, SCHOENECK & KING (AV)

1167 Third Street South, 33940-7098
Telephone: 813-262-6812
Fax: 813-262-6908
Syracuse, New York Office: 18th Floor One Lincoln Center.
Telephone: 315-422-0121.
Fax: 315-422-3598.
Albany, New York Office: 111 Washington Avenue.
Telephone: 518-462-7421.
Fax: 518-462-7441.
Boca Raton, Florida Office: 5355 Town Center Road, Suite 1002.
Telephone: 407-368-1212.
Fax: 407-338-9955.
Oswego, New York Office: 130 East Second Street.
Telephone: 315-343-9116.
Fax: 315-343-1231.

(See Next Column)

Overland Park, Kansas Office: 7500 College Boulevard, Suite 910.
Telephone: 913-345-8001.
Fax: 913-345-9017.

MEMBERS OF FIRM

David N. Sexton
David L. Dawson
D. Fred Garner

RESIDENT ASSOCIATES

Jean A. Ryan
Dennis P. Cronin
Dennis C. Brown

For full biographical listings, see the Martindale-Hubbell Law Directory

CATALANO, FISHER, GREGORY, CROWN & SULLIVAN, CHARTERED (AV)

Northern Trust Building, Suite 404, 4001 Tamiami Trail North, 33940
Telephone: 813-262-8000
Telecopier: 813-262-4372

Anthony J. Catalano
A. Alston Fisher, Jr.
C. Neil Gregory
Howard L. Crown
John L. Sullivan, Jr.

OF COUNSEL

Mark V. Silverio
William deForest Thompson

For full biographical listings, see the Martindale-Hubbell Law Directory

JAMES W. ELKINS, P.A. (AV)

Suite 303 The Fairway Building, 1000 Tamiami Trail North, 33940
Telephone: 813-263-0910
Fax: 813-263-6091

James W. Elkins

Approved Attorney for: Attorneys Title Insurance Fund.

For full biographical listings, see the Martindale-Hubbell Law Directory

MERSHON, SAWYER, JOHNSTON, DUNWODY & COLE (AV)

A Partnership including Professional Associations
Pelican Bay Corporate Centre, Suite 501, 5551 Ridgewood Drive, 33963
Telephone: 813-598-1055
Fax: 813-598-1868
Miami, Florida Office: Suite 4500 First Union Financial Center, 200 South Biscayne Boulevard.
Telephone: 305-358-5100.
Cable Address: "Mercole."
Telex: 515705.
Fax: 305-376-8654.
West Palm Beach, Florida Office: 777 South Flagler Drive, Suite 900.
Telephone: 407-659-5990.
Fax: 407-659-6313.
Key West, Florida Office: 3132 North Side Drive, Suite 102.
Telephone: 305-296-1774.
Fax: 305-296-1715.
London, England Office: Blake Lodge, Bridge Lane, London SW11 3AD, England.
Telephone: 44-71-978-7748.
Fax: 44-71-350-0156.

MEMBERS OF FIRM

Richard C. Grant (P.A.) (Resident)
Robert D. W. Landon, II, (P.A.)
Jeffrey D. Fridkin (Resident)
Richard M. Bezold
William M. Pearson (P.A.)

ASSOCIATES

G. Helen Athan (Resident)
Michael A. Feldman
Kurt E. Lee
Robin C. Thomes

For full biographical listings, see the Martindale-Hubbell Law Directory

PORTER, WRIGHT, MORRIS & ARTHUR (AV)

4501 Tamiami Trail North, 33940-3060
Telephone: 813-263-8898; (800-876-7962)
FAX: 813-436-2990
Telex: 6503213584 MCI
Columbus, Ohio Office: 41 South High Street, 43215-6194.
Telephones: 614-227-2000; (800-533-2794).
Telex: 650321584.
Fax: 614-227-2100.
Dayton, Ohio Office: One Dayton Centre, One South Main Street, 45402.
Telephones: 513-228-2411; (800-533-4434).
Fax: 513-449-6820.
Cincinnati, Ohio Office: 250 E. Fifth Street, 45202-4166.
Telephones: 513-381-4700; (800-582-5813).
Fax: 513-421-0991.
Cleveland, Ohio Office: 925 Euclid Avenue, 44115-1483.
Telephones: 216-443-9000; (800-824-1980).
Fax: 391243909011.
Washington, D.C. Office: 1233 20th Street, N.W., 20036-2395.
Telephones: 202-778-3000; (800-456-7962).
Fax: 202-778-3063.

(See Next Column)

PORTER, WRIGHT, MORRIS & ARTHUR—*Continued*

MEMBERS OF FIRM

Robert M. Buckel (Resident) | Gary K. Wilson (Resident)
W. Jeffrey Cecil (Resident) | Mary Beth Moser Clary
Jeffrey S. Kannensohn | Harry L. Henning
James E. Willis (Resident) | Richard M. Markus
Ronald S. Perlman

OF COUNSEL

John D. Gast

RESIDENT ASSOCIATES

Samara S. Holland | Margaret Racaniello
Stuart A. Thompson

Approved Attorneys for: Attorneys Title Insurance Fund; First American Title Insurance Corporation; Lawyers Title Insurance Corporation.

For full biographical listings, see the Martindale-Hubbell Law Directory

VEGA, BROWN, STANLEY, MARTIN & ZELMAN, P.A. (AV)

2660 Airport Road, South, 33962
Telephone: 813-774-3333
Fax: 813-774-6420

George Vega, Jr. | Lawrence D. Martin
John F. Stanley | Theodore W. Zelman

Thomas J. Wood | John G. Vega
Paula J. Rhoads | Sharon M. Hanlon
Michael G. Moore

OF COUNSEL

Thomas R. Brown

General Counsel for: Lely Estates; Naples Community Hospital.
Local Counsel: Fleischmann Trust; Quail Creek Developments.

For full biographical listings, see the Martindale-Hubbell Law Directory

NEW PORT RICHEY, Pasco Co.

JAMES J. ALTMAN (AV)

5628 Main Street, 34652
Telephone: 813-848-8435
Fax: 813-847-2750

ASSOCIATES

Robert N. Altman | Thomas P. Altman

Approved Attorney for: Attorneys' Title Insurance Fund.
Reference: NationsBank of Florida.

For full biographical listings, see the Martindale-Hubbell Law Directory

NEW SMYRNA BEACH, Volusia Co.

GILLESPIE AND GILLESPIE, P.A. (AV)

Gillespie Building, 233 North Causeway, P.O. Drawer 580, 32170
Telephone: 904-428-2416
Fax: 904-423-8252

W. M. Gillespie (1879-1932) | J. U. Gillespie (1916-1981)
William M. Gillespie

Representative Client: First Federal Savings Bank of New Smyrna.
Approved Attorneys for: Attorneys' Title Insurance Fund.

For full biographical listings, see the Martindale-Hubbell Law Directory

NICEVILLE, Okaloosa Co.

POWELL, JONES & REID (AV)

107 North Partin Drive, P.O. Box 400, 32588-0400
Telephone: 904-678-2118
Fax: 904-678-8336
Destin, Florida Office: Suite 21 Commerce Row, 225 Main Street.
Telephone: 904-837-9099.

MEMBERS OF FIRM

Stanley Bruce Powell | Charles W. Reid
Michael A. Jones | Keith J. Kinderman

References: Peoples National Bank of Niceville; Destin Bank; Barnett Bank of Northwest Florida; Vanguard Bank and Trust Co.

For full biographical listings, see the Martindale-Hubbell Law Directory

NORTH MIAMI BEACH, Dade Co.

BUCHANAN INGERSOLL, PROFESSIONAL CORPORATION (AV)

One Turnberry Place, 19495 Biscayne Boulevard, 33180
Telephone: 305-933-5600
Telecopier: 305-933-2350
Pittsburgh, Pennsylvania Office: 5800 USX Tower, 600 Grant Street.
Telephone: 412-562-8800.
Philadelphia, Pennsylvania Office: Two Logan Square, Twelfth Floor, 18th & Arch Streets.
Telephone: 215-665-8700.

(See Next Column)

Harrisburg, Pennsylvania Office: Vartan Parc, 30 North Third Street.
Telephone: 717-237-4800.
Tampa, Florida Office: Suite 1030, 101 East Kennedy Boulevard.
Telephone: 813-222-8180.
Princeton, New Jersey Office: Buchanan Ingersoll, A Partnership, College Centre, 500 College Road East.
Telephone: 609-452-2666.
Lexington, Kentucky Office: Suite 600, PNC Bank Plaza, 200 West Vine Street.
Telephone: 606-225-5333.

Joshua L. Dubin | Barry A. Nelson
Dennis J. Eisinger | Wayne M. Pathman
Jeremy A. Koss | Gary S. Phillips

SENIOR ATTORNEYS

Ralph B. Bekkevold | Mark J. Neuberger

Kenneth R. Bernstein | Jeffrey M. Goodz
Kevin Carmichael | Kenneth P. Kerr
Steven B. Chaneles | Rose Marie LaFemina
Marcie R. Getelman | Andrea B. Mackson
Richard N. Schermer

For full biographical listings, see the Martindale-Hubbell Law Directory

STERN & TANNENBAUM, P.A. (AV)

17071 West Dixie Highway, 33160
Telephone: 305-945-1851, Broward Line: 305-920-9793
Fax: 305-949-9989

Jerome H. Stern

Counsel for: The First National Bank of Boston; Bankers Trust Co.; Hamptons Development Corp. of Dade; Pembroke Lakes South Associates.
Approved Title Agent for: Ticor Title Insurance Co.

For full biographical listings, see the Martindale-Hubbell Law Directory

*OCALA,** Marion Co.

AYRES, CLUSTER, CURRY, McCALL & BRIGGS, P.A. (AV)

21 Northeast First Avenue, P.O. Box 1148, 34478
Telephone: 904-351-2222
Telecopier: 904-351-0312

Willard Ayres (1910-1988) | Douglas H. Oswald
Edwin C. Cluster | James E. Collins
Landis V. Curry, Jr. | Scott Allan Frick
Wayne C. McCall | Jeffrey L. Sauey
Randy R. Briggs | Steven W. Wingo

Counsel for: Sun Bank/North Central Florida.
Local Counsel for: AMREP Corp.

For full biographical listings, see the Martindale-Hubbell Law Directory

SAVAGE, KRIM & SIMONS, P.A. (AV)

121 N.W. Third Street, 34475-6695
Telephone: 904-732-8944
Fax: 904-867-0504

Charles A. Savage (1898-1994) | Frederick J. Krim
Gary C. Simons

Mark S. Fisher

OF COUNSEL

Richard T. Jones

Approved Attorneys for: Attorneys' Title Insurance Fund; Federal Land Bank, Columbia, S. C.
References: First Union National Bank; Barnett Bank of Marion County, N.A.; Sun Bank of Ocala.

For full biographical listings, see the Martindale-Hubbell Law Directory

*ORLANDO,** Orange Co.

BAKER & HOSTETLER (AV)

SunBank Center, Suite 2300, 200 South Orange Avenue, 32802-3432
Telephone: 407-649-4000
In Cleveland, Ohio: 3200 National City Center, 1900 East Ninth Street.
Telephone: 216-621-0200.
In Columbus, Ohio: Capitol Square, Suite 2100, 65 East State Street.
Telephone: 614-228-1541.
In Denver, Colorado: 303 East 17th Avenue, Suite 1100.
Telephone: 303-861-0600.
In Houston, Texas: 1000 Louisiana, Suite 2000.
Telephone: 713-751-1600.
In Long Beach, California: 300 Oceangate, Suite 620.
Telephone: 310-432-2827.
In Los Angeles, California: 600 Wilshire Boulevard.
Telephone: 213-624-2400.
In Washington, D.C.: Washington Square, Suite 1100, 1050 Connecticut Avenue, N.W., Suite 1100.
Telephone: 202-861-1500.

(See Next Column)

BAKER & HOSTETLER, *Orlando—Continued*

In College Park, Maryland: 9658 Baltimore Boulevard, Suite 206.
Telephone: 301-441-2781.
In Alexandria, Virginia: 437 North Lee Street.
Telephone: 703-549-1294.
In San Francisco, California: One Sansome Street, Suite 2000.
Telephone: 415-951-4705.

MEMBERS OF FIRM IN ORLANDO, FLORIDA

G. Thomas Ball (Managing Partner-Orlando Office)

PARTNERS

Stephen E. Cook
Denis L. Durkin
John W. Foster, Sr.
Richard T. Fulton
Todd M. Hoepker
Jerry R. Linscott
Frank M. Mock
Max F. Morris
Rosemary O'Shea
Hector A. Perez
Joel H. Sharp, Jr.
Robert J. Webb
Kenneth C. Wright

ASSOCIATES

Lea A. Banks
Elise L. Bloom
Jacqueline Bozzuto
John Lee Brewerton, III
Jeffrey E. Decker
James V. Etscorn
Christopher N. Fountas
Kurt P. Gruber
Daniel F. Hogan (Not admitted in FL)
Frank S. Ioppolo, Jr.
Kristine R. Kutz
Joanne Braddock Lambert
Mark S. Lieblich
Brian T. Lower
Andrew T. Marcus
Richard D. Robinson (Not admitted in FL)
Brenda Hartwright Smith
Deni D. Smith
Kathryn L. Sweers
Robert W. Thielhelm, Jr.
Michael J. Thompson
Harkley R. Thornton
Rana Tiwari

OF COUNSEL

Charles R. Harrison
Joseph J. Kadow

RETIRED PARTNER

V. Keith Young

For full biographical listings, see the Martindale-Hubbell Law Directory

BOBO, SPICER, CIOTOLI, FULFORD, BOCCHINO, DEBEVOISE & LE CLAINCHE, P.A. (AV)

Landmark Center One, Suite 510, 315 East Robinson Street, 32801-1949
Telephone: 407-849-1060
Fax: 407-843-4751
West Palm Beach, Florida Office: Esperante, Sixth Floor, 222 Lakeview Avenue, 33401.
Telephone: 407-684-6600.
FAX: 407-684-3828.

John W. Bocchino
D. Andrew DeBevoise

Christopher C. Curry
Robert R. Saunders
Keith A. Scott
J. Clancey Bounds
Sharon A. Chapman
Sophia B. Ehringer
Tyler S. McClay

For full biographical listings, see the Martindale-Hubbell Law Directory

BOROUGHS, GRIMM, BENNETT & MORLAN, P.A. (AV)

201 East Pine Street, Suite 500, P.O. Box 3309, 32802-3309
Telephone: 407-841-3353
Telecopier: 407-843-9587

R. Lee Bennett
Thomas Boroughs
William A. Grimm
Harold E. Morlan, II
John R. Simpson, Jr.
Douglas E. Starcher
Robert J. Stovash

Edward R. Alexander, Jr.
Kenneth P. Hazouri

OF COUNSEL

Robert W. Boyd

General Counsel for: Autonomous Technologies Corporation; Bubble Room, Inc.; The Civil Design Group, Inc.; Datamax Corporation; The Investment Counsel Company; Sawtek Inc.

For full biographical listings, see the Martindale-Hubbell Law Directory

CARLTON, FIELDS, WARD, EMMANUEL, SMITH & CUTLER, P.A. (AV)

Suite 1600 Firstate Tower, 255 South Orange Avenue (32802), P.O. Box 1171, 32801
Telephone: 407-849-0300
Telecopier: (407) 648-9099
Tampa, Florida Office: One Harbour Place, 777 South Harbour Island Drive. P.O. Box 3239.
Telephone: 813-223-7000.
West Palm Beach, Florida Office: Esperanté, 222 Lakeview Avenue, Suite 1400, 33401, P.O. Box 150, 33402.
Telephone: 407-659-7070.

(See Next Column)

Pensacola, Florida Office: Harbourview Building, 4th Floor, 25 West Cedar Street, 32501, P.O. Box 12426, 32582.
Telephone: 904-434-0142.
Tallahassee, Florida Office: Fifth Floor, First Florida Bank Building, 215 South Monroe Street, 32301, P.O. Drawer 190, 32302. .
Telephone: 904-224-1585.
St. Petersburg, Office: Barnett Tower, Suite 2300, One Progress Plaza, 33701, P.O. Box 2861, 33731.
Telephone: 813-821-7000.

Lawrence M. Watson, Jr.
Roger D. Schwenke
George Barford
Laurence E. Kinsolving
Robert L. Young
William D. Palmer
Thomas D. Scanlon
Charles J. Cacciabeve
Laurel E. Lockett
Vernon Swartsel
Daniel C. Johnson

OF COUNSEL

Davisson F. Dunlap
James A. Urban

Alton L. Lightsey
Vivian P. Cocotas
Charles D. Hargrove
Michael S. Popok (Not admitted in FL)
Kathleen Fowler Loerzel
Thomas P. Wert
Thomas H. Justice III
Philip A. Diamond

For full biographical listings, see the Martindale-Hubbell Law Directory

COBB COLE & BELL (AV)

Suite 1428 SunBank Center, 200 South Orange Avenue, 32801
Telephone: 407-843-3337
Fax: 407-843-0553
Daytona Beach, Florida Office: 150 Magnolia Avenue.
Telephone: 904-255-8171.
Fax: 904-258-5068.
Maitland, Florida Office: 900 Winderley Place, Suite 122.
Telephone: 407-661-1123.
Fax: 407-661-5743.
Tallahassee, Florida Office: 131 North Gadsden Street.
Telephone: 904-681-3233.
Fax: 904-681-3241.
Palm Coast, Florida Office: Sun Bank Building, 1 Florida Park Drive South, Suite 350.
Telephone: 904-446-2622.
Fax: 904-446-2654.

Samuel P. Bell, III
Jay D. Bond, Jr.
Jonathan D. Kaney Jr.
J. Lester Kaney
John J. Upchurch
James M. Barclay
C. Allen Watts
Kevin X. Crowley
Kenneth R. Artin
Michael D. Williams

General Counsel for: Daytona Beach Racing & Recreational Facilities District; News Journal Corporation.
Local Counsel for: Canal Insurance Co.; First Union National Bank of Florida; Southern Bell Telephone & Telegraph Co.; United States Fidelity & Guaranty Co.
Approved Attorneys for: American Pioneer Title Insurance Co.; Attorneys' Title Insurance Fund.

For full biographical listings, see the Martindale-Hubbell Law Directory

DEWOLF, WARD, O'DONNELL & HOOFMAN, P.A. (AV)

Suite 2000, 111 North Orange Avenue, 32801-4800
Telephone: 407-841-7000
Telecopy: 407-843-6035

Thomas B. DeWolf
John H. Ward
John L. O'Donnell, Jr.
Robert S. Hoofman
A. Clifton Black
James E. Glatt, Jr.,

Michael W. O. Holihan
Victor A. Diaz

Representative Clients: Andover Companies; Applause, Inc.; Attorney's Title Insurance Co.; Buena Vista Pictures Distribution, Inc.; Chicago Title Insurance Co.; Deutsche Credit Corp.; Eastman Kodak Co.; Employers Insurance of Wausau; Lockheed Missiles & Space Co., Inc.; Walt Disney World Co.

For full biographical listings, see the Martindale-Hubbell Law Directory

JAMES O. DRISCOLL, P.A. (AV)

3222 Corrine Drive, 32803
Telephone: 407-894-8821
Fax: 407-895-5625

James O. Driscoll

Local Counsel for: State Farm Insurance Cos.

For full biographical listings, see the Martindale-Hubbell Law Directory

Orlando—Continued

Eubanks, Hilyard, Rumbley, Meier & Lengauer, A Professional Association (AV)

Suite 1700 - Gateway Center The Travelers Building, 1000 Legion Place, P.O. Box 4973, 32802-4973
Telephone: 407-425-4251
Telecopier: 407-841-8431

Ernest H. Eubanks
Rodney G. Ross (1934-1982)
Sutton G. Hilyard, Jr.
G. Yates Rumbley
George A. Meier, III
Steven F. Lengauer
Jeffrey G. Slater
Robert E. Bonner
Craig L. Brams
Alexander Muszynski, III
Bruce R. Bogan
Bobby G. Palmer, Jr.
Edward L. Fagan
Melissa Arony
Douglas G. Carey
Virginia S. Williams
Wiley A. Rariden
Melinda G. Baum
Perry W. Doran, Jr.
Stephen P. Matzuk

Representative Clients: Chubb & Son; Gallagher-Bassett Insurance Service; Kemper Group; Liberty Mutual Insurance Co.; Orange County, Florida/-City of Orlando; Reliance Insurance Cos.; United Technologies Corp.; Walt Disney World Co.; Zurich Insurance Co.

For full biographical listings, see the Martindale-Hubbell Law Directory

Foley & Lardner (AV)

Suite 1800, 111 North Orange Avenue, P.O. Box 2193, 32802-2193
Telephone: 407-423-7656
Telex: 441781 (HQ ORL)
Facsimile: 407-648-1743
Milwaukee, Wisconsin Office: Firstar Center, 777 East Wisconsin Avenue.
Telephone: 414-271-2400.
Telex: 26-819 (Foley Lard Mil).
Facsimile: 414-297-4900.
Madison, Wisconsin Office: Firstar Plaza, One South Pinckney Street, P.O. Box 1497.
Telephone: 608-257-5035.
Telex: 262051 (F L Madison).
Facsimile: 608-258-4258.
Chicago, Illinois Office: Suite 3300, One IBM Plaza, 330 N. Wabash Avenue.
Telephone: 312-755-1900.
Facsimile: 312-755-1925.
Washington, D.C. Office: Washington Harbour, Suite 500, 3000 K Street, N.W.
Telephone: 202-672-5300.
Telex: 904136 (Foley Lard Wsh).
Facsimile: 202-672-5399.
Annapolis, Maryland Office: Suite 102, 175 Admiral Cochrane Drive.
Telephone: 301-266-8077.
Telex: 899149 (Oldtownpat).
Facsimile: 301-266-8664.
Jacksonville, Florida Office: The Greenleaf Building, 200 Laura Street, P.O. Box 240.
Telephone: 904-359-2000.
Facsimile: 904-359-8700.
Tallahassee, Florida Office: Suite 450, 215 South Monroe Street, P.O. Box 508.
Telephone: 904-222-6100.
Facsimile: 904-224-0496.
Tampa, Florida Office: Suite 2700, One Hundred N. Tampa Street, P.O. Box 3391.
Telephones: 813-229-2300; Pinellas County: 813-442-3296.
Facsimile: 813-221-4210
West Palm Beach, Florida Office: Suite 200, Phillips Point East Tower, 777 South Flagler Drive.
Telephone: 407-655-5050.
Facsimile: 407-655-6925.

RESIDENT PARTNERS

J. Gordon Arkin
Edmund T. Baxa, Jr.
Terence J. Delahunty, Jr.
Richard A. DuRose
Mark C. Extein
James S. Grodin
Richard A. Heinle
Keith James Hesse
John P. Horan
Michael A. Hornreich
Christopher K. Kay
Peter G. Latham
Thomas K. Maurer
K. Rodney May
Sybil Meloy
Joseph R. Panzl
Christopher D. Rolle
Paul E. Rosenthal
John A. Sanders
Ronald M. Schirtzer
Christopher C. Skambis, Jr.
Egerton K. van den Berg
Jon M. Wilson
R. Duke Woodson

RESIDENT SPECIAL COUNSEL

Robert J. Walter

RESIDENT OF COUNSEL

David C. Latham

RETIRED PARTNERS

Norman F. Burke
Francis V. Gay

(See Next Column)

RESIDENT ASSOCIATES

Bradley K. Alley
Anita L. Barber (Not admitted in FL)
David P. Barker
Michael J. Beaudine
W. Bruce DelValle
Mary A. Doty
Martha Hunter Formella
John R. Hamilton
Edward P. Jordan, II
Ometrias Dean Long
Karen A. Lorenzen
Kathleen L. Maloney
Lucy Johnson Mangan
Lili C. Metcalf
Michael Lynn Moore
Laura R. Oleck
James Everett Shepherd V
Andrew V. Showen
Arthur D. Sims, II
J. Walter Spiva
Christi L. Underwood
Steven W. Zelkowitz

General Counsel for: The Greater Orlando Aviation Authority.
Attorneys for: United Parcel Service of America, Inc.; Citrus Central, Inc.

For full biographical listings, see the Martindale-Hubbell Law Directory

Gattis, Hallowes & Carpenter, Professional Association (AV)

130 Hillcrest Street, P.O. Box 3109, 32802
Telephone: 407-843-8470
Fax: 407-843-4436

Donald L. Gattis, Jr.
Walton B. Hallowes, Jr.
Darrell F. Carpenter

For full biographical listings, see the Martindale-Hubbell Law Directory

Gray, Harris and Robinson, Professional Association (AV)

Suite 1200 Southeast Bank Building, 201 East Pine Street, P.O. Box 3068, 32802
Telephone: 407-843-8880
Telecopier: 407-244-5690
Cocoa Beach, Florida Office: Gray, Harris, Robinson, Kirschenbaum & Peeples. Glass Bank Building, 4th Floor, 505 North Orlando Avenue, P.O. Box 320757.
Telephone: 407-783-2218.
Telecopier: 407-783-2297.

G. Wayne Gray (1900-1965)
J. Charles Gray
Gordon H. "Stumpy" Harris
Richard M. Robinson
Phillip R. Finch
Pamela O. Price
James F. Page, Jr.
William A. Boyles
Thomas A. Cloud
Byrd F. Marshall, Jr.
J. Mason Williams III
Leo P. Rock, Jr.
G. Robertson Dilg
Charles W. Sell
Jack A. Kirschenbaum
James W. Peeples III
Richard E. Burke
Guy S. Haggard
Frederick W. Leonhardt
Borron J. Owen, Jr.
Michael K. Wilson

Paul S. Quinn, Jr.
David L. Schick
Jack K. McMullen
Susan Tassell Spradley
Tracy Ann Borgert
Kent Lee Hipp
Lila Ingate McHenry
Michael E. Neukamm
Robert L. Beals
Donald H. Gibson
Kimberly L. Noworyta
Michele R. Plante
N. Scott Novell
Christopher J. Coleman
Margaret (Peggy) R. Hoyt
Russell S. Kent

OF COUNSEL

Malcolm R. Kirschenbaum
Sydney L. Jackowitz
William G. Boltin, III

LEGAL SUPPORT PERSONNEL

Keith W. Houck

Representative Clients: First Union; NationsBank; Jimmy Bryan Enter.; Topeka Group, Inc.; Telesat Cablevision, Inc.; Orange County Health Facilities Authority; Walt Disney World.
Approved Attorneys for: Attorneys' Title Insurance Fund; American Title Insurance Co.; Title Insurance of Minnesota.

For full biographical listings, see the Martindale-Hubbell Law Directory

Gurney & Handley, P.A. (AV)

225 E. Robinson, Suite 450, 32801
Telephone: 407-843-9500

Leon H. Handley
Richard W. Lassiter
John L. Sewell
David W. Roquemore, Jr.
Robert S. Green
W. Marvin Hardy, III
Ronald L. Harrop
Francis E. Pierce, III
Michael F. Sutton
Peter N. Smith
Dennis R. O'Connor

David Brian Falstad
J. Brian Baird
Michael J. Maloney
Michael V. Barszcz
Steven H. Preston

(See Next Column)

GURNEY & HANDLEY P.A., *Orlando—Continued*

LEGAL SUPPORT PERSONNEL

Charles J. Brackett, Jr. (Claims Analyst)

Representative Clients: Atlanta Casualty Company; Beneficial Mortgage Corp.; Ford Consumer Finance Co., Inc.; Government Employees Insurance Co.; Home Savings of America, FSB; John Hancock Mutual Life Insurance Co.; Meritor Credit Corp.; Orlando Utilities Commission; Phoenix Home Life Mutual Insurance Co.; Vistana Resort Development, Inc.

For full biographical listings, see the Martindale-Hubbell Law Directory

HOLLAND & KNIGHT (AV)

A Partnership including Professional Corporations
200 S. Orange Avenue, Suite 2600, 32801
Telephone: 407-425-8500
Fax: 407-244-5288
Mailing Address: P.O. Box 1526, 32802
Fort Lauderdale, Florida Office: One East Broward Boulevard, Suite 1300.
Telephone: 305-525-1000.
Fax: 305-463-2030.
Jacksonville, Florida Office: 50 N. Laura Street, Suite 3900.
Telephone: 904-353-2000.
Fax: 904-358-1872.
Lakeland, Florida Office: 92 Lake Wire Drive.
Telephone: 813-682-1161.
Fax: 813-688-1186.
Miami, Florida Office: 701 Brickell Avenue, 30th Floor.
Telephone: 305-374-8500.
Fax: 305-787-7799.
St. Petersburg, Florida Office: 360 Central Avenue.
Telephone: 813-896-7171.
Fax: 813-822-8048.
Tallahassee, Florida Office: 315 Calhoun Street, Suite 600.
Telephone: 904-224-7000.
Fax: 904-224-8832.
Tampa, Florida Office: 400 North Ashley, Suite 2300.
Telephone: 813-227-8500.
Fax: 813-229-0134.
West Palm Beach, Florida Office: 625 N. Flagler Drive, Suite 700.
Telephone: 407-833-2000.
Fax: 407-650-8399.
Washington, D.C. Office: 2100 Pennsylvania Avenue, N.W.
Telephone: 202-955-3000.
Fax: 202-955-5564.
Atlanta, Georgia Office: 1201 West Peachtree Street, N.W., Suite 3100.
Telephone: 404-817-8500.
Fax: 404-881-0470.
Special Counsel: Shaw, Licitra, Parente, Esernio & Schwartz, P.C., 1010 Franklin Avenue, Garden City, N.Y., 11530, 300 East 42nd Street, New York, N.Y., 10017.

ORLANDO MEMBERS AND ASSOCIATES

Mark J. Buhler
David E. Cardwell
Louis T. M. Conti
Raymond Ehrlich
William O. E. Henry
J. Fraser Himes
Phyllis A. Hood
Jeffry R. Jontz
Terry L. McCollough
C. Parkhill Mays, Jr.
Howell W. Melton, Jr.
Leslie King O'Neal
James A. Park, III
Steven R. Schooley
James L. Simon
Roger W. Sims
Lee Stuart Smith
Richard L. Stockton

Glenn Arthur Adams
Cynthia J. Brennan
Mary Beth Cantrell
Christopher V. Carlyle
Christopher B. Clark
John R. Dierking
Charles J. Hawkins, II
Mac D. Heavener, III
Thomas M. McAleavey
Brian A. McDowell
Robin Uricchio O'Quinn
Rory C. Ryan

OF COUNSEL

Richard L. Fletcher, Jr.

For full biographical listings, see the Martindale-Hubbell Law Directory

HONIGMAN MILLER SCHWARTZ AND COHN (AV)

A Partnership including Professional Corporations
390 North Orange Avenue, Suite 1300, 32801-1632
Telephone: 407-648-0300
Telecopier: 407-648-1155
West Palm Beach, Florida Office: Suite 800 Esperante Building, 222 Lakeview Avenue.
Telephone: 407-838-4500.
Tampa, Florida Office: 2700 Landmark Centre, 401 E. Jackson Street.
Telephone: 813-221-6600.
Detroit, Michigan Office: 2290 First National Building.
Telephone: 313-256-7800.
Lansing, Michigan Office: 222 North Washington Square, Suite 400.
Telephone: 517-484-8282.
Houston, Texas Office: 3100 First Interstate Bank Plaza, 1000 Louisiana.
Telephone: 713-650-2600.

(See Next Column)

Los Angeles, California Office: Watt Plaza, Suite 2200, 1875 Century Park East.
Telephone: 310-789-3800.
Fax: 310-789-3814.

MEMBERS

Wendy Anderson (P.A.)
J. Lindsay Builder, Jr., (P.A.)
Charles V. Choyce, Jr.
Michael J. Grindstaff (P.A.)
J.A. Jurgens (P.A.)
David S. Oliver (P.A.)
Michael J. Sullivan (P.A.)
Brad M. Tomtishen

ASSOCIATES

Jan A. Albanese
Suzanne M. Amaducci
Orlando L. Evora
Roseanna J. Lee
Paul W. Moses II
Vincent J. Profaci

General Counsel For: Wayne Densch, Inc.; Florida Housing Finance Agency.
Representative Clients: Barnett Bank of Central Florida, N.A.; Connecticut Mutual Life Insurance Co.; A.G. Edwards & Sons, Inc.; W.R. Grace & Co.; Paine Webber, Inc.; Pulte Corporation; Sun Bank, N.A.

For full biographical listings, see the Martindale-Hubbell Law Directory

DAVID M. LANDIS, P.A. (AV)

28 East Washington Street, P.O. Box 2209, 32802
Telephone: 407-841-5858
Fax: 407-839-1781

David M. Landis
Jon E. Kane

Reference: United American Bank of Central Florida.

For full biographical listings, see the Martindale-Hubbell Law Directory

MATHEWS SMITH RAILEY & DECUBELLIS, P.A. (AV)

Suite 801, Citrus Center, 255 South Orange Avenue, P.O. Box 4976, 32802-4976
Telephone: 407-872-2200
Telecopier: 407-423-1038

Lawrence G. Mathews, Jr.
Maura T. Smith
Lilburn R. Railey, III
Daniel L. DeCubellis
Frank M. Bedell
Mary Meeks Wills
W. Edward (Ned) McLeod

Representative Clients: American Telephone and Telegraph; Design Professional Insurance Corp.; Florida Lawyers Mutual Insurance Corp.; Great Southwest Corp.; International Game Technology, Inc.; Jennings Environmental Services, Inc.; Mader Southeast, Inc.; Orange County; PGA Tour, Inc.; Sun Banks, Inc.

For full biographical listings, see the Martindale-Hubbell Law Directory

PLEUS, ADAMS, DAVIS & SPEARS, P.A. (AV)

940 Highland Avenue, P.O. Box 3627, 32802
Telephone: 407-422-8116
Fax: 407-648-1044

Robert J. Pleus, Jr.
Richard H. Adams, Jr.
Bradley J. Davis
Douglas C. Spears
Richard D. Connor, Jr.
Paul L. SanGiovanni

Jennifer S. Eden
Reinhard G. Stephan
Deborah B. Ansbro
Kevin E. Mangum

General Counsel for: Lochaven Federal Savings & Loan; Independence Mortgage Corporation of America; Roman Catholic Diocese of Orlando.
Representative Clients: Ensign Property Group, Inc.; Herman J. Heidrich & Sons; Deere Credit Services.

For full biographical listings, see the Martindale-Hubbell Law Directory

SHUTTS & BOWEN (AV)

A Partnership including Professional Associations
20 North Orange Avenue, Suite 1000, P.O. Box 2064, 32801
Telephone: 407-423-3200
Cable Address: "Shuttsbo"
Telefax: 407-425-8316
Key Largo, Florida Office: Suite A206, 31 Ocean Reef Drive.
Telephone: 305-367-2881.
Miami, Florida Office: 1500 Miami Center, 201 South Biscayne Boulevard.
Telephone: 305-358-6300.
Cable Address: "Shuttsbo."
Telefax: 305-381-9982.
West Palm Beach, Florida Office: One Clearlake Centre, 250 Australian Avenue, Suite 500.
Telephone: 407-835-8500.
Fax: 407-650-8530.
Amsterdam, The Netherlands Office: Shutts & Bowen, B.V., Europa Boulevard 59, 1083 AD, Amsterdam.
Telephone: (31 20) 661-0969.
Fax: (31 20) 642-1475.
London, England Office: 48 Mount Street, London W1Y 5RE.
Telephone: 4471493-4840.
Telefax: 4471493-4299.

(See Next Column)

SHUTTS & BOWEN—*Continued*

MEMBERS OF FIRM

Andrew M. Brumby (Resident)
Charles Robinson Fawsett (P.A.)
Robert A. Freyer (Resident)
Michael L. Gore (Resident)
Robert A. Savill (Resident)
Robert C. Sommerville (P.A.)
James G. Willard (Resident)
Kenneth W. Wright (Resident)

RESIDENT ASSOCIATES

Thomas P. Callan
Mary Ruth Houston
Patrick M. Muldowney
Lisa R. Pearson
Daniel J. Weidmann

OF COUNSEL

Rod Jones (Resident)

For full biographical listings, see the Martindale-Hubbell Law Directory

CRAIG B. WARD, P.A. (AV)

Suite 501, 105 East Robinson Street, 32801
Telephone: 407-839-0222
Fax: 407-839-0577

Craig B. Ward

OF COUNSEL

Charles D. Miner

For full biographical listings, see the Martindale-Hubbell Law Directory

WINDERWEEDLE, HAINES, WARD & WOODMAN, P.A. (AV)

Barnett Bank Center, 390 North Orange Avenue, P.O. Box 1391, 32802-1391
Telephone: 407-423-4246
Telecopier: 407-423-7014
Winter Park, Florida Office: Barnett Bank Building 250 Park Avenue, South, P.O. Box 880.
Telephone: 407-644-6312.
Telecopier: 407-645-3728.

Harold A. Ward, III
Victor E. Woodman
William A. Walker II
James L. Fly
Joseph Penn Carolan, III
Tucker H. Byrd
Thomas A. Simser, Jr.
Dykes C. Everett
Robert P. Major
James Edward Cheek, III
William H. Robbinson, Jr.
John H. Dyer, Jr.
Wynne Ellen Franklin
J. Jeffrey Deery
Paula P. Lightsey
Nancy S. Freeman

General Counsel: RoTech Medical Corp.
Counsel for: Barnett Bank of Central Florida, N.A.; Dial Medical of Florida, Inc.; United Southern Bank.
Representative Clients: Security National Bank; United American Bank; Georgia-Pacific Corp.; USX Corp.

For full biographical listings, see the Martindale-Hubbell Law Directory

ZIMMERMAN, SHUFFIELD, KISER & SUTCLIFFE, P.A. (AV)

Landmark Center One, Suite 600, 315 East Robinson Street, P.O. Box 3000, 32802
Telephone: 407-425-7010
Telecopier: 407-425-2747

Bernard J. Zimmerman
W. Charles Shuffield
Wendell J. Kiser
Roland A. Sutcliffe Jr.
Ultima Degnan Morgan
Robert E. Mansbach, Jr.
Robert L. Dietz
Stephen B. Hatcher
Robert W. Peacock, Jr.
Clement L. Hyland
J. Timothy Schulte

Melissa Dubina Kaplan
John C. Bachman
Pamela Lynn Foels
Paul A. Kelley
Edward M. Kuhn III
Eric P. Gibbs
Joseph C. L. Wettach
Edward C. Duncan, III
Derrick E. Cox
Trent W. Ling
Charles H. Leo
Vivian M. Reeves
Joseph A. Regnery
John V. Colvin
Kraig N. Johnson
Gene E. Crick, Jr.
Charles B. Costar III
Kevin G. Malchow
Thomas Warren Sculco
Kevin L. Lienard
Daniel R. Murphy
Michael C. Tyson

LEGAL SUPPORT PERSONNEL

W. Raymond Herod

For full biographical listings, see the Martindale-Hubbell Law Directory

*PALATKA,** Putnam Co. — (Refer to St. Augustine)

PALM BEACH, Palm Beach Co.

CALDWELL & PACETTI (AV)

324 Royal Palm Way, P.O. Box 2775, 33480-2775
Telephone: 407-655-0620
Fax: 407-655-3775

(See Next Column)

MEMBERS OF FIRM

Manley P. Caldwell (1901-1971)
Madison F. Pacetti (1914-1994)
Manley P. Caldwell, Jr.
Kenneth W. Edwards
Mary M. Viator
Charles F. Schoech
Elizabeth S. (Betsy) Burden
John A. Weig

OF COUNSEL

Arthur E. Barrow (Retired)

Representative Clients: Shawano Drainage District; Acme Improvement District; Northern Palm Beach County Water Control District; Indian Trail Water Control District; Siemens Information Systems; Town Of Hypoluxo; Everglades Agricultural Area Environmental Protection District; East County Water Control District; Town of Lake Clarke Shores.

For full biographical listings, see the Martindale-Hubbell Law Directory

MURPHY, REID & PILOTTE, P.A. (AV)

340 Royal Palm Way, 33480
Telephone: 407-655-4060
Facsimile: 407-832-5436
Vero Beach, Florida Office: Plantation Plaza, 6606-20th Street, P.O. Drawer M.
Telephone: 407-567-6480.
Facsimile: 407-562-0220.

Eugene W. Murphy, Jr.
Frank T. Pilotte

OF COUNSEL

Philip H. Reid, Jr.

For full biographical listings, see the Martindale-Hubbell Law Directory

ROZELLE, SULLIVAN AND CALL (AV)

223 Sunset Avenue, Suite 200, P.O. Box 229, 33480
Telephone: 407-655-8585
Fax: 407-655-8663

MEMBERS OF FIRM

Douglas D. Rozelle, Jr.
Paul M. Sullivan, Jr.
John S. Call, Jr.

ASSOCIATES

Stephen W. Stoll, Jr.

Representative Clients: Wal-Mart Stores, Inc.; Motors Insurance Corp.; American Contractors Insurance Group, Inc.; Continental Loss Adjusting Co.; The Equitable Life Assurance Society; Connecticut General Life Insurance Co.; Safeco Insurance Co.; Phar-Mor of Florida, Inc.; World Wide Insurance Group; Chrysler Insurance Co.

For full biographical listings, see the Martindale-Hubbell Law Directory

WINTHROP, STIMSON, PUTNAM & ROBERTS (AV)

125 Worth Avenue, 33480
Telephone: 407-655-7297
Telefax: 407-833-6726
New York, N.Y. Office: One Battery Park Plaza, 10004.
Telephone: 212-858-1000.
Stamford, Connecticut Office: Financial Centre, 695 East Main Street, P.O. Box 6760, 06904-6760.
Telephone: 203-348-2300.
Washington, D.C. Office: 1133 Connecticut Avenue, N.W., 20036.
Telephone: 202-775-9800.
London, England Office: 2 Throgmorton Avenue, London, EC2N 2AP, England.
Telephone: 011-4471-628-4931.
Brussels, Belgium Office: Rue Du Taciturne 42, 1040 Brussels, Belgium.
Telephone: 011-322-230-1392.
Tokyo, Japan Office: 608 Atagoyama Bengoshi Building 6-7, Atago 1-chome, Minato-ku, Tokyo 105 Japan.
Telephone: 011-813-3437-9740.
Hong Kong Office: 2505 Asia Pacific Finance Tower, Citibank Plaza, 3 Garden Road, Central.
Telephone: 011-852-530-3400.

MEMBERS OF FIRM

Philip G. Hull
Michael V. Sterlacci
Douglas F. Williamson, Jr.

COUNSEL

John C. Dotterrer

SENIOR COUNSEL

Howard J. Falcon, Jr. (Retired)

RESIDENT ASSOCIATES

George D. Karibjanian
Guy Rabideau

For full biographical listings, see the Martindale-Hubbell Law Directory

PALM BEACH GARDENS, Palm Beach Co.

SCOTT, ROYCE, HARRIS, BRYAN, BARRA & JORGENSEN, PROFESSIONAL ASSOCIATION (AV)

4400 PGA Boulevard, Suite 900, 33410
Telephone: 407-624-3900
Fax: 407-524-3533

(See Next Column)

SCOTT, ROYCE, HARRIS, BRYAN, BARRA & JORGENSEN PROFESSIONAL ASSOCIATION, *Palm Beach Gardens—Continued*

Robert Claude Scott (1925-1982)	Richard K. Barra
Raymond W. Royce	Robert A. Schaeffer
J. Richard Harris	Mark P. Gagnon
John L. Bryan, Jr.	Barry B. Byrd
John M. Jorgensen	Donna A. Nadeau

LEGAL SUPPORT PERSONNEL

Cherisse C. Roy

Representative Clients: First Union National Bank of Florida, N.A.; John D. & Catherine T. MacArthur Foundation; North Palm Beach County Association of Realtors, Inc.; Lost Tree Village; Jupiter Hills; Art Moran Pontiac, Inc.; Comerica Bank & Trust, FSB; Northern Trust Bank of Florida, N.A.; U.S. Trust Company of Florida.

For full biographical listings, see the Martindale-Hubbell Law Directory

*PANAMA CITY,** Bay Co.

BRYANT AND HIGBY, CHARTERED (AV)

833 Harrison Avenue, P.O. Drawer 860, 32402-0860
Telephone: 904-763-1787
Fax: 904-785-1533

Lynn C. Higby (1938-1992)	Rowlett W. Bryant

Clifford C. Higby

Representative Clients: Florida First Federal Savings Bank; Associated Land Title Group, Inc.; Service First, Inc.; City of Panama City, Florida; Panama City Port Authority; Travelers Insurance Cos.; Cotton States Insurance Co.; Preferred Risk Mutual Insurance Co.

For full biographical listings, see the Martindale-Hubbell Law Directory

RICHARD SMOAK (AV)

103 West 5th Street, P.O. Box 1006, 32402-1006
Telephone: 904-747-1900
Fax: 904-747-1910

Representative Clients: Panama City - Bay County Airport & Industrial District; Continental Insurance Co.; Florida Physicians Insurance Co.; Hartford Insurance Co.; Mutual of Omaha Insurance Co.; Ranger Insurance Co.; St. Paul Fire & Marine Insurance Co.; Seibels Bruce Cos.; Stone Container Corporation.

For full biographical listings, see the Martindale-Hubbell Law Directory

*PENSACOLA,** Escambia Co.

BEGGS & LANE (AV)

Seventh Floor, Blount Building, 3 West Garden Street, P.O. Box 12950, 32576-2950
Telephone: 904-432-2451
Telecopier: 904-469-3330

MEMBERS OF FIRM

E. Dixie Beggs (Retired)	John F. Windham
Bert H. Lane (1917-1981)	J. Nixon Daniel, III
Robert P. Gaines	G. Edison Holland, Jr.
William Guy Davis, Jr.	Ralph A. Peterson
W. Spencer Mitchem	Gary B. Leuchtman
James M. Weber	John P. Daniel
Robert L. Crongeyer	Jeffrey A. Stone

James S. Campbell

ASSOCIATES

Teresa E. Liles	Russell A. Badders
Russell F. Van Sickle	David J. Barberie

For full biographical listings, see the Martindale-Hubbell Law Directory

CARLTON, FIELDS, WARD, EMMANUEL, SMITH & CUTLER, P.A. (AV)

Harbourview Building, 4th Floor, 25 West Cedar Street (32501), P.O. Box 12426, 32582
Telephone: 904-434-0142
Telecopier: (904) 434-5366
Tampa, Florida Office: One Harbour Place, 777 South Harbour Island Drive, 33602. P.O. Box 3239, 33601.
Telephone: 813-223-7000.
West Palm Beach, Florida Office: Esperanté, 222 Lakeview Avenue, Suite 1400, 33401, P.O. Box 150, 33402.
Telephone: 407-659-7070.
Orlando, Florida Office: Suite 1600 Firstate Tower, 255 South Orange Avenue, 32801. P.O. Box 1171, 32802.
Telephone: 407-849-0300.
Tallahassee, Florida Office: Fifth Floor, First Florida Bank Building, 215 South Monroe Street, 32301. P.O. Drawer 190, 32302. .
Telephone: 904-224-1585.
St. Petersburg Office: Barnett Tower, Suite 2300, One Progress Plaza, 33701. P.O. Box 2861, 33731.
Telephone: 813-821-7000.

(See Next Column)

Wright Moulton	George Barford
G. Miles Davis	Laurel E. Lockett
Roger D. Schwenke	Stephen L. Walker
Jacob D. Varn	Bill B. McEachern, Jr.

Sally C. Bussell

Carol A. Ruebsamen	P. Bradford Hathorn

For full biographical listings, see the Martindale-Hubbell Law Directory

SHELL, FLEMING, DAVIS & MENGE, P.A. (AV)

Seventh Floor Seville Tower, P.O. Box 1831, 32598
Telephone: 904-434-2411
Fax: 904-435-1074

Thurston A. Shell	Danny L. Kepner
Fletcher Fleming	Charles L. Hoffman, Jr.
Rollin D. Davis, Jr.	Stephen B. Shell
M. J. Menge	Maureen Duignan

Jan Shackelford

For full biographical listings, see the Martindale-Hubbell Law Directory

SMITH, SAUER, DEMARIA & JOHNSON (AV)

510 East Zaragoza, P.O. Box 12446, 32501
Telephone: 904-434-2761
Fax: 904-438-8860

G. Thomas Smith	Kathleen K. DeMaria
Jeffrey T. Sauer	Carlton M. Johnson, Jr.

Representative Clients: Exxon Corp.; Amerada Hess; EastGroup Properties; American General.

For full biographical listings, see the Martindale-Hubbell Law Directory

*PERRY,** Taylor Co. — (Refer to Madison)

PLANT CITY, Hillsborough Co.

TRINKLE, REDMAN, SWANSON & BYRD, P.A. (AV)

121 North Collins, Drawer TT, 33566
Telephone: 813-752-6133
Fax: 813-754-8957

John R. Trinkle (1901-1969)	Conrad Swanson
Robert S. Trinkle	Johnnie B. Byrd, Jr.
James L. Redman	Daniel M. Coton

General Counsel for: Sunshine State Federal Savings and Loan Assn.; Withlacoochee River Electric Cooperative, Inc.
Local Counsel for: Plant City Steel Co.

For full biographical listings, see the Martindale-Hubbell Law Directory

POMPANO BEACH, Broward Co.

JOHN L. KORTHALS (AV)

1401 East Atlantic Boulevard, 33060
Telephone: 305-783-2999
FAX: 305-783-9832

For full biographical listings, see the Martindale-Hubbell Law Directory

PORT CHARLOTTE, Charlotte Co.

WILKINS, FROHLICH, JONES, HEVIA, RUSSELL & SUTTER, P.A. (AV)

18501 Murdock Circle, Suite 601, 33948
Telephone: 813-625-0700
Telecopier: 813-625-9540

Gary L. Wilkins	Jesus M. Hevia
W. Cort Frohlich	W. Kevin Russell
Phillip J. Jones	Brian O. Sutter
Melissa Green Jones	Louise O. Hanaoka

Joseph G. Cappuccio

For full biographical listings, see the Martindale-Hubbell Law Directory

PORT ST. LUCIE, St. Lucie Co. — (Refer to Fort Pierce)

*PUNTA GORDA,** Charlotte Co.

WOTITZKY & WOTITZKY (AV)

Suite 301, The Professional Center, 201 West Marion Avenue, 33950
Telephone: 813-639-2171
Telecopier: 813-639-8617
Englewood, Florida Office: 579 South Indiana Avenue, Suite B2.
Telephone: 813-473-1700.
Fax: 813-473-2517.

(See Next Column)

WOTITZKY & WOTITZKY—*Continued*

MEMBERS OF FIRM

John B. Mizell
Edward L. Wotitzky
Warren R. Ross
Hal F. Wotitzky
Leo Wotitzky

OF COUNSEL

Frank Wotitzky

General Counsel for: Murdock Florida Bank.
Representative Client: Punta Gorda Corp.
Approved Attorneys for: Attorneys' Title Insurance Fund, Orlando, Florida; Chicago Title Insurance Co.

For full biographical listings, see the Martindale-Hubbell Law Directory

*QUINCY,** Gadsden Co.

LINES, HINSON AND LINES (AV)

121 North Madison Street, P.O. Box 550, 32353-0550
Telephone: 904-875-1300
Telecopier: 904-875-1350

MEMBERS OF FIRM

William D. Lines (1914-1992)
Alexander L. Hinson
Blucher B. Lines

Representative Clients: Talquin Electric Cooperative, Inc.; Quincy State Bank; Quincy Telephone Co.; Georgia Pacific Corp.; Havana State Bank.

For full biographical listings, see the Martindale-Hubbell Law Directory

*ST. AUGUSTINE,** St. Johns Co.

UPCHURCH, BAILEY & UPCHURCH, P.A. (AV)

780 North Ponce de Leon Boulevard, P.O. Drawer 3007, 32085-3007
Telephone: 904-829-9066
Facsimile: 904-825-4862

John D. Bailey, Jr.
Tracy W. Upchurch
Frank D. Upchurch, III
Katherine Gaertner Jones
Michael A. Siragusa

OF COUNSEL

Frank D. Upchurch, Sr. (1894-1987)
Frank D. Upchurch, Jr.
Hamilton D. Upchurch

General Counsel for: Flagler College, Inc.; Marineland, Inc.; Prosperity Bank of St. Augustine.
Local Counsel for: First Union National Bank of Florida; Southern Bell Telephone and Telegraph Co.; Florida Power and Light Co.

For full biographical listings, see the Martindale-Hubbell Law Directory

ST. PETERSBURG, Pinellas Co.

JOHN T. ALLEN, JR., P.A. (AV)

4508 Central Avenue, 33711
Telephone: 813-321-3273
Fax: 813-323-2789

John T. Allen, Jr.

Karen E. Maller
Nicholas C. Glover
Bryan K. McLachlan

Representative Clients: G.J. Apple, Inc.; Federation of Mobile Home Owners; West Coast Regional Water Authority in Pipeline Litigation; Southern Plazas Med.
Special Counsel for: Pinellas County.
Reference: Rutland's Bank, Seminole, FL.

For full biographical listings, see the Martindale-Hubbell Law Directory

CARLTON, FIELDS, WARD, EMMANUEL, SMITH & CUTLER, P.A. (AV)

Barnett Tower, Suite 2300, One Progress Plaza (33701), P.O. Box 2861, 33731
Telephone: 813-821-7000
Fax: 813-822-3768
Tampa, Florida Office: One Harbour Place, 777 South Harbour Island Drive, 33602. P.O. Box 3239, 33601.
Telephone: 813-223-7000.
West Palm Beach, Florida Office: Esperanté, 222 Lakeview Avenue, Suite 1400, 33401, P.O. Box 150, 33402.
Telephone: 407-659-7070.
Orlando, Florida Office: Suite 1600, Firstate Tower, 255 South Orange Avenue, 32801. P.O. Box 1171, 32802.
Telephone: 407-849-0300.
Pensacola, Florida Office: Harbourview Building, 4th Floor, 25 West Cedar Street, 32501. P.O. Box 12426, 32582.
Telephone: 904-434-0142.
Tallahassee, Florida Office: Fifth Floor, First Florida Bank Building, 215 South Monroe Street, 32301. P.O. Drawer 190, 32302.
Telephone: 904-224-1585.

(See Next Column)

Sylvia H. Walbolt
Roy G. Harrell, Jr.
Alan C. Sundberg
John P. Higgins
David G. Mulock
Steven C. Dupré
Gary L. Sasso
David R. Punzak
Jacob D. Varn
Lee H. Rightmyer

OF COUNSEL

Robert L. Ulrich

J. Michael Walls
William L. Grossenbacher
Randall J. Love

For full biographical listings, see the Martindale-Hubbell Law Directory

JOHN R. FOLTZ (AV)

4800 Forty Sixth Avenue North, P.O. Box 60358, 33784
Telephone: 813-527-4111
Approved Attorney for: Attorney's Title Insurance Fund.
Reference: First Union National Bank of Florida; Barnett National Bank of Florida.

For full biographical listings, see the Martindale-Hubbell Law Directory

HOLLAND & KNIGHT (AV)

A Partnership including Professional Corporations
360 Central Avenue, Suite 1500, 33701-3845
Telephone: 813-896-7171
Fax: 813-822-8048
Mailing Address: P.O. Box 3542, 33731-3542
Fort Lauderdale, Florida Office: One East Broward Boulevard, Suite 1300.
Telephone: 305-525-1000.
Fax: 305-463-2030.
Jacksonville, Florida Office: 50 N. Laura Street, Suite 3900.
Telephone: 904-353-2000.
Fax: 904-358-1872.
Lakeland, Florida Office: 92 Lake Wire Drive.
Telephone: 813-682-1161.
Fax: 813-688-1186.
Miami, Florida Office: 701 Brickell Avenue, 30th Floor.
Telephone: 305-374-8500.
Fax: 305-787-7799.
Orlando, Florida Office: 200 S. Orange Avenue, Suite 2600.
Telephone: 407-425-8500.
Fax: 407-244-5288.
Tallahassee, Florida Office: 315 Calhoun Street, Suite 600.
Telephone: 904-224-7000.
Fax: 904-224-8832.
Tampa, Florida Office: 400 N. Ashley.
Telephone: 813-227-8500.
Fax: 813-229-0134.
West Palm Beach, Florida Office: 625 N. Flagler Drive, Suite 700.
Telephone: 407-833-2000.
Fax: 407-650-8399.
Washington, D.C. Office: 2100 Pennsylvania Avenue, N.W.
Telephone: 202-955-3000.
Fax: 202-955-5564.
Atlanta, Georgia Office: 1201 West Peachtree Street, N.W., Suite 3100.
Telephone: 404-817-8500.
Fax: 404-881-0470.
Special Counsel: Shaw, Licitra, Parente, Esernio & Schwartz, P.C., 1010 Franklin Avenue, Garden City, N.Y., 11530, 300 East 42nd Street, New York, N.Y., 10017.

Chester E. Bacheller
William L. Johnson
William H. Bartlett
Douglas S. Jones
Stephen C. Chumbris
S. Curtis Kiser
Allan B. Davis
G. Dennis Lynn, Jr.
James D. Eckert
Bruce Marger
Joseph W. Fleece
Robert Donald Mastry
Joseph W. Fleece, III
Robert L. Paver
Charles W. Ross

Gerald D. Davis
Michael D. D. Geldart
Doreen A. Stone

OF COUNSEL

Hugh E. Reams

For full biographical listings, see the Martindale-Hubbell Law Directory

MARTIN ERROL RICE, P.A. (AV)

696 First Avenue North, Suite 400, P.O. Box 205, 33701
Telephone: 813-821-4884
Fax: 813-821-4987

Martin Errol Rice

For full biographical listings, see the Martindale-Hubbell Law Directory

St. Petersburg—Continued

RIDEN, EARLE & KIEFNER, P.A. (AV)

City Center, North Tower, 100 Second Avenue South, Suite 400, 33701-4336
Telephone: 813-822-6000
Telecopier: 813-821-3721

Thomas K. Riden
James T. Earle, Jr.
John R. Kiefner, Jr.
Paul Castagliola
Robert H. Crawford
Neil G. Kiefer
D. Jay Snyder
Christopher C. Ferguson
Timothy A. Miller
Gary E. Frazier
James C. Rowe
Christopher B. Young
Clifford J. Hunt
Benjamin Felder

Patricia R. Fay
M. Deanna Harris

For full biographical listings, see the Martindale-Hubbell Law Directory

*SANFORD,** Seminole Co.

THOMAS A. SPEER, P.A. (AV)

Speer Building, P.O. Box 1364, 32772
Telephone: 407-322-0681
Fax: 407-322-2674

Thomas A. Speer

For full biographical listings, see the Martindale-Hubbell Law Directory

STENSTROM, MCINTOSH, JULIAN, COLBERT, WHIGHAM & SIMMONS, P.A. (AV)

Suite 22 Sun Bank-Downtown, P.O. Box 4848, 32772-4848
Telephone: 407-322-2171
Fax: 407-330-2379

Thomas E. Whigham (1952-1988)
Douglas Stenstrom (Retired)
Kenneth W. McIntosh
Ned N. Julian, Jr.
William L. Colbert
Franklin C. Whigham
Clayton D. Simmons
Robert K. McIntosh
Donna L. Surratt-McIntosh

William E. Reischmann, Jr.
Catherine D. Reischmann
Martha H. McIntosh

Representative Clients: City of Sanford; Seminole County School Board; City of Oviedo; City of Casselberry; Seminole Community College; City of Lake Mary.

For full biographical listings, see the Martindale-Hubbell Law Directory

*SARASOTA,** Sarasota Co.

WILLIAM H. BEHRENFELD (AV)

2063 Main Street, 34237-6038
Telephone: 813-365-9090
Fax: 813-365-9094

For full biographical listings, see the Martindale-Hubbell Law Directory

BURKET, SMITH, BOWMAN & GEORGE (AV)

22 South Tuttle Avenue-Suite 3, 34237
Telephone: 813-366-5510
Fax: 813-951-0839

MEMBERS OF FIRM

John F. Burket (1875-1947)
John F. Burket, Jr. (1915-1984)
David G. Bowman
Eugene O. George

OF COUNSEL

V. Morris Smith

General Counsel for: Bay Village of Sarasota, Inc. (Life Care Facility); Southern Grocery Co.; Florida Ladder Co.; Siesta Key Utilities Authority, Inc. (S.K.U.A.); Ludwig-Walpole Co. (General Insurance).

For full biographical listings, see the Martindale-Hubbell Law Directory

DICKINSON & GIBBONS, P.A. (AV)

1750 Ringling Boulevard, P.O. Box 3979, 34230
Telephone: 813-366-4680
FAX: 813-953-3136

Francis C. Dart (1902-1972)
G. Hunter Gibbons
Ward E. Dahlgren
Lewis F. Collins, Jr.
Gary H. Larsen
Camden T. French
Ralph L. Marchbank, Jr.
A. James Rolfes
Burwell J. Jones
Richard R. Garland
Stephen G. Brannan
Deborah J. Blue
Mark A. Haskins
Jeffrey D. Peairs
Kim Carlton Bonner
Douglas R. Wight
Stephen R. Kanzer
David S. Preston
Mary Gall Jack
John A. Yanchek

(See Next Column)

OF COUNSEL

Patrick H. Dickinson

LEGAL SUPPORT PERSONNEL

Elliot J. Welch
Christine C. Menzel
Patricia L. Hunter
Nance R. Walker
Krista R. Nero
Diane Schroeder
Janet E. Gadoury (Certified Legal Assistant)

Representative Clients: Ford Motor Co.; Florida Power & Light Co.; Squibb Corp.
Insurance Clients: Liberty Mutual Insurance Co.; Allstate Insurance Co.; Nationwide Insurance Group; Ohio Casualty Insurance Co.; United States Fidelity & Guaranty Co.; State Farm Insurance Company.

For full biographical listings, see the Martindale-Hubbell Law Directory

NELSON HESSE CYRIL SMITH WIDMAN HERB CAUSEY & DOOLEY (AV)

2070 Ringling Boulevard, P.O. Box 2524, 34230
Telephone: 813-366-7550
FAX: 813-955-3708

MEMBERS OF FIRM

Richard E. Nelson
Ronald Alexander Cyril (1938-1988)
Richard L. Smith
Robert C. Widman
F. Steven Herb
Omer S. Causey
William A. Dooley
Michael S. Drews
Frederick J. Elbrecht

ASSOCIATES

Gary W. Peal
Philip Sypula
J. Kal Gibron
J. Neal Mobley

OF COUNSEL

Robert L. Hesse

General Counsel for: Enterprise National Bank; Dooley Mack Construction Co.; Achieve Sports Management, Inc.
Representative Clients: Wellcraft Marine; Attorneys Title Insurance Fund; Crum & Forster Insurance Co.; Radiology, Inc.; The Carlton Ranch, Inc.
References: Southtrust Bank; Enterprise National Bank.

For full biographical listings, see the Martindale-Hubbell Law Directory

SYPRETT, MESHAD, RESNICK & LIEB (AV)

1900 Ringling Boulevard, 34236
Telephone: 813-365-7171
FAX: 813-365-7923

John D. Dumbaugh
Teresa D. Jones
M. Joseph Lieb, Jr.
John W. Meshad
Michael L. Resnick
Jim D. Syprett

Peter J. Krotec
Alan M. Oravec
Philip R. Zimmerman
Melinda A. Delpech

References: First Union National Bank; SouthTrust Bank.

For full biographical listings, see the Martindale-Hubbell Law Directory

DAVID S. WATSON CHARTERED (AV)

1605 Main Street, Suite 612, 34236
Telephone: 813-366-8891
FAX: 813-366-1806

David S. Watson

OF COUNSEL

Richard W. Cooney

For full biographical listings, see the Martindale-Hubbell Law Directory

WILLIAMS, PARKER, HARRISON, DIETZ & GETZEN, PROFESSIONAL ASSOCIATION (AV)

1550 Ringling Boulevard, 34230-3258
Telephone: 813-366-4800
Telecopier: 813-366-5109
Mailing Address: P.O. Box 3258, Sarasota, Florida, 34230-3258

J. J. Williams, Jr. (1886-1968)
W. Davis Parker (1920-1982)
William T. Harrison, Jr.
George A. Dietz
Monte K. Marshall
James L. Ritchey
Hugh McPheeters, Jr.
William G. Lambrecht
John T. Berteau
John V. Cannon, III
Charles D. Bailey, Jr.
J. Michael Hartenstine
Michele Boardman Grimes
James L. Turner
William M. Seider
Elizabeth C. Marshall
Robert W. Benjamin
Frank Strelec
David A. Wallace
Terri Jayne Salt
Jeffrey A. Grebe
John Leslie Moore
Mark A. Schwartz
Stephanie Edwards
Ric Gregoria
Morgan R. Bentley
Susan Barrett Jewell
Linda R. Getzen
Kimberly J. Page
Phillip D. Eck

(See Next Column)

WILLIAMS, PARKER, HARRISON, DIETZ & GETZEN PROFESSIONAL ASSOCIATION—*Continued*

OF COUNSEL

Frazer F. Hilder
William E. Getzen
Elvin W. Phillips

Counsel for: Sarasota-Manatee Airport Authority; Sarasota County Public Hospital Board; William G. & Marie Selby Foundation; Taylor Woodrow Homes Ltd.; The School Board of Sarasota County.
Local Counsel for: NationsBank of Florida; Arvida/JMB Partners.

For full biographical listings, see the Martindale-Hubbell Law Directory

*SEBRING,** Highlands Co.

SWAINE AND HARRIS, P.A. (AV)

425 South Commerce Avenue, 33870
Telephone: 813-385-1549
Fax: 813-471-0008
Lake Placid, Florida Office: 212 Interlake Boulevard. P.O. Box 548.
Telephone: 813-465-2811.
Fax: 813-465-6999.

J. Michael Swaine
Bert J. Harris, III
John K. McClure

Alison B. Copley
William J. Nielander

Representative Clients: Barnett Bank of Highlands County; Lykes Bros., Inc.; City of Sebring; City of Lake Placid; Lakeshore Mall.
Approved Attorneys for: Attorneys' Title InsuranceFund.

For full biographical listings, see the Martindale-Hubbell Law Directory

*STARKE,** Bradford Co. — (Refer to Gainesville)

*STUART,** Martin Co.

OUGHTERSON, OUGHTERSON, PREWITT & SUNDHEIM, P.A. (AV)

310 Southwest Ocean Boulevard, 34994-2007
Telephone: 407-287-0660
FAX: 407-287-0422

T. T. Oughterson (1904-1983)
Wm. A. Oughterson
John E. Prewitt
Frederick G. Sundheim, Jr.

Counsel for: The Hobe Sound Co.; Martin County Taxpayers Assn.; The Jupiter Island Club.
Local Counsel for: Chase Federal Bank.
Approved Attorneys for: Attorneys' Title Insurance Fund; Chicago Title Insurance Co.; Commonwealth Land Title Insurance Co.

For full biographical listings, see the Martindale-Hubbell Law Directory

*TALLAHASSEE,** Leon Co.

* indicates certain Bar Register subscribers whose principal office is located elsewhere in the state and who have arranged for representation as a part of the state capital listings that follow

*** CARLTON, FIELDS, WARD, EMMANUEL, SMITH & CUTLER, P.A. (AV)**

Fifth Floor, First Florida Bank Building, 215 South Monroe Street, P.O. Drawer 190, 32302
Telephone: 904-224-1585
Telecopier: (904) 222-0398
Tampa, Florida Office: One Harbour Place, 777 South Harbour Island Drive, 33602. P.O. Box 3239, 33601.
Telephone: 813-223-7000.
West Palm Beach, Florida Office: Esperanté, 222 Lakeview Avenue, Suite 1400, 33401, P.O. Box 150, 33402.
Telephone: 407-659-7070.
Orlando, Florida Office: Suite 1600 Firstate Tower. 255 South Orange Avenue, 32801. P.O. Box 1171, 32802.
Telephone: 407-849-0300.
Pensacola, Florida Office: Harbourview Building, 4th Floor, 25 West Cedar Street, 32501. P. O. Box 12426, 32582.
Telephone: 904-434-0142.
St. Petersburg, Florida Office: Barnett Tower, Suite 2300, One Progress Plaza, 33701. P.O. Box 2861, 33731.
Telephone: 813-821-7000.

Alan C. Sundberg
Jacob D. Varn
J. Robert McClure, Jr.
George Barford
David S. Dee
Robert W. Pass
Nancy G. Linnan
W. Douglas Hall
F. Townsend Hawkes
Martha Harrell Chumbler

Michael Patrick Donaldson
Paul A. Vazquez
Warren H. Husband

For full biographical listings, see the Martindale-Hubbell Law Directory

COLLINS & TRUETT, P.A. (AV)

2804 Remington Green Circle, Suite 4, Post Office Drawer 12429, 32317-2429
Telephone: 904-386-6060
Telecopier: 904-385-8220

Richard B. Collins
Gary A. Shipman

Brett Q. Lucas (Resident)
Dawn D. Caloca
Joseph E. Brooks
C. Timothy Gray
Rogelio Fontela
Charles N. Cleland, Jr.
Clifford W. Rainey

OF COUNSEL

Edgar C. Booth
James A. Dixon, Jr.

Representative Clients: Agency Rent-A-Car; Agricultural Excess and Surplus Insurance Co.; AIG Life Insurance Co.; Alliance Insurance Group; Allstate Insurance Co.; American Empire Surplus Lines Insurance Co.; American International Underwriters Inc.; Atlanta Casualty Insurance Co.; Avis Rent-A-Car; Bankers and Shippers Insurance Co.

For full biographical listings, see the Martindale-Hubbell Law Directory

ERVIN, VARN, JACOBS, ODOM & ERVIN (AV)

305 South Gadsden Street, P.O. Drawer 1170, 32302
Telephone: 904-224-9135
Telecopier: 904-222-9164

MEMBERS OF FIRM

F. Perry Odom
Thomas M. Ervin, Jr.
C. Everett Boyd, Jr.
Melissa Fletcher Allaman
Charles Gary Stephens
Robert M. Ervin Jr.
Stuart E. Goldberg
J. Stanley Chapman

ASSOCIATES

Elizabeth Fletcher Duffy

COUNSEL CONSULTANT

Robert M. Ervin

OF COUNSEL

Wilfred C. Varn
Joseph C. Jacobs
Richard W. Ervin
B. K. Roberts
Marilyn K. Morris

Representative Clients: Florida Association of Broadcasters; E. I. duPont de Nemours & Co., Inc.; Florida Credit Union League; Atlantic Richfield Co.; Wells Fargo Ag Credit Corp.; American Acceptance Corp.; Coastal Petroleum Co.; General Motors Corp.; Goodyear Tire and Rubber Co.; The Grand Union Co.

For full biographical listings, see the Martindale-Hubbell Law Directory

*** FOLEY & LARDNER (AV)**

Suite 450, 215 South Monroe Street, P.O. Box 508, 32302-0508
Telephone: 904-222-6100
Facsimile: 904-224-0496
Milwaukee, Wisconsin Office: Firstar Center, 777 East Wisconsin Avenue.
Telephone: 414-271-2400.
Telex: 26-819 (Foley Lard Mil).
Facsimile: 414-297-4900.
Madison, Wisconsin Office: Firstar Plaza, One South Pinckney Street, P.O. Box 1497.
Telephone: 608-257-5035.
Telex: 262051 (F L Madison).
Facsimile: 608-258-4258.
Chicago, Illinois Office: Suite 3300, One IBM Plaza, 330 N. Wabash Avenue.
Telephone: 312-755-1900.
Facsimile: 312-755-1925.
Washington, D.C. Office: Washington Harbour, Suite 500, 3000 K Street, N.W.
Telephone: 202-672-5300.
Telex: 904136 (Foley Lard Wsh).
Facsimile: 202-672-5399.
Annapolis, Maryland Office: Suite 102, 175 Admiral Cochrane Drive.
Telephone: 301-266-8077.
Telex: 899149 (Oldtownpat).
Facsimile: 301-266-8664.
Jacksonville, Florida Office: The Greenleaf Building, 200 Laura Street, P.O. Box 240.
Telephone: 904-359-2000.
Facsimile: 904-359-8700.
Orlando, Florida Office: Suite 1800, 111 North Orange Avenue, P.O. Box 2193.
Telephone: 407-423-7656.
Telex: 441781 (HQ ORL).
Facsimile: 407-648-1743.
Tampa, Florida Office: Suite 2700, One Hundred N. Tampa Street, P.O. Box 3391.
Telephones: 813-229-2300; Pinellas County: 813-442-3296.
Facsimile: 813-221-4210.
West Palm Beach, Florida Office: Suite 200, Phillips Point East Tower, 777 South Flagler Drive.
Telephone: 407-655-5050.
Facsimile: 407-655-6925.

(See Next Column)

FOLEY & LARDNER, *Tallahassee—Continued*

RESIDENT PARTNER

Joseph W. Jacobs

RESIDENT ASSOCIATES

Kevin G. Fitzgerald

For full biographical listings, see the Martindale-Hubbell Law Directory

HENRY, BUCHANAN, MICK, HUDSON & SUBER, P.A. (AV)

117 South Gadsden Street P.O. Drawer 1049, 32302
Telephone: 904-222-2920
Telecopier: 904-224-0034

Bryan W. Henry (1925-1986)
John D. Buchanan, Jr.
Robert A. Mick
Edwin R. Hudson
Jesse F. Suber
Harriet W. Williams
J. Steven Carter

Reference: Barnett Bank of Tallahassee, Inc.

For full biographical listings, see the Martindale-Hubbell Law Directory

HOLLAND & KNIGHT (AV)

A Partnership including Professional Corporations
315 Calhoun Street, Suite 600, 32301
Telephone: 904-224-7000
Fax: 904-224-8832
Mailing Address: P.O. Drawer 810, 32302
Fort Lauderdale, Florida Office: One East Broward Boulevard, Suite 1300.
Telephone: 305-525-1000.
Fax: 305-463-2030.
Jacksonville, Florida Office: 50 N. Laura Street, Suite 3900.
Telephone: 904-353-2000.
Fax: 904-358-1872.
Lakeland, Florida Office: 92 Lake Wire Drive.
Telephone: 813-682-1161.
Fax: 813-688-1186.
Miami, Florida Office: 701 Brickell Avenue, 30th Floor.
Telephone: 305-374-8500.
Fax: 305-787-7799.
Orlando, Florida Office: 200 S. Orange Avenue, Suite 2600.
Telephone: 407-425-8500.
Fax: 407-244-5288.
St. Petersburg, Florida Office: 360 Central Avenue.
Telephone: 813-896-7171.
Fax: 813-822-8048.
Tampa, Florida Office: 400 North Ashley, Suite 2300.
Telephone: 813-227-8500.
Fax: 813-229-0134.
West Palm Beach, Florida Office: 625 N. Flagler Drive, Suite 700.
Telephone: 407-833-2000.
Fax: 407-650-8399.
Washington, D.C. Office: 2100 Pennsylvania Avenue, N.W.
Telephone: 202-922-3000.
Fax: 202-955-5564.
Atlanta, Georgia Office: 1201 West Peachtree Street, N.W., Suite 3100.
Telephone: 404-817-8500.
Fax: 404-881-0470.
Special Counsel: Shaw, Licitra, Parente, Esernio & Schwartz, P.C., 1010 Franklin Avenue, Garden City, N.Y., 11530, 300 East 42nd Street, New York, N.Y., 10017.

TALLAHASSEE MEMBERS AND ASSOCIATES

Martha W. Barnett
Julian D. Clarkson
Hume F. Coleman
Lawrence N. Curtin
Harry R. Detwiler, Jr.
James Mann Ervin, Jr.
Robert R. Feagin, III
Mark E. Holcomb
Stephen F. Hanlon
Thomas J. Jones
S. Curtis Kiser
David Bruce May, Jr.
Morris H. Miller
Samuel J. Morley
Lawrence E. Sellers, Jr.
Lawrence P. Stevenson
William D. Townsend
Steven J. Uhlfelder

John Murray Gillies
Cheridah V. Renuart
Susan L. Stephens
Susan L. Turner
Karen D. Walker
Nina M. Zollo

For full biographical listings, see the Martindale-Hubbell Law Directory

HOPPING BOYD GREEN & SAMS (AV)

123 South Calhoun Street, P.O. Box 6526, 32314
Telephone: 904-222-7500
Fax: 904-224-8551

MEMBERS OF FIRM

Carlos Alvarez
James S. Alves
Brian H. Bibeau
Kathleen L. Blizzard
Elizabeth C. Bowman
William L. Boyd, IV
Richard S. Brightman
Peter C. Cunningham
Ralph A. DeMeo
Thomas M. DeRose
William H. Green
Wade L. Hopping
Frank E. Matthews
Richard D. Melson

(See Next Column)

MEMBERS OF FIRM (Continued)

David L. Powell
William D. Preston
Carolyn S. Raepple
Gary P. Sams
Robert P. Smith
Cheryl G. Stuart

ASSOCIATES

Kristin M. Conroy
Charles A. Culp, Jr.
Connie C. Durrence
Jonathan S. Fox
James Calvin Goodlett
Gary K. Hunter, Jr.
Dalana W. Johnson
Jonathan T. Johnson
Angela R. Morrison
Gary V. Perko
Karen Peterson
Michael P. Petrovich
Douglas S. Roberts
R. Scott Ruth
Julie Rome Steinmeyer

OF COUNSEL

W. Robert Fokes

Representative Clients: ITT Community Development Corp.; Florida Power & Light Co.; Florida Electric Power Coordinating Group; Hollywood, Inc.; CF Industries, Inc.; Association of Physical Fitness Centers; Sunniland Pipe Line Company, Inc.; Florida Chemical Industries Council; Mobil Oil Co.; Waste Management, Inc.

For full biographical listings, see the Martindale-Hubbell Law Directory

* MACFARLANE AUSLEY FERGUSON & MCMULLEN (AV)

Washington Square Building, 227 South Calhoun Street, P.O. Box 391, 32302
Telephone: 904-224-9115
Telecopier: 904-222-7560
Clearwater, Florida Office: AmSouth Bank Building, Suite 800, 400 Cleveland Street, 34615.
Telephone: 813-441-8966.
Fax: 813-442-8470.
Palm Harbor, Florida Office: Republic Bank Building, Suite 150, 33920 U.S. Highway 19 North, 34684.
Telephone: 813-785-4402.
Fax: 813-785-0735.
Tampa, Florida Office: 2300 First Florida Tower, 111 Madison Street, 33602.
Telephone: 813-273-4200.
Fax: 813-273-4396.

MEMBERS OF FIRM

John K. Aurell
DuBose Ausley
Margaret B. Ausley
James D. Beasley
John R. Beranek
Kevin J. Carroll
C. Graham Carothers
Robert N. Clarke, Jr.
J. Marshall Conrad
Timothy B. Elliott
Stephen C. Emmanuel
John P. Fons
Van P. Geeker
Michael J. Glazer
Carla A. Green
Kenneth R. Hart
David J. Hull
E. Martin McGehee
Deborah Stephens Minnis
Carolyn D. Olive
R. Stan Peeler
Robert A. Pierce
M. Julian Proctor, Jr.
H. Palmer Proctor
Steven P. Seymoe
William M. Smith
James Harold Thompson
Emily S. Waugh
C. Gary Williams
Lee L. Willis

ASSOCIATES

Michael P. Bruyere
J. Jeffry Wahlen
J. Ben Watkins, III

LEGAL SUPPORT PERSONNEL

GOVERNMENTAL LIAISON

Stephen D. Dyal

ADMINISTRATOR

Ronald C. Callen

Representative Clients: BellSouth Telecommunications, Inc.; Capital City Bank Group, Inc.; CSX Transportation, Inc.; Lykes Bros. Inc. and Subsidiary Companies; Morton Plant Hospital; National Medical Enterprises, Inc.; Peoples Gas System, Inc.; Sprint Corp./United Telephone; Tampa Electric Co.; The Procter & Gamble Co.

For full biographical listings, see the Martindale-Hubbell Law Directory

PENNINGTON & HABEN, P.A. (AV)

215 South Monroe - 2nd Floor, 32301
Telephone: 904-222-3533
FAX: 904-222-2126

D. Andrew Byrne
Bram D. E. Canter
Robert Cintron, Jr.
Robert S. Cohen
Charles L. Cooper, Jr.
Bruce Culpepper
Sonya Krouskop Daws
Peter M. Dunbar
Davisson F. Dunlap, Jr.
John H. French, Jr.
Ralph H. Haben, Jr.
R. Bruce McKibben, Jr.
John C. Pelham, Jr.
Carl R. Pennington, Jr.
Ronald R. Richmond
C. Edwin Rude, Jr.
Nancy Black Stewart
Cynthia S. Tunnicliff
William E. Whitney
Ben H. Wilkinson
Cathi C. Wilkinson

(See Next Column)

PENNINGTON & HABEN P.A.—*Continued*

Barbara D. Auger
William W. Blue
Marc W. Dunbar
Dayten P. Hanson
Michael A. Kliner
Charles W. Murphy
Darren Schwartz
John T. Stemberger

OF COUNSEL

R. Stuart Huff (P.A.)
Christopher W. Kanaga (Not admitted in FL)
William VanDercreek (Not admitted in FL)

SPECIAL CONSULTANTS

Karl Adams
Randy Miller
David L. Swafford

Representative Clients: Columbia/HCA Health Care Corp.; BP America; Time-Warner Ax5; NationsBank of Florida, N.A.; First Union National Bank of Florida; Florida Association of Property Appraisers; Associated Industries of Florida; State Of Florida, Department of Insurance; Sprint Cellular Company of Florida; Phillip Morris U.S.A.

For full biographical listings, see the Martindale-Hubbell Law Directory

BENJAMIN K. PHIPPS (AV)

802 First Florida Bank Tower, P.O. Box 1351, 32302
Telephone: 904-222-2717
FAX: 904-681-6651
(Also Member of Adorno & Zeder)

References: Barnett Bank; Sun Trust Bank.

For full biographical listings, see the Martindale-Hubbell Law Directory

RADEY HINKLE THOMAS & MCARTHUR (AV)

Suite 1000 Monroe-Park Tower, 101 North Monroe Street, P.O. Drawer 11307, 32302
Telephone: 904-681-7766
Telecopier: 904-681-0506

John Radey
Robert L. Hinkle
Harry O. Thomas
Elizabeth Waas McArthur
Ricky L. Polston
Jeffrey L. Frehn
Leslie G. Street

Representative Clients: Ringling Bros. Barnum-Bailey Combined Shows; Johnson & Johnson; Electronic Data Systems Corp.; Commonwealth Land Title Insurance Co.; State Mutual Life Assurance Company of America; Columbia/HCA Healthcare Corp.

For full biographical listings, see the Martindale-Hubbell Law Directory

ROGERS, TOWERS, BAILEY, JONES & GAY, P.A. (AV)

106 South Monroe Street, P.O. Box 1872, 32302
Telephone: 904-222-7200
Facsimile: 904-222-7204
Jacksonville, Florida Office: 1301 Riverplace Boulevard, Suite 1500.
Telephone: 904-398-3911.

Paul P. Sanford
Frank L. Jones (Resident)

LEGAL SUPPORT PERSONNEL

Marvin Arrington

For full biographical listings, see the Martindale-Hubbell Law Directory

TAYLOR, BRION, BUKER & GREENE (AV)

Suite 250, 225 South Adams Street, 32302-3189
Telephone: 904-222-7717
Telecopier: 904-222-3494
Miami, Florida Office: Fourteenth Floor, 801 Brickell Avenue.
Telephone: 305-377-6700.
Telecopier: 305-371-4578; 371-4579.
Telex: 153653 Taybri.
Key West, Florida Office: 500 Fleming Street.
Telephone: 305-292-1776.
Telecopier: 305-292-1982.
Fort Lauderdale, Florida Office: Barnett Bank Plaza, 12th Floor, One East Broward Boulevard.
Telephone: 305-522-6700.
Telecopier: 305-522-6711.
Coral Gables, Florida Office: 2801 Ponce De Leon Boulevard, Suite 707.
Telephone: 305-455-7577.
Telecopier: 305-446-9944.

Wilbur E. Brewton (Resident Partner)
W. Douglas Moody, Jr.
I. Ed Pantaleon
Kelly Brewton Plante

For full biographical listings, see the Martindale-Hubbell Law Directory

*TAMPA,** Hillsborough Co.

ALLEN, DELL, FRANK & TRINKLE (AV)

1240 Barnett Plaza, 101 East Kennedy Boulevard, P.O. Box 2111, 33601
Telephone: 813-223-5351
Telecopier: 813-229-6682

MEMBERS OF FIRM

Ralph C. Dell
Roderick K. Shaw, Jr.
Stewart C. Eggert
Gary M. Witters
Joseph G. Heyck, Jr.
Michael N. Brown
Lynn H. Cole
Marian Priest McCulloch
Robert A. Mora
Benjamin G. Morris
A. Christopher Kasten, II
Richard A. Harrison
James S. Eggert
Trae D. Williams

Representative Clients: CSX Transportation; Bank of Tampa; Florida Citrus Processors Assn.; Florida Steel Corp.; The Coca Cola Co., Foods Division; Montgomery Elevator Co.; Seminole Electric Cooperative Inc.; Hillsborough County Hospital Authority; Tampa General Healthcare f/k/a Tampa General Hospital; Tampa Greyhound Track.

For full biographical listings, see the Martindale-Hubbell Law Directory

BUCHANAN INGERSOLL, PROFESSIONAL CORPORATION (AV)

Suite 1030, 101 East Kennedy Boulevard, 33602
Telephone: 813-222-8180
Telecopier: 813-222-8189
Pittsburgh, Pennsylvania Office: 5800 USX Tower, 600 Grant Street.
Telephone: 412-562-8800.
Philadelphia, Pennsylvania Office: Two Logan Square, Twelfth Floor, 18th & Arch Streets.
Telephone: 215-665-8700.
Harrisburg, Pennsylvania Office: Vartan Parc, 30 North Third Street.
Telephone: 717-237-4800.
North Miami Beach, Florida Office: 19495 Biscayne Boulevard.
Telephone: 305-933-5600.
Princeton, New Jersey Office: Buchanan Ingersoll, A Partnership, College Centre, 500 College Road East.
Telephone: 609-452-2666.
Lexington, Kentucky Office: Suite 600, PNC Bank Plaza, 200 West Vine Street.
Telephone: 606-225-5333.

James J. Kennedy III
J. Jerome Mansmann (Not admitted in FL)

SENIOR ATTORNEYS

Mary Ann Lochner

Dale S. Webber

For full biographical listings, see the Martindale-Hubbell Law Directory

BUSH ROSS GARDNER WARREN & RUDY, P.A. (AV)

220 South Franklin Street, 33602
Telephone: 813-224-9255
Telecopier: 813-223-9620

John R. Bush
James O. Davis, III
Samuel B. Dolcimascolo
Patricia Labarta Douglas
J. Stephen Gardner
John N. Giordano
Richard B. Hadlow
Paul L. Huey
Craig A. Minegar
Jeremy P. Ross
John F. Rudy, II
Edward O. Savitz
Randy K. Sterns
Jeffrey W. Warren

Mahlon H. Barlow
Mark A. Cotter
Jeffrey P. Greenberg
Lisa A. Hoppe
David M. Jeffries
Christine M. Polans
Alicia J. Schumacher
Daniel H. Sherman IV
H. Bradley Staggs
Paul D. Watson

Representative Clients: Boyle Engineering Corporation; The Celotex Corporation; CitiCorp Services, Inc.; Design Professional Insurance Companies, Inc.; Dunkin' Donuts Incorporated; HavaTampa, Incorporated; Hillsborough County Medical Association; Smith Barney Shearson; SouthTrust Bank; Technology Research Corp.

For full biographical listings, see the Martindale-Hubbell Law Directory

CARLTON, FIELDS, WARD, EMMANUEL, SMITH & CUTLER, P.A. (AV)

One Harbour Place, 777 South Harbour Island Drive (33602), P.O. Box 3239, 33601
Telephone: 813-223-7000
Telex: Carfield 52-2520
Telecopier: (813) 229-4133
West Palm Beach, Florida Office: Esperanté, 222 Lakeview Avenue, Suite 1400, 33401, P.O. Box 150, 33402.
Telephone: 407-659-7070.

(See Next Column)

CARLTON, FIELDS, WARD, EMMANUEL, SMITH & CUTLER P.A., *Tampa—Continued*

Orlando, Florida Office: Suite 1600, Firstate Tower, 255 South Orange Avenue, 32801, P.O. Box 1171, 32802.
Telephone: 407-849-0300.
Pensacola, Florida Office: Harbourview Building, 4th Floor, 25 West Cedar Street, 32501, P.O. Box 12426, 32582.
Telephone: 904-434-0142.
Tallahassee, Florida Office: Fifth Floor, First Florida Bank Building, 215 South Monroe Street, 32301, P.O. Drawer 190, 32301.
Telephone: 904-224-1585.
St. Petersburg, Florida Office: Barnett Tower, Suite 2300, One Progress Plaza, 33701, P.O. Box 2861, 33731.
Telephone: 813-821-7000.

Giddings E. Mabry (1877-1968)
O. K. Reaves (1877-1970)
Doyle E. Carlton (1887-1972)
Marvin Green (1904-1986)
D. Wallace Fields (1910-1991)
Michel G. Emmanuel (1918-1992)
Wm. Reece Smith, Jr.
Edward I. Cutler
A. Broaddus Livingston
Leonard H. Gilbert
Peter J. Winders
William F. McGowan, Jr.
Thomas D. Aitken
Sylvia H. Walbolt
Joseph B. Cofer
David G. Mulock
Roger D. Schwenke
Robert R. Vawter, Jr.
Laurence E. Kinsolving
Ruth Barnes Himes
Wayne L. Thomas
Thomas F. Icard, Jr.
Robert W. Pass
Michael F. Nuechterlein
George Barford
J. Bert Grandoff
Steven L. Sparkman
Nathaniel L. Doliner
John P. McAdams
Gwynne A. Young
Thomas A. Snow
Donald E. Hemke
D. Hywel Leonard
Kenneth E. Graves
Chris S. Coutroulis
John W. Boult
Paul C. Davis
Mark A. Brown
Robert A. Soriano
Robert L. Ciotti
Edward W. Gerecke
Robert M. Quinn
Gary L. Sasso
Donald R. Schmidt
Wallace B. Anderson, Jr.
David P. Burke
Edgel C. Lester, Jr.
Nancy J. Faggianelli
Luis Prats
Richard B. Campbell
James R. Wiley
Paula McDonald Rhodes
J. Kevin Carey
Laurel E. Lockett
Michael J. Nolan, II
Richard A. Denmon
David B. Williams
Jeanette M. Flores
Marylin E. Culp
Spencer M. Punnett, II
Michael J. Virgadamo

OF COUNSEL
James W. Ault

Stephen D. Marlowe
Lavinia James Vaughn
Sandra G. Porter
George J. Meyer
W. Patrick Ayers
Morris C. Massey
S. Jane Mitchell
E. Kelly Bittick, Jr.
Mary Stenson Scriven
John J. Lamoureux
Theo J. Karaphillis
Paul J. Ullom
Luis Alvarez, Jr.
Cathleen G. Bell
Suzanne M. Elinger
Linda L. Fleming
Kathleen S. McLeroy
Wm. Cary Wright
Amy Goldin Schneirov
James B. Baldinger
Robert S. Freedman
David Matthew Allen
Susan L. Landy
Ronald J. Tenpas
Joseph V. McNabb
Stephanie J. Young
Edmund S. Whitson, III
Cecilia M. Jorajuria
Victor D. Berg
Stephen D. Hopkins
Thomas P. Barber
Andrew Clifford Greenberg
Terrill F. Jordan
Thaxter A. Cooper
Lorien Smith Johnson
Kaiwen Tseng
Aimee Kemker Elson
Laurie A. Mack

For full biographical listings, see the Martindale-Hubbell Law Directory

CUNNINGHAM LAW GROUP, P.A. (AV)

100 Ashley Drive, South, Suite 100, 33602
Telephone: 813-228-0505
Telefax: 813-229-7982

Anthony W. Cunningham
Donald G. Greiwe
James D. Clark

For full biographical listings, see the Martindale-Hubbell Law Directory

FOLEY & LARDNER (AV)

Suite 2700, One Hundred N. Tampa Street, P.O. Box 3391, 33601-3391
Telephone: 813-229-2300;
Pinellas County: 813-442-3296
Facsimile: 813-221-4210
Milwaukee, Wisconsin Office: Firstar Center, 777 East Wisconsin Avenue.
Telephone: 414-271-2400.
Telex: 26-819 (Foley Lard Mil).
Facsimile: 414-297-4900.

(See Next Column)

Madison, Wisconsin Office: Firstar Plaza, One South Pinckney Street, P.O. Box 1497.
Telephone: 608-257-5035.
Telex: 262051 (F L Madison).
Facsimile: 608-258-4258.
Chicago, Illinois Office: Suite 3300, One IBM Plaza, 330 N. Wabash Avenue.
Telephone: 312-755-1900.
Facsimile: 312-755-1925.
Washington, D.C. Office: Washington Harbour, Suite 500, 3000 K Street, N.W.
Telephone: 202-672-5300.
Telex: 904136 (Foley Lard Wsh).
Facsimile: 202-672-5399.
Annapolis, Maryland Office: Suite 102, 175 Admiral Cochrane Drive.
Telephone: 301-266-8077.
Telex: 899149 (Oldtownpat).
Facsimile: 301-266-8664.
Jacksonville, Florida Office: The Greenleaf Building, 200 Laura Street. P.O. Box 240.
Telephone: 904-359-2000.
Facsimile: 904-359-8700.
Orlando, Florida Office: Suite 1800, 111 North Orange Avenue, P.O. Box 2193.
Telephone: 407-423-7656.
Telex: 441781 (HQ ORL).
Facsimile: 407-648-1743.
Tallahassee, Florida Office: Suite 450, 215 South Monroe Street, P.O. Box 508.
Telephone: 904-222-6100.
Facsimile: 904-224-0496.
West Palm Beach, Florida Office: Suite 200, Phillips Point East Tower, 777 South Flagler Drive.
Telephone: 407-655-5050.
Facsimile: 407-655-6925.

PARTNERS

Russell T. Alba
Kenneth A. Beytin
Daniel N. Burton
Stephen A. Crane
Lewis H. Hill, III
James M. Landis
Thomas E. Lange
Sybil Meloy
David M. Rieth
David L. Robbins
R. Andrew Rock
Stanley A. Tarkow
Martin A. Traber (Not admitted in FL)
Mark J. Wolfson

RETIRED PARTNERS
William J. Kiernan, Jr.

RESIDENT ASSOCIATES

Larry J. Davis, Jr.
Vitauts M. Gulbis
Cindy L. LoCicero
Randall W. Lord
Kenneth J. Meister
Donald A. Mihokovich
Terri Gillis Tucker
Anne J. Williams

For full biographical listings, see the Martindale-Hubbell Law Directory

GIBBONS, SMITH, COHN & ARNETT, A PROFESSIONAL ASSOCIATION (AV)

3321 Henderson Boulevard, P.O. Box 2177, 33601
Telephone: 813-877-9222
FAX: 813-877-9290

Arthur S. Gibbons (1908-1986)
Gary A. Gibbons
Kirk M. Gibbons
Armin H. Smith, Jr.
Roy W. Cohn
Patricia Arnett
John R. Bello, Jr.
R. Wade Wetherington
Gregory E. Mierzwinski
Rod B. Neuman
Elizabeth A. Pereira
Shawn E. Harrison
Theodore Jay Hamilton

OF COUNSEL

Glenn E. Gerhardt
John A. Guyton, Jr.

For full biographical listings, see the Martindale-Hubbell Law Directory

GLENN RASMUSSEN & FOGARTY (AV)

1300 First Union Center, 100 South Ashley Drive, P.O. Box 3333, 33601-3333
Telephone: 813-229-3333
Fax: 813-229-5946

Rod Anderson
David E. Arroyo
Robert W. Bivins
Sharon Docherty Danco
Richard E. Fee
David S. Felman
Michael A. Fogarty
Robert B. Glenn
Donald S. Hart, Jr.
Michael S. Hooker
Erin C. Keleher
Bradford D. Kimbro
Guy P. McConnell
Robert C. Rasmussen
Edwin G. Rice
Steven W. Vazquez

Reference: First Union National Bank of Florida.

For full biographical listings, see the Martindale-Hubbell Law Directory

Tampa—Continued

HOLLAND & KNIGHT (AV)

A Partnership including Professional Corporations
400 North Ashley, Suite 2300, 33602
Telephone: 813-227-8500
Fax: 813-229-0134
Mailing Address: P.O. Box 1288, 33601-1288
Atlanta, Georgia Office: 1201 W. Peachtree Street, N.W., Suite 3100.
Telephone: 404-817-8500.
Fax: 404-881-0470.
Fort Lauderdale, Florida Office: One East Broward Boulevard, Suite 1300.
Telephone: 305-525-1000.
Fax: 305-463-2030.
Jacksonville, Florida Office: 50 N. Laura Street, Suite 3900.
Telephone: 904-353-2000.
Fax: 904-358-1872.
Lakeland, Florida Office: 92 Lake Wire Drive.
Telephone: 813-682-1161.
Fax: 813-688-1186.
Miami, Florida Office: 701 Brickell Avenue, 30th Floor.
Telephone: 305-374-8500.
Fax: 305-787-7799.
Orlando, Florida Office: 200 S. Orange Avenue, Suite 2600.
Telephone: 407-425-8500.
Fax: 407-244-5288.
St. Petersburg, Florida Office: 360 Central Avenue.
Telephone: 813-896-7171.
Fax: 813-822-8048.
Tallahassee, Florida Office: 315 Calhoun Street, Suite 600.
Telephone: 904-224-7000.
Fax: 904-224-8832.
West Palm Beach, Florida Office: 625 N. Flagler Drive, Suite 700.
Telephone: 407-833-2000.
Fax: 407-650-8399.
Washington, D.C. Office: 2100 Pennsylvania Avenue, N.W.
Telephone: 202-955-5550.
Fax: 202-955-5564.
Special Counsel: Shaw, Licitra, Parente, Esernio & Schwartz, P.C., 1010 Franklin Avenue, Garden City, N.Y., 11530, 300 East 42nd Street, New York, N.Y., 10017.
Detroit, Michigan Office: 2290 First National Building.
Telephone: 313-256-7800.
Lansing, Michigan Office: 222 North Washington Square, Suite 400.
Telephone: 517-484-8282.
Houston, Texas Office: 3100 First Interstate Bank Plaza, 1000 Louisiana.
Telephone: 713-650-2600.
Los Angeles, California Office: Watt Plaza, Suite 2200, 1875 Century Park East.
Telephone: 310-789-3800.
Fax: 310-789-3814.

TAMPA MEMBERS AND ASSOCIATES

Robert J. Asti
Chester E. Bacheller
Anderson L. Baldy III
Bernard A. Barton, Jr.
Elizabeth Bevington
Richard M. Blau
Russell S. Bogue, III
David S. Bralow
Karl J. Brandes
Steven L. Brannock
Robert N. Butler
Warren M. Cason
William G. Christopher
Richard E. Davis
William B. deMeza, Jr.
Richard D. Eckhard
Robert R. Feagin, III
John Germany
Frederick J. Grady
Robert J. Grammig
Mark E. Grantham
G. Calvin Hayes
J. Fraser Himes
George B. Howell, III
Michael L. Jamieson
John Arthur Jones
Ellen Neil Kalmbacher
D. Burke Kibler, III
Edward F. Koren
Steven M. Larimore
Jack A. Levine
Byrne Litschgi
Carol J. LoCicero
Bill McBride (Managing Partner)
Jack S. Newsome
Paul E. Parrish
Thomas J. Patka
Stephen J. Powell
Bruce H. Roberson
Frederick M. Rothenberg
Frederick S. Schrils
James H. Shimberg, Jr.
David R. Singleton
Patrick W. Skelton
Lora J. Smeltzly
Brian C. Sparks
Charles L. Stutts
Gregg Darrow Thomas
Robert H. Waltuch
Julia Sullivan Waters
Douglas A. Wright
Barbara M. Yadley

A. Brian Albritton
R. Gregory Bailey (Not admitted in FL)
Stacy D. Blank
Michael L. Chapman
Michael S. Goetz
Lance S. Hamilton
Elizabeth Belsom Johnson
Earl M. Johnson, Jr.
Monta Michelle King
Jeffrey A. Maine
Kelly A. Martin
Susan Tillotson Mills
James L. Olivier
John E. Phillips
Samuel P. Queirolo
Audrey B. Rauchway
Andrew L. Rosenkranz
Theodore Washington Small, Jr.
Marcio W. Valladares

MEMBERS

Robert W. Boos (P.A.)
Michael G. Cooke (P.A.)
Harry Christopher Goplerud (P.A.)
Gregory G. Jones (P.A.)
Maria Maistrellis (P.A.)
Barbara R. Pankau (P.A.)
James B. Soble (P.A.)
Brad M. Tomtishen (P.A.)

ASSOCIATES

Kevin M. Gilhool
Dennis Hernandez
Susan M. Salvatore

Representative Clients: Sun Bank of Tampa Bay; The Sembler Company; Raymond James & Assoc.; Whirlpool Corporation; Wilma South Corp.
Approved Attorneys for: Commonwealth Land Title Insurance Co.; Chicago Title Insurance Co.

For full biographical listings, see the Martindale-Hubbell Law Directory

HONIGMAN MILLER SCHWARTZ AND COHN (AV)

A Partnership including Professional Corporations
2700 Landmark Centre, 401 E. Jackson Street, 33602
Telephone: 813-221-6600
Telecopier: 813-223-4410
West Palm Beach, Florida Office: Suite 800 Esperante Building, 222 Lakeview Avenue.
Telephone: 407-838-4500.
Orlando, Florida Office: 390 North Orange Avenue, Suite 1300.
Telephone: 407-648-0300.

(See Next Column)

JOHNSON, BLAKELY, POPE, BOKOR, RUPPEL & BURNS, P.A. (AV)

100 North Tampa Street Suite 1800, P.O. Box 1100, 33601
Telephone: 813-225-2500
Telecopier: 813-223-7118
Clearwater, Florida Office: 911 Chestnut Street, P.O. Box 1368.
Telephone: 813-461-1818.
Telecopier: 813-441-8617.

John T. Blakely
Bruce H. Bokor
Guy M. Burns
Rebecca A. Henson
Scott C. Ilgenfritz
Frank R. Jakes
Timothy A. Johnson, Jr.
John R. Lawson, Jr.
F. Wallace Pope, Jr.
Dennis G. Ruppel
Philip M. Shasteen
Charles M. Tatelbaum

Bruce W. Barnes
Alexis Pauline Brooks (Resident at Tampa)
Lisa B. Dodge
James W. Humann
Michael C. Markham
Anthony P. Zinge

For full biographical listings, see the Martindale-Hubbell Law Directory

LAU, LANE, PIEPER, CONLEY & MCCREADIE, P.A. (AV)

Suite 1700, 100 South Ashley, P.O. Box 838, 33601
Telephone: 813-229-2121
Telecopier: 813-228-7710
Port Canaveral, Florida Office: 405 Atlantis Road, Suite B.
Telephone: 407-799-3400.
Telecopier: 813-228-7710.

James V. Lau
Charles C. Lane
Nathaniel G. W. Pieper
Mary A. Lau
Timothy C. Conley
David W. McCreadie
Annette Horan
Earl R. McMillin (Resident, Port Canaveral Office)
David F. Pope
Daintry E. Cleary

For full biographical listings, see the Martindale-Hubbell Law Directory

MACFARLANE AUSLEY FERGUSON & MCMULLEN (AV)

2300 First Florida Tower, 111 Madison Street, P.O. Box 1531, 33601
Telephone: 813-273-4200
FAX: 813-273-4396
Clearwater, Florida Office: AmSouth Bank, Suite 800, 400 Cleveland Street, 34615.
Telephone: 813-441-8966.
Fax: 813-442-8470.
Palm Harbor, Florida Office: Republic Bank Building, Suite 150, 33920 U.S. Highway 19 North, 34684.
Telephone: 813-785-4402.
Fax: 813-785-0735.
Tallahassee, Florida Office: Washington Square Building, 227 South Calhoun Street, 32301.
Telephone: 904-224-9115.
Fax: 904-222-7560.

MEMBERS OF FIRM

Howard P. Macfarlane (1888-1967)
Chester H. Ferguson (1908-1983)
John C. Bierley
David M. Boggs
Chad W. Browne
Robert W. Clark
Robert G. Cochran
Cody F. Davis
James Craig Delesie, Sr.
E. John Dinkel, III
Brian D. Forbes
Matthew J. Foster
Susan W. Fox
James W. Goodwin, II

(See Next Column)

MACFARLANE AUSLEY FERGUSON & MCMULLEN, *Tampa—Continued*

MEMBERS OF FIRM (Continued)

David J. Kadyk
D. James Kadyk
David C. G. Kerr
Carole Taylor Kirkwood
Edward J. Kohrs
Andrew K. Macfarlane
Ellen M. Macfarlane
Ted R. Manry, III
Carter B. McCain
David M. Mechanik
Thomas B. Mimms, Jr.
John H. Mueller
Vincent L. Nuccio, Jr.
Lawrence J. O'Neil
Stephen L. Pankau
Charles W. Pittman
Stephen H. Reynolds
Gordon J. Schiff
Stephen H. Sears
T. Terrell Sessums
Nathan B. Simpson
H. Vance Smith
William B. Taylor, IV
Stella Ferguson Thayer
Claude H. Tison, Jr.
Ansley Watson, Jr.

ASSOCIATES

David W. Adams
Denise L. Andersen
Andrew Melton Brown
C. Graham Carothers, Jr.
Edward M. Copeland, IV
Matthew R. Costa
Scott C. Davis
W. Penn Dawson, III
J. Craig Delesie, Jr.
Sandra L. Fanning
Carolyn J. House
Julie Ann Koehne
Patrick T. Lennon
Dan D. McClain
Mark E. McLaughlin
Phillip L. Nelson
David M. Nicholson
Harold D. Oehler
Dale J. Rickert
Bruce M. Rodgers
Staci A. Russ

OF COUNSEL

Janet E. Goldberg

Representative Clients: BellSouth Telecommunications, Inc.; Capital City Bank Group, Inc.; CSX Transportation, Inc.; Lykes Bros. Inc. and Subsidiary Companies; Morton Plant Hospital; National Medical Enterprises, Inc.; Peoples Gas System, Inc.; Sprint Corp./United Telephone; Tampa Electric Co.; The Procter & Gamble Co.

For full biographical listings, see the Martindale-Hubbell Law Directory

MELENDI, GIBBONS & GARCIA, A PROFESSIONAL ASSOCIATION (AV)

408 East Madison Street, 33602
Telephone: 813-228-0853
FAX: 813-229-0220

Joseph E. Melendi
Mark H. Gibbons
Reginald R. Garcia

Reference: Sun Bank of Tampa Bay.

For full biographical listings, see the Martindale-Hubbell Law Directory

SHACKLEFORD, FARRIOR, STALLINGS & EVANS, PROFESSIONAL ASSOCIATION (AV)

Suite 1400, 501 East Kennedy Boulevard, P.O. Box 3324, 33601
Telephone: 813-273-5000
Cable Address: Intrepid, Tampa
Fax: 813-273-5145

R. W. Shackleford (1890-1964)
T. M. Shackleford, Jr. (1884-1973)
J. Rex Farrior (1896-1993)
J. Rex Farrior, Jr.
Thomas C. MacDonald, Jr.
Thomas P. Evans
David G. Hanlon
Warren Frazier
John I. Van Voris
Lucius M. Dyal, Jr.
Stephen F. Myers
William A. Gillen, Jr.
Donald A. Gifford
Joseph W. Clark
Richard M. Zabak
Peter J. Kelly
James B. Murphy, Jr.
Sharyn B. Zuch
David C. Banker
Joseph F. Kinman, Jr.
William R. Lane, Jr.
Ricardo A. Fernandez
Daniel F. Molony
Ronald E. Bush
Donald H. Whittemore
Dennis E. Manelli
Debra Ann Schrils
Gregory P. Hansel
Geoffrey Todd Hodges
John A. Anthony

Donna S. Koch
H. Hamilton Rice, III
Mildred D. Beam-Rucker
Jonathan S. Gilbert

OF COUNSEL

Norman Stallings

Representative Clients: Jack Eckerd Corp.; Barnett Bank, N.A.; Shell Oil Corp.; Publix Supermarkets, Inc.; University of Florida; Sun City Center Corp.; Walter Ind.; John Hancock Mutual Life Insurance Co.; Aetna Casualty & Surety Company.

For full biographical listings, see the Martindale-Hubbell Law Directory

TRENAM, KEMKER, SCHARF, BARKIN, FRYE, O'NEILL & MULLIS, PROFESSIONAL ASSOCIATION (AV)

2700 Barnett Plaza, 101 East Kennedy Boulevard, P.O. Box 1102, 33602
Telephone: 813-223-7474
FAX: 813-229-6553
Telex: 6502251910 MCI
ABA/net 1574
St. Petersburg, Florida Office: One Progress Plaza, Suite 2000.
Telephone: 813-898-7474.
Fax: 813-821-0407.

John J. Trenam (1912-1978)
Harry Kemker (1930-1984)
Marvin E. Barkin
William C. Frye
Albert C. O'Neill, Jr.
Harold W. Mullis, Jr.
William Knight Zewadski
Richard M. Leisner
Keith E. Rounsaville
Richard H. Sollner
Robert H. Buesing
William G. Scott, III
Stanley H. Eleff
Gary I. Teblum
Nelson D. Blank
John Sebastian Vento
Don B. Weinbren
Mary H. Quinlan
David R. Brittain
George E. Nader
Edward C. LaRose
Roberta A. Colton
Roberta Casper Watson
J. Alan Asendorf
John Daniel Goldsmith
Karen E. Lewis
R. Dennis Tweed
John E. Johnson
D. Michael O'Leary
Richard M. Hanchett
Lansing C. Scriven

Marie Tomassi
Elizabeth Pascale Francis
Wendolyn S. Busch
Peter R. Wallace (St. Petersburg Office)
Stephen M. Crawford
J. Cary Ross, Jr.
H. Wayne Porter
Scott E. Rogers
Michael K. Green
Dinita L. James
Robert G. Stern
Todd W. Fennell
J. Eric Taylor
Nelson T. Castellano
Michael A. Peters
William H. Harrell, Jr.
Charles M. Harris, Jr.
Kip P. Roth (Not admitted in FL)
Jeffrey A. Freedman
Laura E. Prather

OF COUNSEL

Leslie D. Scharf
James V. Carideo

For full biographical listings, see the Martindale-Hubbell Law Directory

ZINOBER & MCCREA, P.A. (AV)

Enterprise Plaza, 201 East Kennedy Boulevard Suite 1750, P.O. Box 1378, 33602
Telephone: 813-224-9004
Telecopier: 813-223-4881
Also Available for Consultation at: Summit Building, 13575 58th Street, N., Suite 265, Clearwater, 34620.
Telephone: 813-224-9004.

Peter W. Zinober
Richard C. McCrea, Jr.

Edwin J. Turanchik
Frank E. Brown
D. Michael Pointer, II
Charles A. Powell, IV
Jacqueline Ley Brown
Nancy A. Roslow
Cynthia L. May
Scott T. Silverman

LEGAL SUPPORT PERSONNEL

Debra A. Douglas (Administrator)

For full biographical listings, see the Martindale-Hubbell Law Directory

*TAVARES,** Lake Co.

CAUTHEN AND OLDHAM, P.A. (AV)

131 West Main Street, 32778
Telephone: 904-343-3455
Fax: 904-343-8801

Gordon G. Oldham, Jr.
David E. Cauthen
William A. Milton, III
Timothy S. Keough

References: Florida National Bank; First Federal Savings & Loan Association of Lake County.

For full biographical listings, see the Martindale-Hubbell Law Directory

*TITUSVILLE,** Brevard Co.

HOLLAND, STARLING, SEVERS, STADLER & FRIEDLAND, P.A. (AV)

509 Palm Avenue, P.O. Box 669, 32781-0669
Telephone: 407-267-1711; 407-632-2129
Fax: 407-632-2192

S. Lindsey Holland, Jr. (1921-1989)
John M. Starling
Dwight W. Severs
Richard E. Stadler
Kenneth Friedland
John M. Harris

(See Next Column)

HOLLAND, STARLING, SEVERS, STADLER & FRIEDLAND P.A.—*Continued*

Representative Clients: City of Titusville; Brevard County Clerk of Court; The Goldfield Corp.; Stottler Stagg & Associates; Sun Bank, N.A.; Town of Melbourne Village, AmSouth Bank.
Approved Attorneys for: Attorneys' Title Insurance Fund; Commonwealth Land Title Insurance Co.

For full biographical listings, see the Martindale-Hubbell Law Directory

VERO BEACH,* Indian River Co.

COLLINS, BROWN & CALDWELL, CHARTERED (AV)

756 Beachland Boulevard, P.O. Box 3686, 32964
Telephone: 407-231-4343
FAX: 407-234-5213

George G. Collins, Jr.
Calvin B. Brown
William W. Caldwell
Bruce D. Barkett
Bradley W. Rossway
Michael J. Garavaglia
John E. Moore, III

Reference: First Union Bank of Indian River County, Vero Beach, Florida.

For full biographical listings, see the Martindale-Hubbell Law Directory

GOULD, COOKSEY, FENNELL, BARKETT, O'NEILL & MARINE, PROFESSIONAL ASSOCIATION (AV)

979 Beachland Boulevard, 32963
Telephone: 407-231-1100
Fax: 407-231-2020

John R. Gould (1921-1988)
Byron T. Cooksey
Darrell Fennell
Lawrence A. Barkett
Eugene J. O'Neill
Christopher H. Marine

David M. Carter

Counsel for: Barnett Bank of Indian River County; Indian River National Bank; Citrus Bank, N.A..
Approved Attorneys for: Attorneys' Title Insurance Fund; Commonwealth Land Title Insurance Company; Lawyers Title Insurance Corp.; Federal Land Bank of Columbia.
Local Counsel for: Los Angeles Dodgers, Inc.

For full biographical listings, see the Martindale-Hubbell Law Directory

MOSS, HENDERSON, VAN GAASBECK, BLANTON & KOVAL, P.A. (AV)

817 Beachland Boulevard, P.O. Box 3406, 32964-3406
Telephone: 407-231-1900
Fax: 407-231-4387

George H. Moss, II
Steve L. Henderson
Everett J. Van Gaasbeck
Robin A. Blanton
Thomas A. Koval
Clinton W. Lanier
Kevin S. Doty

Donald E. Feuerbach
Fred L. Kretschmer, Jr.
Margaret Sue Lyon
Lisa D. Harpring
Kathleen W. Stratton
Lewis W. Murphy, Jr.
E. Clayton Yates
Judith Goodman Hill

OF COUNSEL

Charles E. Garris
Ford J. Fegert

Representative Clients: Aetna Life & Casualty; Alcoa Florida, Inc.; Florida Power & Light Co.; Insurance Company of North America; Liberty Mutual Insurance Co.; Sears, Roebuck & Co.; Sugar Cane Growers Cooperative of Florida; Norfolk Southern Corporation/North American Van Lines, Inc.

For full biographical listings, see the Martindale-Hubbell Law Directory

O'HAIRE, QUINN, CANDLER & O'HAIRE (AV)

3111 Cardinal Drive, P.O. Box 4375, 32964
Telephone: 407-231-6900
FAX: 407-231-9729

MEMBERS OF FIRM

Michael O'Haire
Jerome D. Quinn
Richard Boyer Candler
Sean M. O'Haire

References: Barnett Bank of Indian River County; The Beach Bank of Vero Beach.

For full biographical listings, see the Martindale-Hubbell Law Directory

SMITH & SMITH (AV)

Citrus Financial Center, Suite 301, 1717 Indian River Boulevard, 32960
Telephone: 407-567-4351
FAX: 407-567-4298

MEMBERS OF FIRM

Sherman N. Smith, Jr.
Sherman N. Smith, III

References: Barnett Bank of Indian River County; The Beach Bank of Vero Beach.

(See Next Column)

For full biographical listings, see the Martindale-Hubbell Law Directory

WEST PALM BEACH,* Palm Beach Co.

BEVERLY & TITTLE, P.A. (AV)

823 North Olive Avenue, 33401
Telephone: 407-655-6022
Fax: 407-655-6044

Don Beverly
James D. Tittle, Jr.

Reference: Barnett Bank, West Palm Beach, Florida.

For full biographical listings, see the Martindale-Hubbell Law Directory

BOBO, SPICER, CIOTOLI, FULFORD, BOCCHINO, DEBEVOISE & LE CLAINCHE, P.A. (AV)

Esperante, Sixth Floor, 222 Lakeview Avenue, 33401
Telephone: 407-684-6600
Fax: 407-684-3828
Orlando, Florida Office: Landmark Center One, Suite 510, 315 East Robinson Street, 32801-1949.
Telephone: 407-849-1060.
Fax: 407-843-4751.

A. Russell Bobo
David W. Spicer
Eugene L. Ciotoli
Jeffrey C. Fulford
John W. Bocchino (Resident, Orlando Office)
D. Andrew DeBevoise (Resident, Orlando Office)
Stephan A. Le Clainche

Christopher C. Curry (Resident, Orlando Office)
Patti A. Haber
Paul A. Nugent
Joseph A. Osborne
Richard B. Schwamm
Michael S. Smith
Paul M. Adams
Robert A. Zimmerman
Neil A. Deleon
Sharon A. Chapman (Resident, Orlando Office)
J. Clancey Bounds (Resident, Orlando Office)
Robert R. Saunders (Resident, Orlando Office)
Keith A. Scott (Resident, Orlando Office)
Sophia B. Ehringer (Resident, Orlando Office)
Tyler S. McClay (Resident, Orlando Office)
Michael D. Burt
Dominic John "Jack" Scalera, III
Casey D. Shomo
Armando T. Lauritano

For full biographical listings, see the Martindale-Hubbell Law Directory

CARLTON, FIELDS, WARD, EMMANUEL, SMITH & CUTLER, P.A. (AV)

Esperanté, 222 Lakeview Avenue, Suite 1400 (33401), P.O. Box 150, 33402
Telephone: 407-659-7070
Fax: 407-659-7368
Tampa,Florida Office: One Harbour Place, 777 South Harbour Island Drive, 33602. P.O. Box 3239, 33601.
Telephone: 813-223-7000.
Orlando, Florida Office: Suite 1600, Firstate Tower, 255 South Orange Avenue, 32801. P.O. Box 1171, 32802.
Telephone: 407-849-0300.
Pensacola, Florida Office: Harbourview Building, 4th Floor, 25 West Cedar Street, 32501. P.O. Box 12426, 32582.
Telephone: 904-434-0142.
Tallahassee, Florida Office: Fifth Floor, First Florida Bank Building, 215 South Monroe Street, 32301. P.O. Drawer 190, 32302.
Telephone: 904-224-1585.
St. Petersburg, Florida Office: Barnett Tower, Suite 2300, One Progress Plaza, 33701. P.O. Box 2861, 33731.
Telephone: 813-821-7000.

Gary M. Brandenburg
Thomas A. Hanson
Robert N. Gilbert
Michael S. Tammaro
Jacob D. Varn
David S. Dee
Stephen J. Krigbaum
Eric C. Christu
John R. Hart
Lynda J. Harris
Joseph Ianno, Jr.

OF COUNSEL

Thomas J. Schwartz

Patrick Joseph Rooney
Rebecca F. Duke
Diana D. Grana
Mimi McAndrews
Donald Tobyn De Young

For full biographical listings, see the Martindale-Hubbell Law Directory

EASLEY & WILLITS, P.A. (AV)

Suite 800 Forum III, 1655 Palm Beach Lakes Boulevard, 33401
Telephone: 407-684-7300
Facsimile: 407-684-8711

(See Next Column)

EASLEY & WILLITS P.A., *West Palm Beach—Continued*

H. Michael Easley
Richard H. Willits
M. Christopher Edwards

For full biographical listings, see the Martindale-Hubbell Law Directory

FARISH, FARISH & ROMANI (AV)

316 Banyan Boulevard, P.O. Box 4118, 33402
Telephone: 407-659-3500
Fax: 407-655-3158

MEMBERS OF FIRM

Joseph D. Farish (1892-1977)
Joseph D. Farish, Jr.
Robert V. Romani

ASSOCIATES

S. Emory Rogers
Peter Bassaline
Keith R. Taylor

LEGAL SUPPORT PERSONNEL

Ken P. Beelner

References: 1st Union Bank; Clewiston National Bank; Barnett Bank of Palm Beach County.

For full biographical listings, see the Martindale-Hubbell Law Directory

FOLEY & LARDNER (AV)

Suite 200, Phillips Point East Tower, 777 South Flagler Drive, 33401-6163
Telephone: 407-655-5050
Facsimile: 407-655-6925
Milwaukee, Wisconsin Office: Firstar Center, 777 East Wisconsin Avenue.
Telephone: 414-271-2400.
Telex: 26-819 (Foley Lard Mil).
Facsimile: 414-297-4900.
Madison, Wisconsin Office: Firstar Plaza, One South Pinckney Street, P.O. Box 1497.
Telephone: 608-257-5035.
Telex: 262051 (F L Madison).
Facsimile: 608-258-4258.
Chicago, Illinois Office: Suite 3300, One IBM Plaza, 330 N. Wabash Avenue.
Telephone: 312-755-1900.
Facsimile: 312-755-1925.
Washington, D.C. Office: Washington Harbour, Suite 500, 3000 K Street, N.W.,
Telephone: 202-672-5300.
Telex: 904136 (Foley Lard Wsh).
Facsimile: 202-672-5399.
Annapolis, Maryland Office: Suite 102, 175 Admiral Cochrane Drive.
Telephone: 301-266-8077.
Telex: 899149 (Oldtownpat).
Facsimile: 301-266-8664.
Jacksonville, Florida Office: The Greenleaf Building, 200 Laura Street, P.O. Box 240.
Telephone: 904-359-2000.
Facsimile: 904-359-8700.
Orlando, Florida Office: Suite 1800, 111 North Orange Avenue, P.O. Box 2193.
Telephone: 407-423-7656.
Telex: 441781 (HQ ORL).
Facsimile: 407-648-1743.
Tallahassee, Florida Office: Suite 450, 215 South Monroe Street, P.O. Box 508.
Telephone: 904-222-6100.
Facsimile: 904-224-0496.
Tampa, Florida Office: Suite 2700, One Hundred N. Tampa Street, P.O. Box 3391.
Telephones: 813-229-2300; Pinellas County: 813-442-3296.
Facsimile: 813-221-4210.

PARTNERS

Harrison K. Chauncey Jr.
James A. Farrell
Robert P. Marschall
Sybil Meloy
Thomas F. Munro, II
Andrew A. Ostrow
Jack A. Porter
Amy S. Rubin
William P. Sklar

RESIDENT ASSOCIATES

John P. Cole
Marilyn A. Moore
Todd B. Pfister
Susan M. Seigle

For full biographical listings, see the Martindale-Hubbell Law Directory

HOLLAND & KNIGHT (AV)

A Partnership including Professional Corporations
625 N. Flagler Drive Suite 700, 33401
Telephone: 407-833-2000
Fax: 407-650-8399
Mailing Address: P.O. Box 3208, 33402
Fort Lauderdale, Florida Office: One East Broward Boulevard, Suite 1300.
Telephone: 305-525-1000.
Fax: 305-463-2030.

(See Next Column)

Jacksonville, Florida Office: 50 N. Laura Street, Suite 3900.
Telephone: 904-353-2000.
Fax: 904-358-1872.
Lakeland, Florida Office: 92 Lake Wire Drive.
Telephone: 813-682-1161.
Fax: 813-688-1186.
Miami, Florida Office: 701 Brickell Avenue, 30th Floor.
Telephone: 305-374-8500.
Fax: 305-787-7799.
Orlando, Florida Office: 200 S. Orange Avenue, Suite 2600.
Telephone: 407-425-8500.
Fax: 407-244-5288.
St. Petersburg, Florida Office: 360 Central Avenue.
Telephone: 813-896-7171.
Fax: 813-822-8048.
Tallahassee, Florida Office: 315 Calhoun Street, Suite 600.
Telephone: 904-224-7000.
Fax: 904-224-8832.
Washington, D.C. Office: 2100 Pennsylvania Avenue, N.W.
Telephone: 202-955-3000.
Fax: 202-955-5564.
Atlanta, Georgia Office: 1201 West Peachtree Street, N.W., Suite 3100.
Telephone: 404-817-8500.
Fax: 404-881-0470.
Special Counsel: Shaw, Licitra, Parente, Esernio & Schwartz, P.C., 1010 Franklin Avenue, Garden City, N.Y., 11530, 300 East 42nd Street, New York, N.Y., 10017.

MEMBERS AND ASSOCIATES

Martin J. Alexander
W. Reeder Glass
Michael S. Greene
Hank Jackson
Scott B. Newman
Whilden S. Parker
David L. Perry, Jr.

Eunice Tall Baros
William P. Heller
Robert Rivas

OF COUNSEL

Richard S. Weinstein

For full biographical listings, see the Martindale-Hubbell Law Directory

HONIGMAN MILLER SCHWARTZ AND COHN (AV)

A Partnership including Professional Corporations
Suite 800 Esperante Building, 222 Lakeview Avenue, 33401-6112
Telephone: 407-838-4500
Telecopier: 407-832-3036; 832-2645
Tampa, Florida Office: 2700 Landmark Centre, 401 E. Jackson Street.
Telephone: 813-221-6600.
Orlando, Florida Office: 390 North Orange Avenue, Suite 1300.
Telephone: 407-648-0300.
Detroit, Michigan Office: 2290 First National Building.
Telephone: 313-256-7800.
Lansing, Michigan Office: 222 North Washington Square, Suite 400.
Telephone: 517-484-8282.
Houston, Texas: 3100 First Interstate Bank Plaza, 1000 Louisiana.
Telephone: 713-650-2600.
Los Angeles, California Office: Watt Plaza, Suite 2200, 1875 Century Park East.
Telephone: 310-789-3800.
Fax: 310-789-3814.

MEMBERS

Carl Angeloff (P.A.)
Carla L. Brown
Morris C. Brown (P.A.)
J.A. Jurgens (P.A.)
Mark Nussbaum (P.A.)
Steven R. Parson (P.A.)
Neil W. Platock
Donald H. Reed, Jr.
Marvin S. Rosen (P.A.)
Steven L. Schwarzberg (P.A.)
Lloyd R. Schwed
E. Lee Worsham (P.A.)

ASSOCIATES

Jose O. Diaz
Gina Greeson Hyland

OF COUNSEL

Delmer C. Gowing, III, (P.A.)

General Counsel for: Florida Cable Television Association, Inc.; Forbes-Cohen Properties (The Garden Mall); Multivest Real Estate, Inc.; PHM Corp. (Pulte Home Corporation).
Representative Clients: Ford Motor Co.; Rite Aid Corporation; Servico; The Taubman Company, Inc.; The Travelers Insurance Company.

For full biographical listings, see the Martindale-Hubbell Law Directory

JONES, FOSTER, JOHNSTON & STUBBS, P.A. (AV)

Flagler Center Tower, 505 South Flagler Drive, P.O. Box 3475, 33402-3475
Telephone: 407-659-3000
Fax: 407-832-1454

Sidney A. Stubbs, Jr.
John Blair McCracken
John C. Randolph
Herbert Adams Weaver, Jr.
Larry B. Alexander
Thornton M. Henry
Margaret L. Cooper
D. Culver Smith III (P.A.)
Allen R. Tomlinson
Peter S. Holton

(See Next Column)

JONES, FOSTER, JOHNSTON & STUBBS P.A.—*Continued*

Michael P. Walsh
Peter A. Sachs
Michael T. Kranz
John S. Trimper
Mark B. Kleinfeld
Andrew R. Ross
Scott Gardner Hawkins
Steven J. Rothman
Rebecca G. Doane

Joyce A. Conway
Stephen J. Aucamp
Christopher S. Duke
Scott L. McMullen
John C. Rau
Tracey Biagiotti
Edward Diaz

Counsel For: U.S. Trust Co.; NationsBank of Florida, N.A.; Island National Bank; Bankers Trust Company of Florida; Sun Bank/South Florida, N.A.; General Motors Acceptance Corp.

For full biographical listings, see the Martindale-Hubbell Law Directory

---

STUART E. KOCHA, P.A. (AV)

118 Clematis Street, P.O. Box 1427, 33402
Telephone: 407-659-5611
Fax: 407-659-5636

Stuart E. Kocha

LEGAL SUPPORT PERSONNEL

David L. Halderman (Chief Investigator)
Steve L. Sheehy (Investigator)

References: NationsBank; Admiralty Bank.

For full biographical listings, see the Martindale-Hubbell Law Directory

KUBICKI DRAPER (AV)

United National Bank Tower, Suite 1100, 1675 Palm Beach Lakes Boulevard, 33401
Telephone: 407-640-0303
Fax: 407-640-0524
Miami, Florida Office: Penthouse City National Bank Building, 25 West Flagler Street, 33130.
Telephone: 305-374-1212.
Telecopier: 305-374-7846.
Fort Lauderdale, Florida Office: Suite 1600, One East Broward Boulevard, 33301.
Telephone: 305-768-0011.
Fax: 305-768-0514.

David Knight (Resident)
Stephen W. Schwed (Resident)
Michael S. Smith

Laurie J. Adams
Hubert S. McGinley (Resident)

For full biographical listings, see the Martindale-Hubbell Law Directory

ROBERT S. LEVY, P.A. (AV)

Suite 502 Forum III, 1655 Palm Beach Lakes Boulevard, 33401
Telephone: 407-686-6080
Fax: 407-686-6085

Robert S. Levy

Reference: First Union National Bank of Florida.

For full biographical listings, see the Martindale-Hubbell Law Directory

---

MONTGOMERY & LARMOYEUX (AV)

1016 Clearwater Place, Drawer 3086, 33402-3086
Telephone: 407-832-2880
Fax: 407-832-0887

MEMBERS OF FIRM

Robert M. Montgomery, Jr.
Christopher M. Larmoyeux

ASSOCIATES

Rebecca L. Larson
Todd Cash Alofs
Odette Marie Bendeck

For full biographical listings, see the Martindale-Hubbell Law Directory

NASON, GILDAN, YEAGER, GERSON & WHITE, P.A. (AV)

Penthouse Suite United National Bank Tower, 1645 Palm Beach Lakes Boulevard, 33401
Telephone: 407-686-3307
Fax: 407-686-5442

Herbert L. Gildan
Thomas J. Yeager
Gary N. Gerson
John White, II
Phillip C. Gildan
Nathan E. Nason
M. Richard Sapir
Kenneth A. Marra
Gregory L. Scott
Domenick R. Lioce
Alan I. Armour, II
Mark A. Pachman
Elaine Johnson James

(See Next Column)

John M. McDivitt
Howard J. Falcon, III
Susan Fleischner Kornspan

For full biographical listings, see the Martindale-Hubbell Law Directory

---

PETERS, ROBERTSON, LAX, PARSONS & WELCHER (AV)

Suite 300-Pavilion Northbridge Center, 515 North Flagler Drive, 33401-4381
Telephone: Palm Beach: 407-832-9698
Broward: 305-771-7493
Facsimile: 407-832-5654
Miami, Florida Office: Suite 600, Ingraham Building, 25 Southeast 2nd Avenue.
Telephone: 305-374-3103.
Fax: 305-377-9805.
Fort Lauderdale, Florida Office: Suite 600, 600 South Andrews Avenue.
Telephone: 305-761-8999.
Fax: 305-761-8990.
Fort Myers, Florida Office: 1342 Colonial Boulevard, Suite 7, Key West Professional Centre.
Telephone: 813-936-1129.
Fax: 813-936-4036.

Steven Charles Simon (Resident)

Representative Clients: Auto-Owners Insurance Co.; Dade County School Board; Employers Reinsurance Group; Gallagher Bassett Insurance Service; Maryland Casualty Co.

For full biographical listings, see the Martindale-Hubbell Law Directory

---

PRUITT & PRUITT, P.A. (AV)

Suite 400 Flagler Tower, 505 South Flagler Drive, 33401
Telephone: 407-655-8080
Fax: 407-655-4134

William H. Pruitt
William E. Pruitt

Reference: Flagler National Bank.

For full biographical listings, see the Martindale-Hubbell Law Directory

---

DONALD J. SASSER, P.A. (AV)

1800 Australian Avenue, South, Suite 203, P.O. Box 2907, 33402
Telephone: 407-689-4378
Fax: 407-689-4652
Boca Raton, Florida Office: 2200 Corporate Boulevard, N.W., Suite 302, 33431.
Telephone: 407-998-7725.

Donald J. Sasser

Jorge M. Cestero

Reference: First Union National Bank of Florida.

For full biographical listings, see the Martindale-Hubbell Law Directory

SEARCY DENNEY SCAROLA BARNHART & SHIPLEY, PROFESSIONAL ASSOCIATION (AV)

2139 Palm Beach Lakes Boulevard, P.O. Drawer 3626, 33402-3626
Telephone: 407-686-6300
800-780-8607
Fax: 407-478-0754

Christian D. Searcy, Sr.
Earl L. Denney, Jr.
John Scarola
F. Gregory Barnhart
John A. Shipley
Lois J. Frankel
David K. Kelley, Jr.
Lawrence J. Block, Jr.
C. Calvin Warriner, III
William A. Norton
David J. Sales

James N. Nance
Katherine Ann Martinez
T. Michael Kennedy
Todd S. Stewart
Christopher K. Speed

LEGAL SUPPORT PERSONNEL

Deane L. Cady (Paralegal/Investigator)
James E. Cook (Paralegal/Investigator)
Emilio Diamantis (Paralegal/Investigator)
David W. Gilmore (Paralegal/Investigator)
John C. Hopkins (Paralegal/Investigator)
Thaddeus E. Kulesa (Paralegal/Investigator)
J. Peter Love (Paralegal/Investigator)
Marjorie A. Morgan (Paralegal)
Joel C. Padgett (Paralegal/Investigator)
William H. Seabold (Paralegal/Investigator)
Kathleen Simon (Paralegal)
Steve M. Smith (Paralegal/Investigator)
Judson Whitehorn (Paralegal/Investigator)
Marcia Yarnell Dodson (Not admitted in FL; Law Clerk)
Kelly Lynn Hopkins (Paralegal/Investigator)
Frank Cotton (Paralegal/Investigator)

For full biographical listings, see the Martindale-Hubbell Law Directory

West Palm Beach—Continued

SHUTTS & BOWEN (AV)

A Partnership including Professional Associations
One Clearlake Centre, 250 Australian Avenue Suite 500, 33401
Telephone: 407-835-8500
Cable Address: "Shuttsbo"
Fax: 407-650-8530
Key Largo, Florida Office: Suite A206, 31 Ocean Reef Drive.
Telephone: 305-367-2881.
Miami, Florida Office: 1500 Miami Center, 201 South Biscayne Boulevard.
Telephone: 305-358-6300.
Cable Address: "Shuttsbo."
Telefax: 305-381-9982.
Orlando, Florida Office: 20 North Orange Avenue, Suite 1000.
Telephone: 407-423-3200.
Fax: 407-425-8316.
Amsterdam, The Netherlands Office: Shutts & Bowen, B.V., Europa Boulevard 59, 1083 AD, Amsterdam.
Telephone: (31 20) 661-0969.
Fax: (31 20) 642-1475.
London, England Office: 48 Mount Street, London W1Y.
Telephone: 4471493-4840.
Telefax: 4471493-4299.

MEMBERS OF FIRM

Arnold L. Berman (Resident)	Joseph F. McSorley (Resident)
Charles Robinson Fawsett (P.A.)	Arthur J. Menor (Resident)
David A. Gart	Robert D. Miller (Resident)
Robert E. Gunn (P.A.) (Resident)	Robert C. Sommerville (P.A.)
	John B. White (P.A.)
Marvin A. Kirsner (Resident)	Scott G. Williams (Resident)

RESIDENT ASSOCIATES

Jonathan D. Gerber	Robert B. Goldman

Robert Wexler

OF COUNSEL

John R. Day (P.A.)

For full biographical listings, see the Martindale-Hubbell Law Directory

LAW OFFICES OF LOUIS M. SILBER, P.A. (AV)

Reflections II, Suite 855, 400 Australian Avenue, South, 33401
Telephone: 407-655-6640
Fax: 407-659-3345

Louis M. Silber

Philip L. Valente, Jr.

For full biographical listings, see the Martindale-Hubbell Law Directory

WALTON LANTAFF SCHROEDER & CARSON (AV)

A Partnership including Professional Associations
United National Bank Tower, Suite 800, 1645 Palm Beach Lakes Boulevard, P.O. Box 2966, 33401
Telephone: 407-689-6700
Telecopier: 407-689-2647
Miami, Florida Office: One Biscayne Tower, 25th Floor, 2 South Biscayne Boulevard.
Telephone: 305-379-6411.
Telecopier: 305-577-3875.
Fort Lauderdale, Florida Office: Third Floor, Blackstone Building, 707 Southeast Third Avenue.
Telephone: 305-463-8456.
Telecopier: 305-763-6294.
Coral Gables, Florida Office: Suite 1101, Gables International Plaza, 2655 Le Jeune Road.
Telephone: 305-379-6411.
Telecopier: 305-446-9206.

RESIDENT PARTNERS

Wayne T. Gill (P.A.)	Roberta J. Karp
Marla A. Mudano	John G. White, III

RESIDENT ASSOCIATES

Amy L. Smith	George W. Bush, Jr.
Gregory William Coleman	David S. Tadros
Kurt A. Wyland	Steven E. Foor

Ellen S. Malasky

For full biographical listings, see the Martindale-Hubbell Law Directory

WINTER HAVEN, Polk Co.

CRITTENDEN & CRITTENDEN, P.A. (AV)

103 Avenue A., N.W., P.O. Drawer 152, 33882-0152
Telephone: 813-293-2161
Fax: 813-299-3207

H. C. Crittenden (1898-1969)	Robert R. Crittenden

(See Next Column)

LEGAL SUPPORT PERSONNEL

Peggy L. Thompson	Freida G. Hart

Counsel for: City of Lake Alfred, Florida; 400 and 402 Avenue K Prof. Partnerships; Town of Dundee.
Approved Attorney for: Lawyers Title Insurance Corp.; Federal Land Bank of Columbia, South Carolina; Attorneys' Title Insurance Fund.

For full biographical listings, see the Martindale-Hubbell Law Directory

PETERSON, MYERS, CRAIG, CREWS, BRANDON & PUTERBAUGH, P.A. (AV)

Suite 300, 141 5th Street N.W., P.O. Drawer 7608, 33883-7608
Telephone: 813-294-3360
Lake Wales, Florida Office: 130 East Central Avenue, P.O. Box 1079.
Telephones: 813-676-7611; 683-8942.
Lakeland, Florida Office: 100 East Main Street, P.O. Box 24628.
Telephones: 813-683-6511; 676-6934.

Jack P. Brandon	Corneal B. Myers
Beach A Brooks, Jr.	Cornelius B. Myers, III
J. Davis Connor	Robert E. Puterbaugh
Michael S. Craig	Abel A. Putnam
Roy A. Craig, Jr.	Thomas B. Putnam, Jr.
Jacob C. Dykxhoorn	Deborah A. Ruster
Dennis P. Johnson	Stephen R. Senn
Kevin C. Knowlton	Andrea Teves Smith
Douglas A. Lockwood, III	Kerry M. Wilson

General Counsel for: Barnett Bank of Polk County.
Representative Clients: Mutual Wholesale Co.; Sun Bank/Mid-Florida, N.A.; Chase Commercial Corp.; Barnett Banks, Inc.; Ben Hill Griffin, Inc.; Alcoma Association, Inc.
Approved Attorneys for: Attorneys' Title Insurance Fund; Federal Land Bank, Columbia, South Carolina; Equitable Life Assurance Society of the United States.

For full biographical listings, see the Martindale-Hubbell Law Directory

WINTER PARK, Orange Co.

FREDERICK W. PEIRSOL (AV)

280 West Canton Avenue, Suite 305, 32789
Telephone: 407-647-6363
Fax: 407-647-6378

LEGAL SUPPORT PERSONNEL

Susan Koser (Legal Assistant)

Reference: Trust Dept., Sun Bank, N.A., Winter Park & Orlando, Florida.

TROUTMAN, WILLIAMS, IRVIN, GREEN & HELMS, PROFESSIONAL ASSOCIATION (AV)

311 West Fairbanks Avenue, 32789
Telephone: 407-647-2277
FAX: 407-628-2986
Kissimmee, Florida Office: Suite 206, 120 Broadway, 34741.
Telephone: 407-933-8834.
FAX: 407-933-8253.

Russell Troutman	Roger D. Helms
Joseph H. Williams	Joseph J. Polich, Jr.
Paul B. Irvin	Jack E. Bowen
Robert F. Green	David M. Giard

Kim Michael Cullen

For full biographical listings, see the Martindale-Hubbell Law Directory

WINDERWEEDLE, HAINES, WARD & WOODMAN, P.A. (AV)

Barnett Bank Building, 250 Park Avenue, South, P.O. Box 880, 32790-0880
Telephone: 407-644-6312
Telecopier: 407-645-3728
Orlando, Florida Office: Barnett Bank Center, 390 North Orange Avenue, P.O. Box 1391.
Telephone: 407-423-4246.
Telecopier: 407-423-7014.

W. E. Winderweedle (1906-1979)	William A. Walker II
Webber B. Haines (Of Counsel)	C. Brent McCaghren
Harold A. Ward, III	Randolph J. Rush
Victor E. Woodman	Gregory L. Holzhauer
John D. Haines	W. Graham White

General Counsel for: Winter Park Health Foundation, Inc.; City of Winter Park; RoTech Medical Corp.; Schwartz Electro-Optics, Inc.
Counsel for: Barnett Bank of Central Florida, N.A.; Florida Conference of the United Church of Christ, Inc.
Representative Clients: Security National Bank; Georgia Pacific Corp.; USX Corp.

For full biographical listings, see the Martindale-Hubbell Law Directory

WINTER SPRINGS, Seminole Co. — (Refer to Longwood)

GEORGIA

*ABBEVILLE,** Wilcox Co. — (Refer to Eastman)

*ALBANY,** Dougherty Co.

DIVINE, WILKIN, RAULERSON & FIELDS (AV)

600 North Jackson Street, P.O. Box 64, 31702-0064
Telephone: 912-883-1610
Telecopier: 912-883-1647

MEMBERS OF FIRM

William T. Divine, Jr.
Edgar B. Wilkin, Jr.
R. Kelly Raulerson
Richard W. Fields
Keith T. Dorough
W. Douglas Divine

General Counsel for: Security Bank and Trust Co.
Representative Clients: Allstate Insurance Co.; Beck Motor Co.; Freitex, Inc.; Jamison Bedding Co.; M&M/Mars; State Farm Insurance Cos.; Fred Taylor Co., Inc.; The Travelers Insurance Cos.; Liberty Mutual Insurance Co.; Georgia Farm Bureau Mutual Insurance Co.

For full biographical listings, see the Martindale-Hubbell Law Directory

FARKAS, LEDFORD AND PERRY (AV)

Suite 300 Albany Towers, 235 Roosevelt Avenue, P.O. Box 128, 31702
Telephone: 912-435-5621
Fax: 912-436-5930

Leonard Farkas
Thomas G. Ledford
Diane Lindsey Perry

Representative Clients: Allstate Insurance Cos.; Government Employees Insurance Co.

For full biographical listings, see the Martindale-Hubbell Law Directory

*ALMA,** Bacon Co. — (Refer to Douglas)

*AMERICUS,** Sumter Co.

ELLIS & EASTERLIN, A PROFESSIONAL CORPORATION (AV)

410 West Lamar Street, P.O. Box 488, 31709
Telephone: 912-924-9316
Fax: 912-924-6248

George R. Ellis, Sr. (1905-1988)
George R. Ellis, Jr.
Benjamin F. Easterlin, IV
George M. Peagler, Jr.
James C. Gatewood
John V. Harper
James M. Skipper, Jr.
Russ F. Barnes

For full biographical listings, see the Martindale-Hubbell Law Directory

*ASHBURN,** Turner Co. — (Refer to Tifton)

*ATHENS,** Clarke Co.

BLASINGAME, BURCH, GARRARD & BRYANT, P.C. (AV)

440 College Avenue North, P.O. Box 832, 30603
Telephone: 706-354-4000
Telecopier: 706-353-0673

J. Ralph Beaird
Gary B. Blasingame
E. Davison Burch
Henry G. Garrard, III
Everett Clay Bryant
M. Steven Heath
Andrew J. Hill, III
Michael A. Morris
Thomas H. Rogers, Jr.
William D. Harvard
Rikard L. Bridges
William S. Cowsert
Ivan A. Gustafson
Michael C. Daniel
David S. Thomson
Gregory Alexander Daniels
Milton F. Eisenberg
Stephen E.B. Smith
J. David Felt, Jr.
Wayne R. Allen
Amy Lou King

Representative Clients: NationsBank of Georgia, N.A.; Georgia Power Co.; Georgia Natural Gas Co.; Pittsburgh Corning Corp.; Downtown Athens Development Authority; Georgia National Bank; Fowler Products Co., Inc.; St. Paul Fire & Marine Insurance Co.; Athens Newspapers, Inc.; First Commerce Bancorp, Inc.

For full biographical listings, see the Martindale-Hubbell Law Directory

McLEOD, BENTON, BEGNAUD & MARSHALL (AV)

8th Floor, NationsBank Building, P.O. Box 8108, 30603
Telephone: 706-549-9400
Fax: 706-549-9406

MEMBERS OF FIRM

Larry V. McLeod
Terrell W. Benton, Jr.
Jeanette S. Scott
Darrel Begnaud
Andrew H. Marshall
Malcolm C. McArthur
William C. Berryman, Jr.
Daniel C. Haygood
Hilary N. Shuford
David K. Linder
Richard L. Brittain

(See Next Column)

OF COUNSEL

Robert E. Gibson

Counsel for: NationsBank; Athens First Bank & Trust Company; Georgia Power Company; CSX Transportation, Inc.; St. Mary's Hospital; Benson's Inc.; Oconee County School District; Walton County School District.

For full biographical listings, see the Martindale-Hubbell Law Directory

*ATLANTA,** Fulton Co.

ALEMBIK, FINE & CALLNER, P.A. (AV)

Marquis One Tower, Fourth Floor, 245 Peachtree Center Avenue, N.E., 30303
Telephone: 404-688-8800
Telecopier: 404-420-7191

Michael D. Alembik (1936-1993)
Lowell S. Fine
Bruce W. Callner
Kathy L. Portnoy
Ronald T. Gold
G. Michael Banick
Mark E. Bergeson
Russell P. Love

Z. Ileana Martinez
Kevin S. Green
Susan M. Lieppe
T. Kevin Mooney
Bruce R. Steinfeld
Janet Lichiello Franchi

For full biographical listings, see the Martindale-Hubbell Law Directory

ALSTON & BIRD (AV)

A Partnership including Professional Corporations
One Atlantic Center, 1201 West Peachtree Street, 30309-3424
Telephone: 404-881-7000
Telecopier: 404-881-7777
Cable Address: AMGRAM GA
Telex: 54-2996
Easylink: 62985848
Washington, D.C. Office: 700 Thirteenth Street, Suite 350 20005-3960.
Telephone: 202-508-3300.
Telecopier: 202-508-3333.

MEMBERS OF FIRM

G. Conley Ingram
Frazer Durrett, Jr.
Ralph Williams, Jr.
L. Clifford Adams, Jr.
Walter W. Mitchell
Michael A. Doyle
Alexander E. Wilson III
Ronald L. Reid
Neil Williams
John K. Train III
B. Harvey Hill, Jr.
Robert G. Edge
Rawson Foreman
C. David Butler
A. James Elliott (P.C.)
Joseph V. Myers, Jr.
R. Neal Batson
F. Dean Copeland
Sidney J. Nurkin
Alexander W. Patterson
Oscar N. Persons
Benjamin F. Johnson III
Joe T. Taylor
Bernard L. Greer, Jr.
William C. Humphreys, Jr.
James S. Stokes
John M. Edwards, Jr.
Dow N. Kirkpatrick II
H. Sadler Poe
W. Terence Walsh
Philip C. Cook
Robert C. Lower
James F. Nellis, Jr.
Timothy S. Perry
Peter M. Wright
Gerald W. Bowling
Robert H. Buckler
Arnold L. Feinstein
Peter Kontio
Robert D. McCallum, Jr.
Jack S. Schroder, Jr.
T. Michael Tennant
Benjamin T. White
Michael R. Davis
Kevin E. Grady
Jack H. Senterfitt
William H. Avery
Peter Q. Bassett
Judson Graves
Forrest W. Hunter
Jonathan W. Lowe
Patrick M. Norton
Jeffrey P. Adams
Helene Z. Cohen
Peter M. Degnan
Lee A. DeHihns III
Jay D. Bennett
J. William Boone
John L. Coalson, Jr.
Steven M. Collins
John L. Douglas
Anne S. Rampacek
Frank G. Smith III
John C. Weitnauer
J. Vaughan Curtis
Christopher Glenn Sawyer
Glenn R. Thomson
Nill V. Toulme
Pinney L. Allen
James S. Hutchinson
Ralph F. MacDonald III
R. Wayne Thorpe
John A. Buchman
(Not admitted in GA)
John I. Spangler III
Laura Glover Thatcher
Frank M. Conner III
Martin J. Elgison
Terence J. Greene
Ira H. Parker
Grant T. Stein
Gregory C. Braden
Charles A. Brake, Jr.
Keith O. Cowan
H. Stephen Harris, Jr.
George M. Maxwell, Jr.
Robert J. Middleton, Jr.
Theodore E. G. Pound
Bernard Taylor
Albert E. Bender, Jr.
Richard T. Fulton
Mary C. Gill
Lauren G. Grien
William H. Hughes, Jr.
Karol V. Mason
Timothy J. Pakenham
Michael T. Petrik
Donna Potts Bergeson
Bryan E. Davis
Richard W. Grice
Michael P. Kenny
Gerald L. Mize, Jr.
Timothy J. Peaden
Robert P. Riordan
John E. Stephenson, Jr.
Clare H. Draper IV

(See Next Column)

ALSTON & BIRD, *Atlanta—Continued*

MEMBERS OF FIRM (Continued)

R. Steve Ensor
Christopher D. Mangum
Stephen A. Opler
Craig R. Pett
Randall L. Allen
David E. Brown, Jr.
Dennis J. Connolly
Todd R. David
Elizabeth A. Gilley
Richard R. Hays
William R. Klapp, Jr.
Jennifer Brown Moore
Mark C. Rusche
Marci P. Schmerler
Della Wager Wells
Sam K. Kaywood, Jr.

SENIOR COUNSEL

Lawrence P. Klamon
Pierre Howard

COUNSEL

E. Bruce Mather
Lawrie E. Demorest
J. Kennard Neal
Sydney S. Cleland
Janet E. Witt (Not admitted in GA)
Douglas B. Chappell
Homer Lee Walker

ASSOCIATES

Kimberly A. Ackourey
Leon Adams, Jr.
Lori G. Baer
Holly B. Barnett
Karen B. Baynes
Charles J. Biederman
Rick D. Blumen
Christina K. Braisted
R. Gregory Brophy
Lonnie T. Brown, Jr.
Jay B. Bryan
Glenda G. Bugg
B. Davis Butler
Linda G. Carpenter
W. Thomas Carter III
Lisa H. Cassilly
Douglas E. Cloud
Laura J. Coleman
Scott C. Commander
Bradley L. Cooper
Alston D. Correll III
Cynthia L. Counts
Robert L. Crewdson
Paul M. Cushing
Kristen K. Darnell
Frederick C. Dawkins
Jo C. Dearing
Susan B. Devitt
Bobby L. Dexter
Jeffrey A. Dickerson
Johan Droogmans
Lance P. Dunnings
Brian D. Edwards
Sarah V. Elliott
James G. Farris, Jr.
John N. Fleming
John P. Fry
A. McCampbell Gibson
James C. Grant
Ernest LaMont Greer
James W. Hagan
Darren C. Hauck
Jennifer Gimer Hays
John R. Hickman
H. Douglas Hinson
W. Hunter Holliday
Kristin Klausen Howard
Lori P. Hughes
Joel J. Hughey
Susan E. Hurd
Clifton M. Iler
Jeff A. Israel
John A. Jordak, Jr.
Michael D. Kaufman
Daniel A. Kent
Beth E. Kirby
Kimberly A. Knight
Aldo L. LaFiandra
Rebecca McLemore Lamberth
Daniel M. LeBey
Matthew W. Levin
Douglas J. MacGinnitie
David M. Maxwell
Robin Goff Mayer
William S. Mayfield
Michael R. McAlevey
Jennifer Greer McCrory
Mark F. McElreath
Scott A. McLaren
Teri T. McMahon
R. Clay Milling
Charles H. Morgan
Robert D. Mowrey
Ben E. Muraskin
Nicole Fletcher O'Connor
Nils H. Okeson
Laura Lewis Owens
William T. Plybon
Steven L. Pottle
Vionnette Reyes
Daniel L. Rikard
Thomas S. Robinson III
Dawnmarie Rodziewicz
Kimberly Dyslin Rountree
John C. Sawyer
Angie Schilling
Blair G. Schlossberg
Eileen M. G. Scofield
Debra K. Scott (Not admitted in GA)
Candace N. Smith
H. Suzanne Smith
Richard A. Snow
Joseph P. L. Snyder
Robyn Ice Sosebee
K. David Steele
Michael L. Stevens
David J. Stewart
Karen L. Sukin
Teresa D. Thebaut
Paul F. Wellborn III
Timothy G. Werner
Thomas L. West III
Michelle A. Williams
Susan J. Wilson
James J. Wolfson
Karen K. Wolter
Susan L. Wright

OF COUNSEL

Henry J. Miller
Arthur Howell
Eugene T. Branch
Sidney O. Smith, Jr.
Robert L. Foreman, Jr.
Richard A. Allison

For full biographical listings, see the Martindale-Hubbell Law Directory

---

FRANCIS M. BIRD, JR. (AV)

50 Hurt Plaza, Suite 730, 30303
Telephone: 404-525-0885
Fax: 404-523-2806
(Also Of Counsel to Pamela L. Tremayne)

OF COUNSEL

Pamela L. Tremayne

For full biographical listings, see the Martindale-Hubbell Law Directory

---

BONDURANT, MIXSON & ELMORE (AV)

1201 W. Peachtree Street Suite 3900, 30309
Telephone: 404-881-4100
FAX: 404-881-4111

MEMBERS OF FIRM

Emmet J. Bondurant II
H. Lamar Mixson
M. Jerome Elmore
Edward B. Krugman
James C. Morton
Jeffrey O. Bramlett
Dirk G. Christensen
Jane E. Fahey
Jeffrey D. Horst
John E. Floyd
Carolyn R. Gorwitz
Michael A. Sullivan

ASSOCIATES

Scott F. Bertschi
Mary Jo Bradbury
P. Richard Game
Robin M. Hutchinson
Frank M. Lowrey, IV
J. Scott McClain
Keenan Rance Sephus Nix
Jill A. Pryor
Michael B. Terry
Joshua F. Thorpe

Representative Clients: The Aetna Casualty and Surety Company; Bottlers of Coca-Cola, U.S.A.; Brinks Home Security Systems, Inc.; Delta Air Lines, Inc.; Fina Oil and Chemical Company; JMB Realty Corp.; The Paradies Shops, Inc.; Sanifill, Inc.; Trammell Crow Co.

For full biographical listings, see the Martindale-Hubbell Law Directory

---

BOOTH, WADE & CAMPBELL (AV)

Cumberland Center II, 3100 Cumberland Circle, Suite 1500, 30339
Telephone: 404-850-5000
FAX: 404-850-5079

MEMBERS OF FIRM

Allison Wade
Gordon Dean Booth, Jr.
Douglas N. Campbell
L. Dale Owens
Walter E. Jospin
Larry D. Ledbetter
Harry V. Lamon, Jr., (P.C.)
Carl I. Gable, Jr., (P.C.)

ASSOCIATES

Allen Buckley
Steven W. Hardy (Not admitted in GA)
Randolph H. Houchins
Randall W. Johnson
Edward C. Konieczny (Not admitted in GA)
Courtney G. Lytle
Edward H. Nicholson, Jr.
Nancy P. Parson
Scott A. Wharton

Representative Clients: American Airlines, Inc.; Apple South, Inc.; British Airports; Columbia/HCA Healthcare Corporation; Delta Air Lines, Inc.; Life Insurance Company of Georgia; Merrill Lynch & Co.; Prudential Securities Incorporated; Southwire Company.

For full biographical listings, see the Martindale-Hubbell Law Directory

---

R. DAVID BOTTS (AV)

152 Nassau Street, N.W., 30303
Telephone: 404-688-5500
FAX: 404-688-6463

For full biographical listings, see the Martindale-Hubbell Law Directory

---

CARTER & ANSLEY (AV)

Suite 1000 One Ninety One Peachtree Tower, 191 Peachtree Street, 30303-1747
Telephone: 404-658-9220
FAX: 404-658-9726

MEMBERS OF FIRM

Shepard Bryan (1871-1970)
W. Colquitt Carter (1904-1988)
Ben Kingree, III
Tommy T. Holland
H. Sanders Carter, Jr.
A. Terry Sorrells
Robert A. Barnaby, II
Thomas E. Magill
Robert O. McCloud, Jr.
Anthony J. McGinley
Christopher N. Shuman
Elizabeth J. Bondurant

OF COUNSEL

Bonneau Ansley

ASSOCIATES

Michael A. Coval
Rebecca J. Schmidt
Keith L. Lindsay
Burke B. Johnson
Kenton J. Coppage
John H. Zwald
A. Louise Tanner
David M. Atkinson

For full biographical listings, see the Martindale-Hubbell Law Directory

---

CASHIN, MORTON & MULLINS (AV)

Two Midtown Plaza - Suite 1900, 1360 Peachtree Street, N.E., 30309-3214
Telephone: 404-870-1500
Telecopier: 404-870-1529

(See Next Column)

CASHIN, MORTON & MULLINS—*Continued*

MEMBERS OF FIRM

Harry L. Cashin, Jr.
C. Read Morton, Jr.
A. L. Mullins, Jr.
Richard A. Fishman
William T. McKenzie
James Dean Spratt, Jr.
David W. Cranshaw
Richard Gerakitis
Robert Hunt Dunlap, Jr.
Robert O. Ball, III
Steven R. Glasscock
David Tully Hazell

ASSOCIATES

Lisa S. Street
Noel B. McDevitt, Jr.
James Marx Sherman
Kara E. Albert (Not admitted in GA)
Gibson T. Hess

Representative Clients: Alex Brown Realty, Inc.; ARA Food Services; Bank South, N.A.; Carey Paul Cos.; Central Life Insurance Company; Diversified Shelter Group, Ltd.; Dymetrol Co., Inc.; Edwards-Warren Tire Co.; First Union National Bank; Flournoy Development Co.

For full biographical listings, see the Martindale-Hubbell Law Directory

DAVIS, MATTHEWS & QUIGLEY, P.C. (AV)

Fourteenth Floor, Lenox Towers II, 3400 Peachtree Road, 30326
Telephone: 404-261-3900
Telecopier: 404-261-0159

Baxter L. Davis
William M. Matthews
Ron L. Quigley
J. Michael Harrison
Melvin L. Drake, Jr.
Richard W. Schiffman, Jr.
Frank A. DeVincent

Elizabeth Green Lindsey
John Charles Olderman
Chason Lash Harrison, Jr.
Deborah M. Lubin
Sylvia A. Martin

Approved Attorneys for: Lawyers Title Insurance Corp.

For full biographical listings, see the Martindale-Hubbell Law Directory

DREW ECKL & FARNHAM (AV)

880 West Peachtree Street, P.O. Box 7600, 30357
Telephone: 404-885-1400
Facsimile: 404-876-0992

MEMBERS OF FIRM

Charles L. Drew
W. Wray Eckl
Clayton H. Farnham
Arthur H. Glaser
James M. Poe
John A. Ferguson, Jr.
Theodore Freeman
John P. Reale
Stevan A. Miller
H. Michael Bagley
Hall F. McKinley III
G. Randall Moody
B. Holland Pritchard
T. Bart Gary
David A. Smith
Kenneth A. Hindman
Paul W. Burke
Daniel C. Kniffen
John C. Bruffey, Jr.
Benton J. Mathis, Jr.
John G. Blackmon, Jr.
Dennis M. Hall
J. William Haley
Donald R. Andersen
Ann Bishop Byars
Gary R. Hurst
Stephen W. Mooney

ASSOCIATES

Anne M. Landrum
Nena K. Puckett
Nicole D. Tifverman
Jerry C. Carter, Jr.
Phillip E. Friduss
L. Lee Bennett, Jr.
Christopher J. Culp
Katherine D. Dixon
William T. Mitchell
J. Robb Cruser
Philip Wade Savrin
Lucian Gillis, Jr.
Peter H. Schmidt, II
Brooks von Biberstein Powers
April Rich
Maureen M. Middleton
Robert L. Welch
Julie Young John
Jeffrey B. Grimm
Suzanne VonHarten Sanders
Leigh Lawson Reeves
Bruce A. Taylor, Jr.
Douglas T. Lay
Douglas M. Baker
Elizabeth B. Luzuriaga
David R. Bergquist
Charles L. Norton, Jr.
Nancy F. Rigby
Peter A. Law
Douglas G. Smith, Jr.
Terrence T. Rock
Phillip Comer Griffeth
Marian S. Singer
Steven D. Prelutsky
Julianne L. Swilley
Stephen A. Lisle
Paul G. Phillips
Patricia R. Stevens
Carter Allen
Mary H. Hines
Lisa A. Kelehear
A. Bradley Dozier, Jr.
B. Greg Cline
C. Lawrence Meyer
Eryn J. Dawkins
Philip G. Pompilio

Representative Clients: American International Adjustment Co.; Chicago Title Insurance Co.; CIGNA; Crum & Forster Commercial Insurance; Ford Motor Co.; Frito-Lay, Inc.; General Motors; Georgia Pacific Corp.; Liberty Mutual Insurance Co.; Parthenon/Hospital Corporation of America.

For full biographical listings, see the Martindale-Hubbell Law Directory

FAIN, MAJOR & WILEY, P.C. (AV)

The Hurt Building, 50 Hurt Plaza, Suite 300, 30303
Telephone: 404-688-6633
Telecopier: 404-420-1544

Donald M. Fain
Gene A. Major
Charles A. Wiley, Jr.
Christopher E. Penna
Thomas E. Brennan
John K. Miles, Jr.
Darryl G. Haynes
David Wayne Williams
Brian Alligood
Frederic H. Pilch, III
Derek A. Mendicino

Representative Clients: Allstate Insurance Co.; Budget Rent-A-Car; Carolina Freight Carriers Corp.; Chrysler Insurance Co.; Georgia Farm Bureau Mutual Insurance Co.; Great Atlantic & Pacific Tea Co.; Hertz Corp.; Universal Underwriters Insurance Co.; Westfield Insurance co.; Winn-Dixie Stores, Inc.

For full biographical listings, see the Martindale-Hubbell Law Directory

FRANKEL, HARDWICK, TANENBAUM & FINK, P.C. (AV)

359 East Paces Ferry Road, N.E., 30305
Telephone: 404-266-2930
Fax: 404-231-3362

Samuel N. Frankel
Pearce D. Hardwick
Allan J. Tanenbaum
Barry B. McGough
Neal J. Fink
Martha J. Kuckleburg
James J. Brissette
Pepi Friedman
Joel S. Arogeti
Barbara A. Lincoln

Kimberly C. Hodgson
Susan L. Shaver
Stephen E. Parker
Jere Recob

OF COUNSEL

David F. Cooper

Representative Clients: America's Favorite Chicken Co. (Church's and Popeye's); Softlab, Inc.; Basic, Inc.; Buffalo's Franchise Concepts, Inc.; Combustion Engineering, Inc.; Commerical Bank of Georgia; Patients Pharmacies; Hank Aaron Enterprises, Inc.; Nursecare (Nursing Homes); Sundance Products, Inc.; Venture Construction Company; Sobstad Corp.

For full biographical listings, see the Martindale-Hubbell Law Directory

FREEMAN & HAWKINS (AV)

4000 One Peachtree Center, 303 Peachtree Street, N.E., 30308-3243
Telephone: 404-614-7400
Fax: 404-614-750
CompuServe address: 73541,1626
Internet address: 73451.1626@compuserve.com

MEMBERS OF FIRM

Joe C. Freeman, Jr.
Paul M. Hawkins
J. Bruce Welch
Albert H. Parnell
A. Timothy Jones
Alan F. Herman
Howell Hollis, III
Michael J. Goldman
H. Lane Young, II
Joseph R. Cullens
Frank C. Bedinger, III
Julia Bennett Jagger
Stephen M. Lore
William H. Major, III
Edward M. Newsom
T. Ryan Mock, Jr.
Lawrence J. Myers
Jack N. Sibley
Warner S. Fox
Robert U. Wright
Thomas F. Wamsley, Jr.

OF COUNSEL

J. R. Cullens
Oliver B. Dickins, Jr.

ASSOCIATES

Kimberly Houston Ridley
Ollie M. Harton
Michael E. Hutchins
Barry S. Noeltner
Kevin J. Bahr
Joanne Beauvoir Brown
Edwin L. Hall, Jr.
Kenan G. Loomis
Roger M. Goode
Robert Rache Elarbee
Charles R. Beans
Louis E. Bridges III
Dennis J. Manganiello
Peter R. York
Kathryn Anne Thurman
Cullen Christie Wilkerson, Jr.
Allen W. Nelson
T. H. Lyda
Christine Lupo Mast
Blanche Rose Miller
Edward C. Henderson, Jr.
Stephen M. Brooks
Allen L. Broughton
Thomas G. Tidwell
Kristine Berry Morain
Kristen K. Duggan
Michael A. Mills

For full biographical listings, see the Martindale-Hubbell Law Directory

GLASS, MCCULLOUGH, SHERRILL & HARROLD (AV)

1409 Peachtree Street, N.E., 30309
Telephone: 404-885-1500
Telecopier: 404-892-1801
Buckhead Office: Monarch Plaza, 3414 Peachtree Road, N.E., Suite 450, Atlanta, Georgia, 30326-1162.
Telephone: 404-885-1500.
Telecopier: 404-231-1978.

(See Next Column)

GLASS, MCCULLOUGH, SHERRILL & HARROLD, *Atlanta—Continued*

Washington, D.C. Office: 1155 15th Street, N.W., Suite 400, Washington, D.C., 20005.
Telephone: 202-785-8118.
Telecopier: 202-785-0128.

MEMBERS OF FIRM

Peter B. Glass
Kenneth R. McCullough
Jeffrey C. Baxter
Mark A. Block
William D. Brunstad
T. Kennerly Carroll, Jr.
Geoffrey H. Cederholm
William F. Clark
Gardner G. Courson
Luther C. Curtis
C. Walker Ingraham
Ugo F. Ippolito
Susan Kalus
John A. Sherrill
Thomas J. Harrold, Jr.
James H. Kaminer, Jr.
Ross P. Kendall
James W. King
S. Andrew McKay
John J. Scroggin
Jerry A. Shaifer
R. Phillip Shinall, III
W. Clayton Sparrow, Jr.
John M. Stuckey, Jr.
Bradley J. Taylor
Robert M. Trusty
Robert E. Wilson

OF COUNSEL

Glee A. Triplett

ASSOCIATES

Deborah L. Britt
Terence G. Clark
Patrick J. Clarke
Ronald J. Conte
Bryan A. Downs
Neill Edwards
Allen W. Groves
D. Lynn Holliday
Cecilia S. Jackson
Mark L. Kaplan
Laura H. MacElroy
Paul P. Mattingly
Betsy Birns McCall
Lori Ann Olejniczak
Kendal D. Silas
Laura H. Walter (Not admitted in GA; Resident, Washington, D.C. Office)
Lianne M. White

For full biographical listings, see the Martindale-Hubbell Law Directory

GOLDNER, SOMMERS, SCRUDDER & BASS (AV)

2839 Paces Ferry Road, Suite 800, 30339-3774
Telephone: 404-436-4777
Facsimile: 404-436-8777

Stephen L. Goldner
Susan V. Sommers
Henry E. Scrudder, Jr.
Glenn S. Bass
C. G. Jester, Jr.
Alfred A. Quillian, Jr.

Sandra G. Chase
Linda Jacobsen Pollock
Benjamin David Ladner
Marci R. Weston
William W. Horlock, Jr.
Michelle P. Jordan
Tammy Spivack Skinner

For full biographical listings, see the Martindale-Hubbell Law Directory

HISHON & BURBAGE (AV)

Suite 2000 Eleven Hundred Peachtree Building, 1100 Peachtree Street, 30309
Telephone: 404-898-9880
Telecopier: 404-898-9890

MEMBERS OF FIRM

Robert H. Hishon
Jesse S. Burbage, III
Bruce B. Weddell
R. Bradley Carr

ASSOCIATES

Mike Bothwell

OF COUNSEL

James G. Killough

For full biographical listings, see the Martindale-Hubbell Law Directory

HOLT, NEY, ZATCOFF & WASSERMAN (AV)

A Partnership including Professional Corporations
100 Galleria Parkway, Suite 600, 30339
Telephone: 404-956-9600
Facsimile Number: 404-956-1490

MEMBERS OF FIRM

Robert G. Holt (P.C.)
James M. Ney (P.C.)
Sanford H. Zatcoff (P.C.)
Michael G. Wasserman (P.C.)
J. Scott Jacobson
Charles D. Vaughn
Stephen C. Greenberg
Richard P. Vornholt
Barbara J. Schneider

ASSOCIATES

Brian P. Cain
David S. O'Quinn
Jay Frank Castle

Representative Clients: AmeriHealth, Inc.; Citibank, N.A.; Cummins South, Inc.; First American Title Insurance Co.; First National Bank of Chicago; First Union National Bank of Georgia; Georgia Scientific & Technical Research Foundation; NationsBank of Georgia, N.A.; Safety-Kleen Corp.; Trammell Crow Residential.

For full biographical listings, see the Martindale-Hubbell Law Directory

JENKINS & EELLS (AV)

The Rhodes Building, Suite 500, 3005 Chamblee-Tucker Road, 30341
Telephone: 404-457-1850
Fax: 404-458-5894
Cartersville, Georgia Office: 15 Public Square.
Telephone: 404-387-1373.
Fax: 404-387-2396.

MEMBERS OF FIRM

Frank E. Jenkins, III
Gregory M. Eells
G. Carey Nelson
Sharon C. Barnes

ASSOCIATES

Kirk R. Fjelstul
John A. Medina
B. Emory Potter

OF COUNSEL

Bradley M. Hoyt

For full biographical listings, see the Martindale-Hubbell Law Directory

JONES, DAY, REAVIS & POGUE (AV)

3500 One Peachtree Center, 303 Peachtree Street, N.E., 30308-3242
Telephone: 404-521-3939
Cable Address: "Attorneys Atlanta"
Telex: 54-2711
Telecopier: 404-581-8330
In Brussels, Belgium: Avenue Louise 480, 7th Floor, B-1050 Brussels.
Telephone: 011-32-2-645-14-11.
Telecopier: 011-32-2-645-14-45.
In Chicago, Illinois: 77 West Wacker.
Telephone: 312-782-3939.
Telecopier: 312-782-8585.
In Cleveland, Ohio: North Point. 901 Lakeside Avenue.
Telephone: 216-586-3939.
Cable Address: "Attorneys Cleveland".
Telex: 980389.
Telecopier: 216-579-0212.
In Columbus, Ohio: 1900 Huntington Center.
Telephone: 614-469-3939.
Cable Address: "Attorneys Columbus".
Telecopier: 614-461-4198.
In Dallas, Texas: 2300 Trammell Crow Center, 2001 Ross Avenue.
Telephone: 214-220-3939.
Cable Address: "Attorneys Dallas."
Telex: 730852.
Telecopier: 214-969-5100.
In Frankfurt, Germany: Westendstrasse 41, 60325 Frankfurt am Main.
Telephone: 011-49-69-7438-3939.
Telecopier: 011-49-69-741-1686.
In Geneva, Switzerland: 20, rue de Candolle.
Telephone: 011-41-22-320-2339.
Telecopier: 011-41-22-320-1232.
In Hong Kong: 1501 One Exchange Square, 8 Connaught Place.
Telephone: 011-852-526-6895.
Telecopier: 011-852-810-5787.
In Irvine, California: 2603 Main Street, Suite 900.
Telephone: 714-851-3939.
Telex: 194911 Lawyers LSA.
Telecopier: 714-553-7539.
In London, England: One Mount Street.
Telephone: 011-44-71-493-9361.
Cable Address: "Surgoe London WI."
Telecopier: 011-44-71-493-9666.
In Los Angeles, California: 555 West Fifth Street, Suite 4600.
Telephone: 213-489-3939.
Telex: 181439 UD.
Telecopier: 213-243-2539.
In New York, New York: 599 Lexington Avenue.
Telephone: 212-326-3939.
Cable Address: "JONESDAY NEWYORK."
Telex: 237013 JDRP UR.
Telecopier: 212-755-7306.
In Paris, France: 62, rue du Faubourg Saint-Honore.
Telephone: 011-33-1-44-71-3939.
Cable Address: "Surgoe Paris."
Telex: 290156 Surgoe.
Telecopier: 011-33-1-49-24-0471.
In Pittsburgh, Pennsylvania: 500 Grant Street, 31st Floor.
Telephone: 412-391-3939.
Cable Address: "Attorneys Pittsburgh".
Telecopier: 412-394-7959.
In Riyadh, Saudi Arabia: Law Offices of Saud M.A. Shawwaf, P.O. Box 2700.
Telephones: 011 (966-1) 465-6543, 011 (966-1) 464-8534 or 011 (966-1) 464-8540.
Telex: 401831 SAUCON SJ.
Telecopier: (966-1) 464-8480.
In Taipei, Taiwan: 7th Floor, 2 Tun Hwa South Road, Section 2.
Telephone: 011 (886-2) 704-6808 and 704-6809.
Telecopier: 011 (886-2) 704-6791.

(See Next Column)

JONES, DAY, REAVIS & POGUE—*Continued*

In Tokyo, Japan: Shiroyama JT Mori Bldg., 15th Floor, 3-1, Toranomon 4-chome Minato-ku.
Telephone: 011-81-3-3433-3939.
Telecopier: 011-81-3-5401-2725.
In Washington, D.C.: Metropolitan Square, 1450 G Street, N.W.
Telephone: 202-879-3939.
Cable Address: "Attorneys Washington."
Telex: 89-2410 ATTORNEYS WASH.
Telecopier: 202-737-2832. 2-737-2832.

MEMBERS OF FIRM IN ATLANTA

Dom H. Wyant
W. Rhett Tanner
Robert W. Smith
Girard E. Boudreau, Jr.
Russell S. Grove, Jr.
Christopher L. Carson
W. Lyman Dillon
Alvis E. Campbell
Dorothy Yates Kirkley
James H. Landon
David J. Bailey
R. Mason Cargill
Milford B. Hatcher, Jr.
Richard M. Kirby
G. Lee Garrett, Jr.
Paul Burke O'Hearn
Barry J. Stein
James R. Johnson
John E. Zamer
R. Dal Burton
William B. B. Smith
Lisa Anne Stater
R. Matthew Martin
Richard H. Miller (Not admitted in GA)
Lizanne Thomas
Deborah A. Sudbury

OF COUNSEL

L. Travis Brannon, Jr.
James F. McEvoy
Ruth H. Gershon

SENIOR ATTORNEY

L. Trammell Newton, Jr.
Arthur G. Kent (Not admitted in GA)
John E. Taylor

ASSOCIATES

Stephen B. Schrock
David P. Baum
Sidney R. Brown
Gregory Russell Hanthorn
Robert Q. Jones, Jr.
Rory D. Lyons (Not admitted in GA)
Ralph R. Morrison
William V. Bryant
Michael Joseph McConnell
William Baxter Rowland
Cherie M. Fuzzell
Victoria A. George
Kenneth Hayes Harrigan
David M. Monde
Aasia Mustakeem
Eliot William Robinson
Katherine M. Elwood (Not admitted in GA)
E. Elaine Rogers
Steven J. Stewart
Mark L. Hanson
James L. Hayes, Jr.
Robert N. Johnson
Mark A. Loeffler
Mariann Morgan
Douglas D. Selph
Dale Smith Voyles
Janine Cone Metcalf (Not admitted in GA)
Terrill L. Mallory
Richard P. LeVee (Not admitted in GA)
Stefano M. Miele
Diane G. Pulley
John H. Williamson
J. Olen Earl
Kevin A. Hendricks
Kim Purcell Pike
Joel C. Ross
Linzy O. Scott, III
Douglas M. Towns
Gregory M. Cole
Wendy Y. Normandin
J. Christopher York
Sara B. King
T. Robert Reid
Sterling A. Spainhour, Jr.

For full biographical listings, see the Martindale-Hubbell Law Directory

KILPATRICK & CODY (AV)

Suite 2800, 1100 Peachtree Street, 30309-4530
Telephone: 404-815-6500
Telephone Copier: 404-815-6555
Telex: 54-2307
Washington, D.C. Office: Suite 800, 700 13th Street, N.W., 20005.
Telephone: 202-508-5800. Telephone Copier: 202-508-5858.
Brussels, Belgium Office: Avenue Louise 65, BTE 3, 1050 Brussels.
Telephone: (32) (2) 533-03-00.
Telecopier: (32) (2) 534-86-38.
London, England Office: 68 Pall Mall, London, SW1Y 5ES, England.
Telephone: (44) (71) 321 0477.
Telecopier: (44) (71) 930 9733.
Augusta, Georgia Office: Suite 1400 First Union Bank Building, P.O. Box 2043, 30903. Telephone (706) 724-2622. Telecopier (706) 722-0219.

Harold Hirsch (1881-1939)
Alexander Stephens Clay (1905-1945)
Marion Smith (1884-1947)
Welborn B. Cody (1899-1976)
Martin E. Kilpatrick (1905-1980)
Albert C. Tate, Jr. (1938-1983)
Ernest P. Rogers (1903-1985)
William B. Gunter (1919-1986)
Devereaux F. McClatchey (1906-1993)
D. Lurton Massee, Jr. (1936-1993)

OF COUNSEL

Louis Regenstein
Harry S. Baxter
A. Gus Cleveland
George B. Haley
Thomas C. Shelton

(See Next Column)

MEMBERS OF FIRM

Barry Phillips
Harold E. Abrams
Miles J. Alexander
Elliott H. Levitas
Jefferson Davis, Jr. (London, England and Brussels, Belgium Offices)
Matthew H. Patton
William A. Burnham
G. Kimbrough Taylor, Jr.
A. Kimbrough Davis
Joel B. Piassick
Jerre B. Swann
Wyck A. Knox, Jr. (Augusta Office)
Duane C. Aldrich
Richard R. Cheatham
David M. Zacks
Alfred S. Lurey
A. Stephens Clay
Tim Carssow
Susan A. Cahoon
Dennis S. Meir
Joseph M. Beck
R. Alexander Bransford, Jr.
Thomas C. Harney
Richard R. Boisseau
Raymond G. Chadwick, Jr. (Augusta Office)
Frederick K. Heller, Jr. (Resident, Brussels, Belgium Office)
Rupert M. Barkoff
William J. Vesely, Jr.
James H. Coil III
William H. Boice
Suzanne G. Mason
J. William Veatch, III
W. Stanley Blackburn
Edmund M. Kneisel
Virginia S. Taylor
Thomas H. Christopher
M. Andrew Kauss
R. Slaton Tuggle, III
John S. Pratt
Hilary P. Jordan
Mark D. Wincek (Not admitted in GA)
Duncan A. Roush
Gary K. Saidman
Frederick H. von Unwerth
Thomas William Baker
Caroline W. Spangenberg
James E. Blanchard (Augusta Office)
Marc K. Ritzmann
G. William Austin, III
J. Vance Hughes
Robert E. Banta
C. Randall Nuckolls
James L. Ewing, IV
Thompson H. Gooding, Jr.
Keith T. Ott (Resident, London, England Office)
Richard A. Horder
Timothy N. Tucker
Sally Cotter Baxter
Jane E. Jordan
Michael W. Tyler
David A. Stockton
Diane L. Prucino
Alan R. Perry, Jr.
Judith A. Powell
Deborah B. Zink
Mara McRae
Christopher P. Bussert
Thomas K. Bick (Not admitted in GA)
Martha Jo Wagner (Not admitted in GA)
Stephen E. Hudson
Patrea L. Pabst
Dennis L. Zakas
W. Randy Eaddy
Colvin T. Leonard, III
Gary J. Toman
James R. Kanner
Kent E. Mast
Evelyn H. Coats
H. Quigg Fletcher, III
C. Ray Mullins
Ted H. Clarkson (Augusta Office)
Earle R. Taylor, III
Louis A. Aguilar
Gregg E. McDougal (Augusta Office)
Roderick C. Dennehy, Jr.
Neal S. Berinhout
William H. Brewster
Candace L. Fowler
F. Sheffield Hale
Dean W. Russell
J. Henry Walker, IV
Kurt E. Blase (Washington, D.C. Office)

COUNSEL

G. Paris Sykes, Jr.
Michael H. Trotter
Kathryn B. Solley
R. Scott Tewes

ASSOCIATES

Claudia R. Adkison
David K. Anderson
Todd R. Bair
William B. Barkley
John F. Beasley, Jr.
Craig E. Bertschi
James F. Bogan, III
J. Scott Carr
Louis S. Cataland (Not admitted in GA)
Gregory K. Cinnamon
Elizabeth H. Cohen (Not admitted in GA)
Jerome F. Connell, Jr.
Elizabeth P. Cowie
Lexie L. Craven (Not admitted in GA)
Jan Meadows Davidson
Theodore H. Davis, Jr.
Lisa S. Edwards
Daniel M. Epstein
Donald C. Evans, Jr.
Felipe J. Farley
Lynn E. Fowler
Nancy G. Gilreath (Not admitted in GA)
Jamie L. Greene
Richard B. Hankins
Ralph H. Harrison, III
Michael K. Heilbronner
Kevin E. Hooks
Ciannat M. Howett (Resident)
Laura M. Ivey
Steven H. Jackman
Walter E. Johnson
Craig R. Kaufman (Not admitted in GA)
Mark P. Kelly
Paul Vincent Lalli
Michael Dean Langford
William F. Long
Laurel J. Lucey
Stephanie K. Maffett
Melinda A. Marbes
Kenneth J. Markowitz (Washington, D.C. Office)
David R. Martinez
Stephen W. Mazza
Kevin M. McMahon
Todd C. Meyers
John M. Mitnick
Jeffrey F. Montgomery
Reinaldo Pascual
Carolyn A. Peterson
Charles M. Rice
Jane W. Robbins
Brian Leonard Schleicher
Jennifer S. Schumacher
Edwin S. Schwartz (Not admitted in GA)
Lori J. Shapiro
Rebecca L. Sigmund
Trent B. Speckhals
Ann Marie Stack
James D. Steinberg
Mitchell G. Stockwell
Whit F. Stolz
Rebekah G. Strickland
Jeffrey J. Toney
Jeffrey A. Van Detta

(See Next Column)

KILPATRICK & CODY, *Atlanta—Continued*

ASSOCIATES (Continued)

Mary Lillian Walker
Amy Weinstein
Charles D. Weiss
Kevin R. Wolff
Cheryl Knowles Zalesky

Representative Clients: Southern Bell Telephone and Telegraph Co.; Lockheed Aeronautical Systems Co.; Frito-Lay, Inc.; Scientific-Atlanta, Inc.; Scripto-Tokai, Inc.; Bank South Corporation; PepsiCo.

For full biographical listings, see the Martindale-Hubbell Law Directory

KING & SPALDING (AV)

191 Peachtree Street, N.E., 30303-1763
Telephone: 404-572-4600
FAX: 404-572-5100
Cable Address: "Terminus"
Telex: 54-2917 KINSPALD ATL
Washington, D.C. Office: 1730 Pennsylvania Avenue, N.W., 20006.
Telephone: 202-737-0500.
FAX: 202-626-3737.
New York, N.Y. Office: 120 West 45th Street, 10036.
Telephone: 212-556-2100.
FAX: 212-556-2222;
Telex: 6716353; Answerback: Compris.

MEMBERS OF FIRM

Alex C. King (1856-1926)
Jack J. Spalding (1856-1938)
Hughes Spalding (1886-1969)
Furman Smith (1910-1968)
Robert Battey Troutman (1890-1973)
William K. Meadow (1914-1987)
Griffin B. Bell
Frank C. Jones
Byron Attridge
Robert L. Steed
John A. Wallace
Edward J. Hawie
John C. Staton, Jr.
David L. Coker
George Lemuel Hewes
Horace H. Sibley
Charles M. Shaffer, Jr.
W. Donald Knight, Jr.
Robert W. Miller
James H. Wildman (See New York Listing)
Joseph B. Haynes
Herschel M. Bloom
William S. McKee (See Washington, D.C. Listing)
Michael C. Russ
Lloyd Sutter
Walter W. Driver, Jr.
Eugene G. Partain
George H. Lanier
Lanny B. Bridgers
Clarence H. Ridley
William A. Clineburg, Jr.
Richard G. Woodward
William F. Nelson
Joseph R. Bankoff
Theodore M. Hester (See Washington, D.C. Listing)
Mason W. Stephenson
Nolan C. Leake
Ralph B. Levy
John Hays Mershon
Donald S. Kohla
Charles H. Tisdale, Jr.
Russell B. Richards
George S. Branch
Michael E. Ross
Ruth Tinsley West
William B. Fryer
Michael R. Horten
Scott J. Arnold
Bruce N. Hawthorne
Albert H. Conrad, Jr.
Henry L. Bowden, Jr.
Robert G. Woodward
Abraham N. M. Shashy, Jr. (See Washington, D.C. Listing)
Harry L. Gutman (See Washington, D.C. Listing)
Joseph W. Dorn (See Washington, D.C. Listing)
L. Joseph Loveland, Jr.
James D. Miller (See Washington, D.C. Listing)
Chilton Davis Varner
Gilbert D. Porter (See New York Listing)
Glen A. Reed
David G. Epstein
H. Lane Dennard, Jr.
Karl-Erbo Graf von Kageneck (See New York Listing)
Wilfried E. Witthuhn (See New York Listing)
M. Robert Thornton
Jackie S. Levinson (See Washington, D.C. Listing)
William E. Hoffmann, Jr.
Larry D. Thompson
Steven R. Lainoff (See Washington, D.C. Listing)
Eugene M. Pfeifer (See Washington, D.C. Listing)
Gerald T. Woods
William C. Hendricks III (See Washington, D.C. Listing)
Randolph C. Coley
Ralph A. Pitts
John D. Capers, Jr.
J. Kevin Buster
Mark A. Kuller (See Washington, D.C. Listing)
Gordon Travers (See New York Listing)
Isam Salah (See New York Listing)
James H. Lokey, Jr.
E. William Bates, II (See New York Listing)
William A. Holby
Bruce W. Baber
Gordon A. Smith
James A. Pardo, Jr.
Philip A. Theodore
Floyd C. Newton, III
William R. Goodell
Dan L. Heller
Richard L. Shackelford
Richard A. Schneider
W. Clay Gibson
Peter J. Genz
Jeffrey M. Stein
Daniel J. King (See New York Listing)
Jess H. Stribling (See Washington, D.C. Listing)
Edward M. Basile (See Washington, D.C. Listing)
Dwight J. Davis
Eleanor Banister
Michael J. Egan, III
Robert G. Pennington
Robert D. Hays
Michael R. Smith
Stanley H. Abramson (See Washington, D.C. Listing)
Katherine L. Rhyne (See Washington, D.C. Listing)
Joseph Sedwick Sollers III (See Washington, D.C. Listing)

(See Next Column)

MEMBERS OF FIRM (Continued)

Thomas F. Wessel (See Washington, D.C. Listing)
Margaret E. O'Neil (See New York Listing)
Martin M. McNerney (See Washington, D.C. Listing)
William G. Roche
Jon R. Harris, Jr.
Caroline Bensabat Marshall
William R. Spalding
J. Warren Ott
Philip E. Holladay, Jr.
Kathrine A. McLendon (See New York Listing)
Peter K. Storey (See New York Listing)
Patricia Ferrari (See New York Listing)
Brian Rosner (See New York Listing)
Michael E. Norton (See New York Listing)
Bernays Thomas Barclay (See New York Listing)
Patricia T. Barmeyer
Frederick H. Degnan (See Washington, D.C. Listing)
Thomas K. Dotzenrod
Bernadette M. Drankoski
Sandra W. Hallmark (See Washington, D.C. Listing)
Beth Hornbuckle
R. Anthony Howard, Jr. (See Washington, D.C. Listing)
John J. Kelley III
Stephanie E. Parker
Eileen P. Brumback (See New York Listing)
Robert P. Bryant
S. Samuel Griffin
Bond K. Koga (See New York Listing)
Charles K. McKnight, Jr.
Elizabeth M. Schachner
Michael P. Mabile (See Washington, D.C. Listing)
Dan Hall Willoughby, Jr.
Paul K. Ferdinands
William F. Lummus, Jr.
Reginald Ross Smith
Hector E. Llorens, Jr.
Suzanne C. Feese
Michael W. Johnston
Dvorah A. Richman (See Washington, D.C. Listing)

OF COUNSEL

George D. Busbee

COUNSEL

James N. Gorsline
David D. Willoughby
Les Oakes
David A. Nix
William C. Talmadge (See Washington, D.C. Listing)
Susan Jewett (See Washington, D.C. Listing)
Thomas B. Gaines, Jr.
Susan E. Foxworth
Veronica G. Kayne (See Washington, D.C. Listing)
Diane S. White
Harold M. Shaw (See Washington, D.C. Listing)
Joan L. Dillon
Sandra Cohen Kalter (See Washington, D.C. Listing)
James A. Hughes, Jr. (See Washington, D.C. Listing)
John W. Hinchey
Paul J. Larkin, Jr. (See Washington, D.C. Listing)
Erik J. Swenson (See New York Listing)

ASSOCIATES

Jonathan M. Aberman (See New York Listing)
Lynn Ackerman
Leticia D. Alfonso
J. Tucker Alford
Robert R. Ambler, Jr.
Joseph B. Amsbary, Jr.
Catherine L. Amspacher (Not admitted in GA)
Jill Pride Anderson
Deborah J. Andrews (See Washington, D.C. Listing)
Laurence B. Appel
William J. Armstrong
Donald D. Ashley (See Washington, D.C. Listing)
Paul M. Baisier
Ady A. Barkay (See Washington, D.C. Listing)
Sara E. Barton
Susan L. Bassett
W. Randall Bassett
C. William Baxley
Andrew T. Bayman
H. Harris Beall
Matthew L. Bennett (See Washington, D.C. Listing)
Mary A. Bernard
Douglas A. Bird
Michael L. Bishop
Sarah Robinson Borders
Daniel D. Bosis, Jr. (See Washington, D.C. Listing)
James W. Boswell, III
Katherine A. Brokaw
Althea J.K. Broughton
Kelly R. Caffarelli
Jameson B. Carroll
Ellen J. Case (See Washington, D.C. Listing)
Stephanie Barkholz Casteel
Nicole Caucci
C. Paul Chalmers
Han Choi
M. Kristin Ramsey Clyde
Michael J. Cochran
Fred G. Codner
Philip A. Cooper
Peter K. Daniel
Katharine Darnell
Todd P. Davis
Steven J. De Groot
Kerrie Covell Dent (See Washington, D.C. Listing)
Gregory C. Dorris (See Washington, D.C. Listing)
William L. Durham II
Lawrence Slade Eastwood, Jr.
Keith E. Engel (See Washington, D.C. Listing)
Stefan W. Engelhardt (See New York Listing)
Steven J. Estep
Zachary Thomas Fardon (See Washington, D.C. Listing)
Andrew K. Fletcher
C. Constance Fore
Jennifer L. Fox
Mark Edwin Freitag
Joe Garcia, Jr. (See Washington, D.C. Listing)
Timothy J. Goodwin
Jill R. Greaney (See Washington, D.C. Listing)
Ellen K. Greene
Steven J. Greene (See New York Listing)
Alana L. Griffin (Not admitted in GA)
Joan E. Hankin (See Washington, D.C. Listing)
Kenneth R. Hannahs, Jr. (Not admitted in GA)
Lawton W. Hawkins
Susan L. Heilbronner (See Washington Listing)
John C. Herman
William H. (Hal) Hess
Tara A. Higgins (See New York Listing)
James E. Hooper, Jr.
Christopher W. House, III

(See Next Column)

KING & SPALDING—*Continued*

ASSOCIATES (Continued)

Mary Ellen Huckabee
Ginabeth B. Hutchison
Mona Lucille Hymel (See Washington, D.C. Listing)
Louis N. (Woody) Jameson
Robert M. Keenan, III
Edward G. Kehoe (See New York Listing)
Caroline M. Kelly
Robert B. Kinz (See New York Listing)
Stacey A. Kipnis
Lee M. Kirby (See New York Listing)
Jill Swerdloff Klein (See Washington, D.C. Listing)
Leah J. Knowlton
Marilyn J. Kuray (See Washington, D.C. Listing)
Darryl S. Laddin
Scott G. Langerman
Mark A. Lewis
Todd Y. McArthur (See Washington, D.C. Listing)
Letitia A. McDonald
Robert B. McIntosh
Patricia L. McKenney (See Washington, D.C. Listing)
Ann McWhorter
Paul B. Murphy
Roger Eugene Murray
Jeff V. Nelson (See New York Listing)
Alan H. Nichols
Christina Sungyoon Pak
Christina Sungyoon Parker
Michael R. Powers (Not admitted in GA)
D. C. Presten, III
Polly J. Price (See Washington, D.C. Listing)
Alan J. Prince
Stephen Rahaim (Not admitted in GA)
Keith D. Reuben
Lara B. Robinson
Sarah E. Rosenberg
Michael E. Rubinger
William S. Shackelford (See Washington, D.C. Listing)
Shelly Y. Sharp
Helen L. Siegal (Not admitted in GA; See New York Listing)
Lawrence A. Slovensky
Bradley A. Slutsky
Douglas A. Smith
Sean R. Smith
James C. Snyder, Jr. (See Washington, D.C. Listing)
James B. Sowell
Alexander C. S. Spiro (See New York Listing)
M. Jefferson Starling, III
Phyllis B. Sumner
Evelyn S. Tang (See Washington, D.C. Listing)
Janet Taylor (Not admitted in GA)
Mary Jane Theis
Carmen R. Toledo
Anders K. Torning
John P. H. Vigman (See New York Listing)
Kristy Weathers
Jack Williams, Jr.
Loren B. Wimpfheimer
Stephen M. Wiseman (See New York Listing)
Carol M. Wood
Jill M. Wood
Laura L. Woollcott
Christopher A. Wray
Michael Wilson Youtt
Carolyn M. Zander

STAFF ATTORNEYS

Elizabeth K. Dorminey
Jimmy F. Kirkland
Donald E. Meyer (Not admitted in GA)

Representative Clients: BellSouth Corp.; Calloway Foundation; Capital Holding Corp.; Charter Medical Corp.; The Coca-Cola Co.; Crawford & Company; Emory University; Georgia Tech Foundation; Gulf States Paper Corp.; Hardaway Construction Co.

For full biographical listings, see the Martindale-Hubbell Law Directory

KUTAK ROCK (AV)

A Partnership Including Professional Corporations
4400 Georgia-Pacific Center, 133 Peachtree Street, N.E., 30303-1808
Telephone: 404-222-4600
Fax: 404-222-4654
Baton Rouge, Louisiana Office: 300 Four United Plaza, 8555 United Plaza Boulevard, 70809-2251.
Telephone: 504-929-8585.
Facsimile: 504-929-8580.
Denver, Colorado Office: Suite 2900, 717 Seventeenth Street, 80202-3329.
Telephone: 303-297-2400.
Facsimile: 303-292-7799.
Little Rock, Arkansas Office: Suite 1770, 124 West Capitol Avenue, 72201-3719.
Telephone: 501-376-9208.
Facsimile: 501-375-3749.
Kansas City, Missouri Office: United Missouri Bank Building, Third Floor, 9201 Ward Parkway.
Telephone: 816-361-3363.
Telecopier: 816-361-8397.
Los Angeles, California Office: Suite 1330, 2049 Century Park East, 90067-3115.
Telephone: 310-785-3900.
Facsimile: 310-785-3999.
New York, New York Office: Seventh Floor, 505 Park Avenue, 10022-1155.
Telephone: 212-752-0800.
Facsimile: 212-752-2281.
Oklahoma City, Oklahoma Office: 1190 Oklahoma Tower, 210 West Park Avenue, 73102-5618.
Telephone: 405-232-9827.
Facsimile: 405-232-8307.
Omaha, Nebraska Office: The Omaha Building, 1650 Farnam Street, 68102-2186.
Telephone: 402-346-6000.
Facsimile: 402-346-1148.

(See Next Column)

Phoenix, Arizona Office: Suite 650, 3636 North Central Avenue, 85012-1984.
Telephone: 602-285-1700.
Facsimile: 602-285-1868.
Pittsburgh, Pennsylvania Office: 1214 Frick Building, 437 Grant Street, 15219-6002.
Telephone: 412-261-6720.
Facsimile: 412-261-6717.
Washington, D.C. Office: Suite 1000, 1101 Connecticut Avenue, NW, 20036-4374.
Telephone: 202-828-2400.
Facsimile: 202-828-2488.

OF COUNSEL

Edwin L. Sterne
Thomas R. Todd, Jr.
Robert G. Brunton (Not admitted in GA)

MEMBERS OF FIRM

Lawrence L. Thompson
Michael K. Wolensky
Edward M. Ford
David L. Amsden
Paul M. Smith
Gregory R. Crochet
Michael A. Kazamias

ASSOCIATES

Sarah E. Day
Angela M. Gottsche
David J. Gellen
Nanette L. Wesley

For full biographical listings, see the Martindale-Hubbell Law Directory

LIPSHUTZ, GREENBLATT & KING (AV)

2300 Harris Tower-Peachtree Center, 233 Peachtree Street, N.E., 30043
Telephone: 404-688-2300
Fax: 404-588-0648
Washington, D.C. Office: Suite 950, 1275 K Street, N.W.
Telephone: 202-898-4800.

MEMBERS OF FIRM

Robert J. Lipshutz
Edward L. Greenblatt
Randall M. Lipshutz

OF COUNSEL

William R. King
Tito Mazzetta

ASSOCIATES

Paula B. Smith
Timothy L. S. Sitz

For full biographical listings, see the Martindale-Hubbell Law Directory

LONG ALDRIDGE & NORMAN (AV)

A Partnership including Professional Corporations
One Peachtree Center, Suite 5300, 303 Peachtree Street, 30308
Telephone: 404-527-4000
Telecopier: 404-527-4198
Washington, D.C. Office: Suite 950, 1615 L Street, 20036.
Telephone: 202-223-7033.
Telecopier: 202-223-7013.

MEMBERS OF FIRM

John G. Aldridge
Evan Appel
Douglas L. Beresford (Resident, Washington, D.C. Office)
Barbara L. Blackford
Phillip A. Bradley
Bruce P. Brown
David R. Bucey
Stephen L. Camp
Clyde E. Click
F. T. Davis, Jr., (P.C.)
Deborah S. Ebel
James A. Fleming
William L. Floyd
Gordon D. Giffin
Jeffrey K. Haidet
Thomas D. Hall
Robert D. Hancock, Jr.
John E. Holtzinger, Jr. (Resident, Washington, D.C. Office)
W. Stell Huie
R. William Ide III
David M. Ivey
M. Hill Jeffries, Jr.
J. James Johnson
Stanley S. Jones, Jr.
Margaret M. Joslin
Mark S. Kaufman
Edward A. Kazmarek
Paul H. Keck (Resident, Washington, D.C. Office)
Mark S. Lange
Clay C. Long
J. Allen Maines
Patrick M. McGeehan
Barbara A. McIntyre
Philip H. Moise
Bruce W. Moorhead, Jr.
Albert G. Norman, Jr.
John E. Ramsey
Ann Distler Salo
Russell N. Sewell, Jr.
Jacolyn A. Simmons (Resident, Washington, D.C. Office)
Edgar H. Sims, Jr. (P.C.)
Jesse J. Spikes
William F. Stevens
John T. Stough, Jr. (Resident, Washington, D.C. Office)
Patricia E. Tate
James J. Thomas II
William F. Timmons
Russell A. Tolley
Thomas R. B. Wardell (Not admitted in GA)
Jack H. Watson, Jr. (Resident, Washington, D.C. Office)
Robert I. White (Resident, Washington, D.C. Office)
Charles T. Zink

ASSOCIATES

Susan Rappa Bain
David L. Balser
James L. Barkin
R. Daniel Beale
Wayne N. Bradley
David M. Calhoun
Susan E. Dignan
L. Craig Dowdy
Kevin M. Downey (Resident, Washington, D.C. Office)
Alison M. Drummond
Thomas J. Flanigan

(See Next Column)

LONG ALDRIDGE & NORMAN, *Atlanta—Continued*

ASSOCIATES (Continued)

Lynn Gavin
Carol Russell Geiger
Kathleen Griffin
Deborah Stone Grossman
Roy E. Hadley, Jr.
Janet Eifert Haury
Susan L. Hearne (Not admitted in GA)
Eric Charles Lang
W. Scott Laseter
Thomas P. Lauth, III
H. Franklin Layson
Carole A. Loftin
Jennifer D. Malinovsky
Gary W. Marsh
Ann-Marie M. McGaughey
Kyle Michel (Resident, Washington, D.C. Office)
Paula Rafferty Miller
Joel D. Newton (Resident, Washington, D.C. Office)
Laura Fink Nix
W. Gregory Null
Andrew R. Pachman
Brooke Hume Pendleton
J. Michell Philpott
Mindy S. Planer
Melanie McGee Platt
Kenneth B. Pollock
Kellie S. Raiford
John Warner Ray, Jr.
John R. Schneider (Not admitted in GA)
Johnathan H. Short
Gregory Mark Simpson
Janice Nathanson Smith
Wendy A. Strassner
Sheryl L. Thomson
Briggs L. Tobin
Melissa P. Walker
Richard R. Willis

OF COUNSEL

William J. Carney
James W. Culbreth
C. Edward Kuntz
Carl W. Mullis, III
Martin R. Tilson, Jr.
Gerald D. Walling
John L. Watkins
Nancy A. White (Resident, Washington, D.C. Office)
Bruce H. Wynn

Representative Clients: Aladan Corporation; American Business Products, Inc.; Atlanta Gas Light Co.; The Cable Television Association of Georgia; Coca-Cola Enterprises Inc.; Law Companies Group, Inc.; MCI Communications Corp.; Murex Corp.; PNC, N.A.; President Baking Company, Inc.

For full biographical listings, see the Martindale-Hubbell Law Directory

LONG, WEINBERG, ANSLEY AND WHEELER (AV)

A Partnership including Professional Corporations
999 Peachtree Street, N.E., Suite 2700, 30309
Telephone: 404-876-2700
Facsimile: 404-875-9433

MEMBERS OF FIRM

Thomas J. Long (1898-1965)
Palmer H. Ansley (1927-1991)
Ben L. Weinberg, Jr., (P.C.)
Sidney F. Wheeler
J. Kenneth Moorman
John M. Hudgins, IV, (P.C.)
Robert G. Tanner
Joseph W. Watkins
James H. Fisher, II
M. Diane Owens
Robert D. Roll
Kenneth Marc Barré, Jr.
Alan L. Newman
Marvin A. Devlin
Earl W. Gunn
C. Bradford Marsh
Arnold E. Gardner
Lance D. Lourie
Milton B. Satcher, III
David A. Sapp
Stephen H. Sparwath
Kathryn S. Whitlock

ASSOCIATES

Ronald R. Coleman Jr.
Mark E. Robinson
Frederick N. Sager, Jr.
Debra E. LeVorse
Quinton S. Seay
Charles K. Reed
Sharon B. Austin
Patricia M. Peters
Carol P. Michel
John K. Train, IV
Johnathan T. Krawcheck
John C. Bonnie
Emily J. Brantley
Paul L. Weisbecker
Daniel W. Sweat
Margie M. Eget
Joseph N. Crosswhite
William P. Langdale, III
J. Calhoun Harris, Jr.
Laura V. Semonche
Michele L. Davis
Dennis J. Webb, Jr.
Jacquelyn D. Van Tuyl
George A. Koenig

OF COUNSEL

Meade Burns

Representative Clients: Aetna Casualty & Surety Corp.; Chrysler Motors Corp.; Emory University; Dow Corning Corp.; Ford Motor Co.; Freuhauf Trailer Corp.; Merck; Otis Elevator Co.; St. Paul Fire & Marine Insurance Co.; Toyota Motor Sales U.S.A., Inc.

For full biographical listings, see the Martindale-Hubbell Law Directory

LORD, BISSELL & BROOK (AV)

One Atlantic Center, 1201 West Peachtree Street, N.W., Suite 3700, 30309
Telephone: 404-870-4600
Telecopy: 404-872-5547
Chicago, Illinois Office: Suites 2600-3600 Harris Bank Building, 115 South LaSalle Street, 60603.
Telephone: 312-443-0700.
Telecopy: 312-443-0570.
Cable Address: "Lowirco."
Telex: 25-0336.
Los Angeles, California Office: 300 South Grand Avenue, 90071-3200.
Telephone: 213-485-1500.
Telecopy: 213-485-1200.
Telex: 18-1135.

(See Next Column)

Rockford, Illinois Office: 120 West State Street, Suite 200, 61101.
Telephone: 815-963-8050.

RESIDENT PARTNERS

Michael J. Athans
David M. Leonard
J. Robert Persons
Walton N. Smith
Thomas J. Strueber
Richard M. Watson

RESIDENT ASSOCIATES

Jeffrey R. Darby
Andrew R. Diamond
Paul L. Fields, Jr.
Richard J. Fortwengler, Jr.
David G. Greene
Gregory A. Gunter
Terry R. Howell
Carol B. Kiersky
Gilbert M. Malm
Robert E. McLaughlin
Prescott L. Nottingham
M. Joseph Sterner
Corliss L. Worford
James H. Wynn

OF COUNSEL

Marsha Kellman Klevickis

For full biographical listings, see the Martindale-Hubbell Law Directory

MACEY, WILENSKY, COHEN, WITTNER & KESSLER (AV)

Suite 700 Carnegie Building, 133 Carnegie Way, Northwest, 30303
Telephone: 404-584-1200
Telecopier: 404-681-4355
Other Atlanta, Georgia Office: 5784 Lake Forrest Drive, Suite 214, 30328.

MEMBERS OF FIRM

Morris W. Macey
Frank B. Wilensky
H. William Cohen
Sheldon R. Wittner (1943-1988)
Richard P. Kessler, Jr.
Mark L. Golder
Neil C. Gordon
Susan L. Howick
M. Todd Westfall

OF COUNSEL

Lloyd M. Feiler

ASSOCIATES

James R. Sacca
David B. Kurzweil
Michael D. Pinsky
Shayna M. (Salomon) Steinfeld
Robert A. Winter
Pamela Gronauer Hill
Rachel Anderson Snider

For full biographical listings, see the Martindale-Hubbell Law Directory

PAGE & BACEK (AV)

3490 Piedmont Road, N.E., Suite 900, 30305-4801
Telephone: 404-365-9900
Telecopier: 404-264-0221

MEMBERS OF FIRM

J. Boyd Page
Donald A. Bacek
Steven J. Gard
Brian N. Smiley
J. Michael Bishop
Edward J. Dovin
Sandra L. Goddard

ASSOCIATES

Richard L. Heffner, Jr.
Neil D. Lansing

OF COUNSEL

Edward H. Saunders

For full biographical listings, see the Martindale-Hubbell Law Directory

PAUL, HASTINGS, JANOFSKY & WALKER (AV)

A Partnership including Professional Corporations
Firm Established in 1951; Office in 1980.
42nd Floor, Georgia Pacific Center, 133 Peachtree Street, N.E., 30303-1840
Telephone: 404-588-9900
Los Angeles, California Office: Twenty-Third Floor 555 South Flower Street.
Telephone: 213-683-6000.
Cable Address: "Paulhast."
TWX: 910-321-4065.
Orange County, California Office: Seventeenth Floor, 695 Town Center Drive, Costa Mesa.
Telephone: 714-668-6200.
Washington, D.C. Office: Tenth Floor, 1299 Pennsylvania Avenue, N.W.
Telephone: 202-508-9500.
Santa Monica, California Office: Fifth Floor, 1299 Ocean Avenue.
Telephone: 310-319-3300.
Stamford, Connecticut Office: Ninth Floor, 1055 Washington Boulevard.
Telephone: 203-961-7400.
New York, New York Office: 31st Floor, 399 Park Avenue.
Telephone: 212-318-6000.
Tokyo, Japan Office: Toranomon Ohtori Building, 8th Floor, 4-3 Toranomon 1-Chome, Minato-Ku.
Telephone: (03) 3507-0730.

MEMBERS OF FIRM

Richard M. Asbill
R. Lawrence Ashe, Jr., (P.C.)
Jesse H. Austin, III
Keith W. Berglund
Daryl R. Buffenstein
Thomas G. Burch, Jr.
Kevin Conboy
Paul J. Connell
James H. Cox
William E. Eason, Jr.

(See Next Column)

PAUL, HASTINGS, JANOFSKY & WALKER—*Continued*

MEMBERS OF FIRM (Continued)

Weyman T. Johnson, Jr.
Philip J. Marzetti
Chris D. Molen
Julian D. Nealy
John G. Parker
Charles T. Sharbaugh
Wayne H. Shortridge
John H. Steed
C. Geoffrey Weirich

OF COUNSEL

Leslie A. Dent
Renee Lewis Glover
Deborah A. Marlowe
Robert C. Moot, Jr.
Craig K. Pendergrast
W. Andrew Scott
Charles A. Shanor

ASSOCIATES

David J. Burge
Ronald T. Coleman, Jr.
James R. Glenister
Jocelyn J. Hunter
A. Christine Hurt
Janet L. Kishbaugh
Kimberly Martin
Melinda L. Moseley
John J. Neely, III
Tait O. Norton
Dwan E. Packnett
L. Lynne Pulliam
Nancy E. Ryan
Howard J. Schechter (Not admitted in GA)
Mathew Anthony Schuh
Joseph C. Sharp
Kim M. Shipley
E. Gary Spitko (Not admitted in GA)
Kristen K. Swartz
Eric Jon Taylor
Michael T. Voytek (Not admitted in GA)
Stanley F. Wasowski (Not admitted in GA)
Crystal L. Williams (Not admitted in GA)
Jonathan B. Wilson

For full biographical listings, see the Martindale-Hubbell Law Directory

---

POPE, McGLAMRY, KILPATRICK & MORRISON (AV)

A Partnership including Professional Corporations
83 Walton Street, N.W., P.O. Box 1733, 30303
Telephone: 404-523-7706;
Phenix City, Alabama: 205-298-7354
Columbus, Georgia Office: 318 11th Street, 2nd Floor, P.O. Box 2128, 31902-2128.
Telephone: 706-324-0050.

MEMBERS OF FIRM

C. Neal Pope (P.C.)
Max R. McGlamry (P.C.) (Resident, Columbus, Georgia Office)
Paul V. Kilpatrick, Jr. (Resident, Columbus, Georgia Office)
R. Timothy Morrison
Michael L. McGlamry
Earle F. Lasseter
William J. Cornwell
Jay F. Hirsch
Daniel W. Sigelman
Wade H. Tomlinson, III
William Usher Norwood, III

RESIDENT ASSOCIATES

C. Elizabeth Pope

Reference: Columbus Bank & Trust Co.

For full biographical listings, see the Martindale-Hubbell Law Directory

---

POWELL, GOLDSTEIN, FRAZER & MURPHY (AV)

191 Peachtree Street, N.E., Sixteenth Floor, 30303
Telephone: 404-572-6600
Telex: 542864
Telecopier: 404-572-6999
Cable Address: "Pgfm"
Washington, D.C. Office: Sixth Floor, 1001 Pennsylvania Avenue, N.W., 20004.
Telephone: 202-347-0066.

MEMBERS OF FIRM

John Dozier Little (1871-1934)
Arthur Gray Powell (1873-1951)
Max F. Goldstein (1886-1973)
Burket Dean Murphy (1894-1981)
Edward E. Dorsey (1920-1981)
James N. Frazer (1903-1985)
Eric W. Anderson
Gavin S. Appleby
David M. Armitage
David R. Aufdenspring
David S. Baker
Jerry B. Blackstock
Larry I. Bogart
Armin G. Brecher
Virginia A. Bush
Gregory M. Chait (Not admitted in GA)
Frank A. Crisafi
William V. Custer, IV
Dean S. Daskal
V. Robert Denham, Jr.
Gabriel Dumitrescu
Marilyn M. Fish
Elliott Goldstein
C. Scott Greene
Wilbur Gordon Hamlin, Jr.
John W. Harbin
Robert R. Harlin
James W. Hawkins
Jesse W. Hill
Scott M. Hobby
Lewis C. Horne, Jr.
J. Winston Huff
J. Stephen Hufford
Randall L. Hughes
LeeAnn Jones
James H. Keaten
Jeffrey W. Kelley
V. Scott Killingsworth
William L. Kinzer
Kathryn L. Knudson
Kenneth H. Kraft
Bruce R. Larson
William G. Leonard
Jay J. Levin
Robert C. Lewinson
William Joseph Linkous, Jr.
Frank Love, Jr.
John T. Marshall
James J. McAlpin, Jr.
Frank S. McGaughey, III

(See Next Column)

MEMBERS OF FIRM (Continued)

Thomas R. McNeill
Richard C. Mitchell
Walter G. Moeling, IV
Charles Eugene Murphy, Jr.
David C. Nicholson
E. Penn Nicholson
John R. Parks
James C. Rawls
Thomas S. Richey
Robert C. Reynolds, Jr.
Kim H. Roeder
David G. Ross
Joan Boilen Sasine
Steven G. Schaffer
William B. Shearer, Jr., P.C.
Jonathan R. Shils
Leonard A. Silverstein
E. A. Simpson, Jr.
Scott D. Smith
W. Scott Sorrels
G. William Speer
Ronald D. Stallings
William J. Thompson
Robert M. Travis
Rex R. Veal
G. Patrick Watson
Karen Wildau
Gregory H. Worthy
John F. Wymer, III

ASSOCIATES

W. Tinley Anderson, III
Richard L. Arenburg
Brooks S. Baker
Catherine D. Barshay
Thomas J. Biafore
John R. Bielema, Jr.
Linda G. Birchall
Anthony R. Boggs
Mary Williams Bondurant
Cindy A. Brazell
William Bard Brockman
Janine Brown
Edmund B. Burke
Gil Y Burstiner
Norma Lydia Casal
Jayne H. Chapman
Christen E. Civiletto
Paul F. Concannon
W. Scott Creasman
Eric Croone
Santhia L. Curtis
Robert F. Dallas
Michael I. Diamond
James A. Dudukovich
Margaret P. Eisenhauer
Deborah Fleischer
Michael S. French
Christopher P. Galanek
Anthony I. Giacobbe, Jr.
Douglas S. Gosden
Richard Ellett Green
John M. Gross
Daniel J. Grossman
Wendy L. Hagenau
Catherine M. Hall
Hilary Harp
Kimberly C. Harris (Not admitted in GA)
Riccarda Heising
Robyn A. Henry
Joann Gallagher Jones
Todd E. Jones
Caroline S. Katz
Cynthia D. Kennedy
Daniel R. King
Katherine M. Koops
Charles H. Kuck (Not admitted in GA)
Beth Lanier
Anne Maher LaMastra
Jane E. Larimer
Susan I. Lasseter
Daniel P. Leary
Wendolyn Ward Markham
Lisa Sanders Marks
Shawn Martin
Karen D. Martinez
Adrienne E. Marting
Samuel M. Matchett
Erin E. Matthews
Charlene L. McGinty
William Dennis McKinnie
Jona J. Miller (Not admitted in GA)
Rebecca J. Miller
Robin Catherine Murray-Gill
Lynn Hopson Murrell
Mark A. Nelson
Carol D. Newman
Linda C. Odom (Not admitted in GA)
Mark F. Padilla
Jeffrey D. Paquin
Deana K. Pruitt
William M. Ragland, Jr.
Walter E. Riehemann
Raymond P. Sheley
Debra L. Skal
Sara Kay Sledge
Laura Lynn Smith
Amy L. Stafford
Courtney K. Stout
Marc A. Taylor
Anne L. Thompson
Matthew J. Troy (Not admitted in GA)
James K. Wagner, Jr.
James A. Walker, Jr.
Andrew M. Walsh
Joseph D. Wargo
Kathleen A. Wasch
Sheridan M. Watson
Kristen Yadlosky
C. Edward Young

OF COUNSEL

Frank S. Alexander
Robert Hebert (Not admitted in GA)
John H. Horne
Jeffrey L. Raney

For full biographical listings, see the Martindale-Hubbell Law Directory

---

REECE & LANG, P.S.C. (AV®)

The Lenox Building, 3399 Peachtree Road Northeast Suite 2000, 30326
Telephone: 404-365-0456
FAX: 404-365-0629
London, Kentucky Office: 400 South Main St.
Telephone: 606-864-2263.
Fax: 606-878-6426.

A. Douglas Reece (Not admitted in GA)
John M. Lang (Not admitted in GA)
Timothy J. Walker (Not admitted in GA)
Melanie Kay Fields Hensley (Not admitted in GA)
David D. Robinson (Resident)
Thomas S. Gryboski (Resident)

OF COUNSEL

Laurence R. Dry (Not admitted in GA)

Representative Client: First State Bank and Trust Company of Manchester.

For full biographical listings, see the Martindale-Hubbell Law Directory

Atlanta—Continued

ROGERS & HARDIN (AV)

2700 Cain Tower, Peachtree Center, 229 Peachtree Street, N.E., 30303
Telephone: 404-522-4700
Telex: 54-2335
Telecopier: 404-525-2224

MEMBERS OF FIRM

John J. Almond
Miriam J. Dent
Steven E. Fox
Edward J. Hardin
Hunter R. Hughes, III
Dan F. Laney, III
Stephen R. Leeds
Alan C. Leet
Phillip S. McKinney
Robert A. Parker, Jr.
Tony G. Powers
C. B. Rogers
Michael Rosenzweig
Peter W. Schneider
Richard H. Sinkfield
Paul W. Stivers

CORPORATE COUNSEL

Ross Miller (Not admitted in GA)

SENIOR ATTORNEYS

Catherine M. Bennett
James W. Beverage

Gregory J. Giornelli
Lisa Bodenstein Golan
Jessica J-M Hagen
Amy S. Haney
Terry L. Houser
Robert C. Hussle
William M. Joseph
Daniel McGinnis
Eli J. Richardson
Laura H. Robison
Brett A. Rogers
Liane A. Schleifer
Benjamin A. Stone
Linda O. Vinson
Jeffrey W. Willis
Daniel Dragomir Zegura

For full biographical listings, see the Martindale-Hubbell Law Directory

SUTHERLAND, ASBILL & BRENNAN (AV)

999 Peachtree Street, N.E., 30309-3996
Telephone: 404-853-8000
Facsimile: 404-853-8806
Washington, D.C. Office: 1275 Pennsylvania Avenue, N.W., 20004-2404.
Telephone: 202-383-0100.
New York, N.Y. Office: 1270 Avenue of the Americas, 10020-1700.
Telephone: 212-332-3000.
Austin, Texas Office: 111 Congress Avenue, 23rd Floor, 78701-4079.
Telephone: 512-469-3350.

MEMBERS OF THE FIRM IN ATLANTA, GEORGIA

William A. Sutherland (1896-1987)
Alfred G. Adams, Jr.
F. Louise Adams
Peter J. Anderson
William D. Barwick
John W. Bonds, Jr.
William H. Bradley
Thomas M. Byrne
John A. Chandler
Reginald J. Clark
George L. Cohen
Katherine Meyers Cohen
N. Jerold Cohen
Thomas A. Cox
David Robert Cumming, Jr.
Peter H. Dean
Carey P. DeDeyn
B. Knox Dobbins
Michael J. Egan
Herbert R. Elsas
J. D. Fleming, Jr.
John H. Fleming
Stephen F. Gertzman
James P. Groton
C. Christopher Hagy
H. Edward Hales, Jr.
Victor P. Haley
William M. Hames
James K. Hasson, Jr.
Barrett K. Hawks
James L. Henderson, III
Mac Asbill, Sr. (1893-1992)
Joseph B. Brennan (1903-1991)
Thomas C. Herman
Charles D. Hurt, Jr.
J. Patton Hyman, III
Thomas B. Hyman, Jr.
James Bruce Jordan
Edward W. Kallal, Jr.
Mark D. Kaufman
Bennett Lexon Kight
Cada T. Kilgore, III
Charles T. Lester, Jr.
Alfred A. Lindseth
James R. McGibbon
John H. Mobley, II
Richard G. Murphy, Jr.
Judith A. O'Brien
James A. Orr
William R. Patterson
James R. Paulk, Jr.
M. Celeste Pickron
Richard L. Robbins
Haynes R. Roberts
Barbara S. Rudisill
Herbert J. Short, Jr.
George Anthony Smith
Elizabeth Vranicar Tanis
Randolph W. Thrower
C. Christopher Trower
Larry J. White
James H. Wilson, Jr.
Walter H. Wingfield

COUNSEL OF THE FIRM IN ATLANTA, GEORGIA

Patricia Bayer Cunningham
Joycelyn L. Fleming
Patricia Anne Gorham
Charles M. Flickinger
Louise B. Matte
S. Elaine McChesney
S. Lawrence Polk
R. Michael Robinson
Bradley E. Wahl

SPECIAL TRADEMARK AND COPYRIGHT COUNSEL

Paul S. Owens

For full biographical listings, see the Martindale-Hubbell Law Directory

VINCENT, CHOREY, TAYLOR & FEIL, A PROFESSIONAL CORPORATION (AV)

Suite 1700, The Lenox Building, 3399 Peachtree Road, N.E., 30326
Telephone: 404-841-3200
Telex: 650 298-1749
Telecopier: 404-841-3221

Richard H. Vincent
Thomas V. Chorey, Jr.
John L. Taylor, Jr.
Eric D. Ranney
Otto F. Feil III
Robert N. Berg
Thomas J. Stalzer
Susan Shivers Fink
Celeste McCollough

Matthew L. Hess
M. Suellen Henderson
Gregory P. Youra
Jean B. Blumenfeld
Philip M. Rees
David A. Flanigan, Jr.
Karen G. Crenshaw
Jeffery T. Coleman
Lisa Fivars Harper

OF COUNSEL

Zack D. Cravey, Jr.
Ann Arnold Watkins

For full biographical listings, see the Martindale-Hubbell Law Directory

*AUGUSTA,** Richmond Co.

BURNSIDE, WALL, DANIEL, ELLISON & REVELL (AV)

A Partnership including Professional Corporations
454 Greene Street, P.O. Box 2125, 30903
Telephone: 706-722-0768
FAX: 706-722-5984

MEMBERS OF FIRM

Robert C. Daniel, Jr., (P.C.) (1943-1993)
Thomas R. Burnside, Jr. (P.C.)
James B. Wall (P.C.)
James W. Ellison
Harry D. Revell

ASSOCIATES

Thomas R. Burnside, III
Lori S. D'Alessio

Representative Clients: CSRA Regional Development Commission; City of Harlem, Georgia; Liquid Carbonic Corp.; Richmond County, Georgia; Southern Machine & Tool Co.; Jefferson EMC; Southeastern Equipment Co.; SECO Aviation, Inc.; SECO Parts & Equipment, Inc.

For full biographical listings, see the Martindale-Hubbell Law Directory

CAPERS, DUNBAR, SANDERS & BRUCKNER (AV)

Fifteenth Floor, First Union Bank Building, 30901-1454
Telephone: 706-722-7542
Telecopier: 706-724-7776

MEMBERS OF FIRM

John D. Capers
Paul H. Dunbar, III
E. Frederick Sanders
Ziva P. Bruckner

ASSOCIATES

Carl P. Dowling

For full biographical listings, see the Martindale-Hubbell Law Directory

DYE, TUCKER, EVERITT, WHEALE & LONG, A PROFESSIONAL ASSOCIATION (AV)

453 Greene Street, P.O. Box 2426, 30903
Telephone: 706-722-0771
Fax: 706-722-7028

A. Rowland Dye
Thomas W. Tucker
A. Zachry Everitt
Duncan D. Wheale
John B. Long
Benjamin H. Brewton

Troy A. Lanier

OF COUNSEL

A. Montague Miller

Representative Clients: State Farm Insurance Cos.; The Travelers Insurance Co.; Georgia Power Co.; Wachovia National Bank (Augusta Division); Chubb Group; Montgomery Ward; Augusta Board of Realtors; Ryder Truck Rental, Inc.; Canal Insurance Company; K Mart.

For full biographical listings, see the Martindale-Hubbell Law Directory

FLETCHER, HARLEY & FLETCHER (AV)

429 Walker Street, P.O. Box 2084, 30903-2084
Telephone: 706-724-0558
Fax: 706-724-4730

MEMBERS OF FIRM

Leonard O. Fletcher, Jr.
C. Thompson Harley
W. Lawrence Fletcher

For full biographical listings, see the Martindale-Hubbell Law Directory

Augusta—Continued

FULCHER, HAGLER, REED, HANKS & HARPER (AV)

A Partnership including Professional Corporations
520 Greene Street, P.O. Box 1477, 30903-1477
Telephone: 706-724-0171
Telecopier: 706-724-4573

MEMBERS OF FIRM

William M. Fulcher (1902-1993)
Gould B. Hagler (Retired)
William C. Reed (Retired)
David H. Hanks (P.C.)
John I. Harper (P.C.)
Robert C. Hagler (P.C.)
Michael B. Hagler (P.C.)
James W. Purcell (P.C.)
J. Arthur Davison (P.C.)
Mark C. Wilby (P.C.)
Ronald C. Griffeth
N. Staten Bitting, Jr. (P.C.)

ASSOCIATES

David P. Dekle
Sharon R. Blair
J. Edward Enoch, Jr.
Scott W. Kelly
Cynthia A. Gray
Elizabeth McLeod Kitchens
Barry A. Fleming

General Counsel for: GIW Industries, Inc.
Division Counsel for: CSX Transportation; Textron, Inc. (E-Z Go Car Division).
Counsel for: NationsBank; Georgia Natural Gas Co. (a division of Atlanta Gas Light Co.); Champion International Corp.; Aetna Life and Casualty; Liberty Mutual Insurance Company; St. Paul Fire & Marine Insurance Co.; Kimberly Clark Corporation.

For full biographical listings, see the Martindale-Hubbell Law Directory

HULL, TOWILL, NORMAN & BARRETT, A PROFESSIONAL CORPORATION (AV)

Seventh Floor, Trust Company Bank Building, P.O. Box 1564, 30903-1564
Telephone: 706-722-4481
Fax: 706-722-9779

James M. Hull (1885-1975)
George B. Barrett (1894-1942)
Julian J. Willingham (1887-1963)
John Bell Towill (1907-1991)
Robert C. Norman (Retired, 1991)
W. Hale Barrett
Lawton Jordan, Jr.
Patrick J. Rice
Douglas D. Batchelor, Jr.
David E. Hudson
Neal W. Dickert
John W. Gibson
William F. Hammond
Mark S. Burgreen
George R. Hall
James B. Ellington
F. Michael Taylor

Robert A. Mullins
William J. Keogh, III
Edward J. Tarver
J. Noel Schweers, III
Michael S. Carlson
Ralph Emerson Hanna, III
Susan D. Barrett
Timothy Moses

Counsel for: Trust Company Bank of Augusta, N.A.; Georgia Federal Bank, FSB, Augusta Division; Southeastern Newspapers Corp.; Georgia Power Co.; Southern Bell Telephone & Telegraph Co.; St. Joseph Hospital, Augusta, Georgia, Inc.; Norfolk Southern Corp.; Merry Land & Investment Co., Inc.; Housing Authority of the City of Augusta; Georgia Press Association.

For full biographical listings, see the Martindale-Hubbell Law Directory

KILPATRICK & CODY (AV)

Suite 1400, First Union Bank Building, P.O. Box 2043, 30903
Telephone: 706-724-2622
Telephone Copier: 706-722-0219
Atlanta, Georgia Office: Suite 2800, 1100 Peachtree Street.
Telephone: 404-815-6500.
Telecopier: 404-815-6555.
Washington, D.C. Office: Suite 800, 700 13th Street, N.W., 20005.
Telephone: 202-508-5800. Telephone Copier: 202-508-5858.
Brussels, Belgium Office: Avenue Louise 65, BTE 3, 1050 Brussels.
Telephone: (32) (2) 533-03-00.
Telecopier: (32) (2) 534-86-38.
London, England Office: 68 Pall Mall, London, SW1Y 5ES, England.
Telephone: (44) (71) 321 0477.
Telecopier: (44) (71) 930 9733.

Wyck A. Knox, Jr.
Raymond G. Chadwick, Jr.
James E. Blanchard
Ted H. Clarkson
Gregg E. McDougal

R. Perry Sentell, III
Joseph H. Huff
W. Craig Smith

Representative Clients: University Health Services, Inc.; National Cardiovascular Network, Inc.; Atlanta Cardiology, P.C.; First Union National Bank of Georgia; A.A. Friedman Co.; Blanchard & Calhoun Real Estate Co., Inc.; Boardman Petroleum, Inc.; Castleberry's Food Co., Inc.; DSM Chemicals North America, Inc.; Westinghouse Savannah River Company.

For full biographical listings, see the Martindale-Hubbell Law Directory

WARLICK, TRITT & STEBBINS (AV)

15th Floor, First Union Bank Building, 30901
Telephone: 706-722-7543
Fax: 706-722-1822
Columbia County Office: 119 Davis Road, Martinez, Georgia 30907.
Telephone: 706-860-7595.
Fax: 705-860-7597.

MEMBERS OF FIRM

William Byrd Warlick
Roy D. Tritt (Resident, Martinez Office)
Charles C. Stebbins, III
E. L. Clark Speese
Michael W. Terry
D. Scott Broyles
Ross S. Snellings
C. Gregory Bryan

OF COUNSEL

Richard E. Miley

For full biographical listings, see the Martindale-Hubbell Law Directory

*BAINBRIDGE,** Decatur Co.

KIRBO & KENDRICK (AV)

206 West Water Street, P.O. Box 425, 31717
Telephone: 912-246-3900
Telecopier: 912-246-3318

MEMBERS OF FIRM

Bruce W. Kirbo
Bruce W. Kirbo, Jr.
David A. Kendrick

ASSOCIATES

Richard A. Epps

Representative Clients: Southwest Georgia Farm Credit, A.C.A.; Elberta Crate and Box Co.; Engelhard Corp.; Sellers Oil Co.; Farm Credit Bank; City of Bainbridge; Decatur County Board of Education.

For full biographical listings, see the Martindale-Hubbell Law Directory

*BARNESVILLE,** Lamar Co. — (Refer to Forsyth)

*BAXLEY,** Appling Co. — (Refer to Jesup)

*BLACKSHEAR,** Pierce Co. — (Refer to Waycross)

*BRUNSWICK,** Glynn Co.

LAW OFFICES OF JAMES A. BISHOP (AV)

Suite 401, First Federal Plaza, P.O. Box 1396, 31521-1396
Telephone: 912-264-2390
Fax: 912-264-5859

For full biographical listings, see the Martindale-Hubbell Law Directory

FENDIG, MCLEMORE, TAYLOR & WHITWORTH, P.C. (AV)

Suite 200 Trust Company Bank Building, P.O. Box 1996, 31521
Telephone: 912-264-4126
Telecopier: 912-264-0591

Albert Fendig, Jr.
Gilbert C. McLemore, Jr.
Philip R. Taylor
David T. Whitworth
James B. Durham

Donna L. Crossland
Beth B. Mason-O'Neal

Counsel for: Trust Company Bank of S.E. Georgia, N.A.; First Federal Savings Bank; Sea Island Property Owners Assn.; Calsilite Manufacturing Co.; Continental Insurance Cos.; Crum & Forster; Fireman's Fund Insurance Cos.; The Hertz Corp.; Insurance Company of North America; United States Fidelity & Guaranty Co.

For full biographical listings, see the Martindale-Hubbell Law Directory

GILBERT, HARRELL, GILBERT, SUMERFORD & MARTIN, P.C. (AV)

Suite 200 First Federal Plaza, 31521
Telephone: 912-265-6700
Fax: 912-264-3917

Wallace E. Harrell
James B. Gilbert, Jr.
Rees M. Sumerford
M. Fleming Martin, III
Monroe Lynn Frey, III
Jameson L. Gregg
Wallace E. Harrell, III

Charles G. Spalding
Lisa Godbey
Kristi E. Harrison
Mark D. Johnson

OF COUNSEL

James B. Gilbert
Joseph A. Whittle
Ralph T. Skelton, Jr.

Attorneys for: Sea Island Co.; American National Bank; Georgia-Pacific Corp.; Atlanta Gas Light Co.; Sea Harvest Packing Co.; Zurich General Accident & Liability Insurance Co.; Lumbermens Mutual Casualty Co.; BMW of North America.

(See Next Column)

GILBERT, HARRELL, GILBERT, SUMERFORD & MARTIN P.C., *Brunswick—Continued*

Assistant Division Counsel for: Southern Railway Co.
Counsel for: Hercules Inc.

For full biographical listings, see the Martindale-Hubbell Law Directory

NIGHTINGALE, LILES, DENNARD & CARMICAL (AV)

1528 Ellis Street, P.O. Box 1496, 31521
Telephone: 912-265-0220
FAX: 912-264-1716

MEMBERS OF FIRM

Bernard N. Nightingale (1907-1981)
Thomas E. Dennard, Jr.
Lee A. Carmical

OF COUNSEL

Edward B. Liles

Approved Attorneys for: First Federal Savings Bank of Brunswick , Ga.; Georgia Federal Bank, F.S.B.; Trust Company Bank, N.A.; Lawyers Title Insurance Corp.; First Union National Bank.

For full biographical listings, see the Martindale-Hubbell Law Directory

WHELCHEL, BROWN, READDICK & BUMGARTNER (AV)

5 Glynn Avenue, P.O. Box 220, 31521-0220
Telephone: 912-264-8544
Telecopier: 912-264-9667

MEMBERS OF FIRM

J. Thomas Whelchel
Richard A. Brown, Jr.
Terry L. Readdick
John E. Bumgartner
B. Kaye Katz

ASSOCIATES

G. Todd Carter
Richard K. Strickland
Joseph R. Odachowski

Representative Clients: Georgia Power Co.; Sears, Roebuck & Co.; Allstate Insurance Co.; Commercial Union Insurance Co.; Georgia Farm Bureau Mutual Insurance Co.; Government Employees Insurance Co.; Nationwide Insurance Co.; State Farm Insurance Cos.; Wausau Insurance Cos.

For full biographical listings, see the Martindale-Hubbell Law Directory

*BUCHANAN,** Haralson Co. — (Refer to Cedartown)

*BUENA VISTA,** Marion Co. — (Refer to Columbus)

BUFORD, Gwinnett Co.

GIBSON DEAN II, P.C. (AV)

109 Main Street, P.O. Box 939, 30518
Telephone: 404-945-4976
FAX: 404-945-0234

Gibson Dean, II

Representative Clients: John Bailey Oldsmobile-Pontiac-Buick-GMC Truck, Inc.; Blue Circle, Inc.
Approved Attorneys For: Lawyers Title Insurance Corp.; Ticor Title Insurance Corp.
Reference: NationsBank.

For full biographical listings, see the Martindale-Hubbell Law Directory

*BUTLER,** Taylor Co. — (Refer to Macon)

*CAIRO,** Grady Co. — (Refer to Thomasville)

*CALHOUN,** Gordon Co.

CHANCE, MADDOX & SMITH (AV)

204 North Wall Street, P.O. Box 577, 30703-0577
Telephone: 706-629-4407
Fax: 706-625-2488

MEMBERS OF FIRM

J. C. Maddox
David K. Smith

ASSOCIATES

M. Suzanne Hayes Hutchinson

OF COUNSEL

Ronald F. Chance

Representative Clients: Gordon County Board of Education; Gordon County Board of Commissioners; Hiwassee Land Co.; Gordon County Contractor's Builders Supply, Inc.; Development Authority of Gordon County; Ranger Manufacturing, Inc.; Basic Materials, Inc.; Willcan, Inc.
Approved Attorneys for: Lawyers Title Insurance Corp.; Farmers Home Administration; The Federal Land Bank of Columbia.

For full biographical listings, see the Martindale-Hubbell Law Directory

*CAMILLA,** Mitchell Co.

FRANK C. VANN (AV)

47 East Oakland Avenue, P.O. Box 387, 31730
Telephone: 912-336-8231
Fax: 912-336-8542

ASSOCIATES

Gary O. Allen

Representative Clients: Baker County Bank; Mitchell County Board of Education; McNair Farms; Pinecliff Gin, Inc.; Mitchell County Farm Service, Inc.; Casle Foods JV, L.L.C.

For full biographical listings, see the Martindale-Hubbell Law Directory

*CANTON,** Cherokee Co. — (Refer to Jasper)

*CARROLLTON,** Carroll Co.

TISINGER, TISINGER, VANCE & GREER, A PROFESSIONAL CORPORATION (AV)

100 Wagon Yard Plaza, P.O. Box 2069, 30117
Telephone: 404-834-4467
FAX: 404-834-5426

David H. Tisinger
Richard G. Tisinger
J. Thomas Vance
Thomas E. Greer
Kevin B. Buice
C. David Mecklin, Jr.
G. Gregory Shadrix
Robert H. Sullivan
Phillip D. Wilkins
Glenn M. Jarrell
Douglas C. Vassy
J. Branson Parker
Stacey L. Blackmon
Steven T. Minor
John A. Harris
Edith Freeman Rooks
David F. Miceli

Representative Clients: Atlanta Casualty Company; Carroll County Board of Education; Carrollton Federal Bank-Federal Savings Bank; City of Bowdon; City of Villa Rica; Georgia Farm Bureau Mutual Insurance Company; St. Paul Fire and Marine Insurance Company; Southwire Company; State Farm Mutual Automobile Insurance Company; Tanner Medical Center, Inc.

For full biographical listings, see the Martindale-Hubbell Law Directory

*CARTERSVILLE,** Bartow Co.

LAW OFFICES WARREN & WM. MORGAN AKIN, P.C. (AV)

11 West Public Square, P.O. Box 878, 30120
Telephone: 404-382-0780
Fax: 404-386-1452

Warren Akin
Wm. Morgan Akin

Representative Clients: CSX Transportation, Inc.; Georgia Power Co.; Bartow County Bank; Lumbermens Mutual Casualty Co.; Bartow Mutual Insurance Co.; Allstate Insurance Co.; Dan River Mills, Inc.; Phillips Fibers Corp. (Division of Phillips Petroleum Corp.); Nationwide Insurance Co.

For full biographical listings, see the Martindale-Hubbell Law Directory

*CEDARTOWN,** Polk Co.

MUNDY & GAMMAGE, P.C. (AV)

216 Main Street, P.O. Box 930, 30125-0930
Telephone: 706-748-3870
706-688-9416 (Atlanta)
Fax: 706-748-2489
Rome, Georgia Office: The Carnegie Building, 607 Broad Street.
Telephone: 706-290-5180.

Emil Lamar Gammage, Jr.
William D. Sparks
(Mrs.) Gerry E. Holmes
George E. Mundy
Miles L. Gammage
John S. Husser
B. Jean Crane
Kelly A. Benedict

For full biographical listings, see the Martindale-Hubbell Law Directory

YORK, MCRAE & YORK (AV)

York Building, 117 E. Woodland Street, P.O. Box 246, 30125
Telephone: 706-748-3780
FAX: 706-748-1175

MEMBERS OF FIRM

Glenn T. York, Jr.
Michael D. McRae
Michael H. York, Sr.

Local Counsel for: Seaboard Coast Line Railroad Co.; Bowater North American Corp.
Representative Clients: First Federal Savings & Loan Association of Cedartown; Polk School District; City of Cedartown; Cedartown-Polk County Hospital Authority; Cedartown Industrial Development Corp.; Rockmart Development Authority.

For full biographical listings, see the Martindale-Hubbell Law Directory

*CHATSWORTH,** Murray Co. — (Refer to Dalton)

*COCHRAN,** Bleckley Co. — (Refer to Eastman)

*COLUMBUS,** Muscogee Co.

DAVIDSON, CALHOUN & MILLER, P.C. (AV)

The Joseph House, 828 Broadway, P.O. Box 2828, 31902-2828
Telephone: 706-327-2552
Telecopier: 706-323-5838

J. Quentin Davidson, Jr. | Charles W. Miller
Marcus B. Calhoun, Jr. | David A. Buehler
H. Owen Lee

For full biographical listings, see the Martindale-Hubbell Law Directory

HATCHER, STUBBS, LAND, HOLLIS & ROTHSCHILD (AV)

Suite 500 The Corporate Center, 233 12th Street, P.O. Box 2707, 31902-2707
Telephone: 706-324-0201
Telecopier: 706-322-7747

MEMBERS OF FIRM

A. Edward Smith (1902-1962)
S. B. Hatcher (1887-1968)
J. Madden Hatcher (1897-1975)
Howell Hollis (1919-1991)
Aaron J. Land (1911-Retired)
J. Madden Hatcher, Jr. (1937-Retired)
Albert W. Stubbs
Alan F. Rothschild
William B. Hardegree
Morton A. Harris
J. Barrington Vaught
Charles T. Staples
James E. Humes, II
Joseph L. Waldrep
Robert C. Martin, Jr.
George W. Mize, Jr.
John M. Tanzine, III
John McKay Sheftall
Alan F. Rothschild, Jr.
William C. Pound

ASSOCIATES

Mote W. Andrews III
C. Morris Mullin
Theodore Darryl (Ted) Morgan

General Counsel for: Trust Company Bank of Columbus, N.A.; TOM'S Foods Inc.; Muscogee County Board of Education; Burnham Service Corp.; Kinnett Dairies, Inc.; St. Francis Hospital, Inc.
Assistant Division Counsel for: Norfolk Southern Corp.
Local Counsel for: State Farm Insurance Cos.; First Union National Bank of Georgia; AFLAC, Inc.

For full biographical listings, see the Martindale-Hubbell Law Directory

LAYFIELD, ROTHSCHILD & MORGAN (AV)

1030 First Avenue, P.O. Box 2788, 31902-2788
Telephone: 706-324-4167
FAX: 706-324-1969

MEMBERS OF FIRM

Martelle Layfield, Jr. (1937-1989)
Jerome M. Rothschild
W. Donald Morgan, Jr.

ASSOCIATES

Virgil T. Theus
Neal J. Callahan

Reference: Columbus Bank and Trust Company.

For full biographical listings, see the Martindale-Hubbell Law Directory

POPE, MCGLAMRY, KILPATRICK & MORRISON (AV)

A Partnership including Professional Corporations
318 11th Street, 2nd Floor, P.O. Box 2128, 31902-2128
Telephone: 706-324-0050;
Phenix City, Alabama: 205-298-7354
Atlanta, Georgia Office: 83 Walton Street, N.W., P.O. Box 1733, 30303.
Telephone: 404-523-7706.

MEMBERS OF FIRM

C. Neal Pope (P.C.)
Max R. McGlamry (P.C.) (Resident)
Paul V. Kilpatrick, Jr. (Resident)
R. Timothy Morrison (Resident, Atlanta, Georgia Office)
Michael L. McGlamry
Earle F. Lasseter
William J. Cornwell
Jay F. Hirsch
Daniel W. Sigelman
Wade H. Tomlinson, III (Resident, Atlanta Office)
William Usher Norwood, III (Resident, Atlanta Office)

RESIDENT ASSOCIATES

Joan S. Redmond
Teresa Pike Majors

Reference: Columbus Bank & Trust Co.

For full biographical listings, see the Martindale-Hubbell Law Directory

*CONYERS,** Rockdale Co.

MADDOX, STARNES & NIX (AV)

945 Bank Street, P.O. Drawer 1017, 30207-1017
Telephone: 404-922-7700
Fax: 404-760-7600

Robert W. Maddox
Jeffrey M. Starnes
John A. Nix

ASSOCIATES

Michael S Waldrop

(See Next Column)

OF COUNSEL

Thomas A. Bowman
C. McLaurin Sitton

LEGAL SUPPORT PERSONNEL

Cheryl T. Armstrong

For full biographical listings, see the Martindale-Hubbell Law Directory

*CORDELE,** Crisp Co.

DAVIS, GREGORY, CHRISTY & FOREHAND (AV)

708 East Sixteenth Avenue, P.O. Drawer 5230, 31015
Telephone: 912-273-7150
Fax: 912-273-7578
Vienna, Georgia Office: 104 West Union Street, P.O. Box 397.
Telephone: 912-268-4125.
Telecopier: 912-268-6373.

MEMBERS OF FIRM

Hardy Gregory, Jr.
Gary C. Christy
John N. Davis
David A. Forehand, Jr.

OF COUNSEL

T. Hoyt Davis, Jr.

For full biographical listings, see the Martindale-Hubbell Law Directory

ROBERTS, ROBERTS & INGRAM (AV)

122 East Twelfth Avenue, P.O. Box 487, 31015
Telephone: 912-273-5202
Fax: Available Upon Request

Guy V. Roberts, Jr.
Lawrence W. Roberts
Stephen J. Ingram

Representative Clients: City of Cordele, Georgia; Cordele Implement Co., Inc.; Cordele Office Building Authority; Hospital Authority of Crisp County.
Local Counsel: Cordele Sash, Door, & Lumber Co.; Griffin Lumber Co., Inc.; Housing Authority of Cordele, Georgia; Downtown Development Authority of Cordele.

For full biographical listings, see the Martindale-Hubbell Law Directory

*COVINGTON,** Newton Co. — (Refer to Monroe)

*CUMMING,** Forsyth Co.

BOLING, RICE, BETTIS, BOTTOMS & BAGLEY (AV)

123 Tribble Gap Road, P.O. Box 244, 30130
Telephone: 404-887-3162;
Atlanta: 404-688-8895
Fax: 404-889-8824

OF COUNSEL

Leon Boling

MEMBERS OF FIRM

Zachariah A. Rice, Jr.
Barry Phillip Bettis
Dennis J. Bottoms
Jeffrey S. Bagley

ASSOCIATES

Angela F. Martin

Representative Clients: Wachovia Bank of Georgia, N.A., Forsyth County Division; Sawnee Electric Membership Corp.; City of Cumming, Georgia; Forsyth County Board of Education; Fairfield Mortgage Associates of Gainesville; Farm Credit Bank of Columbia; Georgia Farm Bureau Mutual Insurance Co.; The Peoples Bank of Forsyth County; The Mortgage Source d/b/a 1st National Bank of Gainesville.

For full biographical listings, see the Martindale-Hubbell Law Directory

*DAHLONEGA,** Lumpkin Co. — (Refer to Gainesville)

*DALTON,** Whitfield Co.

MINOR, BELL & NEAL, P.C. (AV)

202 West Waugh Street, P.O. Box 2666, 30722-2666
Telephone: 706-226-2666
Telecopier: 706-278-3569

John T. Minor, III
William W. Bell, Jr.
John P. Neal, III
Rickie L. Brown
John T. Minor, IV
Stephen B. Farrow
William F. Jourdain
Harvard H. Kranzlein, Jr.
Michael J. Tuck
Robert D. Jenkins
Robert G. McCurry
M. Shane Lovingood

For full biographical listings, see the Martindale-Hubbell Law Directory

MITCHELL & MITCHELL, P.C. (AV)

101 North Thornton Avenue, 30720
Telephone: 706-278-2040
Fax: 706-278-3040

(See Next Column)

MITCHELL & MITCHELL P.C., *Dalton—Continued*

D. Wright Mitchell (1895-1970)
Douglas W. Mitchell (1921-1984)
Erwin Mitchell
Neil Wester
James H. Bisson, III
Terry L. Miller
Michael C. Cherof
Susan Williams Bisson
Christine Clark Taylor
William J. Kimsey

Counsel for: The City of Dalton, Georgia; Galaxy Carpet Mills, Inc.
Local Counsel for: Bituminous Casualty Corp.; CSX Corp.; NationsBank of Dalton, Georgia.
Reference: Nations Bank of Dalton, Georgia.

For full biographical listings, see the Martindale-Hubbell Law Directory

*DAWSON,** Terrell Co. — (Refer to Albany)

*DECATUR,** De Kalb Co.

HYATT & HYATT, P.C. (AV)

Suite 201, Trust Building, 545 North McDonough Street, 30030
Telephone: 404-377-3635
Fax: 404-377-8304

Charles H. Hyatt (Retired)
John M. Hyatt

For full biographical listings, see the Martindale-Hubbell Law Directory

MCLARTY, ROBINSON & VAN VOORHIES (AV)

One Decatur Towncenter, Suite 330, 150 East Ponce de Leon Avenue, 30030
Telephone: 404-377-6464
Fax: 404-377-6748 or 404-377-3658

Paul M. McLarty, Jr.
John E. Robinson
James C. Van Voorhies, Jr.

Jane B. Nicol
Lorene J. Bombich Fitzgerald
William Michael Hale, Jr.

Reference: Trust Company Bank; Mountain National Bank.

For full biographical listings, see the Martindale-Hubbell Law Directory

ERNEST J. NELSON, JR. (AV)

Suite 201 Trust Building, 545 North McDonough Street, 30030
Telephone: 404-378-3633
FAX: 404-377-8304

For full biographical listings, see the Martindale-Hubbell Law Directory

SIMMONS, WARREN & SZCZECKO, PROFESSIONAL ASSOCIATION (AV)

315 West Ponce de Leon Avenue, Suite 850, 30030
Telephone: 404-378-1711
Fax: 404-377-6101

M. T. Simmons, Jr.
Wesley B. Warren, Jr.
Joseph Szczecko
William C. McFee, Jr.

Representative Clients: David Hocker & Associates (Shopping Center Development); Julian LeCraw & Company (Real Estate); Royal Oldsmobile,; Cotter & Co.; Atlanta Neurosurgical Associates, P.A.; Villager Lodge, Inc.; Troncalli Motors, Inc.

For full biographical listings, see the Martindale-Hubbell Law Directory

*DONALSONVILLE,** Seminole Co. — (Refer to Bainbridge)

DORAVILLE, De Kalb Co.

JOE W. GERSTEIN, P.C. (AV)

6485 Peachtree Industrial Boulevard, 30360
Telephone: 404-458-7606
Fax: 404-457-6082

Joe W. Gerstein

For full biographical listings, see the Martindale-Hubbell Law Directory

*DOUGLAS,** Coffee Co.

COTTINGHAM & PORTER, P.C. (AV)

319 East Ashley Street, P.O. Box 798, 31533
Telephone: 912-384-1616
Fax: 912-384-1775

Sidney L. Cottingham
Robert L. Porter, Jr.
William L. Thompson

Representative Clients: Brooks Auto Parts, Inc.; Coats & Clark, Inc.; Coffee County Bank; Coffee County Board of Education; Coffee County Hospital Authority; Douglas-Coffee County Industrial Authority; First National Bank of Coffee County, N.A.; Fletcher Oil Co., Inc.; Golden Poultry Company, Inc.; Joseph Campbell Co.

(See Next Column)

For full biographical listings, see the Martindale-Hubbell Law Directory

PRESTON & PRESTON, P.C. (AV)

220 East Ward Street, P.O. Box 71, 31533
Telephone: 912-384-4700
Fax: 912-384-5839

Montgomery L. Preston (1910-1991)
Robert H. Preston
Edward L. Bagwell, III

Attorneys for: Georgia Power Co.; Joseph R. Campbell Co.; General Telephone Co.; Trust Company Bank of Coffee County; Lott Builders Supply Co.; All State Ins. Co.; Wal-Mart Stores, Inc.; Woodmen of the World Life Insurance Society; First Railroad Community Federal Credit Union.
Issuing Agents for: Lawyers Title Insurance Corp.; First American Title Insurance Co.

For full biographical listings, see the Martindale-Hubbell Law Directory

*EASTMAN,** Dodge Co.

HARRISON, HARRISON & LLOP (AV)

202 Norman Avenue, P.O. Box 0967, 31023
Telephone: 912-374-4346
Hawkinsville, Georgia Office: 328 Commerce Street, P.O. Box 35.
Telephone: 912-783-2006.

MEMBERS OF FIRM

Milton Harrison
Steven M. Harrison
Rita J. Llop

ASSOCIATES

Sarah F. Wall

Attorneys for: City of Eastman; City of Chester; Town of Rhine.
Local Counsel for: ITT Rayonier, Inc.
Approved Attorneys for: Lawyers Title Insurance Corp.; Ticor Title Insurance Co.; Kansas City Title Insurance Co.; Federal Land Bank of Columbia, S.C.; Central Georgia Federal Land Bank; Georgia Development Authority; American Title Insurance Co.; The Insurance Company of Minnesota.

For full biographical listings, see the Martindale-Hubbell Law Directory

*EATONTON,** Putnam Co. — (Refer to Monticello)

*ELBERTON,** Elbert Co.

HEARD, LEVERETT, PHELPS, WEAVER & CAMPBELL (AV)

25 Thomas Street, P.O. Drawer 399, 30635
Telephone: 706-283-2651
Fax: 706-283-2670

Robert M. Heard
E. Freeman Leverett
R. Chris Phelps
Cynthia G. Weaver
Richard D. Campbell

Robert F. Leverett

General Counsel for: Granite City Bank; Coggins Granite, Inc.
Counsel for: Georgia School Boards Assn.; Georgia Telephone Assn.; Elbert County Board of Education; City of Elberton; Fibers & Fabrics of Georgia, Inc.; Pennsylvania Granite Corp.
Approved Attorneys for: Chicago Title Co.; Minnesota Title Co.; South Carolina Title Co.

For full biographical listings, see the Martindale-Hubbell Law Directory

*ELLAVILLE,** Schley Co. — (Refer to Albany)

*FAYETTEVILLE,** Fayette Co. — (Refer to Griffin)

*FITZGERALD,** Ben Hill Co.

MILLS & CHASTEEN, P.C. ATTORNEYS AT LAW (AV)

315 South Main Street, P.O. Box 408, 31750
Telephone: 912-423-4335
Fax: 912-423-5742

J. C. McDonald (1899-1969)
Ben B. Mills, Jr.
Robert W. Chasteen, Jr.

Attorneys for: The Bank of Fitzgerald; Hospital Authority of Ben Hill County; Board of Commissioners of Ben Hill County; Colony Bank Corp.; Ashburn Bank.
Approved Attorneys: South Georgia Farm Credit Service; Old Republic Title Ins. Co.; Farmers Home Administration; Lawyers Title Insurance Co.

For full biographical listings, see the Martindale-Hubbell Law Directory

*FORSYTH,** Monroe Co.

HAYGOOD, LYNCH, HARRIS & MELTON (AV)

87 North Lee Street, P.O. Box 657, 31029-2120
Telephone: 912-994-5171
Fax: 912-994-4588
Monticello, Georgia Office: 248 W. Green Street, 31064.
Telephone: 706-468-8846.

MEMBERS OF FIRM

Charles B. Haygood, Jr. | Robert L. Harris
Larry Persons Lynch | C. Robert Melton

For full biographical listings, see the Martindale-Hubbell Law Directory

*FORT VALLEY,** Peach Co. — (Refer to Perry)

*GAINESVILLE,** Hall Co.

HARBEN & HARTLEY (AV)

539 Green Street, P.O. Box 2975, 30503
Telephone: 404-534-7341
FAX: 404-532-0399

MEMBERS OF FIRM

Sam S. Harben, Jr. | Phillip L. Hartley
Martha McMasters Pearson

ASSOCIATES

Emily Bagwell Harben

LEGAL SUPPORT PERSONNEL

Barbara J. Smith | Lisa A. Rosetti

For full biographical listings, see the Martindale-Hubbell Law Directory

HULSEY, OLIVER & MAHAR (AV)

200 E.E. Butler Parkway, P.O. Box 1457, 30503
Telephone: 404-532-6312
Fax: 404-531-9230

MEMBERS OF FIRM

E. D. Kenyon (1890-1981) | R. David Syfan
Julius M. Hulsey | Jane A. Range
Samuel L. Oliver | Joseph D. Cooley, III
James E. Mahar, Jr. | Thomas L. Fitzgerald

ASSOCIATES

Thomas D. Calkins | B. Chan Caudell

Counsel for: United Cities Gas Co.; Continental Insurance Cos.; Underwriters Adjusting Co.; Ralston Purina Co.; Carolina Casualty Insurance Co.; Hall County; Lake Lanier Islands Development Authority; Winn-Dixie Stores, Inc.; Gainesville Bank and Trust.

For full biographical listings, see the Martindale-Hubbell Law Directory

SMITH, GILLIAM AND WILLIAMS (AV)

200 Old Coca-Cola Building, 301 Green Street, N.W., P.O. Box 1098, 30503
Telephone: 404-536-3381
Fax: 404-531-1491

MEMBERS OF FIRM

R. Wilson Smith, Jr. (1906-1983) | Jerry A. Williams
John H. Smith | Kelly Anne Miles
Steven P. Gilliam | Bradley J. Patten

ASSOCIATES

M. Tyler Smith | Scott Arthur Ball

General Counsel for: Gainesville Industrial Electric Co.; Georgia Mutual Insurance Co.; L & R Farms; H. Wilson Manufacturing Co.; Goforth Electrical Supply; North Georgia Petroleum Co.; Gibbs Management Group, Inc.

For full biographical listings, see the Martindale-Hubbell Law Directory

STEWART, MELVIN & FROST (AV)

Hunt Tower, Suite 600, 200 Main Street, P.O. Box 3280, 30503
Telephone: 404-536-0101
FAX: 404-532-2171; 532-5071

MEMBERS OF FIRM

J. Douglas Stewart | J. Kenneth Nix
W. Woodrow Stewart | T. Treadwell Syfan
John M. Melvin | G. Allen Broxton
Frank W. Armstrong | Steven A. Cornelison
William H. Blalock, Jr. | J. C. Highsmith, Jr.
J. Randall Frost | Mark W. Alexander

Representative Clients: The First National Bank of Gainesville; First National Bancorp; Gainesville & Hall County Development Authority; Georgia Chair Co.; Cargill, Inc.; McKibbon Bros., Inc.; ConAgra Poultry Company; Nationwide Insurance Cos.; The Travelers Cos.

For full biographical listings, see the Martindale-Hubbell Law Directory

WHELCHEL, DUNLAP & GIGNILLIAT (AV)

(Successors to Dunlap & Dunlap)
405 Washington Street, N.E., P.O. Box 1, 30501
Telephone: 404-532-7211
Telecopier: 404-532-7361

MEMBERS OF FIRM

Edgar B. Dunlap (1892-1955) | John A. Gram
William P. Whelchel (1895-1975) | Edgar B. Dunlap, II
William A. Bagwell | Thomas M. Cole
Wright Willingham | Richard R. Harste
William L. Rogers, Jr. | Thomas S. Bishop
Madeline S. Wirt

ASSOCIATES

Murray J. Kogod | Robert Wakefield Chambers, III
Mary Claffey Smith | John Flanders Kennedy
Charles N. Kelley, Jr.

OF COUNSEL

James A. Dunlap | William R. Gignilliat, Jr.

General Counsel for: Trust Company Bank of North Georgia; Housing Authority of City of Gainesville; The Citizens Bank of Gainesville; Northeast Georgia Medical Center, Inc.
Counsel for: Georgia Power Co.; Milliken & Co.; Johnson & Johnson; Atlanta Gas Light Co.; CSX Transportation Inc.; CIGNA Property and Casualty Cos.

For full biographical listings, see the Martindale-Hubbell Law Directory

*GREENSBORO,** Greene Co. — (Refer to Madison)

*GREENVILLE,** Meriwether Co. — (Refer to La Grange)

*GRIFFIN,** Spalding Co.

JOHN M. COGBURN, JR. (AV)

115 North Sixth Street, P.O. Box 907, 30224
Telephone: 404-228-2148
Telecopier: 404-228-5018
McDonough, Georgia Office: Suite 300E, First Community Bank Building, 12 North Cedar Street.
Telephone: 404-954-9004.
Fax: 404-228-5018.

ASSOCIATES

R. Michelle Denton

Representative Clients: Griffin-Spalding County Hospital Authority; Allstar Knitwear Co., Inc. (Textiles); Atlanta Tees, Inc. (Sportswear Distribution); Industrial Refrigeration Enterprises, Inc. (Refrigeration Engineers and Contractors); Spauchus Associates, Inc. (Chemical Engineering Consultants).

For full biographical listings, see the Martindale-Hubbell Law Directory

CUMMING, CUMMING & ESARY (AV)

322 South Sixth Street, P.O. Box 577, 30224
Telephone: 706-227-3746
Fax: 706-227-3891

MEMBERS OF FIRM

D. R. Cumming (1888-1970) | W. Barron Cumming
Joseph R. Cumming (1906-1990) | Sidney R. Esary

Counsel for: First National Bank of Griffin; United Bank of Griffin; Dundee Mills, Inc.; Rushton Cotton Mills.
Local Counsel for: Thomaston Cotton Mills.
Approved Attorneys for: Lawyers Title Insurance Corp.; Chicago Title Insurance Co.; Title Insurance Company of Minnesota.

For full biographical listings, see the Martindale-Hubbell Law Directory

ROBERT H. SMALLEY, JR. PROFESSIONAL CORPORATION (AV)

115 North Sixth Street, P.O. Box 907, 30224
Telephone: 404-228-2125
Telecopier: 404-228-5018

Robert H. Smalley, Jr. | Thomas E. Baynham, III

Representative Clients: The Bank of Spalding County; Griffin Spalding County Development Authority; Masada Communications, Ltd. (CATV); Union Camp Corp. (Local Counsel).

For full biographical listings, see the Martindale-Hubbell Law Directory

*HARTWELL,** Hart Co.

WALTER JAMES GORDON (AV)

Gordon Building, P.O. Box 870, 30643
Telephone: 706-376-5418
FAX: 706-376-5416

ASSOCIATES

Eleanor Patat Cotton

References: NationsBank of Georgia, N.A.; The Bank of Hartwell; Athens First Bank & Trust Company.

For full biographical listings, see the Martindale-Hubbell Law Directory

*HAWKINSVILLE,** Pulaski Co. — (Refer to Perry)

*HAZLEHURST,** Jeff Davis Co. — (Refer to Eastman)

*HINESVILLE,** Liberty Co.

JONES, OSTEEN, JONES & ARNOLD (AV)

206 East Court Street, P.O. Box 800, 31313
Telephone: 912-876-0111
Cable Address: "JOJA"
Fax: 912-368-2979

MEMBERS OF FIRM

Charles M. Jones
Billy N. Jones
J. Noel Osteen
Jeffery L. Arnold

ASSOCIATES

G. Brinson Williams, Jr.
Linnie L. Darden, III
Mark W. Nickerson

General Counsel for: The Hinesville Bank; The Coastal Bank; Coastal Utilities, Inc.; Coastal Electric Membership Corp.; Liberty County Hospital Authority; Hinesville Area Board of Realtors; Liberty County Industrial Authority; Liberty County, Georgia; City of Riceboro.

For full biographical listings, see the Martindale-Hubbell Law Directory

*JEFFERSON,** Jackson Co. — (Refer to Athens)

*JESUP,** Wayne Co.

HOWARD, CARSWELL & BENNETT, P.C. (AV)

Lawyers Building, 145 N. Brunswick Street, P.O. Box 543, 31545
Telephone: 912-427-4268

Joseph H. Thomas (1909-1984)
Kenneth R. Carswell
Hubert H. Howard
R. Violet Bennett

Representative Clients: Graward General Companies; Independent Fire Insurance Companies; Georgia Insurers Insolvency Pool; The Seibels Bruce Insurance Company; Cigna; ITT Rayonier, Inc.; Georgia Power Co.; Southern Trust Insurance Co.; Cotton States Insurance Co.; Lawyers Title Insurance Corp.;

For full biographical listings, see the Martindale-Hubbell Law Directory

*JONESBORO,** Clayton Co.

DRIEBE & DRIEBE, P.C. (AV)

6 Courthouse Way, P.O. Box 975, 30237
Telephone: 404-478-8894
FAX: 404-478-9606
Atlanta, Georgia Office: 152 Nassau Street, N.W.
Telephone: 404-688-5500.

Charles J. Driebe
Charles J. Driebe, Jr.
J. Ron Stegall

Approved Attorneys for: First American Title Insurance Co.; Attorney's Title Guaranty Fund.
Representative Clients: Atlanta International Records, Inc.; Henry County Airport, Inc.; Clayton News/Daily; Atlanta Beach Sports & Entertainment Park, Inc.

For full biographical listings, see the Martindale-Hubbell Law Directory

OLIVER, DUCKWORTH, SPARGER & WINKLE, P.C. (AV)

146 McDonough Street, P.O. Box 37, 30236
Telephone: 404-478-8883
Fax: 404-473-0872

G. Robert Oliver
Kevin W. Sparger
David P. Winkle

Richard Lord
Kathy Brown Valencia

OF COUNSEL

William H. Duckworth, Jr.

Local Counsel for: Department of Transportation, State of Georgia.
Representative Clients: Clayton County Hospital Authority; Clayton County Water Authority; Clayton College Foundation, Inc.; Clayton County Development Authority; Low Temp Industries, Inc.; Medical Association of Georgia Mutual Insurance Co.

For full biographical listings, see the Martindale-Hubbell Law Directory

*LA FAYETTE,** Walker Co.

WATSON & DANA (AV)

Corner Duke and Withers Streets, P.O. Box 1496, 30728
Telephone: 706-638-5225
Fax: 706-638-8070

MEMBERS OF FIRM

Dennis D. Watson
Joseph F. Dana

(See Next Column)

ASSOCIATES

Melissa D. Gifford

Representative Clients: Bank of Dade, Trenton, Georgia; Walker County, Georgia; Synthetic Industries, Inc.; The Hospital Authority of Walker, Dade and Catoosa Counties; Cuna Mutual Insurance Group; Georgia Farm Bureau Mutual Insurance Company; MMI Companies, Inc.; National Union Fire Insurance Company; Nationwide Mutual Insurance Company; Preferred Risk Mutual Insurance Company.

For full biographical listings, see the Martindale-Hubbell Law Directory

WOMACK & RHYNE (AV)

109 East Patton Avenue, P.O. Box 549, 30728
Telephone: 706-638-2234
FAX: 706-638-3173

MEMBERS OF FIRM

Ronald R. Womack
John W. Rhyne, Jr.

ASSOCIATES

John T. Siess

Counsel for: City of LaFayette; Housing Authority of the City of LaFayette; Walker County Board of Education; City of Trenton; State of Georgia Department of Transportation; Radix Broadcasting, Inc.

For full biographical listings, see the Martindale-Hubbell Law Directory

*LA GRANGE,** Troup Co.

DUNCAN, THOMASSON & ACREE (AV)

18 North LaFayette Square, P.O. Box 1168, 30241
Telephone: 706-882-7731
FAX: 706-845-1717

MEMBERS OF FIRM

Thurman E. Duncan
James T. Thomasson, Jr.
Marc E. Acree

General Counsel for: Mountville Mills, Inc.; Daniel Realty & Insurance Co., Inc.; Commercial Bank and Trust Company of Troup County; Radiology Associates of West Georgia, P.C.; Woodbury Business Forms, Inc.
Approved Attorneys for: Lawyers Title Insurance Corp.; American Title Insurance Co.

For full biographical listings, see the Martindale-Hubbell Law Directory

LEWIS, TAYLOR & TODD, P.C. (AV)

304 Church Street, 30241
Telephone: 706-882-2501
Fax: 706-882-4905

George E. Sims, Jr. (1917-1967)
John M. Taylor
James R. Lewis
Jeffrey M. Todd

Counsel for: Callaway Foundation, Inc.; Nations Bank; Mansour's Inc.; The City of La Grange.
Local Counsel for: State Farm Mutual Automobile Insurance Co.; Liberty Mutual Insurance Co.
Approved Attorneys for: Ticor Title Insurance Co.; Lawyers Title Insurance Corp.

For full biographical listings, see the Martindale-Hubbell Law Directory

*LAWRENCEVILLE,** Gwinnett Co.

ANDERSEN, DAVIDSON & TATE, P.C. (AV)

324 West Pike Street, Suite 200, P.O. Box 265, 30246-0265
Telephone: 404-822-0900
Telecopier: 404-822-9680

Thomas J. Andersen
Thomas T. Tate
Gerald Davidson, Jr.
Jeffrey R. Mahaffey

William M. Ray, II
Kathleen B. Guy
Johnathan D. Crumly

OF COUNSEL

Ethel D. Andersen

References: Trust Company Bank; The Bank of Gwinnett County; Chicago Title Insurance Co.; Title Insurance Company of Minnesota.

For full biographical listings, see the Martindale-Hubbell Law Directory

WEBB, TANNER & POWELL (AV)

Suite 300 Gwinnett Federal Building, 750 South Perry Street, P.O. Box 27, 30246
Telephone: 404-962-8545; 963-3423
Fax: 404-963-3424

MEMBERS OF FIRM

Jones Webb
William G. Tanner
Anthony O. L. Powell

(See Next Column)

WEBB, TANNER & POWELL—*Continued*

ASSOCIATES

Ralph L. Taylor, III
Andrew R. Mertz
Robert Jackson Wilson
Steven A. Pickens

Attorneys for: Gwinnett Federal Savings & Loan Assn.; City of Lawrenceville, Ga.; Water and Sewer Authority of Gwinnett County; West Georgia Farm Credit, ACA; Georgia Power Co.; Lawyers Title Insurance Corp.; Young Harris College, Young Harris, Georgia; Chicago Title Insurance Co.

For full biographical listings, see the Martindale-Hubbell Law Directory

*LOUISVILLE,** Jefferson Co. — (Refer to Waynesboro)

*LYONS,** Toombs Co. — (Refer to Metter)

*MACON,** Bibb Co.

ANDERSON, WALKER & REICHERT (AV)

Suite 404 Trust Company Bank Building, P.O. Box 6497, 31208-6497
Telephone: 912-743-8651
Telecopier: 912-743-9636

MEMBERS OF FIRM

R. Lanier Anderson (1871-1959)
R. Lanier Anderson, Jr. (1899-1984)
Charles W. Walker (1905-1984)
Mallory C. Atkinson, Jr. (1939-1990)
Albert P. Reichert
Thomas L. Bass
Albert P. Reichert, Jr.
John D. Reeves
John W. Collier
Walter H. Bush, Jr.
Eugene S. Hatcher
Robert A. B. Reichert
Elton L. Wall
Susan S. Cole
Jonathan A. Alderman

ASSOCIATES

Brown W. Dennis, Jr.
John P. Cole
Travis M. Trimble
Stephen M. Welsh

Representative Clients: Riverwood International Georgia, Inc.; Hospital Corporation of America; Pepsi-Cola Bottling Company of Macon; Radiology Associates of Macon, P.C.; Thiele Kaolin Company; Trust Company Bank of Middle Georgia, N.A.
General Insurance Clients: Liberty Mutual Insurance Co.; United States Fidelity & Guaranty Co.; Continental Insurance Cos.; Alexis, Inc.

For full biographical listings, see the Martindale-Hubbell Law Directory

CHAMBLESS, HIGDON & CARSON (AV)

Suite 200 Ambrose Baber Building, 577 Walnut Street, P.O. Box 246, 31298-5399
Telephone: 912-745-1181
Telecopier: 912-746-9479

MEMBERS OF FIRM

Joseph H. Davis
Joseph H. Chambless
David B. Higdon
James F. Carson, Jr.
Thomas F. Richardson
Mary Mendel Katz
Emmitte H. Griggs
Marc T. Treadwell

ASSOCIATES

Kim H. Stroup
Christopher Balch
Jon Christopher Wolfe

Local Counsel for: Atlanta Gas Light Co.; First Union National Bank of Georgia; Security National Bank.

For full biographical listings, see the Martindale-Hubbell Law Directory

HALL, BLOCH, GARLAND & MEYER (AV)

1500 Charter Medical Building, P.O. Box 5088, 31213-3199
Telephone: 912-745-1625
Telecopier: 912-741-8822

MEMBERS OF FIRM

J. E. Hall (1876-1945)
Charles J. Bloch (1893-1974)
Ellsworth Hall, Jr. (1908-1984)
J. René Hawkins (1924-1971)
Ellsworth Hall, III
F. Kennedy Hall
Benjamin M. Garland
J. Patrick Meyer, Jr.
J. Steven Stewart
J. Burton Wilkerson, Jr.
Duncan D. Walker, III
Mark E. Toth

ASSOCIATES

Ramsey T. Way, Jr.
Todd C. Brooks

F. Kennedy Hall, Division Counsel (Georgia): Norfolk Southern Corporation; Norfolk Southern Railway Company.
Counsel for: Wachovia Bank of Georgia, N.A.; Charter Medical Corporation; South Georgia Natural Gas Co.; Helena Chemical Corp.; American Druggist Insurance Cop.; Fickling & Walker Asset and Property Management, Inc.; Navistar International Corporation.

For full biographical listings, see the Martindale-Hubbell Law Directory

HARRIS & JAMES (AV)

600 First Liberty Bank Tower, 201 Second Street, P.O. Box 4866, 31208-4866
Telephone: 912-745-9661
Telecopier: 912-745-9824

(See Next Column)

MEMBERS OF FIRM

John B. Harris, Jr.
John E. James
John Burke Harris, III
William C. Harris
Kathryn Weigand Gerhardt

ASSOCIATES

Lisa Neill-Beckmann
Charles E. Johnson, III

OF COUNSEL

Sarah Stevenson Harris

Representative Clients: Dry Branch Kaolin Co.; Georgia Department of Transportation; Jefferson-Pilot Life Insurance Co.; Public Service Telephone Co.; Riverside Cemetery; Hart's Mortuary; Macon Orthopedic & Hand Center, P.A.; Rivoli Orthopedic Assn., P.A.; Southeastern Store Owners Assn.; G C Quality Lubricants, Inc.

For full biographical listings, see the Martindale-Hubbell Law Directory

JONES, CORK & MILLER (AV)

435 Second Street, Fifth Floor, P.O. Box 6437, 31201-2724
Telephone: 912-745-2821
Telecopier: 912-743-9609

MEMBERS OF FIRM

C. Baxter Jones (1895-1968)
Charles M. Cork (1908-1982)
Charles M. Cork, Jr.
Carr G. Dodson
Timothy K. Adams
John C. Cork
H. Jerome Strickland
Hubert C. Lovein, Jr.
W. Warren Plowden, Jr.
Rufus D. Sams, III
Thomas C. James, III
Steve L. Wilson
James M. Elliott, Jr.
Thomas C. Alexander
C. Ashley Royal
Robert C. Norman, Jr.
Jerry A. Lumley
John T. Mitchell, Jr.
W. Carter Bates III
Timothy Harden, III
Howard J. Strickland, Jr.
Cater C. Thompson
Thomas W. Joyce
Brandon A. Oren

ASSOCIATES

W. Kerry Howell
David A. Pope
William T. Prescott
Shawn Marie Story
James E. Messer, Jr.
Timothy K. Hall

OF COUNSEL

Wallace Miller, Jr.
John W. Smith

General Counsel for: The Bibb Co.; Trust Company Bank of Middle Georgia, N.A.; First Liberty Bank; Wesleyan College; Bibb County Board of Education.
Division Counsel for: Georgia Power Co.
Represent Locally: Southern Bell Telephone & Telegraph Co.; Allstate Insurance Co.; The City of Macon; St. Paul Fire & Marine Insurance Co.

For full biographical listings, see the Martindale-Hubbell Law Directory

O'NEAL, BROWN & SIZEMORE, A PROFESSIONAL CORPORATION (AV)

Suite 1001, American Federal Building, 544 Mulberry Street, 31201
Telephone: 912-742-8981
Telecopier: 912-743-5035
Atlanta, Georgia Office: Suite 2600, One Atlanta Plaza, 950 East Paces Ferry Road, N.E.
Telephone: 404-237-6701.
Telecopier: 404-233-1267.

H. T. O'Neal, Jr. (1924-1983)
Manley F. Brown
Lamar W. Sizemore, Jr.

John C. Clark (Associate, Atlanta Office)

OF COUNSEL

James M. Wootan

For full biographical listings, see the Martindale-Hubbell Law Directory

SELL & MELTON (AV)

A Partnership including a Professional Corporation
14th Floor, Charter Medical Building, P.O. Box 229, 31297-2899
Telephone: 912-746-8521
Telecopier: 912-745-6426

Andrew W. McKenna (1918-1981)
E. S. Sell, Jr.
John D. Comer
Buckner F. Melton
Mitchel P. House, Jr.
Joseph W. Popper, Jr.
Doye E. Green
Edward S. Sell, III
John A. Draughon
R. (Chix) Miller
Russell M. Boston (P.C.)
Brian J. Passante

ASSOCIATES

Doye E. Green, Jr.
Jeffrey B. Hanson
Robert D. McCullers
Michelle W. Johnson

General Counsel for: Macon Telegraph Publishing Co. (The Macon Telegraph); Macon-Bibb County Hospital Authority; County of Bibb; County of Twiggs; Smith & Sons Foods, Inc. (S & S Cafeterias); Macon Bibb County Industrial Authority; Burgess Pigment Co.

(See Next Column)

SELL & MELTON, *Macon—Continued*

For full biographical listings, see the Martindale-Hubbell Law Directory

*MADISON,** Morgan Co.

LAMBERT & ROFFMAN (AV)

126 East Washington Street, P.O. Box 169, 30650
Telephone: 706-342-9683
Telecopier: 706-342-3566

MEMBERS OF FIRM

E. R. Lambert
Allan R. Roffman

ASSOCIATES

M. Joseph Reitman, Jr.
Mark W. Dauenhauer

Representative Clients:
Corporate: Walton Electric Membership Corp.; Wellington-Puritan, Inc.; Bank of Madison.
Local Governments: Morgan County Board of Commissioners; City of Madison; City of Social Circle; Walton County Water and Sewage Authority.
Local Counsel: Trust Company Bank of Northeast Georgia; Evergreen Timberlands Corp.

For full biographical listings, see the Martindale-Hubbell Law Directory

*MARIETTA,** Cobb Co.

AWTREY AND PARKER, P.C. (AV)

211 Roswell Street, P.O. Box 997, 30061
Telephone: 404-424-8000
Fax: 404-424-1594

L. M. Awtrey, Jr. (1915-1986)
George L. Dozier, Jr.
Harvey D. Harkness
Mike Harrison
Dana L. Jackel
Donald A. Mangerie (1924-1988)
Michael L. Marsh
Barbara H. Martin
A. Sidney Parker
Toby B. Prodgers
J. Lynn Rainey
Annette M. Risse (Mrs.)
Robert B. Silliman

Gregg A. Landau
Lisa G. Gunn
Alan H. Sheldon

OF COUNSEL

Allan J. Hall
J. Ben Moore
S. Alan Schlact

General Counsel for: Kennesaw Finance Co.; Cobb Electric Membership Corporation; Development Authority of Cobb County.
Local Counsel for: Coats & Clark; Bell South Mobility; Lockheed-Georgia Corp.; Post Properties, Inc.; CSX Transportation, Inc.

For full biographical listings, see the Martindale-Hubbell Law Directory

CUSTER & HILL, P.C. (AV)

241 Washington Avenue, P.O. Box 1224, 30061
Telephone: 404-429-8300
Fax: 404-429-8338

Lawrence B. Custer
Douglas A. Hill

Reference: First Union National Bank.

For full biographical listings, see the Martindale-Hubbell Law Directory

DOWNEY & CLEVELAND (AV)

288 Washington Avenue, 30060
Telephone: 404-422-3233
Fax: 404-423-4199

OF COUNSEL

Lynn A. Downey

MEMBERS OF FIRM

Robert H. Cleveland (1940-1989)
Joseph C. Parker
Y. Kevin Williams
Russell B. Davis
G. Lee Welborn

ASSOCIATES

Rodney S. Shockley
W. Curtis Anderson
Scott D. Clay
Todd E. Hatcher

Representative Clients: Allstate Insurance Co.; St. Paul Insurance Cos.; Georgia Farm Bureau Mutual Insurance Co.; State Farm Insurance Cos.; Cotton States Mutual Insurance Co.; Colonial Insurance Co. of California; Ed Voyles Oldsmobile, Honda and Chrysler-Plymouth; Chuck Clancy Ford; City of Acworth; Lockheed Aeronautical Systems Company, a Division of Lockheed Corporation.

For full biographical listings, see the Martindale-Hubbell Law Directory

*MCDONOUGH,** Henry Co.

SMITH, WELCH & STUDDARD (AV)

41 Keys Ferry Street, P.O. Box 31, 30253
Telephone: 404-957-3937
Fax: 404-957-9165
Stockbridge, Georgia Office: 1231-A Eagle's Landing Parkway.
Telephone: 404-389-4864.
FAX: 404-389-5157.

MEMBERS OF FIRM

Ernest M. Smith (1911-1992)
A. J. Welch, Jr.
Ben W. Studdard, III
J. Mark Brittain (Resident, Stockbridge Office)

ASSOCIATES

Patrick D. Jaugstetter
E. Gilmore Maxwell
J.V. Dell, Jr. (Resident, Stockbridge Office)

Representative Clients: Alliance Corp.; Atlanta Motor Speedway, Inc.; Bellamy-Strickland Chevrolet, Inc.; Ceramic and Metal Coatings Corp.; City of Hampton; City of Locust Grove; City of Stockbridge.

For full biographical listings, see the Martindale-Hubbell Law Directory

*METTER,** Candler Co.

DOREMUS, JONES AND SMITH, P.C. (AV)

21 North Kennedy Street, P.O. Box 296, 30439
Telephone: 912-685-5763
Telecopier: 912-685-4902

Ogden Doremus
Bobby Jones
Julian B. Smith, Jr.

Robert B. Sullivan

Representative Clients: Metter Banking Co.; Wallace Business Forms, Inc.; Cal-Maine Foods, Inc.; Franklin Chevrolet; Federal Land Bank; Georgia Farm Bureau Mutual Insurance Co., Inc.; The Travelers Insurance Co.; Nationwide Insurance Co.

For full biographical listings, see the Martindale-Hubbell Law Directory

*MILLEDGEVILLE,** Baldwin Co. — (Refer to Macon)

*MILLEN,** Jenkins Co. — (Refer to Augusta)

*MONROE,** Walton Co. — (Refer to Decatur)

*MONTICELLO,** Jasper Co.

HAYGOOD, LYNCH, HARRIS & MELTON (AV)

248 West Green Street, 31064
Telephone: 706-468-8846
Forsyth, Georgia Office: 87 North Lee Street, 31029.
Telephone: 912-994-5171.
Fax: 912-994-4588.

Larry Persons Lynch

Representative Clients: Monroe County Industrial Development Authority; Fairfield Financial; Bank South, Jasper County, N.A.; Georgia Timberlands, Inc.
Local Counsel for: Atlanta Gas Light Co.; Georgia Pacific Corp.; Bowater Southern Paper Corp.; Liberty Savings Bank.

For full biographical listings, see the Martindale-Hubbell Law Directory

*MOULTRIE,** Colquitt Co.

MOORE, CHAMBLISS, ALLEN AND TYNDALL (AV)

317 South Main Street, P.O. Box 190, 31776
Telephone: 912-985-1213
Fax: 912-890-1314

L. L. Moore (1880-1962)
R. Lamar Moore
C. Saxby Chambliss
Keith F. Allen
David R. Tyndall

Representative Clients: Moultrie National Bank; Colquitt Electric Membership Corp.; Rich Oil Co.; Moultrie Farm Center; Destiny Industries, Inc.; Moultrie Manufacturing Co.
Local Counsel: The Equitable Life Assurance Society of the United States; Chubb & Son, Inc.; Miller Brewing Company.

For full biographical listings, see the Martindale-Hubbell Law Directory

WHELCHEL, WHELCHEL & CARLTON (AV)

26 Second Avenue, S.W., P.O. Box 768, 31768
Telephone: 912-985-1590
FAX: 912-985-0946

(See Next Column)

WHELCHEL, WHELCHEL & CARLTON—*Continued*

MEMBERS OF FIRM

Hoyt H. Whelchel (1893-1960)
Hoyt H. Whelchel, Jr.
James C. Whelchel
John M. Carlton, Jr.

Representative Clients: Holman Supply Co.; United States Fidelity & Guaranty Co.; Great American Indemnity Co.; City of Moultrie; The St. Paul Cos.; Colquitt County Board of Education; Universal Underwriters Group; Riverside Manufacturing Company; Hospital Authority of Colquitt County.

For full biographical listings, see the Martindale-Hubbell Law Directory

*NASHVILLE,** Berrien Co. — (Refer to Moultrie)

*NEWNAN,** Coweta Co.

GLOVER & DAVIS, P.A. (AV)

10 Brown Street, P.O. Box 1038, 30264
Telephone: 404-253-4330;
Atlanta: 404-463-1100
Fax: 404-251-7152
Peachtree City, Georgia Office: Suite 130, 200 Westpark Drive.
Telephone: 404-487-5834.
Fax: 404-487-3492.

J. Littleton Glover
Welborn B. Davis, Jr. (1922-1974)
J. Littleton Glover, Jr.
Alan W. Jackson
Randy E. Connell
Delia T. Crouch
W. Robert Hancock, Jr. (Resident, Peachtree Office)
Asa M. Powell, Jr.
Felicia Odom Smith (Resident, Peachtree Office)
Jerry Ann Conner
Melissa A. Cordell

Representative Clients: Newnan Savings Bank; Pike Transfer Co.; Batson-Cook Company, General Corporate and Construction Divisions; Coweta County, Georgia; Heard County, Georgia; Putnam-Greene Financial Company; West Georgia.
Local Counsel for: International Latex Corp.; First Union National Bank of Georgia; Farm Credit, ACA.

For full biographical listings, see the Martindale-Hubbell Law Directory

ROSENZWEIG, JONES & MACNABB, P.C. (AV)

32 South Court Square, P.O. Box 220, 30264
Telephone: 404-253-3282;
(Atlanta) 404-577-5376
FAX: 404-251-7262

George C. Rosenzweig
Sidney Pope Jones, Jr.
Joseph P. MacNabb

Charles C. Witcher
Douglas L. Dreyer

Approved Attorneys for: Lawyers Title Insurance Corp.; Commonwealth Land Title Insurance Co.; St. Paul Title Insurance Co.; Chicago Title Insurance Co.

For full biographical listings, see the Martindale-Hubbell Law Directory

SANDERS, HAUGEN & SEARS (AV)

11 Perry Street, P.O. Box 1177, 30263
Telephone: 404-253-3880
Fax: 404-254-0093

MEMBERS OF FIRM

Walter D. Sanders (1909-1989)
Willis G. Haugen
C. Bradford Sears, Jr.
Walter S. Haugen

Attorneys for: Southern Railway System; Georgia Power Co.; City of Newnan; The Bibb Co.; Southern Bell Telephone Co.; Brown Steel Contractors.

For full biographical listings, see the Martindale-Hubbell Law Directory

WOOD, ODOM AND EDGE, P.A. (AV)

15 Jefferson Street, P.O. Drawer 1608, 30264
Telephone: 404-253-9885; 1-800-346-5357
Fax: 404-253-9896
Atlanta Telephone: 404-577-9024
Sharpsburg, Georgia Office: 3091 East Highway 34.
Telephone: 404-251-7266.
Telecopier: 404-251-7266.

Gus L. Wood
H. Parnell Odom
Arthur B. Edge, IV

Jacquelyn L. Kneidel
Kim T. Stephens

For full biographical listings, see the Martindale-Hubbell Law Directory

*NEWTON,** Baker Co. — (Refer to Camilla)

NORCROSS, Gwinnett Co.

THOMPSON & SLAGLE, P.C. (AV)

5335 Triangle Parkway Suite 550, 30092
Telephone: 404-662-5999

(See Next Column)

DeWitte Thompson
Jefferson B. Slagle
David J. Merbaum

Gady Zeewy
David Ian Matthews

For full biographical listings, see the Martindale-Hubbell Law Directory

*OCILLA,** Irwin Co.

WALTERS, DAVIS, MEEKS & PUJADAS, P.C. (AV)

South Cherry Street, P.O. Box 247, 31774
Telephone: 912-468-7472; 468-9433
Fax: 912-468-9022

W. Emory Walters
J. Harvey Davis
W. Edward Meeks, Jr.
Thomas E. Pujadas
C. Vinson Walters, II

LEGAL SUPPORT PERSONNEL

Larry P. Harper

Attorneys for: Irwin County Board of Education; First State Bank of Ocilla; Irwin County; Wilcox County.
Local Counsel for: Georgia Farm Bureau Mutual Insurance Co.
Approved Attorneys for: Kaiser Aluminum & Chemical Sales, Inc.; Lawyers Title Insurance Corp.; Ticor Title Insurance Co.; Farmers Home Administration; Federal Land Bank of Columbia.

For full biographical listings, see the Martindale-Hubbell Law Directory

*PERRY,** Houston Co.

HULBERT, DANIEL & LAWSON (AV)

912 Main Street, P.O. Box 89, 31069
Telephone: 912-987-2622
Fax: 912-987-7037

MEMBERS OF FIRM

Hubert A. Aultman (1920-1977)
David P. Hulbert (Of Counsel)
Tom W. Daniel
Hugh Lawson, Jr.
Robert T. Tuggle, III
William R. Jerles, Jr.

Representative Clients: Flint Electric Membership Corp.; Houston County Board of Education; Tri-County Electric Membership Corp.; Agricultural Investment Management Corp.; The Bank of Perry.
Approved Attorneys for: Lawyers Title Insurance Corp.; Chicago Title Insurance Co.; Ticor Title Insurance Co.; Federal Land Bank of Columbia; Farmers Home Administration.

For full biographical listings, see the Martindale-Hubbell Law Directory

WALKER, HULBERT, GRAY & BYRD (AV)

909 Ball Street, P.O. Box 1234, 31069
Telephone: 912-987-1415
Fax: 912-987-1077

MEMBERS OF FIRM

Lawrence C. Walker, Jr.
David G. Walker
David P. Hulbert, Jr.
Michael G. Gray
Charles W. Byrd

ASSOCIATES

S. E. Moody, III

Representative Clients: City of Perry; City of Reynolds; Houston County Hospital Authority; Perry-Fort Valley Airport Authority; Crossroads Bank of Georgia; Citizens State Bank, Reynolds; World Acceptance Corporation; NavCom Defense Electronics, Inc.; Brown and Williamson Tobacco Corp.

For full biographical listings, see the Martindale-Hubbell Law Directory

*QUITMAN,** Brooks Co. — (Refer to Valdosta)

*REIDSVILLE,** Tattnall Co. — (Refer to Metter)

*RINGGOLD,** Catoosa Co. — (Refer to Dalton)

*ROME,** Floyd Co.

BRINSON, ASKEW, BERRY, SEIGLER, RICHARDSON & DAVIS (AV)

A Partnership including Professional Corporations
Omberg House, 615 West First Street, P.O. Box 5513, 30162-5513
Telephone: 706-291-8853;
Atlanta: 404-521-0908
Telecopier: 706-234-3574

MEMBERS OF FIRM

Robert M. Brinson (P.C.)
C. King Askew (P.C.)
Robert L. Berry
Joseph M. Seigler, Jr.
Thomas D. Richardson
J. Anderson Davis
Hendrick L. Cromartie, III

OF COUNSEL

Wright W. Smith

(See Next Column)

BRINSON, ASKEW, BERRY, SEIGLER, RICHARDSON & DAVIS, *Rome—Continued*

ASSOCIATES

Mark M. J. Webb
Joseph B. Atkins
I. Stewart Duggan, Jr.

Representative Clients: City of Rome; Georgia Power Co.; NationsBank of Georgia, N.A.; News Publishing Company (Rome News Tribune); Redmond Regional Medical Center; Oglethorpe Power Corp.; Suhner Manufacturing, Inc.; The Federal Land Bank of Columbia; AmSouth Bank of Georgia; United States Fidelity & Guaranty Co.

For full biographical listings, see the Martindale-Hubbell Law Directory

ROGERS, MAGRUDER, SUMNER & BRINSON (AV)

701 Broad Street, P.O. Drawer 5187, 30162-5187
Telephone: 706-291-7050;
Atlanta Line: 706-522-5160
Telefax: 706-291-6242

MEMBERS OF FIRM

J. Clinton Sumner, Jr.
Moses E. Brinson
Karl M. Kothe
Raymon H. Cox

ASSOCIATES

Clay White
Kay Ann King

OF COUNSEL

Dudley B. Magruder, Jr.
Jack Rogers
Wade C. Hoyt, Jr.

Counsel for: Citizens Federal Savings & Loan Assn.; State Farm Mutual Insurance Cos.; Atlanta Gas Light Co.; Galey & Lord, Inc.; Best Manufacturing Co.; Georgia Power Co.; West Point-Pepperell Manufacturing Co.; Southern Bell Telephone & Telegraph Co.; Liberty Mutual Insurance Co.

For full biographical listings, see the Martindale-Hubbell Law Directory

SHAW, MADDOX, GRAHAM, MONK & BOLING (AV)

Trust Company Bank Building, P.O. Box 29, 30162-0029
Telephone: 706-291-6223
Telecopier: 706-291-7429

MEMBERS OF FIRM

Charles C. Shaw
James D. Maddox
John M. Graham, III
C. Wade Monk
William H. Boling, Jr.
Jo H. Stegall, III
David F. Guldenschuh
Daniel M. Roper
Jule W. Peek, Jr.
Virginia B. Harman

ASSOCIATES

Scott M. Smith
Thomas H. Manning
David Tomlin
Mather D. Graham

OF COUNSEL

Oscar M. Smith

Representative Clients: Trust Company Bank of Northwest Georgia; Bagby Transfer Co.; Inland-Rome Inc.; Southern Railway Co.; Aetna Casualty & Surety Co.; American Mutual Liability Insurance; Commercial Union Assurance Cos.; Hartford Accident & Indemnity Co.

For full biographical listings, see the Martindale-Hubbell Law Directory

*SANDERSVILLE,** Washington Co. — (Refer to Louisville)

*SAVANNAH,** Chatham Co.

ADAMS & ELLIS, A PROFESSIONAL CORPORATION (AV)

15 Drayton Street, P.O. Box 2364, 31498-2364
Telephone: 912-233-1108
Telecopier: 912-234-5357

A. Pratt Adams, Jr. (1914-1981)
Thomas H. Adams (1917-1986)
J. Wiley Ellis
James R. Gardner
Ronald C. Berry
George L. Lewis
Christopher E. Klein

David W. Adams
Laura Jean Tromly
James K. Austin
Tracy Cullen O'Connell
Thomas L. Cole
Emily Samantha Blumenthal

Representative Clients: Gulfstream Aerospace, Inc.; Colonial Oil Industries, Inc.; Strachan Shipping Co.; Morris Newspaper Corp.; Northwestern National Insurance Group; Green Tree Acceptance; Ford Motor Credit Co.

For full biographical listings, see the Martindale-Hubbell Law Directory

BOUHAN, WILLIAMS & LEVY (AV)

The Armstrong House, 447 Bull Street, P.O. Box 2139, 31498-1001
Telephone: 912-236-2491
FAX: 912-233-0811

MEMBERS OF FIRM

John J. Bouhan (1886-1971)
B. H. Levy (1912-1988)
Frank W. Seiler
Walter C. Hartridge
Edgar Pomeroy Williams
Edwin D. Robb, Jr.
Leamon R. Holliday, III
Lawrence Michael Donovan, Jr.

(See Next Column)

MEMBERS OF FIRM (Continued)

B. H. Levy, Jr.
John G. Lientz
M. Tyus Butler, Jr.
M. Brice Ladson
Roy E. Paul
Joseph A. Mulherin, III
Wilbur D. Owens, III
Peter D. Muller

OF COUNSEL

George W. Williams
Alan S. Gaynor
John Michael Brennan
Samuel A. Cann

ASSOCIATES

Melanie L. Marks
Carlton E. Joyce
Charles V. Loncon
Francis S. Exley
Jane L. Peeples
Timothy H. Edwards

General Counsel for: Savannah Electric and Power Co.; Wachovia Bank of Georgia, N.A.; Southeastern Maritime Co.; Solomons Co.; Fiduciary Services Corp.; Peeples Industry, Inc.; Board of Education of the City of Savannah and County of Chatham; The Branigar Organization, Inc.

For full biographical listings, see the Martindale-Hubbell Law Directory

BRANNEN, SEARCY & SMITH (AV)

22 East Thirty-Fourth Street, P.O. Box 8002, 31412
Telephone: 912-234-8875
Fax: 912-232-1792

Perry Brannen (1903-1984)
Frank P. Brannen
William N. Searcy
David R. Smith
Daniel C. Cohen
Wayne L. Durden

OF COUNSEL

William T. Daniel, Jr.

ASSOCIATES

Robert L. Jenkins
Bernard F. Kistler, Jr.
Fonda L. Jackson

Counsel for: Continental Insurance Co.

For full biographical listings, see the Martindale-Hubbell Law Directory

CHAMLEE, DUBUS & SIPPLE (AV)

Suite 301 Cluskey Building, 127 Abercorn Street, P.O. Box 9523, 31412
Telephone: 912-232-3311
Cable Address: "Floodtide"
Telex: 804733
Telecopier: 912-232-3253

MEMBERS OF FIRM

George H. Chamlee
Gustave R. Dubus, III
David F. Sipple

For full biographical listings, see the Martindale-Hubbell Law Directory

HUNTER, MACLEAN, EXLEY & DUNN, P.C. (AV)

200 East St. Julian Street, P.O. Box 9848, 31412
Telephone: 912-236-0261
Cable Address: "Ancan"
Telecopier: 912-236-4936
Telex: 54-6483
Atlanta, Georgia Office: The Peachtree, 1355 Peachtree Street, N.E., Suite 1175.
Telephone: 404-876-3611.
Fax: 404-870-2025.

Malcolm R. Maclean
William M. Exley, Jr.
Henry M. Dunn, Jr.
John M. Hewson, III
Arnold C. Young
W. Brooks Stillwell, III
F. Saunders Aldridge, III
Robert S. Glenn, Jr.
Lee C. Mundell
Andrew H. Ernst
Roland B. Williams
Don L. Waters
Leonard J. Panzitta
Dorothea Summerell
Jonathan D. Sprague
Joseph R. Ross
Harold B. Yellin
Wade W. Herring, II
Therese Forrester Pindar
Anne Cote Marscher
Marvin A. Fentress
Debra J. Brook
Glen M. Darbyshire
R. Jason D'Cruz
Christopher Weis Phillips
Robert A. Mason
Kirby Clarice Gould
Darrin L. McCullough
Ronnie D. Talley
Thomas Mills Fleming
Edith H. Holloman
Tracy S. Plott
George M. Earle
David M. Hirsberg
Douglas C. Turner
Edward O. Henneman
Steven J. Arsenault (Not admitted in GA)
Thomas Sean Cullen
Timothy N. Toler (Atlanta Office)
Daniel J. Mohan (Atlanta Office)
Jan M. Hunter (Atlanta Office)

OF COUNSEL

Nell C. Pillard
Nancy Patrick Nutting

Representative Clients: Great Dane Trailers, Inc.; Fort Howard Corp.; West of England; Atlantic Wood Industries, Inc.; Home Insurance Co.

For full biographical listings, see the Martindale-Hubbell Law Directory

Savannah—Continued

INGLESBY, FALLIGANT, HORNE, COURINGTON & NASH, A PROFESSIONAL CORPORATION (AV)

300 Bull Street, Suite 302, P.O. Box 1368, 31402-1368
Telephone: 912-232-7000
Telecopier: 912-232-7300

Sam P. Inglesby, Jr.	Dorothy W. Courington, II
J. Daniel Falligant	Thomas A. Nash, Jr.
Kathleen Horne	Dolly Chisholm

Representative Clients: NationsBank of Georgia, N.A.; Intermarine USA; Rotary Corp.; Atlanta Gas Light Co.; Ford Motor Credit Co.; Independent Insurance Agents of Savannah, Inc.; Savannah Christian Preparatory School.

For full biographical listings, see the Martindale-Hubbell Law Directory

MILLER, SIMPSON & TATUM (AV)

Suite 400 Trust Company Bank Building, 33 Bull Street, P.O. Box 1567, 31498
Telephone: 912-233-5722
Telecopier: 912-234-5950

MEMBERS OF FIRM

John B. Miller	M. Lane Morrison
John E. Simpson	J. Reid Williamson, III
John M. Tatum	William E. Dillard III

ASSOCIATES

Robert Alvin Lewallen, Jr.	Michael Jonas Thomerson

General Counsel for: Savannah Foods & Industries, Inc.; Trust Company of Georgia Bank of Savannah, N.A.
Counsel for: Prudential Insurance Co. of America; Historic Savannah Foundation, Inc.; John Hancock Mutual Life Insurance Co.
Assistant Division Counsel for: Norfolk Southern Corporation.

For full biographical listings, see the Martindale-Hubbell Law Directory

PAINTER, RATTERREE & BART (AV)

The Commerce Building, 222 West Oglethorpe Avenue, Suite 401, P.O. Box 9946, 31412
Telephone: 912-233-9700
FAX: 912-233-2281

Paul W. Painter, Jr.	James L. Elliott
R. Clay Ratterree	Sarah Brown Akins
Randall K. Bart	Robert H. Stansfield

For full biographical listings, see the Martindale-Hubbell Law Directory

*SPARTA,** Hancock Co. — (Refer to Thomson)

*STATESBORO,** Bulloch Co.

ALLEN & CLASSENS (AV)

30 North Main Street, P.O. Box 478, 30458
Telephone: 912-764-6221
FAX: 912-764-2724

MEMBERS OF FIRM

Francis W. Allen	Michael J. Classens

Attorneys for: Sea Island Bank.
Approved Attorneys for: Lawyers Title Insurance Corp.; Farmers Home Administration.

For full biographical listings, see the Martindale-Hubbell Law Directory

*SWAINSBORO,** Emanuel Co.

REEVES & PALMER (AV)

117 Court Street, P.O. Box 1347, 30401
Telephone: 912-237-6190

Robert S. Reeves	Kathy S. Palmer

For full biographical listings, see the Martindale-Hubbell Law Directory

SHEPHERD, GARY & MCWHORTER (AV)

SSG Building, 104 East Moring Street, Drawer 99, 30401
Telephone: 912-237-7551

MEMBERS OF FIRM

Felix C. Williams (1899-1972)	Loren Gary, II
George L. Smith, II (1912-1973)	William H. McWhorter, Jr.
Sidney B. Shepherd	Millard B. Shepherd, Jr.

Representative Clients: Cities of Swainsboro, Adrian, Garfield and Nunez; The Citizens Bank of Swainsboro; ITT Raynier Paper Co.; Farm Bureau Insurance Co.
Approved Attorneys for: Lawyers Title Insurance Corp.; Ticor Title Insurance Co.; Title Insurance Company of Minnesota; Chicago Title Insurance Co.; Auto Parts & Supply.

For full biographical listings, see the Martindale-Hubbell Law Directory

*SYLVANIA,** Screven Co. — (Refer to Metter)

*SYLVESTER,** Worth Co. — (Refer to Albany)

*TALBOTTON,** Talbot Co. — (Refer to Columbus)

TALLAPOOSA, Haralson Co. — (Refer to Carrollton)

*THOMASTON,** Upson Co.

ADAMS, BARFIELD, DUNAWAY & HANKINSON (AV)

Atwater Building, 30286
Telephone: 706-647-5466
Fax: 706-647-6434

MEMBERS OF FIRM

Dickson Adams (1919-1975)	David B. Dunaway
Ronald Barfield	Tommy R. Hankinson
Catherine Barfield	

General Counsel for: City of Thomason; Thomaston Federal Savings Bank; Upson County Hospital Authority.
Representative Clients: Thomaston Mills, Inc.; Cincinnati Insurance Co.; City of Thomaston; West Georgia Farm Credit Service, ACA.
Approved Attorneys for: Lawyers Title Insurance Corp.; Chicago Title Insurance Co.

For full biographical listings, see the Martindale-Hubbell Law Directory

*THOMASVILLE,** Thomas Co.

ALEXANDER & VANN (AV)

218 East Jackson Street, P.O. Box 1479, 31799
Telephone: 912-226-2565
Fax: 912-228-0444

MEMBERS OF FIRM

Thomas H. Vann, Jr.	William C. Sanders
Charles H. Watt, III	David E. Wilder
John T. Holt	George R. Lilly, II
James H. Smith	

Allen E. Lockerman, IV

Counsel for: Commercial Bank; Davis Water & Waste Industries, Inc.
District Counsel for: CSX Transportation Inc.
Local Counsel for: St. Paul Fire & Marine Insurance Cos.; State Farm Mutual Automobile Insurance Co.; Insurance Company of North America; Auto-Owners Insurance Co.

For full biographical listings, see the Martindale-Hubbell Law Directory

*THOMSON,** McDuffie Co.

KNOX AND SWAN (AV)

Knox Building, P.O. Box 539, 30824
Telephone: 706-595-1841
Fax: 706-595-2404

MEMBERS OF FIRM

Robert E. Knox (1916-1994)	Robert E. Knox, Jr.
W. Bryant Swan, Jr.	

Representative Clients: Allied Bank of Georgia; First Savings Bank; Kingsley Mill Corp.; Hardware Mutual Casualty Co.; General Accident & Assurance Corp.; Employers Mutual of Wausau; Hartford Accident & Indemnity Co.; Sentry Insurance Group; Hoover Treated Wood Products Co.

For full biographical listings, see the Martindale-Hubbell Law Directory

*TIFTON,** Tift Co.

SIMS & FLEMING, P.C. (AV)

823 Love Avenue, P.O. Box 1165, 31793
Telephone: 912-386-0964
Fax: 912-386-1452

John S. Sims, Jr.	Carlton A. Fleming, Jr.

James M. Walker, III	John C. Spurlin

Representative Clients: First Community Bank of Tifton; Trust Company Bank; Thomson Newspapers, Inc. (The Tifton Gazette); South Georgia Farm Credit Service; Griffin Truck Lines; State Farm Mutual Automobile Insurance Co.; State Farm Fire and Casualty Insurance Co.; Home Insurance Cos.; Georgia Casualty & Surety Co.; Nationwide Insurance Co.

For full biographical listings, see the Martindale-Hubbell Law Directory

*TOCCOA,** Stephens Co.

MCCLURE, RAMSAY & DICKERSON (AV)

400 Falls Road, P.O. Drawer 1408, 30577
Telephone: 706-886-3178
Fax: 706-886-1150

MEMBERS OF FIRM

Clyde M. McClure (1892-1976)	Allan R. Ramsay
George B. Ramsay, Jr.	Martha B. Sikes
John A. Dickerson	Marlin R. Escoe

(See Next Column)

McClure, Ramsay & Dickerson, *Toccoa—Continued*

ASSOCIATES

Alice D. Hayes
Elizabeth Felton Moore
Leon Jourolmon

OF COUNSEL

Knox Bynum

Counsel for: Coats and Clark, Inc.; Stephens Federal Savings & Loan Assn.; St. Paul Insurance Cos.; State Farm Insurance Cos.; Cotton States Insurance Cos.; City of Toccoa; Citizens Bank; Habersham Plantation Corp.; Patterson Pump Co.

For full biographical listings, see the Martindale-Hubbell Law Directory

*VALDOSTA,** Lowndes Co.

Tillman, McTier, Coleman, Talley, Newbern & Kurrie (AV)

910 North Patterson Street, P.O. Box 5437, 31603-5437
Telephone: 912-242-7562
Fax: 912-333-0885

MEMBERS OF FIRM

Henry T. Brice (1925-1976)
B. Lamar Tillman (1912-1990)
John T. McTier
Wade H. Coleman
George T. Talley
C. George Newbern
Thompson Kurrie, Jr.
Richard L. Coleman
Edward F. Preston
William E. Holland
Clay Powell

OF COUNSEL

Dona Scott Laskey

Attorneys for: NationsBank; Georgia Power Co.; Liberty Mutual Insurance Co.; USF&G Co.; Georgia Casualty & Surety Co.; Valdosta-Lowndes County Industrial Authority; City of Valdosta; American Turpentine Farmers Assn.

For full biographical listings, see the Martindale-Hubbell Law Directory

*VIENNA,** Dooly Co.

Davis, Gregory, Christy & Forehand (AV)

104 West Union Street, P.O. Box 397, 31092
Telephone: 912-268-4125
Telecopier: 912-268-6373
Cordele, Georgia Office: 708 East Sixteenth Avenue, P.O. Drawer 5230.
Telephone: 912-273-7150.
Fax: 912-273-7578.

MEMBERS OF FIRM

Hardy Gregory, Jr.
Gary C. Christy
John N. Davis
David A. Forehand, Jr.

OF COUNSEL

T. Hoyt Davis, Jr.

For full biographical listings, see the Martindale-Hubbell Law Directory

WARNER ROBINS, Houston Co.

Roy N. Cowart, P.C. (AV)

1555 Watson Boulevard, P.O. Box 818, 31099
Telephone: 912-922-8515
FAX: 912-922-3184

Roy N. Cowart

Representative Clients: Park Newspapers of Georgia, Inc.; Shaheen Office Supply, Inc.; Dr. F.G. Hernandez, P.C.; C.L. Williams Insurance Agency; Maria H. Bartlett, M.D.; Surgical Associates, P.C.; Robert A. Carter, M.D., P.C.; Golden Key Realty, Inc.; Stalmaker Plastics, Inc.

For full biographical listings, see the Martindale-Hubbell Law Directory

*WASHINGTON,** Wilkes Co. — (Refer to Athens)

*WAYCROSS,** Ware Co. — (Refer to Brunswick)

*WAYNESBORO,** Burke Co. — (Refer to Augusta)

*WRIGHTSVILLE,** Johnson Co. — (Refer to Metter)

*ZEBULON,** Pike Co. — (Refer to Griffin)

HAWAII

*HILO,** Hawaii Co.

CARLSMITH BALL WICHMAN MURRAY CASE & ICHIKI (AV)

A Partnership including Law Corporations
121 Waianuenue Avenue, P.O. Box 686, 96721-0686
Telephone: 808-935-6644
Cable Address: "Carlsmith-Hilo"
Telecopier: 808-935-7975
Honolulu, Hawaii Office: Suite 2200, Pacific Tower, 1001 Bishop Street. P.O. Box 656.
Telephone: 808-523-2500.
Los Angeles, California Office: 555 South Flower Street, 25th Floor.
Telephone: 213-955-1200.
Long Beach, California Office: 301 East Ocean Boulevard, 7th Floor.
Telephone: 310-435-5631.
Washington, D.C. Office: 700 14th Street, N.W., 9th Floor.
Telephone: 202-508-1025.
Mexico City, Mexico Office: Monte Pelvoux 111, Piso 1, Col. Lomas de Chapultepec, 11000 Mexico, D.F.
Telephone: (011-52-5) 520-8514.
Fax: (011-52-5) 540-1545.
Mexico, D.F. Office of Carlsmith Ball Garcia Cacho y Asociados, S.C. (Authorized to practice Mexican Law): Monte Pelvoux 111, Piso 1, Col. Lomas de Chapultepec, 11000, Mexico, D.F.
Telephone: (011-52-5) 520-8514.
Fax: (011-52-5) 540-1545.
Agana, Guam Office: 4th Floor, Bank of Hawaii Building, P.O. Box BF.
Telephone: 671-472-6813.
Saipan, Commonwealth of the Northern Mariana Islands Office: Carlsmith Building, Capitol Hill, P.O. Box 5241.
Telephone: 670-322-3455.
Wailuku, Maui, Hawaii Office: One Main Plaza, Suite 400, 2200 Main Street, P.O. Box 1086.
Telephone: 808-242-4535.
Kailua-Kona, Hawaii Office: Second Floor, Bank of Hawaii Annex Building, P.O. Box 1720.
Telephone: 808-329-6464.
Kapolei, Hawaii Office: Kapolei Building, Suite 318, 1001 Kamokila Boulevard.
Telephone: 808-674-0850.

MEMBERS OF FIRM

Steven S. C. Lim
Tim Lui-Kwan

RESIDENT ASSOCIATE

Sherrill A. Atwood

For full biographical listings, see the Martindale-Hubbell Law Directory

CASE & LYNCH (AV)

A Partnership including Professional Corporations
(Formerly Pratt, Moore, Bortz & Case - 1967 to 1971)
(Formerly Case, Kay & Lynch - 1979 to 1986)
Case & Lynch Business Center, 460 Kilauea Avenue (Hawaii), 96720
Telephone: 808-961-6611
Telecopier: 808-961-4962
Honolulu, Hawaii Office: 2600 Grosvenor Center, Mauka Tower, 737 Bishop Street.
Telephone: 808-547-5400.
Lihue, Kauai, Hawaii Office: Watumull Plaza, Suite 202, 4334 Rice Street.
Telephone: 808-245-4705.
Kilauea, Kauai, Hawaii Office: Kong Lung Center, Kilauea Lighthouse Road, P.O. Box 988.
Telephone: 808-828-2890.
Kahului, Maui, Hawaii Office: The Kahului Building, Suite 470, 33 Lono Avenue.
Telephone: 808-871-8351.
Kailua-Kona, Hawaii Office: Hanama Place, Suite 101, 75-5706 Kuakini Highway.
Telephone: 808-329-4421.

RESIDENT PARTNERS

Robert E. Bethea
Valta A. Cook
Alan S. Konishi

RESIDENT ASSOCIATES

Peter K. Kubota
Ivan M. Torigoe

RESIDENT COUNSEL

Gary N. Hagerman
Sandra E. Pechter Schutte

RESIDENT OF COUNSEL

Ernest H. Kubota

Representative Clients: Bank of Hawaii; C. Brewer & Co., Ltd; Del Monte Corp.; Eastman Kodak Co.; Food Fair Supermarkets; Hawaiian Electric Co., Inc.; Homart Development Co.; Kona Board of Realtors; Realty Finance Co., Ltd.; W.H. Shipman, Ltd.

For full biographical listings, see the Martindale-Hubbell Law Directory

*HONOLULU,** Honolulu Co.

ALSTON, HUNT, FLOYD & ING ATTORNEYS AT LAW, A LAW CORPORATION (AV)

18th Floor Pacific Tower, 1001 Bishop Street, P.O. Box 2281, 96804
Telephone: 808-524-1800
Telecopier: 808-524-4591

Paul D. Alston
William S. Hunt
Shelby Anne Floyd
Louise K. Y. Ing
Ellen Godbey Carson
Bruce S. Noborikawa
Sharon A. Merkle
Everett S. Kaneshige
David A. Nakashima

Mei Nakamoto
Peter C. Hsieh
Theodore D.C. Young
Mary Martin
Hyo-Jin Jeni Lee
Jade Lynne Holck
Marilyn M. L. Chung
Matthew H. Meier
Susan Jameson
Joseph P. Viola

OF COUNSEL

Bruce H. Wakuzawa
Leigh-Ann K. Miyasato

Representative Clients: Kaiser Aluminum and Chemical Co.; Federal Deposit Insurance Corp.; Kaiser Foundation Health Plan, Inc.; Citicorp Savings; International Holdings, Inc.; Chicago Title Insurance Co.; Amfac, Inc.

For full biographical listings, see the Martindale-Hubbell Law Directory

ASHFORD & WRISTON (AV)

A Partnership including Law Corporations
Alii Place, Suite 1400, 1099 Alakea Street, P.O. Box 131, 96810
Telephone: 808-539-0400
Telecopier: 808-533-4945
Kailua-Kona, Hawaii Office: 208 Kuakini Tower, 75-5722 Kuakini Highway.
Telephone: 808-329-7706.
Telecopier: 808-329-7528.

MEMBERS OF FIRM

A. James Wriston, Jr., (A Law Corporation)
Albert H. Ogawa (A Law Corporation)
Galen C. K. Leong
Wayne P. Nasser (A Law Corporation)
Douglas W. MacDougal (A Law Corporation)
John A. Lockwood (A Law Corporation)
Cuyler E. Shaw (A Law Corporation)
Michael W. Gibson
Robert Bruce Graham, Jr.
Rosemary T. Fazio
Diane S. Kishimoto
Paul S. Aoki
Francis P. Hogan
James K. Mee
Lorrin B. Hirano
Kirk W. Caldwell
Marjorie Chun Yung Au
Paul R. Goto

ASSOCIATES

Katharine P. Lloyd
Keith M. N. Yonamine
Charles A. Price
Owen H. Matsunaga
Cynthia K. Ching
Mary Beth M. Wong
Glenn K.C. Ching
Bruce D. Hieneman
Paul D. Fredrick
Lemuel A. Carlos
Shah J. Bento
Ronda K. Kent
Todd K. Apo

COUNSEL

Clinton R. Ashford (A Law Corporation)
Adrian W. Rosehill
Dennis A. Krueger (Resident, Kailua-Kona Office)

For full biographical listings, see the Martindale-Hubbell Law Directory

AYABE, CHONG, NISHIMOTO, SIA & NAKAMURA (AV)

A Partnership including a Professional Corporation
3000 Grosvenor Center, 737 Bishop Street, 96813
Telephone: 808-537-6119
Telecopier: 808-526-3491

MEMBERS OF FIRM

Sidney K. Ayabe (P.C.)
Robert A. Chong
John S. Nishimoto
Richard Nakamura
Jeffrey H. K. Sia
Kenneth T. Goya
Francis M. Nakamoto
Calvin E. Young
Diane W. Wong
Rodney S. Nishida
Patricia T. Fujii
Rhonda Nishimura
Gail M. Kang

Ann H. Aratani
Philip S. Uesato
Ronald M. Shigekane
Robin R. Horner
Nicole Jung-Shin Rhee
Stephen G. Dyer
Steven L. Goto
Daria Ann Loy
Virgil B. Prieto
Kelley G.A. Nakano

(See Next Column)

AYABE, CHONG, NISHIMOTO, SIA & NAKAMURA, *Honolulu—Continued*

Representative Clients: Travelers Insurance Co.; St. Paul Fire and Marine Insurance Co.; The Employers Group of Insurance Companies; TIG Insurance Co.; Pacific Insurance Co.; Hartford Accident and Indemnity Co.; Continental Casualty Co.; First Insurance Company of Hawaii, Ltd.

For full biographical listings, see the Martindale-Hubbell Law Directory

BURKE, SAKAI, MCPHEETERS & BORDNER ATTORNEYS AT LAW, A LAW CORPORATION (AV)

3100 Mauka Tower, Grosvenor Center, 737 Bishop Street, 96813-3222
Telephone: 808-523-9833
Telecopier: 808-528-1656

Edmund Burke
Wayne M. Sakai
Howard F. McPheeters
William A. Bordner
Michiro Iwanaga
James T. Estes, Jr.
Jeffrey T. Ono
Carlton W. T. Chun
Jan M. Tamura
Lance S. Fujisaki
Kunio Kuwabe
Leta H. Price
J. Gerard Lam
Mary L. Lucasse
David A. Gruebner
Madalyn Purcell
Judy Chung (Not admitted in HI)
Allegra R.D. Hyte

Representative Clients: Amfac, Inc.; Bank of Hawaii; Central Pacific Bank; CNA Insurance Co.; Longs Drug Stores, Inc.; Medical Insurance Exchange of California; Pacific Resources, Inc.; Shipowners' Claims Bureau; U.S. Aviation Underwriters.

For full biographical listings, see the Martindale-Hubbell Law Directory

CADES SCHUTTE FLEMING & WRIGHT (AV)

Formerly Smith, Wild, Beebe & Cades
1000 Bishop Street, P.O. Box 939, 96808
Telephone: 808-521-9200
Telex: 7238589
Telecopier: 808-531-8738
Affiliated Law Firm: Udom-Prok Associates Law Offices, 105/36 Tharinee Mansion, Borom Raj Chananee Road Bangkoknoi, Bangkok, Thailand, 10700.
Telephone: 011 660 435-4146.
Kailua-Kona, Hawaii Office: Hualalai Center, Suite B-303, 75-170 Hualalai Road.
Telephone: 808-329-5811.
Telecopier: 808-326-1175.

MEMBERS OF FIRM

Robert B. Bunn
William M. Swope
Douglas E. Prior
E. Gunner Schull
Michael P. Porter
Donald E. Scearce
Richard A. Hicks
Roger H. Epstein
Jeffrey S. Portnoy
Bernice Littman
Nicholas C. Dreher
Mark A. Hazlett
Philip J. Leas
David C. Larsen
Stephen B. MacDonald
Larry T. Takumi
William A. Cardwell
C. Michael Hare
Richard R. Clifton
Roy A. Vitousek, III (Resident, Kona Office)
Nelson N. S. Chun
Darryl H. W. Johnston
Vito Galati
Cary S. Matsushige
David Schulmeister
Thomas E. Crowley, III
Lorraine H. Akiba
Milton M. Yasunaga
Susan Oki Mollway
Gino L. Gabrio
Colin O. Miwa
Martin E. Hsia
Stewart J. Martin
Peter W. Olson
Rhonda L. Griswold
Gail M. Tamashiro
Grace Nihei Kido
Donna Y. L. Leong
David F.E. Banks
Dennis J. Gaughan

ASSOCIATES

Patricia J. McHenry
K. James Steiner, Jr.
Blane T. Yokota
Jeffrey D. Watts
Eric N. Roose
Marjorie A. Lau
Laurie A. Kuribayashi
James H. Ashford
Michele M. Sunahara
Nani Lee (Resident, Kona Office)
Cynthia M. Johiro
John P. Powell (Resident, Kona Office)
Dennis W. Chong Kee
Carlito P. Caliboso
Catherine A. Carey
Daniel H. Devaney IV
Allen R. Wolff
Mark D. Lofstrom
Karen Wong
Michael H. Shikuma
Jeffrey K. Natori
Eric S.T. Young
Dean T. Yamamoto
Lynn Higashi Hiatt (Resident, Kona Office)
Johnnel L. Nakamura (Not admitted in HI)
Kimberly A. O'Neill (Not admitted in HI; Resident, Kona Office)

Arthur G. Smith (1882-1966)
Urban Earl Wild (1891-1952)
Eugene H. Beebe (1889-1966)
Charles A. Gregory (1902-1972)
C. Frederick Schutte (1921-1988)
Milton Cades (1903-1992)
A. Singleton Cagle (1923-1994)
Edward deL. Boyle (1942-1994)

(See Next Column)

OF COUNSEL

J. Russell Cades
William L. Fleming
Harold S. Wright
James S. Campbell

Counsel for: Amfac, Inc.; First Hawaiian Bank; Bishop Trust Co., Ltd.; Alexander & Baldwin, Inc.; Theo. H. Davies & Co., Ltd.; C. Brewer & Company, Ltd.; Bank of America, FSB; The Bank of Tokyo, Ltd.; Haseko (Hawaii), Inc.; The Industrial Bank of Japan, Ltd.

For full biographical listings, see the Martindale-Hubbell Law Directory

CARLSMITH BALL WICHMAN MURRAY CASE & ICHIKI (AV)

A Partnership including Law Corporations
Suite 2200, Pacific Tower, 1001 Bishop Street, P.O. Box 656, 96809-3402
Telephone: 808-523-2500
Cable Address: "CWCMI"
Telecopier: 808-523-0842
Telex: 723-8770 CWCMI HR
Los Angeles, California Office: 555 South Flower Street, 25th Floor.
Telephone: 213-955-1200.
Long Beach, California Office: 301 East Ocean Boulevard, 7th Floor.
Telephone: 310-435-5631.
Washington, D.C. Office: 700 14th Street, N.W., 9th Floor.
Telephone: 202-508-1025.
Mexico City, Mexico Office: Monte Pelvoux 111, Piso 1, Col. Lomas de Chapultepec, 11000 Mexico, D.F.
Telephone: (011-52-5) 520-8514.
Fax: (011-52-5) 540 1545.
Mexico, D.F. Office of Carlsmith Ball Garcia Cacho y Asociados, S.C. (Authorized to practice Mexican Law): Monte Pelvoux 111, Piso 1, Col. Lomas de Chapultepec, 11000 Mexico, D.F.
Telephone: (011-52-5) 520-8514.
Fax: (011-52-5) 540-1545.
Agana, Guam Office: 4th Floor, Bank of Hawaii Building, P.O. Box BF.
Telephone: 671-472-6813.
Saipan, Commonwealth of the Northern Mariana Islands Office: Carlsmith Building, Capitol Hill, P.O. Box 5241.
Telephone: 670-322-3455.
Wailuku, Maui, Hawaii Office: One Main Plaza, Suite 400, 2200 Main Street, P.O. Box 1086.
Telephone: 808-242-4535.
Kailua-Kona, Hawaii Office: Second Floor, Bank of Hawaii Annex Building, P.O. Box 1720.
Telephone: 808-329-6464.
Hilo, Hawaii Office: 121 Waianuenue Avenue, P.O. Box 686.
Telephone: 808-935-6644.
Kapolei, Hawaii Office: Kapolei Building, Suite 318, 1001 Kamokila Boulevard.
Telephone: 808-674-0850.

MEMBERS OF FIRM

Paul H. Achitoff
Robert E. Aitken (Resident at Long Beach, California Office)
Robert A. Alsop (Resident at Los Angeles, California Office)
William E. Atwater, III
Joseph A. Ball (Resident at Long Beach, California Office)
Roger B. Baymiller (Resident at Los Angeles, California Office)
Nancy M. Beckner (Resident at Los Angeles, California Office)
Daniel A. Bent
John F. Biehl (Resident at Saipan Office)
James W. Boyle
Stephen L. Bradford (Resident at Los Angeles, California Office)
Margery S. Bronster
Alfonso Garcia Cacho (Resident, Mexico Office)
Donn W. Carlsmith (A Law Corporation)
Edward E. Case
James H. Case (A Law Corporation)
Grant Y. M. Chun (Resident at Maui Office)
Mary Jane Connell
Richard E. Conway (Resident at Long Beach, California Office)
Brian C. Cuff (Resident at Long Beach, California Office)
Ruth D. Davis (Resident at Agana, Guam Office)
Patricia Devlin
Donn A. Dimichele (Resident at Los Angeles, California Office)
Albert H. Ebright (Resident at Los Angeles, California Office)
Anna M. Elento-Sneed
Terrence A. Everett (Resident at Los Angeles, California Office)
Anne Price Fortney (Resident at Washington, D.C. Office)
Paul Mullin Ganley (A Law Corporation)
Gary G. Grimmer
George G. Grubb (A Law Corporation)
Harman M. Hitt (Resident at Long Beach, California Office)
Jonathan R. Hodes (Resident at Los Angeles, California Office)
David T. W. Huang
Andy M. Ichiki
Michelle C. Imata
Tom C. Ingledue (A Law Corporation)
Philip D. Isaac (Resident at Agana, Guam Office)
Albert Saul Israel (Resident at Long Beach, California Office)
Eric A. James
Patrick H. Jones
Robert N. Katayama
John C. Khil
Karl K. Kobayashi
Robert F. Kull (Resident at Los Angeles, California Office)
Tom C. Leuteneker (Resident at Maui Office)
Steven S. C. Lim (Resident, Hilo and Kailua-Kona, Hawaii Offices)
Ivan M. Lui-Kwan (A Law Corporation)
Tim Lui-Kwan (Resident at Hilo Office)
B. Martin Luna (Resident at Maui Office)
John P. Manaut
Barry W. Marr

(See Next Column)

CARLSMITH BALL WICHMAN MURRAY CASE & ICHIKI—*Continued*

MEMBERS OF FIRM (Continued)

Matthew M. Matsunaga
John R. McDonough (Resident at Los Angeles, California Office)
George T. Mooradian (Resident at Long Beach, California Office)
Garry W. Morse (Resident at Agana, Guam Office)
Lynn E. Moyer (Resident at Long Beach, California Office)
Randolph G. Muhlestein (Resident at Los Angeles, California Office)
Joseph D. Mullender, Jr. (Resident at Long Beach, California Office)
Mark K. Murakami
Anthony Murray (Los Angeles and Long Beach, California Offices)
Steven M. Nagata
Craig G. Nakamura (Resident at Maui Office)
David R. Nevitt (Resident at Saipan Office)
Lawrence S. Okinaga (A Law Corporation)
John D. Osborn (Resident at Saipan Office)
Russell A. Ota
Richard R. Pace (Resident at Los Angeles, California Office)
Presley W. Pang
James Polish (Resident at Los Angeles, California Office)
Sylvester V. Quitiquit (Resident at Kona, Hawaii Office)
Dean H. Robb
Tom E. Roesser
John E. Rogers (Resident, Mexico, D.F., Mexico Office)
Marcia K. Schultz (Resident at Saipan Office)
Peter Starn (A Law Corporation)
James L. Starshak
Robert Edward Strand
Renee L. Stransky (Resident at Washington, D.C. Office)
Gerald A. Sumida (A Law Corporation)
Thomas R. Sylvester
Lance F. Taniguchi
Allan Edward Tebbetts (Resident at Long Beach, California Office)
Robert R. Thornton (Resident at Los Angeles, California Office)
Robert D. Triantos (Resident at Kailua-Kona Office)
Paul M. Ueoka (Resident at Maui Office)
J. Thomas Van Winkle (A Law Corporation)
Charles R. Wichman
Donald C. Williams
William C. Williams, Jr. (Resident at Agana, Guam Office)
David W. K. Wong
Duane H. Zobrist (Resident at Los Angeles, California Office)

ASSOCIATES

Kristen S. Armstrong (Resident, Agana, Guam Office)
Sherrill A. Atwood (Resident at Hilo Office)
Annie Kun Baker (Resident at Los Angeles, California Office)
Philip R. Brown
Lisanne M. Butterfield (Resident, Agana, Guam Office)
William J. Carey
Christopher J. Cole
Gilbert S. Coloma-Agaran (Resident at Maui Office)
Misty L. Colwell (Resident, Long Beach Office)
Duane R. Fisher (Resident at Long Beach, California Office)
Peter N. Greenfeld
Charles M. Heaukulani
Robert D. S. Kim (Resident at Kailua-Kona Office)
Lawrence C. King (Resident at Saipan Office)
David Patrick Ledger
Katherine G. Leonard
Sharon S. Mequet (Resident at Long Beach, California Office)
Kevin E. Moore
Mark K. Mukai
Nathan T. Natori
David S. Olson (Resident at Los Angeles, California Office)
Daniel J. Payne (Resident at Long Beach, California Office)
Andrew L. Pepper
Nancy L. Ribaudo
Sheila L. Y. Sakashita
Ian L. Sandison
Meredith M. Sayre (Resident at Agana, Guam Office)
Jonathan L. Smoller (Resident at Los Angeles, California Office)
Sinforoso M. Tolentino (Resident at Agana, Guam Office)
Ann Luotto Wolf (Resident at Los Angeles, California Office)
Jon T. Yamamura
Curtis B. K. Yuen

OF COUNSEL

Herbert G. Baerwitz (Resident at Los Angeles, California Office)
Roger P. Crouthamel (Resident at Agana, Guam Office)
Douglas Dalton (Resident at Los Angeles, California Office)
Leigh-Wai Doo (Resident at Honolulu, Hawaii Office)
Charles E. Greenberg (Resident at Long Beach, California Office)
Dagmar V. Halamka (Resident at Los Angeles, California Office)
George A. Hart, Jr. (Resident at Long Beach, California Office)
Clark Heggeness (Resident at Long Beach, California Office)
Tom K. Houston (Resident at Los Angeles, California Office)
David L. Irons (1936-1984)
Herman T. F. Lum (Resident, Honolulu, Hawaii Office)
John D. Miller (A Professional Corporation) (Resident at Long Beach, California Office)
Barry R. Ogilby (Resident at Los Angeles, California Office)
Aaron Schildhaus (Resident at Washington, D.C. Office)
James T. Stovall, III (Not admitted in HI; Resident, Washington, D.C. Office)

For full biographical listings, see the Martindale-Hubbell Law Directory

CASE & LYNCH (AV)

A Partnership including Professional Corporations
(Formerly Pratt, Moore, Bortz & Case - 1967 to 1971)
(Formerly Case, Kay & Lynch - 1979 to 1986)
2600 Grosvenor Center, Mauka Tower, 737 Bishop Street, 96813
Telephone: 808-547-5400
Cable Address: "Loio"
Telex: 7238523
Telecopier: 808-523-1920
Lihue, Kauai, Hawaii Office: Watumull Plaza, Suite 202, 4334 Rice Street.
Telephone: 808-245-4705.
Kahului, Maui, Hawaii Office: The Kahului Building, Suite 470, 33 Lono Avenue.
Telephone: 808-871-8351.
Kilauea, Kauai, Hawaii Office: Kong Lung Center, Kilauea Lighthouse Road, P.O. Box 988.
Telephone: 808-828-2890.
Hilo, Hawaii Office: Case & Lynch Business Center, 460 Kilauea Avenue.
Telephone: 808-961-6611.
Kailua-Kona, Hawaii Office: Hanama Place, Suite 101, 75-5706 Kuakini Highway.
Telephone: 808-329-4421.

MEMBERS OF FIRM

W. O. Smith (1848-1929)
Michael J. Belles (Resident at Lihue, Kauai Office)
Robert E. Bethea (Resident at Hilo, Hawaii Office)
Michael L. Biehl (A Law Corporation)
Bruce C. Bigelow (A Law Corporation)
Daniel H. Case (A Law Corporation)
Valta A. Cook (Resident at Hilo, Hawaii Office)
James M. Cribley (A Law Corporation)
Caroline Peters Egli (Resident at Kahului, Maui Office)
David C. Farmer
Wallace H. Gallup, Jr. (Resident at Kailua-Kona Office)
Max W. J. Graham, Jr. (Resident at Lihue, Kauai Office)
Gregory M. Hansen (A Law Corporation)
Wesley W. Ichida (A Law Corporation)
Lyle Minoru Ishida
Matthew G. Jewell (Resident at Kailua-Kona, Hawaii Office)
Alan S. Konishi (Resident at Hilo, Hawaii Office)
Nenad Krek
C. Dudley Pratt (1900-1970)
Dennis M. Lombardi
Vincent J. Lugani
Paul A. Lynch (A Law Corporation)
Paul R. Mancini (A Law Corporation) (Resident at Kahului, Maui Office)
Michael R. Marsh
John R. Myrdal (A Law Corporation)
David W. Proudfoot (A Law Corporation)
Scott Douglas Radovich
Steven L. Rinesmith
Robert E. Rowland (A Law Corporation) (Resident at Kahului, Maui Office)
Robert F. Schneider
Cathy Lee Sekiguchi
R. Clay Sutherland (Resident at Kahului, Maui Office)
Tod Z. Tanaka
Steven E. Thomas
Frederick R. Troncone
J. Gregory Turnbull
Thomas D. Welch, Jr. (Resident at Kahului, Maui Office)
Stephen D. Whittaker (Resident at Kailua-Kona, Hawaii Office)
Gary L. Wixom (A Law Corporation)

ASSOCIATES

David F. Andrew
Stacey W.E. Chong
Jerilynn Ono Hall
Quentin K. Kawananakoa
Steven J. Kim
Peter K. Kubota (Resident at Hilo, Hawaii Office)
David W. Lacy (Resident at Kailua-Kona Office)
Valerie J. Lam
Matthew V. Pietsch (Resident at Kahului, Maui Office)
Stephen M. Teves
Ivan M. Torigoe (Resident at Hilo, Hawaii Office)

COUNSEL

Hartwell H. K. Blake (Resident at Lihue, Kauai Office)
Malvin D. Dohrman (Resident at Kilauea, Kauai Office)
Gary N. Hagerman (Resident at Hilo, Hawaii Office)
Timothy J. Hogan
Dianne G. Jagmin
Frank T. Kanemitsu
Candace McCaslin (Resident at Lihue, Kauai Office)
Peter M. Morimoto (Resident at Lihue, Kauai Office)
Robert A. Richardson (Resident at Kahului, Maui Office)
Sandra E. Pechter Schutte (Resident, at Hilo, Hawaii Office)
Scott D. Whiting

OF COUNSEL

Ernest H. Kubota (Resident at Hilo, Hawaii Office)
Allen M. Stack

Representative Clients: Alexander & Baldwin; Bank of Hawaii; C. Brewer Properties; Chevron Corp.; First Hawaiian Bank; Ford Motor Co.; General Motors Corp.; Hawaiian Electric Industries; Punahou School; Trustees of the Liliuokalani Trust.

For full biographical listings, see the Martindale-Hubbell Law Directory

CHAR SAKAMOTO ISHII & LUM (AV)

Suite 850, 841 Bishop Street, 96813
Telephone: 808-522-5133
Facsimile: 808-522-5144

(See Next Column)

CHAR SAKAMOTO ISHII & LUM, *Honolulu—Continued*

Vernon F. L. Char
Steven Lawrence Ching
Elizabeth Ann Ishii
David M. K. Lum
Charles E. McKay
Denise C. H. Nip
Ronald R. Sakamoto

Earl M. Ching
Jacqueline H. Furuta
Carolyn E. Hayashi
Kery K. Kamita
Elise L.Y. Lee

For full biographical listings, see the Martindale-Hubbell Law Directory

CHUN, KERR, DODD & KANESHIGE (AV)

Suite 900, 745 Fort Street Mall, 96813
Telephone: 808-528-8200
Telecopier: 808-536-5869

MEMBERS OF FIRM

Edward Y. C. Chun
George L. T. Kerr
William H. Dodd
Melvin Y. Kaneshige
Andrew V. Beaman
Ray K. Kamikawa
Danton S. Wong
Leroy E. Colombe

ASSOCIATES

Trudy M. Burns
Kyong-Su Im
Curtis L. Sano

References: Bank of Hawaii; First Hawaiian Bank.

For full biographical listings, see the Martindale-Hubbell Law Directory

DAMON KEY BOCKEN LEONG KUPCHAK ATTORNEYS AT LAW, A LAW CORPORATION (AV)

1600 Pauahi Tower, 1001 Bishop Street, 96813-3480
Telephone: 808-531-8031
Cable Address: ADVOCATES
Facsimile: 808-533-2242

Lee M. Agsalud
R. Charles Bocken
Jennifer Z. Brooks
Clinton K. L. Ching
C. F. Damon, Jr.
Gerhard Frohlich
Diane Deskins Hastert
Charles W. Key
Christine A. Kubota
Kenneth R. Kupchak
Denis C. H. Leong
David P. McCauley
James C. McWhinnie
Anna H. Oshiro
Leon R. Roose
Douglas C. Smith
X. Ben Tao
Alan Van Etten
Michael A. Yoshida

OF COUNSEL

Erik D. Eike
Robert H. Thomas
William F. Thompson, III

Representative Clients: American Express; BHP Petroleum Americas (Hawaii); C Brewer & Co., Ltd.; Leo A. Daly, Inc.; Federal Deposit Insurance Corporation; Fletcher Challenge, Ltd.; Hawaii Baking Co.; Hawaiian Trust Co., Ltd.; Kemper Real Estate Management Co.; Molokai Ranch, Ltd.

For full biographical listings, see the Martindale-Hubbell Law Directory

FUJIYAMA, DUFFY & FUJIYAMA ATTORNEYS AT LAW, A LAW CORPORATION (AV)

2700 Pauahi Tower, Bishop Square, 1001 Bishop Street, 96813
Telephone: 808-536-0802
Telecopier: 808-536-5117

Wallace S. Fujiyama (1925-1994)
James E. Duffy, Jr.
Rodney M. Fujiyama
James J. Stone
Archie T. Ikehara
Ralph R. LaFountaine
Colbert M. Matsumoto
Glenn K. Sato
Steven J. T. Chow
Leslie E. Kobayashi

Nancy J. Ryan
Scott S. Hashimoto
Wynde M. Yamamoto
Douglas H. Knowlton
Ward F. N. Fujimoto
Lynette Mah Matsushima
Brian Aburano
Gregg M. Ushiroda
Jean Polhamus Creadick
Charlotte Chyr
Steven T. Brittain (Resident)
Reese R. Nakamura

Representative Clients: Hartford Accident & Indemnity Co.; Maryland Casualty Co.; New England Mutual Life Insurance Co.; Duty Free Shoppers, Ltd.; West Beach Estates (Ko Olina Resort).

For full biographical listings, see the Martindale-Hubbell Law Directory

GOODSILL ANDERSON QUINN & STIFEL (AV)

Alii Place, Suite 1800, 1099 Alakea Street, P.O. Box 3196, 96801-3196
Telephone: 808-547-5600
FAX: 808-547-5880
Kailua-Kona Office: 75-170 Hualalai Professional Complex, Suite D-216, P.O. Box 2639.
Telephone: 808-329-7731.
FAX: 808-326-2384.

(See Next Column)

MEMBERS OF FIRM

Martin Anderson
Hugh Shearer
C. Jepson Garland
Conrad M. Weiser
David J. Dezzani
Robert G. Hite
Ronald H. W. Lum
David J. Reber
John R. Lacy
Robert F. Hirano
Raymond Shigeo Iwamoto
Ronald K. K. Sakimura
Thomas W. Williams, Jr.
Michael A. Shea
William S. Miller
Jacqueline L. S. Earle
Kenneth A. Ross (Resident, Kailua-Kona Office)
Lani L. Ewart
Randall K. Steverson
Patricia Y. Lee
Gary M. Slovin
Lisa Woods Munger
Kenneth B. Hipp
Ernest J. T. Loo
Bruce L. Lamon
Peter T. Kashiwa
Russell S. Kato
Lant A. Johnson
Steven M. Nakashima
Vincent A. Piekarski
Mark B. Desmarais
Linda Zichittella Leong
Scott G. Leong
Leighton J. H. S. Yuen
Corlis J. Chang
Carl J. Schlack, Jr.
Barbara A. Petrus
Robert J. Hackman
Cynthia M. Nojima
Miki Okumura
Mark F. Ito
Wayne H. Muraoka
Audrey E. J. Ng
Donna A. Tanoue
Gregory R. Kim
Richard K. Mirikitani
Alan S. Fujimoto
Walter C. Davison
David W. Sherman
Gregg J. Kinkley
Raymond K. Okada
Gail Otsuka Ayabe
Dale Edward F.T. Zane
LindaLee K. Farm
P. Roy Catalani
Margaret C. Jenkins
Carol Ann Eblen
Craig I. Nakanishi

COUNSEL

Randall W. Roth
E. Laurence Gay

ASSOCIATES

Jeffrey Scott Piper
Roy John Tjioe
Lynne T. Toyofuku
Judith A. Carrithers
Jennifer Cook Clark
Kurt K. Kawafuchi
Kellie M. N. Sekiya
Judy Y. Lee
Elizabeth A. Strance (Resident, Kailua-Kona Office)
Lennes N. Omuro
Lisa T. Redell
Nora E. Conroy
Moon-Ki Chai
Derek R. Kobayashi (Resident, Kailua-Kona Office)
Mary A. Renfer
Wilma Sur
Howard G. McPherson
Peter Y. Kikuta
Trisha M. Kimura
David W. Lonborg
Karen Lynn Scarborough Stanitz
Edmund K. Saffery
Natalie S. Hiu
Russell K. Kaupu
Sara Shirin Razani
Lisa von der Mehden
Gerald A. Brooks (Not admitted in HI)
Elizabeth B. Croom (Resident, Kailua-Kona Office)
Lisa A. Bail
Mia Y. Teruya

OF COUNSEL

Marshall M. Goodsill
William F. Quinn
Genro Kashiwa

Representative Clients: Aetna Life and Casualty; Argonaut Insurance Co.; Fireman's Fund Insurance Co.; The Home Insurance; Industrial Indemnity Co.; MEDMARC; State Farm Insurance Co.; Tokio Marine Management Inc.; Transamerica Insurance Co.; United States Aviation Underwriters Incorporated.

For full biographical listings, see the Martindale-Hubbell Law Directory

HAMILTON, GIBSON, NICKELSEN, RUSH & MOORE

(See Rush Moore Craven Sutton Morry & Beh)

KOBAYASHI, SUGITA & GODA (AV)

A Partnership including Professional Corporations
8th Floor, Hawaii Tower, 745 Fort Street, 96813
Telephone: 808-539-8700
Telecopier: 808-539-8799
Telex: 6502396585 MCI
MCI Mail: 23 96585
ABA/Net: ABA2281

MEMBERS OF FIRM

Bert T. Kobayashi, Jr., (Atty. at Law, A Law Corp.)
Kenneth Y. Sugita (Atty. at Law, A Law Corp.)
Alan M. Goda (Atty. at Law, A Law Corp.)
Dale W. Lee (Atty. at Law, A Law Corp.)
Lex R. Smith (Atty. at Law, A Law Corp.)
Byron C. Feldman, II (Atty. at Law, A Law Corp.)
David L. Monroy (Atty. at Law, A Law Corp.)
Wendell H. Fuji (Atty. at Law, A Law Corp.)
Robert K. Ichikawa
Charles W. Gall
Alan K. Maeda
Janeen-Ann A. Olds
Wintehn K. T. Park
Darcy L. Endo
Rod S. Aoki
Dawn D. M. Ishihara
Burt T. Lau
Joseph I. N. Kiyose
Ernest H. Nomura
John Kodachi

(See Next Column)

KOBAYASHI, SUGITA & GODA—*Continued*

MEMBERS OF FIRM (Continued)

Christopher T. Kobayashi
Lisa W. Cataldo

OF COUNSEL

Bert T. Kobayashi, Sr.

Reference: First Hawaiian Bank.

For full biographical listings, see the Martindale-Hubbell Law Directory

LYONS, BRANDT, COOK & HIRAMATSU (AV)

841 Bishop Street, Suite 1800, 96813
Telephone: 808-524-7030
Facsimile: 808-533-3011

MEMBERS OF FIRM

Samuel A. B. Lyons
George W. Brandt
Thomas E. Cook
Beverly Lynne K. Hiramatsu
Jeffrey A. Griswold
Bradford F. K. Bliss
Steven Y. Otaguro
Stefan M. Reinke
Paul R. Grable
Edquon Lee

For full biographical listings, see the Martindale-Hubbell Law Directory

MCCORRISTON MIHO MILLER MUKAI (AV)

Five Waterfront Plaza, 4th Floor, 500 Ala Moana Boulevard, 96813
Telephone: 808-529-7300
Facsimile: 808-524-8293
Cable: Attorneys, Honolulu

MEMBERS OF FIRM

William C. McCorriston
Jon T. Miho
Clifford J. Miller
Franklin K. Mukai
Michael D. Tom
William K. Meheula
Donald K. O. Wong
Calvert G. Chipchase, III
D. Scott MacKinnon
Kenneth B. Marcus
Kenneth G. K. Hoo
Patrick K. Lau
Jerrold Y. Chun
Mark J. Bennett
Nadine Y. Ando
Darolyn Hatsuko Lendio
Richard B. Miller
David N. Kuriyama
Eric T. Kawatani
Randall K. Schmitt
Keith K. Suzuka
John Y. Yamano
Randal Keiji Nagatani
Brad S. Petrus

ASSOCIATES

Sharon H. Nishi
Thomas E. Bush
Andrew W. Char
Randall F. Sakumoto
Lynn M. Petry
Lisa M. Ginoza
Alexander R. Jampel
Mark D. Clement
Leslie H. Kondo
K. Rae McCorkle
Peter J. Hamasaki
Darren Patrick Conley
Carrie K. Okinaga
Joel D. Kam
Mark W. Eliashof

COUNSEL

Michael J. O'Malley
Michael Rosenthal

OF COUNSEL

Stanley Y. Mukai

For full biographical listings, see the Martindale-Hubbell Law Directory

PAUL, JOHNSON, PARK & NILES ATTORNEYS AT LAW, A LAW CORPORATION (AV)

Suite 1300 Pacific Tower, 1001 Bishop Street, P.O. Box 4438, 96812-4438
Telephone: 808-524-1212
Telecopier: 808-528-1654
Cable Address: "Pacificlaw"
Wailuku, Maui, Hawaii Office: 203 H.G.E.A. Building, 2145 Kaohu Street, P.O. Box 870. 96793-0870.
Telephone: 808-242-6644.
Fax: 808-244-9775.

James T. Paul
David Arthur Johnson
Corey Y. S. Park
Sheryl L. Nicholson
Robyn B. Chun
Judy A. Tanaka
Richard J Kiefer
Danielle K. Hart
Michael A. Medeiros

For full biographical listings, see the Martindale-Hubbell Law Directory

RUSH MOORE CRAVEN SUTTON MORRY & BEH (AV)

A Partnership including Law Corporations
20th Floor, Hawaii Tower Amfac Center, 745 Fort Street, 96813-3862
Telephone: 808-521-0400
Facsimile: 808-521-0597
Cable Address: "Lawyers Honolulu"
Telex: 7430043
Wailuku, Maui, Hawaii Office: One Main Plaza, 2200 Main Street, Suite 650.
Telephone: 808-244-3332.
Facsimile: 808-244-5322.

MEMBERS OF FIRM

Marshall B. Henshaw (1889-1970)
William R. Loomis (1939-1980)
Don C. Hamilton (1914-1984)
Harold W. Nickelsen (1924-1985)
Frank D. Gibson, Jr. (1920-1990)
Harold W. Conroy (Retired)
Willson C. Moore, Jr., (A Law Corporation)
Anthony B. Craven
Richard C. Sutton, Jr.
G. Richard Morry
Walter Beh, II
Edward M. Sanpei
Michael L. Freed (A Law Corporation)
Stephen K. C. Mau (A Law Corporation)
Earl T. Sato
James P. Brumbaugh (Resident at Maui Office)
J. Stephen Street
Jennifer M. Yusi
David Shibata
Susan Tius
Carol Y. Asai-Sato
Cheryl A. Nakamura
Irene A. Anzai
Patricia Mathias NaPier
Donald Carl Machado, Jr.
Brian R. Jenkins (Resident at Maui Office)
Ray P. Wimberley (Resident at Maui Office)
Tracy G. Chinen
Daniel J. Berman

ASSOCIATES

Thomas L. Benedict
Janice Hee Saito
Lisa K. Strandtman
Caroline S. Otani
Peter K. Thompson
Anders G. O. Nervell
Bradford L. Tannen
Jeffrey C. Johnson

OF COUNSEL

Dwight M. Rush (A Law Corporation)

Representative Clients: Bank of Hawaii; Pioneer Federal Savings Bank; Hyatt Corporation; Kamehameha Schools/Bernice Pauahi Bishop Estate; Government Employees Insurance Co.; Underwriters at Lloyds.

For full biographical listings, see the Martindale-Hubbell Law Directory

TORKILDSON, KATZ, JOSSEM, FONSECA, JAFFE, MOORE & HETHERINGTON ATTORNEYS AT LAW, A LAW CORPORATION (AV)

Amfac Building, 15th Floor, 700 Bishop Street, 96813-4187
Telephone: 808-521-1051
Cable Address: "Counsel"
Telex: RCA 723-8185
Telecopier: 808-521-8239
Kailua-Kona, Hawaii Office: 75-5706 Kuakini Highway, Suite 105.
Telephone: 808-329-8581.
Telecopier: 808-329-3837.
Hilo, Hawaii Office: 100 Pauahi Street, Suite 206.
Telephone: 808-961-0406.
Telecopier: 808-935-1225.

Ernest C. Moore, Jr. (1913-1972)
Raymond M. Torkildson
Robert S. Katz
Jared H. Jossem
Roger W. Fonseca
Edward A. Jaffe
Ernest C. Moore, III
Robert Wm. Hastings, II (Resident, Kailua-Kona Office)
J. George Hetherington
Terrence M. Lee
Richard M. Rand
Jeffrey S. Harris
Craig K. Hirai
Gregory M. Sato
John L. Knorek
Ronald I. Heller
Wilson M. N. Loo
Steven B. Jacobson
Sabrina R. Toma
Perry W. Confalone
Oren T. Chikamoto
Allen H. Sakai
Phillip A. Li
David Waters
A. Scott Leithead (Resident, Hilo Office)
Wayne S. Yoshigai

OF COUNSEL

Jon R. Ono (Resident, Hilo Office)

Steven L. F. Ho
Brian I. Ezuka
Matt A. Tsukazaki
Kitty K. Kamaka
Liane L. Kimura
Stephanie Anne Chin
Timothy A. Walker
Lisa L. Mardon
Steven V. Torkildson
Kelly Ann Patch
Clayton A. Kamida (Not admitted in HI)

For full biographical listings, see the Martindale-Hubbell Law Directory

Honolulu—Continued

WATANABE, ING & KAWASHIMA (AV)

A Partnership including Professional Corporations
Hawaii Tower, 5th & 6th Floors, 745 Fort Street, 96813
Telephone: 808-544-8300
Facsimile: 808-544-8399
Telex: 6502396585 MCI
MCI Mail: 23 96585
ABA/Net: ABA2281

MEMBERS OF FIRM

Jeffrey N. Watanabe (Atty. at Law, A Law Corp.)
James Kawashima (Atty. at Law, A Law Corp.)
J. Douglas Ing (Atty. at Law, A Law Corp.)
Wray H. Kondo (Atty. at Law, A Law Corp.)
John T. Komeiji (Atty. at Law, A Law Corp.)
Ronald Y. K. Leong (Atty. at Law, A Law Corp.)
Robert T. Takamatsu (Atty. at Law, A Law Corp.)
Cynthia Winegar (Atty. at Law, A Law Corp.)
Randall Y. Yamamoto (Atty. at Law, A Law Corp.)
Lyle Y. Harada (Atty. at Law, A Law Corp.)
Michael A. Lorusso (Atty. at Law, A Law Corp.)
Pamela J. Larson (Atty. At Law, A Law Corp.)
William H. Gilardy, Jr.
John R. Aube (Atty. at Law, A Law Corp.)
Jan M.L.Y. Amii (Atty. at Law, A Law Corp.)

ASSOCIATES

Donna Y. Kanemaru
George B. Apter
Marcus B. Sierra
Lani Narikiyo
Seth M. Reiss
George D. Quillin
Charlene K. Ikeda
Peter L. Fritz
Elena J. Onaga
LLoyd S. Yoshioka
Curtis C. Kim
Beth K. Fujimoto
Patsy H. Kirio
Kevin H. Oda
Michael C. Bird
Brian Y. Hiyane
Dennis J. Hwang
Teri Y. Kondo
Jeff N. Miyashiro

OF COUNSEL

George R. Ariyoshi

ASIA PACIFIC CONSULTANT

Victor Hao Li (Not admitted in HI)

LEGAL SUPPORT PERSONNEL

GOVERNMENT AFFAIRS ADVISORS

Jon T. Okudara
Millicent M. Y. H. Kim

References: First Hawaiian Bank; American Savings Bank.

For full biographical listings, see the Martindale-Hubbell Law Directory

VERNON Y. T. WOO (AV)

Suite 205, 1019 Waimanu Street, 96814
Telephone: 808-522-0044
Fax: 808-522-0048

For full biographical listings, see the Martindale-Hubbell Law Directory

KAHULUI, Maui Co.

CASE & LYNCH (AV)

A Partnership including Professional Corporations
(Formerly Pratt, Moore, Bortz & Case - 1967 to 1971)
(Formerly Case, Kay & Lynch - 1979 to 1986)
The Kahului Building, Suite 470, 33 Lono Avenue, 96732
Telephone: 808-871-8351
Telecopier: 1-871-0732
Honolulu, Hawaii Office: 2600 Grosvenor Center, Mauka Tower, 737 Bishop Street.
Telephone: 808-547-5400.
Lihue, Kauai, Hawaii Office: Watumull Plaza, Suite 202, 4334 Rice Street.
Telephone: 808-245-4705.
Kilauea, Kauai, Hawaii Office: Kong Lung Center, Kilauea Lighthouse Road. P.O. Box 988.
Telephone: 808-828-2890.
Hilo, Hawaii Office: Case & Lynch Business Center, 460 Kilauea Avenue.
Telephone: 808-961-6611.
Kailua-Kona, Hawaii Office: Hanama Place, Suite 101, 75-5706 Kuakini Highway.
Telephone: 808-329-4421.

RESIDENT PARTNERS

Caroline Peters Egli
Paul R. Mancini (A Law Corporation)
Robert E. Rowland (A Law Corporation)
R. Clay Sutherland
Thomas D. Welch, Jr.

RESIDENT ASSOCIATE

Matthew V. Pietsch

(See Next Column)

RESIDENT COUNSEL

Robert A. Richardson

Representative Clients: Alexander & Baldwin, Inc.; Amfac/JMB Hawaii, Inc.; Baldwin Pacific Corp.; C. Brewer Properties; Haleakala Ranch Co.; Harry and Jeanette Weinberg Foundation, Inc.; Marriott Corp.; Molokai Ranch; Napili Kai Beach Club; Ulupalakua Ranch.

For full biographical listings, see the Martindale-Hubbell Law Directory

KAILUA-KONA, Hawaii Co.

CADES SCHUTTE FLEMING & WRIGHT (AV)

Hualalai Center, Suite B-303, 75-170 Hualalai Road, 96740
Telephone: 808-329-5811
Telecopier: 808-326-1175
Honolulu, Hawaii Office: 1000 Bishop Street, P. O. Box 939.
Telephone: 808-521-9200.
Affiliated Law Firm: Udom-Prok Associates Law Offices, 105/36 Tharinee Mansion, Bormo Raj Chananee Road Bangkoknoi, Bangkok, Thailand, 10700.
Telephone: 011 662 435-4146.

Roy A. Vitousek, III (Resident Partner)

RESIDENT ASSOCIATES

Nani Lee
John P. Powell
Lynn Higashi Hiatt
Kimberly A. O'Neill (Not admitted in HI)

For full biographical listings, see the Martindale-Hubbell Law Directory

CARLSMITH BALL WICHMAN MURRAY CASE & ICHIKI (AV)

A Partnership including Law Corporations
Second Floor, Bank of Hawaii Annex Building, P.O. Box 1720, 96745-1720
Telephone: 808-329-6464
Telecopier: 808-329-9450
Honolulu, Hawaii Office: Suite 2200, Pacific Tower, 1001 Bishop Street. P.O. Box 656.
Telephone: 808-523-2500.
Los Angeles, California Office: 555 South Flower Street, 25th Floor.
Telephone: 213-955-1200.
Long Beach, California Office: 301 East Ocean Boulevard, 7th Floor.
Telephone: 310-435-5631.
Washington, D.C. Office: 700 14th Street, N.W., 9th Floor.
Telephone: 202-508-1025.
Mexico City, Mexico Office: Monte Pelvoux 111, Piso 1, Col. Lomas de Chapultepec, 11000 Mexico, D.F.
Telephone: (011-52-5) 520-8514.
Fax: (011-52-5) 540-1545.
Mexico, D.F. Office of Carlsmith Ball Garcia Cacho y Asociados, S.C. (Authorized to practice Mexican Law): Monte Pelvoux 111, Piso 1, Col. Lomas de Chapultepec, 11000, Mexico, D.F.
Telephone: (011-52-5) 520-8514.
Fax: (011-52-5) 540-1545.
Agana, Guam Office: 4th Floor, Bank of Hawaii Building, P.O. Box BF.
Telephone: 671-472-6813.
Saipan, Commonwealth of the Northern Mariana Islands Office: Carlsmith Building, Capitol Hill, P.O. Box 5241.
Telephone: 670-322-3455.
Wailuku, Maui, Hawaii Office: One Main Plaza, Suite 400, 2200 Main Street, P.O. Box 1086.
Telephone: 808-242-4535.
Hilo, Hawaii Office: 121 Waianuenue Avenue, P.O. Box 686.
Telephone: 808-935-6644.
Kapolei, Hawaii Office: Kapolei Building, Suite 318, 1001 Kamokila Boulevard.
Telephone: 808-674-0850.

RESIDENT PARTNERS

Steven S. C. Lim
Sylvester V. Quitiquit
Robert D. Triantos

RESIDENT ASSOCIATES

Robert D. S. Kim

For full biographical listings, see the Martindale-Hubbell Law Directory

CASE & LYNCH (AV)

A Partnership including Professional Corporations
(Formerly Pratt, Moore, Bortz & Case - 1967 to 1971)
(Formerly Case, Kay & Lynch - 1979 to 1986)
Hanama Place, Suite 101, 75-5706 Kuakini Highway, 96740
Telephone: 808-329-4421
Telecopier: 808-329-4508
Honolulu, Hawaii Office: 2600 Grosvenor Center, Mauka Tower, 737 Bishop Street.
Telephone: 808-547-5400.
Lihue, Kauai, Hawaii Office: Watumull Plaza, Suite 202, 4334 Rice Street.
Telephone: 808-245-4705.
Kilauea, Kauai, Hawaii Office: Kong Lung Center, Kilauea Lighthouse Road. P.O. Box 988.
Telephone: 808-828-2890.

(See Next Column)

CASE & LYNCH—*Continued*

Kahului, Maui, Hawaii Office: The Kahului Building, Suite 470, 33 Lono Avenue.
Telephone: 808-871-8351.
Hilo, Hawaii Office: Case & Lynch Business Center, 460 Kilauea Avenue.
Telephone: 808-961-6611.

RESIDENT PARTNERS

Wallace H. Gallup, Jr. Matthew G. Jewell
Stephen D. Whittaker

RESIDENT ASSOCIATES

David W. Lacy

Representative Clients: Bank of Hawaii; First Hawaiian Bank; Liliuokalani Trust; Pacific Island Tire, Inc.; G & L Development, Inc.

For full biographical listings, see the Martindale-Hubbell Law Directory

GOODSILL ANDERSON QUINN & STIFEL (AV)

75-170 Hualalai Professional Complex, Suite D-216, P.O. Box 2639, 96745
Telephone: 808-329-7731
FAX: 808-326-2384
Honolulu, Hawaii Office: Alii Place, Suite 1800, 1099 Alakea Street, P.O. Box 3196.
Telephone: 808-547-5600.
FAX: 808-547-5880.

RESIDENT MEMBERS

Kenneth A. Ross

RESIDENT ASSOCIATES

Elizabeth A. Strance Derek R. Kobayashi
Elizabeth B. Croom

For full biographical listings, see the Martindale-Hubbell Law Directory

KILAUEA, Kauai Co.

CASE & LYNCH (AV)

Partnership including Professional Corporations
(Formerly Pratt, Moore, Bortz & Case - 1967-1971)
(Formerly Case, Kay & Lynch - 1979 to 1986)
Kong Lung Center, Kilauea Lighthouse Road, P.O. Box 988, 96754
Telephone: 808-828-2890
Telecopier: 808-828-2114
Honolulu, Hawaii Office: 2600 Grosvenor Center, Mauka Tower, 737 Bishop St.
Telephone: 808-547-5400.
Kahului, Maui, Hawaii Office: The Kahului Building, Suite 470, 33 Lono Avenue.
Telephone: 808-871-8351.
Hilo, Hawaii Office: Case & Lynch Business Center, 460 Kilauea Avenue.
Telephone: 808-961-6611.
Kailua-Kona, Hawaii Office: Hanama Place, Suite 101, 75-5706 Kuakini Highway.
Telephone: 808-329-4421.
Lihue, Kauai, Hawaii Office: Watumull Plaza, Suite 202, 4334 Rice Street.
Telephone: 808-245-4705.

RESIDENT COUNSEL

Malvin D. Dohrman

Representative Clients: Big Save, Inc.; Bank of Hawaii; County of Kauai; First Hawaiian Bank; Grove Farm Co. & Subsidiaries; Pacific Ocean Properties; Obayashi Corp.

For full biographical listings, see the Martindale-Hubbell Law Directory

*LIHUE,** Kauai Co.

CASE & LYNCH (AV)

A Partnership including Professional Corporations
(Formerly Pratt, Moore, Bortz & Case - 1967-1971)
(Formerly Case, Kay & Lynch - 1979 to 1986)
Watumull Plaza, Suite 202, 4334 Rice Street, 96766
Telephone: 808-245-4705
Telecopier: 808-245-3277
Honolulu, Hawaii Office: 2600 Grosvenor Center, Mauka Tower, 737 Bishop St.
Telephone: 808-547-5400.
Kahului, Maui, Hawaii Office: The Kahului Building, Suite 470, 33 Lono Avenue.
Telephone: 808-871-8351.
Hilo, Hawaii Office: Case & Lynch Business Center, 460 Kilauea Avenue.
Telephone: 808-961-6611.
Kailua-Kona, Hawaii Office: Hanama Place, Suite 101, 75-5706 Kuakini Highway.
Telephone: 808-329-4421.
Kilauea, Kauai, Hawaii Office: Kong Lung Center, P.O. Box 988, Kilauea Lighthouse Road.
Telephone: 808-828-2890.

Michael J. Belles David W. Proudfoot (A Law
Max W. J. Graham, Jr. Corporation)

(See Next Column)

RESIDENT COUNSEL

Hartwell H. K. Blake Candace McCaslin
Peter M. Morimoto

Representative Clients: Big Save, Inc.; Bank of Hawaii; County of Kauai; First Hawaiian Bank; Grove Farm Co. & Subsidiaries; Pacific Ocean Properties; Obayashi Corp.

For full biographical listings, see the Martindale-Hubbell Law Directory

*WAILUKU,** Maui Co.

CARLSMITH BALL WICHMAN MURRAY CASE & ICHIKI (AV)

A Partnership including Law Corporations
One Main Plaza, Suite 400, 2200 Main Street, P.O. Box 1086, 96793-2225
Telephone: 808-242-4535
Telecopier: 808-244-4974
Honolulu, Hawaii Office: Suite 2200, Pacific Tower, 1001 Bishop Street. P.O. Box 656.
Telephone: 808-523-2500.
Los Angeles, California Office: 555 South Flower Street, 25th Floor.
Telephone: 213-955-1200.
Long Beach, California Office: 301 East Ocean Boulevard, 7th Floor.
Telephone: 310-435-5631.
Washington, D.C. Office: 700 14th Street, N.W., 9th Floor.
Telephone: 202-508-1025.
Mexico City, Mexico Office: Monte Pelvoux 111, Piso 1, Col. Lomas de Chapultepec, 11000 Mexico, D.F.
Telephone: (011-52-5) 520-8514.
Fax: (011-52-5) 540-1545.
Mexico, D.F. Office of Carlsmith Ball Garcia Cacho y Asociados, S.C. (Authorized to practice Mexican Law): Monte Pelvoux 111, Piso 1, Col. Lomas de Chapultepec, 11000 Mexico, D.F.
Telephone: (011-52-5) 540-8514.
Fax: (011-52-5) 540-1545.
Agana, Guam Office: 4th Floor, Bank of Hawaii Building, P.O. Box BF.
Telephone: 671-472-6813.
Saipan, Commonwealth of the Northern Mariana Islands Office: Carlsmith Building, Capitol Hill, P.O. Box 5241.
Telephone: 670-322-3455.
Kailua-Kona, Hawaii Office: Second Floor, Bank of Hawaii Annex Building, P.O. Box 1720.
Telephone: 808-329-6464.
Hilo, Hawaii Office: 121 Waianuenue Avenue, P.O. Box 686.
Telephone: 808-935-6644.
Kapolei, Hawaii Office: Kapolei Building, Suite 318, 1001 Kamokila Boulevard.
Telephone: 808-674-0850.

RESIDENT PARTNERS

Grant Y. M. Chun B. Martin Luna
Tom C. Leuteneker Craig G. Nakamura
Paul M. Ueoka

RESIDENT ASSOCIATES

Gilbert S. Coloma-Agaran

For full biographical listings, see the Martindale-Hubbell Law Directory

KRUEGER & CAHILL (AV)

2065 Main Street, 96793
Telephone: 808-244-7444; Honolulu: 536-7474
Facsimile: 808-244-4177
Cable Address: "Maulaw"

MEMBERS OF FIRM

James Krueger Peter T. Cahill

LEGAL SUPPORT PERSONNEL

LEGAL ASSISTANTS

Sharon O'Shaughnessy Theresa N. Coletti
Sandra D.H. Stearns

A List of Representative Clients and References will be furnished upon request.

For full biographical listings, see the Martindale-Hubbell Law Directory

PAUL, JOHNSON, PARKS & NILES ATTORNEYS AT LAW, A LAW CORPORATION (AV)

203 H.G.E.A. Building, 2145 Kaohu Street, P.O. Box 870, 96793-0870
Telephone: 808-242-6644
Fax: 808-244-9775
Honolulu, Hawaii Office: Suite 1300 Pacific Tower, 1001 Bishop Street, P.O. Box 4438. 96812-4438.
Telephone: 808-524-1212.
Telecopier: 808-528-1654.

Dennis James Niles William M. McKeon
Carla M. Nakata

For full biographical listings, see the Martindale-Hubbell Law Directory

IDAHO

*AMERICAN FALLS,** Power Co. — (Refer to Pocatello)

*BLACKFOOT,** Bingham Co. — (Refer to Pocatello)

*BOISE,** Ada Co.

CANTRILL, SKINNER, SULLIVAN & KING (AV)

1423 Tyrell Lane, P.O. Box 359, 83701
Telephone: 208-344-8035
Fax: 208-345-7212

MEMBERS OF FIRM

David W. Cantrill
Gardner W. Skinner, Jr.
Willis E. Sullivan, III
John L. King
Robert D. Lewis
Frank P. Kotyk

ASSOCIATES

Tyra Hansen Stubbs
Clinton O. Casey

LEGAL SUPPORT PERSONNEL

Garianne Erwin

Representative Clients: Safeco Insurance Companies; Prudential Property and Casualty Insurance Co.; State Insurance Fund; Farmers Insurance Co.; Jordan-Wilcomb Company; Nature Conservancy; Independent School District of Boise City; Hartford Insurance Group; Stewart Title of Idaho, Inc.
Reference: Key Bank of Idaho.

For full biographical listings, see the Martindale-Hubbell Law Directory

EBERLE, BERLIN, KADING, TURNBOW & MCKLVEEN, CHARTERED (AV)

Capitol Park Plaza, 300 North Sixth Street, P.O. Box 1368, 83701
Telephone: 208-344-8535
Facsimile: 208-344-8542

J. Louis Eberle (1890-1964)
T.H. Eberle (1922-1977)
R.B. Kading, Jr.
R.M. Turnbow
William J. McKlveen
Warren Eugene Jones
Mark S. Geston
Thomas R. Linville
Richard A. Riley
Joseph H. Uberuaga, II
Robert L. Berlin
Scott D. Hess
Bradley G. Andrews
William A. Fuhrman
Richard K. Lierz
Neil D. McFeeley
Stephen A. Bradbury
Kimbell D. Gourley
Steven E. Alkire

Ronald L. Williams
Ann K. Shepard
Derrick J. O'Neill
Stanley J. Tharp
David W. Knotts

OF COUNSEL

James L. Berlin
Gary C. Randall

General Counsel: Key Bank of Idaho; Key Trust Company of the West; Key Mortgage Funding; IdaWest Energy Company; Diamond Sports.
Representative Clients: Key Bank of Idaho; U.S. West Communications; Cessna Aircraft Co.

For full biographical listings, see the Martindale-Hubbell Law Directory

ELAM & BURKE, A PROFESSIONAL ASSOCIATION (AV)

Key Financial Center, 702 West Idaho Street, P.O. Box 1539, 83701
Telephone: 208-343-5454
Telecopier: 208-384-5844

Laurel E. Elam (1888-1974)
Carl A. Burke (1898-1961)
Carl P. Burke
M. Allyn Dingel, Jr.
John Magel
David B. Lincoln
James D. LaRue
Randall A. Peterman
Ryan P. Armbruster
Melville W. Fisher, II
William G. Dryden
Peter C. K. Marshall
Trudy Hanson Fouser
Scott L. Campbell
Bobbi Killian Dominick
William J. Batt
Jeffery J. Ventrella
James A. Ford
Jeffrey A. Thomson

J. Ray Durtschi
Bradlee R. Frazer
Kristen R. Thompson
Margaret S. Schaefer
Eric L. Berliner
Harry M. Lane, Jr.
Paul J. Augustine
Jeffrey W. Pusch

Representative Clients: Morrison-Knudsen, Inc.; Texas Instruments, Inc.; Prudential Securities, Inc.; Pechiney Corp.; Dow Corning Corporation; U.S. West Communications; State Farm Insurance Cos.; Sinclair Oil Company d/b/a Sun Valley Company; Farmers Insurance Group; Hecla Mining Company.

For full biographical listings, see the Martindale-Hubbell Law Directory

EVANS, KEANE (AV)

Suite 200, 1101 West River Street, P.O. Box 959, 83701-0959
Telephone: 208-384-1800
Facsimile: 208-345-3514
Kellogg, Idaho Office: 111 Main Street, P.O. Box 659.
Telephone: 208-784-1105.

MEMBERS OF FIRM

James P. Keane (1925-1988)
Fred M. Gibler (Also at Kellogg)
Charles L. A. Cox (Also at Kellogg)
Rex Blackburn
Bruce C. Jones
Barton L. Kline
William A. McCurdy
Jed W. Manwaring
James D. Hovren
David W. Gratton

OF COUNSEL

Blaine F. Evans
Robert J. Koontz
Will S. Defenbach

John O. Cossel (At Kellogg Office)
Justin W. Julian (Also At Kellogg Office)
K. Heidi Gudgell
Thomas B. Humphrey
Jon M. Bauman
Elizabeth G. Roper
Kara Lee Barton (Not admitted in ID)
Joyce Hettenbach

Representative Clients: American Cyanamid Co.; Chrysler Corp.; Coeur d'Alene Mines Corp.; Crum & Forster; Ford Motor Co.; Hecla Mining Co.; Idaho Power Co.; State Farm Mutual Automobile Insurance Co.; Sunshine Mining & Refining Company; U.S. Bank of Idaho, N.A.

For full biographical listings, see the Martindale-Hubbell Law Directory

JAMES R. GILLESPIE, P.A. (AV)

512 West Bannock, P.O. Box 2337, 83701
Telephone: 208-344-8400
Fax: 208-344-7100

James R. Gillespie

Sandra Meikle Carter

For full biographical listings, see the Martindale-Hubbell Law Directory

HALL, FARLEY, OBERRECHT & BLANTON (AV)

Key Financial Center, 702 West Idaho Street, Suite 700, P.O. Box 1271, 83701-1271
Telephone: 208-336-0404
Facsimile: 208-336-5193

Richard E. Hall
Donald J. Farley
Phillip S. Oberrecht
Raymond D. Powers
Candy Wagahoff Dale
Robert B. Luce
J. Kevin West
Bart W. Harwood

J. Charles Blanton
John J. Burke
Steven J. Hippler
Thorpe P. Orton
Ronald S. Best (Not admitted in ID)

References: Boise State University; Farm Bureau Mutual Insurance Company of Idaho; Medical Insurance Exchange of California; The St. Paul Cos.

For full biographical listings, see the Martindale-Hubbell Law Directory

HOLLAND & HART (AV)

Suite 1400, West One Plaza, 101 South Capitol Boulevard, P.O. Box 2527, 83701
Telephone: 208-342-5000
Telecopier: 208-343-8869
Denver, Colorado Office: Suite 2900, 555 Seventeenth Street. P.O. Box 8749.
Telephone: 303-295-8000.
Cable Address: "Holhart Denver."
Telecopier: 303-295-8261.
TWX: 910-931-0568.
Denver Tech Center, Colorado Office: Suite 1050, 4601 DTC Boulevard.
Telephone: 303-2290-1600
Telecopier: 303-290-1606.
Aspen, Colorado Office: 600 East Main Street.
Telephone: 303-925-3476.
Telecopier: 303-925-9367.
Boulder, Colorado Office: Suite 500, 1050 Walnut.
Telephone: 303-473-2700.
Telecopier: 303-473-2720.
Colorado Springs, Colorado Office: Suite 1000, 90 S. Cascade Avenue.
Telephone: 719-475-7730.
Telex: 820770 SHHTLX.
Telecopier: 719-634-2461.
Washington, D.C. Office: Suite 310, 1001 Pennsylvania Avenue, N.W.
Telephone: 202-638-5500.
Telecopier: 202-737-8998.
Billings, Montana Office: Suite 1400, 175 North 27th Street.
Telephone: 406-252-2166.
Telecopier: 406-252-1669.

(See Next Column)

HOLLAND & HART—*Continued*

Salt Lake City, Utah Office: Suite 880, 111 East Broadway.
Telephone: 801-578-6000.
FAX: 801-578-6010.
Cheyenne, Wyoming Office: Holland & Hart, A Partnership including Professional Corporations, Suite 500, 2020 Carey Avenue, P.O. Box 1347.
Telephone: 307-778-4200.
Telecopier: 307-778-8175.
Jackson, Wyoming Office: Holland & Hart, A Partnership including Professional Corporations, Suite 2, 175 South King Street, P.O. Box 68.
Telephone: 307-739-9741.
Telecopier: 307-739-9744.

RESIDENT PARTNERS

Willis E. Sullivan (1911-1992)
Edith Miller Klein (Retired)
Walter H. Bithell
J. Frederick Mack
Larry E. Prince
B. Newal Squyres, Jr.
Steven B. Andersen

RESIDENT OF COUNSEL

Debra K. Ellers
Brian J. King

RESIDENT ASSOCIATES

Sandra L. Clapp
Kim J. Dockstader
Robert A. Faucher
Murray D. Feldman
Dana Lieberman Hofstetter
Kurt D. Holzer
Linda B. Jones

For full biographical listings, see the Martindale-Hubbell Law Directory

HOPKINS, RODEN, CROCKETT, HANSEN & HOOPES (AV)

802 West Bannock, Suite 900, P.O. Box 2110, 83701-2110
Telephone: 208-336-7930
Fax: 208-336-9154
Idaho Falls, Idaho Office: 428 Park Avenue. P.O. Box 51219. 83405-1219.
Telephone: 208-523-4445.
Fax: 208-523-4474.

MEMBERS OF FIRM

C. Timothy Hopkins
William C. Roden
Gregory L. Crockett
John D. Hansen
D. Fredrick Hoopes
C. Tom Arkoosh
Lary S. Larson
Paul B. Rippel
Teresa L. Sturm
Steven K. Brown

Lane R. Simmons

Representative Clients: First Interstate Bank of Idaho, N.A.; Nature Conservancy of Idaho; Micron Technology, Inc.; Hewlett Packard Co.; U.S. West Communications; Anheuser-Busch Companies, Inc.; Wal-Mart, Inc.; Eastern Idaho Economic Development Council, Inc.; Mutual of Enumclaw; Wausau Insurance Cos.

For full biographical listings, see the Martindale-Hubbell Law Directory

IMHOFF & LYNCH (AV)

1607 West Jefferson Street, P.O. Box 739, 83701
Telephone: 208-336-6900
Facsimile: 208-336-7031

MEMBERS OF FIRM

James B. Lynch
Michael W. Moore
Thomas P. Baskin, III
Paige Alan Parker

Kaaren Lynn Barr
Penny L. Dykas
Mary L. McDougal

OF COUNSEL

Joseph M. Imhoff, Jr.

Representative Clients: United State Aviation Underwriters, Aetna Casualty & Surety, Co., Yellow Freight, Underwriters at Llodys, Willis Coroon Management Co., Inc., National Union Fire Insurance Co., Capital Insurance Co., Coleman Co., Alfa Laval Agri., Inc., Admiral Insurance Co.
Reference: First Security Bank.

For full biographical listings, see the Martindale-Hubbell Law Directory

MANWEILER, BEVIS & CAMERON, P.A. (AV)

Suite 220, 960 Broadway Avenue, P.O. Box 827, 83706
Telephone: 208-345-1040
FAX: 208-345-0365

Howard I. Manweiler
James A. Bevis
Alan D. Cameron, II
Mark H. Manweiler
David D. Manweiler
Kristi Brockway Smith
Gary L. Davis
Michael R. Johnson

Representative Clients: Overland Lumber Co.; State of Idaho Military Division.
Reference: West One Bank.

For full biographical listings, see the Martindale-Hubbell Law Directory

MARTIN, CHAPMAN, SCHILD & LASSAW, CHARTERED (AV)

Suite 100, 476 North 12th Street, P.O. Box 2898, 83701
Telephone: 208-343-6485
Fax: 208-343-9819
Sun Valley, Idaho Office: P.O. Box 744.
Telephone: 208-788-2876.
Fax: 208-788-2818.
Twin Falls, Idaho Office: 834 Falls Avenue, Suite 1020A.
Telephone: 208-734-9629.

John S. Chapman
J. F. Martin (1893-1967)
C. Ben Martin
Raymond D. Schild
Donald A. Lassaw

References: West One Bank, Idaho, N.A. (formerly Idaho First National Bank); First Security Bank of Idaho, N.A.

For full biographical listings, see the Martindale-Hubbell Law Directory

MOFFATT, THOMAS, BARRETT, ROCK & FIELDS, CHARTERED (AV)

First Security Building, 911 West Idaho Street, Suite 300, P.O. Box 829, 83701
Telephone: 208-345-2000
FAX: 208-385-5384
Idaho Falls Office: 525 Park Avenue, Suite 2D, P.O. Box 1367, 83403.
Telephone: 208-522-6700.
FAX: 208-522-5111.
Pocatello, Idaho Office: 1110 Call Creek Drive, P.O. Box 4941, 83201.
Telephone: 208-233-2001.

Willis C. Moffatt (1907-1980)
Eugene C. Thomas
John W. Barrett
R. B. Rock
Richard C. Fields
Robert E. Bakes
Paul S. Street
Larry C. Hunter
Glenna M. Christensen
Mark S. Prusynski
Morgan W. Richards, Jr.
Michael G. McPeek
Stephen R. Thomas
Jon S. Gorski
Gary T. Dance (Idaho Falls and Pocatello Offices)
Gerald T. Husch
Thomas V. Munson
Kirk R. Helvie
Thomas C. Morris
Michael E. Thomas
Patricia M. Olsson
James C. deGlee

Grant T. Burgoyne
Stephen J. Olson
Patrick J. Kole
Andrew P. Doman
David S. Jensen
Ray E. Smith
Allen K. Davis
Bradley J. Williams
Mark A. Ellison
James L. Martin
Alan D. Malone
Josephine P. Beeman
Kelly Greene McConnell

Representative Clients: BMC West Corporation; Chevron, U.S.A.; First Security Bank of Idaho, N.A.; General Motors Corp.; Idaho Potato Commission; Intermountain Gas Co.; John Alden Life Insurance Co.; Micron, Inc.; Royal Insurance Cos.; St. Luke's Regional Medical Center & Mountain States Tumor Institute.

For full biographical listings, see the Martindale-Hubbell Law Directory

***BONNERS FERRY,** Boundary Co. — (Refer to Coeur d'Alene)**

***BURLEY,** Cassia Co. — (Refer to Rupert)**

***CALDWELL,** Canyon Co.**

GIGRAY, MILLER, DOWNEN & WILPER (AV)

9th and Dearborn Streets, P.O. Box 640, 83606-0640
Telephone: 208-459-0091
Fax: 208-459-0096

MEMBERS OF FIRM

Dean E. Miller (1922-1983)
William F. Gigray, Jr.
Donald E. Downen
Ronald J. Wilper

Representative Clients: Albertson College of Idaho; Whittenberger Foundation; Syms Fruit Ranch, Inc.; Ste. Chapelle Wineries; Wilder School District No. 133; Nampa Highway District; Flahiff Funeral Chapels, Inc.; D & B Supply; Twin Cities Broadcasting Co.; Gem State Manufacturing, Inc.; City of Marsing, Idaho.

For full biographical listings, see the Martindale-Hubbell Law Directory

***CHALLIS,** Custer Co. — (Refer to Idaho Falls)**

***EMMETT,** Gem Co. — (Refer to Caldwell)**

***GOODING,** Gooding Co. — (Refer to Twin Falls)**

***HAILEY,** Blaine Co. — (Refer to Ketchum)**

***IDAHO FALLS,** Bonneville Co.**

ANDERSON, NELSON & HALL (AV)

490 Memorial Drive, P.O. Box 51630, 83405-1630
Telephone: 208-522-3001
Telecopier: 208-523-7254

(See Next Column)

ANDERSON, NELSON & HALL, *Idaho Falls—Continued*

MEMBERS OF FIRM

Arthur L. Smith (1916-1988)
Eugene L. Bush (1928-1986)
W. J. Anderson
Douglas R. Nelson
Gregory S. Anderson
Blake G. Hall
Scott R. Hall
Joel E. Tingey

ASSOCIATES

Todd R. Erikson

OF COUNSEL

John M. Sharp

Representative Clients: J. R. Simplot Soil Builders, Inc.; Monroc, Inc.; EG&G Idaho, Inc.; City of Idaho Falls; The Continental Insurance Cos.; United States Fidelity and Guarantee Insurance Co.; Bank of Commerce; The Farm Credit Bank of Spokane; M. K. Ferguson, Inc.

For full biographical listings, see the Martindale-Hubbell Law Directory

HILLER, BENJAMIN & ASSOCIATES (AV)

Suite 2A, Second Floor, The Earl Building, 525 Park Avenue, P.O. Box 52020, 83405-2020
Telephone: 208-525-3200; 800-574-3201
FAX: 208-525-3232

MEMBERS OF FIRM

M. B. "Buck" Hiller
Willis B. Benjamin

Representative Clients: First Security Bank of Idaho, N.A.; Farmers Insurance Group; Fireman's Fund American; Eastern Idaho Regional Medical Center; Pacific Power & Light Co.; Merrill, Lynch, Pierce, Fenner & Smith; State Insurance Fund.

For full biographical listings, see the Martindale-Hubbell Law Directory

HOLDEN, KIDWELL, HAHN & CRAPO (AV)

West One Bank Building, P.O. Box 50130, 83405
Telephone: 208-523-0620
Telefax: 208-523-9518

MEMBERS OF FIRM AND ASSOCIATES

Arthur W. Holden (1877-1967)
Robert Bonnifield Holden (1911-1971)
Terry L. Crapo (1939-1982)
William Sutherland Holden (1907-1988)
Fred Joseph Hahn
Kent W. Foster
Robert E. Farnam
William D. Faler
Stephen E. Martin
Charles A. Homer
Gary Lane Meikle
Gayle A. Sorenson
Donald L. Harris
Dale W. Storer
Marie T. Tyler
John G. Simmons

Robert Marinus Follett
James K. Slavens

Representative Clients: The Equitable Life Assurance Society of the U. S. (Commercial, Farm & City Loans); The Post Register; West One Bank Idaho N.A.; School District #91; John Hancock Mutual Life Insurance Co.; KIFI TV; Melaleuca, Inc.

For full biographical listings, see the Martindale-Hubbell Law Directory

HOPKINS, RODEN, CROCKETT, HANSEN & HOOPES (AV)

Salisbury Building, 428 Park Avenue, P.O. Box 51219, 83405-1219
Telephone: 208-523-4445
Fax: 208-523-4474
Boise, Idaho Office: 802 West Bannock, Suite 900. P.O. Box 2110. 83701-2110.
Telephone: 208-336-7930.
Fax: 208-336-9154.

MEMBERS OF FIRM

Seward H. French, III (1941-1984)
Ted C. Springer (1943-1984)
C. Timothy Hopkins
William C. Roden
Gregory L. Crockett
John D. Hansen
D. Fredrick Hoopes
C. Tom Arkoosh
Lary S. Larson
Paul B. Rippel
Teresa L. Sturm
Steven K. Brown

David H. Shipman
Katherine S. Moriarty
Lane R. Simmons
Reed E. Andrus

LEGAL SUPPORT PERSONNEL

REGISTERED PATENT AGENT

Robert A. deGroot

Representative Clients: First Interstate Bank of Idaho, N.A.; Nature Conservancy of Idaho; Micron Technology, Inc.; Hewlett Packard Co.; U.S. West Communications; Anheuser-Busch Companies, Inc.; Wal-Mart, Inc.; Eastern Idaho Economic Development Council, Inc.; Mutual of Enumclaw; Wausau Insurance Cos.

For full biographical listings, see the Martindale-Hubbell Law Directory

PETERSEN, MOSS, OLSEN, CARR, ESKELSON & HALL (AV)

485 E Street, 83401
Telephone: 208-523-4650
FAX: 208-524-3391

MEMBERS OF FIRM

Dennis M. Olsen (1930-1985)
George C. Petersen, Jr.
Reed L. Moss
Wm. Charles Carr
Scott P. Eskelson
Stephen D. Hall

Representative Client: State Farm Insurance Cos.

For full biographical listings, see the Martindale-Hubbell Law Directory

ST. CLAIR, DALLING & MEACHAM (AV)

A Partnership including Professional Corporations
The Earl Building, 501 Park Avenue, P.O. Box 50050, 83405
Telephone: 208-522-2350
Fax: 208-524-6342

Clency St. Clair (1871-1957)
Robert W. St. Clair (1907-1989)
Richard T. St. Clair (Chartered)
William R. Dalling (Chartered)
Dean Dalling (Chartered)
Gregory P. Meacham (Chartered)
Karl R. Decker (Chartered)

Representative Clients: First Security Bank of Idaho, N.A.; Safeco Insurance Co.; Farmers Insurance Group; Kemper Insurance Cos.; Intermountain Health Care; TransAmerica Insurance Co.; Royal Insurance Co.; Eastern Idaho Regional Medical Center; Pacific Power & Light Co.; Merrill Lynch; Idaho State Insurance Fund; Bombardier Corp.

For full biographical listings, see the Martindale-Hubbell Law Directory

*JEROME,** Jerome Co. — (Refer to Twin Falls)

KELLOGG, Shoshone Co.

EVANS, KEANE (AV)

111 Main Street, P.O. Box 659, 83837
Telephone: 208-784-1105
Facsimile: 208-783-7601
Boise, Idaho Office: Suite 200, 1101 West River Street, P.O. Box 959.
Telephone: 208-384-1800

James P. Keane (1925-1988)
Fred M. Gibler (Also at Boise)
Charles L. A. Cox (Also at Boise)

John O. Cossel
Justin W. Julian

Representative Clients: American Cyanamid Co.; AMOCO; Coeur d'Alene Mines Corp.; Ford Motor Co.; Hecla Mining Co.; Idaho Power Co.; Insurance Company of North America; Sunshine Mining Co.; Volkswagen of America.

For full biographical listings, see the Martindale-Hubbell Law Directory

*MALAD CITY,** Oneida Co. — (Refer to Pocatello)

*MOSCOW,** Latah Co. — (Refer to Lewiston)

*MOUNTAIN HOME,** Elmore Co. — (Refer to Boise)

NAMPA, Canyon Co. — (Refer to Caldwell)

*PAYETTE,** Payette Co. — (Refer to Caldwell)

*POCATELLO,** Bannock Co.

JONES, CHARTERED (AV)

P.O. Box 967, 83204-0967
Telephone: 208-232-5911
FAX: 208-232-5962

Lamont Jones
Jack H. Robison
Thomas J. Holmes
Jesse C. Robison
Kelly Kumm

Representative Clients: First Security Bank of Idaho; Idaho Power Co.; American Land Title Company; City of Pocatello; Pocatello Regional Medical Center; Crossland Credit Corp.
Reference: First Security Bank of Idaho, N.A.

For full biographical listings, see the Martindale-Hubbell Law Directory

MERRILL & MERRILL, CHARTERED (AV)

Key Bank Building, P.O. Box 991, 83204
Telephone: 208-232-2286
Fax: 208-232-2499

A. L. Merrill (1886-1961)
R. D. Merrill (1893-1972)
Wesley F. Merrill
Dave R. Gallafent
Stephen S. Dunn
D. Russell Wight
N. Randy Smith
David C. Nye
Kent L. Hawkins

Representative Clients: Key Bank of Idaho; Phillips Petroleum Co.; The Travelers Insurance Co.; Aetna Casualty & Surety Co.; Hartford Accident & Indemnity Co.; Equitable Life Assurance Society; Utah Power & Light Co.;

(See Next Column)

MERRILL & MERRILL CHARTERED—*Continued*

Pacific Corp.; Porteneuf-Marsh Valley Canal Co.; Farm Bureau Mutual Insurance Co. of Idaho.

For full biographical listings, see the Martindale-Hubbell Law Directory

RACINE, OLSON, NYE, COOPER & BUDGE, CHARTERED (AV)

Center Plaza, Corner First & Center, P.O. Box 1391, 83204
Telephone: 208-232-6101
FAX: 208-232-6109

Louis F. Racine, Jr. — John A. Bailey, Jr.
William D. Olson — John R. Goodell
W. Marcus W. Nye — John B. Ingelstrom
Gary L. Cooper — Daniel C. Green
Randall C. Budge — Reed W. Larsen
Brent O. Roche

Fred J. Lewis — Mitchell W. Brown
Kirk Hadley — Eric S. Hunn
David E. Alexander

Representative Clients: Allstate Insurance Co.; Farmers Insurance Group of Cos.; Idaho Irrigation Pumpers Assn.; Monsanto Co.; North Pacific Insurance Co.; Safeco Insurance Co.; West One Bank.

For full biographical listings, see the Martindale-Hubbell Law Directory

SERVICE, GASSER & KERL (AV)

2043 East Center Street, P.O. Box 6009, 83205-6009
Telephone: 208-232-4471
Fax: 208-232-1808

MEMBERS OF FIRM

Archie W. Service — Steven V. Richert
Clark Gasser — Rudolph E. (Rick) Carnaroli
Ron Kerl — James A. Spinner
Frederick L. Ringe — Kay E. Moore

LEGAL SUPPORT PERSONNEL

LEGAL ASSISTANT

Darcy Taylor

Representative Clients: Key Bank of Idaho; Allied Insurance Group; Union Pacific Railroad Co.; Farm Credit Bank of Spokane; KHD Deutz of America Corp.; Interstate Production Credit Association; D.L. Evans Bank; Cowboy Oil Cos.
References: Key Bank of Idaho; First Security Bank of Idaho.

For full biographical listings, see the Martindale-Hubbell Law Directory

WARD, MAGUIRE & BYBEE (AV)

353 East Lander, P.O. Box 4758, 83205-4758
Telephone: 208-232-5167
FAX: 208-232-5181

MEMBERS OF FIRM

Martin R. Ward — David H. Maguire
D. Kirk Bybee

ASSOCIATES

Kent V. Reynolds

Representative Clients: Farmers Insurance Group (Truck Exchange); The American Insurance Group; Unigard Insurance Group; Hartford Mutual Insurance Co.; Transport Indemnity Co.; Aetna Insurance Co.

For full biographical listings, see the Martindale-Hubbell Law Directory

*PRESTON,** Franklin Co. — (Refer to Pocatello)

*REXBURG,** Madison Co.

RIGBY, THATCHER, ANDRUS, RIGBY, KAM & MOELLER, CHARTERED (AV)

25 North Second East, P.O. Box 250, 83440
Telephone: 208-356-3633
Fax: 208-356-0768

Ray W. Rigby — Jerry R. Rigby
Gordon S. Thatcher (On Leave) — Michael S. Kam
G. Rich Andrus — Gregory W. Moeller

Attorneys For: North Fork Reservoir Co.; Class "A" School Districts 321 & 322; Fall River, Raft River and Lost River Electric Cooperatives; Ultimate Director, Inc.; Madison Cooperative Association, Inc.; W.R. Henderson Construction, Inc.; Committee of Nine of Water District 01.
Representative Clients: Taylor Chevrolet Co.; Madison Cooperative Assn., Inc.; Valley Bank (Headquarter Office).

For full biographical listings, see the Martindale-Hubbell Law Directory

*RIGBY,** Jefferson Co. — (Refer to Rexburg)

*RUPERT,** Minidoka Co.

GOODMAN & BOLLAR, CHARTERED (AV)

717 7th Street, P.O. Box D, 83350
Telephone: 208-436-4774
Fax: 208-436-4837

William T. Goodman — Alan C. Goodman
Rick L. Bollar

Representative Clients: Raft River Highway District; Minidoka County Highway District; First Security Bank (Local Counsel); Minidoka Memorial Hospital; Minidoka County Fire District.
References: First Security Bank of Idaho; West One Bank.

For full biographical listings, see the Martindale-Hubbell Law Directory

*ST. ANTHONY,** Fremont Co. — (Refer to Rexburg)

*SHOSHONE,** Lincoln Co. — (Refer to Ketchum)

*TWIN FALLS,** Twin Falls Co.

COLEMAN, RITCHIE & ROBERTSON (AV)

156 2nd Avenue West, P.O. Box 525, 83303-0525
Telephone: 208-734-1224
Fax: 208-734-3983

MEMBERS OF FIRM

John R. Coleman — John S. Ritchie
Thomas M. Robertson

Representative Clients: First Federal Savings Bank of Twin Falls and Branches in Rupert, Burley, Ketchum & Buhl, Idaho; West One Bank (Twin Falls Office); Connecticut Mutual Life Insurance Co. References: West One Bank (Twin Falls Office); First Security Bank of Idaho, (Twin Falls Office); First Federal Savings Bank of Twin Falls.

For full biographical listings, see the Martindale-Hubbell Law Directory

*WALLACE,** Shoshone Co. — (Refer to Kellogg)

*WEISER,** Washington Co. — (Refer to Caldwell)

ILLINOIS

*ALBION,** Edwards Co. — (Refer to Carmi)

ALTON, Madison Co. — (Refer to Edwardsville)

ASHLAND, Cass Co. — (Refer to Beardstown)

AURORA, Kane Co.

MICKEY, WILSON, WEILER & RENZI, P.C. (AV)
2111 Plum Street, 2nd Floor, P.O. Box 787, 60507-0787
Telephone: 708-801-9699
FAX: 708-801-9715

Gary K. Mickey
Peter K. Wilson, Jr.
Bernard K. Weiler
Constance Burnett Renzi

Steven A. Andersson

For full biographical listings, see the Martindale-Hubbell Law Directory

MURPHY, HUPP, FOOTE, MIELKE AND KINNALLY (AV)
North Island Center, P.O. Box 5030, 60507
Telephone: 708-844-0056
FAX: 708-844-1905

MEMBERS OF FIRM

William C. Murphy
Robert B. Hupp
Robert M. Foote
Craig S. Mielke
Patrick M. Kinnally
Paul G. Krentz
Joseph C. Loran
Gerald K. Hodge

Timothy D. O'Neil
Thomas U. Hipp

OF COUNSEL

Robert T. Olson

Representative Clients: American Telephone & Telegraph Co.; Fox Valley Park District; Lyon Metal Products; Kane County Forest Preserve District; Hollywood Casino; Employers Mutual Insurance Co.; Forty-Eight Insulations, Inc.; UNR Asbestos Disease Trust; Richards-Wilcox Co.; National Bank & Trust Company of Syracuse.

For full biographical listings, see the Martindale-Hubbell Law Directory

BATAVIA, Kane Co.

DRENDEL, TATNALL, HOFFMAN & MCCRACKEN, A PROFESSIONAL CORPORATION (AV)
201 Houston Street, Suite 300, P.O. Box 1808, 60510-6808
Telephone: 708-406-5440
FAX: 708-406-6179

Gilbert X. Drendel, Jr.
Susan B. Tatnall
Thomas J. Hoffman
Thomas G. McCracken
Kate L. McCracken
Kevin G. Drendel
Mark C. Gorham

Reference: The Old Second National Bank of Aurora, Aurora, Illinois.

For full biographical listings, see the Martindale-Hubbell Law Directory

*BELLEVILLE,** St. Clair Co.

DONOVAN, ROSE, NESTER & SZEWCZYK, P.C. (AV)
8 East Washington Street, 62220
Telephone: 618-235-2020
Telecopier: 618-235-9632

Harold A. Donovan, Sr.
Michael J. Nester
Dennis E. Rose
Edward J. Szewczyk
Charles L. Joley

OF COUNSEL

Vincent J. Hatch (Retired)

Douglas R. Heise
Georgiann Oliver
Kenneth M. Nussbaumer
Bret A. Cohen

Representative Clients: State Farm Mutual Auto & Life Co.; Travelers Insurance Co.; Liberty Mutual Insurance Co.; Government Employees Insurance Co.; Great American Insurance Co.; Aetna Casualty & Surety Co.; Royal Globe Insurance Co.; Illinois Founders Insurance Co.; INA (Insurance Company of North America).

For full biographical listings, see the Martindale-Hubbell Law Directory

THE DUCEY LAW FIRM, P.C. (AV)
Richland Executive Plaza II, Suite 201, 521 West Main Street, 62220
Telephone: 618-233-1358; 271-0826
Telecopier: 618-234-9560
St. Louis, Missouri Office: 906 Olive Street.
Telephone: 314-621-5581.

(See Next Column)

Cornelius T. Ducey, Sr.
Cornelius T. Ducey, Jr.
C. Patout Ducey

Timothy L. Donaho, Jr.

For full biographical listings, see the Martindale-Hubbell Law Directory

GUNDLACH, LEE, EGGMANN, BOYLE & ROESSLER (AV)
5000 West Main Street, P.O. Box 23560, 62223-0560
Telephone: 618-277-9000; East St. Louis: 271-8000
Telecopier: 618-277-4594
St. Louis, Mo.
St. Louis, Missouri Office: 1010 Market Street, Suite 1640.
Telephone: 314-231-2084.
Telecopier: 314-231-1960.

PARTNERS

Norman J. Gundlach
Carl W. Lee
Richard E. Boyle
Richard M. Roessler
Kenneth L. Halvachs
Thomas R. Peters
Charles J. Swartwout

ASSOCIATES

Karen E. Mason
Richard J. Mehan, Jr. (Resident, St. Louis, Missouri Office)
Robert D. Andrekanic
Curtis Ray Picou
Michael J. Brunton
Mary G. Sullivan
Ellen M. Edmonds
Terence M. Patton
Mark R. Kurz

OF COUNSEL

Roger M. Fitz-Gerald

District Counsel for: CSX Transportation.
Division Counsel for: Norfolk-Southern Corp.
Attorneys for: Illinois Central Railroad; Illinois Power Co.; Metropolitan, Prudential, Equitable, John Hancock, Northwestern Mutual and General American Life Insurance Cos.

For full biographical listings, see the Martindale-Hubbell Law Directory

HEILIGENSTEIN & BADGLEY, PROFESSIONAL CORPORATION (AV)
30 Public Square, 62220
Telephone: 618-235-1000
Fax: 618-235-1086

Christian E. Heiligenstein
Brad L. Badgley

B. Jay Dowling

Reference: Magna Bank, N.A.

For full biographical listings, see the Martindale-Hubbell Law Directory

THOMPSON & MITCHELL (AV)
525 West Main Street, 62220
Telephone: 618-277-4700; 314-271-1800
Telecopier: 618-236-3434
St. Louis, Missouri Office: One Mercantile Center, Suite 3300.
Telephone: 314-231-7676.
Telecopier: 314-342-1717.
St. Charles, Missouri Office: 200 North Third Street.
Telephone: 314-946-7717.
Telecopier: 314-946-4938.
Washington, D.C. Office: 700 14th Street, N.W., Suite 900.
Telephone: 202-508-1000.
Telecopier: 202-508-1010.

MEMBERS OF FIRM

Joseph R. Lowery
W. Thomas Coghill, Jr.
Donald E. Weihl
Michael D. O'Keefe
Thomas W. Alvey, Jr.
Karl D. Dexheimer
David F. Yates
Garrett C. Reuter
Raymond L. Massey
Gary Mayes
Allan McD. Goodloe, Jr.
Thomas F. Hennessy, III
William A. Schmitt
Robert H. Brownlee
Thomas R. Jayne
Mary M. Bonacorsi
Allen D. Allred
Dan H. Ball
William R. Bay
Mark Sableman
Charles M. Poplstein
Edward S. Bott, Jr.
James G. Blase
Harry W. Wellford, Jr.
Myron A. Hanna
Bradley A. Winters
Mark J. Stegman
Edward A. Cohen
Nicholas J. Lamb
Francis X. Buckley, Jr.
Kurt E. Reitz
Kurt S. Schroeder
James J. Murphy

OF COUNSEL

Robert L. Broderick
James R. Parham

ASSOCIATES

Conny Davinroy Beatty
D. Kimberly Brown
Kelly M. Brown
Tom R. Burcham III
Karen A. Carr
David S. Corwin
Ellen F. Cruickshank
Mary Sue Juen
Crystal M. Kennedy
Cherie K. Harpole MacDonald
Deborah J. Mehrmann
William J. Niehoff

(See Next Column)

THOMPSON & MITCHELL—*Continued*

ASSOCIATES (Continued)

Eric R. Riess (Not admitted in IL)
Donald K. Schoemaker
Mark S. Schuver
Michael J. Scotti III
David A. Stratmann
David F. Szewczyk
T. Bradford Waltrip
Roman P. Wuller

Representative Clients: First Illinois Bank; General Motors Corp.; Harcros Pigments, Inc.; Illinois-American Water Co.; Magna Group, Inc.; Marsh Company; Memorial Hospital of Belleville; Norfolk Southern Corp.; Peabody Coal Company; Union Electric Co.

For full biographical listings, see the Martindale-Hubbell Law Directory

WALKER & WILLIAMS, PROFESSIONAL CORPORATION (AV)

4343 West Main Street, 62223
Telephone: 618-274-1000; 277-1000
Telecopier: 618-233-1637
Edwardsville, Illinois Office: 70 Edwardsville Professional Park.
Telephone: 618-656-9222.
St. Louis, Missouri Office: 906 Olive, Suite 1250.
Telephone: 314-241-2441.
Telecopier: 314-241-7240.

Ralph D. Walker (1906-1988)
Wayne P. Williams (1904-1990)
David B. Stutsman
John B. Gunn
Donald J. Dahlmann
Dale L. Bode
James C. Cook
Thomas E. Jones
Anthony L. Martin (Resident, St. Louis, Missouri Office)
Harlan A. Harla

Michael D. Clark
Paul P. Waller III
James R. Garrison
John E. Sabo
Leslie Offergeld
John C. Craig
Andrew Thomas McCullagh (Resident, St. Louis, Missouri Office)
Terry Ivan Bruckert

General Attorneys in Illinois for: Union Pacific Railroad Co.; CSX Transportation, Inc.; St. Louis Southwestern Railway Co.
Local Attorneys for: Consolidated Rail Corp.
Representative Clients: United States Fidelity & Guaranty Co.; Farmers Insurance Group; Hanover Insurance Co.; The Alton & Southern Railway Co.; Allstate Insurance Co.; Firemen's Fund American Insurance Cos.

For full biographical listings, see the Martindale-Hubbell Law Directory

*BELVIDERE,** Boone Co. — (Refer to Rockford)

*BENTON,** Franklin Co.

HART AND HART (AV)

602 West Public Square, P.O. Box 937, 62812-0937
Telephone: 618-435-8123
Telecopier: 618-435-2962

William H. Hart (1862-1941)
William W. Hart (1894-1968)
Marion M. Hart (1896-1964)
William W. Hart, Jr. (Retired)
Richard O. Hart
Murphy C. Hart
A. Courtney Cox
Pamela Sue Lacey

Representative Clients: Boatmen's Bank of Franklin County; State Bank of Whittington; Magna Bank of Southern Illinois; Benton Park District; Benton Public Library District; HHL Financial Services; Barnes Hospital (St. Louis); St. Lukes Hospital (St. Louis); St. Mary's Hospital (Centralia); Credit Bureau Systems, Inc.

For full biographical listings, see the Martindale-Hubbell Law Directory

*BLOOMINGTON,** McLean Co.

COSTIGAN & WOLLRAB, P.C. (AV)

308 East Washington Street, 61701
Telephone: 309-828-4310
Telecopier: 309-828-4325

James C. Wollrab (1919-1989)
William F. Costigan
Guy C. Fraker
David C. Wochner
Robert W. Neirynck
Paul R. Welch
William S. Bach
Kevin P. Jacobs
Dawn L. Wall

Robert S. White
Todd E. Bugg
John Casey Costigan
Richard D. Fox

Representative Clients: Aetna Life & Casualty Farmland Insurance Group; Allstate Insurance Co.; Marine American State Bank; CNA; Firestone Tire & Rubber Co.; Hartford Insurance Group; CIGNA; The Norfolk and Western Railroad; Pekin Insurance Co.; State Farm Insurance.

For full biographical listings, see the Martindale-Hubbell Law Directory

DUNN, ULBRICH, HUNDMAN, STANCZAK & OGAR (AV)

1001 North Main Street, 61701
Telephone: 309-828-6241
FAX: 309-828-8321

(See Next Column)

MEMBERS OF FIRM

Richard F. Dunn (1888-1963)
Richard T. Dunn
William T. Hundman
Mark T. Dunn
David S. Dunn
David L. Stanczak
Helen E. Ogar

ASSOCIATES

Douglas J. Hundman

OF COUNSEL

William M. Goebel
Louis F. Ulbrich

Representative Clients: Board of Governors of State Colleges and Universities, State of Illinois; Country Mutual Insurance Co.; First Federal Savings & Loan Association of Bloomington; Illinois Wesleyan University; Metropolitan Life Insurance Co., Agricultural Investments and Commercial Investments; The Peoples Bank; Peoples Mid-Illinois Corp.; Illinois Corn Marketing Board; Illinois Soybean Program Operating Board.

For full biographical listings, see the Martindale-Hubbell Law Directory

*CAIRO,** Alexander Co. — (Refer to Marion)

*CAMBRIDGE,** Henry Co.

TELLEEN, TELLEEN, BRAENDLE, HORBERG & THURMAN (AV)

124 West Exchange Street, P.O. Box 179, 61238
Telephone: 309-937-3339
Fax: 309-937-2830
Geneseo, Illinois Office: 137 South State. Suite 208 Cellar Building.
Telephone: 309-944-6866.

Leonard E. Telleen (1877-1966)
Kenneth L. Telleen (Retired)
Leonard W. Telleen
James T. Braendle
Kurt J. Horberg
Virgil A. Thurman
Scott M. Smith

Reference: Peoples Bank of Cambridge.

For full biographical listings, see the Martindale-Hubbell Law Directory

CARBONDALE, Jackson Co.

BRANDON, SCHMIDT & PALMER (AV)

916 West Main Street, P.O. Box 3898, 62902-3898
Telephone: 618-549-0777
Telecopier: 618-457-4691

MEMBERS OF FIRM

Wm. Kent Brandon
Charles E. Schmidt
Phillip G. Palmer

ASSOCIATES

Jeffrey A. Goffinet
Christy W. Solverson
Stephen W. Stone
Thomas E. Margolis

Representative Clients: State Farm Mutual Automobile Insurance Co.; State Farm Fire & Casualty Co.; Milwaukee Insurance Co.; Pekin Insurance Co.; Grinnel Mutual Reinsurance Co.; Western Casualty & Surety Co. (The Western Insurance Cos.); Reliance Insurance Co.; Fireman's Fund American Insurance Co.
Reference: First National Bank of Carbondale.

For full biographical listings, see the Martindale-Hubbell Law Directory

FEIRICH/SCHOEN/MAGER/GREEN (AV)

2001 West Main Street, P.O. Box 1570, 62903-1570
Telephone: 618-529-3000
Telecopier: 618-529-3008

MEMBERS OF FIRM

Paul G. Schoen
T. Richard Mager
Richard A. Green
Mary Lou Rouhandeh
John C. Ryan
Michael F. Dahlen
Kevin L. Mechler
Rebecca Whittington

ASSOCIATES

John S. Rendleman, III
Pieter Noble Schmidt
Gary B. Nelson
Edward Renshaw
Jeffrey Berkbigler

OF COUNSEL

John K. Feirich
John C. Feirich

Representative Clients: Country Mutual Insurance Co.; Sentry Insurance Co.; Great Central Insurance Co.; Consolidation Coal Co.; Heitman Properties, Ltd.; Southern Illinois Hospital Services; Mariah Boats, Inc.; Southern Illinois Airport Authority; Downstate National Banks.

For full biographical listings, see the Martindale-Hubbell Law Directory

*CARLINVILLE,** Macoupin Co.

PHELPS, KASTEN, RUYLE & BURNS (AV)

130 East Main Street, 62626
Telephone: 217-854-3283
FAX: 217-854-9527

(See Next Column)

PHELPS, KASTEN, RUYLE & BURNS, *Carlinville—Continued*

MEMBERS OF FIRM

Edward R. Phelps (1904-1985) Nancy L. Ruyle
Carl E. Kasten Thomas P. Burns

ASSOCIATES

Byron J. Sims

Representative Clients: Carlinville National Bank; Blackburn University; Area Diesel Service, Inc.; Farmers and Merchants Bank; H & H Construction Services, Inc.

For full biographical listings, see the Martindale-Hubbell Law Directory

*CARLYLE,** Clinton Co. — (Refer to Centralia)

*CARMI,** White Co.

CONGER & ELLIOTT, PROF. CORP. (AV)

Farm Bureau Building, 62821
Telephone: 618-382-4187
Fax: 618-384-2452

Chauncey S. Conger (Deceased) Ivan A. Elliott, Jr.
Ivan A. Elliott (Deceased) Robert Michael Drone
Gregory K. Stewart

Representative Clients: First National Bank of Carmi; State Farm Insurance Co.; Country Mutual Insurance Co.; Prudential Insurance Co.; Community Unit School District No. 3; Central Illinois Public Service Co.; Carmi Township Hospital; Egyptian Health Department; Commonwealth Edison.

For full biographical listings, see the Martindale-Hubbell Law Directory

*CARROLLTON,** Greene Co. — (Refer to Carlinville)

*CARTHAGE,** Hancock Co.

HARTZELL, GLIDDEN, TUCKER AND HARTZELL (AV)

Williams Building, P.O. Box 70, 62321
Telephone: 217-357-3121
FAX: 217-357-2027
Macomb, Illinois Office: Old Bailey House, 100 South Campbell Street.
Telephone: 309-833-3121.

MEMBERS OF FIRM

Homer H. Williams (1894-1965) John R. Glidden
Franklin M. Hartzell Stanley L. Tucker
Thomas F. Hartzell

Counsel for: Marine Trust Company of Carthage; Bowen State Bank; Pioneer Lumber Co.;
Local Counsel for: The Atchison, Topeka and Santa Fe Railroad; State Farm Mutual Insurance Co.; The Prudential Insurance Company of America; American States Insurance Co.

For full biographical listings, see the Martindale-Hubbell Law Directory

CHAMPAIGN, Champaign Co.

FLYNN, PALMER & TAGUE (AV)

402 West Church Street, P.O. Box 1517, 61824-1517
Telephone: 217-352-5181
Telecopier: 217-352-7964

MEMBERS OF FIRM

Leonard T. Flynn Charles L. Palmer
Michael J. Tague

ASSOCIATES

John B. Alsterda Richard P. Klaus

Representative Clients: Bituminous Insurance Co.; Home Insurance Co.; Standard Mutual Insurance Co.; Universal Underwriters Co.; BankChampaign N.A.; Champaign National Bank; Champion Federal Savings and Loan; First Federal Savings and Loan of Champaign; Champaign Asphalt Co.; Champaign Board of Education.

For full biographical listings, see the Martindale-Hubbell Law Directory

MEYER, CAPEL, HIRSCHFELD, MUNCY, JAHN & ALDEEN, P.C. (AV)

306 West Church Street, P.O. Box 6750, 61826-6750
Telephone: 217-352-1800
Telecopier: 217-352-1083
Urbana, Illinois Office: 300 West Main Street.
Telephone: 217-328-5520.

James L. Capel, Jr. (1933-1991) David B. Sholem
John C. Hirschfeld Mark D. Lipton
Dennis K. Muncy Tracy J. Nugent
Francis J. Jahn Richard T. West
Donald R. Aldeen Rusty W. Freeland
John H. Elder Glenna J. Weith
Holly W. Jordan

(See Next Column)

Lorna K. Geiler James M. Mullady
Patrick T. Fitzgerald Todd J. Black
Wendy Shields Bauer Mark P. Miller
Neil R. Rafferty Paul J. Fina
Joseph Dwyer Murphy

OF COUNSEL

August C. Meyer, Jr.

Representative Clients: Bank of Illinois in Champaign; Bell Foods, Inc.; Champaign News-Gazette; Christie Clinic; Federal Deposit Insurance Corp.; Illini Cablevision, Inc.; Kuck & Associates, Inc.; Covenant Medical Center of Champaign-Urbana; Midwest Television, Inc.; Parkland College.

For full biographical listings, see the Martindale-Hubbell Law Directory

RENO, O'BYRNE & KEPLEY, P.C. (AV)

501 West Church Street, P.O. Box 800, 61824-0800
Telephone: 217-352-7661
Telecopier: 217-352-2169

Donald M. Reno (1906-1987) Edward H. Rawles
J. Michael O'Byrne Stephen M. O'Byrne
Vance I. Kepley (Retired) Glenn A. Stanko
Brett A. Kepley

Kathleen V. Riccio Timothy S. Jefferson

Local Counsel for: Great Central Insurance Co.; Employers of Wausau; Pekin Insurance Group; Connecticut General Life Insurance Co.; University of Illinois; Union Insurance Group; Maryland Casualty Co.; Covenant Medical Center.
Labor Counsel for: Kerasotes Theatres, Inc.
General Counsel for: Gibson Community Hospital.

For full biographical listings, see the Martindale-Hubbell Law Directory

THOMAS, MAMER & HAUGHEY (AV)

Fifth Floor, First of America Bank Building, 30 Main Street, 61820-3629
Telephone: 217-351-1500
Telecopier: 217-355-0087
Mailing Address: P.O. Box 560, Champaign, Illinois, 61824-0560

James G. Thomas (1901-1990)

MEMBERS OF FIRM

Stuart M. Mamer Craig J. Causeman
Roger E. Haughey Michael R. Cornyn
Lott H. Thomas Richard R. Harden
William J. Brinkmann Robert A. Hoffman
Howard W. Small Dan M. Slack
David A. Bailie David E. Krchak
Bruce E. Warren

ASSOCIATES

Linda L. Laugges John M. Sturmanis

Representative Clients: First of America Bank-Champaign County, N.A.; Board of Trustees of the University of Illinois; American Savings Bank; Illinois Provident Trust; Prudential Insurance Company of America; Thompson Lumber Co.; The Carle Foundation; The Carle Foundation Hospital; Aetna Life and Casualty Co.; St. Paul Insurance Co.

For full biographical listings, see the Martindale-Hubbell Law Directory

*CHARLESTON,** Coles Co.

BRAINARD, BOWER & KRAMER (AV)

Brainard Building, 600 Jackson Avenue, 61920
Telephone: 217-345-3929
Fax: 217-345-6501
Casey, Illinois Office: 14 North Central, Suite 211. 62420.
Telephone: 217-932-5885.
Fax: 217-932-5889.

MEMBERS OF FIRM

H. Ogden Brainard (1905-1992) James M. Grant
J. Leeds Bower William A. Sunderman
Henry E. Kramer Brian L. Bower
William J. Warmoth Kristin L. Wilson

Representative Clients: Boatmen's National Bank of Charleston; Champion Federal Savings and Loan Assn.; Community Bank & Trust (S.B.); Casey National Bank; Charleston Community Unit School District No. 1; ITT Hartford Insurance Co.; Servistar Corp.; The Country Cos.; Aetna Casualty and Surety Co.; Sarah Bush Lincoln Health Center.

For full biographical listings, see the Martindale-Hubbell Law Directory

Charleston—Continued

RYAN, BENNETT & RADLOFF

(See Mattoon)

CHICAGO, Cook Co.*

ALTHEIMER & GRAY (AV)

Suite 4000, 10 South Wacker Drive, 60606
Telephone: 312-715-4000
Fax: 312-715-4800
Telex: RCA 297102 A G UR
Warsaw, Poland Office: ul. Nowogrodzka 50, 00-950 Warsaw.
Telephones: 011-48-39-12-1338; 22-298-357.
Fax: 011-48-2-628-3640.
Telex: 867 817079.
Prague, Czech Republic Office: Platnerska 4, 110 00 Prague 1.
Telephone: 42-2 2481-2782.
Fax: 42-2 2481-0125.
Kiev, Ukraine Office: Kontraktova Ploscha 4, Building 3, Room 304, 254145 Kiev.
Telephone: 7-044-230-2534, Within Kiev: 416-6073.
Fax: 7-044-230-2535.
Bratislava, Slovakia Office: Nam. SNP 15, 81000 Bratislava.
Telephone: 011-42-7-362-736.
Fax: 011-42-7-367-960.
Istanbul, Turkey Office: Tesvikiye Cad. 107, Tesvikiye Palas 7, Tesvikiye 80200 Istanbul, Turkey.
Telephone: 011-90-212-227-6750.
Fax: 011-90-212-227-6759.

Marlene R. Abrams
Alan J. Altheimer
Robert I. Berger
Myles D. (Mush) Berman
Paul P. Biebel, Jr.
Bruce A. Bonjour
Robert P. Bramnik
John J. Buttita
James E. Carroll
Melanie Rovner Cohen
Alexandra R. Cole
George I. Cowell
Kenneth M. Crane
James R. Cruger
Susan J. Daley
Paul M. Daugerdas
Jeffrey P. De Jong
Stephen M. Dorfman
David L. Fargo
Faye B. Feinstein
Robert Feldgreber
David S. Finch
Thomas P. Fitzgerald
Howard Friedman
Kenneth R. Gaines
Françoise Gilbert
Donald A. Gillies
Norman M. Gold
Louis B. Goldman
Phillip Gordon
James S. Gray
Milton H. Gray
Lionel G. Gross
Martha Mahan Haines
Roger B. Harris
Howard M. Helsinger
Richard A. Hinden
Robert M. Horwitch
Peter M. Howard (Not admitted in IL)
Bruce K. Huvard
Robert A. Janoski
Jaroslawa Zelinsky Johnson
David V. Kahn
Robert M. Kalec
Nancy L. Kasko
Mark Thomas Kindelin
George Kovac
Jeffrey T. Kraus
Steve Lawrence
Myron Lieberman
Corey E. Light
Melvin K. Lippe
Theodore J. Low
John E. Lowe
Brian S. Maher
Jeremy D. Margolis
F. John McGinnis
John W. Morrison
Barry B. Nekritz
S. Michael Peck
Steven R. Peltin
Daniel M. Pierce
Anita J. Ponder
John F. Prusiecki
David C. Roston
Robert J. Rubin
Terry M. Schlade
Robert L. Schlossberg
David W. Schoenberg
Benjamin D. Schwartz
Audrey E. Selin
Kenneth C. Shepro
Jeffrey Norman Smith
Judy Ludwig Smith
Gary L. Specks
John C. Stiefel
Sherwin J. Stone
Jeffrey S. Torf
Donald S. Weiss
Edward E. Wicks
Mindy L. Wolin
Donna M. Zak

RETIRED PARTNERS

Jacob Logan Fox
Samuel T. Lawton, Jr.
Joseph J. Strasburger

ASSOCIATES

Cathleen Hainer Albrecht
Rita M. Alliss
Michael H. Altman
Miriam S. Barasch
Anthony Bergamino, Jr.
Sean W. Bezark
Laurence R. Bronska
Peter J. Butler
Curtis R. Calvert
Richard M. Carbonara
Benjamin L. Chu
Rita E. DeBoer
Mary Beth De Bord
Laurence B. Dobkin
Ted A. Donner
Michael M. Eidelman
William S. Ettelson
Bradley M. Falk
Barry Fischer
Daniel Harrison Fogel
Marjorie Kean Fradin
Ania M. Frankowska
Steven A. Gibson
Judith A. Gold
Keith A. Goldberg
Kendy M. Hess
Judson Cary Hite
Bradley W. Johnson
Patricia E. Kaplan
Renee F. Kessel
David S. Klevatt
David H. Latham

(See Next Column)

ASSOCIATES (Continued)

Lori A. Lenard
Peter H. Lieberman
C. Vincent Maloney
Daniel G.M. Marre
Bradley J. Martin
Erwin Mayer
Jane B. McCullough
Andrew W. McCune
Kenneth A. Mckee
Robert J. Mendes
Paul K. Morton
Wm. Keith Myatt
Frank Natanek
Peter A. O'Brien
Carolyn N. Offenbach
Lisa A. Ronga
Alec Rubenstein
Mark J. Rubin
Lisa I. Sandlow
Valerie Schultz
Joshua E. Silverglade
Emily Claire Solberg
Julie A. Swanson
James K. Thurston
Angelo F. Tiesi
Charles A. Valente
Phyllis L. Volk
Anthony L. Wanger
Darren B. Watts
Victoria L. Wendling
Roger Wilen
Deborah L. Zaccarine

COUNSEL

Charles F. Adler, Jr.
Scott A. Bremer
Jules Dashow
F. Alison Dodds
Perry Goldberg
Allen Grossman, Inc., (A Professional Corporation)
Thomas N. Harding
David J. Lester
Alan H. Pollack
Richard A. Prince
Don H. Reuben
Jack M. Siegel
Granvil I. Specks

RETIRED OF COUNSEL

Lester Reinwald

For full biographical listings, see the Martindale-Hubbell Law Directory

ARONBERG GOLDGEHN DAVIS & GARMISA (AV)

Suite 3000 One IBM Plaza, 60611-3633
Telephone: 312-828-9600
Telecopier: 312-828-9635

MEMBERS OF FIRM

Ronald J. Aronberg
Mitchell S. Goldgehn
Steven P. Davis
William J. Garmisa
James S. Jarvis
Melvin A. Blum
Robert N. Sodikoff
Andrew S. Williams
Ned S. Robertson
Nathan H. Lichtenstein
James A. Smith
William W. Yotis III
Gene H. Hansen
Deborah G. Cole

OF COUNSEL

Charles E. Zeitlin

ASSOCIATES

Christopher J. Bannon
Lisa J. Brodsky
James J. Hickey
Eric D. Kaplan
Cynthia B. Lafuente
Carol A. Martin
Marc W. O'Brien
John M. Riccione
David H. Sachs
William J. Serritella, Jr.
William C. Wilder

For full biographical listings, see the Martindale-Hubbell Law Directory

BAKER & MCKENZIE (AV)

One Prudential Plaza, 130 East Randolph Drive, 60601
Telephone: (312) 861-8000
Intn'l. Dialing: (1-312) 861-8000
Cable Address: ABOGADO
Telex: 254425; 206010
Answer Back: ABOGADO CGO; BAKER CGO
Intn'l. Only: 82789; 82790
Answer Back: 82789 ABOGAUI; 82790 ABOGAUI
Facsimiles: (1-312) 861-2898; 861-2899; 861-2900; 861-8080 (Operator)
Associated Offices of Baker & McKenzie in: Amsterdam, Bangkok, Barcelona, Beijing, Berlin, Bogotá, Brasília, Brussels, Budapest, Buenos Aires, Cairo, Caracas, Chicago, Dallas, Frankfurt, Geneva, Guangzhou, Hanoi, Ho Chi Minh City, Hong Kong, Juárez, Kiev, London, Madrid, Manila, Melbourne, México City, Miami, Milan, Monterrey, Moscow, New York, Palo Alto, Paris, Prague, Rio de Janeiro, Riyadh, Rome, St. Petersburg, San Diego, San Francisco, São Paulo, Singapore, Stockholm, Sydney, Taipei, Tijuana, Tokyo, Toronto, Valencia, Warsaw, Washington, D.C. and Zürich.
Affiliated Organizations in: Guangzhou and Shanghai.
Correspondent Law Firm: Hadiputranto, Hadinoto & Partners, Jakarta.

MEMBERS OF FIRM

Robert H. Aland
Peter Almeroth
Russell Baker (1901-1979)
James G. Barnes
Norman J. Barry, Jr.
Ingrid L. Beall
Jack D. Beem
Peter J. H. Bentley
Robert L. Berner, Jr.
Leslie A. Bertagnolli
Neal J. Block
Andrew J. Boling
Thomas F. Bridgman
Donald J. Brown, Jr.
John T. Coleman
Michael L. Coleman
John J. Conroy, Jr.
Robert J. Cunningham
Robert E. Deignan
Robert H. Dilworth
John W. Dondanville
Richard H. Donohue
Thomas A. Doyle
Edwin R. Dunn
David W. Ellis
John C. Filosa

(See Next Column)

BAKER & MCKENZIE, *Chicago—Continued*

MEMBERS OF FIRM (Continued)

Richard B. Foster, III
Richard M. Franklin
Gary W. Fresen
Robert J. Gareis
Michael J. Garvey
David P. Hackett
Thomas M. Haderlein
Lafayette G. Harter, III
Donald J. Hayden
Frederick E. Henry
J. Patrick Herald
James T. Hitch, III
Douglas Hoffman
Akira Ito
Jerome W. Jakubik
Thomas E. Johnson
Sidney M. Kaplan
Mark L. Karasik
Neal A. Klegerman
John A. Krivicich
Karen A. Kuenster
Eric M. Lasry
Gregg D. Lemein
Charles B. Lewis
William Joseph Linklater
Gerald L. Maatman, Jr.
J. Kent Mathewson
Sebastiao de Souza Mattos Neto
Maura Ann McBreen
Paul McCarthy
William S. McDowell, Jr.
John C. McKenzie (1913-1962)
Michael S. Mensik
Marcel J. Molins
Peter J. Mone
Francis D. Morrissey
John E. Morrow
Thomas R. Nelson
James M. O'Brien
Daniel J. O'Connor
Paul B. O'Flaherty, Jr.
Michael A. Pollard
Peter B. Powles
John T. Rank
William Lynch Schaller
Premjit Singh
Paul D. Slocomb
Robert W. Smyth, Jr.
Barbara C. Spudis
James G. Staples
Howard L. Stovall
Thomas W. Studwell
Philip F. Suse
Preston M. Torbert
Michael J. Wagner
Friedrich J. Weinkopf
Philip J. Zadeik
Edward J. Zulkey

LOCAL PARTNERS

Stephen R. Ayres
Patrick T. Navin
Mark A. Oates
Michael P. O'Brien
Kevin C. Parks
David I. Roche
Dieter A. Schmitz
Jia Zhao

SENIOR COUNSEL

David S. Ruder

ASSOCIATES

Regina F. Atkins
Gerald K. Bolkema
Mark H. Boyle
Barrie L. Brejcha
Lisa Sopata Brogan
Mark M. Burden
Adriane W. Burkland
Martin R. Castro
Peter K.M. Chan
Thomas W. Cushing
Moira Ann Dages
David J. Davis
Karen Kies DeGrand
B. Scott Douglass
Adolfo Durañona (Not admitted in United States)
Hillary A. Ebach
Amr A. El Bayoumi
Cristina M. Ladeira Ferreira
Tamara L. Frantzen
Pablo A. Garcia-Moreno
Sebastian Gronstedt (Not admitted United States)
Maria G. Gutierrez
Lawrence F. Haas
Michael R. Hull
Yoong-Neung Kee
Elizabeth E. Lewis
Todd O. Maiden (Not admitted in IL)
Victor M. Marroquin
John D. Martin
John R. McElyea
John M. McGarry
Elizabeth A. Mitchell
Michael L. Morkin
John M. Murphy
David A. Nelson
Glenn W. Newman
Francisco Miguel Noyola
Jeffrey M. O'Donnell
Joan O'Reilly Oh
Jennifer O'Hearne
Ronald L. Ohren
Vincent S. Oleszkiewicz
Nam H. Paik
Oren S. Penn
Michael T. Pfau
Joseph J. Quigley
Ines K. Radmilovic
Taylor S. Reid
Joan M. Richman
Amalia S. Rioja
Brian C. Shea
William M. Sneed
Anthony G. Stamato
Betsy Logan Stelle
James Lee Stetson
L. Michael Tarpey
Yuri A. Timokhov (Not admitted United States)
William E. Vaughan
Thomas J. Vega-Byrnes
Lorrie A. Vick
David A. Waimon
Donna Jordan Williams
Jonathan M. Wilson (Not admitted in United States)
Richard M. Wolfson

For full biographical listings, see the Martindale-Hubbell Law Directory

BELL, BOYD & LLOYD (AV)

Three First National Plaza Suite 3300, 70 West Madison Street, 60602
Telephone: 312-372-1121
FAX: 312-372-2098
Washington, D.C. Office: 1615 L Street, N.W.
Telephone: 202-466-6300.
FAX: 202-463-0678.

MEMBERS OF FIRM

Jeffrey B. Aaronson
Michael J. Abernathy
Gregory R. Andre
Cameron S. Avery
D. Daniel Barr
William L. Barr, Jr.
Paul M. Bauch
Nancy E. Bertoglio
Robert J. Best
John H. Bitner
Jeffrey A. Blevins
John C. Blew

(See Next Column)

MEMBERS OF FIRM (Continued)

William G. Brown
Terrence E. Budny
William R. Carney
James W. Collins
Randy J. Curato
James P. Daley
Lee A. Daniels
William F. Dolan
Raymond H. Drymalski
Steven E. Ducommun
Lawrence C. Eppley
Nicholas J. Etten
Sanford R. Gail
Stanley J. Garber
Lawrence M. Gavin
Durward J. (James) Gehring
Joseph V. Giffin
Victor E. Grimm
D. Scott Hargadon
Warren C. Haskin (Managing Partner)
Thomas Z. Hayward, Jr.
Frank K. Heap
James P. Hemmer
Francis J. Higgins
Thomas C. Homburger
Robert T. Johnson, Jr.
Thomas F. Joyce
Ellen S. Kornichuk
Jeffrey R. Ladd
Daniel Lawler
Alice S. Lonoff
Lawrence M. Mages
Patrick J. Maloney
Brian E. Martin
John T. McCarthy
Brigid M. McGrath
Scott M. Mendel
Rebecca C. Meriwether
Paul T. Metzger
John P. Morrison
John P. (Pete) Morrison
Thomas J. Murphy
John R. Myers
David M. Novak
Michael K. Ohm
Janet D. Olsen
Stephen J. O'Neil
Matthew K. Phillips
William S. Price
Kenneth E. Rechtoris
James A. Romanyak
John W. Rotunno
Peter G. Rush
David M. Saltiel
Gregory J. Schroedter
John P. Scotellaro
Michael Sennett
Alan M. Serwer
Richard L. Sevcik
Robert V. Shannon
Thomas C. Shields
Paul A. Strasen
Edwin C. Thomas, III
Larry L. Thompson
Anita Medina Tyson
John J. Verscaj
John Craig Walker
Neal H. Weinfield
Robert L. Wiesenthal

OF COUNSEL

Stanton H. Berlin
Alan R. Brodie
Richard L. Curry
R. James Gormley
William N. Haddad
William B. Hanley
Rollin C. Huggins, Jr.
John T. Loughlin
Charles T. Martin
James T. Rhind
Keith D. Schulz
Allen R. Smart
Daniel P. Ward
Jack M. Whitney, II
John C. York
Laird Bell (1910-1965)
Darrell S. Boyd (1919-1971)
Glen A. Lloyd (1931-1975)
William G. Burns (1907-1988)
J. William Hayton (1926-1994)

ASSOCIATES

Andrew R. Andreasik
Mark D. Bauer (Not admitted in IL)
W. Thomas Bergerson
Lynne Therese Boehringer
Michelle D, Bowers
Robert Raymond Brown
Timothy R.M. Bryant
J. David Brymesser
G. Nicholas Bullat
Thomas R. Carey
Douglas M. Chalmers
Michael Chimitris
David D. Cleary
Micaela M. Daly
Kathryn A. Finn
Marc D. Fisher (Not admitted in IL)
Brian P. Gallagher
Carol A. Genis
Joanne L. Hyman
Kathryn D. Ingraham
Sarah K. Johnson
Faye L. Katt
Maureen Ward Kirby
Josh M. Leavitt
Cindy S. Mangiaforte
Kevin J. McCarthy
D. Mark McMillan
Kathleen M. Meyers-Grabemann
Nanette M. Norton
Amy L. Ostrander
Randall L. Oyler
Matthew A. Phillips
Amy S. Powers
Ari J. Rosenthal
Julie M. Rubins
Stuart A. Shanus
Melissa Anne Siebert
Woon-Wah Siu
Dawn M. Slamecka
James P. Tutaj
Stephen H. Wenc
Stacy H. Winick
Melanie L. Witt

For full biographical listings, see the Martindale-Hubbell Law Directory

BOWLES, KEATING, HERING & LOWE, CHARTERED (AV)

135 South La Salle Street, Suite 1040, 60603-4295
Telephone: 312-263-6300
Fax: 312-263-0415
Italy Office: 10, Via Pietro Verri, 20121 Milan, Italy.
Telephone: 2-798609.
Fax: 276001473.
European Associated Offices:
Italy Office: Studio Legale Ippolito, viale Astichello, 6, 36100 Vicenza, Italy.
Telephone: 444-300957.
Fax: 444-300827..
Sweden Office: Advokatgruppen i Stockholm AB, Kommendorsgatan 26,114 48 Stockholm, Sweden.
Telephone: 8-667-0765.
Fax: 8-660-9827.

(See Next Column)

BOWLES, KEATING, HERING & LOWE CHARTERED—*Continued*

France Office: Allain - Kaltenbach - Plaisant - Raimon, 14 Rue Lejemptel, 94302 Vincennes (Paris), France.
Telephone: 1-4374 7494.
Fax: 1-4374 3222.
Asian Cooperative Offices:
China Offices: Liaoning Law Office For Foreign Affairs, 11 Liaohe Street, Shenyang Liaoning 110032, China.
Telephone: 652125.
Telex: 808305 LCPIT CN.
FAX: (24) 664791. Dalian Foreign Economic Law Office: No. 2 S. Square, Dalian, Liaoning, China.
Telephone: 332532.
FAX: 332532. Shenyang Foreign Economic Law Office, 230-3, Quingnian Street, Shenhe District, Shenyang Liaoning 110014, China.
Telephone: 290123.

Clyde O. Bowles, Jr. (Chicago Office)
Mario Bruno
Roberto N. Bruno
Nicola Fiordalisi (Chicago Office)
Glenn Z. Hering (Chicago Office)
Kathryn R. Ingrim (Chicago Office)
Christopher L. Ingrim (Chicago Office)
Thomas M. Keating (Chicago Office)
Jung Y. Lowe (Chicago Office)
Lynne R. Ostfeld (Chicago Office)
Arnold A. Silvestri (Chicago Office)

COUNSEL

Malcolm A. Chandler (Chicago Office)

For full biographical listings, see the Martindale-Hubbell Law Directory

CASSIDAY, SCHADE & GLOOR (AV)

Suite 1200, 333 West Wacker Drive, 60606-1289
Telephone: 312-641-3100
Waukegan, Illinois Office: 415 Washington Street.
Telephone: 708-249-0700.
Wheaton, Illinois Office: 128-B South County Farm Road.
Telephone: 708-682-9800.

MEMBERS OF FIRM

Timothy J. Ashe
Richard A. Barrett, Jr. (Resident Partner, Wheaton, Illinois Office)
Peter G. Bell
Marc F. Benjoya (Resident Partner, Waukegan, Illinois Office)
Thomas P. Boylan
Robert S. Burtker
Joseph A. Camarra
John D. Cassiday
Susan E. Seiwert Conner
Michael J. Cucco
John R. Davis (Resident Partner, Waukegan, Illinois Office)
Mary K. Finley
James A. Foster
William J. Furey
Joseph A. Giannelli
D. Patterson Gloor
Jean M. Golden
Michael J. Hennig
Richard C. Huettel
David A. Johnson
James W. Kopriva
Michael J. Morrissey
Martha A. Pagliari
Bradford D. Roth
Rudolf G. Schade, Jr.
Gregory E. Schiller
John N. Seibel
A. Jeffrey Seidman
Brian C. Sundheim
Julie A. Teuscher
Bruce M. Wall

ASSOCIATES

James D. Ahern
Simone R. Asmussen
Mark M. Brennan
Denise G. Brodsky (Resident, Waukegan, Illinois Office)
Michael T. Burnett
Lew J. Campione
Scott R. Ellefsen (Resident, Wheaton, Illinois Office)
Philip J. Fowler
Catherine L. Garvey
Corey H. Grauer (Resident, Waukegan, Illinois Office)
John D. Hackett
Vanessa Walker Hampton
Brian J. Hickey
Patricia J. Hogan
Evan Hughes
Jennifer Ann Keller
Michael S. Komoll
Andrew J. Kovarik
Stuart P. Krauskopf
Sandra E. Kupelian
Beth A. Landau
Morgan A. Milne
Constance R. O'Neill
Richard A. Paulus
Brian Poust
Anne R. Rempe
Kimberly L. Robinson
Jeffrey R. Sandler
Amy F. Schwemer
Therese S. Seeley (Resident, Wheaton, Illinois Office)
Michael Murphy Tannen
David C. Van Dyke
James L. Wilkinson
James C. Zacharski
Sally Jo Zimmerman

Representative Clients: Amerisure, Bituminous Insurance Co.; Chubb Insurance Group; Fireman's Fund; IIT Hartford Insurance Group; Illinois State Medical Insurance Co.; Prudential Insurance Co.; St. Paul Insurance Co.; U.S. Fidelity & Guaranty Insurance; University of Chicago.

For full biographical listings, see the Martindale-Hubbell Law Directory

CHAPMAN AND CUTLER (AV)

111 West Monroe Street, 60603
Telephone: 312-845-3000
TWX: 910-221-2103
Fax: 312-701-2361
Salt Lake City, Utah Office: Suite 800, Key Bank Tower, 50 South Main Street.
Telephone: 801-533-0066.
Fax: 801-533-9595.
Phoenix, Arizona Office: Suite 1100, One Renaissance Square, 2 North Central Avenue.
Telephone: 602-256-4060.
Fax: 602-256-4099.

Ann Acker
Robert D. Aicher
Vincent M. Aquilino
Leah F. Arner
David T. B. Audley
Daniel J. Bacastow
Andrea G. Bacon
Michael P. Barrett
David S. Barritt
Walter P. Begley
Jeffrey D. Berry
Wendy C. Binder
Daniel C. Bird, Jr.
Deborah Thomas Boye
Lee A. Boye
James M. Breen
Edwin S. Brown
Jeffrey A. Burger
James C. Burr (Not admitted in IL; Resident, Salt Lake City Office)
George D. Buzard, III
Theodore S. Chapman (1877-1943)
David J. Cholst
Debra S. Clark
Steven L. Clark
Lynn Leland Coe
Rafael L. Cook
William E. Corbin, Jr.
Richard A. Cosgrove
David S. Crossett
Patricia M. Curtner
Henry E. Cutler (1879-1959)
Robert P. Davis
John M. Dixon
Larry Elkins
Eric F. Fess
J. Richard Fisher, Jr.
C. Robert Foltz
Michael W. Ford
Steven G. Frost
M. David Galainena
Michael J. Gamsky
Lynda K. Given
Richard H. Goss
Wendy A. Grossman
John F. Halbleib
Thomas W. Heenan
Samuel J. Henry
F. B. Hubachek, Jr.
Charles S. Hughes
Howard H. Hush, Jr.
William S. Jardine
Charles L. Jarik
James E. Jenz
Daniel L. Johnson
Charles A. Kelly
Richard F. Klein
Mark J. Kneedy
Jonathan A Koff
Paul C. Kosin
David M. Kozak
Daniel J. Kucera
Harry P. Lamberson
Darrell R. Larsen, Jr. (Not admitted in IL; Resident, Salt Lake City Office)
Edward L. Lembitz, Jr.
Matthew R. Lewin
Robert V. Lewis
William M. Libit
Frederick V. Lochbihler
Robert E. Lockner
James E. Luebchow
Paul R. Madden (Resident, Phoenix Office)
Elizabeth L. Majers
Richard A. Makarski
Neil R. Mann
Michael G. McGee
Timothy V. McGree
Terry A. McIlroy
Michael J. Mitchell
Timothy P. Mohan
Thomas J. Morgan
Robert C. Nash
James P. O'Brien
Terence T. O'Meara
Robert W. Ollis, Jr.
John S. Overdorff (Resident, Phoenix Office)
S. Louise Rankin
James R. Richardson
Ronald E. Rokosz
Aron H. Routman
Richard J. Scott (Resident, Salt Lake City Office)
Steven B. Silverman
William P. Smith
Edward V. Sommer
James E. Spiotto
Stephen F. Stroh
George Penman Sullivan, Jr.
Harold C. Sutter
William M. Taylor
James R. Theiss, Jr.
Kenneth R. M. Thompson
M. John Trofa
John L. Tuohy
Kenneth J. Vaughan
Terrence M. Walsh
John A. Ward
John R. Weiss
David G. Williams
Steven N. Wohl
Richard A. Wohlleber
Steven N. Zaris

Bruce D. Agin
Scott R. Anderson
Steven G. Anderson
Dana Simaitis Armagno
Anthony J. Ashley
Shelley J. Bacastow
Robert M. Baratta, Jr.
Erin P. Bartholomy
Brian A. Bates
José J. Behar
Michael T. Benz
John F. Bibby, Jr.
Stephen R. Boatwright (Resident, Phoenix Office)
Matthew C. Boba
James M. Broeking
Nancy A. Burke
Gregory J. Bynan
William A. Callison
Rosanne Ciambrone
Peter A. Clark
Steven D. Conlon
William R. DeHaan (Resident, Phoenix Office)
Jennifer L. Dressler
Anne Marie Duffy
Lisa M. Engel
Daniel J. Favero
William J. Fellerhoff
Jennifer L. Figler
Marc P. Franson
Brian D. Free
Peter R. Freund
Andre Gamble
Stephen E. Garcia
John E. Garda
Colleen A. Gartland
Jeremy A. Gibson
Basil V. Godellas

(See Next Column)

CHAPMAN AND CUTLER, *Chicago—Continued*

Tara Ann Goff (Not admitted in IL)
Jamie Lou Goldman
Paul K. Haberkamp
Ronald J. Hacker
Steven G. Hastings
John C. Hitt, Jr.
Raymond J. Horn, III
R. William Hunter
Kristine M. Johnson
Marie I. Jordan
Bryan T. D. Jung
Kevin P. Kalinich
Karla L. Kambic
Alan L. Kennard
Barbara C. Klabacha
William M. Kochlefl (Not admitted in IL)
Scott A. Kolar
Kelly K. Kost
Paul J. Kunkel
E. Anthony Lauerman III
Bridget Logterman
Paul E. Lubanski
David A. Lullo
Sean T. Maloney
Carol McAlpine
David B. McMullen
John P. Mundo
Charles W. Nauts
James R. Nelson
Kyle E. Nenninger
Michele Niermann
Kathleen L. Nooney
Ger P. O'Donnell
Brian J. O'Neil
Mary M. Oates
Keith F. Oberkfell
Lisa A. Olsen
Stathy Panopoulos
Michael M. Parham
Thomas G. Park
Kathleen R. Pasulka
Karen E. Patrick
Bradley D. Patterson (Resident, Salt Lake City Office)
Gordon P. Paulson
Edward J. Pelican
Kenneth A. Peterson, Jr.
Stacy K. Pike
Debra Ann Piscitelli
Gary R. Polega
Janet E. Raycraft
Dianne E. Rist
Lisa A. Roatch
Eric M. Roberson
Donald B. Rohbock (Not admitted in IL; Resident, Salt Lake City Office)
Susan E. Rollins
Heather Ross
Anthony R. Rosso
Suzanne M. Russell
W. Michael Ryan
Cynthia A. Rybak
Grace L. Shaff
Bansari M. Shah
Susan Shallenberger
Colleen Shaughnessy
Elizabeth C. Sheil
Todd N. Sheldon
Alizon J. Shuldiner
Laura P. Sorensen
Jonathan L. Stein
Robert D. Stephan
Mark A. Sternberg
David J. Stevens (Resident, Salt Lake City Office)
Elizabeth D. Swanson
Sanjay T. Tailor
Ross D. Taylor
Tedd T. Termunde
Richard K. Tomei
Deanne M. Tomse
Franklin H. Top III
Christopher J. Townsend
Robert G. Tucker
Mary E. Tuuk
George F. Venci, Jr.
Linn M. Visscher
Christopher F. Walrath
Rodney G. Wendt (Not admitted in IL; Resident, Salt Lake City Office)
Karl T. Williams
Pamela Cocalas Wirt
Anthony D. Yager
David H. Zielke

OF COUNSEL

Peter V. Fazio

For full biographical listings, see the Martindale-Hubbell Law Directory

---

CLAUSEN MILLER GORMAN CAFFREY & WITOUS, P.C. (AV)

10 South La Salle Street, 60603-1098
Telephone: 312-855-1010
Telecopier: 312-606-7777
Telex: 27-0647
Wheaton, Illinois Office: 2100 Manchester Road, P.O. Box 1265.
Telephone: 708-668-9100.
Telecopier: 708-668-9169.
European Affiliated Law Firm: Dutaret La Giraudière Larroze, 58, Rue de Monceau, 75008 Paris, France.
Telephone: 33.1.44.95.25.25.
Telecopier: 33.1.44.95.25.00.
Telex: 649 622 F
and: Avenue des Arts, 53, 1040 Brussels, Belgium.
Telephone: 32.2.511.44.66.
Telecopier: 32.2.514.56.62.
New York, N.Y. Office: 100 Maiden Lane.
Telephone: 212-504-6020.
Telecopier: 212-504-6015.
Newark, New Jersey Office: 1 Gateway Center, Suite 2600, 07102-5396.
Telephone: 201-645-0564.
Troy, Michigan Office: 3155 West Beaver Road, 48084-3007.
Telephone: 313-816-0500.

John P. Gorman (1912-1980)
John R. Caffrey (1923-1980)
Donald N. Clausen (1899-1985)
Norman A. Miller (1906-1989)
Patrick J. Navin (1930-1993)
John J. Witous (Retired)
Craig M. Antas
Jeffrey J. Asperger
Ivar R. Azeris
James S. Barber
Diane M. Baron
John F. Brennan
Richard A. Buchanan
Kevin P. Caraher
Richard C. Clark
Michael W. Duffy (Resident, Troy, Michigan Office)
George C. Ellison
James T. Ferrini
Michael L. Foran
David R. Ganfield II
Robert E. Gilmartin III
Michael R. Grimm
John T. Groark
Fredric J. Grossman
William J. Hacker

(See Next Column)

Celeste A. Hill
James M. Hoey
Richard G. Howser
John M. Hynes
Edward M. Kay
Lisa Marco Kouba
Tyler Jay Lory
Stephen D. Marcus
Randall I. Marmor
Joyce M. Maxberry
David B. McAfee
John B. McCabe
Thomas A. McDonald
Richard L. Murphy
James O. Nolan
Frances T. Norek
Steven N. Novosad
William J. Oberts
Mary C. O'Connor
Margaret J. Orbon
Edward J. Ozog
Douglas J. Palandech
Robert L. Reifenberg
Thomas H. Ryerson (Resident, Wheaton Office)
Dominick W. Savaiano
Stephen J. Schlegel
Frank L. Schneider
Gilbert J. Schroeder
Martin C. Sener
Thomas J. Skeffington (Resident, New York, N.Y. Office)
Gregory S. Smith (Resident Principal, New York Office)
Mary F. Stafford
Richard Wm Strawbridge
James R. Swinehart
Harry L. Wilson
Kevin J. Young
Jeffrey R. Zehe
George A. Zelcs

OF COUNSEL

Charles A. Gilmartin

Nick Alexander (Resident, Wheaten Office)
Kurt D. Baer
Michael J. Baughman
Anne L. Blume
Christopher C. Botta (New York, N.Y. and Newark, New Jersey Offices)
Paul Bozych
Laura A. Caldwell
Joan S. Callan
Susan Condon
Robert N. Dunn
Paul T. Falk
Joseph T. Fernim
Dennis D. Fitzpatrick
Steven J. Fried (Resident, New York, N.Y. Office)
David N. Friedland
Ann Ferguson Frolik
Ronald F. Geimer
James B. Glennon
Mary Lu Hahn
Edward F. Hayes III (Not admitted in IL; Resident, New York, N.Y. Office)
David M. Heilmann
Harvey R. Herman
Michael L. Howley
Margaret M. Hupp
Joseph J. Janatka
Cole S. Kain
Richard M. Kaplan
Marc F. Katalinic
Kimbley A. Kearney
Christopher E. Kentra
Paul D. Kerpan
James J. Knibbs
Melinda S. Kollross
Ilene M. Korey
Richard H. Lehman
John Limotte (Resident, New York, N.Y. Office)
Fabrice Lorvo (Resident, New York, N.Y. Office)
Maura K. Lutz (Resident, Troy, Michigan Office)
John J. Malm
Dirk Marschhausen (Not admitted in IL; Resident, New York, N.Y. Office)
James P. Marsh (Resident, Wheaton Office)
Brenda Dunton McNamara
Kevin K. McQuillan
Kevin P. Mohr
Bruce N. Moss (Resident, Troy, Michigan Office)
Mary Blake Nasenbenny
Erik W. Nielsen
Sonia V. Odarczenko
Benjamin E. Patterson
Mark D. Paulson
Amy Rich Paulus
Maryann Peronti (Not admitted in IL; New York, N.Y. and Newark, New Jersey Offices)
Matthew S. Ponzi
Dean S. Rauchwerger
Paul Scott Ritchie
Charles J. Rocco (Resident, New York, N.Y. Office)
William A. Rogers
Miguel A. Ruiz
Amy C. Scalise
Mark J. Seplak
James F. Smith
Jacqueline R. Sparks
Marta A. Stein
Robert A. Stern (Not admitted in IL; Resident, New York, N.Y. Office)
Imelda R. Terrazino
Michael L. Vittori
Sava Alexander Vojcanin
Dale F. Weigand
Mark E. Wilson
Michael E. Zidek (Resident, Wheaton Office)

References: The First National Bank of Chicago; La Salle National Bank.

For full biographical listings, see the Martindale-Hubbell Law Directory

---

DALEIDEN, THOMPSON & TREMAINE, LTD. (AV)

20 North Wacker Drive, 60606
Telephone: 312-899-1044
FAX: 312-899-0878

Norbert A. Daleiden
David F. Thompson
Arthur J. Tremaine

For full biographical listings, see the Martindale-Hubbell Law Directory

DEUTSCH, LEVY & ENGEL, CHARTERED (AV)

Suite 1700, 225 West Washington Street, 60606
Telephone: 312-346-1460
Boynton, Beach Florida Office: 3C Westgate Lane.
Telephone: 407-737-6003.
Wheaton, Illinois Office: Suite B2, 620 West Roosevelt Road.
Telephone: 312-665-9112.

(See Next Column)

DEUTSCH, LEVY & ENGEL CHARTERED—*Continued*

Earl A. Deutsch	Michael J. Devine
Paul M. Levy	Barry R. Katz
Terry L. Engel	Stuart Berks
Frank R. Cohen	LaDonna M. Loitz
Marshall D. Krolick	Kenneth W. Funk
Jerry I. Rudman	Michael B. Kahane

Phillip J. Zisook	Jomarie B. Fredericks
David I. Addis	Stephen A. Viz
Michael J. Antonello	Thomas W. Goedert

Martin P. Ryan

COUNSEL

Edward M. Burke	Irwin Panter

For full biographical listings, see the Martindale-Hubbell Law Directory

DICKINSON, WRIGHT, MOON, VAN DUSEN & FREEMAN (AV)

225 West Washington, Suite 400, 60606-3418
Telephone: 312-220-0300
Facsimile: 312-220-0021
Detroit, Michigan Office: 500 Woodward Avenue, Suite 4000.
Telephone: 313-223-3500.
Facsimile: 313-223-3598.
Bloomfield Hills, Michigan Office: 525 North Woodward Avenue, Suite 2000.
Telephone: 810-433-7200.
Facsimile: 810-433-7274.
Grand Rapids, Michigan Office: 200 Ottawa Avenue, N.W., Suite 900.
Telephone: 616-458-1300.
Facsimile: 616-458-6753.
Lansing, Michigan Office: Suite 200, 215 South Washington Square.
Telephone: 517-371-1730.
Facsimile: 517-371-2939.
Washington, D.C. Office: Suite 800, 1901 L Street, N.W.
Telephone: 202-659-1559.
Facsimile: 02-659-1559.
Warsaw, Poland Office: 46 Wilcza Street, 4th Floor, 00-679.
Telephone: (48-22) 299-241.
Facsimile: (48-2) 628-4107. Komertel Satellite Phone: (48-39) 121-510.

RESIDENT PARTNERS

Robert E. Neiman	Martin L. Greenberg
Robert P. Hurlbert	Stephen S. Herseth
Ronald B. Grais	Daniel F. Gosch
James M. Tervo	Thea D. Dunmire

RESIDENT OF COUNSEL

Steven V. Napolitano	Allan G. Sweig

RESIDENT ASSOCIATES

Randi S. Lipin	Creighton R. Meland, Jr.
Sean D. Major	Daniel James Sheridan
Richard R. McGill, Jr.	Louis Theros

Representative Clients: American Yazaki Corp.; Ameritech International; Ameritech Publishing Inc.; Arthur Andersen & Co.; Ashland Petroleum Co.; Automobile Club of Michigan; Barden Cablevision; Baxter International, Inc.; Chrysler Corp.; Chrysler Realty Corp.

For full biographical listings, see the Martindale-Hubbell Law Directory

FOLEY & LARDNER (AV)

Suite 3300, One IBM Plaza, 330 N. Wabash Avenue, 60611-3608
Telephone: 312-755-1900
Facsimile: 312-755-1925
Milwaukee, Wisconsin Office: Firstar Center, 777 East Wisconsin Avenue.
Telephone: 414-271-2400.
Telex: 26-819 (Foley Lard Mil).
Facsimile: 414-289-3791.
Madison, Wisconsin Office: Firstar Plaza, One South Pinckney Street, P.O. Box 1497.
Telephone: 608-257-5035.
Facsimile: 608-258-4258.
Washington, D.C. Office: Washington Harbour, Suite 500, 3000 K Street, N.W.
Telephone: 202-672-5300.
Telex: 904136 (Foley Lard Wsh.).
Facsimile: 202-672-5399.
Annapolis, Maryland Office: Suite 102, 175 Admiral Cochrane Drive.
Telephone: 301-266-8077.
Telex: 899149 (Oldtownpat).
Facsimile: 301-266-8664.
Jacksonville, Florida Office: The Greenleaf Building, 200 Laura Street, P.O. Box 240.
Telephone: 904-359-2000.
Facsimile: 904-359-0319.
Orlando, Florida Office: Suite 1800, 111 North Orange Avenue, P.O. Box 2193.
Telephone: 407-423-7656.
Telex: 441781 (HQ ORL).
Facsimile: 407-648-1743.

(See Next Column)

Tallahassee, Florida Office: Suite 450, 215 South Monroe Street, P.O. Box 508.
Telephone: 904-222-6100.
Facsimile: 904-224-0496.
Tampa, Florida Offices: Suite 2700, One Hundred N. Tampa Street, P.O. Box 3391.
Telephones: 813-229-2300; Pinellas County: 813-442-3296.
Facsimile: 813-221-4210.
West Palm Beach, Florida Office: Suite 200, Phillips Point East Tower, 777 South Flagler Drive.
Telephone: 407-655-5050.
Facsimile: 407-655-6925.

PARTNERS

Wesley N. Becker	Paul G. Neilan
Suzanne S. Dawson	Michael E. Olsen
Scott E. Early	Nehad S. Othman
Patrick N. Giordano	Mark L. Prager
Joan M. Kubalanza	Randall S. Rapp
John D. Lien	Hoken S. Seki
J. Craig Long	George T. Simon
David S. Lott	Stephen M. Slavin
Edwin D. Mason	Pierre C. Talbert, Jr.
Chris J. Mollet	James A. Winkler
Gerald J. Neal	Robert J. Zimmerman

ASSOCIATES

Evelyn C. Arkebauer	Alice O. Martin
Bradley S. Block	Nancy A. Needlman
Christopher W. Brownell	Jeffery S. Norman
Bruce M. Essen	John G. Rauch
Dean M. Jeske	David T. Rusoff

Becky B. Serafini

For full biographical listings, see the Martindale-Hubbell Law Directory

HYNES JOHNSON & HEALY (AV)

180 North La Salle Street, Suite 1900, 60601
Telephone: 312-407-0200
Facsimile: 312-407-0305

MEMBERS OF FIRM

Robert E. Hynes	Barbara Johnson

Michael T. Healy

For full biographical listings, see the Martindale-Hubbell Law Directory

JONES, DAY, REAVIS & POGUE (AV)

77 West Wacker, 60601-1692
Telephone: 312-782-3939
Telecopier: 312-782-8585
In Atlanta, Georgia: 3500 One Peachtree Center, 303 Peachtree Street, N.E.
Telephone: 404-521-3939.
Cable Address: "Attorneys Atlanta".
Telex: 54-2711.
Telecopier: 404-581-8330.
In Brussels, Belgium: Avenue Louise 480, 7th Floor, B-1050 Brussels.
Telephone: 011-32-2-645-14-11.
Telecopier: 011-32-2-645-14-45.
In Cleveland, Ohio: North Point, 901 Lakeside Avenue.
Telephone: 216-586-3939.
Cable Address: "Attorneys Cleveland."
Telex: 980389.
Telecopier: 216-579-0212.
In Columbus, Ohio: 1900 Huntington Center.
Telephone: 614-469-3939.
Cable Address: "Attorneys Columbus."
Telecopier: 614-461-4198.
In Dallas, Texas: 2300 Trammell Crow Center, 2001 Ross Avenue.
Telephone: 214-220-3939.
Cable Address: "Attorneys Dallas."
Telex: 730852.
Telecopier: 214-969-5100.
In Frankfurt, Germany: Westendstrasse 41, 60325 Frankfurt am Main.
Telephone: 011-49-69-7438-3939.
Telecopier: 011-49-69-741-1686.
In Geneva, Switzerland: 20, rue de Candolle.
Telephone: 011-41-22-320-2339.
Telecopier: 011-41-22-320-1232.
In Hong Kong: 1501 One Exchange Square, 8 Connaught Place.
Telephone: 011-852-526-6895.
Telecopier: 011-852-810-5787.
In Irvine, California: 2603 Main Street, Suite 900.
Telephone: 714-851-3939.
Telex: 194911 Lawyers LSA.
Telecopier: 714-553-7539.
In London, England: One Mount Street.
Telephone: 011-44-71-493-9361.
Cable Address: "Surgoe London WI."
Telecopier: 011-44-71-493-9666.
In Los Angeles, California: 555 West Fifth Street, Suite 4600.
Telephone: 213-489-3939.
Telex: 181439 UD.
Telecopier: 213-243-2539.

(See Next Column)

JONES, DAY, REAVIS & POGUE, *Chicago—Continued*

In New York, New York: 599 Lexington Avenue.
Telephone: 212-326-3939.
Cable Address: "JONESDAY NEWYORK."
Telex: 237013 JDRP UR.
Telecopier: 212-755-7306.
In Paris, France: 62, rue du Faubourg Saint-Honore.
Telephone: 011-33-1-44-71-3939.
Cable Address: "Surgoe Paris."
Telex: 290156 Surgoe.
Telecopier: 011-33-1-49-24-0471.
In Pittsburgh, Pennsylvania: 500 Grant Street, 31st Floor.
Telephone: 412-391-3939.
Cable Address: "Attorneys Pittsburgh."
Telecopier: 412-394-7959.
In Riyadh, Saudi Arabia: Law Offices of Saud M.A. Shawwaf, P.O. Box 2700.
Telephones: 011 (966-1) 465-6543, 011 (966-1) 464-8534 or 011 (966-1) 464-8540.
Telex: 401831 SAUCON SJ.
Telecopier: (966-1) 464-8480.
In Taipei, Taiwan: 7th Floor, 2 Tun Hwa South Road, Section 2.
Telephone: 011 (886-2) 704-6808 and 704-6809.
Telecopier: 011 (886-2) 704-6791.
In Tokyo, Japan: Shiroyama JT Mori Bldg., 15th Floor, 3-1, Toranomon 4-chome, Minato-Ku.
Telephone: 011-81-3-3433-3939.
Telecopier: 011-81-3-5401-2725.
In Washington, D.C.: Metropolitan Square, 1450 G Street, N.W.
Telephone: 202-879-3939.
Cable Address: "Attorneys Washington."
Telex: 89-2410 ATTORNEYS WASH.
Telecopier: 202-737-2832.

MEMBERS OF FIRM IN CHICAGO

Robert L. Lindgren
David J. Rosso
Dan B. Miller
Ronald S. Rizzo (Not admitted in IL)
Robert A. Yolles
Ronald A. Sandler
Douglas H. Walter
Robert H. Baker
Thomas F. Gardner
William P. Ritchie
Paul W. Schroeder
John P. C. Duncan
Daniel E. Reidy
David L. Carden
Gary T. Johnson
James C. Hagy
Boyd J. Springer
Jeffrey J. Baker
David S. Kurtz
James R. Daly
Lee Ann Russo
Lester J. Savit
Michael F. Dolan
Elizabeth Clough Kitslaar
Vicki A. O'Meara
Susan Elliott
June K. Ghezzi
Cory Lipoff
Christopher W. Flynn
Robert J. Graves
Irene Savanis

OF COUNSEL

Theodore R. Scott
Clarence J. Fleming
James B. Raden
Dennis R. Homerin
Christian T. Jones
William S. McKay, Jr.
William J. Harmon
Karl B. Anderson

SENIOR ATTORNEYS

John B. Carothers III
Russell L. McIlwain

ASSOCIATES

Thomas P. McNulty
Sandra Byster Weiss
Suzanne Speyser Greene
Robert C. Lee
Kevin G. McBride
Cheryl Lynn Urbanski
James A. White
Stephanie E. Balcerzak
Nancy M. Kollar
Susan I. Matejcak
Steven M. Taibl
Charles T. Wehland
Joni L. Andrioff
Jeffrey Wiley Linstrom
Timothy J. Melton
Katherine W. Delahunt
Robert C. Micheletto
Mary Jo Quinn (Not admitted in IL)
Nancy A. Tanck
Carol A. Ahern
Ellen Davies Gregory
Julie Marie Olk
Jane K. Murphy
James C. Paschall
Kristin A. Pil
Josef S. Athanas
James C. Dunlop
Elizabeth Haber Lacy
Peter Nels Larson
Timothy R. Pohl
John J. Reidy, III
Arlene Boxerman Rosenberg
Sharyl A. Hirsh
Laurie F. Humphrey
Trisha L. Johnson
James F. Kosciolek
Eileen M. Scanlon
Tina M. Tabacchi
David J. Chorzempa
Gregory J. Henchel
Douglas I. Lewis
Sean D. Malloy
Brian L. Sedlak
Patrick T. Stanton
Michael B. Willian
Mark A. Godsey
Philip R. Strauss

For full biographical listings, see the Martindale-Hubbell Law Directory

KECK, MAHIN & CATE (AV)

A Partnership including Professional Corporations
77 West Wacker Drive Suite 4900, 60601-1693
Telephone: 312-634-7700
Cable Address: "Hamscott"
Telex: 25-3411
Fax: 312-634-5000
Washington, D.C. Office: Penthouse, 1201 New York Avenue, N.W.
Telephone: 202-789-3400.
Telecopier: 202-789-1158.
Peoria, Illinois Office: Suite 640, 331 Fulton Street.
Telephone: 309-673-1681.
Oakbrook Terrace, Illinois Office: Suite 1000, One Mid America Plaza.
Telephone: 708-954-2100.
Telecopier: 708-954-2112.
Schaumburg, Illinois Office: Suite 250 Schaumburg Corporate Center, 1515 East Woodfield Road.
Telephone: 708-330-1200.
Telecopier: 708-330-1220.
Houston, Texas Office: 2800 First City Main Building, 1021 Main Street.
Telephone: 713-951-0990.
Telecopier: 713-951-0987.
Los Angeles, California Office: 2029 Century Park East.
Telephone: 310-284-8771.
Fax: 310-284-8359.
New York, N.Y. Office: 220 E. 42nd Street.
Telephone: 212-682-3060.
Fax: 212-490-3918.
San Francisco, California Office: One Maritime Plaza, Golden Gateway Center, 23rd Floor.
Telephone: 415-392-7077.
Fax: 415-392-3969.

MEMBERS OF FIRM

Michael A. Abbott (Resident, Houston, Texas Office)
Stephen L. Agin
Robert F. Aldrich (Resident, Washington, D.C. Office)
Robert Edward Arroyo
James W. Ashley, Jr.
Elizabeth M. Asperger
John R. F. Baer
David F. Bantleon (Resident, Washington, D.C. Office)
Sharon R. Barner
Lyman D. Bedford (Resident, Los Angeles, California Office)
R. Clay Bennett
Debra Rae Bernard
Christopher A. Bloom
Keith J. Braskich (Resident, Peoria, Illinois Office)
Kenneth D. Brody (Resident, Washington, D.C. Office)
W. Joel Bryant (Resident, Houston, Texas Office)
Jonathan G. Bunge (P.C.)
Mark W. Burns
William H. Campbell (Resident, Peoria, Illinois Office)
James A. Carmody (Resident, Houston, Texas Office)
F. Willis Caruso
James J. Casey
Michael K. Cavanaugh (P.C.)
Edward J. Chalfie
Ronald K. Clausen (Resident, San Francisco, California Office)
Ronald D. Cohn (Resident, Washington, D.C. Office)
Grant Cook (Resident, Houston, Texas Office)
Darryl R. Davidson
Barry Davis (Resident, Houston, Texas Office)
Peter M. Davis
Roy G. Davis (Resident, Peoria, Illinois Office)
Michael J. Dolesh
John S. Elias (Resident, Peoria, Illinois Office)
Geraldine A. Ferraro (Resident, New York, New York Office)
Martin M. Fleisher (Resident, San Francisco, California Office)
Martin Fleit (Resident, Washington, D.C. Office)
Bruce W. Foudree
Shari L. Friedman
Katherine Roulhac Garn (P.C.) (Resident, San Francisco, California Office)
Gary J. Gasper (Resident, Washington, D.C. Office)
Stephen C. Glazier (Resident, Washington, D.C. Office)
Larry S. Goldberg
A. Benjamin Goldgar
Michael A. Gollin (Resident, Washington, D.C. Office)
William C. Graft (Resident, Schaumburg, Illinois Office)
Robert E. Greenberg (Resident, Washington, D.C. Office)
Kenneth C. Greene (Resident, San Francisco, California Office)
Robert M. Grossman
Daniel G. Grove (Resident, Washington, D.C. Office)
Robin W. Grover (Resident, Washington, D.C. Office)
Weston W. Hanscom
Carl F. J. Henninger (Resident, Oakbrook Terrace, Illinois Office)
Minard E. Hulse, Jr.
John T. Huntington (Resident, Oakbrook Terrace, Illinois Office)
William C. Ives
Richard J. Jacobson
Janet L. Jannusch (Resident, Peoria, Illinois Office)
John A. Jeffries (P.C.)
Carol A. Joffe (Resident, Washington, D.C. Office)
David R. Johanson (Resident, San Francisco, California Office)
Gary C. Johnson (Resident, Houston, Texas Office)
Thomas W. Johnston
Thomas R. Jolly (Resident, Washington, D.C. Office)
Patrick W. Jordan (Resident, San Francisco, California Office)
Stanley S. Jutkowitz (Resident, Washington, D.C. Office)
Sheldon Karon
Terence P. Kennedy
Thomas H. Kennerly (Resident, Houston, Texas Office)
John A. Klages
Carl R. Klein
Robert M. Kluchin

(See Next Column)

KECK, MAHIN & CATE—*Continued*

MEMBERS OF FIRM (Continued)

Amy Listick Koenig
James A. Kohlstedt (Resident, Oakbrook Terrace, Illinois Office)
Albert H. Kramer (Resident, Washington, D.C. Office)
Henry S. Landan
Peter C. Langenus (Resident, New York, N.Y. Office)
Patrick J. Leston (Resident, Oakbrook Terrace, Illinois Office)
George William Lewis (Resident, Washington, D.C. Office)
Roger L. Longtin
Janet Otsuka Love
Robin R. Lunn
Lawrence A. Manson
Angela Marsh
Warren J. Marwedel
Beverly D. Mason (Resident, Houston, Texas Office)
Malcolm McCaleb, Jr.
Judith W. McCue
John A. McDonald
Donald J. McNeil
Patrick J. McNerney
Paul M. McNicol (Resident, New York, N.Y. Office)
Thomas J. McNulty
J. Dennis McQuaid (Resident, San Francisco, California Office)
Brian J. Meginnes (Resident, Peoria, Illinois Office)
David R. Melton
Brian Meltzer (Resident, Schaumburg, Illinois Office)
Roger J. Metzler, Jr. (Resident, San Francisco, California Office)
Pamela J. Mills
Dennis Minichello
Anita T. Molano
Charles B. Molster, III (Resident, Washington, D.C. Office)
Michael J. Moriarty (Resident, New York, N.Y. Office)
Curt W. Moy (Resident, Houston, Texas Office)
Donald G. Mulack
Stanley C. Nardoni
Laurance P. Nathan
Catherine A. T. Nelson
Julie Collins Nelson (Resident, San Francisco, California Office)
Mark D. Nelson
Michael C. Neubauer
Carl A. Neumann (Resident, Oakbrook Terrace, Illinois Office)
Blake T. Newton, III (Resident, New York, N.Y. Office)
Dennis M. O'Dea (Resident, New York, N.Y. Office)
Philip L. O'Neill (Resident, Washington, D.C. Office)
Lewis J. Paper (Resident, Washington, D.C. Office)
R. Clyde Parker, Jr. (Resident, Houston, Texas Office)
Jefferson Perkins
Cyrus E. Phillips, IV (Resident, Washington, D.C. Office)
Robert A. Plessala (Resident, Houston, Texas Office)
Dennis J. Powers
Robert W. Pratt
Craig A. Pridgen (Resident, San Francisco, California Office)
John F. Purtill (Resident, Schaumburg, Illinois Office)
Maridee A. Quanbeck
Carlos M. Recio (Resident, Washington, D.C. Office)
Clarence O. Redman
Richard L. Reinish
Robert M. Riffle (Resident, Peoria, Illinois Office)
J. Reed Roesler (Resident, Peoria, Illinois Office)
Douglass F. Rohrman
Carla J. Rozycki
Deborah Schavey Ruff
Donald W. Rupert
Darrell J. Salomon (Resident, San Francisco, California Office)
Cary Brian Samowitz (Resident, New York, N.Y. Office)
Robert J. Schneider
Thomas E. Schnur
Michael R. Seghetti (Resident, Peoria, Illinois Office)
Larry Selander
Peter M. Shannon, Jr.
Howard J. Siegel
Susan Anne Sinclair (Resident, Washington, D.C. Office)
Norman H. Singer (Resident, Washington, D.C. Office)
Michael L. Sklar
Douglas A. Slansky (Resident, Oakbrook Terrace, Illinois Office)
Kenneth S. Slaughter (Resident, Washington, D.C. Office)
Madeleine E. Sloane (Resident, San Francisco, California Office)
Guy E. Snyder
Michael J. Sreenan
Roger T. Stelle (Resident, Schaumburg, Illinois Office)
K. Bruce Stickler
Joan F. Symansky (Resident, Washington, D.C. Office)
Cornelius J. Tanis
Monica L. Thompson
Thomas Thorne-Thomsen
Bedell A. Tippins
Thomas C. Tokos (Resident, San Francisco, California Office)
Kevin Tottis
Janet L. Tracy
John B. Truskowski
Peter K. Trzyna (Not admitted in IL)
Jeffrey A. Usow
Roy M. Van Cleave
Michael J. Van Zandt (Resident, San Francisco, California Office)
Jacqueline W. Vlaming (Resident, Oakbrook Terrace, Illinois Office)
James R. Vogler
Kevin A. Walsh (Resident, New York, N.Y. Office)
Wesley S. Walton
Dorothy Voss Ward
Michael O. Warnecke
Reuben C. Warshawsky
Neil A. Wasserstrom (Resident, Houston, Texas Office)
Steven A. Weiler (Resident, Washington, D.C. Office)
James M. Wetzel
Augustus T. White (Resident, Houston, Texas Office)
Jeffrey B. Whitt
James T. Williams (Resident, New York, N.Y. Office)
Dennis M. Wilson
Lawrence A. Wojcik
Richard K. Wray
Roger T. Yokubaitis (Resident, Houston, Texas Office)
David E. Zajicek (Resident, Oakbrook Terrace, Illinois Office)
Robert L. Zaletel (Resident, San Francisco, California Office)
Howard P. Zweig

(See Next Column)

OF COUNSEL

Harry B. Clark (Resident, New York, N.Y. Office)
Robert S. Cushman
Louis H. Diamond (Resident, Washington, D.C. Office)
Fletcher H. Etheridge (Resident, Houston, Texas Office)
Bruce R. Johnson (Resident Oakbrook Terrace, Illinois Office)
Robert C. Keck
James S. Laing
Charles B. Mahin
Brian P. McGinty
Donald E. McNicol (Resident, New York, N.Y. Office)
Kai Allen Nebel
James T. Otis (Resident, Peoria, Illinois Office)
Elaine M. Postley (Resident, New York, N.Y. Office)
Richard A. Speer (Not admitted in IL)
John Yonco
Carl E. Zwisler III (Resident, Washington, D.C. Office)

ASSOCIATES

James R. Blunk
Matthew T. Bailey (Resident, Washington, D.C. Office)
Troy M. Calkins
Thomas P. Cassidy (Resident, Washington, D.C. Office)
Leslie F. Chard, III
Timothy D. Church (Resident, Peoria, Illinois Office)
Christine C. Coverdale (Resident, San Francisco, California Office)
John M. Craig (Not admitted in IL; Resident, Washington, D.C. Office)
Steven E. Cyranoski
Richard R. Diefendorf (Resident, Washington, D.C. Office)
Stephanie Lee Dodge
Tracy E. Donner
Grant Dunwoody (Resident, Houston, Texas Office)
Catherine Stanton Flanagan
Jon Carl Gealow
Sheila R. Gibbs-Cunningham
Catherine R. Giella
Linda Vernon Goldberg
Glenn W. D. Golding (Resident, Washington, D.C. Office)
Lisa E. Grampo
Mary T. Griffin
David H. Hight (Resident, Oakbrook Terrace, Illinois Office)
Judith A. Hoggan (Resident, Washington, D.C. Office)
Marianne Craigmile Holzhall
Michael J. Hughes
Douglas H. Jackson
David B. Jeppsen (Resident, Washington, D.C. Office)
Nanette Joslyn (Resident, San Francisco, California Office)
Kathleen Hechringer Kane
Myriam Benhamou Kaplan
Kathryn M. Kotel (Resident, Schaumburg, Illinois Office)
Kimberly A. Krueger
Janet M. Kyte
Meena Kang Latta
Dana J. Lesemann (Resident, Washington, DC Office)
Stephen M. Levine (Resident, San Francisco, California Office)
Joan L. Long
David G. Lubben (Resident, Peoria, Illinois Office)
Pamela J. Lyons (Resident, Schaumburg, Illinois Office)
Todd E. Marlette (Resident, Washington, D.C. Office)
Thomas R. Marshall (Resident, New York, N.Y. Office)
David S. Martin
Marsha Dula Matthews (Resident, Washington, DC Office)
Patricia L. Mehler
Joanne K. Mirras (Resident, Los Angeles, California Office)
William J. Mitchell (Resident, Schaumburg, Illinois Office)
Marvin C. Moos (Resident, Houston, Texas Office)
Ruth N. Morduch (Resident, Washington, D.C. Office)
Michael Mueller
Patricia S. Nathan (Resident, Houston, Texas Office)
Jan C. Nielsen (Resident, San Francisco, California Office)
Douglas L. Noren
Kathleen M. O'Laughlin
Michael C. O'Neil
Ayako Onoda (Resident, San Francisco, California Office)
Pamela Lee Peters
David J. Poirier
Stacey L. Prange
Antonia Sexton Pritchard
Robert L. Reeb
Patrick W. Reilly (Resident, Washington, D.C. Office)
Robert S. Rigg
Steven C. Roper
Julie Rosen
Douglas E. Rosenfeld (Resident, Washington, D.C. Office)
Jeffrey A. Roth
Robert A. Roth
David M. Seghetti
Christopher T. Sheean
Eric L. Singer (Resident, Oakbrook Terrace Office)
Andrew W. Sohn (Resident, Oakbrook Terrace, Illinois Office)
Heather C. Steinmeyer
Maureen Calabrese Strauts (Resident, Oakbrook Terrace, Illinois Office)
Wayne L. Tang
Robert J. Vechiola
John S. Vishneski III
Brigitte von Weiss
Adam R. Walker
Jeffrey J. Ward
Warren P. Wenzloff
Shari L. West (Resident, Peoria, Illinois Office)
Bradford T. Yaker
Stephen N. Yang (Resident, San Francisco, California Office)
John F. Young

For full biographical listings, see the Martindale-Hubbell Law Directory

LASER, POKORNY, SCHWARTZ, FRIEDMAN & ECONOMOS, P.C. (AV)

205 North Michigan Avenue, 38th Floor, 60601-5914
Telephone: 312-540-0600
Telecopier: 312-540-0610

(See Next Column)

LASER, POKORNY, SCHWARTZ, FRIEDMAN & ECONOMOS P.C., *Chicago—Continued*

Jules M. Laser
Stephen J. Pokorny
Marc H. Schwartz
Bruce M. Friedman
Peter C. Economos
Joel A. Stein
Brad A. Levin
Alvin J. Helfgot
Bruce E. Bell
Michael M. Lorge

Danni J. Haag
Joshua S. Hyman
David A. Shapiro

For full biographical listings, see the Martindale-Hubbell Law Directory

LORD, BISSELL & BROOK (AV)

Suites 2600-3600 Harris Bank Building, 115 South La Salle Street, 60603
Telephone: 312-443-0700
Telecopy: 312-443-0570
Cable Adress: "Lowirco"
Telex: 25-0336
Los Angeles, California Office: 300 South Grand Avenue, 90071-3200.
Telephone: 213-485-1500.
Telecopy: 213-485-1200.
Telex: 18-1135.
Atlanta, Georgia Office: One Atlantic Center, 1201 West Peachtree Street, N.W., Suite 3700, 30309.
Telephone: 404-870-4600.
Telecopy: 404-872-5547.
Rockford, Illinois Office: 120 West State Street, Suite 200, 61101.
Telephone: 815-963-8050.

MEMBERS OF FIRM

John Solon Lord (1881-1979)
Cushman Brewer Bissell (1900-1987)
Herbert C. Brook (1910-1990)
Charles A. Adamek (Resident, Los Angeles Office)
David J. Adams
Steven H. Adelman
David M. Agnew
John T. Anderson
Margaret M. Anderson
William C. Anderson, III
Simon H. Aronson
Stephen C. Ascher
Michael J. Athans (Resident, Atlanta Office)
Robert B. Austin
Gail M. Baev (Resident, Los Angeles Office)
Carey S. Barney
M. Elizabeth Bennett
Kirk A. Borchardt
George L. Burgett
Thomas J. Burke, Jr.
Evan A. Burkholder
Chad M. Castro
John S. Chapman
Michael P. Comiskey
R. Dean Conlin
Joseph E. Coughlin
Charles L. Crouch, III (Resident, Los Angeles Office)
Michael Davis
Thomas W. Dempsey
Nick J. DiGiovanni
Kirk W. Dillard
Williams P. Dorr
R. Bruce Duffield
James R. Dwyer
David P. Faulkner (Resident, Rockford Office)
Edward C. Fitzpatrick
Don W. Fowler
Lawrence M. Friedman
Roger R. Fross
Mark R. Goodman
Lawrence A. Gray
Hugh C. Griffin
John C. Gurley
John B. Haarlow
Randall A. Hack
David C. Hall
Leisa J. Hamm
Laurence A. Hansen
Louis S. Harrison
Michael R. Hassan
Richard A. Hemmings
Wallye Muzette Hill
Thomas W. Jenkins
Diane I. Jennings
Richard F. Johnson
Raffi Kalousdian
William J. Kelty, III
David L. Kendall
Celeste M. King
Robert A. Knuti
Karen J. Kowal
Jeffrey S. Kravitz (Resident, Los Angeles Office)
Mark A. Kreger
Forrest B. Lammiman
Paul H. LaRue, Jr.
L. Anthony Lehr
David M. Leonard (Resident, Atlanta Office)
Harvey S. Lichterman
Gary L. Lockwood
Kay W. McCurdy
David C. McLauchlan
R. R. McMahan
Hugh L. Moore
Richard E. Mueller
Thomas J. Murnighan
Stephen M. Murray
John K. O'Connor
John N. Oest
Keith D. Parr
Judy Platt Perlman
J. Robert Persons (Resident, Atlanta Office)
Robert J. Pugliese
Robert D. Rasor
David R. Reed
Daniel I. Schlessinger
David R. Schmidt
Rudolf H. Schroeter (Resident, Los Angeles Office)
Michael Schuette
David L. Skelding
David J. Slawkowski
Walter T. Slezak
Walton N. Smith (Resident, Atlanta Office)
Rowe W. Snider
Lyle Wayne Sparks
Jeffry S. Spears (Resident, Rockford Office)
Maynerd I. Steinberg
Thomas L. Stevens
Thomas J. Strueber (Resident, Atlanta Office)
Gerald O. Sweeney, Jr.
Jane H. Veldman
Eugene H. Wachtel
Benjamin Waisbren
Ann Marie Walsh
Thomas C. Walsh
Richard M. Watson (Resident, Atlanta Office)
William T. Weaver
Frederic Weber
Gary W. Westerberg

(See Next Column)

MEMBERS OF FIRM (Continued)

Richard L. Wexler
Mark D. Wilcox
Keith G. Wileman (Resident, Los Angeles Office)
John M. Wulfers
Mary Jane Yardley
Daniel J. Zollner

OF COUNSEL

Paul C. Blume
Richard K. Decker
Dennis J. Fox
David M. Gooder
Thomas J. Healey
Thomas P. Healy
Bobbe Hirsh
Harold L. Jacobson
Stephen P. Kenney
Clark C. King, Jr.
Marsha Kellman Klevickis (Resident, Atlanta Office)
Max E. Meyer
Robert S. Seiler
John S. Shapira
John G. Smith
Forrest L. Tozer
James R. Wimmer

ASSOCIATES

Fred L. Alvarez
Robert P. Arnold
Robert A. Badgley
Tracy Victoria Bare
Patricia J. Barker
Steven M. Bauer
Joseph P. Beckman
Robert J. Berg
Jon Biasetti
Kathleen M. Bickelhaupt
William P. Bila
Brenda Adams Bissett (Resident, Los Angeles Office)
Jessica H. Breitbarth
Timothy W. Brink
Alfred L. Buchanan
John D. Buchanan (Resident, Los Angeles Office)
Mary Ellen Busch
Terrence P. Canade
Cynthia J. Cappello
Christopher K. Carpenter
Deborah Carroll
Donald J. Chenevert (Resident, Atlanta Office)
Marilee Clausing
C. Guerry Collins (Resident, Los Angeles Office)
Robert P. Conlon
Jeffrey R. Darby (Resident, Atlanta Office)
Patrick E. Deady
Andrew R. Diamond (Resident, Atlanta Office)
Franklin T. Dunn (Resident, Los Angeles Office)
William D. Ellison
Mark Scott Fall (Resident, Los Angeles Office)
Paul L. Fields, Jr. (Resident, Atlanta Office)
Kurt W. Florian, Jr.
Patricia J. Foltz
Ann Kettelson Ford
Richard J. Fortwengler, Jr. (Resident, Atlanta Office)
Albert E. Fowerbaugh, Jr.
Cynthia M. Frey (Resident, Los Angeles Office)
Michael J. Gaertner
Brian T. Garelli
Edward P. Gibbons
Laura J. Ginett
Laura S. Golden
Jannis E. Goodnow
Michael Z. Green
David G. Greene (Resident, Atlanta Office)
Gregory A. Gunter (Resident, Atlanta Office)
Michael P. Hannigan
Keith N. Hasty
Catherine C. Hays
Colleen M. Hennessy
Scott E. Herbst
Sarah J. Hewitt
Margaret S. Hickey
Peter F. Higgins
Joseph A. Hinkhouse
Terry R. Howell (Resident, Atlanta Office)
John E. Hrebec
John M. Hughes
Mary Pat Huske
Thomas P. Hyatte
Pamela M. Jimenez
Deborah Jones
Susan P. Jordan
Amy Hoagland Kane
Laura A. Kane
Camille N. Khodadad
Carol B. Kiersky (Resident, Atlanta Office)
Barbara J. Klass (Resident, Los Angeles Office)
Jacqueline Redin Klein (Resident, Los Angeles Office)
Andrew Kochanowski
Scott A. Kogen
Barry Kroot
Susan K. Laing
LouCinda Laughlin (Resident, Los Angeles Office)
Jeri Rouse Looney (Resident, Los Angeles Office)
Mark J. Lura
Sandra K. Macauley
Timothy M. Maggio
Gilbert M. Malm (Resident, Atlanta Office)
Donald J. Manikas
Christopher W. Matern
Paul F. Matousek
C. Kevin McCabe
Susan Magee McColgan
Richard O. McDermott
Molly C. McGinnis
John J. McGuirk
Patrick John Mc Laughlin
Robert E. McLaughlin (Resident, Atlanta Office)
Jan M. Michaels
Dale T. Miller
Darrell D. Miller (Resident, Los Angeles Office)
Thomas P. Minnick
Kathryn G. Montgomery
Joseph J. Morford
William D. Nolen
Prescott L. Nottingham (Resident, Atlanta Office)
Eric B. Noyes
Kevin Michael O'Hagan
Jason A. Parson
Sharon Finegan Patterson
Mitchell J. Popham (Resident, Los Angeles Office)
Michael E. Prangle
J. Brett Pritchard
Matthew W. Rappleye
Robert B. Robinson
Leslie J. Rosen
Eric P. Schoonveld
Robbie Danielle Schwartz
Nancy Shaw
Anthony B. Sherman
Martha E. Sperry
Anne M. Stalder
M. Joseph Sterner (Resident, Atlanta Office)
Richard P. Stowell
Andrea Stulgies-Clauss
Jennifer L. Sucher
Catalina J. Sugayan
Robert E. Sweeney, Jr.
Gregg E. Szilagyi
Ann Caroline Taylor
Kurt T. Temple
Robert D. Tepper
Michael P. Trier

(See Next Column)

LORD, BISSELL & BROOK—*Continued*

ASSOCIATES (Continued)

Anne Kelly Turner
Todd M. Van Baren
Victoria A. Verhagen
Damon N. Vocke
David E. Walker
John T. Williams
Susan M. Witt (Resident, Rockford Office)
Anthony F. Witteman (Resident, Los Angeles Office)
Corliss L. Worford (Resident, Atlanta Office)
Kathryn C. Wyatt
James H. Wynn (Resident, Atlanta Office)
Michael Yetnikoff

For full biographical listings, see the Martindale-Hubbell Law Directory

MANDEL, LIPTON AND STEVENSON LIMITED (AV)

Suite 2900, 120 North La Salle Street, 60602
Telephone: 312-236-7080
Facsimile: 312-236-0781

Richard L. Mandel
Alfred R. Lipton
Leonard M. Malkin
R. Peter Carey
Henry A. Waller
Kathleen Roseborough
Richard A. Lifshitz
Terry Yale Feiertag
Kathleen Hogan Morrison
Uve R. Jerzy
Carolyn E. Winter

Audrey L. Gaynor
Goldie C. Domingue

OF COUNSEL

Nicholas Stevenson

LEGAL SUPPORT PERSONNEL

Jacqueline Steffens (Paralegal)

References: Northern Trust Co.; American National Bank of Chicago.

For full biographical listings, see the Martindale-Hubbell Law Directory

MAYER, BROWN & PLATT (AV)

190 South La Salle Street, 60603-3441
Telephone: (312) 782-0600
Pitney Bowes: (312) 701-7711
Telex: 190404
Cable: LEMAY
Washington, D.C. Office: 2000 Pennsylvania Avenue, N.W., 20006-1882.
Telephone: (202) 463-2000. Pitney Bowes: (202) 861-0484, Pitney Bowes: (202) 861-0473.
Telex: 892603.
Cable: LEMAYDC
New York, New York Office: 787 Seventh Avenue, Suite 2400, 10019-6018.
Telephone: (212) 554-3000. Pitney Bowes: (212) 262-1910.
Telex: 701842.
Cable: LEMAYEN.
Houston, Texas Office: 700 Louisiana Street, Suite 3600, 77002-2730.
Telephone: (713) 221-1651. Pitney Bowes: (713) 224-6410.
Telex: 775809.
Cable: LEMAYHOU.
Los Angeles, California Office: 350 South Grand Avenue, 25th Floor, 90071-1503.
Telephone: (213) 229-9500. Pitney Bowes: (213) 625-0248.
Telex: 188089.
Cable: LEMAYLA.
London, England Office: 162 Queen Victoria Street, EC4V 4DB.
Telephone: 011-44-71-248-1465.
Fax: 011-44-71-329-4465.
Telex: 8811095.
Cable: LEMAYLDN.
Tokyo, Japan Office: (Kawachi Gaikokuho Jimu Bengoshi Jimusho) Urbannet Otemachi Building 13F 2-2, Otemachi 2-chome, Chiyoda-ku, Tokyo 100.
Telephone: 011-81-3-5255-9700.
Facsimile: 011-81-3-5255-9797.
Berlin, Germany Office: Spreeufer 5, 10178.
Telephone: 011-49-30-240-7930.
Fax: 011-49-30-240-79344.
Brussels, Belgium Office: Square de Meeûs 19/20, Bte. 4, 1040.
Telephone: 011-32-2-512-9878.
Fax: 011-32-2-511-3305.
Telex: 20768 MBPBRU B.
Mexico City, Mexico, D.F., Mexico Correspondent: Jáuregui, Navarrete, Nader y Rojas, S.C. Abogados, Paseo de la Reforma 199, Pisos 15, 16 y 17, 06500, Mexico.
Telephone: 011-525-591-16-55.
Fax: 011-525-535-80-62, 011-525-703-22-47.
Cable: JANANE.

MEMBERS OF FIRM

David F. Abbott
Lee N. Abrams
J. Trent Anderson
Diane E. Ambler (Washington, D.C. Office)
Percy L. Angelo
Franklin P. Auwarter
Robert C. Baptista, Jr.
Joseph W. Bartlett (New York, N.Y. Office)
Robert N. Barnard
Gregory L. Barton
Teresa A. Beaudet (Los Angeles, California Office)
Mark H. Berens
Robert M. Berger

(See Next Column)

MEMBERS OF FIRM (Continued)

John C. Berghoff, Jr.
Barbara Bertok
Barry P. Biggar (New York, N.Y. Office)
Christian F. Binnig
Robert E. Bloch (Washington, D.C. Office)
David I. Bloom (Washington, D.C. Office)
John N. Boley
Fern C. Bomchill
Richard S. Brennan
Robert I. Bressman (New York, N.Y. Office)
Joan Edmonds Brophy
Richard F. Broude (New York, N.Y. Office)
Caroline Brower
Mary Rose Brusewitz (New York, N.Y. Office)
Thierry G. F. Buytaert (Brussels Office)
Michael A. Campbell
Michael G. Capatides (New York, N.Y. Office)
James B. Carlson (New York, N.Y. Office)
John M. Carroll
Jean S. Chan (New York, N.Y. Office)
Charles Chu (Washington, D.C. Office)
Diane Citron (Not admitted in IL)
Paul B. Clemenceau (Houston, Texas Office)
Richard A. Cole (London, England Office)
Ian R. Coles (London, England Office)
Joseph P. Collins
Vincent J. Connelly
George W. Craven
Robert E. Curley
David S. Curry
William M. Daley
Peter V. Darrow (New York, N.Y. Office)
Robert P. Davis (Washington, D.C. Office)
Scott J. Davis
Laura A. DeFelice (New York, N.Y. Office)
Debora de Hoyos
William E. Deitrick
Julian C. D'Esposito, Jr.
Edward F. Dobbins, Jr.
Jeff C. Dodd (Houston, Texas Office)
Jerome F. Donohoe
Thomas C. Durham
Thomas M. Durkin
Louis P. Eatman (Los Angeles, California Office)
Russell R. Eggert
Roy T. Englert, Jr. (Washington, D.C. Office)
Tyrone C. Fahner
Rosanne J. Faraci
Richard J. Favretto (Washington, D.C. Office)
Michael R. Feagley
Robert F. Finke
L. Bruce Fischer (Los Angeles, California Office)
Delilah B. Flaum
Mary C. Fontaine
J. Paul Forrester
Andrew L. Frey (Washington, D.C. Office)
Dennis G. Friedman
Peter M. Gaines (London, England Office)
Marc Gary (Washington, D.C. Office)
Barry Gassman (Los Angeles, California Office)
John J. Gearen
Kenneth S. Geller (Washington, D.C. Office)
Bettina Getz
Steven R. Gilford
Michael J. Gill
Mark H. Gitenstein (Washington, D.C. Office)
Ronald B. Given
James W. Gladden, Jr.
Joseph R. Goeke
Jeffrey I. Gordon
Robert E. Gordon
William A. Gordon
Maureen J. Gorman
Arthur I. Gould
A. Duncan Gray, Jr. (Houston, Texas Office)
Ray H. Greenblatt
Lloyd S. Guerci (Washington, D.C. Office)
Catharine A. Haake
Robert K. Hagan
Frederic L. Hahn
S. Alan Hamburger (Brussels, Belgium Office)
Marshall E. Hanbury (Not admitted in IL)
Kevin P. Hawken
Steven K. Hazen (Los Angeles, California Office)
Robert A. Helman
Kathleen M. Hennessey
Leo Herzel
Vincent E. Hillery
Catherine W. Hoeg (Houston, Texas Office)
Robert J. Holz
James D. Holzhauer
Thomas R. Hood (New York, N.Y. Office)
Charles M. Horn (Washington, D.C. Office)
Carrie Kiger Huff
Harley Hutchins
Ronald A. Jacks
Caryn L. Jacobs
Thomas N. Jersild
Erika Z. Jones (Washington, D.C. Office)
Roger J. Jones
James J. Junewicz
Kenneth J. Jurek
Ivan P. Kane
Harold L. Kaplan
Wayne S. Kaplan
Alvin Charles Katz
M. Marvin Katz (Houston, Texas Office)
Michael T. Kawachi (Tokyo, Japan Office)
Robert A. Kelman
Michael F. Kerr
Stanton A. Kessler
Roger J. Kiley, Jr.
Thomas S. Kiriakos
Jeffrey A. Klopf (Los Angeles, California Office)
James E. Knox
William H. Knull, III (Houston, Texas Office)
Kenneth E. Kohler (Los Angeles, California Office)
Arthur J. Kowitt
Jason H. P. Kravitt
Simeon M. Kriesberg (Washington, D.C. Office)
Robert J. Kriss
Herbert W. Krueger
Philip Allen Lacovara (Washington, D.C. and New York Offices)
Stuart M. Litwin
Theodore A. Livingston, Jr.
Wayne R. Luepker
George A. Luscombe, II
Christine Lutgens
George W. Madison (New York, N.Y. Office)
Cary J. Malkin
John D. Marshall
Alan J. Martin
Stephen J. Mattson
Frank D. Mayer, Jr.
Terri A. Mazur
Hugh R. McCombs
Howard M. McCue, III
T. Mark McLaughlin

(See Next Column)

MAYER, BROWN & PLATT, *Chicago—Continued*

MEMBERS OF FIRM (Continued)

James J. McGuire (New York, N.Y. Office)
Thomas B. McNeill
Jonathan C. Medow
Richard S. Millard
Jay Parry Monge (New York, N.Y. Office)
Deborah Alfred Monson
Paula J. Morency
Donna Evensen Morgan
Frank E. Morgan, II (New York, N.Y. Office)
John E. Muench
J. Thomas Mullen
David Narefsky
John H. Nash (Houston, Texas Office)
Alec G. Nedelman (Los Angeles, California Office)
Steven H. Nemerovski
Brian E. Newhouse (Los Angeles, California Office)
C. Mark Nicolaides (Berlin, Germany Office)
Michael E. Niebruegge (Houston, Texas Office)
Harvey Nixon
Patrick W. O'Brien
Michele L. Odorizzi
Anna M. O'Meara
Jerry L. Oppenheimer (Washington, D.C. Office)
Joseph B. Organ
Carolyn P. Osolinik (Washington, D.C. Office)
James E. Padilla (New York, N.Y. Office)
Danuta Bembenista Panich
Stanley J. Parzen
Stuart P. Pergament (Washington, D.C. Office)
Andrew J. Pincus (Washington, D.C. Office)
Douglas A. Poe
Lynne M. Raimondo
George A. Ranney, Jr.
Mitchell D. Raup
Elizabeth A. Raymond
Phillip S. Reed
William J. Reifman (Los Angeles, California Office)
Laura D. Richman
Michael P. Richman (New York, N.Y. Office)
David B. Ritter
M. Ellen Robb (Los Angeles, California Office)
Lawrence S. Robbins (Washington, D.C. Office)
John C. Roebuck (Tokyo, Japan Office)
Eddy J. Rogers, Jr. (Houston, Texas Office)
Howard J. Roin
Matthew A. Rooney
Richard M. Rosenberg
Michael F. Rosenblum
Martin G. Rosenstein
Kenneth M. Rosenzweig
Paul J. N. Roy
Stuart M. Rozen
George Ruhlen (Houston, Texas Office)
Douglas M. Rutherford (London, England Office)
Mark W. Ryan (Washington, D.C. Office)
John R. Sagan
Alan N. Salpeter
Julia R. Sarron
William A. Schmalzl
John P. Schmitz (Washington, D.C. Office)
Edward J. Schneidman
Joseph U. Schorer
James C. Schroeder
David A. Schuette
James A. Serritella
Stephen M. Shapiro
Kevin L. Shaw (Los Angeles, California Office)
Richard W. Shepro
Timothy C. Sherck
Brian W. Smith (Washington, D.C. Office)
Lawrence K. Snider
Neil M. Soltman (Los Angeles, California Office)
Robert A. Southern (Los Angeles, California Office)
David M. Spector
James S. Stanhaus
Adrian L. Steel, Jr. (Washington, D.C. Office)
J. Robert Stoll
Jeffrey M. Strauss
Robert H. Swart (Washington, D.C. Office)
Evan M. Tager (Washington, D.C. Office)
James E. Tancula (Houston, Texas Office)
Paul W. Theiss
Frederick B. Thomas
S. Raymond Tillett
William C. Tompsett
John M. Touhy
Charles S. Triplett (Washington, D.C. Office)
Watson B. Tucker
James J. Tyler (Houston, Texas Office)
George J. Tzanetopoulos
Miguel A. Valdes
Barry Alan Van Dyke
Terry Otero Vilardo (Houston, Texas Office)
Thomas M. Vitale (New York, N.Y. Office)
James R. Walther (Los Angeles, California Office)
Don L. Weaver (Los Angeles, California Office)
Priscilla P. Weaver
David B. Weinberg
Seth J. Weinberger
Barry A. White
Kenneth E. Wile
Joel V. Williamson
Richard S. Williamson
David L. Witcoff
Mark S. Wojciechowski (New York, N.Y. Office)
Steven Wolowitz (New York, N.Y. Office)
Herbert L. Zarov
Michael I. Zinder (New York, N.Y. Office)

OF COUNSEL

Roger W. Barrett
James R. Barry
Stuart Bernstein
Marla Chernof Cohen
Richard C. Cummings, Jr.
Ronald R. Dietrich
David K. Duffee (New York, N.Y. Office)
Albert I. Edelman (New York, N.Y. Office)
Patricia V. Gentry
Marcia E. Goodman
Marian Conroy Haney
Diane M. Huff
Warren L. Jervey (New York, N. Y. Office)
Michele G. Magner
Philip H. Martin
Richard K. Matta (Washington, D.C. Office)
Kevin C. McDonald
Lillian Miller
Donald C. Morris
Amy L. Nathan (Washington, D.C. Office)
Younghee J. Ottley
Rex A. Palmer
Alfred M. Rogers, Jr.

(See Next Column)

OF COUNSEL (Continued)

Charles Rothfeld (Washington, D.C. Office)
Patricia F. Sharkey
Justin A. Stanley
Edmund A. Stephan
Robert L. Stern

SPECIAL CONSULTANT

Michael W. McConnell

ASSOCIATES

Daniel Acosta
Nelson Kyunam Ahn (New York, N.Y. Office)
Courtney D. Allison (Washington, D.C. Office)
Marwan Al-Turki (London, England Office)
Bradley J. Andreozzi (New York, N.Y. Office)
Jennifer T. Ansbro
Jonathan A. Backman
Dorann E. Banks (Washington, D.C. Office)
James H. Bathon (New York, N.Y. Office)
Ira J. Belcove
Douglas M. Belofsky
Audrey Ingber Bender (New York, New York Office)
Gail C. Bent
Benjamin M. Berinstein
Edward S. Best
Michael E. Bieniek
Carol J. Bilzi (Washington, D.C. Office)
Sara A. Biro
Timothy S. Bishop
Richard L. Bjelde (Berlin, Germany Office)
Michael T. Blair
Paul S. Bock (Washington, D.C. Office)
Stephen D. Bohrer (New York, New York Office)
Benjamin A. Bornstein (New York, N.Y. Office)
Kim Marie Kozaczek Boylan (Washington, D. C. Office)
Jacqueline R. Brady (Los Angeles, California Office)
Addison D. Braendel
Patricia K. Brito (Houston, Texas Office)
Ellen M. Bublick
H. Thomas Byron, III (Washington, D.C. Office)
Kimberlee S. Cagle (Houston, Texas Office)
Timothy P. Callahan
Patricia B. Carlson
David A. Carpenter
Jerry C. Carter
Leland H. Chait
Christopher D. Chen (Los Angeles, California Office)
Kelly A. Chesney
M. Lindsay Childress (Washington, D.C. Office)
Barbara A. Clark (Houston, Texas Office)
Gerald P. Cleary (Not admitted in IL)
Edward X. Clinton, Jr.
Barbara E. Cohen
Anthony J. Coleby (London, England Office)
Victoria Russell Collado
Catherine M. Collins (London, England Office)
Martin J. Collins (New York, N.Y. Office)
Rita N. Conroy
Marcia G. Cotler
David C. Crane (Washington, D.C. Office)
Paul Michael Crimmins
June E. Daniel
Raniero D'Aversa, Jr. (New York, N.Y. Office)
Diana L. Davis (Houston, Texas Office)
Sheila D'Cruz
John J. Dedyo (New York, N.Y. Office)
Daniel J. Delaney
Lynn E. Delzell
Thomas DiLenge (Washington, D.C. Office)
Thomas W. Dimond
Douglas A. Doetsch
Kelly J. Doherty
Peter J. Donoghue
Brian G. Donovan
Kira E. Druyan
Ralph P. Dudziak
Daniel Dumezich
James Gregory Duncan (Washington, D.C. Office)
Jeffrey L. Dunetz (New York, N. Y. Office)
John F. Edelbrock, Jr.
Kerry Lynn Edwards (Washington, D.C. Office)
Thomas P. Egan
Robert D. Ellis (New York, N.Y. Office)
Timothy B. Ellwood (Houston, Texas Office)
Carlos R. Escobar (Houston, Texas Office)
Donald M. Falk (Washington, D.C. Office)
Kirsten J. Felling
Robert V. Fitzsimmons
Patricia A. Flaming
Amy B. Folbe
Nicole V.F. Bergman Fong (New York, N.Y. Office)
Jeffrey S. Fowler
David J. Franklyn
Fritz E. Freidinger
Gary D. Friedman (New York, N.Y. Office)
Jeffrey B. Frishman
Laurie A. Gallancy
Kathy Woeber Gardner (Not admitted in IL)
Bruce L. Gelman
James Charles Geoly
Robert H. George (Houston, Texas Office)
Michael I. Gilman (Washington, D.C. Office)
Jill R. Goodman
Glenn Graff
Anthony G. Graham (Los Angeles, California Office)
David W. Grawemeyer
Richard Greta (Los Angeles, California Office)
Terri T. Griffiths (Houston, Texas Office)
Salvatore Guerrera (New York, New York Office)
Sandra M. Guerrero
Karen Hagnell
Keith C. Hannigan
Myles R. Hansen (Washington, D.C. Office)
Andrew G. Haring (Tokyo, Japan Office)
Stacee A. Hasenbalg
Robert G. Harvey (New York, N.Y. Office)
Sally A. T. Hawkins (Houston, Texas Office)
Ronald G. Hayden
Wendy J. Heiman
Michelle M. Henkel
William C. Hermann
Michael L. Hermsen (Not admitted in IL)
Judith Hession (Houston, Texas Office)
Daniel G. Hildebrand
Carol A. Hitselberger
Debra Bedford Hoffman
Robert F. Hugi

(See Next Column)

MAYER, BROWN & PLATT—*Continued*

ASSOCIATES (Continued)

David A. Hyman
Manzer Ijaz (London, England Office)
Susan J. Irion
Gary A. Isaac
Dean Alan Isaacs
Valerie-Leila Jaber (New York, N.Y. Office)
William J. Jackson (Houston, Texas Office)
Josh Jacobson (New York, N.Y. Office)
Molly F. James (Washington, D.C. Office)
John A. Janicik
Jerome J.M.F. Jauffret (Los Angeles, California Office)
Christian A. Johnson
David M. Jones
Paul A. Jorissen
Daniel Kanter
Adam B. Kastner (Los Angeles, California Office)
Daniel G. Kazan
Walter Keneally (Houston, Texas Office)
Terry Kernell (Houston, Texas Office)
Nabil L. Khodadad (London, England Office)
Sally Doubet King
Thomas Kittle-Kamp
Marc L. Klyman
Beth R. Kramer (New York, N. Y. Office)
Stephen A. Kubiatowski
Kathryn A. Kusske (Washington, D.C. Office)
Dennis G. LaGory
Ronald M. Lambert
Bennett W. Lasko
Benjamin W. Lau (New York, N.Y. Office)
Susan J. Launi (Brussels, Belgium Office)
John F. Lawlor
Kim A. Leffert
Stacey N. LeFont (New York, N.Y. Office)
Jerome M. Lehrman
Monte M. Lemann II (Los Angeles, California Office)
Mary B. Lemuth (Houston, Texas Office)
Fredrick S. Levin
Jeffrey C.B. Levine
William A. Levy
Anne K. Lewis
Lori E. Lightfoot
Erik J. Lillya
Nicholas W. Lobenthal (New York, N.Y. Office)
Beth Ann Loeb
Douglas J. Lubelchek
Daniel W. Luther
Kimberly A. Lynch (New York, N.Y. Office)
Edward Skinner Madara, III (New York, N.Y. Office)
Marjorie M. Margolies
Jonathan L. Marks
Andrew S. Marovitz
John F. Marsh (New York, N.Y. Office)
Joseph M. Martin
Tony J. Masciopinto
Andrew Mattei (New York, N.Y. Office)
Travis C. McCullough (Houston, Texas Office)
Marlaine J. McVisk
David E. Metz
Joyce L. Meyer
Paul Meyer
Bruce A. Mitchell
Antonio Molestina (New York, N.Y. Office)
Susan J. Moran
Louis P. Moritz
Christopher P. Murphy (Los Angeles, California Office)
Lucia Nale
Edward S. Nekritz
Amy E. Newman
Caroline Neyrinck (Brussels, Belgium Office)
Philip J. Niehoff
Limor Nissan (New York, N.Y. Office)
Kenneth E. Noble
Frank P. Nocco (New York, N.Y. Office)
Lennine Occhino
Mary Payton O'Hara (New York, New York Office)
Steven J. Olson
Michael C. Overman (Houston, Texas Office)
Rosaria Vivo Owen
Christine Pagac
Susan K. Pavlica (Houston, Texas Office)
Ross Pazzol
George A. Pecoulas
Daniel Penn (New York, N.Y. Office)
Scott P. Perlman (Washington, D.C. Office)
Vytas A. Petrulis (Houston, Texas Office)
Laurie E. Phelan
Jeffrey S. Piell
Edward R. Rabe, Jr.
Stephen K. Racker
Cynthia D. Randell
Shruthi G. Reddy
Charles F. Regan, Jr.
Mari Yamamoto Regnier
N. Neville Reid
Thomas S. Reif
Craig E. Reimer
Gary W. Reinbold
Clisson S. Rexford
Michael P. Rissman
Carol S. Rivers
Walter M. Rogers
Leonard X Rosenberg
Marc E. Rosenthal
Laurie R. Rubenstein (Washington, D.C. Office)
Javier H. Rubinstein
Harvey P. Sanders (New York, New York Office)
Stefan H. Sarles (London, England Office)
Christine A. Scarnecchia
Nina E. Scholtz (Los Angeles, California Office)
Joel Schreier
George B. Schwab (New York, N.Y. Office)
Sharyl L. Schwartz
Jeffrey Seifman
Ronald M. Shoss (Houston, Texas Office)
Kerri Appel Siegel (New York, N.Y. Office)
Jonathan E. Singer
Steven K. Skinner
David F. Sladic (Houston, Texas Office)
Adam C. Sloane (Washington, D.C. Office)
Michael Sloyer (New York, N.Y. Office)
Diane Green Smith
Marc F. Sperber
Mary Ann Spiegel
James M. Spira
Bruce M. Stachenfeld (New York, N.Y. Office)
John P. Starkweather
Miriam B. Stein
William O. Stein (Los Angeles, California Office)
Scott M. Stewart
Glen F. Strong

ASSOCIATES (Continued)

(See Next Column)

John J. Sullivan (Washington, D.C. Office)
Michael T. Sullivan
Edward J. Tabaczyk
Mark R. Taylor
Mark R. Ter Molen
Carl J. Thomas (Los Angeles, California Office)
Richard J. Timmel
Oliver Ott Trumbo, III (New York, N.Y. Office)
Michael L. Tucker
Mark R. Uhrynuk (London, England Office)
Alan E. Untereiner (Washington, D.C. Office)
Stephen Van Dolsen
Robert G. Vanecko
Christopher M. Vidovic
John Voorhees
Kathleen Anne Walsh (New York, N.Y. Office)
Tracy Goad Walter
Barbara Bidell Watkins
Lyman C. Welch
Thomas C. Wexler (London, England Office)
Lawrence E. White
Robert B. White
Edward H. Williams
Gary A. Winters (Washington, D.C. Office)
Nigel A. Wright (London, England Office)
Karen L. Young (London, England Office)
Richard L. Zack (New York, N.Y. Office)
Donald P. Zeithaml, Jr.
Michael T. Zeller (Not admitted in IL)
Scott M. Zemser (New York, N.Y. Office)
Richard G. Ziegler

For full biographical listings, see the Martindale-Hubbell Law Directory

MAYER, FRIEDLICH, SPIESS, TIERNEY, BROWN & PLATT

(See Mayer, Brown & Platt)

McBRIDE BAKER & COLES (AV)

500 West Madison Street 40th Floor, 60661
Telephone: 312-715-5700
Cable Address: "Chilaw"
Telex: 270258
Telecopier: 312-993-9350

MEMBERS OF FIRM

David Ackerman
Henry S. Allen, Jr.
Steven B. Bashaw
Michael J. Boland
Malcolm H. Brooks
Martin J. Campanella
William J. Cooney
Paul D. Frenz
Anthony L. Frink
Andrew R. Gelman
Geoffrey G. Gilbert
Lola Miranda Hale
Kenneth A. Jenero
Francis L. Keldermans
Thomas J. Kinasz
Evan M. Kjellenberg
Sidney C. Kleinman
Clifton A. Lake
David S. Mann
Elias N. Matsakis
Morgan J. Ordman
Elizabeth S. Perdue
Robert W. Queeney
Richard A. Redmond
G. Gale Roberson, Jr.
John P. Ryan, Jr.
Anne Hamblin Schiave
Robert C. Schnitz
Robert I. Schwimmer
David Shayne
Thomas J. Smedinghoff
Mark J. Steger
William M. Stevens
Steven B. Varick
Thomas P. Ward
Michael L. Weissman
Richard R. Winter
Joseph S. Wright, Jr.
Larry M. Zanger

OF COUNSEL

Robert O. Case
Lawrence A. Coles, Jr.
John J. Cresto
N. A. Jim Giambalvo
Thomas R. Leavens

ASSOCIATES

Naomi R. Angel
Adam E. Berman
Robert M. Brawley
Richard P. Emich
Marc L. Fogelberg
Christopher J. Grant
Robert S. Hirschhorn
Jerald Holisky
Patrick W. Kocian
Steven R. Lifson
Joseph S. Messer
Richard F. Nelson
Linda Popovich Nicastro
Carolyn O'Connor
Lorijean G. Oei
Nancy L. Pionk
George Michael Sanders
Paul R. Simons
Thomas R. Stilp
Peter J. Strand
Jonathan E. Strouse

For full biographical listings, see the Martindale-Hubbell Law Directory

McDERMOTT, WILL & EMERY (AV)

A Partnership including Professional Corporations
227 West Monroe Street, 60606-5096
Telephone: 312-372-2000
Telex: 253565 Milam CGO
Facsimile: 312-984-7700
Boston, Massachusetts Office: 75 State Street, Suite 1700.
Telephone: 617-345-5000.
Telex: 951324 MILAM BSN.
Facsimile: 617-345-5077.
Miami, Florida Office: 201 South Biscayne Boulevard.
Telephone: 305-358-3500.
Telex: 441777 LEYES.
Facsimile: 305-347-6500.

(See Next Column)

McDermott, Will & Emery, *Chicago—Continued*

Washington, D.C. Office: 1850 K Street, N.W.
Telephone: 202-887-8000.
Telex: 253565 MILAM CGO.
Facsimile: 202-778-8087.
Los Angeles, California Office: 2049 Century Park East.
Telephone: 310-277-4110.
Facsimile: 310-277-4730.
Newport Beach, California Office: 1301 Dove Street, Suite 500.
Telephone: 714-851-0633.
Facsimile: 714-851-9348.
New York, N.Y. Office: 1211 Avenue of the Americas.
Telephone: 212-768-5400.
Facsimile: 212-768-5444.
St. Petersburg, Russia Office: 2/2 Tchaikovsky Street, #517, 191187 St. Petersburg, Russia.
Telephone: (7) (812) 273-9831.
Facsimile: (7) (812) 273-9831.
Tallinn, Estonia Office: Tallinn Business Center, 6 Harju Street, EE0001 Tallinn, Estonia.
Telephone: 372 6 31-05-53.
Facsimile: 372 6 31-05-54.
Vilnius, Lithuania Office: Smetonos 6, 2600 Vilnius, Lithuania.
Telephone: 370 2 61-43-08.
Facsimile: 370 2 22-79-55.
Associated (Independent) Offices:
Brussels, Belgium: Uettwiller Grelon Lippens Dekeyser, 73 avenue Vandendriessche, 1150 Brussels, Belgium.
Telephone: (32) (2) 772-87-50.
Facsimile: (32) (2) 772-87-52.
London, England: Paisner & Co, Bouverie House, 154 Fleet Street, London EC4A 2DQ, England.
Telephone: (44) (71) 353-0299.
Facsimile: (44) (71) 583-8621.
Paris, France: Uettwiller Grelon Gout Canat & Associes, 68, boulevard de Courcelles, 75017 Paris, France.
Telephone: (33) (1) 48 88 89 00.
Facsimile: (33) (1) 48 88 05 50.

MEMBERS OF FIRM

Edward H. McDermott (1896-1982)
William M. Emery (1907-1966)
John W. Cavanaugh (1906-1969)
Frederick G. Acker
Wendell H. Adair, Jr. *
Michael F. Anthony
Frederick W. Axley *
Julie Badel
W. Timothy Baetz *
Grant A. Bagan
Rita T. Bahr
David A. Baker
George W. Benson
Stuart M. Berkson *
James E. Betke *
Shell J. Bleiweiss
Wilber H. Boies *
Thomas C. Borders *
Robert E. Bouma
Raymond E. Boyle
Alan C. Brown
Michelle C. Burke
William J. Butler
Stephen M. Chiles
Sophia E. Chrusciel
Paul J. Compernolle
Richard L. Dees *
David P. De Yoe
Thomas H. Donohoe
John R. Doyle *
Monte Dube
David J. Duez *
Ann Duker
John M. Eckel *
Scott Ellwood
Stephen D. Erf
Cecilia M. Eytalis
Michael R. Fayhee *
Fred I. Feinstein *
Jerry K. Fellows
Helen R. Friedli *
John Edmund Gaggini *
Richard J. Garvey *
James M. Gaynor, Jr.
Lawrence Gerber *
Scott N. Gierke
Dean C. Gramlich
Byron L. Gregory
Steven P. Handler *
Richard A. Hanson *
Don S. Harnack *
Carol A. Harrington
Mark M. Harris
Alan J. Hawksley
Quentin G. Heisler, Jr. *
John P. Hendrickson *
Carolyn S. Hesse
Robert G. Hoban
Steven H. Hoeft
Brian S. Hucker *
Charles E. Hussey II
Thomas M. Jones *
Gregory W. Kabel
Lisa M. Kaderabek
Stanley R. Kaminski, Jr.
Dean A. Kant
Gary C. Karch
Stewart W. Karge
Howard L. Kastel *
David M. Keller
Melinda M. Kleehamer
Janet M. Koran
Paul J. Kozacky
Andrea S. Kramer
Bernard S. Kramer
Mercedes A. Laing
Marilyn Lamar
Paul L. Langer
Jean M. Langie
Gerard M. Latus *
Wade S. Leathers
Jon R. Lind *
Richard T. Lorenz, Jr. *
James L. Malone III *
H. George Mann *
David Marx, Jr.
Barbara W. Mayers
John H. McDermott *
William J. McGrath *
J. Robert McMenamin *
Cathy Houston McNeil
Stanley H. Meadows *
Jerome B. Meites
Edward F. Michalak
Stephen R. Miller
Elizabeth M. Mills
Nancy A. Mitchell
Sandra R. Murphy *
Lonn W. Myers *
Alan D. Nesburg *
Franklin W. Nitikman *
Gerald M. Offutt *
Alan J. Olson *
Anne M. Pachciarek
Gregory G. Palmer
Joseph H. Paquin, Jr.
Steven F. Pflaum

(See Next Column)

MEMBERS OF FIRM (Continued)

Joan F. Polacheck
William R. Pomierski
James R. Pranger
Gary L. Prior *
William J. Quinlan, Jr.
Barry J. Quirke
Lazar Pol Raynal
Douglas M. Reimer *
James M. Roche *
N. Rosie Rosenbaum
Lewis S. Rosenbloom
Nancy G. Ross
Joseph O. Rubinelli, Jr.
Louis M. Rundio, Jr.
Alan S. Rutkoff
David R. Ryder
Martha V. Sackley
Richard L. Sandler
Harry M. Sangerman *
Steven S. Scholes
Robert A. Schreck, Jr. *
John T. Schriver, III *
William P. Schuman
Harvey M. Sheldon
Karen A. Simonsen
Hugh F. Smart
David J. Stetler
Jeffrey E. Stone
Cornelius J. Sullivan *
Douglas C. Tibble
L. Stanton Towne
James M. Trapp *
Stephen A. Tsoris
Bruce H. Weitzman *
Roger W. Wenthe
Neal J. White
Todd R. Wiener
Scott M. Williams
Mark L. Yeager
Lowell D. Yoder
Daniel N. Zucker

COUNSEL

Norman H. Nachman
M. Kevin Outterson
Joseph Keig, Jr. *

OF COUNSEL

James W. Ashley
Frank E. Babb
Arthur E. Bryan, Jr.
Patrick J. Caraher *
Frank M. Covey, Jr.
Irving S. Fishman *
Charles N. Huber
Robert B. McDermott *
Howard C. Michaelsen, Jr.
Winston C. Moore
Joseph P. Mulhern
Emory S. Naylor, Jr.
John S. Pennell
Stephen C. Sandels *
Warren C. Seieroe
Rainer R. Weigel *
Samuel Weisbard

ASSOCIATES

Joseph S. Adams
Brent R. Austin (Not admitted in IL)
Maria S. Bayer
Michael A. Bezney
John A. Biek (Not admitted in IL)
David S. Blackmar
Michael L. Boykins
Jillisa Brittan
Julie Y. Chen (Not admitted in IL)
Paul E. Chronis
Kevin T. Conroy
Jonathan M. Cyrluk
Terry Darden (Not admitted in IL)
James E. Dickett
Kathryn T. Ditmars
Daniel J. Donnelly
Christine M. Drylie
Margaret M. Duncan
Kevin J. Feeley
John A. Flaherty
Jonathan J. Flaum
David A. Fruchtman
Alfonso Garcia-Mingo (Not admitted in the United States)
Charles M. Gering
Nancy S. Gerrie
Matthew M. Getter
Susan Shaw Gleason
Lisa B. Greenfield
Brooks B. Gruemmer
Kimberly Kelley Gruemmer
Marcelo Halpern
B. Lane Hasler
Kristen E. Hazel
Nancy M. Hoffman
Jeffrey A. Jung
P. André Katz
Judith A. Kelley
Lydia R. B. Kelley
Paula J. Krasny
Marielle V. Lifshitz
Robert D. LoPrete
Lynnette L. Lupia
Scott Martin
Janet A. Marvel
Catherine A. McCain
Gregory A. McConnell
Sandra Parker McGill
David B. Montgomery
Diane M. Morgenthaler
Gail H. Morse
Christopher M. Murphy
Adam J. Narot
Susan M. Nash
Maureen A. Pastika
Carol S. Portman
Anne R. Pramaggiore
Matthew M. Preston
Susan Rifken
Nancy Rodkin Rotering
Jack H. Rottner
Elizabeth A. Rourke
Michael S. Schachter
Heidi J. Steele
Courtney N. Stillman
Jan E. Stone
John P. Tamisiea
Terence J. Venezia
Kevin J. Walsh
Michelle M. Warner
Daniel J. Weissburg (Not admitted in IL)
Wendy Merz Wells
Peggy A. Zemanick
Craig H. Zimmerman

*Denotes a lawyer employed by a Professional Corporation which is a member of the Firm.

For full biographical listings, see the Martindale-Hubbell Law Directory

---

Miller, Shakman, Hamilton, Kurtzon & Schlifke (AV)

Suite 1100, 208 South La Salle Street, 60604
Telephone: 312-263-3700
FAX: 312-263-3270

MEMBERS OF FIRM

Neil H. Adelman
Marc O. Beem
Stephen J. Bisgeier
Geraldine Soat Brown
Derek L. Cottier
Edward W. Feldman
Arthur W. Friedman
Ruth Goldman
R. Dickey Hamilton
Diane F. Klotnia

(See Next Column)

MILLER, SHAKMAN, HAMILTON, KURTZON & SCHLIFKE—*Continued*

MEMBERS OF FIRM (Continued)

Michael S. Kurtzon
Scott M. Lapins
Edward W. Malstrom
Barry A. Miller
Ronald S. Miller
Bernard A. Schlifke
Michael L. Shakman

OF COUNSEL

Morton John Barnard
Theodore Berger
Norman Geis
David J. Krupp
David Parson
Maurice Rosenfield
Stanton Schuman

ASSOCIATES

James P. Bailinson
Julie H. Friedman
Lisa M. Ramsden
Mark A. Segal
John J. Stocker

For full biographical listings, see the Martindale-Hubbell Law Directory

PETERSON & ROSS (AV)

200 East Randolph Drive, Suite 7300, 60601-6969
Telephone: 312-861-1400
Telecopy: 312-565-0832
Telex: 25-4161 EPALAW CGO
Los Angeles, California Office: 333 South Grand Avenue, Suite 1600, 90071-1520.
Telephone: 213-625-3500.
Springfield, Illinois Office: 600 South Second Street, Suite 104, 62704.
Telephone: 217-525-0700.
Morristown, New Jersey Office: 55 Madison Avenue, Suite 200, 07960.
Telephone: 201-993-9668.

MEMBERS OF FIRM

Walter Henry Eckert (1923-1944)
Walter W. Ross, Jr. (1934-1972)
Abe R. Peterson (1923-1983)
Owen Rall (1933-1985)
Theodore Joseph Tsoumas
J. Robert Geiman
Peter M. Sfikas
Lawrence X. Pusateri
Theodore A. Boundas
Norbert J. Wegerzyn
Daniel B. Hales
Joseph J. Hasman
J. Richard Childers
Vincent P. Reilly
Raymond J. Jast
Michael P. Tone
Louis C. Roberts
Terry M. Cosgrove
Thomas A. Reed
Ernest W. Irons
Clay H. Phillips
John M. Duczynski
James A. Skarzynski
Gary E. Wilcox
Bonnie G. Lederman
William K. McVisk
Thomas S. White
Thomas F. Lucas
Daniel A. Engel
John K. Silk
Walter M. Piecewicz
Craig A. Varga
Geoffrey L. Isaac
Jeffrey M. Ammons
Charles D. Thomas
John T. Evrard
David J. Novotny
Tracy C. Beggs
Alexis J. Rogoski
Robert L. Suomala
Regina K. McCabe
William A. Chittenden, III
Anne Fiedler
Rocco J. Spagna
John E. Black, Jr.
Julia M. Core
Christopher J. Graham
Larry A. Hoellwarth
Roderick T. Dunne
Stephen M. Hoke
Tamra S. Kempf
Priscilla A. May
Bruce N. Menkes
Donald A. Murday
David T. Burrowes
Brian A. Frankl
Jeanne M. Lamar
Jonathan N. Ledsky
Donald B. Leventhal
Michael J. Rosen
Oran F. Whiting

OF COUNSEL

Elroy C. Sandquist, Jr.
Robert G. Schloerb
Robert S. Milnikel
Andrew J. Palmer

ASSOCIATES

Noelle Swanson Berg
Lorna Borenstein (Not admitted in IL)
Kathleen A. Brosnan
Cunera M. Buys
Cheryl L. Chavarrie
Ann M. Chilton
Cecilia M. Clarke
Janice L. Cleary
Dennis B. Condon
Carrie E. Cope
Sarah Gaines Grider Cronan
Carol C. Dillard
Elizabeth Gwynn Dobie
Dirk E. Ehlers
Robert E. Fisher
Lee Ann S. Galowich
Felicia Lynn Gerber
Sherri L. Giffin
Jeannine M. Glavas
Kristi Ann Gleim
Edward M. Graham
Karen M. Kopp
Robin J. Korman
David L. Koury
Daniel S. Lambert
David G. Larmore
Sean Patrick MacCarthy
Nick A. Markus
Joanne J. Matousek
Theodore J. May
Arthur J. McColgan, II
Daniel J. McMahon
William M. Monat
S. Ana Perich
Raana C. Rafiullah
R. Nathan Randall
William P. Rector
Rene Robertson
Stephen J. Rosenfeld
Peter G. Ross
David P. Schluckebier
David F. Schmidt
Susan M. Solomon

(See Next Column)

ASSOCIATES (Continued)

Robert H. Sorge
Kira E. Sufalko
Douglas J. Varga
John A. Vasko
Thomas P. Yardley, Jr.

RESIDENT PARTNERS AT SPRINGFIELD, ILLINOIS OFFICE

Zack Stamp

RESIDENT PARTNERS AT LOS ANGELES, CALIFORNIA OFFICE

Richard O. Briggs
Robert B. Leck III
Steven Ray Garcia

RESIDENT PARTNERS AT MORRISTOWN, NEW JERSEY OFFICE

Verice M. Mason
Kenneth D. Merin

RESIDENT OF COUNSEL AT LOS ANGELES, CALIFORNIA OFFICE

Robert C. Haase, Jr.

RESIDENT ASSOCIATES AT LOS ANGELES, CALIFORNIA OFFICE

Amy Boorer
Randall J. Kelley
Daniel J. Kelly
Daniel T. Mosier
Michael J. Partos
Christopher R. Pflug

RESIDENT ASSOCIATES AT SPRINGFIELD, ILLINOIS

Kevin J. McFadden
Kirk H. Petersen

For full biographical listings, see the Martindale-Hubbell Law Directory

PRETZEL & STOUFFER, CHARTERED (AV)

One South Wacker Drive Suite 2500, 60606-4673
Telephone: 312-346-1973
FAX: 312-346-8242; 346-8060

Gemma B. Allen
Richard William Austin
David M. Bennett
Richard L. Berdelle
Audrey A. Berish
Glen R. Bernfield
Paula Meyer Besler
William B. Bower
Michael G. Bruton
Barbara Condit Canning
Maryanne H. Capron
Robert Marc Chemers
Michael A. Clarke
Elizabeth Conkin
Suzanne Marie Crowley
Desmond P. Curran
Jeffery W. Davis
Marilyn Brock Doig
Joseph M. Dooley, III
Matthew J. Egan
Marc I. Fenton
M. Anne Gavagan
David B. Gelman
Timothy J. Gillick (1940-1984)
Michael D. Goodman
Richard J. Gorman
Joyce M. Greene
Sally Oxley Hagerty
Patrick F. Healy, III
Brian T. Henry
Robert J. Heyne
Robert S. Hoover
Heather L. Huthwaite
William E. Kenny
Donald J. Kindwald
James A. Knox, Jr.
Christine M. Koman
Marlene A. Kurilla
James A. LaBarge
Ronald S. Ladden
Steven M. Laduzinsky
Donald B. Lenderman
David J. Loughnane
Patrick Foran Lustig
Steven John Martin
Victoria L. Masciopinto
William P. McGowen, III
John M. McGregor
Daniel B. Mills
James P. Moran
Daniel J. Moriarty
Edward H. Nielsen
Donald J. O'Meara, Jr.
Molly M. O'Reilly
Gary Arthur Peters
Paul L. Price
Neil K. Quinn
Charles F. Redden
Lynn M. Reid
Catherine Coyne Reiter
Mark D. Roth
Roger A. Rubin
Edward B. Ruff, III
Lewis M. Schneider
Betty-Jane Schrum
Alan J. Schumacher
Peter G. Skiko
John V. Smith, II
Jodi M. Smoller
Christine Hough Speranza
Mark P. Standa
Leo M. Tarpey, Jr.
Robert D. Tuerk
Anthony J. Tunney
Stephen C. Veltman
John J. Walsh, III
Richard M. Waris
Timothy A. Weaver
Michael J. Weber
William P. White III
Daniel G. Wills
Richard S. Wisner

OF COUNSEL

Joseph B. Lederleitner
Paul W. Pretzel (1906-1987)
Ralph E. Stouffer, Jr.

Representative Clients: Allstate Insurance Co.; St. Paul Insurance Companies.

For full biographical listings, see the Martindale-Hubbell Law Directory

ROOKS, PITTS AND POUST (AV)

Suite 1500 Xerox Centre, 55 West Monroe Street, 60603
Telephone: 312-372-5600
Telex: MCI/WUI 650-3698534
Facsimile: 312-726-9239 and 312-726-2396
Wheaton, Illinois Office: 201 Naperville Road.
Telephone: 708-690-8500.
Facsimile: 708-690-8553.
Joliet, Illinois Office: 111 North Ottawa Street.
Telephone: 815-727-4511.
Facsimile: 815-727-1586.

(See Next Column)

ROOKS, PITTS AND POUST, *Chicago—Continued*

MEMBERS OF FIRM

Jay A. Lipe	James L. Donnelly
Thomas Feehan	Lee T. Hettinger
Ray F. Drexler	Robert C. Bodach
Alan S. Ganz	Richard J. Kavanagh (Resident, Joliet Office)
Francis A. Heroux	Marc A. Primack
Jerome N. Groark	Marc D. Ginsberg
Robert J. Baron	Michael Gahan
Stephen E. Sward	Terrence M. Burns
Timothy J. Groark	Mark W. Weisbard
John J. Blasi	Robert R. Gorbold
James H. Ihrke	George J. Vosicky
Wayne F. Plaza	Martin A. A. Diestler
Terrence E. Kiwala	David J. Bressler
George N. Gilkerson, Jr.	Michael F. Sexton
Terrence J. Madden	Nancy E. Paridy
John J. Mangan	Mark S. Anderson
Frank C. Rowland	Mary E. Callow
Fred R. McMorris	Thomas R. Hill
James D. Grumley	Patricia Cari Nowak
Ian M. Sherman	Janet A. Stiven
Jeffrey M. Dalebroux	Kenneth W. Clingen
Michael C. Borders	Mitchell E. Jones
Geoffrey A. Bryce	

Chris E. Limperis

Harry N. Arger	Charles A. Le Moine
Diane P. Bartus	Joan D. Lindauer
Richard Capra	J. Barrett Long
Edward P. Dismukes	Nick Marsico
Glennon P. Dolan	Patrick M. McMahon
Maureen J. Hanlon	Paul A. Michalik
Karen Wilson Howard	Frederick F. Richards, III
Carolyn J. Jones	Julie L. Soloway
Gerald T. Karr	Michael R. Stiff (Resident, Joliet, Illinois Office)
Kenneth R. Landis, Jr.	

COUNSEL

John G. Poust	Eugene H. Ruark

OF COUNSEL

Henry L. Pitts	D. Glenn Ofsthun
Robert W. Thomas (Resident Of Counsel, Joliet, Illinois Office)	Daniel P. Socha
	John V. Ryan, III
William W. Fullagar	John P. Hanna
Stuart C. Kroesch	D. Kevin Blair

H. Sam Onoda

For full biographical listings, see the Martindale-Hubbell Law Directory

ROSENTHAL AND SCHANFIELD, PROFESSIONAL CORPORATION (AV)

46th Floor, Mid Continental Plaza, 55 East Monroe Street, 60603
Telephone: 312-236-5622
Telecopier: 312-236-7274

David M. Alin	Henry M. Morris
Joseph A. Baldi	Gerald B. Mullin
Scott E. Becker	Joseph R. Podlewski, Jr.
Francis A. Beninati	Kristen E. Poplar
Martin K. Blonder	Donald A. Robinson
Steven H. Blumenthal	Lester Rosen
David T. Brown	Robert O. Rosenman
Marvin Cohn	William P. Rosenthal
James M. Dash	Norman L. Rothenbaum
I. Walter Deitch	Susan C. Salita
Rochelle Secemsky Dyme	Leonard Schanfield (1921-1990)
Jay Russell Goldberg	Barry E. Semer
David A. Golin	Suzanne M. Soltan
David E. Gordon	Blooma Stark
William H. Kelly, Jr.	Ronald K. Szopa
Stephen P. Kikoler	Michael Viner
Richard F. Lee	Sheri E. Warsh
Ira M. Levin	Mary Prus Wasik
Joel C. Levin	Stanley R. Weinberger
Mark S. Lieberman	David L. Weinstein
Thomas I. Matyas	Thomas M. White

OF COUNSEL

Alex Elson	Richard E. Friedman

Maynard I. Wishner

For full biographical listings, see the Martindale-Hubbell Law Directory

ROSS & HARDIES (AV)

A Partnership including Professional Corporations
Suite 2500, 150 North Michigan Avenue, 60601
Telephone: 312-558-1000
Cable Address: "Daidin"
TWX: 910-221-1154
Telecopier: 312-750-8600
New York, N.Y. Office: 65 East 55th Street.
Telephone: 212-421-5555.
Telecopier: 212-421-5682.
Washington, D.C. Office: 888 - 16th Street, N.W.
Telephone: 202-296-8600.
Telecopier: 202-296-8791.
Somerset, New Jersey Office: 580 Howard Avenue.
Telephone: 908-563-2700.
Telecopier: 908-563-2777.

MEMBERS OF FIRM

CHICAGO, ILLINOIS OFFICE

William P. O'Keefe (1929-1979)	C. Frederick LeBaron, Jr.
Clarence H. Ross (1950-1981)	Larry R. Goldstein
Richard F. Babcock (1957-1993)	Leslie D. Locke
Melvin A. Hardies (1950-1994)	Susan Grob Lichtenfeld
David N. McBride	Monica A. Carroll
William J. Winger	Elizabeth West Speidel
Bruce J. McWhirter	Mark N. Woyar
David F. Sterling *	Bernard Roccanova
William P. O'Keefe, Jr. *	Susan M. Mongillo
Robert J. Pristave *	Daniel P. Hogan
Duane A. Feurer	Robert T. Zielinski
Richard J. Rappaport *	Jeffrey E. Rogers
Robert E. Wangard	T. Stephen Dyer
Michael H. King *	John W. Van Vranken
James K. Toohey	Jacquelyn F. Kidder
William D. Serritella	Patrick E. Brady
Richard E. Lieberman	Alison Cornell Blair Laing
Robert W. Kleinman	John F. Pollick
Keith Philip Schoeneberger	Arnold E. Grant
Paul A. Lutter	Shawn M. Lyden
Robert S. Jacobs	Jon K. Stromsta
Lawrence R. Samuels	Kurt H. Feuer
James T. Harrington	Peter J. Valeta
Barbara Baran	Raymond H. Groble III
Carol Berlin Manzoni	Ira P. Goldberg
James B. Riley, Jr.	David L. Rieser
Louis W. Levit	Elizabeth L. Corey
Richard J. Mason	Sean M. Sullivan
Robert M. Fishman	P. Matthew Glavin
Raymond T. Murphy	Anne M. Beckert
Scott Hodes	Donald C. Pasulka
Gary L. Starkman	Keith A. Dorman
Robert O. Wienke	Patricia K. Smoots
Timothy C. Klenk	Steven M. Taber
Charles M. Chadd	Jules I. Crystal

NEW YORK, NEW YORK OFFICE

Joseph S. Kaplan	J. Joseph Bainton
John B. Pellegrini	Richard A. Wilsker
Yvette Harmon	Michael J. Di Mattia
Christopher P. O'Connell	Robert S. Blaustein
Kenneth Zuckerbrot	Philip L. Guarino
Kevin T. Collins	Jody B. Keltz
Lawrence N. Mullman	Shari L. Pine

WASHINGTON, D.C. OFFICE

Myles J. Ambrose	Steven P. Kersner
Raymond J. Kimball	Stephen R. Ross
John A. Howell	James A. Stenger
John R. Fornaciari	Robert M. Disch
Robert D. McDonald	Evelyn M. Suarez

Jeffrey S. Neeley

SOMERSET, NEW JERSEY OFFICE

Helen Davis Chaitman

COUNSEL

CHICAGO, ILLINOIS OFFICE

Keith I. Parsons	Karl Berolzheimer
Walker Winter	Joan Webster Connor
Maurice P. Wolk	Joann Tansey Angarola

COUNSEL

NEW YORK, NEW YORK OFFICE

Leonard Rovins

COUNSEL

WASHINGTON, D.C. OFFICE

Salvatore E. Caramagno	Thomas Gerald Olp

ASSOCIATES

Roxanne A. Ablan	Kelly J. Bugle
J. Michael Amrein	John M. Callahan
Scott Becker	Andrew D. Crain
Jeffrey A. Berman	Dana D. Deane
Mary Clare Bonaccorsi	Scott P. Downing
Jerome K. Bowman	Thomas D. Drescher

(See Next Column)

ROSS & HARDIES—*Continued*

ASSOCIATES (Continued)

Jeffrey S. Dunlap
Debra L. Duzinskas
Matthew S. Elvin
Robert W. Glantz
Lisa Allen Golant
David S. Guin
Janice K. Hamblin
Julie L. Helenbrook
Kenton L. Hill
Darren J. Hunter
Gail Chaney Kalinich
Kimberly J. Kannensohn
Kathryn M. Kemp
A. Jay Koehler, III
Susan Febles Lifvendahl
Laura A. Lindner
Mary Therese Link
Amy B. Manning
Ginger G. Mayer
John P. McCabe
Lisa I. McCarthy
Kimberly Grossman Metrick
Colleen Elizabeth Moore
Mary Margaret Moore
Helmer J. Nelson
John C. Nishi
Alice G. Owings
Christopher S. Panczner
Jacqueline Rosenberg Peltz
David A. Piech
Christian M. Poland (Not admitted in IL)
Sharon P. Riley
Beth A. Sansiper (Not admitted in IL)
Harry J. Secaras
Brian L. Shaw
Leonora L. Shaw
Sarah Winterhalter Sheehan
Brian A. Sher
Steven K. Sims
George J. Spathis
Kari J. Sperstad
Joel H. Spitz
Anne T. Stinneford
Philip N. Storm
Thomas D. Titsworth, Jr.
Kimberly Ann Warnke
Charles W. Wesselhoft
Neil G. Wolf
Jay A. Yalowitz

NEW YORK, NEW YORK OFFICE

Jose Anibal Baez
Andrew Beatty
Stephen M. De Luca
Carol A. Dunning
Philip Goldstein
Judith A. Hagley
Donald S. Krueger
John G. McCarthy
Theresa K. Nick
David F. Norton
Cleve Marlon Scott
Catherine M. Vaczy
Michael C. Xylas

WASHINGTON, D.C. OFFICE

Roger Banks
Kathryn A. Hutton
Jocelyn R. Roy
John J. Vecchione

SOMERSET, NEW JERSEY OFFICE

Laurence J. Bravman

*Professional Corporation

For full biographical listings, see the Martindale-Hubbell Law Directory

RUDNICK & WOLFE (AV)

A Partnership including Professional Corporations
203 North La Salle Street, Suite 1800, 60601-1293
Telephone: 312-368-4000
Telecopier: 312-236-7516
Telex: 754347
Tampa, Florida Office: 101 East Kennedy Boulevard, Suite 2000.
Telephone: 813-229-2111.
Telecopier: 813-229-1447.
Washington, D.C. Office: 1300 Eye Street, N.W., Suite 280E, 20005-3314.
Telephone: 202-962-8600.
Telecopier: 202-962-8610.

PARTNERS

Stanley J. Adelman
Ross J. Altman
Salvatore A. Barbatano
James L. Beard
Mark A. Berkoff
Brian W. Blaesser
Thomas J. Boodell, Jr.
Michael G. Brennan
Hal M. Brown
William J. Campbell, Jr.
John Chen
Louis S. Cohen
John T. J. Cusack
Gregory R. A. Dahlgren
Byron S. Delman
Charles L. Edwards
Michael H. Elam
Mark I. Feldman
Lawrence J. Fey
Sue Ann Fishbein
Michael B. Fischer
Paul E. Fisher
Bruce A. Fox
Harold W. Francke
Elizabeth H. Friedgut
Roselyn L. Friedman
J. Kevin Garvey
Deborah L. Gersh
Mark A. Gershon
Thomas F. Geselbracht
Allen J. Ginsburg (P.C.)
Edward S. Goldman
Michael R. Goldman
Robert H. Goldman
Kim A. Goodhard
Shepard Gould
Ross Green
George L. Grumley
Errol R. Halperin
Kenneth Hartmann
Stuart Hershman
John H. Heuberger
Paul Homer (P.C.)
Richard S. Homer
Gregory W. Hummel
Richard S. Huszagh
Leroy G. Inskeep
Stacy L. Johnson
Howard E. Kane
David J. Kayner
Sandra Y. Kellman
Kenneth K. Kneubuhler
Mary K. Krigbaum
Stephen A. Landsman
Peter A. Levy
Steven L. Loren
Bruce D. Loring
Gerald B. Lurie
David G. Lynch
John R. Mannix, Jr.
Jerome Marks
Philip V. Martino
Adrianne C. Mazura
Carol A. McErlean

(See Next Column)

PARTNERS (Continued)

William M. McErlean
Charles R. McKirdy
Ralph R. Mickelson
Lee I. Miller
Nicholas R. Minear
David N. Missner
Portia Owen Morrison
Theodore J. Novak (P.C.)
Mark D. Olson
Jeffrey N. Owen
George T. Plumb
Harold B. Pomerantz
Mark A. Rabinowitz
J. Timothy Ramsey
William L. Rawson
Lawrence A. Robins (P.C.)
Merwin S. Rosenberg
Richard S. Rosenstein
Peter B. Ross
Harry L. Rudnick (1936-1973)
Lewis G. Rudnick
Paul D. Rudnick
Renee M. Schoenberg
Stephen W. Schwab
Marc P. Seidler
Theodore A. Shapero
Benjamin P. Shapiro
Mark L. Shapiro
Joseph W. Sheyka
Donald A. Shindler
David B. Sickle
Seymour F. Simon
Gary Mark Sircus
Perry J. Snyderman
Morton M. Steinberg
Gregory A. Thorpe
Sandra J. Wall
Robert I. Wertheimer
Dennis E. Wieczorek
Theodore I. Yi
Mark D. Yura
William A. Zolla

ASSOCIATES

Brooke E. Alexy
Simon B. Anolick
Jeffrey S. Arnold
Earl J. Barnes, II
Michael L. Ben-Isvy
Ian Brenson
John D. Burke
Unah Choi
Fredric A. Cohen
Janet B. Cory
Mary Jane DeWeese
Michele Leslie Dodd
Janice L. Duban
Wayne H. Elowe
Todd A. Fishbein
Jennifer M. Fossland
Julie A. Garvey
Elise A. Gibson
Kathleen M. Gilligan
Thomas A. Gilson
Gail M. Goering
Stephen M. Gordon
Elizabeth A. Graber
David L. Hall
Peter G. Hallam
John W. Harbst
Robert G. Hertel, Jr.
Holly Hirst
Ellen M. Hunt
Michele Ann Jenkins
Scott E. Jordan
Laura A. Josephson
Alan M. Kaplan
Brooke M. Kenevan
Richard Klawiter
Samuel H. Kovitz
Michael P. Kuppersmith (Not admitted in IL)
Jill Clark Laarman
Timothy J. Lambert
Christina King Loundy
Shawn S. Magee
Steven J. Marcus
James T. Mayer
Sally J. McDonald
Keith W. Medansky
David E. Mendelsohn
Alison M. Mitchell
John Eric Mitchell
Michael J. Moran
John R. Mussman
Mark P. Naughton, Jr.
Bruce C. Nelson
David W. Norton
David L. Reifman
Bradley V. Ritter
James D. Roberts
William A. Rudnick
Alan J. Salle
Thomas F. Sax
Scott A. Semenek
M. Gretchen Silver
Carol A. Sobczak
Brett D. Soloway
Samuel B. Stempel
Valeria C. St. Vicina
Howard L. Teplinsky
John F. Verhey
Timothy R. Verrilli
Thomas O. Weeks
Mark R. Williams

OF COUNSEL

Elizabeth H. Belkin
Zhengdong Huang
Sandra L. Oberkfell

For full biographical listings, see the Martindale-Hubbell Law Directory

SACHNOFF & WEAVER, LTD. (AV)

30 South Wacker Drive, Suite 2900, 60606
Telephone: 312-207-1000
Telecopier: 312-207-6400

Frank D. Ballantine
Thomas J. Bamonte
Jack L. Block
Barry S. Cain
Paul D. Carman
Stuart J. Chanen
Beth M. Clark
Nathan H Dardick
Stewart Dolin
Candace J. Fabri
Joel S. Feldman
Michael K. Fridkin
Matthew T. Gensburg
Jeffrey T. Gilbert
Neil Greenbaum
David A. Grossberg
Scott D. Gudmundson
Seth M. Hemming
Austin L. Hirsch
Cynthia Jared
Jeffrey L. London
Michael A. LoVallo
Suzanne McCarthy
Douglas R. Newkirk
Arnold A. Pagniucci
Jonathan S. Quinn
Brian D. Roche
Lance R. Rodgers
James A. Rolfes
Barry S. Rosen
Carolyn Hope Rosenberg
Harry B. Rosenberg
Ellis B. Rosenzweig
Lowell E. Sachnoff
Jeffrey A. Schumacher
Marshall Seeder
Clifford J. Shapiro
Duane F. Sigelko
Richard G. Smolev
Sheldon L. Solow
Abraham J. Stern
Edward V. Walsh, III

(See Next Column)

SACHNOFF & WEAVER LTD., *Chicago—Continued*

William N. Weaver, Jr.
Sarah R. Wolff
Edward J. Wong, Jr. (On Leave)
Eugene F. Zelek, Jr.

Anne K. Berleman
Christine M. Bodewes
Craig T. Boggs
Mary N. Cameli
Gary S. Caplan
William E. Doran
Arthur D. Gunther
Angela Y. Im
Jonathan T. Kamin
Michael M. Kaplan
Marc Kieselstein
James M. Marion
John W. Moynihan
Robert H. Nathan
Joel M. Neuman
Michael D. Richman
Neal D. Rutstein
Howard Schickler
Bradley S. Schmarak
Charles P. Schulman
Susan D. Snyder
Ann M. Spillane
Laura M. Wunder

OF COUNSEL

Jules G. Cogan
Ilene Dobrow Davidson
Morton Denlow
Daniel M. Harris
Richard C. Jones
Lewis Manilow
Leonard Jay Schrager
Burton Silverstein
Ernest D. Simon
Joseph Stein

For full biographical listings, see the Martindale-Hubbell Law Directory

SCHIFF HARDIN & WAITE (AV)

A Partnership including Professional Corporations
Founded 1864
7200 Sears Tower, 60606
Telephone: 312-876-1000; Facsimile: 312-258-5600.
Cable Address: Dallschiff. TWX: 910-221-2463.
Wash., D.C., New York, N.Y., Peoria, Ill. & Merrillville, IN.
Washington, D.C. Office: 1101 Connecticut Avenue, N.W.
Telephone: 202-778-6400.
Facsimile: 202-778-6460.
New York, New York Office: 150 East 52nd Street, Suite 2900.
Telephone: 212-753-5000.
Facsimile: 212-753-5044.
Peoria, Illinois Office: 300 Hamilton Boulevard, Suite 100.
Telephone: 309-673-2800.
Facsimile: 309-673-2801.
Merrillville, Indiana Office: 8585 Broadway, Suite 842.
Telephone: 219-738-3820.
Facsimile: 219-738-3826.

MEMBERS OF FIRM

Max Pam (1904-1925)
Harry B. Hurd (1904-1943)
Alexander F. Reichmann (1905-1948)
Andrew J. Dallstream (1927-1962)
Sydney K. Schiff (1924-1973)
Oscar D. Stern (1911-1973)
Louis S. Hardin (1925-1979)
Querin P. Dorschel (1939-1979)
Lester G. Britton (1924-1983)
Thomas W. Abendroth
John F. Adams
Roy M. Adams
Barry S. Alberts
Thomas L. Aldrich
David F. Allen (P.C.)
Bennett P. Applegate
Bruce Jay Baker
Nancy K. Bellis
Jill B. Berkeley
Scott Bieber
Lawrence Block (P.C.)
Michael L. Brody
Harmon A. Brown
James E. Brown
Kevin J. Byrne
Robert D. Campbell
Joseph A. Cancila, Jr.
James A. Clark
Catherine A. Daubard
Paul E. Dengel
W. Brinkley Dickerson, Jr.
Erica L. Dolgin
Patricia Dondanville
Stephen J. Dragich
Joseph J. Duffy
Marci A. Eisenstein
Catherine Masters Epstein
Kevin D. Evans
Peter V. Fazio, Jr.
J. Mark Fisher
Charles D. Fox, IV
Mark C. Friedlander
Eugene J. Geekie, Jr.
Deborah A. Golden
Stuart L. Goodman
Brent J. Graber
Walter C. Greenough
William M. Hannay
Frederick L. Hartmann, Jr.
Ann Rae Heitland
Barbara E. Hermansen
David A. Herpe
Carrie Jankauer Hightman
David R. Hodgman
Allan Horwich
Richard J. Hoskins
Carter Howard
Lawrence H. Jacobson
C. Richard Johnson
Janet M. Johnson
James M. Kane
Andrew A. Kling
Aaron J. Kramer
Donald J. Kreger
Ruth E. Krugly
Rebecca J. Lauer
Ty D. Laurie
Shirley M. Lukitsch
Joseph R. Lundy
Thomas P. Luning
Paul M. Lurie
Owen E. MacBride
Neal A. Mancoff
James E. Mann
Wayne A. McCoy
James R. McDaniel
W. Donald McSweeney (P.C.)
Michael S. Melbinger
Michael L. Meyer
Robert J. Minkus
Gary L. Mowder (P.C.)
William H. Navin
Joseph H. Nesler
Jeanne L. Nowaczewski
Paul B. O'Flaherty (P.C.)
Joseph J. O'Hara, Jr.
Todd S. Parkhurst
Roger Pascal
Charles H.R. Peters
Guenther M. Philipp (P.C.)

(See Next Column)

MEMBERS OF FIRM (Continued)

Scott E. Pickens
Robert R. Pluth, Jr.
Carol R. Prygrosky
Thomas B. Quinn
Robert John Regan
Paul K. Rhoads
Mitchell S. Rieger
Robert H. Riley
Burton R. Rissman (P.C.)
Kenneth M. Roberts
Gabriel M. Rodriguez
Dan W. Schneider
Keith Shay (P.C.)
Terry J. Smith
Mark D. Snider
Frederick J. Sperling
Charles R. Staley
James M. Van Vliet, Jr.
John J. Voortman (P.C.)
Lisa A. Weiland
Bruce P. Weisenthal
Linda Jeffries Wight
Robert B. Wilcox, Jr.
Ronald Wilder
Jay Williams
James B. Wilson (P.C.)
Mark C. Zaander
Sheldon A. Zabel
Christopher J. Zinski

OF COUNSEL

Dean C. Cameron
Milton H. Cohen
John T. Hayes
Norman Waite
John J. Waldron

ASSOCIATES

Brian K. Abrams
Lawrence C. Bachman
Kim Marie Barker
Lauralyn G. Bengel
Katharine L. Bensen
Stephen J. Bonebrake
Robert J. Brantman
Daniel S. Brennan
Stacey E. Burnham
James R. Carey
Renee Cipriano
Frith C. Crandall
Bryan L. Crino
Carter C. Culver
Heidi Dalenberg
Stephanie H. Denby
Lisa A. Dunsky
Becky M. Elrad
Peter J. Falconer
Steven D. Friedland
James P. Gaughan
Stuart I. Graff
Paul Edwin Greenwalt, III
Jeffrey C. Groulx
Edward J. Hannon
Peter L. Harris
Sondra A. Hemeryck
Andrea L. Horne
David Jacobs
Michael L. Kayman
James G. Keane
Brian D. Kluever
Aphrodite Kokolis
Kevin L. Kolton
Joseph J. Krasovec, III
Rosemary Krimbel
John F. Lapham
Lisa C. Leib
J. Timothy Leslie (Not admitted in IL)
Eric L. Lohrenz
David A. Makarechian
William E. Meyer, Jr.
Jeffrey E. Michael
Hallie J. Miller
Jane Ellen Montgomery
Michael K. Moyers
Thomas J. Pauloski
Andrew C. Porter
Jody Lynn Rudman
Lynn E. Rzonca
Heather Chase Sawyer
Adam C. Smedstad
Debra L. Stetter
Linda K. Stevens
Mary R. Szews
Jayant W. Tambe
Patricia J. Thompson
Francine Norz Tobin
Scott C. Tomassi
Robert W. Unikel
Victoria Karen Van Meter
Darren M. R. VanPuymbrouck
Mary A.M. Walters
Glenn Weinstein
Susan B. Weiss
Helen T. Wilson
Lisa Winger
Edward J. Wong, III
Jacqueline C. Zipser

RESIDENT PARTNERS
WASHINGTON, D.C. OFFICE

Edward J. Finn
Barbara K. Heffernan
Drexel D. Journey
Andrew M. Klein
Gearold L. Knowles
Shaheda Sultan

RESIDENT OF COUNSEL

John W. Glendening, Jr.
Edwin S. Rockefeller
John S. Schmid

RESIDENT ASSOCIATES

Genaro G. Fullano
Cheryl L. Jones
Debra Ann Palmer
M. Thompson Rattray

RESIDENT PARTNER
NEW YORK, NEW YORK OFFICE

Paul A. Scrudato

RESIDENT ASSOCIATE

Paul J. Collins

RESIDENT PARTNER
PEORIA, ILLINOIS OFFICE

Theodore L. Eissfeldt

RESIDENT ASSOCIATES

David G. Kabbes
Jason A. Zellers

RESIDENT PARTNER
MERRILLVILLE, INDIANA OFFICE

Peter L. Hatton

For full biographical listings, see the Martindale-Hubbell Law Directory

Chicago—Continued

SIDLEY & AUSTIN (AV)

A Partnership including Professional Corporations
One First National Plaza, 60603
Telephone: 312-853-7000
Telecopier: 312-853-7036
Los Angeles, California Office: 555 W. Fifth Street, 40th Flr., 90013-1010.
Telephone: 213-896-6000.
Telecopier: 213-896-6600.
New York, New York Office: 875 Third Avenue. 10022.
Telephone: 212-906-2000.
Telecopier: 212-906-2021.
Washington, D.C. Office: 1722 Eye Street, N.W., 20006.
Telephone: 202-736-8000.
Telecopier: 202-736-8711.
London, England Office: Broadwalk House, 5 Appold Street, EC2A 2AA.
Telephone: 011-44-71-621-1616.
Telecopier: 011-44-71-626-7937.
Tokyo, Japan Office: Taisho Seimei Hibiya Building, 7th Floor, 9-1, Yurakucho, 1 Chome, Chiyoda-Ku, 100.
Telephone: 011-81-3-3218-5900.
Facsimile: 011-81-3-3218-5922.

MEMBERS OF FIRM
CHICAGO, ILLINOIS OFFICE

Rolando R. Acosta
Anthony J. Aiello
Thomas W. Albrecht
Geraldine M. Alexis
Gerald A. Ambrose
Gerald L. Angst
James G. Archer
Virginia L. Aronson
Frederic J. Artwick
Richard W. Astle
Larry A. Barden
J. Robert Barr
Susan T. Bart
Sara Elizabeth Bartlett
Frank V. Battle, Jr.
William H. Baumgartner, Jr.
Larry D. Berning
Eugene H. Bernstein
H. Bruce Bernstein
Stephan V. Beyer
Alan P. Bielawski
Jack R. Bierig
Frank L. Bixby *
Kevin F. Blatchford
David J. Boyd
Thomas P. Brown
Willis R. Buck, Jr.
James N. Cahan
Stephen C. Carlson
Walter C. Carlson
David W. Carpenter
James J. Carroll
Patrick S. Casey
Thomas K. Cauley, Jr.
James E. Clark
Richard G. Clemens
Thomas A. Cole
William F. Conlon
Philip J. Crihfield
Robert E. Cronin
Maureen M. Crough
Michael W. Davis
William S. DeCarlo
James C. Dechene
Wilbur C. Delp, Jr. *
J. Douglas Donenfeld
Charles W. Douglas
Robert A. Downing *
Maja Campbell Eaton
Joseph S. Ehrman *
Nathan P. Eimer
Arlene C. Erlebacher
Robert A. Ferencz
William O. Fifield
Stephen P. Fitzell
Neil Flanagin *
Mary Patricia Flood
Todd D. Freer
Gregory H. Furda
Douglas F. Fuson
John M. George, Jr.
Brian J. Gold
Michael L. Gold
William C. Golden
Andrew L. Goldstein
Sara J. Gourley
David F. Graham
Jon M. Gregg
Jack Guthman
Jo Lynn Haley
Pamela R. Hanebutt
James A. Hardgrove
Holly A. Harrison
Joseph H. Harrison, Jr.
Lisa A. Hausten
Janet E. Henderson
Kevin J. Hochberg
Michael G. Hron
Lawrence H. Hunt, Jr.
DeVerille A. Huston
Leland E. Hutchinson
David B. Johnson
James D. Johnson
Linzey D. Jones, Jr.
Richard B. Kapnick
Timothy E. Kapshandy
Jim L. Kaput
Gerard D. Kelly
Janet Langford Kelly
Gina B. Kennedy
William D. Kerr
Sharon L. King
Michael J. Kinn
Lawrence I. Kipperman
Andrew G. Klevorn
Shalom L. Kohn
Jeffrey G. Kraft
Bryan Krakauer
Laurence D. Lasky
Laura L. Leonard
John G. Levi
Anthony R. Licata
William F. Lloyd
James R. Looman
Frederick C. Lowinger
Robert J. Maganuco
Robert A. Malstrom
James L. Marovitz
Prentice H. Marshall, Jr.
R. Eden Martin
Henry L. Mason III
Elizabeth K. McCloy
Joseph T. McCullough IV
John M. McDonough
Robert D. McLean
Thomas M. McMahon
Michael I. Miller
Theodore N. Miller
Paul D. Monson
Thomas H. Morsch *
Jodie L. Nedeau
William J. Nissen
Lawrence J. Nyhan
Richard J. O'Brien, Jr.
John M. O'Hare
Richard F. O'Malley, Jr.
Robert M. Olian
Dennis V. Osimitz
Jules M. Perlberg *
George A. Platz III
David T. Pritikin
Richard D. Raskin
Marc E. Raven
Anne E. Rea
Sarah J. Read
Thomas D. Rein

(See Next Column)

MEMBERS OF FIRM
CHICAGO, ILLINOIS OFFICE (Continued)

Dennis P. Reis
William P. Richmond *
Albert Ritchie
Kathleen L. Roach
Thomas A. Roberts
Martin F. Robinson
Jeffrey S. Rothstein
Priscilla E. Ryan
Thomas F. Ryan
John J. Sabl
David R. Sawyier
David M. Schiffman
J. Andrew Schlickman
Eugene A. Schoon
Charles E. Schrank
Andrew H. Shaw
Michael S. Sigal
John P. Simon
Mary Jacobs Skinner
Lee M. Smolen
Sharp Sorensen
David M. Stahl
Jeffrey C. Steen
Philip P. Steptoe III
Gary B. Stern
David R. Stewart
James R. Stinehart
James R. Stinson
Steven Sutherland
Thomas E. Swaney
Michael J. Sweeney
Dale E. Thomas
Stephen P. Thomas
Jeffrey R. Tone
John W. Treece
Constantine L. Trela, Jr.
Sherry S. Treston
Howard J. Trienens *
J. Ronald Trost
*(Not admitted in IL)
Frank B. Vanker
R. Todd Vieregg *
Deirdre M. von Moltke
Roger A. Vree
James F. Warchall
Robert R. Watson
Lyman W. Welch
H. Blair White *
R. Quincy White *
James S. Whitehead
Douglas H. Williams
John C. Williams *
Latham Williams
Robert R. Wootton

RETIRED PARTNERS
CHICAGO, ILLINOIS OFFICE

Russell M. Baird
James E. S. Baker
Russell O. Bennett
Franklin A. Chanen *
Mark C. Curran *
Howard E. Haynie *
David P. List
Charles E. Lomax
Donald S. Petersen
Henry A. Preston

LOS ANGELES, CALIFORNIA OFFICE

Amy L. Applebaum
David W. Burhenn
Gary J. Cohen
M. Scott Cooper
George Deukmejian
Lori Huff Dillman
James F. Donlan
Edward D. Eddy III
Donald Etra
Robert Fabrikant
Howard D. Gest
Richard J. Grad
Larry G. Gutterridge
Kent A. Halkett
Adam M. Handler
Thomas P. Hanrahan
James M. Harris
Richard W. Havel
Marc I. Hayutin
Stuart L. Kadison
Michael C. Kelley
Daniel G. Kelly, Jr.
Moshe J. Kupietzky
Perry L. Landsberg
Theodore N. Miller
Sally Schultz Neely
J. Robert Nelson
Edwin L. Norris
Peter I. Ostroff
Thomas E. Patterson
Richard T. Peters
Linda S. Peterson
Theodore A. Pianko
Howard J. Rubinroit *
Donald L. Samuels
Joel G. Samuels
Sherwin L. Samuels
J. Ronald Trost
D. William Wagner

RETIRED PARTNER
LOS ANGELES, CALIFORNIA OFFICE

George W. McBurney
Robert H. Shutan *

WASHINGTON, D.C. OFFICE

Christopher L. Bell
Judith Hippler Bello
James F. Bendernagel Jr.
Frederic G. Berner, Jr.
Richard D. Bernstein
David T. Buente, Jr.
C. John Buresh
Ann E. Bushmiller
Daniel M. Davidson
Eugene R. Elrod
Lester G. Fant III
Ronald S. Flagg
Alan C. Geolot
Thomas C. Green
Joseph R. Guerra
Samuel I. Gutter
Mark E. Haddad
Kevin Hawley
Stephen S. Hill
Alan F. Holmer
Mark D. Hopson
Terence M. Hynes
George W. Jones, Jr.
Peter D. Keisler
David M. Levy
David J. Lewis
Angus Macbeth
Marc E. Manly
Lorrie M. Marcil
Robert D. McLean
David Michael Miles
Lawrence A. Miller
G. Paul Moates
Michael A. Nemeroff
Francis J. O'Toole
Carter G. Phillips
Vincent F. Prada
Imad I. Qasim
P. David Richardson, II
Melvin Rishe
Constance Arden Sadler
Gene C. Schaerr
Mark D. Schneider
Langley R. Shook
Joseph B. Tompkins, Jr.
R. Clark Wadlow
Roger D. Wiegley
R. Merinda Wilson
Elroy H. Wolff
Robert R. Wootton
Thomas H. Yancey

NEW YORK, NEW YORK OFFICE

James G. Archer
James D. Arden
Frank V. Battle, Jr.
Steven M. Bierman
Eva Yulan Chan
Shelley C. Chapman
Kelley A. Cornish
Eugene A. Danaher

(See Next Column)

SIDLEY & AUSTIN, *Chicago—Continued*

NEW YORK, NEW YORK OFFICE (Continued)

Daniel S. Dokos
Scott M. Freeman
Susan A. Goldberg
Robert W. Hirth
John G. Hutchinson
James D. Johnson
Ralph E. Lerner
Mir Mahboob Mahmood
Thomas E. Pitts, Jr.
Myles C. Pollin
Andrew C. Quale, Jr.
David Alan Richards
David L. Ridl
Paul K. Risko
Irving L. Rotter
Robert H. Scarborough
Michael J. Schmidtberger
L. Gilles Sion
Shuichi Suzuki
Theodore J. Theophilos
Alan M. Unger
Paul R. Wysocki
Michael H. Yanowitch
Henry R. Zheng

LONDON, ENGLAND OFFICE

Mark A. Angelson

TOKYO, JAPAN OFFICE

John R. Box

COUNSEL

CHICAGO, ILLINOIS OFFICE

Carol A. Doyle
Robert R. Frei
Alan Gabbay
Clifford W. Garstang
Donald J. Gralen *
Loren E. Juhl
Edward P. Kenney
James W. Kissel
Roger F. Lewis
Amy D. Mayber
Thomas W. Merrill
Maurice J. Miller
Newton N. Minow *
Randal C. Picker
A. Bruce Schimberg * (Retired)
Peter Thornton

WASHINGTON, D.C. OFFICE

David R. Ford
Rex E. Lee
Stephen B. Lyons
Gary P. Quigley
Richard E. Young

NEW YORK, NEW YORK OFFICE

Claire Shows Hancock
Nicholas A. Robinson
Richard A. Stanley
Richard B. Stewart
Barbara A. Vrancik

RETIRED COUNSEL

LOS ANGELES, CALIFORNIA OFFICE

Richard Schauer

ASSOCIATES

CHICAGO, ILLINOIS OFFICE

Suresh T. Advani
Susan M. Alkema
Julie O'Donnell Allen
Mary Beth Bailey
Lory A. Barsdate
Marc A. Benjamin
Jennifer L. Billingsley
Tracy Birmingham
Robert T. Biskup
Mark B. Blocker
Gina E. Brock
Michael V. Casaburi
David R. Charles
Linton J. Childs
Paul L. Choi
Ronnie Christou
Mark D. Chutkow
Elizabeth J. Cisar
James F. Conlan
J. Tyson Covey
R. James Cravens, Jr.
Katherine J. D'Amaro
Tracy D. Daw
Jeffrey H. Dean
Richard R. Dennerline
Stephanie L. Dest
William G. Dickett
Beth J. Dickstein
Vilia M. Drazdys
Nancy K. DuCharme
Karen O. Dunlop
Robert E. Easton
William M. Ejzak
Steven J. Ellison
Brad B. Erens
William J. Factor
Brian J. Fahrney
Karen J. Fellows
Joseph Ferguson
D. Cameron Findlay
Thomas S. Finke
Lynn D. Fleisher
Lisa D. Freeman
Robert P. Freeman
Joseph P. Gattuso
Gary D. Gerstman
David A. Goldberg
Alan L. Goldman
Michael A. Gordon
Mark I. Greenberg
Craig A. Griffith
Scott E. Gross
Eric A. Haab
Arlene R. Haas
Jonathan O. Hafen
Jeffrey D. Hanslick
Susan V. Harris
Robert M. Hatch
Michael de León Hawthorne
John A. Heller
Kathleen M. Henry
David R. Hill
James W. Hitzeman
Kathryn Baugh Hofman
Maureen L. Holz
Linda T. Ieleja
Rick L. Jett
Pran Jha
Matthew E. Johnson
Steven F. Katz
Mark L. Kaufmann
Joseph D. Kearney
Timothy J. Kenesey
Colleen M. Kenney
Mark A. Kerber
Phillip J. Kerwin
Robert R. Kimball
Jordan A. Klein
Gary J. Kocher
George C. Kokkines
Kiplund R. Kolkmeier
Ashok K. Lalwani
Brandon D. Lawniczak
Christine A. Leahy
Jeffrey E. Leeb
Sharon K. Legenza
Patricia A. LeVarsky
Mary H. Lindsay
Murray L. Lyon
David E. Manning
John P. McGarrity
M. Kathleen McGowan
Patrick T. McNeil
Christopher J. Menting
Eugene L. Miller
Stephanie N. Mitchell
Katie A. Moertl
Scott J. Moore

(See Next Column)

ASSOCIATES

CHICAGO, ILLINOIS OFFICE (Continued)

Carole A Morey
Kathleen M. Mulligan
George L. Mullin
Leanne Ebert Murphy
Mary C. Niehaus
Bridget M. O'Keefe
Yasko Odagiri
Leah Eisen Pazol
Anastasia M. Polek
John M. Rafkin
Heidi Mallory Rauh
Kathleen A. Ravotti
Daniel S. Reinberg
Suzanne S. Riekes
Linda M. Rio
Ellen S. Robbins
Richard E. Robbins
Matthew F. Roberts
Kelly Jo Rogers
Emily J. Rothman
Kim K. W. Rucker
Alfred N. Sacha
Scott E. Saef
Theodore R. Scarborough
John M. Schloerb
Bryan A. Schneider
David E. Schreibman
John T. Shapiro
Evelyn E. Shockley
Amy K. Singh
Joan E. Slavin
Michael S. Smith
Scott C. Solberg
James B. Speta
Stanley B. Stallworth
Debra J. Stanek
Stephanie D. Stapleton
Susan A. Stone
Sheila A. Sundvall
Paul A. Svoboda
Byron F. Taylor
James E. Taylor
Nancy A. Temple
Thomas M. Thesing
Paul E. Veith
Michael A. Warner, Jr.
Melville W. Washburn
Marc D. Wassermann
William C. Way
Susan A. Weber
William J. Weiss
Evan B. Westerfield
Marian E. Whiteman
Marjorie Golis Wilde
Carolyn Kohn Winick
David W. Wirt
John S. Wirt
Steven W. Young
David J. Zampa
Bruce M. Zessar
Sharon Sobczak Zuiker

*Denotes a lawyer employed by a Professional Corporation which is a member of the Firm.

For full biographical listings, see the Martindale-Hubbell Law Directory

SONNENSCHEIN NATH & ROSENTHAL (AV)

Suite 8000 Sears Tower, 233 South Wacker Drive, 60606
Telephone: 312-876-8000
Cable Address: "Sonberk"
Telex: 25-3526
Telecopier: 312-876-7934
New York, N.Y. Office: 1221 Avenue of the Americas, 24th Floor.
Telephone: 212-768-6700.
Facsimile: 212-391-1247.
Washington, D.C. Office: 1301 K Street, N.W., Suite 600 East Tower.
Telephone: 202-408-6400.
Fax: 202-408-6399.
San Francisco, California Office: 685 Market Street, 10th Floor.
Telephone: 415-882-5000.
Facsimile: 415-543-5472; 882-5038.
Los Angeles, California Office: 601 South Figueroa Street, Suite 1500.
Telephone: 213-623-9300.
Facsimile: 213-623-9924.
St. Louis, Missouri Office: One Metropolitan Square, Suite 3000.
Telephone: 314-241-1800.
Facsimile: 314-259-5959.

Edward Sonnenschein (1881-1935)
Hugo Sonnenschein (1883-1956)

MEMBERS OF FIRM

Neal I. Aizenstein
David Albenda (Not admitted in IL; Resident, New York, N.Y. Office)
Stuart Altschuler
Swanson W. Angle (Not admitted in IL; Resident, St. Louis, Missouri Office)
Reid L. Ashinoff (Not admitted in IL; Resident, New York, N.Y. Office)
Pamela Baker
Michael A. Bamberger (Not admitted in IL; Resident, New York, N.Y. Office)
William T. Barker
Michael A. Barnes (Not admitted in IL; Resident, San Francisco, California Office)
Michael H. Barr (Not admitted in IL; Resident, New York, N.Y. Office)
Larry M. Bauer (Resident, St. Louis, Missouri Office)
Michael J. Bayard (Resident, Los Angeles, California Office)
Carol Anne Been
Susan M. Benton-Powers
Dennis N. Berman (Resident, New York, N.Y. Office)
Frank C. Bernard
Amy L. Bess (Resident, Washington, D.C. Office)
Alan B. Bornstein (Not admitted in IL; Resident, St. Louis, Missouri Office)
Roger T. Brice
Ernest P. Burger (Not admitted in IL; Resident, Los Angeles, California Office)
Charles R. Campbell, Jr. (Not admitted in IL; Resident, Los Angeles, California Office)
Leo J. Carlin (Deceased, 1988)
Lorie A. Chaiten
Dale M. Cohen
John Collen
Sherman P. Corwin
Robert E. Curry, Jr. (Resident, New York, N.Y. Office)
Steven R. Davidson
J. Ross Docksey
Jeffrey L. Dorman
Robin M. Edwards (Not admitted in IL; Resident, San Francisco, California Office)
Kevin J. Egan
Todd R. Eskelsen (Resident, Washington, D.C. Office)
Phyllis A. Ewer

(See Next Column)

SONNENSCHEIN NATH & ROSENTHAL—*Continued*

MEMBERS OF FIRM (Continued)

James B. Fadim
Robert M. Farquharson (Deceased, 1987)
Richard L. Fenton
James R. Ferguson
Elizabeth A. Ferrell (Not admitted in IL; Resident, Washington, D.C. Office)
Samuel Fifer
Sheldon I. Fink
Amy H. Fisher (Not admitted in IL; Resident, New York, N.Y. Office)
Abraham Fishman
Martin J. Foley (Not admitted in IL; Resident, Los Angeles, California Office)
Jeffrey C. Fort
Gary J. Fox
Matthew C. Fragner (Not admitted in IL; Resident, Los Angeles, California Office)
Steven H. Frankel (Resident, San Francisco, California Office)
Louis S. Freeman
Linda E. Friedman (Not admitted in IL; Resident, New York, N.Y. Office)
Michael M. Froy
Francis M. Gaffney (Not admitted in IL; Resident, St. Louis, Missouri Office)
Alan S. Gilbert
Paul E. B. Glad (Not admitted in IL; Resident, San Francisco, California Office)
Robert N. Grant
John I. Grossbart
Peter J. Gurfein (Resident, Los Angeles, California Office)
Philip A. Haber (Resident, New York, N.Y. Office)
Frank H. Hackmann (Resident, St. Louis, Missouri Office)
Elliott J. Hahn (Resident, Los Angeles, California Office)
John S. Hahn (Not admitted in IL; Resident, Washington, D.C. Office)
Wayne R. Hannah, Jr.
Mark T. Hansen (Not admitted in IL; Resident, Los Angeles, California Office)
Linda Chaplik Harris
Richard Harris (Deceased, 1986)
Blake L. Harrop
Roger K. Heidenreich (Resident, St. Louis, Missouri Office)
Carl B. Hillemann III (Resident, St. Louis, Missouri Office)
Harold C. Hirshman
Kenneth H. Hoch
Thomas Holden (Not admitted in IL; Resident, San Francisco, California Office)
Mitchell L. Hollins
Oliver L. Holmes (Not admitted in IL; Resident, San Francisco, California Office)
Donald P. Horwitz
Stuart E. Hunt (Not admitted in IL; Resident, Washington, D.C. Office)
David C. Jacobson
Fruman Jacobson
Marian S. Jacobson
Robert C. Johnson
Gayle M. Jones (Not admitted in IL; Resident, San Francisco, California Office)
Robert T. Joseph
Louis C. Keiler
Ronald D. Kent (Not admitted in IL; Resident, Los Angeles, California Office)
H. Sinclair Kerr, Jr. (Not admitted in IL; Resident, San Francisco, California Office)
Christopher Q. King
Robert H. King, Jr. (Resident, San Francisco, California Office)
Leslie A. Klein
James A. Klenk
Karen Beth Ksander
Frederic S. Lane
David A. Lapins
John J. Lawlor
Mark R. Lehrer (Not admitted in IL; Resident, New York, N.Y. Office)
Edward L. Lembitz (1926-1993)
Jeffrey Lennard
Marc Levenstein
Fred L. Levy (Not admitted in IL; Resident, Washington, D.C. Office)
Steven M. Levy
Julius Lewis
Scott A. Lindquist
Richard M. Lipton
R. Michael Lowenbaum (Not admitted in IL; Resident, St. Louis, Missouri Office)
Donald G. Lubin
David W. Maher
Barry S. Maram
Richard L. Marcus
Sandra R. McCandless (Resident, San Francisco, California Office)
Jacques K. Meguire
Mark F. Mehlman
Michael W. Melendez (Not admitted in IL; Resident, San Francisco, California Office)
Cynthia L. Mellema (Not admitted in IL; Resident, San Francisco, California Office)
Robert F. Messerly
Paul J. Miller
Robert B. Millner
Patrick G. Moran
William C. Morison-Knox (Not admitted in IL; Resident, San Francisco, California Office)
Bernard Nath
Marlene D. Nations
Dustin E. Neumark
Dennis Nathan Newman
Charles F. Newlin
Bernard J. Nussbaum
Philip A. O'Connell, Jr. (Resident, San Francisco, California Office)
Mary Denise O'Connor (Not admitted in IL)
John M. O'Donnell
Eric A. Oesterle
Thomas G. Opferman
Roderick A. Palmore
Lee T. Paterson (Not admitted in IL; Resident, Los Angeles, California Office)
Roger W. Patrick (Not admitted in IL; Resident, Washington, D.C. Office)
Sidney M. Perlstadt
Laura R. Petroff (Resident, Los Angeles, California Office)
Earl E. Pollock
Alan M. Posner
Caryl A. Potter, III (Not admitted in IL; Resident, Washington, D.C. Office)
Duane C. Quaini
Charles A. Redd (Resident, St. Louis, Missouri Office)
Susan K. Reiter
C. Harker Rhodes, Jr.
Andria K. Richey (Not admitted in IL; Resident, Los Angeles, California Office)
Michael W. Ring (Not admitted in IL; Resident, Los Angeles, California Office)
Samuel R. Rosenthal
Edwin A. Rothschild

MEMBERS OF FIRM (Continued)

(See Next Column)

Timothy C. Russell (Not admitted in IL; Resident, Washington, D.C. Office)
Kirk R. Ruthenberg (Resident, Washington, D.C. Office)
Sally Larson Sargent
Charles D. Satinover
David L. Schiavone
Eric M. Schiller
Donald M. Schindel
Michael A. Schlanger (Not admitted in IL; Resident, Washington, D.C. Office)
Arnold P. Schuster (Not admitted in IL; Resident, San Francisco, California Office)
Robert F. Scoular (Not admitted in IL; Resident, Los Angeles, California Office)
Norbert M. Seifert (Not admitted in IL; Resident, Los Angeles, California Office)
Gary Senner
J. A. Shafran (Not admitted in IL; Resident, Los Angeles, California Office)
Harold D. Shapiro
Gerald J. Sherman
Alan H. Silberman
Mark C. Simon
Roger C. Siske
Jane S. Smith (Resident, St. Louis, Missouri Office)
Ronald E. Stauffer (Not admitted in IL; Resident, Washington, D.C. Office)
Thomas M. Stephens
Ellyn J. Steuer (Not admitted in IL; Resident, New York, N.Y. Office)
Errol L. Stone
Leslie Chambers Strohm (Resident, St. Louis, Missouri Office)
Daniel R. Swett
Scott Turow
Thomas K. Vandiver (Resident, St. Louis, Missouri Office)
Elpidio Villarreal
Donna J. Vobornik
Susan M. Walker (Not admitted in IL; Resident, Los Angeles, California Office)
Everett S. Ward
Andrew L. Weil
Margo Weinstein
Jerome P. Weiss (Not admitted in IL; Resident, Washington, D.C. Office)
Linda D. White
James G. Wiehl (Not admitted in IL; Resident, St. Louis, Missouri Office)
Michael S. Wien (Not admitted in IL; Resident, New York, N.Y. Office)
John Leland Williams (Not admitted in IL; Resident, San Francisco, California Office)
Nicholas C. Yost (Resident, San Francisco, California Office)

OF COUNSEL

Jean Allard
Wayne H. Davis (Resident, New York, N.Y. Office)
Marc B. Heller (Resident, New York, N.Y. Office)
Arnold B. Kanter
Robert B. Murphy (Resident, Washington, D.C. Office)
Marshall S. Shapo

SENIOR ATTORNEY

Susan G. Connelly

ASSOCIATES

Jon K. Adams (Not admitted in IL; Resident, San Francisco, California Office)
Gwendolyn S. Andrey
Dana L. Ballinger (Not admitted in IL; Resident, San Francisco, California Office)
Robin Marie Barsky
Ronald S. Bell
Cheryl Dyer Berg (Resident, San Francisco, California Office)
Kirsten K. Bergin
Betsy J. Braack
Adam Scott Bram (Resident, Los Angeles, California Office)
Julie A. Bregande (Resident, St. Louis, Missouri Office)
Ryan R. Brenneman
Debra M. Buhring
William F. Burton (Not admitted in IL; Resident, Washington, D.C. Office)
John J. Calkins (Resident, Washington, D.C. Office)
Anthony Capobianco (Resident, Los Angeles, California Office)
Rick Charles Chessen (Not admitted in IL; Resident, Washington, D.C. Office)
Nargis Choudhry (Resident, Los Angeles, California Office)
Rubin E. Cruse, Jr. (Not admitted in IL; Resident, Los Angeles, California Office)
Stephen J. Curran (Not admitted in IL; Resident, Los Angeles, California Office)
Susan Kay Daniel (Resident, St. Louis, Missouri Office)
Andrew L. DaSilva (Resident, New York, N.Y. Office)
Paul Davis
Sally L. Davis
Shelley R. (Barber) De Leo (Not admitted in IL; Resident, San Francisco, California Office)
Maria Sileno DeLoughry (Resident, Washington, D.C. Office)
Mark L. Dosier
Elizabeth M. Dougal
Kenneth Drake (Not admitted in IL; Resident, New York, New York Office)
Diane V. Dygert
Timothy L. Elliott (Resident, St. Louis, Missouri Office)
Cynthia A. Faur
Karen H. Flax
Gerald E. Fradin
Liza M. Franklin
Lori L. Gaddis (Resident, St. Louis, Missouri Office)
Jeffrey M. Galkin
Karin Mason Garell (Not admitted in IL; Resident, Los Angeles, California Office)
Brent Matthew Giddens (Not admitted in IL; Resident, Los Angeles, California Office)
Barbara J. Gilbert
Steven F. Ginsberg
Kenneth J. Gladish
Bryce P. Goeking (Not admitted in IL; Resident, San Francisco, California Office)
Julie Goldscheid (Not admitted in IL; Resident, New York, N.Y. Office)
Jill Gould (Resident, Washington, D.C. Office)
Lisa R. Green (Resident, New York, N.Y. Office)
Steven Mark Greenbaum
Scott L. Hammel
Mark L. Hanover

(See Next Column)

SONNENSCHEIN NATH & ROSENTHAL, *Chicago—Continued*

ASSOCIATES (Continued)

Michael A. Heller
Carmen Hernandez-Lonstein
Diane L. Hoadley (Resident, St. Louis, Missouri Office)
Peter C. Hoehn (Not admitted in IL; Resident, New York, N.Y. Office)
Richard M. Hoffman
Joseph P. Hornyak (Not admitted in IL; Resident, Washington, D.C. Office)
James A. Huttenhower
Jeffrey S. Isaacs (Resident, New York, N.Y. Office)
Robert J. Isaacson (Resident, St. Louis, Missouri Office)
Benjamin B. Iselin (Resident, New York, N.Y., Office)
Bryan C. Jackson (Resident, Los Angeles, California Office)
Susan J. Jacobson
Scott L. Jones (Not admitted in IL; Resident, Los Angeles, California Office)
Stephanie D. Jones
Matthew I. Kaplan (Resident, Los Angeles, California Office)
Gregory S. Karawan (Not admitted in IL; Resident, New York, N.Y. Office)
Steven R. Karl (Resident, St. Louis, Missouri Office)
Katharine A. Kates (Resident, San Francisco, California Office)
Kenji Kawahigashi (Resident, Los Angeles, California Office)
Keijiro Kimura (Not admitted in IL)
John C. Koski
Paul Kuruk (Resident, Los Angeles, California Office)
Mary Kay Lacey (Not admitted in IL; Resident, San Francisco, California Office)
Elizabeth (Beth) J. Lapham
David C. Layden
Paul A. Leboffe (Not admitted in IL; Resident, San Francisco, California Office)
Pauline Ng Lee (Resident, Los Angeles, California Office)
Bruce H. Leshine (Resident, New York, N.Y. Office)
Kelvin K.F. Leung
David E. Lieberman
Mark J. Linderman (Not admitted in IL; Resident, San Francisco, California Office)
Matthew F. Lintner (Resident, San Francisco, California Office)
Rachel M. Lipschutz (Not admitted in IL; Resident, New York, N.Y. Office)
Andrew R. Livingston (Not admitted in IL; Resident, San Francisco, California Office)
Beverly O. Lobell (Resident, New York, New York Office)
Lisa A. MacVittie (Not admitted in IL; Resident, Washington, D.C. Office)
Rhonda V. Magee (Resident, San Francisco, California Office)
Donna L. Marks
Michael R. Maryn (Not admitted in IL; Resident, Washington, D.C. Office)
Richard J. Mathias (Resident, Los Angeles, California Office)
J. Robert Maxwell (Resident, San Francisco, California Office)
Jane Wells May
Sean McEneaney (Resident, San Francisco, California Office)
Dwayne P. McKenzie (Resident, Los Angeles, California Office)
Diane M. Mellett
Timothy M. Metzger
Mary L. Mills
Karen E. Milner (Resident, St. Louis, Missouri Office)
Kirk M. Minckler
Grace Ellen Mueller (Not admitted in IL; Resident, Los Angeles, California Office)
Stacey L. Murphy (Resident, St. Louis, Missouri Office)
Lisa Reilly Nadler (Resident, St. Louis, Missouri Office)
Gregory R. Naron
Doris Burgett Owens
Mark W. Page
Thomas J. Palazzolo (Resident, St. Louis, Missouri Office)
Sanford M. Pastroff
Dorothy P. Patton (Resident, New York, N.Y. Office)
Laura F. Peters (Not admitted in IL; Resident, Washington, D.C. Office)
Kenneth J. Pfaehler (Not admitted in IL; Resident, Washington, D.C. Office)
Debra McGuire Piliero (Resident, Washington, D.C. Office)
Jonathan Piper
Andrew Eliot Porter
Teresa Dale Pupillo (Resident, St. Louis, Missouri Office)
Mark D. Rabe (Resident, St. Louis, Missouri Office)
Robert E. Richards
Stephanie A. Rigaux (Resident, Washington, D.C. Office)
Lori E. Romley (Not admitted in IL; Resident, San Francisco, California Office)
Jeffrey M. Rose (Resident, New York, N.Y. Office)
Michael D. Rosenthal
Phillip A. Rothermich (Resident, St. Louis, Missouri Office)
Catherine A. Salton (Not admitted in IL; Resident, San Francisco, California Office)
Bin Xue Sang (Resident, Los Angeles, California Office)
Stephen Douglas Sayre
Carole Schecter
Cheryl L. Segal
Tamara Seyler-James (Resident, San Francisco, California Office)
Evan Siegel
Felicia L. Silber (Not admitted in IL; Resident, Washington, D.C. Office)
David Simantob (Resident, Los Angeles, California Office)
Peter A. Smalbach (Resident, San Francisco, California Office)
Barbara Lee Smith
Gregory L. Smith (Resident, San Francisco, California Office)
T. Mark Smith (Not admitted in IL; Resident, Los Angeles, California Office)
Christopher P. Sonderby (Resident, San Francisco, California Office)
Diane Sovereign (Resident, Los Angeles, California Office)
Faith H. Spencer
Charles Spiegel (Not admitted in IL; Resident, San Francisco, California Office)
David J. Stagman
Todd M. Stennes
Craig A. Sterling (Resident, San Francisco, California Office)
Jonathan D. Taft
Pamela J. Tennison (Resident, San Francisco, California Office)

ASSOCIATES (Continued)

(See Next Column)

Jill A. Thompson
Kenda Tomes
Valerie M. Valdez (Resident, New York, New York Office)
Kelly B. Valen (Resident, San Francisco, California Office)
Catherine A. Van Horn
William B. Van lonkhuyzen (Resident, San Francisco, California Office)
Maralee Buttery Vezie (Resident, New York, N.Y. Office)
Jacqueline M. Vidmar
William M. Walsh
Elizabeth E. Ward
Anne Nicholson Weber
Aron G. Weber (Resident, New York, N.Y. Office)
Pamela Grose Welty (Not admitted in IL; Resident, Washington, D.C. Office)
Lisabeth Jacobs Wesselkamper (Resident, San Francisco, California Office)
Rebecca L. Williams
Benjamin E. Wolff III
Debra B. Yale
Paula M. Yost (Not admitted in IL; Resident, San Francisco, California Office)
Lauren M. Yu (Resident, Los Angeles, California Office)

For full biographical listings, see the Martindale-Hubbell Law Directory

TAYLOR, MILLER, SPROWL, HOFFNAGLE & MERLETTI (AV)

33 North La Salle Street, Suite 2222, 60602-2691
Telephone: 312-782-6070
FAX: 312-782-6081

Orville Taylor (1885-1969)
John S. Miller (1888-1965)
James J. Hoffnagle
Roger A. Merletti
Ralph W. F. Lustgarten
Richard W. Oloffson
Frank C. Stevens
Roger LeRoy

OF COUNSEL

Charles R. Sprowl

ASSOCIATES

John R. Adams
Katherine M. Mulroy
Daniel K. Fritz
Robert W. Rohm
Hugh J. Doyle
Jack Bruce Batten
John Anthony DiSalvo
Timothy Couture

For full biographical listings, see the Martindale-Hubbell Law Directory

VEDDER, PRICE, KAUFMAN & KAMMHOLZ (AV)

A Partnership including Vedder, Price, Kaufman & Kammholz, P.C.
222 North La Salle Street, 60601-1003
Telephone: 312-609-7500
Fax: 312-609-5005
Rockford, Illinois Office: Vedder, Price, Kaufman & Kammholz, 4615 East State Street, Suite 201.
Telephone: 815-226-7700.
Washington, D.C. Office: Vedder, Price, Kaufman, Kammholz & Day, 1600 M. Street, N.W.
Telephone: 202-296-0500.
New York, New York Office: Vedder, Price, Kaufman, Kammholz & Day, 805 Third Avenue.
Telephone: 212-407-7700.

MEMBERS OF FIRM

Beverly B. Vedder (1887-1955)
William F. Price (1909-1973)
Charles R. Kaufman (1908-1990)
Theophil C. Kammholz (1909-1992)
William W. McKittrick
William O. Petersen
Robert C. Claus
Stanley B. Block
James S. Petrie
George P. Blake
Frank G. Reeder
Michael G. Beemer
Richard H. Schnadig
John Jacoby
Paul F. Gleeson
Charles H. Wiggins, Jr.
Theodore J. Tierney
Michael E. Reed
Richard H. Sanders
Charles F. Custer
Michael L. Igoe, Jr.
Martin M. Ruken
Allan E. Lapidus
Robert J. Stucker
Thomas L. O'Brien
Richard C. Robin
Robert J. Moran
Robert J. Washlow
David E. Bennett
Donald W. Jenkins
Daniel O'Rourke
William F. Walsh
Robert E. Browne
Richard A. Zachar
Nina Gidden Stillman
Christine M. Rhode
Paul F. Russell
Lawrence L. Summers
Thomas G. Abram
Michael G. Cleveland
Lawrence J. Casazza
Thomas A. Baker
Rene A. Torrado, Jr.
John J. Jacobsen, Jr.
Charles B. Wolf
Michael W. Sculnick
Richard H. Levy
E. Wayne Robinson
Douglas J. Polk
Richard F. Zehnle
John T. McEnroe
James M. Kane
John R. Obiala
Cathy G. O'Kelly
Gregory G. Wrobel
James A. Spizzo
Benjamin J. Baker
Pearl A. Zager
Douglas J. Lipke
Edward C. Jepson, Jr.
Dalius F. Vasys
Norman B. Julius
Bruce R. Alper
William L. Conaghan
Thomas P. Desmond
Douglas M. Hambleton
Daniel T. Sherlock
Igor Potym
Jonathan H. Bogaard
John M. Wolff, Jr.
Edward A. Cohen
Neal A. Crowley
Jennifer R. Evans
Daniel C. McKay, II
Carol L. Van Hal Browne
Diane M. Kehl
Dean N. Gerber

(See Next Column)

VEDDER, PRICE, KAUFMAN & KAMMHOLZ—*Continued*

MEMBERS OF FIRM (Continued)

Janet M. Hedrick
David A. Sturms
Anne M. Murphy
Karen L. Pszanka-Layng

ASSOCIATES

Paul Parker
William C. Glynn
Tami J. Reding-Brubaker
Scott William Ammarell
Andrew M. Gardner
Stuart D. Kenney
Lynne A. Gochanour
Steven J. Gray
Randall Marc Lending
Thomas C. McDonough
Philip L. Mowery
Michael A. Nemeroff
Jeannine M. Pisoni
Patricia J. Moore
Maria A. O'Donnell
Mark J. Handfelt
C. Elizabeth Belmont
Steven G. Rudolf
Malory N. Harriman
Catherine A. Lemmer
Karen L. Taylor
Timothy W. O'Donnell
Lane R. Moyer
Carla Rendina Owen
Geoffrey R. Kass
Steven J. Bridges
Robert J. Patton
Marianne W. Culver
James A. Arpaia
Mark R. Galis
Christine A. Provost
Edward N. Druck
Robert I. Kenny
William J. Bettman
James A. Morsch
Mark A. Steffensen
Michael P. Nicolai
Nancy M. Gerrity
Jeffrey T. Veber
Reed W. Ramsay
Thomas R. Dee
Andrea M. Boado
Mark G. Malven
Paula K. DeAngelo
Ann M. Schlaffman

OF COUNSEL IN CHICAGO

Brainerd Chapman
Bernard J. Echlin
Paul H. LaRue
John J. Cassidy, Jr.

PARTNERS AT ROCKFORD, ILLINOIS

Greg A. Cheney
Paul R. Cicero

ASSOCIATES AT ROCKFORD, ILLINOIS

Mary K. Osborn
Shawn O. Miller

PARTNER AT D.C. AND NEW YORK CITY

Virgil B. Day

PARTNERS AT NEW YORK CITY

Virgil B. Day
John C. Grosz
Dan L. Goldwasser
Alan M. Koral
Donald A. Wassall
Denise L. Blau
John H. Eickemeyer
Neal I. Korval
Ronald Scheinberg
Alfrado D. Donelson

ASSOCIATES AT NEW YORK CITY

Marc S. Wenger
Michael J. Crisafulli
Jonathan A. Wexler
Neil A. Capobianco
Inge H.E. Jonckheer Maki
Boris B. Thomas
Salvatore G. Gangemi

OF COUNSEL AT NEW YORK CITY

James R. Cherry
Edward J. Walsh, Jr.
Edward F. Campbell, Jr. (Not admitted in IL)
Patricia Anne Lind

PARTNERS AT DISTRICT OF COLUMBIA

Edwin H. Seeger
Thomas L. Farmer
George J. Pantos
Thomas A. Brooks
Jane C. Luxton

For full biographical listings, see the Martindale-Hubbell Law Directory

WILDMAN, HARROLD, ALLEN & DIXON (AV)

225 West Wacker Drive, 30th Floor, 60606-1229
Telephone: 312-201-2000
Cable Address: "Whad"
Fax: 312-201-2555
Aurora, Illinois Office: 1851 W. Galena Boulevard, Suite 210.
Telephone: 708-892-7021.
Fax: 708-892-7158.
Waukegan, Illinois Office: 404 West Water, P. O. Box 890.
Telephone: 708-623-0700.
Fax: 708-244-5273.
Lisle, Illinois Office: 4300 Commerce Court.
Telephone: 708-955-0555.
Libertyville, Illinois Office: 611 South Milwaukee Avenue.
Telephone: 708-680-3030.
New York, New York Office: Wildman, Harrold, Allen, Dixon & Smith. The International Building, 45 Rockefeller Plaza, Suite 353.
Telephone: 212-632-3850.
Fax: 212-632-3858.
Toronto, Ontario affiliated Office: Keel Cottrelle. 36 Toronto Street, Ninth Floor, Suite 920.
Telephone: 416-367-2900.
Telefax: 416-367-2791.
Telex: 062-18660.
Mississauga, Ontario affiliated Office: Keel Cottrelle. 100 Matatson Avenue East, Suite 104.
Telephone: 416-890-7700.
Fax: 416-890-8006.

(See Next Column)

MEMBERS OF FIRM

Thomas D. Allen
John J. Arado
Richard C. Bartelt
Michael R. Blankshain
Cal R. Burnton
Edward T. Butt, Jr.
Douglas R. Carlson
Paul S. Chervin (Waukegan and Libertyville Offices)
James A. Christman
Dana S. Connell
John W. Costello
Thomas W. Daggett
Steven E. Danekas
Stewart S. Dixon
Michael Dockterman
James P. Dorr
Thomas P. Duffy
John L. Eisel
Jerald P. Esrick
Roger G. Fein
Ira C. Feldman
James D. Fiffer
Donald E. Figliulo
David J. Fischer
Donald Flayton
Craig Steven Fochler
Kathy Pinkstaff Fox
John E. Frey
Peter H. Fritts
Richard P. Glovka
Michael J. Grant
Jeffrey P. Gray
Charles J. Griffin, Jr.
Robert E. Haley
Robert E. Hamilton
Bernard Harrold
H. Roderic Heard
Ronald M. Hem (Resident, Aurora Office)
Helaine Wachs Heydemann
Mark W. Hianik
Richard J. Hickey, III
Keith C. Hult
Matthew A. Hurd
James C. James, III (Resident, Aurora Office)
Richard C. Johnson (Resident, Lisle Office)
David A. Kanter
Robert E. Kehoe, Jr.
Young Kim
Anne Giddings Kimball
R. Henry Kleeman
Leonard S. Kurfirst
Steven L. Larson (Waukegan and Libertyville Offices)
Dean J. Leffelman (Resident, Lisle Office)
Brian W. Lewis
Joseph F. Madonia
Charles R. Mandly, Jr.
Lee B. McClain
Michael L. McCluggage
Mark J. McCombs
Donald R. McGarrah
John E. McGovern, Jr.
Ellen Beverley McNamara
Sheldon P. Migdal
Mark P. Miller
James R. Morrin
James M. Mulcahy
Robert W. Newman
Timothy G. Nickels
James T. Nyeste
Sarah L. Olson
Richard C. Palmer
David J. Parsons
Thomas E. Patterson
Douglas L. Prochnow
David S. Rees
George S. Rosic
Alan B. Roth
Fred E. Schulz
Robert L. Shuftan
Donald J. Simantz (Resident, Aurora Office)
Thomas H. Snyder
Robert S. Solomon
Linda E. Spring (Waukegan and Libertyville Offices)
Charles S. Stahl, Jr.
Sanford M. Stein
Robert A. Strelecky (Resident Partner, DuPage County Office)
Richard B. Thies
Peter A. Tomaras
Ruth E. VanDemark
Thomas J. Verticchio
Louis P. Vitullo
Georgia L. Vlamis
James B. Vogts
Susan L. Walker
Craig M. White
Max Wildman
Dale G. Wills
John A. Ybarra

COUNSEL

Howard Arvey
Marshall L. Burman
Robert M. Gunn
Bernard D. Hirsh
George W. Overton
Edwin A. Wahlen
Diane G. Elder

Deborah A. Arbogast
Jody A. Ballmer
John W. Barbian
Donald C. Battaglia
Kathryn S. Bedward
John T. Benz
Eric A. Berlin
Kathleen M. Boege
James G. Bonebrake
Troy M. Brethauer
David J. Chroust (Resident, Lisle Office)
William H. Clune
Julie A. Correll
Jill A. Cuba
Leo P. Dombrowski
Rodney L. Drinnon
Gary E. Dyal
Wendy L. Fink
Ira S. Friedrich
Eric W. Gallender
Adam J. Glazer
Lisa I. Gordon
Scott Z. Hochfelder
Gerise M. Hooks
Anthony G. Hopp
Mark A. Huddle
Darryl P. Jacobs
Daniel Steven Kaplan
Elizabeth Keiley
Cheryl A. Kettler
Cynthia A. King
Steven H. Klein
David Alex Korn
Warren C. Laski
John S. Letchinger
Thomas M. Lynch
Rebecca J. McDade
Lauren L. McFarlane
Vania Montero
Kathryn A. Mrkonich
Richard D. Murphy Jr.
Ellen J. Neely
W. Scott Nehs
Gregory S. Norrod
Martha D. Owens
David F. Pardys
Brad L. Peterson
Barbara M. Prohaska (Resident, Lisle Office)
Lori Ann Prokes
Barbara C. Raffaldini
Kartik Kalyan Raman
Kevin B. Reid
John A. Roberts
Kimberly E. Roy
Alan J. Rubenstein
Elizabeth A. Sanders
Frederick L. Schwartz
E. Regan Shepley

(See Next Column)

WILDMAN, HARROLD, ALLEN & DIXON, *Chicago—Continued*

Stephanie B. Shulak
Lisa S. Simmons
David M. Simon
Ada Skyles
Paul A. Slager
Vernon P. Squires
Antigone D. Stoken
R. John Street
Lauren S. Tashma
Jeanne Walker
Bradley Alan Warrick
Susan M. Weis (Not admitted in IL)
Joleen S. Willis
Robin L. Wolkoff
Jonathan W. Young

For full biographical listings, see the Martindale-Hubbell Law Directory

WILLIAMS AND MONTGOMERY, LTD. (AV)

20 North Wacker Drive Suite 2100, 60606
Telephone: 312-443-3200
Telex: 206598
Facsimile: 312-443-1323
Waukegan, Illinois Office: 33 North County Street.
Telephone: 708-360-1220.
Wheaton, Illinois Office: 310 S. County Farm Road.
Telephone: 708-690-3200.
Joliet, Illinois Office: 81 North Chicago Avenue.
Telephone: 815-727-2653.
Miami, Florida Office: Williams, Montgomery & Thompson, Ltd., 25 Southeast Second Avenue.
Telephone: 305-373-7611.
Facsimile: 305-358-1251.

Lloyd E. Williams, Jr.
C. Barry Montgomery
Barry L. Kroll
Thomas H. Neuckranz
Anthony P. Katauskas
David E. Morgans
Craig A. Tomassi
Nunzio C. Radogno
Anthony J. Kiselis
Edward J. Murphy
Alton C. Haynes
James K. Horstman
Patrick F. Klunder
David E. Stevenson
Michael R. La Barge
Kevin Campbell
David P. Boyd
Rodney E. VanAusdal
Lori E. Iwan
Lawrence K. Rynning
Jeffrey H. Lipe
Bruce W. Lyon
Thomas F. Cameli
Manya A. Pastalan Grant
Michael D. Huber

OF COUNSEL

Robert D. McHugh

Lawrence A. Szymanski
Walter S. Calhoun
Gregory J. Bird
Mary Anne Sliwinski
Thomas J. Pontikis
Mark J. Vogg
Brigid E. Kennedy
Perry W. Hoag
Mark R. Misiorowski
Peter J. Szatkowski
Douglas A. Miller
Hall Adams, III
Stephen W. Heil
Thomas J. Popovich
Edward R. Moor
Michael J. Pacer
J. Calvin Downing, III
David E. Neumeister
Sheila M. Reilly
Mark D. Brent
Shimon B. Kahan
Jennifer M. Lundy
Mark E. Winters
Brian J. Hunt
Amy McKeever Toman
Bradley C. Nahrstadt
Charles D. Stone
Brian W. Troglia
Karen M. Talty
Elizabeth Felt Wakeman
Edward O. Pacer
Ralph J. Kooy
Gregory W. Beihl
Douglas W. Lohmar, Jr.

For full biographical listings, see the Martindale-Hubbell Law Directory

WILSON & MCILVAINE (AV)

500 West Madison, Suite 3700, 60661-2511
Telephone: 312-715-5000
Telecopier: 312-715-5155

John P. Wilson (1867-1922)
Wm. B. McIlvaine (1888-1943)

PARTNERS

C. John Anderson
Walter W. Bell
Cynthia A. Bergmann
Richard P. Blessen
Thomas E. Chomicz
Michael F. Csar
Thomas G. Draths
Carrie A. Durkin
Robert F. Forrer
James J. Gatziolis
Douglas R. Hoffman
Richard L. Horn
Jerry D. Jones
Gary H. Kline
Sarah M. Linsley
Thomas J. Magill
Daniel C. McKay
Kendall R. Meyer
Dennis J. O'Hara
Dwight B. Palmer, Jr.
Thomas A. Polachek
John J. Quinlisk
Janice E. Rodgers
Peter A. Sarasek
Quinton F. Seamons
Stephanie B. Shellenback
Leonard S. Shifflett
Steven A. Smith
Alexander Terras
John P. Vail
Brian J. Wanca

(See Next Column)

ASSOCIATES

Cynthia J. Barnes
Patrick J. Bitterman
Marie K. Eitrheim
Timothy S. Harris
William T. McCormick
Alison L. Paul
Anne S. Quinn
Todd A. Rowden
David S. Schaffer, Jr.
Clinton J. Wesolik

OF COUNSEL

Charles W. Boand
Kent Chandler, Jr.
Frank A. Reichelderfer
Kenneth F. Montgomery
Vernon T. Squires

For full biographical listings, see the Martindale-Hubbell Law Directory

WINSTON & STRAWN (AV)

35 West Wacker Drive, 60601
Telephone: 312-558-5600
Cable Address: "Winston Chicago"
Facsimile: 312-558-5700
Washington, D.C. Office: 1400 L Street, N.W.
Telephone: 202-371-5700.
Telecopier: 202-371-5950.
Telex: 440574 INTLAW UI.
New York, N.Y. Office: 175 Water Street.
Telephone: 212-269-2500.
Telecopier: 212-952-1474/5.
Cable Address: "Coledeitz, NYK".
Telex: (RCA) 232459.
Geneva, Switzerland Office: 43 Rue du Rhone, 1204.
Telephone: (4122) 7810506.
Fax: (4122) 7810361.

Frederick H. Winston (1853-1886)
Frederick S. Winston (1878-1909)
Silas Hardy Strawn (1891-1946)

MEMBERS OF FIRM

George B. Christensen (Semi-Retired)
Calvin P. Sawyier
Thomas A. Reynolds, Jr.
Edward L. Foote
Bruce L. Bower
Robert B. Golding (1923-1992)
Richard J. Brennan
M. Finley Maxson
Norman Waite, Jr.
Robert G. Lane
John W. Stack
Stephen C. Bruner
Terry M. Grimm
Dean L. Overman (Washington, D.C. Office)
Scott M. Feldman
Duane M. Kelley
Albert Milstein
Kurt L. Schultz
James L. Fletcher
Paul H. Hensel, Chief Administrative Partner
Columbus R. Gangemi, Jr.
Christopher D. Murtaugh
Robert F. Denvir
Hurd Baruch
Gary A. Goodman
John R. Keys, Jr. (Washington, D.C. Office)
Gregory S. Murray
James M. Neis
Michael V. Hasten
Susan E. Cremin
Robert W. Ericson (New York, N.Y. Office)
Neil E. Holmen
Gerald C. Peterson
Kimball R. Anderson
David G. Crumbaugh
Jerome W. Pope
Thomas A. Reynolds, III
Robert F. Wall
Dan K. Webb
Wayne D. Boberg
Mark G. Henning
Gregory J. Malovance
Scott J. Szala
Clive M. Topol
Charles E. Stahl
James H. Russell
Thomas P. Fitzgerald
Deborah Gage Haude
Timothy J. Rivelli
Stephen C. Schulte
Edward F. Gerwin, Jr. (Washington, D.C. Office)
Gerald F. Munitz
Jim L. Blanco
F. Ellen Duff
W. Kirk Grimm
Terry John Malik
Bruce A. Toth
Robert W. Tarun
Edward J. Buchholz
Jerome H. Gerson
James W. Doran
Arnold G. Gough, Jr.
Dennis J. Kelly
R. Mark McCareins
William J. Ralph
Jeffrey P. Carren
Stephen P. Durchslag
Edward L. Levine (New York, N.Y. Office)
Donald L. Laufer (New York, N.Y. Office)
Richard B. Teiman (New York, N.Y. Office)
Anthony J. D'Auria (New York, N.Y. Office)
Edward N. Meyer (New York, N.Y. Office)
Jonathan Goldstein (New York, N.Y. Office)
Joseph A. DiBenedetto (New York, N.Y. Office)
Jeffrey H. Elkin (New York, N.Y. Office)
Michael Hirschfeld (New York, N.Y. Office)
Howard Seife (New York, N.Y. Office)
Robert Scott Edmonds (New York, N.Y. Office)
James J. Terry (New York, N.Y. Office)
Amy B. Siegel (New York, N.Y. Office)
Susan Berkwitt-Malefakis (New York, N.Y. Office)
Neal L. Wolf
Joseph A. Walsh, Jr.
Janet S. Baer
Andrew H. Connor
Steven F. Molo
Michael G. Robinson
Timothy J. Rooney
Mark M. Heatwole
Deborah C. Costlow (Washington, D.C. Office)
Paul B. Abramson (New York, N.Y. Office)
Kenneth C. H. Willig (New York, N.Y. Office)

(See Next Column)

WINSTON & STRAWN—*Continued*

MEMBERS OF FIRM (Continued)

Robert S. Fischler (New York, N.Y. Office)
John C. Phelan (New York, N.Y. Office)
Robert C. Satrom (New York, N.Y. Office)
Richard S. Talesnick (New York, N.Y. Office)
Leonard W. Belter (Washington, D.C. Office)
Richard C. Browne (Washington, D.C. Office)
Thomas M. Buchanan (Washington, D.C. Office)
Donald K. Dankner (Washington, D.C. Office)
Scott M. DuBoff (Washington, D.C. Office)
Peter N. Hiebert (Washington, D.C. Office)
Eric L. Hirschhorn (Washington, D.C. Office)
William K. Keane (Washington, D.C. Office)
Frederick J. Killion (Washington, D.C. Office)
John C. Kirtland (Washington, D.C. Office)
Joseph B. Knotts, Jr. (Washington, D.C. Office)
Michael R. Lemov (Washington, D.C. Office)
William J. Madden, Jr. (Washington, D.C. Office)
J. Michael McGarry, III (Washington, D.C. Office)
Malcolm H. Philips, Jr. (Washington, D.C. Office)
John P. Proctor (Washington, D.C. Office)
Robert M. Rader (Washington, D.C. Office)
Nicholas S. Reynolds (Washington, D.C. Office)
Daniel F. Stenger (Washington, D.C. Office)
Mark J. Wetterhahn (Washington, D.C. Office)
John E. Williams (Washington, D.C. Office)
Howard M. Pearl
Robert H. Shadur
Lawrence R. Desideri
Leonard Orkin (New York, N.Y. Office)
Herbert J. Deitz (1908-1992)
R. Evan Smith (New York, N.Y. Office)
Loren M. Dollet (New York, N.Y. Office)
Thomas J. Quigley (New York, N.Y. Office)
David A. Repka (Washington, D.C. Office)
Norman Newman (New York, N.Y. Office)
Anthony F. LoFrisco (New York, N.Y. Office)
James R. Thompson, Jr.
Ronald G. Caso (New York, N.Y. Office)
Thomas R. Bearrows (New York, N.Y. Office)
Thomas F. Blakemore
Thomas J. Frederick
George C. Lombardi
Cory E. Friedman (New York, N.Y. Office)
Rex L. Sessions (New York, N.Y. Office)
Peter Kryn Dykema (Washington, D.C. Office)
Margaret A. Hill (Washington, D.C. Office)
John A. Waits, II (Washington, D.C. Office)
Douglas L. Wisner (New York, N.Y. Office)
James H. Burnley IV (Washington, D.C. Office)
LaJuana S. Wilcher (Washington, D.C. Office)
Beryl F. Anthony, Jr. (Washington, D.C. Office)
Christine L. Albright
Norman R. Vander Clute (Washington, D.C. Office)
Marc S. Palay (Geneva, Switzerland Office)
M. Javade Chaudhri (Washington, D.C. Office)
Benjamin P. Fishburne, III (Washington, D.C. Office)
Barry J. Hart (Washington, D.C. Office)
Steven M. Lucas (Washington, D.C. Office)
David W. Roderer (Washington, D.C. Office)
Jane DiRenzo Pigott
Charles L. Kinney (Washington, D.C. Office)
James R. Curtiss (Washington, D.C. Office)
Charles C. Adams, Jr. (Geneva, Switzerland Office)
Nicolas C. Ulmer (Geneva, Switzerland Office)
Julie A. Bauer
Charles B. Boehrer
Deborah K. Boling
Terrence R. Brady
Steven J. Gavin
John MacCarthy
Peter C. McCabe, III
William G. Miossi
Louis J. Weber III
Sheldon L. Trubatch (Washington, D.C. Office)
Bruce Baker
Timothy J. O'Brien
John C. Lorentzen
James M. Reum
Robert A. Mangrum (Washington, D.C. Office)

OF COUNSEL

Robert M. Bor (Washington, D.C. Office)
James T. Pitts (Washington, D.C. Office)
Graham B. Purcell, Jr. (Washington, D.C. Office)
Charles R. Sharp (Washington, D.C. Office)
John H. More (Washington, D.C. Office)
Frank D. Kenney (Retired)
James L. Perkins
Carl J. Peckinpaugh (Washington, D.C. Office)

SENIOR ATTORNEYS

Lee M. Rubenstein
Timothy J. Oxley
Kevin E. White
Helen D. Shapiro
Anne W. Cottingham (Washington, D.C. Office)
Jane E. Croes (New York, N.Y. Office)
E. King Poor
Charles P. Sheets
Barry L. Salkin (New York, N.Y. Office)
Darrell Widen
William A. Horin (Washington, D.C. Office)
Richard W. Pearse
Gregory M. Garger

(See Next Column)

ASSOCIATES

Kimberley R. Anderson
Brian T. Black
Darcy J. Bogenrief
John M. Bowler
Bruce R. Braun
William D. Brewer
Jeffrey A. Brown
James D. Burton
Christopher S. Canning
Andrew R. Cardonick
Nancy L. Carey
John W. Christopher
Mark A. Chudzinski
Gabriela F. Cleveland
Gary Collins
Christina Karcher Corsiglia
Joseph M. Crabb
Timothy S. Crisp
Jack Crowe
Timothy J. Dable
Thomas A. d'Ambrosio
D. Albert Daspin
Oscar A. David
Jennifer J. Demmon
John M. Dickman
W. Gordon Dobie
Daniel G. Dolan
Peter F. Donati
Michael T. Donovan
Patrick O. Doyle
Susan W. Drewke
Dane Drobny
Paul A. Duffy
Todd J. Ehlman
Dena A. Epstein
Teri Lee Ferro
Patrick F. Gordon
Bradley C. Graveline
Douglas N. Greenburg
John R. Grier
John B. Griffith
Brian S. Hart
Kyle L. Harvey
Eric Hobson
James F. Hurst
Carol A. Hyland
Ronald H. Jacobson
Gemia McDearmon Jonscher
Catherine Wozniak Joyce
David E. Koropp
Adam S. Kosh
Alexandra O. Kostiw
Eleni Skoulikas Kouimelis
Kenneth T. Kristl
Stephen J. Legatzke
Alan V. Lindquist
Marie A. Lona
Roger S. Lucas
Alexis MacDowall
Susan L. Mahoney
Donald J. Malloy
Andrew J. McDonough
Donald F. McLellan
Samuel Mendenhall
Hal B. Merck
Richard E. Morgan
R. Cabell Morris, Jr.
Kurt J. H. Mueller
Michael L. Mulhern
Kelly C. Mulholland
Brian E. Neuffer
Jennifer T. Nijman
Daniel A. Ninivaggi
Ronald J. Nye
Timothy P. O'Connor
Peter L. O'Reilly
Philip M. Pinc
Susan A. Pipal
Kenneth P. Purcell
Andrew W. Ratts
Gregg D. Reisman
Michael P. Reynolds
Brian F. Richards
Michael P. Roche
Anita M. Sarafa-Williams
Gay R. Schreiber
Joy Sellstrom
Thomas V. Skinner
Gregory K. Smith
Michael J. Stepek
Kathleen Ann Swien
Cheryl R. Tama
Joseph James Torres
Joseph B. VanFleet
John N. Walker
Brant C. Weidner
Loren A. Weil
Thomas J. Wiegand
Joseph J. Zaknoen
N. Theodore Zink, Jr.
Jonathan E. Zweig

STAFF ATTORNEYS

Robert J. Garrett
Stephen N. Sher

For full biographical listings, see the Martindale-Hubbell Law Directory

*CLINTON,** DeWitt Co.

RUDASILL & RUDASILL (AV)

118 Warner Court, P.O. Box 656, 61727
Telephone: 217-935-8818
Fax: 217-935-8400

MEMBERS OF FIRM

A. J. Rudasill
Thomas J. Rudasill

For full biographical listings, see the Martindale-Hubbell Law Directory

COLLINSVILLE, Madison Co.

DUNHAM, BOMAN & LESKERA (AV)

114 West Main Street, 62234
Telephone: 618-344-7734
Telecopier: 618-344-3853
East St. Louis, Illinois Office: 520 First Illinois Bank Building.
Telephone: 618-271-0535.
Telecopier: 618-271-2800.
Belleville, Illinois Office: 208 North High Street.
Telephone: 618-397-2151.
Telecopier: 618-397-2285.
St. Louis, Missouri Office: 52 Maryland Plaza, Suite 301.
Telephone: 314-367-3030.

John W. Leskera
William L. Berry

For full biographical listings, see the Martindale-Hubbell Law Directory

COLUMBIA, Monroe Co.

CROWDER & SCOGGINS, LTD. (AV)

121 West Legion Avenue, P.O. Box 167, 62236
Telephone: 618-281-7111
Fax: 618-281-7115

(See Next Column)

CROWDER & SCOGGINS LTD., *Columbia—Continued*

Floyd E. Crowder | Mark S. Rohr
Mark C. Scoggins | Alan G. Pirtle
Timothy A. Gutknecht

Counsel for: First Bank, Columbia; Columbia Quarry Co.; Luhr Bros., Inc.; Monroe County Title Co.; City of Waterloo; Chicago Title Co.; Illinois Excavators, Inc.; Rogers Redi-Mix, Inc.; Tower Rock Stone Co.; Gateway FS, Inc.

For full biographical listings, see the Martindale-Hubbell Law Directory

CRYSTAL LAKE, McHenry Co.

MILITELLO, ZANCK & COEN, P.C. (AV)

40 Brink Street, 60014
Telephone: 815-459-8800
FAX: 815-459-8429

James G. Militello | Patrick D. Coen
Thomas C. Zanck | James L. Wright

Mark S. Saladin | James G. Militello, III
Michael L. Orndahl | Barbara H. Switzer

OF COUNSEL

Michael A. Ungvarsky, Jr.

References: Home State Bank of Crystal Lake; First National Bank of Crystal Lake; McHenry State Bank; Amcore Bank N.A., Woodstock.

For full biographical listings, see the Martindale-Hubbell Law Directory

ZUKOWSKI, ROGERS, FLOOD & MCARDLE (AV)

50 Virginia Street, 60014
Telephone: 815-459-2050
Facsimile: 815-459-9057
Chicago, Illinois Office: 100 South Wacker Drive, Suite 1502.
Telephone: 312-407-7700.
Facsimile: 312-332-1901.

MEMBERS OF FIRM

Richard R. Zukowski | David W. McArdle
H. David Rogers | Andrew T. Freund
Richard G. Flood | Jeannine A. Thoms
Stuart D. Gordon

ASSOCIATES

William P. Stanton | Rita W. Garry
Valeree D. Marek | Kelly A. Cahill
Melissa J. Cooney | Michael J. Smoron
Michael J. Chmiel

OF COUNSEL

Timothy J. Curran | Francis S. Lorenz

Representative Clients: Scottsdale Insurance Co.; Illinois Municipal League Risk Management Association-Martin Boyer Companies; Village of Algonquin; Village of Lake in the Hills; Village of Johnsburg; Village of Lakewood; Village of Bull Valley; Village of Hebron; City of Harvard; City of McHenry.

For full biographical listings, see the Martindale-Hubbell Law Directory

*DANVILLE,** Vermilion Co.

ACTON AND SNYDER (AV)

11 East North Street, 61832
Telephone: 217-442-0350; 446-0600
Fax: 217-442-0335

Harvey H. Acton (1913-1994)

MEMBERS OF FIRM

Carroll E. Snyder | Thomas B. Meyer
Robert Dale Acton | Phillip S. Miller
Thomas R. Smith | Thomas M. O'Shaughnessy

ASSOCIATES

Terrence Miles | Laura S. Neshek
Derek J. Girton

Local Attorneys For: Illinois Power Co.; The Chicago, Milwaukee, St. Paul & Pacific Ry. Co.; Prudential Insurance Co.; The Travelers; Liberty Mutual; General Motors Corp.; Palmer-American National Bank; American Savings and Loan Assn.; Lauhoff Grain Co.; CCL Industries, Inc.; Gannett Papers.

For full biographical listings, see the Martindale-Hubbell Law Directory

GUNN & HICKMAN, P.C. (AV)

220 North Vermilion Street, P.O. Box 706, 61832
Telephone: 217-446-0880
Fax: 217-442-3901

(See Next Column)

R.R. Bookwalter (1885-1951) | William R. Kesler
Walter T. Gunn (1879-1956) | John B. Jenkins
I. Ray Carter (1891-1960) | James L. Brougher
Horace E. Gunn | Fred L. Hubbard
Michael C. Upperman, Jr.

OF COUNSEL

Robert Z. Hickman

Counsel for: First Midwest Bank/Danville; Valmont Inc.; Hartford Accident & Indemnity Co.; Nacco Materials Handling Group, Inc.; Insurance Company of North America; Commercial Union Assurance Cos.; Ranger Insurance Co.; Iroquois Federal Savings & Loan Assn.; AgriBank, FCB; Westfield Insurance Companies.

For full biographical listings, see the Martindale-Hubbell Law Directory

HUTTON, LAURY, HESSER, LIETZ & WILCOX (AV)

16 West Madison Street, P.O. Box 1128, 61832
Telephone: 217-446-9436
FAX: 217-446-9462

MEMBERS OF FIRM

Jackson R. Hutton (1914-1991) | Gary D. Hesser
Everett L. Laury | Gregory G. Lietz
Austin W. Buchanan (1928-1973) | Roy G. Wilcox

Representative Clients: General Motors Corp.; Metropolitan Life Insurance Co.; The Equitable Life Assurance Society of the U.S.; Illinois State Medical Insurance Services, Inc.; Pekin Insurance Co.; St. Paul Fire and Marine Insurance Co.; Employers Reinsurance Corp.; Hertz Corp.

For full biographical listings, see the Martindale-Hubbell Law Directory

SEBAT, SWANSON, BANKS, GARMAN & TOWNSLEY (AV)

139 North Vermilion, 61832
Telephone: 217-443-0255
Fax: 217-443-0263

MEMBERS OF FIRM

Walter J. Grant (1874-1962) | Robert J. Banks, Jr.
Paul F. Jones (1898-1953) | Gill M. Garman
John E. Sebat (Retired) | William L. Townsley
Ralph J. Swanson | Randall P. Ray
Arthur J. Kapella

ASSOCIATES

Kristin R. Solberg

Representative Clients: Allied Chemical Co.; First Savings & Loan Assn.; Crows Hybrid Corn Co.; Missouri Pacific Railroad; Argonaut Insurance Co.; Ohio Casualty Co.; Liberty Mutual Insurance Co.; St. Paul-Mercury; U. S. F. & G. Co.; Zurich Insurance Group.

For full biographical listings, see the Martindale-Hubbell Law Directory

*DECATUR,** Macon Co.

ERICKSON, DAVIS, MURPHY, GRIFFITH & WALSH, LTD. (AV)

Suite 200, 225 South Main Street, P.O. Box 25138, 62525-5138
Telephone: 217-428-0948
FAX: 217-428-0996

Wayne E. Armstrong (1916-1977) | Garry E. Davis
W. Scott Murphy
Frederick P. Erickson | Thomas E. Griffith
Michael A. Walsh

Christopher K. Bradley

Representative Clients: Archer-Daniels Midland Company; Associated Physicians Insurance Company; Auto-Owners Insurance; Commercial Union Insurance Co.; Farmers Insurance Group; General Casualty Insurance Companies; Illinois State Medical Insurance Exchange; Millikin University; Procter & Gamble Co.

For full biographical listings, see the Martindale-Hubbell Law Directory

KEHART, SHAFTER, HUGHES & WEBBER, P.C. (AV)

500 First of America Center, P.O. Box 871, 62525-0871
Telephone: 217-428-4689
Telecopier: 217-422-7950

Michael J. Kehart | Mark D. Gibson
A. James Shafter | James E. Peckert
Charles C. Hughes | Catherine L. Mannweiler
Albert G. Webber IV | Gregory Q. Hill
Deanne F. Jones

OF COUNSEL

Albert G. Webber III | T. G. Bolen

Representative Clients: Archer-Daniels-Midland Co.; A.E. Staley Manufacturing Co.; Mueller Co.; Soyland Power Cooperative; Illinois State Medical Insurance Services; Aetna Casualty & Surety Co.; Wagner Castings Co.; Cub Foods; Decatur Newspapers Inc. - Decatur Herald & Review; Lincoln Diagnostics.

(See Next Column)

KEHART, SHAFTER, HUGHES & WEBBER P.C.—*Continued*

For full biographical listings, see the Martindale-Hubbell Law Directory

SAMUELS, MILLER, SCHROEDER, JACKSON & SLY (AV)

406 First of America Center, P.O. Box 1400, 62525
Telephone: 217-429-4325
Telecopier: 217-425-6313
Arthur, Illinois Office: 131 B South Vine Street.
Telephone: 217-543-3403.

MEMBERS OF FIRM

Charles Chambers Le Forgee (1888-1951)
Thomas Walter Samuels (1914-1989)
Carl R. Miller (1930-1986)
E. Wayne Schroeder
Jerald E. Jackson
Nicholas J. Neiers
James W. Alling
John E. Fick
Guy E. Williams
John S. Cobb
Mark E. Jackson
Keith W. Casteel
Darrell A. Woolums
John E. Sanner
Edward Q. Costa
James T. Jackson

ASSOCIATES

Rhonda L. Richards
J. Richard Campbell
Kristen E. Supinie

OF COUNSEL

William M. Rice
Thomas S. Sly

Representative Clients: Illinois Power Company; Norfolk Southern Corporation; Decatur Memorial Hospital; Millikin University; St. Paul Insurance Co.; Kemper Group; Gallagher-Bassett.

For full biographical listings, see the Martindale-Hubbell Law Directory

DE KALB, De Kalb Co.

BOYLE, CORDES AND BROWN (AV)

363 East Lincoln Highway, 60115
Telephone: 815-756-6328
Fax: 815-756-8842

MEMBERS OF FIRM

Gary W. Cordes
Charles G. Brown

OF COUNSEL

John G. Boyle

Representative Clients: DeKalb Park District; First of America Bank-DeKalb; U.S.F. & G. Co.
References: First of America Bank-DeKalb; First National Bank in DeKalb.

For full biographical listings, see the Martindale-Hubbell Law Directory

KLEIN, STODDARD & BUCK (AV)

555 Bethany Road, 60115
Telephone: 815-748-0380
Fax: 815-748-4030
Sycamore, Illinois Office: 122 South Locust, P.O. Box 86.
Telephone: 815-895-4597.
Fax: 815-895-2276.

Ronald G. Klein (Resident)

Representative Clients: The National Bank and Trust Co.; Resource Bank; Pierce Township; Sycamore Fire Protection District; Kishwaukee Community Hospital; DeKalb Area Association of Realtors; Village of Lee; Equitable Agri Business, Inc.; DeKalb County Building Authority.

For full biographical listings, see the Martindale-Hubbell Law Directory

DU QUOIN, Perry Co.

HOHLT, HOUSE, DEMOSS & JOHNSON (AV)

13 North Division, 62832
Telephone: 618-542-4703
Nashville, Illinois Office: Holston Building.
Telephone: 618-327-8241.
Telecopier: 618-327-4079.
Pinckneyville, Illinois Office: 1 North Main Street.
Telephone: 618-357-2178.
Telecopier: 618-357-3314.

MEMBERS

Don E. Johnson
Roger H. Seibert
Donald Bigham

Counsel for: Nashville Savings & Loan Assn.; Murphy-Wall State Bank & Trust Company of Pinckneyville; First National Bank of Pinckneyville; Farmers & Merchants National Bank of Nashville; Oakdale State Bank.
Local Counsel for: Consolidation Coal Co.; Natural Gas Pipeline Company of America; Amax Coal Co.; Zeigler Coal Co.

For full biographical listings, see the Martindale-Hubbell Law Directory

EAST ST. LOUIS, St. Clair Co.

CARR, KOREIN, TILLERY, KUNIN, MONTROY & GLASS (AV)

412 Missouri Avenue, 62201
Telephone: 618-274-0434
Telecopier: 618-274-8369
St. Louis, Missouri Office: 701 Market Street, Suite 300.
Telephone: 314-241-4844.
Telecopier: 314-241-3525.
Belleville, Illinois Office: 5520 West Main.
Telephone: 618-277-1180.

MEMBERS OF FIRM

Rex Carr
Sandor Korein
Stephen M. Tillery
Joel A. Kunin
Gerald L. Montroy
Mark Glass

ASSOCIATES

G. Richard Jones
Mark M. Silvermintz
Martin L. Perron
Staci M. Yandle
Steven M. Wallace
Michael B. Marker
Ferne P. Wolf
Mark A. Brueggemann
Robert L. King
Christine J. Moody

OF COUNSEL

Lawrence Alan Waldman
Katherine J. Tillery

References: Union Bank; First National Bank.

For full biographical listings, see the Martindale-Hubbell Law Directory

DUNHAM, BOMAN & LESKERA (AV)

520 First Illinois Bank Building, 62201
Telephone: 618-271-0535
Telecopier: 618-271-2800
Belleville, Illinois Office: 208 North High Street.
Telephone: 618-397-2151.
Telecopier: 618-397-2285.
Collinsville, Illinois Office: 114 West Main Street.
Telephone: 618-344-7734.
Telecopier: 618-344-3853.
St. Louis, Missouri Office: 52 Maryland Plaza, Suite 301.
Telephone: 314-367-3030.

M.F. Oehmke (1887-1963)
Wm. C. Dunham (1893-1975)
Howard Boman (1917-1985)

MEMBERS OF FIRM

John W. Leskera
William L. Berry
Eric C. Young
Russell K. Scott
Robert D. Francis
John L. Bitzer

ASSOCIATES

Edward L. Adelman
Robert W. Rongey

Attorneys for: Transamerica Insurance Group; The Travelers Indemnity Co.; Wausau Insurance Cos.; American States Insurance Co.; Hanover Insurance Co.

For full biographical listings, see the Martindale-Hubbell Law Directory

*EDWARDSVILLE,** Madison Co.

BURROUGHS, HEPLER, BROOM, MACDONALD & HEBRANK (AV)

Two Mark Twain Plaza, Suite 300, 103 N. Main Street, P.O. Box 510, 62025-0510
Telephone: 618-656-0184
Telecopier: 618-656-1364

MEMBERS OF FIRM

George D. Burroughs (1873-1977)
William G. Burroughs (1872-1952)
Mallory L. Burroughs (1884-1965)
Jesse L. Simpson (1884-1973)
David L. Simpson (Retired)
G. Gordon Burroughs (Of Counsel)
Larry E. Hepler
Gordon R. Broom
Theodore J. MacDonald, Jr.
Jeffrey S. Hebrank

ASSOCIATES

Lisa K. Franke
Gary E. True
Jack H. Humes, Jr.
Marc A. Lapp
Paul W. Johnson
William J. Knapp
Melissa Griggs
L. David Green
J. Todd Hayes
James W. McConkey
J. Robert Edmonds
Daniel W. Farroll
David J. Gerber
Donald J. Ohl
D. Scott Rendleman
Matthew W. Homann

Representative Clients: Ameritech; Travelers Insurance Co.; Fireman's Fund-American Insurance Group; Continental Loss Adjusting Services; Employers Union Insurance Co.; The Hartford; Illinois Power Co.; W.R. Grace; Mark Twain Bank; Prairie Farms.

For full biographical listings, see the Martindale-Hubbell Law Directory

Edwardsville—Continued

HEYL, ROYSTER, VOELKER & ALLEN, PROFESSIONAL CORPORATION (AV)

Suite 100, Mark Twain Plaza II, 103 North Main Street, P.O. Box 467, 62025
Telephone: 618-656-4646
Telecopier: 618-656-7940
Peoria, Illinois Office: Suite 600, Bank One Building, 124 S.W. Adams, 61602.
Telephone: 309-676-0400.
Telecopier: 309-676-3374.
Springfield, Illinois Office: Suite 575, First of America Center, P.O. Box 1687, 62705.
Telephone: 217-522-8822.
Telecopier: 217-523-3902.
Urbana, Illinois Office: Suite 300, 102 East Main Street, P.O. Box 129, 61801.
Telephone: 217-344-0060.
Telecopier: 217-344-9295.
Rockford, Illinois Office: Suite 1015, Talcott Building, P.O. Box 1288, 61105.
Telephone: 815-963-4454.
Telecopier: 815-963-0399.

RESIDENT PERSONNEL

Robert H. Shultz, Jr.
John A. Ess
Kent L. Plotner

RESIDENT OF COUNSEL

Robert T. Bruegge
William J. Becker

Timothy D. Seifert
Mark D. Ward
Robert D. Rowland
Christine M. Giacomini
Daniel M. Reavy
James A. Telthorst
William Robert Miller

For full biographical listings, see the Martindale-Hubbell Law Directory

REED, ARMSTRONG, GORMAN, COFFEY, THOMSON, GILBERT & MUDGE, PROFESSIONAL CORPORATION (AV)

One Mark Twain Plaza, Suite 300, P.O. Box 368, 62025
Telephone: 618-656-0257; 656-2244
Facsimile: 618-692-4416
Other Edwardsville Office: 125 North Buchanan.
Telephone: 618-656-2244.
Fax: 618-658-1307.
Springfield, Illinois Office: One West Old State Capital Plaza, Suite 400, Myers Building.
Telephone: 217-525-1366.
Fax: 217-525-0986.

James L. Reed (Retired)
Stephen W. Thomson
Harry C. Armstrong
John L. Gilbert
James E. Gorman
Stephen C. Mudge
Gary R. Coffey
Charles C. Compton
Martin K. Morrissey

Debra J. Meadows
Rodney W. Phillipe
Kevin J. Babb
Mitchell B. Stoddard
Richard J. Behr
David Laurent
Michael J. Bedesky
Gregory W. Coffey
Bryan L. Skelton

Representative Clients: State Farm Insurance Cos.; Country Companies; Standard Mutual Casualty Co.; General Casualty Company of Wisconsin; Western States Mutual Insurance Co.; Hawkeye-Security Insurance Co.; Shelter Insurance Co.; New Hampshire Insurance Group; Heritage Insurance Co.; Southern Illinois University of Edwardsville.

For full biographical listings, see the Martindale-Hubbell Law Directory

WALKER & WILLIAMS, PROFESSIONAL CORPORATION (AV)

70 Edwardsville Professional Park, 62025
Telephone: 618-656-9222
Belleville, Illinois Office: 4343 West Main Street.
Telephones: 618-274-1000; 277-1000.
Telecopier: 618-233-1637.
St. Louis, Missouri Office: 906 Olive, Suite 1250.
Telephone: 314-241-2441.
Telecopier: 314-241-7240.

Dale L. Bode

For full biographical listings, see the Martindale-Hubbell Law Directory

*EFFINGHAM,** Effingham Co. — (Refer to Vandalia)

ELGIN, Cook & Kane Cos.

ARIANO, ANDERSON, BAZOS, HARDY & CASTILLO (AV)

A Partnership of Professional Corporations
474 Summit Street, 60120
Telephone: 708-695-2400
Telecopy: 708-695-8397
Other Elgin Office: 1250 Larkin Avenue, Suite 100.
Telephone: 708-742-8800.
Fax: 708-742-9777
Huntley, Illinois Office: 10604 North Vine Street, 60142.
Telephone: 708-669-5020.

Frank V. Ariano
William F. Castillo
Allen M. Anderson
Gary M. Vanek
Peter C. Bazos
Daniel A. Weiler
Ralph C. Hardy
Brett E. Anderson

Chadwick I. Buttell

For full biographical listings, see the Martindale-Hubbell Law Directory

BRADY, MCQUEEN, MARTIN, COLLINS & JENSEN (AV)

2425 Royal Boulevard, P.O. Box 807, 60123
Telephone: 708-695-2000

MEMBERS OF FIRM

Wayne M. Jensen
Alfred Y. Kirkland, Jr.
Richard L. Heimberg
Glen T. Dobosz
Loren S. Golden
Diana S. Larson
Roger K. Frandsen
Michael C. Deutsch
Ronald E. Rasmussen
Jane E. Craddock

ASSOCIATES

Keith A. Spong
Marios Nicholas Karayannis
Fred J. Beer

Representative Clients: Prudential Insurance Company of America; NBD Bank Elgin; First Community Bank, Elgin; Union Insurance Group; Chicago Title Insurance Co.; Elgin Corrugated Box Co.; Hoffer Plastics Corp.; Lamp Construction Co.

For full biographical listings, see the Martindale-Hubbell Law Directory

ELIZABETH, Jo Daviess Co. — (Refer to Galena)

*EUREKA,** Woodford Co. — (Refer to Peoria)

FAIRBURY, Livingston Co. — (Refer to Watseka)

*FAIRFIELD,** Wayne Co. — (Refer to Mount Vernon)

FLORA, Clay Co. — (Refer to Mount Vernon)

*FREEPORT,** Stephenson Co.

SCHMELZLE AND KROEGER (AV)

208 West Stephenson Street, P.O. Box 837, 61032
Telephone: 815-235-2500
Facsimile: 815-235-4597
Stockton, Illinois Office: 123 West Front Street.
Telephone: 815-947-3202.

MEMBERS OF FIRM

Robert P. Eckert (1869-1949)
Robert J. Schmelzle
Louis F. Reinhold (1890-1952)
Richard F. Eckert
Robert P. Eckert, Jr. (1903-1966)
Woodruff A. Burt
Peter D. McClanathan
Marvin F. Burt (1905-1983)
Stephen S. Schmelzle
David D. Shockey

OF COUNSEL

Wilbur L. Kroeger

Counsel for: German-American State Bank; Lena State Bank; Midwest Bank of Freeport; State Bank of Davis; State Bank of Freeport; Union Savings Bank.

For full biographical listings, see the Martindale-Hubbell Law Directory

*GALENA,** Jo Daviess Co.

NACK, RICHARDSON & KELLY (AV)

106 North Main Street, 61036
Telephone: 815-777-1218; 777-1219
Fax: 815-777-2609
Elizabeth, Illinois Office: Elizabeth State Bank Building.
Telephone: 815-858-3712.

Jos. M. Nack (1865-1939)
Louis A. Nack, Jr.
Louis A. Nack (1901-1981)
James J. Nack
James W. Richardson (1925-1988)
Roger H. Kelly

(See Next Column)

NACK, RICHARDSON & KELLY—*Continued*

ASSOCIATES

Terry M. Kurt | Joseph E. Nack

Representative Clients: The First National Bank of Galena; Economy Fire & Casualty Co.; Illinois Insurance Guaranty Fund; Chestnut Mountain Lodge; Elizabeth State Bank; Hanover State Bank; City of East Dubuque; Shell Oil Co.; Aetna Insurance Group; American Mutual Insurance Co.

For full biographical listings, see the Martindale-Hubbell Law Directory

*GALESBURG,** Knox Co.

BARASH, STOERZBACH & HENSON, P.C. (AV)

139 South Cherry Street, P.O. Box 1328, 61402-1328
Telephone: 309-343-4193
Telecopier: 309-343-7500

Burrel Barash (1906-1993)
Robert C. Stoerzbach
Barry M. Barash
Dwayne I. Morrison
Daniel B. Stoerzbach
Carl E. Hawkinson
Paul L. Mangieri
John W. Robertson
Pamela Wilcox
Richard Arthur Dahl

Representative Clients: Allstate Insurance Co.; American States; City of Knoxville, Illinois; Community School District No. 208 R.O.W.V.A.; Country Mutual Insurance Co.; Economy Fire & Casualty Co.; Farmers and Mechanics Bank; Galesburg Clinic; Hartford Insurance Co.; Ken Co.

For full biographical listings, see the Martindale-Hubbell Law Directory

HATTERY, SIMPSON & WEST (AV)

Suite 402 Hill Arcade, 61401
Telephone: 309-343-6152
Telecopier: 309-343-5103
Monmouth, Illinois Office: 1025 East Broadway.
Telephone: 309-734-3150.
Telefax: 309-734-4435.
Roseville, Illinois Office: 130 North Main Street.
Telephone: 309-426-2176.
Telefax: 309-426-2177

MEMBERS OF FIRM

Robert E. McLaughlin
John J. Hattery
Roger L. Williamson
S. David Simpson
Thomas G. West
Ronald D. Stombaugh (Resident at Monmouth Office)
Timothy E. Sullivan
Carol Masden Fornander
George M. Hennenfent (Resident at Roseville Office)
Daniel S. Alcorn

For full biographical listings, see the Martindale-Hubbell Law Directory

GALVA, Henry Co.

EVERETT & LUYMES, P.C. (AV)

P.O. Box 165, 61434
Telephone: 309-932-2001

Reynolds M. Everett (1907-1989)
James B. Young (1914-1982)
Reynolds M. Everett, Jr.
Keith A. Luymes

Representative Clients: Norwest Bank N.A., Galva Branch; E.W. Houghton Lumber Co.; Dixline Co., Inc.; Gateway Coop; The Swedish Consultant General; Central Soya Co., Inc.; Wyffels Hybrids, Inc.; Galva, Bishop Hill and Clover Township Fire Districts; Woodhull Cooperative Grain Co.

For full biographical listings, see the Martindale-Hubbell Law Directory

GENESEO, Henry Co. — (Refer to Cambridge)

*GENEVA,** Kane Co.

SMITH, LANDMEIER & SKAAR, P.C. (AV)

15 North Second Street, 60134
Telephone: 708-232-2880
Fax: 708-232-2889

Howard E. Smith, Jr.
Allen L. Landmeier
James D. Skaar

Brian W. Baugh
Vincent J. Elders

References: Firstar Bank, Geneva, N.A., Geneva, Illinois; State Bank of Geneva, Geneva, Illinois.

For full biographical listings, see the Martindale-Hubbell Law Directory

*GOLCONDA,** Pope Co. — (Refer to Harrisburg)

GRANITE CITY, Madison Co.

BERNARD & DAVIDSON (AV)

3600 Nameoki Road, 62040
Telephone: 618-452-6100
Telecopier: 618-451-2051
St. Louis, Missouri Office: 314 N. Broadway.
Telephone: 314-231-4181.

MEMBERS OF FIRM

Burton C. Bernard (1926-1991)
Joseph R. Davidson
Ronald A. Roth
David L. Antognoli

ASSOCIATES

Mervin W. Warren, Jr.
Gary L. Smith
Peter M. Gannott
Kevin J. Davidson
Ronald D. Robinson

A list of Representative Clients will be furnished upon request.

For full biographical listings, see the Martindale-Hubbell Law Directory

LUEDERS, ROBERTSON & KONZEN (AV)

1939 Delmar Avenue, 62040
Telephone: 618-876-8500
Telecopier: 618-876-4534

MEMBERS OF FIRM

Wesley Lueders (1896-1957)
Randall Robertson
Leo H. Konzen
R. Eric Robertson
Edward C. Fitzhenry, Jr.
Brian E. Konzen

ASSOCIATES

Douglas F. Hartman

Representative Clients: Central Banc System, Inc. (Trust Division); Granite City Div., National Steel Corp.; A.O. Smith Corp.; The Nestle Co.; Olin Corp.; Archers-Daniels-Midland Co.; Illinois Industrial Energy Consumers (IIEC) including General Motors Corp.

For full biographical listings, see the Martindale-Hubbell Law Directory

*GREENVILLE,** Bond Co. — (Refer to Hillsboro)

*HARDIN,** Calhoun Co. — (Refer to Carrollton)

*HARRISBURG,** Saline Co.

JELLIFFE, FERRELL & MORRIS (AV)

108 East Walnut Street, 62946
Telephone: 618-253-7153; 253-7647
Telecopier: 618-252-1843

OF COUNSEL

Charles R. Jelliffe

MEMBERS OF FIRM

DeWitt Twente (1904-1976)
Donald V. Ferrell
Walden E. Morris

ASSOCIATES

Michal Doerge
Thomas J. Foster
Timothy L. Fornes

Representative Clients: Auto-Owners Insurance; Country Cos; Metropolitan Life Insurance; Ohio Casualty Group; Standard Mutual Insurance Co.; State Farm Cos.; Redland Insurance Co.; Aetna Casualty & Surety Co.; Kerr-McGee Coal Corp.; Sahara Coal Co.

For full biographical listings, see the Martindale-Hubbell Law Directory

HARVARD, McHenry Co.

ELMAN & EHARDT, LTD. (AV)

205 East Front Street, 60033-2900
Telephone: 815-943-4051
Fax: 815-934-4086

William Elman

Reference: First State Bank of Harvard, Harvard, Illinois.

For full biographical listings, see the Martindale-Hubbell Law Directory

*HAVANA,** Mason Co. — (Refer to Beardstown)

*HENNEPIN,** Putnam Co.

BOYLE, GOLDSMITH & BOLIN (AV)

227 East Court Street, 61327
Telephone: 815-925-7393

MEMBERS OF FIRM

Walter Durley Boyle
Linn C. Goldsmith
Roger C. Bolin

References: Farmers State Bank, McNabb, Illinois; The Putnam County Bank, Hennepin, Illinois.

For full biographical listings, see the Martindale-Hubbell Law Directory

HENRY, Marshall Co. — (Refer to Princeton)

HIGHLAND, Madison Co.

Donald C. Rikli (AV)

914 Broadway, 62249
Telephone: 618-654-2364; 654-2365
Fax: 618-654-4752

For full biographical listings, see the Martindale-Hubbell Law Directory

*HILLSBORO,** Montgomery Co. — (Refer to Vandalia)

*JACKSONVILLE,** Morgan Co.

Bellatti, Fay, Bellatti & Beard (AV)

333 West State Street, P.O. Box 696, 62651
Telephone: 217-245-7111
Fax: 217-245-2832
Office also at Ashland, Illinois. Telephone: 217-476-3318.

OF COUNSEL

William L. Fay

MEMBERS OF FIRM

Walter R. Bellatti
John E. Bellatti
Daniel J. Beard
Timothy E. Ruppel
Thomas L. Veith

General Counsel for: Elliott State Bank; Bound to stay Bound Banks, Inc..
District Counsel for: Illinois Power Company; Norfolk Southern Railroad.
Representative Clients: Mobil Chemical Co.; Equitable Life Assurance Society; Prudential Insurance Co.; Allstate Insurance Co.; Travelers Insurance Co.; Corepak Packaging, Inc.

For full biographical listings, see the Martindale-Hubbell Law Directory

Rammelkamp, Bradney, Dahman, Kuster, Keaton, Fritsche & Lindsay, P.C. (AV)

232 West State Street, P.O. Box 489, 62651
Telephone: 217-245-6177
Fax: 217-243-7322

L.O. Vaught (1865-1955)
Carl E. Robinson (1886-1964)
Orville N. Foreman (1904-1972)
Albert W. Hall (1912-1986)
Theodore C. Rammelkamp (Retired)
Marc Dahman
Larry D. Kuster
Forrest G. Keaton
Barbara Fritsche
Nancy Lindsay
Maria M. Gonzalez
Richard R. Freeman

OF COUNSEL

Robert E. Bradney
Theodore C. Rammelkamp, Jr.

H. Allen Yow

Representative Clients: Country Mutual Insurance Co.; State Farm Mutual Auto Insurance Co.; Home Insurance Co.; Oscar Mayer Co., Inc.; Elliott State Bank; New Hampshire Insurance Group; Pekin Farmers Insurance Co.

For full biographical listings, see the Martindale-Hubbell Law Directory

*JERSEYVILLE,** Jersey Co. — (Refer to Carrollton)

*JOLIET,** Will Co.

Herschbach, Tracy, Johnson, Bertani & Wilson (AV)

Two Rialto Square, 116 North Chicago Street, Sixth Floor, 60431
Telephone: 815-723-8500
Fax: 815-727-4846

Wayne R. Johnson
Thomas R. Wilson
Richard H. Teas
Scherrill W. Weichbrodt (1930-1993)
George F. Mahoney, III
Michael W. Hansen
Raymond E. Meader
A. Michael Wojtak
Kenneth A. Carlson
David J. Silverman
Roger D. Rickmon
John S. Gallo
Thomas R. Osterberger

OF COUNSEL

Donald J. Tracy
Louis R. Bertani
John L. O'Brien

RETIRED PARTNER

Walter O. Herschbach

General Counsel for: First National Bank of Joliet.
Representative Clients: Chicago Title Insurance Co.; Vulcan Materials Company; Dow Chemical, U.S.A.; Marathon Oil Co.; Waste Management, Inc.; General Electric Credit Corp.; The Copley Press, Inc.; Citizens Utilities Co.; Empress River Casino Corporation.

For full biographical listings, see the Martindale-Hubbell Law Directory

McKeown, Fitzgerald, Zollner, Buck, Hutchison & Ruttle (AV)

2455 Glenwood Avenue, 60435
Telephone: 815-729-4800
FAX: 815-729-4711
Frankfort, Illinois Office: 28 Kansas Street.
Telephone: 815-469-2176.
FAX: 815-469-0295.

MEMBERS OF FIRM

Charles J. McKeown (1908-1985)
Paul O. McKeown (1913-1982)
Richard T. Buck (1936-1992)
Joseph C. Fitzgerald
Max E. Zollner
Douglas P. Hutchison
David L. Ruttle
Theodore J. Jarz
Douglas J. McKeown
Timothy J. Rathbun
James B. Harvey
Kenneth A. Grey
Michael R. Lucas

ASSOCIATES

Christopher N. Wise
Gary S. Mueller
Frank S. Cservenyak, Jr.
William P Mullarkey
Arthur J. Wilhelmi

OF COUNSEL

Stewart C. Hutchison

Representative Clients: Caterpillar Tractor Co.; First National Bank of Lockport; Homart Development Co.; First Midwest Bank, N.A.; Silver Cross Hospital; Joliet Township High School District; Villages of: Plainfield and Mokena; Southwest Agency for Risk Management; Joliet Junior College Foundation; Health Service Systems, Inc.

For full biographical listings, see the Martindale-Hubbell Law Directory

Spesia, Ayers, Ardaugh & Wunderlich (AV)

Two Rialto Square, 116 North Chicago Street, Suite 200, 60431
Telephone: 815-726-4311
FAX: 815-726-6828

MEMBERS OF FIRM

Douglas F. Spesia
E. Kent Ayers
John R. Ardaugh
Gary L. Wunderlich

ASSOCIATES

Dinah Lennon Archambeault
John C. Roth
Edward J. Schoen, Jr.

OF COUNSEL

Ralph C. Murphy
Kenneth E. Timm
Arthur T. Lennon (1923-1988)

Counsel For: Commonwealth Edison Co.; Illinois Bell Telephone Co.; Country Mutual Insurance Co.; Northern Illinois Gas Co.; Metropolitan Life Insurance Co.; Indiana Consolidated Insurance Cos.; A.N.R. Pipeline Co.; Amoco Chemical Corp.; Village of New Lenox; Peoples Gas Light & Coke Company.

For full biographical listings, see the Martindale-Hubbell Law Directory

*KANKAKEE,** Kankakee Co.

Ackman, Marek, Boyd & Simutis, Ltd. (AV)

Suite 400, One Dearborn Square, 60901
Telephone: 815-933-6681
FAX: 815-933-9985
Watseka, Illinois Office: 123 South Fourth Street.
Telephone: 815-432-5215.
FAX: 815-432-3186.
Gilman, Illinois Office: 201 S. Crescent.
Telephone: 815-265-4533.

Richard L. Ackman
J. Dennis Marek
Robert W. Boyd
Frank J. Simutis (Watseka and Gilman Offices)
Deborah A. Woodruff

James A. Devine
Jack L. Haan

Representative Clients: American States Insurance Co.; Auto Owners Insurance Co.; Country Mutual Insurance Co.; Farmers Insurance Group; Hartford Accident & Indemnity Co.; Kankakee Water Co.; Medical Protective Co.; State Farm Insurance Co.; Watseka First National Bank; Economy Fire & Casualty Co.

For full biographical listings, see the Martindale-Hubbell Law Directory

Blanke, Norden, Barmann, Kramer & Bohlen, P.C. (AV)

Suite 502, 200 East Court Street, P.O. Box 1787, 60901
Telephone: 815-939-1133
FAX: 815-939-0994

Armen R. Blanke (Deceased)
Paul F. Blanke (Retired)
Dennis A. Norden
Glen R. Barmann
Christopher W. Bohlen
Michael D. Kramer

For full biographical listings, see the Martindale-Hubbell Law Directory

KEWANEE, Henry Co. — (Refer to Cambridge)

*LACON,** Marshall Co. — (Refer to Hennepin)

LA SALLE, La Salle Co.

HERBOLSHEIMER, LANNON, HENSON, DUNCAN AND REAGAN, P.C. (AV)

State Bank Building, Suite 400, 654 First Street, P.O. Box 539, 61301
Telephone: 815-223-0111
FAX: 815-223-5829
Ottawa, Illinois Office: 200 First Federal Savings Bank Building. Ottawa, IL 61350.

George L. Herbolsheimer (1911-1992)
R. James Lannon, Jr.
T. Donald Henson
John S. Duncan, III
Michael T. Reagan (Resident, Ottawa Office)
Douglas A. Gift
Gary R. Eiten

Karen C. Eiten
Jonathan F. Brandt
Michael C. Jansz (Resident, Ottawa Office)
Jill W. Broderick
Murl Tod Melton

Attorneys for: Aetna Insurance Group; St. Paul Fire and Marine Insurance Co.; State Farm Insurance Co.; La Salle State Bank; The Daily News Tribune Company, La Salle; Eureka Savings Bank; Illinois Valley Community Hospital; Community Hospital of Ottawa; Commonwealth Edison, Co.; United States Fidelity & Guaranty, Co.

For full biographical listings, see the Martindale-Hubbell Law Directory

*LAWRENCEVILLE,** Lawrence Co.

GOSNELL, BORDEN & ENLOE, LTD. (AV)

815 12th Street, P.O. Box 737, 62439-0737
Telephone: 618-943-2338
Fax: 618-943-2080

John F. Borden
Douglas A. Enloe

Larry N. Sloss, Jr.
Patrick L. Hahn

OF COUNSEL

Maurice E. Gosnell

General Counsel for: First Bank of Lawrence County; Peoples National Bank.
Local Counsel for: Hartford Accident & Indemnity Co.; Aetna Casualty & Surety Co.; Texaco, Inc.; Country Mutual Insurance Co.; State Farm Insurance Co.; Economy Fire & Casualty Co.; Continental Insurance Co.; Crum & Forster Group.

For full biographical listings, see the Martindale-Hubbell Law Directory

*LEWISTOWN,** Fulton Co. — (Refer to Macomb)

*LINCOLN,** Logan Co.

WOODS & BATES (AV)

306 Clinton Street, 62656
Telephone: 217-735-1234
Fax: 217-735-1236

MEMBERS OF FIRM

Charles H. Woods (1883-1958)
Norman S. Woods (1915-1944)
William B. Bates

OF COUNSEL

Robert J. Woods
William C. Bates, Jr.

Representative Clients: Illico Independent Oil Co.; The Abraham Lincoln Memorial Hospital; Christian Homes, Inc.; Lincoln Firemen's Pension Fund; L & F Products, a Division of Kodak.

For full biographical listings, see the Martindale-Hubbell Law Directory

LITCHFIELD, Montgomery Co. — (Refer to Vandalia)

*LOUISVILLE,** Clay Co. — (Refer to Mount Vernon)

*MACOMB,** McDonough Co.

FLACK, MCRAVEN & STEPHENS (AV)

32 West Side Courthouse Square, 61455
Telephone: 309-837-5000
Fax: 309-836-2335

MEMBERS OF FIRM

J. Dixson McRaven
Charles Haynes Flack
Richard D. Stephens
Lawrence J. Kwacala
Bruce J. Biagini
James Patrick Murphy
Joseph W. McRaven
A. Anthony Ashenhurst

For full biographical listings, see the Martindale-Hubbell Law Directory

MARENGO, McHenry Co.

POLLOCK, MEYERS, EICKSTEADT & WEECH, LTD. (AV)

Marengo State Bank Building, 100 West Washington Street, 60152
Telephone: 815-568-8071
FAX: 815-568-0003

Norman J. Pollock
Harvey A. Meyers
Richard W. Eicksteadt
Charles P. Weech

Representative Clients: Marengo State Bank; The State Bank of Woodstock; Marengo Fire Protection District; Riley Township; Woodstone Co.; Marengo Steel Co.; Marengo Disposal Co.; Key Development Co.; Agrinetics, Inc.; Compost Enterprises.

For full biographical listings, see the Martindale-Hubbell Law Directory

*MARION,** Williamson Co.

MITCHELL & ARMSTRONG, LTD. (AV)

404 North Monroe, P.O. Box 488, 62959
Telephone: 618-993-2134
Telecopier: 618-993-8702

J. C. Mitchell
William A. Armstrong
Bruce W. Mitchell

Stephen R. Green

Representative Clients: St. Paul Fire & Casualty Insurance Company; Illinois State Medical Insurance Exchange; Liberty Mutual Insurance Company; Shelter Insurance Company; Corporate Services, Inc.; Wal-Mart Stores, Inc.; Atlantic Mutual Insurance Company; Farmer's Insurance Exchange; United States Fidelity and Guarantee Company.

For full biographical listings, see the Martindale-Hubbell Law Directory

WINTERS, BREWSTER, CROSBY & PATCHETT (AV)

111 West Main, P.O. Box 700, 62959
Telephone: 618-997-5611
Fax: 618-997-6522

MEMBERS OF FIRM

Charles D. Winters (1917-1992)
John S. Brewster
Thomas F. Crosby, III
John R. (Randy) Patchett

ASSOCIATES

Andrea Lynn McNeill

For full biographical listings, see the Martindale-Hubbell Law Directory

*MARSHALL,** Clark Co. — (Refer to Paris)

MATTOON, Coles Co.

CRAIG & CRAIG (AV)

1807 Broadway, P.O. Box 689, 61938-0689
Telephone: 217-234-6481
Telecopier: 217-234-6486
Mount Vernon, Illinois Office: 227 1/2 South 9th Street.
Telephone: 618-244-7511.

MEMBERS OF FIRM

Craig Van Meter (1895-1981)
Fred H. Kelly (1894-1971)
Robert M. Werden (1908-1969)
George N. Gilkerson (1911-1985)
John H. Armstrong
John P. Ewart
Richard F. Record, Jr.
Stephen L. Corn
Richard Charles Hayden
Robert G. Grierson
Gregory C. Ray
Paul R. Lynch (Resident, Mount Vernon Office)
Kenneth F. Werts (Resident, Mount Vernon Office)
John L. Barger
James M. Dion

ASSOCIATES

Mark R. Karpus
Beverly J. Ring
Joshua N. Rosen (Resident, Mount Vernon Office)
Kathleen M. Kattner
Richard A. Tjepkema

OF COUNSEL

Jack E. Horsley

Counsel for: Monterey Coal Co., a Division of Exxon Coal USA, Inc.; Marathon Oil Co.; Illinois Central R.R. Co.; Okaw Building & Loan Assn., Mattoon, Illinois; The Medical Protective Insurance Co.; Consolidated Communications, Inc.; Lloyds Underwriters at London; Hartford Insurance Co.; Coles Together, a Not-For-Profit Corp.; Coles Building Corporation.

For full biographical listings, see the Martindale-Hubbell Law Directory

HELLER, HOLMES & ASSOCIATES, P.C. (AV)

1101 Broadway, P.O. Box 889, 61938-0889
Telephone: 217-235-2700
FAX: 217-235-0743

(See Next Column)

HELLER, HOLMES & ASSOCIATES, P.C., *Mattoon—Continued*

Harlan Heller H. Kent Heller
Brent D. Holmes Mitchell K. Shick

Teresa K. Righter Maria C. Dunn
Rodney L. Smith Matthew P. Garland
William R. Tapella

Representative Clients: Quantum Chemical Co.; First National Bank of Effingham.
References: First National Bank, Mattoon, Ill.; Central National Bank of Mattoon.

For full biographical listings, see the Martindale-Hubbell Law Directory

RYAN, BENNETT & RADLOFF (AV)

300 Richmond East, P.O. Box 629, 61938-0629
Telephone: 217-234-2000
Fax: 217-234-2001

MEMBERS OF FIRM

Willis P. Ryan (1911-1983) Michael D. Ryan
James A. Bennett Michael K. Radloff
Stephen R. Ryan Christopher A. Koester
Brien J. O'Brien

Counsel For: State Farm Insurance Cos.; American States Insurance Co.; Auto-Owners Insurance Co.; Country Cos.; Economy Fire and Casualty Co.; Bituminous Insurance Cos.; Farmland Insurance; Millers Mutual Insurance; Horace Mann Insurance Co.
Reference: First Mid-Illinois Bank & Trust, Mattoon, Ill.

For full biographical listings, see the Martindale-Hubbell Law Directory

*MCLEANSBORO,** Hamilton Co. — (Refer to Mount Vernon)

*METROPOLIS,** Massac Co. — (Refer to Marion)

MOLINE, Rock Island Co. — (Refer to Rock Island)

*MONMOUTH,** Warren Co.

BEAL, PRATT AND PRATT (AV)

57 Southeast Public Square, P.O. Box 200, 61462-0200
Telephone: 309-734-3193
Telecopier: 309-734-7279

MEMBERS OF FIRM

Edward B. Love (1906-1972) Channing L. Pratt
Marion L. Beal Jane Hartley Pratt

Jonathan C. Wright

Representative Clients: State Farm Mutual Insurance Co.; Western States Insurance; Wolverine Insurance; Aetna Life and Casualty; General Casualty Company of Wisconsin; Hawkeye Security Insurance; CNA Insurance.

For full biographical listings, see the Martindale-Hubbell Law Directory

*MONTICELLO,** Piatt Co. — (Refer to Champaign)

*MORRISON,** Whiteside Co.

LUDENS, POTTER & BURCH (AV)

409 North Cherry, P.O. Box 360, 61270
Telephone: 815-772-2161
Telecopier: 815-772-7440

MEMBERS OF FIRM

Lawrence A. Ludens (1912-1990) William A. Burch
Robert H. Potter Thomas J. Potter
Stanley B. Steines

Representative Clients: Smith Trust & Savings Bank, Morrison, Illinois; Fulton State Bank, Fulton, Illinois; Farmers State Bank, Chadwick and Mount Carroll; First Illinois National Bank, Savanna, Ill.; Federated Insurance Co.; Country Mutual Insurance Co.; Fulton Flood Control District, Fulton, Illinois; Farmers Savings Bank, Preston, Iowa; Miles Savings Bank, Miles, Iowa; Iowa Mutual Insurance Company.

For full biographical listings, see the Martindale-Hubbell Law Directory

MORTON, Tazewell Co. — (Refer to Peoria)

*MOUND CITY,** Pulaski Co. — (Refer to Marion)

*MOUNT CARROLL,** Carroll Co.

LEEMON, WEINSTINE, SHIRK & MELLOTT (AV)

102 1/2 East Market Street, P.O. Box 112, 61053
Telephone: 815-244-3422
Fax: 815-244-3900
Weinstine, Shirk, Mellott & Leemon: 301 East Main Street, Morrison, Illinois, 61270.
Telephone: 815-772-7211.
Fax: 815-772-4599.

(See Next Column)

MEMBERS OF FIRM

John A. Leemon William R. Shirk
Lester S. Weinstine Michael A. Mellott

Representative Clients: First State Bank of Shannon, Shannon, Ill.; Savanna State Bank; Farm Credit Bank of St. Louis; Mt. Carroll Mutual Fire Insurance Co.; Country Mutual Insurance Co.

For full biographical listings, see the Martindale-Hubbell Law Directory

*MOUNT STERLING,** Brown Co. — (Refer to Quincy)

*MOUNT VERNON,** Jefferson Co.

CAMPBELL, BLACK, CARNINE & HEDIN, P.C. (AV)

P.O. Drawer C, 62864
Telephone: 618-242-3310
Fax: 618-242-3735

David A. Campbell Carl L. Favreau
Terry R. Black Howard W. Campbell (1911-1980)
Roy L. Carnine John E. Jacobsen (1922-1985)
Craig R. Hedin Glenn E. Moore (1911-1991)
Mark J. Ballard David E. Furnall (1905-1993)
Jerome E. McDonald

Fred R. Mann

Representative Clients: Kerr-McGee Coal Corp.; Good Samaritan Hospital; Country Mutual Insurance Co.; Southern Illinois Stone Co; Rend Lake Conservancy District; King City Federal Savings Bank; Consolidation Coal Co.; Illinois State Medical Insurance Services; State Farm Automobile Insurance Co.; John Hancock Mutual Life Insurance Co.

For full biographical listings, see the Martindale-Hubbell Law Directory

HOWARD & HOWARD (AV)

P.O. Drawer U, 62864
Telephone: 618-242-6594
FAX: 618-244-7197

MEMBERS OF FIRM

George W. Howard, Jr. David R. Leggans
G. W. Howard, III David L. Piercy
Jeffrey G Howard

Representative Clients: Boatmen's Bank of Mount Vernon; First State Bank of Dix; Tri-County Electric Cooperative; Hamilton County Telephone Co-op.

For full biographical listings, see the Martindale-Hubbell Law Directory

MITCHELL, NEUBAUER, SHAW & HANSON, P.C. (AV)

123 South 10th Street, Mercantile Bank Building, 6th Floor, P.O. Box 1088, 62864
Telephone: 618-242-0705
Telecopier: 618-242-4820

A. Ben Mitchell Robert E. Shaw
Timothy R. Neubauer Leslie James Hanson

Curtis W. Martin Michael D. McHaney

Attorneys for: C. E. Brehm Oil Trust; Mt. Vernon City Schools.
Local Attorneys for: The Citizens National Bank of Evansville; Agri Bank, FCB; Mercantile Bank of Mt. Vernon.

For full biographical listings, see the Martindale-Hubbell Law Directory

NAPERVILLE, Du Page Co.

NADELHOFFER, KUHN, MITCHELL, MOSS, SALOGA & LECHOWICZ, P.C. (AV)

111 East Jefferson Avenue, P.O. Box 359, 60566
Telephone: 708-355-1700
FAX: 708-355-0458

Carleton Nadelhoffer Jonathan Y. Moss
Daniel L. Kuhn James E. Saloga
Paul M. Mitchell Alan E. Lechowicz

Robert I. Mork Annette Christine Corrigan

For full biographical listings, see the Martindale-Hubbell Law Directory

*NASHVILLE,** Washington Co.

HOHLT, HOUSE, DEMOSS & JOHNSON (AV)

Holston Building, P.O. Box 249, 62263
Telephone: 618-327-8241
Telecopier: 618-327-4079
Pinckneyville, Illinois Office: 1 North Main Street.
Telephone: 618-357-2178.
Telecopier: 618-357-3314.
Du Quoin, Illinois Office: 13 North Division.
Telephone: 618-542-4703.

(See Next Column)

HOHLT, HOUSE, DEMOSS & JOHNSON—*Continued*

MEMBERS OF FIRM

Harold H. House (1903-1944)
Byron O. House (1926-1956)
Wilbert J. Hohlt
Clarence W. DeMoss
Don E. Johnson
Roger H. Seibert
Donald Bigham
William C. DeMoss

ASSOCIATES

Robert D. Bowers

OF COUNSEL

James Byron House

Counsel for: Nashville Savings & Loan Assn.; Murphy-Wall State Bank & Trust Company of Pinckneyville; First National Bank of Pinckneyville; Farmers & Merchants National Bank of Nashville; Oakdale State Bank.
Local Counsel for: Consolidation Coal Co.; Natural Gas Pipeline Company of America; Amax Coal Co.; Zeigler Coal Co.

For full biographical listings, see the Martindale-Hubbell Law Directory

*NEWTON,** Jasper Co. — (Refer to Lawrenceville)

*OLNEY,** Richland Co. — (Refer to Lawrenceville)

*OQUAWKA,** Henderson Co. — (Refer to Monmouth)

*OREGON,** Ogle Co.

WILLIAMS & MCCARTHY, A PROFESSIONAL CORPORATION (AV)

607 Washington Street, P.O. Box 339, 61061
Telephone: 815-732-2101
Fax: 815-732-2289
Rockford, Illinois Office: 321 West State Street, P.O. Box 219.
Telephone: 815-987-8900.
Fax: 815-968-0019. ABANET: ABA 5519.

Kim D. Krahenbuhl
Clayton L. Lindsey
Wendy S. Howarter

Representative Clients: Anderson Industries, Inc.; Liberty Mutual Insurance Co.; Atwood Industries, Inc.; The Travelers; American Mutual Insurance Co.; Rockford Memorial Hospital; Chrysler Corp.

For full biographical listings, see the Martindale-Hubbell Law Directory

*OTTAWA,** La Salle Co.

HUPP, LANUTI, IRION & MARTIN, P.C. (AV)

227 West Madison, P.O. Box 768, 61350
Telephone: 815-433-3111
Fax: 815-433-9109

Joseph E. Lanuti
Paul V. Martin
George C. Hupp, Jr.
Richard L. Burton

Michelle Hutson

OF COUNSEL

George C. Hupp

Representative Clients: Country Mutual Insurance Co.; State Farm Mutual Automobile Insurance Co.; State Farm Fire & Casualty Co.; Economy Fire and Casualty Co.; Employee Mutual Casualty Co.; Sentry Insurance Co.; United Fire and Casualty Co.; Allstate Insurance Co.; Millers Mutual Insurance Assn.; Continental Casualty Co.

For full biographical listings, see the Martindale-Hubbell Law Directory

MYERS, DAUGHERITY, BERRY & O'CONOR, LTD. (AV)

130 East Madison Street, 61350
Telephone: 815-434-6206
Fax: 815-434-6203
Streator, Illinois Office: 7 North Point Drive.
Telephone: 815-672-3116.
Fax: 815-672-0738.

John A. Berry (1912-1986)
Stephen C. Myers
Eugene P. Daugherity
Richard J. Berry
Andrew J. O'Conor

Sheryl H. Kuzma

Representative Clients: Auto Owners Insurance, Co.; Union Bank; First National Bank of Ottawa, Illinois; Union Bancorp Inc.; First State Bank; United States Fidelity & Guaranty Co.; St. Mary's Hospital; General Casualty Insurance, Co.

For full biographical listings, see the Martindale-Hubbell Law Directory

*PEORIA,** Peoria Co.

CASSIDY & MUELLER (AV)

1510 First Financial Plaza, 61602
Telephone: 309-676-0591
FAX: 309-676-8036

(See Next Column)

MEMBERS OF FIRM

John E. Cassidy (1896-1984)
John E. Cassidy, Jr.
David B. Mueller
John E. Cassidy, III
Timothy J. Cassidy
Timothy J. Newlin

ASSOCIATES

Andrew D. Cassidy

Representative Clients: Aetna Casualty & Surety Co.; Atchison, Topeka & Santa Fe Railroad Co.; Continental Oil Company; E.I. DuPont-DeNemours & Company; Hartford Accident & Indemnity Company; Illinois-American Water Company; John P. Pearl & Associates, Ltd.; Liberty Mutual Insurance Co.; Occidental Petroleum Company; Warner-Lambert Company; St. Paul Fire and Casualty Co.

For full biographical listings, see the Martindale-Hubbell Law Directory

HEYL, ROYSTER, VOELKER & ALLEN, PROFESSIONAL CORPORATION (AV)

Suite 600, Bank One Building, 124 S.W. Adams, 61602
Telephone: 309-676-0400
Telecopier: 309-676-3374
Springfield, Illinois Office: Suite 575, First of America Center, P.O. Box 1687, 62705.
Telephone: 217-522-8822.
Telecopier: 217-523-3902.
Urbana, Illinois Office: Suite 300, 102 East Main Street, P.O. Box 129, 61801.
Telephone: 217-344-0060.
Telecopier: 217-344-9295.
Rockford, Illinois Office: Suite 1015, Talcott Building, P.O. Box 1288, 61105.
Telephone: 815-963-4454.
Telecopier: 815-963-0399.
Edwardsville, Illinois Office: Suite 100 Mark Twain Plaza II, 103 N. Main Street, P.O. Box 467, 62025.
Telephone: 618-656-4646.
Telecopier: 618-656-7940.

Clarence W. Heyl (1884-1968)
John H. Royster (1907-1985)
William J. Voelker, Jr. (1917-1993)
Lyle W. Allen (Of Counsel)
Richard N. Molchan (Of Counsel)
Gary M. Peplow
Duncan B. Cooper III
Robert V. Dewey, Jr.
Brent H. Gwillim
Rex K. Linder
Timothy L. Bertschy
Gary D. Nelson
David R. Sinn
Roger R. Clayton
Bradford B. Ingram
Nicholas J. Bertschy
Stephen J. Heine
Karen L. Kendall
William I. Covey
Christopher P. Larson
Craig S. Young

RESIDENT OF COUNSEL

John C. Mulgrew, Jr.

Elizabeth Wiese Christensen
James M. Voelker
J. Kevin Wolfe
David A. Perkins
Joseph G. Feehan
Lisa A. LaConte
Matthew S. Hefflefinger
Brad A. Elward
Craig L. Unrath
James J. Manning
Christina S. Hemenway

For full biographical listings, see the Martindale-Hubbell Law Directory

KAVANAGH, SCULLY, SUDOW, WHITE & FREDERICK, P.C. (AV)

301 S.W. Adams Street, Suite 700, 61602
Telephone: 309-676-1381
FAX: 309-676-0324

Jay T. Hunter (1873-1953)
Eugene Davis McLaughlin (1894-1958)
Richard J. Kavanagh (1894-1963)
J. Chase Scully, Jr. (1907-1969)
William McDowell Frederick (1907-1991)
Joseph Z. Sudow
Richard C. Kavanagh
Julian E. Cannell
David J. Walvoord
Charles G. Roth
David J. Dubicki
Phillip B. Lenzini
Karen M. Stumpe
Brian D. Mooty
Douglas S. Slayton
James W. Springer
Gary E. Schmidt
Mark W. Marlott
Michael A. Kraft

OF COUNSEL

Eugene L. White
Julian B. Venezky
Donald G. Beste

Counsel for: First of America Bank - Illinois, N.A.; Farm Credit Bank of St. Louis; Construction Equipment Federal Credit Union; Travelers Insurance Co.; Phoenix Mutual Life Insurance Co.; United States Fidelity & Guaranty Co.; Equitable Life Assurance Society of the U.S.; The Pleasure Driveway and Park District of Peoria; Board of Education of the City of Peoria School District, 150; Anderson State Bank.

For full biographical listings, see the Martindale-Hubbell Law Directory

Peoria—Continued

KINGERY DURREE WAKEMAN & RYAN, ASSOC. (AV)

915 Commerce Bank Building, 61602
Telephone: 309-676-3612
FAX: 309-676-1329

Arthur R. Kingery
Edward R. Durree
Steven A. Wakeman
Christopher P. Ryan
Lindsay W. Wright
Craig J. Reiser

Reference: Commerce Bank of Peoria.

For full biographical listings, see the Martindale-Hubbell Law Directory

QUINN, JOHNSTON, HENDERSON & PRETORIUS, CHARTERED (AV)

(Formerly McConnell, Kennedy, Quinn & Johnston)
227 N. E. Jefferson Street, 61602
Telephone: 309-674-1133
Telecopier: 309-674-6503
Springfield, Illinois Office: Three North, Old State Capitol Plaza, 62701.
Telephone: 217-753-1133.

Lowell R. McConnell (1911-1971)
Golden A. McConnell (1914-1974)
Joseph A. Leimkuehler (1931-1974)
Thomas B. Kennedy, Sr. (1912-1988)
W. Thomas Johnston
R. Michael Henderson
Murvel Pretorius, Jr.
Bradley W. Dunham
Robert H. Jennetten
Gery R. Gasick
Charles D. Knell
Gregory A. Cerulo
Paul P. Gilfillan
John P. Fleming
Mary W. McDade
Stephen P. Kelly

Thomas L. Perkins
Laurie M. Judd
Jeanne L. Wysocki
Joseph J. Bembenek, Jr.
James Andrew Borland
Julie A. Ward
David Blair Collins
John F. Kamin
Stephanie E. Sparks
Scott R. Paulsen
Michael J. Holt
Matthew B. Smith

OF COUNSEL

Richard E. Quinn
William C. Nicol
John C. Newell, Jr.

Representative Clients: Allstate Insurance Co.; American International Group; Bituminous Insurance Co.; City of Peoria; General Motors; Illinois State Medical Insurance Services, Inc.; Pekin Insurance; Peoria Journal Star, Inc.; St. Paul Insurance Co.

For full biographical listings, see the Martindale-Hubbell Law Directory

SCHIFF HARDIN & WAITE (AV)

A Partnership including Professional Corporations
Founded 1864
300 Hamilton Boulevard, Suite 100, 61602
Telephone: 309-673-2800
Facsimile: 309-673-2801
Chicago, Illinois Office: 7200 Sears Tower.
Telephone: 312-876-1000.
Facsimile: 312-258-5600.
TWX: 910-221-2463.
Washington, D.C. Office: 1101 Connecticut Avenue, N.W.
Telephone: 202-778-6400.
Facsimile: 202-778-6460.
New York, New York Office: 150 East 52nd Street, Suite 2900.
Telephone: 212-753-5000.
Facsimile: 212-753-5044.
Merrillville, Indiana Office: 8585 Broadway, Suite 842.
Telephone: 219-738-3820.
Facsimile: 219-738-3826.

RESIDENT PARTNER

Theodore L. Eissfeldt

RESIDENT ASSOCIATES

David G. Kabbes
Jason A. Zellers

For full biographical listings, see the Martindale-Hubbell Law Directory

ROBERT C. STRODEL, LTD. (AV)

927 Commerce Bank Building, 61602
Telephone: 309-676-4500
Fax: 309-676-4566

Robert C. Strodel

For full biographical listings, see the Martindale-Hubbell Law Directory

SUTKOWSKI & WASHKUHN LTD. (AV)

124 Southwest Adams Street, Suite 560, 61602
Telephone: 309-673-4500
Facsimile: 309-673-2195

(See Next Column)

Edward F. Sutkowski
Wilson C. Washkuhn
David B. Daley
Dean B. Rhoads

Robert H. Rhode

Representative Clients: RLI Corp.; Bielfeldt & Company; DMI, Inc.; Kress Corp.; Laidlaw Corp.; Otto Baum & Sons, Inc.; Associated Anesthesiologists, S.C.

For full biographical listings, see the Martindale-Hubbell Law Directory

SWAIN, HARTSHORN & SCOTT (AV)

411 Hamilton Boulevard, Suite 1806, 61602-1104
Telephone: 309-637-1700; Toll Free (USA): 800-728-1806
Fax: 309-637-1708

OF COUNSEL

Timothy W. Swain

MEMBERS OF FIRM

Tim Swain
Donald M. Hartshorn
Robert W. Scott, Jr.

John A. Schellenberg

For full biographical listings, see the Martindale-Hubbell Law Directory

SWAIN, JOHNSON & GARD (AV)

411 Hamilton Boulevard, Suite 1900, 61602
Telephone: 309-673-0741
Facsimile: 309-673-0751

MEMBERS OF FIRM

Arber Johnson (1915-1982)
Frederick D. Johnson
William M. Ahlenius
James H. Bunce
Kent A. Noble
Frederick A. Johnson
Ronald B. Schertz
James P. Johnson
Donald L. Robinson

ASSOCIATES

Michael A. Hall

OF COUNSEL

Mishael O. Gard
Beth J. Fitch
Mark D. Howard

Representative Clients: Federal Deposit Insurance Corporation; The Greater Peoria Sanitary and Sewage Disposal District.

For full biographical listings, see the Martindale-Hubbell Law Directory

WESTERVELT, JOHNSON, NICOLL & KELLER (AV)

14th Floor, First Financial Plaza, 411 Hamilton Boulevard, 61602
Telephone: 309-671-3550
FAX: 309-671-3588

MEMBERS OF FIRM

Frank T. Miller (1873-1948)
O. P. Westervelt (1887-1970)
Eugene R. Johnson (1899-1981)
David A. Nicoll (1913-1993)
Homer W. Keller
Robert D. Jackson
Wayne L. Hanold
Ross E. Canterbury
James D. Broadway
Thomas M. Hayes
Thomas G. Harvel
Roger E. Holzgrafe
Daniel L. Johns
Kevin D. Schneider
James R. Morrison
L. Lee Smith
Thomas W. O'Neal
Charles Couri

ASSOCIATES

Kevin L. Elder
Thomas A. McConnaughay
Barbara Kay Parker
Jennifer Stevens
Scott K. Daines (Not admitted in IL)
J. Phillip Krajewski

COUNSEL

Seth M. Dabney
Arthur G. Greenberg

Representative Clients: Allstate Ins. Cos.; ASARCO, Inc.; Caterpillar Inc.; The Firestone Tire & Rubber Co.; John Deere Co.; The Methodist Medical Center of Illinois; Metropolitan Life Insurance Co.; Peoria and Pekin Union Ry. Co.; Sears, Roebuck and Co.; State Farm Insurance Cos.

For full biographical listings, see the Martindale-Hubbell Law Directory

*PETERSBURG,** Menard Co. — (Refer to Springfield)

*PINCKNEYVILLE,** Perry Co.

HOHLT, HOUSE, DEMOSS & JOHNSON (AV)

1 North Main Street, 62274
Telephone: 618-357-2178
Telecopier: 618-357-3314
Nashville, Illinois Office: Holston Building.
Telephone: 618-327-8241.
Telecopier: 618-327-4079.
Du Quoin, Illinois Office: 13 North Division.
Telephone: 618-542-4703.

(See Next Column)

HOHLT, HOUSE, DEMOSS & JOHNSON—*Continued*

MEMBERS

Don E. Johnson
Roger H. Seibert
Donald Bigham

Counsel for: Nashville Savings & Loan Assn.; Murphy-Wall State Bank & Trust Company of Pinckneyville; First National Bank of Pinckneyville; Farmers & Merchants National Bank of Nashville; Oakdale State Bank.
Local Counsel for: Consolidation Coal Co.; Natural Gas Pipeline Company of America; Amax Coal Co.; Zeigler Coal Co.

For full biographical listings, see the Martindale-Hubbell Law Directory

*PRINCETON,** Bureau Co.

JOHNSON, MARTIN, RUSSELL, ENGLISH, SCOMA & BENEKE, P.C. (AV)

Ten Park Avenue West, 61356
Telephone: 815-875-4555

Watts A. Johnson (1856-1930)
Rolla L. Russell (1864-1952)
Carey R. Johnson (1884-1951)
Joseph R. Peterson (1904-1967)
Fred G. Russell (1911-1994)
Watts C. Johnson
Donald C. Martin
Daniel K. Russell
Robert F. Russell
Michael L. English
Paul M. Scoma
William S. Beneke

For full biographical listings, see the Martindale-Hubbell Law Directory

*QUINCY,** Adams Co.

KEEFE, BRENNAN & BRENNAN (AV)

314 North Sixth Street, 62301
Telephone: 217-223-1555
Fax: 217-223-1570

MEMBERS OF FIRM

James N. Keefe
Jerry L. Brennan
Babette L. Brennan

SCHMIEDESKAMP, ROBERTSON, NEU & MITCHELL (AV)

525 Jersey, P.O. Box 1069, 62306
Telephone: 217-223-3030
Telecopier: 217-223-1005

MEMBERS OF FIRM

Carl G. Schmiedeskamp (1898-1987)
John T. Robertson
Theodore Grant House (1930-1980)
Richard B. Neu
Delmer R. Mitchell, Jr.
William G. Keller, Jr.
Jonathan H. Barnard
William M. McCleery, Jr.
Mark A. Drummond
Ted M. Niemann
Gena J. Awerkamp

Representative Clients: Mercantile Trust & Savings Bank; Moorman Manufacturing Co.; Travelers Insurance Co.; Hartford Accident & Indemnity Co.; Aetna Casualty & Surety Co.; Knapheide Mfg. Co.; Harris Corp.; Bituminous Casualty Corp.; Quincy Compressor Division of Colt Industries, Inc.

For full biographical listings, see the Martindale-Hubbell Law Directory

SCHOLZ, LOOS, PALMER, SIEBERS & DUESTERHAUS (AV)

625 Vermont Street, 62301
Telephone: 217-223-3444; 217-222-7620
FAX: 217-223-3450

MEMBERS OF FIRM

Richard F. Scholz, Sr. (1901-1975)
Delbert Loos (1909-1993)
Charles A. Scholz
James L. Palmer
Steven E. Siebers
Joseph A. Duesterhaus
Christopher G. Scholz

Representative Clients: Heintz Electric Co.; Sunset Home of the United Methodist Church; Quincy Notre Dame Foundation; First Bankers Trust Company, N.A.; Merchants Wholesale, Inc.
Local Counsel: Don M. Casto Organization; York Steak House Systems, Inc.; Associates Commercial Corp.; Gulf and Western Industries, Inc.; Firemen's Fund Insurance.

For full biographical listings, see the Martindale-Hubbell Law Directory

*ROBINSON,** Crawford Co. — (Refer to Lawrenceville)

ROCHELLE, Ogle Co.

FEARER, NYE, AHLBERG & CHADWICK (AV)

420 Fourth Avenue, P.O. Box 117, 61068
Telephone: 815-562-2156
Fax: 815-562-2158
Oregon, Illinois Office: 209 South Fifth Street, P.O. Box 256, 61061.
Telephone: 815-732-6113.
Fax: 815-732-3193.

(See Next Column)

MEMBERS OF FIRM

Philip H. Nye, Jr.
James G. Ahlberg
Robert T. Chadwick

Represent: Del Monte Corp.; John Hancock Mutual Life Insurance Co.; Rochelle Savings and Loan Assoc.; Kishwaukee College; Crawford & Company; First National Bank & Trust Co. of Rochelle.

For full biographical listings, see the Martindale-Hubbell Law Directory

*ROCKFORD,** Winnebago Co.

CONDE, STONER & KILLOREN (AV)

120 West State Street, Suite 400, 61101
Telephone: 815-987-4000
FAX: 815-987-9889
Rochelle, Illinois Office: 400 Maymart Drive, 61068.
Telephone: 815-562-2677.

MEMBERS OF FIRM

Dale F. Conde
Clifford E. Stoner
Thomas A. Killoren
Thomas A. Bueschel
Robert A. Calgaro

James M. Hess
Alan H. Cooper
Kimberly Baker Timmerwilke

OF COUNSEL

Clifford A. Pedderson
Lisle W. Menzimer

References: Rockford School District; Central Commodities Limited; Medical Protective Co.; Wausau Insurance Companies; Caronia Corp.; National Medical Enterprises; Professional Risk Management, Inc.; Krause, Inc.; First of America, North Central N.A.

For full biographical listings, see the Martindale-Hubbell Law Directory

HEYL, ROYSTER, VOELKER & ALLEN, PROFESSIONAL CORPORATION (AV)

Suite 1015, Talcott Building, P.O. Box 1288, 61105
Telephone: 815-963-4454
Telecopier: 815-963-0399
Peoria, Illinois Office: Suite 600, Bank One Building, 124 S.W. Adams, 61602.
Telephone: 309-676-0400.
Telecopier: 309-676-3374.
Springfield, Illinois Office: Suite 575, First Of America Center, P.O. Box 1687, 62705.
Telephone: 217-522-8822.
Telecopier: 217-523-3902.
Urbana, Illinois Office: Suite 300, 102 East Main Street, P.O. Box 129, 61801.
Telephone: 217-344-0060.
Telecopier: 217-344-9295.
Edwardsville, Illinois Office: Suite 100, Mark Twain Plaza II, P.O. Box 467, 62025.
Telephone: 618-656-4646.
Telecopier: 618-656-7940.

RESIDENT PERSONNEL

Douglas J. Pomatto
Kevin J. Luther
Richard K. Hunsaker

Janet E. Lanpher
Mark J. McClenathan
Charles D. McCann
John D. Lanpher
Gregory F. Coplan
Eric C. Pratt

For full biographical listings, see the Martindale-Hubbell Law Directory

LORD, BISSELL & BROOK (AV)

120 West State Street, Suite 200, 61101
Telephone: 815-963-8050
Chicago, Illinois Office: Suites 2600-3600 Harris Bank Building, 115 South LaSalle Street, 60603.
Telephone: 312-443-0700.
Telecopy: 312-443-0570.
Cable Address: "Lowirco."
Telex: 25-0336.
Los Angeles, California Office: 300 South Grand Avenue, 90071-3200.
Telephone: 213-485-1500.
Telecopy: 213-485-1200.
Telex: 18-1135.
Atlanta, Georgia Office: One Atlantic Center, 1201 West Peachtree Street, N.W., Suite 3700, 30309.
Telephone: 404-870-4600.
Telecopy: 404-872-5547.

RESIDENT PARTNERS

David P. Faulkner
Jeffry S. Spears

RESIDENT ASSOCIATES

Susan M. Witt

For full biographical listings, see the Martindale-Hubbell Law Directory

Rockford—Continued

RENO, ZAHM, FOLGATE, LINDBERG & POWELL (AV)

Camelot Tower, 1415 East State Street, 61104
Telephone: 815-987-4050
FAX: 815-987-4092

Shelby L. Large (1911-1960)
Guy B. Reno (1917-1972)
Ralph S. Zahm (1935-1984)
H. Emmett Folgate (1954-1993)
Wesley E. Lindberg
R. Jerome Pfister
Robert A. Fredrickson
Jack D. Ward
Jan H. Ohlander
James D. Zeglis
John H. Young
Jamie J. Swenson Cassel
Craig P. Thomas

ASSOCIATES

Arthur G. Kielty
Suzanne Kiwaiko Robinson

COUNSEL

Roger Reno
William B. Powell
Angus S. More, Jr.
Edward J. Fahy

Representative Clients: Amcore Bank N.A., Rockford; HomeBanc; Amerock Corp.; Elco Industries, Inc.; Rockford Division of Borg-Warner Corp.; Roper Whitney Inc.; Cherry Valley and North Park Fire Protection Districts; Firemen's Fund-American; Kemper; U.S.F. & G.; Traveler's; Crum & Forster.

For full biographical listings, see the Martindale-Hubbell Law Directory

WILLIAMS & MCCARTHY, A PROFESSIONAL CORPORATION (AV)

321 West State Street, P.O. Box 219, 61105-0219
Telephone: 815-987-8900
Fax: 815-968-0019 ABANET: ABA 5519
Oregon, Illinois Office: 607 Washington Street. P.O. Box 339.
Telephone: 815-732-2101.
Fax: 815-732-2289.

John R. Kinley
Elmer C. Rudy
Thomas S. Johnson
Edward R. Telling, III
Russell D. Anderson
John E. Pfau
Richard A. Berman
John W. Rosenbloom
John W. France
John L. Shepherd
Terry D. Anderson
Kim D. Krahenbuhl (Resident Partner, Oregon, Illinois Office)
Scott C. Sullivan
Carol H. Hallock
Jane E. Durgom-Powers
James P. Devine
J. Mark Doherty
John J. Holevas
Timothy J. Rollins
Clayton L. Lindsey (Resident Partner, Oregon, Illinois Office)

Stephen E. Balogh
Robert E. Luedke
Marc C. Gravino
Thomas P. Sandquist
Carl A. Ecklund
Wendy S. Howarter (Resident, Oregon, Illinois Office)
Ronald A. Barch

OF COUNSEL

John C. McCarthy

Representative Clients: Anderson Industries, Inc.; Liberty Mutual Insurance Co.; Atwood Industries, Inc.; The Travelers; American Mutual Insurance Co.; Rockford Memorial Hospital; Chrysler Corp.; USF&G, West Bend.

For full biographical listings, see the Martindale-Hubbell Law Directory

*ROCK ISLAND,** Rock Island Co.

KATZ, MCANDREWS, BALCH, LEFSTEIN & FIEWEGER, P.C. (AV)

200 Plaza Office Building, 1705 Second Avenue, P.O. Box 3250, 61204-3250
Telephone: 309-788-5661
Facsimile: 309-788-5688

John C. McAndrews (1943-1993)
Isador I. Katz
Bruce L. Balch
Stuart R. Lefstein
Martin H. Katz
Peter C. Fieweger
Frank R. Edwards
Robert T. Park
Samuel S. McHard
Dale G. Haake
Linda E. Frischmeyer
Philip E. Koenig
John A. Hoekstra
Brian S. Nelson
Stephen T. Fieweger

John F. Doak
Lori R. Lefstein

Attorneys for: Roy E. Roth Co.; Augustana College.
Local Attorneys for: Aetna Casualty & Surety Co.; Maryland Casualty Co.; Liberty Mutual Insurance Co.; CIGNA Cos.; Country Mutual Insurance Co.; Cincinnati Insurance Co.

For full biographical listings, see the Martindale-Hubbell Law Directory

LANE & WATERMAN (AV)

500 Rock Island Bank Building, 61201
Telephone: 309-786-1600
Fax: 309-786-1794
Davenport, Iowa Office: 220 North Main Street, Suite 600.
Telephone: 319-324-3246.
Fax: 319-324-1616.

Robert A. Van Vooren
Charles E. Miller
Dana M. Craig
Carol A. H. Freeman
Robert V. P. Waterman, Jr.
Peter J. Benson
Constance A. Schriver
John D. Telleen
Richard A. Davidson

ASSOCIATES

Irene Prior Loftus
Jodi K. Plagenz

For full biographical listings, see the Martindale-Hubbell Law Directory

WESSELS, STOJAN & STEPHENS P.C. (AV)

423 Seventeenth Street, P.O. Box 4300, 61204-4300
Telephone: 309-794-9400
Telecopier: 309-794-9386

Pete M. Wessels
Clark J. Stojan
B. Douglas Stephens
Mark A. Tarnow
Joel K. Heriford

Caroline K. Bawden

OF COUNSEL

Henry G. Borden

Representative Clients: First of America Bank-Quad Cities, N.A.; First National Bank of Moline.

For full biographical listings, see the Martindale-Hubbell Law Directory

*RUSHVILLE,** Schuyler Co. — (Refer to Beardstown)
*SALEM,** Marion Co. — (Refer to Centralia)
*SHAWNEETOWN,** Gallatin Co. — (Refer to Harrisburg)
SHEFFIELD, Bureau Co. — (Refer to Mattoon)
*SHELBYVILLE,** Shelby Co. — (Refer to Mattoon)

*SPRINGFIELD,** Sangamon Co.

BROWN, HAY & STEPHENS (AV)

700 First National Bank Building, P.O. Box 2459, 62701-1489
Telephone: 217-544-8491
Fax: 217-544-9609

MEMBERS OF FIRM

Harvey B. Stephens
Edward J. Cunningham
Robert M. Magill
Norman P. Jones
Robert A. Stuart, Jr.
J. Patrick Joyce, Jr.
Eric L. Grenzebach
Jeffery M. Wilday
William F. Trapp
Paul Bown
Almon A. Manson, Jr.
Dwight H. O'Keefe, III
Emmet A. Fairfield
Denise M. Druhot
Harvey M. Stephens

COUNSEL

Ben L. DeBoice
Simon L. Friedman

ASSOCIATES

David R. Reid
Elizabeth W. Anderson
Andrew T. Pribe
John Edward Childress
James W. Bruner

General Counsel for: FirstBank of Illinois Co.; The First National Bank of Springfield; U.S. Electric Co.; Littler Trust Estate; Memorial Medical Center.
Local Counsel for: Consolidation Coal Co.; Panhandle Eastern Pipe Line Co.; The Western Union Telegraph Corp.; AMICA Mutual Insurance Co.

For full biographical listings, see the Martindale-Hubbell Law Directory

GIFFIN, WINNING, COHEN & BODEWES, P.C. (AV)

1 West Old State Capitol Plaza, Suite 600 Myers Building, P.O. Box 2117, 62705
Telephone: 217-525-1571
Facsimile: 217-525-1710

D. Logan Giffin (1890-1980)
Montgomery S. Winning (1892-1966)
C. Terry Lindner (1903-1987)
Alfred F. Newkirk (1904-1980)
James M. Winning
Robert S. Cohen
Herman G. Bodewes
John L. Swartz
Carol Hansen Fines
R. Mark Mifflin
Thomas P. Schanzle-Haskins, III
Gregory K. Harris

Arthur B. Cornell, Jr,
Christine G. Zeman
David A. Herman
Michael Joseph Mannion
Jane N. Denes

(See Next Column)

GIFFIN, WINNING, COHEN & BODEWES P.C.—*Continued*

Representative Clients: Illinois Association of Realtors; Board of Regents of Regency Universities, Magna Bank of Central Illinois, N.A.; Grinnell Mutual Reinsurance Co.; State Employee's Retirement System of Illinois; Illinois League of Savings Institutions; Ohio Casualty Group Insurance Companies; Southern Illinois University School of Medicine; Central Illinois Builders of A.G.C.

For full biographical listings, see the Martindale-Hubbell Law Directory

GRAHAM AND GRAHAM (AV)

1201 South Eighth Street, 62703
Telephone: 217-523-4569

MEMBERS OF FIRM

James M. Graham (1851-1945)
James J. Graham (1880-1965)
Hugh J. Graham (1877-1972)
Hugh J. Graham, Jr.
Hugh J. Graham, III

ASSOCIATES

Richard J. Wilderson
Nancy Eckert Martin
Dean W. Jackson
Bradley E. Huff

Counsel for: Hospital Sisters Health System.
Representative Clients: Chicago and Illinois Midland Railway; SPCSL Railway; St. Anthony's Memorial Hospital, Effingham; St. Mary's Hospital, Decatur; St. John's Hospital, Springfield.

For full biographical listings, see the Martindale-Hubbell Law Directory

HECKENKAMP, SIMHAUSER & LABARRE, P.C. (AV)

509 South Sixth Street, Suite 600, 62701
Telephone: 217-528-5627
Fax: 217-528-2097

Robert G. Heckenkamp
Walter J. Simhauser
William F. Fuiten (1946-1977)
Alfred B. LaBarre
Steven Carl Ward
William M. Taylor
Duane D. Young
Laura Giannone Dietrich

PARALEGALS

Gae A. Kelly
Debbie S. Mohan

Representative Clients: The Travelers Insurance Co.; Springfield Fire & Casualty Insurance Co.; Charles E. Robbins, Real Estate and Development; First Financial Insurance Co.; Illinois Bell Telephone Co.; American Telephone & Telegraph Co.; Kemper Insurance Co.; Allied Signal Corp.; Garrett General Aviation Services.
Reference: First of America Bank, Springfield.

For full biographical listings, see the Martindale-Hubbell Law Directory

HEYL, ROYSTER, VOELKER & ALLEN, PROFESSIONAL CORPORATION (AV)

Suite 575, First of America Center, P.O. Box 1687, 62705
Telephone: 217-522-8822
Telecopier: 217-523-3902
Peoria, Illinois Office: Suite 600, Bank One Building, 124 S.W. Adams, 61602.
Telephone: 309-676-0400.
Telecopier: 309-676-3374.
Urbana, Illinois Office: Suite 300, 102 East Main Street, P.O. Box 129, 61801.
Telephone: 217-344-0060.
Telecopier: 217-344-9295.
Rockford, Illinois Office: Suite 1015, Talcott Building, P.O. Box 1288, 61105.
Telephone: 815-963-4454.
Telecopier: 815-963-0399.
Edwardsville, Illinois Office: Suite 100 Mark Twain Plaza II, 103 N. Main Street, P.O. Box 467, 62025.
Telephone: 618-656-4646.
Telecopier: 618-656-7940.

RESIDENT PERSONNEL

Frederick P. Velde
Gary L. Borah
Gary S. Schwab
Adrian E. Harless
Donald R. Tracy
Francis J. Lynch
Scott D. Spooner

RESIDENT OF COUNSEL

Roy O. Gulley

Daniel R. Simmons
Guy A. Studach
Patrick J. Londrigan
Steven C. Rahn
Kurt M. Koepke
David V. White
John E. Kerley
Daniel P. Schuering
Shannon L. Taylor

For full biographical listings, see the Martindale-Hubbell Law Directory

MOHAN, ALEWELT, PRILLAMAN & ADAMI (AV)

First of America Center, Suite 325, 1 North Old Capitol Plaza, 62701-1323
Telephone: 217-528-2517
Telecopier: 217-528-2553

MEMBERS

Edward J. Alewelt
Fred C. Prillaman
Paul E. Adami
Cheryl Stickel Neal

OF COUNSEL

James T. Mohan

ASSOCIATES

Stephen F. Hedinger
Becky S. McCray

Representative Clients: Andrews Environmental Engineering, Inc.; B & W Land Co.; Browning-Ferris Industries of Illinois, Inc.; Carlinville Area Hospital; Evans Construction Co.; Federal Deposit Insurance Corp.; McLaughlin Manufacturing Co.; Park Realty.

For full biographical listings, see the Martindale-Hubbell Law Directory

SORLING, NORTHRUP, HANNA, CULLEN AND COCHRAN, LTD. (AV)

Formerly Sorling, Catron and Hardin
800 Illinois Building, 607 East Adams Street, P.O. Box 5131, 62705
Telephone: 217-544-1144
Telecopier: 217-522-3173

Carl A. Sorling (1896-1991)
B. Lacey Catron, Jr. (1912-1959)
John H. Hardin (1909-1978)
George William Cullen (1917-1986)
Charles H. Northrup
Philip E. Hanna
Thomas L. Cochran
Patrick V. Reilly
William S. Hanley
R. Gerald Barris
Stephen A. Tagge
Michael A. Myers
Carl Clark Germann
Gary A. Brown
Stephen R. Kaufmann
Frederick B. Hoffmann
William R. Enlow
Craig S. Burkhardt
Michael C. Connelly
Scott C. Helmholz
John A. Kauerauf
James M. Morphew
Stephen J. Bochenek
David A. Rolf

Margaret (Peggy) J. Ryan
Mark K. Cullen
Thomas H. Wilson
Irene H. Gainer
Todd Michael Turner
Charles J. Northrup

Counsel for: Central Illinois Public Service Company; Bank One Springfield; Doctors Hospital, Springfield, Ill; Illini Dairy Queen, Inc.; Springfield Airport Authority.
Representative Clients: Monsanto Agricultural Products Co.; Franklin Life Insurance Co.; WICS-TV, Inc.

For full biographical listings, see the Martindale-Hubbell Law Directory

STREATOR, La Salle Co.

MYERS, DAUGHERITY, BERRY & O'CONOR, LTD. (AV)

7 Northpoint Drive, 61364
Telephone: 815-672-3116
Fax: 815-672-0738
Ottawa, Illinois Office: 130 East Madison Street.
Telephone: 815-434-6206.

John A. Berry (1912-1986)
Stephen C. Myers
Eugene P. Daugherity
Richard J. Berry
Andrew J. O'Conor

For full biographical listings, see the Martindale-Hubbell Law Directory

*SULLIVAN,** Moultrie Co.

MCLAUGHLIN AND FLORINI, LTD. (AV)

16 South Washington Street, P.O. Box 233, 61951
Telephone: 217-728-7325
Fax: 217-728-8122

Joseph L. McLaughlin (1884-1963)
James M. McLaughlin
Joseph V. Florini

Representative Clients: Scott State Bank, Bethany, Ill.; Shank Road Oil & Culvert Co., Mattoon, Ill.; State Bank of Arthur, Ill.; First Mid-Illinois Bank & Trust.

For full biographical listings, see the Martindale-Hubbell Law Directory

*SYCAMORE,** De Kalb Co.

KLEIN, STODDARD & BUCK (AV)

122 South Locust, P.O. Box 86, 60178
Telephone: 815-895-4596
FAX: 815-895-2276
De Kalb, Illinois Office: 555 Bethany Road.
Telephone: 815-748-0380.
Fax: 815-748-4030.

(See Next Column)

KLEIN, STODDARD & BUCK, *Sycamore—Continued*

Ronald G. Klein (Resident, De Kalb Office)
James A. Stoddard
James R. Buck

Philip M. Rice

Representative Clients: The National Bank and Trust Co.; Resource Bank; Squaw Grove and Pierce Township; Cortland and Sycamore Fire Protection District; Kishwaukee Community Hospital; DeKalb Area Association of Realtors; Equitable Agri Business, Inc.; DeKalb County Building Authority; Village of Hinckley; Northern FS, Inc.

For full biographical listings, see the Martindale-Hubbell Law Directory

*TOLEDO,** Cumberland Co. — (Refer to Mattoon)

*TUSCOLA,** Douglas Co.

RAYMOND LEE, JR. (AV)

Route 36 at Ohio Street, 61953
Telephone: 217-253-2100

Representative Clients: Arcola Cooperative Grain Co.; Tuscola Community Unit School District #301; Atwood Fire Protection District; Village of Atwood; Atwood Grain & Supply Co.; Hoke Construction Co.

For full biographical listings, see the Martindale-Hubbell Law Directory

NICHOLS, JONES & MCCOWN (AV)

104 East North Central Avenue, P.O. Box 258, 61953
Telephone: 217-253-2342

George E. Nichols (1893-1974)
Harold C. Jones (1907-1965)
Harrison J. McCown

Attorneys for: First State Bank of Newman; Villa Grove State Bank; Conrail; Illinois Central Railroad; Baltimore & Ohio Railway Co.; Murdock Township; Newman Fire Protection District.

For full biographical listings, see the Martindale-Hubbell Law Directory

*URBANA,** Champaign Co.

HEYL, ROYSTER, VOELKER & ALLEN, PROFESSIONAL CORPORATION (AV)

Suite 300, 102 East Main Street, P.O. Box 129, 61801
Telephone: 217-344-0060
Telecopier: 217-344-9295
Peoria, Illinois Office: Suite 600, Bank One Building, 124 S.W. Adams, 61602.
Telephone: 309-676-0400.
Telecopier: 309-676-3374.
Springfield, Illinois Office: Suite 575, First Of America Center, P.O. Box 1687, 62705.
Telephone: 217-522-8822.
Telecopier: 217-523-3902.
Rockford, Illinois Office: Suite 1015, Talcott Building, P.O. Box 1288, 61105.
Telephone: 815-963-4454.
Telecopier: 815-963-0399.
Edwardsville, Illinois Office: Suite 100 Mark Twain Plaza II, 103 N. Main Street, P.O. Box 467, 62025.
Telephone: 618-656-4646.
Telecopier: 618-656-7940.

RESIDENT PERSONNEL

James C. Kearns
Edward M. Wagner
Michael E. Raub
Bruce L. Bonds

James W. Cox
John D. Flodstrom
John C. Piland
David L. Garner
Bradford J. Peterson
Fred K. Heinrich
Bruce A. Radke

For full biographical listings, see the Martindale-Hubbell Law Directory

PHEBUS, WINKELMANN, WONG & BRAMFELD (AV)

136 West Main Street, P.O. Box 1008, 61801
Telephone: 217-337-1400
Telecopier: 217-337-1607

Darius E. Phebus
Wendell G. Winkelmann
Joseph W. Phebus
Betsy Pendleton Wong
John F. Bramfeld

Thorpe Facer
Nancy J. Glidden
Thomas F. Koester

Representative Clients: Busey Bank; Illinois Central Railroad Co.; Consolidated Rail Corp.; National Railroad Passenger Corp.; Peoples Gas Light and Coke Co.; National Gas Pipeline Company of America; International Brotherhood of Electrical Workers Local Union 601; Plumbers and Steamfitters Local Union 149; Urbana Park District.

For full biographical listings, see the Martindale-Hubbell Law Directory

WEBBER & THIES, P.C. (AV)

202 Lincoln Square, P.O. Box 189, 61801
Telephone: 217-367-1126
FAX: 217-367-3752

Charles M. Webber (1903-1991)
Richard L. Thies
Craig R. Webber
Carl M. Webber
David C. Thies
Holten D. Summers
Daniel P. Wurl
Sheryl A. Bautch
John E. Thies

Alan R. Singleton
Phillip R. Van Ness

For full biographical listings, see the Martindale-Hubbell Law Directory

*VANDALIA,** Fayette Co.

BURNSIDE DEES JOHNSTON & CHOISSER (AV)

First National Bank Building, 62471
Telephone: 618-283-3260
FAX: 618-283-2851

MEMBERS OF FIRM

J. G. Burnside (1873-1969)
Robert G. Burnside
Joe Dees
Jack B. Johnston
Dale F. Choisser

General Counsel for: The First National Bank of Vandalia; The First State Bank of St. Peter; State Bank of Farina; S&S Urethane, Inc.
Local Counsel for: Pekin Insurance Co.

For full biographical listings, see the Martindale-Hubbell Law Directory

*VIENNA,** Johnson Co. — (Refer to Harrisburg)

*WATERLOO,** Monroe Co. — (Refer to Belleville)

*WATSEKA,** Iroquois Co.

ACKMAN, MAREK, BOYD & SIMUTIS, LTD. (AV)

123 South Fourth Street, 60970
Telephone: 815-432-5215
FAX: 815-432-3186
Kankakee, Illinois Office: Suite 400, One Dearborn Square.
Telephone: 815-933-6681.
FAX: 815-933-9985.
Gilman, Illinois Office: 210 N. Central.
Telephone: 815-265-4533.

Frank J. Simutis (Managing Partner)

James A. Devine

Representative Clients: American States Insurance Co.; Country Mutual Insurance Co.; Farmers Insurance Group; Hartford Accident & Indemnity Co.; Kankakee Water Co.; Medical Protective Co.; State Farm Insurance Co.; Economy Fire & Casualty Co.

For full biographical listings, see the Martindale-Hubbell Law Directory

BROCK, MARKWALDER, SUNDERLAND, MURPHY & SPENN (AV)

130 West Cherry Street, P.O. Box 407, 60970
Telephone: 815-432-3936
Milford, Illinois Office: Corner of Axtel & Lyle Streets.
Telephone: 815-889-4928.
Danforth, Illinois Office: 100 South Front Street.
Telephone: 815-269-2744.
Cissna Park, Illinois Office: 102 North Second.
Telephone: 815-457-2136.

OF COUNSEL

Glen W. Brock

MEMBERS OF FIRM

Dale W. Markwalder
Louis B. Sunderland
Patrick J. Murphy
Theodore R. Spenn

Kay Lawfer Johnson

Representative Clients: Central Bank, Ashkum, Illinois; Cissna Park State Bank; Citizens State Bank of Milford; Farmers State Bank of Danforth; Iroquois Title Co.; Iroquois Farmers State Bank; Iroquois Federal Savings and Loan Assn.; Milford Building & Loan Assn.; Watseka Farmers Grain Co.

For full biographical listings, see the Martindale-Hubbell Law Directory

RAZZANO & KINZER (AV)

115 East Walnut Street, P.O. Box 300, 60970
Telephone: 815-432-2100; 432-4987
Piper City, Illinois Office: 12 West Peoria Street.
Telephone: 815-686-2243.
Clifton, Illinois Office: 1st National Bank Building.
Telephone: 815-694-2939.

(See Next Column)

RAZZANO & KINZER—*Continued*

MEMBERS OF FIRM

Wallace J. Bell (1903-1980) | A. William Razzano
Kenneth A. Smith (1909-1971) | James B. Kinzer, III

Representative Clients: First Trust & Savings Bank of Watseka, IL; Iroquois Memorial Hospital, Watseka, IL; Meier Oil Company; Manito Transit Co.; First National Bank of Clifton, IL; Bankers Life Co.; John Hancock Life Insurance Co.; Prudential Insurance Co.; United State Fidelity and Guaranty Co.; American States Insurance Co.

For full biographical listings, see the Martindale-Hubbell Law Directory

*WAUKEGAN,** Lake Co.

DIVER, GRACH, QUADE & MASINI (AV)

First Federal Savings and Loan Building, 111 North County Street, 60085
Telephone: 708-662-8611
FAX: 708-662-2960

MEMBERS OF FIRM

Clarence W. Diver (1883-1962) | David R. Quade
Thomas W. Diver | Robert J. Masini
Brian S. Grach | Sarah P. Lessman

Heidi J. Aavang | Donna-Jo Rodden Vorderstrasse

A list of Representative Clients will be furnished upon request.
Reference: First Midwest Bank of Waukegan.

For full biographical listings, see the Martindale-Hubbell Law Directory

HALL, ROACH, JOHNSTON, FISHER & BOLLMAN (AV)

20 South Utica Street, 60085
Telephone: 708-244-0600
FAX: 708-244-7022

MEMBERS OF FIRM

Michael L. Roach | Ned L. Fisher
Jay J. Johnston | Robert M. Bollman
C. Jeffrey Thut

ASSOCIATES

Julia K. Carpenter

OF COUNSEL

Albert L. Hall | Edward R. Holmberg

Representative Clients: C.M. St. P. & P. Railroad; Commonwealth Edison Co.; Laserage Technology Corp.; Kemper Group; Marino Construction Company, Inc.; HeatherRidge Umbrella Association; Lake Forest High School District; Northern Trust Bank/Lake Forest; Natural Gas Pipeline Co.

For full biographical listings, see the Martindale-Hubbell Law Directory

*WHEATON,** Du Page Co.

CLAUSEN MILLER GORMAN CAFFREY & WITOUS, P.C. (AV)

2100 Manchester Road, P.O. Box 1265, 60187-2402
Telephone: 708-668-9100
Telecopier: 708-668-9169
Chicago, Illinois Office: 10 South La Salle Street.
Telephone: 312-855-1010.
Telecopier: 312-606-7777.
Telex: 27-0647.
European Affiliated Law Firm: Dutaret LaGiraudière Larroze, 58, Rue de Monceau, 75008 Paris, France.
Telephone: 33.1.44.95.25.25.
Telecopier: 33.1.44.95.25.00.
Telex: 649 622 F
and: Avenue des Artes, 53, 1040 Brussels, Belgium.
Telephone: 32.2.511.44.66.
Telecopier: 32.2.514.56.62.
New York, N.Y. Office: 100 Maiden Lane.
Telephone: 212-504-6020.
Telecopier: 212-504-6015.
Newark, New Jersey Office: 1 Gateway Center, Suite 2600, 07102-5396.
Telephone: 201-645-0564.
Troy, Michigan Office: 3155 West Beaver Road, 48084-3007.
Telephone: 313-816-0500.

Thomas H. Ryerson

James P. Marsh | Michael E. Zidek

References: The First National Bank of Chicago; La Salle National Bank.

For full biographical listings, see the Martindale-Hubbell Law Directory

DONOVAN & ROBERTS, P.C. (AV)

104 East Roosevelt Road, Suite 202, P.O. Box 417, 60189-0417
Telephone: 708-668-4211
Fax: 708-668-2076

(See Next Column)

Keith E. Roberts, Sr. | Robert R. Verchota
Keith E. (Chuck) Roberts, Jr. | James J. Konetski

Marie F. Leach | Robert M. Skutt
Mark J. Lyons | Robert J. Lentz
Andrew L. Dryjanski | Rosemarie Calandra

For full biographical listings, see the Martindale-Hubbell Law Directory

RATHJE, WOODWARD, DYER & BURT (AV)

300 East Roosevelt Road, P.O. Box 786, 60189
Telephone: 708-668-8500
Fax: 708-668-9218

MEMBERS OF FIRM

Henry J. Burt, Jr. | Gary L. Taylor
Peter A. Zamis | John F. Garrow
R. Terence Kalina | Reese J. Peck
Henry S. Stillwell, III | Tracy D. Kasson

OF COUNSEL

Robert E. Dyer | Albert C. Koontz

Attorneys for: NBD Wheaton Bank.
Local Attorneys for: Allstate Insurance Co.; Commonwealth Edison Co.; Liberty Mutual Insurance Co.

For full biographical listings, see the Martindale-Hubbell Law Directory

*WINCHESTER,** Scott Co. — (Refer to Jacksonville)

*WOODSTOCK,** McHenry Co.

CALDWELL, BERNER & CALDWELL (AV)

100 1/2 Cass Street, P.O. Box 1289, 60098
Telephone: 815-338-3300
Fax: 815-338-0015

MEMBERS OF FIRM

William I. Caldwell (1908-1971) | William I. Caldwell, Jr.
James E. Berner | Richard T. Jones
Michael T. Caldwell | Jeffrey A. Rouhandeh

Representative Clients: Allstate Insurance Co.; American States Insurance Co.; Maryland Casualty Co.; Kemper Insurance Group; Northwestern National Insurance Group; C.N.A. Group; Universal Underwriters Insurance Co.; American Home Group; City of Woodstock; Dorr Township.

For full biographical listings, see the Martindale-Hubbell Law Directory

KELL, NUELLE & LOIZZO (AV)

121 East Calhoun Street, 60098
Telephone: 815-338-4511
FAX: 815-338-0002

MEMBERS OF FIRM

Vette E. Kell | Thomas F. Loizzo
Thomas D. Nuelle | David R. Missimer

Representative Clients: General Casualty Companies; ITT Hartford; Home Insurance Co.; State Farm Mutual Automobile Insurance Co.; The Travelers Insurance Co.; Ohio Casualty Insurance Co.; Ohio Farmers Insurance Co.; Kemper Insurance Group; American Family Insurance Co.
Reference: State Bank of Woodstock.

For full biographical listings, see the Martindale-Hubbell Law Directory

*YORKVILLE,** Kendall Co. — (Refer to Joliet)

INDIANA

*ALBION,** Noble Co. — (Refer to Kendallville)

*ANGOLA,** Steuben Co. — (Refer to Kendallville)

*AUBURN,** De Kalb Co. — (Refer to Kendallville)

BATESVILLE, Ripley & Franklin Cos.

EATON & ROMWEBER (AV)

13 East George Street, 47006
Telephone: 812-934-5735
Fax: 812-934-6041
Versailles, Indiana Office: 123 South Main Street. P.O. Box 275.
Telephone 812-689-5111.
Fax: 812-689-5165.

MEMBERS OF FIRM

Larry L. Eaton
Anthony A. Romweber

ASSOCIATE

Evelina Coker Brown

For full biographical listings, see the Martindale-Hubbell Law Directory

GREEMAN, KELLERMAN & KOEPCKE (AV)

105 East George Street, P.O. Box 116, 47006
Telephone: 812-934-4334
Fax: 812-934-6144

MEMBERS OF FIRM

Paul V. Wycoff (1896-1973)
William W. Greeman (1914-1993)
John L. Kellerman
F. Kristen Koepcke
John L. Kellerman II

Representative Clients: Hillenbrand Industries, Inc.; PSI Energy; Indiana and Michigan Electric; Batesville Tool & Die, Inc.; Batesville Community School Corp.; Southeastern Career Center; Town of Sunman; Meridian Insurance Co.; Nationwide Insurance Co.; American Family Insurance Co.

For full biographical listings, see the Martindale-Hubbell Law Directory

*BEDFORD,** Lawrence Co.

STEELE, STEELE, MCSOLEY & MCSOLEY (AV)

Bank One Building, Suite One, 1602 I Street, 47421
Telephone: 812-279-3513
Fax: 812-275-3504

MEMBERS OF FIRM

Ruel W. Steele (1908-1992)
Byron W. Steele
Brent E. Steele
Patrick S. McSoley
Darlene Steele McSoley

ASSOCIATES

Sean S. Steele

Representative Clients: Bank One; The First National Bank of Mitchell; The Times Mail (newspaper); Ralph Rogers & Co., Inc.; Indiana Bell Telephone Co.; Texas Gas Transmission Corporation; Edgewood Clinic, Inc. (Medical Professional Corporation); U.S. Gypsum Company and Druthers Restaurant of Mitchell, Inc.

For full biographical listings, see the Martindale-Hubbell Law Directory

BERNE, Adams Co. — (Refer to Fort Wayne)

*BLOOMFIELD,** Greene Co. — (Refer to Bloomington)

*BLOOMINGTON,** Monroe Co.

BARNHART, STURGEON & SPENCER (AV)

313 North Lincoln, P.O. Box 1234, 47402-1234
Telephone: 812-332-9476
Fax: 812-331-8819

MEMBERS OF FIRM

Alfred Evens (1881-1949)
Leroy Baker (1903-1989)
Frank A. Barnhart
Suzanne Sturgeon
Michael J. Spencer

OF COUNSEL

Robert L. Ralston

Local Attorneys for: Home Insurance Co.; Westinghouse Electric Corp.; General Electric Co.; Government Employees Insurance Co.; Bloomington Board of Realtors; The Peoples State Bank, Ellettsville, Indiana; Hawkeye-Security Insurance Co.
Approved Attorney for: Lawyers Title Insurance Corp.

For full biographical listings, see the Martindale-Hubbell Law Directory

BUNGER & ROBERTSON (AV)

226 South College Square, P.O. Box 910, 47402-0910
Telephone: 812-332-9295
Fax: 812-331-8808

(See Next Column)

MEMBERS OF FIRM

Len E. Bunger, Jr. (1921-1993)
Don M. Robertson
Thomas Bunger
Joseph D. O'Connor III
James L. Whitlatch
Samuel R. Ardery

ASSOCIATES

Margaret M. Frisbie
William J. Beggs
John W. Richards

OF COUNSEL

Philip C. Hill

Representative Clients: Aetna Insurance Companies; Bloomington Hospital; Commercial Union Group; Indiana Insurance Co.; Liberty Mutual Insurance; Medical Protective Co.; Monroe County Community School Corp.; Professional Golf Car, Inc.; Prudential Insurance Company of America; State Farm Automobile Insurance Co.

For full biographical listings, see the Martindale-Hubbell Law Directory

MILLER CARSON BOXBERGER & MURPHY (AV)

3100 John Hinkle Place, Suite 106, 47408
Telephone: 812-333-1225
Fax: 812-333-1925
Fort Wayne, Indiana Office: 1400 One Summit Square.
Telephone: 219-423-9411.
Telecopier: 219-423-4329.

Edward J. Liptak

Representative Corporate and Financial Clients: Advanced Machine & Tool Corporation; Ford Motor Credit Company; NBD Bank, N.A.; Wal-Mart Inc.
Representative Insurance Clients: Bliss-McKnight Group; Employer's Mutual Company; Employers Mutual of Wausau; General Accident Fire & Life Assurance Corp., LTD.

For full biographical listings, see the Martindale-Hubbell Law Directory

*BLUFFTON,** Wells Co. — (Refer to Fort Wayne)

*BOONVILLE,** Warrick Co. — (Refer to Evansville)

*BRAZIL,** Clay Co.

THOMAS & THOMAS (AV)

33 West National Avenue, P.O. Box 194, 47834
Telephone: 812-446-2369
Fax: 812-443-5626

MEMBERS OF FIRM

John J. Thomas
Amos P. Thomas

ASSOCIATES

Andrew P. Thomas
David O. Thomas

OF COUNSEL

Edward A. Pease

References: First Bank & Trust Co.; Riddell National Bank.

For full biographical listings, see the Martindale-Hubbell Law Directory

BREMEN, Marshall Co.

KIZER & NEU (AV)

1406 West Plymouth Street, P.O. Box 158, 46506
Telephone: 219-546-2626
FAX: 219-546-2608
Plymouth, Indiana Office: 319 West Jefferson Street. P.O. Box 158.
Telephone: 219-936-2169.
FAX: 219-936-2642.

James H. Neu (1917-1991)
Mark E. Wagner

Counsel for: The First State Bank, Bourbon, Indiana; Bremen Castings, Inc.; Bornemann Products, Inc.; Universal Bearings, Inc., all of Bremen, Indiana.

For full biographical listings, see the Martindale-Hubbell Law Directory

*BROWNSTOWN,** Jackson Co. — (Refer to Seymour)

*CANNELTON,** Perry Co. — (Refer to Tell City)

CARMEL, Hamilton Co.

CAMPBELL KYLE PROFFITT (AV)

Suite 400, 650 East Carmel Drive, 46032
Telephone: 317-846-6514
FAX: 317-843-8097
Noblesville, Indiana Office: 198 South Ninth Street, P.O. Box 2020.
Telephone: 317-773-2090

MEMBERS OF FIRM

John D. Proffitt (Resident)
Robert F. Campbell (Resident)
Deborah L. Farmer (Resident)
William E. Wendling, Jr. (Resident)
Anne Hensley Poindexter (Resident)

(See Next Column)

CAMPBELL KYLE PROFFITT—*Continued*

ASSOCIATES

Christine Crull Altman (Resident)
Todd L. Ruetz (Resident)

Representative Clients: Bridgewater/Firestone, Inc.; Wainwright Bank & Trust Co.; State Automobile Insurance Assn.; Indiana Bell Telephone Co.; Vernon Insurance Cos.; Carmel Clay Schools; Clay Township Regional Waste District.

For full biographical listings, see the Martindale-Hubbell Law Directory

COOTS, HENKE & WHEELER, PROFESSIONAL CORPORATION (AV)

255 East Carmel Drive, 46032
Telephone: 317-844-4693
Fax: 317-573-5385

E. Davis Coots
Steven H. Henke
James K. Wheeler
Jeffrey O. Meunier
Sheila Ann Marshall
T. Jay Curts
James D. Crum
Jeffrey S. Zipes
James E. Zoccola
Elizabeth I. Van Tassel

Representative Clients: Thomas & Skinner, Inc.; MPD, Inc.; Silco Engineering Co., Inc.; Metro Bank.

For full biographical listings, see the Martindale-Hubbell Law Directory

CHESTERTON, Porter Co.

HARRIS, WELSH & LUKMANN (AV)

107 Broadway, 46304
Telephone: 219-926-2114
Fax: 219-926-1503

MEMBERS OF FIRM

Michael C. Harris
Robert A. Welsh
L. Charles Lukmann, III

ASSOCIATES

Scott M. Rafferty

Representative Clients: Pine Township; Northern Indiana Commuter Transportation District; Duneland School Corp.; Town of Burns Harbor, Indiana; Board of Commissioners of Porter County; Town of Pines; Town of Chesterton; Paulson Oil Co.

For full biographical listings, see the Martindale-Hubbell Law Directory

CLARKSVILLE, Clark Co.

HANGER, ENGEBRETSON, MAYER & VOGT (AV)

501 Eastern Boulevard, 47129
Telephone: 812-288-1235
Louisville, Kentucky: 502-584-5800
Fax: 812-288-1240

MEMBERS OF FIRM

John M. Mayer (1913-1986)
Louis G. Mayer (1918-1991)
William J. Hanger (Retired)
William F. Engebretson
John M. Mayer, Jr.
Samuel H. Vogt, Jr.
William E. Smith, III
Steven K. Palmquist

ASSOCIATES

Cara Wells Stigger
Susan Wagner Hynes
Kerstin Ann Schuhmann

Representative Clients: First Federal Savings and Loan Association of Clark County; Ticor Title Insurance Company; Old Republic National Title Insurance Company.
Approved Attorneys for: Commonwealth Land Title Insurance Co.
Reference: First Federal Savings and Loan Association of Clark County; PNC Bank Indiana, Inc.

For full biographical listings, see the Martindale-Hubbell Law Directory

CLINTON, Vermillion Co. — (Refer to Brazil)

*COLUMBUS,** Bartholomew Co.

JONES PATTERSON BOLL & TUCKER, PROFESSIONAL CORPORATION (AV)

330 Franklin Street, P.O. Box 67, 47202
Telephone: 812-376-8266
Fax: 812-376-0981

Harold V. Jones, Jr.
Dan A. Patterson
Cynthia A. Boll
J. Grant Tucker

For full biographical listings, see the Martindale-Hubbell Law Directory

SHARPNACK, BIGLEY, DAVID & RUMPLE (AV)

321 Washington Street, P.O. Box 310, 47202-0310
Telephone: 812-372-1553
Fax: 812-372-1567

(See Next Column)

MEMBERS OF FIRM

Julian Sharpnack (1879-1968)
Lew G. Sharpnack (1905-1968)
Thomas C. Bigley (1912-1978)
Maurice A. David (Retired)
Thomas C. Bigley, Jr.
John R. Rumple
Timothy J. Vrana
John A. Stroh
Jeffrey S. Washburn
Joan Tupin Crites

Representative Clients: Irwin Union Bank and Trust Co.; PSI Energy, Inc.; State Farm Mutual Insurance Cos.; American States Insurance Co.; Home News Enterprises; Cummins Federal Credit Union; Richards Elevator, Inc.

For full biographical listings, see the Martindale-Hubbell Law Directory

*CONNERSVILLE,** Fayette Co. — (Refer to Rushville)

*CRAWFORDSVILLE,** Montgomery Co.

BERRY, CAPPER & TULLEY (AV)

131 North Green Street, P.O. Box 429, 47933
Telephone: 317-362-7340
Fax: 317-362-5023

Andrew N. Foley (1909-1963)
John R. Berry (1907-1986)
Richard G. Tulley
John S. Capper, IV
S. Bryan Donaldson

Representative Clients: Elston Bank & Trust Co.; R. R. Donnelley & Sons Co. (Crawfordsville Division); Linden State Bank; City of Crawfordsville, Ind.

For full biographical listings, see the Martindale-Hubbell Law Directory

HENTHORN, HARRIS AND TAYLOR, P.C. (AV)

122 East Main Street, P.O. Box 645, 47933
Telephone: 317-362-4440
Facsimile: 317-362-4521

Robert B. Harding (1908-1977)
Carl F. Henthorn (Retired)
C. Rex Henthorn
J. Lamont Harris
Daniel L. Taylor

Stuart K. Weliever

Representative Clients: Sommer Metalcraft Corp.; U.S.F. & G. Co.; Indiana Insurance Co.; Bank One, Crawfordsville, N.A.; Farm Credit Services; Montgomery Savings Association; USA Life One Insurance Co. of Indiana; Heartland Co-Op, Inc.; Layne & Myers Grain Co., Inc.; Crawfordsville Journal-Review.

For full biographical listings, see the Martindale-Hubbell Law Directory

WERNLE, RISTINE & AYERS, L.P.C. (AV)

414 Ben Hur Building, 47933
Telephone: 317-362-2640
FAX: 317-362-8796

OF COUNSEL

Robert F. Wernle
Richard O. Ristine

James E. Ayers
Gregory H. Miller
Elizabeth A. Justice
Christopher V. Redmaster
Jeffrey A. Boggess

LEGAL SUPPORT PERSONNEL

PARALEGAL

Louisa I. Blaich

Representative Clients: Wabash College; Lincoln Federal Savings Bank; Terra Products, Inc.; North Montgomery Community School Corp.; Thrifty Wholesale Supply Inc.; United States Fidelity & Guaranty Co.; Ohio Casualty Co.

For full biographical listings, see the Martindale-Hubbell Law Directory

*CROWN POINT,** Lake Co. — (Refer to Merrillville)

*DANVILLE,** Hendricks Co.

HINKLE KECK & GUNDLACH (AV)

35 West Marion Street, 46122
Telephone: 317-745-5441
FAX: 317-745-0490

MEMBERS OF FIRM

Ansel R. Pollard (1884-1971)
Harlan H. Hinkle
Kevin J. Hinkle
Philip L. Gundlach

ASSOCIATES

David E. Kenninger
J. Gordon Gibbs, Jr.

Representative Clients: Hendricks Community Hospital; Town of Lizton; The North Salem State Bank; Hendricks County Bank and Trust Co.; Plainfield Chrysler-Plymouth, Inc.
References: Hendricks County Bank and Trust Co.; The North Salem State Bank.

For full biographical listings, see the Martindale-Hubbell Law Directory

*DELPHI,** Carroll Co.

IVES, EMERSON & MANAHAN (AV)

113 West Franklin Street, 46923
Telephone: 317-564-2078
Telecopier: 317-564-3688

MEMBERS OF FIRM

Joseph T. Ives, Jr.
Barry T. Emerson
Patrick F. Manahan

Representative Clients: NBD Bank N.W.; Public Service Indiana; State Farm Mutual; Farm Bureau Insurance Co.; Salin Bank; Yeoman Telephone Co., Inc.; Globe Valve Corp; Meridian Insurance; Delphi Community School Corp.

For full biographical listings, see the Martindale-Hubbell Law Directory

EAST CHICAGO, Lake Co.

BURKE, MURPHY, COSTANZA & CUPPY (AV)

First National Bank Building, 720 W. Chicago Avenue, 46312
Telephone: 219-397-2401
Telecopier: 219-397-0560
Merrillville, Indiana Office: Suite 600, 8585 Broadway.
Telephone: 219-769-1313.
Telecopier: 219-769-6806.
Palm Harbor, Florida Office: Suite 280, 33920 U.S. Highway 19 North.
Telephone: 813-787-7799.
Telecopier: 813-787-7237.

Lester F. Murphy
Joseph E. Costanza
David K. Ranich
David Cerven
Craig R. Van Schouwen
Edward L. Burke
Frederick M. Cuppy
Gerald K. Hrebec
Andrew J. Kopko
Lambert C. Genetos
George W. Carberry
Kathryn D. Schmidt
Demetri J. Retson
Elizabeth P. Moenning

ASSOCIATES

Paula E. Neff
Lily M. Schaefer
Todd A. Etzler
Craig R. Van Schouwen
Stacia L. Yoon
Kevin E. Steele

Representative Clients: NBD/Gainer N.A.; The Post Tribune (Knight Ridder Publications); Town of Merrillville; Continental Machine & Engineering Co., Inc.; Gary Steel Products Corp.; Superior Construction Co., Inc.; Federal National Mortgage Association; Morrison Construction Co.; St. Catherine Hospital of East Chicago, Indiana.

For full biographical listings, see the Martindale-Hubbell Law Directory

ELKHART, Elkhart Co.

CHESTER, PFAFF & BROTHERSON (AV)

317 West Franklin Street, P.O. Box 507, 46515-0507
Telephone: 219-294-5421
Telecopier: 219-522-1476

MEMBERS OF FIRM

Robert A. Pfaff
James R. Brotherson
Edward J. Chester
Glenn E. Killoren

OF COUNSEL

Willard H. Chester

ASSOCIATES

Robert C. Whippo
Judson Gregory Barce

For full biographical listings, see the Martindale-Hubbell Law Directory

THORNE, GRODNIK, RANSEL, DUNCAN, BYRON & HOSTETLER (AV)

228 West High Street, 46516-3176
Telephone: 219-294-7473
FAX: 219-294-5390
Mishawaka, Indiana Office: 310 Valley American Bank and Trust Building, 310 West McKinley Avenue. P.O. Box 1210.
Telephone: 219-256-5660.
FAX: 219-674-6835.

MEMBERS OF FIRM

William A. Thorne
Charles H. Grodnik
J. Richard Ransel
Glenn L. Duncan
James R. Byron
Steven L. Hostetler

ASSOCIATES

James H. Milstone
Michael A. Trippel
W. Douglas Thorne (Not admitted in IN)

OF COUNSEL

F. Richard Kramer
Joseph C. Zakas

Counsel for: Witmer-McNease Music Co., Inc.; Valley American Bank and Trust Co., Mishawaka, Indiana.

For full biographical listings, see the Martindale-Hubbell Law Directory

*ENGLISH,** Crawford Co. — (Refer to Tell City)

*EVANSVILLE,** Vanderburgh Co.

BAMBERGER, FOREMAN, OSWALD AND HAHN (AV)

7th Floor Hulman Building, P.O. Box 657, 47704-0657
Telephone: 812-425-1591
Fax: 812-421-4936

OF COUNSEL

Charles E. Oswald, Jr.

MEMBERS OF FIRM

Frederick P. Bamberger (1903-1983)
William P. Foreman
Robert H. Hahn
Jeffrey R. Kinney
George A. Porch
Robert M. Becker
Fred S. White
R. Thomas Bodkin
George Montgomery
Terry G. Farmer
Roderick W. Clutter, Jr.

ASSOCIATES

Michele S. Bryant
Douglas W. Patterson
David D. Bell
J. Herbert Davis
Marjorie A. Meeks
Jason Lueking
Catherine A. Nestrick
Christopher Lee
M. Beth Burger

Representative Clients: Aetna Life and Casualty Group; AT&T; CNB Bancshares Inc.; Dow Chemical Co.; Medical Protective Ins. Co.; Southern Indiana Gas and Electric Company; St. Mary's Medical Center of Evansville, Inc.; State Farm Mutual Automobile Ins. Co.; Travelers Ins. Co.; Welborn Clinic/HMO.

For full biographical listings, see the Martindale-Hubbell Law Directory

BOWERS, HARRISON, KENT & MILLER (AV)

25 N.W. Riverside Drive, P.O. Box 1287, 47706-1287
Telephone: 812-426-1231
Fax: 812-464-3676

MEMBERS OF FIRM

F. Wesley Bowers
Joseph H. Harrison
David V. Miller
Paul E. Black
Gary R. Case
Arthur D. Rutkowski
George C. Barnett, Jr.
Terry Noffsinger
David E. Gray
Gregory A. Kahre
Paul J. Wallace
Timothy J. Hubert
James P. Casey
Thomas A. Massey
Greg A. Granger
Joseph H. Harrison, Jr.
Lawrence L. Grimes

ASSOCIATES

Cedric Hustace
Christopher E. Carl
Michelle Agostino Cox
Sara Ann Harrison
William O. Williams, II
Elizabeth Healy Campbell

OF COUNSEL

Addison M. Beavers
K. Wayne Kent

LEGISLATIVE CONSULTANT

William G. Greif

Division Counsel in Indiana for: Southern Railway Co.
District Attorneys for the Southern District of Indiana: CSX Transportation, Inc.
Representative Clients: Permanent Federal Savings Bank; Citizens Realty & Insurance, Inc.

For full biographical listings, see the Martindale-Hubbell Law Directory

FINE & HATFIELD (AV)

520 N.W. Second Street, P.O. Box 779, 47705-0779
Telephone: 812-425-3592
Telecopier: 812-421-4269

MEMBERS OF FIRM

Isadore J. Fine (1897-1975)
Joe S. Hatfield (1908-1993)
Charles H. Sparrenberger (1913-1992)
James E. Marchand
Ronald R. Allen
Thomas H. Bryan
Thomas R. Fitzsimmons
Danny E. Glass
Stephen S. Lavallo
D. Timothy Born
Patricia Kay Woodring

ASSOCIATES

Shannon Scholz Frank
William H. Mullis
Debra S. McGowan

For full biographical listings, see the Martindale-Hubbell Law Directory

KAHN, DEES, DONOVAN & KAHN (AV)

P.O. Box 3646, 47735-3646
Telephone: 812-423-3183
Fax: 812-423-3841

MEMBERS OF FIRM

Isidor Kahn (1887-1963)
Robert Kahn (Retired)
Alan N. Shovers
Thomas O. Magan
Larry R. Downs
Wm. Michael Schiff
Robert H. Brown
Jon D. Goldman
Marilyn R. Ratliff
Brian P. Williams

(See Next Column)

KAHN, DEES, DONOVAN & KAHN—*Continued*

MEMBERS OF FIRM (Continued)

G. Michael Schopmeyer
David L. Clark
Jeffrey A. Wilhite
John E. Hegeman
Jeffrey K. Helfrich
Jeffrey W. Ahlers
Mary Lee Franke

ASSOCIATES

Marjorie J. Scharpf
Richard O. Hawley, Jr.
Kent A. Brasseale, II

OF COUNSEL

Harry P. Dees
Arthur R. Donovan

Counsel for: Deaconess Hospital, Inc.; Keller Crescent Co., Inc.; Windsor Plastics, Inc.; Potter & Brumfield, Division of Siemens; Atlas Van Lines, Inc.; Daughters of Charity of St. Vincent de Paul of Indiana, Inc.; Jasper Engine and Transmission Exchange; Cresline Plastic Pipe Co., Inc.; Orion Electric (American) Inc.; University of Southern Indiana.

For full biographical listings, see the Martindale-Hubbell Law Directory

KIGHTLINGER & GRAY (AV)

One Riverfront Place, Suite 210, 20 N.W. First Street, 47708
Telephone: 812-464-9508
Telecopier: 812-464-9511
Indianapolis, Indiana Office: Market Square Center, Suite 660, 151 North Delaware Street, 46204.
Telephone: 317-638-4521.
Telecopier: 317-636-5917.
New Albany, Indiana Office: Pinnacle Centre, Suite 200, 3317 Grant Line Road, P.O. Box 6727, 47151.
Telephone: 812-949-2300.
Telecopier: 812-949-8556.

RESIDENT PARTNERS

Brent R. Weil

RESIDENT ASSOCIATES

Troy A. Reynolds
Jill Reifinger Marcrum
David R. Sauvey
Timothy A. Klinger
Dirck H. Stahl

Representative Clients: American Family Mutual Insurance Co.; American International Group; American States; Associated Aviation Underwriters; Black & Decker (U.S., Inc.); Government Employees Insurance Co.; Mack Trucks, Inc.; Reliance Insurance Group.
Reference: INB National Bank.

For full biographical listings, see the Martindale-Hubbell Law Directory

STATHAM, JOHNSON & MCCRAY (AV)

215 North West Martin Luther King Jr. Boulevard, P.O. Box 3567, 47734-3567
Telephone: 812-425-5223
Facsimile: 812-421-4238

MEMBERS OF FIRM

Herman L. McCray (1905-1984)
D. Bailey Merrill (1912-1993)
William E. Statham
R. Eugene Johnson
Michael McCray
Thomas J. Kimpel
Stephen Hensleigh Thomas
Donald J. Fuchs
Gerald F. Allega
Douglas V. Jessen

ASSOCIATES

Thomas P. Norton
Keith E. Rounder
Brent Alan Raibley
Bryan S. Rudisill

For full biographical listings, see the Martindale-Hubbell Law Directory

WRIGHT, EVANS AND DALY (AV)

425 Main Street, 47708
Telephone: 812-424-3300
Fax: 812-421-5588

MEMBERS OF FIRM

Claude B. Lynn (Retired)
Donald R. Wright
Gerald H. Evans
R. Lawrence Daly

ASSOCIATES

Christopher L. Lucas
Keith M. Wallace

Representative Clients: Browning-Ferris Industries of Indiana, Inc.; Castle Contracting Co., Inc.; Computing Solutions, Inc.; Happy China Trading Corporation; Manpower Incorporated of Evansville; Need-A-Nurse, Inc.; Mills-Wallace and Associates, Inc. Design Professionals; Servicemaster of Evansville, Inc.; Siemers Glass Company, Inc.; Southwestern Indiana Mental Health Center, Inc.

For full biographical listings, see the Martindale-Hubbell Law Directory

*FORT WAYNE,** Allen Co.

BAKER & DANIELS (AV)

2400 Fort Wayne National Bank Building, 46802
Telephone: 219-424-8000
FAX: (219) 460-1700
Indianapolis, Indiana Office: 300 North Meridian Street.
Telephone: 317-237-0300.
South Bend, Indiana Office: First Bank Building, 205 West Jefferson Boulevard.
Telephone: 219-234-4149.
Elkhart, Indiana Office: 301 South Main Street, Suite 307.
Telephone: 219-296-6000.
Washington, D.C. Office: 1701 K Street, N.W. Suite 400.
Telephone: 202-785-1565.

MEMBERS OF FIRM

F. B. Shoaff (1877-1961)
John D. Shoaff (1908-1982)
Maclyn T. Parker
Martin A. Weissert
George T. Dodd
Robert T. Hoover
Thomas M. Shoaff
John F. Hoffman
Joseph W. Kimmell, II
Anthony Niewyk
David A. Scott
Lawrence E. Shine
N. Reed Silliman
John R Burns, III
Steven H. Hazelrigg
Steven L. Jackson
Richard H. Blaich
Michael L. James
Jon A. Bomberger
Timothy J. Haffner
David P. Irmscher
Albert J. Dahm
Douglas Dormire Powers

OF COUNSEL

Thomas M. Moorhead

ASSOCIATES

Maria C. Campo
Jeffrey O. Davidson (Not admitted in IN)
Kevin R. Erdman
Jeanne E. Longsworth
Robert D. Moreland
Michael J. Nader
Jeffrey A. Townsend
Michael T. Bates
H. John Okeson
Charles J. Heiny
Randall J. Knuth
Holly Demarest Warshauer
Gary D. Johnson
M. Randall Spencer
Debra L. Schroeder
Todd T. Taylor
Edward Sullivan, III
Anthony M. Zirille

Representative Clients: Central Soya Co., Inc.; Essex Group, Inc.; ITT Corp.; Lincoln National Corp.; Lutheran Hospital of Indiana; Norwest Bank, Fort Wayne; Tokheim Corp.; Shambaugh & Son, Inc.; General Motors Corp.; Eli Lilly and Company.

For full biographical listings, see the Martindale-Hubbell Law Directory

BARRETT & MCNAGNY (AV)

215 East Berry Street, P.O. Box 2263, 46801-2263
Telephone: 219-423-9551
Telecopier: 219-423-8924
Huntington, Indiana Office: 429 Jefferson Park Mall, P.O. Box 5156.
Telephone: 219-356-7766.
Telecopier: 219-356-7782.

James M. Barrett (1852-1929)
Phil M. McNagny (1886-1969)
Otto E. Grant, Jr. (1914-1969)
James M. Barrett, Jr. (1895-1979)
Byron F. Novitsky (1909-1988)

MEMBERS OF FIRM

J. Michael O'Hara
Otto M. Bonahoom
Howard L. Chapman
Ted S. Miller (Resident, Huntington Office)
Paul S. Steigmeyer
John M. Clifton, Jr.
Robert S. Walters
John F. Lyons
N. Thomas Horton, II
Richard D. Robinson
William L. Sweet, Jr.
Patrick G. Michaels
Thomas M. Fink
Richard E. Fox
Gary J. Rickner
John D. Walda
James P. Fenton
John P. Martin
Alan VerPlanck
Dennis C. Becker
Thomas P. Yoder
Thomas M. Kimbrough
Ronald J. Ehinger
Stephen L. Chapman
Thomas A. Herr
Thomas J. Markle
Michael P. O'Hara
Joseph G. Bonahoom
Thomas M. Niezer

ASSOCIATES

Robert R. Glenn (Resident, Huntington Office)
Anthony M. Stites
Renee R. Neeld
David R. Steiner
Kevin K. Fitzharris

OF COUNSEL

William F. McNagny
James M. Barrett, III

RETIRED PARTNERS

Mentor Kraus (1905—)
J. A. Bruggeman (1906—)

Counsel for: Aetna Group; B.F. Goodrich Co.; Consolidated Rail Corp.; Franklin Electric Co., Inc.; Fort Wayne National Bank; Hartford Group; Northern Indiana Public Service Co.; Omni-Source Corp.; Phelps Dodge Magnet Wire Corp.; Union Federal Savings Bank of Indianapolis.

For full biographical listings, see the Martindale-Hubbell Law Directory

Fort Wayne—Continued

BECKMAN, LAWSON, SANDLER, SNYDER & FEDEROFF (AV)

800 Standard Federal Plaza, 46802
Telephone: 219-422-0800
Facsimile: 219-420-1013
Syracuse, Indiana Office: 200 West Main Street.
Telephone: 219-457-5727.
Facsimile: 219-457-2056.

MEMBERS OF FIRM

Jack W. Lawson
Neil F. Sandler
Frank J. Gray
Howard B. Sandler
Stephen R. Snyder
James A. Federoff
John H. Brandt
Thomas J. Goeglein
Jon A. Bragalone
Brian J. T'Kindt
David C. Cates

Douglas R. Adelsperger
Travis S. Friend
Jack C. Birch
Deborah Wiers Vincent
Ronald B. Cassidente
Robert L. Nicholson
W. Randall Kammeyer
Timothy E. Ochs
Craig R. Patterson (Not admitted in IN)

OF COUNSEL

Frederick A. Beckman
Douglas E. Miller

Reference: NBD, N.A.

For full biographical listings, see the Martindale-Hubbell Law Directory

HELMKE, BEAMS, BOYER & WAGNER (AV)

300 Metro Building, Berry & Harrison Streets, 46802-2242
Telephone: 219-422-7422
Telecopier: 219-422-6764

MEMBERS OF FIRM

Walter E. Helmke (1901-1976)
Walter P. Helmke
R. David Boyer
Robert A. Wagner
J. Timothy McCaulay
Daniel J. Borgmann

ASSOCIATES

Trina Glusenkamp Gould

OF COUNSEL

Glen J. Beams
John G. Reiber

Representative Clients: Aalco Distributing Co., Inc.; Brotherhood Mutual Insurance Co.; Fremont Community Schools; Teco, Inc.; Air-O-Mat, Inc.; Leo Distributors, Inc.

For full biographical listings, see the Martindale-Hubbell Law Directory

MILLER CARSON BOXBERGER & MURPHY (AV)

1400 One Summit Square, 46802-3137
Telephone: 219-423-9411
Telecopier: 219-423-4329
Bloomington, Indiana Office: 3100 John Hinkle Place, Suite 106.
Telephone: 812-333-1225.
Fax: 812-333-1925.

MEMBERS OF FIRM

Milford M. Miller, Jr.
Philip L. Carson
Bruce O. Boxberger
Edward L. Murphy, Jr.
Thomas W. Yoder
Charles R. Cogdell
John J. Wernet
Richard P. Samek
Phillip A. Renz
Edward J. Liptak (Resident, Bloomington, Indiana Office)
Robert T. Keen, Jr.

ASSOCIATES

Larry L. Barnard
Diana Carol Bauer
James P. Buchholz
Arthur E. Mandelbaum
Timothy A. Manges (Not admitted in IN)
Douglas A. Hoffman
Daniel G. McNamara
Mark E. Witmer
Karl J. Veracco

Representative Corporate and Financial Clients: Advanced Machine & Tool Corporation; Ford Motor Credit Company; NBD Bank, N.A.; Wal-Mart Inc.
Representative Insurance Clients: Bliss-McKnight Group; Employer's Mutual Company; Employers Mutual of Wausau; General Accident Fire & Life Assurance Corp., LTD.

For full biographical listings, see the Martindale-Hubbell Law Directory

ROTHBERG, GALLMEYER, FRUECHTENICHT & LOGAN (AV)

2100 Fort Wayne National Bank Building, 110 West Berry Street, P.O. Box 11647, 46859-1647
Telephone: 219-422-9454
Telefax: 219-422-1622

(See Next Column)

MEMBERS OF FIRM

Sol Rothberg (1910-1993)
Thomas A. Gallmeyer (1922-1981)
Thomas D. Logan
Martin T. Fletcher
F. L. Dennis Logan
Scott T. Niemann
David R. Smelko
Dennis F. Dykhuizen
Catherine C. Ediger
Anne Carney

ASSOCIATES

Gregory Martin Cole
James A. Butz
Michael T. Deam
Brian L. Nehrig
Andrea L. Hermer
J. Rickard Donovan

OF COUNSEL

George E. Fruechtenicht
John H. Heiney

Counsel for: Parkview Memorial Hospital; Cameron Memorial Community Hospital; Norwest Bank Indiana, N.A.; NBD Bank, N.A.; Citizens Banking Company of Anderson; Azar's, Incorporated; Fort Wayne-Allen County Airport Authority; Fort Wayne Public Transportation Corporation; Avis Industrial Corp.; Farm Credit Services of Mid-America, ASA; Slater Fort Wayne Federal Credit Union.

For full biographical listings, see the Martindale-Hubbell Law Directory

SHAMBAUGH, KAST, BECK & WILLIAMS (AV)

600 Standard Federal Plaza, 46802-2405
Telephone: 219-423-1430
FAX: 219-422-9038

MEMBERS OF FIRM

Willard Shambaugh (1897-1976)
Michael H. Kast (Semi-Active)
Stephen J. Williams
Edward E. Beck
Daniel E. Serban
John B. Powell
Timothy L. Claxton
James D. Streit

Counsel for: Hagerman Construction Corp.; Rogers Markets, Inc.; K & H Realty Corp.; Olive B. Cole Foundation; M. E. Raker Foundation, Inc.; Associates Financial Services Co., of Indiana, Inc.; Professional Federal Credit Union; Fort Wayne Education Association; American Ambassador Casualty Company; CBT Credit Services, Inc.

For full biographical listings, see the Martindale-Hubbell Law Directory

*FOWLER,** Benton Co.

BARCE & RYAN (AV)

103 North Jackson Avenue, P.O. Box 252, 47944
Telephone: 317-884-0383
Fax: 317-884-0445
Kentland, Indiana Office: 301 East Graham Street, P.O. Box 338.
Telephone: 219-474-5158.
Fax: 219-474-6610.

MEMBER OF FIRM

John W. Barce
J. Edward Barce (Resident at Fowler Office)

For full biographical listings, see the Martindale-Hubbell Law Directory

WILLIAM B. WEIST (AV)

Weist Building, P.O. Box 101, 47944
Telephone: 317-884-1840
Fax: Available Upon Request

ASSOCIATES

Rex W. Kepner

References: Fowler State Bank, Fowler, Indiana; Farmers and Merchants Bank, Boswell, Indiana.

For full biographical listings, see the Martindale-Hubbell Law Directory

*FRANKLIN,** Johnson Co.

LA GRANGE, FREDBECK & DEPPE (AV)

Nine East Court, 46131
Telephone: 317-736-5138
Fax: 317-736-8268

OF COUNSEL

Richard L. La Grange

MEMBERS OF FIRM

Melvin N. Fredbeck
Brian J. Deppe
Eric W. Fredbeck

Representative Clients: Clark-Pleasant Community School Corp.; Central Nine Vocational-Technical School; Johnson Memorial Hospital; Syndicate Theatres, Inc.; Town of Bargersville; Indiana Masonic Home; Hensley Township; Nineveh Township; Clark Township; Annual Reports, Inc.

For full biographical listings, see the Martindale-Hubbell Law Directory

GARY, Lake Co.

STULTS, STULTS, FORSZT & PAWLOWSKI, A PROFESSIONAL ASSOCIATION (AV)

3637 Grant Street, P.O. Box 15050, 46409-5050
Telephone: 219-887-7000
Fax: 219-884-1179

Fred M. Stults, Jr. — Robert P. Forszt
Frederick M. Stults, III — David R. Pawlowski

Representative Clients: American Road Insurance Co.; Employers Casualty Co.; Indiana Insurance Co.; SAFECO Insurance Co.

For full biographical listings, see the Martindale-Hubbell Law Directory

*GOSHEN,** Elkhart Co.

YODER, AINLAY, ULMER & BUCKINGHAM (AV)

130 North Main Street, P.O. Box 575, 46527-0575
Telephone: 219-533-1171
Telecopier: 219-534-4174

MEMBERS OF FIRM

George L. Pepple (1907-1963) — R. Gordon Lord
John D. Ulmer — Patrick F. O'Leary
George E. Buckingham — Craig M. Buche
Gregory A. Hartzler — Michael F. DeBoni
Alan L. Weldy

ASSOCIATES

B. Douglas Hayes — Mark A. Matthes
Denise C. Davis

OF COUNSEL

Frank E. Yoder — Charles W. Ainlay

Counsel for: CTB, Inc.; Elkhart County Farm Bureau Credit Union; Elkhart County Government; First State Bank of Middlebury; Goshen College; Goshen General Hospital; Goshen Rubber Co.; HomeCrest Corporation; State Farm Insurance Cos.; Town of Middlebury, IN.

For full biographical listings, see the Martindale-Hubbell Law Directory

*GREENCASTLE,** Putnam Co.

J. D. CALBERT (AV)

15 West Franklin Street, Suite A, P.O. Box 644, 46135
Telephone: 317-653-8477

Representative Clients: First Citizens Bank & Trust Co.; Putnam County Hospital; Cincinnati Insurance Cos.; Farm Bureau Insurance Co.; Meridian Mutual Insurance Co.

For full biographical listings, see the Martindale-Hubbell Law Directory

*GREENSBURG,** Decatur Co.

ROLFES, GARVEY, WALKER & ROBBINS (AV)

132 East Washington Street, P.O. Box 468, 47240-0468
Telephone: 812-663-4441
Fax: 812-662-6249

MEMBERS OF FIRM

Raymond B. Rolfes (1898-1986) — Karl F. Walker
Richard H. Garvey (1926-1991) — William H. Robbins

Representative Clients: First Federal Savings & Loan Assn., Greensburg; Don Meyer Ford Mercury, Inc.; Al Reynolds, Inc.; Lowe's Pellets and Grain Inc.; Westfield Insurance Co.; Fifth Third of Southeastern Indiana; Royal-Globe Insurance Co.; Farm Credit Services.

For full biographical listings, see the Martindale-Hubbell Law Directory

GREENWOOD, Johnson Co.

VAN VALER WILLIAMS & HEWITT (AV)

Suite 400 National City Bank Building, 300 South Madison Avenue, P.O. Box 405, 46142
Telephone: 317-888-1121
Fax: 317-887-4069

MEMBERS OF FIRM

Joe N. Van Valer — Jon E. Williams
Brian C. Hewitt

ASSOCIATES

J. Lee Robbins — John M. White
William M. Waltz — Kim Van Valer Shilts
Mark E. Need

For full biographical listings, see the Martindale-Hubbell Law Directory

HAMMOND, Lake Co.

GALVIN, GALVIN & LEENEY (AV)

5231 Hohman Avenue, 46320
Telephone: 219-933-0380
Fax: 219-933-0471

(See Next Column)

MEMBERS OF FIRM

Edmond J. Leeney (1897-1978) — Carl N. Carpenter
Timothy P. Galvin, Sr. (1894-1993) — John E. Chevigny
Timothy P. Galvin, Jr.
Francis J. Galvin, Sr. (Retired) — Patrick J. Galvin
W. Patrick Downes

Brian L. Goins — William G. Crabtree II
John H. Lloyd, IV

Attorneys for: Mercantile National Bank of Indiana; Citizens Financial Services, F.S.B.; State Farm Insurance Co.; Auto Owners Insurance Co.; CIGNA; Armco, Inc.; St. Margaret Mercy Healthcare Centers, Inc.; St. Anthony Hospital and Health Centers (Michigan City); Calumet Council, Inc., Boy Scouts of America; Chicago Title Insurance Company.

For full biographical listings, see the Martindale-Hubbell Law Directory

McHIE, MYERS, McHIE & ENSLEN (AV)

53 Muenich Court, 46320
Telephone: 219-931-1707
Telecopier: 219-932-2417

MEMBERS OF FIRM

G. Edward McHie — James E. McHie
Charles A. Myers — Charles Endicott Enslen

ASSOCIATES

Carol M. Green — Richard A. Hanning
Carolyn N. Fehring

Representative Clients: USX Corp.; Ronwal Transportation, Inc.; Hammond Redevelopment Commission; Raytrans, Inc.; La Salle Steel Co.; The Budd Co.; Emro Marketing Co., A Division of Marathon Oil.

For full biographical listings, see the Martindale-Hubbell Law Directory

*HARTFORD CITY,** Blackford Co. — (Refer to Marion)

HIGHLAND, Lake Co.

BLACKMUN, BOMBERGER & MORAN (AV)

A Partnership including a Professional Corporation
Schuyler Square West, 9006 Indianapolis Boulevard, 46322
Telephone: 219-972-2200
FAX: 219-972-2404

Edwin H. Friedrich (1892-1979) — Peter C. Bomberger
Charles G. Bomberger (1907-1980) — William J. Moran
Leonard M. Holajter
Stanley A. Tweedle (Retired) — Stephen A. Tyler
Gilbert F. Blackmun — Alan R. Faulkner

Counsel for: Amtrak; Indiana Bell Telephone Co.; Metropolitan Life Insurance Co.; Prudential Insurance Co.; United States Fidelity & Guaranty Co.; CSX Transportation; Conrail; Continental National Group; The Methodist Hospitals, Inc.

For full biographical listings, see the Martindale-Hubbell Law Directory

*HUNTINGTON,** Huntington Co.

GORDON BENDALL BRANHAM MCNEELY & DELANEY (AV)

533 Warren Street, P.O. Box 269, 46750-0269
Telephone: 219-356-4100
Telecopier: 219-356-4100
Warren, Indiana Office: 223A North Wayne Street.
Telephone: 219-375-2311.
Roanoke, Indiana Office: First National Bank Building.
Telephone: 219-672-2992.

OF COUNSEL

William S. Gordon

MEMBERS OF FIRM

Theodore L. Bendall — Dennis L. McNeely
John F. Branham — Richard DeLaney
William S. Gordon, Jr. — Scott P. Faurote

Representative Clients: Aetna Casualty & Surety Co.; Bippus State Bank; City of Huntington; First Federal Savings Bank; Huntington College; Indiana Lumbermens Mutual Insurance Co.; Lime City Economic Development Co., Inc.; Schenkel's All Star Dairy, Inc.; Simpson Grain Co., Inc.; Westfield Insurance Cos.

For full biographical listings, see the Martindale-Hubbell Law Directory

*INDIANAPOLIS,** Marion Co.

BAKER & DANIELS (AV)

300 North Meridian Street, 46204
Telephone: 317-237-0300
FAX: 317-237-1000
Fort Wayne, Indiana Office: 2400 Fort Wayne National Bank Building.
Telephone: 219-424-8000.
South Bend, Indiana Office: First Bank Building, 205 West Jefferson Boulevard.
Telephone: 219-234-4149.

(See Next Column)

BAKER & DANIELS, *Indianapolis—Continued*

Elkhart, Indiana Office: 301 South Main Street, Suite 307,
Telephone: 219-296-6000.
Washington, D.C. Office: 1701 K Street, N.W., Suite 400.
Telephone: 202-785-1565.

Albert Baker (1874-1942) Edward Daniels (1877-1918)
Joseph Daniels (1914-1972)

MEMBERS OF FIRM

Joseph B. Carney
Robert L. Jessup
Virgil L. Beeler
William F. Landers, Jr.
Michael R. Maine
Norman P. Rowe
Terrill D. Albright
Fred E. Schlegel
James A. Aschleman
Jerry R. Jenkins
Wendell R. Tucker
Stephen A. Claffey
Norman G. Tabler, Jr.
David R. Frick
H. Patrick Callahan
Rory O'Bryan
Stephen H. Paul
Charles T. Richardson
Michael J. Huston
Lewis D. Beckwith
Donald P. Bennett
Thomas G. Stayton
James M. Carr
James H. Ham, III
Mary Katherine Lisher
David N. Shane
Theodore J. Esping
Brian K. Burke
Daniel F. Evans, Jr.
Robert W. Elzer
John W. Purcell
Thomas A. Vogtner
David C. Worrell
Francina A. Dlouhy
John T. Neighbours
Roberta Sabin Recker
Gregory J. Utken
David W. Miller
J. Daniel Ogren
David Lawther Johnson
Tibor D. Klopfer
Harry F. McNaught, Jr.
George W. Somers
Lawrence A. Steward
David K. Herzog
Randy D. Loser
Christopher G. Scanlon
John B. Swarbrick, Jr.
John R. Schaibley, III
Robert Kirk Stanley
Rebecca A. Richardson
Irene T. Adamczyk
Ben W. Blanton
Jay Jaffe
Alan L. McLaughlin
Gayle L. Skolnik
Brent D. Taylor
Anne Slaughter Andrew
Hudnall A. Pfeiffer
Jeffrey M. Stautz
Joseph H. Yeager, Jr.
Richard T. Freije, Jr.
G. Frederick Glass
Thomas A. Pitman
Byron K. Mason
Daniel L. Boeglin
James W. Clark
Ronald D. Gifford
Karl P. Haas
Jill Harris Tanner
Mitzi Harris Martin
Joseph M. Scimia
Richard C. Starkey
Robert S. Wynne
Mary Booth Miller Stanley
John A. Gardner
Todd Murray Nierman
Kevin M. Toner
J. Jeffrey Brown

COUNSEL

Byron P. Hollett
John D. Cochran
E. Clay Ulen
Dan R. Winchell
Stephen W. Terry, Jr.
Thomas M. Lofton
Richard E. Aikman
Henry B. Blackwell, II
Arthur R. Whale
Daniel E. Johnson
R. Matthew Neff

ASSOCIATES

Robert M. Bond
Debra L. Hinshaw
Marci A. Reddick
Nancy J. Futterknecht
Gregory N. Dale
Sharon A. Hilmes
Wendy W. Ponader
Cynthia L. Ramsey
Bradley Merrill Thompson
David A. Given
John Joseph Tanner
Thomas C. Froehle Jr.
Brant O. Gardner
Scott D. Himsel
Scott M. Kosnoff
Cynthia Pearson Purvis
Andrew Z. Soshnick
Brian S. Fennerty
Mark E. Wright
Nancy G. Bollinger
Ellen E. Boshkoff
Cynthia M. Cormany
Kevin P. Griffith
Paul Lowell Haines
Michael J. MacLean
Kenneth B. Siepman
Mark A. Voigtmann
David V. Ceryak
Stephen L. Foutty
Amy E. Kosnoff
Carl R. Pebworth
MaryAnn Schlegel Ruegger
Michael P. Bigelow
Melissa S. Barnes
Rolanda Moore Haycox
Ji-Qing Liu
Edward J. Prein
Mark J. Sifferlen
Janet Madden Charles
Michael Watters
Patrick S. Cross
Alana Michelle Davis
Jonas Q. Burgett
Charles A. Grandy

FORT WAYNE OFFICE
MEMBERS OF FIRM

Maclyn T. Parker
Martin A. Weissert
George T. Dodd
Robert T. Hoover
Thomas M. Shoaff
John F. Hoffman
Joseph W. Kimmell, II
Anthony Niewyk
David A. Scott
Lawrence E. Shine
N. Reed Silliman
John R. Burns, III
Steven H. Hazelrigg
Steven L. Jackson
Robert H. Blaich
Michael L. James
Jon A. Bomberger
Timothy J. Haffner
David P. Irmscher
Albert J. Dahm
Douglas Dormire Powers

(See Next Column)

OF COUNSEL

Thomas M. Moorhead

ASSOCIATES

Maria C. Campo
Jeffrey O. Davidson
(Not admitted in IN)
Kevin R. Erdman
Jeanne E. Longsworth
Robert D. Moreland
Michael J. Nader
Jeffrey A. Townsend
Michael T. Bates
H. John Okeson
Charles J. Heiny
Randall J. Knuth
Holly Demarest Warshauer
Gary D. Johnson
M. Randall Spencer
Debra L. Schroeder
Todd T. Taylor
Edward Sullivan, III
Anthony M. Zirille

SOUTH BEND, INDIANA OFFICE
MEMBERS OF FIRM

Ronald J. Jaicomo
James D. Hall
Thomas J. Brunner, Jr.
Richard L. Hill
James M. Matthews
Peter G. Trybula
Paul J. Peralta

OF COUNSEL

Ken C. Decker

ASSOCIATES

Mary Ann Boulac
Randolph R. Rompola
Robert A. Wade
Amy Lawrence Mader
Kevin Doyle O'Rear

ELKHART, INDIANA OFFICE
MEMBERS OF FIRM

Kennard R. Weaver
James M. Matthews
Peter G. Trybula

ASSOCIATES

Angella M. Castille
Robert A. Wade

WASHINGTON, D.C. OFFICE
MEMBER OF FIRM

Frank S. Swain

LEGAL SUPPORT PERSONNEL

James L. Turner
Vicki L. Beckenbaugh
Susan L. Davis
Eugene Valanzano

Representative Clients: Associated Insurance Companies, Inc.; Bank One, Indianapolis, N.A.; Borg-Warner Corp.; City of Indianapolis; Cummins Engine Co.; Eli Lilly and Company; General Motors Corp.; Indiana Bell; Indianapolis Public Schools; United Airlines.

For full biographical listings, see the Martindale-Hubbell Law Directory

BOBERSCHMIDT, MILLER, O'BRYAN, TURNER & ABBOTT, A PROFESSIONAL ASSOCIATION (AV)

Bank One Center/Circle, 111 Monument Circle, Suite 302, 46204-5169
Telephone: 317-632-5892
Telecopier: 317-686-3423

Philip F. Boberschmidt
Jerald L. Miller
Berton W. O'Bryan
L. Craig Turner
Tony H. Abbott

OF COUNSEL

John Thomas Drics

A List of Representative Clients will be furnished upon request.

For full biographical listings, see the Martindale-Hubbell Law Directory

BOSE MCKINNEY & EVANS (AV)

2700 First Indiana Plaza, 135 North Pennsylvania Street, 46204
Telephone: 317-684-5000
Facsimile: 317-684-5173
Indianapolis North Office: Suite 1201, 8888 Keystone Crossing, 46240.
Telephone: 317-574-3700.
Facsimile: 317-574-3716.

MEMBERS OF FIRM

William M. Evans (1923-1991)
Robert H. McKinney (Retired)
John W. Wynne (Retired)
Lewis C. Bose
Wayne C. Ponader
James P. Seidensticker, Jr.
Robert P. Kassing
G. Pearson Smith, Jr.
David A. Butcher
Philip A. Nicely
Theodore J. Nowacki
Kendall C. Crook
Ronald E. Elberger
Thomas M. Johnston
David L. Wills
Charles R. Rubright
Daniel C. Emerson
Alan W. Becker
Daniel B. Seitz
Leonard Opperman
David A. Travelstead
Stephen E. Arthur
Linda E. Coletta
Margaret Bannon Miller
Ronald M. Soskin
George E. Purdy
Keith E. White
L. Parvin Price
David L. Swider
James C. Carlino
R. J. McConnell
C. Joseph Russell
Jon M. Bailey
Elizabeth Theobald Young
Michael A. Trentadue
Karl R. Sturbaum
Robert B. Clemens
J. Greg Easter
Kathleen G. Lucas
Roderick H. Morgan

(See Next Column)

BOSE MCKINNEY & EVANS—*Continued*

MEMBERS OF FIRM (Continued)

Dwight L. Miller
E. Victor Indiano
V. Samuel Laurin III
James E. Carlberg

ASSOCIATES

George Thomas Patton, Jr.
Karen Glasser Sharp
Debra Linn Burns
Gregory W. Guevara
Gary L. Chapman
Lisa C. McKinney
Natalie J. Stucky
Alan S. Townsend
Christopher C. Levandoski
Scott A. Weathers
Thomas G. Burroughs
Daniel P. McInerny
Tammy K. Haney
Robert C. Sproule
Jeffrey S. Koehlinger
Robert K. Johnson
J. Scott Enright
William C. Ahrbecker
Susan E. Traynor
Mary Beth Plummer

OF COUNSEL

Peter Lynn Goerges

Representative Clients: Association of Indiana Life Insurance Cos.; Duke Realty Investments; Emmis Broadcasting Corp.; First Indiana Bank; Indianapolis Colts, Inc.; Indiana League of Savings Institutions, Inc.; Prudential Life Insurance Co.; Metropolitan Life Insurance Co.; USX Corp.

For full biographical listings, see the Martindale-Hubbell Law Directory

BUSCHMANN, CARR & SHANKS, PROFESSIONAL CORPORATION (AV)

1020 Market Tower, 10 West Market Street, 46204-2963
Telephone: 317-636-5511
Fax: 317-636-3661
Franklin, Indiana Office: 160 Fairway Lakes Drive.
Telephone: 317-738-9540.
Fax: 317-738-9310.
Fishers, Indiana Office: 9093 Technology Drive, Suite 103.
Telephone: 317-577-0756.
Fax: 317-577-9910.

C. Severin Buschmann (1896-1980)
Stephen R. Buschmann
Charles N. Doberneck
John R. Carr, Jr.
Gary L. Dilk
John R. Carr, III
John N. Shanks II
Bret S. Clement
Lisa T. Hamilton

OF COUNSEL

Bryan B. Davenport (For complete biographical data, see Franklin, Indiana Office)
A. David Meyer
J. Scott Barratt (P.C.)
Jeanette C. Kassebaum (For complete biographical data, see Fishers, Indiana Office)

Representative Clients: Archer-Daniels Midland Co.; Ball Corp.; Industrial Valley Title Insurance; Creative Risk Management, Inc.; Deflecto Corporation; Glenfed Mortgage Corp.; Gates McDonald; Merchants National Bank & Trust Company of Muncie; Monumental Life Insurance Co.; National Council on Compensation Insurance.

For full biographical listings, see the Martindale-Hubbell Law Directory

HACKMAN MCCLARNON HULETT & CRACRAFT (AV)

2400 One Indiana Square, 46204
Telephone: 317-636-5401
Facsimile: 317-686-3288

MEMBERS OF FIRM

James R. McClarnon
Michael B. Cracraft
Marvin L. Hackman
Timothy K. Ryan
Robert S. Hulett
Philip B. McKiernan
Vicki L. Anderson

ASSOCIATES

Jane A. Phillips
Thomas F. Bedsole
Jeffrey G. Jackson
Thomas A. Dickey

OF COUNSEL

John D. Cochran, Jr.
Mark S. Alderfer

Representative Clients: Ameritech Indiana; AT&T Technologies, Inc.; Citizens Gas & Coke Utility; F. C. Tucker Co., Inc.; Texas Eastern Products Pipeline Co.; Indiana Municipal Power Agency; I.V.C. Industrial Coatings, Inc.; McGraw-Hill Broadcasting Co., Inc.; NBD Bank, N.A.; State Farm Mutual Automobile Insurance Company.

For full biographical listings, see the Martindale-Hubbell Law Directory

HALL, RENDER, KILLIAN, HEATH & LYMAN, PROFESSIONAL CORPORATION (AV)

Suite 2000, One American Square Box 82064, 46282
Telephone: 317-633-4884
Telecopier: 317-633-4878
North Office: Suite 820, 8402 Harcourt Road, 46260.
Telephone: 317-871-6222.

(See Next Column)

William S. Hall
Fred J. Bachmann
John C. Render
Kevin P. Speer
Rex P. Killian
Greta E. Gerberding
R. Terry Heath
Doreen Denega
Stephen W. Lyman
Jeffrey W. Short
L. Richard Gohman
Gregory W. Moore
Jeffrey Peek
John C. Meade
Clifford A. Beyler
Jill Workman Martin
Joseph R. Impicciche
Clifton E. Johnson
Timothy C. Lawson
Christine B. Zoccola
Douglas P. Long
Martha B. Wentworth
William H. Thompson
Richard W. McMinn
Timothy W. Kennedy
Rebekah N. Murphy
Steven H. Pratt
Michael B. McMains
N. Kent Smith
Todd J. Selby
Maureen O'Brien Griffin
Gregg M. Wallander
Robert A. Hicks
J. Scott Waters, IV
Mary C. Gaughan
James B. Hogan
Donald R. Russell

For full biographical listings, see the Martindale-Hubbell Law Directory

ICE MILLER DONADIO & RYAN (AV)

One American Square Box 82001, 46282-0002
Telephone: 317-236-2100
Fax: 317-236-2219

MEMBERS OF FIRM

James V. Donadio
James A. Shanahan
Alan H. Lobley
Michael A. Blickman
Jim A. O'Neal
Philip A. Whistler
Donald G. Sutherland
Marcus B. Chandler
John A. Grayson
Jeffrey O. Lewis
Leland B. Cross, Jr.
John F. Prescott, Jr.
Leonard J. Betley
Phillip L. Bayt
Evan E. Steger
Fred R. Biesecker
Berkley W. Duck, III
Thomas K. Downs
William R. Riggs
Mary Nold Larimore
Ralph A. Cohen
E. Van Olson
Jack R. Snyder
Lisa Stone Sciscoe
Charles E. Wilson
Marc W. Sciscoe
Arthur P. Kalleres
Richard A. Smikle
Bruce A. Polizotto
John R. Thornburgh
Jay G. Taylor
Mary Beth Braitman
G. Daniel Kelley, Jr.
Brenda S. Horn
Gordon D. Wishard
Gregory L. Pemberton
S. R. Born
L. Alan Whaley
David M. Mattingly
Robert B. Bush
James D. Kemper
Bonnie L. Gallivan
Martin J. Klaper
John T. Murphy
James R. Fisher
Richard J. Thrapp
Richard E. Parker
Zeff A. Weiss
John P. Ryan
Stephen J. Hackman
Cory Brundage
Steven K. Humke
Harry L. Gonso
Debra Hanley Miller
Terry A. M. Mumford
Todd W. Ponder
W. C. Blanton
Michael A. Wukmer
Michael H. Boldt
Lucy A. Emison
David J. Mallon, Jr.
Michael J. Lewinski
Thomas H. Ristine
Melissa Proffitt Reese
Phillip R. Scaletta, III
Mark J. Richards
Barton T. Sprunger
Elizabeth A. Smith
Susan B. Tabler
Thomas W. Peterson
James L. Petersen
Patricia A. Zelmer
James S. Cunning
Paul B. Overhauser
Gary J. Dankert
Lacy M. Johnson
Philip C. Genetos
Michael D. Marine
Byron L. Myers
Henry A. Efroymson

SENIOR COUNSEL

Timothy W. Sullivan
Gene E. Wilkins

OF COUNSEL

William P. Diener
Mark D. Grant
Bradley L. Williams
Kathleen K. Shortridge
Nancy Menard Riddle
Deborah A. Lawrence
James B. Burroughs
Susan Barnhizer Rivas
Karen Little Arland
Bruce J. Alvarado
C. Daniel Motsinger
Diana Lynn Wann
Gloria A. Aplin
Tianlong Yu (Not admitted in IN)
Roland A. Fuller, III
Daniel E. Fisher

STAFF ATTORNEYS

Sandra K. Bickel
Dana G. Meier
R. Steven Linne
John W. Rowings

RETIRED PARTNERS

Donald F. Elliott, Jr.
Alan T. Nolan
Kenneth Foster
Edward J. Ohleyer
George B. Gavit
Robert D. Risch
Robert D. McCord
Geoffrey Segar
Merle H. Miller
Jerome M. Strauss
James S. Telfer

(See Next Column)

ICE MILLER DONADIO & RYAN, *Indianapolis—Continued*

ASSOCIATES

Terri Ann Czajka
Bette J. Dodd
Joseph E. Whitsett, Jr.
Sherry A. Fabina-Abney
Bruce W. Longbottom
Kelly Bauman Pitcher
Donald M. Snemis
Dale E. Stackhouse
Edward P. Steegmann
Michael A. Wilkins
Kristin L. Altice
Catherine R. Beck
Dodd Joseph Gray
Jane Neuhauser Herndon
Matthew C. Hook
Michael R. Kerr
Peggy J. Naile
Elizabeth P. Rippy
Kevin C. Woodhouse
Robert A. Anderson
Daniel S. Corsaro
James Scott Fanzini
Laure V. Flaniken
Kevin R. Knight
Dominic F. Polizzotto
Brian G. Steinkamp
Timothy A. Brooks
Gerald B. Coleman
Christopher J. Franzmann
Robert W. Horner, III
Terrence J. Keusch
Michael J. Melliere
John J. Morse
Judy Starobin Okenfuss
Michael E. Schrader
Stephanie Alden Smithey
Michael L. Tooley
Angela K. Wade
Barbara J. Weigel
Kathleen Weyher Kiefer
Curtis W. McCauley
Dean T. Burger
Charles A. Compton
Laura B. Daghe
Philippa M. Guthrie
Brian L. McDermott
Jodie L. Miner
Thomas E. Mixdorf
Heather K. Olinger
R. Brock Jordan
Antje C. Petersen
Adam Arceneaux
Amanda Enayati
Dan L. O'Korn
Paul H. Sinclair
Ann L. Colussi
Ann L. Theobald
Anita M. Hodgson
Nicholas C. Deets
Melissa J. Garrard

Counsel for: American United Life Insurance Co.; Chrysler Corp.; Ford Motor Company; General Electric Company; Indiana Bankers Assn.

For full biographical listings, see the Martindale-Hubbell Law Directory

JOHNSON, SMITH, DENSBORN, WRIGHT & HEATH (AV)

One Indiana Square Suite 1800, 46204
Telephone: 317-634-9777
Telecopier: 317-636-9061

MEMBERS OF FIRM

John F. Joyce (1948-1994)
Wayne O. Adams, III
Robert M. Baker, III
Thomas A. Barnard
David J. Carr
Peter D. Cleveland
David R. Day
Donald K. Densborn
Thomas N. Eckerle
Mark W. Ford
G. Ronald Heath
Robert B. Hebert
John David Hoover
Andrew W. Hull
Dennis A. Johnson
Richard L. Johnson
Michael J. Kaye
John R. Kirkwood
David Williams Russell
James T. Smith
Martha Taylor Starkey
David E. Wright

ASSOCIATES

Robert C. Wolf (1949-1993)
Carolyn H. Andretti
Maureen F. Barnard
David G. Blachly
Robert T. Buday
Sean Michael Clapp
Jeffrey S. Cohen
Charles M. Freeland
David W. Givens, Jr.
Gary P. Goodin
Patricia L. Marshall
Bradley C. Morris
Steven J. Moss
Padric K. J. O'Brien
Cathleen J. Perry
David D. Robinson
Ronald G. Sentman
David A. Tucker
Sally Franklin Zweig

OF COUNSEL

Earl Auberry (1923-1989)
Larry A. Conrad (1935-1990)
Bruce W. Claycombe
Laura S. Cohen
Paul D. Gresk
William T. Lawrence
Mark A. Palmer
Lawrence W. Schmits
Catherine A. Singleton

For full biographical listings, see the Martindale-Hubbell Law Directory

KATZMAN KATZMAN & PYLITT, A PROFESSIONAL CORPORATION (AV)

3905 Vincennes Road, Suite 100, 46268
Telephone: 317-872-5700
Telecopier: 317-872-5769

Alvin J. Katzman
Mariellen Katzman
Bernard L. Pylitt

Jeffrey A. Hearn

OF COUNSEL

Daniel B. Altman

A list of representative clients will be furnished upon request.

For full biographical listings, see the Martindale-Hubbell Law Directory

KIGHTLINGER & GRAY (AV)

Market Square Center, Suite 660, 151 North Delaware Street, 46204
Telephone: 317-638-4521
Telecopier: 317-636-5917
Evansville, Indiana Office: One Riverfront Place, Suite 210, 20 N.W. First Street, 47708.
Telephone: 812-464-9508.
Telecopier: 812-464-9511.
New Albany, Indiana Office: Pinnacle Centre, Suite 200, 3317 Grant Line Road, P.O. Box 6727, 46151.
Telephone: 812-949-2300.
Telecopier: 812-949-8556.

MEMBERS OF FIRM

Vayne M. Armstrong (1894-1959)
Harry L. Gause (1898-1964)
Paul B. Hudson (1907-1970)
Aribert L. Young (1923-1980)
Mark William Gray
Robert J. Wampler
Donald L. Dawson
Peter G. Tamulonis
Richard A. Young
J. Randall Aikman
Michael E. Brown
Mark D. Gerth
Steven E. Springer
Joan Fullam Irick
Richard T. Mullineaux (Resident, New Albany Office)
Robert M. Kelso
Brent R. Weil (Resident, Evansville Office)
Philip Linnemeier
John B. Drummy
James W. Roehrdanz
Samuel A. Day (Resident, New Albany Office)
Peter A. Velde
Thomas B. Blackwell
Briane M. House
Thomas J. Jarzyniecki, Jr.
Jeffrey A. Doty
Thomas E. Wheeler II
Rodney L. Scott (Resident, New Albany Office)

OF COUNSEL

Erle A. Kightlinger

ASSOCIATES

S. Michael Woodard
Troy A. Reynolds (Resident, Evansville Office)
Jill Reifinger Marcrum (Resident, Evansville Office)
Mary M. Nord (Resident, New Albany Office)
John K. Baird
William L. O'Connor
Van T. Willis (Resident, New Albany Office)
Scott L. Tyler (Resident, New Albany Office)
Laura E. Moenning
Paul F. Lottes
Christopher C. Hagenow
Roger H. Schmelzer
David R. Sauvey (Resident, Evansville Office)
Eric D. Johnson
Joseph M. Perkins, Jr.
Timothy A. Klinger (Resident, Evansville Office)
Dirck H. Stahl (Resident, Evansville Office)

Representative Clients: American Family Mutual Insurance Co.; American International Group; American States; Associated Aviation Underwriters; Black & Decker (U.S., Inc.); Government Employees Insurance Co.; Mack Trucks, Inc.; Reliance Insurance Group.
Reference: INB National Bank.

For full biographical listings, see the Martindale-Hubbell Law Directory

LEWIS & KAPPES, PROFESSIONAL CORPORATION (AV)

Suite 1210 One American Square, P.O. Box 82053, 46282
Telephone: 317-639-1210
Telecopier: 317-639-4882

Ted B. Lewis (1919-1991)
Philip S. Kappes
Terence L. Eads
David W. Gray
John F. Wickes, Jr.
Gary P. Price
Steven L. Tuchman
Thomas R. Ruge
C. Duane O'Neal
Brett James Miller
James L. Turner

Richard T. Trettin
Todd A. Richardson
Rhonda L. Fuller
Peter S. French
Pamela H. Sherwood

OF COUNSEL

Samuel A. Fuller
Kevin W. Dogan

For full biographical listings, see the Martindale-Hubbell Law Directory

LOCKE REYNOLDS BOYD & WEISELL (AV)

1000 Capital Center South, 201 North Illinois Street, 46204
Telephone: 317-237-3800
Telecopier: 317-237-3900

Theodore L. Locke (1891-1981)
Hugh E. Reynolds (1900-1968)
Emerson Boyd (1914-1986)
Hugh E. Reynolds, Jr.
Lloyd H. Milliken, Jr.
James S. Haramy
William V. Hutchens
James J. McGrath
David S. Allen
David M. Haskett
Michael A. Bergin
David T. Kasper
Stephen J. Dutton
Steven J. Strawbridge
Thomas L. Davis
Robert A. Fanning
Randall R. Riggs
Alan S. Brown
Michael D. Moriarty
Glenn T. Troyer
Paul S. Mannweiler
Mark J. Roberts

(See Next Column)

LOCKE REYNOLDS BOYD & WEISELL—*Continued*

Kevin Charles Murray
Julia M. Blackwell
Michael T. Bindner
Michael J. Schneider
Kim F. Ebert
David E. Jose
Terrence L. Brookie
Michael J. Rusnak
Richard A. Huser
Jeffrey B. Bailey
Paul G. Reis
Thomas J. Campbell
Diane L. Parsons
Burton M. Harris
Howard R. Cohen
Charles B. Baldwin
Andrew James Richardson
Thomas W. Farlow
Karl M. Koons, III
Julia F. Crowe
James Dimos

Stephen L. Vaughan
Kristen K. Rollison
Thomas R. Schultz
Todd J. Kaiser
Peter H. Donahoe
Eric A. Riegner
Kevin C. Schiferl
Ariane Schallwig Johnson
Peter H. Pogue
John H. Daerr
James O. Waanders
John K. McDavid
Lisa Drees Tobin
Robert A. Burtzlaff
Robert W. Wright
Robert T. Dassow
Jeffrey J. Mortier
Kevin M. Boyle
Nicholas C. Pappas
Mary A. Schopper
Susan E. Cline
Dirk Wallsmith
Jerrilyn Powers Ramsey
Katherine Coble Dassow
Lisa A. McCallum
Charles S. Eberhardt, II
Kathleen A. Hash
Kathryn Weymouth Williams
Mary Margaret Ruth Feldhake
Nelson D. Alexander
Curt W. Hidde

OF COUNSEL

William B. Weisell
William H. Vobach
Robert C. Riddell
Rodney E. Corson
David S. Klinestiver
Sarah R. Galvarro
Jeffrey R. Gaither
Jeffrey S. Dible

Counsel for: American Honda Motor Co., Inc.; CNA Insurance Cos.; General Motors Corp.; Montgomery Ward & Co., Inc.; I.D.S./American Express, Inc.; Kroger Co.; NBD Bank, N.A.; Navistar International Transportation Corp.; PEPSICO, Inc.; Resort Condominiums International, Inc.

For full biographical listings, see the Martindale-Hubbell Law Directory

PARR RICHEY OBREMSKEY & MORTON (AV)

1600 Market Tower, Ten West Market Street, 46204
Telephone: 317-269-2500
FAX: 317-269-2514
Lebanon, Indiana Office: Parr Building. 225 West Main Street. P.O. Box 666.
Telephone: 317-482-0110; 269-2509.
FAX: 317-483-3444.

MEMBERS OF FIRM

A. A. Parr (1910-1959)
W. H. Parr (1878-1967)
William R. Nichols (1946-1980)
W. H. Parr, Jr. (1903-1988)
David S. Richey
Peter L. Obremskey
Don F. Morton
Kent M. Frandsen
Charles W. Ritz, III
Paul S. Kruse
Carol Sparks Drake
Larry J. Wallace

ASSOCIATES

James A. L. Buddenbaum
Anthony W. Patterson

Counsel For: Wabash Valley Power Association; Indiana Statewide Association of Rural Electric Cooperatives, Inc.; AT&T Communications; Ohio Valley Gas Corp.; Bell South Cellular Corp.; Cellular One; Bartholomew County REMC; Boone County REMC; Hendricks County REMC; Jasper County REMC.
Local Attorneys for: A.T.&T. Communications, Inc.; GTE Mobilnet.

For full biographical listings, see the Martindale-Hubbell Law Directory

ROCAP, WITCHGER & THRELKELD (AV)

700 Union Federal Building, 45 North Pennsylvania Street, 46204
Telephone: 317-639-6281
FAX: 317-637-9056

James E. Rocap, Sr. (1881-1969)
John T. Rocap (1909-1980)
Keith C. Reese (1920-1993)

MEMBERS OF FIRM

James E. Rocap, Jr.
James D. Witchger
W. Brent Threlkeld
Richard A. Rocap
James C. Todderud
Thomas Todd Reynolds

ASSOCIATES

Robert S. O'Dell
Nancy Grannan Curless
Michael D. Ramsey
Tara L. Becsey
Bette J. Peterson
Robert A. Durham
Jeffrey V. Crabill

OF COUNSEL

Joseph F. Quill

Counsel for: Phillips Petroleum Co.; State Farm Mutual Auto Insurance Co.; Principal Casualty & Insurance; Cessna Finance Corp.; American Family Insurance Group; The Travelers Insurance Co.

(See Next Column)

For full biographical listings, see the Martindale-Hubbell Law Directory

RUCKELSHAUS, ROLAND, HASBROOK & O'CONNOR (AV)

Suite 1100, 129 East Market Street, 46204
Telephone: 317-634-4356
Fax: 317-634-8635

MEMBERS OF FIRM

John C. Ruckelshaus
Paul G. Roland
William A. Hasbrook
John F. Kautzman
David T. Hasbrook

ASSOCIATES

Leo T. Blackwell
M. Elizabeth Bemis

OF COUNSEL

John C. O'Connor

Representative Clients: State Lodge Fraternal Order of Police; Professional Firefighters Union of Indiana AFL-CIO; Indianapolis Yellow Cab, Inc.; Roselyn Bakeries, Inc.; United Consulting Engineers, Inc. St. Vincent Hospital.

SOMMER & BARNARD, ATTORNEYS AT LAW, PC (AV)

4000 Bank One Tower, 111 Monument Circle, P.O. Box 44363, 46244-0363
Telephone: 317-630-4000
FAX: 317-236-9802
North Office: 8900 Keystone Crossing, Suite 1046, Indianapolis, Indiana, 46240-2134.
Telephone: 317-630-4000.
FAX: 317-844-4780.

James K. Sommer
William C. Barnard
James E. Hughes
Edward W. Harris, III
Frederick M. King
Jerald I. Ancel
Eric R. Johnson
Gordon L. Pittenger
Lynn Brundage Jongleux
Frank J. Deveau
John E. Taylor
Michael C. Terrell
Marlene Reich
Richard C. Richmond, III
Julianne S. Lis-Milam
Steven C. Shockley
Stephen B. Cherry
Robert J. Hicks
Lawrence A. Vanore
Donald C. Biggs
Debra McVicker Lynch

Gayle A. Reindl
Ann Carr Mackey
Gregory J. Seketa
Sandra L. Gosling
Edwin J. Broecker
Thomas R. DeVoe
Mary T. Doherty
William K. Boncosky

OF COUNSEL

Jerry Williams
Glenn Scolnik
Philip L. McCool
Charles E. Valliere
Verl L. Myers

Representative Clients: Comerica Bank; Excel Industries; Federal Express; Kimball International; Monsanto; Renault Automation; Repport International; TRW, Inc.

For full biographical listings, see the Martindale-Hubbell Law Directory

STARK DONINGER & SMITH (AV)

Suite 700, 50 South Meridian Street, 46204
Telephone: 317-638-2400
Fax: 317-633-6618; 633-6619

MEMBERS OF FIRM

John C. Stark
Bruce E. Smith
John W. Van Buskirk
Richard W. Dyar
Patricia Seasor Bailey
Brian J. Tuohy
Mark A. Bailey
Lewis E. Willis, Jr.

ASSOCIATES

Neil E. Lucas
Richard B. Kaufman
Patrick J. Dietrick

COUNSEL

Clarence H. Doninger
Gregory S. Fehribach
John F. Hoehner
Robert D. Maas
William K. Byrum

Reference: Huntington National Bank of Indiana.

For full biographical listings, see the Martindale-Hubbell Law Directory

WOODEN MCLAUGHLIN & STERNER (AV)

1600 Capital Center South, 201 North Illinois Street, 46204
Telephone: 317-639-6151
Fax: 317-639-6444

(See Next Column)

WOODEN MCLAUGHLIN & STERNER, *Indianapolis—Continued*

MEMBERS OF FIRM

William P. Wooden
Robert L. McLaughlin
Dan G. Sterner
Michael C. Cook
Ronald G. Salatich
Thomas W. Dinwiddie
John D. Nell
Douglas B. King
Dale W. Eikenberry
Andrew C. Charnstrom
Daniel D. Trachtman
Julie L. Michaelis
Thomas M. Hanahan
Erick D. Ponader
Mary L. Titsworth

ASSOCIATES

Kent M. Broach
David A. Pesel
Jeffrey L. McKean
Andrea L. Cohen
Therese Fehribach Coffey
Stephen J. Akard
Holly Hapak Betz
Caroline Lingelbach Young
Michael A. Schoening
Kurt A. Webber
Derek D. Murphy
Stephen E. Ferrucci
Michael A. Moffatt

OF COUNSEL

Thomas D. Titsworth
Katherine L. Shelby

Representative Clients: AT&T; Amoco Oil Co.; Cook Group; Eaton & Lauth Development Co.; Exxon Corp.; Hospital Corporation of America; Merrell Dow Pharmaceutical, Inc.; Monroe Guaranty Insurance Company; Peabody Coal Company; Playtex Family Products, Inc.

For full biographical listings, see the Martindale-Hubbell Law Directory

*JEFFERSONVILLE,** Clark Co.

SMITH, BARTLETT, HEEKE & CARPENTER (AV)

Holzbog House, 209 East Chestnut Street, P.O. Box 98, 47131-0098
Telephone: 812-282-7736
FAX: 812-284-8388

MEMBERS OF FIRM

Wilmer T. Fox (1881-1946)
Charles C. Fox (1912-1975)
Ernest W. Smith
Rick E. Bartlett
Sandra L. Heeke
Cheryl A. Carpenter

ASSOCIATES

Sandra Winnett Lewis
Pamela K. Thompson
Mary E. Fondrisi

Representative Clients: NBD Bank, N.A.; Liberty Mutual Insurance Co.; Geo. Pfau's Sons Co., Inc.; General Accident Group; American Family Insurance; PSI Energy; American States Insurance Co.

For full biographical listings, see the Martindale-Hubbell Law Directory

KENDALLVILLE, Noble Co.

EMERICK & DIGGINS, P.C. (AV)

218 South Main Street, 46755-1796
Telephone: 219-347-1050
Fax: 219-347-5927
Ligonier, Indiana Office: 310 South Cavin Street, 46767.
Telephone: 219-894-4150.
Fax: 219-894-4152.

Rex S. Emerick (1910-1946)
R. Stan Emerick
Daniel F. Diggins

Howard F. Hanson
Jerry L. Carson (Resident at Ligonier Office)
James Abbs

OF COUNSEL

Merritt W. Diggins

General Counsel for: Frick Lumber Co., Inc.; J.O. Mory Stores, Inc.; East Noble School Corp.; Reliable Tool & Machine Co.; Kendallville Iron & Metal, Inc.;
Approved Attorneys for: Louisville Title Insurance Co.; Lawyers Title Insurance Corp.
Reference: Society Bank, Kendallville, Indiana.

For full biographical listings, see the Martindale-Hubbell Law Directory

*KENTLAND,** Newton Co.

BARCE & RYAN (AV)

301 East Graham Street, P.O. Box 338, 47951
Telephone: 219-474-5158
Fax: 219-474-6610
Fowler, Indiana Office: 103 North Jackson Avenue, P.O. Box 252.
Telephone: 317-884-0383.
Fax: 317-884-0445.

(See Next Column)

MEMBERS OF FIRM

John W. Barce
R. Steven Ryan
J. Edward Barce (Resident at Fowler Office)

Representative Clients: USX Corporation; Metropolitan Life Insurance Company; Goodland State Bank; Bank of Oxford; DeMotte State Bank; Newton County Stone; Northern Indiana Public Service Company; DeMeter, Inc; Town of Boswell; Town of Brook.

For full biographical listings, see the Martindale-Hubbell Law Directory

*KOKOMO,** Howard Co.

BAYLIFF, HARRIGAN, CORD & MAUGANS, P.C. (AV)

The Security Building, 123 North Buckeye, P.O. Box 2249, 46904-2249
Telephone: 317-459-3941
Fax: 317-459-3974

Edgar W. Bayliff
Daniel J. Harrigan
C. Michael Cord
J. Conrad Maugans

Mark A. Scott

Reference: Society National Bank, Indiana; First Federal Savings Bank of Kokomo, Indiana.

For full biographical listings, see the Martindale-Hubbell Law Directory

FELL, MCGARVEY, TRAURING & WILSON (AV)

515 West Sycamore Street, P.O. Box 958, 46903-0958
Telephone: 317-457-9321
Telecopier: 317-452-0882

MEMBERS OF FIRM

John E. Fell, Jr.
Eugene J. McGarvey, Jr.
Thomas J. Trauring
Alan D. Wilson

Representative Clients: Big R Stores; First National Bank, Kokomo; Haynes International, Inc.; Hospital Authority of the City of Kokomo; Kokomo City Hall Building Corp.; PPG Industries, Inc.; Star Building Supply, Inc.; Mervis Industries, Inc.; G-W Invader, Inc.; Taylor Community School Corp.
References: First National Bank; Society Bank of Howard County.

For full biographical listings, see the Martindale-Hubbell Law Directory

LACEY, O'MAHONEY, MAHONEY, SAGER & KING (AV)

208 E. Mulberry Street, P.O. Box 805, 46903-0805
Telephone: 317-459-0751
Fax: 317-459-5950
ABA Net: 1722

OF COUNSEL

LeRoy M. Lacey
Edward S. Mahoney

MEMBERS OF FIRM

William P. O'Mahoney
Sally A. Sager
Corbin K. King

ASSOCIATES

Mark A. McCann

Representative Clients: Adept Custom Molders, Inc.; Adonis Manufacturing Corp.; Atlantic Insurance Group; BMJ Mold & Engineering, Co., Inc.; Empire Insurance Cos.; Globe Insurance Co.; Kokomo Common Council; John Hancock Insurance Co.; St. Joseph Hospital and Health Center; Society National Bank, Indiana; Taylor Township Trustee; Town of Greentown; Lloyds of London.

For full biographical listings, see the Martindale-Hubbell Law Directory

*LAFAYETTE,** Tippecanoe Co.

BALL, EGGLESTON, BUMBLEBURG & MCBRIDE (AV)

810 Bank One Building, P.O. Box 1535, 47902
Telephone: 317-742-9046
Fax: 317-742-1966

Cable G. Ball (1904-1981)
Owen Crook (1908-1977)
Warren N. Eggleston (1923-1991)

MEMBERS OF FIRM

Joseph T. Bumbleburg
John K. McBride
Jack L. Walkey
Michael J. Stapleton
Jeffrey J. Newell
James T. Hodson
Brian Wade Walker

ASSOCIATES

Cheryl M. Knodle
Randy J. Williams
Norman G. Printer

General Counsel for: The Lafayette Union Railway Co.; Bank One, Lafayette, N.A.
Representative Clients: Farmers Insurance Group; General Accident Fire & Life Assurance Corp.; City of Lafayette Board of Parks and Recreation; West Lafayette Community School Corp.; Travelers Insurance Co.; Trustees, West Lafayette Public Library.

For full biographical listings, see the Martindale-Hubbell Law Directory

Lafayette—Continued

BENNETT, BOEHNING, POYNTER & CLARY (AV)

6th Floor, Lafayette Bank & Trust Building, 133 North Fourth Street, P.O. Box 469, 47902-0469
Telephone: 317-742-9066
Telecopier: 317-742-7641

MEMBERS OF FIRM

William K. Bennett
Richard A. Boehning
Robert E. Poynter
Brent E. Clary
Roger Wm. Bennett

ASSOCIATES

Christine A. DeSanctis
Marianne M. Owen
James A. Gothard

General Counsel for: Lafayette Surgical Clinic, Inc.; West Lafayette Regional Sewer District; Fred Gutwein Seed Co.; Dunn & Hargitt, Inc.; Industrial Plating, Inc.; Pizza King, Inc.; Goldden Corporation; Grauel Enterprises, Inc.; Lafayette Bank and Trust Company; Journal and Courier; Lafayette Masonry Supply, Inc.; Lafayette Obstetrics & Gynecology, Inc.; PowerMark, Ltd.; Resources Industry, Inc.; Solidex Technologies, Inc.; Endoplus Inc.; Med Institute, Inc.
Area and County Counsel for: Cedar Run Limited Limited; ALCOA.
Approved Title Attorneys for: Lawyers Title Insurance Co.; First American Title Ins. Co.; National Attorneys' Title Assurance Fund, Inc.

For full biographical listings, see the Martindale-Hubbell Law Directory

HOFFMAN, LUHMAN & BUSCH (AV)

300 Main Street, Suite 700, P.O. Box 99, 47902
Telephone: 317-423-5404
Fax: 317-742-6448

MEMBERS OF FIRM

J. Frederick Hoffman
David W. Luhman
Thomas H. Busch

OF COUNSEL

Richard Donahue

Representative Clients: Farm Bureau Mutual Insurance Co.; Bank of Wolcott; Bright National Bank; American States Insurance Co.; Haywood Publishing Co., Inc.; American Yorkshire Club.
References: Lafayette Bank & Trust Co., Lafayette, Indiana; Farmers & Merchants Bank, Rochester, Indiana; Lafayette Savings Bank, Lafayette, Indiana.

For full biographical listings, see the Martindale-Hubbell Law Directory

MAYFIELD AND BROOKS (AV)

322 Main Street, P.O. Box 650, 47902
Telephone: 317-423-5454
FAX: 317-742-8666

Ambrose R. Mayfield (1907-1980)
Thomas L. Brooks

Phillip J. Scaletta, Jr.
Thomas L. Brooks, Jr.

Representative Clients: DeFouw Chevrolet, Inc.; Kendrick Buick-Cadillac, Inc.; Century 21 Bouwkamp Agency; Lafayette Real Estate Marketing Corp.; Smith Office Equipment, Inc.; American Vending Corp.; Sun Industries, Inc.; National Attorneys' Title Insurance Fund, Inc.
Reference: NBD Bank, N.A.

STUART & BRANIGIN (AV)

The Life Building, 300 Main Street, Suite 800, 47902
Telephone: 317-423-1561
Telecopier: 317-742-8175

MEMBERS OF FIRM

Allison Ellsworth Stuart (1886-1950)
Roger D. Branigin (1902-1975)
Russell H. Hart
Roger D. Branigin, Jr.
Thomas L. Ryan
James V. McGlone
Carl W. Kloepfer
Thomas R. McCully
Larry R. Fisher
Nina B. Kirkpatrick
Mark Lillianfeld
Stephen R. Pennell
Anthony S. Benton
Erik D. Spykman
William E. Emerick
John C. Duffey
Mark E. DeYoung
Thomas B. Parent
Laura L. Bowker
Kevin D. Nicoson

COUNSEL

George A. Rinker
John F. Bodle

ASSOCIATES

Susan K. Holtberg
John M. Stuckey
Deborah B. Trice
Brent W. Huber
David A. Starkweather
Geoffrey Blazi
A. James Chareq

General Counsel for: The Lafayette Life Insurance Co.; INB National Bank, N.W.; Lafayette Home Hospital, Inc.

(See Next Column)

State Counsel for: Norfolk & Western Railway Co.
Mr. Ryan is Counsel to: The Trustees of Purdue University.
Representative Clients: Aluminum Company of America; Liberty Mutual Insurance Group.

For full biographical listings, see the Martindale-Hubbell Law Directory

*LAGRANGE,** LaGrange Co. — (Refer to Elkhart)

*LA PORTE,** La Porte Co.

NEWBY, LEWIS, KAMINSKI & JONES (AV)

916 Lincoln Way, 46350
Telephone: 219-362-1577
Direct Line Michigan City: 219-879-6300
Fax: 219-362-2106
Mailing Address: P.O. Box 1816, La Porte, Indiana, 46352-1816

MEMBERS OF FIRM

John E. Newby (1916-1990)
Daniel E. Lewis, Jr.
Gene M. Jones
John W. Newby
Perry F. Stump, Jr.
Edward L. Volk
Mark L. Phillips
Martin W. Kus
Marsha Schatz Volk
Mark A. Lienhoop
James W. Kaminski

ASSOCIATES

John F. Lake
William S. Kaminski
Christine A. Sulewski
David P. Jones

SENIOR COUNSEL

Leon R. Kaminski

OF COUNSEL

Daniel E. Lewis

Counsel for: U. S. F. & G. Co.; State Farm Mutual Insurance Co.; Auto Owners Insurance Co.; La Porte Bank & Trust Co.; Liberty Mutual Insurance Co.; Sullair Corp.; La Porte Community School Corp.; United Farm Bureau Mutual Insurance Co.; Physicians Insurance of Indiana.

For full biographical listings, see the Martindale-Hubbell Law Directory

*LEBANON,** Boone Co.

PARR RICHEY OBREMSKEY & MORTON (AV)

Parr Building, 225 West Main Street, P.O. Box 666, 46052
Telephone: 317-482-0110; 269-2509
FAX: 317-483-3444
Indianapolis, Indiana Office: 1600 Market Tower, Ten West Market Street.
Telephone: 317-269-2500.
FAX: 317-269-2514.

MEMBERS OF FIRM

David S. Richey
Peter L. Obremskey
Kent M. Frandsen
Paul S. Kruse
Carol Sparks Drake
Anthony W. Patterson

Counsel For: Wabash Valley Power Association; Indiana Statewide Association of Rural Electric Cooperatives, Inc.; AT&T Communications; Ohio Valley Gas Corp.; Bell South Cellular Corp.; Cellular One; Bartholomew County REMC; Boone County REMC; Hendricks County REMC; Jasper County REMC.
Local Attorneys for: A.T.&T. Communications, Inc.; GTE Mobilnet.

For full biographical listings, see the Martindale-Hubbell Law Directory

*LOGANSPORT,** Cass Co.

MILLER, TOLBERT, MUEHLHAUSEN, MUEHLHAUSEN & GROFF, P.C. (AV)

216 Fourth Street Caller Box: 7010, 46947-7010
Telephone: 219-722-4343
FAX: 219-722-1936

Glenn L. Miller (1902-1992)
George R. Wildman (1932-1994)
Frank E. Tolbert
John C. Muehlhausen
James K. Muehlhausen
R. Tod Groff

John S. Damm

Counsel for: The Home Insurance Co.; Prudential Property & Casualty Insurance Co.; United Farm Bureau Mutual Insurance Co.; United State Fidelity & Guaranty Co.; Vernon Fire & Casualty Insurance Co.; Hastings Mutual Insurance Co.; Milwaukee Insurance Co.; Hartford Insurance; Tracer Trailer, Inc.

For full biographical listings, see the Martindale-Hubbell Law Directory

*MADISON,** Jefferson Co.

COOPER, COX, BARLOW AND JACOBS (AV)

201 East Main Street, 47250-3493
Telephone: 812-273-4440
FAX: 812-273-2329

(See Next Column)

COOPER, COX, BARLOW AND JACOBS, *Madison—Continued*

MEMBERS OF FIRM

Charles W. Cooper
Joe E. Cox
Robert L. Barlow, II
Nancy C. Jacobs

Representative Clients: Indiana-Kentucky Electric Corp.; Indiana Gas Co.; PSI Energy, Inc.; Madison Bank & Trust Co.; Liberty Mutual Insurance Co.; Safeco Insurance Co.; Meridian Mutual Insurance Co.; Farmers Bank of Milton.

For full biographical listings, see the Martindale-Hubbell Law Directory

JENNER & AUXIER (AV)

508 East Main Street, 47250
Telephone: 812-265-5132
Fax: 812-265-5691

MEMBERS OF FIRM

William Edward Jenner
Darrell M. Auxier

ASSOCIATES

Greg May

Representative Clients: United States Fidelity and Guaranty Co.; Morrow Tobacco Warehouse; Madison Consolidated School Corp.; Ohio Valley Opportunities, Inc.; Residential Management Systems, Inc.
Reference: Madison Bank and Trust Co.

*MARION,** Grant Co.

BROWNE, SPITZER, HERRIMAN, STEPHENSON, HOLDEREAD & MUSSER (AV)

One Twenty Two East Fourth Street, P.O. Box 927, 46952-0927
Telephone: 317-664-7307
Fax: 317-662-0574

MEMBERS OF FIRM

James R. Browne (1940-1993)
John R. Browne, Jr.
Herbert A. Spitzer, Jr.
Charles E. Herriman
Phillip E. Stephenson
Jerome T. Holderead
Josef D. Musser
Michael D. Conner

ASSOCIATES

Mark E. Spitzer

OF COUNSEL

Jerry W. Torrance (Semi-Retired)

Representative Clients: State Farm Mutual Insurance Company; United Farm Bureau Mutual Insurance Company; Star Financial Group; Ford Motor Company; Tulox Plastics Corp.

For full biographical listings, see the Martindale-Hubbell Law Directory

*MARTINSVILLE,** Morgan Co.

WEHRLE & SMITH, P.C. (AV)

359 East Morgan Street, P.O. Box 1452, 46151
Telephone: 317-342-7148; 831-5922
FAX: Avaliable Upon Request

William H. Wehrle
Phillip R. Smith

F. Daniel Gettelfinger

For full biographical listings, see the Martindale-Hubbell Law Directory

MERRILLVILLE, Lake Co.

BURKE, MURPHY, COSTANZA & CUPPY (AV)

Suite 600 8585 Broadway, 46410
Telephone: 219-769-1313
Telecopier: 219-769-6806
East Chicago, Indiana Office: First National Bank Building. 720 W. Chicago Avenue.
Telephone: 219-397-2401.
Telecopier: 219-397-0506.
Palm Harbor, Florida Office: Suite 280, 33920 U.S. Highway 19 North.
Telephone: 813-787-7799.
Telecopier: 813-787-7237.

MEMBERS OF FIRM

Edward L. Burke
Lester F. Murphy (East Chicago, Indiana and Palm Harbor, Florida Offices)
Joseph E. Costanza
Frederick M. Cuppy
Gerald K. Hrebec
Andrew J. Kopko
Lambert C. Genetos
George W. Carberry
David K. Ranich
Kathryn D. Schmidt
David Cerven
Demetri J. Retson
Elizabeth P. Moenning

ASSOCIATES

Paula E. Neff
Lily M. Schaefer
Todd A. Etzler
Craig R. Van Schouwen
Stacia L. Yoon
Kevin E. Steele

(See Next Column)

Representative Clients: NBD/Gainer N.A.; Centier Bank; Town of Merrillville; Whiteco Industries; Continental Machine & Engineering Co., Inc.; Gary Steel Products Corp.; Superior Construction Co., Inc.; Federal National Mortgage Association; Morrison Construction Co.; St. Catherine Hospital of East Chicago, Indiana.

For full biographical listings, see the Martindale-Hubbell Law Directory

HODGES & DAVIS, P.C. (AV)

5525 Broadway, 46410
Telephone: 219-981-2557
Fax: 219-980-7090
Portage, Indiana Office: 6508 U.S. Highway 6.
Telephone: 219-762-9129.
Fax: 219-762-2826.

William F. Hodges (1877-1954)
Claude V. Ridgely (1881-1963)
Thomas M. Hodges (1906-1969)
Herschel B. Davis (1901-1990)
Gilbert Gruenberg (1902-1989)
Bruce E. Sayers (1939-1990)
Clyde D. Compton
William B. Davis
Earle F. Hites
R. Lawrence Steele
Gregory A. Sobkowski
Bonnie C. Coleman
Jill M. Madajczyk
Laura B. Brown
David H. Kreider

OF COUNSEL

Edward J. Hussey

Representative Clients: The Methodist Hospitals, Inc.; City of Portage, Indiana; Jewel Cos., Inc.; Osco Drug, Inc.; Porter County Plan Commission.

For full biographical listings, see the Martindale-Hubbell Law Directory

HOEPPNER WAGNER AND EVANS (AV)

Twin Towers, Suite 606 South, 1000 East 80th Place, 46410
Telephone: 219-769-6552; 465-0432
FAX: 219-738-2349
Valparaiso, Indiana Office: 103 East Lincolnway, P.O. Box 2357.
Telephone: 219-464-4961; 769-8995.
Fax: 219-465-0603.

RESIDENT MEMBERS

F. Joseph Jaskowiak

RESIDENT ASSOCIATES

James L. Clement, Jr.
J. Brian Hittinger

For full biographical listings, see the Martindale-Hubbell Law Directory

LUCAS, HOLCOMB & MEDREA (AV)

300 East 90th Drive, 46410
Telephone: 219-769-3561
Fax: 219-756-7409

MEMBERS OF FIRM

James A. Holcomb
John O. Stiles
Daniel A. Medrea
Robert F. Peters
Stephen R. Place
Nick Katich
Mary Linda Casey
Mark S. Lucas

ASSOCIATES

Karen L. Hughes
George S. Brasovan
David E. Woodward
Edward G. Zaknoen

OF COUNSEL

Robert A. Lucas
Robert J. Addison

Representative Clients: Bank One, Merrillville, N. A.; U. S. F. & G. Co.; Montgomery Ward Co.; Calumet Securities Corp. (Mortgage Bankers); Munster Medical Research Foundation, Inc. (Operating "The Community Hospital"); Hammond Clinic.

For full biographical listings, see the Martindale-Hubbell Law Directory

SPANGLER, JENNINGS & DOUGHERTY, P.C. (AV)

8396 Mississippi Street, 46410-6398
Telephone: 219-769-2323
Facsimile: 219-769-5007
Valparaiso, Indiana Office: 150 Lincolnway, Suite 3001.
Telephone: 219-462-6151.
FAX: 219-477-4935.

Ronald T. Spangler
Harry J. Jennings
Patrick J. Dougherty (Valparaiso Office)
Duane V. Stoner (1923-1982)
Samuel J. Furlin
Richard A. Mayer
Jay A. Charon
John P. McQuillan
Samuel J. Bernardi, Jr. (Valparaiso Office)
Jon F. Schmoll
Robert D. Hawk
Joseph E. McDonald
Peter G. Koransky
David J. Hanson
Robert P. Kennedy
Allen B. Zaremba
James T. McNiece
Daniel A. Gioia
James D. McQuillan
David L. Abel, II
Harold G. Hagberg
Lawrence A. Kalina
Robert P. Stoner (Valparaiso Office)
Theresa Lazar Springmann

(See Next Column)

SPANGLER, JENNINGS & DOUGHERTY P.C.—*Continued*

Gregory J. Tonner
Kathleen M. Maicher
Paul B. Poracky
Robert D. Brown
Robert J. Dignam
David R. Phillips
Kristin A. Mulholland
Feisal Amin Istrabadi
Anthony F. Tavitas
Lloyd P. Mullen
Kisti Good Risse
Jeff J. Shaw
Tammy S. Sestak
Terry R. Boesch
Mark D. Geheb
James E. Brammer
Greg A. Bouwer
Ginamarie Gaudio-Graves
Victor H. Prasco
Carl A. Greci
James M. Portelli

OF COUNSEL

Clarence Borns

Representative Clients: Allstate Insurance Cos.; Bank One, Merriville, N.A.; First National Bank of Valparaiso; Ford Motor Credit Co.; Inland Steel Co.; Munster Calumet Shopping Center; School Town of Munster; St. Paul Insurance Cos.; State Farm Cos.; Volkswagen of America.

For full biographical listings, see the Martindale-Hubbell Law Directory

MICHIGAN CITY, La Porte Co.

SWEENEY, DABAGIA, DONOGHUE, THORNE, JANES & PAGOS (AV)

709 Franklin Square, P.O. Box 769, 46360
Telephone: 219-879-5321
Fax: 219-879-2942

MEMBERS OF FIRM

Clarence T. Sweeney (1899-1980)
John H. Sweeney
Lee W. Dabagia
Patrick E. Donoghue
Jeffrey L. Thorne
William Janes
Donald W. Pagos

References: First Citizens Bank, N.A.

For full biographical listings, see the Martindale-Hubbell Law Directory

MISHAWAKA, St. Joseph Co.

SCHINDLER AND OLSON (AV)

122 South Mill Street, P.O. Box 100, 46544
Telephone: 219-259-5461
Fax: 219-259-5462

MEMBERS OF FIRM

John W. Schindler, Jr.
James J. Olson
John W. Schindler (1884-1971)
Leo VanTilbury (1900-1966)

Representative Clients: Penn-Harris-Madison School Corp.; School City of Mishawaka.
Reference: 1st Source Bank of Mishawaka.

For full biographical listings, see the Martindale-Hubbell Law Directory

*MONTICELLO,** White Co. — (Refer to Delphi)

*MT. VERNON,** Posey Co.

HAWLEY, HUDSON & ALMON (AV)

309 Main Street, P.O. Box 716, 47620
Telephone: 812-838-4495

MEMBERS OF FIRM

K. Richard Hawley
Henry C. Hudson
S. Brent Almon
Marc E. Hawley

ASSOCIATES

Beth Ann Folz

Representative Clients: People's Bank & Trust Co., Mt. Vernon; Babcock & Wilcox Co.; General Electric Co., MSD of Mt. Vernon; Continental Grain Co.; Stephans', Inc.; Warehouse Services, Inc.; Mt. Vernon Barge Service, Inc.

For full biographical listings, see the Martindale-Hubbell Law Directory

*MUNCIE,** Delaware Co.

SHIREY, EDWARDS & GLASS (AV)

Century Building, Suite Four, 330 East Main Street, 47305
Telephone: 317-288-0207

MEMBERS OF FIRM

Wayne A. Shirey
Joseph G. Edwards
Todd Irwin Glass

ASSOCIATES

David B. Roesner

Reference: American National Bank & Trust Co.

For full biographical listings, see the Martindale-Hubbell Law Directory

MUNSTER, Lake Co.

LAW OFFICES OF EUGENE M. FEINGOLD (AV)

707 Ridge Road, Suite 204, 46321
Telephone: 219-836-8800
Fax: 219-836-8944

ASSOCIATES

Steven P. Kennedy
Barbara Richards Campbell

For full biographical listings, see the Martindale-Hubbell Law Directory

LAW OFFICES OF TIMOTHY F. KELLY (AV)

Suite 2A, 9250 Columbia Avenue, 46321
Telephone: 219-836-4062
Telecopier: 219-836-0167

MEMBERS OF FIRM

Timothy F. Kelly
Karl K. Vanzo

ASSOCIATES

Harvey Karlovac
Douglas George Amber

LEGAL SUPPORT PERSONNEL
LEGAL ASSISTANTS

Kristen Cook Faso
Kathleen E. Peek

For full biographical listings, see the Martindale-Hubbell Law Directory

*NASHVILLE,** Brown Co. — (Refer to Bloomington)

*NEW ALBANY,** Floyd Co.

MATTOX & MATTOX (AV)

Suite 420 Elsby Building, P.O. Box 1203, 47151-1203
Telephone: 812-944-8005
Facsimile: 812-944-2255

MEMBERS OF FIRM

Richard L. Mattox
S. Frank Mattox

ASSOCIATES

Linda A. Mattox
Derrick H. Wilson
Karen R. Goodwell

Representative Clients: AAOMS National Insurance; Cablelink, Inc.; Floyd Memorial Hospital; John Deere Co.; Kimball International, Inc.; The Medical Protective Co.; Papa Johns Intl., Inc.; PHICO Insurance Co.; Physicians Group, Inc.; Robinson Nugent, Inc.

For full biographical listings, see the Martindale-Hubbell Law Directory

WYATT, TARRANT & COMBS (AV)

(Formerly Orbison, O'Connor, MacGregor & Mattox)
The Elsby Building, 117 East Spring Street, 47150
Telephone: 812-945-3561
Telecopier: 812-949-2524
Louisville, Kentucky Office: Citizens Plaza.
Telephone: 502-589-5235.
Telecopier: 502-589-0309.
Lexington, Kentucky Office: 1700 Lexington Financial Center.
Telephone: 606-233-2012.
Telecopier: 606-259-0649.
Frankfort, Kentucky Office: The Taylor-Scott Building, 311 West Main Street, P.O. Box 495.
Telephone: 502-223-2104.
Telecopier: 502-227-7681.
Nashville, Tennessee Office: 1500 Nashville City Center, 511 Union Street.
Telephone: 615-244-0020.
Telecopier: 615-256-1726.
Music Row Office: 29 Music Square East.
Telephone: 615-255-6161.
Telecopier: 615-254-4490.
Hendersonville, Tennessee Office: 313 E. Main Street, Suite 1.
Telephone: 615-822-8822.
Telecopier: 615-824-4684.

MEMBERS OF FIRM

Telford B. Orbison (1901-1990)
Charles E. MacGregor
James E. Bourne
Thomas W. Sinex
J. Spencer Harmon
Richard A. Bierly
Janet K. Martin

ASSOCIATES

Barbara Wetzel Gernert
John W. Woodard, Jr.

OF COUNSEL

Richard C. O'Connor

Representative Clients: Allstate Insurance Co.; Amoco Oil Co.; Ford Motor Credit Corp.; Green Banner Publications, Inc.; Gettelfinger Popcorn Company, Inc.; Joe Huber Farms, Inc.; Indiana Bell Telephone Co.; Province of Our Lady of Consolation, Inc.; Public Service Indiana; United Farm Bureau Mutual Insurance Co.

For full biographical listings, see the Martindale-Hubbell Law Directory

*NEW CASTLE,** Henry Co.

Scotten & Hinshaw (AV)

214 South Main Street, 47362-4286
Telephone: 317-529-2100
Fax: 317-529-3532

MEMBERS OF FIRM

E. G. Scotten (1877-1957)
J. R. Hinshaw (1883-1970)
James R. Stanley (1910-1980)
R. Scott Hayes
David L. Copenhaver
Gregory L. Crider

OF COUNSEL

George W. Hand

General Counsel For: Ameriana Savings Bank.
Representative Clients: Farm Bureau Mutual Insurance Co.; General Accident & Indemnity Co.; City of New Castle.

For full biographical listings, see the Martindale-Hubbell Law Directory

NEW HAVEN, Allen Co. — (Refer to Ft. Wayne)

*NEWPORT,** Vermillion Co. — (Refer to Brazil)

*NOBLESVILLE,** Hamilton Co.

Campbell Kyle Proffitt (AV)

198 South Ninth Street, P.O. Box 2020, 46060-2020
Telephone: 317-773-2090
FAX: 317-776-5051
Carmel, Indiana Office: Suite 400, 650 East Carmel Drive.
Telephone: 317-846-6514.
Fax: 317-843-8097.

MEMBERS OF FIRM

Frank S. Campbell (1880-1964)
Frank W. Campbell (1916-1991)
John M. Kyle
John D. Proffitt (Resident, Carmel Office)
Robert F. Campbell (Resident, Carmel Office)
Jeffrey S. Nickloy
Deborah L. Farmer (Resident, Carmel Office)
William E. Wendling, Jr. (Resident, Carmel Office)
Anne Hensley Poindexter (Resident, Carmel Office)

ASSOCIATES

Christine Crull Altman (Resident, Carmel Office)
Andrew M. Barker
Karen R. McClure
Todd L. Ruetz (Resident, Carmel Office)

Representative Clients: Bridgestone/Firestone Inc.; Indiana Bell Telephone Co.; Statesman Insurance Group; Mobil Oil Corp.; PSI Energy, Inc.

For full biographical listings, see the Martindale-Hubbell Law Directory

Church, Church, Hittle & Antrim (AV)

938 Conner Street, P.O. Box 10, 46060-0010
Telephone: 317-773-2190
Telecopier: 317-773-5320

MEMBERS OF FIRM

Manson E. Church
Douglas D. Church
Jack G. Hittle
J. Michael Antrim
Martin E. Risacher
Bruce M. Bittner

ASSOCIATES

Brian J. Zaiger
David Joseph Barker
Leslie Craig Henderzahs

OF COUNSEL

Gary D. Beerbower

Representative Clients: Noblesville Schools; Westfield-Washington Schools; Indiana School Finance Corp.; Community Bank; Metrobank; Towns of Westfield, Fishers and Noblesville; Reynolds Farm Equipment Co.; Weihe Engineering.

For full biographical listings, see the Martindale-Hubbell Law Directory

NORTH VERNON, Jennings Co.

McConnell and Finnerty (AV)

38 North 5th Street, P.O. Box 90, 47265
Telephone: 812-346-5201
FAX: 812-346-8470

MEMBERS OF FIRM

Ira B. Hamilton (1899-1982)
Harold H. McConnell
Corinne R. Finnerty

ASSOCIATES

Alan L. Marshall

Representative Clients: Union Bank & Trust Co.; Farm Bureau Mutual Insurance Co.; Home Federal Savings Bank; Lees Inns of America, Inc.; Rose Acre Farms, Inc.; Pekin Insurance.

For full biographical listings, see the Martindale-Hubbell Law Directory

*PAOLI,** Orange Co.

Tucker and Tucker (AV)

188 South Court Street, 47454
Telephone: 812-723-2313
Fax: 812-723-3789

James L. Tucker (1873-1960)
James C. Tucker

OF COUNSEL

James M. Tucker

Counsel for: Orange County Bank; Bank of Orleans; Springs Valley Bank and Trust Co.; First National Bank of Paoli; Town of Paoli; The Orleans Community Schools; The Springs Valley Community Schools; Paoli Community Schools; Reynolds, Inc.
Local Counsel for: Kimball International, Inc.; Texas Eastern Transmission Co.

*PETERSBURG,** Pike Co. — (Refer to Vincennes)

*PLYMOUTH,** Marshall Co.

Kizer & Neu (AV)

319 West Jefferson Street, P.O. Box 158, 46563
Telephone: 219-936-2169
FAX: 219-936-2642
Bremen, Indiana Office: 1406 West Plymouth Street, P.O. Box 158.
Telephone: 219-546-2626.
FAX: 219-546-2608.

MEMBERS OF FIRM

Marshall F. Kizer (1907-1988)
James H. Neu (1917-1991)
Richard F. Joyce
Harold L. Wyland
Jere L. Humphrey
Mark E. Wagner (Resident at Bremen)
Ronald D. Gifford
James N. Clevenger

Counsel for: The First State Bank, Bourbon, Indiana; 1st Source Bank of Marshall County; Prudential Insurance Company of America; Bremen Castings, Inc.; Bornemann Products, Inc.; Universal Bearings, Inc., all of Bremen, Indiana; Society Bank, South Bend, Indiana; 4th District Farm Credit Services.

For full biographical listings, see the Martindale-Hubbell Law Directory

PORTAGE, Porter Co.

Hodges & Davis, P.C. (AV)

6508 U.S. Highway 6, 46368
Telephone: 219-762-9129
Fax: 219-762-2826
Merrillville, Indiana Office: 5525 Broadway.
Telephone: 219-981-2557.
Fax: 219-980-7090.

Clyde D. Compton
Earle F. Hites
R. Lawrence Steele
Gregory A. Sobkowski
Bonnie C. Coleman

Representative Clients: The Methodist Hospitals, Inc.; City of Portage, Indiana; Jewel Cos., Inc.; Osco Drug, Inc.; Porter County Plan Commission.

For full biographical listings, see the Martindale-Hubbell Law Directory

*PORTLAND,** Jay Co. — (Refer to Fort Wayne)

*PRINCETON,** Gibson Co.

Hall, Partenheimer & Kinkle (AV)

219 North Hart Street, P.O. Box 313, 47670
Telephone: 812-386-0050
FAX: 812-385-2575

MEMBERS OF FIRM

Verner P. Partenheimer
J. Robert Kinkle
R. Scott Partenheimer

Representative Clients: Interlake Inc.; Gibson County Bank; Old Ben Coal Co.
Approved Attorneys for: Lawyers Title Insurance; Ticor Title Insurance.

For full biographical listings, see the Martindale-Hubbell Law Directory

*RISING SUN,** Ohio Co. — (Refer to Lawrenceburg)

*ROCHESTER,** Fulton Co. — (Refer to Plymouth)

*ROCKVILLE,** Parke Co. — (Refer to Terre Haute)

*RUSHVILLE,** Rush Co.

Earnest, Foster, Eder, Levi & Northam (AV)

114 West Third Street, P.O. Box 430, 46173
Telephone: 317-932-4118
Fax: 317-932-4486

OF COUNSEL

Kenneth L. Earnest
James S. Foster

(See Next Column)

EARNEST, FOSTER, EDER, LEVI & NORTHAM—*Continued*

MEMBERS OF FIRM

Robert J. Eder
Richard K. Levi
David E. Northam

Representative Clients: Rush County REMC; First Federal Savings and Loan Association of Rushville; Rush Memorial Hospital; Farm Bureau Insurance Co.; Farmers State Bank; The Sampler, Inc.; Ticor Title Insurance Co.

For full biographical listings, see the Martindale-Hubbell Law Directory

*SALEM,** Washington Co.

MEAD, MEAD & THOMPSON (AV)

Mead Building, 108 East Market, P.O. Box 468, 47167
Telephone: 812-883-4693
Fax: 812-883-2207

MEMBERS OF FIRM

Walter G. Mead (1879-1976)
Willis C. Mead (1914-1992)
John W. Mead
Trent Thompson

ASSOCIATE

Mark D. Clark

A List of References will be furnished upon Request.

For full biographical listings, see the Martindale-Hubbell Law Directory

*SCOTTSBURG,** Scott Co.

THOMAS E. EVERITT, P.C. (AV)

59 1/2 East Wardell, 47170
Telephone: 812-752-7190

Thomas E. Everitt

For full biographical listings, see the Martindale-Hubbell Law Directory

HOUSTON AND THOMPSON, P.C. (AV)

49 East Wardell Street, 47170
Telephone: 812-752-5920
Fax: 812-752-6989

Robert L. Houston, III
Kerry L. Thompson

References: Liberty National Bank & Trust Company of Indiana; Scott County State Bank.

For full biographical listings, see the Martindale-Hubbell Law Directory

*SHELBYVILLE,** Shelby Co.

ADAMS & CRAMER (AV)

33 West Washington Street, 46176
Telephone: 317-398-6626
FAX: 317-392-1962

Ralph Adams (1901-1986)

MEMBERS OF FIRM

Fred V. Cramer
Robert W. Adams

ASSOCIATES

David A. Mack (Not admitted in IN)

Counsel for: Mickey's T-Mart; Town of Morristown, Indiana; Southwestern Consolidated Schools; Brewer Design Services; Fiddler's Three.

For full biographical listings, see the Martindale-Hubbell Law Directory

*SHOALS,** Martin Co. — (Refer to Jasper)

*SOUTH BEND,** St. Joseph Co.

BAKER & DANIELS (AV)

First Bank Building, 205 West Jefferson Boulevard, 46601
Telephone: 219-234-4149
Fax: 219-239-1900
Indianapolis, Indiana Office: 300 North Meridian Street.
Telephone: 317-237-0300.
Fort Wayne, Indiana Office: 2400 Fort Wayne National Bank Building.
Telephone: 219-424-8000.
Elkhart, Indiana Office: 301 South Main Street, Suite 307.
Telephone: 219-296-6000.
Washington, D.C. Office: 1701 K Street, N.W., Suite 400.
Telephone: 202-785-1565.

MEMBERS OF FIRM

Ronald J. Jaicomo (Resident)
James D. Hall (Resident)
Thomas J. Brunner, Jr. (Resident)
Richard L. Hill (Resident)
James M. Matthews
Peter G. Trybula
Paul J. Peralta (Resident)

RESIDENT OF COUNSEL

Ken C. Decker

(See Next Column)

ASSOCIATES

Mary Ann Boulac (Resident)
Randolph R. Rompola (Resident)
Robert A. Wade
Amy Lawrence Mader (Resident)
Kevin Doyle O'Rear (Resident)

Representative Clients: City of South Bend; 1st Source Bank; Jack-Post Corp.; Society Corp.; South Bend Drug Co.; WSBT, Inc.; General Motors Corp.; Indiana Bell; Eli Lilly and Company; Borg-Warner Corporation.

For full biographical listings, see the Martindale-Hubbell Law Directory

DIAMOND AND DIAMOND (AV)

405 West Wayne Street, P.O. Box 1875, 46634-1875
Telephone: 219-232-6918

Arthur M. Diamond
Eric L. Diamond
Jeffrey M. Jankowski

Representative Clients: Creed Excavating Co., Inc.; Eslinger Furniture & Appliances, Inc.; Ideal Consolidated, Inc.; International Bakers Service, Inc.; Lithotone Inc.; Louie's Tux Shop, Inc.; Portage Realty Corp.; Radiology, Inc.; Van Overberghe Builders, Inc.
References: Norwest Bank Indiana, N.A., South Bend.

For full biographical listings, see the Martindale-Hubbell Law Directory

EDWARD N. KALAMAROS & ASSOCIATES PROFESSIONAL CORPORATION (AV)

129 North Michigan Avenue, P.O. Box 4156, 46634
Telephone: 219-232-4801
Telecopier: 219-232-9736

Edward N. Kalamaros
Timothy J. Walsh
Thomas F. Cohen
Joseph M. Forte
Robert Deane Woods
Peter J. Agostino
Patrick J. Hinkle
Bernard E. Edwards
Philip E. Kalamaros
Sally P. Norton
Kevin W. Kearney
Lynn E. Arnold

Representative Clients: South Bend Medical Foundation, Inc.; Powell Tool Supply, Inc.; Cooper Industries/Anco Division; Orthopedic & Sports Medicine Center of Northern Indiana, Inc.; Edward J. DeBartolo Corporation; University Park Mall; Marriott Corporation; Employers Reinsurance Corporation; Orion Group.

For full biographical listings, see the Martindale-Hubbell Law Directory

ROWE, FOLEY & GARDNER (AV)

Suite 900 Society Bank Building, 46601
Telephone: 219-233-8200

R. Kent Rowe
R. Kent Rowe, III
Edmond W. Foley
Martin J. Gardner

ASSOCIATES

Gregory J. Haines
Timothy J. Maher
Lee Korzan
Steven D. Groth
Evan S. Roberts
William James O'Mahony

For full biographical listings, see the Martindale-Hubbell Law Directory

*SPENCER,** Owen Co.

CHARLES W. EDWARDS (AV)

64 East Market Street, P.O. Box 108, 47460
Telephone: 812-829-2209
FAX: 812-829-2200

Approved Attorney for: Ticor Title Insurance Co.
Reference: Owen County State Bank.

For full biographical listings, see the Martindale-Hubbell Law Directory

*SULLIVAN,** Sullivan Co. — (Refer to Terre Haute)

*TERRE HAUTE,** Vigo Co.

COX, ZWERNER, GAMBILL & SULLIVAN (AV)

511 Wabash Avenue, P.O. Box 1625, 47808-1625
Telephone: 812-232-6003
Fax: 812-232-6567

MEMBERS OF FIRM

Ernest J. Zwerner (1918-1980)
Benjamin G. Cox (1915-1988)
Gilbert W. Gambill, Jr.
James E. Sullivan
Benjamin G. Cox, Jr.
David W. Sullivan
Robert L. Gowdy
Louis F. Britton
Robert D. Hepburn
Carroll D. Smeltzer
Jeffry A. Lind

ASSOCIATES

Ronald E. Jumps

Counsel for: Terre Haute First National Bank; Farmers Insurance Group; Indiana-American Water Co.; Indiana State University; Merchants National Bank of Terre Haute; Rose-Hulman Institute of Technology; Tribune-Star Publishing Co., Inc.; Weston Paper & Manufacturing Co.

For full biographical listings, see the Martindale-Hubbell Law Directory

DAY SWANGO BRATTAIN & NATTKEMPER (AV)

322 South Sixth Street, P.O. Box 1444, 47808
Telephone: 812-232-9571
Fax: 812-234-1688

MEMBERS OF FIRM

Howard T. Batman (1906-1985) J. Morton Swango (1913-1990)
David I. Day, Jr. (1914-1990) George A. Brattain
C. Don Nattkemper

ASSOCIATES

David R. Bolk

Representative Clients: Terre Haute Savings Bank; Wabash Valley Broadcasting Corp; Indianapolis Motor Speedway Corp.; Texas Gas Transmission Corp.; The Morris Plan Company of Terre Haute, Inc.
Approved Title Attorneys for: Ticor Title Insurance Co.

For full biographical listings, see the Martindale-Hubbell Law Directory

LEWIS AND LEWIS (AV)

629 Cherry Street, P.O. Box 1506, 47808
Telephone: 812-232-2382
Fax: 812-232-2383

MEMBERS OF FIRM

Jerdie D. Lewis (1904-1993) Michael J. Lewis
Jordan D. Lewis Elizabeth Lewis Rodway

Representative Clients: United Farm Bureau Mutual Insurance Companies; Consolidated Rail Corp.; The Statesman Group; Sentry Insurance Co.; General Casualty Cos.; Inter-Insurance Exchange of the Chicago Motor Club.
Reference: The Merchants National Bank of Terre Haute, Indiana.

For full biographical listings, see the Martindale-Hubbell Law Directory

WILKINSON, GOELLER, MODESITT, WILKINSON & DRUMMY (AV)

333 Ohio Street, P.O. Box 800, 47808-0800
Telephone: 812-232-4311
Fax: 812-235-5107

MEMBERS OF FIRM

Myrl O. Wilkinson Kelvin L. Roots
David H. Goeller John C. Wall
Raymond H. Modesitt William M. Olah
B. Curtis Wilkinson Craig M. McKee
William W. Drummy Scott M. Kyrouac
Jeffrey A. Boyll

ASSOCIATES

David P. Friedrich Anthony R. Jost

Representative Corporate Clients: Merchants National Bank; Owens Corning Fiberglass; CSX, Inc.; General Housewares Corp.; MAB Paints; Chicago Title Insurance Co.; Terre Haute Board of Realtors; Union Hospital; Associated Physicians and Surgeons Clinic, Inc.; PSI Energy, Inc.

For full biographical listings, see the Martindale-Hubbell Law Directory

*TIPTON,** Tipton Co. — (Refer to Kokomo)

*VALPARAISO,** Porter Co.

BLACHLY, TABOR, BOZIK & HARTMAN (AV)

Suite 401 Indiana Federal Building, 46383
Telephone: 219-464-1041

MEMBERS OF FIRM

Quentin A. Blachly David L. Hollenbeck
Glenn J. Tabor David L. DeBoer
James S. Bozik Thomas F. Macke
Duane W. Hartman Randall J. Zromkoski
Richard J. Rupcich

ASSOCIATES

Roger A. Weitgenant Timothy E. Balko

Reference: First National Bank.

For full biographical listings, see the Martindale-Hubbell Law Directory

DOUGLAS, ALEXA, KOEPPEN & HURLEY (AV)

14 Indiana Avenue, P.O. Box 209, 46384-0209
Telephone: 219-462-2126
Fax: 219-477-4408

MEMBERS OF FIRM

Herbert K. Douglas R. Bradley Koeppen
William E. Alexa Brian J. Hurley

ASSOCIATE

Mark A. Gland

(See Next Column)

OF COUNSEL

George W. Douglas Leo J. Clifford

Attorneys for: Urschel Laboratories, Inc.; Northern Indiana Public Service Co.; Midwest Steel Division, National Steel; McGill Manufacturing Co., Inc.; Park District, City of Valparaiso.

For full biographical listings, see the Martindale-Hubbell Law Directory

HOEPPNER WAGNER AND EVANS (AV)

103 East Lincolnway, P.O. Box 2357, 46384-2357
Telephone: 219-464-4961; 769-8995
Fax: 219-465-0603
Merrillville, Indiana Office: Twin Towers, Suite 606 South, 1000 East 80th Place.
Telephone: 219-769-6552. Porter County: 219-465-0432.
Fax: 219-738-2349.

RETIRED

Delmar R. Hoeppner (Retired)

MEMBERS OF FIRM

William H. Wagner James L. Jorgensen
Larry G. Evans Ronald P. Kuker
William F. Satterlee, III Richard A. Browne
Gordon A. Etzler F. Joseph Jaskowiak
John E. Hughes (Resident, Merrillville Office)
Morris A. Sunkel Richard M. Davis
James A. Cheslek Mark E. Schmidtke

ASSOCIATES

Todd A. Leeth Jonathan R. Hanson
Michael P. Blaize Robert L. Clark
Mary Jill Sisson J. Brian Hittinger
Heidi B. Jark Lauren K. Kroeger
James L. Clement, Jr. Jeffrey W. Clymer
(Resident, Merrillville Office)

Attorneys for: Bethlehem Steel Corp.; Chester, Inc.; Hunt-Wesson Foods, Inc.; NBD Gainer; Owens-Corning Fiberglas Corp.; Valparaiso University; State Farm Insurance; Allstate Insurance Co.

For full biographical listings, see the Martindale-Hubbell Law Directory

SPANGLER, JENNINGS & DOUGHERTY, P.C. (AV)

150 Lincolnway, Suite 3001, 46303
Telephone: 219-462-6151
FAX: 219-477-4935
Merrillville, Indiana Office: 8396 Mississippi Street.
Telephone: 219-769-2323.

RESIDENT PERSONNEL

Patrick J. Dougherty Samuel J. Bernardi, Jr.
Duane V. Stoner (1923-1982) Robert P. Stoner

Jeff J. Shaw James E. Brammer

Reference: First National Bank of Valparaiso.

For full biographical listings, see the Martindale-Hubbell Law Directory

LAW OFFICES OF JAMES V. TSOUTSOURIS (AV)

Five Lincolnway, 46383
Telephone: 219-462-4148
Fax: 219-477-4932

ASSOCIATES

Joann Tsoutsouris John Edward Martin
G. Anthony Bertig Lori L. Ferngren

A list of Representative Clients and References will be furnished upon request.

For full biographical listings, see the Martindale-Hubbell Law Directory

*VERSAILLES,** Ripley Co.

EATON & ROMWEBER (AV)

123 South Main Street, P.O. Box 275, 47042
Telephone: 812-689-5111
Fax: 812-689-5165
Batesville, Indiana Office: 13 East George Street. Telephone 812-934-5735.
Fax: 812-934-6041.

MEMBERS OF FIRM

Larry L. Eaton Anthony A. Romweber

ASSOCIATES

W. Gregory Coy

For full biographical listings, see the Martindale-Hubbell Law Directory

*VINCENNES,** Knox Co.

EMISON, DOOLITTLE, KOLB & ROELLGEN (AV)

Eighth & Busseron Streets, P.O. Box 215, 47591
Telephone: 812-882-2280
FAX: 812-885-2308

(See Next Column)

EMISON, DOOLITTLE, KOLB & ROELLGEN—*Continued*

MEMBERS OF FIRM

Rabb Emison
Robert P. Doolittle, Jr.
Jeffrey B. Kolb
J. David Roellgen

Clients Include: Security Bank & Trust Co.; Sun-Commercial Newspaper; Amoco Pipeline; Tenneco; United Farm Bureau Mutual Insurance Co.

For full biographical listings, see the Martindale-Hubbell Law Directory

HART, BELL, DEEM, EWING & STUCKEY (AV)

513 Main Street, P.O. Box 979, 47591
Telephone: 812-882-8935

Clarence B. Kessinger (1859-1940)
William H. Hill (1876-1942)

OF COUNSEL

Arthur L. Hart

MEMBERS OF FIRM

Donald G. Bell
David A. Deem
Nathaniel Mark Ewing
H. Brent Stuckey

ASSOCIATE

Thomas W. Washburne

General Counsel for: First Federal Bank, a Federal Savings Bank; Security Bank & Trust Co.; Vincennes University; Good Samaritan Hospital; H.G. Heinz, Inc.; McKim's Foods, Inc.
District or Local Counsel for: Prudential Insurance Co.; Shelter Insurance; Indiana Insurance Co.
Local Counsel for: CSX Transportation, Inc.

For full biographical listings, see the Martindale-Hubbell Law Directory

*WABASH,** Wabash Co. — (Refer to Huntington)

*WARSAW,** Kosciusko Co.

HARRIS & HARRIS (AV)

222 North Buffalo Street, 46580
Telephone: 219-267-2111
Fax: 219-268-2277

Philip J. Harris
Stephen P. Harris
Marcus Kosins, Jr.

Representative Clients: Mutual Federal Savings Bank; Akron Foundry, Inc.; Bertsch Food Service Co.; Carey Realty, Inc.; Miller & Sons Structures, Inc.; Patona Bay Boat Service; Union Tool Corp.; Sun Metal Products, Inc.; Warsaw Plating Works, Inc.; U.C.C. Coffee Company (Japan).

For full biographical listings, see the Martindale-Hubbell Law Directory

LEMON, REED, ARMEY, HEARN & LEININGER (AV)

210 North Buffalo Street, P.O. Box 770, 46581-0770
Telephone: 219-268-9111
Telecopier: 219-267-8647

MEMBERS OF FIRM

Thomas R. Lemon
Rex L. Reed
Michael E. Armey
R. Steven Hearn
Daniel K. Leininger

ASSOCIATES

Jane L. Kauffman
Katharine Mull Carter

OF COUNSEL

Robert L. Rasor

Representative Clients: Lake City Bank; Zimmer Inc.; The Dalton Foundries, Inc.; Grace Schools, Inc.; Kosciusko Community Hospital, Inc.; Othy, Inc.

For full biographical listings, see the Martindale-Hubbell Law Directory

*WASHINGTON,** Daviess Co. — (Refer to Vincennes)

*WILLIAMSPORT,** Warren Co. — (Refer to Covington)

*WINAMAC,** Pulaski Co. — (Refer to Logansport)

*WINCHESTER,** Randolph Co. — (Refer to Richmond)

IOWA

*ADEL,** Dallas Co. — (Refer to Dallas Center)

*ALBIA,** Monroe Co. — (Refer to Ottumwa)

*ALGONA,** Kossuth Co. — (Refer to Ft. Dodge)

AMES, Story Co.

NEWBROUGH, JOHNSTON, BREWER, MADDUX AND NADLER (AV)
612 Kellogg Avenue, P.O. Box 847, 50010
Telephone: 515-232-1761
Fax: 515-232-8962

MEMBERS OF FIRM

D. R. Newbrough
Frank B. Johnston
James A. Brewer
Jere C. Maddux
Barry Nadler

ASSOCIATES

Deborah S. Krauth
Todd M. Boothroyd

Local Counsel: Todd & Sargent, Inc.; Ames Community School District; Ames Daily Tribune-Times, Inc.; Continental Western Insurance Co.; American Home Assurance Co.; New Hampshire Insurance Group; Economy Fire & Casualty Co.; The American Home Group.

For full biographical listings, see the Martindale-Hubbell Law Directory

SINGER, PASLEY, HOLM, TIMMONS, MATHISON & CURTIS (AV)
323 Sixth Street, P.O. Box 664, 50010
Telephone: 515-232-4732
Fax: 515-232-4756

MEMBERS OF FIRM

William A. Singer
Clarke A. Pasley
Stevan A. Holm
John L. Timmons
Jane Melson Mathison
Larry R. Curtis

References available upon request.

For full biographical listings, see the Martindale-Hubbell Law Directory

SMITH, SHARP, BENSON, JAHN & FEILMEYER (AV)
618 Douglas, P.O. Box 270, 50010-0270
Telephone: 515-239-5000
Fax: 515-239-5010

MEMBERS OF FIRM

John E. Nutty (Retired)
Donald L. Smith
Dale E. Sharp
David W. Benson
Lawrence E. Jahn
Franklin J. Feilmeyer

References: First National Bank, Ames, Iowa; Brenton Savings Bank, FSB.

For full biographical listings, see the Martindale-Hubbell Law Directory

*ANAMOSA,** Jones Co. — (Refer to Cedar Rapids)

*ATLANTIC,** Cass Co.

CAMBRIDGE, FEILMEYER, LANDSNESS, CHASE & JONES (AV)
707 Poplar Street, P.O. Box 496, 50022
Telephone: 712-243-1663
Fax: 712-243-3799
Griswold, Iowa Office: 206 Montgomery Street.
Telephone: 712-778-2776.
Massena, Iowa Office: 207 Main Street.
Telephone: 712-779-3735.

Boyd M. Cambridge (1908-1990)
Ronald W. Feilmeyer
Roland K. Landsness
David W. Chase
Lawrence S. Jones

Representative Clients: First Whitney Bank & Trust, Atlantic, Iowa; Walnut Grove Products Division of W.R. Grace & Co.; Travelers Ins.; Farm Bureau Mutual Insurance Co.; Norwest Bank Iowa, N.A.; Grinnell Mutual Insurance Co.; Cass County Memorial Hospital; Atlantic Community School District.

For full biographical listings, see the Martindale-Hubbell Law Directory

*AUDUBON,** Audubon Co. — (Refer to Atlantic)

*BEDFORD,** Taylor Co. — (Refer to Mt. Ayr)

BETTENDORF, Scott Co.

WELLS, GALLAGHER, ROEDER & MILLAGE (AV)
(Not a Partnership)
1989 Spruce Hills Drive, 52722
Telephone: 319-355-5303
Fax: 319-359-7711

Robert D. Wells (1904-1990)
Robert H. Gallagher
Michael L. Roeder
David A. Millage

(See Next Column)

Matthew D. Hatch

For full biographical listings, see the Martindale-Hubbell Law Directory

*BLOOMFIELD,** Davis Co. — (Refer to Ottumwa)

*BURLINGTON,** Des Moines Co. — (Refer to Fort Madison)

*CARROLL,** Carroll Co.

BRUNER & BRUNER (AV)
225 East Seventh Street, 51401
Telephone: 712-792-3480
Fax: 712-792-6981

MEMBERS OF FIRM

Robert S. Bruner
Barry T. Bruner

Represents: Principal Mutual Life Insurance Co., Des Moines, Iowa; Metropolitan Life Insurance Co.; Carroll County State Bank; Farner-Bocken Co.; City of Halbur; F & H Foods; Carroll Manufacturing, Inc.; Region XII Council of Governments; Auen Distributing Co.

NEU, MINNICH, COMITO & HALL, P.C. (AV)
721 North Main Street, 51401
Telephone: 712-792-3508
Fax: 712-792-3563
Glidden, Iowa Office: 118 Idaho Street.
Telephone: 712-659-3740.

G. Arthur Minnich (1920-1984)
Arthur A. Neu
Jeffrey R. Minnich
Frank J. Comito
Patrick W. Hall

Represent: First Federal Savings Bank; Farm Bureau Mutual Insurance Co.; American Family Insurance Group; Iowa Kemper Insurance Co.; Grinnell Mutual Reinsurance Co.; Economy Fire and Casualty Co.

For full biographical listings, see the Martindale-Hubbell Law Directory

CEDAR FALLS, Black Hawk Co.

REDFERN, MASON, DIETER, LARSEN & MOORE (AV)
315 Clay Street, P.O. Box 627, 50613
Telephone: 319-277-6830
Facsimile: 319-277-3531

MEMBERS OF FIRM

James B. Newman (1870-1958)
George F. Newman (1908-1988)
William W. McKinley (1926-1981)
LeRoy H. Redfern
David R. Mason
Robert J. Dieter
John C. Larsen
Steven D. Moore
Donald B. Redfern
Mark W. Fransdal
Mark S. Rolinger

ASSOCIATES

Susan Bernau Staudt

Representative Clients: Norwest Bank Iowa; The National Bank of Waterloo; Don R. Havens Co.; Control-O-fax Corp.; Cedar Falls Community School District; University of Northern Iowa Foundation; United States Fidelity and Guaranty Co.; The Travelers Insurance Cos.; Fireman's Fund Insurance Companies.

For full biographical listings, see the Martindale-Hubbell Law Directory

*CEDAR RAPIDS,** Linn Co.

LYNCH, DALLAS, SMITH & HARMAN, P.C. (AV)
526 Second Avenue SE, P.O. Box 2457, 52406-2457
Telephone: 319-365-9101
Facsimile: 319-365-9512

Charles J. Lynch (1905-1983)
William M. Dallas (1905-1981)
Ralph V. Harman (Retired)
Donald E. Smith
Donald G. Ribble
H. Edward Beatty
Gerald Lyell Fatka
Scott E. McLeod
Robert R. Rush
John M. Titler
Hugo C. Burdt
Edward J. Krug
Wilford H. Stone
Sean W. McPartland
Matthew J. Nagle

Jana L. Happel
Elizabeth D. Jacobi
Thomas D. Wolle

Representative Clients: American States Insurance Co.; Blue Cross and Blue Shield of Iowa; Chicago Central & Pacific Railroad Co.; Deere & Co.; Electric Mutual Insurance Co.; Farm Credit Bank of Omaha; Rockwell International Corp.; State Farm Insurance Cos.; The Travelers Insurance Cos.

For full biographical listings, see the Martindale-Hubbell Law Directory

SHUTTLEWORTH & INGERSOLL, P.C. (AV)
500 Firstar Bank Building, P.O. Box 2107, 52406-2107
Telephone: 319-365-9461
Fax: 319-365-8443

(See Next Column)

SHUTTLEWORTH & INGERSOLL P.C.—*Continued*

Thomas M. Collins
James C. Nemmers
Michael O. McDermott
John M. Bickel
Robert D. Houghton
Richard S. Fry
Richard C. Garberson
Gary J. Streit
Carroll J. Reasoner
Steven J. Pace
Glenn L. Johnson
Thomas P. Peffer
Kevin H. Collins
William P. Prowell
Diane Kutzko
Mark L. Zaiger
Douglas R. Oelschlaeger
Constance M. Alt
William S. Hochstetler
Kurt L. Kratovil

LeeAnn M. Ferry
Christine L. McLaughlin
William H. Courter
Dean D. Carrington
Nancy J. Penner

OF COUNSEL

Ralph W. Gearhart
W. R. Shuttleworth

COUNSEL

Joan Lipsky
James D. Hodges, Jr.
Theodore J. Collins

Representative Clients: Amana Society; Archer-Daniels-Midland Co.; Cargill, Inc.; Cryovac, Inc., a Division of W. R. Grace & Co.; Firstar Bank Cedar Rapids, N.A.; General Mills, Inc.; General Motors Corp.; MCI; PMX Industries, Inc.; Rockwell International - Graphic Systems Division.

For full biographical listings, see the Martindale-Hubbell Law Directory

SIMMONS, PERRINE, ALBRIGHT & ELLWOOD, L.L.P. (AV)

A Partnership including a Professional Corporation
115 Third Street S.E. Suite 1200, 52401
Telephone: 319-366-7641
Telecopier: 319-366-1917 (I,II,III)

RETIRED

Justin W. Albright

PARTNERS

Haven Y. Simmons (1888-1975)
Beahl T. Perrine (1902-1989)
James R. Snyder
Darrel A. Morf
James E. Shipman
Stephen J. Holtman
Robert M. Jilek (P.C.)
Iris E. Muchmore
Dennis J. McMenimen
Gregory M. Lederer
James A. Gerk
Richard G. Hileman, Jr.
Roger W. Stone
David A. Hacker
Dean R. Einck
David W. Kubicek
Linda M. Kirsch
Matthew J. Petrzelka
Matthew J. Brandes
James M. Peters

ASSOCIATES

Winfrid Schellin
Leonard T. Strand
Gilda L. Boyer
Lon D. Moeller
Donald R. Schoonover
Webb L. Wassmer
Michael J. Frey
Jeffrey T. Ramsey
Mark A. Roberts
Chad M. Von Kampen

COUNSEL

Larry D. Helvey

OF COUNSEL

William P. Ellwood
John R. Carpenter

Representative Clients: Amana Refrigeration, Inc.; Norwest Bank Iowa, N.A.; Sheaffer Pen; Weyerhaeuser Co.; Grand Wood Area Education Agency; Howard R. Green Co.; Varied Investments, Inc.; Norand Corp.; Universal Gym Equipment Co.; Hall Foundation.

For full biographical listings, see the Martindale-Hubbell Law Directory

*CENTERVILLE,** Appanoose Co. — (Refer to Ottumwa)

*CHARITON,** Lucas Co. — (Refer to Knoxville)

*CHEROKEE,** Cherokee Co.

HERRICK, ARY, COOK, COOK, COOK & COOK (AV)

209 West Willow Street, P.O. Box 209, 51012
Telephone: 712-225-5175
FAX: 712-225-5178

MEMBERS OF FIRM

William K. Herrick (1878-1944)
Lester C. Ary (1893-1962)
John Howard Cook
John H. Cook, Jr.
Richard Ary Cook
William D. Cook

Attorneys for: Cherokee State Bank; Cherokee Community School District; Lundell Construction Co., Inc.; Tiel Sanford Memorial Fund; Simonsen Mill Inc.; Sioux Valley Memorial Hospital; Obeco Inc.; Christensen Brothers Concrete.

For full biographical listings, see the Martindale-Hubbell Law Directory

SAYRE & WITTGRAF (AV)

223 Pine Street, P.O. Box 535, 51012
Telephone: 712-225-6481
FAX: 712-225-5300

(See Next Column)

MEMBERS OF FIRM

Lew McDonald (1884-1963)
David L. Sayre
George W. Wittgraf

Representative Clients: Central Trust and Savings Bank, Cherokee, Iowa; Wilson Foods Corp.; Grundman-Hicks Construction Co., Inc.; C-M-L Telephone Cooperative Association of Meriden, Iowa; Jesse's Fine Meats, Inc.; Beck Ranch Inc.; Continental Western Insurance Co.; United Fire and Casualty Co.

For full biographical listings, see the Martindale-Hubbell Law Directory

*CLARINDA,** Page Co.

TURNER, JONES & BITTING (AV)

301 East Main Street, P.O. Box 231, 51632
Telephone: 712-542-2151
FAX: 712-542-2031

MEMBERS OF FIRM

Clinton H. Turner (1909-1969)
Sanford A. Turner
Paul W. Jones
Ronny M. Bitting

Representative Clients: Citizens State Bank, Clarinda, Iowa; City of Clarinda; South Page School District; Cities of Coin, Braddyville, Shambaugh, Blanchard and Northboro, Iowa; Lisle Corp., Clarinda, Iowa; Page County Savings & Loan Assn.
References: Citizens State Bank; Page County State Bank of Clarinda, Iowa.

For full biographical listings, see the Martindale-Hubbell Law Directory

*CLARION,** Wright Co. — (Refer to Hampton)

*CLINTON,** Clinton Co. — (Refer to Maquoketa)

COLUMBUS JUNCTION, Louisa Co. — (Refer to Muscatine)

*CORNING,** Adams Co. — (Refer to Clarinda)

*CORYDON,** Wayne Co. — (Refer to Mt. Ayr)

*COUNCIL BLUFFS,** Pottawattamie Co.

PERKINS, SACKS, HANNAN, REILLY AND PETERSEN (AV)

215 South Main Street, P.O. Box 1016, 51502-1016
Telephone: 712-328-1575
Fax: 712-328-1562

MEMBERS OF FIRM

Proctor R. Perkins (Retired)
Kenneth Sacks (Retired)
C. R. Hannan
Michael G. Reilly
Deborah L. Petersen

ASSOCIATES

Kellie Rae Taylor

References: First National Bank; Firstar Bank of Council Bluffs; State Bank and Trust.

For full biographical listings, see the Martindale-Hubbell Law Directory

PETERS LAW FIRM, P.C. (AV)

233 Pearl Street, P.O. Box 1078, 51502-1078
Telephone: 712-328-3157
FAX: 712-328-9092

James A. Campbell
Dennis Leu
Dennis M. Gray
James A. Thomas
Lyle W. Ditmars
Scott H. Peters
John M. McHale
Jacob J. Peters
Leo P. Martin
Scott J. Rogers

Jon E. Heisterkamp
Edean Wetherell
Matthew G. Woods

RETIRED

John M. Peters

Representative Clients: Hawkeye Bank & Trust; Grinnell Mutual Reinsurance Co.; Iowa West Racing Association; Rockwell International; Shelter Insurance; State Farms Insurance; Midlands Mall; Kemper Group; The Pillsbury Co.; The Cities of Crescent.

For full biographical listings, see the Martindale-Hubbell Law Directory

PETERSON & KOCOUREK (AV)

Suite 406-408 First Federal Savings and Loan Building, 51501
Telephone: 712-323-5880
FAX: 712-323-9575

MEMBERS OF FIRM

Richard W. Peterson
John W. Kocourek

ASSOCIATES

Susan M. Conroy

Reference: Council Bluffs Savings Bank.

For full biographical listings, see the Martindale-Hubbell Law Directory

Council Bluffs—Continued

STUART, TINLEY, PETERS, THORN & HUGHES (AV)

Northwestern Bell Building, 310 West Kanesville Boulevard, Second Floor, P.O. Box 398, 51502-0398
Telephone: 712-322-4033
Fax: 712-322-6243

MEMBERS OF FIRM

James E. Thorn — Oscar E. Johnson (1901-1993)
William R. Hughes, Jr. — Robert M. Stuart (1914-1986)
Gary R. Faust — Jack W. Peters (1931-1993)
Kristopher K. Madsen — Emmet Tinley (Retired)

ASSOCIATES

Richard D. Crowl, Jr.

Representative Clients: Chicago, Burlington Northern Railroad Co.; Firstar Bank Council Bluffs; Fireman's Fund-American; Hartford Insurance Group; Royal; St. Paul Fire & Marine Group; Liberty Mutual Insurance Company.

For full biographical listings, see the Martindale-Hubbell Law Directory

TELPNER, SMITH & RUESCH (AV)

25 Main Place, Suite 200, P.O. Box 248, 51502-0248
Telephone: 712-325-9000
Fax: 712-328-1946

MEMBERS OF FIRM

Maynard S. Telpner — Charles L. Smith
Jack E. Ruesch

Reference: Firstar Bank, Council Bluffs, Iowa.

For full biographical listings, see the Martindale-Hubbell Law Directory

*CRESCO,** Howard Co.

ELWOOD, O'DONOHOE, O'CONNOR & STOCHL (AV)

217 North Elm Street, P.O. Box 377, 52136
Telephone: 319-547-3321
Fax: 319-547-3189
New Hampton, Iowa Office: 101 North Locust Avenue, P.O. Box 310.
Telephone: 515-394-5943.
Fax: 515-394-5945.

MEMBERS OF FIRM

Henry L. Elwood — Christopher F. O'Donohoe
Richard D. Stochl

ASSOCIATES

Darin Neely

OF COUNSEL

James D. O'Connor — James E. O'Donohoe

Representative Clients: Grinnell Mutual Reinsurance Co.; Security State Bank, New Hampton, Iowa; United Fire & Casualty Insurance Co.; Board of Trustees, New Hampton Municipal Light Plant; Citizens National Bank, New Hampton, Iowa; Farmers Cooperative, New Hampton, Iowa; Cresco Union Savings Bank, Cresco, Iowa; Boatmen's Bank, Cresco, Iowa; Featherlite Mfg., Inc.; Decorah State Bank, Protivin, Iowa.

*CRESTON,** Union Co. — (Refer to Mt. Ayr)

DALLAS CENTER, Dallas Co.

McDONALD, BROWN & FAGEN (AV)

502-15th Street, P.O. Box 250, 50063
Telephone: 515-992-3728
Fax: 515-992-3971

John C. McDonald — Ralph R. Brown
Charles H. Fagen

ASSOCIATE

Duane P. Hagerty

Representative Clients: Brenton State Bank; Dallas Mutual Insurance Co.; City of Dallas Center; City of Granger; Dallas Center-Grimes Community School District; Spurgeon Manor, Inc.; Synhorst & Schraad, Inc.; Direct Connect, Inc.

*DAVENPORT,** Scott Co.

CARLIN, HELLSTROM & BITTNER (AV)

A Partnership including Professional Corporations
1000 Firstar Center, 52801
Telephone: 319-328-3333
Fax: 319-328-3352

John A. Hellstrom (1921-1992) — Robert D. Lambert (P.C.)
John J. Carlin (Retired, 1993) — Michael J. Motto
R. Richard Bittner (P.C.) — Michael K. Bush
J. Hobart Darbyshire — Jeffrey S. Bittner
James D. Hoffman

(See Next Column)

ASSOCIATES

William J. Bush — James T. Carlin

Representative Clients: First Federal Savings; Firstar Bank Davenport, N.A.; Lawyers Title Insurance Co.; Iowa Mutual Insurance Co.; Palmer Communications, Inc.; Palmer College Foundation; Allied Mutual Insurance Co.; Farm & City Insurance Co.; Signal Hill Communications, Inc. (WOC-AM, KUUL-FM); Pekin Insurance Co.

For full biographical listings, see the Martindale-Hubbell Law Directory

HENINGER AND HENINGER, PROFESSIONAL CORPORATION (AV)

Suite 501, 101 West Second Street, 52801
Telephone: 319-324-0418
Fax: 319-324-5808

Ralph U. Heninger (1908-1993) — Ralph W. Heninger
Ralph H. Heninger — Peter W. Church

Representative Clients: Crescent Laundry; Davenport Medical Education Foundation, Inc.; Genesis Health Services Foundation; Genesis Health System; Genesis Medical Center; Genesis Self Insurance Trust; Jumer's Rock Island Casino; Northwest Bank & Trust; Wyffels Hybrids, Inc.

For full biographical listings, see the Martindale-Hubbell Law Directory

LANE & WATERMAN (AV)

220 North Main Street, Suite 600, 52801
Telephone: 319-324-3246
Fax: 319-324-1616
Rock Island, Illinois Office: 500 Rock Island Bank Building.
Telephone: 309-786-1600.
Fax: 309-786-1794.

MEMBERS OF FIRM

Joe R. Lane (1902-1931) — Carol A. H. Freeman
Charles M. Waterman (1902-1924) — Curtis E. Beason
Robert V. P. Waterman — Robert V. P. Waterman, Jr.
Robert A. Van Vooren — Peter J. Benson
Thomas N. Kamp — Constance A. Schriver
William C. Davidson — R. Scott Van Vooren
C. Dana Waterman, III — Thomas D. Waterman
Charles E. Miller — John D. Telleen
Thomas J. Shields — Richard A. Davidson
James A. Mezvinsky — Carole J. Anderson
David A. Dettmann — Hallie E. Still-Caris
Dana M. Craig — Michael P. Byrne
Terry M. Giebelstein — Edmund H. Carroll, Jr.
Rand S. Wonio — Maria Mihalakis Waterman
John D. DeDoncker

ASSOCIATES

Jeffrey W. Paul — Mary Woodburn Patch
Irene Prior Loftus — Tracy L. Polaschek
Amy H. Snyder — R. Clay Thompson
Jodi K. Plagenz — Bruce F. Bright

OF COUNSEL

Donald H. Sitz

Representative Clients: Iowa-Illinois Gas and Electric Co.; Davenport Bank and Trust Co. N.A.; Lee Enterprises, Inc.; Iowa-American Water Co.; Aluminum Company of America; Northwestern Bell Telephone Co.; ANR Pipeline Co.; Hartford Insurance Group; Aetna Life and Casualty Co.

For full biographical listings, see the Martindale-Hubbell Law Directory

WEHR, BERGER, LANE & STEVENS (AV)

Suite 900, Kahl Building, 326 West Third Street, 52801-1280
Telephone: 319-326-1000
Fax: 319-326-4701

MEMBERS OF FIRM

Edward N. Wehr — Harold John Dane, III
A. Fred Berger — John R. Newman
Gary M. Lane — Steven A. Berger

OF COUNSEL

Richard L. Stevens — Charles K. Peart

Representative Clients: Per Mar Security & Research Corp.; Childs Construction Co., Inc.; Riverside Products; Sivyer Steel Corp.; Deco Tool Supply Co.; Gless Brothers Trucking; Hillebrand Construction Co.; Econo-Methods Engineering, Inc.; Davenport Bell Credit Union; Scott County Homebuilders Assn.

For full biographical listings, see the Martindale-Hubbell Law Directory

*DECORAH,** Winneshiek Co.

MILLER, PEARSON, GLOE, BURNS, BEATTY & COWIE, P.C. (AV)

301 West Broadway, 52101
Telephone: 319-382-4226
FAX: 319-382-3783

(See Next Column)

MILLER, PEARSON, GLOE, BURNS, BEATTY & COWIE P.C.—*Continued*

Frank R. Miller (1915-1977)
Donald H. Gloe
James Burns
Marion L. Beatty
Robert J. Cowie, Jr.

OF COUNSEL

Floyd S. Pearson

Counsel For: Luther College; Decorah Community School District; Winneshiek County Memorial Hospital; Decorah State Bank.
Local Counsel for: Farmers Mutual Reinsurance Co.; Ohio Casualty Insurance Co.; Iowa Farm Mutual Insurance Cos.; Employers Mutual Liability Insurance Co. of Wisconsin; Continental Casualty Co.; Employers Mutual Casualty Co.

For full biographical listings, see the Martindale-Hubbell Law Directory

*DENISON,** Crawford Co. — (Refer to Carroll)

*DES MOINES,** Polk Co.

AHLERS, COONEY, DORWEILER, HAYNIE, SMITH & ALLBEE, P.C. (AV)

100 Court Avenue, Suite 600, 50309-2231
Telephone: 515-243-7611
Fax: 515-243-2149

Philip J. Dorweiler
Kenneth H. Haynie
H. Richard Smith
Robert G. Allbee
John F. McKinney, Jr.
L. W. Rosebrook
Richard G. Santi
Edgar H. Bittle
Ronald L. Sutphin
Terry L. Monson
Lance A. Coppock
David H. Luginbill
Mark W. Beerman
Edward W. Remsburg
Randall H. Stefani
Elizabeth Gregg Kennedy
Wade R. Hauser III
William J. Noth
David M. Swinton
Linda L. Kniep
Peter L. J. Pashler
Ivan T. Webber
Serge H. Garrison
Jane B. McAllister
R. Mark Cory
Ronald L. Peeler

OF COUNSEL

Paul F. Ahlers
James Evans Cooney

Andrew J. Bracken
Steven L. Serck
Jeffrey M. Lamberti
Michael J. Eason
Carole A. Tillotson
Garth D Adams
Debra Townsend Lind
Steven Michael Nadel
Merle W. Fleming

Representative Clients: Drake University; Insurance Company of North America; West Des Moines State Bank; Koss Construction Co.; Pittsburgh-Des Moines Steel Co.; Sears, Roebuck & Co.; Iowa Association of Municipal Utilities; Iowa State Board of Regents; Kirke Van Orsdel, Inc.; Travelers Insurance Group; WestBank.

For full biographical listings, see the Martindale-Hubbell Law Directory

BELIN HARRIS LAMSON MCCORMICK, A PROFESSIONAL CORPORATION (AV)

2000 Financial Center, 50309
Telephone: 515-243-7100
Telecopier: 515-282-7615

David W. Belin
Charles E. Harris
Jeffrey E. Lamson
Mark McCormick
Steven E. Zumbach
Thomas L. Flynn
Roger T. Stetson
Jon L. Staudt
Richard W. Lozier, Jr.
James V. Sarcone, Jr.
James R. Swanger
Jeffrey A. Krausman
Jeremy C. Sharpe
Charles D. Hunter
John T. Seitz
Robert A. Mullen
David L. Charles
William D. Bartine, II
Quentin R. Boyken
Charles F. Becker
Mark E. Weinhardt
Eric W. Burmeister
Dennis P. Ogden
Margaret C. Callahan
Robert D. Sharp
John M. Bouslog
Timothy P. Willcockson

OF COUNSEL

Sue Luettjohann Seitz
Gerard D. Neugent
Lawrence E. Pope

For full biographical listings, see the Martindale-Hubbell Law Directory

BROWN, WINICK, GRAVES, BASKERVILLE AND SCHOENEBAUM, P.L.C. (AV)

Suite 1100, Two Ruan Center, 601 Locust Street, 50309
Telephone: 515-242-2400
FAX: 515-283-0231
Pella, Iowa Office: 706 Washington Street, 50219.
Telephone: 515-628-4513.
Fax: 515-628-8494.

(See Next Column)

John G. Fletcher
Marvin Winick
Richard W. Baskerville
Bruce Graves
Steven C. Schoenebaum
E. Ralph Walker
Harold N. Schneebeck
Richard K. Updegraff
Paul D. Hietbrink
William C. Brown
Jill Thompson Hansen
James H. Gilliam
Charles J. Kalinoski
Paul E. Carey
David J. Darrell
Robert R. Smith
Margaret M. Chaplinsky
Steven P. Wandro
Michael R. Blaser
Douglas E. Gross
John D. Hunter
Robert D. Andeweg
Stuart I. Feldstein
Alice Eastman Helle
CeCelia C. Ibson
Daniel L. Stockdale

Barbara Brooker Burnett
Thomas D. Johnson
Sean P. Moore
Christopher R. Sackett

OF COUNSEL

Walter R. Brown

For full biographical listings, see the Martindale-Hubbell Law Directory

CONNOLLY, O'MALLEY, LILLIS, HANSEN & OLSON (AV)

820 Liberty Building, 6th & Grand Avenue, 50309
Telephone: 515-243-8157
Fax: 515-243-3919

MEMBERS OF FIRM

William J. Lillis
Russell J. Hansen
Michael W. O'Malley
Eugene E. Olson
Peter S. Cannon
Streetar Cameron
Douglas A. Fulton
Daniel L. Manning

ASSOCIATES

Christopher R. Pose

OF COUNSEL

John Connolly, III

A list of Representative Clients will be furnished upon request.
References will be furnished upon request.

For full biographical listings, see the Martindale-Hubbell Law Directory

DAVIS, HOCKENBERG, WINE, BROWN, KOEHN & SHORS, P.C. (AV)

The Financial Center, 666 Walnut Street, Suite 2500, 50309-3993
Telephone: 515-288-2500
Cable: Davis Law
Facsimile: 515-243-0654
Affiliated London, England Office: Vizards, Solicitors, 42 Bedford Row. London WC1R 4JL England.
Telephone: 071-405-6302.
Facsimile: 071-405-6248.

A. Arthur Davis
Harlan D. Hockenberg
Donald J. Brown
William J. Koehn
John D. Shors
Stephen W. Roberts
William R. King
Robert F. Holz, Jr.
Dennis D. Jerde
C. Carleton Frederici
George W. Sullivan
Michael G. Kulik
Richard E. Ramsay
F. Richard Thornton
Thomas E. Salsbery
Frank J. Carroll
Bruce I. Campbell
Jonathan C. Wilson
Patricia A. Shoff
Steven L. Nelson
David B. VanSickel
Gene R. La Suer
Diane M. Stahle
Deborah M. Tharnish
Brian L. Wirt
Frank A. Camp
Kent A. Herink
Robert J. Douglas, Jr.
Nicholas H. Roby
Mark D. Walz
Gary M. Myers
Stanley J. Thompson
David A. Tank
David M. Erickson
Lori Torgerson Chesser
Jo Ellen Whitney
Richard S. Jenkins
David W. Body
Becky S. Knutson
M. Daniel Waters
Christopher P. Jannes
Brian J. Laurenzo

Sharon K. Malheiro
Kris Holub Smith
William A. Boatwright
Brett J. Trout
Mitchell L. DeStigter
Scott M. Brennan
Bryan A. Glinton
Carla Jensen Hamborg

OF COUNSEL

Donald A. Wine
A. J. Greffenius
Richard F. Stageman
William D. Thomas
Jamie A. Wade
David W. Dunn
Jean McNeil Dunn
Sally A. Reavely

For full biographical listings, see the Martindale-Hubbell Law Directory

DICKINSON, MACKAMAN, TYLER & HAGEN, P.C. (AV)

Suite 1600 Hub Tower, 699 Walnut Street, 50309-3986
Telephone: 515-244-2600
Telecopier: 515-246-4550

(See Next Column)

DICKINSON, MACKAMAN, TYLER & HAGEN, P.C., *Des Moines—Continued*

L. J. Dickinson (1873-1968)
L. Call Dickinson (1905-1974)
Addison M. Parker (Retired)
John H. Raife (Retired)
Robert B. Throckmorton (Retired)
Helen C. Adams
Brent R. Appel
Barbara G. Barrett
John W. Blyth
L. Call Dickinson, Jr.
Jeanine M. Freeman
David J. Grace
Craig F. Graziano
Howard O. Hagen
J. Russell Hixson
Paul E. Horvath
F. Richard Lyford
John R. Mackaman
Richard A. Malm
James W. O'Brien
Arthur F. Owens
Rebecca Boyd Parrott
David M. Repp
Robert C. Rouwenhorst
Russell L. Samson
David S. Steward
Philip E. Stoffregen
Francis (Frank) J. Stork
Jon P. Sullivan
Celeste L. Tito (Not admitted in IA)
Paul R. Tyler
John K. Vernon
J. Marc Ward
Linda S. Weindruch

OF COUNSEL

Robert E. Mannheimer

Representative Clients: Archer-Daniels-Midland Co.; Board of Water Works Trustees, Des Moines, Iowa; Merchants Bonding Co. (Mutual); Norwest Bank, N.A.

For full biographical listings, see the Martindale-Hubbell Law Directory

DUNCAN, GREEN, BROWN, LANGENESS & ECKLEY, A PROFESSIONAL CORPORATION (AV)

380 Capital Square, 400 Locust Street, 50309-2331
Telephone: 515-288-6440
Fax: 515-288-6448

Hearst R. (Randy) Duncan, Jr.
Brent B. (Chris) Green
Gregory R. Brown
James B. Langeness
Stephen R. Eckley

Randolph Mathieson Duncan
Mariclare Thinnes Culver
Scott P. Duncan
Emily McAllister

Representative Clients: American Republic Insurance Co.; Bridgestone/Firestone, Inc.; City of Des Moines; Coca Cola Corp.; Charles Gabus Ford, Inc.; The Coleman Co.; Federated Rural Electric Insurance Cooperative; Fruehauf Trailer Corp.; The Goodyear Co.; Heller Financial, Inc.

For full biographical listings, see the Martindale-Hubbell Law Directory

FINLEY, ALT, SMITH, SCHARNBERG, MAY & CRAIG, P.C. (AV)

Fourth Floor Equitable Building, 50309
Telephone: 515-288-0145
Telecopier: 515-288-2724

Hubert C. Jones (1913-1974)
Robert G. Riley (1916-1992)
Thomas A. Finley
Jerry P. Alt
Glenn L. Smith
Steven K. Scharnberg
Lorraine J. May
David C. Craig
John D. Hilmes
R. Todd Gaffney
Glenn Goodwin

Dawn R. Siebert
Kerry Finley
Thomas P. Murphy

Representative Clients: Aetna Casualty & Surety Co.; Aetna Life Insurance Co.; ALAS; American Society of Composers, Authors and Publishers; Equitable Life Assurance Society of the U.S.; Federated Insurance Co.; Meredith Corp.
Iowa Attorneys for: Midwest Medical Insurance Co.
District Attorneys for: Norfolk & Southern Railroad; CP Rail Systems.

For full biographical listings, see the Martindale-Hubbell Law Directory

GREFE & SIDNEY (AV)

2222 Grand Avenue, P.O. Box 10434, 50306
Telephone: 515-245-4300
Fax: 515-245-4452

MEMBERS OF FIRM

Rolland E. Grefe
Ross H. Sidney
Thomas W. Carpenter
Henry A. Harmon
Claude H. Freeman
Stephen D. Hardy
Robert C. Thomson
Craig S. Shannon
John Werner
Patrick J. McNulty
Iris J. Post
Mark W. Thomas
Guy R. Cook

ASSOCIATES

Ken A. Winjum
David C. Duncan
Andrew D. Hall
Kevin W. Techau
Stephanie L. Glenn
Mark A. Schultheis
Debra L. Scorpiniti

(See Next Column)

Representative Clients: Easter Stores; Freeman Decorating Co.; Iowa-Nebraska Farm Equipment Association, Inc.; Pella Corp.; State Farm Mutual Insurance Companies of Bloomington, Ill.; Liberty Mutual Insurance Co.; United States Fidelity and Guaranty Co.; Koehring Co.

For full biographical listings, see the Martindale-Hubbell Law Directory

HANSEN, MCCLINTOCK & RILEY (AV)

Eighth Floor - Fleming Building, 218 Sixth Avenue, 50309
Telephone: 515-244-2141
Fax: 515-244-2931

MEMBERS OF FIRM

Haemer Wheatcraft (1904-1983)
J. Rudolph Hansen
John A. McClintock
Ronald A. Riley
Chester C. Woodburn, III
William D. Scherle
David L. Brown
Richard G. Blane, II
John E. Swanson

Representative Clients: The St. Paul Companies; Bituminous Insurance Companies; Northwestern National Insurance Co.; The Travelers Insurance Companies; United States Aviation Insurance Group; American International Companies; Iowa Credit Union League; The McAninch Corp.; R. J. Reynolds Tobacco Co.; Brown Bros., Inc. Electrical Contractors.

For full biographical listings, see the Martindale-Hubbell Law Directory

HERRICK, LANGDON & LANGDON (AV)

1800 Financial Center, Seventh and Walnut, 50309
Telephone: 515-282-8150
Telecopier: 515-282-8226

MEMBERS OF FIRM

Allan A. Herrick (1896-1989)
Herschel G. Langdon
Richard G. Langdon
William R. Clark, Jr.
Richard N. Winders
Richard A. Steffen
Eric F. Turner
Kermit B. Anderson
Kathleen L. Nutt

ASSOCIATES

Michael B. O'Meara

Representative Clients: Norwest Bank Iowa, N.A.; Hy-Vee Food Stores, Inc.; MAPCO Inc.; The Principal Financial Group; Continental Insurance; Mercedes Benz of North America; American Home Assurance Co.

For full biographical listings, see the Martindale-Hubbell Law Directory

PATTERSON, LORENTZEN, DUFFIELD, TIMMONS, IRISH, BECKER & ORDWAY (AV)

729 Insurance Exchange Building, 50309
Telephone: 515-283-2147
Fax: 515-283-1002

MEMBERS OF FIRM

G. O. Patterson (1914-1982)
James A. Lorentzen
Theodore T. Duffield
William E. Timmons
Roy M. Irish
Gary D. Ordway
Robin L. Hermann
Harry Perkins, III
Michael F. Lacey, Jr.
Gregory J. Wilson
Jeffrey A. Boehlert
Douglas A. Haag
Charles E. Cutler
Ronald M. Rankin
Michael D. Huppert
Martin C. Sprock
Frederick M. Haskins
William A. Wickett

ASSOCIATES

Jeffrey A. Baker
Janice M. Herfkens
Coreen K. Bezdicek
Scott S. Bellis

OF COUNSEL

F. H. Becker

Representative Clients: Allied Mutual Insurance Company; CNA Insurance Company; Chubb Insurance Group; Continental Western Insurance Co.; Farmers Insurance Group; Farmland Insurance Company; Grinnell Mutual Reinsurance Company; Hawkeye Security Insurance Company; Iowa Insurance Institute, St. Paul Fire & Marine Insurance Company.

For full biographical listings, see the Martindale-Hubbell Law Directory

THE ROSENBERG LAW FIRM (AV)

1010 Insurance Exchange Building, 505 Fifth Avenue, 50309
Telephone: 515-243-7600

MEMBERS OF FIRM

Raymond Rosenberg
Paul H. Rosenberg

ASSOCIATES

Dean A. Stowers
Brent D. Rosenberg

Reference: Firstar Bank, Des Moines, Iowa.

For full biographical listings, see the Martindale-Hubbell Law Directory

Des Moines—Continued

Shearer, Templer, Pingel & Kaplan, A Professional Corporation (AV)

Suite 437 3737 Woodland Avenue (West Des Moines, 50266), P.O. Box 1991, 50309
Telephone: 515-225-3737
Fax: 515-225-9510

Ronni F. Begleiter
Thomas M. Cunningham
Becky S. Goettsch
Jeffrey L. Goodman
Ronald M. Kaplan
Lawrence L. Marcucci
Mark L. McManigal
John R. Perkins
G. Brian Pingel
Leon R. Shearer
Brenton D. Soderstrum
Jeffrey D. Stone
David G. Stork
John A. Templer, Jr.
Ann M. Ver Heul

For full biographical listings, see the Martindale-Hubbell Law Directory

Sullivan & Ward, P.C. (AV)

801 Grand, Suite 3500, 50309-2719
Telephone: 515-244-3500
Telecopier: 515-244-3599

John T. Ward
Michael P. Joynt
Louis R. Hockenberg
Richard R. Chabot
Robert M. Holliday
Mark Landa
John V. Donnelly

Dennis L. Puckett
Amy Christensen Couch
James G. Sawtelle
Jill Mataya Corry

Representative Clients: Iowa Association of Electric Cooperatives; Central Iowa Power Cooperative; Prudential Insurance Company of America; National Rural Utilities Cooperative Finance Corp.; Norwest Bank Des Moines, N.A.; First Union Mortgage Corp.; Travelers Insurance Co.; Siegwerk, Inc.

For full biographical listings, see the Martindale-Hubbell Law Directory

Wasker, Dorr, Wimmer & Marcouiller, P.C. (AV)

801 Grand Avenue, Suite 3100, 50309-8036
Telephone: 515-283-1801
Facsimile: 515-283-1802

Charles F. Wasker
Fred L. Dorr
William J. Wimmer
D. Mark Marcouiller

Robert A. Sims
David A. Bolte
Jennifer Ann Tyler
Matthew D. Kern

OF COUNSEL

Russell H. Laird

For full biographical listings, see the Martindale-Hubbell Law Directory

Whitfield & Eddy, P.L.C. (AV)

317 6th Avenue, Suite 1200 Locust at 6th, 50309-4110
Telephone: 515-288-6041
Fax: 515-246-1474

Allen Whitfield (1904-1984)
John C. Eddy
Harley A. Whitfield
A. Roger Witke
Gary Gately
Timothy J. Walker
David L. Phipps
Benjamin B. Ullem
Robert M. Kreamer
Robert L. Fanter
Bernard L. Spaeth, Jr.
Rodney P. Kubat
William L. Fairbank
Robert G. Bridges
Jaki K. Samuelson
Kevin M. Reynolds
Thomas H. Burke
Thomas Henderson
George H. Frampton
Charles E. Gribble
Megan Manning Antenucci
Wendy L. Carlson
Robert J. Blink
Gary A. Norton
Mark V. Hanson
Maureen Roach Tobin

Jeffrey William Courter
August B. Landis
Kent Thomas Kelsey
Richard J. Kirschman
John F. Fatino
Jason M. Casini
Nancy P. O'Brien
Pamela J. Prager

OF COUNSEL

Dean Dutton

General Counsel For: American Life and Casualty Co.; Hawkeye-Security Insurance Co.; Iowa Funeral Directors Assn.; The Statesman Group, Inc.; United Security Insurance Co.
Representative Clients: Brenton National Bank, N.A.; Crum & Forster Commercial Insurance; Decker Truck Line, Inc.; General Motors Co.

For full biographical listings, see the Martindale-Hubbell Law Directory

DE WITT, Clinton Co. — (Refer to Maquoketa)

*DUBUQUE,** Dubuque Co.

O'Connor & Thomas, P.C. (AV)

700 Locust Street, Suite 200, CyCare Plaza, 52001-6874
Telephone: 319-557-8400
Telecopier: 319-556-1867

Robert M. Bertsch
Gary K. Norby
John C. O'Connor
Brendan T. Quann
Les V. Reddick
A. John Arenz
Chad C. Leitch
Richard K. Whitty
Stephen C. Krumpe

Todd L. Stevenson
Brenda Stine-Reiher
James E. Goodman, Jr.

Representative Clients: Interstate Power Co.; American Trust & Savings Bank; First National Bank of Dubuque; The Archdiocese of Dubuque; A.Y. McDonald Industries, Inc.; Hartford Accident & Indemnity Co.

For full biographical listings, see the Martindale-Hubbell Law Directory

*ELDORA,** Hardin Co.

Wilson, Hall & Craig, Professional Corporation (AV)

1305 Twelfth Street, P.O. Box 431, 50627-0431
Telephone: 515-858-5475
Fax: 515-858-3157
Hubbard, Iowa Office: 213 East Maple.
Telephone: 515-864-3338. Tuesday and Thursday A.M. only.

Donald C. Wilson
Jack A. Hall
Patrick J. Craig
Mitchel T. Behr

Representative Clients: Hardin County Savings Bank, Eldora, Iowa; Security Bank, Eldora, Iowa; Security State Bank, Hubbard, Iowa; Cities of Hubbard and Union, Iowa; Harold H. Luiken & Sons, Inc., Steamboat Rock, Iowa; Dodger Industries, Inc., Eldora, Iowa; Whink Products Co., Eldora, Iowa; Hardin County Mutual Ins. Assn., New Providence, Iowa; Heart of Iowa Telephone Cooperative, Union, Iowa; Farmers Cooperative Company, Hubbard, Iowa.

*ELKADER,** Clayton Co. — (Refer to Waukon)

*EMMETSBURG,** Palo Alto Co. — (Refer to Algona)

*ESTHERVILLE,** Emmet Co.

Fitzgibbons Brothers (AV)

A Partnership including a Professional Corporation
108 North 7th Street, P.O. Box 496, 51334
Telephone: 712-362-7215
Fax: 712-362-3526

MEMBERS OF FIRM

Leo E. Fitzgibbons
Francis Fitzgibbons
Joseph L. Fitzgibbons
Harold W. White (P.C.)
Ned A. Stockdale
David A. Lester

For full biographical listings, see the Martindale-Hubbell Law Directory

*FAIRFIELD,** Jefferson Co. — (Refer to Ottumwa)

*FOREST CITY,** Winnebago Co. — (Refer to Mason City)

*FORT DODGE,** Webster Co.

Johnson, Erb, Gibb, Bice & Carlson, P.C. (AV)

600 Boston Centre, P.O. Box 1396, 50501-1396
Telephone: 515-573-2181
Fax: 515-573-2548
Gowrie, Iowa Office: 1103 Market Street.
Telephone: 515-352-3111.
Fax: 515-352-3113.

Arthur H. Johnson
Dean P. Erb (Gowrie Office)
William S. Gibb
Craig E. Carlson
Thomas J. Bice
James L. Kramer
William J. Good
Neven J. Mulholland
Stuart J. Cochrane

Eric J. Eide

OF COUNSEL

Wilbur J. Latham

District Counsel for: Iowa-Illinois Gas & Electric Co.
Representative Clients: Cigna Property & Casualty Co.; City of Lehigh; Farmland Mutual Insurance Co. New Cooperative, Inc.; Trinity Regional Hospital; Boatmen's Bank of Fort Dodge.

For full biographical listings, see the Martindale-Hubbell Law Directory

Kersten & Carlson (AV)

Seventh Floor, Snell Building, P.O. Box 957, 50501
Telephone: 515-576-4127
Fax: 515-576-6340

(See Next Column)

KERSTEN & CARLSON, *Fort Dodge—Continued*

MEMBERS OF FIRM

Don N. Kersten
Stephen G. Kersten
Claire F. Carlson (Retired)
Steven W. Hendricks
Mark S. Brownlee

ASSOCIATES

Angela J. Ostrander

General Counsel for: Farmers Coop, Co., Gilmore City, Iowa.
Local Attorneys for: Sears Roebuck & Co.; General Motors Corp.
Representative Clients: Employers Mutual Cos.; Liberty Mutual Insurance Co.; Farmers Casualty Co.; Allied Insurance Co.; Farm Bureau; C.N.A.; Empire Fire & Marine; Employers Insurance of Wausau; Mutual Fire & Auto.

For full biographical listings, see the Martindale-Hubbell Law Directory

*GARNER,** Hancock Co. — (Refer to Algona)

*GLENWOOD,** Mills Co. — (Refer to Council Bluffs)

*GREENFIELD,** Adair Co. — (Refer to Winterset)

*GRUNDY CENTER,** Grundy Co.

KLIEBENSTEIN, HERONIMUS, SCHMIDT & GEER (AV)

630 G Avenue, 50638
Telephone: 319-824-6951
FAX: 319-824-6953

Don Kliebenstein
Kirby D. Schmidt
Thomas J. Heronimus
Todd A. Geer

Counsel For: Grundy National Bank, Grundy Center; Grundy Center Community School District; Kruger Seed Co.; Beaman Cooperative Co.
Local Counsel For: The Travelers Insurance Co. (Farm Mortgage Loan Department); Western Dressing, Inc.; R.S. Bacon Veneer Co.; Mutual Benefit Life Insurance Co. (Farm Mortgage Loan Department).

For full biographical listings, see the Martindale-Hubbell Law Directory

*GUTHRIE CENTER,** Guthrie Co. — (Refer to Perry)

*HAMPTON,** Franklin Co.

HOBSON, CADY & CADY (AV)

9 First Street S.W., 50441
Telephone: 515-456-2555
Fax: 515-456-3315

MEMBERS OF FIRM

A. J. Hobson (1903-1972)
G. Arthur Cady
G. A. Cady, III

General Counsel for: Ag Services of America, Inc.
A list of Representative Clients will be furnished upon request.
References: First National Bank of Hampton; Liberty Bank & Trust.

For full biographical listings, see the Martindale-Hubbell Law Directory

*HARLAN,** Shelby Co.

KOHORST LAW FIRM (AV)

602 Market Street Building, P.O. Box 722, 51537-0722
Telephone: 712-755-3156
Fax: 712-755-7404

Robert Kohorst
Kathleen Schomer Kohorst

ASSOCIATES

William T. Early
Steven Elza Goodlow

Representative Clients: Employers Mutual Insurance Companies of Des Moines, Iowa; Farm Service Co-op., Harlan, Iowa; Mapco Natural Gas Liquids, Inc., Tulsa, Oklahoma; United Fire & Casualty Co.; Farmers Mutual Telephone Co., Harlan, Iowa.

For full biographical listings, see the Martindale-Hubbell Law Directory

HUBBARD, Hardin Co. — (Refer to Eldora)

HUMBOLDT, Humboldt Co. — (Refer to Fort Dodge)

*IDA GROVE,** Ida Co. — (Refer to Cherokee)

*INDEPENDENCE,** Buchanan Co. — (Refer to Waterloo)

*INDIANOLA,** Warren Co.

ELGIN, CLOGG & PATIN (AV)

106 East Salem Avenue, P.O. Box 215, 50125
Telephone: 515-961-2574
FAX: 515-961-2577

P. F. Elgin
Richard B. Clogg
Claire B. Patin

A List of Representative Clients will be furnished on request.

For full biographical listings, see the Martindale-Hubbell Law Directory

*IOWA CITY,** Johnson Co.

MEARDON, SUEPPEL, DOWNER & HAYES P.L.C. (AV)

122 South Linn Street, 52240
Telephone: 319-338-9222
Fax: 319-338-7250

William L. Meardon
Mark T. Hamer
William F. Sueppel
Thomas D. Hobart
Robert N. Downer
Margaret T. Lainson
James P. Hayes
Douglas D. Ruppert
James D. McCarragher
Paul J. McAndrew, Jr.
Timothy J. Krumm

William J. Sueppel
Charles A. Meardon
Steven A. Michalek

Representative Clients: United Technologies-Automotive; Perpetual Savings Bank; Farmers Savings Bank of Kalona; Metro Pavers, Inc.; League of Iowa Municipalities; Hills Bank and Trust Co.; J.M. Swank Co.; City of Muscatine; McComas-Lacina Construction Co., Inc.; Diamond Dave's Taco Company, Inc.

For full biographical listings, see the Martindale-Hubbell Law Directory

IOWA FALLS, Hardin Co.

WHITESELL LAW FIRM (AV)

Law House, 410 Washington Avenue, P.O. Box 336, 50126
Telephone: 515-648-4646
FAX: 515-648-3283

John P. Whitesell

ASSOCIATES

Bruce T. Smith

General Counsel for: Ellsworth College Trustees; PBW Broadcasting Corp. (KIFG, AM-FM); Jonathan, Ltd.; Ellsworth College Dormitories, Inc.; Farmers Mutual Insurance Co.; Competitive Capital Resources, Inc.; River Hills Financial Services, Inc.

For full biographical listings, see the Martindale-Hubbell Law Directory

*JEFFERSON,** Greene Co. — (Refer to Carroll)

*KEOSAUQUA,** Van Buren Co. — (Refer to Ottumwa)

LENOX, Taylor Co. — (Refer to Mt. Ayr)

*LEON,** Decatur Co. — (Refer to Mt. Ayr)

*LOGAN,** Harrison Co. — (Refer to Harlan)

*MANCHESTER,** Delaware Co. — (Refer to Dubuque)

MAPLETON, Monona Co. — (Refer to Sioux City)

*MARENGO,** Iowa Co.

HARNED & MCMEEN (AV)

888 Court Avenue, P.O. Box 267, 52301
Telephone: 319-642-5521

MEMBERS OF FIRM

F. Paul Harned (1892-1973)
L. C. McMeen

ASSOCIATES

Edward D. Jorgensen

Representative Clients: Benton County State Bank; Boatmen's Bank of Marengo; I.M.T. Insurance Co.; Iowa Valley Community School District.
References: Boatmen's Bank of Marengo; Benton County State Bank, Blairstown, Iowa.

For full biographical listings, see the Martindale-Hubbell Law Directory

*MARSHALLTOWN,** Marshall Co.

CARTWRIGHT, DRUKER & RYDEN (AV)

112 West Church Street, P.O. Box 496, 50158
Telephone: 515-752-5467
Fax: 515-752-4370

MEMBERS OF FIRM

H. G. Cartwright (1902-1982)
John F. Veldey
Rex J. Ryden
Joel T. S. Greer
John B. Grier
Sharon Soorholtz Greer
Gregory D. Thompson

OF COUNSEL

Harry Druker

Representative Clients: Fisher Controls International Inc.; Hawkeye Bank; Marshalltown Savings Bank, FSB; Travelers Insurance Co.; Lennox Industries Inc.; State Farm Mutual Insurance Co., Bloomington, Ill.; Farm Bureau Mutual Insurance Co.; Allied Group; Employers Group.

For full biographical listings, see the Martindale-Hubbell Law Directory

Marshalltown—Continued

JOHNSON, SUDENGA, LATHAM & PEGLOW (AV)

118 East Main Street, P.O. Box 1180, 50158-1180
Telephone: 515-752-8800
Telecopier: 515-752-8095

MEMBERS OF FIRM

Craig L. Johnson
W. J. Latham, Jr.
George W. Sudenga
Paul C. Peglow
Kevin M. O'Hare

Representative Clients: Aetna Insurance Co.; Economy Fire & Casualty Co.; John Hancock Mutual Life Insurance Co.; The Hartford Insurance Group; Ottilie Seeds; Plaza Family Dental Services; R. D. Stewart, Inc.; Northwestern National Insurance Co.; United Fire & Casualty Co.; United States Fidelity & Guaranty Co.

WELP, HARRISON, BRENNECKE & MOORE (AV)

302 Masonic Temple Building, P.O. Box 618, 50158
Telephone: 515-752-4271
Fax: 515-752-5266

MEMBERS OF FIRM

G. A. Mote (1874-1965)
Leslie E. Smaha
Arley J. Wilson (1913-1982)
Larry E. McKibben
Roger E. Harrison
James L. Goodman
Allen E. Brennecke
William J. Lorenz
James R. Moore
James C. Ellefson
Douglas W. Beals

ASSOCIATES

Michael R. Horn

OF COUNSEL

William L. Welp

Representative Clients: Farmers Savings Bank; Beaman, Iowa; Brenner Trust; Ottilie Farms, Inc.; Arbie Mineral Feed Co.; Cooper Farms, Inc.

For full biographical listings, see the Martindale-Hubbell Law Directory

*MASON CITY,** Cerro Gordo Co.

WINSTON, REUBER & BYRNE, LAWYERS, A PROFESSIONAL CORPORATION (AV)

119 Second Street, N.W., 50401
Telephone: 515-423-1913
FAX: 515-423-8998

Harold R. Winston
John H. Reuber
Michael G. Byrne

Representative Clients: Libbey-Owens Ford Glass Co.; Goodyear Tire and Rubber; Skelly Oil; United Guernsey Co-op; Norwest Bank; First Interstate Bank of Mason City.

For full biographical listings, see the Martindale-Hubbell Law Directory

*MONTEZUMA,** Poweshiek Co. — (Refer to Newton)

*MT. PLEASANT,** Henry Co. — (Refer to Washington)

NASHUA, Chickasaw Co. — (Refer to Charles City)

*NEVADA,** Story Co. — (Refer to Ames)

*NEW HAMPTON,** Chickasaw Co.

ELWOOD, O'DONOHOE, O'CONNOR & STOCHL (AV)

101 North Locust Avenue, P.O. Box 310, 50659
Telephone: 515-394-5943
Fax: 515-394-5945
Cresco, Iowa Office: 217 North Elm Street. P.O. Box 377.
Telephone: 319-547-3321.
Fax: 319-547-3189.

MEMBERS OF FIRM

Henry L. Elwood
Christopher F. O'Donohoe
Richard D. Stochl

ASSOCIATES

Darin Neely

OF COUNSEL

James D. O'Connor
James E. O'Donohoe

Representative Clients: Grinnell Mutual Reinsurance Co.; Security State Bank, New Hampton, Iowa; United Fire & Casualty Insurance Co.; Board of Trustees, New Hampton Municipal Light Plant; Citizens National Bank, New Hampton, Iowa; Farmers Cooperative, New Hampton, Iowa; Cresco

(See Next Column)

Union Savings Bank, Cresco, Iowa; Boatmen's Bank, Cresco, Iowa; Featherlite Mfg., Inc.; Decorah State Bank, Protivin, Iowa.

*NEWTON,** Jasper Co.

BRIERLY LAW OFFICE (AV)

211 First Avenue West, 50208
Telephone: 515-792-4160
Fax: 515-792-2410
Grinnell, Iowa Office: Fifth Avenue Plaza, 924 West Street.
Telephone: 515-236-8622.
Sully, Iowa Office: 618 4th Street.
Telephone: 515-594-4420.

MEMBERS OF FIRM

Laurence L. Brierly (1903-1984)
Dennis F. Chalupa
Ennis McCall (1912-1987)
Bradley McCall
Lewis M. Girdner
Mark A. Otto

ASSOCIATES

John H. Terpstra

Representative Clients: Thombert, Inc. (Plastics); Edwards Publications, Inc.; Mid-Iowa Savings Bank, FSB; First Newton National Bank; Pleasantville State Bank; Hawkeye Bank and Trust, N.A.; J. H. McKlveen and Co.; Mid-west Manufacturing Co.; City of Mitchellville; City of Prairie City.

For full biographical listings, see the Martindale-Hubbell Law Directory

DIEHL & CLAYTON (AV)

309 First Avenue West, 50208
Telephone: 515-792-6121
Fax: 515-792-4384

MEMBERS OF FIRM

H.C. Korf (1876-1936)
J.N. Diehl (1913-1984)
E.O. Korf (1889-1949)
James W. Cleverley (1925-1989)
Benjamin C. Clayton

ASSOCIATES

Michael K. Jacobsen

Representative Clients: First State Bank, Lynnville, Iowa; Iowa Southern Utilities Co.; Economy Fire & Casualty Co.; Travelers Insurance Co.; Newton Clinic; Exchange State Bank, Mingo and Collins, Iowa; City of Lynnville, Iowa; City of Lambs Grove, Iowa.

For full biographical listings, see the Martindale-Hubbell Law Directory

*NORTHWOOD,** Worth Co. — (Refer to Mason City)

*ORANGE CITY,** Sioux Co. — (Refer to Le Mars)

*OSAGE,** Mitchell Co. — (Refer to Charles City)

*OSCEOLA,** Clarke Co. — (Refer to Indianola)

*OTTUMWA,** Wapello Co.

JOHNSON, HESTER & WALTER (AV)

111 West Second Street, P.O. Box 716, 52501-0716
Telephone: 515-684-5481
Telecopier: 515-684-5487

MEMBERS OF FIRM

David J. Hester
Thomas M. Walter

ASSOCIATES

Gayla R. Harrison
Robert E. Breckenridge, II

OF COUNSEL

Walter F. Johnson

Representative Clients: Firstar Bank Ottumwa; Deere and Co.; Lee Enterprises Inc.; Liberty Mutual Insurance Co.; John Deere Ottumwa Works.

For full biographical listings, see the Martindale-Hubbell Law Directory

KIPLE, KIPLE, DENEFE, BEAVER & GARDNER (AV)

104 South Court Street, P.O. Box 493, 52501
Telephone: 515-683-1626
FAX: 515-683-3597

MEMBERS OF FIRM

James L. Kiple
J. Terrence Denefe
Charles M. Kiple
Jerome M. Beaver
Steven Gardner

General Counsel for: Firstar Bank Ottumwa; Winger Contracting Co.; Ideal Ready-Mix Co., Inc.; Wapello Rural Water Association, Inc.; Norris Asphalt Paving Co.

Representative Clients: Pafco Insurance Co.; Hawkeye Security Insurance Co.; The Travelers Insurance Companies; Farm Bureau Mutual Insurance Co.

For full biographical listings, see the Martindale-Hubbell Law Directory

PERRY, Dallas Co.

WILLIS & SACKETT (AV)

1212 Second Street, P.O. Box 310, 50220
Telephone: 515-465-5331
Telecopier: 515-465-5333

MEMBERS OF FIRM

Blake Willis (1892-1961)
George H. Sackett (1900-1983)
Ned Willis
G. Robert Sackett

Counsel for: Perry State Bank; City of Perry; Perry Community Schools.
Local Counsel: Farm Credit Bank of Omaha.

*POCAHONTAS,** Pocahontas Co. — (Refer to Rockwell City)

*RED OAK,** Montgomery Co. — (Refer to Clarinda)

*ROCK RAPIDS,** Lyon Co. — (Refer to Spirit Lake)

*ROCKWELL CITY,** Calhoun Co.

LEWIS S. HENDRICKS (AV)

408 Fifth Street, P.O. Box 111, 50579
Telephone: 712-297-7567
Fax: 712-297-5407

Reference: National Bank of Rockwell City.

For full biographical listings, see the Martindale-Hubbell Law Directory

*SAC CITY,** Sac Co. — (Refer to Rockwell City)

*SIBLEY,** Osceola Co. — (Refer to Rock Rapids)

*SIDNEY,** Fremont Co. — (Refer to Hamburg)

*SIGOURNEY,** Keokuk Co. — (Refer to Ottumwa)

*SIOUX CITY,** Woodbury Co.

BERENSTEIN VRIEZELAAR MOORE MOSER & TIGGES (AV)

300 Commerce Building, P.O. Box 1557, 51102
Telephone: 712-252-3226
Fax: 712-252-4873
Dakota Dunes, South Dakota Office: One River Place, Suite 111, 600 Stevens Port Drive, 57049.
Telephone: 605-232-9464.
Fax: 712-252-4873.

MEMBERS OF FIRM

Marvin S. Berenstein
Kent Vriezelaar
Dan A. Moore
Cynthia C. Moser
Dale C. Tigges
Ray H. Edgington
Karen M. McCarthy
Craig S. Berenstein
Maureen Brown Heffernan

ASSOCIATES

David J. King
Jeffrey A. Johnson
Elizabeth A. Row
Louis S. Goldberg (1897-1984)

Representative Clients: Aalfs Manufacturing, Inc.; Briar Cliff College; Canal Capital Corp.- Sioux City Stockyards; Firstar Bank-Sioux City, N.A.; Gateway 2000, Inc.; Metropolitan Life Insurance Co.; Metz Baking Co.; Sioux Tools, Inc.; Sisters of Mercy-Marian Health Center; Wells Dairy & Blue Bunny Ice Cream.

For full biographical listings, see the Martindale-Hubbell Law Directory

CORBETT, ANDERSON, CORBETT, POULSON, FLOM & VELLINGA (AV)

400 Security Building, P.O. Box 3527, 51102
Telephone: 712-277-1261
Fax: 712-277-6631

MEMBERS OF FIRM

Edward M. Corbett (1868-1940)
Edward V. Corbett (1904-1973)
Carlton M. Corbett (1901-1976)
Stanley M. Corbett
John B. Anderson
Charles L. Corbett
Jeffrey L. Poulson
Douglas E. Flom
Rodney D. Vellinga
Maxine M. Buckmeier
James N. Daane

ASSOCIATES

Kathleen D. Saltzman
James E. Walker

Attorneys for: First Federal Savings Bank of Siouxland; North American Manufacturing Co.
Local Attorneys for: Fidelity & Deposit Company of Maryland; Seaboard Surety Co.; Continental Oil Co.; Hawkeye Bank & Trust Co.; Commercial Federal Savings & Loan Assn.; St. Lukes Regional Medical Center of Sioux City.

For full biographical listings, see the Martindale-Hubbell Law Directory

EIDSMOE, HEIDMAN, REDMOND, FREDREGILL, PATTERSON & SCHATZ (AV)

A Partnership including Professional Corporations
701 Pierce Street, Suite 200, P.O. Box 3086, 51102
Telephone: 712-255-8838
Fax: 712-258-6714

MEMBERS OF FIRM

Marvin F. Heidman
James W. Redmond
Alan E. Fredregill (P.C.)
Charles T. Patterson
Kenneth C. Schatz (P.C.)
Thomas M. Plaza
Daniel D. Dykstra
Lance D. Ehmcke
Margaret M. Prahl
John Ackerman
Gregg E. Williams
Judith A. Higgs
John C. Gray
Daniel B. Shuck

ASSOCIATES

Rita C. Grimm
Ryan K. Crayne
Charles E. Trullinger
John W. Gleysteen (Retired)
Robert R. Eidsmoe (Retired)
Jacob C. Gleysteen (1883-1943)
H. Clifford Harper (1891-1959)

Representative Clients: Aetna Casualty & Surety Co.; Irving F. Jensen Co., Inc.; Marian Health Center; Medical Protective Co.; John Morrell & Co.; Pig Improvement Co.; State Farm Mutual Insurance Co.; Terra International, Inc.; The Security National Bank of Sioux City; Wal-Mart Stores, Inc.

For full biographical listings, see the Martindale-Hubbell Law Directory

GILES AND GILES (AV)

322 Frances Building, 505 Fifth Street, 51101
Telephone: 712-252-4458
FAX: 712-252-3400
Crofton, Nebraska Office: P. O. Box 88.
Telephone: 402-388-4215.

MEMBERS OF FIRM

W. Jefferson Giles, III
William J. Giles, IV

ASSOCIATES

Gregory Gifford Giles

Representative Clients: Security National Bank, Firstar Bank, Boatmen's Bank, all in Sioux City, Iowa; Live Stock State Bank, Yankton, SD.

For full biographical listings, see the Martindale-Hubbell Law Directory

MARKS & MADSEN (AV)

Suite 303, United Federal Plaza Building, P.O. Box 3226, 51102
Telephone: 712-258-1200
Fax: 712-258-2012

MEMBERS OF FIRM

Bernard B. Marks
George F. Madsen

Representative Clients: Briar Cliff College; Dennis Supply Co.; The Equitable Life Assurance Society of the U.S.; First Federal Savings Bank of Siouxland; First National Bank in Le Mars; Hirschbach Motor Lines, Inc.; Pioneer Bank; Restoration Trust Corp.; Sioux City Brick and Tile Co.; The Security National Bank of Sioux City, Iowa.

For full biographical listings, see the Martindale-Hubbell Law Directory

MAYNE & MAYNE (AV)

400 Home Federal Building, P.O. Box 5049, 51102
Telephone: 712-252-3220
FAX: 712-252-1535

MEMBERS OF FIRM

Wiley Mayne
John D. Mayne

ASSOCIATES

Robert J. Pierson

Representative Clients: American Home Insurance; American Telephone & Telegraph Co.; Amoco Oil Co.; Chubb Insurance; Federated Mutual Insurance Co.; Ford Motor Credit Co.; Fremont Indemnity Co.; Ranger Insurance; Metz Baking Co.; Shell Chemical Co.

For full biographical listings, see the Martindale-Hubbell Law Directory

RAWLINGS, NIELAND, PROBASCO, KILLINGER, ELLWANGER, JACOBS & MOHRHAUSER (AV)

300 Toy Building, 51101
Telephone: 712-277-2373
FAX: 712-277-3304

James W. Kindig (1879-1950)
Lowell C. Kindig (1913-1992)
Robert E. Beebe (1913-1988)

MEMBERS OF FIRM

William J. Rawlings
Maurice B. Nieland
Gene A. Probasco
Sam S. Killinger
Michael W. Ellwanger
Michael P. Jacobs
Jeffrey R. Mohrhauser
M. Anthony Rossi
Timothy S. Bottaro
Richard H. Moeller
Suzan E. Boden

(See Next Column)

RAWLINGS, NIELAND, PROBASCO, KILLINGER, ELLWANGER, JACOBS & MOHRHAUSER—*Continued*

ASSOCIATES

Jeffrey D. Garreans

Representative Clients: Arnold Motor Supply; Chesterman Co.; CNA Insurance Co.; Farmers Savings Bank of Remsen; Iowa Farm Bureau Insurance Co.; Maryland Casualty Co.; Norwest Iowa Pork, Inc.; Norwest Bank Iowa, National Association; St. Paul Fire and Marine Insurance Co.; United Fire and Casualty Co.

For full biographical listings, see the Martindale-Hubbell Law Directory

SHULL, COSGROVE, HELLIGE, DU BRAY & LUNDBERG (AV)

700 Frances Building, 505 Fifth Street, P.O. Box 1828, 51102
Telephone: 712-255-4444
Telecopier: 712-255-4465

MEMBERS OF FIRM

James M. Cosgrove
Michael R. Hellige
F. Joseph Du Bray
Paul D. Lundberg
M. James Daley
Robert F. Meis
Scott A. Hindman
James W. Radig
Christopher K. Miller

OF COUNSEL

D. Carlton Shull

Representative Clients: Burlington Northern Inc.; Employers Mutual Cos.; Ford Motor Co.; The Hartford; Liberty Mutual Insurance Co.; Prince Manufacturing Corp.; Sioux City Journal; The Travelers; Western Iowa Tech Community College.

For full biographical listings, see the Martindale-Hubbell Law Directory

*SPENCER,** Clay Co. — (Refer to Spirit Lake)

*SPIRIT LAKE,** Dickinson Co.

NAREY, CHOZEN AND SAUNDERS (AV)

Narey Building, 832 Lake Street, P.O. Box E, 51360-0605
Telephone: 712-336-3410
Fax: 712-336-0668

MEMBERS OF FIRM

Harry E. Narey (1885-1962)
Peter B. Narey
Michael J. Chozen
Lonnie B. Saunders

Representative Clients: First Bank and Trust, Spirit Lake, Iowa; Iowa Electric Light and Power Co., Spirit Lake, Iowa; State Bank of Terril, Terril, Iowa; State Bank, Spirit Lake, Iowa; Smith-Lumber, Inc.; Dickinson County Savings Bank; City of Okoboji; United Fire and Casualty Co.; Home Insurance Co.; City of Orleans.

For full biographical listings, see the Martindale-Hubbell Law Directory

*STORM LAKE,** Buena Vista Co. — (Refer to Cherokee)

*TIPTON,** Cedar Co. — (Refer to Iowa City)

*TOLEDO,** Tama Co. — (Refer to Marshalltown)

VICTOR, Iowa Co. — (Refer to Marengo)

*VINTON,** Benton Co. — (Refer to Cedar Rapids)

*WAPELLO,** Louisa Co. — (Refer to Muscatine)

*WATERLOO,** Black Hawk Co.

BEECHER, RATHERT, ROBERTS, FIELD, WALKER & MORRIS, P.C. (AV)

Suite 300 Court Square Building, 620 Lafayette Street, P.O. Box 178, 50704
Telephone: 319-234-1766
Telecopier: 319-234-1225

W. L. Beecher (1891-1976)
W. Louis Beecher
John W. Rathert
Jay P. Roberts
Hugh M. Field
John R. Walker, Jr.
Richard R. Morris
Carter J. Stevens

Eric W. Johnson
Theresa E. Hoffman
Heidi L. Noonan

General Counsel for: American Black Hawk Broadcasting Co.
Representative Clients: Deere & Company; Chubb/Pacific Indemnity Group; The Equitable Life Assurance Society of the United States; The National Bank of Waterloo.

For full biographical listings, see the Martindale-Hubbell Law Directory

DUTTON, BRAUN, STAACK, HELLMAN & IVERSEN, P.L.C. (AV)

3151 Brockway Road, P.O. Box 810, 50704
Telephone: 319-234-4471
Fax: 319-234-8029

(See Next Column)

Hal M. Mosier (1890-1966)
Craig H. Mosier (Retired 1982)
Sydney A. Thomas (Retired 1988)
Samuel T. Beatty (Retired 1990)
David J. Dutton
Robert W. Braun
Thomas L. Staack
James R. Hellman
Gary D. Iversen
Michael A. Mc Enroe
Cheryl L. Weber
Steven K. Daniels
Bruce L. Braley
John J. Hines
James F. Kalkhoff

James Scott Bayne
David C. Thompson
Elizabeth A. Lounsberry
Lisa R. Schmitt
Kevin D. Ahrenholz

Representative Clients: Kemper Insurance Group; Auto Owners Insurance Co.; Grinnell Mutual Reinsurance Co.; CNA Insurance Cos.; The Travelers Insurance Co.; Economy Fire & Casualty Co.; Hawkeye Community College; Crossroads Ford, Ltd.; Iowa Communications Community Credit Union; Black Hawk County Solid Waste Management Commission.

For full biographical listings, see the Martindale-Hubbell Law Directory

GALLAGHER, LANGLAS & GALLAGHER, P.C. (AV)

Law Building, 405 East Fifth Street, P.O. Box 2615, 50704
Telephone: 319-233-6163
Fax: 319-233-6435

Edward J. Gallagher, Jr.
Thomas W. Langlas
Edward J. Gallagher, III
George L. Weilein
Timothy C. Boller
Cynthia A. Scherrman
Thomas C. Verhulst

Jeffrey C. Peterzalek
David A. Roth

References: The National Bank of Waterloo; The Waterloo Savings Bank; Norwest Bank Iowa NA, Waterloo, Iowa.

For full biographical listings, see the Martindale-Hubbell Law Directory

SWISHER & COHRT (AV)

528 West Fourth Street, P.O. Box 1200, 50704
Telephone: 319-232-6555
FAX: 319-232-4835

MEMBERS OF FIRM

Benjamin F. Swisher (1878-1959)
L. J. Cohrt (1898-1974)
Charles F. Swisher (1919-1986)
Eldon R. McCann
Steven A. Weidner
Larry J. Cohrt
J. Douglas Oberman
Stephen J. Powell
Jim D. DeKoster
Jeffrey J. Greenwood
Samuel C. Anderson
Robert C. Griffin
Kevin R. Rogers

ASSOCIATES

Beth E. Hansen
Mark F. Conway
Natalie Williams Burr

Firm is Counsel for: Koehring Corp.; Clay Equipment; Chamberlain Manufacturing Co.; Waterloo Courier.
Local Counsel for: Allied Group; John Deere Insurance; Liberty Mutual Insurance Co.

For full biographical listings, see the Martindale-Hubbell Law Directory

*WAUKON,** Allamakee Co.

JACOBSON, BRISTOL, GARRETT & SWARTZ (AV)

Jacobson-Bristol Building, 25 First Avenue, N.W., P.O. Box 49, 52172
Telephone: 319-568-3439
Fax: 319-568-3210

MEMBERS OF FIRM

Arthur H. Jacobson (1910-1986)
James D. Bristol
James E. Thomson (Retired, 1992)
James A. Garrett
Jeffrey L. Swartz

Representative Clients: Farmers & Merchants Savings Bank, Waukon, Iowa; Allied Group; Grinnell Mutual Reinsurance Co.; Mutual Fire and Casualty; United Fire & Casualty Co.

For full biographical listings, see the Martindale-Hubbell Law Directory

*WEBSTER CITY,** Hamilton Co. — (Refer to Fort Dodge)

WEST DES MOINES, Polk Co. — (Refer to Des Moines)

*WEST UNION,** Fayette Co. — (Refer to Waukon)

WILLIAMSBURG, Iowa Co. — (Refer to Marengo)

*WINTERSET,** Madison Co.

JORDAN, OLIVER & WALTERS (AV)

Farmers & Merchants Bank Building, P.O. Box 230, 50273
Telephone: 515-462-3731
Fax: 515-462-3734

(See Next Column)

JORDAN, OLIVER & WALTERS, *Winterset—Continued*

MEMBERS OF FIRM

Shirley A. Webster (1909-1989)	Jerrold B. Oliver
Lewis H. Jordan	G. Stephen Walters

Reference: Farmers & Merchants State Bank, Winterset, Iowa.

For full biographical listings, see the Martindale-Hubbell Law Directory

KANSAS

*ABILENE,** Dickinson Co. — (Refer to Salina)

*ALMA,** Wabaunsee Co. — (Refer to Manhattan)

ARKANSAS CITY, Cowley Co. — (Refer to Winfield)

*ASHLAND,** Clark Co. — (Refer to Dodge City)

*ATCHISON,** Atchison Co. — (Refer to Leavenworth)

*ATWOOD,** Rawlins Co. — (Refer to Oberlin)

*BELLEVILLE,** Republic Co. — (Refer to Concordia)

*BURLINGTON,** Coffey Co. — (Refer to Emporia)

CHANUTE, Neosho Co.

HENSHALL, PENNINGTON & BRAKE (AV)

Lower Level Suite New Bank of Commerce Building, 101 West Main Street, P.O. Box 667, 66720
Telephone: 316-431-2600
Fax: 316-431-1505

Charles E. Henshall (1916-1982)
Robert Pennington
David S. Brake

Representative Clients: Lancer Oil, Inc.; Fireman's Fund American Insurance Companies; Church Mutual Insurance Co.; Eastern Savings Bank; Shelter Insurance Cos.; Farmers Casualty Cos.; Mid-Continent Casualty Co.; City of Chanute; Neosho Memorial Regional Medical Center; Federal Deposit Insurance Corporation.

*CIMARRON,** Gray Co. — (Refer to Dodge City)

*CLAY CENTER,** Clay Co. — (Refer to Junction City)

*COLBY,** Thomas Co. — (Refer to Goodland)

*COLDWATER,** Comanche Co. — (Refer to Pratt)

*COLUMBUS,** Cherokee Co.

ARMSTRONG & PRAUSER (AV)

101 East Elm Street, P.O. Box 47, 66725
Telephone: 316-429-3107
FAX: 316-429-2335

Paul L. Armstrong (1918-1991)
Larry A. Prauser

Representative Clients: Citizens State Bank of Weir; Empire District Electric Co.; Ace Electric Co., Inc.

For full biographical listings, see the Martindale-Hubbell Law Directory

*CONCORDIA,** Cloud Co. — (Refer to Salina)

*COUNCIL GROVE,** Morris Co. — (Refer to Emporia)

*DODGE CITY,** Ford Co.

MANGAN, DALTON, TRENKLE, REBEIN & DOLL, CHARTERED (AV)

208 West Spruce Street, 67801-1147
Telephone: 316-227-8126
Fax: 316-227-8451

Jim Mangan (Retired)
Jack E. Dalton (Retired)
William P. Trenkle, Jr.
David J. Rebein
Michael A. Doll

Shane Bangerter
Cheryl L. Jackson

For full biographical listings, see the Martindale-Hubbell Law Directory

WILLIAMS, STROBEL, MALONE, MASON & RALPH, P.A. (AV)

Second Floor, Bank IV Building, P.O. Box 39, 67801
Telephone: 316-225-4168
FAX: 316-225-7261

Carl Van Riper (1879-1950)
James A. Williams
C. W. Hughes (1910-1960)
Ken W. Strobel
Terry J. Malone
Ronald C. Mason
Bradley C. Ralph

Representative Clients: Fidelity State Bank & Trust Co., Dodge City; Roto-Mix, Inc.; Hartford Accident & Indemnity Co.; Travelers Insurance Co.; Farmers State Bank, Bucklin; Dodge City Board of Education; City of Dodge City; West Plains Regional Hospital.

For full biographical listings, see the Martindale-Hubbell Law Directory

*EL DORADO,** Butler Co. — (Refer to Eureka)

*ELLSWORTH,** Ellsworth Co. — (Refer to Salina)

*EMPORIA,** Lyon Co.

ATHERTON & ATHERTON (AV)

304 Bank IV Building, Suite 400, P.O. Box 624, 66801
Telephone: 316-342-1277; 342-1278
FAX: 316-342-2343

MEMBERS OF FIRM

John G. Atherton
Stephen J. Atherton

Representative Clients: Bank IV, Emporia, Kansas; Unified School District #253; American States Insurance Cos.; Manufacturers and Wholesalers Indemnity Co.; American Casualty Cos.; Universal Underwriters Insurance Co.; Travelers Insurance Co.; Maryland Casualty Co.

For full biographical listings, see the Martindale-Hubbell Law Directory

*EUREKA,** Greenwood Co.

FORBES & POHL (AV)

417 North Main Street, 67045
Telephone: 316-583-5508; 583-5509
Fax: 316-583-6503

MEMBERS OF FIRM

Harold G. Forbes (1912-1984)
Dale L. Pohl
Patrick T. Forbes

General Counsel for: Emprise Banks, Eureka & Toronto; Home Bank & Trust of Eureka; Jackson Brothers Oil Co.
Representative Clients: Burlington Northern Railway Co.; Farm Bureau Mutual Insurance Co.; Travelers Insurance Co.; Prudential Insurance; Purkeypile Construction.

For full biographical listings, see the Martindale-Hubbell Law Directory

*FORT SCOTT,** Bourbon Co.

SHORT, GENTRY & BISHOP, P.A. (AV)

Suite 100 Security Professional Center, Fourth and Judson, 66701
Telephone: 316-223-0530
Facsimile: 316-223-6956

Forrest E. Short
Charles H. Gentry
Patrick S. Bishop

Counsel for: Bruce Marble & Granite Co., Inc.; Key Industries, Inc.; KMDO Broadcasting, Inc.; Bourbon County Consolidated Rural Water District #2; KVCY; National Indemnity Co.; Chicago Title Insurance Co.; Tri State Insurance Co.

For full biographical listings, see the Martindale-Hubbell Law Directory

*FREDONIA,** Wilson Co. — (Refer to Chanute)

*GARDEN CITY,** Finney Co.

HOPE, MILLS, BOLIN, COLLINS & RAMSEY (AV)

607 North Seventh Street, P.O. Box 439, 67846
Telephone: 316-276-3203
Fax: 316-276-3300

MEMBERS OF FIRM

Wm. Easton Hutchison (1860-1952)
C. E. Vance (1878-1958)
A. M. Fleming (1888-1971)
Clifford R. Hope, Jr.
Jim D. Mills
William B. Bolin
Michael E. Collins
Michael K. Ramsey

General Counsel: Garden City Production Credit Assn.; The Garden City Co-op, Inc.; Lane-Scott Electric Co-Operative, Inc.; Geier's, Inc.
Representative Clients: Farm Bureau Mutual Insurance Co.; Federated Mutuals; Lawyers Title Insurance Co.; Prudential Insurance Company of America.

For full biographical listings, see the Martindale-Hubbell Law Directory

*GARNETT,** Anderson Co.

STEVEN B. DOERING (AV)

111 East Fourth Street, P.O. Box 345, 66032
Telephone: 913-448-5493
FAX: 913-448-5458

Reference: Kansas State Bank.

For full biographical listings, see the Martindale-Hubbell Law Directory

*GIRARD,** Crawford Co. — (Refer to Pittsburg)

*GREAT BEND,** Barton Co.

CONNER & OPIE (AV)

Suite 102, 2015 Forest Avenue, Drawer E, 67530
Telephone: 316-793-5455
Fax: 316-793-5456

(See Next Column)

CONNER & OPIE, *Great Bend—Continued*

Samuel Maher (1849-1918)
Elrick C. Cole (1856-1937)
Theodore Cole (1852-1890)
William Osmond (1853-1947)
T.B. Kelly (1889-1965)

MEMBERS OF FIRM

Fred L. Conner
Glenn E. Opie

General Counsel For: Straub Oilfield Services Inc-Case/International; Tretbar Farms.
Local Counsel For: Atchison, Topeka & Santa Fe Railway Co.; Continental Oil Co.; Texaco, Inc.; The Prudential Insurance Co. of America; Natural Gas Pipeline Company of America; General Motors Corp.; Coachman Industries; John Hancock Mutual Life Insurance Company.

For full biographical listings, see the Martindale-Hubbell Law Directory

*HAYS,** Ellis Co.

DREILING, BIEKER & HOFFMAN (AV)

111 West 13th Street, P.O. Box 579, 67601
Telephone: 913-625-3537
FAX: 913-625-8129

MEMBERS OF FIRM

Norbert R. Dreiling
Dennis L. Bieker
Donald F. Hoffman

ASSOCIATES

Melvin J. Sauer, Jr.

General Counsel: Dreiling Oil Company, Hays, Kansas; Golden Belt Bank, FSA, Ellis, Kansas; Midland Marketing, Inc., Hays, Kansas; St. John's Rest Home, Victoria & Hays, Kansas.
Representative Clients: Farm Bureau Mutual Insurance Company of Kansas; Midwest Energy of Hays, Kansas.

For full biographical listings, see the Martindale-Hubbell Law Directory

*HIAWATHA,** Brown Co. — (Refer to Troy)

*HOWARD,** Elk Co. — (Refer to Eureka)

*HOXIE,** Sheridan Co. — (Refer to Oberlin)

*HUGOTON,** Stevens Co. — (Refer to Liberal)

*HUTCHINSON,** Reno Co.

GILLILAND & HAYES, P.A. A PROFESSIONAL CORPORATION (AV)

335 N. Washington, Suite 260, P.O. Box 2977, 67504-2977
Telephone: 316-662-0537
Facsimile: 316-669-9426
Wichita, Kansas Office: Suite 121 The Quarters, 310 West Central.
Telephone: 316-262-2266.
Kansas City, Missouri Office: 1234 Penntower, 3100 Broadway.
Telephone: 816-753-3100.
Facsimile: 816-753-2271.

Robert J. Gilliland
Gerald L. Green
John F. Hayes
David N. Zimmerman (Not admitted in KS; Resident, Kansas City, Missouri Office)
James R. Gilliland
John S. Schmidt
Scott J. Mann
Bruce B. Waugh (Not admitted in KS; Resident, Kansas City, Missouri Office)
John K. Sherk, III (Resident, Kansas City, Missouri Office)
Michael R. O'Neal
Carol Zuschek Smith (Resident, Kansas City, Missouri Office)
Bradley D. Dillon

C. J. Wahrman, III (Resident, Kansas City, Missouri Office)
Matthew L. Bretz
Cinda L. Smith
Laura A. Hederstedt

Representative Clients: Central Bank and Trust Co.; Dillon Cos., Inc.; AT&SF Railway Co.; Farm Bureau Mutual Insurance Co.; Hartford Insurance Cos.; Hutchinson Clinic, P.A.; Hutchinson Hospital Corp.; Southwestern Bell Telephone Co.; Stuckey Lumber & Supply, Inc.

For full biographical listings, see the Martindale-Hubbell Law Directory

MARTINDELL, SWEARER & SHAFFER (AV)

811 East Thirtieth Street, P.O. Box 1907, 67504-1907
Telephone: 316-662-3331
Fax: 316-662-9978
Kingman, Kansas Office: 120 East A Avenue, P.O. Box 415.
Telephone: 316-532-5158,
Fax: 316-532-2303.

MEMBERS OF FIRM

Robert C. Martindell
Charles D. Lee
John H. Shaffer
Francis E. Meisenheimer (Resident, Kingman, Kansas Office)
William B. Swearer
Elwin F. Cabbage
Jerry L. Ricksecker
John B. Swearer
Gerald E. Hertach
Carolyn H. Patterson
Jess W. Arbuckle

(See Next Column)

Representative Clients: Emprise Bank, N.A.; Charles E. Carey Foundation, Inc.; Krause Plow Corporation; J.H. Shears Sons, Inc. (Contractors); Hutchinson Industrial District #1.

For full biographical listings, see the Martindale-Hubbell Law Directory

REYNOLDS, FORKER, BERKLEY, SUTER, ROSE & DOWER (AV)

Suite 200, 129 West 2nd Avenue, P.O. Box 1868, 67504-1868
Telephone: 316-663-7131
Fax: 316-669-0714

MEMBERS OF FIRM

Roy C. Davis (1890-1959)
John T. Suter
Robert Y. Jones (1912-1963)
Trish Rose
H. Newlin Reynolds
Thomas A. Dower
Dan W. Forker, Jr.
Raymond F. Berkley
Gregory G. Meredith

For full biographical listings, see the Martindale-Hubbell Law Directory

*INDEPENDENCE,** Montgomery Co. — (Refer to Coffeyville)

*IOLA,** Allen Co.

TALKINGTON AND CHASE (AV)

20 North Washington Avenue, P.O. Box 725, 66749
Telephone: 316-365-5125
FAX: 316-365-8066

MEMBERS OF FIRM

J. D. (Dave) Conderman (1915-1978)
Robert V. Talkington
Robert F. Chase

Representative Clients: State Farm Mutual Insurance Co.; Medical Protective Co.; Allen County Hospital.

For full biographical listings, see the Martindale-Hubbell Law Directory

*JETMORE,** Hodgeman Co. — (Refer to Dodge City)

*JOHNSON,** Stanton Co. — (Refer to Garden City)

*JUNCTION CITY,** Geary Co.

HARPER, HORNBAKER, ALTENHOFEN & OPAT, CHARTERED (AV)

715 North Washington Street, P.O. Box 168, 66441
Telephone: 913-762-2100
Fax: 913-762-2291

Howard W. Harper (1912-1988)
Charles W. Harper, II
Lee Hornbaker
Craig Altenhofen
Steven Hornbaker
Steven L. Opat

Representative Clients: First State Bank; City of Grandview Plaza; Commercial Union Insurance Co.; Dodson Group; State Farm Insurance Cos.; Reliance Insurance Co.; Employers Mutual; U.S.F.&G.
Approved Attorneys for: Chicago Title & Trust; Columbian Title & Trust.

For full biographical listings, see the Martindale-Hubbell Law Directory

WEARY, DAVIS, HENRY, STRUEBING & TROUP (AV)

819 North Washington Street, P.O. Box 187, 66441
Telephone: 913-762-2210
Telefax: 913-238-3880

MEMBERS OF FIRM

Ulysses S. Weary (1885-1977)
Keith R. Henry
Robert K. Weary
Steven R. Struebing
Victor A. Davis, Jr.
David P. Troup

LEGAL SUPPORT PERSONNEL

Lydia Barth (Legal Assistant)

Representative Clients: Central National Bank; Unified School District #475; First State Bank of Junction City; Mid-America & Kansas CATV Assns.; First Page, Inc.
Local Counsel for: United Telephone Company of Kansas; Robertson & Penn, Inc.; Continental Grain, Inc.; Wal-Mart Stores, Inc.; Douglas Cable Communications.

For full biographical listings, see the Martindale-Hubbell Law Directory

*KANSAS CITY,** Wyandotte Co.

BODDINGTON & BROWN, CHTD. (AV)

Suite 100 Security Bank Building, Minnesota Avenue at 7th Street, 66101
Telephone: 913-371-1272
FAX: 913-371-5726

N. Jack Brown
John L. Hampton
Kenneth E. Holm
Joseph R. Ebbert
Leo L. Logan
D. Scott Brown
David W. Hauber
Stephen P. Doherty
Glenn B. Brown

(See Next Column)

BODDINGTON & BROWN CHTD.—*Continued*

OF COUNSEL

Albert M. Ross
Edward M. Boddington, Jr. (Retired)

For full biographical listings, see the Martindale-Hubbell Law Directory

HOLBROOK, HEAVEN & FAY, P.A. (AV)

757 Armstrong, P.O. Box 171927, 66117
Telephone: 913-342-2500
Fax: 913-342-0603
Merriam, Kansas Office: 6700 Antioch Street.
Telephone: 913-677-1717.
Fax: 913-677- 0403.

Reid F. Holbrook
Lewis A. Heaven, Jr. (Resident, Merriam Office)
Ted F. Fay, Jr. (Resident, Merriam Office)
Thomas E. Osborn
Robert L. Kennedy
Janet M. Simpson
John D. Tongier (Resident, Merriam Office)
Thomas M. Sutherland
Thomas S. Busch (Resident, Merriam Office)
Vincent K. Snowbarger (Resident, Merriam Office)
Kurt S. Brack
Sally A. Howard
Brent G. Wright
Damian Hornick (Resident, Merriam Office)
Henry F. Sonday, Jr.

OF COUNSEL

Donald H. Corson, Jr.
Darrel E. Johnson (Resident, Merriam Office)

For full biographical listings, see the Martindale-Hubbell Law Directory

MCANANY, VAN CLEAVE & PHILLIPS, P.A. (AV)

Fourth Floor, 707 Minnesota Avenue, P.O. Box 1300, 66117
Telephone: 913-371-3838
Facsimile: 913-371-4722
Lenexa, Kansas Office: Suite 200, 11900 West 87th Street Parkway.
Telephone: 913-888-9000.
Facsimile: 913-888-7049.
Kansas City, Missouri Office: Suite 304, 819 Walnut Street.
Telephone: 816-556-9417.

Edwin S. McAnany (1871-1954)
Thomas M. Van Cleave (1887-1961)
Willard L. Phillips (1905-1989)
John J. Jurcyk, Jr.
Robert D. Benham
Clifford T. Mueller (Resident, Lenexa Office)
James R. Goheen
Patrick D. McAnany (Resident, Lenexa Office)
Frank D. Menghini
David M. Druten (Resident, Lenexa Office)
Daniel B. Denk
Charles A. Getto
William P. Coates, Jr. (Resident, Lenexa Office)
Frederick J. Greenbaum
Nancy S. Anstaett (Resident, Lenexa Office)
Jeanne Gorman Rau
Wade A. Dorothy (Resident, Lenexa Office)
Robert F. Rowe, Jr. (Resident, Lenexa Office)
Lawrence D. Greenbaum
John David Jurcyk (Resident, Lenexa Office)
Douglas M. Greenwald
Daniel F. Church
Anton C. Andersen
Rosemary Podrebarac Case
Terri L. Savely Bezek
Joseph W. Hemberger
Gregory D. Worth (Resident, Lenexa Office)
Gregory S. Brown
Deryl William Wynn
Rex Wayne Henoch
Clifford K. Stubbs (Resident, Lenexa Office)
Henry E. Couchman, Jr.
Tracy D. Venters
Eric Thomas Lanham
Kristine Anne Purvis
Gregory P. Goheen
Paul K. Thoma
Stephen A. McManus

OF COUNSEL

Patrick Bevan McAnany (Resident, Lenexa Office)
Thomas M. Van Cleave, Jr. (Resident, Lenexa Office)
George T. O'Laughlin (Not admitted in KS)

Reference: UMB Commercial National Bank.

For full biographical listings, see the Martindale-Hubbell Law Directory

*KINGMAN,** Kingman Co. — (Refer to Pratt)

*KINSLEY,** Edwards Co. — (Refer to Dodge City)

*LA CROSSE,** Rush Co. — (Refer to Hays)

*LARNED,** Pawnee Co. — (Refer to Great Bend)

*LAWRENCE,** Douglas Co.

ALLEN, COOLEY & ALLEN (AV)

201 Mercantile Bank Tower, 900 Massachusetts, 66044-2868
Telephone: 913-843-0222
Fax: 913-843-0254

(See Next Column)

MEMBERS OF FIRM

Milton P. Allen, Sr. (1914-1988)
Gerald L. Cooley
Milton P. Allen, Jr.

ASSOCIATES

John M. Cooley
Michelle Ann Davis
Paul A. Seymour, III
Randall F. Larkin

Representative Clients: LRM Industries, Inc.; Shelter Insurance Cos.; Fireman's Fund Insurance Co.; B.A. Green Construction Co.; Westheffer Co., Inc.; The World Co., Inc.; Sunflower Cable TV; City of Lawrence.

For full biographical listings, see the Martindale-Hubbell Law Directory

BARBER, EMERSON, SPRINGER, ZINN & MURRAY, L.C. (AV)

1211 Massachusetts Street, P.O. Box 667, 66044
Telephone: 913-843-6600
Fax: 913-843-8405

John A. Emerson
Byron E. Springer
Richard L. Zinn
Thomas V. Murray
Calvin J. Karlin
Todd N. Thompson
Jane M. Eldredge

Mark A. Andersen
William N. Fleming
Charles F. Blaser

COUNSEL

Richard A. Barber
Martin B. Dickinson, Jr.
Glee S. Smith, Jr.

Representative Clients: Mercantile Bank of Lawrence, N.A., Lawrence, Kansas; University National Bank of Lawrence; FMC Corp.; Mine Safety Appliances Co.; Equitable Life Assurance Society of the U.S.; The Travelers Insurance Co.; Farm Bureau Mutual Insurance Co.

For full biographical listings, see the Martindale-Hubbell Law Directory

PETEFISH, CURRAN, IMMEL & HEEB (AV)

842 Louisiana Street, P.O. Box 485, 66044
Telephone: 913-843-0450
Fax: 913-843-0407

MEMBERS OF FIRM

C. C. Stewart (1884-1960)
Olin K. Petefish
Peter K. Curran
John J. Immel
Jeffrey O. Heeb

Representative Clients: The Lawrence National Bank & Trust Co.; Kansas University Endowment Assn.; Unified School Districts #491 and #497, Douglas County, Kansas; Kansas Public Service Co., Inc.; Columbia Savings Assn.; Lawrence Memorial Hospital; Presbyterian Manor of Lawrence.
Reference: The Lawrence National Bank & Trust Co.

For full biographical listings, see the Martindale-Hubbell Law Directory

STEVENS, BRAND, GOLDEN, WINTER & SKEPNEK (AV)

502 First National Bank Tower, P.O. Box 189, 66044-8200
Telephone: 913-843-0811
Fax: 913-843-0341

MEMBERS OF FIRM

John W. Brand, Jr.
Webster L. Golden
Winton A. Winter, Jr.
Diane W. Simpson
Scott J. Bloch
William J. Skepnek

ASSOCIATE

Nanette M. Kraus

Representative Clients: The Bank of Kansas/Lawrence; First Savings Bank; Peoples's National Bank & Trust; The Medical Protective Co.; Maupintour, Inc.; Bankers Life; Alvamar, Inc.; Economy Fire and Casualty Co.; Pennsylvania Casualty Co.; Laird Noller Ford, Inc.

For full biographical listings, see the Martindale-Hubbell Law Directory

*LEAVENWORTH,** Leavenworth Co.

DAVIS, BEALL, MCGUIRE & THOMPSON, CHARTERED (AV)

117 Cherokee, P.O. Box 69, 66048
Telephone: 913-682-3822
Fax: 913-682-7136

T. Homer Davis (1903-1992)
Robert D. Beall
John F. Thompson

OF COUNSEL

H. Lee McGuire, Jr.
Terence A. Lober

Representative Clients: First National Bank & Trust Co.; Army National Bank; Great Western Manufacturing Co.; Delaware Township; St. John Hospital; St. Mary College.

For full biographical listings, see the Martindale-Hubbell Law Directory

LENEXA, Johnson Co.

McAnany, Van Cleave & Phillips, P.A. (AV)

Suite 200, 11900 West 87th Street Parkway, 66215
Telephone: 913-888-9000
Facsimile: 913-888-7049
Kansas City, Kansas Office: Fourth Floor, 707 Minnesota Avenue, P.O. Box 1300.
Telephone: 913-371-3838.
Facsimile: 913-371-4722.
Kansas City, Missouri Office: Suite 304, 819 Walnut Street.
Telephone: 816-556-9417.

RESIDENT ATTORNEYS

Clifford T. Mueller, Wade A. Dorothy, Patrick D. McAnany, Robert F. Rowe, Jr., David M. Druten, John David Jurcyk, William P. Coates, Jr., Gregory D. Worth, Nancy S. Anstaett, Clifford K. Stubbs

OF COUNSEL

Patrick Bevan McAnany, Thomas M. Van Cleave, Jr.

Reference: UMB Commercial National Bank.

For full biographical listings, see the Martindale-Hubbell Law Directory

*LYNDON,** Osage Co. — (Refer to Ottawa)

*LYONS,** Rice Co. — (Refer to McPherson)

*MANKATO,** Jewell Co. — (Refer to Beloit)

*MARION,** Marion Co. — (Refer to McPherson)

*MARYSVILLE,** Marshall Co.

Galloway, Wiegers & Heeney (AV)

1114 Broadway, P.O. Box 468, 66508
Telephone: 913-562-2375
Fax: 913-562-5348

MEMBERS OF FIRM

Robert F. Galloway (1918-1986), Richard D. Heeney, Edward F. Wiegers, Michael W. Murphy, Charles Thomas Kier

Representative Clients: Citizens State Bank and Exchange National Bank, Maryville, Kansas; Landoll Corp; Bremen Farmers Mutual Insurance Co.; State Bank of Axtell; State Bank of Blue Rapids; Farm Credit Bank of Wichita.

*MCPHERSON,** McPherson Co.

Bremyer & Wise, P.A. (AV)

The Bremyer Building, P.O. Box 1146, 67460
Telephone: 316-241-0554
Telefax: 316-241-7692

Robert W. Wise, Brett A. Reber, J. Thomas Marten, Casey R. Law, Jill Bremyer-Archer, Randee Koger

OF COUNSEL

John K. Bremyer, Jay K. Bremyer

For full biographical listings, see the Martindale-Hubbell Law Directory

*MEADE,** Meade Co. — (Refer to Dodge City)

*NEWTON,** Harvey Co. — (Refer to Wichita)

*NORTON,** Norton Co. — (Refer to Oberlin)

*OAKLEY,** Logan Co. — (Refer to Goodland)

*OBERLIN,** Decatur Co.

Lund Law Firm, Chartered, A Professional Corporation (AV)

118 West Hall Street, P.O. Box 267, 67749
Telephone: 913-475-2312; 475-3540

Elmo Lund

Representative Clients: Sauvage Oil Co.; Brown Motor Co.
Reference: The Bank, Oberlin, Kansas.

*OSBORNE,** Osborne Co. — (Refer to Beloit)

*OSKALOOSA,** Jefferson Co. — (Refer to Valley Falls)

*OSWEGO,** Labette Co. — (Refer to Parsons)

*OTTAWA,** Franklin Co.

Anderson, Byrd, Richeson & Flaherty (AV)

216 South Hickory, P.O. Box 17, 66067
Telephone: 913-242-1234
Fax: 913-242-1279
Wellsville, Kansas Office: Wellsville Bank Building, P.O. Box 516.
Telephone: 913-883-2230.

MEMBERS OF FIRM

Robert A. Anderson, James G. Flaherty, Richard C. Byrd, Robert L. Bezek, Jr., John L. Richeson, Dee A. Henrichs

Representative Clients: Board of Education, Unified School Districts 289, 290 and 456; The City of Ottawa, Kansas; Empire District Electric Co.; Mesa Operating Co.; Ottawa University; First National Bank, Ottawa; Wellsville Bank; Kansas State Bank, Ottawa; Atmos.

For full biographical listings, see the Martindale-Hubbell Law Directory

Richard O. Skoog, P.A. (AV)

Title Building, P.O. Box 307, 66067-0307
Telephone: 913-242-2157

John B. Pierson (1911-1967), Richard O. Skoog

Counsel for: Ninth District; Southeast Kansas Production Credit Assn.; Federal Land Bank; Unified School District #287.
Local Counsel for: St. Paul Fire & Marine; Northwestern National Casualty Co.; Travelers Insurance Co.; Aetna Casualty & Surety Co.; Hartford Accident & Indemnity Co.; Farm Credit Bank of Wichita.

For full biographical listings, see the Martindale-Hubbell Law Directory

OVERLAND PARK, Johnson Co.

Blackwell Sanders Matheny Weary & Lombardi L.C. (AV)

40 Corporate Woods, Suite 1200, 9401 Indian Creek Parkway, 66210
Telephone: 913-345-8400
Telecopier: 913-344-6375
Kansas City, Missouri Office: Suite 1100, Two Pershing Square. 2300 Main Street.
Telephone: 816-274-6800.
Telecopier: 816-274-6914.

RESIDENT MEMBERS

Stephen T. Adams, James D. Griffin, James D. Conkright, Timothy W. Triplett, J. Michael Grier, James M. Warden

OF COUNSEL

Barton P. Cohen, Donald F. Martin (Not admitted in KS), Stephen C. Harmon

RESIDENT ASSOCIATES

Jeffrey S. Austin, Kristopher A. Kuehn, Victoria Henges Bonavia, James D. Langner (Not admitted in KS), Diane Breneman, B. K. Christopher, Diana D. Moore, William F. High, Peter S. Obetz, Lori H. Hill, Steven K. O'Hern, Sean K. Hogan, Kathryn A. Regier, Phillip D. Kline, Jana V. Richards, Michael J. Kuckelman, Curtis O. Roggow, Roger Warren

For full biographical listings, see the Martindale-Hubbell Law Directory

Lathrop & Norquist, L.C. (AV)

1050/40 Corporate Woods, 9401 Indian Creek Parkway, 66210-2007
Telephone: 913-451-0820
Telecopier: 913-451-0875
Kansas City, Missouri Office: 2345 Grand Boulevard, Suite 2500.
Telephone: 816-842-0820.
Telecopier: 816-421-0500.

Jeffrey O. Ellis (Resident), John L. Vratil (Resident), W. Joseph Hatley (Resident), William K. Waugh III (Resident), William G. Howard, Frederick K. Starrett (Resident), Gordon E. Wells, Jr. (Resident), Curtis L. Tideman, Harry E. Wigner, Jr. (Resident)

OF COUNSEL

Charles F. Zarter (Resident)

Laura J. Bond (Resident), J. Anthony Frazier (Resident), Denise E. Farris (Resident), Patrick J. Gregory (Resident), Mark Allen Ferguson (Resident), Charles W. McKee (Resident)

For full biographical listings, see the Martindale-Hubbell Law Directory

Overland Park—Continued

PAYNE & JONES, CHARTERED (AV)

Commerce Terrace, College Boulevard at King 11000 King, P.O. Box 25625, 66225
Telephone: 913-469-4100
FAX: 913-469-8182

Howard E. Payne (1901-1976)
W. C. Jones (1908-1970)
Robert P. Anderson
Keith Martin
H. Thomas Payne
John H. Johntz, Jr.
Edward M. Boyle
Michael G. Norris
Barry W. McCormick
Thomas K. Jones
David K. Martin
Jodde Olsen Lanning
Thomas L. Griswold
Susan S. Baker
Bruce Keplinger
T. Bradley Manson
John M. Klamann
Kip A. Kubin
Donald R. Whitney
Jon W. Gilchrist
Michael W. Lucansky
Michael B. Lowe
Julie A. N. Sample
Dirk L. Hubbard
Steven L. Passer
J. Tyler Peters
Scott M. Adam
Scott C. Long
Deborah A. Moeller
Roger Hadley Templin

Representative Clients: First Federal Savings & Loan Association of Olathe, Kansas; Aetna Casualty & Surety Co.; Commercial Union Insurance Cos.; Farmers Insurance Group; The Hartford Insurance Group; United States Fidelity & Guaranty Co.; Continental Insurance Co.

For full biographical listings, see the Martindale-Hubbell Law Directory

SHUGHART THOMSON & KILROY, A PROFESSIONAL CORPORATION (AV)

Suite 1100, 32 Corporate Woods, 9225 Indian Creek Parkway, 66210
Telephone: 913-451-3355
Kansas City, Missouri Office: Twelve Wyandotte Plaza, 120 West 12th Street.
Telephone: 816-421-3355.

KANSAS OFFICE ATTORNEYS

William V. North
Steven D. Ruse
James P. O'Hara
Anthony F. Rupp
Robert B. Keim
Gregory L. Musil
Donald A. Culp
Roger M. Phillips
Charles J. Hyland

For full biographical listings, see the Martindale-Hubbell Law Directory

WALLACE, SAUNDERS, AUSTIN, BROWN & ENOCHS, CHARTERED (AV)

10111 West 87th Street, P.O. Box 12290, 66282-2290
Telephone: 913-888-1000
Fax: 913-888-1065
Wichita, Kansas Office: 600 Epic Center, 301 North Main Street.
Telephone: 316-269-2100.
Fax: 316-269-2479.
Springfield, Missouri Office: 1201 Hammons Tower, 901 East St. Louis Street.
Telephone: 417-866-2300.
Fax: 417-866-2444.
Kansas City, Missouri Office: 1200 East 104th Street, Second Floor.
Telephone: 913-888-1000.
Fax: 913-888-1065.

Frank Saunders, Jr.
Barton Brown
Richmond M. Enochs
James G. Butler, Jr.
James O. Schwinn
Richard T. Merker
Jerome V. Bales
H. Wayne Powers
Rod L. Richardson
Paul Hasty, Jr.
Barry E. Warren
Sally H. Harris
Mark W. McKinzie
Michael P. Oliver
James L. Sanders
Rudolf H. Beese
Michael J. Dutton
Thomas D. Billam
Kevin L. Bennett
Gary R. Terrill
Timothy G. Lutz
Mark V. Bodine
Norman I. Reichel, Jr.
Leonard R. Frischer
Bradley S. Russell
Ben W. Ansley

OF COUNSEL

Gary M. Cupples (Not admitted in KS)
Jeffrey W. Bruce (Not admitted in KS)
Larry J. Austin (Retired)
Kenneth B. Wallace (1912-1982)

Patrick E. McGrath
Robert A. Mintz
D'Ambra Howard
Timothy J. Mudd
Karl Kuckelman
John M. Ross
Eric A. Van Beber
Patrick F. Hulla
Tina A. Smith
Jay B. Brown
Karen A. Seymour
Derrick A. Pearce
Chad K. Gillam
John Graham, Jr.
Arlen L. Tanner
Gavin Fritton
W. Eugene Cox

For full biographical listings, see the Martindale-Hubbell Law Directory

PARSONS, Labette Co.

DEARTH, MARKHAM & JACK, CHARTERED (AV)

1712 Broadway, P.O. Box 1034, 67357
Telephone: 316-421-1970; 421-3650
Fax: 316-421-8846

Glenn Jones (1911-1985)
Richard C. Dearth
David K. Markham
Jeffry L. Jack

OF COUNSEL

John B. Markham

Representative Clients: First National Bank and Trust Co.; Commercial Bank; Day & Zimmerman International, Inc.; Liberty Mutual Insurance Co.; American States Insurance Co.; Federated Insurance Co.

For full biographical listings, see the Martindale-Hubbell Law Directory

*PHILLIPSBURG,** Phillips Co. — (Refer to Oberlin)

PITTSBURG, Crawford Co.

WILBERT AND TOWNER, P.A. (AV)

506 North Pine, P.O. Box V, 66762
Telephone: 316-231-5620
Fax: 316-231-5812

Paul L. Wilbert
Garry W. Lassman
Robert J. Fleming
A. J. Wachter
J. Gordon Gregory
William B. Wachter
William J. Morin
Craig R. Richey

OF COUNSEL

John B. Towner

For full biographical listings, see the Martindale-Hubbell Law Directory

PRAIRIE VILLAGE, Johnson Co.

BENNETT, LYTLE, WETZLER, MARTIN & PISHNY, L.C. (AV)

Suite 300 Greenview Place, 5000 West 95th Street, P.O. Box 8030, 66208
Telephone: 913-642-7300
Fax: 913-642-0520

Robert F. Bennett
Robert F. Lytle
Charles E. Wetzler
P. Stephen Martin
Lyle D. Pishny
Richard S. Wetzler
Bruce F. Landeck
James R. Orr
Andrew F. Sears
Janice S. Martin
Patrick D. Gaston
David J. Adkins
Mark C. Owens
Patricia A. Bennett

Nathan M. Sutton
David C. Wetzler

OF COUNSEL

Peter A. Martin, P.C.

Representative Clients: Bank IV Kansas; Johnson County Community College; Unified School District 512 (Shawnee Mission Public Schools); City of Prairie Village, Kansas; City of Leawood, Kansas.

For full biographical listings, see the Martindale-Hubbell Law Directory

HOLMAN, McCOLLUM & HANSEN, P.C. (AV(T))

9400 Mission Road Suite 205, 66206
Telephone: 913-648-7272
Fax: 913-383-9596
Kansas City, Missouri Office: 644 West 57th Terrace.
Telephone: 816-333-8522.
Fax: 913-383-9596.

Joseph Y. Holman
Frank B. W. McCollum
Eric L. Hansen
Dana L. Parks
Nancy Merrill Wilson
Amy L. Brown
E. John Edwards III (Not admitted in KS)
Katherine E. Rich

For full biographical listings, see the Martindale-Hubbell Law Directory

*PRATT,** Pratt Co.

HAMPTON & HAMPTON (AV)

Professional Building, 113 East Third, Drawer H, 67124-1108
Telephone: 316-672-5533
Fax: 316-672-6713

MEMBERS OF FIRM

B.V. Hampton
Bill V. Hampton, Jr.

General Counsel For: First National Bank in Pratt; Pratt Feeders, Inc.; Pratt Community College/Area Vocational School; M-C Company; Unified School District 438; Pratt Ag Aviation, Inc.; J.V.J. Irrigation Services.

For full biographical listings, see the Martindale-Hubbell Law Directory

*RUSSELL,** Russell Co. — (Refer to Hays)

*ST. FRANCIS,** Cheyenne Co. — (Refer to Goodland)

*ST. JOHN,** Stafford Co.

SHIELDS LAW OFFICE, P.A. (AV)

106 East Third Street, P.O. Box 427, 67576
Telephone: 316-549-3212
Fax: 316-549-3268

Emerson H. Shields

Representative Clients: Farmers and Merchants State Bank, Macksville; First National Bank & Trust of St. John.

*SALINA,** Saline Co.

CLARK, MIZE & LINVILLE, CHARTERED (AV)

129 South Eighth, P.O. Box 380, 67402-0380
Telephone: 913-823-6325
Fax: 913-823-1868

James P. Mize (1910-1988)
L. O. Bengtson
Peter L. Peterson
John W. Mize
Greg A. Bengtson
Lawton M. Nuss
Mickey W. Mosier
Robert M. Adrian
Steven W. Brown
Dana P. Ryan
Paula J. Wright
Eric N. Anderson
Donald G. Reinsch

OF COUNSEL

C. L. Clark
Aubrey G. Linville

Representative Clients: Asbury-Salina Regional Medical Center, Inc.; Coldwell-Banker, Antrim, Piper, Wenger Realtors, Inc.; Crestwood, Inc.; Kansas Wesleyan University; Premier Pneumatics; City of Salina; Sunflower Bank, N.A.; Tony's Pizza Service; Unified School District 305; Wilson & Company, Engineers & Architects.

For full biographical listings, see the Martindale-Hubbell Law Directory

HAMPTON, ROYCE, ENGLEMAN & NELSON (AV)

Ninth Floor United Building, 67401
Telephone: 913-827-7251
Fax: 913-827-2815

MEMBERS OF FIRM

C. W. Burch (1869-1945)
B. I. Litowich (1883-1949)
LaRue Royce (1891-1954)
E. S. Hampton (1905-1982)
Tom W. Hampton (1935-1984)
C. Stanley Nelson
Jack N. Stewart
W. Dean Owens
N. Royce Nelson
Sidney A. Reitz
David D. Moshier
J. Stan Sexton
David R. Klaassen
Debra Egli James
Jeffrey E. King
Terry Criss

OF COUNSEL

John Q. Royce (1918-1991)
Howard Engleman
Clarence L. King, Jr.

ASSOCIATES

John Andrew O'Leary

Representative Clients: Altman Construction and Supply, Inc.; Bank IV, Salina; Farmers & Merchants Bank of Colby; First Bank and Trust of Salina; First National Bank of Beloit; Kansas Chemical & Fertilizer Assn.; Kansas Grain & Feed Assn.; Morrison Enterprises; Salina Supply Co.; Sellers Tractor Co., Inc.

For full biographical listings, see the Martindale-Hubbell Law Directory

*SCOTT CITY,** Scott Co. — (Refer to Garden City)

*SEDAN,** Chautauqua Co. — (Refer to Coffeyville)

*SENECA,** Nemaha Co. — (Refer to Marysville)

*SHARON SPRINGS,** Wallace Co. — (Refer to Goodland)

*SMITH CENTER,** Smith Co. — (Refer to Beloit)

STERLING, Rice Co. — (Refer to Hutchinson)

*STOCKTON,** Rooks Co. — (Refer to Hays)

*SYRACUSE,** Hamilton Co. — (Refer to Garden City)

*TOPEKA,** Shawnee Co.

BENNETT & DILLON (AV)

1605 Southwest 37th Street, 66611
Telephone: 913-267-5063
Fax: 913-267-2652

MEMBERS OF FIRM

Mark L. Bennett, Jr.
Wilburn Dillon, Jr.
Glenda L. Cafer
Ann L. Hoover

References: Commerce Bank and Trust; Columbian National Bank and Trust; Silver Lake State Bank.

For full biographical listings, see the Martindale-Hubbell Law Directory

COSGROVE, WEBB & OMAN (AV)

1100 Bank IV Tower, One Townsite Plaza, 66603
Telephone: 913-235-9511
Fax: 913-235-2082

MEMBERS OF FIRM

M. F. Cosgrove (1889-1961)
Robert L. Webb (1890-1975)
Ralph W. Oman (1897-1984)
Philip E. Buzick (1918-1970)
William B. McElhenny (1920-1976)
Donald J. Horttor
Edward L. Bailey
Robert L. Baer
Charles T. Engel
Carol B. Bonebrake

ASSOCIATE

Susan L. Mauch

OF COUNSEL

James D. Waugh

For full biographical listings, see the Martindale-Hubbell Law Directory

DAVIS, UNREIN, HUMMER, MCCALLISTER & BUCK (AV)

100 East Ninth Street, Third Floor, P.O. Box 3575, 66601-3575
Telephone: 913-354-1100
Fax: 913-354-1113

MEMBERS OF FIRM

Byron M. Gray (1901-1986)
Maurice D. Freidberg (1902-1965)
Charles L. Davis, Jr. (1921-1992)
Michael J. Unrein
J. Franklin Hummer
Mark A. Buck
James B. Biggs
Christopher M. Rohrer
Brenda L. Head

OF COUNSEL

Gary D. McCallister

Representative Clients: Adams Business Forms; Bettis Asphalt Co., Inc.; Blue Cross & Blue Shield of Kansas; Cooper Tire & Rubber Co.; Deere & Co.; Famous Brands; Jostens, Inc.; Kansas Association of Realtors; McElroys, Inc.; McPherson Contractors.

For full biographical listings, see the Martindale-Hubbell Law Directory

FISHER, PATTERSON, SAYLER & SMITH (AV)

534 Kansas Avenue, Suite 400, 66603-3463
Telephone: 913-232-7761
Fax: 913-232-6604
Overland Park, Kansas Office: Suite 210, 11050 Roe Street. 66211.
Telephone: 913-339-6757.
Fax: 913-339-6187.

MEMBERS OF FIRM

Donald Patterson
Charles Keith Sayler
Edwin Dudley Smith (Resident, Overland Park Office)
Larry G. Pepperdine
James P. Nordstrom
Justice B. King
J. Steven Pigg
Steve R. Fabert
Ronald J. Laskowski
Michael K. Seck (Resident, Overland Park Office)
David P. Madden (Resident, Overland Park Office)
Steven K. Johnson

ASSOCIATES

Kristine A. Larscheid
Michael L. Bennett
Kurt A. Level (Resident, Overland Park Office)
Betty J. Mick

OF COUNSEL

David H. Fisher

Representative Clients: Gage Shopping Center, Inc.; Fireman's Fund-American Insurance Cos.; United States Fidelity and Guaranty Co.; Hartford Insurance Group.; The Procter & Gamble Company; American Cyanamid Company; Commercial Union Insurance Companies; Kansas Fire & Casualty Co.; National Casualty/Scottsdale Insurance Co.

For full biographical listings, see the Martindale-Hubbell Law Directory

GOODELL, STRATTON, EDMONDS & PALMER (AV)

515 South Kansas Avenue, 66603-3999
Telephone: 913-233-0593
Telecopier: 913-233-8870

MEMBERS OF FIRM

Gerald L. Goodell
Wayne T. Stratton
Robert E. Edmonds (Retired)
Arthur E. Palmer
H. Philip Elwood
Harold S. Youngentob
Gerald J. Letourneau
Charles R. Hay
Patrick M. Salsbury
Michael W. Merriam
John H. Stauffer, Jr.
Les E. Diehl
David E. Bruns
Daniel J. Gronniger
N. Larry Bork
John D. Ensley

OF COUNSEL

Robert A. McClure
Samuel D. Brownback

(See Next Column)

GOODELL, STRATTON, EDMONDS & PALMER—*Continued*

ASSOCIATES

Curtis J. Waugh
Catherine Walberg
Craig S. Kendall
Steve A Schwarm

SPECIAL COUNSEL

Joseph E. McKinney
Marta Fisher Linenberger

Local Counsel for: Farm Bureau Mutual Insurance Co.; Metropolitan Life Insurance Co.; St. Paul Fire & Marine Insurance Co.
General Counsel for: American Home Life Insurance Co.; Columbian National Title Insurance Co.; The Menninger Foundation; Stauffer Communications, Inc.; Kansas Association of Realtors; Kansas Medical Society; Kansas Hospital Association.

For full biographical listings, see the Martindale-Hubbell Law Directory

PORTER, FAIRCHILD, WACHTER & HANEY, P.A. (AV)

Suite 1000, Bank IV Tower, 534 South Kansas Avenue, P.O. Box 1833, 66601-1833
Telephone: 913-235-2200
Facsimile: 913-235-8950

James W. Porter
Ronald W. Fairchild
John H. Wachter
Thomas D. Haney

Douglas F. Martin
Sheldon J. Moss

For full biographical listings, see the Martindale-Hubbell Law Directory

WRIGHT, HENSON, SOMERS, SEBELIUS, CLARK & BAKER (AV)

Commerce Bank Building, 100 Southeast Ninth Street, 2nd Floor, P.O. Box 3555, 66601-3555
Telephone: 913-232-2200
FAX: 913-232-3344

MEMBERS OF FIRM

Thomas E. Wright
Charles N. Henson
Dale L. Somers
K. Gary Sebelius
Bruce J. Clark
Anne Lamborn Baker

ASSOCIATES

Catherine A. Walter
Evelyn Zabel Wilson
Theron L. Sims, Jr.
J. Lyn Entrikin Goering

For full biographical listings, see the Martindale-Hubbell Law Directory

*TRIBUNE,** Greeley Co. — (Refer to Garden City)

*TROY,** Doniphan Co.

EULER & McQUILLAN (AV)

137 South Main Street, P.O. Box 326, 66087
Telephone: 913-985-3561
FAX: 913-985-2322

MEMBERS OF FIRM

Jack R. Euler
William R. McQuillan

ASSOCIATES

Robyn Euler Johnson
Joel Euler

Representative Clients: Bank of Denton; Farmers State Bank, Wathena, Kansas; Burr Oak Drainage Districts No. 2 and 3; Elwood-Gladden Drainage District; Rural Fire Districts No. 1 and 4; Cities of Denton, Elwood and Wathena.
References: The Bank of Denton, Denton, Kansas; Farmers State Bank, Wathena, Kansas.

For full biographical listings, see the Martindale-Hubbell Law Directory

VALLEY FALLS, Jefferson Co.

LOWRY & JOHNSON (AV)

323 Broadway Avenue, P.O. Box 10, 66088
Telephone: 913-945-3281
Facsimile: 913-945-6255

MEMBERS OF FIRM

Gordon K. Lowry
Rick A. Johnson
Stuart S. Lowry

Attorneys for: Kendall State Bank, Valley Falls, Kansas; Leavenworth-Jefferson Electric Cooperative, Inc.; Unified School District #338, Valley Falls, Kansas; Delaware Watershed Joint District #10; Cities of Nortonville and Valley Falls, Kansas; Kaw Valley Electric Cooperative, Topeka, Kansas.
General Counsel for: Kansas Electric Co-operatives, Inc.

For full biographical listings, see the Martindale-Hubbell Law Directory

*WA KEENEY,** Trego Co. — (Refer to Hays)

*WASHINGTON,** Washington Co. — (Refer to Marysville)

WELLSVILLE, Franklin Co.

ANDERSON, BYRD, RICHESON & FLAHERTY (AV)

Wellsville Bank Building, P.O. Box 516, 66092
Telephone: 913-883-2230
Ottawa, Kansas Office: 216 South Hickory, P.O. Box 7.
Telephone: 913-242-1234.
Fax: 913-242-1279.

John L. Richeson

Representative Clients: Board of Education, Unified School Districts 289, 290 and 456; The City of Ottawa, Kansas; Empire District Electric Co.; Mesa Operating Co.; Ottawa University; First National Bank, Ottawa; Wellsville Bank; Kansas State Bank, Ottawa; Atmos.

For full biographical listings, see the Martindale-Hubbell Law Directory

*WICHITA,** Sedgwick Co.

ADAMS, JONES, ROBINSON AND MALONE, CHARTERED (AV)

600 Market Centre, 155 North Market, P.O. Box 1034, 67201-1034
Telephone: 316-265-8591
Telecopier: 316-265-9719

Mark H. Adams (1897-1984)
Charles E. Jones (1908-1992)
William I. Robinson (1909-1993)
J. Ashford Manka (1911-1970)
Clifford L. Malone
Philip L. Bowman
Donald W. Bostwick
Mert F. Buckley
John W. Sumi
Monte Vines
Teresa J. James
Laura L. Ice
Larry D. Spurgeon
Michael T. Metcalf

OF COUNSEL

John S. Seeber

Representative Clients: Financial: Intrust Bank, N.A.; Metropolitan Federal Bank, fsb; Bank IV, Kansas; Travelers Insurance Co.; Citizens State Bank of Hugoton; Mulvane State Bank. Oil and Gas: Williams Natural Gas Co.; BHP Petroleum (Americas) Inc. General: Ameri-Kart Corp.; Clark Equipment, Co.

For full biographical listings, see the Martindale-Hubbell Law Directory

DEPEW & GILLEN (AV)

151 North Main, Suite 700, 67202-1408
Telephone: 316-265-9621
Facsimile: 316-265-3819

MEMBERS OF FIRM

Spencer L. Depew
Dennis L. Gillen
Jack Scott McInteer
David W. Nickel
Nicholas S. Daily
David E. Rogers
Charles Christian Steincamp

For full biographical listings, see the Martindale-Hubbell Law Directory

FLEESON, GOOING, COULSON & KITCH, L.L.C. (AV)

125 North Market Street, Suite 1600, P.O. Box 997, 67201-0997
Telephone: 316-267-7361
Telecopier: 316-267-1754

Howard T. Fleeson (1895-1957)
Homer V. Gooing (1894-1986)
Wayne Coulson (1910-1985)
Paul R. Kitch (1911-1987)
Carl A. Bell, Jr.
Gerrit H. Wormhoudt
Willard B. Thompson
Richard I. Stephenson
Thomas D. Kitch
J. Eric Engstrom
Stephen M. Joseph
Stephen E. Robison
Mark F. Anderson
Ronald Campbell
Timothy P. O'Sullivan
Gregory J. Stucky
Charles E. Millsap
Edward J. Healy
Linda K. Constable
William P. Tretbar
Susan P. Selvidge
Dixie F. Madden
Thomas J. Lasater
David G. Seely
Mary E. May
Stephen M. Stark
Lyndon W. Vix

John T. Steere
William Townsley
Scott Jensen
Jordan Clay
John R. Gerdes
Joan M. Bowen
John E. Rees, II
Kent A. Meyerhoff

OF COUNSEL

Dale M. Stucky
Donald R. Newkirk
James R. Boyd

Attorneys for: Bank IV, Wichita, N.A; Intrust Bank, N.A.; Wichita Eagle and Beacon Publishing Co., Inc.; Southwest Kansas Royalty Owners Assn.; Liberty Mutual Insurance Co.; Grant Thornton; The Law Company; Vulcan Materials Co.; The Wichita State University Board of Trustees.

For full biographical listings, see the Martindale-Hubbell Law Directory

Wichita—Continued

FOULSTON & SIEFKIN (AV)

(Formerly Foulston, Siefkin, Powers & Eberhardt)
700 Fourth Financial Center, Broadway at Douglas, 67202
Telephone: 316-267-6371
Facsimile: 316-267-6345
Topeka, Kansas Office: 1515 Bank IV Tower, 534 Kansas Avenue. 66603.
Telephone: 913-233-3600.
FAX: 913-233-1610.
Member: Lex Mundi, A Global Association of Independent Firms

MEMBERS OF FIRM

Richard C. Harris
Gerald Sawatzky
Robert L. Howard
Charles J. Woodin
Mikel L. Stout
Benjamin C. Langel
William H. Dye
Phillip S. Frick
Stanley G. Andeel
Frederick L. Haag
Richard D. Ewy
Darrell L. Warta
Harvey R. Sorensen
James M. Armstrong
Mary Kathleen Babcock
Charles P. Efflandt
James D. Oliver
Gary L. Ayers
Gloria G. Farha Flentje
Larry G. Rapp
R. Douglas Reagan
Jay F. Fowler
Stephen M. Kerwick
Gary E. Knight
Christopher M. Hurst
Vaughn Burkholder
Terry C. Cupps
Susan L. Smith
Wyatt M. Wright
Jim H. Goering
Wyatt A. Hoch
Amy S. Lemley
James P. Rankin (Resident, Topeka Office)
Douglas L. Hanisch
Douglas L. Stanley
J. Steven Massoni
Timothy B. Mustaine
Jeffery A. Jordan
Trisha A. Thelen
William R. Wood, II
Eric F. Melgren
Kevin J. Arnel
Craig W. West
Carol A. Beier

SPECIAL COUNSEL

Robert L. Heath
Nancy M. Clifton
James L. Grimes, Jr. (Resident, Topeka Office)
David M. Traster
Matthew C. Hesse
Robert A. Fox (Resident, Topeka Office)

ASSOCIATES

Mark D. Anstoetter
Mark A. Biberstein
Boyd A. Byers
Jeffrey P. DeGraffenreid
John V. Dwyer
William N. Kirk
Eric K. Kuhn
J. May Liang
James Scott MacBeth
Rowdy B. Meeks
Kelly W. Milligan
Jay M. Rector
Gaye B. Tibbets
Stewart T. Weaver
Thomas W. Young

Representative Clients: Fourth Financial Corp. (Bank IV Kansas); The Boeing Company; The Coleman Co.; Koch Industries, Inc.; Pizza Hut, Inc.; State Farm Mutual Insurance Co.; Shelter Insurance Company; Atlantic Richfield Co.; The Sisters of St. Joseph of Wichita; The Wichita Clinic.

For full biographical listings, see the Martindale-Hubbell Law Directory

GOTT, YOUNG & BOGLE, P.A.

(See Young, Bogle, McCausland, Wells & Clark)

HERSHBERGER, PATTERSON, JONES & ROTH, L.C. (AV)

600 Hardage Center, 100 South Main, 67202-3779
Telephone: 316-263-7583
Fax: 316-263-7595

A. W. Hershberger (1897-1976)
J. B. Patterson (1895-1957)
Richard Jones (1914-1988)
Jerome E. Jones
Robert J. Roth
William R. Smith
Greer Gsell
J. Michael Kennalley
Evan J. Olson
John A. Vetter
Jeffrey A. Roth
David J. Morgan
Ken W. Dannenberg

Tracy A. Applegate
Marc P. Clements

OF COUNSEL

H. E. Jones
John L. Kratzer, Jr.

Counsel For: First National Bank in Wichita; Andarko Petroleum Corporation; Chinese Industries; Mobil Oil Corp.; CNA Insurance; Royal Exchange Group; Central National Insurance Group; Transamerica Insurance Group; Northwestern National Insurance Group.

For full biographical listings, see the Martindale-Hubbell Law Directory

HINKLE, EBERHART & ELKOURI, L.L.C. (AV)

Suite 2000 Epic Center, 301 North Main Street, 67202
Telephone: 316-267-2000
Fax: 316-264-1518

(See Next Column)

Winton M. Hinkle
Max E. Eberhart
David S. Elkouri
John E. Caton
John R. Stallings
Eric S. Namee
John Terry Moore
David M. Rapp
Thomas R. Powell
William F. Bradley, Jr.
Dan C. Peare

J. T. Klaus
L. Dale Ward
Connie D. Tatum
Kim A. Bell
Kathryn D. Griffith

OF COUNSEL

Roger M. Theis

Representative Clients: Farm Credit Bank of Wichita; City of Wichita, Kansas; Wichita Public Schools; Beech Aircraft Corporation; Hugoton Energy Corporation; Rand Graphics, Inc.; Cessna Aircraft Company; St. Francis Regional Medical Center; The Colemen Co., Inc.; Universal Products Inc.

For full biographical listings, see the Martindale-Hubbell Law Directory

KAHRS, NELSON, FANNING, HITE & KELLOGG (AV)

Suite 630, 200 West Douglas Street, 67202-3089
Telephone: 316-265-7761
Telecopier: 316-267-7803

MEMBERS OF FIRM

William A. Kahrs (1904-1989)
Robert H. Nelson (1904-1977)
Darrell D. Kellogg (1931-1992)
Richard C. Hite
Richard L. Honeyman
Larry A. Withers
Gary A. Winfrey
Robert Hall
Clark R. Nelson
Steven D. Gough
Scott J. Gunderson
Randy Troutt
Arthur S. Chalmers
Marc A. Powell
Kim R. Martens
Linda S. Parks
Forrest James Robinson, Jr.
Don D. Gribble, II
John G. Pike
Vince P. Wheeler
Alan R. Pfaff
Dennis V. Lacey

ASSOCIATES

Dana D. Preheim
Donald N. Peterson, II
Curtis L. Perry
Todd M. Connell
J. Scott Pohl

OF COUNSEL

H. W. Fanning

Representative Clients: Advance Chemical Dist., Inc.; Learjet Corp.; Hahner, Foreman & Harness, Contractors; New York Life Ins. Co.; United States Fidelity & Guaranty Co; General Motors Corp.; St. Paul Ins. Cos.; Ruffin Hotel Corp.; Central Detroit Diesel Allison, Inc.

For full biographical listings, see the Martindale-Hubbell Law Directory

KLENDA, MITCHELL, AUSTERMAN & ZUERCHER (AV)

1600 Epic Center, 301 North Main Street, 67202-4888
Telephone: 316-267-0331
Telecopier: 316-267-0333

MEMBERS OF FIRM

L. D. Klenda
Alexander B. Mitchell, II
Bruce W. Zuercher
Gary M. Austerman
Michael R. Biggs
Alan D. Herman
John V. Wachtel
J. Michael Morris
David D. Broomfield
Jeffrey D. Peier
Ron Dean Beal
Scott A. Eads
Mark J. Lazzo
John B. Gilliam
Gregory B. Klenda
Christopher A. McElgunn

ASSOCIATES

Brett C. Bogan
Deborah L. Mahoney
Mary T. Malicoat
Daniel C. Schulte
Robert (Rocky) D. Wiechman, Jr.

OF COUNSEL

Vincent L. Bogart
Patricia J. Coffey
Ronald M. Gott

Representative Clients: Beechcraft Employees Credit Union; Bombardier Capital Inc.; Halliburton Co.; Mid-America World Trade Center; National Cooperative Refinery Assn.; Petroleum, Inc.; Physicians Corporation of America; St. Francis Regional Medical Center, Inc.; United States Aviation Underwriters.
Franchise Client: ALCF, Inc. (Association of Little Caesars Franchisees).

For full biographical listings, see the Martindale-Hubbell Law Directory

MARTIN, PRINGLE, OLIVER, WALLACE & SWARTZ, L.C. (AV)

300 Page Court, 220 West Douglas Street, 67202-3194
Telephone: 316-265-9311
Telefax: 316-265-2955

Robert Martin
William L. Oliver, Jr.
Paul B. Swartz
Dwight D Wallace
Larry B. Spikes
Martin W. Bauer
Douglas S. Pringle
David S. Wooding

(See Next Column)

MARTIN, PRINGLE, OLIVER, WALLACE & SWARTZ L.C.—*Continued*

George C. Bruce
Terry L. Malone
Jeff C. Spahn, Jr.
Jeff Kennedy
Terry L. Mann
Terry J. Torline
Stuart M. Kowalski
Brian S. Burris
Ann T. Rider
William S. Woolley

Kathryn Gardner
Michael G. Jones
Richard K. Thompson
Ellen Tracy
Brent A. Mitchell
Angela L. Reed
Roger E. McClellan

OF COUNSEL

Orval J. Kaufman
Kenneth Pringle (Retired)

LEGAL SUPPORT PERSONNEL

Patricia A. Gorham

General Counsel for: Beech Aircraft Corp.; Travel Air Insurance Co., Ltd.; Mull Drilling Co.
Representative Clients: K N Energy, Inc.; Multimedia Cablevision, Inc.; Peoples Natural Gas Co.; Raytheon Company; Union National Bank; United Beechcraft, Inc.; Rose America.

For full biographical listings, see the Martindale-Hubbell Law Directory

MORRIS, LAING, EVANS, BROCK & KENNEDY, CHARTERED (AV)

Fourth Floor, 200 West Douglas, 67202-3084
Telephone: 316-262-2671
FAX: 316-262-6226; 262-5991
Topeka Office: 800 S.W. Jackson, Suite 914. 66612-2214.
Telephone: 913-232-2662.
Fax: 913-232-9983.

Lester L. Morris (1901-1966)
Verne M. Laing (Retired)
Ferd E. Evans, Jr. (1919-1991)
Ralph R. Brock
Joseph W. Kennedy
Robert I. Guenthner
David C. Adams
Ken M. Peterson
Richard D. Greene
A. J. Schwartz, Jr.
Donald E. Schrag
William B. Sorensen, Jr.
Dennis M. Feeney
Jeffery L. Carmichael
Robert W. Coykendall
Robert K. Anderson
Susan R. Schrag
Robert E. Nugent
Michael Lennen
Karl R. Swartz
Roger L. Theis
Jana Deines Abbott
Richard F. Hayse (Resident, Topeka Office)
Thomas R. Docking
Gerald N. Capps
Diane S. Worth
Eva Powers (Resident, Topeka Office)
Tim J. Moore
Bruce A. Ney
Janet Huck Ward

OF COUNSEL

Robert B. Morton

References: The Emprise Banks of Kansas; Mellon Bank; N.A.; The Merchants National Bank of Topeka; Southwest National Bank; Twin Lakes Bank & Trust.

For full biographical listings, see the Martindale-Hubbell Law Directory

TRIPLETT, WOOLF & GARRETSON (AV)

Suite 800 Centre City Plaza, 151 North Main, 67202-1409
Telephone: 316-265-5700
Telecopy: 316-265-6165

MEMBERS OF FIRM

Thomas C. Triplett
John P. Woolf
Thomas P. Garretson
James A. Walker
Timothy E. McKee
Theron E. Fry
Eric B. Metz
Ron H. Harnden
Lee Thompson
Eric S. Strickler
Tad Patton
Bradley A. Stout

ASSOCIATES

Rachael K. Pirner
Jeffrey Don Leonard
Nancy J. Strouse

Representative Clients: Brite Voice Systems, Inc.; Beech Aircraft Corp.; Coleman Company, Inc.; Colorado Interstate Gas Co.; Dow Chemical Co.; Friends University; KPMG Peat Marwick; Mid-America Pipeline Co.; Travelers Insurance Co.; Willis Coroon of Kansas, Inc.

For full biographical listings, see the Martindale-Hubbell Law Directory

YOUNG, BOGLE, McCAUSLAND, WELLS & CLARK, P.A. (AV)

106 West Douglas, Suite 923, 67202
Telephone: 316-265-7841
Facsimile: 316-265-3956

Glenn D. Young, Jr.
Jerry D. Bogle
Paul S. McCausland
William A. Wells
Kenneth M. Clark
Patrick C. Blanchard

Mark R. Maloney

(See Next Column)

OF COUNSEL

Orlin L. Wagner

Representative Clients: Bridgestone/Firestone Inc.; Deere & Co.; Citibank; Metropolitan Life Insurance Co.; Equitable Life Assurance Society of the United States; New York Life Insurance Co.

For full biographical listings, see the Martindale-Hubbell Law Directory

*YATES CENTER,** Woodson Co. — (Refer to Chanute)

KENTUCKY

*ALBANY,** Clinton Co. — (Refer to Glasgow)

ASHLAND, Boyd Co.

Martin, Picklesimer, Justice & Vincent (AV)

431 Sixteenth Street, P.O. Box 2528, 41105-2528
Telephone: 606-329-8338
Fax: 606-325-8199

Richard W. Martin
Max D. Picklesimer
David Justice
John F. Vincent

ASSOCIATES

Thomas Wade Lavender, II
P. Kimberly Watson

Representative Clients: City of Ashland; FIVCO Area Development District; Boyd County Sanitation District No. 2; Mid-America Distributors, Inc.
Insurance Counsel for: State Farm Mutual Automobile Insurance Co.; State Farm Fire and Casualty Co.; Aetna Casualty Insurance Co.; Grange Mutual Insurance Co.; Great American Insurance Co.

For full biographical listings, see the Martindale-Hubbell Law Directory

VanAntwerp, Monge, Jones & Edwards (AV)

1544 Winchester Avenue Fifth Floor, P.O. Box 1111, 41105-1111
Telephone: 606-329-2929
Fax: 606-329-0490
Ironton, Ohio Office: Cooper & VanAntwerp, A Legal Professional Association, 407 Center Street.
Telephone: 614-532-4366.

MEMBERS OF FIRM

Howard VanAntwerp, III
Gregory Lee Monge
William H. Jones, Jr.
Carl D. Edwards, Jr.
Kimberly Scott McCann

ASSOCIATES

Matthew J. Wixsom
William Mitchell Hall
James D. Keffer
Stephen S. Burchett

Representative Clients: Armco; Bank of Ashland; Calgon Carbon Corp.; King's Daughters' Hospital; Allstate Insurance Co.; Kemper Insurance Group; Commercial Union Cos.; The Mayo Coal Cos.; Maryland Casualty Co.; Merck & Co.

For full biographical listings, see the Martindale-Hubbell Law Directory

*BARBOURVILLE,** Knox Co. — (Refer to Middlesboro)

*BARDWELL,** Carlisle Co. — (Refer to Mayfield)

*BEATTYVILLE,** Lee Co. — (Refer to Richmond)

*BENTON,** Marshall Co. — (Refer to Murray)

*BOWLING GREEN,** Warren Co.

Bell, Orr, Ayers & Moore, P.S.C. (AV)

1010 College Street, P.O. Box 738, 42102-0738
Telephone: 502-781-8111
Telecopier: 502-781-9027

Chas. R. Bell (1891-1976)
Joe B. Orr (1914-1987)
Reginald L. Ayers
Ray B. Buckberry, Jr.
Quinten B. Marquette
George E. Strickler, Jr.
Kevin C. Brooks
Timothy L. Mauldin
Barton D. Darrell
Timothy L. Edelen

James S. Weisz

General Counsel for: First American National Bank of Kentucky; Farm Credit Services of Mid-America, ACA.; Houchens Industries, Inc. (Food Markets and Shopping Centers); Warren County Board of Education; Bowling Green Municipal Utilities.
Representative Clients: Chicago Title Insurance Co.; Commonwealth Land Title Insurance Co.; Kentucky Farm Bureau Mutual Insurance Co.; Martin Automotive Group; Home Insurance Group.

(See Next Column)

For full biographical listings, see the Martindale-Hubbell Law Directory

Broderick, Thornton & Pierce (AV)

921 College Street, Phoenix Place, P.O. Box 1137, 42102-1137
Telephone: 502-782-6700
Facsimile: 502-782-3110

David F. Broderick
Steven O. Thornton
Darell R. Pierce

ASSOCIATES

Pamela Carolyn Bratcher
B. Alan Simpson
Kenneth P. O'Brien

Representative Clients: Allstate Insurance Co.; National City Bank; American States Insurance Co.; Capital Enterprise Insurance; Fireman's Fund Insurance Co.; Imperial Casualty & Indemnity; Indiana Lumbermen's Mutual Insurance; Kentucky Medical Insurance Co.; Scotty's Contracting & Stone, Inc.; St. Paul Insurance Co.

For full biographical listings, see the Martindale-Hubbell Law Directory

Campbell, Kerrick & Grise (AV)

1025 State Street, P.O. Box 9547, 42102-9547
Telephone: 502-782-8160
FAX: 502-782-5856

MEMBERS OF FIRM

Joe Bill Campbell
Thomas N. Kerrick
John R. Grise
Gregory N. Stivers
H. Brent Brennenstuhl
Deborah Tomes Wilkins

ASSOCIATES

H. Harris Pepper, Jr.
Lanna Martin Kilgore
Laura Hagan

Representative Clients: Dollar General Corp.; Greenview Hospital; Hospital Corporation of America; Hardin Memorial Hospital; Monarch Environmental, Inc.; Mid-South Management Group, Inc.; Western Kentucky University; Service One Credit Union; Trans Financial Bank; TKR Cable.

For full biographical listings, see the Martindale-Hubbell Law Directory

Cole, Moore & McCracken (AV)

921 College Street-Phoenix Place, P.O. Box 10240, 42102-7240
Telephone: 502-782-6666
FAX: 502-782-8666

MEMBERS OF FIRM

John David Cole
Frank Hampton Moore, Jr.
John H. McCracken
Matthew J. Baker

ASSOCIATES

Howard E. Frasier, Jr.
Douglas W. Gott
Dov Moore
C. Terrell Miller
Michael D. Lindsey

OF COUNSEL

Frank R. Goad

Counsel for: Western Kentucky Cola-Cola Bottling Co.; Clark Distributing Co., Inc.; Scotty's Contracting & Stone Co.
Local Counsel for: General Electric Co.; Bucyrus-Erie Company; Wal-Mart Stores, Inc.; Kroger/Country Oven.
Representative Insurance Clients: Liberty Mutual Insurance Co.; Travelers Insurance Co.; Wausau Insurance Co.

For full biographical listings, see the Martindale-Hubbell Law Directory

English, Lucas, Priest & Owsley (AV)

1101 College Street, P.O. Box 770, 42102-0770
Telephone: 502-781-6500
Telecopier: 502-782-7782

MEMBERS OF FIRM

Charles E. English
James H. Lucas
Whayne C. Priest, Jr.
Michael A. Owsley
Keith M. Carwell
Murry A. Raines
Kurt W. Maier
Charles E. English, Jr.
Wade T. Markham, II

ASSOCIATES

D. Gaines Penn
Robert A. Young
Vance Cook
W. Cravens Priest, III
Marc Allen Lovell
Regina Abrams

For full biographical listings, see the Martindale-Hubbell Law Directory

Harlin & Parker, P.S.C. (AV)

519 East Tenth Street, P.O. Box 390, 42102-0390
Telephone: 502-842-5611
Telefax: 502-842-2607
Smiths Grove, Kentucky Office: Old Farmers Bank Building.
Telephone: 502-563-4701.

(See Next Column)

HARLIN & PARKER P.S.C.—*Continued*

William Jerry Parker
Max B. Harlin, III
James David Bryant
Jerry A. Burns
James D. Harris, Jr.
Scott Charles Marks
Michael K. Bishop
Mark D. Alcott (Resident, Smith Grove Office)

OF COUNSEL

Maxey B. Harlin
Jo T. Orendorf

Insurance Clients: Allstate Insurance Co.; American Hardware Mutual Insurance Co.; CNA Insurance Companies; Maryland Casualty Company; Government Employees Insurance Co.; American International Group.
Railroad and Utilities Clients: District Attorneys for South Central Bell Telephone Co.; CSX Transportation, Inc.
Local Counsel for: General Motors Corp.; Ford Motor Co.; Chrysler Corp.

For full biographical listings, see the Martindale-Hubbell Law Directory

MILLIKEN LAW FIRM (AV)

426 East Main Street, P.O. Box 1640, 42102-1640
Telephone: 502-843-0800
Fax: 502-842-1237

W. Currie Milliken
Morris Lowe

Reference: Trans Financial Bank, Bowling Green, Kentucky.

For full biographical listings, see the Martindale-Hubbell Law Directory

*BURKESVILLE,** Cumberland Co. — (Refer to Glasgow)

*CADIZ,** Trigg Co. — (Refer to Hopkinsville)

*CALHOUN,** McLean Co. — (Refer to Owensboro)

*CAMPBELLSVILLE,** Taylor Co. — (Refer to Glasgow)

*CARLISLE,** Nicholas Co. — (Refer to Lexington)

*CLINTON,** Hickman Co. — (Refer to Mayfield)

*COLUMBIA,** Adair Co. — (Refer to Glasgow)

CORBIN, Knox & Whitley Cos.

LEICK, HAMMONS AND BRITTAIN (AV)

First National Bank & Trust Company Building, P.O. Box 1388, 40702
Telephone: 606-528-5252; 528-2442
Fax: 606-528-2491

MEMBERS OF FIRM

Herman E. Leick
Robert P. Hammons
Gary W. Brittain

LEGAL SUPPORT PERSONNEL

Flora M. McFadden

Counsel for: The First National Bank & Trust Company of Corbin; Pepsi-Cola Bottling Company of Corbin; Corbin Board of Education.

For full biographical listings, see the Martindale-Hubbell Law Directory

COVINGTON, Kenton Co.

ADAMS, BROOKING, STEPNER, WOLTERMANN & DUSING (AV)

421 Garrard Street, P.O. Box 861, 41012
Telephone: 606-291-7270
FAX: 606-291-7902
Florence, Kentucky Office: 8100 Burlington Pike, Suite 400, 41042.
Telephone: 606-371-6220.
FAX: 606-371-8341.

Charles S. Adams (1906-1971)
John R. S. Brooking
Donald L. Stepner
James G. Woltermann (Resident at Florence Office)
Gerald F. Dusing (Resident at Florence Office)
Michael M. Sketch (Resident at Florence Office)
Dennis R. Williams (Resident at Florence Office)
James R. Kruer
Jeffrey C. Mando

ASSOCIATES

Marc D. Dietz (Resident at Florence Office)
Gregory S. Shumate
John S. "Brook" Brooking (Resident at Florence Office)
Stacey L. Graus
Lori A. Schlarman (Resident, Florence Office)
Paul J. Darpel (Resident, Florence Office)
Chandra S. Baldwin (Not admitted in KY)

Representative Clients: CSX Transportation; Balluff, Inc., Wampler, Inc., Kisters, Inc., Krauss-Maffei, Inc., A group of German companies; State Automobile Mutual Insurance Co.; Chevron of California; Great American Insurance Co.; Grange Mutual Insurance Co.; Meridian Mutual Insurance Co.; Fifth-Third Bank of Northern Ky.; Northern Kentucky University.

For full biographical listings, see the Martindale-Hubbell Law Directory

GREENEBAUM DOLL & MCDONALD (AV)

A Partnership including Professional Service Corporations
50 East Rivercenter Boulevard, P.O. Box 2050, 41012-2050
Telephone: 606-655-4200
Telecopier: 606-655-4239
Louisville, Kentucky Office: 3300 National City Tower.
Telephone: 502-589-4200.
Fax: 502-587-3695.
Lexington, Kentucky Office: 1400 Vine Center Tower.
Telephone: 606-231-8500.
Fax: 606-255-2742.
Cincinnati, Ohio Office: 832 Main Street.
Telephone: 513-421-8087.
Fax: 513-421-8089.

MEMBERS OF FIRM

Wm. T. Robinson, III
Edwin H. Perry
Thomas A. Brown
Michael M. Fleishman *
Phillip D. Scott
Charles Fassler
Eric L. Ison
P. Richard Anderson, Jr.
Lloyd R. Cress
James A. Kegley
Hiram Ely, III
Peggy B. Lyndrup
Nicholas R. Glancy
Harry D. Rankin
Richard S. Cleary
H. Douglas Jones
Henry C. T. Richmond, III
William L. Montague
Jeffrey A. McKenzie
Roger N. Braden (Resident)
Michael H. Brown (Resident)

ASSOCIATES

J. Kevin King
Robert D. Hudson
Sheryl E. Heeter
K. Lance Lucas
Christopher P. Finney
David A. Reisman
Kenneth J. Dietz

OF COUNSEL

Edward B. Weinberg *
Henry L. Stephens, Jr.

Representative Clients: Aetna Life Insurance Co.; ANDALEX Resources, Inc.; Ashland Oil, Inc.; A T & T Communications, Inc.; Bethlehem Steel Corp.; Brown-Forman Corp.; Citizens Fidelity Bank & Trust Co.; Humana, Inc.; KFC National Cooperative Advertising Program, Inc.
*A Professional Service Corporation

For full biographical listings, see the Martindale-Hubbell Law Directory

KLETTE AND KLETTE (AV)

250 Grandview Drive, Suite 250, Ft. Mitchell, 41017-5610
Telephone: 606-344-9966
Fax: 606-344-9900
Cincinnati, Ohio Office: 3905 Brigadoon Drive, 45255.
Telephone: 513-421-6699.

MEMBERS OF FIRM

John H. Klette, Jr.
V. Ruth Klette
Debra S. Fox

LEGAL SUPPORT PERSONNEL

Evelyn Richard (Paralegal)

General Counsel for: The Northern Kentucky Motor Club; First Federal Savings & Loan Association of Covington.

For full biographical listings, see the Martindale-Hubbell Law Directory

O'HARA, RUBERG, TAYLOR, SLOAN AND SERGENT (AV)

Suite 209 C, Thomas More Park, P.O. Box 17411, 41017-0411
Telephone: 606-331-2000
Fax: 606-578-3365

MEMBERS OF FIRM

John J. O'Hara
Robert E. Ruberg
Arnold S. Taylor
Donald J. Ruberg
David B. Sloan
Gary J. Sergent
Michael K. Ruberg
Michael O'Hara

ASSOCIATES

Lisa Kalker
Anne Marie Mielech
Suzanne Cassidy

Representative Clients: Cincinnati Bell; American Transportation Enterprises; Union Light, Heat & Power Co.; Crum & Forster; American States Insurance Co.; Ohio Casualty Co.; Monticello Insurance Co.; United States Aviation Underwriters, Inc.
Local Counsel for: Lloyds of London.

For full biographical listings, see the Martindale-Hubbell Law Directory

SMITH, WOLNITZEK, SCHACHTER & ROWEKAMP, P.S.C. (AV)

502 Greenup Street, P.O. Box 352, 41012-0352
Telephone: 606-491-4444
Fax: 606-491-1001
Fort Mitchell, Kentucky Office: 250 Grandview Avenue., Suite 500.
Telephone: 606-578-4444.
Fax: 606-578-4440.

(See Next Column)

SMITH, WOLNITZEK, SCHACHTER & ROWEKAMP P.S.C., *Covington—Continued*

Thomas C. Smith
Stephen D. Wolnitzek
Paul J. Schachter
Leonard G. Rowekamp
J. David Bender
Barbara Dahlenburg Bonar

Penny Unkraut Hendy
John J. Garvey, III
Timothy B. Schenkel
David A. Shearer

Representative Clients: Hartford Insurance Co.; Nationwide Insurance Co.

For full biographical listings, see the Martindale-Hubbell Law Directory

STRAUSS & TROY A LEGAL PROFESSIONAL ASSOCIATION (AV)

Suite 1400, 50 East Rivercenter Boulevard, 41011
Telephone: 513-621-8900; 513-621-2120
Telecopier: 513-629-9444
Cincinnati, Ohio Office: 2100 PNC Center, 201 East Fifth Street.
Telephone: 513-621-2120.
Telecopier: 513-241-8259.

Samuel M. Allen (Resident)
Gordon H. Hood (Resident)
Martin C. Butler (Resident)
Timothy B. Theissen (Resident)

Marshall K. Dosker (Resident)

OF COUNSEL

Paul J. Theissen (Resident)

For full biographical listings, see the Martindale-Hubbell Law Directory

WARE, BRYSON, WEST & KUMMER (AV)

157 Barnwood Drive, 41017
Telephone: 606-341-0255
FAX: 606-341-1876

MEMBERS OF FIRM

Rodney S. Bryson
Larry C. West
John R. Kummer
Mark W. Howard
Greg D. Voss
Robert B. Cetrulo

ASSOCIATES

Susanne M. Cetrulo
W. L. (Skip) Hammons, Jr.
James M. West
Orie S. Ware (1882-1974)
William O. Ware (1908-1961)
James C. Ware (1913-1991)

Attorneys for: First National Bank of Northern Ky.; State Farm Insurance Co.; Reliance Insurance Group; Maryland Casualty Insurance Co.; Kemper Insurance Co.; Prudential Insurance Co.; State Farm Fire & Casualty Insurance Co.; Shelby Mutual Insurance Co.; Cincinnati Insurance Co.

For full biographical listings, see the Martindale-Hubbell Law Directory

CRESTVIEW HILLS, Kenton Co.

TAFT, STETTINIUS & HOLLISTER (AV)

Thomas More Centre, 2670 Chancellor Drive, 41017-3491
Telephone: 606-331-2838; 513-381-2838
Facsimile: 513-381-6613
Cincinnati, Ohio Office: 1800 Star Bank Center, 425 Walnut Street.
Telephone: 513-381-2838.
Washington, D.C. Office: Suite 500, 625 Indiana Avenue, N.W.
Telephone: 202-628-2838.
Columbus, Ohio Office: Twelfth Floor, 21 East State Street.
Telephone: 614-221-2838.

RESIDENT MEMBERS

Richard D. Spoor
Donald M. Hemmer
Robert B. Craig

RESIDENT ASSOCIATES

Robert A. Winter Jr.
Timothy L. Coyle
Joseph A. Rectenwald

Counsel for: Clarion Mfg. Corp.; The David J. Joseph Company; Duro Bag Mfg. Co.; Equitable Bag Co., Inc.; G & J Pepsi Cola Bottlers, Inc.; Gibson Greetings, Inc.; James Graham Brown Foundation; Klockner Ferromatic Desma, Inc.; Liberty National Bank; Paul Hemmer Construction Co.

For full biographical listings, see the Martindale-Hubbell Law Directory

*CYNTHIANA,** Harrison Co.

SWINFORD & SIMS, P.S.C. (AV)

40 East Pike Street, P.O. Box 397, 41031
Telephone: 606-234-5820

M. C. Swinford (1857-1952)
J. Thaxter Sims (1904-1978)
Ron Mahoney (1942-1987)
John Swinford
E. Douglas Miller

(See Next Column)

Dorothy Jo Mastin
W. Kelly Caudill

Representative Clients: First Federal Savings Bank of Cynthiana; Hurst Home Insurance Co.; Kentucky Farm Breau Insurance Co.; Kentucky Growers Insurance Co.; The National Bank of Cynthiana; United States Fidelity and Guaranty Co.
Approved Attorneys for: Farm Credit Services of Mid-America, ACA; Commonwealth Land Title Insurance Co. (Agents); Farmers Home Administration (Escrow Agents).

For full biographical listings, see the Martindale-Hubbell Law Directory

*DANVILLE,** Boyle Co.

SHEEHAN, BARNETT & HAYS, P.S.C. (AV)

114 South Fourth Street, P.O. Box 1517, 40422
Telephone: 606-236-2641; 606-734-7552
FAX: 606-236-1483

James G. Sheehan, Jr.
James William Barnett
Edward D. Hays

Representative Clients: Bank One; Bank of Danville and Trust Co.; Great Financial Federal; Kentucky Farm Bureau Mutual Insurance Co.; Motorist Mutual Insurance Co.; R.R. Donnelley & Sons, Inc.; State Automobile Mutual Insurance Co.; City of Danville; Shelter Insurance Co.; Trim Masters, Inc.

For full biographical listings, see the Martindale-Hubbell Law Directory

*DIXON,** Webster Co. — (Refer to Madisonville)

*EDMONTON,** Metcalfe Co. — (Refer to Glasgow)

*ELIZABETHTOWN,** Hardin Co.

REFORD H. COLEMAN AND ASSOCIATES (AV)

2907 Ring Road, P.O. Box 4030, 42702-4030
Telephone: 502-737-0499
Fax: 502-737-0488

Michael L. Stevens
Steven B. Mulrooney

Representative Clients: American States Insurance Cos.; Coca-Cola Bottling Co.; Federated Rural Elec. Insurance Co.; Firemans Fund Insurance Cos.; General Motors Corp.; Indiana Insurance Co.; Kentucky Farm Bureau Mutual Insurance Corp.; Liberty Mutual Insurance Co.; Ohio Casualty Insurance Group; United Services Automobile Association (State Counsel).

For full biographical listings, see the Martindale-Hubbell Law Directory

COLLIER, ARNETT, QUICK & COLEMAN (AV)

128 West Dixie Avenue, P.O. Box 847, 42701
Telephone: 502-765-4112
Fax: 502-769-3081

MEMBERS OF FIRM

James M. Collier
John L. Arnett
Kim F. Quick
Jerry M. Coleman

ASSOCIATES

Deborah Lewis Shaw

Counsel for: City of Elizabethtown; PNC Bank; Elizabethtown Independent School District.
Representative Clients: Nationwide Insurance Co.; Shelter Insurance Co.; State Farm Insurance Co.; Government Employees Insurance Co.; Liberty Mutual Insurance Co.; Kemper Insurance Group; Motorist Mutual Insurance Co.

For full biographical listings, see the Martindale-Hubbell Law Directory

LEWIS, PRESTON & EASTON (AV)

102 West Dixie Avenue, 42701
Telephone: 502-765-4106
Fax: 502-737-0443

MEMBERS OF FIRM

Paul M. Lewis
Dwight Preston
Kelly Mark Easton

Approved Attorneys For: Commonwealth Land Title.
Reference: Cecilian Bank.

*ELKTON,** Todd Co. — (Refer to Russellville)

*FALMOUTH,** Pendleton Co. — (Refer to Newport)

*FLEMINGSBURG,** Fleming Co. — (Refer to Morehead)

FLORENCE, Boone Co.

Adams, Brooking, Stepner, Woltermann & Dusing (AV)

8100 Burlington Pike, Suite 400, 41042-0576
Telephone: 606-371-6220
FAX: 606-371-8341
Covington, Kentucky Office: 421 Garrard Street.
Telephone: 606-291-7270.
FAX: 606-291-7902.

Donald L. Stepner
James G. Woltermann (Resident)
Gerald F. Dusing (Resident)
Michael M. Sketch (Resident)
Dennis R. Williams (Resident)
Jeffrey C. Mando

ASSOCIATES

Marc D. Dietz (Resident)
John S. "Brook" Brooking (Resident)
Lori A. Schlarman
Paul J. Darpel

Representative Clients: CSX Transportation; State Automobile Mutual Insurance Co.; Standard Oil Co. (Ky.); Great American Insurance Co.; Grange Mutual Insurance Co.; Meridian Mutual Insurance Co.; Fifth-Third Bank of Boone County; Northern Kentucky University.

For full biographical listings, see the Martindale-Hubbell Law Directory

FORT THOMAS, Campbell Co.

Don Johnson, P.S.C. (AV)

20 North Grand Avenue, Suite 15, 41075
Telephone: 606-441-3900
Telecopier: 606-441-3018

Donald L. Johnson

Richard G. Johnson

Reference: Northern Kentucky Bank & Trust Co.; Alexandria IGA; D. Schneider Const. Co.; Bluegrass Carryout, Inc.; Kees Medical Speciality Co.; Ralph Long Concrete Pumping, Inc.; El Jiroto Enterprises; HASCO, Inc.; West Side Baber Cab Co.

For full biographical listings, see the Martindale-Hubbell Law Directory

*FRANKFORT,** Franklin Co.

* indicates certain Bar Register subscribers whose principal office is located elsewhere in the state and who have arranged for representation as a part of the state capital listings that follow

McBrayer, McGinnis, Leslie & Kirkland (AV)

Suite 300, State National Bank Building, 305 Ann Street, P.O. Box 1100, 40602
Telephone: 502-223-1200
Telecopier: 502-227-7385
Greenup, Kentucky Office: Main & Harrison Streets, P.O. Box 347.
Telephone: 606-473-7303.
Telecopier: 606-473-9003.
Lexington, Kentucky Office: 163 West Short Street.
Telephone: 606-231-8780.
Telecopier: 606-231-6518.

MEMBERS OF FIRM

W. Terry McBrayer
William D. Kirkland
Christopher M. Hill (Resident)
Charles C. Simms, III

LEGAL SUPPORT PERSONNEL

Mike D. Helton

References: Farmers Bank & Capitol Trust Co., Frankfort, Ky.; State National Bank, Frankfort, Ky.; National City Bank, Lexington, Ky.

For full biographical listings, see the Martindale-Hubbell Law Directory

*** Stites & Harbison (AV)**

Formerly Stites, McElwain & Fowler and Harbison, Kessinger, Lisle & Bush
421 West Main Street, 40601
Telephone: 502-223-3477
Louisville, Kentucky Office: 400 West Market Street, Suite 1800.
Telephone: 502-587-3400.
Lexington, Kentucky Office: 2300 Lexington Financial Center.
Telephone: 606-226-2300.
Jeffersonville, Indiana Office: 323 East Court Avenue.
Telephone: 812-282-7566.

MEMBERS OF FIRM

Ben B. Fowler (1916-1990)
Bruce F. Clark
Elizabeth K. Broyles
Mark R. Overstreet
Judith A. Villines
Timothy C. Kimmel (Frankfort and Louisville Offices)

Representative Clients: South Central Bell Telephone Co.; New York Life Insurance Co.; Chrysler Financial Corp.

(See Next Column)

For full biographical listings, see the Martindale-Hubbell Law Directory

Stoll, Keenon & Park (AV)

(Formerly Johnson & Judy)
326 West Main Street, 40601
Telephone: 502-875-6000
Telecopier: 502-875-6008
Lexington, Kentucky Office: 201 E. Main Street, Suite 1000.
Telephone: 606-231-3000.
Telecopier: 606-253-1093; 606-253-1027.
Louisville, Kentucky Office: 400 West Market Street, Suite 2650, 40202.
Telephone: 502-568-9100.
Telecopier: 502-568-6340.

William E. Johnson
Michael L. Judy
Robert W. Kellerman
J. Guthrie True
Richard M. Guarnieri

ASSOCIATES

Paul C. Harnice

OF COUNSEL

Squire N. Williams, Jr.

Representative Clients: Kentucky State University; Kentucky Press Assn.; Plantmix Asphalt Industry of Kentucky, Inc.; Kentucky Optometric Assn.; Kentucky Podiatry Assn.; Frankfort Scrap Metal Co.; Lexington Scrap Metal Co.; Lowes, Inc. (Retail Stores); Farmers Bank and Capital Trust Co.; Kentucky Retirement Systems.

For full biographical listings, see the Martindale-Hubbell Law Directory

Wyatt, Tarrant & Combs (AV)

The Taylor-Scott Building, 311 West Main Street, 40602
Telephone: 502-223-2104
Telecopier: 502-227-7681
Louisville, Kentucky Office: Citizens Plaza.
Telephone: 502-589-5235.
Telecopier: 502-589-0309.
Lexington, Kentucky Office: 1700 Lexington Financial Center.
Telephone: 606-233-2012.
Telecopier: 606-259-0649.
New Albany, Indiana Office: The Elsby Building, 117 East Spring Street.
Telephone: 812-945-3561.
Telecopier: 812-949-2524.
Nashville, Tennessee Office: 1500 Nashville City Center, 511 Union Street.
Telephone: 615-244-0020.
Telecopier: 615-256-1726.
Music Row, Nashville Office: 29 Music Square East.
Telephone: 615-255-6161.
Telecopier: 615-254-4490.
Hendersonville, Tennessee Office: 313 E. Main Street, Suite 1.
Telephone: 615-822-8822.
Telecopier: 615-824-4684.

MEMBERS OF FIRM

George L. Seay, Jr.
Joseph J. Zaluski

ASSOCIATES

Lesly Ann Reisenfeld-Davis
Martha Nash-Caywood

Representative Client: Arch Mineral Corporation; Centran Corp.; David J. Joseph Company; Goodyear; Huscoal, Inc.; Hillshire Farms & Hahn's; Kentucky Criterion Coal; Nutone, Inc.; Sara Lee Corporation; Zeigler Coal Holding Co., Inc.

For full biographical listings, see the Martindale-Hubbell Law Directory

*GEORGETOWN,** Scott Co.

Bradley & Bradley (AV)

Bradley Building, 102 West Main Street, 40324
Telephone: 502-863-1464

MEMBERS OF FIRM

Victor A. Bradley, Sr. (1885-1969)
J. Craig Bradley, Sr. (1881-1961)
Victor A. Bradley, Jr. (1913-1984)
J. Craig Bradley, Jr.
Clay M. Brock
James B. Wooten, Jr.

Vice Division Counsel: Cincinnati, New Orleans & Texas Pacific Railway.
Assistant Division Counsel for: Southern Railway System.
Attorneys for: Louisville & Nashville Railroad Co.; Kentucky Utilities Co.; First National Bank & Trust Co.; Farmers Bank & Trust Company of Georgetown, Ky.; The Chesapeake & Ohio Railroad Co.; South Central Bell Telephone Co.; Georgetown College; State Farm Mutual Insurance Co.

For full biographical listings, see the Martindale-Hubbell Law Directory

Georgetown—Continued

E. DURWARD WELDON (AV)

217 East Main Street, 40324
Telephone: 502-863-1285

Approved Attorney For: Lawyers Title Insurance Corporation of Richmond, Virginia; Louisville Title Division of Commonwealth Land Title Insurance Co. (Binder Agent); The Equitable Life Assurance Society of the United States.

For full biographical listings, see the Martindale-Hubbell Law Directory

*GLASGOW,** Barren Co.

GARMON & GOODMAN (AV)

139 North Public Square, P.O. Box 663, 42142-0663
Telephone: 502-651-8812
Telecopier: 502-651-8846

MEMBERS OF FIRM

Larry D. Garmon — Charles A. Goodman III

Representative Clients: United Farm Tools, Inc.; James N. Gray Construction Co., Inc.; Pedigo-Lessenberry Insurance Agency, Inc.; Manning Motor Express, Inc.; Commonwealth Relocation Services; Central Soya, Inc.; Chrysler Credit Corp.
Approved Attorneys For: Chicago Title Insurance Co.; Commonwealth Land Title Insurance Co. (Agent).
Reference: Trans Financial Bank, N.A., Glasgow, Ky.

For full biographical listings, see the Martindale-Hubbell Law Directory

HERBERT & HERBERT (AV)

135 North Public Square, P.O. Box 1000, 42141
Telephone: 502-651-9000
FAX: 502-651-3317

MEMBERS OF FIRM

H. Jefferson Herbert, Jr. — Betty Reece Herbert

Representative Clients: Alliance Corp. (Construction); Eaton Corp.; Glasgow Foods, Inc.; Supreme Mills, Inc.; T.J. Samson Community Hospital.
Approved Attorneys for: Fireman's Fund Insurance Companies; Indiana Insurance Co.; Agway Insurance Co.; Travelers Insurance Co.
Reference: South Central Bank, Glasgow, Kentucky.

For full biographical listings, see the Martindale-Hubbell Law Directory

RICHARDSON, BARRICKMAN, DICKINSON & TRAVIS (AV)

125 East Main Street, P.O. Box 368, 42142-0368
Telephone: 502-651-2116
Telefax: 502-651-8056

MEMBERS OF FIRM

John Evans Richardson (1896-1957)
Brents Dickinson, Jr. (1904-1981)
Uhel O. Barrickman
Thomas L. Travis

Representative Clients: Tenneco, Inc.; Liberty Mutual Insurance Co.; Aetna Casualty & Surety Co.; CSX; State Automobile Mutual Insurance Co.; The Travelers Insurance Co.; U.S. Fidelity & Guaranty Co.; Kentucky Farm Bureau Insurance Co.
Counsel for: New Farmers National Bank of Glasgow.

For full biographical listings, see the Martindale-Hubbell Law Directory

*GREENUP,** Greenup Co.

MCBRAYER, MCGINNIS, LESLIE & KIRKLAND (AV)

Main & Harrison Streets, P.O. Box 347, 41144-0347
Telephone: 606-473-7303
Telecopier: 606-473-9003
Lexington, Kentucky Office: McBrayer, McGinnis, Leslie & Kirkland. 163 West Short Street.
Telephone: 606-231-8780.
Telecopier: 606-231-6518.
Frankfort, Kentucky Office: McBrayer, McGinnis, Leslie & Kirkland. Suite 300 State National Bank Building, 305 Ann Street, P.O. Box 1100.
Telephone: 502-223-1200.
Telecopier: 502-227-7385.

MEMBERS OF FIRM

W. Terry McBrayer
John R. McGinnis
Phillip Bruce Leslie
William D. Kirkland
Oscar Sammons (1908-1985)
J. D. Atkinson, Jr.
William R. Palmer, Jr.
Bruce W. MacDonald
Luke Bentley, III

References: Kentucky Bank & Trust Company of Greenup County; Commercial Bank of Grayson; Star Bank of Ironton, Ohio.

For full biographical listings, see the Martindale-Hubbell Law Directory

WARNOCK & WARNOCK (AV)

221 Main Street, P.O. Box 617, 41144
Telephone: 606-473-5381

(See Next Column)

Frank H. Warnock — Frank K. Warnock

*GREENVILLE,** Muhlenberg Co. — (Refer to Madisonville)

*HARDINSBURG,** Breckinridge Co. — (Refer to Owensboro)

*HARLAN,** Harlan Co.

RICE & HENDRICKSON (AV)

127 Woodland Hills, P.O. Box 980, 40831
Telephone: 606-573-3955
Fax: 606-573-3956

MEMBERS OF FIRM

William A. Rice — H. Kent Hendrickson

Representative Clients: USX Corp.; Navistar International Transportation Corp.; Bituminous Casualty Corp.; Kentucky Utilities Co.; Aetna Casualty & Surety Co.; Nationwide Insurance; The Hartford Insurance Group; Arch Mineral Corp.

For full biographical listings, see the Martindale-Hubbell Law Directory

*HARTFORD,** Ohio Co. — (Refer to Owensboro)

*HAZARD,** Perry Co.

BARRET, HAYNES, MAY, CARTER AND ROARK, P.S.C. (AV)

113 Lovern Street, P.O. Box 1017, 41701
Telephone: 606-436-2165; 436-4824
Fax: 606-439-1450

Maxwell P. Barret (1918-1988)
Hoover Haynes (Retired)
Randall Scott May
Ralph D. Carter
J. L. Roark
William Engle, III

Denise Moore Davidson
Thomas S. Miller
Deborah Lewis Bailey

Representative Clients: Citizens State Bank; Virginia Iron, Coal & Coke Co.; Blue Diamond Coal Co.; Kentucky Power Co.; Royal Globe Insurance Co.; Firemen's Fund; American Insurance Group; Old Republic Insurance Co.; Nationwide Insurance Co.; Kentucky Farm Bureau Mutual Insurance Co.

For full biographical listings, see the Martindale-Hubbell Law Directory

GULLETT & COMBS (AV)

109 Broadway, Second Floor, P.O. Box 1039, 41702-5039
Telephone: 606-439-1373
Fax: 606-439-4450

MEMBERS OF FIRM

Asa P. Gullett, III — Ronald G. Combs

ASSOCIATES

Teresa C. Reed — Matthew Lawton Bowling

Reference: Peoples Bank and Trust Co.

For full biographical listings, see the Martindale-Hubbell Law Directory

*HENDERSON,** Henderson Co.

DEEP & WOMACK (AV)

790 Bob Posey Street, P.O. Box 50, 42420
Telephone: 502-827-2522
FAX: 502-826-2870

MEMBERS OF FIRM

Charles David Deep
Zack N. Womack
James G. Womack

For full biographical listings, see the Martindale-Hubbell Law Directory

KING, DEEP AND BRANAMAN (AV)

127 North Main Street, P.O. Box 43, 42420
Telephone: 502-827-1852
FAX: 502-826-7729

MEMBERS OF FIRM

Leo King (1893-1982)
William M. Deep (1920-1990)
William Branaman
Harry L. Mathison, Jr.
W. Mitchell Deep, Jr.
H. Randall Redding
Dorin E. Luck

ASSOCIATES

Leslie M. Newman
Robert Khuon Wiederstein
Greg L. Gager

Counsel for: Ohio Valley National Bank of Henderson; Fireman's Fund; Reynolds Metals Co.; Medical Protective Co.; Allstate Insurance Co.; Able Energy Co.; Western Casualty & Surety Co.; Commercial Casualty Insurance Co.

For full biographical listings, see the Martindale-Hubbell Law Directory

Henderson—Continued

SHEFFER, HOFFMAN, THOMASON & MORTON (AV)

300 First Street, 42420
Telephone: 502-826-3300
Telecopier: 502-827-5070
Owensboro, Kentucky Office: 101 East Second Street.
Telephone: 502-684-3700.
Telecopier: 502-684-3881.
Paducah, Kentucky Office: 401 Broadway.
Telephone: 502-443-9401.
Telecopier: 502-443-3624.

OF COUNSEL

Charles B. West

MEMBERS OF FIRM

Ronald G. Sheffer
John Stanley Hoffman (Resident)
David H. Thomason (Resident)
John C. Morton (Resident)
Jacqueline C. Kingsolver (Resident, Owensboro Office)
Peter B. Lewis
J. Christopher Hopgood (Resident)
Michael W. Alvey
James A. Sigler (Resident)
John A. Sheffer (Resident, Owensboro Office)
Andrew T. Coiner (Resident, Paducah Office)
Karen L. Wilson (Resident)
Jane E. Hanner (Resident, Paducah Office)
Leslie W. Moore (Resident, Owensboro Office)
C. Thomas Miller (Resident, Paducah Office)
Samuel John Bach (Resident, Owensboro Office)
Tina R. McFarland Jones (Not admitted in KY; Resident, Owensboro Office)
E. Dawn Smith (Resident)
Christopher D. Miller (Resident, Owensboro Office)

For full biographical listings, see the Martindale-Hubbell Law Directory

*HICKMAN,** Fulton Co. — (Refer to Murray)

*HINDMAN,** Knott Co.

WEINBERG, CAMPBELL, SLONE & SLONE, P.S.C. (AV)

Main Street, P.O. Box 727, 41822
Telephone: 606-785-5048; 785-5049
FAX: 606-785-3021

William R. Weinberg
Randy A. Campbell
Jerry Wayne Slone
Randy G. Slone

References: Bank of Hindman; Thacker & Grigsby Telephone Co.

For full biographical listings, see the Martindale-Hubbell Law Directory

*HOPKINSVILLE,** Christian Co.

KEMP AND KEMP (AV)

608 South Main Street, P.O. Box 648, 42241
Telephone: 502-886-8272
Fax: 502-885-5207

MEMBERS OF FIRM

J. Daniel Kemp
Judy Hall Kemp

Counsel for: Pennyrile Rural Electric Cooperative Corp.; Hopkinsville Sewerage & Water Works Commission; Southern States Cooperative.
References: NationsBank, Hopkinsville, Kentucky; First City Bank & Trust Co., Hopkinsville, Kentucky; Commercial Bank of Dawson, Dawson Springs, Kentucky.
Approved Attorney for: Farm Credit Services; Commonwealth Land Title Insurance Co. (Agent).

For full biographical listings, see the Martindale-Hubbell Law Directory

LAW OFFICE OF PAUL K. TURNER (AV)

521 Weber Street, P.O. Box 627, 42241-0627
Telephone: 502-886-9453
Telecopier: 502-886-7732

Counsel for: Kentucky Finance Co.; Kentucky New Era (Newspaper); Flynn Enterprises.
Representative Clients: Bethlehem Steel; Pillsbury, Inc.
Approved Attorneys for: Commonwealth Land Title Insurance Co.; Trans Financial Bank; Trigg County Farmers Bank; First City Bank and Trust Company.
References: Nations Bank of Kentucky; Trigg County Farmers Bank, Cadiz, Ky.; First City Bank & Trust Co., Hopkinsville, Kentucky; Trans Financial Bank, Bowling Green, Scottsville and Dawson Springs, Kentucky.

For full biographical listings, see the Martindale-Hubbell Law Directory

WHITE, WHITE, ASKEW & CRENSHAW (AV)

707 South Main Street, P.O. Box 2, 42241
Telephone: 502-885-5377
Fax: 502-885-5383

(See Next Column)

MEMBERS OF FIRM

Pollard White
Lee T. White
Logan B. Askew
Julia T. Crenshaw

Counsel for: First City Bank & Trust Co.; Jennie Stuart Medical Center; Hopkinsville Milling Co., Inc.; White Hydraulics, Inc.; Plymouth Tube Co.; Pennyrile Collection, Inc.
Representative Clients: Farm Credit Services; The Equitable Life Assurance Society; Government Employees Insurance Co.; NationsBank of Kentucky, Inc.

For full biographical listings, see the Martindale-Hubbell Law Directory

HORSE CAVE, Hart Co.

HENSLEY, DUNN, ROSS & HOWARD (AV)

Professional Arts Building, P.O. Box 350, 42749
Telephone: 502-786-2155
FAX: 502-786-2118
Bowling Green, Kentucky Office: 1725 Ashley Circle, Suite 208.
Telephone: 502-781-8880.

MEMBERS OF FIRM

Robert B. Hensley
Gregory Y. Dunn
Patrick A. Ross
James I. Howard

Representative Clients: Kentucky Farm Bureau Mutual Insurance Co.; Liberty Mutual Insurance Co.; Ohio Casualty Insurance Co.; United States Fidelity & Guaranty Co.; Home Insurance Co.; Caverna Memorial Hospital; Westfield Cos.; State Auto Mutual Insurance Co.; Kentucky Central Insurance Co.; CIGNA Insurance Co.

For full biographical listings, see the Martindale-Hubbell Law Directory

*HYDEN,** Leslie Co. — (Refer to Hazard)

*IRVINE,** Estill Co. — (Refer to Richmond)

*JACKSON,** Breathitt Co. — (Refer to Hazard)

*JAMESTOWN,** Russell Co. — (Refer to Somerset)

*LA GRANGE,** Oldham Co. — (Refer to Frankfort)

*LANCASTER,** Garrard Co. — (Refer to Danville)

*LAWRENCEBURG,** Anderson Co. — (Refer to Versailles)

*LEBANON,** Marion Co. — (Refer to Harrodsburg)

*LEITCHFIELD,** Grayson Co. — (Refer to Elizabethtown)

*LEXINGTON,** Fayette Co.

BOEHL STOPHER & GRAVES (AV)

444 West Second Street, 40508
Telephone: 606-252-6721
FAX: 606-253-1445
Louisville, Kentucky Office: Suite 2300, Providian Center, 400 West Market Street.
Telephone: 502-589-5980.
Fax: 502-561-9400.
Paducah, Kentucky Office: Suite 340 Executive Inn Riverfront, One Executive Boulevard.
Telephone: 502-442-4369.
Fax: 502-442-4689.
Prestonsburg, Kentucky Office: 125 Court Street.
Telephone: 606-886-8004.
Fax: 606-886-9579.
New Albany, Indiana Office: Elsby East, Suite 204, 400 Pearl Street.
Telephone: 812-948-5053.
Fax: 812-948-9233.

RESIDENT PARTNERS

W. T. Adkins
Nolan Carter, Jr.
Gregory K. Jenkins
Ronald L. Green
Steven G. Kinkel
Kim Martin Wilkie
Guillermo A. Carlos

RESIDENT ASSOCIATES

James B. Cooper
Michael J. Cox
Garry R. Kaplan

Counsel for: Ford Motor Co.; Texas Eastern Transmission Corp.; Coca-Cola Bottling Co.; National Collegiate Athletic Assn.; Hartford Accident and Indemnity Co.; Continental Insurance Group; St. Paul Fire & Marine Insurance Co.; Lloyds of London; Old Republic Insurance Co.

For full biographical listings, see the Martindale-Hubbell Law Directory

BROCK, BROCK & BAGBY (AV)

190 Market Street, P.O. Box 1630, 40592-1630
Telephone: 606-255-7795
Fax: 606-255-6198

MEMBERS OF FIRM

Walter L. Brock, Jr.
Daniel N. Brock
Glen S. Bagby
J. Robert Lyons, Jr.
Beverly Benton Polk

(See Next Column)

BROCK, BROCK & BAGBY, *Lexington—Continued*

ASSOCIATE

Bruce A. Rector

LEGAL SUPPORT PERSONNEL

PARALEGALS

Pamela H. Brown
Freda Greer Grubbs

For full biographical listings, see the Martindale-Hubbell Law Directory

BUCHANAN INGERSOLL, PROFESSIONAL CORPORATION (AV)

Suite 1210, Vine Center Office Tower, 333 West Vine Street, 40507
Telephone: 606-225-5333
Telecopier: 606-225-5334
Pittsburgh, Pennsylvania Office: 5800 USX Tower, 600 Grant Street.
Telephone: 412-562-8800.
Philadelphia, Pennsylvania Office: Two Logan Square, Twelfth Floor, 18th & Arch Streets.
Telephone: 215-665-8700.
Harrisburg, Pennsylvania Office: Vartan Parc, 30 North Third Street.
Telephone: 717-237-4800.
Tampa, Florida Office: 101 East Kennedy Boulevard, Suite 1030.
Telephone: 813-222-8180.
North Miami Beach, Florida Office: 19495 Biscayne Boulevard.
Telephone: 305-933-5600.
Princeton, New Jersey Office: Buchanan Ingersoll, A Partnership, College Centre, 500 College Road East.
Telephone: 609-452-2666.

John R. Leathers

Stephen G. Allen
Sam P. Burchett

For full biographical listings, see the Martindale-Hubbell Law Directory

FERRERI & FOGLE (AV)

500 Quality Place, 300 East Main Street, 40507
Telephone: 606-253-4700
Telefax: 606-253-4702
Louisville, Kentucky Office: 203 Speed Building, 333 Guthrie Green.
Telephone: 502-582-1381.
Telefax: 502-581-9887.

MEMBERS OF FIRM

Thomas L. Ferreri
Ronald J. Pohl
Joel W. Aubrey

ASSOCIATES

Roberta K. Kiser
Robert S. Jones
Stanley S. Dawson
Sherri P. Brown
Hugh Brett Stonecipher

For full biographical listings, see the Martindale-Hubbell Law Directory

FOWLER, MEASLE & BELL (AV)

Kincaid Towers, 300 West Vine Street, Suite 650, 40507-1660
Telephone: 606-252-6700
Fax: 606-255-3735

MEMBERS OF FIRM

Dan E. Fowler (1908-1991)
Thomas P. Bell (1922-1986)
Darrell B. Hancock (1923-1988)
Grover C. Thompson, Jr. (1911-1988)
Taft A. McKinstry
Guy R. Colson
E. Patrick Moores
John E. Hinkel, Jr.
Robert S. Ryan
T. Bruce Bell
Michael W. Troutman
Elizabeth S. Feamster
R. Craig Reinhardt

ASSOCIATES

Susan S. Kennedy
Dianne P. Allison
Barry M. Miller
Brendan M. Turney
Michael E. Liska

OF COUNSEL

Walter C. Cox, Jr.

Representative Clients: General Electric Co.; Kentucky Farm Bureau Mutual Ins. Co.; Liberty Mutual Ins. Co.; State Farm Ins. Co.; Allstate Ins. Co.; Progressive Casualty Ins. Co.; Bank One, Lexington, N.A.; Kentucky Medical Services; PNC Bank, Kentucky, Inc.

For full biographical listings, see the Martindale-Hubbell Law Directory

GERALDS, MOLONEY & JONES (AV)

259 West Short Street, 40507
Telephone: 606-255-7946

R. P. Moloney (1902-1963)
Donald P. Moloney (1921-1972)
Richard P. Moloney (1929-1972)
Oscar H. Geralds, Jr.
Michael R. Moloney
Ernest H. Jones, II
Billy W. Sherrow
John P. Schrader
E. Douglas Stephan
Robert L. Swisher
John G. Rice
Frances Geralds Rohlfing
Kathryn Ann Walton
Gail Luhn Pyle

(See Next Column)

Representative Clients: Aetna Life and Casualty Co.; Allstate Insurance Co.; State Farm Mutual Automobile Insurance Co.; Nationwide Insurance Co.
Reference: Commerce National Bank.

For full biographical listings, see the Martindale-Hubbell Law Directory

GESS MATTINGLY & ATCHISON, P.S.C. (AV)

201 West Short Street, 40507-1269
Telephone: 606-255-2344
Facsimile: 606-233-4269

William B. Gess (1906-1985)
John G. Atchison, Jr.
Charles G. Wylie
Natalie S. Wilson
Carl Timothy Cone
Joseph H. Miller
Richard E. Fitzpatrick
William W. Allen
William R. Hilliard, Jr.
Guy M. Graves
Winifred L. Bryant
Walter R. Morris, Jr.
Robert E. Maclin, III
Linda W. Christian
Gary L. Rohrer
Jeffrey R. Walker
Elizabeth Hughes Spears
Christel Schrader Nash
Jennifer Sartor Smart

OF COUNSEL

Jack F. Mattingly
Leslie G. Phillips

Representative Clients: National City Bank; WLEX-TV, Inc.; Prudential Insurance Company of America; Central Kentucky Agricultural Credit Assn.; B.F. Saul Real Estate Investment Trust; American Hardware Mutual Insurance Co.; Navistar Financial Corp.; The Proctor & Gamble Co.; University of Kentucky; Federal Credit Union; Prudential Securities, Inc.

For full biographical listings, see the Martindale-Hubbell Law Directory

GREENEBAUM DOLL & McDONALD (AV)

A Partnership including Professional Service Corporations
1400 Vine Center Tower, 40508
Telephone: 606-231-8500
Telecopier: 606-255-2742
Telex: 213029
Louisville, Kentucky Office: 3300 National City Tower.
Telephone: 502-589-4200.
Fax: 502-587-3695.
Covington, Kentucky Office: 50 East River Center Boulevard, P.O. Box 2050.
Telephone: 606-655-4200.
Fax: 606-655-4239.
Cincinnati, Ohio Office: 832 Main Street.
Telephone: 513-421-8087.
Fax: 513-421-8089.

MEMBERS OF FIRM

Edward L. McDonald (1870-1961)
Angus W. McDonald (1912-1980)
W. VanMeter Alford (1916-1981)
Laramie L. Leatherman (1932-1994)
Phillip D. Scott
A. Robert Doll *
Edwin H. Perry
Thomas A. Brown
Ivan M. Diamond
Michael M. Fleishman *
Lawrence K. Banks *
Wm. T. Robinson, III
Charles Fassler
John A. West
Michael L. Ades (Resident)
Eric L. Ison
Robert C. Stilz, Jr. (Resident)
John R. Cummins
Lloyd R. Cress
James A. Kegley
Marcus P. McGraw (Resident)
James G. LeMaster (Resident)
Job D. Turner, III (Resident)
John S. Sawyer (Resident)
Hiram Ely, III
John V. Wharton (Resident)
Peggy B. Lyndrup
J. Whitney Wallingford, II (Resident)
Nicholas R. Glancy
V. Thomas Fryman, Jr. (Resident)
Bruce E. Cryder
Richard S. Cleary
Danny C. Reeves (Resident)
H. Douglas Jones
Carolyn M. Brown (Resident)
Henry C. T. Richmond, III
Susan J. Hoffmann (Resident)
Deborah H. Tudor (Resident)
Mark T. Hayden (Resident)
Stephen W. Switzer (Resident)
John C. Bender (Resident)
David A. Owen (Resident)

ASSOCIATES

Anne A. Chesnut (Resident)
Margaret A. Miller (Resident)
Virginia H. Underwood
D. Barry Stilz (Resident)
J. Kevin King
John A. Kolanz (Resident)
Kenneth A. Jackson (Resident)
Erin Brisbay McMahon (Resident)
Bryan R. Reynolds (Resident)
Gregory R. Schaaf (Resident)
Benjamin D. Crocker
Molly C. Foree
Edward A. Receski

OF COUNSEL

Glen M. Krebs (Resident)
Richard W. Spears
Henry L. Stephens, Jr. (Resident in Covington, Kentucky)
Vickie Yates Brown (Resident in Louisville, Kentucky)

Representative Clients: Aetna Life Insurance Co.; ANDALEX Resources, Inc.; Ashland Oil, Inc.; AT&T Communications, Inc.; Bethlehem Steel Corp.; Brown-Forman Corp.; Columbia Gas & Transmission Co.; Commonwealth Aluminum Corp.; Consolidation Coal Co.; Costain Coal, Inc.
*A Professional Service Corporation

For full biographical listings, see the Martindale-Hubbell Law Directory

HARBISON, KESSINGER, LISLE & BUSH

(See Stites & Harbison)

JACKSON & KELLY (AV)

175 East Main Street, Suite 500, P.O. Box 2150, 40595
Telephone: 606-255-9500
Fax: 606-281-6478
Charleston, West Virginia Office: 1600 Laidley Tower, P.O. Box 553.
Telephone: 304-340-1000.
Washington, D.C. Office: 2401 Pennsylvania Avenue, N.W., Suite 400.
Telephone: 202-973-0200.
Martinsburg, West Virginia Office: 300 Foxcroft Avenue, P.O. Box 1068.
Telephone: 304-263-8800.
Charles Town, West Virginia Office: 700 East Washington Street, P.O. Box 983.
Telephone: 304-728-6088.
Clarksburg, West Virginia Office: 203 Main Street.
Telephone: 304-623-3002.
Morgantown, West Virginia Office: 6000 Hampton Center, P.O. Box 619.
Telephone: 304-599-3000.
New Martinsville, West Virginia Office: 256 Russell Avenue, P.O. Box 68.
Telephone: 304-455-1751.
Denver, Colorado Office: Suite 2700, 1660 Lincoln Street.
Telephone: 303-837-0003.

MEMBERS OF FIRM

James L. Gay
William K. Bodell, II
W. Henry Jernigan, Jr.
William A. Hoskins, III
Barry S. Settles
Jeffrey J. Yost
A. Stuart Bennett
William E. Doll, Jr.
Martin E. Hall
Kevin M. McGuire
W. Rodes Brown
Natalie D. Brown
Dean K. Hunt

ASSOCIATES

Jacqueline Syers Duncan
Stanton L. Cave
Timothy Ray Coleman
Shannon Upton Johnson
Sannie Overly

OF COUNSEL

John S. Palmore

Representative Clients: Bank One; Consol of Kentucky; Contel Cellular; Cyprus Amex Minerals Co.; Electric Fuels Corp.; Kentucky Association of Counties and the Kentucky Municipal League; Kentucky Medical Assn.; Lane's End Farm; St. Joseph Hospital; TECO Energy, Inc.

For full biographical listings, see the Martindale-Hubbell Law Directory

LANDRUM & SHOUSE (AV)

106 West Vine Street, P.O. Box 951, 40588-0951
Telephone: 606-255-2424
Facsimile: 606-233-0308
Louisville, Kentucky Office: 400 West Market Street, Suite 1550, 40202.
Telephone: 502-589-7616.
Facsimile: 502-589-2119.

MEMBERS OF FIRM

John H. Burrus
George P. Parker (Resident, Louisville Office)
Thomas M. Cooper
William C. Shouse
Pierce W. Hamblin
Mark L. Moseley
Leslie Patterson Vose
John R. Martin, Jr. (Resident, Louisville Office)
James W. Smirz
Larry C. Deener
Sandra Mendez Dawahare
Mark J. Hinkel
Delores Hill Pregliasco (Resident, Louisville Office)
Benjamin Cowgill, Jr.
John Garry McNeill
Jack E. Toliver
Michael J. O'Connell (Resident, Louisville Office)
R. Kent Westberry (Resident, Louisville Office)
J. Denis Ogburn (Resident, Louisville Office)
Jane Durkin Samuel

ASSOCIATES

Stephen D. Milner
Stephen R. Chappell
Julie Muth Goodman
David G. Hazlett (Resident, Louisville Office)
Charles E. Christian
Thomas E. Roma, Jr. (Resident, Louisville Office)
Virginia W. Gregg
Timothy D. Martin (Resident, Louisville Office)
Douglas L. Hoots
Dave Whalin (Resident, Louisville Office)
G. Bruce Stigger (Resident, Louisville Office)
Daniel E. Murner
Joy Anna Anderson
Courtney T. Baxter (Resident, Louisville Office)
Julie A. Butcher
Frank M. Jenkins, III
D. Sean Nilsen (Resident, Louisville Office)
Sheila P. Hiestand
Cynthia K. Lowe
Wende C. Morris

(See Next Column)

OF COUNSEL

Weldon Shouse
Frank J. Dougherty, Jr. (Resident, Louisville Office)

District Attorneys: CSX Transportation, Inc.
Special Trial Counsel: Ford Motor Co. and Affiliates (Eastern Kentucky); Clark Equipment Co.
Representative Clients: The Continental Insurance Cos.; U.S. Insurance Group; U.S. Fidelity & Guaranty Co.; Ohio Casualty Insurance Co.; CIGNA; Royal Insurance Cos.

For full biographical listings, see the Martindale-Hubbell Law Directory

MARTIN, OCKERMAN & BRABANT (AV)

200 North Upper Street, 40507
Telephone: 606-254-4401

MEMBERS OF FIRM

Hogan Yancey (1881-1960)
William B. Martin (1895-1975)
Thomas C. Brabant
Foster Ockerman, Jr.
Madeleine B. Eldred

OF COUNSEL

Foster Ockerman

Counsel for: Lexington Federal Savings Bank; Good Samaritan Hospital; Newmarket Bloodstock Agency, Ltd.; Equity Property and Development Co.; Park Communications of KY (WTVQ); AAA Blue Grass/Kentucky; Good Samaritan Foundation.
Reference: Bank One, Lexington, N.A.

For full biographical listings, see the Martindale-Hubbell Law Directory

MCBRAYER, MCGINNIS, LESLIE & KIRKLAND (AV)

163 West Short Street, 40507-1361
Telephone: 606-231-8780
Telecopier: 606-231-6518
Greenup, Kentucky Office: Main & Harrison Streets, P.O. Box 347.
Telephone: 606-473-7303.
Telecopier: 606-473-9003.
Frankfort, Kentucky Office: Suite 300 State National Bank Building, 305 Ann Street, P.O. Box 1100.
Telephone: 502-223-1200.
Telecopier: 502-227-7385.

MEMBERS OF FIRM

W. Terry McBrayer
John R. McGinnis
Phillip Bruce Leslie
William D. Kirkland
James G. Amato
George D. Gregory
Fred E. Fugazzi, Jr.
W. Brent Rice
James H. Frazier, III
Dennis J. Conniff
John G. Irvin, Jr.
Megan Lake Thornton
Lisa E. Hord
Thomas C. Lyons
Susan Pugh Chaplin
Cheryl H. Anderson
Mary Wis Estes
Matthew W. Breetz
Julia F. Costich

For full biographical listings, see the Martindale-Hubbell Law Directory

MOYNAHAN, BULLEIT, KINKEAD & IRVIN (AV)

201 West Vine Street, 40507
Telephone: 606-233-3550
Nicholasville, Kentucky Office: 110 North Main Street.
Telephone: 606-887-1200.

Bernard T. Moynahan, Jr.
Thomas E. Bulleit, Jr.
Shelby C. Kinkead, Jr.
David R. Irvin
Wayne F. Collier
Susan Speare Durant
Jay R. Garrett

OF COUNSEL

Robert W. Heaton

For full biographical listings, see the Martindale-Hubbell Law Directory

NEWBERRY, HARGROVE & RAMBICURE, P.S.C. (AV)

2800 Lexington Financial Center, 250 West Main Street, 40507-1743
Telephone: 606-231-3700
Facsimile: 606-259-1092
Washington, D.C. Office: 1211 Connecticut Avenue, N.W. Suite 300. 20036-2701.
Telephone: 202-466-3700.
Fax: 202-466-2007.

James H. Newberry, Jr.
James E. Hargrove
William C. Rambicure
Forrest W. Ragsdale, III
Brian C. Gardner
David William Regan (Resident, Washington, D.C. Office)
David C. Trimble
S. Dianne Blanford
T. Renee Mussetter Montague
Garry A. Perry
Susan C. Sears

(See Next Column)

NEWBERRY, HARGROVE & RAMBICURE P.S.C., *Lexington—Continued*

OF COUNSEL

Stephen L. Miller

Representative Clients: Airdrie Stud, Inc.; Bank One Lexington, N.A.; Kentucky Medical Insurance Co.; Kentucky Highlands Investment Corp.; Lehman Brothers; Long John Silver's, Inc.; Racing Corporation of America; Toyota Tsusho America, Inc.; University of Kentucky; Underwriters at Lloyds, London.

For full biographical listings, see the Martindale-Hubbell Law Directory

JAMES R. ODELL, P.S.C. (AV)

171 North Upper Street, 40507
Telephone: 606-231-0210
FAX: 606-252-2917

James R. Odell
George D. Smith

For full biographical listings, see the Martindale-Hubbell Law Directory

PIPER, WELLMAN & BOWERS (AV)

200 North Upper Street, 40507
Telephone: 606-231-1012
FAX: 606-231-7367

MEMBERS OF FIRM

George C. Piper
Dean T. Wellman
Barbara J. Bowers

ASSOCIATES

Johann F. Herklotz
Paula J. Holbrook

Representative Clients: Kentucky Hospital Assn. Trust; Woodford Hospital; Garrard Memorial Hospital; Century American Insurance Co.; Guaranty National Ins. Co.; Rhone Pharmaceuticals; Glaxo; Hillhaven Corp.; Sisters of Charity of Nazareth Health System, Inc.; Ky. River Medical Center; St. Josephs Hospital.

For full biographical listings, see the Martindale-Hubbell Law Directory

ROBERTS & SMITH (AV)

167 West Main Street Suite 200, 40507
Telephone: 606-233-1104

MEMBERS OF FIRM

Larry S. Roberts
Kenneth W. Smith

For full biographical listings, see the Martindale-Hubbell Law Directory

ROSENBAUM & ROSENBAUM, P.S.C. (AV)

Suite 300 The Lexington Building, 40507
Telephone: 606-259-1321
Fax: 606-259-1324

Elwood Rosenbaum (1908-1991)
Barbara M. Rosenbaum
Robert Leslie Rosenbaum
Linda Gosnell
Joseph L. Rosenbaum
Henry Nicholls

Representative Clients: Federal Insurance Co.; Ryder System, Inc.

For full biographical listings, see the Martindale-Hubbell Law Directory

STITES & HARBISON (AV)

Formerly Stites, McElwain & Fowler and Harbison, Kessinger, Lisle & Bush
2300 Lexington Financial Center, 40507
Telephone: 606-226-2300
Louisville, Kentucky Office: 400 West Market Street, Suite 1800.
Telephone: 502-587-3400.
Frankfort, Kentucky Office: 421 West Main Street.
Telephone: 502-223-3477.
Jeffersonville, Indiana Office: 323 East Court Avenue.
Telephone: 812-282-7566.

MEMBERS OF FIRM

James W. Stites (1897-1975)
Clinton M. Harbison (1886-1975)
Ben B. Fowler (1916-1990)
Richard Bush, Jr. (1915-1991)
Kent McElwain (1927-1992)
Calvert T. Roszell
Charles E. Palmer, Jr.
Sidney C. Kinkead, Jr.
George W. Mills
Steven L. Beshear
Bruce M. Reynolds
Buckner Hinkle, Jr.
J. David Porter
Stephen M. Ruschell
Robert M. Beck, Jr.
Charles J. Lisle
John M. Famularo
Thomas E. Meng
Walter R. Byrne, Jr.
Janet A. Craig
Gregory P. Parsons
Kenneth R. Sagan
Richard G. Griffith
J. Clarke Keller
Laura D. Keller
James W. Taylor
Ashley W. Ward
W. Bradford Boone

(See Next Column)

Andrew R. Jacobs
Philip L. Hanrahan
Lynn C. Stidham
Cheryl Ulene Lewis
Bonnie Campbell Kittinger
William T. Gorton III
Margaret M. Pisacano
Benjamin Lee Kessinger, III
Lissa Wathen
Erica L. Horn
Don A. Pisacano
Anne E. Gorham
William T. Shier
Lisa M. Kleopfel
Rebecca B. Stephenson
Lloyd C. Chatfield II (Lexington, Kentucky Office)

OF COUNSEL

Rufus Lisle
Nathan Elliott, Jr.
Ralph F. Kessinger

COUNSEL

Ben L. Kessinger, Jr.
Thomas J. Stipanowich

For full biographical listings, see the Martindale-Hubbell Law Directory

STOLL, KEENON & PARK (AV)

201 E. Main Street, Suite 1000, 40507-1380
Telephone: 606-231-3000
Telecopier: 606-253-1093; 606-253-1027
Frankfort, Kentucky Office: 326 West Main Street.
Telephone: 502-875-6000.
Telecopier: 502-875-6008.
Louisville, Kentucky Office: 400 West Market Street, Suite 2650, 40202.
Telephone: 502-568-9100.
Telecopier: 502-568-6340.

MEMBERS OF FIRM

Wallace Muir (1878-1947)
Richard C. Stoll (1876-1949)
Rodman W. Keenon (1883-1966)
William H. Townsend (1890-1964)
James Park (1892-1970)
John L. Davis (1913-1970)
Gladney Harville (1921-1978)
Gayle A. Mohney (1906-1980)
G. Lee Langston (1942-1983)
C. William Swinford (1921-1986)
Robert F. Houlihan
William E. Johnson
Leslie W. Morris, II
Lindsey W. Ingram, Jr.
William L. Montague
Bennett Clark
Spencer D. Noe
William T. Bishop, III
Joseph M. Scott, Jr.
Michael L. Judy
Richard C. Stephenson
Charles E. Shivel, Jr.
Robert M. Watt, III
J. Peter Cassidy, Jr.
Samuel D. Hinkle, IV
Maxwell P. Barret, Jr.
R. David Lester
Robert F. Houlihan, Jr.
William M. Lear, Jr.
Gary L. Stage
Herbert A. Miller, Jr.
Gary W. Barr
Donald P. Wagner
Douglas P. Romaine
Frank L. Wilford
Harvie B. Wilkinson
Robert W. Kellerman
Lizbeth Ann Tully
J. David Smith, Jr.
Eileen M. O'Brien
David C. Schwetschenau
Anita M. Britton
Rena Gardner Wiseman
C. Joseph Beavin
Diane M. Carlton
Kendall S. Barret
Larry A. Sykes
P. Douglas Barr
Perry M. Bentley
Dan M. Rose
J. Guthrie True
Denise Kirk Ash
Bonnie Hoskins
Gregory D. Pavey
J. Mel Camenisch, Jr.
Richard M. Guarnieri
John Wesley Walters, Jr.

ASSOCIATES

Mary Beth Griffith
Laura Day DelCotto
Lea Pauley Goff
Culver V. Halliday
James L. Thomerson
David E. Fleenor
James D. Allen
Susan Beverly Jones
Melissa Anne Stewart
Todd S. Page
John Browning Park
Richard A. Nunnelley
Paul C. Harnice
Roger W. Madden
William L. Montague, Jr.
Robert E. Wier
Matthew D. Nelson
Tammy C. Snyder

OF COUNSEL

Squire N. Williams, Jr.

Representative Clients: Bank One, Lexington, NA; Farmers Capital Bank Corp.; The Tokai Bank Ltd.; Link Belt Construction Equipment Co.; General Motors Corp.; International Business Machines Corp.; Ohbayashi Corp.; R. J. Reynolds Tobacco Co.; Rockwell International Corp.; Square D Co.

For full biographical listings, see the Martindale-Hubbell Law Directory

STURGILL, TURNER & TRUITT (AV)

155 East Main Street, 40507
Telephone: 606-255-8581
Fax: 606-231-0851

MEMBERS OF FIRM

Don S. Sturgill
Gardner L. Turner
Jerry D. Truitt
Stephen L. Barker
Donald P. Moloney, II
Ann D. Sturgill
Phillip M. Moloney
Douglas L. McSwain
Kevin G. Henry
Gina S. McCann

(See Next Column)

STURGILL, TURNER & TRUITT—*Continued*

MEMBERS OF FIRM (Continued)

Gene Lynn Humphreys
R. Temple Juett
Jennifer L. Fletcher
Edmund J. Benson
Mary Gumbert Moloney
Katherine M. Coleman

For full biographical listings, see the Martindale-Hubbell Law Directory

VIMONT & WILLS (AV)

Suite 300, 155 East Main Street, 40507-1317
Telephone: 606-252-2202
Telecopier: 606-259-2927

MEMBERS OF FIRM

Richard E. Vimont
Timothy C. Wills
Bernard F. Lovely, Jr.
Richard M. Wehrle

ASSOCIATES

Barbara Booker Wills
Kimberly D. Lemmons
J. Thomas Rawlings
J. Stan Lee

For full biographical listings, see the Martindale-Hubbell Law Directory

WILSON, DECAMP & TALBOTT, P.S.C. (AV)

155 East Main Street, Suite 200, 40507-1332
Telephone: 606-225-1191
Fax: 606-225-5176

Philip E. Wilson
Earl S. Wilson, Jr.
Patterson A. DeCamp
John S. Talbott, III

Representative Clients: All-Phase Electric Supply Co.; American International Group; America Resources Insurance Company, Inc.; AZUR US, Inc.; Bluegrass Famous Recipe Fried Chicken, Inc.; Campbell House Inn; Codeco, Inc.; d/b/a Papa John's Pizza; Commonwealth Land Title Insurance Company; Community Bank of Lexington Inc.

For full biographical listings, see the Martindale-Hubbell Law Directory

WYATT, TARRANT & COMBS (AV)

1700 Lexington Financial Center, 40507
Telephone: 606-233-2012
Telecopier: 606-259-0649
Louisville, Kentucky Office: Citizens Plaza.
Telephone: 502-589-5235.
Telecopier: 502-589-0309.
Frankfort, Kentucky Office: The Taylor-Scott Building, 311 West Main Street.
Telephone: 502-223-2104.
Telecopier: 502-227-7681.
New Albany, Indiana Office: The Elsby Building, 117 East Spring Street.
Telephone: 812-945-3561.
Telecopier: 812-949-2524.
Nashville, Tennessee Office: 1500 Nashville City Center, 511 Union Street.
Telephone: 615-244-0020.
Telecopier: 615-256-1726.
Music Row, Nashville Office: 29 Music Square East.
Telephone: 615-255-6161.
Telecopier: 615-254-4490.
Hendersonville, Tennessee Office: 313 E. Main Street, Suite 1.
Telephone: 615-822-8822.
Telecopier: 615-824-4684.

MEMBERS OF FIRM

Bert T. Combs (1911-1991)
C. Kilmer Combs
William H. McCann
Herbert D. Sledd
H. Foster Pettit
Richard C. Ward
Stewart E. Conner
James T. Hodge
Joseph H. Terry
James D. Ishmael, Jr.
Jeff A. Woods
Thomas J. Luber
Bradford L. Cowgill
Barbara B. Edelman
Mark T. MacDonald
J. Mark Burton
Paul J. Cox
Chauncey S.R. Curtz
John R. Rhorer, Jr.
Judge B. Wilson II
Vanessa M. Berge
Debra H. Dawahare
George J. Miller
David A. Smart
Lisa E. Underwood
Karen J. Greenwell
William B. Owsley

ASSOCIATES

Penny R. Warren
Bruce B. McElvein
Gayle B. McGrath
Solomon Lee Van Meter
Marco M. Rajkovich, Jr.
John M. Williams
Jennifer Leigh Sapp
Janet M. Graham
Henry L. Hipkens
John C. Miller
Troy D. Reynolds
Charles D. Webb, Jr.
Mary G. Barfield
Bruce R. Smith

COUNSEL

Edward T. Breathitt, Jr.
Jack G. Jones, Jr.
Henry E. Kinser

Representative Clients: Arch Mineral Corp.; Ashland Coal, Inc.; Baptist Healthcare System, Inc.; Berwind Corp.; Design Professional Insurance Co.; Fasig-Tipton Company, Inc.; GRW Engineers, Inc.; Kentucky Coal Assn.; Lexington-Fayette Urban County Government; PNC Bank, Kentucky, Inc.

(See Next Column)

For full biographical listings, see the Martindale-Hubbell Law Directory

*LIBERTY,** Casey Co. — (Refer to Danville)

*LONDON,** Laurel Co.

CRABTREE & GOFORTH (AV)

120 East Fourth Street, 40741-1414
Telephone: 606-878-8888
Fax: 606-878-8899

Wm. Gary Crabtree
Michael A. Goforth

Representative Clients: Nationwide Insurance Co.; National Casualty Insurance Co.; Scottsdale Insurance Co.; CIGNA Insurance Co.; Coronet Insurance Co.; Protective Insurance Co.; Sedgwick James of Illinois, Inc.; Crum & Forster Underwriters Group; Grange Mutual Cos.; Lloyds of London.

For full biographical listings, see the Martindale-Hubbell Law Directory

FARMER, KELLEY & FARMER (AV)

502 West Fifth Street, Drawer 490, 40743
Telephone: 606-878-7640
Fax: 606-878-2364
Lexington Office: 121 Prosperous Place, Suite 13 B, 40509-1834.
Telephone: 606: 263-2567.
Facsimile: 606: 263-2567.

MEMBERS OF FIRM

F. Preston Farmer
John F. Kelley, Jr.
Michael P. Farmer

ASSOCIATES

Martha L. Brown
Jeffrey T. Weaver

References: The First National Bank; Cumberland Valley National Bank & Trust Company of London, Ky.; London Bank & Trust Co.

For full biographical listings, see the Martindale-Hubbell Law Directory

HAMM, MILBY & RIDINGS (AV)

120 North Main Street, 40741
Telephone: 606-864-4126
Fax: 606-878-8144

MEMBERS OF FIRM

Robert L. Milby
Marcia Milby Ridings
Kenneth H. Gilliam

James A. Ridings
Gregory A. Lay
LaDonna Lynn Koebel

Representative Clients: Acceleration National; Aetna Life & Casualty Ins. Co.; All Risk Claims Service, Inc.; Allstate Insurance Co.; Alexis; American Automobile Mutual Ins.; American Bankers; American Hardware Ins. Co.

For full biographical listings, see the Martindale-Hubbell Law Directory

REECE & LANG, P.S.C. (AV)

London Bank & Trust Building, 400 South Main Street, P.O. Drawer 5087, 40745-5087
Telephone: 606-864-2263
Fax: 606-878-6426
Atlanta, Georgia Office: The Lenox Building, 3399 Peachtree Road N.E., Suite 2000.
Telephone: 404-365-0456.
FAX: 404-365-0629.

A. Douglas Reece
John M. Lang
Timothy J. Walker
Melanie Kay Fields Hensley
David D. Robinson (Not admitted in KY; Resident, Atlanta, Georgia Office)
Leona A. Power
Mary-Ann Garrison
Gary W. Napier
William E. Johnson, Jr.
J. Follace Fields, III
Thomas S. Gryboski (Not admitted in KY; Resident, Atlanta, Georgia Office)

OF COUNSEL

John F. Lang
Laurence R. Dry (Not admitted in KY)

Representative Client: Transco Coal Company; First State Bank and Trust Company of Manchester; London Bank & Trust Company; Leeco, Inc.; Interstate Coal Company; Impac Hotel Group; Head Sports, Inc.; G & M Oil Co, Inc.; Acordia of Lexington, Inc.

For full biographical listings, see the Martindale-Hubbell Law Directory

TAYLOR, KELLER & DUNAWAY (AV)

802 North Main Street, P.O. Box 905, 40743-0905
Telephone: 606-878-8844
Facsimile: 606-878-5547

Boyd F. Taylor
J. Warren Keller
Bridget L. Dunaway

OF COUNSEL

Pamela Adams Chesnut

(See Next Column)

TAYLOR, KELLER & DUNAWAY, *London—Continued*

LEGAL SUPPORT PERSONNEL

Berneda Baker (Paralegal)

Representative Clients: Chubb Group; Coronet Insurance Group; ITT Hartford; Mutual of Omaha; American General Property Ins. Co.; State Farm Fire & Casualty; State Farm Mutual Automobile Insurance Co.
Local Counsel for: Kentucky Utilities Co.
References: The First National Bank; Cumberland Valley National Bank & Trust Company of London, Kentucky.

For full biographical listings, see the Martindale-Hubbell Law Directory

TOOMS & HOUSE (AV)

310 West Fifth Street, P.O. Box 520, 40743-0520
Telephone: 606-864-4145
FAX: 606-864-4279

MEMBERS OF FIRM

Murray L. Brown (1894-1980)
Roy E. Tooms (1917-1986)
R. William Tooms
Brian C. House

ASSOCIATES

Amy V. Barker

Representative Clients: State Auto Mutual Insurance Co.; Grange Mutual Casualty Co.; Kentucky Farm Bureau Mutual Insurance Co.

For full biographical listings, see the Martindale-Hubbell Law Directory

*LOUISA,** Lawrence Co. — (Refer to Paintsville)

*LOUISVILLE,** Jefferson Co.

BEALE & HUMPHREY, P.S.C. (AV)

1906 Kentucky Home Life Building, 40202
Telephone: 502-584-5246
FAX: 502-585-4301
Lexington, Kentucky Office: Suite 310, Merrill-Lynch Building, 100 East Vine Street.
Telephone: 606-233-1527.
Jeffersonville, Indiana Office: 521 East Seventh Street.
Telephone: 812-283-7672.

Robert J. Beale
Herman L. Humphrey

OF COUNSEL

Corneal L. Domeck, III
Sidney N. White

Representative Clients: Carolina Casualty Insurance Co.; Amerisure Cos.; Guaranty National Insurance Co.; Occidental Fire & Casualty Co.; Equity Mutual Insurance Co.; Casualty Reciprocal Exchange; U-Haul Co.; Yellow Freight Systems; Lumber Mutual; National American Insurance Co.

For full biographical listings, see the Martindale-Hubbell Law Directory

BENNETT, BOWMAN, TRIPLETT & VITTITOW (AV)

First Trust Centre, Suite 400 South, 200 South Fifth Street, 40202
Telephone: 502-583-5581
Fax: 502-583-9622
Owensboro, Kentucky Office: 209 West Second Street, P.O. Box 765.
Telephone: 502-683-5308.
Fax: 502-685-1797.

MEMBERS OF FIRM

John L. Bennett (1918-1988)
James G. Bowman
Chester A. Vittitow, Jr.
Douglas B. Taylor
Robert R. deGolian
Robert Vic Bowers, Jr. (Resident at Owensboro Office)
D. Thomas Hansen
James P. Dilbeck, Jr.
Michael T. Lee (Resident at Owensboro Office)

OF COUNSEL

Henry A. Triplett

Representative Clients: State Farm Mutual Automobile Ins. Co.; State Farm Fire & Casualty Co.; State Farm Life Insurance Co.; Ohio Casualty Insurance Co.; West American Insurance Co.; Ohio Security Insurance Co.; American International Group; Meridian Mutual Insurance Co.; Prudential Insurance Co.; Ranger Insurance Co.

For full biographical listings, see the Martindale-Hubbell Law Directory

BOEHL STOPHER & GRAVES (AV)

Suite 2300 Providian Center, 400 West Market Street, 40202-3354
Telephone: 502-589-5980
FAX: 502-561-9400
Lexington, Kentucky Office: 444 West Second Street.
Telephone: 606-252-6721.
Fax: 606-253-1445.
Paducah, Kentucky Office: Suite 340 Executive Inn Riverfront, One Executive Boulevard.
Telephone: 502-442-4369.
Fax: 502-442-4689.

(See Next Column)

Prestonsburg, Kentucky Office: 125 Court Street.
Telephone: 606-886-8004.
Fax: 606-886-9579.
New Albany, Indiana Office: Elsby East, Suite 204, 400 Pearl Street.
Telephone: 812-948-5053.
Fax: 812-948-9233.

OF COUNSEL

Joseph E. Stopher
George R. Effinger (Resident at Paducah)

MEMBERS OF FIRM

Herbert F. Boehl (1894-1986)
Arthur J. Deindoerfer (1907-1990)
Raymond O. Harmon (1918-1990)
James M. Graves (1912-1994)
William O. Guethlein
Galen J. White, Jr.
William P. Swain
Larry L. Johnson
W. T. Adkins (Resident at Lexington)
Edward H. Stopher
Nolan Carter, Jr. (Resident at Lexington)
Jefferson K. Streepey
Wesley G. Gatlin
George R. Carter
Robert E. Stopher
Philip J. Reverman, Jr.
Jonathan Freed (Resident at Paducah)
Peter J. Glauber
Gregory K. Jenkins (Resident at Lexington)
Raymond G. Smith
Walter E. Harding
William M. Newman, Jr.
Thomas M. Smith (Resident at Prestonsburg)
Robert M. Brooks
John W. Phillips
Susan D. Phillips
Ronald L. Green (Resident at Lexington)
Richard L. Walter (Resident at Paducah)
Douglas A. U'Sellis
Steven G. Kinkel (Resident at Lexington)
John P. Rall (Resident at Paducah)
Kim Martin Wilkie (Resident at Lexington)
John Harlan Callis, III (Resident at Prestonsburg)
Charles D. Walter (Resident at Paducah)
Janie C. McKenzie (Resident at Prestonsburg)
Guillermo A. Carlos (Resident at Lexington)
William B. Orberson
John F. Parker Jr.
Jeffrey L. Hansford (Not admitted in KY; Resident at New Albany, Indiana)
Matthew Hunter Jones (Resident at New Albany, Indiana)

ASSOCIATES

James B. Cooper (Resident at Lexington)
Martin H. Kinney, Jr.
Mary Ann Kiwala
Richard W. Edwards
Frank Miller, Jr.
Teresa M. Groves (Resident at Paducah)
John B. Moore
Kimberly S. May-Downey (Resident at Prestonsburg)
Robert D. McClure
Michael J. Cox (Resident at Lexington)
William J. Crowe
Denise Bashford Askin
Garry R. Kaplan (Resident at Lexington)
David Sean Ragland
Jenifer A. Tarter
James T. Crain, III
David B. Wrinkle (Resident at Paducah)
Daniel S. Stratemeyer (Resident at Paducah)
Palmer G. Vance, II
J. Bradley Sanders (Resident at New Albany, Indiana)
Michael S. Maloney
E. Michael Ooley (Resident at New Albany, Indiana)
Joe F. Wright

John C. Talbott

Counsel for: Ford Motor Co.; Texas Eastern Transmission Corp.; Coca-Cola Bottling Co.; Hartford Accident and Indemnity Co.; Continental Insurance Group; St. Paul Fire & Marine Insurance Co.; Lloyds of London; Old Republic Insurance Co.

For full biographical listings, see the Martindale-Hubbell Law Directory

CHAUVIN & CHAUVIN (AV)

Twentieth Floor, Kentucky Home Life Building, 239 South Fifth Street, 40202
Telephone: 502-583-6580
Fax: 502-584-0904

MEMBERS OF FIRM

L. Stanley Chauvin, Jr.
L. Stanley Chauvin, III

For full biographical listings, see the Martindale-Hubbell Law Directory

CONLIFFE, SANDMANN & SULLIVAN (AV)

621 West Main Street, 40202
Telephone: 502-587-7711
Telecopier: 502-587-7756
Other Louisville Office: 4169 Westport Road, Suite 111, 40207.
Telephone: 502-896-2966.
Jeffersonville, Indiana Office: 141 E. Spring Street, 47150.
Telephone: 812-949-7711.

Charles I. Sandmann (1936-1992)

MEMBERS OF FIRM

I. G. Spencer, Jr.
Karl N. Victor, Jr.
Michael E. Conliffe
Richard M. Sullivan
Sam Deeb
Jack R. Underwood, Jr.
E. Bruce Neikirk
Victoria Ann Ogden
Robert A. Donald, III
Sally Hardin Lambert

(See Next Column)

CONLIFFE, SANDMANN & SULLIVAN—*Continued*

MEMBERS OF FIRM (Continued)

Steven J. Kriegshaber
Edwin J. Lowry, Jr.
Olivia Morris Fuchs
James A. Babbitz
Kenneth A. Bohnert
James T. Mitchell
Wm. Dennis Sims
Edward F. Busch
Laura J. Ensor
Richard B. Taylor
John R. Broadway

OF COUNSEL

Allen P. Dodd, III
Alan R. Miller

For full biographical listings, see the Martindale-Hubbell Law Directory

THOMAS M. CRAWFORD, P.S.C. (AV)

200 Hart Block Building, 730 West Main, 40202-2640
Telephone: 502-589-6190
Fax: 502-584-1744

Thomas M. Crawford

For full biographical listings, see the Martindale-Hubbell Law Directory

EWEN, HILLIARD & BUSH (AV)

The Starks Building Suite 1090, 455 S. 4th Street, 40202
Telephone: 502-584-1090
Fax: 502-584-4707

MEMBERS OF FIRM

Victor W. Ewen (1924-1989)
A. Campbell Ewen
Frank P. Hilliard
John M. Bush

ASSOCIATES

Kevin P. Kinney
Scott F. Scheynost
Lawrence W. Cook
Richard G. Sloan

For full biographical listings, see the Martindale-Hubbell Law Directory

FERRERI & FOGLE (AV)

203 Speed Building, 333 Guthrie Green, 40202
Telephone: 502-582-1381
Telefax: 502-581-9887
Lexington, Kentucky Office: 500 Quality Place, 300 East Main Street.
Telephone: 606-253-4700.
Telefax: 606-253-4702.

MEMBERS OF FIRM

Thomas L. Ferreri
James G. Fogle
Judson F. Devlin
C. Patrick Fulton
Phillipe W. Rich

ASSOCIATES

Brian Timothy Gannon
Walter C. Jobson
John G. Grohmann
Katherine K. Kitchen
William A. Lyons

OF COUNSEL

William A. Miller
Glenn L. Schilling

Representative Clients: Aetna Life and Casualty; Alexsis; American International Adjustment Co.; American Resources Insurance Co.; American States Insurance Co.; Bituminous Insurance Co.; Chubb Group of Insurance Cos.; Commercial Union Insurance Co.; Commonwealth of Kentucky; Compensation Hospital Association Trust.

For full biographical listings, see the Martindale-Hubbell Law Directory

JOSEPH G. GLASS (AV)

Suite 200, 235 South Fifth Street, 40202
Telephone: 502-584-7288
FAX: Available Upon Request

References: Citizens Fidelity Bank & Trust; Liberty National Bank.

For full biographical listings, see the Martindale-Hubbell Law Directory

GOLDBERG & SIMPSON, P.S.C. (AV)

3000 National City Tower, 40202
Telephone: 502-589-4440
Telefax: 502-581-1344
Washington, D.C. Office: 1200 G Street, N.W. - Suite 800, 20005.
Telephone: 202-434-8968.
Telefax: 202-737-5822.

Fred M. Goldberg
David B. Ratterman
Jonathan D. Goldberg
James S. Goldberg
Mitchell A. Charney
Steven A. Goodman
A. Courtney Guild, Jr.
Edward L. Schoenbaechler
Samuel H. DeShazer
R. Thomas Carter
Cathy S. Pike
Gerald L. Stovall
Stephen E. Smith
Mary Alice Maple
Marva M. Gay
Douglas S. Haynes
Scott P. Zoppoth
Cynthia Buss Maddox
Jan M. West
Charles H. Cassis

(See Next Column)

OF COUNSEL

Ronald V. Simpson
David A. Brill
Kenneth G. Lee (Not admitted in KY; Resident, Washington, D.C. Office)

Representative Clients: First National Bank; Liberty Mutual Insurance Co.; Jewish Hospital Healthcare Services, Inc.; Louisville & Jefferson County Board of Health; Capital Holding Corp.

For full biographical listings, see the Martindale-Hubbell Law Directory

GREENEBAUM DOLL & MCDONALD (AV)

A Partnership including Professional Service Corporations
3300 National City Tower, 40202
Telephone: 502-589-4200
Fax: 502-587-3695
Lexington, Kentucky Office: 1400 Vine Center Tower.
Telephone: 606-231-8500.
Fax: 606-255-2742.
Covington, Kentucky Office: 50 East River Center Boulevard, P.O. Box 2050.
Telephone: 606-655-4200.
Fax: 606-655-4239.
Cincinnati, Ohio Office: 832 Main Street.
Telephone: 513-421-8087.
Fax: 513-421-8089.

S. L. Greenebaum (1902-1973)
Edward L. McDonald (1870-1961)
Angus W. McDonald (1912-1980)
W. VanMeter Alford (1916-1981)
Laramie L. Leatherman (1932-1994)
A. Robert Doll *
Edwin H. Perry
Thomas A. Brown
Michael G. Shaikun *
Ivan M. Diamond
Michael M. Fleishman *
Lawrence K. Banks *
Phillip D. Scott (Covington and Lexington, Kentucky)
Wm. T. Robinson, III
R. Van Young
Charles Fassler
John A. West (Lexington, Kentucky and Cincinnati, Ohio)
Michael L. Ades (Resident at Lexington, Kentucky)
W. Plumer Wiseman, Jr.
Eric L. Ison
John H. Stites, III
Robert C. Stilz, Jr. (Resident at Lexington, Kentucky)
John R. Cummins
P. Richard Anderson, Jr.
Lloyd R. Cress
Charles J. Lavelle
Mark S. Ament *
James A. Kegley (Lexington and Covington Offices)
Marcus P. McGraw (Resident at Lexington, Kentucky)
James G. LeMaster (Resident at Lexington, Kentucky)
Job D. Turner, III (Resident at Lexington, Kentucky)
John S. Sawyer (Resident at Lexington, Kentucky)
Hiram Ely, III
John V. Wharton (Resident at Lexington, Kentucky)
Peggy B. Lyndrup
J. Whitney Wallingford, II (Resident at Lexington, Kentucky)
Nicholas R. Glancy (Lexington and Covington, Kentucky)
V. Thomas Fryman, Jr. (Resident at Lexington, Kentucky)
Bruce E. Cryder (Lexington, Kentucky and Cincinnati, Ohio)
John W. Ames
Harry D. Rankin (Covington, Kentucky and Cincinnati, Ohio)
Barbara Reid Hartung
Richard S. Cleary
Danny C. Reeves (Resident at Lexington, Kentucky)
H. Douglas Jones (Lexington and Covington, Kentucky and Cincinnati, Ohio)
Carolyn M. Brown (Resident at Lexington, Kentucky)
Carmin D. Grandinetti
Janet P. Jakubowicz
Margaret E. Keane
Tandy C. Patrick
Henry C. T. Richmond, III
Roger N. Braden (Resident at Covington, Kentucky)
William L. Montague (Covington, Kentucky and Cincinnati, Ohio Offices)
Mary G. Eaves
Mark S. Riddle
Philip C. Eschels
Susan J. Hoffmann (Resident at Lexington, Kentucky)
Patrick J. Welsh
Holland N. McTyeire, V
Deborah H. Tudor (Resident at Lexington, Kentucky)
Mark T. Hayden (Resident at Lexington, Kentucky)
Jeffrey A. McKenzie
Jeffrey A. Savarise
Stephen W. Switzer (Resident at Lexington, Kentucky)
John C. Bender (Resident at Lexington, Kentucky)
Michael H. Brown (Resident, Covington, Kentucky)
Glenn A. Price, Jr.
Bradley E. Dillon
Daniel E. Fisher
David A. Owen (Resident at Lexington, Kentucky)

ASSOCIATES

Anne A. Chesnut (Resident at Lexington, Kentucky)
Margaret A. Miller (Resident at Lexington, Kentucky)
J. Mark Grundy
D. Barry Stilz (Resident at Lexington, Kentucky)
Mark F. Sommer
J. Kevin King (Lexington and Covington, Kentucky and Cincinnati, Ohio)
Thomas J. Birchfield
John A. Kolanz (Resident at Lexington, Kentucky)
Kenneth A. Jackson (Resident at Lexington, Kentucky)
Mark H. Oppenheimer
Daniel P. Cherry
Daniel L. Waddell
Thomas M. Williams
John P. Fendig
Angela McCormick Bisig

(See Next Column)

GREENEBAUM DOLL & MCDONALD, *Louisville—Continued*

ASSOCIATES (Continued)

Robert D. Hudson (Resident, Covington, Kentucky and Cincinnati Offices)
Erin Brisbay McMahon (Resident at Lexington, Kentucky)
Bryan R. Reynolds (Resident at Lexington, Kentucky)
Gregory R. Schaaf (Resident at Lexington, Kentucky)
Damien M. Prather
Nora J. Clevenger
Benjamin D. Crocker (Resident, Lexington Office)
Jerrold R. Perchik
John S. Lueken
Sheryl E. Heeter (Covington and Cincinnati Offices)
J. Kent Wicker
Paul E. Porter
Brent R. Baughman
Henry S. Alford
Tracy S. Byrd
Lori R. Hollis
Mary Beth Siggelkow
J. René Toadvine
Audra J. Eckerle
Christopher P. Finney
Kenneth J. Dietz (Resident at Covington, Kentucky)
David A. Reisman (Resident at Covington, Kentucky)
Molly C. Foree (Resident at Lexington, Kentucky)
Edward A. Receski (Resident at Lexington, Kentucky)
Virginia H. Underwood (Resident at Lexington, Kentucky)

OF COUNSEL

Glen M. Krebs (Resident at Lexington, Kentucky)
William C. Ballard, Jr.
Martin S. Weinberg
Edward B. Weinberg *
Henry L. Stephens, Jr. (Resident in Covington, Kentucky)
Vickie Yates Brown

Representative Clients: Aetna Life Insurance Co.; ANDALEX Resources, Inc.; Ashland Oil, Inc.; A T & T Communications, Inc.; Bethlehem Steel Corp.; Brown-Forman Corp.; Humana, Inc.; Kentucky Kingdom, Inc.; KFC National Cooperative Advertising Program, Inc.
*A Professional Service Corporation

For full biographical listings, see the Martindale-Hubbell Law Directory

HIRN DOHENY REED & HARPER (AV)

A Partnership including a Professional Service Corporation
2000 Meidinger Tower, 40202
Telephone: 502-585-2450
Telecopiers: 502-585-2207; 585-2529

MEMBERS OF FIRM

Marvin J. Hirn
Frank P. Doheny, Jr.
John S. Reed
David W. Harper
James R. Cox
Gary R. Weitkamp
Scott W. Brinkman
John E. Selent
Ivan J. Schell (P.S.C.)
Robert B. Vice
William G. Strench
T. Richard Riney
Lisabeth Hughes Abramson
B. Todd Thompson

ASSOCIATES

Maxine E. Bizer
James Nitsche
Rosann Dolle Tafel
William D. Roberts
Steven A. Edwards
Michael A. Valenti
Mary R. Harville
Michael W. Oyler
Benjamin C. Fultz

OF COUNSEL

Thomas J. Flynn

Representative Clients: Humana, Inc.; Louisville Gas and Electric Co; Presbyterian Church (U.S.A.); Lantech, Inc.; Mid-America Bank of Louisville; Indiana United Bancorp.; National City Bank, Kentucky; PNC Bank; Columbia/HCA; J.J.B. Hilliard, W.L. Lyons, Inc.

For full biographical listings, see the Martindale-Hubbell Law Directory

HUMMEL & COAN (AV)

Kentucky Home Life Building, The Seventeenth Floor, 239 South Fifth Street, 40202-3268
Telephone: 502-585-3084
Fax: 502-585-3548

OF COUNSEL

Washer Kaplan Rothschild Aberson & Miller

MEMBERS OF FIRM

Dennis J. Hummel
Marvin L. Coan

ASSOCIATES

David L. Sage, II

Representative Clients: Georgia Pacific Corp.; Safeco Insurance Cos.; The Aetna Casualty & Surety Co.; Dr. Bizer's Vision World; GRE Insurance Group; Calvert Insurance Co.; Western Heritage Insurance Co.

For full biographical listings, see the Martindale-Hubbell Law Directory

LANDRUM & SHOUSE (AV)

400 West Market Street Suite 1550, 40202
Telephone: 502-589-7616
Facsimile: 502-589-2119
Lexington, Kentucky Office: 106 West Vine Street, P.O. Box 951.
Telephone: 606-255-2424.
Facsimile: 606-233-0308.

(See Next Column)

RESIDENT MEMBERS OF THE FIRM

George P. Parker
John R. Martin, Jr.
Delores Hill Pregliasco
Michael J. O'Connell
R. Kent Westberry
J. Denis Ogburn

RESIDENT ASSOCIATES

David G. Hazlett
Thomas E. Roma, Jr.
Timothy D. Martin
Dave Whalin
G. Bruce Stigger
Courtney T. Baxter
D. Sean Nilsen

OF COUNSEL

Frank J. Dougherty, Jr.

For full biographical listings, see the Martindale-Hubbell Law Directory

MACKENZIE & PEDEN, P.S.C. (AV)

650 Starks Building, 455 South Fourth Avenue, 40202-2509
Telephone: 502-589-1110
Fax: 502-589-1117

Thomas G. Mooney (1939-1991)
Wm. A. MacKenzie
John G. Crutchfield
Wayne J. Carroll
James C. Hickey
B. Carlton Neat, III
Robert W. Dickey
James T. Lobb
Valerie T. Mayer
Edward H. Bartenstein
Sidney L. Hymson
Lee Ann Risner
Charles T. Baxter

OF COUNSEL

William B. Peden
Walker C. Cunningham, Jr.
Lawrence J. Phillips
Stephen A. Schwager
Jerry L. Ulrich

Representative Clients: Allstate Insurance Co.; American States Insurance Co.; The Fund Insurance Companies; State Automobile Mutual Insurance Co..

For full biographical listings, see the Martindale-Hubbell Law Directory

FRANK MASCAGNI, III (AV)

Suite 200, Second Floor, Morrissey Building, 304 West Liberty Street, 40202-3012
Telephone: 502-583-2831
Fax: 502-583-3701

Reference: PNC Bank, Ky.

For full biographical listings, see the Martindale-Hubbell Law Directory

MIDDLETON & REUTLINGER, P.S.C. (AV)

2500 Brown and Williamson Tower, 40202-3410
Telephone: 502-584-1135
Fax: 502-561-0442
Jeffersonville, Indiana Office: 605 Watt Street, 47130.
Telephone: 812-282-4886.

O. Grant Bruton
Kenneth S. Handmaker
Ian Y. Henderson
James N. Williams, Jr.
Charles G. Middleton, III
Charles D. Greenwell
Brooks Alexander
John W. Bilby
C. Kent Hatfield
Timothy P. O'Mara
Stewart L. Prather
D. Randall Gibson
G. Kennedy Hall, Jr.
James R. Higgins, Jr.
Mark S. Fenzel
Kathiejane Oehler
Charles G. Lamb
Thomas W. Frentz
William Jay Hunter, Jr.
James E. Milliman
David J. Kellerman
John M. Franck II
Kipley J. McNally

Margaret E. Thorp
Beach A. Craigmyle
Julie A. Gregory
Karen M. Campbell
Amy B. Berge
David W. Carrithers
James C. Eaves, Jr.
Dennis D. Murrell
Michael R. Shumate
Augustus S. Herbert
Dana L. Lucas
William K. Oldham
Thomas P. O'Brien III

OF COUNSEL

Albert F. Reutlinger (Retired)
Henry Meigs, II
Philip M. Lanier
J. Paul Keith, III

Counsel for: Chevron USA; Liberty National Bank; Logan Aluminum, Inc.; Louisville Gas & Electric Co.; MCI Telecommunications Corp.; Metropolitan Life Insurance Co.; Kosmos Cement Co.; Porcelain Metal Corp.; The Home Insurance Co.; The Kroger Co.; Demars Haka Development, Inc.

For full biographical listings, see the Martindale-Hubbell Law Directory

J. BRUCE MILLER LAW GROUP (AV)

621 West Main Street, Third Floor, 40202
Telephone: 502-587-0900
Telecopier: 502-587-9008

(See Next Column)

J. BRUCE MILLER LAW GROUP—*Continued*

J. Bruce Miller
Evan G. Perkins
Norma C. Miller
Anthony L. Schnell
Denis B. Fleming, Jr.
Michael J. Kitchen

Representative Clients: Anson Machine Mfg. Co.; Biddinger Investment Capital Corp. (Indiana); Carneal Enterprises, Inc. (Kentucky/Florida); Jefferson County, Kentucky; MPD Inc. (Owensboro, Kentucky); Motion Picture Association of America; Packaging Unlimited Group (Kentucky/North Carolina); Paducah Medical Supply, Inc. (Kentucky/Tennessee/Florida); Sun Group Broadcasting, Inc. (Indiana/Tennessee); Thurman Development Co. (Kentucky/Florida).

For full biographical listings, see the Martindale-Hubbell Law Directory

MORGAN & POTTINGER, P.S.C. (AV)

601 West Main Street, 40202
Telephone: 502-589-2780
Telecopier: 502-585-3498
Lexington, Kentucky Office: 133 West Short Street.
Telephone: 606-253-1900.
Telecopier: 606-255-2038.
New Albany, Indiana Office: 400 Pearl Street, Suite 100.
Telephone: 812-948-0008.
Telecopier: 812-944-6215.

Patrick E. Morgan
John T. McGarvey
C. Edward Hastie (Resident, Lexington Office)
M. Deane Stewart
James I. Murray (Resident, Lexington Office)
Douglas Gene Sharp
John A. Majors
Mark J. Sandlin
J. Jeffrey Cooke
Robert Louis Goodin, Jr.
Jerry L. Kelly (Resident, Lexington Office)
Scott T. Rickman (Resident, Lexington Office)
Judith B. Hoge
Ruthanne Q. Whitt
M. Thurman Senn
Garret B. Hannegan (Not admitted in KY; Resident, New Albany, Indiana Office)
Julia A. Gilbert (Resident, New Albany, Indiana Office)
Hal D. Friedman
Stephen B. Humphress
Rebecca K. Kuster

SENIOR COUNSEL

David C. Pottinger

COUNSEL

Elmer E. Morgan

For full biographical listings, see the Martindale-Hubbell Law Directory

MORRIS, GARLOVE, WATERMAN & JOHNSON (AV)

Established 1925 as Morris and Garlove.
Suite 1000, One Riverfront Plaza, 40202-2959
Telephone: 502-589-3200
Fax: 502-589-3219

Charles W. Morris (1892-1961)
Frank A. Garlove (1907-1981)
Matt L. Garlove (1931-1989)
Nicholas Johnson (Retired)
Louis N. Garlove
David L. Waterman
Irwin G. Waterman
Allan Weiss
Joseph H. Cohen
Alan N. Linker
Robert V. Waterman
Joseph C. Spalding
Michael T. Hymson
J. D. Raine, Jr.
Sheryl Kramer Smith
Louis I. Waterman
Lawrence H. Belanger

ASSOCIATES

J. Gregory Troutman

For full biographical listings, see the Martindale-Hubbell Law Directory

MULLOY, WALZ, WETTERER, FORE & SCHWARTZ (AV)

First Trust Centre, Suite 700N, 200 South Fifth Street, 40202
Telephone: 502-589-5250
Fax: 502-589-1637

MEMBERS OF FIRM

William P. Mulloy
Karl M. Walz
William S. Wetterer, Jr.
F. Larkin Fore
Dan T. Schwartz
B. Mark Mulloy
Mary Anne Wetterer Watkins
William S. Wetterer, III
Bryan J. Dillon
J. Gregory Clare
Ronda Hartlage
T. Lee Sisney

OF COUNSEL

Stephen H. Miller

Reference: American States Insurance Co.; Crawford & Company; Paragon Group, Inc.; Queens Group; Southeastern Dairies, Inc.; Ticor Title Co.; First National Bank of Louisville; Stockyards Bank; Arrow Electric Co.

For full biographical listings, see the Martindale-Hubbell Law Directory

NASH, NASH, STOESS & BROWN (AV)

Third Floor, 235 South Fifth Street, 40202
Telephone: 502-584-6394
FAX: 502-584-0208

Edward G. Gildersleeve, Jr. (1937-1985)
Richard H. Nash, Sr.
Richard H. Nash, Jr.
Ray H. Stoess, Jr.
Donald Killian Brown

Reference: Citizens Fidelity Bank & Trust Company of Louisville.

For full biographical listings, see the Martindale-Hubbell Law Directory

OGDEN NEWELL & WELCH (AV)

1200 One Riverfront Plaza, 40202-2973
Telephone: 502-582-1601
Fax: 502-581-9564

MEMBERS OF FIRM

Squire R. Ogden (1898-1984)
Richard F. Newell
James S. Welch
John T. Ballantine
Joseph C. Oldham
James L. Coorssen
Stephen F. Schuster
Scott T. Wendelsdorf
John G. Treitz, Jr.
Walter Lapp Sales
Ernest W. Williams
David A. Harris
Gregory J. Bubalo
D. Brian Rattliff
W. Gregory King
Kendrick R. Riggs
Robert E. Thieman
James B. Martin, Jr.
Lisa Ann Vogt
Turney P. Berry

ASSOCIATES

Lynn H. Wangerin
John Wade Hendricks
James G. Campbell
Teresa C. Buchheit
Susan C. Bybee
Douglas C. Ballantine
Lady Evelyn Booth
Tracy S. Prewitt
Thomas E. Rutledge
Sharon A. Mattingly
Jennifer J. Hall
Allyson K. Sturgeon

OF COUNSEL

John S. Greenebaum

Counsel for: KU Energy Corp.; Kentucky Utilities Co.; Brown-Forman Corp.; B. F. Goodrich Co.; Brown & Williamson Tobacco Corp.; J.J.B. Hilliard, W.L. Lyons, Inc.; Interlock Industries, Inc.; Akzo Coatings, Inc.; United Medical Corp.; Bank of Louisville.

For full biographical listings, see the Martindale-Hubbell Law Directory

OLDFATHER & MORRIS (AV)

One Mezzanine The Morrissey Building, 304 West Liberty Street, 40202
Telephone: 502-589-5500
Fax: 502-589-5338

Ann B. Oldfather
Douglas H. Morris, II
William F. McMurry
James Barrett
Teresa A. Talbott

For full biographical listings, see the Martindale-Hubbell Law Directory

RUBIN HAYS & FOLEY (AV)

First Trust Centre 200 South Fifth Street, 40202
Telephone: 502-569-7550
Telecopier: 502-569-7555

MEMBERS OF FIRM

Wm. Carl Fust
Harry Lee Meyer
David W. Gray
Irvin D. Foley
Joseph R. Gathright, Jr.
Lisa Koch Bryant
Sharon C. Hardy
Charles S. Musson
W. Randall Jones
K. Gail Russell

ASSOCIATES

Christian L. Juckett

OF COUNSEL

James E. Fahey
Newman T. Guthrie

Representative Clients: J.C. Bradford & Co., Inc.; J.J.B. Hilliard, W.L. Lyons, Inc.; Huntington National Bank; Liberty National Bank and Trust Company; National City Bank; PNC Bank; Prudential Bache & Co., Inc.; Prudential Securities, Inc.; Society Bank; Stock Yards Bank and Trust Co.

For full biographical listings, see the Martindale-Hubbell Law Directory

SEILLER & HANDMAKER (AV)

2200 Meidinger Tower, 40202
Telephone: 502-584-7400
Telecopier: 502-583-2100
Paris, Kentucky Office: Seiller, Handmaker & Blevins, P.S.C., 1431 South Main Street.
Telephone: 606-987-3980.
Telecopier: 606-987-3982.
New Albany, Indiana Office: 204 Pearl Street, Suite 200.
Telephone: 812-948-8307.
Telecopier: 812-948-8383.

Edward F. Seiller (1897-1990)

(See Next Column)

SEILLER & HANDMAKER, *Louisville—Continued*

MEMBERS OF FIRM

Stuart Allen Handmaker
Bill V. Seiller
David M. Cantor
Neil C. Bordy
Kyle Anne Citrynell
Maury D. Kommor
Cynthia Compton Stone

ASSOCIATES

Glenn A. Cohen
Pamela M. Greenwell
Tomi Anne Blevins Pulliam (Resident, Paris Office)
Linda Scholle Cowan
Mary Zeller Wing Ceridan
Michael C. Bratcher
John E. Brengle
Patrick R. Holland, II
Edwin Jon Wolfe
Donna F. Townsend
William C. Robinson

OF COUNSEL

Robert S. Frey

For full biographical listings, see the Martindale-Hubbell Law Directory

STITES & HARBISON (AV)

Formerly Stites, McElwain & Fowler and Harbison, Kessinger, Lisle & Bush
400 West Market Street, Suite 1800, 40202
Telephone: 502-587-3400
Frankfort, Kentucky Office: 421 West Main Street.
Telephone: 502-223-3477.
Lexington, Kentucky Office: 2300 Lexington Financial Center.
Telephone: 606-226-2300.
Jeffersonville, Indiana Office: 323 East Court Avenue.
Telephone: 812-282-7566.

MEMBERS OF FIRM

James W. Stites (1897-1975)
Clinton M. Harbison (1886-1980)
S. Lloyd Cardwell (1909-1987)
Ben B. Fowler (1916-1990)
Richard Bush, Jr. (1915-1991)
Kent McElwain (1927-1992)
Lively M. Wilson
Calvert T. Roszell (Lexington, Kentucky Office)
Ronald R. Fifer (Jeffersonville, Indiana Office)
Charles E. Palmer, Jr. (Lexington, Kentucky Office)
Winfrey P. Blackburn, Jr.
David C. Brown
Sidney C. Kinkead, Jr. (Lexington, Kentucky Office)
George W. Mills (Lexington, Kentucky Office)
C. Dant Kearns
W. Robinson Beard
Ralston W. Steenrod
Robert W. Lanum (Jeffersonville, Indiana Office)
Alfred S. Joseph, III
Steven L. Beshear (Lexington, Kentucky Office)
J. Bissell Roberts
Bruce M. Reynolds (Lexington, Kentucky Office)
Charles J. Cronan, IV
T. Kennedy Helm, III
Buckner Hinkle, Jr. (Lexington, Kentucky Office)
William H. Haden, Jr.
J. David Porter (Lexington, Kentucky Office)
Stephen M. Ruschell (Lexington, Kentucky Office)
Cecile Anne Blau (Jeffersonville, Indiana Office)
James D. Moyer
Robert M. Beck, Jr. (Lexington, Kentucky Office)
Charles J. Lisle (Lexington, Kentucky Office)
Jamieson G. McPherson
Bruce F. Clark (Frankfort, Kentucky Office)
William E. Hellmann
James R. Williamson
John M. Famularo (Lexington, Kentucky Office)
Thomas E. Meng (Lexington, Kentucky Office)
Douglass C. E. Farnsley
Robert W. Griffith
Walter R. Byrne, Jr. (Lexington, Kentucky Office)
W. Kennedy Simpson
Philip W. Collier
C. Craig Bradley, Jr.
Mark R. Overstreet (Frankfort, Kentucky Office)
W. Patrick Stallard
John A. Bartlett
Robert M. Connolly
John L. Tate
Jefferey M. Yussman
Joseph L. Hamilton
Janet A. Craig (Lexington, Kentucky Office)
James C. Seiffert
Gregory P. Parsons (Lexington, Kentucky Office)
Judith A. Villines (Frankfort, Kentucky Office)
Kenneth R. Sagan (Lexington, Kentucky Office)
Richard G. Griffith (Lexington, Kentucky Office)
Michael D. Risley
J. Clarke Keller (Lexington, Kentucky Office)
Laura D. Keller (Lexington, Kentucky Office)
James W. Taylor (Lexington, Kentucky Office)
Alex P. Herrington, Jr.
Byron N. Miller
Richard A. Vance
Ashley W. Ward (Lexington, Kentucky Office)
Allen L. Morris (Jeffersonville, Indiana Office)
W. Bradford Boone (Lexington, Kentucky Office)

Rebecca F. Schupbach
Brooks D. Kubik
Philip L. Hanrahan (Lexington, Kentucky Office)
Samuel G. Gaines
Alan M. Applegate (Jeffersonville, Indiana Office)
Andrew R. Jacobs (Lexington, Kentucky Office)
Carol Dan Browning
Cynthia L. Coffee
Lynn C. Stidham (Lexington, Kentucky Office)
Cheryl Ulene Lewis (Lexington, Kentucky Office)
Shannon Antle Hamilton
Elizabeth K. Broyles (Frankfort, Kentucky Office)

(See Next Column)

Bonnie Campbell Kittinger (Lexington, Kentucky Office)
Kathleen O. McKune
William T. Gorton III (Lexington, Kentucky Office)
Susan S. Armstrong
Margaret M. Pisacano (Lexington, Kentucky Office)
Jeffrey C. Filcik
Benjamin Lee Kessinger, III (Lexington, Kentucky Office)
T. Morgan Ward, Jr.
Lissa Wathen (Lexington, Kentucky Office)
Rita E. Williams
Brian A. Cromer
Scot A. Duvall
Martha J. Hasselbacher
Erica L. Horn (Lexington, Kentucky Office)
Don A. Pisacano (Lexington, Kentucky Office)
Brenda J. Runner
Catharine C. Young
W. Bryan Hudson
James M. McDonough
Jacqueline K. Armstrong
David Domene
Anne E. Gorham (Lexington, Kentucky Office)
Angela Hendricks Davis
William T. Shier (Lexington, Kentucky Office)
Catherine Murr Young
W. Thomas Halbleib, Jr.
Douglas B. Bates (Jeffersonville, Indiana Office)
Mary M. Boaz
Monique R. Hunt
Timothy C. Kimmel (Louisville and Frankfort Offices)
Lisa M. Kleopfel (Lexington, Kentucky Office)
Rebecca B. Stephenson (Lexington, Kentucky Office)
Catherine Tang
James W. Proud
Lloyd C. Chatfield II (Lexington, Kentucky Office)
Barry A. Hines
James Kennedy Murphy

OF COUNSEL

Rufus Lisle (Lexington, Kentucky Office)
Nathan Elliott, Jr. (Lexington, Kentucky Office)
T. Kennedy Helm, Jr.
Ralph F. Kessinger (Lexington, Kentucky Office)
James W. Stites, Jr.

COUNSEL

Ben L. Kessinger, Jr. (Lexington, Kentucky Office)
Thomas J. Stipanowich (Lexington, Kentucky Office)
J. Scott Greene

Representative Clients: South Central Bell Telephone Co.; Glenmore Distilleries Co.; New York Life Insurance Co.; Chrysler Financial Corp.; ARCO Metals Co.; Aetna Life & Casualty Insurance Cos.; Illinois Central Railroad Co.

For full biographical listings, see the Martindale-Hubbell Law Directory

STITES, McELWAIN & FOWLER

(See Stites & Harbison)

STOLL, KEENON & PARK (AV)

400 West Market Street Suite 2650, 40202
Telephone: 502-568-9100
Telecopier: 502-568-6340
Frankfort, Kentucky Office: 326 West Main Street.
Telephone: 502-875-6000.
Telecopier: 502-875-6008.
Lexington, Kentucky Office: 210 E. Main Street, Suite 1000, 40507-1380.
Telephone: 606-231-3000.
Telecopier: 606-253-1093; 606-253-1380.

MEMBERS OF FIRM

Samuel D. Hinkle, IV
Robert W. Kellerman

ASSOCIATES

Lea Pauley Goff
Culver V. Halliday
Tammy C. Snyder

For full biographical listings, see the Martindale-Hubbell Law Directory

TILFORD, DOBBINS, ALEXANDER & BUCKAWAY (AV)

Suite 1406, One Riverfront Plaza, 40202
Telephone: 502-584-6137

MEMBERS OF FIRM

Charles W. Dobbins (1916-1992)
Henry J. Tilford (1880-1968)
George S. Wetherby (1905-1954)
Lawrence W. Wetherby (1908-1994)
John T. Metcalf (1890-1974)
Stuart E. Alexander
William A. Buckaway, Jr.
Charles W. Dobbins, Jr.
Mark Wesley Dobbins
Stuart E. Alexander, III
John M. Nader
Sandra F. Keene
Thomas J.B. Hurst

OF COUNSEL

Randolph Noe
Carolyn K. Balleisen

LEGAL SUPPORT PERSONNEL

Jennifer Olvey

For full biographical listings, see the Martindale-Hubbell Law Directory

Louisville—Continued

WOODWARD, HOBSON & FULTON (AV)

2500 National City Tower, 101 South Fifth Street, 40202
Telephone: 502-581-8000
Fax: 502-581-8111
Lexington, Kentucky Office: National City Plaza, 301 East Main Street, Suite 650.
Telephone: 606-244-7100.
Telecopier: 606-244-7111.

MEMBERS OF FIRM

Ernest Woodward (1877-1968)
Robert P. Hobson (1893-1966)
Will H. Fulton (1888-1953)
John P. Sandidge
Ernest Woodward II (1917-1990)
John A. Fulton (1919-1987)
Kenneth L. Anderson
William D. Grubbs
Lionel A. Hawse (Resident, Lexington, Kentucky Office)
Harry K. Herren
William A. Blodgett, Jr.
David R. Monohan
Will H. Fulton
Robert L. Hallenberg
Bradley R. Hume
Richard H. C. Clay
Thomas A. Hoy
Mary Jo Wetzel
John F. Gleason
Gregory L. Smith
Gregory A. Bölzle
J. Michael Dalton
Elizabeth Ullmer Mendel
Jann B. Logsdon
Arthur L. Williams
Linsey W. West (Resident, Lexington, Kentucky Office)

ASSOCIATES

Ellen M. Hesen
David T. Schaefer
Patrick Michael
Eric M. Jensen
I. Johan Trengove
D. Craig York
Susan B. Booker
T. Kevin Flanery (Resident, Lexington, Kentucky Office)
Kathryn A. Quesenberry
Sandra Tremper O'Brien
Mark L. Watts
Christopher R. Cashen (Resident, Lexington, Kentucky Office)
L. Jay Gilbert
C. Dean Furman

OF COUNSEL

Fielden Woodward
Robert C. Hobson
Robert J. Schumacher

Representative Clients: General Motors Corp.; Fischer Packing Co.; Ralston Purina Co.; Sears, Roebuck & Co.; Greyhound Lines; Liberty Mutual Insurance Co.; Kitchen Kompact; Sts. Mary & Elizabeth; Kemper Insurance Co.

For full biographical listings, see the Martindale-Hubbell Law Directory

WYATT, TARRANT & COMBS (AV)

Citizens Plaza, 40202
Telephone: 502-589-5235
Telecopier: 502-589-0309
Lexington, Kentucky Office: 1700 Lexington Financial Center.
Telephone: 606-233-2012.
Telecopier: 606-259-0649.
Frankfort, Kentucky Office: The Taylor-Scott Building, 311 West Main Street.
Telephone: 502-223-2104.
Telecopier: 502-227-7681.
New Albany, Indiana Office: The Elsby Building, 117 East Spring Street,
Telephone: 812-945-3561.
Telecopier: 812-949-2524.
Nashville, Tennessee Office: 1500 Nashville City Center, 511 Union Street.
Telephone: 615-244-0020.
Telecopier: 615-256-1726.
Music Row, Nashville Office: 29 Music Square East.
Telephone: 615-255-6161.
Telecopier: 615-254-4490.
Hendersonville, Tennessee Office: 313 E. Main Street, Suite 1.
Telephone: 615-822-8822.
Telecopier: 615-824-4684.

MEMBERS OF FIRM

Telford B. Orbison (1901-1990)
John E. Tarrant (1898-1990)
Stuart E. Lampe (1906-1994)
Bert T. Combs (1911-1991)
John S. Osborn, Jr.
Robert L. Maddox
Edgar A. Zingman
Gordon B. Davidson
Lawrence L. Jones, III
Richard W. Iler
Clay L. Morton
Russell H. Riggs
Robert C. Ewald
A. Wallace Grafton, Jr.
Samuel G. Bridge, Jr.
H. Alexander Campbell
Stewart E. Conner
R. Lawrence Baird
J. Larry Cashen
Parker W. Duncan, Jr.
Robert I. Cusick
Charles R. Simons
Edwin S. Hopson
Grover C. Potts, Jr.
John P. Reisz
Jon L. Fleischaker
K. Gregory Haynes
M. Stephen Pitt
Stephen D. Berger
Francis J. Mellen, Jr.
Martin P. Duffy
Walter M. Jones
Michael B. Vincenti
Mark C. Blackwell
Frank F. Chuppe, Jr.
Thomas J. Luber
Allison Joseph Maggiolo
Richard Northern
Merrill S. Schell
Raymond M. Burse
J. Michael Brown
Paul J. Cox
Kimberly K. Greene
G. Alexander Hamilton
Patrick W. Mattingly
Theodore T. Myre, Jr.

(See Next Column)

MEMBERS OF FIRM (Continued)

Parker W. Eads
David W. Seewer
Virginia Hamilton Snell
Arthur Adams Rouse
Gordon B. Wright
Cynthia W. Young
Byron E. Leet
Mary Ann Main
Caryn F. Price
Leo F. Camp
J. Anthony Goebel
Robert A. Heath
William H. Hollander
Holliday Hopkins Thacker
Joan Lloyd Cooper
Christopher R. Fitzpatrick
Mark A. Robinson
Michelle Turner

ASSOCIATES

Michael Keith Kirk
Stephen R. Price
Rita L. McDonald
Cornelius E. Coryell, II
Jane C. Fousheé
Jeffrey E. Wallace
Carole Douglas Christian
Denise St. Clair Kaiser
Donald J. Kelly
Gail C. Oppenheimer
Jean W. Bird
Beverly J. Glascock
Jeffrey A. Hamilton
Todd A. Hauss
James W. Lee
Caroline Miller Oyler
Clara M. Passafiume
David L. Reichert
Joseph L. Landenwich
G. Christopher Van Bever
Cynthia Blevins Doll
Priscilla K. Garland
Lori E. Harris
Martha Jo Klosterman
Deborah H. Patterson
Steven L. Snyder
Michelle D. Wyrick
Mitzi D. Wyrick
Gregory S. Berman
Craig A. Hawley
Rickey A. Walton

COUNSEL

Frank W. Burke, Sr.
E. Frederick Zopp
Martin Rockwell
Frank W. Burke, Jr.

OF COUNSEL

Wilson W. Wyatt, Sr.

Representative Clients: Alliant Health System, Inc.; Ashland Oil, Inc.; Brown & Williamson Tobacco Corp.; Churchill Downs, Inc.; Ford Motor Co.; Gannett Co., Inc./The Courier-Journal & Louisville Times; General Electric Co.; Henry Vogt Machine Co.; PNC Bank, Kentucky, Inc. & its affiliates; PNC Bank Corp; United Catalysts, Inc.

For full biographical listings, see the Martindale-Hubbell Law Directory

LOWMANSVILLE, Lawrence Co.

MARCUM & TRIPLETT (AV)

U.S. 23, P.O. Box 178, 41232
Telephone: 606-297-6403
Telecopier: 606-297-6405

MEMBERS OF FIRM

Leo A. Marcum
John R. Triplett

Reference: Inez Deposit Bank, Inez, Kentucky.

For full biographical listings, see the Martindale-Hubbell Law Directory

*MADISONVILLE,** Hopkins Co.

MITCHELL, JOINER, HARDESTY & LOWTHER (AV)

113 East Center Street, Drawer 659, 42431-0659
Telephone: 502-825-4455
Telefax: 502-825-9600

Thomas A. Mitchell
Richard M. Joiner
Randall L. Hardesty
Charles E. Lowther
Sheila C. Lowther
Karen W. Imboden

Representative Clients: Aetna Life and Casualty; American Resources Insurance Co., Inc.; Anchor Packing Company; Willis Corroon Administrative Services Corp.; Fireman's Fund Insurance Co.; Indiana Insurance Co.; Liberty Mutual Insurance Co.; MAPCO, Inc.; Costain Coal, Inc.; Western Kentucky Gas Co.

For full biographical listings, see the Martindale-Hubbell Law Directory

MOORE, MORROW & FRYMIRE

(See Frymire, Evans, Peyton, Teague & Cartwright)

*MANCHESTER,** Clay Co.

SMITH & WELLS (AV)

110 Lawyer Street, P.O. Box 447, 40962
Telephone: 606-598-2113
Fax: 606-598-8029

MEMBERS OF FIRM

Chas. C. Smith (1903-1975)
Neville Smith
Timothy L. Wells
Harold Rader

Counsel for: Greenleaf Trucking Co.; Shamrock Coal Co.; Red Bird Hospital; Clay County Board of Education; Mid South Electrics, Inc.; Elk River Resources, Inc.
Local Counsel for: Kentucky Farm Bureau Insurance Cos.
Approved Attorney for: Louisville Title Division of Commonwealth Land Title Insurance Co.; Title Insurance Company of Minnesota.

For full biographical listings, see the Martindale-Hubbell Law Directory

*MARION,** Crittenden Co. — (Refer to Madisonville)

*MAYFIELD,** Graves Co.

NEELY & BRIEN (AV)
238 North Seventh Street, 42066
Telephone: 502-247-9333
Fax: 502-247-7143

MEMBERS OF FIRM
Sam Boyd Neely
James B. Brien, Jr.
S. Boyd Neely, Jr.

ASSOCIATES
Robert C. Brown
R. Brent Vasseur

Representative Clients: Liberty Bank & Trust Co.; General Tire Inc. Kentucky Farm Bureau Mutual Insurance Co.; Mayfield City Board of Education; State Auto Insurance Co.; Hospital Corporation of America.; Fancy Farm Credit Union; Ingersoll-Rand Co.
Approved Attorneys for: Louisville Title Division of Commonwealth Land Title Insurance Co.; Lawyers Title Insurance Corp.; Ticor Title Insurance Co.; Chicago Title Ins. Co.

For full biographical listings, see the Martindale-Hubbell Law Directory

*MAYSVILLE,** Mason Co. — (Refer to Morehead)

*MONTICELLO,** Wayne Co. — (Refer to Somerset)

*MORGANFIELD,** Union Co. — (Refer to Henderson)

*MORGANTOWN,** Butler Co. — (Refer to Bowling Green)

*MOUNT OLIVET,** Robertson Co. — (Refer to Lexington)

*MOUNT STERLING,** Montgomery Co.

WHITE, PECK, CARRINGTON AND MCDONALD (AV)
26 Broadway, P.O. Box 304, 40353
Telephone: 606-498-2872
Telecopier: 606-498-2877

MEMBERS OF FIRM
Lewis A. White
Grover A. Carrington
Alan B. Peck
Michelle "Shelly" R. McDonald

Counsel for: Bob's Food Service, Inc; Kentucky Farm Bureau Insurance Cos.; Mt. Sterling Advocate; Montgomery & Traders Bank & Trust Co.; Commonwealth Bank F.S.B.; Owingsville Banking Co.; Po Folks, Inc.; McCormick Lumber Co.; Walker Construction Co.; Warren Builders, Inc.

For full biographical listings, see the Martindale-Hubbell Law Directory

*MOUNT VERNON,** Rockcastle Co.

CLONTZ & COX (AV)
Courthouse, 205 Main Street, P.O. Box 1350, 40456
Telephone: 606-256-5111
Fax: 606-256-2036

MEMBERS OF FIRM
Carl R. Clontz
Jerry J. Cox
John E. Clontz

Representative Clients: The Bank of Mt. Vernon; Citizens Bank, Brodhead, Kentucky; Kentucky Farm Bureau Mutual Insurance Co.; Louisville Title Division of Commonwealth Land Title Insurance Co.
Reference: The Bank of Mt. Vernon, Mt. Vernon, Kentucky.

For full biographical listings, see the Martindale-Hubbell Law Directory

*MUNFORDVILLE,** Hart Co. — (Refer to Horse Cave)

*MURRAY,** Calloway Co.

GREGORY, EASLEY AND BLANKENSHIP (AV)
Hughes Building, 204 South Sixth Street, P.O. Box 230, 42071
Telephone: 502-753-2633
Fax: 502-753-1825

MEMBERS OF FIRM
Nat R. Hughes (1906-1981)
R. Sidney Easley
John A. Gregory, Jr.
C. Mark Blankenship

ASSOCIATES
Dennis J. Courtney

Representative Clients: Kentucky Medical Insurance Co.; Kentucky Farm Bureau Mutual Insurance Co.; State Farm Mutual Automobile Insurance; R. T. Vanderbilt Co.; Briggs and Stratton Corp.; State Auto Insurance; Meridian Insurance Co.; Peoples Bank of Murray; Murray State University Credit Union.

For full biographical listings, see the Martindale-Hubbell Law Directory

NEWPORT, Campbell Co.

JOLLY & BLAU (AV)
3699 Alexandria Pike, P.O. Box 249, 41076
Telephone: 606-441-5400
Fax: 606-441-8428

MEMBERS OF FIRM
A. J. Jolly (1924-1989)
Bernard J. Blau
Robert E. L. Blau

ASSOCIATES
Gregory B. Kriege
Kenneth L. Foltz
Carl Turner
Steven Plummer

Representative Clients: American Mutual Insurance Co.; Chubb-Pacific Indemnity Group; Firemen's Fund Insurance Co.; Beacon Insurance Co.; Kemper Insurance Co.; U.S. Insurance Group.
Approved Attorneys and Issuing Agent for: Louisville Title Division of Commonwealth Land Title Insurance Co.; Lawyers Title Insurance Corp.
References: Huntington Bank of Kenton County; Provident Bank of Campbell County.

For full biographical listings, see the Martindale-Hubbell Law Directory

*NICHOLASVILLE,** Jessamine Co. — (Refer to Lexington)

*OWENSBORO,** Daviess Co.

BAMBERGER & ABSHIER (AV)
111 West 2nd Street, 42303-4113
Telephone: 502-926-4545
Fax: 502-684-0064

MEMBERS OF FIRM
Ronald J. Bamberger
Phillip G. Abshier

ASSOCIATES
Steven S. Crone
Angela L. Wathen

For full biographical listings, see the Martindale-Hubbell Law Directory

LOVETT & LAMAR (AV)
208 West Third Street, 42303-4121
Telephone: 502-926-3000
FAX: 502-685-2625

MEMBERS OF FIRM
Wells T. Lovett
John T. Lovett
Charles L. Lamar
Marty G. Jacobs

Representative Clients: Farm Credit Services of Mid-America, ACA; Galante Manufacturing Co.; Hocker Developments, Inc.; National-Southwire Aluminum; Willamette Industries, Inc.; Bel-Cheese; Sterett Construction Co.; Green River Steel, Inc.

For full biographical listings, see the Martindale-Hubbell Law Directory

MCCARROLL, NUNLEY & HARTZ (AV)
111 East Third Street, P.O. Box 925, 42302-0925
Telephone: 502-683-3535
FAX: 502-926-6056

MEMBERS OF FIRM
Clarence McCarroll (1916-1989)
Marvin P. Nunley
Max S. Hartz

ASSOCIATE
Victoria L. Yevincy

Representative Clients: Aetna Casualty & Surety Company; Allstate Insurance Company; American Hardware Mutual Insurance Company; American Motorists Insurance Company; Automobile Club Insurance Company; Celina Mutual Insurance Company; Chubb Group of Insurance Companies; CIGNA Insurance Companies; Citizens Insurance Company of America; CNA Insurance Company.

For full biographical listings, see the Martindale-Hubbell Law Directory

RUMMAGE, KAMUF, YEWELL, PACE & CONDON (AV)
Great Financial Federal Building, 322 Frederica Street, 42301
Telephone: 502-685-3901
FAX: 502-926-2005

MEMBERS OF FIRM
William E. Rummage
David L. Yewell
Charles J. Kamuf
Patrick D. Pace
David C. Condon

ASSOCIATES
John M. Mischel

Representative Clients: Owensboro Municipal Utilities Commission; Lincoln Service Corp.; Hancock County Planning Commission; Daviess County Board of Education; Barmet Aluminum Corp.; Owensboro Sewer Commission; TICOR Title Insurance Co.; Chicago Title Insurance Co.; Owensboro Riverport Authority; Housing Authority of Owensboro.

For full biographical listings, see the Martindale-Hubbell Law Directory

Owensboro—Continued

SHEFFER, HOFFMAN, THOMASON & MORTON (AV)

101 East Second Street, 42303
Telephone: 502-684-3700
Telecopier: 502-684-3881
Henderson, Kentucky Office: 300 First Street.
Telephone: 502-826-3300.
Telecopier: 502-827-5070.
Paducah, Kentucky Office: 401 Broadway.
Telephone: 502-443-9401.
Telecopier: 502-443-3624.

OF COUNSEL

Charles B. West (Resident, Henderson Office)

MEMBERS OF FIRM

Ronald G. Sheffer
John Stanley Hoffman (Resident, Henderson Office)
David H. Thomason (Resident, Henderson Office)
John C. Morton (Resident, Henderson Office)
Jacqueline C. Kingsolver (Resident)
Peter B. Lewis
J. Christopher Hopgood (Resident, Henderson Office)
Michael W. Alvey
James A. Sigler (Resident, Henderson Office)
Andrew T. Coiner (Resident, Paducah Office)
Karen L. Wilson (Resident, Henderson Office)
Jane E. Hanner (Resident, Paducah Office)
Leslie W. Moore
C. Thomas Miller (Resident, Paducah Office)
Samuel John Bach (Resident)
Tina R. McFarland Jones (Not admitted in KY; Resident)
E. Dawn Smith (Resident, Henderson Office)

For full biographical listings, see the Martindale-Hubbell Law Directory

WILSON, WILSON & PLAIN (AV)

414 Masonic Building, 42301
Telephone: 502-926-2525
Telecopier: 502-683-3812

MEMBERS OF FIRM

George S. Wilson, Jr. (1902-1966)
William L. Wilson (1912-1993)
George S. Wilson, III
R. Scott Plain
William L. Wilson, Jr.
Thomas S. Poteat
R. Scott Plain, Jr.

Representative Clients: Liberty National Bank, Owensboro, Ky.; Owensboro Board of Education; Owensboro River Sand & Gravel Co.; The Prudential Ins. Co.; Kentucky Farm Bureau Mutual Insurance Co.; Baskin Robbins; Motorist Mutual Insurance Co.; Yager Materials, Inc.
Approved Attorneys for: Louisville Title Division of Commonwealth Land Title Insurance Co.

For full biographical listings, see the Martindale-Hubbell Law Directory

*PADUCAH,** McCracken Co.

BOEHL STOPHER & GRAVES (AV)

Suite 340 Executive Inn Riverfront, One Executive Boulevard, 42001
Telephone: 502-442-4369
FAX: 502-442-4689
Louisville, Kentucky Office: Providian Center, Suite 2300, 400 West Market Street.
Telephone: 502-589-5980.
Fax: 502-561-9400.
Lexington, Kentucky Office: 444 West Second Street.
Telephone: 606-252-6721.
Fax: 606-253-1445.
Prestonsburg, Kentucky Office: 125 Court Street.
Telephone: 606-886-8004.
Fax: 606-886-9579.
New Albany, Indiana Office: Elsby East, Suite 204, 400 Pearl Street.
Telephone: 812-948-5053.
Fax: 812-948-9233.

RESIDENT OF COUNSEL

George R. Effinger

RESIDENT PARTNERS

Jonathan Freed
Richard L. Walter
John P. Rall
Charles D. Walter

RESIDENT ASSOCIATES

Teresa M. Groves
David B. Wrinkle
Daniel S. Stratemeyer

Counsel for: Ford Motor Co.; Texas Eastern Transmission Corp.; Coca-Cola Bottling Co.; National Collegiate Athletic Assn.; Hartford Accident and Indemnity Co.; Continental Insurance Group; St. Paul Fire & Marine Insurance Co.; Lloyds of London; Old Republic Insurance Co.

For full biographical listings, see the Martindale-Hubbell Law Directory

HARDY, TERRELL, BOSWELL & SIMS (AV)

425 South 6th Street, P.O. Box 1265, 42001
Telephone: 502-442-9237
Fax: 502-442-9411

MEMBERS OF FIRM

Adrian H. Terrell (1904-1970)
James L. Hardy (1918-1993)
Burke B. Terrell
J. David Boswell
Van Sims

ASSOCIATES

Georgia Mae Nelson Dunn (Mrs.)
Brian R. Fleming

Local Counsel for: Energas Co.
Insurance Clients: Kemper Group; Indiana Insurance Cos.; State Automobile Insurance Co.; Farmers Insurance Group; American States Insurance Co.; Kentucky Hospital Trust Association; Farmland Insurance Co.; Scottsdale Insurance Co.; Canal Insurance Co.

For full biographical listings, see the Martindale-Hubbell Law Directory

MCMURRY & LIVINGSTON (AV)

7th Floor, Citizens Bank Building, P.O. Box 1700, 42001
Telephone: 502-443-6511
Telefax: 502-443-6548

MEMBERS OF FIRM

W. Pelham McMurry
Milton M. Livingston, Jr.
W. Fletcher McMurry Schrock
M. Greg Rains
David C. Booth
Stephen E. Smith, Jr.
Phillip L. Little
G. Kent Price

ASSOCIATES

Kerry D. Smith
Louis Keith Myers

Counsel for: Citizens Bank & Trust Co. of Paducah; Paducah Power System.
Representative Clients: Reliance Insurance Co.; Home Insurance Co.; Lowes Companies, Inc.

For full biographical listings, see the Martindale-Hubbell Law Directory

SHEFFER, HOFFMAN, THOMASON & MORTON (AV)

401 Broadway, 42001
Telephone: 502-443-9401
Telecopier: 502-443-3624
Henderson, Kentucky Office: 300 First Street.
Telephone: 502-826-3300.
Telecopier: 502-827-5070.
Owensboro, Kentucky Office: 101 East Second Street.
Telephone: 502-684-3700.
Telecopier: 502-684-3881.

OF COUNSEL

Charles B. West (Resident, Henderson Office)

MEMBERS OF FIRM

Ronald G. Sheffer
John Stanley Hoffman (Resident, Henderson Office)
David H. Thomason (Resident, Henderson Office)
John C. Morton (Resident, Henderson Office)
Jacqueline C. Kingsolver (Resident, Owensboro Office)
Peter B. Lewis
J. Christopher Hopgood (Resident, Henderson Office)
Michael W. Alvey
James A. Sigler (Resident, Henderson Office)
John A. Sheffer (Resident, Owensboro Office)
Andrew T. Coiner (Resident)
Karen L. Wilson (Resident, Henderson Office)
Jane E. Hanner (Resident)
Leslie W. Moore (Resident, Owensboro Office)
C. Thomas Miller (Resident)
Samuel John Bach (Resident, Owensboro Office)
Tina R. McFarland Jones (Not admitted in KY; Resident, Owensboro Office)
E. Dawn Smith (Resident, Henderson Office)
Christopher D. Miller (Resident, Owensboro Office)

For full biographical listings, see the Martindale-Hubbell Law Directory

WHITLOW, ROBERTS, HOUSTON & RUSSELL (AV)

Old National Bank Building, 300 Broadway, P.O. Box 995, 42001
Telephone: 502-443-4516
FAX: 502-443-4571

Thomas S. Waller (1890-1975)
Thomas W. Threlkeld (1905-1985)

MEMBERS OF FIRM

Henry O. Whitlow
Richard C. Roberts
Gary B. Houston
Thomas B. Russell
Mark C. Whitlow
E. Frederick Straub, Jr.
Randy L. Treece
Mark S. Medlin
R. Christion Hutson

ASSOCIATES

Anne Fowler Gwinn
Ronald F. Kupper

Counsel for: The BFGoodrich Company; Peoples First National Bank & Trust Co.; Kentucky Medical Insurance Co.; Aetna Life & Casualty; State Farm Mutual Insurance Cos.; Westvaco Corp.; Crounse Corp.; Liberty Mutual Insurance; The Medical Protective Co.; Paxton Media Group, Inc.

For full biographical listings, see the Martindale-Hubbell Law Directory

*PAINTSVILLE,** Johnson Co.

WELLS, PORTER & SCHMITT (AV)

327 Main Street, 41240
Telephone: 606-789-3747; 789-3749; 789-3775
Fax: 606-789-3790

MEMBERS OF FIRM

Z. Wells (1890-1946)
R. L. Wells (1894-1953)
J. K. Wells
John V. Porter, Jr.
Michael J. Schmitt
Donald L. Jones
Roger L. Massengale

ASSOCIATES

Sandra Spurgeon
Johnny L. Griffith

Representative Clients: Columbia Gas Transmission Corp.; Columbia Gas of Kentucky; C. & O. Railway Co.; Ashland Oil, Inc.; Travelers Insurance Co.; United States Fidelity & Guaranty Co.; Fireman's Fund-American Insurance Co.

For full biographical listings, see the Martindale-Hubbell Law Directory

*PARIS,** Bourbon Co. — (Refer to Lexington)

*PIKEVILLE,** Pike Co.

BAIRD, BAIRD, BAIRD AND JONES, P.S.C. (AV)

415 Second Street, P.O. Box 351, 41501
Telephone: 606-437-6276
Fax: 606-437-6383

William J. Baird (1913-1987)
William J. Baird, III
John H. Baird
Charles J. Baird
Paul Edward Jones
Terri L. Smith
James B. Ratliff
Russell H. Davis, Jr.
Billy R. Shelton
Sam A. Carter
Lois A. Kitts

Representative Clients: Pikeville National Bank & Trust Co.; LP Big Sandy Co., Massachusetts; Coal Operators & Associates; Norfolk & Southern Railway Co.; Maryland Casualty Co.; Nationwide Insurance Co.; Royal Globe Insurance Co.; The St. Paul Cos.
Approved Attorneys for: Lawyers Title Insurance Corp.

For full biographical listings, see the Martindale-Hubbell Law Directory

STRATTON, MAY, HAYS & HOGG, P.S.C. (AV)

232 Second Street Ward Building, P.O. Box 851, 41502
Telephone: 606-437-7300
Fax: 606-437-7569
Whitesburg, Kentucky Office: By-Pass Highway 15. 41858.
Telephone: 606-633-9922.

Henry D. Stratton (1925-1989)
Marrs Allen May
John D. Hays
Edgar N. Venters
David C. Stratton
Stephen L. Hogg
F. Byrd Hogg (Resident, Whitesburg, Kentucky Office)

LEGAL SUPPORT PERSONNEL

PARALEGALS

Carol Rowe Potter (Real Estate Paralegal)
Brenda Hays (Personnel Injury Paralegal)

General Counsel For: The Citizens Bank of Pikeville.
Representative Clients: Republic Steel Corp.; Island Creek Coal Co.; Virginia Iron Coal & Coke Co.; Commercial Union Insurance Co.; The Travelers Insurance Co.; Universal Underwriters Insurance Co.; Bituminous Casualty Co.; Enterprise Coal Company. Reference: Citizens Bank, Pikeville.

For full biographical listings, see the Martindale-Hubbell Law Directory

*PRESTONSBURG,** Floyd Co.

COMBS AND STEVENS (AV)

99 North Lake Drive, P.O. Box 189, 41653
Telephone: 606-886-2391; 886-1000
Fax: 606-886-2776

MEMBERS OF FIRM

James A. Combs
Ralph H. Stevens

ASSOCIATES

Gregory A. Isaac

For full biographical listings, see the Martindale-Hubbell Law Directory

FRANCIS, KAZEE & FRANCIS (AV)

119 East Court Street, P.O. Box 700, 41653
Telephone: 606-886-2361; 886-2362
FAX: 606-886-9603
Paintsville, Kentucky Office: 103 Main Street, P.O. Box 1275.
Telephone: 606-789-3059.

(See Next Column)

MEMBERS OF FIRM

D. B. Kazee
William G. Francis
William S. Kendrick
David H. Neeley
Mitchell D. Kinner
John T. Chafin
C. V. Reynolds
P. Franklin Heaberlin
Martin Lee Osborne
Brett D. Davis

ASSOCIATES

Robert J. Patton
William C. Mullins
Anthony Craig Davis

OF COUNSEL

Fred G. Francis (Retired)

Representative Clients: Island Creek Coal Co.; The Elk Horn Coal Corp.; First Commonwealth Bank; Old Republic Insurance Co.; Zurich American Insurance Co.; Maryland Casualty Co.; Bituminous Casualty Corp.; Mack Financial Corp.; Nationwide Insurance; Kentucky May Coal Co., Inc.

For full biographical listings, see the Martindale-Hubbell Law Directory

*PRINCETON,** Caldwell Co. — (Refer to Madisonville)

*RICHMOND,** Madison Co.

COY, GILBERT & GILBERT (AV)

212 North Second Street, 40475
Telephone: 606-623-3877
Fax: 606-624-5435

MEMBERS OF FIRM

Charles R. Coy
James T. Gilbert
Jerry W. Gilbert
Sandra A. Bolin

ASSOCIATES

Mark A. Shepherd

General Counsel: Peoples Bank and Trust Co. of Madison County.

For full biographical listings, see the Martindale-Hubbell Law Directory

SHUMATE, FLAHERTY & EUBANKS (AV)

Formerly Shumate, Shumate & Flaherty
225 West Irvine Street, P.O. Box 157, 40476-0157
Telephone: 606-623-3049
FAX: 606-623-6406

MEMBERS OF FIRM

Hunter M. Shumate (1893-1971)
Thomas D. Shumate (1906-1978)
Peter J. Flaherty (1920-1978)
Peter J. Flaherty III
Michael F. Eubanks

General Counsel for: Peoples Rural Telephone Cooperative Corp., McKee, Ky.
Local Counsel for: Ashland Oil & Transportation Co.

For full biographical listings, see the Martindale-Hubbell Law Directory

*RUSSELLVILLE,** Logan Co.

JESSE L. RILEY, JR. (AV)

Kirkpatrick Building, Winter Street, P.O. Box 428, 42276
Telephone: 502-726-7554; 726-8740
Fax: 502-726-2733

Counsel for: Citizens National Bank; Western Kentucky Gas Co.; E. R. Carpenter, Inc.; South Logan Water Association; Brown's Tobacco Warehouse, Inc.; Russellville Warehousing Inc.
Representative Clients: United States Fidelity and Guaranty Insurance Co.; Southern Deposit Bank.
Approved Attorney for: Farm Credit Services.

For full biographical listings, see the Martindale-Hubbell Law Directory

*SALYERSVILLE,** Magoffin Co. — (Refer to Paintsville)

*SANDY HOOK,** Elliott Co. — (Refer to Paintsville)

*SCOTTSVILLE,** Allen Co. — (Refer to Bowling Green)

*SHELBYVILLE,** Shelby Co. — (Refer to Frankfort)

*SMITHLAND,** Livingston Co. — (Refer to Paducah)

SMITHS GROVE, Warren Co.

HARLIN & PARKER, P.S.C. (AV)

Old Farmers Bank Building, 42171
Telephone: 502-563-4701
Bowling Green, Kentucky Office: 519 East Tenth Street.
Telephone: 502-842-5611.
Telefax: 502-842-2607. ABA-NET-9014.

Max B. Harlin, III
Mark D. Alcott (Resident)

Insurance Clients: American Hardware Mutual Insurance Co.; Allstate Insurance Co.; Transamerica Insurance Group; American International Group.
Railroad and Utilities Clients: District Attorneys for CSX Transportation, Inc.; South Central Bell Telephone Co.

(See Next Column)

HARLIN & PARKER P.S.C.—*Continued*

Local Counsel for: General Motors Corp.; Ford Motor Co.; AMC/Jeep.

For full biographical listings, see the Martindale-Hubbell Law Directory

*SOMERSET,** Pulaski Co.

ADAMS & ADAMS (AV)

Suite 106 First Federal Building, 107 South Main Street, P.O. Box 35, 42502-0035
Telephone: 606-679-6741; 678-4916
FAX: 606-679-3691

MEMBERS OF FIRM

Charles C. Adams — Norma B. Adams

ASSOCIATES

Jane Adams Venters — Jeffrey Scott Lawless

Counsel for: First and Farmers Bank of Somerset, Inc.; Aluminum Wheel Technology, Inc.
Representative Clients: First Federal Savings Bank; Aluminum Wheel Technology, Inc.; Tecumseh Products Co.; Food Fair Cos.; Kentucky Farm Bureau Mutual Insurance Cos.; Cumberland Valley Communications; Shamrock Coal Co.; Railum, Inc.

For full biographical listings, see the Martindale-Hubbell Law Directory

THE FIRM OF JOHN G. PRATHER (AV)

Prather Building, P.O. Box 106, 42502
Telephone: 606-679-1626; 679-4838; 678-5604
FAX: 606-679-8204

MEMBERS OF FIRM

John G. Prather — John G. Prather, Jr.
Winter R. Huff (Ms.)

Representative Clients: First & Farmers Bank of Somerset; Aetna Casualty & Surety Co.; Continental Group; Sentry-Dairyland Insurance; Employers Group; Hartford Accident & Indemnity; Kemper Insurance Co.; Underwriters Adjusting Co.; Pulaski County Water District #2; Security Insurance Group.

For full biographical listings, see the Martindale-Hubbell Law Directory

*SPRINGFIELD,** Washington Co. — (Refer to Bardstown)

*STANFORD,** Lincoln Co. — (Refer to Danville)

*STANTON,** Powell Co. — (Refer to Mount Sterling)

*TAYLORSVILLE,** Spencer Co. — (Refer to Bardstown)

*TOMPKINSVILLE,** Monroe Co. — (Refer to Glasgow)

*WARSAW,** Gallatin Co. — (Refer to Frankfort)

*WHITESBURG,** Letcher Co. — (Refer to Pikeville)

*WHITLEY CITY,** McCreary Co. — (Refer to Somerset)

*WICKLIFFE,** Ballard Co. — (Refer to Mayfield)

*WINCHESTER,** Clark Co. — (Refer to Lexington)

LOUISIANA

*ABBEVILLE,** Vermilion Parish — (Refer to New Iberia)

*ALEXANDRIA,** Rapides Parish

GOLD, WEEMS, BRUSER, SUES & RUNDELL, A PROFESSIONAL LAW CORPORATION (AV)

2001 MacArthur Drive, P.O. Box 6118, 71307-6118
Telephone: 318-445-6471
Telecopier: 318-445-6476

Leo Gold (1907-1987)
George B. Hall (1924-1971)
Charles S. Weems, III
Henry B. Bruser, III
Eugene J. Sues
Edward E. Rundell
Robert G. Nida
Dee Dodson Drell
Sam N. Poole, Jr.
Peggy Dean St. John
Thomas K. Brocato
Kenneth O. Ortego
Raymond L. Brown, Jr.
James Ogden Middleton, II
Randall L. Wilmore
Dorrell Jarrell Brister
Jan C. Holloway
Joseph R. Ballard
Carolyn J. Smilie
Gregory B. Upton
Randall M. Seeser
Julie R. Wilkerson
John C. Davidson
J. Michael Chamblee
Charles D. Elliott
Darrell K. Hickman
J. Kendall Rathburn

OF COUNSEL

Camille F. Gravel

Representative Clients: Roy O. Martin Lumber Co., Inc.; Rapides Bank & Trust Company in Alexandria; Rapides Regional Medical Center; Aetna Casualty Group; Allstate Insurance Co.; Texas Industries, Inc.; International Paper Company; Louisiana-Pacific Corporation; Crest Industries, Inc.

For full biographical listings, see the Martindale-Hubbell Law Directory

PROVOSTY, SADLER & DELAUNAY (AV)

7th Through 10th Floors, Hibernia National Bank Building, 934 Third Street, P.O. Drawer 1791, 71309-1791
Telephone: 318-445-3631
Telecopier: 318-445-9377

MEMBERS OF FIRM

LeDoux R. Provosty (1894-1980)
Richard B. Sadler, Jr. (1912-1990)
LeDoux R. Provosty, Jr.
William H. deLaunay, Jr.
Albin A. Provosty, III
H. Brenner Sadler
David P. Spence
Frederick B. Alexius
Ronald J. Fiorenza
Ricky L. Sooter
Michael L. Glass
Andrew E. Schaffer
Stephen D. Wheelis
David R. Sobel
Jeffrey A. Riggs

ASSOCIATES

H. Bradford Calvit
Joseph J. Bailey
Catherine G. Brame
Gregory L. Jones
John P. Doggett
Bryan Scott Cowart
Raymond B. Landry
Monique F. Rauls

Local Counsel for: Central Louisiana Electric Company Inc.; Prudential Insurance Company of America; Dresser Industries, Inc.; The St. Paul Fire & Marine Ins. Co.; Missouri Pacific Railroad Co.; Louisiana Intrastate Gas Co.; Insurance Company of North America; American Indemnity Group; The Haliburton Cos.; E. I. DuPont DeNemours Co.

For full biographical listings, see the Martindale-Hubbell Law Directory

STAFFORD, STEWART & POTTER (AV)

3112 Jackson Street, P.O. Box 1711, 71309
Telephone: 318-487-4910
Fax: 318-487-9417

MEMBERS OF FIRM

Grove Stafford, Jr.
Larry A. Stewart
Russell L. Potter
Paul Boudreaux, Jr.
Bradley J. Gadel
James D. Kirk
Andrew P. Texada
Mark Alan Watson
Gary B. Tillman

ASSOCIATES

Mark Pearce
Randall B. Keiser

Representative Clients: Admiral Insurance Co.; Allied Insurance Co.; Asplundh Manufacturing Company; Bankers & Shippers Insurance Company of New York; Bic Corporation; John Deere Insurance Company; Government Employees Insurance Co.; Sentry Insurance Co.; Trinity Universal Insurance Company; U.S. Fidelity & Guaranty Co.

For full biographical listings, see the Martindale-Hubbell Law Directory

*AMITE,** Tangipahoa Parish — (Refer to Hammond)

*ARCADIA,** Bienville Parish — (Refer to Ruston)

*BASTROP,** Morehouse Parish — (Refer to Monroe)

*BATON ROUGE,** East Baton Rouge Parish

BREAZEALE, SACHSE & WILSON, L.L.P. (AV)

Twenty-Third Floor, One American Place, P.O. Box 3197, 70821-3197
Telephone: 504-387-4000
Fax: 504-387-5397
New Orleans, Louisiana Office: Place St. Charles, Suite 4214, 201 St. Charles Avenue.
Telephone: 504-582-1170.
Fax: 504-582-1164.

MEMBERS OF FIRM

H. Payne Breazeale (1886-1990)
Victor A. Sachse, Jr. (1903-1979)
Maurice J. Wilson (1919-1990)
H. Payne Breazeale, Jr. (1920-1979)
Victor A. Sachse, III
Gordon A. Pugh
James E. Toups, Jr.
Paul M. Hebert, Jr.
Van R. Mayhall, Jr.
Leonard R. Nachman, II
Claude F. Reynaud, Jr.
John J. Cooper (Resident, New Orleans Office)
Murphy J. Foster, III
David R. Cassidy
Robert T. Bowsher
Christine Lipsey
David R. Kelly
Cecil J. Blache
Robert L. Atkinson
David M. Charlton
Douglas K. Williams
Stephen F. Chiccarelli
Emile C. Rolfs, III
John F. Whitney (Resident, New Orleans Office)
John E. Heinrich
Joseph E. Friend (Resident, New Orleans Office)
John W. Barton, Jr.
Richard D. Leibowitz
Michael R. Hubbell
Jude C. Bursavich
Gary L. Laborde (Resident, New Orleans Office)
Jon C. Adcock

ASSOCIATES

William F. Ridlon, II
Leo C. Hamilton
Gayla M. Moncla
Steven B. Loeb
James R. Chastain, Jr.
J. Mark Robinson
Linda Perez Clark
Trenton J. Oubre
Gwen P. Harmon
Luis A. Leitzelar
Erin M. Hart

Counsel for: Hibernia National Bank; South Central Bell Telephone Co.; Allied-Signal Corp.; Reynolds Metal Co.; Illinois Central Railroad Co.; The Continental Insurance Cos.; Fireman's Fund American Group; Chicago Bridge & Iron Co.; Montgomery Ward & Co.

For full biographical listings, see the Martindale-Hubbell Law Directory

KANTROW, SPAHT, WEAVER & BLITZER, A PROFESSIONAL LAW CORPORATION (AV)

Suite 300, City Plaza, 445 North Boulevard, P.O. Box 2997, 70821-2997
Telephone: 504-383-4703
Fax: 504-343-0630; 343-0637

Byron R. Kantrow
Carlos G. Spaht
Geraldine B. Weaver
Sidney M. Blitzer, Jr.
Paul H. Spaht
Lee C. Kantrow
John C. Miller
Vincent P. Fornias
David S. Rubin
Diane L. Crochet
Richard F. Zimmerman, Jr.
Bob D. Tucker
Martin E. Golden
Joseph A. Schittone, Jr.

S. Layne Lee
J. Michael Robinson, Jr.
Connell L. Archey
Richard D. Moreno
Randal J. Robert

Representative Clients: CNA Insurance Cos.; Federal Deposit Insurance Corp.; Hartford Insurance Group; Air Products and Chemicals, Inc.; CF Industries, Inc.; AT&T; United Companies Financial Corp.

For full biographical listings, see the Martindale-Hubbell Law Directory

KEAN, MILLER, HAWTHORNE, D'ARMOND, MCCOWAN & JARMAN, L.L.P. (AV)

22nd Floor, One American Place, P.O. Box 3513, 70821
Telephone: 504-387-0999
Fax: 504-388-9133
New Orleans, Louisiana Office: Energy Centre, Suite 1470, 1100 Poydras Street.
Telephone: 504-585-3050.
Fax: 504-585-3051.

MEMBERS OF FIRM

R. Gordon Kean, Jr. (1919-1992)
Ben R. Miller, Jr.
Robert A. Hawthorne, Jr.
William R. D'Armond
Charles S. McCowan, Jr.
G. William Jarman
Leonard L. Kilgore III
Gary A. Bezet
Carey J. Messina
Michael C. Garrard
Vance A. Gibbs
Isaac M. Gregorie, Jr.
Maureen N. Harbourt
G. Blane Clark, Jr.
M. Dwayne Johnson
James R. Lackie
David K. Nelson
J. Carter Wilkinson
Sandra Louise Edwards
Bradley C. Myers
Melanie M. Hartmann
Linda Sarradet Akchin
Erich P. Rapp

(See Next Column)

KEAN, MILLER, HAWTHORNE, D'ARMOND, MCCOWAN & JARMAN L.L.P.—*Continued*

MEMBERS OF FIRM (Continued)

Charles L. Patin, Jr.
Mathile W. Abramson
Cynthia M. Chemay
Todd A. Rossi
Katherine W. King

Kelly Wilkinson
Ray C. Dawson
Gregg R. Kronenberger
Charles S. McCowan III
D. Scott Landry
Jay M. Jalenak, Jr.
Belinda B. LeBlanc
Linda G. Rodrigue
Theresa R. Hagen
Glenn M. Farnet
Esteban Herrera, Jr.
Susan Knight Carter (Resident, New Orleans Office)
Catherine A. Filhiol
James Randy Young
John F. Jakuback
Janelle Caire Devillier
Barrye Kay Panepinto
William Ellis Latham II
Mary Dougherty Jackson
L. Victor Gregoire
Marie R. Parent
Mark D. Mese
Robert Neill Aguiluz
Robert M. Hoyland
Mark A. Marionneaux
Gary P. Graphia

SPECIAL COUNSEL

Gerald Le Van

LEGAL SUPPORT PERSONNEL

Yuxian Wang

Representative Clients: DSM Copolymer, Inc., Baton Rouge, LA; Exxon Corporation, Baton Rouge, LA; Georgia-Pacific Corporation, Atlanta, GA; Hancock Bank of Louisiana, Baton Rouge, LA.; Lamar Advertising Company, Baton Rouge, LA; Louisiana Municipal Risk Management Agency, Baton Rouge, LA; Piccadilly Cafeterias, Inc., Baton Rouge, LA; Premier Bank, National Association, Baton Rouge LA.; Texaco Inc.; White Plains, NY; Transcontinental Gas Pipeline Co., Houston, TX.

For full biographical listings, see the Martindale-Hubbell Law Directory

MATHEWS, ATKINSON, GUGLIELMO, MARKS & DAY (AV)

(Registered Limited Liability Partnership)
320 Somerulos Street, P.O. Box 3177, 70821-3177
Telephone: 504-387-6966
Fax: 504-387-8338

G. T. Owen, Jr. (1905-1972)
E. Leland Richardson (1904-1977)
Robert C. Taylor (1910-1983)
George Mathews (1914-1987)
Daniel R. Atkinson
Carey J. Guglielmo
Paul Marks, Jr.
Judith R. Atkinson
Ben L. Day
Thomas E. Balhoff
Richard G. Creed, Jr.
Charles A. Schutte, Jr.
John W. Perry, Jr.
Henry G. Terhoeve
Glen Scott Love
Leonard Cardenas, III
Daniel R. Atkinson, Jr.
Geraldine E. Fontenot
Daniel J. Balhoff
Lindsey J. Leavoy
Dawn T. Trabeau-Mire
Joseph W. Mengis

OF COUNSEL

Doug Moreau

Representative Clients: City National Bank; American Insurance Assn.; Greyhound Corp.; The Travelers Insurance Co.; Chrysler Corp.; State Farm Insurance Co's.; Allstate Insurance Co.; Aetna Life & Casualty Co.

For full biographical listings, see the Martindale-Hubbell Law Directory

PHELPS DUNBAR, L.L.P. (AV)

Suite 701, City National Bank Building, P.O. Box 4412, 70821-4412
Telephone: 504-346-0285
Telecopier: 504-381-9197
New Orleans, Louisiana Office: Texaco Center, 400 Poydras Street. Telephone 504-566-1311.
Telecopier: 504-568-9130; 504-568-9007.
Cable Address: "Howspencer."
Telex: 584125 WU.
Telex: 6821155 WUI.
Jackson, Mississippi Office: Suite 500, Security Centré North, 200 South Lamar Street, P.O. Box 23066.
Telephone: 601-352-2300.
Telecopier: 601-360-9777.
Tupelo, Mississippi Office: Seventh Floor, One Mississippi Plaza, P.O. Box 1220.
Telephone: 601-842-7907.
Telecopier: 601-842-3873.
Houston, Texas Office: Suite 501, 4 Houston Center, 1331 Lamar Street.
Telephone: 713-659-1386.
Telecopier: 713-659-1388.
London, England Office: Suite 976, Level 9, Lloyd's, 1 Lime Street, London EC3M 7DQ England.
Telephone: 011-44-71-929-4765.
Telecopier: 011-44-71-929-0046.
Telex: 987321.

OF COUNSEL

Frank S. Craig, Jr.

(See Next Column)

RESIDENT PARTNERS

H. Alston Johnson, III
Michael D. Hunt
Jennifer Bowers Zimmerman
F. Scott Kaiser
Steven J. Levine
Allen D. Darden
Jonathan C. Benda
Thomas H. Kiggans
Marshall M. Redmon

MEMBERS OF FIRM

John P. Manard, Jr., Resident, New Orleans, Louisiana Office)

COUNSEL

J. Michael Cutshaw
E. Jane Sherman

RESIDENT ASSOCIATES

Jane H. Barney
Michael David Ferachi
Susan W. Furr
Darrell J. Loup
Patrick O'Hara
Jane A. Robert
Diane Fagan Robinson
John R. Trahan
Patricia Hill Wilton

Representative Clients: Citibank, N.A.; City National Bank of Baton Rouge; Ford Motor Credit Company; Hartford Insurance Group; Hibernia National Bank; Louisiana Companies; Missouri Pacific Railroad Co.; Rubicon Inc.; The Travelers Insurance Company; Underwriters at Lloyd's, London.

For full biographical listings, see the Martindale-Hubbell Law Directory

POWERS, CLEGG & WILLARD (AV)

7967 Office Park Boulevard, P.O. Box 15948, 70895
Telephone: 504-928-1951
Telecopier: 504-929-9834

MEMBERS OF FIRM

John Dale Powers
Michael V. Clegg
William E. Willard

ASSOCIATES

Neil H. Mixon
Troy J. Charpentier
Mary A. Cazes

General Counsel for: Audubon Insurance Co.
Louisiana Counsel for: Hancock Bank & Trust Co.; Hertz Corp.; Ciba-Geigy Corp.; Utica Mutual Insurance Co.

For full biographical listings, see the Martindale-Hubbell Law Directory

TAYLOR, PORTER, BROOKS & PHILLIPS (AV)

Premier Bank Building, 8th Floor, 451 Florida Street, P.O. Box 2471, 70821
Telephone: 504-387-3221
Telecopier: 504-346-8049
New Orleans, Louisiana Office: Pan-American Life Center, 601 Poydras Street, Suite 2415.
Telephone: 504-524-1956.
Fax: 504-522-1810.

OF COUNSEL

Charles Worsham Phillips
Robert J. Vandaworker

MEMBERS OF FIRM

Benjamin Brown Taylor (1885-1959)
Charles Vernon Porter (1885-1962)
Laurance Waddill Brooks (1900-1971)
Benjamin Brown Taylor, Jr. (1913-1990)
Frank W. Middleton, Jr. (1919-1993)
Tom F. Phillips
Frank M. Coates, Jr.
John I. Moore
William H. McClendon, III
William A. Norfolk
William Shelby McKenzie
John S. Campbell, Jr.
Robert H. Hodges
John L. Glover
John R. Tharp
W. Luther Wilson
J. Clayton Johnson
G. Michael Pharis
Eugene R. Groves
A. Michael Dufilho
W. Arthur Abercrombie, Jr.
Fredrick R. Tulley
Vernon P. Middleton
James L. Ellis
John Michael Parker
Nancy C. Dougherty
Mary E. Tharp
J. Ashley Moore
Edwin W. Fleshman
Vicki M. Crochet
Harry J. Philips, Jr.
Lloyd J. Lunceford
Thomas R. Peak
C. Michael Hart
John F. McDermott
Brett P. Furr
M. Lenore Feeney

ASSOCIATES

Kathleen C. Mason
Marc S. Whitfield
John H. Runnels
David J. Messina (Resident, New Orleans Office)
Gregory E. Bodin
James C. Carver
Margaret L. Tooke
Deborah E. Lamb
T. MacDougall Womack
David H. Hanchey
David M. Bienvenu, Jr.
Paul J. Ory (Resident, New Orleans Office)
Tamara D. Simien
David J. Shelby, II
Erick Y. Miyagi
Jayne L. Middleton

General Counsel for: Baton Rouge Broadcasting Co.; Baton Rouge Water Works Co.; Cablevision of Baton Rouge, Ltd.; Louisiana State University and A. and M. College; Louisiana Television Broadcasting Co.; Our Lady of the Lake Hospital, Inc.; Pennington Biomedical Research Foundation; The Newton Group.

For full biographical listings, see the Martindale-Hubbell Law Directory

WATSON, BLANCHE, WILSON & POSNER (AV)

505 North Boulevard, P.O. Drawer 2995, 70821-2995
Telephone: 504-387-5511
Fax: 504-387-5972
Other Baton Rouge, Louisiana Office: 4000 South Sherwood Forest Boulevard, Suite 504.
Telephone: 504-291-5280.
Fax: 504-293-8075.

Warren O. Watson (1893-1973)
Fred A. Blanche (1898-1977)
Charles W. Wilson (1910-1981)
Harvey H. Posner
Robert L. Roland
Alton J. Reine, Jr.
Peter T. Dazzio
Felix R. Weill
Richard S. Dunn
William E. Scott, III
Mary H. Thompson
Michael M. Remson
P. Chauvin Wilkinson, Jr.
Randall L. Champagne
René J. Pfefferle

ASSOCIATES

P. Scott Jolly
Raymond A. Daigle, Jr.

Representative Clients: Citizens Savings and Loan Association; Community Coffee Company, Inc.; Louisiana Hospital Association; Prudential Insurance Company of America (The).

For full biographical listings, see the Martindale-Hubbell Law Directory

BUNKIE, Avoyelles Parish — (Refer to Marksville)

*CAMERON,** Cameron Parish — (Refer to Lake Charles)

*CLINTON,** East Feliciana Parish — (Refer to Baton Rouge)

*COLUMBIA,** Caldwell Parish — (Refer to Monroe)

*COUSHATTA,** Red River Parish — (Refer to Natchitoches)

*COVINGTON,** St. Tammany Parish

GARIC KENNETH BARRANGER (AV)

200 North Columbia Street, 70433
Telephone: 504-892-4024; 892-4084
Fax: 504-892-1246

ASSOCIATE

Grace Phyllis Gremillion

Reference: Citizens Bank & Trust Co.

For full biographical listings, see the Martindale-Hubbell Law Directory

*DE RIDDER,** Beauregard Parish

HALL, LESTAGE & LANDRENEAU (AV)

205 Second Street, P.O. Box 880, 70634
Telephone: 318-463-8692
Fax: 318-463-2272

MEMBERS OF FIRM

William E. Hall, Jr.
H. O. Lestage, III
David R. Lestage
F. Steve Landreneau
Brian S. Lestage

Representative Clients: Boise Cascade Corp.; City Savings & Trust Co.; Crosby Land Resources; Firemen's Fund-American Cos.; Great American Insurance Co.; The Hartford Insurance Group; Pacific Marine Insurance Co.; State Farm Mutual Automobile Insurance Co.; The Travelers Insurance Co.; United States Fidelity & Guaranty Co.

For full biographical listings, see the Martindale-Hubbell Law Directory

*DONALDSONVILLE,** Ascension Parish — (Refer to Plaquemine)

*FRANKLINTON,** Washington Parish — (Refer to Bogalusa)

*GRETNA,** Jefferson Parish — (Refer to New Orleans)

*JENA,** La Salle Parish

GAHARAN & WILSON (AV)

Gaharan-Wilson Building, 107 East Courthouse, P.O. Box 1356, 71342
Telephone: 318-992-2104
Fax: 318-992-5110

Leonard W. Richey (1918-1975)
P. S. Gaharan, Jr. (1902-1989)
Joseph Wilson
Donald R. Wilson

Representative Clients: Justiss Oil Co., Inc.; Placid Oil Co.; Hunt Petroleum Corp.; International Paper Co.; Louisiana-Pacific Corp.; Cooper Industries; Liberty Mutual.
Reference: Jonesville Bank & Trust, Bank of Jena.

*JENNINGS,** Jefferson Davis Parish — (Refer to Lake Charles)

*JONESBORO,** Jackson Parish — (Refer to Ruston)

*LAFAYETTE,** Lafayette Parish

DAVIDSON, MEAUX, SONNIER, McELLIGOTT & SWIFT (AV)

810 South Buchanan Street, P.O. Drawer 2908, 70502
Telephone: 318-237-1660
Fax: 318-237-3676

MEMBERS OF FIRM

James J. Davidson, Jr. (1904-1990)
V. Farley Sonnier (1942-1988)
Richard C. Meaux, Sr.
James J. Davidson, III
John E. McElligott, Jr.
John G. Swift
Jeffrey A. Rhoades
Philip A. Fontenot
Kyle L. Gideon
Theodore G. Edwards, IV
Stacey L. Knight

ASSOCIATES

Jhan C. Boudreaux Beaullieu
Tracy P. Curtis

OF COUNSEL

Jan Whitehead Swift

General Counsel: Southwest Louisiana Electric Membership Corp.; Power Rig Drilling Co.; Inc.; Macro Oil Co., Inc.; Dwight W. Andrus Insurance Agency; Lafayette Airport Commission.
Local Counsel: Southern Pacific Transportation Co.
Representative Clients: Highlands Insurance Co.; Wal-Mart Stores, Inc.; USAA.

For full biographical listings, see the Martindale-Hubbell Law Directory

RICHARD R. KENNEDY A PROFESSIONAL LAW CORPORATION (AV)

309 Polk Street, P.O. Box 3243, 70502-3243
Telephone: 318-232-1934
Fax: 318-232-9720

Richard R. Kennedy

For full biographical listings, see the Martindale-Hubbell Law Directory

MANGHAM, DAVIS AND OGLESBEE (AV)

Suite 1400 First National Bank Towers, 600 Jefferson Street, P.O. Box 93110, 70509-3110
Telephone: 318-233-6200
Fax: 318-233-6521

Michael R. Mangham
Louis R. Davis
Michael G. Oglesbee
Herman E. Garner, Jr.

ASSOCIATES

Dawn Mayeux Fuqua
Lisa Hanchey Sevier

SPECIAL COUNSEL

Michael J. O'Shee

OF COUNSEL

George W. Hardy, III
Robert E. Rowe

Reference: The First National Bank of Lafayette, Lafayette, Louisiana.

For full biographical listings, see the Martindale-Hubbell Law Directory

ONEBANE, DONOHOE, BERNARD, TORIAN, DIAZ, McNAMARA & ABELL (AV)

Suite 600, Versailles Centre, 102 Versailles Boulevard, P.O. Box 3507, 70502
Telephone: 318-237-2660
Telecopier: 318-266-1232
Cable Address: "Ondob"
Telex: 311283

Joseph Onebane (1917-1987)
John G. Torian, II (1936-1991)
Lawrence E. Donohoe, Jr.
John Allen Bernard
James E. Diaz
Timothy J. McNamara
Edward C. Abell, Jr.
Helen Onebane Mendell
Lawrence L. Lewis, III
Robert M. Mahony
Daniel G. Fournerat
Douglas W. Truxillo
Randall C. Songy
Chris G. Robbins
Michael G. Durand
Greg Guidry
Joseph L. Lemoine, Jr.
Mark L. Riley
Graham N. Smith
Gordon T. Whitman
Gary P. Kraus
Richard J. Petre, Jr.
Thomas G. Smart
James E. Diaz, Jr.
Roger E. Ishee
R. Thomas Jorden, Jr.
Kevin R. Rees
John W. Penny, Jr.
John A. Keller

Jennifer McDaniel Kleinpeter
Steven C. Lanza
Christopher H. Hebert
John W. Kolwe
Sue Nations
Joel P. Babineaux
Michael W. Landry
Ted M. Anthony
Carolyn Trahan Bertrand
Alison M. Brumley

Representative Clients: Allstate Insurance Co.; CIGNA; Continental Insurance Co.; Employers-Commercial; Fireman's Fund American Insurance Co.; Highlands Insurance Co.; Travelers Insurance Co.

For full biographical listings, see the Martindale-Hubbell Law Directory

Roy, Bivins, Judice & Henke, A Professional Law Corporation (AV)

600 Jefferson Street, Suite 800, P.O. Drawer Z, 70502
Telephone: 318-233-7430
Telecopier: 318-233-8403
Telex: 9102505130

Harmon F. Roy
John A. Bivins
Ronald J. Judice
Kenneth M. Henke
W. Alan Lilley
Philip E. Roberts
Patrick M. Wartelle

Representative Clients: Employers Insurance of Wausau; Louisiana Medical Mutual Ins. Co.; C.N.A.; Aetna Casualty & Surety; Zurich Ins. Co.; Our Lady of Lourdes Regional Medical Center, Inc.; St Paul Fire & Marine Ins. Co.; First Financial Insurance Company.

For full biographical listings, see the Martindale-Hubbell Law Directory

*LAKE CHARLES,** Calcasieu Parish

Baggett, McCall & Burgess, A Professional Law Corporation (AV)

3006 Country Club Road, P.O. Drawer 7820, 70606-7820
Telephone: 318-478-8888
Fax: 318-478-8946

William B. Baggett
Robert C. McCall
Roger G. Burgess
William B. Baggett, Jr.
Wells T. Watson
Jeffrey T. Gaughan

For full biographical listings, see the Martindale-Hubbell Law Directory

Bergstedt & Mount (AV)

Second Floor, Magnolia Life Building, P.O. Drawer 3004, 70602-3004
Telephone: 318-433-3004
Facsimile: 318-433-8080

MEMBERS OF FIRM

Thomas M. Bergstedt
Benjamin W. Mount

ASSOCIATES

Van C. Seneca
Thomas J. Gayle
Gregory P. Marceaux
Joseph R. Pousson

OF COUNSEL

Charles S. Ware

Representative Clients: Armstrong World Industries; Ashland Oil Co.; CIGNA Property & Casualty Companies; Homequity; Lake Area Medical Center; Leach Company; Olin Corporation; Terra Corporation; Town of Iowa; R. D. Werner Company.

For full biographical listings, see the Martindale-Hubbell Law Directory

Brame, Bergstedt & Brame (AV)

426 Kirby Street, 70601
Telephone: 318-439-4571
Fax: 318-439-4556

MEMBERS OF FIRM

Frank M. Brame
John E. Bergstedt
Joseph A. Brame
David B. McCain
J. Gregory Bergstedt

ASSOCIATE

Carlyn Bettinger Bergstedt

Representative Clients: American Hardware Mutual Insurance Co.; Commercial Union Insurance Cos.; Employers Insurance of Wausau; Equitable Life Assurance Company of America; Louisiana Medical Mutual Insurance Company; Maryland-American General Insurance Group; Mutual of Omaha; Ryder System, Inc.; Scottsdale Insurance Co.; Zurich Insurance Co.

For full biographical listings, see the Martindale-Hubbell Law Directory

Jones, Tête, Nolen, Hanchey, Swift & Spears, L.L.P. (AV)

First Federal Building, P.O. Box 910, 70602
Telephone: 318-439-8315
Telefax: 436-5606; 433-5536

MEMBERS OF FIRM

Sam H. Jones (1897-1978)
William R. Tête
William M. Nolen
James C. Hanchey
Carl H. Hanchey
William B. Swift
Kenneth R. Spears
Edward J. Fonti
Charles N. Harper
Gregory W. Belfour
Robert J. Tête
Yul D. Lorio

OF COUNSEL

John A. Patin
Edward D. Myrick

(See Next Column)

ASSOCIATES

Lilynn A. Cutrer
Lydia Ann Guillory-Lee
Clint David Bischoff

General Counsel for: First Federal Savings & Loan Association of Lake Charles; Beauregard Electric Cooperative, Inc.

Representative Clients: Atlantic Richfield Company; CITGO Petroleum Corp.; Conoco Inc.; HIMONT U.S.A., Inc.; ITT Hartford; Olin Corporation; OXY USA Inc.; Premier Bank, National Association; W.R. Grace & Co.

For full biographical listings, see the Martindale-Hubbell Law Directory

Plauché Smith & Nieset, A Professional Law Corporation (AV)

1123 Pithon Street, P.O. Drawer 1705, 70602
Telephone: 318-436-0522
Facsimile: 318-436-9637

S. W. Plauché (1889-1952)
S. W. Plauché, Jr. (1915-1966)
A. Lane Plauché
Allen L. Smith, Jr.
James R. Nieset
Frank M. Walker, Jr.
Michael J. McNulty, III
Jeffrey M. Cole
Andrew R. Johnson, IV
Charles V. Musso, Jr.
Christopher P. Ieyoub
H. David Vaughan, II
Rebecca S. Young
Stephanie A. Landry

Representative Clients: CIGNA; CNA Insurance Cos.; Commercial Union Insurance Cos.; Crum & Forster; General Motors Corp.; Reliance Insurance Cos.; Royal Insurance Group; State Farm; U.S. Insurance Group.

For full biographical listings, see the Martindale-Hubbell Law Directory

Raggio, Cappel, Chozen & Berniard (AV)

500 Magnolia Life Building, P.O. Box 820, 70601
Telephone: 318-436-9481
Fax: 318-436-9499

MEMBERS OF FIRM

Alvin O. King (1890-1958)
Thomas C. Hall (1919-1973)
Thomas L. Raggio
Richard B. Cappel
Frederick L. Cappel
Richard A. Chozen
Stephen A. Berniard, Jr.
Christopher M. Trahan
L. Paul Foreman
M. Keith Prudhomme

ASSOCIATES

Kevin J. Koenig

Counsel for: Aetna Casualty & Surety Co.; Allstate Insurance Co.; Hercules Incorporated; Liberty Mutual Insurance Co.; Southern Pacific Co.; United States Fidelity and Guaranty Co.; Crowley Maritime Corp.; General Motors Corp.; Sabine Towing & Transportation Co.; E. I. duPont de Nemours & Co., Inc.

For full biographical listings, see the Martindale-Hubbell Law Directory

Scofield, Gerard, Veron, Singletary & Pohorelsky, A Professional Law Corporation (AV)

1114 Ryan Street, P.O. Drawer 3028, 70601
Telephone: 318-433-9436
Telefax: 318-436-0306

John B. Scofield
Richard E. Gerard, Jr.
J. Michael Veron
C. Eston Singletary
John R. Pohorelsky
Scott J. Scofield
Patrick D. Gallaugher, Jr.
Robert E. Landry
Russell J. Stutes, Jr.

Representative Clients: Admiral Insurance Co.; Amoco Production Co.; Browning-Ferris Industries, Inc.; Cosmos Broadcasting Corp.; Ford Motor Co.; Dresser Industries, Inc.; Kansas City Southern Railway Co.; Mobil Exploration & Producing U.S., Inc.; Phillips Petroleum Co.; Premier Bank, N.A.

For full biographical listings, see the Martindale-Hubbell Law Directory

Stockwell, Sievert, Viccellio, Clements & Shaddock (AV)

One Lakeside Plaza, P.O. Box 2900, 70601
Telephone: 318-436-9491
FAX: 318-493-7210

MEMBERS OF FIRM

Oliver P. Stockwell (1907-1993)
Fred H. Sievert, Jr. (1923-1988)
Charles D. Viccellio
Robert W. Clements
William E. Shaddock
Emmett C. Sole
John Stanton Bradford
Stephen C. Polito
Robert S. Dampf
William B. Monk
Jeanne M. Sievert
H. Alan McCall
Brian L. Coody
Paul Veazey
James Anthony Blanco
Andrew D. McGlathery, III

OF COUNSEL

Thomas G. Henning

(See Next Column)

STOCKWELL, SIEVERT, VICCELLIO, CLEMENTS & SHADDOCK, *Lake Charles—Continued*

ASSOCIATES

H. Aubrey White, III
Benjamin J. Guilbeau, Jr.
Susan Gay Viccellio

Representative Clients: The Continental Insurance Cos.; State Farm Insurance Cos.; PPG Industries, Inc.; Gulf States Utilities Co.; Lakeside National Bank of Lake Charles; Lake Charles Memorial Hospital; Texaco, Inc.; St. Patrick Hospital of Lake Charles; Firestone-Bridgestone, Inc.; Reliance Insurance Co.

For full biographical listings, see the Martindale-Hubbell Law Directory

*LEESVILLE,** Vernon Parish — (Refer to De Ridder)

*MANSFIELD,** De Soto Parish — (Refer to Shreveport)

*MARKSVILLE,** Avoyelles Parish

LABORDE & LAFARGUE (AV)

Laborde Building, 308 North Main, P.O. Box 277, 71351
Telephone: 318-253-7521; 253-7522

MEMBERS OF FIRM

Cliffe E. Laborde, Jr. (1913-1983)
Edwin L. Lafargue
David E. Lafargue
Carol M. Lafargue

General Counsel for: Tidewater, Inc.; Tidex, Inc.; Haas Investment Co., Inc.; Hamburg Mills; Guaranty Seed Co.
Representative Clients: Pan American Petroleum Corp.; Murphy Oil Corp.; Ocean Drilling & Exploration Co.; Hilliard Oil & Gas, Inc.

For full biographical listings, see the Martindale-Hubbell Law Directory

METAIRIE, Jefferson Parish

BERNARD, CASSISA & ELLIOTT, A PROFESSIONAL LAW CORPORATION (AV)

1615 Metairie Road, P.O. Box 55490, 70055-5490
Telephone: 504-834-2612
Telecopier: 504-838-9438

Peter L. Bernard, Jr. (1920-1991)
Frank L. Micholet (1913-1972)
Paul V. Cassisa, Sr.
Stephen N. Elliott
Benjamin Franklin Davis, Jr.
Eugene M. McEachin, Jr.
Robert A. McMahon, Jr.
Albert C. Miranda
Mickey S. deLaup
Patricia Schuster Le Blanc
Carl J. Giffin, Jr.
Paul V. Cassisa, Jr.
Howard B. Kaplan
John D. Sileo
William L. Brockman
Jeffrey K. Warwick
Robert A. Knight

Representative Clients: Royal Insurance Group; General Motors Corp.; Hartford Insurance Group; Nissan Motor Corp.; Toyota Motor Sales, U.S.A., Inc.; Honda North America, Inc.

For full biographical listings, see the Martindale-Hubbell Law Directory

HAILEY, MCNAMARA, HALL, LARMANN & PAPALE (AV)

A Partnership including Law Corporations
Suite 1400, One Galleria Boulevard, P.O. Box 8288, 70011
Telephone: 504-836-6500
Fax: 504-836-6565

MEMBERS OF FIRM

James W. Hailey, Jr., (P.L.C.)
Henry D. McNamara, Jr., (P.L.C.)
W. Marvin Hall (P.L.C.)
Antonio E. Papale, Jr., (P.L.C.)
Laurence E. Larmann (P.L.C.)
Richard A. Chopin (P.L.C.)
Kevin L. Cole
Michael P. Mentz
Richard T. Simmons, Jr.,(P.L.C.)
Nelson W. Wagar, III, (P.L.C.)
Michael J. Vondenstein
Brian ReBoul
David K. Persons
Thomas M. Richard
Dominic J. Ovella
Elizabeth Smyth Sirgo
C. Kelly Lightfoot
John T. Culotta (P.L.C.)
John E. Unsworth, Jr.
Julie DiFulco Robles

ASSOCIATES

William R. Seay, Jr.
Cyril B. Burck, Jr.
Claude A. Greco
Valerie T. Schexnayder
John Price McNamara
W. Evan Plauche
Brian T. Carr
Kurt D. Engelhardt
W. Glenn Burns

OF COUNSEL

John P. Volz

Representative Clients: Certain Underwriters at Lloyds of London; Diamond Offshore Drilling Inc.; First American Title Insurance Company; The Flintkote Co.; Litton Industries; Martin Marietta Manned Space Systems; Rheem Manufacturing Co.; Rowan Companies, Inc; State Farm Fire & Casualty Co.; Textron, Inc; Travelers Companies.

For full biographical listings, see the Martindale-Hubbell Law Directory

*MINDEN,** Webster Parish

KITCHENS, BENTON, KITCHENS & WARREN, A PROFESSIONAL LAW CORPORATION (AV)

420 Broadway, P.O. Box 740, 71055
Telephone: 318-377-5331
Fax: 318-377-5361

Graydon K. Kitchens, Sr. (1903-1988)
John B. Benton, Jr.
Paul E. Kitchens
William Rick Warren
Graydon K. Kitchens, III

Representative Clients: State Farm Insurance Co.; Howard Lumber & Supply Co., Inc.; Minden Building & Loan Assn.; Mister Twister, Inc.; Minden Housing Authority.
Reference: Minden Bank & Trust Co.

For full biographical listings, see the Martindale-Hubbell Law Directory

*MONROE,** Ouachita Parish

DAVENPORT, FILES & KELLY (AV)

1509 Lamy Lane, P.O. Box 4787, 71211-4787
Telephone: 318-387-6453
FAX: 318-323-6533

MEMBERS OF FIRM

Thos. W. Davenport (1909-1962)
Wm. G. Kelly, Jr.
Thomas W. Davenport, Jr.
Jack B. Files
Mike C. Sanders
Ramsey L. Ogg
Michael J. Fontenot

ASSOCIATES

M. Shane Craighead

STAFF ATTORNEY

Stacy L. Guice

Representative Clients: American International Group (AIG); Burlington Motor Carriers; Chubb Group; Crum & Forster Group; Delta Airlines, Inc.; GAINSCO; Government Employees Insurance Co.; Highlands Ins. Co.; Trinity Universal Ins. Co.; Zurich-American Insurance Companies.

For full biographical listings, see the Martindale-Hubbell Law Directory

HAYES, HARKEY, SMITH & CASCIO, L.L.P. (AV)

2811 Kilpatrick Boulevard, P.O. Box 8032, 71211-8032
Telephone: 318-387-2422
FAX: 318-388-5809

Haynes L. Harkey, Jr.
Louis D. Smith
Joseph D. Cascio, Jr.
Charles S. Smith
Thomas M. Hayes, III
Bruce McKamy Mintz
C. Joseph Roberts, III

OF COUNSEL

Thomas M. Hayes, Jr.

John B. Saye
Karen L. Hayes

Representative Clients: Ford Motor Co.; Hanover Insurance Co.; Cigna, Inc.; St. Francis Medical Center, Inc.; St. Paul Insurance Group; Travelers Ins. Co.; Cooper Industries; Lawyers Title Insurance Corp.; Riverwood International Corp.

For full biographical listings, see the Martindale-Hubbell Law Directory

HUDSON, POTTS & BERNSTEIN (AV)

10th Floor, Premier Bank Building, 130 DeSiard Street, Drawer 3008, 71210
Telephone: 318-388-4400
Fax: 318-322-4194

MEMBERS OF FIRM

Murray Hudson (1920-1971)
John J. Potts (1894-1935)
Henry Bernstein, Jr. (1930-1978)
Robert C. Downing (1952-1991)
Jesse D. McDonald
Paul K. Kirkpatrick, Jr.
Ben R. Hanchey
James A. Rountree
W. Craig Henry
Gordon L. James
Robert M. Baldwin
Charles W. Herold, III
William T. McNew
Brady Dean King, II

ASSOCIATES

W. Lee Perkins, Jr.
Jay P. Adams
Jan Peter Christiansen
Brian P. Bowes
Stephen Adam North

General Attorneys for: Missouri Pacific Railroad Co.
Attorneys for: Premier Bank, Monroe; General Motors; Allstate Insurance Co.; State Farm Fire & Casualty Co.; Hartford Insurance Group; Royal Globe Insurance Cos.; Dodson Insurance Group.

For full biographical listings, see the Martindale-Hubbell Law Directory

Monroe—Continued

McLeod, Verlander, Eade & Verlander (AV)

A Partnership including Professional Law Corporations
1900 North 18th Street, Suite 610, P.O. Box 2270, 71207-2270
Telephone: 318-325-7000
Telecopier: 318-324-0580

MEMBERS OF FIRM

Robert P. McLeod (P.L.C.)
David E. Verlander, III (P.L.C.)
Ellen R. Eade
Paul J. Verlander
Rick W. Duplissey
Pamela G. Nathan

For full biographical listings, see the Martindale-Hubbell Law Directory

Snellings, Breard, Sartor, Inabnett & Trascher (AV)

1503 North 19th Street, P.O. Box 2055, 71207-2055
Telephone: 318-387-8000
Fax: 318-387-8200

MEMBERS OF FIRM

George M. Snellings, Jr. (1910-1984)
Daniel Ryan Sartor, Jr.
Carrick R. Inabnett
Charles C. Trascher, III
E. Frank Snellings
L. Kent Breard, Jr.
Clara Moss Sartor
William Brooks Watson
David C. McMillin

ASSOCIATES

Jon Keith Guice
Carrick B. Inabnett

OF COUNSEL

Kent Breard

Representative Clients: Central Bank; Delta Air Lines, Inc.; Federal Deposit Insurance Co.; Glenwood Regional Medical Center; John Hancock Mutual Life Insurance Company; Kemper Insurance Group; Horace Mann Insurance Cos.; Resolution Trust Corp.

For full biographical listings, see the Martindale-Hubbell Law Directory

MORGAN CITY, St. Mary Parish

Lippman, Mahfouz & Martin (AV)

Inglewood Mall, P.O. Box 2526, 70381
Telephone: 504-384-1833
Telecopy: 504-385-4632

MEMBERS OF FIRM

Alfred S. Lippman
Thomas L. Mahfouz
Dale P. Martin

ASSOCIATES

Brian M. Tranchina

For full biographical listings, see the Martindale-Hubbell Law Directory

*NATCHITOCHES,** Natchitoches Parish

McCoy, Hawthorne, Roberts & Begnaud, Ltd., A Law Corporation (AV)

300 St. Denis Street, P.O. Box 1369, 71458-1369
Telephone: 318-352-6495
Telecopier: 318-352-9982

Kenneth D. McCoy, Jr.
Dee A. Hawthorne
Mark L. Roberts
Mark A. Begnaud

Representative Clients: American Service Life Ins. Co.; Central Bank; Farm Credit Bank of Texas; First Bank of Natchitoches (general counsel); First South PCA; Natchitoches Parish Port Commission; Northwestern State University of Louisiana; Red River Waterway District; Reserve Life Ins. Co.; Riverwood International Corporation.

For full biographical listings, see the Martindale-Hubbell Law Directory

*NEW IBERIA,** Iberia Parish

Armentor & Wattigny, A Professional Law Corporation (AV)

101 West Main Street, Suite B, P.O. Box 10030, 70562-0030
Telephone: 318-369-3826
Fax: 318-369-6572

Minos H. Armentor
Gerard B. Wattigny
Dean M. Wattigny

Representative Clients: Cajun Sugar Co-op, Inc.; Voorhies Supply Co., Inc.; Voorhies Machine Shop; Konriko Rice Co.; D&B Boat Rentals, Inc.; Stockstill Boat Rentals, Inc.; Century 21 Shadows Real Estate.
Agents For: Lawyers Title Ins.

For full biographical listings, see the Martindale-Hubbell Law Directory

*NEW ORLEANS,** Orleans Parish

Breazeale, Sachse & Wilson, L.L.P. (AV)

Place St. Charles, Suite 4214, 201 St. Charles Avenue, 70170
Telephone: 504-582-1170
Fax: 504-582-1164
Baton Rouge, Louisiana Office: Twenty-Third Floor, One American Place, P.O. Box 3197.
Telephone: 504-387-4000.
Fax: 504-387-5397.

MEMBERS OF FIRM

Gordon A. Pugh
Van R. Mayhall, Jr.
John J. Cooper (Resident)
Cecil J. Blache
John F. Whitney (Resident)
Joseph E. Friend (Resident)
Gary L. Laborde (Resident)

For full biographical listings, see the Martindale-Hubbell Law Directory

Chaffe, McCall, Phillips, Toler & Sarpy (AV)

A Partnership including a Professional Law Corporation
2300 Energy Centre, 1100 Poydras Street, 70163-2300
Telephone: 504-585-7000
Telecopier: 504-585-7075
Cable Address: "Denegre"
Telex: (AT&T) 460122 CMPTS
Baton Rouge, Louisiana Office: 202 Two United Plaza, 8550 United Plaza Boulevard.
Telephone: 504-922-4300.
Fax: 504-922-4304.

MEMBERS OF FIRM

John Lemuel Toler (1895-1985)
Leon Sarpy
Felix H. Lapeyre
Donald A. Lindquist
Robert B. Deane
Peter A. Feringa, Jr.
Nolan Kammer
B. Lloyd Magruder
J. Dwight LeBlanc, Jr.
Charles L. Chassaignac
G. Phillip Shuler, III
James A. Barton, III
Robert B. Fisher, Jr.
Corinne Ann Morrison
James A. Babst
William F. Grace, Jr.
Robert S. Rooth
Harry R. Holladay
Marc G. Shachat
L. Havard Scott, III
Derek Anthony Walker
Jonathan C. McCall
Kenneth J. Servay
Andrew Rinker, Jr.
Raymond G. Hoffman, Jr.
Kathleen S. Plemer
Daniel L. Daboval
Thomas D. Forbes
Julie D. Livaudais
John F. Olinde
Carmelite M. Bertaut
John H. Clegg
David R. Richardson
Dona J. Dew
Jose S. Canseco
E. Howell Crosby
Keith Eric Gisleson
Henry D. Salassi, Jr. (Resident Partner, Baton Rouge)
John Neely Kennedy
W. Anthony Toups, III
Douglas L. Grundmeyer
Betty F. Mullin
J. Gregory Wyrick
Merle F. Shoughrue
Charles P. Blanchard
Robert B. Landry, III
Brent A. Talbot
James C. Young
Andrew C. Partee, Jr.
Ronald L. Naquin
Paul E. Ramoni, Jr.
Hervin A. Guidry
H. Evans Scobee (Resident Special Partner, Baton Rouge)
Guy Wootan
John C. Saunders, Jr.

ASSOCIATES

Rebecca A. Stulb
Mark L. Gundlach
Mary L. Meyer
Skye C. Henry
Daphne P. McNutt
Donald J. Cazayoux, Jr. (Resident Associate, Baton Rouge)
Eric J. Simonson
Scott C. Barney
Scott A. Soule
G. Wade Wootan

OF COUNSEL

E. Harold Saer, Jr.
George W. Pigman, Jr.
Gordon O. Ewin
Paul A. Nalty
Nathaniel P. Phillips, Jr.

Representative Clients: CSX Transportation, Inc. (formerly, Louisville & Nashville Railroad Co.); Alerion Bank; Hibernia Corp.; The Allstate Insurance Co.; The Equitable Life Assurance Society of the United States; Liverpool and London Steamship Protection and Indemnity Assn. Ltd.; The West of England Steam Ship Owners Mutual Insurance Assn. (Luxembourg); Associated Builders and Contractors, Inc.; Resolution Trust Corp.; Brown & Williamson Tobacco Corp.

For full biographical listings, see the Martindale-Hubbell Law Directory

Christovich and Kearney, L.L.P. (AV)

Suite 2300 Pan American Life Center, 601 Poydras Street, 70130-6078
Telephone: 504-561-5700
FAX: 504-561-5743
Houston, Texas Office: 700 Louisiana, Suite 4550, 77002.
Telephone: 713-225-2255.
Fax: 713-225-1112.

(See Next Column)

CHRISTOVICH AND KEARNEY L.L.P., *New Orleans—Continued*

MEMBERS OF FIRM

Alvin R. Christovich, Jr.
William K. Christovich
J. Walter Ward, Jr.
Lawrence J. Ernst
James F. Holmes
Robert E. Peyton
C. Edgar Cloutier
Charles W. Schmidt, III
Richard K. Christovich
Terry Christovich Gay
Paul G. Preston
Michael M. Christovich
E. Phelps Gay
Thomas C. Cowan
Geoffrey P. Snodgrass
J. Warren Gardner, Jr.
Kevin R. Tully
Lance R. Rydberg
Elizabeth S. Cordes
John K. Leach
Fred T. Hinrichs
Daniel A. Rees
Charles M. Lanier, Jr.

ASSOCIATES

Lyon H. Garrison
Philip J. Borne
Anthony Reginelli, Jr.
Paige F. Rosato
J. Roslyn Lemmon
James Aristide Holmes
Richard J. Garvey, Jr.
Scott P. Yount
Patricia Broussard
Patrick W. Drouilhet (Not admitted in LA)
Cheryl A. Smith (Not admitted in LA)

OF COUNSEL

Nannette Jolivette-Brown

Representative Clients: Associated Aviation Underwriters; Brown & Root, Inc.; Chubb/Pacific Indemnity Group; Continental Insurance Company; Crawford & Co.; Crum & Forster; Highlands Insurance Company; Insurance Company of North America; Liberty Mutual Insurance Company; Southern Pacific Transportation Co.

For full biographical listings, see the Martindale-Hubbell Law Directory

DEUTSCH, KERRIGAN & STILES (AV)

A Partnership including Professional Law Corporations
755 Magazine Street, 70130-3672
Telephone: 504-581-5141
Cable Address: "Dekest"
Telex: 584358
Telecopier: 504-566-1201

MEMBERS OF FIRM

Eberhard P. Deutsch (1897-1980)
R. Emmett Kerrigan (1902-1980)
Harry F. Stiles (1902-1953)
David C. Treen
Bernard Marcus (P.L.C.)
Frederick R. Bott (P.L.C.)
William W. Messersmith, III, (P.L.C.)
Charles K. Reasonover (P.L.C.)
David L. Campbell
Charles F. Seemann, Jr., (P.L.C.)
Robert E. Kerrigan, Jr., (P.L.C.)
Bertrand M. Cass, Jr.
Harry S. Anderson (P.L.C.)
Raymon G. Jones (P.L.C.)
Francis J. Barry, Jr.
Victor E. Stilwell, Jr., (P.L.C.)
Allen F. Campbell
Matt J. Farley (P.L.C.)
Philip D. Lorio, III
G. Alex Weller
A. Wendel Stout, III
Daniel A. Smith
Terrence L. Brennan
Marc J. Yellin (P.L.C.)
Howard L. Murphy
Darrell K. Cherry (P.L.C.)
Richard B. Montgomery III
William E. Wright, Jr.
Nancy J. Marshall
James G. Wyly, III
Ellis B. Murov (P.L.C.)
Joseph L. McReynolds
Joseph L. Spilman, III
Duris L. Holmes
Janet L. MacDonell
William Lee Kohler
Theodore L. White
William C. Harrison, Jr.
Judy L. Burnthorn
L. Paul Hood, Jr.

OF COUNSEL

Brunswick G. Deutsch (P.L.C.)
Marian Mayer Berkett
Ralph L. Kaskell, Jr.
Malcolm W. Monroe
Francis G. Weller (P.L.C.)

ASSOCIATES

Gary B. Roth
Michael W. Boleware
Gene Ray Smith
Barbara L. Malik
Garald P. Weller
Karyn J. Vigh
Reneé Clark McGinty
Herman J. Gesser, III
Lisa C. Winter
Karen Wells Roby
Victor J. Franckiewicz, Jr.
W. Christopher Beary
Sheldon W. Snipe

LEGAL SUPPORT PERSONNEL

Dalton L. Woolverton

For full biographical listings, see the Martindale-Hubbell Law Directory

FRASER, WHITE & DES ROCHES (AV)

530 Natchez Street, Suite 200, 70130
Telephone: 504-581-4726
Facsimile: 504-581-1190

MEMBERS OF FIRM

Richard A. Fraser, III
J. Ralph White
Cary A. Des Roches

(See Next Column)

OF COUNSEL

William R. Campbell, Jr.
Lisa K. Tanet

For full biographical listings, see the Martindale-Hubbell Law Directory

GORDON, ARATA, MCCOLLAM & DUPLANTIS, L.L.P. (AV)

A Partnership including Professional Law Corporations
Place St. Charles, Suite 4000, 201 St. Charles Avenue, 70170-4000
Telephone: 504-582-1111
Fax: 504-582-1121
Lafayette, Louisiana Office: 625 East Kaliste Saloom Road.
Telephone: 318-237-0132.
Fax: 318-237-3451.
Baton Rouge, Louisiana Office: 1710 One American Place.
Telephone: 504-381-9643.
Fax: 504-336-9763.

MEMBERS OF FIRM

John A. Gordon (A P.L.C.)
Blake G. Arata (A P.L.C.)
John M. McCollam (A P.L.C.)
Ewell E. Eagan, Jr., (A P.L.C.)
Marcel Garsaud, Jr.
Philip N. Asprodites
Jeanne Provosty Breckinridge
Guy E. Wall
Cynthia A. Nicholson
Cathy E. Chessin
William T. D'Zurilla
Alan C. Wolf
Paul E. Bullington
Deborah Cunningham Foshee
Steven W. Copley
James L. Weiss
Loulan J. Pitre, Jr.
Jason A. T. Jumonville
Marion D. Welborn Weinstock
Ernest E. Svenson
William N. Norton

ASSOCIATES

Anthony C. Marino
Martin E. Landrieu
Kathryn Manchester Borbas
A. Gregory Grimsal
Donna Phillips Currault
Scott A. O'Connor
C. Peck Hayne, Jr.
Douglas H. McCollam
Elizabeth L. Gordon
Clarence J. (Clancy) DuBos, III
Camille Bienvenu Poche
Marcy V. Massengale

LAFAYETTE OFFICE

RESIDENT MEMBERS OF FIRM

B. J. Duplantis (A P.L.C.)
Benjamin B. Blanchet
Margaret D. Swords
William F. Bailey
James E. Slatten, III
Samuel E. Masur

RESIDENT ASSOCIATES

Rebecca Wormser Comeaux
Denis C. Swords

BATON ROUGE OFFICE

RESIDENT MEMBER OF FIRM

Richard E. Matheny

RESIDENT ASSOCIATE

Teanna West Neskora

Representative Clients: Amoco Production Co.; McMoran Oil & Gas Co., Inc.; First National Bank of Commerce of New Orleans; Universal Health Services, Inc.; Cox Cable Communications, Inc.; W.R. Grace & Co.; Lorillard, Inc.; First City Bancorporation; Pan-American Life Insurance Co.

For full biographical listings, see the Martindale-Hubbell Law Directory

GUSTE, BARNETT & SHUSHAN, L.L.P. (AV)

One Poydras Plaza, 25th Floor, 639 Loyola Avenue, 70113-3125
Telephone: 504-529-4141
Telecopier: 504-561-0326

MEMBERS OF FIRM

Roy F. Guste
William M. Barnett
William J. Guste, III
Sidney L. Shushan (P.C.)
J. Harrison Henderson, III
Richard L. Weil
Robert A. Barnett
Joseph B. Landry
Paul M. Lavelle
Claude A. Schlesinger

Gideon T. Stanton, III
Mary E. Brennan
Rachel I. Becker
Jonathan M. Shushan
Jeffery M. Lynch

Representative Clients: National Tea Co.; Figgie International, Inc.; Volvo-GM Heavy Truck Corp.; Colony Insurance Co.; Cardinal Insurance Co.; National/Canal-Villere Supermarkets, Inc.; Aetna Life & Casualty Insurance Co.; Winn Dixie Stores, Inc.; Cooper Tire Co.; Johnson Controls, Inc.; Medical Malpractice Protection Plan, Inc.

For full biographical listings, see the Martindale-Hubbell Law Directory

HEBERT, MOULEDOUX & BLAND, A PROFESSIONAL LAW CORPORATION (AV)

Pan-American Life Center, Suite 1650, 601 Poydras Street, 70130
Telephone: 504-525-3333
Cable Address: "HMBL"
Telex: 588-092;
Fax: 504-523-4224

(See Next Column)

HEBERT, MOULEDOUX & BLAND A PROFESSIONAL LAW CORPORATION—*Continued*

Maurice C. Hebert, Jr.
André J. Mouledoux
Wilton E. Bland, III
Georges M. Legrand
Roch P. Poelman
Alan Guy Brackett
David M. Flotte
C. William Emory
Franck F. LaBiche, Jr.
C. Michael Parks
Daniel J. Hoerner
John H. Musser, V

Representative Clients: Archer-Daniels Midland Company; Bisso Marine Company, Inc.; Carline Geismar Fleet, Inc.; Cooper/T. Smith Stevedoring Company, Inc.; Delta Queen Steamboat Co.; Diamond Offshore Drilling, Inc.; LOOP INC.; Marine Equipment Management Corporation; McDermott Incorporated; Olympic Marine Company.

For full biographical listings, see the Martindale-Hubbell Law Directory

JONES, WALKER WAECHTER, POITEVENT CARRÈRE & DENÈGRE (AV)

Place St. Charles, 201 St. Charles Avenue, 70170-5100
Telephone: 504-582-8000
Telecopiers: Xerox 7033, 504-582-8549, 504-582-8574, 504-582-8583
Baton Rouge, Louisiana Office: One American Place, Suite 1700, 70825-0001.
Telephone: 504-346-5500.
Telecopiers: Xerox 7021, 504-346-5517 and Xerox 295, 504-336-1644. ABA Net 3792.
Lafayette, Louisiana Office: 201 Rue Iberville, Suite 210, 70508-3281.
Telephone: 318-232-5353.
Telecopier: Xerox 7021, 318-232-5415.
Washington, D.C. Office: Republic Place, Suite 245, 1776 Eye Street, N.W., 20006-3700.
Telephone: 202-828-8363.
Telecopier: Xerox 7021, 202-828-6907.

MEMBERS OF FIRM

Joseph Merrick Jones (1903-1963)
J. Mort Walker, Jr. (1904-1983)
Arthur J. Waechter, Jr.
Edward B. Poitevent
Ernest A. Carrère, Jr.
George Denègre
John V. Baus
Robert B. Acomb, Jr.
Edward B. Benjamin, Jr.
Patrick W. Browne, Jr.
Charles W. Lane, III
John J. Weigel
Donald L. King
James Larkin Selman, II
John R. Peters, Jr.
Thomas C. Keller
Donald O. Collins
John C. Combe, Jr.
R. Henry Sarpy, Jr.
Robert M. Contois, Jr.
Michael K. Tarver
Edward F. Martin
Carl C. Hanemann
Raymond J. Salassi, Jr.
Stewart E. Niles, Jr.
John D. Kitchen
Janice M. Foster
Harry S. Hardin, III
John J. Broders
Glenn G. Goodier
Robert R. Casey
Edward J. Koehl, Jr.
Thomas M. Nosewicz
David F. Edwards
L. Richards McMillan, II
Reilly L. Stonecipher (Resident, Baton Rouge Office)
Howard E. Sinor, Jr.
R. Patrick Vance
Charles E. Leche
John G. Gomila, Jr.
Robert B. Bieck, Jr.
Rudolph R. Ramelli
Madeleine Fischer
David G. Radlauer
John C. Blackman (Resident, Baton Rouge Office)
J. Kelly Duncan
Stanhope B. Denègre
Edward H. Bergin
Grady S. Hurley
Edward Dirk Wegmann
William M. Backstrom, Jr.
George R. Alvey, Jr.
Alex P. Trostorff
James E. Wright, III
Joseph J. Lowenthal, Jr.
Margaret F. Murphy
Alton E. Bayard, III (Resident, Baton Rouge Office)
Robert T. Lemon, II
H. Mark Adams
Elizabeth Jones Futrell
Michael A. Chernekoff
Richard J. Tyler
William H. Hines
W. Philip Clinton
William B. Masters
Thomas A. Casey, Jr.
R. Lewis McHenry
Curtis R. Hearn
Gary H. Miller
Carl D. Rosenblum
Bruce J. Toppin
Covert J. Geary
Pauline F. Hardin
Patrick H. Patrick
R. Christian Johnsen (Resident, Washington, D.C. Office)
Kenneth J. Najder
Thomas K. Potter, III
Jefferson R. Tillery
Patrick J. Veters
John L. Duvieilh
Richard D. Bertram
Lisa Manget Buchanan
Wayne G. Zeringue, Jr.

SPECIAL COUNSEL

Julian P. Brignac
John Clark Boyce (Resident, Baton Rouge Office)
Thomas A. Casey (Resident, Baton Rouge Office)
Stanley A. Millan
A. Justin Ourso III (Resident, Baton Rouge Office)

OF COUNSEL

Edward L. Merrigan (Resident, Washington, D.C. Office)
N. Hunter Johnston (Not admitted in LA; Resident, Washington, D.C. Office)

(See Next Column)

ASSOCIATES

Robert L. Walsh
Virginia W. Gundlach
M. Richard Schroeder
Rosemarie Falcone
J. Marshall Page, III
Thomas Y. Roberson, Jr.
Robin D. McGuire (Resident, Lafayette Office)
William J. Joyce
Judith V. Windhorst
Elizabeth Hardy Noe
Douglas N. Currault II
Deborah A. Van Meter
S. Michele Ray
Nan Roberts Eitel
Michele Whitesell Crosby (Resident, Baton Rouge Office)
Mary Ellen Jordan
Susan K. Chambers
Donna Thompson Mueller
F. Rivers Lelong
Dionne M. Rousseau
T. Michael Twomey
David R. Nicholson
William H. Hardie, III
Tracy R. Bishop
L. Barbee Ponder IV
H. Hughes Grehan
Patricia A. Bethancourt
Jacquelyn L. Morton
Andrew R. Lee
Edward J. Briscoe
Philip S. Clark
Jessica Livingston
Gavin P. Mahlie
Louis S. Nunes III
Katy Kimbell Theriot
Laura Leigh Blackston
Richard C. Badeaux
Michelle A. Bourque
Timothy S. Cragin
Elizabeth Slatten Healy
Stephen M. Robinson (Resident, Baton Rouge Office)
Roderick K. West

Representative Clients: Avondale Industries, Inc.; Century Telephone Enterprises, Inc.; Entergy Corp.; First Commerce Corp.; International Shipholding Corp.; Offshore Pipelines, Inc.; South Central Bell; Texaco, Inc.; Tidewater, Inc.; The Travelers Companies.

For full biographical listings, see the Martindale-Hubbell Law Directory

LEAKE & ANDERSSON (AV)

1700 Energy Centre, 1100 Poydras Street, 70163-1701
Telephone: 504-585-7500
Telecopier: 504-585-7775

MEMBERS OF FIRM

Robert E. Leake, Jr.
W. Paul Andersson
Lawrence A. Mann
Marta-Ann Schnabel O'Bryon
Kevin O'Bryon
George D. Fagan
Donald E. McKay, Jr.

ASSOCIATES

Stanton E. Shuler, Jr.
Rebecca Olivier Hand
Guy D. Perrier

Representative Clients: Commercial Credit Services Corp.; First Financial Insurance Co.; Government Employees Insurance Co.; National Union Fire Insurance Co.; National Food Processors, Inc.; Nationwide Insurance Co.; Professional Construction Services, Inc.

For full biographical listings, see the Martindale-Hubbell Law Directory

LEMLE & KELLEHER, L.L.P. (AV)

A Partnership including Professional Law Corporations
21st Floor, Pan-American Life Center, 601 Poydras Street, 70130-6097
Telephone: 504-586-1241
FAX: 504-584-9142
Cable Address: "Lemmor"
Telex: WU 584272
Baton Rouge, Louisiana Office: One American Place, 301 Main Street, Suite 1800, 70825.
Telephone: 504-387-5068.
FAX: 504-387-4995.
London, England Office: 1 Seething Lane, EC3N 4AX.
Telephone: 071-702-1446.
FAX: 071-702-1447.

MEMBERS OF FIRM

Harry B. Kelleher
Moïse Dennery
H. Martin Hunley, Jr.
George A. Frilot, III (A Professional Law Corp.)
Thomas W. Thorne, Jr.
Albert H. Hanemann, Jr.
Paul B. Deal
Julian H. Good
John M. Page
William S. Penick (A Professional Law Corporation)
James H. Daigle (A Professional Law Corporation)
J. William Vaudry, Jr.
William R. Forrester, Jr.
Ernest L. Edwards, Jr. (A Professional Law Corp.)
Ashton R. O'Dwyer, Jr. (A Professional Law Corp.)
Alan H. Goodman (A Professional Law Corporation)
James M. Petersen
Edward F. Kohnke, IV
George Frazier
James R. Conway, III
Stephen R. Remsberg
Richard B. Foster
Michael A. McGlone
Sherry Marcus Wise
Hal C. Welch
David S. Kelly
Douglas P. Matthews
James H. Brown, Jr.
Roger A. Stetter
Joseph N. Mole
David A. Olson
Deborah C. Faust
Donald H. McDaniel
Peter L. Koerber
Darryl J. Foster
George E. Cain, Jr.
W. L. West
Miles P. Clements
Scott S. Partridge
Patrick Johnson, Jr.
C. William Bradley, Jr.
Michael T. Cali
James F. Shuey
L. Eades Hogue

(See Next Column)

LEMLE & KELLEHER L.L.P., *New Orleans—Continued*

MEMBERS OF FIRM (Continued)

B. Richard Moore, Jr.
Charles R. Talley
James R. Silverstein
Michael J. Furman
Gerald J. Talbot
Andrew S. de Klerk
Christopher J. Dicharry
Walter F. Marcus, III
Stephen G. Lindsey
Randall A. Fish
James C. Butler
William O. Jaynes, Jr.
Allen J. Krouse, III
Francis H. Brown, III
Elizabeth Wall Magner
Amy L. Baird
Susan Northrop Ryan
Peter E. Sperling
Lawrence W. DaGate
J. Dwight LeBlanc, III
Maryann Liuzza Cote
James C. Exnicios
Richard A. Aguilar
Gerald J. Huffman, Jr.

OF COUNSEL

Albert J. Flettrich

SPECIAL COUNSEL

Samuel B. LaVergne
Timothy W. Hardy

ASSOCIATES

Deborah I. Schroeder
John J. Hainkel, III
E. John Heiser
Thomas M. Benjamin
Kent B. Ryan
Patrick J. McShane
Kenneth A. Mayeaux
Dwight C. Paulsen, III
Glenn P. Orgeron
H. Dunbar Healy
David F. Waguespack
Wayne K. McNeil
Michael R. Phillips
Robert P. Hutchinson
David M. Whitaker
Kenneth M. Klemm
Richard E. Gruner, Jr.
Brandon E. Mary
Nicole D. Martin
Greg A. Pellegrini
S. Scott Bluestein

Counsel for: Aetna Life & Casualty; Illinois Central Gulf Railroad; Kaiser Aluminum & Chemical Corp.; Merrill Lynch, Pierce, Fenner & Smith; Valley Line Co.

For full biographical listings, see the Martindale-Hubbell Law Directory

LOWE, STEIN, HOFFMAN, ALLWEISS & HAUVER, L.L.P. (AV)

One Shell Square, 701 Poydras Street Suite 3600, 70139-3600
Telephone: 504-581-2450
Telecopier: 504-581-2461

MEMBERS OF FIRM

Robert C. Lowe
Mark S. Stein
Mitchell J. Hoffman
Michael R. Allweiss
Terence L. Hauver
David H. Bernstein
Ellen Widen Kessler
Max J. Cohen

Judith A. Kaufman
Suzette Marie Smith
Steven A. Glaviano
David M. Prados
Marynell L. Piglia

For full biographical listings, see the Martindale-Hubbell Law Directory

MILLING, BENSON, WOODWARD, HILLYER, PIERSON & MILLER (AV)

A Partnership including Professional Law Corporations
Suite Twenty-Three Hundred, 909 Poydras Street, 70112-1017
Telephone: 504-569-7000
Cable Address: "Milling"
Telex: 58-4211
Telecopier: 504-569-7001
ABA net: 15656
MCI Mail: "Milling"
Lafayette, Louisiana Office: 101 LaRue France, Suite 200.
Telephone: 318-232-3929.
Telecopier: 318-233-4957.
Baton Rouge, Louisiana Office: Suite 402, 8555 United Plaza Blvd.
Telephone: 504-928-688.
Fax: 504-928-6881.

PARTNER EMERITUS

M. Truman Woodward, Jr., (P.C.)

MEMBERS OF FIRM

Haywood H. Hillyer, Jr., (P.C.)
G. Henry Pierson, Jr., (P.C.)
Joseph B. Miller
David J. Conroy (P.C.)
Wilson S. Shirley, Jr., (P.C.)
Guy C. Lyman, Jr., (P.C.)
Neal D. Hobson (P.C.)
F. Frank Fontenot (P.C.)
William C. Gambel (P.C.)
Charles A. Snyder (P.C.)
Richard A. Whann (P.C.)
Emile A. Wagner, III, (P.C.)
Charles D. Marshall, Jr. (P.C.)
James K. Irvin (P.C.)
Hilton S. Bell (P.C.)
Katherine Goldman (P.C.)
John W. Colbert (P.C.)
Bruce R. Hoefer, Jr. (P.C.)
David N. Schell, Jr. (P.C.)
Patrick A. Talley (P.C.)
Mary L. Grier Holmes (P.C.)
Jean M. Sweeney (P.C.)

SPECIAL COUNSEL

J. Clifford Rogillio (P.C.)
Patrick J. Butler, Jr.
Timothy T. Roniger
Peter M. Meisner

(See Next Column)

ASSOCIATES

Mark P. Dauer
Julia M. Pearce
Jay Corenswet
Ann C. Dowling
Alanna S. Arnold
Benjamin O. Schupp
J. Timothy Betbeze
F. Paul Simoneaux, III
Robert T. Lorio
Mary Sprague Langston

LAFAYETTE OFFICE
RESIDENT MEMBERS OF FIRM

Jack C. Caldwell
Robert L. Cabes (P.C.)

SPECIAL COUNSEL

John E. Castle, Jr.

RESIDENT ASSOCIATES

Karen T. Bordelon
Thomas C. Stewart

BATON ROUGE OFFICE
RESIDENT OF COUNSEL

Stephen C. Carleton

Counsel for: Arthur Andersen & Co.; Chevron U.S.A., Inc.; The Dow Chemical Co.; The Louisiana Land & Exploration Co.; McDermott International Inc.; Phillips Petroleum; Whitney National Bank.

For full biographical listings, see the Martindale-Hubbell Law Directory

NESSER, KING & LEBLANC (AV)

Suite 3800 Place St. Charles, 201 St. Charles Avenue, 70170
Telephone: 504-582-3800
Telecopier: 504-582-1233

John T. Nesser, III
Henry A. King
Joseph E. LeBlanc, Jr.
David S. Bland
Patricia Ann Krebs
Robert J. Burvant
Eric Earl Jarrell
Liane K. Hinrichs

Jeffrey M. Burmaster
Jeffrey A. Mitchell
Margaret M. Sledge
Josh M. Kantrow
Elton A. Foster
Elizabeth S. Wheeler
Robert J. Bergeron
Timothy S. Madden
Elizabeth A. Meek

OF COUNSEL

Clare P. Hunter
George B. Jurgens, III
J. Grant Coleman
Len R. Brignac
George Farber, Jr.

For full biographical listings, see the Martindale-Hubbell Law Directory

PHELPS DUNBAR, L.L.P. (AV)

Texaco Center, 400 Poydras Street, 70130-3245
Telephone: 504-566-1311
Telecopier: 504-568-9130, 504-568-9007
Cable Address: "Howspencer"
Telex: 584125 WU
Telex: 6821155 WUI
Baton Rouge, Louisiana Office: Suite 701, City National Bank Building, P.O. Box 4412.
Telephone: 504-346-0285.
Telecopier: 504-381-9197.
Jackson, Mississippi Office: Suite 500, Security Centré North, 200 South Lamar Street, P.O. Box 23066.
Telephone: 601-352-2300.
Telecopier: 601-360-9777.
Tupelo, Mississippi Office: Seventh Floor, One Mississippi Plaza, P.O. Box 1220.
Telephone: 601-842-7907.
Telecopier: 601-842-3873.
Houston, Texas Office: Suite 501, 4 Houston Center, 1331 Lamar Street.
Telephone: 713-659-1386.
Telecopier: 713-659-1388.
London, England Office: Suite 976, Level 9, Lloyd's, 1 Lime Street, London EC3M 7DQ England.
Telephone: 011-44-71-929-4765.
Telecopier: 011-44-71-929-0046.
Telex: 987321.

OF COUNSEL

Louis B. Claverie
John W. Sims
Frank S. Craig, Jr. (Resident, Baton Rouge, Louisiana Office)
Charles Edward Dunbar, III
J. Barbee Winston
John G. Weinmann

MEMBERS OF FIRM

George W. Healy, III
James Bradley Kemp, Jr.
Harry S. Redmon, Jr.
Fred M. Bush, Jr. (Not admitted in LA; Jackson and Tupelo, Mississippi Offices)
James H. Roussel
Philip deV. Claverie
Robert U. Soniat
Charles M. Steen
Harry Rosenberg
F. M. Bush, III (Not admitted in LA; Jackson and Tupelo, Mississippi Offices)
John P. Manard, Jr.
Harvey D. Wagar, III
H. Alston Johnson, III (Resident, Baton Rouge, Louisiana Office)
Walker W. (Bill) Jones, III (Not admitted in LA; Jackson and Tupelo, Mississippi Offices)

(See Next Column)

PHELPS DUNBAR L.L.P.—*Continued*

MEMBERS OF FIRM (Continued)

David W. Mockbee (Not admitted in LA; Resident, Jackson, Mississippi Office)
Ross F. Bass, Jr. (Not admitted in LA; Resident, Jackson, Mississippi Office)
E. Clifton Hodge, Jr. (Not admitted in LA; Resident, Jackson, Mississippi Office)
C. Delbert Hosemann, Jr. (Not admitted in LA; Resident, Jackson, Mississippi Office)
Paul O. Miller, III (Not admitted in LA; Resident, Jackson, Mississippi Office)
Armin J. Moeller, Jr. (Resident, Jackson, Mississippi Office)
Kent E. Westmoreland (Not admitted in LA; Resident, Houston, Texas Office)
Claude LeRoy Stuart, III (Not admitted in LA; Resident, Houston, Texas Office)
Roy C. Cheatwood
Edward B. Poitevent, II
Danny G. Shaw
Reuben V. Anderson (Not admitted in LA; Resident, Jackson, Mississippi Office)
George B. Hall, Jr.
Robert C. Clotworthy
Richard N. Dicharry
Frank W. Trapp (Not admitted in LA; Resident, Jackson, Mississippi Office)
Michael D. Hunt (Resident, Baton Rouge, Louisiana Office)
Arthur F. Jernigan, Jr. (Not admitted in LA; Resident, Jackson, Mississippi Office)
Luther T. Munford (Not admitted in LA; Resident, Jackson, Mississippi Office)
Dan M. McDaniel, Jr. (Not admitted in LA; Resident, Jackson, Mississippi Office)
George M. Gilly
Christopher O. Davis
William H. Howard, III
Robert W. Nuzum
Gary E. Friedman (Not admitted in LA; Resident, Jackson, Mississippi Office)
Robert P. McCleskey, Jr.
Shaun B. Rafferty
Brent B. Barriere
Michael B. Wallace (Not admitted in LA; Resident, Jackson, Mississippi Office)
Bruce V. Schewe
J. Clifton Hall, III
G. Bruce Parkerson
Jean Magee Hogan (Not admitted in LA; Jackson and Tupelo, Mississippi Offices)
Julia Marie Adams (Not admitted in LA; Resident, Houston, Texas Office)
William D. Aaron, Jr.
Glover A. Russell, Jr. (Not admitted in LA; Resident, Jackson, Mississippi Office)
Stephen P. Hall
James A. Stuckey
Stephen H. Leech, Jr. (Not admitted in LA; Resident, Jackson, Mississippi Office)
W. Thomas Siler, Jr. (Not admitted in LA; Jackson and Tupelo, Mississippi Offices)
R. Pepper Crutcher, Jr. (Jackson and Tupelo, Mississippi Offices)
Nancy Scott Degan
Virginia Boulet
Jennifer Bowers Zimmerman (Resident, Baton Rouge, Louisiana Office)
John P. Sneed (Resident, Jackson, Mississippi Office)
F. Scott Kaiser (Resident, Baton Rouge, Louisiana Office)
Deborah Shelby Nichols (Not admitted in LA; Resident, Jackson, Mississippi Office)
Brian D. Wallace
M. Nan Alessandra
Dana E. Kelly (Not admitted in LA; Resident, Jackson, Mississippi Office)
William C. Brabec (Not admitted in LA; Resident, Jackson, Mississippi Office)
David M. Hunter
Steven J. Levine (Resident, Baton Rouge, Louisiana Office)
Allen D. Darden (Resident, Baton Rouge, Louisiana Office)
Mary Ellen Roy
William I. Gault, Jr. (Not admitted in LA; Resident, Jackson, Mississippi Office)
Susan Fahey Desmond (Not admitted in LA; Resident, Jackson, Mississippi Office)
Charles D. Porter (Not admitted in LA; Resident, Jackson, Mississippi Office)
David P. Webb (Not admitted in LA; Resident, Jackson, Mississippi Office)
Sessions Ault Hootsell III
Mark C. Dodart
Jonathan C. Benda (Resident, Baton Rouge, Louisiana Office)
Paul L. Peyronnin
Thomas H. Kiggans (Resident, Baton Rouge, Louisiana Office)
Raymond J. Pajares
Marshall M. Redmon (Resident, Baton Rouge, Louisiana Office)

COUNSEL

Edwin K. Legnon
Jane E. Armstrong
J. Michael Cutshaw (Resident, Baton Rouge, Louisiana Office)
Floyd A. Wisner
Barbara L. Arras
Mary Elizabeth Hall (Not admitted in LA; Resident, Jackson, Mississippi Office)
Alissa J. Allison
E. Jane Sherman (Resident, Baton Rouge, Louisiana Office)
Paul H. Johnson, III (Not admitted in LA; Resident, Jackson, Mississippi Office)
G. Kay L. Trapp (Not admitted in LA; Jackson and Tupelo, Mississippi Offices)
Linda Bounds Sherman (Not admitted in LA; Resident, Jackson, Mississippi Office)
Gregory D. Pirkle (Not admitted in LA; Jackson and Tupelo, Mississippi Offices)
Gary Meringer

(See Next Column)

ASSOCIATES

David A. Abramson
Lee R. Adler
Louis G. Authement
Laura Ann Baity
Chuck D. Barlow (Not admitted in LA; Resident, Jackson, Mississippi Office)
Jane H. Barney (Resident, Baton Rouge, Louisiana Office)
Gerardo R. Barrios
Scott W. Bates (Not admitted in LA; Resident, Jackson, Mississippi Office)
John B. Beard (Not admitted in LA; Resident, Jackson, Mississippi Office)
M. Lea Beaty (Not admitted in LA; Jackson and Tupelo, Mississippi Offices)
Sheryl Bey (Resident, Jackson, Mississippi Office)
Wendy T. Blanchard
Kyle Brackin
Evan T. Caffrey (Not admitted in LA; Resident, Houston, Texas Office)
Laurie Dearman Clark
Diane Hollenshead Copes (Not admitted in LA)
Laura E. Cormier (Not admitted in LA; Resident, Houston, Texas Office)
Malinda York Crouch (Not admitted in LA; Resident, Houston, Texas Office)
John C. Cunningham (Not admitted in LA; Resident, Houston, Texas Office)
Warren A. Cuntz, Jr.
Kimberly Ward Diaz
Julia A. Dietz
Danny A. Drake (Not admitted in LA; Resident, Jackson, Mississippi Office)
Charles G. Duffy, III
John Wilson Eaton III (Not admitted in LA; Jackson and Tupelo, Mississippi Offices)
Robert S. Eitel
Ken Fairly (Not admitted in LA; Resident, Jackson, Mississippi Office)
Tanza C. Farr (Not admitted in LA; Resident, Houston, Texas Office)
Michael David Ferachi (Resident, Baton Rouge, Louisiana Office)
Peter N. Freiberg
Susan W. Furr (Resident, Baton Rouge, Louisiana Office)
Kevin M. Grace
N. Eleanor Graham
Robert W. Graves (Not admitted in LA; Resident, Jackson, Mississippi Office)
Gregory D. Guida (Not admitted in LA; Resident, Jackson, Mississippi Office)
Eric P. Halber
Jennifer L. Hantel
Richard Leo Harrell (Resident, Houston, Texas Office)
L. Tiffany Hawkins
William B. Hidalgo
Robert T. Higginbotham Jr. (Not admitted in LA; Resident, Jackson, Mississippi Office)
James M. Jacobs
Danatus N. King
David M. Korn
Kent A. Lambert
John B. Landry, Jr. (Not admitted in LA; Resident, Jackson, Mississippi Office)
Darrell J. Loup (Resident, Baton Rouge, Louisiana Office)
Patricia Ann Lynch
Angela M. McLain (Not admitted in LA; Resident, Jackson, Mississippi Office)
Melissa M. McMillan
Stephanie G. McShane
John A. Meynardie (Not admitted in LA; Resident, Jackson, Mississippi Office)
Pamela G. Michiels
Karen Klaas Milhollin (Not admitted in LA; Resident, Houston, Texas Office)
Jeffrey S. Moore (Not admitted in LA; Jackson and Tupelo, Mississippi Offices)
Wendy L. Moore (Not admitted in LA; Resident, Jackson, Mississippi Office)
Julie Sneed Muller (Not admitted in LA; Resident, Jackson, Mississippi Office)
L. Elizabeth Weathington Nance
Dinetia M. Newman (Not admitted in LA; Jackson and Tupelo, Mississippi Offices)
Patrick O'Hara (Resident, Baton Rouge, Louisiana Office)
Daniel T. Pancamo
Adair Draughn Freeman Parr
Chelye E. Prichard (Not admitted in LA; Resident, Jackson, Mississippi Office)
Carlton W. Reeves (Not admitted in LA; Resident, Jackson, Mississippi Office)
Todd C. Richter (Not admitted in LA; Resident, Jackson, Mississippi Office)
William J. Riviere
Jane A. Robert (Resident, Baton Rouge, Louisiana Office)
Diane Fagan Robinson (Resident, Baton Rouge, Louisiana Office)
Daniel C. Rodgers
Mary Frances Lindquist Rosamond
James A. Rowell
Andrew L. Schwarcz
William F. Selph III (Not admitted in LA; Resident, Jackson, Mississippi Office)
David B. Sharpe
William Carter Smallwood, III (Not admitted in LA; Jackson and Tupelo, Mississippi Offices)
David P. Steiner
David M. Thomas, II (Not admitted in LA; Resident, Jackson, Mississippi Office)
John R. Trahan (Resident, Baton Rouge, Louisiana Office)
Sheila T. Walet
Michael F. Walther (Resident, Houston, Texas Office)
G. Benjamin Ward
Ronald J. White
Stephen M. Wilson (Not admitted in LA; Jackson and Tupelo, Mississippi Offices)
Patricia Hill Wilton (Resident, Baton Rouge, Louisiana Office)
Mark E. Young
Dawei Zhang
Joseph A. Ziemianski (Not admitted in LA; Resident, Jackson, Mississippi Office)

Representative Clients: The Britannia Steamship Insurance Assn., Ltd.; Citibank, N.A.; Freeport-McMoRan Inc.; General Electric Company and Subsidiaries; Hibernia National Bank; Hilton Hotels Corp.; Louisiana Gas Service Co., Inc.; Missouri Pacific Railroad Co.; The Southern Farm Bureau Companies; Underwriters at Lloyd's, London.

For full biographical listings, see the Martindale-Hubbell Law Directory

SESSIONS & FISHMAN, L.L.P. (AV)

A Registered Limited Liability Partnership including Professional Corporations
Place St. Charles, 201 St. Charles Avenue, 70170-3500
Telephone: 504-582-1500
Telex: 58364NLN
Fax: 504-582-1555

MEMBERS OF FIRM

Frank J. Stich, Jr.
Max Nathan, Jr. (P.C.)
Robert E. Winn
Donald R. Mintz (P.C.)
Owen A. Neff
L. K. Clement, Jr.
William M. Lucas, Jr.
Michael J. Molony, Jr. (P.C.)
Jack M. Alltmont
J. David Forsyth
James Ryan, III
M. Shael Herman
Peter S. Title
Mark A. Fullmer
Carole Cukell Neff
Stephen R. Doody
Louis Leonard Galvis
Robert A. Redwine
Reuben I. Friedman
Sally A. Shushan
Camilo K. Salas, III
Dorothy S. Jacobs (P.C.)
Joy Goldberg Braun
Andrew A. Braun
Joyce M. Dombourian (P.C.)
Alan D. Ezkovich
Juan J. Lizarraga
John William Hite, III
Sharon Cormack Mize

OF COUNSEL

James F. Pinner
Robert J. Skinner

SENIOR COUNSEL

Ralph H. Fishman
Leonard H. Rosenson (1917-1994)

ASSOCIATES

Edward J. Rivera
David N. Corkern
Julie A. Scheib
David P. Salley
Valerie Welz Jusselin
Raymond P. Ward
Michael A. Berenson
Robert L. Waddle (Not admitted in LA)
Cary J. Amann
Dana F. Dausch (P.C.)
M. Suzanne Montero

Representative Clients: Air Products & Chemicals, Inc.; Bethlehem Steel Corp.; Employer's Reinsurance Corp.; The Equitable Life Assurance Society of the United States; Holiday Inns, Inc.; J.C. Penney Co., Inc.; State Farm Insurance Cos.; The American Tobacco Co.; United Services Automobile Assn.; Volkswagen of America, Inc.

For full biographical listings, see the Martindale-Hubbell Law Directory

STONE, PIGMAN, WALTHER, WITTMANN & HUTCHINSON (AV)

A Partnership including Professional Corporations
546 Carondelet Street, 70130-3588
Telephone: 504-581-3200
Telecopier: 504-581-3361
Baton Rouge, Louisiana Office: City National Bank Building, 445 North Boulevard, Suite 640, Baton Rouge, Louisiana 70802.
Telephone: 504-387-4211.
Telecopier: 504-387-4254.

MEMBERS OF FIRM

Saul Stone
Paul O. H. Pigman (P.C.)
Ewell P. Walther, Jr. (1932-1990)
Phillip A. Wittmann
Campbell C. Hutchinson (P.C.)
David L. Stone (P.C.)
William D. Treeby (P.C.)
Paul M. Haygood (P.C.)
Hirschel T. Abbott, Jr., (P.C.)
Michael R. Fontham (P.C.)
Anthony M. DiLeo (P.C.)
Esmond Phelps, II (P.C.)
Jack M. Weiss (P.C.)
Wayne J. Lee (P.C.)
Clinton W. Shinn (P.C.)
Robert M. Walmsley, Jr. (P.C.)
James C. Gulotta, Jr., (P.C.)
Paul L. Zimmering
John M. Landis
Stephen H. Kupperman (P.C.)
Stephen G. Bullock
Sarah S. Vance (P.C.)
Kyle Schonekas
Kay Wolfe Eagan (P.C.)
Steven W. Usdin (P.C.)
Judy Y. Barrasso (P.C.)
Susan Gayle Talley (P.C.)
Douglas D. Dodd
Randall A. Smith (P.C.)
Noel J. Darce
C. Lawrence Orlansky (P.C.)
Richard C. Stanley
Calvin P. Brasseaux (P.C.)
Michael R. Schneider (P.C.)
Scott T. Whittaker
Denise M. Pilié(P.C.)
Sterling Scott Willis (P.C.)
Ellen M. Chapin
Barry W. Ashe (P.C.)
George C. Freeman, III
Joseph L. Caverly (P.C.)
Nelea A. Absher (P.C.)
David J. Lukinovich (P.C.)
Cecilia C. Woodley (P.C.)
Marc D. Winsberg

SPECIAL COUNSEL

Warren M. Faris

(See Next Column)

ASSOCIATES

Linda R. Gallagher
Mary Modenbach White
Dorothy Hudson Wimberly
Tondra Netherton Heiman
Michael D. Landry
Marcus V. Brown
Mary L. Dumestre
Mark B. Holton
Robert E. Harrington
Karen H. Freese
Laurie Barcelona Halpern
David K. Hall
John P. Cerise
Paul J. Masinter
Thomas M. Flanagan
Angela J. Crowder
James R. Swanson
Andrew R. Thomas
Dane S. Ciolino
Lynda C. Friedmann
Rachel Wendt Wisdom
Edwin H. Neill, III
William L. Geary, Jr.
Elizabeth M. McCarron
Louis L. Plotkin
Victoria de Lisle Blanks
Mary L. Coyne
John Michael Harlow
Stephanie D. Shuler
Kelly McNeil Legier
Deborah Pearce-Reggio

For full biographical listings, see the Martindale-Hubbell Law Directory

TERRIBERRY, CARROLL & YANCEY, L.L.P. (AV)

3100 Energy Centre, 1100 Poydras Street, 70163-3100
Telephone: 504-523-6451
Cable Address: "Terrib"
Telex: 6821224 (WUI)
Fax: 504-524-3257

MEMBERS OF FIRM

Benjamin W. Yancey (1906-1991)
Walter Carroll, Jr. (Retired)
Maurie D. Yager
G. Edward Merritt
James L. Schupp, Jr.
John A. Bolles
Charles F. Lozes
Robert J. Barbier
Rufus C. Harris, III
Hugh Ramsay Straub
Robert S. Reich
David B. Lawton
Roger D. Allen
Janet Wessler Marshall
D. Kirk Boswell
Gary A. Hemphill
Laurence R. De Buys, IV
Kevin J. LaVie
Stephen E. Mattesky

COUNSEL

Andrew T. Martinez
Cynthia Anne Wegmann

ASSOCIATES

Robert B. Acomb, III
Gerald M. Baca
Michael M. Butterworth
John A. Scialdone

Representative Clients: Assuranceforeningen Gard; Assuranceforeningen Skuld; Certain Underwriters at Lloyd's; The London Steam-Ship Owners' Mutual Insurance Assn. Ltd.; Lykes Bros. Steamship Co., Inc.; New Orleans Steamship Assn.; Nordisk Skibsrederforening (Northern Shipowners Defence Club); Scandinavian Marine Claims Office, Inc.; Steamship Mutual Underwriting Assn. Ltd.; United Kingdom Mutual Steam Ship Assurance Assn. Ltd.

For full biographical listings, see the Martindale-Hubbell Law Directory

*NEW ROADS,** Pointe Coupee Parish — (Refer to Baton Rouge)

*OPELOUSAS,** St. Landry Parish

DAUZAT, FALGOUST, CAVINESS, BIENVENU & STIPE (AV)

510 S. Court Street, P.O. Box 1450, 70571
Telephone: 318-942-5811
Fax: 318-948-9512

MEMBERS OF FIRM

Jimmy L. Dauzat
Jerry J. Falgoust
Peter F. Caviness
Steven J. Bienvenu
Jeigh L. Stipe

For full biographical listings, see the Martindale-Hubbell Law Directory

DUBUISSON AND DUBUISSON (AV)

345 South Court Street, P.O. Box 230, 70570
Telephone: 318-942-6506
Fax: 318-942-8774

MEMBERS OF FIRM

E. B. Dubuisson (1865-1943)
Edward Dubuisson (1902-1966)
James G. Dubuisson
Edward B. Dubuisson

Representative Clients: The Travelers Insurance Co.; Missouri Pacific Railroad Co.; South Central Bell Telephone & Telegraph Co.; Pennsylvania Manufacturers Association Insurance Co.; Millers Mutual Insurance Association of Illinois; Connecticut General Life Insurance Co.; American Home Assurance Co.; Shell Oil Co.
Local Attorneys for: St. Landry Bank & Trust Co. (General Counsel); Cabot Carbon Co.

For full biographical listings, see the Martindale-Hubbell Law Directory

*PLAQUEMINE,** Iberville Parish

BORRON, DELAHAYE, EDWARDS & DORÉ (AV)

58065 Meriam Street, P.O. Box 679, 70765-0679
Telephone: 504-687-3571; 343-3148
Fax: 504-687-9695

(See Next Column)

BORRON, DELAHAYE, EDWARDS & DORÉ—*Continued*

MEMBERS OF FIRM

Paul G. Borron (1874-1960)
Charles Ory Dupont (1919-1976)
Paul G. Borron, III
Allen M. Edwards
James P. Doré
John L. Delahaye

OF COUNSEL

Paul G. Borron, Jr.
J. Evan Delahaye

Representative Clients: Iberville Building & Loan Assn.; American Sugar Cane League; Iberville Trust & Savings Bank; South Central Bell Telephone Co.; Citizens Bank & Trust Co.; Iberville Motors, Inc.; A. Wilbert's Sons Limited Partnership; Hebert Brothers Engineers; Surgical Associates of Baton Rouge, Inc.; First American Title Insurance Co.

For full biographical listings, see the Martindale-Hubbell Law Directory

*PORT ALLEN,** West Baton Rouge Parish — (Refer to Plaquemine)

*RUSTON,** Lincoln Parish

GOFF AND GOFF (AV)

612 North Vienna Street, P.O. Box 2050, 71270
Telephone: 318-255-1760

A. Kennon Goff, III
Addison K. Goff, IV

Representative Clients: Ruston State Bank & Trust Co.; South Central Bell Telephone Co.; Jones-O'Brien Oil Co.

For full biographical listings, see the Martindale-Hubbell Law Directory

*ST. MARTINVILLE,** St. Martin Parish — (Refer to New Iberia)

*SHREVEPORT,** Caddo Parish

BARLOW AND HARDTNER L.C. (AV)

Tenth Floor, Louisiana Tower, 401 Edwards Street, 71101-3289
Telephone: 318-227-1131
Telecopier: 318-227-1141
Mailing Address: P.O. Box 8, Shreveport, Louisiana, 71161-0008

Ray A. Barlow
Quintin T. Hardtner, III
Malcolm S. Murchison
Kay Cowden Medlin
Joseph L. Shea, Jr.
David R. Taggart
Clair F. White
Stephen E. Ramey
Philip E. Downer, III
Michael B. Donald
Jay A. Greenleaf

OF COUNSEL

Cecil E. Ramey, Jr.
Paula Hazelrig Hickman

Bruce A. Bannon
Charles F. Boyd

Representative Clients: Kelley Oil Corporation; NorAm Energy Corp. (formerly Arkla, Inc.); Central and South West; Panhandle Eastern Corp.; Pennzoil Producing Co.; Johnson Controls, Inc.; Ashland Oil, Inc.; Southwestern Electric Power Company; Brammer Engineering, Inc.; General Electric Co.

For full biographical listings, see the Martindale-Hubbell Law Directory

COOK, YANCEY, KING & GALLOWAY, A PROFESSIONAL LAW CORPORATION (AV)

1700 Commercial National Tower, 333 Texas Street, P.O. Box 22260, 71120-2260
Telephone: 318-221-6277
Telecopier: 318-227-2606

Clarence L. Yancey (1909-1982)
John F. Cassibry (1950-1987)
Sidney E. Cook (1927-1989)
A. Richard Gear (1941-1992)
Sidney B. Galloway
Edwin L. Blewer, Jr.
James Robert Jeter
Herschel E. Richard, Jr.
Stephen R. Yancey II
Samuel W. Caverlee
J. William Fleming
James H. Campbell
F. Drake Lee, Jr.
Charles G. Tutt
Frank M. Dodson
Albert M. Hand, Jr.
Jerald R. Harper
Cynthia C. Anderson
Brian A. Homza
Bernard S. Johnson
Glenn L. Langley
Sidney E. Cook, Jr.
Eskridge E. Smith, Jr.
Timothy B. Burnham
Curtis R. Shelton
Kenneth Mascagni
James R. Sterritt
J. Benjamin Warren, Jr.
Leland H. Ayres
Bryce J. Denny
Lance P. Havener
William C. Kalmbach, III
S. Price Barker
Lisa Dunn Folsom
S. Curtis Mitchell
Gregg A. Wilkes
Julia E. Blewer
Laura A. Merkler
Tracy A. Burch
Mary D. Bicknell
Robert Kennedy Jr.

OF COUNSEL

Benjamin C. King

Counsel for: Aetna Life and Casualty Co.; Caddo Bossier Port Commission; Commercial National Bank in Shreveport; Specialty Oil Co.; First American Title Insurance Co.; Hunt Oil Co.; International Paper Co.; Maryland-American General Insurance Co.; Missouri Pacific Railroad Co.; Schumpert Medical Center.

(See Next Column)

For full biographical listings, see the Martindale-Hubbell Law Directory

MAYER, SMITH & ROBERTS, L.L.P. (AV)

1550 Creswell, 71101
Telephone: 318-222-2135, 222-2268
Fax: 318-222-6420

MEMBERS OF FIRM

Caldwell Roberts
Walter O. Hunter, Jr.
Mark A. Goodwin
Ben Marshall, Jr.
Alexander S. Lyons
Kim Purdy Thomas
Richard G. Barham
David Butterfield
Vicki C. Warner
Henry N. Bellamy
John C. Turnage
Paul R. Mayer, Jr.
Steven E. Soileau

ASSOCIATES

Deborah Shea Baukman
Caldwell Roberts, Jr.
Frank K. Carroll
Dalton Roberts Ross

STAFF ATTORNEY

J. Thomas Butler

OF COUNSEL

Charles L. Mayer
Paul R. Mayer

Representative Clients: CNA Insurance Companies; Liberty Mutual Insurance Company; The St. Paul Companies; United States Fidelity and Guaranty Company; Schumpert Medical Center; Travelers Insurance Company; Great American Insurance Company; Insurance Corporation of America; Highlands Insurance Company; Ohio Casualty Group of Insurance Companies.

For full biographical listings, see the Martindale-Hubbell Law Directory

SIMON, FITZGERALD, COOKE, REED & WELCH (AV)

Suite 200, 4700 Line Avenue, 71106
Telephone: 318-868-2600
Telecopier: 318-868-8966

MEMBERS OF FIRM

Fred Simon (1904-1993)
Archie M. Simon
Thomas P. Fitzgerald (1914-1993)
Paul M. Cooke
Chatham H. Reed
Keith M. Welch
Kevin R. Molloy

A list of Representative Clients will be furnished upon request.

For full biographical listings, see the Martindale-Hubbell Law Directory

TUCKER, JETER, JACKSON AND HICKMAN, L.L.P. (AV)

Louisiana Tower, 401 Edwards Street Suite 905, 71101-3146
Telephone: 318-425-7764 to 425-7767
Telecopier: 318-425-7792

MEMBERS OF FIRM

John H. Tucker, Jr. (1891-1984)
Horace M. Holder (1913-1989)
Robert McLean Jeter, Jr.
T. Haller Jackson, Jr.
Katherine Leslie Brash Jeter
T. Haller Jackson, III
Kenneth L. Hickman

Attorneys for: Curtis Parker Oil Co.; Gannett River States Publishing Corporation.
Local Attorneys for: South Central Bell Telephone Co.; Morton-Thiokol, Inc.

For full biographical listings, see the Martindale-Hubbell Law Directory

WIENER, WEISS, MADISON & HOWELL, A PROFESSIONAL CORPORATION (AV)

333 Texas Street, Suite 2350, P.O. Box 21990, 71120-1990
Telephone: 318-226-9100
Fax: 318-424-5128

Jacques L. Wiener (1909-1988)
Donald P. Weiss
John M. Madison, Jr.
James Fleet Howell
James R. Madison
Neil T. Erwin
Lawrence Russo, III
Susie Morgan
Larry Feldman, Jr.
Allen P. Jones
Katherine Clark Hennessey
Jeffrey W. Weiss
R. Joseph Naus
Mark L. Hornsby
Donald B. Wiener

Representative Clients: Pioneer Bank & Trust Co.; Ford Motor Credit Corp.; CNA Insurance Companies; International Paper Companies; Louisiana Homebuilders Association Self Insurers Fund; LSU-Shreveport; Sealy Realty, Inc.; Palmer Petroleum, Inc.; Brookshire Grocery Company (Louisiana); Northwest Louisiana Production Credit Association.

For full biographical listings, see the Martindale-Hubbell Law Directory

WILKINSON, CARMODY & GILLIAM (AV)

1700 Beck Building, 400 Travis Street, P.O. Box 1707, 71166
Telephone: 318-221-4196
Telecopier: 318-221-3705

(See Next Column)

WILKINSON, CARMODY & GILLIAM, *Shreveport—Continued*

MEMBERS OF FIRM

John D. Wilkinson (1867-1929)
William Scott Wilkinson (1895-1985)
Arthur R. Carmody, Jr.
Bobby S. Gilliam
Mark E. Gilliam
Penny D. Sellers
Brian D. Landry

Representative Clients: Farmers Insurance Group; Home Federal Savings & Loan Association of Shreveport; The Kansas City Southern Railway Co.; KTAL-TV; Lincoln National Life Insurance Co.; Mobil Oil Co.; Schumpert Medical Center; Sears, Roebuck & Co.; Southern Pacific Transportation Co.; Southwestern Electric Power Co.

For full biographical listings, see the Martindale-Hubbell Law Directory

*VILLE PLATTE,** Evangeline Parish — (Refer to Opelousas)

*WINNFIELD,** Winn Parish

SIMMONS AND DERR (AV)

Simmons Building, Church Street, P.O. Box 525, 71483
Telephone: 318-628-3951

MEMBERS OF FIRM

Kermit M. Simmons
Jacque D. Derr

Reference: Bank of Winnfield & Trust Co.

For full biographical listings, see the Martindale-Hubbell Law Directory

*WINNSBORO,** Franklin Parish — (Refer to Rayville)

MAINE

*AUBURN,** Androscoggin Co.

SKELTON, TAINTOR & ABBOTT, A PROFESSIONAL CORPORATION (AV)

95 Main Street, P.O. Box 3200, 04212-3200
Telephone: 207-784-3200
Fax: 207-784-3345

Frederick G. Taintor (Retired)
Charles H. Abbott
Stephen P. Beale
Peter M. Garcia
Bryan M. Dench
John B. Cole
Jill A. Checkoway
Stephen B. Wade
Michael R. Poulin
Norman J. Rattey
June D. Zellers

Harold N. Skelton
Douglas Gravel
Jonathan Doolittle

OF COUNSEL

William B. Skelton, II

General Counsel for: Androscoggin Savings Bank; Bates College; Central Maine Medical Center; Auburn Savings & Loan Association; Auburn Housing Authority; Maine School Administrative District No. 52; W. S. Libbey Co.; Lewiston Sun-Journal.

For full biographical listings, see the Martindale-Hubbell Law Directory

*AUGUSTA,** Kennebec Co.

* indicates certain Bar Register subscribers whose principal office is located elsewhere in the state and who have arranged for representation as a part of the state capital listings that follow

DOYLE & NELSON (AV)

150 Capitol Street, 04330
Telephone: 207-622-6124
Telefax: 207-623-1358
Toll Free: 800-639-3165

MEMBERS OF FIRM

Jon R. Doyle
Craig H. Nelson

ASSOCIATES

Mark R. Zobel
Daniel P. Riley, Jr.
Janet P. Welch (Not admitted in ME)

Local Counsel for: Citicorp and its subsidiaries; R.J. Reynolds Tobacco Co.; British Consulate General.
Counsel for: Financial Institutions Service Corp.; Miles Memorial Hospital; Maine Medical Records Assn.; Citicorp Acceptance Corp.; Citicorp Homeowners, Inc.

For full biographical listings, see the Martindale-Hubbell Law Directory

*** PIERCE, ATWOOD, SCRIBNER, ALLEN, SMITH & LANCASTER (AV)**

77 Winthrop Street, 04330
Telephone: 207-622-6311
Fax: 207-623-9367
Portland, Maine Office: One Monument Square.
Telephone: 207-773-6411.
Camden, Maine Office: 36 Chestnut Street, P.O. Box 780.
Telephone: 207-236-4333.

MEMBERS OF FIRM

Warren E. Winslow, Jr.
Malcolm L. Lyons
Joseph M. Kozak
Michael D. Seitzinger
John C. Nivison

ASSOCIATES

Daniel J. Stevens
Benjamin P. Townsend
Christine F. Burke

For full biographical listings, see the Martindale-Hubbell Law Directory

*** PRETI, FLAHERTY, BELIVEAU & PACHIOS (AV)**

45 Memorial Circle, P.O. Box 1058, 04332-1058
Telephone: 207-623-55300
Telecopier: 207-623-2914
Portland, Maine Office: 443 Congress Street, P.O. Box 11410, 04104-7410.
Telephone: 207-791-3000.
Telecopier: 207-791-3111.
Rumford, Maine Office: 150 Congress Street, P.O. Drawer L, 04276-2035.
Telephone: 207-364-4593.
Telecopier: 207-369-9421.

RESIDENT MEMBERS OF FIRM

Severin M. Beliveau
Michael J. Gentile
Bruce C. Gerrity
Anthony W. Buxton
James C. Pitney, Jr.
Virginia E. Davis
Joseph G. Donahue

(See Next Column)

RESIDENT ASSOCIATES

Mark B. LeDuc
Stephen E. F. Langsdorf
Ann R. Robinson
Deirdre M. O'Callaghan
Charles F. Dingman
Jeffrey P. Russell

For full biographical listings, see the Martindale-Hubbell Law Directory

*BANGOR,** Penobscot Co.

EATON, PEABODY, BRADFORD & VEAGUE, P.A. (AV)

Fleet Center-Exchange Street, P.O. Box 1210, 04402-1210
Telephone: 207-947-0111
Telecopier: 207-942-3040
Augusta, Maine Office: 2 Central Plaza.
Telephone: 207-622-3747.
Telecopier: 207-622-9732.
Brunswick, Maine Office: 167 Park Row.
Telephone: 207-729-1144.
Telecopier: 207-729-1140.
Camden, Maine Office: 7-9 Washington Street.
Telephone: 207-236-3325.
Telecopier: 207-236-8611.
Dover-Foxcroft, Maine Office: 30 East Main Street.
Telephone: 207-564-8378.
Telecopier: 207-564-7059.

Malcolm E. Morrell, Jr.
John W. Conti
Robert J. Eaton
Thomas M. Brown
Edward D. Leonard, III
Calvin E. True
Bernard J. Kubetz
Thomas C. Johnston
Clarissa B. Edelston
Douglas M. Smith (Resident, Dover-Foxcroft and Augusta Offices)
Daniel G. McKay
Stephen G. Morrell (Resident, Brunswick Office)
Glen L. Porter
Gordon H. S. Scott (Resident, Augusta Office)
Martin L. Wilk (Resident, Brunswick Office)
Clare Hudson Payne
Michael B. Trainor
John A. Cunningham (Resident, Brunswick Office)
William B. Devoe
Karen A. Huber
P. Andrew Hamilton
George Franklin Eaton, II
Terry W. Calderwood (Resident, Camden Office)
Paul L. Gibbons (Resident, Camden Office)
Gregory A. Brodek

OF COUNSEL

George F. Peabody
Donald A. Spear (Resident, Brunswick Office)
John E. McKay

John M. Monahan (Resident, Dover-Foxcroft Office)
Laurie A. Dart
Jonathan B. Huntington (Resident, Dover-Foxcroft Office)
Judy A.S. Metcalf (Resident, Brunswick Office)
R. Lee Ivy
David C. Webb
Thad B. Zmistowski
Lorena R. Rush
Dorisann B. W. Wagner (Resident, Augusta Office)
Allison C. Lucy
Roger Lang Huber
David W. Kesner
Michael A. Duddy

A List of Representative Clients available upon request.

For full biographical listings, see the Martindale-Hubbell Law Directory

GROSS, MINSKY, MOGUL & SINGAL, P.A. (AV)

Key Plaza, 23 Water Street, P.O. Box 917, 04402-0917
Telephone: 207-942-4644
Telecopier: 207-942-3699
Ellsworth, Maine Office: 26 State Street.
Telephone: 207-667-4611.
Telecopier: 207-667-6206.

Jules L. Mogul (1930-1994)
Norman Minsky
George Z. Singal
Louis H. Kornreich
George C. Schelling
Edward W. Gould
Steven J. Mogul
James R. Wholly

Wayne P. Libhart (Resident, Ellsworth, Maine Office)
Daniel A. Pileggi
Philip K. Clarke
Christopher R. Largay (Resident, Ellsworth Office)
Hans G. Huessy
William B. Entwisle
Sandra L. Rothera

OF COUNSEL

Edward I. Gross

Representative Clients: Dahl Chase Pathology Associates; Superior Paper Products.
Local Counsel for: The St. Paul Insurance Cos.; Aetna Life & Casualty Co.; Imperial Casualty & Indemnity Co.

For full biographical listings, see the Martindale-Hubbell Law Directory

Bangor—Continued

RICHARDSON, TROUBH & BADGER, A PROFESSIONAL CORPORATION (AV)

82 Columbia Street, P.O. Box 2429, 04402-2429
Telephone: 207-945-5900
Telecopier: 207-945-0758
Portland, Maine Office: Richardson & Troubh, A Professional Corporation, 465 Congress Street. P.O. Box, 9732.
Telephone: 207-774-5821.
Telecopier: 207-761-2056.

Frederick J. Badger, Jr. (Resident)
Ann M. Murray (Resident)

Frederick F. Costlow (Resident)
John B. Lucy (Resident)

Representative Clients: Royal Globe Insurance; Travelers Insurance; Peerless Insurance; CIGNA; General Motors Corp.; Hanover Insurance; Liberty Mutual Insurance;
Local Counsel for: General Motors Corp.; Beloit Corp./Harnischfeger; Winnebago Industries.

For full biographical listings, see the Martindale-Hubbell Law Directory

VAFIADES, BROUNTAS & KOMINSKY (AV)

Key Plaza, 23 Water Street, P.O. Box 919, 04402-0919
Telephone: 207-947-6915
Telecopier: 207-941-0863

MEMBERS OF FIRM

Nicholas P. Brountas
Susan R. Kominsky
Marvin H. Glazier
Eugene C. Coughlin, III

ASSOCIATES

Amy L. Faircloth
Lisa Cohen Lunn
Louise M. Davis
Terence M. Harrigan
Rosalind S. Prince
James C. Munch, III

OF COUNSEL

Lewis V. Vafiades

For full biographical listings, see the Martindale-Hubbell Law Directory

BAR HARBOR, Hancock Co.

FENTON, CHAPMAN, FENTON, SMITH & KANE, P.A. (AV)

109 Main Street, P.O. Box B, 04609
Telephone: 207-288-3331
FAX: 207-288-9326

William Fenton
Hancock Griffin, Jr. (1912-1980)
Douglas B. Chapman
Nathaniel R. Fenton
Chadbourn H. Smith
Daniel H. Kane

Margaret A. Timothy
Eric Lindquist

OF COUNSEL

David Einhorn
Edwin R. Smith

Reference: Bar Harbor Banking and Trust Co.

For full biographical listings, see the Martindale-Hubbell Law Directory

*BATH,** Sagadahoc Co.

CONLEY, HALEY & O'NEIL (AV)

Thirty Front Street, 04530
Telephone: 207-443-5576
Telefax: 207-443-6665

J. Michael Conley
Mark L. Haley
Constance P. O'Neil
Arlyn H. Weeks
Laura M. O'Hanlon

Representative Clients: Bath Iron Works Corporation; Central Maine Power Company; Saco Defense, Inc.; Sugarloaf Mountain Corporation.
References: Casco Northern Bank, N.A.; First Federal Savings & Loan Association of Bath; Shawmut Bank.

For full biographical listings, see the Martindale-Hubbell Law Directory

BIDDEFORD, York Co.

JENSEN BAIRD GARDNER & HENRY (AV)

(Successor to Walker, Bradford & LaBrique)
419 Alfred Street, 04005
Telephone: 207-282-5107
Telecopier: 207-282-6301
Portland, Maine Office: Ten Free Street.
Telephone: 207-775-7271.
Telecopier: 207-775-7935.

RESIDENT MEMBERS OF FIRM

John D. Bradford
David J. Jones
Ralph W. Austin
Joan LaBrique Cook
Keith R. Jacques

(See Next Column)

RESIDENT ASSOCIATES

Milda A. Castner
Anne H. Jordan

Representative Clients: General Motors Acceptance Corp.; Sedgwick James; Owens Corning Fiberglas; S.D. Warren Corp.; Key Bank of Maine.

For full biographical listings, see the Martindale-Hubbell Law Directory

CAMDEN, Knox Co.

PIERCE, ATWOOD, SCRIBNER, ALLEN, SMITH & LANCASTER (AV)

36 Chestnut Street, P.O. Box 780, 04843
Telephone: 207-236-4333
Fax: 207-236-6247
Portland, Maine Office: One Monument Square.
Telephone: 207-773-6411.
Augusta, Maine Office: 77 Winthrop Street.
Telephone: 207-622-6311.

MEMBERS OF FIRM

Richard A. McKittrick
Peter G. Warren

For full biographical listings, see the Martindale-Hubbell Law Directory

*DOVER-FOXCROFT,** Piscataquis Co.

C. W. & H. M. HAYES, P.A. (AV)

5 Lincoln Street, P.O. Box 189, 04426
Telephone: 207-564-3314
Telecopier: 207-564-7015

Charles W. Hayes (1865-1940)
Harold M. Hayes (1894-1963)
John L. Easton, Jr. (1926-1988)
James H. H. White (1932-1992)
Stuart E. Hayes
Kevin L. Stitham

Representative Clients: The Fleet Bank of Maine; Moosehead Manufacturing Co. (Hardwood Furniture); Hardwood Products Co.; Automobile Legal Assn.
Approved Attorneys for: New York TRW Title Insurance Inc.; Commonwealth Land Title Insurance Co.

For full biographical listings, see the Martindale-Hubbell Law Directory

*ELLSWORTH,** Hancock Co.

HALE & HAMLIN (AV)

10 State Street, P.O. Box 729, 04605
Telephone: 207-667-2561
Telefax: 207-667-8790

Eugene Hale (1836-1918)
Hannibal E. Hamlin (1858-1938)
Philip R. Lovell (1899-1961)
Charles J. Hurley (1908-1981)

OF COUNSEL

Atherton Fuller

MEMBERS OF FIRM

Barry K. Mills
Dale L. Worthen
Jeffrey W. Jones
Melissa Moll

ASSOCIATES

Laura Yustak Smith

Approved Attorneys for: Commonwealth Title Insurance Company; American Title Insurance Company.

For full biographical listings, see the Martindale-Hubbell Law Directory

FORT FAIRFIELD, Aroostook Co. — (Refer to Presque Isle)

GARDINER, Kennebec Co. — (Refer to Augusta)

KENNEBUNK, York Co.

SMITH ELLIOTT SMITH & GARMEY, P.A. (AV)

Webhannet Place, Route One South, P.O. Box 980, 04043
Telephone: 207-985-4464
Telefax: 207-985-3946
Saco, Maine Office: 199 Main Street, P.O. Box 1179.
Telephone: 207-282-1527.
Telefax: 207-283-4412. Sanford
Telephone: 207-324-1560. Portland
Telephone: 207-774-3199. Wells
Telephone: 207-646-0970.
Portland, Maine Office: 100 Commercial Street, Suite 304.
Telephone: 207-774-3199.
Telefax: 207-774-2235.

Alan S. Nelson
Karen B. Lovell

Robert M. Nadeau

Representative Clients: Towns of Waterboro and Kennebunk, Maine; City of Biddeford; Saco and Biddeford Savings Institution; Ocean Communities Federal Credit Union;
Local Counsel for: Mutual Fire Insurance Company.
References: Casco Northern Bank, N. A. (Saco Kennebunk Branches); Saco & Biddeford Savings Institution.

For full biographical listings, see the Martindale-Hubbell Law Directory

LEWISTON, Androscoggin Co.

Brann & Isaacson (AV)

184 Main Street, P.O. Box 3070, 04243-3070
Telephone: 207-786-3566
Telecopier: 207-783-9325

MEMBERS OF FIRM

Louis J. Brann (1876-1948)
Peter A. Isaacson (1895-1980)
Irving Isaacson
George S. Isaacson
Alfred C. Frawley, III
Martin I. Eisenstein
Martha E. Greene
David W. Bertoni

ASSOCIATES

Benjamin W. Lund
Peter D. Lowe
Daniel C. Stockford
Roy T. Pierce
David C. Pierson

Representative Clients: L.L. Bean, Inc.; Direct Marketing Assn.; Readers Digest Assn.; The Sharper Image; Bantam Doubleday Dell, Inc.; Supreme Slipper Manufacturing Company, Inc.; Livermore Falls Trust Co.; Dow Chemical Co.; United Egg Producers; Miller Hydro Group.

For full biographical listings, see the Martindale-Hubbell Law Directory

Platz & Thompson, P.A. (AV)

95 Park Street, P.O. Box 960, 04243
Telephone: 207-783-8558
Telecopier: 207-783-9487

John A. Platz (1913-1980)
J. Peter Thompson
Philip K. Hargesheimer
Paul S. Douglass
Roger J. O'Donnell, III
Robert V. Hoy
Michael J. LaTorre
James B. Main

Representative Clients: Maine Education Assoc.; Androscoggin Savings Bank; BayBank; Key Bank of Maine; Pioneer Plastics, Inc.; Conifer Industries (KFC franchises for State of Maine); Getty Oil Co.; Livermore Falls Trust; Platz Assoc.; H.P. Cummings, Const. Co.

For full biographical listings, see the Martindale-Hubbell Law Directory

*MACHIAS,** Washington Co. — (Refer to Ellsworth)

*PORTLAND,** Cumberland Co.

Amerling & Burns, A Professional Association (AV)

193 Middle Street, 04101
Telephone: 207-775-3581
Facsimile: 207-775-3814
Affiliated St. Croix Office: Coon & Sanford, P.O. Box 25918, Six Chandlers's Wharf, Suite 202, 00824-0918.

W. John Amerling
George F. Burns
David P. Ray
John R. Coon
Arnold C. Macdonald
Mary DeLano
Joanne F. Cole
A. Robert Ruesch

OF COUNSEL

Bruce M. Jervis

Representative Clients: H.E. Sargent, Inc. (construction); Merrill Trust; J.M. Huber, Inc.; Jackson Laboratories; Hague International (engineering); Aetna Life & Casualty Co.; The Hartford; Great American Insurance Co.; Wausau Insurance Co.

For full biographical listings, see the Martindale-Hubbell Law Directory

Herbert H. Bennett and Associates, P.A. (AV)

Suite 300, 121 Middle Street, P.O. Box 7799, 04112-7799
Telephone: 207-773-4775
Telecopier: 207-774-2366

Herbert H. Bennett (1928-1992)
Peter Bennett
Jeffrey Bennett
Frederick B. Finberg
Melinda J. Caterine
Hilary A. Rapkin

Counsel for: Associated Grocers of New England; Casco Northern Bank, N.A.; Coca Cola Bottling Company of Northern New England, Inc.; Northern Utilities/Bay State Gas; Pratt & Whitney (Division of United Technologies); Primerica Financial Services; Sprague Energy (C.H. Sprague & Son); Perrier Group of America, Inc.; Lepage Bakeries, Inc. (Country Kitchen); Table Talk Pies, Inc.; Texaco, Inc.

For full biographical listings, see the Martindale-Hubbell Law Directory

Bernstein, Shur, Sawyer and Nelson, A Professional Corporation (AV)

100 Middle Street, P.O. Box 9729, 04104-5029
Telephone: 207-774-1200
Telecopier: 207-774-1127 Telecommunications: 761-2974
Augusta, Maine Office: 146 Capitol Street, Box 5057.
Telephone: 207-623-1596.
Telecopier: 626-0200.

(See Next Column)

Kennebunk, Maine Office: 62 Portland Road.
Telephone: 207-985-7152.
Telecopier: 985-3174.

Israel Bernstein (1890-1967)
Louis Bernstein (1900-1993)
Barnett I. Shur (1905-1992)
Sumner Thurman Bernstein
Leonard M. Nelson
William W. Willard
Gregory A. Tselikis
F. Paul Frinsko
Peter J. Rubin
Alan R. Atkins
Richard P. LeBlanc
Eric F. Saunders
Gordon F. Grimes
Philip H. Gleason
Geoffrey H. Hole
James H. Young, II
Mary L. Schendel
John M. R. Paterson
Linda A. Monica
Charles E. Miller
Richard M. Schade (Resident, Augusta Office)
Lee K. Bragg (Resident, Augusta Office)
John H. Montgomery, III
Christopher L. Vaniotis
Nathan H. Smith
Robert H. Stier, Jr.
James A. Houle
Catherine A. Lee
Durward W. Parkinson (Resident, Kennebunk Office)
John L. Carpenter
Patrick J. Scully
Anthony E. Perkins
Catherine O'Connor (Resident, Kennebunk Office)
Joseph J. Hahn
Diane S. Lukac
Nelson A. Toner
David A. Soley
Lester F. Wilkinson, Jr. (Resident, Augusta Office)
Kenneth W. Lehman
C. Wesley Crowell (Resident, Kennebunk Office)
Kate S. Debevoise

Margaret C. Lavoie (Resident, Kennebunk Office)
Patricia A. Peard
Robert J. Perna
Robert J. Crawford
Neal F. Pratt
Kenneth D. Pierce (Resident, Kennebunk Office)
Christian L. Barner (Resident, Kennebunk Office)
Robert F. Macdonald, Jr.
Mary Elizabeth Fougere
Lawrence H. Bryant
Jaimie Paul Schwartz
Abigail D. King
Lisa A. Ernst
Scott E. Schul
Paul S. Veidenheimer
Glenn Israel

OF COUNSEL

Herbert H. Sawyer

Representative Clients: University of Maine; Fleet Bank of Maine; First NH Banks, Inc.; Sebago, Inc.; Greater Portland Transit District.

For full biographical listings, see the Martindale-Hubbell Law Directory

Drummond & Drummond (AV)

One Monument Way, 04101
Telephone: 207-774-0317
Telefax: 207-761-4690

MEMBERS OF FIRM

David N. Fisher, Jr.
Horace W. Horton
John B. Emory
Arthur A. Cerullo
James B. Barns
Robert C. Santomenna

ASSOCIATES

Andrew W. Sparks
Alexandra E. Caulfield
Paul E. Peck
Patricia B. McNamara

OF COUNSEL

Peter W. Greenleaf
Wadleigh B. Drummond (1885-1979)
Josiah H. Drummond (1914-1991)

Representative Clients: W. L. Blake & Co.; Keeley Construction Co., Inc.; Maine Surgical Supply Co.; Olympia Sport Center, Inc.

For full biographical listings, see the Martindale-Hubbell Law Directory

Jensen Baird Gardner & Henry (AV)

Ten Free Street, P.O. Box 4510, 04112
Telephone: 207-775-7271
Telecopier: 207-775-7935
York County Office: 419 Alfred Street, Biddeford, Maine.
Telephone: 207-282-5107.
Telecopier: 207-282-6301.

OF COUNSEL

Raymond E. Jensen
M. Donald Gardner
Merton G. Henry

MEMBERS OF FIRM

Kenneth Baird (1914-1987)
N. B. Walker (1851-1935)
Thomas B. Walker (1882-1968)
John D. Bradford (Resident, York County Office)
Walter E. Webber
Donald A. Kopp
Kenneth M. Cole, III
Nicholas S. Nadzo
Frank H. Frye
David J. Jones (Resident, York County Office)
Michael A. Nelson
Ralph W. Austin (Resident, York County Office)
Joan LaBrique Cook (Resident, York County Office)
Ronald A. Epstein
William H. Dale
Joseph H. Groff, III
F. Bruce Sleeper
Deborah M. Mann
Leslie E. Lowry, III

(See Next Column)

JENSEN BAIRD GARDNER & HENRY, *Portland—Continued*

MEMBERS OF FIRM (Continued)

Keith R. Jacques (Resident, York County Office)
Patricia McDonough Dunn
Michael J. Quinlan
Elizabeth T. High
James N. Katsiaficas
Peter B. LaFond
John R. Goldsbury

ASSOCIATES

Milda A. Castner (Resident, York County Office)
Emily A. Bloch
Anne H. Jordan (Resident, York County Office)
Scott A. Robertson
Barry P. Fernald
Bernadette Ann Bolduc
Karen McGee Hurley
Sally J. Daggett
Matthew A. Woodward

Representative Clients: General Motors Acceptance Corp.; York Mutual Insurance Co.; Knutson Mortgage Corp.; Owens Corning Fiberglass.

For full biographical listings, see the Martindale-Hubbell Law Directory

McCANDLESS & HUNT (AV)

57 Exchange Street, 04101
Telephone: 207-772-4100
Telecopier: 207-772-1300

MEMBERS OF FIRM

Eileen M. L. Epstein
David E. Hunt
Elizabeth T. McCandless

ASSOCIATES

Dennis J. O'Donovan

For full biographical listings, see the Martindale-Hubbell Law Directory

PERKINS, THOMPSON, HINCKLEY & KEDDY, P.A. (AV)

One Canal Plaza, P.O. Box 426, 04112-0426
Telephone: 207-774-2635

Thomas Schulten
Bruce E. Leddy
Owen W. Wells
Douglas S. Carr
Andrew A. Cadot
Thomas B. Wheatley
John R. Opperman
Philip C. Hunt
John S. Upton
Peggy L. McGehee
Melissa Hanley Murphy
John H. Rich III
John A. Ciraldo
John A. Hobson
Helen I. Muther
Timothy P. Benoit

Fred W. Bopp III
Craig N. Denekas
Mark P. Snow
William J. Sheils

For full biographical listings, see the Martindale-Hubbell Law Directory

PETRUCCELLI & MARTIN (AV)

50 Monument Square, P.O. Box 9733, 04104-5033
Telephone: 207-775-0200
Telecopier: 207-775-2360

MEMBERS OF FIRM

Gerald F. Petruccelli
Joel C. Martin
Daniel W. Bates

ASSOCIATES

Michael K. Martin
James B. Haddow
Linda C. Russell
Kenneth D. Keating
Thomas C. Bradley

Representative Clients: Bangor Hydro-Electric Co.; Chubb Insurance Co.; Coopers & Lybrand; Cumberland Farms; General Electric Capital Corp.; Maine Medical Center; Pine Tree Telephone & Telegraph Co.; KPMG Peat Marwick; Union Mutual Fire Insurance Co.; Vermont Mutual Insurance Co.

For full biographical listings, see the Martindale-Hubbell Law Directory

PIERCE, ATWOOD, SCRIBNER, ALLEN, SMITH & LANCASTER (AV)

One Monument Square, 04101
Telephone: 207-773-6411
Fax: 207-773-3419
Augusta, Maine Office: 77 Winthrop Street.
Telephone: 207-622-6311.
Camden, Maine Office: 36 Chestnut Street, P.O. Box 780.
Telephone: 207-236-4333.

MEMBERS OF FIRM

Leonard A. Pierce (1885-1960)
Edward W. Atwood (1897-1977)
Jotham D. Pierce (1918-1990)
Fred C. Scribner, Jr. (1908-1994)
Sigrid E. Tompkins
William C. Smith
Ralph I. Lancaster, Jr.
Jeremiah D. Newbury
Gerald M. Amero
Bruce A. Coggeshall
S. Mason Pratt, Jr.
Daniel E. Boxer
Jotham D. Pierce, Jr.
Warren E. Winslow, Jr. (Resident, Augusta Office)
Everett P. Ingalls
Malcolm L. Lyons (Resident, Augusta Office)
James B. Zimpritch
James G. Good
John O'Leary
Peter W. Culley
Jeffrey M. White

(See Next Column)

MEMBERS OF FIRM (Continued)

Joseph M. Kozak (Resident, Augusta Office)
George J. Marcus
Louise K. Thomas
John W. Gulliver
John D. Delahanty
Charles S. Einsiedler, Jr.
Richard A. McKittrick (Resident, Camden Office)
Peter H. Jacobs
Michael D. Seitzinger (Resident, Augusta Office)
Daniel M. Snow
Richard P. Hackett
Robert A. Moore
Michael R. Currie
William J. Kayatta, Jr.
Peter G. Warren (Resident, Camden Office)
Gordon K. Gayer
Thomas R. Doyle
Christopher E. Howard
Wayne R. Douglas
Dennis C. Keeler
Philip F. W. Ahrens, III
James R. Erwin, II
Kevin F. Gordon
Jacob A. Manheimer
Gregory D. Woodworth
Elaine S. Falender
Scott T. Maker
John C. Nivison (Resident, Augusta Office)
Margaret Coughlin LePage
Kenneth Fairbanks Gray
Elizabeth R. Butler
John J. Aromando
David J. Champoux
William H. Nichols
Gloria A. Pinza
William E. Taylor
Catherine R. Connors
David E. Barry

OF COUNSEL

Charles W. Allen
Vincent L. McKusick

ASSOCIATES

Sarah H. Beard
Stephen G. Grygiel
Gisele M. Nadeau
Dixon P. Pike
Barbara K. Wheaton
Jennie L. Clegg
Anthony R. Derosby
Daniel J. Stevens (Resident, Augusta Office)
Michael N. Ambler, Jr.
Kate L. Geoffroy
Matthew D. Manahan
Michael S. Wilson
Eric D. Altholz
Steven W. Abbott
Richard P. Olson
Nancy V. Savage
Benjamin P. Townsend
Mary McQuillen
Adam H. Steinman
Deborah L. Shaw
James M. Saffian
David P. Littell
Jonathan A. Block
Jared S. des Rosiers
Foster A. Stewart, Jr
Barney Simeon Goldstein
Pamela C. Morris
Allan M. Muir
William L. Worden
Debra L. Brown
Christine F. Burke (Resident, Augusta Office)
David Allen Brenningmeyer
Marcia A. Metcalf

STAFF ATTORNEY

Judith A. Fletcher Woodbury

For full biographical listings, see the Martindale-Hubbell Law Directory

PRETI, FLAHERTY, BELIVEAU & PACHIOS (AV)

443 Congress Street, P.O. Box 11410, 04104-7410
Telephone: 207-791-3000
Telecopier: 207-791-3111
Augusta, Maine Office: 45 Memorial Circle, P.O. Box 1058, 04332-1058.
Telephone: 207-623-5300.
Telecopier: 207-623-2914.
Rumford, Maine Office: 150 Congress Street, P.O. Drawer L, 04276-2035.
Telephone: 207-364-4593.
Telecopier: 207-369-9421.

MEMBERS OF FIRM

John J. Flaherty
Albert J. Beliveau, Jr. (Rumford Office)
Severin M. Beliveau (Augusta Office)
Harold C. Pachios
Michael J. Gentile (Augusta Office)
Richard H. Spencer, Jr.
Keith A. Powers
Christopher D. Nyhan
Eric P. Stauffer
Jonathan S. Piper
Daniel Rapaport
John P. Doyle, Jr.
Bruce C. Gerrity (Augusta Office)
Anthony W. Buxton (Augusta Office)
Jeffrey T. Edwards
Michael G. Messerschmidt
Randall B. Weill
James C. Pitney, Jr. (Augusta Office)
Evan M. Hansen
Virginia E. Davis (Augusta Office)
Edward R. Benjamin, Jr.
Leonard M. Gulino
Dennis C. Sbrega
Geoffrey K. Cummings
Estelle A. Lavoie
Susan E. LoGiudice
Michael Kaplan
Michael L. Sheehan
Joseph G. Donahue (Augusta Office)
David B. Van Slyke

OF COUNSEL

Robert F. Preti
Robert W. Smith

ASSOCIATES

Nelson J. Larkins
Mark B. LeDuc (Augusta Office)
Stephen E. F. Langsdorf (Augusta Office)
James E. Phipps
Jeanne T. Cohn-Connor
John P. McVeigh
Marilyn E. Mistretta
Elizabeth A. Olivier
Ann R. Robinson (Augusta Office)
Deirdre M. O'Callaghan (Augusta Office)
Jeffrey M. Sullivan
Scott T. Rodgers
Kevin J. Beal
Penny St. Louis

(See Next Column)

PRETI, FLAHERTY, BELIVEAU & PACHIOS—*Continued*

ASSOCIATES (Continued)

Charles F. Dingman (Augusta Office)
Richard L. Suter
Jeffrey P. Russell (Augusta Office)
Carl W. Tourigny
Jennifer F. Kreckel (Rumford Office)
Timothy J. Bryant
Maureen Tsao
Kimberley S. New

Representative Clients: The St. Paul Companies; Key Bank of Maine; Maine Municipal Assn.; Guy Gannett Publishing Co.; Maine Turnpike Authority; American International Group; Southern Maine Medical Center; NRG Barriers, Inc.; Maine Automobile Dealers Assn.; Bangor Hydro-Electric Co.

For full biographical listings, see the Martindale-Hubbell Law Directory

RICHARDSON & TROUBH, A PROFESSIONAL CORPORATION (AV)

465 Congress Street, P.O. Box 9732, 04104-5032
Telephone: 207-774-5821
Telecopier: 207-761-2056
Bangor, Maine Office: Richardson Troubh & Badger, A Professional Corporation, 82 Columbia Street.
Telephone: 207-945-5900.
Telecopier: 207-945-0758.

Harrison L. Richardson
William B. Troubh
Edwin A. Heisler
John S. Whitman
Robert J. Piampiano
Richard J. Kelly
Wendell G. Large
Frederick J. Badger, Jr. (Resident, Bangor Office)
Kevin M. Gillis
Michael P. Boyd
Thomas E. Getchell
John W. Chapman
Michael Richards
William K. McKinley
Elizabeth G. Stouder
Barri Bloom
Daniel F. Gilligan
Paul S. Bulger
Ann M. Murray (Resident, Bangor Maine)

Frederick F. Costlow (Resident, Bangor Office)
John B. Lucy (Resident, Bangor Office)
M. Thomasine Burke
John G. Richardson
Linda L. Sears
Kevin G. Anderson
Anne H. Cressey
Daniel R. Felkel
Thomas R. McKeon

Representative Clients: Fireman's Fund American Insurance Companies; Ford Motor Company; Great American Insurance Co.; CIGNA; Kemper Insurance Group; Liberty Mutual Insurance Co.; Norfolk & Dedham Mutual Fire Insurance Co.; Security Insurance Group; Scott Paper Co.; United Parcel Service.

For full biographical listings, see the Martindale-Hubbell Law Directory

SMITH ELLIOTT SMITH & GARMEY, P.A. (AV)

100 Commercial Street, Suite 304, 04101
Telephone: 207-774-3199
Telefax: 207-774-2235
Kennebunk, Maine Office: Route One South, P.O. Box 980.
Telephone: 207-985-4464.
Telefax: 207-985-3946.
Saco, Maine Office: 199 Main Street, P.O. Box 1179.
Telephone: 207-282-1527.
Telefax: 207-283-4412. Sanford
Telephone: 207-324-1560. Wells
Telephone: 207-464-0970.

Randall E. Smith
Terrence D. Garmey
Richard P. Romeo
Robert H. Furbish

Michael J. Waxman

Representative Clients: Towns of Waterboro and Kennebunk, Maine; City of Biddeford; Saco and Biddeford Savings Institution; Ocean Communities Federal Credit Union.
Local Counsel for: Mutual Fire Insurance Company.
Reference: Casco Northern Bank, N. A. (Saco Branch); Saco & Biddeford Savings Institution.

For full biographical listings, see the Martindale-Hubbell Law Directory

VERRILL & DANA (AV)

One Portland Square, P.O. Box 586, 04112-0586
Telephone: 207-774-4000
Fax: 207-774-7499
Augusta, Maine Office: 45 Memorial Circle, P.O. Box 957.
Telephone: 207-623-3889.
Fax: 207-622-3117.
Kennebunk, Maine Office: Lafayette Center, P.O. Box 266.
Telephone: 207-985-7193.
Fax: 207-985-3957.

(See Next Column)

COUNSEL

John A. Mitchell
Robert B. Williamson, Jr.
Louis A. Wood
John L. Sullivan
Frank C. Royer, Jr.
Marianne McGettigan
Suzanne E. Meeker
Martin S. Amick
Claudia D. Raessler

MEMBERS OF FIRM

Roger A. Putnam
Peter B. Webster
Charles R. Oestreicher
Michael T. Healy
Christopher J. W. Coggeshall
Robert B. Patterson, Jr.
Bruce W. Bergen (Resident Partner, Kennebunk Office)
Charles A. Harvey, Jr.
Judith M. Coburn
Christopher S. Neagle
David C. Hillman
James T. Kilbreth, III
John D. Duncan
Andrew M. Horton
William S. Harwood
William S. Wilson, Jr.
James G. Goggin
Beth Dobson
Peter R. Kraft
Gregory S. Fryer
Gregory L. Foster
Gregg H. Ginn
David E. Warren
Lawrence C. Winger
William C. Knowles
Gene R. Libby (Resident Partner, Kennebunk Office)
Robert S. Frank
James C. Palmer
S. Catherine Longley
Mark K. Googins
Matthew L. Caras
David C. Boyer, Jr.
Douglas P. Currier
Kimberly S. Couch
James A. McCormack
Alan D. MacEwan
Charles C. Soltan (Resident Partner, Augusta Office)

ASSOCIATES

Charles P. Bacall
Lisa S. Boehm
Robert C. Brooks
Vickie A. Caron
Robert E. Cleaves
Roger A. Clement, Jr.
James I. Cohen
Michael J. Donlan (Resident Associate, Kennebunk Office)
K. Douglas Erdmann
S. Carter Friend
David L. Galgay, Jr.
Matthew H. Herndon
Carl E. Kandutsch
Michael W. MacLeod-Ball (Resident Associate, Kennebunk Office)
Roy Steven McCandless
Jacqueline W. Rider
William J. Ryan, Jr. (Resident Associate, Augusta Office)
Alexandra L. Treadway
Thomas A. Welch (Resident Associate, Kennebunk Office)

LEGAL SUPPORT PERSONNEL

David A. Nicklas

Counsel for: American Maize-Products Co.; ASCAP; Bowdoin College; Casco Northern Bank, N.A.; Fleet Bank; Hannaford Bros. Co.; Maine Blue Cross and Blue Shield; Maine Public Service Co.; Peoples Heritage Bank; Portland Water District.

For full biographical listings, see the Martindale-Hubbell Law Directory

PRESQUE ISLE, Aroostook Co.

PHILLIPS, OLORE & DUNLAVEY, P.A. (AV)

Key Bank Building, 480 Main Street, P.O. Box 1087, 04769
Telephone: 207-769-2361
Fax: 207-769-2381

Wendell L. Phillips (1913-1972)
Hugo A. Olore, Jr.
David A. Dunlavey
Brent A. York

Local Counsel For: Casco Northern Bank, N.A.
Representative Clients: City of Presque Isle; Town of Mapleton; Maine School Administrative Districts #32 and #45; Maine Potato Growers, Inc.; Government Employees Insurance Co.; United Services Automobile Assn.; Lomas Mortgage, U.S.A., Inc.; KeyCorp Mortgage Co.
Approved Attorneys And Agents For: Chicago Title Insurance Co.

For full biographical listings, see the Martindale-Hubbell Law Directory

STEVENS, ENGELS, BISHOP & SPRAGUE (AV)

428 Main Street, P.O. Box 311, 04769
Telephone: 207-768-5481
Telefax: 207-764-1663

MEMBERS OF FIRM

Albert M. Stevens
Richard C. Engels
Frank H. Bishop, Sr.
Jonathan W. Sprague
Michael L. Dubois

Representative Clients: Commercial Union Cos.; Travelers Insurance Co.; Aetna Insurance Co.; Firemans Fund Group; Hartford Insurance Group; Home Indemnity Co.; Maine Bonding and Casualty Co.; New Hampshire Group; Liberty Mutual Insurance Co.; Peoples Heritage Bank.

For full biographical listings, see the Martindale-Hubbell Law Directory

*ROCKLAND,** Knox Co.

STROUT & PAYSON, P.A. (AV)

10 Masonic Street, P.O. Box 248, 04841-0248
Telephone: 207-594-8400
Fax: 207-594-2724

(See Next Column)

STROUT & PAYSON P.A., *Rockland—Continued*

Arthur E. Strout
Joseph B. Pellicani (1936-1988)
Robert J. Levine
Esther R. Barnhart
Carol Ann Lundquist
Randal E. Watkinson
Elizabeth Biddle Jennings

OF COUNSEL

Curtis M. Payson
John Knight

Approved Attorneys For: First American Title Insurance Co.; Chicago Title Insurance Co.

For full biographical listings, see the Martindale-Hubbell Law Directory

RUMFORD, Oxford Co.

PRETI, FLAHERTY, BELIVEAU & PACHIOS (AV)

150 Congress Street, P.O. Drawer L, 04276-2035
Telephone: 207-364-4593
Telecopier: 207-369-9421
Portland, Maine Office: 443 Congress Street, P.O. Box 11410, 04104-7410.
Telephone: 207-791-3000.
Telecopier: 207-791-3111.
Augusta, Maine Office: 45 Memorial Circle, P.O. Box 1058, 04332-1058.
Telephone: 207-623-5300.
Telecopier: 207-623-2914.

RESIDENT MEMBER OF FIRM

Albert J. Beliveau, Jr.

RESIDENT ASSOCIATE

Jennifer F. Kreckel

For full biographical listings, see the Martindale-Hubbell Law Directory

SACO, York Co.

SMITH ELLIOTT SMITH & GARMEY, P.A. (AV)

199 Main Street, P.O. Box 1179, 04072
Telephone: 207-282-1527
Telefax: 207-283-4412
Sanford Telephone: 207-324-1560
Portland Telephone: 207-774-3199
Wells Telephone: 207-646-0970
Kennebunk, Maine Office: Route One South, P.O. Box 980.
Telephone: 207-985-4464.
Telefax: 207-985-3946.
Portland, Maine Office: 100 Commercial Street, Suite 304.
Telephone: 207-774-3199.
Telefax: 207-774-2235.

Charles W. Smith (1915-1983)
Roger S. Elliott
Alan S. Nelson
Randall E. Smith
Charles W. Smith, Jr.
Terrence D. Garmey
Karen B. Lovell
Peter W. Schroeter
Richard P. Romeo
Robert H. Furbish
William S. Kany
John H. O'Neil, Jr.
Harry B. Center, II
David S. Abramson

Robert M. Nadeau
Michael J. Waxman
Barbara J. Petitti

Representative Clients: City of Biddeford; Towns of Waterboro and Kennebunk, Maine; Saco and Biddeford Savings Institution; Ocean Communities Federal Credit Union;
Local Counsel for: Mutual Fire Insurance Company.
References: Casco Northern Bank, N.A. (Saco Branch); Saco & Biddeford Savings Institution.

For full biographical listings, see the Martindale-Hubbell Law Directory

SANFORD, York Co. — (Refer to Biddeford)

*SKOWHEGAN,** Somerset Co.

EAMES & STERNS (AV)

65 Cross Street, P.O. Box 959, 04976-0959
Telephone: 207-474-8105; 474-2626
Telefax: 207-474-8106

Clayton E. Eames (1891-1966)
Donald E. Eames
Richard S. Sterns

Representative Clients: Farrin Bros. & Smith, Contractors; Towns of Skowhegan, Madison and Starks; Key Bank; Fleet Bank; Candian Chains; Goodwill Home Assn.; Moose River Lumber Co., Inc.; T.R. Dillon Logging, Inc.; De Long Sportswear, Inc. (Clothing Mfg.); Ambrose G. McCarthy, Jr.

For full biographical listings, see the Martindale-Hubbell Law Directory

WRIGHT & MILLS, P.A. (AV)

218 Water Street, P.O. Box 9, 04976
Telephone: 207-474-3324
Telefax: 207-474-3609

(See Next Column)

Carl R. Wright
S. Peter Mills, III
Paul P. Sumberg
Kenneth A. Lexier
Dale F. Thistle

Representative Clients: Design Professionals Insurance Company, New Jersey; Solon Manufacturing Company, Solon, Maine; Kleinschmidt Associates-Engineers, Pittsfield, Maine; Acheron Engineering, Newport, Maine; E.W. Littlefield-Contractors, Hartland, Maine; WBRC-Architects, Bangor, Maine.

For full biographical listings, see the Martindale-Hubbell Law Directory

VAN BUREN, Aroostook Co. — (Refer to Presque Isle)

WATERVILLE, Kennebec Co.

WEEKS & HUTCHINS (AV)

Two Park Place, P.O. Box 417, 04903-0417
Telephone: 207-872-2783
Telefax: 207-872-5749

Thomas N. Weeks (1895-1985)
Bradford H. Hutchins (1907-1992)
Roger A. Welch (1930-1993)

OF COUNSEL

Miles P. Frye

MEMBERS OF FIRM

Timothy R. O'Donnell
Waldemar G. Buschmann
Jonathan G. Rogers

ASSOCIATES

Cheryl Hotchkiss Fasse

Representative Clients: C. F. Hathaway Co.; Scott Paper Co.; Colby College; Fleet Bank; Nationwide Insurance Group; First American Title Insurance Co.; Lawyers Title Insurance Corp.; Kennebec Water District; Waterville Osteopathic Hospital.

For full biographical listings, see the Martindale-Hubbell Law Directory

WELLS, York Co. — (Refer to Kennebunk)

*WISCASSET,** Lincoln Co. — (Refer to Brunswick)

YORK, York Co.

STRATER & STRATER, P.A. (AV)

266 York Street, P.O. Box 69, 03909
Telephone: 207-363-2900
Telefax: 207-363-2902

David Strater
Nicholas S. Strater

Representative Clients: Kennebunk Savings Bank; York Sewer District.
Approved Attorneys For: National Attorneys Title Insurance Co.; Lawyers Title Insurance Corp.; American Title Insurance Co.; Chicago Title Insurance Co.; Commonwealth Land Title Insurance Co.
Reference: Kennebunk Savings Bank; York Sewer District.

For full biographical listings, see the Martindale-Hubbell Law Directory

MARYLAND

*ANNAPOLIS,** Anne Arundel Co.

Council, Baradel, Kosmerl & Nolan, P.A. (AV)

125 West Street, Fourth Floor, P.O. Box 2289, 21404-2289
Telephone: 410-268-6600
Baltimore: 410-269-6190
Washington, D.C.: 301-261-2247
FAX: 410-269-8409

Ronald E. Council
Ronald A. Baradel
Wayne T. Kosmerl
James P. Nolan
William F. Flood, III
Kevin M. Schaeffer
Charles Bagley, IV
John Ralph Greiber, Jr.

John P. Rhody, Jr.
Donna McCabe Schaeffer
John Naumann Strange
Susan T. Ford
Edwin H. Staples, II

OF COUNSEL

George N. Manis
Nicholas Goldsborough

Representative Clients: Farmers National Bank; Bank of Maryland; State Farm Mutual Automobile Insurance Co.; American Republic Insurance Co.; Liberty Mutual Insurance Co.; Annapolis Yacht Sales, Inc.; Chesapeake Harbour Condominium; Maryland Marine Contractors Assn.

For full biographical listings, see the Martindale-Hubbell Law Directory

Foley & Lardner (AV)

Suite 102, 175 Admiral Cochrane Drive, 21401-7367
Telephone: 410-266-8077
Telex: 899149 (Oldtownpat)
Facsimile: 410-266-8664
Milwaukee, Wisconsin Office: Firstar Center, 777 East Wisconsin Avenue.
Telephone: 414-271-2400.
Telex: 26-819 (Foley Lard Mil).
Facsimile: 414-289-3791.
Madison, Wisconsin Office: Firstar Plaza, One South Pinckney Street, P.O. Box 1497.
Telephone: 608-257-5035.
Facsimile: 608-258-4258.
Chicago, Illinois Office: Suite 3300, One IBM Plaza, 330 N. Wabash Avenue.
Telephone: 312-755-1900.
Facsimile: 312-755-1925.
Washington, D.C. Office: Washington Harbour, Suite 500, 3000 K Street, N.W.
Telephone: 202-672-5300.
Telex: 904136 (Foley Lard Wsh.)
Facsimile: 202-672-5399.
Jacksonville, Florida Office: The Greenleaf Building, 200 Laura Street. P.O. Box 240.
Telephone: 904-359-2000.
Facsimile: 904-359-0319.
Orlando, Florida Office: Suite 1800, 111 North Orange Avenue, P.O. Box 2193.
Telephone: 407-423-7656.
Telex: 441781 (HQ ORL).
Facsimile: 407-648-1743.
Tallahassee, Florida Office: Suite 450, 215 South Monroe Street, P.O. Box 508.
Telephone: 904-222-6100.
Facsimile: 904-224-0496.
Tampa, Florida Office: Suite 2700, One Hundred N. Tampa Street, P.O. Box 3391.
Telephones: 813-229-2300; Pinellas County: 813-442-3296.
Facsimile: 813-221-4210. County: 813-446-9641.
West Palm Beach, Florida Office: Suite 200, Phillips Point East Tower, 777 South Flagler Drive.
Telephone: 407-655-5050.
Facsimile: 407-655-6925.

PARTNERS

Arthur Schwartz
Brian J. McNamara

ASSOCIATES

John P. Veschi

For full biographical listings, see the Martindale-Hubbell Law Directory

P. James Underwood (AV)

9A Maryland Avenue, P.O. Box 2335, 21404
Telephone: 410-268-4247

Wharton, Levin, Ehrmantraut, Klein & Nash, A Professional Association (AV)

104 West Street, 21404-0551
Telephone: 800-322-1984; 410-263-5900
Baltimore, Maryland Office: 400 East Pratt Street.
Telephone: 410-269-7529.

(See Next Column)

Bethesda, Maryland Office: 7200 Wisconsin Avenue, Suite 308.
Telephone: 301-656-1001.

James T. Wharton
David A. Levin
William A. Ehrmantraut
Robert Dale Klein
Brian J. Nash
A. Gwynn Bowie, Jr.
Jack L. Harvey
Michael T. Wharton
Andrew E. Vernick
D. Lee Rutland

David A. Roling
Brian F. Holeman (Not admitted in MD)
Debra S. Block
Daniel C. Costello
Christian A. Lodowski
Douglas K. Schrader
Linda G. Wales
Stuart N. Herschfeld
Denise Elizabeth Atkinson
Marian L. Hogan
Mary C. Jockel

For full biographical listings, see the Martindale-Hubbell Law Directory

*BALTIMORE,** (Independent City)

Allen, Johnson, Alexander & Karp, P.A. (AV)

Suite 1540, 100 East Pratt Street, 21202
Telephone: 410-727-5000
Fax: 410-727-0861
Washington, D.C. Office: 1707 L Street, N.W., Suite 1050.
Telephone: 202-828-4141.

Donald C. Allen
John D. Alexander, Jr.
Daniel Karp
D'Ana E. Johnson (Resident, Washington, D.C. Office)

Anne Marie McGinley (Resident, Washington, D.C. Office)
Denise Ramsburg Stanley
George B. Breen (Not admitted in MD; Resident, Washington, D.C. Office)
Robert G. McGinley (Resident, Washington, D.C. Office)
James X. Crogan, Jr.
Yvette M. Bryant
Kevin Bock Karpinski
Brett A. Balinsky

Representative Clients: Scottsdale Insurance Co.; Nautilus Insurance Co.; Jefferson Insurance Co.; Liberty Mutual Insurance Co.; Avis Rent-A-Car; Otis Elevator Co.; Montgomery Elevator Co.; Admiral Insurance Co.; Local Government Insurance Trust; Lancer Insurance Co.

For full biographical listings, see the Martindale-Hubbell Law Directory

Anderson, Coe & King (AV)

201 North Charles Street, Suite 2000, 21201
Telephone: 410-752-1630
Cable Address: ABKO
Fax: 752 0085
Ocean City, Maryland Office: 7904 Coastal Highway, Suite 5, P.O. Box 535.
Telephone: 301-524-6411.
Fax: 301-524-9479.

COUNSEL

G. C. A. Anderson (1898-1985)
Ward B. Coe, Jr.
Frank J. Vecella
John F. King

MEMBERS OF FIRM

Robert H. Bouse, Jr.
E. Dale Adkins, III
James A. Rothschild
M. Bradley Hallwig
J. Michael Sloneker
G. Macy Nelson
E. Philip Franke, III
T. Michael Preston
Philip C. Jacobson
Lynn B. Malone
Gregory L. Van Geison

ASSOCIATES

Barbara McC. Stanley
Matthew T. Angotti
Hugh Cropper, IV (Resident, Ocean City Office)
Jill R. Leiner
James S. Aist
Kimberly E. Rice
Russell Sherlock Woodward
Jacqueline S. Russell

Representative Clients: Hartford Accident & Indemnity Co.; The St. Paul Insurance Cos.; Medical Mutual Liability Society of Maryland; Chrysler Corp.; Provident Life and Accident Insurance Co.; Emerson Electric Co.; Pennsylvania Hospital Ins. Co.; Maryland Association of Boards of Education Group Insurance Pool; Pittsburg Corning Corp.; Sierra Club.

For full biographical listings, see the Martindale-Hubbell Law Directory

Gordon, Feinblatt, Rothman, Hoffberger & Hollander (AV)

The Garrett Building, 233 East Redwood Street, 21202
Telephone: 410-576-4000
Telex: 908041 BAL

MEMBERS OF FIRM

Donald N. Rothman
Lewis A. Kann
Edward E. Obstler
Sander L. Wise
Zelig Robinson
David H. Fishman (Chairman)
Allan J. Malester
Lawrence S. Greenwald
Lester D. Bailey
Herbert Goldman
Robert E. Sharkey
Alan Richard Sachs

(See Next Column)

GORDON, FEINBLATT, ROTHMAN, HOFFBERGER & HOLLANDER, *Baltimore—Continued*

MEMBERS OF FIRM (Continued)

Thomas J. Doud, Jr.
Lawrence D. Coppel (Chairman)
Nancy E. Paige
Marc P. Blum
Barry F. Rosen (Chairman)
Sheila K. Sachs
Timothy D. A. Chriss
Robert C. Kellner (Chairman)
George K. Reynolds, III
Robert W. Katz
Abba David Poliakoff
Jerrold A. Thrope (Chairman)
J. Ronald Shiff
Neil J. Schechter
Elliott Cowan
Jay A. Shulman
Lynn B. Sassin
Matthew P. Mellin
Henry E. Schwartz
Thomas X. Glancy, Jr.
Hillel Tendler
Michael C. Powell
Bradford W. Warbasse
Barbara Holtz Levine
Michael J. Jack
John Martin Klein II

OF COUNSEL

David P. Gordon
Eugene M. Feinblatt
LeRoy E. Hoffberger
Evan Alevizatos Chriss
Loring E. Hawes

ASSOCIATES

Claire A. Smearman
Mary Beth Beattie
Ned T. Himmelrich
Sharon D. Credit
Susan A. Nachman
Caroline G. Ellis
Seth M. Rotenberg
Karen M. Crabtree
David W. Lease
Edward N. Kane, Jr.
John R. Severino
Catherine A. Bledsoe
Nancy M. Juda
Gregory S. Reynolds
Cheryl F. Kitt
Richard D. Stevens
Jonathan J. Biedron
Charles A. Borek
Rebecca L. Dietz
Sigmund R. Kallins

For full biographical listings, see the Martindale-Hubbell Law Directory

HYLTON & GONZALES (AV)

Suite 418 Equitable Building, 10 North Calvert Street, 21202
Telephone: 410-547-0900
Telecopier: 410-625-1560

MEMBERS OF FIRM

William A. Hylton, Jr.
Louise Michaux Gonzales

ASSOCIATES

Robin Belville Chapman

For full biographical listings, see the Martindale-Hubbell Law Directory

KRAMON & GRAHAM, P.A. (AV)

Commerce Place, One South Street, Suite 2600, 21202-3201
Telephone: 410-752-6030
Facsimile: 410-539-1269
Bel Air, Maryland Office: The Emmorton Professional Building. 2107 Laurel Bush Road.
Telephones: 410-515-0040; 410-569-0299.
Facsimile: 410-569-0298.

Andrew Jay Graham
James M. Kramon
Lee H. Ogburn
Jeffrey H. Scherr
Nancy E. Gregor
James P. Ulwick
Philip M. Andrews
Gertrude C. Bartel
Marilyn Hope Fisher
Max H. Lauten
Kathleen A. Birrane
Kevin F. Arthur
Aron U. Raskas
Perry F. Sekus
Geoffrey H. Genth
Regina M. Dufresne
Ian Gallacher

Representative Clients: Allstate Insurance Co.; Georgia-Pacific Corp.; Glass Mental Health Centers, Inc.; INAPRO; Sacred Heart Hospital; Toll Brothers, Inc.; United States Fidelity & Guaranty Company.

For full biographical listings, see the Martindale-Hubbell Law Directory

MILES & STOCKBRIDGE, A PROFESSIONAL CORPORATION (AV)

10 Light Street, 21202-1487
Telephone: 410-727-6464
Telecopier: 385-3700
Towson, Maryland Office: 600 Washington Avenue, Suite 300.
Telephone: 410-821-6565.
Telecopier: 823-8123.
Easton, Maryland Office: 101 Bay Street.
Telephone: 410-822-5280.
Telecopier: 822-5450.
Cambridge, Maryland Office: 300 Academy Street.
Telephone: 410-228-4545.
Telecopier: 228-5652.
Rockville, Maryland Office: 22 West Jefferson Street.
Telephone: 301-762-1600.
Telecopier: 762-0363.
Frederick, Maryland Office: 30 West Patrick Street.
Telephone: 301-662-5155.
Telecopier: 662-3647.

(See Next Column)

Washington, D.C. Office: 1450 G. Street, N.W., Suite 445.
Telephone: 202-737-9600.
Telecopier: 737-0097.
Fairfax, Virginia Office: Fair Oaks Plaza, 11350 Random Hills Road.
Telephone: 703-273-2440.
Telecopier: 273-4446.

Clarence W. Miles (1897-1977)
Enos S. Stockbridge (1888-1963)
Lowell R. Bowen
James P. Garland
Theodore W. Hirsh
Richard M. Hall
James R. Eyler
William T. Define
Timothy R. Casgar
James P. Gillece, Jr.
James C. Doub
Robert L. Doory, Jr.
Richard D. Bennett
Charles T. Bowyer
Frederick W. Runge, Jr.
Edward J. Adkins
John P. Sweeney
Samuel H. Clark, Jr.
Richard E. Levine
Harold Altscher
John A. Stalfort
Katherine L. Bishop
Patrick K. Arey
Anthony W. Kraus
Mark D. Gately
Irving E. Walker
Charles B. Schelberg
Kathleen M. Donahue
Timothy L. Mullin, Jr.
J. W. Thompson Webb
Steven D. Frenkil
Kathleen Pontone
Stephen M. Silvestri
Jefferson V. Wright
Timothy K. Hogan
Jeffrey H. Seibert
Shaun F. Carrick
David Seidl
Cynthia Collins Allner
John B. Frisch
John R. Rutledge
Kristine A. Crosswhite
William S. Liebman
Glenn C. Campbell
Jerome T. Miraglia
Thomas J. St. Ville
Clement D. Erhardt, III
Jeffrey A. Markowitz
Douglas M. Topolski
Douglas B. Pfeiffer
Marian C. Hwang
Daniel R. Lanier
Mark S. Demilio

OF COUNSEL

John S. Hebb, III

COUNSEL

Julien A. Hecht
Carolyn Jacobs

ASSOCIATE COUNSEL

Susan L. Spence
Lydia Belknap Duff
Donald S. Meringer

Thomas D. Renda
Theodore A. Shields
Mauricio E. Barreiro
Robert S. Brennen
John R. Devine
Gary B. Eidelman
Edgar C. Snow, Jr.
J. Mitchell Kearney
Craig A. Enck
Linda V. Donhauser
Kathleen DeSales Gast Smith
Marc E. Shach
Michael A. Brown
Deborah Lee Zimic
Susan Chapman Durbin
Matthew S. Sturtz
Steven F. Barley
Gregory L. Lockwood
Henry J. Suelau
Gerard D. St. Ours
Lisa Petti Ellis
Charles R. Schaller, Jr.
James H. Fields
John J. Leidig
J. Mark Coulson
David A. Gibbons
George A. Kohutiak
John E. McCann, Jr.
John R. Mentzer, III
Ann M. Sheridan
Barron L. Stroud, Jr.
Donna Preston
Eric M. Davis
Nicole M. Maddrey
Margaret A. Jacobsen
Virginia A. Stuelpnagel
Stephen E. Whitted (Not admitted in MD)
Lisa J. Kahn
Stephen J. Cullen
E. Hutchinson Robbins, Jr.
William D. Hugo
William Taylor, IV
Renee Nacrelli
Joseph W. Havermill
Andrea R. Macintosh

STAFF ATTORNEYS

Francina Critzman
Paige Lescure

Representative Clients: Maryland National Bank; Lloyd's of London; The Black & Decker Corp.; Aetna Life & Casualty Co.; Martin Marietta Corp.; Employers Mutual Casualty Co.; Transcontinental Gas Pipeline Corp.; Westinghouse Electric Corp.; Crum & Forster Group; NationsBank Corporation.

For full biographical listings, see the Martindale-Hubbell Law Directory

NILES, BARTON & WILMER (AV)

1400 Legg Mason Tower, 111 South Calvert Street, 21202-6185
Telephone: 410-783-6300
Cable Address: "Nilwo"
Telecopier: 410-783-6363

MEMBERS OF FIRM

A. Adgate Duer
John Gill Wharton
Forrest F. Bramble, Jr.
Patrick J. B. Donnelly
Edgar H. Gans
Paul B. Lang
Larry J. Albert
V. Timothy Bambrick
Robert F. Scholz
Robert P. O'Brien
John L. Wood
Paul W. Grimm
Steven E. Leder
C. Laurence Jenkins, Jr.
Matthew L. Kimball
R. Wayne Pierce
Carl F. Ameringer
David D. Gilliss

(See Next Column)

NILES, BARTON & WILMER—*Continued*

OF COUNSEL

Carlyle Barton, Jr.

ASSOCIATES

Susan D. Baker
April U. Hogsten
John C. Wetzel
Timothy T. Smith
Susan B. Austin
George E. Reede, Jr
Gina M. Harasti
Mary Alice McNamara
Paul McDermott Finamore
Jeffrey A. Wothers
Andrew L. Jiranek
Craig D. Roswell
Tracy A. Mays

For full biographical listings, see the Martindale-Hubbell Law Directory

PHILLIPS P. O'SHAUGHNESSY, P.A. (AV)

22 East Fayette Street, 7th Floor, 21202-1706
Telephone: 410-685-0300
FAX: 410-659-6945

Phillips P. O'Shaughnessy

For full biographical listings, see the Martindale-Hubbell Law Directory

PIERSON, PIERSON & NOLAN (AV)

Suite 1600 Redwood Tower, 217 East Redwood Street, 21202
Telephone: 410-727-7733
FAX: 410-625-0253

MEMBERS OF FIRM

Leon H. A. Pierson (1901-1981)
Edward Pierson (1906-1990)
W. Michel Pierson
James J. Nolan, Jr.
Robert L. Pierson

OF COUNSEL

David S. Sykes

For full biographical listings, see the Martindale-Hubbell Law Directory

PIPER & MARBURY (AV)

Charles Center South, 36 South Charles Street, 21201-3010
Telephone: 410-539-2530
FAX: 410-539-0489
Washington, D.C. Office: 1200 Nineteenth Street, N.W., 20036-2430.
Telephone: 202-861-3900.
FAX: 202-223-2085.
Easton, Maryland Office: 117 Bay Street, 21601-2703.
Telephone: 410-820-4460.
FAX: 410-820-4463.
Garrison, New York Office: Garrison Landing.
Telephone: 914-424-3711.
Fax: 914-424-3045.
New York, N.Y. Office: 31 West 52nd Street, 10019-6118.
Telephone: 212-261-2000.
FAX: 212-261-2001.
Philadelphia, Pennsylvania Office: Suite 1500, 2 Penn Center Plaza, 19102-1715.
Telephone: 215-656-3300.
FAX: 215-656-3301.
London, England Office: 14 Austin Friars, EC2N 2HE.
Telephone: 071-638-3833.
FAX: 071-638-1208.

MEMBERS OF FIRM

Andre W. Brewster
George L. Russell, Jr.
Nathan B. Feinstein (Resident, Washington, D.C. Office)
Charles T. Albert
Roger D. Redden
Shale D. Stiller
Charles C. Abeles (Resident, Washington, D.C. Office)
Leonard E. Cohen
Wilbert H. Sirota
Robert B. Barnhouse
L. P. Scriggins
Lewis A. Noonberg (Resident, Washington, D.C. Office)
Sheldon Krantz (Resident, Washington, D.C. Office)
Joseph G. Finnerty, Jr.
Donald E. Sharpe
Henry Robbins Lord
Toni K. Allen (Resident, Washington, D.C. Office)
Thomas H. Truitt (Resident, Washington, D.C. Office)
Richard K. White, Jr.
Stuart A. Smith (Resident, New York Office)
Robert E. Young
William R. Weissman (Resident, Washington, D.C. Office)
Donald P. McPherson, III
Edwin M. Martin, Jr. (Resident, Washington, D.C. Office)
Lawrence M. Katz
Philip L. Cohan (Resident, Washington, D.C. Office)
George A. Nilson
Broughton M. Earnest (Resident, Easton Office)
Steven K. Yablonski (Resident, Washington, D.C. Office)
John E. Kratz, Jr.
Francis X. Wright
James J. Winn, Jr.
Russell H. Gardner
Geoffrey R. W. Smith (Resident, Washington, D.C. Office)
J. Brian Molloy (Resident, Washington, D.C. Office)
Ronald L. Plesser (Resident, Washington, D.C. Office)
Charles J. Raubicheck (Resident, New York, N.Y. Office)
Steven D. Shattuck
Mark Pollak
Stanard T. Klinefelter
Michael Esher Yaggy
Jay I. Morstein
Jeffrey D. Herschman
Joseph H. Langhirt

(See Next Column)

MEMBERS OF FIRM (Continued)

Neil J. Dilloff
Edward C. Sledge
Mark J. Tauber (Resident, Washington, D.C. Office)
Anthony L. Young (Resident, Washington. D.C. Office)
Richard M. Kremen
E. Miles Prentice, III (Resident, New York, New York Office)
Randall B. Lowe (Resident, Washington, D.C. Office)
Virginia Knoop Adams
Francis B. Burch, Jr.
Deborah E. Jennings
George E. Rahn, Jr. (Resident, Philadelphia, Pennsylvania Office)
Francis X. Markey (Resident, Washington, D.C. Office)
Joseph A. Fanone (Resident, Washington, D.C. Office)
Earl S. Wellschlager
Richard C. Tilghman, Jr.
Jeffrey F. Liss (Resident, Washington, D.C. Office)
Ronald B. Sheff
Richard J. Hafets
Edward J. Levin
George P. Stamas
Stephen R. Mysliwiec (Resident, Washington, D.C. Office)
Daniel J. Carrigan (Resident, Washington, D.C. Office)
Alan C. Porter (Resident, Washington, D.C. Office)
I. Scott Bass
Alfred Ferrer III (Resident, New York, N.Y. Office)
William F. Kiniry, Jr. (Resident, Philadelphia, Pennsylvania Office)
Robert W. Smith, Jr.
Kenneth L. Thompson
Elizabeth Grieb
John P. Machen
Mark J. Friedman
William D. Blakely (Resident, Washington, D.C. Office)
Michael F. Brockmeyer
Stephen L. Owen
Joyce J. Gorman (Resident, Washington, D.C. Office)
Stewart K. Diana
Lee A. Sheller
John E. Griffith, Jr.
Jay Gary Finkelstein (Resident, Washington, D.C. Office)
C. Lamar Garren
Elizabeth A. McKennon
Sandra P. Gohn
Jonathan D. Smith
William L. Henn, Jr.
Henry D. Kahn
Paul A. Tiburzi
Joel A. Dewey
Robert J. Mathias
David S. Musgrave
Marianne Schmitt Hellauer
Mark Muedeking
Cynthia J. Morris (Resident, Washington, D.C. Office)
David H. Bamberger (Resident, Washington, D.C. Office)
David Clarke, Jr. (Resident, Washington, D.C. Office)
Paul D. Shelton
Mary F. Edgar (Resident, Washington, D.C. Office)
John B. Watkins V
Charles P. Scheeler
Christopher E. O'Brien (Not admitted in MD; Resident, New York Office)
James M. Brogan
Anthony H. Rickert (Resident, Washington, D.C. Office)
Susan J. Klein
Nancy Doerr O'Neil
Donna Hill Staton
Kurt J. Fischer
James A. Gede, Jr.
Wm. Roger Truitt
Douglas H. Green (Resident, Washington, D.C. Office)
Raymond G. Mullady, Jr.
Steven J. Mandell (Resident, Washington, D.C. Office)
Ronald P. Schiller (Resident, Philadelphia, Pennsylvania Office)
David N. Baumann (Resident, Washington, D.C. Office)
Emmett F. McGee, Jr.
Sheila Mosmiller Vidmar
Theodore D. Segal
Kristin H. R. Franceschi

OF COUNSEL

Robert M. Goldman
Robert B. Watts
Frank T. Gray
M. Peter Moser
Edward Owen Clarke, Jr.
Decatur H. Miller
William L. Reynolds
Robert N. McKay (Resident, New York, N.Y. Office)
Richard T. Kortright (Resident, New York, N.Y. Office)
Daniel R. Mackesey (Resident, Washington, D.C. Office)
Evelyn W. Pasquier
Peter H. McCallion (Resident, Garrison, New York Office)

SENIOR ATTORNEY

Richard C. Walters (Resident, Washington, D.C. Office)

ASSOCIATES

John P. White (Resident, Easton Office)
Barbara Ann Frouman (Not admitted in MD)
Cynthia S. Amling
Deborah Topper Garren
James P. Rathvon (Resident, Washington, D.C. Office)
Lynette M. Phillips
Deborah Singer Howard
H. Mark Stichel
Nora E. Garrote (Resident, Washington, D.C. Office)
Emilio W. Cividanes (Resident, Washington, D.C. Office)
Craig J. Hornig
Cyd Beth Wolf
Ray L. Earnest (Resident, Easton Office)
John J. Kuchno
Paul Stanley Novak
Michael C. Carter (Resident, Washington, D.C. Office)
James B. Reach (Resident, Washington, D.C. Office)
Stephen H. Kaufman
Stephen B. Lebau
Gina Monath Zawitoski
Michael S. Barranco
Christine M. Barilla
John F. Kaufman
Eric B. Miller
Elizabeth C. Kelley
Kathleen A. Ellis
Thomas P. Lloyd
Barbara C. Woods
Carolyn M. Bamberger (Resident, Washington, D.C. Office)
Len Matsunaga (Resident, New York, N.Y. Office)
Mitchell S. Marder (Resident, Washington, D.C. Office)
Mark A. Dewire
Stephen M. Sharkey
Jane A. Wilson

(See Next Column)

PIPER & MARBURY, *Baltimore—Continued*

ASSOCIATES (Continued)

Benjamin S. Boyd (Resident, Washington, D.C. Office)
Thomas E. D. Millspaugh
Jill Cantor Nord
Gretchen L. Lowe (Resident, Washington, D.C. Office)
Donna F. Triscoli
Thomas L. Totten
Glen K. Allen
Cristin Carnell Lambros
Diane M. Lank
Robert C. Douglas
Susan K. Datesman
Eric Paltell
Jay G. Cohen
Ann L. Lamdin
Joseph V. Gote (Resident, Washington, D.C. Office)
O. Daniel Ansa (Resident, Philadelphia, Pennsylvania Office)
John E. Benedict (Resident, Washington, D.C. Office)
Randall D. Sones
Theodore L. Charnley
Leonard L. Gordon (Resident, Washington, D.C. Office)
Brigit A. McCann
Anthony L. Meagher
Stephen A. Riddick
Mary E. Gately (Resident, Washington, D.C. Office)
David A. Franchina (Resident, Washington, D.C. Office)
James D. Mathias
Leila B. Boulton (Resident, Washington, D.C. Office)
Timothy P. Branigan (Resident, Washington, D.C. Office)
Diane Crosson McEnroe (Resident, New York, N.Y. Office)
Susan C. Stolzer (Resident, New York, N.Y. Office)
JoAnn E. Levin
Jeffrey A. Sharpe
Simone Brych (Resident, London, England Office)
Susan S. Sands
Timothy U. Sharpe
Norman L. Rave, Jr. (Resident, Washington, D.C. Office)
Katrina C. Kamantauskas-Holder
Marta D. Harting
Pamela McDade Johnson
James D. Gette (Resident, Philadelphia, Pennsylvania Office)
Tracey Gann Turner
Carville B. Collins
Louise S. Hertz
Joseph Kernen (Resident, Philadelphia, Pennsylvania Office)
Deborah P. Nason (Resident, Philadelphia, Pennsylvania Office)
John A. Washington, Jr. (Resident, Washington, DC Office)
Nancy A. Spangler (Resident, Washington, D.C. Office)
Robert G. Blue
Charles Kevin Kobbe
Richard D. Moore
J. Benjamin Unkle, Jr.
Joseph J. Bellinger, Jr.
Yolanda Stefanou Faerber
William Single, IV
Anne-Therese Bechamps
Devethia Nichols-Thompson
Pamela A. Long
Martin E. Wolf
Kimberly E. Wolod (Resident, Washington, D.C. Office)
Sarah Jean Curtis
John Caleb Dougherty
Marianne Mancino Thiede (Resident, Washington, D.C. Office)
Susannah M. Bennett
Stephanie D. Pullen Brown
Jordan I. Bailowitz
Eric L. Keller (Resident, Washington, D.C. Office)
Judith Altenberg (Resident, Washington, D.C. Office)
Barry P. McDonald (Resident, Washington, D.C. Office)
Edward F. Maluf (Resident, New York, N.Y. Office)
John J. Giblin, Jr.
Timothy M. Cramer (Resident, Washington, D.C. Office)
Lawrence R. Seidman
Caryn A. Jackson
Kathleen C. Jones
Paul J. Day
Kathy A. Murphy
Carla G. Pennington-Cross (Resident, Washington, D.C. Office)
Sheryl N. Stephenson
Karen M. Valentine
Denise Giraldez (Resident, Washington, D.C. Office)
Jennifer A. White (Resident, Washington, D.C. Office)
Joan E. Quigley
Scott V. Kamins
Wayne E. Tumlin (Resident, Washington, D.C. Office)
Chase J. Sanders
Mark J. O'Connor (Resident, Washington, D.C. Office)
Wm. David Chalk
Brian D. Henderson (Resident, Washington, D.C. Office)
LaRue E. Cook
Edith F. Webster
F. Joseph Gormley
Manuel E. Maisog
Lydia Kay Griggsby
Richard J. Marks
David H. Schnabel
Keara M. O'Donnell (Resident, Washington, D.C. Office)
Guy E. Flynn
Jack William Merritt
W. Brachshaw Sitton (Not admitted in MD)

For full biographical listings, see the Martindale-Hubbell Law Directory

---

SEMMES, BOWEN & SEMMES (AV)

A Partnership of Professional Corporations
250 West Pratt Street, 21201
Telephone: 410-539-5040
Facsimile: 410-539-5223
Washington D.C. Office: Suite 900, 1025 Connecticut Avenue, N.W.
Telephone: 202-822-8250.
Wilmington, Delaware Office: 1220 North Market Street.
Telephone: 302-427-2227.
Towson, Maryland Office: Eleventh Floor, 401 Washington Avenue.
Telephone: 410-296-4400.
Hagerstown, Maryland Office: 339 E. Antietam Street, Suite 5.
Telephone: 301-739-4558.

(See Next Column)

MEMBERS OF FIRM

John E. Semmes (1851-1925)
Jesse N. Bowen (1879-1938)
John E. Semmes, Jr. (1881-1967)
Franklin Goldstein (P.C.)
Gilbert B. Lessenco (P.C.) (Resident, Washington, D.C. Office)
Thomas J. S. Waxter, Jr. (P.C.)
Cleaveland D. Miller (P.C.)
David E. Belcher (P.C.)
Robert P. Mittelman (P.C.)
David C. Daneker (P.C.)
Thomas W. W. Haines (P.C.)
Alan N. Gamse (P.C.)
Geoffrey S. Mitchell (P.C.)
Charles E. Iliff, Jr. (P.C.)
Francis J. Gorman (P.C.)
J. Snowden Stanley, Jr., (P.C.)
Robert E. Scott, Jr., (P.C.)
Irving P. Cohen (P.C.) (Resident, Washington, D.C. Office)
Charles R. Moran (P.C.)
Richard T. Sampson (P.C.)
Mark J. Daneker (P.C.)
Rudolph L. Rose (P.C.)
Robert A. McIntire (P.C.)
Thomas J. Manning, Jr. (P.C.)
Lawrence R. Liebesman (P.C.)
Kevin M. O'Connell (P.C.)
David McI. Williams (P.C.)
James Wm. Morrison (P.C.) (Resident, Washington, D.C. Office)
Herman B. Rosenthal (P.C.)
Donald L. Bradfield (P.C.)
Barry A. Friedman (P.C.) (Resident, Washington, D.C. Office)
Kathleen Howard Meredith (P.C.)
George S. Lawler (P.C.)
Michael W. Prokopik (P.C.)
William J. Jackson (P.C.)
Daniel J. Moore (P.C.) (Resident, Towson, Maryland Office)
Timmy F. Ruppersberger (P.C.)
Wendy Widmann (P.C.)
JoAnne Zawitoski (P.C.)
Aline C. Ryan (P.C.)
Thomas G. Hagerty (P.C.) (Resident, Washington, D.C. Office)
Richard W. Scheiner (P.C.)
Pamela A. Bresnahan (P.C.) (Resident, Washington, D.C. Office)
Brooke Schumm III (P.C.)
Maxine Adler (P.C.)
Deborah H. Diehl (P.C.)
Donna L. Jacobs (P.C.)
Jeffrey P. McCormack (P.C.)
Perry E. Darby (P.C.)
Scott D. Goetsch (P.C.) (Resident, Towson, Maryland Office)
James A. Johnson (P.C.)
Patti Gilman West (P.C.)
Walter R. Calvert (P.C.)
Robert T. Franklin (P.C.)
Stan M. Haynes (P.C.)
Michael F. Bonkowski (P.C.) (Resident, Wilmington, Delaware Office)
Robert W. Hesselbacher, Jr. (P.C.) (Resident, Washington, D.C. Office)
Frank S. Jones, Jr. (P.C.)
Patrick M. Shelley (P.C.)
David J. Shaffer (P.C.) (Resident, Washington, D.C. Office)
Gary L. Bohlke (P.C.) (Not admitted in MD)
William H. Kable (P.C.)
Kenneth L. Samuelson (P.C.) (Resident, Washington, D.C. Office)
Joanne M. Dicus (P.C.)
Douglas M. Fox (P.C.)
David B. Goldstein (P.C.)
Kristine Kappeler Howanski (P.C.)
James G. Prince (P.C.)

OF COUNSEL

Thomas E. Cinnamond
David R. Owen
James D. Peacock

COUNSEL

Cory M. Amron (Resident, Washington, D.C. Office; See Washington, D.C.)
James Bremer (Resident, Washington, D.C. Office)
William R. Dorsey, III
Kenneth S. Kamlet (Not admitted in MD)
Larry S. Snowhite (Not admitted in MD; Resident, Washington, D.C. Office)
William C. Trimble, Jr.

SENIOR ASSOCIATES

Jeffrey P. Buhrman
Sandra Howard Darby
Wendell Finner
Denise A. Greig
E. Bernard Justis
Heather Holt Kraus
Stephen S. McCloskey
Dana S. J. Nangle
Robert E. Rockwell (Resident, Hagerstown, Maryland Office)
Brent C. Shaffer
David Arthur Skomba
Ferrier Stillman
Margaret Fonshell Ward

Brian A. Balenson
Elizabeth W. Benet
Curtis A. Boykin
Stephan Y. Brennan
Randolph M. Collins
Duane J. Desiderio (Not admitted in MD)
Joseph M. English, IV
Willis Gunther Ferlise
Stacy E. Finn
Richard A. Froehlinger, III
Thomas A. Hauser
Frederick M. Hopkins
Bethany Jackson
Maija B. Jackson
Debra I. Lubman
Kent Koji Matsumoto
Thomas V. McCarron
Severn E.S. Miller
S. Keith Moulsdale
Christopher W. Poverman
Jennifer S. Pressman
Carolyn E. Ryan
Roberta C. Sinopole
Gay Ann Spahn
Stephen M. Springer
Patricia A. Sumner
J. Charles Szczesny
Ronald J. Travers
Glen H. Tschirgi
Dominick M. Valencia, Jr.
David J. Wildberger
Jerusa Carl Wilson, Jr. (Resident, Washington, D.C. Office)
Anthony Jackson Zaccagnini

Representative Clients: Aetna Life & Casualty Co.; Associated Aviation Underwriters; Bethlehem Steel Corp.; E.I. du Pont de Nemours & Co.; General Electric Co.; Liberty Mutual Insurance Co.; MBNA, Inc.; Merrill, Lynch, Pierce, Fenner & Smith, Inc.; Metropolitan Life Insurance Co.; Provident Bank of Maryland.

For full biographical listings, see the Martindale-Hubbell Law Directory

SMITH, SOMERVILLE & CASE (AV)

100 Light Street, 21202
Telephone: 410-727-1164
Panafax Direct Dial: 410-385-8060
Washington, D.C. Office: 1100 Connecticut Avenue, N.W., Suite 410, 20036.
Telephone: 202-833-1164.
Fax: 202-833-8125.

MEMBERS OF FIRM

Clater W. Smith (1901-1980)
William B. Somerville (1916-1983)
Richard W. Case (1918-1984)
Robert E. Powell
Robert J. Carson
Theodore B. Cornblatt
Douglas G. Worrall
Barbara Ann Spicer
Laurence Schor (Resident at Washington, D.C. Office)
Barry Bach
Howard G. Goldberg
Gary F. Florence
Michael James Kelly
Ronald G. Dawson
S. Woods Bennett
Susan L. Schor (Resident at Washington, D.C. Office)
Brett L. Antonides (Resident at Washington, D.C. Office)
John R. Penhallegon
John J. Boyd, Jr.
James E. Baker, Jr.
Jeffrey J. Plum
Patrick M. Pike
Leslie J. Polt
Harry E. Silverwood, Jr.
Michael J. Baxter
Ralph L. Arnsdorf
Patricia McHugh Lambert
Gordon R. Calvert
Randall M. Lutz
Bennett Gilbert Gaines
Deborah K. Besche
Catherine A. Potthast
Cheryl O'Donnell Guth
Brian S. Jablon
Craig F. Ballew
Allen F. Loucks
Maryanne Dubbs
Patrick A. Roberson
Daryl J. Sidle
A. Michael Sidle
Lawrence S. Conn
David J. McManus, Jr.

OF COUNSEL

M. King Hill, Jr.
Glenn C. Parker
David Bielawski

ASSOCIATES

Sharon K. Engelhard
Jeffrey Y. Laynor
John M. Seeberger
Gary R. Jones
Zvi Guttman
Gary T. Lathrop
Steven E. Schenker
Roderick R. Barnes
Michael E. Cross
David B. Applefeld
Stanley Turk
Keri F. Kretschmann
James E. Myers
Jonathan E. Goldberg
Steven J. Meltzer
Thomas J. S. Waxter, III
James A. Frederick
Deborah Dawes Tayman
Honora Wohlgemuth Sutor
Stephen S. Burgoon
Jessica S. Schaffer
Cynthia D. Penny-Ardinger

For full biographical listings, see the Martindale-Hubbell Law Directory

THIEBLOT, RYAN, MARTIN & FERGUSON, P.A. (AV)

4th Floor, The World Trade Center, 21202-3091
Telephone: 410-837-1140
Washington, D.C. Line: 202-628-8223
Fax: 410-837-3282

Robert J. Thieblot
Anthony W. Ryan
J. Edward Martin, Jr.
Robert L. Ferguson, Jr.
Bruce R. Miller
Robert D. Harwick, Jr.
Thomas J. Schetelich
Christopher J. Heffernan

M. Brooke Murdock
Anne M. Hrehorovich
Donna Marie Raffaele
Michael N. Russo, Jr.
Jodi K. Ebersole
Hamilton Fisk Tyler
Peter Joseph Basile

Representative Clients: Ford Motor Credit Co.; USF & G Co.; The American Road Insurance Co.; Fidelity Engineering Corp.; The North Charles Street Design Organization; Record Collections, Inc.; Toyota Motor Credit Co.

For full biographical listings, see the Martindale-Hubbell Law Directory

TYDINGS & ROSENBERG (AV)

100 East Pratt Street, 21202
Telephone: 410-752-9700
FAX: 410-727-5460
Cable Address: "Tyla"

MEMBERS OF FIRM

Millard E. Tydings (1890-1961)
Morris Rosenberg (1905-1992)
Paul Walter
J. Hardin Marion
Marc J. Lipchin
Edward J. Lopata
J. Michael McWilliams
A. Lee Lundy, Jr.
William C. Sammons
Thomas M. Wilson, III
Thomas C. Lederman
John B. Isbister
Alan M. Grochal
Claude Edward Hitchcock
Paul W. Grace
Lawrence L. Hooper, Jr.
Paul D. Trinkoff
Robert S. Downs

(See Next Column)

MEMBERS OF FIRM (Continued)

Robert A. Gordon
Harold M. Walter
William Willis Carrier, III
Diane V. D'Aiutolo
Gerry H. Tostanoski

ASSOCIATES

Theresa Burian Shea
Mary Ann Fenner Medema
Joseph M. Bellew
Frederick C. Leiner
Anthony J. Breschi
Lawrence J. Quinn
Scott Patrick Burns
Kimberly Hale Carney
Mary Frances Ebersole
Timothy A. Hodge, Jr.
Scott A. Thomas
Melissa C. Giove
Lynn A. Kohen
Jeffrey K. Sands (Not admitted in MD)
David R. Finn
Stephanie G. Posner
Jon M. Laria
Jeffrey H. Cohen
Jennifer C. Holmes
Michael H. Tow

COUNSEL

David O. Whitman

Representative Clients: Chubb Group of Insurance Cos.; First National Bank of Maryland; IBM Corp.; Johnson & Johnson; Joseph E. Seagrams & Sons, Inc.; Kaiser Foundation Health Plan of the Mid-Atlantic States, Inc.; Kemper Insurance Co.; Mercedes-Benz of North America, Inc.; Inc.; Texas Instruments, Inc.; W.R. Grace & Co.

For full biographical listings, see the Martindale-Hubbell Law Directory

VENABLE, BAETJER AND HOWARD (AV)

A Partnership including Professional Corporations
1800 Mercantile Bank & Trust Building, 2 Hopkins Plaza, 21201
Telephone: 410-244-7400
Washington, D.C. Office: Venable, Baetjer, Howard & Civiletti. Suite 1000, 1201 New York Avenue, N.W.
Telephone: 202-962-4800.
McLean, Virginia Office: Suite 400, 2010 Corporate Ridge.
Telephone: 703-760-1600.
Rockville, Maryland Office: Suite 500, One Church Street, P. O. Box 1906.
Telephone: 301-217-5600.
Towson, Maryland Office: 210 Allegheny Avenue, P. O. Box 5517.
Telephone: 410-494-6200.

MEMBERS OF FIRM

Richard M. Venable (1839-1910)
Edwin G. Baetjer (1868-1945)
Charles McH. Howard (1870-1942)
Jacques T. Schlenger (P.C.)
William J. McCarthy (P.C.)
Russell Ronald Reno, Jr. (P.C.)
Thomas P. Perkins, III (P.C.)
James A. Cole
Benjamin R. Civiletti (P.C.) (Also at Washington, D.C. and Towson, Maryland Offices)
John B. Howard (Resident, Towson, Maryland Office)
David D. Downes (Resident, Towson, Maryland Office)
Anthony M. Carey (Also at Washington, D.C. Office)
George Cochran Doub (P.C.)
John Henry Lewin, Jr. (P.C.)
Stanley Mazaroff (P.C.)
Lee M. Miller (P.C.)
Alan D. Yarbro (P.C.)
Neal D. Borden (Also at Washington, D.C. Office)
Robert A. Shelton
Thomas J. Kenney, Jr. (P.C.) (Also at Washington, D.C. Office)
Roger W. Titus (Resident, Rockville, Maryland Office)
Daniel O'C. Tracy, Jr. (Also at Rockville, Maryland Office)
Jan K. Guben (Also at Washington, D. C Office)
Ian D. Volner (Not admitted in MD; Resident, Washington, D.C. Office)
N. Peter Lareau (P.C.)
Thomas J. Madden (Not admitted in MD; Resident, Washington, D.C. Office)
William L. Walsh, Jr. (P.C.) (Not admitted in MD; Resident, McLean, Virginia Office)
Ronald R. Glancz (Not admitted in MD; Resident, Washington, D.C. Office)
David J. Levenson (Not admitted in MD; Resident, Washington, D.C. Office)
Robert P. Bedell (Not admitted in MD; Resident, Washington, D.C. Office)
Dennis J. Whittlesey (Not admitted in MD; Resident, Washington, D.C. Office)
Robert G. Smith (P.C.)
Douglas D. Connah, Jr. (P.C.) (Also at Washington, D.C. Office)
James D. Wright (P.C.)
Joe A. Shull (Resident, Washington, D.C. Office)
David T. Stitt (Not admitted in MD; Resident, McLean, Virginia Office)
Robert E. Madden (Not admitted in MD; also at Washington, D.C. and McLean, Virginia Offices)
Kenneth C. Bass, III (Not admitted in MD; Also at Washington, D.C. and McLean, Virginia Offices)
John H. Zink, III (Resident, Towson, Maryland Office)
Lars E. Anderson (Not admitted in MD; Resident, McLean, Virginia Office)
John G. Milliken (Not admitted in MD; Also at Washington, D.C. and McLean, Virginia Offices)
Bruce E. Titus (Resident, McLean, Virginia Office)
Joel Z. Silver (Not admitted in MD; Resident, Washington, D.C. Office)
Paul F. Strain (P.C.)
Alexander I. Lewis, III (P.C.) (Also at Towson, Maryland Office)
Max Stul Oppenheimer (P.C.) (Also at Washington, D.C. and Towson, Maryland Offices)

(See Next Column)

VENABLE, BAETJER AND HOWARD, *Baltimore—Continued*

MEMBERS OF FIRM (Continued)

William D. Dolan, III (P.C.) (Not admitted in MD; Resident, McLean, Virginia Office)
Paul T. Glasgow (Resident, Rockville, Maryland Office)
Joseph C. Wich, Jr. (Resident, Towson, Maryland Office)
Joseph G. Block (Not admitted in MD; Resident, Washington, D.C. Office)
Sondra Harans Block (Resident, Rockville, Maryland Office)
Jeffrey J. Radowich
Edward F. Glynn, Jr. (Not admitted in MD; Resident, Washington, D.C. Office)
Craig E. Smith
Robert G. Ames (Also at Washington, D.C. Office)
Thomas B. Hudson (Also at Washington, D.C. Office)
Michael Schatzow (Also at Washington, D.C. and Towson, Maryland Offices)
John F. Cooney (Not admitted in MD; Resident, Washington, D.C. Office)
Bryson L. Cook (P.C.) (Also at Washington, D.C. Office)
Nell B. Strachan
Barbara E. Schlaff
David G. Lane (Resident, McLean, Virginia Office)
N. Frank Wiggins (Resident, Washington, D.C. Office)
L. Paige Marvel
Susan K. Gauvey (Also at Towson, Maryland Office)
Richard L. Wasserman (P.C.)
James K. Archibald (Also at Washington, D.C. and Towson, Maryland Offices)
G. Stewart Webb, Jr.
George W. Johnston (P.C.)
Judson W. Starr (Not admitted in MD; Also at Washington, D.C. and Towson, Maryland Offices)
Constance H. Baker
H. Russell Frisby, Jr.
James R. Myers (Not admitted in MD; Resident, Washington, D.C. Office)
Jeffrey D. Knowles (Not admitted in MD; Resident, Washington, D.C. Office)
F. Dudley Staples, Jr. (Also at Towson, Maryland Office)
Edward L. Wender (P.C.)
David M. Fleishman
Jana Howard Carey (P.C.)
Jeffrey A. Dunn (also at Washington, D.C. Office)
George F. Pappas (Also at Washington, D.C. Office)
Mitchell Kolkin
William D. Coston (Not admitted in MD; Resident, Washington, D.C. Office)
Peter P. Parvis
James L. Shea (Also at Washington, D.C. Office)
Jeffrey P. Ayres (P.C.)
Brigid E. Kenney
Nathaniel E. Jones, Jr.
Ellen F. Dyke (Not admitted in MD; Resident, McLean, Virginia Office)
Elizabeth C. Honeywell
Maurice Baskin (Resident, Washington, D.C. Office)
John J. Pavlick, Jr. (Not admitted in MD; Resident, Washington, D. C. Office)
Amy Berman Jackson (Not admitted in MD; Resident, Washington, D.C. Office)
William D. Quarles (Also at Washington, D.C. and Towson, Maryland Offices)
C. Carey Deeley, Jr. (Also at Towson, Maryland Office)
Kathleen Gallogly Cox (Resident, Towson, Maryland Office)
Christopher R. Mellott
David Eugene Rice
W. Robert Zinkham
Cynthia M. Hahn (Resident, Towson, Maryland Office)
Jeffrey L. Ihnen (Not admitted in MD; Resident, Washington, D. C. Office)
M. King Hill, III (Resident, Towson, Maryland Office)
James A. Dunbar (Also at Washington, D.C. Office)
Elizabeth R. Hughes
Ronald W. Taylor
Robert L. Waldman
Robert A. Cook
Mary E. Pivec (Also at Washington, D.C. Office)
Thomas J. Kelly, Jr. (Not admitted in MD; Resident, Washington, D. C. Office)
John A. Roberts (Also at Rockville, Maryland Office)
Robert A. Hoffman (Resident, Towson, Maryland Office)
Robert J. Bolger, Jr. (Also at Washington, D.C. Office)
David J. Heubeck
J. Michael Brennan (Resident, Towson, Maryland Office)
Joel J. Goldberg (Not admitted in MD; Washington, D.C. and McLean, Virginia Offices)
James F. Worrall (Not admitted in MD; Resident, Washington, D.C. Office)
Bruce H. Jurist (Also at Washington, D.C. Office)
Linda L. Lord (Not admitted in MD; Resident, Washington, D.C. Office)
John M. Gurley (Not admitted in MD; Resident, Washington, D.C. Office)
Paul A. Serini (Also at Washington, D.C. Office)
Herbert G. Smith, II (Not admitted in MD; Resident, McLean, Virginia Office)
Patrick J. Stewart (Also at Washington, D.C. Office)
Ariel Vannier
Gary M. Hnath (Resident, Washington, D.C. Office)
Kevin L. Shepherd
James E. Cumbie
Michael H. Davis (Resident, Towson, Maryland Office)
Darrell R. VanDeusen

OF COUNSEL

A. Samuel Cook (P.C.) (Resident, Towson, Maryland Office)
Arthur W. Machen, Jr. (P.C.)
Robert M. Thomas (P.C.)
Frank Horton (Not admitted in MD; Resident, Washington, D.C. Office)
Robert R. Bair (P.C.)
Herbert R. O'Conor, Jr. (Resident, Towson, Maryland Office)
Richard H. Mays (Not admitted in MD; Mclean, Virginia and Washington, D.C.)
Robert A. Beizer (Resident, Washington, D.C. Office)
Emried D. Cole, Jr.

(See Next Column)

OF COUNSEL (Continued)

Judith A. Armold
Thomas J. Cooper (Not admitted in MD; Resident, Washington, D. C. Office)
Jerome S. Gabig, Jr. (Not admitted in MD; Resident, Washington, D.C. Office)
Joyce K. Becker
Geoffrey R. Garinther (Also at Washington, D.C. Office)
Mary T. Flynn (Not admitted in MD; Resident, McLean, Virginia Office)
Fred W. Hathaway (Not admitted in MD; Resident, Washington, D.C. Office)

ASSOCIATES

Michael J. Baader
Scharon L. Ball
Paul D. Barker, Jr.
Elizabeth Marzo Borinsky
Gregory S. Braker (Resident, Washington, D.C. Office)
Julian Sylvester Brown (Not admitted in MD; Resident, McLean, Virginia Office)
Courtney G. Capute
Daniel William China
Wallace E. Christner (Not admitted in MD)
Patrick L. Clancy (Resident, Rockville, Maryland Office)
Christine J. Collins
Kevin B. Collins
Michael W. Conron
Patricia Gillis Cousins (Resident, Rockville, Maryland Office)
Carla Draluck Craft (Resident, Washington, D.C. Office)
Royal W. Craig (Resident, Washington, D.C. Office)
Donald P. Creston (Not admitted in MD; Resident, Washington, D.C. Office)
Gregory A. Cross
Marina Lolley Dame (Resident, Towson, Maryland Office)
David S. Darland (Not admitted in MD; Resident, Washington, D.C. Office)
J. Van L. Dorsey (Resident, Towson, Maryland Office)
Wm. Craig Dubishar (Not admitted in MD; Resident, McLean, Virginia Office)
John P. Edgar
Fred Joseph Federici, III (Resident, Washington, D.C. Office)
Ellen Berkow Feldman
Ellen Finlay (Not admitted in MD)
Newton B. Fowler, III
Rochelle Block Fowler
Francis X. Gallagher, Jr. (Not admitted in MD)
Robert H. Geis, Jr.
David W. Goewey (Not admitted in MD; Resident, Washington, D.C. Office)
Jeffrey K. Gonya
D. Brent Gunsalus (Not admitted in MD; Resident, Washington, D.C. Office)
E. Anne Hamel
Lisa H. Rice Hayes
James W. Hedlund (Not admitted in MD; Resident, Washington, D.C. Office)
Andrew R. Herrup (Resident, Washington, D.C. Office)
Cynthia A. Hickey
David R. Hodnett (Not admitted in MD; Resident, McLean, Virginia Office)
J. Scott Hommer, III (Not admitted in MD; Resident, McLean, Virginia Office)
Todd J. Horn
Maria F. Howell
Matthew L. Iwicki
Mary-Dulany James (Resident, Towson, Maryland Office)
Paula Titus Laboy (Resident, Rockville, Maryland Office)
Gregory L. Laubach (Resident, Rockville, Maryland Office)
Fernand A. Lavallee (Not admitted in MD; Resident, Washington, D. C. Office)
Thomas M. Lingan
Jon M. Lippard (Not admitted in MD; Resident, McLean, Virginia Office)
Wingrove S. Lynton
Edward Brendan Magrab (Resident, Washington, D.C. Office)
Patricia A. Malone (Resident, Towson, Maryland Office)
Valerie K. Mann (Not admitted in MD; Resident, Washington, D.C. Office)
Vicki Margolis
Laura K. McAfee
Christine M. McAnney (Not admitted in MD; Resident, McLean, Virginia Office)
John A. McCauley
Timothy J. McEvoy
Lindsay Beardsworth Meyer (Not admitted in MD; Resident, Washington, D.C. Office)
Mitchell Y. Mirviss
Samuel T. Morison (Not admitted in MD; Resident, Washington, D.C. Office)
Michael J. Muller
Traci H. Mundy (Not admitted in MD; Resident, Washington, D.C. Office)
Vadim A. Mzhen
Valerie Floyd Portner
John T. Prisbe
Lawrence C. Renbaum
Michael W. Robinson (Not admitted in MD; Resident, McLean, Virginia Office)
Dino S. Sangiamo
John Peter Sarbanes
Myriam Judith Schmell
Joseph C. Schmelter
Karen A. Schultz (Not admitted in MD; Resident, Washington, D.C. Office)
Catherine L. Schuster
Robert A. Schwinger
Davis V. R. Sherman
Nathan E. Siegel
Todd K. Snyder
Melissa Landau Steinman (Resident, Washington, D.C. Office)
Neal H. Strum
Linda Marotta Thomas
Brian R. Trumbauer
J. Preston Turner
Terri L. Turner
Barbara L. Waite (Not admitted in MD; Resident, Washington, D.C. Office)
Paul N. Wengert (Not admitted in MD; Resident, Washington, D.C. Office)
G. Page Wingert (Resident, Towson, Maryland Office)
Karen D. Woodard (Resident, Washington, D.C. Office)
Robin L. Zimelman

For full biographical listings, see the Martindale-Hubbell Law Directory

Baltimore—Continued

WHARTON, LEVIN, EHRMANTRAUT, KLEIN & NASH, A PROFESSIONAL ASSOCIATION (AV)

400 East Pratt Street, 21202
Telephone: 800-322-1984; 410-269-7529
Annapolis, Maryland Office: 104 West Street, P.O. Box 551, Annapolis.
Telephone: 800-322-1984; 410-263-5900.
Bethesda, Maryland Office: 7200 Wisconsin Avenue, Suite 308.
Telephone: 301-656-1001.

James T. Wharton
David A. Levin
William A. Ehrmantraut
Robert Dale Klein
Brian J. Nash
A. Gwynn Bowie, Jr.
Jack L. Harvey
Michael T. Wharton
Andrew E. Vernick
D. Lee Rutland

David A. Roling
Brian F. Holeman (Not admitted in MD)
Debra S. Block
Daniel C. Costello
Christian A. Lodowski
Douglas K. Schrader
Linda G. Wales
Stuart N. Herschfeld
Denise Elizabeth Atkinson
Marian L. Hogan
Mary C. Jockel

For full biographical listings, see the Martindale-Hubbell Law Directory

WHITEFORD, TAYLOR & PRESTON (AV)

7 Saint Paul Street, 21202-1626
Telephone: 410-347-8700
Telex: 5101012334
Fax: 410-752-7092
Towson, Maryland Office: 210 West Pennsylvania Avenue.
Telephone: 410-832-2000.
Washington, D.C. Office: 888 17th Street, N.W.
Telephone: 202-659-6800.

MEMBERS OF FIRM

Paul F. Due (1896-1972)
Palmer R. Nickerson (1898-1969)
W. Hamilton Whiteford (1903-1992)
B. Conway Taylor, Jr. (1918-1993)
Wilbur D. Preston, Jr.
John H. Somerville
Harvey M. Lebowitz
Richard C. Whiteford
Daniel H. Honemann
Larry M. Wolf
Arthur P. Rogers (Resident Washington, D.C. Office)
Louis G. Close, Jr.
Joseph K. Pokempner
Robert S. Hillman
Fenton L. Martin
William B. Whiteford (Managing Partner)
Robert M. Wright
B. Ford Davis
Ascanio S. Boccuti (Resident Towson Office)
Thomas C. Beach, III
Ransom J. Davis
Kenneth J. Ingram (Resident Washington, D.C. Office)
John A. Hayden, III (Resident Towson Office)
Richard J. Magid
Robert Sloan, III
Ward B. Coe, III
Frederick Singley Koontz
George J. Bachrach
Stephen B. Caplis
Robert B. Curran
Dale B. Garbutt
Paul W. Madden
Priscilla C. Caskey
Stephen F. Fruin
James R. Chason (Resident Towson Office)
James F. Rosner (Resident Towson Office)
James C. Holman
Joseph D. Douglass (Resident Washington, D.C. Office)
Harry S. Johnson
William F. Ryan, Jr.
Gerard P. Sunderland
Steven E. Bers
William M. Davidow, Jr.
Thomas P. Kimmitt, Jr. (Resident Towson Office)
Albert J. Matricciani, Jr.
Jeanne M. Phelan
Kevin C. McCormick
John V. Church
Jonathan E. Claiborne (Resident Towson Office)
Albert J. Mezzanotte, Jr. (Resident Towson Office)
Douglas F. Murray
Deborah Sweet Byrnes (Resident Towson Office)
Warren N. Weaver
Barbara Lee Ayres (Resident Towson Office)
Charles A. Berardesco
Carol A. Zuckerman
Paul M. Nussbaum
G. Scott Barhight (Resident Towson Office)
Edward M. Buxbaum (Resident Towson Office)
Kenneth Oestreicher
John P. Evans
Dana C. Petersen
Anne Talbot Brennan (Resident Towson Office)
Gerard J. Gaeng
Philip B. Barnes (Resident Towson Office)
John J. Hathway (Resident Washington, D.C. Office)
Glenn R. Bonard (Resident Washington, D.C. Office)

OF COUNSEL

Roger A. Clapp
J. Royall Tippett, Jr.
Ernest C. Trimble (Resident Towson Office)
Edward A. Johnston (Resident Towson Office)
George D. Solter (Resident Towson Office)
C. William Tayler (Resident Washington, D.C. Office)
Jeffrey M. Glosser (Resident Washington, D.C. Office)
Lee A. Satterfield (Resident Washington, D.C. Office)

(See Next Column)

COUNSEL

Joseph V. Truhe, Jr.
Colleen R. Cross
Eric W. Cowan

ASSOCIATES

Nancy S. Allen
Lisa A. Lett
Gardner M. Duvall
Mary Gately Bodley (Resident Towson Office)
Peter D. Guattery
Natalie C. Magdeburger (Resident Towson Office)
Joseph N. Schaller
Judith C. Ensor (Resident Towson Office)
Howard R. Feldman
Jonathan Z. May
Kristine L. Meyer (Resident Washington, D.C. Office)
Gary S. Posner
Lawrence J. Yumkas
Joseph J. Mezzanotte
Michael D. Oliver
Andrew J. Terrell (Resident Washington, D.C. Office)
Robert F. Carney
Julia Kingsley Evans
Sandra Harlen Benzer
Eva H. Hill
Karl J. Nelson (Resident Towson Office)
Adam C. Harrison
Mark C. Kopec
Padraic McSherry Morton
John L. Senft
Catherine Whitehurst Steiner
Lynn Bozentka Taylor
Brendan P. Bunn (Resident Washington, D.C. Office)
Julianne Erin Dymowski (Resident Washington, D.C. Office)
Christopher M. Hoffmann
Elise Davison
Steven E. Tiller (Resident Towson Office)
Mary Claire Chesshire
Gail Donovan Chester
George L. Russell III
D. Scott Freed (Not admitted in MD)
John F. Carlton
Christine K. McSherry (Resident Towson Office)

For full biographical listings, see the Martindale-Hubbell Law Directory

WRIGHT, CONSTABLE & SKEEN (AV)

250 West Pratt Street, 13th Floor, 21201-2423
Telephone: 410-539-5541
Telex: 710 234-2383 CALDAS
Fax: 301-659-1350
Elkton, Maryland Office: 138 East Main Street.
Telephone: 301-398-1844.

MEMBERS OF FIRM

Wm. Pepper Constable (1882-1976)
John D. Wright (1903-1976)
George W. Constable (Retired)
Read A. McCaffrey (Retired)
William A. Skeen (Retired)
C. Gordon Haines
Thomas F. Comber, 3rd (Resident, Elkton Office)
John A. Scaldara
John Brentnall Powell, Jr.
B. Marvin Potler
Michael J. Abromaitis
Monte Fried
James W. Constable
Michael C. Warlow
David W. Skeen
John Philip Miller
James D. Skeen
Kenneth F. Davies
Sharon L. Guida
Stephen F. White
Brian S. Goodman
Frederick L. Kobb
Paul F. Evelius

ASSOCIATES

Richard J. Rogers
Lois A. Fenner McBride
Douglas H. Seitz
Mary Alice Smolarek
Donald J. Walsh
Catherine H. Bellinger

COUNSEL

Emma S. Robertson
Francis N. Iglehart, Jr.
P. McEvoy Cromwell

Representative Clients: AAI Corp.; Conowingo Power Co.; Weyerhaeuser Co.; Baltimore's International Culinary College, Inc.; Commercial Credit Corp.; Noxell Corp.; Consolidated Rail Corp.; Murray Corp.; Atlantic Mutual Insurance Co.; Sea Containers, Ltd.

For full biographical listings, see the Martindale-Hubbell Law Directory

*BEL AIR,** Harford Co.

BROWN, BROWN & BROWN, A PROFESSIONAL ASSOCIATION (AV)

200 South Main Street, 21014
Telephone: 410-838-5500
Baltimore: 410-879-2220
FAX: 410-893-0402

A. Freeborn Brown
T. Carroll Brown
Augustus F. Brown
Albert J. A. Young

Harold Douglas Norton
Christopher R. vanRoden
Timothy A. Cook
David E. Carey

Attorneys For: Baltimore Gas & Electric Co.; Chesapeake & Potomac Telephone Co.; Aberdeen Proving Ground Federal Credit Union; First Virginia Bank-Central Maryland; First National Bank of Maryland; Bell Atlantic Mobile Systems; First Harbor Securities.
Approved Counsel For: The Chicago Title Insurance Co. of Maryland, Inc.; Maryland Tortable Concrete, Inc.

For full biographical listings, see the Martindale-Hubbell Law Directory

Bel Air—Continued

STARK & KEENAN, A PROFESSIONAL ASSOCIATION (AV)

30 Office Street, 21014
Telephone: 410-838-5522
Baltimore: 410-879-2222
Fax: 410-879-0688

Elwood V. Stark, Jr.
Charles B. Keenan, Jr.
Thomas E. Marshall
Edwin G. Carson
Judith C. H. Cline
Gregory A. Szoka
Robert S. Lynch

Claire Prin Blomquist
Kimberly Kahoe Muenter
Paul W. Ishak

For full biographical listings, see the Martindale-Hubbell Law Directory

BETHESDA, Montgomery Co.

CONROY, BALLMAN & DAMERON, CHARTERED (AV)

4809 St. Elmo Avenue, 20814
Telephone: 301-654-6860
FAX: 301-654-3840
Gaithersburg, Maryland Office: Suite 402, Six Montgomery Village Avenue.
Telephone: 301-921-1900.
Fax: 301-948-9020.
Rockville, Maryland Office: 5870 Hubbard Drive.
Telephone: 301-984-3100.
Fax: 301-984-3434.
Bowie, Maryland Office: 4201 Northview Drive.
Telephone: 301-805-1400.
Fax: 301-805-0952.

B. George Ballman
J. Michael Conroy, Jr.
Rollie Feuchtenberger (Resident)

Representative Clients: NationsBank; Maryland National Bank; Norwest Mortgage Co.; U.S. Home, Inc.; The Ryland Group, Inc.; Montgomery County Association of REALTORS, Inc.; Citibank (Md.) N.A.; NVHomes; Elm Street Development, Inc.; Security Pacific Mortgage Corp.

For full biographical listings, see the Martindale-Hubbell Law Directory

PALEY, ROTHMAN, GOLDSTEIN, ROSENBERG & COOPER, CHARTERED (AV)

Seventh Floor, One Bethesda Center, 4800 Hampden Lane, 20814
Telephone: 301-656-7603
Telecopier: 301-654-7354

Glenn M. Cooper
Victor J. Rosenberg
Mark S. Goldstein
Mark S. Rothman
Stephen H. Paley
Paula A. Calimafde
Ronald A. Dweck
Arthur H. Blitz
Robert H. Maclay
Steven A. Widdes
Hope Eastman
Dennis L. Sharp
R. Thomas Hoffmann
Albert D. Pailet
Diane A. Fox
Theodore P. Stein
Jeffrey A. Kolender
Wendelin I. Lipp

Mark A. Binstock
Patricia M. Weaver
David A. Glauber
Alan D. Eisler
Donna G. Pearlman (Not admitted in MD)
David M. Rothenstein
Brent M. Goldstein

OF COUNSEL
Alan S. Mark

For full biographical listings, see the Martindale-Hubbell Law Directory

WHARTON, LEVIN, EHRMANTRAUT, KLEIN & NASH, A PROFESSIONAL ASSOCIATION (AV)

7200 Wisconsin Avenue, Suite 308, 20814
Telephone: 301-656-1001
Baltimore, Maryland Office: 400 East Pratt Street.
Telephone: 410-269-7529.
Annapolis, Maryland Office: 104 West Street, P.O. Box 551, Annapolis.
Telephone: 800-322-1984; 410-263-5900.

James T. Wharton
David A. Levin
William A. Ehrmantraut
Robert Dale Klein
Brian J. Nash
A. Gwynn Bowie, Jr.
Jack L. Harvey
Michael T. Wharton
Andrew E. Vernick
D. Lee Rutland

David A. Roling
Brian F. Holeman (Not admitted in MD)
Debra S. Block
Daniel C. Costello
Christian A. Lodowski
Douglas K. Schrader
Linda G. Wales
Stuart N. Herschfeld
Denise Elizabeth Atkinson
Marian L. Hogan
Mary C. Jockel

For full biographical listings, see the Martindale-Hubbell Law Directory

BLADENSBURG, Prince Georges Co. — (Refer to Hyattsville)

BOWIE, Prince Georges Co.

CONROY, BALLMAN & DAMERON, CHARTERED (AV)

4201 Northview Drive, 20716
Telephone: 301-805-1400
Fax: 301-805-0952
Gaithersburg, Maryland Office: Suite 402, Six Montgomery Village Avenue.
Telephone: 301-921-1900.
Fax: 301-948-9020.
Rockville, Maryland Office: 5870 Hubbard Drive.
Telephone: 301-984-3100.
Fax: 301-984-3434.
Bethesda, Maryland Office: 4809 St. Elmo Avenue.
Telephone: 301-654-6860.
FAX: 301-654-3840.

J. Michael Conroy, Jr.
Lynn R. Kromminga (Resident)

Representative Clients: NationsBank; Maryland National Bank; Norwest Mortgage Co.; U.S. Home, Inc.; The Ryland Group, Inc.; Montgomery County Association of REALTORS, Inc.; Citibank (Md.) N.A.; NVHomes; Elm Street Development, Inc.; Security Pacific Mortgage Corp.

For full biographical listings, see the Martindale-Hubbell Law Directory

*CENTREVILLE,** Queen Annes Co.

THOMPSON & THOMPSON (AV)

118 North Commerce Street, 21617
Telephone: 410-758-0877
Fax: 410-758-2305

James E. Thompson, Jr.
Jeffrey E. Thompson

References: The Centreville National Bank; The Security Title Guaranty Co.

For full biographical listings, see the Martindale-Hubbell Law Directory

COLLEGE PARK, Prince Georges Co.

WILLONER, CALABRESE & ROSEN, P.A. (AV)

4603 Calvert Road, 20740-3421
Telephone: 301-699-1400
Fax: 301-779-2213

Ronald A. Willoner
John F. Calabrese
Steven Rosen

Stephen F. Shea
Thomas J. Love

Reference: Allegiance Bank, N.A., Bethesda, Maryland.

For full biographical listings, see the Martindale-Hubbell Law Directory

*CUMBERLAND,** Allegany Co. — (Refer to Hagerstown)

*DENTON,** Caroline Co. — (Refer to Easton)

*EASTON,** Talbot Co.

COWDREY, THOMPSON & KARSTEN, P.A. (AV)

130 N. Washington Street, P.O. Box 1747, 21601
Telephone: 410-822-6800
Fax: 410-820-6586
Annapolis, Maryland Office: 621 Ridgely Avenue, Suite 402.
Telephone: 410-841-1938.
Fax: 410-841-1940.

Roy B. Cowdrey, Jr.
Paul J. Jones, Jr.
David R. Thompson
Kurt D. Karsten

Robert J. Merriken
Robert M. Messick, Jr.
Cecilia I. Lavrin
Scott G. Patterson
Diane M. Janulis

Representative Clients: The St. Paul Cos.; Princeton Insurance Co.; Medical Mutual Liability Insurance Society of Maryland; Talbot County, Maryland; Chesapeake Publishing Corp.

For full biographical listings, see the Martindale-Hubbell Law Directory

WHEELER, THOMPSON, PARKER & COUNTS (AV)

129 North Washington Street, P.O. Box 1209, 21601
Telephone: 410-822-1122
Fax: 410-822-3635

MEMBERS OF FIRM

Edward T. Miller (1895-1968)
Ernest M. Thompson (1921-1989)
Charles E. Wheeler
Dorothy H. Thompson
Willard C. Parker, II
Richard L. Counts, III
Douglas A. Collison

ASSOCIATES
John Whitelaw Ong

(See Next Column)

WHEELER, THOMPSON, PARKER & COUNTS—*Continued*

OF COUNSEL

David C. Mielke

Representative Clients: Nationwide Insurance Co.; Home Indemnity Co.; Chicago Title Insurance Company of Maryland; State Farm Mutual Insurance Co.; Chesapeake College; Habitat for Humanity of Talbot County; Talbot County Board of Education; Fuller Motor Sales, Inc.; St. Michaels Housing Authority.
Reference: Maryland National Bank, Easton Branch.

For full biographical listings, see the Martindale-Hubbell Law Directory

*ELKTON,** Cecil Co.

WRIGHT, CONSTABLE & SKEEN (AV)

138 East Main Street, 21921
Telephone: 301-398-1844
Baltimore, Maryland Office: 250 West Pratt Street, 13th Floor.
Telephone: 410-539-5541.
Fax: 410-659-1350.

MEMBERS OF FIRM

Wm. Pepper Constable (1882-1976)
Thomas F. Comber, 3rd (Resident)

Representative Clients: Delaware Trust Co.; Whirlpool Financial; B&G Automotive, Inc.

For full biographical listings, see the Martindale-Hubbell Law Directory

*ELLICOTT CITY,** Howard Co. — (Refer to Columbia)

*FREDERICK,** Frederick Co.

MILLER, MILLER & CANBY, CHARTERED (AV)

129-13 West Patrick Street, 21701
Telephone: 301-696-1380
FAX: 301-696-1385
Rockville, Maryland Office: 200-B Monroe Street.
Telephone: 301-762-5212.
FAX: 301-762-6044.

Robert L. Burchett
Diane M. Poole
Bruce N. Dean (Resident)

Representative Clients: Montgomery General Hospital, Inc.; Sandy Spring National Bank of Maryland.

For full biographical listings, see the Martindale-Hubbell Law Directory

OFFUTT, HORMAN, BURDETTE & FREY, P.A. (AV)

Offutt Building, 22 West Second Street, 21701
Telephone: 301-662-8248;
Hagerstown: 301-293-6032;
Montgomery Co., D.C./Va. line: 301-948-5633
Fax: 301-663-8968

W. Jerome Offutt
John N. Burdette
George T. Horman
Charles Burton Frey
Scott D. Miller
Barry A. Farmer

Representative Clients: Donald B. Rice Tire Co., Inc.; Meadows Van and Storage Co.; Central Maryland Farm Credit.
Local Counsel: Agristar Corp.; First National Bank of Maryland.
Co-Counsel for: Central Maryland Farm Credit.
Reference: Middletown Valley Bank.

For full biographical listings, see the Martindale-Hubbell Law Directory

GAITHERSBURG, Montgomery Co.

CONROY, BALLMAN & DAMERON, CHARTERED (AV)

Suite 402, Six Montgomery Village Avenue, 20879
Telephone: 301-921-1900
FAX: 301-948-9020
Bethesda, Maryland Office: 4809 St. Elmo Avenue.
Telephone: 301-654-6860.
Fax: 301-654-3840.
Bowie, Maryland Office: 4201 Northview Drive.
Telephone: 301-805-1400.
Fax: 301-805-0952.
Rockville, Maryland Office: 5870 Hubbard Drive.
Telephone: 301-984-3100.
Fax: 301-984-3434.

John M. Conroy (1916-1986)
B. George Ballman
J. Michael Conroy, Jr. (Bethesda, Rockville and Bowie Offices)
Thomas D. Gibbons
Stephen J. Orens
Donna M. McMillan
Glenn C. Etelson
Robert H. Haslinger (Resident, Rockville Office)
Charles M. Cockerill
Wendy D. Pullano
Terrence M. Sullivan
Lynn R. Kromminga (Resident, Bowie Office)
Lisa Beth Winer

(See Next Column)

Rollie Feuchtenberger (Resident, Bethesda Office)
Benjamin C. Winn, Jr. (Not admitted in MD)
G. Michael DuFour
Elizabeth A. White
Ronald Allen Sutton
Charles E. Kohlhoss, III
Sarah M. Eckert (Resident, Rockville Office)
Teresa M. Kelly

OF COUNSEL

James L. Dameron, III

Representative Clients: NationsBank; Maryland National Bank; Norwest Mortgage Co.; U.S. Home, Inc.; The Ryland Group, Inc.; Montgomery County Association of REALTORS, Inc.; Citibank (Md.) N.A.; NVHomes; Elm Street Development, Inc.; Security Pacific Mortgage Corp.

For full biographical listings, see the Martindale-Hubbell Law Directory

GREENBELT, Prince Georges Co.

JOSEPH, GREENWALD AND LAAKE, P.A. (AV)

Capital Office Park, 6404 Ivy Lane, Suite 400, 20770
Telephone: 301-220-2200
Telecopier: 301-220-1214

Fred R. Joseph
Andrew E. Greenwald
Walter E. Laake, Jr.
Stephen A. Friedman
Burt M. Kahn
Michael D. Jackley
Steven M. Pavsner
John Shay Parker
Peggy Crespi Kaplan
Barbara J. Gorinson
Timothy P. O'Brien
Michael V. Statham
Jay P. Holland
Lisa S. Segel
Michael T. M. Shannon
Daryl Sue Caplan
Kenneth A. Gelfarb
Peter S. Fayne
Eric Rosenberg

For full biographical listings, see the Martindale-Hubbell Law Directory

STANLEY S. PICKETT (AV)

Suite 414 Capital Office Park, 6411 Ivy Lane, 20770
Telephone: 301-513-0613

Stanley Sinclair Pickett

ASSOCIATES

Gordon J. Brumback

Representative Clients: B.F. Saul Co.; McDonald and Eudy Printers, Inc.; Condominium Management, Inc.; Long & Foster Realtors; Mitron Systems Corp.; Coldwell Banker; Eastern Property Group, Inc.; Glenanden Housing Authority; Koones & Montgomery, Inc.; Trans America Management, Inc.

For full biographical listings, see the Martindale-Hubbell Law Directory

REICHELT, NUSSBAUM, DUKES, LAPLACA & MILLER (AV)

The Maryland Trade Center, Suite 1000, 7500 Greenway Center Drive, P.O. Box 627, 20768-0627
Telephone: 301-474-9000
Fax: 301-345-0565

MEMBERS OF FIRM

Herbert W. Reichelt (1908-1993)
Charles A. Dukes, Jr.
Ronald M. Miller
T. Summers Gwynn, III
Gary Greenwald
Andrew W. Nussbaum
Sheldon L. Gnatt
Raymond G. LaPlaca
Daniel A. LaPlaca

ASSOCIATES

Gail Borjeson Viens
Roger C. Thomas
Wanda G. Caporaletti

OF COUNSEL

Paul M. Nussbaum

Representative Clients: Tower Federal Credit Union; Suburban Bank of Maryland.
Reference: NationsBank of Maryland, N.A.

For full biographical listings, see the Martindale-Hubbell Law Directory

LANHAM, Prince Georges Co.

McCARTHY, BACON & COSTELLO (AV)

Washington Business Park, Suite 300, 4640 Forbes Boulevard, 20706-4323
Telephone: 301-306-1900
Fax: 301-306-1988

MEMBERS OF FIRM

Kevin J. McCarthy
Edward C. Bacon
John F. X. Costello
Michael McGowan
Patricia M. Thornton
Mark D. Palmer
Stan Derwin Brown

ASSOCIATES

John Bradley Kaiser
Matthew J. Turner
John T. Bergin

OF COUNSEL

Michael G. Trainer
Charles E. Channing, Jr.

For full biographical listings, see the Martindale-Hubbell Law Directory

*LA PLATA,** Charles Co.

THOMAS C. HAYDEN, JR., P.A. (AV)

105 La Grange Avenue, P.O. Box 1039, 20646
Telephone: 301-934-9531; 301-870-3477
Fax: 301-934-5473

Thomas C. Hayden, Jr. H. A. Turner, IV
Thomas R. Simpson, Jr.

Representative Clients: County First Bank.
Reference: County First Bank, La Plata, Maryland.

For full biographical listings, see the Martindale-Hubbell Law Directory

MUDD, MUDD & FITZGERALD, P.A. (AV)

106 St. Mary's Avenue, P.O. Box 310, 20646
Telephone: 301-934-9541
FAX: 301-934-8178

John F. Mudd (1907-1950) Thomas F. Mudd
F. DeSales Mudd (1933-1972) John F. Mudd
Stephen P. Fitzgerald

Richard A. Cooper Robert M. Burke

Local Counsel for: Maryland National Bank (La Plata); Potomac Electric Power Co.; The Hartford Insurance Group; Maryland Bank & Trust Co.; Chicago Title Insurance Co,; Peninsula Title Insurance Co.; Colonial Farm Credit Agric. Credit Assn.
Counsel for: Interstate General Corporation; SMO, Inc.

For full biographical listings, see the Martindale-Hubbell Law Directory

*LEONARDTOWN,** St. Marys Co. — (Refer to Upper Marlboro)

LEXINGTON PARK, St. Marys Co. — (Refer to Upper Marlboro)

*OAKLAND,** Garrett Co. — (Refer to Hagerstown)

OCEAN CITY, Worcester Co.

ADKINS, POTTS & SMETHURST

(See Salisbury)

*PRINCE FREDERICK,** Calvert Co.

PITROF & STARKEY (AV)

30 Industry Lane, 20678
Telephone: 410-535-0708; 301-855-1943
Fax: 301-855-9145
Upper Marlboro, Maryland Office: 14713 Main Street, P.O. Box 130.
Telephone: 301-627-4300; 800-862-6221.
Fax: 301-627-9084.

MEMBERS OF FIRM

Eugene Edward Pitrof Thomas L. Starkey

ASSOCIATES

Richard D. Lloyd Justin J. Sasser

Reference: Maryland National Bank.

For full biographical listings, see the Martindale-Hubbell Law Directory

*PRINCESS ANNE,** Somerset Co. — (Refer to Salisbury)

RIVERDALE, Prince Georges Co.

MEYERS, BILLINGSLEY, SHIPLEY, RODBELL & ROSENBAUM, P.A. (AV)

Suite 400 Berkshire Building, 6801 Kenilworth Avenue, 20737-1385
Telephone: 301-699-5800
Fax: 301-779-5746

William V. Meyers Joseph B. Chazen
Lance W. Billingsley Michele LaRocca
Russell W. Shipley Frederick Stichnoth
Paul B. Rodbell Arthur J. Horne, Jr.
Robert H. Rosenbaum Leslie A. Pladna
Russell E. Warfel Rita Kaufman Grindle
Linda C. Carter Juliane Corroon Miller
Gina Marie Smith

Reference: First National Bank of Maryland.

For full biographical listings, see the Martindale-Hubbell Law Directory

*ROCKVILLE,** Montgomery Co.

ANDERSON & QUINN (AV)

The Adams Law Center, 25 Wood Lane, 20850
Telephone: 301-762-3303
FAX: 301-762-3776
Washington, D.C. Office: 1220 L Street, N.W., Suite 540.
Telephone: 202-371-1245.

(See Next Column)

MEMBERS OF FIRM

Charles C. Collins (1900-1973) Donald P. Maiberger
Robert E. Anderson (Not admitted in MD; Retired) Robert P. Scanlon (Resident, Washington, D.C. Office)
Francis X. Quinn James G. Healy
William Ray Scanlin (Resident, Washington, D.C. Office)

ASSOCIATES

John A. Rego Donald J. Urgo, Jr.
Richard L. Butler (Resident, Washington, D.C. Office) Laura A. Garufi
Kelly D. Vanstrom
Marie M. Gavigan (Mrs.) Alice Kelly Scanlon

Representative Clients: C & P Telephone; Commercial Union Insurance Cos.; Allstate Insurance Co.; State Farm Mutual Automobile Insurance Co.; Liberty Mutual Insurance Co.; Northbrook Insurance Cos.; Travelers Insurance Co.; National General Insurance Co.; American International Adjustment Co.; Marriott Corp.

For full biographical listings, see the Martindale-Hubbell Law Directory

BRAULT, GRAHAM, SCOTT & BRAULT (AV)

101 South Washington Street, 20850
Telephone: 301-424-1060
Fax: 301-424-7991
Washington, D.C. Office: 1906 Sunderland Place, N.W.
Telephone: 202-785-1200.
FAX: 202-785-4301.
Arlington, Virginia Office: Suite 1201, 2300 North Clarendon Boulevard, Courthouse Plaza.
Telephone: 703-522-1781.

OF COUNSEL

Laurence T. Scott

MEMBERS OF FIRM

Denver H. Graham (1922-1987) Ronald G. Guziak (Resident)
Albert E. Brault (Retired) Daniel L. Shea (Resident)
Albert D. Brault (Resident) Keith M. Bonner
Leo A. Roth, Jr. M. Kathleen Parker (Resident)
James S. Wilson (Resident) Regina Ann Casey (Resident)
James M. Brault (Resident)

ASSOCIATES

David G. Mulquin (Resident) Eric A. Spacek
Sanford A. Friedman (Not admitted in MD)
Holly D. Shupert (Resident) Rhonda Ann Hurwitz (Resident)
Joan F. Brault (Resident)

Representative Clients: American Oil Co.; Crum & Forster Group; Fireman's Fund American Insurance Cos.; Kemper Group; Reliance Insurance Cos.; Safeco Group; Government Employees Insurance Co.; Medical Mutual Insurance Society of Maryland; Legal Mutual Liability Insurance Society of Maryland.

For full biographical listings, see the Martindale-Hubbell Law Directory

CHEN, WALSH, TECLER & MCCABE (AV)

Suite 300, 200-A Monroe Street, 20850
Telephone: 301-279-9500
FAX: 301-294-5195

MEMBERS OF FIRM

William James Chen, Jr. Kenneth B. Tecler
John Burgess Walsh, Jr. John F. McCabe, Jr.

For full biographical listings, see the Martindale-Hubbell Law Directory

CONROY, BALLMAN & DAMERON, CHARTERED (AV)

5870 Hubbard Drive, 20852
Telephone: 301-984-3100
FAX: 301-984-3434
Gaithersburg, Maryland Office: Suite 402, Six Montgomery Village Avenue.
Telephone: 301-921-1900.
Fax: 301-948-9020.
Bethesda, Maryland Office: 4809 St. Elmo Avenue.
Telephone: 301-654-6860.
Fax: 301-654-3840.
Bowie, Maryland Office: 4201 Northview Drive.
Telephone: 301-805-1400.
Fax: 301-805-0952.

B. George Ballman Robert H. Haslinger (Resident)
J. Michael Conroy, Jr. Sarah M. Eckert (Resident)

Representative Clients: NationsBank; Maryland National Bank; Norwest Mortgage Co.; U.S. Home, Inc.; The Ryland Group, Inc.; Montgomery County Association of REALTORS, Inc.; Citibank (Md.) N.A.; NVHomes; Elm Street Development, Inc.; Security Pacific Mortgage Corp.

For full biographical listings, see the Martindale-Hubbell Law Directory

Rockville—Continued

McCarthy, Wilson & Ethridge (AV)

100 South Washington Street, 20850
Telephone: 301-762-7770
FAX: 301-762-0374

MEMBERS OF FIRM

Joseph S. McCarthy (1918-1983)
Charles E. Wilson, Jr.
Paul H. Ethridge
Thomas Patrick Ryan
Robert B. Hetherington

ASSOCIATES

D. Elizabeth Walker
Rocco C. Nunzio
Edward J. Brown
Charles Elliot Wilson, III
Juli Martin Tweedy
Carolyn J. Hodges
Donna S. Brennan

Representative Clients: Allstate Insurance Co.; Erie Insurance Exchange; Horace Mann Insurance Co.; Leaseway Transportation System, Inc.; Lloyd's of London; Massachusetts Mutual Life Insurance Co; Sears Roebuck & Co.

For full biographical listings, see the Martindale-Hubbell Law Directory

Miller, Miller & Canby, Chartered (AV)

200-B Monroe Street, 20850
Telephone: 301-762-5212
FAX: 301-762-6044
Frederick, Maryland Office: 129-13 West Patrick Street.
Telephone: 301-696-1380.
FAX: 301-696-1385.

Robert L. Burchett
James L. Thompson
Lewis R. Schumann
Joel S. Kline
Diane M. Poole
Joseph P. Suntum

OF COUNSEL

James R. Miller, Jr.
William M. Canby
Patrick C. McKeever

Ellen S. Walker
Susan W. Carter
Bruce N. Dean (Resident, Frederick Office)
Glenn M. Anderson

Representative Clients: Asbury Methodist Home Inc.; Montgomery General Hospital, Inc.; Sandy Spring National Bank of Maryland.

For full biographical listings, see the Martindale-Hubbell Law Directory

Miller & Steinberg (AV)

Suite 414, 414 Hungerford Drive, 20850
Telephone: 301-424-1180
FAX: 301-424-8459

MEMBERS OF FIRM

James Robert Miller
Harvey B. Steinberg
Kevin G. Hessler

Reference: NationsBank, Rockville Branch.

For full biographical listings, see the Martindale-Hubbell Law Directory

Rowan & Quirk (AV)

The Adams Law Center, 27 Wood Lane, 20850
Telephone: 301-762-4050
FAX: 301-762-9189

MEMBERS OF FIRM

William J. Rowan, III
Joseph M. Quirk

ASSOCIATES

John G. Nalls

For full biographical listings, see the Martindale-Hubbell Law Directory

Shulman, Rogers, Gandal, Pordy & Ecker, P.A. (AV)

Third Floor, 11921 Rockville Pike, 20852-2743
Telephone: 301-230-5200
Telecopier: 301-230-2891
Washington, D.C. Office: 1120-19th Street, N.W., Eighth Floor.
Telephone: 202-872-0400.

Lawrence A. Shulman
Donald R. Rogers
Larry N. Gandal
Karl L. Ecker
David A. Pordy
David D. Freishtat
Martin P. Schaffer
Christopher C. Roberts
Jeffrey A. Shane
Edward M. Hanson, Jr.
David M. Kochanski
Walter A. Oleniewski
Lawrence L. Bell
James M. Kefauver
Rebecca Oshoway
Robert B. Canter
Edward F. Schiff
Philip J. McNutt
Daniel S. Krakower
Kevin P. Kennedy
James P. Sullivan
Ashley Joel Gardner
Alan B. Sternstein
Nancy P. Regelin

(See Next Column)

OF COUNSEL

Martin Levine
Lawrence J. Eisenberg
Solomon L. Margolis
William Robert King
Fred S. Sommer

Michael J. Froehlich
James M. Hoffman
William C. Davis, III
James A. Powers
Elizabeth N. Shomaker
Michael V. Nakamura
Paul A. Bellegarde
Gregory J. Rupert
Samuel M. Spiritos
Sandra E. Brusca
Jonathan M. Forster
Douglas K. Hirsch
Patrick M. Martyn
Kim A. Viti
Joan A. Pisarchik
Steven M. Curwin (Not admitted in MD)
Holloway B. Lefkowitz (Not admitted in MD)
John J. McKenna, Jr.

Reference: Maryland National Bank, Montgomery County Regional Office.

For full biographical listings, see the Martindale-Hubbell Law Directory

Stein, Sperling, Bennett, De Jong, Driscoll, Greenfeig & Metro, P.A. (AV)

25 West Middle Lane, 20850
Telephone: 301-340-2020; 800-435-5230
Telecopier: 301-340-8217

Millard S. Bennett
David S. De Jong
David C. Driscoll, Jr.
Jack A. Garson
Stuart S. Greenfeig
Ann G. Jakabcin
A. Howard Metro
Jeffrey M. Schwaber
Donald N. Sperling
Paul T. Stein

Beth H. McIntosh
Kieyasien K. Moore
James D. Dalrymple
Ann H. Sablosky
Fred A. Balkin
Jeffrey D. Goldstein

For full biographical listings, see the Martindale-Hubbell Law Directory

Venable, Baetjer and Howard (AV)

A Partnership including Professional Corporations
Suite 500, One Church Street, P.O. Box 1906, 20850-4129
Telephone: 301-217-5600
FAX: 301-217-5617
Baltimore, Maryland Office: 1800 Mercantile Bank & Trust Building, 2 Hopkins Plaza.
Telephone: 410-244-7400.
Washington, D.C. Office: Venable, Baetjer, Howard & Civiletti. Suite 1000, 1201 New York Avenue, N.W.
Telephone: 202-962-4800.
McLean, Virginia Office: Suite 400, 2010 Corporate Ridge.
Telephone: 703-760-1600.
Towson, Maryland, Office: 210 Allegheny Avenue, P. O. Box 5517.
Telephone: 410-494-6200.

MEMBERS OF FIRM

Roger W. Titus
Daniel O'C. Tracy, Jr. (Also at Baltimore, Maryland Office)
Paul T. Glasgow
Sondra Harans Block
John A. Roberts (Also at Baltimore, Maryland Office)

ASSOCIATES

Patrick L. Clancy
Patricia Gillis Cousins
Paula Titus Laboy
Gregory L. Laubach

For full biographical listings, see the Martindale-Hubbell Law Directory

*SALISBURY,** Wicomico Co.

Adkins, Potts & Smethurst (AV)

Suite 600, One Plaza East, P.O. Box 4247, 21803-4247
Telephone: 410-749-0161
Fax: 410-749-5021
Snow Hill, Maryland Office: 102A Market Street.
Telephone: 301-632-2025.

MEMBERS OF FIRM

E. Dale Adkins, Jr. (1915-1982)
Charles J. Potts (1910-1994)
Raymond Stevens Smethurst, Jr.
Robert B. Taylor
Sally D. Adkins
John C. Seipp
L. Richard Phillips
Albert Gillis Allen, II

ASSOCIATES

Barbara R. Trader
Paula A. Price
Karen Sherwood Payne

OF COUNSEL

Benjamin L. Willey

Representative Clients: Associated Builders and Contractors (Eastern Shore Chapter); Atlantic Wood Industries, Inc.; Bank of Delaware; Delmarva Power & Light Co.; Lawyers Title Insurance Corp.; Nature Conservancy; Pepsi Cola Bottling Company of Salisbury, Inc.; Shopco Group; WBOC, Inc.; Wicomico County Housing Authority.

For full biographical listings, see the Martindale-Hubbell Law Directory

Salisbury—Continued

DUVALL & DUVALL (AV)

108 East Market Street, P.O. Box 4077, 21803-4077
Telephone: 410-548-1010
Fax: 410-548-1045

MEMBERS OF FIRM

William G. Duvall
Richard M. Duvall

Reference: Nations Bank.

For full biographical listings, see the Martindale-Hubbell Law Directory

WEBB, BURNETT, JACKSON, CORNBROOKS, WILBER, VORHIS & DOUSE (AV)

115 Broad Street, P.O. Box 910, 21801
Telephone: 410-742-3176
Fax: 410-742-0438
Cambridge, Maryland Office: Suite 301, First Cambridge Building, 601 Locust Street.
Telephone: 410-476-3610.

MEMBERS OF FIRM

Frederick W. C. Webb (1889-1956)
John W. T. Webb (1918-1990)
K. King Burnett
W. Newton Jackson, 3rd
Ernest I. Cornbrooks, III
Paul D. Wilber
David A. Vorhis
David B. Douse

ASSOCIATES

Chris Schiller Mason
J. Scott Robertson

Counsel for: First National Bank of Maryland (Salisbury branch); K & L Microwave, Inc.; Peninsula General Hospital Medical Center.
Local Attorneys for: State Farm Insurance Cos.; Nationwide Insurance Cos.; Travelers Insurance Co.; United States Fidelity & Guaranty Co.; Aetna Casualty & Surety Co.; Insurance Company of North America.

For full biographical listings, see the Martindale-Hubbell Law Directory

SEABROOK, Prince Georges Co.

FOSSETT & BRUGGER, CHARTERED (AV)

The Aerospace Building, 10210 Greenbelt Road, 20706
Telephone: 301-794-6900
Telecopy: 301-794-7638
La Plata, Maryland Office: 105 LaGrange Avenue, P.O. Box F.
Telephone: 301-934-4200. Washington Line: 301-753-9600.
FAX: 301-870-2884.

George A. Brugger
Clarence L. Fossett
Jonathan I. Kipnis
Nancy L. Slepicka
Diane O. Leasure
Midgett S. Parker, Jr.
William M. Shipp
John C. Fredrickson
Lorraine J. Webb (Resident, La Plata Office)
Michael A. Faerber
Michael F. Canning, Jr.
Harold Gregory Martin
Mary A. Liano

LEGAL SUPPORT PERSONNEL

Dean Armstrong

Representative Clients: Banyan Management Corp.; Capital Office Park; Coscan Washington, Inc.; Citizens Bank & Trust Company of Maryland; Greenhorne & O'Mara, Inc.; Kettler Brothers; Michael T. Rose Cos.; The Mutual Life Insurance Company of New York; Richmond-American Homes; Winchester Homes, Inc.

For full biographical listings, see the Martindale-Hubbell Law Directory

SILVER SPRING, Montgomery Co.

GINGELL & JENKINS (AV)

Suite 506 Wheaton Plaza South, 11160 Veirs Mill Road, 20902
Telephone: 301-949-0100
Telecopier: 301-949-0467

MEMBERS OF FIRM

Robert A. Gingell
Donn K. Jenkins

Terry William McConnaughey
C. Lawrence Holcomb
Sebastian G. Wright

Representative Clients: Air Flow Co. (Industrial Air Conditioning); Bethesda Realty Co.; Photo Science, Inc.
References: Sovran Bank; First National Bank of Maryland (Rockville, Maryland, Branch); Signet Bank Maryland.

For full biographical listings, see the Martindale-Hubbell Law Directory

LINOWES AND BLOCHER (AV)

Suite 1000, 1010 Wayne Avenue, 20910
Telephone: 301-588-8580
Telecopier: 301-495-9044
TTY/TDD: 301-588-3380
Washington, D.C. Office: Suite 840, 800 K Street, N.W.
Telephone: 202-408-3220.
Telecopier: 202-408-1719.
Greenbelt, Maryland Office: Suite 402, 6411 Ivy Lane.
Telephone: 301-982-3382.
Telecopier: 301-982-0595.
Annapolis, Maryland Office: 145 Main Street, P.O. Box 31.
Telephone: 410-268-0881.
Telecopier: 301-261-2603.
Frederick, Maryland Office: Suite 102, 228 W. Patrick Street.
Telephone: 301-695-0244.
Telecopier: 301-663-6656.
Columbia, Maryland Office: Suite B215, 10015 Old Columbia Road.
Telephone: 410-312-5457.
Fax: 410-290-5285.

MEMBERS OF FIRM

Joseph P. Blocher
John J. Carmody, Jr. (Not admitted in MD)
David M. Cohen
Kathryn J. Dahl (Resident Partner, Annapolis, Maryland office)
C. Robert Dalrymple
John J. Delaney
Stephen P. Elmendorf
Phil T. Feola (Resident Partner, Washington, D.C. office)
Cynthia A. Giordano (Not admitted in MD; Resident Partner, Washington, D.C. office)
Andrew M. Goldstein
Larry A. Gordon
Gerald W. Heller
William M. Hoffman, Jr.
John L. Hollingshead
Andrew L. Isaacson
Stephen Z. Kaufman
William Kominers
Robert H. Metz
Jerry A. Moore III (Not admitted in MD; Resident Partner, Washington, D.C. office)
John R. Orrick, Jr.
Robert C. Park, Jr.
Leslie Moore Romine (Resident Partner, Greenbelt, Maryland office)
Barbara A. Sears
James A. Vidmar, Jr.
Roger D. Winston
James B. Witkin
Richard M. Zeidman

SENIOR COUNSEL

R. Robert Linowes

PARTNER EMERITUS

Charles G. Dalrymple

OF COUNSEL

Gary Altman
David L. Cahoon
Bradford F. Englander (Not admitted in MD)
Myles Hannan

ASSOCIATES

Todd D. Brown
James E. Gilbert
Moia T. Gruber
Elizabeth M. Hosford
Douglas M. Irvin
Bruce C. Johnson
Amy C. Kwak
Dorothy H. Moore (Not admitted in MD)
David M. Plott (Resident, Annapolis, Maryland office)
Lynn A. Robeson
David W. Rowan
Scott R. Smith
Paul-Michael Sweeney
Emily J. Vaias

Representative Clients: Boston Properties; CenterMark Properties, Inc.; First National Bank of Maryland; Foulger/Pratt Development; Hechinger Co.; Manufacturers Life Insurance Co.; Manekin Corporation; National Geographic Society; Wal-Mart, Inc.

For full biographical listings, see the Martindale-Hubbell Law Directory

LIPSHULTZ AND HONE, CHARTERED (AV)

Suite 108 Montgomery Center, 8630 Fenton Street, 20910
Telephone: 301-587-8500
Fax: 301-495-9759
Washington, D.C. Office: Suite 200, 2000 L Street, N.W.
Telephone: 202-872-0909.

Leonard L. Lipshultz
John Llewellyn Hone
Stanley L. Lipshultz
Frank L. Lipshultz
Ronald G. DeWald
Michael T. O'Bryant (Not admitted in MD)
Stephen S. Brown
James R. Schraf
Victor I. Weiner
Christopher A. Conte
Mark Feinroth
Joseph J. Bottiglieri
Renee R. Nebens
Andrew R. Simonson
Suzanne L. Ingersoll

For full biographical listings, see the Martindale-Hubbell Law Directory

WHEELER & KORPECK (AV)

Suite 700, 8601 Georgia Avenue, 20910
Telephone: 301-587-6200
Telecopier: 301-589-6324

(See Next Column)

WHEELER & KORPECK—*Continued*

MEMBERS OF FIRM

William B. Wheeler (Retired)
Jerome E. Korpeck
William T. Wheeler
Robert L. Brownell
Mark W. Kugler
Roger K. Bain
Robert L. Flynn, III

ASSOCIATES

Robin M. Nicholson

Representative Clients: Potomac Investment Associates; Inter-American Development Bank Federal Credit Union; F.O. Day Paving Co.; U.S. Home Corporation; Rocky Gorge Communities, Inc.; CSX Realty, Inc.; The Tower Companies; Kay Management; Polinger Companies.
Reference: Nations Bank/Maryland.

For full biographical listings, see the Martindale-Hubbell Law Directory

*TOWSON,** Baltimore Co.

HOWELL, GATELY, WHITNEY & CARTER (AV)

401 Washington Avenue, Twelfth Floor, 21204
Telephone: 410-583-8000
FAX: 410-583-8031

MEMBERS OF FIRM

H. Thomas Howell
William F. Gately
Benjamin R. Goertemiller
Daniel W. Whitney
David A. Carter
William R. Levasseur

ASSOCIATES

Una M. Perez
John S. Bainbridge, Jr.
George D. Bogris
Wendy A. Lassen
Kathleen D. Leslie

For full biographical listings, see the Martindale-Hubbell Law Directory

MILES & STOCKBRIDGE, A PROFESSIONAL CORPORATION (AV)

600 Washington Avenue, Suite 300, 21204-3965
Telephone: 410-821-6565
Telecopier: 823-8123
Baltimore, Maryland Office: 10 Light Street.
Telephone: 410-727-6464.
Telecopier: 385-3700.
Easton, Maryland Office: 101 Bay Street.
Telephone: 410-822-5280.
Telecopier: 822-5450.
Cambridge, Maryland Office: 300 Academy Street.
Telephone: 410-228-4545.
Telecopier: 228-5652.
Rockville, Maryland Office: 22 West Jefferson Street.
Telephone: 301-762-1600.
Telecopier: 762-0363.
Frederick, Maryland Office: 30 West Patrick Street.
Telephone: 301-662-5155.
Telecopier: 662-3647.
Washington, D.C. Office: 1450 G. Street, N.W., Suite 445.
Telephone: 202-737-9600.
Telecopier: 737-0097.
Fairfax, Virginia Office: Fair Oaks Plaza, 11350 Random Hills Road.
Telephone: 703-273-2440.
Telecopier: 273-4446.

Milton R. Smith, Jr.
Stephen C. Winter
K. Donald Proctor
Gary C. Duvall
John B. Sinclair
Lawrence F. Haislip
Kenneth F. Spence, III

Jeffrey P. Reilly
Charles R. Diffenderffer
Daniel Nuzzi
Kevin J. Pascale
Richard A. Dellheim

Representative Clients: The Black & Decker Corp.; Colonial Pipeline Co.; Crum & Forster Commercial Insurance; Fidelity Management Co.; First National Bank of Maryland; Henry Adams, Inc.; Maryland National Bank; MNC Commercial Corp.; MacKenzie Properties, Inc.

For full biographical listings, see the Martindale-Hubbell Law Directory

NOLAN, PLUMHOFF & WILLIAMS, CHARTERED (AV)

Suite 700 Court Towers, 210 West Pennsylvania Avenue, 21204
Telephone: 410-823-7800
Fax: 410-296-2765

James D. Nolan (Retired, 1980)
J. Earle Plumhoff (1940-1988)
Ralph E. Deitz (1918-1990)
Newton A. Williams
Thomas J. Renner
William P. Englehart, Jr.
Stephen J. Nolan
Robert L. Hanley, Jr.
Robert S. Glushakow
Stephen M. Schenning
Douglas L. Burgess
Robert E. Cahill, Jr.
E. Bruce Jones
J. Joseph Curran, III

(See Next Column)

OF COUNSEL

T. Bayard Williams, Jr.

Representative Clients: Baltimore County, Maryland; Bituminous Insurance Companies; Board of Education of Anne Arundel County; Carolina Freight Carriers Corporation; Patapsco Federal Savings & Loan Association; Pulte Home Corporation; Royal Oak Federal Savings Bank, F.S.B.; Shelter Development Corporation; Summit Broadcasting Corporation; Wyman Park Federal Savings and Loan Association.

For full biographical listings, see the Martindale-Hubbell Law Directory

ROYSTON, MUELLER, MCLEAN & REID (AV)

Suite 600, 102 West Pennsylvania Avenue, 21204
Telephone: 410-823-1800
Fax: 410-828-7859

MEMBERS OF FIRM

R. Taylor McLean
Richard A. Reid
E. Harrison Stone
Carroll S. Klingelhofer III
Thomas F. McDonough
Eugene W. Cunningham, Jr.
Laurel Paretta Evans
Keith R. Truffer
Robert S. Handzo
Edward J. Gilliss
C. Larry Hofmeister, Jr.
John W. Browning

ASSOCIATES

Julia O'Hara Berk
Christine J. Saverda
Laura L. Henninger

OF COUNSEL

Charles F. Stein, III

Representative Clients: Atlantic Residential Mortgage Corporation, a Subsidiary of the Bank of Baltimore; Baltimore County Revenue Authority; Bell Atlantic-MD; The Reuben H. Donnelley Corporation; Genstar Stone Products Co.; Mercantile-Safe Deposit and Trust Co.; Morrison Restaurants, Inc.; Rosedale Federal Savings and Loan Assn.; Royal Insurance Co.; The Williams Companies, Inc.

For full biographical listings, see the Martindale-Hubbell Law Directory

VENABLE, BAETJER AND HOWARD (AV)

A Partnership including Professional Corporations
210 Allegheny Avenue, P.O. Box 5517, 21204
Telephone: 410-494-6200
FAX: 410-821-0147
Baltimore, Maryland Office: 1800 Mercantile Bank & Trust Building, 2 Hopkins Plaza.
Telephone: 410-244-7400.
Washington, D.C. Office: Venable, Baetjer, Howard & Civiletti. Suite 1000, 1201 New York Avenue, N.W.
Telephone: 202-962-4800.
McLean, Virginia Office: Suite 400, 2010 Corporate Ridge.
Telephone: 703-760-1600.
Rockville, Maryland Office: Suite 500, One Church Street, P. O. Box 1906.
Telephone: 301-217-5600.

PARTNERS

James D. C. Downes (1906-1979)
James H. Cook (1918-1993)
Benjamin R. Civiletti (P.C.) (Also at Washington, D.C. and Baltimore, Maryland Offices)
John B. Howard
David D. Downes
John H. Zink, III
Alexander I. Lewis, III (P.C.) (Also at Baltimore, Maryland Office)
Max Stul Oppenheimer (P.C.) (Also at Baltimore, Maryland and Washington, D.C. offices)
Joseph C. Wich, Jr.
Michael Schatzow (Also at Baltimore, Maryland and Washington, D.C. Offices)
Susan K. Gauvey (Also at Baltimore, Maryland Office)
James K. Archibald (Also at Baltimore, Maryland and Washington, D.C. Offices)
Judson W. Starr (Not admitted in MD; Also at Baltimore and Towson, Maryland Offices)
F. Dudley Staples, Jr. (Also at Baltimore, Maryland Office)
William D. Quarles (Also at Washington, D.C. Office)
C. Carey Deeley, Jr. (Also at Baltimore, Maryland Office)
Kathleen Gallogly Cox
Cynthia M. Hahn
M. King Hill, III
Robert A. Hoffman
J. Michael Brennan
Michael H. Davis

OF COUNSEL

A. Samuel Cook (P.C.)
Herbert R. O'Conor, Jr.

ASSOCIATES

Marina Lolley Dame
J. Van L. Dorsey
Mary-Dulany James
Patricia A. Malone
G. Page Wingert

For full biographical listings, see the Martindale-Hubbell Law Directory

WHITEFORD, TAYLOR & PRESTON (AV)

210 West Pennsylvania Avenue, 21204-4515
Telephone: 410-832-2000
Baltimore, Maryland Office: 7 Saint Paul Street.
Telephone: 410-347-8700.
Telex: 5101012334.
Fax: 410-752-7092.

(See Next Column)

WHITEFORD, TAYLOR & PRESTON, *Towson—Continued*

Washington, D.C. Office: 888 17th Street, N.W.
Telephone: 202-659-6800.

RESIDENT PARTNERS

Ascanio S. Boccuti
John A. Hayden, III
James R. Chason
James F. Rosner
Thomas P. Kimmitt, Jr.
Jonathan E. Claiborne
Albert J. Mezzanotte, Jr.
Deborah Sweet Byrnes
Barbara Lee Ayres
G. Scott Barhight
Edward M. Buxbaum
Anne Talbot Brennan
Philip B. Barnes

OF COUNSEL

Ernest C. Trimble
Edward A. Johnston
George D. Solter

RESIDENT ASSOCIATES

Mary Gately Bodley
Natalie C. Magdeburger
Judith C. Ensor
Karl J. Nelson
Steven E. Tiller
Christine K. McSherry

For full biographical listings, see the Martindale-Hubbell Law Directory

*UPPER MARLBORO,** Prince Georges Co.

KNIGHT, MANZI, BRENNAN, OSTROM AND HAM, A PROFESSIONAL ASSOCIATION (AV)

14440 Old Mill Road, 20772
Telephone: 301-952-0100
Annapolis/Baltimore: 410-269-0336
Fax: 301-952-0221
Crofton, Maryland Office: 26 Crofton Lane.
Telephones: 301-261-0808; Annapolis: 410-721-9377.
Fax: 301-261-6945.
Mitchellville, Maryland Office: 12164 Central Avenue, Suite 228.
Telephone: 301-390-0577.
Fax: 301-390-8464.

William E. Knight
Robert A. Manzi
William C. Brennan, Jr.
Robert B. Ostrom
Richard J. Ham
John F. Shay, Jr.
Stuart R. Hammett
Martin J. Shuham

Monica M. Haley-Pierson
Daniel F. Lynch III
Norman D. Rivera

OF COUNSEL

Francine Silver Taylor

For full biographical listings, see the Martindale-Hubbell Law Directory

MENG & UREY (AV)

14604 Elm Street, P.O. Box 549, 20773
Telephone: 301-627-1600
FAX: 301-627-2838

George E. Meng
Paul K. Urey, III

ASSOCIATES

Mary Ann Ryan
Thomas Richard Kirvin

For full biographical listings, see the Martindale-Hubbell Law Directory

PITROF & STARKEY (AV)

14713 Main Street, P.O. Box 130, 20773-0130
Telephone: 301-627-4300; 800-862-6221
Fax: 301-627-9084
Prince Frederick, Maryland Office: 30 Industry Lane.
Telephones: 410-535-0708; 301-855-1943.
Fax: 301-855-9145.

MEMBERS OF FIRM

Eugene Edward Pitrof
Thomas L. Starkey

ASSOCIATES

Richard D. Lloyd
Justin J. Sasser

Reference: First National Bank of Maryland.

For full biographical listings, see the Martindale-Hubbell Law Directory

SASSCER, CLAGETT & BUCHER (AV)

14803 Pratt Street, 20772
Telephone: 301-627-5500
FAX: 301-627-4156

MEMBERS OF FIRM

Lansdale G. Sasscer (1893-1964)
James R. Bucher
William N. Zifchak
Phillip R. Zuber
Thomas A. McManus

ASSOCIATES

Giancarlo M. Ghiardi
Jeffrey L. Harding
Mark T. Foley
Catherine C. Collins

(See Next Column)

OF COUNSEL

Hal C. B. Clagett
Lansdale G. Sasscer, Jr.

Local Counsel for: Allstate Insurance Co.; Continental Insurance Co.; Home Indemnity Insurance Co.; Liberty Mutual Insurance Co.; Montgomery Mutual Insurance Co.; Nationwide Insurance Co.; Potomac Electric Power Co.

For full biographical listings, see the Martindale-Hubbell Law Directory

*WESTMINSTER,** Carroll Co.

DAVIS & MURPHY (AV)

237 East Main Street, 21157
Telephone: 410-848-5411
Baltimore: 410-876-2757
Fax: 410-876-9158
Mount Airy, Maryland Office: 1512 Ridgeside Drive. P.O.Box 380.
Telephone: 301-831-7272; 410-549-1010.
Fax: 301-831-0724.

MEMBERS OF FIRM

James Willard Davis
Daniel Murphy

ASSOCIATES

Michael D. Zimmer
Andrew C. Stone

Representative Clients: Masonry Contractors, Inc.; Westminster Bank and Trust Co.; Woodhaven Building and Developers, Inc.; Koren Development Inc.
References: Carroll County Bank and Trust Co.; Union National Bank; Westminster Bank and Trust Co.; Chicago Title Insurance.

For full biographical listings, see the Martindale-Hubbell Law Directory

DULANY & LEAHY (AV)

127 East Main Street, P.O. Box 525, 21158-0525
Telephone: 410-848-3333; Baltimore Line: 876-2117
FAX: 410-876-0747

MEMBERS OF FIRM

William B. Dulany
J. Brooks Leahy

ASSOCIATES

Amber Dahlgreen Curtis
Kenneth M. Williams

Representative Clients: Carroll County Bank and Trust Co.; Lehigh Portland Cement Co.; Pizza Hut of Maryland, Inc.; McGregor Printing Corporation; Mutual Fire Insurance Company of Carroll County.
Reference: Carroll County Bank and Trust Co.

For full biographical listings, see the Martindale-Hubbell Law Directory

WALSH & FISHER, A PROFESSIONAL ASSOCIATION (AV)

179 East Main Street, 21157
Telephone: 410-848-9200; 876-2135
Telecopier: 410-848-9313

D. Eugene Walsh (1895-1980)
Charles O. Fisher
Charles O. Fisher, Jr.
Richard C. Murray
David B. Weisgerber

Representative Clients: Genstar Stone Products Co., Conewago Contractors, Inc.; Town of Mt. Airy; Town of Hampstead; Town of Manchester; Westminster Bank and Trust Co.; Carroll County General Hospital, Inc.; Adams County National Bank.

For full biographical listings, see the Martindale-Hubbell Law Directory

MASSACHUSETTS

ADAMS, Berkshire Co. — (Refer to Pittsfield)

AMESBURY, Essex Co.

HAMEL, DESHAIES & GAGLIARDI (AV)

Five Market Square, P.O. Box 198, 01913
Telephone: 508-388-3558
Telecopier: 508-388-0441

MEMBERS OF FIRM

Richard P. Hamel
Robert J. Deshaies
Paul J. Gagliardi

ASSOCIATES

H. Scott Haskell
Roger D. Turgeon
Peter R. Ayer, Jr.
Charles E. Schissel

Representative Clients: Essex County Gas Co., Amesbury, MA; First and Ocean National Bank, Newburyport, MA; Amesbury Co-Operative Bank, Amesbury, MA.
Approved Attorneys for: Chicago Title Insurance; Old Republic Title Insurance Co.

For full biographical listings, see the Martindale-Hubbell Law Directory

AMHERST, Hampshire Co. — (Refer to Northampton)

ANDOVER, Essex Co.

SHERMAN AND CREGG (AV)

15 Central Street, 01810
Telephone: 508-475-4595

Roland H. Sherman (1948-1971)
Edward F. Cregg

Representative Clients: Phillips Academy, Andover; Prudential Life Insurance Co.; The Pike School; Doyle Lumber Co., Inc.; Voltek, Inc.; Lawrence Savings Bank.

For full biographical listings, see the Martindale-Hubbell Law Directory

ATTLEBORO, Bristol Co.

COOGAN, SMITH, BENNETT, McGAHAN, LORINCZ & JACOBI (AV)

144 Bank Street, P.O. Box 2320, 02703
Telephone: 508-222-0002
Telecopier: 508-222-9095

MEMBERS OF FIRM

Peirce B. Smith
Paul F. Lorincz
Charles E. Bennett
Michael T. McGahan
James Jerome Coogan
John F. D. Jacobi, III
Timothy J. McGahan

ASSOCIATES

Edward Kieran Shanley
Kimberly G. Barrett

For full biographical listings, see the Martindale-Hubbell Law Directory

*BARNSTABLE,** Barnstable Co. — (Refer to Hyannis)

BEVERLY, Essex Co.

GLOVSKY & GLOVSKY (AV)

8 Washington Street, 01915
Telephone: 508-922-5000
FAX: 508-921-7809

MEMBERS OF FIRM

Abraham Glovsky (1896-1973)
John E. Glovsky
C. Henry Glovsky
Mark B. Glovsky
Bertram Glovsky
Kevin M. Dalton
Charles R. Richey, Jr.

ASSOCIATES

Hildy M. Feuerbach
Donald K. Freyleue

Representative Clients: Warren Five Cents Savings Bank; Rose's Oil Service, Inc.; Medical Group, Inc.; Associates in OBGYN, Inc.; Pewter Pot, Inc.; Leslie S. Ray Insurance Agency, Inc.; Professional Relations and Research Institute, Inc.
Reference: Beverly National Bank.

For full biographical listings, see the Martindale-Hubbell Law Directory

*BOSTON,** Suffolk Co.

* indicates certain Bar Register subscribers whose principal office is located elsewhere in the state and who have arranged for representation as a part of the state capital listings that follow

BARRON & STADFELD, P.C. (AV)

Two Center Plaza, 02108
Telephone: 617-723-9800
Telecopier: 617-523-8359
Hyannis, Massachusetts Office: 258 Winter Street.
Telephone: 617-778-6622.

Bernard A. Dwork
John J. Yagjian
Hertz N. Henkoff
Julie Taylor Moran
Peter P. Myerson
Mitchell J. Notis
Enid M. Starr
Robert J. Hoffer
Thomas V. Bennett
Joseph G. Butler
Edward E. Kelly
Denise L. Page
Kevin F. Moloney
Mark W. Roberts
David P. Dwork
Rosemary Purtell

Dorothy M. Bickford
Donna M. Pisciotta
Alison L. Berman
Warren E. Agin
Roger T. Manwaring
Christine Ann Gardner
Judith C. Knight
Shawn P. O'Rourke
Kevin P. Scanlon

For full biographical listings, see the Martindale-Hubbell Law Directory

BINGHAM, DANA & GOULD (AV)

150 Federal Street, 02110
Telephone: 617-951-8000
Cable Address: "Blodgham Bsn"
Telex: 275147 BDGBSN UR
Telecopy: 617-951-8736
Hartford, Connecticut Office: 100 Pearl Street.
Telephone: 203-244-3770.
Telecopy: 203-527-5188.
London, England Office: 39 Victoria Street, SWIH 0EE.
Telephone: 011-44-71-799-2646.
Telecopy: 011-44-71-799-2654.
Telex: 888179 BDGLDN G.
Cable Address: "Blodgham Ldn".
Washington, D.C. Office: 1550 M Street, N.W.
Telephone: 202-822-9320.
Telecopy: 202-833-1506.

MEMBERS OF FIRM

Donald-Bruce Abrams
John F. Adkins
Jonathan M. Albano
Mark A. Andrew (Resident in London, England Office)
Cynthia Faye Barnett
Robert A. J. Barry, Jr.
Alan W. Beloff
William N. Berkowitz
Jonathan K. Bernstein (Resident in Hartford, Connecticut Office)
David C. Boch
Vicki Van Velson Bonnington
Jeremiah J. Bresnahan, Jr.
John S. Brown
Marijane Benner Browne
John H. Chu
Lea Anne Copenhefer
Stephen J. Coukos
Neal J. Curtin
John J. Curtin, Jr.
James S. Davis
Louis J. Duval
M. Gordon Ehrlich
Frederick F. Eisenbiegler
David L. Engel
Randal A. Farrar
Roger D. Feldman
Sula R. Fiszman
Jody E. Forchheimer
Francis H. Fox
Daniel L. Goldberg
Gordon B. Greer
Linda J. Groves
Paul R. Gupta
Steven W. Hansen
Richard M. Harter
William A. Hazel
Henry S. Healy
Douglas M. Henry
Joe H. Hicks
Russell E. Isaia
Charles L. Janes
David O. Johanson
Richard H. Johnson
Roger P. Joseph
Gerald J. Kehoe
William D. Kirchick
John R. Kirk
Joseph L. Kociubes
Diane M. Kottmyer
Ben M. Krowicki (Resident in Hartford, Connecticut Office)
Amy L. Kyle
Paul J. Lambert (Resident in Washington, D.C. Office)
Richard D. Leggat
George P. Mair
Colin S. Marshall
S. Elaine McChesney
William A. McCormack, Jr.
Robert E. McDonnell
Neal C. Mizner (Resident in Hartford, Connecticut Office)
James F. Monahan
Scott Carson Moriearty
Justin P. Morreale
Guy B. Moss
David J. Murphy
Michael P. O'Brien
Victor J. Paci
Victor H. Polk, Jr.
Gerald F. Rath
Marc A. Reardon
James N. Rice
Marcia Robinson
Neal A. Rosen
Vincent M. Sacchetti
Edward A. Saxe
James G. Scantling (Resident in Hartford, Connecticut Office)
Peter D. Schellie (Resident in Washington, D.C. Office)
Scott M. Schooley (Resident in Hartford, Connecticut Office)
Norman J. Shachoy
Leslie H. Shapiro

(See Next Column)

BINGHAM, DANA & GOULD, *Boston—Continued*

MEMBERS OF FIRM (Continued)

Lawrence I. Silverstein
Edwin E. Smith
John R. Snyder (Resident in Hartford, Connecticut Office)
William G. Southard
Lee A. Spielman (Resident in Hartford, Connecticut Office)
James C. Stokes
John R. Utzschneider
Paul M. Vaughn
Thomas H. Walsh, Jr.
Judy K. Weinstein (Resident in Hartford, Connecticut Office)
Sabin Willett
Robert M. Wolf
Joseph C. Zengerle, III (Resident in Washington D.C. Office)
Jay S. Zimmerman (Resident in London, England Office)
Peter F. Zupcofska

OF COUNSEL

Austin S. Ashley
Hugh J. Ault
Sumner H. Babcock
Kenneth W. Bergen
J. Patrick Dowdall
Joseph H. B. Edwards
Joseph Ford
David R. Glissman (Resident in Hartford, Connecticut Office)
Robert J. Hallisey
Burton M. Harris
Robert Haydock, Jr.
Joseph F. Hunt
Catherine E. LaMarr (Resident in Hartford, Connecticut Office)
William J. McNally
Francis S. Moulton, Jr.
James P. Rowles
James M. White, Jr.
Mari Anne Wilson

ASSOCIATES

Peter Alley
Rebecca Federman Alperin
Frank A. Appicelli (Resident in Hartford, Connecticut Office)
Marion Giliberti Barish
Mark W. Batten
James L. Black, Jr.
Robert M. Borden (Resident in Hartford, Connecticut Office)
Johan Van't Hul Brigham
Robert A. Buhlman
Dianne S. Burden
Teresa Burke (Resident in Washington, D.C. Office)
James E. Cobery
John J. Concannon, III
Sherry L. Countryman
Paula G. Curry
Susan Walsh Davis
Loraine de Jong (Resident in London, England Office)
Mary Kathryn DeNevi
Deidre A. Doherty
Timothy J. Fallon
Carol A. Fantozzi (Resident in Hartford, Connecticut Office)
John J. Finn
Marcy Friedman
Walter F. Garger (Resident in Hartford, Connecticut Office)
Gregory J. Getschman
Michael E. Gibney
Gerald B. Goldberg (Resident in Hartford, Connecticut Office)
Jon C. Gonzales
Jonathan D. Gworek
Thomas J. Hennessey
Patricia J. Hill
Thomas John Holton
Meerie M. Joung
Sandra E. Kahn
Scott H. Kapilian
Brian Keeler
Richelle S. Kennedy
Jeffrey S. King
Connie L. Kolb
Julie E. Korostoff
Carolyn M. Landever (Resident in Washington, D.C. Office)
James D. Leroux
Michael W. Leslie
Peter J. Mancusi
Robert G. Martin
Patricia M. McCarthy
James C. McGrath
Marianne Meacham
Stephen M. Miklus
Wendy Adams Miklus
Robert A. Miley
Patricia M. Natale
Karen E. Nelson
Sonia Y. Norman-Johnson
Douglas E. Onsi
Michael P. Panagrossi (Resident in Hartford, Connecticut Office)
Daniel I. Papermaster (Resident in Hartford, Connecticut Office)
Maria M. Park
Martin J. Pasqualini
Joseph P. Pelican (Resident in Washington, D.C. Office)
Julie Scallen Reed
Donald P. Richards
Paul M. Robertson
James Scott Rollins (Resident in Hartford, Connecticut Office)
Peter C. L. Roth
Laurie F. Rubin
Darcy A. Ryding
T. Malcolm Sandilands (Resident in London, England Office)
Daniel S. Savrin
Toby R. Serkin
John R. Skelton
Charles L. Solomont
Susan Spring (Resident in London, England Office)
Jeffrey P. Steele
E. Clothier Tepper
Richard A. Toelke
Neil W. Townsend
Sonya M. Tsiros
Matthew J. Tuttle
Julio E. Vega
Ian M. Wenniger
Shelbey D. Webbe Wright
David Yamin

LEGAL SUPPORT PERSONNEL

William A. Bachman

For full biographical listings, see the Martindale-Hubbell Law Directory

BROWN & STADFELD (AV)

66 Long Wharf, 02110
Telephone: 617-720-4200
Fax: 617-720-0240

Harold Brown
L. Seth Stadfeld

(See Next Column)

L. Michael Hankes
Linda J. Keogh
Catherine M. Keenan
Susan J. Assad

For full biographical listings, see the Martindale-Hubbell Law Directory

BURNS & LEVINSON (AV)

125 Summer Street, 02110-1624
Telephone: 617-345-3000
Telecopier: 617-345-3299
Rockland, Massachusetts Office: 1001 Hingham Street.
Telephone: 617-749-1023; 982-4100.
Telecopier: 617-982-4141.

MEMBERS OF FIRM

Lawrence M. Levinson
Thomas D. Burns
Robert W. Weinstein
William H. Clancy
Barry L. Solar
Howard D. Medwed
John A. Donovan
Norman C. Spector
Charles Mark Furcolo
Martin B. Shulkin
Steven C. Goodwin
George E. Christodoulo
David J. Hatem
William E. Moderi
Traver Clinton Smith, Jr.
Melvin A. Warshaw
Paul E. Stanzler
Chester A. Janiak
Michael Weinberg
Susan M. Barnard
Stuart M. Van Tine (Resident, Rockland Office)
Nancy R. Van Tine (Resident, Rockland Office)
David E. Grossman
Frederick S. Paulsen
John J. McGivney
David P. Rosenblatt
Elliot M. Sherman
Joel S. Freedman
Barbara S. Hamelburg
Michael Ross Gottfried
Evelyn A. Haralampu
Dennis J. Kelly
Mark J. Levinson
Michael H. Goshko
Richard A. Savrann
Raymond E. Baxter
Margot Ames Clower
Jeffrey D. Sternklar
Michael G. Tracy
Robert C. Rives, Jr.
Warren D. Hutchison
Dana C. Blakslee
Darrell Mook
Jeffrey R. Martin
Robin Patrick Daniels
Gary Wm. Smith
Richard L. Wulsin
Jay S. Gregory
Cheryl A. Waterhouse
Randy Kaplan

ASSOCIATES

Lawrence J. McNally, Jr.
Steven L. Charlip
Kevin G. Kenneally
Elizabeth J. Maillett
Michael P. Giunta (Resident, Rockland Office)
Michelle F. Rosenberg (Resident, Rockland Office)
Maura A. Greene
Ralph G. Picardi
Mark C. DiVincenzo
Mark Ventola
Ann M. Donovan
Maria-Eugenia Recalde
Michelle S. Labrecque
Dennis J. Bannon
Clifford R. Cohen
Henry T.A. Moniz
Frank C. Muggia
Walter M. Foster
Luigi Leo
Pamela G. Smith
Jeffrey L. Alitz
Cathleen S. Dinsmore
Robert S. Halpern
Joni F. Katz
Victoria L. Karlson
Harris K. Weiner
Andrew W. Daniels
William H. DiAdamo
Andrew P. Botti
Maureen S. Kelley
Maureen S. Jones (Resident, Rockland Office)
Duane G. Sullivan
Sean F. O'Connor
Holly A. Ditchfield
Patricia B. Gary
Beverly A. Kogut
Curtis R. Diedrich
Mary P. Sharon
Steven J. Bolotin
Julie S. Crozier
Ellen Donahue
Maura McCaffery
Pavel H. Wonsowicz
Elizabeth L.S. Dana
Ellen C. Peckham
David J. Gorman
Arlene Mainster Holtzman
Scott P. Murphy
Linda R. Coffey
Anthony J. Fitzpatrick
Thomas P. Hagen
Renee Inomata
Andrew J. McBreen
Michelle Macken Zavez

OF COUNSEL

Karl Greenman
Edmund J. O'Brien
Warren E. Tolman
David M. Thomas
Herbert M. Weiss
George N. Tobia, Jr.

For full biographical listings, see the Martindale-Hubbell Law Directory

CASNER & EDWARDS (AV)

1 Federal Street, 27th Floor, 02110
Telephone: 617-426-5900
Telecopier: 617-426-8810
Cable Address: "Fedlaw"

MEMBERS OF FIRM

Thomas D. Edwards (1931-1987)
Andrew J. Casner, Jr.
Walter H. Mayo, III
Martin E. Greenblatt
Charles M. Hamann
Robert A. Murphy
Robert E. Cowden, III
John H. Ashby
Douglas K. Mansfield
Andrew M. Higgins
Terrance J. Hamilton
Robert S. Kutner
David J. Chavolla
Robert L. Ciociola

(See Next Column)

CASNER & EDWARDS—*Continued*

MEMBERS OF FIRM (Continued)

Stephen M. Perry
Gary L. Hoff
Anita W. Robboy
Robert M. Mendillo

ASSOCIATES

Gaynor D. Casner
Jo-Ann Charak
Donna Brewer MacKenna
Gary L. Kemp
Peter A. Caro
Joan M. Griffin
Matthew T. Murphy
Thomas R. Holland
Thomas J. Walsh
Jeffrey M. Lovely
Cathy M. Judd-Stein
Cristina V. Coletta

For full biographical listings, see the Martindale-Hubbell Law Directory

LAW OFFICES OF ANSEL B. CHAPLIN (AV)

31 State Street, 02109
Telephone: 617-227-0272
Truro, Massachusetts Office: P.O. Box 867.
Telephone: 508-487-1190.

Ansel B. Chaplin
Frederick Kuhn
Anne C. Kenney

For full biographical listings, see the Martindale-Hubbell Law Directory

CHERWIN & GLICKMAN (AV)

A Partnership including Professional Corporations
One International Place, 02110-2622
Telephone: 617-330-1625
FAX: 617-330-1642

Stanley A. Glickman (1937-1994)
Joel I. Cherwin (P.C.)
Marshall D. Stein
Douglas L. Jones
Alfred D. Ellis (P.C.)
Emilie F. Athanasoulis
Lisa Lee Foster
Elizabeth J. McGlynn

OF COUNSEL

Jay F. Theise (P.C.)

For full biographical listings, see the Martindale-Hubbell Law Directory

CHOATE, HALL & STEWART (AV)

Exchange Place, 53 State Street, 02109
Telephone: 617-248-5000
Cable Address: "Chohalste".
Telecopier: 617-248-4000
Telex: 49615860. MCI Mail #: 5536395.

MEMBERS OF FIRM

Paul W. Allison
David L. Arnheim
Pamela E. Berman
Allen M. Bornheimer
Samuel B. Bruskin
Robert M. Buchanan, Jr.
Lyman G. Bullard, Jr.
Mark D. Cahill
Sandra Jesse Carter
Stephen M. L. Cohen
Sarah Chapin Columbia
John M. Cornish
F. Davis Dassori, Jr.
Roslyn G. Daum
David S. Davenport
Brian A. Davis
Ailsa DePrada Deitemeyer
Kathy A. Faulk
Scott A. Faust
Stephen K. Fogg
Robert S. Frank, Jr.
Marion R. Fremont-Smith
Robert M. Gargill
William P. Gelnaw, Jr.
Frank Giso III
Charles L. Glerum
Laura C. V. W. Glynn
Myra J. Green
William F. Grieco
Andrew C. Griesinger
John R. Grumbacher
Jeffrey L. Heidt
James C. Heigham
Weld S. Henshaw
Carla B. Herwitz
Edward F. Hines, Jr.
Richard N. Hoehn
Christopher M. Jedrey
Mitchell H. Kaplan
Alan H. Kaufman
Alicia M. Colarte Kelly
Larry C. Kenna
W. Brewster Lee
Howard J. Levitan
Thomas F. Maffei
James A. McDaniel
Arnold P. Messing
Mark A. Michelson
Paul D. Moore
John A. Nadas
Andrew L. Nichols
Joseph E. O'Leary
Jeremiah T. O'Sullivan
Peter M. Palladino
Sam Pasternack
Frank B. Porter, Jr.
Cameron Read
William C. Rogers
James Roosevelt, Jr.
A. Hugh Scott
Thomas E. Shirley
Jo Ann Shotwell
M. James Shumaker
David F. Slottje
John R. Walkey
Michael Arthur Walsh
Willie J. Washington
Thomas H. P. Whitney, Jr.
Eric W. Wodlinger

OF COUNSEL

Joseph T. Baerlein
Nathaniel T. Dexter
Kevin P. Light

SENIOR ATTORNEY

Kathleen King Parker

(See Next Column)

ASSOCIATES

Oliver F. Ames, Jr.
Ruth R. Aronson
David A. Attisani
Diane L. Azarian
Jane A. Bell
Brian A. Berube
Julie B. Brennan
Lorraine M. Brennan
Douglas S. Brown
Tina A. Campbell
Paul F. Carroll
Christopher H.M. Carter
Karen L. Cartotto
Katherine A. Chaurette
David A. Cifrino
Frank J. Cimler, Jr.
Shane K. Cobb
Lynn Toney Collins
Jeanne C. Conerly
Christine Conley
Nolly Elisabeth Corley
David M. Corwin
Timothy J. Courville
David B. Currie
Paul G. Cushing
Steven P. Eakman
Timothy R. Epp
Bret A.S. Fausett
Cecilia Kim Finnerty
Frank N. Gaeta
Deborah Kantar Gardner
Kathleen M. Genova
Douglas R. Gooding
James W. Hackett, Jr.
Gerald M. Haines, II
Jonathan W. Harlow, Jr.
James P. Hawkins
Stephen G. Hennessy
Anne Rickard Jackowitz
Robert V. Jahrling, III
Kurt A. James
Michael G. Jones
Warren A. Kaplan
Gregory Keating
Peter G. Koback
Michael C. Koffman
Monica Levine Lacks
Kevin J. Lesinski
Jeffrey A. Levinson
Marni Smilow Levitt
Lloyd Lipsett (Not admitted in MA)
Diana K. Lloyd
Jodie M. Lolik
Theodore A. Lund
Cynthia Thomas MacLean
Paul M. Mahoney, Jr.
Richard J. Maloney
Thomas F. Maloney
Steven L. Manchel
Eric J. Marandett
Sam A. Mawn-Mahlau
Nicholas J. Nesgos
Liam T. O'Connell
Miranda R. Pickells
Laurence D. Pierce
Michael R. Reinemann
James R. Richards
Douglas D. Robinow
Sarah Wolcott Saunders
Heidi A. Schiller
Nora J. Schneider
Stephanie N. Shanley
James S. Shorris
Melanie S. Sommer
John S. Tuohy
Christopher Umana
James T. Vradelis
Sara A. Walker
Lisa Fishbone Wallack
Keith Wexelblatt
Miriam A. Widmann
Stephanie M. Williams
Susan L. Williams

For full biographical listings, see the Martindale-Hubbell Law Directory

CORNELL AND GOLLUB (AV)

75 Federal Street, 02110
Telephone: 617-482-8100
Telecopier: 617-482-3917

MEMBERS OF FIRM

Robert W. Cornell (1910-1988)
Karl L. Gollub (1934-1985)
David H. Sempert
Philip J. Foley
Peter M. Durney
Paul F. Lynch

ASSOCIATES

Susan Geyer Malloy
Jane Treen Brand
Hugh M. Coxe
Janet J. Bobit
Thomas A. Pursley
David W. McGough
Susan M. Donaldson
Marie E. Chadeayne
Bruce E. Hopper
Thomas H. Dolan
Eric B. Goldberg
Kelly L. Wilkins
Martha Jane Dickey

For full biographical listings, see the Martindale-Hubbell Law Directory

CRAIG AND MACAULEY, PROFESSIONAL CORPORATION (AV)

Federal Reserve Plaza, 600 Atlantic Avenue, 02210
Telephone: 617-367-9500
Telecopier: 617-742-1788; 617-248-0886

John C. Craig
William F. Macauley
David F. Hannon
Mary P. Brody
A. Van C. Lanckton
Richard E. Quinby
Stephen Wald
William R. Moorman, Jr.

OF COUNSEL

Charles C. Craig
Donald W. Suchma

John G. Snyder
Martin P. Desmery
Beth S. Stomberg
Alan D. Hoch
Andrew M. Porter
R. Paul Faxon
Christopher J. Panos
Peter J. Roberts
Diane M. Crawford-Kelly
Mark W. Manning
Anthony D. Rizzotti
Laurie A. Parrott
Christopher S. Dalton
Michael J. Degnan

For full biographical listings, see the Martindale-Hubbell Law Directory

Boston—Continued

CUDDY BIXBY (AV)

One Financial Center, 02111
Telephone: 617-348-3600
Telecopier: 617-348-3643
Wellesley, Massachusetts Office: 60 Walnut Street.
Telephone: 617-235-1034.

Francis X. Cuddy (Retired)
Wayne E. Hartwell
Brian D. Bixby
Anthony M. Ambriano
William E. Kelly
Paul G. Boylan
Robert A. Vigoda
Paul J. Murphy
Alexander L. Cataldo
Duncan S. Payne
Stephen T. Kunian
Arthur P. Menard
Joseph H. Walsh
Michael J. Owens
Robert J. O'Regan
Andrew R. Menard
David F. Hendren
Glenn B. Asch
Timothy E. McAllister
William R. Moriarty
Kevin P. Sweeney
Denise I. Murphy

For full biographical listings, see the Martindale-Hubbell Law Directory

DAY, BERRY & HOWARD (AV)

Twenty First Floor, 260 Franklin Street, 02110
Telephone: 617-345-4600
Telex: 990686
Telecopier: 617-439-4453
Hartford, Connecticut Office: City Place.
Telephone: 203-275-0100.
Telecopier: 203-275-0343.
Stamford, Connecticut Office: One Canterbury Green.
Telephone: 203-977-7300.
Telecopier: 203-977-7301.

MEMBERS OF FIRM IN BOSTON

James L. Ackerman
Joseph W. Ambash
Glenn E. Brace (Not admitted in MA)
David B. Broughel
Lewis A. Burleigh
Daniel J. Carragher
Jeffrey A. Clopeck
Nancy M. Cullen
George L. Cushing
Lisa J. Damon
Charles Donelan
Thomas D. Gill, Jr.
William A. Hunter
J. Charles Mokriski
Ross A. Pascal
William Shields
H. Lawrence Tafe, III
Kenneth E. Werner
Cynthia J. Williams

ASSOCIATES OF FIRM IN BOSTON

Jonathan T. Baer
Colin Hugh Buckley
David C. Camp
Bruce D. Hickey
Carol F. Liebman
Kathleen S. Moore
Kenneth B. Newton
Kathryn A. O'Leary
Nancy M. Reimer
Mark C. Rosenthal
Lisa A. Stephanian
Daniel P. Sullivan
Maura D. Sullivan
Danielle Y. Vanderzanden
James E. Venable, Jr.
Mary Ellen C. Whiteman
Mark C. Wilson
G. Perry Wu
Anne Magill Ziebarth

OF COUNSEL

Richard C. Csaplar, Jr.

COUNSEL

Kenneth A. Reich

For full biographical listings, see the Martindale-Hubbell Law Directory

*** DECHERT PRICE & RHOADS (AV)**

Ten Post Office Square South, 12th Floor, 02109
Telephone: 617-728-7100
Telefax: 617-426-6567
Philadelphia, Pennsylvania: 4000 Bell Atlantic Tower, 1717 Arch Street.
Telephone: 215-994-4000.
New York, N.Y.: 477 Madison Avenue.
Telephone: 212-326-3500.
Washington, D.C.: 1500 K Street, N. W.
Telephone: 202-626-3300.
Harrisburg, Pennsylvania: Thirty North Third Street.
Telephone: 717-237-2000.
Princeton, New Jersey: Princeton Pike Corporate Center, P.O. Box 5218.
Telephone: 609-520-3200.
London, England: 2 Serjeants' Inn, EC4Y 1LT.
Telephone: (071) 583-5353. (Also see Titmuss Sainer Dechert).
Brussels, Belgium: 65 Avenue Louise, 1050.
Telephone: (02) 535-5411.

RESIDENT PARTNERS

Adrienne M. Baker
Timothy C. Blank
Bernard J. Bonn III
Joseph R. Fleming
Sheldon A. Jones
Alan L. Lefkowitz

RESIDENT OF COUNSEL

James M. Storey

RESIDENT COUNSEL

Susan M. Camillo

(See Next Column)

RESIDENT ASSOCIATES

Terrie J. Hanna
Deborah W. Kirchwey
Caroline Pearson
David A. Rozenson
Richard A. Stamm
Kara W. Swanson
Jason A. Tucker
Dina Warner

For full biographical listings, see the Martindale-Hubbell Law Directory

ESDAILE, BARRETT & ESDAILE (AV)

75 Federal Street, 02110
Telephone: 617-482-0333
FAX: 617-426-2978

MEMBERS OF FIRM

J. Newton Esdaile
Charles W. Barrett, Jr.
James N. Esdaile, Jr.
Norman I. Jacobs
Michael E. Mone
Patricia L. Kelly
Robert J. Rutecki

ASSOCIATES

Shaun Spencer Forsyth
Rhonda Traver Maloney
Hilary R. Weinert
Steven J. Ryan
C. William Barrett
Mary J. Moynihan-Conneely
Jon M. Jacobs

OF COUNSEL

Charles J. Murray

For full biographical listings, see the Martindale-Hubbell Law Directory

FERRITER, SCOBBO, SIKORA, SINGAL, CARUSO & RODOPHELE, P.C. (AV)

One Beacon Street, 02108
Telephone: 617-589-0700
Fax: 617-589-0701
Newton, Massachusetts Office: 73 Lexington Street.
Telephone: 617-965-3220.
Fax: 617-969-9159.

Maurice J. Ferriter
Nicholas J. Scobbo, Jr.
Mitchell J. Sikora, Jr.
Gerald J. Caruso
Bruce A. Singal
Robert P. Rodophele

Francesco Mercuri
Robert M. Granger
Ann Ryan-Small
Vincent L. DiCianni
Robert Wolkon
Lynn Peterson Read
Lauren E. Duca
Laurie Ellen Weisman
James Erickson Fitzgerald

OF COUNSEL

Alan L. Kovacs
Richard E. Connolly

For full biographical listings, see the Martindale-Hubbell Law Directory

FOLEY, HOAG & ELIOT (AV)

One Post Office Square, 02109
Telephone: 617-482-1390
Cable Address: "Foleyhoag"
Telex: 94-0693
Telecopier: 617-482-7347
Washington, D.C. Office: 1615 L Street, N.W.
Telephone: 202-775-0600.
Telecopier: 202-857-0140.

MEMBERS OF FIRM

David L. Weltman
Verne W. Vance, Jr.
Hanson S. Reynolds
David B. Ellis
David W. Walker
Mark F. Clark
John D. Patterson, Jr.
James K. Brown
Robert L. Birnbaum
William J. Cheeseman
Christian M. Hoffman
Michael B. Keating
Adam Sonnenschein
Leonard Schneidman
Edward N. Gadsby, Jr.
Peter B. Ellis
Paul E. Tsongas
John H. Henn
Barry B. White
Arnold M. Zaff
Louis P. Georgantas
Philip Burling
John M. Stevens, Jr.
Peter W. Coogan
Sandra Shapiro
Paul V. Lyons
Kenneth L. Grinnell
Deborah A. Willard
John L. Burke, Jr. (Managing Partner, Washington, D.C. Office)
Charles J. Beard
Deborah B. Breznay
Richard W. Benka
Stanley B. Bernstein
Arthur G. Telegen
Thomas M. S. Hemnes
Stephen B. Deutsch
Donald R. Ware
Peter M. Rosenblum
Dennis R. Kanin
Paul R. Murphy
Marc K. Temin
Toni G. Wolfman
Jacob N. Polatin
Steven W. Phillips
Laurie Burt
William B. Koffel
Kevin J. Fitzgerald
David R. Pierson
Dean F. Hanley
Stefanie D. Cantor
Robert W. Sweet, Jr.
Brandon F. White
David R. Geiger
Bruce A. Kinn

(See Next Column)

FOLEY, HOAG & ELIOT—*Continued*

MEMBERS OF FIRM (Continued)

Robert S. Sanoff
James A. Smith
Wendy B. Jacobs
Gary C. Crossen
Richard Belin
James T. Montgomery, Jr. (Resident at Washington, D.C. Office)
Andrew Z. Schwartz
Ellyn R. Weiss (Resident at Washington, D.C. Office)
Arlene L. Bender
Jonathan H. Hulbert
Mark L. Johnson
Bruce R. Parker
Carol Hempfling Pratt
Michael N. Glanz
Nicholas C. Theodorou
Richard R. Schaul-Yoder

Herbert L. Berman
H. Kenneth Fish
Hans F. Loeser
Jerome Preston, Jr.

OF COUNSEL

John F. Bok
Donald L. Connors

COUNSEL

Diane E. Bissonnette

ASSOCIATES

Feriale Abdullah
Michael A. Albert
Andrew D. Beard
Leslie Beth Bellas (Resident, Washington, D.C. Office)
Steven A. Bercu
Jonathan E. Book
Michael Parker Boudett
Richard M. Brunell
James W. Bucking
Mara D. Calame
Vincent J. Canzoneri
Timothy G. Caron
Peter M. Casey
Charles H. Cella
Michael Thomas Chaffers
Karen B. Cheyney
Monica E. Conyngham
Robert L. Cowdrey
Stephanie Cutler (Resident at Washington, D.C. Office)
Dan Danielsen
Amy P. Dennin
Deborah Drosnin
Jonathan M. Ettinger
David H. Feinberg
Kathleen Freeman
Lynda B. Furash
Mary Beth Gentleman
C. Erik Gustafson (Resident, Washington, D.C. Office)
Jeffrey M. Hahn
John D. Hancock
Elline Hildebrandt
Seth D. Jaffe
Michael I. Joachim
David Kahan
Adam P. Kahn
Amy B. G. Katz
Jonathan A. Keselenko
William R. Kolb
Claire Laporte
Harry F. Lee
George N. Lester
Matthew B. Lowrie
Audrey C. Mark
Teresa A. Martland
Gerald A. Mc Donough
Douglas M. McGarrah
Laurie M. McTeague
Earl W. Mellott, II
Anthony D. Mirenda
Gregory T. Moffatt
Susan Barbieri Montgomery
Marcia L. Moore
Jeffrey B. Mullan
Kathryn Partridge
Alexander H. Pyle
Sarah Burgess Reed
Toby B. Richard
Sarah M. Richards
Paul R. Rocklin
Michael L. Rosen
David H. Ruttenberg
John A. Shope
Thomas E. Stoddard
Bradford Gram Swing
James E. Tucker
David D. Vanspeybroeck
Charles E. Weinstein
Michele A. Whitham
Miles Archer Woodlief

For full biographical listings, see the Martindale-Hubbell Law Directory

---

FRIEDMAN & ATHERTON (AV)

(Formerly Friedman, Atherton, King & Turner)
(Formerly Friedman, Atherton, Sisson & Kozol)
Exchange Place, 53 State Street, 02109-2803
Telephone: 617-227-5540
Telecopier: 617-523-1559

Lee M. Friedman (1895-1957)
Percy A. Atherton (1903-1940)
Frank L. Kozol (1927-1993)

OF COUNSEL

Frank H. Shapiro

MEMBERS OF FIRM

Joel A. Kozol
Lee H. Kozol
William I. Cowin
Robert D. Kozol
Richard M. Zinner
Matthew S. Kozol
Alan M. Spiro
David L. Kelston
Victor Bass

ASSOCIATES

Thomas C. Bailey
Andrew D. Cummings
Paula F. Donahue
John J. Ellis
Michele L. King
David M. Kozol
Penny Kozol
Joseph B. Lichtblau
David A. Rich
Marie C. Vaccarelli
Herbert Weinberg

COUNSEL

Paul Bork

For full biographical listings, see the Martindale-Hubbell Law Directory

GADSBY & HANNAH (AV)

125 Summer Street, 02110
Telephone: 617-345-7000
Telex: 6817512 GADHAN BSN
Telefax: 617-345-7050
Washington, D.C. Office: 1747 Pennsylvania Avenue, N.W., Suite 800.
Telephone: 202-429-9600.

PARTNERS

Richard K. Allen
David M. Amidon
Ronald G. Busconi
Wendell Robert Carr, Jr.
Harold J. Carroll
Paul E. Clifford
Thomas G. Collins
Allan R. Curhan
Marianne Gilleran
Augusto F. Grace
Harry R. Hauser
Peter S. Johnson
Robert J. Kaler
Cynthia B. Keliher
Daniel J. Kelly
Wesley J. Marshall, Jr.
Stanley A. Martin
James J. Myers
Michael N. Sheetz
Jeffrey P. Somers
Kevin J. Toomey
Patrick C. Toomey
Robert A. Trevisani
Walter D. Wekstein
Burton Winnick
William A. Zucker

OF COUNSEL

John B. Miller

ASSOCIATES

Joseph M. Centofanti
Peter M. Coppinger
Michael W. Dingle
Robert J. Foley
Leigh A. Gilligan
John R. Hallal
Rosa C. Hallowell
Paul Marshall Harris
Jason M. Holt
Jill Rosen Hyde
Lawrence R. Katz
Diane M. McDermott
Michael T. McInerny
Richard P. Quinn
Ellen Borkum Scult
Steven M. Shishko
Lisa G. Sorkin
Linda A. Surdacki
Peter F. Trotter
Kathleen B. Woodard
David L. Woronov

WASHINGTON, D.C. OFFICE

RESIDENT PARTNERS

Robert S. Brams (Not admitted in MA)
Mary Ann Gilleece
Michael A. Hordell
Paul F. Kilmer (Not admitted in MA)
Carol L. B. Matthews (Not admitted in MA)

RESIDENT ASSOCIATES

Thomas W. Brooke (Not admitted in MA)
Robert F. Garcia, Jr. (Not admitted in MA)

RESIDENT OF COUNSEL

Jeffrey B. Mulhall (Not admitted in MA)

For full biographical listings, see the Martindale-Hubbell Law Directory

---

GILMAN, MCLAUGHLIN & HANRAHAN (AV)

A Partnership including a Professional Corporation
Harbor Plaza, 470 Atlantic Avenue, 02210
Telephone: 617-482-1900
Cable Address: Gilmac

MEMBERS OF FIRM

Arthur M. Gilman
Walter H. McLaughlin, Jr.
Robert E. McLaughlin
David G. Hanrahan
John B. Shevlin, Jr.
William F. York
Michael Eby
James W. Murphy
J. David Moran (P.C.)
Fredric L. Ellis
David L. Klebanoff

COUNSEL

Walter H. McLaughlin, Sr.
Donna E. Cohen

ASSOCIATES

Robert E. Moran
Timothy M. Corcoran
Nora J. Mann
Leigh A. McLaughlin
Marla B. Kirk
Bernice McPhillips
Ross D. Ginsberg

For full biographical listings, see the Martindale-Hubbell Law Directory

---

GOODWIN, PROCTER & HOAR (AV)

A Partnership including Professional Corporations
Exchange Place, 02109-2881
Telephone: 617-570-1000
Cable Address: "Goodproct, Boston"
Telex: 94-0640
Telecopier: 617-523-1231
Washington, D.C. Office: 901 Fifteenth Street, N.W., Suite 410.
Telephone: 202-414-6160.
Telecopier: 202-789-1720.
Albany, New York Office: One Steuben Place.
Telephone: 518-472-9460.
Telecopier: 518-472-9472.

(See Next Column)

GOODWIN, PROCTER & HOAR, *Boston—Continued*

MEMBERS OF FIRM

Robert E. Goodwin (1878-1971)
Joseph O. Procter (1880-1932)
Samuel Hoar (1877-1952)
Donald J. Evans (P.C.)
Robert B. Fraser (P.C.)
Preston H. Saunders (P.C.)
Marshall Simonds (P.C.)
William B. King (P.C.)
Samuel L. Batchelder, Jr., (P.C.)
William H. Gorham (P.C.)
Edward T. O'Dell, Jr., (P.C.)
Allan van Gestel
Joseph W. Haley (P.C.)
A. Jeffrey Dando (P.C.)
Donald P. Quinn (P.C.)
George W. Butterworth, III
David P. Ries (P.C.)
Richard E. Floor (P.C.)
Michael Steinberg (P.C.)
Jerome H. Somers (P.C.)
Shepard M. Remis (P.C.)
Steven J. Comen
Jeremiah S. Buckley (Resident, Washington D.C. Office)
Wayne A. Budd
Jon D. Schneider (P.C.)
Robert C. Pomeroy (P.C.)
Stephen W. Carr (P.C.)
Paul F. Ware, Jr., (P.C.)
Don M. Kennedy (P.C.)
Richard A. Soden
Edward L. Glazer (P.C.)
William V. Buccella
Raymond P. Boulanger (P.C.)
Thomas J. Griffin, Jr.
Michael S. Elder (Resident, Albany, New York Office)
Paul F. McDonough, Jr., (P.C.)
Robert F. Houser (P.C.)
Howard A. Cubell
Kenneth A. Cohen (P.C.)
John J. Cleary (P.C.)
Michael H. Glazer (P.C.)
Francis W. Dubreuil (P.C.)
Anthony M. Feeherry
F. Beirne Lovely, Jr.
Paul R. Gauron (P.C.)
Susan M. Cooke (P.C.)
James J. Dillon (P.C.)
John Kenneth Felter (P.C.)
Lawrence R. Cahill (P.C.)
Lawrence E. Kaplan (P.C.)
David F. Dietz (P.C.)
Paul W. Lee (P.C.)
Edward Matson Sibble, Jr., (P.C.)
Jeffrey C. Bates
William P. Mayer
Daniel M. Glosband (P.C.)
Henry C. Dinger (P.C.)
Stuart M. Cable
Susan Hall Mygatt
Paul D. Schwartz (P.C.)
Diane L. Currier (P.C.)
Thomas P. Storer (P.C.)
James W. Nagle
Lynne B. Barr
Michael J. Pappone (P.C.)
Paul E. Nemser
Marian A. Tse
Martin Carmichael III (P.C.)
Raymond C. Zemlin (P.C.)
Christopher P. Davis
Stephen D. Poss (P.C.)
Laura C. Hodges Taylor (P.C.)
John R. LeClaire (P.C.)
Regina M. Pisa (P.C.)
William H. Whitledge (P.C.)
Richard A. Oetheimer
Philip H. Newman
Alexander A. Randall
Kevin M. Dennis
John J. Egan III
Geoffrey R. T. Kenyon
Gilbert G. Menna (P.C.)
Adam N. Weisenberg (P.C.)
Nancer Ballard
Sandra Sue McQuay
Wilfred J. Benoit, Jr.
Trudy A. Ernst (P.C.)
Stephen H. Schroeder
Donald S. Berry (P.C.)
Kevin J. Handly
Daniel Patrick Condon
Robert M. Hale
E. Michael Paul Thomas
Christopher T. Katucki (P.C.)
F. Dennis Saylor, IV
John C. Englander
Andrew E. Shipley
Christopher B. Barker
Ettore A. Santucci (P.C.)
Gregory A. Bibler
R. Todd Cronan
Jeffrey D. Plunkett
Ann D. Dexter
Michael C. Hanson
H. David Henken
Joseph L. Johnson III
Paul C. Nightingale
Joseph M. Kolar (Resident, Washington, D.C. Office)
Cerise H. Lim-Epstein
Matthew T. Giuliani
Elizabeth McDermott
Minta E. Kay
Ross D. Gillman
J. Anthony Downs
Steven M. Ellis
Jeffrey C. Hadden
H. Neal Sandford
Bradford J. Smith
Mark E. Tully
Keith D. Shugarman (Resident, Washington, D.C. Office)

OF COUNSEL

Leonard Wheeler
Charles D. Post
Carl F. Schipper, Jr.
Frederick J. Robbins (P.C.)
William J. Pechilis (P.C.)
Russell G. Simpson (P.C.)
Arthur L. Stevenson
Donald B. Gould

COUNSEL

Henry B. Shepard, Jr., (P.C.)
Evan Jones
Daniel J. Mullen
Michael J. Meagher

ASSOCIATES

Mary-Kathleen O'Connell
Joan Garrity Flynn
Gordon H. Piper
Anette Seltzer Lewis
Michael J. Litchman
Kristina Hansen Wardwell
A. Lauren Carpenter
John O. Newell
Theresa A. Cook
Nina Raginsky Mishkin
Paula M. Bagger
Meredeth A. Beers
Alan Dankner
Thomas M. Hefferon
Joseph M. Herlihy
Terrence J. Cullen
Oliver C. Colburn
Margaret B. Crockett
Thomas J. Phillips
Raymond D. Hiley
Kenneth J. Parsigian
Scott L. Robertson
Donna Stoehr Hanlon
Marc A. Silver
Jeffrey M. Wolf
Thomas P. LaFrance
Robert J. Gilbert
Gregg S. Levin
Marsha Weinerman
Janice L. Sherman

(See Next Column)

ASSOCIATES (Continued)

Jennifer Hilton Weiss
Michael L. Andresino
Stephen V. Loughlin
Deirdre C. Ryan Menoyo
David L. Ruediger
Judy Newberne
Kim M. Rubin
John B. Steele
David W. Watson
Robert P. Whalen, Jr.
Peter R. DeFeo
Michael J. Wall
William R. Moore
Gerard A. Caron
John B. Daukas
Robert A. Freeman
Kerry S. Kehoe
Barbara Healy Smith
Deirdre A. Cunnane
Mary A. Daly
Patricia D. Popov
Elizabeth Shea Fries
Catherine W. Gill
Lori Henderson
Peter F. Neronha
Andrew S. Josef
Andrew C. Sucoff
Melissa Dyan Smith
David M. Barlow
James J. Berriman
James M. Broderick
Elliot J. Mark
Kathryn I. Murtagh
Loraine Parkinson
Judith A. Solomon
Christopher T. Vrountas
Mary M. Diggins
John G. Loughnane
Yvette C. Mendez
Michelle R. Peirce
Christopher N. Popov
Jeremy M. Sternberg
Peter T. Fariel
Edward M. Schulman
Mark F. Cavanaugh
Carol S. Warren
Bruce I. Tribush
Celia S. Byler
Cindy H. Rose
Gregory J. Lyons
Robert G. Kester
Jeffrey P. Naimon (Resident, Washington, D.C. Office)
Joseph A. Piacquad (Not admitted in MA)
Douglas Alexander Batt
Nathaniel Dalton
Maura Griffith Moffatt
Daniel P. Karnovsky
Ann C.M. Leafstedt
Felix S. Riccio
Winifred Lynn Swan
Reginald F. Thors
David R. Zipps
Carol R. Lev
Neil McLaughlin
Margaret M. Ross
Duc Nguyen (Resident, Washington D.C. Office)
Giles A. Birch
J. Todd Hahn
Rebecca A. Lee
Jennifer Locke
Robert G. Schwartz, Jr.
Steven E. Skwara
Ellen S. Winer
Jennifer M. Bott
Carla Folz Brigham
Glenn D. Burlingame (Not admitted in MA)
Patricia A. Albright
Stephen G. Charkoudian
Jonathan I. Handler
Brenna B. Jordan
James A. Matarese
Kendal B. Price
Andrew F. Viles
Nuria del Pilar Rivera
Robert J. Waeldner
Domenic P. Gaeta
Susan M. Cullina
B. Dane Dudley
Samuel L. Richardson
Scott F. Duggan
Samantha J. Kim
Nancy L. Sholes
Joseph Alexander, Jr.
Janet M. Dunlap
Jennifer Merrigan Fay
Michael J. Kendall
Jeffrey D. Scheman
Paula D. Leca
David L. Permut
Melissa L. Roy
Kevin F. Slayne
Daniel C. Winston
Patricia A. Lipoma
Laura J. Moloney
Andrew J. Weidhaas
U. Gwyn Williams
Stephen C. Kolocotronis

For full biographical listings, see the Martindale-Hubbell Law Directory

GOULSTON & STORRS, A PROFESSIONAL CORPORATION (AV)

400 Atlantic Avenue, 02110-3333
Telephone: 617-482-1776
Telecopy: 617-574-4112

H. Edward Abelson
David M. Abromowitz
Steven R. Astrove
Mark D. Balk
Thomas P. Bloch
Harry S. Dannenberg
Nancy Mammel Davids
Robert C. Davis
Jack A. Eiferman
Matthew E. Epstein
Lester J. Fagen
Leonard H. Freiman
Martin A. Glazer
Alan S. Goldberg
Michael A. Hammer
Michael J. Haroz
Philip A. Herman
William A. Horne
Douglas M. Husid
Denis M. King
Jordan P. Krasnow
Richard Langerman
William A. Levine
Phillip G. Levy
Darline M. Lewis
Julia C. Livingston
Deborah R. Lunder
Kenneth E. MacKenzie
Adrienne M. Markham
Richard A. Marks
Patricia Ann Metzer (Miss)
Anne H. Meyer
Phillip J. Nexon
James F. O'Brien
Rudolph F. Pierce
Michael M. Robinson
Philip R. Rosenblatt
Alan W. Rottenberg
Eli Rubenstein
Daniel C. Sacco
Nancy B. Samiljan
Thomas J. Sartory
Kitt Sawitsky
Joseph R. Schmidt
Barbara E. (Shaeffer) Schmitt
Carole Miner Schuman
Joel B. Sherman
Donald L. Shulman
Ronald B. Shwartz
Thomas G. Sitzmann
Marvin Sparrow
Marilyn L. Sticklor
Robert S. Towsner
John E. Twohig
Arthur S. Waldstein
James F. Wallack

(See Next Column)

GOULSTON & STORRS A PROFESSIONAL CORPORATION—*Continued*

Robert A. Weiland
David S. Weiss
Hynrich W. Wieschhoff
Jeffrey S. Wolfson

Daniel R. Avery
Lisa J. Avery-Peck (Not admitted in MA)
Herman T. Bayless
Patrick C. Bennison
Peter D. Corbett
Christopher A. Ditunno (Not admitted in MA)
Martin M. Fantozzi
Julie A Frohlich
Robert P. Goldman
Barry D. Green
Charlotte M. Hartwell
Jacqueline Jourdain Haynes (Not admitted in MA)
Deborah S. Horwitz
Lawrence M. Kraus
Kathryn A. Lachelt (Not admitted in MA)
Frank E. Litwin
Pamela M. Maloney
Jane A. Materazzo
Lynne Alix Morrison
Kathryn A. Murphy
Emily Nozick
Kevin P. O'Flaherty
Jonathan M. Pearlstein
Jennifer C. Platt
Roslyn Poznansky
David W. Price
Douglas B. Rosner
Steven Schwartz
William M. Seuch
Joel Sklar
Steven J. Snyder
B. Andrew Zelermyer

OF COUNSEL

William O. Flannery
Patricia McGovern

Herbert B. Ehrmann (1891-1970)
David H. Greenberg (1905-1988)
Thomas Kaplan (1916-1993)
Samuel Markell (1888-1992)
Jay E. Orlin (1936-1993)

For full biographical listings, see the Martindale-Hubbell Law Directory

HALE AND DORR (AV)

A Partnership including Professional Corporations
60 State Street, 02109
Telephone: 617-526-6000
Cable Address: "Hafis."
Telex: 94-0472
Telecopier: Domestic 617-526-5000; 617-742-9108
Washington, D.C. Office: 1455 Pennsylvania Avenue, N.W.
Telephone: 202-942-8400.
Cable Address: "Hafis Wsh."
Telecopier: 202-942-8484.
Manchester, New Hampshire Office: 1155 Elm Street.
Telephone: 603-628-7400.
Telecopier: 603-627-3880.

MEMBERS OF FIRM

Samuel S. Dennis, 3rd, (P.C.)
James D. St. Clair (P.C.)
John F. Cogan, Jr. (P.C.)
Norman B. Asher
Jerome P. Facher
James A. Brink
Robert J. Richards, Jr.
Paul P. Brountas
John D. Hamilton, Jr., (P.C.)
Robert E. Fast
Harold Hestnes
Ernest V. Klein
S. Donald Gonson
Martin S. Kaplan (P.C.)
Hugh R. Jones, Jr.
Philip D. Stevenson
Alexander A. Bernhard (P.C.)
Vincent P. McCarthy (P.C.)
Louis H. Hamel, Jr.
John G. Fabiano
C. Hall Swaim
John H. Morton
John M. Westcott, Jr.
Richard W. Giuliani
Stephen H. Oleskey
Richard L. Berkman
Thomas E. Neely
Robert Tuchmann
Harry T. Daniels
Robert W. Mahoney
Joseph P. Barri
Paul P. Daley
Richard J. Innis
Linda K. Sherman
James L. Quarles, III (Resident, Washington, D.C. Office)
Joel H. Sirkin
Joan A. Lukey
Robert D. Keefe
Jeffrey B. Rudman
Robert S. Mueller, III (Resident, Washington, D.C. Office)
David E. Redlick
Edward Young
John A. Burgess
Edwin A. James
William F. Lee
Roger M. Ritt
Mark G. Borden
Neil H. Jacobs
Michael L. Fay
Richard A. Johnston
John J. Regan
James C. Burling
Andrew H. Cohn
William H. Schmidt
Peter B. Tarr
Katharine E. Bachman
Mark N. Polebaum
Allen H. Fox (Resident, Washington, D.C. Office)
William C. Benjamin
James B. Lampert
Steven D. Singer
David H. Erichsen
Paul G. Wallach (Resident, Washington, D.C. Office)
Robert D. Burke
Joseph J. Christian
William R. O'Reilly, Jr.
John D. Sigel
Thomas N. O'Connor
Steven S. Snider (Resident, Washington, D.C. Office)
Geoffrey S. Stewart (Resident, Washington, D.C. Office)
Michelle D. Miller
Merriann M. Panarella
Jay E. Bothwick
Sarah Rothermel
Jeffrey N. Carp
Philip P. Rossetti
David Sylvester (Resident, Washington, D.C. Office)
Jay P. Urwitz (Resident, Washington, D.C. Office)
Jeffrey J. Davidson (Resident, Washington, D.C. Office)

(See Next Column)

MEMBERS OF FIRM (Continued)

John W. Delaney
Richard V. Wiebusch (Resident, Manchester, New Hampshire Office)
Jennifer C. Snyder
Thomas L. Barrette, Jr.
William G. McElwain (Resident, Washington, D.C. Office)
John F. Batter III
Melvin R. Shuman
Gilbert B. Kaplan (Resident, Washington, D.C. Office)
John K. P. Stone, III
Michael R. Heyison
Christopher J. Perry
Michael J. Bevilacqua
Rekha D. Packer
Pamela J. Wilson
David A. Westenberg
Patrick J. Rondeau
Peter J. Macdonald
Mark G. Matuschak
Robert C. Kirsch (Resident, Manchester, New Hampshire Office)
Stephen A. Jonas
Olivia A. O'Neill
Wayne M. Kennard (Not admitted in MA)
Kenneth H. Slade (Not admitted in MA)
Richard M. Tardiff
Jeffrey A. Stein (Resident, Manchester, New Hampshire Office)
Hollie L. Baker (Resident, Washington, D.C. Office)
Jeffrey A. Hermanson
Hal J. Leibowitz
Paul V. Rogers
A. Silvana Giner
Christopher P. Harvey
William F. Leahy (Resident, Washington, D.C. Office)
Susan W. Murley
Brent B. Siler (Resident, Washington, D.C. Office)
Brenda J. Fingold
Jude A. Curtis (Resident, Manchester, New Hampshire Office)
Richard L. Hoffman
Daniel Levin (Resident, Washington, D.C. Office)
Robyn B. Klinger
Wayne L. Stoner
Susan M. Curtin
Henry N. Wixon (Resident, Washington, D.C. Office)
A. William Caporizzo
William H. Paine
James A. Perley, Jr.
David C. Phelan (Not admitted in MA)
Scott A. Roberts
Kenneth R. Meade (Resident, Washington, D.C. Office)
Elizabeth M. Leonard
Charles J. Gray
David K. Wanger
Jonathan D. Rosenfeld
Paul G. Igoe
Andrea J. Robinson
Nancy J. Kelley
Mary E. Cavanaugh
David Marder
James W. Prendergast
John H. Chory
Mary Jo Johnson
Paul Jakubowski
Susan M. Kincaid
Gary P. Brady
David B. Bassett
David A. Wilson (Resident, Washington, D.C. Office)
Donald R. Steinberg
Donald J. Williamson (Resident, Manchester, New Hampshire Office)
Paul W. Jameson (Resident, Washington, D.C. Office)
Robert P. Nault
Ann K. Bernhardt
Charles P. Kindregan
Virginia H. Kingsley
Stephen C. Reilly
Brian E. Whiteley
Jonathan Wolfman
Michael F. Zullas

COUNSEL

Herbert W. Vaughan (P.C.)
James Segel
Catherine V. Mannick
James F. Millea, Jr.
Peter A. Spaeth
Daniel W. Halston
Kenneth A. Hoxsie
Jane Cetlin Pickrell (Resident, Manchester, New Hampshire Office)

ASSOCIATES

Stephanie Monaghan O'Brien
Carol A. Hannigan
Erik P. Kimball
Michael J. LaCascia
Brian W. Robinson
N. Roland Savage
Anthony A. Scibelli
Daniel P. Tighe
Kathleen M. Weinstein (Not admitted in MA; Resident, Washington, D.C. Office)
Albert P. Parker, II (Resident, Washington D.C. Office)
Sean P. Sherman (Resident, Washington, D.C. Office)
Stuart M. Falber
Deborah C. Segal
Anne Marie Tanin
Michael J. Gartland
S. Tara Miller
Keith R. Barnett
Erik P. Belt
Michael G. Bongiorno
James R. Burke
William S. Gehrke
Richard N. Kimball
B. J. Krintzman
Daniel W. McCarthy
Michael J. Nathanson
W. Scott O'Connell (Resident, Manchester, New Hampshire Office)
Heidi C. Paulson
Leonard A. Pierce
Joseph L. Stanganelli (Not admitted in MA)
Kerry J. Tomasevich
Elaine M. Hartnett
Frank W. Getman Jr.
Lisa A. Rydin
Michael P. Scanlon
Eve Stolov Vaudo
Mitchel Appelbaum
Jane E. Price
Wendy E. Anderson (Resident, Washington, D.C. Office)
Jorge L. Contreras, Jr.
Pamela A. Harbeson
William J. Healey (Resident, Washington, D.C. Office)
Susan McWhan Tobin (Resident, Washington, D.C. Office)
Lisa B. Newlin
Keith M. Roberts
Laura E. Schneider
Kelly J. Voight
Cris R. Revaz (Resident, Washington, D.C. Office)
Carolyn S. Ballan
Sean T. Boulger
Jamie N. Class
Glenn M. Martin
Michael J. Moody
Julia A. Rossetti
Sloane Elizabeth Anders (Resident, Washington, D.C. Office)
Alicia Afalonis

(See Next Column)

HALE AND DORR, *Boston—Continued*

ASSOCIATES (Continued)

Sarah Curtis
Robert F. Fitzpatrick Jr.
Scott A. Lively
Lisa J. Pirozzolo
Patrick Shin
Rusty Wilson (Resident, Washington, D.C. Office)
Michael D. Bain
Judith A. Evans (Resident, Washington, D.C. Office)
Dominic E. Massa
James J. Nicklaus
Scott E. Pueschel
Wendy Rae Rodano (Resident, Washington, D.C. Office)
Jason Tate Sherwood
Cynthia Tanner
Mark R. Young
Joseph E. Mullaney, III
Nicholas Carter

Laurence D. Shind
Patricia Anne Whalen
William A. Caldwell
Carolyn P. Partan
David J. Shapiro
Susanne M. Hopkins-Klima (Resident, Washington, D.C. Office)

For full biographical listings, see the Martindale-Hubbell Law Directory

HEMENWAY & BARNES (AV)

60 State Street, 02109
Telephone: 617-227-7940
Fax: 617-227-0781

MEMBERS OF FIRM

Alfred Hemenway (1863-1927)
Charles B. Barnes (1893-1956)
George H. Kidder
David H. Morse
Roy A. Hammer
Lawrence T. Perera
John J. Madden
George T. Shaw
Timothy F. Fidgeon
Ruth R. Budd
Michael B. Elefante
Michael J. Puzo
Thomas L. Guidi
Edward Notis-McConarty
Diane C. Tillotson
Susan Hughes Banning
Frederic J. Marx
Deborah J. Hall
Kurt F. Somerville
Stephen W. Kidder
Teresa A. Belmonte

COUNSEL

Michael L. Leshin

ASSOCIATES

Andrea H. Maislen
Barbara Zicht Richmond
Marsha K. Zierk
Charles Fayerweather
Christopher Denn
James P. Warner
Brian C. Broderick

OF COUNSEL

Guido R. Perera

For full biographical listings, see the Martindale-Hubbell Law Directory

HILL & BARLOW, A PROFESSIONAL CORPORATION (AV)

One International Place, 02110
Telephone: 617-439-3555
Telex: 94-0916
Telecopier: 439-3580

Arthur Dehon Hill (1869-1947)
Robert Shaw Barlow (1869-1943)
Richard L. Alfred
Charles C. Ames
R. Hale Andrews, Jr.
Thomas H. Belknap
Gregory P. Bialecki
Nonnie Steer Burnes
Thomas C. Chase
Richard S. Chute
Penny P. Cobey
Frances Cohen
Timothy J. Dacey, III
Charles R. Dougherty
Bruce E. Falby
John G. Gillis
John A. D. Gilmore
Michael S. Greco
Joseph D. Hinkle
David A. Hoffman
John M. Kahn
Peter Katz
Richard L. Levine
Winifred I. Li
Terrence W. Mahoney
Gael Mahony
Wayne H. Miller
W. Hugh M. Morton
Christopher L. Noble
Stephen M. Nolan
Gregory D. Peterson
Joseph R. Ramrath
Richard W. Renehan
Richard D. Rudman
Carl M. Sapers
Miriam Vock Sheehan
Joseph D. Steinfield
Jonathan Strong
Elliot M. Surkin
Daniel A. Taylor
Thomas G. Taylor
Dennis W. Townley
William A. Truslow
E. Randolph Tucker
John C. Vincent, Jr.
Barbara Freedman Wand
Michael D. Weisman
Richard M. Zielinski

OF COUNSEL

Kingsbury Browne, Jr.
Benjamin H. Lacy
James R. Repetti
John L. Sullivan

ASSOCIATE OF COUNSEL

Josephine Foehrenbach Brown
Diane diIanni

(See Next Column)

Sarah H. Arnholz (Not admitted in MA)
Charles A. Baker, III
Peter E. Ball
Linda Gillenwater Bauer
Robert A. Bertsche
Sara Miron Bloom
Martha Born
Elizabeth Brendze
Joshua M. Davis
Susan C. Dawson
Nancy E. Dempze
Joseph L. Faber
William B. Forbush, III
John C.P. Goldberg
Michael J. Goldberg
Lisa C. Goodheart
Gail A. Goolkasian
David P. Horne
Ilana C. Hurwitz
Mark J. Johnston
Renee M. Jones
Theos D. McKinney, III
Neil V. McKittrick
Alexander W. Moore
Valerie L. Moore
Judith E. Norton
Christopher Patusky
Michael J. Pineault
Heather M. Quay
Michael D. Ricciuti
David W. Tarbet
Andrea M. Teichman
Cornelia R. Tenney
Timothy B. Tomasi
Timothy Veeser
Michael D. Vhay (Not admitted in MA)
Audrey K. Wang

For full biographical listings, see the Martindale-Hubbell Law Directory

HINCKLEY, ALLEN & SNYDER (AV)

(Formerly Hinckley, Allen, Tobin & Silverstein and Snyder, Tepper & Comen)
One Financial Center, 02111-2625
Telephone: 617-345-9000
Providence, Rhode Island Office: 1500 Fleet Center.
Telephone: 401-274-2000.

MEMBERS OF FIRM

Susan H. Alexander
Paula K. Andrews
Richard C. Arrighi
E. Jerome Batty (Not admitted in MA)
Jonathan Bell
Edmund C. Bennett (Not admitted in MA)
Thomas C. Carey
Stephen J. Carlotti (Not admitted in MA)
Gordon A. Carpenter
Sean O. Coffey (Not admitted in MA)
Scott E. Cooper
Thomas Roberts Courage
Thomas S. Crane
Joseph P. Curran (Not admitted in MA)
Michael P. DeFanti
Kristin A. DeKuiper
Joseph M. Di Orio (Not admitted in MA)
Malcolm Farmer, III
Margaret D. Farrell (Not admitted in MA)
Noel M. Field, Jr. (Not admitted in MA)
Pasco Gasbarro Jr.
Alan P. Gottlieb
Gerard R. Goulet
William R. Grimm
Paul A. Hedstrom
Jacques V. Hopkins (Not admitted in MA)
James A. Jackson (Not admitted in MA)
James E. Keeley (Not admitted in MA)
Robert J. Kerwin
Joel Lewin
Doris Jami Licht
Sandra Matrone Mack (Not admitted in MA)
Matthew T. Marcello, III (Not admitted in MA)
Frederick P. McClure
Michael B. Nulman
H. Peter Olsen (Not admitted in MA)
John J. Pendergast, III (Not admitted in MA)
Gerald J. Petros
Richard H. Pierce
Debra G. Reece
Brian P. Richards (Not admitted in MA)
David J. Rubin (Not admitted in MA)
Dennis M. Ryan
Charles E. Schaub, Jr.
Frank A. Segall
Paul A. Silver
Michael A. Silverstein (Not admitted in MA)
Evan Slavitt
Richard G. Small
Herman Snyder
Robert F. Sylvia
Richard J. Tetrault
Edwin G. Torrance (Not admitted in MA)
Howard E. Walker (Not admitted in MA)
Richard D. Wayne
Joachim A. Weissfeld (Not admitted in MA)

ASSOCIATES

Jeffrey D. Abbey (Not admitted in MA)
John W. Bishop, Jr.
Joseph S. U. Bodoff
Leon C. Boghossian III
Sarah J. Bulger
Beth Ann Carlson (Not admitted in MA)
David Barry Connolly
Robin A. DeAugustinis
Lynne Barry Dolan
Susan F. Donahue
Bradley P. Dorman (Not admitted in MA)
Robert M. Duffy
Eric F. Eisenberg
Robert D. Emerson
Michael C. Fee
Joseph P. Ferrucci
Michelle A. Ruberto Fonseca
Hugh J. Gorman, III
Kim Herman Goslant
Gloria Maria Gutierrez
Richard L. E. Jocelyn (Not admitted in MA)
James S. Judd
Michael S. McSherry
Toni Ann Motta (Not admitted in MA)
Mary Powers Murray
Christopher W. Nelson (Not admitted in MA)
Christopher M. Neronha
Paul F. O'Donnell, III
Elena B. Olson
Gardner H. Palmer, Jr.
Julianne Palumbo
Susan E. Raitt
James O. Reavis
Steven A. Remsberg

(See Next Column)

HINCKLEY, ALLEN & SNYDER—*Continued*

ASSOCIATES (Continued)

Mark Resnick
Claire J.V. Richards
Jeremy Ritzenberg
Craig Michael Scott
Michael F. Sweeney
Susan B. Tuchman

OF COUNSEL

David D. Barricelli (Not admitted in MA)
Anthony J. Buccitelli
Willard Krasnow
Willard R. Pope
Edward W. Powers
Bentley Tobin

For full biographical listings, see the Martindale-Hubbell Law Directory

HUTCHINS, WHEELER & DITTMAR, A PROFESSIONAL CORPORATION (AV)

101 Federal Street, 02110
Telephone: 617-951-6600

STOCKHOLDERS/MEMBERS

Katherine L. Babson, Jr.
Mark N. Berman
Laura L. Carroll
John H. Clymer
Donald D. Cooper
David T. Dinwoodey
James S. Dittmar
Alan H. Einhorn
Jack H. Fainberg
Francis J. Feeney, Jr.
Ronald Garmey
Frederick H. Grein, Jr.
John J. Griffin, Jr.
William E. Halmkin
Harry A. Hanson, III
Lori J. Holik
John D. Hughes
Franklin C. Huntington, IV
Carolyn P. Jacoby
Jonathan R. Karis
Deborah S. Kay
James A. Kobe
Richard R. Lavin
Leonard G. Learner
Philip C. Lombardo, Jr.
Anthony J. Medaglia, Jr. (P.C.)
James L. Messenger
Arthur S. Meyers, Jr. (Not admitted in MA)
Evelyn Venables Moreno
Richard S. Nicholson
Mary Ellen O'Mara
Sanford F. Remz
Michael J. Riccio, Jr.
Sander A. Rikleen
Charles W. Robins (P.C.)
Regina Strazulla Rockefeller
David S. Rosenthal
Robert P. Sherman
Adrienne Smith
Richard M. Stein
Joseph C. Tanski
Robert A. Thompson
John C. Thomson
Richard L. Trembowicz
Andrew M. Troop
Sally A. VanderWeele
James R. Westra
James G. Wheeler
Jeffrey S. Wieand
Charles A. Wry, Jr.
Richard J. Yurko

ASSOCIATES

John M. Baker
Robert G. Bannish
John W. Banse
R. Hitz Burton (Not admitted in MA)
Thomas M. Camp
Alan Jay Cooke
William Brett Davis
David Ross De Veau (Not admitted in MA)
Mark William Eagle
Marilyn Emack (Not admitted in MA)
Laurie Ilene Gelb
Thomas A. Giacchetto
Geoffrey Hargreaves-Heald
Meredith A. Helmer
John F. Hemenway
Julie Huston
Robert L. Kirby, Jr.
David P. Kreisler
Ronald LaRussa
Maureen A. MacFarlane
Joseph C. Marrow
Mary Beth Martin
Robert Orsi
Karen M. O'Toole
Donald W. Parker
Gregory A. Pastore (Not admitted in MA)
Steven M. Peck
Kim E. Perry
Laura Michelle Pritzker
Mark D. Robins
Samuel C. Sichko
Jeffrey Michael Snider
Jill M.E. Sullivan
Patrick G. Sullivan
John M. Timperio
Susan M. Valente
Seth R. Weissman
Shannon D. Whisenant

OF COUNSEL

Ernest G. Angevine (P.C.)
Michael T. Gengler
William F. Kehoe
Rainer M. Kohler (P.C.)
Nicholas U. Sommerfeld
Henry Wheeler

For full biographical listings, see the Martindale-Hubbell Law Directory

KOPELMAN AND PAIGE, P.C. (AV)

101 Arch Street, 02110
Telephone: 617-951-0007
Cable Address: "Lawkope"
Fax: 617-951-2735

Leonard Kopelman
Donald G. Paige
Elizabeth A. Lane
Joyce F. Frank
John W. Giorgio
Barbara J. Saint Andre
Joel B. Bard
Everett Joseph Marder
Patrick J. Costello

(See Next Column)

Joseph L. Tehan, Jr.
William Hewig, III
Theresa M. Dowdy
Deborah Eliason
Jeanne S. McKnight
Judith Chanoux Cutler
Anne-Marie M. Hyland
Richard Bowen
Cheryl Ann Banks
David J. Doneski
Sandra M. Charton
Brian W. Riley
Mary L. Giorgio
Kathleen Elisabeth Connolly
John G. Gannon

For full biographical listings, see the Martindale-Hubbell Law Directory

ARTHUR F. LICATA, P.C. (AV)

20 Custom House Street, Suite 1010, 02110
Telephone: 617-345-9588
Fax: 617-261-4570

Arthur F. Licata

For full biographical listings, see the Martindale-Hubbell Law Directory

LOONEY & GROSSMAN (AV)

A Partnership including Professional Corporations
101 Arch Street, 02110
Telephone: 617-951-2800
Fax: 617-951-2819

William F. Looney, Jr.
Stewart F. Grossman (P.C.)
Richard J. Grahn
Bertram E. Snyder
Robert Cushman Barber
Richard J. Levin
Bradley W. Snyder

OF COUNSEL

Wesley S. Chused
Melvin S. Hoffman (P.C.)
Joseph H. Matzkin
Paul D. McCarthy
Sherman H. Starr, Jr.

ASSOCIATES

Susan F. Drogin
Seth Salinger
Erin M. Gilligan
David Yanofsky
Neil D. Warrenbrand
Maria Galvagna
Lisa Sternschuss
Keir J. Beadling

For full biographical listings, see the Martindale-Hubbell Law Directory

MARTIN, MAGNUSON, MCCARTHY & KENNEY (AV)

133 Portland Street, 02114
Telephone: 617-227-3240
Telecopier: 617-227-3346

MEMBERS OF FIRM

Ephraim Martin (1900-1988)
Clement McCarthy (1921-1985)
Raymond J. Kenney, Jr. *
Charles P. Reidy, III *
Daniel J. Griffin, Jr. *
Philip E. Murray, Jr. *
Joseph L. Doherty, Jr. *
Neal M. Lerer *
Paul R. Keane *
John P. Mulvey *
Paul M. McTague *
Carol A. Kelly *
Gail L. Anderson *
Edward F. Mahoney *

COUNSEL

Harold E. Magnuson
Edward F. Hennessey

Joan L. Atlas *
Joseph B. Bertrand *
Martha A. Driscoll *
Douglas A. Robertson *
Mary T. Gibbons *
Teresa J. Farris *
Elizabeth A. Cushing *
Mark A. Newcity
Marie G. Leary *

Representative Clients: Allstate Insurance Company; American International Adjustment Company; Browning - Ferris Industries, Inc.; Fireman's Fund Insurance Companies; Fireman's Fund; Joint Underwriting Association of Massachusetts; Liability Limited; Multi Systems Agency LTD.; Murray Ohio Manufacturing Company; Risk Management Foundation; Shand Morhan Company.
References: Fleet Bank; Shawmut Bank, N.A.
*Employees of The Professional Corporation of McCarthy, Kenney & Reidy.

For full biographical listings, see the Martindale-Hubbell Law Directory

MCDERMOTT, WILL & EMERY (AV)

A Partnership including Professional Corporations
75 State Street, Suite 1700, 02109-1807
Telephone: 617-345-5000
Telex: 951324 MILAM BSN
Facsimile: 617-345-5077
Chicago, Illinois Office: 227 West Monroe Street.
Telephone: 312-372-2000.
Telex: 253565 MILAM CGO.
Facsimile: 312-984-7700.
Miami, Florida Office: 201 South Biscayne Boulevard.
Telephone: 305-358-3500.
Telex: 441777 LEYES.
Facsimile: 305-347-6500.

(See Next Column)

McDermott, Will & Emery, *Boston—Continued*

Washington, D.C. Office: 1850 K Street, N.W.
Telephone: 202-887-8000.
Telex: 253565 MILAM CGO.
Facsimile: 202-778-8087.
Los Angeles, California Office: 2049 Century Park East.
Telephone: 310-277-4110.
Facsimile: 310-277-4730.
Newport Beach, California Office: 1301 Dove Street, Suite 500.
Telephone: 714-851-0633.
Facsimile: 714-851-9348.
New York, N.Y. Office: 1211 Avenue of the Americas.
Telephone: 212-768-5400.
Facsimile: 212-768-5444.
St. Petersburg, Russia Office: 2/2 Tchaikovsky Street, #517, 191187 St. Petersburg, Russia.
Telephone: (7) (812) 273-9831.
Facsimile: (7) (812) 273-9831.
Tallinn, Estonia Office: Tallinn Business Center, 6 Harju Street, EE0001 Tallinn, Estonia.
Telephone: 372 6 31-05-53.
Facsimile: 372 6 31-05-54.
Vilnius, Lithuania Office: Smetonos 6, 2600 Vilnius, Lithuania.
Telephone: 370 2 61-43-08.
Facsimile: 370 2 22-79-55.
Associated (Independent) Offices:
Brussels, Belgium: Uettwiller Grelon Lippens Dekeyser, 73 avenue Vandendriessche, 1150 Brussels, Belgium.
Telephone: (32) (2) 772-87-50.
Facsimile: (32) (2) 772-87-52.
London, England: Paisner & Co, Bouverie House, 154 Fleet Street, London EC4A 2DQ, England.
Telephone: (44) (71) 353-0299.
Facsimile: (44) (71) 583-8621.
Paris, France: Uettwiller Grelon Gout Canat & Associes, 68, Boulevard de Courcelles, 75017 Paris, France.
Telephone: (33) (1) 48 88 89 00.
Facsimile: (33) (1) 48 88 05 50.

MEMBERS OF FIRM

Arthur I. Anderson
Linda D. Bentley
Michael L. Blau
Peter Braun
Cornelius J. Chapman, Jr.
Christopher J. Donovan
David A. Fazzone *
Mary Belle Feltenstein
Walter A. Foskett
Donald R. Frederico
Harvey W. Freishtat
Adolfo R. Garcia *
Dustin F. Hecker
Timothy D. Jaroch
Martin R. Leinwand
Peter R. Leone
Erich Luschei
James J. Marcellino
Christopher W. Parker
Stephen C. Ploszaj
John R. Pomerance
Peter L. Resnik
Marjory D. Robertson
Thomas H. Sullivan *
Gordon T. Walker

COUNSEL

Robert J. Cordy
Doron F. Ezickson

OF COUNSEL

Andrew M. Wood

Anthony A. Bongiorno
Rudolph F. DeFelice
Amy J. Gould
James J. Haggerty
Robert H. Hoaglund II
Nicholas P. Holder
Susan M. Insoft
Steven W. Kasten
Cherie L. Krigsman
Sally Kaplan Levy
Andrew C. Liazos
Jill Braunwald Porter
V. Denise Saunders
Michelle S. Wolf
Alicia M. V. Wyman

*Denotes a lawyer employed by a Professional Corporation which is a member of the Firm.

For full biographical listings, see the Martindale-Hubbell Law Directory

---

Mintz, Levin, Cohn, Ferris, Glovsky and Popeo, P.C. (AV)

One Financial Center, 02111
Telephone: 617-542-6000
FAX: 617-542-2241
Washington, D.C. Office: 701 Pennsylvania Avenue, N.W. Suite 900.
Telephone: 202-434-7300.
Fax: 202-434-7400.

Herman A. Mintz (1886-1979)
Benjamin Levin (1899-1991)
Haskell Cohn (1901-1993)
Milton C. Wasby (1907-1993)
A. Morris Kobrick (1909-1976)
William M. Glovsky (1921-1990)
William H. Wolf (1924-1975)
Jerome S. Hertz (1928-1993)

OF COUNSEL

Francis X. Bellotti

(See Next Column)

Richard G. Mintz
Jerome Gotkin
Francis X. Meaney
Charles D. Ferris (Resident, Washington, D.C. Office)
R. Robert Popeo
Peter Van
Sidney A. Slobodkin
William C. Brashares (Resident, Washington, D.C. Office)
Kenneth J. Novack
Frank W. Lloyd (Resident, Washington, D.C. Office)
Thomas J. Kelly
Stephen Weiner
David A. Gilbert
Thomas R. Murtagh
Frederick J. Pittaro
Paul D. Bishop
Irwin M. Heller
Stephen M. Leonard
Howard E. Cohen
Robert M. Gault
David H. Halpert
Martha J. Koster
Michael P. Last
Thomas M. Reardon
Jeffrey M. Wiesen
Joel R. Bloom
Richard E. Mikels
George L. Chimento
Dennis I. Greene
Richard R. Kelly
John K. Markey
Christopher H. Milton
Gregory A. Sandomirsky
Bruce D. Sokler (Resident, Washington, D.C. Office)
Maxwell D. Solet
Michael S. Gardener
Gregor P. Kudarauskas
C. Stephen Parker, Jr.
Alvin J. Lorman
Michael L. Lieberman (Not admitted in MA)
John R. Regier
David G. Spackman
Andrew R. Urban
John F. Donohue
Stuart A. Offner
Michael D. Sinclair
Rebecca L. Jackson (Not admitted in MA; Resident, Washington, D.C. Office)
Cameron F. Kerry
Charles Alan Samuels (Resident, Washington, D.C. Office)
Patrick J. Sharkey
Howard J. Symons (Resident, Washington, D.C. Office)
Stanley A. Twarog
Douglas A. Zingale
Elizabeth B. Burnett
Jonathan L. Kravetz
Craig H. Campbell
Ann-Ellen Marcus Hornidge
Eve T. Horwitz
Whitton E. Norris III
Kenneth M. Bello
Peter A. Biagetti
Rachael Macindoe Dorr
Ann K. Friedman (Resident, Washington, D.C. Office)
H. Joseph Hameline
Stephen T. Langer
Bruce F. Metge
Kenneth B. Schwartz
Paul D. Wilson
Mary Lee Moore
Paul J. Ricotta
Jeffrey S. Robbins
Susan F. Schwartz
Samuel M. Starr
Leocadia Irine Zak
Lee H. Glickenhaus
David E. Lurie
Bruce E. Rogoff
Steven P. Rosenthal
Leonard Weiser-Varon
Joshua Davis
Peter F. Demuth
Peter Kimm, Jr. (Resident, Washington, D.C. Office)
James A. Kirkland (Resident, Washington, D.C. Office)
Elizabeth P. Knauss
Henry A. Sullivan
Kim V. Marrkand
William W. Kannel
Tracy A. Miner
Richard H. Moche
Rosemary M. Allen
Kathleen M. Sheehan

Judith S. Lidsky
John Paul Sullivan (Not admitted in MA)
Robert J. Ryan
Marilyn Newman
William P. McDermott
Ellen L. Janos
Catherine S. Stamps
Marie Lefton (Director of Professional Practice)
David S. Szabo
Susan Englander Hislop
John C. Plotkin
James A. Durham (Director of Practice Development and Community Service)
Timothy J. Langella
David S. Lintz
Jodi M. Landau
Susan J. Cohen
William M. Hill
Joanne A. Robbins
Constance D. Sprauer
Bert H. Ware
John J. Brunelli (Not admitted in MA)
Christopher J. Harvie (Not admitted in MA)
Andrew Nathanson
Barbara D. Dallis
Kathleen C. Tulloh Brink
Michael F. Connolly
Meryl J. Epstein
Lewis J. Geffen (Not admitted in MA)
Cynthia J. Helenek
Cherie R. Kiser (Resident, Washington, D.C. Office)
Judith Slovin Levenfeld
Rick M. Olin
Susan P. Phillips
Anne L. Tully
Joel D. Beeders (Not admitted in MA)
Beth I. Z. Boland
Noam Ayali (Not admitted in MA)
Carleasa A. Coates
Richard A. Goldman
Elizabeth Kagan Cooper
Rebecca E. Kotkin
Shari A. Levitan
E. Peter Parker
Linda B. Port
Jeffrey R. Porter
Robert S. Steinberg
Kecia Boney (Resident, Washington, D.C. Office)
Marie J. Buttarazzi
Navjeet K. Bal
Joseph P. Crawford-Kelly
Donna M. Evans
Alan S. Gale
Mary-Laura Greely
Peter S. Lawrence
Richard Mirabito
Ann M. O'Rourke
John F. Sylvia
John A. Sym
Julie E. Bahret
Joseph P. Curtin
Shepard Davidson

(See Next Column)

MINTZ, LEVIN, COHN, FERRIS, GLOVSKY AND POPEO P.C.—*Continued*

Andrea M. Fish
Karen C. McCusker
Kevin M. McGinty
Stephen T. Murray
M. Daria Niewenhous
Richard W. Rose
Thomas C. Walsh
Richard P. Zermani
Marion K. Antonucci
Michael R. B. Balfe
Kimberly S. Budd
Meghan B. Burke
Peter T. Butterfield
Maryann Civitello
Patrick T. Clendenen
Jeffrey A. Dretler
Susan M. Finegan
Allan M. Green
Judith I. Jacobs
Joseph P. Messina
Valerie B. Robin
Joseph L. Demeo
Elizabeth Brody Gluck
Anne Kinnane
Karen W. Levy (Resident, Washington, D.C. Office)
Elizabeth F. Mason
Mark A. Merante
Elizabeth J. Moshang
Jennifer P. Sacon
Anthony E. Varona (Resident, Washington, D.C. Office)
Martha M. Bailey
Joan E. Cirillo
Tara M. Corvo (Resident, Washington, D.C. Office)
Margaret A. Gilleran
Joanne C. Griffin
Kimberly H. Kelley
Michael F. Kleine (Resident, Washington, D.C. Office)
Paige A. Manning
Thomas S. Moffatt

For full biographical listings, see the Martindale-Hubbell Law Directory

NUTTER, MCCLENNEN & FISH (AV)

A Partnership including a Professional Corporation
One International Place, 02110-2699
Telephone: 617-439-2000
Telex: 94-0790
Facsimile: 617-973-9748
Hyannis, Massachusetts Office: Route 28, 1185 Falmouth Road, P.O. Box 1630.
Telephone: 508-790-5400.
Telecopier: 508-771-8079.

MEMBERS OF FIRM

Murray S. Freeman
Edward C. Mendler
Dana C. Coggins
John P. Driscoll, Jr.
Edward F. McHugh, Jr.
Charles B. Abbott
Duane R. Batista
Charles R. Parrott
Constantine Alexander
Robert L. Dancy
James W. Hackett
Augustus F. Wagner, Jr.
Miriam H. Kanter
Michael E. Mooney
Andrew J. McElaney, Jr.
Daniel J. Gleason
William T. Sherry, Jr.
William H. Baker
Michael J. Bohnen
Louis J. Marett
Charles A. Rosebrock
Robert A. Fishman
Edward P. Leibensperger
Alan D. Rose
Jonathan R. Harris
Stephen M. Andress
Thomas P. Jalkut
Neil P. Motenko
Anne Smiley Rogers
Mary K. Ryan
David E. Watson
Gary D. Zanercik
Peter Nils Baylor
Sharon R. Burger
Zdislaw W. Wieckowski
Patrick M. Butler
Paul R. Eklund
James H. Simon
Michael T. Cetrone
Arthur R Hofmann, Jr.
David R. Schmahmann
Nelson G. Apjohn
Peter R. Brown
Joseph G. Blute
Martin C. Pentz
Dianne Hobbs
Stephen J. Brake
Lisa Cameron Wood
Marianne Ajemian
Michael K. Krebs

OF COUNSEL

Irving J. Helman (P.C.)
Nathan Newbury III
John L. Thompson
William H. MacCrellish, Jr.
Bancroft R. Wheeler
Norman T. Byrnes
Frances H. Miller

JUNIOR PARTNERS

Susan Leonard Repetti
Richard H. Durben
Mark S. La Conte
Deirdre M. Murphy
James E. Dawson
Beth H. Mitchell
Donald Robert Peck
Diane Rosse
Michael Joseph Engelberg
Deborah J. Manus
Richard P. Schwartz
Timothy M. Smith
Michael L. Chinitz
Michelle J. Lipton

ASSOCIATES

Allison W. Allen
Nanette A. Avril
James N. Boudreau
Julia Satti Cosentino
Charles F. Cronin
Kevin J. Curtin
Glenn E. Deegan
Patricia H. DiRuggiero
Daniel J. Driscoll
Marc F. Dupré
John C. Fitzpatrick
Sheila M. Flaherty
Gary L. Gill-Austern
Suzanne L. Glassburn
Nicholas Halpern
Daniel Ross Harris
David C. Henderson
Ann Marie Holder
John Hunt (Not admitted in MA)
Ronald M. Jacobs
Allison B. Kaplan
Regina P. Kornfield
Douglas G. Kott
Paul G. Lannon, Jr.
Lauren A. Liss
Shari L. Lobe
Sarah M. Manning
Nancy A. McGuire
Susan C. Murphy

(See Next Column)

ASSOCIATES (Continued)

Hugh A. O'Reilly
Jonathan Z. Pearlson
Eve Grace Penoyer
Lori Jean Polacheck
Suzanne M. Quill
Andrée M. Saulnier
Erik A. Schmidt
Joseph F. Shea
Cheray G. Shein
Julie A. Trachten
Robert D. Webb
Richard M. Wong

HYANNIS, MASSACHUSETTS OFFICE
PARTNERS

Augustus F. Wagner, Jr.
Patrick M. Butler

OF COUNSEL

Edward F. McLaughlin, Jr.

JUNIOR PARTNER

Marian S. Wossum

For full biographical listings, see the Martindale-Hubbell Law Directory

PALMER & DODGE (AV)

(Storey Thorndike Palmer & Dodge)
One Beacon Street, 02108
Telephone: 617-573-0100
Telecopier: 617-227-4420
Telex: 951104
Cable Address: "Storeydike," Boston

MEMBERS OF FIRM

Moorfield Storey (1887-1929)
John L. Thorndike (1887-1920)
Bradley W. Palmer (1893-1946)
Robert G. Dodge (1910-1964)
F. Andrew Anderson
Neil P. Arkuss
F. Kingston Berlew
Michael R. Brown
Robert W. Buck
Acheson H. Callaghan, Jr.
Abigail A. Cheever
Ralph A. Child
Lawrence B. Cohen
Norman P. Cohen
Matthew C. Dallett
Jeanne P. Darcey
Jean M. DeLuca
Ralph C. Derbyshire
Casimir de Rham, Jr.
Robert Duggan
Andrew L. Eisenberg
Lynnette C. Fallon
Steven N. Farber
John G. Faria
Ruth E. Fitch
David R. Friedman
Karl P. Fryzel
Ralph D. Gants
Nathaniel S. Gardiner
Michael T. Gass
Laurie S. Gill
Leon J. Glazerman
Robert H. Hale
Laurie J. Hall
Richard Hiersteiner
Malcolm E. Hindin
Robert G. Holdway
George M. Hughes
Jeffrey F. Jones
Stanley Keller
Ronald H. Kessel
Jerry V. Klima
Michael J. Lacek
William L. Lahey
Scott P. Lewis
Francis C. Lynch
Michael Lytton
Judith A. Malone
Maureen P. Manning
Eric F. Menoyo
Thomas W. Merrill
Robert P. Moncreiff
Raymond M. Murphy
Arthur B. Page
David R. Pokross, Jr.
John E. Rattigan, Jr.
David E. Rideout
David R. Rodgers
Richard S. Rosenstein
Walter J. St. Onge, III
Peter M. Saparoff
Thomas G. Schnorr
Steven L. Schreckinger
Thane D. Scott
Thomas M. Spera
Craig E. Stewart
Henry G. Stewart
Robert E. Sullivan
Jeffrey Swope
Peter S. Terris
James L. Terry
John M. Thomas
George Ticknor
Roger P. Vacco
Jerome N. Weinstein
James M. Whalen
William T. Whelan
John L. Whitlock
John Taylor Williams
Donald F. Winter
Peter Wirth
Tamara S. Wolfson
R. Robert Woodburn, Jr.
Jackson W. Wright, Jr.

COUNSEL

Stephen J. Abarbanel
David J. Corrsin
Charles E. DeWitt, Jr.
Richard L. Farr (Not admitted in MA)
Jay E. Gruber
Kevin R. McNamara
Alan S. Musgrave
Zick Rubin
Russell B. Swapp
Pamela M. Veasy
Cassandra Warshowsky

ASSOCIATES

Mary Ellen Alessandro
Mystica M. Alexander
John J. Aquino
Marsha Phillips Beatrice
Mark L. Belanger
Amy Berman
Kevin W. Blanton
Grace Blea-Nuñez (Not admitted in MA)
Darca L. Boom
Gregory J. Britz, Jr.
Maureen A. Broe
Katherine Keeton Carter
John G. Casagrande, Jr.
Suzanne V. Cocca
Stephen L. Coco
Mark J. Enyedy
Eileen Finan
Susan V. Fried
Jordana B. Glasgow
Elizabeth A. Grammer
Michele E. Granda
Mary E. Greenwald
Jane M. Guevremont
Joseph F. Hardcastle
Nancy T. Harrington
Anne Marie Hill
Mark A. Kablack
John C. Kacoyannakis (Not admitted in MA)

(See Next Column)

PALMER & DODGE, *Boston—Continued*

ASSOCIATES (Continued)

Pamela Johnson Knauer
Joseph J. Laferrera
Daryl J. Lapp
Carmel Anne Leonard
Tracey L. McCain
Stephen C. McEvoy
Kathleen E. McGrath
Mary C. Moran
Eileen F. Morrison
Susan Murphy
Harvey Nosowitz
Mary Clements Pajak
Prasan A. Pandite
Kirsten C. Poler
Salvatore Ricciardone
Michael D. Rivard
Anne Robbins
Marc A. Rubenstein
Kenneth W. Salinger
Elizabeth P. Seaman
Richard B. Smith
G. Thacher Storm
Betsey Sue
Doris F. Tennant
Joshua M. Thayer
James G. Topetzes
Mary S. Tracy
Aaron C. von Staats
Alison Sweet Zieff
Janet M. Zipin

OF COUNSEL

Virginia Aldrich
Theodore Chase
Ann C. King
Robert J. McGee
Robert W. Meserve
James W. Perkins
John A. Perkins
Mary G. Sullivan
John P. Weitzel
John M. Woolsey, Jr.

For full biographical listings, see the Martindale-Hubbell Law Directory

PEABODY & ARNOLD (AV)

50 Rowes Wharf, 02110-3342
Telephone: 617-951-2100
Telecopier: 617-951-2125
Providence, Rhode Island Office: One Citizens Plaza, Suite 840.
Telephone: 401-831-8330.
Fax: 401-831-8359.

MEMBERS OF FIRM

Francis Peabody (1899-1938)
Edward K. Arnold (1899-1937)
Samuel H. Batchelder (1909-1966)
Willard B. Luther (1909-1962)
Paul J. Ayoub
Jonathan Bangs
James H. Belanger
Michael F. Burke
Donald S. Burnham
Philip H. Cahalin
Bert J. Capone
James E. Carroll
Lawrence G. Cetrulo
Robert J. Coughlin
Philip M. Cronin
Linda S. Dalby
Allen N. David
Paul R. Devin
John K. Dineen
Michael P. Duffy
Ann C. Egan
David W. Fitts
R. Alan Fryer
Michael J. Glazerman
Deborah S. Griffin
David A. Grossbaum
Ripley E. Hastings
Peter G. Hermes
Joseph D. S. Hinkley
James A. P. Homans
John A. Kessler, Jr.
Anil Khosla
Mark C. McCrystal
Robert W. Monaghan
Alexander H. Pratt, Jr.
Douglas C. Reynolds
Samuel S. Robinson
George C. Rockas
Suanne C. St. Charles
John B. Savoca
Peter B. Seamans
Peter M. Shapland
Molly Haynes Sherden
Randolph L. Smith
Donald E. Vaughan
Edward E. Watts, III
Harvey Weiner
Gregory L. White
Thomas A. Wooters
Kevin E. Young
Mark E. Young
Stephen Ziobrowski

OF COUNSEL

John R. Gowell, Jr. (Resident, Providence, Rhode Island Office)
Frank N. Ray (Resident, Providence, Rhode Island Office)
Ralph F. Tuller (P.C.)

COUNSEL

John G. Brooks
Robert D. Power

ASSOCIATES

Barry D. Ramsdell
Peter C. Netburn
Amanda D. Darwin
John P. Connelly
Elizabeth Z. Holmes
Michael J. Rauworth
Suzanne Sheldon
Michael F. Sommerville
Jennifer L. Lauro
Frank S. Hamblett
Robert A. McCall
Shelia High King
Thomas Frisardi
Annette M. Boelhouwer
Kevin J. O'Connor
Amelia M. Charamba
Maureen E. Kane
Denise E. Pedulla
Sean N. Egan
Robert Payne Fox, Jr.
Chantal M. Healey
Maureen Mulligan
John J. O'Connor
Thomas H. Hayman
Sandra P. Criss
Sarah E. Batt
Thomas C. Farrell
CharCretia V. DiBartolo
William J. Dellea
Anna M. Magliocco
Scott S. Spearing
William R. Freeman
Kirsten A. Beske
David B. Frederick
Elsie Bennett Kappler
Amalie Tuffin
Kristine E. George

(See Next Column)

ASSOCIATES (Continued)

Mark W. McCarthy (Not admitted in MA)
Kirsten M. Lacovara
John P. Dougherty
David W. Fanikos
Robin E. Folsom
Rita D. Lu

For full biographical listings, see the Martindale-Hubbell Law Directory

POWERS & HALL, PROFESSIONAL CORPORATION (AV)

(Powers, Hall & Jones 1897-1903)
(Powers & Hall 1903-1957).
(Powers Hall, Montgomery & Weston 1957-1970)
100 Franklin Street, 02110
Telephone: 617-728-9600
Facsimile: 617-728-9633

DIRECTORS

Richard A. Wiley
Walter G. Van Dorn
William Williams II
Douglas A. Nadeau
Gene A. Blumenreich
John V. Woodard
Robert W. Holmes, Jr.
Gregory J. Englund
Andrew D. Frieze
Sydelle Pittas
Pamela J. Anderson
Benjamin W. Moulton
Stephen J. Small
Philip S. Mehall
David A. Broadwin

OF COUNSEL

John Clarke Kane

COUNSEL

Robert L. Nessen

Philip R. Reilly
Richard W. Mable
Michael K. Barron
Kathleen M. Bildzok
Marc C. Laredo
James T. Barrett
Mark G. Maher
Marcia Beth Stairman Wagner
David L. McEvoy
Gail Eagan
Eileen Smith Ewing (Not admitted in MA)

For full biographical listings, see the Martindale-Hubbell Law Directory

RACKEMANN, SAWYER & BREWSTER, PROFESSIONAL CORPORATION (AV)

One Financial Center, 02111
Telephone: 617-542-2300
Telecopier: 617-542-7437

William B. Tyler
George V. Anastas
Henry H. Thayer
Stephen Carr Anderson
Albert M. Fortier, Jr.
Michael F. O'Connell
Stuart T. Freeland
Raymond J. Brassard
Alan B. Rubenstein
Martin R. Healy
James R. Shea, Jr.
Brian M. Hurley
Janet M. Smith
Peter Friedenberg
Richard S. Novak
J. David Leslie
Alexander H. Spaulding
Sanford M. Matathia
Anne P. Zebrowski

OF COUNSEL

Albert B. Wolfe
August R. Meyer
Richard H. Lovell

COUNSEL

Ronald S. Duby
Ross J. Hamlin

Margaret L. Hayes
Daniel J. Ossoff
Mary B. Freeley
Gordon M. Orloff
Donald R. Pinto, Jr.
Lucy West Behymer
Richard J. Gallogly
Melissa Langer Ellis
James A. Wachta
Susan Dempsey Baer
Daniel J. Bailey, III
Michael S. Giaimo
Maura E. Murphy
Mary L. Gallant
Peter A. Alpert
Lauren D. Armstrong
Robert B. Foster
Elizabeth A. Gibbons

For full biographical listings, see the Martindale-Hubbell Law Directory

RICH, MAY, BILODEAU & FLAHERTY, P.C. (AV)

The Old South Building, 294 Washington Street, 02108-4675
Telephone: 617-482-1360
FAX: 617-556-3889

John F. Rich (1908-1987)
Thomas H. Bilodeau (1915-1987)
Gerald May
Harold B. Dondis
Walter L. Landergan, Jr.
Edwin J. Carr
Arthur F. Flaherty
Franklin M. Hundley
Michael F. Donlan
Joseph F. Sullivan, Jr.
Owen P. Maher
Nicolas A. Kensington
Daniel T. Clark
Gerald V. May, Jr.
Eric J. Krathwohl
Michael J. McHugh
James M. Behnke
James M. Avery
Stephen M. Kane
Mark C. O'Connor
Walter A. Wright, III
Emmett E. Lyne

(See Next Column)

RICH, MAY, BILODEAU & FLAHERTY P.C.—*Continued*

Nicholas F. Kourtis
James T. Finnigan
Carol E. Kazmer
Robert P. Snell

For full biographical listings, see the Martindale-Hubbell Law Directory

ROCHE, CARENS & DEGIACOMO (AV)

A Partnership including Professional Corporations
One Post Office Square, 02109
Telephone: 617-451-9300
Facsimile: 617-482-3868
Woburn, Massachusetts Office: 400 Unicorn Park Drive.
Telephone: 617-933-5505.
Saugus, Massachusetts Office: 605 Broadway.
Telephone: 617-233-4074.
Vineyard Haven, Massachusetts Office: P.O. Box 2165.
Telephone: 508-693-7333.
Braintree, Massachusetts Office: 51 Commercial Street.
Telephone: 617-356-4210.

MEMBERS OF FIRM

Frederick W. Roche (1914-1971)
James R. DeGiacomo
Robert J. Sherer
Michael T. Putziger (P.C.)
Judith K. Wyman (P.C.)
John C. Wyman (P.C.)
Richard J. Saletta
John W. Gahan, III
Frank M. Capezzera
Loring A. Cook, III
John J. O'Connor, Jr.
Thomas K. Zebrowski
Susan J. Baronoff
Johanna Smith
Mary S. Parker
Anne Hanford Stossel
Mark G. DeGiacomo
Joseph R. Tarby III (Resident, Woburn Office)
Lynne Callahan DeGiacomo
Joan P. Armstrong
Maury E. Lederman
Brian R. Cook
Tracie L. Longman
Jacqueline Holmes Haley
Francis A. DiLuna (Resident, Woburn Office)

ASSOCIATES

William M. Healy (Resident, Vineyard Haven Office)
Cynthia H.N. Post
Thomas S. Vangel
Elizabeth B. Ornstein
Mark J. Warner
James B. Pratt
John F. Brosnan
Rachel S. Gerny
Allen A. Lynch, III (Resident, Saugus Office)
David A. Kelly (Resident, Braintree Office)
Edward J. Rozmiarek
Nancy M. Harris
Timothy P. Cox
Peter Carbone, III (Resident, Woburn Office)

OF COUNSEL

Thomas J. Carens
Daniel J. Johnedis

For full biographical listings, see the Martindale-Hubbell Law Directory

ROPES & GRAY (AV)

One International Place, 02110
Telephone: 617-951-7000
Fax: 617-951-7050
Washington, D.C. Office: Suite 1200, 1001 Pennsylvania Avenue, N.W.
Telephone: 202-626-3900.
Telecopy: 202-626-3961.
Providence, Rhode Island Office: 30 Kennedy Plaza.
Telephone: 401-455-4400.
Telecopy: 401-455-4401.

MEMBERS OF FIRM

Thomas L. P. O'Donnell
George C. Caner, Jr.
A. Lane McGovern
George H. Lewald
Richard W. Southgate
Champe A. Fisher
John E. Beard
Truman S. Casner
John A. Ritsher
John A. Pike
Edward A. Benjamin
George T. Finnegan
W. Lincoln Boyden
Arthur G. Siler
Howard K. Fuguet
C. Dean Dusseault
Peter MacDougall
David J. Blattner, Jr.
Charles P. Normandin
Henry L. Hall, Jr.
Jerome M. Leonard
David M. Donaldson
Thomas G. Dignan, Jr.
Fred R. Becker
Nicholas A. Grace
Paul B. Galvani
Nelson G. Ross
Robert F. Hayes
William G. Meserve
Philip J. Smith
Francis X. Hanlon
Edward P. Lawrence
Richard P. Ward
G. Marshall Moriarty
William L. Patton
Ruth R. O'Brien
Ronald L. Groves
Thomas W. Taylor
Peter H. Dodson
Ronald B. Schram
Carolyn M. Osteen
Russell A. Gaudreau, Jr. (Washington, D.C. Office)
William F. McCarthy
Robert L. Nutt
Stephen B. Perlman
Francis L. Coolidge
John C. Kane, Jr.
Robert K. Gad, III
Douglas N. Ellis, Jr.
Stephen P. Lindsay
Steven J. Simons
Susan R. Shapiro
Mary E. Weber
John H. Mason
David L. Raish
Thomas M. Susman (Washington, D.C. Office)

(See Next Column)

MEMBERS OF FIRM (Continued)

Roscoe Trimmier, Jr.
William S. Eggeling (Providence, Rhode Island Office)
Lawrence D. Bragg, III
Virginia F. Coleman
R. Hardin Matthews
John W. Gerstmayr
Daniel T. Roble
Steven T. Hoort
Kenneth W. Erickson
Harvey J. Wolkoff
Edward J. Joyce
Gregory E. Moore
David M. Mandel
Nancy E. Ator
Christopher A. Klem
Robert D. Guiod
Nancy R. Rice
Jeffrey B. Storer
James L. Sigel
Martin E. Lybecker (Washington, D.C. Office)
Stephen E. Shay (Not admitted in MA)
Susan A. Johnston
Dwight W. Quayle
Robert N. Shapiro
R. Bradford Malt
Winthrop G. Minot
Geoffrey B. Davis (Providence, Rhode Island Office)
Colburn T. Cherney (Washington, D.C. Office)
Joseph B. Kittredge, Jr.
Thomas H. Hannigan, Jr.
Don S. DeAmicis
David O. Stewart (Washington, D.C. Office)
Claire R. McGuire
Thomas B. Draper
David C. Chapin
David B. Walek
Steven A. Wilcox
Gregory D. Sheehan
John C. Bartenstein
Douglas H. Meal
Eric M. Elfman
Deborah J. Weiss
Richard J. Lettieri
Steven A. Kaufman
John D. Donovan, Jr.
Adelbert L. Spitzer
David A. Fine
Brett A. Robbins
Jonathan M. Zorn
William A. Knowlton
Keith F. Higgins
Alfred O. Rose
Samuel J. Buffone (Washington, D.C. Office)
J. Daniel Berry (Washington, D.C. Office)
Karen Kemper Henson
John M. Loder
Timothy W. Diggins
John T. Montgomery
Dennis M. Coleman (Providence, Rhode Island Office)
Mark V. Nuccio
Martin J. Newhouse
Larry J. Rowe
Hemmie Chang
R. Newcomb Stillwell
John O. Chesley, II
Susan M. Galli
Anne Phillips Ogilby
Mark P. Szpak
Rom P. Watson
Alan G. Priest (Washington, D.C. Office)
Peter M. Brody (Washington, D.C. Office)
Michael K. Fee
Joan McPhee (Providence, Rhode Island Office)

COUNSEL

Samuel Frankenheim
Daniel I. Halperin (Washington, D.C. Office)
Donald W. Glazer
William W. Park
Daniel Steiner

ASSOCIATES

Loretta W. Holway
Arthur W. Hughes, III
W. Thomas Moulton, Jr.
Robert C. Macaulay, Jr.
David J. Kerman
Margaret W. Chambers
John Billings French (Not admitted in MA)
Peter N. Rosenberg
Susan T. Nicholson
Clayton S. Marsh (Not admitted in MA)
John E. McElhinney
Joseph M. Eagan
David A. McKay
Kathryn Selleck Shea
Paul J. O'Donnell
Lee C. Rubin
Daniel S. Evans
Ann Pauly
Lauren I. Norton
Michael R. Pontrelli
David A. Martland
Richard A. Szczebak
Randall W. Bodner
Michael P. Duffy
Walter R. McCabe, III
Martin A. Cameron-Hall
Steven F. Scott
Ann L. Milner
Robert B. Gordon
Andrew C. Pickett
Laurie R. Wallach
Thomas B. Smith (Washington, D.C. Office)
Jeffrey P. Trout
Bryan Chegwidden
Christopher M. Leich
Jay B. Smith
John B. Ayer
Michele M. Garvin
Howard J. Castleman
Akiyo Fujii
Brenda Sweeny Diana
Anne E. Craige McNay
Pamela J. Perun
Patrick Diaz (Not admitted in MA)
Peter M. DelVecchio
Stephen W. Bernstein
John R. Baraniak, Jr.
Jacqueline E. Camp
Mark R. DiOrio
Raj Marphatia
Marc J. Bloostein
Mark P. Goshko
David A. Brown
Raymond C. Ortman, Jr. (Washington, D.C. Office)
Loretta R. Richard
Margaret A. Sheehan (Washington, D.C. Office)
Alyson B. Gal
C. Richard Elam
Jane D. Goldstein
Timothy M. McCrystal
Diana L. Cooper
Lisa M. Ropple
David P. Lucey
Kevin J. O'Connor
Kyle S. Chase
Eric Jaeger
Thomas P. Smith
Patrick O'Brien
Jonathan C. Wilk
Ivan B. Knauer
Richard E. Manley
Claudia Leis Bolgen
Matthew M. Burke
Deborah J. Coleman
Ellen Page DelSole
Paula Drake
Pamela D. Everhart
James B. Haines
Timothy J. Hinkle
James M. Lichtman (Washington, D.C. Office)
Colin J. Zick

(See Next Column)

ROPES & GRAY, *Boston—Continued*

ASSOCIATES (Continued)

Collin J. Beecroft
Linda Dallas Rich (Washington, D.C. Office)
Karen A. Johnson
Caroline R. Elliott
Zachary J. Shulman
Richard D. Batchelder, Jr.
Peter L. Ebb
Theodore M. Hess-Mahan
Daniel J. Klau
James M. Wilton
Bonnie B. Edwards
James W. Matthews
Paul R. Noe (Washington, D.C. Office)
Gary M. Bishop
Todd H. Shuster
William J. Ballou
Kenneth A. Galton
Gregory S. Gilman
Marjorie Harris Loeb
James R. Brown, Jr.
Christopher Ceruolo
Colleen M. Granahan
Sarah G. Manchester
Amy A. Null
Tisa K. Hughes
Nancy E. Taggart
Kurt S. Kusiak
David T. Lyons
Sara Goldsmith Schwartz
Maryellen M. Lundquist (Washington, D.C. Office)
Julie A. Brogan
James S. DeGraw
Michael J. Savitz
Felice C. Wagner (Not admitted in MA; Washington, D.C. Office)
Françoise M. Haan (Washington, D.C. Office)
Michael S. Sher
Josephine M. Higgins
Michael P. Allen
Debra Brown Allen
William George III
Brigid K. Hurley
Susan M. Landers
Joann S. Nestor
Michael A. O'Hara
William R. Royer
Jennifer N. Samsel
Joseph T. Turo, Jr.
William P. Wall
Darlene C. Lynch
David R. Baron
Margaret C. Curtin (Not admitted in MA; Washington, D.C. Office)
Luke T. Cadigan
Peter F. May
Michael F. Sexton
William S. Elias II
Joshua S. Levy
Madeleine C. Timin (Not admitted in MA)
Christopher J. Austin (Not admitted in MA)
Michael E. DeFao
John Jay Althoff
Lee S. Feldman
Ana M. Francisco
Suzanne M. Lambert
Brian D. McCabe
Sean W. Mullaney
Ellen H. Solomon
Caroline R. Rogers
Nicole R. Hartje
Betsy Fishman Rosenfeld

OF COUNSEL

H. Brian Holland
Allen O. Eaton
James B. Ames
Warren E. Carley
Edward B. Hanify
Francis J. Vaas (On leave)
Francis H. Burr
Andrew H. Cox
Wilson C. Piper
Ernest J. Sargeant
Douglas Mercer
Harry K. Mansfield
Henry S. Streeter
Peter Leffingwell Albrecht
Oscar W. Haussermann, Jr.
Paul F. Perkins
John M. Harrington, Jr.
Alfred W. Fuller
Joan D. Fuller

For full biographical listings, see the Martindale-Hubbell Law Directory

RUBIN AND RUDMAN (AV)

50 Rowes Wharf, 02110
Telephone: 617-330-7000
Telecopier: 617-439-9556

Stanley H. Rudman
Howard Rubin
Milton Bordwin
Myrna Putziger
Charles J. Speleotis
W. Bradley Ryan
Peter B. Finn
Andrew J. Newman
Harold Stahler
Michael R. Coppock
J. Robert Casey
John D. Kalish
Raymond M. Kwasnick
Jason A. Sokolov
Robert S. Walker
Dana F. Rodin
Lawrence E. Uchill
Kenneth M. Barna
Selig A. Saltzman
Edward R. Zaval
Peter F. Granoff
Gene T. Barton, Jr.
Jonathan D. Canter
Alan K. Posner
Philip L. Sussler
Jacob Aaron Esher
James H. Greene
John A. DeTore

Michael L. Altman
Stephen C. Flashenberg
Alan D. Mandl
Robert D. Shapiro
Jane Elizabeth Jones
Leonard M. Davidson
Dale Ann Kaiser
Donald J. Quill
Robert J. Mack
Michael K. Crossen
Mark W. Corner
David C. Fixler
Suzanne L. King
Diedre T. Lawrence
Helen E. Morgan
Susan A. Bernstein
Margaret A. Robbins
Edward R. Hill, Jr.
Donna C. Sharkey
Michael C. Bainum
Susan M. Caruso

For full biographical listings, see the Martindale-Hubbell Law Directory

SHERBURNE, POWERS & NEEDHAM, P.C. (AV)

One Beacon Street, 02108
Telephone: 617-523-2700
Fax: 617-523-6850

William D. Weeks
John T. Collins
Allan J. Landau
John L. Daly
Stephen A. Hopkins
Alan I. Falk
C. Thomas Swaim
James Pollock
William V. Tripp III
Stephen S. Young
William F. Machen
W. Robert Allison
Jacob C. Diemert
Philip J. Notopoulos
Richard J. Hindlian
Paul E. Troy
Harold W. Potter, Jr.
Dale R. Johnson
Philip S. Lapatin
Pamela A. Duckworth
Mark Schonfeld
James D. Smeallie
Paul Killeen
Gordon P. Katz
Joseph B. Darby, III
Richard M Yanofsky
James E. McDermott
Robert V. Lizza
Miriam Goldstein Altman
John J. Monaghan
Margaret J. Palladino
Mark C. Michalowski
David Scott Sloan
M. Chrysa Long
Lawrence D. Bradley
Miriam J. McKendall

Cynthia A. Brown
Cynthia M. Hern
Dianne R. Phillips
Paul M. James
Theodore F. Hanselman
Joshua C. Krumholz
Ieuan G. Mahony
Kenneth L. Harvey
Christopher J. Trombetta
Edwin F. Landers, Jr.
Amy J. Mastrobattista
William Howard McCarthy, Jr.
Douglas W. Clapp
Tamara E. Goulston
Nicholas J. Psyhogeos

COUNSEL

Haig Der Manuelian
Mason M. Taber, Jr.
Karl J. Hirshman
Benjamin Volinski
Kenneth P. Brier

OF COUNSEL

John Barr Dolan

For full biographical listings, see the Martindale-Hubbell Law Directory

SHERIN AND LODGEN (AV)

100 Summer Street, 02110
Telephone: 617-426-5720
Telecopier: 617-542-5186
Los Angeles, California Office: 11300 W. Olympic Boulevard, Suite 700.
Telephone: 310-914-7891.
Fax: 310-552-5327.
Nashua New Hampshire Office: One Indian Head Plaza.
Telephone: 603-595-4511.
Fax: 603-595-4968.
Providence, Rhode Island Office: 55 Pine Street.
Telephone: 401-274-8060.

MEMBERS OF FIRM

Arthur L. Sherin (1946-1964)
George E. Lodgen (1946-1971)
Morton B. Brown
George Waldstein
John M. Reed
Robert J. Muldoon, Jr.
Alette E. Reed
Edward M. Bloom
Thomas J. Raftery
Joshua M. Alper
Gary M. Markoff
Bryan G. Killian
David A. Guberman
Kenneth R. Berman
Frank J. Bailey
Thomas P. Gorman
Dorothy Nelson Stookey
Mark A. Nowak
Ronald W. Ruth
Steven D. Eimert
Daniel B. Winslow
Barbara A. O'Donnell
Brian C. Levey
A. Neil Hartzell
Kenneth J. Mickiewicz
Craig M. Brown
Andrew Royce
Daniel O. Gaquin
Thomas A. Hippler
Rhonda B. Parker
John J. Slater, III (Resident)

ASSOCIATES

Joanna E. Scannell
Nereyda Garcia
John C. La Liberte
Karen Elise Berman
Margaret H. Leeson
Joseph M. Kerwin
Christopher A. Kenney
David Benfield
Michael C. Giardiello

OF COUNSEL

Paul Melrose
Michael S. Strauss

LEGAL SUPPORT PERSONNEL

Marilyn Stewart

For full biographical listings, see the Martindale-Hubbell Law Directory

SIMONDS, WINSLOW, WILLIS & ABBOTT, A PROFESSIONAL ASSOCIATION (AV)

50 Congress Street, 02109
Telephone: 617-523-5520
Fax: 617-523-4619

(See Next Column)

SIMONDS, WINSLOW, WILLIS & ABBOTT A PROFESSIONAL ASSOCIATION—*Continued*

William S. Abbott
William L. Eaton
Marc A. Elfman
Robert S. Gulick
Peter R. Johnson
Brenda G. Levy
Robert Torrence Morrison
Hugh V. A. Starkey
Dudley H. Willis
Byron E. Woodman, Jr.
John L. Worden III
Edward J. Wynne III

For full biographical listings, see the Martindale-Hubbell Law Directory

SUGARMAN AND SUGARMAN, P.C. (AV)

One Beacon Street, 02108
Telephone: 617-542-1000
Telecopier: 617-542-1359

Nathan Fink (1920-1974)
Paul R. Sugarman
Neil Sugarman
W. Thomas Smith
Steven L. Hoffman
Robert W. Casby
Kerry Paul Choi
Valerie A. Yarashus
Charlotte E. Glinka

Jodi M. Petrucelli
Darin Michael Colucci
Kimberly Ellen Nelson Winter
Marianne Camille LeBlanc

For full biographical listings, see the Martindale-Hubbell Law Directory

SULLIVAN & WORCESTER (AV)

One Post Office Square, 02109
Telephone: 617-338-2800
Telecopier: 617-338-2880
TWX: 710-321-1976
Washington, D.C. Office: 1025 Connecticut Avenue, N.W.
Telephone: 202-775-8190.
New York, New York Office: 767 Third Avenue.
Telephone: 212-486-8200.

John B. Sullivan, Jr. (1876-1952)
John N. Worcester (1899-1976)

MEMBERS OF FIRM

Frederic G. Corneel
John Hand
Roger B. Hunt
Charles C. Cabot, Jr.
John B. French
Marshall L. Tutun
John A. Dudley (Resident Partner at Washington, D.C.)
John C. Emery
Thomas E. Weesner
Christopher M. Weld
Norman A. Bikales
Robert M. Buchanan
Richard H. Goldman
Kenneth J. Seaman
Michael M. Davis
Paul F. Beatty
W. Lee H. Dunham
William L. Fishman (Resident Partner at Washington, D.C.)
Robert N. Hickey (Resident Partner at Washington, D.C.)
G. Michael Hawkey
Peter G. Johannsen
Joseph L. Serafini
Howard C. Buschman, III (Resident Partner at New York, New York)
Alan R. Feldman
Mark L. Levine (Resident Partner at New York, New York)
Edward Woll, Jr.
Harvey E. Bines
Andra R. Hotchkiss
J. Randolph MacPherson (Resident Partner at Washington, D.C.)
Joseph H. Newberg
Barry M. Portnoy
Laura Steinberg
Christopher C. Curtis
Charles M. Dubroff (Resident Partner at New York, New York)
George P. Lindsay (Resident Partner at New York, New York)
Ira K. Gross
Richard Teller
Dennis J. White
Diane L. Beauchesne
Christopher Cabot
Lena Genello Goldberg
Timothy T. Hilton
Alexander A. Notopoulos, Jr.
Louis A. Rodriques
Richard J. Steets
Victor N. Baltera
Jonathan B. Dubitzky
John K. Graham
Joseph G. Hadzima, Jr.
Paul R. Wiener (Resident Partner at New York, New York)
Eshel Bar-Adon (Not admitted in MA; Resident Partner at Washington, D.C.)
Harry E. Ekblom, Jr.
Timothy M. Lindamood
Patrick P. Dinardo
Barbara D. Gilmore
Karen L. Linsley
Patrick K. Miehe
Larry L. Varn
Cynthia M. Clarke
Warren M. Heilbronner
Cornelius J. Murray III
Joel R. Carpenter
David M. Leahy (Resident Partner at Washington, D.C.)
Deborah Anne O'Malley
Michael A. Matzka
Alan H. Pleskow (Resident Partner at New York, New York)
Martha Juelich Gordon
Jennifer Babbin Clark
Richard D. Lieberman (Resident Partner at Washington, D.C.)

COUNSEL

Charles M. Goldman
Joseph Auerbach
Robert B. Luick
Augustus W. Soule, Jr.
Jas. Murray Howe
Joseph C. Robbins
Philip H. Suter
David M. Schwartz (Resident Counsel at Washington, D.C.)
Robert L. Calhoun (Resident Counsel at Washington, D.C.)
Paul G. Kirk, Jr.

(See Next Column)

COUNSEL (Continued)

Susan M. McCraw
Ilene Robinson
Michael D. Bliss
Nicole Laccetti Rives

ASSOCIATES

Simon B. Posner (Resident Associate at New York, New York)
Rosemary Wilson
Linda Lyons Warren (Resident Associate at New York, New York)
Steve M. Bederman (Resident Associate at New York, New York)
Katherine J. Ross
Donald P. Board
Molly Cochran
Gayle P. Ehrlich
Suzanne L'Hernault (Resident Associate at New York, New York)
Nancy S. Lucas
Bryan G. Tyson
Elizabeth S. Wigon
William J. Curry
Marcy H. Kammerman (Resident Associate at New York, New York)
Jean Pagliuca Smith
Christopher Bertschmann
Susan J. Forest
David A. Guadagnoli
Rosa Prestia (Resident Associate at New York, New York)
John J. Cheney
Erik Hestnes
Miriam G. Kosowsky
Kathleen Provost
Melina M. T. Murphy
Gregory S. Getschow
John P. Zavez
Priscilla E. Johnson
Joseph D. McGlinchey, II
Nathan Newman
Bruce C. Seyboth
Carter L. Vinson
Roger F. Assad
Richard A. Calame
Kathleen M. Miskiewicz
Robert M. O'Connell, Jr.
Elizabeth M. Suntken
Lisa Whitney Lahey
Ameek Ashok Ponda
Martin Ris
Lisa F. Sherman
Joan L. Yanofsky
Jesse M Fried
Ronald S. Eppen
David H. Johnson
David G. Mitchell
Mathew J. Nicolella
Frank Polverino (Resident Associate at New York, New York)

For full biographical listings, see the Martindale-Hubbell Law Directory

TAYLOR, ANDERSON & TRAVERS (AV)

75 Federal Street, 02110
Telephone: 617-654-8200
Fax: 617-482-5350
Providence, Rhode Island Office: The Wilcox Building, 42 Weybosset Street.
Telephone: 401-273-7171.
Fax: 401-273-2904.

MEMBERS OF FIRM

Allan E. Taylor
James H. Anderson
Margaret S. Travers
James J. Duane, III
Sidney W. Adler
John J. Barton
Susan H. Williams
Ellen Epstein Cohen
Pamela Slater Gilman
Alexandra B. Harvey

ASSOCIATES

Edward D. Shoulkin
Jennifer Ellis Burke
Melanie J. Gargas
A. Bernard Guekguezian
Francis A. Connor, III
Gina Witalec Verdi
Robert C. Shindell

For full biographical listings, see the Martindale-Hubbell Law Directory

TESTA, HURWITZ & THIBEAULT (AV)

Exchange Place, 53 State Street, 02109
Telephone: 617-248-7000
Telecopier: 617-248-7100

MEMBERS OF FIRM

Donald L. Anglehart
William B. Asher, Jr.
Steven M. Bauer
Jason Berger
Scott A. Birnbaum
Margaret W. Brill
Mark H. Burnett
David J. Byer
Edmund C. Case
E. Michael Collins
Henry W. Comstock, Jr.
Leslie E. Davis
Linda DeRenzo
Eric A. Deutsch
Daniel P. Finkelman
Margaret A. Flanagan
David S. Godkin
Dean C. Gordanier, Jr.
Gordon H. Hayes, Jr.
John M. Hession
Joseph A. Hugg
Stephen A. Hurwitz
Jin-Kyung (Kay) Kim
Rufus C. King
Katherine M. Kneeland
Kevin T. Lamb
Mark J. Macenka
Timothy C. Maguire
Edwin L. Miller, Jr.
James P. O'Hare
Robin A. Painter
Brian E. Pastuszenski
Edmund R. Pitcher
Howard S. Rosenblum
William J. Schnoor, Jr.
William B. Simmons, Jr.
Mark D. Smith
Andrew E. Taylor, Jr.
Richard J. Testa
George W. Thibeault
John F. Welsh
Lawrence S. Wittenberg

COUNSEL

John A. Doernberg
Anne G. Plimpton

(See Next Column)

TESTA, HURWITZ & THIBEAULT, *Boston—Continued*

ASSOCIATES

Alan J. Applebaum
Jocelyn M. Arel
Kevin M. Barry
Thomas A. Beaudoin
David C. Berry
Mitchell S. Bloom
Eric A. Blumsack
Thomas A. Bockhorst
Marie H. Bowen
Dean J. Breda
Steven C. Browne (Not admitted in MA)
Debra A. Buxbaum
Paula A. Campbell
Michael J. Cayer
Kimberly M. Collins
William J. Corcoran
Loletta L. Darden
F. George Davitt (Not admitted in MA)
Deborah L. Drexler
Marla Dubin
Lois Brommer Duquette
Roy D. Edelstein
Douglas R. Ederle
Barbara M. Fagan
Gillian M. Fenton
Kathy A. Fields
Adam P. Forman
Suanne M. Garnier
Kenneth J. Gordon
Pamela B. Greene
Gregg Allen Griner
John E. Henry
Jordan D. Hershman
Laurie S. Jamieson
Amy M. Karp
Erin E. Karzmer (Not admitted in MA)
Arie P. Katz
Douglas J. Kline
Susan J. Krueger
Roger A. Lane
George W. Lloyd (Not admitted in MA)
Robert B. Lovett
Dana A. Lukens
Peter E. Markman
Kevin M. McKenna
Stephen T. Mears
John A. Meltaus
Carl E. Metzger
Jonathan M. Moulton
John M. Mutkoski
Minnie S. Park (Not admitted in MA)
Deborah Peckham
Harold Francis Pfister
Mark D. Pomfret
Jennifer A. Post
William L. Prickett
Kevin M. Royer
Susan P. Ruch
Richard S. Sanders
Mark K. Schonfeld
Mark C. Schueppert
Heather M. Stone
John J. Stout
David W. Tegeler
Miguel J. Vega
Christine C. Vito
Stephen D. Whetstone
Babak (Bo) Yaghmare
Xinhua (Howard) Zhang

LEGAL SUPPORT PERSONNEL
REGISTERED PATENT AGENTS
TECHNOLOGY SPECIALISTS

Duncan A. Greenhalgh
Madeline I. Johnston
Robin D. Kelley
Robert J. Tosti

For full biographical listings, see the Martindale-Hubbell Law Directory

WARNER & STACKPOLE (AV)

75 State Street, 02109
Telephone: 617-951-9000
Cable Address: "Warstack"
Telecopier: 617-951-9151
Telex: 940139

MEMBERS OF FIRM

Joseph B. Warner (1848-1923)
Pierpont L. Stackpole (1875-1936)
E. Barton Chapin (1885-1967)
Samuel Adams
William B. Hetzel, Jr.
John J. McCarthy
Willard G. McGraw, Jr.
Stephen E. Moore
John C. Hutchins
Gordon M. Stevenson, Jr.
Henry T. Goldman
Stanley V. Ragalevsky
Kenneth S. Boger
Ronald F. Kehoe
Joseph J. Leghorn
Michael A. Leon
Ralph T. Lepore, III
Christopher E. Nolin
Leon J. Lombardi
Edward J. Brennan, Jr.
John A. Dziamba
Janice Kelley Rowan
Judith G. Dein
Elizabeth F. Potter
James G. Ward
Linda A. Ouellette
Timothy B. Bancroft
Paul C. Bauer
Antoinette D. Hubbard
Patricia R. Hurley
Keith C. Long
Stephen L. Palmer
Steven L. Paul
Douglas F. Seaver
Michael DeMarco

ASSOCIATES

Richard R. Loewy
Charlene D. Andros
Deborah K. Blum-Shore
Gilbert R. Hoy, Jr.
Robert A. Whitney
Deborah E. Barnard
Kevin M. Meuse
Peter T. Wechsler
Michael A. Hickey
Ellen S. Rosenberg
B. Minde Kornfeld
James J. Arguin
Kenneth R. Brown
Laurie C. Buck
David J. Powers
Alexis L. Smith
John T. Smolak
Karen R. Sweeney
Christa A. Arcos
Stephanie L. Dadaian
Daniel E. Rosenfeld
Geoffrey E. Proulx
William P. Corbett, Jr.
Jill M. Pechacek
Anne T. Zecha

COUNSEL

Jerold S. Kayden
George E. Curtis
Andrew F. Lane
David W. Lewis, Jr.
Howard A. Levine

(See Next Column)

OF COUNSEL

Melville Chapin
Endicott Smith
Norman A. Hubley

For full biographical listings, see the Martindale-Hubbell Law Directory

WHITE, INKER, ARONSON, P.C. (AV)

One Washington Mall, 02108
Telephone: 617-367-7700
Telecopier: 617-523-5085

Monroe L. Inker
Martin L. Aronson
John P. White, Jr.
Ann E. Wagner
Leilah Anne Keamy
John Newman Flanagan
Frances M. Giordano
Kim D. Vo
Robert J. Rivers, Jr.
Laura J. DiPasquale
Kevin R. Connelly
Libby G. Fulgione, II
Amy Lyn Blake
Bryna S. Klevan

OF COUNSEL

Sanford N. Katz

For full biographical listings, see the Martindale-Hubbell Law Directory

WILLCOX, PIROZZOLO AND MCCARTHY, PROFESSIONAL CORPORATION (AV)

50 Federal Street, 02110
Telephone: 617-482-5470
Telecopier: 617-423-1572
Worcester, Massachusetts Office: 421 Main Street.
Telephone: 508-799-7446.

Harold M. Willcox (1925-1975)
Jack R. Pirozzolo
Richard F. McCarthy

Richard L. Binder
Richard E. Bennett
Judith Seplowitz Ziss
Kelly M. Bird

OF COUNSEL

Richard P. Crowley
Thomas A. Kahrl

For full biographical listings, see the Martindale-Hubbell Law Directory

BRAINTREE, Norfolk Co.

LANE, LANE AND KELLY (AV)

836 Washington Street, 02184
Telephone: 617-848-0040
Fax: 617-380-4136

Myron N. Lane (1907-1972)
Richard B. Lane
Robert P. Kelly

ASSOCIATES

Evelyn V. Henry
David B Lane

Representative Client: The Braintree Cooperative Bank.

For full biographical listings, see the Martindale-Hubbell Law Directory

*CAMBRIDGE,** Middlesex Co.

GEORGE F. GORMLEY, P.C. (AV)

One Main Street, P.O. Box 965, 02142-0090
Telephone: 617-349-3750
Fax: 617-661-2576

George F. Gormley

Jackie L. Segel
John D. Colucci

For full biographical listings, see the Martindale-Hubbell Law Directory

WILLIAM M. O'BRIEN (AV)

Suite 216, 186 Alewife Brook Parkway, 02138
Telephone: 617-661-2600
Fax: 617-864-0654

For full biographical listings, see the Martindale-Hubbell Law Directory

CONCORD, Middlesex Co.

LAW OFFICE OF HENRY J. DANE .(AV)

37 Main Street, P.O. Box 540, 01742
Telephone: 508-369-8333
Fax: 508-369-3106
Cable Address: Danelaw

ASSOCIATES

Trevor A. Haydon, Jr.

OF COUNSEL

Mark D. Shuman

For full biographical listings, see the Martindale-Hubbell Law Directory

*DEDHAM,** Norfolk Co.

GELERMAN & CASHMAN (AV)

270 Bridge Street, 02026-1798
Telephone: 617-329-8300
Telecopier: 617-329-0387

MEMBERS OF FIRM

Michael C. Donahue
Richard A. Gelerman
Daniel F. Cashman
Gail M. Buschmann
John M. Lovely

OF COUNSEL

Richard A. Feigenbaum

For full biographical listings, see the Martindale-Hubbell Law Directory

*EDGARTOWN,** Dukes Co. — (Refer to Osterville)

FRAMINGHAM, Middlesex Co.

HARGRAVES, KARB, WILCOX & GALVANI (AV)

The Corporate Center, 550 Cochituate Road, 01701
Telephone: 508-620-0140
Fax: 508-875-7728

MEMBERS OF FIRM

Francis P. Wilcox, Jr.
William H. Mayer
Victor H. Galvani
Dana L. Mason
Edward J. Mahan
William M. Pezzoni
Paul V. Galvani
Mark R. Haranas
Robert P. Jachowicz

OF COUNSEL

Arthur M. Mason
Brenda S. Steinberg

Counsel for: Framingham Cooperative Bank; Lind-Farquhar Co.; Strathmore Machine Toole Co.; Framingham Housing Authority.
Local Counsel for: International Paper Co.; General Motors Corp. (Framingham, Mass.); Bose Corp.; Consolidated Rail Corp.

For full biographical listings, see the Martindale-Hubbell Law Directory

GLOUCESTER, Essex Co. — (Refer to Beverly)

HARWICH PORT, Barnstable Co. — (Refer to Truro)

HINGHAM, Plymouth Co.

GILLIS & ANGLEY (AV)

Suite 227, 160 Old Derby Street, 02043
Telephone: 617-749-2432
Telecopier: 617-740-0768

MEMBERS OF FIRM

Ralph J. Gillis
Edward T. Angley

OF COUNSEL

Sally Skees-Helly (Not admitted in MA)

For full biographical listings, see the Martindale-Hubbell Law Directory

HOLYOKE, Hampden Co.

BEGLEY & FERRITER, P.C. (AV)

One Court Plaza, P.O. Box 711, 01041
Telephone: 413-536-1646
Telecopier: 413-536-0323

William E. Begley
John J. Ferriter
Maurice J. Ferriter
Michael O. Shea

OF COUNSEL

Thomas N. Wilson

For full biographical listings, see the Martindale-Hubbell Law Directory

CHARTIER, OGAN, BRADY & LUKAKIS (AV)

850 Building, 850 High Street, 01040
Telephone: 413-536-1395
Fax: 413-532-9583

MEMBERS OF FIRM

Louis Y. Chartier (1912-1993)
Peter F. Brady
Jane M. Bartello (1950-1994)
Michael J. Lukakis
Jacob Ogan (1895-1991)
Robert W. Shute
Charles J. Emma

ASSOCIATES

Andrea L. Brunault
Daniel M. Glanville
Michael T. Sarnacki
Niki A. Lukakis

OF COUNSEL

Norman Ogan (Retired)

Representative Clients: Holyoke Credit Union; Trust Insurance Co.; Commercial Union Insurance Co.; Commonwealth Packaging Corp.; Marcus Printing Co.; Greater Holyoke-Chicopee Board of Realtors; Westfield Gas and Electric Department Management Guild; Western Massachusetts Girl Scout Council, Inc.; AM Marketing, Inc.

(See Next Column)

For full biographical listings, see the Martindale-Hubbell Law Directory

LYON, SCULLY & FITZPATRICK (AV)

Whitney Place, 14 Bobala Road, 01040
Telephone: 413-536-4236
Fax: 413-536-3773

MEMBERS OF FIRM

George B. Scully (1919-1992)
Charles P. Lavelle
Clarke S. Lyon
James F. Donnelly
William D. Fitzpatrick
Peter C. Connor
Priscilla Fifield Chesky

ASSOCIATES

Deborah D.A. Jeffrey

Representative Clients: Mount Holyoke College; Newspapers of New England, Inc.; Loomis House Retirement Community; Atlas Copco Compressors Inc.; Hazen Paper Company, Town of South Hadley.

For full biographical listings, see the Martindale-Hubbell Law Directory

LAWRENCE, Essex Co. — (Refer to Andover)

LEOMINSTER, Worcester Co. — (Refer to Worcester)

LOWELL, Middlesex Co.

DONAHUE & DONAHUE ATTORNEYS, P.C. (AV)

21 George Street, 01852
Telephone: 508-458-6887
Fax: 508-458-3424

Daniel J. Donahue (1860-1939)
Peter V. Lawlor
Joseph P. Donahue (1889-1973)
Bradford P. Fortin
Charles A. Donahue (1891-1964)
Richard K. Donahue, Jr.
Richard K. Donahue
Andrea S. Barisano
Joseph P. Donahue, Jr.
Matthew C. Donahue
Joseph D. Regan
Richard E. Cavanaugh
Michael W. Gallagher
Kelly R. Spencer

Representative Clients: The Travelers Insurance Co.; L'Energia Cogeneration, Inc.

For full biographical listings, see the Martindale-Hubbell Law Directory

GOLDMAN & CURTIS (AV)

Lowell Place, 144 Merrimack Street, 01852
Telephone: 508-454-8804, 729-2625

MEMBERS OF FIRM

Frank Goldman (1890-1965)
James T. Curtis
Robert H. Goldman (1918-1991)
Cornelia C. Adams

Gregory T. Curtis
Carolyn L. Greenberg

OF COUNSEL

Efthemios J. Bentas
James T. Curtis, Jr.
Matthew P. Demaras

For full biographical listings, see the Martindale-Hubbell Law Directory

MIDDLEBORO, Plymouth Co. — (Refer to Fall River)

NATICK, Middlesex Co.

ZALTAS, MEDOFF & RAIDER (AV)

74 West Central Street, 01760
Telephone: 508-655-1960, Boston: 617-235-0217
FAX: 508-655-4347

Arnold I. Zaltas
Irving I. Medoff
Mark H. Raider

ASSOCIATES

Kathryn A. Sanderson
George E. Levoy, III
A. David Zaltas

For full biographical listings, see the Martindale-Hubbell Law Directory

NEW BEDFORD, Bristol Co.

PRESCOTT, BULLARD & McLEOD (AV)

558 Pleasant Street, 02740
Telephone: 508-999-1351; 999-2381
General Office: 508-999-1351
Title Office: 508-999-2381
Fax: 508-999-9433

MEMBERS OF FIRM

John M. Bullard (1921-1965)
Davis C. Howes
Raymond McLeod (1948-1978)
Richard C. Borges
Bryant Prescott (1929-1982)
Peter M. Nicholson
Oliver Prescott, Jr. (1927-1984)
John M. Janiak
Michael A. Kehoe

(See Next Column)

PRESCOTT, BULLARD & MCLEOD, *New Bedford—Continued*

ASSOCIATES

David A. French, Jr.
Richard C. Borges, Jr.

Representative Clients: New Bedford Institution for Savings; Compass Bank for Savings; Citizens Bank of Massachusetts; Atlantic Refining Co.; National Bank of Fairhaven; BayBank Southeast, National Association; Ashley Ford Sales, Inc.
Approved Attorneys for: Lawyers Title Insurance Corp.; Chicago Title Insurance Co.; Commonwealth Land Title Insurance Co.

For full biographical listings, see the Martindale-Hubbell Law Directory

NEWBURYPORT, Essex Co. — (Refer to Lawrence)

*NORTHAMPTON,** Hampshire Co.

EDWARD D. ETHEREDGE LAW OFFICES (AV)

64 Gothic Street, 01060
Telephone: 413-584-1600
Fax: 413-585-8406

Shelley Steuer

For full biographical listings, see the Martindale-Hubbell Law Directory

GROWHOSKI, CALLAHAN, KUNDL & KUZMESKI (AV)

60 State Street, 01060
Telephone: 413-584-1500
Fax: 413-584-1670

MEMBERS OF FIRM

John M. Callahan
Thomas M. Growhoski
Judith Kundl
David C. Kuzmeski

For full biographical listings, see the Martindale-Hubbell Law Directory

OSTERVILLE, Barnstable Co. — (Refer to Hyannis)

*PITTSFIELD,** Berkshire Co.

CAIN, HIBBARD, MYERS & COOK, A PROFESSIONAL CORPORATION (AV)

66 West Street, 01201
Telephone: 413-443-4771
Telecopier: 413-443-7694
Great Barrington, Massachusetts Office: 309 Main Street, 01230.
Telephone: 413-528-4771.
Fax: 413-528-5553.

SENIOR COUNSEL

Frederick M. Myers

Leonard H. Cohen
C. Jeffrey Cook
Brian J. Quinn (Resident, Great Barrington Office)
F. Sydney Smithers, IV
David O. Burbank
John F. Rogers
Michael E. MacDonald
John A. Agostini
William B. Roberts

RETIRED

Lincoln S. Cain

Stephen B. Hibbard (1907-1987)

Virginia Stanton Smith
William A. Rota
Diane M. DeGiacomo
Steven T. Smith
Nancy A. Lyon
Jennifer L. Gerrard
Benjamin Smith
Kevin M. Kinne

OF COUNSEL

William F. Mufatti
Thomas D. McCann

Representative Clients: Bank of Boston/First Agricultural Bank; Metropolitan Life Insurance Co.; Prudential Insurance Co.; Home Insurance Co.; Berkshire Medical Center; The Berkshire Gas Co.; Western Massachusetts Electric Co.
Local Counsel for: General Electric Co.

For full biographical listings, see the Martindale-Hubbell Law Directory

RONALD E. OLIVEIRA (AV)

74 North Street, Suite 208, 01201
Telephone: 413-499-3832
Facsimile: 413-447-9127

ASSOCIATES

Dawn M. Rich

Representative Clients: Aetna Life & Casualty Insurance Company; St. Paul Insurance Company; Vermont Mutual Insurance Company; Plymouth Rock Assurance Company; Pilgrim Insurance Company; Massachusetts Medical Professional Insurance Association; Travelers Insurance Company; Berkshire Gas Company; Andover Insurance Company; Hospital Underwriters Insurance Company.

(See Next Column)

For full biographical listings, see the Martindale-Hubbell Law Directory

*SALEM,** Essex Co.

PLUNKETT & PLUNKETT, P.C. (AV)

120 Washington Street, 01970
Telephone: 508-744-2444
FAX: 508-744-7961

Barry W. Plunkett
Christopher L. Plunkett

Laura L. Deorocki
Elizabeth W. Dailey

Representative Clients: Salem Five Cents Savings Bank; The Northshore Corp.; Graves Yacht Yard.
Agents for: Commonwealth Land Title Insurance Co.; Title Insurance Company of Minnesota; Lawyers Title Insurance Corp.

For full biographical listings, see the Martindale-Hubbell Law Directory

*SPRINGFIELD,** Hampden Co.

COOLEY, SHRAIR P.C. (AV)

5th Floor, 1380 Main Street, 01103
Telephone: 413-781-0750
Telecopier: 413-733-3042

David A. Shrair
Irving D. Labovitz
Robert L. Dambrov
Alan S. Dambrov
Alice E. Zaft
Rona S. Fingold
Peter W. Shrair
Norman C. Michaels
Mark A. NeJame
Mary E. Hurley
Mark D. Mason

OF COUNSEL

Edward B. Cooley
Sidney M. Cooley

Reference: Fleet Bank.

For full biographical listings, see the Martindale-Hubbell Law Directory

DOHERTY, WALLACE, PILLSBURY AND MURPHY, P.C. (AV)

19th Floor, One Monarch Place, 1414 Main Street, 01144
Telephone: 413-733-3111
Telecopier: 413-734-3910

Dudley B. Wallace (1900-1987)
Louis W. Doherty (1898-1990)
Robert E. Murphy
Paul S. Doherty
Samuel A. Marsella
Philip J. Callan, Jr.
Gary P. Shannon
Robert L. Leonard
A. Craig Brown
L. Jeffrey Meehan
David J. Martel
John James McCarthy
Joan Ho Bond
William P. Hadley
Barry M. Ryan
Deborah A. Basile
Paul M. Maleck
Claire L. Thompson
W. Garth Janes

Christopher M. Browne
Michael J. Rye
Elizabeth N. Clarke
Michael K. Callan
Kevin M. Walkowski

OF COUNSEL

Frederick S. Pillsbury
Matthew J. Ryan, Jr.
Lewis A. Whitney, Jr.

Local Counsel for: Nationwide Mutual Insurance Co.; Liberty Mutual Insurance Co.; General Motors Corp.; Wausau Insurance Cos.; Royal Insurance; Metropolitan Property & Liability Insurance Co.
Representative Clients: Fontaine Bros.; F.L. Roberts and Company Inc.; Town of Longmeadow.

For full biographical listings, see the Martindale-Hubbell Law Directory

EGAN, FLANAGAN AND COHEN, P.C. (AV)

67 Market Street, P.O. Box 9035, 01102
Telephone: 413-737-0260
Fax: 413-737-0121

James F. Egan (1896-1986)
William C. Flanagan
Charles S. Cohen
Mary Egan Boland
John J. Egan
Theodore C. Brown
Edward J. McDonough, Jr.
Maurice M. Cahillane
Charles W. Danis, Jr.
John G. Bagley
Bart W. Heemskerk
Henry M. Downey
Robert L. Quinn
Jessica B. Young
Eileen Z. Sorrentino

David G. Cohen

OF COUNSEL

J. David Keaney
Edward T. Collins

Counsel for: Mercy Hospital; Roman Catholic Diocese of Springfield; McKinstry, Incorporated.

For full biographical listings, see the Martindale-Hubbell Law Directory

Springfield—Continued

Ely & King (AV)

One Financial Plaza, 1350 Main Street, 01103
Telephone: 413-781-1920
Telecopier: 413-733-3360

MEMBERS OF FIRM

Joseph Buell Ely (1905-1956)
Raymond T. King (1919-1971)
Frederick M. Kingsbury (1924-1968)
Hugh J. Corcoran (1938-1992)
Richard S. Milstein
Donald A. Beaudry
Richard F. Faille
Leland B. Seabury
Gregory A. Schmidt
Pamela Manson
Anthony T. Rice
Russell J. Mawdsley

ASSOCIATES

Donna M. Brown

Representative Clients: Hartford Accident & Indemnity Co.; Albert Steiger Cos.; Shawmut Bank N.A.; Springfield Institution for Savings; St. Paul Fire & Marine Insurance Co.; The Rouse Co.; Tighe & Bond, Inc.; Northeast Utilities.

For full biographical listings, see the Martindale-Hubbell Law Directory

Pellegrini & Seeley, P.C. (AV)

1145 Main Street, 01103
Telephone: 413-785-5300
Fax: 413-731-0626

Gilbert W. Baron (1911-1987)
Gerard L. Pellegrini
Earlon L. Seeley, Jr.
Donald W. Blakesley
Phyllis P. Ryan
Paul F. Schneider

Steven D. Rose
Michael J. Chieco
Charles R. Casartello, Jr.
Thomas E. Casartello
Patrick C. Gable
Catherine L. Watson

For full biographical listings, see the Martindale-Hubbell Law Directory

Robinson Donovan Madden & Barry, P.C. (AV)

Suite 1600, Baybank Tower, 1500 Main Street, 01115
Telephone: 413-732-2301
Fax: 413-785-4658

Homans Robinson (1894-1973)
Lawrence M. Sinclair (1942-1986)

OF COUNSEL

Milton J. Donovan
John H. Madden, Jr.
Edward J. Barry

Gordon H. Wentworth
James H. Tourtelotte
Charles K. Bergin, Jr.
Victor Rosenberg
Ronald C. Kidd
Jeffrey W. Roberts
Jeffrey L. McCormick
James M. Rabbitt
James F. Martin
Robert P. Cunningham
John C. Sikorski
Nancy Frankel Pelletier
Paul S. Weinberg
Frederica H. McCarthy
Matthew J. King

James K. Bodurtha
Douglas F. Boyd
Susan L. Cooper
Kimberly Davis Crear
Russell F. Denver
Edmund J. Gorman
Keith A. Minoff
Patricia M. Rapinchuk
Jonathan P. Rice
Neva Kaufman Rohan

Counsel for: Shawmut Bank, N.A.; The First National Bank of Boston; United Cooperative Bank; Sunshine Art Studios.
Representative Clients: American Policyholders' Insurance Co.; C.N.A.; Commercial Union Insurance Co.; Hanover Insurance Co.

For full biographical listings, see the Martindale-Hubbell Law Directory

Ryan, Martin, Costello, Allison & Leiter, P.C. (AV)

Suite 2500, BayBank Tower, 1500 Main Street, P.O. Box 15629, 01115-5629
Telephone: 413-739-6971
Fax: 413-739-1441

Charles V. Ryan
Philip J. Ryan
Bradford R. Martin, Jr.
Mary K. Downey Costello
Donald J. Allison
Bruce L. Leiter
Joan C. Steiger
Timothy J. Ryan
William J. Cass
Michael P. Ryan

For full biographical listings, see the Martindale-Hubbell Law Directory

*TAUNTON,** Bristol Co. — (Refer to Fall River)

TRURO, Barnstable Co.

Law Offices of Ansel B. Chaplin (AV)

P.O. Box 867, 02652
Telephone: 508-487-1190
Boston, Massachusetts Office: 31 State Street.
Telephone: 617-227-0272.

Ansel B. Chaplin

For full biographical listings, see the Martindale-Hubbell Law Directory

WALTHAM, Middlesex Co.

Flynn, Hardy & Cohn (AV)

Sterling Bank Building, One Moody Street, 02254-9181
Telephone: 617-893-3610
Telecopier: 617-893-1494

MEMBERS OF FIRM

John J. Flynn, Sr. (1881-1969)
Paul L. Flynn (1893-1971)
John J. Flynn, III (1917-1989)
Robert S. Flynn
Peter C. Hardy
A. Richard Cohn

John G. Lamb

COUNSEL

Laurence S. Flaherty

LEGAL SUPPORT PERSONNEL

Peter M. Flynn

Counsel for: Waltham Weston Hospital & Medical Center, Center for Mental Health; Plywood Supply, Inc. Waltham Savings Bank; Waltham Chemical Co.; Crover Cronin, Inc. (Department Store).

For full biographical listings, see the Martindale-Hubbell Law Directory

Harnish, Jenney, Mitchell and Resh (AV)

675 Main Street, 02154
Telephone: 617-894-0000
Telecopier: 617-893-8357

MEMBERS OF FIRM

Francis E. Jenney
David L. Mitchell
Harvey J. Resh
Joseph Melone
Robert C. Mann
Margaret Manzon Skinner
Rhonda B. Fogel
Cynthia Spahl

For full biographical listings, see the Martindale-Hubbell Law Directory

WELLESLEY, Norfolk Co.

Nicholas B. Soutter (AV)

One Washington Street, Suite 208, 02181
Telephone: 617-237-6300
Fax: 617-237-6143

ASSOCIATE

Paul S. McGovern

For full biographical listings, see the Martindale-Hubbell Law Directory

WESTFIELD, Hampden Co. — (Refer to Springfield)

*WORCESTER,** Worcester Co.

Fletcher, Tilton & Whipple, P.C. (AV)

370 Main Street, 01608
Telephone: 508-798-8621
Telecopier: 508-791-1201

Sumner B. Tilton (1904-1981)
Paris Fletcher (1903-1989)
Robert J. Whipple
George Avery White
Henry C. Horner
John E. Hodgson
Sumner B. Tilton, Jr.
Phillips S. Davis
Robert R. Kimball
Douglas Q. Meystre
Alexander E. Drapos
Warner S. Fletcher
Robert F. Dore, Jr.
Arthur H. Miller (Not admitted in MA)
James M. Burgoyne
William D. Jalkut
Patricia Finnegan Gates
Mark L. Donahue
Stuart A. Hammer
Lucille B. Brennan
Sheila Campbell Murphy
Kirk A. Carter
Dennis F. Gorman
David J. Officer
Donna Toman Salvidio

For full biographical listings, see the Martindale-Hubbell Law Directory

Glickman, Sugarman & Kneeland (AV)

11 Harvard Street, P.O. Box 2917, 01613
Telephone: 508-756-6206
Fax: 508-831-0443

MEMBERS OF FIRM

Melvyn Glickman
David W. Sugarman
David J. Kneeland, Jr.

(See Next Column)

GLICKMAN, SUGARMAN & KNEELAND, *Worcester—Continued*

ASSOCIATES

Joe Boynton
Wayne M. LeBlanc

For full biographical listings, see the Martindale-Hubbell Law Directory

MACCARTHY, POJANI & HURLEY (AV)

Worcester Plaza, 446 Main Street, 01608
Telephone: 508-798-2480
Fax: 508-797-9561

Philip J. MacCarthy
Dennis Pojani
John F. Hurley, Jr.
Howard E. Stempler
John Macuga, Jr.

ASSOCIATES

William J. Ritter

Representative Clients: Shawmut Bank N.A.; Melville Corp.; Travelers Insurance Co.; Liberty Mutual Co.; United States Fidelity & Guaranty Co.; Commerce Insurance Co.; Worcester Mutual Insurance Co.; Fleet Bank of Massachusetts, N.A.; Health Plans, Inc.; Marane Oil Corp.

For full biographical listings, see the Martindale-Hubbell Law Directory

MCGUIRE & MCGUIRE, P.C. (AV)

340 Main Street, Suite 910, 01608
Telephone: 508-754-3291
Fax: 508-752-0553

John K. McGuire (1952-1985)
Joseph E. McGuire
John K. McGuire, Jr.

Penelope A. Kathiwala
Christine Griggs Narcisse
Paul Durkee
Teresa Brooks

For full biographical listings, see the Martindale-Hubbell Law Directory

MIRICK, O'CONNELL, DEMALLIE & LOUGEE (AV)

Bank of Boston Tower, 100 Front Street, Suite 1700, 01608-1477
Telephone: 508-799-0541
Fax: 508-752-7305

MEMBERS OF FIRM

Robert J. Martin
Bayard T. DeMallie
David L. Lougee
Robert V. Deiana
John O. Mirick
Demitrios M. Moschos
Robert P. Lombardi
Edward C. Bassett, Jr.
James C. Donnelly, Jr.
Stephen J. Doyle
Karen E. Ludington
Richard C. Van Nostrand
Jeffrey L. Donaldson
Paul J. D'Onfro
Janet Wilson Moore
Andrew B. O'Donnell
Alden J. Bianchi
Robert L. Hamer
Michael R. Mosher
David E. Surprenant
Peter J. Dawson
Joseph M. Hamilton

OF COUNSEL

Laurence H. Lougee
Gardener G. DeMallie
Richard W. Mirick

ASSOCIATES

Larry E. Salem
Robert S. Heppe, Jr.
Russell J. Hallisey
Charles B. Straus, III
John S. Chinian
Joseph H. Baldiga
William S. Rogers, Jr.
Pamela H. Sager
Joan O. Vorster
Paul R. Greenberg
Robert J. Travers
Sharon A. De Louchrey
Kenneth R. Kohlberg
Glen M. Mair
Michael G. Donovan

References: Shawmut Bank, N.A., Worcester; The First National Bank of Boston, Worcester.

For full biographical listings, see the Martindale-Hubbell Law Directory

MOUNTAIN, DEARBORN & WHITING (AV)

370 Main Street, 01608
Telephone: 508-756-2423
Fax: 508-755-6640

MEMBERS OF FIRM

John D. Sharpe (1941-1979)
Alfred N. Whiting (1920-1989)
Thomas R. Mountain
Richard W. Dearborn
Samuel R. DeSimone
Henry W. Beth
Francis J. Russell
Dale R. Harger
Mark W. Bloom
Donald J. O'Neil

ASSOCIATES

Lawrence S. Delaney
Ellen M. O'Connor
Ann K. Molloy

References: Shawmut Bank N.A.; Flagship Bank and Trust Company; Worcester County Institution for Savings; Mechanics Bank of Worcester.

For full biographical listings, see the Martindale-Hubbell Law Directory

REARDON & REARDON (AV)

One Exchange Place, 01608
Telephone: 508-754-1111
Fax: 508-797-6176
Boston, Massachusetts Office: 69 Beacon Street.
Telephone: 617-248-6998.

MEMBERS OF FIRM

James G. Reardon
Edward P. Reardon
Frank S. Puccio, Jr.

ASSOCIATES

Austin M. Joyce
James G. Haddad
Margaret Reardon Suuberg
James G. Reardon, Jr.
Julie E. Reardon
Michael J. Akerson
Francis J. Duggan

References: Mechanics National Bank; Shawmut Worcester County Bank N.A.; Bank of New England, Worcester.

For full biographical listings, see the Martindale-Hubbell Law Directory

MICHIGAN

*ADRIAN,** Lenawee Co.

WALKER, WATTS, JACKSON & MCFARLAND (AV)

160 North Winter Street, 49221
Telephone: 517-265-8138
Fax: 517-265-8286

MEMBERS OF FIRM

William H. Walker
Prosser M. Watts, Jr.
Mark A. Jackson
Michael McFarland

Attorneys for: Adrian State Bank; Bank of Lenawee; Consumers Power Co.; Norfolk & Western Railway Co.; Citizens Gas Fuel Co.; Auto Owners Insurance Co.; Amerisure Co.; Blissfield Manufacturing Co.; Adrian College.

For full biographical listings, see the Martindale-Hubbell Law Directory

*ALLEGAN,** Allegan Co.

ORTON, TOOMAN, HALE AND MCKOWN, P.C. (AV)

Court House Square, North, Drawer 239, 49010
Telephone: 616-673-2136
Fax: 616-673-2898

Rex W. Orton (1914-1988)
Lester J. Tooman
Gregory D. Hale
Stephen B. McKown
David F. Kiel

Representative Clients: Allegan Public Schools; Dorr Township; Allegan General Hospital; Allegan Medical Clinic, P.C.; Kalamazoo Ferry Company; Allegan Foundation.

For full biographical listings, see the Martindale-Hubbell Law Directory

ALMA, Gratiot Co.

FORTINO, PLAXTON & MOSKAL (AV)

Warwick Professional Center, 175 Warwick Drive, P.O. Box 578, 48801
Telephone: 517-463-2101
Fax: 517-463-2104

MEMBERS OF FIRM

Charles M. Fortino
Anthony G. Costanzo
MaryAnn Fry

OF COUNSEL

Alfred J. Fortino
Kenneth D. Plaxton

RETIRED

John J. Moskal

Attorneys for: Farmers State Bank, Breckenridge; State Farm Mutual Insurance Co.; Auto Owners Insurance Co.; Hastings Mutual Ins. Co.; The Ohio Casualty Ins. Co.; Commercial National Bank; Bear Truss and Components Co.; Alma Iron and Metal; Powell Fabrication & Mfg.; City of Alma; Gratiot Community Credit Union.

For full biographical listings, see the Martindale-Hubbell Law Directory

*ALPENA,** Alpena Co. — (Refer to Petoskey)

*ANN ARBOR,** Washtenaw Co.

BARNETT & RICH, P.C. (AV)

415 Detroit Street, 48104
Telephone: 313-769-0200
Fax: 313-769-1989

Gordon J. Barnett, Jr.
Kenneth Alan Rich
Eugene V. Douvan
Michael G. Kramer

Reference: Comerica Bank, Ann Arbor, Michigan.

For full biographical listings, see the Martindale-Hubbell Law Directory

BOOTHMAN, HEBERT & ELLER, P.C. (AV)

300 N. Fifth Avenue, Suite 140, 48108
Telephone: 313-995-9050
Fax: 313-995-8966
Detroit, Michigan Office: One Kennedy Square, Suite 2006.
Telephone: 313-964-0150.
Fax: 313-964-2226.

Richard C. Boothman (Resident)

For full biographical listings, see the Martindale-Hubbell Law Directory

BUTZEL LONG, A PROFESSIONAL CORPORATION (AV)

Suite 400, 121 West Washington, 48104-1345
Telephone: 313-995-3110
Telecopier: 313-995-1777
Detroit, Michigan Office: Suite 900, 150 West Jefferson.
Telephone: 313-225-7000.
Telecopier: 313-225-7080.

(See Next Column)

Birmingham, Michigan Office: Suite 200, 32270 Telegraph Road.
Telephone: 810-258-1616.
Telecopier: 810-258-1439.
Lansing, Michigan Office: 118 West Ottawa Street.
Telephone: 517-372-6622.
Telecopier: 372-6672.
Grosse Pointe Farms, Michigan Office: Suite 260, 21 Kercheval.
Telephone: 313-886-5446.
Telecopier: 313-886-2114.

Robert B. Foster (Resident)
John Henry Dudley, Jr.
Robert M. Vercruysse
James E. Stewart
David W. Sommerfeld
James L. Hughes
E. William S. Shipman
Leonard M. Niehoff
Robert A. Boonin

COUNSEL

John F. McCuen, Jr. (Resident)
Robert F. Magill, Jr. (Resident)
Ralph S. Rumsey (Resident)

OF COUNSEL

Martha Ellen Dennis (Resident)
Robin S. Phillips (Resident)

J. Michael Huget
Jordan S. Schreier
Robert E. Norton II

For full biographical listings, see the Martindale-Hubbell Law Directory

CONLIN, MCKENNEY & PHILBRICK, P.C. (AV)

700 City Center Building, 48104-1994
Telephone: 313-761-9000
Fax: 313-761-9001

Edward F. Conlin (1902-1953)
John W. Conlin (1904-1972)
Albert J. Parker (1901-1970)
Chris L. McKenney
Karl R. Frankena
Allen J. Philbrick
Phillip J. Bowen
Richard E. Conlin
Michael D. Highfield
Bruce N. Elliott
Neil J. Juliar
Robert M. Brimacombe
David S. Swartz
James A. Schriemer
Elizabeth M. Petoskey
Bradley J. MeLampy
Joseph W. Phillips
William M. Sweet
Lori A. Buiteweg
Douglas G. McClure
Thomas B. Bourque
Marjorie M. Dixon
Bonnie H. Keen

OF COUNSEL

John W. Conlin

Representative Clients: Fingerle Lumber Co.; Ann Arbor Area Board of Realtors; Borders, Inc.; Society Bank, Michigan; Auto-Owners Insurance Co.; Wolverine Title Co.
Approved Attorneys for: American Title Insurance Co.; Ticor Title Insurance Co.

For full biographical listings, see the Martindale-Hubbell Law Directory

DAVIS AND FAJEN, P.C. (AV)

Suite 400, 320 North Main Street, 48104
Telephone: 313-995-0066
Facsimile: 313-995-0184
Grand Haven, Michigan Office: Davis, Fajen & Miller. Harbourfront Place, 41 Washington Street, Suite 260.
Telephone: 616-846-9875.
Facsimile: 616-846-4920.

Peter A. Davis
James A. Fajen
Nelson P. Miller
Richard B. Bailey
Catherine G. Tennant

Reference: First of America Bank-Ann Arbor.

For full biographical listings, see the Martindale-Hubbell Law Directory

DYKEMA GOSSETT (AV)

315 East Eisenhower Parkway, Suite 100, 48108-3306
Telephone: 313-747-7660
Telex: 23-0121
Fax: 313-747-7696
Detroit, Michigan Office: 400 Renaissance Center, 48243-1668.
Telephone: 313-568-6800.
Fax: 313-568-6594.
Bloomfield Hills, Michigan Office: 1577 North Woodward Avenue, Suite 300, 48304-2820.
Telephone: 810-540-0700.
Fax: 810-540-0763.
Grand Rapids, Michigan Office: 200 Oldtown Riverfront Building, 248 Louis Campau Promenade, N.W., 49503-2668.
Telephone: 616-776-7500.
Fax: 616-776-7573.
Lansing, Michigan Office: 800 Michigan National Tower, 48933-1707.
Telephone: 517-374-9100.
Fax: 517-374-9191.

(See Next Column)

DYKEMA GOSSETT, *Ann Arbor—Continued*

Washington, D.C. Office: Franklin Square, Suite 300 West Tower, 1300 I Street, N.W.. 20005-3306.
Telephone: 202-522-8600.
Fax: 202-52208669.
Chicago, Illinois Office: Three First National Plaza, Suite 1400, 70 W. Madison, 60602-4270.
Telephone: 312-214-3308.
Fax: 312-214-3441.

RESIDENT MEMBERS

Raynold A. Schmick
Raymond T. Huetteman, Jr.
E. Edward Hood
Bettye S. Elkins
Jack C. Radcliffe, Jr.
James M. Cameron, Jr.
James P. Greene
Jonathan D. Rowe
Daniel J. Stephenson
Janet L. Neary
Sharon M. Kelly
Richard J. Landau
Bruce G. Davis

RESIDENT ASSOCIATES

Marie R. Deveney
Kathleen A. Reed
Thomas R. Stevick
Andrew J. McGuinness
Anne E. MacIntyre
Bradley L. Smith

For full biographical listings, see the Martindale-Hubbell Law Directory

GARAN, LUCOW, MILLER, SEWARD, COOPER & BECKER, P.C. (AV)

101 North Main Street, Suite 801, 48104-1400
Telephone: 313-930-5600
Fax: 313-930-0043
Detroit, Michigan Office: 1000 Woodbridge Place.
Telephone: 313-446-1530.
Fax: 313-259-0450.
Port Huron, Michigan Office: Port Huron Office Center, 511 Fort Street, Suite 505.
Telephone: 810-985-4400.
Fax: 810-985-4107.
Grand Blanc, Michigan Office: 8332 Office Park Drive.
Telephone: 810-695-3700.
Fax: 810-695-6488.
Troy, Michigan Office: 2301 West Big Beaver Road, Suite 212.
Telephone: 810-649-7600.
Fax: 810-649-5438.
Mount Clemens, Michigan Office: Towne Square Development, 10 South Main Street, Suite 307.
Telephone: 810-954-3800:
Fax: 810-954-3803.

Judith A. Moskus (Resident)

John W. Whitman (Resident)

For full biographical listings, see the Martindale-Hubbell Law Directory

HOOPER, HATHAWAY, PRICE, BEUCHE & WALLACE (AV)

126 South Main Street, 48104
Telephone: 313-662-4426
Fax: 313-662-9559

Joseph C. Hooper (1899-1980)
John R. Hathaway (Retired)
Alan E. Price
James R. Beuche
Bruce T. Wallace
Charles W. Borgsdorf
Mark R. Daane
Gregory A. Spaly
Robert W. Southard
William J. Stapleton
Bruce C. Conybeare, Jr.
Anthony P. Patti
Marcia J. Major

OF COUNSEL

James A. Evashevski
Roderick K. Daane

Representative Clients: Chem-Trend, Inc.; Dundee Cement Co.; Ervin Industries, Inc.; First Martin Corp.; Group 243 Design, Inc.; Honeywell; Microwave Sensors, Inc.; Shearson Lehman Hutton; O'Neal Construction Co.; Pittsfield Products, Inc.

For full biographical listings, see the Martindale-Hubbell Law Directory

KITCH, DRUTCHAS, WAGNER & KENNEY, P.C. (AV)

303 Detroit Street, Suite 400, P.O. Box 8610, 48107-8610
Telephone: 313-994-7600
Fax: 313-994-7626
Detroit, Michigan Office: One Woodward, Tenth Floor, 48226-3412.
Telephone: 313-965-7403.
Fax: 313-965-7403.
Lansing, Michigan Office: 120 Washington Square, North, Suite 805, One Michigan Avenue, 48933-1609.
Telephone: 517-372-6430.
Fax: 517-372-0441.
Macomb County Office: Towne Square Development, 10 South Main Street, Suite 301, Mount Clemens, 48043-7903.
Telephone: 810-463-9770.
Fax: 810-463-8994.

(See Next Column)

Toledo, Ohio Office: 405 Madison Avenue, Suite 1500, 43604-1235.
Telephone: 419-243-4006.
Fax: 419-243-7333.
Troy, Michigan Office: 3001 West Big Beaver Road, Suite 200, 48084-3103.
Telephone: 810-637-3500.
Fax: 810-637-6630.

Clyde M. Metzger, III (Principal)
William A. Tanoury (Principal)
Daniel J. Niemann (Associate Principal)
Richard J. Joppich
Ellen M. Keefe-Garner
Roselyn R. Parmenter
Carole S. Empey
Carol S. Allis
Kathleen P. Knol
Bridget Kerry Quinn
John J. Koselka

For full biographical listings, see the Martindale-Hubbell Law Directory

MILLER, CANFIELD, PADDOCK AND STONE, P.L.C. (AV)

A Professional Limited Liability Company
Founded in 1852 by Sidney Davy Miller
101 North Main Street, Seventh Floor, 48104-1400
Telephone: 313-663-2445
Fax: 313-747-7147
Detroit, Michigan Office: 150 West Jefferson, Suite 2500, 48226-4415.
Telephone: 313-963-6420.
Fax: 313-496-7500.
Cable Address: "Stem Detroit."
Bloomfield Hills, Michigan Office: Suite 100, Pinehurst Office Center, 1400 North Woodward, 48303-2014.
Telephone: 313-645-5000.
Fax: 313-645-1917.
Grand Rapids, Michigan Office: 1200 Campau Square Plaza, 99 Monroe, N.W., 49503-2639.
Telephone: 616-454-8656.
Fax: 616-776-6322.
Howell, Michigan Office: 121 South Barnard Street, Suite 4, 48843-2305.
Telephone: 517-546-7600.
Telecopier: 517-546-6974.
Kalamazoo, Michigan Office: 444 West Michigan Avenue, 49007-3752.
Telephone: 616-381-7030.
Fax: 616-382-0244.
Lansing, Michigan Office: One Michigan Avenue, Suite 900, 48933-1609.
Telephone: 517-487-2070.
Fax: 517-374-6304.
Monroe, Michigan Office: The Executive Centre, 214 East Elm Avenue, 48161-2682.
Telephone: 313-243-2000.
Fax: 313-243-0901.
Washington, D.C. Office: 1225 Nineteenth Street, N.W., Suite 400. 20036.
Telephone: 202-429-5575; 785-0600.
Fax: 202-331-1118; 785-1234.
Pensacola, Florida Office: 25 West Cedar, 32501.
Telephone: 904-469-1088.
Fax: 904-432-0677.
St. Petersburg, Florida Office: 100 Second Avenue S., Suite 7045, 33701.
Telephone: 813-982-6000.
Fax: 813-892-6002.
Gdansk, Poland Office: Suite 322, Dom Technika Building, Ul. Rajska 6, 80-850.
Telephone: 011-485-831-2808.
Fax: 011-485-831-4719.
Warsaw, Poland Office: Ul. Marszalkowska 82, Suite 561, 00-517.
Telephone: 011-482-623-6457 and 6458.
Fax: 011-482-623-6459.

RESIDENT PARTNERS

John B. DeVine
Robert E. Gilbert
Allyn D. Kantor
Erik H. Serr
Timothy D. Sochocki
Gary A. Bruder
Susan Hedges Patton
David A. French
J. David Reck
David N. Parsigian

OF COUNSEL

Edmond F. DeVine

SENIOR ATTORNEYS

Charles A. Duerr, Jr.
Ronald D. Gardner
Marta A. Manildi

RESIDENT ASSOCIATES

A. Paul Thowsen
John O. Renken
Diane B. Cabbell
Linda M. Ledbetter
Suzanne L. DeVine
Amy J. Broman

Representative Firm Clients: Chrysler Corp.; Comerica, Inc.; City of Detroit, Mich.; Detroit Tigers, Inc.; First of Michigan; Fretter, Inc.; Ford Motor Co.; Ford Motor Credit Co.; Great Lakes Bancorp; Henry Ford Hospital.

For full biographical listings, see the Martindale-Hubbell Law Directory

Ann Arbor—Continued

Pear Sperling Eggan & Muskovitz, P.C. (AV)

Domino's Farms, 24 Frank Lloyd Wright Drive, 48105
Telephone: 313-665-4441
Fax: 313-665-8788
Ypsilanti, Michigan Offices: 5 South Washington Street.
Telephone: 313-483-3626 and 2164 Bellevue at Washtenaw.
Telephone: 313-483-7177.

Edwin L. Pear
Lawrence W. Sperling
Andrew M. Eggan
Melvin J. Muskovitz
Thomas E. Daniels
Joel F. Graziani
Paul R. Fransway
Francyne Stacey
Helen Conklin Vick
Scott H. Mandel
David E. Kempner

Counsel for: Domino's Pizza, Inc.; Townsend and Bottum, Inc.; Gelman Sciences, Inc.; Victory Lane Quick Oil Change Inc.; Bank One, Ypsilanti, N.A.; Ann Arbor Transportation Authority; Meadowbrook Insurance Group; Michigan Municipal Liability & Property Pool.
Approved Attorneys for: Lawyers Title Insurance Corp.

For full biographical listings, see the Martindale-Hubbell Law Directory

*BAD AXE,** Huron Co. — (Refer to Port Huron)

BATTLE CREEK, Calhoun Co.

Sullivan, Hamilton, Schulz, Letzring, Simons, Kreter, Toth & Lebeuf (AV)

Tenth Floor Comerica Building 25 West Michigan Mall, 49017
Telephone: 616-965-3216

Maxwell B. Allen (1884-1942)
John M. Allen (1914-1985)
Ronald H. Ryan (1901-1988)
James M. Sullivan
Robert P. Hamilton
Bert W. Schulz
Kurt F. Letzring
Stephen L. Simons
Mark E. Kreter
Michael J. Toth
Ronald A. Lebeuf

OF COUNSEL

Raymond R. Allen

General Counsel for: Michigan Woodwork and Specialties.
Local Counsel for: The Medical Protective Co.; Gannett, Inc.; Automobile Club of Michigan Insurance Group and Insurance Assn. (AAA); Michigan Physicians Mutual Liability Co.; State Farm Mutual Insurance Co.; Auto Owners Ins. Co.; Cincinnati Ins. Co.; Nationwide Ins. Co.

For full biographical listings, see the Martindale-Hubbell Law Directory

Varnum, Riddering, Schmidt & Howlett (AV)

4950 West Dickman Road, Suite B-1, 49015
Telephone: 616-962-7144
Grand Rapids, Michigan Office: Bridgewater Place, P.O. Box 352, 49501-0352.
Telephone: 616-336-6000; 800-262-0011.
Facsimile: 616-336-7000.
Telex: 1561593 VARN.
Lansing, Michigan Office: The Victor Center, Suite 810, 201 North Washington Square, 48933.
Telephone: 517-482-6237.
Facsimile: 517-482-6937.
Kalamazoo, Michigan Office: 350 East Michigan Avenue, 49007.
Telephone: 616-382-2300.
Facsimile: 616-382-2382.
Grand Haven, Michigan Office: 321 Washington Street, P.O. Box 288, 49417.
Telephone: 616-846-7100.
Facsimile: 616-846-7101.
Detroit, Michigan Office: 440 East Congress, Fourth Floor, 48226.
Telephone: 313-961-1600.
Facsimile: 313-961-1636.

MEMBER OF FIRM

Carl E. Ver Beek

For full biographical listings, see the Martindale-Hubbell Law Directory

*BAY CITY,** Bay Co.

Braun Kendrick Finkbeiner (AV)

201 Phoenix Building, P.O. Box 2039, 48708
Telephone: 517-895-8505
Telecopier: 517-895-8437
Saginaw, Michigan Office: 8th Floor Second National Bank Building.
Telephone: 517-753-3461.
Telecopier: 517-753-3951.

MEMBERS OF FIRM

Ralph J. Isackson
Patrick D. Neering
George F. Gronewold, Jr.
Frank M. Quinn
Gregory E. Meter
Daniel S. Opperman
Gregory T. Demers
Jeffrey C. Wilson

(See Next Column)

ASSOCIATES

Michael E. Wooley

Representative Clients: APV Chemical Machinery, Inc.; Bay Health Systems; Berger and Co.; Catholic Federal Credit Union; Charter Township of Bridgeport; City of Saginaw; City of Vassar; City of Zilwaukee; Corporate Service; Cox Cable.

For full biographical listings, see the Martindale-Hubbell Law Directory

Higgs Law Offices (AV)

302 Chemical Bank Building, 213 Center Avenue, P.O. Box 2099, 48707
Telephone: 517-892-1499
Fax: 517-892-1443

Milton E. Higgs

ASSOCIATES

J. Edmund (Jack) Frost

OF COUNSEL

F. Norman Higgs (Retired)

Seward, Tally & Piggott, P.C. (AV)

1009 Washington Avenue, P.O. Box 795, 48707-0795
Telephone: 517-892-6551
Fax: 517-892-1568

B. J. Tally, Jr.
Webster C. Tally
Mark J. Brissette
John M. Morosi
Kenneth K. Wright
Lewis M. Seward
Barbara F. Livingston

OF COUNSEL

John W. Grigg
John W. Piggott

Representative Clients: Bay Medical Care Facility; Dunlop Pontiac; Euclid Tool & Machine; Euclid Industries; Williams Cheese Co.; General Housing Corp.; Bank of Alma; Commercial National Bank of Ithaca; Farmers State Bank; First of America Bank-Mid Michigan, N.A.; Farwell State Bank; Bay Governmental Credit Union.
Reference: First of America Bank-Mid Michigan, N.A.

For full biographical listings, see the Martindale-Hubbell Law Directory

Smith & Brooker, P.C. (AV)

703 Washington Avenue, P.O. Box X-921, 48707-0921
Telephone: 517-892-2595
Saginaw, Michigan Office: 3057 Davenport Avenue.
Telephone: 517-799-1891.
Flint, Michigan Office: 3506 Lennon Road.
Telephone: 810-733-0140.

Carl H. Smith (1898-1981)
James K. Brooker (1902-1973)

RESIDENT ATTORNEYS

Carl H. Smith, Jr.
Albert C. Hicks
Glenn F. Doyle
Richard C. Sheppard
George B. Mullison
Charles T. Hewitt

Representative Clients: Allen Medical Building Co.; Charter Township of Hampton; CIGNA; Medical Protective Insurance Co.; Monitor Sugar Co.; Region VII Area Agency on Aging; State Farm Mutual Automobile Insurance Co.; Sterling Area Health Center; Medical Staff of Bay Medical Center; Secura Insurance.

For full biographical listings, see the Martindale-Hubbell Law Directory

*BEULAH,** Benzie Co.

Murchie, Calcutt & Boynton

(See Traverse City)

BIRMINGHAM, Oakland Co.

Butzel Long, A Professional Corporation (AV)

Suite 200, 32270 Telegraph Road, 48025
Telephone: 810-258-1616
Telecopier: 810-258-1439
Detroit, Michigan Office: Suite 900, 150 West Jefferson.
Telephone: 313-225-7000.
Telecopier: 313-225-7080.
Lansing, Michigan Office: 118 West Ottawa Street.
Telephone: 517-372-6622.
Telecopier: 517-372-6672.
Ann Arbor, Michigan Office: Suite 400, 121 West Washington.
Telephone: 313-995-3110.
Telecopier: 313-995-1777.
Grosse Pointe Farms, Michigan Office: Suite 260, 21 Kercheval.
Telephone: 313-886-5446.
Telecopier: 313-886-2114.

(See Next Column)

BUTZEL LONG A PROFESSIONAL CORPORATION, *Birmingham—Continued*

Stephen A. Bromberg (Resident)
Allan Nachman (Resident)
Abba I. Friedman (Resident)
Edward D. Gold (Resident)
Paul L. Triemstra (Resident)
Frederick G. Buesser, III (Resident)
T. Gordon Scupholm II (Resident)
David W. Sommerfeld
Michael M. Jacob (Resident)
Thomas B. Radom (Resident)
David W. Berry (Resident)
D. Stewart Green (Resident)
Gordon J. Walker (Resident)
Gordon W. Didier
Diane M. Soubly
Alan S. Levine
Gary J. Abraham (Resident)
James Y. Stewart
Eric J. Flessland (Resident)
Lawrence A. Lichtman
Brian P. Henry

OF COUNSEL

Sidney L. Cohn (Resident)
William A. Penner, Jr.
James M. Wienner (Resident)

Katherine B. Albrecht (Resident)
Anthony J. Saulino, Jr. (Resident)
Patrick A. Karbowski (Resident)
Ronald E. Reynolds
Robert P. Perry (Resident)
Susan Klein Friedlaender (Resident)

For full biographical listings, see the Martindale-Hubbell Law Directory

---

AUSTIN HIRSCHHORN, P.C. (AV)

251 East Merrill Street, 2nd Floor, 48009-6150
Telephone: 810-646-9944
FAX: 810-647-8596

Austin Hirschhorn

For full biographical listings, see the Martindale-Hubbell Law Directory

---

MILLER, CANFIELD, PADDOCK AND STONE, P.L.C.

(See Bloomfield Hills)

BLOOMFIELD HILLS, Oakland Co.

CLARK, KLEIN & BEAUMONT (AV)

1533 North Woodward Avenue, Suite 220, 48304
Telephone: 810-258-2900
Facsmile: 810-258-2949
Detroit, Michigan Office: 1600 First Federal Building. 1001 Woodward Avenue.
Telephone: 313-965-8300.
Facsimile: 313-962-4348.

MEMBERS OF FIRM

Michael D. Mulcahy
Edward C. Dawda
Curtis J. Mann
Susan J. Sadler
Tyler D. Tennent
Sherwin E. Zamler

ASSOCIATES

Amy Bateson
Todd A. Schafer
Joseph K. Hart, Jr.

For full biographical listings, see the Martindale-Hubbell Law Directory

---

DICKINSON, WRIGHT, MOON, VAN DUSEN & FREEMAN (AV)

525 North Woodward Avenue, Suite 2000, 48304-2970
Telephone: 810-433-7200
Facsimile: 810-433-7274
Detroit, Michigan Office: 500 Woodward Avenue, Suite 4000.
Telephone: 313-223-3500.
Facsimile: 313-223-3598.
Grand Rapids, Michigan Office: 200 Ottawa Avenue, N.W., Suite 900.
Telephone: 616-458-1300.
Facsimile: 616-458-6753.
Lansing, Michigan Office: Suite 200, 215 South Washington Square.
Telephone: 517-371-1730.
Facsimile: 517-487-4700.
Washington, D.C. Office: Suite 800, 1901 L Street, N.W.
Telephone: 202-457-0160.
Facsimile: 202-659-1559.
Chicago, Illinois Office: 225 West Washington, Suite 400.
Telephone: 312-220-0300.
Facsimile: 312-220-0021.
Warsaw, Poland Office: 46 Wilcza Street, 4th Floor, 00-679.
Telephone: (48-22) 299-241.
Facsimile: (48-2) 628-4107. Komertel Satellite Phone: (48-39) 121-510.

RESIDENT PARTNERS

Ward Randol, Jr.
Charles F. Clippert
Robert V. Peterson
Frank G. Pollock
Joyce Q. Lower
Charles T. Harris
John H. Norris
Stephen E. Dawson
Edward H. Pappas
Henry W. Saad
George R. Ashford
Erik J. Stone
David R. Bruegel
Maureen H. Burke
Jon Robert Steiger
Zan M. Nicolli
Deborah L. Grace
Robert A. LaBelle

(See Next Column)

RESIDENT PARTNERS (Continued)

Elizabeth M. Pezzetti
Judith E. Gowing
Cynthia A. Moore
Daniel M. Brinks
Joseph W. DeLave
Mary A. Pearson
Margaret Van Meter

OF COUNSEL

Douglas L. Mann
Vivian Perry-Johnston
Thomas D. McLennan
Bethany E. Hawkins

RESIDENT ASSOCIATES

Michelle Stahl Ausdemore
Terrence A. Barr
Jeffrey J. Brown
Robert E. Carr
Sara Anne Engle
Nanci J. Grant
Robert B. Hotchkiss
Deborah A. Hulse (Not admitted in MI)
Lauren M. Hurwitz
Kelli L. Kerbawy
Karen Raitt Modell
John T. Panourgias
Gregory J. Parry
Andrew H. Thorson

Representative Clients: Federal-Mogul Corp.; Florists' Transworld Delivery Assn.; GMF Robotics Corp.; Kmart Corp.; Kuhlman Corp.; Michigan Consolidated Gas Co.; NBD Bank, N.A.

For full biographical listings, see the Martindale-Hubbell Law Directory

---

DYKEMA GOSSETT (AV)

1577 North Woodward Avenue Suite 300, 48304-2820
Telephone: 810-540-0700
Telex: 23-0121
Fax: 810-540-0763
Detroit, Michigan Office: 400 Renaissance Center, 48243-1668.
Telephone: 313-568-6800.
Fax: 313-568-6594.
Ann Arbor, Michigan Office: 315 East Eisenhower Parkway, Suite 100, 48108-3306.
Telephone: 313-747-7660.
Fax: 313-747-7696.
Grand Rapids, Michigan Office: 200 Oldtown Riverfront Building, 248 Louis Campau Promenade, N.W., 49503-2668.
Telephone: 616-776-7500.
Fax: 616-776-7573.
Lansing, Michigan Office: 800 Michigan National Tower, 48933.
Telephone: 517-374-9100.
Fax: 517-374-9191.
Washington, D.C. Office: Franklin Square, Suite 300 West Tower, 1300 I Street, N.W., 20005-3306.
Telephone: 202-522-8600.
Fax: 202-522-86697
Chicago, Illinois Office: Three First National Plaza, Suite 1400, 70 W. Madison, 60602-4270.
Telephone: 312-214-3380.
Fax: 312-214-3441.

RESIDENT MEMBERS

Bowden V. Brown
B. Kingsley Buhl
John K. Cannon
J. Bruce Donaldson
Robert L. Duty
Fred J. Fechheimer
Michael D. Fishman
Dennis M. Gannan
Richard D. Grauer
Alan M. Greene
Dennis M. Haffey
Craig L. John
Louis W. Kasischke
Robert L. Kelly
Stuart D. Logan
D. Richard McDonald
William T. Myers
Ralph T. Rader
Ronald L. Rose (Resident, Bloomfield Hills Office)
David M. Rosenberger
Mary Elizabeth Royce
Charles R. Rutherford
Rex E. Schlaybaugh, Jr.
Robert L. Schwartz
Thomas B. Spillane, Jr.
Mark H. Sutton
Randy W. Tung

OF COUNSEL

John J. Slavin
Donald E. Shely

RETIRED MEMBERS

William H. Baldwin
William T. Gossett
Robert A. Sloman
Brian Sullivan

RESIDENT ASSOCIATES

Jeffrey B. Conner
Joseph V. Coppola, Sr.
Donald M. Crawford (Not admitted in MI)
Nancy L. Farnam
David John Gaskey
Joseph H. Hickey
Kevin M. Hinman
Howard N. Luckoff
John W. Rees
William C. Roush
Stephen L. Scharf
Catherine Kim Shierk
Michael B. Stewart
Michael Tucker
Sally A. York

For full biographical listings, see the Martindale-Hubbell Law Directory

---

FEENEY KELLETT & WIENNER, PROFESSIONAL CORPORATION (AV)

950 N. Hunter Boulevard, Third Floor, 48304-3927
Telephone: 810-258-1580
Fax: 810-258-0421

(See Next Column)

FEENEY KELLETT & WIENNER PROFESSIONAL CORPORATION—*Continued*

James P. Feeney
S. Thomas Wienner
Peter M. Kellett
Cheryl A. Bush
Linda M. Galante
Deborah F. Collins
David N. Goltz
G. Gregory Schuetz
Tracy D. Knox (Not admitted in MI)
Patrick G. Seyferth
Mark A. Fisher

For full biographical listings, see the Martindale-Hubbell Law Directory

HOWARD & HOWARD ATTORNEYS, P.C. (AV)

The Pinehurst Office Center, Suite 101, 1400 North Woodward Avenue, 48304-2856
Telephone: 810-645-1483
Telecopier: 810-645-1568
Kalamazoo, Michigan Office: The Kalamazoo Building, Suite 400, 107 West Michigan Avenue.
Telephone: 616-382-1483.
Telecopier: 616-382-1568.
Lansing, Michigan Office: The Phoenix Building, Suite 500, 222 Washington Square, North.
Telephone: 517-485-1483.
Telecopier: 517-485-1568.
Peoria, Illinois Office: Howard & Howard, P.C., The Creve Coeur Building, Suite 200, 321 Liberty Street.
Telephone: 309-672-1483.
Telecopier: 309-672-1568.

Kelly A. Allen
Gustaf R. Andreasen
William G. Asimakis, Jr.
Daniel L. Baker
Antoinette Beuche
Robert L. Biederman
Lori Belden Bobbitt
Walter J. Borda
Fernando A. Borrego
Tammy L. Brown
Philip T. Carter
Kevin M. Chudler
Carolyn M. Claerhout
William J. Clemens
Michael G. Cruse
Thomas R. Curran, Jr.
Chris T. Danikolas
Mark A. Davis
John Gerald Gleeson
Paul Green
Roger M. Groves
Wade E. Haddad
John G. Hayward
William H. Honaker
Robert B. Johnston
J. Michael Kemp
Daniel N. King
Jon H. Kingsepp
Steven C. Kohl
Timothy E. Kraepel
D. Craig Martin
Claude Henry Miller
Robert D. Mollhagen
Theodore W. Olds III
Susan E. Padley
Gary A. Peters
Martha A. Proctor
Jeffrey G. Raphelson
Brad A. Rayle
Brian J. Renaud
Blake K. Ringsmuth
Deborah M. Schneider
Raymond E. Scott
Michael V. Sucaet
Thomas J. Tallerico
Laura A. Talt
Donald F. Tucker
Jacqueline K. Vestevich
James C. Wickens
Timothy M. Wittebort
John E. Young
Marla Gottlieb Zwas

Representative Clients: First of America Bank Corporation; W.R. Grace & Co.; Chrysler Corp.; Indian Head Industries; Coopers & Lybrand; United Technologies.

For full biographical listings, see the Martindale-Hubbell Law Directory

MAY, SIMPSON & STROTE, A PROFESSIONAL CORPORATION (AV)

100 West Long Lake Road Suite 200, P.O. Box 541, 48303-0541
Telephone: 810-646-9500

Richard H. May
Thomas C. Simpson
Ronald P. Strote
Steven M. Raymond
John A. Forrest
David K. McDonnell

Steven F. Alexsy
Marilynn K. Arnold
Michele A. Lerner

Representative Clients: Aamco Transmission; American Annuity Life Insurance; Container Corporation of America; Citicorp Financial Center; Century 21 Real Estate Corp.; Oak Hills Mortgage Corp.; Ziebart International Corp.
Reference: NBD Bank, N.A.

For full biographical listings, see the Martindale-Hubbell Law Directory

MEYER, KIRK, SNYDER & SAFFORD (AV)

Suite 100, 100 West Long Lake Road, 48304
Telephone: 810-647-5111
Telecopier: 810-647-6079
Detroit, Michigan Office: 2500 Penobscot Building.
Telephone: 313-961-1261.

George H. Meyer
John M. Kirk
George E. Snyder
Ralph R. Safford
Donald H. Baker, Jr.
Patrick K. Rode

ASSOCIATES

Christopher F. Clark
Boyd C. Farnam
Debra S. Meier

(See Next Column)

OF COUNSEL

Mark R. Solomon

Representative Clients: Chemical Waste Management; Ervin Advertising; The Michigan and S.E. Michigan McDonald's Operators Assn.; The Southland Corp. (7-Eleven Food Stores); Stauffer Chemical Co.; Techpoint, Inc.

For full biographical listings, see the Martindale-Hubbell Law Directory

MILLER, CANFIELD, PADDOCK AND STONE, P.L.C. (AV)

A Professional Limited Liability Company
Founded in 1852 by Sidney Davy Miller
Suite 100 Pinehurst Office Center, 1400 North Woodward, P.O. Box 2014, 48303-2014
Telephone: 810-645-5000
Fax: 810-645-1917
Fax: 810-258-3036
Detroit, Michigan Office: 150 West Jefferson, Suite 2500, 48226-4415.
Telephone: 313-963-6420.
Fax: 313-496-7500.
Cable Address: "Stem Detroit."
Ann Arbor, Michigan Office: 101 North Main Street, 7th Floor, 48104-1400.
Telephone: 313-663-2445.
Fax: 313-747-7147.
Grand Rapids, Michigan Office: 1200 Campau Square Plaza, 99 Monroe, N.W., 49503-2639.
Telephone: 616-454-8656.
Fax: 616-776-6322.
Howell, Michigan Office: 121 South Barnard Street, Suite 4, 48843-2305.
Telephone: 517-546-7600.
Telecopier: 517-546-6974.
Kalamazoo, Michigan Office: 444 West Michigan Avenue, 49007-3752.
Telephone: 616-381-7030.
Fax: 616-382-0244.
Lansing, Michigan Office: One Michigan Avenue, Suite 900, 48933-1609.
Telephone: 517-487-2070.
Fax: 517-374-6304.
Monroe, Michigan Office: The Executive Centre, 214 East Elm Avenue, 48161-2682.
Telephone: 313-243-2000.
Fax: 313-243-0901.
Washington, D.C. Office: 1225 Nineteenth Street, N.W., Suite 400. 20036.
Telephone: 202-429-5575; 785-0600.
Fax: 202-331-1118; 785-1234.
Pensacola, Florida Office: 25 West Cedar, 32501.
Telephone: 904-469-1088.
Fax: 904-432-0677.
St. Petersburg, Florida Office: 100 Second Avenue S., Suite 7045, 33701.
Telephone: 813-982-6000.
Fax: 813-892-6002.
Gdansk, Poland Office: Suite 322, Dom Technika Building, Ul. Rajska 6, 80-850.
Telephone: 011-485-831-2808.
Fax: 011-485-831-4719.
Warsaw, Poland Office: Ul. Marszalkowska 82, Suite 561, 00-517.
Telephone: 011-482-623-6457 and 6458.
Fax: 011-482-623-6459.

RESIDENT MEMBERS

Lawrence A. King (P.C.)
Richard A. Jones (P.C.)
John A. Thurber (P.C.)
John A. Marxer (P.C.)
Kenneth E. Konop
Ronald H. Riback
James W. Williams
Frank L. Andrews
J. Kevin Trimmer
Gregory V. Di Censo
Brad B. Arbuckle

RESIDENT OF COUNSEL

John A. Gilray, Jr., (P.C.)
Henry R. Nolte, Jr.

RESIDENT ASSOCIATES

Ronald E. Hodess
Jereen G. Trudell
William L. Rosin
Dawn M. Schluter
Anna M. Maiuri

Representative Firm Clients: Chrysler Corp.; Comerica, Inc.; City of Detroit, Mich.; Detroit Tigers, Inc.; First of Michigan; Fretter, Inc.; Ford Motor Co.; Ford Motor Credit Co.; Great Lakes Bancorp; Henry Ford Hospital.

For full biographical listings, see the Martindale-Hubbell Law Directory

SHANTZ AND BOOKER, PROFESSIONAL CORPORATION (AV)

525 N. Woodward Avenue, Suite 1100, 48304
Telephone: 810-644-2266
Fax: 810-644-2810

John F. Shantz
James H. Booker

George A. Contis

OF COUNSEL

Constance M. Ettinger

Representative Clients: William Crook Fire Protection Co.; West Bloomfield School District; Clarenceville School District; Madison School District; Progressive Metal Manufacturing Co.; Marco Wood Products, Inc.; Dunn's,

(See Next Column)

SHANTZ AND BOOKER PROFESSIONAL CORPORATION, *Bloomfield Hills—Continued*

Inc.; Craftmation Inc.; Akins Construction Co.; School District of the City of Royal Oak; Radio Distributing Co.

For full biographical listings, see the Martindale-Hubbell Law Directory

STROBL AND MANOOGIAN, P.C. (AV)

300 East Long Lake Road, Suite 200, 48304-2376
Telephone: 810-645-0306
Facsimile: 810-645-2690

Thomas J. Strobl
Brian C. Manoogian
John Sharp
James A. Rocchio
Kieran F. Cunningham
Michael E. Thoits
James D. Wilson

James T. Dunn
Sara S. Lisznyai
Brian M. Gottry
Thomas H. Kosik
Keith S. King
Pamela S. Ritter
Robert F. Boesiger
Douglas Young

OF COUNSEL

Glenn S. Arendsen

Representative Clients: Masco Corporation; MascoTech; American Speedy Printing Centers; Bohn Aluminum Corporation; Flat Rock Metal, Inc.; Sherwood Metal Products, Inc.; Capitol Bancorp, Ltd.; Access Bidco.

For full biographical listings, see the Martindale-Hubbell Law Directory

*CADILLAC,** Wexford Co.

MURCHIE, CALCUTT & BOYNTON

(See Traverse City)

*CASSOPOLIS,** Cass Co. — (Refer to Niles)

*CHARLEVOIX,** Charlevoix Co.

MURCHIE, CALCUTT & BOYNTON

(See Traverse City)

*CHARLOTTE,** Eaton Co. — (Refer to Lansing)

*CORUNNA,** Shiawassee Co. — (Refer to Flint)

*DETROIT,** Wayne Co.

BODMAN, LONGLEY & DAHLING (AV)

34th Floor 100 Renaissance Center, 48243
Telephone: 313-259-7777
Fax: 313-393-7579
Troy, Michigan Office: Suite 2020, 755 West Big Beaver Road.
Telephone: 810-362-2110.
Ann Arbor, Michigan Office: 110 Miller, Suite 300.
Telephone: 313-761-3780.
Northern Michigan Office: 229 Court Street, P.O. Box 405, Cheboygan.
Telephone: 616-627-4351.

MEMBERS OF FIRM

Henry E. Bodman (1874-1963)
Clifford B. Longley (1888-1954)
Louis F. Dahling (1892-1992)
Pierre V. Heftler
Richard D. Rohr
Theodore Souris
Joseph A. Sullivan
Carson C. Grunewald
Walter O. Koch (Troy Office)
Alfred C. Wortley, Jr.
Michael B. Lewiston
George D. Miller, Jr.
Mark W. Griffin (Ann Arbor Office)
Thomas A. Roach (Ann Arbor Office)
Kenneth R. Lango (Troy Office)
James T. Heimbuch
Herold McC. Deason
James A. Smith
James R. Buschmann
George G. Kemsley
Joseph N. Brown
David M. Hempstead
Joseph J. Kochanek
Randolph S. Perry (Ann Arbor Office)
James J. Walsh
David G. Chardavoyne
David W. Hipp
Robert G. Brower
Larry R. Shulman
Charles N. Raimi
Terrence B. Larkin (Troy Office)
Thomas Van Dusen (Troy Office)
Fredrick J. Dindoffer
Robert J. Diehl, Jr.
John C. Cashen (Troy Office)
James C. Conboy, Jr. (Northern Michigan Office)
Lloyd C. Fell (Northern Michigan Office)
F. Thomas Lewand
Michael A. Stack (Northern Michigan Office)
Kathleen A. Lieder (Northern Michigan Office)
Karen L. Piper
Martha Bedsole Goodloe (Troy Office)
Harvey W. Berman (Ann Arbor Office)
Barbara Bowman Bluford
R. Craig Hupp
Lawrence P. Hanson (Northern Michigan Office)
Christopher J. Dine (Troy Office)
Henry N. Carnaby (Troy Office)
Jerold Lax (Ann Arbor Office)
Linda J. Throne (Northern Michigan Office)
Diane L. Akers
Ralph E. McDowell

(See Next Column)

MEMBERS OF FIRM (Continued)

Susan M. Kornfield (Ann Arbor Office)
Stephen I. Greenhalgh
Kathleen O'Callaghan Hickey
Patrick C. Cauley
Dennis J. Levasseur
David P. Larsen
Gail Pabarue Bennett (Troy Office)
Kay E. Malaney (Troy Office)

COUNSEL

Robert A. Nitschke
John S. Dobson (Ann Arbor Office)
Lewis A. Rockwell
Patricia D. White (Ann Arbor Office)

ASSOCIATES

Gary D. Reeves (Troy Office)
Joseph W. Girardot
Barnett Jay Colvin
David W. Barton (Northern Michigan Office)
Susan E. Conboy (Northern Michigan Office)
Sandra L. Sorini (Ann Arbor Office)
Stephen K. Postema (Ann Arbor Office)
Bonnie S. Sherr
Lisa M. Panourgias
R. Carl Lanfear
Louise-Annette Marcotty
William L. Hoey
Laurie A. Allen (Troy Office)
Marc M. Bakst
A. Craig Klomparens (Northern Michigan Office)
Kim M. Williams
David P. Rea
Jodee Fishman Raines
Nicholas P. Scavone, Jr.
Lydia Pallas Loren (Ann Arbor Office)
Robert C. Skramstad
Deanna L. Dixon
Arthur F. deVaux (Troy Office)

Representative Clients: Abitibi Price Group; Archdiocese of Detroit; Comerica Bank; The Detroit Lions, Inc.; Ford Estates; General Motors Corporation; Charles Stewart Mott Foundation; Norfolk Southern Corporation; Panhandle Eastern Corporation; State Farm Mutual Automobile Insurance Company.

For full biographical listings, see the Martindale-Hubbell Law Directory

BOOTHMAN, HEBERT & ELLER, P.C. (AV)

One Kennedy Square, Suite 2006 719 Griswold, 48226
Telephone: 313-964-0150; 1-800-572-8022
Fax: 313-964-2226
Ann Arbor, Michigan Office: 300 N. Fifth Avenue, Suite 140.
Telephone: 313-995-9050.
Fax: 313-995-8966.

Dale L. Hebert
Richard C. Boothman (Resident, Ann Arbor Office)
Gary S. Eller

George D. Moustakas
Roy A. Luttmann
Marta J. Hoffman
Sharon E. Hollins
Joyce E. Taylor

OF COUNSEL

L. Stewart Hastings, Jr.
Kathryn A. Kerka

Representative Clients: University of Michigan; CNA Insurance Companies; Michigan Physicians Mutual Liability Co.; Emergency Physicians Medical Group; Kaiser Permanente; Physicians Insurance Co. of Michigan.
Reference: Comerica Bank-Detroit.

For full biographical listings, see the Martindale-Hubbell Law Directory

BRADY HATHAWAY, PROFESSIONAL CORPORATION (AV)

1330 Buhl Building, 48226-3602
Telephone: 313-965-3700
Telecopier: 313-965-2830

John F. Brady
Thomas M. J. Hathaway
Thomas P. Brady
Daniel J. Bretz
Liliana A. Ciccodicola
Connie M. Cessante

Representative Clients: Beam Stream, Inc.; Bundy Tubing Company; Century 21 Real Estate Corp.; Datamedia Corporation; Energy Conversion Devices, Inc.; Michigan Gas Utilities; Pony Express Courier Corp,; Schering Corporation; Warner-Lambert; Wolverine Technologies.

For full biographical listings, see the Martindale-Hubbell Law Directory

BUESSER, BUESSER, BLACK, LYNCH, FRYHOFF & GRAHAM, P.C. (AV)

Suite 1750, 100 Renaissance Center, 48243
Telephone: 313-259-5220
Bloomfield Hills, Michigan Office: Suite 2000, 4190 Telegraph Road.
Telephone: 810-642-7880.

Frederick G. Buesser, Jr. (1916-1993)
Charles E. Blank
William R. Buesser
William O. Lynch
Timothy T. Fryhoff
Ronald F. Graham
Michael J. Black
John L. Hopkins, Jr.
L. James Wilson
Betty L. Lowenthal
Charles D. Brown
Maureen B. Connaughton
Kevin P. Kavanagh

Representative Clients: Wayne County Medical Society; Francis P. Rhoades Memorial Foundation; Detroit Country Day School; Air-Way Manufacturing Co.; American States Insurance Co.; Holiday Inns, Inc.; The Promus Companies Incorporated; Premo Pharmaceutical Co.; Citizens Insurance Co. of America; Michigan Rivet Corp.

For full biographical listings, see the Martindale-Hubbell Law Directory

Butzel Long, A Professional Corporation (AV)

Suite 900, 150 West Jefferson, 48226
Telephone: 313-225-7000
Telecopier: 313-225-7080
Birmingham, Michigan Office: Suite 200, 32270 Telegraph Road.
Telephone: 810-258-1616.
Telecopier: 810-258-1439.
Lansing, Michigan Office: 118 West Ottawa Street.
Telephone: 517-372-6622.
Telecopier: 517-372-6672.
Ann Arbor, Michigan Office: Suite 400, 121 West Washington.
Telephone: 313-995-3110.
Telecopier: 313-995-1777.
Grosse Pointe Farms, Michigan Office: Suite 260, 21 Kercheval.
Telephone: 313-886-5446.
Telecopier: 313-886-2114.

Leo M. Butzel (1874-1961)
Thomas G. Long (1883-1973)
William M. Saxton
Harold A. Ruemenapp
Stephen A. Bromberg (Birmingham)
Morris Milmet
Douglas G. Graham
Robert J. Battista
Frank B. Vecchio
Allan Nachman (Birmingham)
William R. Ralls (Lansing)
John P. Williams
Xhafer Orhan
John B. Weaver
George H. Zinn, Jr.
C. Peter Theut
John Henry Dudley, Jr.
Robert M. Vercruysse
Richard E. Rassel
Abba I. Friedman (Birmingham)
Edward D. Gold (Birmingham)
Robert B. Foster (Ann Arbor)
Paul L. Triemstra (Birmingham)
Jack D. Shumate
Edward M. Kronk
Philip J. Kessler
Thomas E. Sizemore
Donald B. Miller
John P. Hancock, Jr.
James E. Stewart
Virginia F. Metz
Frederick G. Buesser, III (Birmingham)
Leonard F. Charla
T. Gordon Scupholm II (Birmingham)
James C. Bruno
Mark S. Smallwood
David W. Sommerfeld (Birmingham, Grosse Pointe Farms and Ann Arbor)
Michael M. Jacob (Birmingham)
Thomas B. Radom (Birmingham)
David W. Berry (Birmingham)
Carl Rashid, Jr.
D. Stewart Green (Birmingham)
Dennis B. Schultz
Gregory V. Murray
Mark T. Nelson
Daniel P. Malone
Keefe A. Brooks
Justin G. Klimko
Michael D. Guzick
James E. Wynne
Barbara S. Kendzierski
Raymond J. Carey
David B. Calzone
Mark R. Lezotte
Michael J. Lavoie
Michael F. Golab
Edward M. Kalinka
Gordon J. Walker (Birmingham)
James L. Hughes
Arthur Dudley II
E. William S. Shipman
Richard P. Saslow
Gordon W. Didier
Dennis K. Egan
Jack J. Mazzara
Bruce L. Sendek
Lynne E. Deitch
Peter D. Holmes
Diane M. Soubly
Daniel B. Tukel
Susan Carino Nystrom
Alan S. Levine
Darlene M. Domanik
Leonard M. Niehoff
Carey A. DeWitt
Gary J. Abraham (Birmingham)
James Y. Stewart
Eric J. Flessland (Birmingham)
Lawrence A. Lichtman
Brian P. Henry (Birmingham and Lansing)
Lynn Abraham Sheehy
Robert A. Boonin
Sheldon H. Klein
Andrea Roumell Dickson

COUNSEL

Oscar H. Feldman
David F. DuMouchel
John F. McCuen, Jr. (Ann Arbor)
Robert F. Magill, Jr. (Ann Arbor)
Ralph S. Rumsey (Ann Arbor)

INTERNATIONAL PRACTICE ADVISOR

Akira Hara (Not admitted United States)

OF COUNSEL

George E. Brand, Jr.
Sidney L. Cohn (Birmingham)
Martha Ellen Dennis (Ann Arbor)
David M. Gaskin
Jere D. Johnston
John J. Kuhn
William A. Penner, Jr.
Robin S. Phillips (Ann Arbor)
Erwin S. Simon
Malcolm J. Sutherland
James M. Wienner (Birmingham)

William D. Vanderhoef
J. Michael Huget
Barbara T. Pichan
Katherine B. Albrecht (Birmingham)
Anthony J. Saulino, Jr. (Birmingham)
James S. Rosenfeld
David K. Tillman
Brian J. Miles

(See Next Column)

Clara DeMatteis Mager
Patrick A. Karbowski (Birmingham)
Ronald E. Reynolds
Kenneth H. Adamczyk
Phillip C. Korovesis
Jordan S. Schreier
Richard T. Hewlett
Robert P. Perry (Birmingham)
Michael R. Poterala
Joshua A. Sherbin
Nicholas J. Stasevich
Susan Klein Friedlaender (Birmingham)
James J. Urban (Lansing)
Leland R. Rosier (Lansing)
Daniel R. W. Rustmann
Eugene H. Boyle, Jr.
Bernice M. Tatarelli
Jeffrey S. Wilke
Guglielmo A. Pezza
Debra Auerbach Clephane
Timothy M. Labadie
Paul S. Lewandowski
Susan Hartmus Hiser
Elizabeth A. Dumouchelle
Stacy D. Holloman
Robert E. Norton II
James J. Giszczak
Lois E. Walker
Maria T. Harshe
Sherri A. Krause
Robin K. Luce
Patricia E. Nessel
Ann M. Kelly
Barbara L. McQuade
Laurie J. Michelson
Barbara Dodenhoff Urlaub
Herbert C. Donovan (Not admitted in MI)
Caridad Pastor-Klucens
Timothy E. Galligan (Not admitted in MI)
Wendel Vincent Hall (Lansing)

Representative Clients: Bridgestone/Firestone, Inc.; The Detroit News, Inc.; Detroit Diesel Corp.; Kelly Services; Kelsey Hayes Co.; Merrill Lynch & Co., Inc.; Stroh Brewery Co.; Takata Corp.; United Parcel Services of America, Inc.; The University of Michigan.

For full biographical listings, see the Martindale-Hubbell Law Directory

Clark, Klein & Beaumont (AV)

1600 First Federal Building, 1001 Woodward Avenue, 48226
Telephone: 313-965-8300
Facsimile: 313-962-4348
Bloomfield Hills Office: 1533 North Woodward Avenue, Suite 220, 48304.
Telephone: 810-258-2900.
Facsimile: 810-258-2949.

Joseph H. Clark (1860-1941)
George H. Klein (1881-1968)
John W. Beaumont (1858-1941)

MEMBERS OF FIRM

Patrick J. Keating
David P. Wood
Dwight H. Vincent
Laurence M. Scoville, Jr.
Henry Earle, III
William B. Dunn
J. Walker Henry
Douglas J. Rasmussen
D. Kerry Crenshaw
David M. Hayes
Robert G. Buydens
Richard C. Marsh
John F. Burns
Michael D. Mulcahy (Resident Bloomfield Hills, Michigan Office)
Fred W. Batten
P. Robert Brown, Jr.
Robert L. Weyhing, III
David E. Nims, III
Thomas S. Nowinski
David H. Paruch
Dennis G. Bonucchi
Edward C. Dawda (Resident Bloomfield Hills, Michigan Office)
Curtis J. Mann (Resident Bloomfield Hills, Michigan Office)
James E. Baiers
Duane L. Tarnacki
Suanne Tiberio Trimmer
Jonathan T. Walton, Jr.
Susan J. Sadler (Resident Bloomfield Hills, Michigan Office)
Michael S. Khoury
Mark L. McAlpine
Joseph A. Bonventre
Timothy M. Koltun
Michael G. Cumming
Michael J. Sullivan
Tyler D. Tennent (Resident, Bloomfield Hills, Michigan Office)
Rachelle G. Silberberg
Cynthia L.M. Johnson
John J. Hern, Jr.
Sherwin E. Zamler (Resident Bloomfield Hills, Michigan Office)
Dorothy Hanigan Basmaji
Paul E. Scheidemantel
J. Thomas MacFarlane
Edward C. Hammond
John E. Berg
Andrea M. Kanski

COUNSEL

Charles M. Bayer
Byron D. Walter

OF COUNSEL

Gerald L. Stoetzer
John C. Donnelly
Sidney W. Smith, Jr.
Leonard W. Smith

ASSOCIATES

Jennifer M. Sweeney Buckley
Maureen A. Darmanin
Thomas M. Dixon
Amy Bateson (Resident Bloomfield Hills, Michigan Office)
Thomas D. Dyze
Judith Greenstone Miller
Edward J. Hood
Keith James
Michael I. Conlon
David A. Foster
Patricia Bordman
Robin D. Ferriby
Kerry A. Anderson (Not admitted in MI)
Katrina I. Crawley
David A. Breuch
Patrice A. Villani
Todd A. Schafer (Resident, Bloomfield Hills, Michigan Office)
Georgette Borrego Dulworth
Joseph K. Hart, Jr. (Resident, Bloomfield Hills, Michigan Office)
Laura S. Stafford
Jennifer Crawford
M. Maureen McHugh
Donica Tolee Thomas

(See Next Column)

CLARK, KLEIN & BEAUMONT, *Detroit—Continued*

For full biographical listings, see the Martindale-Hubbell Law Directory

DICKINSON, WRIGHT, MOON, VAN DUSEN & FREEMAN (AV)

500 Woodward Avenue, Suite 4000, 48226-3425
Telephone: 313-223-3500
Facsimile: 313-223-3598
Bloomfield Hills, Michigan Office: 525 North Woodward Avenue, Suite 2000.
Telephone: 810-433-7200.
Facsimile: 810-433-7274.
Grand Rapids, Michigan Office: 200 Ottawa Avenue, N.W., Suite 900.
Telephone: 616-458-1300.
Facsimile: 616-458-6753.
Lansing, Michigan Office: Suite 200, 215 South Washington Square.
Telephone: 517-371-1730.
Facsimile: 517-487-4700.
Washington, D.C. Office: Suite 800, 1901 L Street, N.W.
Telephone: 202-457-0160.
Facsimile: 202-659-1559.
Chicago, Illinois Office: 225 West Washington, Suite 400.
Telephone: 312-220-0300.
Facsimile: 312-220-0021.
Warsaw, Poland Office: 46 Wilcza Street, 4th Floor, 00-679.
Telephone: (48-22) 299-241.
Facsimile: (48-2) 628-4107. Komertel Satellite Phone: (48-39) 121-510.

MEMBERS OF FIRM

Selden S. Dickinson (1892-1964)
Edward P. Wright (1894-1962)
Richard C. Van Dusen (1925-1991)
Fred W. Freeman
Patrick J. Ledwidge
Verne C. Hampton II
Ward Randol, Jr. (Bloomfield Hills Office)
Charles F. Clippert (Bloomfield Hills Office)
Russell A. McNair, Jr.
John E. S. Scott
Herbert G. Sparrow, III
John Corbett O'Meara
Judson Werbelow (Lansing Office)
Charles R. Kinnaird
Michael T. Platt (Washington, D.C. Office)
John A. Krsul, Jr.
Douglas D. Roche
John A. Everhardus
Robert V. Peterson (Bloomfield Hills Office)
Edgar C. Howbert
Peter S. Sheldon (Lansing Office)
Robert S. Krause
Frank G. Pollock (Bloomfield Hills Office)
Robert E. Neiman (Chicago, Illinois Office)
Joseph A. Fink (Lansing Office)
Joyce Q. Lower (Bloomfield Hills Office)
Robert P. Hurlbert (Chicago, Illinois Office)
Thomas G. Kienbaum
Lawrence G. Campbell
Charles T. Harris (Bloomfield Hills Office)
David L. Turner
John H. Norris (Bloomfield Hills Office)
Ronald B. Grais (Chicago, Illinois Office)
William J. Fisher, III (Grand Rapids Office)
James N. Candler, Jr.
Kenneth J. McIntyre
Julia Donovan Darlow
J. Bryan Williams
Stephen E. Dawson (Bloomfield Hills Office)
Richard J. Meyers
Edward H. Pappas (Bloomfield Hills Office)
Jeffrey M. Petrash (Washington, D.C. Office)
Michael Gary Vartanian
Henry W. Saad (Bloomfield Hills Office)
John K. Lawrence
C. Beth DunCombe
James A. Samborn
Philip M. Frost
Timothy H. Howlett
James M. Tervo (Chicago, Illinois Office)
Terence M. Donnelly
Thomas D. Carney
Roger H. Cummings
Stuart F. Cheney (Grand Rapids Office)
Richard L. Braun, II
Joseph C. Marshall, III
Richard M. Bolton
Steven C. Nadeau
Jerome M. Schwartz
Richard A. Glaser (Grand Rapids Office)
George R. Ashford (Bloomfield Hills Office)
Henry M. Grix
James W. Bliss (Lansing Office)
Erik J. Stone (Bloomfield Hills Office)
Gregory L. McClelland (Lansing Office)
Richard W. Paul
David R. Bruegel (Bloomfield Hills Office)
Bruce C. Thelen
Peter H. Ellsworth (Lansing Office)
Noel D. Massie
Richard L. Caretti
Theodore R. Opperwall
Kirk Howard Betts (Washington, D.C. Office)
Margaret A. Coughlin
William E. Elwood (Washington, D.C. Office)
Martin L. Greenberg (Chicago, Illinois Office)
Keith J. Lerminiaux
Kester K. So (Lansing Office)
John M. Lichtenberg (Grand Rapids Office)
Francis R. Ortiz
Thomas J. Manganello
W. Anthony Jenkins
Larry J. Stringer
Robert E. Kinchen
Daniel M. Katlein
Robert W. Powell
Thomas D. Hammerschmidt, Jr.
Thomas V. Yates
Mark R. High
Richard A. Wilhelm
Peter Swiecicki (Warsaw, Poland Office)
Paul M. Wyzgoski
Barbara Hughes Erard
Maureen H. Burke (Bloomfield Hills Office)
Dwight D. Ebaugh (Lansing Office)

(See Next Column)

MEMBERS OF FIRM (Continued)

Samuel D. Littlepage (Washington, D.C. Office)
Conrad J. Clark (Washington, D.C. Office)
Stephen S. Herseth (Chicago, Illinois Office)
Jon Robert Steiger (Bloomfield Hills Office)
Kenneth T. Brooks (Lansing Office)
Kathleen A. Lang
Tomoaki Ikenaga
Daniel F. Gosch (Chicago, Illinois Office)
William P. Shield, Jr.
Brian K. Cullin
Thomas G. McNeill
Elizabeth Phelps Hardy
William T. Burgess
Zan M. Nicolli (Bloomfield Hills Office)
Jeffery V. Stuckey (Lansing Office)
Deborah L. Grace (Bloomfield Hills Office)
Gail A. Anderson (Lansing Office)
Andrea Andrews Larkin (Lansing Office)
Robert A. LaBelle (Bloomfield Hills Office)
Christopher L. Rizik
Elizabeth M. Pezzetti (Bloomfield Hills Office)
Judith E. Gowing (Bloomfield Hills Office)
Cynthia A. Moore (Bloomfield Hills Office)
Claudia Rast
David E. Pierson (Lansing Office)
Linda V. Parker
Johanna H. Armstrong
Dustin P. Ordway (Grand Rapids Office)
Mary Elizabeth Kelly
Danna Marie Kozerski
Andrew S. Boyce
Eric J. Pelton
Mark K. Riashi
Daniel M. Brinks (Bloomfield Hills Office)
Cynthia M. York
Steven H. Hilfinger
Joel M. Shere
Thea D. Dunmire (Chicago, Illinois Office)
Krzysztof Wierzbowski (Warsaw, Poland Office)
Joseph W. DeLave (Bloomfield Hills Office)
Jerry L. Johnson
Mary A. Pearson (Bloomfield Hills Office)
Brian K. Zahra
Margaret Van Meter (Bloomfield Hills Office)

CONSULTING PARTNERS

Charles R. Moon
Ernest Getz
W. Gerald Warren
Grady Avant, Jr.

OF COUNSEL

Lucien N. Nedzi (Washington, D.C. Office)
Bruce A. Tassan (Washington, D.C. Office)
Thomas D. McLennan (Bloomfield Hills Office)
T. R. Knecht (Grand Rapids Office)
Steven V. Napolitano (Chicago, Illinois Office)
Douglas L. Mann (Bloomfield Hills Office)
Vivian Perry-Johnston (Bloomfield Hills Office)
Piotr J. Strawa (Warsaw, Poland Office)
John A. Ziegler, Jr.
Bethany E. Hawkins (Bloomfield Hills Office)
Douglas J. Van Der Aa (Grand Rapids Office)
Allan G. Sweig (Chicago, Illinois Office)
Mitchell J. Rapp (Lansing Office)
Marc A. Bergsman (Washington, D.C. Office)
Jill M. Barker (Washington, D.C. Office)

ASSOCIATES

Michelle Stahl Ausdemore (Bloomfield Hills Office)
Terrence A. Barr (Bloomfield Hills Office)
William R. Beekman (Lansing Office)
William C. Bertrand, Jr. (Lansing Office)
Jeffrey J. Brown (Bloomfield Hills Office)
Bruce R. Byrd
Robert E. Carr (Bloomfield Hills Office)
Kim D. Crooks (Lansing Office)
Michael S. Daar
Stephanie Dawkins Davis
Mark Alan Densmore
David R. Deromedi
Andrew S. Doctoroff
Julie T. Emerick
Sara Anne Engle (Bloomfield Hills Office)
Christine R. Essique
James P. Evans (Lansing Office)
Sherisse Eddy Fiorvento
Michelle Thurber Freese
Todd K. Garvelink
Kirk E. Grable (Lansing Office)
Nanci J. Grant (Bloomfield Hills Office)
Erin E. Gravelyn (Grand Rapids Office)
Melissa A. Hagen (Lansing Office)
K. Scott Hamilton
Michael C. Hammer
Craig W. Hammond
Douglas D. Hampton
Jana L. Henkel-Benjamin
Robert B. Hotchkiss (Bloomfield Hills Office)
Deborah A. Hulse (Not admitted in MI; Bloomfield Hills Office)
Lauren M. Hurwitz (Bloomfield Hills Office)
Kyle M. H. Jones
Mary Keizer Kalmink
Kelli L. Kerbawy (Bloomfield Hills Office)
Monica J. Labe
Douglas P. Lane
Deborah A. Lee (Lansing Office)
Mi Young Lee
Sandra J. LeFevre
Randi S. Lipin (Chicago, Illinois Office)
Edwin J. Lukas
Elizabeth Virginia Main
Sean D. Major (Chicago, Illinois Office)
Linda S. McAlpine
Clara Scholla McCarthy
Mark A. McDowell (Lansing Office)
Richard R. McGill, Jr. (Chicago, Illinois Office)
Sarah A. McLaren
Richard D. McNulty (Lansing Office)
Creighton R. Meland, Jr. (Chicago, Illinois Office)
Karen Raitt Modell (Bloomfield Hills Office)

(See Next Column)

DICKINSON, WRIGHT, MOON, VAN DUSEN & FREEMAN—*Continued*

ASSOCIATES (Continued)

Sharon R. Newlon
James Gavan O'Connor (Grand Rapids Office)
Richard W. Paige
John T. Panourgias (Bloomfield Hills Office)
Gregory J. Parry (Bloomfield Hills Office)
Matthew V. Piwowar (Warsaw, Poland Office)
James A. Plemmons
Daniel D. Quick
Henryk Romanczuk (Not admitted in United States) (Warsaw, Poland Office)
Jeffrey S. Ruprich
Diane G. Schwartz
Marian Keidan Seltzer
Daniel James Sheridan (Chicago, Illinois Office)
Colleen M. Shevnock
Delmas A. Szura (Lansing Office)
John L. Teeples (Grand Rapids Office)
Louis Theros (Chicago, Illinois Office)
Jeffrey E. Thompson (Lansing Office)
Andrew H. Thorson (Bloomfield Hills Office)
James M. Toner
Linda J. Truitt
Rock A. Wood (Grand Rapids Office)
Jennifer A. Zinn

LEGAL SUPPORT PERSONNEL

COMPUTER LITIGATION SUPPORT

Valerie L. Hanafee

JAPANESE CLIENT SUPPORT

Yukiko Sato

Representative Clients: Federal-Mogul Corp.; Florists' Transworld Delivery Assn.; GMF Robotics Corp.; Kmart Corp.; Kuhlman Corp.; Michigan Consolidated Gas Co.; NBD Bank, N.A.

For full biographical listings, see the Martindale-Hubbell Law Directory

DYKEMA GOSSETT (AV)

400 Renaissance Center, 48243-1668
Telephone: 313-568-6800
Cable Address: "Dyke-Detroit"
Telex: 23-0121
Fax: 313-568-6594
Ann Arbor, Michigan Office: 315 East Eisenhower Parkway, Suite 100, 48108-3306.
Telephone: 313-747-7660.
Fax: 313-747-7696.
Bloomfield Hills, Michigan Office: 1577 North Woodward Avenue, Suite 300, 48304-2820.
Telephone: 810-540-0700.
Fax: 810-540-0763.
Grand Rapids, Michigan Office: 200 Oldtown Riverfront Building, 248 Louis Campau Promenade, N.W., 49503-2668.
Telephone: 616-776-7500.
Fax: 616-776-7573.
Lansing, Michigan Office: 800 Michigan National Tower, 48933-1707.
Telephone: 517-374-9100.
Fax: 517-374-9191.
Washington, D.C. Office: Franklin Square, Suite 300 West Tower, 1300 I Street, N.W., 20005-3306.
Telephone: 202-522-8600.
Fax: 202-522-8669.
Chicago, Illinois Office: Three First National Plaza, Suite 1400, 70 W. Madison, 60602-4270.
Telephone: 312-214-3380.
Fax: 312-214-3441.

MEMBERS OF FIRM

Maria B. Abrahamsen
Ted T. Amsden
Susan Artinian
Joseph C. Basta
Richard B. Baxter (Resident at Grand Rapids Office)
J. Michael Bernard
James T. Blake
William J. Brennan (Resident at Grand Rapids Office)
Teresa A. Brooks (Resident at Washington, D.C. Office)
Bowden V. Brown (Resident at Bloomfield Hills Office)
B. Kingsley Buhl (Resident at Bloomfield Hills Office)
James M. Cameron, Jr. (Resident at Ann Arbor Office)
John K. Cannon (Resident at Bloomfield Hills Office)
Timothy K. Carroll
James W. Collier
Laurence D. Connor
Michael P. Cooney
John B. Curcio (Resident at Lansing Office)
Bruce G. Davis (Resident at Ann Arbor Office)
Joseph F. Dillon
J. Terrance Dillon (Resident at Grand Rapids Office)
Alan R. Dominick (Resident at Lansing Office)
J. Bruce Donaldson (Resident at Bloomfield Hills Office)
David E. Doran (Resident at Grand Rapids Office)
Robert L. Duty (Resident at Bloomfield Hills Office)
Bettye S. Elkins (Resident at Ann Arbor Office)
James M. Elsworth
John A. Entenman
Albert Ernst (Resident at Lansing Office)
J. Theodore Everingham
Fred J. Fechheimer (Resident at Bloomfield Hills Office)
J. Kay Felt
John A. Ferroli (Resident at Grand Rapids Office)
William E. Fisher
Michael D. Fishman (Resident at Bloomfield Hills Office)
Jane Forbes
Robert J. Franzinger
Martin Jay Galvin
Dennis M. Gannan (Resident at Bloomfield Hills Office)

(See Next Column)

MEMBERS OF FIRM (Continued)

Barbara L. Goldman
Richard D. Grauer (Resident at Bloomfield Hills Office)
Alan M. Greene (Resident at Bloomfield Hills Office)
James P. Greene (Resident at Ann Arbor Office)
Steven E. Grob
Dennis M. Haffey (Resident at Bloomfield Hills Office)
Mark E. Hauck
Patrick F. Hickey
J. Timothy Hobbs (Not admitted in MI; Resident at Washington, D.C. Office)
E. Edward Hood (Resident at Ann Arbor Office)
Raymond T. Huetteman, Jr. (Resident at Ann Arbor Office)
Kathryn J. Humphrey
Margaret Adams Hunter
Craig L. John (Resident at Bloomfield Hills Office)
Louis W. Kasischke (Resident at Bloomfield Hills Office)
Robert L. Kelly (Resident at Bloomfield Hills Office)
Sharon M. Kelly (Resident at Ann Arbor Office)
James P. Kiefer (Resident at Lansing Office)
Gregory M. Kopacz
Kathrin E. Kudner
Richard J. Landau (Resident at Ann Arbor Office)
J. Thomas Lenga
Michael A. Lesha
Kathleen McCree Lewis
Seth M. Lloyd
Stuart D. Logan (Resident at Bloomfield Hills Office)
Stewart L. Mandell
Richard M. Matthews
Bonnie L. Mayfield
Richard J. McClear
Debra M. McCulloch
Bruce A. McDonald (Not admitted in MI; Resident at Washington, D.C. Office)
D. Richard McDonald (Resident at Bloomfield Hills Office)
Thomas J. McGraw
Richard D. McLellan (Resident at Lansing Office)
Patrick E. Mears (Resident at Grand Rapids Office)
Derek I. Meier
Sandra Lea Meyer
Fredrick M. Miller
Aleksandra A. Miziolek
Stephen S. Muhich (Resident at Grand Rapids Office)
William T. Myers (Resident at Bloomfield Hills Office)
Janet L. Neary (Resident at Ann Arbor Office)
Robert L. Nelson (Resident at Grand Rapids Office)
Katherine S. Nucci (Not admitted in MI; Resident at Washington, D.C. Office)
Theodore H. Oldham
Howard E. O'Leary, Jr. (Resident at Washington, D.C. Office)
Judy A. O'Neill
Brian J. Page (Resident at Grand Rapids Office)
William J. Perrone (Resident at Lansing Office)
Marilyn A. Peters
Cameron H. Piggott
Thomas W. B. Porter
Richard E. Rabbideau
Jack C. Radcliffe, Jr. (Resident at Ann Arbor Office)
Ralph T. Rader (Resident at Bloomfield Hills Office)
Paul R. Rentenbach
Joseph A. Ritok, Jr.
Ronald L. Rose (Resident at Bloomfield Hills Office)
David M. Rosenberger (Resident at Bloomfield Hills Office)
Jonathan D. Rowe (Resident at Ann Arbor Office)
Mary Elizabeth Royce (Resident at Bloomfield Hills Office)
Charles R. Rutherford (Resident at Bloomfield Hills Office)
Brad S. Rutledge (Resident at Lansing Office)
Suzanne Sahakian
Ronald J. Santo
Rex E. Schlaybaugh, Jr. (Resident at Bloomfield Hills Office)
Raynold A. Schmick (Resident at Ann Arbor Office)
Robert L. Schwartz (Resident at Bloomfield Hills Office)
Daniel J. Scully, Jr.
Lloyd A. Semple
Lori M. Silsbury (Resident at Lansing Office)
Leamon R. Sowell, Jr.
Thomas B. Spillane, Jr. (Resident at Bloomfield Hills Office)
Wilfred A. Steiner, Jr.
Daniel J. Stephenson (Resident at Ann Arbor Office)
Timothy Sullivan (Not admitted in MI; Resident at Washington, D.C. Office)
Mark H. Sutton (Resident at Bloomfield Hills Office)
Roger K. Timm
Paul H. Townsend, Jr.
David L. Tripp
Randy W. Tung (Resident, Bloomfield Hills Office)
Thomas Stephen Vaughn
Stephen D. Winter
Fred L. Woodworth (Resident at Washington, D.C. Office)
Daniel G. Wyllie
Donald S. Young
Stephen H. Zimmerman (Resident at Lansing Office)
Frank K. Zinn

OF COUNSEL

George W. Ash
Eugene A. Gargaro, Jr.
Mary Steck Kershner
G. Mark McAleenan, Jr. (Resident at Grand Rapids Office)
Donald E. Shely
John J. Slavin (Resident at Bloomfield Hills Office)

RETIRED PARTNERS

William H. Baldwin
Earl R. Boonstra
Henry A. Clay (Not admitted in MI)
James W. Draper
Clifford H. Domke
John R. Dykema
E. James Gamble
William T. Gossett
Robert N. Hammond (Resident at Grand Rapids Office)
Edward C. Hanpeter
Robert A. Sloman
Brian Sullivan
James D. Tracy
Paul R. Trigg, Jr.
H. Gordon Wood

(See Next Column)

DYKEMA GOSSETT, *Detroit—Continued*

Raymond K. Dykema (1889-1971)
Elroy O. Jones (1889-1973)
Renville Wheat (1893-1968)
James H. Spencer (1908-1970)
Nathan B. Goodnow (1906-1985)

ASSOCIATES

John F. Birmingham, Jr.
Paul Francis Bohn
Kevin J. Bonner
Scott D. Broekstra (Resident at Grand Rapids Office)
Daniel J. Brondyk (Resident at Grand Rapids Office)
Michael J. Brown (Resident at Lansing Office)
James R. Bruinsma (Resident at Grand Rapids Office)
Sean M. Carty
Jeffrey B. Conner (Resident at Bloomfield Hills Office)
Joseph V. Coppola, Sr. (Resident at Bloomfield Hills Office)
Margaret A. Costello
Sandra Miller Cotter (Resident at Lansing Office)
Donald M. Crawford (Resident at Bloomfield Hills Office)
Willis R. Davis, Jr.
Marie R. Deveney (Resident at Ann Arbor Office)
Krishna S. Dighe
Dennis M. Doherty
Phyllis G. Donaldson
Elizabeth M. Donovan
Laura J. Eisele
Joseph K. Erhardt
Nancy L. Farnam (Resident at Bloomfield Hills Office)
Ann D. Fillingham (Resident at Lansing Office)
Martin R. Fischer (Not admitted in MI; Resident at Washington, D.C. Office)
Cheryl Anne Fletcher
Brion J. Fox
Lee S. Fruman
Kevin P. Fularczyk
David John Gaskey (Resident at Bloomfield Hills Office)
Grant P. Gilezan
Margaret M. Gillis
Julia A. Goatley Moreno (Resident at Lansing Office)
Marguerite Marie Gritenas
Joseph H. Hickey (Resident at Bloomfield Hills Office)
Kevin M. Hinman (Resident at Bloomfield Hills Office)
Jennifer J. Howe
Mark D. Jacobs
Cathleen C. Jansen
Judy Parker Jenkins (Not admitted in MI; Resident at Washington, D.C. Office)
Zora E. Johnson
Jeffrey S. Jones
Sheri B. Katzman
Barbara A. Kaye
Susan Allene Kovach
Nicole Yvette Lamb-Hale
Mark C. Larson
Joanne R. Lax
Gerald T. Lievois
Howard N. Luckoff (Resident at Bloomfield Hills Office)
Douglas L. Lutz (Resident at Grand Rapids Office)
Anne E. MacIntyre (Resident at Ann Arbor Office)
Bryan D. Marcus
Jerome I. Maynard (Resident at Chicago, Illinois Office)
Andrew J. McGuinness (Resident at Ann Arbor Office)
Mark A. Metz
Gregory S. Narsh
Ava K. Ortner
Mark W. Osler
James C. Partridge (Not admitted in MI)
Thomas M. Pastore
Dennis M. Pousak
Kathleen A. Reed (Resident at Ann Arbor Office)
John W. Rees (Resident at Bloomfield Hills Office)
Paul W. Ritsema (Resident at Grand Rapids Office)
Carol H. Rodriguez
Steven J. Rollins (Resident at Chicago, Illinois Office)
Ann Marie Ronchetto
William C. Roush (Resident at Bloomfield Hills Office)
James R. Saalfeld (Resident at Grand Rapids Office)
Stephen L. Scharf (Resident at Bloomfield Hills Office)
Rosemary G. Schikora
Steven H. Schwartz
Catherine Kim Shierk (Resident at Bloomfield Hills Office)
Todd J. Shoudy
Jeffrey N. Silveri
Bradley L. Smith (Resident at Ann Arbor Office)
John F. Smart (Resident at Grand Rapids Office)
Micheal A. Smith
Thomas R. Stevick (Resident at Ann Arbor Office)
Michael B. Stewart (Resident at Bloomfield Hills Office)
Cynthia B. Summerfield (Resident at Washington, D.C. Office)
Troy R. Taylor
Gina M. Torielli (Resident at Lansing Office)
Michael Tucker (Resident at Bloomfield Hills Office)
Jill M. Wheaton
Leonard C. Wolfe (Resident at Lansing Office)
Sherrill D. Wolford
Sally A. York (Resident at Bloomfield Hills Office)
Nicholas G. Zotos

For full biographical listings, see the Martindale-Hubbell Law Directory

FEIKENS, VANDER MALE, STEVENS, BELLAMY & GILCHRIST, P.C. (AV)

One Detroit Center Suite 3400, 500 Woodward Avenue, 48226-3406
Telephone: 313-962-5909
Fax: 313-962-3125

Robert E. Dice (1922-1983)
Jon Feikens
Jack E. Vander Male
Frederick B. Bellamy
Alan Gordon Gilchrist
L. Neal Kennedy
Bruce A. VandeVusse
Lee A. Stevens
William C. Hurley
Linda M. Galbraith
Michael S. Cafferty
Robert H. Feikens

(See Next Column)

Roger L. Wolcott
Richard G. Koefod
Joseph E. Kozely, Jr.
Jeffrey Feikens
Keith J. Soltis
Michael B. Barey
Gary T. Tandberg
Susan Tillotson Mills
Thomas H. Schram

OF COUNSEL

Sam W. Thomas (P.C.)
Walter Vincent Bernard III
Robert N. Foster

For full biographical listings, see the Martindale-Hubbell Law Directory

FILDEW, HINKS, MILLER, TODD & WANGEN (AV)

3600 Penobscot Building, 48226-4291
Telephone: 313-961-9700
Telecopier: 313-961-0754

MEMBERS OF FIRM

Stanley L. Fildew (1896-1978)
Frank T. Hinks (1887-1974)
Richard E. Hinks (1916-1990)
John H. Fildew
Alan C. Miller
Charles D. Todd III
Randall S. Wangen
Mary Jane Ruffley
Robert D. Welchli
William P. Thorpe
Colleen A. Kramer
Stephen J. Pokoj

ASSOCIATES

Charles S. Kennedy, III
Gerald M. Swiacki

References: First of America Bank-Detroit, N.A.; Comerica Bank-Detroit; National Bank of Detroit.

For full biographical listings, see the Martindale-Hubbell Law Directory

FOSTER, MEADOWS & BALLARD, P.C. (AV)

3200 Penobscot Building, 48226
Telephone: 313-961-3234
Cable Address: "Foster"
Telex: 23-5823
Facsimile: 313-961-6184

Sparkman D. Foster (1897-1967)
John L. Foster
Charles R. Hrdlicka
Paul D. Galea
Richard A. Dietz
Robert H. Fortunate
Robert G. Lahiff
Camille A. Raffa-Dietz

Michael J. Liddane
Paul A. Kettunen

OF COUNSEL

John F. Langs
John A. Mundell, Jr.

Counsel for: Air Canada; Canadian National Railways; Grand Trunk Western Railroad; Alexander and Alexander; Shand Morahan; Utica Mutual.
Admiralty Counsel for: Ford Motor; Bob Lo Co.

For full biographical listings, see the Martindale-Hubbell Law Directory

GARAN, LUCOW, MILLER, SEWARD, COOPER & BECKER, P.C. (AV)

1000 Woodbridge Place, 48207-3192
Telephone: 313-446-1530
Fax: 313-259-0450
Grand Blanc, Michigan Office: 8332 Office Park Drive.
Telephone: 810-695-3700.
Fax: 810-695-6488.
Port Huron, Michigan Office: Port Huron Office Center, 511 Fort Street, Suite 505.
Telephone: 810-985-4400.
Fax: 810-985-4107.
Ann Arbor, Michigan Office: 101 North Main Street, Suite 801.
Telephone: 313-930-5600.
Fax: 313-930-0043.
Troy, Michigan Office: 2301 West Big Beaver Road, Suite 212.
Telephone: 810-649-7600.
Fax: 810-649-5438.
Mount Clemens Office: Towne Square Development, 10 S. Main Street, Suite 307.
Telephone: 810-954-3800.
Fax: 810-954-3803.

Matthew A. Seward
David J. Cooper
James L. Borin
Thomas F. Myers
Dennis P. Partridge
John E. McSorley
Lamont E. Buffington
Thomas L. Misuraca
Rosalind Rochkind
James J. Hayes, Jr.
James C. Rabaut
Thomas W. Emery
Joseph Crystal
Jon P. Desenberg
Boyd E. Chapin, Jr.
James S. Goulding
Frederick B. Plumb
Mark C. Smiley

Ian C. Simpson
Patricia L. Patterson
Daniel S. Saylor
Peter B. Worden, Jr.
Charlotte H. Johnson
David M. Shafer
Lloyd G. Johnson
John J. Gillooly
Robert D. Goldstein
Michael J. Paolucci

(See Next Column)

GARAN, LUCOW, MILLER, SEWARD, COOPER & BECKER P.C.—*Continued*

Michael J. Severyn
Michael J. DePolo
C. David Miller, II
Robert J. Squiers, Jr.
David J. Langford
Anne K. Newcomer
Robert A. Obringer
Eun (Ellen) G. Ha

OF COUNSEL

Daniel L. Garan
Albert A. Miller
Roy E. Castetter
Beth A. Andrews
Nancy J. Bourget

Counsel for: Allstate Insurance Co.; Sears, Roebuck & Co.; Liberty Mutual Insurance Co.; Continental Insurance Companies.

For full biographical listings, see the Martindale-Hubbell Law Directory

HONIGMAN MILLER SCHWARTZ AND COHN (AV)

A Partnership including Professional Corporations
2290 First National Building, 48226
Telephone: 313-256-7800
Telecopier: 313-962-0176
Telex: 235705
Lansing, Michigan Office: Phoenix Building, 222 North Washington Square, Suite 400.
Telephone: 517-484-8282.
West Palm Beach, Florida Office: Suite 800 Esperante Building, 222 Lakeview Avenue.
Telephone: 407-838-4500.
Tampa, Florida Office: 2700 Landmark Centre, 401 E. Jackson Street.
Telephone: 813-221-6600.
Orlando, Florida Office: 390 North Orange Avenue, Suite 1300.
Telephone: 407-648-0300.
Houston, Texas Office: 3100 First Interstate Bank Plaza, 1000 Louisiana.
Telephone: 713-650-2600.
Los Angeles, California Office: McNeill Plaza, Suite 820, 15260 Ventura Boulevard, 91403.
Telephone: 818-784-2900.

MEMBERS OF FIRM

Richard J. Aaron (Lansing, Michigan Office)
Joel S. Adelman
Peter M. Alter
John E. Amerman
Norman C. Ankers
Joseph T. Aoun
Elizabeth A. Baergen
Frederick M. Baker, Jr. (Lansing, Michigan Office)
C. Leslie Banas
Donald F. Baty, Jr.
Thomas J. Beale
Norman H. Beitner
Maurice S. Binkow
Richard Bisio
Jonathan R. Borenstein
Jay E. Brant
Keith B. Braun
Ingrid K. Brey
Lee W. Brooks
Richard J. Burstein
Therese Byrnes
Judy B. Calton
William M. Cassetta
Carol A. Clark
Gerald S. Cook
Roger Cook
Gregory J. DeMars
Daniel J. Demlow (Lansing, Michigan Office)
Patrick T. Duerr
Christopher J. Dunsky
John H. Eggertsen
David A. Ettinger
Robert A. Fineman
Herschel P. Fink
David Foltyn
Frederick J. Frank
William F. Frey
H. Alan Gocha
Kenneth C. Gold
Mark A. Goldsmith
Philip A. Grashoff, Jr.
Margaret E. Greene
Gerald M. Griffith
Michael A. Gruskin
Norman D. Hawkins
Raymond W. Henney
Carl W. Herstein
William O. Hochkammer
Steven G. Howell
Kimberly K. Hudolin
Alan M. Hurvitz
Robert A. Hykan
Jeffrey A. Hyman
Norman Hyman
Linn A. Hynds
Howard B. Iwrey
Robert M. Jackson
Sandra L. Jasinski (Lansing, Michigan Office)
James H. Kabcenell
John M. Kamins
Edward F. Kickham
Timothy Sawyer Knowlton (Lansing, Michigan Office)
Kevin M. Kohls
Jeffrey R. Kravitz
Robert J. Krueger, Jr.
Donald J. Kunz
Robert H. Kurnick, Jr.
Mary Jo Larson
Marguerite Munson Lentz
Denise J. Lewis
Stuart M. Lockman
Ronald S. Longhofer
Frank T. Mamat
Gerard Mantese
Kenneth R. Marcus
Lawrence D. McLaughlin
Mitchell R. Meisner
A. David Mikesell
Mark Morton (Lansing, Michigan Office)
Cyril Moscow
Brian Negele
David B. Nelson
Charles Nida
James H. Novis
Joseph G. Nuyen, Jr.
Nancy M. Omichinski
David K. Page
Lisa M. Panepucci
Alex L. Parrish
John D. Pirich (Lansing, Michigan Office)
Joseph M. Polito
Paul Revere, III
G. Scott Romney
Linda S. Ross
Chris E. Rossman
J. Adam Rothstein
Phyllis G. Rozof
Roberta R. Russ
Jerome M. Salle
William D. Sargent
Laurence J. Schiff
Edward R. Schonberg
Alan E. Schwartz

(See Next Column)

MEMBERS OF FIRM (Continued)

Alan Stuart Schwartz
Benjamin O. Schwendener, Jr. (Lansing, Michigan Office)
Mark Shaevsky
Margaret Shannon
Michael B. Shapiro
Sherill Siebert
John Sklar
Richard S. Soble
Samuel T. Stahl
Mark A. Stern
Theodore B. Sylwestrzak
Stuart H. Teger
Sheryl L. Toby
Sheldon S. Toll
Gary A. Trepod (Lansing, Michigan Office)
Grant R. Trigger
Andronike A. Tsagaris
Alan M. Valade (Lansing, Michigan Office)
John W. Voelpel
Stephen Wasinger
Robert B. Weiss
Mark R. Werder
Randall P. Whately
William C. Whitbeck (Lansing, Michigan Office)
William A. Wichers II
Sheldon P. Winkelman
I. W. Winsten
Ruth E. Zimmerman (Lansing, Michigan Office)
William J. Zousmer
Richard E. Zuckerman

ASSOCIATES

Ann L. Andrews (Lansing, Michigan Office)
Gary K. August
Stanford P. Berenbaum
Rebecca L. Burtless-Creps
Sally J. Churchill
Cameron J. Evans
William L. Fealko, III (Not admitted in MI)
Michael J. Friedman
Seth D. Gould
Daniel M. Halprin
Gregory D. Hanley (Not admitted in MI)
Andrea Hansen (Lansing, Michigan Office)
Daniel G. Helton
Samina R. Hurst
S. Lee Johnson
John S. Kane (Lansing, Michigan Office)
Walter J. Kramarz
Melissa Leigh Markey
Lawrence J. Murphy
Claudia D. Orr
Tracy E. Silverman
Steven M. Ribiat
Julie E. Robertson
Michelle Epstein Taigman
Cynthia G. Thomas
Barbara A. Van Zanten
Lisa M. Waits
Jeffrey L. Woolstrum
Roy H. Wyman, Jr.

OF COUNSEL

Milton J. Miller
Rodman N. Myers
Jason L. Honigman (1904-1990)
Irwin I. Cohn (1896-1984)

RESIDENT IN WEST PALM BEACH, FLORIDA OFFICE

MEMBERS

Carl Angeloff (P.A.)
Carla L. Brown
Morris C. Brown (P.A.)
J.A. Jurgens (P.A.)
Mark Nussbaum (P.A.)
Steven R. Parson (P.A.)
Neil W. Platock
Donald H. Reed, Jr.
Marvin S. Rosen (P.A.)
Steven L. Schwarzberg (P.A.)
Lloyd R. Schwed
E. Lee Worsham (P.A.)

ASSOCIATES

Jose O. Diaz
Gina Greeson Hyland

OF COUNSEL

Delmer C. Gowing, III, (P.A.)

RESIDENT IN TAMPA, FLORIDA OFFICE

MEMBERS

Robert W. Boos (P.A.)
Michael G. Cooke (P.A.)
Harry Christopher Goplerud (P.A.)
Gregory G. Jones (P.A.)
Maria Maistrellis
Barbara R. Pankau
James B. Soble (P.A.)
Brad M. Tomtishen (P.A.)

ASSOCIATES

Kevin M. Gilhool
Dennis Hernandez

RESIDENT IN ORLANDO, FLORIDA OFFICE

MEMBERS

Thomas R. Allen (P.A.)
Wendy Anderson (P.A.)
J. Lindsay Builder, Jr., (P.A.)
Charles V. Choyce, Jr.
Donald J. Curotto (P.A.)
Michael J. Grindstaff (P.A.)
J.A. Jurgens (P.A.)
Thomas F. Lang (P.A.)
David S. Oliver (P.A.)
Michael J. Sullivan (P.A.)
Brad M. Tomtishen (P.A.)

ASSOCIATES

Jan A. Albanese
Suzanne M. Amaducci
Brian Stuart Chilton
Orlando J. Evora
Roseanna J. Lee
Paul W. Moses II
Vincent J. Profaci

RESIDENT IN HOUSTON, TEXAS OFFICE

MEMBERS

Louis Karl Bonham (P.C.)
John T. Klug (P.C.)
Sid Leach (P.C.)

ASSOCIATES

Anne E. Brookes
John G. Flaim
Joy Jacobson
Paul N. Katz

OF COUNSEL

Asher Rabinowitz
James Popp
William F. Ikard

(See Next Column)

HONIGMAN MILLER SCHWARTZ AND COHN, *Detroit—Continued*

RESIDENT IN LOS ANGELES, CALIFORNIA OFFICE
MEMBERS

Robert C. Danner | Daniel E. Martyn, Jr.
George E. Schulman

ASSOCIATES

Melanie J. Bingham | Adryane R. Omens
Michael D. Schulman

General Counsel for: Arbor Drugs Inc.; The Detroit Free Press; The Detroit Medical Center; Handleman Co.; PHM Corporation (Pulte Home Corp.); William C. Roney & Co.
Local or Special Counsel for: American Society of Composers, Authors and Publishers (ASCAP); AutoAlliance International Inc. (formerly Mazda Motor Manufacturing (USA) Corporation); NBD Bank, N.A.; The Taubman Company, Inc.

For full biographical listings, see the Martindale-Hubbell Law Directory

JAFFE, RAITT, HEUER & WEISS, PROFESSIONAL CORPORATION (AV)

One Woodward Avenue, Suite 2400, 48226
Telephone: 313-961-8380
Telecopier: 313-961-8358
Cable Address: "Jafsni"
Southfield,Michigan Office: Travelers Tower, Suite 1520.
Telephone: 313-961-8380.
Monroe, Michigan Office: 212 East Front Street, Suite 3.
Telephone: 313-241-6470.
Telefacsimile: 313-241-3849.

Judith Lowitz Adler
Gail A. Anderson
Christopher A. Andreoff
Julia Blakeslee
Robert S. Bolton
Alexander B. Bragdon
Penny L. Carolan
R. Christopher Cataldo
Thomas E. Coughlin
Jeffrey L. Forman
Wallace H. Glendening
Gary R. Glenn
Joel S. Golden
Robert J. Gordon
Larry K. Griffis
Jeffrey G. Heuer
John A. Hohman, Jr. (Resident, Monroe, Michigan Office)
Blair B. Hysni
Lisa Biddinger Hysni
Ira J. Jaffe
Robin H. Krueger
Mark P. Krysinski
Sharon J. LaDuke
Melanie LaFave
Robert E. Lewis
Eric A. Linden
Ralph R. Margulis
Joel J. Morris
Lawrence C. Patrick, Jr.
James G. Petrangelo (Resident, Monroe, Michigan Office)
Steven C. Powell
Victor F. Ptasznik
Mark K. Rabidoux
Cecil G. Raitt
David H. Raitt
Michael A. Rajt
Louis P. Rochkind
Mark D. Rubenfire
Stephen G. Schafer
Linda C. Scheuerman
Brian G. Shannon
Joseph J. Shannon
Lawrence R. Shoffner
William E. Sider
Arthur H. Siegal
Elliot A. Spoon
George A. Sumnik
Susan M. Sutton
David D. Warner
Arthur A. Weiss
Jeffrey D. Weisserman
Jay L. Welford
Cynthia A. White
Thomas H. Williams
Janet G. Witkowski
Richard A. Zussman

Derek S. Adolf
David P. Armstrong
Susan Michelle Bakst
Harolyn D. Beverly
Mark E. Crane
Lesley A. Gaber
Carolyn J. Griem
Kerry Gross-Bondy (Resident, Monroe, Michigan Office)
Stephen S. Laplante
Susan S. Lichterman
Jane Derse Quasarano
Gerald F. Reinhart
Daniella Saltz
Thomas L. Shaevsky
Jon A. Sherk
Nancy L. Waldmann
Jeffrey M. Weiss
Laith L. Yaldoo
Wendy L Zabriskie

OF COUNSEL

David Griem | Nathan L. Milstein

Representative Clients: Allnet Communications Services, Inc.; Fretter, Inc.; Michigan State Hospital Finance Auth.; The Stroh Brewery Company; Unisys Corporation; Weiss Construction Co.

For full biographical listings, see the Martindale-Hubbell Law Directory

KASIBORSKI, RONAYNE & FLASKA, A PROFESSIONAL CORPORATION (AV)

3066 Penobscot Building, 48226
Telephone: 313-961-1900
Telecopier: 313-961-1556

Chester E. Kasiborski, Jr. | Kenneth A. Flaska
John J. Ronayne, III | Joseph John Bernardi
L. Jean Benoit

(See Next Column)

OF COUNSEL

Chester Kasiborski | Diane Hubel Delekta

For full biographical listings, see the Martindale-Hubbell Law Directory

KELLER, THOMA, SCHWARZE, SCHWARZE, DUBAY & KATZ, P.C. (AV)

440 E. Congress, 5th Floor, 48226
Telephone: 313-965-7610
Bloomfield Hills, Michigan Office: Suite 122, 100 West Long Lake Road.
Telephone: 313-647-3114.

Leonard A. Keller (1906-1970)
Charles E. Keller
Frederick B. Schwarze
Thomas H. Schwarze
Dennis B. DuBay
James R. Miller
Stewart J. Katz
Anthony J. Heckemeyer
Thomas L. Fleury
Terrence J. Miglio
Gary P. King
Donna R. Nuyen
Robert A. Lusk
Linda M. Foster
Bruce M. Bagdady
Carl F. Schwarze
George P. Butler, III
Christopher M. Murray
Brian A. Kreucher
Kenneth C. Howell
Mark C. Knoth
Patrice L. Baker
John J. Rabaut

OF COUNSEL

Richard J. Thoma

Counsel for: Livonia Public Schools; Ludington News Co., Inc.
Representative Clients: Borg-Warner Corp.; E & L Transport Co.; The Kroger Co.; Holnam, Inc.
Public Employer Clients: City of Farmington Hills; City of Flint; City of Grosse Pointe Woods; Saginaw Public Schools.

For full biographical listings, see the Martindale-Hubbell Law Directory

KERR, RUSSELL AND WEBER (AV)

One Detroit Center, 500 Woodward Avenue, Suite 2500, 48226-3406
Telephone: 313-961-0200
Telecopier: 313-961-0388
Bloomfield Hills, Michigan Office: 3883 Telegraph Road.
Telephone: 810-649-5990.
East Lansing, Michigan Office: 1301 North Hagadorn Road.
Telephone: 517-336-6767.

Richard D. Weber
Roy H. Christiansen
William A. Sankbeil
Robert Royal Nix, II
Monte D. Jahnke
Patrick McLain
Michael B. Lewis
Curtis J. DeRoo
Michael D. Gibson
Daniel G. Beyer
James R. Case
George J. Christopoulos
Paul M. Shirilla
Stephen D. McGraw
Kurt R. Vilders
James R. Cambridge
Thomas R. Williams
Edward C. Cutlip, Jr.
Mark M. Cunningham
Mark J. Stasa
Joanne Geha Swanson
Robert J. Pineau
Jeffrey A. Brantley
Catherine Bonczak Edwards
David E. Sims
Christopher A. Cornwall
Dennis A. Martin
Patrick J. Haddad
Richard C. Busleep
Eric I. Lark
James E. DeLine
Daniel J. Schulte
John D. Gatti
Susan I Chae

OF COUNSEL

Robert G. Russell

For full biographical listings, see the Martindale-Hubbell Law Directory

KITCH, DRUTCHAS, WAGNER & KENNEY, P.C. (AV)

One Woodward, Tenth Floor, 48226-3412
Telephone: 313-965-7900
Fax: 313-965-7403
Lansing, Michigan Office: 120 Washington Square, North, Suite 805, One Michigan Avenue, 48933-1609.
Telephone: 517-372-6430.
Fax: 517-372-0441.
Macomb County Office: Towne Square Development, 10 South Main Street, Suite 301, Mount Clemens, 48043-7903.
Telephone: 810-463-9770.
Fax: 810-463-8994.
Toledo, Ohio Office: 405 Madison Avenue, Suite 1500, 43604-1235.
Telephone: 419-243-4006.
Fax: 419-243-7333.
Troy, Michigan Office: 3001 West Big Beaver Road, Suite 200, 48084-3103.
Telephone: 810-637-3500.
Fax: 810-637-6630.
Ann Arbor, Michigan Office: 303 Detroit Street, Suite 400, P.O. Box 8610, 48107-8610.
Telephone: 313-994-7600.
Fax: 313-994-7626.

(See Next Column)

KITCH, DRUTCHAS, WAGNER & KENNEY P.C.—*Continued*

Richard A. Kitch	Elizabeth I. Huldin
Gregory G. Drutchas (Principal, Troy Office)	Roselyn R. Parmenter (Resident, Ann Arbor Office)
Ronald E. Wagner	Susan Marie Beutel
Jeremiah J. Kenney (Managing Principal)	Carole S. Empey (Ann Arbor Office)
Ralph F. Valitutti, Jr.	Debra S. Hirsch (Lansing Office)
Richard R. DeNardis	Ellen M. Keefe-Garner (Ann Arbor Office)
Mona K. Majzoub	David R. Nauts
Harry J. Sherbrook	Carol Ann Tarnowsky (Troy Office)
Anthony G. Arnone	Richard T. Counsman
Mark D. Willmarth (Principal)	Kenneth G. Frantz (Troy Office)
Charles W. Fisher	Karen Ann Smyth
Clyde M. Metzger, III (Principal, Ann Arbor Office)	Robert J. Bradfield III
Thomas J. Foley	Mark A. Wisniewski
Victor J. Abela (Principal, Troy Office)	Julia Kelly McNelis
Jeffrey H. Chilton	J. Mark Trimble (Toledo, Ohio Office)
James H. Hughesian	Sharon A. DeWaele
John P. Ryan (Principal, Lansing Office)	Arthur F. Brandt
William D. Chaklos	Dean A. Etsios
Steve N. Cheolas (Principal, Macomb County Office)	Michael K. McCoy
Richard S. Baron	Stephen R. Brzezinski
Susan Healy Zitterman	Kent Riesen (Toledo, Ohio Office)
David L. Kaser (Principal, Troy Office)	Joseph P. McGill
William Vertes (Principal, Lansing Office)	Paula M. Burgess (Toledo, Ohio Office)
William A. Tanoury (Principal, Ann Arbor Office)	Lisa M. Iulianelli
R. Michael O'Boyle (Associate Principal, Troy Office)	Fred J. Fresard
John J. Ramar	Maureen Rouse-Ayoub
John Stephen Wasung (Principal, Toledo, Ohio Office)	Matthew M. Walton (Mount Clemens Office)
Bruce R. Shaw	Barbara A. Martin
Karen Bernard Berkery (Associate Principal)	Carol S. Allis (Ann Arbor Office)
Susan M. Ramage (Associate Principal, Lansing Office)	Terese L. Farhat
Pamela Hobbs	Christopher J. Valeriote
Daniel R. Corbet	Richard P. Cuneo
Brian R. Garves	Kim J. Sveska
Daniel R. Shirey	Kathleen P. Knol (Ann Arbor Office)
Daniel J. Niemann (Associate Principal, Ann Arbor Office)	David A. Schoolcraft (Lansing Office)
John M. Sier (Associate Principal)	Lauri A. Read (Troy Office)
John Paul Hessburg	Lisa DiPonio
Philip Cwagenberg (Troy Office)	Bridget Kerry Quinn (Resident, Ann Arbor Office)
William P. O'Leary	John J. Koselka (Ann Arbor Office)
David M. Kraus	David J. Allen
Verlin R. Nafziger	Richard M. Mitchell
Robert A. Fehniger (Macomb County Office)	Mary Catherine Storen
Richard J. Joppich (Ann Arbor Office)	Diane M. Carpentier
Christopher P. Dinverno	Julia S. Hoffert-Rosen (Troy Office)
Kenneth M. Essad	Robert W. Lipp, III
Steven Waclawski	Cullen B. McKinney
Gregory P. Sweda (Troy Office)	Christine G. Strasser
Ronald S. Bowling	Norman P. Moore, Jr.
Sara Mae Gerbitz	Carla M. Calabrese
Linda M. Garbarino	Fredericia J. Craig
Antonio Mauti	Pamela A. Boland
Lawrence David Rosenstock	Michael M. McNamara
Thomas R. Shimmel	Jeffrey T. Gorcyca
	Laura L. Witty
	Christina L. Gill
	Gail E. Kinney

For full biographical listings, see the Martindale-Hubbell Law Directory

LOPATIN, MILLER, FREEDMAN, BLUESTONE, HERSKOVIC & HEILMANN, A PROFESSIONAL CORPORATION (AV)

1301 East Jefferson, 48207
Telephone: 313-259-7800

Albert Lopatin	Saul Bluestone
Sheldon L. Miller	Maurice Herskovic
Stuart G. Freedman	Michael G. Heilmann

Michael A. Gantz (1939-1990)	David R. Berndt
David F. Dickinson	Stephen I. Kaufman
Richard E. Shaw	Jeffrey S. Cook
Ronald Robinson	Robert J. Boyd, III
Jeffrey A. Danzig	Patrick M. Horan
B. J. Belcoure	Richard R. Mannausa

Alan Wittenberg

(See Next Column)

OF COUNSEL

Harry Okrent (1912-1990) — Lee R. Franklin (Ms.)
Bernard L. Humphrey

For full biographical listings, see the Martindale-Hubbell Law Directory

MAY, SIMPSON & STROTE, A PROFESSIONAL CORPORATION

(See Bloomfield Hills)

MEYER, KIRK, SNYDER & SAFFORD (AV)

2500 Penobscot Building, 48226
Telephone: 313-961-1261
Fax: 810-647-6079
Bloomfield Hills, Michigan Office: Suite 100, 100 West Long Lake Road.
Telephone: 313-647-5111.
Telecopier: 313-647-6079.

George H. Meyer	Ralph R. Safford
John M. Kirk	Donald H. Baker, Jr.
George E. Snyder	Patrick K. Rode

ASSOCIATES

Christopher F. Clark	Boyd C. Farnam

Debra S. Meier

OF COUNSEL

Mark R. Solomon

Representative Clients: Chemical Waste Management, Inc.; Ervin Advertising; The Michigan and S.E. Michigan McDonald's Operators Assn.; The Southland Corp. (7-Eleven Food Stores); Stauffer Chemical Co.; Techpoint, Inc.

For full biographical listings, see the Martindale-Hubbell Law Directory

MILLER, CANFIELD, PADDOCK AND STONE, P.L.C. (AV)

A Professional Limited Liability Company
Founded in 1852 by Sidney Davy Miller
150 West Jefferson, Suite 2500, 48226-4415
Telephone: 313-963-6420
Fax: 313-496-7500
Cable Address: "Stem Detroit"
Detroit, Michigan Office: 150 West Jefferson, Suite 2500, 48226-4415.
Telephone: 313-963-6420.
Fax: 313-496-7500.
Cable Address: "Stem Detroit."
Ann Arbor, Michigan Office: 101 North Main Street, 7th Floor, 48104-1400.
Telephone: 313-663-2445.
Fax: 313-747-7147.
Bloomfield Hills, Michigan Office: Suite 100, Pinehurst Office Center, 1400 North Woodward, 48303-2014.
Telephone: 313-645-5000.
Fax: 313-645-1917.
Grand Rapids, Michigan Office: 1200 Campau Square Plaza, 99 Monroe, N.W., 49503-2639.
Telephone: 616-454-8656.
Fax: 616-776-6322.
Howell, Michigan Office: 121 South Barnard Street, Suite 4, 48843-2305.
Telephone: 517-546-7600.
Telecopier: 517-546-6974.
Kalamazoo, Michigan Office: 444 West Michigan Avenue, 49007-3752.
Telephone: 616-381-7030.
Fax: 616-382-0244.
Lansing, Michigan Office: One Michigan Avenue, Suite 900, 48933-1609.
Telephone: 517-487-2070.
Fax: 517-374-6304.
Monroe, Michigan Office: The Executive Centre, 214 East Elm Avenue, 48161-2682.
Telephone: 313-243-2000.
Fax: 313-243-0901.
Washington, D.C. Office: 1225 Nineteenth Street, N.W., Suite 400. 20036.
Telephone: 202-429-5575; 785-0600.
Fax: 202-331-1118; 785-1234.
Pensacola, Florida Office: 25 West Cedar, 32501.
Telephone: 904-469-1088.
Fax: 904-432-0677.
St. Petersburg, Florida Office: 100 Second Avenue S., Suite 7045, 33701.
Telephone: 813-982-6000.
Fax: 813-892-6002.
Gdansk, Poland Office: Suite 322, Dom Technika Building, Ul. Rajska 6, 80-850.
Telephone: 011-485-831-2808.
Fax: 011-485-831-4719.
Warsaw, Poland Office: Ul. Marszalkowska 82, Suite 561, 00-517.
Telephone: 011-482-623-6457 and 6458.
Fax: 011-482-623-6459.

MEMBERS OF FIRM

Lawrence A. King (P.C.) (Bloomfield Hills Office)	Joseph F. Maycock, Jr.
John B. DeVine (Ann Arbor Office)	Allen Schwartz
Robert E. Hammell	John W. Gelder
	George E. Parker, III

(See Next Column)

MILLER, CANFIELD, PADDOCK AND STONE P.L.C., *Detroit—Continued*

MEMBERS OF FIRM (Continued)

Richard A. Jones (P.C.) (Bloomfield Hills Office)
Stevan Uzelac (P.C.)
Gilbert E. Gove
Robert S. Ketchum
Samuel J. McKim, III, (P.C.)
Rocque E. Lipford (P.C.) (Monroe Office)
Joel L. Piell
Robert E. Gilbert (Ann Arbor Office)
Eric V. Brown, Jr. (Kalamazoo Office)
Bruce D. Birgbauer
George T. Stevenson
John A. Thurber (P.C.) (Bloomfield Hills Office)
Orin D. Brustad
Carl H. von Ende
Erik H. Serr (Ann Arbor Office)
Allyn D. Kantor (Ann Arbor Office)
Mark E. Schlussel
Charles E. Ritter (Kalamazoo Office)
Thomas G. Parachini
John A. Campbell (Kalamazoo Office)
David D. Joswick (P.C.)
Charles L. Burleigh, Jr.
John A. Marxer (P.C.) (Bloomfield Hills Office)
Gregory L. Curtner
Dennis R. Neiman
Kenneth E. Konop (Bloomfield Hills Office)
Leonard D. Givens
W. Mack Faison
Joseph F. Galvin
Thomas J. Heiden (Grand Rapids Office)
Ronald H. Riback (Bloomfield Hills Office)
James W. Williams (Bloomfield Hills Office)
Thomas P. Hustoles (Kalamazoo Office)
William J. Danhof (Lansing Office)
Clarence L. Pozza, Jr.
Jerry T. Rupley
Michael W. Hartmann
Kent E. Shafer
James C. Foresman
John J. Collins, Jr.
John R. Cook (Kalamazoo Office)
Lawrence D. Owen (Lansing Office)
Thomas W. Linn
Stephen G. Palms
Jerome R. Watson
Frank L. Andrews (Detroit and Bloomfield Hills Offices)
Donna J. Donati
Donald W. Keim
Larry J. Saylor
Mark E. Putney (Grand Rapids Office)
James G. Vantine, Jr. (Kalamazoo and Grand Rapids Offices)
Richard J. Seryak
Michael R. Atkins (Lansing Office)
Leland D. Barringer
Timothy D. Sochocki (Ann Arbor Office)
Thomas C. Phillips (Grand Rapids and Lansing Offices)
Christopher J. Dembowski (Lansing Office)
Marjory G. Basile
Terrence M. Crawford
Ryan H. Haywood
Michael J. Hodge (Lansing Office)
J. Kevin Trimmer (Bloomfield Hills Office)
Steven D. Weyhing (Lansing Office)
Richard A. Gaffin (Grand Rapids Office)
Kevin M. McCarthy (Kalamazoo Office)
Ronald E. Baylor (Kalamazoo Office)
Gary A. Bruder (Ann Arbor Office)
Beverly Hall Burns
Charles S. Mishkind (Grand Rapids, Lansing and Kalamazoo Offices)
Stephen J. Ott
Amanda Van Dusen
Peter W. Waldmeir
Thomas G. Appleman
Thomas H. Van Dis (Kalamazoo Office)
Walter Briggs Connolly, Jr.
Michael P. Coakley
Cynthia B. Faulhaber
Jeffrey M. McHugh
Susan Hedges Patton (Ann Arbor Office)
Robert F. Rhoades
James E. Spurr (Kalamazoo Office)
Gregory V. Di Censo (Bloomfield Hills Office)
Michael L. Lencione
Stephen M. Tuuk (Grand Rapids Office)
Robert D. VanderLaan (Grand Rapids Office)
Brad B. Arbuckle (Bloomfield Hills Office)
Mark T. Boonstra
Harold W. Bulger, Jr.
Michael G. Campbell (Grand Rapids Office)
David A. French (Ann Arbor Office)
Michael A. Limauro
Karen Ann McCoy
Kevin J. Moody (Lansing Office)
Steven M. Stankewicz (Kalamazoo Office)
Robert E. Lee Wright
Andrea L. Fischer
Michael A. Indenbaum
Alison B. Marshall (Washington, D.C. Office)
J. David Reck (Ann Arbor and Howell Offices)
Michael H. Traison
Jonathan S. Green
Le Roy L. Asher, Jr.
Vernon Bennett III (Grand Rapids and Kalamazoo Offices)
Douglas W. Crim (Grand Rapids Office)
Pamela Chapman Enslen (Kalamazoo Office)
Michael P. McGee
David N. Parsigian (Ann Arbor Office)
Jay B. Rising (Lansing Office)
Deborah W. Thompson
Richard T. Urbis
Richard F. X. Urisko
Steven A. Roach
Richard A. Walawender

OF COUNSEL

William G. Butler
John A. Gilray, Jr., (P.C.) (Bloomfield Hills Office)
Eric V. Brown, Sr. (Kalamazoo Office)
Edmond F. DeVine (Ann Arbor Office)
James E. Tobin
Stratton S. Brown
Richard B. Gushée
Peter P. Thurber
George J. Slykhouse (Grand Rapids Office)
Gerard Thomas (Kalamazoo Office)
George E. Bushnell, Jr.

(See Next Column)

OF COUNSEL (Continued)

Henry R. Nolte, Jr. (Bloomfield Hills Office)
Donald B. Lifton
Anne H. Hiemstra
Richard I. Lott (Pensacola, Florida Office)
Nicholas P. Miller (Washington, D.C. Office)
Joseph Van Eaton (Washington, D.C. Office)
Tillman L. Lay (Washington, D.C. Office)
William R. Malone (Washington, D.C. Office)
Steven C. Kahn (Washington, D.C. Office)
Stephen J. Markman
David K. McLeod

SENIOR ATTORNEYS

Charles E. Scholl (Grand Rapids Office)
David E. Hathaway (Grand Rapids Office)
Julianna B. Miller
Leo P. Goddeyne (Kalamazoo Office)
Charles A. Duerr, Jr. (Ann Arbor Office)
Michael J. Taylor (Grand Rapids Office)
Don M. Schmidt (Kalamazoo Office)
Ronald D. Gardner (Ann Arbor Office)
Elise Levasseur Rohn
William B. Beach
Abigail Elias
David F. Dixon
Robert J. Sandler
Lawrence M. Dudek
Irene Bruce Hathaway
Sherry Katz-Crank (Lansing Office)
Marta A. Manildi (Ann Arbor Office)
Gary W. Faria
David J. Hasper (Grand Rapids Office)
Susan E. Juroe (Washington, D.C. Office)
Michael A. Alaimo
David A. Gatchell (St. Petersburg Office)
John G. VanSlambrouck
Celeste M. Moy (Washington, D.C. Office)

ASSOCIATES

Brian J. Doren
Ilana A. Stein Ben-Ze'ev
Walter A. Payne, III
Ronald E. Hodess (Bloomfield Hills Office)
Ellen M. Tickner
George D. Mesritz
John C. Shea (Lansing Office)
Kathryn L. Ossian
Donald J. Hutchinson
Megan P. Norris
Kurt N. Sherwood (Kalamazoo Office)
Patricia D. Lott (Pensacola Office)
Frederick E. Ellrod III (Washington, D.C. Office)
Jereen G. Trudell (Bloomfield Hills Office)
Richard I. Loebl
Gary E. Mitchell (Grand Rapids Office)
Matthew C. Ames (Washington, D.C. Office)
Ballard Jay Yelton III (Kalamazoo Office)
Michael A. Luberto, Jr.
Clifford T. Flood (Lansing Office)
Linda M. Bruton
William L. Rosin (Bloomfield Hills Office)
Thomas R. Cox
Lori L. Purkey (Kalamazoo Office)
L. Jeffrey Zauberman
Joanne B. Faycurry
Janet R. Chrzanowski
Dawn M. Schluter (Bloomfield Hills Office)
A. Paul Thowsen (Ann Arbor Office)
Robert J. Haddad
John H. Willems
Erich H. Hintzen
James R. Lancaster, Jr. (Lansing Office)
Carol A. Jizmejian
Joan L. Kramlich (Lansing Office)
John O. Renken (Ann Arbor and District of Columbia Offices)
Terry Xiaotian Gao (Washington, D.C. Office)
Frederick A. Acomb
Joseph G. Sullivan
Lisa D. Pick
Elizabeth J. Partington (Pensacola Office)
Louise B. Wright (Kalamazoo Office)
John C. Arndts
Brian S. Westenberg
Amy S. Davis
A. Michael Palizzi
Sally A. Hamby
Patrick F. McGow
Brian K. Telfair
Paul G. Machesky
Mark A. Randon
Michael C. Fayz
Jeffrey S. Starman
Anna M. Maiuri (Bloomfield Hills Office)
Thomas D. Colis
Dean M. Altobelli (Lansing Office)
Derek T. Montgomery
Amy J. Broman (Ann Arbor Office)
Diane B. Cabbell (Ann Arbor Office)
Steven G. Cohen
Kristin M. Neun (Washington, D.C. Office)
David A. Nacht
Bradley C. White (Grand Rapids Office)
Sean P. Culliton (Pensacola Office)
Jeffrey D. Adelman
Meg Hackett Carrier (Grand Rapids Office)
Linda M. Ledbetter (Ann Arbor Office)
Catherine M. Patterson
Suzanne L. DeVine (Ann Arbor Office)
Karen M. Hassevoort (Kalamazoo Office)

Representative Firm Clients: Chrysler Corp.; Comerica, Inc.; City of Detroit, Mich.; Detroit Tigers, Inc.; First of Michigan; Fretter, Inc.; Ford Motor Co.; Ford Motor Credit Co.; Great Lakes Bancorp; Henry Ford Hospital.

For full biographical listings, see the Martindale-Hubbell Law Directory

Detroit—Continued

PEPPER, HAMILTON & SCHEETZ (AV)

100 Renaissance Center, 36th Floor, 48243-1157
Telephone: 313-259-7110
Telecopy: 313-259-7926
Philadelphia, Pennsylvania Office: 3000 Two Logan Square, Eighteenth and Arch Streets, 19103-2799.
Telephone: 215-981-4000.
Fax: 215-981-4750.
Washington, D.C. Office: 1300 Nineteenth Street, N.W., 20036-1685.
Telephone: 202-828-1200.
Fax: 202-828-1665.
Harrisburg, Pennsylvania Office: 200 One Keystone Plaza, North Front and Market Streets, P.O. Box 1181, 17108-1181.
Telephone: 717-255-1155.
Fax: 717-238-0575.
Berwyn, Pennsylvania Office: 1235 Westlakes Drive, Suite 400, 19312-2401.
Telephone: 610-640-7800.
Fax: 610-640-7835.
New York, New York Office: 450 Lexington Avenue, Suite 1600, 10017-3904.
Telephone: 212-878-3800.
Fax: 212-878-3835.
Wilmington, Delaware Office: 1201 Market Street, Suite 1401, P.O. Box 1709, 19899-1709.
Telephone: 302-571-6555.
Fax: 302-656-8865.
Westmont, New Jersey Office: Sentry Office Plaza, Suite 321, 216 Haddon Avenue, 08108-2811.
Telephone: 609-869-9555.
Fax: 609-869-9595.
London, England Office: City Tower, 40 Basinghall Street, EC2V 5DE.
Telephone: 011-44-71-628-1122.
Fax: 011-44-71-628-6010.
Moscow, Russia Office: 19-27 Grokholsky Pereulok, 129010.
Telephone: 011-7-095-280-4493.
Fax: 011-7-095-280-5518.

PARTNERS

Abraham Singer (Managing Partner)
Joel D. Applebaum
Hugh Douglas Camitta
I. William Cohen
Michael A. Fleming
Scott L. Gorland
Lisa Sommers Gretchko
Richard D. Grow
Vicki R. Harding
Stuart E. Hertzberg
Dennis S. Kayes
Robert C. Ludolph
David L. Maurer
Phyllis Golden Morey
David Murphy
Erica E. Peresman
Barbara Rom
Richard A. Rossman
Michael B. Staebler
Thomas P. Wilczak

ASSOCIATES

Judith E. Caliman
Todd A. Caraway
AnnMarie Black Dahms
René M. L. Hanseman
Kay Standrige Kress
Matthew J. Lund
Catherine C. Lynem
John Mucha, III
Drew S. Norton
Marianne Lebeuf Wade
Sarah C. Zearfoss

For full biographical listings, see the Martindale-Hubbell Law Directory

PRATHER & ASSOCIATES, P.C. (AV)

3800 Penobscot Building, 48226-4220
Telephone: 313-962-7722
Facsimile: 313-962-2653

Kenneth E. Prather

Jan Rewers McMillan

For full biographical listings, see the Martindale-Hubbell Law Directory

RILEY AND ROUMELL, P.C. (AV)

7th Floor, Ford Building, 48226-3986
Telephone: 313-962-8255
Telefax: 313-962-2937

Wallace D. Riley
George T. Roumell, Jr.
William F. Dennis
Steven M. Zarowny
Amy E. Newberg
Alfred John Eppens
Wilber M. Brucker III
Allen J. Lippitt
Gregory T. Schultz

OF COUNSEL

Wilber M. Brucker, Jr.
William D. Cohan
Emmet E. Tracy, Jr.

Representative Clients: Comerica Bank-Detroit; Peoples State Bank; Federal National Mortgage Assn.; Federal Home Loan Mortgage Corp.; SCOR S.A.; Chas. Verheyden, Inc.; Detroit Board of Education; County of Wayne; City of Livonia.

For full biographical listings, see the Martindale-Hubbell Law Directory

SCHUREMAN, FRAKES, GLASS & WULFMEIER (AV)

440 East Congress, Fourth Floor, 48226
Telephone: 313-961-1500
Telecopier: 313-961-1087
Harbor Springs, Michigan Office: One Spring Street Sq., 49740.
Telephone: 616-526-1145.
Telecopier: 616-526-9343.

MEMBERS OF FIRM

Jeptha W. Schureman
John C. Frakes, Jr.
Charles F. Glass
LeRoy H. Wulfmeier, III
Cheryl L. Chandler
David M. Ottenwess

ASSOCIATES

Daniel J. Dulworth
John J. Moran
Paul A. Salyers
Erane C. Washington

Reference: Comerica.

For full biographical listings, see the Martindale-Hubbell Law Directory

SHANTZ AND BOOKER, PROFESSIONAL CORPORATION

(See Bloomfield Hills)

TIMMIS & INMAN (AV)

300 Talon Centre, 48207
Telephone: 313-396-4200
Telecopier: 313-396-4228

MEMBERS OF FIRM

Michael T. Timmis
Wayne C. Inman
Robert E. Graziani
George A. Peck
Charles W. Royer
Richard L. Levin
Henry J. Brennan, III
Mark W. Peyser
Richard M. Miettinen
Lisa R. Gorman

ASSOCIATES

Bradley J. Knickerbocker
George M. Malis
Amy Lynn Ryntz
Mark Robert Adams
Daniel G. Kielczewski
Michael F. Wais
Kevin S. Kendall
John P. Kanan
David J. Galbenski

OF COUNSEL

William B. Fitzgerald
W. Clark Durant, III

Representative Clients: Stylecraft Printing Company; Stylerite Label Corporation; Retail Resources, Inc.; Deneb Robotics, Inc.; Peabody Management, Inc.; Ferndale Honda, Inc,; Applied Process, Inc.; Insilco Corporation; Variety Foods, Inc.; Certain Underwriters at Lloyds of London.

For full biographical listings, see the Martindale-Hubbell Law Directory

VANDEVEER GARZIA, PROFESSIONAL CORPORATION (AV)

Suite 1600, 333 West Fort Street, 48226
Telephone: 313-961-4880
Fax: 313-961-3822
Oakland County Office: 220 Park Street, Suite 300, Birmingham, Michigan.
Telephone: 810-645-0100.
Fax: 810-645-2430.
Macomb County Office: 50 Crocker Boulevard, Mount Clemens, Michigan.
Telephone: 810-468-4880.
Fax: 810-465-7159.
Kent County Office: 510 Grand Plaza Place, 220 Lyon Square, Grand Rapids, Michigan.
Telephone: 616-366-8600.
Fax: 616-786-9095.
Holland, Michigan Office: 1121 Ottawa Beach Road, Suite 140.
Telephone: 616-399-8600.
Fax: 616-786-9095.

Fred L. Vandeveer (1879-1972)
James E. Haggerty, Sr. (1900-1966)
Leroy G. Vandeveer (1902-1981)
Buelle A. Doelle (1902-1985)
Thomas P. Rockwell
James A. Sullivan
James E. Plastow, Jr.
Michael M. Hathaway
John J. Lynch, III (Resident, Oakland County Office)
Thomas M. Peters
James K. Thome (Resident, Oakland County Office)
Cecil F. Boyle, Jr. (Resident, Oakland County Office)
Ronald L. Cornell (Resident, Macomb County Office)
William J. Heaphy (Kent County and Holland Offices)
Gary Alan Miller
William L. Kiriazis
Cynthia E. Merry
Dennis B. Cotter
Daniel P. Steele
Shelley K. Miller (Resident, Oakland County Office)
Terrance P. Lynch
Lynda D. Barbat
Leonard A. Krzyzaniak, Jr.
David P. Grunewald
Bruce E. Pearce
Hal O. Carroll

OF COUNSEL

Samuel A. Garzia
Richard J. Tonkin
Ivin E. Kerr
John M. Heaphy
Roy C. Hebert

(See Next Column)

VANDEVEER GARZIA PROFESSIONAL CORPORATION, *Detroit—Continued*

Paul C. Pfister (Resident, Oakland County Office)
David B. Timmis (Resident, Oakland County Office)
Lauren Elizabeth Meyer
Nancy A. Hensley (Resident, Oakland County Office)
Dawn Twydell Gladhill
Jason J. Thompson
C. Edward Hildebrandt (Resident, Oakland County Office)
Renee Richardson
Theodore A. Metry
Donald C. Brownell
Laurie S. Raab (Resident, Oakland County Office)

Representative Clients: Aetna Casualty and Surety Co.; Bic Corp.; CNA Insurance Group; Travelers Insurance Co.; United States Aviation Underwriters; Goodyear Tire & Rubber Co.

For full biographical listings, see the Martindale-Hubbell Law Directory

EAST LANSING, Ingham Co.

FARHAT, STORY & KRAUS, P.C. (AV)

Beacon Place, 4572 South Hagadorn Road, Suite 3, 48823
Telephone: 517-351-3700
Fax: 517-332-4122

Leo A. Farhat
James E. Burns (1925-1979)
Monte R. Story
Richard C. Kraus
Max R. Hoffman Jr.
Chris A. Bergstrom
Kitty L. Groh
Charles R. Toy
David M. Platt

Lawrence P. Schweitzer
Jeffrey J. Short
Kathy A. Breedlove
Thomas L. Sparks

Representative Clients: Big L. Corp.; Michigan Automotive Wholesalers Association.; Hartman-Fabco, Inc.; Lansing Electric Motors, Inc.; Mike Miller Lincoln Mercury; Edward Rose Realty, Inc.; Jackson National Life Insurance; Squires School and Commercial Sales; GTE Directory Services Corp.
Reference: Capitol National Bank, City Bank, Old Kent Bank & Trust.

For full biographical listings, see the Martindale-Hubbell Law Directory

SMITH, HAUGHEY, RICE & ROEGGE, P.C. (AV)

1301 North Hagadorn, 48823-2320
Telephone: 517-332-3030
Telecopier: 517-332-3468
Grand Rapids, Michigan Office: 200 Calder Plaza Building, 250 Monroe Avenue, N.W., 49503-2251.
Telephone: 616-774-8000.
Telecopier: 616-774-2461.
Traverse City, Michigan Office: 241 East State Street, P.O. Box 848, 49685-0848.
Telephone: 616-929-4878.
Telecopier: 616-929-4182.

Douglas G. Powe

Loretta B. Passanante
Daniel N. Stephens
James R. Duby, Jr.
Veronica A. Marsich

Representative Clients: Chevron; Cincinnati Insurance Co.; General Motors Corp.; Kemper Insurance Group; Michigan Hospital Assn.; Navistar International; St. Paul Insurance Cos.; Steelcase, Inc.; Sears Roebuck & Co.; Dow Elanco.

For full biographical listings, see the Martindale-Hubbell Law Directory

*ESCANABA,** Delta Co.

BUTCH, QUINN, ROSEMURGY, JARDIS, BUSH, BURKHART & STROM, P.C. (AV)

816 Ludington Street, 49829
Telephone: 906-786-4422
Fax: 906-786-5128
Gladstone, Michigan Office: 201 First National Bank Building.
Telephone: 906-428-3123.
Marquette, Michigan Office: 300 South Front Street.
Telephone: 906-228-4440.
Iron Mountain, Michigan Office: 500 South Stephenson Avenue.
Telephone: 906-774-4460.
Marinette, Wisconsin Office: 2008 Ella Court.
Telephone: 715-732-4154.

Torval E. Strom (1885-1946)
Wheaton L. Strom (1914-1974)
Thomas L. Butch
Michael B. Quinn
Robert S. Rosemurgy
Terrill S. Jardis
Allen S. Bush
Terry F. Burkhart
Peter W. Strom
Paul L. Strom
Steven C. Parks
John A. Lewandowski
Bonnie Lee Hoff
James E. Soderberg
JoJean A. Miller

(See Next Column)

LEGAL SUPPORT PERSONNEL

Katherine Anne LeDuc

Representative Clients: MFC First National Bank, Escanaba, Michigan; United States Fidelity & Guaranty Co.; City of Gladstone; Baybank; Bresnan Cable Communications Co.; Engineered Machined Products, Inc.; Upper Peninsula Association of Realtors.

For full biographical listings, see the Martindale-Hubbell Law Directory

*FLINT,** Genesee Co.

DEAN, DEAN, SEGAR, HART & SHULMAN, P.C. (AV)

1616 Genesee Towers, One East First Street, 48502
Telephone: 810-235-5631
Fax: 810-235-8983

Max Dean
Robert Abram (1934-1967)
Robert L. Segar
Clifford H. Hart
Leonard B. Shulman
James Hallem
Sherri L. Katz

OF COUNSEL

Cameron Dean

Representative Clients: Flint Industrial Sales & Equipment Co.; P&H Plumbing & Heating, Inc.; Genesee County Dental Society; City of Montrose; Royalite Electric Co.; King of All Manufacturing, Inc.; Executive Travel Service.
Local Counsel for: Detroit Automobile Inter-Insurance Exchange.
References: NBD Bank, N.A.; Citizens Bank.

For full biographical listings, see the Martindale-Hubbell Law Directory

GAULT DAVISON (AV)

A Partnership including Professional Corporations
Tenth Floor, North Bank Center, 48502
Telephone: 810-234-3633
Fax: 810-233-3387
Fenton, Michigan Office: 14165 N. Fenton Road.
Telephone: 313-750-6644.
Fax: 313-750-6679.

MEMBERS OF FIRM

Harry G. Gault (1892-1975)
Matthew Davison, Jr. (1916-1989)
Russell E. Bowers
Guy H. Hill (Retired)
Bernard L. McAra
F. Robert Schmelzer (P.C.) (Resident, Fenton, Michigan Office)
Frederick L. Schmoll, III, (P.C.)
Kendall B. Williams
Edward B. Davison

OF COUNSEL

Richard J. Figura
Patric A. Parker
Allan L. Parker

ASSOCIATES

Richard C. Hohenstein
Kathy L. Weir
Kevin A. Lavalle
John R. Moynihan
Gary Spinning Casey
Brooke Burroughs Moynihan
Abner J. Tansil
Michael J. Gildner

Representative Clients: Automobile Club Insurance Assn.; State Farm Insurance Cos.; Farm Bureau Insurance Group; Governmental Casualty Insurance Co.; Howard Delivery Service, Inc.; MagnaTek Universal; Electric co.; K-mart Corp.

For full biographical listings, see the Martindale-Hubbell Law Directory

MACDONALD, FITZGERALD, MACDONALD & SIMON, P.C. (AV)

200 McKinnon Building, 48502
Telephone: 810-232-3184; 234-2204
Fax: 810-232-9632

Robert J. MacDonald (1914-1987)
John J. FitzGerald
R. Duncan MacDonald
Timothy J. Simon
Timothy J. MacDonald

References: Michigan National Bank; Genesee Merchants Bank & Trust Co.

For full biographical listings, see the Martindale-Hubbell Law Directory

SMITH & BROOKER, P.C. (AV)

3506 Lennon Road, P.O. Box 7650, 48507
Telephone: 810-733-0140
Bay City, Michigan Office: 703 Washington Avenue.
Telephone: 517-892-2595.
Saginaw, Michigan Office: 3057 Davenport Avenue.
Telephone: 517-799-1891.

RESIDENT ATTORNEYS

Thomas A. Connolly
Peter L. Diesel

Representative Clients: CIGNA; Ford Motor Co.; State Farm Mutual Automobile Insurance Co.; State Farm Fire & Casualty; Employers Mutual Companies; Michigan Lawyers Mutual; Auto Owners Insurance; Michigan Municipal Risk Authority; Monumental General Insurance; Lake State Railway Co.

For full biographical listings, see the Martindale-Hubbell Law Directory

Flint—Continued

WINEGARDEN, SHEDD, HALEY, LINDHOLM & ROBERTSON (AV)

501 Citizens Bank Building, 48502-1983
Telephone: 810-767-3600
Telecopier: 810-767-8776

MEMBERS OF FIRM

Myron Winegarden (1906-1986)
William C. Shedd
Dennis M. Haley
John T. Lindholm
Donald H. Robertson
L. David Lawson
John R. Tucker

ASSOCIATES

Alan F. Himelhoch
Suellen J. Parker
Damion Frasier
Peter T. Mooney

OF COUNSEL

Howard R. Grossman

Representative Clients: Citizens Commercial and Savings Bank; R. L. White Development Corporation; Interstate Traffic Consultants (Intracon) Inc.; Downtown Development Authority of Flint; Young Olds-Cadillac, Inc.; First American Title Insurance Co.; Sorensen Gross Construction Co.; Genesee County; Insight, Inc.; Modern Industries, Inc.

For full biographical listings, see the Martindale-Hubbell Law Directory

GRAND BLANC, Genesee Co.

GARAN, LUCOW, MILLER, SEWARD, COOPER & BECKER, P.C. (AV)

8332 Office Park Drive, 48439
Telephone: 810-695-3700
Fax: 810-695-6488
Detroit, Michigan Office: 1000 Woodbridge Place.
Telephone: 313-446-1530.
Fax: 313-259-0450.
Port Huron, Michigan Office: Port Huron Office Center, 511 Fort Street, Suite 505.
Telephone: 810-985-4400.
Fax: 810-985-4187.
Ann Arbor, Michigan Office: 101 North Main Street, Suite 801.
Telephone: 313-930-5600.
Fax: 313-930-0043.
Troy, Michigan Office: 2301 West Big Beaver Road, Suite 212.
Telephone: 810-649-7600.
Fax: 810-649-5438.
Mount Clemens Office: Towne Square Development, 10 S. Main Street, Suite 307.
Telephone: 810-954-3800.
Fax: 810-954-3803.

Joseph Kochis (Resident)
William J. Brickley (Resident)

Kenneth V. Klaus (Resident)
Denise M. Granzow (Resident)
David L. Lattie

For full biographical listings, see the Martindale-Hubbell Law Directory

*GRAND RAPIDS,** Kent Co.

ALLABEN, MASSIE, VANDER WEYDEN & TIMMER (AV)

Suite 850, Commerce Building, 5 Lyon Street, N.W., 49503
Telephone: 616-774-2182
Fax: 616-774-0602

MEMBERS OF FIRM

Fred Roland Allaben (1901-1985)
Sam F. Massie, Jr.
Keith A. Vander Weyden
John J. Timmer
Robert W. Bandeen

John R. Allaben

Representative Clients: Auto Club Insurance Association; American States Insurance Co.; Michigan Mutual Liability Co.; Fidelity & Casualty Company of New York; U.S. Aircraft Insurance Group; Security Mutual Casualty Co.; Nationwide Mutual Insurance Co.; Security Mutual Casualty Co.; Nationwide Mutual Insurance Co.; Union Insurance Co.

For full biographical listings, see the Martindale-Hubbell Law Directory

BORRE, PETERSON, FOWLER & REENS, P.C. (AV)

The Philo C. Fuller House, 44 Lafayette, N.E., P.O. Box 1767, 49501-1767
Telephone: 616-459-1971
FAX: 616-459-2393

Glen V. Borre
James B. Peterson
Ben A. Fowler
William C. Reens
Frank H. Johnson
Mark D. Sevald
William R. Vander Sluis
William G. Krupar

Reference: Old Kent Bank & Trust Co.

For full biographical listings, see the Martindale-Hubbell Law Directory

CHOLETTE, PERKINS & BUCHANAN (AV)

900 Campau Square Plaza Building, 99 Monroe Avenue, N.W., 49503
Telephone: 616-774-2131
Fax: 616-774-7016

Paul E. Cholette (1897-1974)
William A. Perkins (1905-1986)
William D. Buchanan (1909-1992)

MEMBERS OF FIRM

Calvin R. Danhof
Frederick W. Bleakley
Reynolds A. Brander, Jr.
Bruce M. Bieneman
William J. Warren
Donald C. Exelby
Thomas H. Cypher
William A. Brengle
Alfred J. Parent
Charles H. Worsfold
Michael P. McCasey
Marc A. Kidder
Michael C. Mysliwiec
Evan L. MacFarlane
John A. Quinn
Albert J. Engel, III
Stephen C. Oldstrom
William E. McDonald, Jr.
Mark E. Fatum
Richard K. Grover, Jr.
David J. DeGraw

ASSOCIATES

Kenneth L. Block
William J. Yob
Robert E. Attmore
Martin W. Buschle
Miles J. Murphy, III
Martha P. Forman
Kathrine M. West
Robert A. Kamp

Counsel for: Aetna Casualty & Surety Co.; Argonaut Insurance Co.; Auto-Owners Insurance Co.; Employers Mutual; Liberty Mutual Insurance Co.; Sentry Group; State Farm Insurance; Eastern Aviation and Marine Underwriters; Home Insurance Co.; Nationwide Insurance.

For full biographical listings, see the Martindale-Hubbell Law Directory

CLARY, NANTZ, WOOD, HOFFIUS, RANKIN & COOPER (AV)

500 Calder Plaza, 250 Monroe Avenue, N.W., 49503-2244
Telephone: 616-459-9487
Telecopier: 616-459-5121

MEMBERS OF FIRM

Jack R. Clary
Philip W. Nantz
Philip F. Wood
Leonard M. Hoffius
Robert P. Cooper
Robert L. DeJong
Richard A. Wendt
Stephen J. Mulder
Leo H. Litowich
Harold E. Nelson
Stanley J. Stek
John H. Gretzinger
Edward J. Inman
Daniel R. Kubiak
Scott G. Smith
Mark R. Smith
Marshall W. Grate
Steven K. Girard
Jeffrey VanHorne Sluggett
George R. Ciampa

OF COUNSEL

Richard J. Rankin, Jr.

ASSOCIATES

Mark D. Pakkala
Dale R. Rietberg
Douglas H. Wiegerink
Jack C. Clary
Sandra S. Hamilton
Peter H. Peterson
Thomas J. Dempsey (Not admitted in MI)
Philip G. Henderson
Fred J. Posont
Michael J. Distel
Terry E. Tobias
Kathryn Kraus Nunzio

Representative Clients: United Bank of Michigan; D&W Food Centers, Inc.; FMB First Michigan Bank-Grand Rapids; Goodrich Theatres & Radio, Inc.; S. Abraham & Sons, Inc.; Garb-Ko, Inc., d/b/a 7-Eleven; Weather Shield Mfg., Inc.; JET Electronics & Technology, Inc.; Westinghouse Credit Corp.

For full biographical listings, see the Martindale-Hubbell Law Directory

DICKINSON, WRIGHT, MOON, VAN DUSEN & FREEMAN (AV)

200 Ottawa Avenue, N.W., Suite 900, 49503-2423
Telephone: 616-458-1300
Facsimile: 616-458-6753
Detroit, Michigan Office: 500 Woodward Avenue, Suite 4000.
Telephone: 313-223-3500.
Facsimile: 313-223-3598.
Bloomfield Hills, Michigan Office: 525 North Woodward Avenue, Suite 2000.
Telephone: 810-433-7200.
Facsimile: 810-433-7274.
Lansing, Michigan Office: Suite 200, 215 South Washington Square.
Telephone: 517-371-1730.
Facsimile: 517-487-4700.
Washington, D.C. Office: Suite 800, 1901 L Street, N.W.
Telephone: 202-457-0160.
Facsimile: 202-659-1559.
Chicago, Illinois Office: 225 West Washington, Suite 400.
Telephone: 312-220-0300.
Facsimile: 312-220-0021.
Warsaw, Poland Office: 46 Wilcza Street, 4th Floor, 00-679.
Telephone: (48-22) 299-241.
Facsimile: (48-2) 628-4107. Komertel Satellite Phone: (48-39) 121-510.

(See Next Column)

DICKINSON, WRIGHT, MOON, VAN DUSEN & FREEMAN, *Grand Rapids—Continued*

RESIDENT PARTNERS

William J. Fisher, III — Richard A. Glaser
Stuart F. Cheney — John M. Lichtenberg
Dustin P. Ordway

OF COUNSEL

T. R. Knecht — Douglas J. Van Der Aa

RESIDENT ASSOCIATES

Erin E. Gravelyn — John L. Teeples
James Gavan O'Connor — Rock A. Wood

Representative Clients: Federal-Mogul Corp.; Florists' Transworld Delivery Assn.; GMF Robotics Corp.; Kmart Corp.; Kuhlman Corp.; Michigan Consolidated Gas Co.; NBD Bank, N.A.

For full biographical listings, see the Martindale-Hubbell Law Directory

DYKEMA GOSSETT (AV)

200 Oldtown Riverfront Building, 248 Louis Campau Promenade, N.W., 49503-2668
Telephone: 616-776-7500
Telex: 23-0121
Fax: 616-776-7573
Detroit Michigan Office: 400 Renaissance Center, 48243-1668.
Telephone: 313-568-6800.
Fax: 313-568-6594.
Ann Arbor, Michigan Office: 315 East Eisenhower Parkway, Suite 100, 48108-3306.
Telephone: 313-747-7660.
Fax: 313-747-7696.
Bloomfield Hills, Michigan Office: 1577 North Woodward Avenue, Suite 300, 48304-2820.
Telephone: 810-540-0700.
Fax: 810-540-0763.
Lansing, Michigan Office: 800 Michigan National Tower, 48933-1707.
Telephone: 517-374-9100.
Fax: 517-374-9191.
Washington, D.C. Office: Franklin Square, Suite 300 West Tower, 1300 I Street, N.W., 20005-3306.
Telephone: 202-522-8600.
Fax: 202-522-8669.
Chicago, Illinois Office: Three First National Plaza, 70 W. Madison, Suite 1400, 60602-4270.
Telephone: 312-214-3380.
Fax: 312-214-3441.

RESIDENT MEMBERS

Robert L. Nelson — Stephen S. Muhich
Richard B. Baxter — William J. Brennan
J. Terrance Dillon — John A. Ferroli
Patrick E. Mears — Brian J. Page
David E. Doran

OF COUNSEL

G. Mark McAleenan, Jr.

RETIRED MEMBERS

Robert N. Hammond

RESIDENT ASSOCIATES

Daniel J. Brondyk — John F. Smart
Paul W. Ritsema — James R. Saalfeld
Douglas L. Lutz — Scott D. Broekstra
James R. Bruinsma

For full biographical listings, see the Martindale-Hubbell Law Directory

FARR & OOSTERHOUSE (AV)

Suite 400, Ledyard Building, 125 Ottawa Avenue, N.W., 49503
Telephone: 616-459-3355
Fax: 616-235-3350

MEMBERS OF FIRM

William S. Farr — Joel E. Krissoff
Kenneth R. Oosterhouse — John R. Oostema
Charles E. Chamberlain, Jr.

ASSOCIATES

Michelene B. Pattee

For full biographical listings, see the Martindale-Hubbell Law Directory

GRUEL, MILLS, NIMS AND PYLMAN (AV)

50 Monroe Place, Suite 700 West, 49503
Telephone: 616-235-5500
Fax: 616-235-5550

MEMBERS OF FIRM

Grant J. Gruel — Scott R. Melton
William F. Mills — Brion J. Brooks
J. Clarke Nims — Thomas R. Behm
Norman H. Pylman, II — J. Paul Janes

(See Next Column)

Representative Clients: Aquinas College; Bell Helmet Co.; Blodgett Memorial Medical Center; Butterworth Hospital; Chem Central, Inc.; Cook Pump Co.; Grove, Inc.; NBDC; Heim Corp.

For full biographical listings, see the Martindale-Hubbell Law Directory

GARY J. MCINERNEY, P.C. (AV)

330 East Fulton, 49503
Telephone: 616-458-6111
Telecopier: 616-458-9268

Gary J. McInerney

Michael A. McInerney — Adna H. Underhill

For full biographical listings, see the Martindale-Hubbell Law Directory

MCSHANE & BOWIE (AV)

540 Old Kent Building, P.O. Box 360, 49503-2481
Telephone: 616-774-0641
Fax: 616-774-2366

MEMBERS OF FIRM

T. Gerald McShane (1902-1982) — Gary G. Love
Thomas C. Shearer — John R. Grant
David L. Smith — Dan M. Challa
William H. Bowie — John F. Shape
Keith P. Walker — Wayne P. Bryan
Terry J. Mroz — Michael W. Donovan

OF COUNSEL

Jack M. Bowie

ASSOCIATES

Denise D. Twinney — Miri L. Goldman

Representative Clients: West Side Federal Savings & Loan Assn.; Hartger & Willard Mortgage Associates, Inc.

For full biographical listings, see the Martindale-Hubbell Law Directory

MILLER, CANFIELD, PADDOCK AND STONE, P.L.C. (AV)

A Professional Limited Liability Company
Founded in 1852 by Sidney Davy Miller
1200 Campau Square Plaza, 99 Monroe, N.W., P.O. Box 329, 49503-2639
Telephone: 616-454-8656
Fax: 616-776-6322
Detroit, Michigan Office: 150 West Jefferson, Suite 2500, 48226-4415.
Telephone: 313-963-6420.
Fax: 313-496-7500.
Cable Address: "Stem Detroit."
Ann Arbor, Michigan Office: 101 North Main Street, 7th Floor, 48104-1400.
Telephone: 313-663-2445.
Fax: 313-747-7147.
Bloomfield Hills, Michigan Office: Suite 100, Pinehurst Office Center, 1400 North Woodward, 48303-2014.
Telephone: 313-645-5000.
Fax: 313-645-1917.
Howell, Michigan Office: 121 South Barnard Street, Suite 4, 48843-2305.
Telephone: 517-546-7600.
Telecopier: 517-546-6974.
Kalamazoo, Michigan Office: 444 West Michigan Avenue, 49007-3752.
Telephone: 616-381-7030.
Fax: 616-382-0244.
Lansing, Michigan Office: One Michigan Avenue, Suite 900, 48933-1609.
Telephone: 517-487-2070.
Fax: 517-374-6304.
Monroe, Michigan Office: The Executive Centre, 214 East Elm Avenue, 48161-2682.
Telephone: 313-243-2000.
Fax: 313-243-0901.
Washington, D.C. Office: 1225 Nineteenth Street, N.W., Suite 400. 20036.
Telephone: 202-429-5575; 785-0600;
Fax: 202-331-1118; 785-1234.
Pensacola, Florida Office: 25 West Cedar 32501.
Telephone: 904-469-1088.
Fax: 904-432-0677.
St. Petersburg Florida Office: 100 Second Avenue S., Suite 7045, 33701.
Telephone: 813-982-6000.
Fax: 813-892-6002.
Gdansk, Poland Office: Suite 322, Dom Technika Building, Ul. Rajska 6, 80-850.
Telephone: 011-485-831-2808.
Fax: 011-485-831-4719.
Warsaw, Poland Office: Ul. Marszalkowska 82, Suite 561, 00-517.
Telephone: 011-482-623-6457 and 6458.
Fax: 011-482-623-6459.

(See Next Column)

MILLER, CANFIELD, PADDOCK AND STONE P.L.C.—*Continued*

MEMBERS OF FIRM

Thomas J. Heiden (Resident)
Mark E. Putney (Resident)
Thomas C. Phillips
Richard A. Gaffin
Charles S. Mishkind (Detroit, Lansing and Kalamazoo Offices)
Stephen M. Tuuk (Resident)
Robert D. VanderLaan (Resident)
Michael G. Campbell (Resident)
Robert E. Lee Wright
Vernon Bennett III
Douglas W. Crim (Resident)

OF COUNSEL

George J. Slykhouse (Resident)

SENIOR ATTORNEYS

Charles E. Scholl (Resident)
David E. Hathaway (Resident)
Michael J. Taylor (Resident)
David J. Hasper (Resident)

ASSOCIATES

Gary E. Mitchell (Resident)
John C. Arndts (Resident)
Bradley C. White
Meg Hackett Carrier (Resident)

Representative Firm Clients: Chrysler Corp.; Comerica, Inc.; City of Detroit, Mich.; Detroit Tigers, Inc.; First of Michigan; Fretter, Inc.; Ford Motor Co.; Ford Motor Credit Co.; Great Lakes Bancorp; Henry Ford Hospital.

For full biographical listings, see the Martindale-Hubbell Law Directory

SMITH, HAUGHEY, RICE & ROEGGE, P.C. (AV)

200 Calder Plaza Building, 250 Monroe Avenue, N.W., 49503-2251
Telephone: 616-774-8000
Telecopier: 616-774-2461
East Lansing, Michigan Office: 1301 North Hagadorn, 48823-2320.
Telephone: 517-332-3030.
Telecopier: 517-332-3468.
Traverse City, Michigan Office: 241 East State Street, P.O. Box 848, 49685-0804.
Telephone: 616-929-4878.
Telecopier: 616-929-4182.

Clifford A. Mitts (1902-1962)
Laurence D. Smith (1913-1980)
Robert V.V. Rice (1899-1982)
Michael S. Barnes (1944-1989)
L. Roland Roegge
Thomas F. Blackwell
P. Laurence Mulvihill
Lawrence P. Mulligan
Thomas R. Tasker
Paul H. Reinhardt
Lance R. Mather
Charles F. Behler
Gary A. Rowe
William W. Jack, Jr.
William J. Hondorp
Thomas M. Weibel
James G. Black
E. Thomas Mc Carthy, Jr.
Glenn W. House, Jr.
Thomas R. Wurst
Craig R. Noland
Paul M. Oleniczak
Craig S. Neckers
Thomas E. Kent
Leonard M. Hickey
David N. Campos
Anthony J. Quarto
Bruce P. Rissi
John C. O'Loughlin
John M. Kruis
Paul G. Van Oostenburg
Dale Ann Iverson
William R. Jewell
Jon D. Vander Ploeg
Patrick F. Geary
Terence J. Ackert
Brian J. Kilbane
Dan C. Porter
Brian J. Plachta
Phillip K. Mowers
Carol D. Carlson

Kay L. Griffith Hammond
Ann M. Stuursma
Richard E. Holmes, Jr.
Marilyn S. Nickell
Christopher R. Genther
Beth Suzanne Kromer
Lois Marie Ens
Paul D. Fox
Robert M. Kruse
Harriet M. Hageman
John B. Combs
Aileen M. Simet
Scott W. Morgan
Matthew L. Meyer
Bret M. Hanna
Carine J. Joachim
Todd W. Millar
Elizabeth Roberts VerHey
Jennifer Jane Nasser

OF COUNSEL

A. B. Smith, Jr.
David O. Haughey
Susan Bradley Jakubowski
Thomas P. Scholler

Representative Clients: Chevron; Cincinnati Insurance Co.; General Motors Corp.; Kemper Insurance Group; Michigan Hospital Assn.; Navistar International; St. Paul Insurance Cos.; Steelcase, Inc.; Sears Roebuck & Co.; Dow Elanco.

For full biographical listings, see the Martindale-Hubbell Law Directory

VANDEVEER GARZIA, PROFESSIONAL CORPORATION (AV)

510 Grand Plaza Place, 220 Lyon Square, 49503
Telephone: 616-366-8600
Fax: 616-786-9095
Wayne County Office: Suite 1600, 333 West Fort Street, Detroit, Michigan.
Telephone: 313-961-4880.
Fax: 313-961-3822.
Oakland County Office: 220 Park Street, Suite 300, Birmingham, Michigan.
Telephone: 810-645-0100.
Fax: 810-645-2430.

(See Next Column)

Macomb County Office: 50 Crocker Boulevard, Mount Clemens, Michigan.
Telephone: 810-468-4880.
Fax: 810-465-7159.
Holland, Michigan Office: 1121 Ottawa Beach Road, Suite 140.
Telephone: 616-399-8600.
Fax: 616-786-9095.

William J. Heaphy

Representative Clients: Aetna Casualty and Surety Co.; Chubb Insurance ; Farmers Insurance Group; Goodyear Tire & Rubber Co.; Transamerica Insurance Group.

For full biographical listings, see the Martindale-Hubbell Law Directory

VARNUM, RIDDERING, SCHMIDT & HOWLETT (AV)

Bridgewater Place, P.O. Box 352, 49501-0352
Telephone: 616-336-6000
800-262-0011
Facsimile: 616-336-7000
Telex: 1561593 VARN
Lansing, Michigan Office: The Victor Center, Suite 810, 210 North Washington Square, 48933.
Telephone: 517-482-6237.
Facsimile: 517-482-6937.
Kalamazoo, Michigan Office: 350 East Michigan Avenue, 49007.
Telephone: 616-382-2300.
Facsimile: 616-382-2382.
Grand Haven, Michigan Office: 321 Washington Street, P.O. Box 288, 49417.
Telephone: 616-846-7100.
Facsimile: 616-846-7101.
Battle Creek, Michigan Office: 4950 West Dickman Road, Suite B-1, 49015.
Telephone: 616-962-7144.
Detroit, Michigan Office: 440 East Congress, Fourth Floor, 48226.
Telephone: 313-961-1600.
Facsimile: 313-961-1636.

OF COUNSEL

John L. Wierengo, Jr.
F. William Hutchinson
R. Stuart Hoffius
Gordon B. Boozer

COUNSEL

William J. Halliday, Jr.
Eugene Alkema
Terrance R. Bacon
Peter Visserman
H. Raymond Andrews, Jr.
Karen S. Kienbaum (Resident at Detroit Office)
Michelle Engler (Resident at Lansing Office)
James R. Viventi (Resident at Lansing Office)

MEMBERS OF FIRM

James N. DeBoer, Jr.
William K. Van't Hof
Hilary F. Snell
Peter Armstrong
Robert J. Eleveld
Kent J. Vana
Carl E. Ver Beek
Jon F. DeWitt
John C. Carlyle (Resident at Grand Haven Office)
Donald L. Johnson
Daniel C. Molhoek
Gary P. Skinner
Thomas T. Huff (Resident at Kalamazoo Office)
Timothy J. Curtin
H. Edward Paul
John E. McGarry
Dirk Hoffius
J. Terry Moran
Thomas J. Mulder
Thomas J. Barnes
Robert D. Kullgren
Richard A. Kay
Larry J. Titley
Bruce A. Barnhart
Fredric A. Sytsma
Jack D. Sage
Jeffrey L. Schad
Thomas G. Demling
John W. Pestle
Robert P. Cooper
Frank G. Dunten
Nyal D. Deems
Richard A. Hooker (Resident at Kalamazoo Office)
Randall W. Kraker
Peter A. Smit
Mark C. Hanisch
Marilyn A. Lankfer
Thomas L. Lockhart
Robert L. Diamond
Bruce G. Hudson (Resident at Lansing Office)
Bruce Goodman
Joseph J. Vogan
Eric J. Schneidewind (Resident at Lansing Office)
Teresa S. Decker
Jeffrey R. Hughes
Richard W. Butler, Jr.
Lawrence P. Burns
Matthew D. Zimmerman
William E. Rohn
John Patrick White
Charles M. Denton II
Paul M. Kara
Jeffrey D. Smith (Resident at Kalamazoo Office)
H. Lawrence Smith
Thomas C. Clinton
Mark L. Collins
Jonathan W. Anderson
Carl Oosterhouse
William J. Lawrence III
Gregory M. Palmer
Susan M. Wyngaarden
Kaplin S. Jones
Stephen P. Afendoulis
Robert A. Hendricks
David E. Khorey
Michael G. Wooldridge
Timothy J. Tornga
Perrin Rynders
Mark S. Allard
Timothy E. Eagle
David A. Rhem
Donald P. Lawless
Michael S. McElwee (Resident at Kalamazoo Office)
George B. Davis
Jacqueline D. Scott
N. Stevenson Jennette III
David E. Preston

(See Next Column)

VARNUM, RIDDERING, SCHMIDT & HOWLETT, *Grand Rapids—Continued*

MEMBERS OF FIRM (Continued)

Jeffrey W. Beswick (Resident at Grand Haven Office)
Elizabeth Joy Fossel
Joel E. Bair
Joan E. Schleef
Scott A. Huizenga

ASSOCIATES

Richard J. McKenna
Michael F. Kelly
Kathleen P. Fochtman
Jeffrey J. Fraser
James R. Stadler
Richard R. Symons
Jinya Chen
Jeffery S. Crampton
Ronald G. DeWaard
Maureen Potter
Vicki S. Young
Mark A. Davis
Andrew J. Kok
Patrick A. Miles, Jr.
Eric J. Guerin (Kalamazoo Office)
Steven J. Morren
Kevin Abraham Rynbrandt
Thomas J. Augspurger
Randy A. Bridgeman
Michael X. Hidalgo
Thomas G. Kyros
Pamela J. Tyler
Mary C. Bonnema
Jon M. Bylsma
Joseph B. Levan
Edward J. McNeely
Linda L. Oldford

STAFF ATTORNEYS

Beverly Holaday (Resident at Lansing Office)
Randall J. Groendyk
Robert C. Rutgers, Jr.
Terri L. Shapiro
Bruce H. Vanderlaan
Marc Daneman

Counsel for: First Michigan Bank Corp.; Herman Miller, Inc.

For full biographical listings, see the Martindale-Hubbell Law Directory

WARNER, NORCROSS & JUDD (AV)

900 Old Kent Building, 111 Lyon Street, N.W., 49503-2489
Telephone: 616-752-2000
Fax: 616-752-2500
Muskegon, Michigan Office: 400 Terrace Plaza, P.O. Box 900.
Telephone: 616-727-2600.
Fax: 616-727-2699.
Holland, Michigan Office: Curtis Center, Suite 300, 170 College Avenue.
Telephone: 616-396-9800.
Fax: 616-396-3656.

OF COUNSEL

Lawson E. Becker
Conrad A. Bradshaw
Harold F. Schumacher
Charles C. Lundstrom

MEMBERS OF FIRM

David A. Warner (1883-1966)
George S. Norcross (1889-1960)
Siegel W. Judd (1895-1982)
Platt W. Dockery (1906-1974)
J. M. Neath, Jr. (1928-1974)
Leonard D. Verdier, Jr. (1915-1989)
Thomas J. McNamara (1936-1989)
Phil R. Johnson (1908-1990)
Thomas R. Winquist
George L. Whitfield
Wallson G. Knack
Charles E. McCallum
Jerome M. Smith
John D. Tully
R. Malcolm Cumming
William K. Holmes
Roger M. Clark
Edward Malinzak
John H. Logie
Donald J. Veldman (Resident at Muskegon Office)
I. John Snider, II (Resident at Muskegon Office)
Jack B. Combs
Joseph F. Martin
John R. Marquis (Resident at Holland Office)
John H. Martin (Resident at Muskegon Office)
James H. Breay
Ernest M. Sharpe
Vernon P. Saper
Hugh H. Makens
Joseph M. Sweeney
Gordon R. Lewis
Robert J. Chovanec
Peter L. Gustafson
Roger H. Oetting
J. A. Cragwall, Jr.
Stephen R. Kretschman
W. Michael Van Haren
Richard A. Durell
Michael L. Robinson
Eugene E. Smary
Douglas E. Wagner
Robert W. Sikkel (Muskegon and Holland Offices)
Thomas H. Thornhill (Resident at Muskegon Office)
Jeffrey O. Birkhold
Timothy Hillegonds
Blake W. Krueger
John G. Cameron, Jr.
John H. McKendry, Jr. (Resident at Muskegon Office)
Paul T. Sorensen
Carl W. Dufendach
Stephen C. Waterbury
Rodney D. Martin
Richard E. Cassard
Alex J. DeYonker
Charles E. Burpee
John D. Dunn
William W. Hall
Bruce C. Young
Shane B. Hansen
F. William McKee
Louis C. Rabaut
Paul R. Jackson (Resident at Muskegon Office)
Douglas A. Dozeman
John V. Byl
Janet Percy Knaus
Kathleen M. Hanenburg
Tracy T. Larsen
Sue O. Conway
Steven R. Heacock
Cameron S. DeLong
Jeffrey B. Power
Scott D. Hubbard
Stephen B. Grow
Richard L. Bouma
Daniel R. Gravelyn
Robert J. Jonker
Devin S. Schindler
Michael H. Schubert (Resident at Muskegon Office)

(See Next Column)

ASSOCIATES

Valerie Pierre Simmons
James Moskal
Robert J. Buchanan
Mark K. Harder (Resident at Holland Office)
Kenneth W. Vermeulen
Mark E. Brouwer
Mark R. Lange
Jeffrey S. Battershall
Jeffrey A. Ott
Eric S. Richards
Martha Walters Atwater
Rodrick W. Lewis
Kevin G. Dougherty
Scott J. Gorsline
Melvin G. Moseley, Jr.
James J. Rabaut
James P. Enright
Timothy L. Horner
Richard D. Cornell, Jr. (Resident at Muskegon Office)
R. Paul Guerre
Loren M. Andrulis
Karen J. Vanderwerff
Susan Gell Meyers
Gordon J. Toering
Frank E. Berrodin (Resident at Muskegon Office)
Steven A. Palazzolo (Resident at Muskegon Office)
Norbert F. Kugele
Eric D. Stubenvoll
Shaun M. Murphy
Kevin P. McDowell (Resident at Holland Office)
Mark J. Wassink
Richard J. Suhrheinrich
David Paul Trummel
Dennis J. Donohue
Michael I. Kleaveland (Resident at Muskegon Office)
Elizabeth M. Topliffe
Susan N. McFee
Julie H. Sullivan
Molly E. McFarlane
William P. Dani
Andrew D. Hakken
Andrea J. Bernard
Brian S. Felton
Lori L. Gibson
Mark T. Ostrowski
Michael P. Lunt

General Counsel for: Bissell Inc.; Blodgett Memorial Medical Center; Guardsman Products, Inc.; Haworth, Inc.; Kysor Industrial Corp.; Michigan Bankers Assn.; Old Kent Financial Corp.; Steelcase Inc.; Wolverine World Wide, Inc.

For full biographical listings, see the Martindale-Hubbell Law Directory

WHEELER UPHAM, A PROFESSIONAL CORPORATION (AV)

Second Floor, Trust Building, 40 Pearl Street, N.W., 49503
Telephone: 616-459-7100
Fax: 616-459-6366

Gordon B. Wheeler (1904-1986)
Buford A. Upham (Retired)
Robert H. Gillette
Geoffrey L. Gillis
John M. Roels
Gary A. Maximiuk
Timothy J. Orlebeke
Kenneth E. Tiews
Jack L. Hoffman
Janet C. Baxter
Peter Kladder, III
James M. Shade
Thomas A. Kuiper

Counsel for: Travelers Insurance Co.; Prudential Insurance Co. of America; Farmers Insurance Group; Metropolitan Life Insurance Co.; Conrail Trans.; Monsanto Co.; Firestone Tire & Rubber Co.; Navistar, Inc.; Medtronic, Inc.; Westdale Better Homes and Gardens.

For full biographical listings, see the Martindale-Hubbell Law Directory

GROSSE POINTE, Wayne Co.

DOLD, SPATH & MCKELVIE, P.C. (AV)

17190 Denver Avenue, P.O. Box 36786, 48236-0786
Telephone: 313-886-7500
Fax: 313-886-7505
Troy, Michigan Office: 5445 Corporate Drive, Suite 170.
Telephone: 313-952-5100.
Fax: 313-952-5138.

Douglas H. Dold

Elisabeth Hessheimer Gregory

Representative Clients: New Bright Industries; U.S. Chemical Co.; Ford Motor Co.; Dinverno Waste Disposal; Allpoints Warehousing Corp.; Atlantic Mutual Insurance Co.; Conquest Construction Co.; General Motors Corp.; Triad Financial, Inc.; U.S. Maintenance Corp.

For full biographical listings, see the Martindale-Hubbell Law Directory

GROSSE POINTE FARMS, Wayne Co.

BUTZEL LONG, A PROFESSIONAL CORPORATION (AV)

Suite 260, 21 Kercheval Avenue, 48236-3695
Telephone: 313-886-5446
Telecopier: 313-886-2114
Detroit, Michigan Office: Suite 900, 150 West Jefferson.
Telephone: 313-225-7000.
Telecopier: 313-225-7080.
Birmingham, Michigan Office: Suite 200, 32270 Telegraph Road.
Telephone: 810-258-1616.
Telecopier: 810-258-1439.
Lansing, Michigan Office: 118 West Ottawa Street.
Telephone: 517-372-6622.
Telecopier: 517-372-6672.
Ann Arbor, Michigan Office: Suite 400, 121 West Washington.
Telephone: 313-995-3110.
Telecopier: 313-995-1777.

(See Next Column)

BUTZEL LONG A PROFESSIONAL CORPORATION—*Continued*

Douglas G. Graham
George H. Zinn, Jr.
Mark S. Smallwood
David W. Sommerfeld
Carl Rashid, Jr.

OF COUNSEL

David M. Gaskin
William A. Penner, Jr.

For full biographical listings, see the Martindale-Hubbell Law Directory

*HART,** Oceana Co. — (Refer to Ludington)

*HILLSDALE,** Hillsdale Co.

PARKER, HAYES & LOVINGER, P.C. (AV)

14-16 South Howell Street, P.O. Box 358, 49242
Telephone: 517-437-7210
Fax: 517-437-0260

James B. Parker
Lawrence L. Hayes, Jr.
John P. Lovinger

Representative Clients: Hillsdale County National Bank; Village of Jonesville; Ann Arbor Associates; Hillsdale & Branch Counties (Labor Counsel); Hillsdale College; Powell Petroleum Co.; Foulke Construction Co.; Helton & Associates; Somerset Township; Hillsdale Tool & Mfg. Co.

For full biographical listings, see the Martindale-Hubbell Law Directory

HOLLAND, Ottawa Co.

CUNNINGHAM DALMAN, P.C. (AV)

321 Settlers Road, P.O. Box 1767, 49422-1767
Telephone: 616-392-1821
Fax: 616-392-4769

Gordon H. Cunningham
Ronald L. Dalman
Max R. Murphy
James A. Bidol
Andrew J. Mulder
Joel G. Bouwens
Kenneth B. Breese
Jeffrey K. Helder
Ronald J. Vander Veen
David M. Zessin
Mark H. Zietlow
James W. Bouwens
Randall S. Schipper

Peter A. Handy
Susan E. Vroegop
Melinda M. Abney

OF COUNSEL

Vernon D. Ten Cate
Kenneth B. Peirce, Jr.

Representative Clients: FMB-First Michigan Bank; First of America Bank-Holland; Ottawa Savings & Loan, F.A.; City of Holland; Detroit Auto Inter-Insurance Exchange (AAA); American States Insurance Co.; Economic Development Corp.; Hope College; Western Theological Seminary.
Reference: FMB-First Michigan Bank.

For full biographical listings, see the Martindale-Hubbell Law Directory

WARNER, NORCROSS & JUDD (AV)

Curtis Center, Suite 300, 170 College Avenue, 49423-2920
Telephone: 616-396-9800
Fax: 616-396-3656
Grand Rapids, Michigan Office: 900 Old Kent Building, 111 Lyon Street, N.W.
Telephone: 616-752-2000.
Fax: 616-752-2500.
Muskegon, Michigan Office: 400 Terrace Plaza, P.O. Box 900.
Telephone: 616-727-2600.
Fax: 616-727-2699.

MEMBERS OF FIRM

John R. Marquis (Resident)
Robert W. Sikkel

ASSOCIATES

Mark K. Harder (Resident)
Kevin P. McDowell (Resident)

General Counsel for: Atmosphere Processing, Inc.; Dew-El Corp.; Draw Form, Inc.; First of America Bank-Holland; Holland Community Hospital; Howard Miller Clock Co.; J.B. Laboratories, Inc.; Lamb, Inc.; Lumir Corp.; Manpower Temporary Services.

For full biographical listings, see the Martindale-Hubbell Law Directory

*HOUGHTON,** Houghton Co.

VAIRO, MECHLIN, TOMASI, JOHNSON & MANCHESTER (AV)

400 East Houghton Street, 49931
Telephone: 906-482-0770
Fax: 906-482-2938
Calumet, Michigan Office: 200 5th Street.
Telephone: 906-337-0312.

MEMBERS OF FIRM

Gerald G. Vairo
David R. Mechlin
Paul J. Tomasi
Frederick N. Johnson
Jeryl A. Manchester

(See Next Column)

Michael J. Mannisto

Representative Clients: Accident Fund of Michigan; Auto Club Insurance Association; Auto Owners Insurance Co.; Citizens Insurance Company of America; Fireman's Fund Insurance Co.; First of America Bank; Hartford Group; Michigan Technological University; South Range State Bank; Upper Peninsula Power Co.

For full biographical listings, see the Martindale-Hubbell Law Directory

*HOWELL,** Livingston Co.

PAUL L. DECOCQ (AV)

408 West Grand River Avenue, 48843
Telephone: 517-546-6620
Fax: 517-546-0330

For full biographical listings, see the Martindale-Hubbell Law Directory

PETER B. VAN WINKLE, P.C. (AV)

105 East Grand River, 48843
Telephone: 517-546-2680

William P. Van Winkle (1858-1920)
Don W. Van Winkle (1887-1971)
Charles K. Van Winkle (Retired)
Peter B. Van Winkle

Reference: First National Bank in Howell, Howell, Mich.

For full biographical listings, see the Martindale-Hubbell Law Directory

*IONIA,** Ionia Co. — (Refer to Grand Rapids)

IRA, St. Clair Co. — (Refer to Ishpeming)

*IRON MOUNTAIN,** Dickinson Co. — (Refer to Ishpeming)

*ITHACA,** Gratiot Co. — (Refer to Alma)

*JACKSON,** Jackson Co.

BULLEN, MOILANEN, KLAASEN & SWAN, P.C. (AV)

402 South Brown Street, 49203
Telephone: 517-788-8500
Fax: 517-788-8507

Lawrence L. Bullen
Philip M. Moilanen
Terry J. Klaasen
David W. Swan

Robert M. Gordon

OF COUNSEL

T. Harrison Stanton
J. Adrian Rosenburg (1896-1983)
Frank C. Painter (1905-1976)

Counsel for: Comerica Bank-Jackson; C.N.A. Insurance Group; Employers of Wausau Insurance Co.
General Counsel For: Decker Manufacturing Corp., Albion; Weatherwax Investment Co.; Dawlen Corp.; Photo Marketing Association International.
Local Counsel For: Marathon Oil Co.; Sears Roebuck & Co.; Montgomery Ward.

For full biographical listings, see the Martindale-Hubbell Law Directory

POTTER & HAMILTON (AV)

404 South Jackson Street, P.O. Box 764, 49204
Telephone: 517-788-6290
Fax: 517-784-7188

George E. Potter
Janet L. Hamilton

ASSOCIATES

Frederick Girodat, II

Reference: City Bank & Trust Company, N.A.

For full biographical listings, see the Martindale-Hubbell Law Directory

*KALAMAZOO,** Kalamazoo Co.

DEMING, HUGHEY, LEWIS, ALLEN & CHAPMAN, P.C. (AV)

800 Old Kent Bank Building, 49007
Telephone: 616-349-6601
Fax: 616-349-3831

Ned W. Deming
Richard M. Hughey
Dean S. Lewis
W. Fred Allen, Jr.
Ross E. Chapman
Winfield J. Hollander
John A. Scott
Bruce W. Martin (Resident)
Daniel L. Conklin
William A. Redmond
Stephen M. Denenfeld
Thomas C. Richardson
Gregory G. St. Arnauld
Roger G. Allen (Retired)
Anne McGregor Fries
Amy J. Glass
Richard M. Hughey, Jr.
Richard J. Bosch
Thomas P. Lewis
Christopher T. Haenicke

(See Next Column)

DEMING, HUGHEY, LEWIS, ALLEN & CHAPMAN P.C., *Kalamazoo—Continued*

LEGAL SUPPORT PERSONNEL

Dorothy B. Kelly

General Counsel for: The Old Kent Bank of Kalamazoo; Gilmore Brothers, Inc.; Root Spring Scraper Co.; Kalamazoo County Road Commission; Loftenberg Educational Scholarship Trust; Farm Credit Services of West Michigan; Irving S. Gilmore Foundation; National Meals on Wheels Foundation; Irving S. Gilmore International Keyboard Festival.

For full biographical listings, see the Martindale-Hubbell Law Directory

EARLY, LENNON, PETERS & CROCKER, P.C. (AV)

900 Comerica Building, 49007-4752
Telephone: 616-381-8844
Fax: 616-349-8525

George H. Lennon, III
John T. Peters, Jr.
David G. Crocker
Harold E. Fischer, Jr.
James E. Beck
Lawrence M. Brenton
Gordon C. Miller
Blake D. Crocker
Robert M. Taylor
Corenn I. Wright
Patrick D. Crocker
Andrew J. Vorbrich

OF COUNSEL

Vincent T. Early
C. H. Mullen
Thompson Bennett

Attorneys for: General Motors Corp.; Wal-Mart Stores; Borgess Medical Center; Aetna Insurance: Kemper Group; Medical Protective Co.; Zurich Insurance; AAA; Liberty Mutual; Home Insurance.

For full biographical listings, see the Martindale-Hubbell Law Directory

HOWARD & HOWARD ATTORNEYS, P.C. (AV)

The Kalamazoo Building, Suite 400, 107 West Michigan Avenue, 49007-3956
Telephone: 616-382-1483
Telecopier: 616-382-1568
Bloomfield Hills, Michigan Office: The Pinehurst Office Center, Suite 101, 1400 North Woodward Avenue.
Telephone: 810-645-1483.
Telecopier: 810-645-1568.
Lansing, Michigan Office: The Phoenix Building, Suite 500, 222 Washington Square North.
Telephone: 517-485-1483.
Telecopier: 517-485-1568.
Peoria, Illinois Office: Howard & Howard, P.C., The Creve Coeur Building, Suite 200, 321 Liberty Street.
Telephone: 309-672-1483.
Telecopier: 309-672-1568.

John W. Allen
Gerry Bartlett-McMahon
Robert C. Beck
Eric E. Breisach
Jeffrey P. Chalmers
Michael L. Chojnowski
William A. Dornbos
Richard D. Fries
James H. Geary
Edgar G. Gordon
Bruce R. Grubb
Richard L. Halpert
Joseph B. Hemker
David L. Holmes
John C. Howard
J. Michael Kemp
James H. Koning
Peter J. Livingston
D. Craig Martin
Lawrence J. Murphy
Charles C.S. Park
David E. Riggs
Bonnie Y. Sawusch
Shamra M. Van Wagoner
Steven H. Weston
Myra L. Willis
Thomas J. Wuori

Representative Clients: First of America Bank Corp.; Simpson Paper Company; W.R. Grace & Co.; Stryker Corp.; Kalamazoo Valley Community College.
Local Counsel for: Chrysler Motors Corp.
International Counsel for: Sony Corp.

For full biographical listings, see the Martindale-Hubbell Law Directory

KREIS, ENDERLE, CALLANDER & HUDGINS, A PROFESSIONAL CORPORATION (AV)

One Moorsbridge, 49002
Telephone: 616-324-3000
Telecopier: 616-324-3010

Thomas L. Combs (1932-1976)
Robert A. Palmer (1918-1984)
Russell A. Kreis
Alan G. Enderle
Douglas L. Callander
C. Reid Hudgins III
Robert B. Borsos
Jeffrey C. O'Brien
Stephen J. Hessen
Jeffery S. Rubel
Thomas G. King
Daniel P. Mc Glinn
Raymond C. Schultz
Jeffrey D. Swenarton
John F. Koryto
Julie A. Sullivan

For full biographical listings, see the Martindale-Hubbell Law Directory

LILLY & LILLY, P.C. (AV)

505 South Park Street, 49007
Telephone: 616-381-7763
Fax: 616-344-6880

Charles M. Lilly (1990-1903)
Terrence J. Lilly

For full biographical listings, see the Martindale-Hubbell Law Directory

MILLER, CANFIELD, PADDOCK AND STONE, P.L.C. (AV)

A Professional Limited Liability Company
Founded in 1852 by Sidney Davy Miller
444 West Michigan Avenue, 49007-3752
Telephone: 616-381-7030
Fax: 616-382-0244
Detroit, Michigan Office: 150 West Jefferson, Suite 2500, 48226-4415.
Telephone: 313-963-6420.
Fax: 313-496-7500.
Cable Address: "Stem Detroit."
Ann Arbor, Michigan Office: 101 North Main Street, 7th Floor, 48104-1400.
Telephone: 313-663-2445.
Fax: 313-747-7147.
Bloomfield Hills, Michigan Office: Suite 100, Pinehurst Office Center, 1400 North Woodward, 48303-2014.
Telephone: 313-645-5000.
Fax: 313-645-1917.
Grand Rapids, Michigan Office: 1200 Campau Square Plaza, 99 Monroe, N.W., 49503-2639.
Telephone: 616-454-8656.
Fax: 616-776-6322.
Howell, Michigan Office: 121 South Barnard Street, Suite 4, 48843-2305.
Telephone: 517-546-7600.
Telecopier: 517-546-6974.
Lansing, Michigan Office: One Michigan Avenue, Suite 900, 48933-1609.
Telephone: 517-487-2070.
Fax: 517-374-6304.
Monroe, Michigan Office: The Executive Centre, 214 East Elm Avenue, 48161-2682.
Telephone: 313-243-2000.
Fax: 313-243-0901.
Washington, D.C. Office: 1225 Nineteenth Street, N.W., Suite 400. 20036.
Telephone: 202-429-5575; 785-0600.
Fax: 202-331-1118; 785-1234.
Pensacola, Florida Office: 25 West Cedar, 32501.
Telephone: 904-469-1088.
Fax: 904-432-0677.
St. Petersburg, Florida Office: 100 Second Avenue S., Suite 7045,33701.
Telephone: 813-982-6000.
Fax: 813-892-6002.
Gdansk, Poland Office: Suite 322, Dom Technika Building, Ul. Rajska 6, 80-850.
Telephone: 011-485-831-2808.
Fax: 011-485-831-4719.
Warsaw, Poland Office: Ul. Marszalkowska 82, Suite 561, 00-517.
Telephone: 011-482-623-6457 and 6458.
Fax: 011-482-623-6459.

MEMBERS OF FIRM

Eric V. Brown, Jr. (Resident)
Charles E. Ritter (Resident)
John A. Campbell (Resident)
Thomas P. Hustoles (Resident)
John R. Cook (Resident)
James G. Vantine, Jr. (Resident)
Kevin M. McCarthy (Resident)
Ronald E. Baylor (Resident)
Charles S. Mishkind (Grand Rapids, Detroit and Lansing Offices)
Thomas H. Van Dis (Resident)
James E. Spurr (Resident)
Steven M. Stankewicz (Resident)
Vernon Bennett III (Resident)
Pamela Chapman Enslen (Resident)

RESIDENT OF COUNSEL

Eric V. Brown, Sr.
Gerard Thomas

RESIDENT SENIOR ATTORNEYS

Leo P. Goddeyne
Don M. Schmidt

RESIDENT ASSOCIATES

Kurt N. Sherwood
Ballard Jay Yelton, III
Lori L. Purkey
Louise B. Wright
Karen M. Hassevoort

Representative Firm Clients: Chrysler Corp.; Comerica, Inc.; City of Detroit, Mich.; Detroit Tigers, Inc.; First of Michigan; Fretter, Inc.; Ford Motor Co.; Ford Motor Credit Co.; Great Lakes Bancorp; Henry Ford Hospital.

For full biographical listings, see the Martindale-Hubbell Law Directory

VARNUM, RIDDERING, SCHMIDT & HOWLETT (AV)

350 East Michigan Avenue, 49007
Telephone: 616-382-2300
Facsimile: 616-382-2382
Grand Rapids, Michigan Office: Bridgewater Place, P.O. Box 352, 49501-0352.
Telephone: 616-336-6000; 800-262-0011.
Facsimile: 616-336-7000.
Telex: 1561593 VARN.

(See Next Column)

VARNUM, RIDDERING, SCHMIDT & HOWLETT—*Continued*

Lansing, Michigan Office: The Victor Center, Suite 810, 210 North Washington Square, 48933.
Telephone: 517-482-6237.
Facsimile: 517-482-6937.
Grand Haven, Michigan Office: 321 Washington Street, P.O. Box 288.
Telephone: 616-846-7100.
Facsimile: 616-846-7101.
Battle Creek, Michigan Office: 4950 West Dickman Road, Suite B-1, 49015.
Telephone: 616-962-7144.
Detroit, Michigan Office: 440 East Congress, Fourth Floor, 48226.
Telephone: 313-961-1600.
Facsimile: 313-961-1636.

COUNSEL

Peter Visserman

MEMBERS OF FIRM

Thomas T. Huff (Resident) — Jeffrey D. Smith (Resident)
Richard A. Hooker (Resident) — Robert A. Hendricks
Michael S. McElwee (Resident)

ASSOCIATES

Eric J. Guerin

Counsel For: AgriStor Credit Corp.; ASMO Manufacturing (Japan); Armstrong International; Arvco Container Corp.; Bond Supply Co.; Bowers Manufacturing Co.; Channel 41, Inc.; Comerica Bank-Kalamazoo; Getman Corp.; Michigan National Bank.

For full biographical listings, see the Martindale-Hubbell Law Directory

LANSING, Ingham Co.

* indicates certain Bar Register subscribers whose principal office is located elsewhere in the state and who have arranged for representation as a part of the state capital listings that follow

BUTZEL LONG, A PROFESSIONAL CORPORATION (AV)

118 West Ottawa Street, 48933
Telephone: 517-372-6622
Telecopier: 517-372-6672
Detroit, Michigan Office: Suite 900, 150 West Jefferson.
Telephone: 313-225-7000.
Telecopier: 313-225-7080.
Birmingham, Michigan Office: Suite 200, 32270 Telegraph Road.
Telephone: 810-258-1616.
Telecopier: 810-258-1439.
Ann Arbor, Michigan Office: Suite 400, 121 West Washington.
Telephone: 313-995-3110.
Telecopier: 313-995-1777.
Grosse Pointe Farms, Michigan Office: Suite 260, 21 Kercheval.
Telephone: 313-886-5446.
Telecopier: 313-886-2114.

William R. Ralls (Resident) — Brian P. Henry

James J. Urban (Resident) — Leland R. Rosier (Resident)
Wendel Vincent Hall (Resident)

For full biographical listings, see the Martindale-Hubbell Law Directory

DENFIELD, TIMMER, JAMO & O'LEARY (AV)

521 Seymour Avenue, 48933
Telephone: 517-371-3500
Fax: 517-371-4514

George H. Denfield — James S. Jamo
James A. Timmer — James S. O'Leary
Kathleen A. Lopilato

Representative Clients: Auto-Owners Insurance Co.; National Indemnity Insurance Co.; Travelers Insurance Co.; Ohio Farmers Insurance Co.; Bankers Life & Casualty Co.; Western Casualty & Surety Co.; Indiana Insurance Group; Western Surety Co.; Michigan Municipal League; Preston Trucking.

For full biographical listings, see the Martindale-Hubbell Law Directory

*** DICKINSON, WRIGHT, MOON, VAN DUSEN & FREEMAN (AV)**

Suite 200, 215 South Washington Square, 48933-1816
Telephone: 517-371-1730
Facsimile: 517-487-4700
Detroit, Michigan Office: 500 Woodward Avenue, Suite 4000.
Telephone: 313-223-3500.
Facsimile: 313-223-3598.
Bloomfield Hills, Michigan Office: 525 North Woodward Avenue, Suite 2000.
Telephone: 810-433-7200.
Facsimile: 810-433-7274.
Grand Rapids, Michigan Office: 200 Ottawa Avenue, N.W., Suite 900.
Telephone: 616-458-1300. Facsimile 616-458-6753.
Washington, D.C. Office: Suite 800, 1901 L Street, N.W.
Telephone: 202-457-0160.
Facsimile: 202-659-1559.

(See Next Column)

Chicago, Illinois Office: 225 West Washington, Suite 400.
Telephone: 312-220-0300.
Facsimile: 312-220-0021.
Warsaw, Poland Office: 46 Wilcza Street, 4th Floor, 00-679.
Telephone: (48-22) 299-241.
Facsimile: (48-2) 628-4107. Komertel Satellite Phone: (48-39) 121-510.

RESIDENT PARTNERS

Judson Werbelow — Kester K. So
Peter S. Sheldon — Dwight D. Ebaugh
Joseph A. Fink — Kenneth T. Brooks
James W. Bliss — Jeffery V. Stuckey
Gregory L. McClelland — Gail A. Anderson
Peter H. Ellsworth — Andrea Andrews Larkin
David E. Pierson

RESIDENT OF COUNSEL

Mitchell J. Rapp

RESIDENT ASSOCIATES

William R. Beekman — Melissa A. Hagen
William C. Bertrand, Jr. — Deborah A. Lee
Kim D. Crooks — Mark A. McDowell
James P. Evans — Richard D. McNulty
Kirk E. Grable — Delmas A. Szura
Jeffrey E. Thompson

Representative Clients: Federal-Mogul Corp.; Florists' Transworld Delivery Assn.; GMF Robotics Corp.; Kmart Corp.; Kuhlman Corp.; Michigan Consolidated Gas Co.; NBD Bank, N.A.

For full biographical listings, see the Martindale-Hubbell Law Directory

DUNNINGS & FRAWLEY, P.C. (AV)

Duncan Building, 530 South Pine Street, 48933-2299
Telephone: 517-487-8222
Fax: 517-487-2026

Stuart J. Dunnings, Jr. — John J. Frawley

Stuart J. Dunnings, III — Steven D. Dunnings

Representative Clients: Lansing Board of Education; Lansing Housing Commission; Ford Motor Co.
References: First of America; Michigan National Bank.

For full biographical listings, see the Martindale-Hubbell Law Directory

*** DYKEMA GOSSETT (AV)**

800 Michigan National Tower, 48933-1707
Telephone: 517-374-9100
Telex: 23-0121
Fax: 517-374-9191
Detroit, Michigan Office: 400 Renaissance Center, 48243-1668.
Telephone: 313-568-6800.
Fax: 313-568-6594.
Ann Arbor, Michigan Office: 315 East Eisenhower Parkway, Suite 100, 49108-3306.
Telephone: 313-747-7660.
Fax: 313-747-7696.
Bloomfield Hills, Michigan Office: 1577 North Woodward Avenue, Suite 300, 48304-2820.
Telephone: 810-540-0700.
Fax: 810-540-0763.
Grand Rapids, Michigan Office: 200 Oldtown Riverfront Building, 248 Louis Campau Promenade, N.W., 49503-2668.
Telephone: 616-776-7500.
Fax: 616-776-7573.
Washington, D.C. Office: Franklin Square, Suite 300 West Tower, 1300 I Street, N.W., 20005-3306.
Telephone: 202-522-8600.
Fax: 202-522-8669.
Chicago, Illinois Office: Three First National Plaza, Suite 1400, 70 W. Madison, 60602-4270.
Telephone: 312-214-3380.
Fax: 312-214-3441.

RESIDENT MEMBERS

Richard D. McLellan — Albert Ernst
John B. Curcio — William J. Perrone
Alan R. Dominick — Brad S. Rutledge
Stephen H. Zimmerman — James P. Kiefer
Lori M. Silsbury

RESIDENT ASSOCIATES

Michael J. Brown — Julia A. Goatley Moreno
Ann D. Fillingham — Gina M. Torielli
Sandra Miller Cotter — Leonard C. Wolfe

For full biographical listings, see the Martindale-Hubbell Law Directory

Lansing—Continued

FOSTER, SWIFT, COLLINS & SMITH, P.C. (AV)

313 South Washington Square, 48933-2193
Telephone: 517-371-8100
Telecopier: 517-371-8200
Farmington Hills, Michigan Office: 32300 Northwestern Highway, Suite 230.
Telephone: 810-851-7500.
Fax: 810-851-7504.

Walter S. Foster (1877-1961)
Richard B. Foster
Lawrence B. Lindemer
Thomas G. McGurrin, Jr.
Theodore W. Swift
John L. Collins
Webb A. Smith
Allan J. Claypool
Gary J. McRay
Robert J. McCullen
David VanderHaagen
Stephen I. Jurmu
William K. Fahey
Stephen O. Schultz
William R. Schulz
David H. Aldrich
Scott A. Storey
Charles A. Janssen
Charles E. Barbieri
James B. Jensen, Jr.
Scott L. Mandel
Robert E. McFarland (Resident, Farmington Hills Office)
Kathryn M. Niemer (Resident, Farmington Hills Office)
James B. Croom
Michael D. Sanders
David J. Houston
Brian A. Kaser
Steven L. Owen
Sherry A. Stein
Brent A. Titus
Stephen J. Lowney
Frank A. Fleischmann
Louis K. Nigg
Glen A. Schmiege
Patricia A. Calore
Kevin T. McGraw
Michael J. Bommarito
Deanna Swisher
Jean G. Schtokal
Mark H. Canady
Eric E. Doster
Michael W. Puerner
Stephen J. Rhodes
Matt G. Hrebec
Brian G. Goodenough
Robert L. Knechtel
Melissa J. Jackson
Mark J. Burzych
Thomas R. Meagher
Douglas A. Mielock
Scott R. Forbush
Peter R. Albertins
Scott A. Chernich
Lisa E. Claypool
Todd A. Smith
Matthew W. Collins
Nina McMenamin (Not admitted in MI)

OF COUNSEL

Steven H. Lasher

LEGAL SUPPORT PERSONNEL

LEGAL ASSISTANTS

Laurie A. Delaney
Sandra L. De Santis
Julie M. Hill
Kelly A. LaGrave
Nancy O'Shea
Jeanne M. Phillips
Constance G. Powis
Lisa J. Silverthorn
Theresa G. Solberg
Janice Underwood
Jaxine L. Wintjen

General Counsel for: First American Bank-Central; Story, Inc.; Michigan Milk Producers Assn.; Edward W. Sparrow Hospital; St. Lawrence Hospital; Demmer Corp.; Michigan Financial Corp.
Local Counsel for: Shell Oil Co.; Michigan-Mutual Insurance Co.; Century Cellunet.

For full biographical listings, see the Martindale-Hubbell Law Directory

FRASER TREBILCOCK DAVIS & FOSTER, P.C. (AV)

1000 Michigan National Tower, 48933
Telephone: 517-482-5800
Fax: 517-482-0887
Okemos, Michigan Office: 2188 Commons Parkway.
Telephone: 517-349-1300.
Fax: 517-349-0922.

Joe C. Foster, Jr.
Eugene Townsend (1926-1982)
Ronald R. Pentecost
Donald A. Hines
Peter L. Dunlap
Everett R. Zack
Douglas J. Austin
Robert W. Stocker, II
Michael E. Cavanaugh
John J. Loose
David E. S. Marvin
Stephen L. Burlingame
C. Mark Hoover
Darrell A. Lindman
Ronald R. Sutton
Iris K. Socolofsky-Linder
Brett Jon Bean
Richard C. Lowe
Gary C. Rogers
Mark A. Bush
Michael H. Perry
Brandon W. Zuk
David D. Waddell
Thomas J. Waters

John E. Bos
Michael C. Levine
Mark R. Fox
Nancy L. Little
Sharon A. Bruner
Michael S. Ashton
Michael James Reilly
Michelyn E. Pastuer
Patrick K. Thornton
Charyn K. Hain
Brian D. Herrington
Michael J. Laramie
Marcy R. Meyer

(See Next Column)

OF COUNSEL

Archie C. Fraser
Everett R. Trebilcock
James R. Davis

Counsel for: Auto Club Insurance Assn. (ACIA); Auto Owners Insurance Co.; City of Mackinac Island; Federal Insurance Co.; General Motors Corp.; Grand Trunk Ry. Co.; Prudential Insurance Company of America; State Farm Automobile Insurance Co.

For full biographical listings, see the Martindale-Hubbell Law Directory

* HONIGMAN MILLER SCHWARTZ AND COHN (AV)

A Partnership including Professional Corporations
222 North Washington Square, Suite 400, 48933
Telephone: 517-484-8282
Telecopier: 517-484-8286
Detroit, Michigan Office: 2290 First National Building.
Telephone: 313-256-7800.
West Palm Beach, Florida Office: Suite 800 Esperante Building, 222 Lakeview Avenue.
Telephone: 407-838-4500.
Tampa, Florida Office: Suite 350 One Harbour Place, 777 South Harbour Island Boulevard.
Telephone: 813-221-6600.
Orlando, Florida Office: 390 North Orange Avenue, Suite 1300.
Telephone: 407-648-0300.
Houston, Texas Office: 3100 First Interstate Bank Plaza, 1000 Louisiana.
Telephone: 713-650-2600.
Los Angeles, California Office: McNeill Plaza, Suite 820, 15260 Ventura Boulevard, 91403.
Telephone: 818-784-2900.

MEMBERS

Richard J. Aaron
Frederick M. Baker, Jr.
Daniel J. Demlow
Sandra L. Jasinski
Timothy Sawyer Knowlton
Mark Morton
John D. Pirich
Benjamin O. Schwendener, Jr.
Gary A. Trepod
Alan M. Valade
William C. Whitbeck
Ruth E. Zimmerman

ASSOCIATES

Ann L. Andrews
Andrea Hansen
John S. Kane

General Counsel for: Dart Container Corp; Forbes-Cohen Properties (The Lansing Mall); Granger Land Development Co.; Michigan Hospital Association.
Legal or Special Counsel for: Champion International; Greater Detroit Resource Recovery Authority; First American Title Insurance Company of the Midwest; Indiana Michigan Power Co.

For full biographical listings, see the Martindale-Hubbell Law Directory

HOWARD & HOWARD ATTORNEYS, P.C. (AV)

The Phoenix Building, Suite 500, 222 Washington Square, North, 48933-1817
Telephone: 517-485-1483
Telecopier: 517-485-1568
Kalamazoo, Michigan Office: The Kalamazoo Building, Suite 400, 107 West Michigan Avenue.
Telephone: 616-382-1483.
Telecopier: 616-382-1568.
Bloomfield Hills, Michigan Office: The Pinehurst Office Center, Suite 101, 1400 North Woodward Avenue.
Telephone: 810-645-1483.
Telecopier: 810-645-1568.
Peoria, Illinois Office: Howard & Howard, P.C., The Creve Coeur Building, Suite 200, 321 Liberty Street.
Telephone: 309-672-1483.
Telecopier: 309-672-1568.

Todd D. Chamberlain
Chistopher C. Cinnamon
David C. Coey
Matthew J. Coffey
Thomas L. Cooper
Michele LaForest Halloran
Patrick D. Hanes
Ellen M. Harvath
J. Michael Kemp
James E. Lozier
D. Craig Martin
C. Douglas Moran
Donald F. Tucker
Patrick R. Van Tiflin

Representative Clients: First of America Bank Corporation; W.R. Grace & Co.; Chrysler Corp.; Indian Head Industries; Cooper & Lybrand; United Technologies.
Local Counsel for: General Motors Corp.; American Cyanamid Co.

For full biographical listings, see the Martindale-Hubbell Law Directory

KITCH, DRUTCHAS, WAGNER & KENNEY, P.C. (AV)

One Michigan Avenue, 120 Washington Square, North, Suite 805, 48933-1609
Telephone: 517-372-6430
Fax: 517-372-0441
Detroit, Michigan Office: One Woodward, Tenth Floor, 48226-3412.
Telephone: 313-965-7900.
Fax: 313-965-7403.

(See Next Column)

KITCH, DRUTCHAS, WAGNER & KENNEY P.C.—*Continued*

Macomb County Office: Towne Square Development, 10 South Main Street, Suite 301, Mount Clemens, 48043-7903.
Telephone: 810-463-9770.
Fax: 810-463-8994.
Toledo, Ohio Office: 405 Madison Avenue, Suite 1500, 43604-1235.
Telephone: 419-243-4006.
Fax: 419-243-7333.
Troy, Michigan Office: 3001 West Big Beaver Road, Suite 200, 48084-3103.
Telephone: 810-637-3500.
Fax: 810-637-6630.
Ann Arbor, Michigan Office: 303 Detroit Street, Suite 400, P.O. Box 8610. 48107-8610.
Telephone: 313-994-7600.
Fax: 313-994-7626.

John P. Ryan (Principal)
William Vertes (Principal)
Susan M. Ramage (Associate Principal)
Debra S. Hirsch
David A. Schoolcraft

For full biographical listings, see the Martindale-Hubbell Law Directory

LOOMIS, EWERT, EDERER, PARSLEY, DAVIS & GOTTING, P.C. (AV)

232 South Capitol Avenue, Suite 1000, 48933
Telephone: 517-482-2400
Facsimile: 517-482-0070

Plummer Snyder (1900-1974)
Rodger T. Ederer
William D. Parsley
Jack C. Davis (P.C.)
Karl L. Gotting (P.C.)
David M. Lick
Harvey J. Messing
James R. Neal
Kenneth W. Beall
Michael G. Oliva
Jeffrey W. Bracken
Catherine A. Jacobs
Ronald W. Bloomberg
Michael H. Rhodes
Howard J. Soifer
Jeffrey L. Green
Gary L. Field

Sherri A. Wellman
Kelly K. Reed
Jeffrey S. Theuer
Marc D. Matlock

OF COUNSEL

George W. Loomis (P.C.)
Quentin A. Ewert

Representative Clients: Altman Development Co.; Century Telephone Enterprises; Columbian Distribution, Inc.; Comerica Bank; Consumers Power Co.; The Douglas Company; Southeastern Michigan Gas Enterprises, Inc.; Upper Peninsula Energy Corp.; Wal-Mart Stores, Inc.; Wisconsin Electric Power Co.

For full biographical listings, see the Martindale-Hubbell Law Directory

MILLER, CANFIELD, PADDOCK AND STONE, P.L.C. (AV)

A Professional Limited Liability Company
Founded in 1852 by Sidney Davy Miller
Suite 900, One Michigan Avenue, 48933-1609
Telephone: 517-487-2070
Fax: 517-374-6304
Detroit, Michigan Office: 150 West Jefferson, Suite 2500, 48226-4415.
Telephone: 313-963-6420.
Fax: 313-496-7500.
Cable Address: "Stem Detroit."
Ann Arbor, Michigan Office: 101 North Main Street, 7th Floor, 48104-1400.
Telephone: 313-663-2445.
Fax: 313-747-7147.
Bloomfield Hills, Michigan Office: Suite 100, Pinehurst Office Center, 1400 North Woodward, 48303-2014.
Telephone: 313-645-5000.
Fax: 313-645-1917.
Grand Rapids, Michigan Office: 1200 Campau Square Plaza, 99 Monroe, N.W., 49503-2639.
Telephone: 616-454-8656.
Fax: 616-776-6322.
Howell, Michigan Office: 121 South Barnard Street, Suite 4, 48843-2305.
Telephone: 517-546-7600.
Telecopier: 517-546-6974.
Kalamazoo, Michigan Office: 444 West Michigan Avenue, 49007-3752.
Telephone: 616-381-7030.
Fax: 616-382-0244.
Monroe, Michigan Office: The Executive Centre, 214 East Elm Avenue, 48161-2682.
Telephone: 313-243-2000.
Fax: 313-243-0901.
Washington, D.C. Office: 1225 Nineteenth Street, N.W., Suite 400. 20036.
Telephone: 202-429-5575; 785-0600.
Fax: 202-331-1118; 785-1234.
Pensacola, Florida Office: 25 West Cedar, 32501.
Telephone: 904-469-1088.
Fax: 904-432-0677.

(See Next Column)

St. Petersburg Office: 100 Second Avenue S., Suite 7045, 33701.
Telephone: 813-982-6000.
Fax: 813-892-6002.
Gdansk, Poland Office: Suite 322, Dom Technika Building, Ul. Rajska 6, 80-850.
Telephone: 011-485-831-2808.
Fax: 011-485-831-4719.
Warsaw, Poland Office: Ul. Marszalkowska 82, Suite 561, 00-517.
Telephone: 011-482-623-6457 and 6458.
Fax: 011-482-623-6459.

MEMBERS OF FIRM

William J. Danhof (Resident)
Lawrence D. Owen (Resident)
Michael R. Atkins (Resident)
Thomas C. Phillips
Christopher J. Dembowski (Resident)
Michael J. Hodge (Resident)
Steven D. Weyhing (Resident)
Kevin J. Moody (Resident)
Jay B. Rising (Resident)

RESIDENT SENIOR ATTORNEY

Sherry Katz-Crank

RESIDENT ASSOCIATES

John C. Shea
Clifford T. Flood
James R. Lancaster, Jr.
Joan L. Kramlich
Dean M. Altobelli

Representative Firm Clients: Chrysler Corp.; Comerica, Inc.; City of Detroit, Mich.; Detroit Tigers, Inc.; First of Michigan; Fretter, Inc.; Ford Motor Co.; Ford Motor Credit Co.; Great Lakes Bancorp; Henry Ford Hospital.

For full biographical listings, see the Martindale-Hubbell Law Directory

STREET & GRUA (AV)

2401 East Grand River, 48912
Telephone: 517-487-8300
Fax: 517-487-8306

MEMBERS OF FIRM

Victor C. Anderson (1904-1981)
Cassius E. Street, Jr.
Remo Mark Grua

Representative Clients: Applegate Insulation Manufacturing; General Aviation, Inc.; Classic Aircraft Corp.; General White GMC; Old Kent Bank of Lansing.
References: First of America-Central; Old Kent Bank of Lansing, N.A.

For full biographical listings, see the Martindale-Hubbell Law Directory

*LAPEER,** Lapeer Co.

TAYLOR, CARTER, BUTTERFIELD, RISEMAN, CLARK AND HOWELL, P.C. (AV)

407 Clay Street, 48446
Telephone: 810-664-5921
Fax: 313-664-0904

Robert L. Taylor (1909-1992)
Carl M. Riseman
Thomas K. Butterfield
Emory W. Clark
Gary W. Howell
David J. Churchill

OF COUNSEL

Michael L. Carter

Steven D. Jarvis
Michael C. Ewing

Representative Clients: Lapeer County Bank & Trust Co.; State Mutual Insurance Co.; Kirk Construction Co.; Lapeer County & City Economic Development Corp.; Lapeer County Co-op; Lapeer Co. Abstract & Title Co.; Carl M. Schultz, Inc.; Lapeer Metal Products, Inc.; Capac State Bank.

For full biographical listings, see the Martindale-Hubbell Law Directory

*LELAND,** Leelanau Co.

MURCHIE, CALCUTT & BOYNTON

(See Traverse City)

*MANISTEE,** Manistee Co. — (Refer to Ludington)

*MANISTIQUE,** Schoolcraft Co. — (Refer to Escanaba)

*MARQUETTE,** Marquette Co.

KENDRICKS, BORDEAU, ADAMINI, KEEFE, SMITH, GIRARD AND SEAVOY, P.C. (AV)

128 West Spring Street, 49855
Telephone: 906-226-2543
Fax: 906-226-2819

(See Next Column)

KENDRICKS, BORDEAU, ADAMINI, KEEFE, SMITH, GIRARD AND SEAVOY P.C., *Marquette—Continued*

George T. Kendricks (1918-1991)
Robert M. Bordeau
Stephen F. Adamini
Ronald D. Keefe
William R. Smith
Dennis H. Girard
Kenneth J. Seavoy
Tami M. Seavoy
D. Gregor MacGregor, III
Michael J. Kolasa

For full biographical listings, see the Martindale-Hubbell Law Directory

*MARSHALL,** Calhoun Co. — (Refer to Battle Creek)

*MENOMINEE,** Menominee Co. — (Refer to Escanaba)

*MIDLAND,** Midland Co.

CURRIE & KENDALL, P.C. (AV)

6024 Eastman Avenue, P.O. Box 1846, 48641-1846
Telephone: 517-839-0300
Fax: 517-832-0077

Gilbert A. Currie (1882-1960)
James A. Kendall
William C. Collins
Thomas L. Ludington
Ramon F. Rolf, Jr.
Daniel J. Cline
Peter A. Poznak
Julia A. Close
Peter J. Kendall
Jeffrey N. Dyer

OF COUNSEL

Gilbert A. Currie
I. Frank Harlow
William D. Schuette

LEGAL SUPPORT PERSONNEL

Barbara J. Byron

Counsel for: Chemical Financial Corp.; Chemical Bank & Trust Co.; Saginaw Valley State University; Northwood University; The Midland Foundation; Elsa U. Pardee Foundation; Rollin M. Gerstacker Foundation; Charles J. Strosacker Foundation.

For full biographical listings, see the Martindale-Hubbell Law Directory

HANDLON, EASTMAN & DEWITT, P.C. (AV)

Suite 1100 Courthouse Square Building, 240 West Main Street, 48640
Telephone: 517-631-5490
Fax: 517-631-1777

Richard M. Handlon
Tad J. Eastman
David S. DeWitt

Representative Clients: Comerica Bank-Midland Co.; Household Finance; Remax, Inc.; Masco Industries, Inc.; Cherryview Development Corp.; Buckingham Computer Services, Inc.
References: Comerica Bank-Midland; Chemical Bank & Trust Co.

For full biographical listings, see the Martindale-Hubbell Law Directory

RIECKER, VAN DAM, GANNON, LOOBY & BARKER, P.C. (AV)

414 Townsend Street, P.O. Box 632, 48640
Telephone: 517-631-1025
Facsimile: 517-631-9880

John E. Riecker
Philip Van Dam
John E. Gannon
Lynn S. Looby
Richard William Barker

General Counsel for: Herbert H. and Grace A. Dow Foundation; Harry A. and Margaret D. Towsley Foundation; Midland Center for the Arts; Dow-Howell-Gilmore Associates, Inc.
Counsel for: Comerica Bank N.A.; MidMichigan Regional Health System; Wolverine Bank, F.B.S.; Midway Connection Airlines, Inc; Midland County Growth and Economic Development Corp.; Bresnan Communications, Inc.

For full biographical listings, see the Martindale-Hubbell Law Directory

*MONROE,** Monroe Co.

JAFFE, RAITT, HEUER & WEISS, PROFESSIONAL CORPORATION (AV)

212 East Front Street, Suite 3, 48161
Telephone: 313-241-6470
Telefacsimile: 313-241-3849
Detroit, Michigan Office: One Woodward Avenue, Suite 2400.
Telephone: 313-961-8380.
Telecopier: 313-961-8358.
Southfield, Michigan Office: Suite 1520, Travelers Tower.
Telephone: 313-961-8380.

Alexander B. Bragdon
John A. Hohman, Jr. (Resident)
James G. Petrangelo (Resident)
Lawrence R. Shoffner

Kerry Gross-Bondy (Resident)

Representative Clients: Berlin Township; Frenchtown Charter Township.

For full biographical listings, see the Martindale-Hubbell Law Directory

MILLER, CANFIELD, PADDOCK AND STONE, P.L.C. (AV)

A Professional Limited Liability Company
Founded in 1852 by Sidney Davy Miller
The Executive Centre, 214 East Elm Avenue, 48161-2682
Telephone: 313-243-2000
Fax: 313-243-0901
Detroit, Michigan Office: 150 West Jefferson, Suite 2500, 48226-4415.
Telephone: 313-963-6420.
Fax: 313-496-7500.
Cable Address: "Stem Detroit."
Ann Arbor, Michigan Office: 101 North Main Street, 7th Floor, 48104-1400.
Telephone: 313-663-2445.
Fax: 313-747-7147.
Bloomfield Hills, Michigan Office: Suite 100, Pinehurst Office Center, 1400 North Woodward, 48303-2014.
Telephone: 313-645-5000.
Fax: 313-645-1917.
Grand Rapids, Michigan Office: 1200 Campau Square Plaza, 99 Monroe, N.W., 49503-2639.
Telephone: 616-454-8656.
Fax: 616-776-6322.
Howell, Michigan Office: 121 South Barnard Street, Suite 4, 48843-2305.
Telephone: 517-546-7600.
Telecopier: 517-546-6974.
Kalamazoo, Michigan Office: 444 West Michigan Avenue, 49007-3752.
Telephone: 616-381-7030.
Fax: 616-382-0244.
Lansing, Michigan Office: One Michigan Avenue, Suite 900, 48933-1609.
Telephone: 517-487-2070.
Fax: 517-374-6304.
Washington, D.C. Office: 1225 Nineteenth Street, N.W., Suite 400. 20036.
Telephone: 202-429-5575; 785-0600.
Fax: 202-331-1118; 785-1234.
Pensacola, Florida Office: 25 West Cedar, 32501.
Telephone: 904-469-1088.
Fax: 904-432-0677.
St. Petersburg, Florida Office: 100 Second Avenue S., Suite 7045, 33701.
Telephone: 813-982-6000.
Fax: 813-892-6002.
Gdansk, Poland Office: Suite 322, Dom Technika Building, Ul. Rajska 6, 80-850.
Telephone: 011-485-831-2808.
Fax: 011-485-831-4719.
Warsaw, Poland Office: Ul. Marszalkowska 82, Suite 561, 00-517.
Telephone: 011-482-623-6457 and 6458.
Fax: 011-482-623-6459.

RESIDENT MEMBERS

Rocque E. Lipford (P.C.)

Representative Firm Clients: Chrysler Corp.; Comerica, Inc.; City of Detroit, Mich.; Detroit Tigers, Inc.; First of Michigan; Fretter, Inc.; Ford Motor Co.; Ford Motor Credit Co.; Great Lakes Bancorp; Henry Ford Hospital.

For full biographical listings, see the Martindale-Hubbell Law Directory

READY, SULLIVAN & READY (AV)

204 South Macomb Street, 48161
Telephone: 313-242-7600
Fax: 313-242-0366

MEMBERS OF FIRM

Thomas D. Ready
Michael L. Heller
Durward L. Hutchinson
John F. Ready

ASSOCIATES

Conly K. Crossley
Christina D. Hunt

Representative Client: Motorists Insurance Cos.

For full biographical listings, see the Martindale-Hubbell Law Directory

*MOUNT CLEMENS,** Macomb Co.

GARAN, LUCOW, MILLER, SEWARD, COOPER & BECKER, P.C. (AV)

Towne Square Development, 10 S. Main Street Suite 307, 48043-2370
Telephone: 810-954-3800
Fax: 810-954-3803
Detroit, Michigan Office: 1000 Woodbridge Place.
Telephone: 313-446-1530.
Fax: 313-259-0450.
Grand Blanc, Michigan Office: 8332 Office Park Drive.
Telephone: 810-695-3700.
Fax: 810-695-6488.
Ann Arbor, Michigan Office: 101 North Main Street, Suite 801.
Telephone: 313-930-5600.
Fax: 313-930-0043.
Troy, Michigan Office: 2301 West Big Beaver Road, Suite 212.
Telephone: 810-649-7600.
Fax: 810-649-5438.

(See Next Column)

GARAN, LUCOW, MILLER, SEWARD, COOPER & BECKER P.C.—*Continued*

Port Huron, Michigan Office: Port Huron Office Center, 511 Fort Street, Suite 505.
Telephone: 810-985-4400.
Fax: 810-985-4107.

Millard W. H. Becker, Jr. Richard E. Eaton

Timothy E. O'Neill

For full biographical listings, see the Martindale-Hubbell Law Directory

KITCH, DRUTCHAS, WAGNER & KENNEY, P.C. (AV)

Towne Square Development, 10 South Main Street, Suite 301, 48043-7903
Telephone: 810-463-9770
Fax: 810-463-8994
Detroit, Michigan Office: One Woodward, Tenth Floor, 48226-3412.
Telephone: 313-965-7900.
Fax: 313-965-7403.
Lansing, Michigan Office: 120 Washington Square, North, Suite 805, One Michigan Avenue, 48933-1609.
Telephone: 517-372-6430.
Fax: 517-372-0441.
Toledo, Ohio Office: 405 Madison Avenue, Suite 1500, 43604-1235.
Telephone: 419-243-4006.
Fax: 419-243-7333.
Troy, Michigan Office: 3001 West Big Beaver Road, Suite 200, 48084-3103.
Telephone: 810-637-3500.
Fax: 810-637-6630.
Ann Arbor, Michigan Office: 303 Detroit Street, Suite 400, P.O. Box 8610, 48107-8610.
Telephone: 313-994-7600.
Fax: 313-994-7626.

Ralph F. Valitutti, Jr. (Principal)
Steve N. Cheolas (Principal)
Robert A. Fehniger
Matthew M. Walton

For full biographical listings, see the Martindale-Hubbell Law Directory

VANDEVEER GARZIA, PROFESSIONAL CORPORATION (AV)

50 Crocker Boulevard, 48043
Telephone: 810-468-4880
Fax: 810-465-7159
Wayne County Office: Suite 1600, 333 West Fort Street, Detroit, Michigan.
Telephone: 810-961-4880.
Fax: 810-961-3822.
Oakland County Office: 220 Park Street, Suite 300, Birmingham, Michigan.
Telephone: 810-645-0100.
Fax: 810-645-2430.
Kent County Office: 555 Grand Plaza Place, 220 Lyon Square, Grand Rapids, Michigan.
Telephone: 616-366-8600.
Fax: 616-786-9095.
Holland, Michigan Office: 1121 Ottawa Beach Road, Suite 140.
Telephone: 616-399-8600.
Fax: 616-786-9095.

RESIDENT PERSONNEL

Ronald L. Cornell

Representative Clients: Aetna Casualty and Surety Co.; Chubb Insurance; Farmers Insurance Group; Goodyear Tire & Rubber Co.; Transamerica Insurance Group.

For full biographical listings, see the Martindale-Hubbell Law Directory

*MOUNT PLEASANT,** Isabella Co.

HALL AND LEWIS (AV)

300 South University Avenue, 48858
Telephone: 517-773-0004
Fax: 517-772-1512

Thomas W. Hall, Jr. John W. Lewis

Representative Clients: Blodgett Oil Co., Inc.; Clark's Manufactured Homes, Inc.; Curtice Lumber Company; DeWitt Lumber Co.; The Embers, Inc.; Exploration Enterprises, Inc.; Family Home Health Care; Fast Environmental, Inc.; Isabella Community Credit Union; Midland Area Credit Union.

For full biographical listings, see the Martindale-Hubbell Law Directory

LYNCH, GALLAGHER, LYNCH & MARTINEAU (AV)

555 North Main Street, P.O. Box 446, 48858
Telephone: 517-773-9961
Fax: 517-773-2107
Lansing, Michigan Office: 2400 Lake Lansing Road, Suite B.
Telephone: 517-485-0400.
Fax: 517-485-0402.

(See Next Column)

MEMBERS OF FIRM

Edward N. Lynch (1908-1984)
Byron P. Gallagher
John J. Lynch
Steven W. Martineau
Sue A. Jeffers
Paula K. Manis (Resident at Lansing Office)
William M. McClintic
Michael J. Hackett
Byron P. Gallagher, Jr. (Resident at Lansing Office)
Denise A. Koehler

Representative Clients: Amoco Production, Co.; Liquid Transport, Inc.; Central Concrete Products; Central Michigan University; Northern Michigan Oil and Gas Corp.

For full biographical listings, see the Martindale-Hubbell Law Directory

*MUNISING,** Alger Co. — (Refer to Marquette)

*MUSKEGON,** Muskegon Co.

CULVER, KNOWLTON, EVEN & FRANKS (AV)

250 Terrace Plaza, P.O. Box 629, 49443
Telephone: 616-724-4320
Telecopier: 616-724-4330

MEMBERS OF FIRM

Fred C. Culver, Jr.
Michael M. Knowlton
Kevin B. Even
Eugene A. Franks

Representative Clients: SPx Corporation; First of America Bank-West Michigan; Old Kent Bank of Grand Haven; Comerica Bank; East Shore Chemical Company; Muskegon County Association of Realtors; Midland Groceries.

For full biographical listings, see the Martindale-Hubbell Law Directory

LAGUE, NEWMAN & IRISH, A PROFESSIONAL CORPORATION (AV)

600 Terrace Plaza, P.O. Box 389, 49443
Telephone: 616-725-8148
Telecopier: 616-726-3404

Eric R. Gielow
Michael W. Irish
Karen L. Kayes
Anthony J. Kolenic, Jr.
Richard C. Lague
Chris Ann McGuigan
David R. Munroe
William M. Newman
Chris D. Slater
Philip M. Stoffan
J. Scott Timmer
Alvin D. Treado

General Counsel: Hackley Hospital & Medical Center; Kaydon Corp.; Cole's Quality Foods; Kudziel Industries.
Local Counsel: First of American Bank, West Michigan; Booth Newspapers, Inc.; Occidental Petroleum Corp.; SPX Corp.; Spring Manufacturers Institute, Inc.

For full biographical listings, see the Martindale-Hubbell Law Directory

PARMENTER O'TOOLE (AV)

175 West Apple Street, P.O. Box 786, 49443-0786
Telephone: 616-722-1621
Telecopier: 616-728-2206; 722-7866

MEMBERS OF FIRM

G. Thomas Johnson
George D. Van Epps
Eric J. Fauri
John M. Briggs, III
Michael L. Rolf
George W. Johnson
Robert D. Eklund
W. Brad Groom
Timothy G. Hicks
John C. Schrier
Christopher L. Kelly

ASSOCIATES

Linda Sue Kaare
Shawn P. Davis

OF COUNSEL

Robert L. Forsythe
Arthur M. Rude
Thomas J. O'Toole
Cyrus M. Poppen (Retired)
Harold M. Street (Retired)
Foster D. Potter (Retired)
George A. Parmenter (1903-1993)
Henry L. Wierengo (1905-1983)
Paul T. Sorensen (1920-1966)
Edward C. Farmer (1889-1975)
Joseph T. Riley (1895-1975)
Raymond J. Engle (1904-1982)

General Counsel for: FMB Lumberman's Bank; AmeriBank Federal Savings Bank; City of Muskegon; Quality Tool & Stamping Co., Inc.; Radiology Muskegon, P.C.
Local Counsel for: General Electric Capital Corp.; Paine-Webber; Teledyne Industries, Inc. (Continental Motors Division); Westinghouse Electric Corporation (Knoll Group).

For full biographical listings, see the Martindale-Hubbell Law Directory

WARNER, NORCROSS & JUDD (AV)

400 Terrace Plaza, P.O. Box 900, 49443-0900
Telephone: 616-727-2600
Fax: 616-727-2699
Grand Rapids, Michigan Office: 900 Old Kent Building, 111 Lyon Street, N.W.
Telephone: 616-752-2000.
Fax: 616-752-2500.

(See Next Column)

WARNER, NORCROSS & JUDD, *Muskegon—Continued*

Holland, Michigan Office: Curtis Center, Suite 300, 170 College Avenue.
Telephone: 616-396-9800.
Fax: 616-396-3656.

MEMBERS OF FIRM

Donald J. Veldman (Resident)
I. John Snider, II (Resident)
John H. Martin (Resident)
Robert W. Sikkel
Michael L. Robinson
Thomas H. Thornhill (Resident)
John H. McKendry, Jr. (Resident)
Paul R. Jackson (Resident)
Michael H. Schubert (Resident)

ASSOCIATES

Rodrick W. Lewis
Richard D. Cornell, Jr. (Resident)
Frank E. Berrodin (Not admitted in MI; Resident)
Steven A. Palazzolo (Resident)
Michael I. Kleaveland (Resident)

Representative Clients: Amstore Corp.; Andrie, Inc.; Bristol-Myers Squibb; Cannon-Muskegon Corp.; Comerica Bank; Cordova Chemical Co.; First Michigan Bank Corp.; First of America Bank - West Michigan; Fisher Steel and Supply Co.; Hastings Manufacturing Co.

For full biographical listings, see the Martindale-Hubbell Law Directory

*NEWBERRY,** Luce Co. — (Refer to Marquette)

NILES, Berrien Co.

HADSELL, LANDGRAF & LYNCH (AV)

19 South 3rd Street, P.O. Box 610, 49120
Telephone: 616-683-6500
Fax: 616-683-0600

MEMBERS OF FIRM

Philip A. Hadsell, Jr.
Robert L. Landgraf, Jr.
Christopher J. Lynch
René J. VanSteelandt

Representative Clients: National Standard Co.; French Paper Co.; Simplicity Pattern Co.; Lawyers' Title Insurance Corp.; Fairplain Plaza Co.; Cincinnati Ins. Co.; American Electric Power Co.

For full biographical listings, see the Martindale-Hubbell Law Directory

OWOSSO, Shiawassee Co. — (Refer to Flint)

*PAW PAW,** Van Buren Co. — (Refer to Kalamazoo)

*PETOSKEY,** Emmet Co.

STROUP, JOHNSON & TRESIDDER, P.C. (AV)

Pennsylvania Plaza, P.O. Box 809, 49770
Telephone: 616-347-3907
Fax: 616-347-2499

Nathaniel W. Stroup
Charles W. Johnson
Stephen J. Tresidder
Joel D. Wurster

Representative Clients: NBD of Petoskey, N.A.; Hodgkiss & Douma, Inc.; Michigan Physicians Mutual Liability Co.; Public Schools of Petoskey, Michigan; Top O'Michigan Rural Electric Cooperative; Emmet County Road Commission.

For full biographical listings, see the Martindale-Hubbell Law Directory

*PONTIAC,** Oakland Co.

BOOTH, PATTERSON, LEE, NEED & ADKISON, P.C. (AV)

1090 West Huron Street, 48328
Telephone: 810-681-1200
FAX: 810-681-1754

Douglas W. Booth (1918-1992)
Calvin E. Patterson (1913-1987)
Parvin Lee, Jr.
J. Timothy Patterson
David J. Lee
Gregory K. Need
Phillip G. Adkison
Martin L. Kimmel
Allan T. Motzny
Ann DeCaminada Christ
Kathryn Niazy Nichols

For full biographical listings, see the Martindale-Hubbell Law Directory

*PORT HURON,** St. Clair Co.

GARAN, LUCOW, MILLER, SEWARD, COOPER & BECKER, P.C. (AV)

Port Huron Office Center, 511 Fort Street, Suite 505, 48060-3922
Telephone: 810-985-4400
Fax: 810-985-4107
Detroit, Michigan Office: 1000 Woodbridge Place.
Telephone: 313-446-1530.
Fax: 313-259-0450.
Grand Blanc, Michigan Office: 8332 Office Park Drive.
Telephone: 810-695-3700.
Fax: 810-695-6488.
Ann Arbor, Michigan Office: 101 North Main Street, Suite 801.
Telephone: 313-930-5600.
Fax: 313-930-0043.

(See Next Column)

Troy, Michigan Office: 2301 West Big Beaver Road, Suite 212.
Telephone: 810-649-7600.
Fax: 810-649-5438.
Mount Clemens Office: Towne Square Development, 10 S. Main Street, Suite 307.
Telephone: 810-954-3800.
Fax: 810-954-3803.

John P. Seyfried (Resident)

David E. Oppliger (Resident)
Randolph J. Martinek
David J. Roe

For full biographical listings, see the Martindale-Hubbell Law Directory

NICHOLSON, FLETCHER & DEGROW (AV)

522 Michigan Street, 48060-3893
Telephone: 810-987-8444
Facsimile: 810-987-8149

MEMBERS OF FIRM

David C. Nicholson
Gary A. Fletcher
Dan L. DeGrow

ASSOCIATES

Mark G. Clark
John D. Tomlinson
Gregory T. Stremers

Representative Clients: Fremont Mutual Insurance Co.; Westfield Insurance Co.; Michigan Municipal Risk Management Authority; City of Port Huron; City of Marysville; Port Huron Area School District; Marysville Public Schools; Wirtz Manufacturing Co.; Raymond Excavating; Relleum Real Estate Development Co.

For full biographical listings, see the Martindale-Hubbell Law Directory

O'SULLIVAN, BEAUCHAMP, KELLY & WHIPPLE (AV)

627 Fort Street, 48060-5488
Telephone: 810-987-4111
Telecopier: 810-987-8763

MEMBERS OF FIRM

Joseph F. Walsh (1868-1955)
William R. Walsh (1886-1965)
W. Grafton Sharp (1913-1979)
Clifford Patrick O'Sullivan
Norman D. Beauchamp
Charles G. Kelly
David C. Whipple
David A. Keyes

Counsel for: The Times Herald Co. (a Gannett newspaper); Port Huron Hospital; Huron Plastics, Inc.; Commercial and Savings Bank of St. Clair County; Michigan National Bank; General Motors Corp.; Massey-Ferguson Credit Corp.; Community Foundation of St. Clair County.

For full biographical listings, see the Martindale-Hubbell Law Directory

*REED CITY,** Osceola Co. — (Refer to Big Rapids)

*SAGINAW,** Saginaw Co.

BRAUN KENDRICK FINKBEINER (AV)

8th Floor Second National Bank Building, 48607
Telephone: 517-753-3461
Telecopier: 517-753-3951
Bay City, Michigan Office: 201 Phoenix Building, P.O. Box 2039.
Telephone: 517-895-8505.
Telecopier: 517-895-8437.

MEMBERS OF FIRM

Hugo E. Braun (1894-1973)
Russell A. Schafer (1906-1982)
J. Richard Kendrick
James V. Finkbeiner
Hugo E. Braun, Jr.
Edward J. McArdle (1938-1989)
Thomas F James (1940-1990)
Morton E. Weldy
C. Patrick Kaltenbach
Harold J. Blanchet, Jr.
Kenneth W. Kable
E. Louis Ognisanti
Bruce L. Dalrymple
Michael H. Allen
Robert A. Kendrick
Charles A. Gilfeather
Thomas R. Luplow
John A. Decker
Michael J. Sauer
Timothy L Curtiss
Scott C. Strattard
Craig W. Horn
Francis J. Keating
Barry M. Levine
Brian F. Bauer

ASSOCIATES

Judith A. Lincoln
Irenna M. Garapetian
Carolyn Pollock Cary
Brian S. Makaric
William G. Tishkoff
Glenn L. Fitkin
Brian S. Fleetham
Jamie C. Hecht Nisidis

OF COUNSEL

Thomas M. Murphy

Representative Clients: The Dow Chemical Co.; General Motors Corp.; Lobdell Emery Manufacturing Co.; Merrill, Lynch, Inc.; Saginaw General Hospital; Saginaw News; The Wickes Foundation.

For full biographical listings, see the Martindale-Hubbell Law Directory

Saginaw—Continued

O'NEILL, WALLACE & DOYLE, P.C. (AV)

Suite 302 Four Flags Office Center, 300 St. Andrews Road, P.O. Box 1966, 48605
Telephone: 517-790-0960
Fax: 517-790-6902
Flint, Michigan Office: 611 West Court Street.
Telephone: 810-235-4031.
Fax: 810-235-5715.

Terence J. O'Neill
David A. Wallace
Thomas J. Doyle
Charles F. Filipiak

Richard L. Alger, Jr.
James D. Henke
David Carbajal
James E. O'Neill, III
John J. Danieleski, Jr.

Representative Clients: Home Insurance Co.; Great American Insurance Co.; Farmers Insurance Co.; Cincinnati Insurance Co.; Ohio Casualty Insurance Co.; Safeco Insurance Co.; Liberty Mutual Insurance Co.; CUNA Mutual Insurance.; Pioneer State Mutual Insurance Co.; Michigan Mutual Insurance Co.

For full biographical listings, see the Martindale-Hubbell Law Directory

SMITH & BROOKER, P.C. (AV)

3057 Davenport Avenue, 48602
Telephone: 517-799-1891
Bay City, Michigan Office: 703 Washington Avenue.
Telephone: 517-892-2595.
Flint, Michigan Office: 3506 Lennon Road.
Telephone: 810-733-0140.

RESIDENT ATTORNEYS

Francis B. Drinan
Michael J. Huffman

Representative Clients: CIGNA; Citizens Insurance Co.; City of Saginaw; Saginaw Township Community Schools; State Farm Mutual Automobile Insurance Co.; CSX Transportation.

For full biographical listings, see the Martindale-Hubbell Law Directory

*ST. IGNACE,** Mackinac Co.

BROWN AND BROWN (AV)

First National Bank Building, 49781
Telephone: 906-643-7800
Fax: 906-643-7157

MEMBERS OF FIRM

James J. Brown (Retired)
Charles M. Brown
Tom H. Evashevski

Counsel for: Union Terminal and Piers, Mackinac Island, Michigan; First National Bank, St. Ignace; Mackinac Island Carriage Tours; McGregor Oil Co.; City of St. Ignace.

For full biographical listings, see the Martindale-Hubbell Law Directory

*ST. JOSEPH,** Berrien Co.

BUTZBAUGH & DEWANE (AV)

Law and Title Building, 811 Ship Street, P.O. Box 27, 49085
Telephone: 616-983-0191
Fax: 616-983-5078

OF COUNSEL

Lester E. Page
David Vander Ploeg
James B. McQuillan

MEMBERS OF FIRM

Alfred M. Butzbaugh
John E. Dewane
Mark A. Miller
Randall L. Juergensen
Michael J. Roberts

ASSOCIATES

Philip J. Paarleberg

Representative Clients: SJS Federal Savings Bank; American Society of Agricultural Engineers; Whirlpool Corp.; Transamerica Insurance Group; Automobile Club Insurance Assn.; Imperial Printing Co.

For full biographical listings, see the Martindale-Hubbell Law Directory

FISHER LAW OFFICE (AV)

Law & Title Building, P.O. Box 83, 49085
Telephone: 616-983-5511
Telecopier: 616-893-5571

Vance A. Fisher

For full biographical listings, see the Martindale-Hubbell Law Directory

SPELMAN, SAUER, BURDICK & METZGER, P.C. (AV)

414 Main Street, P.O. Box 378, 49085
Telephone: 616-983-0531
Telecopier: 616-983-1936

(See Next Column)

John H. Spelman
Jonathan B. Sauer
Carl R. Burdick
Michael L. Metzger
Frances P. Chickering

Representative Clients: Sears, Roebuck & Co.; Foremost Insurance Co.; Whirlpool Corp.; The City of Watervliet; Southeast Berrien County Landfill Authority; Fremont Mutual Insurance Co.; North Pointe Insurance Co.; MonoCeramics, Inc.; Lincoln Charter Township; First Resource Federal Credit Union.

For full biographical listings, see the Martindale-Hubbell Law Directory

*SAULT STE. MARIE,** Chippewa Co.

MOHER & CANNELLO, P.C. (AV)

150 Water Street, P.O. Box 538, 49783
Telephone: 906-632-3397
FAX: 906-632-0479
Newberry, Michigan Office: 200 East John.
Telephone: 906-293-3600.

Thomas G. Moher
Steven J. Cannello
Timothy S. Moher

Representative Clients: City of Sault Ste. Marie, Michigan; Sault Bank; Sault Ste. Marie Economic Development Corp.; State of Michigan; Michigan Department of Transportation; Tendercare Nursing Homes of Michigan; Chippewa County, Village of De Tour; Pickford Township.

For full biographical listings, see the Martindale-Hubbell Law Directory

SHELBY, Oceana Co. — (Refer to Muskegon)

SOUTHFIELD, Oakland Co.

JAFFE, RAITT, HEUER & WEISS, PROFESSIONAL CORPORATION (AV)

Travelers Tower, Suite 1520, 48076
Telephone: 313-961-8380
Detroit, Michigan Office: One Woodward Avenue, Suite 2400.
Telephone: 313-961-8380.
Telecopier: 313-961-8358.
Monroe, Michigan Office: 212 East Front Street, Suite 3.
Telephone: 313-241-6470.
Telefacsimile: 313-241-3849.

Ira J. Jaffe

Representative Clients: Alfa Romeo, Inc.; Allnet Communications Services, Inc.; Amurcon Corp.; Erb Lumber Co.; Major Pharmaceutical Corp.; Michigan State Hospital Finance Authority; New York Carpet World, Inc.; Riverside Metal Products, Inc.; Weiss Construction Co.

For full biographical listings, see the Martindale-Hubbell Law Directory

MASON, STEINHARDT, JACOBS & PERLMAN, PROFESSIONAL CORPORATION (AV)

Suite 1500, 4000 Town Center, 48075-1415
Telephone: 810-358-2090
Fax: 810-358-3599

Gordon I. Ginsberg
Irving I. Boigon
Jack Schon
Walter B. Mason, Jr.
Frederick D. Steinhardt
John E. Jacobs
Michael B. Perlman
Jerome P. Pesick
Anthony Ilardi, Jr.
Richard A. Barr
Jeannine F. Gleeson-Smith
Robert G. Schuch
Jay W. Tower
Jonathan B. Frank

Carolyn J. Crawford
Michael C. Azar
Diane Flagg Goldstein
H. Adam Cohen

OF COUNSEL

Erwin B. Ellmann
Randolph J. Friedman
Marvin C. Daitch
John M. Roche

Representative Clients: Citibank, N.A.; City of Dearborn; DeMattia Development Co.; Forest City Enterprises; Michigan Wholesale Drug Assn.; Mortgage Bankers Association of Michigan; Nationwide Insurance Co.; City of Taylor; Union Labor Life Insurance Co.; Yellow Freight Systems, Inc.

For full biographical listings, see the Martindale-Hubbell Law Directory

SOMMERS, SCHWARTZ, SILVER & SCHWARTZ, P.C. (AV)

2000 Town Center, Suite 900, 48075
Telephone: 810-355-0300
Telecopier: 810-746-4001
Plymouth, Michigan Office: 747 South Main Street.
Telephone: 313-455-4250.

Stanley S. Schwartz
Leonard B. Schwartz
Lawrence Warren
Steven J. Schwartz
Paul Groffsky
Donald R. Epstein
John F. Vos, III
Jeffrey N. Shillman
Jeremy L. Winer
David R. Getto

(See Next Column)

SOMMERS, SCHWARTZ, SILVER & SCHWARTZ P.C., *Southfield—Continued*

Norman D. Tucker
Robert H. Darling
Paul W. Hines
Donald J. Gasiorek
Patrick B. McCauley
Justin C. Ravitz
Kenneth V. Cockrel (1938-1988)
Gary A. Taback
Allen J. Kovinsky
David L. Nelson
Robert G. Portnoy
Joseph A. Golden
William M. Brukoff
Stephen N. Leuchtman
Richard D. Toth
Allen J. Wall
Richard D. Fox
Frank Mafrice
James J. Vlasic
Victor A. Coen
Richard L. Groffsky
David J. Winter
Joseph E. Grinnan
David M. Black
B. A. Tyler
Daniel D. Swanson
Michael J. Cunningham
J. Lee Tilson
James D. Ledbetter
Patrick Burkett
Jon J. Birnkrant
David A. Kotzian
Matthew G. Curtis
Charles R. Ash, III
Helen K. Joyner
Robert J. Schwartz
John L. Runco
Patricia A. Stamler
Susanne Pryce
Lisa K. Pernick
Joseph H. Bourgon
Stephen S. Birnkrant
Tracy L. Allen
Antonia Fletcher Grinnan
Sam G. Morgan
Saulius K. Mikalonis
Frank T. Aiello
David J. Shea
Murray C. Slomovitz
Anne M. Schoepfle
Carl B. Downing
Alan B. Koenig
David B. Deutsch
Gary D. Dodds
Jabran G. Yasso
Kenneth T. Watkins
Gary E. Abeska
James A. Carlin

OF COUNSEL

Norman Samuel Sommers
Howard Silver
H. Rollin Allen
Charles S. Farmer
Sherwin M. Birnkrant

General Counsel for: City of Taylor; Foodland Distributors; C.A. Muer Corporation; Vlasic & Company; Nederlander Corporation; Woodland Physicians; Midwest Health Centers, P.C.
Representative Clients: Crum & Forster Insurance Company; City of Pontiac; Michigan National Bank; Perry Drugs.

For full biographical listings, see the Martindale-Hubbell Law Directory

*STANDISH,** Arenac Co. — (Refer to Bay City)

*STANTON,** Montcalm Co.

MIEL MIEL & PERRY (AV)

125 West Main Street, P.O. Box 8, 48888
Telephone: 517-831-5208; 831-4727
Fax: 517-831-8854

OF COUNSEL

C. Homer Miel

MEMBERS OF FIRM

Charles H. Miel
C. Robert Perry

Counsel for: Chemical Bank Montcalm; Montcalm Community College; City of Stanton; Montcalm Title Co.; Townships of Belvidere, Maple Valley, Pine, Sidney; Village of McBride.

For full biographical listings, see the Martindale-Hubbell Law Directory

STERLING HEIGHTS, Macomb Co.

O'REILLY, RANCILIO, NITZ, ANDREWS & TURNBULL, P.C. (AV)

One Sterling Town Center, 12900 Hall Road, Suite 350, 48313-1151
Telephone: 810-726-1000
Fax: 810-726-1560

Paul J. O'Reilly
Kenneth L. Rancilio
John A. Nitz
Clark A. Andrews
Charles E. Turnbull
Neil J. Lehto
Craig S. Schoenherr, Sr.
Michael J. Piatek
Bert T. Ross
Pauline Stoey Baleda
Christopher P. Baker
Gary W. Wilds
David B. Viar
Sean A. Fraser
Susan A. Rancilio
Michael F. Goethals

OF COUNSEL

Gary J. Collins

For full biographical listings, see the Martindale-Hubbell Law Directory

STURGIS, St. Joseph Co.

DRESSER LAW OFFICE, P.C. (AV)

112 South Monroe Street, 49091
Telephone: 616-651-3281
Fax: 616-651-3261

Raymond H. Dresser (1901-1968)
John E. Oster (1948-1981)
Raymond H. Dresser, Jr.
John R. Dresser
Robert P. Brothers
Walter H. Gilbert
Patrick Joseph Haas, Jr.

(See Next Column)

LEGAL SUPPORT PERSONNEL

Mary G. Dresser (Legal Assistant)

Attorneys for: Freeman Manufacturing Co.; Burr Oak Tool and Gauge, Inc.; Kirsch Co.; Society Bank-Michigan, Sturgis, Michigan; Sturgis Federal Savings Bank; Midwest Tool & Cutlery, Inc.

For full biographical listings, see the Martindale-Hubbell Law Directory

THREE RIVERS, St. Joseph Co. — (Refer to Sturgis)

*TRAVERSE CITY,** Grand Traverse Co.

MURCHIE, CALCUTT & BOYNTON (AV)

109 East Front Street, Suite 300, 49684
Telephone: 616-947-7190
Fax: 616-947-4341

Robert B. Murchie (1894-1975)
Harry Calcutt
Jack E. Boynton
William B. Calcutt
Mark A. Burnheimer
Dawn M. Rogers

ASSOCIATES

George W. Hyde, III
Ralph J. Dilley (Not admitted in MI)

General Counsel for: Old Kent Bank-Grand Traverse; Northwestern Savings Bank & Trust; Central-State Bancorp; Traverse City Record Eagle; WPNB-7 & WTOM-4; Emergency Consultants, Inc.; National Guardian Risk Retention Group, Inc.; Farmers Mutual Insurance Co.; Environmental Solutions, Inc.
Local Counsel For: Consumers Power Co.

For full biographical listings, see the Martindale-Hubbell Law Directory

SMITH, HAUGHEY, RICE & ROEGGE, P.C. (AV)

241 East State Street, P.O. Box 848, 49685-0848
Telephone: 616-929-4878
Telecopier: 616-929-4182
Grand Rapids, Michigan Office: 200 Calder Plaza Building, 250 Monroe Avenue, N.W., 49503-2251.
Telephone: 616-774-8000.
Telecopier: 616-774-2461.
East Lansing, Michigan Office: 1301 North Hagadorn, 48823-2320.
Telephone: 517-332-3030.
Telecopier: 517-332-3468.

George Frederick Bearup
Mark P. Bickel
P. David Vinocur
R. Jay Hardin
Robert W. Tubbs
Robert M. Faulkner

Thomas C. Kates
John R. Vander Veen
Mark D. Williams
Jeffrey R. Wonacott
Ann M. Kling

Representative Clients: Chevron; Cincinnati Insurance Co.; General Motors Corp.; Kemper Insurance Group; Michigan Hospital Assn.; Navistar International; St. Paul Insurance Cos.; Steelcase, Inc.; Sears Roebuck & Co.; Dow Elanco.

For full biographical listings, see the Martindale-Hubbell Law Directory

SMITH, JOHNSON & BRANDT, ATTORNEYS, P.C. (AV)

603 Bay Street, P.O. Box 705, 49684
Telephone: 616-946-0700
Fax: 616-946-1735
Lansing, Michigan Office: Suite 402, 116 West Ottawa Street.
Telephone: 517-482-5142.

Louis A. Smith
H. Wendell Johnson
Donald A. Brandt
Allen G. Anderson
Edgar Roy III

Barbara Ann Assendelft
Paul T. Jarboe
Thomas A. Pezzetti
Joseph E. Quandt

Representative Clients: Alden State Bank; Empire National Bank of Traverse City; First of America Bank-Northern Michigan; Garland; Grand Traverse Mall Limited Partnership; Green Tree Acceptance, Inc.; Lansing Automakers' Federal Credit Union; Michigan Automobile Dealers Association; Cherry Capital Oldsmobile Cadillac L.L.C.; Elmer's Crane and Dozer, Inc.

For full biographical listings, see the Martindale-Hubbell Law Directory

TROY, Oakland Co.

CAMPBELL, O'BRIEN & MISTELE, P.C. (AV)

850 Stephenson Highway Suite 410, 48083-1163
Telephone: 810-588-5800
Fax: 810-588-6669

Edwin G. O'Brien (1907-1983)
Dale C. Campbell
Henry E. Mistele
Arthur R. Spears, Jr.
Paul W. Loock
Robert J. Figa
Curtis H. Mistele

(See Next Column)

CAMPBELL, O'BRIEN & MISTELE P.C.—*Continued*

References: First of America, Comerica Bank.

For full biographical listings, see the Martindale-Hubbell Law Directory

CHANDLER, BUJOLD & CHANDLER (AV)
755 West Big Beaver Road Suite 1114, 48084
Telephone: 810-362-2277
Telecopier: 810-362-3760

Dan W. Chandler
Frank J. Bujold
W. Robert Chandler
R. Joseph Chandler
Francis X. Bujold, II

For full biographical listings, see the Martindale-Hubbell Law Directory

DOLD, SPATH & MCKELVIE, P.C. (AV)
5445 Corporate Drive, Suite 170, 48098
Telephone: 810-952-5100
Fax: 810-952-5138
Grosse Pointe, Michigan Office: 17190 Denver Avenue, P.O. Box 36786.
Telephone: 313-886-7500.

Douglas H. Dold (Resident, Grosse Pointe, Michigan Office)
John M. Spath
Charles L. McKelvie

David P. Neveux (Resident, Grosse Pointe, Michigan Office)
Frank M. DeLuca
Elisabeth Hessheimer Gregory
Edward L. Ewald
Julie C. Canner
John Hodges
Tony F. Di Ponio

Representative Clients: New Bright Industries; U.S. Chemical Co.; Ford Motor Co.; Dinverno Waste Disposal; Allpoints Warehousing Corp.; Atlantic Mutual Insurance Co.; Conquest Construction Co.; General Motors Corp.; Triad Financial, Inc.; U.S. Maintenance Corp.

For full biographical listings, see the Martindale-Hubbell Law Directory

GARAN, LUCOW, MILLER, SEWARD, COOPER & BECKER, P.C. (AV)
2301 W. Big Beaver Road, Suite 212, 48084
Telephone: 810-649-7600
Fax: 810-649-5438
Detroit, Michigan Office: 10000 Woodbridge Place.
Telephone: 313-446-1530.
Fax: 313-259-0450.
Grand Blanc, Michigan Office: 8332 Office Park Drive.
Telephone: 810-695-3700.
Fax: 810-695-6488.
Port Huron, Michigan Office: Port Huron Office Center, 511 Fort Street, Suite 505.
Telephone: 810-985-4400.
Fax: 810-985-4107.
Ann Arbor, Michigan Office: 101 North Main Street, Suite 801.
Telephone: 313-930-5600.
Fax: 313-930-0043.
Mount Clemens, Michigan Office: Suite 307, Towne Square Development, 10 South Main Street.
Telephone: 810-954-3800.
Fax: 810-954-3803.

Milton Lucow (Resident)
Roger A. Smith (Resident)
Mark Shreve (Resident)
James W. Heckman (Resident)
Edward M. Freeland (Resident)
Steven A. Matta (Resident)

Susan M. Williams (Resident)
Steven E. Nurenberg (Resident)
Meri E. Craver (Resident)

Counsel for: Allstate Insurance Co.; Sears, Roebuck & Co.; Liberty Mutual Insurance Co.; Continental Insurance Companies.

For full biographical listings, see the Martindale-Hubbell Law Directory

KITCH, DRUTCHAS, WAGNER & KENNEY, P.C. (AV)
3001 West Big Beaver Road Suite 200, 48084-3103
Telephone: 810-637-3500
FAX: 810-637-6630
Detroit, Michigan Office: One Woodward, Tenth Floor, 48226-3412.
Telephone: 313-965-7900.
Fax: 313-965-7403.
Lansing, Michigan Office: 120 Washington Square, North, Suite 805, One Michigan Avenue, 48933-1609.
Telephone: 517-372-6430.
Fax: 517-372-0441.
Macomb County Office: Towne Square Development, 10 South Main Street, Suite 301, Mount Clemens, 48043-7903.
Telephone: 810-463-9770.
Fax: 810-463-8994.
Toledo, Ohio Office: 405 Madison Avenue, Suite 1500, 43604-1235.
Telephone: 419-243-4006.
Fax: 419-243-7333.

(See Next Column)

Ann Arbor, Michigan Office: 303 Detroit Street, Suite 400, P.O. Box 8610, 48107-8610.
Telephone: 313-994-7600.
Fax: 313-994-7626.

Gregory G. Drutchas (Resident Principal)
Victor J. Abela (Principal)
David L. Kaser (Principal)
R. Michael O'Boyle (Associate Principal)
Philip Cwagenberg
Gregory P. Sweda
Carol Ann Tarnowsky
Kenneth G. Frantz
Lauri A. Read
Julia S. Hoffert-Rosen
Gail E. Kinney

For full biographical listings, see the Martindale-Hubbell Law Directory

MATHESON, PARR, SCHULER, EWALD, ESTER & JOLLY (AV)
2555 Crooks Road, Suite 200, 48084
Telephone: 810-643-7900
Telecopier: 810-643-0417

MEMBERS OF FIRM

George S. Dixon (1906-1973)
Albert D. Matheson (1912-1990)
Robert Alan Parr
Eugene C. Ewald
Robert D. Schuler
John W. Ester
Terence K. Jolly
James D. Osmer
John A. Stevens
Marta D. Remeniuk

Representative Clients: National Automobile Transporters Labor Division; Brink's Inc.; Expertec, Inc.; Advance Technology, Inc.; Digital Electronic Automation, Inc.; Frito-Lay, Inc.
Reference: Comerica Bank.

For full biographical listings, see the Martindale-Hubbell Law Directory

YPSILANTI, Washtenaw Co.

PEAR SPERLING EGGAN & MUSKOVITZ, P.C. (AV)
5 South Washington Street, 48197
Telephone: 313-483-3626
Fax: 313-483-1107
Ann Arbor, Michigan Office: Domino's Farms, 24 Frank Lloyd Wright Drive.
Telephone: 313-665-4441
Other Ypsilanti, Michigan Office: 2164 Bellevue at Washtenaw.
Telephone: 313-483-7177.

Lawrence W. Sperling
Andrew M. Eggan
Thomas E. Daniels
Helen Conklin Vick

Counsel for: Domino's Pizza, Inc.; Bank One, Ypsilanti, N.A.; Townsend and Bottum, Inc.; Ann Arbor Housing Commission; The Credit Bureau of Ypsilanti; City of Ypsilanti (Labor Counsel); Michigan Municipal Worker's Compensation; Self-Insurance Fund.
Approved Attorneys for: Lawyers Title Insurance Corp.

For full biographical listings, see the Martindale-Hubbell Law Directory

MINNESOTA

ADRIAN, Nobles Co.

HEDEEN, HUGHES & WETERING (AV)

Adrian State Bank Building, 56110
Telephone: 507-483-2033
Worthington, Minnesota Office: 421-10th Street.
Telephones: 507-376-3181; 376-3182.

William T. Hedeen

*AITKIN,** Aitkin Co.

RYAN, RYAN & ZIMMERMAN (AV)

4 Second Street, N.W., P.O. Box 388, 56431
Telephone: 218-927-2136

MEMBERS OF FIRM

Joseph W. Ryan
Michael F. Ryan
Richard A. Zimmerman

Representative Clients: The First National Bank of Aitkin; First National Bank of Deerwood; State Bank of McGregor; United Power Assn.; Mille Lacs Electric Cooperative; Farm Bureau Mutual Insurance Co.; Aitkin Independent School Dist. #1; City of Aitkin; City of Deerwood.

For full biographical listings, see the Martindale-Hubbell Law Directory

*ALEXANDRIA,** Douglas Co.

THORNTON, HEGG, REIF, JOHNSTON & DOLAN (AV)

1017 Broadway, P.O. Box 819, 56308
Telephone: 612-762-2361
FAX: 612-762-1638

MEMBERS OF FIRM

R. S. Thornton (1892-1960)
Joseph G. Thornton (Retired)
Robert M. Hegg
Thomas J. Reif
Scott T. Johnston
Michael J. Dolan
Bruce R. Rubbelke

Representative Clients: National Farmers Union Property & Casualty Co.; Austin Mutual Insurance Co.; North Star Mutual Insurance Co.; American Family; Western Natl.; Milwaukee Mutual; Grinnell Mutual.
General Counsel for: Nodland Construction Co.; Buttweiler Do-All, Inc.

For full biographical listings, see the Martindale-Hubbell Law Directory

*ANOKA,** Anoka Co. — (Refer to Minneapolis)

AURORA, St. Louis Co. — (Refer to Springfield)

*AUSTIN,** Mower Co.

ALDERSON, ONDOV, LEONARD, SWEEN & RIZZI, P.A. (AV)

105 East Oakland Avenue, P.O. Box 366, 55912-0366
Telephone: 507-433-7394
Facsimile: 507-433-8890
Blooming Prairie Office: 348 East Main.
Telephone: 507-583-4526.

Rollin C. Alderson (1893-1986)
Raymond B. Ondov, Of Counsel
Gary E. Leonard
Paul V. Sween
Steven T. Rizzi, Jr.

Dean K. Adams
Michael C. Zender

Representative Clients: First Bank Southeast, National Association, Austin, Minnesota; Geo. A. Hormel & Co.; Maryland Casualty Co..

For full biographical listings, see the Martindale-Hubbell Law Directory

BAUDLER, BAUDLER, MAUS & BLAHNIK (AV)

110 North Main Street, 55912
Telephone: 507-433-2393
FAX: 507-433-9530
Spring Valley, Minnesota Office: 304 So. Broadway.
Telephone: 507-346-7301.
FAX: 507-346-2537.

MEMBERS OF FIRM

Otto Baudler (1881-1970)
William J. Baudler (1914-1992)
Bryan J. Baudler
Lawrence E. Maus
Robert M. Maus
Robert E. Blahnik (Resident at Spring Valley Office)
Thomas C. Baudler

ASSOCIATES

David L. Forman
Lee A. Bjorndal

Representative Clients: Farmers Insurance Group; Twin City Federal; Home Federal Bank; Western National Mutual Insurance Co.; The Kemper Insurance Group; Federated Insurance Cos.; First Bank Austin; Norwest Mortgage, Inc.; Grinnell Mutual Insurance; Northbrook Property & Casualty Insurance Co.

For full biographical listings, see the Martindale-Hubbell Law Directory

HOVERSTEN, STROM, JOHNSON & RYSAVY (AV)

807 West Oakland Avenue, 55912
Telephone: 507-433-3483
Fax: 507-433-7889

MEMBERS OF FIRM

Kermit F. Hoversten
Craig W. Johnson
Donald E. Rysavy
David V. Hoversten
John S. Beckmann
Fred W. Wellmann
Steven J Hovey

ASSOCIATES

Mary Carroll Leahy
Daniel Loren Scott

OF COUNSEL

Kenneth M. Strom

Representative Clients: Hartford Insurance Co.; Allied Insurance Group; Travelers Insurance; American States Insurance; Royal Milbank Insurance; Prudential Insurance Co.; Independent School District 756; St. Olaf Hospital; Austin Medical Clinic; Norwest Bank, Austin.

For full biographical listings, see the Martindale-Hubbell Law Directory

*BAUDETTE,** Lake of the Woods Co. — (Refer to Bemidji)

*BENSON,** Swift Co. — (Refer to Montevideo)

*BRECKENRIDGE,** Wilkin Co. — (Refer to Fergus Falls)

*CALEDONIA,** Houston Co. — (Refer to Spring Valley)

*CAMBRIDGE,** Isanti Co. — (Refer to Minneapolis)

*CHASKA,** Carver Co. — (Refer to Minneapolis)

*DETROIT LAKES,** Becker Co. — (Refer to Moorhead)

*DULUTH,** St. Louis Co.

BYE BOYD AGNEW, LTD. (AV)

200 Sellwood Building, 202 West Superior Street, 55802-1960
Telephone: 218-727-8451
Fax: 218-727-6081

Richard L. Bye
Robert W. Boyd
Jerome P. Agnew
R. Craft Dryer
Elizabeth A. Storaasli
Mark L. Knutson
Gerald A. Pommerville

John H. Bray

General Counsel: Independent School District 709, Duluth.
Representative Clients: Superwood Corp.; Ulland Brothers, Inc.; Western National Bank of Duluth; Zenith Dredge Co.; Zenith Products, Inc.; Arrowhead Blacktop; Duluth Steel Fabricators.
Reference: Norwest Bank Minnesota North, N.A.

For full biographical listings, see the Martindale-Hubbell Law Directory

CRASSWELLER, MAGIE, ANDRESEN, HAAG & PACIOTTI, P.A. (AV)

1000 Alworth Building, P.O. Box 745, 55801
Telephone: 218-722-1411
Telecopier: 218-720-6817

Donald B. Crassweller
Robert H. Magie, III
Charles H. Andresen
Michael W. Haag
James P. Paciotti
Sandra E. Butterworth
Brian R. McCarthy
Bryan N. Anderson
Robert C. Barnes
Kurt D. Larson
Gerald T. Anderson

COUNSEL

John M. Donovan
Robert K. McCarthy (1915-1986)

Representative Clients: Inland Steel Co.; Allstate Insurance Co.; Liberty Mutual Insurance Co; State Farm Insurance Cos.; Great Lakes Gas Transmission Co.; Lakehead Pipe Line Co.; Trans-Canada Gas Pipeline, Ltd.

For full biographical listings, see the Martindale-Hubbell Law Directory

FRYBERGER, BUCHANAN, SMITH & FREDERICK, P.A. (AV)

700 Lonsdale Building, 302 West Superior Street, 55802
Telephone: 218-722-0861
Fax: 218-722-9568
St. Paul Office: Capitol Center, 386 N. Wabasha.
Telephone: 612-221-1044.

(See Next Column)

FRYBERGER, BUCHANAN, SMITH & FREDERICK P.A.—*Continued*

Bruce Buchanan
Nick Smith
Harold A. Frederick
Dexter A. Larsen
James H. Stewart
Robert E. Toftey
Michael K. Donovan
Neal J. Hessen
Joseph J. Mihalek
Shawn M. Dunlevy
Anne Lewis
David R. Oberstar
Abbot G. Apter
Michael Cowles
Martha M. Markusen

Daniel D. Maddy
Stephanie A. Ball
Paul B. Kilgore
Mary Frances Skala
Rolf A. Lindberg (Resident, St. Paul Office)
Kevin T. Walli (Resident, St. Paul Office)
Kevin J. Dunlevy (Resident, St. Paul Office)
Teresa M. O'Toole
Dean R. Borgh
James F. Voegeli (Resident, St. Paul Office)
James A. Lund
Mark D. Britton (Resident, St. Paul Office)
Judith A. Zollar

OF COUNSEL

Herschel B. Fryberger, Jr.

Representative Clients: North Shore Bank of Commerce; General Motors Acceptance Corp.; Western Lake Superior Sanitary District; City of Duluth; First Bank Minnesota (N.A.); Norwest Bank Minnesota North N.A.; Airport State Bank; Park State Bank; M & I First National Bank of Superior; St. Lukes Hospital Duluth.

For full biographical listings, see the Martindale-Hubbell Law Directory

HALVERSON, WATTERS, BYE, DOWNS, REYELTS & BATEMAN, LTD. (AV)

700 Providence Building, 55802
Telephone: 218-727-6833
FAX: 218-727-4632

G. W. Halverson
W. D. Watters
Don L. Bye
Anthony S. Downs
Steven L. Reyelts
Charles B. Bateman
Steven W. Schneider
Eric L. D. Hylden

Sonia M. Sturdevant
Aaron Bransky
Timothy W. Andrew, Sr.

LEGAL SUPPORT PERSONNEL

William R. Crom (Investigator/Paralegal)

Representative Clients: Northern Drug Co.; WDIO-TV.; Duluth Teachers Retirement Fund; Duluth Teachers Credit Union; Duluth Clinic, Ltd.; American States Insurance Cos.; CIGNA Cos.; CNA Group; Farm Bureau Mutual Ins. Co.

For full biographical listings, see the Martindale-Hubbell Law Directory

HANFT, FRIDE, O'BRIEN, HARRIES, SWELBAR & BURNS, P.A. (AV)

1000 First Bank Place, 130 West Superior Street, 55802-2094
Telephone: 218-722-4766
Fax: 218-720-4920

Edward T. Fride (1927-1986)
Gilbert W. Harries
Gaylord W. Swelbar
William M. Burns
Richard R. Burns
John D. Kelly
Richard J. Leighton
Frederick A. Dudderar, Jr.
John R. Baumgarth
J. Kent Richards
Tim A. Strom
R. Thomas Torgerson
Cheryl M. Prince
Robin C. Merritt

Jennifer L. Crook
Kathleen Small Bray
Mark D. Pilon
Amy J. Hunt

Counsel for: Canadian National Railways; Duluth, Winnipeg & Pacific Railroad; First Bank North, N.A.; Great American Insurance Companies; Johnson-Wilson Constructors, Inc.; Minnesota Power; Northern Minnesota Utilities; Oglebay Norton Co.; United States Fidelity and Guaranty Company; U.S. Insurance Group.

For full biographical listings, see the Martindale-Hubbell Law Directory

*ELBOW LAKE,** Grant Co.

FLUEGEL, HELSETH, MCLAUGHLIN, ANDERSON & BRUTLAG, CHARTERED (AV)

12 Central Avenue South, P.O. Box 180, 56531-0180
Telephone: 218-685-5400
Fax: 218-685-4321
Morris Office: 215 Atlantic Avenue; P.O. Box 527.
Telephone: 612-589-4151.
Ortonville Office: 212 Second St., N.W.
Telephone: 612-839-2922.

(See Next Column)

Dennis J. Helseth
Paul Brutlag
Michael M. Fluegel (Resident, Morris, Minnesota Office)
Warrenn C. Anderson (Resident, Morris, Minnesota Office)
Robert V. Dalager (Resident, Morris, Minnesota Office)
Robert R. Pflueger (Resident, Ortonville, Minnesota Office)
Germain B. Kunz (Resident, Ortonville, Minnesota Office)
David C. McLaughlin (Resident, Ortonville, Minnesota Office)

*ELK RIVER,** Sherburne Co. — (Refer to St. Cloud)

ELLENDALE, Steele Co. — (Refer to St. Cloud)

*FARIBAULT,** Rice Co. — (Refer to Owatonna)

*FERGUS FALLS,** Otter Tail Co.

HOFF, SVINGEN, ATHENS & RUSSELL (AV)

125 South Mill Street, P.O. Box 697, 56537
Telephone: 218-736-5456 - Fax: 218-739-5331

MEMBERS OF FIRM

Peter A. Hoff
R. Kristian Svingen
Thomas C. Athens
Robert L. Russell, III

General Counsel for: Otter Tail Power Co.; Bois de Sioux Watershed; N.F. Field Abstract Company.
Representative Clients: Colonial Ins. Co. of America; Farm Bureau Ins. Co.; Western National Mutual; Colonial Penn Ins.; Nationwide Ins.; First National Bank of Battle Lake; K-Mart; Crawford & Co.; Old Republic National Title Ins. Co.

For full biographical listings, see the Martindale-Hubbell Law Directory

DAVID F. LUNDEEN (AV)

107 Court Street, 56537
Telephone: 218-736-4866
FAX: 218-736-7747

For full biographical listings, see the Martindale-Hubbell Law Directory

*FOLEY,** Benton Co. — (Refer to St. Cloud)

*GAYLORD,** Sibley Co. — (Refer to New Ulm)

*GLENWOOD,** Pope Co. — (Refer to Alexandria)

*GRAND RAPIDS,** Itasca Co.

LANO, NELSON, O'TOOLE & BENGTSON, LTD. (AV)

115 East Fifth Street, P.O. Box 20, 55744
Telephone: 218-326-9603
Fax: 218-326-1565

Neal A. Lano
Leif A. Nelson
Dennis L. O'Toole
Brian C. Bengtson

Representative Clients: State Farm Mutual Automobile Insurance Co.; Allstate Insurance Co.; Great American Insurance Co.; Independent School District No. 316; Fireman's Fund; Transamerica Insurance Co.; City of Grand Rapids; City of Habbing.

For full biographical listings, see the Martindale-Hubbell Law Directory

*GRANITE FALLS,** Yellow Medicine Co. — (Refer to Olivia)

*HALLOCK,** Kittson Co.

BRINK, SOBOLIK, SEVERSON, VROOM & MALM, P.A. (AV)

217 South Birch Avenue, P.O. Box 790, 56728
Telephone: 218-843-3686
FAX: 218-843-2724

Lyman A. Brink (1909-1972)
Dennis M. Sobolik
Robert K. Severson
Ronald C. Vroom
Roger C. Malm
Robert M. Albrecht
Blake S. Sobolik
Jeffrey W. Hane

Representative Clients: Northwestern State Bank, Hallock, Minn.; Karlstad State Bank, Karlstad, Minn.; Argyle State Bank, Argyle, Minn.; City of Hallock; American Federal Savings & Loan Assn.; State Farm Insurance Co.; Minnesota Rice Growers, Inc.

For full biographical listings, see the Martindale-Hubbell Law Directory

HIBBING, St. Louis Co.

NAUGHTIN, MULVAHILL AND MURRAY (AV)

2007 Fourth Avenue East, 55746
Telephone: 218-262-3891
Fax: 218-263-7706
Buhl, Minnesota Office: First National Bank Building.
Telephone: 218-258-3213.

(See Next Column)

NAUGHTIN, MULVAHILL AND MURRAY, *Hibbing—Continued*

Peter J. Mulvahill
Gail N. Murray

Representative Clients: First Bank Minnesota; First National Bank of Buhl; Ryan Construction Company of Minnesota, Inc.; Mesabi Regional Medical Center; L & M Radiator, Inc.; Dom-Ex, Inc.

HUTCHINSON, McLeod Co.

KRAFT, WALSER, NELSON, HETTIG & HONSEY (AV)

131 Main Street South, P.O. Box 129, 55350-0129
Telephone: 612-587-8150
Olivia, Minnesota Office: 107 North Ninth Street, P.O. Box 148.
Telephone: 612-523-1322.
Renville, Minnesota Office: 338 North Main Street.
Telephone: 612-329-3474.

John H. Kraft
Paul A. Nelson
Donald H. Walser
Steven E. Hettig
Daniel B. Honsey

Representative Clients: American State Bank of Olivia; Duininck Companies; Southern Minnesota Beet Sugar Cooperative; Buffalo Lake Nursing Home; Brandt Electric, Inc.; Renville Farmers Co-op Credit Union; State Bank of Bird Island; Farm Credit Services; Richard Larson Builders, Inc.

For full biographical listings, see the Martindale-Hubbell Law Directory

*INTERNATIONAL FALLS,** Koochiching Co. — (Refer to Bemidji)

*JACKSON,** Jackson Co.

MUIR, COSTELLO & CARLSON (AV)

603 Second Street, 56143
Telephone: 507-847-4200
Fax: 507-847-3028
Lakefield, Minnesota Office: 310 Main Street, P.O. Box 929.
Telephone: 507-662-6621.
Fax: 507-662-6623.
Heron Lake, Minnesota Office: 265 Tenth Street, P.O. Box 287.
Telephone: 507-793-2285.
Fax: 507-793-0081.

MEMBERS OF FIRM

Maylon G. Muir (Retired)
Hans K. Carlson
Patrick K. Costello (Lakefield and Heron Lake Offices)

Representative Clients: Banks: Bank Midwest, Minnesota - Iowa, N.A.; First National Bank - Lakefield; Farmers and Merchants State Bank of Alpha; Heron Lake State Bank; First State Bank of Okabena; Southwest State Bank; Community First National Bank - Lakefield.
Municipalities: Cities of Lakefield, Alpha.
Other Representative Clients: Kruse Paving, Inc.

For full biographical listings, see the Martindale-Hubbell Law Directory

*LE CENTER,** Le Sueur Co.

CHRISTIAN, SPARTZ, KEOGH & CHRISTIAN (AV)

65 South Park Avenue, P.O. Box 156, 56057
Telephone: 612-357-2278
Fax: 612-357-2270

MEMBERS OF FIRM

Harry F. Christian
Michael T. Keogh
Donald H. Spartz
Douglas J. Christian

Representative Clients: First National Bank, Le Center, Minnesota; Elysian State Bank, Elysian, Minnesota; First State Bank, Le Center, Minnesota.
Reference: First National Bank, Le Center, Minnesota.

For full biographical listings, see the Martindale-Hubbell Law Directory

*LITCHFIELD,** Meeker Co. — (Refer to Willmar)

*LITTLE FALLS,** Morrison Co. — (Refer to Brainerd)

*LONG PRAIRIE,** Todd Co. — (Refer to St. Cloud)

*LUVERNE,** Rock Co. — (Refer to Worthington)

*MANKATO,** Blue Earth Co.

BLETHEN, GAGE & KRAUSE (AV)

127 South Second Street, P.O. Box 3049, 56001
Telephone: 507-345-1166
Fax: 507-345-8003

OF COUNSEL

Kelton Gage

(See Next Column)

MEMBERS OF FIRM

Samuel B. Wilson (1873-1954)
Randall C. Berkland
Arthur H. Ogle (1916-1975)
David T. Peterson
William C. Blethen (Retired)
James H. Turk
Raymond C. Krause (Retired)
Stephen P. Rolfsrud
Bailey W. Blethen
Michael C. Karp
Richard J. Corcoran
Kevin M. Connelly
Wm. David Taylor III

General Counsel For: Mankato Citizens Telephone Co.; Norwest Bank Minnesota South Central, N.A.: Waseca Mutual Insurance Co.; Hickory Tech Corporation; Winco, Inc.
Local Counsel For: American States Insurance Co.; ConAgra Fertilizer Co.; Northern Natural Gas Co., a division of Enron Corp.; General Motors Corp.; Millers Mutual Insurance Co.

For full biographical listings, see the Martindale-Hubbell Law Directory

FARRISH, JOHNSON & MASCHKA (AV)

200 Union Square Business Center, 201 North Broad Street, P.O. Box 550, 56002-0550
Telephone: 507-387-3002
Fax: 507-625-4002

MEMBERS OF FIRM

Robert G. Johnson
William S. Partridge
Gerald L. Maschka
Kenneth R. White
David A. Salsbery
Mary Anne Wray
Charles W. Ries
Paul J. Simonett
Scott V. Kelly
Margaret H Culp

OF COUNSEL

Penny L. Herickhoff

Representative Clients: Travelers Insurance Co.; American State Bank of Mankato, Mankato, Minn.; Hartford Insurance Group; St. Paul Insurance Cos.; Employers Mutual of Wausau; State Farm Co.; Federated Insurance Co.; Firemen's Fund American Insurance Co.; Maryland Casualty Co.; American Family Insurance Group.

For full biographical listings, see the Martindale-Hubbell Law Directory

JOHNSON, ANDERSON & ZELLMER (AV)

600 South Second Street, P.O. Box 637, 56001
Telephone: 507-387-4002
FAX: 507-345-5001

MEMBERS OF FIRM

C. A. (Gus) Johnson, II
Randy J. Zellmer
Jerome T. Anderson
Suzette E. Johnson

For full biographical listings, see the Martindale-Hubbell Law Directory

MCLEAN PETERSON LAW FIRM, CHARTERED (AV)

Twin City Federal Building, 325 South Broad Street, P.O. Box 1360, 56002
Telephone: 507-387-3155
Fax: 507-387-3166
St. Clair, Minnesota Office: State Bank of St. Clair.
Telephone: 507-245-3785.
Lake Crystal, Minnesota Office: Highway 60.
Telephone: 507-726-2200.
Vernon Center, Minnesota Office:
Telephone: 507-549-3416.

Gordon P. Smith (1890-1961)
Bruce G. Miller (1943-1992)
Edward D. McLean
John M. Riedy
Charles T. Peterson
Bradley C. Walker
Thomas R. Sullivan
John C. Peterson
Howard F. Haugh
Jeffrey D. Gednalske
Steven H. Fink

Representative Clients: CNA Insurance Co.; Katolight Corp.; The Family Bank F.S.B.; Robert W. Carlstrom Construction Co.; Condux International, Inc.; Independent School District #77 (Mankato); Immanuel-St. Joseph's Hospital of Mankato, Inc.; Jones Metal Products, Inc.; North Star Concrete Co.; Western National Insurance Company.

For full biographical listings, see the Martindale-Hubbell Law Directory

*MILACA,** Mille Lacs Co. — (Refer to St. Cloud)

*MINNEAPOLIS,** Hennepin Co.

ABDO AND ABDO, P.A. (AV)

710 Northstar West, 625 Marquette Avenue, 55402
Telephone: 612-333-1526
Fax: 612-342-2608

E. John Abdo (1912-1993)
Keith J. Broady
Robert P. Abdo
Kenneth J. Abdo
Steven R. Hedges
Timothy C. Matson

Representative Clients: ADT Security Systems, Inc.; Cold Spring Brewing Co., Cold Spring, Minn.

For full biographical listings, see the Martindale-Hubbell Law Directory

Minneapolis—Continued

ARNOLD & McDOWELL (AV)

5881 Cedar Lake Road, 55416-1492
Telephone: 612-545-9000
Minnesota Wats Line: 800-343-4545
Fax: 612-545-1793
Princeton, Minnesota Office: 501 South Fourth Street.
Telephone: 612-389-2214.
Hutchinson, Minnesota Office: 101 Park Place.
Telephone: 612-587-7575.

MEMBERS OF FIRM

David B. Arnold
Gary D. McDowell
Steven A. Anderson
G. Barry Anderson
Steven S. Hoge
Paul D. Dove
Laura K. Fretland
David A. Brueggemann

ASSOCIATES

Richard G. McGee
Cathryn D. Reher
Gina M. Brandt
Brett D. Arnold

OF COUNSEL

William W. Cameron
Raymond C. Lallier
Jane Van Valkenburg

For full biographical listings, see the Martindale-Hubbell Law Directory

ARTHUR, CHAPMAN, McDONOUGH, KETTERING & SMETAK, P.A. (AV)

500 Young Quinlan Building, 81 South Ninth Street, 55402
Telephone: 612-339-3500
Fax: 612-339-7655

Lindsay G. Arthur, Jr.
John T. Chapman
Michael P. McDonough
Robert W. Kettering, Jr.
Theodore J. Smetak
Donna D. Geck
Patrick C. Cronan
Thomas A. Pearson
Colby B. Lund
Michael R. Quinlivan
Sally J. Ferguson
James S. Pikala
Jeremiah P. Gallivan
Katherine L. MacKinnon
Blake W. Duerre
Karen Melling van Vliet
Richard C. Nelson
Eugene C. Shermoen, Jr.
David L. Christianson
Paul J. Rocheford
Lee J. Keller
Gregory J. Johnson
Joseph D. O'Brien, Jr.
Paula Duggan Vraa
Joseph W. Waller
Elizabeth Truesdell Smith
Anne Elizabeth Betts
Christine L. Tuft
Roger J. Stelljes

Representative Clients: American International Group; American States; Bristol Myers-Squibb, Inc.; Continental Insurance Co.; General Casualty; Home Insurance Co.; Metropolitan Property & Liability Insurance Co.; Navistar International; Safeco Insurance Co.; USAA.

For full biographical listings, see the Martindale-Hubbell Law Directory

AUSTIN & ABRAMS, A PROFESSIONAL ASSOCIATION (AV)

700 Northstar West, 55402
Telephone: 612-332-4273; 800-659-2679
FAX: 612-342-2107

Harold J. Carroll (1901-1978)
Frank X. Cronan (1912-1975)
Robert M. Austin
Jerome B. Abrams
Paul R. Smith
Lauris Heyerdahl
Keith J. Goar
Paul V. Kieffer
Timothy J. Wilson

Representative Clients: Hawkeye Security Ins. Co.; CNA Insurance; Employer's Mutual Ins. Co.

For full biographical listings, see the Martindale-Hubbell Law Directory

BASSFORD, LOCKHART, TRUESDELL & BRIGGS, P.A. (AV)

(Formerly Richards, Montgomery, Cobb & Bassford, P.A.)
3550 Multifoods Tower, 55402-3787
Telephone: 612-333-3000
Telecopier: 612-333-8829

Fred B. Snyder (1859-1951)
Edward C. Gale (1862-1943)
Frank A. Janes (1908-1959)
Nathan A. Cobb, Sr. (1905-1976)
Bergmann Richards (1888-1978)
Edmund T. Montgomery (1904-1987)
Charles A. Bassford (1914-1990)
Greer E. Lockhart
Lynn G. Truesdell
Jerome C. Briggs
Frederick E. Finch
John M. Degnan
Lewis A. Remele, Jr.
Kevin P. Keenan
James O. Redman
Rebecca Egge Moos
John M. Anderson
Charles E. Lundberg
Gregory P. Bulinski
Donna J. Blazevic
Mary E. Steenson
Mark P. Hodkinson
Thomas J. Niemiec
Andrew L. Marshall
Michael A. Klutho
Kathryn H. Davis
Gregory W. Deckert

(See Next Column)

Kevin P. Hickey
John P. Buckley
Bradley J. Betlach
Mark Whitmore
Christopher R. Morris
Kelly Christensen

Representative Clients: Chubb/Pacific Indemnity Group; Greyhound Lines, Inc.; John Hancock Mutual Life Insurance Co.; Medical Protective Co.; Metropolitan Life Insurance Co.; The Travelers Insurance Cos.

For full biographical listings, see the Martindale-Hubbell Law Directory

BEST & FLANAGAN (AV)

4000 First Bank Place, 601 Second Avenue South, 55402-4331
Telephone: 612-339-7121
Fax: 612-339-5897

James I. Best (1902-1966)
Robert J. Flanagan (1898-1974)

MEMBERS OF FIRM

Robert L. Crosby
Leonard M. Addington
Robert R. Barth
N. Walter Graff
Allen D. Barnard
Richard A. Peterson
Robert J. Christianson, Jr.
Frank J. Walz
Frank E. Vogl
Marinus W. Van Putten, Jr.
David B. Morse
John A. Burton, Jr.
James C. Diracles
Robert L. Meller, Jr.
Judith A. Rogosheske
Scott D. Eller
Charles C. Berquist
George O. Ludcke
E. Joseph LaFave
Gregory D. Soule
Cathy E. Gorlin
Patrick B. Hennessy
Timothy A. Sullivan
Brian F. Rice
Tracy J. Van Steenburgh
David J. Zubke
Steven R. Kruger
James P. Michels
Paul E. Kaminski
Daniel R. Nelson
John P. Boyle
Ross C. Formell

ASSOCIATES

Cindy J. Larson
Caryn Scherb Glover
Mary E. Shearen
Catherine J. Courtney
Keith J. Nelsen
Barbara M. Ross
Tracy Falck Kochendorfer
Jeannice M. Reding
Sarah C. Madison
Robert D. Maher
David H. Johnson
Paul J. Harmon
William J. Morris, Jr.
Michael Luther Diggs
Michael Howard Pink

OF COUNSEL

John R. Carroll
James D. Olson
Robert M. Skare
Archibald Spencer
Ward B. Lewis
C. William Franke

References: First Bank Minneapolis; Norwest Bank Minnesota.

For full biographical listings, see the Martindale-Hubbell Law Directory

BRENNER & GLASSMAN, LTD. A PROFESSIONAL ASSOCIATION (AV)

Suite 170, 2001 Killebrew Drive, 55425-1822
Telephone: 612-854-7600
Telecopier: 612-854-0502

Louis W. Brenner, Sr.
Richard A. Glassman

William D. Turkula
Michael J. Orme
Thomas W. Larkin

OF COUNSEL

John J. Todd

For full biographical listings, see the Martindale-Hubbell Law Directory

BRIGGS AND MORGAN, PROFESSIONAL ASSOCIATION (AV)

2400 IDS Center, 80 South Eighth Street, 55402
Telephone: 612-334-8400
Telecopier: 612-334-8650
St. Paul, Minnesota Offices: 2200 First National Bank Building.
Telephone: 612-223-6600.
Telecopier: 612-223-6450.

RESIDENT PERSONNEL

Brian G. Belisle
John A. Cairns
Christopher C. Cleveland
R. Scott Davies
William T. Dolan
Marian M. Durkin
Jonathan L. Eisenberg
Avron L. Gordon
Joel H. Gottesman
Michael J. Grimes
Nils F. Grossman
Trudy J. Halla
Samuel L. Hanson
Charles R. Haynor
Jeffrey J. Keyes
Joseph T. Kinning
Andrew R. Kintzinger
Michael C Krikava
Thomas A. Larson
David M. Lebedoff
Matthew J. Levitt
John H. Lindstrom
Lauren E. Lonergan
Richard G. Mark
J. Patrick McDavitt
Michael Thomas Miller
James E. Nelson
Carolyn S. Nestingen
Joseph P. Noack
Robert J. Pratte
James G. Ray
Charles B. Rogers

(See Next Column)

BRIGGS AND MORGAN PROFESSIONAL ASSOCIATION, *Minneapolis—Continued*

RESIDENT PERSONNEL (Continued)

David B. Sand
Margaret K. Savage
Andrew C. Selden
David J. Spencer
David J. Steingart
Gregory J. Stenmoe
Timothy R. Thornton
Brian D. Wenger
Karin L. Wille
Steven W. Wilson
Stephen Winnick
Nancy J. Wolf
Robert E. Woods

Nancy Chaffee Aiken
Donna J.T. Bailey
Gregory M. Bistram
Linda L. Boss
Scott G. Bowman
Denise P. Brennan (Not admitted in MN)
Karen J. Evans
Mark J. Frenz
Alison S. Kaardal
Janel E. LaBoda
Michelle C. Leighton
Anthony M. Marick
Kristin S. Melby
Jack Y. Perry
Diane B. Ray
Eric J. Rucker
Jay W. Schlosser
H. Torbjorn Svensson
Paul C. Thissen
Vincent A. Thomas
Philip J. Tilton
Michael J. Tostengard

OF COUNSEL

Donald R. Johnston
Jerry F. Rotman
Robert G. Share
John Troyer

For full biographical listings, see the Martindale-Hubbell Law Directory

FRED BURSTEIN & ASSOCIATES, P.A. (AV)

5450 Norwest Center, 90 South Seventh Street, 55402
Telephone: 612-339-6561
Fax: 612-337-5572

Fred Burstein

Dylan J. McFarland
Eric J. Olsen

Reference: Firstar Bank of Minnesota, N.A.

For full biographical listings, see the Martindale-Hubbell Law Directory

DORSEY & WHITNEY (AV)

A Partnership including Professional Corporations
220 South 6th Street, 55402
Telephone: 612-340-2600
Facsimile: 612-340-2868
Cable Address: "Dorow"
Telex: 290605
Answer-back: "Dorsey Law MPS"
Rochester, Minnesota Office: 201 First Avenue, S.W., Suite 340, P.O. Box 848, 55902.
Telephone: 507-288-3156.
Des Moines, Iowa Office: 801 Grand, Suite 3900, 50309.
Telephone: 515-283-1000.
New York, New York Office: 350 Park Avenue, 10022.
Telephone: 212-415-9200.
Washington, D.C. Office: Suite 200, 1330 Connecticut Avenue, N.W., 20036.
Telephone: 202-452-6900.
Brussels, Belgium Office: 35 Square De Meeûs B-1040.
Telephone: 011-32-2-504-4611.
London, England Office: 3 Gracechurch Street, EC3V OAT.
Telephone: 011-44-71-929-3334.
Billings, Montana Office: 1200 First Interstate Center, 401 North 31st Street, P.O. Box 7188, 59103.
Telephone: 406-252-3800.
Great Falls, Montana Office: 507 Davidson Building, 8 Third Street North, P.O. Box 1566, 59401.
Telephone: 406-727-3632.
Missoula, Montana Office: 127 East Front Street, Suite 310, 59802.
Telephone: 406-721-6025.
Denver, Colorado Office: 370 Seventeenth Street, Republic Plaza Building, Suite 4400, 80202-5644.
Telephone: 303-629-3400.
Orange County, California Office: Center Tower, 650 Town Center Drive, Suite 1930, P.O. Box 5066, Costa Mesa, 92626.
Telephone: 714-662-7300.
Fargo, North Dakota Office: Dakota Center, 51 North Broadway, Suite 210, P.O. Box 1344, 58107-1344.
Telephone: 701-235-6000.

MEMBERS OF FIRM

Stewart D. Aaron (Resident, New York, New York Office)
Jonathan B. Abram
James D. Alt
Joseph H. Andersen
Kim A. Anderson
Leslie J. Anderson
Emery W. Bartle
Stephen D. Bell (Resident, Denver, Colorado Office)
William J. Berens
James M. Bergen (Resident, New York, New York Office)
David A. Bieging (Resident, Washington, D.C. Office)
Philip F. Boelter

(See Next Column)

MEMBERS OF FIRM (Continued)

Richard L. Bond (Resident, New York, New York Office)
Virginia Walker Boylan (Resident, Washington, D.C. Office)
Timothy E. Branson
Richard A. Brekke (Resident, Billings, Montana Office)
Ronald J. Brown
Dennis P. Buratti
Robert A. Burns
Diane T. Butler
Richard O. Campbell (Resident, Denver, Colorado Office)
Don D. Carlson
Steven E. Carlson (Resident, London, England Office)
Robert E. Cattanach, Jr.
Steven K. Champlin
David L. Claypool (Resident, Des Moines, Iowa Office)
John S. Clifford
Rebecca A. Comstock
Katherine A. Constantine
Jay F. Cook
John A. Cooney
John Crist (Resident, Billings, Montana Office)
Kevin A. Cudney (Resident, Denver, Colorado Office)
Craig A. Currie
Kenneth L. Cutler
Scott M. Desmond (Resident, New York, New York Office)
Steven J. Dickinson (Resident, Des Moines, Iowa Office)
Craig D. Diviney
Nelson G. Dong
Robert J. Dwyer, Jr. (Resident, New York, New York Office)
J. Marquis Eastwood
George G. Eck
Mae Nan Ellingson (Resident, Missoula, Montana Office)
Verlane L. Endorf
Gregory A. Fontaine
Donald S. Franke
David N. Fronek
L. Joseph Genereux
Jerome P. Gilligan
Mark Ginder
Roy A. Ginsburg
Barry D. Glazer (Resident, Brussels, Belgium Office)
Joseph C. Gonnella
Elizabeth A. Goodman
Stephen E. Gottschalk
G. Larry Griffith (P.A.)
Munford Page Hall, II (Resident, Washington, D.C. Office)
Mark E. Hamel
Joseph W. Hammell
Thomas S. Hay
Raymond A. Hayward (Resident, Rochester, Minnesota Office)
Timothy S. Hearn
Robert A. Heiberg
Robert H. Helmick (Resident, Des Moines, Iowa Office)
Stuart R. Hemphill
Peter S. Hendrixson
J. Andrew Herring
John S. Hibbs (P.A.)
William R. Hibbs
Charles W. Hingle (Billings, Montana Office)
William H. Hippee, Jr.
Robert L. Hobbins
Jean F. Holloway
Virginia Anne Housum (Resident, Denver, Colorado Office)
J David Jackson
Norene D. Jacobs (Resident, Des Moines, Iowa Office)
Mark A. Jarboe
Eugene L. Johnson (P.A.)
Gary M. Johnson
Larry W. Johnson
William A. Johnstone
William A. Jonason (Resident, Rochester, Minnesota Office)
James L. Jones (Billings and Great Falls, Montana Offices)
Robert E. Josten (Resident, Des Moines, Iowa Office)
James R. Kahn (Resident, New York, New York Office)
Stephen A. Kals (Resident, New York, New York Office)
Mark R. Kaster
Thomas O. Kelly III
William J. Keppel
Michael D. Killin (Resident, Denver, Colorado Office)
John D. Kirby
Paul B. Klaas
Loren R. Knott
George A. Koeck
Peter E. Kohl (Resident, London, England Office)
John T. Kramer
Peter M. Lancaster
James K. Langdon II
W. Charles Lantz (Resident, Rochester, Minnesota Office)
David J. Lauth
Michael A. Lindsay
Thomas S. Llewellyn (Resident, Washington, D.C. Office)
Bridget A. Logstrom
David J. Lubben
Stephen P. Lucke
James B. Lynch
Bruce A. MacKenzie (Resident, Great Falls, Montana Office)
Roger J. Magnuson
Jerry C. D. Mahoney (P.A.)
Diane D. Malfeld
John W. Manning (Resident, Great Falls, Montana Office)
Thomas R. Manthey
Phillip H. Martin (P.A.)
Thomas O. Martin
Owen C. Marx (Resident, New York, New York Office)
John M. (Jack) Mason
David L. McCuskey
Michael J. McDonnell
Edwin N. McIntosh (Resident, Des Moines, Iowa Office)
Patrick J. McLaughlin
Lee R. Mitau
Thomas O. Moe (P.A.)
Norman Moloshok (Resident, New York, New York Office)
L. Daniel Mullaney (Resident, Washington, D. C. Office)
Steven C. Nelson
Daniel P. O'Keefe
Brian E. Palmer
William B. Payne
Laurence W. Petersen (Resident, Billings, Montana Office)
Carol A. Peterson
Edward J. Pluimer
Thomas R. Pollock (Resident, New York, New York Office)
Charles L. Potuznik
Michael Prichard
Kathleen L. Prudhomme
Michael J. Radmer
John G. Rainey, Jr. (Resident, New York, New York Office)
David A. Ranheim
Michael E. Reeslund
John B. Rehm (Resident, Washington, D.C. Office)
Stanley M. Rein
Leonard S. Rice
Paula S. Rindels
Robert A. Rosenbaum
Michael J. Rufkahr (Resident, New York, New York Office)
Jeffrey M. Samberg (Resident, New York, New York Office)
Charles F. Sawyer
Paul J. Scheerer
Robert A. Schwartzbauer
William F. Schwitter, Jr. (Resident, New York, New York Office)

(See Next Column)

DORSEY & WHITNEY—*Continued*

MEMBERS OF FIRM (Continued)

Kathleen Dunn Sheehy
Bruce J. Shnider
Jeffrey L. Sikkema (Resident, Costa Mesa, California Office)
Richard H. Silberberg (Resident, New York, New York Office)
Robert J. Silverman
Joel M. Simon (Resident, New York, New York Office)
David C. Singer (Resident, New York, New York Office)
Peter W. Sipkins
Nicholas J. Spaeth (Resident, Fargo, North Dakota Office)
William R. Soth (P.A.)
Warren R. Spannaus
William R. Stoeri
Mary J. Streitz
R. Keith Strong (Resident, Great Falls, Montana Offices)
Robert J. Struyk
George Y. Sugiyama (Resident, Washington, D.C. Office)
Jay L. Swanson
Richard G. Swanson
Janice M. Symchych
Thomas W. Tinkham
Thomas F. Topel (Resident, Billings, Montana Office)
Paul M. Torgerson
James E. Townsend
Michael Trucano
Jon F. Tuttle (Resident, Washington, D.C. Office)
Gary L. Tygesson
Kenneth T. Tyra
Thomas D. Vander Molen
Suzanne B. Van Dyk
Michael J. Wahoske
Lenora Walker
Steven J. Wells
William J. Wernz
William A. Whitlock (Resident, Denver, Colorado Office)
John R. Wicks (Resident, Rochester, Minnesota Office)
Perry M. Wilson, III
John W. Windhorst, Jr.
Zhao Zhang
John C. Zwakman

SENIOR ATTORNEY

Robert L. Sterup (Resident, Billings, Montana Office)

ASSOCIATES

Clifford S. Anderson
John T. Arnason
Stephen R. Baird
Amy C. Becker
Jeffrey R. Benson
Scott Allen Benson
Michael G. Bohn (Resident, Denver, Colorado Office)
Bethany S. Brand
Robert W. Bras (Resident, Washington, D.C. Office)
B. Andrew Brown
LeFleur C. Browne
David E. Bruhn
Philippe M. Bruno (Resident, Washington, D.C. Office)
Elizabeth C. Buckingham
Forrest G. Burke
Suzanne M. Burke (Resident, New York, New York Office)
Theodore C. Cadwell, Jr.
Peter W Carter
Sarah M. Casserly
James L. Chosy
Douglas R. Christensen
Steven M. Christenson
Karen L. Clauson (Resident, Denver, Colorado Office)
Andrew J. Cohen
William A. Cole (Resident, Billings, Montana Office)
Steven F. Coleman
Rosario Conde-Johanek (Resident, New York, N.Y. Office)
Patrick F. Courtemanche
Holly H. Cox (Resident, New York, New York Office)
Richard K. Cozine
James H. Curtin
David G. Dennis (Resident, Great Falls, Montana Office)
Paul R. Dieseth
Sharon McDonnell Dobbs
William A. Dossett
Scott W. Doyle (Resident, Washington, D.C. Office)
Vernle C. (Skip) Durocher, Jr.
Janene B. Duthie (Resident, Denver, Colorado Office)
Holly S.A. Eng
Patrick J. Feeley (Resident, New York, New York Office)
Sharon L. Ferko (Resident, New York, New York Office)
Michael E. Florey
Lori Elison Freeman (Resident, Billings, Montana Office)
Arnold H. Frishman
Stacey M. Fuller
Cynthia A. Geiwitz
Lisa D. Genovese (Resident, New York, New York Office)
Catherine A. Gnatek
William R. Goetz
Bernd Ulrich Graf (Resident, Brussels, Belgium Office)
Melinda K. Greer
David D. Grossklaus (Resident, Des Moines, Iowa Office)
George A. Hagerty (Resident, Denver, Colorado Office)
David G. Hagopian (Resident, Costa Mesa, California Office)
Maren L. Hed
Sharon J. Hester (Resident, Billings, Montana Office)
Gordon P. Heinson
Peggy L. Hicks
Kenneth E. Higgins (Not admitted in MN)
Frederic F. Hillier
Elizabeth Cardle Hinck
Lisa C. Hondros
Lance R. Hoskins (Resident, Billings, Montana Office)
Alison C. Humphrey
Holly Fife Hunter (Not admitted in MN; Resident, New York, New York Office)
Jeffrey M. Hurlburt (Resident, Des Moines, Iowa Office)
Thomas M. Johnston
Jana L. Julsrud
Patricia Hill Kelley (Resident, Denver, Colorado Office)
Steven J. Kemps
Alexandra B. Klass
Sally Klemperer (Not admitted in MN)
James D. Kremer
Elaine M. Kumpula
Anthony A. Kuznik
Malcolm E. Landau (Not admitted in MN)
Catherine R. Landman
Amy E. Lange
Bricker L. Lavik
Sonja G. Lemmer
Laura M. Lestrade (Resident, New York, New York Office)
Kenneth E. Levitt (Not admitted in MN)
Jay R. Lindgren
Norman C. Linnell
John G. Lubitz (Resident, Denver, Colorado Office)
David C. Lundsgaard
Wilson K. Lundsgaard
David J. MacLaughlin
Edward B. Magarian
Creighton R. Magid

(See Next Column)

ASSOCIATES (Continued)

A. Melinda Maher
J. Eric Maki (Resident, New York, New York Office)
Robert G. Manson (Resident, New York, New York Office)
Lawrence T. Martinez
Zappa J. Mathew
Katherine M. Mattson
Francis J. McAnulty (Resident, Rochester, Minnesota Office)
Jeffrey G. McGuire
Michael D. Michaux
Lance G. Morgan
James A. Neal
John D. Nelson
Robert G. Newkirk (Not admitted in MN)
Eric M. Nicholson
Aldo Noto (Resident, Washington, D.C. Office)
Steven B. Nyquist
Devan V. Padmanabhan
Linda R. Pagnano
Thomas A. Pantalion
James V. Parravani (Resident, New York, New York Office)
Todd C. Pearson
Julia L. Rau
Jean L. Rausch (Not admitted in MN)
John P. Rhodes
Amy Hallman Rice
Frederick S. Richards II
Paul Robbennolt
James A. Rogers
David G. Ronald
Elizabeth J. Ruffing (Resident, Denver, Colorado Office)
Kevin Saville
James E. Schmeckpeper
Joan M. Schroeder
Robert A. Seng
John L. Seymour, III (Not admitted in MN)
Christopher T. Shaheen (Not admitted in MN)
Wayne A. Shammel (Resident, Denver, Colorado Office)
Thomas Skelton (Not admitted in MN; Resident, New York, New York Office)
Nancy B. Smith
John O. Somers
Allan M. Soobert (Resident, Washington, D.C. Office)
Jill E. Strawbridge (Resident, New York, New York Office)
Gerald H. Sullivan, Jr.
Daniel R. Sundell
Mary B. Thomas
Susan Thompson
Claire H. Topp
David Y. Trevor
Salvatore J. Vitiello (Resident, New York, New York Office)
J. Thomas Vitt
Nicholas A.J. Vlietstra
Kevin J. Wadzinski
Kristyn Walker
Jacqueline J. Warner
Yosef B. Weinstock (Resident, New York, New York Office)
Mark A. Wolfe
Elizabeth S. Wright
Kenneth S. Yudell (Resident, New York, New York Office)
Bianca Zick
Karen A. Zughaib (Resident, Washington, D.C. Office)
Todd E. Zimmerman (Resident, Fargo, North Dakota Office)
Margaret M. Zverinova

SENIOR ATTORNEY

Darryl L. Meyers

OF COUNSEL

Michael E. Bress (P.A.)
David Busby (Resident, Washington, D.C. Office)
Douglas W. Fix, Resident, Denver, Colorado Office)
Duane E. Joseph (P.A.)
John D. Levine
Raymond A. Reister
Jane Evans Roberts (Resident, Denver, Colorado Office)
George A. Skoler (Not admitted in MN)
James B. Vessey (P.A.)

RETIRED PARTNERS

Craig A. Beck (Resident, Rochester, Minnesota Office)
David R. Brink
Thomas M. Brown
Peter Dorsey
Thomas S. Erickson (P.A.)
John F. Finn
George P. Flannery
Robert O. Flotten (P.A.)
Maynard B. Hasselquist
Charles J. Hauenstein
Horace Hitch
Russell W. Lindquist
Waldo F. Marquart
Curtis L. Roy
John J. Taylor
Arthur E. Weisberg (P.A.)

Representative Clients: ADC Telecommunications, Inc.; Dain Bosworth Inc.; First Bank Systems, Inc.; Green Tree Acceptance Inc.; Inter-Regional Financial Group; Kraus Anderson, Inc.; Little Six, Inc.; Mayo Clinic; SUPERVALU INC.; United Healthcare Corp.

For full biographical listings, see the Martindale-Hubbell Law Directory

FAEGRE & BENSON (AV)

2200 Norwest Center, 90 South Seventh Street, 55402-3901
Telephone: 612-336-3000
Facsimile: 612-336-3026
Denver, Colorado Office: 2500 Republic Plaza, 370 Seventeenth Street.
Telephone: 303-592-5900.
Facsimile: 303-592-5693.
Des Moines, Iowa Office: 400 Capital Square, 400 Locust Street.
Telephone: 515-248-9000.
Facsimile: 515-248-9010.
Washington, D.C. Office: The Homer Building, Suite 450 North, 601 Thirteenth Street, N.W.
Telephone: 202-783-3880.
Facsimile: 202-783-3899.
London, England Office: 10 Eastcheap.
Telephone: 44-71-623-6163.
Facsimile: 44-71-623-3227.
Frankfurt, Germany Office: Westendstrasse 24, 6000 Frankfurt am Main 1, EC3M 1ET.
Telephone: 49-69-1743 43.
Facsimile: 49-69-1743 49.

(See Next Column)

FAEGRE & BENSON, *Minneapolis—Continued*

MEMBERS OF FIRM

MINNEAPOLIS, MINNESOTA OFFICE

G. Alan Cunningham
Gerald T. Flom
James Fitzmaurice
Gordon G. Busdicker
John D. French
Ronald B. Hemstad
Norman R. Carpenter
Lawrence C. Brown
Martin N. Burke
John E. Harris
Paul T. Birkeland
David M. Beadie
David R. Brennan
Richard C. Schmoker
Thomas M. Crosby, Jr.
Philip L. Bruner
Duane W. Krohnke
James A. Dueholm
Hubert V. Forcier
James M. Samples
Gale R. Mellum
Jerry W. Snider
Timothy M. O'Brien
Stephen Rosholt
Frank B. Butler
Gordon B. Conn, Jr.
Bruce A. Ackerman
Michael H. Harper, Jr.
Thomas L. Kimer
Joseph M. Price
W. Smith Sharpe, Jr.
Philip S. Garon
John F. Beukema
Walter J. Duffy, Jr.
James P. Stephenson
Reid Carron
John K. Steffen
John B. Gordon
Thomas M. Mayerle
Thomas G. Morgan
Kent E. Richey
John H. Hinderaker
Robert L. Schnell, Jr.
Richard A. Nelson
Brian B. O'Neill
Gary L. Gandrud
Michael E. Murphy
Charles E. Steffey
William R. Busch, Jr.
Bonnie M. Fleming
Henry F. Frisch
Winthrop A. Rockwell
Jack M. Fribley
Steven C. Schroer
John P. Borger
Richard A. Helde
Steven R. Anderson
Jay D. Christiansen
Charles S. Ferrell
David B. Miller
James E. Nicholson
Rebecca L. Rom
Richard A. Forschler
Robert C. Hentges
James A. O'Neal
Sally A. Johnson
Walter H. Rockenstein, II
Robert L. Collins
Bruce M. Engler
Susan L. Jacobson
Walter A. Pickhardt
Donald C. Shepard
Wendy J. Wildung
Scott W. Johnson
Mary Trippler
James L. Volling
Kenneth A. Liebman
Thomas H. Bennin
Gerard M. Nolting
Michael R. Stewart
David M. Vander Haar
Peter J. Withoff
Marianne T. Remedios
Daniel G. Wilczek
Charles T. Parks, Jr.
Mary E. Stumo
Peter C. Halls
Patrick J. O'Connor, Jr.
Daniel J. Amen
Jeff H. Eckland
Douglas J. Heffernan
Jennifer R. Mewaldt
Kirk O. Kolbo
John M. Haurykiewicz
Lyle G. Ward
Bruce M. Batterson
Delmar R. Ehrich
James M. Pfau
Steven L. Severson
David M. Morehouse
Calvin L. Litsey
Diana Young Morrissey
D. Charles Macdonald
John R. Wheaton
Douglas P. Long
Terri K. Simard
Valerie M. Welch
Dennis M. Ryan
Gregory J. Schaefer
John W. Polley
J. Hazen Graves
William R. Joyce
Bruce Jones
Daniel C. Gerhan
Steven C. Kennedy
Patrick J. Schiltz
David J. Goldstein
Paul S. Moe
Mark D. Savin
Linda S. Svitak
Lori Ann Wagner
Andrew G. Humphrey
Jeffrey D. Hedlund

DENVER, COLORADO OFFICE

Joseph M. Montano
Frederic K. Conover, II
John D. Shively
Bruce W. Sattler
Dirk W. De Roos
Michael S. McCarthy
Michael J. Cook
Gerald A. Niederman
Christian Carl Onsager
Harlan S. Abrahams
Leslie A. Fields
Catherine A. Lemon
Elizabeth A. MacDonald
Daniel F. Warden
Russell O. Stewart
Diane B. Davies
Charlotte Wiessner

DES MOINES, IOWA OFFICE

Thomas J. Miller
Michael A. Giudicessi
Kimberly J Walker
Kasey W. Kincaid
Terri L. Combs

WASHINGTON, D.C. OFFICE

G. Daniel Miller
Charles D. Ablard

LONDON, ENGLAND OFFICE

Thomas E. Johnson
Scott M. James

FRANKFURT, GERMANY OFFICE

Philip B. Haleen

(See Next Column)

SPECIAL COUNSEL

MINNEAPOLIS, MINNESOTA OFFICE

James E. Bowlus
Elizabeth L. Taylor
Luke R. Komarek
Sharon L. Reich
R. Carl Moy
Kathleen Gregor Wenger

SPECIAL PROJECT COUNSEL

Emad Tinawi

STAFF ATTORNEY

Kristin A. Jameson

DENVER, COLORADO

OF COUNSEL

Jo Frances Walsh

COUNSEL

WASHINGTON, D.C. OFFICE

Morton Pomeranz

EUROPEAN COMMUNITY COUNSEL

LONDON, ENGLAND OFFICE

Paul Egerton-Vernon

EASTERN EUROPEAN COUNSEL

FRANKFURT, GERMANY OFFICE

Olga Iliana Bachvarova

J. B. Faegre (1887-1986)
John C. Benson (1890-1986)
Paul Christopherson (1902-1987)
Robert J. Christianson (1908-1981)
Everett A. Drake (Retired)
Donald L. Robertson (Retired)
George D. McClintock (Retired)
Rodger L. Nordbye (Retired)
George E. Harding
John S. Holten (Retired)
Robert W. Oelke (Retired)
James A. Halls (Retired)
Charles L. Horn (Retired)
Jack D. Gage (Retired)

ASSOCIATES

MINNEAPOLIS, MINNESOTA OFFICE

Bridget M. Ahmann
Paula Weseman Theisen
Peggy Steif Abram
Paul W. Heiring
Sheri A. Ahl
Karin J. Birkeland
Felicia J. Boyd
Laura S. Carlson
Kathlyn E. Noecker
Daniel J. Connolly
Susan B. Grupe
Michael T. McCormick
Andrea M. Fike
Ronald J. Lee
Thomas J. Vollbrecht
Michael S. Sherrill
Walter C. Linder
Karen J. Canon
Sarah Armstrong
Richard A. Duncan
Ann Marie Hanrahan
David J. Shannon
Sonia A. Shewchuk
Michael F. Kelly, Jr.
Kathleen H. Sanberg
Elizabeth R. Schiltz
Michael L. Cheever
Randy L. Gegelman
John P. Mandler
Scott A. Anderegg
Gretchen S. Gates
Michael A. Ponto
James R. Steffen
Steven E. Suckow
Mary Cullen Yeager
David A. Pearson
Theresa H. Keninger
James B. Sheehy
Matthew R. Bogart
Randall E. Kahnke
Michael J. Macaluso
David B. Clark
Stephen M. Mertz
Daniel A. Tysver
Charles F. Webber
Marit Westman Zosel
Eric E. Jorstad
William L. Roberts
Richard Yoshiharu Sako (Not admitted in MN)
Joseph C. Baker
John D. Bessler
Susan C. Davis
Erik P. Dove
Charles F. Knapp
Kelly L. Phillips
Thomas S. Schroeder
Jerome T. Will
Gail Chang Bohr
Jacqueline A. Layton
Brendan W. Randall
Sidney J. Spaeth
Jacqueline R. Rolfs
Graham van der Leeuw
Paul R. Jevnick (Not admitted in MN)
Nathan Zietlow (Not admitted in MN)
Peter J. Berrie
Christin Eaton Garcia
Madhulika Jain
Jane Elizabeth Kiker
Patricia K. Oakes
Jason D. Topp
Thomas S. Bottern
John Edward Connelly
Elizabeth M. Hendricks
Wayne J. Rice
Andrew J. Ritten
Karen Wilson
Dharminder S. Devgun
Stephen A. Donovan
James J. Hartnett, IV
Nestor F. Ho
Laura A. Lundquist
Kim J. Patrick
Gary S. Weinstein
Robert T. Magill
Chad M. Oldfather
Thomas R. Ragatz
Timothy C. Rank
Samuel Rosenstein

DENVER, COLORADO OFFICE

Colin C. Deihl
Adrienne O'Connell McNamara
Steven N. Jacobs
Natalie Hanlon-Leh
Mary B. Tribby
Arthur G. Woodward
Michael J. Pankow
Michel L. Glawe
Matthew Nelson
John R. Sperber

DES MOINES, IOWA OFFICE

Susan M. Boe
Melissa Shafter

(See Next Column)

FAEGRE & BENSON—*Continued*

WASHINGTON, D.C. OFFICE

Melanie Julian Muckle
David W. Powell

FRANKFURT, GERMANY OFFICE

Ralph W. Hummel
Vinzenz Bödeker

Counsel for: Norwest Bank Minnesota, N.A.; Northwestern National Life Insurance Co.; Cowles Media Co.; Dayton Hudson Corp.
Local Counsel for: Aetna Casualty & Surety Co.; Chrysler Corp.; Insurance Company of North America; U.S. WEST Communications.

For full biographical listings, see the Martindale-Hubbell Law Directory

FELHABER, LARSON, FENLON AND VOGT, PROFESSIONAL ASSOCIATION (AV)

Suite 4200, First Bank Place 601 2nd Avenue South, 55402-4302
Telephone: 612-339-6321
Facsimile: 612-338-0535
St. Paul, Minnesota Office: Suite 2100, Minnesota World Trade Center.
Telephone: 612-222-6321. Facsimilie: 612-222-8905.

Robert L. Bach
Richard A. Beens
James A. Blomquist
Edward J. Bohrer
Stephen J. Burton
Paul H. Cady
Edward Q. Cassidy
Christopher P. Chilstrom
David M. Cremons
James J. Cronin
Terrance M. Cullen
James M. Dawson
Thomas J. Doyle
Stanley J. Duran
William K. Ecklund
Robert J. Fenlon
Robert S. Halagan
Jan Douglas Halverson
Angela D. Hansen
Christopher S. Hayhoe
Brad J. Heying
(Not admitted in MN)
David R. Hols
Ronald R. Kirchoff
Jona K. Klibanoff
Lee A. Lastovich
Dennis J. Merley
William F. Mohrman
Byron D. Olsen
Penelope J. Phillips
Thomas M. Regan
Steven L. Ross
Karen G. Schanfield
Russell J. Sudeith, Jr.
Thomas M. Vogt
Honnen S. Weiss
Paul J. Zech

OF COUNSEL

Samuel Bearmon
Charles F. Bisanz
Kareen R. Ecklund

For full biographical listings, see the Martindale-Hubbell Law Directory

FOSTER, WALDECK, LIND & GRIES, LTD. (AV)

Suite 2300 Metropolitan Centre, 333 South Seventh Street, 55402
Telephone: 612-375-1550
Facsimile: 612-375-0647
St. Michael, Minnesota Office: 100 East Central, P.O. Box 35, 55376.
Telephone: 612-497-3099. Facsimilie: 612-497-3639.

Thomas A. Foster
Timothy W. Waldeck
Peter E. Lind
John R. Gries
Rolf E. Sonnesyn
David J. Lenhardt
Byron M. Peterson
Steven E. Tomsche

Gregory J. Van Heest
Jennifer L. Kjos
Philip J. Danen

Reference: Firstar Bank of Minnesota, N.A.

For full biographical listings, see the Martindale-Hubbell Law Directory

FREDRIKSON & BYRON, P.A. (AV)

1100 International Centre, 900 Second Avenue South, 55402-3397
Telephone: 612-347-7000
Telex: 290569 FREDRIKSON MPS
Telecopier: 612-347-7077
European Office: 79 Knightsbridge, London SW1X 7RB England.
Telephone: 44-71-823-2338.
Telecopier: 44-71-235-2683.

Wells J. Wright (1912-1985)
John P. Byron
Bertin A. Bisbee, Jr.
Richard R. Hansen
Jerome B. Pederson
Robert G. Weber
Robert P. Sands
Keith A. Libbey
Robert B. Whitlock
Howard G. Stacker
Raymond M. Lazar
Thomas R. King
John H. Stout
James L. Baillie
R. Bertram Greener
Warren E. Mack
John L. Powers
Charles F. Diessner
Quentin T. Johnson
Timothy M. Heaney
James R. Haller
Leo G. Stern
Thomas W. Garton
Dobson West
John A. Satorius
Michael A. Stern
Neil A. Weikart
William J. Brody
John H. Merkle
Thomas S. Fraser
Glenn R. Ayres
Stephen R. Bergerson
John A. Grimstad
Eric S. Anderson

(See Next Column)

David R. Busch
John E. Drawz
Adrian E. Herbst
Dennis M. Coyne
David C. Grorud
Konrad J. Friedemann
Larry J. Berg
John J. Erhart
John G. Kost
Kathleen A. Hughes
John M. Koneck
Thomas R. Wilhelmy
Paul L. Landry
Kent G. Harbison
Sue Halverson
Thomas R. Muck
Linda C. Schwartz
James B. Platt
David P. Bunde
Faye Knowles
Richard A. Ross
Gregory P. Kaihoi
Sharon K. Freier
Robert K. Ranum
Mary S. Ranum
Larry D. Hause
Clinton E. Cutler
John P. James
Laurie J. Miller
Robert C. Boisvert, Jr.
Anne M. Radolinski
Gerald R. Giombetti
(Not admitted in MN)
Simon C. Root
Mary E. Strand
Lynn M. Gardin
John F. Wurm
Philip M. Goldman
Daniel J. Maertens
Lawrence E. Koslow
Steven N. Beck
Ann M. Ladd
Gregory G. Freitag
Mary Anne Colovic
Jon C. Nuckles
Steven Z. Kaplan
David R. Marshall
F. Chet Taylor
Cynthia D. Stricker
Todd A. Wind
Jay M. Quam
Richard D. Snyder
Bronwen L. Cound
Edward S. Hotchkiss
William E. Connors
Christopher J. Dolan
Timothy P. Dordell
Thomas B. Archbold
James E. Dorsey
Gail F. Brandt
Elizabeth Beach Bryant
Cynthia A. Jokela
Mary M. Krakow
Debra J. Linder
Melodie R. Rose
Joseph G. Springer
David C. West
Mark W. Greiner
Susan D. Steinwall
Elizabeth McGraw Reiskytl
Rebecca A. Raleigh
Kimberly J. Nordby
Mary E. Hanton
Michelle M. Boynton
Dean R. Karau
Theresa M. Harris
David M. Glaser
Corinna Vecsey
Jean T. Paltzer-Fleming
Paul T. Parker
Terri A. Georgen
Daniel A. Yarano
Robin Powers Kinning

OF COUNSEL

John M. Palmer

For full biographical listings, see the Martindale-Hubbell Law Directory

GILMORE, AAFEDT, FORDE, ANDERSON & GRAY, P.A. (AV)

150 South Fifth Street, Suite 3100, 55402
Telephone: 612-339-8965
Fax: 612-349-6839

Curtis C. Gilmore (Retired)
John R. de Lambert (Retired)
Michael D. Aafedt
Michael Forde
Donald W. Anderson
James R. Gray
Jay T. Hartman
Roderick C. Cosgriff
Janet Monson
Steven C. Gilmore
Mary Marvin Hager

Peter M. Banovetz
Robin D. Simpson
Kirk C. Thompson
Kathy A. Endres
Miriam P. Rykken
Janet Scheel Stellpflug
Lawrence C. Miller
Adam S. Wolkoff
David J. Klaiman
David Brian Kempston
Charles S. Bierman
Sheryl A. Zaworski
Kathryn M. Hipp

Representative Client: General Casualty/Reliance.

For full biographical listings, see the Martindale-Hubbell Law Directory

HENSON & EFRON, P.A. (AV)

1200 Title Insurance Building, 400 Second Avenue South, 55401
Telephone: 612-339-2500
FAX: 612-339-6364

Robert F. Henson
Stanley Efron
Wellington W. Tully, Jr.
Joseph T. Dixon, Jr.
Alan C. Eidsness
William F. Forsyth
Stuart T. Williams
Bruce C. Recher
Louis L. Ainsworth
Stephen L. Hopkins
Susan E. Vandenberg
Clark D. Opdahl

Karen S. Johnston
David Bradley Olsen
Jeffrey N. Saunders
Cheryl Hood Langel
Daniel A. Bueide
Cassandra Phillips Chaffee
John A. Mack
Scott A. Neilson
Sherilyn K. Beck

Representative Clients: Pentair, Inc.; Juran & Moody, Inc.; H.B. Fuller Co.

For full biographical listings, see the Martindale-Hubbell Law Directory

Minneapolis—Continued

HVASS, WEISMAN & KING, CHARTERED (AV)

Suite 450, 100 South Fifth Street, 55402
Telephone: 612-333-0201
FAX: 612-342-2606

Charles T. Hvass (Retired)
Si Weisman (1912-1992)
Robert J. King
Frank J. Brixius
Richard A. Williams, Jr.
Charles T. Hvass, Jr.
Robert J. King, Jr.
Michael W. Unger

John E. Daly
John M. Dornik
Mark T. Porter

For full biographical listings, see the Martindale-Hubbell Law Directory

KAPLAN, STRANGIS AND KAPLAN, P.A. (AV)

5500 Norwest Center, 90 South Seventh Street, 55402
Telephone: 612-375-1138
Fax: 612-375-1143

Sheldon Kaplan
Samuel L. Kaplan
Ralph Strangis
Harvey F. Kaplan
Andris A. Baltins
David Karan
Bruce J. Parker
Catherine A. Bartlett
Robert T. York
Margery K. Otto
Nancy S. Bender-Kelner
Karlin S. Symons
James C. Melville

OF COUNSEL

John H. Matheson

Representative Clients: Affinity Group, Inc.; Allianz Life Insurance Company of North America; Damark International, Inc.; Davisco International, Inc.; LifeUSA Insurance Company; National Presto Industries, Inc.; Payless Cashways, Inc.; Polaris Industries, Inc.; TCF Bank Savings fsb; Trailer Life Enterprises, Inc.

For full biographical listings, see the Martindale-Hubbell Law Directory

LEONARD, STREET AND DEINARD, PROFESSIONAL ASSOCIATION (AV)

Suite 2300, 150 South Fifth Street, 55402
Telephone: 612-335-1500
Telecopier: 612-335-1657

George B. Leonard (1872-1956)
Arthur L. H. Street (1877-1961)
Benedict S. Deinard (1899-1969)
Amos S. Deinard (1898-1985)
Harold D. Field, Jr., (P.A.)
Allen I. Saeks (P.A.)
Thomas D. Feinberg
Morris M. Sherman
George F. Reilly
Charles K. Dayton
Stephen R. Pflaum
Charles A. Mays
Lowell J. Noteboom (P.A.)
George F. McGunnigle
Richard G. Pepin, Jr.
Byron E. Starns, Jr.
Steven M. Rubin
John H. Herman (P.A.)
Steven D. DeRuyter
James R. Dorsey
Stephen J. Davidson
Stephen R. Litman (P.A.)
Edward M. Moersfelder
Robert L. Barrows
Richard J. Wegener (P.A.)
Daniel J. McInerney, Jr.
Frederick W. Morris
John C. Kuehn (P.A.)
Bradley J. Gillan
Michael A. Nekich
Martha C. Brand
David N. Haynes
James V. Roth
Richard H. Martin
Robyn Hansen
Robert L. DeMay
Angela M. Bohmann
Timothy J. Pabst
Robert P. Thavis
James G. Bullard
Joseph M. Finley, Jr.
Lawrence J. Field
David W. Kelley
Mark S. Weitz
Robert J. Huber
David Kantor
John M. Sheran
Angela Mulkerin Christy
Lowell V. Stortz
Douglas B. Greenswag
Ellen G. Sampson
Joan Ericksen Lancaster
Rosanne Nathanson
Michael G. Taylor
John W. Getsinger
Thomas P. Sanders
Robert Zeglovitch
Timothy Welch
Gregg J. Cavanagh
Susan M. Robiner
Bradley J. Gunn
Blake Shepard, Jr.
Nancy A. Wiltgen
William L. Greene
Steven L. Belton
Marc D. Simpson
Shaun C. McElhatton
James J. Bertrand

Debra G. Strehlow
Peter E. Schifsky
Carolyn V. Wolski
Steven R. Lindemann
William H. Koch
Ronald J. Schultz
Ellen Goldberg Luger
Jerry S. Podkopacz
Steven J. Rindsig
Jama M. Kriz
Wendy C. Skjerven
Loren A. Unterseher
Robert H. Torgerson
Edward A. Murphy
Thomas J. Conley
Gregory L. Poe
Joshua J. Kanassatega
Jann M. Eichlersmith
Ruth B. O'Neill
Andrew P. Lee
I. Daniel Colton
Nicole A. Engisch
Tammie S. Ptacek
Michael J. Wurzer

(See Next Column)

Jeffrey E. Grell
Barbara Podlucky Berens
Keith S. Moheban
Alan W. Van Dellen
Jane F. Godfrey
Eric H. Galatz
Dwight A. Larson
Rosanne Jacuzzi
Daniel L. Palmquist
Catherine A. McEnroe
Kathleen A. Roberge (Not admitted in MN)
Sheri Kasper Hank
John E. King
Daniel Oberdorfer
Jeffrey A. Eyers
Steven P. Zabel
James R. Frey
Kathryn A. McCauley
Amy L. Barton
Jeanne M. Cochran
Robert L. Striker (Not admitted in MN)

OF COUNSEL

Sidney Lorber
Sidney Barrows (P.A.)
Peter H. Bachman
Michelle A. Miller

Representative Clients: Hubbard Broadcasting, Inc.; Midcontinent Media, Inc.

For full biographical listings, see the Martindale-Hubbell Law Directory

LOVETT & SMITH, LTD. (AV)

100 South Fifth Street, Suite 2250, 55402
Telephone: 612-339-4567

Thomas G. Lovett, Jr.
Glenn L. Smith
Larry B. Ricke

For full biographical listings, see the Martindale-Hubbell Law Directory

MASLON EDELMAN BORMAN & BRAND (AV)

3300 Norwest Center, 90 South Seventh Street, 55402-4140
Telephone: 612-672-8200
Fax: 612-672-8397

MEMBERS OF FIRM

Samuel H. Maslon (1901-1988)
Hyman Edelman (1905-1993)
Sidney J. Kaplan (1909-1962)
Roger E. Joseph (1917-1966)
Irving R. Brand (1918-1990)
Marvin Borman
Charles Quaintance, Jr.
Neil I. Sell
Martin G. Weinstein
William E. Mullin
William Z. Pentelovitch
Joseph Alexander
Gary J. Haugen
Thomas H. Borman
Rebecca A. Palmer
Mark Eric Baumann
David F. Herr
R. Lawrence Purdy
James Duffy O'Connor
Richard G. Wilson
Leon I. Steinberg
Lawrence M. Shapiro
Howard B. Tarkow
William M. Mower
Larry A. Koch
Virginia Ann Bell
Justin H. Perl
Cooper S. Ashley
Sally Stolen Grossman
Terri Krivosha
Mary R. Vasaly
Edwin Chanin
Clark T. Whitmore
Wayne S. Moskowitz
Mallory K. Mullins
Susan D. Holappa
Charles A. Hoffman
Russell F. Lederman

ASSOCIATES

Richard A. Kempf
Mark W. Lee
Lorrie L. Salzl
Susan E. Oliphant
Alain Marc Baudry
Patricia I. Reding
Anna L. Korinko
Jonathan S. Parritz
Brian J. Klein
James F. Killian
James F. Hanneman
Jeanmarie T. Sales
David T. Quinby
Kevin M. Koepke
Douglas T. Holod
Carleton B. Crutchfield
John D. Darling (Not admitted in MN)
Neil P. Ayotte
Rachel U. Gibbs
Brenda J. Arndt
Laurie K. Fett
Cynthia F. Gilbertson

OF COUNSEL

Robert A. Engelke
Michael L. Snow

Reference: National City Bank, Minneapolis, Minnesota.

For full biographical listings, see the Martindale-Hubbell Law Directory

MEAGHER & GEER (AV)

4200 Multifoods Tower, 33 South Sixth Street, 55402
Telephone: 612-338-0661
Telecopier: 612-338-8384

MEMBERS OF FIRM

I. E. Meagher (1905-1979)
Arthur B. Geer (1908-1977)
Burr B. Markham (1915-1991)
Clyde F. Anderson (Retired)
Oscar C. Adamson, II (Retired)
Mark C. Brennan (Retired)
Arthur W. Nelson (Retired)
Carlyn D. Knudson (Retired)
William D. Flaskamp
Roderick D. Blanchard
Thomas L. Adams
David B. Orfield
Gary W. Hoch
James M. Riley
John Richard Bland
James F. Roegge
R. Gregory Stephens
Donald Chance Mark, Jr.
Robert M. Frazee
Kenneth W. Dodge
Gary M. Hagstrom
Steven C. Eggimann
Bradley M. Jones
Douglas J. Muirhead
Charles E. Spevacek
Charles H. Becker

(See Next Column)

MEAGHER & GEER—*Continued*

MEMBERS OF FIRM (Continued)

Robert E. Salmon
Robert R. Fafinski, Jr.
William M. Hart
Shirley Okrent Lerner
Timothy W. Ridley
Laura J. Hanson
Rodger A. Hagen
John J. McDonald, Jr.
Mark J. Heley
Michael D. Hutchens
Karl J. Yeager
Mary M. O'Brien

ASSOCIATES

Victoria L. Wagner
Christian Andrew Preus
Robert E. Diehl
Galen L. Bruer
Thomas H. Crouch
Cortney S. Le Neave
Leatha Grein Wolter
John C. Hughes
Mark A. Bloomquist
Randy A. Sharbono
Kerry M. Evensen
Robert L. Graff
Barbara A. Zurek
Michael J. Tomsche
Brian R. Sattler
Stacy A. Broman
Eric L. Marhoun
Richard L. Pemberton, Jr.
Thomas E. Propson
Priti R. Patel
Trudi Noel Trysla
Susan M. Radde
Jana M. Sulpizio
Julie L. Levi
Joseph W.E. Schmitt
Cecilie Morris Loidolt
Peter G. Lennington
Robert G. Mork
Christopher J. Schulte
Jeffrey M. Thompson
Brian E. Stevens
Aaron B. Latto
David Hollingshead Anderson
Jennifer Ball Mohlenhoff
Kimberly Hewitt Boyd
Sherry L.S. Trudeau

Insurance Clients: Federated Mutual Insurance Co.; Allstate Insurance Cos.; State Farm Insurance Cos.

For full biographical listings, see the Martindale-Hubbell Law Directory

MESHBESHER & SPENCE, LTD. (AV)

1616 Park Avenue, 55404
Telephone: 612-339-9121
Fax: 612-339-9188
St. Paul, Minnesota Office: World Trade Center.
Telephone: 612-227-0799.
St. Cloud, Minnesota Office: 400 Zapp Bank Plaza.
Telephone: 612-656-0484.

Kenneth Meshbesher
Ronald I. Meshbesher
Russell M. Spence (Resident, St. Paul Office)
James H. Gilbert
John P. Clifford
Dennis R. Johnson
Jack Nordby
Paul W. Bergstrom (Resident, St. Paul Office)
Patrick K. Horan (Resident, St. Paul Office)
Daniel J. Boivin
Michael C. Snyder
James A. Wellner
John P. Sheehy
Mark D. Streed
Randall Spence
Howard I. Bass
Daniel C. Guerrero
Katherine S. Flom
Pamela R. Finney
Jeffrey P. Oistad (Resident, St. Cloud Office)
Jeffrey A. Olson
Daniel E. Meshbesher
Anthony J. Nemo
Colleen M. Christianson
Russell Spence, Jr.

For full biographical listings, see the Martindale-Hubbell Law Directory

MOSS & BARNETT, A PROFESSIONAL ASSOCIATION (AV)

4800 Norwest Center, 90 South Seventh Street, 55402-4129
Telephone: 612-347-0300
Telecopier: 612-339-6686

Herman J. Ratelle
Patrick F. Flaherty
Wayne A. Hergott
Paul Van Valkenburg
Michael L. Flanagan
Thomas A. Keller III
W. Scott Herzog
James E. O'Brien
Paul G. Neimann
Edward L. Winer
William N. Koster
William A. Haug
Charles A. Parsons, Jr.
Richard J. Johnson
Robert J. Lukes
James A. Rubenstein
Thomas R. Sheran
J. Michael Hirsch
Edward J. Blomme
Ann K. Newhall
Michael J. Ahern
Jeffrey L. Watson
Thomas J. Shroyer
Dale M. Wagner
David P. Jendrzejek
Curtis D. Smith
Dave F. Senger
Robert A. Brunig
Louis J. Speltz
Mitchell H. Cox
Michael J. Bradley
Peter A. Koller
Richard J. Kelber
Laura J. McKnight
Kevin M. Busch
Susan C. Rhode
Thomas M. Hughes
Nick Hay

OF COUNSEL

Milda K. Hedblom

J. Michael Colloton
Thomas A. Judd
Deanne M. Greco
Douglas M. Lawrence
Cass S. Weil
M. Cecilia Ray
Joseph R. Klein
Vincent J. Fahnlander
Paul B. Zisla
Timothy E. Wuestenhagen

(See Next Column)

Nancy M. Kiskis
Charles E. Jones
JoAnn K. Barbetta
Brian T. Grogan
Michael J. Luzum
Cory Larsen Bettenga
Daniel P. Damond
Scott A. Abdallah
Klay C. Ahrens

RETIRED

Verne W. Moss
Fremont C. Fletcher
James H. Hennessy
Stanley R. Stasel
Howard S. Cox

Representative Clients: Chubb Group of Insurance Companies; First Bank System, Inc.; Mayo Foundation; Northern States Power; Norwest Bank Minnesota; United Hardware Distributing Co. (Hardware Hank Stores); Vista Telephone Company of Minnesota.

For full biographical listings, see the Martindale-Hubbell Law Directory

O'CONNOR & HANNAN (AV)

3800 IDS Center, 80 South Eighth Street, 55402-2254
Telephone: 612-343-1200
Telecopy: 612-343-1256
Washington, D.C. Office: 1919 Pennsylvania Avenue, N.W., Suite 800.
Telephone: 202-887-1400.
Telecopy: 202-466-2198.

MEMBERS OF FIRM

Frederick W. Thomas (1911-1986)
William C. Kelly (1918-1970)
Patrick J. O'Connor
Joe A. Walters
Robert J. Tennessen
John S. Jagiela

OF COUNSEL

Michael E. McGuire

WASHINGTON, D.C. OFFICE

William T. Hannan (1911-1985)
John J. Flynn (1925-1990)
H. Robert Halper (1931-1988)
Patrick J. O'Connor
Edward W. Brooke *
Thomas H. Quinn *
David R. Melincoff *
Hope S. Foster *
Patrick E. O'Donnell *
Joseph H. Blatchford *
F. Gordon Lee *
George J. Mannina, Jr. *
John J. McDermott *
James W. Symington *
Donald R. Dinan *
Michael Colopy **
Thomas J. Schneider *
David L. Hill *
Thomas J. Corcoran **
Peter M. Kazon *
Christina W. Fleps *
Timothy W. Jenkins *
Gary C. Adler *
Wayne M. Zell *
J. Timothy O'Neill *
Mark R. Paoletta *
David L. Anderson *
Audrey P. Rasmussen *

Stephen C. Fogleman *
Elissa Garber Kon *
Craig A. Koenigs *

OF COUNSEL

David C. Treen *
E. William Crotty *
Charles R. McCarthy, Jr. *
William W. Nickerson *
H. George Schweitzer *

A List of Representative Clients will be furnished upon request.
*Not admitted in Minn.
**Non-Lawyer Partner

For full biographical listings, see the Martindale-Hubbell Law Directory

PARSINEN BOWMAN & LEVY, A PROFESSIONAL ASSOCIATION (AV)

100 South 5th Street Suite 1100, 55402
Telephone: 612-333-2111
FAX: 612-333-6798

Dennis A. Bowman
John Parsinen
Robert A. Levy
Jack A. Rosberg
John F. Bonner, III
David A. Gotlieb
Karen Ciegler Hansen
Jeffrey C. Robbins
E. Burke Hinds, III
Howard J. Rubin
David A. Orenstein
Diane L. Kroupa
Jeanne K. Stretch
John C. Levy
Joseph M. Sokolowski
Randy B. Evans
Brian R. Martens
Steven R. Katz

Rebecca McDaniel
Ann Marks Sanford
Timothy R. Ring
Robert A. Hill
W. James Vogl, Jr.
Bradley Allen Kletscher
John R. Bedosky
Roben D. Hunter
Jeffrey R. Johnson (Not admitted in MN)

OF COUNSEL

Bruce B. James

For full biographical listings, see the Martindale-Hubbell Law Directory

Minneapolis—Continued

POPHAM, HAIK, SCHNOBRICH & KAUFMAN, LTD. (AV)

222 South 9th Street, Suite 3300, 55402
Telephone: 612-333-4800
Denver, Colorado Office: Suite 2400, 1200 17th Street.
Telephone: 303-893-1200.
Washington, D.C. Office: 655 Fifteenth Street, N.W., Suite 800.
Telephone: 202-824-8000.
Miami, Florida Office: 4000 International Place, 100 Southeast 2nd Street.
Telephone: 305-530-0050.
Affiliated Offices: Kasper, Knacke, Schauble and Wintterlin
Stuttgart, Germany Office: Schützenstrasse 13, 70182 Stuttgart.
Telephone: 0-1149-711-22363.
Fax: 011-49-711-223-6410.
Leipzig, Germany Office: Könneritzstrasse 43, 04229 Leipzig.
Telephone: 00149-341-491-8429.
Fax: 01149-341-491-8215.
Beijing, China Office: Tianping Law Office, 20, Wangfujing Avenue, P.O. Code 100006.
Telephone: 861-513-5261.

Wayne G. Popham
Raymond A. Haik
Roger W. Schnobrich
Robert A. Minish
Rolfe A. Worden
G. Marc Whitehead
Bruce D. Willis
G. Robert Johnson
Robert S. Burk
Hugh V. Plunkett, III
Frederick C. Brown, Jr.
Thomas K. Berg
Bruce D. Malkerson
James R. Steilen
James B. Lockhart
Allen W. Hinderaker
D. William Kaufman
Paul H. Tietz
Howard S. (Sam) Myers, III
Janie S. Mayeron
Thomas J. Barrett
James A. Payne
David A. Jones
Lee E. Sheehy
Michael T. Nilan
Thomas M. Sipkins
Robert C. Moilanen
Thomas F. Nelson
Thomas J. Radio
David L. Hashmall
James W. Rockwell
Kathleen M. Martin
John C. Childs
Douglas P. Seaton
Thomas E. Sanner
Scott K. Goldsmith
Frank A. Taylor
Madge S. Thorsen
Richard A. Kaplan
Bruce B. McPheeters
Scott E. Richter
Paul J. Linstroth
Scott A. Smith
Brian N. Johnson
Bradley A. Fuller
Michael S. Gilliland
Donald M. Lewis
Girard P. Miller
Elizabeth Ann Thompson
Keith J. Halleland
Mark B. Peterson
Bruce A. Peterson
Janna R. Severance
Thomas C. Mielenhausen
J. Michael Schwartz
Jeffrey P. Cairns
Ellen L. Maas
Lewis J. Rotman
Louis N. Smith
Bruce H. Little
Mark F. Palma
Russell S. Ponessa
Bryan L. Crawford
Matthew E. Damon
Paul B. Jones
William D. Hittler
John W. Provo
Gregory G. Scott
Gary P. Gengel, II
Cecilia M. Michel
Robert C. Castle
Shane R. Kelley
Robert R. Ribeiro
Kathryn Walker-Torgerson
Karen Hansen
Suesan Lea Pace
Steven M. Phillips
William R. Skallerud
Patricia O'Leary Kiscoan
Andrew D. Parker

SPECIAL COUNSEL

George J. Socha, Jr.
Deborah J. Klein

Karen Rae Cole
Robert B. MacDonald
Kevin P. Staunton
Daniel D. Hill
Andrea Mitchell Walsh
Michael A. Putnam
John Mark Elliott
Bruce L. McLellan
Donald R. McNeil Jr.
Bryan J. Leary
Michael V. Seifert
Jeffrey J. Weill
Anne W. Awsumb
Thaddeus R. Lightfoot (Not admitted in MN)
Robert K. Shelquist
Todd M. Kleinhuizen
Jeffrey D. Pflaum
Steven A. Kaye
Leslye DeRoos Rood
Patrick A. Reinken
Julie M. Friedman
Thomas W. Macleod, III
David H. Wright
Elizabeth M. Richter
Kelley M. Sohler
Polly A. Maier
Peter L. Tester
Andrew H. Seitel
Meredith M. McQuaid
Elaine J. Erickson
S. Lata Setty
Sheila T. Kerwin
Denise M. Ellis
Pamela Elaine Bethel
Aaron M. Rodriguez
Courtney E. Ward
Caroline A. Simenson
Joseph Schmitt
Janell M. Gabor
Tracy Lessman McGuire
Christopher A. Lidstad
Sandra L. Schlafge
David M. Hudson
John M. Jackson
Liane M. Wong
James A. Mennell
Rosanne G. Zaidenweber
Shirley J. Qual

(See Next Column)

OF COUNSEL

Fred L. Morrison
Judith T. Younger
Thomas M. Libera
Yi Qian

Representative Clients: Ashland Oil, Inc.; Cargill, Inc.; E.F. Hutton, Inc.; Iowa Beef Processors, Inc.; Northern States Power Co.; SciMed Life Systems, Inc.; Underwriters Adjustment Co.

For full biographical listings, see the Martindale-Hubbell Law Directory

ROBERT MERRILL ROSENBERG, P.A. (AV)

Suite 2500 One Financial Plaza, 120 South Sixth Street, 55402-1826
Telephone: 612-349-5290
Facsimile: 612-349-9962

Robert Merrill Rosenberg

For full biographical listings, see the Martindale-Hubbell Law Directory

SALITERMAN & SIEFFERMAN LAW FIRM (AV)

Suite 1000 Northstar Center East, 608 Second Avenue South, 55402
Telephone: 612-339-1400
Fax: 612-349-2908

Richard A. Saliterman
Floyd E. Siefferman, Jr.
John R. Heine
Nicholas M. Wenner
Bretton J. Horttor

LEGAL SUPPORT PERSONNEL

Darryl R. Fenley

For full biographical listings, see the Martindale-Hubbell Law Directory

SIEGEL, BRILL, GREUPNER & DUFFY, P.A. (AV)

1300 Washington Square, 100 Washington Avenue South, 55401
Telephone: 612-339-7131
Telecopier: 612-339-6591

Richard Siegel
Josiah E. Brill, Jr.
James R. Greupner
Gerald S. Duffy
Wood R. Foster, Jr.
Thomas H. Goodman
John S. Watson
Wm. Christopher Penwell
Susan M. Voigt
Anthony James Gleekel
Joel H. Jensen

Sherri L. Rohlf
Brian E. Weisberg
Rosemary Tuohy
Jordan M. Lewis
James A. Yarosh

RETIRED

Maurice L. Grossman (P.A.)
Sheldon D. Karlins (P.A.)

Representative Clients: Champion Auto Stores, Inc.; Holiday Inns; Ron-Vik, Inc.; Super America Stations, Inc.; Ashland Oil, Inc.; Aveda Corporation; Applied Spectrum Technology, Inc.; Richard Manufacturing Co.; Mann Theaters; Homecraft Builders, Inc.

For full biographical listings, see the Martindale-Hubbell Law Directory

WAGNER, FALCONER & JUDD, LTD. (AV)

2650 IDS Center, 80 South Eighth Street, 55402-2113
Telephone: 612-339-1421
Telecopier: 612-349-6691

C. J. Wagner (1905-1988)
Alan W. Falconer
Robert A. Judd
James K. Sander
Mark O. Anderson
Rodney A. Honkanen
Michael J. DuPont

LEGAL SUPPORT PERSONNEL

Gary Lawrence (Commercial Account Manager)

Representative Clients: Honeywell, Inc.; United Electric Co.; Trane Co.; Alexander & Alexander, Inc.; Marsh & McLennan; American Insurance Agency; C. H. Carpenter Lumber Co.; L.S.B. Industries, Inc.; Snyder General Corporation.

For full biographical listings, see the Martindale-Hubbell Law Directory

ZELLE & LARSON (AV)

33 South Sixth Street, City Center, Suite 4400, 55402
Telephone: 612-339-2020
Telecopier: 612-336-9100
Waltham, Massachusetts Office: 3 University Office Park, 95 Sawyer Road, Suite 500.
Telephone: 617-891-7020.
Dallas, Texas Office: 1201 Main Street, Suite 3000.
Telephone: 214-742-3000.
San Francisco, California Office: One Market Plaza, Steuart Street Tower, 15th Floor.
Telephone: 415-978-9788.

(See Next Column)

ZELLE & LARSON—*Continued*

MEMBERS OF FIRM

Lowry Barfield (Resident, Dallas, Texas Office)
Stanley G. DeLaHunt
Alex M. Duarte (Resident, San Francisco, California Office)
Mark J. Feinberg
H. Jerome Gette (Resident, Dallas, Texas Office)
Rolf E. Gilbertson
Paul L. Gingras
Richard M. Hagstrom
John T. Harding, Jr. (Resident, Waltham, Massachusetts Office)
Lawrence T. Hofmann
Philip C. Hunsucker (Resident, San Francisco, California Office)
Dale I. Larson
David S. Markun (Resident, San Francisco, California Office)
John Buck Massopust
William Gerald McElroy, Jr. (Resident, Waltham, Massachusetts Office)
Terrence C. McRea (Resident, Dallas, Texas Office)
Steven D. Meier (Resident, San Francisco, California Office)
Janet L. R. Menna (Resident Waltham, Massachusetts Office)
Michael S. Quinn (Resident, Dallas, Texas Office)
James S. Reece
Timothy W. Regan
Jeff Ross
Patricia St. Peter
Lyle B. Sinell (Resident, San Francisco, California Office)
James E. Speier (Resident, Dallas, Texas Office)
Richard L. Voelbel
Sandra Wallace
Robert M. Wattson
Anthony R. Zelle (Resident, Waltham, Massachusetts Office)
Lawrence Zelle

ASSOCIATES

Steven J. Badger (Resident, Dallas, Texas Office)
Bryan M. Barber (Resident, San Francisco, California Office)
Michelle R. Bernard (Resident, San Francisco, California Office)
Karen Ann Brandstrader (Resident, San Francisco, California Office)
Brad E. Brewer (Resident, Dallas, Texas Office)
Kerry K. Brown (Resident, Dallas, Texas Office)
Michael R. Cashman
Thomas B. Caswell, III
Catherine M. Colinvaux (Resident, Waltham, Massachusetts Office)
Thomas H. Cook, Jr. (Resident, Dallas, Texas Office)
Veronica Czuchna (Resident, Dallas, Texas Office)
Thomas M. Darden
Matthew K. Davis (Resident, Dallas, Texas Office)
Keith A. Dotseth
Michelle Kathleen Enright
Greg S. Farnik (Resident, Dallas, Texas Office)
Rosemary A. Frazel
Felicia F. Goldstein (Resident, San Francisco, California Office)
Robert L. Gonser (Resident, San Francisco, California Office)
John C. Goodnow
Lisa F. Graul (Resident, San Francisco, California Office)
Andrea J. Greenberg (Resident, San Francisco, California Office)
Colleen C. Hammer (Resident, San Francisco, California Office)
Lesley M. James
Jonathan D. Jay
Mark C. Kareken
Ronald S. Kravitz (Resident, San Francisco, California Office)
David C. Linder (Not admitted in MN)
Brian E. Mahoney (Resident, San Francisco, California Office)
Robert D. Martinez (Resident, Dallas, Texas Office)
Kristin E. McIntosh (Resident, Waltham, Massachusetts Office)
Robert F. McKenna (Resident, San Francisco, California Office)
Daniel J. Millea
Natalie S. Monroe (Resident, Waltham, Massachusetts Office)
Joanne Munro (Resident, Dallas, Texas Office)
Kathleen B. O'Neill (Resident, Waltham, Massachusetts Office)
Joseph P. Pozen
Ranjani Ramakrishna (Resident, San Francisco, California Office)
Brian L. Ripperger
Andrew H. Roberts (Resident, Dallas, Texas Office)
Charles J. Rothstein
Scott J. Ryskoski (Not admitted in MN)
Denise Schardein (Resident, San Francisco, California Office)
Dana Shelhimer (Resident, Dallas, Texas Office)
Scott A. Slomiak (Resident, San Francisco, California Office)
Gillian Small, G.M. (Resident, San Francisco, California Office)
Paul K. Smith
T. Joe Snodgrass
L. Kimberly Steele (Resident, Dallas, Texas Office)
Michael J. Steinlage
Karl S. Vasiloff (Resident, Waltham, Massachusetts Office)
Terese S. Wallschlaeger
Daniel S. Weiss

For full biographical listings, see the Martindale-Hubbell Law Directory

*MONTEVIDEO,** Chippewa Co.

NELSON OYEN TORVIK (AV)

221 North First Street, P.O. Box 656, 56265
Telephone: 612-269-6461
Fax: 612-269-8024
Clarkfield, Minnesota Office:
Telephone: 612-669-4447.

(See Next Column)

MEMBERS OF FIRM

John P. Nelson (Retired)
Sigvald B. Oyen (Retired)
Stephen S. Torvik
David M. Gilbertson
Janice M. Nelson
Kevin K. Stroup

ASSOCIATES

Geoffrey J. Hathaway

Representative Clients: Minnwest Bank Montevideo; Minnesota Valley Cooperative Light & Power Assn.; Co-op Credit Union; Metropolitan Federal Bank Montevideo.
References: Minnwest Bank Montevideo; General Adjustment Bureau, Inc.

For full biographical listings, see the Martindale-Hubbell Law Directory

PRINDLE, MALAND, SELLNER, STENNES AND KNUTSEN, CHARTERED (AV)

102 Parkway Drive, P.O. Box 591, 56265
Telephone: 612-269-6491
Fax: 612-269-5433
Clara City, Minnesota Office: Telephone 612-847-2418.

W. D. Prindle (Retired)
Donald L. Maland
John P. Sellner
Stephen L. Stennes
Dwayne N. Knutsen

General Counsel for: First National Bank in Montevideo, Minn.
Representative Clients: Citizens State Bank, Clara City, Minn.; Mutual Service Casualty Insurance Co., St. Paul, Minn.; Milbank Mutual Insurance Co., Milbank, S. Dakota; National Farmers Union Property & Casualty Co., Denver, Colo.

For full biographical listings, see the Martindale-Hubbell Law Directory

*MOORHEAD,** Clay Co.

DOSLAND, NORDHOUGEN, LILLEHAUG & JOHNSON, P.A. (AV)

Suite 203 American Bank Moorhead Building, 730 Center Avenue, P.O. Box 100, 56561-0100
Telephone: 218-233-2744
Fax: 218-233-1570

C. A. Nye (1886-1910)
C. G. Dosland (1898-1945)
G. L. Dosland (1927-1983)
W. B. Dosland (1954-1990)
John P. Dosland
Curtis A. Nordhougen
Duane A. Lillehaug
Joel D. Johnson
Bruce Romanick

General Counsel For: American Crystal Sugar Co.; American Bank Moorhead, Moorhead, Minnesota.
Representative Clients: Auto Owners Insurance Co.; Wausau Insurance Cos.; Gethsemane Episcopal Cathedral; Swift-Eckrich, Inc.; Barrett Mobile Home Transport, Inc.; Moorhead Economic Development Authority; Eventide.
Reference: American Bank Moorhead, Moorhead, Minnesota.

For full biographical listings, see the Martindale-Hubbell Law Directory

GUNHUS, GRINNELL, KLINGER, SWENSON & GUY, LTD. (AV)

512 Center Avenue, P.O. Box 1077, 56561-1077
Telephone: 218-236-6462
Telecopier: 218-236-9873
Fargo, North Dakota Office: 514 Gate City Building, P.O. Box 2783.
Telephone: 701-235-2506.
Telecopier: 701-235-9862.

ATTORNEYS

Gunder Gunhus
Paul E. Grinnell
Edward F. Klinger
Robert H. Swenson
William L. Guy, III
Dean A. Hoistad
Craig R. Campbell
Jon E. Strinden
Bernard E. Reynolds
Eric K. Fosaaen
Gregory P. Hammes
Bruce A. Schoenwald
Mary C. Locken
David M. Petrocchi (Not admitted in MN)

Insurance Clients: Aetna Life and Casualty Co.; Crum & Forster; Home Insurance Co.; Royal Insurance—USTU; St. Paul Cos.; United States Fidelity and Guaranty Co.
Representative Clients: Certainteed Corp.; Farm Credit Services; Heartland Medical Center; U.S. West Communications.

For full biographical listings, see the Martindale-Hubbell Law Directory

JEFFRIES, OLSON, FLOM, OPPEGARD & HOGAN, P.A. (AV)

403 Center Avenue, P.O. Box 9, 56561-0009
Telephone: 218-233-3222
FAX: 218-233-7065
Fargo, North Dakota Office: 1325 23rd Street SW, 58103.
Telephone: 701-280-2300.

Richard N. Jeffries
Thomas R. Olson
Joel A. Flom
Paul R. Oppegard
Barry P. Hogan

(See Next Column)

JEFFRIES, OLSON, FLOM, OPPEGARD & HOGAN P.A., *Moorhead—Continued*

James R. Bullis | Ronald James Knoll

Representative Clients: American International Adjustment Co.; American States/Western Insurance Co.; Farmers Insurance Group; Federated Mutual Insurance Co.; Fireman's Fund Insurance Co.; Hartford Insurance Co.; Midwest Medical Insurance Co.; St. Paul Fire & Marine Insurance Co.

For full biographical listings, see the Martindale-Hubbell Law Directory

*MORA,** Kanabec Co. — (Refer to St. Cloud)

*MORRIS,** Stevens Co. — (Refer to Alexandria)

*NEW ULM,** Brown Co.

GISLASON, DOSLAND, HUNTER AND MALECKI (AV)

A Partnership including a Professional Association
State and Center Streets, P.O. Box 458, 56073-0458
Telephone: 507-354-3111
Telecopier: 507-354-8447
Minneapolis, Minnesota Office: Opus Center, Suite 215E. 9900 Bren Road East, P.O. Box 5297.
Telephone: 612-933-9900.
Telecopier: 612-933-0242.
Mankato, Minnesota Office: 75 Teton Lane, P.O. Box 4157.
Telephone: 507-387-1115.
Fax: 507-387-4413.
Chanhassen, Minnesota Office: Americana Community Bank Building, 600 West 79th Street, P.O. Box 950.
Telephone: 612-934-7754.
Fax: 612-934-7793.

MEMBERS OF FIRM

Sidney P. Gislason (1908-1985)
C. Allen Dosland
Daniel A. Gislason
Robert M. Halvorson (1945-1993)
C. Thomas Wilson
Ruth Ann Webster
Gary W. Koch
William A. Moeller
Kurt D. Johnson
Reed H. Glawe
Noel L. Phifer
Jeffry C. Braegelmann

ASSOCIATES

David W. Sturges (Not admitted in MN)
Mark S. Ullery
Michael S. Dove

Regional Counsel for: Associated Milk Producers, Inc.
Representative Clients: Travelers Insurance Co.; CIGNA; St. Paul Insurance Cos.; Farmers Insurance Group; Auto-Owners Insurance Co.; Midwest Medical Insurance Co.; Minnesota Lawyers Mutual Insurance Co.; Wausau Insurance Co.; Wal-Mart.

For full biographical listings, see the Martindale-Hubbell Law Directory

NORTHFIELD, Rice Co.

SCHMITZ & OPHAUG (AV)

220 Division Street, P.O. Box 237, 55057
Telephone: Northfield 507-645-9541
Twin Cities 612-333-1831
Fax: 507-645-8232

MEMBERS OF FIRM

Peter J. Schmitz | John M. Ophaug

For full biographical listings, see the Martindale-Hubbell Law Directory

*OLIVIA,** Renville Co.

KRAFT, WALSER, NELSON, HETTIG & HONSEY (AV)

107 North Ninth Street, P.O. Box 148, 56277-0148
Telephone: 612-523-1322
Hutchinson, Minnesota Office: 131 Main Street South. P.O. Box 129.
Telephone: 612-587-8150.
Renville, Minnesota Office: 338 North Main Street.
Telephone: 612-329-3474.

John H. Kraft
Donald H. Walser
Paul A. Nelson
Steven E. Hettig
Daniel B. Honsey

Representative Clients: American State Bank of Olivia; Duininck Cos.; Southern Minnesota Beet Sugar Cooperative; Buffalo Lake Nursing Home; Brandt Electric, Inc.; Renville Farmers Co-op Credit Union; State Bank of Bird Island; City of Renville; Farm Credit Services; Richard Larson Builders, Inc.

For full biographical listings, see the Martindale-Hubbell Law Directory

*OWATONNA,** Steele Co.

NELSON, CASEY, TRIPP & DOW, P.A. (AV)

Parrott Building, 202 North Cedar Street, P.O. Box 545, 55060
Telephone: 507-451-3580
Fax: 507-451-3532

(See Next Column)

Harold S. Nelson (1890-1972)
Otto J. Nelson (1894-1947)
George E. Dow, Jr.
David L. Einhaus
Eric J. Mattison

OF COUNSEL

Byron J. Casey | Wallace M. Tripp (Retired)

Representative Clients: First Bank of Owatonna; Owatonna School District; Central Co-op Oil Assn.; Kraay Bros., Inc.; Blount Inc.; Gopher Sport; Budget Oil Co.; Owatonna Clinic, P.A.; Security Archives.

*PIPESTONE,** Pipestone Co. — (Refer to Montevideo)

*PRESTON,** Fillmore Co. — (Refer to Spring Valley)

*RED LAKE FALLS,** Red Lake Co. — (Refer to Thief River Falls)

*RED WING,** Goodhue Co.

RICHARDSON AND RICHARDSON (AV)

Goodhue County National Bank Building, 55066
Telephone: 612-388-4796

MEMBERS OF FIRM

Charles Richardson | Charles O. Richardson

Reference: Goodhue County National Bank.

For full biographical listings, see the Martindale-Hubbell Law Directory

*REDWOOD FALLS,** Redwood Co. — (Refer to Montevideo)

RENVILLE, Renville Co.

KRAFT, WALSER, NELSON, HETTIG & HONSEY (AV)

338 North Main Street, P.O. Box 617, 56284
Telephone: 612-329-3474

John H. Kraft
Donald H. Walser
Paul A. Nelson
Steven E. Hettig

*ROCHESTER,** Olmsted Co.

DUNLAP & SEEGER, P.A. (AV)

Marquette Bank Building, 206 South Broadway, Suite 505, P.O. Box 549, 55903-0549
Telephone: 507-288-9111
Fax: 507-288-9342

Robert R. Dunlap (1915-1992)
Franklin Michaels
Ronald L. Seeger
Milton A. Rosenblad
Paul A. Finseth
Daniel E. Berndt
John B. Arnold
Peter C. Sandberg
Tina L. Mohr
Jeffrey A. Hanson
Kenneth R. Moen
William J. Ryan
Paul W. Bucher
Nancy Brostrom Vollertsen
Douglas A. Boese
Thomas W. Jacobson
Mary H. Dunlap
William P. Volkmar
Mark E. Fosse
Ken D. Schueler
Gregory J. Griffiths
Michael S. Dietz
Eric D. Larson

Representative Clients: Norwest Bank Minnesota Southeast N.A.; Marquette Bank Rochester; Farm Credit Services of Southern Minnesota, ACA; Minnesota Lawyers Mutual Insurance Co.; Allied Mutual Insurance Co.; State Farm Mutual Automobile Insurance Co.; Auto-Owners Insurance Co.; Farmers Insurance Group; County of Olmsted; Rochester Independent School District No. 535.

For full biographical listings, see the Martindale-Hubbell Law Directory

O'BRIEN, EHRICK, WOLF, DEANER & MAUS (AV)

206 South Broadway, Suite 611, 55904-6558
Telephone: 507-289-4041
Fax: 507-281-4778

MEMBERS OF FIRM

F. J. O'Brien (1904-1992)
Richard V. Ehrick
Thomas Wolf
Ted E. Deaner
Terence L. Maus
Steven S. Fuller
Joseph F. Chase
Jill I. Frieders

ASSOCIATES

David J. Jones
Julia E. Utz
Jerrold E. Anderson

OF COUNSEL

Allan R. DeBoer

Representative Clients: City of Rochester; County of Olmsted; Mayo Clinic; Rochester Public Schools; Crawford and Company; Farm Credit Services; First Bank National Association; Sentry Insurance; Travelers Insurance Cos.; Pepsi Cola Bottling Co. of Rochester.

For full biographical listings, see the Martindale-Hubbell Law Directory

*ROSEAU,** Roseau Co. — (Refer to Hallock)

*ST. CLOUD,** Stearns, Benton & Sherburne Cos.

HUGHES, MATHEWS & DIDIER, P.A. (AV)

110 South Sixth Avenue, Suite 200, P.O. Box 548, 56302-0548
Telephone: 612-251-4397
Fax: 612-251-5781

Kevin J. Hughes
Thomas E. Mathews
Jean M. Didier

Paul R. Harris
Timothy S. Murphy

Representative Clients: The First American National Bank of St. Cloud; The St. Cloud Hospital; St. John's University; College of St. Benedict; Tanner Systems, Inc.; Anderson Trucking Service, Inc.

For full biographical listings, see the Martindale-Hubbell Law Directory

HUGHES, THOREEN & KNAPP, P.A. (AV)

110 South Sixth Avenue, Suite 200, P.O. Box 1718, 56302-1718
Telephone: 612-251-6175
Fax: 612-251-6857

Keith F. Hughes
Gerald L. Thoreen
Thomas P. Knapp
Jerry O. Relph
Bradley W. Hanson

Representative Clients: The First American Bank of St. Cloud; North American State Bank of Belgrade, Minnesota; Holiday Inn of St. Cloud, Inc.; Catholic Charities of the Diocese of St. Cloud; Central Minnesota Mental Health Center; Central Minnesota Community Foundation; D.H. Blattner & Sons, Inc.; St. John's Abbey and University; College of St. Benedict; Sisters of the Order of St. Benedict.

For full biographical listings, see the Martindale-Hubbell Law Directory

*ST. JAMES,** Watonwan Co. — (Refer to New Ulm)

*ST. PAUL,** Ramsey Co.

BRIGGS AND MORGAN, PROFESSIONAL ASSOCIATION (AV)

2200 First National Bank Building, 55101
Telephone: 612-223-6600
Telecopier: 612-223-6450
Minneapolis, Minnesota Office: 2400 IDS Center, 80 South Eighth Street.
Telephone: 612-334-8400.
Telecopier: 612-334-8650.

RESIDENT PERSONNEL

Richard D. Anderson
Frederick P. Angst
Kevin A. Berg
Andrea M. Bond
Neal T. Buethe
Daniel J. Cole, Jr.
John L. Devney
Terence N. Doyle
Mary M. Dyrseth
Martin H. Fisk
David C. Forsberg
Bernard P. Friel
Michael J. Galvin, Jr.
Jerome A. Geis
David G. Greening
R. Ann Huntrods
Mary L. Ippel
Paul S. Jacobsen
John R. Kenefick
Scott G. Knudson
A. Patrick Leighton, III
James J. Long
Alan H. Maclin
David C. McDonald
M. Brigid McDonough
Michael J. McEllistrem
John J. McNeely
James P. O'Meara
Cole Oehler
Elena L. Ostby
Peter S. Popovich
Jeffrey A. Redmon
Mark G. Schroeder
Sally A. Scoggin
Peter H. Seed
McNeil V. Seymour, Jr.
Jeffrey F. Shaw
Douglas L. Skor
Terry L. Slye
Ronald L. Sorenson
Tony R. Stemberger
Michael H. Streater
John B. Van de North, Jr.
James A. Vose
Daniel R. Wachtler

Philip G. Alden
Mark J. Ayotte
Karna A. Berg
Thomas L. Bray
Darlene M. Cobian
Margo L. Coyle
Lydia P. Crawford
Kathleen Erickson DiGiorno
David L. Donlin
Craig M. Gregersen
Toni L. Halleen
W. Patrick Judge
Patrick T. Kampmeyer
Eric L. Leonard
Patrick E. Mascia
Robin L. Phillips
Ellen M. Smith

OF COUNSEL

Frank Hammond
Leonard J. Keyes
Burt E. Swanson

MINNEAPOLIS OFFICE

Nancy Chaffee Aiken
Donna T.J. Bailey
Brian G. Belisle
Gregory M. Bistram
Linda L. Boss
Scott G. Bowman
John A. Cairns
Christopher C. Cleveland
R. Scott Davies
William T. Dolan
Marian M. Durkin
Jonathan L. Eisenberg
Karen J. Evans
Mark J. Frenz
Avron L. Gordon
Joel H. Gottesman

(See Next Column)

MINNEAPOLIS OFFICE (Continued)

Michael J. Grimes
Nils F. Grossman
Trudy J. Halla
Samuel L. Hanson
Charles R. Haynor
Jeffrey J. Keyes
Joseph T. Kinning
Andrew R. Kintzinger
Michael C Krikava
Janel E. LaBoda
Thomas A. Larson
David M. Lebedoff
Michelle C. Leighton
Matthew J. Levitt
John H. Lindstrom
Lauren E. Lonergan
Anthony M. Marick
Richard G. Mark
J. Patrick McDavitt
Kristin S. Melby
Michael Thomas Miller
James E. Nelson
Carolyn S. Nestingen
Joseph P. Noack
Jack Y. Perry
Robert J. Pratte
Diane B. Ray
James G. Ray
Charles B. Rogers
David B. Sand
Margaret K. Savage
Jay W. Schlosser
Andrew C. Selden
David J. Spencer
David J. Steingart
Gregory J. Stenmoe
H. Torbjorn Svensson
Vincent A. Thomas
Timothy R. Thornton
Philip J. Tilton
Michael J. Tostengard
Brian D. Wenger
Karin L. Wille
Steven W. Wilson
Stephen Winnick
Nancy J. Wolf
Robert E. Woods

OF COUNSEL

Donald R. Johnston
Jerry F. Rotman
Robert G. Share
John Troyer

For full biographical listings, see the Martindale-Hubbell Law Directory

COLLINS, BUCKLEY, SAUNTRY AND HAUGH (AV)

West 1100 First National Bank Building, 332 Minnesota Street, 55101
Telephone: 612-227-0611
Telecopier: 612-227-0758

MEMBERS OF FIRM

Eugene D. Buckley
Theodore J. Collins
Michael J. Sauntry
William E. Haugh, Jr.
Mark W. Gehan, Jr.
Patrick T. Tierney
Thomas J. Germscheid
John R. Schulz
Thomas R. O'Connell
Dan C. O'Connell
Christine L. Stroemer
Sarah J. Batzli

ASSOCIATES

Bonnie J. Bennett
Thomas E. McEllistrem

Reference: First National Bank of St. Paul.

For full biographical listings, see the Martindale-Hubbell Law Directory

FELHABER, LARSON, FENLON AND VOGT, PROFESSIONAL ASSOCIATION (AV)

Suite 2100, Minnesota World Trade Center, 55101
Telephone: 612-222-6321
Facsimile: 612-222-8905
Minneapolis, Minnesota Office: Suite 4200, First Bank Place, 601 2nd Avenue South.
Telephone: 612-339-6321.
Facsimile: 612-338-0535.

Robert L. Bach
Richard A. Beens
James A. Blomquist
Edward J. Bohrer
Stephen J. Burton
Paul H. Cady
Edward Q. Cassidy
Christopher P. Chilstrom
David M. Cremons
James J. Cronin
Terrance M. Cullen
James M. Dawson
Thomas J. Doyle
Stanley J. Duran
William K. Ecklund
Robert J. Fenlon
Robert S. Halagan
Jan Douglas Halverson
Angela D. Hansen
Christopher S. Hayhoe
Brad J. Heying (Not admitted in MN)
David R. Hols
Ronald R. Kirchoff
Jona K. Klibanoff
Lee A. Lastovich
Dennis J. Merley
William F. Mohrman
Byron D. Olsen
Penelope J. Phillips
Thomas M. Regan
Steven L. Ross
Karen G. Schanfield
Russell J. Sudeith, Jr.
Thomas M. Vogt
Honnen S. Weiss
Paul J. Zech

OF COUNSEL

Samuel Bearmon
Charles F. Bisanz
Kareen R. Ecklund

For full biographical listings, see the Martindale-Hubbell Law Directory

JARDINE, LOGAN & O'BRIEN (AV)

2100 Piper Jaffray Plaza, 444 Cedar Street, 55101
Telephone: 612-290-6500
Fax: 612-223-5070

(See Next Column)

JARDINE, LOGAN & O'BRIEN, *St. Paul—Continued*

MEMBERS OF FIRM

Donald M. Jardine
Jerre F. Logan (1923-1983)
John R. O'Brien
Gerald M. Linnihan
Alan R. Vanasek
John M. Kennedy, Jr.
Eugene J. Flick
Charles E. Gillin
James J. Galman
Pierre N. Regnier
Mark A. Fonken
Gregory G. Heacox
George W. Kuehner
James A. Jardine
Patti J. Skoglund
Sean E. Hade
Gregg A. Johnson
Timothy S. Crom
Lawrence M. Rocheford

ASSOCIATES

Thomas M. Countryman
James G. Golembeck
Kerry C. Koep
David J. Hoekstra
James K. Helling
Thomas A. Harder
Marsha E. Devine
Leonard J. Schweich
Kimberly K. Hobert
Katherine E. Sprague
Michael A. Rayer
Marlene S. Garvis
Mary Patricia Rowe
Karen R. Cote
Randall S. Lane
Jane Lanoue Binzak
Nathan W. Hart
Joseph E. Flynn
Ronald R. Envall
William R. Hauck

Representative Clients: American Hardware Mutual Insurance Co.; Ohio-Casualty Group; Farmers Insurance Group; Maryland-Casualty Co; CIGNA; Federated Insurance Co.; American International Group; Lumbermen's Underwriting Alliance; Dodson Insurance Group; Safeco Insurance Co.

For full biographical listings, see the Martindale-Hubbell Law Directory

MURNANE, CONLIN, WHITE & BRANDT, P.A. (AV)

1800 Piper Jaffray Plaza, 444 Cedar Street, 55101
Telephone: 612-227-9411
FAX: 612-223-5199

E. Willard Murnane (1907-1976)
Charles R. Murnane (1913-1982)
Thomas M. Conlin
Robert W. Murnane
Robert T. White
John E. Brandt
John D. Hirte
Steven J. Kirsch
Andrew T. Shern
Michael S. Ryan
James F. Baldwin
C. Todd Koebele
Michael P. Tierney
John R. Shoemaker
Daniel A. Haws
William L. Moran

Thomas A. Gilligan, Jr.
David C. Anastasi
Joel D. Hedberg
Thomas J Norby
Anne F. Baker
Kammey M.K. Mahowald
Nicole B. Surges
Peter B. Tiede

Representative Clients: Aetna Life & Casualty Co.; Amoco; BIC Corporation; Combustion Engineering; Dresser Industries; Northland Companies; State Farm Mutual Insurance Company; Travelers Insurance Company; Wausau Insurance Co.

For full biographical listings, see the Martindale-Hubbell Law Directory

WINTHROP & WEINSTINE, A PROFESSIONAL ASSOCIATION (AV)

3200 Minnesota World Trade Center, 30 East Seventh Street, 55101
Telephone: 612-290-8400
FAX: 612-292-9347
Minneapolis Office: 3000 Dain Bosworth Plaza, 60 South Sixth Street.
Telephone: 612-347-0700.
Fax: 612-347-0600.

Sherman Winthrop
Robert R. Weinstine
Richard A. Hoel
Roger D. Gordon
Steven C. Tourek
Stephen J. Snyder
Marvin C. Ingber
Hart Kuller
David P. Pearson
Thomas M. Hart, IV
Darron C. Knutson
John A. Knapp
Eric O. Madson
Michele D. Vaillancourt
David E. Moran, Jr.
Donald J. Brown
Jon J. Hoganson
Sandra J. Martin
Gary W. Schokmiller
Todd B. Urness
Timothy M. Barnett
Scott J. Dongoske
Peter J. Gleekel
Edward J. Drenttel
Jeffrey R. Ansel
Laurie A. Knocke
Lloyd W. Grooms, Jr.
Julie K. Williamson
Betsy J. Loushin
Mark T. Johnson

Jennifer Wirick Breitinger
Brooks F. Poley
Julie Widley Schnell
Thomas H. Boyd
Jeffrey L. Shlosberg
Joseph C. Nauman
Daniel C. Beck
Eric J. Nystrom
Kristin Peterson LeBre
Joanne L. Matzen
Evan D. Coobs
Thomas A. Walker
Gina M. Grothe Follen
Patrick W. Weber
Charles A. Durant
Timothy J. Bettenga
Craig A. Brandt
Michael A. Duffy
James W. Dierking
Catherine A. Dominguez
Therese Marie Marso
Melissa Arndt Galindo

(See Next Column)

Suzanne M. Spellacy
Trevor V. Gunderson
Blair A. Rosenthal
Michael P. North
Rachel A. Armstrong
Matthew T. Boos

OF COUNSEL

Joseph S. Friedberg
Daniel W. Hardy

Representative Clients: Aero Systems Engineering, Inc.; American National Bank and Trust Co.; Bremer Financial Corporation and subsidiary banks; Otto Bremer Foundation; Juran & Moody, Inc.; St. Paul Progress Corp.; Wick Building Systems, Inc.

For full biographical listings, see the Martindale-Hubbell Law Directory

*SLAYTON,** Murray Co. — (Refer to Worthington)

SOUTH ST. PAUL, Dakota Co.

LEVANDER, GILLEN & MILLER, P.A. (AV)

633 South Concord Street, Suite 402, P.O. Box 298, 55075
Telephone: 612-451-1831
Fax: 612-450-7384

Harold LeVander (1910-1992)
Arthur F. Gillen
Roger C. Miller
Timothy J. Kuntz
Daniel J. Beeson
Rollin H. Crawford
Kenneth J. Rohlf
Elizabeth J. Wolf
Joseph P. Lally
Tonetta E. Tollefson
Stephen H. Fochler
Thomas R. Lehmann

Representative Clients: Mid Continent Area Power Pool; City of Sunfish Lake; Censtone Products; United Power Assn.; City of South St. Paul; Wally McCarthy Oldsmobile, Inc.; Minnesota Dental Assn.; City of Inver Grove Heights.
Reference: First American Bank Metro, Minnesota.

For full biographical listings, see the Martindale-Hubbell Law Directory

SPRING VALLEY, Fillmore Co.

BAUDLER, BAUDLER, MAUS & BLAHNIK (AV)

304 South Broadway, 55975
Telephone: 507-346-7301
FAX: 507-346-2537
Austin, Minnesota Office: 110 North Main Street.
Telephone: 507-433-2393.
FAX: 507-433-9530.

Otto Baudler (1881-1970)
Lawrence E. Maus
Robert E. Blahnik

Representative Clients: Ostrander State Bank; First National Bank of Spring Valley; Twin City Federal Savings & Loan Assn.; First American State Bank of Grand Meadow, Minn.; Farmers Insurance Group; Mutual Service Casualty Co.; Indemnity Company of North America; Western National Mutual Insurance Co.; The Kemper Insurance Group.; Home Federal Savings & Loan Assn.

*STILLWATER,** Washington Co.

ECKBERG, LAMMERS, BRIGGS, WOLFF & VIERLING (AV)

1835 Northwestern Avenue, 55082
Telephone: 612-439-2878
Fax: 612-439-2923

MEMBERS OF FIRM

Lyle J. Eckberg
James F. Lammers
Robert G. Briggs
Paul A. Wolff
Mark J. Vierling
Gregory G. Galler
Kevin K. Shoeberg

ASSOCIATES

Thomas J. Weidner
Susan Danner Olson

For full biographical listings, see the Martindale-Hubbell Law Directory

*THIEF RIVER FALLS,** Pennington Co.

CHARLSON, MARBEN & JORGENSON, P.A. (AV)

119 West Second Street, P.O. Box 506, 56701
Telephone: 218-681-4002
Fax: 218-681-4004

Kurt J. Marben
Michael L. Jorgenson

Representative Clients: Northern State Bank of Thief River Falls; American Hardware Mutual Insurance Co.; American Family Insurance Co.; Employers Mutual of Wausau; Milbank Mutual Insurance Co.; National Family Insurance Co.; Wikstrom Telephone Co.; Dairyland Mutual Insurance Co.; Preferred Risk Mutual Insurance Co.; North Star Mutual Insurance Co.

For full biographical listings, see the Martindale-Hubbell Law Directory

*TWO HARBORS,** Lake Co. — (Refer to Duluth)

VIRGINIA, St. Louis Co.

TRENTI LAW FIRM (AV)

1000 Lincoln Building, 55792
Telephone: 218-749-1962
Fax: 218-749-4308
Edina, Minnesota Office: 6600 France Avenue, Suite 465.
Telephone: 612-929-7512.
Fax: 612-929-2464.
Cook, Minnesota Office: 219 South River St., Box 1177, 55723.
Telephone: 218-666-5781.
Fax: 218-666-5782.

John A. Trenti
Patrick J. Roche, Jr.
Robert H. Stephenson
Carver Richards
Sam A. Aluni
Gordon C. Pineo
Joseph Lyons-Leoni (Resident, Edina Office)
Scott C. Neff
Gina M. Palokangas

Representative Clients: St. Paul Cos.; Queen City Federal Savings & Loan Assn.; First Bank, Virginia, Minnesota; Eveleth Fee Office (Mineral Interests).

For full biographical listings, see the Martindale-Hubbell Law Directory

*WABASHA,** Wabasha Co. — (Refer to Winona)

*WADENA,** Wadena Co.

KENNEDY & NERVIG (AV)

503 Jefferson Street South, P.O. Box 647, 56482-0647
Telephone: 218-631-2505
Fax: 218-631-9078

MEMBERS OF FIRM

Charles R. Kennedy
Luther P. Nervig

Sally Ireland Robertson
Daniel T. Carlisle
Katherine R. Carlson
Brent Eliot Walz

OF COUNSEL

Charles W. Kennedy

Representative Clients: Wadena State Bank; First National Bank of Menagha; First National Bank of Bertha-Verndale; Security State Bank of Sebeka; Todd-Wadena Electric Co-op (REA); Merickel Lumber Mills; West Central Telephone Co.; Wadena Public Schools; Dorn and Company; Mason Brothers Company; Wadena DAC; Gores Company; Northern Cooperatives.

For full biographical listings, see the Martindale-Hubbell Law Directory

*WARREN,** Marshall Co. — (Refer to Thief River Falls)

*WASECA,** Waseca Co. — (Refer to Mankato)

*WHEATON,** Traverse Co. — (Refer to Ortonville)

*WILLMAR,** Kandiyohi Co.

HULSTRAND ANDERSON LARSON & HANSON (AV)

331 Professional Plaza, 331 Third Street S.W., P.O. Box 130, 56201
Telephone: 612-235-4313; 235-4314

MEMBERS OF FIRM

George E. Hulstrand
Ronald C. Anderson
L. Wayne Larson
Gregory R. Anderson
Rodney C. Hanson
Jon C. Saunders

ASSOCIATES

LeeAnn Clayton

Representative Clients: Heritage Bank, N.A., Willmar; Northland Greyhound Lines; Citizens State Bank of Clara City; Milwaukee Insurance Co.; Clinic Associates, Inc.
References: Heritage Bank, N.A., Willmar; First National Bank of Willmar; First American Bank and Trust Company of Willmar.

For full biographical listings, see the Martindale-Hubbell Law Directory

SCHMIDT, THOMPSON, JOHNSON & MOODY, P.A. (AV)

707 Litchfield Avenue, S.W., Suite 100, P.O. Box 913, 56201-0913
Telephone: 612-235-1980; 1-800-733-7057

Henry W. Schmidt
Joe E. Thompson
William W. Thompson
Thomas G. Johnson
David C. Moody

Bradley J. Schmidt
Kathryn N. Smith

Representative Clients: First American Bank of Willmar; First Bank Central, N.A.; Willmar School District # 347; Holiday Inn of Willmar; Hormel Foods Corp.; Roth Chevrolet, Inc.; Auto Owners Insurance Co.; American Hardware Mutual Insurance Co.; American Family Insurance Co.

For full biographical listings, see the Martindale-Hubbell Law Directory

*WINDOM,** Cottonwood Co. — (Refer to Worthington)

*WINONA,** Winona Co.

STREATER, MURPHY, GERNANDER, FORSYTHE & TELSTAD, P.A. (AV)

64-68 East Fourth Street, 55987
Telephone: 507-454-2925
FAX: 507-454-2929

Leo F. Murphy, Jr.
Kent A. Gernander
James R. Forsythe
Cindy K. Telstad

OF COUNSEL

Harold S. Streater

Representative Clients: Winona National & Savings Bank; Lanoga Corp.; United Building Centers, Inc.; Winona Daily News; City of Rollingstone; Boelter Industries Inc.; Winona Agency, Inc.

For full biographical listings, see the Martindale-Hubbell Law Directory

*WORTHINGTON,** Nobles Co.

HEDEEN, HUGHES & WETERING (AV)

421-10th Street, P.O. Box 9, 56187
Telephone: 507-376-3181
Telecopier: 507-376-9404
Adrian, Minnesota Office: Adrian State Bank Building.
Telephone: 507-483-2033.

MEMBERS OF FIRM

Arnold W. Brecht (Deceased)
William T. Hedeen
Laurence B. Hughes
William J. Wetering

ASSOCIATES

Bruce N. Kness

Representative Clients: Norwest Bank of Worthington; First State Bank of Rushmore; Rickbeil's, Inc.; Worthington Federal Savings & Loan Assn.; State Automobile & Casualty Underwriters; Farm Bureau Mutual Insurance Co.; Consolidated Co-ops.

For full biographical listings, see the Martindale-Hubbell Law Directory

MISSISSIPPI

*ABERDEEN,** Monroe Co.

HOLCOMB, DUNBAR, CONNELL, CHAFFIN & WILLARD, A PROFESSIONAL ASSOCIATION (AV)

109 1/2 West Commerce Street, P.O. Box 866, 39730
Telephone: 601-369-8800
Facsimile: 601-369-9404
Jackson, Mississippi Office: 111 East Capitol Street, Suite 290, P.O. Box 2990, 39207-2990.
Telephone: 601-948-0048.
Facsimile: 601-948-0050.
Clarksdale, Mississippi Office: 152 Delta Avenue, P.O. Box 368, 38614.
Telephone: 601-627-2241.
Facsimile: 601-627-9788.
Oxford, Mississippi Office: 1217 Jackson Avenue, P.O. Drawer 707, 38655.
Telephone: 601-234-8775.
Facsimile: 601-234-8638.
Southhaven, Mississippi Office: Suite 1, 8727 Northwest Drive, P.O. Box 190, 38671.
Telephone: 601-342-6806.
Facsimile: 601-342-6792.

Jack F. Dunbar
Craig M. Geno
Guy T. Gillespie, III
John H. Dunbar
David C. Dunbar
Robert H. Faulks
James T. McCafferty, III
Barry C. Blackburn

OF COUNSEL

Ralph E. Pogue

Counsel for: United Southern Bank; Mississippi Power & Light Co.; Mississippi Valley Gas Co.; Aetna Casualty & Surety Co.; Southern Farm Bureau Casualty Insurance Co.; South Central Bell Telephone Co.; State Farm Mutual Automobile Insurance Co.; Fireman's Fund Insurance Cos.; Deere & Co.; Navistar International Transportation Corp.

For full biographical listings, see the Martindale-Hubbell Law Directory

PATTERSON & PATTERSON (AV)

304 East Jefferson Street, P.O. Box 663, 39730
Telephone: 601-369-2476
1-800-523-9975
FAX: 601-369-9806

MEMBERS OF FIRM

Robert D. Patterson
Jan P. Patterson

LEGAL SUPPORT PERSONNEL

Raye Long

Local Counsel for: National Bank of Commerce of Mississippi; American Colloid Company; Vista Chemical Co.; Pruet Production Co.; Arco Oil & Gas Co.; Chemical Corporation; Unimin Corporation.

For full biographical listings, see the Martindale-Hubbell Law Directory

*BATESVILLE,** Panola Co. — (Refer to Oxford)

*BAY ST. LOUIS,** Hancock Co. — (Refer to Gulfport)

*BAY SPRINGS,** Jasper Co. — (Refer to Laurel)

*BELZONI,** Humphreys Co. — (Refer to Greenwood)

BILOXI, Harrison Co.

CORBAN & GUNN (AV)

770 Water Street, P.O. Drawer 1916, 39533
Telephone: 601-432-7826
Telecopier: 601-435-5702

MEMBERS OF FIRM

Lawrence C. Corban, Jr.
Clyde H. Gunn, III

Representative Clients: Dees Chevrolet Co.; Savings & Loan Association of Pascagoula-Moss Point; Frank P. Corso & Co., Inc.; Munro Petroleum & Terminal Corp.; Ship Services Corp.

For full biographical listings, see the Martindale-Hubbell Law Directory

PAGE, MANNINO & PERESICH (AV)

759 Vieux Marché Mall, P.O. Drawer 289, 39530
Telephone: 601-374-2100
Telecopier: 601-432-5539
Jackson, Mississippi Office: One LeFleurs Square, 4735 Old Canton Road, P.O. Box 12159.
Telephone: 601-364-1100.
Telecopier: 601-364-1118.
Gulfport, Mississippi Office: Markham Building, 2301 - 14th Street, Suite 600, Drawer 660.
Telephone: 601-863-8861.
Telecopier: 601-863-8871.

(See Next Column)

MEMBERS OF FIRM

Lyle M. Page
Frederick J. Mannino
Ronald G. Peresich
Michael B. McDermott
Stephen G. Peresich
Jess H. Dickinson
Tere Richardson Steel
David S. Raines
Michael P. Collins
Randolph Cook Wood
Mary A. Nichols
Joseph Henry Ros
Thomas William Busby
Michael E. Whitehead
Katharine Malley Samson
Douglas J. Wise

Representative Clients: United States Fidelity & Guaranty Co.; St. Paul Fire & Marine Insurance Co.; Crawford & Co.; Anheuser-Busch Corp.
General Counsel for: Peoples Bank of Biloxi, Mississippi; Biloxi Regional Medical Center; Bank of Mississippi (Gulf Coast Division).

For full biographical listings, see the Martindale-Hubbell Law Directory

RUSHING & GUICE (AV)

683 Water Street, P.O. Box 1925, 39533-1925
Telephone: 601-374-2313
Telecopier: 601-374-8155

MEMBERS OF FIRM

Charles L. Rushing (1881-1923)
William L. Guice (1887-1971)
William Lee Guice III

OF COUNSEL

Jacob D. Guice

ASSOCIATES

Edgar F. Maier
R. Scott Wells

LEGAL SUPPORT PERSONNEL

Antonia Strong

For full biographical listings, see the Martindale-Hubbell Law Directory

*BOONEVILLE,** Prentiss Co. — (Refer to Tupelo)

*BRANDON,** Rankin Co. — (Refer to Jackson)

*BROOKHAVEN,** Lincoln Co. — (Refer to Hazlehurst)

CALHOUN CITY, Calhoun Co. — (Refer to Oxford)

*CANTON,** Madison Co. — (Refer to Jackson)

*CARROLLTON,** Carroll Co. — (Refer to Greenwood)

*CHARLESTON,** Tallahatchie Co. — (Refer to Clarksdale)

*CLARKSDALE,** Coahoma Co.

CHAPMAN, LEWIS & SWAN (AV)

501 First Street, P.O. Box 428, 38614
Telephone: 601-627-4105
FAX: 601-627-4171

Ralph E. Chapman
Richard B. Lewis
Dana J. Swan

For full biographical listings, see the Martindale-Hubbell Law Directory

HOLCOMB, DUNBAR, CONNELL, CHAFFIN & WILLARD, A PROFESSIONAL ASSOCIATION (AV)

152 Delta Avenue, P.O. Box 368, 38614
Telephone: 601-627-2241
Facsimile: 601-627-9788
Jackson, Mississippi Office: 111 East Capitol Street, Suite 290, P.O. Box 2990, 39207-2990.
Telephone: 601-948-0048.
Facsimile: 601-948-0050.
Aberdeen, Mississippi Office: 109 1/2 West Commerce Street, P.O. Box 866, 39730.
Telephone: 601-369-8800.
Facsimile: 601-369-9404.
Oxford, Mississippi Office: 1217 Jackson Avenue, P.O. Drawer 707, 38655.
Telephone: 601-234-8775.
Facsimile: 601-234-8638.
Southaven, Mississippi Office: Suite 1, 8727 Northwest Drive, 38671.
Telephone: 601-342-6806.
Facsimile: 601-342-6792.

William M. Chaffin
William G. Willard, Jr.
William A. Baskin
Jeffrey S. Dilley
David A. Burns
Barry C. Blackburn

OF COUNSEL

Pat D. Holcomb
Chester H. Curtis
Edward P. Connell

Counsel for: United Southern Bank; Mississippi Power & Light Co.; Mississippi Valley Gas Co.; Aetna Casualty & Surety Co.; Southern Farm Bureau Casualty Insurance Co.; South Central Bell Telephone Co.; State Farm Mutual Fire & Casualty Insurance Co.; Fireman's Fund Insurance Cos.; Deere & Co.; Navistar International Transportation Corp.

For full biographical listings, see the Martindale-Hubbell Law Directory

Clarksdale—Continued

LUCKETT LAW FIRM, A PROFESSIONAL ASSOCIATION (AV)

143 Yazoo Avenue, P.O. Drawer 1000, 38614-1000
Telephone: 601-624-2591
Telecopier: 601-627-5403

William O. Luckett — William O. Luckett, Jr.

John B. Gillis — Betty W. Maynard
Nathan J. McMullen, Jr.

District and Local Counsel for: Employers Group; Firemen's Fund; Liberty Mutual Insurance Co.; CNA Group; Deere & Co.; Indiana Lumbermens Insurance Co.; Texas Gas Transmission Corp.; American Interstate Insurance Company of Georgia; Elliston, Inc.; Graward General Insurance.

For full biographical listings, see the Martindale-Hubbell Law Directory

ROSS, HUNT, SPELL & ROSS, A PROFESSIONAL ASSOCIATION (AV)

123 Court Street, P.O. Box 1196, 38614
Telephone: 601-627-5251
Telecopier No.: 601-627-5254
Clinton, Mississippi Office: 203 Monroe Street.
Telephone: 601-924-2655.

Tom T. Ross (1903-1993) — David R. Hunt
Tom T. Ross, Jr.

Thomas W. Allen — Patricia W. Burchell

OF COUNSEL

William E. Spell

Representative Client: Beech Aircraft Corp., Wichita, Kansas.

For full biographical listings, see the Martindale-Hubbell Law Directory

*CLEVELAND,** Bolivar Co.

JACKS, ADAMS & WESTERFIELD, P.A. (AV)

106 South Pearman Avenue, P.O. Box 1209, 38732
Telephone: 601-843-6171
FAX: 601-843-6176

Gerald H. Jacks — Richard L. Kimmel
William S. Adams, Jr. — S. David Norquist
Andrew M. W. Westerfield — Thomas B. Janoush

General Counsel For: The Valley Bank; Cleveland School District 4; Commonwealth National Life Insurance Co.
Area Counsel For: Commercial Union; United States Fidelity & Guaranty Co.; Baxter Travenol Laboratories, Inc.; New Hampshire Insurance Co.; American International Adjustment Co.; Imperial Casualty Co.; Self Insurers Service, Inc.

For full biographical listings, see the Martindale-Hubbell Law Directory

LEVINGSTON & LEVINGSTON (AV)

201 South Pearman Avenue, P.O. Box 1327, 38732
Telephone: 601-843-2791
Fax: 601-843-2797

MEMBERS OF FIRM

Alfred A. Levingston — Jeffrey A. Levingston

General Counsel for: Bolivar County Drainage Commissioners; Bolivar County Hospital; City of Shelby.
Local Counsel for: Commercial Union; Maryland Casualty Co.; Federated Mutual Implement & Hardware Insurance Co.; Baxter-Travenol Laboratories, Inc.

For full biographical listings, see the Martindale-Hubbell Law Directory

*COLLINS,** Covington Co. — (Refer to Hattiesburg)

*COLUMBIA,** Marion Co.

AULTMAN, TYNER, MCNEESE & RUFFIN, LTD., A PROFESSIONAL LAW CORPORATION (AV)

329 Church Street, P.O. Drawer 707, 39429
Telephone: 601-736-2222
Hattiesburg, Mississippi Office: 315 Hemphill Street, P.O. Drawer 750.
Telephone: 601-583-2671.
Gulfport, Mississippi Office: 1201 25th Avenue, Suite 300, P.O. Box 607.
Telephone: 601-863-6913.

Thomas D. McNeese — Richard F. Yarborough, Jr.

Lawrence E. Hahn

(See Next Column)

OF COUNSEL

Ernest Ray Duff

Representative Clients: Hercules, Inc.; United States Steel Corp.; Ford Motor Co.; International Paper Co.; Phillips Petroleum Co.; Aetna Casualty & Surety Co.; CNA Group; Liberty Mutual Insurance Co.; St. Paul Fire & Marine Insurance Co.; Fireman's Fund.

For full biographical listings, see the Martindale-Hubbell Law Directory

DANTIN & DANTIN (AV)

Suite 301 Citizens Bank Building, P.O. Box 604, 39429
Telephone: 601-736-5378
Telecopier: 601-736-8603

MEMBERS OF FIRM

Maurice Dantin — Forest M. Dantin

Representative Clients: Crosby Land & Resources; Justin Wilson Co.; Taylor Energy Co.; Citizens Bank; Crosby Trading Co.; Circle Bar Ranch; Crosby Forest Products Co.; Johnnie Stringer Moving and Storage, Inc.

For full biographical listings, see the Martindale-Hubbell Law Directory

*COLUMBUS,** Lowndes Co.

GHOLSON, HICKS, NICHOLS & WARD, A PROFESSIONAL ASSOCIATION (AV)

Court Square Towers, 605 Second Avenue North, P.O. Box 1111, 39703-1111
Telephone: 601-327-0662
Fax: 601-327-6217
Starkville, Mississippi, Office: 121 North Jackson Street, P.O. Drawer 59, 39759-0059.
Telephone: 601-323-1912.
Fax: 601-324-4795.

William Ward — Katherine S. Kerby
Hunter M. Gholson — David B. Jolly
Dewitt T. Hicks, Jr. — P. Nelson Smith, Jr.
Aubrey E. Nichols — John Franklin Williams
Ralph E. Rood — William R. Couch
John W. Crowell — William Thomas Cooper
J. Gordon Flowers — Marc Darren Amos
H. Russell Rogers — David Tyler Lewis

Counsel for: National Bank of Commerce of Mississippi; Trustmark National Bank; United States Fidelity and Guaranty Co.; Fireman's Fund American Insurance Cos.; Cargill, Inc.; Kerr-McGee Corp.; City of Columbus; Gulf States Manufacturers, Inc.; Airline Manufacturing Co.; Lowndes County Port Authority.

For full biographical listings, see the Martindale-Hubbell Law Directory

MITCHELL, MCNUTT, THREADGILL, SMITH & SAMS, P.A. (AV)

215 Fifth Street North, P.O. Box 1366, 39701
Telephone: 601-328-2316
Facsimile: 601-328-8035
Tupelo, Mississippi Office: 105 South Front Street, P.O. Box 7120.
Telephone: 601-842-3871.
Facsimile: 601-842-8450.
Corinth, Mississippi Office: 508 Waldron Street, P.O. Box 1200.
Telephone: 601-286-9931.
Facsimile: 601-286-8984.
Oxford, Mississippi Office: 1216 Van Buren, P.O. Box 430.
Telephone: 601-234-4843.
Facsimile: 601-234-9071.
Jackson, Mississippi Office: Deposit Guaranty Plaza, 210 East Capitol, Suite 1540, P.O. Box 1005.
Telephone: 601-948-8505.
Facsimile: 601-948-8537.
Memphis, Tennessee Office: 1255 Lynnfield Road, Building A, Suite 123.
Telephone: 901-767-5185.
Facsimile: 901-767-5918.

L. F. Sams, Jr. — Ronald I. Loeb
Taylor B. Smith — Michael D. Ferris
Guy W. Mitchell, III — Richard H. Spann
William C. Spencer — W. Scott Collins
W. H. (Hank) Jolly, Jr. (Resident) — Lauren J. Hutchins
Otis R. Tims
David L. Sanders — Martha Bost Stegall
Claude F. Clayton, Jr. — Jeffry M. Cox
William C. Murphree — Timothy M. Threadgill
Ronald L. Roberts — J. Douglas Ford
John S. Hill — Jeffrey J. Turnage (Resident)

OF COUNSEL

William J. Threadgill — Burney F. Threadgill

Representative Clients: Ceco Buildings Division, Robertson-Ceco Corporation; First Columbus National Bank; The General Tire & Rubber Co.; Weyerhaeuser Co.; The Commercial Dispatch Publishing Co.; St. Paul Insurance Cos.; Imes Communication Group; Sanderson Plumbing Products Corp.; Federated Mutual Insurance Co.; Southern Farm Bureau Casualty Insurance Co.

(See Next Column)

MITCHELL, MCNUTT, THREADGILL, SMITH & SAMS P.A., *Columbus—Continued*

MEMBERS OF FIRM

Stanny Sanders (1918-1972) — Sam N. Fonda
Webb Franklin — Thomas M. Flanagan, Jr.

OF COUNSEL

Hardy Lott

Attorneys for: Deposit Guaranty National Bank; Delta Electric Power Assn.; Sentry Insurance Co.; Zurich American Insurance Co.; Kemper Insurance Group; The Western Insurance Cos; Coca-Cola Bottling Works of Greenwood; J.J. Ferguson Enterprises; Old River Development Casino, Inc. (Lady Luck Casino); Innovative Gaming, Inc.

For full biographical listings, see the Martindale-Hubbell Law Directory

*CORINTH,** Alcorn Co. — (Refer to Tupelo)

*DE KALB,** Kemper Co. — (Refer to Meridian)

*FAYETTE,** Jefferson Co. — (Refer to Natchez)

*FOREST,** Scott Co. — (Refer to Meridian)

*FULTON,** Itawamba Co. — (Refer to Tupelo)

*GREENVILLE,** Washington Co.

CAMPBELL, DELONG, HAGWOOD & WADE (AV)

923 Washington Avenue, P.O. Box 1856, 38702-1856
Telephone: 601-335-6011
Fax: 601-334-6407

Fred C. DeLong, Jr. (1931-1993)

MEMBERS OF FIRM

Roy D. Campbell, Jr. — James T. Milam
L. Carl Hagwood — Harold H. Mitchell, Jr.
Lawrence D. Wade — John F. Davis, Jr.
Roy D. Campbell, III — Robert N. Warrington

William Lee Hon — Vikki Jeanell Jones-Spencer
Randall E. Day

OF COUNSEL

J. Walker Sturdivant

Counsel for: Trustmark National Bank; Sunburst Bank; Mississippi Marine Corp. Local Counsel for: Mississippi Power & Light Co.; Commercial Union Assurance Cos.; Mississippi Farm Bureau Insurance Cos.; United States Fidelity & Guaranty Insurance Co.; St. Paul Cos.; Liberty Mutual Insurance Co.; Medical Assurance Company of Mississippi.

For full biographical listings, see the Martindale-Hubbell Law Directory

LAKE, TINDALL & THACKSTON (AV)

Formerly Firm of Wynn, Hafter, Lake & Tindall
127 South Poplar Street, P.O. Box 918, 38701
Telephone: 601-378-2121
Facsimile: 601-378-2183
Paducah, Kentucky Office: One Executive Boulevard, Suite 318, P.O. Box 30.
Telephone: 502-442-1900.
Facsimile: 502-442-8247.
Jackson, Mississippi Office: 350 Security Centre North, 200 South Lamar Street, P.O. Box 1787.
Telephone: 601-948-2121.
Facsimile: 601-948-0603.

William T. Wynn (1890-1959) — Clinton W. Walker, III
Jerome S. Hafter (1895-1969) — Carl J. Marshall (Resident Paducah Office)
Franklin S. Thackston, Jr. — Marian S. Alexander
Charles S. Tindall, III — Jenny M. Virden
Edwin Spivey Gault (Resident Paducah Office) — Paul Mathis, Jr.
Jerome C. Hafter — David J. Puddister
Stephen L. Thomas — Shawn Neill Sullivan
Edwin W. Tindall — Laura Limerick Gibbes (Resident Jackson Office)
W. Wayne Drinkwater, Jr. (Resident Jackson Office) — Paul P. Bouler, Jr.
Andrew N. Alexander, III — Margaret S. Oertling (Resident Jackson Office)

OF COUNSEL

J. A. Lake — Charles S. Tindall, Jr.

General Counsel for: Greenville Bank (Branch of Deposit Guaranty National Bank of Jackson); Bunge Towing, Inc.; SUPERVALU INC., Lewis Grocer Division; Greenville Port Commission; Stein Mart Inc.; Delta and Pine Land Co.
Local Counsel For: Insurance: Aetna Casualty & Surety Co.; Cigna-Aetna Insurance Co.; Allstate Insurance Co.; Shelter Insurance Co.

For full biographical listings, see the Martindale-Hubbell Law Directory

*GREENWOOD,** Leflore Co.

JOHN P. HENSON (AV)

105 West Market Street, P.O. Box 494, 38930
Telephone: 601-453-6227
Telefax: 601-453-6228

For full biographical listings, see the Martindale-Hubbell Law Directory

LOTT, FRANKLIN, FONDA & FLANAGAN (AV)

202 West Market, P.O. Box 1176, 38930
Telephone: 601-453-6576
Telecopier: 601-453-2777

(See Next Column)

UPSHAW, WILLIAMS, BIGGERS, PAGE & KRUGER (AV)

309 Fulton Street, P.O. Drawer 8230, 38930
Telephone: 601-455-1613
Facsimile: 601-453-9245
Jackson, Mississippi Office: One Jackson Place, 188 East Capitol Street, Suite 600. P.O. Drawer 1163, 39215.
Telephone: 601-944-0005.
Facsimile: 601-355-4269.

MEMBERS OF FIRM

James E. Upshaw — Lonnie D. Bailey
Tommie G. Williams — Robert S. Upshaw
Marc A. Biggers — Clinton M. Guenther
Thomas Y. Page (Resident, Jackson Office) — Roger C. Riddick (Resident, Jackson Office)
Stephen P. Kruger (Resident, Jackson Office) — Edley H. Jones, III (Resident, Jackson Office)
Glenn F. Beckham — C. Richard Benz, Jr.
James D. Holland (Resident, Jackson Office) — Richard C. Williams, Jr.
F. Ewin Henson, III — Wes Peters (Resident, Jackson Office)

ASSOCIATES

Brent E. Southern (Resident, Jackson Office) — Mark C. Carroll (Resident, Jackson Office)
R.H. Burress, III — Paul L. Goodman
Kathleen S. Gordon (Resident, Jackson Office) — Walter C. Morrison, IV (Resident, Jackson Office)
W. Hugh Gillon, IV (Resident, Jackson Office) — Patrick C. Malouf (Resident, Jackson Office)
William C. Helm (Resident, Jackson Office) — David C. Meadors
Bryan H. Callaway — Stuart B. Harmon (Resident, Jackson Office)

OF COUNSEL

B. L. Riddick (Resident, Jackson Office) — John R. Countiss, III (Resident, Jackson Office)

Representative Clients: U.S.F. & G. Co.; State Farm Mutual Automobile Ins. Co.; ; Continental Insurance Co.; St. Paul Fire & Marine Insurance Co.; Aetna Casualty & Surety Co.; Kemper Insurance Co.; Zurich-American Ins. Group; Home Ins. Co.; Illinois Central Railroad Co.; Allstate Insurance Co.

For full biographical listings, see the Martindale-Hubbell Law Directory

*GRENADA,** Grenada Co.

LISTON/LANCASTER

(See Winona)

*GULFPORT,** Harrison Co.

AULTMAN, TYNER, MCNEESE & RUFFIN, LTD., A PROFESSIONAL LAW CORPORATION (AV)

1201 25th Avenue, Suite 300, P.O. Box 607, 39502
Telephone: 601-863-6913
Hattiesburg, Mississippi Office: 315 Hemphill Street, P.O. Drawer 750.
Telephone: 601-583-2671.
Columbia, Mississippi Office: 329 Church Street, P.O. Drawer 707.
Telephone: 601-736-2222.

Ben E. Sheely — Paul J. Delcambre, Jr.
Dorrance (Dee) Aultman, Jr.

For full biographical listings, see the Martindale-Hubbell Law Directory

EATON AND COTTRELL, P.A. (AV)

1310 Twenty Fifth Avenue, P.O. Box 130, 39502
Telephone: 601-864-9900; 601-863-9821
Telecopier: 601-864-8221

Barney E. Eaton (1878-1944) — Terese T. Wyly
James S. Eaton — Annette E. Ball
Ben H. Stone — Paul Richard Lambert
Luther R. Boyd — William V. Westbrook, III
H. Rodger Wilder — William S. Boyd, III
John M. Harral — D. Mitchell McCranie

(See Next Column)

EATON AND COTTRELL P.A.—*Continued*

Brenda Vanover Znachko
Donna S. Negrotto
J. Adrian Smith
G. Martin Warren, Jr.
Jennifer West Signs
Kenneth R. Flottman
Scott E. Andress
Ricky J. Cox

OF COUNSEL

David Cottrell, Jr.
Eaton A. Lang, Jr.
Carl B. Carruth

General Counsel for: Mississippi Power Co.; Mississippi State Port Authority at Gulfport.
Representative Clients: E. I. DuPont de Nemours & Co.; Ford Motor Co.; Hertz Corporation; Ryder Truck Rental, Inc.; Waste Management of Mississippi, Inc.; Goldin Industries, Inc.; Cavenham Forest Industries, Inc.

For full biographical listings, see the Martindale-Hubbell Law Directory

GALLOWAY & GALLOWAY, P.A. (AV)

Suite 204 Merchants Bank Building, 1300 Twenty Fifth Avenue, P.O. Drawer 4248, 39502
Telephone: 601-864-1170
Telecopier: 601-868-1531

Robert C. Galloway
James B. Galloway
John L. Galloway
Ann Bowden-Hollis
Susan V. Pittman

OF COUNSEL

Charles R. Galloway

General Counsel for: Memorial Hospital at Gulfport; Gulfport Community Development Commission.
Local Counsel for: Cellular South.
Attorneys for: Nissan Motor Corporation in U.S.A.; Farmers Insurance Group; TerChemicals, Inc.; Bristol-Myers-Squibb Co.; W.C. Fore Trucking, Inc.; Orange Grove Utilities, Inc.

For full biographical listings, see the Martindale-Hubbell Law Directory

BOYCE HOLLEMAN A PROFESSIONAL CORPORATION (AV)

1913 15th Street, P.O. Drawer 1030, 39502
Telephone: 601-863-3142
Telecopier: 601-863-9829

Boyce Holleman

Michael B. Holleman
Timothy C. Holleman
Leslie Dean Holleman
David J. White

References: Hancock Bank, Gulfport; Merchants Bank & Trust Co., Gulfport; Bank of Wiggins, Wiggins, Mississippi.

For full biographical listings, see the Martindale-Hubbell Law Directory

MEADOWS, RILEY, KOENENN AND TEEL, P.A. (AV)

1720 23rd Avenue, P.O. Box 550, 39502
Telephone: 601-864-4511
Telecopier: 601-868-2178

Joseph R. Meadows
Donnie D. Riley
Alfred R. Koenenn
Walter W. Teel
Jerry D. Riley
Karen J. Young

Representative Clients: Bubba Oustalat Lincoln Mercury, Inc.; Lee Tractor Co. of Mississippi.
Reference: Hancock Bank.

For full biographical listings, see the Martindale-Hubbell Law Directory

PAGE, MANNINO & PERESICH (AV)

Markham Building, 2301 14th Street, Suite 600, Drawer 660, 39501-2095
Telephone: 601-863-8861
Telecopier: 601-863-8871
Biloxi, Mississippi Office: 759 Vieux MarchéMall, P.O. Drawer 289.
Telephone: 601-374-2100.
Telecopier: 601-432-5539.
Jackson, Mississippi Office: One Lefleurs Square, 4735 Old Canton Road, P.O. Box 12159.
Telephone: 601-364-1100.
Telecopier: 601-364-1118.

MEMBERS OF FIRM

Lyle M. Page
Frederick J. Mannino
Ronald G. Peresich
Michael B. McDermott
Stephen G. Peresich
Jess H. Dickinson
Tere Richardson Steel
David S. Raines
Michael P. Collins
Randolph Cook Wood
Mary A. Nichols
Joseph Henry Ros
Thomas William Busby
Michael E. Whitehead
Katharine Malley Samson
Douglas J. Wise

Representative Clients: United States Fidelity & Guaranty Co.; St. Paul Fire & Marine Insurance Co.; Crawford & Co.; Anheuser-Busch Corp.
General Counsel for: Peoples Bank of Biloxi, Mississippi; Biloxi Regional Medical Center; Bank of Mississippi (Gulf Coast Division).

(See Next Column)

For full biographical listings, see the Martindale-Hubbell Law Directory

*HATTIESBURG,** Forrest Co.

AULTMAN, TYNER, MCNEESE & RUFFIN, LTD., A PROFESSIONAL LAW CORPORATION (AV)

315 Hemphill Street, P.O. Drawer 750, 39403-0750
Telephone: 601-583-2671
Columbia, Mississippi Office: 329 Church Street, P.O. Drawer 707.
Telephone: 601-736-2222.
Gulfport, Mississippi Office: 1201 25th Avenue, Suite 300, P.O. Box 607.
Telephone: 601-863-6913.

Dorrance Aultman
Thomas W. Tyner
Thomas D. McNeese (Resident, Columbia Office)
Louie F. Ruffin
Richard F. Yarborough, Jr. (Resident, Columbia Office)
Ben E. Sheely (Resident, Gulfport Office)
Patrick H. Zachary
Paul J. Delcambre, Jr. (Resident, Gulfport Office)
Robert J. Dambrino, III
Vicki R. Leggett
R. Curtis Smith, II
Dorrance (Dee) Aultman, Jr. (Resident, Gulfport Office)
William Nelson Graham

James L. Quinn
Walter J. Eades
Lawrence E. Hahn (Resident, Columbia Office)
Carol Ann Estes
Victor A. DuBose

OF COUNSEL

Ernest Ray Duff (Resident, Columbia Office)

Representative Clients: Hercules, Inc.; U.S. Steel Corp.; Ford Motor Co.; Phillips Petroleum Co.; Aetna Casualty & Surety Co.; CNA Group; Liberty Mutual Insurance Co.; St. Paul Fire & Marine Insurance Co.; Fireman's Fund.

For full biographical listings, see the Martindale-Hubbell Law Directory

MONTAGUE, PITTMAN & VARNADO, A PROFESSIONAL ASSOCIATION (AV)

525 Main Street, P.O. Drawer 1975, 39403-1975
Telephone: 601-544-1234
Telecopier: 601-544-1276

Reginald A. Gray, Jr. (1919-1979)
Frank D. Montague, Jr.
James C. Pittman, Jr.
F. Douglas Montague, III
Carey R. Varnado

Brian A. Montague
Bob W. Pittman, Jr.
William R. Newman
Stacy S. Ruffin

General Counsel for: Hattiesburg American (Gannett); Wesley Health System (Methodist Hospital).
Representative Clients: Georgia Pacific Corp.; South Central Bell; General Motors Acceptance Corp.; The Home Insurance Cos.; Fidelity & Deposit Company of Maryland; Canal Ins. Co.; Deposit Guaranty N.B.; Laurel Regional Corporate Association.

For full biographical listings, see the Martindale-Hubbell Law Directory

*HAZLEHURST,** Copiah Co.

ARMSTRONG, PATTEN, THOMAS & LEACH (AV)

246 West Gallatin Street, P.O. Box 190, 39083
Telephone: 601-894-4061
Telecopier: 601-894-4792

MEMBERS OF FIRM

John T. Armstrong
Harry O. Hoffman, Jr. (1921-1981)
John T. Armstrong, Jr.
Edward E. Patten, Jr.
J. Cliff Thomas, Jr.
Howard O. Leach

Representative Clients: Sun Co.; International Paper Co.
Approved Attorneys for: Lawyers Title Insurance Corp.; Mississippi Valley Title Insurance Co.; Chicago Title Insurance Co.

For full biographical listings, see the Martindale-Hubbell Law Directory

*HERNANDO,** De Soto Co.

GERALD W. CHATHAM, SR. (AV)

291 Losher Street, 38632
Telephone: 601-429-9871
Telecopier: 601-429-0242

ASSOCIATES

Claude M. Purvis

Representative Clients: Allstate Insurance Co.; Ranger Insurance Co.; Paracelsus Senatobia Community Hospital; National Bank of Commerce, Memphis, TN; Balboa Insurance Co.; Wausau Insurance Co.; Premier Alliance Insurance Co.; Nationwide Insurance Co.; Alumax Extrusions, Inc.; National Home Insurance Co.

For full biographical listings, see the Martindale-Hubbell Law Directory

*HOLLY SPRINGS,** Marshall Co. — (Refer to Oxford)

*IUKA,** Tishomingo Co. — (Refer to Tupelo)

*JACKSON,** Hinds Co.

* indicates certain Bar Register subscribers whose principal office is located elsewhere in the state and who have arranged for representation as a part of the state capital listings that follow

ALSTON, RUTHERFORD, TARDY & VAN SLYKE (AV)

121 North State Street, P.O. Drawer 1532, 39215-1532
Telephone: 601-948-6882
Fax: 601-948-6902

MEMBERS OF FIRM

Alex A. Alston, Jr.
William S. Mendenhall
Kenneth A. Rutherford
Julie E. Chaffin
Thomas W. Tardy, III
Patrick D. McMurtray
Leonard D. Van Slyke, Jr.
Terryl K. Rushing
Barry H. Powell
C. Jackson Williams

ASSOCIATES

John Howard Shows
Richard L. Jones
Denise Foster Schreiber
Terry S. Williamson
David M. Loper

OF COUNSEL

Beth C. Clay
Rowan H. Taylor

Counsel for: Anheuser-Busch Companies, Inc.; Motion Picture Association of America, Inc.; E. I. Du Pont de Nemours & Co.; The Dow Chemical Co.; Dean Witter Reynolds Inc.; Ford Motor Co.; Yellow Freight System, Inc.; Xerox Corp.; Gannett Co. Inc.; Mississippi Baptist Foundation.

For full biographical listings, see the Martindale-Hubbell Law Directory

BUTLER, SNOW, O'MARA, STEVENS & CANNADA (AV)

17th Floor, Deposit Guaranty Plaza, 210 E. Capitol Street, P.O. Box 22567, 39225-2567
Telephone: 601-948-5711
Telecopier: 601-949-4555

Geo. Butler (1877-1948)
Chas. B. Snow (1894-1960)
J. Morgan Stevens (1876-1951)
Junior O'Mara (1914-1986)

MEMBERS OF FIRM

Harold D. Miller, Jr.
J. Stevenson Ray
Lawrence J. Franck
E. Marcus Wiggs III
C. Eugene McRoberts, Jr.
Jamie Planck Martin
John A. Crawford
Paula A. Graves
D. Carl Black, Jr.
Leslie Joyner Bobo
Lauch M. Magruder, Jr.
Ann Fortenberry Corso
Hugh C. Montgomery, Jr.
O. Kendall Moore
James W. O'Mara
Robert M. Frey
W. Scott Welch, III
Gilbert C. Van Loon
Jay A. Travis, III
Thomas A. Webb
Lee Davis Thames
A. Camille Henick
Charles L. Brocato
Ronald G. Taylor
Kenneth W. Barton
J. Collins Wohner Jr.
Charles F. Johnson, III
Donna Brown Jacobs
Stephen W. Rosenblatt
J. Cal Mayo, Jr.
James S. Overstreet, Jr.
George Randle Thomas
Herbert C. Ehrhardt
J. Lee Woodruff
Christy D. Jones
Selby Allen Ireland
Don B. Cannada
E. Barry Bridgforth
Phil B. Abernethy
William Massie Gage
William Eugene Magee
Michael E. McWilliams
Thomas E. Williams
Stephanie M. Rippee
Edward A. Wilmesherr
Arthur Dennis Spratlin, Jr.
R. Barry Cannada
Nancy Morse Parkes
Thomas C. Lacey, Jr.
Brooks R. Buchanan
John C. Henegan
E. Barney Robinson III
J. Carter Thompson, Jr.
L. Lee Tyner, Jr.
Daniel G. Hise
J. Clifton Johnson II
Jeffrey A. Walker
Daniel P. Jordan III
Paul N. Davis
James L. Henley Jr.
J. Paul Varner
John J. Healy III

OF COUNSEL

Robert C. Cannada
George H. Butler
Phineas Stevens
Dan McCullen

Counsel for: American Cyanamid Co.; Beneficial Corp.; Deposit Guaranty National Bank; Eli Lilly & Co.; Ergon Energy Group; Gulf Guaranty Insurance Co.; McRae's Department Stores; Miller Transporters, Inc.; Reliance Insurance Co.; South Central Bell Telephone Co.

For full biographical listings, see the Martindale-Hubbell Law Directory

FRASCOGNA, COURTNEY, WRIGHT, BIEDENHARN & SMITH (AV)

Suite 1390, One Jackson Place, P.O. Box 23126, 39225-3126
Telephone: 601-969-1737
Telecopier: 601-969-1739
Telex: 705446

(See Next Column)

Xavier M. Frascogna, Jr.
Richard E. Biedenharn
Richard A. Courtney
Stanley Q. Smith
J. Stephen Wright
Glen K. Till, Jr.

Reference: Deposit Guaranty National Bank.

For full biographical listings, see the Martindale-Hubbell Law Directory

GREEN, CHENEY AND HUGHES (AV)

100 South Congress Street, 39201
Telephone: 601-969-1969
Telecopier: 601-948-3019

MEMBERS OF FIRM

Joshua Green
Charles E. Hughes

Representative Clients: Deposit Guaranty National Bank; National American Insurance Co.; The Dial Corporation; Lowe's Companies, Inc.; Melvin Simon and Associates, Inc.
Approved Attorneys For: Lawyers Title Insurance Corp.; Mississippi Valley Title Insurance Co.; Title Insurance Co. of Minnesota.

For full biographical listings, see the Martindale-Hubbell Law Directory

HOLCOMB, DUNBAR, CONNELL, CHAFFIN & WILLARD, A PROFESSIONAL ASSOCIATION (AV)

111 East Capitol Street, Suite 290, P.O. Box 2990, 39207-2990
Telephone: 601-948-0048
Facsimile: 601-948-0050
Clarksdale, Mississippi Office: 152 Delta Avenue, P.O. Box 368, 38614.
Telephone: 601-627-2241.
Facsimile: 601-627-9788.
Aberdeen, Mississippi Office: 109 1/2 West Commerce Street, P.O. Box 866, 39730.
Telephone: 601-369-8800.
Facsimile: 601-369-9404.
Oxford, Mississippi Office: 1217 Jackson Avenue, P.O. Drawer 707, 38655.
Telephone: 601-234-8775.
Facsimile: 601-234-8638.
Southaven, Mississippi Office: Suite 1, 8727 Northwest Drive, P.O. Box 190, 38671.
Telephone: 601-342-6806.
Facsimile: 601-342-6792.

Jack F. Dunbar
C. Michael Pumphrey
William M. Chaffin
Robert H. Faulks
William G. Willard, Jr.
Robert F. Wood
W. Larry Harris
James T. McCafferty, III
Craig M. Geno
Jeffrey S. Dilley
Guy T. Gillespie, III
David A. Burns
Edward A. Moss
T. Swayze Alford
Thomas J. Suszek
Nancy M. Maddox
John H. Dunbar
Robert S. Mink
Wylene W. Dunbar
Jeffrey Kyle Tyree
David C. Dunbar
Stephan L. McDavid
Michael N. Watts
Barry C. Blackburn
Janet G. Arnold
John Ramsey McCarroll, III
William A. Baskin
Lynn Fitch Mitchell
Thomas T. Dunbar
Louis H. Watson, Jr.

OF COUNSEL

Pat D. Holcomb
Edward P. Connell
Chester H. Curtis
Ralph E. Pogue

Counsel for: United Southern Bank; Mississippi Power & Light Co.; Mississippi Valley Gas Co.; Aetna Casualty & Surety Co.; Southern Farm Bureau Casualty Insurance Co.; South Central Bell Telephone Co.; State Farm Fire & Casualty Insurance Co.; Fireman's Fund Insurance Cos.; Deere & Co.; Navistar International Transportation Corp.

For full biographical listings, see the Martindale-Hubbell Law Directory

PAGE, MANNINO & PERESICH (AV)

One LeFleurs Square, 4735 Old Canton Road, P.O. Box 12159, 39236-2159
Telephone: 601-364-1100
Telecopier: 601-364-1118
Biloxi, Mississippi Office: 759 Vieux MarchéMall, P.O. Drawer 289.
Telephone: 601-374-2100.
Telecopier: 601-432-5539.
Gulfport, Mississippi Office: Markham Building, 2301 - 14th Street, Suite 600, P.O. Drawer 660.
Telephone: 601-863-8861.
Telecopier: 601-863-8871.

MEMBERS OF FIRM

Lyle M. Page
Michael P. Collins
Frederick J. Mannino
Randolph Cook Wood
Ronald G. Peresich
Mary A. Nichols
Michael B. McDermott
Joseph Henry Ros
Stephen G. Peresich
Thomas William Busby
Jess H. Dickinson
Michael E. Whitehead
Tere Richardson Steel
Katharine Malley Samson
David S. Raines
Douglas J. Wise (Not admitted in MS)

(See Next Column)

PAGE, MANNINO & PERESICH—*Continued*

Representative Clients: United States Fidelity & Guaranty Co.; St. Paul Fire & Marine Insurance Co.; Crawford & Co.; Anheuser-Busch Corp.
General Counsel for: Peoples Bank of Biloxi, Mississippi; Biloxi Regional Medical Center; Bank of Mississippi (Gulf Coast Division).

For full biographical listings, see the Martindale-Hubbell Law Directory

PHELPS DUNBAR, L.L.P. (AV)

Suite 500, Security Centré North, 200 South Lamar Street, P.O. Box 23066, 39225-3066
Telephone: 601-352-2300
Telecopier: 601-360-9777
New Orleans, Louisiana Office: Texaco Center, 400 Poydras Street.
Telephone: 504-566-1311.
Telecopier: 504-568-9130; 504-568-9007.
Cable Address: "Howspencer."
Telex: 584125 WU.
Telex: 6821155 WUI.
Baton Rouge, Louisiana Office: Suite 701, City National Bank Building, P.O. Box 4412.
Telephone: 504-346-0285.
Telecopier: 504-381-9197.
Tupelo, Mississippi Office: Seventh Floor, One Mississippi Plaza, P.O. Box 1220.
Telephone: 601-842-7907.
Telecopier: 601-842-3873.
Houston, Texas Office: Suite 501, 4 Houston Center, 1331 Lamar Street.
Telephone: 713-659-1386.
Telecopier: 713-659-1388.
London, England Office: Suite 976, Level 9, Lloyd's, 1 Lime Street, London EC3M 7DQ England.
Telephone: 011-44-171-929-4765.
Telecopier: 011-44-171-929-0046.
Telex: 987321.

MEMBERS OF FIRM

Fred M. Bush, Jr. (Also at Tupelo, Mississippi Office)
F. M. Bush, III (Also at Tupelo, Mississippi Office)
Walker W. (Bill) Jones, III (Also at Tupelo, Mississippi Office)
David W. Mockbee
Ross F. Bass, Jr.
E. Clifton Hodge, Jr.
C. Delbert Hosemann, Jr.
Paul O. Miller, III
Armin J. Moeller, Jr.
Reuben V. Anderson
Frank W. Trapp
Arthur F. Jernigan, Jr.
Luther T. Munford
Dan M. McDaniel, Jr.
Gary E. Friedman
Michael B. Wallace
Jean Magee Hogan (Also at Tupelo, Mississippi Office)
Glover A. Russell, Jr.
Stephen H. Leech, Jr.
W. Thomas Siler, Jr. (Also at Tupelo, Mississippi Office)
R. Pepper Crutcher, Jr. (Also at Tupelo, Mississippi Office)
John P. Sneed
Deborah Shelby Nichols
Dana E. Kelly
William C. Brabec
William I. Gault, Jr.
Susan Fahey Desmond
Charles D. Porter
David P. Webb

COUNSEL

Mary Elizabeth Hall
Paul H. Johnson, III
G. Kay L. Trapp (Also at Tupelo, Mississippi Office)
Linda Bounds Sherman
Gregory D. Pirkle (Also at Tupelo, Mississippi Office)

ASSOCIATES

Chuck D. Barlow
Scott W. Bates
John B. Beard
M. Lea Beaty (Also at Tupelo, Mississippi Office)
Sheryl Bey
Heather J. Camp
Danny A. Drake
John Wilson Eaton III (Also at Tupelo, Mississippi Office)
Ken Fairly
Robert W. Graves
Gregory D. Guida
Robert T. Higginbotham Jr.
John B. Landry, Jr.
Angela M. McLain
John A. Meynardie
Jeffrey S. Moore (Also at Tupelo, Mississippi Office)
Wendy L. Moore
Julie Sneed Muller
Dinetia M. Newman (Also at Tupelo, Mississippi Office)
A. Matt Pesnell
Chelye E. Prichard
Carlton W. Reeves
Todd C. Richter
Wendy L. Russell
William F. Selph III
William Carter Smallwood, III (Also at Tupelo, Mississippi Office)
David M. Thomas, II
Stephen M. Wilson (Also at Tupelo, Mississippi Office)
Joseph A. Ziemianski

Representative Clients: Bank of Mississippi; Beech Aerospace Services; Blue Cross & Blue Shield of Mississippi; Cellular South, Inc.; General Motors Corporation; The Kroger Co.; Mississippi Municipal Liability Plan; Philip Morris Incorporated; Underwriters at Lloyd's, London; Westinghouse Electric.

For full biographical listings, see the Martindale-Hubbell Law Directory

PRICE & ZIRULNIK (AV)

Suite 1150 Capital Towers, 125 South Congress Street, P.O. Box 3439, 39207-3439
Telephone: 601-353-3000
Telecopier: 601-353-3007

John H. Price, Jr.
Barry S. Zirulnik

ASSOCIATES

William G. Cheney, Jr.

Representative Clients: Yellow Freight System, Inc.; Mississippi Dairy Products Association, Inc.; LuVel Dairy Products, Inc.; Mississippi Farm Bureau Federation; Mississippi Department of Transportation; Mississippi High School Activities Association, Inc.; Variety Wholesalers, Inc.; Mississippi Bankers Association; Metal Rolling, Inc.

For full biographical listings, see the Martindale-Hubbell Law Directory

STEEN REYNOLDS DALEHITE & CURRIE (AV)

Mississippi Valley Title Building, 315 Tombigbee Street, P.O. Box 900, 39205
Telephone: 601-969-7054
Telecopier: 601-969-5120

MEMBERS OF FIRM

Jimmie B. Reynolds, Jr.
William M. Dalehite, Jr.
Edward J. Currie, Jr.
Whitman B. Johnson, III
William C. Griffin
Philip W. Gaines
Michael F. Myers

ASSOCIATES

Frances R. Shields
William H. Creel, Jr.
James C. Smallwood, III
F. Keith Ball
Shannon S. Clark
Lisa L. Williams
Le Robinson Brown

OF COUNSEL

Jerome B. Steen

Mississippi Counsel for: State Farm Insurance Co.
Representative Clients include: Allstate Insurance Co.; St. Paul Insurance Cos.; Indiana Lumbermens Mutual Insurance Co.; United Services Automobile Assn.; Empire Fire & Marine Ins.; Sears Roebuck & Co.
References: Trustmark National Bank, Jackson, Mississippi.

For full biographical listings, see the Martindale-Hubbell Law Directory

STENNETT, WILKINSON & PEDEN, A PROFESSIONAL ASSOCIATION (AV)

100 Congress Street South, P.O. Box 22627, 39225-2627
Telephone: 601-948-3000
Telefax: 601-948-3019

E. W. Stennett (1899-1979)
Horace Steele (1907-1980)
J. C. Stennett (1903-1987)
Gene A. Wilkinson
James A. Peden, Jr.
Derryl W. Peden
James C. Martin
Richard C. Bradley, III

LEGAL SUPPORT PERSONNEL

Stacey L. Smith

Representative Clients: Frito-Lay, Inc.; Laws Construction Co., Inc.; McCullough Environmental Services, Inc.; Mississippi Bankers Association; Mississippi Commissioner of Insurance; Protective Service Life Insurance Co.; The Mitchell Company; The Promus Companies, Incorporated; Thorn, Alvis, Welch Investment Securities, Inc.; United Mississippi Bank.

For full biographical listings, see the Martindale-Hubbell Law Directory

* **UPSHAW, WILLIAMS, BIGGERS, PAGE & KRUGER** (AV)

One Jackson Place, 188 East Capitol Street, Suite 600, P.O. Drawer 1163, 39215
Telephone: 601-944-0005
Facsimile: 601-355-4269
Greenwood, Mississippi Office: 309 Fulton Street, P.O. Drawer 8230, 38930.
Telephone: 601-455-1613.
Facsimile: 601-453-9245.

RESIDENT MEMBERS

Thomas Y. Page
Stephen P. Kruger
James D. Holland
Roger C. Riddick
Edley H. Jones, III
Wes Peters

RESIDENT ASSOCIATES

Brent E. Southern
Kathleen S. Gordon
W. Hugh Gillon, IV
William C. Helm
Mark C. Carroll
Walter C. Morrison, IV
Patrick C. Malouf
Stuart B. Harmon

OF COUNSEL

B. L. Riddick
John R. Countiss, III

Representative Clients: U.S.F. & G. Co.; State Farm Mutual Automobile Ins. Co.; Continental Insurance Co.; St. Paul Fire & Marine Insurance Co.; Aetna Casualty & Surety Co.; Kemper Insurance Co.; Zurich-America Ins. Group; Home Ins. Co.; Illinois Central Railroad Co.; Allstate Insurance Co.

For full biographical listings, see the Martindale-Hubbell Law Directory

Jackson—Continued

WATKINS & EAGER (AV)

Suite 300 The Emporium Building, P.O. Box 650, 39205
Telephone: 601-948-6470
Facsimile: (601) 354-3623

William H. Watkins (1871-1959)
Pat H. Eager, Jr. (1892-1970)
Elizabeth Watkins Hulen (1899-1977)
Hassell H. Whitworth (1925-1991)
Thomas H. Watkins (1933-1994)

OF COUNSEL

William E. Suddath, Jr.
Vardaman S. Dunn
Thomas M. Murphree, Jr.

MEMBERS OF FIRM

William F. Goodman, Jr.
Charles Clark
James A. Becker, Jr.
William H. Cox, Jr.
P. Nicholas Harkins, III
John G. Corlew
George R. Fair
Kenneth E. Milam
John L. Low, IV
Michael W. Ulmer
Paul H. Stephenson, III
William F. Goodman, III
Clifford B. Ammons
Jamie G. Houston, III
Frank J. Hammond, III
Richard T. Lawrence
Robert H. Pedersen
Steven D. Orlansky
Robert A. Miller
Douglas J. Gunn
Paul J. Stephens
David L. Ayers
Frank A. Wood, Jr.
Virginia T. Munford
Rebecca Lee Wiggs
William F. Ray
Michael O. Gwin
M. Binford Williams, Jr.
James A. Lowe, III
Lewis W. Bell
J. Fred Spencer, Jr.
Mildred M. Morris

ASSOCIATES

Edwin Y. Hannan
Walter J. Brand
Louis B. Lanoux
Myles A. Parker
J. Grant Sellers
Walter T. Johnson
Mark D. Jicka
Kathleen D. Patrick
Susan Latham Steffey
Gaines Michael Massey
Richard G. Peaster
Lynn Plimpton Risley
Leah Draayer McDowell
Stacey T. Earnest
Christopher B. Bradford
C. Maison Heidelberg

Representative Clients: Ashland Oil, Inc.; Chevron U.S.A. Inc.; CIGNA Property and Casualty Companies; Ford Motor Co.; Ingersoll-Rand Co.; Jitney Jungle Stores of America, Inc.; Shell Oil Co.; Sterling Winthrop Inc.; Trustmark National Bank.

For full biographical listings, see the Martindale-Hubbell Law Directory

WELLS MARBLE & HURST (AV)

Suite 400, Lamar Life Building, 317 East Capitol Street, P.O. Box 131, 39205-0131
Telephone: 601-355-8321
Telecopier: 601-355-4217

William Calvin Wells (1844-1914)
Major W. Calvin Wells (1878-1957)
William Calvin Wells, Jr. (1908-1988)

MEMBERS OF FIRM

Erskine W. Wells
Roland D. Marble
Joe Jack Hurst
J. Jerry Langford
John Edward Hughes, III
James S. Armstrong
William H. Glover, Jr.
Wendell H. Cook, Jr.
Kenna L. Mansfield, Jr.
Steven H. Begley
Daniel H. Fairly
Roy H. Liddell
Walter D. Willson

ASSOCIATES

Kelly D. Simpkins
Lana Edwards Gillon

Counsel for: General Motors Corp.; United States Steel Corp.; International Business Machines Corp.; Illinois Central Railroad Co.; Lamar Life Insurance Co.; Metropolitan Life Insurance Co.; Prudential Insurance Company of America; Southern Natural Gas Co.; Trustmark National Bank of Jackson.

For full biographical listings, see the Martindale-Hubbell Law Directory

WELLS, MOORE, SIMMONS & NEELD (AV)

1300 Deposit Guaranty Plaza, P.O. Box 1970, 39215-1970
Telephone: 601-354-5400
Telecopier: 601-355-5850

MEMBERS OF FIRM

Calvin Lowell Wells
James H. Neeld, III
Frank T. Moore, Jr.
Eugene A. Simmons
Thomas Calvin Wells
Michael Farrell
Arthur M. Edwards, III
Jeffrey P. Hubbard
Peter L. Doran

(See Next Column)

ASSOCIATES

Susan McEuen Lawler
W. Jeff Hamm
John M. Desmond (Not admitted in MS)

Representative Clients: Chase Manhattan Bank; Deposit Guaranty National Bank; First Interstate Bankcorp; Western Surety Co.; Delta Pipeline Co.
General Counsel for: Cal-Maine Foods, Inc.

For full biographical listings, see the Martindale-Hubbell Law Directory

WISE CARTER CHILD & CARAWAY, PROFESSIONAL ASSOCIATION (AV)

600 Heritage Building, 401 East Capitol Street, P.O. Box 651, 39205
Telephone: 601-968-5500
FAX: 601-968-5519

Natie P. Caraway
James K. Child, Jr.
Louis H. Watson
James L. Robertson
George Q. Evans
A. Spencer Gilbert III
Henderson S. Hall, Jr.
Charles T. Ozier
Robert B. McGehee
W. McDonald Nichols
Henry E. Chatham, Jr.
Richard D. Gamblin
David W. Clark
John D. Price
Margaret H. Williams
Robert P. Wise
Douglas E. Levanway
F. Hall Bailey
Barbara Childs Wallace
Clifford K. Bailey, III
Andrew D. Sweat
Mark P. Caraway
George H. Ritter
R. Mark Hodges
Betty Toon Collins
Charles E. Ross

OF COUNSEL

Sherwood W. Wise
William O. Carter, Jr.

John W. Robinson, III.
Ronald J. Artigues, Jr.
Rachael Hetherington Lenoir
L. Jager Smith, Jr.
Douglas T. Miracle
Philip W. Thomas
Joanne S. Samson
James W. Manuel

Representative Clients: General Motors Corp.; Sanderson Farms, Inc.; Sunburst Bank; Energy Operations, Inc.; Illinois Central Railroad Co.; McCaw Cellular Communications, Inc.; Mississippi Power & Light Co.; Mississippi Hospital Assn.; St. Paul Cos.

For full biographical listings, see the Martindale-Hubbell Law Directory

*KOSCIUSKO,** Attala Co. — (Refer to Winona)

*LAUREL,** Jones Co.

GIBBES GRAVES MULLINS BULLOCK & FERRIS (AV)

1107 West Sixth Street, P.O. Box 1409, 39441-1409
Telephone: 601-649-8611
FAX: 601-649-6062

MEMBERS OF FIRM

William S. Mullins, III
E. Brooke Ferris, III
Norman Gene Hortman, Jr.
Eugene M. Harlow
Richard O. Burson

ASSOCIATES

Romney H. Entrekin
Deidra D. Jones

Representative Clients: Norfolk Southern Corp.; Travelers Insurance Co.; Masonite Corp., a Division of International Paper Co.; National Railroad Passenger Corp.(AMTRAK); COHO Resources, Inc.; St. Paul Insurance; The Virginia Insurance Reciprocal; Chevron USA, Inc.; South Central Bell; Medical Assurance Co. of Ms.

For full biographical listings, see the Martindale-Hubbell Law Directory

*LEAKESVILLE,** Greene Co. — (Refer to Lucedale)

*LEXINGTON,** Holmes Co. — (Refer to Greenwood)

*LIBERTY,** Amite Co. — (Refer to Tylertown)

*LOUISVILLE,** Winston Co. — (Refer to Columbus)

*LUCEDALE,** George Co.

MURPHY & SHEPARD (AV)

235 Ratliff Street, 39452-2246
Telephone: 601-947-7575; 947-7576
Fax: 601-947-4425

MEMBERS OF FIRM

Williams S. Murphy
Robert P. Shepard

Attorneys for: City of Lucedale.
Approved Attorneys for: Mississippi Valley Title Insurance Co.; Lawyers Title Insurance Corp.; Chicago Title Insurance Co.
Representative Client: TRW Title Insurance Company

*MACON,** Noxubee Co. — (Refer to Columbus)

*MAGNOLIA,** Pike Co. — (Refer to Tylertown)

MC COMB, Pike Co. — (Refer to Tylertown)

*MEADVILLE,** Franklin Co. — (Refer to Natchez)

*MERIDIAN,** Lauderdale Co.

BOURDEAUX AND JONES (AV)

505 Constitution Avenue, P.O. Box 2009, 39302-2009
Telephone: 601-693-2393
Fax: 601-693-0226

Thomas D. Bourdeaux
Thomas R. Jones
William C. Hammack
Thomas L. Webb
J. Richard Barry
E. Gregory Snowden
Michael D. Herrin
Lee Thaggard

General Counsel for: Dixie Oil Co. of Alabama; Great Southern National Bank; Meridian Housing Authority; Mississippi Loggers Purchasing Group, Inc.; New South Communications, Inc.; City of Meridian; Lauderdale County Board of Supervisors.
Local Counsel for: Chrysler Corporation; Louisiana-Pacific Corp.; Hartford Insurance Group; Fireman's Fund American Insurance Cos.; Mississippi Loggers Assn.-S.I.F.; United States Fidelity and Guaranty Co.; Town of Marion.

For full biographical listings, see the Martindale-Hubbell Law Directory

EPPES, WATTS & SHANNON (AV)

4805 Poplar Springs Drive, P.O. Box 3787, 39303-3787
Telephone: 601-483-3968
Telecopier: 601-693-0416

MEMBERS OF FIRM

Walter W. Eppes, Jr.
T. Kenneth Watts
John Rex Shannon
Grace Watts Mitts
William B. Carter

Representative Clients: Allstate Insurance Co.; American International Adjusting Co.; CIGNA; Liberty Mutual Insurance Co.; Royal Globe Insurance Co.; St. Paul Insurance Cos.; State Farm Insurance Co.; General Motors Corporation; Medical Assurance Corp.; Sears, Roebuck and Co.

For full biographical listings, see the Martindale-Hubbell Law Directory

HAMILTON & LINDER (AV)

2713 Seventh Street, P.O. Box 2146, 39302-2146
Telephone: 601-693-5548
FAX: 601-693-2949

MEMBERS OF FIRM

Joe Clay Hamilton
David H. Linder

For full biographical listings, see the Martindale-Hubbell Law Directory

*NATCHEZ,** Adams Co.

GWIN, LEWIS & PUNCHES (AV)

319 Market Street, P.O. Box 1344, 39120
Telephone: 601-446-6621
FAX: 601-442-6175
Woodville, Mississippi Office: 457 Main Street.
Telephone: 601-446-6621.

MEMBERS OF FIRM

Lucien C. Gwin, Jr.
W. Bruce Lewis
Robert R. Punches
Lucien C. Gwin, III
Christopher E. Kelley

Mississippi Counsel for: International Paper Company.
Representative Clients: Sammons Communications, Inc.; Britton & Koontz First National Bank; Mississippi Farm Bureau Insurance Co.

For full biographical listings, see the Martindale-Hubbell Law Directory

*NEW ALBANY,** Union Co.

SUMNERS, CARTER & McMILLIN, P.A. (AV)

104 North Central Avenue, P.O. Drawer 730, 38652
Telephone: 601-534-6326
Telecopier: 601-534-5205

Robert L. Smallwood, Jr. (1909-1954)
Leslie Darden (1910-1982)
Lester F. Sumners
Robert M. Carter
Roger H. McMillin, Jr.

Representative Clients: First National Bank; Union County Board of Supervisors, U.S.F. & G. Co.; Maryland Casualty Co.

For full biographical listings, see the Martindale-Hubbell Law Directory

*OKOLONA,** Chickasaw Co. — (Refer to Tupelo)

*OXFORD,** Lafayette Co.

HOLCOMB, DUNBAR, CONNELL, CHAFFIN & WILLARD, A PROFESSIONAL ASSOCIATION (AV)

1217 Jackson Avenue P.O. Drawer 707, 38655
Telephone: 601-234-8775
Facsimile: 601-234-8638
Jackson, Mississippi Office: 111 East Capitol Street, Suite 290. P.O. Box 2990, 39207-2990.
Telephone: 601-948-0048.
Facsimile: 601-948-0050.
Clarksdale, Mississippi Office: 152 Delta Avenue, P.O. Box 368, 38614.
Telephone: 601-627-2241.
Facsimile: 601-627-9788.
Aberdeen, Mississippi Office: 109 1/2 West Commerce Street, P.O. Box 866, 39730.
Telephone: 601-369-8800.
Facsimile: 601-369-9404.
Southaven, Mississippi Office: Suite 1, 8727 Northwest Drive, P.O. Box 190, 38671.
Telephone: 601-342-6806.
Facsimile: 601-342-6792.

Jack F. Dunbar
Craig M. Geno
Guy T. Gillespie, III
Edward A. Moss
Thomas J. Suszek
John H. Dunbar
Wylene W. Dunbar
Michael N. Watts
Janet G. Arnold
Thomas T. Dunbar
T. Swayze Alford
Nancy M. Maddox
Robert S. Mink
Stephan L. McDavid
Barry C. Blackburn
John Ramsey McCarroll, III
Louis H. Watson, Jr.

OF COUNSEL

Edward P. Connell

Counsel for: United Southern Bank; Mississippi Power & Light Co.; Mississippi Valley Gas Co.; Aetna Casualty & Surety Co.; Southern Farm Bureau Casualty Insurance Co.; South Central Bell Telephone Co.; State Farm Mutual Fire & Casualty Insurance Co.; Fireman's Fund Insurance Cos.; Deere & Co.; Navistar International Transportation Corp.

For full biographical listings, see the Martindale-Hubbell Law Directory

*PASCAGOULA,** Jackson Co.

COLINGO, WILLIAMS, HEIDELBERG, STEINBERGER & McELHANEY, P.A. (AV)

711 Delmas Avenue, P.O. Box 1407, 39568-0240
Telephone: 601-762-8021
FAX: 601-762-7589

Joe R. Colingo
Roy C. Williams
James H. Heidelberg
Karl R. Steinberger
Michael J. McElhaney, Jr.
James H. Colmer, Jr.
Robert W. Wilkinson
Brett K. Williams

Carol S. Noblitt
Karen N. Haarala
Stephen Walker Burrow
Scott D. Smith
Gina L. Bardwell

LEGAL SUPPORT PERSONNEL

Harry H. Carpenter

Representative Clients: International Paper Co.; R.J. Reynolds; Westinghouse Corp.; St. Paul Fire & Marine Ins. Co.; Kemper Group; Singing River Hospital System.

For full biographical listings, see the Martindale-Hubbell Law Directory

*PHILADELPHIA,** Neshoba Co. — (Refer to Meridian)

PICAYUNE, Pearl River Co.

WILLIAMS, WILLIAMS AND MONTGOMERY, P.A. (AV)

900 Highway 11 South, P.O. Box 1058, 39466
Telephone: 601-798-0480
FAX: 601-798-5481
Poplarville, Mississippi Office: 109 Erlanger Street, P.O. Box 113.
Telephone: 601-795-4572.
FAX: 601-795-8382.

E. B. Williams (1890-1976)
E. B. Williams, Jr. (1917-1990)
Lampton O'Neal Williams
Joseph H. Montgomery
E. Bragg Williams, III
L. O'Neal Williams, Jr.

Michael E. Patten
Anne M. Parker

Representative Clients: Hancock Bank, Bank of Commerce Branch; Wesley's Fertilizer Plant, Inc.; Bass Pecan Co., Lumberton, Mississippi; Joe N. Miles & Sons Lumber Co., Lumberton and Silver Creek, Mississippi, and Bogalusa, Louisiana.

For full biographical listings, see the Martindale-Hubbell Law Directory

*PONTOTOC,** Pontotoc Co. — (Refer to Tupelo)

*POPLARVILLE,** Pearl River Co.

WILLIAMS, WILLIAMS AND MONTGOMERY, P.A. (AV)

109 Erlanger Street, P.O. Box 113, 39470
Telephone: 601-795-4572
FAX: 601-795-8382
Picayune, Mississippi Office: 900 Highway 11 South, P.O. Box 1058.
Telephone: 601-798-0480.
FAX: 601-798-5481.

E. B. Williams (1890-1976)
E. B. Williams, Jr. (1917-1990)
Lampton O'Neal Williams
Joseph H. Montgomery
E. Bragg Williams, III
L. O'Neal Williams, Jr.

Michael E. Patten
Anne M. Parker

Representative Clients: Hancock Bank, Bank of Commerce Branch; Wesley's Fertilizer Plant, Inc.; Wesley Oil and Gas Co., Inc.; Garrett Industries, Inc.; Bass Pecan Co., Lumberton, Miss.; Joe N. Miles & Sons Lumber Co., Inc., Lumberton and Silver Creek, Miss. and Bogalusa, La.
Reference: Hancock Bank, Bank of Commerce Branch, Poplarville, Mississippi.

For full biographical listings, see the Martindale-Hubbell Law Directory

*PORT GIBSON,** Claiborne Co. — (Refer to Vicksburg)

*PRENTISS,** Jefferson Davis Co. — (Refer to Columbia)

*QUITMAN,** Clarke Co. — (Refer to Meridian)

*RIPLEY,** Tippah Co. — (Refer to Tupelo)

*ROLLING FORK,** Sharkey Co. — (Refer to Yazoo City)

*ROSEDALE,** Bolivar Co. — (Refer to Cleveland)

*SARDIS,** Panola Co. — (Refer to Clarksdale)

SOUTHAVEN, De Soto Co.

BRIDGFORTH & BUNTIN (AV)

1607 State Line Road, P.O. Box 241, 38671
Telephone: 601-393-4450
Fax: 601-342-5646

MEMBERS OF FIRM

Dudley B. Bridgforth, Jr.
Taylor D. Buntin, III

For full biographical listings, see the Martindale-Hubbell Law Directory

HOLCOMB, DUNBAR, CONNELL, CHAFFIN & WILLARD, A PROFESSIONAL ASSOCIATION (AV)

Suite 1, 8727 Northwest Drive, P.O. Box 190, 38671
Telephone: 601-342-6806
Facsimile: 601-342-6792
Jackson, Mississippi Office: 111 East Capitol Street, Suite 290, P.O. Box 2990, 39207-2990.
Telephone: 601-948-0048.
Facsimile: 601-948-0050.
Clarksdale, Mississippi Office: 152 Delta Avenue, P.O. Box 368, 38614.
Telephone: 601-627-2241.
Facsimile: 601-627-9788.
Aberdeen, Mississippi Office: 109 1/2 West Commerce Street, P.O. Box 866, 39730.
Telephone: 601-369-8800.
Facsimile: 601-369-9404.
Oxford, Mississippi Office: 1217 Jackson Avenue, P.O. Drawer 707, 38655.
Telephone: 601-234-8775.
Facsimile: 601-234-8638.

Jack F. Dunbar
William M. Chaffin
Thomas J. Suszek
Michael N. Watts
William A. Baskin
David A. Burns
Barry C. Blackburn
John Ramsey McCarroll, III

OF COUNSEL

Edward P. Connell

Counsel For: United Southern Bank; Mississippi Power & Light Co.; Mississippi Valley Gas Co.; Aetna Casualty & Surety Co.; Southern Farm Bureau Casualty Insurance Co.; South Central Bell Telephone Co.; State Farm Mutual Fire & Casualty Insurance Co.; Deere & Co.; Navistar International Transportation Corp.; Sunburst Bank.

For full biographical listings, see the Martindale-Hubbell Law Directory

*STARKVILLE,** Oktibbeha Co.

GHOLSON, HICKS, NICHOLS & WARD, A PROFESSIONAL ASSOCIATION (AV)

121 North Jackson Street, P.O. Drawer 59, 39759-0059
Telephone: 601-323-1912
Fax: 601-324-4795
Columbus, Mississippi, Office: Court Square Towers, 605 Second Avenue North, P.O. Box 1111.
Telephone: 601-327-0662.
Fax: 601-327-6217.

William Ward
Hunter M. Gholson
Dewitt T. Hicks, Jr.
Aubrey E. Nichols
Ralph E. Rood
John W. Crowell
J. Gordon Flowers
H. Russell Rogers
Katherine S. Kerby
David B. Jolly
P. Nelson Smith, Jr.
John Franklin Williams
William R. Couch
William Thomas Cooper
Marc Darren Amos
David Tyler Lewis

Counsel for: National Bank of Commerce of Mississippi; Trustmark National Bank; United States Fidelity and Guaranty Co.; Fireman's Fund American Insurance Cos.; Cargill, Inc.; Kerr-McGee Corp.; City of Columbus; Gulf States Manufacturers, Inc.; Airline Manufacturing Co.; Lowndes County Port Authority.

For full biographical listings, see the Martindale-Hubbell Law Directory

*SUMNER,** Tallahatchie Co. — (Refer to Clarksdale)

*TUNICA,** Tunica Co. — (Refer to Clarksdale)

*TUPELO,** Lee Co.

HOLLAND, RAY & UPCHURCH, P.A. (AV)

322 Jefferson Street, P.O. Drawer 409, 38802
Telephone: 601-842-1721
Facsimile: 601-844-6413

Sam E. Lumpkin (1908-1964)
Ralph L. Holland
James Hugh Ray
Robert K. Upchurch
W. Reed Hillen, III
Thomas A. Wicker

Michael D. Tapscott

Representative Clients: The Travelers; Continental Casualty Co.; South Central Bell Telephone Co.; The Greyhound Corp.; Mississippi Valley Gas Co.; Bryan-Rogers, Inc.; The Housing Authority of the City of Tupelo; Action Industries, Inc.; American Cable Systems, Inc.; American Funeral Assurance Co.

For full biographical listings, see the Martindale-Hubbell Law Directory

MITCHELL, MCNUTT, THREADGILL, SMITH & SAMS, P.A. (AV)

105 South Front Street, P.O. Box 7120, 38802
Telephone: 601-842-3871
Facsimile: 601-842-8450
Columbus, Mississippi Office: 215 Fifth Street North, P.O. Box 1366.
Telephone: 601-328-2316.
Facsimile: 601-328-8035.
Corinth, Mississippi Office: 508 Waldron Street, P.O. Box 1200.
Telephone: 601-286-9931.
Facsimile: 601-286-8984.
Oxford, Mississippi Office: 1216 Van Buren, P.O. Box 430.
Telephone: 601-234-4845.
Facsimile: 601-234-9071.
Jackson, Mississippi Office: Deposit Guaranty Plaza, 210 East Capitol, Suite 1540, P.O. Box 1005.
Telephone: 601-948-8505.
Facsimile: 601-948-8537.
Memphis, Tennessee Office: 1255 Lynnfield Road, Building A, Suite 123.
Telephone: 901-767-5185.
Facsimile: 901-767-5918,

Guy W. Mitchell, Sr. (1881-1969)
Guy W. Mitchell, Jr. (1912-1986)
L. F. Sams, Jr.
Taylor B. Smith
Guy W. Mitchell, III
William C. Spencer
W. H. (Hank) Jolly, Jr. (Resident at Columbus Office)
David L. Sanders (Resident at Columbus Office)
S. T. Rayburn (Resident at Oxford Office)
James L. Carroll
Claude F. Clayton, Jr.
Wendell H. Trapp, Jr. (Resident at Corinth Office)
Thomas D. Murry
William C. Murphree
Ronald L. Roberts
Albert G. Delgadillo
Michael D. Greer
John S. Hill
Ronald I. Loeb
Michael D. Ferris
Richard H. Spann (Columbus and Jackson Offices)
W. Scott Collins
James A. Barnett, Jr.
Lauren J. Hutchins (Resident, Columbus and Memphis Office)
Otis R. Tims
Donna M. Barnes
H. Richmond Culp, III
Michael D. Chase
Martha Bost Stegall

(See Next Column)

MITCHELL, MCNUTT, THREADGILL, SMITH & SAMS P.A.—*Continued*

John G. Wheeler
Jeffry M. Cox
Ronald Henry Pierce (Resident at Oxford Office)
Timothy M. Threadgill (Resident, Columbus and Oxford Offices)
Tacey Clark Humphrey (Resident at Corinth Office)
D. Andrew Phillips
Gregg A. Caraway
J. Douglas Ford (Resident at Columbus Office)
A. Rhett Wise
Jeffrey J. Turnage (Resident at Columbus Office)
Bo Russell
M. Alison Farese
Paige B. Rayburn

OF COUNSEL

Robert N. McNutt
William J. Threadgill
Wade H. Lagrone
Burney F. Threadgill

Representative Clients: State Farm Mutual Insurance Co.; Aetna Casualty and Surety; Burlington Northern Railroad; City of Tupelo; Community Federal Savings & Loan Assn.; Cummins Engine Co.; North Mississippi Health Services, Inc. (North Mississippi Medical Center); Medical Assurance Company of Mississippi; United States Fidelity & Guaranty Co.

For full biographical listings, see the Martindale-Hubbell Law Directory

MITCHELL, VOGE, BEASLEY AND CORBAN (AV)

108 North Broadway, P.O. Box 29, 38802
Telephone: 601-842-4231
Telecopier: 601-842-2689

W. P. Mitchell
Jess B. Rogers (1924-1975)
Dennis W. Voge
William M. Beasley
Stephen M. Corban

ASSOCIATES

Stephen H. Morris
Edwin H. Priest
Leslie W. Smith

For full biographical listings, see the Martindale-Hubbell Law Directory

PHELPS DUNBAR, L.L.P. (AV)

Seventh Floor, One Mississippi Plaza, P.O. Box 1220, 38802-1220
Telephone: 601-842-7907
Telecopier: 601-842-3873
New Orleans, Louisiana Office: Texaco Center, 400 Poydras Street.
Telephone: 504-566-1311.
Telecopier: 504-568-9130; 504-568-9007.
Cable Address: "Howspencer."
Telex: 584125 WU.
Telex: 6821155 WUI.
Baton Rouge, Louisiana Office: Suite 701, City National Bank Building, P.O. Box 4412.
Telephone: 504-346-0285.
Telecopier: 504-381-9197.
Jackson, Mississippi Office: Suite 500, Security Centré North, 200 South Lamar Street, P.O. Box 23066.
Telephone: 601-352-2300.
Telecopier: 601-360-9777.
Houston, Texas Office: Suite 501, 4 Houston Center, 1331 Lamar Street.
Telephone: 713-659-1386.
Telecopier: 713-659-1388.
London, England Office: Suite 976, Level 9, Lloyd's, 1 Lime Street, London EC3M 7DQ England.
Telephone: 011-44-171-929-4765.
Telecopier: 011-44-171-929-0046.
Telex: 987321.

MEMBERS OF FIRM

Fred M. Bush, Jr.
F. M. Bush, III (Also at Jackson, Mississippi Office)
Walker W. (Bill) Jones, III (Also at Jackson, Mississippi Office)
Jean Magee Hogan
W. Thomas Siler, Jr. (Also at Jackson, Mississippi Office)
R. Pepper Crutcher, Jr. (Also at Jackson, Mississippi Office)

COUNSEL

G. Kay L. Trapp
Gregory D. Pirkle

ASSOCIATES

M. Lea Beaty
John Wilson Eaton III (Also at Jackson, Mississippi Office)
Jeffrey S. Moore
Dinetia M. Newman
William Carter Smallwood, III
Stephen M. Wilson

Representative Clients: AMCA International Limited (Jesco Division); Bank of Mississippi; Blue Cross & Blue Shield of Mississippi; CBI Equifax; General Motors Corporation; The Kroger Co.; Mississippi Municipal Liability Plan; North Mississippi Medical Center, Inc. (and affiliated hospitals); Philip Morris Incorporated; Underwriters at Lloyd's, London.

For full biographical listings, see the Martindale-Hubbell Law Directory

WEBB, SANDERS, DEATON, BALDUCCI & SMITH (AV)

363 North Broadway, P.O. Box 496, 38802-0496
Telephone: 601-844-2137
Facsimile: 601-842-3863
Oxford, Mississippi Office: 2154 South Lamar Boulevard, P.O. Box 148.
Telephone: 601-236-5700.
Facsimile: 601-236-5800.

MEMBERS OF FIRM

Dan W. Webb
Benjamin H. Sanders
Dana Gail Deaton
Chris H. Deaton
Timothy R. Balducci
Kent E. Smith
Danny P. Hall, Jr.
B. Wayne Williams

OF COUNSEL

Rachael Howell Webb

Representative Clients: Allstate Insurance Company; Georgia Casualty & Surety Company; GAB Business Services, Inc.; The Kroger Company; Ohio Casualty Insurance Company; Phillips and Associates; State Auto Insurance Company; State Farm Fire & Casualty Company; Transport Life Insurance Company; United States Fidelity & Guaranty Company.

For full biographical listings, see the Martindale-Hubbell Law Directory

*TYLERTOWN,** Walthall Co.

JOSEPH M. STINSON (AV)

1108 Beulah Avenue, 39667
Telephone: 601-876-5121; 876-5122
FAX: 601-876-5882

Representative Clients: Stringer Industries, Inc.; Jones Lumber Co., Inc.
Approved Attorney for: Mississippi Valley Title Insurance Co.; Farm Credit Bank of Texas.

For full biographical listings, see the Martindale-Hubbell Law Directory

*VICKSBURG,** Warren Co.

TELLER, MARTIN, CHANEY & HASSELL (AV)

Suite 500 Merchants Bank, 820 South Street, P.O. Box 789, 39181
Telephone: 601-636-6565
FAX: Available Upon Request

MEMBERS OF FIRM

Landman Teller, Jr.
M. James Chaney, Jr.
Douglas E. Hassell
J. Allen Derivaux, Jr.
Frank J. Campbell
B. Blake Teller

OF COUNSEL

Landman Teller
Burkett H. Martin

Representative Clients: International Paper Co.; Vicksburg Business Investment Co.; Coca-Cola Bottling Company of Vicksburg; Bank of Mississippi; Merchants Bank, National Association; Anderson-Tully Co.; Vicksburg Warren School District.
Approved Attorneys for: Mississippi Valley Title Insurance Co.; First American Title Insurance Co.; Lawyers Title Insurance Corp.

For full biographical listings, see the Martindale-Hubbell Law Directory

*WEST POINT,** Clay Co. — (Refer to Columbus)

*WINONA,** Montgomery Co.

LISTON/LANCASTER (AV)

126 North Quitman Avenue, P.O. Box 645, 38967
Telephone: 601-283-2132
Fax: 601-283-3742

William H. Liston
Alan D. Lancaster
William Liston, III
Lee B. Hazlewood

For full biographical listings, see the Martindale-Hubbell Law Directory

*WOODVILLE,** Wilkinson Co.

GWIN, LEWIS & PUNCHES (AV)

457 Main Street, 39669
Telephone: 601-446-6621
Natchez, Mississippi Office: 319 Market Street.
Telephone: 601-446-6621.
FAX: 601-442-6175.

W. Bruce Lewis
Lucien C. Gwin, III

Mississippi Counsel for: International Paper Company.
Representative Clients: Sammons Communications, Inc.; Britton & Koontz First National Bank; Mississippi Farm Bureau Insurance Co.

MISSOURI

*ALBANY,** Gentry Co.

Fred Kling (AV)

109 North Smith, 64402
Telephone: 816-726-3210

For full biographical listings, see the Martindale-Hubbell Law Directory

*AVA,** Douglas Co. — (Refer to West Plains)

*BENTON,** Scott Co. — (Refer to Sikeston)

*BOLIVAR,** Polk Co. — (Refer to Springfield)

*BOONVILLE,** Cooper Co. — (Refer to Columbia)

*BOWLING GREEN,** Pike Co. — (Refer to Hannibal)

*BUFFALO,** Dallas Co. — (Refer to Springfield)

*BUTLER,** Bates Co. — (Refer to Nevada)

*CALIFORNIA,** Moniteau Co. — (Refer to Jefferson City)

*CAMDENTON,** Camden Co. — (Refer to Lebanon)

CAPE GIRARDEAU, Cape Girardeau Co.

Finch, Bradshaw, Strom & Steele, L.C. (AV)

3113 Independence, P.O. Box 1300, 63702-1300
Telephone: 314-334-0555
Fax: 314-334-2947

James A. Finch (1883-1953)
Lehman Finch (1916-1991)
John P. Bradshaw
Stephen E. Strom
Richard G. Steele
James A. Cochrane, III
Paul H. Berens
Daniel P. Finch
Dale E. Gerecke
Craig M. Billmeyer

OF COUNSEL

William S. Rader

Representative Clients: Royal-Globe Insurance Co; R. B. Potashnick, General Contractor; United States Fidelity & Guaranty Co.; KFVS-TV; Liberty Mutual Insurance Co.; Southern Illinois Stone Co.; Cape Central Airways; St. Francis Medical Center, AmeriFirst Bank of Cape Girardeau.

For full biographical listings, see the Martindale-Hubbell Law Directory

Oliver, Oliver & Waltz, P.C. (AV)

400 Broadway, P.O. Box 559, 63702-0559
Telephone: 314-335-8278
Fax: 314-334-6375

R. B. Oliver (1850-1934)
R. B. Oliver, Jr. (1880-1971)
Allen Laws Oliver (1886-1970)
John (Jack) L. Oliver (1916-1978)
John L. Oliver, Jr.
James Frederick Waltz
Richard K. Kuntze
Jeffrey P. Hine

J. Michael Ponder
Jonah Ted Yates

OF COUNSEL

A. J. Seier

Representative Clients: Mercantile Bank of Cape Girardeau; Union Electric Co.; Soutwestern Bell Corp.; Ford Motor Co.; Consolidated Drainage District No. 1; City of Charleston; MOMEDICO; CNA; The Travelers; The Hartford.

For full biographical listings, see the Martindale-Hubbell Law Directory

Thomasson, Gilbert, Cook, Remley & Maguire (AV)

715 Clark Avenue, P.O. Box 1180, 63702-1180
Telephone: 314-335-6651
Fax: 314-335-6182

MEMBERS OF FIRM

Donald P. Thomasson
Paul V. Gilbert
John L. Cook
David M. Remley
Jeffrey S. Maguire

Representative Clients: Aetna Life & Casualty; Allstate Insurance Cos.; American Family Insurance; Cameron Mutual Insurance Co.; Farmers Insurance Group; Hospital Services Group; John Deere Insurance Co.; St. Paul Insurance Co.; State Farm Insurance Cos.

For full biographical listings, see the Martindale-Hubbell Law Directory

*CARROLLTON,** Carroll Co. — (Refer to Kansas City)

*CARTHAGE,** Jasper Co.

Flanigan, McCanse & Lasley (AV)

400 Grant Street, 64836
Telephone: 417-358-2127
FAX: 417-358-5335

MEMBERS OF FIRM

John H. Flanigan (1889-1974)
John H. Flanigan, Jr. (1910-1976)
Laurence H. Flanigan
William Joseph Lasley
David B. Mouton

OF COUNSEL

Thad C. McCanse

ASSOCIATES

Dean G. Dankelson

Attorneys for: Allstate Insurance Co.; American States Insurance Co.; Burlington, Northern Railroad Co.; Chicago Title Insurance Co.; The Farmers Group; Grace Oil Co.; The Hartford; Mid Continent Casualty Co. The Travelers Group; Union Pacific Railroad Co.

For full biographical listings, see the Martindale-Hubbell Law Directory

*CARUTHERSVILLE,** Pemiscot Co. — (Refer to Kennett)

*CASSVILLE,** Barry Co. — (Refer to Carthage)

*CHARLESTON,** Mississippi Co. — (Refer to Sikeston)

CHESTERFIELD, St. Louis Co. — (Refer to St. Louis)

*CHILLICOTHE,** Livingston Co. — (Refer to Trenton)

*CLAYTON,** St. Louis Co.

Tremayne, Lay, Carr & Bauer (AV)

Suite 1510, Chromalloy Plaza, 120 South Central Avenue (St. Louis), 63105
Telephone: 314-863-4151
Telecopier: 314-863-0720

MEMBERS OF FIRM

A. Wimmer Carr (1929-1993)
Bertram W. Tremayne, Jr. (Retired)
Kenneth S. Lay
Helen Graefe Bauer
Eric F. Tremayne
Eugene E. Coon, Jr.
Jerome C. Coleman
Thomas G. Lemley

ASSOCIATES

Belinda B. Burnworth

Reference: Boatmen's Bank of St. Louis County.

For full biographical listings, see the Martindale-Hubbell Law Directory

*CLINTON,** Henry Co.

Poague, Wall, Eshelman & Cox (AV)

116 West Jefferson, P.O. Box 226, 64735
Telephone: 816-885-2221
FAX: 816-885-2792

MEMBERS OF FIRM

Barkley M. Brock (1915-1978)
Haysler Allen Poague (1898-1982)
Julius F. Wall
Ross Eshelman
Robert L. Cox

General Counsel for: Union State Bank; Plow Realty of Texas; Golden Valley Memorial Hospital; Citizens State Bank of Clinton/Calhoun; Union State Bank; Hilty Quarries, Inc.

For full biographical listings, see the Martindale-Hubbell Law Directory

*COLUMBIA,** Boone Co.

Knight, Ford, Wright, Atwill, Parshall & Baker (AV)

609 East Walnut Street, 65201
Telephone: 314-449-2613
Telecopier: 314-875-8154

MEMBERS OF FIRM

David L. Knight
Hamp Ford
Marvin E. Wright
Daniel K. Atwill
Jeffrey O. Parshall
Michael R. Baker
Glen R. Ehrhardt

ASSOCIATES

David W. Walker
Jeffrey H. Blaylock
Susan Ford Robertson
Mariam Decker
Edward L. Guinn
James R. Green
Lawrence W. Ferguson
Richard L. Montgomery, Jr.

General Counsel for: Commerce Bank; Boone Hospital Center and Boone Clinic.
Representative Clients: Hartford Insurance Group; Aetna Insurance Co.; Automobile Club Inter-Insurance Exchange; Medical Protective Co.; Stephens College; Boone County Fire Protection District; Columbia College.

For full biographical listings, see the Martindale-Hubbell Law Directory

Columbia—Continued

OLIVER, WALKER, CARLTON AND WILSON (AV)

Suite 406, 401 Locust Street, P.O. Box 977, 65205
Telephone: 314-443-3134
Telecopier: 314-442-6323

MEMBERS OF FIRM

David A. Oliver | Edwin J. Carlton
Roland P. Walker | Betty K. Wilson

ASSOCIATES

John D. Smith | Helen M. Cripps

Representative Clients: Aetna Insurance Co.; Allied Group; Allstate Insurance Co.; American Family Insurance Group; Chrysler Corp.; Aviation Adjustment Bureau; CNA Insurance; Federated Insurance Co.; Old Republic; Shelter Insurance Cos.

For full biographical listings, see the Martindale-Hubbell Law Directory

SMITH, LEWIS, BECKETT, POWELL & ROARK (AV)

Haden Building, 901 East Broadway, Suite 100, 65201-4894
Telephone: 314-443-3141
FAX: 314-442-6686

MEMBERS OF FIRM

Robert C. Smith (Retired) | William Jay Powell
Raymond C. Lewis, Jr. | John L. Roark
Bruce H. Beckett | Colly Durley

ASSOCIATES

Andrew S. Flach | James B. Lowery
Timothy W. Burns

Representative Clients: Union Electric Co.; Boone National Savings & Loan Assn.; Missouri Press Assn.; First National Bank and Trust Co.; Medical Protective Co. of Fort Wayne; Central Electric Power Cooperative; Pepsi Cola Bottling Co.; Pennsylvania National Mutual Casualty Insurance Co.; First American Title Insurance Corp.; United Fire & Casualty Co.

For full biographical listings, see the Martindale-Hubbell Law Directory

DEXTER, Stoddard Co. — (Refer to Bloomfield)

*DONIPHAN,** Ripley Co. — (Refer to Poplar Bluff)

*EDINA,** Knox Co. — (Refer to Kirksville)

*FARMINGTON,** St. Francois Co. — (Refer to Fredericktown)

*FAYETTE,** Howard Co. — (Refer to Columbia)

*FREDERICKTOWN,** Madison Co.

SCHNAPP, GRAHAM, REID & FULTON (AV)

135 East Main Street, 63645
Telephone: 314-783-7212
Telecopier: 314-783-7812

MEMBERS OF FIRM

J. B. Schnapp (1920-1994) | Maurice B. Graham
John W. Reid, II (1940-1991) | Robin E. Fulton
Daniel P. Fall

ASSOCIATES

Brian J. McNamara | Mike D. Murphy
David R. Sallee

General Counsel for: New Era Bank; Black River Electric Cooperative; Belgrade State Bank, Belgrade, Mo.; Purcell Tire & Rubber Co.
Local and Regional Counsel for: ASARCO, Inc.; Mississippi River Transmission Corp.

For full biographical listings, see the Martindale-Hubbell Law Directory

*FULTON,** Callaway Co. — (Refer to Columbia)

*GALENA,** Stone Co. — (Refer to Springfield)

*GALLATIN,** Daviess Co. — (Refer to Chillicothe)

*GRANT CITY,** Worth Co. — (Refer to Maryville)

*GREENFIELD,** Dade Co. — (Refer to Springfield)

HANNIBAL, Marion Co.

ELY, CARY, WELCH & HICKMAN (AV)

1000 Center Street, P.O. Box 710, 63401
Telephone: 314-221-0080
Fax: 314-221-3856

MEMBERS OF FIRM

Ben Ely (1898-1987) | Joseph D. Welch
James E. Cary | Charles L. Hickman

ASSOCIATE

Karina Q. Borromeo

Representative Clients: Great River Gas Company of Hannibal; Burlington and Northern Railway Co.; Norfolk & Western Railroad; Travelers Insurance Co.; Dodson Insurance Group; Royal Insurance Cos.; Farmers and Merchants Bank of Hannibal; Federated Insurance Co.; National Life and Accident Group.

For full biographical listings, see the Martindale-Hubbell Law Directory

RENDLEN, RENDLEN, REDINGTON AND BASTIAN, P.C. (AV)

800 Broadway, P.O. Box 1255, 63401
Telephone: 314-221-4060
Fax: 314-221-2371

Charles E. Rendlen, Sr. (1878-1957) | Charles E. Rendlen, Jr.
Branham Rendlen (1906-1985) | Charles E. Rendlen, III
| Thomas P. Redington
Donald M. Bastian

General Counsel For: Commerce Bank of Hannibal; Wells Abstract Co.; American Loan & Savings Assn.

For full biographical listings, see the Martindale-Hubbell Law Directory

*HERMANN,** Gasconade Co. — (Refer to Jefferson City)

*HILLSBORO,** Jefferson Co.

THURMAN, HOWALD, WEBER, BOWLES & SENKEL (AV)

One Thurman Court, 63050
Telephone: 314-789-2601, 797-2601
Telecopier: 314-797-2904

MEMBERS OF FIRM

J. W. Thurman (1902-1986) | James E. Bowles
John W. Howald | David P. Senkel
Louis J. Weber | Floyd T. Norrick

ASSOCIATES

Nanci R. Wisdom | Valerie L. Polites
Emily C. Aschinger

For full biographical listings, see the Martindale-Hubbell Law Directory

WEGMANN, GASAWAY, STEWART, SCHNEIDER, DIEFFENBACH, TESREAU, STOLL & SHERMAN, P.C. (AV)

Court House Square, P.O. Box 740, 63050
Telephone: 314-797-2665
Direct Dial, St. Louis: 296-5769 Telecopier: 314-797-3505

Will B. Dearing (1902-1975) | Nicholas G. Gasaway, Jr.
Samuel Richeson (1904-1976) | Jack C. Stewart
J. Richard Roberts (1928-1975) | Albert W. Dieffenbach, Jr.
John A. Schneider (1942-1992) | Dennis H. Tesreau
Roland A. (Ray) Wegmann | Mark T. Stoll
Randall D. Sherman

Darrell E. Missey | Nathan B. Stewart
Joy I. Hannel

For full biographical listings, see the Martindale-Hubbell Law Directory

*HOUSTON,** Texas Co. — (Refer to Rolla)

*INDEPENDENCE,** Jackson Co.

CONSTANCE, STEWART & COOK (AV)

501 West Lexington Avenue, 64050
Telephone: 816-833-1800
FAX: 816-833-1805

MEMBERS OF FIRM

Byron Constance | David H. Cook
Byron A. Stewart, Jr. | Bradley A. Constance
Byron G. Stewart

Representative Clients: Amresco; Jackson County Board of Election Commissioners.
Approved Attorneys for: Farmers Home Administration; Security-Pacific Mortgage Co.; Commonwealth Land Title Insurance Co.

For full biographical listings, see the Martindale-Hubbell Law Directory

*IRONTON,** Iron Co. — (Refer to Fredericktown)

*JEFFERSON CITY,** Cole Co.

BRYDON, SWEARENGEN & ENGLAND, PROFESSIONAL CORPORATION (AV)

The Hammond Building, 312 East Capitol Avenue, P.O. Box 456, 65102-0456
Telephone: 314-635-7166
Facsimile: 314-635-0427

David V. G. Brydon | Paul A. Boudreau
James C. Swearengen | Sondra B. Morgan
William R. England, III | Sarah J. Maxwell
Johnny K. Richardson | Charles E. Smarr
Gary W. Duffy | Mark G. Anderson
Dean L. Cooper

(See Next Column)

BRYDON, SWEARENGEN & ENGLAND PROFESSIONAL CORPORATION, *Jefferson City—Continued*

Representative Clients: The Empire District Electric Co.; St. Joseph Light & Power Co.; Union Electric Co.; United Cities Gas Co.; U.S. Water/Lexington, Missouri; Utilicorp United, Inc.; Fidelity Telephone Company; Mid-Missouri Telephone Co.; Citizens Telephone Company of Higginsville, Missouri; GTE North Incorporated.

For full biographical listings, see the Martindale-Hubbell Law Directory

HENDREN AND ANDRAE (AV)

Monroe House, 235 East High Street, P.O. Box 1069, 65102
Telephone: 314-636-8135
Telecopier: 314-636-5226

OF COUNSEL

Henry Andrae

MEMBERS OF FIRM

Charles H. Howard (1925-1970)
John E. Burruss, Jr. (1933-1985)
John H. Hendren (1907-1988)
Richard S. Brownlee, III
Michael A. Dallmeyer
Duane E. Schreimann
J. Kent Lowry
Douglas L. Van Camp
Gerald E. Roark
Donald C. Otto, Jr.
Michael G. Berry
Hallie H. Gibbs, II

ASSOCIATES

John W. Kuebler
Susan Turner
Sherry L. Doctorian
Christopher P. Rackers

Representative Clients: United States Fidelity & Guaranty; Chesebrough-Pond's, Inc.; Union Pacific Railroad; Purina Mills, Inc.; American Cancer Society; Cargill, Inc.

For full biographical listings, see the Martindale-Hubbell Law Directory

WESNER, KEMPTON, RUSSELL AND DOMINIQUE (AV)

623 East McCarty Street, P.O. Box 1108, 65102-1108
Telephone: 314-635-7241
Fax: 314-635-2631
Sedalia, Missouri Office: 114 East 5th Street, P.O. Box 815.
Telephone: 816-827-0314,
Fax: 816-827-1200.

P. Pierre Dominique
Mark T. Kempton (Resident at Sedalia, Mo.)
Robert G. Russell (Resident at Sedalia, Mo.)
Andrew S. Carroll (Resident at Sedalia, Mo.)
J. Christopher Spangler (Resident at Sedalia, Mo.)

Representative Clients: Home Savings and Loan Assn.; Professional Medical Insurance Co.; St. Paul Title Insurance Corp.; Missouri Association of Osteopathic Physicians and Surgeons; State Farm Mutual Insurance Co.; Kemper Insurance Co.; U. S. F. & G.; Great American Insurance Co.

For full biographical listings, see the Martindale-Hubbell Law Directory

JOPLIN, Jasper Co.

BLANCHARD, VAN FLEET, MARTIN, ROBERTSON & DERMOTT (AV)

320 West Fourth Street, P.O. Box 1626, 64802
Telephone: 417-623-1515
Facsimile: 417-623-6865

MEMBERS OF FIRM

Karl W. Blanchard
John R. Martin (1922-1982)
Malcolm L. Robertson
Jon Dermott
Karl W. Blanchard, Jr.
Ronald E. Mitchell
Greg B. Carter

OF COUNSEL

Herbert Van Fleet

ASSOCIATES

Ronald G. Sparlin
Theresa L. Ohler
John R. Mollenkamp

Representative Clients: Chubb Group; First National Bank of Sarcoxie; First State Bank; Liberty Mutual Insurance Co.; Missouri Southern State College; St. Paul Insurance Co.; State Farm Insurance Cos.; Southwestern Bell Telephone Co.; Tamko Asphalt Products; United States Fidelity & Guaranty Co..

For full biographical listings, see the Martindale-Hubbell Law Directory

KANSAS CITY, Jackson, Clay & Platte Cos.

ARMSTRONG, TEASDALE, SCHLAFLY & DAVIS (AV)

A Partnership including Professional Corporations
1700 City Center Square, 1100 Main Street, 64105
Telephone: 816-221-3420
Facsimile: 816-221-0786
Olathe, Kansas Office: 100 East Park.
Telephone: 913-345-0706.

(See Next Column)

St. Louis, Missouri Office: One Metropolitan Square.
Telephone: 314-621-5070.
Facsimile: 314-621-5065.
Twx: 910-761-2246.
Cable: ATKV LAW.
Belleville, Illinois Office: 23 South First Street.
Telephone: 618-397-4411.

MEMBERS OF FIRM

Ilus W. Davis
Edward E. Schmitt
Ford R. Nelson, Jr.
Truman K. Eldridge, Jr.
Thomas M. Bradshaw (P.C.)
Thomas H. Stahl (P.C.)
Roy R. Darke
Edward R. Spalty
Christopher J. Anderson
John A. Vering, III
Lynn W. Hursh
Donald G. Scott
Philip A. Klawuhn
Jennifer Putman Kyner
Charles F. Speer

ASSOCIATES

Jerald S. Meyer
Douglas R. Richmond
Daniel Owen Herrington
Gerald A. King
Renana B. Abrams
Robert P. Wray
Dianne M. Hansen
Wayde S. Kindiger
Darren S. Black

Representative Clients: American International Group; Boatmen's First National Bank of Kansas City; Bunzl Building Supply Co., Inc.; Century 21 Real Estate Corp.; Dow Corning Corp.; General Mills, Inc.; Great American Insurance Cos.; Missouri Easter Seal Society; The Public School Retirement System of Missouri; Faultless Starch/Bon Ami Company.

For full biographical listings, see the Martindale-Hubbell Law Directory

BLACKWELL SANDERS MATHENY WEARY & LOMBARDI L.C. (AV)

Suite 1100, Two Pershing Square, 2300 Main Street, 64108
Telephone: 816-274-6800
Telecopier: 816-274-6914
Overland Park, Kansas Office: 40 Corporate Woods, Suite 1200, 9401 Indian Creek Parkway.
Telephone: 913-345-8400.
Telecopier: 913-344-6375.

MEMBERS OF FIRM

Stephen T. Adams (Resident, Overland Park, Kansas Office)
James M. Ash
Jeffrey D. Ayers
Timothy M. Aylward
James Bandy
Toni Hays Blackwood
James Borthwick
John Keith Brungardt
Bruce Campbell
James D. Conkright (Resident, Overland Park, Kansas Office)
Henry R. Cox
David R. Erickson
David A. Fenley
Floyd R. Finch, Jr.
Robin V.W. Foster
Gary D. Gilson
J. Michael Grier (Resident, Overland Park, Kansas Office)
James D. Griffin (Resident, Overland Park, Kansas Office)
Allan V. Hallquist
Winn W. Halverhout
Jeffrey T. Haughey
Robert A. Horn
Charles D. Horner
Shirley Ward Keeler
William W. LaRue
Martin M. Loring
William A. Lynch
Benjamin F. Mann
Robert E. Marsh
Larry L. McMullen
Peter T. Niosi
Leslie J. Parrette, Jr.
Robert Penninger
John R. Phillips
Beverlee J. Roper (Not admitted in MO)
William H. Sanders, Jr.
William H. Sanders, Sr.
Randy P. Scheer
Douglas J. Schmidt
Roger W. Slead
Peter B. Sloan
Sally B. Surridge
Michael J. Thompson
Timothy W. Triplett (Resident, Overland Park, Kansas Office)
Thomas W. Wagstaff
James M. Warden (Resident, Overland Park, Kansas Office)
Maurice A. Watson
Daniel C. Weary
Mark D. Welker
David L. West
Dennis P. Wilbert
John P. Williams
Ralph G. Wrobley
Karl Zobrist

SENIOR COUNSEL

Katharine S. Bunn
Hibberd V. B. Kline, III
Neil J. Recker
Gaylord G. Smith

OF COUNSEL

Menefee D. Blackwell
Barton P. Cohen (Resident, Overland Park, Kansas Office)
Ernest M. Fleischer
Stephen C. Harmon (Resident, Overland Park, Kansas Office)
Cornelius E. Lombardi, Jr.
Donald F. Martin (Resident, Overland Park, Kansas Office)
Edward T. Matheny, Jr.

STAFF ATTORNEYS

Lori H. Hill (Resident, Overland Park, Kansas Office)
Heather Nye

(See Next Column)

BLACKWELL SANDERS MATHENY WEARY & LOMBARDI L.C.—*Continued*

ASSOCIATES

Gary E. Armbrust
Jeffrey S. Austin (Resident, Overland Park, Kansas Office)
Elizabeth R. Tyndall Baucum
Richard M. Beheler (Not admitted in MO)
Kristi D. Bohling
Victoria Henges Bonavia (Resident, Overland Park, Kansas Office)
Diane Breneman (Resident, Overland Park, Kansas Office)
Kathryn B. Bussing (Not admitted in MO)
B. K. Christopher (Resident, Overland Park, Kansas Office)
J. Randall Coffey
Robert S. Conway
Marcia S. Cook
Daryl J. Douglas
Kyle W. Drefke (Not admitted in MO)
Philip Dupont
Merry Evans
Shelly L. Freeman
Michael J. Furlong
George A. Hanson
William F. High (Resident, Overland Park, Kansas Office)
Sean K. Hogan (Resident, Overland Park, Kansas Office)
Tessa K. Jacob
Phillip D. Kline (Resident, Overland Park, Kansas Office)
M. Courtney Koger
Christopher A. Koster
Michael J. Kuckelman (Resident, Overland Park, Kansas Office)
Kristopher A. Kuehn (Resident, Overland Park, Kansas Office)
James D. Langner (Resident, Overland Park, Kansas Office)
Christopher C. Lewis
John David Mandelbaum
Scott Martin
Sarah D. Mathews
John G. Mazurek
Douglas P. McLeod
Mary Elizabeth Metz
Gregory J. Minana
Diana D. Moore (Resident, Overland Park, Kansas Office)
Steven K. O'Hern (Resident, Overland Park, Kansas Office)
Peter S. Obetz (Resident, Overland Park, Kansas Office)
Michelle Y. Patterson
Cynthia L. Payseur
Michael C. Phillips
Julianne Popper
David B. Raymond
Kathryn A. Regier (Resident, Overland Park, Kansas Office)
Dora E. Reid
David L. Rein Jr.
Jana V. Richards (Resident, Overland Park, Kansas Office)
William W. Richerson, Jr.
Curtis O. Roggow (Resident, Overland Park, Kansas Office)
Robert G. Rooney
Shelley Ann Runion
Brock A. Shealy
Jeffrey J. Simon
Michael A. Slaney
Price A. Sloan
Christopher S. Stachowiak
Terrance M. Summers
Michael M. Tamburini
Linda K. Tiller (Not admitted in MO)
Roger Warren
Shari L. Wright
Cori Leonard Young

Representative Clients: Black & Veatch; Carter Waters Corp.; The Coca-Cola Bottling Company of Mid-America; Commerce Bancshares, Inc.; Cook Paint and Varnish Co.; Fairbanks Morse Pump Corp.; Payless Cashways, Inc.; Puritan-Bennett Corp.; UtiliCorp United Inc.

For full biographical listings, see the Martindale-Hubbell Law Directory

---

FIELD, GENTRY & BENJAMIN, P.C. (AV)

210 Plaza West Building, 4600 Madison, 64112-3012
Telephone: 816-561-5580
Telecopy: 816-561-5080
Overland Park, Kansas Office: Suite 306, 6811 West 63rd. Street, 66202. Telephone 913-384-9599.

Lyman Field
Reed O. Gentry
James W. Benjamin
Douglas N. Ghertner
John R. Loss
Lee M. Baty
Robert R. Barton

Laura M. Rowzee
John M. Huff
Theresa A. Otto
Brian J. Doherty

Representative Clients: The Travelers Ins. Cos.; Liberty Mutual Insurance Co.; U. S. Aviation Underwriters; J.C. Nichols Co.

For full biographical listings, see the Martindale-Hubbell Law Directory

---

FRENSLEY & TOWERMAN, P.C. (AV)

Suite 105 Park Plaza Building, 801 West 47th Street, 64112-1253
Telephone: 816-531-5262
FAX: 816-531-5380

David R. Frensley
Craig Towerman
Robert E. Pinnell

OF COUNSEL

David P. Hargrave

For full biographical listings, see the Martindale-Hubbell Law Directory

---

HILLIX, BREWER, HOFFHAUS, WHITTAKER & WRIGHT, L.L.C. (AV)

Fourth Floor, Two Crown Center, 2420 Pershing Road, 64108-2574
Telephone: 816-421-6767; 816-221-0355
Telecopier: 816-421-2896

(*See Next Column*)

Albert F. Hillix (1896-1982)
Charles E. Hoffhaus
Kent E. Whittaker
Lynn C. Hoover
R. Dennis Wright
Whitney F. Miller
Norman E. Beal
Dennis L. Davis
Terrence Ahern
David E. Bass
C. Brooks Wood
M. Michael Gill
Thomas E. Carew
Kirk H. Doan
William M. Modrcin
Joseph C. Benage
Kent V. Stallard
V. Edwin Stoll
Charles F. Jensen
Tamra Wilson Setser
David G. Watkins
James S. Swenson
J. Richard Crawford
Timothy J. Feathers

Kimberly A. Shell
S. Margene Childress
Tim S. Haverty
Cheryl Bloethe Linder
Julia A. Riggle
James R. Hess
Kurt Stohlgren
Gregory M. Power
William M. Davison
Melissa C. Hinton

OF COUNSEL

Oscar S. Brewer
Thomas E. King
Allen W. Blair

LEGAL SUPPORT PERSONNEL

Melanie S. Bacon (Certified Public Accountant)
Kathryn A. Brinser
Patricia L. Crabtree
Jennifer Crisp
Judith M. Dent
Dan Drake (Certified Public Accountant)
L. Jane Jacobs
Virginia M. Martin
Sharon L. Oldham
Suzanne M. Orf

Representative Clients: Aetna Life & Casualty; American States Insurance; Arthur Andersen & Co.; Nebraska Public Power District; Orscheln Farm & Supply Co.; The Southgate Bank; The Vendo Co.; United Savings Bank.

For full biographical listings, see the Martindale-Hubbell Law Directory

---

JACKSON, LILLA & MCFERRIN, P.C. (AV)

800 Bryant Building, 1102 Grand Avenue, 64106
Telephone: 816-474-1900
Fax: 816-474-0217

John M. Lilla
Lindsay K. McFerrin (Bates)

Brian A. Snyder

OF COUNSEL

Don M. Jackson
Jesse L. Childers

LEGAL SUPPORT PERSONNEL

Rebecca S. Wortman (Legal Assistant/Investigator)

References: Available upon request.

For full biographical listings, see the Martindale-Hubbell Law Directory

---

LATHROP & NORQUIST, L.C. (AV)

2345 Grand Boulevard, Suite 2500, 64108
Telephone: 816-842-0820
Telecopier: 816-421-0500
Overland Park, Kansas Office: 1050/40 Corporate Woods, 9401 Indian Creek Parkway.
Telephone: 913-451-0820.
Telecopier: 913-451-0875.

Gardiner Lathrop (1850-1938)
Paul G. Koontz (1894-1988)
Robert M. Adams
C. David Barrier
William H. Bates
William G. Beck
Irwin E. Blond
Sherman A. Botts
Harlan D. Burkhead
John H. Calvert
David V. Clark
Douglas R. Dalgleish
Peter F. Daniel
Paul S. DeFord
Daniel M. Dibble
Jeffrey O. Ellis (Resident, Overland Park, Kansas Office)
James C. Fitter, Jr.
Charles Frisbie
H. Steven Graham
Jonathan R. Haden
W. Joseph Hatley (Resident, Overland Park, Kansas Office)
Jack W. R. Headley
Sue M. Honegger
William G. Howard (Resident, Overland Park, Kansas Office)
Alfred R. Hupp, Jr.
Curtis A. Krizek
Scott A. Long
Ronald E. Manka
Maribeth S. McMahon
Thomas J. McMahon
Timothy K. McNamara
Roland B. Miller III
Stephen G. Mitchell
Brian B. Myers
Charles F. Myers
Maurice J. O'Sullivan, Jr.
Michael W. Rhodes
Jerome D. Riffel
Jack D. Rowe
Thomas A. Ryan
Terry J. Satterlee (Ms.)
William M. Stapleton
Frederick K. Starrett (Resident, Overland Park, Kansas Office)
Thomas S. Stewart
Curtis L. Tideman (Resident, Overland Park, Kansas Office)
James P. Tierney
Robert J. Virden
John L. Vratil (Resident, Overland Park, Kansas Office)
William K. Waugh III (Resident, Overland Park, Kansas Office)

(*See Next Column*)

LATHROP & NORQUIST L.C., *Kansas City—Continued*

Gordon E. Wells, Jr. (Resident, Overland Park, Kansas Office)
Harry E. Wigner, Jr. (Resident, Overland Park, Kansas Office)
Brian N. Woolley

OF COUNSEL

Jerald K. Bales
Angela M. Bennett
Michael K. Glenn (Not admitted in MO)
David V. Kenner
Ann Mesle
William M. Symon, Jr.
Charles F. Zarter (Resident, Overland Park, Kansas Office)

RETIRED

Howard A. Crawford
Carl A. Hummel
Elliot Norquist
Thomas J. Wheatley

Alok Ahuja
Stacy M. Andreas
Laura J. Bond (Resident, Overland Park, Kansas Office)
L. J. Buckner, Jr.
Denise E. Farris (Resident, Overland Park, Kansas Office)
J. A. (Jay) Felton
Brian T. Fenimore
Mark Allen Ferguson (Resident, Overland Park, Kansas Office)
J. Anthony Frazier (Resident, Overland Park, Kansas Office)
Jennifer S. Graham
Patrick J. Gregory (Resident, Overland Park, Kansas Office)
John J. Hogerty II
Gary D. Justis
Eliot L. Kaplan (Not admitted in MO)
Linfei Liu
Brian J. Madden
Jennifer Hamilton McCoy
Charles W. McKee (Resident, Overland Park, Kansas Office)
Christine M. McKee
William C. Odle
Jeffrey P. Ray
Teresa J. Stewart
J. Michael Stradinger
Joan Dungey Toomey
Michael R. Tripp
John E. Tyler III

Representative Clients: The Atchison, Topeka & Santa Fe Railway Co.; Colgate-Palmolive Co.; Ford Motor Co.; GST Steel Inc.; Massachusetts Mutual Life Insurance Co.; Miles Inc.

For full biographical listings, see the Martindale-Hubbell Law Directory

NIEWALD, WALDECK & BROWN, A PROFESSIONAL CORPORATION (AV)

One Kansas City Place, 1200 Main, Suite 4100, 64105
Telephone: 816-471-7000
Telecopier: 816-474-0872
Overland Park, Kansas Office: Suite 550 Corporate Woods Building #40. 9401 Indian Creek Parkway. P.O. Box 25790, 66225.
Telephone: 913-451-1717.

Paul H. Niewald
Michael E. Waldeck
Stephen S. Brown
Kenton C. Granger
Kevin E. Glynn
John L. Hayob
Terry Karnaze
Gary A. Schafersman
William J. DeBauche
Randa Rawlins
Michael D. Matteuzzi
Alice G. Amick
Patrick J. Doran
Angela K. Green
Vincent F. O'Flaherty
Melodie A. Powell

Jill Frost
Kevin J. Driscoll
Christina Magee (Not admitted in MO)
Lisa A. Dunbar
Julie J. Gibson
Laura Elizabeth Thompson
Jonathan L. Laurans
Deborah R. Swank

OF COUNSEL

John Patrick O'Connor
G. Steven Ruprecht

For full biographical listings, see the Martindale-Hubbell Law Directory

SHUGHART THOMSON & KILROY, A PROFESSIONAL CORPORATION (AV)

Twelve Wyandotte Plaza, 120 West 12th Street, 64105
Telephone: 816-421-3355
Overland Park, Kansas Office: Suite 1100, 32 Corporate Woods, 9225 Indian Creek Parkway 66210.
Telephone: 913-451-3355.

Henry M. Shughart (1897-1962)
Harry P. Thomson (1917-1988)
William P. Eckels (1946-1987)
Ralph G. Trogdon (1910-1993)
John M. Kilroy
Donald L. Shughart
Thomas J. Leittem
Ben L. Guenther
R. Lawrence Ward
William B. Jensen
J. Harlan Stamper
Robert R. Raymond
George E. Leonard
William V. North
Joel Pelofsky
William B. Prugh
Perry M. Toll
Thomas F. Fisher
Thomas G. Kokoruda
Jack L. Campbell
John M. Kilroy, Jr.
W. James Foland
Timothy D. O'Leary
Roy Bash
Donald H. Loudon
Steven H. Goodman
Dennis D. Palmer
William E. Quirk
Jennifer Gille Bacon
W. Terrence Kilroy
William L. Yocum
Steven D. Ruse

(See Next Column)

Robert A. Henderson
John S. Conner
J. Douglas Irmen
P. John Brady
Jacob W. Bayer, Jr.
Russell S. Jones, Jr.
Bradley J. Baumgart
Robert T. Schendel
Norris E. Greer
James P. O'Hara
David L. McMurray
Daniel T. Murphy
Kirk J. Goza
Joel R. Mosher
Gregory M. Bentz
Philip W. Bledsoe
Anthony F. Rupp
Robert B. Keim
Judith S. Heeter
Ted R. Osburn
Randal L. Schultz
Bart E. Eisfelder
Tommy W. Taylor
Claudia J. York
Gregory L. Musil
Michael J. Gorman
Joseph J. Roper
Donald A. Culp
Lawrence A. Swain
Dean Kuckelman
Robert W. Pohl
Kathleen A. Forsyth
G. William Quatman
Lynn Deal Cockle
Roger M. Phillips
Christopher F. Pickering
Lisa D. Eckold
Janice E. Stanton
Sheryl Feutz-Harter
Brian D. Doerr
Roger P. Wright
David E. Shay
Thomas A. Sheehan
Mary A. Schmitt
Mark A. Olthoff
David B. Pursell
Michael P. Allen
Bradley D. Honnold
Ralph K. Phalen
Joseph Conrad Smith
Mary Owensby Thompson
Karen R. Glickstein
James C. Sullivan
Andrew L. McMullen
Ellen S. Martin
Charles J. Hyland
Michael S. Ketchmark
Bradley D. Holmstrom
Randall W. Schroer
David W. Norburg
Scott E. Vincent
James D. George
Michael D. Moeller
S. Meigs Jones, III
Brett Davis
Adam P. Sachs
Leah M. Gagne
William Clayton Crawford
Jack M. Epps
Ann C. Abercrombie

OF COUNSEL

William C. Nulton
George W. Harlan
David E. Pierce (Not admitted in MO)

For full biographical listings, see the Martindale-Hubbell Law Directory

SPENCER FANE BRITT & BROWNE (AV)

1400 Commerce Bank Building, 1000 Walnut Street, 64106-2140
Telephone: 816-474-8100
Overland Park, Kansas Office: Suite 500, 40 Corporate Woods, 9401 Indian Creek Parkway.
Telephone: 913-345-8100.
Washington, D.C. Office: 1133 Connecticut Avenue, N.W., Suite 1000.
Telephone: 202-775-2376.

MEMBERS OF FIRM

Byron Spencer (1893-1964)
Irvin Fane (1904-1982)
Harry L. Browne (1911-1985)
James H. Andreasen
J. Nick Badgerow (Resident, Overland Park, Kansas Office)
James G. Baker
Russell W. Baker, Jr.
James T. Britt
Bruce E. Cavitt
Paul D. Cowing
Stanley E. Craven
Gardiner B. Davis
Michael F. Delaney
David D. Gatchell
Donald W. Giffin
Scott J. Goldstein
Carl H. Helmstetter
Richard H. Hertel (Resident, Overland Park, Kansas Office)
Michael D. Hockley
James R. Hudek
Mark P. Johnson
James W. Kapp, Jr.
Brian N. Kaufman
Basil W. Kelsey
Michael C. Kirk
Elaine Drodge Koch
Ronald L. Langstaff
Gregory C. Lawhon
Robert P. Lyons
I. Edward Marquette
William C. Martucci
Kenneth A. Mason
Jacob F. May, Jr. (Resident, Overland Park, Kansas Office)
James T. Price
Michael F. Saunders
Richard W. Scarritt
Terry W. Schackmann
Sandra L. Schermerhorn
Edward A. Setzler
Mendel Small
Gad Smith
Lowell L. Smithson
James A. Snyder
Richard H. Spencer
Mark A. Thornhill
John L. Utz
Michaela M. Warden (Resident, Overland Park, Kansas Office)
James R. Willard
David L. Wing
Jack L. Whitacre
Jerome T. Wolf
Curtis E. Woods
William H. Woodson
Teresa A. Woody

OF COUNSEL

Georgann H. Eglinski
Mitchell S. Pettit (Resident, Washington, D.C. Office)
Charles S. Schnider (Resident, Overland Park, Kansas Office)

SPECIAL COUNSEL

Shirley Edmonds Goza
Stephanie A. Mathews

ASSOCIATES

Gregory L. Ash (Not admitted in MO)
Daniel B. Boatright
Elizabeth A. Brand
Denise D. Clemow
Lynne Marie Douglas
Marilyn P. Dunn
Mary Nan Dupont
Edward C. Fensholt
Jan P. Helder, Jr.

(See Next Column)

SPENCER FANE BRITT & BROWNE—*Continued*

ASSOCIATES (Continued)

Aaron C. Johnson
Elizabeth J. Keenan
Timothy J. Kuester
Nancy M. Landis (Resident, Overland Park, Kansas Office)
J. Bradley Leitch
Samuel P. Logan
Christine Y. Martin
Michael L. McCann
Barry L. Pickens
Dale K Ramsey
Kenneth A. Schifman
Therese M. Schuele
Mary S. Shafer
Brian F. Stayton (Resident, Overland Park, Kansas Office)
Douglas M. Weems
Thomas J. Wilcox

Representative Clients: Allsop Venture Partners; AT&T Technologies, Inc.; Baird Kurtz & Dobson; Bedford Properties; Builders Association of Missouri; City of Kansas City, Missouri; Daniels-McCray Lumber Co.; Heavy Constructors Assn.; Kansas City Power and Light Co.; Missouri Hospital Assn.

For full biographical listings, see the Martindale-Hubbell Law Directory

SWANSON, MIDGLEY, GANGWERE, KITCHIN & MCLARNEY, L.L.C. (AV)

1500 Commerce Trust Building, 922 Walnut, 64106-1848
Telephone: 816-842-6100
Overland Park, Kansas Office: The NCAA Building, Suite 350, 6201 College Boulevard.
Telephone: 816-842-6100.

Roy P. Swanson (1896-1985)
Kenneth E. Midgley (1903-1990)
Henry G. Eager (1923-1972)
Richard K. Andrews (1936-1993)
George H. Gangwere, Jr.
John J. Kitchin
James H. McLarney
Robert W. McKinley
C. W. Crumpecker, Jr.
John S. Black
Lawrence M. Maher
Rodney V. Hipp
Richard N. Bien
Neil Loren Johnson
W. Ann Hansbrough
Allen R. Slater

Craig T. Kenworthy
Linda J. Salfrank
James A. Durbin
Tedrick A. Housh, III

OF COUNSEL

Daniel V. Hiatt

Counsel for: General Electric Co.; Chrysler Corp.; Conoco, Inc.; Yellow Freight System, Inc.; The Prudential Insurance Co. of America; Metropolitan Life Insurance Co.; National Collegiate Athletic Assn.; Land Title Insurance Co.; Safeway Stores, Inc.; The Lee Apparel Co.

For full biographical listings, see the Martindale-Hubbell Law Directory

WYRSCH ATWELL MIRAKIAN LEE & HOBBS, P.C. (AV)

1300 Mercantile Tower 1101 Walnut, 64106-2122
Telephone: 816-221-0080
Fax: 816-221-3280

James R. Wyrsch
Stephen G. Mirakian
Ronald D. Lee
Charles E. Atwell
James R. Hobbs
Keith E. Drill
Michael P. Joyce
Marilyn B. Keller
Cheryl A. Pilate
W. Brian Gaddy

LEGAL SUPPORT PERSONNEL

Phillip A. Thompson (Investigative and Paralegal)
Darlene Wyrsch (Paralegal)
Dru A. Colhour (Paralegal)
Al Tolentino (Paralegal and Videographer/Photographer)
Kathy Vetsch (Paralegal)

For full biographical listings, see the Martindale-Hubbell Law Directory

*KENNETT,** Dunklin Co.

CROW, REYNOLDS, PREYER AND SHETLEY (AV)

Cotton Exchange Bank Building, P.O. Box 189, 63857-0189
Telephone: 314-888-4664; 888-4665
Facsimile: 314-888-0322

MEMBERS OF FIRM

Elbert L. Ford (1899-1975)
James F. Ford (1925-1979)
Wendell W. Crow
James R. Reynolds
H. Mark Preyer
Matthew R. Shetley

Representative Clients: Merchants and Planters Bank; State Farm Mutual Auto Insurance Co.; Farm Bureau Mutual Insurance Co.; Fireman's Fund Insurance Cos.; Bank of Bootheel; Security Insurance Group; Universal Underwriters Insurance Co.; Columbia Mutual Insurance Co.; Cotton Exchange Bank; Metropolitan Life Insurance Co.; Hartford Insurance Group.

For full biographical listings, see the Martindale-Hubbell Law Directory

DALTON, TREASURE & MOWRER (AV)

203 College Street, P.O. Box 529, 63857
Telephone: 314-888-4631
Facsimile: 314-888-2127

(See Next Column)

MEMBERS OF FIRM

John Hall Dalton
Harold B. Treasure
J. Michael Mowrer
John Hall Dalton, Jr.

General Counsel: Kennett National Bank; Riggs Wholesale Co.
Representative Clients: The Equitable Life Assurance Society; Aetna Insurance Group; John Hancock Mutual Life Insurance Co.; The Travelers; International Association of Aviation Underwriters; Shelter Insurance Cos.; Liberty Mutual Insurance Cos.; Hanover Insurance Co.; Southern Missouri Savings & Loan Assn.

For full biographical listings, see the Martindale-Hubbell Law Directory

WELMAN, BEATON, MCVEY, HIVELY & GODLEY (AV)

206 St. Francis Street, P.O. Box 269, 63857
Telephone: 314-888-4566
Telecopier: 314-888-3413
Malden, Missouri Office: Four Towne Square.
Telephone: 314-276-5768.

MEMBERS OF FIRM

William O. Welman
John M. Beaton
Terry M. McVey
Brian D. Hively
Barbara A. Godley

General Counsel for: Boatmen's Bank of Kennett.
Representative Clients: Associated Natural Gas Co.; Continental Loss Adjusting Service; Twin Rivers Regional Medical Center; Kennett School District.; First Community Bank; Emerson Electric Co.; Home Insurance Co.; Malden School District; Underwriters Adjusting Co.

For full biographical listings, see the Martindale-Hubbell Law Directory

*KIRKSVILLE,** Adair Co.

OSWALD & COTTEY, A PROFESSIONAL CORPORATION (AV)

Suite A, 210 North Elson, P.O. Box K, 63501
Telephone: 816-665-5628
Fax: 816-665-6035

Thomas R. Oswald
Louis F. Cottey

Brenda Wall-Swedberg
Scott L. Templeton
Susan R. Barrow

For full biographical listings, see the Martindale-Hubbell Law Directory

*LAMAR,** Barton Co. — (Refer to Carthage)

*LEBANON,** Laclede Co.

DONNELLY, BALDWIN AND WILHITE, P.C. (AV)

112 North Madison, P.O. Box D, 65536
Telephone: 417-532-3177
Facsimile: 417-532-3727

Phil M. Donnelly (1891-1961)
James E. Baldwin
David E. Wilhite
Mark E. Rector

OF COUNSEL

David Donnelly

District Attorneys for: Burlington Northern Railroad Company.
Counsel for: Boatmen's National Bank of Lebanon; Central Bank of Lebanon, Mo.; Detroit Tool and Engineering Co.; Detroit Tool Metal Products Co.
Local Counsel for: State Farm Mutual Insurance Co.; Royal-Globe Insurance Cos.; Southwestern Bell Telephone Co.; Continental Insurance Cos.; Shelter Mutual Insurance Co.

For full biographical listings, see the Martindale-Hubbell Law Directory

*LEXINGTON,** Lafayette Co. — (Refer to Kansas City)

*LIBERTY,** Clay Co.

HALE, KINCAID & SKINNER, P.C. (AV)

17 West Kansas Street, 64068
Telephone: 816-781-4757
Fax: 816-781-1953

Martin E. Lawson (1867-1957)
Francis G. Hale (1889-1977)
Robert E. Coleberd (1896-1971)
William B. Waters (1916-1985)
Thomas E. Allen (1938-1991)
Arthur R. Kincaid
Leary G. Skinner
Patricia L. Hughes
Michael S. Shipley
William E. Shull
Patricia D. Reynolds

For full biographical listings, see the Martindale-Hubbell Law Directory

WITHERS, BRANT, IGOE & MULLENNIX, P.C. (AV)

Two South Main, 64068
Telephone: 816-781-4788
FAX: 816-792-2807

(See Next Column)

WITHERS, BRANT, IGOE & MULLENNIX P.C., *Liberty—Continued*

Conn Withers (1907-1993)
Jerome E. Brant
Vincent F. Igoe, Jr.
Ronald C. Mullennix
Victor C. Panus, Jr.
Steven D. Wolcott
John M. Crossett
Thomas C. Capps

Alison K. Blessing
Mark E. Kelly
Martin J. Weishaar
Kett R. Craven

OF COUNSEL

Nancy A. Norton

For full biographical listings, see the Martindale-Hubbell Law Directory

*MACON,** Macon Co.

COLLINS AND GRIMM, A PROFESSIONAL CORPORATION (AV)

107 1/2 North Rollins Street, 63552
Telephone: 816-385-2115
Fax: 816-385-2200

John D. Collins
Hadley E. Grimm

Jill Whitehead Creed

Representative Clients: State Farm Mutual Automobile Insurance Co.; Shelter Insurance Co.; American States Insurance; American Family Insurance Co.; Royal-Globe Insurance Co.; Hartford Indemnity and Accident Co.; Macon Electric Cooperative.

For full biographical listings, see the Martindale-Hubbell Law Directory

MALDEN, Dunklin Co.

WELMAN, BEATON, MCVEY, HIVELY & GODLEY (AV)

Four Towne Square, 63863
Telephone: 314-276-5768
Kennett, Missouri Office: 206 St. Francis Street, P.O. Box 269.
Telephone: 314-888-4566.
Telecopier: 314-888-3413.

MEMBERS OF FIRM

William O. Welman
John M. Beaton
Terry M. McVey
Brian D. Hively

General Counsel for: Boatmen's Bank of Kennett.
Representative Clients: Associated Natural Gas Co.; Continental Insurance Co.; Twin Rivers Regional Medical Center; Kennett School District.; First Community Bank; Emerson Electric Co.; Home Insurance Co.; Malden School District; Underwriters Adjusting Co.

For full biographical listings, see the Martindale-Hubbell Law Directory

*MARYVILLE,** Nodaway Co.

STRONG, STRONG & PROKES, A PROFESSIONAL CORPORATION (AV)

124 East Third Street, 64468
Telephone: 816-582-3133
FAX: 816-582-3145

Frank H. Strong
Frank H. Strong, Jr.
Roger M. Prokes

Barry L. Anderson
Robert E. Sundell

OF COUNSEL

John W. Baker, Jr.

General Counsel for: Bank Midwest N.A., Maryville, Mo.; Dempsey-Hardin L-P Gas; St. Francis Hospital; Loch Sand & Construction Co.
Counsel for: Eveready Battery Co., Inc.; New England Business Services, Inc.; The Daily Forum.
Representative Insurance Client: Farmers Insurance Group.

For full biographical listings, see the Martindale-Hubbell Law Directory

ZAHND, DIETRICH & ROSS (AV)

408 North Market Street, 64468
Telephone: 816-582-7468
FAX: 816-582-8790

MEMBERS OF FIRM

Larry L. Zahnd
Glen A. Dietrich
Scott Ross

Representative Clients: Nodaway Valley Bank, Maryville, Mo.; First Bank of Maryville; Summa Implement Co.; West Nodaway R-1 School District; Consumers Oil Company of Maryville; Cities of Barnard, Ravenwood, Skidmore, Maitland, and Guilford; Phoenix Mutual Life Insurance Co.; Robbins Lighting, Inc.; Belcher and Long, Midland Engineering, Inc.; Middlefork Water Company; Woodruff Arnold, Inc.
Approved Attorneys for: Farmers Home Administration; Veterans Administration; Farm and Home Savings Assoc.

For full biographical listings, see the Martindale-Hubbell Law Directory

*MEMPHIS,** Scotland Co. — (Refer to Kirksville)

*MEXICO,** Audrain Co.

SEIGFREID, RUNGE, LEONATTI, POHLMEYER & SEIGFREID, P.C. (AV)

123 East Jackson Street, 65265
Telephone: 314-581-2211
Telecopier: 314-581-6577

G. Andy Runge (1930-1991)
Louis J. Leonatti
Michael J. Pohlmeyer
Paul A. Seigfreid
Randall P. Baker
Daniel J. Monte

OF COUNSEL

Jerome W. Seigfreid

Counsel for: Commerce Bank N.A.; Aetna Casualty & Surety Co.; State Farm Mutual Insurance Cos.; National Refractories and Minerals Corp.; City of Mexico, Mo.; Central Electric Co.; U. S. Fidelity & Guaranty Co; Audrain Medical Center.

For full biographical listings, see the Martindale-Hubbell Law Directory

*MILAN,** Sullivan Co. — (Refer to Kirksville)

MOBERLY, Randolph Co.

TATLOW & GUMP (AV)

110 North Fifth Street, 65270
Telephone: 816-263-3100
Fax: 816-263-0660

MEMBERS OF FIRM

C. M. Hulen, Sr. (1894-1975)
C. M. Hulen, Jr. (Retired)
Gary A. Tatlow
Rex V. Gump

ASSOCIATES

Vickie Kaye Davis

For full biographical listings, see the Martindale-Hubbell Law Directory

*MOUNT VERNON,** Lawrence Co. — (Refer to Springfield)

*NEVADA,** Vernon Co.

EWING, SMITH & HOBEROCK (AV)

123 North Main Street, P.O. Box 287, 64772
Telephone: 417-667-3318
Fax: 417-667-9503

MEMBERS OF FIRM

Lynn M. Ewing, Jr.
Ortrie D. Smith
Christopher Hoberock
Lynn M. Ewing, III

ASSOCIATES

Malia M. Haskins

OF COUNSEL

Howard C. Gosnell, Jr.

General Counsel for: Cottey College; Sac Osage Electric Cooperative; Joseph L. Pohl, Inc.
Attorneys for: Community Bank of Eldorado Springs; Allstate Insurance Co.; Hartford Insurance Co.; Kemper Insurance Group; El Dorado Springs School District.

For full biographical listings, see the Martindale-Hubbell Law Directory

RUSSELL, BROWN, BICKEL & BRECKENRIDGE (AV)

108 West Walnut Street, P.O. Drawer J, 64772
Telephone: 417-667-5076
Fax: 417-667-3013

MEMBERS OF FIRM

Donald B. Russell
Keith Brown
James R. Bickel
Bryan C. Breckenridge

ASSOCIATE

Anita Donaldson Conboy

For full biographical listings, see the Martindale-Hubbell Law Directory

*NEW LONDON,** Ralls Co. — (Refer to Hannibal)

*NEW MADRID,** New Madrid Co. — (Refer to Sikeston)

*OREGON,** Holt Co. — (Refer to Maryville)

*OZARK,** Christian Co. — (Refer to Springfield)

*PALMYRA,** Marion Co. — (Refer to Hannibal)

*PARIS,** Monroe Co. — (Refer to Mexico)

*PERRYVILLE,** Perry Co. — (Refer to Fredericktown)

*PLATTSBURG,** Clinton Co. — (Refer to St. Joseph)

*POPLAR BLUFF,** Butler Co.

Bloodworth & Bloodworth (AV)

Highway 60 East and B Street, P.O. Box 909, 63901
Telephone: 314-785-6425; 785-6426; 785-6427
Fax: 314-785-4198

MEMBERS OF FIRM

C. T. Bloodworth, Sr. (1878-1956)
C. T. Bloodworth, Jr. (1909-1956)
Ralph R. Bloodworth (1916-1982)
Wm. H. Bloodworth
Ralph R. Bloodworth, Jr.
John H. Bloodworth

ASSOCIATES

Bobby D. Peterson

A List of Representative Clients or References will be furnished upon request.

For full biographical listings, see the Martindale-Hubbell Law Directory

*POTOSI,** Washington Co. — (Refer to Hillsboro)

*RICHMOND,** Ray Co. — (Refer to Kansas City)

*ROCK PORT,** Atchison Co. — (Refer to Maryville)

*ROLLA,** Phelps Co.

Thomas, Birdsong & Clayton, P.C. (AV)

1100 North Elm Street, P.O. Box 248, 65401
Telephone: 314-364-4097
Telecopier: 314-364-0664
Waynesville, Missouri Office: 200 N. Lynn Street.
Telephone: 314-774-5252.
Telecopier: 314-774-2801.

Dewey A. Routh (1898-1981)
W. H. (Tom) Thomas, Jr.
Dan L. Birdsong
John A. Clayton

William R. Sachs
Ina Ruth McKune
Howard Benson Becker

Representative Clients: Phelps County Regional Medical Center; Mercantile Bank; Ozark Equipment Co.; Sellers-Sexton Motors.
Representative Insurance Clients: U.S.F. & G.; Medical Protective Company; Safeco Insurance Co.; Royal Insurance Co.; Aetna Life & Casualty;
References: Mercantile Bank; Phelps County Bank.

For full biographical listings, see the Martindale-Hubbell Law Directory

Williams, Robinson, Turley & White, A Professional Corporation (AV)

Suite 404, 202 West Ninth Street, P.O. Box 47, 65401
Telephone: 314-341-2266
Facsimile: 314-341-5864
Salem, Missouri Office: Public Square, 110 East 5th Street.
Telephone: 314-729-3612.
Fax: 314-729-5125.

John Z. Williams
J. Kent Robinson
J. William Turley
Mark E. Turley
Ronald White
Cynthia L. Turley
Joseph W. Rigler (Resident, Salem Office)
Larry V. Swall, II

Lisa Van Steenbergh

OF COUNSEL

B. B. Turley

For full biographical listings, see the Martindale-Hubbell Law Directory

*ST. CHARLES,** St. Charles Co.

Thompson & Mitchell (AV)

200 North Third Street, 63301
Telephone: 314-946-7717
Telecopier: 314-946-4938
St. Louis, Missouri Office: Suite 3300, One Mercantile Center.
Telephone: 314-231-7676.
Telecopier: 314-342-1717.
Belleville, Illinois Office: 525 West Main Street.
Telephone: 618-277-4700; 314-271-1800.
Telecopier: 618-236-3434.
Washington, D.C. Office: 700 14th Street, N.W., Suite 900.
Telephone: 202-508-1000.
Telecopier: 202-508-1010.

MEMBERS OF FIRM

Rollin J. Moerschel
John C. Hannegan
Keith W. Hazelwood
James J. Hennelly
Wm. Randolph Weber
Tracy Mathis

(See Next Column)

ASSOCIATES

Steven C. Schwendemann
V. Scott Williams

Representative Clients: BJC Health System; City of St. Charles, Missouri; City of St. Peters, Missouri; GTE Corporation; The Industrial Development Authority of St. Charles County, Missouri; Magna Bank of St. Charles County; RehabCare Corporation; St. Anthon's Medical Center; St. Charles County Community College; Station Casinos, Inc.

For full biographical listings, see the Martindale-Hubbell Law Directory

*STE. GENEVIEVE,** Ste. Genevieve Co. — (Refer to Fredericktown)

*ST. JOSEPH,** Buchanan Co.

Brown, Douglas & Brown (AV)

Pioneer Building, 510 Francis Street, 64501
Telephone: 816-232-7748
Fax: 816-232-6915

Robert A. Brown (1899-1981)
Robert E. Douglas (Retired)

MEMBERS OF FIRM

Robert A. Brown, Jr.
John P. Beihl
Wendell E. Koerner, Jr.
Suzanne Bocell Bradley
Richard J. Yocum
Errol D. Taylor
Keith W. Ferguson
Keith J. Schieber

Representative Clients: Commercial Union Insurance Companies; State Farm Mutual Insurance Companies; Farmers Insurance Group; The Western Companies; The Medical Protective Company; Missouri Medical Insurance Co.; United Missouri Bank of St. Joseph; School District of St. Joseph; Gray Manufacturing Co.

For full biographical listings, see the Martindale-Hubbell Law Directory

Morton, Reed & Counts (AV)

Suite 320, Robidoux Center, 64501
Telephone: 816-232-8411
Fax: 816-232-8418

MEMBERS OF FIRM

William M. Morton (1892-1979)
Ronald S. Reed (1904-1970)
David H. Morton (1922-1986)
Ronald S. Reed, Jr.
James H. Counts
Stephen J. Briggs
Creath S. Thorne
Michael J. Ordnung

Representative Clients: Commerce Bank of St. Joseph; C. D. Smith Drug Co.; Chicago Title Insurance Co.; Fireman's Insurance Company of Newark, N.J.; St. Joseph Board of Realtors; Exchange Bank of Mound City; Farmers Home Administration; Empire Gas Corporation.

For full biographical listings, see the Martindale-Hubbell Law Directory

Strop, Thomas, Burns & Holliday (AV)

Suite 302 Robidoux Center, 64501
Telephone: 816-279-0861; 233-5430
Fax: 816-279-5586

MEMBERS OF FIRM

William H. Strop
John K. Thomas
John F. Burns
Clarence G. Strop (1909-1986)
Ronald R. Holliday

ASSOCIATES

Scott Burns

Representative Clients: Southwestern Bell (litigation); Wausau Insurance Co.; Sentry Insurance Group; Hartford Fire Insurance Co.; Continental Insurance Cos.; American National Bank; Midwest Federal Savings & Loan; Clark Construction Co.

For full biographical listings, see the Martindale-Hubbell Law Directory

Utz, Litvak, Summers, Powers & Manring (AV)

Suite 500 Frederick Towers, 2400 Frederick Avenue, 64506
Telephone: 816-233-0257
Telecopier: 816-233-9411

MEMBERS OF FIRM

Thomas R. Summers
G. Brent Powers
John Manring

ASSOCIATES

David R. Schmitt

OF COUNSEL

W. H. Utz, Jr.
Milton Litvak

Representative Clients: Travelers Insurance Co.; KQTV; Boehringer-Ingelheim Animal Health, Inc.; Citizens Bank of Oregon, Mo.; Mercantile Bank of St. Joseph; Criswell Oil Co.; The Blueside Cos.; Heaton-Bowman-Smith Funeral Home, Inc.

For full biographical listings, see the Martindale-Hubbell Law Directory

St. Joseph—Continued

WATKINS, BOULWARE, LUCAS, MINER, MURPHY & TAYLOR (AV)

3101 Frederick Avenue, 64506
Telephone: 816-364-2117
Telecopier: 816-279-3977

MEMBERS OF FIRM

Thomas D. Watkins
R. Dan Boulware
Gregory C. Lucas
Robert B. Miner
R. Edward Murphy
Michael L. Taylor
Joseph W. Elliott
Mark R. Woodbury

ASSOCIATES

Carol C. Barnett
Craig D. Ritchie
Kenneth Eric Siemens

OF COUNSEL

O. W. Watkins, Jr.

For full biographical listings, see the Martindale-Hubbell Law Directory

ST. LOUIS, (Independent City)

ANDERSON & GILBERT (AV)

The Boatmen's Bank Building, Sixth Floor, 7800 Forsyth Boulevard (Clayton), 63105
Telephone: 314-721-2777
Telecopier: 314-721-3515

MEMBERS OF FIRM

Roscoe Anderson (1884-1951)
William R. Gilbert (1886-1963)
Jesse A. Wolfort (1882-1967)
Norman Bierman (1907-1987)
Norris H. Allen (1904-1991)
Robert G. Burridge
Francis X. Duda
Stuart M. Haw
Fortis M. Lawder
Joel D. Monson
D. Paul Myre

OF COUNSEL

Patrick M. Duggan
John P. Sullivan (Retired)

Representative Clients: St. Paul Fire & Marine Insurance Co.; Jewish Hospital of St. Louis; Foremost Insurance Co.; Medical Defense Associates; Risk Control Associates; Symons Int'l; Schneider Nat'l, Inc.; Bank of Chesterfield; Mega Bancshares, Inc.

For full biographical listings, see the Martindale-Hubbell Law Directory

ARMSTRONG, TEASDALE, SCHLAFLY & DAVIS (AV)

A Partnership including Professional Corporations
One Metropolitan Square, 63102-2740
Telephone: 314-621-5070
Facsimile: 314-621-5065
Twx: 910 761-2246
Cable: ATKV LAW
Kansas City, Missouri Office: 1700 City Center Square. 1100 Main Street, 64105.
Telephone: 816-221-3420.
Facsimile: 816-221-0786.
Belleville, Illinois Office: 23 South First Street, 62220.
Telephone: 618-397-4411.
Olathe, Kansas Office: 100 East Park, 66061.
Telephone: 913-345-0706.

MEMBERS OF FIRM

Edwin S. Baldwin (P.C.)
Donald U. Beimdiek (P.C.)
Bruce E. Woodruff (P.C.)
John R. Barsanti, Jr., (P.C.)
Kenneth F. Teasdale (P.C.)
Fred Leicht, Jr., (P.C.)
Frank N. Gundlach (P.C.)
Robert Lewis Jackson (P.C.)
Justin C. Cordonnier (P.C.)
John L. Gillis, Jr., (P.C.)
Frederick O. Hanser (P.C.)
James J. Virtel
Joseph S. von Kaenel (P.C.)
Thomas Cummings (P.C.)
John J. Inkley, Jr.
Larry M. Sewell (P.C.)
Robert G. Schwendinger
Thomas H. Bottini
Richard B. Scherrer (P.C.)
Denis P. McCusker
Peter L. Clark (P.C.)
Jay A. Summerville
Edwin L. Noel (P.C.)
Theodore H. Hellmuth (P.C.)
Byron E. Francis (P.C.)
Jeffrey D. Fisher (P.C.)
John H. Quinn III, (P.C.)
McPherson D. Moore
O. Kirby Colson, III
Steven P. Sanders
Theodore J. Williams, Jr.
Jonathan W. Igoe
Timothy K. Kellett (P.C.)
Thomas B. Weaver (P.C.)
John L. Sullivan
Daniel R. Wofsey (P.C.)
Wilbur L. Tomlinson (P.C.)
Raymond R. Fournie
Clark H. Cole
Daniel J. Godar
Steven N. Cousins
Paul N. Venker
Robert C. Graham, III
Stephen C. Jones
Jordan B. Cherrick
John F. Cowling
Ann E. Buckley
Timothy J. Tryniecki
Diane E. Felix
Glenn E. Davis
George M. von Stamwitz
Michael A. Chivell
Mary C. Kickham
Bryan K. Wheelock
Peter J. Krane
David L. Going
A. J. Chivetta
Donald G. Mueller, Jr.
Philip G. Louis, Jr.
Sally J. McKee
Richard L. Waters
Joan Z. Cohen

(See Next Column)

MEMBERS OF FIRM (Continued)

Gary L. Rutledge
Susan Bradley Buse
John Talbot Sant, Jr.
Mark D. Sophir
William M. Corrigan, Jr.
Albert F. Bender, III

ASSOCIATES

Norella V. Huggins
David G. Loseman
Deirdre C. Gallagher
Scott Hunt
Richard W. Engel, Jr.
John S. Metzger
Therese Rolufs Trelz
Andrew B. Mayfield
Christopher W. Dysart
Michelle Suzanne House
Michael L. Skinner
James L. Stockberger
Keith A. Rabenberg
Marlene C. Archey-Crim
James G. Nowogrocki
Thomas L. Orris
Lauren L. Holloway
Timothy R. McFadden
Daniel D. Doyle
Lisa M. Wood
Susan B. Knowles
Richard L. Saville, Jr.
Douglas R. Sprong
Mitchell L. Crain
Karen A. Menghini
James E. Mello
Patrick J. Kenny
Timothy J. Prosser
Petree A. Eastman
Mary C. Parker
Matthew R. Byer
Virginia H. Howell
Daniel C. Nelson
Michael F. Roche
Hengtao "Hank" Wang
Marshall R. Hoekel
Janelle D. Strode
Michael J. Miller
John J. O'Brien
Countess W. Price
Craig A. Wilson
James V. Hetzel
Jennifer A. Auer
Mark A. Boatman
Dennis C. Bremer
Stanley W. Crosley
Cornell Foggie Jr.
Christine M. Gibson
Jennifer S. Lohman
Patrick J. Whalen

OF COUNSEL

August L. Griesedieck
Robert F. Schlafly
John J. Cole (P.C.)
Bourne Bean (P.C.)
Frederick H. Mayer (P.C.)
John P. Emde (P.C.)
Charles E. Dapron

Representative Clients: Anheuser-Busch, Inc.; Blue Cross and Blue Shield of Missouri, Inc.; Christian Hospitals; McDonalds Corp.; Petrolite Corp.; Procter & Gamble, Inc.; Southwestern Bank of St. Louis; Southwestern Bell Telephone; Toyota Motor Company; Union Electric Co.

For full biographical listings, see the Martindale-Hubbell Law Directory

COBURN & CROFT (AV)

One Mercantile Center, 63101
Telephone: 314-621-8575
Telecopier: 314-621-2989
Houston, Texas Office: 2400 NationsBank Center, 700 Louisiana.
Telephone: 713-225-3800.
Telecopier: 713-225-3828.
Belleville, Illinois Office: Suite 202, 120 West Main.
Telephone: 618-277-1020.

MEMBERS OF FIRM

Richmond C. Coburn
Thomas L. Croft (1913-1980)
Gerald J. Zafft
John R. Musgrave
Kenneth R. Heineman
Kent D. Kehr
J. William Newbold
Thomas E. Douglass
James L. Fogle
Louis F. Bonacorsi
Richard A. Mueller
Richard S. Cornfeld
Guy A. Schmitz
Ellen E. Bonacorsi
Michael B. Minton
Bruce D. Ryder
Paul M. Brown
Joseph G. Nassif
Daniel T. Engle
Timothy F. Noelker
James R. Keller
Dale R. Joerling
Timothy E. Hayes
Ronald L. Hack
Edwin G. Harvey
Mark A. Bayles
Dean L. Franklin
Ketrina G. Bakewell
Larry A. Reed
Vincent H. Venker, II
Paul A. Streiff
Frank B. Janoski
Linda L. Shapiro
John B. Kinsella
Dudley W. Von Holt
Kenneth J. Mallin
Anne-Marie Kienker
Carl L. Rowley
Jon M. Moyers

ASSOCIATES

Cathryn A. Conrad
Linda W. Tape
James M. Cox
Eleanor A. Maynard
Judith Lynne Garner
Joseph C. Orlet
Kirk R. Crowder
Raymond W. Gruender
Margaret Hart-Mahon
Wendy W. Walsh
James R. Walsh
Wendy Wiedemann Hudson
Richard P. Jacobs
Kevin M. Barry
Steven E. Garlock
Kathy A. Wisniewski
Carl J. Pesce
Jane Fedder Lazaroff
Neal C. Stout
Robert T. Mills
Jonathan F. Andres
Adam E. Miller
Todd G. Zimmerman
Joseph M. Kellmeyer
Ann M. Jones
Veronica A. Gioia
Jeffrey E. Asbed
Eric J. Lindhorst
Allen P. Press
Beverly S. Davis
Thomas D. Brown
Thomas C. Burke
Stacey L. Stater
Daniel J. Carpenter
Nicholas B. Clifford, Jr.
William F. Sasser III

(See Next Column)

COBURN & CROFT—*Continued*

OF COUNSEL

Edwin J. Putzell, Jr. James H. Drake

Representative Clients: Allied Signal; American Cyanamid Co.; American Telephone and Telegraph Co.; Burlington Northern Railroad; Emerson Electric Co.; Ingersoll-Rand Kawasaki Motors Corp., U.S.A.; Monsanto Co.; Shell Oil Co.; Southern Pacific Transportation Co.

For full biographical listings, see the Martindale-Hubbell Law Directory

DOHENY & DOHENY (AV)

Suite 230, 2458 Old Dorsett Road, P.O. Box 2547, 63043-2400
Telephone: 314-298-9000
Telecopier: 314-298-9009

MEMBERS OF FIRM

John V. Lee (1890-1951)
Frank Lee (1895-1962)
Donald A. Doheny, Sr.

OF COUNSEL

John V. Doheny
Donald A. Doheny, Jr. (Not admitted in MO)

For full biographical listings, see the Martindale-Hubbell Law Directory

EVANS & DIXON (AV)

1200 Saint Louis Place, 200 North Broadway, 63102-2749
Telephone: 314-621-7755
Kansas City, Missouri Office: City Center Square, 1100 Main Street, Suite 2000, 64105-2119.
Telephone: 816-472-4600.
Edwardsville, Illinois Office: 17 Ginger Creek Meadows, P.O. Box 405. 62025-3508.
Telephone: 618-656-8505.
Leawood, Kansas Office: 8016 State Line Road, Suite 207. 66208-3713.
Telephone: 913-649-5386.

MEMBERS OF FIRM

John F. Evans (1897-1964)
John R. Dixon (1914-1984)
James V. Gallen (1925-1985)
Ralph C. Kleinschmidt (1921-1982)
Edward W. Warner
Eugene K. Buckley
Henry D. Menghini
Robert M. Evans
Robert W. Wilson (Resident, Edwardsville, Illinois Office)
Sam P. Rynearson
Edward M. Vokoun
Harvey G. Schneider
James B. Kennedy
Jeffry S. Thomsen
James A. Thoenen
Gerre S. Langton
John A. Michener
Raymond J. Flunker
Stefan J. Glynias
James M. Gallen
Robert E. Bidstrup
Edward S. Meyer
Bradley V. Spaunhorst
Gerard T. Noce
K. Steven Jones
Robert J. Krehbiel
Robert N. Hendershot, II
Robert P. Numrich (Kansas City, Missouri and Leawood, Kansas Offices)
William F. Ringer (Resident, Kansas City, Missouri Office)
Marilyn C. Phillips
Richard F. Huck, III
David S. Ware
John F. Cooney
George T. Floros
Robert W. Haeckel
Michael F. Banahan
Carl D. Lothman
Robert D. Tucker (Resident, Edwardsville, Illinois Office)
Betsy J. Levitt
Kathi L. Chestnut
Michael Reda (Resident, Edwardsville, Illinois Office)
Brian J. Fowler (Kansas City, Missouri and Leawood, Kansas Offices)
Don A. Shaffer (Not admitted in MO; Resident, Edwardsville, Illinois Office)
Priscilla F. Gunn
Jeffrey K. Suess
Kevin P. Schnurbusch
Maurice D. Early
Thomas Clinkenbeard (Resident, Kansas City, Missouri Office)

OF COUNSEL

William W. Evans

ASSOCIATES

Scott C. Annunziata
Brenda G. Baum
Michael D. Bean (Resident, Edwardsville, Illinois Office)
Joan B. Bernstein
Martin J. Buckley
Thomas M. Buckley
Ann Marie Butler
Debbie S. Champion
Paul D. Chesterton
Teresa L. Cotton
Susan E. Decker (Kansas City, Missouri and Leawood, Kansas Offices)
Joseph L. Engelhard
Kim M. Fenton
Kevin L. Fritz
Philip C. Graham
Lisa A. Green
Stacey R. Hancock-Robinson
Cynthia M. Hennessey
John W. Hoffman (Resident, Edwardsville, Illinois Office)
Scott E. Huber
Amy E. Kaiser
Jill E. Kapp
Paul F. Keeven
John P. Kemppainen, Jr.
Carl Kessinger
Martin A. Klug
David C. Knieriem
Mark R. Kornblum
Paul D. Larimore
Mary Anne Lindsey
Bruce J. Magnuson
James D. Maschhoff
Cynthia A. Masterson
John S. McCollough

(See Next Column)

ASSOCIATES (Continued)

Jacqueline E. Moore
Susan M. Moore
James K. Muhlenbruch
Karen A. Mulroy
James M. Neimann
Patrick A. Patterson
David G. Phoenix
Carl C. Pohle
Jeffrey M. Proske
David J. Reynolds, Jr.
Betsy S. Schmidt
Steven R. Sharp
Laura E. Smith
Paul Joseph Stingley (Resident, Kansas City, Missouri Office)
Adrian P. Sulser
Timothy M. Tierney
Joy R. Urbom
Kenneth L. Voigt
Martha Madden Weast (Kansas City, Missouri and Leawood, Kansas Offices)
Alexander M. Wilson (Resident, Edwardsville, Illinois Office)
Stephen E. Winborn
Kurt E. Wolfgram

Attorneys for: Allstate Insurance Co.; Chrysler Corp.; Chubb & Son, Inc.; Kemper Insurance Group; Southwestern Bell Telephone Co.; Travelers Insurance Co.; Zurich Insurance Co.

For full biographical listings, see the Martindale-Hubbell Law Directory

GALLOP, JOHNSON & NEUMAN, L.C. (AV)

Interco Corporate Tower, 101 S. Hanley, 63105
Telephone: 314-862-1200
Telecopier: 314-862-1219

MEMBERS OF FIRM

Philip Gallop (1906-1984)
Donald P. Gallop
Alan G. Johnson
Sanford S. Neuman
Harold S. Goodman
William E. Buckley
Michael N. Newmark
Stephen W. Skrainka
Charles M. Tureen
Edwin D. Akers, Jr.
Thomas G. Lewin
Robert H. Wexler
Steven E. Kushner
John J. Temporiti
David W. Harlan
John P. Walsh
Thomas H. Mug
Richard W. Hokamp
Randy S. Gerber
Marvin O. Young
David T. Hamilton
Thomas M. Newmark
Michael A. Kahn
Jason M. Rugo
Stuart Symington, Jr.
Thomas B. Kinsock
Peter D. Kerth
Patrick M. Sanders
Cawood K. Bebout
Barbara J. Hartung-Wendel
Linda C. Shubow
Kurtis B. Reeg
Alan C. Witte
Nancy J. Dilley
Bethe M. Growe
Thomas P. Hohenstein

Todd J. Aschbacher
Kurt A. Baca
Mary M. Bannister
Douglas J. Bates
Linda K. Baxter
Thomas J. Campbell
Carl R. Desenberg (Not admitted in MO)
David J. Harris
Jennifer Goldberg Low
Mary S. McMath
Sandra L. Nugent
Harold B. Oakley
Rosalie Wacker O'Brien
Tod J. O'Donoghue
Timothy J. Sarsfield
Lucy A. Singer
David A. Streubel
Nick H. Varsam
Daniel G. Vogel
John T. Walsh
Rebecca Epstein Walsh
Patricia S. Williams

COUNSEL

Barbara L. Behrens
Carolyn A. Haimann
Kay R. Sherman

Representative Clients: Data Research Associates, Inc.; Falcon Products, Inc.; KV Pharmaceutical Co.; Ciba Giegy Corp.; Magna Group, Inc. and subsidiary banks; Medicine Shoppe International, Inc.; Missouri Research Laboratories, Inc.; Raskas Foods, Inc.; Paric Corp.; Safeco and General Insurance Companies of America.

For full biographical listings, see the Martindale-Hubbell Law Directory

LEWIS, RICE & FINGERSH (AV)

A Partnership including Partnerships and Individuals
500 North Broadway, Suite 2000, 63102-2147
Telephone: 314-444-7600
Telecopier: 314-241-6056
Clayton, Missouri Office: Suite 400, 8182 Maryland Avenue.
Telephone: 314-444-7600.
Belleville, Illinois Office: 325 South High Street.
Telephone: 618-234-8636.
Hays, Kansas Office: 201 W. 11th St.
Telephone: 913-625-3997.
Leawood, Kansas Office: Suite 375, 8900 State Line.
Telephone: 913-381-8898.
Kansas City, Missouri Office: 1010 Walnut, Suite 500.
Telephone: 816-421-2500.

RESIDENT PARTNERS

Robert Smith Allen
Walter J. Taylor
John M. Drescher, Jr.
Eugene J. Gabianelli
Henry F. Luepke, Jr.
Robert B. Hoemeke
John Torrey Berger, Jr.
Henry H. Stern, Jr.
James W. Herron
John K. Pruellage
Bernard N. Frank
Joseph H. Weyhrich
Lawrence H. Weltman
Michael P. Casey

(See Next Column)

LEWIS, RICE & FINGERSH, *St. Louis—Continued*

RESIDENT PARTNERS (Continued)

Allen S. Boston
Barry A. Short
Michael R. Turley
Jacob W. Reby
Michael D. Mulligan
Mark T. Keaney
Andrew Rothschild
John J. Gazzoli, Jr.
Richard A. Ahrens
Kimball R. McMullin
Larry L. Deskins
John J. Moellering
John M. Hessel
Robert N. Kahn
John D. Valentine
Thomas C. Erb
Richard A. Wunderlich
Douglas D. Hommert
James V. O'Brien
James F. Sanders
Marian V. Mehan
Joseph J. Trad
John J. Riffle
Joseph E. Martineau
Curtis C. Calloway
David L. Coffman
Lori W. Jones
Rosemarie M. Karcher
Richard B. Walsh, Jr.
Jeffrey B. Hunt

RETIRED PARTNERS

James A. Singer
Abe J. Garland
Philip A. Maxeiner
Edmonstone F. Thompson
Daniel J. Sullivan
F. Wm. McCalpin
Charles C. Allen, Jr.

ASSOCIATES

Daniel E. Claggett
John E. Hall
Mary B. Schultz
Angela Fick Braly
Kelly A. Bridges
Cordell P. Schulten
Duane L. Coleman
Alan H. Kandel
Thomas L. Caradonna
Robert J. Golterman
Catherine R. Phillips
Robert J. Will
Beverly A. Marcin
Ronald A. Norwood
Lawrence E. Parres
Eric D. Paulsrud
Kimberly N. Springer
Tom W. Zook
Brian D. Bouquet
Mark S. Hentschell
Timothy E. Kastner
Leonard J. Essig (Not admitted in MO)
Theodore H. Lucas
Jon A. Santangelo
Lynn Ann Hinrichs
Elizabeth Webster Lane
Robert H. Lattinville
Scott J. Luedke
William S. Sanderson (Not admitted in MO)
David N. Barnes
Mary L. Frontczak
Benjamin A. Lipman
Jeana D. McFerron
Robert S. Moore
Gregory M. Otto
Gary M. Smith
Neal F. Perryman
Thomas P. Berra, Jr.
Yvette M. Guerra
Ann M. Salamon
Beth L. Dreitler (Not admitted in MO)
J. Daniel Patterson
Thomas J. Niemann
Joseph F. Hipskind, Jr.
Christine Marie Comer
MaryAnn Nessel
James E. Duffy (Not admitted in MO)
Michael A. Schuldt
Robert G. Guller

For full biographical listings, see the Martindale-Hubbell Law Directory

LOWENHAUPT & CHASNOFF, L.L.C. (AV)

10 South Broadway, Suite 600, 63102-1733
Telephone: 314-241-5950
Telefax: 314-436-2667

Abraham Lowenhaupt (1878-1958)
Jacob Chasnoff (1883-1977)
Henry C. Lowenhaupt (1913-1990)
Bernard Mellitz (1912-1993)
Owen T. Armstrong
Jules Chasnoff
Hugh R. Law
Charles A. Lowenhaupt
Jerrold D. Rosen
Douglas M. Baron

Peter A. Smith
Helen Frances Parker Newcomb

OF COUNSEL

Jack M. Chasnoff

LEGAL SUPPORT PERSONNEL

William F. Neal (Office Administrator)

For full biographical listings, see the Martindale-Hubbell Law Directory

MOSER AND MARSALEK, P.C. (AV)

Suite 700, St. Louis Place, 200 North Broadway, 63102-2730
Telephone: 314-421-5364
Telecopier: 314-421-5640

W. Edwin Moser (1894-1969)
G. W. Marsalek (1913-1963)
Frank X. Cleary (1900-1975)
John S. Marsalek (1887-1980)
Julian C. Jaeckel (1924-1984)
Joseph H. Mueller
F. Douglas O'Leary
John J. Horgan
William L. Davis
David L. Zwart
Michael R. Noakes
Jerome C. Simon
Peter F. Spataro
Brian R. Plegge
Philip L. Willman
Thomas Carter, II
Thomas J. Magee
J. Steven Erickson
Doreen G. Powell
Kevin M. Leahy

(See Next Column)

Robyn G. Fox
Kimberly A. Maschmeyer
Seth G. Gausnell
Laurie S. Wright
Terry L. Pijut
Brian D. Winer
Ann Gaylor Rucker
Gregory T. Mueller
Jill M. Young
Patrick J. Horgan
John F. Padberg
Karie E. Casey
Robert G. Pennell
Mark A. Cordes
Mark D. Madden
Jeannette S. Graviss
Thomas Edward Fagan
Bradlee L. Blake
Sherry Alisa Gutnick (Not admitted in MO)

OF COUNSEL

Byron G. Carpenter
Parks G. Carpenter

Representative Clients: Aetna Casualty & Surety; American Ind. Group; American International Group; Chubb Group Insurance Cos.; Fireman's Fund Insurance Co.; Goodyear Tire & Rubber Co.; Jewish Hospital; Lancer Claims; Medical Protective Ins. Co.

For full biographical listings, see the Martindale-Hubbell Law Directory

PEPER, MARTIN, JENSEN, MAICHEL AND HETLAGE (AV)

720 Olive Street, Twenty-Fourth Floor, 63101
Telephone: 314-421-3850
Fax: 314-621-4834
Fort Myers, Florida Office: 2080 McGregor Boulevard, Third Floor.
Telephone: 813-337-3850.
Fax: 813-337-0970.
Punta Gorda, Florida Office: 1625 West Marion Avenue, Suite 2.
Telephone: 813-637-1955.
Fax: 813-637-8485.
Naples, Florida Office: 850 Park Shore Drive, Suite 202.
Telephone: 813-261-6525.
Fax: 813-649-1805.
Belleville, Illinois Office: 720 West Main Street, Suite 140.
Telephone: 618-234-9574.
Fax: 618-234-9846.

MEMBERS OF FIRM

Wm. McChesney Martin (1875-1955)
George A. Jensen (1929-1990)
Richard A. Hetlage
William A. Richter
Robert O. Hetlage
Lewis R. Mills
Robert C. Johnson
John R. Short
Marshall D. Hier
Arthur L. Smith
John C. Rasp
J. Neil Huber, Jr.
Ronald O. Schowalter
John W. Brickler
Richard E. Jaudes
Mark R. Leuchtmann
Paul G. Griesemer
Albert S. Rose
James E. Moore, III (At Punta Gorda, Florida Office)
Richard P. Sher
Stephen H. Rovak
Deborah I. Conrad
Thomas A. Mickes
Thomas E. Tueth
Kenneth A. Jones (At Fort Myers, Punta Gorda and Naples, Florida Offices)
Beverly Grady (At Fort Myers and Punta Gorda, Florida Offices)
Craig S. Biesterfeld
Michael D. Hart
Jeffrey J. Kalinowski
Bradley S. Hiles
Richard J. Pautler
Kathleen T. Mueller
Joanne D. Martin
Mark S. Packer
Kathleen S. Schoene
Steven W. Hubbard (At Fort Myers and Punta Gorda, Florida Offices)
Gary D. McConnell
Michael A. Clithero
Matthew G. Perlow
Ian P. Cooper
Robert L. Jackstadt (At Belleville, Illinois Office)
Raymond S. Kreienkamp
Clifford A. Godiner
Terry L. Lister
G. Carson McEachern (At Fort Myers and Naples, Florida Offices)
Peter H. Ruger
Andrew T. Hoyne
Mark Steinbeck (At Fort Myers, Florida Office)
John P. McNearney

COUNSEL

Cleon L. Burt
Warren R. Maichel
Malcolm W. Martin
Christian B. Peper
Thomas F. Schlafly

SENIOR ATTORNEY

Robert Schultz

ASSOCIATES

Craig A. Adoor
Stephen T. Bee
Celynda L. Brasher
Lisa J. Browman
Cathleen S. Bumb
Thomas A. A. Cook
Christopher L. Craig
David Lee Fleisher, Jr.
Stuart E. Funderburg
Donna M. Goelz
Teri B. Goldman
Benjamin H. Hulsey
Catherine Hope Johnson
Peter C. Johnson
Melanie Gurley Keeney
Daniel J. Lett
Alphonse McMahon
James R. Myers (At Fort Myers and Punta Gorda, Florida Offices)
Stephen J. O'Brien
Robert G. Oesch
Thomas E. Proost
Laura K. W. Rebbe

(See Next Column)

PEPER, MARTIN, JENSEN, MAICHEL AND HETLAGE—*Continued*

ASSOCIATES (Continued)

David L. Schenberg
David L. Schlapbach
Diana M. Schmidt
Ruth A. Streit
Ellen L. Theroff
James G. Thomeczek
Randall S. Thompson
Robert J. Tomaso
Sally Herr Townsley
M. Celeste Vossmeyer
Geri L. Waksler (At Fort Myers and Punta Gorda, Florida Offices)
B. Michelle Ward
Peter G. Yelkovac

For full biographical listings, see the Martindale-Hubbell Law Directory

RABBITT, PITZER & SNODGRASS, P.C. (AV)

One Boatmen's Plaza, Suite 2300, 800 Market Street, 63101-2608
Telephone: 314-421-5545
Facsimile: 314-421-3144
Belleville, Illinois Office: 23 South First Street.
Telephone: 618-236-0626.

Daniel T. Rabbitt
Michael J. Pitzer
Gary E. Snodgrass
Richard J. Zalasky
Louis J. Basso
Peter J. Dunne
Steven J. Hughes
Donald L. O'Keefe
Sandra A. Steiniger
Robyn R. Lundt
Joseph P. Whyte
Matthew T. Willaert
Gary S. Wolfe
Matthew J. Sauter
Meg Marshall Thomas
Evan D. Buxner
Suzanne Woodard

For full biographical listings, see the Martindale-Hubbell Law Directory

ANTHONY B. RAMIREZ, P.C. (AV)

1221 Locust Street, Suite 503, 63103
Telephone: 314-621-5237
Fax: 314-621-2778

Anthony B. Ramirez

For full biographical listings, see the Martindale-Hubbell Law Directory

SELNER, GLASER, KOMEN, BERGER & GALGANSKI, P.C. (AV)

7700 Bonhomme Avenue, Suite 700 (Clayton), 63105-1924
Telephone: 314-721-7272
Fax: 314-721-1668

Norman A. Selner
A Fuller Glaser, Jr.
Leonard Komen
Corey S. Berger
Thomas R. Galganski

Steven M Cohen
Deborah L. Doak
Ann Bodewes Stephens
Brian P. Seltzer
William B. Langenbacher
Jill M. Palmquist
Brian Stokes
Laura L. Harrison

OF COUNSEL

Stanley E. Goldstein
Jonathan E. Sloane

For full biographical listings, see the Martindale-Hubbell Law Directory

SONNENSCHEIN NATH & ROSENTHAL (AV)

One Metropolitan Square, Suite 3000, 63102
Telephone: 314-241-1800
Telecopier: 314-259-5959
Chicago, Illinois Office: Suite 8000 Sears Tower, 233 South Wacker Drive.
Telephone: 312-876-8000.
Cable Address: "Sonberk".
Telex: 25-3526.
Facsimile: 312-876-7934.
New York, N.Y. Office: 1221 Avenue of the Americas, 24th Floor.
Telephone: 212-768-6700.
Facsimile: 212-391-1247.
Washington, D.C. Office: 1301 K Street, N.W., Suite 600, East Tower.
Telephone: 202-408-6400.
Facsimile: 202-408-6399.
Los Angeles, California Office: Suite 1500, 601 South Figueroa Street.
Telephone: 213-623-9300.
Facsimile: 213-623-9924.
San Francisco, California Office: 685 Market Street, 10th Floor.
Telephone: 415-882-5000.
Facsimile: 415-543-5472; 882-5038.

Swanson W. Angle
Larry M. Bauer
Alan B. Bornstein
Francis M. Gaffney
Frank H. Hackmann
Roger K. Heidenreich
Carl B. Hillemann III
R. Michael Lowenbaum
Charles A. Redd
Jane S. Smith
Leslie Chambers Strohm
Thomas K. Vandiver
James G. Wiehl

(See Next Column)

ASSOCIATES

Julie A. Bregande
Susan Kay Daniel
Timothy L. Elliott
Lori L. Gaddis
Diane L. Hoadley
Robert J. Isaacson
Steven R. Karl
Karen E. Milner
Stacey L. Murphy
Lisa Reilly Nadler
Thomas J. Palazzolo
Teresa Dale Pupillo
Mark D. Rabe
Phillip A. Rothermich

For full biographical listings, see the Martindale-Hubbell Law Directory

SUELTHAUS & KAPLAN, P.C. (AV)

7733 Forsyth Boulevard, Twelfth Floor, 63105
Telephone: 314-727-7676
Telecopier: 314-727-7166
Belleville, Illinois Office: 23 Public Square, Suite 450, 62220.
Telephone: 618-277-5550.
Telecopier: 618-277-5610.

George H. Suelthaus (1901-1984)
Albert D. Krueger (1903-1992)
Kenneth H. Suelthaus
Lawrence P. Kaplan
Thomas M. Walsh
Kenneth E. Hand
Stuart H. Zimbalist
Ronald L. Pallmann (Resident, Belleville, Illinois Office)
Mark W. Weisman
Jamie Zveitel Kwiatek
Craig A. Smith
Bradley G. Kafka
Richard D. Lageson
Kyler L. Humphrey
Larry K. Harris
John D. Ashcroft
Scot W. Boulton
Helmut Starr
Harold G. Belsheim II (Resident, Belleville, Illinois Office)

OF COUNSEL

Steven G. Schumaier
Richard J. Stahlhuth
Wayne Braxton Wright
Henry M. Ordower

Bruce R. Bartlett
Gino F. Battisti
Anne E. Billings
Julia M. Bruemmer
Nicole M. Chaput
David C. Davis
Mary F. Giacoma
Steven B. Gorin
Valerie Held
David M. Hofele
S. H. Gregory Overstreet (Resident, Belleville, Illinois Office)
Robert J. Selsor
William D. Shultz, Jr. (Resident, Belleville, Illinois Office)
Sarah A. Siegel
Lori L. Underberger
David R. Weaver
Mark B. Weinheimer

Representative Clients: Archer Daniels Midland Company; Citation Computer Systems, Inc.; Didion Manufacturing Company; Hilton Hotels Corporation; Holten Meat Company; Kuhlman Design Group; John Fabick Tractor Co.; Miss Elaine's, Inc.; Marion Pepsi-Cola Bottling Company; Navistar Financial Corp.; Nestle Enterprises, Inc.; Painting and Decorating Contractors of America; St. Louis Regional Convention and Sports Complex Authority; Health Technologies, Inc.; Whelan Security Company.

For full biographical listings, see the Martindale-Hubbell Law Directory

THOMPSON & MITCHELL (AV)

One Mercantile Center, Suite 3300, 63101
Telephone: 314-231-7676
Telecopier: 314-342-1717
Belleville, Illinois Office: 525 West Main Street.
Telephone: 618-277-4700; 314-271-1800.
Telecopier: 618-236-3434.
St. Charles, Missouri Office: 200 North Third Street.
Telephone: 314-946-7717.
Telecopier: 314-946-4938.
Washington, D.C. Office: 700 14th Street, N.W., Suite 900.
Telephone: 202-508-1000.
Telecopier: 202-508-1010.

MEMBERS OF FIRM

William G. Guerri
Joseph P. Logan
Charles B. Baron
David F. Ulmer
Thomas F. Eagleton
William J. McNamara
W. Stanley Walch
James J. Raymond
Millard Backerman
Michael D. O'Keefe
Fred E. Arnold
David Wells
Gerard K. Sandweg, Jr.
Charles M. Babington III
David A. Lander
David F. Yates
Thomas R. Corbett
Paul F. Pautler
Joan M. Newman
Charles A. Newman
Michael F. Lause
Gordon L. Ankney
Rhonda C. Thomas
Donald B. Dorwart
Raymond L. Massey
Gary Mayes
Peter A. Fanchi
Claire Halpern
Michael Lazaroff
Robert H. Brownlee
James W. Erwin
Thomas R. Jayne
Stephen B. Higgins
Mary M. Bonacorsi
Allen D. Allred
William J. Falk
Dan H. Ball
Kenton E. Knickmeyer
William R. Bay
Thomas J. Minogue
Mark Sableman
Henry A. Bettendorf
Charles M. Poplstein
Robert M. LaRose
John W. Finger
James G. Blase

(See Next Column)

THOMPSON & MITCHELL, *St. Louis—Continued*

MEMBERS OF FIRM (Continued)

Harry W. Wellford, Jr.
Bradley A. Winters
Jan Robey Alonzo
Michael J. Morris
Liza S. Forshaw
Thomas A. Litz
Edward A. Cohen
Patricia L. Cohen
Charles R. Saulsberry
Paul M. Macon
Mark L. Kaltenrieder
Nicholas J. Lamb
Francis X. Buckley, Jr.
Lawrence C. Friedman
Ronald E. Haglof
Richard L. Lawton
Harris A. Maynord
James J. Murphy
Peter S. Strassner
Charles H. Binger

OF COUNSEL

Stanley T. Bjurstrom
John N. Ehlers
Michael Jos. Hart

ASSOCIATES

Martin P. Akins
Mike W. Bartolacci
Conny Davinroy Beatty
Mark V. Bossi
Lisa M. Braun
Kelly M. Brown
John J. Carey
J. Powell Carman
David S. Corwin
Tracy J. Cowan
Ellen F. Cruickshank
Jonathan F. Dalton
Joseph P. Danis
Mark J. Drish
William J. Dubinsky
Matthew J. Fairless
David D. Farrell
Lorna L. Frahm
Janet M. Franklin
Steven D. Graham
William D. Hakes
Melissa Anne Hall
Ruthanne C. Hammett
Jennifer J. Herner
Diane M. Hoelzl
Stephen G. Jeffery
Bettina Lynn Joist
Roger A. Keller, Jr.
Cheryl A. Kelly
Abigail T. Kelman
Crystal M. Kennedy
Melvin D. Kennedy
Andrew J. Klinghammer
Michele Campbell Kloeppel
Katherine G. Knapp
A. Laurie Koller
Sara E. Kotthoff
Denette C. Kuhlman
Tomea C. Mayer
Steven B. Mitchell
David F. Morris
Jane M. Moul
Robert L. Norton
Christopher B. Reid
Linda Carroll Reisner
Gerard K. Rodriguez
Deborah K. Rush
T. Evan Schaeffer
Anthony G. Simon
Martin B. Sipple
Stephen D. Smith
David A. Stratmann
Kevin A. Sullivan
Bryan L. Sutter
David F. Szewczyk
Stephen R. Welby
Roman P. Wuller

BELLEVILLE, ILLINOIS OFFICE

RESIDENT MEMBERS OF FIRM

Joseph R. Lowery
W. Thomas Coghill, Jr.
Donald E. Weihl
Thomas W. Alvey, Jr.
Karl D. Dexheimer
Garrett C. Reuter
Allan McD. Goodloe, Jr.
Thomas F. Hennessy, III
William A. Schmitt
Edward S. Bott, Jr.
Myron A. Hanna
Mark J. Stegman
Kurt E. Reitz
Kurt S. Schroeder

RESIDENT OF COUNSEL

Robert L. Broderick
James R. Parham

RESIDENT ASSOCIATES

D. Kimberly Brown
Tom R. Burcham, III
Karen A. Carr
Mary Sue Juen
CHERIE K. HARPOLE MACDONALD
Deborah J. Mehrmann
William J. Niehoff
Eric R. Riess
Donald K. Schoemaker
Mark S. Schuver
Michael J. Scotti, III
T. Bradford Waltrip

ST. CHARLES, MISSOURI OFFICE

MEMBERS OF FIRM

Rollin J. Moerschel
John C. Hannegan
Keith W. Hazelwood
James J. Hennelly
Wm. Randolph Weber
Tracy Mathis

ASSOCIATES

Steven C. Schwendemann
V. Scott Williams

WASHINGTON, D.C. OFFICE

MEMBERS OF FIRM

Murray J. Belman
Milton D. Andrews (Not admitted in MO)
Michael A. Greenspan
John V. Austin
Barbara B. Powell
Gerald D. Stoltz
Marjorie F. Krumholz
Richard A. Schaberg

ASSOCIATES

Catherine M. Beresovski
Halpin J. Burke
Randall K. Hulme

Representative Clients: American Commercial Lines, Inc.; A.P. Green Industries, Inc.; Chrysler Corporation; Enterprise Rent-A-Car; Magna Banks; Mallinckrodt, Inc.; Mercantile Banks; Missouri Pacific Railroad Company; Peabody Coal Co.; RehabCare Corporation.

For full biographical listings, see the Martindale-Hubbell Law Directory

WEIER, HOCKENSMITH & SHERBY, P.C. (AV)

Bel Aire Office Park, 12801 Flushing Meadow Drive, 63131
Telephone: 314-965-2255
Fax: 314-965-6653

G. William Weier
Dana Hockensmith
James W. Sherby
J. Richard McEachern
Mark H. Zoole
LaRee M. DeFreece
Phillip A. Tatlow

OF COUNSEL

Robert A. Bedell
Robert H. McRoberts, Jr.
Martin T. Sigillito

Representative Clients: National American Corp. Inc.; St. John's Mercy Medical Center; Curtis Transport, Inc.; State Bank of De Soto; Missouri Council of the Blind; HEI, Inc.; Public Water Supply District No. 7; Essex Contracting, Inc.; Christian Hospitals Northeast-Northwest.

For full biographical listings, see the Martindale-Hubbell Law Directory

ZIERCHER & HOCKER, P.C. (AV)

231 South Bemiston Avenue, Suite 800 (Clayton), 63105
Telephone: 314-727-5822
FAX: 314-727-2824

Edgar G. Boedeker
William J. Bruin, Jr.
George J. Bude
Edgar T. Farmer
Gary H. Feder
Edward K. Fehlig
Jeffrey E. Fine
Daniel L. Human
David R. Human
F. William Human, Jr.
Christopher Karlen
Steven W. Koslovsky
Albert A. Michenfelder, Jr.
Jeffrey S. Morgan
Richard A. Roth
G. Carroll Stribling, Jr.
Thomas E. Toney, III
Gary L. Vincent
Richard A. Yawitz
Erwin Tzinberg (1912-1974)
Herbert W. Ziercher (1902-1988)

OF COUNSEL

Lon Hocker
James L. Nouss
Howard J. Smith

John J. Diehl, Jr.
Jill M. Farmer
Mark F. (Thor) Hearne, II
Mary Webster Murphy
Jeffrey D. Sigmund

Counsel for: Chrysler Realty Corp.; Clayton School District; First National Bank of St. Louis; The Funny Bone Comedy Clubs of America, Inc.; The Jones Company; McDonalds' Corp.; The National Credit Union Administration; St. John's Mercy Medical Center; St. Louis County Library; St. Louis Science Center.

For full biographical listings, see the Martindale-Hubbell Law Directory

*SALEM,** Dent Co. — (Refer to Rolla)

*SAVANNAH,** Andrew Co. — (Refer to St. Joseph)

*SEDALIA,** Pettis Co.

GARDNER, GARDNER & GARDNER (AV)

416 South Ohio Avenue, 65301-4432
Telephone: 816-827-0204
Telex: ABA/net: rsgardner
Compuserve: 76146-1533
Fax: 816-826-4443

MEMBERS OF FIRM

John T. Martin (1904-1974)
Robert S. Gardner
R. Scott Gardner
Anne C. Gardner

Representative Clients: CNA Insurance Cos.; United Fire & Casualty Co.; Third National Bank of Sedalia; St. Paul Fire & Marine Insurance Co.; Silvey Cos.; United States Fidelity & Guaranty Co.; Viking Insurance Co. of Wisconsin.

For full biographical listings, see the Martindale-Hubbell Law Directory

WESNER, KEMPTON, RUSSELL AND DOMINIQUE (AV)

114 East 5th Street, P.O. Box 815, 65302-0815
Telephone: 816-827-0314
Fax: 816-827-1200
Jefferson City, Missouri Office: 623 East McCarty Street, P.O. Box 1108.
Telephone: 314-635-7241,
Fax: 816-635-2631.

Fred F. Wesner (1898-1974)
Robert L. Wesner (1924-1988)
Mark T. Kempton
Robert G. Russell
Andrew S. Carroll
J. Christopher Spangler
P. Pierre Dominique (Resident at Jefferson City, Mo.)

Representative Clients: State Farm Mutual Automobile Insurance Co.; Shelter Insurance Co.; Continental Insurance Cos.; Great American Insurance Cos.
Reference: Third National Bank, Sedalia.

For full biographical listings, see the Martindale-Hubbell Law Directory

SIKESTON, Scott Co.

Blanton, Rice, Sidwell & Ottinger (AV)

219 South Kings Highway, P.O. Box 805, 63801
Telephone: 314-471-1000
Facsimile: 314-471-1012

MEMBERS OF FIRM

Harry C. Blanton (1891-1973)
Thomas R. Gilmore (1939-1984)
David E. Blanton
Bernard C. Rice
King E. Sidwell
Terry R. Ottinger
Bruce A. Lawrence
Joseph C. Blanton, Jr.
James A. Pinkston
Timothy P. Gilmore

Representative Clients: St. Louis Southwestern Railway Lines; Employers Mutuals of Wausau; The Travelers Insurance Co.; Cigna; Commercial Union Insurance Group; Kemper Group; Continental-National Insurance Group; Shelter Insurance Cos.; First National Bank, Sikeston, Mo.; Columbia Mutual Insurance Company.

For full biographical listings, see the Martindale-Hubbell Law Directory

Drumm, Winchester & Gleason (AV)

113 West North Street, P.O. Box 40, 63801
Telephone: 314-471-1207
Fax: 314-971-1050

MEMBERS OF FIRM

Manuel Drumm
William H. Winchester, III
Stephanie Mitchell Gleason

Representative Clients: Aetna Casualty & Surety Co.; Cameron Mutual Insurance Co.; Boyer Construction Co.; Risk Control Associates; Missouri Medical Insurance Co.

For full biographical listings, see the Martindale-Hubbell Law Directory

*SPRINGFIELD,** Greene Co.

Carnahan, Evans, Cantwell & Brown, P.C. (AV)

Four Corporate Centre, Suite 410, 1949 East Sunshine, P.O. Box 10009 G.S.S., 65808
Telephone: 417-887-8490
Fax: 417-887-8935

John M. Carnahan, Jr. (Retired 1987)
John M. Carnahan, III
William E. Evans
C. Bradford Cantwell
Clifford S. Brown
Frank C. Carnahan

Representative Clients: Aaron's Automotive Products, Inc.; Aire-Master of America, Inc.; Connell-Howe Insurers, Inc.; Ozark Neonatal Associates, Inc.; Oxford Health Care Corp.; PAS, Inc.; Plastic Surgery Clinic of Springfield, Inc.; Smith-Glynn-Callaway Clinic, Inc.; Underwood Oil Co.
Reference: Trust Department of The Boatmen's Bank of Southern Missouri.

For full biographical listings, see the Martindale-Hubbell Law Directory

Farrington & Curtis, P.C. (AV)

750 North Jefferson, 65802
Telephone: 417-862-6726
Telecopier: 417-862-6948

John S. Farrington (1875-1946)
Arthur M. Curtis (1886-1950)
Richard Farrington
Jack S. Curtis
E. C. Curtis (Retired)
Lincoln J. Knauer
William J. Hart
Gary A. Powell
Charles B. Cowherd
Lee J. Viorel, III
Debra Mallonee Shantz
Mark D. Pfeiffer

Bryan O. Wade
Jeffrey Alan McFarland

District Attorneys for: Union Pacific Railroad Co.
Attorneys for: Boatmen's Bank of Southern Missouri; Paul Mueller Co.; Montgomery Ward & Co.; Acme Structural, Inc.; Silver Dollar City, Inc.; Drury College; Meek Building Centers; Walmart Stores, Inc.

For full biographical listings, see the Martindale-Hubbell Law Directory

Mann, Walter, Burkart, Weathers & Walter, L.C. (AV)

Suite 600 John Q. Hammons Building, 300 John Q. Hammons Parkway, 65806-2593
Telephone: 417-862-7037
FAX: 417-862-7528

Edgar P. Mann (1858-1953)
Frank C. Mann (1888-1971)
C. Wallace Walter (1911-1992)
Glenn A. Burkart
Buell F. Weathers
Kenneth T. Walter
Bruce E. Hunt
Gary E. Bishop

LEGAL SUPPORT PERSONNEL

Luann L. Mattson

Representative Clients: Southwestern Bell Telephone Co.; Mercantile Bank of Springfield; Burlington Northern Railroad Co.; Phillips Petroleum Co.; Prudential Insurance Co.; CNA Insurance; Federated Mutual Insurance Co.; Employers Mutual Cos.; Medical Protective Co.; Roadway Express Inc.

(See Next Column)

For full biographical listings, see the Martindale-Hubbell Law Directory

Miller & Sanford, A Professional Corporation (AV)

1845 South National Avenue, P.O. Box 4288, 65808-4288
Telephone: 417-886-2000
Fax: 417-886-9126

John Weston Miller (1900-1981)
John F. Carr (1911-1990)
Wm. P. Sanford
Vincent Tyndall
Frank M. Evans, III
James F. McLeod
Craig R. Oliver
Douglas R. Nickell
Mark A. Powell
Ed. L. Payton
Cynthia B. McGinnis
Jerry A. Harmison, Jr.

Stacey A. Stenger
Daniel R. Wichmer
Bob Lawson, Jr.

OF COUNSEL

James H. Arneson

Counsel for: ITT Hartford; Home Insurance Co.; Boatmen's National Bank Springfield, N.A.; Liberty Mutual Insurance Co.; St. John's Regional Health Center; Maryland Casualty Co.; Great West Casualty Co.; American International Group.

For full biographical listings, see the Martindale-Hubbell Law Directory

Reynolds & Conway, P.C. (AV)

406 McDaniel Building, 318 Park Central East, 65806
Telephone: 417-869-0768
FAX: 417-869-6007

Jerry L. Reynolds
Ronald A. Conway

References: Boatmens National Bank.

For full biographical listings, see the Martindale-Hubbell Law Directory

Woolsey, Fisher, Whiteaker & McDonald, A Professional Corporation (AV)

300 S. Jefferson, Suite 600, P.O. Box 1245, 65801
Telephone: 417-869-0581
Telecopier: 417-831-7852

Clarence O. Woolsey (1911-1984)
Harold J. Fisher (Retired)
Raymond E. Whiteaker
William H. McDonald
Bradley J. Fisher
John E. Price
Virginia L. Fry
David A. Childers
Richard C. Miller
Thomas Y. Auner
Richard E. Davis
William G. Todd
Joseph Dow Sheppard, III
William Craig Hosmer
Brent S. Bothwell
Lee Ann Miller

OF COUNSEL

Richard K. Wilson
Don G. Busch
James H. Wesley, II
Connie L. Wible

Rana L. Faaborg
Carol Taylor Aiken
Stuart H. King
William R. Robb
James R. Royce
William G. Petrus, Jr.
Joseph L. Johnson
Eric G. Jensen
Marjorie M. Wallace

Representative Clients: AT&T/Paradyne/MRAC, Inc.; Bass Pro Shops/-Tracker Marine, Inc.; Emerson Electric Companies; Enron Liquid Fuels; Unisys; American States Insurance Company; Kemper Insurance Group; Wausau Insurance Group; Zurich-American Insurance Company.

For full biographical listings, see the Martindale-Hubbell Law Directory

*STEELVILLE,** Crawford Co. — (Refer to Rolla)

*STOCKTON,** Cedar Co. — (Refer to Nevada)

*TROY,** Lincoln Co. — (Refer to Hannibal)

*TUSCUMBIA,** Miller Co. — (Refer to Jefferson City)

*VERSAILLES,** Morgan Co. — (Refer to Jefferson City)

*WARRENSBURG,** Johnson Co. — (Refer to Clinton)

WASHINGTON, Franklin Co. — (Refer to St. Louis)

*WAYNESVILLE,** Pulaski Co. — (Refer to Lebanon)

*WEST PLAINS,** Howell Co.

Brill, Moore & Wagoner, P.C. (AV)

204 West Main Street, P.O. Box 527, 65775
Telephone: 417-256-6174
Fax: 417-256-0928

(See Next Column)

BRILL, MOORE & WAGONER P.C., *West Plains—Continued*

Newton C. Brill
Rich D. Moore
Kenneth A. Wagoner

Representative Clients: Boatmen's First National Bank of West Plains; Amyx Manufacturing Co.
Insurance Clients: American Family Insurance Co. Shelter Mutual Insurance Co.; Federated Insurance.
References: Boatmen's First National Bank of West Plains; Mercantile Bank of Willow Springs.

For full biographical listings, see the Martindale-Hubbell Law Directory

MONTANA

*ANACONDA,** Deer Lodge Co.

Knight, Dahood, McLean, Everett & Dayton (AV)

P.O. Box 727, 59711
Telephone: 406-563-3424
Fax: 406-563-7519

MEMBERS OF FIRM

J. B. C. Knight (1889-1967)
Wade J. Dahood
David M. McLean
Bernard J. Everett
Ray J. Dayton

ASSOCIATES

Douglas J. DiRe

Reference: Security Bank.

For full biographical listings, see the Martindale-Hubbell Law Directory

*BAKER,** Fallon Co. — (Refer to Miles City)

*BIG TIMBER,** Sweet Grass Co. — (Refer to Livingston)

*BILLINGS,** Yellowstone Co.

Brown, Gerbase, Cebull, Fulton, Harman & Ross, P.C. (AV)

315 North 24th Street, P.O. Drawer 849, 59103-0849
Telephone: 406-248-2611
FAX: 406-248-3128
Bozeman, Montana Office: 510 South 23rd Street.
Telephone: 406-587-8486.
Fax: 406-587-4524.

Rockwood Brown
Claude J. Gerbase, Jr.
Richard F. Cebull
Angus B. Fulton
Steven J. Harman
John Walker Ross
John J. Russell
John A. Dostal
Michael W. Tolstedt
Timothy A. Filz
Michael P. Heringer
Guy W. Rogers

Scott G. Gratton

For full biographical listings, see the Martindale-Hubbell Law Directory

Crowley, Haughey, Hanson, Toole & Dietrich (AV)

500 Transwestern II, 490 North 31st Street, P.O. Box 2529, 59103
Telephone: 406-252-3441
Fax: 406-259-4159
Helena, Montana Office: IBM Building, 100 North Park Avenue, Suite 300, 59601.
Telephone: 406-449-4165.
Fax: 406-449-5149.

RETIRED

Cale J. Crowley
Stuart W. Conner

OF COUNSEL

James M. Haughey
Norman Hanson
Bruce R. Toole
Neil S. Keefer

MEMBERS OF FIRM

Henry J. Coleman (1885-1961)
Arthur F. Lamey (1892-1963)
James H. Kilbourne (1912-1974)
Frank A. Gallagher (1907-1976)
John M. Dietrich
Louis R. Moore
Gareld F. Krieg
Arthur F. Lamey, Jr.
Myles J. Thomas
George C. Dalthorp
David L. Johnson
Kemp J. Wilson
Herbert I. Pierce, III
Terry B. Cosgrove
Ronald R. Lodders
Charles R. Cashmore
Lawrence B. Cozzens
Steven P. Ruffatto
Allan L. Karell
James P. Sites
Carolyn S. Ostby
Steven J. Lehman
Laura A. Mitchell
Christopher Mangen, Jr.
Michael E. Webster
Daniel N. McLean
Robert G. Michelotti, Jr.
John R. Alexander
Donald L. Harris
William D. Lamdin, III
William J. Mattix
Peter F. Habein
Michael S. Dockery
Malcolm H. Goodrich
Mary Scrim
Jon T. Dyre
Eric K. Anderson
Bruce A. Fredrickson
Renee L. Coppock
Janice L. Rehberg
Joe C. Maynard, Jr.

ASSOCIATES

John R. Lee
Steven Robert Milch
Scott M. Heard
Leonard H. Smith
Neil G. Westesen
Michael S. Lahr
Lori A. Harper
Robert T. Bell

(See Next Column)

LEGAL SUPPORT PERSONNEL

Jolyn Beringer (Litigation Legal Assistant)
Lori H. Cornish (Litigation Legal Assistant)
Katherine Honaker (Probate Legal Assistant)
Marilyn J. Bennett (Commercial Paralegal and Marketing Coordinator)
Donna Meehan (Legal Assistant/Certified Public Accountant)
Stephen R. Regimbal (Natural Resources Legal Assistant)
Jane Thomas (Litigation Legal Assistant)
Margaret Webster (Librarian)

Representative Clients: Montana Power Co.; First Interstate Bank of Commerce; MDU Resources Group, Inc.; Chevron U.S.A., Inc.; Noranda Minerals Corp.; United Parcel Service.
Insurance Clients: Farmers Insurance Group; New York Life Insurance Co.

For full biographical listings, see the Martindale-Hubbell Law Directory

Holland & Hart (AV)

Suite 1500, First Interstate Center, 401 North 31st Street, P.O. Box 639, 59101
Telephone: 406-252-2166
Telecopier: 406-252-1669
Denver, Colorado Office: Suite 2900, 555 Seventeenth Street. P.O. Box 8749.
Telephone: 303-295-8000.
Cable Address: "Holhart Denver."
Telecopier: 303-295-8261.
TWX: 910-931-0568.
Denver Tech Center, Colorado Office: Suite 1050, 4601 DTC Boulevard.
Telephone: 303-290-1600.
Telecopier: 303-290-1606.
Aspen, Colorado Office: 600 East Main Street.
Telephone: 303-925-3476.
Telecopier: 303-925-9367.
Boulder, Colorado Office: Suite 500, 1050 Walnut.
Telephone: 303-473-2700.
Telecopier: 303-473-2720.
Colorado Springs, Colorado Office: Suite 1000, 90 S. Cascade Avenue.
Telephone: 719-475-7730.
Telex: 820770 SHHTLX.
Telecopier: 719-634-2461.
Washington, D.C. Office: Suite 310, 1001 Pennsylvania Avenue, N.W.
Telephone: 202-638-5500.
Telecopier: 202-737-8998.
Boise, Idaho Office: Suite 1400, West One Plaza, 101 South Capitol Boulevard, P.O. Box 2527.
Telephone: 208-342-5000.
Telecopier: 208-343-8869.
Salt Lake City, Utah Office: Suite 880, 111 East Broadway.
Telephone: 801-578-6000.
FAX: 801-578-6010.
Cheyenne, Wyoming Office: Holland & Hart, A Partnership including Professional Corporations, Suite 500, 2020 Carey Avenue, P.O. Box 1347.
Telephone: 307-778-4200.
Telecopier: 307-778-8175.
Jackson, Wyoming Office: Holland & Hart, A Partnership including Professional Corporations, Suite 2, 175 South King Street, P.O. 68.
Telephone: 307-739-9741.
Telecopier: 307-739-9744.

PARTNERS

Stephen H. Foster
Paul D. Miller
Donald W. Quander
Jeanne Matthews Bender
James M. Ragain
David R. Chisholm

SPECIAL COUNSEL

Kyle A. Gray
Robert A. Lorenz

RESIDENT ASSOCIATES

Bruce F. Fain
W. Scott Mitchell
Patricia D. Peterman

For full biographical listings, see the Martindale-Hubbell Law Directory

Moulton, Bellingham, Longo & Mather, P.C. (AV)

Suite 1900 Sheraton Plaza, 27 North 27th Street, P.O. Box 2559, 59103
Telephone: 406-248-7731

Fredric D. Moulton (1912-1989)
William H. Bellingham
Ward Swanser
Brent R. Cromley
Gerald B. Murphy
Randy H. Bellingham
Robert H. Prigge
Sidney R. Thomas
Konrad Kent Koolen
Gregory G. Murphy
William A. Forsythe
Doug James
Brad H. Anderson
Thomas E. Smith
John T. Jones
T. Thomas Singer

OF COUNSEL

Bernard E. Longo
William S. Mather

(See Next Column)

MOULTON, BELLINGHAM, LONGO & MATHER P.C., *Billings—Continued*

Ramona Heupel Stevens
Martha Sheehy
Harlan B. Krogh
Duncan Albert Peete

Counsel for: First Bank-Montana; Lee Enterprises, Inc. (Billings Gazette); Fireman's Fund Insurance Cos.; Kampgrounds of America, Inc.; State Farm Mutual Automobile Insurance Co.; General Motors Corp.; MDU Resources Group, Inc.; Western Energy; Bechtel Construction Co.; Shell Oil Co.

For full biographical listings, see the Martindale-Hubbell Law Directory

*BOULDER,** Jefferson Co. — (Refer to Butte)

*BOZEMAN,** Gallatin Co.

KOMMERS, KASTING & ROTH (AV㊣)

Martel Financial Center, 215 West Mendenhall, Suite A-1, P.O. Box 1267, 59715
Telephone: 406-587-7717
FAX: 406-587-9461

MEMBERS OF FIRM

James M. Kommers
Kent M. Kasting
Daniel J. Roth

ASSOCIATES

John M. Kauffman

OF COUNSEL

Elizabeth S. Lewis

For full biographical listings, see the Martindale-Hubbell Law Directory

LANDOE, BROWN, PLANALP & BRAAKSMA, P.C. (AV)

27 North Tracy, P.O. Box One, 59771-0001
Telephone: 406-586-4351
Fax: 406-586-7877

Hjalmar B. Landoe (1907-1990)
Gene I. Brown
J. Robert Planalp
Calvin L. Braaksma
Steven W. Reida
John H. Tarlow
Mark E. Miller

OF COUNSEL

Joseph B. Gary

Representative Clients: Fireman's Fund Insurance Co.; Mountain West Farm Bureau Insurance Co.; USAA Insurance Co.; Safeco Insurance Co.; Allstate Insurance Co.; National Chiropractic Mutual Insurance Company; First Security Bank of Bozeman; First Security Bank of West Yellowstone; Montana Bank of Bozeman; Metropolitan Mortgage and Securities Company, Inc.

For full biographical listings, see the Martindale-Hubbell Law Directory

MORROW, SEDIVY & BENNETT, PROFESSIONAL CORPORATION (AV)

First Security Bank Building, P.O. Box 1168, 59771
Telephone: 406-586-4311

J. H. Morrow (1908-1992)
Edmund P. Sedivy, Jr.
Lyman H. Bennett, III
Thomas M. White
David L. Weaver
Lynda S. Weaver

Representative Clients furnished upon request.
Reference: First Security Bank of Bozeman.

For full biographical listings, see the Martindale-Hubbell Law Directory

*BROADUS,** Powder River Co. — (Refer to Miles City)

*BUTTE,** Silver Bow Co.

CORETTE POHLMAN ALLEN BLACK & CARLSON, A PROFESSIONAL CORPORATION (AV)

Mayer Building, 129 West Park Street, P.O. Box 509, 59703
Telephone: 406-723-3205
FAX: 406-723-8919

R. D. Corette
Dolphy O. Pohlman
Gerald R. Allen
Gregory C. Black
Robert M. Carlson
Marshal L. Mickelson
John T. Johnston

Marvin James Knapstad, Jr.
William M. O'Leary
Helen Waldbillig McCarthy
Ann M. Monaghan

State Counsel for: Union Pacific Railroad Co.
Representative Clients: CNA; Dow Elanco; Allstate Insurance Co.; Kemper Insurance Group; Ford Motor Company; Safeway Stores; Eli Lily Co.; Wyath Laboratories, Inc.

For full biographical listings, see the Martindale-Hubbell Law Directory

*CHINOOK,** Blaine Co. — (Refer to Great Falls)

*CHOTEAU,** Teton Co. — (Refer to Great Falls)

*CIRCLE,** McCone Co. — (Refer to Sidney)

*COLUMBUS,** Stillwater Co. — (Refer to Billings)

*CONRAD,** Pondera Co. — (Refer to Great Falls)

*CUT BANK,** Glacier Co. — (Refer to Great Falls)

*DEER LODGE,** Powell Co. — (Refer to Anaconda)

*DILLON,** Beaverhead Co. — (Refer to Butte)

*EKALAKA,** Carter Co. — (Refer to Miles City)

*FORSYTH,** Rosebud Co. — (Refer to Billings)

*FORT BENTON,** Chouteau Co. — (Refer to Great Falls)

*GLASGOW,** Valley Co.

GALLAGHER & ARCHAMBEAULT, A PROFESSIONAL CORPORATION (AV)

605 Third Avenue South, P.O. Box 512, 59230
Telephone: 406-228-9331
Fax: 406-228-9335

Francis Gallagher
Gerald T. Archambeault

Attorneys for: Bank of Montana-Glasgow; Valley Bank-Glasgow; Braden-Pehlke Construction Co., Inc.; Fort Peck Federal Credit Union; Hinsdale Livestock Co.; Markels Inc.; Page Whitman Land and Cattle; Phillips County Veterinary Clinic, P.S.C.; Town of Fort Peck.

For full biographical listings, see the Martindale-Hubbell Law Directory

*GLENDIVE,** Dawson Co. — (Refer to Sidney)

*GREAT FALLS,** Cascade Co.

JARDINE, STEPHENSON, BLEWETT AND WEAVER, P.C. (AV)

Seventh Floor, First National Bank Building, P.O. Box 2269, 59403
Telephone: 406-727-5000
FAX: 406-727-5419

John H. Weaver (Retired)
John D. Stephenson, Sr. (1907-1992)
George N. McCabe
John D. Stephenson, Jr.
Jack L. Lewis
Donald J. Hamilton
James E. Aiken
K. Dale Schwanke
Lon T. Holden
Gary W. Bjelland
Gregory A. Luinstra
J. Michael Young
Judith Ames Bartram
Sue Ann Love
Francis X. Clinch
Steven T. Potts
Robert B. Pfennigs

Alex Blewett
Joseph G. Mudd
Patrick R. Watt

SPECIAL COUNSEL

Timothy J. Wylder

Attorneys for: General Motors Corp.; Great Falls Clinic; First Bank-Great Falls; Aetna Life & Casualty; Safeco Insurance; General Mills, Inc.; Ford Motor Co.; Burlington Northern Railroad Co.; Exxon; Union Oil Co..

For full biographical listings, see the Martindale-Hubbell Law Directory

*HAMILTON,** Ravalli Co.

KOCH, JOHNSON, WEBER & GOHEEN (AV)

345 West Main Street, Drawer 433, 59840
Telephone: 406-363-2722; 363-1655
Fax: 406-363-2972

MEMBERS OF FIRM

Thomas P. Koch
Lawrence D. Johnson
Richard A. Weber, Jr.
Gail Hafner Goheen

Representative Clients: Ravalli County Bank; Ravalli County Electric Co-Op; Bitter Root Irrigation District.
Reference: Ravalli County Bank, Hamilton, Montana.

For full biographical listings, see the Martindale-Hubbell Law Directory

*HARDIN,** Big Horn Co. — (Refer to Billings)

*HARLOWTON,** Wheatland Co. — (Refer to Billings)

*HAVRE,** Hill Co. — (Refer to Great Falls)

*HELENA,** Lewis and Clark Co.

BROWNING, KALECZYC, BERRY & HOVEN, P.C. (AV)

139 North Last Chance Gulch, P.O. Box 1697, 59624
Telephone: 406-449-6220
Telefax: 406-443-0700

R. Stephen Browning
Stanley T. Kaleczyc
Leo Berry
J. Daniel Hoven
Oliver H. Goe
John H. Maynard

(See Next Column)

BROWNING, KALECZYC, BERRY & HOVEN P.C.—*Continued*

Katharine S. Donnelley
Leo S. Ward
Marcia J. Davenport
Catherine A. Laughner
Ken C. Crippen
Sharon A. O'Leary
Mark D. Etchart
Page Carroccia Dringman
Kimberly A. Bernard

Reference: First Bank Helena, Helena, Montana.

For full biographical listings, see the Martindale-Hubbell Law Directory

GOUGH, SHANAHAN, JOHNSON & WATERMAN (AV)

33 South Last Chance Gulch, P.O. Box 1715, 59624
Telephone: 406-442-8560
Telecopier: 406-442-8783

MEMBERS OF FIRM

T. B. Weir (1883-1962)
Edwin S. Booth (1907-1976)
Newell Gough, Jr.
William H. Coldiron
Ward A. Shanahan
Cordell Johnson
Ronald F. Waterman
Jock O. Anderson
Alan L. Joscelyn
William P. Driscoll
Thomas E. Hattersley, III
Sarah M. Power
Holly J. Franz
Michael S. Lattier

ASSOCIATES

James B. Lippert
David C. Dalthorp
William L. MacBride, Jr. (Not admitted in MT)

Representative Clients: Ash Grove Cement; Borden, Inc.; Case Corporation; Chevron Companies; Farmers Insurance Group; Golden Sunlight Mines; Montana Power Company; Noranda Minerals Corporation; Pegasus Gold Corporation; United States Fidelity and Guaranty Company.

For full biographical listings, see the Martindale-Hubbell Law Directory

LUXAN & MURFITT (AV)

4th Floor, Montana Club Building, 24 West Sixth Avenue, P.O. Box 1144, 59624
Telephone: 406-442-7450
Fax: 406-442-7361

H. J. Luxan (1918-1984)

MEMBERS OF FIRM

Michael J. Mulroney
Gary L. Davis
Dale E. Reagor
Patrick E. Melby
Michael J. Rieley
Michael S. Becker
Tom K. Hopgood

ASSOCIATES

Gregory A. Van Horssen

OF COUNSEL

Walter S. Murfitt
Roger W. Tippy

Representative Clients: Norwest Bank, Helena; Norwest Capital Management and Trust Co.; Nicholson Cos.; St. Peter's Community Hospital; Montana Life and Health Insurance Guaranty Assn.; CIGNA Insurance Co.; First Montana Title Co.; Lee Enterprises, Inc.
References: Norwest Bank Helena; First Montana Title Co.

For full biographical listings, see the Martindale-Hubbell Law Directory

*JORDAN,** Garfield Co. — (Refer to Miles City)

*KALISPELL,** Flathead Co.

HASH, O'BRIEN & BARTLETT (AV)

Plaza West, 136 First Avenue, West, P.O. Box 1178, 59901
Telephone: 406-755-6919
Fax: 406-755-6911

MEMBERS OF FIRM

Charles L. Hash
Kenneth E. O'Brien
James C. Bartlett
C. Mark Hash

General Counsel for: Glacier Bank F.S.B.; Budget Finance; Flathead County Title Co.
Representative Clients: Western Surety Co.; Liberty Mutual Insurance Co.; Allstate Insurance Co.; Hillsteads Department Store; Montana Brokers, Inc.
Reference: Glacier Bank F.S.B.

For full biographical listings, see the Martindale-Hubbell Law Directory

MURPHY, ROBINSON, HECKATHORN & PHILLIPS, P.C. (AV)

431 1st Avenue West, 59901
Telephone: 406-752-6644
FAX: 406-752-5108

James E. Murphy (1910-1990)
C. Eugene Phillips (1932-1993)
I. James Heckathorn
John B. Dudis, Jr.
Daniel D. Johns
Donald R. Murray, Jr.
Dana L. Christensen
Steven E. Cummings
Debra D. Parker
Mikel L. Moore

(See Next Column)

OF COUNSEL

Calvin S. Robinson
James A. Robischon
M. Dean Jellison

LEGAL SUPPORT PERSONNEL

Douglas W. Wardinsky (Legal Assistant)

Representative Clients: First Interstate Bank of Montana, N.A.; Pacific Corp.; Farmers Insurance Exchange; Northwestern Telephone Systems, Inc.; Semitool, Inc.; Winter Sports, Inc. (Big Mountain); The Doctors Company; Attorneys Liability Practice Society; Kandall Insurance Company.
Reference: First Interstate Bank of Montana, N.A.

For full biographical listings, see the Martindale-Hubbell Law Directory

*LIBBY,** Lincoln Co. — (Refer to Kalispell)

*LIVINGSTON,** Park Co.

HUPPERT & SWINDLEHURST, P.C. (AV)

420 South Second Street, P.O. Box 523, 59047
Telephone: 406-222-2023

Arnold Huppert, Jr. (Retired)
Joseph T. Swindlehurst

Jeffrey N. Pence

Counsel for: Empire Federal Savings & Loan Assn.; First National Park Bank; Park Electric Co-operative, Inc.; Park Clinic.
References: First Security Bank of Livingston; First National Park Bank.

For full biographical listings, see the Martindale-Hubbell Law Directory

*MALTA,** Phillips Co. — (Refer to Glasgow)

*MILES CITY,** Custer Co.

LUCAS & MONAGHAN, P.C. (AV)

513 Main Street, P.O. Box 728, 59301
Telephone: 406-232-4070
Fax: 406-232-4093
Broadus, Montana Office: 121 East Wilson.
Telephone: 406-436-2864.

James P. Lucas
Thomas M. Monaghan
A. Lance Tonn
Gary L. Day

Representative Clients: United States Fidelity and Guaranty Company; St. Paul Insurance Companies; INA; Montana Municipal Insurance Authority.

For full biographical listings, see the Martindale-Hubbell Law Directory

*MISSOULA,** Missoula Co.

BOONE, KARLBERG AND HADDON (AV)

Suite 301 Central Square, 201 West Main Street, P.O. Box 9199, 59807
Telephone: 406-543-6646
FAX: 406-549-6804

MEMBERS OF FIRM

Jack W. Rimel (1916-1958)
William T. Boone (1910-1984)
Karl R. Karlberg (1923-1988)
James J. Benn (1944-1992)
Thomas H. Boone
Sam E. Haddon
William L. Crowley
Randy J. Cox
Robert J. Sullivan
David B. Cotner
Dean A. Stensland
David H. Bjornson

ASSOCIATES

Steven C. Haddon
Cynthia K. Staley

Insurance Clients: The Travelers Companies; Prudential Insurance Company of America; Metropolitan Life Insurance Co; St. Paul Fire & Marine Insurance Co.; Fireman's Fund; Commerce Mortgage Co.; Industrial Indemnity Co.; Underwriters at Lloyds.
Counsel For: First Interstate Bank of Commerce, Missoula, N.A.; Montana Bank of South Missoula.

For full biographical listings, see the Martindale-Hubbell Law Directory

GARLINGTON, LOHN & ROBINSON (AV)

199 West Pine Street, P.O. Box 7909, 59807
Telephone: 406-523-2500
Telefax: 406-523-2595

OF COUNSEL

J. C. Garlington
R. H. Robinson

PARTNERS

Sherman V. Lohn
William Evan Jones
George D. Goodrich
Larry E. Riley
Robert E. Sheridan
Lawrence F. Daly
Gary L. Graham
Gregory L. Hanson
Gary B. Chumrau
Bradley J. Luck
Candace C. Fetscher
E. Craig Daue
John O. Mudd
W. Dennis Starkel
Paul C. Meismer
William T. Wagner
Charles E. McNeil
Susan P. Roy
Steven S. Carey

(See Next Column)

GARLINGTON, LOHN & ROBINSON, *Missoula—Continued*

ASSOCIATES

Kelly M. Wills
Terry J. MacDonald
Maureen H. Lennon
Michael C. Prezeau
Anita Harper Poe
Stephen Ross Brown
Lucy T. France

LEGAL SUPPORT PERSONNEL

Bonnie L. March

Counsel For: First Banks-Missoula; Columbia Falls Aluminum Co.
Local Attorneys for: Stone Container Co.; Western Montana Clinic; Montana Power Co.; The Daily Missoulian; Community Medical Center; Amtrak; Allstate Insurance Co.; State Farm Mutual Insurance Co.

For full biographical listings, see the Martindale-Hubbell Law Directory

KNIGHT, MACLAY & MASAR (AV)

The Florence, Suite 300, 111 North Higgins Avenue, P.O. Box 8957, 59807-8957
Telephone: 406-721-5440
Fax: 406-721-8644

MEMBERS OF FIRM

Robert M. Knight
Helena S. Maclay
James J. Masar

ASSOCIATES

Andrew C. Dana

Representative Clients: Zenchiku Land and Livestock, Inc.; Heart Bar Heart Ranch; Monture Hereford Ranch; Rocking Chair Ranch; The Nature Conservancy; Bank of Montana; Pioneer Federal Savings & Loan; Flint Creek Valley Bank; First American Title Insurance Co.; Old Republic National Title Insurance Co.

For full biographical listings, see the Martindale-Hubbell Law Directory

WORDEN, THANE & HAINES, P.C. (AV)

Suite 600, 111 N. Higgins, P.O. Box 4747, 59806
Telephone: 406-721-3400
Fax: 406-721-6985

Donovan Worden (1893-1968)
Jeremy G. Thane
Harry A. Haines
Ronald A. Bender
Molly R. Shepherd
Patrick G. Frank
Ralph B. Kirscher
Martin S. King
Patrick D. Dougherty

W. Carl Mendenhall
Gail M. Haviland
Shane A. Vannatta
Bradley D. Dantic
Peter S. Dayton

OF COUNSEL

Donovan Worden, Jr.
Robert W. Minto, Jr.

Counsel for: Employers Association of Western Montana; Bank of Montana-Missoula; Western Federal Savings Bank; Chrysler Credit Corporation; General Motors Corp.
Insurance Clients: Allstate Insurance; Farmers Insurance Group; Millers Insurance Group; The St. Paul Companies; Royal Insurance.

For full biographical listings, see the Martindale-Hubbell Law Directory

*PHILIPSBURG,** Granite Co. — (Refer to Anaconda)

*PLENTYWOOD,** Sheridan Co. — (Refer to Sidney)

*POLSON,** Lake Co. — (Refer to Kalispell)

*RED LODGE,** Carbon Co. — (Refer to Billings)

*ROUNDUP,** Musselshell Co. — (Refer to Billings)

*SCOBEY,** Daniels Co. — (Refer to Glasgow)

*SHELBY,** Toole Co. — (Refer to Great Falls)

*SIDNEY,** Richland Co.

HABEDANK, CUMMING, BEST & SAVAGE (AV)

302 West Main Street, P.O. Box 1250, 59270
Telephone: 406-482-1802
Fax: 406-482-6411

MEMBERS OF FIRM

Jacque W. Best
Robert J. Savage

ASSOCIATES

Diane Savage

OF COUNSEL

Otto T. Habedank
Wayne K. Cumming

Counsel for: Holly Sugar Corp.; Community Memorial Hospital; Richland National Bank; Lower Yellowstone R.E.A.; Montana-Dakota Utility.
Insurance Clients: Royal-Milbank Insurance Co.; Milbank Mutual Insurance Co.; Farmer's Union Insurance Co.; State Farm Insurance Co.; Phico Insurance Co.

For full biographical listings, see the Martindale-Hubbell Law Directory

*STANFORD,** Judith Basin Co. — (Refer to Great Falls)

*SUPERIOR,** Mineral Co. — (Refer to Missoula)

*THOMPSON FALLS,** Sanders Co. — (Refer to Kalispell)

*TOWNSEND,** Broadwater Co. — (Refer to Helena)

*VIRGINIA CITY,** Madison Co. — (Refer to Butte)

*WHITE SULPHUR SPRINGS,** Meagher Co. — (Refer to Helena)

*WIBAUX,** Wibaux Co. — (Refer to Sidney)

*WOLF POINT,** Roosevelt Co. — (Refer to Glasgow)

NEBRASKA

*AINSWORTH,** Brown Co. — (Refer to Valentine)

*ALBION,** Boone Co. — (Refer to Norfolk)

*ALLIANCE,** Box Butte Co.

ALBERT T. REDDISH (AV)

510 Box Butte Avenue, P.O. Box 827, 69301-0827
Telephone: 308-762-1150
Fax: Available Upon Request

Counsel for: Gentry Land Co.
Local Attorneys for: Prudential Life Insurance Co.; Railcar Maintenance Co.; Southwestern Electric Power Co.; Woolrich Woolen Mills, Inc.

For full biographical listings, see the Martindale-Hubbell Law Directory

*ALMA,** Harlan Co. — (Refer to Kearney)

*AUBURN,** Nemaha Co. — (Refer to Beatrice)

*AURORA,** Hamilton Co.

WHITNEY, NEWMAN, MERSCH & OTTO (AV)

Professional Building, P.O. Box 228, 68818
Telephone: 402-694-3161
Fax: 402-694-4426
Henderson, Nebraska Office: 1012 North Main Street.
Telephone: 402-723-4684.

OF COUNSEL

Charles L. Whitney

MEMBERS OF FIRM

John W. Newman (1917-1981) William L. Mersch
Timothy J. Otto

Representative Clients: Aurora Dental Clinic, P.C.; Wortman Enterprises; Henderson Telephone Co.; Doctors Medical Services; Midwest Irrigation Co.; Henderson Irrigation; Aurora Publishing Co.; Aurora Cooperative Elevator Co.

For full biographical listings, see the Martindale-Hubbell Law Directory

*BASSETT,** Rock Co. — (Refer to Valentine)

*BRIDGEPORT,** Morrill Co. — (Refer to Scottsbluff)

*BROKEN BOW,** Custer Co.

SCHAPER & STEFFENS (AV)

345 South 10th Avenue, P.O. Box 586, 68822
Telephone: 308-872-6481
Fax: 308-872-6385

MEMBERS OF FIRM

William C. Schaper (1890-1977) Carlos E. Schaper
William Vern Steffens

General Counsel for: Custer Federal Savings & Loan Assn., Broken Bow; United Nebraska Bank, Broken Bow, Nebraska; Security State Bank, Ansley.
Local Counsel for: Federated Mutual Implement and Hardware Insurance Co.; Shield of Shelter Insurance Co.; John Hancock Mutual Life Insurance Co.; Prudential Life Insurance Co.; Massey-Ferguson, Inc.; F.D.I.C.; Resolution Trust Corporation.

For full biographical listings, see the Martindale-Hubbell Law Directory

*BUTTE,** Boyd Co. — (Refer to Valentine)

CAMBRIDGE, Furnas Co.

EISENHART & EISENHART (AV)

Eisenhart Building, P.O. Box 250, 69022
Telephone: 308-697-3737
Fax: 308-697-3631

Hugh W. Eisenhart (Retired) Eric B. Eisenhart

Represent: First National Bank; Cambridge Telephone Co.

*CENTRAL CITY,** Merrick Co. — (Refer to Grand Island)

*CHADRON,** Dawes Co.

BUMP AND BUMP (AV)

P.O. Box 1140, 69337-2358
Telephone: 308-432-4411
Fax: 308-432-4412

MEMBERS OF FIRM

Leo Bump (1900-1958) Bevin B. Bump
Rex C. Nowlan

General Counsel For: City of Chadron; Chadron State College; Chadron Medical Clinic, P.C.; Manning OO Ranches, Inc.; Village of Hemingford.

For full biographical listings, see the Martindale-Hubbell Law Directory

*CHAPPELL,** Deuel Co. — (Refer to Ogallala)

*COLUMBUS,** Platte Co.

GRANT, ROGERS, MAUL & GRANT (AV)

1464 27th Avenue, P.O. Box 455, 68601
Telephone: 402-564-3274
Fax: 402-564-7055
Albion, Nebraska Office: West Highway 92.
Telephone: 402-395-6026.

MEMBERS OF FIRM

Warren G. Albert (1904-1981) Noyes W. Rogers
Vance E. Leininger (Retired) Thomas M. Maul
William H. Grant Clark J. Grant

ASSOCIATES

James M. Dake

Representative Clients: First National Bank and Trust Co.; Travelers Insurance Co.; Nebraska Public Power District; Behlen Manufacturing Co.; Lindsay Mfg. Co.; Farm Credit Services of Omaha; Columbus United Federal Credit Union; Fleischer Mfg. Co.; United Nebraska Bank; Nebraska Electric G & T.

For full biographical listings, see the Martindale-Hubbell Law Directory

CURTIS, Frontier Co. — (Refer to North Platte)

*DAVID CITY,** Butler Co. — (Refer to Columbus)

*FAIRBURY,** Jefferson Co. — (Refer to Beatrice)

*FRANKLIN,** Franklin Co. — (Refer to Kearney)

*FREMONT,** Dodge Co. — (Refer to Omaha)

*FULLERTON,** Nance Co. — (Refer to Columbus)

*GENEVA,** Fillmore Co. — (Refer to York)

*GERING,** Scotts Bluff Co.

HOLTORF, KOVARIK, ELLISON & MATHIS, P.C. (AV)

1715 11th Street, P.O. Box 340, 69341-0340
Telephone: 308-436-5297
FAX: 308-436-2297

Hans J. Holtorf, Jr. (1914-1992) James W. Ellison
Leland K. Kovarik James M. Mathis

Michelle M. Dreibelbis

Representative Clients: Travelers Insurance Co.; State Farm Mutual Auto Insurance Co.; Liberty Mutual Insurance Co.; Farmers Insurance Group; Hawkeye Security Insurance Co.; Aetna Life & Casualty Co.; Casualty Underwriters.
Counsel: North Platte Natural Resources District.
References: First State Bank of Gering; Gering State Bank.

For full biographical listings, see the Martindale-Hubbell Law Directory

*GRAND ISLAND,** Hall Co.

CUNNINGHAM, BLACKBURN, FRANCIS, BROCK & CUNNINGHAM (AV)

222 North Cedar Street, P.O. Box 2280, 68802-2280
Telephone: 308-384-2636
FAX: 308-384-6556

MEMBERS OF FIRM

B. J. Cunningham (1888-1977) William A. Francis
B. J. Cunningham, Jr. Patrick A. Brock
William G. Blackburn John M. Cunningham

Representative Clients: Five Points Bank; Skag-Way Discount Dept. Stores, Inc.; Johnson Cashway Lumber Company of Grand Island; Spelts-Schultz Lumber Co.; City of Wood River Nebraska; Norwest Financial Services; Platte River Whooping Crane Maintenance Trust, Inc.; Catholic Diocese of Grand Island, Nebraska; Toner's Inc. of Grand Island; Ord Equipment, Inc.

SHAMBERG, WOLF, MCDERMOTT & DEPUÉ (AV)

Norwest Bank Building, P.O. Box 460, 68802
Telephone: 308-384-1635; 308-384-0770
Fax: 308-384-1759

MEMBERS OF FIRM

C. E. Cronin (1908-1977) John A. Wolf
James I. Shamberg John B. McDermott
Ronald S. Depué

Attorneys for: Northwestern Public Service; Norwest Bank Nebraska, N.A.; Union Pacific Railroad Co.; Central Platte Natural Resources District;
Representative Clients: Royal Globe Group; The Equitable Life Assurance Society; Federated Mutual Insurance Cos.; Iowa Mutual Insurance Co.; Allstate Insurance Co.; Universal Underwriters Insurance Co.

For full biographical listings, see the Martindale-Hubbell Law Directory

Grand Island—Continued

THE LEGAL PROFESSIONAL CORPORATION OF TRACY & McQUILLAN (AV)

706 West Koenig Street, 68801-6556
Telephone: 308-382-5154
Fax: 308-382-3242

Howard E. Tracy
Michael J. McQuillan

For full biographical listings, see the Martindale-Hubbell Law Directory

*GREELEY,** Greeley Co. — (Refer to Grand Island)

*HARRISON,** Sioux Co. — (Refer to Scottsbluff)

*HARTINGTON,** Cedar Co. — (Refer to Norfolk)

*HEBRON,** Thayer Co. — (Refer to Beatrice)

*HOLDREGE,** Phelps Co. — (Refer to Kearney)

*IMPERIAL,** Chase Co. — (Refer to McCook)

*LEXINGTON,** Dawson Co. — (Refer to Kearney)

*LINCOLN,** Lancaster Co.

BARLOW, JOHNSON, FLODMAN, SUTTER, GUENZEL & ESKE (AV)

1227 Lincoln Mall, P.O. Box 81686, 68501-1686
Telephone: 402-475-4240
Fax: 402-475-0329

MEMBERS OF FIRM

Robert A. Barlow (1921-1986)
Kile W. Johnson
Steven J. Flodman
William D. Sutter
Steven E. Guenzel
James A. Eske

ASSOCIATES

Mark T. Gokie
Tony James Brock

OF COUNSEL

Gene D. Watson

Special Counsel: Nebraska Public Power District.
Representative Clients: Allied Group; Chubb/Pacific Indemnity Group; Citizens State Bank, Polk, Nebraska; Crum & Foster; Federated Rural Electric Insurance Corp.; Runza Drive-Inns of America; United States Fidelity & Guaranty Co.; Viking Insurance Company of Wisconsin.

For full biographical listings, see the Martindale-Hubbell Law Directory

BAYLOR, EVNEN, CURTISS, GRIMIT & WITT (AV)

Suite 1200, 206 South 13th Street, 68508
Telephone: 402-475-1075
Telecopier: 402-475-9515

MEMBERS OF FIRM

F. B. Baylor (1884-1967)
H. B. Evnen (1905-1988)
J. Arthur Curtiss
Robert T. Grimit
Donald R. Witt
M. Douglas Deitchler
Walter E. Zink, II
Randall L. Goyette
Stephen S. Gealy
Scott A. Burcham
Gail S. Perry
Dallas D. Jones
Jill Gradwohl Schroeder

ASSOCIATES

David A. Dudley
John W. Ballew, Jr.
Brenda S. Spilker
David D. Zwart
Thomas B. Wood
Stephanie F. Stacy
Allan E. Wallace

OF COUNSEL

John R. Baylor

Representative Clients: Allstate Insurance Co.; The Employers-Commercial Union Insurance Group; Employers Mutual of Wausau; Continental Insurance Group; Continental National American Group; Farmers Insurance Group; Farmland Insurance; Government Employees Insurance Co.; J. S. Kemper Group; State Farm.

For full biographical listings, see the Martindale-Hubbell Law Directory

CROSBY, GUENZEL, DAVIS, KESSNER & KUESTER (AV)

400 Lincoln Benefit Building, 134 South 13th Street, 68508
Telephone: 402-434-7300
Fax: 402-434-7303

Thomas R. Pansing (1917-1973)

OF COUNSEL

Robert C. Guenzel (Retired)

MEMBERS OF FIRM

Robert B. Crosby
Donn E. Davis
Theodore L. Kessner
William D. Kuester
Steven G. Seglin
Rocky C. Weber
Rick G. Wade

(See Next Column)

ASSOCIATES

Sylvester J. Orsi
Marti J. Brockmeier

Representative Clients: Lincoln Chamber Industrial Development Corporation; Lincoln Catholic Diocese; Nebraska School Activities Association; Norris Public Power District; Lower Platte South Natural Resources District; Nebraska Cooperative Council; Associated General Contractors; Provident Federal Savings Bank; Metromail Corp.; Lincoln Benefit Life Co.

For full biographical listings, see the Martindale-Hubbell Law Directory

DEMARS, GORDON, OLSON, RECKNOR & SHIVELY (AV)

Suite 400 Centre Terrace Building, 1225 L Street, P.O. Box 81607, 68501-1607
Telephone: 402-438-2500
Fax: 402-438-6329

MEMBERS OF FIRM

James J. DeMars
James E. Gordon
William E. Olson, Jr.
John F. Recknor
Robert W. Shively
James C. Zalewski
Danene J. Tushar

ASSOCIATES

Bruce A. Smith

For full biographical listings, see the Martindale-Hubbell Law Directory

ERICKSON & SEDERSTROM, P.C. (AV)

Suite 400, Cornhusker Plaza, 301 South 13th Street, 68508
Telephone: 402-476-1000
Fax: 402-476-6167
Omaha, Nebraska Office: Regency Westpointe, 10330 Regency Parkway Drive.
Telephone: 402-397-2200.
Fax: 402-390-7137.

Charles Thone
Charles D. Humble
Alan M. Wood
Douglas L. Curry
Mark M. Schorr
Linda W. Rohman
David C. Mussman

Representative Clients: California Public Employees Retirement Plan (CALPERS); Chase Manhattan Leasing Co.; Albertson's, Inc.; Baker's Supermarkets, Inc.; Osco Drug, Inc.; Lincoln General Hospital; Martin Luther Home; Lincoln Electric System.

For full biographical listings, see the Martindale-Hubbell Law Directory

JAMES W. HEWITT (AV)

1815 Y Street, P.O. Box 80268, 68501
Telephone: 402-434-1212
FAX: 402-434-1799

Representative Clients: Universal Surety Co.; Inland Insurance Co.; Ready Mixed Concrete Co.; Kerford Limestone Co.; Western Sand and Gravel Co.

For full biographical listings, see the Martindale-Hubbell Law Directory

KNUDSEN, BERKHEIMER, RICHARDSON & ENDACOTT (AV)

1000 NBC Center, 68508
Telephone: 402-475-7011
Facsimile: 402-475-8912
Capitol Office: 1233 Lincoln Mall, Suite 202.
Telephone: 402-434-3399.
Facsimile: 402-434-3390.
Denver, Colorado Office: Suite 510, Alamo Plaza, 1401 - 17th Street.
Telephone: 303-395-4250.
Facsimile: 303-295-4243.

MEMBERS OF FIRM

Wallace A. Richardson
Richard R. Endacott
Robert J. Routh
James A. Snowden
Kenneth C. Stephan
Larry L. Ruth (Resident Capitol Office)
Rodney M. Confer
Richard C. Reier
Robert A. Cannon
Paula J. Metcalf
Terry C. Dougherty
John R. Hoffert
Trev E. Peterson
William L. Tannehill
William J. Mueller (Resident Capitol Office)
David R. Wilson
Shirley K. Williams
Thomas L. Beam (Resident, Denver, Colorado Office)
Cheryl R. Zwart

ASSOCIATES

Douglas J. Peterson
Andrew S. Pollock
Walter J. Downing (Resident, Denver, Colorado Office)
Dean J. Sitzmann
Fredrick T. Martinez (Resident, Denver, Colorado Office)
Jeanelle R. Robson (Not admitted in NE)
Brett W. Berg

OF COUNSEL

Richard A. Knudsen
Richard L. Berkheimer

Representative Clients: Burlington Northern Railroad Company; National Bank of Commerce Trust and Savings Association; Stuart Enterprises; Cooper Foundation; American Express; Dain Bosworth, Inc.

(See Next Column)

KNUDSEN, BERKHEIMER, RICHARDSON & ENDACOTT—*Continued*

Insurance Clients: Aetna Casualty and Surety Co.; General Casualty Company of Wisconsin; The Prudential Insurance Company of America; St. Paul Insurance Co.; United States Fidelity & Guaranty Co.

For full biographical listings, see the Martindale-Hubbell Law Directory

MATTSON, RICKETTS, DAVIES, STEWART & CALKINS (AV)

1401 FirsTier Bank Building, 233 South 13th Street, 68508
Telephone: 402-475-8433
FAX: 475-0105

MEMBERS OF FIRM

C. Russell Mattson (1905-1988) | Lawayne L. Feit
Lewis R. Ricketts (1910-1990) | Randall V. Petersen
Thomas M. Davies | J. L. Spray
Daniel E. Wherry | Reginald Scott Kuhn

ASSOCIATE

Stephen D. Mossman

OF COUNSEL

John W. Stewart

RETIRED PARTNER

Raymond K. Calkins

General Counsel: American Cancer Society, Nebraska Division; Nebraska Wesleyan University; The Tabitha Foundation; The Sunderbruch Corporation, Nebraska; State of Nebraska Real Estate Commission; Security National Bank.
Representative Clients: Texaco, Inc.; American Combined Insurance Company; Old Republic Surety Company; Commercial State Bank, Clay Center, Nebraska.

For full biographical listings, see the Martindale-Hubbell Law Directory

WOODS & AITKEN (AV)

Suite 1500, 206 South 13th Street, 68508
Telephone: 402-474-0321
FAX: 402-474-5777

MEMBERS OF FIRM

Frank H. Woods (1868-1952) | Edward H. Tricker
Thomas C. Woods (1895-1958) | Gary B. Schneider
William I. Aitken (1896-1978) | Wm. Lee Merritt
Philip M. Aitken | Joseph H. Badami
Richard W. Smith | Kerry L. Kester
J. Taylor Greer | Victor E. Covalt, III
Richard L. Spangler, Jr. | Tyler J. Sutton
Allen L. Overcash | Robert B. Evnen
Paul M. Schudel | Joel D. Heusinger
Nana G. H. Smith

ASSOCIATES

David A. Hecker | Jennifer J. Strand
Craig C. Dirrim

OF COUNSEL

Bert L. Overcash | John H. Ziegenbein

For full biographical listings, see the Martindale-Hubbell Law Directory

*LOUP CITY,** Sherman Co. — (Refer to Broken Bow)

*MADISON,** Madison Co. — (Refer to Norfolk)

*MC COOK,** Red Willow Co.

COLFER, WOOD, LYONS & WOOD (AV)

124 West C Street, P.O. Box 100, 69001
Telephone: 308-345-2580; 345-5063
FAX: 308-345-2426

MEMBERS OF FIRM

Joseph D. Wood, Jr. | Philip P. Lyons
Paul M. Wood

RETIRED

Thomas F. Colfer

For full biographical listings, see the Martindale-Hubbell Law Directory

HANSON & HANSON (AV)

316 Norris Avenue, 69001
Telephone: 308-345-5120
FAX: 308-345-3812

Fred T. Hanson (1902-1990) | John F. Hanson

Representative Clients: Bank of Indianola; AMFirst Bank of Hayes Center.
References: Bank of Indianola; Mc Cook National Bank.

For full biographical listings, see the Martindale-Hubbell Law Directory

*MINDEN,** Kearney Co. — (Refer to Hastings)

*NEBRASKA CITY,** Otoe Co. — (Refer to Lincoln)

*NELIGH,** Antelope Co. — (Refer to Norfolk)

NORFOLK, Madison Co.

BROGAN & STAFFORD, P.C. (AV)

1400 North 9th Street, P.O. Box 667, 68702
Telephone: 402-371-9688
Fax: 402-371-2256
Tilden, Nebraska Office:
Telephone: 402-368-5600.

Thomas E. Brogan | Michael T. Brogan
Richard D. Stafford | Timothy E. Brogan

Representative Clients: City of Tilden; The Tilden Bank; General Motors Acceptance Corp.; Norfolk Daily News; Coldwell Banker Dover Realtors; Cornhusker Casualty Co.; The Equitable Life Assurance Society of the United States; Travelers Insurance Co.; United Fire and Casualty Co.; United States Fidelity & Guaranty Co.

For full biographical listings, see the Martindale-Hubbell Law Directory

JEWELL, GATZ, COLLINS, FITZGERALD & DELAY (AV)

105 South 2nd Street, P.O. Box 1367, 68701
Telephone: 402-371-4844
Fax: 402-371-5673

MEMBERS OF FIRM

Daniel D. Jewell | Dennis W. Collins
Clinton J. Gatz | Mark D. Fitzgerald
Thomas H. DeLay

ASSOCIATES

J. Mark Barnett | Michael J. Plambeck
Michele L. Moser | Todd B. Vetter

Insurance Company Clients: Aetna Life & Casualty Group; Employers Mutual of Wausau; St. Paul Insurance Cos.; State Farm Insurance Companies; John Hancock Life Insurance Co.; Travelers Insurance Co.
Local Counsel for: Nucor Corp.; Minnesota Mining and Manufacturing Co.; Federal Land Bank of Omaha; Norwest Bank Nebraska, N.A., Norfolk, Nebraska (Member, Norwest Bancorporation, Minneapolis, Minnesota).

For full biographical listings, see the Martindale-Hubbell Law Directory

*NORTH PLATTE,** Lincoln Co.

BASKINS & ROEDER (AV)

Fourth & Sycamore Streets, P.O. Box 865, 69103-0865
Telephone: 308-532-1136
Fax: 308-532-1137

MEMBERS OF FIRM

C. L. Baskins (1889-1973) | Charles W. Baskins
Robert E. Roeder

General Counsel for: United Nebraska Bank, North Platte, Nebr.; Bank of Paxton, Paxton, Nebr.; Hershey State Bank, Hershey, Nebr.; Village of Hershey, Nebr.; Village of Stapleton, Stapleton, Nebr.
Approved Attorneys for: American Title Insurance Co.; Lawyers Title Insurance Co.

For full biographical listings, see the Martindale-Hubbell Law Directory

KELLEY, SCRITSMIER & BYRNE, P.C. (AV)

221 West Second Street, P.O. Box 1669, 69103-1669
Telephone: 308-532-7110
FAX: 308-534-0248

Donald H. Kelley | Royce E. Norman
Gary L. Scritsmier | Burnell E. Steinmeyer, Jr.
Gary D. Byrne | Larry R. Baumann
James R. McClymont | Tim W. Thompson
Larry A. Todd | James J. Paloucek

Steven P. Vinton | Martin J. Troshynski

Representative Clients: First National Bank and Trust Company of North Platte; Production Credit Association of The Midlands; James E. Simon Co.; State Farm Insurance Cos.; Allied Insurance Services; Ticor Title Insurance Co.; Nebraska Public Power District; The Farm Credit Bank of Omaha; Western Publishing; North Platte Public Schools.

For full biographical listings, see the Martindale-Hubbell Law Directory

MURPHY, PEDERSON, WAITE & WILLIAMS (AV)

112 North Dewey Street, P.O. Box 38, 69103
Telephone: 308-532-2202
Fax: 308-532-2741

MEMBERS OF FIRM

Donald W. Pederson | David W. Pederson
Frank E. Piccolo (1929-1987) | Terrance O. Waite
Milton C. Murphy (1901-1990) | Susan Catherine Williams
Todd R. McWha

Representative Clients: North Platte National Bank; Western Publishing Co.; North Platte Air Authority; North Platte Telegraph; Employers Mutual Insurance Cos.; Federated Insurance Co.; IBP, Inc.; KNOP-TV; Shelter Insurance Co.; Universal Surety Co.

For full biographical listings, see the Martindale-Hubbell Law Directory

*OGALLALA,** Keith Co.

McGinley, Lane, Mueller, O'Donnell & Reynolds, P.C. (AV)

McGinley & Lane Building, 401 North Spruce Street, P.O. Box 119, 69153
Telephone: 308-284-4001
FAX: 308-284-8319

Gerald J. McGinley (1904-1981)
Raymond L. McClory (1904-1993)
William P. Mueller (Retired)
James A. Lane
R. Kevin O'Donnell
Robert B. Reynolds

J. Blake Edwards
Robert S. Harvoy

Representative Clients: Employers-Commercial Union Cos.; State Farm Mutual Insurance Co.; John Hancock Mutual Life Insurance Co.; Hawkeye-Security Insurance Co.; Maryland Casualty Co.; Hartford Insurance Group; Stromberg Carlson Corp.; Adams Bank & Trust, Ogallala, Nebr.

For full biographical listings, see the Martindale-Hubbell Law Directory

*OMAHA,** Douglas Co.

Abrahams, Kaslow & Cassman (AV)

8712 West Dodge Road, Suite 300, 68114
Telephone: 402-392-1250
Telecopier: 402-392-0816

MEMBERS OF FIRM

Ben E. Kaslow (1907-1993)
Frederick S. Cassman
Howard J. Kaslow
Frank F. Pospishil
Ronald K. Parsonage
William H. Coates
John W. Herdzina
Randall C. Hanson
Harvey B. Cooper
R. Craig Fry
Timothy M. Kenny
Terrence P. Maher
Teresa A. Beaufait
Eric H. Lindquist
Sandra L. Maass
Thomas J. Malicki

ASSOCIATES

Aaron D. Weiner
Todd A. Richardson
Michael D. McClellan
Tamara Greunke Brehmer

OF COUNSEL

Milton R. Abrahams

Representative Clients: American National Bank; Data Transmission Network Corp.; First Data Corp.; Lozier Corp. (store fixture manufacturer); Noddle Development Co. (shopping center development); Omaha Steaks International, Inc.; Pamida, Inc. (discount stores); Scoular Grain Co.; Tenaska, Inc. (cogeneration and independent power plants); United Mortgage Corp.

For full biographical listings, see the Martindale-Hubbell Law Directory

Andersen, Berkshire, Lauritsen & Brower (AV)

A Partnership including a Professional Corporation
Suite 200, 8805 Indian Hills Drive, 68114-4070
Telephone: 402-397-0666
Facsimile: 397-4633

Robert K. Andersen (1921-1988)
Robert H. Berkshire
Thomas C. Lauritsen
Sam R. Brower (P.C.)
Richard N. Berkshire
John C. Hewitt
Robert J. Kirby
Thomas M. Houston

ASSOCIATES

Eric L. Nipp
Laurie B. Meyers
Angela L. Burmeister

OF COUNSEL

Dean W. Wallace

Representative Clients: The Chicago Lumber Company of Omaha; Hunt Transportation, Inc.; Great Plains Natural Gas Co.; Durham Resources, Inc.; Johnson Hardware Co.; Bekins Van & Storage Co.; The Swanson Corp.; Paxton & Vierling Steel Co.; May Broadcasting Co.

For full biographical listings, see the Martindale-Hubbell Law Directory

Berens & Tate, P.C. (AV)

Suite 400, 10050 Regency Circle, 68114
Telephone: 402-391-1991
Fax: 402-391-7363

Kelvin C. Berens
Joseph Dreesen
Timothy D. Loudon
Christopher E. Hoyme
Mark E. McQueen
Jerylyn R. Bridgeford
Christopher R. Hedican
Scott S. Moore
Mark A. Fahleson
Michelle Pribil

(See Next Column)

OF COUNSEL

John E. Tate
Donald E. Leonard (1933-1994)

For full biographical listings, see the Martindale-Hubbell Law Directory

Brashear & Ginn (AV)

800 Metropolitan Federal Plaza, 1623 Farnam Street, 68102-2106
Telephone: 402-348-1000; 800-746-4444
Telecopier: 402-348-1111

Kermit A. Brashear
Robert V. Ginn
Julia L. Gold
Mark J. Daly
Craig A. Knickrehm
Richard A. Drews
Mitchell L. Pirnie

Donald J. Straka
Paul J. Halbur
Kermit A. Brashear III
Brad C. Epperly

OF COUNSEL

MaryBeth Frankman

Representative Clients: American International Group, New York, New York; Bay Enterprises, Inc., Los Angeles, California; Crawford & Company, Dallas, Texas; Federal Deposit Insurance Corporation, Washington, D.C.; Green Tree Financial Corp., Sioux Falls, South Dakota; Guild Cooperative, Danville, California; Lutheran Ministry Foundation, Omaha, Nebraska; Omniflight Helicopters, Inc., Dallas, Texas; Scottsdale Insurance Company, Scottsdale, Arizona; TransWood Carriers, Inc., Omaha, Nebraska.

For full biographical listings, see the Martindale-Hubbell Law Directory

Cassem, Tierney, Adams, Gotch & Douglas (AV)

Suite 300, 8805 Indian Hills Drive, 68114
Telephone: 402-390-0300
Telecopier: 402-390-9676

MEMBERS OF FIRM

Edwin Cassem (1902-1980)
Lawrence J. Tierney
Robert K. Adams
Charles F. Gotch
John R. Douglas
Daniel J. Duffy
Theodore J. Stouffer
Michael F. Kinney
Terry J. Grennan
Patrick B. Donahue
Ronald F. Krause
Dennis R. Riekenberg
David A. Blagg
Brien M. Welch
Michael K. Huffer

ASSOCIATES

Michael F. Scahill
Leif D. Erickson
Helarie H. Hollenbeck
Melany S. Chesterman

OF COUNSEL

Edward Shafton

Representative Clients: Aetna Casualty & Surety Co.; Chrysler Corp.; Eli Lilly & Co.; G. D. Searle & Co.; Hartford Accident & Indemnity Co.; Johnson & Johnson; Litigation Management Specialists; Merck & Co., Inc.; Safeco Insurance Co.; Travelers Insurance Co.

For full biographical listings, see the Martindale-Hubbell Law Directory

Dwyer, Pohren, Wood, Heavey, Grimm, Goodall & Lazer (AV)

A Partnership including Professional Corporations
Suite 400, 8712 West Dodge Road, 68114
Telephone: 402-392-0101
Telefax: 402-392-1011

MEMBERS OF FIRM

Robert V. Dwyer, Jr.
Edward F. Pohren
W. Eric Wood (P.C.)
Michael W. Heavey (P.C.)
Andrew E. Grimm
Mark L. Goodall
Michael L. Lazer
James D. Loerts
Lisa A. Sarver
Shawn M. Ilg

Representative Clients: K-Products, Inc.; Deutsche Credit Corp.; Purina Mills, Inc.; Bishop Clarkson Memorial Hospital, Omaha, Nebraska; Nebraska Hospital Association; Strategic Air Command Federal Credit Union; Heller Financial, Inc.; Fordmotor Credit Company; National Medical Enterprises, Inc.; CETAC Technologies, Inc.

For full biographical listings, see the Martindale-Hubbell Law Directory

Erickson & Sederstrom, P.C. (AV)

Regency Westpointe, 10330 Regency Parkway Drive, 68114
Telephone: 402-397-2200
Fax: 402-390-7137
Lincoln, Nebraska Office: Suite 400, Cornhusker Plaza, 301 South 13th Street.
Telephone: 402-476-1000.
Fax: 402-476-6167.

Lewis R. Leigh
Ray R. Simon
Donald H. Erickson
Daniel D. Koukol
Wm. E. Morrow, Jr.
Soren S. Jensen
Daniel B. Kinnamon
Joel Davis

(See Next Column)

ERICKSON & SEDERSTROM P.C.—*Continued*

Virgil K. Johnson
Charles V. Sederstrom, Jr.
Michael C. Washburn
John C. Brownrigg
Thomas J. Culhane
Richard J. Gilloon
Samuel Earle Clark
Gary L. Hoffman
J Russell Derr
Jerald L. Rauterkus
William T. Foley
Mark Peterson
Sherry L. Hubert
Lane D. Edenburn
Leroy D. Peterson

OF COUNSEL

Leo Eisenstatt
Roland J. Santoni
Michael A. Fortune
Anne O. Fortune

Representative Clients: Nebraska State Bank of Omaha; Berkshire Hathaway, Inc.; Bozell, Inc.; IBP, Inc.; Quaker Oats Co.; United A-G Cooperative, Inc.; Immanuel Medical Center; Cornhusker Casualty Co.; Hartford Accident & Indemnity Co.; Mortgage Guaranty Insurance Corp. (MGIC).

For full biographical listings, see the Martindale-Hubbell Law Directory

FRASER, STRYKER, VAUGHN, MEUSEY, OLSON, BOYER & BLOCH, P.C. (AV)

500 Energy Plaza, 409 South 17th Street, 68102
Telephone: 402-341-6000
Telecopier: 402-341-8290

Peter J. Vaughn
Joseph K. Meusey
Stephen G. Olson
John K. Boyer
Steven Bloch
Wayne J. Mark
George C. Rozmarin
James L. Quinlan
Norman H. Wright
Michael L. Schleich
Thomas F. Flaherty
George F. Heiden
Kenneth W. Sharp
Joseph E. Jones
Robert L. Freeman
Robert W. Rieke
Robert F. Rossiter, Jr.
Stephen M. Bruckner
Mary Kay Frank
Michael F. Coyle
Robert M. Yates
Rex A. Rezac

John M. Ryan
Dwight E. Steiner
Lon A. Licata
Lori L. Cleary
Roger L. Shiffermiller
Mark C. Laughlin
Eric A. Anderson
James A. Mullen
Michael J. Mooney
John J. McCarthy

OF COUNSEL

Robert G. Fraser
Hird Stryker
Robert R. Veach

For full biographical listings, see the Martindale-Hubbell Law Directory

HANSEN, ENGLES & LOCHER, P.C. (AV)

800 Exchange Building, 1905 Harney Street, 68102
Telephone: 402-348-0900
Telecopier: 402-348-0904

Melvin C. Hansen, Jr.
Albert M. Engles
Thomas M. Locher
Brian D. Nolan
Donald J. Pavelka, Jr.
Robert Vinson Roach
Dan H. Ketcham
Stephen G. Olson, II

Kevin J. Dostal
Matthew J. Buckley
Scott A. Lautenbaugh
Michael T. Findley
S. Patrick Ingram
Christopher Aupperle
Amy LaFollette
Thomas H. Cellilli, III

For full biographical listings, see the Martindale-Hubbell Law Directory

KATSKEE, HENATSCH & SUING (AV)

10404 Essex Court, Suite 100, 68114
Telephone: 402-391-1697
Fax: 402-391-8932

MEMBERS OF FIRM

Milton A. Katskee
Dean F. Suing
Jerry W. Katskee

ASSOCIATES

Francis T. Belsky
David A. Castello
John B. Henley
Kristine K. Kluck

OF COUNSEL

Harry R. Henatsch

References: Mid-City Bank; FirsTier Bank N.A., Omaha.

For full biographical listings, see the Martindale-Hubbell Law Directory

KENNEDY, HOLLAND, DELACY & SVOBODA (AV)

Kennedy Holland Building, 10306 Regency Parkway Drive, 68114-3743
Telephone: 402-397-0203
Telecopier: 402-397-7824
Council Bluffs, Iowa Office: 119 South Main Street, Suite 150, 51503-9036.
Telephone: 712-323-1600.
Facsimile: 712-323-9251.

(See Next Column)

Robert A. Skochdopole
Thomas R. Burke
C. E. Heaney, Jr.
Lyman L. Larsen
William T. Oakes
William M. Lamson, Jr.
Jeffrey D. Toberer
Robert J. Murray
Robert F. Craig
Jon S. Reid
Daniel P. Chesire
William R. Johnson
Neil B. Danberg, Jr.
Michael J. Dugan
Patricia A. Zieg
Diane C. Sonderegger
Frank M. Schepers
Steven D. Johnson
Karen M. Shuler
Patrick G. Vipond
John M. French
Raymond E. Walden
Mark E. Novotny
Donald L. Erftmier, Jr.
David J. Schmitt
James E. McGill, II
William Robert Settles
Conal L. Hession
Jennifer Wolfe Jerram
Matthew G. Dunning
James W. Ambrose, II
Michael S. Degan
Charles F. Maxwell, III
William J. Bianco
Frederick T. Harris

OF COUNSEL

Frank J. Barrett
Rodney K. Vincent

Representative Clients: FirsTier Bank; E. I. Dupont de Nemours; Eli Lilly and Co., Inc.; Farmers Insurance Group; General Motors Corp.; Volkswagen of America, Inc.; Campbell Soup Co.; Westinghouse Corp.; Uniroyal, Inc.

For full biographical listings, see the Martindale-Hubbell Law Directory

KOLEY, JESSEN, DAUBMAN & RUPIPER, PROFESSIONAL CORPORATION (AV)

One Pacific Place, Suite 800, 1125 South 103 Street, 68124
Telephone: 402-390-9500
Telecopier: 402-390-9005

James L. Koley
Paul C. Jessen
Allen E. Daubman
Arden J. Rupiper (1951-1991)
Mara L. Rasure
Michael M. Hupp
Donald L. Swanson
M. Shaun McGaughey
Michael C. Cox
Jay A. Vankat
Gregory C. Scaglione
Marlon M. Lofgren
Margaret Coyle Hershiser
James J. Theisen, Jr.
Max J. Burbach
Terrance S. DeWald
Kurt F. Tjaden
Michael J. King
Rochelle A. Mullen
Thomas Edward Powell, II
Roberta J. Loberg
David L. Heim

For full biographical listings, see the Martindale-Hubbell Law Directory

KUTAK ROCK (AV)

A Partnership including Professional Corporations
The Omaha Building, 1650 Farnam Street, 68102-2186
Telephone: 402-346-6000
Fax: 402-346-1148
Atlanta, Georgia Office: 4400 Georgia-Pacific Center, 133 Peachtree Street, NE, 30303-1808.
Telephone: 404-222-4600.
Facsimile: 404-222-4654.
Baton Rouge, Louisiana Office: 300 Four United Plaza, 8555 United Plaza Boulevard, 70809-2251.
Telephone: 504-929-8585.
Facsimile: 504-929-8580.
Denver, Colorado Office: Suite 2900, 717 Seventeenth Street, 80202-3329.
Telephone: 303-297-2400.
Facsimile: 303-292-7799.
Kansas City, Missouri Office: United Missouri Bank Building, Third Floor, 9201 Ward Parkway.
Telephone: 816-361-3363.
Telecopier: 816-361-8397.
Little Rock, Arkansas Office: Suite 1770, 124 West Capitol Avenue, 72201-3719.
Telephone: 501-376-9208.
Facsimile: 501-375-3749.
Los Angeles, California Office: Suite 1330, 2049 Century Park East, 90067-3115.
Telephone: 310-785-3900.
Facsimile: 310-785-3999.
New York, New York Office: Seventh Floor, 505 Park Avenue, 10022-1155.
Telephone: 212-752-0800.
Facsimile: 212-752-2281.
Oklahoma City, Oklahoma Office: Suite 475, 6305 Waterford Boulevard, 73118-1116.
Telephone: 405-232-9827.
Facsimile: 405-232-8307.
Phoenix, Arizona Office: 16th Floor, 3300 North Central Avenue, 85012-1984.
Telephone: 602-285-1700.
Facsimile: 602-285-1868.
Pittsburgh, Pennsylvania Office: 1214 Frick Building, 437 Grant Street, 15219-6002.
Telephone: 412-261-6720.
Facsimile: 412-261-6717.

(See Next Column)

KUTAK ROCK, *Omaha—Continued*

Washington, D.C. Office: Suite 1000, 1101 Connecticut Avenue, NW, 20036-4374.
Telephone: 202-828-2400.
Facsimile: 202-828-2488.

OF COUNSEL

Harold L. Rock
Roman L. Hruska
David K. Karnes
William Grodinsky (1894-1985)
Frank L. Burbridge (1903-1988)
Gail E. Burbridge (1909-1993)
Allan Jay Garfinkle
John J. Cavanaugh
Allan L. Grauer
P. Thomas Pogge
Robert M. Slovek
Debbie Sinclair Ruskin

MEMBERS OF FIRM

Robert J. Kutak (1932-1983)
John E. Musselman
Steven S. Huff
George H. Krauss
John J. Wagner
J. Michael Gottschalk
Joe E. Armstrong
David A. Jacobson
Walter L. Griffiths
Michael L. Curry
Katherine A. Carey
Richard C. Anderl
Patricia A. Burdyny
Jerre A. Tritsch
John E. Hubbard
Lauren M. Ronald
Steven W. Seline
Patrick W. Kennison, Jr.
Michael G. Connery
Robert L. Cohen
Denis P. Burke
Kenneth R. Dodds (1949-1986)
Curtis L. Christensen
Patricia Schuett Peterson
Fred Bunker Davis
Sheila Phillips Hawes
Jane Erdenberger
Jo Bass
Wayne B. Henry
William H. McCartney
Dennis L. Holsapple
Judith A. Schweikart
Karilyn E. Kober
Raymond J. Fehringer
Steven P. Amen
Tracy T. Bridges
Richard K. Bonness
Bartholomew L. McLeay
Gregg S. Yeutter
Alissa G. Sandin
Jerry M. Slusky
Jeff A. Anderson
Kathleen M. Quinn
Patrick B. Griffin
Tory M. Bishop
James K. Perkins
Jeffrey T. Wegner
Mark A. Ellis
John L. Petr
Cynthia L. Sanders

ASSOCIATES

Christopher D. Phillips
Bradley J. Nielsen
Joel W. VanderVeen
Mark R. Nethers
Paul M. O'Hanlon
Thomas J. Kenny
Gregory M. Gorski
John Detisch
Kyle L. Hanson
Clare M. Tande
Diana J. Vogt
Bruce A. Wilson
Todd A. Foje
Susan G. O'Hanlon
Marlon A. Polk
Margaret A. Falck
Michelle S. Mapes
Michael J. Mills
Margaret A. Nelson
Michael K. Bydalek
John E. Higgins
Joan C. Jackson-Polk
Dianne E. Pierson
Randal S. Putnam
Emily K. Smith
Thomas D. Waldman
Lisa Y. Roskens
James H. Baird
Bernadette A. Lally
David A. Stage
David A. Weill
John M. Wightman, Jr.
Richard P. Jeffries
Kristine R. Victor

For full biographical listings, see the Martindale-Hubbell Law Directory

LAUGHLIN, PETERSON & LANG (AV)

11306 Davenport Street, 68154
Telephone: 402-330-1900
Fax: 402-330-0936

MEMBERS OF FIRM

Mark L. Laughlin
Robert F. Peterson
James E. Lang

Representative Clients: Andersen Electric Co.; General Electric Capital Corp.; Sears, Roebuck & Co.; Dodge Land Co.; Security Mutual Life Insurance Co. of Lincoln, NE; Century Development Co.

For full biographical listings, see the Martindale-Hubbell Law Directory

MCCORMACK, COONEY, HILLMAN & ELDER (AV)

Suite 650, 7171 Mercy Road, 68106
Telephone: 402-397-8051
FAX: 402-397-2868
Denver, Colorado Office: Dominion Plaza, 600 17th Street, Suite 905 North.
Telephone: 303-825-3305.
Fax: 303-825-3669.

MEMBERS OF FIRM

Robert E. McCormack (1906-1984)
Patrick L. Cooney (1930-1984)
Michael McCormack
Eugene L. Hillman
William J. Elder (Resident, Denver, Colorado Office)
John S. Lingo

(See Next Column)

OF COUNSEL

John R. McCormack

Representative Clients: American Family Insurance Group; Great West Casualty Co.; Horace Mann Insurance Co.; Independent Realty Co.; Upper Missouri Trading Co.
Reference: Norwest Bank, Omaha, Nebraska.

For full biographical listings, see the Martindale-Hubbell Law Directory

MCGILL, GOTSDINER, WORKMAN & LEPP, P.C. (AV)

Suite 500 - First National Plaza, 11404 West Dodge Road, 68154
Telephone: 402-492-9200
Telecopier: 402-492-9222

Stephen T. McGill
R. Thomas Workman
Gary M. Gotsdiner
Robert Lepp
Howard N. Kaplan
Paul D. Kratz
Michael S. Mostek
Paul R. Elofson
Robert J. Kmiecik
George O. Rebensdorf
Keith A. Green
Kevin M. Keegan
Mark A. Pieper
Mary L. Hewitt

OF COUNSEL

Ronald R. Volkmer
G. Michael Fenner

LEGAL SUPPORT PERSONNEL

LEGAL ASSISTANTS

Linda A. Walker

Representative Clients: Norwest Bank Nebraska N.A.; Mutual of Omaha; Nebraska Health Care Assn.; Bethesda Care Centers; Behlen Mfg. Co.; Metz Baking Company.

For full biographical listings, see the Martindale-Hubbell Law Directory

MCGRATH, NORTH, MULLIN & KRATZ, P.C. (AV)

Suite 1400, One Central Park Plaza, 68102
Telephone: 402-341-3070
Telecopy: 402-341-0216
Telex: 797122 MNMKOM

George B. Boland (1897-1975)
Raymond E. McGrath (1905-1986)
Thomas A. Walsh (1920-1972)
John A. O'Malley (1914-1990)
John E. North
Dean G. Kratz
Robert D. Mullin, Sr.
David L. Hefflinger
Richard L. Gordon
Bruce C. Rohde
James P. Fitzgerald
Leo A. Knowles
Terrence D. O'Hare
John F. Thomas
Jeffrey J. Pirruccello
John P. Passarelli
Lee H. Hamann
Randal M. Limbeck
Mark F. Enenbach
Roger J. Miller
Timothy J. Pugh
Robert D. Mullin, Jr.
James D. Wegner
Thomas C. McGowan
John E. North, Jr.
A. Stevenson Bogue
William F. Hargens
Roger W. Wells
Robert J. Bothe
Edward G. Warin
J. Terry Macnamara
Michael G. Mullin
Nicholas K. Niemann
Pamela K. Black
Patrick J. Barrett
Steven P. Case
James G. Powers
Barbara Jark Goodbarn
Ronald L. Comes
Gary F. Wence
David G. Anderson
David H. Roe
Robert G. Dailey
Douglas E. Quinn
J. Scott Paul
James J. Frost
Guy Lawson
John A. Andreasen
Martel J. Bundy
Sandra D. Morar
David C. Nelson
James J. Niemeier
Keith P. Larsen
Patrick C. Stephenson
Patrick E. Brookhouser, Jr.
Daniel C. Pape
Michael J. Weaver, Jr.
Ronald G. Fleming
James M. Sulentic
Daniel G. Jarlenski, Jr.
Thomas J. Kelley
Terry A. Bauman
John J. Schirger
Matthew W. McGrory
W. Gregory O'Kief
Patrick J. Straka
Aaron A. Clark
Jean M. Connolly
Kristin N. Schelwat

OF COUNSEL

Donald B. da Parma
David J. Nielsen
Rodney Shkolnick
Daniel J. Monen, Jr.

General Counsel for: ConAgra, Inc.; InaCom Corp.; Omaha Airport Authority; Physicians Mutual Insurance Co.; Valmont Industries.
Representative Clients: Ag America FCB; Ag Processing, Inc.; Dow Chemical.
Insurance Clients: Admiral Insurance Co.; American Family Insurance Group.

For full biographical listings, see the Martindale-Hubbell Law Directory

*O'NEILL,** Holt Co. — (Refer to Norfolk)

*ORD,** Valley Co. — (Refer to Broken Bow)

*OSCEOLA,** Polk Co. — (Refer to Columbus)

OXFORD, Furnas Co. — (Refer to Cambridge)

*PAWNEE CITY,** Pawnee Co. — (Refer to Beatrice)

*PIERCE,** Pierce Co. — (Refer to Norfolk)

*PLATTSMOUTH,** Cass Co. — (Refer to Omaha)

*PONCA,** Dixon Co. — (Refer to Norfolk)

*RED CLOUD,** Webster Co. — (Refer to Hastings)

*ST. PAUL,** Howard Co. — (Refer to Grand Island)

*SCHUYLER,** Colfax Co. — (Refer to Columbus)

SCOTTSBLUFF, Scotts Bluff Co.

SIMMONS, OLSEN, EDIGER AND SELZER, P.C. (AV)

Professional and Business Center, 1502 Second Avenue, P.O. Box 1949, 69361
Telephone: 308-632-3811
Fax: 308-635-0907

Howard P. Olsen, Jr. — Rick L. Ediger
John F. Simmons — John A. Selzer
Steven W. Olsen

Jeffrey L. Hansen — James M. Worden

OF COUNSEL

Robert G. Simmons, Jr.

Representative Clients: FirsTier Bank, Scottsbluff and Gering, Nebraska; First State Bank; Continental Western Insurance Co.; Allied Insurance Group; John Deere Credit Corporation; Navistar Financial Corporation; Farm Credit Services; Security Pacific Finance Corporation; City of Scottsbluff; The Travelers Companies.

For full biographical listings, see the Martindale-Hubbell Law Directory

VAN STEENBERG, CHALOUPKA, MULLIN, HOLYOKE, PAHLKE, SMITH, SNYDER & HOFMEISTER, P.C. (AV)

1904 1st Avenue, P.O. Box 1204, 69363-1204
Telephone: 308-635-3161
Telecopier: 308-632-3128

Robert Paul Chaloupka — Robert G. Pahlke
Robert W. Mullin — Steven C. Smith
Thomas T. Holyoke — Paul W. Snyder
Paul E. Hofmeister

Tylor J. Petitt — David B. Eubanks

OF COUNSEL

Richard M. Van Steenberg

For full biographical listings, see the Martindale-Hubbell Law Directory

*SEWARD,** Seward Co. — (Refer to Lincoln)

*SIDNEY,** Cheyenne Co.

MARTIN, MATTOON, MATZKE & MATTOON (AV)

907 Jackson Street, P.O. Box 316, 69162
Telephone: 308-254-5595

MEMBERS OF FIRM

Paul L. Martin (1891-1985) — Gerald E. Matzke
Frank J. Mattoon — Steven F. Mattoon

ASSOCIATES

J. Todd Weber

Local Counsel for: American National Bank; Cabela's, Inc.; Sidney & Lowe Railroad, Inc.; Burlington-Northern Inc.; General Motors; Pfizer Inc.
Representative Clients: Exxon Corp.; Platte Pipeline Co.; Hartford Insurance Group; K-N Energy.

For full biographical listings, see the Martindale-Hubbell Law Directory

*STANTON,** Stanton Co. — (Refer to Norfolk)

SUPERIOR, Nuckolls Co. — (Refer to Hastings)

*TECUMSEH,** Johnson Co. — (Refer to Beatrice)

*TEKAMAH,** Burt Co. — (Refer to West Point)

*VALENTINE,** Cherry Co.

QUIGLEY, DILL & QUIGLEY (AV)

229 North Main Street, 69201
Telephone: 402-376-3001; 376-3002
FAX: 402-376-1422

MEMBERS OF FIRM

William S. Dill — William Byron Quigley

(See Next Column)

OF COUNSEL

William B. Quigley

Reference: The Abbott Bank - Valentine.

For full biographical listings, see the Martindale-Hubbell Law Directory

*WAHOO,** Saunders Co. — (Refer to Omaha)

*WEST POINT,** Cuming Co.

MOODIE & MOODIE (AV)

Moodie Building, P.O. Box 15, 68788
Telephone: 402-372-5436
Fax: Available upon request

MEMBERS OF FIRM

P. M. Moodie — Robert D. Moodie

Representative Clients: Farmers & Merchants National Bank; First National Bank; Cuming County Public Power District; United States Fidelity and Guaranty Co.; State Farm Mutual Insurance Cos.; General Insurance Co. of America; The Prudential Insurance Co. of America; Charter West National Bank, West Point, Nebr.

For full biographical listings, see the Martindale-Hubbell Law Directory

*YORK,** York Co.

ANGLE, MURPHY, VALENTINO & CAMPBELL, P.C. (AV)

Suite 200 York State Bank Building, 68467
Telephone: 402-362-7725
FAX: 402-362-3875

Wallace W. Angle — Vincent Valentino
Michael J. Murphy — Charles William Campbell

Representative Clients: York State Bank & Trust Co.; County of York; City of York; State Troopers Association of Nebraska; E & O Professionals Underwriting Administrators.

For full biographical listings, see the Martindale-Hubbell Law Directory

NEVADA

*CARSON CITY,** (Independent City)

ALLISON, MACKENZIE, HARTMAN, SOUMBENIOTIS & RUSSELL, LTD. (AV)

402 North Division Street, P.O. Box 646, 89702
Telephone: 702-882-0202
Telecopier: 702-882-7918

George V. Allison
Andrew MacKenzie
Mike Soumbeniotis
James T. Russell
Mike Pavlakis
Joan C. Wright
Patrick V. Fagan
Karen A. Peterson
Mark E. Amodei

Stephen D. Hartman
Michael A. Pintar
Roy L. Farrow
James R. Cavilia
Audrey P. Damonte
Christopher MacKenzie

Representative Clients: Carson City Nugget Casino; Carson City School District; Carsonite International; Contel of California, Inc.; Frehner Trucking Services Conrad H. Hilton Foundation; Nevada Geothermal Council, Inc.; Public Employees Retirement System of Nevada (Mortgage and Real Estate); The Ridge Tahoe; Rockwell International Corp.; United States Fidelity of Guaranty Co.

For full biographical listings, see the Martindale-Hubbell Law Directory

SCARPELLO & ALLING, LTD. A PROFESSIONAL CORPORATION (AV)

Formerly Manoukian, Scarpello & Alling, Ltd., A Professional Corporation
Bank of America Center Suite 300, 600 East William Street, 89701
Telephone: 702-882-4577
FAX: 702-882-0810
Stateline (Lake Tahoe), Nevada Office: Kingsbury Square, Suite 2000. P.O. Box 3390.
Telephone: 702-588-6676.
Fax: 702-588-4970.

Fred V. Scarpello (Resident)
Ronald D. Alling (Resident, Stateline-Lake Tahoe Office)
W. F. "Bill" Huss (Resident)
Richard Glasson (Resident, Stateline-Lake Tahoe Office)
Jeff E. Parker (Resident)

Chris D. Nichols (Resident, Stateline-Lake Tahoe Office)
James R. Hales (Resident)
Peter P. Adamco (Resident, Stateline-Lake Tahoe Office)
Richard A. Oshinski
David R. Cochran (Resident, Stateline-Lake Tahoe Office)

Representative Clients: Western Title Company, Inc. (formerly Lawyers Title Insurance Corp.); General Electric Credit Corp.; El Dorado Savings Bank; Caesars Tahoe Hotel & Casino (Lake Tahoe); Harvey's Resort Hotel & Casino (Lake Tahoe); Blue Cross and Blue Shield of Nevada; Lift Engineering & Manufacturing Co.; Heavenly Valley Ski Resort; Bruce Industries; Nevada Occupational Safety and Health Review Board (OSHA).

For full biographical listings, see the Martindale-Hubbell Law Directory

*ELKO,** Elko Co.

LAW OFFICES GOICOECHEA & DI GRAZIA, LTD. A PROFESSIONAL CORPORATION (AV)

In Association with
Vaughan & Hull, Ltd.
A Professional Corporation
P.O. Box 1358, 89803
Telephone: 702-738-8091
Fax: 702-738-4220

Robert B. Goicoechea
Gary E. Di Grazia

Thomas J. Coyle, Jr.

Representative Clients: Independence Minning Co., Inc.; Alpark Petroleum, Inc.; Nevada Bank & Trust; Metropolitan Life Ins.

For full biographical listings, see the Martindale-Hubbell Law Directory

PUCCINELLI & PUCCINELLI (AV)

700 Idaho Street, 89801
Telephone: 702-738-7293
FAX: 702-738-0454
Mailing Address: P.O. Box 530, 89803

MEMBERS OF FIRM

Leo J. Puccinelli
Andrew J. Puccinelli

(See Next Column)

John A. Collier

Representative Clients: Credit Bureau of Elko County; First Interstate Bank of Nevada.
References: First Interstate Bank of Nevada, N.A.; Bank of America.

For full biographical listings, see the Martindale-Hubbell Law Directory

LAW OFFICES VAUGHAN & HULL, LTD. A PROFESSIONAL CORPORATION (AV)

In Association with
Goicoechea & Di Grazia, Ltd.
A Professional Corporation
530 Idaho Street, P.O. Box 1420, 89803
Telephone: 702-738-4031
Fax: 702-738-4036

Robert O. Vaughan
Jack E. Hull

Representative Clients: Ellison Ranching Co.; Stockmen's Hotel, Inc.; George Gund III; Metropolitan Life Insurance Co.; Wells Rural Electric Co.
Reference: First Interstate Bank of Nevada, N.A., (Elko Main Branch).

For full biographical listings, see the Martindale-Hubbell Law Directory

WILSON AND BARROWS, LTD. (AV)

442 Court Street, P.O. Box 389, 89801
Telephone: 702-738-7271
FAX: 702-738-5041

Stewart R. Wilson
Richard G. Barrows

OF COUNSEL

Orville R. Wilson

Representative Clients: Petan Company of Nevada, Inc. (Cattle); Idaho Power Co.; Upper Humbolt Water Users Assn.; Salmon River Cattlemen's Assn.; El Aero Services, Inc.; Red Lion Casino; Club 93 Casino; Elko County School District; Casino Express Airlines.

For full biographical listings, see the Martindale-Hubbell Law Directory

*ELY,** White Pine Co. — (Refer to Elko)

*LAS VEGAS,** Clark Co.

BECKLEY, SINGLETON, DE LANOY, JEMISON & LIST, CHARTERED, A PROFESSIONAL LAW CORPORATION (AV)

530 Las Vegas Boulevard South, 89101
Telephone: 702-385-3373
Telecopier: 702-385-9447
Reno, Nevada Office: 100 West Liberty Street, Suite 700.
Telephone: 702-323-8866.
Telecopier: 702-323-5523.

W. Bruce Beckley (1915-1986)
René C. Arceneaux (1947-1990)
Rex A. Jemison
Mark C. Scott, Jr.
J. Mitchell Cobeaga
Bruce A. Leslie
Daniel F. Polsenberg
Robert Aaron Callaway (Resident, Reno Office)
Carol Davis Zucker
Elizabeth Goff Gonzalez
Randal A. De Shazer
Philip M. Hymanson
Norman Patrick Flanagan, III (Resident, Reno Office)
J. Kenneth Creighton (Resident, Reno Office)

Layne T. Rushforth
Tamela L. Kahle
Paul A. Acker
Kwasi Nyamekye
James L. Edwards
Todd N. Nelson
Imanuel B. Arin
Tracey Brice Howard
Ike Lawrence Epstein
Darin R. Savage
Naomi R. Arin

OF COUNSEL

William Singleton
Jack C. Cherry
Drake De Lanoy

For full biographical listings, see the Martindale-Hubbell Law Directory

CROCKETT & MYERS, LTD. A PROFESSIONAL CORPORATION (AV)

700 South Third Street, 89101
Telephone: 702-382-6711
Fax: 702-384-8102

J. R. Crockett, Jr.
Richard W. Myers
James V. Lavelle III
Eleissa C. Lavelle
Michael P. Villani

Laura E. Wunsch Stubberud

Reference: Sun State Bank.

For full biographical listings, see the Martindale-Hubbell Law Directory

Las Vegas—Continued

DEANER, DEANER, SCANN, CURTAS & MALAN (AV)

Suite 300, 720 South Fourth Street, 89101
Telephone: 702-382-6911
Fax: 702-386-6048

MEMBERS OF FIRM

Charles W. Deaner
J. Douglas Deaner (1944-1990)
Susan Williams Scann
John A. Curtas
Douglas R. Malan
Steven J. Mack

Representative Client: California Federal Bank.
Reference: Nevada State Bank.

For full biographical listings, see the Martindale-Hubbell Law Directory

GOOLD, PATTERSON, DEVORE & RONDEAU (AV)

905 Bank of America Plaza, 300 South Fourth Street, 89101
Telephone: 702-386-0038
Telecopier: 702-385-2484

Barry Stephen Goold
Jeffrey D. Patterson
Thomas J. DeVore
Thomas Rondeau

ASSOCIATES

Wilbur M. Roadhouse
Bryan K. Day
Kathryn S. Wonders

Representative Clients: Gateway Development Group; Hanshaw Partnership; Jack Tarr Development; Meridian Point Properties, Inc.; NationsBank; Pacific Cellular; Plaster Development Co.; RS Development; U.S.A. Capital Land Fund.
Reference: Bank of America.

For full biographical listings, see the Martindale-Hubbell Law Directory

HALE, LANE, PEEK, DENNISON AND HOWARD (AV)

Suite 800, Nevada Financial Center, 2300 West Sahara Avenue, Box 8, 89102
Telephone: 702-362-5118
Fax: 702-365-6940
Reno, Nevada Office: Porsche Building, 100 West Liberty Street, Tenth Floor, P.O. Box 3237.
Telephone: 702-786-7900.
Telefax: 702-786-6179.

MEMBERS OF FIRM

Edward Everett Hale (1929-1993)
Steve Lane
J. Stephen Peek
Karen D. Dennison
R. Craig Howard
Stephen V. Novacek
Richard L. Elmore
Marilyn L. Skender
Lenard E. Schwartzer
Alex J. Flangas
Donald L. Christensen
William C. Davis, Jr.
Robert D. Martin
Patricia J. Curtis

ASSOCIATES

Tracy L. Chase
I. Scott Bogatz
James L. Kelly
Jeremy J. Nork
Georganne W. Bradley
Kimberly A. Chatlin
J. Robert Parke
Shannon J. Flake

OF COUNSEL

Gary B. Gelfand

Representative Clients: Lenders: Bank of America Nevada; U.S. Bank of Nevada. Title Companies: Chicago Title Insurance Co. Shopping Centers: Moana West Shopping Center. Construction and Development: Trammell Crow Co.; Caughlin Ranch; McKenzie Construction, Inc.; Western Water Development Co.; Lake at Las Vegas Joint Venture.

For full biographical listings, see the Martindale-Hubbell Law Directory

HILBRECHT & ASSOCIATES, CHARTERED (AV)

723 South Casino Center Boulevard, 89101-6716
Telephone: 702-384-1036
Telefax: 702-384-2LAW

Norman Ty Hilbrecht

Morgan Drew Davis
Eric A. Daly (Not admitted in NV)

Representative Clients: Bell Trans; Bell United Insurance; Bristol-Myers Squibb; Calzona Tankways; Coldwell Banker; Desert Chrysler-Plymouth; Enstrom Helicopter Co.; Paul Revere Insurance; United Companies.
Reference: American Bank of Commerce.

For full biographical listings, see the Martindale-Hubbell Law Directory

JOLLEY, URGA, WIRTH & WOODBURY (AV)

Suite 800 Bank of America Plaza, 300 South Fourth Street, 89101
Telephone: 702-385-5161
Telecopier: 702-382-6814
Boulder City, Nevada Office: Suite 105, 1000 Nevada Highway.
Telephone: 702-293-3674.

(See Next Column)

MEMBERS OF FIRM

R. Gardner Jolley
William R. Urga
Roger A. Wirth
Bruce L. Woodbury
Jay Earl Smith
Stephanie M. Smith
Kathryn Elizabeth Stryker
Mark A. James
Donald E. Brookhyser
J. Douglas Driggs, Jr.

ASSOCIATES

Allen D. Emmel
Troy E. Peyton
Brian E. Holthus
Craig M. Murphy
John T. Steffen
Elissa F. Cadish
Mark J. Wenker
Gregory J. Walch
Lee K. Hartman
Mark E. Konrad
Gregory G. Gordon
Laura J. Thalacker
Ronald J. Thompson

Representative Client: First Interstate Bank of Nevada; Nevada State Bank; Chicago Title Insurance Co.; Melvin Simon & Associates, Inc.; General Motors Acceptance Corp.; Toyota Motor Credit Corporation; Owens-Corning Fiberglas Corp.; Champion Home Builders Co.; Circus Circus Casinos, Inc.; Southwest Gas Corp.

For full biographical listings, see the Martindale-Hubbell Law Directory

JONES, JONES, CLOSE & BROWN, CHARTERED (AV)

Suite 700, Bank of America Plaza, 300 South Fourth Street, 89101-6026
Telephone: 702-385-4202
Telecopier: 702-384-2276
Reno, Nevada Office: 290 South Arlington.
Telephone: 702-322-3811.
Telecopier: 702-348-0886.

Clifford A. Jones (Retired)
Herbert M. Jones
Melvin D. Close, Jr.
Joseph W. Brown
Gary R. Goodheart
Michael E. Buckley
Douglas G. Crosby
Richard F. Jost
Charles H. McCrea, Sr.
Janet L. Chubb (Resident, Reno Office)
Douglas M. Cohen
Kirk B. Lenhard
Kevin R. Stolworthy
Stephen M. Rice
Richard F. Holley

Kriston (Kris) T. Ballard
Philip M. Ballif
John W. Field
Gary T. Foremaster
Anthony C. Gordon
Dawn R. Hinman
R. Douglas Kurdziel
Paul A. Lemcke
Kenneth K. Liu
M. Celeste Luce
Michael D. Merchant
Karl L. Nielson
Dennis L. Olson
Renee R. Reuther
Thomas F. Smock
Diana L. Sullivan
John M. Sullivan
Carol L. Wetzel

OF COUNSEL

Thomas A. Thomas

Representative Clients: Bank of America-Nevada; First Interstate Bank of Nevada; Lawyers Title; Chrysler Credit Corporation; Western Acceptance Corporation; Southern Farm Bureau; Life Insurance Company; Federal Deposit Insurance Corporation; Resolution Trust Corporation; Southwest Gas Corporation.

For full biographical listings, see the Martindale-Hubbell Law Directory

JOHN PETER LEE, LTD. (AV)

830 Las Vegas Boulevard South, 89101
Telephone: 702-382-4044
Telecopy: 702-383-9950

John Peter Lee

Barney C. Ales
Nancy L. Allf
Theresa M. Dowling
Paul C. Ray
E. Brent Bryson
Timothy P. Thomas

For full biographical listings, see the Martindale-Hubbell Law Directory

LIONEL SAWYER & COLLINS (AV)

1700 Bank of America Plaza, 300 South Fourth Street, 89101
Telephone: 702-383-8888
Fax: 702-383-8845
Reno, Nevada Office: Suite 1100, Bank of America Plaza, 50 West Liberty Street.
Telephone: 702-788-8666.
Fax: 702-788-8682.

MEMBERS OF FIRM

Samuel S. Lionel
Grant Sawyer
Jeffrey P. Zucker
Paul Hejmanowski
Robert D. Faiss
David N. Frederick
Dennis L. Kennedy
Richard W. Horton (Resident, Reno Office)
Dan C. Bowen (Resident, Reno Office)
Mark A. Solomon
Rodney M. Jean
Evan J. Wallach
Harvey Whittemore (Resident, Reno Office)
Todd M. Touton
David C. Whittemore

(See Next Column)

LIONEL SAWYER & COLLINS, *Las Vegas—Continued*

MEMBERS OF FIRM (Continued)

Cam Ferenbach
Lynda Sue Mabry
Mark H. Goldstein
Anthony N. Cabot
Kirby J. Smith
Paul D. Bancroft (Resident, Reno Office)
Colleen A. Dolan (Resident, Reno Office)
Jennifer A. Smith (Resident, Reno Office)
John R. Bailey
Kristin Burt McMillan
Gary Wayne Duhon (Resident, Reno Office)
Laurel Elizabeth Davis
Dan R. Reaser (Resident, Reno Office)

OF COUNSEL

Robert M. Buckalew
Brian McKay (Resident, Reno Office)
Bert M. Goldwater (Resident)

ASSOCIATES

Jeffrey D. Menicucci (Resident, Reno Office)
Gordon H. Warren
Louis E. Garfinkel
Donald L. Soderberg (Resident, Reno Office)
Deborah L. Earl
Carl D. Savely
Layne J. Butt
Ellen F. Whittemore
Mark Lemmons
Paul E. Larsen
Christopher R. Hooper (Resident, Reno Office)
Suvinder S. Ahluwalia
Madelene C. Amendola (Resident, Reno Office)
Angelia M. Forister
Mark A. McIntire
Mark H. Fiorentino
Jack R. Hanifan
Howard E. Cole
P. Gregory Giordano
Stephen R. Hackett
Robert P. Spretnak
Allen Jay Wilt (Resident, Reno Office)
Elaine S. Guenaga (Resident, Reno Office)
Lynn S. Fulstone
Robert J. Daskas (Resident, Reno Office)
E.A. Rosenfeld
Susan Leigh Myers
Bryan M. Williams
Jeffrey D. Baustert
Michael D. Rawlins
Etta L. Walker (Resident, Reno Office)
Kevin D. Doty
Sandra D. Turner
Daniel Clay McGuire
Morgan Baumgartner (Resident, Reno Office)
Christopher R. Coley (Resident, Reno Office)

Representative Clients: Caesars Palace; Humana, Inc.; General Motors Corporation; Kerr McGee Corporation; Lewis Homes of Nevada; Citicorp; Hilton Hotels Corporation; Sprint/Central Telephone-Nevada; Tropicana Hotel and Country Club.

For full biographical listings, see the Martindale-Hubbell Law Directory

---

MCDONALD, CARANO, WILSON, MCCUNE, BERGIN, FRANKOVICH & HICKS (AV)

Suite 1000, 2300 West Sahara Avenue, 89102
Telephone: 702-873-4100
Telecopier: 702-873-9966
Reno, Nevada Office: 241 Ridge Street.
Telephone: 702-322-0635.
Telecopier: 702-786-9532.

MEMBERS OF FIRM

David W. Huston (Resident)
Thomas R. C. Wilson, II
John J. McCune
Leo P. Bergin, III
John J. Frankovich
Larry R. Hicks
Alvin J. (Bud) Hicks
Robert E. Armstrong
William A. S. Magrath, II
James W. Bradshaw
Lenard T. Ormsby
Deborah E. Schumacher
Sylvia L. Harrison
George F. Ogilvie III (Resident)

ASSOCIATES

Pat Lundvall
Matthew C. Addison
James P. Stefflre
Scott A. Swain (Resident)
Andrew P. Gordon (Resident)
Bryan R. Clark
Shawn Jay Young
Miranda Mai Du

OF COUNSEL

William S. Boyd (Resident)
Charles E. Huff (Resident)

Representative Clients: AT&T Communications of Nevada; Bally Gaming, Inc.; Boomtown, Inc.; Boyd Gaming Corporation; First Interstate Bank of Nevada; Jackpot Enterprises, Inc.; Primadonna Resorts, Inc.; Shaver Construction.

For full biographical listings, see the Martindale-Hubbell Law Directory

---

GEORGE F. OGILVIE (AV)

Fourteenth Floor, 3800 Howard Hughes Parkway, 89109
Telephone: 702-796-5555
FAX: 702-369-2666
(Also of Counsel to Gordon & Silver, LTD.)

For full biographical listings, see the Martindale-Hubbell Law Directory

OSHINS & GIBBONS (AV)

Suite G-46, 501 South Rancho Drive, 89106
Telephone: 702-386-1935
Fax: 702-386-6823
Santa Ana, California Office: Oshins & Inouye, 3 Imperial Promenade, Suite 11 D.
Telephone: 714-850-4828.

MEMBERS OF FIRM

Richard A. Oshins
Mark W. Gibbons

OF COUNSEL

Edward S. Inouye (Not admitted in NV)

For full biographical listings, see the Martindale-Hubbell Law Directory

---

PICO & MITCHELL (AV)

2000 South Eastern Avenue, 89104
Telephone: 702-457-9099
FAX: 702-457-8451

MEMBERS OF FIRM

James F. Pico
Bert O. Mitchell
Christy Brad Escobar

ASSOCIATES

James R. Rosenberger
Gary L. Myers
E. Breen Arntz
Robert W. Cottle
Cory Hilton
Lawrence Davidson
Thomas A. Ericsson
Linda M. Graham

Representative Clients: Home Insurance Co.; State Farm Mutual Insurance Co.; Industrial Indemnity Ins. Co.; Great American Insurance Co.; Argonaut Insurance Cos.; Clark County Medical Society; Rose de Lima Hospital; Fairway Chevrolet; American States Insurance Co.; Hartford Ins.

For full biographical listings, see the Martindale-Hubbell Law Directory

---

*LOVELOCK,** Pershing Co.

BELANGER & PLIMPTON (AV)

1440 Cornell Avenue, P.O. Box 580, 89419
Telephone: 702-273-2631
Fax: 702-273-2278

MEMBERS OF FIRM

Roland W. Belanger
Todd A. Plimpton

Representative Clients: Dravo Corp.; First Interstate Bank of Nevada, Lovelock Office.
Reference: First Interstate Bank of Nevada (Lovelock Office).

For full biographical listings, see the Martindale-Hubbell Law Directory

---

*MINDEN,** Douglas Co. — (Refer to Carson City)

*RENO,** Washoe Co.

BECKLEY, SINGLETON, DE LANOY, JEMISON & LIST, CHARTERED, A PROFESSIONAL LAW CORPORATION (AV)

100 West Liberty Street, Suite 700, 89501
Telephone: 702-323-8866
Telecopier: 702-323-5523
Las Vegas, Nevada Office: 530 Las Vegas Boulevard South.
Telephone: 702-385-3373.
Telecopier: 702-385-9447.

Robert Aaron Callaway (Resident)
Stephen S. Kent (Resident)
Philip M. Hymanson
Norman Patrick Flanagan, III (Resident)
J. Kenneth Creighton (Resident)

Layne T. Rushforth
Lisa E. Anderson (Resident)

OF COUNSEL

Robert F. List (Resident)

For full biographical listings, see the Martindale-Hubbell Law Directory

---

ERICKSON, THORPE & SWAINSTON, LTD. (AV)

601 S. Arlington Avenue, P.O. Box 3559, 89505
Telephone: 702-786-3930
Fax: 702-786-4160

Roger L. Erickson
Donald A. Thorpe
George W. Swainston
William G. Cobb
James L. Lundemo
Gary A. Cardinal
Thomas Peter Beko
John A. Aberasturi

Representative Clients: Albertson's, Inc.; Allstate Insurance Co.; Avis Rent-A-Car System; Chrysler Corp.; Firestone Tire and Rubber Co.; Industrial Indemnity Co.; Airport Authority of Washoe County; Dow Corning; Peppermill Hotel & Casino; Bank of America Nevada.

For full biographical listings, see the Martindale-Hubbell Law Directory

Reno—Continued

Guild, Russell, Gallagher & Fuller, Ltd. (AV)

100 West Liberty, Suite 800, P.O. Box 2838, 89505
Telephone: 702-786-2366
Telecopier: 702-322-9105

Clark J. Guild (1887-1971)
Clark J. Guild, Jr.
C. David Russell
John K. Gallagher
Gary M. Fuller
Craig M. Burkett

OF COUNSEL

Reese H. Taylor, Jr.

Representative Clients: Southwest Gas Corp.; Fred H. Dressler; City of Los Angeles, Department of Water & Power; Metropolitan Water District of Southern California; Plymouth Land and Stock Co.

For full biographical listings, see the Martindale-Hubbell Law Directory

Hale, Lane, Peek, Dennison and Howard (AV)

Porsche Building, 100 West Liberty Street, Tenth Floor, P.O. Box 3237, 89501
Telephone: 702-786-7900
Telefax: 702-786-6179
Las Vegas, Nevada Office: Suite 800, Nevada Financial Center, 2300 West Sahara Avenue, Box 8.
Telephone: 702-362-5118.
Fax: 702-365-6940.

MEMBERS OF FIRM

Edward Everett Hale (1929-1993)
Steve Lane
J. Stephen Peek
Karen D. Dennison
R. Craig Howard
Stephen V. Novacek
Richard L. Elmore
Marilyn L. Skender
Lenard E. Schwartzer
Alex J. Flangas
Donald L. Christensen
William C. Davis, Jr.
Robert D. Martin
Patricia J. Curtis

ASSOCIATES

Tracy L. Chase
I. Scott Bogatz
James L. Kelly
Jeremy J. Nork
Georganne W. Bradley
Kimberly A. Chatlin
J. Robert Parke
Shannon J. Flake

OF COUNSEL

Gary B. Gelfand

Representative Clients: Lenders: Bank of America Nevada; U.S. Bank of Nevada; First Western Bank. Title Companies: Chicago Title Insurance Co. Shopping Centers: Moana West Shopping Center. Construction and Development: Trammell Crow Co.; Caughlin Ranch; McKenzie Construction, Inc.; Western Water Development Co.

For full biographical listings, see the Martindale-Hubbell Law Directory

Jeppson & Lee, A Professional Corporation (AV)

(A Partner with Van Cott, Bagley, Cornwall & McCarthy)
100 West Liberty, Suite 990, 89501
Telephone: 702-333-6800
Facsimile: 702-333-6809
Salt Lake City, Utah Office: Van Cott, Bagley, Cornwall & McCarthy, 50 South Main Street, Suite 1600.
Telephone: 801-532-3333.
Ogden, Utah Office: Van Cott, Bagley, Cornwall & McCarthy, Suite 900, 2404 Washington Boulevard.
Telephone: 801-394-5783.
Park City, Utah Office: Van Cott, Bagley, Cornwall & McCarthy, 314 Main Street, Suite 205.
Telephone: 801-649-3889.

John A. Snow
Roger W. Jeppson
Keith L. Lee

OF COUNSEL

Richard K. Sager
J. Holmes Armstead, Jr. (Not admitted in NV)

Andrew S. Gabriel
Mark G. Simons (Resident, Reno, Nevada Office)
R. Blain Andrus

For full biographical listings, see the Martindale-Hubbell Law Directory

Lionel Sawyer & Collins (AV)

Suite 1100, Bank of America Plaza, 50 West Liberty Street, 89501
Telephone: 702-788-8666
Fax: 702-788-8682
Las Vegas, Nevada Office: 1700 Bank of America Plaza, 300 South Fourth Street.
Telephone: 702-383-8888.
Fax: 702-383-8845.

(*See Next Column*)

MEMBERS OF FIRM

Samuel S. Lionel
Grant Sawyer
Jon R. Collins (1923-1987)
Richard W. Horton (Resident)
Dan C. Bowen (Resident)
Harvey Whittemore (Resident)
Paul D. Bancroft (Resident)
Colleen A. Dolan (Resident)
Jennifer A. Smith (Resident)
Gary Wayne Duhon (Resident)
Dan R. Reaser (Resident)

OF COUNSEL

Brian McKay (Resident)

ASSOCIATES

Jeffrey D. Menicucci (Resident)
Donald L. Soderberg (Resident)
Christopher R. Hooper (Resident)
Madelene C. Amendola (Resident)
Allen Jay Wilt (Resident)
Elaine S. Guenaga (Resident)
Robert J. Daskas (Resident)
Etta L. Walker (Not admitted in NV)
Morgan Baumgartner
Christopher R. Coley

Representative Clients: Caesars Palace; Humana Inc.; General Motors Corporation; Kerr McGee Corporation; Lewis Homes of Nevada; Citicorp; Hilton Hotels Corporation; Sprint/Central Telephone-Nevada; Tropicana Hotel and Country Club.

For full biographical listings, see the Martindale-Hubbell Law Directory

McDonald, Carano, Wilson, McCune, Bergin, Frankovich & Hicks (AV)

241 Ridge Street, 89505
Telephone: 702-322-0635
Telecopier: 702-786-9532
Las Vegas, Nevada Office: Suite 1000, 2300 West Sahara Avenue.
Telephone: 702-873-4100.
Telecopier: 702-873-9966.

MEMBERS OF FIRM

Robert L. McDonald
John J. McCune
Thomas R. C. Wilson, II
Leo P. Bergin, III
John J. Frankovich
Larry R. Hicks
Alvin J. (Bud) Hicks
Robert E. Armstrong
William A. S. Magrath, II
Timothy E. Rowe
James W. Bradshaw
Lenard T. Ormsby
Deborah E. Schumacher
David W. Huston (Resident, Las Vegas Office)
John B. Galvin
Sylvia L. Harrison
George F. Ogilvie III (Resident, Las Vegas Office)

ASSOCIATES

James C. Giudici
Valerie Cooke Skau
Pat Lundvall
Matthew C. Addison
James P. Stefflre
Gerard L. Oskam
Scott A. Swain (Resident, Las Vegas Office)
Andrew P. Gordon (Resident, Las Vegas Office)
Bryan R. Clark (Resident, Las Vegas Office)
David F. Grove
Paul J. Georgeson
S. Jay Young (Resident, Las Vegas Office)
Miranda Mai Du (Resident, Las Vegas Office)

OF COUNSEL

Donald L. Carano
William S. Boyd (Resident, Las Vegas Office)
Charles E. Huff (Resident, Las Vegas Office)

Representative Clients: AT&T Communications of Nevada; Associated General Contractors of America; Eldorado Hotel & Casino; First Interstate Bank of Nevada; Intermountain Federal Land Bank Association; James Hardie (USA), Inc.; Primadonna Resorts, Inc.; Scolari's Warehouse Markets; Shaver Construction; Time Oil Company (Nevada Counsel).

For full biographical listings, see the Martindale-Hubbell Law Directory

Mortimer Sourwine Mousel & Sloane, Ltd. (AV)

333 Marsh Avenue, P.O. Box 460, 89504
Telephone: 702-323-8633
Facsimile: 702-323-8668

Wayne L. Mortimer
Julien G. Sourwine
David L. Mousel
Douglas A. Sloane

Representative Clients: American International Group; Bradford White Corporation; California Casualty; Capital Ford; General Motors Corp.; Holcomb Construction Co.; Martin Iron Works, Inc.; United States Fidelity and Guaranty Co.
Reference: First Interstate Bank of Nevada.

For full biographical listings, see the Martindale-Hubbell Law Directory

Robison, Belaustegui, Robb and Sharp, A Professional Corporation (AV)

71 Washington Street, 89503
Telephone: 702-329-3151
FAX: 702-329-7941

(*See Next Column*)

ROBISON, BELAUSTEGUI, ROBB AND SHARP A PROFESSIONAL CORPORATION, *Reno—Continued*

Kent R. Robison
Thomas L. Belaustegui
Walter Bruce Robb
F. DeArmond Sharp
Keegan Graham Low
Susan Ball Rothe

Barry L. Breslow
Hal Taylor
Brian E. Sandoval
Michelle Marie Erlach

LEGAL SUPPORT PERSONNEL

PARALEGALS

James Stewart
V. Jayne Ferretto

Representative Clients: Great Western Bank; Young Electric Sign Company; Allstate Life Ins. Co.; Pacific Mutual Life Insurance Company; The Equitable Life Assurance Society of the U.S.; John Alden Life Insurance Co.; Circus Circus Enterprises, Inc.; General Star Management Co.; State of Nevada Board of Registered Professional Engineers and Land Surveyors; Red Lion Inns.

For full biographical listings, see the Martindale-Hubbell Law Directory

VARGAS & BARTLETT (AV)

201 West Liberty Street, P.O. Box 281, 89504
Telephone: 702-786-5000
Cable Address: "Varbadix"
Fax: 702-786-1177

MEMBERS OF FIRM

George L. Vargas (1909-1985)
John C. Bartlett (1910-1982)
James P. Logan (1920-1984)
Louis Mead Dixon (1919-1993)
Albert F. Pagni
Frederic R. Starich
John P. Sande, III
William J. Raggio
Phillip W. Bartlett
Scott A. Glogovac
Linda A. Bowman
Michael R. Kealy
C. Thomas Burton, Jr.
Michael P. Lindell
Clinton E. Wooster
Karen M. Ayarbe
J. William Ebert

ASSOCIATES

Jeffrey J. Whitehead
Debra B. Robinson
James G. Sanford
Michael G. Alonso
Stacey A. Upson
Gregory J. Livingston

For full biographical listings, see the Martindale-Hubbell Law Directory

STATELINE, Douglas Co.

SCARPELLO & ALLING, LTD. A PROFESSIONAL CORPORATION (AV)

Formerly Manoukian, Scarpello & Alling, Ltd., A Professional Corporation
Kingsbury Square Suite 2000, P.O. Box 3390 (Lake Tahoe), 89449-3390
Telephone: 702-588-6676
FAX: 702-588-4970
Carson City, Nevada Office: Bank of America Center, Suite 300, 600 East William Street.
Telephone: 702-882-4577.
Fax: 702-882-0810.

Ronald D. Alling (Resident)
Richard Glasson (Resident)

Chris D. Nichols (Resident)
Peter P. Adamco (Resident)
David R. Cochran (Resident)

Representative Clients: Harvey's Resort Hotel & Casino (Lake Tahoe); Western Title Company, Inc. (formerly Lawyers Title Insurance Corp.); El Dorado Savings Bank; Caesars Tahoe Hotel & Casino (Lake Tahoe); Blue Cross and Blue Shield of Nevada; Lift Engineering & Manufacturing Co.; Heavenly Valley Ski Resort; Nevada Occupational Safety and Health Review Board (OSHA); Aetna Surety Co.; Hartford Casualty Insurance Company.

For full biographical listings, see the Martindale-Hubbell Law Directory

*TONOPAH,** Nye Co. — (Refer to Carson City)

*WINNEMUCCA,** Humboldt Co. — (Refer to Elko)

*YERINGTON,** Lyon Co. — (Refer to Carson City)

ZEPHYR COVE, Douglas Co. — (Refer to Carson City)

NEW HAMPSHIRE

BERLIN, Coos Co. — (Refer to Lancaster)

CLAREMONT, Sullivan Co.

Leahy & Denault (AV)

178 Broad Street, P.O. Box 829, 03743
Telephone: 603-543-3185
Fax: 603-543-1514

Raymond V. Denault (1908-1983)
Albert D. Leahy (1903-1994)

MEMBERS OF FIRM

Albert D. Leahy, Jr.
Thomas P. Connair
James G. Feleen

Counsel for: Claremont Savings Bank.
Approved Attorneys for: American Title Insurance Co.; Chicago Title Insurance Co.; Lawyers Title Insurance Corp.; USLIFE Title Insurance Co.; Stewart Title Guaranty Co.
Representative Clients: First Vermont Bank & Trust Co.; Vermont National Bank; Diversified Products, Inc.

For full biographical listings, see the Martindale-Hubbell Law Directory

*CONCORD,** Merrimack Co.

Orr & Reno, Professional Association (AV)

One Eagle Square, P.O. Box 3550, 03302-3550
Telephone: 603-224-2381
Fax: 603-224-2318

Malcolm McLane
Ronald L. Snow
Charles F. Leahy
Richard B. Couser
Neil F. Castaldo
Mary Susan Leahy
William L. Chapman
Howard M. Moffett
James E. Morris
David W. Marshall
John A. Malmberg
Thomas C. Platt, III
Connie L. Rakowsky
Jill K. Blackmer
Cordell A. Johnston
James P. Bassett
Bradford W. Kuster
Mark S. McCue
Charles A. Szypszak
Steven L. Winer
Peter F. Burger
R. James Steiner
Lisa Snow Wade
Megan R. MacMullin
Ellen M. Burger
Susan MacDonald Hatem
Virginia Symmes Sheehan
Jennifer A. Eber
Marcia Hennelly Moran
Molly Ganger
Matthew D. Njaa
Laura E. Tobin
Gayle Morrell Braley
Jonathan A. Charlain
Pamela E. Phelan

OF COUNSEL

Dudley W. Orr
Robert H. Reno

Representative Clients: Beach Aircraft Corporation; Chubb Life America; Fleet Bank; Dartmouth-Hitchcock Medical Center; EnergyNorth, Inc.; National Grange Mutual Co.; New England College; New England Electric System Co.; Newspapers of New England, Inc.; St. Paul's School.

For full biographical listings, see the Martindale-Hubbell Law Directory

Ransmeier & Spellman, Professional Corporation (AV)

One Capitol Street, P.O. Box 600, 03302-0600
Telephone: 603-228-0477
Telecopier: 603-224-2780

Joseph S. Ransmeier
Lawrence E. Spellman
John C. Ransmeier
Dom S. D'Ambruoso
Lawrence S. Smith
Michael Lenehan
Steven E. Hengen
Garry R. Lane
Jeffrey J. Zellers
Timothy E. Britain
Charles P. Bauer

Thomas N. Masland
Harold T. Judd
R. Stevenson Upton
R. Matthew Cairns
Lisa L. Biklen
Carol J. Holahan
John T. Alexander
Paul H. MacDonald
Kristin E. Martin
James B. Godfrey (1909-1992)

For full biographical listings, see the Martindale-Hubbell Law Directory

Sulloway & Hollis (AV)

9 Capitol Street, P.O. Box 1256, 03302-1256
Telephone: 603-224-2341
Fax: 603-224-2557; 226-2404; 226-2405; 228-0787
Laconia, New Hampshire Office: The Belknap Mill, 25 Beacon Street East.
Telephone: 603-528-3190.
Fax: 603-528-3197.

MEMBERS OF FIRM

Frank J. Sulloway (1883-1981)
Franklin Hollis (1904-1980)
Irving H. Soden (1919-1989)
Charles F. Sheridan, Jr.
Martin L. Gross
Michael M. Lonergan
Edward M. Kaplan
Warren C. Nighswander

(See Next Column)

MEMBERS OF FIRM (Continued)

Irvin D. Gordon
Michael P. Lehman
Peter F. Imse
R. Carl Anderson
Robert M. Larsen
John W. Mitchell
Margaret Harrington Nelson
David F. Conley
Eleanor Holmes MacLellan
John M. Sullivan
James O. Barney
James E. Owers
Robert J. Lanney
Jeffrey S. Cohen
Peter T. Beach
Peter Alexander Meyer
John Ray Harrington
Daniel P. Luker

ASSOCIATES

William D. Pandolph
Gregory A. Moffett
Jeanine L. Poole
Seán Mann Dunne
Kimberlee J. Grillo
W. Kirk Abbott
Carol A. Fiore
Philip R. Braley
Douglas D. Byrd
Elizabeth V. Killeen
Richard P. McCaffrey
Edward C. Mosca
Ross W. Weisman
Todd C. Fahey
Kerry M. Casey
Jennifer Shea Moeckel
Ryan K. Stafford

OF COUNSEL

Guy A. Swenson, Jr.
John P. Chandler (Resident at Laconia Office)
Edward B. Hamlin

Representative Clients: Aetna Casualty & Surety Co.; Public Service Company of N. H.; First New Hampshire Bank, N.A.; New Hampshire Savings Bank; Lawyers Title Insurance Corp.; New Hampshire Medical Society.

For full biographical listings, see the Martindale-Hubbell Law Directory

*DOVER,** Strafford Co.

Burns, Bryant, Hinchey, Cox & Rockefeller, P.A. (AV)

Burns Building, 255 Washington Street, P.O. Box 608, 03820
Telephone: 603-742-2332
Fax: 603-749-4970

George T. Hughes (1873-1943)
Stanley M. Burns (1902-1967)
Robert P. Shea (1936-1983)
Paul Richard Cox
Donald R. Bryant (Of Counsel)
Robert E. Hinchey (Of Counsel)
Christine M. Rockefeller
Jennifer Rosenfeld (Not admitted in NH)
Matthew B. Cox

Representative Clients: Metropolitan Life Insurance Co.; Prudential Insurance Company of America; Concord Group Insurance Cos.

For full biographical listings, see the Martindale-Hubbell Law Directory

*EXETER,** Rockingham Co.

Holland, Donovan, Beckett & Hermans, Professional Association (AV)

151 Water Street, P.O. Box 1090, 03833
Telephone: 603-772-5956
Fax: 603-778-1434

John W. Perkins (1902-1973)
Everett P. Holland (1915-1993)
Robert B. Donovan
William H. M. Beckett
Stephen G. Hermans

Ronald G. Sutherland

For full biographical listings, see the Martindale-Hubbell Law Directory

HAMPTON, Rockingham Co.

Casassa and Ryan (AV)

459 Lafayette Road, 03842
Telephone: 603-926-6336
Fax: 603-926-4127

MEMBERS OF FIRM

H. Alfred Casassa
John J. Ryan
Peter J. Saari
Kenneth D. Murphy
Robert A. Casassa

ASSOCIATES

Faye R. Goldberg
Daniel R. Hartley

General Counsel: Foss Manufacturing Company.
Representative Clients: Town of Hampton Falls; Town of North Hampton; Rye Beach Village District; Hampton School District; Susan Conway Enterprises; Clipper Nursing Homes; Wal-Mart Inc.

For full biographical listings, see the Martindale-Hubbell Law Directory

*KEENE,** Cheshire Co.

Bell, Falk & Norton, P.A. (AV)

8 Middle Street, P.O. Box F, 03431
Telephone: 603-352-5950
FAX: 603-352-5930

(See Next Column)

BELL, FALK & NORTON P.A., *Keene—Continued*

Ernest L. Bell, Jr. (1925-1961)
Ernest L. Bell
Arnold R. Falk
John C. Norton

William James Robinson

For full biographical listings, see the Martindale-Hubbell Law Directory

FAULKNER, PLAUT, HANNA, FREUND & WORTHEN, P.C. (AV)

91 Court Street, P.O. Box 527, 03431-0527
Telephone: 603-352-3630
Fax: 603-352-2940

Philip H. Faulkner (1907-1959)
N. Michael Plaut (Retired)
George R. Hanna
George R. Freund, Jr.
Joseph W. Worthen, II
Cynthia L. Worthen

OF COUNSEL

Francis F. Faulkner

Representative Clients: Granite State Bankshares, Inc.; Granite Bank; Savings Bank of Walpole; Nationwide Mutual Insurance Co.; MPB Corp.; Kingsbury Corp.; Travelers Insurance Co.; Peerless Insurance Co.; Prudential Property and Casualty Insurance Co.; The Hitchcock Clinic.

For full biographical listings, see the Martindale-Hubbell Law Directory

*LACONIA,** Belknap Co.

NORMANDIN, CHENEY & O'NEIL (AV)

Normandin Square, 213 Union Avenue, P.O. Box 575, 03247-0575
Telephone: 603-524-4380

MEMBERS OF FIRM

Fortunat Ernest Normandin (1890-1967)
Fortunat A. Normandin (1909-1967)
Thomas Perkins Cheney (1918-1970)
A. Gerard O'Neil
Paul L. Normandin
John D. O'Shea, Jr.
A.G. O'Neil, Jr.
Robert A. Dietz
James F. LaFrance

ASSOCIATES

Duncan J. Farmer
Susanne M. Strong

Counsel for: Laconia Savings Bank; Lakes Region Mental Health Center; Laconia Airport Authority; Community TV Corp.; Central New Hampshire Realty, Inc.; All Metals Industries, Inc.; Lakes Region Anesthesiology, P.A.; Cormier Corp.; Scotia Technology; Vemaline Products.

For full biographical listings, see the Martindale-Hubbell Law Directory

*LANCASTER,** Coos Co.

DONOVAN & DESJARDINS, P.C. (AV)

133 Main Street, P.O. Box 438, 03584
Telephone: 603-788-2525
FAX: 603-788-3942

Paul F. Donovan
Paul D. Desjardins

Representative Clients: Portland Pipeline Corp.; Lancaster National Bank; Greyhound Lines, Inc.; Merchants Mutual Casualty Co.; Lumbermens Mutual Casualty Co.; Metropolitan Life Insurance Co.; Town of Northumberland.

For full biographical listings, see the Martindale-Hubbell Law Directory

LEBANON, Grafton Co.

DASCHBACH, KELLY & COOPER, PROFESSIONAL ASSOCIATION (AV)

8 South Park Street, P.O. Box 191, 03766
Telephone: 603-448-2211

Charles F. Tesreau (1916-1978)
Joseph F. Daschbach
Lawrence A. Kelly
Deborah Jones Cooper

Tim Caldwell

Local Counsel for: Dartmouth College.
Approved Attorneys for: Chicago Title Insurance Co.; First American Title Insurance Co.
References: Ledyard National Bank, Hanover, N.H.; First N H Bank.

For full biographical listings, see the Martindale-Hubbell Law Directory

*MANCHESTER,** Hillsborough Co.

DEVINE, MILLIMET & BRANCH, PROFESSIONAL ASSOCIATION (AV)

111 Amherst Street, P.O. Box 719, 03105
Telephone: 603-669-1000
FAX: 603-669-8547

(See Next Column)

Joseph A. Millimet (Retired)
Matthias J. Reynolds
John S. Holland
E. Donald Dufresne
Joseph M. McDonough, III
Richard E. Galway, Jr.
Paul C. Remus
Andrew D. Dunn
David H. Barnes
George R. Moore
Susan Vercillo Duprey
Donald E. Gardner
Daniel J. Callaghan
Frederick J. Coolbroth
Steven Cohen
Nancy V. Sisemoore
Robert C. Dewhirst
Richard E. Mills
Newton H. Kershaw, Jr.
Laurence W. Getman
James N. Tamposi, Jr.
Karen Solomon McGinley
Stephen J. Schulthess
Donald R. Stacey
Douglas N. Steere
Donald A. Burns
Steven E. Grill
Ovide M. Lamontagne
Thomas Quarles, Jr.
Paul L. Salafia
Robert E. McDaniel
Mark T. Broth
Cynthia J. Larose
Cynthia Andras Satter
Nelson A. Raust
Eric G. Falkenham
Charles T. Giacopelli
Camille H. Di Croce
Richard W. Head
Jon B. Sparkman
Anu R. Mullikin
Ronald D. Ciotti
Melinda S. Gehris
Julie Ann Boyle
Alexander J. Walker, Jr.
Gregory D. H. Jones
James T. Sullivan
Ruth A. Shapiro (Not admitted in NH)
Dyana J. Crahan
Patrick C. McHugh
Christopher R. Goddu
Scott W. Ellison
Stephen H. Faberman
Bret D. Gifford
Marjorie E. Lanier

For full biographical listings, see the Martindale-Hubbell Law Directory

HALE AND DORR (AV)

A Partnership including Professional Corporations
1155 Elm Street, 03101
Telephone: 603-628-7400
Telecopier: 603-627-3880
Washington, D.C. Office: 1455 Pennsylvania Avenue, N.W.
Telephone: 202-942-8400.
Cable Address: "Hafis Wsh."
Telecopier: 202-942-8484.
Boston, Massachusetts Office: 60 State Street.
Telephone: 617-526-6000.
Cable Address: "Hafis."
Telex: 94-0472.
Telecopier: Domestic 617-526-5000; 617-742-9108.

MEMBERS OF FIRM

Richard V. Wiebusch (Resident)
Alexander A. Bernhard (P.C.)
Robert C. Kirsch (Resident)
Jeffrey A. Stein (Resident)
Jude A. Curtis (Resident)
Donald J. Williamson (Resident)

COUNSEL

Jane Cetlin Pickrell (Resident)

ASSOCIATES

Michael G. Bongiorno
W. Scott O'Connell (Resident)

For full biographical listings, see the Martindale-Hubbell Law Directory

MCLANE, GRAF, RAULERSON & MIDDLETON, PROFESSIONAL ASSOCIATION (AV)

City Hall Plaza, 900 Elm Street, P.O. Box 326, 03105
Telephone: 603-625-6464
Telecopier: 603-625-5650
Concord, New Hampshire Office: Bicentennial Square, 15 North Main Street.
Telephone: 603-226-0400.
Portsmouth, New Hampshire Office: 30 Penhallow Street.
Telephone: 603-436-2818.

John R. McLane (1886-1969)
Ralph W. Davis (1890-1951)
John P. Carleton (1899-1977)
Peter Guenther (1931-1986)
Harriet E. Mansfield (1899-1986)
Kenneth F. Graf (1906-1992)
Robert A. Raulerson (1926-1994)
John A. Graf (1935-1994)
Arthur A. Greene, Jr. (Retired)
John R. McLane, Jr.
Jack B. Middleton
Charles A. DeGrandpre (Resident Partner, Portsmouth Office)
James R. Muirhead
Peter B. Rotch
Arthur G. Greene
Robert A. Wells
R. David DePuy
Bruce W. Felmly
James C. Hood
J. Christopher Marshall
Robert E. Jauron
Thomas J. Donovan
Linda Crandall Connell
Wilbur A. Glahn, III
William V. A. Zorn
Gregory H. Smith (Resident Partner, Concord Office)
Richard A. Samuels
Steven V. Camerino
Joseph A. Foster
Connie Boyles Lane
Ralph F. Holmes
Kathleen M. Robinson (Resident Partner, Portsmouth Office)
Michael L. Henry (Resident Partner, Portsmouth Office)
Peter D. Anderson
David Wolowitz (Resident Partner, Portsmouth Office)

(See Next Column)

McLane, Graf, Raulerson & Middleton Professional Association—
Continued

Maria Holland Law
Alice K. Page (Resident, Portsmouth Office)
Thomas W. Hildreth
Michael B. Tule
Kevin M. Leach
Joseph D. Leverone
Michael J. Quinn (Resident, Concord Office)
Christine S. Anderson
Suzanne M. Gorman
Mark C. Rouvalis
Anne M. Edwards
Linda S. Johnson
Steven M. Burke
J. Kirk Trombley (Resident, Portsmouth Office)
James J. Tenn, Jr.
Mark A. Wright
Ellen L. Arnold (Resident, Concord Office)
Peter G. Ness
Byrne J. Decker
Suzanne M. Woodland (Resident, Portsmouth Office)
Daniel G. Russo
John P. Beals
John M. Curran
Deborah F. Morazzi
Barry Needleman (Resident, Concord Office)
Kelly A. Ayotte
Jeffrey Kovalik

OF COUNSEL

Jacqueline L. Killgore

LEGAL SUPPORT PERSONNEL

James E. Karlovich (Managing Director)

Representative Clients: Action Equipment Co., Inc.; Agfa Gavaert, Inc.; BankEast Corp.; Child & Family Services of New Hampshire; EnergyNorth Inc.; Hitchner Manufacturing; Manchester Water Works; New England Telephone & Telegraph Co.; New Hampshire Automobile Dealers Assn.; Shearson, Lehman/American Express, Inc.

For full biographical listings, see the Martindale-Hubbell Law Directory

---

Sheehan Phinney Bass + Green, Professional Association (AV)

Hampshire Plaza, 1000 Elm Street, P.O. Box 3701, 03105-3701
Telephone: 603-668-0300
800-625-SPBG
Concord Telephone: 603-224-5541
Fax: 603-627-8121
Portsmouth, New Hampshire Office: One Harbour Place.
Telephone: 603-433-2111.
Fax: 603-433-3126.

John J. Sheehan (1899-1993)
William L. Phinney (1909-1977)
William S. Green
Kimon S. Zachos
Robert E. Dastin
Alan L. Reische
James E. Higgins
Thomas H. Richards
Jon S. Richardson
W. Michael Dunn
Peter F. Kearns (Resident, Portsmouth, New Hampshire Office)
James Q. Shirley
John E. Peltonen
Robert B. Field, Jr. (Resident, Portsmouth, New Hampshire Office)
William J. Donovan
Bradford E. Cook (President and Managing Director, 1993—)
John D. Colliander (Resident, Portsmouth, New Hampshire Office)
Alan P. Cleveland
Claudia Cords Damon
Edward A. Haffer
Michael C. Harvell (Resident, Portsmouth, New Hampshire Office)
Henry B. Stebbins
Stephen E. Weyl
Nicholas J. Lazos
Thomas J. Flygare
Susan A. Galvin
Peter S. Cowan
Michael S. DeLucia
Suzanne E. Groff (Resident, Portsmouth, New Hampshire Office)
David P. Van Der Beken
David S. Brown (Resident, Portsmouth, New Hampshire Office)
Daniel N. Gregoire
Daniel S. Coolidge
Bruce A. Harwood
James T. Cain
Robert P. Cheney, Jr.
Denise A. Poulos (Resident, Portsmouth, New Hampshire Office)
Douglas G. Verge
David L. Dubrow
Peter W. Leberman
Colleen Lyons
F. Anne Ross
Daniel P. Schwarz (Resident, Portsmouth, New Hampshire Office)
Kenneth A. Viscarello
Vasiliki M. Canotas
Ann Meissner Flood
Michael Jeffrey Drooff
Joseph A. DiBrigida, Jr.
Christopher Cole (Resident, Portsmouth, New Hampshire Office)
Thomas S. Burack
Michael S. Cunningham
Margaret E. Probish
James P. Reidy
Joel T. Brighton
Daniel J. Lynch
Bonnie S. Palmer
Robert R. Lucic
Matthew J. Lapointe
George B. Pressly, Jr.
David W. McGrath
James F. Ogorchock
John J. Tenn
Raquel S. Colby
Thomas M. Closson (Resident, Portsmouth, New Hampshire Office)
Anna Barbara Hantz
Richard P. Hazelton
Priscilla E. Kimball
Ferdinand J. Molak, Jr.
Michael Jay Kasten
Kerry T. Scarlott

(See Next Column)

OF COUNSEL

Perkins Bass
Joseph F. Devan
Katherine M. Hanna

LEGAL SUPPORT PERSONNEL

John E. Cooperider

Representative Clients: Anheuser-Busch, Inc.; Bank of New Hampshire Corp.; The Elliot Hospital of Manchester; First NH Banks, Inc.; Granite State Packing Co.; Moore Business Forms, Inc.; New Hampshire College; New Hampshire Dental Service Corp.; New Hampshire Yankee Electric Corp.; Numerica Financial Corp.

For full biographical listings, see the Martindale-Hubbell Law Directory

---

Wadleigh, Starr, Peters, Dunn & Chiesa (AV)

Formerly Wadleigh, Langdell, Starr, Peters & Dunn
95 Market Street, 03101
Telephone: 603-669-4140
Telecopy: 603-669-6018

OF COUNSEL

William Joseph Starr

MEMBERS OF FIRM

Philip G. Peters
Charles J. Dunn
Theodore Wadleigh
Robert L. Chiesa
William C. Tucker
Eugene M. Van Loan, III
John E. Friberg
James C. Wheat
William S. Gannon
John A. Lassey
Ronald J. Lajoie
Kathleen N. Sullivan
Jeffrey H. Karlin
Donald J. Perrault
Marc R. Scheer
Gregory G. Peters
Robert E. Murphy, Jr.
Dean B. Eggert
Michael R. Mortimer
Neil P. Guion

ASSOCIATES

Kathleen C. Peahl
Richard Thorner
Charles F. Cleary
Peter R. Chiesa
David C. Dunn
Lee R. Allman
Christine Desmarais-Gordon

Representative Clients: Aetna Life Insurance Co.; American Motors Corp.; First Deposit National Bank; Hartford Insurance Co.; John Hancock Mutual Life Insurance Co.; Liberty Mutual Insurance Co.; Metropolitan Life Insurance Co.; St. Paul Insurance Co.; Travelers Insurance Co.

For full biographical listings, see the Martindale-Hubbell Law Directory

---

Wiggin & Nourie, P.A. (AV)

20 Market Street, P.O. Box 808, 03105
Telephone: 603-669-2211
Facsimile: 603-623-8442
Nashua, New Hampshire Office: 146 Main Street.
Telephone: 603-889-2212.
Facsimile: 603-598-8442.

J. Walker Wiggin (Retired)
Paul E. Nourie (1908-1978)
T. William Bigelow (Retired)
Dort S. Bigg
William S. Orcutt
W. Wright Danenbarger
L. Jonathan Ross
John R. Monson
Jeffrey B. Osburn
Benjamin F. Gayman
Gordon A. Rehnborg, Jr.
Douglas R. Chamberlain
Wilfred J. Desmarais
Richard B. McNamara
Gregory A. Holmes
Gary Ellis Hicks
Stephen J. Patterson
James G. Cook (Resident, Nashua Office)
Curtis W. Little, Jr.
Andrew A. Merrill
James W. Donchess
Mark A. Langan
Anthony C. Marts (Resident, Nashua, New Hampshire Office)
Eric P. Bernard
Andrew L. Isaac
Peter E. Hutchins
John E. Lucas
Arnold Rosenblatt
Thomas John Pappas (Resident, Nashua, New Hampshire Office)
Thomas P. Manson (Resident, Nashua, New Hampshire Office)
Dennis T. Ducharme
James W. Latshaw
Gary M. Burt
Debra Dyleski-Najjar (Resident, Nashua Office)
Doreen F. Connor
Scott Ames Ewing
Stephanie A. Bray
Shari M. Jankowski

Andrea Grilli Chatfield (Resident, Nashua Office)
Barbara J. Abbott
John P. Fagan
Steven M. Notinger (Resident, Nashua Office)
Gena Cohen Moses
John B. Kenison, Jr.
Alicia A. Papke
Ellen M. Palange
Edrea M. Grabler
David W. Johnston
Helen E. Holden (Resident, Nashua Office)
Mary B. Hardiman
Richard P. Creedon
Ronald W. Cox, Jr.
Maureen K. Bogue (Resident, Nashua Office)
Barbara J. Hann (Resident, Nashua, New Hampshire Office)
Richard W. Evans

(See Next Column)

WIGGIN & NOURIE P.A., *Manchester—Continued*

LEGAL SUPPORT PERSONNEL

Richard D. M. Strawbridge

Representative Clients: National/Regional Firms: Anheuser-Busch Co.; Exxon Company, U.S.A.

For full biographical listings, see the Martindale-Hubbell Law Directory

*NEWPORT,** Sullivan Co. — (Refer to Claremont)

PORTSMOUTH, Rockingham Co.

SHAINES & MCEACHERN, PROFESSIONAL ASSOCIATION (AV)

25 Maplewood Avenue, P.O. Box 360, 03801
Telephone: 603-436-3110
FAX: 603-436-2993
Kittery, Maine Office: McEachern & Thornhill. 10 Walker Street.
Telephone: 207-439-4881.

Robert A. Shaines
John H. McEachern
Paul McEachern
Duncan A. McEachern (Resident at Kittery, Maine Office)
Gregory D. Robbins
Dan W. Thornhill (Resident at Kittery, Maine Office)
Jonathan M. Flagg
Jonathan S. Springer
Christopher A. Johnson (Resident at Kittery, Maine Office)

Peter V. Doyle
Susannah Colt

Counsel for: Seaward Corporation; Town of Kittery.
Representative Clients: C. H. Sprague; Continental Cablevision; Kittery History & Naval Museum; New England Homes; Tudor Insurance.

For full biographical listings, see the Martindale-Hubbell Law Directory

ROCHESTER, Strafford Co.

COOPER, HALL, WHITTUM AND SHILLABER, P.C. (AV)

76 Wakefield Street, P.O. Box 1200, 03867
Telephone: 603-332-1234; 1-800-339-2958 (in New Hampshire)
Fax: 603-332-5797

Burt R. Cooper (1888-1959)
Richard F. Cooper (1915-1985)
Donald F. Whittum
C. Russell Shillaber
Mark S. Moeller
Daniel J. Harkinson

Carl W. Potvin

SENIOR COUNSEL

Fred W. Hall, Jr.

Representative Clients: Fiduciary Trust Company of New Hampshire; Town of Farmington.

For full biographical listings, see the Martindale-Hubbell Law Directory

NEW JERSEY

ASBURY PARK, Monmouth Co.

CARTON, WITT, ARVANITIS & BARISCILLO (AV)

(Formerly Durand, Ivins & Carton)
4001 Route 66 At Garden State Parkway, P.O. Box 1229, 07712
Telephone: 908-922-9500
Telecopier: 908-922-1625
Manasquan, New Jersey Office: 40 Union Avenue, P.O. Box 367.
Telephones: 908-223-1800; 449-5311.

MEMBERS OF FIRM

J. Gerard Carton
Robert V. Carton
George N. Arvanitis
George A. Bariscillo, Jr.
James D. Carton, III (Manasquan Office)
Thomas F. Heaney, Jr.
John C. Carton (Manasquan Office)
Stephen C. Carton
H. Frank Carpentier
Dana C. Argeris
Martin J. McGreevy
Albert A. Zager
Mark R. Aikins
K. Edward Jacobi
James D. Carton (1868-1943)
Forman T. Bailey (1887-1964)
J. Victor Carton (1900-1982)
Thomas D. Nary (1904-1985)
Robert R. Witt (1921-1988)

ASSOCIATES

David R. Leahy
Suzanne White Ballou (Manasquan Office)
Gary L. Edelson
Susan J. F. Weiss
James D. Carton, IV
Aaron J. Rosenfeld

OF COUNSEL

James D. Carton, Jr.

Attorneys for: New Jersey National Bank; Midlantic National Bank/Merchants; New Jersey Bell Telephone Co.
Local Attorneys for: Travelers Insurance Co.; Aetna Casualty & Surety Co.; New Jersey Manufacturers Insurance Co.; Liberty Mutual; Prudential Insurance Co.; Chubb & Son.

For full biographical listings, see the Martindale-Hubbell Law Directory

ATLANTIC CITY, Atlantic Co.

COOPER PERSKIE APRIL NIEDELMAN WAGENHEIM & LEVENSON, A PROFESSIONAL ASSOCIATION (AV)

1125 Atlantic Avenue, 08401-4891
Telephone: 609-344-3161
FAX: 609-344-0939
Northfield, New Jersey Office: 2111 New Road.
Telephone: 609-383-1300.
FAX: 609-383-1375.
Cherry Hill, New Jersey Office: 1415 Route 70 East, Cherry Hill Plaza, Suite 305.
Telephone: 609-795-9110.
FAX: 609-795-8641.
Wildwood, New Jersey Office: 3200 Pacific Avenue, P.O. Box 333.
Telephone: 609-729-1212.
FAX: 609-522-2544.

James L. Cooper
Lawrence M. Perskie (Retired)
Lewis B. April
Louis Niedelman
Ronald A. Wagenheim
Lloyd D. Levenson
Michael Jacobson (Resident, Northfield Office)
Frank A. Petro
Kenneth D. Wolfe
Charles A. Matison
Alan I. Gould (Resident, Wildwood Office)
Barry D. Cohen
Gerard W. Quinn
Russell L. Lichtenstein
Robert E. Salad
Steven D. Scherzer (Resident, Northfield Office)
Paul Tendler
Susan Petro
Eric A. Browndorf (Resident, Northfield Office)
John F. Collins
Rona Zucker Kaplan
Michael R. Litke

Arthur Korth
Anthony P. Monzo
William J. Kohler
Laura L. McAllister
Christine M. Coté
Christopher M. Baylinson
Scott R. Silverman
Joseph D. Deal (Resident, Cherry Hill Office)
Kevin S. Smith
Geralyn A. Furphy (Resident, Cherry Hill Office)
Pacifico S. Agnellini
James S. Weiss (Resident, Northfield Office)
Alan R. Angelo (Resident, Northfield Office)
Renata D. Lowenbraun
Lisa J. Abramson
Epiphany McGuigan

OF COUNSEL

Emanuel L. Levin
Liane P. Levenson

Representative Clients: Aetna Casualty Assurety Co.; Alexsis, Inc.; Commercial Union General Accident; Hartford Insurance Group; Prudential Insurance Co. of America; Reliance Insurance Co.

For full biographical listings, see the Martindale-Hubbell Law Directory

HORN, GOLDBERG, GORNY, DANIELS, PLACKTER & WEISS, A PROFESSIONAL CORPORATION (AV)

Suite 500 Citicenter Building, 1300 Atlantic Avenue, 08401
Telephone: 609-348-4515
Facsimile: 609-348-6834
Voorhees, New Jersey Office: Laurelwood, Suite 155, 1200 Laurel Oak Road.
Telephone: 609-346-8600.
Facsimile: 609-346-9866.
Philadelphia, Pennsylvania Office: 10th Floor, 230 South Broad Street.
Telephone: 215-732-8300.
Facsimile: 215-732-8368.
Trenton, New Jersey Office: 156 West State Street.
Telephone: 609-396-4500.
Fax: 609-396-9111.

Leonard C. Horn
Jack Gorny
Mark Soifer
A. Michael Barker
David J. Weiss
Nicholas Casiello, Jr.
David S. Lieberman
Michael J. Viscount, Jr.
Jill T. Ojserkis
Robert I. Tuteur
Daniel S. Ojserkis
Howard E. Drucks
Joel M. Fleishman
Howard E. Freed
Kevin J. Thornton
Daniel A. Corey
Howard A. Goldberg
John Walker Daniels
David A. Sacks
Edward R. Knight
Jack Plackter
Marc L. Hurvitz
William M. Honan
Melvyn J. Tarnopol
Timothy M. Crammer
Frederick F. Fitchett, III (At Trenton and Voorhees, New Jersey Offices)
John P. Leon (Resident, Voorhees Office)
Mark R. Sander
L. Patricia Sampoli

Barth F. Aaron
Rudi Grueneberg (Resident, Philadelphia, Pennsylvania Office)
Steven M. Horn
Patrick Madamba, Jr.
Sharon Moran-Pennington
Michele B. Ginieczki
Deborah L. Mason
Steven M. Kessler
Eric M. Wood
Grace Bruther
Sally E. Heckeroth
William J. Downey, III
Maneesha S. Joshi
Kathleen A. Worley
Michael A. Koplowitz
Anne Marie P. Kelley
Kathleen Vella
Steven L. Rothman
Joseph G. Antinori
Ellen M. Nicholson
Nicholas F. Talvacchia
Jodi L. Cohen (Resident, Voorhees, Office)
Joel M. Chipkin
Peter M. Sarkos
Barbara Ayars
Michael S. Affanato
Jill Manuel-Coughlin (Resident, Voorhees Office)
India P. Still
Joseph M. Garemore (Resident, Voorhees Office)
James F. Mogan, III

COUNSEL TO THE FIRM

Herbert Horn

OF COUNSEL

Alfred H. Katzman

Representative Clients: Travelers Insurance Co.; Allstate Insurance Co.; Miss America Pageant; Aetna Casualty & Surety Co.; St. Paul Insurance Company; New Jersey Hotel/Motel Association; Atlantic County Builders Association; Princeton Insurance Company; Harrah's Marina Hotel Casino; Sands Hotel and Casino and Country Club.

For full biographical listings, see the Martindale-Hubbell Law Directory

MCALLISTER, WESTMORELAND, VESPER & SCHWARTZ, A PROFESSIONAL CORPORATION (AV)

Bayport One, Yacht Club Drive, 08232
Telephone: 609-645-1111
Fax: 609-646-2781

Robert N. McAllister
Rudolph C. Westmoreland
Thomas J. Vesper
Mark G. Schwartz
Lars S. Hyberg
Joseph B. White
Dara A. Quattrone

Christine T. Jones
Keith T. Smith
David I Sinderbrand
John A. Talvacchia
Alan A. Arsenis

Representative Clients: National Community Bank; United Services Automobile Assn.; Continental Insurance Co.; U.S. Fidelity & Guaranty Co.; Western Union; Johns-Manville; Shell Oil Co.
Reference: National Community Bank of New Jersey.

For full biographical listings, see the Martindale-Hubbell Law Directory

MCGAHN & FRISS (AV)

26 South Pennsylvania Avenue, P.O. Box 1137, 08404
Telephone: 609-345-3261
Telefax: 609-347-7983
Longport, New Jersey Office: P.O. Box 566, 1600 Atlantic Avenue.
Telephone: 609-823-2635.

(See Next Column)

MCGAHN & FRISS, *Atlantic City—Continued*

MEMBER OF FIRM

Patrick T. McGahn, Jr.

OF COUNSEL

Solomon Friss — Solomon Forman

For full biographical listings, see the Martindale-Hubbell Law Directory

SILLS CUMMIS ZUCKERMAN RADIN TISCHMAN EPSTEIN & GROSS, A PROFESSIONAL CORPORATION (AV)

17 Gordon's Alley, 08401-7406
Telephone: 609-344-2800
Fax: 609-344-7035
Telex: 820630 Sillsbeck Nwk
Newark, New Jersey Office: One Riverfront Plaza.
Telephone: 201-643-7000.
New York, N.Y. Office: 250 Park Avenue.
Telephone: 212-643-7000.

Clive S. Cummis — Noah Bronkesh (Resident)
Michael B. Tischman — Cecil J. Banks
Stanley Tannenbaum — Kenneth F. Oettle
Charles J. Walsh — Philip R. Sellinger
Gerald Span — James D. Toll (Resident)
Alan J. Cohen (Resident)

Eric D. Mann (Resident) — N. Lynne Hughes (Resident)

Representative Clients: Bally's Park Place Hotel & Casino; The Claridge at Park Place, Inc.; Resorts International Hotel, Inc.; Arawak Paving Co.; Cumberland Mutual Fire Insurance Co.; The Press & Sunday Press; Ameritelephone, Inc.; Crestmont Federal Savings.

For full biographical listings, see the Martindale-Hubbell Law Directory

VALORE LAW FIRM, P.C. (AV)

Commerce Building Suite 220, 1200 Atlantic Avenue, 08401
Telephone: 609-348-0588
Telecopier: 609-348-0582
Linwood, New Jersey Office: Linwood Commons, Suite C-4, 2106 New Road.
Telephone: 609-926-8866.
FAX: 609-926-8544.

Carl J. Valore — Jeffrey H. Sutherland
Beverly L. Valore — David R. Castellani
Patrick M. McVeigh

For full biographical listings, see the Martindale-Hubbell Law Directory

BAYONNE, Hudson Co.

FITZPATRICK & WATERMAN (AV)

90 West 40th Street, P.O. Box 1227, 07002
Telephone: 201-339-4000
1-800 BOND LAW
Secaucus, New Jersey Office: 400 Plaza Drive, 07096-3159.
Telephone: 201-865-9100.
Facsimile: 201-865-4805.

Harold F. Fitzpatrick

For full biographical listings, see the Martindale-Hubbell Law Directory

BERNARDSVILLE, Somerset Co.

SHAIN, SCHAFFER & RAFANELLO, A PROFESSIONAL CORPORATION (AV)

150 Morristown Road, 07924
Telephone: 908-953-9300
Fax: 908-953-2969

Joel L. Shain — Jeffrey A. Donner
Marguerite M. Schaffer — Joyce Wilkins Pollison
Richard A. Rafanello — Todd R. Staretz

OF COUNSEL

Elliott L. Katz

For full biographical listings, see the Martindale-Hubbell Law Directory

BORDENTOWN, Burlington Co.

WELLS AND SINGER, P.A. (AV)

6 East Park Street, P.O. Box 226, 08505
Telephone: 609-298-1350
Mount Holly, New Jersey Office: 135 High Street, P.O. Box 100.
Telephone: 609-267-0070.
Robbinsville, New Jersey Office: Bank Plaza, Suite C, 14 Main Street (Rt. 526).
Telephone: 609-587-3434.

(See Next Column)

William H. Wells — Paul Rubin
Jonas Singer — Robin E. Echevarria

Christopher R. Musulin — Deborah J. Merriam
Jennifer Lepow Kaminer

OF COUNSEL

Jeffrey Goldman

Counsel for: Bank of Mid-Jersey; The Bordentown Peoples Savings & Loan Assn.; Church Brick Co.; Ariston Airlines Catering Service, Inc.; Belasco Petroleum, Inc.; Arlene's Travel, Inc.; Walnridge Farms, Inc.; Walnridge Equine Clinic.

For full biographical listings, see the Martindale-Hubbell Law Directory

BRICK, Ocean Co.

STARKEY, KELLY, BLANEY & WHITE (AV)

522 Brick Boulevard, P.O. Box 610, 08723
Telephone: 908-477-1610
Fax: 908-477-2225

MEMBERS OF FIRM

Charles E. Starkey — William V. Kelly
James M. Blaney

ASSOCIATES

Natalie Pouch — Therese A. Nestor
Anthony Mancuso — Robert A. Bauer
Christopher J. Carkhuff

Representative Clients: Hartford Insurance Co.; New Jersey Education Assn.; New Jersey Psychiatric Assn.; Ocean County Utilities Authority; Prudential Property & Casualty Insurance Co.; Hanover Insurance Co.; Westinghouse Corp.; John Hancock Insurance Co.

For full biographical listings, see the Martindale-Hubbell Law Directory

*BRIDGETON,** Cumberland Co.

RITTER, HANFORD AND PRYOR (AV)

55 Fayette Street, P.O. Box 320, 08302
Telephone: 609-451-3030
FAX: 609-453-0911

MEMBERS OF FIRM

Theodore Henry Ritter — Eleanor B. Hanford
Robert J. Pryor

References: Farmers & Merchants National Bank of Bridgeton; United Jersey Bank/South.

For full biographical listings, see the Martindale-Hubbell Law Directory

BRIELLE, Monmouth Co.

KORDES, CLAYTON & AMBROSE, P.A. (AV)

2444 Route 34, P.O. Box 365, 08730
Telephone: 908-528-5557
Fax: 908-223-5191

Henry E. Kordes — Donald R. Ambrose
James H. Clayton — Kevin Georgetti

OF COUNSEL

Thomas F. Kelly — Lawrence Iannaccone

For full biographical listings, see the Martindale-Hubbell Law Directory

BURLINGTON, Burlington Co.

SMITH, GOLDSTEIN & MAGRAM, A PROFESSIONAL CORPORATION (AV)

415 High Street, P.O. Box 603, 08016-0603
Telephone: 609-386-2633
Fax: 609-386-8674

Louis A. Smith — Jeffrey N. Goldstein
Edward J. Magram

Elizabeth D. Berenato

Reference: First Fidelity Bank of South Jersey, Burlington, New Jersey.

For full biographical listings, see the Martindale-Hubbell Law Directory

*CAMDEN,** Camden Co.

BROWN & CONNERY (AV)

518 Market Street, P.O. Box 1449, 08101
Telephone: 609-365-5100
Facsimile: 609-858-4967
Westmont, New Jersey Office: 360 Haddon Avenue. P.O. Box 539.
Telephone: 609-854-8900.

(See Next Column)

BROWN & CONNERY—*Continued*

MEMBERS OF FIRM

Horace G. Brown (1902-1990)
Edward T. Curry (1890-1972)
George Purnell (1896-1979)
J. Lawrence Finlayson (1908-1986)
Howard G. Kulp, Jr. (1906-1987)
Thomas F. Connery, Jr.
William J. Cook
Warren W. Faulk
Steven G. Wolschina
Paul Mainardi
John L. Conroy, Jr.
Dennis P. Blake
Michael J. Vassalotti
John J. Mulderig
William M. Tambussi
Bruce H. Zamost
Mark P. Asselta
Stephen J. DeFeo
Jane A. Lorber

ASSOCIATES

Isabel C. Balboa
Joseph A. Zechman
Michael J. Fagan
Karen A. Peterson
Jeffrey E. Ugoretz
Christine O'Hearn
Christine A. Campbell
Joseph T. Carney

Representative Clients: Delaware River Port Authority; Underwood-Memorial Hospital; Garden State Water Company; Philadelphia Newspapers, Inc.; Port Authority Transit Co.; Resolution Trust Corp.; General Electric; Mercedes-Benz Credit Corp.; American Red Cross; Honeywell, Inc.

For full biographical listings, see the Martindale-Hubbell Law Directory

CHATHAM, Morris Co.

EICHLER, FORGOSH, GOTTILLA AND RUDNICK, A PROFESSIONAL CORPORATION (AV)

97 Main Street, P.O. Box 970, 07928
Telephone: 201-701-0500
Fax: 201-701-0333

Peter A. Forgosh
Lawrence A. Rudnick
Roger R. Gottilla
Douglas A. Kent
Michael P. Turner
Linda K. Connolly

OF COUNSEL

A. Albert Eichler
Edwin N. Gross

Miriam E. Cahn
Gary D. Nissenbaum
Scott A. Zuber
Steven D. Grossman
James A. Dempsey
Craig Macauley

Representative Clients: United Jersey Banks; Midlantic National Bank; First Fidelity Bank, N.A., New Jersey; Universal Automotive Distributors; First Commercial Corporation.

For full biographical listings, see the Martindale-Hubbell Law Directory

CHERRY HILL, Camden Co.

FORKIN, McSHANE & ROTZ, A PROFESSIONAL ASSOCIATION (AV)

750 Kings Highway North, 08034-1581
Telephone: 609-779-8500
Fax: 609-779-8030

Thomas S. Forkin
Joseph Patrick McShane, III
Richard B. Rotz
George W. Stevenson, III

For full biographical listings, see the Martindale-Hubbell Law Directory

JUBANYIK, VARBALOW, TEDESCO, SHAW & SHAFFER (AV)

Commerce Atrium Building, 1701 Route 70 East, P.O. Box 2570, 08034
Telephone: 609-751-8500
Telefax: 609-751-9030
Philadelphia, Pennsylvania Office: The Fidelity Bank Building, 123 Broad Street, Thirteenth Floor.
Telephone: 215-732-8546.

Raymond J. Jubanyik (1910-1985)

MEMBERS OF FIRM

Richard J. Jubanyik
Michael D. Varbalow
Frank V. Tedesco
Barry N. Shaw
Hal Jonathan Shaffer
Arnold L. Bartfeld (Not admitted in NJ; Resident, Philadelphia, Pennsylvania Office)
Vincent D'Elia
Suzette D. Bonfiglio

ASSOCIATES

Francis P. Maneri
Gregg M. Wolff
Catherine M. Ward
Aimee L. Manocchio Nason
Francine G. Raichlen (Not admitted in NJ; Resident, Philadelphia, Pennsylvania Office)
William H. Karp
Sharon Goldin-Didinsky
Dean Stuart Reiche (Not admitted in NJ)

Representative Clients: Fidelity Bank; Continental Bank.

For full biographical listings, see the Martindale-Hubbell Law Directory

McCARTER & ENGLISH (AV)

1810 Chapel Avenue West, 08002
Telephone: 609-662-8444
Telecopier: 609-662-6203
Newark, New Jersey Office: Four Gateway Center, 100 Mulberry Street. P.O. Box 652.
Telephone: 201-622-4444.
Telecopier: 201-624-7070.
Cable Address: "McCarter" Newark.
New York, New York Office: Suite 1519, One World Trade Center.
Telephone: 212-466-9018.
Telecopier: 212-432-6568.
Boca Raton, Florida Office: 2255 Glades Road, Suite 319-A.
Telephone: 407-994-6262.
Telecopier: 407-241-0798.
Wilmington, Delaware Office: Mellon Bank Center, 919 Market Street.
Telephone: 302-654-8010
Telecopier: 302-654-0795

RESIDENT PARTNERS

James F. Hammill
Therese M. Keeley
Nathan A. Schachtman

RESIDENT ASSOCIATES

Mary S. Cook
Carol L. Widemon
David L. DaCosta
Evolea C. Watson
Eric J. Kadish
David A. Cohen
Kimberly Waldron
Patricia M. Nigro

For full biographical listings, see the Martindale-Hubbell Law Directory

MONTANO, SUMMERS, MULLEN, MANUEL, OWENS AND GREGORIO, A PROFESSIONAL CORPORATION (AV)

Two Executive Campus, Suite 400, Route 70 and Cuthbert Boulevard, 08002
Telephone: 609-665-9400
Fax: 609-665-0006
Northfield, New Jersey Office: The Executive Plaza, 2111 New Road, Suite 105.
Telephone: 609-383-8900.
Philadelphia, Pennsylvania Office: 1700 Market Street - Suite 2628.
Telephone: 215-732-3900.

Carl Kisselman (1899-1975)
James A. Mullen, Jr.
G. Wesley Manuel, Jr.
F. Herbert Owens, III
Carl J. Gregorio
Gary L. Jakob
Lawrence D. Lally
Paul F. Gilligan, Jr.
David D. Duffin
Michael G. B. David

Craig W. Summers
Mary C. Brennan
James A. Nolan, Jr.
Alfred J. Quasti, Jr.
Robert H. Ayik
Stephen D. Holtzman (Resident, Northfield Office)
Arthur E. Donnelly, III
Bruce C. Truesdale
Ronald S. Collins, Jr.
Matthew P. Lyons
William J. Rudnik (Resident, Northfield Office)

OF COUNSEL

Arthur Montano
William W. Summers

Local Counsel for: Indemnity Insurance Company of North America; Royal Group; General Motors Corp.
Reference: Midlantic National Bank, Cherry Hill, New Jersey.

For full biographical listings, see the Martindale-Hubbell Law Directory

PARKER, McCAY & CRISCUOLO, P.A. (AV)

Commerce Atrium, Suite 500, 1701 Route 70 East, P.O. Box 1806, 08034
Telephone: 609-424-4300
Telecopier: 609-424-1006
Marlton, New Jersey Office: Suite 401 Three Greentree Center, Route 73 & Greentree Road.
Telephone: 609-596-8900.
Telecopier: 609-596-9631.
Philadelphia, Pennsylvania Office: 3700 Bell Atlantic Tower, 1717 Arch Street.
Telephone: 215-994-5315.
Telecopier: 215-994-3100.

Robert C. Beck

Richard M. Berman
Emmanuel J. Argentieri

Local Counsel for: Aetna Casualty & Surety Co.; U.S. Fidelity & Guaranty Co.; Keystone Insurance Co.; Eagle Dyeing & Finishing Co.; Zurich-American Insurance Co.; Commerce Bank, N.A.; First Fidelity Bank; Midlantic Bank.

For full biographical listings, see the Martindale-Hubbell Law Directory

CLINTON, Hunterdon Co.

GEBHARDT & KIEFER, P.C. (AV)

1318 Route 31 CN 4001, 08809
Telephone: 908-735-5161
Telecopier: 908-735-9351
Bridgewater, New Jersey Office: 1170 Route 22 East.
Telephone: 908-725-5157.

William C. Gebhardt (1884-1929)
W. Reading Gebhardt (1919-1980)
Philip R. Gebhardt (1924-1986)
E. Herbert Kiefer (1933-1988)
Richard Dieterly
James H. Knox
Richard P. Cushing
Mark H. Chazin
William W. Goodwin, Jr.
Sharon H. Moore
Robert C. Ward

Judith A. Kopen
Lori Kopf MacWilliam
Jacob A. Papay, Jr.
Joseph F. Trinity
Patricia A. Colabella
Robert G. Engelhart
Steven P. Gruenberg
Darren J. Leotti
Mark Andrew Saloman
Deborah B. Rosenthal

Representative Clients: Summit Bank; Meridian Bank; United National Bank; American Telephone & Telegraph Co; Atlantic Development and Management Corp.; Republic Steel Corp.; Spectrum Technology Group, Inc.; The Henderson Corp.; Adcock Air Drilling; Republic Financial Services.

For full biographical listings, see the Martindale-Hubbell Law Directory

DENVILLE, Morris Co.

EINHORN, HARRIS, ASCHER & BARBARITO, A PROFESSIONAL CORPORATION (AV)

165 East Main Street, P.O. Box 541, 07834-0541
Telephone: 201-627-7300
FAX: 201-627-5847

Theodore E. B. Einhorn
Peter T. Harris
Michael R. Ascher
Patricia M. Barbarito
Victor B. Matthews
Robert A. Scirocco
Bonnie C. Frost

Michael J. Rowland
David H. Ironson
Ann T. Scucci
Janet Block
Lee Ann McCabe
Brett R. Fielo
Jodi F. Tish

Representative Client: Saint Clare's/Riverside Medical Center, Inc.

For full biographical listings, see the Martindale-Hubbell Law Directory

EATONTOWN, Monmouth Co.

ANSELL ZARO BENNETT & GRIMM, A PROFESSIONAL CORPORATION (AV)

(Formerly Abramoff, Fox, Zaro & Mc Govern and Anschelewitz, Barr & Ansell)
615 Hope Road, Entrance 4B CN One, 07724
Telephone: 908-542-6300
Telecopier: 908-542-7305
Newark, New Jersey Office: The Military Park Building, 60 Park Place.
Telephone: 201-642-1801.
Telecopier: 201-642-0310.

Leon Anschelewitz (1905-1986)
Max M. Barr (1902-1993)
David K. Ansell
Richard B. Ansell
Jerold L. Zaro
John O. Bennett, III
Peter B. Grimm
Robert I. Ansell

Joseph L. Foster
Steven J. Kaplan
Mitchell J. Ansell
Donna L. Maul
Marilyn S. Lance
Jeffrey A. Warsh
Brian B. Smith
Stephanie Markos Hodach
Brian E. Ansell
Joseph H. Orlando
Kevin E. Kennedy
Frederick C. Raffetto
Denise E. Totaro
Allison Ansell Ryan
Carmine R. Villani
Edward J. Ahearn

OF COUNSEL

Gordon N. Litwin (Resident, Newark Office)
Steven J. Denholtz
Milton M. Abramoff

Representative Clients: American Express Bank Ltd.; Midlantic National Bank/Merchants; Central Jersey Bank and Trust Co.; Ocean Independent Bank; K. Hovnanian Cos. (Real Estates Developers).

For full biographical listings, see the Martindale-Hubbell Law Directory

WILENTZ, GOLDMAN & SPITZER, A PROFESSIONAL CORPORATION (AV)

Meridian Center I, Two Industrial Way West, 07724
Telephone: 908-493-1000
Telecopier: 908-493-8387
Woodbridge, New Jersey Office: 90 Woodbridge Center Drive, Suite 900, Box 10, 07095.
Telephone: 908-636-8000.
Telecopier: 908-855-6117.
New York, New York Office: Wall Street Plaza, 88 Pine Street, 9th Floor, 10005.
Telephone: 212-267-3091.
Telecopier: 212-267-3828.

Francis V. Bonello
Peter C. Paras

Noel S. Tonneman

For full biographical listings, see the Martindale-Hubbell Law Directory

*ELIZABETH,** Union Co. — (Refer to Union)

ELMWOOD PARK, Bergen Co.

ANDORA, PALMISANO & GEANEY, A PROFESSIONAL CORPORATION (AV)

303 Molnar Drive, P.O. Box 431, 07407-0431
Telephone: 201-791-0100
Fax: 201-791-8922

Anthony D. Andora
John P. Palmisano
John F. Geaney, Jr.
Vincent A. Siano
Joseph M. Andresini
Patrick J. Spina
Melissa A. Muilenburg
Joseph A. Venti

Representative Client: Interchange State Bank, Saddle Brook, New Jersey.

For full biographical listings, see the Martindale-Hubbell Law Directory

ENGLEWOOD, Bergen Co.

CHAZEN & CHAZEN (AV)

75 Grand Avenue, P.O. Box 470, 07631
Telephone: 201-567-5500
Telefax: 201-567-4282

Bernard Chazen
David K. Chazen

For full biographical listings, see the Martindale-Hubbell Law Directory

*FLEMINGTON,** Hunterdon Co.

LARGE, SCAMMELL & DANZIGER, A PROFESSIONAL CORPORATION (AV)

117 Main Street, 08822
Telephone: 908-782-5313
Fax: 908-782-4816

Robert F. Danziger
C. Gregory Watts
Richard L. Tice
Kenneth J. Skowronek
Joseph H. Mulherin

Christine Naples Little

OF COUNSEL

Edwin K. Large, Jr.
Scott Scammell, II (1918-1984)

Representative Clients: Agway, Inc.; Algonquin Gas Transmission Co.; E. I. duPont; Flemington National Bank and Trust Company; Prestige State Bank; Summit Bank.

For full biographical listings, see the Martindale-Hubbell Law Directory

FLORHAM PARK, Morris Co.

CARLIN, MADDOCK, FAY & CERBONE, P.C. (AV)

25 Vreeland Road, P.O. Box 751, 07932
Telephone: 201-377-3350
Fax: 201-377-5626

John J. Carlin, Jr.
Laurence R. Maddock
Donald J. Fay
Richard R. Cerbone

Arthur G. Warden, III
Paul F. Liebman

For full biographical listings, see the Martindale-Hubbell Law Directory

D'ALESSANDRO & JACOVINO (AV)

147 Columbia Turnpike, 07932
Telephone: 201-966-1910
Fax: 201-966-6774
New York, N.Y. Office: 342 Madison Avenue.
Telephone: 212-608-7500

MEMBERS OF FIRM

Edward G. D'Alessandro
Amedeo C. Jacovino

(See Next Column)

D'ALESSANDRO & JACOVINO—*Continued*

ASSOCIATES

Frederick E. Gerson
Edward G. D'Alessandro, Jr.
Ramona A. Santiago

Reference: Midatlantic Bank.

For full biographical listings, see the Martindale-Hubbell Law Directory

GEDNEY, SEAMAN & HILGENDORFF (AV)

248 Columbia Turnpike, P.O. Box 166, 07932-0166
Telephone: 201-377-9120
Fax: 201-377-9126
Morristown, New Jersey Office: 15 James Street.
Telephone: 201-539-3088.
Fax: 201-539-0163

MEMBERS OF FIRM

Stanley L. Gedney, Jr. (1889-1977)
Hugo A. Hilgendorff, Jr. (1914-1991)
Bradford C. Seaman (1898-1986)
Hugo A. Hilgendorff, III

ASSOCIATES

Peter B. Hilgendorff
George B. Wright

For full biographical listings, see the Martindale-Hubbell Law Directory

HACK, PIRO, O'DAY, MERKLINGER, WALLACE & MCKENNA, P.A. (AV)

30 Columbia Turnpike, P.O. Box 941, 07932-0941
Telephone: 201-301-6500
Fax: 201-301-0094

David L. Hack
Peter A. Piro
William J. O'Day
M. Richard Merklinger
Joseph V. Wallace
John M. McKenna
Peter T. Melnyk
Patrick M. Sages

Bonny G. Rafel
Darlene D. Steinhart
Robert G. Alencewicz
Angela J. Mendelsohn
Michelle M. Monte
John T. West
Scott D. Samansky
Douglas J. Olcott
John J. Petrizzo
William F. Murphy
Thomas M. Madden
John F. Lanahan
Rosemarie Deehan Berard

OF COUNSEL

William D. Dougherty

Representative Clients: Aetna Life & Casualty Co.; Avis Rent-a-Car Systems; Eastman Kodak Co.; State Farm Insurance Cos.; Trans World Airlines, Inc.; Travelers Insurance Co.; Westinghouse Electric Co.; Weyerhauser Co.

For full biographical listings, see the Martindale-Hubbell Law Directory

FORKED RIVER, Ocean Co.

LAW OFFICES ARTHUR STEIN & ASSOCIATES (AV)

1041 West Lacey Road, P.O. Box 131, 08731
Telephone: 609-693-6200
Telefax: 609-693-0121

Maria Ann Stork
David A. Semanchik
Gary J. Brower

Representative Clients: Exxon Corp.; Exxon Company, U.S.A.; Citizens First National Bank of New Jersey; Summit Bank; TransAmerican Title Insurance Co.; Lacey Township Board of Education.

For full biographical listings, see the Martindale-Hubbell Law Directory

FORT LEE, Bergen Co.

LOWEN & ABUT, P.A. (AV)

One Executive Drive, 07024
Telephone: 201-592-1700

Charles C. Abut
Lawrence T. Lowen

For full biographical listings, see the Martindale-Hubbell Law Directory

*FREEHOLD,** Monmouth Co.

CERRATO, DAWES, COLLINS, SAKER & BROWN, A PROFESSIONAL CORPORATION (AV)

Wemrock Professional Mall, 509 Stillwells Corner Road, P.O. Box 6009, 07728
Telephone: 908-431-5000; 462-0480
FAX: 908-462-0483

Dominick A. Cerrato
John I. Dawes
James E. Collins
Mark F. Saker
Sanford D. Brown

(See Next Column)

Kerry E. Higgins
Helen M. Wilder
Paul K. Hennessy

OF COUNSEL

Barry William Messinger (Not admitted in NJ)

Representative Clients: The Central Jersey Bank & Trust Co.; Farm Credit Service; Freehold Regional High School; Centrastate Medical Center; New Jersey Conservation Foundation; United Methodist Monmouth Council, Boy Scouts of America; First Fidelity Bank; Ford Motor Co.; Bayliner Marine Corp.; Interlaken Board of Adjustments; Allenhurst Board of Education.

For full biographical listings, see the Martindale-Hubbell Law Directory

*HACKENSACK,** Bergen Co.

BRESLIN AND BRESLIN, P.A. (AV)

41 Main Street, 07601
Telephone: 201-342-4014; 342-4015
Fax: 201-342-0068; 201-342-3077

John J. Breslin, Jr. (1899-1987)
James A. Breslin, Sr. (1900-1980)
Charles Rodgers
E. Carter Corriston
Donald A. Caminiti

Michael T. Fitzpatrick
Angelo A. Bello
Terrence J. Corriston
Kevin C. Corriston
Karen Boe Gatlin
Lawrence Farber
E. Carter Corriston, Jr.

LEGAL SUPPORT PERSONNEL

Gertrude F. Hecht

Representative Clients: Bergen County Housing Authority; Phillips Fuel Co.; Prudential Insurance Co.; Rent Leveling Board of Township of North Bergen; Housing Authority of Passaic.
Reference: United Jersey Bank.

For full biographical listings, see the Martindale-Hubbell Law Directory

CUCCIO AND CUCCIO (AV)

45 Essex Street, 07601
Telephone: 201-487-7411
Fax: 201-487-6574
Mailing Address: P.O. Box 2223, South Hackensack, New Jersey, 07606

MEMBERS OF FIRM

Frank J. Cuccio
Emil S. Cuccio

ASSOCIATES

Pamela Beth Keitz

Representative Clients: TCI of Northern New Jersey; Huffman Koos, Inc.; The Actors Fund of America; Blue Circle-Raia, Inc.; Zimpro, Inc., Division of Sterling Drug; Honig Chemical and Processing Corp.; Napp Technologies, Inc.; River Terrace Gardens Assoc.; Franklin Lakes P.B.A. Local 150.

For full biographical listings, see the Martindale-Hubbell Law Directory

DEENER, FEINGOLD & STERN, A PROFESSIONAL CORPORATION (AV)

2 University Plaza, Suite 602, 07601
Telephone: 201-343-8788
Fax: 201-343-4640

Jerome A. Deener
Cal R. Feingold
Robert A. Stern

Debra T. Hirsch
David M. Edelblum
Anthony M. Vizzoni
James J. Costello, Jr. (Not admitted in NJ)

References: United Jersey Bank; Midlantic Bank; Midland Bank and Trust Co. (Trust Department); Fidelity Bank; Hudson United Bank.

For full biographical listings, see the Martindale-Hubbell Law Directory

DUNN, PASHMAN, SPONZILLI, SWICK & FINNERTY (AV)

411 Hackensack Avenue, 07601
Telephone: 201-489-1500; 845-4000
Fax: 201-489-1512

COUNSEL

Morris Pashman
Murray L. Cole
Paul D. Rosenberg

MEMBERS OF FIRM

Joseph Dunn
Louis Pashman
John E. Finnerty
Edward G. Sponzilli
Daniel A. Swick
Robert E. Rochford
Warren S. Robins

(See Next Column)

DUNN, PASHMAN, SPONZILLI, SWICK & FINNERTY, *Hackensack—Continued*

ASSOCIATES

Nicholas F. Pellitta
Laura S. Kirsch
Danya A. Grunyk
Richard P. Jacobson
Jeffrey M. Shapiro
Deborah L. Ustas
Mark E. Lichtblau
Edward B. Stevenson
Stephen F. Roth

References: United Jersey Bank; Valley National Bank.

For full biographical listings, see the Martindale-Hubbell Law Directory

HARWOOD LLOYD (AV)

130 Main Street, 07601
Telephone: 201-487-1080
Facsimile: 487-4758; 487-8410
East Brunswick, New Jersey Office: Two Tower Center, 10th Floor.
Telephone: 908-214-1010.
Facsimile: 908-214-1818.
Ridgewood, New Jersey Office: 41 Oak Street.
Telephone: 201-447-1422.
Facsimile: 201-447-1926.

MEMBERS OF FIRM

Victor C. Harwood, III
Frank V. D. Lloyd
Brian J. Coyle
Michael B. Oropollo
Richard J. Ryan
Leonard P. Rosa
John D. Allen, III
Frank Holahan
Russell A. Pepe
Gregory J. Irwin
Anthony M. Carlino
Thomas B. Hanrahan
Brian R. Ade
Brian C. Gallagher
Bernadette N. Gordon
Edward Zampino
Jonathan Bubrow

OF COUNSEL

David F. McBride
Theodore W. Trautwein
August Schedler
Francis V. D. Lloyd (1896-1974)
John W. Griggs (1929-1980)
Charles C. Shenier (1905-1970)
Emil M. Wulster (1907-1978)
Daniel Gilady (1927-1975)
George A. Brown (1913-1986)

Alan G. White
Charles E. Powers, Jr.
John W. Albohm
David T. Robertson
Linda A. Olsen
Martha M. Brougham
Peter E. Mueller
Richard W. LeBlancq
Michael J. Brady
Thomas A. Keenan
Paul E. Kiel
David M. Repetto
Curtis J. Turpan
Bernadette M. Peslak
Donald M. Barone
William H. Gowen
Robert F. McAnanly, Jr.
Kathleen M. Berenbroick
Patricia Van Tassel-Cromie
Elizabeth F. Williams
Patricia M. Barrow
Kim E. Sparano
Kathleen Kelly Lang
Andrew J. Naideck
Rose A. Peligri
Ann M. McGuffin
John J. Robertelli
Linda S. Baumann
Mark H. Plager
Ann C. Viscomi
Doreen A. Kunz
Linda M. Mesce
James X. Sattely, Jr.
John D. Kocher
Kristine Denning

Local Counsel for: Aetna Casualty & Surety Co.; Allstate Insurance Co.; Midlantic National Bank/North; United Jersey Bank; Gulf Oil Corp.; Volvo North America Corp.; Kemper Group.

For full biographical listings, see the Martindale-Hubbell Law Directory

HEIN, SMITH, BEREZIN, MALOOF & ROGERS (AV)

Court Plaza East, 19 Main Street, 07601-7023
Telephone: 201-487-7400
Telecopier: 201-487-4228

MEMBERS OF FIRM

Robert J. Maloof
Sidney Berezin
Allan H. Rogers
Robert L. Baum
Alan A. Davidson
Lawrence H. Jacobs

ASSOCIATES

John L. Shanahan
Ellen W. Smith
Carla H. Madnick
Marian H. Speid

OF COUNSEL

Seymour A. Smith
Milton Gurny

Representative Clients: Aetna Insurance Co.; Commercial Union of New York; Employers of Wausau; Great American Insurance Cos.; Hanover Insurance Co.; Health Care Insurance Co.; Merchants Mutual Insurance Co.; St. Paul Fire & Marine Insurance Co.; U.S. Fidelity & Guaranty Co.
Reference: United Jersey Bank.

For full biographical listings, see the Martindale-Hubbell Law Directory

PEARCE & MASSLER (AV)

Court Plaza North, 25 Main Street, 07601-7025
Telephone: 201-342-3400
Facsimile: 201-342-0612

(See Next Column)

Randy T. Pearce
Howard A. Massler

OF COUNSEL

Anthony J. Riposta
Michael Phillips
Gregory M. Gennaro

ASSOCIATES

Brian Fleisig
MaryAnn Borrello

For full biographical listings, see the Martindale-Hubbell Law Directory

SOKOL, BEHOT AND FIORENZO (AV)

39 Hudson Street, 07601
Telephone: 201-488-1300
Fax: 201-488-6541

MEMBERS OF FIRM

Leon J. Sokol
Joseph F. Behot, Jr.
Joseph B. Fiorenzo
Jeffrey A. Zenn

ASSOCIATES

Siobhan C. Spillane
Susan I. Wegner
Jeffrey M. Kahan

COUNSEL

Arthur Bergman
Alan Prigal

For full biographical listings, see the Martindale-Hubbell Law Directory

HACKETTSTOWN, Warren Co.

COURTER, KOBERT, LAUFER & COHEN, P.A. (AV)

1001 Route 517, 07840
Telephone: 908-852-2600
FAX: 908-852-8225
Morristown, New Jersey Office: 10 Park Place.
Telephone: 201-285-1444.
FAX: 201-285-0271.

James A. Courter
Joel A. Kobert
William M. Laufer
Lawrence P. Cohen
Robert A. Smith
Edward S. Nagorsky
Gregory P. Luhn
John J. McLaughlin
Fredric M. Knapp
Jane Ellen Doran
Donald A. Richards (Resident, Morristown Office)
Lynn Fontaine Newsome

Kevin M. Hahn
Vincent W. Rickey
Michael McLaughlin
Christine M. Dalena
Thomas J. Gaynor
Michael S. Selvaggi
Dana A. Roscioli
Laura Lencses McLester
Glenn J. Williams

Representative Clients: M & M Mars Candy Co.; Century 21 of the Northeast, Inc.; National Kitchen & Bath Assn.; Sir Speedy, Inc.; Vanguard Cellular Telephone.

For full biographical listings, see the Martindale-Hubbell Law Directory

HADDONFIELD, Camden Co.

FREEMAN, MINTZ, HAGNER & DEICHES, P.A. (AV)

34 Tanner Street, 08033-2482
Telephone: 609-795-1234

A. David Epstein (1910-1975)
Stanton D. Freeman
Robert D. Mintz
Thomas J. Hagner
Ira R. Deiches

James P. Pierson

Representative Clients: United Jersey Bank, South, NA; Eastern Brewing Corp.; 20th Century Construction; American Credit Indemnity Co.; Lyons Furniture Mercantile Agency; Dun & Bradstreet; Systems & Information Dynamics, Inc.; American Continental Property of New Jersey, Inc.
Reference: Chemical Bank.

For full biographical listings, see the Martindale-Hubbell Law Directory

GERSTEIN, COHEN & GRAYSON (AV)

Twenty Kings Highway West, 08033
Telephone: 609-795-6700
Fax: 609-354-0020

Samuel Gerstein
Diane B. Cohen
Mitchell T. Grayson
Sandford F. Schmidt

Richard M. Chiumento
Suzanne E. Bragg
Andrew B. Cohen
Cheryl Ann Santaniello
Meridee R. Duddleston
Andrew P. Aronson

For full biographical listings, see the Martindale-Hubbell Law Directory

Haddonfield—Continued

Green, Lundgren & Ryan, A Professional Corporation (AV)

227 Kings Highway East, 08033
Telephone: 609-428-5800
Telecopier: 609-428-9802

Peter P. Green
William L. Lundgren, III
Francis X. Ryan
Daniel J. DiStasi
Charles F. Blumenstein, II

James E. Mulroy
Joseph T. Walsh, Jr.
Edward R. Gallagher
Jon M. Demasi
Laurence Todd Bennett
Ward Shaffer Taggart
Michael M. Lamb

Counsel for: Penn Central Co.; Allstate Insurance Co.; New Jersey Bell Telephone Co.; Hartford Accident & Indemnity Co.; Continental Casualty Co.; Sentry Insurance Co.; The Travelers Insurance Co.; Coldwell Banker Real Estate Corp.; Amtrak Conrail.

For full biographical listings, see the Martindale-Hubbell Law Directory

Madden, Madden and Del Duca, P.A. (AV)

108 Kings Highway East, P.O. Box 210, 08033
Telephone: 609-428-9520
Telecopier: 609-428-7335

James J. Madden
Michael P. Madden
Joseph A. Del Duca
Anthony M. Pugliese

Damien O. Del Duca
William H. Dengler, Jr.

For full biographical listings, see the Martindale-Hubbell Law Directory

HAWTHORNE, Passaic Co.

Jeffer, Hopkinson, Vogel, Coomber & Peiffer (AV)

(Formerly Jeffer, Walter, Tierney, DeKorte, Hopkinson & Vogel)
Law Building, 1600 Route 208N, P.O. Box 507, 07507
Telephone: 201-423-0100
Fax: 201-423-5614
Tequesta, Florida Office: 250 Tequesta Drive.
Telephone: 407-747-6000.
Fax: 407-575-9167.
New York, N.Y. Office: Suite 2206, 150 Broadway.
Telephone: 212-406-7260.

MEMBERS OF FIRM

Peter Hofstra (1886-1961)
George Tierney (1895-1976)
Joseph V. Fumagalli (1901-1965)
Richard W. DeKorte (1936-1975)
Robert Walter (1908-1990)
Herman M. Jeffer
Reginald F. Hopkinson
Jerome A. Vogel
Donald J. Coomber
Gary D. Peiffer

ASSOCIATES

Melinda B. Maidens
Peter E. Riccobene
Darryl W. Siss
I. Barbara Cecere

LEGAL SUPPORT PERSONNEL

Janet Faber (Office Administrator)

Counsel for: Brioschi, Inc.; Opici Wine Co.; Gas Pumpers of America Corp.; The Paterson Market Growers Assn.; Jupiter Tequesta National Bank; Dowling Fuel Oil Co.; Becton, Dickinson; JFC International, Inc.; Loews Theaters; Christian Health Care Center.

For full biographical listings, see the Martindale-Hubbell Law Directory

HOBOKEN, Hudson Co. — (Refer to Jersey City)

*JERSEY CITY,** Hudson Co.

Sheehy & Sheehy (AV)

Suite 206, 665 Newark Avenue, 07306
Telephone: 201-795-5500
Fax: 201-795-5172
Toms River, New Jersey Office: 121 Washington Street.
Telephone: 908-505-1919.

MEMBERS OF FIRM

John J. Sheehy
John J. Sheehy
Marian V. Rooney-Sheehy (1926-1984)

References: First Fidelity Bank; Trust Company of New Jersey; Provident Savings.

For full biographical listings, see the Martindale-Hubbell Law Directory

KENILWORTH, Union Co.

Aldan O. Markson (AV)

726 Boulevard, P.O. Box 236, 07033-0236
Telephone: 908-241-5555
Fax: 908-241-5529

Reference: United Counties Trust.

For full biographical listings, see the Martindale-Hubbell Law Directory

LAKEWOOD, Ocean Co.

Bathgate, Wegener, Dugan & Wolf, P.C. (AV)

One Airport Road, P.O. Box 2043, 08701
Telephone: 908-363-0666
Telecopier: 908-363-9864
Newark, New Jersey Office: Three Gateway Center, Fifteenth Floor, Newark, New Jersey 07102.
Telephone: 201-623-6663.
Telecopier: 201-623-5464.

Lawrence E. Bathgate, II
Peter H. Wegener
James P. Dugan
William J. Wolf
Ross D. Gertner
Edward B. Kasselman
Stephan R. Leone
Dominic J. Aprile
Nancy G. Wright
Joseph A. DiCroce
Michael M. DiCicco

James A. Maggs
Robert L. Gutman
Neil Brodsky
Michael I. Halfacre

For full biographical listings, see the Martindale-Hubbell Law Directory

LINDEN, Union Co.

Winetsky and Winetsky (AV)

401 North Wood Avenue, P.O. Box 67, 07036
Telephone: 908-486-2761; 486-2762
Fax: 908-486-2661

MEMBERS OF FIRM

Lewis Winetsky (1929-1986)
Charles N. Winetsky

Reference: United Counties Trust Co., Linden, New Jersey.

For full biographical listings, see the Martindale-Hubbell Law Directory

LIVINGSTON, Essex Co.

Morgan, Melhuish, Monaghan, Arvidson, Abrutyn & Lisowski (AV)

(Formerly Schneider and Morgan)
651 West Mount Pleasant Avenue, 07039
Telephone: 201-994-2500
Fax: 201-994-3375
New York, N.Y. Office: 39 Broadway, 35th Floor.
Telephone: 212-809-1111.
Fax: 212-509-3422.

MEMBERS OF FIRM

Jacob Schneider (1910-1949)
Louis Schneider (1921-1965)
Henry G. Morgan
James L. Melhuish
Robert E. Monaghan
William F. Perry
Richard E. Arvidson
John I. Lisowski
Elliott Abrutyn
Jeffrey M. Kadish
Paul A. Tripodo
John J. Agostini
Robert J. Aste
Mary Adele Hornish
Richard E. Snyder
David M. Welt
Michael A. Sicola
Joseph DeDonato
Robert A. Assuncao

Richard Micliz
Roger C. Schechter
Richard J. Hull
Leonard C. Leicht
Nina Lynn Caroselli
Anthony M. Santoro, Jr.
Robert J. Machi
Michael H. Cohen
Timothy K. Saia
Mary Ellen Scalera
Robert G. Klinck
Linda G. O'Connell
Elizabeth A. Brewster
Barry S. Brownstein
Sandra Lawrence Paz
Nancy J. Platkin
John I. Lisowski, Jr.
Dean Constantine
Andrew A. Elman
Warren C. Nitti
Arthur J. Raimon
John C. Macce
Michelle M. Schott
Charles H. Smith, Jr.
Daniel E. Serata
Daniel T. Hughes (Resident, New York, N.Y. Office)
Heidi P. Rubin Cohen
Joseph G. Dolan
Joseph J. Fell
Michele D. Sullivan
Gina M. Sorge
Joseph G. Racioppi
Deborah J. Banfield
Michael Dolich
Robert F. Schillberg, Jr. (Resident, New York, N.Y. Office)
Warren Usdin
Meredith Kaplan Stoma
Matthew J. Titone (Resident, New York, N.Y. Office)

(See Next Column)

MORGAN, MELHUISH, MONAGHAN, ARVIDSON, ABRUTYN & LISOWSKI, *Livingston—Continued*

OF COUNSEL

Vincent J. Cirlin

LEGAL SUPPORT PERSONNEL

Maria DePascale (Administrator) James J. Murphy (Comptroller)

Represent: The Home Insurance Co.; The Insurance Company of North American Cos.; General Accident Fire & Life Assurance Corp., Ltd.; Zurich Insurance Co.; Trans America Insurance Group; Allstate Insurance Co.; Penn Mutual Insurance Co.; State Farm Insurance; Ohio Casualty Co.; American Mutual Liability Insurance Co.

For full biographical listings, see the Martindale-Hubbell Law Directory

MANASQUAN, Monmouth Co.

CARTON, WITT, ARVANITIS & BARISCILLO (AV)

(Formerly Durand, Ivins & Carton)
40 Union Avenue, P.O. Box 367, 08736
Telephone: 908-223-1800
Asbury Park, New Jersey Office: 4001 Route 66 at Garden State Parkway, P.O. Box 1229.
Telephone: 908-922-9500.
Telecopier: 908-922-1625.

RESIDENT PARTNERS

James D. Carton, III
John C. Carton

RESIDENT ASSOCIATE

Suzanne White Ballou

Attorneys for: New Jersey National Bank; Midlantic National Bank/Merchants; New Jersey Bell Telephone Co.
Local Attorneys for: Travelers Insurance Co.; Cigna Insurance Co.; Aetna Casualty & Surety Co.; New Jersey Manufacturers Insurance Co.; Liberty Mutual; Prudential Insurance Co.; Chubb & Son.

For full biographical listings, see the Martindale-Hubbell Law Directory

MAPLEWOOD, Essex Co.

FIELD & OLESNYCKY (AV)

2040 Millburn Avenue, 07040
Telephone: 201-763-2001
Fax: 201-763-1574

MEMBERS OF FIRM

Robert S. Field
Nestor L. Olesnycky

Reference: The Maplewood Bank & Trust Co.

For full biographical listings, see the Martindale-Hubbell Law Directory

MARLTON, Burlington Co.

PARKER, MCCAY & CRISCUOLO, P.A. (AV)

Suite 401 Three Greentree Centre, Route 73 & Greentree Road, 08053
Telephone: 609-596-8900
Telecopier: 609-596-9631
Cherry Hill, New Jersey Office: Commerce Atrium, Suite 500, 1701 Route 70 East, P.O. Box 1806.
Telephone: 609-424-4300.
Telecopier: 609-424-1006.
Philadelphia, Pennsylvania Office: 3700 Bell Atlantic Tower, 1717 Arch Street.
Telephone: 215-994-5315.
Telecopier: 215-994-3100.

Harold T. Parker (1903-1983)
Albert McCay (1901-1969)
Robert W. Criscuolo (1909-1977)
Barry T. Parker
Robert C. Beck (Resident at Cherry Hill, New Jersey Office)
David A. Parker
Robert J. Partlow
John Michael Devlin
Yves C. Veenstra
Lowell F. Raeder (Resident at Philadelphia, Pennsylvania Office)
Thomas M. Masick
Marc M. Baldwin
Ronald C. Morgan
Joseph G. DeRespino (Not admitted in NJ; Resident at Philadelphia, Pennsylvania Office)
Jeffrey P. Heppard
Timothy J. Hinlicky
Stacy L. Moore, Jr.
Drew J. Parker
Thomas D. Romando
Thomas M. Walsh
Gary F. Piserchia
Philip A. Norcross
Suzanne M. Kourlesis

Robert D. Bernardi
Irving G. Finkel
Mary Ann C. O'Brien
Richard M. Berman (Resident at Cherry Hill, New Jersey Office)
Brian M. Brodowski
Thomas S. Harty
Lynn S. Besancon
Todd A. Beck
Thomas J. Coleman, III
Thomas J. Walls, Jr.
Emily M. Clay (Not admitted in NJ)
John D. Borbi
Robert C. Beck, Jr.
J. Brooks DiDonato
Michael C. Cascio
Lisa M. Kmiec
Pina M. Vricella
Francine M. Cracker
Emmanuel J. Argentieri (Resident at Cherry Hill, New Jersey Office)
Christopher F. Costello
Elena B. Zuares
Brad A. Parker
Craig W. Kugler
Nancy R. Hatch
Megan C. Farrell
Douglas J. Yocum

OF COUNSEL

William V. Webster, Jr.
Richard J. Dill
John P. Lippincott

Local Counsel for: Aetna Casualty & Surety Co.; U.S. Fidelity & Guaranty Co.; Keystone Insurance Co.; Eagle Dyeing & Finishing Co.; Zurich-American Insurance Co.; Rider Insurance Co.; Continental Insurance Co.; Commerce Bank, N.A.

For full biographical listings, see the Martindale-Hubbell Law Directory

MIDDLETOWN, Monmouth Co.

GIORDANO, HALLERAN & CIESLA, A PROFESSIONAL CORPORATION (AV)

125 Half Mile Road, P.O. Box 190, 07748
Telephone: 908-741-3900
Telefax: 908-224-6599
Trenton, New Jersey Office: 441 East State Street.
Telephone: 609-695-3900.
Toms River, New Jersey Office: 200 Main Street.
Telephone: 908-341-9600.

John C. Giordano, Jr.
John R. Halleran
Frank R. Ciesla
Bernard J. Berry, Jr.
Thomas A. Pliskin
John A. Aiello
Michael J. Gross
Richard L. Friedman
George J. Tyler
Lois D. Shafir
John A. Giunco, Jr.
Norman M. Hobbie
Edward S. Radzely
Steven M. Berlin
Sharlene A. Hunt
Vicki Jan Isler
Philip D. Forlenza
William J. Bowe
Tobi E. Graff
Michael J. Canning
Richard D. Stanzione
Paul H. Schneider
M. Scott Tashjy
Michele A. Querques
David P. Corrigan
Anthony R. Caruso
John F. Varley III
Robert A. Olkowitz
Anne Covey Sarch

Brian D. Gillet
Steven J. Brodman
Andrew B. Robins
Michael A. Bruno
Susan D. Davis
Margaret B. Carmeli
Kurt E. Anderson
Paul T. Colella
Jody V. Sackett
David M. Epstein
Laura Nigris Anderson
Joanne S. Gray
Robert J. Blackwell
Lisa A. Butto
Gregg M. Hobbie
Laura A. Lane
Paul V. Fernicola
Lawrence J. Sharon
Tracy A. Armstrong
Sean E. Regan
Debra J. Rubenstein
William H. Healey
Gerald Patrick Lally
Michele Shoueka
Timothy R. Couch
Peter L. Benza
J. Scott Anderson
M. Kristine Lynch
James L. Petsche
Jodi L. Rosenberg
Nancy Steadman-Martin
Jeffrey S. Beenstock

COUNSEL

Elizabeth Hellmers Dusaniwskyj

OF COUNSEL

S. Thomas Gagliano

Representative Clients: Monmouth Medical Center; New Jersey Shore Builders Assn.; Bayshore Community Hospital; American Oil & Supply Co.; South Jersey Hospital; Utica Mutual Insurance Co.; Roberts Pharmaceutical Corp.; Torcon.

For full biographical listings, see the Martindale-Hubbell Law Directory

MILLBURN, Essex Co.

MCDERMOTT & MCGEE (AV)

64 Main Street, P.O. Box 192, 07041-0192
Telephone: 201-467-8080
FAX: 201-467-0012

MEMBERS OF FIRM

John L. McDermott
John P. McGee
Richard P. Maggi
Thomas A. Wester
Richard A. Tango
Frank P. Leanza
John L. McDermott, Jr.

ASSOCIATES

Lawrence G. Tosi
David J. Dickinson
A. Charles Lorenzo
Robert A. McDermott
Kevin John McGee

(See Next Column)

McDermott & McGee—*Continued*

OF COUNSEL

Daniel K. Van Dorn

Representative Clients: Allstate Insurance Co.; American Hardware Mutual Insurance Co.; Argonaut Insurance Cos.; Continental Insurance Cos.; Commercial Union Insurance Cos.; General Accident Group; Maryland-American General Group; Zurich-American Insurance Co.; P.C.M. Intermediaries, Ltd.; The Hanover Insurance Cos.

For full biographical listings, see the Martindale-Hubbell Law Directory

MONTVALE, Bergen Co.

Beattie Padovano (AV)

50 Chestnut Ridge Road, P.O. Box 244, 07645-0244
Telephone: 201-573-1810
Fax: (DEX) 201-573-9736

MEMBERS OF FIRM

James R. Beattie
Ralph J. Padovano
Roger W. Breslin, Jr.
Thomas W. Dunn
Martin W. Kafafian
Adolph A. Romei
Brian R. Martinotti

ASSOCIATES

Emery C. Duell
Brenda J. McAdoo
Kathleen Smyth Cook
Francis B. Sheehan
Susan Calabrese
Antimo A. Del Vecchio
Dean J. Obeidallah
Jeffrey L. Love
Steven A. Weisfeld
S. Joseph Oey
Edward S. Kiel
Christopher Heyer
JoAnne C. Gerber
Robert A. Blass

OF COUNSEL

John J. Lamb

Reference: United Jersey Bank.

For full biographical listings, see the Martindale-Hubbell Law Directory

*MORRISTOWN,** Morris Co.

Clemente, Dickson & Mueller, P.A. (AV)

218 Ridgedale Avenue, P.O. Box 1296, 07962-1296
Telephone: 201-455-8008
Fax: 201-455-8118

William F. Mueller
Jonathan D. Clemente
Joseph A. Dickson
Patrick D. Tobia
Daniel E. Somers
Kathleen Kane Morrison
Jeffrey H. Clott
Christina A. Luancing

For full biographical listings, see the Martindale-Hubbell Law Directory

McElroy, Deutsch and Mulvaney (AV)

1300 Mount Kemble Avenue, P.O. Box 2075, 07962-2075
Telephone: 201-993-8100
Fax: 201-425-0161
Denver, Colorado Office: 1099 18th Street, Suite 3120.
Telephone: 303-293-8800.
Fax: 303-293-3116.

MEMBERS OF FIRM

Lorraine M. Armenti (Resident Partner, Denver Colorado Office)
Grace C. Bertone
John P. Beyel
William C. Carey
Margaret F. Catalano
Stephen H. Cohen (1938-1992)
Kevin T. Coughlin
Edward B. Deutsch
Timothy I. Duffy
Robert J. Kelly
Joseph P. La Sala
Paul A. Lisovicz
Fred A. Manley, Jr.
Michael J. Marone
William T. McElroy
Laurence M. McHeffey
Joseph P. McNulty, Jr.
James M. Mulvaney
Moira E. O'Connell
Loren L. Pierce
Warren K. Racusin
John H. Suminski
Kevin E. Wolff

OF COUNSEL

Richard G. McCarty (Not admitted in NJ)
John F. Whitteaker

ASSOCIATES

Caroline L. Beers
Christopher Robert Carroll
Edward V. Collins
Billy J. Cooper (Resident, Denver, Colorado Office)
John Thomas Coyne
Nada Leslie Wolff Culver (Resident, Denver, Colorado Office)
John J. Cummings
Anthony J. Davis
John Paul Gilfillan
Kevin M. Haas
Gary S. Kull
Matthew J. Lodge
Tracey L. Matura
Nancy McDonald
Robert McGuire
Suzanne Cocco Midlige
Robert W. Muilenburg
Gary Potters
Kathleen M. Quinn
Vincent E. Reilly
Agnes A. Reiss
Barbara C. Zimmerman Robertson
Samuel J. Samaro
Laura A. Sanom

(See Next Column)

ASSOCIATES (Continued)

Thomas P. Scrivo
Dennis T. Smith
Patricia Leen Sullivan
Pamela A. Tanis
Christine L. Thieman
Catharine Acker Vaughan

Representative Clients: ADT Security Systems, Inc.; Yale Materials Handling Corp; Crum & Forster Insurance Co.; Eaton Corp.; Fireman's Fund Insurance Cos.; New Jersey Manufacturers Insurance Co.; The Home Indemnity Co.; Ingersoll-Rand Company; The Pittston Company; Security Pacific Finance Corporation.

For full biographical listings, see the Martindale-Hubbell Law Directory

Pitney, Hardin, Kipp & Szuch (AV)

Park Avenue at Morris County, P.O. Box 1945, 07962-1945
Telephone: 201-966-6300
New York City: 212-926-0331
Telex: 642014
Telecopier: 201-966-1550

MEMBERS OF FIRM

James C. Pitney
William D. Hardin
Clyde A. Szuch
S. Joseph Fortunato
David J. Connolly, Jr.
William H. Hyatt, Jr.
Lawrence F. Reilly
Murray J. Laulicht
Robert C. Neff
Richard Kahn
Edward P. Lynch
Joseph Lunin
Richard L. Plotkin
Timothy R. Greiner
Robert L. Hollingshead
Frederick L. Whitmer
Gregory C. Parliman
Robert G. Rose
Patrick J. McCarthy
James E. Tyrrell, Jr.
Anthony J. Marchetta
Mary Lou Parker
Paul E. Graham
J. Michael Nolan, Jr.
Warren J. Casey
Kevin J. O'Donnell
Peter J. Herzberg
Ronald H. Janis
Glenn C. Geiger
Dennis R. LaFiura
Gail H. Allyn
Henry Nelson Massey
Robert S. Burrick
Dennis T. Kearney
Kenneth J. Norcross
Donald W. Kiel
Joel M. Rosen
Kathy A. Lawler
Harriett Jane Olson
Elizabeth J. Sher
Theresa Donahue Egler
Michael J. Dunne
Stephen G. Traflet
Hope S. Cone
John C. Maloney, Jr.
Lori J. Braender

OF COUNSEL

Philip G. Barber (Not admitted in NJ)
Michael W. Zelenty

COUNSEL

Jane H. Hardin
Paul E. Flanagan
Thomas J. Malman
David P. Doyle
David W. Payne

ASSOCIATES

Kathy Dutton Helmer
Charles P. Abraham
Mark H. Daaleman
David Michael Fabian
L. Allison Garde
Benjamin E. Haglund
Debra H. Katz
William J. O'Shaughnessy, Jr.
Sean T. Quinn
John B. Rutherford
Sheryl M. Schwartz
Joy Harmon Sperling
Ellen M. Boyle
Colleen R. Donovan
Jerrold I. Langer
Jeanmarie McMahon
Kelley J. Newton
Christopher Mark DiMuro
Jonathan E. Hill
Theresa A. Kelly
Donna M. Murphy
Loryn Patricia Riggiola
James T. Ryan, Jr.
John Patrick Scordo
Christina Smith
Christopher John Stracco
Virginia Benton Bailey
Sandra L. Bograd
Kathryn M. Decker
Anne Baglivo Fitzpatrick
Peter James Herrigel
Kathleen T. Kneis
John McGahren
Deirdre E. Moore
Ronald T. Nagle
Patrice M. Renner
Richard J. Wolf
Charles Allen Yuen
Lois A. Yurow
Elizabeth Anne Barba
Paula Block
Young J. Choe (Not admitted in NJ)
Rosemarie DaSilva
Edward J. Hansen
Maxine Harelick Levitan
James M. McKnight
Brian S. Montag
Barbara Ann Moran
Tim J. Robinson
Sally A. Roll
Catherine E. Tamasik
Christopher P. Anton
Kathryn S. Geib
Marco A. Gonzalez, Jr.
Paul J. Halasz
Ivan J. Kaplan
Florina A. Moldovan
Maureen C. Pavely
Rosalie J. Shoeman
Frances B. Stella
Maritza D. Berdote
Joseph E. Hopkins
Jennifer B. Krevitt
Deborah A. Marrone
Paul B. Milcetic
Michael L. Minaides
Charles N. Panzer
Christopher M. Santomassimo
Bruce D. Taterka
William J. Tinsley, Jr.
Richard H. Brown, III
Stanley M. Cichinski
Alan S. Golub
Pamela A. Humbert
David L. Isabel
Susan R. Kohn
Robert W. Mauriello, Jr.
Rina Pedroza
Lisa Ann T. Ruggiero
Scott Louis Weber
Denise Vicente Tighe

(See Next Column)

PITNEY, HARDIN, KIPP & SZUCH, *Morristown—Continued*

Representative Clients: AlliedSignal Inc.; AT&T; Base Ten Systems, Inc.; Exxon Corp.; Ford Motor Co.; Midlantic National Bank; Sony Electronics, Inc.; Union Carbide Corp.; United Parcel Services, Inc.; Warner-Lambert Co.

For full biographical listings, see the Martindale-Hubbell Law Directory

PORZIO, BROMBERG & NEWMAN, A PROFESSIONAL CORPORATION (AV)

163 Madison Avenue, 07962-1997
Telephone: 201-538-4006
Facsimile: 201-538-5146
New York, New York Office: 655 Third Avenue, 10017-5617.
Telephone: 212-986-0600.
Facsimile: 212-986-6491.

Steven P. Benenson
Robert J. Brennan
Lisa Murtha Bromberg
Myron J. Bromberg
D. Jeffrey Campbell
Thomas R. Chesson
Roy Alan Cohen
Alexander J. Drago (Resident, New York Office)
Lauren E. Handler
Edward A. Hogan
Anita Hotchkiss
Kenneth R. Meyer
John M. Newman
Howard J. Schwartz

COUNSEL

Stewart A. Cunningham
Charles E. Erway, III
Thomas Spiesman

Maura E. Blau
Howard P. Davis
Christopher P. DePhillips
Garineh S. Dovletian
Peter A. Drucker
Frank Fazio
Karen A. Kaplan
Vanessa M. Kelly
Jonathan M. Korn
William A. Krais
Jonathan R. Kuhlman
Coleen McCaffery
Jay R. McDaniel
Nancy Gail Minikes
Dean M. Monti (Resident Associate, New York Office)
Randi N. Pomerantz
Robert T. Quackenboss
Cynthia D. Richardson
Gregory J. Schwartz
Diane M. Siana
Charles J. Stoia
Janet A. Sullivan
Morna L. Sweeney
Stephen L. Willis

Representative Clients: American Cyanamid Co.; American Home Products Corp.; ASARCO Inc.; Ayerst Laboratories; Johnson & Johnson; Pfizer Inc.; Warner-Lambert Co.

For full biographical listings, see the Martindale-Hubbell Law Directory

RIKER, DANZIG, SCHERER, HYLAND & PERRETTI (AV)

Headquarters Plaza, One Speedwell Avenue, 07962-1981
Telephone: 201-538-0800
Fax: 201-538-1984
Trenton, New Jersey Office: 170 West State Street.
Telephone: 609-396-2121.
Fax: 609-396-4578.

MEMBERS OF FIRM

Irving Riker (1921-1969)
William I. Riker (1951-1973)
Charles Danzig (1934-1992)
Peter N. Perretti, Jr.
William C. Connelly
Edward A. Zunz, Jr.
Peter F. Eld
Peter L. Berkley
Benjamin P. Michel
Gerald A. Liloia
John P. Sheridan, Jr.
Robert Fischer, III
James S. Rothschild, Jr.
Vincent J. Sharkey, Jr.
Dennis J. O'Grady
Michael K. Furey
Michael R. Cole
Gary E. Walsh
Susan Scott
Robert D. Borteck
Edward K. DeHope
Shawn L. Kelly
Mark S. Rattner
Dennis J. Krumholz
Alan E. Kraus
Glenn A. Clark
Robert J. Schoenberg
Stuart Peim
Maryann Dougherty Kicenuik
Samuel P. Moulthrop
Victoria A. Morrison
Andrew J. Stamelman
Kenneth M. Van Deventer
Jan L. Bernstein
Sigrid S. Franzblau
Anne M. Patterson
John M. Pellecchia
Anthony J. Sylvester
Peter C. Harvey
Craig J. Donaldson
Glenn D. Curving
Robert J. Gilson

OF COUNSEL

Everett M. Scherer
William F. Hyland
Sidney M. Schreiber
Howard F. Casselman

COUNSEL

Charles F. Waskevich, Jr.
Sandra Brown Sherman
John Melicharek, Jr.

ASSOCIATES

Nancy Stewart
Stuart M. Lederman
Jeffrey B. Wagenbach
Jeffrey J. Miller
Janet Falletti Moss
Linda H. Prentiss
Robert C. Daleo
Warren J. Martin Jr.
Mark J. Warshauer
Marilynn R. Greenberg

(See Next Column)

ASSOCIATES (Continued)

Barbara Scheader
David P. Arciszewski
Sabrina Hodges Perel
Edward J. McCartin III
Stephanie Sherman
Gail E. Govelitz
Richard D. Sanders
Martin J. Milita, Jr.
James P. Anelli
Lynne Anne Anderson
Lori A. Ciarrocca
Sarah Locantore Monaghan
James C. Meyer
Michael J. Rossignol
Beatrix W. Shear
Susan Morgan Foster
Abby Harlan Landau
Michael R. O'Donnell
Karen Patruno Sheehy
Brian W. Moore
Nicholas Racioppi, Jr.
James A. Raborn
Sheila M. Nugent
Kenneth O. Bradley
Carol T. Wortmann
Anthony J. Zarillo, Jr.
Vito A. Gagliardi, Jr.
Donald F. MacMaster
Brian E. O'Donnell
Louise A. Johnson
Seth D. Geldzahler
Julian W. Wells
David Fernandez
Judy L. Cavet
Gary A. Greene
Gary N. Wilcox
Liza M. Kirschenbaum
J. Alex Kress
Roberta N. Samuels
John G. Valeri, Jr.
Kevin G. Smith
Deborah J. Fennelly
Stella M. Strelzik
David A. Wolff
Marianne S. Conklin (Not admitted in NJ)
Esther S. Bondy
Nancy C. Eberhardt
Harold L. Kofman
Barbara L. Farricker
Milena S. Quaglietta
Laura M. Massaia
Jeffrey M. Siminoff
Charles A. Weiss
Nadine M. Sarajian
Scott A. Ohnegian
William G. Connolly
Frank C. Welzer
Harold S. Atlas
Brian E. Bragg
Mary Kathryn Palladino
Patricia Roche Sunar
Joseph L. Schwartz
Thomas Byrne
Gloria Lynn Buxbaum
Jeffrey A. Durney
Cathleen H. Giuliana
Bruce A. Harris
Meri-Beth Robertson
Marci L. Sacco
Craig L. Steinfeld
John A. Sheehy
James L. Lott Jr.
Gregory K. Smith
John P. Berkery
Christopher J. McAuliffe
David A. Rockman
Deborah Farber Sonnenberg
Larisa L. Van Kirk
Janice Ng
Steven K. Parness
Shari H. Chertoff
Edwin F. Chociey
Kelly S. Crawford
Lisa M. Dorio

Representative Clients: American Telephone & Telegraph Co.; Chrysler-/AMC; E. I. duPont de Nemours & Co.; First Fidelity Bank, N.A.; General Public Utilities Corp.; International Business Machines Corp.; Jersey Central Power & Light Co.; Johnson & Johnson; New Jersey Health Care Facilities Financing Authority; Rust International Corp.

For full biographical listings, see the Martindale-Hubbell Law Directory

SCHENCK, PRICE, SMITH & KING (AV)

(Formerly King and Vogt)
10 Washington Street, P.O. Box 905, 07963-0905
Telephone: 201-539-1000
Fax: 201-540-7300
New York, N.Y. Office: 101 Park Avenue.
Telephone: 212-986-6482.

MEMBERS OF FIRM

Clinton J. Curtis
James E. Davidson
Julius J. Denzler
William C. Dodd
Willard Bergman, Jr.
Edward W. Ahart
Stephen Sepaniak
Thomas C. C. Humick
Douglas S. Brierley
Edward John Trawinski
Howard P. Shaw
Gilbert S. Leeds
Anita Joy Siegel
Lisa K. Pantel
James P. Wyse
Michael K. Mullen
M. Sheilah O'Halloran
Anne E. Aronovitch
John M. DeMarco
John M. Elias
Michael A. Moroney
Gregory J. Coffey

ASSOCIATES

James B. Garland
Anthony F. Della Pelle
Lauri L. Orfanelli
James A. Rybka
Nancy M. Bangiola
Ivan J. Whittenburg
Paul S. Weidlich
Barbara W. Stoller
Jeffrey T. La Rosa

OF COUNSEL

Clifford W. Starrett
Ben D. White
Patti S. Liberman

For full biographical listings, see the Martindale-Hubbell Law Directory

Morristown—Continued

SHANLEY & FISHER, A PROFESSIONAL CORPORATION (AV)

131 Madison Avenue, 07962-1979
Telephone: 201-285-1000
Telecopier: 1-201-285-1098
Telex: 475-4255 (I.T.T.)
Cable Address: "Shanley"
New York, N.Y. Office: 89th Floor, One World Trade Center.
Telephone: 212-321-1812.
Telecopier: 1-212-466-0569.

L. Bruce Puffer, Jr.
William G. Becker, Jr.
John Kandravy
Raymond M. Tierney, Jr.
Arthur R. Schmauder
Thomas F. Campion
John J. Francis, Jr.
Gerald W. Hull, Jr.
A. Dennis Terrell
Richard E. Brennan
Thomas J. Alworth
William K. Lewis, II
Jeffrey A. Peck
James H. Freis
Matthew Farley
Daniel F. O'Connell
I. Leo Motiuk
Richard A. Levao
Ronald Gould
John D. Clemen
Charles A. Reid, III
Stewart E. Lavey
Paul G. Nittoly
Robert A. Boutillier
Glenn S. Pantel
Walter J. Fleischer, Jr.
Lydia C. Stefanowicz
Susan M. Sharko
Kevin M. Kilcullen
Stephen R. Long
Mary E. Tracey
Brian F. McDonough
James M. Altieri
Patrick M. Stanton
Andrew V. Ballantine
Richard D. Prentice
Robert M. Leonard
John A. Schaff
Robert A. Gladstone
Nan Bernardo
Theodore S. Smith
Michael O. Adelman
Robert K. Malone
Michael Osterman
Neil S. Cartusciello (Not admitted in NJ)

OF COUNSEL

Alvin C. Martin
Michael J. Faigen
Louis L. D'Arminio

COUNSEL

Charles D. Donohue, Jr. (Resident, New York, N.Y. Office)
Stephanie C. Rosen

Jodi Sydell Rosenzweig
Emily A. Schultz
Peter O. Hughes
Joan M. Neri
Bruce L. Shapiro
Margery F. Nathanson
Michaela O'Brien
Kenneth J. Wilbur
Arthur P. Havighorst, II
Michael E. Helmer
Michael J. Nita
Thomas A. Roberts (Resident, New York, N.Y. Office)
Sean Monaghan
Sheila G. Gruber
Lisa Deitsch Taylor
Mark Diana
Joseph M. Cerra
Kathleen H. Dooley
William R. Brown, Sr.
Kathleen B. Harden
Robert A. DelVecchio
Lynn Ciolino Boyajian
Maureen L. Nesbitt
Andrew S. Turkish
Ieva I. Rogers
Clare Maria Begley
Joan E. Pearson
Harry M. Baumgartner
Douglas S. Zucker
Robert A. Burke
Carole A. Hafferty
Lawrence E. Behning
Jeffrey S. Lipkin
Stephanie A. Mergel
Lisa M. Plinio
Nicholas J. Taldone
Edward A. Gramigna, Jr.
Robert A. Klausner
Russell J. Passamano
Stephen C. Hunt
Carla Marie Mascaro
Dawn R. SanFilippo
Rita C. Burghardt
Suzanne Cerra
Stephen R. Fitzpatrick
William J. Mendrzycki
Michael E. Rothpletz, Jr.
Tanya M. Taylor
Mary Jane Armstrong (Resident, New York, N.Y. Office)
Francis J. Quinn
Michael R. Clarke
John M. O'Reilly
Jayne A. Pritchard
Stephen A. Urban
John L. Buckheit
James A. Kozachek

For full biographical listings, see the Martindale-Hubbell Law Directory

*MOUNT HOLLY,** Burlington Co.

WELLS AND SINGER, P.A. (AV)

135 High Street, P.O. Box 100, 08060
Telephone: 609-267-0070
Bordentown, New Jersey Office: 6 East Park Street, P.O. Box 226.
Telephone: 609-298-1350.
Robbinsville, New Jersey Office: Bank Plaza, Suite C, 14 Main Street (Rt. 526).
Telephone: 609-587-3434.

William H. Wells
Jonas Singer
Paul Rubin
Robin E. Echevarria

Christopher R. Musulin
Deborah J. Merriam
Jennifer Lepow Kaminer

(See Next Column)

OF COUNSEL

Jeffrey Goldman

Counsel for: Bank of Mid-Jersey; The Bordentown Peoples Savings & Loan Assn.; Church Brick Co.; Ariston Airlines Catering Service, Inc.; Belasco Petroleum, Inc.; Arlenes Travel, Inc.; Walnridge Farms, Inc.; Walnridge Equine Clinic.

For full biographical listings, see the Martindale-Hubbell Law Directory

*NEWARK,** Essex Co.

BATHGATE, WEGENER, DUGAN & WOLF, P.C. (AV)

Three Gateway Center, Fifteenth Floor, 07102
Telephone: 201-623-6663
Telecopier: 201-623-5464
Lakewood, New Jersey Office: One Airport Road, Lakewood, New Jersey 08701.
Telephone: 908-363-0666.
Telecopier: 908-363-9864.

Lawrence E. Bathgate, II
Peter H. Wegener
James P. Dugan
William J. Wolf
Ross D. Gertner
Edward B. Kasselman
Stephan R. Leone
Dominic J. Aprile
Nancy G. Wright
Joseph A. DiCroce
Michael M. DiCicco

James A. Maggs
Robert L. Gutman
Neil Brodsky
Michael I. Halfacre

For full biographical listings, see the Martindale-Hubbell Law Directory

BROWN & BROWN, P.C. (AV)

One Gateway Center, Fifth Floor, 07102
Telephone: 201-622-1846
Fax: 201-622-2223
Jersey City, New Jersey Office:
Telephone: 201-656-2381.

Raymond A. Brown
Raymond M. Brown

Reference: National Westminster Bank, NJ.

For full biographical listings, see the Martindale-Hubbell Law Directory

CARPENTER, BENNETT & MORRISSEY (AV)

(Formerly Carpenter, Gilmour & Dwyer)
Three Gateway Center, 17th Floor, 100 Mulberry Street, 07102-4079
Telephone: 201-622-7711
New York City: 212-943-6530
Telex: 139405
Telecopier: 201-622-5314
EasyLink: 62827845
ABA/net: CARPENTERB

MEMBERS OF FIRM

James D. Carpenter (1885-1972)
Laurence Reich
John C. Heavey
John E. Keale
Edward F. Ryan
James J. Crowley, Jr.
John P. Dwyer
Michael S. Waters
Anthony C. Famulari
James G. Gardner
John F. Lynch, Jr.
Francis X. O'Brien
Donald A. Romano
Francis X. Dee
Rudy B. Coleman
Edward F. Day, Jr.
Irving L. Hurwitz
Rosemary J. Bruno
William A. Carpenter, Jr.
John J. Peirano
Linda B. Celauro
John D. Goldsmith
John K. Bennett
Patrick G. Brady
Louis M. DeStefano
Michael J. Greenwood
Thomas F. McGuane
Joseph D. Rasnek
Robert J. Stickles
Robert M. Goodman
Lynn D. Healy
Robert L. Heugle, Jr.
Jane Andrews
Thomas M. Moore
James E. Patterson
Scott J. Sheldon
Stephen F. Payerle

OF COUNSEL

Elmer J. Bennett
Thomas L. Morrissey
Warren Lloyd Lewis

ASSOCIATES

Glenn F. Corbett
Jane A. Rigby
Joel L. Botwick
Jennifer L. Kapell
Kevin C. Donovan
James Peter Lidon
Hans G. Polak
Lois H. Goodman
David J. Reilly
Dennis M. Helewa
John J. Shea
Douglas S. Witte
Michelle M. Hydrusko
Jeffrey Bernstein
Kevin F. Murphy
Joseph Gerard Lee
Patrick J. McNamara
Daniel J. O'Hern, Jr.
Matthew Q. Berge
Laura D. Castner
Margaret R. Bennett
Dawn M. Felipe
Bonnie E. Bershad
Michele L. Fliegel
Matthew Gitterman
L. Julius M. Turman

(See Next Column)

CARPENTER, BENNETT & MORRISSEY, *Newark—Continued*

ASSOCIATES (Continued)

Steven J. Santarsiero
Marc E. Wolin
C. Brian Kornbrek
Lisa A. Breen
Karen L. Mayer
Deborah L. Neilan
John M. O'Connor
David A. Cohen
Vimal K. Shah (Not admitted in NJ)
Judith A. Eisenberg

Representative Clients: General Motors Corp.; E. I. du Pont de Nemours and Company; Texaco Inc.; AT&T; Litton Industries; ITT Corp.; International Flavors & Fragrances Inc.; New Jersey Hospital Association; Prudential Insurance Company of America; United Jersey Bank.

For full biographical listings, see the Martindale-Hubbell Law Directory

CRUMMY, DEL DEO, DOLAN, GRIFFINGER & VECCHIONE, A PROFESSIONAL CORPORATION (AV)

One Riverfront Plaza, 07102
Telephone: 201-596-4500
Telecopier: 201-596-0545
Cable-Telex: 138154
Brussels, Belgium Office: Crummy, Del Deo, Dolan, Griffinger & Vecchione. Avenue Louise 475, BTE. 8, B-1050.
Telephone: 011-322-646-0019.
Telecopier: 011-322-646-0152.

Andrew B. Crummy (1895-1981)
Ralph N. Del Deo
John T. Dolan
Michael R. Griffinger
Frank J. Vecchione
Richard E. Cherin
Michael D. Loprete
Barry A. Osmun
Peter J. Carton
John A. Ridley
David J. Sheehan (Managing Partner)
Frank E. Lawatsch, Jr.
Frank B. Reilly, Jr.
James B. Keenan
Richard S. Zackin
Donald H. Steckroth
David M. Hyman
Arnold B. Calmann
Thomas N. Lyons
John H. Klock
Ann G. McCormick
Alyce Cesare Halchak
Brian J. McMahon
Terry R. Broderick (Not admitted in NJ; Resident, Brussels, Belgium Office)
Russell B. Bershad
Paul R. DeFilippo
Karen A. Giannelli
Paul M. Antinori
Philip W. Crawford
Ira J. Hammer
Susanne Peticolas
Kerry M. Parker
Michael F. Quinn
Mary Anne McDonald
Geraldine E. Ponto
Anthony P. La Rocco
John D. Draikiwicz
Gary F. Werner
Michael J. Lerner
Kevin J. McKenna
Stephen R. Reynolds
Jeffrey P. Flynn
Lawrence S. Lustberg
Christine A. Amalfe
Douglas J. Janacek
Guy V. Amoresano

SPECIAL COUNSEL

John J. Gibbons

COUNSEL

Henry J. Walsh
Lawrence A. Goldman
Steven H. Sholk
John V. Jacobi

Gemma M. Lury
John J. Reilly
Thomas R. Dean
Robert E. David
Kathleen M. Peregoy
Michael D. Grohman
David N. Crapo
John M. Marmora
Anthony J. Cincotta
David G. Uffelman
Kim Marie Uva
Sylvia M. Orenstein
Michael N. Aquino
Peter J. Ulrich
Ann Marie Dooley
Michael R. McDonald
Diane C. McDevitt
James M. Lee
Dale E. Barney
Alison Stewart Kerber
Frederick W. Alworth
Mark S. Sidoti
John T. Wolak
H. John Schank, II
Paul F. Cullum, III
Jacqueline N. Lumley
Mary Rose Migliazza
Robin A. Newman
David H. Wollmuth (Not admitted in NJ)
Evan A. Baker
Matthew S. Quinn
David E. De Lorenzi
Mary B. Holovacs
Stephen A. Santola
J. Timothy Mc Donald
Rita M. Nichols
Elizabeth Sarah Kardos
Patricia A. Szakats
Patricia A. Barbieri
Kim M. Catullo
Tanya D. Holcomb
Patrick C. Dunican, Jr.
Carole R. White-Connor
Sam Della Fera, Jr.
Lynn Dolan-Del Vecchio
James N. Lawlor
Robert J. Brener
Anthony J. Kacmarsky
April A. Savoye
Courtney E. Redfern
Jonathan Romberg
Robert F. D'Alessandro
Paul S. Doherty

LEGAL SUPPORT PERSONNEL

Thomas L. Simpson
Sylvia Reuben

Representative Clients: American Telephone & Telegraph Co.; Audit Bureau of Circulation; Hoffmann-La Roche Inc.; McGraw-Hill, Inc.; Mitsubishi Electric Corp.; Mobil Oil Corp.; The Gillette Co.; United Parcel Service, Inc.; Suzuki Motor Corp.

(See Next Column)

For full biographical listings, see the Martindale-Hubbell Law Directory

DEMARIA, ELLIS, HUNT, SALSBERG & FRIEDMAN (AV)

Suite 1400, 744 Broad Street, 07102
Telephone: 201-623-1699
Telecopier: 201-623-0954

MEMBERS OF FIRM

H. Reed Ellis
Ronald H. DeMaria
William J. Hunt
Richard M. Salsberg
Paul A. Friedman
Brian N. Flynn
Richard H. Bauch
Lee H. Udelsman

ASSOCIATES

Mitchell A. Schley
Joseph D. Olivieri
Joanne M. Maxwell
Robyn L. Aversa
George W. Rettig
David S. Catuogno
Debra S. Friedman
Kathryn A. Calista

For full biographical listings, see the Martindale-Hubbell Law Directory

FOX AND FOX (AV)

570 Broad Street, 07102
Telephone: 201-622-3624
Telecopier: 201-622-6220

MEMBERS OF FIRM

David I. Fox
Arthur D. Grossman
Paul I. Rosenberg
Kenneth H. Fast
Martin Kesselhaut
Dennis J. Alessi
Gabriel H. Halpern
Steven A. Holt
Nancy C. McDonald

OF COUNSEL

Jacob Fox (1898-1992)
Martin S. Fox
Robert J. Rohrberger
Robert S. Catapano-Friedman

ASSOCIATES

Robert P. Donovan
Stacey B. Rosenberg
Susan R. Fox
Virginia S. Ryan
Ronnie Ann Powell
Katherine J. Welsh
Craig S. Gumpel
Brett Alison Rosenberg
Alfred V. Acquaviva
Anthony F. Vitiello

For full biographical listings, see the Martindale-Hubbell Law Directory

GREENBERG DAUBER AND EPSTEIN, A PROFESSIONAL CORPORATION (AV)

Suite 600, One Gateway Center, 07102-5311
Telephone: 201-643-3700
Telecopier: 201-643-1218

Melvin Greenberg
Edward J. Dauber
Stanley A. Epstein
H. Glenn Tucker
Paul J. Dillon
Linda G. Harvey
Brenda J. Rediess-Hoosein
Adam W. Jacobs
Jeffrey S. Berkowitz
Kathryn Van Deusen Hatfield

For full biographical listings, see the Martindale-Hubbell Law Directory

HELLRING LINDEMAN GOLDSTEIN & SIEGAL (AV)

One Gateway Center, 07102-5386
Telephone: 201-621-9020
Telecopier: 201-621-7406

Bernard Hellring (1916-1991)
Philip Lindeman, II
Joel D. Siegal
Jonathan L. Goldstein
James A. Scarpone
Michael Edelson
Margaret Dee Hellring
Richard D. Shapiro
Charles Oransky
Richard B. Honig
Richard K. Coplon
Robert S. Raymar
Ronny Jo Greenwald Siegal
Stephen L. Dreyfuss
John A. Adler
Judah I. Elstein
Ronnie F. Liebowitz
Bruce S. Etterman
Matthew E. Moloshok
Rachel N. Davidson
Val Mandel
Sarah Jane Jelin
Eric A. Savage
David N. Narciso
Sheryl E. Koomer

For full biographical listings, see the Martindale-Hubbell Law Directory

LEVITAN & FRIELAND, P.C. (AV)

The Legal Center, Fifth Floor, One River Front Plaza, 07102
Telephone: 201-565-0011
Telecopier: 201-565-0451
Boca Raton, Florida Office: 7301A Palmetto Road, Suite 305C. 33433.
Telephone: 407-367-0626.
Telecopier: 407-367-0669.
Tampa, Florida Office: 3825 Henderson Boulevard, Suite 605A. 33629.
Telephone: 813-276-1788.
Telecopier: 813-276-1866.

Philip I. Levitan
Harry Frieland

(See Next Column)

LEVITAN & FRIELAND P.C.—*Continued*

David Goodman

Reference: Midlantic National Bank.

For full biographical listings, see the Martindale-Hubbell Law Directory

LEVY, EHRLICH & KRONENBERG, A PROFESSIONAL CORPORATION (AV)

60 Park Place, 07102
Telephone: 201-643-0040
Telecopier: 201-596-1781
Hackensack, New Jersey Office: 1 University Plaza, Suite 501, 07601.
Telephone: 301-342-4445.

Ira A. Levy
Arthur Kronenberg
Alan Ehrlich
John J. Petriello
David L. Eisbrouch

Janet Edelman
Daniel I. Hirsch
Bruce E. Gudin
Jeffrey A. Rizika

OF COUNSEL

Michael Antoniewicz
Alan E. Heckler (Not admitted in NJ)

Representative Clients: Panasonic Co.; Transamerica; General Electric.
Reference: First Fidelity Bank.

For full biographical listings, see the Martindale-Hubbell Law Directory

LOWENSTEIN, SANDLER, KOHL, FISHER & BOYLAN, A PROFESSIONAL CORPORATION

(See Roseland)

MATTSON, MADDEN & POLITO (AV)

One Gateway Center, 10th Floor, 07102-5311
Telephone: 201-621-7000
Fax: 201-621-7065

MEMBERS OF FIRM

Le Roy H. Mattson
John R. Leith
Edward G. Madden, Jr.
Mark L. Czyz
Joseph M. Soriano

OF COUNSEL

Andrew S. Polito
Francis T. Giuliano

ASSOCIATES

Charles J. Hayden
Raymond S. Gurak
Angelo A. Cuonzo

Representative Clients: New Jersey Manufacturers Insurance Co.; Chubb & Son, Inc.; Shell Oil Co.; Ford Motor Co.; North American Van Lines.

For full biographical listings, see the Martindale-Hubbell Law Directory

MCCARTER & ENGLISH (AV)

Four Gateway Center, 100 Mulberry Street, P.O. Box 652, 07101-0652
Telephone: 201-622-4444
Telecopier: 201-624-7070
Cable Address: "McCarter" Newark
Cherry Hill, New Jersey Office: 1810 Chapel Avenue West.
Telephone: 609-662-8444.
Telecopier: 609-662-6203.
New York, New York Office: Suite 1519, One World Trade Center.
Telephone: 212-466-9018.
Telecopier: 212-432-6568.
Boca Raton, Florida Office: 2255 Glades Road, Suite 319-A.
Telephone: 407-994-6262.
Telecopier: 407-241-0798.
Wilmington, Delaware Office: Mellon Bank Center, 919 Market Street.
Telephone: 302-654-8010.
Telecopier: 302-654-0795.

MEMBERS OF FIRM

Thomas N. McCarter (1845-1901)
Robert H. McCarter (1882-1941)
Conover English (1902-1963)
Francis E. P. McCarter (1947-1988)
Eugene M. Haring
George C. Witte, Jr.
Steven Barrett Hoskins
Rodney N. Houghton
Thomas F. Daly
Alfred L. Ferguson
Charles R. Merrill
Andrew T. Berry
John L. McGoldrick
Richard C. Cooper
Michael M. Horn
Richard W. Hill
William H. Horton
James F. Hammill (Resident Partner, Cherry Hill, New Jersey Office)
William J. O'Shaughnessy
William S. Greenberg
Frederick B. Lehlbach
Bart J. Colli
Richard M. Eittreim
John E. Flaherty
John A. McKinney, Jr.
William T. Reilly
Hayden Smith, Jr.
John B. Brescher, Jr.
Todd M. Poland
John J. Scally, Jr.
George W. C. McCarter
Roslyn S. Harrison

(See Next Column)

MEMBERS OF FIRM (Continued)

Gita F. Rothschild
David R. Kott
Lois M. Van Deusen
Jeffrey H. Aminoff (Resident Partner, New York, New York Office)
Michael A. Guariglia
Lanny S. Kurzweil
David A. Ludgin
Richard J. Webb
Rosemary Alito
John F. Brenner
Frank E. Ferruggia
Keith E. Lynott
Michael A. Tanenbaum
Richard P. O'Leary
Theodore D. Moskowitz
Scott A. Kobler
Therese M. Keeley (Resident, Cherry Hill, New Jersey Office)
Nathan A. Schachtman (Resident, Cherry Hill, New Jersey Office)
Seth T. Taube
Robert B. Anderson (Resident, Wilmington, Delaware Office)
Stephen M. Vajtay, Jr.
Myrna L. Wigod
Joseph Lubertazzi, Jr.
Mark A. Daniele
Carol C. Stern
Peter S. Twombly
David F. Broderick
James H. Keale
B. John Pendleton, Jr.
Stephen B. Pearlman
Lisa M. Goldman
Martin F. Dowd
Frederick T. Smith
Paul A. Bradley (Resident Partner, Wilmington, Delaware Office)
George H. Kendall
Jacqueline P. Shanes
Charles F. Rysavy
James J. Maron (Resident, Wilmington, Delaware Office)
John C. Garde, Jr.
Anthony Bartell
Linda A. Willett

OF COUNSEL

Woodruff J. English
Arthur C. Hensler, Jr.
Peter C. Aslanides
Nicholas Conover English
Julius B. Poppinga
Ward J. Herbert

COUNSEL

Joseph F. Falgiani
Gary Duescher
Steven A. Beckelman
Jerry P. Sattin
Beth Yingling
J. Forrest Jones
Gary T. Hall
Curtis A. Johnson
Robert W. Smith

SPECIAL COUNSEL

Allen N. Friedman

ASSOCIATES

John R. Drosdick
Charles J. Benjamin, Jr.
Brenda C. Liss
Kathleen O'Connell Keating
Kevin J. Connell
Steven N. J. Wlodychak
Claudia J. Keefe
Mary S. Cook (Resident, Cherry Hill, New Jersey Office)
Karen S. Brehm (Resident, Wilmington, Delaware Office)
Ellen Horowitz Dale
Edward S. Nathan
Robert K. Gunn
Robert A. Fishbein
David C. Apy
Mindy Jacobowitz
Alan C. Thomas
Phyllis Gutto
Paul C. Dritsas
Carol L. Widemon (Resident, Cherry Hill, New Jersey Office)
David L. DaCosta (Resident, Cherry Hill, New Jersey Office)
John C. McGuire
Teresa L. Moore
Joseph M. Aronds
Richard A. Beran
Lisa W.S. Bonsall
David S. Osterman
David S. Garber
Evolea C. Watson (Resident, Cherry Hill, New Jersey Office)
Mark Weissmann
William D. Wallach
Penelope M. Taylor
Eric J. Kadish (Resident, Cherry Hill, New Jersey Office)
Theresa Borzelli
D. Mark Leonard
Gerard G. Brew
Sherilyn Pastor
Gary M. DeFazio
Rosanne C. Baxter
Suzanne M. LaRobardier
Todd Mark Galante
Steven L. Wittels (Resident, New York, New York Office)
Walter A. Effross
Wayne A. Marvel (Resident, Wilmington, Delaware Office)
David E. Wilks (Resident, Wilmington, Delaware Office)
Mark David Lurie
Patrick J. Perrone
Susan C.G. Ericksen
Vito A. Pinto
Arnold L. Natali, Jr.
David A. Cohen (Resident, Cherry Hill, N.J. Office)
Valerie J. Tamburo
William P. Higgins, Jr.
Thomas D. Robertson
Andrew O. Bunn
Debra M. Perry
Edward J. Butler, Jr.
David J. Cooner
Malke Borow
Robin L. Goldfischer
Peter J. Ganz
Debra S. Groisser
Susan A. Feeney
Kimberly Waldron (Resident, Cherry Hill, New Jersey Office)
Katie A. Gummer
Deborah S. Verderame
Kathleen A. Pierce
David J. Adler
Annemarie DuPont
Quedel Principal
Andrew J. Schwartz
Jennifer D. Subryan
Mary W. Unger
David W. Opderbeck
Kenneth E. Thompson
Michael D. Siegel
Anthony Palmisano Jr.
Sheila E. Calello
Karen Depaola
Gregory M. Dyer
Karen L. Blinder
Dror Futter
Thomas W. Ladd
Sean F. Byrnes

(See Next Column)

McCARTER & ENGLISH, *Newark—Continued*

ASSOCIATES (Continued)

Anthony J. Del Piano
Diane Janofsky Rooney
Melanie Leslie
Richard T. Nolan, Jr.
Patricia M. Nigro (Resident, Cherry Hill, New Jersey Office)
Joseph T. Boccassini
Stephen E. Donahue
Barbara A. Favate
Bernadette Mary Wroblak
Robert A. Schwartz
Gayle D. Bernhaut
John K. Bradley
Nancy A. Washington
Stacy A. Silkworth
Robert A. Briedis
Cynthia Spera Neff
Susan C. Brodbeck
Lisa A. Chiappetta
Joseph L. Koerwer
Stephen Hauck
Lori S. Whittaker
Douglas S. Cohen
Emily J. Crowell
J. Wylie Donald
Francis A. Henry
Susan M. Mello
James E. Salitan
Mark A. Schuman
David L. Taylor, Jr.
Audrey A. Hale
Harvey C. Kaish
Cynthia Beagles
Anthony R. Higgins
John Carl Mills

For full biographical listings, see the Martindale-Hubbell Law Directory

McMANIMON & SCOTLAND (AV)

One Gateway Center, 18th Floor, 07102-5311
Telephone: 201-622-1800
Fax: 201-622-7333; 201-622-3744
Atlantic City, New Jersey Office: 26 South Pennsylvania Avenue.
Telephone: 609-347-0040.
Fax: 609-347-0866.
Trenton, New Jersey Office: 172 West State Street.
Telephone: 609-278-1800.
Fax: 609-278-9222.
Washington, D.C. Office: 1275 Pennsylvania Avenue, N.W.
Telephone: 202-638-3100.
Fax: 202-638-4222.

MEMBERS OF FIRM

Joseph P. Baumann, Jr.
Carla J. Brundage
John V. Cavaliere
Edward F. Clark
Christopher H. Falcon
Felicia L. Garland
James R. Gregory
John B. Hall
Thomas A. Hart, Jr. (Resident, Washington, D.C. Office)
Leah C. Healey
Ronald J. Ianoale
Andrea L. Kahn
Jeffrey G. Kramer
Michael A. Lampert
Joseph J. Maraziti, Jr.
Edward J. McManimon, III
Steven P. Natko
Martin C. Rothfelder
Steven Schaars (Resident, Washington, D.C. Office)
Glenn F. Scotland
Michael A. Walker

ASSOCIATES

Carl E. Ailara, Jr.
Diane Alexander-McCabe
Leslie G. London
Cheryl A. Maier
Daniel E. McManus
Sheryl L. Newman
Steven J. Reed
Erik F. Remmler
David J. Ruitenberg
Bradford M. Stern

OF COUNSEL

John R. Armstrong
Carl H. Fogler (Not admitted in NJ)

LEGAL SUPPORT PERSONNEL

Helen Lysaght

PARALEGALS

Jane Folmer
Zulmira Donahue

References: First Fidelity Bank, N.A., New Jersey; Midlantic National Bank.

For full biographical listings, see the Martindale-Hubbell Law Directory

MEDVIN & ELBERG (AV)

One Gateway Center, 16th Floor, 07102
Telephone: 201-642-1300
Fax: 201-642-8613

MEMBERS OF FIRM

Philip Elberg
Alan Y. Medvin

Robert A. Jones
Edna Y. Baugh

For full biographical listings, see the Martindale-Hubbell Law Directory

ROBINSON, ST. JOHN & WAYNE (AV)

Two Penn Plaza East, 07105-2249
Telephone: 201-491-3300
Fax: 201-491-3333
Rochester, New York Office: Robinson, St. John & Curtin. First Federal Plaza.
Telephone: 716-262-6780.
Fax: 716-262-6755.
New York, New York Office: 245 Park Avenue.
Telephone: 212-953-0700.
Fax: 212-880-6555.

(See Next Column)

MEMBERS OF FIRM

Lee A. Albanese
Timothy R. Curtin (Resident at Rochester, New York Office)
Bernard S. Davis
Paul D. Drobbin
W. Hunt Dumont
Bruce S. Edington
David C. Freinberg
Walter J. Greenhalgh
Steven B. Harz
Mark F. Hughes, Jr.
Joseph F. Lagrotteria
Steven L. Lapidus
Paul J. Linker
Kevin H. Marino
Timothy R. McGill (Resident at Rochester, New York Office)
Edward R. McGlynn
John J. Oberdorf
William P. Oberdorf
Daniel F. Peck, Jr.
Bryan G. Petkanics (Resident at New York, New York Office)
Donald A. Robinson
Thomas D. Ruane (Resident, New York, New York Office)
Jerome M. St. John (Resident, New York, New York Office)
Peter G. Seiden (Resident, New York, New York Office)
Peter B. Van Deventer, Jr.
Robert A. Wayne (Resident, New York, New York Office)
E. Kenneth Williams, Jr.

ASSOCIATES

Bryant Kenneth Aaron
Douglas H. Amster
Felicia Nigro Ballard
Kathleen M. Barnett
Allen V. Brown
Claire C. Cecchi
Nicholas J. DeFabrizio (Resident, New York, New York Office)
Gerard S. DiFiore
Cecelia A. Donato
Mary Ann T. Dubiel
H. Scott Ellis
Louis R. Franzese (Resident, New York, New York Office)
Kate T. Gallagher
Kevin P. Galvin
Donna duBeth Gardiner
Bruce Gieseman
Carolyn A. Greene
Cheryl J. Gross
Serene M. Hennion
Donna M. Hughes
Joseph A. Infantolino
Leslie Ann Lajewski
John P. Maloney
Steve Manley
Keith J. Miller
David W. Phillips
Darin D. Pinto
William M. A. Porter
John Patrick Reilly
John J. Sarno
James T. Seery
Andrew Shakalis
Ross W. Smith
David H. Stein
David E. Strand
Gregory G. Tole
Karol Corbin Walker
John S. Wisniewski

OF COUNSEL

Charles D. Hellman
John B. Livelli
Patrick M. Malgieri (Resident, Rochester, New York Office)
Mark B. Rosenman
James I. Wyer

For full biographical listings, see the Martindale-Hubbell Law Directory

SAIBER SCHLESINGER SATZ & GOLDSTEIN (AV)

One Gateway Center, 13th Floor, 07102-5311
Telephone: 201-622-3333
Telecopier: 201-622-3349

MEMBERS OF FIRM

David M. Satz, Jr.
Bruce I. Goldstein
William F. Maderer
David J. D'Aloia
James H. Aibel
Sean R. Kelly
John L. Conover
Lawrence B. Mink
Michael L. Allen
Michael L. Messer
Jeffrey W. Lorell
Jeffrey M. Schwartz
David J. Satz
Joan M. Schwab
Jennine DiSomma
James H. Forte
Vincent F. Papalia

OF COUNSEL

Samuel S. Saiber
Norman E. Schlesinger

COUNSEL

Andrew Alcorn
Robin B. Horn
Randi Schillinger

ASSOCIATES

Audrey M. Weinstein
Robert B. Nussbaum
Michael J. Geraghty
Jonathan S. Davis
Paul S. DeGiulio
Diana L. Sussman
Deanna M. Beacham
Robert W. Geiger
William S. Gyves
Barry P. Kramer
Susan Rozman
Michelle Viola

LEGAL SUPPORT PERSONNEL

DIRECTOR OF FINANCE AND ADMINISTRATION

Ronald Henry

For full biographical listings, see the Martindale-Hubbell Law Directory

SILLS CUMMIS ZUCKERMAN RADIN TISCHMAN EPSTEIN & GROSS, A PROFESSIONAL CORPORATION (AV)

One Riverfront Plaza, 07102-5400
Telephone: 201-643-7000
Fax: 201-643-6500
Telex: 820630 Sillsbeck Nwk
Atlantic City, New Jersey Office: 17 Gordon's Alley.
Telephone: 609-344-2800.

(See Next Column)

Sills Cummis Zuckerman Radin Tischman Epstein & Gross A Professional Corporation—*Continued*

New York, N.Y. Office: 250 Park Avenue.
Telephone: 212-643-7000.

Arthur J. Sills (1917-1982)
Clive S. Cummis
Steven S. Radin
Herbert L. Zuckerman
Michael B. Tischman
Morton S. Bunis
Stanley Tannenbaum
Barry M. Epstein
Steven E. Gross
Thomas J. Demski
Jeffrey Hugh Newman
Lawrence S. Horn
Charles J. Walsh
Jeffrey J. Greenbaum
Simon Levin
Stephen J. Moses
Morris Yamner
Gerald Span
Jeffrey Barton Cahn
Noah Bronkesh (Resident at Atlantic City, N.J. Office)
Lester Aron
Steven M. Goldman
Cecil J. Banks
Kenneth F. Oettle
Alan E. Sherman
Robert J. Alter
Ira A. Rosenberg
Robert Crane
Marc S. Klein
Philip R. Sellinger
Jack M. Zackin
Nelson C. Johnson (Resident at Atlantic City Office)
Thomas S. Novak
Jerry Genberg
Stuart M. Feinblatt
Margaret F. Black
Robert M. Axelrod
Brian S. Coven
Trent S. Dickey
Richard J. Schulman (Not admitted in NJ)
Bernard I. Flateman
William M. Russell
Joseph L. Buckley
Kathleen Gengaro
David J. Rabinowitz
Stanley U. North, III
James D. Toll (Resident at Atlantic City, N.J. Office)
James M. Hirschhorn
Allan C. Bell
Ronald C. Rak
Mark S. Olinsky
Richard J. Sapinski
Victor H. Boyajian
Philip R. White
Alan J. Cohen (Resident at Atlantic City, N.J. Office)
Mark J. Blunda
Lori G. Singer

Noel D. Humphreys
Patricia M. Kerins
Diane M. Lavenda
Wayne B. Heicklen (Not admitted in NJ)
Cherie L. Maxwell
Glenn E. Davis
Harry B. Noretsky
Steven B. Jackman (Not admitted in NJ)
Stuart Rosen
Eileen O'Donnell
Nathan E. Arnell
Steven R. Rowland
Jack Wenik
Eric D. Mann (Resident at Atlantic City, N.J. Office)
Stephen McNally
Mark E. Duckstein
Beth S. Rose
Scott N. Rubin
Frederic M. Tudor
Kenneth L. Moskowitz
Steven Shapiro (Not admitted in NJ)
Alma Lutjen Abrams
A. Ross Pearlson (Not admitted in NJ)
Jeffrey M. Pollock
Bennet Susser
Jodi S. Brodsky
Robert W. Burke
Scott T. Gruber
Jay A. Soled
Steven S. Katz
Linda Badash Katz
Richard S. Schkolnick
Ted Zangari
N. Lynne Hughes (Resident at Atlantic City Office)
Derlys Maria Gutierrez
Sally H. Atkins
Lester Chanin
Paul P. Josephson
Douglas R. Weider
Patricia Brown Fugee
Paul F. Doda
Lora L. Fong
Joshua D. Goodman
Helen E. Kleiner
Rhonda Sobral
Bryan S. Greenberg
Jeffrey M. Weinhaus
Adam Kaiser
Alissa Pyrich
Robert Rosenberg
Keith J. Weingold
Gayle N. Wolkenberg
Garry Rogers
Jennifer L. Borofsky
Joseph D. Glazer
Vaughn L. McKoy
Gwen L. Posner
Susanne K. Rosenzweig
Michele-Lee Berko
Lorraine M. Potenza

OF COUNSEL

David Beck
Victor Futter (Resident at New York, N.Y. Office)
Dena L. Wolf
Jay J. Miller (Resident at New York, N.Y. Office)
Mitchel E. Ostrer

LEGAL SUPPORT PERSONNEL

William P. Rebarick (Executive Director)
Carol J. Allen (Director of Business Development)
Ann E. Freeh (Personnel Manager)
Harvey Kaplowitz (Office Operations Manager)
John A. White (Chief Financial Officer)
Matthew Larkin (Records Manager)
Roberta George (Library Director)
Paul Sutton (MIS Manager)

Representative Clients: Bally's Entertainment Corp.; Blue Cross/Blue Shield of New Jersey; Bristol-Myers Squibb Co.; FIAT U.S.A., Inc.; Jersey City Medical Center; Margaretten Financial Corp.; Marvin Davis Companies; Newark Performing Arts Center; Six Flags Corporation; WWOR-TV, Inc.

For full biographical listings, see the Martindale-Hubbell Law Directory

Stryker, Tams & Dill (AV)

Two Penn Plaza East, 07105
Telephone: 201-491-9500
Fax: 201-491-9692
New York, N.Y. Office: One World Trade Center, Suite 7967.
Telephone: 212-432-9180.

MEMBERS OF FIRM

George A. Aguilar
Melvyn H. Bergstein
Charles M. Costenbader
Ellen S. Delo
Harold Friedman
Charles H. Friedrich, III
Martin G. Gilbert
Joseph E. Kinsella, Jr.
Stephen H. Knee
Dennis C. Linken
Edward N. Lippincott
Ellen O'Connell
Basil F. O'Connor
Edith K. Payne
John J. Rizzo
Virginia G. White

COUNSEL

John H. Awerdick
John R. Kettle, III
Robert A. Marsico
Thomas E. Moseley
Patricia M. Talbert
Alan N. Walter

OF COUNSEL

Burtis W. Horner

ASSOCIATES

Janice L. Birnbaum
Frances Farber-Walter
Martin B. Gill
Sandra Durant Herbert
John P. Leonard
Janice Manganello
John P. O'Toole
Diane Stolbach
Edgar M. Whiting, III

Counsel for: AMP, Incorporated; American International Group, Inc.; Bankers Trust Company; Brunswick Corporation; Eastman Kodak Company; Navistar Financial Corporation; The Prudential Insurance Company of America; USX Corporation.

For full biographical listings, see the Martindale-Hubbell Law Directory

Tompkins, McGuire & Wachenfeld (AV)

A Partnership including a Professional Corporation
Four Gateway Center, 100 Mulberry Street, 07102-4070
Telephone: 201-622-3000
Telecopier: 201-623-7780

MEMBERS OF FIRM

William F. Tompkins (1913-1989)
William B. McGuire (P.A.)
Howard G. Wachenfeld
Francis X. Crahay
Theodore L. Abeles
William J. Prout, Jr.
Rex K. Harriott
Michael F. Nestor
James F. Flanagan, III
Marianne Espinosa Murphy
Christopher James Carey
Marianne M. De Marco
Patrick M. Callahan
John J. Henschel
Michael S. Miller
Douglas E. Motzenbecker
Frederic S. Kessler

ASSOCIATES

Evelyn A. Donegan
Joseph K. Cobuzio
George G. Campion
Leonore C. Lewis
Richard F. Connors, Jr.
Richard A. Ulsamer
Anthony E. Bush
Gina G. Milestone
John R. Watkins, II
Angelo Giacchi
Nadia M. Walker
Diane E. Sugrue
Brian M. English
Cynthia K. Stroud
Lisa W. Santola
David S. Blatteis
Whitney W. Bremer
Carol J. Gismondi
Albert Wesley McKee

OF COUNSEL

William T. Wachenfeld
Paul B. Thompson
Frances S. Margolis
William J. McGee

COUNSEL

Ellen Nunno Corbo
Evelyn R. Storch
William H. Trousdale

Representative Clients: Corbo Jewelers, Inc.; General Electric Co.; Hartford Insurance Group; Marriott Corp.; National Union Fire Insurance Co.; Underwriters at Lloyd's, London.

For full biographical listings, see the Martindale-Hubbell Law Directory

Zazzali, Zazzali, Fagella & Nowak, A Professional Corporation (AV)

One Riverfront Plaza, 07102-5410
Telephone: 201-623-1822
Telecopier: 201-623-2209
Trenton, New Jersey Office: 150 West State Street.
Telephone: 609-392-8172.
Telecopier: 609-392-8933.

Andrew F. Zazzali (1925-1969)
Andrew F. Zazzali, Jr.
James R. Zazzali
Robert A. Fagella
Kenneth I. Nowak

(See Next Column)

ZAZZALI, ZAZZALI, FAGELLA & NOWAK A PROFESSIONAL CORPORATION, *Newark—Continued*

Paul L. Kleinbaum
Richard A. Friedman
Kathleen Anne Naprstek
Michael J. Buonoaguro
Aileen M. O'Driscoll
Charles J. Farley, Jr.
Edward H. O'Hare

For full biographical listings, see the Martindale-Hubbell Law Directory

*NEW BRUNSWICK,** Middlesex Co.

BORRUS, GOLDIN & FOLEY, A PROFESSIONAL CORPORATION

(See Borrus, Goldin, Foley, Vignuolo, Hyman & Stahl, A Professional Corporation, North Brunswick)

HOAGLAND, LONGO, MORAN, DUNST & DOUKAS (AV)

40 Paterson Street, P.O. Box 480, 08903
Telephone: 908-545-4717
Fax: 908-545-4579

MEMBERS OF FIRM

John J. Hoagland
Bartholomew A. Longo
James B. Moran
Alan I. Dunst
Kenneth J. Doukas, Jr.
Michael John Stone
Donald D. Davidson
Thaddeus J. Hubert, III
Joan Alster Weisblatt
Karen M. Buerle
Robert G. Kenny
Michael J. Baker
Robert J. Young
Andrew J. Carlowicz, Jr.
Gary J. Hoagland
Jeffrey S. Intravatola
Jamie D. Happas
Thomas J. Walsh
Robert S. Helwig
Michael F. Dolan
Douglas M. Fasciale
Carol Lonergan Perez
Marc S. Gaffrey

OF COUNSEL

Herman L. Breitkopf

ASSOCIATES

John Charles Simons
Susan K. O'Connor
Stephen G. Perrella
Jacquelyn L. Poland
Gary S. Shapiro
Douglas Susan
Anne M. Weidenfeller
Edward Hoagland, Jr.
Patrick J. McDonald
Susan M. Pierce
Andrew N. Kessler
Ashley C. Paul
R. Michael Keefe
Robert B. Rogers
Carleen M. Steward
Claire N. Gallagher
Dennis P. Liloia
John P. Barnes
Daniel J. Cogan
Judith B. Moor
Kevin Nerwinski

Representative Clients: American International Group; Brush Wellman, Inc.; CNA/Continental Casualty; K. Hovnanian Companies; National Westminster Bank; St. Peter's Medical Center; Underwriters Adjusting Co.; U.S. Healthcare; Xerox; Yellow Freight System.

For full biographical listings, see the Martindale-Hubbell Law Directory

NORTH BRUNSWICK, Middlesex Co.

BORRUS, GOLDIN, FOLEY, VIGNUOLO, HYMAN & STAHL, A PROFESSIONAL CORPORATION (AV)

2875 U.S. Highway 1, Route 1 & Finnigans Lane, P.O. Box 1963, 08902
Telephone: 908-422-1000
Fax: 908-422-1016

Jack Borrus
Martin S. Goldin
David M. Foley
Anthony B. Vignuolo
Jeffrey M. Hyman
James E. Stahl
James F. Clarkin III
Anthony M. Campisano
Aphrodite C. Koscelansky
Robert C. Nisenson
Michael L. Marcus
Eileen Mary Foley
Rosalind Westlake

OF COUNSEL

Gerald T. Foley (1903-1976)

Representative Clients: United Jersey Bank/Franklin State; R. J. Reynolds Tobacco Co.; N.J. Aluminum Co.; K. Hovnanian Enterprises, Inc.; Chicago Title Insurance Co.; Transamerica Title Insurance Co.

For full biographical listings, see the Martindale-Hubbell Law Directory

BUSCH AND BUSCH (AV)

215 North Center Drive, Commerce Center - U.S. #1 South, P.O. Box 7448, 08902-7448
Telephone: 908-821-2300
Telecopier: 908-821-5588

OF COUNSEL

Henry Busch

(See Next Column)

MEMBERS OF FIRM

Lewis D. Busch (1901-1986)
Malcolm R. Busch
Ronald J. Busch
Bertram E. Busch
Mark N. Busch
Leonard R. Busch
Steven F. Satz

Donald J. Sears
Kenneth A. Levine

Representative Clients: Littman Jewelers; Middlesex County Mosquito Extermination Commission; Utica Mutual Insurance Co.; New Brunswick Tomorrow; Township of East Brunswick; Minnesota Mutual Life Insurance Co.; Township of Monroe, Board of Education.

For full biographical listings, see the Martindale-Hubbell Law Directory

NUTLEY, Essex Co.

STRASSER & ASSOCIATES, A PROFESSIONAL CORPORATION (AV)

391 Franklin Avenue, P.O. Box 595, 07110-0107
Telephone: 201-661-5000
Fax: 201-661-0056
Saddle River, New Jersey Office: 70 East Allendale Road, 07458.
Telephone: 201-236-1861.
Fax: 201-236-1863.

William I. Strasser

Robert J. Bavagnoli
Stephen J. Morrone

For full biographical listings, see the Martindale-Hubbell Law Directory

ORADELL, Bergen Co.

NICOLETTE & PERKINS, P.A. (AV)

555 Kinderkamack Road, P.O. Box 549, 07649
Telephone: 201-261-9300
Telecopier: 201-261-8855

David A. Nicolette, Jr.
Eric R. Perkins

Evelyn J. Marose
Jeanette A. Odynski

For full biographical listings, see the Martindale-Hubbell Law Directory

PENNSAUKEN, Camden Co.

SHERMAN, SILVERSTEIN, KOHL, ROSE & PODOLSKY, A PROFESSIONAL CORPORATION (AV)

Fairway Corporate Center, Suite 311, 4300 Haddonfield Road, 08109
Telephone: 609-662-0700
Fax: 609-662-0165
Lakewood, New Jersey Office: 395 Route 70, Suite 205.
Telephone: 908-901-7878.
Bala Cynwyd, Pennsylvania Office: 11 Bala Avenue.
Telephone: 215-923-2513.

Lee S. Sherman
Lee Silverstein
John W. Kohl
M. Zev Rose
Steven M. Podolsky
Andrew J. Karcich
Barry E. Yellin
Alan C. Milstein
Nan S. Famular
John R. Lolio, Jr.
Robert W. Lynch
Phyllis Z. Sherman
R. David Danziger
Michael J. Curry
Daniel J. Barrison (Not admitted in NJ)
Thomas J. Tamburelli
Rhonda R. Feld
Leon H. Rose
Robert E. Schwartz

Leonard R. Rossetti
Harris L. Pogust
Roy D. Ruggiero

OF COUNSEL

Robert M. Washburn

For full biographical listings, see the Martindale-Hubbell Law Directory

PERTH AMBOY, Middlesex Co.

WILENTZ, GOLDMAN & SPITZER, A PROFESSIONAL CORPORATION

(See Woodbridge)

PRINCETON, Mercer Co.

BUCHANAN INGERSOLL (AV)

A Partnership
College Centre, 500 College Road East, 08540-6615
Telephone: 609-452-2666
Telecopier: 609-520-0360
Pittsburgh, Pennsylvania Office: Buchanan Ingersoll, Professional Corporation, 5800 USX Tower, 600 Grant Street.
Telephone: 412-562-8800.

(See Next Column)

BUCHANAN INGERSOLL—*Continued*

Philadelphia, Pennsylvania Office: Buchanan Ingersoll, Professional Corporation, Two Logan Square, Twelfth Floor, 18th & Arch Streets.
Telephone: 215-665-8700.
Harrisburg, Pennsylvania Office: Buchanan Ingersoll, Professional Corporation, Vartan Parc, 30 North Third Street.
Telephone: 717-237-4800.
Tampa, Florida Office: Buchanan Ingersoll, Professional Corporation, 101 East Kennedy Boulevard, Suite 1030.
Telephone: 813-222-8180.
North Miami Beach, Florida Office: Buchanan Ingersoll, Professional Corporation, 19495 Biscayne Boulevard.
Telephone: 305-933-5600.
Lexington, Kentucky Office: Buchanan Ingersoll, Professional Corporation, 1210 Vine Center Office Tower, 333 West Vine Street.
Telephone: 606-225-5333.

Frank S. Chow
Steven S. Goldenberg
David J. Sorin

SENIOR ATTORNEY

William J. Thomas

Michael C. Gibbs (Not admitted in NJ)
Andrew P. Gilbert
Catherine M. Verna

For full biographical listings, see the Martindale-Hubbell Law Directory

DECHERT PRICE & RHOADS (AV)

Princeton Pike Corporate Center, P.O. Box 5218, 08543
Telephone: 609-520-3200
Telefax: 609-520-3259
Philadelphia, Pennsylvania: 4000 Bell Atlantic Tower, 1717 Arch Street.
Telephone: 215-994-4000.
Harrisburg, Pennsylvania: Thirty North Third Street.
Telephone: 717-237-2000.
New York, N.Y.: 477 Madison Avenue.
Telephone: 212-326-3500.
Washington, D.C.: 1500 K Street, N.W.
Telephone: 202-626-3300.
Boston, Massachusetts: Ten Post Office Square South, 12th Floor.
Telephone: 617-728-7100.
London, England: 2 Serjeants' Inn, EC4Y 1LT.
Telephone: (071) 583-5353. (Also see Titmuss Sainer Dechert).
Brussels, Belgium: 65 Avenue Louise, 1050.
Telephone: (02) 535-5411.

RESIDENT PARTNERS

Allen Bloom
Todd D. Johnston
James J. Marino
A. Patrick Nucciarone
George G. O'Brien
Gil C. Tily
Jay L. Zagoren

RESIDENT COUNSEL

Susan M. Hendrickson

RESIDENT ASSOCIATES

Bruce W. Clark
Eric A. Cohn
Matthew V. Del Duca
Raffaella De Trizio
Paul A. Devlin
Mariellen Harrington
Arthur E. Jackson (Not admitted in NJ)
Robert D. Rhoad

For full biographical listings, see the Martindale-Hubbell Law Directory

JAMIESON, MOORE, PESKIN & SPICER, A PROFESSIONAL CORPORATION (AV)

300 Alexander Park CN 5276, 08543-5276
Telephone: 609-452-0808
Fax: 609-452-1147; 452-0943; 951-0096
Trenton, New Jersey Office: Capitol View Building, 150 West State Street.
Telephone: 609-396-5511.

Nola R. Bencze
James J. Britt, Jr.
Dennis R. Casale
Arthur F. Herrmann
Thomas Crawford Jamieson, Jr.
Ann F. Kiernan
Edwin S. Leavitt-Gruberger
Thomas M. Letizia
Ross A. Lewin
Kevin L. Lilly
Michael J. Mann
Thomas G. McMahon
John D. McQuarrie, Jr.
Arthur Meisel
Herbert F. Moore
Kevin J. Moore
Timothy J. O'Neill
Jay Samuels
Neal L. Schonhaut
Mark Solomon
Michael F. Spicer
Thomas P. Weidner
Audrey Wisotsky

OF COUNSEL

Dominick A. Mazzagetti

Leslie A. Adelman
Susan Peper Boudreau
Stephen J. Cusma
John J. Englert
Patricia Urken Herst
Lainie L. Kernis
Anna S. Mendelsohn
Jonathan M. Preziosi
Howard Schachter
Julie Riley Tattoni
John W. Verlaque

(See Next Column)

Representative Clients: New Jersey Bankers Assn.; New Jersey Dental Assn.; Midlantic National Bank; Garden State Land; New Jersey School Boards Insurance Group; Cenlar Federal Savings Bank; Resolution Trust Corp. (RTC); Bristol-Meyers/Squibb; Rider College; Johnson & Johnson.

For full biographical listings, see the Martindale-Hubbell Law Directory

MASON, GRIFFIN & PIERSON, A PROFESSIONAL CORPORATION (AV)

101 Poor Farm Road, 08540
Telephone: 609-921-6543
Fax: 609-683-7978
Hoboken, New Jersey Office: 625 Washington Street, 07030.
Telephone: 201-222-8000.
Fax: 201-222-3292.

Ralph S. Mason (1913-1988)
Gordon D. Griffin
Kester R. Pierson
Edwin W. Schmierer
Craig H. Davis
Kristina Pike Hadinger
George W. Fisher
Donald B. Veix, Jr.
Edward D. Penn
Charles F. Harris
John L. Thurman
James M. Farrell
James J. Burke

Valerie L. Howe
Thomas J. Irwin
Barbara J. Morgan
Shawn M. Neufeld
Elizabeth Zuckerman

OF COUNSEL

Edmond M. Konin
Henry L. Kent-Smith

Representative Clients: Aetna Casualty & Surety Co.; BP America, Inc.; Crestmont Federal Savings; FMC Corporation; InfoMed, Inc.; John Hancock Mutual Life Insurance Co.; Mobil Oil; Taco Bell; Township of Princeton; United Jersey Bank/Central, N.A.

For full biographical listings, see the Martindale-Hubbell Law Directory

MCCARTHY AND SCHATZMAN, P.A. (AV)

228 Alexander Street, P.O. Box 2329, 08543-2329
Telephone: 609-924-1199
Fax: 609-683-5251

John F. McCarthy, Jr.
Richard Schatzman
G. Christopher Baker
John F. McCarthy, III
Michael A. Spero
Barbara Strapp Nelson
W. Scott Stoner

James A. Endicott
Angelo J. Onofri

Representative Clients: Trustees of Princeton University; The Linpro Co.; United Jersey Bank; Chemical Bank, New Jersey, N.A.; Carnegie Center Associates; Merrill Lynch Pierce Fenner & Smith, Inc.; Prudential Insurance Co.

For full biographical listings, see the Martindale-Hubbell Law Directory

MILLER, PORTER & MULLER (AV)

Suite 540, One Palmer Square, 08542
Telephone: 609-921-6077
Fax: 609-497-1439

MEMBERS OF FIRM

William Miller (1913-1977)
Allen D. Porter
Gerald J. Muller

References: Chemical Bank New Jersey, N.A.; United Jersey Bank; Trust Company of Princeton.

For full biographical listings, see the Martindale-Hubbell Law Directory

SMITH, STRATTON, WISE, HEHER & BRENNAN (AV)

600 College Road East, 08540
Telephone: 609-924-6000
FAX: 609-987-6651

MEMBERS OF FIRM

John Robert Heher
William J. Brennan, III
Christopher S. Tarr
Ann Reichelderfer
Wendy L. Mager
Richard J. Pinto
Brian P. Sullivan
Suzanne M. McSorley
Marsha E. Novick
Robert C. Johnston
Peter R. Freed
Thomas E. Hastings
Elizabeth R. Salasko
Diane M. Frenier

ASSOCIATES

Jay A. Ganzman
Megan E. Thomas
Penny A. Bennett
Jay M. Tuckerman
Edward P. Bromley, III
Seth G. Park
Thomas E. Schorr
Grayson Barber
Yale H. Bohn
Carol M. Bianchi
Douglas S. Worthington

(See Next Column)

SMITH, STRATTON, WISE, HEHER & BRENNAN, *Princeton—Continued*

OF COUNSEL

Hugh D. Wise, Jr.
James Scott Hill
Arthur S. Lane
Robert D. Frawley

Representative Clients: Alteon, Inc.; Bristol-Myers Squibb Co.; Princeton Bank & Trust; Princeton University; The Medical Center at Princeton; Princeton Theological Seminary; New Jersey Hospital Assn.; Allstate Insurance Co.

For full biographical listings, see the Martindale-Hubbell Law Directory

RAMSEY, Bergen Co.

FRANCIS T. GIULIANO (AV)

102 Hilltop Road, P.O. Box 340, 07446
Telephone: 201-825-7675
Fax: 201-825-2672
(Also Of Counsel to Mattson, Madden & Polito, Newark, New Jersey)

For full biographical listings, see the Martindale-Hubbell Law Directory

DONALD C. OHNEGIAN (AV)

88 West Main Street, P.O. Box 360, 07446
Telephone: 201-327-7000
Telefax: 201-327-6651

ASSOCIATE

Diane K. Gaylinn

Representative Clients: Upon Request.

For full biographical listings, see the Martindale-Hubbell Law Directory

WEBER, MUTH & WEBER (AV)

One Cherry Lane, P.O. Box 912, 07446-0912
Telephone: 201-327-5000
Telecopier: 201-327-6848

MEMBERS OF FIRM

Walter W. Weber, Jr.
Irwin B. Klugman
Clinton A. Poff

ASSOCIATES

Carole Ann Geronimo
Cynthia A. Kasica
Andrea A. Angera, Jr.
Margaret G. Weber (1925-1990)

For full biographical listings, see the Martindale-Hubbell Law Directory

RED BANK, Monmouth Co.

PHILIP G. AUERBACH A PROFESSIONAL CORPORATION (AV)

231 Maple Avenue, P.O. Box Y, 07701
Telephone: 908-842-6660

Philip G. Auerbach

Edward A. Genz
John J. Ryan

For full biographical listings, see the Martindale-Hubbell Law Directory

DRAZIN AND WARSHAW (AV)

25 Reckless Place, 07701
Telephone: 908-747-3730
Fax: 908-741-0865
Brick, New Jersey Office: 937 Cedar Bridge Road.
Telephone: 908-477-1700.
Hazlet, New Jersey Office: 3315 Highway 35.
Telephone: 908-264-6900.

MEMBERS OF FIRM

Louis M. Drazin (1915-1988)
Thomas T. Warshaw
Dennis A. Drazin
Ronald S. Drazin
Brian D. Drazin

ASSOCIATES

Thomas J. DiChiara
Christopher R. Brown
Vincent L. Stripto
Ralph E. Polcari
Steven L. Kessel
Vincent N. Falcetano, Jr.
John R. Connelly, Jr.
Philip S. Rosenzweig
Roy D. Curnow
Thomas F. Shebell, III
Richard A. Amdur, Jr.

Approved Attorneys for: First Fidelity Bank N.A.; Fidelity Union Trust Co.; Prudential Insurance Company of America; Shadowlawn Savings & Loan Assn.; Carteret Savings & Loan Assn.; Howard Savings & Loan Assn.; United Counties Trust Co.; Midlantic/Merchants.

For full biographical listings, see the Martindale-Hubbell Law Directory

EVANS, OSBORNE, KREIZMAN & BONNEY (AV)

P.O. Box BB, 07701-0569
Telephone: 908-741-9550
Telecopier: 908-741-6536
New York, N.Y. Office: Suite 7967, One World Trade Center.
Telephone: 212-466-1207.

(See Next Column)

MEMBERS OF FIRM

Harry S. Evans
Robert S. Bonney, Jr.
Harry V. Osborne, II
Mary Patricia Magee
Joel N. Kreizman
Mary O'Keefe Massey
John P. Croake
Kevin E. Hoffman

ASSOCIATES

Joseph J. Colao, Jr.
Marie A. Accardi
Susan P. Friedel

OF COUNSEL

R. Gale Rhodes, Jr.
Burton L. Fundler
Lewis H. Robertson
Chester Apy

Representative Clients: United Kingdom P&I Club (Thomas R. Miller & Son, London; Transport Mutual Services Inc., New York); Through Transport Club (New Jersey Correspondent); American Marine Underwriters, Inc.; Continental Insurance Cos.; Hartford Insurance Cos.; Insurance Company of North America (CIGNA Cos.); Jersey Central Power & Light Co.; First Fidelity Bank.

For full biographical listings, see the Martindale-Hubbell Law Directory

LEBENSFELD & ASSOCIATES, P.C. (AV)

140 Broad Street, 07701
Telephone: 908-530-4600
Fax: 908-530-4601
New York, N.Y. Office: 342 Madison Avenue, Suite 1800, 10173.
Telephone: 212-856-9530.
Fax: 212-856-9601.

Alan M. Lebensfeld

Shari D. Nisenson (Resident)
David M. Grill (Resident, New York, NY Office)
Hope G. Brodsky (Resident)
Richard L. Blatt (Resident, New York City Office)

OF COUNSEL

Stephen Sussman

Bank Reference: Bank of New York.

For full biographical listings, see the Martindale-Hubbell Law Directory

REUSSILLE, MAUSNER, CAROTENUTO, BRUNO & BARGER (AV)

365 Broad Street, 07701
Telephone: 908-741-1800
Fax: 908-758-9724
Lakewood, New Jersey Office: 718-A Buckingham Drive.
Telephone: 908-364-4900.
Whiting, New Jersey Office: 38-B Whiting Shopping Center.
Telephone: 908-350-3200.

MEMBERS OF FIRM

John S. Applegate, Sr. (1837-1916)
E. Allaire Cornwell (1902-1978)
John S. Applegate, Jr. (1872-1950)
Alston Beekman, Jr. (1911-1985)
William E. Foster (1887-1952)
Samuel Carotenuto
Leon Reussille, Jr. (1890-1980)
Anthony T. Bruno
Martin M. Barger
Donald B. Steel

ASSOCIATES

John Mercadante
Joel A. Davies

OF COUNSEL

Milton A. Mausner

Representative Clients: Monmouth Regional High School; Borough of Shrewsbury; Colonial State Bank; Borough of Fair Haven; Brookdale Community College, Original Leisure Village; Leisure Village East Association, Leisuretown Association.

For full biographical listings, see the Martindale-Hubbell Law Directory

RIDGEWOOD, Bergen Co.

HARWOOD LLOYD (AV)

41 Oak Street, 07450
Telephone: 201-447-1422
Facsimile: 201-447-1926
Hackensack, New Jersey Office: 130 Main Street.
Telephone: 201-487-1080.
Facsimile: 201-487-4758;201-487-8410.
East Brunswick, New Jersey Office: Two Tower Center, 10th Floor.
Telephone: 908-214-1010.
Facsimile: 908-214-1818.

OF COUNSEL

Theodore W. Trautwein
August Schedler

John W. Albohm
David M. Repetto

Local Counsel for: Aetna Casualty & Surety Co.; Allstate Insurance Co.; Midlantic National Bank/North; United Jersey Bank; Ensign Bank, F.B.; Gulf Oil Corp.; Volvo North America Corp.

(See Next Column)

HARWOOD LLOYD—*Continued*

Reference: United Jersey Bank.

For full biographical listings, see the Martindale-Hubbell Law Directory

ROBBINSVILLE, Mercer Co.

WELLS AND SINGER, P.A. (AV)

Bank Plaza, Suite C , 14 Main Street (Rt. 526), 08691
Telephone: 609-587-3434
Mount Holly, New Jersey Office: 135 High Street, P.O. Box 100.
Telephone: 609-267-0070.
Bordentown, New Jersey Office: 6 East Park Street, P.O. Box 226.
Telephone: 609-298-1350

William H. Wells
Paul Rubin
Jonas Singer
Robin E. Echevarria

Christopher R. Musulin
Deborah J. Merriam
Jennifer Lepow Kaminer

OF COUNSEL

Jeffrey Goldman

Counsel for: Bank of Mid-Jersey; The Bordentown Peoples Savings & Loan Assn.; Church Brick Co.; Ariston Airlines Catering Service, Inc.; Belasco Petroleum, Inc.; Arlenes Travel, Inc.; Walnridge Farms, Inc.; Walnridge Equine Clinic.

For full biographical listings, see the Martindale-Hubbell Law Directory

ROSELAND, Essex Co.

BRACH, EICHLER, ROSENBERG, SILVER, BERNSTEIN, HAMMER & GLADSTONE, A PROFESSIONAL CORPORATION (AV)

101 Eisenhower Parkway, 07068
Telephone: 201-228-5700
Telecopier: 201-228-7852

Alan H. Bernstein
William L. Brach
Todd C. Brower
James T. Davis, II
Richard J. Driver
Burton L. Eichler
John D. Fanburg
William J. Friedman
Stuart M. Gladstone
Charles X. Gormally
Joseph M. Gorrell
Alan R. Hammer
Bruce Kleinman
Brian R. Lenker
Alan S. Pralgever
David J. Ritter
Paul F. Rosenberg
Michael I. Schneck
Harris R. Silver
Alexander J. Tafro

Bruce L. Wolff (Not admitted in NJ)
Alois V. Habjan
David J. Klein
Thomas M. Badenhausen
Frank S. Baldino
Wilma M. Kenny
David S. Bernstein
Georgette J. Siegel
Robert C. Mignella
Debora Laurano Eisen
Gary W. Herschman
Regina A. McGuire
Stephen R. Farber
Kelly A. Waters
John P. Inglesino
Daniel L. Schmutter
Jill Daitch Rosenberg
Kevin M. Lastorino
Michael A. Weiss
Heidi M. Zaslow
Susan L. Miller
Melissa E. Flax
Vicki Sue Hull
John P. Wyciskala, III
Michael S. Zicherman
Jill A. Cohen
Louis P. Lagios
Carl J. Soranno
Bruce J. Schanzer
Dennis P. Powers
Henry J. Aratow, Jr.
Simone E. Handler Hutchinson
Helen A. Nau

OF COUNSEL

Lance A. Posner
George Y. Sodowick
Stuart L. Pachman
Dorothy G. Black

Representative Clients: The Kushner Companies; Saint Barnabas Medical Center; The New Jersey Society of Pathologists; Drexel Heritage By Dover; Valley National Bank; Wondercamp Entertainment Co.; Brounell-Kramer-Waldor-Kane Agency; New Jersey Association of Renal Physicians; Medical Society of New Jersey; New Jersey Academy of Ophthalmology.

For full biographical listings, see the Martindale-Hubbell Law Directory

CARELLA, BYRNE, BAIN, GILFILLAN, CECCHI, STEWART & OLSTEIN, A PROFESSIONAL CORPORATION (AV)

Six Becker Farm Road, 07068-1739
Telephone: 201-994-1700
Telecopier: 201-994-1744
Lyndhurst, New Jersey Office: Carella, Byrne, Bain, Gilfillan, Cecchi, Stewart & Olstein. 37 Park Avenue.
Telephone: 201-935-6900;
Telecopier: 201-804-9414.

Charles C. Carella
Brendan T. Byrne
John N. Bain
John G. Gilfillan, III
James D. Cecchi, Jr.
Herbert M. Rinaldi
Peter G. Stewart
Elliot M. Olstein

(See Next Column)

Arthur T. Vanderbilt, II
Jan Alan Brody
John M. Agnello
James T. Byers
Alfred C. Constants, III
Donald F. Miceli
A. Richard Ross
Kenneth L. Winters
Jeffrey A. Cooper
Carl R. Woodward, III

Raymond J. Lillie
Walter G. Luger
Charles M. Carella
Rosemarie Sherman
Cynthia A. Petrowsky
Charles J. Herron (Not admitted in NJ)
G. Glennon Troublefield
William Squire
Patricia F. Del Baglivo
Lance T. Howard
Gregory D. Ferraro
Dennis F. Gleason
David G. Gilfillan
Brian H. Fenlon
Vincent J. Politan
Kevin L. Leahy
James E. Cecchi

OF COUNSEL

Richard K. Matanle, II
Donald S. Brooks

Representative Clients: American Funding Limited, Montvale, N.J.; Archdiocese of Newark; Carter-Wallace, Inc., New York, N.Y.; Ingersoll-Rand; Johnson Controls, Milwaukee, Wi.; Roselle Savings and Loan Assn., Roselle, N.J.; Russ Berrie and Company, Inc.; Witco Corporation, New York, N.Y.; Johnson Controls World Services & Subsidiaries; Trustee/Receiver Assets of "Crazy Eddie" Antar.

For full biographical listings, see the Martindale-Hubbell Law Directory

CHAPMAN, HENKOFF, KESSLER, PEDUTO & SAFFER (AV)

425 Eagle Rock Avenue, P.O. Box F, 07068
Telephone: 201-403-8800
Fax: 201-403-9444

MEMBERS OF FIRM

Philip L. Chapman
Isaac Henkoff
Leonard A. Peduto, Jr.
Andrew S. Kessler
Michael A. Saffer

Patricia A. Cauldwell
Peter Safirstein
Gary L. Koenigsberg
Diane Bongiovanni

Reference: Valley National Bank.

For full biographical listings, see the Martindale-Hubbell Law Directory

CONNELL, FOLEY & GEISER (AV)

85 Livingston Avenue, 07068
Telephone: 201-535-0500
Telefax: 201-535-9217

MEMBERS OF FIRM

John A. Pindar (1948-1969)
George W. Connell
Adrian M. Foley, Jr.
Theodore W. Geiser
John B. Lavecchia
George J. Kenny
Kenneth F. Kunzman
Samuel Darrow Lord
Richard D. Catenacci
Richard J. Badolato
Peter D. Manahan
John B. Murray
Mark L. Fleder
Jerome M. Lynes
Kevin J. Coakley
Linda A. Palazzolo
John F. Neary
Raymond T. Lyons, Jr.
Thomas S. Cosma
Kathleen S. Murphy
Keith A. Krauss
Patrick J. McAuley
Peter J. Pizzi
Kevin R. Gardner
Robert E. Ryan
Michael X. McBride
Jeffrey W. Moryan
Donald S. Maclachlan
Patricia J. Pindar
Peter J. Smith
Brian G. Steller
Frank A. Lattal
Judith A. Wahrenberger
Philip F. McGovern, Jr.
Karen Munster Cassidy
Stephen D. Kinnard
Karen Painter Randall
Liza M. Walsh
John P. Lacey

ASSOCIATES

Maureen A. Mahoney-Madarasz
Timothy E. Corriston
Ernest W. Schoellkopff
Heidi Willis Currier
John D. Cromie
Guy T. Lytle
John W. Fitzgibbon
Angela A. Iuso
Patrick J. Hughes
George H. Parsells, III
John H. Denton
Pamela M. Kapsimalis
Edward Delesky
Paul T. Fader
Kathleen M. Cehelsky
Kenneth E. Kobylowski
Glenn T. Dyer
Bette A. Hughes
Thomas P. Lihan
Vincent E. McGeary
William T. McGloin
Brendan Judge
Margaret M. Cadigan
William J. Gross
James P. McBarron
Catherine S. Nietzel
Stephen V. Falanga
Wendy Johnson Lario
Jeffrey L. O'Hara
Amrita D. Master
Tricia Bevelock O'Reilly
Thomas A. Sparno

OF COUNSEL

Morris M. Schnitzer
Margaret L. Moses

Representative Clients: Bethlehem Steel Corp.; Borden Inc.; Chase Manhattan Bank; CNA Insurance; Conrail; Hilton Hotels Corp.; Merrill Lynch; Microsoft; New Jersey Manufacturers Insurance.

For full biographical listings, see the Martindale-Hubbell Law Directory

HANNOCH WEISMAN, A PROFESSIONAL CORPORATION (AV)

4 Becker Farm Road, 07068-3788
Telephone: 201-535-5300
New York: 212-732-3262
Telecopier: 201-994-7198
Mailing Address: P.O. Box 1040, Newark, New Jersey, 07101-9819
Washington, D.C. Office: Suite 600, 1150 Seventeenth Street, N.W.
Telephone: 202-296-3432.

Shirley L. Berger
Bernard S. Berkowitz
Albert G. Besser
William D. Bierman
Eric R. Breslin
Kevin J. Bruno
Sanders M. Chattman
Jeffrey A. Cohen
Richard J. Conway, Jr.
Bernard J. D'Avella, Jr.
Lawrence W. Diamond
Nina Laserson Dunn
Robert C. Epstein
Richard S. Finkelstein
Sheldon M. Finkelstein
Joseph J. Fleischman
Irvin M. Freilich
Dean A. Gaver
Stuart J. Glick
Jonathan M. Gross
Herbert J. Hannoch (1890-1983)
William J. Heller
Lee Henig-Elona
Richard J. Hughes (1909-1992)
Carmine A. Iannaccone
Howard A. Kantrowitz
Michael G. Keating
Carleton Richard Kemph
Samuel M. Kinney, Jr. (1925-1987)
Gene R. Korf
Stephen P. Lichtstein
Ira B Marcus
Theodore Margolis
Gary Mazart
Arlene Elgart Mirsky
William S. Myers (1907-1965)
Lawrence T. Neher
William W. Robertson
Todd M. Sahner
James J. Shrager
Richard M. Slotkin
Milton H. Stern (1924-1992)
Ronald M. Sturtz
Diane P. Sullivan
Carl G. Weisenfeld

OF COUNSEL

Joseph A. Weisman

SPECIAL COUNSEL

Geralyn G. Humphrey
Angela D. Slater
David P. Wadyka

Loretta Barnes
Lesley Anne Broomall
Ritaelena Marie Casavechia
Suzanne Quinn Chamberlin
Sandra L. Cohen
Christina E. Di Francesco
Mary Jane McNicholas Dobbs
Jane Dobson
James P. Flynn
Terri L. Freeman
Michael J. Geiger
Suzanne Stahl Heyer
Sanford J. Hodes
Marie A. Latoff
Sheri Faith London
Kathleen M. Maher
Jeffrey D. Mallinger
David S. Mao
Jurij Mykolajtchuk
Christopher W. Nanos
Julie A. Parker
David J. Paulin
Rachelle A. Peluso
Robert H. Solomon
Gerald F. Spada
Nina E. Stone
Anthony J. Tomari
Cynthia L. Warren

For full biographical listings, see the Martindale-Hubbell Law Directory

---

LOWENSTEIN, SANDLER, KOHL, FISHER & BOYLAN, A PROFESSIONAL CORPORATION (AV)

65 Livingston Avenue, 07068
Telephone: 201-992-8700
Telefax: 201-992-5820
Somerville, New Jersey Office: 600 First Avenue. P.O. Box 1113.
Telephone: 201-526-3300.

Alan V. Lowenstein
Richard M. Sandler
Benedict M. Kohl
Arnold Fisher
Joseph LeVow Steinberg
Matthew P. Boylan
Bruce D. Shoulson
John R. MacKay, 2nd
Martin R. Goodman
John D. Schupper
Stephen N. Dermer
Michael L. Rodburg
Allen B. Levithan
R. Barry Stiger
Gregory B. Reilly
Peter H. Ehrenberg
Steven B. Fuerst (Resident at Somerville Office)
Theodore V. Wells, Jr.
William S. Katchen
Michael Dore
John L. Kraft
Ashley Steinhart
Douglas S. Eakeley
Gerald Krovatin
Richard D. Wilkinson
Alan Wovsaniker
Kenneth J. Slutsky
David L. Harris
Zulima V. Farber
William P. Munday
Daniel J. Barkin
George J. Mazin
James Stewart
Laura R. Kuntz
Robert D. Chesler
Richard F. Ricci
Kevin Kovacs (Resident at Somerville Office)
John L. Berger
David W. Field
Martha L. Lester (Resident at Somerville Office)
Linda Pickering

(See Next Column)

John D. Hogoboom
Terry E. Thornton
Robert G. Minion
Jeffrey J. Wild

OF COUNSEL

Robert L. Krakower
Norman W. Spindel
Stuart S. Yusem (Resident at Somerville Office)
Bonnie K. Levitt
Jeffrey M. Davis
Harvey Smith
Diane K.G. Weeks
Richard P. Boehmer

Phyllis F. Pasternak (Resident at Somerville Office)
Marc B. Kramer
John M. Nolan (Resident at Somerville Office)
Eileen M. Clark (Resident at Somerville Office)
Allen P. Langjahr
John B. McCusker
Paul F. Koch, II
Bruce S. Rosen
Darryl Everett Gugig
Samuel B. Santo, Jr.
Jonathan T.K. Cohen
Susan Youdovin Leonard
Paul F. Carvelli
Gary F. Eisenberg
Rosemary E. Ramsay
Vincent P. Browne
Jeffrey B. Gracer
Lawrence M. Rolnick
Neale R. Bedrock
Karim G. Kaspar
Robert M. Lapinsky
Henry M. Price
David A. Thomas
Andrew E. Anselmi
Michael N. Gooen
Peter E. Nahmias
Jeri L. Abrams
Sheila Y. Maddox
Richard C. Szuch
Thomas M. FitzGibbon
Stephen R. Buckingham
Stephanie Wilson
Virginia A. Lazala
Michael J. McDonald
Geoffrey A. Price
Peter L. Skolnik
Neslihan S. Montag
Nancy Lake Martin
Alex Moreau
William J. VonDerHeide
Edward T. Arnold
Thomas E. Mesevage
Joyce A. Davis
Michael D. Lichtenstein
Howard A. Matalon
Brian Weeks
Veronica Smith Lewis (Not admitted in NJ)
Edward M. Zimmerman
Amy C. Grossman
Richard A. Levitan
Maureen E. Montague (Resident at Somerville Office)
Gavin J. Rooney
Jeremy I. Silberman
Christopher L. Weiss
Charisse A. Carney
Nelson D. Johnson
Abby Ages
Tina M. Niehold
Lauren M. Hollender
Sarah B. Levinson (Not admitted in NJ)

For full biographical listings, see the Martindale-Hubbell Law Directory

---

ORLOFF, LOWENBACH, STIFELMAN & SIEGEL, A PROFESSIONAL CORPORATION (AV)

101 Eisenhower Parkway, 07068
Telephone: 201-622-6200
Telecopier: 201-622-3073

Joel D. Siegel
Frank L. Stifelman
Ralph M. Lowenbach
Laurence B. Orloff
Stanley Schwartz
Jeffrey M. Garrod
Floyd Shapiro
Alan F. Kornstein
Samuel Feldman
Edmund A. Mikalauskas
Susan Medinets Holzman
Michael S. Haratz
William J. Adelson
Eileen A. Lindsay

James A. Mohoney
David B. Katz
Linda B. Lewinter
Laura Valenti Studwell
Valerie Jacobson Kelleher
Linda S. Moore
Jonathan R. Gamza

For full biographical listings, see the Martindale-Hubbell Law Directory

---

CHARLES A. ROSEN (AV)

280 Corporate Center, 5 Becker Farm Road, 07068
Telephone: 201-535-2800
Telecopier: 201-535-9777
New York, New York Office: 60 East 42nd Street, Suite 1217.
Telephone: 212-921-2236.

ASSOCIATES

Cecilia M.E. Lindenfelser

Reference: United Jersey Bank.

For full biographical listings, see the Martindale-Hubbell Law Directory

---

WOLFF & SAMSON, P.A. (AV)

280 Corporate Center, 5 Becker Farm Road, 07068
Telephone: 201-740-0500
Fax: 201-740-1407

Joel A. Wolff
David Samson
Ronald E. Wiss
Arthur S. Goldstein
Armen Shahinian
Martin L. Wiener
Gage Andretta
Daniel A. Schwartz
Karen L. Gilman
Edward S. Snyder
Daniel D. Caldwell
Roger J. Breene
Kenneth N. Laptook
David L. Schlossberg

(See Next Column)

WOLFF & SAMSON P.A.—*Continued*

Paul M. Colwell
Robert E. Nies
Morris Bienenfeld
Dennis Brodkin
Dennis M. Toft
M. Jeremy Ostow
Bruce H. Dickstein
John F. Casey

OF COUNSEL

Angelo A. Mastrangelo
Richard L. Amster

James D. Ferrucci
Darryl Weissman
James J. Ross
Harlan L. Cohen
Aaron D. Bassan
Mark A. Kreitman
John M. Simon
Jonathan E. Stark
Laurence M. Smith
Howard K. Uniman
Roxanna Epling Hammett
Donna Jean Nance
Lauren Mileo O'Sullivan
Cynthia Borsella Lindemann
Mark R. Dimaria
Joseph Monaghan
Robert Tchack
Joseph Zawila
Alberto Romero
David Schrader
Stephen H. Bier
Thomas W. Sabino
Catherine P. Wells
Christine Romeo
Sandra P. Nachshen
Sherri C. Shapiro
Jennifer E. Morris
Sean M. Aylward
Kathleen M. Fitzgerald
Mark J. Hontz
Douglas M. Cohen
Mary Jean Riordan

Representative Clients: International Fidelity Insurance Co.; Celentano Brothers, Inc.; Chicago Title Insurance Co.; Hartz Mountain Industries; The Hillier Group; Foster Wheeler Corp.

For full biographical listings, see the Martindale-Hubbell Law Directory

SADDLE RIVER, Bergen Co.

STRASSER & ASSOCIATES, A PROFESSIONAL CORPORATION (AV)

70 East Allendale Rd., 07458
Telephone: 201-236-1861
Fax: 201-236-1863
Nutley, New Jersey Office: 391 Franklin Avenue, 07110-0107.
Telephone: 201-661-5000.
Fax: 201-661-0056.

William I. Strasser

*SALEM,** Salem Co. — (Refer to Woodbury)

SECAUCUS, Hudson Co.

FITZPATRICK & WATERMAN (AV)

400 Plaza Drive, P.O. Box 3159, 07096-3159
Telephone: 201-865-9100
1-800 BOND LAW
Facsimile: 201-865-4805
Bayonne, New Jersey Office: 90 West 40th Street. 07002,
Telephone: 201339-4000; 1-800 BOND LAW.

Harold F. Fitzpatrick
Stephen P. Waterman

ASSOCIATES

James F. McDonough
Glenn C. Merritt
Jeanette M. Samra

OF COUNSEL

Andre Shramenko

For full biographical listings, see the Martindale-Hubbell Law Directory

WATERS, MCPHERSON, MCNEILL, P.C. (AV)

300 Lighting Way, 7th Floor, 07096
Telephone: 201-863-4400
Telecopy: 201-863-2866
Trenton, New Jersey Office: 224 West State Street.
Telephone: 609-599-1000.
New York, N.Y. Office: The Woolworth Building, 233 Broadway, Suite 970.
Telephone: 212-227-7878.

David A. Waters
Kenneth D. McPherson
John H. McNeill
John J. Kot
Daniel E. Horgan
Jack Rosen
(Not admitted in NJ)
William J. Ward
Gregory J. Castano
Frank G. Capece
Steven R. Gray
Lawrence Z. Kotler
E. Neal Zimmermann
Joseph Lesser
(Not admitted in NJ)
George T. Imperial
Nicholas I. Filocco
Kenneth D. McPherson, Jr.
Thomas J. O'Connor
Joseph G. Ragno
Edward G. Imperatore
Michael J. Mehr
Virginia M. Edwards
David J. Mahoney, Jr.
(Not admitted in NJ)
James A. Kosch
James P. Bruno
Frank J. Zazzaro
Charles J. Harriman
Patrick J. Arre
David A. McPherson

(See Next Column)

Joanne Clark
David S. Comito
Paul A. Conciatori
Anthony Coppola-Russo
Randall L. Currier
Blake S. Davis
Marc S. Faecher
Glenn A. Farrell
Perry Florio
Patricia M. Forsyth
Salvatore A. Giampiccolo
Jason K. Gross
Riley E. Horton, Jr.
Lucille Jane Karp
Joseph M. Kennedy
Andrea A. Lipuma
Matthew Malfa
Robert M. Marshall
Mark J. McPherson
John A. O'Shaughnessy
Barbara Packer
Daniel J. Pollak
Giovanni Regina
James J. Seaman
Michael A. Sirgado
Maurice L. Stone
Joseph J. Trefurt
Michael E. Waller

OF COUNSEL

Morton Goldfein
Bernard M. Jaffe
(Not admitted in NJ)
John B. Wefing
Barbara E. Cowen

COUNSEL

Edward Pesin

Representative Clients: American Institute of Certified Public Accountants; Bally Gaming International, Inc.; Cablevision Systems Corp.; The Edward J. DeBartolo Corporation; Hartz Mountain Industries, Inc.; Jones, Lang, Wootton U.S.A.; Liberty Mutual Insurance Co.; Tropicana Products, Inc.

For full biographical listings, see the Martindale-Hubbell Law Directory

SHIP BOTTOM, Ocean Co.

SHACKLETON, HAZELTINE AND BISHOP (AV)

22nd Street and Long Beach Boulevard, P.O. Box 410, 08008
Telephone: 609-494-2136
Telefax: 609-494-0870
Fairfield, New Jersey Office: 253 Passaic Avenue.
Telephone: 201-882-4646.
Telefax: 201-882-4620.

MEMBERS OF FIRM

Richard J. Shackleton
Colin R. Hazeltine
James E. Bishop

ASSOCIATES

Michael T. Collins
James Den Uyl
Laura M. O'Regan
Mary Jane Lidaka
Marc Baden Powell
Eric J. Miller
Robert Emmet Rue

References: Citizens State Bank of New Jersey; Ocean National Bank; Bay State Bank.

For full biographical listings, see the Martindale-Hubbell Law Directory

SHREWSBURY, Monmouth Co.

CHRISTIANSEN, JUBE & KEEGAN, A PROFESSIONAL CORPORATION (AV)

1129 Broad Street, 07702
Telephone: 908-389-0330
Fax: 908-544-0779

Albert R. Jube (1888-1970)
Howard G. Kafer (1923-1985)
Paul J. Christiansen
John P. Keegan

For full biographical listings, see the Martindale-Hubbell Law Directory

*SOMERVILLE,** Somerset Co.

KLAUSNER HUNTER & SEID (AV)

63 East High Street, P.O. Box 1012, 08876
Telephone: 908-685-1552
Fax: 908-526-8233
Skillman Office: 144 Tamarack Circle, Montgomery Knoll, U.S. Hwy. 206 N.
Telephone: 609-921-3747.
Fax: 609-921-3936.

MEMBERS OF FIRM

Stephen E. Klausner
Stephen B. Hunter
Gerald P. Seid (Resident, Skillman, New Jersey Office)

ASSOCIATES

Lawrence J. Van Wess

For full biographical listings, see the Martindale-Hubbell Law Directory

LOWENSTEIN, SANDLER, KOHL, FISHER & BOYLAN, A PROFESSIONAL CORPORATION (AV)

600 First Avenue, P.O. Box 1113, 08876
Telephone: 908-526-3300
Roseland, New Jersey Office: 65 Livingston Avenue.
Telephone: 201-992-8700.
Telefax: 201-992-5820.

(See Next Column)

LOWENSTEIN, SANDLER, KOHL, FISHER & BOYLAN A PROFESSIONAL CORPORATION, *Somerville—Continued*

Steven B. Fuerst
Kevin Kovacs
Martha L. Lester

OF COUNSEL

Stuart S. Yusem
Richard P. Boehmer

Phyllis F. Pasternak
John M. Nolan
Eileen M. Clark
Vincent P. Browne
Jeri L. Abrams
Maureen E. Montague

For full biographical listings, see the Martindale-Hubbell Law Directory

OZZARD WHARTON, A PROFESSIONAL PARTNERSHIP (AV)

75-77 North Bridge Street, P.O. Box 938, 08876
Telephone: 908-526-0700
Telecopier: 908-526-2246

William E. Ozzard
Victor A. Rizzolo
George A. Mauro, Jr.
William B. Savo
Edward M. Hogan
Michael V. Camerino
Alan Bart Grant

Arthur D. Fialk
Kam S. Minhas
Ellen M. Gillespie
Michael G. Friedman
Suzette Nanovic Berrios
Frederick H. Allen, III
Wendy L. Wiebalk
Lori E. Salowe
Denise M. Marra

OF COUNSEL

T. Girard Wharton (1904-1992)
A. Arthur Davis, 3rd
Louis A. Imfeld
John H. Beekman, Jr.
Mark F. Strauss
Miles S. Winder, III

Representative Clients: American Cyanamid; Science Management Corp; New Jersey Manufacturers Insurance Co.; Travelers Insurance Co.; Mack Development Co.; New Jersey Savings Bank.

For full biographical listings, see the Martindale-Hubbell Law Directory

RAYMOND R. AND ANN W. TROMBADORE A PROFESSIONAL CORPORATION (AV)

33 East High Street, 08876
Telephone: 908-722-7555
Fax: 908-722-6269

Raymond R. Trombadore

Megan C. Seel

OF COUNSEL

Ann W. Trombadore

References: Summit Bank; New Jersey Savings Bank; Somerset Savings & Loan Assn.

For full biographical listings, see the Martindale-Hubbell Law Directory

SPARTA, Sussex Co. — (Refer to Sparta)

SPRINGFIELD, Union Co.

McDONOUGH, KORN & EICHHORN, A PROFESSIONAL CORPORATION (AV)

Park Place Legal Center, 959 South Springfield Avenue, P.O. Box 712, 07081-0712
Telephone: 201-912-9099
Fax: 201-912-8604

Peter L. Korn
R. Scott Eichhorn
James R. Korn
William S. Mezzomo

Timothy J. Jaeger
Dona Feeney
Karen M. Lerner
Wilfred P. Coronato
Gail R. Arkin
Nancy Crosta Landale
Christopher K. Costa

OF COUNSEL

Robert P. McDonough

Representative Client: Meeker Sharkey & MacBean.
Reference: United Counties Trust Company.

For full biographical listings, see the Martindale-Hubbell Law Directory

SUMMIT, Union Co.

BOURNE, NOLL & KENYON, A PROFESSIONAL CORPORATION (AV)

382 Springfield Avenue, 07901
Telephone: 908-277-2200
Telecopier: 908-277-6808

(See Next Column)

Donald Bourne (1903-1987)
Edward T. Kenyon
Cary R. Hardy
Charles R. Berman
Kenneth R. Johanson
Martin Rubashkin
David G. White
Roger Mehner
James R. Ottobre

OF COUNSEL

Robert B. Bourne
Clyde M. Noll (Retired)

Lauren K. Harris
Jaime A. O'Brien
Ellyn A. Draikiwicz
Dean T. Bennett
Craig M. Lessner
Michael O'B. Boldt
Christopher D. Boyman
Paul Ramirez
Timothy A. Kalas
Robert F. Moriarty
Mary E. Scrupski

For full biographical listings, see the Martindale-Hubbell Law Directory

COOPER ROSE & ENGLISH (AV)

480 Morris Avenue, 07901-1527
Telephone: 908-273-1212
Fax: 908-273-8922
Rumson, New Jersey Office: 20 Bingham Avenue. 07760.
Telephone: 908-741-7777.
Fax: 908-758-1879.

MEMBERS OF FIRM

John W. Cooper
Frederick W. Rose
Jerry Fitzgerald English
Joseph E. Imbriaco
Roger S. Clapp
Arthur H. Garvin, III
Peter M. Burke
Gary F. Danis
John J. DeLaney, Jr.
David G. Hardin

OF COUNSEL

Harrison F. Durand
Russell T. Kerby, Jr.
Ronald J. Tell

ASSOCIATES

Fredi L. Pearlmutter
Kristi Bragg
Stephen R. Geller
Peter W. Ulicny
Thomas J. Sateary
Gianfranco A. Pietrafesa
Donna M. Russo
J. Andrew Kinsey
Jonathan S. Chester
Daniel Jon Kleinman
Holly English
Margaret R. Kalas
Mary T. Zdanowicz
Robert A. Meyers
Richard F. Iglar

Counsel for: Ciba-Geigy Corp.; Witco Corp.; New Jersey American Water Co.; Mikropul Corp.; AT&T Bell Laboratories; Aircast.

For full biographical listings, see the Martindale-Hubbell Law Directory

HAGGERTY, DONOHUE & MONAGHAN, A PROFESSIONAL ASSOCIATION (AV)

One Springfield Avenue, 07901
Telephone: 908-277-2600
Fax: 908-273-1641

James C. Haggerty
George J. Donohue
Walter E. Monaghan

Rose Ann Haggerty
Thomas J. Haggerty
Alfred F. Carolonza, Jr.
William A. Wenzel
Mahlon H. Ortman
Michael A. Conway
James C. Haggerty, Jr.

OF COUNSEL

Joseph D. Haggerty

LEGAL SUPPORT PERSONNEL

Teresa Romeo

Representative Clients: American International Group; Chubb/Pacific Indemnity Co.; Crawford & Co.; Crum & Forster; Hertz Corp.; Jefferson Insurance Group; Material Damage Adjustment Corp.; New Jersey Manufacturers; New Jersey Property Liability Guaranty Association; Royal Insurance Co.

For full biographical listings, see the Martindale-Hubbell Law Directory

THOROFARE, Gloucester Co.

CHARLES J. SPRIGMAN, JR. (AV)

Suite 803 Sherwood Professional Building, 800 Jessup Road, 08086
Telephone: 609-845-8081
FAX: 609-853-8330
Mailing Address: P.O. Box 682, Woodbury, New Jersey, 08096

Representative Client: Woodbury Daily Times Co., Inc.

*TOMS RIVER,** Ocean Co.

BERRY, KAGAN AND SAHRADNIK, A PROFESSIONAL CORPORATION (AV)

212 Hooper Avenue, P.O. Box 757, 08754
Telephone: 908-349-4800

(See Next Column)

BERRY, KAGAN AND SAHRADNIK A PROFESSIONAL CORPORATION—*Continued*

Franklin H. Berry (1904-1975)
Franklin H. Berry, Jr.
Seymour J. Kagan
John C. Sahradnik

Robert D. Budesa
Steven F. Nemeth
Dina R. Khajezadeh

Attorneys for: County of Ocean; N.J. State Funeral Directors Assn.; Ocean County College; Southern Regional High School District of Ocean County; Admiral Farragut Academy; Boards of Education of Pt. Pleasant Beach, Seaside Park, Beach Haven and Bay Head; National Westminster Bank NJ; Berkeley Sewerage Authority; Ocean Township Municipal Utilities Authority.

For full biographical listings, see the Martindale-Hubbell Law Directory

CURRY & SALZER (AV)

611 Main Street, P.O. Box 1225, 08753
Telephone: 908-240-4200
Fax: 908-349-2674

MEMBERS OF FIRM

James J. Curry, Jr.
Frank S. Salzer
John Marut

LEGAL SUPPORT PERSONNEL

R.N. Sheila Hudak

For full biographical listings, see the Martindale-Hubbell Law Directory

HIERING & DUPIGNAC, A PROFESSIONAL CORPORATION (AV)

64 Washington Street, Court House Square, CN 2015, 08754-2015
Telephone: 908-349-1212
Telefax: 908-349-1217

William T. Hiering
Frank J. Dupignac, Jr.

OF COUNSEL

Richard H. Woods

Representative Clients: Ocean County Utilities Authority; Sambol Construction Co.; Perlmart, Inc.; Venice Amusement Corporation and Subsidiaries; Foodarama ShopRite; 3M Corp.; Crestwood Village, Inc.; Union Valley, Inc.; Heyco Stamped Products.

For full biographical listings, see the Martindale-Hubbell Law Directory

NOVINS, YORK & PENTONY, A PROFESSIONAL CORPORATION (AV)

202 Main Street, 08753
Telephone: 908-349-7100

Robert J. Novins (1910-1973)
Robert F. Novins
Harvey L. York
Kenneth R. Pentony
Lorna S. Scanlon
Ann K. Haskell
S. Karl Mohel
Michael S. Paduano

Robert M. McKeon
Barry K. Odell
Leslie A. Dadourian

OF COUNSEL

William E. O'Connor

Counsel for: Allstate Insurance Co.; Motor Club of America.

For full biographical listings, see the Martindale-Hubbell Law Directory

SCHUMAN & BUTZ (AV)

1130 Hooper Avenue, P.O. Box 608, 08753
Telephone: 908-349-4400
Fax: 908-341-5199
Tuckerton, New Jersey Office: 405 U.S. Highway 9, P.O. Box 7.
Telephone: 609-296-5400.

MEMBERS OF FIRM

Edward W. Haines (1907-1974)
Harold A. Schuman
Thomas P. Butz
Richard C. Butz

Representative Clients: Ciba Geigy Corp.; Township of Little Egg Harbor M.U.A.; American Smelting & Refining Co. (ASARCO, Inc.); Southern Ocean State Bank.
Reference: The First National Bank of Toms River, New Jersey.

For full biographical listings, see the Martindale-Hubbell Law Directory

*TRENTON,** Mercer Co.

* indicates certain Bar Register subscribers whose principal office is located elsewhere in the state and who have arranged for representation as a part of the state capital listings that follow

BACKES & HILL (AV)

(Originally Backes & Backes)
(Formerly Backes, Waldron & Hill)
15 West Front Street, 08608-2098
Telephone: 609-396-8257
Telefax: 609-989-7323

Peter Backes (1858-1941)
Herbert W. Backes (1891-1970)
William Wright Backes (1904-1980)
Michael J. Nizolek (1950-1994)

OF COUNSEL

Robert Maddock Backes

PARTNERS

Harry R. Hill, Jr.
Robert C. Billmeier
Brenda Farr Engel

ASSOCIATES

Susan E. Bacso
Michele N. Siekerka
Henry A. Carpenter II
Lawrence A. Reisman

Representative Clients: New Jersey National Bank; Mercer Medical Center; Catholic Diocese of Trenton; Roller Bearing Company of America; New Jersey Manufacturers Insurance Co.; St. Francis Medical Center; The Trenton Savings Bank; Richie & Page Distributing Co., Inc.; Hill Refrigeration Corporation; General Sullivan Group, Inc.; A-1 Collections, Inc.

For full biographical listings, see the Martindale-Hubbell Law Directory

FOX, ROTHSCHILD, O'BRIEN & FRANKEL (AV)

Princeton Pike Corporate Center, 997 Lenox Drive, Building 3 (Lawrenceville), 08648-2311
Telephone: 609-896-3600
Telecopier: 609-896-1469
Philadelphia, Pennsylvania Office: 10th Floor, 2000 Market Street, 19103-3291.
Telephone: 215-299-2000.
Cable Address: "Frof".
Telecopier: 215-299-2150.
Exton, Pennsylvania Office: Eagleview Corporate Center, 717 Constitution Drive, Suite 111, P.O. Box 673, 19341-0673.
Telephone: 610-458-2100.
Telecopier: 610-458-2112.

Victor Walcoff
Richard M. Kohn
Jonathan D. Weiner
Phillip E. Griffin
Steven C. Levitt
Ezra D. Rosenberg
Simon Kimmelman
Jay S. Ruder
James F. X. Rudy
Roberta DeAngelis
Allison E. Accurso
June H. Millington

ASSOCIATES

Jon C. Martin
H. Lee Schwartzberg, Jr.
R. James Kravitz
Douglas J. Zeltt
Thomas J. Heitzman
Sue A. Gambaccini
Lynn B. McDougall
Magdalena Schardt
Richard E. Wegryn

SPECIAL COUNSEL

Elaine C. Britt

For full biographical listings, see the Martindale-Hubbell Law Directory

* JAMIESON, MOORE, PESKIN & SPICER, A PROFESSIONAL CORPORATION (AV)

Capitol View Building, 150 West State Street, 08628
Telephone: 609-396-5511
Princeton, New Jersey Office: 300 Alexander Park CN-5276.
Telephone: 609-452-0808.
Fax: 609-452-1147; 452-0943; 951-0096.

Nola R. Bencze
James J. Britt, Jr.
Dennis R. Casale
Thomas Crawford Jamieson, Jr.
Ann F. Kiernan
Edwin S. Leavitt-Gruberger
Thomas M. Letizia
Kevin L. Lilly
Thomas G. McMahon
John D. McQuarrie, Jr.
Arthur Meisel
Herbert F. Moore
Kevin J. Moore
Timothy J. O'Neill
Jay Samuels
Neal L. Schonhaut
Michael F. Spicer
Audrey Wisotsky
Thomas P. Weidner

Susan Peper Boudreau
Stephen J. Cusma
John J. Englert
Arthur F. Herrmann
Patricia Urken Herst
Lainie L. Kernis
Michael J. Mann
Julie Riley Tattoni
Howard Schachter
Mark Solomon
John W. Verlaque

(See Next Column)

JAMIESON, MOORE, PESKIN & SPICER A PROFESSIONAL CORPORATION, *Trenton—Continued*

Crawford Jamieson (1902-1967) Burton Peskin (1921-1989)

Representative Clients: New Jersey Bankers Assn.; Cybis; New Jersey Dental Assn.; Trenton Times; SCA Services, Inc.; Atlantic Mutual Insurance Co.; Educational Testing Service; Johnson & Johnson.

For full biographical listings, see the Martindale-Hubbell Law Directory

MCLAUGHLIN & COOPER, A PROFESSIONAL CORPORATION (AV)

949 West State Street, 08607
Telephone: 609-989-8050
Fax: 609-393-3565

Albert Cooper, Jr. (1904-1993) Albert Cooper, III
James J. McLaughlin Joseph E. Choquette
William F. Hartigan, Jr.

Edward A. Hoffman Anthony J. Paulazzo
Kevin M. Shanahan Kathleen G. Waldron
Mary Siobhan Brennan John J. Gentile

OF COUNSEL
Clarence I. Lord

Representative Clients: Fireman's Fund Insurance Cos.; New Jersey Manufacturers Insurance Co.
References: New Jersey National Bank; Capitol State Bank.

For full biographical listings, see the Martindale-Hubbell Law Directory

*** RIKER, DANZIG, SCHERER, HYLAND & PERRETTI (AV)**

170 West State Street, 08608-1102
Telephone: 609-396-2121
Fax: 609-396-4578
Morristown, New Jersey Office: Headquarters Plaza, One Speedwell Avenue.
Telephone: 201-538-0800.
Fax: 201-538-1984.

John P. Sheridan, Jr. John M. Pellecchia

OF COUNSEL
William F. Hyland

For full biographical listings, see the Martindale-Hubbell Law Directory

SCHRAGGER, LAVINE & NAGY, A PROFESSIONAL CORPORATION (AV)

The Atrium at Lawrence, 133 Franklin Corner Road (Lawrenceville), 08648
Telephone: 609-896-9777
Fax: 609-895-1373

Alan S. Lavine Raymond L. Nagy
Bruce M. Schragger James A. Schragger
Jonathan S. Robinson

OF COUNSEL
Henry C. Schragger A. Jerome Moore

Representative Clients: Sears, Roebuck & Co.; New Jersey Manufacturers Insurance Co.; Mercer County Community College; Mercer Mutual Insurance Co..

For full biographical listings, see the Martindale-Hubbell Law Directory

SMITH, STRATTON, WISE, HEHER & BRENNAN

(See Princeton)

STERNS & WEINROTH (AV)

50 West State Street, Suite 1400, P.O. Box 1298, 08607-1298
Telephone: 609-392-2100
Fax: 609-392-7956
Atlantic City, New Jersey Office: 2901 Atlantic Avenue, Suite 201, 08401.
Telephone: 609-340-8300.
Fax: 609-340-8722.
Washington, D.C. Office: 1150 Seventeenth Street, N.W., Suite 600, 20036.
Telephone: 202-296-3432.

William J. Bigham Jeffrey S. Posta
Joseph A. Fusco (Resident, Atlantic City) Michael L. Rosenberg
Elmer M. Matthews David M. Roskos
Paul M. O'Gara Mark D. Schorr
Vincent J. Paluzzi Joel H. Sterns
Frank J. Petrino Susan Stryker
Richard K. Weinroth
Robert Paul Zoller

OF COUNSEL
Joseph Feldstein (Not admitted in NJ)

(See Next Column)

Karen A. Confoy Michael S. Stein
Brian J. Mulligan Bernadette Fallows
Edgar Alden Dunham, IV Richard J. Van Wagner
Marshall D. Bilder C. Lauren Graham

For full biographical listings, see the Martindale-Hubbell Law Directory

VERONA, Essex Co.

SALERNO, COZZARELLI, MAUTONE, DE SALVO & NUSSBAUM, A PROFESSIONAL CORPORATION (AV)

155 Pompton Avenue, 07044
Telephone: 201-239-2222
Fax: 201-239-0463

Ralph J. Salerno Dennis M. Mautone
Frank J. Cozzarelli Peter De Salvo, Jr.
Gary Nussbaum

Robert Ricci John Motta

OF COUNSEL
Frank Cozzarelli, Jr.

References: Peoples Bank, N.A.; The Howard Savings Bank.

For full biographical listings, see the Martindale-Hubbell Law Directory

VINELAND, Cumberland Co.

BASILE, TESTA & TESTA, A PROFESSIONAL CORPORATION (AV)

424 Landis Avenue, P.O. Box 460, 08360
Telephone: 609-691-2300
Telefax: 609-691-5655

Francis G. Basile Joseph P. Testa
Michael L. Testa

Todd W. Heck Michelle J. Douglass
Diane Vari Harold U. Johnson, Jr.
Michael J. Gruccio Walter A. Schultz, Jr.

OF COUNSEL
Frank J. Testa

Representative Client: U.S. Insurance Group.

For full biographical listings, see the Martindale-Hubbell Law Directory

EISENSTAT, GABAGE, BERMAN & FURMAN, A PROFESSIONAL CORPORATION (AV)

1179 East Landis Avenue, P.O. Box O, 08360
Telephone: 609-691-1200
Telecopier: 609-691-0414

Gerald (Jere) M. Eisenstat Mitchell S. Berman
Charles W. Gabage Harry Furman

Patricia Powell

For full biographical listings, see the Martindale-Hubbell Law Directory

GRUCCIO, PEPPER, GIOVINAZZI, DESANTO & FARNOLY, P.A., A PROFESSIONAL CORPORATION (AV)

817 Landis Avenue, P.O. Box CN 1501, 08360
Telephone: 609-691-0100
Fax: 609-692-4095
Associated with: Stradley, Ronon, Stevens & Young, a Philadelphia Law Firm.
Woodbury, New Jersey Office: 21 Delaware Street.
Telephone: 609-848-5558.
Fax: 609-384-1181.
Avalon, New Jersey Office: 2878 Dune Drive.
Telephone: 609-967-4040.
Other New Jersey Offices:
Atlantic City Area: 609-347- 0909.
Salem Area: 609-935-3559.

James J. Gruccio Walter F. Gavigan
Lawrence Pepper, Jr. E. Edward Bowman
Cosmo A. Giovinazzi, III Gerald R. Spall
Robert A. DeSanto Stephen D. Barse
Thomas P. Farnoly Joseph E. Ruth
James J. Gruccio, Jr.

Representative Clients: State Farm Mutual Automobile Insurance Cos.; United States Fidelity & Guaranty Co.; Atlantic City Expressway Authority; County of Salem; County of Cape May; CNA Insurance Co.; Cumberland Mutual Fire Insurance Co.; Cumberland County Guidance Center; Pizza Hut Inc.; Farmers and Merchants National Bank of Bridgeton.

For full biographical listings, see the Martindale-Hubbell Law Directory

Vineland—Continued

LIPMAN, ANTONELLI, BATT, DUNLAP, WODLINGER & GILSON, A PROFESSIONAL CORPORATION (AV)

110 North Sixth Street, P.O. Box 280, 08360
Telephone: 609-692-8000
Telecopier: 609-692-7580

Philip L. Lipman
Americo Antonelli
Gerald J. Batt
Robert F. Dunlap
Gary D. Wodlinger
William M. Gilson
Donna M. Taylor
Robert G. Malestein

COUNSEL

Daniel J. Grosso
Vera B. Lipman (1910-1965)
Adolph Stern (1896-1964)
Arthur L. Joseph (1903-1977)

Representative Client: New Jersey National Bank.

For full biographical listings, see the Martindale-Hubbell Law Directory

RIESENBURGER & KIZNER, P.C. (AV)

190 South Main Road, P.O. Box 640, 08360
Telephone: 609-691-6200
Telecopier: 609-696-8150

Franklin J. Riesenburger
Mitchell H. Kizner

Teresa Marie Munson
William C. Mills, IV
Jeffrey R. Owens

For full biographical listings, see the Martindale-Hubbell Law Directory

SHAPIRO AND SHAPIRO, P.A. A PROFESSIONAL ASSOCIATION (AV)

1063 East Landis Avenue, P.O. Box 787, 08360
Telephone: 609-691-6800
Telecopier: 609-794-3326

Samuel L. Shapiro
Harold B. Shapiro
Dana Davis Teague

Reference: Sun National Bank.

For full biographical listings, see the Martindale-Hubbell Law Directory

WALL TOWNSHIP, Monmouth Co.

MAGEE, PAGANO & ISHERWOOD (AV)

Mirne & Simmill
Mirne, Nowels, Fundler Magee & Kirschner
1937 Route 35 at Allaire Road, P.O. Box 1200, 07719
Telephone: 908-449-2500
Telecopier: 908-449-4005

MEMBERS OF FIRM

Granville D. Magee
Philip G. Pagano
Thomas Isherwood

ASSOCIATES

Lisa M. Richford
Russell Macnow

OF COUNSEL

Michael B. Kirschner

Representative Clients: Wall Township Board of Education; Royal Insurance Cos.
References: Central Jersey Bank & Trust Co.; Commerce Bank Shore N.A.

For full biographical listings, see the Martindale-Hubbell Law Directory

WAYNE, Passaic Co.

DEYOE, HEISSENBUTTEL & MATTIA (AV)

401 Hamburg Turnpike, P.O. Box 2449, 07474-2449
Telephone: 201-595-6300
Fax: 201-595-0146; 201-595-9262

MEMBERS OF FIRM

Charles P. DeYoe (1923-1973)
Wood M. DeYoe
Frederick C. Heissenbuttel
Philip F. Mattia
Gary R. Matano
Scott B. Piekarsky

ASSOCIATES

Anne Hutton
Glenn Z. Poosikian
Jo Ann G. Durr
Frank D. Samperi
Frank A. Campana
John E. Clarke
Jason T. Shafron
Maura Waters Brady

LEGAL SUPPORT PERSONNEL

Marilyn Moore (Office Manager)

Representative Clients: INA/Aetna Insurance Co. (Cigna); Medical Inter-Insurance Companies; Hanover-Amgro, Inc.; Maryland Casualty Co.; Ohio Casualty Insurance Co.; Motor Club of America; Selected Insurance Co.

For full biographical listings, see the Martindale-Hubbell Law Directory

WILLIAMS, CALIRI, MILLER & OTLEY, A PROFESSIONAL CORPORATION (AV)

1428 Route 23, P.O. Box 995, 07474-0995
Telephone: 201-694-0800
Telecopier: 201-694-0302

Walter E. Williams (1904-1985)
David J. Caliri (Retired)
Richard S. Miller
Victor C. Otley, Jr.
Peter B. Eddy
William S. Robertson, III
David Golub
David C. Wigfield
Samuel G. Destito
John H. Hague
Stuart M. Geschwind
Steven A. Weisberger
Lawrence J. McDermott, Jr.
Darlene J. Pereksta
Hope M. Pomerantz
Cheryl H. Burstein
Joanne M. Sarubbi
Daniel Arent Colfax
David T. Miller

Representative Clients: Anchor Savings Bank, FSB; Federal Deposit Insurance Corporation (FDIC): The Hartford Accident and Indemnity Co.; The Ramapo Bank; Reliance Insurance Co.; Resolution Trust Corporation (RTC); Time-Warner Communications, Inc.; New Jersey Sports and Exposition Authority.

For full biographical listings, see the Martindale-Hubbell Law Directory

WEST ATLANTIC CITY, Atlantic Co.

MCALLISTER, WESTMORELAND, VESPER & SCHWARTZ, A PROFESSIONAL CORPORATION

(See Atlantic City)

WESTFIELD, Union Co.

BUTTERMORE, MULLEN, JEREMIAH AND PHILLIPS (AV)

445 East Broad Street, P.O. Box 2189, 07091
Telephone: 908-232-0292
Telecopier: 908-232-3277

MEMBERS OF FIRM

Grant M. Buttermore
Susan N. Mullen
William S. Jeremiah, II
John C. Phillips
Georgette E. David

ASSOCIATES

James F. O'Grady, Jr.

OF COUNSEL

Cuddie E. Davidson, Jr.

Reference: First Fidelity Bank, N.A., New Jersey.

For full biographical listings, see the Martindale-Hubbell Law Directory

LINDABURY, MCCORMICK & ESTABROOK, A PROFESSIONAL CORPORATION (AV)

53 Cardinal Drive, P.O. Box 2369, 07091
Telephone: 908-233-6800
Fax: 908-233-5078

Joseph S. Lindabury (1898-1984)
Richard R. Width
Anthony J. LaRusso
Peter A. Somers
William R. Watkins
Edward J. Frisch
John R. Blasi
John H. Schmidt, Jr.
Donald F. Nicolai
J. Ferd Convery III
Bruce P. Ogden
James K. Estabrook
James D. DeRose
Barry J. Donohue
Robert S. Burney
David R. Pierce
Jay Lavroff
Robert W. Anderson

Marlene Browne Berg
Raymond A. Grimes
Joseph G. Wood
Richard J. Cino
Dina G. Kugel
Timothy D. Lyons
Colleen D. Brennan
Kurt Olender
Lisa A. Freidenrich
Kelly A. Hardy

COUNSEL

Robert S. Schwartz

OF COUNSEL

Kenneth L. Estabrook
Francis X. McCormick
Robert M. Read

Representative Clients: Elizabeth General Medical Center; Great American Insurance Co.; Kessler Institute for Rehabilitation; Kuehne Chemical Co., Inc.; Mechanical Contractors Association of New Jersey; New Jersey Industrial Energy Users; Summit Bank; United Jersey Bank; Western Industries, Inc.

For full biographical listings, see the Martindale-Hubbell Law Directory

WESTMONT, Camden Co.

BROWN & CONNERY (AV)

360 Haddon Avenue, P.O. Box 539, 08108
Telephone: 609-854-8900
Facsimile: 609-858-4967
Camden, New Jersey Office: 518 Market Street, P.O. Box 1449.
Telephone: 609-365-5100.
Telecopier: 609-858-4967.

MEMBERS OF FIRM

Thomas F. Connery, Jr.
William J. Cook
Warren W. Faulk
Steven G. Wolschina
Paul Mainardi
John L. Conroy, Jr.
Dennis P. Blake
Michael J. Vassalotti
John J. Mulderig
William M. Tambussi
Bruce H. Zamost
Mark P. Asselta
Stephen J. DeFeo
Jane A. Lorber

ASSOCIATES

Isabel C. Balboa
Joseph A. Zechman
Michael J. Fagan
Karen A. Peterson
Jeffrey E. Ugoretz
Christine O'Hearn
Christine A. Campbell
Joseph T. Carney

Representative Clients: Delaware River Port Authority; Garden State Water Company; Philadelphia Newspapers, Inc.; Resolution Trust Corp.; General Electric; Mercedez-Benz Credit Corp.; American Red Cross; Associated Services Financial Co., Inc.; Independence Blue Cross; Honeywell, Inc.

For full biographical listings, see the Martindale-Hubbell Law Directory

MARTIN, GUNN & MARTIN, A PROFESSIONAL CORPORATION (AV)

Sentry Office Plaza, Suite 420, 216 Haddon Avenue, P.O. Box 358, 08108
Telephone: 609-858-0900
Telecopier: 609-858-1278

Burchard V. Martin
Bruce M. Gunn
Burchard S. Martin
William J. Martin
Patricia Holden

OF COUNSEL

Kevin J. Kehner

Counsel for: Chubb & Son; Employers Mutual of Wausau; Federal Insurance Co.; Liberty Mutual Insurance Co.; Lumberman's Mutual Casualty Co.; Metropolitan Life Insurance Co.; United States Fidelity & Guaranty Co.; Crawford & Co.

For full biographical listings, see the Martindale-Hubbell Law Directory

WEST ORANGE, Essex Co.

BURSIK, KURITSKY & GIASULLO (AV)

443 Northfield Avenue, 07052
Telephone: 201-325-7800
Telecopier: 201-325-7930

MEMBERS OF FIRM

David H. E. Bursik
Stuart M. Kuritsky
Robert J. Giasullo

ASSOCIATES

Amy Bard
John Messina
Barbara Koerner Craig

For full biographical listings, see the Martindale-Hubbell Law Directory

HOWARD M. DAVIS, P.C. (AV)

743 Northfield Avenue, 07052
Telephone: 201-325-8383
Telefax: 201-325-1159

Howard M. Davis

David A. Stern

Reference: Midlantic National Bank, West Orange.

For full biographical listings, see the Martindale-Hubbell Law Directory

GOLDBERG, MUFSON & SPAR, A PROFESSIONAL CORPORATION (AV)

200 Executive Drive, 07052
Telephone: 201-736-0100
Telecopier: 201-736-0961

Leonard M. Goldberg
Ann Mufson
Michael R. Spar
Kenneth J. Isaacson
Eric W. Olson

OF COUNSEL

Jerome E. Sharfman

For full biographical listings, see the Martindale-Hubbell Law Directory

YOUNG, DIMIERO & SAYOVITZ, A PROFESSIONAL CORPORATION (AV)

Skyline Plaza, 414 Eagle Rock Avenue, 07052
Telephone: 201-736-5200
Telecopier: 201-669-8149

Gary S. Young
Alfred D. Dimiero
Sidney A. Sayovitz
Monica E. Peck
Brian E. Mahoney
Barbara Ann Sgro

Joanne L. Butler
Celia S. Bosco
Marilyn B. Katz

OF COUNSEL

Robert H. Greenwood

Representative Clients: Ferrostaal Corp.; PBA Local 53.

For full biographical listings, see the Martindale-Hubbell Law Directory

ALAN L. ZEGAS (AV)

20 Northfield Avenue, 07052
Telephone: 201-736-1011
Fax: 201-325-2248

For full biographical listings, see the Martindale-Hubbell Law Directory

WEST PATERSON, Passaic Co.

EVANS HAND (AV)

One Garret Mountain Plaza, Interstate 80 at Squirrelwood Road, 07424-3396
Telephone: 201-881-1100
Fax: 201-881-1369

MEMBERS OF FIRM

Peter Vandervoort
W. Fletcher Hock, Jr.
Douglas C. Borchard, Jr.
Charles D. LaFiura
Thomas F. Craig, II
Roy J. Evans
Harry D. Norton, Jr.
Douglas E. Arpert

ASSOCIATES

William M. Sheehy
Mariano H. Picardi
Brian T. Higgins
Janet Connery
Florence Amato Scrivo
Lynda S. Korfmann
Karen Santo Tracy
Deirdre Rafferty Thompson

LEGAL SUPPORT PERSONNEL

Karen A. Baccollo

Representative Clients: Midlantic National Bank; The Bank of New York/National Community Division; The Prudential Insurance Co. of America; Connecticut General Life Insurance Co.; Travelers Insurance Co.; New Jersey Manufacturers Insurance Co.; Bell Atlantic; Algonquin Gas Transmission Co.; Tenneco, Inc.; Corning Glass Works.

For full biographical listings, see the Martindale-Hubbell Law Directory

WOODBRIDGE, Middlesex Co.

GREENBAUM, ROWE, SMITH, RAVIN AND DAVIS (AV)

Metro Corporate Campus I, P.O. Box 5600, 07095-0988
Telephone: 908-549-5600
Cable Address: "Greelaw"
Telecopier: 908-549-1881
ABA Net: 2 529

MEMBERS OF FIRM

Wm. L. Greenbaum (1914-1983)
Robert S. Greenbaum
Arthur M. Greenbaum
Allen Ravin
Paul A. Rowe
Wendell A. Smith
Alan E. Davis
David L. Bruck
Michael B. Himmel
Michael A. Backer
Robert C. Schachter
Martin L. Lepelstat
Dennis A. Estis
William D. Grand
Donald Katz
Benjamin D. Lambert, Jr.
Alan S. Naar
Harriet Farber Klein
Mark H. Sobel
Hal W. Mandel
Barry S. Goodman
Peter A. Buchsbaum
Thomas J. Denitzio, Jr.
Robert S. Goldsmith
Kenneth T. Bills
Thomas C. Senter
Margaret Goodzeit
Robert J. Kipnees
W. Raymond Felton
Christine F. Li
Bruce D. Greenberg
Meryl Ann Greenhause Gonchar
Michael K. Feinberg
Gary A. Kotler
Carlton T. Spiller
Joseph M. Oriolo
Jeffrey L. Kantowitz
Lloyd H. Tubman
Kerry Brian Flowers
Sabrina A. Kogel
Jacqueline M. Printz
Marjorie F. Chertok
Lawrence H. Wertheim

ASSOCIATES

Nancy Isaacson
Susan Okin Goldsmith
Tyrone M. McDonnell
Gary Keith Wolinetz
Michael L. Konig
Matthew E. Power
Jessica R. Mayer
Michael F. Bodrato
Richard L. Hertzberg
Ellen Ann Silver

(See Next Column)

GREENBAUM, ROWE, SMITH, RAVIN AND DAVIS—*Continued*

ASSOCIATES (Continued)

Andrea J. Sullivan
Kathleen Meehan DalCortivo
Christine F. Marks
Marc Jonathan Gross
Marc D. Policastro
Nigel I. Farinha
Andrew J. Rothman
Stephanie Kay Austin
Shirleen A. Roberts
Luke John Kealy
Diane V. Garrity
Christopher S. Porrino
Kathleen Curran Brown
Mary Jean Pizza

OF COUNSEL

Daniel L. Golden

For full biographical listings, see the Martindale-Hubbell Law Directory

WILENTZ, GOLDMAN & SPITZER, A PROFESSIONAL CORPORATION (AV)

90 Woodbridge Center Drive Suite 900, Box 10, 07095
Telephone: 908-636-8000
Telecopier: 908-855-6117
Eatontown, New Jersey Office: Meridian Center I, Two Industrial Way West, 07724.
Telephone: 908-493-1000.
Telecopier: 908-493-8387.
New York, New York Office: Wall Street Plaza, 88 Pine Street, 9th Floor, 10005.
Telephone: 212-267-3091.
Telecopier: 212-267-3828.

David T. Wilentz (1894-1988)
Roger B. Kaplan
G. George Goldman (1922-1959)
Philip A. Pahigian
Henry M. Spitzer (1903-1988)
Brian J. Molloy
Warren W. Wilentz
Randall J. Richards
Matthias D. Dileo
Barry T. Albin
Robert A. Petito
Bonnie M. S. Reiss
Morris Brown
Sheldon E. Jaffe
Harold G. Smith
Stuart T. Cox, Jr.
Frederic K. Becker
Norman J. Peer
Nicholas L. Santowasso
Joseph J. Jankowski
Alfred J. Hill
Frederick J. Dennehy
Richard F. Lert
Roy H. Tanzman
John A. Hoffman
Robert C. Holmes
Stephen E. Barcan
Hal L. Baume
Robert J. Cirafesi
Steven J. Tripp
Francis V. Bonello
Christopher M. Placitella
Vincent P. Maltese
Paul T. Swanicke
David M. Wildstein
Charles S. Zucker
Alan M. Darnell
Jay J. Ziznewski
Gordon J. Golum
James E. Trabilsy
Frank M. Ciuffani
Maureen S. Binetti
Marvin J. Brauth
Anthony J. Pannella, Jr.
Stuart A. Hoberman
Michael J. Barrett
Nicholas Willard Mc Clear
Jeffrey R. Rich
Stephen A. Spitzer
Michael F. Schaff
Richard R. Bonamo
Angelo J. Cifaldi
Sidney D. Weiss
Leslie Jeddis Lang
Peter C. Paras (Resident, Eatontown Office)
Francis X. Journick, Jr.
Anne S. Babineau
Kevin M. Berry (Resident, New York, New York, Office)
Christine D. Petruzzell
Louis T. DeLucia

OF COUNSEL

Matthew F. Fitzgibbon (Not admitted in NJ)
Frank J. Barbaro (Resident, New York, N.Y. Office)

Linda Lashbrook
Ruth D. Marcus (Not admitted in NJ; Resident New York, New York Office)
Steven P. Marshall
Jean R. Campbell
LiliAnn Messina
Lynne M. Kizis
Eric J. Marcy
Kevin A. Calamoneri
Glen D. Savits
Richard J. Byrnes
David S. DeBerry
Jonathan P. Falk
Yvonne Marcuse
Georgia C. Haglund
Robert C. Kautz
Richard A. Catalina, Jr.
Douglas Watson Lubic
Mark F. Curley
Viola S. Lordi
Holly Lichtenstein Goldberg
Susanne Salzer O'Donohue
Edith A. Tobia
Jeffrey K. Epstein
Robert T. Haefele
Elizabeth Connolly Dell
Patricia S. Gardner
Noel S. Tonneman (Resident, Eatontown Office)
Lisa A. Gorab
Amy H. Soled
George L. Kimmel
Donald E. Taylor
Jon G. Kupilik
John E. Keefe, Jr.
Peter R. Herman
Steven P. Knowlton
Cheryl J. Oberdorf
Barry R. Sugarman
Deborah D. Tanenbaum
Melissa L. Klipp
Eric S. Mandelbaum
Andrea I. Bazer
Robert Watson Smith
Fred Hopke
Frank M. Ortiz (Resident, New York, New York Office)
Anita J. Dupree
Alfred Michael Anthony
Risa A. Kleiner
Laura J. Bogaards
Edward T. Kole
Mark S. Lichtenstein
Hesser G. McBride, Jr.
Michael R. Scinto

(See Next Column)

Peter J. Tober
Joseph O'Neil, Jr.
Richard B. Becker
Linda A. Tancs
Jean M. Shanley
Michael J. Conlan
Theodore B. Choi
Timothy E. Burke

Representative Clients: Amerada Hess Corp.; Chevron, U.S.A.; Constellation Bancorp; Cumberland Farms, Inc.; Middlesex County Utilities Authority; New Jersey Automobile Dealers Assn.; Raritan River Steel Co.; The Rouse Co.

For full biographical listings, see the Martindale-Hubbell Law Directory

*WOODBURY,** Gloucester Co.

ANGELO J. FALCIANI, P.A. A PROFESSIONAL CORPORATION (AV)

35 South Broad Street, P.O. Box 379, 08096
Telephone: 609-845-8333
Fax: 609-845-9441

Angelo J. Falciani

Scott J. Lewis
Antoinette L. Falciani
Angelo John Falciani
Carol Tenney

For full biographical listings, see the Martindale-Hubbell Law Directory

LABRUM AND DOAK (AV)

66 Euclid Street, P.O. Box 836, 08096
Telephone: 609-845-8855
Telecopier: 609-848-2694
Philadelphia, Pennsylvania Office: Suite 2900, 1818 Market Street.
Telephone: 610-561-4400.
Telecopier: 610-587-5350.
Norristown, Pennsylvania Office: One Montgomery Plaza, Suite 700.
Telephone: 610-277-7997.
Telecopier: 610-277-2852.
Bethlehem, Pennsylvania Office: 561 East Market Street, P.O. Box 1306.
Telephone: 610-865-2644.
Telecopier: 610-865-2713.
New York, N.Y. Office: 17 Battery Place.
Telephone: 212-809-7870.
Telecopier: 212-785-9279.

RESIDENT MEMBERS

John L. White
Michael G. Brennan
Ronald J. Uzdavinis
Thomas C. Kaczka

RESIDENT ASSOCIATES

Michael D. Dankanich
Sarannah L. McMurtry
John H. Osorio
Gregg L. Zeff
Steven J. Blumenthal
Kenneth H. Kell
Raymond M. LaSalle
Tracy L. Burnley
Gregory H. Melick
Steven Antonelli
Eileen Warner Strulson
Denise Lynn Werner
Teresa Gerlock Hanni
Kevin M. Bothwell

RESIDENT COUNSEL

Jane A. Kenney

Representative Clients: Crum and Forster Insurance Cos.; Insurance Company of North America; Tenneco, Inc.; Employers' Self Insurance Service, Inc.; Insurance Company of North America; Transport Insurance Co.; Woodbury Board of Education.
Reference: First Fidelity Bank/South.

For full biographical listings, see the Martindale-Hubbell Law Directory

NEW MEXICO

*ALAMOGORDO,** Otero Co.

CHARLES W. DURRETT A PROFESSIONAL CORPORATION (AV)

307-11th Street, P.O. Box 750, 88310
Telephone: 505-437-1840
Fax: 505-437-1891

Charles W. Durrett

Representative Clients: Texas-New Mexico Power Company; Government Employees Insurance; International Service Insurance Company; Kemper Insurance Group; Mutual of Omaha; Security Insurance Group; Southland Life Insurance Company; State Farm Insurance Companies; Underwriters at Lloyds, London; Mountain States Mutual Casualty Company.

For full biographical listings, see the Martindale-Hubbell Law Directory

WAYNE A. JORDON (AV)

1200 B New York Avenue, P.O. Box GG, 88311-7516
Telephone: 505-434-2700
Fax: 505-434-5510

Representative Clients: United New Mexico Bank at Alamogordo; United New Mexico Bank at Vaughn; Texas-New Mexico Power Co.; Alamogordo Abstract & Title Co.; Guaranty Abstract & Title Co.; United Services Automobile Assn.; Sudderth Nelson, Inc.
Reference: United New Mexico Bank at Alamogordo.

For full biographical listings, see the Martindale-Hubbell Law Directory

*ALBUQUERQUE,** Bernalillo Co.

BUTT, THORNTON & BAEHR, P.C. (AV)

7000 CityPlace, 2155 Louisiana Boulevard, N.E., P.O. Box 3170, 87190
Telephone: 505-884-0777
FAX: 505-889-8870

Paul L. Butt
J. Duke Thornton
Raymond A. Baehr
Carlos G. Martinez
Norman L. Gagne
John A. Klecan
Alfred L. Green, Jr.
James H. Johansen
Rodney L. Schlagel
Martin Diamond
J. Douglas Compton
Donald E. Lepley, Jr.
John S. Stiff
David N. Whitham
Emily A. Franke
James P. Lyle
Jane A. Laflin
Paul T. Yarbrough
Glenna Hayes

Sherrill K. Filter
Michael P. Clemens
Agnes Fuentevilla Padilla

Representative Clients: Ford Motor Co.; Home Insurance Co.; Reliance Insurance Cos.; Royal Insurance Co.; CIGNA; Norwest Bank; Mayflower Transit; Federal Express Corp.
Reference: Norwest Bank.

For full biographical listings, see the Martindale-Hubbell Law Directory

CIVEROLO, WOLF, GRALOW & HILL, A PROFESSIONAL ASSOCIATION (AV)

500 Marquette, N.W., Suite 1400, P.O. Drawer 887, 87103
Telephone: 505-842-8255
Telecopier: 505-764-6099

Richard C. Civerolo
Wayne C. Wolf
William P. Gralow
Lawrence H. Hill
Kathleen Davison Lebeck
Dennis E. Jontz
W. R. Logan
Roberto C. Armijo
Paul L. Civerolo
Ross L. Crown
Julia C. Roberts
Ellen M. Kelly
R. Thomas Dawe
Thomas P. Gulley
Robert James Curtis
Clinton W. Thute
Kathleen Schaechterle
Nickay B. Manning
Gary J. Cade
M. Clea Gutterson
Judith M. O'Neil
Lisa Entress Pullen
Leslie McCarthy Apodaca

COUNSEL

Donald E. Swaim
Robert W. Becker
Tracy Ahr

General Counsel for: Western Bank.
Counsel for: Home Insurance Co.; Hartford Accident and Indemnity Co.; Farmers Insurance Group; Northwestern National Group; Transamerica Insurance Co.; United Services Automobile Assn.; Chubb & Sons, Inc.; Bell Atlantic Tricon Leasing Corp.
Representative Client: AMREP Corp.

For full biographical listings, see the Martindale-Hubbell Law Directory

HINKLE, COX, EATON, COFFIELD & HENSLEY (AV)

Suite 800, 500 Marquette, N.W., P.O. Box 2043, 87103
Telephone: 505-768-1500
FAX: 505-768-1529
Roswell, New Mexico Office: Suite 700, United Bank Plaza, P.O. Box 10, 88202.
Telephone: 505-622-6510.
FAX: 505-623-9332.
Midland, Texas Office: 6 Desta Drive, Suite 2800, P.O. Box 3580, 79705.
Telephone: 915-683-4691.
FAX: 915-683-6518.
Amarillo, Texas Office: 1700 Bank One Center. P.O. Box 9238, 79105-9238.
Telephone: 806-372-5569.
FAX: 806-372-9761.
Santa Fe, New Mexico Office: 218 Montezuma, P.O. Box 2068, 87504.
Telephone: 505-982-4554.
FAX: 505-982-8623.
Austin, Texas Office: 401 West 15th Street, Suite 800, 78701.
Telephone: 512-476-7137.
FAX: 512-476-5431.
Associated Office: Hoffman & Stephens, P.C., 401 West 15th Street, Suite 800, 78701.
Telephone: 512-476-5434.
Fax: 512-476-5431.

Lewis C. Cox, Jr. (1924-1993)
Roy C. Snodgrass, Jr. (1914-1987)
Clarence E. Hinkle (1901-1985)
W. E. Bondurant, Jr. (1913-1973)
Paul W. Eaton (Amarillo Office)
Conrad E. Coffield (Santa Fe Office)
Harold L. Hensley, Jr. (Roswell Office)
Stuart D. Shanor (Roswell Office)
Eric D. Lanphere
C. D. Martin (Midland Office)
Robert P. Tinnin, Jr.
Marshall G. Martin
Maston C. Courtney (Amarillo Office)
Don L. Patterson (Amarillo Office)
Douglas L. Lunsford (Roswell Office)
Nicholas J. Noeding
T. Calder Ezzell, Jr. (Roswell Office)
William B. Burford (Midland Office)
Richard E. Olson (Roswell Office)
Richard R. Wilfong (Amarillo Office)
Thomas J. McBride
James J. Wechsler (Santa Fe Office)
Nancy S. Cusack (Roswell Office)
Jeffrey L. Fornaciari (Santa Fe Office)
Jeffrey D. Hewett (Midland Office)
James Bruce (Santa Fe Office)
Jerry F. Shackelford (Amarillo Office)
Jeffrey W. Hellberg (Amarillo Office)
William F. Countiss (Amarillo Office)
Albert L. Pitts (Roswell Office)
Thomas M. Hnasko (Santa Fe Office)
John C. Chambers (Amarillo Office)
Gary D. Compton (Amarillo and Austin Offices)
W. H. Brian, Jr. (Amarillo Office)
Russell J. Bailey (Amarillo Office)
Charles R. Watson, Jr. (Amarillo Office)
Thomas D. Haines, Jr. (Roswell Office)
Gregory J. Nibert (Roswell Office)
Mark C. Dow
Fred W. Schwendimann
James M. Hudson (Midland Office)
Jeffrey S. Baird (Amarillo Office)
Thomas E. Hood (Amarillo Office)
Rebecca Nichols Johnson (Roswell Office)
William Paul Johnson (Roswell Office)
Stanley K. Kotovsky, Jr.
Howard R. Thomas
Ellen S. Casey (Santa Fe Office)
Margaret Carter Ludewig
S. Barry Paisner (Santa Fe Office)
Coleman Young (Amarillo Office)
Martin P. Meyers
Wyatt L. Brooks (Amarillo Office)
David M. Russell (Amarillo Office)
Andrew J. Cloutier (Roswell Office)
Stephanie Landry
Kirt E. Moelling (Amarillo Office)
Diane Fisher
Julie P. Neerken
William P. Slattery (Santa Fe Office)

ASSOCIATES

James A. Gillespie (Roswell Office)
Margaret R. McNett
Lisa K. Smith (Amarillo Office)
Norman D. Ewart (Roswell Office)
Darren T. Groce (Midland Office)
Molly B. McIntosh
Marcia Brown Lincoln
Scott A. Shuart (Amarillo Office)
Paul G. Nason
Cathryn D. McClanahan
R. Trey Arvizu, III (Roswell Office)
Amy C. Wright (Amarillo Office)
Ellen T. Louderbough
Karolyn King Nelson (Roswell Office)
Barbara Gregg Glenn (Santa Fe Office)

OF COUNSEL

O. M. Calhoun (Amarillo Office)
Joe W. Wood (Santa Fe Office)
Richard L. Cazzell (Amarillo Office)
Raymond W. Richards (Amarillo Office)
Lahroy Alward White (Amarillo Office)

(See Next Column)

HINKLE, COX, EATON, COFFIELD & HENSLEY—*Continued*

Representative Clients: Anadarko Petroleum Corp.; Atlantic Richfield Co.; Bass Enterprises Production Co.; BHP Petroleum; Caroon & Black Management, Inc.; Chevron, USA, Inc.; CIGNA; City of Albuquerque; Coastal Oil & Gas Corp. Co.; Ethicon Inc., A Johnson & Johnson, Co.; Diagnostik; Conoco; Texaco; Presbyterian Healthcare Services.

For full biographical listings, see the Martindale-Hubbell Law Directory

KELLY, RAMMELKAMP, MUEHLENWEG, LUCERO & LEÓN, A PROFESSIONAL ASSOCIATION (AV)

Simms Tower, 400 Gold Avenue S.W., Suite 500, P.O. Box 25127, 87125-5127
Telephone: 505-247-8860
Fax: 505-247-8881

Henry A. Kelly
David A. Rammelkamp
Robert J. Muehlenweg
Orlando Lucero
Alberto A. León

Todd M. Stafford
David A. Finlayson
Paige G. Leslie

Representative Clients: John L. Rust Co. (Caterpillar); Ponderosa Products, Inc.; Rehobeth-McKinley Christian Healthcare Services; Basis International, Ltd.; Bridgers & Paxton Consulting Engineers, Inc.; D.W.B.H., Inc. (Nissan, Mitsubishi and Hyundai); Envirco Corporation; Mega Corp.; Zanios Foods, Inc.; Albuquerque Truck Center, Ltd.

For full biographical listings, see the Martindale-Hubbell Law Directory

KEMP, SMITH, DUNCAN & HAMMOND, A PROFESSIONAL CORPORATION (AV)

500 Marquette, N.W., Suite 1200, P.O. Box 1276, 87103
Telephone: 505-247-2315
Fax: 505-764-5480
El Paso, Texas Office: 2000 State National Bank Plaza, P.O. Drawer 2800.
Telephone: 915-533-4424.
Fax: 915-546-5360.

John P. Eastham
Robert A. Johnson
Donald B. Monnheimer
Thomas Smidt, II
Bruce E. Castle
James L. Rasmussen
Stephen R. Nelson
A. Drew Hoffman

OF COUNSEL

Paul A. Cooter

Alan Hall
Clinton W. Marrs
James T. Reist
Karla K. Poe
David J. Abell

Representative Clients: Amoco Production Company; Arthur Andersen & Co.; First Security Bank of New Mexico, N.A., Trust Department; Horizon Healthcare Corporation; Leprino Foods Company; Loewen Group International, Inc.; Property Trust of America; SBS Engineering; The Circle K Corporation.

For full biographical listings, see the Martindale-Hubbell Law Directory

MILLER, STRATVERT, TORGERSON & SCHLENKER, P.A. (AV)

500 Marquette Avenue, N.W., Suite 1100, P.O. Box 25687, 87102
Telephone: 505-842-1950
Facsimile: 505-243-4408
Farmington, New Mexico Office: Suite 300, 300 West Arrington. P.O. Box 869.
Telephone: 505-326-4521.
Facsimile: 505-325-5474.
Las Cruces, New Mexico Office: Suite 300, 277 East Amador. P.O. Drawer 1231.
Telephone: 505-523-2481.
Facsimile: 505-526-2215.
Santa Fe, New Mexico Office: 125 Lincoln Avenue, Suite 221. P.O. Box 1986.
Telephone: 505-989-9614.
Facsimile: 505-989-9857.

Ranne B. Miller
Alan C. Torgerson
Kendall O. Schlenker
Alice Tomlinson Lorenz
Gregory W. Chase
Alan Konrad
Margo J. McCormick
Lyman G. Sandy
Stephen M. Williams
Stephan M. Vidmar
Robert C. Gutierrez
Seth V. Bingham (Resident at Farmington Office)
Michael H. Hoses
James B. Collins (Resident at Farmington Office)
Timothy Ray Briggs
Walter R. Parr (Resident at Santa Fe Office)
Rudolph A. Lucero
Daniel E. Ramczyk
Dean G. Constantine
Deborah A. Solove
Gary L. Gordon
Lawrence R. White (Resident at Las Cruces Office)
Sharon P. Gross
Virginia Anderman

(See Next Column)

Marte D. Lightstone
Bradford K. Goodwin
John R. Funk (Resident at Las Cruces Office)
J. Scott Hall (Resident at Santa Fe Office)
Thomas R. Mack
Michael J. Happe (Resident at Farmington Office)
Denise Barela Shepherd
Nancy Augustus
Jill Burtram
Terri L. Sauer
Joel T. Newton (Resident at Las Cruces Office)
Judith K. Nakamura
Thomas M. Domme
David H. Thomas, III
C. Brian Charlton
Ruth O. Pregenzer
Matthew Urrea
Karen Lloyd Acosta (Resident at Las Cruces Office)
Jeffrey E. Jones (Resident at Santa Fe Office)
Leonard D. Sanchez (Not admitted in NM)
Manuel I. Arrieta (Resident at Las Cruces Office)

COUNSEL

William K. Stratvert
Paul W. Robinson

Representative Clients: St. Paul Insurance Cos.; State Farm Mutual Automobile Insurance Co.; The Travelers; United States Fidelity & Guaranty Co.; New Mexico Physicians Mutual Liability Insurance Co.; Farmers Insurance Group; U.S. West Communications; Dona Ana Savings and Loan Assn.; Citizens Bank of Las Cruces; Sunrise Healthcare.

For full biographical listings, see the Martindale-Hubbell Law Directory

MODRALL, SPERLING, ROEHL, HARRIS & SISK, P.A. (AV)

500 Fourth Street, N.W., Sunwest Building, Suite 1000, P.O. Box 2168, 87103-2168
Telephone: 505-848-1800
Fax: 505-848-1889
Santa Fe, New Mexico Office: 119 East Marcy, Suite 200, P.O. Box 9318.
Telephone: 505-983-2020.
Fax: 505-988-8996.
Las Cruces, New Mexico Office: 505 South Main Street, Loretto Towne Centre, Suite 103, P.O. Box 578.
Telephone: 505-526-6655.
Fax: 505-526-6656.

John F. Simms (1885-1954)
Augustus T. Seymour (1907-1965)
J. R. Modrall (1902-1977)
George T. Harris, Jr. (1922-1985)
Leland S. Sedberry, Jr. (1930-1985)
George J. Hopkins (1945-1989)
James E. Sperling (1917-1991)
Allen C. Dewey, Jr.
John R. Cooney
Kenneth L. Harrigan
James M. Parker
Charles I. Wellborn
Dennis J. Falk
Arthur D. Melendres
James P. Houghton
Judy A. Fry
Paul M. Fish
R. E. Thompson
Curtis W. Schwartz (Resident, Santa Fe Office)
Thomas L. Johnson
Lynn H. Slade
Douglas A. Baker
Susan R. Stockstill
Larry P. Ausherman
J. Douglas Foster
Douglas R. Vadnais
Randall J. McDonald
Walter E. Stern, III
Patrick J. Rogers
John A. Darden, III (Resident, Las Cruces Office)
Duane E. Brown
Martha G. Brown
Janet R. Braziel
George F. Koinis
Kevin T. Riedel (Resident, Las Cruces Office)
Eleanor Katherine Bratton
William C. Scott
Tim L. Fields
Douglas G. Schneebeck
Kyle H. Moberly (Resident, Las Cruces Office)
Charles A. Armgardt
Timothy R. Van Valen
Earl E. DeBrine, Jr.
Timothy C. Holm
George R. McFall
Bonnie J. Paisley
Joseph Frontino
Roberta Cooper Ramo
Suzanne M. Barker
Michael D. Hughes (Not admitted in NM)

Kathryn D. Lucero
William R. Keleher
Lisa Mann Burke
Stuart R. Butzier
Donald A. DeCandia
R. Alfred Walker
Timothy J. De Young
Margaret L. Meister
Michael L. Carrico
K. Joseph Cervantes (Resident, Las Cruces Office)
Angelo J. Artuso
Christopher A. Riehl
Gregory C. Ridgley
Nancy F. Arenson (Resident, Santa Fe Office)
James T. Giel
Daniel W. Long
Max J. Madrid
Christine C. Heath (Not admitted in NM)

OF COUNSEL

Joseph E. Roehl
Daniel A. Sisk

COUNSEL

Joe C. Diaz

Representative Clients: Albuquerque Public Schools; The Atchison, Topeka & Santa Fe Railway Co,; Commercial Union Insurance Cos.; Lovelace Medical Foundation; Meridian Oil Inc.; Mountain States Mutual Casualty Co.; Santa Fe Pacific Gold Corporation.
General Counsel for: Boatmen's Sunwest, Inc.; Sunwest Bank of Albuquerque, N.A.

For full biographical listings, see the Martindale-Hubbell Law Directory

Albuquerque—Continued

RODEY, DICKASON, SLOAN, AKIN & ROBB, P.A. (AV)

Albuquerque Plaza, Suite 2200, 201 Third Street, N.W., P.O. Box 1888, 87103-1888
Telephone: 505-765-5900
Fax: 505-768-7395
Santa Fe, New Mexico Office: Suite 101 Marcy Plaza, 123 East Marcy Street, P.O. Box 1357, 87504-1357.
Telephone: 505-984-0100.
Fax: 505-989-9542.

Pearce C. Rodey (1889-1958)
William A. Sloan (1910-1993)
John D. Robb
James C. Ritchie
Robert M. St. John
Joseph J. Mullins
Duane C. Gilkey
Mark K. Adams
Robert G. McCorkle
Bruce Hall
John P. Salazar
William S. Dixon
John P. Burton (Resident, Santa Fe Office)
Rex D. Throckmorton
Jonathan W. Hewes
W. Robert Lasater, Jr.
Mark C. Meiering
Catherine T. Goldberg
Travis R. Collier
Jo Saxton Brayer
S. I. Betzer, Jr.
Edward Ricco
W. Mark Mowery (Resident, Santa Fe Office)
Patrick M. Shay
Nancy J. Appleby
David C. Davenport, Jr. (Resident, Santa Fe Office)
Debra Romero Thal
Ellen G. Thorne
Tracy E. McGee
Charles E. Stuckey
Henry M. Bohnhoff
Charles Kipps Purcell
James P. Fitzgerald
Andrew G. Schultz
John M. Brant
Joseph B. Rochelle
Scott D. Gordon
Susan S. Throckmorton
Angela M. Martinez
Patricia M. Taylor
DeWitt Michael Morgan
Brian H. Lematta
Mark A. Smith
R. Nelson Franse
Theresa W. Parrish
Paul R. Koller
James P. Bieg (Resident, Santa Fe Office)
Barbara G. Stephenson

Jay D. Hill
Charles J. Vigil
Mary P. Keleher
Sheryl S. Mahaney
Mark L. Allen
Thomas L. Stahl
David W. Bunting
Susan K. Barger
Charles W. Weese, III
Paul C. Collins

COUNSEL

Jeffrey W. Loubet

OF COUNSEL

Don L. Dickason
Jackson G. Akin
Ray H. Rodey

Representative Clients: Albuquerque Publishing Co.; ASCAP; Associated Aviation Underwriters Co.; Automobile Club Insurance Co.; Avonite, Inc.; Canal Insurance Co.; General Electric Co.; KOAT-TV; Liberty Mutual Insurance Co.; Sandia Corporation.

For full biographical listings, see the Martindale-Hubbell Law Directory

SUTIN, THAYER & BROWNE, A PROFESSIONAL CORPORATION (AV)

Two Park Square, Suite 1000, 6565 Americas Parkway, N.E., P.O. Box 1945, 87103
Telephone: 505-883-2500
Fax: 505-888-6565
Santa Fe, New Mexico Office: 300 First Interstate Plaza, 150 Washington, P.O. Box 2187, 87504.
Telephone: 505-988-5521.
Fax: 505-982-5297.

Irwin S. Moise (1906-1984)
Lewis R. Sutin (1908-1992)
Saul Cohen (Resident at Santa Fe Office)
Michael G. Sutin (Resident at Santa Fe Office)
Stephen Charnas
Norman S. Thayer, Jr.
Graham Browne
Jonathan B. Sutin
Robert J. Werner
Ray H. Shollenbarger, Jr. (Resident, Santa Fe Office)
Robert G. Heyman
Steven K. Moise
Ronald Segel
Jay D. Hertz
Charles P. Price III
David P. Buchholtz
Mary E. McDonald (Resident at Santa Fe Office)
Gail Gottlieb
Jay D. Rosenblum
Perry E. Bendicksen III
Frank C. Salazar
Suann Hendren
Hope Mead Wynn
Jeffery L. Graves
Bevin C. Owens
David W. Peterson
Stephen Edward Lopez
Michael J. Cadigan
Steven Pacitti
MaryLiz A. Geffert (Resident at Santa Fe Office)
Jean M. Bannon
Pamela Lord Matthews (Resident at Santa Fe Office)
Andrew J. Simons

Representative Clients: Coca-Cola Bottling Co.; Crum & Forster; Ford Motor Credit Co.; The Galles Companies; General Electric Co.; Trammell Crow Co.; United New Mexico Financial Corp.; University of New Mexico; Walgreen Co.

(See Next Column)

For full biographical listings, see the Martindale-Hubbell Law Directory

USSERY & PARRISH, P.A. (AV)

200 Rio Grande Valley Building, 501 Tijeras Avenue, N.W., P.O. Box 487, 87103-0487
Telephone: 505-247-0145
Fax: 505-843-6912

Albert T. Ussery
L. Lamar Parrish

Kathleen Baca

Counsel for: Isleta Pueblo; Sandia Pueblo; San Juan Pueblo; Zia Pueblo.
Representative Client: Auerbach Financial, Inc.
Reference: United New Mexico Bank, Albuquerque.

For full biographical listings, see the Martindale-Hubbell Law Directory

ARTESIA, Eddy Co. — (Refer to Rosewell)

*AZTEC,** San Juan Co. — (Refer to Farmington)

*CARLSBAD,** Eddy Co. — (Refer to Hobbs)

*CLAYTON,** Union Co. — (Refer to Santa Fe)

*CLOVIS,** Curry Co.

ROWLEY LAW FIRM, P.C. (AV)

305 Pile, P.O. Box 790, 88101
Telephone: 505-763-4457
Fax: 505-763-4450

Richard F. Rowley (1908-1980)
Richard F. Rowley, II
Richard F. Rowley, III

Representative Clients: Northwestern Mutual Life Insurance Co.; Prudential Insurance Company of America; Equitable Life Assurance Society; Farm Credit Services; Cigna Capitol Advisors, Inc.; New Mexico American Water Co.; Feed Bag, Inc.; Portal Hay Group Association.
Counsel for: SunWest Bank of Clovis, N.A.

For full biographical listings, see the Martindale-Hubbell Law Directory

TATUM & McDOWELL (AV)

Suite D, Sagebrush Professional Office Complex, 921 East 21st Street, P.O. Drawer 1270, 88101
Telephone: 505-762-7756
Fax: 505-769-1606

MEMBERS OF FIRM

Edwin B. Tatum
James F. McDowell, III

Representative Clients: High Plains Federal Credit Union; Friona Industries Inc.; Valley Rendering Co.; A & M Building Systems Inc.; Citizens Bank of Clovis; American Cattle Feeders, Inc.; Clovis Feedyard, Inc.; Borden's Peanut Co., Inc.
Reference: Sunwest Bank of Clovis, N.A.; First National Bank of Clovis.

For full biographical listings, see the Martindale-Hubbell Law Directory

*DEMING,** Luna Co. — (Refer to Las Cruces)

FARMINGTON, San Juan Co.

BRIONES LAW FIRM, A PROFESSIONAL ASSOCIATION (AV)

333 East Main Street, 87401
Telephone: 505-325-0258
Fax: 505-325-3311

Felix Briones, Jr.

Thomas Roman Briones

Reference: Sunwest Bank of Farmington, Farmington, New Mexico.

For full biographical listings, see the Martindale-Hubbell Law Directory

MILLER, STRATVERT, TORGERSON & SCHLENKER, P.A. (AV)

Suite 300, 300 West Arrington, P.O. Box 869, 87401
Telephone: 505-326-4521
Facsimile: 505-325-5474
Albuquerque, New Mexico Office: 500 Marquette Avenue, N.W., Suite 1100. P.O. Box 25687.
Telephone: 505-842-1950.
Facsimile: 505-243-4408.
Las Cruces, New Mexico Office: Suite 300, 277 East Amador. P.O. Drawer 1231.
Telephone: 505-523-2481.
Facsimile: 505-526-2215.
Santa Fe, New Mexico Office: 125 Lincoln Avenue, Suite 221. P.O. Box 1986.
Telephone: 505-989-9614.
Facsimile: 505-989-9857.

(See Next Column)

MILLER, STRATVERT, TORGERSON & SCHLENKER P.A.—*Continued*

James B. Collins
Seth V. Bingham
Michael J. Happe

Representative Clients: St. Paul Insurance Cos.; State Farm Mutual Automobile Insurance Co.; The Travelers; United States Fidelity & Guaranty Co.; New Mexico Physicians Mutual Liability Insurance Co.; Mountain States Mutual Casualty Co.; Farmers Insurance Group; Amoco Production Co.; Sunrise Healthcare.

For full biographical listings, see the Martindale-Hubbell Law Directory

TANSEY, ROSEBROUGH, GERDING & STROTHER, P.C. (AV)

621 West Arrington Street, P.O. Box 1020, 87499
Telephone: 505-325-1801
Telecopier: 505-325-4675

Haskell D. Rosebrough
Austin E. Roberts (1921-1983)
Richard L. Gerding
Robin D. Strother
Douglas A. Echols
James B. Payne
Michael T. O'Loughlin
Tommy Roberts
Karen L. Townsend

OF COUNSEL

Charles M. Tansey, Jr.

Representative Clients: American International Adjustment Co.; New Mexico Newspapers, Inc.; CIGNA Insurance Co.; Commercial Union Insurance Cos.; United Indian Traders Association, Inc.; Farmington Municipal Schools; Risk Management Division, State of New Mexico; San Juan Regional Medical Center; Merrion Oil & Gas Co; Giant Exploration and Production Co.

For full biographical listings, see the Martindale-Hubbell Law Directory

*FORT SUMNER,** De Baca Co. — (Refer to Clovis)

HOBBS, Lea Co.

MADDOX LAW FIRM, PROFESSIONAL CORPORATION (AV)

220 West Broadway, Suite 200, P.O. Box 2508, 88241
Telephone: 505-393-0505
Fax: 505-397-2646

Don Maddox
James M. Maddox
Scotty Holloman
Gary L. Clingman

General Counsel for: Bravo Energy, Inc.; Star Tool Co.
Representative Clients: College of the Southwest; Sun Publishing Co. (Hobbs News-Sun).

For full biographical listings, see the Martindale-Hubbell Law Directory

J. W. NEAL, P.C. (AV)

Neal Building, 419 West Cain, P.O. Box 278, 88240
Telephone: 505-397-3614
Fax: 505-393-7405

C. Melvin Neal (1907-1968)
J. W. Neal

LEGAL SUPPORT PERSONNEL

PARALEGALS

Bes Castleman

Representative Clients: Highland Insurance Co., Houston, Texas; New Mexico Junior College.

For full biographical listings, see the Martindale-Hubbell Law Directory

STOUT & STOUT (AV)

218 West Lea, P.O. Box 716, 88240
Telephone: 505-393-1555; 393-2211
Fax: 505-393-1825

MEMBERS OF FIRM

Lowell Stout
Mark Stout

For full biographical listings, see the Martindale-Hubbell Law Directory

*LAS CRUCES,** Dona Ana Co.

MARTIN, LUTZ & BROWER, P.C. (AV)

2100 North Main Street, Suite 3, P.O. Drawer W, 88004-1837
Telephone: 505-526-2449
Fax: 505-526-0946

R. Wilson Martin
Hugh T. Brower
William L. Lutz

Representative Clients: Citizens Bank, Las Cruces, New Mexico; Western Bank, Lordsburg, New Mexico; Mesilla Valley Land Title Co., Inc.; Metal Craft, Co.; Newman Outdoor Advertising of New Mexico, Inc.; Century 21 Hollingshead Realty; Equitable Agri-Business.

For full biographical listings, see the Martindale-Hubbell Law Directory

MODRALL, SPERLING, ROEHL, HARRIS & SISK, P.A. (AV)

505 South Main Street Loretto Towne Centre, Suite 103, P.O. Box 578, 88004-0578
Telephone: 505-526-6655
Fax: 505-526-6656
Albuquerque, New Mexico Office: 500 Fourth Street, N.W., Sunwest Building, Suite 1000, P.O. Box 2168.
Telephone: 505-848-1800.
FAX: 505-848-1889.
Santa Fe, New Mexico Office: 119 East Marcy, Suite 200, P.O. Box 9318.
Telephone: 505-983-2020.
Fax: 505-988-8996.

John A. Darden, III
Kevin T. Riedel
Kyle H. Moberly

K. Joseph Cervantes

Representative Clients: El Paso Bell Federal Credit Union; L & P Building Supply, Inc.; L & P Building Supply of Las Cruces, Inc.; Las Cruces Abstract & Title Company; Las Cruces Builders Supply; Las Cruces Sun News; New Mexico Department of Agriculture; Sunwest Bank of Las Cruces, N.A.; Wallace Westwind Chevrolet-Oldsmobile-Cadillac-Geo.

For full biographical listings, see the Martindale-Hubbell Law Directory

WEINBRENNER, RICHARDS, PAULOWSKY & RAMIREZ, P.A. (AV)

8th Floor, First National Tower, P.O. Drawer O, 88004-1719
Telephone: 505-524-8624
Fax: 505-524-4252

Neil E. Weinbrenner
Ralph Wm. Richards
Florencio (Larry) Ramirez
David McNeill, Jr.
Michael T. Murphy
Fred Schiller
Robert Ikard

OF COUNSEL

Michael G. Paulowsky

LEGAL SUPPORT PERSONNEL

Helen Pauline Lemelin

General Counsel for: Stahmann Farms, Inc.; First National Bank of Dona Ana County.
Representative Clients: American General Cos.; Hartford Group; CNA Insurance; Fireman's Fund; United States Fidelity & Guaranty Co.; Travelers Insurance Co.; General Accident Group.

For full biographical listings, see the Martindale-Hubbell Law Directory

*LAS VEGAS,** San Miguel Co. — (Refer to Santa Fe)

*LORDSBURG,** Hidalgo Co. — (Refer to Silver City)

*LOVINGTON,** Lea Co. — (Refer to Hobbs)

*PORTALES,** Roosevelt Co. — (Refer to Clovis)

*RATON,** Colfax Co. — (Refer to Santa Fe)

*ROSWELL,** Chaves Co.

ATWOOD, MALONE, MANN & TURNER, A PROFESSIONAL ASSOCIATION (AV)

Suite 1100, United Bank Plaza, 400 North Pennsylvania Avenue, P.O. Drawer 700, 88202-0700
Telephone: 505-622-6221
Fax: 505-624-2883

Jefferson Davis Atwood (1883-1960)
Ross L. Malone (1910-1974)
Russell D. Mann (P.A.)
Bob F. Turner
John W. Bassett, Jr.
Robert E. Sabin
Brian W. Copple
Steven Lynn Bell
William P. Lynch
Rod M. Schumacher
John S. Nelson
Freddie J. Romero
Lee M. Rogers, Jr.
Timothy A. Lucas
Victoria S. Arends

Jeffery Dean Tatum
Bryan Evans
Richard J. Valle
Barbara A. Reddy

OF COUNSEL

Charles F. Malone

Representative Clients: Amoco Production Co.; Marathon Oil Co.; Sunwest Bank of Roswell; General Motors Corp.; State Farm Insurance Cos.; Commercial Union Assurance Cos.; Mountain States Mutual Casualty Co.; New Mexico Physicians Mutual.

For full biographical listings, see the Martindale-Hubbell Law Directory

*SANTA FE,** Santa Fe Co.

* indicates certain Bar Register subscribers whose principal office is located elsewhere in the state and who have arranged for representation as a part of the state capital listings that follow

CAMPBELL, CARR, BERGE & SHERIDAN, P.A. (AV)

110 North Guadalupe, P.O. Box 2208, 87504-2208
Telephone: 505-988-4421
Telecopier: 505-983-6043

Michael B. Campbell
Bradford C. Berge
William F. Carr
Mark F. Sheridan

Michael H. Feldewert
Tanya M. Trujillo
Nancy A. Rath

OF COUNSEL

Jack M. Campbell

For full biographical listings, see the Martindale-Hubbell Law Directory

CARPENTER, COMEAU, MALDEGEN, BRENNAN, NIXON & TEMPLEMAN (AV)

Coronado Building, 141 East Palace Avenue, P.O. Box 669, 87504-0669
Telephone: 505-982-4611
Telecopier: 505-988-2987

MEMBERS OF FIRM

Richard N. Carpenter
Michael R. Comeau
Larry D. Maldegen
Michael W. Brennan
Sunny J. Nixon
William P. Templeman
Jon J. Indall
Stephen J. Lauer
Paula Ann Cook
Grey Handy
Joseph E. Manges

Representative Clients: Homestake Mining Co.; First National Bank of Santa Fe; N. M. Electric Cooperatives; Plains Electric G & T Cooperative; United Nuclear Corp.; Uranium Producers of America; BHP Minerals; Great American Insurance Co.; GTE; State of New Mexico.

For full biographical listings, see the Martindale-Hubbell Law Directory

CATRON, CATRON & SAWTELL, A PROFESSIONAL ASSOCIATION (AV)

2006 Botulph Road, P.O. Box 788, 87504-0788
Telephone: 505-982-1947
Telecopier: 505-986-1013

Thomas B. Catron (1840-1921)
Charles C. Catron (1879-1951)
Fletcher A. Catron (1890-1964)
Thomas B. Catron III
John S. Catron
William A. Sawtell, Jr.
Fletcher R. Catron
W. Anthony Sawtell
Forrest S. Smith
Michael T. Pottow
Kathrin M. Kinzer-Ellington

LEGAL SUPPORT PERSONNEL

Peggy L. Feldt (Certified Public Accountant)

Attorneys for: Santa Fe Board of Education; American Express Co.; The Santa Fe Opera; Sunwest Bank of Santa Fe; VNS Health Services, Inc.; Santa Maria El Mirador Rehabilitation Services, Inc.; Rancho del Oso Pardo.

For full biographical listings, see the Martindale-Hubbell Law Directory

JONES, SNEAD, WERTHEIM, RODRIGUEZ & WENTWORTH, P.A. (AV)

215 Lincoln Avenue, P.O. Box 2228, 87504-2228
Telephone: 505-982-0011
Fax: 505-989-6288

O. Russell Jones (1912-1978)
James E. Snead
Jerry Wertheim
Manuel J. Rodriguez
John Wentworth
Arturo L. Jaramillo
Peter V. Culbert
James G. Whitley
Francis J. Mathew

Jerry Todd Wertheim
Carol A. Clifford

LEGAL SUPPORT PERSONNEL

PARALEGALS

Linda A. Zieba

General Counsel for: Charter Bank for Savings, F.S.B.; National Education Association of New Mexico.
Representative Clients: Century Bank, F.S.B.; 3M; Scurlock Permian Corp.; Merchants' Fast Motor Lines; Billy Walker Trucking, Inc.; Sprint Cellular, Inc.; Santa Fe Properties, Inc.
Reference: Bank of Santa Fe.

For full biographical listings, see the Martindale-Hubbell Law Directory

MODRALL, SPERLING, ROEHL, HARRIS & SISK, P.A. (AV)

119 East Marcy, Suite 200, P.O. Box 9318, 87504-9318
Telephone: 505-983-2020
Fax: 505-988-8996
Albuquerque, New Mexico Office: 500 Fourth Street, N.W., Sunwest Building, Suite 1000, P.O. Box 2168.
Telephone: 505-848-1800.
Fax: 505-848-1889.
Las Cruces, New Mexico Office: 505 South Main Street, Loretto Towne Centre, Suite 103, P.O. Box 578.
Telephone: 505-526-6655.
Fax: 505-526-6656.

Curtis W. Schwartz

Nancy F. Arenson

Representative Clients: Jackalope, Inc.; Martin Marietta; NCR Corporation; Sierra Telcom Services, Inc; Thornburg Management Co., Inc.

For full biographical listings, see the Martindale-Hubbell Law Directory

MONTGOMERY & ANDREWS, PROFESSIONAL ASSOCIATION (AV)

325 Paseo de Peralta, P.O. Box 2307, 87504-2307
Telephone: 505-982-3873
Albuquerque, New Mexico Office: Suite 1300 Albuquerque Plaza, 201 Third Street, N.W., P.O. Box 26927.
Telephone: 505-242-9677.
FAX: 505-243-2542.

J. O. Seth (1883-1963)
A. K. Montgomery (1903-1987)
Frank Andrews (1914-1981)
Victor R. Ortega
John B. Pound
Bill Chappell, Jr. (Resident, Albuquerque Office)
Richard K. Barlow (Resident, Albuquerque Office)
Gary Kilpatric
Thomas W. Olson
Walter J. Melendres
Bruce Herr
John B. Draper
Nancy M. Anderson King
Sarah Michael Singleton
John D. Phillips (Resident, Albuquerque Office)
Stephen S. Hamilton
Galen M. Buller
Edmund H. Kendrick
Deborah A. Peacock (Resident, Albuquerque Office)
Suzanne B. Kinney (Resident, Albuquerque Office)
Paula G. Maynes
R. Michael Shickich
Rod D. Baker (Resident, Albuquerque Office)
Louis W. Rose
David Carroll Johnson
Paul S. Grand
Scott K. Atkinson (Resident, Albuquerque Office)
Jeffrey D. Myers (Resident, Albuquerque Office)
Thomas A. Clayton
Dana L. Cox (Resident, Albuquerque Office)
Grace Philips
Alex M. Gabaldon
Richard M. Krumbein (Resident, Albuquerque Office)
R. Bruce Frederick
M. Marie Franse (Resident, Albuquerque Office)
Donovan F. Duggan (Not admitted in NM; Resident, Albuquerque Office)

OF COUNSEL

William R. Federici

COUNSEL

Roberta Marie Price (Resident, Albuquerque Office)
Marvin E. Pollock

Representative Clients: Burlington Resources, Inc.; El Paso Natural Gas Co.; Mobil Exploration and Producing, U.S., Inc.; St. Vincent Hospital; Travelers Insurance Co.; United States Fidelity and Guaranty Co.; U S WEST Communications.

For full biographical listings, see the Martindale-Hubbell Law Directory

* **RODEY, DICKASON, SLOAN, AKIN & ROBB, P.A.** (AV)

Suite 101 Marcy Plaza, 123 East Marcy Street, 87501
Telephone: 505-984-0100
Fax: 505-989-9542
Mailing Address: P.O. Box 1357, Santa Fe, New Mexico, 87504-1357
Albuquerque, New Mexico Office: Albuquerque Plaza, Suite 2200, 201 Third Street, N.W..
Telephone: 505-765-5900.
Fax: 505-768-7395.

John P. Burton (Resident)
W. Mark Mowery (Resident)
David C. Davenport, Jr. (Resident)
James P. Bieg (Resident)

OF COUNSEL

Ray H. Rodey

For full biographical listings, see the Martindale-Hubbell Law Directory

SCHEUER, YOST & PATTERSON, A PROFESSIONAL CORPORATION (AV)

125 Lincoln Avenue, Suite 223, P.O. Drawer 9570, 87504
Telephone: 505-982-9911
Fax: 505-982-1621

(See Next Column)

SCHEUER, YOST & PATTERSON A PROFESSIONAL CORPORATION—*Continued*

Ralph H. Scheuer	Roger L. Prucino
Mel E. Yost	Elizabeth A. Jaffe
John N. Patterson	Tracy Erin Conner
Holly A. Hart	Ruth M. Fuess

OF COUNSEL

Melvin T. Yost

Representative Clients: Cyprus-AMAX, Inc.; Century Bank, FSB; Chicago Insurance Co.; GEICO; Pepsico, Inc.; Rocky Mountain Bankcard System; St. John's College; Sun Loan Companies; Territorial Abstract & Title Co.; Tosco Corporation.

For full biographical listings, see the Martindale-Hubbell Law Directory

*** SUTIN, THAYER & BROWNE, A PROFESSIONAL CORPORATION (AV)**

300 First Interstate Plaza, 150 Washington, P.O. Box 2187, 87504
Telephone: 505-988-5521
Fax: 505-982-5297
Albuquerque, New Mexico Office: Two Park Square, Suite 1000, 6565 Americas Parkway, N.E., P.O. Box 1945, 87103.
Telephone: 505-883-2500.
Fax: 505-888-6565.

Saul Cohen (Resident)	Mary E. McDonald (Resident)
Michael G. Sutin (Resident)	MaryLiz A. Geffert (Resident)
Robert J. Werner	Pamela Lord Matthews
Ray H. Shollenbarger, Jr. (Resident)	

Representative Clients: Coca-Cola Bottling Co.; Crum & Forster; Ford Motor Credit Co.; Furr's, Inc.; The Galles Companies; General Electric Co.; Trammell Crow Co.; United New Mexico Financial Corp.; University of New Mexico; Walgreen Co.

For full biographical listings, see the Martindale-Hubbell Law Directory

WHITE, KOCH, KELLY & McCARTHY, A PROFESSIONAL ASSOCIATION (AV)

433 Paseo De Peralta, P.O. Box 787, 87504-0787
Telephone: 505-982-4374
ABA/NET: 1154
Fax: 505-982-0350; 984-8631

William Booker Kelly	Janet Clow
John F. McCarthy, Jr.	Kevin V. Reilly
Benjamin J. Phillips	Charles W. N. Thompson, Jr.
David F. Cunningham	M. Karen Kilgore
Albert V. Gonzales	Sandra J. Brinck

SPECIAL COUNSEL

Paul L. Bloom

Aaron J. Wolf	Carolyn R. Glick

Representative Clients: Southern Pacific Transportation Co.; Nationwide Insurance Co.; Risk Management Division of New Mexico General Services Department; Alliance of American Insurers; Santa Fe Community College; First American Title Insurance Co.; Century Bank; Public Service Company of New Mexico; AT&SF Railway Co.; Gallager Bassett.

For full biographical listings, see the Martindale-Hubbell Law Directory

*SANTA ROSA,** Guadalupe Co. — (Refer to Clovis)

*SILVER CITY,** Grant Co.

J. WAYNE WOODBURY (AV)

214 North Bullard, P.O. Box 857, 88062
Telephone: 505-538-3729
Fax: 505-538-3956
Representative Clients: Pacific Western Land Co.; Phelps Dodge Corp.; Laney Ranches, Inc.; The American National Bank, Silver City, New Mexico.
Reference: The American National Bank, Silver City, New Mexico.

*TAOS,** Taos Co. — (Refer to Santa Fe)

*TUCUMCARI,** Quay Co. — (Refer to Clovis)

NEW YORK

*ALBANY,** Albany Co.

* indicates certain Bar Register subscribers whose principal office is located elsewhere in the state and who have arranged for representation as a part of the state capital listings that follow

AINSWORTH, SULLIVAN, TRACY, KNAUF, WARNER & RUSLANDER (AV)

Brandon Place, 403 New Karner Road, P.O. Box 12849, 12212-2849
Telephone: 518-464-0600
Fax: 518-464-0679

MEMBERS OF FIRM

Danforth E. Ainsworth (1908-1927)
Charles B. Sullivan (1881-1975)
Thomas F. Tracy (1914-1994)
Frank J. Warner, Jr.
Robert K. Ruslander
James E. McHenry
John W. Bailey
Frank M. Pell
Elizabeth M. Dumas
Margaret Comard Lynch
Michael J. Murphy
Timothy J. O'Connor

ASSOCIATES

Dennis W. Habel
Betsy R. Ruslander
Colleen M. O'Connell
Kyran Nigro
Anthony V. Cardona, Jr.
Mary Beth Hynes

OF COUNSEL

Bruce R. Sullivan
John E. Knauf

Local Counsel for: Montgomery Ward & Co.; Liberty Insurance Co.; United Service Auto Assn.; Continental Insurance Cos.; American International Ins. Co.; Aetna Insurance Co.; Kemper Insurance Co.; Sears Roebuck & Co.; Commercial Union Assurance Cos.; Chubb & Sons, Inc.; American Home Assurance Co.

For full biographical listings, see the Martindale-Hubbell Law Directory

* **BOND, SCHOENECK & KING** (AV)

111 Washington Avenue, 12210
Telephone: 518-462-7421
Fax: 518-462-7441
Syracuse, New York Office: 18th Floor One Lincoln Center.
Telephone: 315-422-0121.
Fax: 315-422-3598.
Boca Raton, Florida Office: 5355 Town Center Road, Suite 1002.
Telephone: 407-368-1212.
Fax: 407-338-9955.
Naples, Florida Office: 1167 Third Street South.
Telephone: 813-262-6812.
Fax: 813-262-6908.
Oswego, New York Office: 130 East Second Street.
Telephone: 315-343-9116.
Fax: 315-343-1231.
Overland Park, Kansas Office: 7500 College Boulevard, Suite 910.
Telephone: 913-345-8001.
Fax: 913-345-9017.

RESIDENT MEMBERS

John A. Beach
Richard L. Smith
Richard C. Heffern
Carl Rosenbloom
John M. Freyer
David R. Sheridan
Nicholas J. D'Ambrosio, Jr.
Richard A. Reed
Susan Phillips Read
Joseph P. Van De Loo
Louis A. Alexander
Arthur J. Siegel

RESIDENT ASSOCIATES

Thomas J. Collura
John E. Higgins
Hermes A. Fernandez, III
Michael J. Grygiel
Gregory J. Champion
Thomas Patrick Mc Quade
Patrick L. Seely, Jr.
Robert P. Storch

For full biographical listings, see the Martindale-Hubbell Law Directory

CARTER, CONBOY, CASE, BLACKMORE, NAPIERSKI AND MALONEY, P.C. (AV)

20 Corporate Woods Boulevard, 12211-2350
Telephone: 518-465-3484
Fax: 518-465-1843

J. S. Carter (1920-1954)
M. James Conboy (1920-1969)
James S. Carter
James M. Conboy
Forrest N. Case, Jr.
James C. Blackmore
Eugene E. Napierski
John T. Maloney
Gregory S. Mills
Edward D. Laird, Jr.
Susanna L. Martin
Brian P. Krzykowski
Terence S. Hannigan

John W. VanDenburgh
William J. Greagan
Anne M. Hurley
John J. Gable
Susan DiBella Harvey
Shirley Clouser Greagan
James Anthony Resila
James P. Trainor
David A. Rikard
Nancy E. May-Skinner

(See Next Column)

Christopher Lyons
Eugene Daniel Napierski
Joseph T. Perkins
Colleen H. Whalen
Paul C. Marthy
Christine M. Napierski
Kent B. Sprotbery
Noreen D. Grimmick
Kathleen A. McCaffrey
Victor C. Garlock

Reference: Key Bank of New York.

For full biographical listings, see the Martindale-Hubbell Law Directory

COUCH, WHITE, BRENNER, HOWARD & FEIGENBAUM (AV)

540 Broadway, P.O. Box 22222, 12201
Telephone: 518-426-4600
Telecopier: 518-426-0376
Palm Beach, Florida Office: 2875 South Ocean Boulevard. 33480.
Telephone: 407-586-7109.
Telecopier: 407-586-1496.

MEMBERS OF FIRM

Leslie F. Couch
Algird F. White, Jr.
Barbara S. Brenner
Joel M. Howard, III
Paul A. Feigenbaum
Robert M. Loughney
Harold N. Iselin
Leonard H. Singer
Keith B. Rose

SENIOR COUNSEL

Lawrence H. Cooke

COUNSEL

Christopher A. Cernik

ASSOCIATES

James J. Barriere
Richard A. Breunig
Michael L. Koenig
Pamela Madeiros-Thomson
Michael B. Mager
Richard Joseph Miller, Jr.
Wendy L. Ravitz
Doreen M. Unis

Reference: Key Bank, N.A.

For full biographical listings, see the Martindale-Hubbell Law Directory

DONOHUE, SABO, VARLEY & ARMSTRONG, P.C. (AV)

18 Computer Drive East, P.O. Box 15056, 12212-5056
Telephone: 518-458-8922
Telecopier: 518-438-4349

Paul F. Donohue, Sr. (Retired)
Alvin O. Sabo
Kenneth Varley, Jr.
Robert J. Armstrong
Fred J. Hutchison
Bruce S. Huttner
Kathleen L. Werther

Christine M. D'Addio
Walter M.B. Spiro

Representative Clients: CNA Insurance Cos.; Continental Loss Adjusting Services; Electric Insurance Co.; Electric Mutual Insurance Co.; General Accident Assurance Co.; General Electric Co.; NY Central Mutual Fire Insurance Co.; Preferred Mutual Insurance Co.; State Insurance Fund; Zurich-American Insurance Co.

For full biographical listings, see the Martindale-Hubbell Law Directory

HERZOG, ENGSTROM & KOPLOVITZ, P.C. (AV)

Capital Center, 99 Pine Street, 12207
Telephone: 518-465-7581
Telecopier: 518-462-2743

Jacob H. Herzog
Carl W. Engstrom
Sholom B. Koplovitz
Edwin J. Tobin
James M. Reilly
Harry V. B. Miller
David J. Pollitzer

Germaine A. Curtin
Frederick B. Galt
Frank W. Lang
Victor A. Oberting III
Phillip M. Tribble

General Counsel for: Command Security Corp.; Independent Cement Corp.; Mace Security, Inc.; Hartwick College; Garden Way Inc.; Central National Bank of Canajoharie; Memorial Hospital; First Albany Corporation.
References: Key Bank, N.A.; Fleet Bank of New York; Chemical Bank.

For full biographical listings, see the Martindale-Hubbell Law Directory

KOHN, BOOKSTEIN & KARP, P.C. (AV)

Ninety State Street Suite 929, 12207-1888
Telephone: 518-449-8810
Fax: 518-449-1029

Isadore Bookstein (1891-1973)
Reuben H. Kohn (1903-1994)
Edward L. Bookstein
Eugene M. Karp
Richard A. Kohn

James Blendell
Amy S. O'Connor

OF COUNSEL

Irving I. Waxman
Karen Martino Valle

Representative Clients: Adirondack Transit Lines, Inc.; Amfast Corp.; Simmons Fastener Corp.; Tagsons Papers, Inc.; Thermo Products, Inc.

(See Next Column)

KOHN, BOOKSTEIN & KARP P.C.—*Continued*

For full biographical listings, see the Martindale-Hubbell Law Directory

O'CONNELL AND ARONOWITZ, P.C. (AV)

100 State Street, 12207-1885
Telephone: 518-462-5601
Telecopier: 518-462-2670
Plattsburgh, New York Office: Grand Plaza Building, Suite 204, 159 Margaret Street.
Telephone: 518-562-0600.
Fax: 518-562-0657.
Saratoga Springs, New York Office: Suite 202, 358 Broadway.
Telephone: 518-587-0425.
Fax: 518-587-0565.

Cornelius D. Murray
Daniel M. Sleasman
Neil H. Rivchin
Peter Danziger
Fred B. Wander
Stephen R. Coffey
Dean J. Higgins (Resident, Saratoga Springs Office)
William A. Favreau (Resident, Plattsburgh Office)
Sarah Walker Birn
Thomas J. Di Novo

David J. Demeter
James E. Braman
Gloria Herron Arthur
Ralph W. Bandel
James L. Coffin
Leigh Elizabeth P. Cole (Resident, Plattsburgh Office)
Lori A. Cantwell (Resident, Plattsburgh, Office)
Keith M. Bruno (Resident, Plattsburgh Office)
Michael R. Monahan
Pamela A. Nichols
Polly J. Feigenbaum (Resident, Saratoga Springs Office)
Keith J. Brennan
Raymond M. Ranellucci
Lisa Fenakel Lesser

OF COUNSEL

Francis H. Neverett (Resident, Plattsburgh Office)
Max Gordon
Barbara Gott Billet
John H. Farrell
Andrew T. McEvoy, Jr.

Representative Clients: Capital Newspapers Division of the Hearst Corp.; The New York State Health Facilities Association, Inc.; Time Warner Entertainment; Midcoast Mortgage Corporation; First Albany Corporation (Retirement Plan Counsel).

For full biographical listings, see the Martindale-Hubbell Law Directory

ROCHE CORRIGAN MCCOY & BUSH (AV)

The Wilem Van Zandt Building, 36 South Pearl Street, 12207
Telephone: 518-436-9370

MEMBERS OF FIRM

Robert P. Roche
Peter J. Corrigan
Joseph M. McCoy
Scott W. Bush

Reference: 1st American Bank, Albany.

For full biographical listings, see the Martindale-Hubbell Law Directory

ROWLEY, FORREST, O'DONNELL & HITE, P.C. (AV)

90 State Street Suite 729, 12207-1715
Telephone: 518-434-6187
Fax: 518-434-1287

Richard R. Rowley
Thomas J. Forrest
Brian J. O'Donnell
Robert S. Hite
John H. Beaumont
Mark S. Pelersi
David C. Rowley

James J. Seaman
David P. Miranda
Kevin S. Casey
Richard W. Bader
Daniel W. Coffey
Thomas D. Spain

OF COUNSEL

Rush W. Stehlin

Reference: Norstar Bank.

For full biographical listings, see the Martindale-Hubbell Law Directory

SHANLEY, SWEENEY & REILLY, P.C. (AV)

The Castle at Ten Thurlow Terrace, 12203
Telephone: 518-463-1415
Saratoga Springs, New York Office: 480 Broadway.
Telephone: 518-583-0777.
Fax: 518-583-1184.

Michael P. Shanley, Jr.
Robert L. Sweeney
J. Stephen Reilly (Resident, Saratoga Springs Office)
John L. Allen
Frank P. Milano
Gregory D. Faucher
J. Michael Naughton
Mark R. Marcantano
Patricia Hart Nessler
Lisa M. Peraza
Bonnie J. Riggi
Scott P. Olson

For full biographical listings, see the Martindale-Hubbell Law Directory

TABNER, LAUDATO AND RYAN (AV)

26 Computer Drive West, P.O. Box 12605, 12212-2605
Telephone: 518-459-9000
Telecopier: 518-459-9165

MEMBERS OF FIRM

John W. Tabner
Paul J. Laudato
William F. Ryan, Jr.

OF COUNSEL

C. Theodore Carlson
David S. Mackay

ASSOCIATES

William J. Keniry
Eric N. Dratler
John H. Fisher

Special Counsel for: Water and Sewer Districts; Towns of Colonie, Coxsackie, Guilderland, Johnstown, Queensbury, Rotterdam and Village Castleton.
Reference: Norstar Bank of Upstate New York.

For full biographical listings, see the Martindale-Hubbell Law Directory

THUILLEZ, FORD, GOLD & CONOLLY (AV)

90 State Street, Suite 1500, 12207-1797
Telephone: 518-455-9952
Facsimile: 518-462-4031

MEMBERS OF FIRM

Dale M. Thuillez
Donald P. Ford, Jr.
Barry A. Gold
Henry Neal Conolly

ASSOCIATES

Jonathan B. Summers
Ann C. Crowell
Scott T. Johnson

OF COUNSEL

Thomas A. Ford

SPECIAL COUNSEL

Michael J. Hutter, Jr.
Susan L. Lore

Representative Clients: Kemper Insurance Group; Hospital Underwriters Mutual Insurance Co.; Crum & Forster; Government Employees Insurance Co.; Ellis Hospital; Hartford Insurance Co.; United States Fidelity & Guaranty Co.; The Worcester Insurance Co.; Sofc-Mead; Prudential Property and Casualty Co.

For full biographical listings, see the Martindale-Hubbell Law Directory

TOBIN AND DEMPF (AV)

33 Elk Street, 12207
Telephone: 518-463-1177
Telecopier: 518-463-7489

MEMBERS OF FIRM

Charles J. Tobin (1882-1954)
Charles J. Tobin, Jr. (1915-1987)
James W. Sanderson (1937-1992)
Louis Dempf, Jr.
Michael L. Costello
John W. Clark
John T. Mitchell
David A. Ruffo
Kevin A. Luibrand
R. Christopher Dempf

ASSOCIATES

Mark A. Mainello
Gayle E. Hartz
William H. Reynolds
Raul A. Tabora, Jr.

General Counsel for: Adirondack Beverages, Inc.; MLB Industries, Inc.; College of St. Rose; Siena College; Orange Motor Co., Inc.; The Roman Catholic Diocese of Albany, New York; Teresian House Nursing Home Co.

For full biographical listings, see the Martindale-Hubbell Law Directory

*ALBION,** Orleans Co. — (Refer to Holley)

AMITYVILLE, Suffolk Co. — (Refer to Islandia)

*AUBURN,** Cayuga Co.

BOYLE & ANDERSON, P.C. (AV)

120 Genesee Street, 13021
Telephone: 315-253-0326
Fax: 315-253-4968

Edward T. Boyle (1901-1975)
Herbert T. Anderson
Robert E. Barry
Robert K. Bergan
Richard A. Gleason
P. Alex Lipski
Charles H. Lynch, Jr.
John P. McLane
Ross M. Tisci

Jeffrey S. Woodard

Representative Clients: Columbian Foundation, Inc.; Cayuga Savings Bank; Wells College, Aurora, New York; O. Mustad & Son (U.S.A.), Inc.; W. E. Bouley Co., Inc.; Cooperative Feed Dealers, Inc.; R.P.M. Industries, Inc.; Port Byron Telephone Co.; The Stanley W. Metcalf Foundation; Welch Allyn.

For full biographical listings, see the Martindale-Hubbell Law Directory

Auburn—Continued

CONTIGUGLIA & GIACONA (AV)

The Federal House, 7 William Street, 13021
Telephone: 315-253-9746

MEMBERS OF FIRM

Anthony J. Contiguglia (1897-1986)
Louis P. Contiguglia
Samuel P. Giacona

Representative Clients: Cayuga Savings Bank; Cayuga Homesite Development Corp.; Statewide Funding Corp.; American Residential Mortgage Corp.; GE Capital Home Equity Services; Commonwealth Mortgage Company, Inc.
References: Marine Midland Bank (Auburn Office); Cayuga Savings Bank; The Key Bank of Central New York.

For full biographical listings, see the Martindale-Hubbell Law Directory

BABYLON, Suffolk Co. — (Refer to Islandia)

*BALLSTON SPA,** Saratoga Co. — (Refer to Amsterdam)

*BATAVIA,** Genesee Co. — (Refer to Warsaw)

*BATH,** Steuben Co. — (Refer to Geneva)

BAY SHORE, Suffolk Co. — (Refer to Islandia)

*BELMONT,** Allegany Co. — (Refer to Jamestown)

*BINGHAMTON,** Broome Co.

ASWAD & INGRAHAM (AV)

46 Front Street, 13905
Telephone: 607-722-3495
Fax: 607-722-2566; 722-7269

MEMBERS OF FIRM

Richard N. Aswad
Charles O. Ingraham
Thomas A. Saitta

ASSOCIATES

James F. Haley, Jr.
Angelina C. Beehm
William M. Thomas

Reference: Binghamton Savings Bank.

For full biographical listings, see the Martindale-Hubbell Law Directory

COUGHLIN & GERHART (AV)

One Marine Midland Plaza, P.O. Box 2039, 13902-2039
Telephone: 607-723-9511
Fax: 607-772-6093
Afton, New York Office: 190 Main Street, 13730.
Telephone: 607-639-2222.
Johnson City, New York Office: 257 Main Street, 13790.
Telephone: 607-770-0894.
Unadilla, New York Office: Main Street, 13849.
Telephone: 607-369-3811.

OF COUNSEL

Eugene C. Gerhart
Edward S. Dermody
George L. Ingalls
Carl R. Gitlitz
William L. Gibson, Jr.
George G. Coughlin (1900-1986)

MEMBERS OF FIRM

Loren W. Guy
Richard B. Long
Robert J. Smith
Henry J. Rode, II
Peter H. Bouman
Gordon E. Thompson
Frank W. Miller
Mark S. Gorgos
James P. O'Brien
Richard W. Mertens
Carl A. Kieper
Jeffrey A. Brown
David H. Guy
Beth E. Westfall

ASSOCIATES

Gary B. Kline
Susan L. English
Todd D. Kilpatrick
Robert R. Jones
Paul J. Sweeney
Susan A. Inneo

General Counsel for: Stow Manufacturing Co.; Crowley Foods, Inc.; Stickley Corp.
Representative Clients: Marine Midland Bank, N.A.; National Bank and Trust Company of Norwich; GAF Corporation; Columbian Mutual Life Insurance Co.; Binghamton City School District; New Channels Corp.

For full biographical listings, see the Martindale-Hubbell Law Directory

HINMAN, HOWARD & KATTELL (AV)

700 Security Mutual Building, 80 Exchange Street, 13901
Telephone: 607-723-5341
Fax: 607-723-6605
Norwich, New York Office: 600 South Broad Street, Suite 200.
Telephone: 607-334-5896.
Fax: 607-336-6240.

COUNSEL

George Lyon Hinman
Joseph P. Minnich, Jr.
A. Edward Hill
Erik Edward Joh

(See Next Column)

SPECIAL COUNSEL

Clarence D. Rappleyea, Jr. (Resident, Norwich Office)
Donald R. Campbell
Richard S. Ringwood
David G. Stearns

MEMBERS OF FIRM

Harvey D. Hinman (1864-1954)
Archibald Howard (1872-1962)
Thomas B. Kattell (1875-1947)
Dana B. Hinman (1874-1970)
Roger P. Clark (1869-1934)
C. Addison Keeler (1897-1979)
Thomas H. Fogarty (1902-1966)
Prescott D. Perkins (1902-1969)
Morris Gitletz (1902-1984)
Charles F. Fish (1910-1987)
William L. Ransom, Jr. (1918-1967)
Edward L. Tirrell, Jr. (1917-1993)
John M. Keane (1914-1994)
John M. Keeler
A. Lawrence Abrams
Clayton M. Axtell, Jr.
Warren M. Anderson
C. Addison Keeler, Jr.
John S. Davidge
Keith E. Osber
Colin T. Naylor, III
Richard H. Pille
N. Theodore Sommer
Eugene E. Peckham
John C. Fish
James L. Chivers
James M. Hayes
Peter J. Vivona
Lawrence C. Anderson
James S. Gleason
Clayton M. Axtell, III
M. Elizabeth Bradley
James F. Lee
John G. Dowd
Lee R. Cirba
Katherine A. Fitzgerald
James R. Franz
Albert J. Millus, Jr.
Lillian L. Levy
Wilbur D. Dahlgren
James W. Orband
Kenneth F. Tomko
Paul T. Sheppard

ASSOCIATES

Robert W. Carey
Louis J. Callea (Resident, Norwich Office)
John E. Jones
Thomas W. Cusimano, Jr.
Harvey D. Mervis
Leslie Prechtl Guy
Amy Shapiro
Eugene D. Faughnan
Allen J. Hall
Thomas A. Conlon, Jr.
Daniel D. Reynolds
Michael S. Sinicki
John D. Denmon
Alyssa M. Barreiro

Representative Clients: First-City Division, Chase Lincoln First Bank, N.A.; Binghamton Savings Bank; International Business Machines Corp.; Universal Instruments Corp.; Security Mutual Life Insurance Company of New York; New York Telephone Co.; Travelers Insurance Co.; New York State Electric & Gas Corp.; Exxon Corp.; Columbia Gas System, Inc.

For full biographical listings, see the Martindale-Hubbell Law Directory

BROCKPORT, Monroe Co. — (Refer to Rochester)

*BRONX,** Bronx Co.

MAXWELL S. PFEIFER (AV)

714 East 241st Street, 10470
Telephone: 718-325-5000
Fax: 718-324-0333
Hallandale, Florida Office: 1920 East Hallandale Beach Boulevard, Suite 606.
Telephone: 305-454-1550.

ASSOCIATES

Steven E. Millon
Robert S. Summer

OF COUNSEL

Hon. Alexander A. Dellecese
Sandra Krevitsky Janin
Anthony J. Hatab

LEGAL SUPPORT PERSONNEL

Jay S. Zwerling

For full biographical listings, see the Martindale-Hubbell Law Directory

BRONXVILLE, Westchester Co.

GRIFFIN, COOGAN & VENERUSO, P.C. (AV)

51 Pondfield Road, 10708
Telephone: 914-961-1300
Telecopier: 914-961-1476; 914-961-9385

William E. Griffin
James M. Coogan
James J. Veneruso
Robert W. Wolper

Karen J. Walsh
Joseph A. Ruhl
Daniel J. Griffin
Phyllis Knight Marcus
Paul G. Amicucci
Paul V. Greco
Paul R. Herrick

Approved Closing Attorneys: Hudson Valley Bank; Hudson Valley Mortgage Corp.; American Savings and Loan Association.

For full biographical listings, see the Martindale-Hubbell Law Directory

NOBILE, MAGARIAN & DISALVO (AV)

111 Kraft Avenue, 10708
Telephone: 914-337-6300
Facsimile: 914-337-6913

(See Next Column)

NOBILE, MAGARIAN & DISALVO—*Continued*

Nazareth Magarian | Ralph R. Nobile
Joseph A. DiSalvo

Avis W. Effinger

LEGAL SUPPORT PERSONNEL

Terry Piccillo (Legal Assistant)

Representative Clients: Hudson Valley National Bank; St. Matthew's R.C. Church; St. John's Episcopal Church; Village Lutheran Church.

For full biographical listings, see the Martindale-Hubbell Law Directory

*BROOKLYN,** Kings Co.

CULLEN AND DYKMAN (AV)

177 Montague Street, 11201
Telephone: 718-855-9000
Telecopier: 718-855-4282
Garden City, New York Office: Garden City Center, 100 Quentin Roosevelt Boulevard.
Telephone: 516-357-3700.
Telecopier: 516-357-3792.
Washington, D.C. Office: 1225 Nineteenth Street, N.W., Suite 320.
Telephone: 202-223-8890.
Telecopier: 202-457-1405.
Newark, New Jersey Office: One Riverfront Plaza, Suite 1410.
Telephone: 201-622-1545.
Telecopier: 201-622-4563.

MEMBERS OF FIRM

Alvin Adelman
John J. Bishar, Jr. *
Antonia M. Donohue *
Thomas J. Douglas, Jr. *
Joseph C. Fegan
Gerard Fishberg *
Timothy J. Flanagan
Paul A. Golinski
Michael W. Hall **
William R. Hoatson
***(Not admitted in NY)
Thomas M. Lamberti *
James L. Larocca
(Not admitted in NY)
Kenneth T. Maloney **
Peter J. Mastaglio *
David T. Metcalfe
Paul A. Michels
Lance D. Myers
F. Peter O'Hara
Cynthia B. Okrent
Frederick W. Peters
**(Not admitted in NY)
Joseph D. Simon *
James P. Slattery
Robert J. Sorge
Joseph P. Stevens
William P. Tucker *
Steven L. Zelkowitz

PARTNERS EMERITUS

Harry G. Hill *
Herman Meltzer *
Frederick E. Willits *

OF COUNSEL

Robert G. Hardy
**(Not admitted in NY)
Peter M. Metzger
James R. Lacey ***

ASSOCIATES

Richard H. Funk *
C. Gayden Wren *
Robert C. Nielsen
Daniel D. McLaughlin
Robert D. Aronin *
William E. Bandon
Peter T. Bauer *
Dan M. Blumenthal *
Joseph J. Borges *
Deborah A. Bryant
Angela N. Cascione
Craig H. Cohen *
Diane H. Collins *
Patrick M. Collins
Thomas G. Connolly
Marc A. Deitch ***
Paula Styles Dorman
Michael L. Dornbaum *
Kathleen L. Douglas *
Michael J. Ende *
Robert E. Fernandez
William A. Fox
***(Not admitted in NY)
Deborah M. Franco
Teresa A. Gaffney *
Peter A. Gioia *
James P. Haggerty
Gordon T. Hall *
Jacqueline Hardy ***
Amy F. Hecht *
Nicola R. Jobson ***
Stephanie A. Johnson
Edward C. Klein *
William G. Krejci
Carl A. Laske *
Cheri A. Lawson
Karen I. Levin
Eileen Lin *
Frank J. Lourenso
Doris Lum *
Kirk W. Mackey
Evan J. Mandery *
Peter S. Marchelos *
Sheila K. Maron
Marianne McCarthy *
Peter J. McCarthy *
John P. McEntee *
Kevin M. McEwen
***(Not admitted in NY)
Jennifer A. McNamara *
Brian E. Murray
David B. Owens
Paul J. Patacca *
Rita Piazza-Ryan *
Kelly A. Poole *
Lori Ann Puleo *
Pamela Richman
Joseph S. Rosato
Patricia A. Rossi *
Pasqualino Russo *
James G. Ryan *
David A. Schwartzberg *
Lisa M. Scully *
Richard A. Shannon
Peter G. Sheridan ***
Lisa B. Singer *
Bernard M. Soebke *
John M. Tangel *
Edward J. Tindell *
Kenneth von Schaumburg ***
Thomas B. Wassel *
John M. Wassem
Dona Rita Zino *

(See Next Column)

*Resident, Garden City Office
**Resident, Washington, D.C. Office
***Resident, Newark, New Jersey Office

For full biographical listings, see the Martindale-Hubbell Law Directory

WINGATE & CULLEN (AV)

142 Pierrepont Street, 11201
Telephone: 718-875-3652
Fax: 718-596-6750
Other Brooklyn Office: Bay Ridge, 8804 4th Avenue.
Telephone: 718-745-8844.
Fax: 718-680-0598.
Melville, New York Office: Fleet Financial Plaza, 290 Broad Hollow Road.
Telephone: 516-427-5400.
Fax: 516-427-5402.

MEMBERS OF FIRM

Thomas O. Rice
Peter N. Zogas
Richard H. Freeman
Jonathan R. Frank
Michael F. O'Shea
Robert P. Knapp, III

SENIOR COUNSEL

Claudia C. Conway
Calliope Manis

ASSOCIATES

Jani M. Foley
Kenneth V. Babi
Kevin G. Condon
Paula A. Miller
Marc A. Rapaport

For full biographical listings, see the Martindale-Hubbell Law Directory

*BUFFALO,** Erie Co.

ALBRECHT, MAGUIRE, HEFFERN & GREGG, P.C. (AV)

2100 Main Place Tower, 14202
Telephone: 716-853-1521
Fax: 716-852-2609

George M. Zimmermann
Charles H. Dougherty
James M. Beardsley
Arthur A. Russ, Jr.
David C. Horan
Raymond H. Barr
Philip John Szabla
Gary J. Gleba
Alan J. Bozer
John M. Curran

Laurice A. Ghougasian
William P. Keefer
Glenn J. Bobeck

OF COUNSEL

Ralph J. Gregg
Thomas R. Beecher, Jr.
(200 Theatre Place Office)

For full biographical listings, see the Martindale-Hubbell Law Directory

BERMINGHAM & COOK, P.C. (AV)

1300 Statler Towers, 14202-3066
Telephone: 716-854-6800
Fax: 716-854-3020

Joseph D. Bermingham, Jr.
Donald T. Cook

Geralyn A. Schiffler

OF COUNSEL

Henry W. Cornell III
W. Barry Mallon

For full biographical listings, see the Martindale-Hubbell Law Directory

BLOCK & COLUCCI, P.C. (AV)

1250 Statler Towers, 14202
Telephone: 716-854-4080; 1-800-388-2595
Telex: 919-186
Fax: 716-854-0059
Litigation Fax: 716-854-4070
Jupiter, Florida Office: 1001 N. U.S. Highway One, Suite 400.
Telephone: 407-747-0110.
Fax: 407-743-0046.
Albany, New York Office: 12 Century Hill Drive, P.O. Box 1160, (Latham).
Telephone: 518-783-0535.
Fax: 518-783-5670.
Binghamton, New York Office: The Press Building, 19 Chenago Street.
Telephone: 607-724-3138.
Fax: 607-724-6227.
Rochester, New York Office: 30 West Broad Street, Suite 200.
Telephone: 716-454-1660.
Fax: 716-454-7134.
Syracuse, New York Office: 5786 Widewaters Parkway.
Telephone: 315-445-1272.
Fax: 315-445-9530.

(See Next Column)

BLOCK & COLUCCI P.C., *Buffalo—Continued*

Ernest L. Colucci (1909-1989)
David Simon Brown
Steven S. Brown
Anthony J. Colucci, Jr.
Anthony J. Colucci, III
Mark K. Cramer
William P. Hessney, Jr. (Resident at Albany Office)
William T. Jebb, II
Cheryl A. Short

Elpiniki M. Bechakas
Frank M. Cassara
Dennis H. Cleary
Frank V. Fontana
Marie L. Gallagher
Kathleen M. Kaczor
Scott J. Leitten
John J. Marchese
John K. McAndrew
Kathleen F. McGovern (Resident, Albany Office)
Melanie C. Mecca
Natalie A. Napierala
Margaret Logan Noonan
Michael W. Schafer
Lawrence R. Schwach
Damon H. Serota
Debra A. Spellman
Maureen Tucker
Frederick R. Xlander (Resident Binghamton Office)

OF COUNSEL

Lester H. Block
Joseph F. Crangle

SPECIAL COUNSEL

Richard D. Nadel (Not admitted in NY; Resident, Jupiter, Florida Office)

References: Manufacturers & Traders Trust Co.; Palm Beach National Bank & Trust Co.

For full biographical listings, see the Martindale-Hubbell Law Directory

BROWN & KELLY (AV)

1500 Liberty Building, 14202
Telephone: 716-854-2620
Telecopier: 716-854-0082

MEMBERS OF FIRM

Mark N. Turner (1897-1985)
Thomas J. Kelly
James T. Duggan
Frederick D. Turner
Paul Michael Hassett
Peter E. Klaassesz
Donald B. Eppers
Andrew D. Merrick
Gordon D. Tresch
William E. Nitterauer
William P. Wiles
William D. Harrington
Rodney O. Personius
Paula L. Feroleto
Daniel J. Marren
Lisa T. Sofferin

COUNSEL

Ogden R. Brown
Charles F. Harrington
William E. Nowakowski
Roland R. Benzow

OF COUNSEL

Philip B. Abramowitz

ASSOCIATES

Raymond C. Stilwell
Carlton K. Brownell, III
David S. Zygaj
Kathleen F. Smith
Karen L. Cook
Colleen P. Doyle
Aileen M. Mcnamara

Representative Clients: Exchange Insurance Co.; Aetna Life & Casualty Co.; Fidelity & Deposit Company of Maryland; Consolidated Freightways, Inc.; United States Aviation Underwriters; Maryland Casualty Co.; Herbert F. Darling, Inc.; H.M. Foundation, Inc.

For full biographical listings, see the Martindale-Hubbell Law Directory

DAMON & MOREY (AV)

(Formerly Damon, Morey, Sawyer & Moot)
1000 Cathedral Place, 298 Main Street, 14202-4096
Telephone: 716-856-5500
Facsimile: 716-856-5510
New York, New York Office: 53 Wall Street, Fifth Floor.
Telephone: 212-878-7715.
Facsimile: 212-858-7750.
Rochester, New York Office: Water Tower Park, 1099 Jay Street.
Facsimile: 716-328-2139.
Telephone: 716-328-4500.

MEMBERS OF FIRM

Mason O. Damon (1905-1983)
James S. Marvin (1932-1994)
Robert J. Plache
F. James Kane, Jr.
Malcolm K. Buckley, Jr.
James N. Schmit
Christopher T. Greene
Robert W. Constantine
Franklin W. Heller
Gregory C. Yungbluth
James W. Gormley
James M. Mucklewee
Melinda G. Disare
Robert J. Portin
Joseph J. Schoellkopf, Jr.
Peter F. Brady
William F. Savino
Thomas J. Drury
Patrick B. Curran
Peter S. Marlette
Vincent J. Moore
Gust P. Pullman
John P. Walsh
Sharyn G. Rogers
Carol Guck Snider
Barbara L. Schifeling
Gerard A. Strauss
Michael J. Willett
Joseph W. Dunbar
Steven M. Zweig
Kenneth W. Africano
Julie M. Bargnesi
Daniel F. Brown

(See Next Column)

ASSOCIATES

Amy M. Archer
Hedwig Maria Auletta
Susan A. Benz
Charles S. Carra
Lawrence C. Di Giulio
Kevin S. Doyle
Rodger P. Doyle, Jr.
Anthony L. Eugeni
Maryjo C. Falcone
Henry Gitter
Mary Jo Herrscher
Marjorie E. Klein
Richard M. Lipinski
Kathleen M. Mann
Brendan P. McCafferty
Michael R. Moore
Diane C. Piotrowski
Mary Powers
Marylou K. Roshia
Steven I. Rubinstein
Michael J. Russo
Alyson E. Spaulding
Michelle Wood

OF COUNSEL

Joseph H. Morey, Jr.
Norman R. Stewart

SPECIAL COUNSEL

Mark G. Farrell
George F. Gabel, Jr.
Richard E. Moot
Arthur A. Marrapese III (Resident, Rochester Office)
Paul M. Samson

Counsel for: Aurora Park Health Care Center, Inc.; F.N. Burt Co., Inc.; Graphic Controls Corp.; Niagara Frontier Transit Metro System, Inc.; Sheehan Memorial Hospital.
Local Counsel for: American Insurance Group.; Bell Aerospace Division of Textron, Inc.; Chase Lincoln First Bank, N.A.; CIGNA (INA/Aetna); Metropolitan Life Insurance Co.

For full biographical listings, see the Martindale-Hubbell Law Directory

GOLDSTEIN, NAVAGH, BULAN & CHIARI (AV)

Suite 1440 Rand Building, 14203
Telephone: 716-854-1332
Telecopier: 716-854-1370

MEMBERS OF FIRM

George J. Navagh
Harold P. Bulan
Gerald Chiari

Toby-Lee G. Bulan
Geralyn M. Swenson

For full biographical listings, see the Martindale-Hubbell Law Directory

GROSS SHUMAN BRIZDLE & GILFILLAN, P.C. (AV)

600 Lafayette Court, 465 Main Street, 14203
Telephone: 716-854-4300
Telecopier: 716-854-2787

Gordon R. Gross
Irving M. Shuman
Leonard J. Brizdle (1905-1987)
Peter S. Gilfillan
David H. Alexander
Robert J. Feldman
Leslie M. Greenbaum
Jeffrey A. Human
Robert A. Dean
Hugh C. Carlin
Howard B. Cohen
Herschel Gelber
Cindy Algase Gradl

SPECIAL COUNSEL

Frank R. Bayger
Arnold N. Zelman

Leslie Shuman Zalis
John K. Rottaris
John F. Leone
Dawn A. Foshee
Jonathan D. Schechter

Reference: Key Bank of Western New York, N.A.

For full biographical listings, see the Martindale-Hubbell Law Directory

HEIMERL, KEENAN & LONGO (AV)

1566 Statler Towers, 14202
Telephone: 716-854-5063
Telecopier: 716-854-1069

MEMBERS OF FIRM

Herbert J. Heimerl, Jr.
William F. Keenan
Nicholas J. Longo

ASSOCIATES

W. Clark Trow
Lisa P. Meyers
Scott C. Billman

For full biographical listings, see the Martindale-Hubbell Law Directory

HODGSON, RUSS, ANDREWS, WOODS & GOODYEAR (AV)

A Partnership including Professional Associations
Suite 1800, One M & T Plaza, 14203
Telephone: 716-856-4000
Cable Address: "Magna Carta" Buffalo, N.Y.
Telecopier: 716-849-0349
Albany, New York Office: Three City Square.
Telephone: 518-465-2333.
Telecopier: 518-465-1567.
Rochester, New York Office: 400 East Avenue.
Telephone: 716-454-6950.
Telecopier: 716-454-4698.

(See Next Column)

HODGSON, RUSS, ANDREWS, WOODS & GOODYEAR—*Continued*

Boca Raton, Florida Office: Suite 400, Nations Bank Building, 2000 Glades Road.
Telephone: 407-394-0500.
Telecopier: 305-427-4303.
Mississauga, Ontario, Canada Office: Suite 880, 3 Robert Speck Parkway.
Telephone: 905-566-5061.
Telecopier: 905-566-2049.
New York, New York Office: 330 Madison Avenue, 11th Floor. Telephone 212-297-3370.
Telecopier: 212-972-6521.

MEMBERS OF FIRM
(ALPHABETICALLY BY YEAR OF ADMISSION TO BAR)

Victor T. Fuzak
Edwin T. Bean, Jr.
Richard E. Heath (Boca Raton, Florida Office)
James A. Porter (P.A.) (Boca Raton, Florida Office)
Richard B. Dopkins
William H. Gardner
Charles J. Hahn
H. Kenneth Schroeder, Jr.
John C. Barber, Jr.
Robert M. Walker
Anthony L. Dutton (P.A.) (Boca Raton, Florida Office)
Michael H. Gora (P.A.) (Boca Raton, Florida Office)
David E. Hall
James M. Wadsworth (Managing Partner)
Robert W. Keller
Paul D. Pearson
Robert B. Conklin
Richard A. Goetz (P.A.) (Boca Raton, Florida Office)
Karl W. Kristoff
Thomas E. Sliney (P.A.) (Boca Raton, Florida Office)
Martin G. Linihan
Stephen M. Newman
F. William Gray, III
Harry G. Meyer
Christian G. Koelbl, III
Jerome D. Schad
Richard J. Evans (Rochester Office)
Lance J. Madden
Paul R. Comeau
Cormac C. Conahan (P.A.) (Resident, Boca Raton, Florida Office)
Donald R. Fox (Rochester Office)
Todd M. Joseph
Tricia Thomas Semmelhack
Dianne Bennett
Allen H. Beroza
Richard F. Campbell
Pamela Davis Heilman
Ward B. Hinkle (Rochester Office)
Daniel R. Sharpe
Mark G. Spelman
John P. Amershadian
Ellen V. Weissman
Anne Smith Simet
Charles T. Barker (P.A.) (Boca Raton, Florida Office)
Kenneth F. Barone
David A. Farmelo
Robert B. Fleming, Jr.
Garry M. Graber
Richard L. Weisz (Albany Office)
Jerrold S. Brown (Albany Office)
Kenneth P. Friedman
Paul I. Perlman
Gary M. Schober
Edward C. Northwood
Melvin L. Olver (Rochester Office)
Larry Corman (P.A.) (Boca Raton, Florida Office)
Rick W. Kennedy
Mark S. Klein
Lawrence F. Beyer (Boca Raton, Florida Office)
Alice Accola Joseffer
Robert J. Lane, Jr.
A. Joseph Scott, III (Albany Office)
David M. Stark
Jeffrey W. Stone
Kathleen A. Wall
Benjamin M. Zuffranieri, Jr.
Joseph L. Braccio
Elizabeth G. Clark
Patrick J. Maxwell
Thomas W. Nelson
Bonnie A. Redder
Kevin A. Szanyi
John J. Zak
David V.L. Bradley
Kevin M. Kearney
Janet H. Korts (Rochester Office)
Michael P. Murphy
Hugh M. Russ, III
Cheryl R. Storie
Anthony R. Palermo (Rochester Office)
George W. Cregg, Jr. (Albany Office)
James M. Hankins (Boca Raton, Florida Office)
James C. Simmons
Dennis M. Hyatt (Rochester Office)
Robert D. Plattner (Albany Office)
Peter A. Muth
Richard W. Kaiser
Wendy K. Fechter
Paul Groenwegen (Albany Office)
Hildegard Neubauer
Peter K. Bradley
John L. DeMarco (Rochester Office)
Douglas R. Edwards
Craig L. McGrain (Rochester Office)
Ellen S. Roesch (Albany Office)
Suzanne P. Stern
Carol Anne Fitzsimmons
John F. Donogher
Karen S. Martell (Albany Office)
John J. Christopher
Christopher L. Doyle
Deborah L. Kelly (Albany Office)
Terrence M. Gilbride
Michael E. Maxwell
Paul D. Meosky
Frank J. Notaro
Deborah A. Waldbillig
Lisa C. Saurer

SPECIAL COUNSEL

John C. Courtin

COUNSEL

Laurence R. Goodyear
John E. Dickinson
Edwin O. Tilton
Arnold T. Olena
Gordon A. MacLeod
Samuel Klafter (Rochester Office)

(See Next Column)

ASSOCIATES
(ALPHABETICALLY BY YEAR OF ADMISSION TO BAR)

Matthew M. Korona (Rochester Office)
Anna L. Case
Louis J. Micca (Rochester Office)
Mary Thomas Scott
Michel Pierre Cassier
Michael R. Deming
Cheryl B. Fisher (Albany Office)
Sharon M. Kelly
Wayne J. McChesney
Michael F. Scalise
Mary J. Edwards
Theresa J. Puleo (Albany Office)
Tim Sawers
Amy J. Vigneron
John C. Krenitsky
Sally B. Logan
Diane H. Nowak
Kimberly P. Russell (Rochester Office)
Margot L. Watt
Thomas R. Hyde
R. Anthony Rupp III
Judith A. Shanley
Timothy P. Sheehan (Rochester Office)
Charles E. Graney
M. Bud Nelson
Daniel A. Spitzer
Jeffrey F. Swiatek

For full biographical listings, see the Martindale-Hubbell Law Directory

HURWITZ & FINE, P.C. (AV)

1300 Liberty Building, 14202-3613
Telephone: 716-849-8900
Telecopier: 716-855-0874

Sheldon Hurwitz
Robert P. Fine
Theodore J. Burns
James D. Gauthier
Lawrence C. Franco
Dan D. Kohane
Harry F. Mooney
Ann E. Evanko
Paul J. Suozzi
Roger L. Ross
Christopher J. Hurley
Lawrence M. Ross
Robert M. Lippman
John C. Garas

David P. Lazenski
Diane E. Katz
Amy J. Ziegler
Theresa A. Drew
Donna L. Burden
Daniel R. Archilla
Dennis J. Bischof
Paula Marie Eade Newcomb
Timothy J. Quinlivan
Thomas P. Cunningham

For full biographical listings, see the Martindale-Hubbell Law Directory

KOREN, BERTELL & HOEY (AV)

Suite 1820 Liberty Building, 14202
Telephone: 716-856-3631
Fax: 716-856-5457

MEMBERS OF FIRM

M. Robert Koren (1920-1992)
John T. Bertell
Benjamin J. Hoey
Bruce Kevin Koren

ASSOCIATES

Marc J. Hopkins
Richard J. Lutzel

For full biographical listings, see the Martindale-Hubbell Law Directory

LIPSITZ, GREEN, FAHRINGER, ROLL, SALISBURY & CAMBRIA (AV)

42 Delaware Avenue, Suite 300, 14202
Telephone: 716-849-1333
Fax: 716-855-1580
New York, N.Y. Office: 110 East 59th Street.
Telephone: 212-909-9670.
East Aurora, New York Office: 164 Quaker Road.
Telephone: 716-652-4290.
Alden, New York Office: 1472 Exchange Street.
Telephone: 716-937-9494.

MEMBERS OF FIRM

Raymond F. Roll, Jr.
Carl A. Green
Eugene W. Salisbury
Paul J. Cambria, Jr.
James T. Scime
Herbert L. Greenman
Patrick C. O'Reilly
Michael Schiavone
Laraine Kelley
William M. Feigenbaum
Joseph J. Gumkowski
Vincent A. Tobia
Michael A. Ponterio
Joseph M. LaTona
Sharon M. Heim
Richard P. Weisbeck, Jr.
Cherie L. Peterson
Mark L. Stulmaker
John A. Collins
Barry Nelson Covert

Jeremy M. Schnurr
Daniel J. Sperrazza
MaryBeth Scarcello
Neil J. McKinnon
Robert L. Voltz
Asalyn DuBois
Christopher S. Mattingly
Paul J. Cieslik
Cheryl Meyers
John R. Kresse
Mark F. Steiner
Henry J. Nowak
Robert R. Radel
Catherine Creighton
Mark G. Pearce

OF COUNSEL

Richard Lipsitz

(See Next Column)

LIPSITZ, GREEN, FAHRINGER, ROLL, SALISBURY & CAMBRIA, *Buffalo—Continued*

SPECIAL COUNSEL

Frank J. Parlato
Gerard R. Fornes
James W. Kirkpatrick
George E. Riedel, Jr.
Earl K. Cantwell
Laurie Boreanaz Carra
Robert L. Boreanaz

Representative Clients: Buffalo Bills; Marine Midland Bank, N.A.
Reference: Marine Midland Bank.

For full biographical listings, see the Martindale-Hubbell Law Directory

MALONEY, GALLUP, ROACH, BROWN & McCARTHY, P.C. (AV)

1620 Liberty Building, 14202
Telephone: 716-852-0400
Fax: 716-852-2535

Arthur J. Maloney
John Y. Gallup
Daniel T. Roach
Edmund S. Brown, Jr.
T. Alan Brown
Joseph V. McCarthy
J. Mark Gruber
Donald P. Chiari
Brian Sutter
J. Gregory Hoelscher
Colleen P. Cartonia
Mary J. Murray
John P. Danieu

Elizabeth G. Redmond

Local Attorneys for: American International Group; Chubb Group of Insurance Co.; Healthcare Underwriters Mutual Insurance Co.; Peter J. McBreen and Associates; Medical Liability Mutual Insurance Co.; Medical Malpractice Insurance Association; Merrill Dow; Reliance Insurance Group; Travelers Group.

For full biographical listings, see the Martindale-Hubbell Law Directory

McGEE & GELMAN (AV)

200 Summer Street, 14222
Telephone: 716-883-7272
Fax: 716-883-7084

MEMBERS OF FIRM

Michael R. McGee
Warren B. Gelman
F. Brendan Burke, Jr.
James P. Giambrone, Jr.
Laura A. Colca

For full biographical listings, see the Martindale-Hubbell Law Directory

OFFERMANN, CASSANO, PIGOTT & GRECO (AV)

1776 Statler Towers, 14202
Telephone: 716-856-4800
Telecopier: 716-856-4839

MEMBERS OF FIRM

Francis J. Offermann, Jr.
Thomas R. Cassano
Eugene F. Pigott, Jr.
Josephine A. Greco

ASSOCIATES

Camille P. Wicher
Richard C. Slisz
Andrew G.S. O'Brien
Andrew B. Isenberg
Sheryl A. Lee

Representative Clients: American Nuclear Insurers; American Steamship Co.; Brothers of Mercy Health Facilities; Buffalo Board of Education; Don Davis Auto World, Inc.; Inter-Residence Council Businesses, Inc.; Niagara Frontier Transportation Authority; Park Eye Foundation, Inc.; Rockwell International, Inc.; State Insurance Fund.

For full biographical listings, see the Martindale-Hubbell Law Directory

PHILLIPS, LYTLE, HITCHCOCK, BLAINE & HUBER (AV)

(Formerly Kenefick, Letchworth, Baldy, Phillips & Emblidge)
3400 Marine Midland Center, 14203
Telephone: 716-847-8400
Telecopier: 716-852-6100
Jamestown, New York Office: 307 Chase Bank Building, 8 E. Third Street.
Telephone: 716-664-3906.
Telecopier: 716-664-4230.
Rochester, New York Office: 1400 First Federal Plaza.
Telephone: 716-238-2000.
Telecopier: 716-232-3141.
New York, New York Office: 437 Madison Avenue.
Telephone: 212-759-4888.
Telecopier: 212-308-9079.
Fredonia, New York Office: 11 East Main Street.
Telephone: 716-672-2164.
FAX: 716-672-7979.

John F. Huber, Jr. (1906-1969)
George F. Phillips (1892-1971)
Robert M. Hitchcock (1904-1981)
William E. Lytle (1905-1989)

(See Next Column)

OF COUNSEL

William A. Bain, Jr.
Richard G. Birmingham
Charles G. Blaine
Irving D. Brott, Jr.
Alexander C. Cordes
John F. Donovan
David K. Floyd
Gerard R. Haas
John K. McCormick
William L. Rieth
Edward L. Robinson
Solon J. Stone

PARTNERS

Frederick G. Attea
Thomas M. Barney
Allen R. Bivens
Edward S. Bloomberg
Peter D. Braun
William J. Brown
Caroline Hassett Buerk
Thomas R. Burns (Resident, Rochester Office)
David A. Clemens
James J. Contino
James D. Donathen
John B. Drenning
Kevin J. English
Michael C. Foley (Resident, Jamestown Office)
Annabelle Irey Forrestel
Robert E. Glanville
Morgan G. Graham
George R. Grasser
Robert M. Greene
Richard F. Griffin
Tamar P. Halpern
Waldron S. Hayes, Jr.
John J. Hurley
Martin F. Idzik (Resident, Jamestown Office)
Hugh M. Jones
Paul F. Jones
David H. Kernan
Gary F. Kotaska
James A. Locke
Kenneth A. Manning
Jeremiah J. McCarthy
James G. Meagley
Michael R. Moravec
Paul Morrison-Taylor
Gerald L. Paley (Resident, Rochester Office)
John A. Pappano
Michael B. Powers
Joseph Ritzert
Victoria J. Saxon
Joseph V. Sedita
Raymond H. Seitz
Arthur M. Sherwood
Ronald S. Shubert
James W. Smyton
Peter K. Sommer
Robert M. Spaulding
John C. Spitzmiller
Paul K. Stecker
Paul A. Vick (Resident, Rochester Office)
James H. Watz
Sharon L. Wick
Alan M. Wishnoff
Thomas S. Wiswall
Jacek A. Wysocki
Robert F. Zogas (Resident, Rochester Office)
Paul B. Zuydhoek

SPECIAL COUNSEL

Mary B. Ferguson
Linda L. Kaumeyer
James W. Whitcomb

ASSOCIATES

Cindy Kaplan Bennes
Mark E. Brand
Charles R. Chase
William D. Christ
Robert A. Colón (Resident, Rochester Office)
Douglas W. Dimitroff
Deborah A. Doxey
Paul N. Edwards
Sebastian W. Fasanello
Kimberly A. Ferris
David P. Flynn
Trevor M. Fuller
James R. Grasso
Jeffrey J. Hagen
David R. Hayes
Andrea D. Heinbach-Whaley
Kevin M. Hogan
Brenda Jean Joyce
Joseph P. Kieffer
Janice B. Kirk
Donna M. Lanham
Susan M. Lankenau
Christopher M. Marks
Joseph M. Marris
Lisa McDougall
David J. McNamara
John A. Moscati, Jr.
Kim S. Murphy
David J. Murray
Patricia A. Obstarczyk
Margaret L. Phillips
Martha L. Salzman
Lisa L. Smith
Mark L. Suher (Resident, Rochester Office)
David S. Teske
Cynthia E. Vance
John J. Weinholtz

General Counsel for: Astronics Corporation; Bryant & Stratton Business Institute; Canisius College; Chase Manhattan Bank, N.A.; Columbus McKinnon Corp.
Local Counsel for: A.O. Smith Corp.; Allied Signal; Bethleham Steel Corp.; Chrysler Motor Corp.; E.I. DuPont deNemours Co., Inc.

For full biographical listings, see the Martindale-Hubbell Law Directory

RAICHLE, BANNING, WEISS & STEPHENS (AV)

410 Main Street, 14202
Telephone: 716-852-7587
Telecopier: 716-852-7599

MEMBERS OF FIRM

Frank G. Raichle (1898-1986)
Derrick C. Banning
Arnold Weiss
R. William Stephens

ASSOCIATES

Alan Donatelli
Carl Tronolone
Lisa A. Parlato
John Jablonski

OF COUNSEL

Thomas C. Mack

Representative Client: General Motors Corp.

For full biographical listings, see the Martindale-Hubbell Law Directory

Buffalo—Continued

RODGERS, MENARD & COPPOLA (AV)

1630 Liberty Building, 420 Main Street, 14202-3616
Telephone: 716-852-4100
Facsimile: 716-852-0002

MEMBERS OF FIRM

Douglas S. Coppola
Michael Menard
Mark C. Rodgers

ASSOCIATES

Patricia S. Stroman
Patricia S. Ciccarelli

For full biographical listings, see the Martindale-Hubbell Law Directory

SMITH, MURPHY & SCHOEPPERLE (AV)

786 Ellicott Square, 14203
Telephone: 716-852-1544
Telecopier: 716-852-3559

MEMBERS OF FIRM

Clayton M. Smith (1884-1967)
Esmond D. Murphy (1903-1960)
Richard K. Schoepperle
Frank G. Godson
Peter M. Collard
Lynn D. Gates
Bonnie T. Hager
Janice A. Barber
Linda J. Marsh
Robert A. Baker, Jr.
Norton T. Lowe
Edward J. Murphy, III
Dennis P. Mescall
Stephen P. Brooks

SPECIAL COUNSEL

Dennis C. Vacco

ASSOCIATES

Daniel H. Dillon
Ross J. Runfola
Susan W. Schoepperle
Michael T. Glascott

LEGAL SUPPORT PERSONNEL

LEGAL ADMINISTRATOR

Marybeth Cerrone

PARALEGALS

Michelle M. Wojciechowicz
Janice M. Beyer
Tamara Montaldi
Laurie A. Tripp

Representative Clients: Hartford Insurance Group; Dominion of Canada General Insurance Co.; Casualty Company of Canada; Royal Insurance Cos.; Chrysler Corp.; Merchants Inc., Group; Associated Aviation Underwriters; U.S. Aviation Underwriters.

For full biographical listings, see the Martindale-Hubbell Law Directory

CANAJOHARIE, Montgomery Co. — (Refer to Amsterdam)

*CANTON,** St. Lawrence Co. — (Refer to Ogdensburg)

CARLE PLACE, Nassau Co.

DOLLINGER, GONSKI, GROSSMAN, PERMUT & HIRSCHHORN (AV)

One Old Country Road, 11514
Telephone: 516-747-1010
Telecopier: 516-747-2494

MEMBERS OF FIRM

Matthew Dollinger
Dennis M. Gonski
Floyd G. Grossman
Michael Permut
Alan K. Hirschhorn

ASSOCIATES

Leslie Ann Foodim
Michael J. Spithogiannis
Jessica M. Seidman
Bruce N. Roberts
Alicia B. Devins
Bryan J. Holzberg
Mindy Anne Wallach
Rachel L. Hollander

Reference: Marine Midland National Bank, Carle Place, New York.

For full biographical listings, see the Martindale-Hubbell Law Directory

*CARMEL,** Putnam Co. — (Refer to Beacon)

CARTHAGE, Jefferson Co.

CONBOY, MCKAY, BACHMAN & KENDALL (AV)

307 State Street, 13619
Telephone: 315-493-0030
Watertown, New York Office: 407 Sherman Street.
Telephone: 315-788-5100.
Clayton, New York Office: 342 Riverside Drive.
Telephone: 315-686-3487.
Canton, New York Office: 24 Court Street, P.O. Box 650.
Telephone: 315-386-4539.

RESIDENT PARTNER

Lawrence D. Hasseler

For full biographical listings, see the Martindale-Hubbell Law Directory

*CATSKILL,** Greene Co.

ORESTE VINCENT (AV)

Three Twenty-Nine Main Street, 12414
Telephone: 518-943-3330
(Also Of Counsel to Kingsley & Towne, P.C.)

Reference: Schenectady Trust Co.

CHATHAM, Columbia Co. — (Refer to Kingston)

*COOPERSTOWN,** Otsego Co.

GOZIGIAN, WASHBURN & CLINTON (AV)

Orange L. Van Horne (1907-1946)
Van Horne & Feury (1946-1970)
Van Horne, Feury & Gozigian (1970-1979)
Feury, Gozigian & Washburn (1979-1992)
201-204 Key Bank Building, P.O. Box 431, 13326
Telephone: 607-547-2522
Fax: 607-547-2845

MEMBERS OF FIRM

Edward Gozigian
Philip L. Washburn
David J. Clinton

Counsel for: New York Central Mutual Insurance Co.; Susquehanna Valley Farm Credit ACA; InterKnitting Ltd.
Local Counsel for: Key Bank, N.A.; Astoria Savings & Loan Assn.

For full biographical listings, see the Martindale-Hubbell Law Directory

*CORTLAND,** Cortland Co. — (Refer to Syracuse)

*DELHI,** Delaware Co. — (Refer to Kingston)

EAST MEADOW, Nassau Co.

CERTILMAN BALIN ADLER & HYMAN, LLP (AV)

90 Merrick Avenue, 11554
Telephone: 516-296-7000
Telecopier: 516-296-7111

MEMBERS OF FIRM

Ira J. Adler
Dale Allinson
Herbert M. Balin
Bruce J. Bergman
Michael D. Brofman
Morton L. Certilman
Murray Greenberg
David Z. Herman
Richard Herzbach
M. Allan Hyman
Bernard Hyman
Donna-Marie Korth
Steven J. Kuperschmid
Thomas J. McNamara
Fred S. Skolnik
Louis Soloway
Harold Somer
Howard M. Stein
Brian K. Ziegler

OF COUNSEL

Daniel S. Cohan
Norman J. Levy
Marilyn Price

ASSOCIATES

Howard B. Busch
Scott M. Gerber
Jodi S. Hoffman
Glenn Kleinbaum
Michael C. Manniello
Jaspreet S. Mayall
Stacey R. Miller
Lawrence S. Novak
Kim J. Radbell

For full biographical listings, see the Martindale-Hubbell Law Directory

EAST SYRACUSE, Onondaga Co.

OOT LAW OFFICES (AV)

Medical East, 5900 North Burdick Street, 13057
Telephone: 315-656-2265
Fax: 315-656-5239

MEMBERS OF FIRM

Earl L. Oot
Suzanne E. Oot

References: Onbank & Trust Co.

ELLENVILLE, Ulster Co.

BERGER, FRIEDMAN & CHRISTIANA, P.C. (AV)

129 South Main Street, 12428
Telephone: 914-647-4000

Louis Berger (1915-1988)
Joseph Friedman
Peter L. Berger
Mary Lou P. Christiana

OF COUNSEL

Jay L. Samoff
Jay A. Kaplan

Counsel for: Ellenville National Bank; V.A.W. of America, Inc.; General Sportwear Co., Inc.; Fallsview Hotel, Inc.; Granit Hotel and Country Club; Ukrainian National Assn.; Town of Rochester; Town of Wawarsing Planning and Zoning Boards; Village of Ellenville Zoning Board and Planning Commission; Pine Grove Resort Ranch, Inc.

For full biographical listings, see the Martindale-Hubbell Law Directory

*ELMIRA,** Chemung Co. — (Refer to Endicott)

*FONDA,** Montgomery Co. — (Refer to Amsterdam)

FREDONIA, Chautauqua Co. — (Refer to Jamestown)

GARDEN CITY, Nassau Co.

ALBANESE, ALBANESE & FIORE LLP (AV)

1050 Franklin Avenue, 5th Floor, 11530
Telephone: 516-248-7000

MEMBERS OF FIRM

Vincent M. Albanese
Joseph R. Albanese
Joseph A. Fiore
Gary R. Steinberg
Thomas G. Sherwood
Arthur L. Colozzi

ASSOCIATES

Barry A. Oster
Richard H. Ferriggi
Rachel M. Harari
Laura Paglia Sikorski
Diana Centrella Prevete
Hyman Hacker
Vincent A. Albanese
Jack A. Horn

COUNSEL

Theodore D. Hoffmann
W. Hubert Plummer

LEGAL SUPPORT PERSONNEL

Linda Cristando
Deborah J. Dolan
Demitra Koliokotas Lynch
Florence M. McGoey

References: Apple Bank for Savings; Bank of New York; North Fork Bank; First American Title Insurance Company; American Title Insurance Company; Greater Jamaica Development Corp.; United Nations Plaza Tower Associates, Ltd.; Fidelity National Title Insurance Company of New York.

For full biographical listings, see the Martindale-Hubbell Law Directory

COLLERAN, O'HARA & MILLS (AV)

1225 Franklin Avenue, 11530
Telephone: 516-248-5757
Telecopier: 516-742-1765

Walter M. Colleran (Retired)
Richard L. O'Hara
John F. Mills
Edward J. Groarke
Christopher P. O'Hara

ASSOCIATES

Scott P. Shelkin
Carol L. O'Rourke
James A. Brown
Jennifer Berlingieri
John W. Dunne

COUNSEL

Glenn A. Krebs
Elizabeth Pollina Donlon

LEGAL SUPPORT PERSONNEL

Stephanie Suarez
Robin Young
Madeleine Olaciregui
Ann Carolan
Laura Harrington

For full biographical listings, see the Martindale-Hubbell Law Directory

CULLEN AND DYKMAN (AV)

Garden City Center, 100 Quentin Roosevelt Boulevard, 11530-4850
Telephone: 516-357-3700
Telecopier: 516-357-3792
Brooklyn, New York Office: 177 Montague Street.
Telephone: 718-855-9000.
Telecopier: 718-855-4282.
Washington, D.C. Office: 1225 Nineteenth Street, N.W., Suite 320.
Telephone: 202-223-8890.
Telecopier: 202-457-1405.
Newark, New Jersey Office: One Riverfront Plaza, Suite 1410.
Telephone: 201-622-1545.
Telecopier: 201-622-4563.

MEMBERS OF FIRM

John J. Bishar, Jr.
Antonia M. Donohue
Thomas J. Douglas, Jr.
Gerard Fishberg
Thomas M. Lamberti
James L. Larocca (Not admitted in NY)
Peter J. Mastaglio
F. Peter O'Hara
Joseph D. Simon
William P. Tucker

PARTNERS EMERITUS

Harry G. Hill
Herman Meltzer
Frederick E. Willits

ASSOCIATES

Richard H. Funk
C. Gayden Wren
Thomas B. Wassel
Doris Lum
James G. Ryan
John P. McEntee
Kathleen L. Douglas
Carl A. Laske (Not admitted in NY)
Marianne McCarthy
Paul J. Patacca
Teresa A. Gaffney
Amy F. Hecht
Michael J. Ende
Jennifer A. McNamara
Peter T. Bauer
Michael L. Dornbaum
Diane H. Collins

(See Next Column)

ASSOCIATES (Continued)

Evan J. Mandery
Peter A. Gioia
Lori Ann Puleo
Robert D. Aronin
Dan M. Blumenthal
Craig H. Cohen
Edward C. Klein
Eileen Lin
Peter J. McCarthy
Kelly A. Poole
Patricia A. Rossi
Pasqualino Russo
David A. Schwartzberg
Lisa B. Singer
Bernard M. Soebke
John M. Tangel
Dona Rita Zino
Gordon T. Hall
Peter S. Marchelos
Rita Piazza-Ryan
Joseph J. Borges
Lisa M. Scully
Edward J. Tindell

For full biographical listings, see the Martindale-Hubbell Law Directory

GALLAGHER GOSSEEN & FALLER (AV)

1010 Franklin Avenue, Suite 400, 11530-2927
Telephone: 516-742-2500
Fax: 516-742-2516
Cable: COMPROAIR
New York, New York Office: 350 Fifth Avenue.
Telephone: 212-947-5800.
FAX: 212-967-4965.

MEMBERS OF FIRM

James A. Gallagher, Jr.
Robert I. Gosseen (Resident, New York City Office)
Robert A. Faller
Alan D. Kaplan
Michael J. Crowley
William E. Vita

ASSOCIATES

David H. Arnsten
William A. Bales, Jr.
Jennifer Greenberg
Jeanne M. Gonsalves-Lloyd
Brian P. Morrissey
Leslie A. Rosenstein
Robert A. Sparer (Resident, New York City Office)

OF COUNSEL

Edward M. O'Brien (Resident, New York City Office)
Peter F. Vetro
Daniel F. Hayes
John P. Coogan

For full biographical listings, see the Martindale-Hubbell Law Directory

GOLDEN, WEXLER & SARNESE, P.C. (AV)

(Formerly Golden, Upton & Wexler, P.C.)
377 Oak Street, 11530-9998
Telephone: 516-745-6830
Telecopier: 516-745-6844
Elmsford, New York Office: 570 Taxter Road. 10523
Telephone: 914-347-8060.

Christopher A. Golden
Joel G. Wexler
Regina M. Sarnese

Maryanne Buatti
Kevin M. McDermott
Randi E. Taub
Mary T. Goetz
Warren J. Share
Jill B. Garfinkel
Amy O. Eisenberg
Jody Fay
Patricia A. Kavanagh
Heather M. Levi
Arnold M. Bottalico
Robert J. Ansell
Alma-Lillian Kinn
Patricia A. Amato

For full biographical listings, see the Martindale-Hubbell Law Directory

JASPAN, GINSBERG, SCHLESINGER, SILVERMAN & HOFFMAN (AV)

300 Garden City Plaza, 11530
Telephone: 516-746-8000
Telecopier: 516-746-0552

MEMBERS OF FIRM

Arthur W. Jaspan
Eugene S. Ginsberg
Steven R. Schlesinger
Kenneth P. Silverman
Carol M. Hoffman
Stanley A. Camhi
Eugene P. Cimini, Jr.
Holly Juster
Stephen P. Epstein
Gary M. Schwartz (1945-1985)
Gary F. Herbst
Allen Perlstein
Janet F. Brunell

Alice J. Hollmuller
Laurel Row Kretzing
Leonard M. Fischer
Marci S. Zinn
Salvatore LaMonica
Lawrence J. Tenenbaum
Michael G. McAuliffe
Suzanne Stadler
Randi-Sue Weinberg
Andrew S. Muller
Carol A. Melnick
John O. Fronce

OF COUNSEL

Leo L. Hoffman
Joseph Jaspan
Harold D. Berger
Michael E. White
Horace Z. Kramer (1918-1988)
Harry J. Winick (1899-1988)
Theodore W. Firetog

For full biographical listings, see the Martindale-Hubbell Law Directory

Garden City—Continued

Kase & Druker (AV)

Suite 225, 1325 Franklin Avenue, 11530
Telephone: 516-746-4300
Telecopier: 516-742-9416
Mamaroneck, New York Office: 136 Palmer Avenue.
Telephone: 914-834-4600.
Telecopier: 914-698-3807.

MEMBERS OF FIRM

John L. Kase | James O. Druker

OF COUNSEL

Philip J. Luongo

LEGAL SUPPORT PERSONNEL

Marie T. DeBonis

For full biographical listings, see the Martindale-Hubbell Law Directory

L'Abbate, Balkan, Colavita & Contini, L.L.P. (AV)

1050 Franklin Avenue, 11530
Telephone: 516-294-8844
Telecopier: 516-294-8202; 742-6563

MEMBERS OF FIRM

Donald R. L'Abbate
Kenneth J. Balkan
Anthony P. Colavita
Peter L. Contini
Monte E. Sokol
Douglas L. Pintauro
Richard P. Byrne
Ronald C. Burke
Harry Makris
Marie Ann Hoenings
Jane M. Myers
Dean L. Milber
James Plousadis

OF COUNSEL

Paula M. Gart

ASSOCIATES

Anna M. DiLonardo
David B. Kosakoff
Lewis A. Bartell
Ralph A. Catalano
Gay B. Levine
Victoria Roberts Drogin
Douglas R. Halstrom
Joseph A. Barra
Stephane Jasmin
Lawrence A. Kushnick
Diane H. Miller
Barbara Jean Romaine
Joseph V. Cambareri
Christine Andreoli

A list of References and Representative Clients will be furnished upon request.

For full biographical listings, see the Martindale-Hubbell Law Directory

Montfort, Healy, McGuire & Salley (AV)

1140 Franklin Avenue, 11530
Telephone: 516-747-4082
Telecopier: 516-746-0748

MEMBERS OF FIRM

E. Richard Rimmels, Jr.
Frank J. Cafaro
Philip J. Catapano
Fredric C. Montfort
Donald S. Neumann, Jr.
James J. Keefe, Jr.
Michael A. Baranowicz
James Michael Murphy

OF COUNSEL

Fredric H. Montfort
Edward M. Salley, Jr.
David J. Fleming

ASSOCIATES

Raymond J. Geoghegan
Robert J. Mettalia
Henry J. Wheller
Claudia C. Glacken
Marcie K. Glasser
Bruce A. Cook
Jeffrey D. Present
Joan E. Resnik
Susan H. Dempsey
Camille L. Hansen
Joseph F. Ferrette
Pui C. Cheng
Kathleen Dumont
Christopher T. Cafaro
Edward R. Rimmels
Jeffrey B. Siler

For full biographical listings, see the Martindale-Hubbell Law Directory

Redmond, Pollio & Pittoni, P.C. (AV)

1461 Franklin Avenue, 11530
Telephone: 516-248-2500
Telecopier: 516-248-2348

Benedict J. Pollio
M. John Pittoni
Peter R. Bonchonsky

Mark E. Costello
Kathleen M. Galgano
Rachel Cohen Quaid
Stephen E. Zaino
Ronald A. Pollio

OF COUNSEL

Aldo A. Trabucchi
Frederick Arthur Ross
John T. Redmond
Leonard P. Marinello

For full biographical listings, see the Martindale-Hubbell Law Directory

Sawyer, Davis & Halpern (AV)

600 Old Country Road, 11530
Telephone: 516-222-4567
Telecopier: 516-222-4585

MEMBERS OF FIRM

James Sawyer
Jay Davis
Kenneth J. Halpern

ASSOCIATES

Adam C. Demetri | Ralph W. Lee

For full biographical listings, see the Martindale-Hubbell Law Directory

Shaw, Licitra, Parente, Esernio & Schwartz, P.C. (AV)

1010 Franklin Avenue, 11530
Telephone: 516-742-0610
Cable Address: Lawbanc.
Telex: 143227
Telecopier: 516-742-2670
New York City Office: 300 East 42nd Street.
Telephone: 212-338-0970.
Special Counsel: Holland & Knight 400 North Ashley, P.O. Box 1288, Tampa, Florida, 33602 and 2100 Pennsylvania Avenue, N.W., Washington, D.C., 20037.

Joseph Licitra (1930-1987)
J. Stanley Shaw
C. Albert Parente
George P. Esernio
Jeffrey L. Schwartz
Anton J. Borovina
Edward M. Flint
Stuart I. Gordon
Sarah M. Keenan
Frank J. Livoti
Alan E. Marder
Peter Marullo
Jeffrey M. Zalkin

Francesca Cellese
Caroline Leon Cona
Frank A. Cuoco
Michael C. DeLisa
David P. Gesser
John H. Hall, Jr.
Jeffrey A. Hill
Gaetana Liantonio-McBride
Bradley A. Max
Donald R. Shields
Roberta L. Slattery

SPECIAL COUNSEL

Edward D. Re | Louis D. Laurino

COUNSEL

Victor G. Beaudet (1919-1993)
Louis M. Laurino
Alan M. Parente
Frank Rossetti, III

For full biographical listings, see the Martindale-Hubbell Law Directory

*GENESEO,** Livingston Co. — (Refer to Warsaw)

GLEN COVE, Nassau Co.

Payne, Wood & Littlejohn (AV)

Three School Street, 11542
Telephone: 516-676-0700
Telefax: 516-676-0823
Melville, New York Office: 290 Broad Hollow Road.
Telephone: 516-547-8400.
Telefax: 516-547-0501.
Bridgehampton, New York Office: 1936 Montauk Highway. P.O. Box 1980.
Telephone: 516-537-3100.
Telefax: 516-537-0560.

MEMBERS OF FIRM

Stephen P. Conlon (Managing Partner)

For full biographical listings, see the Martindale-Hubbell Law Directory

GLENS FALLS, Warren Co.

McPhillips, Fitzgerald & Meyer (AV)

(Successors to McPhillips, Fitzgerald & McCarthy)
288 Glen Street, P.O. Box 299, 12801
Telephone: 518-792-1174

MEMBERS OF FIRM

James McPhillips (1872-1949)
C. E. Fitzgerald (1885-1960)
Thomas J. McCarthy (1892-1970)
Gerald P. McPhillips (1902-1982)
Bernard F. McPhillips
Martin A. Meyer
Dennis J. Phillips
William E. Fitzgerald
James E. Cullum
Richard V. Meath

ASSOCIATES

William J. White | Daniel James Hogan

OF COUNSEL

Joseph R. Brennan | Lawrence E. Corbett, Jr.

Local Counsel for: International Paper Co.; Nationwide Insurance Co.; Hartford Insurance Cos.; CNA Insurance.
Attorneys for: Glens Falls National Bank & Trust Co.; Genpak Corp.; Finch Pruyn & Co., Inc.

For full biographical listings, see the Martindale-Hubbell Law Directory

Glens Falls—Continued

MILLER, MANNIX & PRATT, P.C. (AV)

One Broad Street Plaza, P.O. Box 765, 12801
Telephone: 518-793-6611
New York: 800-421-6166
Facsimile: 518-793-6690

John W. Miller (1908-1968)
John C. Mannix
Benjamin R. Pratt, Jr.
Mark Schachner

John C. Mannix, Jr.
Jeffrey J. Friedland
Kellie A. Tripodi
Robert Hall Hafner

Representative Clients: Associates of Glens Falls, Inc.; Fort William Henry Corp.; Insurance Company of North America; Utica Mutual Insurance Co.

For full biographical listings, see the Martindale-Hubbell Law Directory

GLOVERSVILLE, Fulton Co.

MAIDER & SMITH (AV)

37 East Fulton Street, 12078
Telephone: 518-725-7195
Fax: 518-773-3343

MEMBERS OF FIRM

Wesley H. Maider (1879-1955)
Lydon F. Maider
Robert L. Maider
Peter K. Smith

General Counsel for: City National Bank & Trust Co.; St. Thomas, Inc.
Local Counsel for: Sentry Insurance Co.
Reference: City National Bank & Trust Co.

For full biographical listings, see the Martindale-Hubbell Law Directory

*GOSHEN,** Orange Co.

NORTON & CHRISTENSEN (AV)

Goshen Executive Building, 60 Erie Street, P.O. Box 308, 10924
Telephone: 914-294-7949
Telecopier: 914-294-7791
Rochelle Park, New Jersey Office: 151 West Passaic Street, 07662.
Telephone: 201-909-3735.
Fax: 201-368-2102.

MEMBERS OF FIRM

Stanley J. Norton
Henry N. Christensen, Jr.
Harold M. Pressberg

OF COUNSEL

John T. Mayo

For full biographical listings, see the Martindale-Hubbell Law Directory

GOWANDA, Cattaraugus & Erie Cos. — (Refer to Jamestown)

GREAT NECK, Nassau Co.

MARTIN, VAN DE WALLE, DONOHUE, MANDRACCHIA & McGAHAN (AV)

17 Barstow Road, P.O. Box 222074, 11022
Telephone: 516-482-6100
Telecopier: 516-482-6969

MEMBERS OF FIRM

Jules Martin
Charles R. Van de Walle
Joseph A. Guarino (1946-1991)
Nicholas J. Donohue
Stephen P. Mandracchia
James M. McGahan

ASSOCIATES

Ted J. Feldman

Representative Clients: Fidelity National Title Insurance Company of New York; Bancker Construction Corp.; Biener Pontiac-Nissan, Inc.; Festo Corp.; First Investors Corp.; Lighting Horizons, Inc.; Prime Realty Holdings Co.; First Financial Savings Bank, S.L.A.; Chaminade High School; Oppenheimer Management Corp.

For full biographical listings, see the Martindale-Hubbell Law Directory

PEGALIS & WACHSMAN, P.C. (AV)

175 East Shore Road, 11023
Telephone: 718-895-7492; 212-936-2662; 516-487-1990
Outside New York: 1-800-522-0170
Telecopier: 516-487-4304
Philadelphia, Pennsylvania Office: 1601 Market Street, Suite 1040.
Telephone: 215-564-6838.
FAX: 215-564-6840.

Steven E. Pegalis
Harvey F. Wachsman

(See Next Column)

Kathryn M. Wachsman
Alice F. Collopy
Annamarie Bondi-Stoddard
Michael A. Carlucci
Gilbert G. Spencer, Jr.
James B. Baydar
Sanford Nagrotsky
Rhonda L. Meyer
Glenn C. McCarthy (Not admitted in NY)
Michael Aronoff
Daniel Albert Thomas

For full biographical listings, see the Martindale-Hubbell Law Directory

HAMBURG, Erie Co. — (Refer to Buffalo)

HANCOCK, Delaware Co. — (Refer to Binghamton)

HARRISON, Westchester Co.

CLUNE, HAYES, FREY, BENTZEN & CLUNE, P.C. (AV)

480 Mamaroneck Avenue, 10528
Telephone: 914-698-8200
Telecopier: 914-698-8248
Garden City, New York Office: 350 Old Country Road, Suite 103.
Telephone: 516-248-6600. Greenwich, Connecticut Office: 55 Old Field Point Road.
Telephone: 203-629-8313.
Fax: 203-629-8216.

J. Russell Clune
Edward A. Frey
Alfred E. Page, Jr.
Richard D. Bentzen
Martin F. Hayes
Kevin P. Clune
James H. O'Brien, Jr.

Rafael Otero
Robert P. Kelly
Sharon Ann Scanlan
Kenneth E. Mangano
Stephen J. Lo Presti
Nicholas P. Barone
Michael P. Farley

For full biographical listings, see the Martindale-Hubbell Law Directory

HAUPPAUGE, Suffolk Co.

ERIC H. HOLTZMAN (AV)

330 Vanderbilt Motor Parkway, P.O. Box 11005, 11788-0903
Telephone: 516-435-8800
Fax: 516-435-8832

Richard E. Trachtenberg

Reference: European-American Bank & Trust Co.

For full biographical listings, see the Martindale-Hubbell Law Directory

REYNOLDS, CARONIA & GIANELLI (AV)

200 Motor Parkway, P.O. Box 11177, 11788
Telephone: 516-231-1199
Telecopier: 516-231-1334

MEMBERS OF FIRM

James T. Reynolds
Peter R. Caronia
Paul Gianelli

ASSOCIATES

James F. Hagney

OF COUNSEL

John J. J. Jones

Reference: Chemical Bank.

For full biographical listings, see the Martindale-Hubbell Law Directory

HAVERSTRAW, Rockland Co.

MILLER & MILLER, P.C. (AV)

90 New Main Street, P.O. Box 360, 10927
Telephone: 914-429-5371

Samuel Miller
Daniel Miller

Phyllis Weinstein Shandler

For full biographical listings, see the Martindale-Hubbell Law Directory

HEMPSTEAD, Nassau Co.

LAW FIRM OF DONALD E. DEEGAN (AV)

550 Front Street, 11550
Telephone: 516-486-0700
Telecopier: 516-486-2854

MEMBERS OF FIRM

Donald E. Deegan
Marian C. Rice
Walter J. Lundahl
Joseph R. Crafa
James V. Deegan

(See Next Column)

LAW FIRM OF DONALD E. DEEGAN—*Continued*

ASSOCIATES

Mary E. Hayes | Gregg M. McGrath

For full biographical listings, see the Martindale-Hubbell Law Directory

FUREY, FUREY, LAPPING, DEMARIA & PETROZZO, P.C. (AV)

A Partnership including a Professional Corporation
600 Front Street, 11550
Telephone: 516-538-2500
Telecopier: 516-489-5056

James M. Furey
James M. Furey, Jr.
Robert K. Lapping
William D. Demaria
Vincent J. Petrozzo

Susan B. Williams
Susan W. Darlington
Patricia M. Meisenheimer
Jane Himelfarb
Thomas G. Leverage
Judith Pilatsky
Garyn Gdanian
Stuart J. Manzione
Linda A. Henninger
Michael T. Colavecchio
Elena R. Lanza
Christina A. Marotto
Lydia J. Keenan
Joseph M. Nador
David Stephen Wilck
Adam B. Rosen
James W. Jankowski

Reference: Fleet Bank, Hempstead.

For full biographical listings, see the Martindale-Hubbell Law Directory

*HERKIMER,** Herkimer Co. — (Refer to Utica)

HIGHLAND, Ulster Co. — (Refer to Poughkeepsie)

HOLLEY, Orleans Co.

HEATH & MARTIN (AV)

66 Village Square, P.O. Box 200, 14470
Telephone: 716-638-6331
Fax: 716-638-7221

MEMBERS OF FIRM

Edward N. Heath (1859-1940)
Mark Heath (1895-1966)
Robert E. Heath
Jeffrey R. Martin
Douglas M. Heath

Representative Clients: Towns of Clarendon, Gaines, Kendall and Murray; Village of Holley; Albion and Holley Central School Districts; Diaz Chemical Corp.; Holley Cold Storage Fruit and Produce Co., Inc.; Lake Ridge Fruit Co.
Approved Closing Attorneys for: Albion Federal Savings & Loan Assn.; Farmers Home Administration; Sibley Mortgage Corp.; Fleet Bank of New York.

For full biographical listings, see the Martindale-Hubbell Law Directory

*HUDSON,** Columbia Co.

CONNOR, CURRAN & SCHRAM, P.C. (AV)

441 East Allen Street, P.O. Box 77, 12534
Telephone: 518-828-1521
Fax: 518-828-2686
Chatham, New York Office: Fleet Bank Building.
Telephone: 518-392-3641.

William E. J. Connor (1905-1985)
John J. Curran (1921-1975)
Earl Schram, Jr.
Theodore Guterman, II (Resident at Chatham Office)
Nelson R. Alford, Jr. (Resident at Chatham Office)
Daniel J. Tuczinski
Jonathan D. Nichols
Paul M. Freeman

Dawn Kristen Holt
James A. Carlucci
Virginia D. Smith
Sharon D. Freyer
Andrew B. Howard

Representative Client: The Hudson City Savings Institution.

For full biographical listings, see the Martindale-Hubbell Law Directory

RAPPORT, MEYERS, GRIFFEN & WHITBECK (AV)

436 Union Street, 12534
Telephone: 518-828-9444
Telecopier: 518-828-9719
Poughkeepsie, New York Office: 110 Main Street. 12601.
Telephone: 914-473-7766.
Telecopier: 914-473-7790.

Carmi Rapport
Victor M. Meyers
Thomas G. Griffen
Carl G. Whitbeck, Jr.
Jason L. Shaw
George A. Rodenhausen
Seth L. Rapport
Rachel L. Samuels
Shannon Lynn Martin

(See Next Column)

OF COUNSEL

John J. Faso | Stephen M. Saland

References: Key Bank of New York; Hudson City Savings Institution; Trustco Bank; Fleet Bank of New York.

For full biographical listings, see the Martindale-Hubbell Law Directory

HUNTINGTON, Suffolk Co.

CORWIN & MATTHEWS (AV)

71 New Street, P.O. Box 800, 11743
Telephone: 516-421-2400

MEMBERS OF FIRM

Robert L. Corwin
Charles T. Matthews
Nathaniel L. Corwin

For full biographical listings, see the Martindale-Hubbell Law Directory

SMYTH & LACK (AV)

202 East Main Street, 11743
Telephone: 516-271-7500
Telecopier: 516-271-7504

MEMBERS OF FIRM

Vincent A. Smyth | James J. Lack

ASSOCIATES

Thomas P. Solferino
Dana M. Barberis
Stephen I. Witdorchic

Reference: Chemical Bank.

For full biographical listings, see the Martindale-Hubbell Law Directory

ILION, Herkimer Co. — (Refer to Utica)

ISLANDIA, Suffolk Co.

BRACKEN & MARGOLIN (AV)

Suite 300, One Suffolk Square, 11722
Telephone: 516-234-8585
Telecopier: 516-234-8702

MEMBERS OF FIRM

John P. Bracken | Linda U. Margolin

ASSOCIATES

John K. Diviney
Jennifer A. Juengst
Olympia Gouvis

OF COUNSEL

Kenneth Cooperstein
Jon Noel Santemma
Edward P. Schroeder
Jacqueline M. Skubik

Representative Clients: Rason Asphalt, Inc.; S & H Building Materials Corp.
Reference: Marine Midland Bank, N.A.

For full biographical listings, see the Martindale-Hubbell Law Directory

ISLIP, Suffolk Co.

SHLIMBAUM, SHLIMBAUM AND JABLONSKI (AV)

265 Main Street, P.O. Box 8, 11751-0008
Telephone: 516-277-4300
Telecopier: 516-277-4350

MEMBERS OF FIRM

C. Donald Shlimbaum
Lark J. Shlimbaum
Edward C. Jablonski, Jr.

ASSOCIATES

Laura M. Mc Kenna | John H. Edwards

For full biographical listings, see the Martindale-Hubbell Law Directory

*ITHACA,** Tompkins Co.

BARNEY, GROSSMAN, ROTH & DUBOW (AV)

Seneca Building West, Suite 400, 119 East Seneca Street, 14850
Telephone: 607-273-6841
Facsimile: 607-272-8806 (Not for service of papers)

MEMBERS OF FIRM

John C. Barney
Peter G. Grossman
Nelson E. Roth
David A. Dubow
Randall B. Marcus

ASSOCIATES

Hugh C. Kent

Attorneys for: Citizens Savings Bank, F.S.B.; Cayuga Mortgage Company; Town of Ithaca; Town of Danby; Village of Groton; Village of Lansing; Cornell University; Syracuse Telephone Company/Cellular One; Utica Telephone Company/Cellular One; McGuire & Bennett, Inc., Construction Contractors.

For full biographical listings, see the Martindale-Hubbell Law Directory

Ithaca—Continued

HARRIS BEACH & WILCOX (AV)

119 East Seneca Street, P.O. Box 580, 14851
Telephone: 607-273-6444
Washington, DC Office: 1200 18th Street, Suite 210.
Telephone: 202-861-0001.
Fax: 202-861-0011.
Rochester, New York Office: Granite Building, 130 East Main Street.
Telephone: 716-232-4440.
Telecopier: 716-546-2571.
Albany, New York Office: 20 Corporate Woods Boulevard.
Telephone: 518-427-9700.
Fax: 518-427-0235.
Hamburg, New York Office (Buffalo area): One Grimsby Drive.
Telephone: 716-646-5050.
Fax: 716-648-8201.
Syracuse, New York Office: Suite 300, Fleet Bank Building, One Clinton Square.
Telephone: 315-426-4520.
Fax: 315-426-4529.
Other Syracuse, New York Office: The Hills Building, 7th Floor, 217 Montgomery Street.
Telephone: 315-422-7383.
Fax: 315-422-9331.

OF COUNSEL

James J. Clynes, Jr.

MEMBERS OF FIRM

Robert J. Holdsworth, Jr. Edward C. Hooks
Mark B. Wheeler

ASSOCIATES

Joan B. Harman Mark G. Masler
Laurie M. Johnston Marianne W. Young

For full biographical listings, see the Martindale-Hubbell Law Directory

WIGGINS & MASSON (AV)

308 North Tioga Street, P.O. Box 399, 14851
Telephone: 607-272-0479
Telecopier: 607-273-0502

MEMBERS OF FIRM

Walter J. Wiggins Robin Abrahamson Masson

ASSOCIATES

Eileen M. McGlinchey Fahey

Approved Attorneys for: Ticor Title Guaranty Corp.
References: Tompkins County Trust Co.; Citizens Savings Bank.

For full biographical listings, see the Martindale-Hubbell Law Directory

JAMESTOWN, Chautauqua Co.

BURGETT & ROBBINS (AV)

15 East Fifth Street, P.O. Box 3090, 14702-3090
Telephone: 716-488-3090
Fax: 716-483-3765
1-800-832-6582

Dalton J. Burgett Dale C. Robbins

ASSOCIATES

Kenneth M. Lasker Mary Speedy Hajdu
Marlene Toni Brigiotta

References: Fleet Bank, Jamestown, New York; Marine Midland Bank, Jamestown, New York.

For full biographical listings, see the Martindale-Hubbell Law Directory

ERICKSON, WEBB & SCOLTON (AV)

111 West Second Street, 14701
Telephone: 716-488-1178

MEMBERS OF FIRM

Alton R. Erickson (1904-1968) Paul V. Webb, Jr.
Philip A. Erickson Bruce S. Scolton

Reference: Marine Midland Bank, N.A.

For full biographical listings, see the Martindale-Hubbell Law Directory

PHILLIPS, LYTLE, HITCHCOCK, BLAINE & HUBER (AV)

307 Chase Bank Building, 8 E. Third Street, 14702-1279
Telephone: 716-664-3906
Telecopier: 716-664-4230
Buffalo, New York Office: 3400 Marine Midland Center.
Telephone: 716-847-8400.
Telecopier: 716-852-6100.
Rochester, New York Office: 1400 First Federal Plaza.
Telephone: 716-238-2000.
Telecopier: 716-232-3141.
New York, New York Office: 437 Madison Avenue.
Telephone: 212-759-4888.
Telecopier: 212-308-9079.

(See Next Column)

Fredonia, New York Office: 11 East Main Street.
Telephone: 716-672-2164.
FAX: 716-672-7979.

OF COUNSEL

Sherwood S. Cadwell

PARTNERS

Michael C. Foley Martin F. Idzik
Gregory L. Peterson

For full biographical listings, see the Martindale-Hubbell Law Directory

JEFFERSONVILLE, Sullivan Co. — (Refer to Liberty)

*JOHNSTOWN,** Fulton Co. — (Refer to Gloversville)

KATONAH, Westchester Co.

COVEY, ROBERTS, BUCHANAN & LONERGAN (AV)

Village Commons East, 200 Katonah Avenue, 10536
Telephone: 914-232-5161
Telecopier: 914-232-0574
North Palm Beach, Florida Office: Crystal Tree Plaza, 1201 U.S. No. 1, Suite 240.
Telephone: 407-622-8151.
Telecopier: 407-627-0225.

Edwin B. Covey (1908-1975) George Hunter Roberts
Jeffrey D. Buchanan (1943-1994) William R. Lonergan, Jr.

OF COUNSEL

Arthur R. Covey

Representative Clients: New York State Electric & Gas Co.; Katonah-Lewisboro Schools; Goldens Bridge Fire District; Katonah Fire District.
Reference: Chase Bank/NBW.

For full biographical listings, see the Martindale-Hubbell Law Directory

*KINGSTON,** Ulster Co.

COOK, TUCKER, NETTER & CLOONAN, P.C. (AV)

85 Main Street, P.O. Box 3939, 12401
Telephone: 914-331-0702

Andrew J. Cook (1884-1958) William N. Cloonan
Francis X. Tucker (1923-1987) Robert D. Cook
Andrew J. Cook, Jr. Eric M. Kurtz
Robert E. Netter Thomas A. Murphy

Counsel for: Town of Rochester.
Representative Clients: Central Hudson Gas & Electric Corp.; CNA Insurance Co.; Covenant Group; Hanover Insurance Co.; CIGNA; Inapro; Metropolitan Property & Liability Insurance Co.; Norstar Bank; Prudential Insurance Co.; Travelers Insurance Co.

For full biographical listings, see the Martindale-Hubbell Law Directory

HOWARD C. ST. JOHN AND ASSOCIATES (AV)

280 Wall Street, 12401
Telephone: 914-338-4500

ASSOCIATES

Richard A. Anthony Michael Francis Jordan
Joseph L. Canino Stephanie M. Whidden
John J. Cook Kenneth A. Redding
Jill M. Darwak

General Counsel for: Ulster Savings Bank.
Representative Clients: Government Employees Insurance Co.; National Grange Insurance Co.; New York Central Mutual Fire Insurance Co.; AT&T (local counsel); Volkswagen of America, Inc. (local counsel); Inland Steel (local counsel).

For full biographical listings, see the Martindale-Hubbell Law Directory

*LAKE GEORGE,** Warren Co. — (Refer to Glens Falls)

LARCHMONT, Westchester Co.

MCMILLAN, CONSTABILE, MAKER & MURPHY (AV)

2180 Boston Post Road, 10538
Telephone: 914-834-3500
FAX: 914-834-0620

MEMBERS OF FIRM

Thomas R. Constabile, Jr. William Maker, Jr.
Stewart J. McMillan Keith J. McMillan
James G. Murphy

COUNSEL

Robert D. Costello Timothy M. Costello
Rita J. Miller Charles L. Siddons

For full biographical listings, see the Martindale-Hubbell Law Directory

LIBERTY, Sullivan Co.

APPELBAUM, EISENBERG, BAUMAN & APPELBAUM (AV)

6 North Main Street, 12754
Telephone: 914-292-4444

MEMBERS OF FIRM

Sidney Appelbaum
Harold J. Bauman
Bertram W. Eisenberg
Joel R. Appelbaum

ASSOCIATES

Steven M. Pivovar
Michael Frey

Representative Clients: Public Service Mutual Insurance Co.; Aetna Life and Casualty Co.; Allstate Insurance Co.; State Farm Mutual Insurance Co.; Employers-Commercial Union Insurance Group; Royal Globe Indemnity Co.; Pearl Assurance Co.; National Grange Insurance Co.
Reference: Marine Midland Bank.

For full biographical listings, see the Martindale-Hubbell Law Directory

LITTLE FALLS, Herkimer Co. — (Refer to Utica)

*LOCKPORT,** Niagara Co.

SACCA AND SACCA (AV)

102 East Avenue, 14094
Telephone: 716-434-5518
Fax: 716-434-8050

MEMBERS OF FIRM

Stephen A. Sacca
Gerald Stephen Sacca

LEGAL SUPPORT PERSONNEL

Anna Marie Holman (Paralegal)

Representative Clients: Lawyers Title Insurance Corp. (Virginia); Village of Wilson.
References: Manufacturers & Traders Trust Co.; Marine Midland Bank; Lockport Savings Bank.

For full biographical listings, see the Martindale-Hubbell Law Directory

*LOWVILLE,** Lewis Co. — (Refer to Watertown)

*LYONS,** Wayne Co. — (Refer to Seneca Falls)

*MALONE,** Franklin Co.

FISCHER, BESSETTE & MULDOWNEY (AV)

Country Club Road, P.O. Box 420, 12953
Telephone: 518-481-5000
Fax: 518-481-5203

William J. Herron (1905-1993)

OF COUNSEL

Henry A. Fischer

MEMBERS OF FIRM

James P. Bessette
John J. Muldowney

ASSOCIATES

Richard F. Hunter (Not admitted in NY)

For full biographical listings, see the Martindale-Hubbell Law Directory

MAMARONECK, Westchester Co. — (Refer to Port Chester)

MANHASSET, Nassau Co.

FLETCHER, SIBELL, MIGATZ & BURNS, P.C. (AV)

Molloy Building, 22 Bayview Avenue, P.O. Box N, 11030
Telephone: 516-627-6600
Facsimile: 516-627-5241

James H. Fletcher
Bruce W. Migatz
Stanley J. Sibell
John A. Burns, Jr.

OF COUNSEL

Lloyd K. Chanin

Representative Clients: Joseph Eletlo Transfer Co., Inc.; Shearson Lehman Hutton; Micro Contacts, Inc.; Manhasset-Lakeville Water District; Manhasset-Lakeville Fire District; Ulster Savings Bank.
References: National Westminster Bank, U.S.A.; European-American Bank; Norstar Bank; First American Title Insurance Co.

For full biographical listings, see the Martindale-Hubbell Law Directory

MASPETH, Queens Co.

EDWARD M. MCGOWAN (AV)

68-15 Borden Avenue, 11378
Telephone: 718-651-7360
Telecopier: 718-446-0796

For full biographical listings, see the Martindale-Hubbell Law Directory

MASSENA, St. Lawrence Co. — (Refer to Ogdensburg)

MELVILLE, Suffolk Co.

CAHN WISHOD & LAMB, L.L.P. (AV)

534 Broadhollow Road-CS 9034, 11747-9034
Telephone: 516-694-2300
Telecopier: 516-694-2309

Richard C. Cahn
Eugene L. Wishod
P. L. Lamb
Eugene R. Barnosky
Todd A. Knauer
Conley E. Brian, Jr.
Robert H. Cohen
Joel M. Markowitz
Scott M. Karson
Frederick Eisenbud

OF COUNSEL

Joseph H. Wishod

COUNSEL

Joseph J. Salvatore
Patrice Dowd Shenn
Robert L. Folks

ASSOCIATES

Frederick D. Kremer
Marcia Lyn Finkelstein
Kevin P. Mulry
James F. Gesualdi
Howard M. Miller
Carol L. Moore
Jacqueline T. C. Colclough
Catherine M. Healy

Representative Clients: Asia Bank, N.A.; Banco Exterior de Espana; Commack, Comsewogue, Hauppauge and Miller Place Union Free School Districts; Commack and Harborfields Public Libraries; Extebank; Fleet Bank; Huntington Hospital; International Telephone & Telegraph Corp.; Marine Midland Bank, N.A.

For full biographical listings, see the Martindale-Hubbell Law Directory

PAYNE, WOOD & LITTLEJOHN (AV)

290 Broad Hollow Road, 11747
Telephone: 516-547-8400
Telefax: 516-547-0501
Glen Cove, New York Office: Three School Street.
Telephone: 516-676-0700.
Fax: 516-676-0823.
Bridgehampton, New York Office: 1936 Montauk Highway. P.O. Box 1980.
Telephone: 516-537-3100.
Telefax: 516-537-0560.

MEMBERS OF FIRM

Stephen P. Conlon (Managing Partner)
Stephen Van R. Ulman
Philip C. Kilian
Daren A. Rathkopf
Beverly J. Bell
Alan C. Polacek
Robert M. Saltzstein
Thomas L. Costa
Jed C. Albert
Peter B. Colgrove
Theresa K. Quigley
Janet Ganio

OF COUNSEL

Victor C. McCuaig, Jr.
Warren I. Titus, Jr.
Edwin F. Hendrickson
James A. Eisenman
Joseph L. Tobin, Jr.
Waldo Hutchins, III
Estelle S. Roberts

COUNSEL

James M. Marrin
Kevin J. Barry

ASSOCIATES

R. Patrick Quinn
Marlene L. Budd
Mark A. Cuthbertson
Susan H. Jannace

For full biographical listings, see the Martindale-Hubbell Law Directory

WINGATE & CULLEN (AV)

Fleet Financial Plaza, 290 Broad Hollow Road, 11747-4805
Telephone: 516-427-5400
Fax: 516-427-5402
Brooklyn, New York Office: 142 Pierrepont Street.
Telephone: 718-875-3652.
Fax: 718-596-6750.
Other Brooklyn Office: Bay Ridge, 8804 4th Avenue.
Telephone: 718-745-8844.
Fax: 718-680-0598.

MEMBERS OF FIRM

Thomas O. Rice
Peter N. Zogas
Richard H. Freeman
Jonathan R. Frank
Michael F. O'Shea
Robert P. Knapp, III

SENIOR COUNSEL

Claudia C. Conway
Calliope Manis

ASSOCIATES

Jani M. Foley
Kenneth V. Babi
Kevin G. Condon
Paula A. Miller
Marc A. Rapaport

For full biographical listings, see the Martindale-Hubbell Law Directory

MIDDLETOWN, Orange Co.

MacVean, Lewis, Sherwin & McDermott, P.C. (AV)

34 Grove Street, P.O. Box 310, 10940
Telephone: 914-343-3000
Fax: 914-343-3866

Kenneth A. MacVean
Kermit W. Lewis
Louis H. Sherwin
Paul T. McDermott
Jeffrey D. Sherwin

George F. Roesch, III
Michael F. McCusker
Thomas P. Clarke, Jr.
Kevin F. Preston
John Ingrassia
Samuel W. Eager, Jr.

OF COUNSEL

V. Frank Cline

Counsel for: Orange County Trust Co.; Middletown Savings Bank; First Federal Savings & Loan Association of Middletown; Goshen Savings Bank; Advest Bank.

For full biographical listings, see the Martindale-Hubbell Law Directory

*MINEOLA,** Nassau Co.

Kelly, Rode & Kelly, LLP (AV)

330 Old Country Road, 11501
Telephone: 516-739-0400
FAX: 516-739-0434
Riverhead, New York Office: 218 Griffing Avenue.
Telephone: 516-727-0110.

MEMBERS OF FIRM

Joseph F. O'Brien (1956-1968)
George L. Ryan (1968-1976)
John D. Kelly
John Kenneth Rode
Shawn P. Kelly
George J. Wilson

ASSOCIATES

Francis J. Tierney
David S. Pallai
Charles C. Nicholas
Arthur Simuro
Ann Willoughby
MaryBeth Cameron
Edward J. Kelly, IV
Jeffrey C. Gerson
Lisa C. Ceraulo
John P. Boyle
Charles B. Weber
Frank L. Pellegrini
Carolyn Mcquade
Brian J. Noonan

Representative Clients: The New York Hospital Medical Center of Queens; Nationwide Insurance Co.; State Farm Insurance Co.; Motorist Mutual Insurance Co.; Medical Liability Mutual Insurance Co.; New York State Insurance Dept.-Liquidation Bureau; Preferred Physicians Mutual Risk Insurance Co.; McDonnell-Douglas Corp.; Physicians Reciprocal Insurers.
Reference: Citibank.

For full biographical listings, see the Martindale-Hubbell Law Directory

Kennedy & Comerford (AV)

200 Old Country Road, 11501
Telephone: 516-741-8818
Fax: 516-741-1703
New York, N.Y. Office: 805 Third Avenue.
Telephone: 212-750-1614.
Fax: 212-750-2885.

Bernard P. Kennedy
Michael J. Comerford

ASSOCIATES

Anne Marie Caradonna

OF COUNSEL

William J. Poisson
Patrick J. Hackett

For full biographical listings, see the Martindale-Hubbell Law Directory

MOUNT KISCO, Westchester Co.

Anderson, Banks, Curran & Donoghue (AV)

61 Smith Avenue, 10549
Telephone: 914-666-2161
Telecopier: 914-666-3292

MEMBERS OF FIRM

Stanley E. Anderson (1928-1965)
William F. Banks
Stanley E. Anderson, Jr.
Maurice F. Curran
Lawrence W. Thomas
John M. Donoghue
Gregory Keefe
James P. Drohan
Rochelle J. Auslander

ASSOCIATES

Barbara Banks Schwam
Suzanne Johnston
Daniel Petigrow
Stuart Waxman

OF COUNSEL

Margaret A. Clark

Representative Clients: The Centennial Life Insurance Company of America.

For full biographical listings, see the Martindale-Hubbell Law Directory

Shamberg Marwell Cherneff Hocherman Davis & Hollis, P.C. (AV)

55 Smith Avenue, 10549
Telephone: 914-666-5600
Telecopier: 914-666-6267
Goshen, New York Office: 40 Matthews Street, 10924.
Telephone: 914-294-1300.
Fax: 914-294-2001.

Stuart R. Shamberg
John S. Marwell
Peter R. Cherneff
Henry M. Hocherman
Robert F. Davis
P. Daniel Hollis, III
Kenneth J. Frank
David S. Steinmetz
Adam L. Wekstein
Sharon Guss Pollack
Geraldine N. Tortorella

Gregg S. Baker
Rosemary Scariati
Christine Moccia

OF COUNSEL

James G. Sweeney
Daniel A. Piloseno

For full biographical listings, see the Martindale-Hubbell Law Directory

Thomas J. Singleton (AV)

50 Main Street, 10549
Telephone: 914-666-4400
Telecopier: 914-666-6442

For full biographical listings, see the Martindale-Hubbell Law Directory

NANUET, Rockland Co.

Schwartz, Kobb & Scheinert (AV)

404 East Route 59, P.O. Box 220, 10954
Telephone: 914-623-0883
New York City Telephone: 718-562-6509; FAX: 914-623-0966

MEMBERS OF FIRM

Sidney Schwartz
Frank J. Kobb
Joel L. Scheinert

ASSOCIATES

James S. Kobb
Hal B. Patterson

General Counsel for: Finkelstein Memorial Library.
Representative Clients: Chemical Bank; First Fidelity Bank.

For full biographical listings, see the Martindale-Hubbell Law Directory

*NEW CITY,** Rockland Co.

Hurley, Fox, Selig & Kelleher (AV)

60 Pine Street, 10956
Telephone: 914-634-2050
Stony Point, New York Office: Liberty Building, Route 9W, 10980.
Telephone: 914-942-2222.

Paul Anthony Hurley

Representative Clients: Bradlees, Inc.; Amerishare Insurance Co.; American Mutual Insurance Co.; Continental Insurance Cos.; Wausau Insurance Co.; Federal Insurance Co.; Chubb & Son; Commercial Union Group of Insurance Cos.; Empire Insurance Co.

For full biographical listings, see the Martindale-Hubbell Law Directory

NEW ROCHELLE, Westchester Co.

Cooper & Cooper (AV)

175 Memorial Highway, 10801
Telephone: 914-636-5100
Telecopier: 914-636-6553

MEMBERS OF FIRM

Burton S. Cooper
Douglas A. Cooper

Burton J. Lasky
Joseph R. Harbeson
Deborah R. Beckmann

For full biographical listings, see the Martindale-Hubbell Law Directory

McGovern, Connelly & Davidson (AV)

145 Huguenot Street, P.O. Box 0, 10801
Telephone: 914-632-9300
Telecopier: 914-632-1615

MEMBERS OF FIRM

J. Raymond McGovern (1898-1974)
Frank H. Connelly, Sr. (1907-1989)
Harry G. Davidson (1912-1981)
Frank H. Connelly, Jr.
John A. Vasile
Francis B. Orlando
Margaret M. Fitzpatrick
Scott Weinberger

Representative Clients: Capital Sports Inc.; City of New Rochelle; Halpern-Stillman, Inc.; Marine Midland Bank; Samson Management, Co.; The Rawlplug Company, Inc.; Pace Oldsmobile, Inc.; Flynn Burner Corp.

(See Next Column)

McGOVERN, CONNELLY & DAVIDSON—*Continued*

For full biographical listings, see the Martindale-Hubbell Law Directory

*NEW YORK,** New York Co.

ANDREWS & KURTH L.L.P. (AV)

A Registered Limited Liability Partnership
425 Lexington Avenue, 10th Floor, 10017
Telephone: 212-850-2800
Telecopier: 212-850-2929
Telex: 960534 AKLAW NYC
Houston, Texas Office: 4200 Texas Commerce Tower.
Telephone: 713-220-4200.
Telecopier: 713-220-4285.
Washington, D.C. Office: Suite 200, 1701 Pennsylvania Avenue, N.W.
Telephone: 202-662-2700.
Telecopier: 202-662-2739.
Dallas, Texas Office: 4400 Thanksgiving Tower.
Telephone: 214-979-4400.
Telecopier: 214-979-4401.
The Woodlands, Texas Office: Suite 150, 2170 Buckthorne Place, 77380.
Telephone: 713-364-9199.
Telecopier: 713-364-9538.
Los Angeles, California Office: Suite 4200, 601 S. Figueroa Street.
Telephone: 213-896-3100.
Telecopier: 213-986-3137.

MEMBERS OF FIRM

Stuart Bressman
Emanuel S. Cherney
Simon D. Cices
Arthur D. Felsenfeld
Lynne M. Fischman Uniman
Robert D. Frick (Not admitted in NY)
A. Sidney Holderness, Jr.
Hugh M. Ray
Michael Q. Rosenwasser (Not admitted in NY)
Paul N. Silverstein
Avery I. Stok
Walter L. Stratton
R. Donald Turlington
Mark Zvonkovic

OF COUNSEL

Stephan G. Bachelder
Jonathan P. Cramer
Robert D. Simon
Michael Swidler

ASSOCIATES

Maura Fecher Carlin
Inna Fayenson
Peter W. Ghitman
Peter S. Goodman
James D. Higgason, Jr.
Kenneth A. Louard
Allan D. Reiss
Charles D. Rubenstein
Marianne T. Spinelli
Laurence E. Wiseman

STAFF ATTORNEY

Meric A. Underweiser

For full biographical listings, see the Martindale-Hubbell Law Directory

BADIAK WILL & MALOOF (AV)

Suite 1040 120 Broadway, 10271
Telephone: 212-376-6767
Telecopier: 212-376-6770
Telex: 6716686 BANDW
North Miami Beach, Florida Office: Badiak, Will & Kallen, 17071 West Dixie Highway, P.O. Box 600550.
Telephone: 305-945-1851.

MEMBERS OF FIRM

Roman Badiak
Alfred J. Will
Charles C. Goodenough
James J. Ruddy
John D. Kallen (Not admitted in NY; Resident, North Miami, Florida Office)
David L. Maloof (1924-1992)

ASSOCIATES

Paul A. Walsh
Stephen A. Frank
Lynn S. Waterman (Not admitted in NY; Resident, North Miami, Florida Office)

OF COUNSEL

Joseph B. McDonald

For full biographical listings, see the Martindale-Hubbell Law Directory

BAER MARKS & UPHAM (AV)

A Partnership including a Professional Corporation
805 Third Avenue, 10022
Telephone: 212-702-5700
Fax: 212-702-5941
Cable Address: "Julibaer"; "Sellew"

David Aronson
Neal S. Barlia
Donald J. Bezahler
Stanley E. Bloch
Michael V. Blumenthal
Jeffrey M. Cole
James M. Coughlin
Ivan W. Dreyer
Bernard A. Feuerstein
James E. Frankel
Brian R. Gallagher
Eric L. Goldberg
Steven M. Goldman
Howard Graff
Joel M. Handel
Larry D. Henin
Paul M. Kaplan
Gary S. Kleinman

(See Next Column)

Christopher J. Lagno
Kenneth H. Lazaruk
Leslie J. Levinson
Eric D. Martins
Allan E. Mayefsky
Herbert S. Meeker
William B. Norden
Samuel F. Ottensoser
Steven S. Pretsfelder
Lisa Printz Roday
Eugene R. Scheiman
Howard R. Shapiro
Norman M. Sheresky (P.C.)
Donald S. Snider
Morris A. Wirth

ASSOCIATES

Danal F. Abrams
Averlyn M. Archer
Terese L. Arenth
Stuart W. Berg
Jennifer Bush
Frank G. Cernigliaro
Barbara E. Champoux
Edward S. Feig
Daniel J. Friedman
Arlyn B. Goldberg
Ofira Gordon
Sari E. Greenberg
Dorothy F. Henderson
Russell J. Kutell
Beth D. Lesser
Yakir M. Lubowsky
Joseph A. Marinello
David C. Markatos
David L. Mathus
Charles R. Pierce, Jr.
Anne E. Pitter
Jennifer D. Port
Michael T. Rogers
Jonathan J. Russo
Deborah A. Skakel
Paul H. Slaney
Gary M. Tischler
Bruce J. Zabarauskas

OF COUNSEL

Andrew M. Crisses
Aaron L. Danzig
Justin W. D'Atri
Milton B. Eulau
Walter Feldesman (P.C.)
Leon Finley
Arnold Forster
Jay L. Gottlieb
Joseph Korff
Lawrence W. Milas
Gloria E. Pollack
Herman Sassower
Stephen F. Selig

For full biographical listings, see the Martindale-Hubbell Law Directory

BAKER & BOTTS, L.L.P. (AV)

885 Third Avenue Suite 2000, 10022
Telephone: 212-705-5000
Fax: 212-705-5125
Washington, D.C. Office: The Warner, 1299 Pennsylvania Avenue, N.W.
Telephone: 202-639-7700.
Austin, Texas Office: 1600 San Jacinto Center, 98 San Jacinto Boulevard.
Telephone: 512-322-2500.
Dallas, Texas Office: 2001 Ross Avenue.
Telephone: 214-953-6500.
Houston, Texas Office: One Shell Plaza, 910 Louisiana.
Telephone: 713-229-1234.
Moscow, Russian Federation Office: 10 ul. Pushkinskaya, 103031.
Telephone: 7095/921-5300 (Local); 7095/929-7070 (International).

MEMBERS OF FIRM

Jerome H. Kern
Kenneth M. Bialo
Henry B. Gutman
James A. Hime (Not admitted in NY)
Kerry L. Konrad
Karen Leslye Wolf (Not admitted in NY)
Elizabeth M. Markowski
Frederick H. McGrath
Robert W. Murray Jr.
Kenneth S. Siegel

OF COUNSEL

Marc A. Leaf
Bertram Perkel
Ronald D. Sernau

ASSOCIATES

Lee D. Charles
Karen F. Conway
Thomas V. D'Ambrosio
Nancy E. Field (Not admitted in NY)
Laura S. Franco
C. Ben Garren
John L. Graham (Not admitted in NY)
Robert S. Langley, Jr.
Michael A. Lippert
Paul A. Manuel
Jeffrey E. Ostrow
Alice W. Turinas (Not admitted in NY)

For full biographical listings, see the Martindale-Hubbell Law Directory

BAKER & MCKENZIE (AV)

805 Third Avenue, 10022
Telephone: (212) 751-5700
Intn'l. Dialing: (1-212) 751-5700
Cable Address: ABOGADO
Telex: 62572
Answer Back: ABOGADO
Facsimile: (1-212) 759-9133
Associated Offices of Baker & McKenzie in: Almaty, Amsterdam, Bangkok, Barcelona, Beijing, Berlin, Bogotá, Brasília, Brussels, Budapest, Buenos Aires, Cairo, Caracas, Chicago, Dallas, Frankfurt, Geneva, Hanoi, Ho Chi Minh City, Hong Kong, Juárez, Kiev, London, Madrid, Manila, Melbourne, México City, Miami, Milan, Monterrey, Moscow, Palo Alto, Paris, Prague, Rio de Janeiro, Riyadh, Rome, St. Petersburg, San Diego, San Francisco, São Paulo, Singapore, Stockholm, Sydney, Taipei, Tijuana, Tokyo, Toronto, Valencia, Warsaw, Washington, D.C. and Zürich.
Correspondent Law Firm: Hadiputranto, Hadinoto & Partners, Jakarta.

(See Next Column)

BAKER & MCKENZIE, *New York—Continued*

MEMBERS OF FIRM

Janna H. J. Bellwin
Michael Burrows
James R. Cameron
Charles J. Conroy
Robert B. Davidson
Monique S. de Zagon
José W. Fernandez
Stephan H. Haimo
Gerald J. Hayes
Steven R. Howard
Lawrence Walker Newman
Norman J. Resnicow
Malcolm I. Ross
Arthur W. Rovine
Michael I. Saltzman
Vincent A. Sama
Joseph Samet
Benedict J. Sciortino
Alan Siegel
Robert W. Toan
David W. Welles

LOCAL PARTNERS

Robert L. Dumont
Mitchell S. Kaplan
Steven H. Scheinman
Nicholas J. Serwer
David Zaslowsky

OF COUNSEL

Peter D. Lederer
Anthony G. Petrello

SENIOR ATTORNEY

Charles B. Cummings

COUNSEL

Barbara T. Kaplan
Curtis E. Pew

ASSOCIATES

Howard M. Berkower
Leslie M. Book
Everett S. Carbajal
Craig I. Celniker
Maria Chedid (Not admitted in NY)
William L. Clydesdale
Jonathan E. Cohen
Brian S. Cousin
C. Valerie Dabady
Charles M. Davidson
Walda Decreus
John Francis Fitzpatrick
Brett L. Gold
Grant Hanessian
Roger I. R. James
Jon D. Karnofsky
Robert J. Kashtan
Stuart B. Katz
Irwin M. Latner
Robert P. Lewis
Kevin J. Liss
Scott R. MacLeod
Michael S. Novins
Carol M. O'Driscoll
Douglas M. Polley
Yvonne E. Schlaeppi
Martin J. Waters III
Alysia M. White
Andres Williamson (Not admitted in the United States)

For full biographical listings, see the Martindale-Hubbell Law Directory

BANGSER KLEIN ROCCA & BLUM (AV)

230 Park Avenue, 10169-0069
Telephone: 212-856-5800
Telecopier: 212-972-7896

MEMBERS OF FIRM

Darren S Berger
Robert M. Blum
Robert M. Dubow
Jonathan J. Fink
Bettina D. Hindin
Frank H. Klein
James G. Samson
Giacomo Rocca (1932-1992)

GENERAL COUNSEL

Lawrence S. Bangser

COUNSEL

Leo Goldsmith, Jr.
Harold Greenwald

ASSOCIATES

Mark W. Smith
Richard Klein

For full biographical listings, see the Martindale-Hubbell Law Directory

PAUL A. BATISTA A PROFESSIONAL CORPORATION (AV)

950 Third Avenue, Suite 3200, 10022
Telephone: 212-980-0070
Telecopier: 212-758-2809

Paul A. Batista

For full biographical listings, see the Martindale-Hubbell Law Directory

BATTLE FOWLER LLP (AV)

A Limited Liability Partnership
75 East 55th Street, 10022
Telephone: 212-856-7000
Cable Address: "Counsellor"
Telex: 127053
Telecopier: (212) 986-5135

MEMBERS OF FIRM

George Gordon Battle (1897-1949)
Ludlow S. Fowler (1924-1961)
Charles H. Baker
Charles Burton *
Robert J. DeAngelis
Carl A. de Brito
Howard S. Denburg
David E. Eagan
Gerald A. Eppner
Gerald J. Fields *
David Fleischer *
David J. Freeman
Kenneth J. Friedman
Douglas L. Furth
Robert W. Gelfman *
Thomas V. Glynn
Charles J. Hamilton, Jr.

(See Next Column)

MEMBERS OF FIRM (Continued)

William Bruce Johnson
Steven Koch
Thomas E. Kruger *
Eric R. Landau
Jonathan M. Lehr *
John J. Malloy
Michael J. P. Malone, III
William J. McSherry, Jr.
Lawrence Mittman
Donald C. Moss
James Kendrick Noble, III
Richard L. O'Toole
Edward L. Peck *
Douglas A. Raelson
Michael R. Rosella
Michael J. Saltser *
Alvin J. Sarter
Walter F. Schleimer
Paul D. Selver
Eric W. Shaw
Ann Shipley
Dean A. Stiffle
John N. Turitzin
Mary Ann Villari
Alan S. Weil
Robert J. Wertheimer
Joanne M. Wilson
Jordan E. Yarett

OF COUNSEL

Hyman L. Battle, Jr.
Martin L. Edelman *
David D. Griffin *
Charles L. Jaffin *
Theodore W. Kheel

SPECIAL COUNSEL

Peter W. LaVigne
Raymond J. Soffientini
Elise Wagner
David M. Warburg

ASSOCIATES

Billy P. Ascione
Gregory R. Belcamino
Robert B. Brofman
John A. Cahill
Frank T. Cannone
Steven B. Carlin
Elizabeth E. Swire Falker
Edward C. Fargis
James R. Foggo
Robin M. Freundlich
Sharyn Gibau-Heyman
Scott J. Gordon
Vicki S. Gruber
Luke P. Iovine, III
Lori B. Katz
Taro J. Kawamura
Stewart Klein
M. Andica Kunst
James Lawless, IV
Margaret Elias Lehman
Andrew E. Lewin
Michelle Mann
Michael J. Maratea
Colleen M. McIntosh
Mary Mc Kenna
Gregg Miller
Michael A. Mishaan
Lois Nitti-Verlen
Peter Conrad Olsen
Madlyn Gleich Primoff
Gary D. Rawitz
Patrick J. Rohan
Jeffrey E. Romanow
Andrew W. Scher
Gloria M. Skigen
Paul Allan Straus
Edward D. Thomas
Vasilia H.A. Tsismenakis
Carla P.S. Vogel
Michael L. Zuppone

*A Professional Corporation

For full biographical listings, see the Martindale-Hubbell Law Directory

BECKER, GLYNN, MELAMED & MUFFLY (AV)

299 Park Avenue, 10171
Telephone: 212-888-3033
Telex: 254893
Facsimile: (212) 888-0255

David J. Melamed (1930-1990)

MEMBERS OF FIRM

Joseph D. Becker
Robert B. Glynn
Robert C. Muffly
Richard N. Chassin
Kenneth L. Everett
Peter M. Hosinski
Peter Van Nuys
Rachel Korn Wasserman

Alfred S. Farha
Karin P. E. Gustafson
Judith M. Passannante
Matthew W. Woodruff

OF COUNSEL

Paul J. O'Neill, Jr.

For full biographical listings, see the Martindale-Hubbell Law Directory

BECKMAN & MILLMAN, P.C. (AV)

116 John Street, 10038
Telephone: 212-227-6777
Telecopier: 212-227-1486
Midtown Office: 666 Fifth Avenue, New York, New York 10103.

Michael Beckman
Debra J. Millman

For full biographical listings, see the Martindale-Hubbell Law Directory

BEVERIDGE & DIAMOND, P.C. (AV)

40th Floor, 437 Madison Avenue, 10022-7380
Telephone: 212-702-5400
Telecopier: 212-702-5450
Washington, D.C. Office: 1350 I Street, N.W., Suite 700, 20005-3311.
Telephone: 202-789-6000.
Telecopier: 202-789-6190.
Fort Lee, New Jersey Office: Beveridge & Diamond, Suite 400, One Bridge Plaza, 07024-7502.
Telephone: 201-585-8162.
Telecopier: 201-592-7720.

(See Next Column)

BEVERIDGE & DIAMOND P.C.—*Continued*

San Francisco, California Office: Beveridge & Diamond, One Sansome Street, Suite 3400, 94204-4438.
Telephone: 415-397-0100.
Telecopier: 415-397-4238.

Stephen L. Gordon

OF COUNSEL

John French III

Kathryn B. Fuller
Sy Gruza
Craig B. Kravit
David S. Langer
Christopher J. McKenzie
Bernard A. Weintraub

For full biographical listings, see the Martindale-Hubbell Law Directory

BIGHAM ENGLAR JONES & HOUSTON (AV)

14 Wall Street, 10005-2140
Telephone: 212-732-4646
Cable: "Kedge"
RCA Telex: 235332 BEJHUR
Telefax: 2126190781 GR I II III; 2122279491 GR I II III
London, England Office: Lloyd's Suite 699, 1 Lime Street.
Telephone: 71-283-9541.
Telex: 893323 BEJH G.
Telefax: 016262382 GR I II III.
Newark, New Jersey Office: One Gateway Center.
Telephone: 201-643-1303.
Telecopier: 201-643-1124.
Washington, D.C. Office: 1919 Pennsylvania Avenue, N.W., Suite 300.
Telephone: 202-736-2150.
Telefax: 202-223-6739.
Long Beach, California Office: 301 Ocean Boulevard, Suite 800.
Telephone: 310-437-5155.
Telefax: 310-495-3273.

MEMBERS OF FIRM

Douglas A. Jacobsen
Joseph A. Kilbourn
James J. Taylor
James B. McQuillan
James S. McMahon, Jr.
John T. Kochendorfer
Louis G. Juliano
Jay Levine
George R. Daly
John E. Cone, Jr.
John MacCrate, III
Francis A. Montbach
Robert J. Phillips, Jr.
Stephen M. Marcusa
William R. Connor, III
Robert E. Hirsch
Thomas R. Pattison
Marilyn L. Lytle
Peter I. Broeman
Donald T. Rave, Jr.
Stephen V. Rible
William C. Brown, III
Adrian Mecz (Resident, London, England Office)
Helen M. Benzie
Chris Christofides
Paul Ambos
Lawrence B. Brennan
Martin J. Flannery, Jr.
John V. Coulter, Jr.
Karin A. Schlosser
Martin J. Nilsen

Frederick J. Pomerantz

COUNSEL

Alfred J. Morgan, Jr.
Laurence W. Levine

William P. Sullivan, Jr.

ASSOCIATES

Brian D. Bornstein (Resident Associate, Newark, New Jersey)
Barbara D. Burke (Not admitted in NY; Resident Associate, Washington, D.C.)
Joseph T. Caufield
Elaine P. Chryssochoos
Patrick J. Corbett
George S. Evans, Jr.
Paul C. Fonseca (Resident Associate, Newark, New Jersey)
Aileen J. Fox
Christopher J. Keegan (Resident Associate, London, England)
Edward F. Kenny, III (Resident Associate, Long Beach, California)
Timothy P. Lennon
Frederick A. Lovejoy
Gregory J. Mayer
Michael K. Rappaport
Brian H. Reis
Giselle M. Samuely
Frank G. Sinatra
Christopher F. Smith
Douglas E. Szulman
Stacey Tranchina
Michelle L. Wilson (Resident Associate, London, England)

For full biographical listings, see the Martindale-Hubbell Law Directory

BOBROW GREENAPPLE SKOLNIK & SHAKARCHY, P.C. (AV)

630 Third Avenue, 10017
Telephone: 212-953-6633
Fax: 212-949-6943
New Rochelle, New York Office: Suite 1115, 271 North Avenue.
Telephone: 914-632-5050.
Fax: 914-576-1614.

Henry B. Bobrow
Lawrence Greenapple
Steven D. Skolnik
Jacob S. Shakarchy

Steven J. Brog

Peter J. A. O'Hanlon
Marsha Weitz Rotheim

(*See Next Column*)

OF COUNSEL

Walter A. Bobrow (Resident, New Rochelle Office)
Byron K. Burnett

For full biographical listings, see the Martindale-Hubbell Law Directory

BONDY & SCHLOSS (AV)

6 East 43rd Street, 10017
Telephone: 212-661-3535
FAX: 212-972-1677
Cable Address: "Lawfirm"

Eugene L. Bondy (1886-1977)
Norman P.S. Schloss (1887-1956)
Jules N. Bloch (1918-1983)
Edward Lee (1908-1986)
I. Russell Stein (1897-1987)

MEMBERS OF FIRM

Joel I. Berson
John Catterson
Joel S. Forman
Robert Jay Haber
Mark A. Harmon
Shira Nadich Levin
Earle K. Moore
David E. Nierenberg
Joseph S. Rosenthal
Gerald L. Sobol

OF COUNSEL

Martin A. Stoll

For full biographical listings, see the Martindale-Hubbell Law Directory

BRAUNSCHWEIG RACHLIS FISHMAN & RAYMOND, P.C. (AV)

1114 Avenue of the Americas, 10036
Telephone: 212-944-5200
Telecopier: 212-944-5210

Robert Braunschweig
Stephen P. H. Rachlis
Bernard H. Fishman
Richard C. Raymond

OF COUNSEL

Jeffrey M. Herrmann
Jeffrey H. Teitel (Not admitted in NY)
William G. Halby
Gerard C. Smetana (P.C.)
Martin W. McCormack
Jacob Dolinger (Not admitted in NY)

Bruce D. Osborne

LEGAL SUPPORT PERSONNEL

William Hershkowitz

For full biographical listings, see the Martindale-Hubbell Law Directory

BROBECK, PHLEGER & HARRISON (AV)

A Partnership including a Professional Corporation
1301 Avenue of the Americas, 30th Floor, 10019
Telephone: 212-581-1600
Fax: 212-586-7878
San Francisco, California Office: Spear Street Tower, One Market.
Telephone: 415-442-0900.
Telecopier: 415-442-1010.
Los Angeles, California Office: 550 South Hope Street.
Telephone: 213-489-4060.
Telecopier: 213-745-3345.
Palo Alto, California Office: Two Embarcadero Place, 2200 Geng Road.
Telephone: 415-424-0160.
Telecopier: 415-496-2885.
San Diego, California Office: 550 West C Street, Suite 1300.
Telephone: 619-234-1966.
Telecopier: 619-236-1403.
Orange County, California Office: 4675 MacArthur Court, Suite 1000, Newport Beach.
Telephone: 714-752-7535.
Facsimile: 714-752-7522.
Austin, Texas Office: 620 Congress Avenue, Suite 320.
Telephone: 512-477-5495.
Fax: 512-477-5813.
Denver, Colorado Office: 1125 Seventeenth Street, 15th Floor.
Telephone: 303-293-0760.
Fax: 303-299-8819.
Brobeck Hale and Dorr International Offices:
London, England Office: Veritas House, 125 Finsbury Pavement, London EC2A 1NQ.
Telephone: 44 071 638 6688.
Facsimile: 44 071 638 5888.
Prague, Czech Republic Office: Brehova 1, 110 00 Praha 1,
Telephone: 422 232-8461.
Facsimile: 422 232-8444.

MANAGING PARTNER

Richard R. Plumridge

PARTNERS

Ellen B. Corenswet
Robert P. Wessely

OF COUNSEL

Joy F. Forster
Bonnie Garone

(*See Next Column*)

BROBECK, PHLEGER & HARRISON, *New York—Continued*

ASSOCIATES

Luci Staller Altman
Andrew Cadel
Courtney A. Dinsmore
Nigel L. Howard
Alexander D. Lynch
Kenneth L. Metzner

For full biographical listings, see the Martindale-Hubbell Law Directory

BROWN RAYSMAN & MILLSTEIN (AV)

120 West Forty-Fifth Street, 10036
Telephone: 212-944-1515
Fax: 212-840-2429
Los Angeles, California Office: 550 South Hope Street, 20th Floor.
Telephone: 213-624-1616.
Fax: 213-624-4663.
Hartford, Connecticut Office: City Place I, 185 Asylum Street.
Telephone: 203-769-6810.
Fax: 203-769-6816.
Newark, New Jersey Office: One Gateway Center.
Telephone: 201-596-1480.
Fax: 201-622-3317.

MEMBERS OF FIRM

Richard Raysman
Peter Brown
Julian S. Millstein
Michael Hirschberg
Barry G. Felder
Sylvia Khatcherian
Jeffrey B. Steiner
Robert M. Unger
Edward A. Pisacreta
Scott A. Steinberg
Gerard R. Boyce
Kenneth M. Block
Catherine M. McGrath
John H. Reid (Resident, Los Angeles, California)
Dan C. Aardal (Resident, Los Angeles, California)
Thomas C. Clark (Resident, Hartford, Connecticut)

COUNSEL

Michael A. Gerber
Michael I. Chakansky
Gabriela P. Cacuci

ASSOCIATES

John J. Lynch
John S. Rosania (Resident, Hartford, Connecticut)
George S. Trisciuzzi
James K. Landau
Paul J. Pollock
Kenneth A. Adler
Rand G. Boyers
Bruce A. Levy
Jeffrey D. Neuburger
Andrew L. Kramer
Melanie Finkel
Scott A. Weinberg
Robert Anthony Miller
Dov H. Scherzer
Nicholas Tanelli
Jeffrey P. Weingart
John C. Eichenberger
Nanette Claire Heide
David P. Stich
Robert R. Kiesel
Joseph William Chouinard
Susan B. Kalman (Resident, Los Angeles Office)
John C. Ohman
Martin Hillery
T. Anthony Howell
Catherine Termini
Horace H. Ng
Morlan Ty Rogers

For full biographical listings, see the Martindale-Hubbell Law Directory

BROWN & WOOD (AV)

One World Trade Center, 10048-0557
Telephone: 212-839-5300
Cable Address: "Browoodlaw"
Telex: 127324.
Telecopier: 212-839-5599
San Francisco, California Office: 555 California Street, 94104-1715.
Telephone: 415-772-1200.
Washington, D.C. Office: 815 Connecticut Avenue, N.W., Suite 701, 20006-4004.
Telephone: 202-973-0600.
Los Angeles, California Office: 10900 Wilshire Boulevard, 90024-3959.
Telephone: 310-443-0200.
London, England Office: Blackwell House, Guildhall Yard.
Telephone: 0171-606-1888.
Trenton, New Jersey Office: 172 West State Street, 08608-1104.
Telephone: 609-393-0303.
Tokyo, Japan Office: Shiroyama JT Mori Building, 3-1 Toranomon 4-chome, Minato-Ku.
Telephone: 011-813-5472-5360.
Hong Kong Office: Suite 2606, Asia Pacific Finance Tower, Citibank Plaza, 3 Garden Road, Central.
Telephone: 011-852-2509-7888.

MEMBERS OF FIRM

Gundars Aperans
Joseph W. Armbrust, Jr.
John Arnholz (Resident at Washington, D.C. Office)
Lawrence A. Bauer
I. Scott Bieler
Koren Blair
James A. Blalock III (Resident at Washington, D.C. Office)
E. Michael Bradley
Michael P. Braun
Douglas S. Brown (Resident at Los Angeles Office)
Frank P. Bruno
Regina L. Bryant-Fields (Resident at San Francisco Office)
David G. Casnocha (Resident at San Francisco Office)
Richard A. Cassell (Resident at London, England Office)

(See Next Column)

MEMBERS OF FIRM (Continued)

Craig E. Chapman (Resident at Tokyo, Japan Office)
James L. Copeland (Resident at San Francisco Office)
John M. Costello, Jr.
Kenneth T. Cote
Robert J. Donatucci
Walter T. Eccard (Resident at Washington, D. C. Office)
Stephen B. Esko
Mitchell Fenton
Edward J. Fine
Michael L. Fitzgerald
A. J. Alexis Gelinas
Clifford M. Gerber (Resident at San Francisco Office)
Richard L. Goard
Howard G. Godwin, Jr.
Martin E. Gold
William M. Goldman
James A. Gouwar
Eric S. Haueter (Resident at San Francisco Office)
Roger J. Hawke
Thomas A. Humphreys
Alan L. Jakimo
David J. Johnson, Jr. (Resident at Los Angeles Office)
Robert T. Jones (Resident at London, England Office)
Cathy M. Kaplan
Brian M. Kaplowitz
Ross Kaufman
John L. Kelly
Henry S. Klaiman
Mitchell Kleinman
Sharon A. Knight
Kenneth J. Kornblau
Robert M. Kreitman
Allan Neil Krinsman
Susan D. Lewis
F. Lee Liebolt, Jr.
Kenneth C. Lind (Resident at Los Angeles Office)
Dale W. Lum (Resident at Los Angeles Office)
John A. MacKinnon
Andrew J. Maloney
Renwick D. Martin
William R. Massey
Gerald J. McGovern (Resident at San Francisco Office)
Joseph McLaughlin
Wilson C. McLeod (Resident at London, England Office)
Christopher B. Mead (Resident at London, England Office)
Peter J. Michel
Henry F. Minnerop
Patricia A. Murphy
James E. Murray (Resident at Washington, D.C. Office)
John H. Newman
Michael P. Peck
A. Robert Pietrzak
Paul C. Pringle (Los Angeles and San Francisco Offices)
John A. Quisenberry
A. Francis Robinson, Jr.
Carlos A. Rodriguez
Daniel M. Rossner
R. J. Ruble
James J. Sabella
Charles J. Sanders
Mark R. Saunders
Homer D. Schaaf
Richard B. Schreiber (Los Angeles and San Francisco Offices)
Eileen Caulfield Schwab
Douglas A. Sgarro
Yoshiki Shimada
Peter T. Simor
Daniel J. Sitomer
Norman D. Slonaker
Thomas R. Smith, Jr.
Thomas McCarthy Souther
Eric D. Tashman (Resident at San Francisco Office)
Michael F. Taylor
Lawrence C. Tondel
Richard A. Van Dusen
Max Von Hollweg
E. Mark Walsh (Resident at Hong Kong Office)
Gail G. Watson
Judith Welcom
Karel Westerling
L. Markus Wiltshire (Resident at Hong Kong Office)
Michael G. Wolfson
Thomas G. Wood (Resident at San Francisco Office)
Patti T. Wu
James D. Zirin

OF COUNSEL

Richard Conway Casey
Philip W. Clark
Charles J. Johnson, Jr.
Robert L. Mitchell

COUNSEL

Christina Nelson Crosby (Resident at San Francisco Office)
Michael S. Danko (Resident at San Francisco Office)
Louis A. Evans
Catherine S. Gallagher (Resident at Washington, D.C. Office)
William L. Gormley (Resident at Trenton, New Jersey Office)
Laurin Blumenthal Kleiman
Susan Litwer
Steven A. Malsin
Christopher J. McCarthy
Michael S. Sackheim
Robert L. Vitale
James D. Yellen

ASSOCIATES

Amanda E. Allen
Alicia M. Alvarez
Thomas J. Amico
Stephen Wade Angus
Peter D. Arnold
A. Rick Atwood, Jr. (Resident at Los Angeles Office)
Julie Barnes
Jason M. Barnett
Ann P. Bienstock
Mark D. Blake (Resident at San Francisco Office)
Nicholas R. Brown
M. Rosalie Locsin Buenaventura
Lauren Z. Burnham
J. McGinnis Caldwell
James W. C. Canup (Resident at Washington, D.C. Office)
Nancy Marie Chilelli
Cedric Tienwei Chou (Resident at Hong Kong Office)
George Chung
Marie-Anne Clarke
Jennifer Coates
Maureen N. Coleman
J. Gerard Cummins
Patricia R. Cunningham
Michael Minxiang Dai (Resident at Hong Kong Office)
Dyke M. Davies (Resident at London, England Office)
W. Clay Deanhardt (Resident at San Francisco Office)
Keith B. DeLeon
Rosemarie Delgado-Krebs (Resident at Los Angeles Office)
Bennett I. Deutsch
Henry H. Ding
Elaine Donato
James Kevin Dougherty
Madeleine J. Dowling (Not admitted in NY)

(See Next Column)

BROWN & WOOD—*Continued*

ASSOCIATES (Continued)

Patricia L. Duffy (Resident at San Francisco Office)
R. Michael Durrer
Cecilia P. Dyba (Resident at San Francisco Office)
Barbara Jean Endres
Victoria A. Espinel
Richard B. Evans (Resident at Los Angeles Office)
Leslie K. Fairbanks
Karen M. Feher
John C. Feldkamp (Not admitted in NY)
John C. Fernando
John P. Fielding (Resident at Washington, D.C. Office)
Barbara A. Fiske (Resident at San Francisco Office)
Hugh V. Frame
Thomas L. Fraser
Thomas H. French
Christine R. Fryer
Edward E. Gainor (Resident at Washington D.C. Office)
Samir A. Gandhi (Resident at Washington, D.C. Office)
William J. Gannon
Robert A. Giallombardo
Susan M. Girard (Resident at London, England Office)
Javier Gonzalez-Sfeir
John A. Goodman
Alexandra I. Graf
Joshua G. Grunat (Resident at Los Angeles Office)
Jaea F. Hahn
Ellen W. Harris
Paul J. Housey
Brian M. Hoye (Resident at Los Angeles Office)
Bruce William Hurwitz
Thomas J. Jackamo, III
Emilio Jiménez
Sylvia R. Johnson (Resident at San Francisco Office)
David H. Kanefsky
Jack I. Kantrowitz
Neil J. Kaplan
Kevin James Kelly (Resident at Washington, D.C. Office)
Lynnette Kelly
Gordon S. Kiesling
Michael A. King
Howard M. Kleinman
Sheila Kles
Charles Gustaf Klink
Siegfried P. Knopf
Susanne M. Kogut (Resident at Washington, D.C. Office)
Michael T. Kohler
Brian P. Koscelansky
Mark J. Kowal
Jason Tzu-cheng Kuo (Resident at Hong Kong Office)
Nancy S. Kupfer (Not admitted in NY)
Scott E. Lehrer
Stephanie K. Leiter
Ria A. Levine
Huanting "Tim" Li
Elizabeth B. Lynch
Livia L. Maghiar
John C. Maguire (Not admitted in NY)
Mark S. Mandel
Gahmk S. Markarian (Not admitted in NY)
Jeanne M. Quinn Marks
Taisa Markus
William S. Martin (Resident at London, England Office)
Bridget McCarthy (Resident at San Francisco Office)
David Martin McCarthy (Resident at Los Angeles Office)
María De Los Angeles Meléndez
Gregory K. Miller (Resident at San Francisco Office)
Jonathan B. Miller
Russell A. Miller (Resident at San Francisco Office)
Neda N. Morvillo
David J. Moses
Andrew Novak
Stephanie M. Oana (Resident at Tokyo, Japan Office)
James O'Connor
Robert G. O'Connor (Resident at San Francisco Office)
Hedwig O'Hara
Daniel A. Osborn
Stephen Thomas Paine
Daniel F. Passage
Jonathan S Pearlroth
Edward F Petrosky, Jr
Teresa A. Polenz
David C. Powell (Resident at San Francisco Office)
John Quinones
Gisele C. Rainer (Resident at San Francisco Office)
William C. Rand
Gregory Raykher
Robert Charles Reuland
Daniel J. Rieken (Not admitted in NY)
K. Peter Ritter
Albert M. Rodriguez
Jane E. Rohrer (Resident at Los Angeles Office)
James N. Rosen
James Robert Roth (Resident at San Francisco Office)
Conrad P. Rubin (Not admitted in NY)
William E. Ryan III
Drew D. Salvest (Resident at London, England Office)
James P. Sawicz
Michael J. Schiavone
Henry C. Schmeltzer
Patricia A. Seddon
Diane D. Shulman
Gregory Slamowitz
Laurel J. Southworth
Lawrence J. Steele
Elizabeth Storch
Ruth Ann Strauss (Resident at San Francisco Office)
Y. Ping Sun
Brenda F. Szydlo
Michele Elise Taub
R. Blair Thomas (Not admitted in NY)
Cathleen M. Tiernan
Laura A. Tierney
Sean Tierney (Resident at San Francisco Office)
Reed W. Topham
Vincent C. Travagliato
Diana L. Weaver
David J. Weinberger
Keith A. Weller
Jane Welsh
Anne H. West (Resident at Los Angeles Office)
Jorge S. Young (Resident at San Francisco Office)
F. Michael Zachara

For full biographical listings, see the Martindale-Hubbell Law Directory

CAHILL GORDON & REINDEL (AV)

A Partnership including a Professional Corporation
(Cotton & Franklin)
80 Pine Street, 10005
Telephone: 212-701-3000
Cable Address: "Cottofrank New York"
Telex: (ATT) 127068 Cottofrank NYK; (MCI) 232184 CAGO UR
Facsimile: 212-269-5420
Confirmation: 212-701-3557
European Office: 19 rue Francois 1er, 75008, Paris, France.
Telephone: 33.1-47.20.10.50.
Facsimile: 33.1-47.23.06.38.
Telex: 842-642331; CGR 642331F.
Cable Address: "Cottofrank Paris."
District of Columbia Office: 1990 K Street, N.W., Washington, D.C., 20006.
Telephone: 202-862-8900.
Facsimile: 202-862-8958.
Cable Address: "Cottofrank Washington."

MEMBERS OF FIRM

Floyd Abrams
Robert A. Alessi
Roger Andrus
Michael A. Becker
Susan Buckley
Kevin J. Burke
P. Kevin Castel
James J. Clark
Walter C. Cliff (P.C.)
Benjamin J. Cohen
Marshall Cox
Thomas F. Curnin
W. Leslie Duffy
Patricia Farren
Bart Friedman
Joan Murtagh Frankel
Ciro A. Gamboni
William B. Gannett
Charles A. Gilman
Stephen A. Greene
Robert M. Hallman
William M. Hartnett
Thomas R. Jones
Allen S. Joslyn
Thomas J. Kavaler
Lawrence A. Kobrin
Immanuel Kohn
Edward P. Krugman
William T. Lifland
Michael Macris
Jonathan I. Mark
Gerard M. Meistrell
Roger Meltzer
Clifford L. Michel
John P. Mitchell
Mathias E. Mone
Donald J. Mulvihill (Resident Partner, Washington, D.C. Office)
Kenneth W. Orce
Roy L. Regozin
Richard L. Reinhold
Dean I. Ringel
Thorn Rosenthal
Richard J. Sabella
Jonathan A. Schaffzin
H. Richard Schumacher
John J. Schuster
Laurence A. Silverman
Howard G. Sloane
Laurence T. Sorkin
Leonard A. Spivak
Gerald S. Tanenbaum
Jonathan D. Thier
Michael P. Tierney
Robert Usadi
John R. Vaughan
George Wailand
Glenn J. Waldrip, Jr.
Gary W. Wolf
John R. Young
Daniel J. Zubkoff

SENIOR COUNSEL

Joseph P. Conway
David R. Hyde
Denis McInerney
Irwin Schneiderman
Ralph O. Winger

COUNSEL

Corydon B. Dunham
Samuel Estreicher
Philip A. Heimowitz
John J. Stanton, Jr.

EUROPEAN COUNSEL

Freddy Dressen (Paris, France Office)

SENIOR ATTORNEYS

L. Howard Adams
John H. de Boisblanc
Rory M. Deutsch
Joanne M. Hawkins
Kirsten Emigholz
Eric Hellerman
David Kelly
Marc J. Korpus
Dorothy Donahue Petras

For full biographical listings, see the Martindale-Hubbell Law Directory

CARTER, LEDYARD & MILBURN (AV)

2 Wall Street, 10005
Telephone: 212-732-3200
Facsimile: 212-732-3232
Telex: 226609 CLM UR
Cable Address: "Ledyard" NewYork
Midtown Office: 114 West 47th Street, New York, New York 10036.
Telephone: 212-944-7711.
Fax: 212-944-9738.
Washington, D.C. Office: Suite 870, 1350 I Street, N.W. 20005.
Telephone: 202-898-1515.
Fax: 202-898-1521.

MEMBERS OF FIRM

James E. Abbott
John K. Armstrong
Howard J. Barnet, Jr.
Charles L. Brock
Lawrence F. Carnevale
Clifford P. Case, III
Jerome J. Caulfield
Bernard Cedarbaum
Jerome J. Cohen
Richard B. Covey
William E. Donovan
Timothy J. Fitzgibbon (Not admitted in NY; Resident, Washington, D.C. Office)
Michael I. Frankel
James Gadsden

(See Next Column)

CARTER, LEDYARD & MILBURN, *New York—Continued*

MEMBERS OF FIRM (Continued)

Peter P. McN. Gates
Steven J. Glusband
Robert R. Grew
Robert L. Hoegle
(Not admitted in NY)
Beth D. Jacob
M. Davis Johnson
Jack Kaplan
Bernard J. Karol
Stephen L. Kass
Robert A. McTamaney
Vincent Monte-Sano
Neil R. Pearson
James W. Rayhill
Robert M. Riggs
Joseph M. Ryan
Heywood Shelley
Leo Silverstein
William H. Sloane
William F. Sondericker
John C. Sparkman
Marie A. Thomas
Theodore R. Wagner
John K. Whelan

GENERAL COUNSEL

Devereux Milburn

OF COUNSEL

William A. Cameron
Robert S. Erskine, Jr.
Jean M. McCarroll
George Minkin
Stanley F. Reed, Jr.

ASSOCIATES

Walker Mayo Allen, III
Thomas F. Bardo
Stanley D. Baum
Edmund J. Behan
Jeffrey Boxer
Barbara Block Brown
Stephen V. Burger
Patricia Z. Carpenter
John R. Casolaro
Kenneth P. Clark
Drake A. Colley
Elizabeth M. Cursio
Raymond R. Ferrell
Lisa Factor Fox
John F. Haire
Macculloch M. Irving
Peter K. Killough
Judy Kramer
Stephen F. Lappert
Robert G Lennon
Michelle A. Locher
Jonathan F. Mack
Robert C. Malaby
Lee A. Ohliger
Richard G. Pierson
Adam M. Shaw
Steven Sibol
(Not admitted in NY)
Christopher Hale Smith
Craig J.J. Snyder
Eric R. Wapnick
Joseph P. Yamin

For full biographical listings, see the Martindale-Hubbell Law Directory

CHADBOURNE & PARKE (AV)

30 Rockefeller Plaza, 10112
Telephone: 212-408-5100
Telecopier: 212-541-5369
Washington, D.C. Office: Suite 900, 1101 Vermont Avenue, N.W., 20005.
Telephone: 202-289-3000.
Telecopier: 202-289-3002.
Los Angeles, California Office: 601 South Figueroa Street, 90017.
Telephone: 213-892-1000.
Telecopier: 213-622-9865.
London, England Office: 86 Jermyn Street, SW1 6JD.
Telephone: 44-171-925-7400.
Telecopier: 44-171-839-3393.
Moscow, Russia Office: 38 Maxim Gorky Naberezhnaya, 113035.
Telephone: 7095-974-2424.
Telecopier: 7095-974-2425. International satellite lines via U.S.:
Telephone: 212-408-1190.
Telecopier: 212-408-1199.
Hong Kong Office: Suite 3704, Peregrine Tower, Lippo Centre, 89 Queensway.
Telephone: (852) 2842-5400.
Telecopier: (852) 2521-7527.
New Delhi, India Office: Chadbourne & Parke Associates, A16-B Anand Niketan, 110 021.
Telephone: 91-11-301-7568/7581/7582.
Telecopier: 91-11-301-7351.

MEMBERS OF FIRM

Donald Schapiro
Peter M. Ward
Michael B. Weir
David R. Tillinghast
Stuart D. Baker
Zachary Shimer
George E. Zeitlin
Norman Sinrich
Donald I Strauber
Richard M. Leder
Daniel J. O'Neill
Malcolm E. Martin
Edward P. Smith
Charles F. Gibbs
Eugene R. Sullivan, Jr.
Donald S. Rice
Whitney I. Gerard
Michael D. Hess
Bernard W. McCarthy
Morton E. Grosz
Robert J. Gillispie
Leslie John Schreyer
Henry J. Oechler, Jr.
Philip D. Beaumont
Charles K. O'Neill
Rigdon H. Boykin
Roy K. Meilman
Thomas E. Bezanson
William E. Holland
Jerome C. Katz
Peter R. Kolyer
Charles E. Hord, III
Eric J. Lobenfeld
Thomas C. Meriam
Barry H. Nemmers
Lorraine Massaro
Nancy W. Pierce
Peter N. Hillman
Steven L. Williamson
William G. Cavanagh
Mark E. Brossman
Richard Sonkin
Robert W. Sheehan
Andrew C. Coronios
Chaim Wachsberger
Emily F. Johnson
Robert J. Hausen
John J. Sarchio

(See Next Column)

MEMBERS OF FIRM (Continued)

Thomas J. Hall
Peter K. Ingerman
Kenneth P. Coleman
Thomas E. Riley
Ronald E. Richman
John T. Baecher
A. Robert Colby
Bruce G. Sheffler
Thomas J. McCormack
Deborah L. Guider
Garyowen P. Morrisroe
Robert A. Schwinger
Lawrence Rosenberg
Andrea N. Satty
Marc A. Alpert

COUNSEL

Arthur M. Mitchell, III
H. Hedley Stothers, Jr.
Richard G. Liskov
Mary Louise Guttmann
James C. La Forge
Mary T. Yelenick
Steven C. Schwartz

OF COUNSEL

Charles B. Lauren
Frank B. Stone
Harold L. Warner, Jr.
William H. Mathers
John Wilcox
Donald L. Deming
Robert A. Howes
Paul G. Pennoyer, Jr.
William M. Bradner, Jr.
Stephen L. Buchman
William J. Geen
David D. Brown, III

NEW YORK ASSOCIATES

Carole V. Aciman
Marian Baldwin
Peter N. Bassano
Gail C. Bassett
Christopher L. Beers
Brian J. Buttigieg
Patricia M. Carroll
John F. Cinque
Lorraine M. Cody
Marjorie L. Cohen
Philip H. Cohen
Philip J. Costa
Michael David
Barry A. Dinaburg
Vincent Dunn
Sarah E. Efroymson
Barry S. Eisler
John P. Ekberg, III
(Not admitted in NY)
Daniel E. Estrin
Arthur C. Fahlbusch, Jr.
Edmund J. Ferdinand III
Eileen M. Fields
Douglas M. Fried
Kathleen E. Gardner
John O. Gerald, Jr.
Marjorie M. Glover
William A. Greason
Toni C. Hamburg
Cindy D. Hanson
Brian G. Hart
Karina Haum
Richard A. Horodeck
Timothy M. Hughes
Dean L. Jarmel
Lauren D. Kelly
Rebecca Kramnick
Chet A. Kronenberg
Charles F. Lacina
Juliette M. La Chapelle
Robert J. Laughlin
Morton I. Lorge
Monique A. Mc Clure
Hugh G. McCrory, Jr.
W. Colm McKeveny
Neil E. Mellen
David M. Mellgard
Lisa Ann Menelly
Brian A. Miller
Anthony L. Millin
James Mirro
Sean M. Mitts
Nancy L. Montmarquet
Jose Luis Murillo, Jr.
Joseph J. Nauman
Rachel H. Park
Debra M. Patalkis
Robert S. Pruyne
Bruce J. Rader
Gregory B. Reilly, III
(Not admitted in NY)
John P. Reilly
Amy J. Roberts
Jeffrey A. Robins
Lester Ross
Ralph A. Rossi, II
(Not admitted in NY)
Margherita L. Russo
Lawrence E. Savell
Richard E. Signorelli
Gregg D. Smith
Kevin C. Smith
Richard G. Sobel
Susan J. Stromberg
Dennis M. Sughrue
Stephen Turano
M. Corina Vegas
Steven L. Vollins
David L. Wallace
Paul L. Weber
Eric D. Welsh
Cindy Wenig
Austin T. Wilkie
Phoebe A. Wilkinson
Nicholas R. Williams

WASHINGTON, D.C. OFFICE
RESIDENT PARTNERS

Edmund S. Muskie
William S. D'Amico
John B. O'Sullivan
Keith Martin
Cornelius J. Golden, Jr.
Robert F. Shapiro
Russell S. Frye
David M. Raim
Nancy M. Persechino
Thomas E. Hirsch III
William K. Perry
Ellen H. Woodbury
Andrew A. Giaccia
Peter F. Fitzgerald
Keith W. Kriebel
Kenneth R. Pierce

RESIDENT COUNSEL

Lynn N. Hargis
Leslie S. Ritts

RESIDENT OF COUNSEL

Edmund E. Harvey

LOS ANGELES, CALIFORNIA OFFICE
RESIDENT PARTNERS

Richard J. Ney
Jonathan F. Bank
Peter R. Chaffetz
Jay R. Henneberry
Linda S. Dakin

RESIDENT COUNSEL

Kenneth J. Langan
Stuart M. de Haaff

LONDON, ENGLAND OFFICE
RESIDENT PARTNER

Paul A. Randour

(See Next Column)

CHADBOURNE & PARKE—*Continued*

RESIDENT COUNSEL

Peter K. Eck

MOSCOW, RUSSIA OFFICE

PARTNER

William E. Holland

GENERAL DIRECTOR

Genrikh P. Padva (Not admitted in NY)

RESIDENT COUNSEL

John T. Connor, Jr.
Robert E. Langer

RESIDENT ASSOCIATES

Alexander J. Buyevitch (Not admitted in NY)
Mikhail A. Rozenberg (Not admitted in NY)
Melissa J. Schwartz
Natalie Menshikova Whitman (Not admitted in NY)

HONG KONG OFFICE

RESIDENT PARTNERS

Peter D. Cleary
Robert J. Bohme

RESIDENT COUNSEL

Martin C.M. Bashall (Not admitted in the United States)

RESIDENT ASSOCIATES

Kerin Cantwell
Mitchell A. Silk
George He Zhu

NEW DELHI, INDIA OFFICE

RESIDENT PARTNER

Gregory N. Ullman

RESIDENT ASSOCIATES

Anand S. Dayal
Sadhana Kaul
Meaghan McGrath
Jeffrey B.L. Meller

For full biographical listings, see the Martindale-Hubbell Law Directory

CLEARY, GOTTLIEB, STEEN & HAMILTON (AV)

One Liberty Plaza, 10006
Telephone: 212-225-2000
Cable Address: "Clearglaw New York"
Telex:
WUI 62985
Facsimile: 212-225-3999
Washington, D.C. Office: 1752 N Street, N.W., Washington, D.C. 20036.
Telephone: 202-728-2700.
Paris, France Office: 41, Avenue de Friedland, 75008 Paris, France.
Telephone: 33-1-4074-6800.
Brussels, Belgium Office: Rue de la Loi 23, Bte 5, 1040 Brussels, Belgium.
Telephone: 32-2-287-2000.
London, England Office: City Place House, 55 Basinghall Street, London EC2V 5EH England.
Telephone: 44-71-614-2200.
Hong Kong Office: 56th Floor, Bank of China Tower, One Garden Road, Hong Kong.
Telephone: 852-521-4122.
Tokyo, Japan Office: Morgan Carroll Terai Gaikokuho Jimubengoshi Jimusho, 20th Floor, Shin Kasumigaseki Building, 3-2, Kasumigaseki 3-Chome, Chiyoda-Ku, Tokyo 100, Japan.
Telephone: 81-3-3595-3911.
Frankfurt, Germany Office: Ulmenstrasse 37-39, 60325 Frankfurt am Main, Germany.
Telephone: 49-69-971-03-0.

George E. Cleary (1890-1981)
Leo Gottlieb (1896-1989)
Melvin C. Steen (1907-1992)
Fowler Hamilton (1911-1984)

COUNSEL

George W. Ball (Not admitted in NY)
Lyman M. Tondel, Jr.
James G. Johnson, Jr.
George DeSipio
Jerome E. Hyman
Mark W. Frawley, Jr.
Walter S. Rothschild
Richard Crawford Pugh
Thomas H. Hagoort
Peter S. Paine, Jr.

MEMBERS OF FIRM

Richard W. Hulbert
George Weisz
Ned B. Stiles
Alan Appelbaum
Edwin B. Mishkin
George M. Cohen
Stephen L. Dinces
J. Speed Carroll
Anthony C. Gooch
Roger W. Thomas
George J. Grumbach, Jr.
Peter Karasz
Louis Kahn
Mark A. Walker
Allan G. Sperling
Peter H. Darrow
James F. Munsell
Sandra S. Weiksner
Evan A. Davis
J. Webb Moniz
Robert T. Greig
Alan S. Dunning
Christopher H. Lunding
Laurent Alpert
Barry M. Fox
Victor I. Lewkow
Leslie N. Silverman
Robert L. Tortoriello
A. Richard Susko
Stephen H. Shalen
Richard F. Ziegler
Lee C. Buchheit
James M. Peaslee
Thomas J. Moloney
Edward D. Kleinbard
Alan L. Beller

(See Next Column)

MEMBERS OF FIRM (Continued)

Jonathan I. Blackman
William F. Gorin
Michael L. Ryan
Yaron Z. Reich
Richard S. Lincer
Jaime A. El Koury
Steven G. Horowitz
Andrea G. Podolsky
Steven M. Loeb
Donald A. Stern
Craig B. Brod
Jacques Reding (Not admitted in United States)
Sheldon H. Alster
Wanda J. Olson
Mitchell A. Lowenthal
Deborah M. Buell
Edward J. Rosen
James E. Millstein
Lawrence B. Friedman
Nicolas Grabar
Seth Grosshandler
William A. Groll
Janet F. Plache
David L. Sugerman
Howard Zelbo
David E. Brodsky
Arthur H. Kohn
Ana Demel
James R. Modrall
Raymond B. Check
Richard J. Cooper
Jeffrey S. Lewis

SPECIAL COUNSEL

Sandra M. Rocks
Bruce D. Gallant
Ellen M. Creede
S. Douglas Borisky

NEW YORK OFFICE

ASSOCIATES

Gail M. Aidinoff
Martin F. Arias
Gustavo Arnavat
John Berton
Taina Bien-Aime
Carl S. Bjerre
Elizabeth L. Blair
Catherine A. Borneo
Carol R. Bouchner
James L. Bromley
Beverly Lisa Brown
Juan Pablo Cappello
Anupam Chander
Michael R. Chayet
Anne Chwat
Alexander F. Cohen
Richard V. Conza
Carmen A. Corrales
Donna Costa
Stephanie Cotsirilos
Peter L. Critchell
Andrés de la Cruz (Not admitted in the United States; Legal Consultant on the Laws of Argentina)
Yves P. Denizé
Charles B. Deull
Ayala Deutsch
Juliet A. Drake (Not admitted in NY)
Amy G. Dulin
Lynn A. Dummett
Peter R. Eccles
Frank L. Eppes
Howard M. Erichson
Norman Menachem Feder
Daniel Feit
Dana G. Fleischman
Barry Dwayne Ford
Theresa A. Foudy
Mark P. Friedman
Sandra J. Galvis (Not admitted in NY)
Fern S. Ginsberg
Astrid B. Gloade
Paul E. Glotzer
Shawn A. Golden
David M. Goldman
Avi Goldstein
Lindsee P. Granfield
Lawrence T. Gresser
Scott H. Griff
Ellen J. Harvey
Steven M. Hecht
Burr Henly
Robin A. Henry
David H. Herrington
Mary S. Holland
Masahisa Ikeda
Michael S. Isikow
Jorge U. Juantorena (Not admitted in NY)
Lech R. Kalembka
Judith Kassel
Steven M. Knecht
Deborah P. Kubiak
Katharine Lauer
Martha A. Lees (Not admitted in NY)
Michele K. Leibson
David Leinwand
Joan J. Lewis-Osborne
Steven D. Lofchie
Raymond J. Lohier
David C. Lopez
Dorian M. B. Lowell
William Mackey
Patrick G. Marette
Mary M. McDonald
David S. Miller
Bernadette Miragliotta
Denise C. Morgan
Jonathan S. Mothner
Yolande I. Nicholson
Erika W. Nijenhuis
Michelle D. Onello
Elisabeth Z. Ostrow
David Parish
Stanley T. Park (Not admitted in NY)
Janine A. Pearce
John D. Perris
Alfred C. Perry
Roslyn I. Powell
Ya Qin
Leila Rachlin
Joshua H. Rawson
Matthew M. Ricciardi
Jeffrey A. Rosenthal
James E. Rossman
Rafael A. Ruiz-Ayala
Alberto G. Santos
Amy W. Schulman
Roger E. Schwed
Scott C. Senecal
Carol S. Shahmoon
Clive D. Sheldon
Michael E. Sherman
Paul J. Shim
Stephen M. Siderow
Shari Siegel
Colette G. Smith
John E. Smith
H. Christian Sorensen
Jacob C. Sun
Shahriar Tadjbakhsh
Fumihiro Takagi
Bonnie A. Teller
Margaret Thomas
Rekha Vemireddy
Melissa C. Vogel
James W. von Atzingen
James Q. Walker
Elizabeth H. Wang
Mary P. Watson
David E. Webb
Chaya F. Weinberg-Brodt
Michael D. Weinberger
Noreen R. Weiss
Sarah Leah Whitson
Neil Q. Whoriskey
Timothy A. Wilkins
Jonathan A. Willens
Alan S. Wilmit
Steven L. Wilner
Stephen P. Wink
Alicia E. Yamin
Martha S. Zawacki

(See Next Column)

CLEARY, GOTTLIEB, STEEN & HAMILTON, *New York—Continued*

WASHINGTON, D.C. OFFICE

COUNSEL

Robert C. Barnard
Fred D. Turnage

MEMBERS OF FIRM

J. Eugene Marans
Douglas E. Kliever
Daniel B. Silver
Kenneth L. Bachman, Jr.
Charles F. Lettow
Richard deC. Hinds
Sara D. Schotland
Mark Leddy
John C. Murphy, Jr.
Henry J. Plog, Jr.
Dana L. Trier
Eugene M. Goott
Janet L. Weller
Mitchell S. Dupler
Linda J. Soldo
Giovanni P. Prezioso
John T. Byam
John C. Palenberg
Matthew D. Slater
Steven N. Robinson
Michael R. Lazerwitz

SPECIAL COUNSEL

Scott N. Benedict
W. Richard Bidstrup
Linda S. Matlack

ASSOCIATES

Ricardo A. Anzaldúa-Montoya
William A. Baten
Barbara W. Bernstein
Julie B. Bloch
Matthew P. Blischak
Frank R. Borchert, III
Elizabeth M. Burke
Michael J. Byrnes
Robert W. Cook
George R. A. Doumar
Michael G. Egge
David I. Gelfand
Brandt J. Goldstein
Scott R. Goodwin
Kevin A. Griffin
Katherine C. Hall
Mitchell E. Herr
Jean E. Kalicki
Karen A. Kerr
Constance B. Kiggins
John M. Kincaid
Daniel C. Kolb
Jennifer M. Lester
Peter S. Levitt
Kristin S. Mackert
Judith R. Margolin
Michael A. Mazzuchi
Joyce E. McCarty
David H. McClain
Robert J. Mueller
Mark W. Nelson
Jon S. Nicholas
Michael F. O'Connor
Ruth E. Olson
Mitchell L. Rabinowitz
Charles E. Rhodes
Michael P. Shea
Steven K. Shevick
Andra J. Shuster
Mark A. Singley
Christopher G. Smith
Michael S. Steele
Kristen A. Stilt
Michael J. Sussman
Jo Anne Swindler
Sandra E. Trimble
Kirk Van Brunt
James G. Votaw
Julie A. Waddell
Amy Deen Westbrook
Carla L. Wheeler

For full biographical listings, see the Martindale-Hubbell Law Directory

COOPER & DUNHAM (AV)

1185 Avenue of the Americas, 10036
Telephone: 212-278-0400
Facsimile: 212-391-0525

MEMBERS OF FIRM

Gerald W. Griffin
Christopher C. Dunham
Ivan S. Kavrukov
Norman H. Zivin
Peter D. Murray
John P. White
Thomas G. Carulli
Lewis H. Eslinger
Jay H. Maioli
Robert B. G. Horowitz
Donald S. Dowden
Robert D. Katz
William E. Pelton
Peter J. Phillips
Donna A. Tobin

ASSOCIATES

Wendy E. Miller
Richard S. Milner
Robert M. Bauer
Albert Wai-Kit Chan
Matthew J. Golden
Matthew B. Tropper
Lewis J. Kreisler
Jeffrey L. Snow
Jeffrey A. Hovden
Kristina L. Konstas
Robert T. Maldonado
Mark S. Cohen

OF COUNSEL

John N. Cooper
Thomas F. Moran

LEGAL SUPPORT PERSONNEL

SCIENTIFIC ADVISORS

Nathan P. Letts
Elizabeth Ann Bogosian
A. David Joran
Thomas E. Phalen
Adrian Gerard Looney
Keum A. Yoon
Victor DeVito (Patent Agent)

For full biographical listings, see the Martindale-Hubbell Law Directory

COUDERT BROTHERS (AV)

The Grace Building, 1114 Avenue of the Americas, 10036-7794
Telephone: 212-626-4400
Cable Address: "Treduoc"
Telecopier: 212-626-4120
Washington, D.C. 20006: 1627 I Street, N.W.
Los Angeles, California 90017: 1055 West Seventh Street, Twentieth Floor.
San Francisco, California 94111: 4 Embarcadero Center, Suite 3300.
San Jose, California 95113: Suite 1250, Ten Almaden Boulevard.
Paris 75008, France: 52 Avenue des Champs-Elysees.
London, EC4M 7JP, England: 20 Old Bailey.
Brussels B-1050, Belgium: Tour Louise. 149 Avenue Louise, Box 8.
Beijing, People's Republic of China 100020: Suite 2708-09, Jing Guang Centre, Hu Jia Lou, Choa Yang Qu.
Shanghai, People's Republic of China 200002: c/o Suite 1804, Union Building, 100 Yanan Road East.
Hong Kong: 25th Floor, Nine Queen's Road Central.
Singapore 0104: Tung Centre, 20 Collyer Quay.
Sydney N.S.W. 2000, Australia: Suite 2202 State Bank Centre, 52 Martin Place.
Tokyo 107, Japan: 1355 West Tower, Aoyama Twin Towers, 1-1-1 Minami-Aoyama, Minato-ku.
Moscow, Russia: Ulitsa Staraya Basmannaya 14.
01301 Sao Paulo, SP, Brazil: Machado, Meyer, Sendacz, e Opice, Advogados, Rua da Consolacao, 247, 8 Andar.
Bangkok 10500, Thailand: Bubhajit Building, 20 North Sathorn Road, 10th Floor.
Ho Chi Minh City, Vietnam: c/o Saigon Business, 49-57 Dong Du Street, District 1.

MEMBERS OF FIRM

Frederic Rene Coudert (1871-1955)
Alexis C. Coudert (1914-1980)
Wendy L. Addiss
Charles E. Aster
Steven H. Becker
Dean C. Berry
David A. Boillot
Thomas D. Brislin
Peter S. Britell
Douglas F. Broder
Pamela T. Church
Edmund S. Cohen
Jeffrey E. Cohen
James C. Colihan
Frederic R. Coudert, III
Charles H. Critchlow
Michael G. Davies
Emilio A. Dominianni
Thomas J. Drago
Jonathan D. DuBois
Robert L. Eisen
James R. Eiszner, Jr.
Carolyn T. Ellis
Paul D. Friedland
Kevin W. Goering
Gerard V. Hannon
Andrew S. Hedden
Samuel Locke Highleyman, III
Elinor R. Hoffmann
Stephen Hogan
Robert N. Hornick
Stephen M. Hudspeth
Anthony C. Kahn
Frederick P. Konta
Mark D. Lebow
James Ross Macdonald, IV
Edwin Spencer Matthews, Jr.
E. Timothy McAuliffe
John N. McBaine
Timothy J. McCarthy
John Edward McDermott, Jr.
Brian E. McGunigle
Marvin E. Milbauer
Timothy J. O'Brien
Pamela Goodman Ostrager
Kenneth R. Page
Katheryn Clews Patterson
Darrell Prescott
William Rand
Clyde E. Rankin, III
A. James Redway (Resident)
Richard R. Reilly
Thomas J. Rice
Stuart Rubin
Edward T. Schorr
David A. Schwartz-Leeper
James B. Sitrick
Gordon B. Spivack
William Preston Tollinger, Jr.
Charles H. Wagner
Thomas J. Weber
Christopher M. Wells
Anthony Williams

OF COUNSEL

Robert C. Ciricillo
Ernst C. Stiefel

SPECIAL COUNSEL

Donald L. Magnetti

SENIOR ATTORNEY

Deborah Joan Goldstein

ASSOCIATES

John B. Allen
Daniela Amzel
Michael F. Anderson
Patricia M. Angus
Dana James Bolton
Scott C. Budlong
Geoffrey P. Burgess (Not admitted in NY)
Karen Bysiewicz
Jeffrey M. Cohen
Paul J. Crowley
Robert A. Day
S. Adam Deery
Richard A. De Palma
Russell A. Divak
C. Stefan Dombrowski
Mark G. Douglas
Brian C. Dunning
Jay A. Friedman
Maryann Gallagher
Robert G. Gibbons
Daniel Glaser
Evan W. Gray
Jonathan Green
Robin Ellyn Gruber
Jeanne M. Hamburg
Moon-Young Han
Elizabeth Ellis Harris
Lawrence S. Hartman
Steven John Hawes
Christine M. Hoey
Marshall P. Horowitz
Bradford Ted Howes
Mary Louise Johnson
Scott Thompson Jones
Claire R. Kelly
Marianna R. Kennedy
Remy N. Kormos
Thomas J. Mazzarisi
Lateef Mtima
Matthew J. Murabito
Kathleen M. Pacheco
Christopher C. Paci
Jeremy D. Platek

(See Next Column)

COUDERT BROTHERS—*Continued*

ASSOCIATES (Continued)

Francis C. Porada
Adelita C. Press
David George Richardson
Joshua D. Rievman
Albert J. Rim
Jane C. Rubens
Susan K. Rushing
Seth H. Ruzi
Gordon Schnell
Luigi Sensi
Peter Shimamoto
Michael Bradley Shulman
Debra T. Siton
Theodore Snyder
Patrice D. Stavile
Timothy A. Steinert
Suzanne St. Pierre
Tracey Fitzgerald Sullivan
Yodon Thonden
Mark S. Vecchio
Alexandra von Ferstel

WASHINGTON, D.C. OFFICE
RESIDENT PARTNERS

Milo G. Coerper
Richard N. Dean
Robert F. Pietrowski, Jr.
Arthur F. Sampson, III

RESIDENT ASSOCIATES

Kay Georgi
Mary E. Hartnett
James S. Keller
Rebecca A. Matthias
Susan M. Muchmore
Nancy J. Rosenfeld

LOS ANGELES, CALIFORNIA OFFICE
PARTNERS

Ronald W. Buckly
Richard J. Garzilli
R. David Jacobs
Victoria E. Marmorstein
Ralph C. Navarro
Seth A. Ribner
John A. St. Clair
Barrye L. Wall
Richard G. Wallace

RESIDENT ASSOCIATES

Francisco Javier Aparicio
Katherine Fleming Ashton
Bryan D. Biesterfeld
James Bryce Clark
Lillian Hou
David Huebner
Robert R. Jesuele
J. Monica Kim
Edward C. Meara
Nikola M. Mikulicich, Jr.
M. Nicole van Dam

SAN FRANCISCO, CALIFORNIA OFFICE
RESIDENT PARTNERS

Gary L. Benton (San Francisco Office Administrative Partner)
Ronald S. Katz (Managing Partner of California Offices)
Lillian K. Nakagawa
Peter G. Platt
Anthony Theophilos

ASSOCIATES

Victoria E. Brieant
Jeremy A. Cody
Janet A. Hart
Mary B. Neumayr
Melissa Obegi
Joakim E. Parker
Paul S. Schmidtberger
Diane L. Stewart
Mark H. Wildasin

SAN JOSE, CALIFORNIA OFFICE
PARTNERS

Gary L. Benton
Robert A. Christopher
Ronald S. Katz (Managing Partner of California Offices)

ASSOCIATES

Adam R. Bernstein
Richard J. Hart
Richard A. Jones
Bradley Nicholson
Perpetua B. Tranlong

PARIS, FRANCE OFFICE
RESIDENT PARTNERS

Jacques Buhart
Catherine Charpentier
William Laurence Craig
Jean-Patrice de la Laurencie
Charles Kaplan
Eric Laplante
Van Kirk Reeves
Robin Trevor Tait
Jonathan M. Wohl
George T. Yates, III (Managing Partner)

OF COUNSEL

Hubert de Mahuet
Didier Nedjar (European Counsel)
Jean-Claude Petilon

RESIDENT ASSOCIATES

Delphine Abellard
Monique R. Beguiachvili
Jean-Mathieu Cot
Olivier de Précigout
Laure Givry
Aline Gladiline
Arnaud Guérin
Hélène Lepetit
Michael G. Pekowsky
Michael Polkinghorne
Pascale Rouast-Bertier
Catherine Santoul
Philippe Shin
Elisabeth Terron

LONDON, ENGLAND OFFICE
RESIDENT PARTNERS

Barry Metzger
Steven R. Beharrell
Philip Anthony Burroughs
Hugh E. Thompson
Julian D.M. Lew (Resident)
Colin D. Long
Jeremy McCallum
Peter F. Simpson

(See Next Column)

RESIDENT ASSOCIATES

Stuart Blythe
Sara Bond
Jonathan Bor
Michael P. Chissick
Samantha Crowfoot
Richard Kennedy Guelff
Julian E. James
Jeffrey J. Miller
Dean Poster
Julian Stait
Kim Hoa To

BRUSSELS, BELGIUM OFFICE
PARTNERS

Jacques Buhart
Stephen O. Spinks
Paulette Vander Schueren

RESIDENT ASSOCIATES

Peter Alexiadis
Jean-Yves Art
Kent Karlsson
David Chijner
Hervé F. Cogels
Nathalie Gilson
Roland P. Montfort
Dr. Karl H. Pilny
Olivier Prost
Dirk Van Liedekerke

SPECIAL CONSULTANT

Prof. Valentine Korah

HONG KONG OFFICE
RESIDENT PARTNERS

Vivienne Bath
David Richard Halperin
W. Gage McAfee
Owen D. Nee, Jr. (Managing Partner)
Henry J. Uscinski
Sook Young Yeu

RESIDENT ASSOCIATES

Elizabeth A. Bowler
John C. Cole, Jr.
Cornelia S. Edelman
Jong-Dae Lee
Rupert X. Li
Jeffrey J. Miller
Steven L. Toronto (Not admitted in NY)

SINGAPORE OFFICE
RESIDENT PARTNERS

Irwin L. Gubman
Jeffrey Leow

SENIOR ATTORNEY

Richard L. Cassin, Jr.

RESIDENT ASSOCIATES

M. Tamara Box (Not admitted in NY)
Michael S. Horn
Efi Kremetis
Mark A. Nelson
Eleanor Siew-Yin Wong

SAO PAULO, BRAZIL
PARTNER

Ross Kaufman

SYDNEY OFFICE
RESIDENT PARTNERS

Peter Gregory Noble
Peter J. Norman

RESIDENT ASSOCIATES

Maria Theresa Polczynski
Mark S. Williamson

RESIDENT CONSULTANT

W. Warren Scott, III

BEIJING OFFICE
PARTNER

Douglas R. Aden

RESIDENT ASSOCIATES

Phillip William Chritton
Bruce R. Schulberg
Jingzhou Tao
Ning Zhu

SHANGHAI OFFICE
PARTNER

Adam Fremantle

RESIDENT ASSOCIATES

Kenneth Tung

TOKYO OFFICE
RESIDENT PARTNERS

Greg L. Pickrell (Resident)

RESIDENT ASSOCIATES

Julie N. Mack
Marilyn Selby Okoshi

MOSCOW OFFICE
RESIDENT PARTNERS

John F. Sheedy

MOSCOW OFFICE
RESIDENT ASSOCIATES

Andrew J. Fletcher
Marian M. Hagler
Yevgeny V. Nikiforov
Michael G. Pekowsky
Olga N. Sirodoeva

BANGKOK, THAILAND OFFICE
RESIDENT PARTNER

Lance J. Miller

RESIDENT ASSOCIATES

Vilaiporn Chalermlapasadorn
Chatchai Inthasuwan (Not admitted in the United States)
Yongsith Kosawititkul
Orasa Leelataweewud
Dr. Chanvitaya Suvarnapunya
Narissara Udomvongsa
Chayut Vichuprapa
Kamonmit Vudhijumnonk
Craig Alan Wilson

(See Next Column)

COUDERT BROTHERS, *New York—Continued*

VIETNAM OFFICE

RESIDENT PARTNERS

Michael J. Hagan

For full biographical listings, see the Martindale-Hubbell Law Directory

---

CRAVATH, SWAINE & MOORE (AV)

Worldwide Plaza, 825 Eighth Avenue, 10019
Telephone: 212-474-1000
Facsimile: 212-474-3700
Cable Address: "Cravath, New York"
Telex: 1-25547
International Telex: 620-976
London, England Office: 33 King William Street, 10th Floor, London, EC4R 9DU.
Telephone: 071-606-1421.
Facsimile: 071-860-1150.
Hong Kong Office: Suite 2609, Asia Pacific Finance Tower, Citibank Plaza, 3 Garden Road, Central, Hong Kong.
Telephone: 852-509-7200.
Facsimile: 852-509-7272.

Paul Drennan Cravath (1861-1940)
Robert Taylor Swaine (1886-1949)
Hoyt Augustus Moore (1870-1958)

MEMBERS OF FIRM

Allen F. Maulsby
John R. Hupper
Samuel C. Butler
John F. Hunt
George J. Gillespie, III
Thomas D. Barr
Melvin L. Bedrick
George T. Lowy
Robert Rosenman
Alan J. Hruska
John E. Young (Resident Partner, London Office)
James M. Edwards
David G. Ormsby
Richard J. Hiegel
Frederick A.O. Schwarz, Jr.
Christine Beshar
Robert S. Rifkind
David Boies
David O. Brownwood
Paul M. Dodyk
Richard M. Allen (Resident Partner, Hong Kong Office)
Thomas R. Brome
Robert D. Joffe
Herbert L. Camp
Allen Finkelson
Ronald S. Rolfe
Paul C. Saunders
Martin L. Senzel
Douglas D. Broadwater
Alan C. Stephenson
Max R. Shulman
Stuart W. Gold
John W. White
John E. Beerbower
Evan R. Chesler
Patricia Geoghegan
D. Collier Kirkham
Michael L. Schler
Daniel P. Cunningham
Kris F. Heinzelman
B. Robbins Kiessling
Roger D. Turner
Philip A. Gelston
Rory O. Millson
Neil P. Westreich
Francis P. Barron
Richard W. Clary
William P. Rogers, Jr.
James D. Cooper
Stephen L. Gordon
Robert A. Kindler
Daniel L. Mosley
Gregory M. Shaw
Peter S. Wilson
James C. Vardell, III
Robert H. Baron
Kevin J. Grehan
W. Clayton Johnson (Resident Partner, Hong Kong Office)
Stephen S. Madsen
C. Allen Parker
Marc S. Rosenberg
William B. Brannan
Lewis R. Steinberg
Susan Webster
William H. Widen
Timothy G. Massad
David Mercado
Rowan D. Wilson
John T. Gaffney
Peter T. Barbur
Paul Michalski
Sandra C. Goldstein
Thomas G. Rafferty

RETIRED PARTNERS

Roswell L. Gilpatric
Albert R. Connelly
Frank H. Detweiler
John H. Morse
Charles R. Linton
Allen H. Merrill
William J. Schrenk, Jr.
Henry P. Riordan
James H. Duffy
Steward R. Bross, Jr.
Benjamin F. Crane

EUROPEAN COUNSEL

Sarah C. Murphy (Resident, London Office)

SENIOR ATTORNEYS

Patsy Abelle
Constance M. Ayars
Peter M. Crevi
John Gerhard
Richard S. Lasker
Martin R. Levine
Paul D. Siniawer
William J. Whelan, III

SPECIALIST ATTORNEY-HONG KONG

Su Lin Han (Resident, Hong Kong Office)

For full biographical listings, see the Martindale-Hubbell Law Directory

CURTIS, MALLET-PREVOST, COLT & MOSLE (AV)

101 Park Avenue, 10178
Telephone: 212-696-6000
Telecopier: 212-697-1559
Cable Address: "Migniar d New York"
Telex: 12-6811 Migniard; ITT 422127 MGND
Washington, D.C. Office: Suite 1205 L, 1801 K Street, N.W.
Telephone: 202-452-7373.
Telecopier: 202-452-7333.
Telex: ITT 440379 CMPUI.
Newark, New Jersey Office: One Gateway Center, Suite 403.
Telephone: 201-622-0605.
Telecopier: 201-622-5646.
Houston, Texas Office: 2 Houston Center, 909 Fannin Street, Suite 3725.
Telephone: 713-759-9555.
Telecopier: 713-759-0712.
Mexico City, D.F., Mexico Office: Torre Chapultepec, Ruben Dario 281, Col. Bosques de Chapultepec, 11530 Mexico, D.F.
Telephone: 525-282-0444.
Telecopier: 525-282-0637.
Paris, France Office: 8 Avenue Victor Hugo.
Telephone: 45-00-99-68.
Telecopier: 45-00-84-06.
London, England Office: Two Throgmorton Avenue, EC2N 2DL.
Telephone: 71-638-7957.
Telecopier: 71-638-5512.
Frankfurt am Main 1 Office: Staufenstrasse 42.
Telephone: 069-971-4420.
Telecopier: 69-17 33 99.

MEMBERS OF FIRM

J. Dinsmore Adams, Jr.
Mark H. Barth
Alan Berlin
Marco A. Blanco
Roman A. Bninski
William L. Bricker, Jr.
Preston Brown (Resident Partner, Washington, D.C. Office)
Charles L. O. Buderi (Resident Partner, Mexico City, Mexico Office)
Morgan A. Casey, Jr.
Miner D. Crary, Jr.
Philip T. Davies
Ricardo J. Diez Hidalgo (Resident Partner, Houston, Texas Office)
John F. Egan
Anthony W. Fitzgerald (Resident Partner, Newark, New Jersey Office)
Peter E. Fleming, Jr.
Albert Francke, III
Edgar H. Garza-Morales
Robert J. Gruendel
Richard C. Hamlin
Lynn P. Harrison, III
George Kahale, III
Peter A. Kalat
T. Barry Kingham
Townsend J. Knight
Eliot Lauer
Daniel R. Lenihan
Yves E. Lepage
David R. Lindskog
Robert S. Lipton
Herbert M. Lord
Jeffrey D. Mamorsky
John N. Marden
Eileen P. Matthews
Jeremiah T. Mulligan
Mark H. O'Donoghue (Resident Partner, Mexico City Office)
Jeffrey N. Ostrager
Bruce B. Palmer (Resident Partner, London, England Office)
Joseph D. Pizzurro
Benard V. Preziosi, Jr.
Samuel Rosenthal (Resident Partner, Washington, D.C. Office)
Carl A. Ruggiero
Frank A. Russo (Resident Partner, Houston, Texas Office)
Jacques Semmelman
William B. Sherman
Turner P. Smith
Matias Alfonso Vega
Martin Wendel (Resident Partner, Newark, New Jersey Office)
Robert D. Whoriskey
Paulette S. Wolfson (Resident Partner, Houston, Texas Office)
Peter M. Wolrich (Resident Partner, Paris, France Office)
Laishley P. Wragg, Jr.
Jeffrey I. Zuckerman (Resident Partner, Washington, D.C. Office)

COUNSEL

Benjamin H. Balkind
Roger V. Barth (Resident, Washington, D.C. Office)
John M. Cochran, III (Resident Counsel, Paris, France Office)
Antonio M. Prida Peon Del Valle
Miguel I. Estrada Sámano (Not admitted in the United States)
Keith Highet (Resident Counsel, Washington, D.C. Office)
Alexander C. Hoagland, Jr.
Charles E. Stewart, III (Resident Counsel, Frankfurt, Germany Office)
Herbert Stoller

OF COUNSEL

Manuel R. Angulo
John P. Campbell
C. Thomas Godfrey
Ernest A. Gross
Kenneth N. LaVine

SPECIAL COUNSEL

Jan Marcantonio
Charles D. Riviezzo
Beth Turtz

ASSOCIATES

Leila S. Anglade (Resident, Paris, France Office)
Joseph J. Aragonés
Harold J. Bacon
James R. Banko
David M. Beilin
Alan Brody
Lisa A. Bronikowski

(See Next Column)

CURTIS, MALLET-PREVOST, COLT & MOSLE—*Continued*

ASSOCIATES (Continued)

Frances B. Carlisle
Antoinette N. Ceisler
Joseph F. Clyne
Eduardo A. Cukier
Robert N. Dawbarn
Christopher L. Deininger
Nancy E. Delaney
Neil Alan Dellar
Diana Derycz
Rena G. Donin
Erik Ellner
H. Douglas Garfield
Joseph P. Goldberg
Lawrence Goodman
Miriam K. Harwood
Jill A. Imparato
Christina M. Krescanko
Geoffroy P. Lyonnet (Not admitted in the United States; Resident, Paris France Office)
Albrecht S. Münch (Resident, Frankfurt, Germany Office)
Linda A. McGuire
Sarah E. Morgenthau
Michael J. Moscato
Anne Penachio
Graziella Pruiti
Michael C. Quinn
Santiago C. Rabassa (Resident, Mexico City, Mexico Office)
Steven J. Reisman
Michelle A. Rice
Kemal A. Sheikh
David B. Spanier
Robert E. Stemmons (Resident, London, England Office)
Ute Tünnermann-Kasch (Resident, Frankfurt, Germany Office)
Marc S. Taub
Philip H. Thomas
Harold Ullman
Philip T. von Mehren
Andrea Walker-Modu
Jeri C. Weber
Jim Y. Wilon

For full biographical listings, see the Martindale-Hubbell Law Directory

DAVIS POLK & WARDWELL (AV)

450 Lexington Avenue, 10017
Telephone: 212-450-4000
Cable Address: "DavisPolk, New York"
Telex: ITT-421341; ITT-423356
Telecopier: 212-450-4800.
Washington, D.C. Office: 1300 I Street, N.W.
Telephone: 202-962-7000.
Telecopier: 202-962-7111.
Paris, France Office: 4, Place de la Concorde, 75008.
Telephone: 011-331-40.17.36.00
Telecopier: 011-331-42.65.22.34.
Cable Address: "Davispolk Paris."
London, England Office: 1 Frederick's Place, EC2R 8AB.
Telephone: 011-44-71-418-1300.
Telex: 888238.
Telecopier: 011-44-71-418-1400.
Tokyo, Japan Office: In Tokyo practicing as Reid Gaikokuho-Jimu-Bengoshi Jimusho. Tokio Kaijo Building Annex, 2-1, Marunouchi 1-Chome, Chiyoda-Ku, 100.
Telephone: 011-81-3-201-8421.
Telecopier: 011-81-3-201-8444.
Telex: 2224472 DPWTOK.
Frankfurt, Germany Office: MesseTurm, 60308 Frankfurt am Main, Federal Republic of Germany.
Telephone: 011-49-69-97-57-03-0.
Telecopier: 011-49-69-74-77-44.
Hong Kong Office: The Hong Kong Club Building, 3A Chater Road.
Telephone: 852 533 3300.
Fax: 852 533 3388.

SENIOR COUNSEL

D. Nelson Adams
John P. Carroll, Jr.
Joseph Chubb **
Christopher Crowley
Allan A. A. Flynn
S. Hazard Gillespie
William A. Kaynor
Herbert M. Lobl
Bartlett H. McGuire ***
Richard E. Nolan
Donaldson C. Pillsbury
Philip C. Potter, Jr.
Andrew Y. Rogers
Richard B. Smith
Peter O. A. Solbert
William D. Tucker, Jr.

RETIRED PARTNERS

Lawrence E. Walsh
Jonathan M. Clark
Richard Moe

MEMBERS OF FIRM

Henry L. King
Edwin Deane Leonard
Samuel F. Pryor, III
Robert B. Fiske, Jr.
Edward S. Reid ****
James F. Dolan
Milton Carr Ferguson, Jr.
John A. Corry
Richard D. Spizzirri
Charles S. Hoppin
Troland S. Link
Lydia E. Kess
James W. B. Benkard
Colin E. Harley
Daniel F. Kolb
David J. Strupp
Guy Miller Struve
James Woodman Lloyd
Stephen H. Case ***
Francis J. Morison
Frank S. Moseley
Jeffrey Small
David C. Oxman
William Parsons, Jr.
Charles S. Whitman, III
Lewis B. Kaden
William Carleton Gifford
Arthur F. Golden
Steven F. Goldstone
Dennis S. Hersch
Winthrop B. Conrad, Jr.
Lowell Gordon Harriss
William F. Kroener, III ***
Richard Jay Sandler
Robert F. Wise, Jr.
John P. Cooney, Jr.
Robert Lee Heckart ******
Ogden N. Lewis
Bradley Y. Smith
Mikel M. Rollyson

(See Next Column)

MEMBERS OF FIRM (Continued)

Marlene J. Alva *
Peter R. Douglas
John Fouhey
Christopher Mayer
Pierre de Saint Phalle
Robert Jay Levine
John J. McCarthy, Jr.
Jerome G. Snider
William E. Wurtz
Howard A. Ellins
Patrick S. Kenadjian *****
William H. Weigel
Beverly Fanger Chase
Keith L. Kearney
Peter C. Kornman
James P. Lawton
Scott W. Muller ***
William L. Rosoff
George R. Bason, Jr.
Donald S. Bernstein
Alan Dean
John R. Ettinger
Gary G. Lynch
James Duncan Phyfe ******
E. Waide Warner, Jr.
Thomas Patrick Dore, Jr.
David W. Ferguson
Avishai Shachar
Linda A. Simpson
David M. Wells **
D. Scott Wise
Paul W. Bartel, II
Richard A. Drucker ******
Dennis E. Glazer
Paul Kumleben **
Karen E. Wagner
Laureen F. Bedell
John M. Brandow
Michael P. Carroll ***(Not admitted in NY)
Diane G. Kerr
Peter S. W. Levin
Carolyn E. C. Paris
Dennis E. Ross
Andrés V. Gil
Paul R. Kingsley
Joseph Rinaldi
John A. Bick
Thomas P. Ogden
Barbara Nims
Lawrence E. Weiman
Samuel Dimon ***(Not admitted in NY)
Carey Richard Dunne
Randall D. Guynn ***
Phillip R. Mills
Mark L. Shifke
Richard D. Truesdell, Jr.
Sarah Jones Beshar
John W. Buttrick
David L. Caplan
Bruce K. Dallas
James A. Florack
Ronan P. Harty
Yukako Kawata
Susan L. Merrill
Randal K. Quarles
Danforth Townley

COUNSEL

Charles H. B. Braisted
Theodore A. Doremus, Jr. ***(Not admitted in NY)
Jordan Luke ***(Not admitted in NY)
John D. Paton **

SENIOR ATTORNEYS

Margaret Miles Ayres ***(Not admitted in NY)
Julia L. Brickell
Lynn Earl Busath
Juliet Cain
Sue Ann Dillport
Thomas F. Godfrey
Marcie Ann Goldstein
Gary L. Granik
George R. Ince, Jr.
Sharon Katz
James L. Kerr
James D. Liss
James M. Lurie
James P. Mc Intyre
Jeffrey M. Oakes **
Laura J. Siegel
Joseph J. Sperber
Linda Chatman Thomsen ***

ASSOCIATES
NEW YORK OFFICE

Maryellen Abely
Cecilia T. Absher (Not admitted in NY)
David B. Aidelson
Tomoko Akashi
Leslie Hoffman Altus
Avraham Azrieli
M. Katherine Baird
Witold Balaban
Harry Ballan
Gregory G. Ballard
John W. Banes
Laura Rubenstein Barzilai
Richard M. Baumann
Karl H. Bazin
William Bergin
Kenneth M. Bernstein
Norwood P. Beveridge, III
Susan M. Boccardi
Caitlin E. Borgmann
Katrin Borland
Patrick A. Bradford
Peter H. Bresnan
Nicholas P. Brountas
Irene W. Bruynes
Karen Walker Bryce
Daniel N. Budofsky
Bradley J. Butwin
Norman B. Champ, III
Vincent T. Chang
Kenneth H. Chase
Loyti Cheng
Ada Clapp
John J. Clarke, Jr.
Joel M. Cohen
Joseph S. Cohn
J. Edmund Colloton, Jr.
John W. Connolly, III
Mary B. Conway (Not admitted in NY)
Jane Hewett Cooney
Rita M. Costabile
William E. Craco
Jonathan Crawford
William H. Crosby
John G. Crowley
Catherine V. Curry
Karin Seifert Day
Pieter J. de Jong
Donald N. Dirks
Patricia L. Doran
Mason H. Drake
Sarah Eaton
Ulrika Ekman
Kate B. Enroth
Marie T. Farrelly
Michael Feigenbaum
Robert M. Finkel
Laurel FitzPatrick
Gail A. Flesher
Rebecca E. Fletcher
Marianne Fogarty
Andrew G. Fossett
Douglas M. Fuchs
Craig P. Fynn
Norman C. Gillespie
Linda A. Ginsberg
Louis L. Goldberg
Stephen P. Goldberg
Alfredo S. Gomez
Eugene C. Gregor
Joseph P. Hadley
Joseph A. Hall
Tira Harpaz
Rachel C. Heyman
Stephen D. Hibbard
Joy Henry Hinton
Stephanie A. Holmes
Elizabeth A. Hone
Anne Berry Howe
David E. Izhakoff
Nora M. Jordan

(See Next Column)

DAVIS POLK & WARDWELL, *New York—Continued*

ASSOCIATES

NEW YORK OFFICE (Continued)

Veronica Jordan
Keenan R. Keller
Susan D. Kennedy
Elizabeth T. Kessenides
Frederick R. Kessler
Tracy Kimmel
Eleazer Klein
Stephen J. Kloepfer
Delphine Winthrop Knight
John K. Knight, Jr.
John Kole
Leonard Kreynin
William B. Kuesel
Marilyn C. Kunstler
Angelica Kwan
Lisa L. Lang
Nancy L. Lazar
Cathy Leef
Niall Lenihan
Seth R. Lesser
Jacqueline O. LiCalzi
Nancy B. Ludmerer
Keith F. Maxfield
(Not admitted in NY)
Timothy J. Mayopoulos
Tara E. McCaffrey
Patricia McLernon
K. Heather McRay
Jonathan E. Meyer
Linda Carol Mischel Eisner
Warren Motley
Peter Muller
Paul D. Murphy
James E. Murray
Eliseo E. Neuman
Caroline Coleman O'Neill
Patrick C. O'Reilly
Michael Fitzgerald Orman
Michael F. Osborne
Richard N. Osborne
Toni Ann Palter
Marjorie M. Pierre
Lawrence J. Portnoy
Marc J. Posner
Richard Charles Potok
Robert T. Powell
Mary Humes Quillen
Virginia Ann Quinn
Louise Rembar Radin
Thomas J. Reid
Marcelo L. Riffaud
Judith R. Rom
David Rosenfeld
James T. Rothwell
James P. Rouhandeh
Katrin N. Rouner
Kirsten E. Rutnik
Nancy L. Sanborn
Ian S. Schachter
Carole Schiffman
Elizabeth E. Schriever
Elizabeth Schutz
Jeffrey N. Schwartz
Terri A. Sewell
Everett H. Seymour, Jr.
Ayal Shenhav
Carol S. Silverman
Charles Simon
Paula M. Simpkins
Alexander G. Simpson
Po Y. Sit
Barry Sklar
Patrick J. Smith
Tat Man J. So
Elenne Song
Edward Daniel Sopher
Adina T. Spiro
Irene Steiner
James Steinthal
Robert R. Strang
Pimkaeo Sundaravej
Tiziana M. Tabucchi
William L. Taylor
William A. Torres
Deborah A. Torrisi
Wendy Lynn Trugman
Stephen T. Vehslage Jr.
Mario J. Verdolini, Jr.
Michael K. Vernier
Christine Vickery
Jonathan Walcoff
Joseph F. Warganz, Jr.
Michele S. Warman
Erika Diane White
Sharon J. Whitt
James H. R. Windels
D. Antony Wright
Raul F. Yanes
Soo Kyong Yi
Naoko Yoshimura
Dina V. Zissimopoulos

WASHINGTON, D.C. OFFICE

Jeffrey D. Berman
(Not admitted in NY)
Steven L. Chuslo
(Not admitted in NY)
Kathleen L. Ferrell
(Not admitted in NY)
David C. Finn
Beth Louise Golden
James Kent Lehman
(Not admitted in NY)
Jeanine P. McGuinness
Catherine M. O'Neil
Michael H. Pryor
(Not admitted in NY)
Graciela M. Rodriguez
Suzanne E. Rowe
(Not admitted in NY)
Arnon D. Siegel
Amy J. St. Eve
Margaret E. Tahyar
(Not admitted in NY)
Thomas E. Vita
Robert W. Weaver

PARIS, FRANCE OFFICE

Kathleen de Carbuccia
Arthur P. Morin
M. Elizabeth Pauchet
Joseph S. Roslanowick
Deborah Frank Shabecoff
Craig E. Sherman
Laurence Yansouni

LONDON, ENGLAND OFFICE

Julia K. Cowles
Lisa F. Firenze
Miriam Haber
Marcelle R. Joseph
Stowell R. R. Kelner
Deanna L. Kirkpatrick
Reinhard B. Koester
Nicholas Adams Kronfeld
Michael T. Mollerus

TOKYO, JAPAN OFFICE

Theodore A. Paradise
Steven C. Susser
Kaoru Umino

FRANKFURT, GERMANY OFFICE

Hannah L. Buxbaum
Richard A. Kahn
Mark G. Strauch

(See Next Column)

HONG KONG OFFICE

John D. Anderson
William F. Barron
Sandip C. Bhattacharji
Catherina Celosse
Show-Mao Chen
James B. Gatehouse
Yusing Ko
(Not admitted in NY)
Vivien Y. Liu
Averill L. Powers
Anthony Root
Raymond J. Simon

*Resident Paris Office
**Resident London Office
***Resident Washington, D.C. Office
****Resident Tokyo Office
*****Resident Frankfurt Office
******Resident Hong Kong Office

For full biographical listings, see the Martindale-Hubbell Law Directory

DEBEVOISE & PLIMPTON (AV)

875 Third Avenue, 10022
Telephone: 212-909-6000
Domestic Telex: 148377 DEBSTEVE NYK
Telecopier: (212) 909-6836
Los Angeles, California Office: 601 South Figueroa Street, Suite 3700, 90017.
Telephone: 213-680-8000.
Telecopier: 213-680-8100.
Washington, D.C. Office: 555 13th Street, N.W., 20004.
Telephone: 202-383-8000.
Telecopier: (202) 383-8118.
Paris, France Office: 21 Avenue George V 75008.
Telephone: (33-1) 40 73 12 12.
Telecopier: (33-1) 47 20 50 82.
Telex: 648141F DPPAR.
London, England Office: 1 Creed Court, 5 Ludgate Hill, EC4M 7AA.
Telephone: (44-171) 329-0779.
Telex: 88 4569 DPLON G.
Telecopier: (44-171) 329-0860.
Budapest, Hungary Office: 1065 Budapest, Révay Köz 2.III/2.
Telephone: (36-1)112-8067.
Telecopier: (36-1) 132-7995.
Hong Kong Office: 13/F Entertainment Building, 30 Queen's Road Central.
Telephone: (852) 2810-7918.
Fax: (852) 2810-9828.

Eli Whitney Debevoise
(1899-1990)
Francis T. P. Plimpton
(1900-1983)

MEMBERS OF FIRM

Roswell B. Perkins
William B. Matteson
Barry R. Bryan
George B. Adams
(Resident, London Office)
Andrew C. Hartzell, Jr.
Louis Begley
David V. Smalley
Cecil Wray, Jr.
Judah Best
(Washington, D.C. Office)
Robert L. King (Los Angeles, California Office)
Bevis Longstreth
Stephen J. Friedman
Meredith M. Brown
Bruce D. Haims
Standish Forde Medina, Jr.
Edward A. Perell
Theodore A. Kurz
Hugh Rowland, Jr.
(Resident, London Office)
Robert J. Gibbons
Barbara Paul Robinson
Jonathan A. Small
Vincent M. Smith
Paul H. Wilson, Jr.
Wolcott B. Dunham, Jr.
Jeffrey S. Wood
(Resident, Hong Kong Office)
Steven M. Alden
John H. Hall
John G. Koeltl
Ralph C. Ferrara
(Washington, D.C. Office)
James A. Kiernan III
(Resident, Paris Office)
Robert R. Bruce
(Resident, London Office)
Hans Bertram-Nothnagel
Martin Frederic Evans
Steven R. Gross
Roger E. Podesta
Woodrow W. Campbell, Jr.
Marcus H. Strock
Ralph Arditi
David A. Duff
Loren Kieve
(Washington, D.C. Office)
Bruce G. Merritt (Los Angeles, California Office)
Alan H. Paley
Robert J. Cubitto
Eric D. Roiter
(Washington, D.C. Office)
Robert N. Shwartz
Robert J. Staffaroni
Darius Tencza
John M. Allen, Jr. (Los Angeles, California Office)
Franci J. Blassberg
John B. Brady, Jr.
Steven Klugman
Richard D. Bohm
Peter L. Borowitz
Barry Mills
Deborah F. Stiles
Andrew N. Berg
Marcia L. MacHarg
(Washington, D.C. Office)
Steven M. Ostner
Robert F. Quaintance, Jr.
Michael E. Wiles
Daniel M. Abuhoff
Bruce P. Keller
John S. Kiernan
David W. Rivkin
Burt Rosen
Christopher Smeall
William B. Beekman
Michael W. Blair
Jeffrey P. Cunard
(Washington, D.C. Office)
John T. Curry, III
Seth L. Rosen
Edwin G. Schallert
Lawrence K. Cagney
Joseph P. Moodhe
Donald Francis Donovan
Gary M. Friedman
Richard F. Hahn
Lorna G. Schofield

(See Next Column)

DEBEVOISE & PLIMPTON—*Continued*

MEMBERS OF FIRM (Continued)

Andrew L. Sommer
David A. Brittenham
John M. Vasily
Anne E. Cohen
Thomas M. Kelly
Ivan E. Mattei
George E. B. Maguire
Peter R. Schwartz (Los Angeles, California Office)
Bruce E. Yannett

OF COUNSEL

James C. Goodale
Robert B. von Mehren
Philip S. Winterer

SPECIAL COUNSEL

Neil Kaplan (Resident, Hong Kong Office)

INTERNATIONAL COUNSEL AND COUNSEL

Thomas A. Ferrigno (Washington, D.C. Office)
Barbara W. Friedman
Jonathan H. Hines
Adele M. Karig
Linda B. Klein
Gary W. Kubek
Ellen Lieberman
Jane W. Meisel
Daniel G. Murphy (Los Angeles, California Office)
Nathan Ihru Nahm
Paul C. Palmer (Washington, D.C. Office)
A. David Reynolds
John B. Reynolds, III (Washington, D.C. Office)
Jonathan E. Richman
Stewart G. Rosenblum
Francis J. Sailer (Washington, D.C. Office)
David J. Schwartz
Gerald M. Shea (Paris, France Office)
James Cecil Swank (Paris, France Office)
Kirk P. Thornton
Ronald J. Weiss
Raymond G. Wells

RETIRED PARTNERS

Joseph Barbash
Stephen Benjamin
Chester Billings, Jr.
D. Bret Carlson
A. Fairfield Dana
Sidney G. Edwards
William Everdell
Robert J. Geniesse (Washington, D.C. Office)
Michael Harper Goff
Harold H. Healy, Jr.
John F. Johnston, 2nd
Guy Paschal
Richard D. Kahn
George N. Lindsay
Stanley R. Resor
Thomas T. Richmond
Asa Rountree
Oscar M. Ruebhausen
James B. Welles, Jr.

ASSOCIATES

Kevin T. Abikoff (Washington, D.C. Office)
V. Mary Abraham
Nicholas S. Acker
Khadija Amsrouy
Ann M. Ashton (Not admitted in NY)
Katherine Ashton (London, England Office)
Ann G. Baker (Paris Office)
Timothy K. Beeken
Nancy E. Berkeley
David H. Bernstein
Merril R. Bernstein
E. Raman Bet-Mansour (Paris Office)
Lisa B. Bialkin
Paul S. Bird
Craig A. Bowman
Julie Brandfield
David Brewster (London Office)
Kyra K. Bromley
Paul D. Brusiloff
Elizabeth Buckley
Philomena A. Burke
Angela Olivia Burton
Bridget M. Bush (Washington, D.C. Office)
Michele R.M. Campbell
Thomas C. Canfield
David A. Chalfin
Ch'in Lien Chang
Jacqueline C. Charlesworth
Deborah A. Chew
Judith L. Church
Timothy J. Clark
Barbara M. Cohen
Mark A. Cohen
Lance Cole (Washington, D.C. Office)
Mark A. Conley (Los Angeles, California Office)
Marianne Consentino
Blake M. Cornish
Nicholas A. Crincoli (Los Angeles, California Office)
E. Christi Cunningham
Margaret Andrews Davenport
Kevin C. Davis (Washington, D.C. Office)
John Dembeck
Sylvie DeParis-Maze (Paris Office)
Russell G. D'Oench, III
Elizabeth P. Donnem
Antoine d'Ornano (Paris Office)
Michael D. Dorum
Mary Ann Doyle
Giuliana H. Dunham
Peter M. Dwoskin
L. Kate Ellis
Alexander Ewing
Jeremy Feigelson
Linda Filardi
Isaac Finkle
Sara Watkins Fitts
Mark W. Friedman
Frank A. Fritz, III
Philip Galanes
Adam D. Gale
Lawrence M. Garrett (Washington, D.C. Office)
Michael J. Gillespie
Matthew T. Golden
Daniel J. Goldstein
Gregory V. Gooding (Hong Kong Office)
Robert D. Goodman
John A. Grossman
Stuart Hammer
Giselle P. Hantz
Michael P. Harrell
Russell Hartman
Ann L. Heilman
Steven P. Heineman
Stephen R. Hertz
David Hickok (Budapest Office)
Mary Beth Hogan
Judith Taft Horowitz
Abraham B. Hsuan
John P. Irwin, III
Charles E. Joseph
Philip J. Kahn
Roberta R. W. Kameda (Washington, D.C. Office)
Nancy Kane Curreri

(See Next Column)

ASSOCIATES (Continued)

Maidi S. Katz
Frances L. Kellner
Millie Kim
David D. Klein (Los Angeles Office)
Lothar A. Kneifel (Washington, D.C. Office)
Deborah E. Kurtzberg
Marc A. Kushner
Gerard Lacroix (Paris Office)
Barton C. Legum
Maurizio Levi-Minzi
Sandra L. Levy
Lisa H. Lewin
Xiaoming Li (Hong Kong Office)
Byungkwon Lim
Nancy L. Lomazzo
Luz M. Lopez
Vera Losonci
Peter J. Loughran (London Office)
Emmanuel Lulin (Paris Office)
L. Ashley Lyu
Ariadne Dawn Makris (Washington, D.C. Office)
Lena Mandel
Barbara M. Manning
Michael Der Manuelian
Lisa Green Markoff
Anne Marichez (Paris Office)
Theresa A. Marmo
Bonnie L. Martinolich
David P. Mason
Marcellus A. McRae (Los Angeles, California Office)
Carl J. Micarelli
Eniko (Szami) Mikscho
Frettra M. Miller
Kenneth T. Monteiro
Christopher A. Murphy
Mary Beth Navin
Harold A. Neu
Richard L. Nevins
Carl W. Oberdier
P. Bradley O'Neill
Michael T. O'Reilly (Los Angeles, California Office)
Andrew M. Ostrognai
Rodney W. Ott
Peter W. Paulsen
Jennifer L. Pariser
Marc Porosoff
Edmund H. Price (Washington, D.C. Office)
Richard Price
Thomas H. Prochnow
Ellen P. Quackenbos
Paul B. Radvany
Sarah M. Rechter
Robert M. Rosh
Thomas C. Rubin
David W. Runtz
Melissa G. Salten
Leigh R. Schachter
Laura J. Schisgall
Peter F.G. Schuur
Jacqueline Geller Scalisi
James C. Scoville (London Office)
Elizabeth S. Pagel Serebransky
Peter Shabecoff (Paris, France Office)
Rebecca F. Silberstein
Brian D. Simon
Eric Simonson
Steven J. Slutzky
Colby A. Smith
Joan M. Stout
Laura Taylor Swain
Herbert C. Thomas (Washington, D.C.)
Maxine C. Tusa
Harry Waizer
Stephen N. Waldman
Jennifer K. Weidman
Albert L. Wells
Andrea G. Wolfe
Naomi Wolfensohn
Christine A. Worrell
Alicia R. Zalesin
Louise Anne Zeller
Harry Zirlin

For full biographical listings, see the Martindale-Hubbell Law Directory

DECHERT PRICE & RHOADS (AV)

477 Madison Avenue, 10022
Telephone: 212-326-3500
Telefax: 212-308-2041
Philadelphia, Pennsylvania: 4000 Bell Atlantic Tower, 1717 Arch Street.
Telephone: 215-994-4000.
Washington, D.C.: 1500 K Street, N. W.
Telephone: 202-626-3300.
Harrisburg, Pennsylvania: Thirty North Third Street.
Telephone: 717-237-2000.
Princeton, New Jersey: Princeton Pike Corporate Center, P.O. Box 5218.
Telephone: 609-520-3200.
Boston, Massachusetts: Ten Post Office Square South, 12th Floor.
Telephone: 617-728-7100.
London, England: 2 Serjeants' Inn, EC4Y 1LT.
Telephone: (0171) 583-5353. (Also see Titmuss Sainer Dechert).
Brussels, Belgium: 65 Avenue Louise, 1050.
Telephone: (02) 535-5411.

PARTNERS IN NEW YORK

Margaret A. Bancroft
Claude A. Baum
Robert A. Cohen
Leonard J. Connolly
William K. Dodds
Malcolm S. Dorris
William F. Downey
Paul Gluck
Richard A. Goldman
William Goodwin
Ronald R. Jewell
Barbara J. Kelly
Fredric J. Klink
Roger Mulvihill
Thomas F. Munno
Harriet Orol
Paul Wm. Putney
Melvin A. Schwarz
Timothy A. Stafford
James E. Tolan
Bruce B. Wood
Robert D. Wurwarg

COUNSEL IN NEW YORK

Abbe G. Shapiro

OF COUNSEL IN NEW YORK

Paul A. Landsman

ASSOCIATES IN NEW YORK

Joseph Patrick Archie
Judith L. Bachman
George P. Barbaresi
Rose M. Burke
Catherine A. Duke
G. Monique Escudero (Not admitted in NY)
James M. Esposito

(See Next Column)

DECHERT PRICE & RHOADS, *New York—Continued*

ASSOCIATES IN NEW YORK (Continued)

Richard N. Golden
Anke C. Kramer
Joel H. Levitin
Bruce J. Lieber
Glyndwr P. Lobo
Jeffrey S. Lyons
John R. Marcil
Andrea Masley
Lisa M. Nasoff
Edward J. O'Connell
Debra DuBritz O'Gorman
Nina Peters
Nancy Prahofer
Lawrence B. Stoller
Rodney M. Zerbe

For full biographical listings, see the Martindale-Hubbell Law Directory

DEWEY BALLANTINE (AV)

1301 Avenue of the Americas, 10019-6092
Telephone: 212-259-8000
Cable Address: "Dewbalaw"
Telex: 12-6825
Facsimile: 212-259-6333
Washington, D.C. Office: 1775 Pennsylvania Avenue, N.W., 20006-4605.
Telephone: 202-862-1000.
Fax: 202-862-1093.
Los Angeles, California Office: 333 South Hope Street, 90071-1406.
Telephone: 213-626-3399.
Fax: 213-625-0562.
London, England Office: 150 Aldersgate Street, London EC1A 4EJ, England.
Telephone: 011-44-71-606-6121.
Fax: 011-44-71-600-3754.
Hong Kong Office: Asia Pacific Finance Tower, Suite 3907, Citibank Plaza, 3 Garden Road, Central, Hong Kong.
Telephone: 011-852-2509-7000.
Fax: 011-852-2509-7088.
Budapest, Hungary Office: Dewey Ballantine Theodore Goddard, Vadasz utca 31, H-1054 Budapest Hungary.
Telephone: (36-1) 111-9620.
Fax: (36-1) 112-2272.
Prague, Czech Republic Office: Dewey Ballantine Theodore Goddard, Revolucni 13, 110 00 Prague 1, Czech Republic.
Telephone: (42-2) 2481-0283.
Fax: (42-2) 231-0983.
Warsaw, Poland Office: Dewey Ballantine Theodore Goddard, ul. Klonowa 8, 00-591 Warsaw, Poland.
Telephone: 48-22-49-32-88.
Fax: 48-22-49-80-23.
Kraków, Poland Office: Dewey Ballantine Theodore Goddard, Pl. Axentowicza 6. 30-034 Kraków Poland.
Telephone: 48-12-340-339.
Fax: 48-12-333-624.

Thomas E. Dewey (1955-1971)
Arthur A. Ballantine (1919-1960)
Wilkie Bushby (1928-1970)
William P. Palmer (1926-1989)
John E. F. Wood (1940-1987)

MEMBERS OF FIRM

Alan M. Albright (Not admitted in NY; Resident Partner, Los Angeles, California Office)
Timothy J. Alvino
Joseph Angland
Emil Arca
Glenn S. Arden
Bradford J. Badke
Mark R. Baker
Fredric K. Bass
J. Goodwin Bennett (Resident Partner, Washington, D.C. Office)
William K. Bortz
James F. Bowe, Jr. (Resident Partner, Washington, D.C. Office)
David H. Brockway (Resident Partner, Washington, D.C. Office)
Richard J. Burdge, Jr. (Resident Partner, Los Angeles, California Office)
George T. Caplan (Resident Partner, Los Angeles, California Office)
John C. Chappell
Junaid H. Chida
Michael J. Close
John F. Collins
Wayne A. Cross
Christopher J. DiAngelo
C. Brooke Dormire
Joseph K. Dowley (Resident Partner, Washington, D.C. Office)
Lee Smalley Edmon (Resident Partner, Los Angeles, California Office)
Matt E. Egger (Resident Partner, Washington, D.C. Office)
Zori G. Ferkin (Resident Partner, Washington, D.C. Office)
Robert W. Fischer, Jr. (Resident Partner, Los Angeles, California Office)
James A. FitzPatrick, Jr.
Jonathan L. Freedman
John M. Friedman, Jr.
John G. Fritzinger, Jr.
L. Robert Fullem
Fred R. Gander (Resident, London Office)
David C. Garlock (Resident Partner, Washington, D.C. Office)
Douglas L. Getter
Thomas W. Giegerich
E. Ann Gill
Eileen B. Gordon
Charles R. Hager
Russel T. Hamilton
Stuart Hirshfield
Graham R. Hone
Thomas R. Howell (Resident Partner, Washington, D.C. Office)
Peter S. Humphreys
David M. Irwin
Carol W. Trencher Ivanick
Everett L. Jassy
Joseph M. Juhas (Resident Partner, Hong Kong Office)
Kevin A. Juran
Gerald A. Kafka (Resident, Washington, D.C. Office)

(See Next Column)

MEMBERS OF FIRM (Continued)

Frederick W. Kanner
Jack Kaufmann
Alicia M. Kershaw (Resident Partner, Washington, D.C. Office)
Bernard E. Kury
Harvey Kurzweil
Leonard P. Larrabee, Jr.
Felix B. Laughlin (Resident Partner, Washington, D.C. Office)
Jeff S. Liebmann
Stanton J. Lovenworth
Steven P. Lund
Myles V. Lynk (Resident Partner, Washington, D.C. Office)
Stephen R. MacDonald
Thomas C. Mazza
Kevin G. McAnaney (Resident Partner, Washington, D.C. Office)
Robert J. McDermott
W. Clark McFadden II (Resident Partner, Washington, D.C. Office)
David S. McLeod (Resident Partner, Los Angeles, California Office)
Jonathan W. Miller
Richard S. Miller
Saul P. Morgenstern
Sanford W. Morhouse
Brian J. Morris (Resident Partner, London Office)
Donald John Murray
Robert C. Myers
Paul L. Nash
Earle H. O'Donnell (Resident Partner, Washington, D.C.)
Stuart I. Odell
William J. Phillips
Morton A. Pierce
John A. Ragosta (Resident, Washington, D.C. Office)
Richard B. Romney
William W. Rosenblatt
Howard J. Rosenstock (Resident Partner, Washington, D.C. Office)
Peter J. Sacripanti
John J. Salmon (Resident Partner, Washington, D.C. Office)
Charles A. Severs, III
Richard Shutran
Rupert Alan Simpson
Robert M. Smith (Resident Partner, Los Angeles, California Office)
Val A. Soupios
John P. Spuches
Michael H. Stein (Resident Partner, Washington, D.C. Office)
Richard A. Stenberg
Donald W. Stever, Jr.
Joanna Ruth Swomley
Martha J. Talley (Resident Partner, Washington, D.C. Office)
Rodger W. Tighe
John K. Van De Kamp (Resident Partner, Los Angeles, California Office)
Kathy TeStrake Wales (Resident Partner, Los Angeles, California Office)
Clark E. Walter
Josephine C. Wang-Ho (Resident Partner, Hong Kong Office)
Gordon E. Warnke
William B. Warren
Alan Wayte (Resident Partner, Los Angeles, California Office)
Hershel Wein
George C. Weiss
Joe W. Williams
Jeffrey R. Witham (Resident Partner, Los Angeles, California Office)
Alan Wm. Wolff (Resident and Managing Partner, Washington, D.C. Office)
Donald F. Woods, Jr. (Resident Partner, Los Angeles, California Office)
Gary A. York (Resident Partner, Los Angeles, California Office)

COUNSEL

Laurel W. Glassman (Resident Counsel, Washington, D.C. Office)
B. Thomas Mansbach (Resident Counsel, Washington, D.C. Office)
O. Julia Weller (Resident Counsel, Washington, D.C. Office)

OF COUNSEL

Philip W. Buchen (Not admitted in NY)
Frank W. Crabill
Robert H. Haggerty
John J. Hogan, Jr.
Leonard Joseph
Kenneth R. La Voy, Jr.
C. Gorham Phillips
A. James Roberts III (Not admitted in NY; Resident Partner, Los Angeles, California Office)
Horace B. B. Robinson
E. Deane Turner
David E. Watts
William Wemple
Everett I. Willis

For full biographical listings, see the Martindale-Hubbell Law Directory

DONOVAN LEISURE NEWTON & IRVINE (AV)

30 Rockefeller Plaza, 10112
Telephone: 212-632-3000
Cable Address: "Donlard, New York"
Telecopiers: 212-632-3315; 212-632-3321; 212-632-3322.
Washington, D.C. Office: 1250 Twenty-Fourth Street, N.W.
Telephone: 202-467-8300.
Telecopier: 202-467-8484.
Los Angeles, California Office: 333 South Grand Avenue.
Telephone: 213-253-4000.
Cable Address: "Donlard, L.A."
Telecopier: 213-617-2368; 213-617-3246.
Paris, France Office: 130, rue du Faubourg Saint-Honoré, 75008, Paris.
Telephone: (011-33-1) 42-25-47-10.
Telecopier: 011-33-1-42-56-08-06.
Palm Beach, Florida Office: 450 Royal Palm Way.
Telephone: 407-833-1040.
Telecopier: 407-835-8511.

(See Next Column)

DONOVAN LEISURE NEWTON & IRVINE—*Continued*

MEMBERS OF FIRM

Richard D. Belford
Matthew E. Brady
William J. T. Brown
Andrew M. Calamari
Leah Campbell
James J. Capra, Jr.
A. Vernon Carnahan
Michael C. Cohen (Resident at Los Angeles, California Office)
J. Peter Coll, Jr.
Jeffrey A. Conciatori
James P. Corcoran
Edward F. Cox
Frank W. Cuiffo
Peter J. Gartland
Charles W. Gerdts, III
Kenneth N. Hart
Dana W. Hiscock
David R. Jewell
Douglas V. Lewis
A. Peter Lubitz
Louis C. Lustenberger, Jr.
John J. McCann
Aileen C. Meehan
Thomas A. Melfe
René de Monseignat (Not admitted in N.Y.; Resident at Paris, France Office)
Daniel R. Murdock
Kenneth E. Newman
Peter J. Norton
Joseph J. Onufrak
Gordon C. Osmond
Stuart B. Peerce
Linda E. Ransom
Kenneth G. Ray
Mitchell Rogovin (Resident at Washington, D.C. Office)
Hollis F. Russell (Resident, Palm Beach, Florida Office)
Peter G. Smith
Howard B. Soloway (Resident at Los Angeles, California Office)
James L. Stengel
Daniel J. Thomasch
Andrew J. Trubin
David S. Versfelt
John H. Wilkinson

ASSOCIATES

Frank R. Adams
Deborah A. Barnhart
Carolyn E. Bassani
Emmanuel K. Bentil
Laura Benzoni
Alison S. Berger
James J. Bergin
Peter A. Bicks
Mark E. Bokert (Not admitted in NY)
Sandrine M. Bonnet (Not Admitted in United States; Resident at Paris, France Office)
John R. Brautigam (Resident at Washington, D.C. Office)
Lawrence H. Cooke, II
Carol M. Degener
Richard J. DeMarco, Jr.
Laurie Strauch Dix
Michelle C. Dreyfus (Resident at Los Angeles, California Office)
Elyse D. Echtman
Lauren Elliot
Stephen G. Foresta
Jodi E. Freid
Kevin C. George
Andrew T. Hahn
Carolyn B. Handler
Christopher S. Harvey
Christoph C. Heisenberg
Deborah Lynn Hewitt
Klas S. D. Holm
Alan B. Howard
Joan M. Howe
Christine Huang
Marianna O. Huryn (Resident at Los Angeles, California Office)
Jeffrey A. Jakubowicz
Christopher P. Johnson
Sundria R. Lake
Anthony S. Lukaszewski
Christopher J. March
Karen M. McCarthy
Colette Kai Meyer (Resident, Palm Beach, Florida Office)
Vanessa E. Montag
Nina Sumers Myers
Fusae Nara
Michael C. Nicholson
Melissa A. Offen
L. Kevin O'Mara, Jr.
David F. Owens
David B. Pitofsky
Paolo A. Ramundo
Susan B. Reuben
Kathleen D. Rooney
Peter J. Schaeffer
Andrew W. Schilling
J. Michael Schroeder (Not admitted in NY)
Lindal L. Scott
Mithra Sheybani (Resident at Los Angeles, California Office)
Michael T. Stolper
Elizabeth A. Stradar
John T. Sutton
Laurence A. Tosi
Nicole M. van Ackere
Diana L. Weiss
Ilse Padegs Willems
Lesley E. Woodberry
John D. Worland, Jr. (Resident at Washington, D.C. Office)
Henri-Fréd éric Hibon

COUNSEL

William E. Colby (Resident at Washington, D.C. Office)
Hewitt A. Conway (Resident, Palm Beach, Florida Office)
Edward Everett
Reid L. Feldman (Resident at Paris, France Office)
Margaret Katherine Holihan
Arthur J. Mahon
Owen McGivern
Tuuli-Ann Ristkok

OF COUNSEL

Theodore S. Hope, Jr.
George S. Leisure, Jr.
David Teitelbaum

For full biographical listings, see the Martindale-Hubbell Law Directory

DRANOFF & JOHNSON (AV)

950 3rd Avenue
Telephone: 212-643-5351
Pearl River Office: Suite 900, One Blue Hill Plaza. P.O. Box 1629. 10965-8629.
Telephone: 914-735-6200.
Fax: 914-735-7585.
Tarrytown, New York Office: 220 White Plains Road.
Telephone: 914-631-1900.

MEMBERS OF FIRM

Sanford S. Dranoff
Sylvia Goldschmidt

(See Next Column)

Donna M. Genovese

DUANE, MORRIS & HECKSCHER (AV)

112 E. 42nd Street, Suite 2125, 10165
Telephone: 212-499-0410
Fax: 212-499-0420
Philadelphia, Pennsylvania Office: Suite 4200 One Liberty Place.
Telephone: 215-979-1000.
Fax: 215-979-1020.
Harrisburg, Pennsylvania Office: 305 North Front Street, 5th Floor, P.O. Box 1003.
Telephone: 717-237-5500.
Fax: 717-232-4015.
Wilmington, Delaware Office: Suite 1500, 1201 Market Street.
Telephone: 302-571-5550.
Fax: 302-571-5560.
Wayne, Pennsylvania Office 735 Chesterbrook Boulevard, Suite 300.
Telephone: 610-647-3555.
Allentown, Pennsylvania Office: 968 Postal Road, Suite 200.
Telephone: 610-266-3650.
Fax: 610-640-2619.
Cherry Hill, New Jersey Office: 51 Haddonfield Road, Suite 340.
Telephone: 609-488-7300.
Fax: 609-488-7021.

MEMBERS OF FIRM

Robert J. Hasday *
Michael H. Margulis *

*Hasday & Margulis, A Professional Corporation

For full biographical listings, see the Martindale-Hubbell Law Directory

DWIGHT, ROYALL, HARRIS, KOEGEL & CASKEY

(See Rogers & Wells)

EMMET, MARVIN & MARTIN, LLP (AV)

120 Broadway, 10271
Telephone: 212-238-3000
Cable Address: EMMARRO
Fax: 212-238-3100
Morristown, New Jersey Office: 10 Madison Avenue.
Telephone: 201-538-5600.
Fax: 201-538-6448.

MEMBERS OF FIRM

Thomas B. Fenlon
Thomas F. Noone (P.C.)
Lawrence B. Thompson
William A. Leet
David M. Daly
Peter B. Tisne
Michael C. Johansen
Robert W. Viets
Dennis C. Fleischmann
Eric M. Reuben
Jeffrey S. Chavkin
J. Christopher Eagan
Jesse Dudley B. Kimball
Stephen P. Cerow
Ellen J. Bickal
Edward P. Zujkowski
John P. Uehlinger
Irving C. Apar
Julian A. McQuiston
Maria-Liisa Lydon
Christine B. Cesare
Patrick A. McCartney
Matthew P. D'Amico
Brian D. Obergfell

OF COUNSEL

Guy B. Capel
Bernard F. Joyce (P.C.)
Richard P. Bourgerie
George H. P. Dwight

ASSOCIATES

Eunice M. O'Neill
Joseph M. Samulski
Sean M. Carlin
Alfred W. J. Marks
Eileen Chin-Bow
John M. Ryan
Francine M. Kors
Wendy E. Kramer
James C. Hughes, IV
Patricia C. Caputo
Bennett E. Josselsohn
Stephen I. Frank
Mildred Quinones
Anthony M. Harvin
Lynn D. Barsamian
Margaret H. Walker
Robert L. Morgan
Sally Shreeves
Michael Fotios Mavrides
Matthew A. Wieland
Eric E. Schneck (Resident, Morristown Office)
Lisa B. Lerner
Elizabeth K. Somers
Steven M. Berg
Michael E. Cavanaugh
Nancy J. Cohen
Peter L. Mancini
Stephen M. Ksenak

For full biographical listings, see the Martindale-Hubbell Law Directory

FINKELSTEIN BRUCKMAN WOHL MOST & ROTHMAN (AV)

575 Lexington Avenue, 10022-6102
Telephone: 212-754-3100
Telecopier: 212-371-2980
Stamford, Connecticut Office: 1 Landmark Square.
Telephone: 203-358-9200.
Telecopier: 203-969-6140.
Hackensack, New Jersey Office: 20 Court Street.
Telephone: 201-525-1800.
Telecopier: 201-489-4509.

(See Next Column)

FINKELSTEIN BRUCKMAN WOHL MOST & ROTHMAN, *New York—Continued*

MEMBERS OF FIRM

Allen L. Finkelstein
George T. Bruckman
Ronald Gene Wohl
Jack L. Most
Bernard Rothman
Richard M. Schwartz
Harold A. Horowitz
Bernard Ferster
Samuel R. Dolgow
Joel A. Fruchter
David T. Harmon
Joan Levin
Joseph Milano
Sidney Orenstein
T. Lawrence Tabak

ASSOCIATES

Michael R. Fleishman
Marlene Zarfes
David W. Wankoff
Gavin C. Grusd
David B. Bruckman
Maurice L. Miller

OF COUNSEL

Stuart Abrams
Eugenia M. Ballesteros
Sylvan J. Schaffer
Robert S. Barnett
James B. Rosenblum
Patrick J. Filan
Jacob H. Zamansky
Earle R. Tockman

SENIOR COUNSEL

Arthur S. Bruckman

For full biographical listings, see the Martindale-Hubbell Law Directory

FORD MARRIN ESPOSITO WITMEYER & GLESER (AV)

Wall Street Plaza, 88 Pine Street, 10005
Telephone: 212-269-4900
Facsimile: 212-344-4294
Cable Address: "Formarew-New York"

MEMBERS OF FIRM

Michael L. Anania
Charles A. Booth
Cushing O'Malley Condon
Elizabeth M. De Cristofaro
Thomas R. Esposito
William P. Ford
Victor G. Gleser (1948-1992)
Stuart C. Levene
Richard B. Marrin
Philip S. Plexico (1931-1983)
John J. Witmeyer III

ASSOCIATES

James M. Adrian
David A. Beke
Suzanne M. Bernard
Christopher G. Brown
Henry G. Burnett
James S. Felt
Justin M. Kinney
Edward M. Pinter
Stephen M. Reck
John J. Rossetti, Jr.
Michael J. Tricarico

For full biographical listings, see the Martindale-Hubbell Law Directory

FRIED, FRANK, HARRIS, SHRIVER & JACOBSON (AV)

A Partnership including Professional Corporations
One New York Plaza, 10004
Telephone: 212-859-8000
Cable Address: "Steric New York" W.U. Int.
Telex: 620223 W.U. Int.
Telex: 662119 W.U. Domestic: 128173
Telecopier: 212-859-4000 (Dex 6200).
Washington, D.C. Office: Suite 800, 1001 Pennsylvania Avenue.
Telephone: 202-639-7000.
Los Angeles, California Office: 725 South Figueroa Street.
Telephone: 213-689-5800.
London, England Office: 4 Chiswell Street, London EC1Y 4UP.
Telephone: 011-44-171-972-9600.
Fax: 011-44-171-972-9602.
Paris, France Office: 7, Rue Royale, 75008.
Telephone: (+331) 40 17 04 04.
Fax: (+331) 40-17-08-30.

MEMBERS OF FIRM

Charles A. Riegelman (1879-1950)
Arthur L. Strasser (1880-1967)
Hermann E. Simon (1900-1990)
George A. Spiegelberg (1897-1979)
Sam Harris (1912-1980)
William I. Riegelman (1913-1984)
Arnold Hoffman (1921-1993)
Howard B. Adler
Rachel L. Arfa
Marvin V. Ausubel (P.C.)
Jeffrey Bagner
Barry S. Berger
Kenneth R. Blackman
Linda R. Blumkin
Diane E. Burkley (Not admitted in NY)
Donald P. Carleen
Robert Cassanos
Marc P. Cherno
Peter v.Z. Cobb
Gary P. Cooperstein
Terrence A. Corrigan
Robert L. Cunningham, Jr.
Warren S. de Wied
Aviva F. Diamant
E. Donald Elliott (Not admitted in NY)
Lawrence A. First
Douglas H. Flaum
Arthur Fleischer, Jr. (P.C.)
Frederick H. Fogel
Stephen Fraidin (P.C.)
Victor S. Friedman (P.C.)
Herbert L. Galant (P.C.)
Stuart H. Gelfond
Robert E. Gerber
Matthew Gluck
David C. Golay
Peter S. Golden
Howard W. Goldstein
Franklin L. Green
Kevin R. Hackett
Jean E. Hanson

(See Next Column)

MEMBERS OF FIRM (Continued)

Edwin Heller (P.C.)
Lois F. Herzeca
Allen I. Isaacson (P.C.)
Valerie Ford Jacob
Jack L. Jacobson
Gregory P. Joseph
William Josephson
Robert E. Juceam
Stanley I. Katz
Stuart Z. Katz
Arthur S. Kaufman
Allen Kezsbom
Sanford Krieger
Meyer Last
Ann Berger Lesk
Richard O. Loengard, Jr. (P.C.)
William G. McGuinness
Jonathan L. Mechanic
Joshua Mermelstein
Craig F. Miller
Lee S. Parker
Lee S. Parks
Timothy E. Peterson
Harvey L. Pitt
Sheldon Raab (P.C.)
Jed S. Rakoff
Michael H. Rauch
F. William Reindel
Paul M. Reinstein
Harold E. Rosen
Laraine S. Rothenberg
Bruce D. Saber
Ira S. Sacks
Anthony E. Satula, Jr.
Joel Scharfstein
Daniel P. Schechter
Brad Eric Scheler
Richard M. Schwartz
Robert C. Schwenkel
David N. Shine
Peter L. Simmons
Bonnie Kayatta Steingart
Joseph A. Stern
Lewis A. Stern (P.C.)
Audrey Strauss
John C. Sullivan
Alexander R. Sussman
Debra M. Torres
Maxim H. Waldbaum
Gail L. Weinstein

COUNSEL

Milton R. Ackman (P.C.)
Franklin L. Bass (P.C.)
Arthur A. Feder (P.C.)
Hans J. Frank
Walter J. Fried
Herbert Hirsch
Leslie A. Jacobson
Frederick Lubcher (P.C.)
Benjamin Nassau
Robert H. Preiskel (P.C.)
Alan N. Resnick
Leon Silverman (P.C.)

ASSOCIATES

Ben I. Adler
Edward M. Alterman
Stuart M. Altman
Kenneth J. Applebaum
Marcie S. Balint
Lawrence N. Barshay
Demet Basar
James T. Bellerjeau
Gerald C. Bender
Rami A. Beracha
Andrew D. Beresin
Ira P. Berman
John M. Bibona
Laura Grossfield Birger
John A. Borek
James L. Brochin
Christopher C. Cambria
Jonathan H. Canter
Claudia Cantarella
Andrew T. Chalnick
Lily Chang
Jennifer Clarke
Andrew I. Cohen
Eric L. Cohen
Jennifer L. Colyer
Jeanette L. Cotting
Andrew J. Dady
Kimberley A. Danzi
Susan M. Davies
Aryeh Davis
Joanne Clifford Eaton
Mitchell L. Engler
Marcus A. Ernst
Christopher Ewan
Anne-Marie Feeley
Elia Fischer
Edmond T. Fitzgerald
Rachel S. Fleishman
Jessica Forbes
David Frank
Harvey Fuchs
JoAnne D. Ganek
Andrew T. Gardner
Alyssa E. Gelper
James P. Gerkis
Alan V. Goldman
Stephanie J. Goldstein
Jason D. Greenblatt
Emanuel C. Grillo
Paget Hope Gross
Lisa Gulick
Fabian Alejandro Guzman
Margaret R. Hamilton
Nancy Guller Hayt
Douglas W. Henkin
Joseph A. Herz
Seth R. Horowitz
Reinhard Humburg
Gregory J. Ikonen
Jocelyn L. Jacobson
Carine Jean-Claude
Mark Brent Joachim
Lynne A. Johnson
Chavie N. Kahn
Debra A. Karlstein
Susan J. Kent
Charlie King
Kim J. Kirk
Daniel J. Klotz
Honey L. Kober
Mark Kozlowski
William D. Lay
Corynne A. Lebetkin
Maura B. Leeds
Ronald A. Lehmann
Mark D. Lehrman
Cassandra F. Lentchner
Beth E. Levine
Deborah G. Levine
Tajlei Zöe Levis
Lisa A. Levy
Michael A. Levitt
Robert C. Lewis
Alex Lipman
Cara I. Londin
Joel L. London
Janice Mac Avoy
John P. MacDonald
Cynthia M. Martins
David McMillin
Edward O. Mehrfar
Richard M. Michaelson
Lora A. Moffatt
David M. Morris
Susana M. Namnum (Not admitted in NY)
David C. Plache
Margaret Pritchard
Eric H. Queen
Jay Harris Rabin
David C. Radulescu
Craig L. Reicher
Shimon A. Rosenfeld
Kenneth I. Rosh
Marian J. Rothman
Audrey M. Samers
Alan A. Samson
George E. Scargle (Not admitted in NY)
Jeffrey Schreiber
David I. Shapiro
Patrick J. Sheil
Barry G. Sher
Joseph J. Shmidman

(See Next Column)

FRIED, FRANK, HARRIS, SHRIVER & JACOBSON—*Continued*

ASSOCIATES (Continued)

Ross Z. Silver
David E. Sipiora
Joanne Galett Sperling
Paul Steinberg
Steven J. Steinman
Jeffrey S. Tolk
Jane C. W. Tse
Ann Tyson
Michael A. Ungar
Nancy J. Walker
Jane G. Wasman
Gregg L. Weiner
Jill L. Weintraub
Stephen A. Weiss
Matthew M. Weissman
Robin Wenig
Howard D. Westrich
Perry Wildes
Thea Ann Winarsky
Daniel A. Wuersch
Anthony S. Yoo (Not admitted in NY)
Judy Zecchin

For full biographical listings, see the Martindale-Hubbell Law Directory

GIBNEY, ANTHONY & FLAHERTY, L.L.P. (AV)

665 Fifth Avenue, 10022
Telephone: 212-688-5151
Telecopier: (212) 688-8315

MEMBERS OF FIRM

Wilson J. Gibney (1917-1987)
John F. Flaherty
Barry Zalaznick
James H. McGivney
Frederick W. Anthony
Robert V. Okulski
Stephen F. Ruffino
Gerald J. Dunworth
Stephen J. O. Maltby
Kenneth N. Sacks
Brian W. Brokate
Pierre Cournot
Wm. Lee Kinnally, Jr.
Peter Cousins
Melville Southard, Jr.
James Marshall Rae
Robert J. Costello
Bernard J. Ruggieri (P.C.)
Robert J. Bishop

ASSOCIATES

Ivan K. Blumenthal
Joseph Di Cesare
Beth M. Frenchman
Kenneth S. Horowitz
Paul G. Kelly
John Macaluso
Jill Marans
Angelo Egidio Paolo Mazza
Heather J. McDonald
Maria Mejia-Opaciuch
Anthony P. Piscitelli
Marc Ragovin
Sharon D. Simon
Gregory S. Torborg
Alan M. Weintraub

COUNSEL

Ralph F. Anthony
Robert L. Follick
John A. Bessich
Donald J. Williamson
Christopher Magrath
Richard L. Fisch
Stuart H. Brody
Frederick W. McNabb, Jr.
Paolo S. Grassi
Matthew H. Mataraso

For full biographical listings, see the Martindale-Hubbell Law Directory

GOLENBOCK, EISEMAN, ASSOR & BELL (AV)

437 Madison Avenue, 10022
Telephone: 212-907-7300
Telecopier: 212-754-0330
Telex: 291357 Answerback: GEAB UR

MEMBERS OF FIRM

Nathan E. Assor
Lawrence M. Bell
David J. Eiseman
Jeffrey T. Golenbock
Andrew C. Peskoe
Richard S. Taffet
Robert B. Goebel
Leonard Eisenberg

OF COUNSEL

Paul D. Siegfried
Charles D. Schmerler
Jeffrey S. Berger

ASSOCIATES

Andrew S. Bogen
Andrew M. Singer
Jacqueline G. Veit
Tracy J. Brosnan
Peter C. Moskowitz
Jonathan A. Adelsberg
Howard L. Meyerson
Sofia C. Hubscher
Martin S. Hyman
Lawrence R. Haut
John E. Page
Claudia M. Freeman

For full biographical listings, see the Martindale-Hubbell Law Directory

WILLIAM GOODSTEIN (AV)

444 Madison Avenue Suite 2302, 10022
Telephone: 212-888-3100
Cable Address: "Goodlegis New York"
Telex: 620525
Telecopier: (212) 888-0779

For full biographical listings, see the Martindale-Hubbell Law Directory

HALPERIN & HALPERIN, P.C. (AV)

18 East 48th Street, 10017
Telephone: 212-935-2600
Facsimile: 212-753-9173

(See Next Column)

David Halperin
Steven T. Halperin

For full biographical listings, see the Martindale-Hubbell Law Directory

HAWKINS, DELAFIELD & WOOD (AV)

67 Wall Street, 10005
Telephone: 212-820-9300
Cable Address: "Hawkdel, New York"
Telecopier: 212-514-8425
Hartford, Connecticut Office: City Place.
Telephone: 203-275-6260.
Newark, New Jersey Office: One Gateway Center.
Telephone: 201-642-8584.
Los Angeles, California Office: First Interstate World Center, 633 West Fifth Street, Suite 3550.
Telephone: 213-236-9050.
Fax: 213-236-9060.
Washington, D.C. Office: 1015 15th Street, N.W., Suite 930.
Telephone: 202-682-1480.

MEMBERS OF FIRM

Roger J. Bagley
Arto C. Becker (Resident, Los Angeles, California Office)
Howard I. Berkman
Ralph G. Brown
Kevin M. Civale (Resident, Los Angeles, California Office)
Arthur M. Cohen
John J. Cross, III (Resident, Washington, D.C. Office)
John V. Connorton, Jr.
C. Steven Donovan (Resident, New York, New York and Newark, New Jersey Office)
James R. Eustis, Jr.
Martin A. Geiger
Patricia G. Goins
Ronald C. Grosser
Donald G. Gurney
Robert I. Halpern
Wayne W. Hasenbalg (Resident, Newark, New Jersey Office)
Samuel I. Hellman
Brad C. Johnson (Resident, Washington, D.C. Office)
Stanley R. Kramer
W. Cullen MacDonald
Edward J. McCormick
Robert M. McCulloch, Jr.
John M. McNally (Not admitted in NY; Resident, Washington, D.C. Office)
C. Todd Miles
Brendan O'Brien
Elizabeth M. O'Connell
Beatty Barfield Page
Eric S. Petersen
John B. Pirog
Kenneth B. Roberts
Joseph P. Rogers, Jr.
Jeffrey B. Rosen
Robert C. Rosenberg
Elliot J. Schreiber
Richard L. Sigal
Lisa P. Soeder (Resident, Hartford, Connecticut Office)
Steven I. Turner
Bruce D. Van Dusen
Kam Wong
Howard Zucker

COUNSEL

Vanessa L. Bryant (Not admitted in NY; Resident, Hartford, Connecticut Office)

OF COUNSEL

Thomas J. Baer
Gerard Fernandez, Jr.
Charles L. Kades
John T. Sullivan

For full biographical listings, see the Martindale-Hubbell Law Directory

HERZFELD & RUBIN, P.C. (AV)

40 Wall Street, 10005
Telephone: 212-344-5500
Telefax: 212-344-3333
Los Angeles, California Office: Herzfeld & Rubin, 1925 Century Park East.
Telephone: 310-553-0451.
Telefax: 310-553-0648.
Miami, Florida Office: Herzfeld & Rubin, 801 Brickell Avenue, Suite 1501.
Telephone: 305-381-7999.
Telefax: 305-381-8203.
Fort Lauderdale, Florida Office: Herzfeld & Rubin, Gulf Atlantic Center, 1901 West Cypress Creek Road, Suite 415.
Telephone: 305-772-3599.
Telefax: 305-772-2469.
Boca Raton, Florida Office: Herzfeld & Rubin, Boca Bank Corporate Centre, 7000 West Palmetto Park Road, Suite 400.
Telephone: 407-394-2180.
Telefax: 407-394-2582.
Tampa, Florida Office: Barr, Murman, Tonelli, Herzfeld & Rubin, Enterprise Plaza, Suite 901, 201 East Kennedy Boulevard.
Telephone: 813-223-3951.
Telefax: 813-229-2254.
Edison, New Jersey Office: Hanlon, Lavigne, Topchik, Herzfeld & Rubin, Suite 200 Executive Plaza, 10 Parsonage Road.
Telephone: 908-549-9880.
Telefax: 908-549-3068.
Fairfield, New Jersey Office: Hanlon, Lavigne, Topchik, Herzfeld & Rubin, 30 Two Bridges Road.
Telephone: 201-808-0186.

Walter Herzfeld (1907-1968)
Herbert Rubin
Bernard J. Wald
Michael Hoenig
Edward L. Birnbaum
Ian Ceresney
Theodore Ness
Fred W. Rauskolb, III
John A. Schultz
Ellin M. Mulholland
Leonard M. Polisar
Daniel V. Gsovski

(See Next Column)

HERZFELD & RUBIN P.C., *New York—Continued*

Jeffrey L. Chase
Terry Myers
Harry P. Braunstein
Roger Arentzen
Larry S. Reich
Edward P. Speiran
David B. Hamm
Kenneth M. Greenfield
Jerome R. Hellerstein
Jonathan Herlands
William B. Randolph
John M. Schwartz
C. Thomas Schweizer
Howard L. Wexler
Harold J. McKay
Cary Stewart Sklaren
Eugene P. Feit
William C. Guida
Carl T. Grasso
Peter J. Kurshan
Jeffrey Golkin
Mark D. Rosenzweig
Risa G. Dickstein
Patricia Zincke
Isaac D. Szpilzinger
William H. Cox
Joseph B. Rosenberg

RESIDENT PARTNERS, LOS ANGELES, CALIFORNIA OFFICE

Richard L. Ackerman
Martin S. Friedlander
Seymour Kagan
Nicholas Browning, III
Craig L. Winterman
Michael A. Zuk
Richard W. Greenbaum

RESIDENT PARTNERS, NEW JERSEY OFFICES

Robert M. Hanlon
Lawrence N. Lavigne
Meryl J. Topchik

RESIDENT PARTNERS, MIAMI, FLORIDA OFFICE

Myron Shapiro
Jeffrey B. Shapiro
Michael D. Lozoff
Alfredo Marquez-Sterling
David I. Weiss
Luis R. Figueredo
David M. Krause
Stephen E. Nagin
Louis C. Thomas
Stuart A. Rosenfeldt
Gregory J. Ritter

Howard S. Edinburgh
Miriam Skolnik
Leslie T. Williams (Not admitted in NY)
Donna S. Friedman
Michael B. Gallub
Janet O'Connor Cornell
Noreen M. Giusti
Edward V. Schwendemann
Nancy Hershey Lord
Steven A. Steigerwald
Pamela L. Kleinberg
Linda Genero Sklaren
Clifford B. Aaron
Sharon Hyman
Michelle Russo
Eric B. Bettelheim
Linda Marie Brown
Maureen Doerner Fogel
Sandra K. Rotter
Alan D. Stewart
Michael L. Stonberg
John Edozie
Christian Hammerl
Wendy L. Prince
Kathleen Gill Miller
Peter E. Bentley
Elisabeth St. Blaise McCarthy
Michael E. Stern
Jeannine LaPlace
Julia S. Kim
Jeanie V. Lu
Daniel M. Erlij

OF COUNSEL

Cecelia H. Goetz
Gisella Levi Caroti
Martin A. Roeder
Charles A. Crum
Emanuel R. Gold
John J. Driscoll
Allen Murray Myers
Nicholas T. Kuzmack
Kevin J. Vernick
Arthur M. Strauss
Mortimer N. Felsinger
Martin Evans
Joseph E. Donat

SPECIAL COUNSEL

Aaron D. Twerski

For full biographical listings, see the Martindale-Hubbell Law Directory

HOLTZMANN, WISE & SHEPARD (AV)

1271 Avenue of the Americas, 10020
Telephone: 212-554-8000
Cable Address: "Lawise"
International Telex: 422664
Telecopier: 212-554-8181
Palo Alto, California Office: 3030 Hansen Way.
Telephone: 415-856-1200.
Telecopier: 415-856-1344.

Jacob L. Holtzmann (1888-1963)
Henry M. Wise (1880-1965)
Woolsey A. Shepard (1880-1960)
Robert H. Altman
Thomas L. Barton (Resident, Palo Alto, California office)
Steven D. Brown-Inz
Stephen M. Charme
Kevin F. Clancy
Susan Blackfield Crawford (Resident, Palo Alto, California office)
Jay H. Diamond
M. Scott Donahey (Resident, Palo Alto, California office)
George M. Duff, Jr.
Robert F. Ebin
David R. Foley
Bradley F. Gandrup, Jr.
Alan Gettner
John E. Grimmer
David W. Herbst (Resident, Palo Alto, California office)
Howard M. Holtzmann
Philip R. Hyde (Resident, Palo Alto, California office)
Christopher B. Kende
Alan S. Liebman
Arthur B. Malman
Benjamin C. O'Sullivan
Jerrold F. Petruzzelli (Resident, Palo Alto, California Office)
David A. Rosen
Robert M. Sedgwick
Stephen L. Sheinfeld

(See Next Column)

RETIRED PARTNERS

Eliot Bailen
William H. Brayer, Jr.
David Hawkins

ASSOCIATES

Alan J. Bernstein
Timothy R. Curry (Resident, Palo Alto, California Office)
Neal D. Frishberg
Amy L. Gilson (Resident, Palo Alto, California Office)
Gregg H. Kanter
Michelle E. Lentzner (Resident, Palo Alto, California Office)
Robert D. Lillienstein
Michael G. McClory (Resident, Palo Alto, California Office)
Susan K. Meyer (Resident, Palo Alto, California Office)
Edward L. Quevedo (Resident, Palo Alto, California Office).
James M. Smith (Resident, Palo Alto, California Office)
Benjamin F. Spater (Resident, Palo Alto, California Office)
Alison E. Spong (Resident, Palo Alto, California Office)

COUNSEL

Lorraine A. Clasquin (Resident, Palo Alto, California office)
Harvey J. Goldschmid
David S. Lindau
Marla B. Rubin
David N. Schachter (Resident, Palo Alto, California Office)

Representative Clients: Illegheny & Wstn. Engy. Corp.; Allen & Company; Ames Department Stores, Inc.; Coopers & Lybrand; Dax & Coe; Excalibur Technologies Corp.; F A O Schwarz; Fay's Incorporated; Lonza, Inc.; M/A-Com, Inc.

For full biographical listings, see the Martindale-Hubbell Law Directory

HUGHES HUBBARD & REED (AV)

One Battery Park Plaza, 10004
Telephone: 212-837-6000
Cable Address: "Hughreed, New York"
Telex: 427120
Telecopier: 212-422-4726
Paris, France Office: 47, Avenue Georges Mandel, 75116.
Telephone: 33.1.44.05.80.00.
Cable Address: "Hughreed, Paris."
Telex: 645440.
Telecopier: 33.1.45.53.15.04.
Los Angeles, California Office: 350 South Grand Avenue, Suite 3600, 90071-3442.
Telephone: 213-613-2800.
Telecopier: 213-613-2950.
Miami, Florida Office: 801 Brickell Avenue, 33131.
Telephone: 305-358-1666.
Telex: 51-8785.
Telecopier: 305-371-8759.
Washington, D.C. Office: 1300 I Street, N.W., 20005.
Telephone: 202-408-3600.
Telex: 89-2674.
Telecopier: 202-408-3636.
Berlin, Germany Office: Kurfürstendamm 44, W-1000 Berlin 15.
Telephone: 49030-8800080.
Telefax: 49030-88000865.
Telex: 185803KNAPA D.

Charles Evans Hughes (1862-1948)
Charles Evans Hughes, Jr. (1889-1950)
Francis C. Reed (1903-1974)
Allen S. Hubbard (1891-1981)
Orville H. Schell, Jr. (1908-1987)

MEMBERS OF FIRM

Ronald Abramson
Garett J. Albert
John S. Allee
Laura H. Allen
Joël Alquezar (Resident at Paris, France Office)
Bruce E. Aronson
Charles Avrith (Resident at Los Angeles, California Office)
Claire S. Ayer (Resident at Paris, France Office)
Lawrence F. Bates (Resident at Washington, D.C. Office)
Axel H. Baum (Resident at Paris, France and Berlin, Germany Offices)
Candace Krugman Beinecke
William T. Bisset (Resident at Los Angeles, California Office)
James H. Bluck
Anita L. Boomstein
Andrew H. Braiterman
Robert W. Brundige, Jr.
George A. Davidson
Edward S. Davis
Ellen S. Friedenberg
Richard S. Friedman (Resident at Los Angeles, California Office)
George A. Furst (Resident at Los Angeles, California Office)
Jeff H. Galloway
James W. Giddens
Thomas Gilroy
Robert Goldfarb (Resident at Miami, Florida Office)
Gilson B. Gray III
Jane F. Greenman
Rita M. Haeusler (Resident at Los Angeles, California Office)
Merrikay S. Hall
Steven A. Hammond
Spencer L. Harrison (Resident at Los Angeles, California Office)
Vilia B. Hayes
John K. Hoyns
Randall A. Huffman
Michael Iovenko
Claude E. Johnston
Gordon R. Kanofsky (Resident at Los Angeles, California Office)
Richard J. Kaplan (Resident at Los Angeles, California Office)
Howard Kaufman
Ed Kaufmann
Elizabeth J. Keefer (Resident at Washington, D.C. Office)
Dennis S. Klein (Resident at Washington, D.C. Office)
Norman C. Kleinberg
James B. Kobak, Jr.

(See Next Column)

HUGHES HUBBARD & REED—*Continued*

MEMBERS OF FIRM (Continued)

Ralph J. Kreitzman
Peter M. Langenberg (Resident at Los Angeles, California Office)
Theodore H. Latty (Resident at Los Angeles, California Office)
Kenneth A. Lefkowitz
David M. LeMay
James J. Lightburn (Resident at Paris, France Office)
Stephen Luger
William R. Maguire
Michael J. Maloney (Los Angeles, California Office)
Theodore V. H. Mayer
Dominique Mendy (Resident at Paris, France Office)
Beverly G. Miller
Mark R. Moskowitz (Resident at Los Angeles, California Office)
Gloria W. Nusbacher
Yasuo Okamoto
John E. Pearson (Resident at Miami, Florida Office)
Robert P. Reznick (Resident at Washington, D.C. Office)
Jerome I. Rosenberg
Kathleen M. Russo (Resident at Washington, D.C. Office)
Michael E. Salzman
Charles H. Scherer
Thomas G. Schueller
Jonathan A. Schur (Resident at Paris, France Office)
Jerome G. Shapiro
Richard M. Siegel
Robert J. Sisk
Vincent Sol (Resident at Paris, France Office)
Herschel E. Sparks, Jr. (Resident at Miami, Florida Office)
William R. Stein (Resident at Washington, D.C. Office)
John M. Townsend
Wayne L. Warnken
William A. Weber (Resident at Miami, Florida Office)
Thomas Henry Webster (Resident at Paris, France and Berlin, Germany Offices)
Daniel H. Weiner
David W. Wiltenburg

COUNSEL

John Westbrook Fager
John C. Fontaine
Allen S. Hubbard, Jr.
Richard A. Kimball, Jr.
Kalman A. Oravetz
Powell Pierpoint
Edward S. Redington
L. Homer Surbeck

OF COUNSEL

George W. Balkind
Andrea H. Bricker (Resident at Los Angeles, California Office)
Edward W. Forrester
Robert Hajdu
Albert P. Lindemann, Jr. (Resident at Washington, D.C. Office)
Clarence J. McGowan
L. Edwin Smart
Claude Suleyman (Resident, Paris, France Office)
Samuel Sultanik
John F. Walsh
John H. Young (Resident at Miami, Florida Office)
Antonio R. Zamora (Resident at Miami, Florida Office)

LITIGATION COUNSEL

Nicolas Swerdloff

SPECIAL COUNSEL

Andrew Alpern
Paul E. Hanau
Jeffrey H. Lapidus (Resident at Miami, Florida Office)
James J. Pastore
Lydia Tugendrajch

BANKING COUNSEL

Carolyn B. Levine

SENIOR ATTORNEY

Alan G. Kashdan (Resident at Washington, D.C. Office)

ASSOCIATES

Derek J. T. Adler
Michael P. Barbee (California Office)
William A. Barrett (Washington, D.C. Office)
Kimber K. Bell (California Office)
Bouziane Behillil (Paris, France Office)
Eveline Beltzung (Paris, France Office)
Anne P. Birge
Ira J. Blumberg (Washington, D.C. Office)
Nancy C. Braverman-Blume
Pamela R. Champine
Adam B. Cohen
Elaine M. Cohen (Florida Office)
Jeffrey R. Coleman
Laure Colli-Patel (Paris, France Office)
Melissa A. Crane
Patrick M. Creaven
Andrea deGorgey
Alexandre De Goüyon Matignon (Paris, France Office)
James F. Delaney
Laurence Dumure-Lambert (Paris, France Office)
Mark H. Duesenberg (Washington, D.C. Office)
Jodi L. Edelson
Juan J. Farach, Jr. (Miami, Florida Office)
Deena K. Feller
Jean S. Firestone
Peter C.W. Flory (Washington, D.C. Office)
J. Mario Fontes, Jr. (Florida Office)
Robert B. Funkhouser (Washington, D.C. Office)
Jack W. Geckler (Florida Office)
Leslie R. Gibson (Washington, D.C. Office)
Noah Graff
Zdenka S. Griswold
John G. Heard (Paris, France Office)
Joelle Herschtel (Paris, France Office)
Randy B. Holman (California Office)
Zvi Joseph
Scott A. Kamber
Carla A. Kerr
Walter T. Killmer, Jr.
Theodor W. Krauss (Paris, France Office)
Richard A. Lepowsky
Mark H. Levine (California Office)
Ross Lipman

(See Next Column)

ASSOCIATES (Continued)

Roberta R. Loomar (Florida Office)
Charles Lozow
Daniel S. Lubell
Andrew E. Lund
John J. Mandler (Washington, D.C. Office)
Romy Martin
Winston J. Maxwell (Paris, France Office)
John J. McGreevy
Tamara D. McKeown (Florida Office)
Claudia G. McMullin
James M. Modlin
Holly G. Moetell (Washington, D.C. Office)
Lois C. Moonitz (California Office)
Hazen A. Moore
Rachel L. Moritt
Donald J. Mosher
Laure Mottet (Paris, France Office)
Nalene Nath
Serge D. Nehama
Jorge A. Neri
Mary Kathleen O'Connor (Washington, D.C. Office)
Harry Packman, Jr.
Kolleen O. Pasternack (Florida Office)
Laura F. Patallo (Florida Office)
Robb W. Patryk
Patrick T. Perkins
Florence Perrot (Paris, France Office)
Tracy E. Poole
Mary E. Pratt
Eric D. Rapkin (Florida Office)
William D. Riedman
Ella L. Roberts
Pierre-Yves Romain (Paris, France Office)
Jacqueline L. Ross
Seth D. Rothman
Colleen Ryan (California Office)
Angela M. Santoro
Michael J. Scheer
Allen V. Scheiner
Daniel C. Schneider
Cheryl B. Schreiber
Debra B. Schupper
Alan N. Shapiro (Not admitted in NY)
David J. Shladovsky (California Office)
David L. Sorgen
Carol B. Stubblefield
Peter A. Sullivan
Bertrand Thouny (Paris, France Office)
George A. Tsougarakis
Chizuko S. Ueno
L. Mark Weeks
Marc A. Weinstein
Daniel Wolf (Washington, D.C. Office)
Stephanie Young

For full biographical listings, see the Martindale-Hubbell Law Directory

HUTTON INGRAM YUZEK GAINEN CARROLL & BERTOLOTTI (AV)

250 Park Avenue, 10177
Telephone: 212-907-9600
Facsimile: 212-907-9681

MEMBERS OF FIRM

Ernest J. Bertolotti
Daniel L. Carroll
Roger Cukras
Larry F. Gainen
G. Thompson Hutton
Samuel W. Ingram, Jr.
Paulette Kendler
Steven Mastbaum
Dean G. Yuzek
David G. Ebert
Shane O'Neill

ASSOCIATES

Warren E. Friss
Patricia Hewitt
Gail A. Buchman
Stuart A. Christie
Beth N. Green
Timish K. Hnateyko
Jeanne F. Pucci
Jane Drummey
Adam L. Sifre
Susan Ann Fennelly
Marc J. Schneider

For full biographical listings, see the Martindale-Hubbell Law Directory

JONES, DAY, REAVIS & POGUE (AV)

599 Lexington Avenue, 10022
Telephone: 212-326-3939
Cable Address: "JONESDAY NEWYORK"
Telex: 237013 JDRP UR
Telecopier: 212-755-7306
In Atlanta, Georgia: 3500 One Peachtree Center, 303 Peachtree Street, N.E.
Telephone: 404-521-3939.
Cable Address: "Attorneys Atlanta".
Telex: 54-2711.
Telecopier: 404-581-8330.
In Brussels, Belgium: Avenue Louise 480, 7th Floor, B-1050 Brussels.
Telephone: 011-32-2-645-14-11.
Telecopier: 011-32-2-645-14-45.
In Chicago, Illinois: 77 West Wacker.
Telephone: 312-782-3939.
Telecopier: 312-782-8585.
In Cleveland, Ohio: North Point, 901 Lakeside Avenue.
Telephone: 216-586-3939.
Cable Address: "Attorneys Cleveland."
Telex: 980389.
Telecopier: 216-579-0212.
In Columbus, Ohio: 1900 Huntington Center.
Telephone: 614-469-3939.
Cable Address: "Attorneys Columbus."
Telecopier: 614-461-4198.

(See Next Column)

JONES, DAY, REAVIS & POGUE, *New York—Continued*

In Dallas, Texas: 2300 Trammell Crow Center, 2001 Ross Avenue.
Telephone: 214-220-3939.
Cable Address: "Attorneys Dallas."
Telex: 730852.
Telecopier: 214-969-5100.
In Frankfurt, Germany: Triton Haus, Bockenheimer Landstrasse 42, 60323 Frankfurt am Main.
Telephone: 49-69-9726-3939.
Telecopier: 49-69-9726-3993.
In Geneva, Switzerland: 20, rue de Candolle.
Telephone: 011-41-22-320-2339.
Telecopier: 011-41-22-320-1232.
In Hong Kong: 1501 One Exchange Square, 8 Connaught Place.
Telephone: 011-852-2526-6895.
Telecopier: 011-852-2810-5787.
In Irvine, California: 2603 Main Street, Suite 900.
Telephone: 714-851-3939.
Telex: 194911 Lawyers LSA.
Telecopier: 714-553-7539.
In London, England: One Mount Street.
Telephone: 011-44-71-493-9361.
Cable Address: "Surgoe London WI."
Telecopier: 011-44-71-493-9666.
In Los Angeles, California: 555 West Fifth Street, Suite 4600.
Telephone: 213-489-3939.
Telex: 181439 UD.
Telecopier: 213-243-2539.
In Paris, France: 62, rue du Faubourg Saint-Honore.
Telephone: 011-33-1-44-71-3939.
Cable Address: "Surgoe Paris."
Telex: 290156 Surgoe.
Telecopier: 011-33-1-49-24-0471.
In Pittsburgh, Pennsylvania: 500 Grant Street, 31st Floor.
Telephone: 412-391-3939.
Cable Address: "Attorneys Pittsburgh".
Telecopier: 412-394-7959.
In Riyadh, Saudi Arabia: Law Offices of Saud M.A. Shawwaf, P.O. Box 2700.
Telephones: 011 (966-1) 465-6543, 011 (966-1) 464-8534 or 011 (966-1) 464-8540.
Telex: 401831 SAUCON SJ.
Telecopier: (966-1) 464-8480.
In Taipei, Taiwan: 8th Floor, 2 Tun Hwa South Road, Section 2.
Telephone: 011 (886-2) 704-6808.
Telecopier: 011 (886-2) 704-6791.
In Tokyo, Japan: Toranomon MT Building, 4th Floor, 10-3, Toranomon 3-Chome, Minato-Ku, Tokyo 105, Japan.
Telephone: 011-81-3-3433-3939.
Telecopier: 011-81-3-5401-2725.
In Washington, D.C.: Metropolitan Square, 1450 G Street, N.W.
Telephone: 202-879-3939.
Cable Address: "Attorneys Washington."
Telex: 89-2410 ATTORNEYS WASH.
Telecopier: 202-737-2832.

MEMBERS OF FIRM IN NEW YORK

Thomas V. Heyman
Marc S. Kirschner
Dennis W. LaBarre (Not admitted in NY)
David M. Mahle
Fredrick E. Sherman
Leonard C. Pojednic
Michael D. Shumate
Donald F. Devine
Susanna S. Fodor
Karl G. Herold
Robert J. Shansky
Thomas H. Sear
William F. Henze, II
Alan S. Kleiman
Theresa M. Gillis
Robert A. Profusek
Barry Michael Cass
Barry R. Satine
James F. Stomber, Jr.
Charles M. Carberry
John J. Hyland
Mary Ellen Kris
Joanne L. Bober (Not admitted in NY)
Dean M. Erger
Michael J. Templeton (Not admitted in NY)
Steven D. Guynn (Not admitted in NY)
Thomas J. Kelly
Richard E. Andersen
K. C. McDaniel
Wanda N. Payne
Cindy E. Tzerman
Robert W. Gaffey
Dan A. Kusnetz
Peter M. Lieb
Richard H. Sauer
Robert A. Zuccaro
Robert P. Hardy (Not admitted in NY)
Lawrence P. Gottesman
Jane A. Rue

OF COUNSEL

Masatami Otsuka
Robert W. Sparks
Ann F. Vinci
Linda L. D'Onofrio

SENIOR ATTORNEYS

Steven R. Golden
G. Warren Whitaker
Robert Iscaro

ASSOCIATES

Elaine H. Mandelbaum
Eric L. Rosedale
Steven C. Bennett
Brian F. Doran
M. Michèle Faber
Carol A. Surgens (Not admitted in NY)
Sally C. Carroll

(See Next Column)

ASSOCIATES (Continued)

Craig S. Gatarz
Michael B. Guss
Cathy Hershcopf
Randi L. Strudler
David K. Zacharisen
Michael R. Bassett
Harold K. Gordon
David F. Sternlieb
Christopher S. Visick (Not admitted in NY)
Marla S. K. Gale
Kenneth R. Goldberg
Kenneth R. Puhala
Robert K. Smits
Elizabeth H. Evans
Dyan L. Gershman
Andrew G. Kent
Emily S. Lau
Woon L. Kang
A. Michael Covino
Leon B. Friedfeld
Blaney Harper
James P. Jeffry
Torsten M. Marshall
Cara E. Mitnick
Gary D. Fromer
Steven D. Hutensky
Jason W. Kaplan
Jonathan L. Lederman
Brett M. Lev
Sean A. Low
M. Sharmini Mahendran
Daniel R. Milstein
Heidi Wendel
Haleh F. Bakhash
Robert J. Bush
Bradley E. Turk

For full biographical listings, see the Martindale-Hubbell Law Directory

KAYE, SCHOLER, FIERMAN, HAYS & HANDLER (AV)

425 Park Avenue, 10022
Telephone: 212-836-8000
Telex: 234860 KAY UR.
Facsimile: 212-836-8689
Washington, D.C.: McPherson Building, 901 Fifteenth Street, N.W., Suite 1100, 20005.
Telephone: 202-682-3500.
Telex: 897458 KAYSCHOL WSH.
Facsimile: 202-682-3580.
Los Angeles, California: 1999 Avenue of the Stars, Suite 1600, 90067.
Telephone: 213-788-1000.
Facsimile: 213-788-1200.
Hong Kong: 9 Queen Road Centre, 18th Floor.
Telephone: 852-8458989.
Telex: 62816 KAY HX.
Facsimile: 852-8453682; 852-8452389.
Beijing (Peking), People's Republic of China: Scite Tower, Suite 708, 22 Jianguomenwai Dajie, 100004.
Telephone: 861-5124755.
Telex: 222540 KAY CN.
Facsimile: 861-5124760.

MEMBERS OF FIRM

Benj. M. Kaye (1883-1970)
Harold L. Fierman (1898-1978)
Jacob Scholer (1887-1983)
James S. Hays (1901-1989)
Roger E. Berg
Julius Berman
Warren J. Bernstein
Alfred J. Bianco
Michael D. Blechman
Dominic A. Capolongo
Seymour H. Chalif
Sheldon A. Chanales
Andrea S. Christensen
David S. Copeland
T. Brent Costello
Michael J. Crames
Thomas L. Creel
Paul J. Curran
Donald J. Currie
Herbert S. Edelman
Edmund M. Emrich
Jeffrey M. Epstein
Peter L. Faber
Peter M. Fass
Albert M. Fenster
Nancy R. Finkelstein
Robert S. Finley
Peter M. Fishbein
Lynn Toby Fisher
Judith D. Fryer
Nancy E. Fuchs
Edmond Gabbay
Steven J. Glassman
Donen Gleick
Steven J. Glickstein
Alan Franklin Goott
Joel I. Greenberg
Joshua F. Greenberg
Rory A. Greiss
Louis J. Hait
Milton Handler
Joseph D. Hansen
Robert C. Helander
James D. Herschlein
Ellen R. Joseph
Joel Katcoff
Karen E. Katzman
Myron Kirschbaum
Lester M. Kirshenbaum
David Klingsberg
Stephen C. Koval
Andrew A. Kress
Ruthanne Kurtyka
Steven L. Lichtenfeld
Leslie H. Loffman
Andrew Macdonald
Michael Malina
Barry P. Marcus
Eric P. Marcus
Fred H. Marcusa
Kenneth G. M. Mason (Not admitted in NY)
Terry D. Novetsky
Jane W. Parver
Allan M. Pepper
Mitchel H. Perkiel
Thomas C. Ragan
Susan Berkman Rahm
Renée E. Ring
Stanley Rosenberg
Stuart L. Rosow
Aaron Rubinstein
Martin S. Saiman
Sanford J. Schlesinger
Willys H. Schneider
Milton J. Schubin
Madelaine L. Schwab
Steven L. Schwarcz
Richard C. Seltzer
Milton Sherman
Randolph S. Sherman
Thomas A. Smart
Gerald Sobel
Arthur J. Steinberg
Richard M. Steuer
Aaron Stiefel
Jay G. Strum
Sydney E. Unger
Jay W. Waks
Peter A. Walker
William E. Wallace, Jr.
Gregory J. Wallance
Peter H. Weil
Barry A. Willner

(See Next Column)

KAYE, SCHOLER, FIERMAN, HAYS & HANDLER—*Continued*

MEMBERS OF FIRM (Continued)

Arthur F. Woodard
Alice Young
Fredric W. Yerman
William C. Zifchak

SPECIAL COUNSEL

Peter J. DeLuca
Sheldon Oliensis
Stanley H. Fuld
Abraham A. Ribicoff
Stanley D. Waxberg

OF COUNSEL

Ezra J. Doner
Eugene L. Girden
Mary Elizabeth Freeman
Arlene Harris
Robert A. Kandel

RETIRED PARTNERS

Joseph G. Connolly
Melvin Michaelson
Gerald Feller
Bernard William Nimkin
Fred N. Fishman
Stanley D. Robinson
Fred A. Freund
Sidney J. Silberman
Nathaniel H. Jackson
Henry K. Uman
Stuart Marks
Ronald L. Unger

NEW YORK COUNSEL

Scott M. Berman
Brian E. Kriger
Gary B. Bernstein
Steven Lavner
Robert B. Bernstein
Donald M. Levinsohn
Michael D. Braff
Michael A. Lynn
Richard A. De Sevo
Steven T. Marom (Not admitted in NY)
Roger Du Broff
Kathleen M. Faccini
Leonard Lee Podair
Phillip A. Geraci
Mark Schonberger
Stephen Gliatta
Mark Selinger
Mark D. Godler
Bert L. Slonim
Lois B. Gordon
Louis Tuchman
Richard G. Greco
Maris Veidemanis
Donald B. Zief

NEW YORK ASSOCIATES

Laurie Abramowitz
Lori B. Leskin
David Addis (Not admitted in the United States)
Anne Susan Levin
Seth I. Levin
Sara R. Adler
Harold Levine
David Albalah
Deborah S. Lewis
Arlene Rene Alves
Judie Lifton
John C. Amabile
Joseph M. Manak
Howard A. Becker
Kenneth P. Marin
Lori Bienstork
Mark W. Masters
Richard E. Bierman
Thomas J. McGahren
Steven G. Canner
Andrew J. Melnick
Cindy M. Caranella
Stephan W. Milo
Elan S. Carr
Natalia Nicolaidis
Adam D. Cole
David S. Pegno
Daniel P. DiNapoli
Ilene Dalinka Penn
Bea Krain Drechsler
Craig P. Rieders
Martin Feinstein
Julie J. Roach
Elizabeth A. Forman
David W. Robinson
Steven E. Fox
Marc D. Rosenberg
Claudia Abitol Freeman
Barry M. Rosenfeld
Jeffrey A. Fuisz
Marjorie Lynn Roth
Linda Marcelle Gadsby
Steven D. Roth
Thomas P. Gannon, Jr.
Alan E. Rothman
John D. Geelan
Debra Schaumberger
Sheryl M. Gittlitz
Trudi Seery
Adam H. Golden
Marci Guttentag Settle
Robin Golomb
Bonni L. Sheran
Robert Grass
Michael V. Simio
Richard J. Halloran
Kurt Skonberg
Jonathan Lee Hochman
Sebastian A. Soler
Cary S. Hoffman
Lisa M. Solomon
Robert K. Howard
David B. Soskin
John J. P. Howley
Fredric Sosnick
Stephanie Hsieh
Silvia C. Souto
Edward B. Johnson
Jennifer Anne Tafet
Ellyn B. Kaplan
Robin A. Tauber
Cherise Wolas Kasica (Not admitted in NY)
Carlton Thompson
Louis Vitali
Yoon Hi Kim-Greene
Naomi Brufsky Waltman
Mark S. Kingsley
Eli S. Weber
Samuel Kirschner
Fran Tolins Weingast
Barbara A. Lane
Michael R. Williams
Scott B. Zucker

WASHINGTON, D.C. OFFICE
RESIDENT PARTNERS

Terrence B. Adamson
Ronald K. Henry
David O. Bickart
Michael P. House
David J. Branson
Jonathan D. Schiller
Alan W. Granwell
Jason L. Shrinsky
G. Christopher Griner
Randall L. Speck (Not admitted in NY)

WASHINGTON, D.C. SPECIAL COUNSEL

William D. Eberle (P.A.)
Abraham A. Ribicoff

(See Next Column)

WASHINGTON, D.C. COUNSEL

Robert C. Bell, Jr. (Not admitted in NY)
Bruce Alan Eisen
Irving Gastfreund
Christopher R. Brewster
John W. Schryber
James M. Weitzman

WASHINGTON, D.C. ASSOCIATES

Tracy E. Ballard
Farhad Jalinous
Sylvia M. Becker
Laura E. Jehl
John G. Bickerman
William A. Isaacson
Annette M. Capretta
Nancy L. Kiefer
Peter C. Condron
Kenneth L. Marcus
Daniel J. Culhane
John R. Miles
Jana DeSirgh
Allan Gary Moskowitz
Nancy Evert
Raymond Paretzky
Timothy J. Feighery
R. Will Planert
Gary S. Thompson

HONG KONG OFFICE
PARTNER

Franklin D. Chu

COUNSEL

Frank L. Gniffke

HONG KONG OFFICE ASSOCIATES

Rongwei Cai (Not admitted in NY)
Neil L. Meyers (Not admitted in NY)
Bridget Chi
Juan E. Zuniga

BEIJING (PEKING) OFFICE
PARTNER

Franklin D. Chu

LOS ANGELES, CALIFORNIA OFFICE
PARTNERS

Gary Apfel (Resident)
Barry H. Lawrence (Resident)
Aton Arbisser (Resident)
Ronald L. Leibow
Gregory S. Dovel
Pierce O'Donnell (Resident)
Kenneth A. Freeling
Sanford C. Presant
Jeffrey S. Gordon (Resident)
Hushmand Sohaili (Resident)
Channing D. Johnson
William E. Thomson, Jr.

LOS ANGELES, CALIFORNIA OFFICE
SPECIAL COUNSEL

Cruz Reynoso

LOS ANGELES, CALIFORNIA OFFICE
OF COUNSEL

Susan A. Grode
M. Kenneth Suddleson

LOS ANGELES, CALIFORNIA OFFICE
ASSOCIATES

Robert Barnes
Sean Aaron Luaer
Lynne M. O. Brickner
Sean Aarow Luner
Russ Alan Cashdan
Ann Marie Mortimer
Hoon Chun
A. Ken Okamoto
Brian T. Corrigan
Belynda Reck
R. Scott Feldman
Rex T. Reeves, Jr.
Alan L. Friel
Anthony R. Salandra
Peter L. Haviland
John J. Shaeffer
Lillie Hsu
Mitchell J. Steinberger
Lisa Ilona Karsai
Bonnie Stylides
Ronald E. Levinson
W. Casey Walls
Michael A. Lloyd
Renee I. Wolf
Juan E. Zuniga

For full biographical listings, see the Martindale-Hubbell Law Directory

KAYSER & REDFERN (AV)

25 West 39th Street, 16th Floor, 10018
Telephone: 212-391-4960
Fax: 212-391-6917

Leo Kayser, III
Declan P. Redfern

For full biographical listings, see the Martindale-Hubbell Law Directory

KING & SPALDING (AV)

120 West 45th Street, 10036-4003
Telephone: 212-556-2100
FAX: 212-556-2222
Atlanta, Georgia Office: 191 Peachtree Street, N.E., 30303-1763.
Telephone: 404-572-4600.
FAX: 404-572-5100.
Washington, D.C. Office: 1730 Pennsylvania Avenue, N.W., 20006-4706.
Telephone: 202-737-0500.
FAX: 202-626-3737.

RESIDENT PARTNERS

James H. Wildman (Not admitted in NY)
E. William Bates, II (Not admitted in NY)
Gilbert D. Porter
Daniel J. King
Karl-Erbo Graf von Kageneck
Margaret E. O'Neil
Wilfried E. Witthuhn
Kathrine A. McLendon
Isam Salah
Peter K. Storey

(See Next Column)

KING & SPALDING, *New York—Continued*

RESIDENT PARTNERS (Continued)

Patricia Ferrari
Brian Rosner
Michael E. Norton
Bernays Thomas Barclay
Eileen P. Brumback (Not admitted in NY)
Bond K. Koga

RESIDENT COUNSEL

Erik J. Swenson

RESIDENT ASSOCIATES

Stefan W. Engelhardt
Steven J. Greene
Tara A. Higgins
Edward G. Kehoe
Mansoor H. Khan (Not admitted in the United States; Legal Consultant on the Laws of Pakistan)
Lee M. Kirby
Kandis M. Koustenis
Jeff V. Nelson
David Onorato
Christopher B. Price
Andrew D. Schifrin
Helen L. Siegal
Alexander C. S. Spiro
John P. H. Vigman
Stephen M. Wiseman

For full biographical listings, see the Martindale-Hubbell Law Directory

KRAMER, LEVIN, NAFTALIS, NESSEN, KAMIN & FRANKEL (AV)

919 Third Avenue, 10022
Telephone: 212-715-9100
Cable Address: "Nickral"
TWX: 710 581-5340
Telex: 645041
Telecopier: 212-688-2119

MEMBERS OF FIRM

Arthur H. Aufses III
Thomas D. Balliett
Martin Balsam
Jay G. Baris
Thomas E. Constance
Michael J. Dell
Kenneth H. Eckstein
Charlotte Moses Fischman
David S. Frankel
Marvin E. Frankel
Alan R. Friedman
Carl Frischling
Robert M. Heller
Philip S. Kaufman
Peter S. Kolevzon
Kenneth P. Kopelman
Michael Paul Korotkin
Arthur B. Kramer
Kevin B. Leblang
David P. Levin
Ezra G. Levin
Larry M. Loeb
Monica C. Lord
Richard Marlin
Thomas H. Moreland
Ellen R. Nadler
Gary P. Naftalis
Michael J. Nassau
Michael S. Nelson
Maurice N. Nessen
Jay A. Neveloff
Michael S. Oberman
Paul S. Pearlman
Susan J. Penry-Williams
Bruce Rabb
Allan E. Reznick
Scott S. Rosenblum
Michele D. Ross
Max J. Schwartz
Howard A. Sobel
Steven C. Todrys
Jeffrey S. Trachtman
D. Grant Vingoe
Harold P. Weinberger
E. Lisk Wyckoff, Jr.

COUNSEL

Joshua M. Berman
Jules Buchwald
Haig M. Casparian
Rudolph de Winter
Meyer Eisenberg
Arthur D. Emil
Sherwin Kamin
Maxwell M. Rabb
James Schreiber

SPECIAL COUNSEL

M. Frances Buchinsky
Debora K. Grobman
Christian S. Herzeca
Alvin D. Knott
Pinchas Mendelson
David Robbins
Lynn R. Saidenberg
Jonathan M. Wagner
Thomas R. Westle

ASSOCIATES

Philip Bentley
David G. Blaivas
Saul Eliot Burian
Mark I. Chass
Louis S. Citron
Lora S. Collins
Jeffrey W. Davis
Abbe L. Dienstag
Joanne Doldo (Not admitted in NY)
Leda E. Dunn
Mark S. Fawer
Marilyn Feuer
Michael Friedman
J. Russell George
David Michael Gold
Marc A. Goodman
Ronald S. Greenberg
Aviva L. Grossman
Mark J. Headley
Barry Herzog
Rena G. Hoffman
Robert N. Holtzman
Gregory Aaron Horowitz
Eva Izsak-Niimura
Lawrence Evan Jacobs
Susan Jacquemot
Susan Kantor
Shari Kahn Krouner
Karen Y. Kusko
Jodie Lane
Cheryl Lappen
Jane Lee
Louise E. Lipman
Heidi Liss
Trebor Lloyd
Sheri Faith London
Jonathan D. Lupkin
J. Michael Mayerfeld
Izabel Pasagian McDonald
Richard Kolb Milin
Thomas E. Molner
Mary Jane Mona
Peter J. O'Rourke
Robert E. Payne
Geoffrey Potter
Daniel A. J. Rayner
Benjamin S. Reichel
Robin Joan Ridless
Margaret Rowe

(See Next Column)

ASSOCIATES (Continued)

Michael J. Sage (Not admitted in NY)
Robert T. Schmidt
Marc A. Schuman
Mark B. Segall
Dana Ellen Shanler
Stephen Paul Shea
Marjorie E. Sheldon
Judith Singer
Susan A. Stark
Helayne Oberman Stoopack
Marlene Stulbach
Eric Tirschwell
Nicole Elise Toran
Alexander M. Vasilescu
Catherine Verhoff
William R. Wright
Eugenia Oshman Yudanin

STAFF ATTORNEY

Lee D. Caney

Stephen DiCarmine (Managing Attorney)

For full biographical listings, see the Martindale-Hubbell Law Directory

KROLL & TRACT (AV)

A Partnership including a Professional Corporation
520 Madison Avenue, 10022
Telephone: 212-921-9100
Telex: WUI 668838 KROLAWNY; WU 645461 KROLAWNY
Telecopier: 212-869-3657
Los Angeles, California Office: 6500 Wilshire Boulevard.
Telephone: 213-857-5080.
Telex: 181723.
Telecopier: 213-857-5090.
San Francisco, California Office: 120 Montgomery Street, Suite 340.
Telephone: 415-989-2494.
Fax: 415-989-2496.
Houston, Texas Office: 700 Louisiana Street.
Telephone: 713-228-3100.
Telex: 430265.
Telecopier: 713-228-2219.
Baltimore, Maryland Office: 201 North Charles Street.
Telephone: 410-539-1171.
Telecopier: 410-539-1171.
Telex: 5101010278.
Miami, Florida Office: 201 South Biscayne Boulevard.
Telephone: 305-577-4848.
Telex: 808094.
Telecopier: 305-577-3417.
Washington, D.C. Office: 1155 Connecticut Ave. N.W., Suite 500.
Telephone: 202-467-4730.
Telecopier: 202-467-4731.
Mineola, New York Office: Suite 330, 120 Mineola Boulevard, Box 10.
Telephone: 516-747-7333.
Telecopier: 516-747-3540.
London, England Office: Asia House, 31/33 Lime Street, EC3M 7HR.
Telephone: 621-1142.
Telex: 8955700 KROLAW LDN.
Telecopier: 283-6391.
Paris, France Office: 32 Rue la Boétie, 75008.
Telephone: 4563.18.10.
Telex: 643752 F.
Telecopier: 45633494.
Boston, Massachusetts Office: 60 State Street, Suite 2080.
Telephone: 617-742-3530.
Telecopier: 617-227-0201.
White Plains, New York Office: 11 Martine Avenue.
Telephone: 914-946-0773.
Telecopier: 914-946-2216.
Newark, New Jersey Office: One Gateway Center, 17th Floor.
Telephone: 201-622-3955.
Telecopier: 201-622-1112.

MEMBERS OF FIRM

Harold M. Tract (1926-1991)
Sol Kroll
Elliott M. Kroll
James W. Carbin
Kenneth S. Fiorella (Resident, Mineola Office)
Bruce M. Friedman
Patrick J. Moynihan (Resident, White Plains Office)
Charles T. Rubin
Robert J. Ryniker (Resident, Houston, Texas Office)
Gary C. Sachs
Hyman Hillenbrand (Resident, Miami, Florida Office)
Kenneth E. Cohen (Resident, Miami, Florida Office)
Neil B. Connelly
John P. Dearie, Jr.
Maureen Rothschild DiTata
Patricia Kay Dube (Resident, Houston, Texas Office)
Mark S. Fragner
John B. Geddie (Resident, Houston, Texas Office)
Daniel Hardick (Resident, Mineola Office)
Richard A. Levine (Resident, Los Angeles, California Office)
Lori M. Meyers
Stanley E. Orzechowski (Resident, Mineola Office)
Jeffrey N. Rejan
George W. Wright (Resident, Newark, New Jersey Office)
George S. Balis
Joseph Brenner

(See Next Column)

KROLL & TRACT—*Continued*

Stephen A. Aschettino
Gregg M. Bieber (Resident, Miami, Florida Office)
John K. Bosee, 4th
James J. Braze (Resident, San Francisco, California Office)
Kevin J. Bryant
Deborah T. Busby (Resident, Houston, Texas Office)
Joseph A. Clark (Resident, Mineola Office)
Edward M. Cuddy, III
Joseph A. French
Henry R. Gaxiola (Resident, Los Angeles, California Office)
Robert A. Glick
Stewart B. Greenspan
Gary M. Hellman (Resident, Miami, Florida Office)
Dale E. Hibbard
Daniel E. Hoffman (Resident, Los Angeles, California Office)
Thomas J. Hogan (Resident, Boston, Massachusetts Office)
W. Michael Jacobs (Not admitted in NY)
Nora Abatelli Johnson
Bertram G. Kaminski
Ann E. Knight (Resident, Houston, Texas Office)
Adam G.L. Kominsky
Paul Kovner
Andrew B. Lane
David A. Laughlin (Resident, Newark, New Jersey Office)
Shelley Lipman (Resident, Los Angeles, California Office)
Anthony P. Listrom
Salvatore P. LoPiccolo, II (Resident, Houston, Texas Office)
Frank A. Luceri (Resident, Miami, Florida Office)
Melanie S. Marks
Stacy Plotz Maza
James E. Mercante
Julia A. Meyer
Michele J. Mittleman
Steven Jay Monn
Charles H. Mostov (Resident, Los Angeles, California Office)
Michael G. Mucha (Resident, Miami, Florida Office)
Philip A. Nemecek
David Kam Ng (Resident, Los Angeles, California Office)
William F. O'Rourke (Resident, Houston, Texas Office)
Stephen J. Penino (Resident, White Plains Office)
James L. Ray (Resident, Houston, Texas Office)
Judy Sue Robinson (Resident, Houston, Texas Office)
Julius A. Rousseau, III
Nicolas G. Sakellis (Resident, Miami, Florida Office)
Reneé Simon
Christopher A. South
Christopher B. Turcotte
Jennifer A. Williams
David H. Wood (Resident, Houston, Texas Office)

OF COUNSEL

Morton Greenspan
Scott A. Lazar (Resident, Newark, New Jersey Office)
Vito J. Cassan

For full biographical listings, see the Martindale-Hubbell Law Directory

KRONISH, LIEB, WEINER & HELLMAN (AV)

1114 Avenue of the Americas, 10036-7798
Telephone: 212-479-6000
Facsimile: 212-479-6275

MEMBERS OF FIRM

Celia Goldwag Barenholtz
Russell S. Berman
William L. Castleberry
Robert J. Feinstein
Jack K. Feirman
Justin N. Feldman
Brian J. Gallagher
Stephen D. Gardner
John Hartje
Joseph S. Hellman
Harold M. Hoffman
Irwin R. Karassik
Michael E. Katzenstein
Herbert Kronish
Mark S. Levenson
Alan Levine
Jerome T. Levy
Richard Lieb
William Jay Lippman
Mark W. Lipschutz
Chet F. Lipton
William H. O'Brien
Ann-Elizabeth Purintun
Paul M. Ritter
David R. Rogol
Richard S. Rothberg
Renee Schwartz
William J. Schwartz
Donald E. Sonnenborn
Ralph J. Sutcliffe
Steven K. Weinberg
Henry Welt

COUNSEL

James S. Eustice
George J. Solomon
Robert Wolf

SPECIAL COUNSEL

Michael S. Feldman
Barbara J. Scheiner

ASSOCIATES

Suzanne D. Abair
A. Ari Afilalo (Not admitted in NY)
Daniel R. Alcott
Julie E. Barland
Benjamin B. Bedell
Cindi R. Brandt
Stephen Brodsky
Hyman Buchwald
Michelle A. Carey
Siu Lan Chan
Peter L. Ente
Christine Fahey
Joshua B. Gillon
David L. Goldberg
Maureen E. Hannon
Tara Hannon
Genesia Perlmutter Kamen
Susan V. Kayser
Sara Krauss (Not admitted in NY)
John Andrew Morris
M. Jeanne Nelson (Not admitted in NY)
Jill Michele Orlich
Michael Paley
Aaron J. Polak
Nancy H. Richardson
Jeffrey S. Rogoff
Judith A. Saxe

(See Next Column)

ASSOCIATES (Continued)

Michael S. Schiff
Deborah K. Sorell
William A. Ubert
Amy Walsh
Isaiah Weiss
Stephen A. Wieder

For full biographical listings, see the Martindale-Hubbell Law Directory

LA ROSSA, MITCHELL & ROSS (AV)

41 Madison Avenue, 10010
Telephone: 212-696-9700

MEMBERS OF FIRM

James M. La Rossa
John W. Mitchell
Michael S. Ross

ASSOCIATES

Andrew J. Weinstein
Susan G. LaRossa
Evan Glassman
Wendy Z. Brenner
Kenneth Michaels

For full biographical listings, see the Martindale-Hubbell Law Directory

LOEB AND LOEB (AV)

A Partnership including Professional Corporations
345 Park Avenue, 10154-0037
Telephone: 212-407-4000
Facsimile: 212-407-4990
Los Angeles, California Office: Suite 1800, 1000 Wilshire Boulevard, 90017-2475.
Telephone: 213-688-3400.
Cable Address: "Loband LSA".
Telecopier: 213-688-3460; 688-3461; 688-3462.
Century City (Los Angeles), California Office: Suite 2200, 10100 Santa Monica Boulevard, Los Angeles, 90067-4164.
Telephone: 310-282-2000.
Telecopier: 310-282-2191; 282-2192.
Nashville, Tennessee Office: 45 Music Square West, 37203-3205.
Telephone: 615-749-8300.
Facsimile: 615-749-8308.
Rome, Italy Office: Piazza Digione 1, 00197.
Telephone: 011-396-808-8456.
Telecopier: 011-396-674-8223.

MEMBERS OF FIRM

Mortimer H. Hess (1889-1968)
Christopher K. Aidun
Kenneth B. Anderson
Donald L. B. Baraf
Michael D. Beck
David H. Carlin
Marc A. Chamlin
David B. Eizenman
Frank E. Feder (A P.C.)
David C. Fischer
Kenneth D. Freeman
Abraham S. Guterman
Irv Hepner
John F. Lang
Jerome L. Levine
Andrew E. Lippmann
William J. Marlow
Charles H. Miller
Robert L. Pelz
Martin R. Pollner
Robert S. Reich
Andrew M. Ross
Fredric M. Sanders
David M. Satnick
David S. Schaefer
P. Gregory Schwed
David B. Shontz
Lee N. Steiner
Richard P. Streicher
Bruce J. Wexler
Michael P. Zweig

OF COUNSEL

Harry First
Harold I. Kahen
Arthur A. Segall

ASSOCIATES

Sheila E. Acker
Jean-Marie L. Atamian
Michael E. Beloff
Paula K. Colbath
Kathryn Lee Crawford
Anne P. Donovan
Carla Fels
Jay Fenster
John J. Fleming
Kenneth R. Florin
Helen Gavaris
Adrienne Halpern
Gerard A. Hefner
Michael Bryce Kinney
Allison D. Klayman
Maarten B. Kooij
Robert B. Lachenauer
Jonathan E. Ladd
Eric W. McCormick
Harry S. Prawer
Robert B. Rosen
Laurie S. Ruckel
Roni Schneider
Scott I. Schneider
Terri J. Seligman
James D. Taylor
Rebecca E. White
Jan Stephen Wimpfheimer

For full biographical listings, see the Martindale-Hubbell Law Directory

MARKS & MURASE (AV)

399 Park Avenue, 10022-4689
Telephone: 212-318-7700
Telex: 236562
FAX: (212) 752-5378
Washington, D.C. Office: Suite 750, 2001 L Street, N.W.
Telephone: 202-955-4900.
Los Angeles, California Office: Suite 1570, The Wells Fargo Center, 333 South Grand Avenue.
Telephone: 213-620-9690.

(See Next Column)

MARKS & MURASE, *New York—Continued*

PARTNERS IN NEW YORK, NEW YORK

Gary Allyn Adler
Kenneth D. Arbeeny
Carlos J. Bianchi
Eric S. Brown
Michael Z. Brownstein
Ta-Kuang (T.K.) Chang
Andrew J. Cosentino
Douglas J. Danzig
Kymson F. Des Jardins
Peter Figdor
Wallace L. Ford II
Lawrence M. Harnett
Gerald T. Hathaway
Ashby G. Hilsman
In-Young Lee
Ramon P. Marks
Gene Yukio Matsuo
Neil E. McDonell
Barbara R. Mendelson
Manes M. Merrit
Fumiaki Mizuki
Jiro Murase
Satoru Murase
Martin J. Murphy
John C. Rosengren
Roger L. Selfe
Robert Y. Stebbings
Steven M. Swirsky
John B. Wade III
Stephen D. Wayne

COUNSEL IN NEW YORK, NEW YORK

Edward J. LoBello

SPECIAL COUNSEL IN NEW YORK, NEW YORK

Eric L. Gilioli
Mark Lowell Lubin

ASSOCIATES IN NEW YORK, NEW YORK

Marcia E. Connolly
Brian H. Corcoran
Ann Marie Curd
Philip H. Ehrlich
Mark M. Elliott
Jeffrey A. Feit
Diane C. Hertz
Glenn Toshio Ikeda
Ann Gardner Kayman
Jane M. Piehler
Samantha Rosen
Anthony Michael Sabino
Jerrold A. Siskin
Akinobu Yorihiro

PARTNERS IN WASHINGTON, D.C.

Michael D. Bednarek (Not admitted in NY)
Paul Devinsky (Not admitted in NY)
Ronald P. Kananen (Not admitted in NY)
Richard Linn (Not admitted in NY)
George T. Marcou (Not admitted in NY)
Ramon P. Marks
Neil E. McDonell
Roger L. Selfe

OF COUNSEL IN WASHINGTON, D.C.

Matthew J. Marks

ASSOCIATE IN WASHINGTON, D.C.

George C. Beck (Not admitted in NY)

PARTNERS IN LOS ANGELES, CALIFORNIA

Matthew E. Digby
Dane Lee Miller (Not admitted in NY)
Shu Tokuyama
Robert A. West (Not admitted in NY)

ASSOCIATES IN LOS ANGELES, CALIFORNIA

Margaret C. Carroll
Tanya K. Danforth (Not admitted in NY)
John J. Del Propost (Not admitted in NY)
Douglas H. Morseburg (Not admitted in NY)
Craig L. Sheldon

For full biographical listings, see the Martindale-Hubbell Law Directory

MAYER, BROWN & PLATT (AV)

787 Seventh Avenue, Suite 2400, 10019-6018
Telephone: (212) 554-3000
Pitney Bowes: (212) 262-1910
Telex: 701842
Cable: LEMAYEN
Chicago, Illinois Office: 190 South LaSalle Street, 60603-3441.
Telephone: (312) 782-0600. Pitney Bowes: (312) 701-7711.
Telex: 190404.
Cable: LEMAY.
Washington, D.C. Office: 2000 Pennsylvania Avenue, N.W., 20006-1882.
Telephone: (202) 463-2000. Pitney Bowes: (202) 861-0484, Pitney Bowes: (202) 861-0473.
Telex: 892603.
Cable: LEMAYDC.
Houston, Texas Office: 700 Louisiana Street, Suite 3600, 77002-2730.
Telephone: (713) 221-1651. Pitney Bowes: (713) 224-6410.
Telex: 775809.
Cable: LEMAYHOU.
Los Angeles, California Office: 350 South Grand Avenue, 25th Floor, 90071-1503.
Telephone: (213) 229-9500. Pitney Bowes: (213) 625-0248.
Telex: 188089.
Cable: LEMAYLA.
London, England Office: 162 Queen Victoria Street, EC4V 4DB.
Telephone: 011-44-71-248-1465.
Fax: 011-44-71-329-4465.
Telex: 8811095.
Cable: LEMAYLDN.
Tokyo, Japan Office: (Kawachi Gaikokuho Jimu Bengoshi Jimusho), Urbannet Otemachi Building 13F 2-2, Otemachi 2-chome, Chiyoda-ku, Tokyo 100.
Telephone: 011-81-3-5255-9700.
Facsimile: 011-81-3-5255-9797.

(See Next Column)

Berlin, Germany Office: Spreeufer 5, 10178.
Telephone: 011-49-30-240-7930.
Facsimile: 011-49-30-240-79344.
Brussels, Belgium Office: Square de Meeûs 19/20, Bte. 4, 1040.
Telephone: 011-32-2-512-9878.
Fax: 011-32-2-511-3305.
Telex: 20768 MBPBRU B.
Mexico City, Mexico, D.F., Mexico Correspondent: Jáuregui, Navarrete, Nader y Rojas, S.C., Abogados, Paseo de la Reforma 199, Pisos 15, 16 y 17, 06500, Mexico.
Telephone: 011-525-591-16-55.
Facsimile: 011-525-535-80-62; 011-525-703-22-47.
Cable: JANANE.

PARTNERS

Joseph W. Bartlett
Barry P. Biggar
Robert I. Bressman
Richard F. Broude
Mary Rose Brusewitz
Michael G. Capatides
James B. Carlson
Jean S. Chan
Peter V. Darrow
Laura A. DeFelice
Thomas R. Hood
Philip Allen Lacovara
George W. Madison
James J. McGuire
Jay Parry Monge
Frank E. Morgan, II
James E. Padilla
Michael P. Richman
Thomas M. Vitale
Mark S. Wojciechowski
Steven Wolowitz
Michael I. Zinder

OF COUNSEL

David K. Duffee
Albert I. Edelman
Warren L. Jervey

ASSOCIATES

Nelson Kyunam Ahn
Bradley J. Andreozzi
James H. Bathon
Audrey Ingber Bender
Stephen D. Bohrer
Benjamin A. Bornstein
Martin J. Collins
Raniero D'Aversa, Jr.
John J. Dedyo
Robert D. Ellis
Nicole V.F. Bergman Fong
Gary D. Friedman
Salvatore Guerrera
Sandra M. Guerrero
Robert G. Harvey
Valerie-Leila Jaber
Josh Jacobson
Beth Kramer
Benjamin W. Lau
Stacey N. LeFont
Nicholas W. Lobenthal
Kimberly A. Lynch (Not admitted in NY)
Edward Skinner Madara, III
John F. Marsh
Andrew Mattei
Antonio Molestina
Limor Nissan
Frank P. Nocco
Mary Payton O'Hara
Daniel Penn
Harvey P. Sanders
George B. Schwab
Kerri Appel Siegel
Michael N. Sloyer
Bruce M. Stachenfeld
Oliver Ott Trumbo
Kathleen Anne Walsh
Richard L. Zack (Not admitted in NY)
Scott M. Zemser

For full biographical listings, see the Martindale-Hubbell Law Directory

McCARTER & ENGLISH (AV)

Suite 1519, One World Trade Center, 10048
Telephone: 212-466-9018
Telecopier: 212-432-6568
Newark, New Jersey Office: Four Gateway Center, 100 Mulberry Street. P.O. Box 652.
Telephone: 201-622-4444.
Telecopier: 201-624-7070.
Cable Address: "McCarter" Newark.
Cherry Hill, New Jersey Office: 1810 Chapel Avenue West.
Telephone: 609-662-8444.
Telecopier: 609-662-6203.
Boca Raton, Florida Office: 2255 Glades Road, Suite 319-A.
Telephone: 407-994-6262.
Telecopier: 407-241-0798.
Wilmington, Delaware Office: Mellon Bank Center, 919 Market Street.
Telephone: 302-654-8010
Telecopier: 302-654-0795

RESIDENT PARTNER

Jeffrey H. Aminoff

RESIDENT ASSOCIATES

Steven L. Wittels

For full biographical listings, see the Martindale-Hubbell Law Directory

McDERMOTT, WILL & EMERY (AV)

A Partnership including Professional Corporations
1211 Avenue of the Americas, 10036-8701
Telephone: 212-768-5400
Facsimile: 212-768-5444
Chicago, Illinois Office: 227 West Monroe Street.
Telephone: 312-372-2000.
Telex: 253565 MILAM CGO.
Facsimile: 312-984-7700.

(See Next Column)

McDERMOTT, WILL & EMERY—*Continued*

Boston, Massachusetts Office: 75 State Street, Suite 1700.
Telephone: 617-345-5000.
Telex: 951324 MILAM BSN.
Facsimile: 617-345-5077.
Miami, Florida Office: 201 South Biscayne Boulevard.
Telephone: 305-358-3500.
Telex: 441777 LEYES.
Facsimile: 305-347-6500.
Washington, D.C. Office: 1850 K Street, N.W.
Telephone: 202-887-8000.
Telex: 253565 MILAM CGO.
Facsimile: 202-778-8087.
Los Angeles, California Office: 2049 Century Park East.
Telephone: 310-277-4110.
Facsimile: 310-277-4730.
Newport Beach, California Office: 1301 Dove Street, Suite 500.
Telephone: 714-851-0633.
Facsimile: 714-851-9348.
St. Petersburg, Russia Office: 2/2 Tchaikovsky Street, #517, 191187 St. Petersburg, Russia.
Telephone: (7) (812) 273-9831.
Facsimile: (7) (812) 273-9831.
Vilnius, Lithuania Office: Smetonos 6, 2600 Vilnius, Lithuania.
Telephone: 370 2 61-43-08.
Facsimile: 370 2 22-79-55.
Associated (Independent) Offices:
Brussels, Belgium: Uettwiller Grelon Lippens Dekeyser, 73 avenue Vandendriessche, 1150 Brussels, Belgium.
Telephone: (32) (2) 772-87-50.
Facsimile: (32) (2) 772-87-52.
London, England: Paisner & Co, Bouverie House, 154 Fleet Street, London EC4A 2DQ, England.
Telephone: (44) (71) 353-0299.
Facsimile: (44) (71) 583-8621.
Paris, France: Uettwiller Grelon Gout Canat & Associes, 68, boulevard de Courcelles, 75017 Paris, France.
Telephone: (33) (1) 48 88 89 00.
Facsimile: (33) (1) 48 88 05 50.

MEMBERS OF FIRM

Banks Brown
Jeffrey L. Dunetz
Lawrence I. Fox
C. David Goldman (Not admitted in NY)
Gregor F. Gregorich
Cecil R. House
William L. Kandel
Jane Lembeck Kuesel
Sander Lehrer
John D. Lovi
Michele A. Masucci
Sandra E. Mayerson (Not admitted in NY)
Richard J. Reibstein
Andrew B. Roth
Joseph E. Sarachek
Phillip E. Sloan
Mark Thoman
Brien D. Ward
Dean A. Weber
Robert A. Weiner
Harvey Z. Werblowsky

COUNSEL

Maximilian W. Kempner

John J. Calandra
Tracy Hope Davis
Edwin M. Larkin
Amy Serper Leder
Julie A. Day Marion
P. Bradford Ockene
Bryan T. West
Richard A. Wright
Lynette Remen Zinberg

For full biographical listings, see the Martindale-Hubbell Law Directory

HENRY S. MIDDENDORF, JR. (AV)

Suite 201, 36 West 44th Street, 10036
Telephone: 212-575-0350

For full biographical listings, see the Martindale-Hubbell Law Directory

MILBANK, TWEED, HADLEY & McCLOY (AV)

1 Chase Manhattan Plaza, 10005
Telephone: 212-530-5000
Cable Address: "Miltweed NYK"
Fax: 212-530-5219
MCI Mail: MilbankTweed ABA/net Milbank NY
Midtown Office: 50 Rockefeller Plaza, 10020.
Telephone: 212-530-5800.
Fax: 212-530-0158.
Los Angeles, California Office: 601 South Figueroa Street, 30th Floor, 90017.
Telephone: 213-892-4000.
Fax: 213-629-5063.
Telex: 678754. ABA/net: Milbank LA.
Washington, D.C. Office: International Square Building, Suite 1100, 1825 Eye Street, N.W., 20006.
Telephone: 202-835-7500.
Cable Address: "Miltweed Wsh". ITT 440667.
Fax: 202-835-7586. ABA/net: Milbank DC.

(See Next Column)

Tokyo, Japan Office: Nippon Press Center Building, 2-1, Uchisaiwai-cho 2-chome, Chiyoda-ku, Tokyo 100, Japan.
Telephone: 011-81-3-3504-1050.
Fax: 011-81-3-3595-2790, 011-81-3-3502-5192.
London, England Office: Ropemaker Place, 25 Ropemaker Street, EC2Y 9AS.
Telephone: 011-44-171-374-0423.
Cable Address: "Miltuk G."
Fax: 011-44-171-374-0912.
Hong Kong Office: 3007 Alexandra House, 16 Chater Road.
Telephone: 011-852-2526-5281.
Fax: 011-852-2840-0792; 011-852-2845-9046. ABA/net: Milbank HK.
Singapore Office: 14-02 Caltex House, 30 Raffles Place, 0104.
Telephone: 011-65-534-1700.
Fax: 011-65-534-2733. ABA/net: EDNANG.
Moscow, Russia Office: 24/27 Sadovaya-Samotyochnya, Moscow, 103051.
Telephone: 011-7-502-258-5015.
Fax: 011-7-502-258-5014.

MEMBERS OF FIRM

Paul S. Aronzon (Resident Partner, Los Angeles, California Office)
John Cooley Baity
W. Rogers Benson, Jr.
Charles G. Berry
Jonathan G. Blattmachr
Kevin C. Blauch
Stephen J. Blauner
Squire N. Bozorth
Richard S. Brach
George Ian Brandon
Donald B. Brant, Jr.
Barbara J. Briggs
Jeffrey K. Brinck
Russell E. Brooks
Nicholas Buckworth (Partner in an Affiliated Partnership); (Resident, London, England Office)
Theodore D. Burke
Carolyn C. Clark
Warren F. Cooke
Douglas R. Davis
Trayton M. Davis
M. Douglas Dunn
Mark S. Edelstein
Celia A. Felsher
Edwin F. Feo (Resident Partner, Los Angeles, California Office)
Phillip D. Fletcher (Resident, London, England Office)
George J. Forsyth
Wilbur F. Foster, Jr.
David C. L. Frauman (Resident Partner, Los Angeles, California Office)
Cynthia Futter (Resident Partner, Los Angeles, California Office)
Guilford W. Gaylord
John G. Gellene
Joseph S. Genova
Glenn S. Gerstell (Resident Partner, Hong Kong Office)
Elliot Gewirtz
Michael W. Goroff
Richard M. Gray
Jonathan J. Green
Jay D. Grushkin (Resident Partner, Tokyo, Japan Office)
John K. Halvey
L. Douglas Harris
Peter Windley Herman
Anne L. Himes
Joris M. Hogan
G. Malcolm Holderness
C. Stephen Howard (Resident Partner, Los Angeles, California Office)
Geoffrey K. Hurley
Mel M. Immergut
Robert A. Jacobs
John J. Jerome
Douglas W. Jones
Mark A. Kantor (Resident Partner, Washington, D.C. Office)
Bruce E. Kayle
Frederick C. Kneip
David A. Lamb (Resident Partner, Los Angeles, California Office)
Lawrence Lederman
Toni C. Lichstein
Albert F. Lilley
Francis D. Logan
Kenneth MacRitchie (Partner in an Affiliated Partnership); Resident, London, England Office)
William J. Mahoney
Gregory Evers May (Resident Partner, Washington, D.C. Office)
Katherine J. Moore
Peter M. Mortimer
Robert W. Mullen, Jr.
Donal C. O'Brien, Jr.
Ted Obrzut (Resident Partner, Los Angeles, California Office)
John T. O'Connor
Robert S. O'Hara, Jr.
Charles D Peet, Jr.
Arnold B. Peinado, III
Samuel S. Polk
Dale L. Ponikvar
Frank C. Puleo
Barry G. Radick
Brian D. Rance
Robert S. Reder
Mark L. Regante
Robert E. Rice
Elihu F. Robertson
Jonathan R. Rod
Peter D. Rowntree
Eric H. Schunk (Resident Partner, Los Angeles, California Office)
John E. Shockey (Resident Partner, Washington, D.C. Office)
Thomas B. Siebens (Resident Partner, Singapore Office)
David C. Siegfried
Eric F. Silverman
David R. Slade
James S. Sligar
Robert E. Spring
David A. Stagliano
Douglas A. Tanner (Resident Partner, Hong Kong Office)
Richard C. Tufaro (Resident Partner, Washington, D.C. Office)
Peter P. Wallace (Resident Partner, Los Angeles, California Office)
Tsugumichi D. Watanabe
William H. Webster (Resident Partner, Washington, D.C. Office)
Mark L. Weissler
Adam Wenner (Resident Partner, Washington, D.C. Office)
Harry E. White, Jr.
Richard J. Wight
Gary S. Wigmore (Resident Partner, Singapore Office)
Robert B. Williams

(See Next Column)

MILBANK, TWEED, HADLEY & MCCLOY, *New York—Continued*

CONSULTING PARTNERS

Alexander D. Forger
William E. Jackson
Roger B. Oresman
William Parsons
Carroll L. Wainwright, Jr.

OF COUNSEL

Morris H. Bergreen
Martin Blackman
Robert R. Douglass
Scott A. Edelman
Simon Friedman
Adlai S. Hardin, Jr.
Rodrigo J. Howard
David S. Katz (Resident, Washington, D.C. Office)
John H. Kelly
Young Joon Kim (Resident, Hong Kong Office)
Robert F. Lawrence (Resident, Washington, D.C. Office)
John J. McCarthy, Jr.
Joseph M. Persinger
Amy G. Rudnick (Resident, Washington, D.C. Office)
Gregory J. Shrock
Michael J. Simon
David C. Stoller
Peter James Thompson (Resident, Hong Kong Office)
Peter F. Tufo
Hisayo Yasuda (Resident, Tokyo, Japan Office)

SENIOR ATTORNEYS

Eugene F. Farabaugh
Bruce T. Gardner
Charles W. Westland

ASSOCIATES

Steven J. Abrams
Richard I. Alvarez
Joseph A. Anderson
Christos T. Antoniou (Resident, Washington, D.C. Office)
Su Sun Bai
James H. Ball, Jr.
Michael C. Banks
Tia Barancik
Kenneth J. Baronsky (Resident, Los Angeles, California Office)
Nancy Barr
Dino Barajas (Resident, Los Angeles Office)
Daniel D. Bartfeld
Steven J. Bass
Devan D. Beck (Resident, Los Angeles, California Office)
Crayton L. Bell
Michael J. Bellucci
Oleg Berger
Philip Berkowitz
Charles D. Bethill
J. Keith Biancamano (Resident, Los Angeles, California Office)
Laurie R. Binder
Andrea J. Brantner
Mary F. Budig
Anne M. Buscaglia
Bernard C. Byrnes
Mark Caterini
Jaeyoung L. Chang
Helen F. Choi (Resident, Washington, D.C. Office)
Robert Claassen
Evan Jay Cohen
Lynda R. Cohen
Andrea Coles-Bjerre
John M. Conlon
Philip Corsello
John Crow
Pamela Czewska
Michael Dayen (Resident, Los Angeles, California Office)
Jose M. Deetjan (Resident, Los Angeles, California Office)
Daniel M. Dunn
Chieko Eda (Resident, Tokyo, Japan Office)
Michael J. Edelman
Richard K. Elbaum
Christopher R. Epes
Mary C. Ericson (Resident, Washington, D.C. Office)
Mechelle Evans
Jessica A. Feder
Marc-Philip Ferzan (Not admitted in NY)
Drew S. Fine
Edward J. Finley, II
Michael T. Fisher (Resident, Los Angeles, California Office)
Raymond J. Fisher
Deanna Flores (Resident, Washington, D.C. Office)
J. Nixon Fox III (Resident, Hong Kong Office)
Belinda Maughan Foxworth (Resident, Los Angeles, California Office)
Joy K. Gallup
R. Lee Garner III (Resident, Los Angeles, California Office)
David R. Gelfand
Gila E. Gellman
Jonathan S. Gitlin
David A. Godfrey (Resident, Los Angeles, California Office)
Esther Goldbas
Christine C. Griff
James R. Gunther, Jr. (Resident, Washington, D.C. Office)
Kristin Halvey
Jane L. Hanson
William A. Harris
Roland Hlawaty
Gary A. Hobart
William B. Hobbs
John S. Hodgkins (Resident, Los Angeles, California Office)
Kathryn E. Hoff-Patrinos (Resident, Washington, D.C. Office)
C. Thomas Hopkins (Resident, Los Angeles, California Office)
Michael D. Hornstein (Resident, Washington, D.C. Office)
David M. Hudanish (Resident, London, England Office)
Elizabeth Hunt (Resident, Los Angeles, California Office)
Frederick Hyman
Saburabi Nila Ibrahim (Resident, Singapore Office)
David J. Impastato (Resident, Tokyo, Japan Office)
Timothy M. Ison (Resident, Los Angeles, California Office)
Julie M. Jacobs (Resident, Washington, D.C. Office)
Jayson Jarushewsky
David A. Jones (Resident, Los Angeles, California Office)
Mitchell W. Karsch
Robert D. Kartheiser, Jr.
Robert L. Katz
Alexander Kaye
Joseph J. Kelleher
Shazia Khawaja
Jane E. Kineke
Rohit H. Kirpalani (Resident, Washington, D.C. Office)
B. Kelly Kiser
Joseph F. Kishel
Brian Krisberg
Thomas C. Lee
Jacqueline Leung (Resident, Hong Kong Office)
Pamela L. Lewis

(See Next Column)

ASSOCIATES (Continued)

Valerie Longmire (Resident, Los Angeles, California Office)
Guy A. Longobardo
Sara A. Magovern (Not admitted in NY)
Jonathan A. Maizel
Dean A. Manson (Resident, Washington, D.C. Office)
Yibing Mao (Resident, Hong Kong Office)
Allan T. Marks (Resident, Los Angeles, California Office)
Patricia Matzye
Christopher C. McIsaac (Resident, Washington, D.C. Office)
Diane Meyers
Sharon L. Meymarian (Resident, Los Angeles, California Office)
Mark Michigan
Gabrielle Miller
Gail Miranda-Schmidt
Richard S. Mitchell
Jack H. Moore
Timothy Moran
Jane B. Morgan (Resident, Washington, D.C. Office)
Eric K. Moser
Marcelo A. Mottesi (Not admitted in NY)
Robert S. Mower
Daniel R. Mummery
Barbara J. Murphy
Perry J. Nagle
Fred Neufeld (Resident, Los Angeles, California Office)
Dao Nguyen (Resident, Tokyo, Japan Office)
Lisa M. O'Brien
John J. O'Connor (Resident, Los Angeles, California Office)
Alisa Odeen
Patricia O'Kicki
Regina K. O'Shea
Sharon Parella
Morela Z. Paris
Mee Jung Park
A. Nicholas Purrington
Melissa Y. Raciti
Gregory K. Ranslam
Eric R. Reimer (Resident, Los Angeles, California Office)
Fred W. Reinke (Resident, Washington, D.C. Office)
Mark A. Rhodes
Sean K. Richardson
Nancy S. Rights
Robert A. Ripin
Madeline J. Rivlin
Anne M. Ronan
Louis J. Royer
Eileen Driscoll Rubens (Resident, Los Angeles, California Office)
Peter E. Ruhlin
Kathryn Basile Russell
Paula A. Ryan
Jeffrey D. Saferstein
John P. Sare
Deborah Scott Savage
Perry M. Sayles
Joseph Schohl (Resident, Los Angeles, California Office)
Kathy Schumacher
Caleb A. Schwartz
Helfried J. Schwarz (Resident, London, England Office)
Frederick Sembler
Mary E. Shepard
Hee-Jung Shin
Allan B. Silver
Stephen W. Skonieczny
Georgiana J. Slade
Theodore S. Stamas
Jamie Steinfink
Susanna V. Stern
Doreen A. Sullivan
Lazarus N. Sun
Sheryl A. Susser
Jay W. Swanson
Linda Z. Swartz
Jean M. Tabberson
Craig H. Thaler
Susanne M. Toes
Scot Tucker (Resident, Los Angeles, California Office)
Lisa A. Turiel
Thomas Valle
Langdon Van Norden
Marc J. Veilleux
Kathrin A. Wanner
David J. Webb
Anne Wells (Resident, Los Angeles, California Office)
Susan P. Widule (Resident, Los Angeles, California Office)
John D. Wilmore (Resident, Los Angeles, California Office)
David J. Wolfson
Karen B. Wong (Resident, Los Angeles, California Office)
Desiree Woo (Resident, Los Angeles, California Office)
Brent Vardeman Woods (Resident, Hong Kong Office)
Wade R. Wright (Resident, Washington, D.C. Office)
Kym R. Wulfe (Resident, Los Angeles, California Office)
Anthony Chan Wing Yuen (Resident, Hong Kong Office)

For full biographical listings, see the Martindale-Hubbell Law Directory

---

MORVILLO, ABRAMOWITZ, GRAND, IASON & SILBERBERG, P.C. (AV)

565 Fifth Avenue, 10017
Telephone: 212-856-9600
Fax: 212-856-9494
Cable Address: "Litigator, New York"

Robert G. Morvillo
Elkan Abramowitz
Paul R. Grand
Lawrence Iason
Michael C. Silberberg
John J. Tigue, Jr.
Richard D. Weinberg
Barry A. Bohrer
Lawrence S. Bader
Edward M. Spiro
Robert J. Anello
Diana D. Parker
Catherine M. Foti

OF COUNSEL

Michael W. Mitchell

Stephen L. Ascher
Michael F. Buchanan
Elizabeth Jahncke Carroll
Christopher H. Downey
Nicole L. Felton
Tom Firestone
Christopher J. Gunther
John T. Hecht
Ross N. Herman
Craig A. Isaacs
Jill K. Israeloff
Jamie L. Kogan
Linda A. Lacewell
Monique LaPointe
Emily Maranjian
Laurie J. McPherson
Jodi M. Peikin
Sabrina Shroff

For full biographical listings, see the Martindale-Hubbell Law Directory

New York—Continued

MUDGE ROSE GUTHRIE ALEXANDER & FERDON (AV)

(Mudge, Stern, Baldwin & Todd)
(Caldwell, Trimble & Mitchell)
180 Maiden Lane, 10038
Telephone: 212-510-7000
Cable Address: "Baltuchins, New York"
Telex: 127889 & 703729
Telecopier: 212-248-2655/57
Los Angeles, California Office: 21st Floor, 333 South Grand Avenue, 90071.
Telephone: 213-613-1112.
Telecopier: 213-680-1358.
Washington, D.C. Office: 2121 K Street, N.W., 20037.
Telephone: 202-429-9355.
Telecopier: 202-429-9367.
Telex: MRGA 440264.
Cable Address: "Baltuchins, Washington, DC"
West Palm Beach, Florida Office: Suite 900, 515 North Flagler Drive, 33401.
Telephone: 407-650-8100.
Telecopier: 407-833-1722.
Telex: 514847 MRWPB.
Parsippany, New Jersey Office: Morris Corporate Center Two, Building D, One Upper Pond Road, 07054-1075.
Telephone: 201-335-0004.
Telecopier: 201-402-1593.
European Office: 12, Rue de la Paix, 75002 Paris, France.
Telephone: 42.61.57.71.
Telecopier: 42.61.79.21.
Cable Address: "Baltuchins, Paris".
Tokyo, Japan Office: Infini Akasaka, 8-7-15 Akasaka, Minato-Ku, Tokyo 107, Japan.
Telephone: (03) 3423-3970.
Fax: (03) 3423-3971.

MEMBERS OF FIRM

Nathan Abramowitz
Ned H. Bassen
Isaac D. Benkin (Resident Partner, Washington, D.C. Office)
Jonathan Birenbaum
Julia Christine Bliss (Resident Partner, Washington, D.C. Office)
John G. Bove
Timothy T. Brock
Paul G. Burns
Susan Millington Campbell
Nicholas J. Capozzoli, Jr. (Resident Partner, Parsippany, New Jersey Office)
V. Anthony Carbonar (Not admitted in NY)
Charles E. Carey (Resident Partner, Los Angeles California Office)
Alan F. Cariddi (Resident Partner, Paris Office)
Joseph J. Carroll
Joel E. Cohen
Stephen T. Cole (Resident Partner, Los Angeles, California Office)
Elwood F. Collins, Jr.
Kenneth Conboy
Terrence J. Connolly
Michael P. Daniels (Resident Partner, Washington, D.C. Office)
J. William Dantzler, Jr.
Frederick M. Danziger
Francis K. Decker, Jr.
Martin J. Dockery
Richard K. Eaton (Resident Partner, Washington, D.C. Office)
Donald H. Elliott
Theodore N. Farris
Robert E. Ferdon
James J. Florio (Resident Partner, Parsippany, New Jersey Office)
James G. Frangos
Thomas G. Gallatin, Jr.
Leonard Garment (Resident Partner, Washington, D.C. Office)
Gerrit Gillis
Thomas J. Gormley
F. Susan Gottlieb
Judah Gribetz
Robert J. Gunther, Jr.
Michael J. Hannigan
Eugene W. Harper, Jr.
John D. Hawkins, Jr.
Rita A. Hernandez
Carla Anderson Hills (Resident Partner, Washington D.C. Office)
Roderick M. Hills (Resident Partner, Washington, D.C. Office)
Jeffrey Hirsch
H. Sidney Holmes III
David P. Houlihan (Resident Partner, Washington, D.C. Office)
Donald L. Hunt (Resident Partner, Los Angeles, California Office)
James V. Kearney
Charles B. Keefe
John J. Kirby, Jr.
Richard L. Kornblith (Resident Partner, Los Angeles, California Office)
Stanford G. Ladner
Harold G. Levison (Resident Partner, Parsippany, New Jersey Office)
I. Lewis Libby (Resident Partner, Washington, D.C. Office)
Robert A. Longman
Walter P. Loughlin (Not admitted in NY)
Carl F. Lyon, Jr.
James P. Marlin
George J. Martin, Jr.
Takashi Matsumoto (Resident Partner, Tokyo, Japan Office)
Arthur F. McMahon, Jr.
Bruce C. Mee (Resident Partner, Paris, France Office)
Robert B. Michel (Not admitted in NY)
Richard J. Miller (Resident Partner, West Palm Beach, Florida Office)
Shelley B. O'Neill
Catherine E. Palmer
N. David Palmeter (Resident Partner, Washington, D.C. Office)

(See Next Column)

MEMBERS OF FIRM (Continued)

Michael J. Perrucci (Resident Partner, Parsippany, New Jersey Office)
Jeffrey L. Piemont
Anne Adams Rabbino
Clayton S. Reynolds
Fabrice Rué (Resident Partner, Paris, France Office)
Thomas C. Russler
Malcolm R. Schade
Craig M. Scully
Stuart D. Sender
Laurence V. Senn, Jr.
Robert Sidorsky
Timothy M. Toy
Arnold H. Tracy
David A. Vaughan (Resident Partner, Washington, D.C. Office)
Mary Ann Walker (Resident Partner, Washington, D.C. Office)
Christopher M. Waterman
Neil T. Wolk
Donald J. Zoeller

COUNSEL

Joseph J. Aronica (Resident Counsel, Washington, D.C. Office)
Geoffrey Berman
Joseph R. Bock (Resident Counsel, Parsippany, New Jersey Office)
Robert A. Boresta
Walter E. Breen
Winston J. Churchill, Jr.
Thomas W. Evans
Milton Gwirtzman (Resident Counsel, Washington, D.C. Office)
Joseph A. Hoffman (Resident Counsel, Parsippany, New Jersey Office)
William H. Hogeland, Jr.
Norman A. Jenkins, III (Resident Counsel, Los Angeles, California Office)
John T. Kelly (Resident Counsel, Parsippany, New Jersey Office)
Bruce H. Levitt (Resident Counsel, Parsippany, New Jersey Office)
John V. Lindsay
Edward W. Long (Resident Counsel, Los Angeles, California Office)
Joseph T. Lynyak, III (Resident Counsel, Los Angeles, California Office)
Richard H. Nicholls
Christopher Norgaard (Resident Counsel, Los Angeles, California Office)
Ralph Oman (Resident Counsel, Washington, D.C. Office)
Douglas M. Parker
Paul A. Pensig (Resident Counsel, Los Angeles, California Office)
Milton C. Rose
C. Kenneth Shank (Resident Counsel, Parsippany, New Jersey Office)
Harry G. Silleck, Jr.
James M. Spears (Resident Counsel, Washington, D.C. Office)
Vuong Van Bac (Resident Counsel, Paris, France Office)

LEGAL SUPPORT PERSONNEL

Gary B. Fiebert
Frank Badart Kemp
David Barnes
Mitchell Emmett Ward, III

ASSOCIATES

Frederick A. Avila
Peter R. Batten
Mark D. Beckett
James S. Blank
Kenneth M. Breen
John T. Brennan
Brian P. Campbell
Patrick J. Carty
Mark P. Chioffi
Phyllis Harris Clements
James O. Copley
Robert P. Coyne
Patrick J. Della Valle
Edward T. DeSilva
Elizabeth R. Devine
Anthony M. D'Iorio
David L. Dubrow
Lisa K. Eastwood
Ilana Elbaz
A. Mariana Freyre
Wendy K. Gelfand-Chaite
Mitchell S. Gendel
Anthony V. Giancana
Jeffrey M. Goodman
Elisabeth L. Goot
Shari Leigh Gordon
Patricia A. Griffin
Caryn Hemsworth
Russell C. Hochman
Andrew S. Holmes
Elizabeth I. Hook
John P. Iorillo (Not admitted in NY)
Jacqueline M. James
Stephanie L. Jones
Thomas N. Kendris
N. Peter Knoll
James R. Levine
Eric N. Litzky
Judith A. Lockhart (Not admitted in NY)
Stephen M. Lukow
Elinore C. Lyon
Gail A. Matthews
Kathleen E. McKay
Pamela J. McNair
Christopher J. Moore
Jonathan B. Morris
Anthony R. G. Nolan (Not admitted in NY)
Mark O. Norell
Virginia O'Connell
Nicole S. Polley
Stuart S. Poloner
James P. Prenetta, Jr.
Mark R. Pronk
Richard J. Reilly, Jr.
Marc S. Reisler
Susan Leland Safko
Timothy K. Saunders, Jr.
John F. Schaller
Keri Schiowitz
Steven D. Schwartz
Regina Lynn Scinta
Brendan R. Sheehan
Mark A. Simko
Nancy I. Solomon
Joyce J. Sun
Marc H. Supcoff
Debra J. Terry
Jack V. Valinoti
Mark Vasco
Robert R. Viducich
Jeffrey T. Wald
Lore E. Wall
Dennis M. Walsh
Stephen J. Watson
Abby M. Wenzel
Paul F. Wells
James Whelan
Russell G. Wohl
Anne R. Wolfson (Not admitted in NY)
Richard C. Wong
Nancy A. Zajac

(See Next Column)

MUDGE ROSE GUTHRIE ALEXANDER & FERDON, *New York—Continued*

LOS ANGELES, CALIFORNIA
RESIDENT PARTNERS

Charles E. Carey
Stephen T. Cole
Donald L. Hunt
Richard L. Kornblith

LOS ANGELES, CALIFORNIA
RESIDENT COUNSEL

Norman A. Jenkins, III
Edward W. Long
Joseph T. Lynyak, III
Christopher Norgaard
Paul A. Pensig

RESIDENT ASSOCIATES

Carolyn L. Clark
Christopher L. Driscoll
Leeanna Izuel
Frederick S. Kuhlman
Mitchell F. Ludwin
Mary H. Neale
Samuel Poss
Valerie A. Smith
Timothy J. Toohey
Fred G. Yanney

WASHINGTON, D.C.
RESIDENT PARTNERS

Isaac D. Benkin
Julia Christine Bliss
Michael P. Daniels
Richard K. Eaton
Leonard Garment
Carla Anderson Hills
Roderick M. Hills
David P. Houlihan
I. Lewis Libby
N. David Palmeter
David A. Vaughan
Mary Ann Walker

WASHINGTON, D.C.
RESIDENT COUNSEL

Joseph J. Aronica
Milton Gwirtzman
Ralph Oman
James M. Spears

RESIDENT ASSOCIATES

Peter D. Bernstein
Christopher F. Corr
Edith A. Eisner
Richard G. King
Edward N. Leavy
Chen Ma
David M. Morris
Renee J. O'Brien
Robert S. Pothier
Stanley R. Scheiner
Gregory J. Spak
Kristina Zissis

WEST PALM BEACH, FLORIDA
RESIDENT PARTNERS

Richard J. Miller

RESIDENT ASSOCIATES

Mark-David Adams
William G. Capko

PARSIPPANY, NEW JERSEY
RESIDENT PARTNERS

Nicholas J. Capozzoli, Jr.
James J. Florio
Harold G. Levison
Michael J. Perrucci

PARSIPPANY, NEW JERSEY
RESIDENT COUNSEL

Joseph R. Bock
Joseph A. Hoffman
John T. Kelly
Bruce H. Levitt
C. Kenneth Shank

RESIDENT ASSOCIATES

Richard D. Ballot
Lisa Barré-Quick
Edward J. Boccher
Glenn A. Clouser
Willie E. Dennis
Michael S. Herman
Donald E. Souders, Jr.
Christopher M. Troxell
Jennifer A. Wolland

PARIS, FRANCE
RESIDENT PARTNERS

Alan F. Cariddi
Bruce C. Mee
Fabrice Rué

INTERNATIONAL COUNSEL

Vuong Van Bac

RESIDENT ASSOCIATES

Christine Bougis
Michael S. Carter
Hervé De Kervasdoué
Bijan-Emmanuel Eghbal
Carol A. Umhoefer

TOKYO, JAPAN
RESIDENT PARTNER

Takashi Matsumoto

For full biographical listings, see the Martindale-Hubbell Law Directory

MARTIN MUSHKIN (AV)

2nd Floor South, 470 Park Avenue South, 10016
Telephone: 212-779-4233
Fax: 212-779-4241

OF COUNSEL

Barbara Reader

For full biographical listings, see the Martindale-Hubbell Law Directory

NELSON, GORDON & BURSTEIN (AV)

605 Third Avenue, 10158
Telephone: 212-883-1950
Telecopier: 212-983-5048

(See Next Column)

Robert A. Burstein
Bernard S. Gordon
Lester Nelson

For full biographical listings, see the Martindale-Hubbell Law Directory

O'MELVENY & MYERS (AV)

Citicorp Center, 153 East 53rd Street, 54th Floor, 10022-4611
Telephone: 212-326-2000
Facsimile: 212-326-2061
Los Angeles, California Office: 400 South Hope Street.
Telephone: 213-669-6000.
Cable Address: "Moms".
Facsimile: 213-669-6407.
Century City, California Office: 1999 Avenue of the Stars, 7th Floor.
Telephone: 310-553-6700.
Facsimile: 310-246-6779.
Newport Beach, California Office: 610 Newport Center Drive, Suite 1700.
Telephone: 714-760-9600.
Cable Address: "Moms".
Facsimile: 714-669-6994.
San Francisco, California Office: Embarcadero Center West Tower, 275 Battery Street, Suite 2600.
Telephone: 415-984-8700.
Facsimile: 415-984-8701.
Washington, D.C. Office: 555 13th Street, N.W., Suite 500 West.
Telephone: 202-383-5300.
Cable Address: "Moms".
Facsimile: 202-383-5414.
Newark, New Jersey Office: One Gateway Center, 7th Floor, 07102.
Telephone: 201-639-8600.
Facsimile: 201-639-8630.
London, England Office: 10 Finsbury Square, London, EC2A 1LA.
Telephone: 011-44-171-256-8451.
Facsimile: 011-44-171-638-8205.
Tokyo, Japan Office: Sanbancho KB-6 Building, 6 Sanbancho, Chiyoda-ku, Tokyo 102, Japan.
Telephone: 011-81-3-3239-2800.
Facsimile: 011-81-3-3239-2432.
Hong Kong Office: 1104 Lippo Tower, Lippo Centre, 89 Queensway, Central Hong Kong.
Telephone: 011-852-523-8266.
Facsimile: 011-852-522-1760.

NEW YORK, N.Y.
MEMBERS OF FIRM

John L. Altieri, Jr.
Francis J. Burgweger, Jr.
Dale M. Cendali
Theresa A. Cerezola
Alan M. Cohen
Michael A. Curley
Cliff H. Fonstein
(Not admitted in NY)
Andrew J. Frackman
Martin Glenn
Steven L. Grossman
(Not admitted in NY)
L. Jane Hamblen
Marc Hanrahan
Adam C. Harris
Robert S. Insolia
Louis B. Kimmelman
Paul R. Koepff
Jeffrey I. Kohn
C. Douglas Kranwinkle
(Not admitted in NY)
Perry A. Lerner
Charles F. Niemeth
Jeffery L. Norton
Peter V. Pantaleo
Laurence G. Preble
Drake S. Tempest
Ko-Yung Tung
Ulrich Wagner
Jacqueline A. Weiss
Joel B. Zweibel

SPECIAL COUNSEL

Ira M. Belsky
Rosemary B. Boller
Thomas G. Carruthers
Charles W. Fournier
Daniel M. Freedman
Kathleen A. Gallagher
Joseph G. Giannola
Robert A. Grauman
Daniel M. Jochnowitz
Stephanie I. Splane
(Not admitted in NY)
Jane Taylor

RESIDENT ASSOCIATES

Paul M. Alfieri
James D. Arbogast
W. Kirk Baker
(Not admitted in NY)
Robert H. Bienstock
Nadia St. George Burgard
Ralph P. DeSanto
Thomas J. Di Resta
Erica K. Doran
Benjamin D. Feder
Aaron F. Fishbein
Kenneth A. Goldberg
Eugene P. Hanson
J. Michael Harty
Peter R. Herman
(Not admitted in NY)
Richard J. Holmstrom
Gloria Ching-hua Jan
(Not admitted in NY)
Patricia H. Kim
Stephen V. Kovarik
Robert F. Kramer
Malcolm M. Kratzer
Elizabeth Leckie
Dennis J. Martin
Susan M. McNeill
(Not admitted in NY)
Anthony L. Morrison
Maureen O'Connor
Gregory P. Patti, Jr.
Achilles M. Perry
Simon H. Prisk
Claudia E. Ray
Eric Reid
James Gerard Rizzo
Stephanie R. Rosen
Tancred V. Schiavoni, III
Scott Schrader
Darrel M. Seife
Jeanne C. Serocke
Sam S. Shaulson
Jan P. Shelburne
(Not admitted in NY)
James P. Sileneck

(See Next Column)

O'MELVENY & MYERS—*Continued*

RESIDENT ASSOCIATES (Continued)

Sheryl O. Silver
Gary M. Smith
Albert J. Solecki, Jr.
Mark E. Thierfelder
Kenneth J. Turnbull
Kenneth S. Ziman
(Not admitted in NY)

For full biographical listings, see the Martindale-Hubbell Law Directory

OTTERBOURG, STEINDLER, HOUSTON & ROSEN, P.C. (AV)

230 Park Avenue, 10169
Telephone: 212-661-9100
Cable Address: "Otlerton";
Telecopier: 212-682-6104
Telex: 960916

Kurt J. Wolff
Donald N. Gellert
William M. Silverman
Morton L. Gitter
Peter H. Stolzar
Alan R. Weiskopf
Bernard Beitel
Jonathan N. Helfat
Daniel Wallen
Scott L. Hazan
Glenn B. Rice
Albert F. Reisman
Kenneth J. Miller
Richard J. Rubin
Anthony M. Piccione
Steven B. Soll
Alan Kardon
Eugene V. Kokot
Mitchell M. Brand
Stanley L. Lane, Jr.
David W. Morse
Peter L. Feldman

COUNSEL

Lawrence B. Milling
Stephen B. Weissman

Diane B. Kaplan
Lloyd M. Green
Bruce P. Levine
Richard G. Haddad
Lauri Blum Regan
Enid Nagler Stuart
Stephen H. Alpert
Craig D. Zlotnick
Andrew M. Kramer
Jeanne-Marie Marziliano
Jenette A. Barrow
Brett H. Miller
Matthew J. Miller
John J. Kenny
Steven H. Weitzen
Richard L. Stehl
Gary G. Michael
Marc E. Schneider
Susan A. Joyce
Howard M. Sendrovitz

For full biographical listings, see the Martindale-Hubbell Law Directory

PARKER CHAPIN FLATTAU & KLIMPL, L.L.P. (AV)

1211 Avenue of the Americas, 10036
Telephone: 212-704-6000
Telecopier: 212-704-6288
Cable Address: "Lawpark"
Telex: 640347
Great Neck, New York Office: 175 Great Neck Road.
Telephone: 516-482-4422.
Telecopier: 516-482-4469.

MEMBERS OF FIRM

Mark Abramowitz
James Alterbaum
Andrea Paretts Ascher
Christopher Stewart Auguste
Barry J. Brett
Carol F. Burger
Robert M. Carmen
Aurora Cassirer
Elliot Cohen
Lloyd Frank
William D. Freedman
Michael D. Friedman
Jesse J. Graham, II
Charles P. Greenman
Stephen F. Harmon
Mark S. Hirsch
Karen F. Lederer
Michael A. Leichtling
Joel Lewittes
Edward R. Mandell
Peter M. Panken
Kevin D. Porter
Mitchell P. Portnoy
David E. Richman
Stephen G. Rinehart
Herbert L. Rosedale
Henry I. Rothman
Richard A. Rubin
Will Burt Sandler
Michael J. Shef
Gary J. Simon
Alvin M. Stein
Lee W. Stremba
Lawrence David Swift
Alan J. Tarr
B. Michael Thrope
Patricia Lynne Truscelli
Angela D. Vitali
Melvin Weinberg
Martin Eric Weisberg
Jeffrey S. Wolk
Joel M. Wolosky

SENIOR COUNSEL

Emanuel Klimpl
Seymour Levine
Irving Rosenzweig

OF COUNSEL

Edward J. Babb
Harvey M. Boneparth
Monroe Chapin
Henry Condell
Susan A. Dennehy
Raymond W. Dusch
Stuart B. Glover
Paul Goldstein
Daniel S. Greenfeld
Philip J. Hoblin, Jr.
Donald R. Levin
Mark I. Schlesinger
Flora Schnall
Michael Starr

(See Next Column)

ASSOCIATES

Amos Alter
Elyse J. Angelico
Katherine Cooney Ash
Stacey B. Babson-Smith
Bryna R. Beckler-Knoll
Susan M. Bernhardi
Jason I. Bitsky
Miles M. Borden
John Carlson
Joel A. Chernov
Leslie W. Chervokas
Rebecca M. Flynn
James D. Garbus
Miriam B. Gottesfeld
Susan E. Greenwald
E. Mark Gross
Etta M. Gumbs
Angela K. Hellard
(Not admitted in NY)
Gilbert C. Hoover, IV
Jordan A. Horvath
Debra A. Jaret
Timothy I. Kahler
Sheon Karol
Jaime L. Katcher
Elyse Lori Dranoff Kovar
Scott Lechner
Edward P. Liang
Ira Lustbader
Aleena B. Maher
Paul D. Malek
Jonathan O. Margolis
Stephen McLaughlin
Sidnie S. Menkes
Elaine S. Moshe
Robert B. Nourian
Paul J. Nozick
Amianna Pytel
Carolyn S. Reinach
Edward D. Ricchiuto
Andrew H. Sherman
Sharon H. Stern
Judith D. Szokol
Beth Housman Tenzer
Terry Marie Toto
Michael Weinsier
Ronald E. Wilhelm
(Not admitted in NY)
Christine L. Wilson
Jeffrey Wiseman
Glenn P. Zarin

For full biographical listings, see the Martindale-Hubbell Law Directory

PATTERSON, BELKNAP, WEBB & TYLER, LLP (AV)

1133 Avenue of the Americas, 10036-6710
Telephone: 212-336-2000
Fax: 212-336-2222
Moscow, Russia Office: Konushkovskaya 26 Moscow 123242, Russian Federation.
Telephone: 011-7095-253-9607. Telephone/
Fax: 011-7502-221-1857; 011-7095-564-8063.

MEMBERS OF FIRM

Christopher C. Angell
Susan Frank Bloom
Henry P. Bubel
William F. Cavanaugh, Jr.
Herbert H. Chaice
Lisa E. Cleary
Thomas R. deRosa
Gregory L. Diskant
David F. Dobbins
David W. Dykhouse
Robert J. Egan
Robert H. M. Ferguson
Philip R. Forlenza
Eugene M. Gelernter
David M. Glaser
Antonia M. Grumbach
Scott Horton
Jane B. Jacobs
Jeffrey E. LaGueux
Robert P. LoBue
Mary M. Luria
Ellen M. Martin
Thomas C. Morrison
Bernard F. O'Hare
Robert M. Pennoyer
Peter J. Pettibone
Thomas W. Pippert
James H. Powell
Andrew D. Schau
John Emile Schmeltzer, III
John P. Schmitt
Stephen W. Schwarz
Arthur D. Sederbaum
Karl E. Seib, Jr.
Richard R. Upton
Theodore B. Van Itallie, Jr.
John Winter
Stephen P. Younger
Steven A. Zalesin

OF COUNSEL

Harold R. Tyler, Jr.
John P. Persons
Robert B. Shea
Constantine Sidamon-Eristoff
Warren J. Sinsheimer
Ira T. Wender

COUNSEL

Blair Axel
Catherine B. Andreycak
Janet L. Blakeman
Frederick B. Campbell
John Delli-Venneri
Michael O. Finkelstein
Marilyn F. Friedman
Van Z. Krikorian
Jeffrey I. D. Lewis
Cecilia Loving-Sloane
Maureen W. McCarthy
W. B. McKeown
Robert M. McLaughlin
Christine H. Miller
Stephen J. Schreiber
Saul B. Shapiro
David J. Wilfert
Robert D. Wilson, Jr.

ASSOCIATES

Ronald W. Adelman
Susan D. Brown
Laura E. Butzel
Lauren S. Cahn
Lisa C. Cohen
Gordon L. DeMario
John M. DiMatteo
Avrohom P. Dubin
Richard S. Eisert
Jeffrey B. Elikan
Nina Farber
Stephanie W. Fell
Philip L. Hirschhorn
Michael R. Hobbie
Genise Jackson
Robert B. Kambic
Joel A. Kirsch
Timothy J. Klapak
Peter G. Koffler
Robin Krause
Carrie Lamitie
Robert W. Lehrburger
Mark H. Levine
Barbara A. McCormick
Christopher J. McDonald
Pedro Medina
Michael J. Mellis
Edward H. Mills Jr.
Diane Reese Moriarty
Mary Mulligan
Lisa M. Napoletano
Roosevelt N. Nesmith
Juliette M. Passer-Muslin
Diane M. Pompei

(See Next Column)

PATTERSON, BELKNAP, WEBB & TYLER LLP, *New York—Continued*

ASSOCIATES (Continued)

Ellen A. Rothschild
Sarah Greenlee Rubin
Catherine Grevers Schmidt
Joseph P. Scorese
Randall K. Short
Margaret R. Sparks
J. Andrew Stephenson
Gail F. Stone
Kimberly Sweet
Andrew L. Tureff
David M. Walker
Frederick B. Warder, III
Jennifer C. Warren
Bruce L. Wolff

MOSCOW OFFICE

ASSOCIATES

Natasha Antonova (Not admitted in the United States)
Alexander G. Dneprovski (Not admitted in the United States)
Mikhail Y. Galyatin (Not admitted in the United States)
Ludmilla Jackova (Not admitted in the United States)
Galina F. Strikhanova (Not admitted in the United States)

For full biographical listings, see the Martindale-Hubbell Law Directory

PAUL, HASTINGS, JANOFSKY & WALKER (AV)

A Partnership including Professional Corporations
Firm Established in 1951; Office in 1986
31st Floor, 399 Park Avenue, 10022-4697
Telephone: 212-318-6000
Facsimile: 212-319-4090
Los Angeles, California Office: Twenty-Third Floor, 555 South Flower Street.
Telephone: 213-683-6000.
Cable Address: "Paulhast."
Twx: 910-321-4065.
Orange County, California Office: Seventeenth Floor, 695 Town Center Drive, Costa Mesa.
Telephone: 714-668-6200.
Washington, D.C. Office: Tenth Floor, 1299 Pennsylvania Avenue, N.W.
Telephone: 202-508-9500.
Atlanta, Georgia Office: 42nd Floor, Georgia Pacific Center, 133 Peachtree Street, N.E.
Telephone: 404-588-9900.
Santa Monica, California Office: Fifth Floor, 1299 Ocean Avenue.
Telephone: 310-319-3300.
Stamford, Connecticut Office: Ninth Floor, 1055 Washington Boulevard.
Telephone: 203-961-7400.
Tokyo, Japan Office: Toranomon Ohtori Building, 8th Floor, 4-3 Toranomon 1-Chome, Minato-Ku.
Telephone: (03) 3507-0730.

MEMBERS OF FIRM

Daniel G. Bergstein
Barry A. Brooks
Victoria A. Cundiff
R. Bruce Dickson
Alfred G. Feliu
George L. Graff
William M. Hart
John P. Howitt
Euclid A. Irving
Marguerite R. Kahn
James W. Kennedy
Ronald Kreismann
Thomas R. Lamia
Roger M. Milgrim
Brendan J. O'Rourke
Charles B. Ortner
Kevin J. O'Shea
Samuel D. Rosen
Leigh P. Ryan
Robert L. Sherman
Andrew M. Short
Marc L. Silverman
Harvey A. Strickon
Lawrence I. Weinstein
Seth M. Zachary

OF COUNSEL

Kevin C. Logue
Joseph T. Moldovan
John L. Sander
Lucy Prashker
Neil A. Torpey

ASSOCIATES

Donna R. Besteiro
David Boyd Booker
Janet D. Booth
Robert L. Boyd
Peter S. Canelias
Beverly A. Chaney
Justin C. Choi
Sandra A. Crawshaw
David S. Denenberg
Elizabeth A. Fealy
Lisa M. Gigliotti
Joel A. Goldberg
Jill Greenwald
James Che-Ming Hsu
Steven D. Johnson
Roy S. Kaufman
Ken Kimura
Patricia A. Krieg
Michelle A. Leftwich
Katherine B. Lipton
Andrew M. Mayer
Michael T. Mervis
Joseph P. Opich
Suzanne Marie Pepe-Robbins
Lauren S. Peterson
Alexis Pinto
Alesia Selby Regan
Cheryl R. Saban
Nancy L. Sommer
Benjamin S. Strouse
Linda Trembicki
Angela Tung
Philip R. Weingold
Melinda C. Witmer
Lori Zablow

For full biographical listings, see the Martindale-Hubbell Law Directory

PAUL, WEISS, RIFKIND, WHARTON & GARRISON (AV)

1285 Avenue of the Americas, 10019-6064
Telephone: 212-373-3000
TDD 212-373-2000
Cable Address: "Longsight, New York".
Facsimile: 212-757-3990
Washington, D.C. Office: 1615 L Street, N.W., Suite 1300.
Telephones: 202-223-7300, TDD 202-223-7490.
Facsimile: 202-223-7420.
Cable Address: "Longsight, Washington".
Paris, France Office: 199, Boulevard Saint-Germain, 75007.
Telephone: (33-1) 45.49.33.85.
Facsimile: (33-1) 42-22-64-38.
Cable: "Longsight, Paris".
Tokyo, Japan Office: 11th Floor, Main Tower, Akasaka Twin Tower, 17-22, Akasaka 2-chome, Minato-Ku. 107.
Telephone: (81-3) 3505-0291.
Facsimile: (81-3) 3505-4540.
Beijing, People's Republic of China Office: Suite 1910, Scite Tower, 22 Jianguomenwai Dajie, 100004.
Telephones: (86-1) 5123628-30, (86-1) 5122288X.1910.
Facsimile: (86-1) 5123631.
Hong Kong Office: 13th Floor, Hong Kong Club Building, 3A Chater Road, Central Hong Kong.
Telephone: (852) 2536-9933.
Facsimile: (852) 2536-9622.

Lloyd K. Garrison (1946-1991)
Randolph E. Paul (1946-1956)
Louis S. Weiss (1927-1950)
John F. Wharton (1927-1977)

COUNSEL

Morris B. Abram
David C. Brodhead
Edward N. Costikyan
Adrian W. DeWind
Bernard H. Greene
Jay Greenfield
A. Leon Higginbotham, Jr.
Anthony B. Kuklin
James B. Lewis
Robert H. Montgomery, Jr.
Paul J. Newlon
Mordecai Rochlin
Brian L. Schorr
Howard A. Seitz
Samuel J. Silverman
John C. Taylor, 3rd
Jay Topkis
Norman Zelenko

EUROPEAN COUNSEL

Richard Dehé (Resident at Paris, France Office)
Joseph S. Iseman (Resident at Paris, France Office)
Philippe Jambrun (Resident at Paris, France Office)
Pierre E. Petit (Resident at Paris, France Office)

MEMBERS OF FIRM

Neale M. Albert
Mark H. Alcott
Allan J. Arffa
Jonathan R. Bell
Daniel J. Beller
Mark A. Belnick
Mitchell L. Berg
Mark S. Bergman
Bruce A. Birenboim
Allan Blumstein
Richard S. Borisoff
John F. Breglio
Richard J. Bronstein
Joseph E. Browdy
Cameron Clark
Lewis R. Clayton
Jay Cohen
Jerome Alan Cohen
Russell E. Colwell
Robert D. Drain
James M. Dubin
Leslie Gordon Fagen
Dominique Fargue (Resident at Paris, France Office)
Peter L. Felcher
George P. Felleman
Bernard Finkelstein
Mitchell S. Fishman
Robert C. Fleder
Martin Flumenbaum
Terence J. Fortune (Resident at Washington, D.C. Office)
Max Gitter
Eric S. Goldstein
Bruce A. Gutenplan
Gaines Gwathmey, III
Albert P. Hand
Gerard E. Harper
Seymour Hertz
Robert M. Hirsh
Jeh Charles Johnson
Arthur Kalish
Meredith J. Kane
Brad S. Karp
Alan W. Kornberg
Ruben Kraiem
David K. Lakhdhir (Resident at Tokyo, Japan Office)
Steven E. Landers (Resident at Paris, France Office)
John E. Lange (Resident, Hong Kong Office)
Robert L. Laufer
Daniel J. Leffell
Walter F. Leinhardt
Arthur L. Liman
Martin London
Edwin S. Maynard
John P. McEnroe
Colleen McMahon
Robert E. Montgomery, Jr. (Resident at Washington, D.C. Office)
Donald F. Moore
Toby S. Myerson
Matthew Nimetz
Kevin J. O'Brien
Lionel H. Olmer (Not admitted in NY; Resident at Washington, D.C. Office)
John J. O'Neil
Marc E. Perlmutter
Deborah S. Prutzman
James L. Purcell
Leonard V. Quigley
Carey R. Ramos
Carl L. Reisner
Walter Rieman
Simon H. Rifkind
Stuart Robinowitz
Sidney S. Rosdeitcher
Richard A. Rosen
Steven B. Rosenfeld
Peter J. Rothenberg
Ernest Rubenstein
Warren B. Rudman (Not admitted in NY; Resident at Washington, D.C. Office)
Jeffrey B. Samuels
Terry E. Schimek
Kenneth M. Schneider
Robert B. Schumer
Stephen J. Shimshak
David R. Sicular
John A. Silberman
Moses Silverman

(See Next Column)

PAUL, WEISS, RIFKIND, WHARTON & GARRISON—*Continued*

MEMBERS OF FIRM (Continued)

Steven Simkin
Robert S. Smith
Marilyn Sobel
Theodore C. Sorensen
Phillip L. Spector (Not admitted in NY; Resident, Washington, D.C. Office)
Judith Reinhardt Thoyer
David T. Washburn
Alfred D. Youngwood

PRINCIPAL ATTORNEYS

Martha Gray Billman
Colleen M. Codey
Carole S. Davie
Saul H. Finkelstein
Jay L. Himes
Michèle R. Jenkinson
Edwin C. Laurenson
Richard A. Mandel
Andrew J. Peck
Jonathan J. Rikoon
Norman J. Sloane
Allen M. Wieder

SPECIAL COUNSEL

Jeanette K. Chan
Richard S. Elliott (Resident at Washington, D.C. Office)
Anthony McClellan (Resident at Paris, France Office)
Jeffrey H. Olson (Resident at Washington, D.C. Office)

ASSOCIATES

Christine M. Alvarez (Not admitted in NY)
George E. Anhang
Rick B. Antonoff
Jaime A. Areizaga-Soto (Resident, Washington, D.C. Office)
John R. Ashmead
Dean S. Asofsky
Robert A. Atkins
Rory A. Babich (Resident, Hong Kong Office)
Christopher M. Basile
John F. Baughman
Ellen Friedman Bender
Jordan S. Bernstein
Marc E. Bernstein
Nancy L. Bertolino
Alan Birnbaum
Deborah E. Birnbaum
Jerome D. Blake
Jeffrey M. Bloom
Michael P. Bowen
Gidon M. Caine
Donald Gray Carden
Curtis Carmack
Sheree L. Carter
Katia Chéron (Resident at Paris, France Office)
Yvonne Y. F. Chan
Charles S. Chen
Douglas A. Cifu
Gregory A. Clarick
Stuart M. Cobert
Helen M. Corcoran
Isaac D. Corre
Cynthia E. Cunningham
Jodi A. Danzig
Marcella David
Eric R. Dinallo
Terence A. Dixon
Shari E.B. Dreier
Jay L. Dubiner
Alan Effron
Jeffrey M. Eilender
Matthew J. Epstein
Andrew M. Felner
Peter E. Fisch
Aderson Bellegarde François
Jonathan J. Freedman
Harris B Freidus
Lesley K. Friedman
Bertrand C. Fry
Diane C. Gaylor (Resident, Washington, D.C. Office)
Paul D. Ginsberg
Henri Glaser (Resident at Paris, France Office)
Marina Goland
Barry D. Goldberg
Scott A. Goldfarb
Charles F. Goldsmith (Resident, Hong Kong Office)
Charles H. Googe, Jr.
Evan R. Gottesman (Resident at Washington, D.C., Office)
Robert E. Goudie, Jr.
Glenda Gail Grace
Scott P. Grader
Jeffrey A. Greenbaum
Bruce Gruder
Jacqueline S. Guenego
Cheryl E. Hader
Claudia Hammerman
Carl W. Hampe (Resident at Washington D.C. Office)
Stephanie A. Hand
Susan L. Harris
Norman J. Harrison (Resident at Washington, D.C. Office)
Deborah Hartnett
Donald W. Hawthorne
Dina R. Hellerstein
Joanna C. Hendon
Andrew B. Herwitz
Steven C. Herzog
Howard C. Hill
Aubrey I. Holder
Elizabeth Holland
Robert E. Holo
Darrel J. Holstein (Resident at Tokyo, Japan Office)
Nicholas C. Howson (Resident at Beijing, PRC Office)
Dina G. Huebner
Jonathan H. Hurwitz
Julie V. Jacobson
Howard H Jiang
Annaliese S. Kambour
Jennifer A. Kasmin
Maria H. Keane
John C. Kennedy
Karen S. Kennedy
Helen B. Kim
George D. Kleinfeld (Resident at Washington, D.C. Office)
Helena K. Kolenda (Resident at Beijing, PRC Office)
Paul J. Kollmer (Resident at Washington, D.C. Office)
David L. Kornblau
Robert N. Kravitz
Nikolai Krylov (Not admitted in the United States)
Soon-Yub Samuel Kwon (Resident at Washington, D.C. Office)
Judith Landis
Melissa B. Lautenberg
Hang C. Lee
Matthew L. Levine
Marc O. Litt (Not admitted in NY)
Beth Rachel Lobel
Judith Stern Lobel
Erik C. Luchs (Resident, Washington, D.C. Office)
Paul J. Mahoney
Didier Malaquin
John J. Manna, Jr.
Jeffrey S. Marcus
Robert D. Marcus
Marco V. Masotti
Valérie Masset-Branche (Resident at Paris, France Office)

(See Next Column)

ASSOCIATES (Continued)

Jean Helen McMahon
Christian Merkling
Roya M. Moadel-Obedian
Brian Griffin Murphy
Jay K. Musoff
Janet F. Nezhad
Bruce E. Nussbaum (Resident, Tokyo, Japan Office)
William J. O'Brien
John F. O'Sullivan
Lynn B. Oberlander
Lori Wentworth Odierno
Sara Orenstein
Steven D. Pacht
Nicole T. Pappas
Robert P. Parker (Resident at Washington, D.C. Office)
David Jon Pester
Audrey E. Prashker
Deborah E. Proner
Valerie E. Radwaner
Conrad M. Rippy
Brian D. Robbins
Andrew N. Rosenberg
Fay Rosenfeld
Margot S. Rubin
Sherrie L. Russell-Brown
Susan E. Ryan (Resident at Washington, D.C. Office)
Dominique M. Ryder (Resident at Paris, France Office)
Dale M. Sarro
Stephen L. Saxl
Laura M. Schachter
Marc Schachter
Kara Scheinmann
Karyn S. Schiller
Lee A. Schneider
Elliott J. Schuchardt
Frank Schuchat (Resident at Washington, D.C. Office)
Adam H. Schuman
James H. Schwab
Elizabeth J. Schwartz
Jordana G. Schwartz
Laura J. Schwartz
Laura L. Segal
Bradford H. Sewell
Marina L. Sheriff
Charles C. Shulman
David M. Siegal
Mark A. Silberman
William C. Silverman
Adam C. Silverstein
Stephen M. Sinaiko
Gary Stein
Jane B. Stewart
Lori Sullivan
Wenlong Sun
Andrée Sylvestre
Aidan Synnott
Kimberly S. Templeton
Talitha Thurau
Susan A. Tobias
Patrick J. Trostle
Miori Tsubota
Jess A. Velona
Joseph P. Verdon
Maria T. Vullo
Kathleen M. Walker
William A. Walker
Linda J. Wank
Deborah B. Weiss
Richard A. Weissman
Peter D. Weitzner
Mark D. West
Sylvia Wong
Anita Chu Yelland (Not admitted in the United States) (Resident, Hong Kong Office)
Barbara A. Yellen (Resident at Washington, D.C. Office)
Eric D. Young
Donn B. Zaretsky
Edward S. Zas
Jennifer H. Zimmerman
Andrew E. Zobler

For full biographical listings, see the Martindale-Hubbell Law Directory

PHILLIPS, LYTLE, HITCHCOCK, BLAINE & HUBER (AV)

437 Madison Avenue, 10022
Telephone: 212-759-4888
Telecopier: 212-308-9079
Buffalo, New York Office: 3400 Marine Midland Center.
Telephone: 716-847-8400.
Telecopier: 716-852-6100.
Jamestown, New York Office: 307 Chase Bank Building, 8 E. Third Street.
Telephone: 716-664-3906.
Telecopier: 716-664-4230.
Rochester, New York Office: 1400 First Federal Plaza.
Telephone: 716-238-2000.
Telecopier: 716-232-3141.
Fredonia, New York Office: 11 East Main Street.
Telephone: 716-672-2164.
FAX: 716-672-7979.

PARTNERS

William J. Brennan
William J. Brown
Chester L. Cobb
Kenneth R. Crystal
Frank Maas

SPECIAL COUNSEL

Michael G. Shannon

ASSOCIATES

Bruce A. Brown
Robert J. Chanis
Christopher G. Dorman
Beth Gebeloff
Lauri Goodwyn
Ira L. Herman
Ellen R. Moring
William M. Rossi-Hawkins
John E. Stackpole
Milan K. Tyler

For full biographical listings, see the Martindale-Hubbell Law Directory

PROSKAUER ROSE GOETZ & MENDELSOHN LLP (AV)

1585 Broadway, 10036
Telephone: 212-969-3000
Cable Address: "Roput"
Telex: TRT 175719 ROPUT NY
FAX: 212-969-2900
Washington, D.C. Office: 1233 Twentieth Street, N.W., Suite 800.
Telephone: 202-416-6800.
Los Angeles, California Office: 2121 Avenue of the Stars, Suite 2700.
Telephone: 310-557-2900.
San Francisco, California Office: 555 California Street, Suite 4604.
Telephone: 415-956-2218.

(See Next Column)

PROSKAUER ROSE GOETZ & MENDELSOHN LLP, *New York—Continued*

Boca Raton, Florida Office: One Boca Place, Suite 340 West, 2255 Glades Road.
Telephone: 407-241-7400.
Clifton, New Jersey Office: 1373 Broad Street. P.O. Box 4444.
Telephone: 201-779-6300.
Paris, France Office: 9 rue Le Tasse.
Telephone: (33-1) 45 27 43 01

MEMBERS OF FIRM

Joseph M. Proskauer (1877-1971)
Alfred L. Rose (1886-1981)
Norman S. Goetz (1887-1972)
Bertram A. Abrams
Ira Akselrad
Rory Judd Albert
Alfred Appel
L. Robert Batterman
Joseph Baumgarten
Irwin M. Birnbaum
Franklin S. Bonem
Edward A. Brill
Edward Brodsky
Lawrence H. Budish
Arnold I. Burns
Perry A. Cacace
Robert A. Cantone
Michael A. Cardozo
Stuart M. Cohen
Peter D. Conrad
David H. Diamond
Robert Dillof
Charles E. Dropkin
Klaus Eppler
Paul H. Epstein
Joseph Erdman
Bruce E. Fader
Allen I. Fagin
Glenn M. Feit
Michael E. Feldman
Michael E. Foreman
Jacob I. Friedman
Wilbur H. Friedman
James J. Fuld
George G. Gallantz
Howard L. Ganz
Murray Gartner
Bernard Gold
Leon Phillip Gold
Sarah S. Gold
Richard L. Goldberg
David I. Goldblatt
Richard M. Goldstein
Ira M. Golub
Claire P. Gutekunst
Andrew D. Heineman
Kenneth S. Hilton
Philip J. Hirsch
Sheldon I. Hirshon
Jeffrey A. Horwitz
Alan B. Hyman
Jacob Imberman
Arnold S. Jacobs
Jerold D. Jacobson
Alan S. Jaffe
Robert J. Kafin
Robert M. Kaufman
Stephen R. Kaye
Steven M. Kayman
Edward W. Kerson
Nancy A. Kilson
Steven L. Kirshenbaum
Stanley Komaroff
Edward S. Kornreich
Saul G. Kramer
Steven C. Krane
Larry M. Lavinsky
Joseph M. Leccese
David M. Lederkramer
Howard N. Lefkowitz
Arnold J. Levine
Robert J. Levinsohn
Jeffrey W. Levitan
Bruce L. Lieb
Lawrence J. Lipson
Charles Looker
Morton M. Maneker
Gregg M. Mashberg
Kathleen M. McKenna
Walter Mendelsohn
Thomas C. Moore
Carole O'Blenes
Steven E. Obus
Martin J. Oppenheimer
Ronald R. Papa
Alan P. Parnes
Bettina B. Plevan
Bernard M. Plum
Sara S. Portnoy
Andrea S. Rattner
Ronald S. Rauchberg
Alan S. Rosenberg
Lawrence J. Rothenberg
Stephen W. Rubin
Myron D. Rumeld
Bradley I. Ruskin
Paul Salvatore
Peter G. Samuels
Gail Sanger
Donald W. Savelson
Ronald S. Schacht
Neal S. Schelberg
Aaron J. Schindel
Minna Schrag
Dale A. Schreiber
Wendy J. Schriber
George M. Shapiro
Howard A. Shapiro
Edward Silver
Charles S. Sims
Michael S. Sirkin
David W. Sloan
Ronald F. Storette
Philip M. Susswein
Bernard Tannenbaum
Solomon L. Warhaftig
Jay D. Waxenberg
Herbert T. Weinstein
Allan R. Williams
Jerold Zieselman
M. David Zurndorfer

COUNSEL

Mark L. Friedman
Daniel R. Kaplan
Aaron C. Kinderlehrer
Jerome S. Traum

SPECIAL COUNSEL

Stephen A. Albert
Mark Barnes
Elana R. Butler
Alan S. Cohen
Mark E. Davidson
Mary A. Donovan
Remy J. Ferrario
Martha E. Gifford
Marc J. Goldstein
Abraham Gutwein
William E. Hellerstein
Toby R. Hyman
Jack P. Jackson
Stephen P. Kramer
Francis D. Landrey
Fredric C. Leffler
Richard A. Levin
James F. Parver
Gail S. Port
John W. Ritchie
Henry O. Smith, III
Richard L. Spinogatti
Lynn E. Usdan
Lowell D. Willinger
Marya Lenn Yee

CONSULTANTS

Susan G. Curtis
Carole Simon

(See Next Column)

ASSOCIATES

Neil H. Abramson
Cigdem A. Acar
Jeffrey S. Agnew
Bela P. Amladi
Walter Eliot Bard
Steven A. Beede
G. Michael Bellinger
Lisa A. Berkowitz
Gregg L. Bienstock
Martin Bienstock
Lawrence S. Block
Allegra H. Blumfield
Ira G. Bogner
Jennifer A. Borg
Gregory A. Brehm
Genevieve Cannon
Andre C. Castaybert
Sean C. Cenawood
Roberta K. Chevlowe
Karen E. Clarke
Allan H. Cohen
Christopher J. Collins
John E. Daly (Not admitted in NY)
Michael D. Davis
Orrie Dinstein
Pamela L. Dreizen
Lauren J. Drooker
Mitchell A. Drossman
Scott A. Eggers
Matthew L. Eilenberg
Nancy B. Errichetti
Gary I. Fields
Jeffrey N. Fink
Michael A. Freeman
Glenda L. Fussa
Maria F. Gandarez
Fredric J. Glass
Deborah L. Goldman
Herman L. Goldsmith
Steven M. Golub
Sheila M. Gowan
Daniel J. Greaney
Eliot P. Green
Sanford H. Greenberg
Daniel R. Halem
Bruce G. Hart, Jr.
Eric P. Heichel
Gary E. Herzlich
Samuel R. Hill
Jonathan M. Hoffman
Katharine L. Huth
Deborah J. Jacobs
Wayne D. Katz
Paul Kaufman
Lillian R. Kessler
Michael Ik-Hee Kim
Martin Klein
Phyllis A. Klein
Howard S. Koh
Wendy L. Kornreich
Israel E. Kornstein
Stephen B. Kuhn
James W. Langham
Daniel M. Laudor
Lee A. Lazarus
Diane E. Lederman
Henry J. Leibowitz
Joanne K. Lelewer
Eric R. Levine
Jane A. Levine
Steven M. Levy
Gwen J. Lourie
Julie Langer Lowitz
Jeffrey M. Lubell
Robert A. Mandel
Carter M. Mann
Bruce L. McDermott (Not admitted in NY)
James D. Meade
Francine E. Menaker
Bernard J. Michael
Francine Miller
Isaac Montal
Meyer Muschel
Alex S. Navarro
Andrea B. Neuman
Daniel A. Novak
Joseph C. O'Keefe
Elise Anne Olgin (Not admitted in NY)
Vera Ovadia (Not admitted in NY)
Michele M. Ovesey
Mitchell S. Padover
Douglas L. Perlman
Michelle E. Phillips
Dominic J. Picca
David A. Picon
Miouly E. Pongnon
Seth M. Popper
Jennifer T. Radding
Andrew W. Reich
Deborah J. Renard
Michael H. Roffer
Xavier E. Romeu
Allan B. Rothschild
John Rousakis
Samuel H. Rudman
Scott K. Rutsky
Leslie S. Safian
Richard S. Samson
Juliet Sarkessian
Susan F. Scharf
Janet Elizabeth Scherl
Edward W. Scheuermann
Wendy H. Schwartz
Ellen L. Shapiro
Mitchell C. Shelowitz
Peter J. W. Sherwin
Jeffrey L. Shuchat
John Siegal
Rosaria Sinisi
Lori S. Smith
Stephen D. Solomon
Benedicta Stampe (Not admitted in NY)
Karen L. Stefflre
Jeffrey G. Stein
Abby Sternschein
Elizabeth Susser
Michael A. Sussmann
Aaron W. Tandy
Sharif Touray
David A. Tucker (Not admitted in NY)
Rafael A. Vargas (Not admitted in NY)
Royce Wain (Not admitted in NY)
Elissa A. Weiner
Bernard Weinreb
Stephen L. Weinstein
Steven D. Weinstein
William G. Wright (Not admitted in NY)
Miriam Wugmeister

WASHINGTON, D.C. PARTNERS

Jon A. Baumgarten
Mark J. Biros
Arnold I. Burns
Joseph E. Casson
Warren L. Dennis
Malcolm J. Harkins, III
Ian K. Portnoy
Richard H. Rowe
Christopher Wolf

WASHINGTON, D.C.
SPECIAL COUNSEL

David C. Beck
Thomas H. Brock
Bradley L. Kelly
Peter B. Robb (Not admitted in NY)
Eric J. Schwartz
Duane K. Thompson
Michael K. Wyatt

(See Next Column)

PROSKAUER ROSE GOETZ & MENDELSOHN LLP—*Continued*

WASHINGTON, D.C. ASSOCIATES

William M. Altman
Margaret J. Babb
Donald L. Bell, II
Richard S. Binstein
Robert S. Canterman
Stephen B. Fabrizio
James P. Holloway
Dorothy M. Ingalls
David M. Levine
Elizabeth A. Lewis
Laura J. Oberbroeckling
Matthew J. Oppenheim
Cheralyn E. Schessler
Pamela Beth Small
Michael D. Smith

LOS ANGELES, CALIFORNIA PARTNERS

Howard D. Behar
Henry Ben-Zvi
Jeffrey A. Berman
Harold M. Brody
Scott P. Cooper
Thomas W. Dollinger
Steven G. Drapkin
Howard D. Fabrick
Mitchell M. Gaswirth
Bernard D. Gold
Carole E. Handler
Paul D. Rubenstein
Marvin Sears
Lois D. Thompson
Martin S. Zohn

SPECIAL COUNSEL

Walter Cochran-Bond
Kenneth Krug

LOS ANGELES, CALIFORNIA ASSOCIATES

Aaron P. Allan
Nicholas P. Connon
Julie M. Doyle
Alan H. Finkel
Robert M. Gorman
Dana Hirsch Lipman
David S. Lippman
Guy A. Mason
Seth A. Miller
Antonia Ozeroff
Mary H. Rose
Adam J. Rosen
James W. Ryals
Lori E. Sambol
David R. Scheidemantle
Karen L. Stefflre
Leslie A. Wederich
Michael R. Wilner
Scott J. Witlin

SAN FRANCISCO, CALIFORNIA PARTNERS

Dennis T. Daniels
Thomas J. Dowdalls
John H. Feldmann, III
William E. Horwich
Robert V. Kuenzel
J. Mark Montobbio
Joseph W. Russell

SAN FRANCISCO, CALIFORNIA ASSOCIATES

Kenneth G. Downs
Matthew K. Fawcett
Robert B. Mison
Ingrid P. Mittermaier
Ioana Petrou
Philip L. Ross
Michael J. Shpizner

BOCA RATON, FLORIDA PARTNERS

Joseph Erdman
Albert W. Gortz
Allan H. Weitzman
Christopher C. Wheeler

BOCA RATON, FLORIDA SPECIAL COUNSEL

Donn A. Beloff

BOCA RATON, FLORIDA ASSOCIATES

Edward L. Artau
Christine A. Butler
Howard K. Coates, Jr.
Paul J. Geller
Stuart T. Kapp
George A. Pincus
Ellen Laird Royal
Donald E. Thompson, II
Matthew H. Triggs

PARIS, FRANCE PARTNERS

William E. Krisel
Delia B. Spitzer

CLIFTON, NEW JERSEY PARTNER

Kathleen M. McKenna

SPECIAL COUNSEL

Donald B. Shanin

CLIFTON, NEW JERSEY ASSOCIATES

Pamela Davis-Clarke
David W. MacGregor

For full biographical listings, see the Martindale-Hubbell Law Directory

PUTNEY, TWOMBLY, HALL & HIRSON (AV)

Bar Building, 36 West 44th Street, 10036
Telephone: 212-704-0300
Telecopier: 212-575-0595
New Jersey Office: 120 Wood Avenue South, Suite 600, Iselin, New Jersey, 08830.
Telephone: 908-632-2502.
Telecopier: 908-632-2506.
Long Island Office: 29 Park Avenue, Manhasset, New York, 11030.
Telephone: 516-365-3329.
Telecopier: 516-627-8631.

MEMBERS OF FIRM

Edward F. Callan (1918-1986)
Miles W. Hirson (1921-1987)
Howard F. Ordman (1914-1988)
Louis H. Hall, Jr. (1909-1991)
Charles J. Groppe
Joseph R. Parauda
Louis A. Trapp, Jr.
James J. Dean (Resident Partner, New Jersey Office)
Alexander Neave
Daniel F. Murphy, Jr.
Francis E. Lake, Jr.
Winifred D. Morio
Michael T. McGrath
Robert J. Pape, Jr.
Thomas A. Martin
William M. Pollak
Leon Choate, Jr.

(See Next Column)

MEMBERS OF FIRM (Continued)

Dustan T. Smith
John L. Amabile
James E. McGrath, III
Mark E. Haranzo

COUNSEL

Charles O. Strahley
Donald J. Maroldy
John P. Hale
Norman Fassler

ASSOCIATES

Craig M. Bonnist
John Derek Wales
Beverly M. Barr
E. Parker Neave
Shari B. Lash

For full biographical listings, see the Martindale-Hubbell Law Directory

REAVES & YATES (AV)

545 Madison Avenue, 10022
Telephone: 212-308-4600
Fax: 212-308-4851

James A. Reaves

OF COUNSEL

Joan Goodwin Zooper

For full biographical listings, see the Martindale-Hubbell Law Directory

REID & PRIEST LLP (AV)

40 West 57th Street, 10019
Telephone: 212-603-2000
Fax: 212-603-2298
Washington, D.C. Office: Market Square, 701 Pennsylvania Avenue, N.W., 20004.
Telephone: 202-508-4000.
FAX: 202-508-4321.

MEMBERS OF FIRM

Gerald Aksen
Peter K. Anglum
William T. Baker, Jr.
Kathleen M. Balderston
Martin G. Bunin
Jeffrey B. Cobb
Howard A. Cooper (Resident in Washington, D.C. Office)
Raymond F. Dacek (Resident in Washington, D. C. Office)
Deborah A. DeMasi (Resident in Washington, D.C. Office)
Emmett N. Ellis, IV
Richard M. Farmer
Adin C. Goldberg
Marvin G. Goldman
Alan S. Goldstein
Lee M. Goodwin (Resident in Washington, D.C. Office)
Richard S. Green
Robert S. Greenbaum
Leonard Gubar
Robert T. Hall, III (Resident in Washington, D.C. Office)
David R. Hardy
Patricia M. Healy (Resident in Washington, D.C. Office)
Harry G. Heching
Jeanne Simkins Hollis (Washington, D.C. Office)
John T. Hood
Thomas J. Igoe, Jr.
David E. Jacobson (Resident in Washington, D.C. Office)
Richard J. Kane
James N. Karas, Jr.
Gregory Katz
Thomas C. Kent
Stephen H. Kinney, Jr.
Peter M. Kirby (Resident in Washington, D.C. Office)
William A. Kirk, Jr. (Resident in Washington, D.C. Office)
Richard J. Leidl (Resident in Washington, D.C. Office)
Steven R. Loeshelle
Phillip G. Lookadoo (Resident in Washington, D.C. Office)
Jeffrey A. Lowin
Sean S. Macpherson
John D. McGrane (Resident in Washington, D. C. Office)
H. Joseph Mello
Tedson J. Meyers (Resident in Washington, D.C. Office)
Stephan M. Minikes (Resident in Washington, D.C. Office)
Floyd L. Norton, IV (Resident in Washington, D.C. Office)
Judith D. O'Neill (Resident in Washington, D.C. Office)
Elizabeth W. Powers
Courtney M. Price (Not admitted in NY; Resident in Washington, D.C. Office)
Robert J. Reger, Jr.
Bruce A. Rich
Mark J. Riedy (Resident in Washington, D.C. Office)
David S. Robbins
Audrey A. Rohan
John R. Schaefgen, Jr. (Resident in Washington, D.C. Office)
Robert G. Schuur
Arthur C. Silverman
Garrett K. Smith
Richard Ian Solomon
Kevin Stacey
Diana A. Steele
Richard P. Swanson
Marc D. Teitelbaum
Bruce A. Templeton (Resident in Washington, D.C. Office)
J. Anthony Terrell
Ronald G. Todd
Robert B. Viner
James I. Warren
Steven L. Wasserman
Evan S. Widlitz
Louis H. Willenken
Peter C. Williams
Timothy S. Wright
Michael J. Zimmer (Resident in Washington D.C. Office)

SENIOR COUNSEL

Richard M. Merriman (Washington, D. C. Office)
Harry A. Poth, Jr.
William H. Saltsman

(See Next Column)

REID & PRIEST LLP, *New York—Continued*

OF COUNSEL

Jeffrey G. Berman (Washington, D.C. Office)
Robert M. Fields
David A. Gantz
Michele R. Jawin
K. William Kolbe
David E. LeFevre
Edward J. Martin, III
Herbert B. Max
Margaret P. Nastro
Susan L. Robbins
Rohit Sabharwal
Vincent D. Salvatore, Jr.
Charles F. Schirmeister

LEGAL CONSULTANTS

Tetsuya Araseki (Not admitted in United States)
Luis H. Vizioli (Not admitted in United States)

ASSOCIATES

Douglas F. Allen, Jr.
Susan L. Bedford
Joseph J. Blecher
Sandra J. Blitz
Bradford C. Brown
Lawrence B. Brownridge
Nina R. Cannon
Margaret Carfagno
Sharon P. Carlstedt
Peter B. Cohen
Jonathan W. Cole
Dean M. Colucci (Washington, DC Office)
Brendan M. Connell, Jr.
Christopher Connolly
Pamela A. Curran
Laura M. D'Orsi (Washington, D.C. Office)
M. Christine Cornett Drummond (Not admitted in NY; Washington, D.C. Office)
William M. Dudley (Not admitted in NY; Washington, D.C. Office)
Jeffrey E. Dupler
George Dwight, II
Gerald P. Farano (Not admitted in NY; Washington, D.C. Office)
Stephen W. Feingold
Kevin C. Fitzgerald (Not admitted in NY; Washington, D.C. Office)
Michael F. Fitzpatrick
Louise M. Fitzsimons
Christopher J. Foreman (Not admitted in NY)
Evan M. Foulke
Jill R. Franco (Not admitted in NY)
Frederick R. Fucci
Tara Kalagher Giunta (Not admitted in NY; Washington, D.C. Office)
Walter J. Godlewski, III
Michael R. Gordon
Jonathan W. Gottlieb (Not admitted in NY; Washington, D.C. Office)
Christina G. Grasso
Thomas M. Griffin
Daniel Guetta
Thomas C. Havens
Janet Hernandez (Washington, D.C. Office)
Lawrence S. Hirsh
Alan S. Hoffman
Janna E. M. Honig
Catherine Hood
Mary Ann K. Huntington (Washington, D.C. Office)
Charles P. Juster
Jennifer L. Karas (Not admitted in NY; Washington, D.C. Office)
Franziska Klebe
Jodi F. Krieger
Alan Lescht (Washington, D.C. Office)
Joseph H. Lilly, III
Laura E. Longobardi
Laurie S. Marsh
Monica P. McCabe
Brian J. McManus (Not admitted in NY; Washington, D.C. Office)
Douglas B. Miller (Washington, D.C. Office)
Josefa Sicard Mirabal
Manuel A. Miranda (Washington, D.C. Office)
James K. Mitchell (Washington, D. C. Office)
William M. Muller
Timothy M. Murphy (Washington, D.C. Office)
Gregory L. Nelson (Not admitted in NY; Washington, D.C. Office)
Peter K O'Brien
Christopher P. Parnagian
Gregory G. Pavin
Rosanne Pennella
Kimberly M. Phillips
Michelle H. Phillips (Washington, D.C. Office)
Mary M. Popper
Bruce L. Richardson (Not admitted in NY; Washington, D.C. Office)
Carla L. Romita
Maria Ross
Robin A. Roth
Warren S. Sacks
Lynnette M. Santin
Peter Seiden
Donald L. Smith
Pamela C. Tames
Brian L. Taylor
Ronit Tenzer-Gross
Linda M. Terner
Mary Louise Weber
Kenneth B. Weiner (Washington, D.C. Office)
Michael C. Weinstein
Robin M. Weintraub
Allison Jo Wertheim
Charles M. Yoon

For full biographical listings, see the Martindale-Hubbell Law Directory

---

ROGERS & WELLS (AV)

Two Hundred Park Avenue, 10166-0153
Telephone: 212-878-8000
Facsimile: 212-878-8375
Telex: 234493 RKWUR
Washington, D.C. Office: 607 Fourteenth Street, N.W., Washington, D.C. 20005-2011.
Telephone: 202-434-0700.
Facsimile: 202-434-0800.
Los Angeles, California Office: 444 South Flower Street, Los Angeles, California 90071-2901.
Telephone: 213-689-2900.
Facsimile: 213-689-2999.

(See Next Column)

Paris, France Offices: 47, Avenue Hoche, 75008-Paris, France.
Telephone: 33-1-44-09-46-00.
Facsimile: 33-1-42-67-50-81.
Telex: 651617 EURLAW.
London, England Office: 58 Coleman Street, London EC2R 5BE, England.
Telephone: 44-71-628-0101.
Facsimile: 44-71-638-2008.
Telex: 884964 USLAW G.
Frankfurt, Germany Office: Lindenstrasse 37, 60325 Frankfurt/Main, Federal Republic of Germany. Telephone 49-69-97-57-11-0.
Facsimile: 49-69-97-57-11-33.

SENIOR PARTNER

William P. Rogers

EXECUTIVE COMMITTEE

James N. Benedict
David W. Bernstein
Laurence E. Cranch
Thomas A. McGavin, Jr.
Mark F. Pomerantz
James B. Weidner

MANAGING PARTNER

James M. Asher

PARTNERS

Roy C. Andersen
Kevin J. Arquit
Thomas W. Avent, Jr.
Walter R. Bailey
Eileen Bannon
Brad R. Becker
Leora Ben-Ami
James N. Benedict
David W. Bernstein
Jay L. Bernstein
David J. H. Billington
G. David Brinton
Thomas M. Britt, III
Nancy A. Brown
Alejandro E. Camacho
John K. Carroll
Alan M. Christenfeld
John M. Christian
Richard A. Cirillo
Nicholas L. Coch
Laurence E. Cranch
John D. Dadakis
John E. Daniel
Roberto Dañino
Dennis J. Drebsky
Samuel M. Feder (Not admitted in NY)
Joanne Feil
Joseph Ferraro
Johannes K. Gäbel
L. Martin Gibbs
Alan L. Gosule (Not admitted in NY)
Allen Curtis Greer, II
Robert C. Hammerling
William D. Haney, III
Sara P. Hanks (Not admitted in NY)
John A. Healy
George P. Hoare, Jr.
Steven A. Hobbs
Mark Holland
Paul M. Hopkins
Klaus H. Jander
Cynthia L. Kahn
John K. Keitt, Jr.
John E. Kidd
Robert E. King, Jr.
Steven T. Kolyer
Joseph H. Levie
David B. Levinson
Robert A. Lindgren
Donald F. Luke
Leonard B. Mackey, Jr.
Richard T. McDermott
Thomas A. McGavin, Jr.
Craig S. Medwick
Shephard W. Melzer
Paul C. Meyer
James W. Paul
Fioravante G. Perrotta
Stephen E. Poltrack
Mark F. Pomerantz
John M. Quitmeyer
Charles S. Rich
James M. Ringer
David A. Schulz
Melvin L. Schweitzer
Robert K. Sharp
John J. Sheehy
Louise Sommers
Margaret Blair Soyster
Joseph H. Spain
Ward B. Stevenson, Jr.
Lewis Bart Stone
David L. Taub
Frederick B. Utley, III
Norman J. Wachtel
Craig M. Walker
James B. Weidner
Jeffrey H. Weitzman
Peter Whitridge Williams
Richard N. Winfield
David J. Yeres

SENIOR COUNSEL

Loren C. Berry
Eugene L. Bondy, Jr.
Frank X. Clair
Craig L. Collins
Robert E. Frisch
William R. Glendon
Frederick P. Glick
William F. Koegel
Leo P. Larkin, Jr.
Robert D. Larsen
Frederick W. P. Lorenzen
John B. Loughran
Caesar L. Pitassy
James V. Ryan
Frederick G. Tate

COUNSEL AND OF COUNSEL

Helayne L. Baron
Vincent J. Coyle, Jr.
Warren L. Feldman
Edward J. FitzPatrick
Barbara M. Goodstein
Yukio Kashiba
C. Joseph Laughon, II
Selinda A. Melnik
Andrew L. Oringer
Guy C. Quinlan
Joel S. Rublin
Jerome L. Wilson

ASSOCIATES

Joseph A. Adams
Jack G. Alfandary
Gerald T. Balacek
Bari M. Balber
Véronique P. Bardach (Not admitted in NY)
Thomas I. Barnett
Bonnie A. Barsamian
John M. Basnage
Joseph C. Benedetti
David L. Bernstein
Elizabeth Q. Boehmcke
Frank J. Bruttomesso
Gary R. Carney, Jr.
Dr. Patricia A. Carson
Ellen J. Casey
Michele E. Cassidy
Richard S. Catalano
James G. Cavoli
Stefanie V. Chang
Heidi C. Chen
Stacey B. Chervin

(See Next Column)

ROGERS & WELLS—*Continued*

ASSOCIATES (Continued)

Philip G. Chiaramonte
Lena K. Chung
Shannon R. Clark
William J. Cohane (Not admitted in NY)
Jeffrey P. Cohen
Neil G. Cohen
Jerry P. Coleman
S. H. Spencer Compton
Dawn M. Conry
Robert E. Creese
Tammy A. Davis (Not admitted in NY)
Patricia A. De Meyere
Bret S. Derman
Teresa A. DeTurris
Maria B. Diaz
David C. Djaha
Thomas Dolan
Nadia A. Dombrowski
Grace M.F.P. Dos Santos
David J. Duquette, Jr.
Robert J. Edwards
Adam M. Fiore
Thomas F. Fleming
Carolyn K. Foley
Lawrence H. Fox
Theodore E. Francis
Vivian A. Fried
Michael P. Gaughan
David A. Gold
Dawn E. Goldberg
Steven R. Goodman
Paul B. Goucher
Louis Greco
Laura S. Greenstein
Christopher J. Haas
James S. Hassan
Carol A. Mateer Hessler
Peter M. Hoffman
Brian T. Hourihan
Laura L. Icken
Judith B. Jobin
Joy J. Kaplan
Margaret B. Kelley
John S. Kim
Y. Maggie Kim
Michael F. Klein
Mark A. Kornfeld
Timothy W. Korth
Michael B. Kupin
John D. Lamb
Hilary Lane
Susan Lee
Frederick A. Leone
Jon R. Lewis
David I. Lewittes
Craig M. Lieberman
Jeffrey A. Lieberman
John T. Lutz
Louis T. Mangan
Lori A. Martin
Carlos E. Martinez
David F. Matlin
Joan B. Mazur
Matthew E. McCabe (Not admitted in NY)
David E. McCraw
Larry P. Medvinsky
David Meister
James D. Miller
Kenneth L. Miller
Monica G. Mittelstadt
Francis S. Moezinia
David T. Moldenhauer
Alan J. Morrison
James F. Moyle
Paul G. Murphy
Steven J. Musumeci
Christina L. Nargolwala
John A. Nathanson
Gerard P. Norton
Rosanne Notaro
Gol C. Ophir
Christopher J. O'Rourke
Michael A. O'Shea
Chul Pak
Nicholas G. Papastavros
Chandra R. Patel
Andrew Y. Pau
Robert Penchina
Michelle M. Pfeiffenberger
Tristan Pivacek
Richard G. Price
Stephen J. Quine
David P. Rankin
Barry W. Rashkover
Juergen R.H. Reemers
Judith M. Reilly
Stephen B. Reynolds
Jeong-Won Rhee
Donald L. Rhoads
Michael J. Richter
Karl A. Roessner
Jack J. Rose
Mark H. Rose
Elissa M. Rosenburgh (Not admitted in NY)
Maurice N. Ross
Joseph Rotella
Philip E. Roux
Mario V. Salandra
Julie B. Salzman
Ronald M. Sanders
Joanne M. Scalard
Robert D. Schaffer
Mark D. Scheinblum
Thomas K. Schulte
Deborah R. Schwartz
Martin L. Seidel
Sungjean Seo
Thomas G. Sharpe
William T. Slamkowski
Jeffrey Sonnabend
John A. Squires
Craig S. Stein
Rita McCloy Stephanz
Mary Tang
David K. Thornquist
Vincent B. Tritto
Andrew M. Tucker
Herbert S. Washer
Mark D. Weinberger
Kathleen L. Werner
Bruce R. Wilde
Kelly P. Wilson
Alice F. Yurke
Earl S. Zimmerman

WASHINGTON, D.C. OFFICE

SENIOR PARTNER

William P. Rogers

PARTNERS

Kevin J. Arquit
John H. C. Barron, Jr.
Robert T. Carney
Roger A. Clark
Roberto Dañino
Anthony F. Essaye (Resident)
Brandon J. Fields
Ira D. Hammerman
John Paul Ketels
Steven A. Newborn
William Silverman
Ryan Trainer
Dale C. Turza
Charles A. Zielinski

SENIOR COUNSEL

Eugene T. Rossides

COUNSEL AND OF COUNSEL

Whitney Adams
James M. Lynch
William Morris
Thomas R. Petty
Stuart Rothman
Carrie A. Simon
Samuel A. Stern (Not admitted in NY)

(See Next Column)

CONSULTANTS

Barbara J. Covell
Rinaldo Petrignani
Virginia L. Snider

LOS ANGELES, CALIFORNIA OFFICE

PARTNERS

Jeffrey S. Allen
Michael D. Berk
Allan E. Ceran
G. Howden Fraser
John A. Karaczynski
Terry O. Kelly
Michael A. McAndrews
Carl W. Sonne
I. Bruce Speiser

COUNSEL

Randolph H. Elkins
Edward Lasker
Aaron M. Peck

PARIS, FRANCE OFFICE

PARTNERS

Philippe X. Ledoux
Alexander Marquardt
Christian Orengo
Antoine Paszkiewicz

CONSULTANT

Souham El Harati

LONDON, ENGLAND OFFICE

PARTNERS

Eric C. Bettelheim
Daniel Bushner
Sidney Charles Kurth

CONSULTANT

Hugh Dykes

FRANKFURT, GERMANY OFFICE

PARTNERS

Johannes K. Gäbel
Klaus H. Jander

COUNSEL

Dr. Michael F. Griesbeck
Dieter G. Zwicker

For full biographical listings, see the Martindale-Hubbell Law Directory

ROSENMAN & COLIN (AV)

575 Madison Avenue, 10022
Telephone: 212-940-8800
Telecopiers: (212) 940-8776; (212) 935-0679
Cable Address: "Rocokay New York"
Telex: 427571 ROSCOL (ITT); 971520 RCFLC NYK (WU)
Washington, D.C. Office: 1300 19th Street, N.W., 20036.
Telephone: 202-463-7177.
Telecopier: 202-429-0046.
New Jersey Office: Suite 2600, 1 Gateway Center, Newark, New Jersey 07102-5397.
Telephone: 201-645-0572.
Telecopier: 201-645-0573.

MEMBERS OF FIRM

Samuel I. Rosenman (1896-1973)
Ralph F. Colin (1900-1985)
Gordon M. Alpert
Eleanor Breitel Alter
Mal L. Barasch
Franklin F. Bass
Paul A. Baumgarten
Paul L. Bindler
Jerome S. Boros
Lawrence I. Brandes
Howard J. Braun (Resident, Washington, D.C. Office)
Jeffrey L. Braun
Helene Brezinsky
Lauren Reiter Brody
H. Paul Burak
Herman A. Bursky
Lawrence B. Buttenwieser
James J. Calder
Edward H. Cohen
Harry P. Cohen
Saul S. Cohen
Jill E. Darrow
Gilbert S. Edelson
Lawrence D. Eisenberg
Nancy K. Eisner
John F. Finnegan
Mark I. Fisher
Robert I. Fisher
Marshall H. Fishman
Richard H. Fortmann
Jeff J. Friedman
Robert E. Friedman
Joseph L. Getraer
Robert W. Gottlieb
Andrew J. Green
Peter N. Greenwald
Richard A. Gross (Resident, Washington, D.C. Office)
Albert L. Jacobs, Jr.
Howard S. Jacobs
Stephen T. Kelton
Robert L. Kohl
Richard G. Leland
Eric M. Lerner
Arthur S. Linker
Alfred Miller
Merril A. Mironer
Peter F. Nadel
Robert M. Raives
Stephen L. Ratner
Alan I. Raylesberg
Lee H. Robinson
Gerald A. Rosenberg
David E. Ross
Arnold I. Roth
Howard J. Rothman
Joshua S. Rubenstein
Gilbert A. Samberg
Fred M. Santo
Howard Schneider
Clifford H. Schoenberg
Stephen R. Senie
Michael T. Sillerman
Donald H. Siskind
Robert E. Smith
Marybeth Sorady (Resident, Washington, D.C. Office)
Joel W. Sternman
Marc M. Tract
Calvin D. Trowbridge, Jr.
Eugene L. Vogel
Eric J. Wallach
Gerald Walpin
Lisa Weiss
Joel Allen Yunis
David J. Zinberg
Howard Alan Zipser
Joseph Zuckerman

(See Next Column)

ROSENMAN & COLIN, *New York—Continued*

COUNSEL

Arthur M. Borden
Stanley Diamond
Lawrence R. Eno
Max Freund
Maurice H. Goetz
Maurice C. Greenbaum
Maria T. Jones
William M. Kaplan
Howard J. Kashner
Natalie I. Koether
Samuel H. Lindenbaum
Michael V. P. Marks
Manuel Maxwell
William Natbony
Lionel E. Pashkoff (Resident, Washington, D.C. Office)
Benet Polikoff, Jr.
Jesse D. Reingold
Michael Roth
William S. Rubinstein
Andrew J. Schoen
Lloyd I Singer
Mark H. Sparrow

SPECIAL COUNSEL

Charles Harper Anderson, Jr.
Francis R. Angelino
Henry Beck
Philippe Bennett
Linda D. Crawford
Pamela Ehrenkranz
David A. Florman
Theodore A. Howard (Resident, Washington, D.C. Office)
Richard A. Ifft (Resident, Washington, D.C. Office)
Jerold L. Jacobs (Resident, Washington, D.C. Office)
Martin D. Juvelier
Milton J. Kain
Brant K. Maller
Barbara Brooke Manning
Robert A. Mazer (Resident, Washington, D.C. Office)
Kelly L. Morron
Donald M. Nisonoff
Barry M. Okun
Leila J. Rubler
Judi Scott
Jay A. Segal
Sandra L. Spalletta (Resident, Washington, D.C. Office)
Joseph V. Willey

SENIOR ATTORNEYS

Sylvia Arnowich
Ronni G. Davidowitz
Mark A. Greenstein
John F. Settineri

Richard M. Appel
Julie C. Bachelor
Neil S. Belloff
David Bolen
Kenneth C. Brown
Michael J. Brown
Frances Kulka Browne
Karen J. Buchsbaum
Loree Buksbaum (Not admitted in NY)
Mary Cademartori
Pamela M. Capps
Jennifer A. Coen
Stephen H. Cohen
Wendy E. Cohen
Xiomara Corral (Not admitted in NY)
Diane P. da Cunha
Timothy J. Eaton
Sharon R. Egilinsky
Janet Ellis-Meiman
Todd J. Emmerman
Sharon I. Farman
Jonathan J. Faust
Kevin T. Fingeret
Avery S. Fischer
Mark D. Fischer
Mary B. Fisher
Marla Franzese
Michael Dean Gaffney (Resident, Washington, D.C. Office)
Sheryl B. Galler
Philip B. Gerson
Nancy K. Goldsmith
Amy M. Grabino
Garrett L. Gray
Rosemary Halligan
Michael R. Halsband
David B. Horn
Iqbal S. Ishar
Steve E. Issacs (Not admitted in NY)
Austin Jacobson
Nancy Alyse Jacobson
Steven M. Judelson
Perry V. Kalajian
Sharon Kantrowitz
Judith Z. Katz
Andrew L. Klauber
Jonathan J. Konoff
Daniel A. Ladow
Donna L. LaMagna
David H. Landau
Lisa B. Lapinski (Resident, Washington, D.C. Office)
Heidi Lichthardt
Dale J. Lois
Lauri B. London (Not admitted in NY)
Philip J. Loree Jr.
Regina A. Loughran
Lisa D. Love
Kenneth K. Lowenstein
David J. Mark
Leslie Marlow
Helen Collier Mauch
Joel Maxman
Robin S. Meister
Jill L. Miller
Diane L. Mooney (Resident, Washington, D.C. Office)
Edward T. Moy
Joshua C. Nathan
Israel Nissenbaum
Karla A. Olivier
Patience Jane O'Neil
Brian J. O'Sullivan
David J. Papier
Jayshree Parthasarathy
Andrew J. Perel
Michael Peskowitz
Steven E. Plotnick
William M. Popalisky
Barbara Quackenbos
Leslie Roth-Reider
Sharon Rothner-Klein
Bruce M. Sabados
Shelley Sadowsky (Resident, Washington, D.C. Office)
Bret R. Salzer (Not admitted in NY)
Kathleen E. Schaaf
James E. Scranton
Maxine R. Shapiro
Jerome S. Silber
John D. Singer
Martha N. Steinman
Robert H. Strongin
Patricia M. Suh
Mitchell E. Sussman
Gary R. Tarnoff
James P. Tenney
Maria E. Valero
Michael I. Verde
Lori Vinciguerra
Wayne A. Wald
Darren B. Watson
Gail Wheeler
Susan Wiener
J. Mark Young (Resident, Washington, D.C. Office)

For full biographical listings, see the Martindale-Hubbell Law Directory

ROYALL KOEGEL & WELLS

(See Rogers & Wells)

RUBIN BAUM LEVIN CONSTANT & FRIEDMAN (AV)

A Partnership including Professional Corporations and Professional Associations
30 Rockefeller Plaza, 10112
Telephone: 212-698-7700
Cable Address: "Rubaleco, New York"
Telex: 147264
Miami, Florida Office: Rubin Baum Levin Constant Friedman & Bilzin. Suite 2500 First Union Financial Center, 200 South Biscayne Boulevard.
Telephone: 305-374-7580.
Woodbridge, New Jersey Office: 90 Woodbridge Center Drive, Suite 150.
Telephone: 855-2220.
Fax: 908-855-2221.

MEMBERS OF FIRM

Ronald Greenberg
Michael J. Weinberger
Gerald Harris
Stephen A. Marshall
Edward Klimerman
Jeffrey R. Mann
Allan M. Rosenbloom
Thomas G. Barrett
Barry A. Adelman
Brian L. Bilzin (P.A.) (Resident Partner at Miami, Florida Office)
Irwin M. Rosenthal
David A. Mandel (P.C.)
John C. Sumberg (P.A.) (Resident Partner at Miami, Florida Office)
Richard D. Mondre (P.A.) (Resident Partner at Miami, Florida Office)
Alvin J. Goldman
Larry A. Stumpf (P.A.) (Resident Partner at Miami, Florida Office)
Alan D. Axelrod (P.A.) (Resident Partner at Miami, Florida Office)
Martin J. Schwartz
Michael J. Emont
Martin P. Michael
Paul A. Gajer
Brit Geiger
Stewart H. Wahrsager
Denise M. Tormey
Arlene G. Dubin
Richard L. Sadowsky
Martin A. Schwartz (P.A.) (Resident Partner at Miami, Florida Office)
David W. Trench (P.A.) (Resident Partner at Miami, Florida Office)
Robert B. Zimmerman
Norman A. Moscowitz (P.A.) (Resident Partner at Miami, Florida Office)
Paul H. Aloe
Gregg S. Lerner
Richard M. Goldstein (P.A.) (Resident Partner at Miami, Florida Office)
Marc J. Stone (P.A.) (Resident Partner at Miami, Florida Office)
Jonathan D. Drucker
Marina Rabinovich

COUNSEL

Max J. Rubin
Abraham G. Levin (P.C.)
Jack G. Friedman (P.C.)
Irving Constant (P.C.)
Martin A. Coleman (P.C.)
Burton R. Rubin (P.C.)
Burton Joel Ahrens
Walter M. Epstein

SPECIAL COUNSEL

David M. Goldberg

ASSOCIATES

Norman Alpert
Darin S. Billig (Not admitted in NY)
Howard S. Bonfield
Arnold A. Brown (Resident Associate at Miami, Florida Office)
Faith L. Charles
Lawrence M. Devine
Audrey Alterman Ellis (Resident Associate at the Miami, Florida Office)
H. Leigh Feldman
Kenneth David Friedman
Jacob J. Givner (Resident Associate at Miami, Florida Office)
Jeffrey H. Glassover (Resident Association, Miami, Florida Office)
Sharon H. Jacoby
Keith Moskowitz
Mindy L. Pallot (Resident Associate at the Miami, Florida Office)
Richard G. Primoff
Charles H. Ratner (Resident Associate at Miami, Florida Office)
Michael C. Rosenstein
Saul B. Rosenthal (Resident Associate, Miami, Florida Office)
Dov Schwell
Joel Slawotsky
Susan J. Toepfer (Resident Associate at Miami, Florida Office)
Craig Weiner

For full biographical listings, see the Martindale-Hubbell Law Directory

---

SATTERLEE STEPHENS BURKE & BURKE (AV)

230 Park Avenue, 10169-0079
Telephone: 212-818-9200
Cable Address: "Saterfield," New York
Telex: 233437
Telecopy or Facsimile: (212) 818-9606 or 818-9607
Summit, New Jersey Office: 47 Maple Street.
Telephone: 908-277-2221.
Westfield, New Jersey Office: 105 Elm Street.
Telephone: 908-654-4200.

(See Next Column)

SATTERLEE STEPHENS BURKE & BURKE—*Continued*

MEMBERS OF FIRM

Randolph G. Abood
Bernard M. Althoff
Peter A. Basilevsky
Gilman S. Burke
Robert M. Callagy
Robert W. Cockren
Seth H. Dubin
Mark A. Fowler
Robert H. Goldie
Daniel G. Gurfein
William M. Jackson
Dwight A. Kinsey
Stanley Mailman
Howard A. Neuman
Denis R. Pinkernell
Paul J. Powers, Jr.
James F. Rittinger
John Gregory Saver
Kenneth A. Schultz

COUNSEL

Henry J. Formon, Jr. (1921-1993)
James T. Boyle, Jr. (Not admitted in NY)
Maurice Hahn
Robert C. Hubbard
Karen C. Hunter
Wallace B. Liverance, Jr.
Thomas V. Manahan
William A. Moore
Bryan Webb
Barbara L. Zinsser

ASSOCIATES

Barbara B. Cadigan (Not admitted in NY; Resident, Summit, New Jersey Office)
Geraldine Donovan (Not admitted in NY)
William T. McCue
Kirk H. O'Ferrall
Carla N. Barone
Jan R. Uhrbach
Joshua M. Rubins
Careen Brett Shannon
Ted J. Chiappari
James J. Coster
Gregory W. Herbert
Darcy M. Katris
Andrea Peyser
Steven K. Warner (Resident, Summit, New Jersey Office)
Christopher V. Albanese
John L. Slafsky
J. Allison Strickland
Paige K. Grossman
Catherine L. Woodman
Frances M. Bradley (Not admitted in NY)
Maureen Martin Smith (Not admitted in NY)

For full biographical listings, see the Martindale-Hubbell Law Directory

SAUL, EWING, REMICK & SAUL (AV)

Twenty-First Floor, 237 Park Avenue, 10017
Telephone: 212-551-3502
TWX: 425170
Telecopier: 697-8486
Philadelphia, Pennsylvania Office: 3800 Centre Square West.
Telephone: 215-972-7777.
Cable Address: "Bidsal".
TWX: 83-4798.
Telecopier: XEROX 7020 215-972-7725.
Wilmington, Delaware Office: 222 Delaware Avenue, P.O. Box 1266, 19899-1266. For Courier Delivery: 222 Delaware Avenue, Suite 1200, 19801.
Telephone: 302-421-6800.
Cable Address: "Bidsal".
TWX: 83-4798.
Telecopier: XEROX 7020 302-421-6813.
Malvern, Pennsylvania Office: Suite 200, Great Valley Corporate Center, 300 Chester Field Parkway.
Telephone: 215-251-5050.
Cable Address: "BIDSAL".
TWX: 83-4798.
Telecopier: 215-651-5930.
Voorhees, New Jersey Office: Plaza 1000, Main Street, Suite 206 Evesham & Kresson Roads.
Telephone: 609-424-0098.
Telecopier: XEROX 7020 609-424-2204.
Harrisburg, Pennsylvania Office: 240 North 3rd Street, P.O. Box 1291, 17108-1291. For Courier Delivery: 240 N. 3rd Street, Suite 700, 17101.
Telephone: 717-238-8300.
Telecopier: 717-238-4622.
Trenton, New Jersey Office: Capital Center, 50 East State Street, 08608.
Telephone: 609-393-0057.
Fax: 609-393-5962.

MEMBERS OF FIRM

Spencer W. Franck, Jr.
Charles C. Freyer
Pamela S. Goodwin (Managing Resident Partner, Trenton, New Jersey Office)
Alan R. Gordon
Maurice D. Lee, III
Herbert S. Riband, Jr.
Gregory J. Rice
Robert N. Sandler
Miles H. Shore
Anthony F. Walsh

SPECIAL COUNSEL

Robert S. Price
Sondra K. Slade

ASSOCIATES

Gail Cummings Levan

For full biographical listings, see the Martindale-Hubbell Law Directory

SCHEKTER RISHTY GOLDSTEIN & BLUMENTHAL P.C. (AV)

1500 Broadway, 21st Floor, 10036
Telephone: 212-768-3000
Fax: 212-944-7372

(See Next Column)

David M. Blumenthal
Neil S. Goldstein
Joel Rishty
Leon Schekter

Cheryl R. Bloomberg
Ronald A. Fishman
Jeremy J. Satkiewicz
Phylis D. Sherman

OF COUNSEL

Morton A. Frankfurt
Stephen J. Kornreich
David N. Milner
Albert N. Podell
David H. Wander

For full biographical listings, see the Martindale-Hubbell Law Directory

SCHIFF HARDIN & WAITE (AV)

A Partnership including Professional Corporations
Founded 1864
150 East 52nd Street, Suite 2900, 10022
Telephone: 212-753-5000
Facsimile: 212-753-5044
Chicago, Illinois Office: 7200 Sears Tower.
Telephone: 312-876-1000.
Facsimile: 312-258-5600.
TWX: 910-221-2463.
Washington, D.C. Office: 1101 Connecticut Avenue, N.W.
Telephone: 202-778-6400.
Facsimile: 202-778-6460.
Peoria, Illinois Office: 300 Hamilton Boulevard, Suite 100.
Telephone: 309-673-2800.
Facsimile: 309-673-2801.
Merrillville, Indiana Office: 8585 Broadway, Suite 842.
Telephone: 219-738-3820.
Facsimile: 219-738-3826.

RESIDENT PARTNER

Paul A. Scrudato

RESIDENT ASSOCIATES

Paul J. Collins

For full biographical listings, see the Martindale-Hubbell Law Directory

SCHNADER, HARRISON, SEGAL & LEWIS (AV)

330 Madison Avenue, 10017
Telephone: 212-973-8000
Cable Address: "Dejuribus, New York"
Fax: 212-972-8798
Philadelphia, Pennsylvania Office: Suite 3600, 1600 Market Street.
Telephone: 215-751-2000.
Cable Address: "Walew."
Fax: 215-751-2205; 215-751-2313.
Washington, D.C. Office: Suite 600, 1913 Eye Street, N.W.
Telephone: 202-463-2900.
Cable Address: "Dejuribus, Washington."
Fax: 202-296-8930; 202-775-8741.
Harrisburg, Pennsylvania Office: Suite 700, 30 North Third Street.
Telephone: 717-231-4000.
Fax: 717-231-4012.
Norristown, Pennsylvania Office: Suite 901, One Montgomery Plaza.
Telephone: 215-277-7700.
Fax: 215-277-3211.
Pittsburgh, Pennsylvania Office: Suite 2700, Fifth Avenue Place, 120 Fifth Avenue.
Telephone: 412-577-5200.
Fax: 412-765-3858.
Scranton, Pennsylvania Office: Suite 700, 108 North Washington Avenue.
Telephone: 717-342-6100.
Fax: 717-342-6147.
Washington, Pennsylvania Office: 8 East Pine Street.
Telephone: 412-222-7378.
Fax: 412-222-0771.
Cherry Hill, New Jersey Office: Suite 200, Woodland Falls Corporate Park, 220 Lake Drive East.
Telephone: 609-482-5222.
Fax: 609-482-6980.
Atlanta, Georgia Office: Suite 2550 Marquis Two Tower, 285 Peachtree Center Avenue, N.E.
Telephone: 404-215-8100.
Fax: 404-223-5164.

MEMBERS OF THE FIRM IN NEW YORK

John N. Adams
John E. Bradley
M. Christine Carty
Alan A. D'Ambrosio
Isaac E. Druker
W. Michael Garner
Allan D. Goodridge
Emery W. Harper
Greggory B. Mendenhall (Not admitted in NY)
Francis X. Nolan, III
John M. Wyser-Pratte

COUNSEL TO THE FIRM IN NEW YORK

John A. Astorina
Lisa J. Savitt
Leo S. Ullman

SENIOR COUNSEL

Donald H. Rivkin

(See Next Column)

SCHNADER, HARRISON, SEGAL & LEWIS, *New York—Continued*

SENIOR ATTORNEY

Stephen C. F. Diamond

ASSOCIATES IN NEW YORK

Mario M. Kranjac
Joseph R. Manghisi
Nina Massen
Peter J. Schankowitz
David J. Zarfes
(Not admitted in NY)
Nancy D. Zehner

For full biographical listings, see the Martindale-Hubbell Law Directory

SCHULTE ROTH & ZABEL (AV)

900 Third Avenue, 10022
Telephone: 212-758-0404; 800-346-9644
Cable Address: "Olympus NewYork"
Telex: 426775
West Palm Beach, Florida Office: 777 South Flagler Drive.
Cable Address: "P. B. Olympus."
Telephone: 407-659-9800.

MEMBERS OF FIRM

Robert M. Abrahams
Kim E. Baptiste
Lester M. Bliwise
David M. Brodsky
Bonnie Lynn Dixon
Edward G. Eisert
Howard B. Epstein
Michael J. Feinman
Michael S. Feldberg
Steven J. Fredman
Stuart D. Freedman
Susan C. Frunzi
Alan R. Glickman
Lawrence S. Goldberg
Howard O. Godnick
Ronald S. Kochman (Resident, West Palm Beach Office)
Daniel J. Kramer
Burton Lehman
Andrew H. Levy
Isaac B. Lustgarten
John G. McGoldrick
Michael C. Mulitz
Robert S. Nash
Stephen R. Nelson
Mark A. Neporent
James M. Peck
Martin L. Perschetz
Gregory P. Pressman
Frederic L. Ragucci
Kurt F. Rosell
Robert Rosenberg
Paul N. Roth
William A. Ruskin
Jeffrey S. Sabin
Catherine Samuels
Frederick P. Schaffer
Stephen J. Schulte
Charles L. Shapiro
Daniel S. Shapiro
Chaye Zuckerman Shapot (Partner in Charge of Professional Development)
Howard F. Sharfstein
Joseph R. Simone
Irwin J. Sugarman
Shlomo C. Twerski
Janet C. Walden
Alan S. Waldenberg
Paul N. Watterson, Jr.
Paul E. Weber
Marc Weingarten
Andre Weiss
William D. Zabel

SPECIAL COUNSEL

Stephen C. Corriss
Fred R. Green

ASSOCIATES

Debra R. Anisman
Jeffrey A. Aronson
Eric Asmundsson
Michelle S. Babbitt
Conrad G. Bahlke
Hollis Anne Bart
Karen Baseman
Scott V. Beechert
Philippe Benedict
Dean S. Benjamin
Ethan E. Benovitz
Stephanie R. Breslow
Kirk L. Brett
Mark Allen Broude
Michael A. Bucci II
Lisa K. Buckser
Brooks R. Burdette
Glenn Eric Butash
Linda J. Cahn
Bridget E. Calhoun
Jane H. Carmody
Jason E. Carter
Gary Claar
Robert M. Denicola
Mark K. Dowd (Not admitted in NY)
Brian Dunefsky
Janie H. Farkas
Lynn R. Feldman
M. Soledad Feliciano
Martin Fineberg
Richard D. Fox
Deborah Lynn Freedman
David J. Furman
Andrew L. Gaines
Susan R. Galligan
Ilana Hoschander Goldberg
Daniel S. Gluck
Steven D. Gorelick
Gary R. Greenman
Maureen A. Hanlon
Marcy Ressler Harris
Yonina Z. Helman (Not admitted in NY)
Douglas R. Hirsch
Christine Y. Homer
Kelley K. Hwang
Aimée P. Jalazo
Lynn S. Kaplan
Mark E. Kaplan
Charlotte Anne Kelley
Todd Kesselman
Theodore A. Keyes
Robin J. Klar
Roxanne Lagano
Karen E. Lanci
Adam G. Landis
Seth R. Landau
Scott D. Levin
Audrey Hope Levine
Carol Weiner Levy
Caroline Krass Levy
Junling Ma
Vinita K. Mendiratta
Jill R. Mindlin
Richard M. Morris
David J. Murray
Norris Nissim
Peter A. Nussbaum
Alexander J. Ornstein
Mark R. Palmermo
Anthony L. Perricone
Julie Petrow
F. Peter Phillips
F. Barbara Gluck Reid
James K. Rinzler
Christopher P. Ronan
Frederick B. Rosner

(See Next Column)

ASSOCIATES (Continued)

Karen P. Ross
Jesse R. Rubin
Leslie A. Rubin
Jay H. Rubinstein
Marcia S. Ruskin
Jennifer K. Schecter
Lawrence P. Schnapf
Harold E. Schwartz
Sara L. Silbiger
Sharon Beth Soloff
Darnley Dickinson Stewart
John P. Stigi III
Kevin C. Sullivan
Jonathan Taylor
Susan Blackman Tilson
Adam Blaine Toft
Osvaldo F. Torres
Jennifer Trahan
Han-Hsien Tuan
Andris J. Vizbaras
Elise S. Wagner
Susan S. Wallach
William Zeena, Jr. (Resident, West Palm Beach, Florida Office)

For full biographical listings, see the Martindale-Hubbell Law Directory

SEWARD & KISSEL (AV)

(Smith & Martin 1890)
One Battery Park Plaza, 10004
Telephone: 212-574-1200
Cable Address: "Sewkis New York"
Telex: 23-9046; 62-0982
Facsimile: 212-480-8421
Washington, D.C. Office: 1200 G Street, N.W., Suite 350.
Telephone: 202-737-8833.
Facsimile: 202-737-5184.
Representative Office: Nádor utca 11, 1051 Budapest, Hungary.
Telephone: 361-132-7115.
Facsimile: 361-132-7940.

MEMBERS OF FIRM

Eugene P. Souther
Blaise G. A. Pasztory
Albert A. Walsh
Arrial S. Cogan
Bruce D. Senzel
Marlene D. Daniels
James H. Hancock
Anthony R. Mansfield
Anthony C. J. Nuland (Resident, Washington, D.C.)
M. William Munno
Bradford J. Race, Jr.
Peter E. Pront
Dale C. Christensen, Jr.
David L. Fobes
Hadley S. Roe
Russell C. Prince
Craig Thomas Hickernell
Janet R. Zimmer
Robert A. Walder
John Eric Tavss
William F. Kuntz, II
Gary J. Wolfe
Lawrence Rutkowski
Ronald L. Cohen
Mark J. Hyland
Paul T. Clark (Resident, Washington, D.C.)
Jonathan Berger
Thomas G. MacDonald
Mark A. Brody
Paul M. Gottlieb
John J. Cleary
Michael J. McNamara
Kalyan Das
John F. Rigney
Patricia A. Poglinco

SENIOR COUNSEL

George C. Seward

COUNSEL

Lester Kissel
Richard H. Valentine
Edward W. Beuchert
Robert B. Simon
Dr. Péter Komáromi (Resident, Budapest Hungary)
Keith H. Ellis (Resident, Washington, D.C.)
Alberto L. Calafell
Richard H. Metsch

ASSOCIATES

Peter L. Allen
A. Tyson Arnedt (Not admitted in NY)
Hector Becil
Brad L. Berman
Kathryn L. Boyne
Colin T. Burke
Patrick J. Burke
Michael J. Campanelli
Greg B. Cioffi
Billie Cook
John E. Denneen
Michael P. Enright
William J. Ferri
Alison M. Fuller (Resident, Washington, D.C.)
John J. Galban
James F. X. Hiler
Lisa A. Klar
Catherine E.M. Kortlandt
Mark D. Kotwick
Michael E. Kreitman
Wendy Lebowitz-Prager
Susan J. Leong
Susan J. Lorin
Robert E. Lustrin
Francis R. McGann
Darren McSpedon
Peter C. Mester
Eileen C. Murphy
Kevin E. O'Brien
Meryl S. Rosenblatt
Dan J. Schulman
Michael B. Siller
Andrew Silverstein
Jeffrey D. Silverstein
Karen G. Singer
Scott R. Smith
Patricia A. Spraguer
Andrew Stewart
Monica A. Treitmeier-McCarthy
Elizabeth Warner (Resident, Washington, D.C.)

For full biographical listings, see the Martindale-Hubbell Law Directory

New York—Continued

SHEARMAN & STERLING (AV)

599 Lexington Avenue New York, New York 10022-6069 and Citicorp Center, 153 East 53rd Street, 10022-4676
Telephone: (212) 848-4000
Telex: 667290 Num Lau
Fax: 599 Lexington Avenue: (212) 848-7179
Citicorp Center: (212) 848-5252
Abu Dhabi, United Arab Emirates Office: P.O. Box 2948.
Telephone: (971-2) 324477.
Fax: (971-2) 774533.
Beijing, People's Republic of China Office: Suite #2205, Capital Mansion, No. 6, Xin Yuan Nan Road. Chao Yang District Beijing, 100004.
Telephone: (861) 465-4574.
Fax: (861) 465-4578.
Budapest, Hungary Office: Szerb utca 17-19, 1056 Budapest.
Telephone: (36-1) 266-3522.
Fax: (36-1) 266-3523.
Düsseldorf, Federal Republic of Germany Office: Königsallee 46, D-40212 Düsseldorf.
Telephone: (49-211) 13 62 80.
Telex: 8 588 294 NYLO.
Fax: (49-211) 13 33 09.
Frankfurt, Federal Republic of Germany Office: Bockenheimer Landstrasse 55, D-60325 Frankfurt am Main.
Telephone: (49-69) 97-10-70.
Fax: (49-69) 97-10-71-00.
Hong Kong, Hong Kong Office: Standard Chartered Bank Building, 4 Des Voeux Road Central, Hong Kong.
Telephone: (852) 2978-8000.
Fax: (852) 2978-8099.
London, England Office: 199 Bishopsgate, London EC2M 3TY.
Telephone: (44-71) 920-9000.
Fax: (44-71) 920-9020.
Los Angeles, California Office: 725 South Figueroa Street, 21st Floor, 90017-5421.
Telephone: (213) 239-0300.
Fax: (213) 239-0381, 614-0936.
Paris, France Office: 12 rue d'Astorg, 75008.
Telephone: (33-1) 44-71-17-17.
Telex: 282964 Royale.
Fax: (33-1) 44-71-01-01.
San Francisco, California Office: 555 California Street, 94104-1522.
Telephone: (415) 616-1100.
Fax: (415) 616-1199.
Taipei, Taiwan Office: 7th Floor, Hung Kuo Building, 167 Tun Hwa North Road.
Telephone: (886-2) 545-3300.
Fax: (866-2) 545-3322.
Tokyo, Japan Office: Shearman & Sterling (Thomas Wilner Gaikokuho-Jimu-Bengoshi Jimusho), Fukoku Seimei Building, 5th Fl. 2-2-2, Uchisaiwaicho, Chiyoda-ku, Tokyo 100, Japan.
Telephone: (81 3) 5251-1601.
Fax: (81 3) 5251-1602.
Toronto, Ontario, Canada Office: Commerce Court West, Suite 4405, P.O. Box 247, M5L 1E8.
Telephone: (416) 360-8484.
Fax: (416) 360-2958.
Washington, D.C. Office: 801 Pennsylvania Avenue, N.W., Suite 900, 20004-2604.
Telephone: (202) 508-8000.
Fax: (202) 508-8100.

MEMBERS OF FIRM

Stephen R. Volk (Senior Partner)
Lee A. Kuntz (Managing Partner)
Robert E. Dineen, Jr. (New York and Washington)
Mark Kessel
Robert H. MacKinnon
Joseph T. McLaughlin
Whitney D. Pidot
Jaculin T. Aaron (Los Angeles)
Richard S. Aldrich, Jr.
Laurence M. Bambino
Alexander C. Bancroft
Roger J. Baneman
Laura B. Bartell
Douglas P. Bartner
Stuart J. Baskin
Ronald M. Bayer (Los Angeles)
Robert A. Bergquist (Washington, D.C.)
Emily Berlin
Henry C. Blackiston, III
David L. Bleich
Peter H. Blessing
William M. Burke (Los Angeles)
Paul M. Butler, Jr.
John J. Cannon, III
Thomas J. Carlson
Sheri P. Chromow
Wayne Dale Collins
Kathleen M. Comfrey
Creighton O'M. Condon
Frederick T. Davis
Ronald DeKoven
Alan F. Denenberg (Hong Kong)
Thomas A. Dieterich
Joseph A. Doyle
Philip B. Dundas, Jr. (New York and Abu Dhabi)
Cornelius J. Dwyer, Jr.
Jerry V. Elliott
Elizabeth Hazlitt Emerson
Jeremy G. Epstein
Jeffrey S. Facter (San Francisco)
Arthur Norman Field
Stuart K. Fleischmann
William E. Flowers
William M. Friedrich
Pamela M. Gibson (Managing Partner, Toronto)
Stephen T. Giove
William R. Giusti
Donald A. Goldsmith
Bonnie Greaves
Jonathan L. Greenblatt (Washington, D.C.)
Alfred C. Groff (San Francisco)
Faith D. Grossnickle

(See Next Column)

MEMBERS OF FIRM (Continued)

Michael Gruson (New York and Germany)
James T. Halverson
David W. Heleniak
John S. Herbert
Robert E. Herzstein (Washington, D.C)
William H. Hinman (Managing Partner, San Francisco)
William E. Hirschberg
E. Bradford Holbrook, III
Phillip L. Jackson
Andrew B. Jánszky
Jonathan Jewett
Lucian C. Jones
Thomas Joyce (Managing Partner, London)
Richard B. Kendall (Los Angeles)
Michael J. Kennedy (San Francisco)
Joel S. Klaperman
John N. Kramer, Jr.
Kenneth M. Kramer
Dean S. Krystowski (San Francisco)
W. Jeffrey Lawrence
Timothy G. Little
Peter D. Lyons
John J. Madden (Managing Partner, Europe; Paris)
Thomas S. Martin (Washington, D.C.)
John A. Marzulli, Jr. (London)
David A. McCabe
Debra D. McCullough
John A. Millard
Franklin H. Moore, Jr.
John D. Morrison, Jr.
Alfred Mudge
Margaret Murphy
Danforth Newcomb
Jeanne C. Olivier
Clarence W. Olmstead, Jr.
John L. Opar, Jr.
Dennis P. Orr (New York and Washington)
Werner L. Polak
Albert Theodore Powers (Managing Partner, Hong Kong)
Rebecca Foster Prentice (Los Angeles)
Kenneth S. Prince
Daniel L. Rabinowitz
Clark T. Randt, Jr. (Hong Kong)
Linda E. Rappaport
Andrew W. Regan
Gerald Rokoff
William J. F. Roll, III
Alfred J. Ross, Jr.
Marc M. Rossell
Vladimir R. Rossman
Reade H. Ryan, Jr. (Los Angeles)
Paul S. Schreiber
Steven E. Sherman (Managing Partner, San Francisco)
Chris M. Smith
Darryl Snider (Los Angeles)
Justin J. Stevenson III
Elise I. Strauss
Hubertus V. Sulkowski (Managing Partner, Paris and Budapest)
James P. Tallon
Arbie R. Thalacker
Georg F. Thoma (Dusseldorf)
Edward L. Turner III (Hong Kong; Managing Partner, Asia)
Cynthia E. Urda Kassis
Brice T. Voran (Los Angeles)
George J. Wade
Rohan S. Weerasinghe
Henry Weisburg
Jonathan M. Weld
Benzion J. Westreich
Torrey L. Whitman
R. Paul Wickes
William J. Wiegmann (Frankfurt)
Thomas B. Wilner (Tokyo and Washington, D.C.)
John D. Wilson
Mark R. Wingerson
Mary Kate Wold
William Yaro

OF COUNSEL

Hans H. Angermueller
William F. Baxter (San Francisco)
Edward Bransilver (Washington, D.C.)
Robert Carswell
Robert L. Clare, Jr.
Robert M. Feely
Henry B. Guthrie
Henry Harfield
Arne Hovdesven
C. Bedford Johnson
Gilbert Kerlin
Robert H. Knight
Robert A. MacCrindle (Paris)
David T. McGovern (Paris)
Stanley I. Rubenfeld
John T. Schmidt
Edward Hallam Tuck
Henry S. Ziegler

EUROPEAN COUNSEL

Norbert Andreae (Paris)
John E. Baltay (Budapest)
James M. Bartos (London)
Emmanuel Gaillard (Paris)
Andrea K. Muller (Paris)
Robert C. Treuhold (Paris)

FRENCH COUNSEL

Hervé Letréguilly (Paris)

OTHER COUNSEL

Dennis Ardi (Entertainment Law Counsel, Los Angeles)
Stephan E. Becker (Not admitted in NY; International Trade Counsel, Washington, D.C.)
Charles E. Biggio (Antitrust Counsel)
Robert W. Fagiola (Real Estate Counsel, New York)
Charles S. Gittleman (Counsel, New York)
Mark J. Harty (Asian Counsel, Taipei)
Joyce E. Heinzerling (Counsel, New York)
Chu Liu
Bradley Kent Sabel (Counsel, New York)
Joanna Shally (Litigation Counsel, New York)
Michael W. Smith (Middle East Counsel, Abu Dhabi)
George T. Spera, Jr. (Compensation and Benefits Counsel, New York)
John G. Stewart (International Financial Counsel, London)

SENIOR ATTORNEYS

Jeffrey P. Crandall
Helen Doo
Jack D. Gunther, Jr.
Judith S. Leonard
John M. Sykes, III
David J. Wray

For full biographical listings, see the Martindale-Hubbell Law Directory

New York—Continued

SIDLEY & AUSTIN (AV)

A Partnership including Professional Corporations
875 Third Avenue, 10022
Telephone: 212-906-2000
Telecopier: 212-906-2021
Chicago, Illinois Office: One First National Plaza 60603.
Telephone: 312-853-7000.
Telecopier: 312-853-7036.
Los Angeles, California Office: 555 W. Fifth Street, 40th Flr., 90013-1010.
Telephone: 213-896-6000.
Telecopier: 213-896-6600.
Washington, D.C. Office: 1722 Eye Street, N.W. 20006.
Telephone: 202-736-8000.
Telecopier: 202-736-8711.
London, England Office: Broadwalk House, 5 Appold Street, EC2A 2AA.
Telephone: 011-44-71-621-1616.
Telecopier: 011-44-71-626-7937.
Tokyo, Japan Office: Taisho Seimei Hibiya Building, 7th Floor, 9-1, Yurakucho, 1 Chome, Chiyoda-ku, 100.
Telephone: 011-81-3-3218-9500.
Facsimile: 011-81-3-3218-5922.
Singapore Office: 36 Robinson Road, #18-01 City House, Singapore 0106.
Telephone: 011-65-224-5000.
Telecopier: 011-65-224-0530.

RESIDENT PARTNERS

James G. Archer
James D. Arden
Frank V. Battle, Jr. (Not admitted in NY)
Steven M. Bierman
Eva Yulan Chan
Shelley C. Chapman
Kelley A. Cornish
Maureen M. Crough (Not admitted in NY)
Eugene A. Danaher
Daniel S. Dokos
Scott M. Freeman
Susan A. Goldberg
Robert W. Hirth
John G. Hutchinson
James D. Johnson
Ralph E. Lerner
Angus Macbeth
Mir Mahboob Mahmood
Thomas E. Pitts, Jr.
Myles C. Pollin
Andrew C. Quale, Jr.
David Alan Richards
David L. Ridl
Paul K. Risko
Irving L. Rotter
Robert H. Scarborough
Michael J. Schmidtberger
L. Gilles Sion
Shuichi Suzuki
Theodore J. Theophilos
Alan M. Unger
Paul R. Wysocki
Michael H. Yanowitch
Henry R. Zheng

COUNSEL

Claire Shows Hancock
Nicholas A. Robinson
Richard A. Stanley
Richard B. Stewart (Not admitted in NY)
Barbara A. Vrancik

ASSOCIATES

Jill M. Barlow
Richard E. Bartok
Steven B. Berkow
Allan J. Borkow
Stephen Cogut (Not admitted in NY)
Sumy C. Daeufer
M. Zita Ezpeleta
Gary B. Friedman
Robert L. Golub
Christopher J. McCaffrey
Steven D. Meyers
Gary D. Mitchell
Roshelle A. Nagar
Bridget R. O'Neill
Robert M. Plehn
Keila D. Ravelo
Elizabeth M. Sacksteder
Claudia G. Sayre
Simon A. Steel (Not admitted in the United States)
Lee M. Stein
Donald D. Sung
Harold M. Weidenfeld

For full biographical listings, see the Martindale-Hubbell Law Directory

SILLS CUMMIS ZUCKERMAN RADIN TISCHMAN EPSTEIN & GROSS, A PROFESSIONAL CORPORATION (AV)

250 Park Avenue, 10022
Telephone: 212-643-7000
Fax: 212-319-0578
Atlantic City, New Jersey Office: 17 Gordon's Alley.
Telephone: 609-344-2800.
Newark, New Jersey Office: One Riverfront Plaza.
Telephone: 201-643-7000.

Clive S. Cummis
Steven S. Radin
Herbert L. Zuckerman
Michael B. Tischman
Morton S. Bunis
Stanley Tannenbaum
Barry M. Epstein
Steven E. Gross
Thomas J. Demski
Jeffrey Hugh Newman
Lawrence S. Horn
Charles J. Walsh
Jeffrey J. Greenbaum
Simon Levin
Stephen J. Moses
Morris Yamner
Gerald Span
Jeffrey Barton Cahn
Steven M. Goldman
Alan E. Sherman
Robert J. Alter
Ira A. Rosenberg
Robert Crane
Marc S. Klein
Philip R. Sellinger
Jack M. Zackin (Not admitted in NY)
Stuart M. Feinblatt
Margaret F. Black
Trent S. Dickey
Bernard I. Flateman
William M. Russell

(See Next Column)

Joseph L. Buckley
Stanley U. North, III
James M. Hirschhorn
Mark S. Olinsky
Philip R. White

Nathan E. Arnell
Jennifer L. Borofsky
Lester Chanin
Jodi S. Brodsky
Glenn E. Davis
Paul F. Doda
Lora L. Fong
Patricia Brown Fugee
Bryan S. Greenberg
Wayne B. Heicklen
Noel D. Humphreys
Adam Kaiser
Linda Badash Katz
Steven S. Katz
Stephen McNally
Kenneth L. Moskowitz
A. Ross Pearlson
Gwen L. Posner
Beth S. Rose
Stuart Rosen
Robert Rosenberg
Susanne K. Rosenzweig
Scott N. Rubin
Richard S. Schkolnick
Steven Shapiro
Rhonda Sobral
Jay A. Soled
Bennet Susser
Jack Wenik
Gayle N. Wolkenberg

OF COUNSEL

David Beck
Victor Futter (Resident)
Jay J. Miller (Resident)
Dena L. Wolf

Representative Clients: Bally Manufacturing Corp.; Becton Dickinson & Co., Inc.; BMW of North America; Bristol-Myers Squibb Co.; Citibank, N.A.; Margaretten Financial Corporation; FIAT USA, Inc.; WWOR-TV, Inc.; Rotschild Realty, Inc.; Short Line Bus Co.

For full biographical listings, see the Martindale-Hubbell Law Directory

SIMPSON THACHER & BARTLETT (AV)

A Partnership which includes Professional Corporations
425 Lexington Avenue, 10017-3954
Telephone: 212-455-2000
Cable Address: "Xydsink"
Telex: 129158 (SIMPTHBAR NYK) 232622 (S TBBP UR)
Telecopier: 212-455-2502
ESL 62928462
Columbus, Ohio Office: One Riverside Plaza, 43215.
Telephone: 614-461-7799.
Telecopier: 614-461-0040.
London Office: 100 New Bridge Street, London EC4V 6JE, England.
Telephone: 0171 246 8000.
Telecopier: 0171 329 3883.
Tokyo Office: Ark Mori Building, 29th Floor, 12-32 Akasaka 1-Chome, Minato-Ku, Tokyo 107, Japan.
Telephone: 81-3-5562-8601.
Telecopier: 81-3-5562-8606. ESL 62765846.
Hong Kong Office: Asia Pacific Finance Tower - 32nd Floor, 3 Garden Road, Central, Hong Kong.
Telephone: 852-2514-7600.
Telecopier: 852-2869-7694.

MEMBERS OF FIRM

Andrew S. Amer
Bruce D. Angiolillo
James P. Barrett
Richard I. Beattie
Thomas H. Bell
Richard C. Blake
Robert A. Bourque
D. Rhett Brandon (Resident Partner, London, England Office)
Alvin H. Brown
Dickson G. Brown
John R. Cannell
Melvyn L. Cantor
Richard Capelouto
John W. Carr
Charles F. Carroll
David B. Chapnick
Michael J. Chepiga
Sarah E. Cogan
Charles I. Cogut
Michael V. Corrigan
James M. Cotter
Mark G. Cunha
Paul C. Curnin
Robert F. Cusumano
Kenneth C. Edgar, Jr.
David M. Eisenberg
Stephan J. Feder
Joseph J. Feit
John G. Finley
Paul B. Ford, Jr.
John M. Forelle
Robert L. Friedman
Steven M. Fuhrman
Peter J. Gordon
James C. Gorton
Michael P. Graney (Resident Partner, Columbus, Ohio Office)
James J. Hagan (P.C.)
Harold R. Handler (P.C.)
Gail B. Harris
Joel S. Hoffman
Gary I. Horowitz
L. Francis Huck
G. Hartwell Hylton
David W. Ichel
Martin D. Jacobson
Mildred Kalik
Joseph Kartiganer
Andrew R. Keller
John J. Kenney
John J. Kerr, Jr.
Glenn D. Kesselhaut
Alan M. Klein (Resident Partner, London, England Office)
James T. Knight
Charles E. Koob
Lillian E. Kraemer
George R. Krouse, Jr.
John D. Lobrano (Resident Partner, London, England Office)
Kenneth R. Logan
Walter A. Looney, Jr. (Resident Partner, Hong Kong Office)
Edgar M. Masinter (P.C.)
David E. Massengill
Mary Elizabeth McGarry
Edward C. Mendrzycki
Lee Meyerson

(See Next Column)

SIMPSON THACHER & BARTLETT—*Continued*

MEMBERS OF FIRM (Continued)

George Keith Miller (Resident Partner, Hong Kong Office)
Richard Allen Miller
Stephen G. Mills
Gary F. Mottola
Michael D. Nathan
Wilson S. Neely
George M. Newcombe
John W. Ohlweiler
Barry R. Ostrager
Vincent Pagano, Jr.
Laura Palma
Charles O. Rappaport
Roy L. Reardon (P.C.)
Glenn M. Reiter
Gary Rice
Thomas C. Rice
John E. Riley
C. Tanner Rose, Jr.
Philip T. Ruegger III
Gary S. Schpero
Gary L. Sellers
(Mike) Myer O. Sigal, Jr.
Michael H. Simonson
David A. Sneider (Resident Partner, Tokyo, Japan Office)
David J. Sorkin
Robert E. Spatt
John W. Spollen
John B. Tehan
Jeremiah L. Thomas, III
Peter C. Thomas
Mark Thompson
Joseph F. Tringali
Cyrus R. Vance
Mary Kay Vyskocil
Raymond W. Wagner
John L. Walker
Joseph F. Wayland
Richard Chadbourn Weisberg
Gregory A. Weiss
Marissa C. Wesely
David L. Williams
James Ronald Wolfe

COUNSEL

Marcia D. Alazraki
Victoria B. Bjorklund
James J. Burns
J. Scott Dyer
Pamela L. Rollins

ASSOCIATE COUNSEL

Thomas J. Agnello, Jr.
Lilian F. B. Andrews
Adeeb R. Fadil
Michael Isby
David M. Katz
James S. Lanigan, Jr.
Timothy J. Malin
Robert Y. Pelgrift, Jr.

For full biographical listings, see the Martindale-Hubbell Law Directory

SKADDEN, ARPS, SLATE, MEAGHER & FLOM (AV)

919 Third Avenue, 10022
Telephone: 212-735-3000
Telex: 645899 SKARSLAW
Fax: 212-735-2000; 212-735-2001
Boston, Massachusetts Office: One Beacon Street, 02108.
Telephone: 617-573-4800.
Fax: 617-573-4822.
Washington, D.C. Office: 1440 New York Avenue, N.W., 20005.
Telephone: 202-371-7000.
Fax: 202-393-5760.
Wilmington, Delaware Office: One Rodney Square, 19899.
Telephone: 302-651-3000.
Fax: 302-651-3001.
Los Angeles, California Office: 300 South Grand Avenue, 90071.
Telephone: 213-687-5000.
Fax: 213-687-5600.
Chicago, Illinois Office: 333 West Wacker Drive, 60606.
Telephone: 312-407-0700.
Fax: 312-407-0411.
San Francisco, California Office: Four Embarcadero Center, 94111.
Telephone: 415-984-6400.
Fax: 415-984-2698.
Houston, Texas Office: 1600 Smith Street, Suite 4460, 77002.
Telephone: 713-655-5100.
Fax: 713-655-5181.
Newark, New Jersey Office: One Riverfront Plaza, 07102.
Telephone: 201-596-4440.
Fax: 201-596-4444.
Tokyo, Japan Office: 12th Floor, The Fukoku Seimei Building, 2-2-2, Uchisaiwaicho, Chiyoda-ku, 100.
Telephone: 011-81-3-3595-3850.
Fax: 011-81-3-3504-2780.
London, England Office: 25 Bucklersbury EC4N 8DA.
Telephone: 011-44-71-248-9929.
Fax: 011-44-71-489-8533.
Hong Kong Office: 30/F Peregrine Tower, Lippo Centre, 89 Queensway, Central.
Telephone: 011-852-820-0700.
Fax: 011-852-820-0727.
Sydney, New South Wales, Australia Office: Level 26-State Bank Centre, 52 Martin Place, 2000.
Telephone: 011-61-2-224-6000.
Fax: 011-61-2-224-6044.
Toronto, Ontario Office: Suite 1820, North Tower, P.O. Box 189, Royal Bank Plaza, M5J 2J4.
Telephone: 416-777-4700.
Fax: 416-777-4747.
Paris, France Office: 105 rue du Faubourg Saint-Honoré, 75008.
Telephone: 011-33-1-40-75-44-44.
Fax: 011-33-1-49-53-09-99.
Brussels, Belgium Office: 523 avenue Louise, Box 30, 1050.
Telephone: 011-32-2-648-7666.
Fax: 011-32-2-640-3032.

(See Next Column)

Frankfurt, Germany Office: MesseTurm, 27th Floor, 60308.
Telephone: 011-49-69-9757-3000.
Fax: 011-49-69-9757-3050.
Beijing, China Office: 1605 Capital Mansion Tower, No. 6 Xin Yuan Nan Road, Chao Yang District, 100004.
Telephone: 011-86-1-466-8800.
Fax: 011-86-1-466-8822.
Budapest, Hungary Office: Mahart Building, H-1052 Apáczai Csere János u.11, VI.em.
Telephone: 011-36-1-266-2145.
Fax: 011-36-1-266-4033.
Prague, Czech Republic Office: Revolucni 16, 110 00.
Telephone: 011-42-2-231-75-18.
Fax: 011-42-2-231-47-33.
Moscow, Russia Office: Pleteshkovsky Pereulok 1, 107005.
Telephone: 011-7-501-940-2304.
Fax: 011-7-501-940-2511.

MEMBERS OF FIRM

Marshall K. Skadden (1907-1958)
John H. Slate (1913-1967)
William R. Meagher (1903-1981)
Leslie H. Arps (1907-1987)
Joseph H. Flom
Barry H. Garfinkel
Peter P. Mullen
James A. Levitan
James C. Freund
Stephen M. Axinn
Blaine V. Fogg
Robert C. Vincent, Jr.
James F. O'Rorke, Jr.
Roger S. Aaron
Peter Allan Atkins
William P. Frank
Morris J. Kramer
Henry P. Wasserstein
Thomas J. Schwarz
William C. Pelster
Milton G. Strom
Daniel E. Stoller
Robert C. Sheehan
Edward J. Yodowitz
Edmund C. Duffy
Kenneth A. Plevan
Vaughn C. Williams
Mark N. Kaplan
Jeffrey Glekel
Michael L. Cook
Franklin M. Gittes
Douglas M. Kraus
Jonathan J. Lerner
Barnet Phillips, IV
Neal R. Stoll
Benjamin F. Needell
Peter E. Greene
Jerome S. Hirsch
Irene A. Sullivan
Jeffrey W. Tindell
Robert E. Zimet
Matthew J. Mallow
Michael M. Connery
Richard L. Easton
Shepard Goldfein
J. Gregory Milmoe
Alan C. Myers
Stuart N. Alperin
Richard R. Kalikow
Christopher J. Kell
Matthew A. Rosen
J. Michael Schell
Sheila L. Birnbaum
Stephen M. Banker
Samuel Kadet
Lou R. Kling
Martha E. McGarry
Richard T. Prins
Alesia Ranney-Marinelli
Wallace L. Schwartz
Joseph W. Halliday
Michael E. Gizang
Clifford W. Losh (Not admitted in NY)
Charles M. Morgan, III
Vincent J. Pisano
Isaac Shapiro
Fred B. White, III
C. Thomas Kunz
Jonathan M. Bowie
Robert M. Chilstrom
David J. Friedman
Nancy A. Lieberman
Kayalyn A. Marafioti
Peter J. Neckles
Mitchell J. Solomon
Harvey R. Uris
Margaret L. Wolff
George A. Zimmerman
Kenneth J. Bialkin
Sheldon S. Adler
Katherine M. Bristor
Randall H. Doud
Jay B. Kasner
James M. Schell
Eileen Nugent Simon
Miriam L. Siroky
Alan G. Straus
Barbara Wrubel
Clifford H. Aronson
Susan M. Curtis
James M. Douglas
F. Eugene Hiigel
Constance S. Huttner
Thomas H. Kennedy
William S. Rubenstein
Paul Thomas Schnell
David M. Zornow
Joseph A. Coco
Martha Feltenstein
David Fox
Richard F. Kadlick
Phyllis G. Korff
Diana M. Lopo
Harold F. Moore
Marco E. Schnabl
Mark C. Smith
Eduardo R. Vidal
Michael L. Weiner
Utz P. Toepke
Charles M. Fox
Barry E. Hawk
Sally M. Henry
Peter J. McKenna
Seth M. Schwartz
Bertil P-H Lundqvist
John P. Furfaro
Linda C. Hayman
Timothy G. Reynolds
Jonathan L. Koslow
Stuart M. Finkelstein
Richard S. Fortunato
Philip H. Harris
Stacy J. Kanter
Robert J. Sullivan
Patrick J. Foye
Eric L. Cochran
Andrew M. Faulkner
Gregory A. Fernicola
Dana H. Freyer
Neil M. Leff
Jeffrey S. Lichtman
Sally A. Thurston
Sarah M. Ward

OF COUNSEL

Edwin Robbins
Henry P. Baer
Helene L. Kaplan
Joseph Diamond
Charles W. Ufford, Jr.
Evelyn M. Sommer
Harold Einhorn

(See Next Column)

SKADDEN, ARPS, SLATE, MEAGHER & FLOM, *New York—Continued*

COUNSEL

Mary Susan Butch | John B. Kennedy
Peter S. Julian | David J. Fisher
Michael S. Himmel | Susan J. Sutherland
Kenju Watanabe | Richard J. Grossman
Carlene J. Gatting | Richard D. Pritz

SPECIAL COUNSEL

Costa Constantine | Allen L. Weingarten
Nancy Lowe Henry | Steven J. Kolleeny
Bruce J. Prager | Joseph A. Guglielmelli
Ronald J. Tabak | Jeremy A. Berman
Jay S. Berke | Michael G. Valentini
Erskine D. Henderson | Paul Dutka
Angela D. Works | Gail Kendall
Barbara Mendel Mayden

BOSTON, MASSACHUSETTS OFFICE

PARTNERS

Louis A. Goodman | Margaret A. Brown
Thomas R. Bateman | David T. Brewster
Thomas J. Dougherty | Kent A. Coit
George J. Skelly

CHICAGO, ILLINOIS OFFICE

PARTNERS

Charles W. Mulaney, Jr. | William R. Kunkel
Arthur S. Rollin | David E. Springer
Wayne W. Whalen | John Wm. Butler, Jr.
Timothy A. Nelsen | Edward M. Crane
Marian P. Wexler | Thomas A. Hale
Jonathan J. Everett | Randall J. Rademaker
Warren G. Lavey | Christina M. Tchen
Susan Getzendanner | Gary P. Cullen
Ronald J. Clapham | John André LeDuc
N. Lynn Hiestand | Ann H. Pollock
Andrew S. Kenoe | Peter C. Krupp

OF COUNSEL

Lawrence M. Nagin

SPECIAL COUNSEL

Patricia A. Needham

COUNSEL

Susan J. Levine

LOS ANGELES, CALIFORNIA OFFICE

PARTNERS

Jerome L. Coben | Rodrigo A. Guerra, Jr.
Rand S. April | Martha W. Hammer
Joseph J. Giunta | Darrel J. Hieber
John A. Donovan | Thomas C. Janson, Jr.
Frank Rothman | John D. Rayis
Douglas B. Adler | Michael V. Gisser
Brian J. McCarthy | Gregg A. Noel
Richard S. Volpert | Eric S. Waxman
Phillip R. Pollock | Jeffrey B. Valle
Edward E. Gonzalez | Jeffrey H. Dasteel
Nicholas P. Saggese | Harriet S. Posner
Glenn J. Berger | Michael A. Woronoff
Peter Simshauser

SPECIAL COUNSEL

Michael A. Lawson

COUNSEL

Peter W. Clapp | Barry A. L. Hoffman

OF COUNSEL

Warren L. Ettinger

SAN FRANCISCO, CALIFORNIA OFFICE

PARTNERS

Theodore J. Kozloff | Phillip R. Pollock
James E. Lyons | Jose R. Allen

WASHINGTON, D.C. OFFICE

PARTNERS

Neal S. McCoy | Erica A. Ward
J. Phillip Adams | Gilbert T. Schwartz
John M. Nannes | Clifford M. Naeve
Rodney O. Thorson | Martin Klepper
Lynn R. Coleman | Paul W. Oosterhuis
Leslie J. Goldman | Richard L. Brusca
Douglas G. Robinson | Marcia R. Nirenstein
C. Benjamin Crisman, Jr. | Douglas E. Nordlinger
Michael P. Rogan | Thomas J. Casey
Thomas R. Graham | Robert S. Bennett
Robert E. Lighthizer | Carl S. Rauh
Fred T. Goldberg, Jr | Alan Kriegel
Ronald C. Barusch | Janet L. Goetz
Stephen W. Hamilton | Pamela F. Olson
Dorothy A. Darrah | Jeanine L. Matte
William J. Sweet, Jr. | John J. Mangan
Enid L. Veron | William S. Scherman

(See Next Column)

WASHINGTON, D.C. OFFICE

PARTNERS (Continued)

Antoinette Cook Bush | Kenneth Berlin
Albert H. Turkus | Mitchell S. Ettinger
Kenneth A. Gross

OF COUNSEL

Stephen E. McGregor | Philip McBride Johnson

SPECIAL COUNSEL

Robert B. Greenbaum | Kenneth F. Kraus
Edward D. Ross, Jr.

COUNSEL

Thomas E. Weil, Jr. | Mona E. Ehlenberger
Leonard Rawicz | Matthew W. S. Estes
June P. Broadstone | Mark C. Del Bianco
Brian C. Mohr | David Scott Nance

WILMINGTON, DELAWARE OFFICE

PARTNERS

Rodman Ward, Jr. | Thomas J. Allingham II
Steven J. Rothschild | Anthony W. Clark
Richard L. Easton | Robert B. Pincus
Stephen P. Lamb | Marc B. Tucker
Edward P. Welch | Patricia Moran Chuff

OF COUNSEL

Irving S. Shapiro

SPECIAL COUNSEL

Andrew J. Turezyn | Randolph K. Herndon

HOUSTON, TEXAS OFFICE

PARTNER

Lyndon C. Taylor

NEWARK, NEW JERSEY OFFICE

PARTNER

Robert J. Del Tufo

TOKYO, JAPAN OFFICE

PARTNER

E. Anthony Zaloom

LONDON, ENGLAND OFFICE

PARTNERS

Bruce M. Buck | Douglas E. Nordlinger
Richard L. Muglia | Scott V. Simpson

SYDNEY, AUSTRALIA OFFICE

PARTNER

Robert C. Hinkley

HONG KONG OFFICE

PARTNERS

Raymond W. Vickers | Jonathan F. Pedersen
Michael V. Gisser | Gregory G.H. Miao

COUNSEL

Jeffrey S. Christie

TORONTO, ONTARIO, CANADA OFFICE

PARTNERS

Milton G. Strom

BRUSSELS, BELGIUM OFFICE

PARTNERS

Patrick J. Foye

COUNSEL

Fernand Keuleneer | Henry L. Huser
Hendrik J. Cornelis

FRANKFURT, GERMANY OFFICE

ASSOCIATES

Hilary S. Foulkes

PARIS, FRANCE OFFICE

PARTNERS

Isaac Shapiro | Christopher L. Baker

BUDAPEST, HUNGARY OFFICE

PARTNER

Patrick J. Foye

PRAGUE, CZECH REPUBLIC OFFICE

COUNSEL

Marc R. Packer

BEIJING, CHINA OFFICE

PARTNER

Gregory G.H. Miao

MOSCOW, RUSSIA OFFICE

ASSOCIATES

André DeCort

(See Next Column)

SKADDEN, ARPS, SLATE, MEAGHER & FLOM—*Continued*

NEW YORK, N.Y. OFFICE
ASSOCIATES

Aisha H. Abdur-Rahman
David J. Abrams
John Agar
(Not admitted in NY)
Michele Akselrod-Ifrah
Thomas W. Alfano
Barbara Del Pilar Alonso
Liore Z. Alroy
(Not admitted in NY)
Yao Apasu
Katherine A. Armstrong
Marvin A. Artis
(Not admitted in NY)
Brad J. Axelrod
Madeline Baer
Patricia C. Ball
(Not admitted in NY)
Lisa A. Barkan
Steven L. Barnett
Elizabeth M. Bartolo
Anne Beckman
Heather Benedict
Mark A. Berman
Richard T. Bernardo
Adam T. Bernstein
Jonathan D. Bisgaier
Ann Bickford
Lonny R. Block
Eric J. Bock
Stanley D. Brener
Timothy E. Brog
Peretz Bronstein
Mark C. Brooks
Michael L. Bunder
Jane Bello Burke
Emily Campbell
Jeffrey P. Cantrell
Julie B. Carlin-Sasaki
Kelly C. Carr
John A. Caruso
Kevin J. Cassidy
Laura A. Cecere
Alec Y. Chang
Mark S. Cheffo
Owen Chen
Judy H. Chin
Kenneth Chin
Stanley A. Chinitz
Harlan L. Cohen
Ellen M. Collins
Steven M. Cooperman
Robert A. Copen
Ruth L. Cove
Mason L. Crocker
William L. Daly, III
Shoshana R. Davids
John Williams Davie
Patricia Dobberstein
Lisa S. Dorushkin
Stephen H. Douglas
Sean C. Doyle
Carolyn M. Duffy
Douglas W. Dunham
Dennis F. Dunne
Kenneth E. Ehemon, Jr.
Sylvia Einhorn
Lloyd M. Eisenberg
Ronald B. Emanuel
John C. Ertman
Nilene R. Evans
Kevin G. Fales
Arthur F. Fama, Jr.
Judith R. Feder
Loring I. Fenton
Howard A. Fine
Tom M. Fini
Daniel Jeremy Fish
Walker G. Flanary, III
Wendy Fleishman
David Alan Fleissig
George M. Flint, III
Pamela K. Fox
Thomas E. Fox
Kathleen A. Frederick
Neil M. Freeman
Christopher J. French
Eric J. Friedman
Lawrence D. Frishman

Mark N. Froeba
(Not admitted in NY)
Francis M. Fryscak
Angela G. Garcia
John L. Gardiner
Steven Garfinkel
Lawrence V. Gelber
(Not admitted in NY)
Marc S. Gerber
Christopher R. Gette
Dan Geva
Kenneth Gilison
(Not admitted in NY)
David S. Glatt
Jonathan R. Goldblatt
Arthur L. Goldfrank
David J. Goldschmidt
Heidi B. Goldstein
Elihu Gordis
Rita Werner Gordon
Keith E. Gottfried
(Not admitted in NY)
Louis Gottlieb
Thomas W. Gowan
Paul Greenan
Thomas Greenberg
Ira A. Greenstein
Maura Barry Grinalds
Jonathan Gross
Mark Gross
Michael H. Gruengles
Paula M. Guibault
Gilbert Hahn, III
Peter J. Halasz
David W. Hansen
(Not admitted in NY)
Christopher A. Harkins
John D. Harkrider
Lloyd S. Harmetz
Asher A. Harris
George E. Hellman
Allison Hilf
Atsuko Hirose
Jay Bruce Horowitz
Lisa K. Howlett
Steven R. Isko
Steven Isser
James Russell Jackson
Neal Jacobson
David A. Jaffe
Scott R. Jaffe
John J. Jones
Maury B. Josephson
Barbara Jakubowicz
Cheryl Kabalkin
Stephanie J. Kamerow
Kosha Kantharia
Michal Katz
Barbara K. Kelly
James A. Keyte
Christopher J. King
Steffi R. Kipperman
Scott A. Kislin
Kenneth F. Koen
Lisa C. Koff
Susan L. Kone
Sven E. Krogius
Steven Kronengold
Lea Haber Kuck
Robert C. LaMont
Jonathan H. Lander
Ruth Lautt
Jerome J. Lawton
Stuart Lazar
James M. Leahy
H. Soo Lee
Jung-Jin Lee
Loren R. Lembo
Stephen G. Lioce
Steven Litvack
Andrew H. Lo
Michael K. Lowman
Diana Villarnovo Lopez
Caroline S. Lovelace
Mary J. Mace
Joy Elaine Maddox
Eileen M. Maguire
Christopher P. Malloy

NEW YORK, N.Y. OFFICE

(See Next Column)

ASSOCIATES (Continued)

Lawrence A. Marcus
Joseph M. Marger
Joan K. Martin
Thomas A. Martin
Matthew C. Mason
Ira Brad Matetsky
Christy L. McElhaney
Peter G. McGonagle
John Bruce McGuirk
Patricia A. McNulty
Richard S. Meisner
David H. Midvidy
Joel M. Mitnick
Steven J. Moore
Thomas Wynne Morriss, Jr.
Dina Joy Moskowitz
Karen M. Muchunas
Mary E. Mullin
David L. Nagler
Steven F. Napolitano
Sandra E. Nickel
Kathleen Ninivaggi
(Not admitted in NY)
Joseph Philip Nisa
Ilan S. Nissan
Randall L. Nixon
Richard G. Norden
Thomas M. Obermaier
Regina Olshan
Joshua M. Olshin
George N. Oti
Mercedes M. Pacheco
Thomas Pak
Chiahua Pan
Seth L. Pearlstein
Debra A. Post
Illana Post
Nicholas F. Potter
David Alan Powar
Cedric Merlin Powell
Mauro Premutico
Philip A. Ragonetti
Wayne James Rapozo
David C. Reamer
David M. Rees
Michael J. W. Rennock
David M. Rievman
Carl J. Riley
Joel M. Roberto
Neil L. Rock
Anastasia T. Rockas
Rita A. Rodin
Mindy Kapner Roller
Adam C. Rosenberg
Julie C. Ross
Lissa Steele Roth
Audrey Peltz Rubin
Mary-Jo V. Saeli
Lawrence I. Safran
Susan L. Saltzstein
James G. Salzman
Jon E. Santemma
Eric S. Sarner

Rudy E. Scarpa
Barbara J. Schassar
Jeffrey L. Schaub
Jonathan B. Schindel
Leah Schlesinger
Ellen J. Schneider
Allison R. Schneirov
Robbin Schulsohn
David A. Schwartz
Walter Scott
Samuel D. Scruggs
Rona E. Senior
Dan Shamgar
Rona G. Shamoon
Gary Shapiro
Joseph H. Shaulson
Stefani J. Shavel
Daniel Shefter
Mark T. Shehan
Anne Y. Shields
Rosalie B. Shields
Dean S. Shulman
Calvin Siemer
Patricia E. Sindel
Steven M. Skolnick
Linda SooHoo
Felix Sotomayor
Lawrence S. Spiegel
Richard P. Spinelli
Carl E. Stetz
Sandra L. Strange
Kathryn R. Stokes
James Stewart Stringfellow
Andrew F. Strobert
(Not admitted in NY)
Polly S. Swartzfager
Kenneth M. Tallering
Patricia Lim Tan
James R. Tandler
Rosa Anna Testani
Andrea R. Tigar
Michael P. Trolman
Valerie J. Wald
David A. Walden
W. Kirk Wallace
Daniel Gerard Walsh
Erick Phillip Michael Walter
(Not admitted in NY)
Romina Field Weiss
Robert H. Williams
Elizabeth H. Winchester
Jeffrey P. Wofford
Bert L. Wolff
Wendy J. Wolff
Beth R. Wolmer
Robert G. Wray
Kenneth A. Wright, Jr.
Nir D. Yarden
Richard B. Yates
Sabine Zerarka
Diana S.C. Zeydel
Elaine D. Ziff
Gail R. Zweig

CHICAGO, ILLINOIS OFFICE
ASSOCIATES

Steven E. Boyce
Ronald J. Clapham
Marguerite M. Elias
Nicholas L. Giampietro

Eric David Hargan
Robert W. Kadlec
Andrew S. Morrison
Maris M. Rodgon

LOS ANGELES, CALIFORNIA
ASSOCIATES

Karen Leili Corman

Robert J. Mrofka

WILMINGTON, DELAWARE
ASSOCIATES

Mark S. Chehi

Gregg M. Galardi

WASHINGTON, D.C. OFFICE
ASSOCIATES

Bonnie J. Austin
Gregory C. C. Burton
Leo J. Kane

Benjamin B. Klubes
Saul M. Pilchen
Abigail J. Raphael

For full biographical listings, see the Martindale-Hubbell Law Directory

New York—Continued

SONNENSCHEIN NATH & ROSENTHAL (AV)

1221 Avenue of the Americas 24th Floor, 10020
Telephone: 212-768-6700
Facsimile: 212-391-1247
Chicago, Illinois Office: Suite 8000 Sears Tower, 233 South Wacker Drive.
Telephone: 312-876-8000.
Cable Address: "Sonberk".
Telex: 25-3526.
Facsimile: 312-876-7934.
Washington, D.C. Office: 1301 K Street, N.W., Suite 600, East Tower.
Telephone: 202-408-6400.
Facsimile: 202-408-6399.
San Francisco, California Office: 685 Market Street, 10th Floor.
Telephone: 415-882-5000.
Facsimile: 415-543-5472; 882-5038.
Los Angeles, California Office: Suite 1500, 601 South Figueroa Street.
Telephone: 213-623-9300.
Facsimile: 213-623-9924.
St. Louis, Missouri Office: One Metropolitan Square, Suite 3000.
Telephone: 314-241-1800.
Facsimile: 314-259-5959.

RESIDENT PARTNERS

David Albenda
Reid L. Ashinoff
Michael A. Bamberger
Michael H. Barr
Dennis N. Berman
Robert E. Curry, Jr.
Amy H. Fisher
Linda E. Friedman
Philip A. Haber
Mark R. Lehrer
Ellyn J. Steuer
Michael S. Wien

OF COUNSEL

Wayne H. Davis
Marc B. Heller

RESIDENT ASSOCIATES

Andrew L. DaSilva
(Not admitted in NY)
Kenneth Drake
Julie Goldscheid
Lisa R. Green
Peter C. Hoehn
Jeffrey S. Isaacs
Benjamin B. Iselin
Gregory S. Karawan
Bruce H. Leshine
(Not admitted in NY)
Rachel M. Lipschutz
Beverly O. Lobell
Dorothy P. Patton
Jeffrey M. Rose
Valerie M. Valdez
Maralee Buttery Vezie
(Not admitted in NY)
Aron G. Weber

For full biographical listings, see the Martindale-Hubbell Law Directory

STROOCK & STROOCK & LAVAN (AV)

Seven Hanover Square, 10004-2696
Telephone: 212-806-5400
Telecopier: (212) 806-6006
Telexes: Stroock, UT 177693 and Plastroock NYK 177077 (International)
Cable Address: "Plastroock, NYK"
New York Conference Center: 767 Third Avenue, 10017-2023.
Telephones: 212-806-5767; 5768; 5769; 5770.
Telecopier: (212) 421-6234.
Washington, D.C. Office: 1150 Seventeenth Street, N.W., Suite 600, 20036-4652.
Telephone: 202-452-9250.
Telecopier: (202) 421-6234.
Cable Address: "Plastroock, Washington."
Telex: 64238 STROOCK DC; 89401 STROOCK DC.
Los Angeles, California Office: 2029 Century Park East, Floors 16 & 18, 90067-3086.
Telephone: 310-556-5800.
Telecopier: (310) 556-5959.
Cable Address: "Plastroock L.A."
Telex: Plastroock LSA 677190 (Domestic and International).
Miami, Florida Office: 200 South Biscayne Boulevard, Suite 3000, First Union Financial Center, 33131-2385.
Telephone: 305-358-9900.
Telecopier: (305) 789-9302.
Telex: 803133 Stroock Mia (Domestic and International); Broward Line: 527-9900.
Budapest, Hungary Office: East-West Business Center, Rákóczi ut 1-3, H-1088.
Telephone: 011-361-266-9520; 011-361-266-7770.
Telecopier: 001-361-266-9279.

MEMBERS OF FIRM

Robert Abrams
Reed D. Auerbach
Martin S. Baker
Jacob Bart
Robert C. Bata
Hillel M. Bennett
Martin J. Beran (P.C.)
Micah W. Bloomfield
Stanley B. Blumberg
Leonard Boxer
Martin I. Bresler
Melvin A. Brosterman
Brian M. Cogan
Joel Cohen
Lewis G. Cole
Stuart H. Coleman
Brian Diamond
James F. Downey
Melvin Epstein
Jay R. Fialkoff
Thomas Field
David L. Finkelman
Joseph L. Forstadt
Richard L. Fried
Donald D. Gabay
Laura E. Goldbard
Daniel H. Golden
Marvin J. Goldstein

(See Next Column)

MEMBERS OF FIRM (Continued)

Laurence Greenwald
Alan S. Halperin
Lawrence M. Handelsman
Bridget M. Healy
Thomas E. Heftler
Alvin K. Hellerstein
Charles B. Hochman
Fred S. Hodara
David H. Kaufman
Robin E. Keller
Alan M. Klinger
Barbara D. Klippert
Richard H. Kronthal
Lewis Kruger
Jonathan S. Kusko
William D. Latza
Howard S. Lavin
Mark A. Levy
Robert Lewin
Randy Lipsitz
Jeffrey S. Lowenthal
Theodore S. Lynn
Jerome A. Manning
Jay P. Mayesh
Curtis C. Mechling
Peter A. Miller
Martin Minkowitz
Charles G. Moerdler
Elizabeth A. Mullins
Martin H. Neidell
Richard M. Ornitz
William A. Perlmuth
Marvin G. Pickholz
Steven B. Pokotilow (P.C.)
Susan O. Posen
David A. Rahm
Robert A. Raskin
Roger M. Roisman
Mark A. Rosenbaum
Anita S. Rosenbloom
Lawrence Rosenthal (P.C.)
Norman K. Samnick
Bruce H. Schneider
George R. Shockey, Jr.
Richard Siegler
Kevin L. Smith
Mark A. Speiser
Ronald J. Stein
Eva Coben Talel
James R. Tanenbaum
Stuart Troy
Jeffrey D. Uffner
Lois L. Weinroth
Mark S. Wintner
Robert C. Wipperman

SPECIAL COUNSEL

Albert M. Appel
Madelaine R. Berg
Etta Brandman
Michel S. Evanusa
Abbey L. Keppler
Ellen R. Kozlowski
Arlene G. Krieger
Jeffrey H. Roth
Laurel S. Rotker
David Stephens
Starr L. Tomczak

COUNSEL

Rita E. Hauser
Harold I. Kaplan
William J. vanden Heuvel

RETIRED PARTNERS

Bernard E. Brandes
Morton L. Deitch
Martin D. Eile
Franklin Feldman
Jack Gross
Norman Hammer
Gilbert Lazerus
Erwin Millimet
Vivienne W. Nearing
Julius H. Sherman

Natalie Abrams
Ernest E. Badway
Steven Balasiano
Lisa G. Beckerman
Julie A. Beyers
Deborah A. Bigel
Deborah Sager Birnbach
David Bolton
David H. Botter
Julie E. Bowker
Daniel Braun
James L. Burns
William Campbell
Adam J. Chill
Yvonne Lee Clayton
Peter G. Danias
Matthew Jacob Day
Amy B. de Lannoy
Eleni Demetriou
Andrew Reid Dominus
Charles C. Dorego
Maria B. Douvas
Steven Feinstein
Faith A. Firestone
Stephanie Franco
James A. Frechter
David Gershman
Howard M. Gitten
Joseph J. Giamboi
Philip A. Gilman
Louis Ginsberg
Michael A. Golden
Karen A. Gottlieb
Adam S. Grace
Sandra Jefferson Grannum
Mayer Greenberg
Steven M. Greenspan
Edward P. Grosz
Robert A. Grundstein
Leah L. Hanlon
Susan Y. Harrigan
Marcia S. Helbling
Richard Horowitz
Michele L. Jacobson
Maria A. Acevedo Jarme
David A. Javdan
Calvin A. Jones
Rowain Kalichstein
Leslie G. Kanter
Barbara G. Kaplan
David M. Kaston
Joy A. Katz
Richard S. Katz
Robert C. Kern, Jr.
Mark P. Kesslen
Gordon M. Kessler
Julia H. Kim
Vickie Kokkalenois
Amir I. Kornblum
John P. Kraljic
Bradley G. Kulman
Daniel Laifer
Scott P. Landman
Karen Leo
Donald Liebman
Burton N. Lipshie
David W. Lowden
Andrea A. D. Marber
Mark D. Marderosian
Elise C. Masiée
Matthew Mayers
Lisa K. McClelland
James M. McGovern
Edward G. Milgrim
Sherry J. Millman
Irving E. Minkin
Kelli L. Moll
(Not admitted in NY)
Steven P. Moskowitz
Gretchen P. Mullins
John R. Murphy
Steven M. Nachman
David Neier
Carole W. Nimaroff
June A. O'Hea
Todd Orlich
Michele Pahmer
Kenneth Pasquale
Leslie E. Payson
John Petrowski
Anna T. Pinedo
Lauren Pruzan

(See Next Column)

STROOCK & STROOCK & LAVAN—*Continued*

Lisa M. Rafanelli
Karen A. Rich
William A. Rome
Richard C. Rosenzweig
Kenneth J. Ross
Marie V. Santacroce
Vanessa Scaglione
Arthur Schaier
Jeanne B. Schmid
Anthony H. N. Schnelling
Steven L. Schultz
Andrew W. Schwartz
James E. Schwartz
Michele P. Schwartz
Mary Scranton
Randy L. Shapiro
Laura R. Shaw
James A. Shrifren
Barbara J. Shulman
Regan A. Shulman
Jonathan A. Siegel
Matthew W. Siegal
David A. Sifre
David P. Simonds
David P. Simonetti
Douglas E. Singer
Alice J. Solomon
Saundra R. Steinberg
Jay Strauss
Jill Sung
Kenneth H. Theil
Susan Tiffany
Gail B. Wallach
Denise K. Wildes
James R. Wilson
Robert S. Wolmer
Rhonda Yacker
Anita Ka-Wai Yeung
Alan Z. Yudkowsky

WASHINGTON, D.C.
PARTNERS

Barry J. Israel
Will E. Leonard
George G. Lorinczi
Marvin G. Pickholz
Walter Pozen
Mark N. Rae
James Taylor, Jr.

OF COUNSEL

Howard L. Hills

ASSOCIATES

Panagiotis C. Bayz
Alexei J. Cowett
Matthew H. McCarthy
Linda P. Reppert

LOS ANGELES
PARTNERS

Barry L. Dastin
David L. Gersh
Rick S. Kirkbride
Joel M. Kozberg
Gerald J. Mehlman
Schuyler M. Moore
Margaret A. Nagle
Michael F. Perlis
Arnold M. Quittner (P.C.)
Henry J. Silberberg
Julia B. Strickland
Michael M. Umansky
Bennett J. Yankowitz

RETIRED PARTNERS

Merrill E. Jenkins
William H. Levit (P.C.)
Robert M. Shafton

ASSOCIATES

Judith L. Anderson
Lynda Attenborough
Erik A. Christiansen
James W. Denison
Richard S. Forman
Anna M. Graves
Sheri Jeffrey
Nicholas F. Klein
Kevin J. Leichter
David S. Lippes
Mary D. Manesis
Karynne G. Popper
Denise K. Russell
Craig S. Seligman
Lisa Simonetti
Glenn D. Smith
John E. Somorjai
Chauncey M. Swalwell
Robin Van Es

MIAMI
PARTNERS

Scott L. Baena
Michael Basile
Jeffrey Bercow
Robert K. Jordan
Daniel Lampert
David C. Pollack
Arnold D. Shevin
Robert L. Shevin
Paul Steven Singerman
Robert W. Turken

OF COUNSEL

Richard S. Savitt

SPECIAL COUNSEL

Mindy A. Mora
Robert M. Siegel
Carey A. Stiss

RETIRED PARTNER

Charles R. Taine

ASSOCIATES

Ben J. Fernandez
Manuel A. Fernandez
Brent A. Friedman
Ilyse Wrubel Homer
Judith A. Jarvis
John M. Kuhn
Nee M. Laurita
Jana K. McDonald
Jorge J. Perez
Susan Johnson Pontigas
Michael E. Radell
Ivan J. Reich
Jeff C. Schneider
Richard B. Simring
Jerry Jay Sokol
Steven J. Solomon
Steven M. Stoll

BUDAPEST, HUNGARY
PARTNERS

Robert C. Bata
George G. Lorinczi
Richard M. Ornitz
George R. Shockey, Jr.
Dr. Ivan Szasz

(See Next Column)

ASSOCIATES

Krisztina L. Holtzman
Laszlo Tokai
György Udvardi

For full biographical listings, see the Martindale-Hubbell Law Directory

SULLIVAN & CROMWELL (AV)

125 Broad Street, 10004-2498
Telephone: 212-558-4000
Cable Address: "Ladycourt, New York"
Telex: 62694 (International); 12-7816 (Domestic)
Telecopier: 212-558-3588
Midtown Office: 250 Park Avenue, 10177-0021.
Telecopier: 212-558-3792.
Washington, D.C. Office: 1701 Pennsylvania Avenue, N.W., 20006-5805.
Telephone: 202-956-7500.
Telex: 89625.
Telecopier: 202-293-6330.
Los Angeles, California Office: 444 South Flower Street, 90071-2901.
Telephone: 213-955-8000.
Telecopier: 213-683-0457.
Paris Office: 8, Place Vendôme, Paris 75001, France.
Telephone: (011)(331)4450-6000.
Telex: 240654.
Telecopier: (011)(331)4450-6060.
London Office: St. Olave's House, 9a Ironmonger Lane, London EC2V 8EY, England.
Telephone: (011)(44171)710-6500.
Telecopier: (011)(44171)710-6565.
Melbourne, Australia Office: 101 Collins Street, Melbourne, Victoria 3000.
Telephone: (011)(613)654-1500.
Telecopier: (011)(613)654-2422.
Tokyo Office: Gaikokuho Jimu Bengoshi Office of Robert G. DeLaMater, a member of the firm of Sullivan & Cromwell, Tokio Kaijo Building Shinkan, 2-1, Marunouchi, 1-chome Chiyoda-ku, Tokyo 100, Japan.
Telephone: (011)(813)3213-6140.
Telecopier: (011)(813)3213-6470.
Hong Kong Office: 28th Floor, Nine Queen's Road, Central, Hong Kong.
Telephone: (011)(852)826-8688.
Telecopier: (011)(852)522-2280.

MEMBERS OF FIRM

M. Bernard Aidinoff *(Also at Washington, D.C. Office)
John W. Dickey (London Office)
Stephen K. West *
Donald R. Osborn
John E. Merow
Frederick A. Terry, Jr.
W. Loeber Landau
Michael A. Cooper
Robert B. Hiden, Jr.
Ricardo A. Mestres, Jr.
William J. Williams, Jr.
John F. Cannon
Irvine D. Flinn
Michael M. Maney *
Edwin D. Williamson * (Washington, D.C. Office)
Richard E. Carlton
Stephen A. Grant
David M. Huggin
Willard B. Taylor
John L. Warden
Richard R. Howe
William R. Norfolk
Michael W. Weir
Robert M. Thomas, Jr.
Allan M. Chapin
Stanley F. Farrar ** (Los Angeles Office)
William F. Indoe
David M. Kies
Robert M. Osgood (London Office)
Earl D. Weiner
James H. Carter, Jr.
Henry Christensen III
H. Rodgin Cohen (Also at Washington, D.C. Office)
Robert H. Craft, Jr. * (Washington, D.C. Office)
Philip L. Graham, Jr.
Benjamin F. Stapleton
Neil T. Anderson
Daniel Dunson
Charles F. Rechlin ** (Los Angeles Office)
Richard G. Asthalter (Paris Office)
Bruce E. Clark
Richard J. Urowsky
Donald C. Walkovik (Hong Kong Office)
William M. Dallas, Jr.
Margaret K. Pfeiffer * (Washington, D.C. Office)
David B. Tulchin
John E. Baumgardner, Jr.
Jeffrey F. Browne (Melbourne, Australia Office)
D. Stuart Meiklejohn
Mark J. Welshimer
James I. Black III
Ann Bailen Fisher
John P. Mead
Yvonne S. Quinn
Kenneth M. Raisler *
Gandolfo V. DiBlasi
Frank H. Golay, Jr. ** (Los Angeles Office)
Robinson B. Lacy
Michael M. Wiseman
John T. Bostelman
James C. Morphy
David F. Morrison ** (Paris Office)
William A. Plapinger (London Office)
Joseph C. Shenker
Andrew D. Soussloff **
Garrard Russ Beeney
Robert E. Buckholz, Jr.
Eliyahu David Jacobson
Richard H. Klapper
Theodore O. Rogers, Jr. *
Andrew S. Rowen
Erik D. Lindauer
Andrew S. Mason
Frederic C. Rich
Alan J. Sinsheimer
George H. White, III ** (London Office)
Arthur S. Adler
John L. Hardiman
Robert A. Sacks ** (Los Angeles Office)
Donald J. Toumey *
Theodore Edelman
Sergio J. Galvis
Steven L. Holley
Alison S. Ressler ** (Los Angeles Office)
Francis J. Aquila
Patricia A. Ceruzzi
Donald R. Crawshaw

(See Next Column)

SULLIVAN & CROMWELL, *New York—Continued*

MEMBERS OF FIRM (Continued)

Robert G. DeLaMater (Tokyo Office)
David B. Harms
Duncan C. McCurrach (Melbourne, Australia Office)
Richard C. Morrissey (London Office)
Joseph E. Neuhaus *
Robert Samuel Risoleo
William J. Snipes
Andrew P. Solomon
David H. Braff
Robert W. Reeder III
Mark F. Rosenberg
John Evangelakos (Hong Kong Office)
Joseph B. Frumkin
David P. Hariton
Alexandra Davern Korry
Daryl A. Libow (Washington, D.C. Office)
Mark J. Menting
Scott D. Miller (London Office)
Samuel W. Seymour
Basil P. Zirinis, III
Michael H. Steinberg ** (Not admitted in NY; Los Angeles Office)
William D. Torchiana

OF COUNSEL

Donald C. Christ
Janet Thiele Geldzahler * (Washington, D.C. Office)
Douglas Mark McCall * (Washington, D.C. Office)

SPECIAL COUNSEL

Richard L. Alpern
Carol I. Buckmann
Shlomo Cohen
Patricia Diaz Dennis * (Not admitted in NY; Washington, D.C. Office)
Douglas Hayward Evans
William L. Farris
David J. Gilberg *
Jeffrey W. Jacobs * (Not admitted in NY; Washington, D.C. Office)
Lynne R. Malina
Peter C. Manbeck
Mark A. Nouss
Gerald T. Slevin
Dennis C. Sullivan * (Washington, D.C. Office)
Osamu Watanabe (Tokyo Office)

EUROPEAN COUNSEL

Kathryn Ann Campbell (London Office)
Pierre Servan-Schreiber (Paris Office)

RETIRED MEMBERS OF FIRM

John F. Arning
Mitchell Brock
Walter J. Coakley (Washington, D.C. Office)
Norris Darrell, Jr.
Henry N. Ess, III
David S. Henkel
Garfield H. Horn
John C. Jaqua
Edward W. Keane
George C. Kern, Jr.
William J. Kirby
Robert MacCrate *
Robert J. McDonald
Kendyl K. Monroe
William Piel, Jr.
William C. Pierce
Hamilton F. Potter, Jr.
Richard G. Powell
Vincent A. Rodriguez
Marvin Schwartz *
John R. Stevenson
Roy H. Steyer
William E. Willis
William A. Ziegler

ASSOCIATES

Mark D. Alexander (London Office)
Lee Ann Anderson
Leta L. Applegate
Ari Assayag (Paris Office)
Barbara A. Bayliss (London Office)
W. Gary Beeson (Not admitted in NY)
Paul J. Bento
Johan O. Bill
Elizabeth S. Bluestein (Los Angeles Office)
Michael J. Bowe
Michael P. Brady
Garth W. Bray
Matthew J. Brennan *
Ellen Bresler
Alexia E. Brown
William J. Brown * (Washington, D.C. Office)
Gabrielle S. Brussel
Hugh L. Burns
Andrew M. Burton (Los Angeles Office)
Ghislaine Celsa Madeleine Chávez de Arnavat
Rosita Cheung
Corey R. Chivers * (London Office)
John Nelson Chrisman (Not admitted in NY; Hong Kong Office)
Patricia M. Clarke
Scott D. Clemens (Hong Kong Office)
Cristina Cobb
Gary W. Cobbledick (Melbourne, Australia Office)
Craig B. Coben
Philip Leonard Colbran
Stephen C. Connor
John T. Corcoran
Ronald E. Creamer
Francis P. Crispino (London Office)
Dorothy E. Cumby
Diane D'Arcangelo **
Faraz Daneshgar (Not admitted in NY)
Lisamichelle Davis
Robert A. de By
Marc De Leeuw
Dominick P. DeChiara
Maureen B.A. Denton
John C. L. Dixon
Michal Dlouhy (Paris Office)
Robert Wilson Downes
James C. Dugan
Brad Eastman
Marcus P. Efthimiou
Mitchell S. Eitel
Richard A. Ely (London Office)
Samantha Evans (Not admitted in NY; Washington, D.C. Office)
Guy Even-Ezra
William G. Farrar
Alison H. Feagin
Tamar Feder
Jose Ignacio Fernandez * (Not admitted in NY; Washington, D.C. Office)
Robin D. Fessel
Alice Stevens Fisher * (Not admitted in NY; Washington, D.C. Office)
Ari Q. Fitzgerald * (Washington, D.C. Office)
Adam L. Frank
Brian T. Frawley
Berit Freeman

(See Next Column)

ASSOCIATES (Continued)

Edward R. Gallion
David Gaukrodger
Joseph Ginsberg
Robert J. Giuffra, Jr. *
Deborah S. Gordon
Alison M. Gregory
Arunas E. Gudaitis
Edward A. Harris *
Michael E. Hatchett
Jessica Hausknecht
Georgina Elspeth Hayden
Kenneth P. Held
Timothy J. Helwick
Laura Ayn Holleman (London Office)
Douglas E. Holtz (London Office)
Kerry J. Houghton
Fraser L. Hunter, Jr.
Matthew G. Hurd
Sung Jin Hwang (Not admitted in NY; Hong Kong Office)
Gayle M. Hyman
José Ibietatorremendía (Not admitted in NY)
Ken Ikari
Gary Israel **
Nancy C. Jackson ** (Not admitted in NY; Paris Office)
Michael E. Johnson
Ralph Erich Jones
Waldo D. Jones, Jr.
Bernard A. Joseph (Washington, D.C. Office)
Howard J. Kaplan
Peter D. Karol
Sarah R. Katz
Michael S. Katzke
Ann T. Kenny
David S.J. Kim * (Washington, D.C. Office)
Paul M. Kinsella ** (Los Angeles Office)
John E. Kirklin
Joseph C. Kopec
Stephen M. Kotran
Eric M. Krautheimer
Kimberly Krawiec
Adam M. Kupitz
Nicole A. LaBarbera
Michael Lacovara
Jeannette C. Laidlaw
Eric K. Laumann
Kevin J. Lavin (Washington, D.C. Office)
Jonathan T. Lebow
Werner R. Lehfellner
Stuart Leichenko
Joseph Arthur Leopardi
Scott L. Lessing
Thomas R. Leuba * (Washington, D.C. Office)
Robert W. Leung
Susan Silverman Liautaud (Paris Office)
Peter P.H. Lin (Hong Kong Office)
J. Michael Locke * (Washington, D.C. Office)
Lorena P. Lopes
Leslie Lowenbraun
Steven R. Lowson
Steven S. Lucas (Not admitted in NY; Los Angeles Office)
Alison C. Malin
Christopher L. Mann (London Office)
Michael W. Martin
James V. Masella, III
Paul J. McElroy * (Washington, D.C. Office)
Graceann McKeon
Marianne McKeon
Peter T. McKeon, Jr.
Cathleen E. McLaughlin * (Los Angeles Office)
Sara M. Mcleod
Kevin Miller
Michael B. Miller (London Office)
Steven J. P. Miller (London Office)
Paul Mitrokostas
Alexandre A. Montagu
Mary C. Moynihan (Washington, D.C. Office)
Michael F. Mundaca
Tariq Mundiya
Ellen C. Nachtigall (Los Angeles Office)
Keith C. Nashawaty (Not admitted in NY; Los Angeles Office)
Dimitri Nikolakakos (Paris Office)
Elizabeth A. O'Connor
John O'Connor
Jack O'Kelley * (Not admitted in NY; Washington, D.C. Office)
Michael J. O'Sullivan (Los Angeles Office)
Harry A. Olivar, Jr. ** (Los Angeles Office)
Taneki Ono (Tokyo Office)
Nelle Pace (Not admitted in NY)
Nicolas A. Paglietti (London Office)
Keith A. Pagnani
James J. Panella **
Richard C. Pepperman, II
Richard A. Pollack
Jay L. Pomerantz
Andreas F. Pour (Not admitted in NY)
Michael L. Preston (Not admitted in NY; Los Angeles Office)
Cecil D. Quillen III *
Jean Raby (Paris Office)
Osvaldo A. Ramos
Samuel Ramos
John B. Reid-Dodick
Stewart M. Robertson
David B. Rockwell (London Office)
Kathryn E. Rorer (Washington, D.C. Office)
Gilbert E. Rotkin
Adam S. Rubinson (London Office)
Susan Lea Sack
Ivan A. Sacks
George J. Sampas
Michael Sansevero, Jr.
Richard H. Sauer * (Washington, D.C. Office)
John L. Savva ** (Not admitted in NY; Los Angeles Office)
Brett G. Scharffs (Washington, D.C. Office)
Michael D. Schecter (Not admitted in NY; Melbourne, Australia Office)
William E. Schroeder
Lisa B. Schwartz
Evelyn H. Seidman
Dev R. Sen
Penny Shane
Loretta Shaw-Lorello
Timothy E. Sheil * (Washington, D.C. Office)
Gerald D. Shepherd
Lori S. Sherman
Richard H. Siegel (Melbourne, Australia Office)
Rebecca J. Simmons
Irene Skidan
Richard D. Smith
Steven Spielvogel
Sara Kathryn Stadler
John C. Stellabotte
Steven B. Stokdyk (Not admitted in NY; Los Angeles Office)
Michael E. Swartz
Avi I. Szenberg
Yoichiro Taniguchi * (Hong Kong Office)
Stephen A. Thierbach
Brian P. Thomas *(Not admitted in NY)
Steven W. Thomas ** (Los Angeles Office)
Roslyn Tom

(See Next Column)

SULLIVAN & CROMWELL—*Continued*

ASSOCIATES (Continued)

Michael T. Tomaino, Jr.
Teresa Tsai
Maria E. Tsoukalas *
Mathias Turck (Paris Office)
Ayesha K. Waheed
Michael P. Walutes
Benjamin R. Weber
Chun Wei (Hong Kong Office)
Holly Hexter Weiss
Noah M. Weissman
Frederick W. Wertheim
Stephanie G. Wheeler
Karen Doeblin Whetzle
R. Scott Widen
E. Marcellus Williamson
Mark V. Wilson
Paul C. Wilson (Not admitted in NY)
Mitchell J. Wolfe
Diana L. Wollman *
Anna Yang
Sienho Yee
John D. Young, Jr. (Hong Kong Office)
Beth N. Zeiger

David Liebov (Managing Clerk)

*Attorneys also admitted to the District of Columbia Bar
**Attorneys also admitted to the California Bar

For full biographical listings, see the Martindale-Hubbell Law Directory

ROBERT M. TANENBAUM (AV)

767 Fifth Avenue, 43rd Floor, 10153
Telephone: 212-832-8500

For full biographical listings, see the Martindale-Hubbell Law Directory

THACHER PROFFITT & WOOD (AV)

Two World Trade Center, 10048
Telephone: 212-912-7400
Cable Address: "Wallaces, New York"
Telex: 226733TPCW; 669578TPW
Facsimile: 212-912-7751; 912-7752
Washington, D.C. Office: 1500 K Street, N.W.
Telephone: 202-347-8400.
Facsimile: 202-347-6238.
White Plains, New York Office: 50 Main Street.
Telephone: 914-421-4100.
Facsimile: 914-421-4150/4151.

MEMBERS OF FIRM

Kofi Appenteng
Tricia K. Bonner
W. Edward Bright
Robert F. Brodegaard
Charles D. Brown
Diana G. Browne
Jean E. Burke
Albert J. Cardinali
William T. Collins
Kathryn Cruze
William J. Cullen
Charles A. Dietzgen
Joseph Philip Forte
Christopher F. Graham
Joel B. Harris
Stephen S. Kudenholdt
Edward R. Leahy (Resident at Washington, D.C. Office)
Thomas M. Leslie (Resident, White Plains Office)
Douglas J. McClintock
David C. Miller
Lisa M. Miller
Jeffrey J. Murphy
Randal A. Nardone
George J. Petrow
Lauris G. L. Rall
James R. Shorter, Jr.
Donald F. Simone
Francis X. Sulger
Donald B. Susswein (Resident at Washington, D.C. Office)
Lawrence A. Swenson
Thomas N. Talley
Paul D. Tvetenstrand
Stephen T. Whelan
Mitchell G. Williams
Omer S. J. Williams
Stephen B. Wilson (Resident, White Plains Office)
John M. Woods

COUNSEL

Phillip C. Broughton
Dwight B. Demeritt, Jr.
O. Gerard Gjertsen (Resident at White Plains Office)
Lawrence W. Golde
Raymond S. Jackson, Jr.
Edward C. Kalaidjian
Stuart H. Pringle, Jr.
John C. Van Bomel (Resident at White Plains Office)
Cornelius S. Van Rees

SENIOR ATTORNEYS

Raymond T. Field
Michael V. Kaprelian

SPECIAL COUNSEL

Robert M. Zinman

ASSOCIATES

Christopher A. Ambrose
David Philip Ansel
Sharon H. Anson
Oliver J. Armas
Daphne H. Aronson
Jill H. Ashman
Robert C. Azarow
Marla G. Berger
Michael A. Berkowitz
James C. Blakemore
William H. Boericke
Brant Brooks
Joseph Buonanno
Francis M. Caesar
Kenneth F. Cogland
Lisa K. Cohen
A. James Cotins
Amanda M. Demers
Mary Seminara Diemer (Resident at Washington, D.C. Office)
Deirdre A. Dillon
William B. Doniger
Paul S. Donohue (Resident at White Plains Office)
Scott M. Drago

(See Next Column)

ASSOCIATES (Continued)

Barry Edinburg (Not admitted in NY)
Christina L. Feege
Gerald J. Ferguson
Jonathan D. Forstot
Joe L. Fulwiler
Andrew J. Garger
Kevin R. Garlitz
John J. Ginley III
Ellen M. Goodwin
Steven J. Gordon
Joseph G. Grasso
James L. Gregory, III
Penny Matthews Groel
Robert B. Grotch
Adam W. Gurwitz (Resident at Washington, D.C. Office)
Geoffrey E. Hader
Gene A. Haldeman
Christopher J. Hawke
Richard M. Horowitz
Clark C. Huang
Ana C. Iacovetta
Thomas J. Infurna (Resident at White Plains Office)
John A. Jasey
Charles K. Jones
Anthony Juliano
Elizabeth M. Keogh
John J. Kim
Yunah Kim
Erik D. Klingenberg
Keith L. Krasney
Julia H. Lee
Matthew C. Lefferts
Gary N. Levine
Joan A. Lieberman
Maria M. Livanos
Andrea Nancy Mandell
Danielle M. Maratea
Douglas J. Mazer
Colleen Graham McCabe
Paul B. McCarthy
Robert E. McCarthy
Andrew G. McCormick
Michael C. McGrath
Richard L. Mendles
Lynn B. Mesuk (Not admitted in NY)
Sheila M. Murphy
Joseph S. Nicotra
Elton F. Norman (Not admitted in NY)
Evelyn L. Ochman
Douglas H. Olin
Bola Oloko
Stephen F. Ornstein (Resident at Washington, D.C. Office)
Lauren A. Pearlmutter
Michael E. Peeples (Resident at White Plains Office)
Frank J. Peraza
Renata C. Pompa
William S. Presti
Claudia L. Psome
Gregory R. Salathé
Alejandro R. San Miguel
Jason M. Scherr
Lisa R. Schwartz
Erica G. Sharf
Jeffrey Alan Sherman
Richard D. Simonds, Jr.
Mark I. Sokolow
Lisa Dodman Treanor
Alberto J. Troncoso
Sandra L. Tsang (Resident at White Plains Office)
Peter M. Tzelios
Steven Wasser
John C. Weber
Kathleen A. Wechter
Usher T. Winslett
Michael B. Wolk

For full biographical listings, see the Martindale-Hubbell Law Directory

TOWNLEY & UPDIKE (AV)

A Partnership including a Professional Corporation
Chrysler Building, 405 Lexington Avenue, 10174
Telephone: 212-973-6191
Telecopier: (212) 370-1348
Paramus, New Jersey Office: East 80 and Route 4.
Telephone: 201-712-0991.
Fax: 201-712-9444.
Garden City, New York Office: Garden City Center, Suite 506, 100 Quentin Roosevelt Boulevard.
Telephone: 516-227-3737.
Fax: 516-227-3746.

MEMBERS OF FIRM

Louis F. Burke (P.C.)
John D. Canoni
Carl J. Chiappa
Jerome P. Coleman
Mario Diaz-Cruz, III
Sandra Edelman
Perez C. Ehrich
Douglas C. Fairhurst
Cory E. Friedman
Mark D. Geraghty
Michael F. Griffin
Jon H. I. Grouf
William O'C. Harnisch
Jonathan M. Herman
Richard Koo
Jayne M. Kurzman
Harry A. LeBien
Evelyn J. Lehman
Matthew L. Lifflander
Richard R. Lutz
Robert C. Miller
James P. O'Neill
Philip D. Pakula
Robert E. Peduzzi
Robert Lloyd Raskopf
John Paul Reiner
Daniel A. Rizzi
Danforth W. Rogers
Barbara M. Roth
Richard L. Russell
Ralph K. Smith, Jr.
James B. Swire
P. Jay Wilker

COUNSEL

Paul M. Bochner
Helene M. Freeman
Steven I. Himelstein

OF COUNSEL

Elliot Paskoff
John J. Leighton

SPECIAL COUNSEL

Frederick A. Nicoll (Resident, Paramus, New Jersey Office)

ASSOCIATES

Kenneth A. Becker
Michael S. Belohlavek
Alan Blum
John P. Bruynes
James P. Colliton
Christopher A. D'Angelo
Sherri F. Dratfield
George C. Duran
Bruce R.M. Ewing
Nadine Flynn

(See Next Column)

TOWNLEY & UPDIKE, *New York—Continued*

ASSOCIATES (Continued)

Kelly A. Glidden	Ingrid Morning
Andrew D. Goldsmith	Bret I. Parker
Avrom E. Greenberg	David M. Proper
Joan B. Gross	Zvi N. Raskin
Francis J. Hearn, Jr.	Elizabeth Regan
James M. Hershler	Stacy G. Rom-Jensen
Steven Horowitz	Robert A. Rossi
Jason P. Isralowitz	Louis R. Satriale, Jr.
David Gordon Jacoby	Marcie L. Schlanger
Blaire F. Kagan	Robert P. Schlossberg
Edward K. Lenci	Bruce A. Schoenberg
Deborah L. Magnotta	Mark S. Sullivan
Peter Mendelson	Elizabeth A. Tucker
Tanya L. Menton	Donald E. Watnick

For full biographical listings, see the Martindale-Hubbell Law Directory

VARET & FINK P.C. (AV)

(Formerly Milgrim Thomajan & Lee P.C.)
53 Wall Street, 10005-2899
Telephone: 212-858-5300
Cable Address: "Milatom NYK"
Telex: WUI 662124
Telecopier: 212-858-5301
Washington, D.C. Office: 1110 Vermont Avenue, N.W., Suite 600.
Telephone: 202-628-6200.
Fax: 202-628-2288.

David B. Buss	James R. Ledley
Andrew L. Deutsch	Raymond A. Mantle
Robert F. Fink	Garry P. McCormack
James A. Guadiana	Stanley McDermott, III
Leo G. Kailas	Robert A. Meister
James D. Kleiner	Raymond F. Steckel
David P. Langlois	Michael A. Varet

COUNSEL

Christopher J. Clay (Resident, Washington, D.C. Office)	Mitchell E. Radin
	Cindy V. Schlaefer

Peter M. Corrigan	David A. McManus
Carol M. Fischer	John L. Moore, Jr. (Resident, Washington, D.C. Office)
Michael R. Hepworth	
Ellen H. Klestzick	Robert Weiss
Hope P. Krebs	Diane S. Wolfson

For full biographical listings, see the Martindale-Hubbell Law Directory

WALTER, CONSTON, ALEXANDER & GREEN, P.C. (AV)

90 Park Avenue, 10016
Telephone: 212-210-9400
Facsimile: 212-210-9444
Telex: 234436
Washington, D.C. Office: 1140 Connecticut Avenue, N.W., Suite 250, 20036.
Telephone: 202-775-3955.
Facsimile: 202-775-3956.
Darien, Connecticut Office: 30 Center Street, 06820.
Telephone: 203-655-6046.
Facsimile: 203-656-1407.
Munich, Germany Office: Brienner Strasse 11, 80333 Munich.
Telephone: (89) 238070.
Facsimile: (89) 23807110.
Telex: 522957.

Henry M. Alexander (1822-1899)	Heidi B. Duerbeck
	Daniel C. Edmundson
Ashbel Green (1825-1898)	Paul M. Frank
Henry S. Conston	Gregory F. Hauser
William Schurtman	Rudolph S. Houck III
George Berlstein	W. Macy Johnson
Marie-Therese F. Naylor Allen	Alan Kanzer
William M. Barron	Christoph Lange
Saul Ben-Meyer	William H. Miller, Jr.
J. Frederick Berg, Jr.	Michael C. Nissim
Aydin S. Caginalp	Daniel J. O'Neill
Joan-Elisse Carpentier	Thomas Sauermilch
James R. Cogan	John Joseph Sullivan
Stephanie Denkowicz	Ram Sundar
David W. Detjen	David J. Sweet

Edward Tanenbaum

SENIOR COUNSEL

Otto L. Walter	Donald Vail

COUNSEL

Frank C. Bateman, III	Noel J. Para
Ken W. Chin	Jenik Radon
Franz S. Leichter	Philippe S. E. Schreiber
Eric S. Malm	Paul H. Silverman
David J. Mugford	Eric Stenshoel

(See Next Column)

RESIDENT COUNSEL
MUNICH, GERMANY
Elizabeth A. Voight

Rodolfo Arauz	James F. Kelly
John Ford Baron	Wayne R. Landesman
Kathleen M. Bender	Leily Lashkari
Daniel R. Boehnk	Joann M. Longobardi
MichÈle J. Briançon	Sylvie G. Motz
Renēe Brissette	Mitchel C. Pahl
Elyce Friedfeld	Guy A. Reiss
Karl Geercken	John M. Retting
Elizabeth Gonzalez	Lloyd L. Rothenberg
Bea Grossman	Susan M. Smith
Stephen S. Hart	David P. Speciner
Frank G. Helman	Christine A. Spletzer

For full biographical listings, see the Martindale-Hubbell Law Directory

WATSON, FARLEY & WILLIAMS (AV)

380 Madison Avenue, 10017
Telephone: 212-922-2200
Telex: 6790626 WFW NY
Fax: 212-922-1512
London, England Office: 15 Appold Street, London EC2A 2HB.
Telephone: (44 71) 814 8000.
Telex: 8955707 WFW LON G.
Fax: (44 71) 814 8141.
Paris, France Office: 19 rue de Marignan, 75008 Paris.
Telephone: (33 1) 45 63 15 15.
Telex: WFW PAR 651096 F.
Fax: (33 1) 45 61 09 01.
Oslo, Norway Office: Beddingen 8, Aker Brygge, 0250 Oslo.
Telephone: (47 22) 83 83 08.
Telex: 79209 WFW N.
Fax: (47 22) 83 83 13.
Athens, Greece Office: Alassia Building, Defteras Merarchias 13, 185-35 Piraeus.
Telephone: (30 1) 422 3660.
Telex: 24 1311 WFW GR.
Fax: (30 1) 422 3664.
Moscow, Russia Office: 36 Myaskovskovo Street, Moscow 121019.
Telephone: (7 502) 224 1700 (international only); (7 095) 291 8046/5968.
Fax: (7 502) 224 1701 (international only); (7 095) 202 9027.
Copenhagen, Denmark Office: Lille Kongensgade 20 DK-1074 Copenhagen K.
Telephone: (45 33) 91 33 03.
Fax: (45 33) 91 49 12.

MEMBERS OF FIRM

Derick W. Betts, Jr.	Thatcher A. Stone
Leo Chang	Joseph G. Braunreuther
John E. Nelson II	Peter S. Smedresman
David N. Osborne	Philip H. Spector
John S. Osborne, Jr.	R. Jay Fortin
Alfred E. Yudes, Jr.	Robert P. Schreiner

ASSOCIATES

Samuel W. Adams	John G. Kissane
J. Jorge Barrieu	Arthur T. Kolios
Christopher P. Belisle	Susan Hamilton Mac Cormac
Jonathan Ferstenberg	Laura Ellen Savage
Jane M. Freeberg	Craig E. Stearns
Jane S. Hetherington	James K. Wall

LONDON, ENGLAND
RESIDENT PARTNERS
(NOT ADMITTED IN NEW YORK)

A. H. Farley	N. A. D. Thomas
M. A. Watson	M. M. Llewellyn
G. C. Williams	R. P. Whish
D. J. Warder	J. A. Vaughan
C. A. L. Preston	M. J. Lawson
C. St. C. Smallwood	M. J. Davis
W. G. Fossick	A. J. W. Muriel
G. L. Wynne	J. A. D. Watters
F. Dunne	J. H. Surgeoner
N. D. Cuthbert	P. J. Flint
S. R. Curtis	J. M. Kirkland
C. M. H. Walford	R.W. Muir
O. A. Whitty	J.D. Wardle

N.A. Towle

OSLO, NORWAY
RESIDENT PARTNERS
M.L. Vernell (Not admitted in NY)

PARIS, FRANCE
RESIDENT PARTNERS

A. H. Wettern (Not admitted in NY)	D. I. Syed (Not admitted in NY; Avocats à la Cour de Paris)
N. R. D. Moss (Not admitted in NY)	Edward J. Nalbantian

(See Next Column)

WATSON, FARLEY & WILLIAMS—*Continued*

ATHENS, GREECE
RESIDENT PARTNERS
R. A. Rice (Not admitted in NY)

MOSCOW, RUSSIA
RESIDENT PARTNERS
M.G.S. Greville (Not admitted in NY)

COPENHAGEN, DENMARK
RESIDENT PARTNER
Christopher Lowe

For full biographical listings, see the Martindale-Hubbell Law Directory

WHITE & CASE (AV)

1155 Avenue of the Americas, 10036-2787
Telephone: 212-819-8200
Telex: 233188 WHCA UR
Facsimile: 212-354-8113
Washington, D.C.:
Telephone: 202-872-0013.
Facsimile: 202-872-0210.
Los Angeles, California:
Telephone: 213-620-7700.
Facsimile: 213-687-0758; 213-617-2205.
Miami, Florida:
Telephone: 305-371-2700.
Facsimile: 305-358-5744.
Mexico City, Mexico:
Telephone: (52-5) 207-9717.
Facsimile: (52-5) 208-3628.
Tokyo, Japan:
Telephone: (81-3) 3239-4300.
Facsimile: (81-3) 3239-4330.
Hong Kong:
Telephone: (852) 2822-8700.
Facsimile: (852) 2845-9070; Grice & Co., Solicitors,
Telephone: (852) 2826-0333.
Facsimile: (852) 2526-7166.
Singapore, Republic of Singapore:
Telephone: (65) 225-6000.
Facsimile: (65) 225-6009.
Bangkok, Thailand: Pacific Legal Group Ltd., In Association With White & Case,
Telephone: (662) 236-6154/7.
Facsimile: (662) 237-6771.
Hanoi, Viet Nam: Representative Office,
Telephone: (84-4) 227-575/6/7.
Facsimile: (84-4) 227-297.
Bombay, India:
Telephone: (91-22) 282-6300.
Facsimile: (91-22) 282-6305.
London, England:
Telephone: (44-171) 726-6361.
Facsimile: (44-171) 726-4314; (44-171) 726-8558.
Paris, France:
Telephone: (33-1) 42-60-34-05.
Facsimile: (33-1) 42-60-82-46.
Brussels, Belgium:
Telephone: (32-2) 647-05-89.
Facsimile: (32-2) 647-16-75.
Stockholm, Sweden:
Telephone: (46-8) 679-80-30.
Facsimile: (46-8) 611-21-22.
Helsinki, Finland:
Telephone: (358-0) 631-100.
Facsimile: (358-0) 179-477.
Moscow, Russia:
Telephone: (7-095) 201-9292/3/4/5.
Facsimile: (7-095) 201-9284.
Budapest, Hungary:
Telephone: (36-1) 269-0550; (36-1) 131-0933.
Facsimile: (36-1) 269-1199.
Prague, Czech Republic:
Telephone: (42-2) 2481-1796.
Facsimile: (42-2) 232-5522.
Warsaw, Poland: Telephone/
Facsimile: (48-22) 26-80-53; (48-22) 27-84-86. International Telephone/
Facsimile: (48-39) 12-19-06.
Istanbul, Turkey:
Telephone: (90-212) 275-68-98; (90-212) 275-75-33.
Facsimile: (90-212) 275-75-43.
Ankara, Turkey:
Telephone: (90-312) 446-2180.
Facsimile: (90-312) 437-9677.
Jeddah, Saudi Arabia: Law Office of Hassan Mahassni,
Telephone: (966-2) 651-3535.
Facsimile: (966-2) 651-3636.
Riyadh, Saudi Arabia: Law Office of Hassan Mahassni,
Telephone: (966-1) 476-7099.
Facsimile: (966-1) 479-0110.

(See Next Column)

Almaty, Kazakhstan:
Telephone: (7-3272) 50-7491/2.
Facsimile: (7-3272) 61-0842.

MEMBERS OF FIRM

Victor M. Alvarez (Miami, Florida Office)
Aldo A. Badini
Jeffrey Barist
Kevin F. Barnard
Howard S. Beltzer
Eric L. Berg
Scott A. Berger
J. Truman Bidwell, Jr.
Charles N. Brower (Washington, D.C. Office)
Maureen Smyth Brundage
Paul J. Bschorr
Duncan G. Calder III
Lauriston Castleman, Jr.
Sylvia Fung Chin
Robert L. Clare, III
J. D. Clayton
William J. Clinton (Washington, D.C. Office)
Stephen M. Corse (Miami, Florida Office)
Ronald W. Davis
Darryl B. Deaktor (Miami, Florida Office)
Andrew De Natale
Victor J. DeSantis (Washington, D.C. Office)
John M. Donovan
Maureen D. Donovan
Dimitrios Drivas
Alan M. Dunn (Washington, D.C. Office)
John W. Erickson
Edward V. Filardi
C. Randolph Fishburn (Los Angeles, California Office)
Vincent R. FitzPatrick, Jr.
Burton H. Fohrman (Los Angeles, California Office)
Lawrence J. Gannon
Sean J. Geary
J. Alberto Gonzalez-Pita (Miami, Florida Office)
Timothy B. Goodell
Eugene W. Goodwillie, Jr.
David C. Goss
K. Lawrence Gragg (Miami, Florida Office)
Neal F. Grenley
Allan L. Gropper
Rayner M. Hamilton
James F. Hayden
Thomas P. Higgins
Laura B. Hoguet
Brian L. Holman (Los Angeles, California Office)
Richard J. Holwell
Richard A. Horsch
David L. Huber
James B. Hurlock
David G. Johnson (Los Angeles, California Office)
David E. Joyce
Anthony F. Kahn
Kevin Keogh
David S. Klafter
Charles C. Kline (Miami, Florida Office)
P. B. Konrad Knake (1934-1992)
I. Fred Koenigsberg
David N. Koschik
Alexander S. Kritzalis
Carolyn B. Lamm (Washington, D.C. Office)
John T. Lillis
Nels T. Lippert
Francis J. MacLaughlin (Los Angeles, California Office)
Donald T. MacNaughton
Donald P. Madden
John J. McAvoy (Washington, D.C. Office)
Thomas McGanney
John J. McNally
Harry G. Melkonian (Los Angeles, California Office)
Mitchell E. Menaker
John E. Mendez (Los Angeles, California Office)
Janis M. Meyer
Neal S. Millard (Los Angeles, California Office)
Clyde Mitchell
Morton Moskin
Vernon Munroe (1908-1993)
Elizabeth P. Munson
Roger W. Noble
Thomas J. O'Sullivan
Casimir C. Patrick, II
Owen C. Pell
Kenneth A. Raskin
Richard W. Reinthaler
John M. Reiss
Paul C. Rooney, Jr.
Marianne Rosenberg
Edward F. Rover
Winthrop Rutherfurd, Jr.
Robert M. Safron
Arthur A. Scavone
Philip H. Schaeffer
Sandra J. Schecter
Frank L. Schiff
Richard K. Smith, Jr. (Los Angeles, California Office)
Robert Thornton Smith
Walter J. Spak (Washington, D.C. Office)
John A. Sturgeon (Los Angeles, California Office)
Richard B. Sypher
Gwynne H. Wales
H. William Walker, Jr. (Miami, Florida Office)
Duane D. Wall
Travers D. Wood (Los Angeles, California Office)
William F. Wynne, Jr.
Abraham L. Zylberberg

Jay H. Grodin (Los Angeles, California Office)
Lenard H. Mandel
Willis McDonald, IV

RETIRED PARTNERS

Richard H. Appert
Thomas C. Burke
Malcolm J. Edgerton, Jr.
Marion J. Epley, III
Haliburton Fales, 2d
C. Sims Farr
Macdonald Flinn
Philip H. Hedges
Joseph Hinsey, IV
Thomas A. Hopkins
John M. Johnston
Thomas Kiernan
James J. Marshall, Jr.
Andrew O. Miller
Stephen M. Piga
John C. Provine
Thomas M. Ramseur, Jr.
John G. Reed
David Sachs
David W. Swanson
Donald M. Wilkinson, Jr.
William L. Williams
Edward Wolfe

OF COUNSEL

David Bender
Gerard T. Drumm
Paul K. Milmed
Tetsuya Morimoto (Los Angeles, California Office)
Robert B. Smith
James M. Stillwaggon

(See Next Column)

WHITE & CASE, *New York—Continued*

COUNSEL

Robert H. Bloom
Margery A. Colloff
Dwight A. Healy
Steven K. Ross
Jeffrey J. Temple

ASSOCIATES

Troy Alexander
Priscilla Almodovar
Emilio J. Alvarez-Farré (Miami, Florida Office)
Nancy A. Ameen
Peggy Gowan Angelone
S. Ward Atterbury
Andrew S. Auchincloss
Donald E. Baker (Miami, Florida Office)
Robin D. Ball (Los Angeles, California Office)
David H. Bate (Los Angeles, California Office)
Cyrus Benson III
Steven M. Betensky
David Bilkis
David E. Bond (Washington, D.C. Office)
Gil J. Bonwitt (Miami, Florida Office)
Vincent Bowen (Washington, D.C. Office)
Lisa R. Brant (Los Angeles, California Office)
Peter S. Brodsky
Joseph G. Brosnan
Megan M. Bruce (Los Angeles, California Office)
N. Christopher Butler
James R. Cairns (Los Angeles, California Office)
Carlos B. Castillo (Miami, Florida Office)
John A. Catron (Los Angeles, California Office)
Gregory B. Cerbone
Sarka Cerna
Daniel S. Chen (Washington, D.C. Office)
Glenn I. Chernigoff (Los Angeles, California Office)
Anna-Marie Christello-Roop (Washington, D.C. Office)
Thomas W. Christopher (Not admitted in NY)
Gad J. Cohen
Jane D. Connolly
Bethany L. Conybeare
Ellen M. Cotter
Paul J. Crath
Karen Burns Cummings
Christopher M. Curran (Washington, D.C. Office)
G. William Currier
Cori E. Daggett
Kimberly A. Daine
Andrew M. Dansicker (Not admitted in NY)
Peter L. Dedesma (Miami, Florida Office)
Mark DeGennaro
Susan J. De Witt (Los Angeles, California Office)
Darin A. DiBello (Miami, Florida Office)
William P. DiSalvatore
David C. Downie, Jr.
Sophia J. Drewnowski
Michael P. Dunworth
Janeth Duque
John D. Early (Los Angeles, California Office)
Anne L. Eu
Karen R. Fagerstrom
Helen A. Feuer
Christopher P. Frampton
Claire M. Gallagher (Not admitted in NY)
Steven M. Garten
Frances H. George
James A. Gerard
Robert Glouberman (Los Angeles, California Office)
Patricia M. Godoy
Michael S. Goetz
Daniel A. Goldberger
Barbara J. Goodman
John M. Grimes
William S. Haft
Matthew Hagopian
Vincent M. Haley
Kevin A. Hall
E. Bayard Halsted
Charlotte J. Hart (Washington, D.C. Office)
Michael L. Herman
Eric J. Hoechstetter
William C. Holland (Washington, D.C. Office)
Evan C. Hollander
T. Douglas Hollowell
John P. Hornbostel
Jane A. Houk (Miami, Florida Office)
Louis T. Hsieh (Los Angeles, California Office)
Lisa L. Hubbard (Washington, D.C. Office)
Joseph H. Hunt (Washington, D.C. Office)
Elisa F. Hyman
Laura C. Janke
Diana Jarvis
Marcos D. Jimenez (Miami, Florida Office)
M. Elaine Johnston
David J. Kaplan
Raymund G. Kawasaki (Los Angeles, California Office)
Raymond J. Kayal, Jr. (Miami, Florida Office)
Sanford B. Kaynor, Jr.
Robert M. Kelly
Zoltan Kerekes
Stuart Y. Kim (Los Angeles, California Office)
Eric L. Klar
M. Adriana Koeck de Schmidt (Miami, Florida Office)
Glenn M. Kurtz
Jeffrey D. Lapin
Patrick W. Lawler
Patricia Y. Lee (Washington, D.C. Office)
Scott L. Lenz
Matthew P. Lewis (Los Angeles, California Office)
Cecilia O'Brien Lofters
Noël C. Lohr (Los Angeles, California Office)
Lalit K. Loomba
Felix J. Lopez (Miami, Florida Office)
Ole W. Lyngklip, III
Barry N. Machlin (Washington, D.C. Office)
Cecily P. Maguire
Philip L. Maloney (Los Angeles, California Office)
Rachel Mariner (Washington, D.C. Office)
A. Grant McCrea
Deirdre M. McDonald
Joan Morgan McGivern
Sean P. McGrath
Thomas P. McGrath
Patricia L. McKeogh
Michael J. McMillen
Bryan A. Merryman (Los Angeles, California Office)
Enrique Antonio Miguez (Miami, Florida Office)
Steven L. Miller (Los Angeles, California Office)
Robert A. Milne
Beth Jarrett Moffitt (Miami, Florida Office)
Ellen S. Moore (Washington, D.C. Office)
Elizabeth G. Moreno (Los Angeles, California Office)

(See Next Column)

ASSOCIATES (Continued)

Robert J. Morrow
Curt C. Myers
John Narducci
William L. Neilson
Robert A. Nisi
Anna J. Obayashi
Deirdre O'Connor Quinn
Fouad S. Onbargi
Ann L. Parsons (Los Angeles, California Office)
Susan E. Patsalos
George L. Paul (Washington, D.C. Office)
James W. Perkins
Lori J. Perlman
Carole C. Peterson (Los Angeles, California Office)
Laurence Pettit
Corinne M. Plummer
Gregory Pryor
Michael L. Quigley
Adam Ratner
William A. Redfern, III
Dorothea W. Regal
Henry J. Ricardo
Harriet A. Robinson (Washington, D.C. Office)
Catherine D. Rosati
Hillary Barbara Rossman (Miami, Florida Office)
Eric S. Roth (Miami, Florida Office)
Renee M. Rubin (Los Angeles, California Office)
Christopher L. Rudd (Los Angeles, California Office)
Neil W. Rust (Los Angeles, California Office)
Ann M. St.Peter-Griffith (Miami, Florida Office)
Edward E. Sawyer (Miami, Florida Office)
Mary Schinke
William A. Schoneman
Alice A. Seebach (Los Angeles, California Office)
Jennifer L. Sheppard
J. Christopher Shore
Michael S. Shuster
Jill H. Silfen (Los Angeles, California Office)
Edmund W. Sim (Washington, D.C. Office)
Katherine Simonetti (Washington, D.C. Office)
Sami Sindi
Susanne Corey Sizer
Robert L. Skinner (Los Angeles, California Office)
Anne D. Smith (Washington, D.C. Office)
Ellen W. Smith
Geoffrey W. Smith
Abbey P. Cohen Smutny (Washington, D.C. Office)
Glenn E. Solomon (Los Angeles, California Office)
Isaac E. Sperka
Robert F. Sprouls
Sarah M. Starkweather
David S. Starr (Los Angeles, California Office)
Leanne K. Steele
David R. Stepp (Washington, D.C. Office)
Nelson Suit
Andrew C. Svarre
Marina C. Szteinbok
Ichizo Takayama
Helena M. Tavares
Jefferson C. Taylor (Miami, Florida Office)
Robert E. Tiedemann, III
Steven W. Turnbull (Los Angeles, California Office)
Gary L. Urwin (Los Angeles, California Office)
Francis A. Vasquez (Washington, D.C. Office)
Katherine T. Ward
Ted S. Ward (Los Angeles, California Office)
Ian D. Watson
Andrew C. Weiler
Adam K. Weinstein
Mary L. Weiss
Mara S. Weissmann
Dansby White
Meghan A. White (Los Angeles, California Office)
James M. Wicks
Robert Lee Wilkerson (Los Angeles, California Office)
John S. Willems
David J. Wilson (Los Angeles, California Office)
Carol A. Witschel
J. Stefan Wood
Eric S. Yoon
Kenneth K. Yoon
Patrick G. Zabatta

RESIDENT PARTNER, MEXICO CITY OFFICE

Pedro A. Alvarez

RESIDENT PARTNERS, TOKYO OFFICE

Robert F. Grondine
Gary M. Thomas
Christopher P. Wells

RESIDENT PARTNERS, HONG KONG OFFICE

George K. Crozer, IV
Lawrence S. Yee

PARTNER, GRICE & CO., SOLICITORS

R. Geoffrey Grice

RESIDENT PARTNERS, SINGAPORE OFFICE

J. Haywood Blakemore, IV
Kenneth C. Ellis
Wendell C. Maddrey

DIRECTOR, PACIFIC LEGAL GROUP LTD.

Paul G. Russell

RESIDENT PARTNER HANOI OFFICE

K. Minh Dang

RESIDENT PARTNERS, LONDON OFFICE

John M. H. Bellhouse
William E. Butler
Peter Finlay
Francis Fitzherbert-Brockholes
Bernard E. Nelson
H. Philip T. Stopford

(See Next Column)

WHITE & CASE—*Continued*

RESIDENT PARTNERS,
PARIS OFFICE

Stephen R. Bond
Jean-Luc Boussard
Anthony Giustini
Rosine Lorotte
Gilles Peigney
John H. Riggs, Jr.
Christopher R. Seppala

RESIDENT PARTNERS,
STOCKHOLM OFFICE

Göran Åseborn
Rolf Olofsson
Claes Zettermarck

RESIDENT PARTNERS,
MOSCOW OFFICE

Alison M. Dreizen
Maryann E. Gashi-Butler

PARTNER,
BUDAPEST OFFICE

Carl H. Amon III

PARTNERS,
PRAGUE OFFICE

Carl H. Amon III
Daniel J. Arbess

RESIDENT PARTNER,
WARSAW OFFICE

Witold Danilowicz

RESIDENT PARTNER,
ISTANBUL OFFICE

Asli F. Basgoz

RESIDENT PARTNER,
ANKARA OFFICE

Hugh Verrier

PARTNERS,
JEDDAH OFFICE

Alexander S. Kritzalis
Hassan Mahassni

PARTNER,
RIYADH OFFICE

Hassan Mahassni

RESIDENT COUNSEL,
PARIS OFFICE

Nicholas Budd
Pierre-Yves Corrieu

RESIDENT COUNSEL,
SINGAPORE OFFICE

Kimberley R. Landon

RESIDENT COUNSEL,
STOCKHOLM OFFICE

Jan Gregorsson
Lars G. Kjellman

RESIDENT OF COUNSEL,
HELSINKI OFFICE

Petri Yrjo Johannes Haussila

RESIDENT OF COUNSEL,
WARSAW OFFICE

Andrzej Burzynski
Witold Jurcewicz

RESIDENT COUNSEL,
WARSAW OFFICE

Grzegorz E. Domanski
Janusz Fiszer

RESIDENT COUNSEL,
HANOI OFFICE

Paul D. Q. Nguyen

RESIDENT COUNSEL,
ISTANBUL OFFICE

M. Fadlullah Cerrahoğlu

RESIDENT ASSOCIATES,
MEXICO CITY OFFICE

Susan E. Grisso De Ortega
Christian W. Hansen
Michael W. Hein
Kenneth R. Lee

RESIDENT ASSOCIATES,
TOKYO OFFICE

Jonathan M. Heimer
Glen Sugimoto
Osamu Umejima

RESIDENT ASSOCIATES,
HONG KONG OFFICE

Steven P. Allen
Andrew Hin Chi Chan
Isabella de la Houssaye
Mei-Ying Hao
Sharon E. Hartline
Jack H. Su
Alex Y. Wong

RESIDENT ASSOCIATES,
GRICE & CO., SOLICITORS

Steven P. Allen
Andrew Hin Chi Chan
Andrew P. McLean
Kim Margaret Rooney
Alex Y. Wong

RESIDENT ASSOCIATES,
SINGAPORE OFFICE

Michael R. Barz
Alistair A. Duffield
John-Michael Lind
Brian M. Miller
Kevin J. Murphy
Madhurani Powar Garg
Neela Ramanathan
Michael R. Reading
S. M. Edwin Tham
Brian J. Wesol

(See Next Column)

RESIDENT ASSOCIATES,
PACIFIC LEGAL GROUP LTD.

Peangpanor Boonklum
Pongpitak Sawetnant
Dol Bunnag
Suparerk Auychai
Therdtham Pianpicharn
Wannee Arttavitworakarn

RESIDENT ASSOCIATE,
HANOI OFFICE

Tanya G. Pullin

RESIDENT MANAGING ATTORNEY,
BOMBAY OFFICE

Raj Pande

RESIDENT ASSOCIATES,
LONDON OFFICE

Ruth Ambrose
Carolyn M. Brzezinski
Jonathan M. Clark, Jr.
Gerard N. Cranley
Gregory J. Hammond
Thomas A. Hartnett
Kaya H. Proudian
Jeffrey A. Washenko

RESIDENT ASSOCIATES,
PARIS OFFICE

Paule Biensan
Robert Brada, Jr.
Bertrand Caradet
Rémy Cottage-Stone
Dr. Reinhard Dammann
Jean-Charles De Daruvar
Philippe Deneux
Carroll S. Dorgan
Suzanne Durdevic
François Farmine
Pierre Forget
Eric Gastinel
Ronald E. M. Goodman
Clifford J. Hendel
Caroline Kahn
Jean-Francois LeCorre
Anne-France Marmot
Philippe Metais
Mark G. Milford
Vincent Morin
Marie-Helene Peres
Laura Restelli
Mark B. Richards
Peter Rosher
Stewart Robert Shackleton

RESIDENT ASSOCIATES,
BRUSSELS OFFICE

Pontus Lindfelt
Margaret G. Wachenfeld

RESIDENT ASSOCIATES,
STOCKHOLM OFFICE

Cecilia Ahrbom
Penelope E. Codrington
Thomas Engwall
Jan Gustavsson
Ulf Johansson
André Lindekrantz
Fredrik Schultz

RESIDENT ASSOCIATES,
HELSINKI OFFICE

Pia T. Hellman
James G. Hunt
Pekka J. Lehtinen
Laura A. Susi-Gamba
Ala Michael Tarazi

RESIDENT ASSOCIATES,
MOSCOW OFFICE

Natalya Artemyeva
Sergei M. Baranchenkov
Maya Fishkin
Eric Michailov
Kalinka H. Moudrova
Denis Vinokurov

RESIDENT ASSOCIATES,
BUDAPEST OFFICE

David M. Eisenberg
Dr. Klara Honti
Eva Imrik
Phoebe A. Kornfeld
Marie Theresa O'Connor
Jessica Glass Pollack
Szabolcs Posta

RESIDENT ASSOCIATES,
PRAGUE OFFICE

James R. Cowan
Robert B. Irving
Carlo L. Kostka
Monika B. Krizek
Radan Kubr
John C. Leary
Emil Nemec
Monika Rutland

RESIDENT ASSOCIATES,
WARSAW OFFICE

Alexander G. Fraser
Joanna Gomula
Stephen Harder
Barbara Jasniewska
Antoni Tomasz Minkiewicz
Marek Wisniewski
Julita Zimoch

RESIDENT ASSOCIATES,
ISTANBUL OFFICE

Sebnem Isik Kaplanoglu
Refika Tulay Tuzun
Aldoru Uluatam
Deniz Ulusoy
Meltem Usluakol
Can Verdi
Christopher G. Wilkinson
Serap Zuvin

RESIDENT ASSOCIATES,
ANKARA OFFICE

Mesut Cakmak
Anne E. Lederer
Zeynep Onalan

RESIDENT ASSOCIATES,
JEDDAH OFFICE

E. William Cattan, Jr.
Imad Ai-Dine Ghazi
Anas Kailani
Farouk Kouatli
Walid Labadi
Amin Munajed
Gassim Zanoon

RESIDENT ASSOCIATE,
RIYADH OFFICE

James R. Billingsley, Jr.

(See Next Column)

WHITE & CASE, *New York—Continued*

RESIDENT ASSOCIATE,
ALMATY OFFICE

James B. Varanese

LEGAL CONSULTANT,
PACIFIC LEGAL GROUP LTD.

Joseph E. Stumpf

For full biographical listings, see the Martindale-Hubbell Law Directory

WHITMAN BREED ABBOTT & MORGAN (AV)

200 Park Avenue, 10166
Telephone: 212-351-3000
Cable Address: "Whitsom" or "Bengoshi New York"
Telex: 12-5109 (WU); 238436 (RCA)
Telecopier: 212-351-3131
Los Angeles, California Office: 633 West Fifth Street.
Telephone: 213-896-2400.
Sacramento, California Office: Senator Hotel Building, 1121 L Street.
Telephone: 916-441-4242.
Greenwich, Connecticut Office: 2 Greenwich Plaza.
Telephone: 203-869-3800.
Washington, D.C. Offices: 1215 17th Street, N.W.
Telephone: 202-887-0353; 1818 N Street, N.W.
Telephone: 202-466-1100.
Newark, New Jersey Office: One Gateway Center.
Telephone: 201-621-2230.
Palm Beach, Florida Office: 220 Sunrise Avenue.
Telephone: 407-832-5458.
London, England Office: 11 Waterloo Place.
Telephone: 01-839-3226.
Telex: 917881.
Tokyo, Japan Office: Suite 450, New Otemachi Building, 2-2-1 Otemachi, Chiyoda-Ku, Tokyo 100.
Telephone: 81-3-3242-1289.
Associated with: Tyan & Associes, 22, La Sagesse Street, Beirut, Lebanon.
Telephone: 337968.
Fax: 200969.
Telex: 43928.

MEMBERS OF FIRM

Camille Abousleiman
Elizabeth A. Alcorn
Robert J. Bagdasarian
Thomas Goodall Bailey, Jr.
David H. Bamberger
Robert A. Bicks
Anne T. Brower
Paul Andrew Cable
Tracy A. Caras
Hollace Topol Cohen
Richard Crystal
D.F.X. de La Chapelle
Alexander T. Deland
John H. Denne
Judith A. Gelb
Jay Gladis
Brian E. Gledhill
John M. Hadlock
Edward H. Hein
Hans F. Kaeser
Charles H. Kaplan
W. Michael Kelly
Norman N. Kinel
Kevin F. Kostyn
David F. Kroenlein
Paul C. Lambert
Stephen R. Lang
Richard F. Lawler
George K. C. Lee
William M. Loafman
Richard F. Markert
Randolph J. Mayer
C. MacNeil Mitchell
Henry G. Morriello
David E. Morse
Eric M. Nelson
John M. Newell
Scott D. Newman
James S. Normile
George J. Noumair
John O'Callahan
John C. Oram, Jr.
David S. Patterson
Benjamin M. Polk
F. Herbert Prem, Jr.
Maged F. Riad
Sander B. Ross
David H. Schmidt
Joseph W. Schmidt
David W. Scott
Berge Setrakian
Alan J. Sorkowitz
Christopher A. Stack
Christopher H. Stephens
Brian L. Sullivan
Loran T. Thompson
John S. Twomey
Neil Underberg
Mary F. Voce
John F. Walsh, Jr.
Kevin Walsh
Monte E. Wetzler
Howard S. Wolfson
Joseph J. Zedrosser

RETIRED PARTNERS

James B. Anderson
J. Sinclair Armstrong
Frederick H. Bruenner
Archibald H. Cashion
Richard R. Dailey
Paul E. Doherty
Ellis J. Freedman
Robert S. Newman
F. Van Siclen Parr
John A. Pateracki, Jr.
Herbert P. Polk
Patrick H. Sullivan

COUNSEL

Hugh L. Carey
Paul J. Chase
Charles R. Foy
Daniel R. Goodman
William D. Hart, Jr.
David Jaffe
Ernest H. Lorch
Carol Lyttle, Jr.
John J. Marchi
Winthrop R. Munyan
William Rubin
John V. Thornton
James M. Waddington

(See Next Column)

ASSOCIATES

Gina Armstrong
Louise R. Bernstein
Sally S. Blinken
Patricia M. Brannick
Jill I. Braverman
Robert C. Brighton, Jr.
John C. Canoni
Joseph Blaise Cartafalsa
Margaret Civetta
Paul D. Connuck
Lester J. Czukor
Steven Paul DeRicco
Martin J. Dever, Jr.
Brian Philip Donnelly
William F. Dudine, III
Joseph DuPont
Christopher M. Flanagan
Adam J. Freedman
Barbara T. Friedman
Michael W. Galligan
Dawn E. Glynn
Lisa Gomberg
James W. Harmon, Jr.
Dean J. M. Heitner
Sarah Hewitt
Greg A. Hodes
Pamela Christine Holly
Anthony C. Kaye
Michael T. Kiesel
Patricia Anne Kuhn
Teresa T. Kuo
Norman M. Leon
Richard Levine
Julie Ann Lynch
Michael K. Madden
Patricia V.B. Madsen
Graziella B. Mahler
Dean N. Menegas
John J. Meyler
Christian H. W. Mittweg
Howard F. Mulligan, Jr.
Karen Ostad
Ellen M. O'Toole
Mark C. Prybylski
Gary P. Rosenthal
Diane K. Roskies
Regina Clark Salathe
Geraldine G. Sanchez
Jonathan S. Sanoff
Danielle Schanz
Loren Selznick
George A. Smith
Phillip M. Smith
Olga Sorkin
James T. Southwick
Ivy B. Stempel
Alice B. Stock
William M. Sunkel
John E. Tardera
Eric P. Taylor
Sarah W. Thomas
Richard A. Walderman
Ralph A. Walter
Clare C.L. Wee
David J. Weisenfeld
Steven J. Young
Harry Zelcer
Peter B. Zlotnick
Catherine M. Zucal

LOS ANGELES, CALIFORNIA OFFICE
RESIDENT PARTNERS

Jorge Arciniega
Christopher A. Burrows
Francis W. Costello
Joseph P. Dailey
Richard A. Eastman
Thomas F. Hanley, III
Lawrence H. Heller
Robert L. Ivey
Gerold W. Libby
Maita Deal Prout
Mark S. Shipow
Richard T. Williams
Paul C. Workman

RESIDENT ASSOCIATES

Alex R. Baghdassarian
Christopher Bryan
Donald M. Clary
Vito A. Costanzo
Roger B. Coven
Alisa J. Freundlich
Daniel W. Lee
Paul S. Marks
Melanie L. McCall
Ann Bridget McCarthy
Tasha D. Nguyen
Michael Okada
Eddie Rodriquez
Jack S. Sholkoff
Kimberly Winer

SACRAMENTO, CALIFORNIA OFFICE
RESIDENT PARTNER

Rodney J. Blonien

GREENWICH, CONNECTICUT OFFICE
PARTNERS

Frank Lewis Baker, III
Mark R. Carta
Charles E. Coates, III
Bruce F. Cohen
James A. Fulton
Kenneth M. Gammill
Charles E. Janson
Richard F. Lawler
Thomas J. McKee
Robert C. O'Brien
Harry E. Peden, Jr.
Harry E. Peden, III
Leland C. Selby
Christopher A. Stack
David P. Tuttle

RETIRED PARTNERS

Mortimer P. Barnes
William T. Cahill
Joseph Mitchell Kaye
Jacob R. Lynch
Alan M. MacCracken
Richard Joyce Smith
Clark McK. Whittemore, Jr.

COUNSEL

Jennifer N. Boyd
Everett Fisher
Brian D. Forrow
Richard L. Rose

RESIDENT ASSOCIATES

Sarah O. Conrades
Joseph V. Cuomo
Joseph C. Gasparrini
Elizabeth M. Grant
Deborah S. Gordon
Maurice H. Hartigan, III
L. Page Heslin
Richard E. Mancuso
Elizabeth B. Palache
Charles W. Pieterse
James C. Riley
J. Michael Schroeder
Douglas S. Skalka
William Bradford Smith, Jr.
Margaret Ann Triolo
Sujata Yalamanchili

WASHINGTON, D.C. OFFICE
RESIDENT PARTNERS

Michael G. Carey
Donald O. Clark
William N. Hall
Marcia A. Wiss

RESIDENT ASSOCIATES

John Fehrenbach

(See Next Column)

WHITMAN BREED ABBOTT & MORGAN—*Continued*

NEWARK, NEW JERSEY OFFICE
RESIDENT PARTNERS

Andrew Muscato
John M. Scagnelli
Joseph J. Zedrosser

RESIDENT ASSOCIATES

Eric S. Aronson
Michael B. Barry
Michael J. Caffrey
Katherine Heras Creenan
Warren A. Koshofer
Julia C. Mallalieu
Christina A. Rallo
David A. Roth

LONDON, ENGLAND OFFICE
RESIDENT PARTNERS

Gordon L. Jaynes
Michael J. McNulty
Elwood A. Rickless
Elton Shane

RESIDENT ASSOCIATES

Lucinda M. Williams

TOKYO, JAPAN
RESIDENT PARTNER

Richard A. Eastman

For full biographical listings, see the Martindale-Hubbell Law Directory

---

WILLKIE FARR & GALLAGHER (AV)

One Citicorp Center, 153 East 53rd Street, 10022-4669
Telephone: 212-821-8000
Fax: 212-821-8111
Telex: RCA 233780-WFGUR; RCA 238805-WFGUR
Washington, D.C. Office: Three Lafayette Centre, 1155 21st Street, N.W., 6th Floor, 20036-3384.
Telephone: 202-328-8000.
Fax: 202-887-8979; 202-331-8187.
Telex: RCA 229800-WFGIG; WU 89-2762.
Paris, France Office: 6, Avenue Velasquez 75008.
Telephone: 011-33-1-44-35-44-35.
Fax: 011-331-42-89-87-01.
Telex: 652740-WFG Paris.
London, England Office: 3rd Floor, 35 Wilson Street, EC2M 2SJ.
Telephone: 011-44-71-696-9060.
Fax: 011-44-71-417-9191.

MEMBERS OF FIRM

Marc Abrams
Peter A. Appel
Mitchell J. Auslander
Joseph T. Baio
William H. Barringer (Resident Partner, Washington, D.C. Office)
Jonathan D. Bassett
Roger D. Blanc
Sue D. Blumenfeld (Resident Partner, Washington, D.C. Office)
John B. Cairns
Thomas M. Cerabino
Kevin B. Clark (Resident Partner, Washington, D.C. Office)
Henry M. Cohn
Dale S. Collinson
Brian Conboy (Resident Partner, Washington, D.C. Office)
Louis A. Craco
Jean-Luc Cuadrado (Resident Partner, Paris, France Office)
John S. D'Alimonte
Monty Davis
John P. Dean (Resident Partner, Washington, D.C. Office)
Richard K. DeScherer
Dennis R. Deveney
Rose F. DiMartino
Robert M. Drillings
Christopher A. Dunn (Resident Partner, Washington, D.C. Office)
James P. Durling (Resident Partner, Washington, D.C. Office)
William N. Dye
Dwight W. Ellis III
Cornelius T. Finnegan, III
Eric J. Fleury (Resident Partner, Paris, France Office)
David L. Foster
Michel Frieh (Resident Partner, Paris, France Office)
Alexander T. Galloway II
Steven J. Gartner
William J. Grant, Jr.
Stephen W. Greiner
Yaacov M. Gross
Dan S. Grossman
Michael H. Hammer (Resident Partner, Washington, D.C. Office)
Peter J. Hanlon
William E. Hiller
Tonny K. Ho
Robert B. Hodes
Peter H. Jakes
Lawrence O. Kamin
Thomas F. Kaufman (Resident Partner, Washington, D.C. Office)
Peter J. Kenny
Gerald Kerner
Robert J. Kheel
Charles I. Kingson
Richard L. Klein
Steven D. Klein
Bruce R. Kraus
Jay F. Leary (Resident Partner, Paris, France Office)
Burton M. Leibert
Bernard Le-Pezron (Resident Partner, Paris, France Office)
Stephen T. Lindo
Alan J. Lipkin
Jeanne M. Luboja
Ira H. Lustgarten
Richard Mancino
Christopher E. Manno
Michael G. Marks
Leslie M. Mazza
David J. McCabe
Francis J. Menton, Jr.
Raymond W. Merritt
Bruce M. Montgomerie
David P. Murray (Resident Partner, Washington, D.C. Office)
Roger D. Netzer
Neil Novikoff
Jack H. Nusbaum
Brian E. O'Connor
John R. Oller
Steven M. Oster (Resident Partner, Washington, D.C. Office)

(See Next Column)

MEMBERS OF FIRM (Continued)

Daniel Payan (Resident Partner, Paris, France Office)
Anthony F. Phillips
Kenneth J. Pierce (Resident Partner, Washington, D.C. Office)
Eugene A. Pinover
Richard L. Posen
Jon S. Rand
Steven H. Reisberg
Benito Romano
William H. Rooney
Emmanuel Rosenfeld (Resident Partner, Paris, France Office)
Thomas M. Rothman
Daniel D. Rubino
Richard D. Rudder
Philippe M. Salomon
Richard C. Sammis
Anthony D. Schlesinger
Daniel Schloendorn
Peter W. Schmidt
Matthew R. Schneider (Resident Partner, Washington, D.C. Office)
Michael A. Schwartz
Michael J. Segal
Barry N. Seidel
Patricia S. Skigen
Harvey L. Sperry
Duncan J. Stewart
Elizabeth S. Stong
Chester J. Straub
Susan P. Thomases
Myron Trepper
Kristen van Riel (Resident Partner, Paris, France Office)
Philip L. Verveer (Resident Partner, Washington, D.C. Office)
Nora Ann Wallace
Laurence D. Weltman
Brent W. White
Theodore C. Whitehouse (Resident Partner, Washington, D.C. Office)
Michael R. Young
Emily M. Zeigler

COUNSEL

Armando T. Belly
Walston S. Brown
Noel Hemmendinger (Resident, Washington, D.C. Office)
Anna De Nerciat-Lascar (Resident Paris, France Office)
Robert M. Saunders
Russell L. Smith (Resident, Washington, D.C. Office)

ASSOCIATES

Daniel J. Aaron
Steven I. Abrams
Peter J. Allman
Nicole N. Anderson
Sean Anderson
Scott A. Arenare
Sander Ash
Gregory B. Astrachan
Michael Bailey
Thomas W. Bark (Paris, France Office)
Kathryn L. Barrett
Blake A. Bell
Colin Bell
Serge Benchetrit
Guy Benda (Paris, France Office)
Kim A. Berger
Eliott M. Berman
Amy L. Berns
James H. Bicks
Alexandra Bigot (Paris, France Office)
Karen E. Blaustein
Kenneth M. Blumberg
William J. Borner
David K. Boston
John J. Bowers
Randy Branitsky (Washington, D.C. Office)
Laura U. Brett
Susan W. Brodkin
Francis M. Buono (Washington, D.C. Office)
Christopher W. Burden
Adrien Cadieux (Paris, France Office)
Thomas J. Cahill
Christina E. Callahan (Not admitted in NY)
Joseph A. Callari
Maryann Canfield
Patrick J. Carmody
Jean-Christophe Castera (Paris, France Office)
Pascal Chadenet (Paris, France Office)
Sarah T. Chasson
Joanne M. Chormanski
Kerwin Chung
Alice M. Clark
Michael G. Clateman (Not admitted in NY)
Michael P. Collins
Carolyn W. Conkling (Washington, D.C. Office)
Gregory M. Cooke
Carolyn C. Cornell
Franck Courmont (Paris, France Office)
Frank A. Daniele
Marie B. Darienzo
Franklin R. Davis
Michael de Cordova
Robert J. Dehney (Not admitted in NY)
Randolph A. DelFranco
Michael Dermer
Allard De Waal (Paris, France Office)
George C. Dolatly
Jennifer A. Donaldson (Washington, D.C. Office)
Renaud DuBois (Paris, France Office)
Patrick S. Dunleavy
Claire Duval (Paris, France Office)
Neil J. Eckstein
Robert H. Edwards, Jr. (Washington, D.C. Office)
Elvin Esteves
Lisa W. Feinman
Matthew A. Feldman
Colette Fergusson
John Fikre
Arlena B. Filipowicz
Brian Finley (Washington, D.C. Office)
Jeffrey B. Finnell
Nancy A. Fischer (Washington, D.C. Office)
John R. Flanigan (Paris, France Office)
Jeffrey W. Fouts (Paris, France Office)
William C. Fredericks
Christophe Garaud (Paris, France Office)
Nicholas S. Gatto
Mary L. Gerdes
Kathleen M. Golden
Thomas H. Golden
Douglas E. Goodfriend
Stephen G. Gorell
Jennifer L. Gray (Not admitted in NY)
Isaac P. Grossman
Jacqueline A. Grundei
Evan M. Gsell
William H. Gump (London, England Office)
John J. Halloran, Jr.
Gregory L. Harris
Matthew Herenstein

(See Next Column)

WILLKIE FARR & GALLAGHER, *New York—Continued*

ASSOCIATES (Continued)

Michael W. Hile
(Not admitted in NY)
Gary Hirsch
Kelly M. Hnatt
Jeffrey S. Hochman
Jeffrey D. Hoeh
Daniel R. Hunter
(Washington, D.C. Office)
Michael S. Immordino
Elizabeth L. Inglehart
Loretta A. Ippolito
James J. Jackson
Andrew D. Jaeger
Catherine Jeancolas
(Paris, France Office)
Thomas Jones
(Washington, D.C. Office)
Pierre Karpik
(Paris, France Office)
Avi Katz
Bonni Fine Kaufman
(Washington, D.C. Office)
Ira S. Kaufman
Scott L. Kaufman
Michael J. Kelly
Leila Khazaneh
Christine M. Kim
David R. King (D.C. Office)
Adam M. Klein
Martin B. Klotz
Jonathan H. Kopp
(Washington, D.C. Office)
Mark T. Lab
Robert L. LaFrankie
(Washington, D.C. Office)
Eric Laget
(Not admitted in NY)
Adams Chi-Peng Lee
(Washington, D.C. Office)
Maurice M. Lefkort
Janice E. Levine
Joshua M. Levine
Joseph J. Lewczak
Donna H. Lieberman
William B. Lindsey
(Washington, D.C. Office)
Josephine B. Link
Steven I. Loew
(Not admitted in NY)
Sharon Makower
Sean P. Maloney
Janna Manes
Alexandra Margolis
Jonathan E. Marsh
(Paris, France Office)
Jil Mazer-Marino
J. Kevin McCarthy
Mary-Lynn McDevitt
John L. McGrew
(Washington, D.C. Office)
Edgar B. Miller
(Washington, D.C. Office)
Eric J. Mitnick
Steven M. Monroe
Thomas E. Myers
Andrew W. Needham
(Not admitted in NY)
Melissa E. Newman
(Washington, D.C. Office)
Matthew R. Nicely
(Washington, D.C. Office)
Mitchel Ochs
Masaaki Ogawa
(Washington, D.C. Office)
Sarah C. Osborn
Stephen A. Overton
Reza Arman Pahlavan
Stacey E. Paradise
Gregory G. Patchen
David C. Peck
Jorge Pedreira
Adam Pelzman
Kirstan Penasack
Didier Penot
(Paris, France Office)
Carlisle E. Perkins
(Washington, D.C. Office)
Brenda Perrotti
Louis T. Petrillo
Michele R. Pistone
(Washington, D.C. Office)
Lawrence R. Plotkin
Etty M. Pollack
Anthony P. Polito
Jeremy Pomeroy
Daniel L. Porter
(Washington, D.C. Office)
Jeffrey R. Poss
(London, England Office)
David E. Rabin
Linda S. Rahnema
(Washington, D.C. Office)
Douglas A. Rappaport
John M. Ratino
(Washington, D.C. Office)
Edward J. Reznik
Mary Anne Richmond
Emily A. Rixinger
Kimberly A. Roeder
Richard C. Rosen
Matthew W. Runkel
Mark R. Salamon
Arlene Sanders
Gabriel R. Sanz-Rexach
(Washington, D.C. Office)
Jordan B. Savitch
Linda G. Schechter
Beth J. Schlegel
John M. Scott
Stewart M. Scott
Steven A. Seidman
Muriel Serre-Prevost
(Paris, France Office)
Paul V. Shalhoub
Gregg B. Shulklapper
Joseph H. Smolinsky
Conrad J. Smucker
(Washington, D.C. Office)
Neil Squillante
Robert Stebbins
Laurence C. Stein
Jennifer L. Stevens
(Washington, D.C. Office)
Carl L. Stine
Christopher S. Stokes
(Washington, D.C. Office)
J. Pasco Struhs
Raymond F. Sullivan, Jr.
Thomas M. Sweeney Jr.
Gordon Y. Synn
Andrew V. Tenzer
Patricia E. Torrente
Beth D. Tractenberg
Jeffrey L. Traum
Shawna R. Tunnell
Douglas Ulene
George Vuoso
Nicole E. Waldbaum
Kim A. Walker
Susan F. Wegner
(Washington, D.C. Office)
Sharon J. Weinberg
Jacqueline Weisman
(Washington, D.C. Office)
David S. Wolin
(Not admitted in NY)
Lois Wye
(Washington, D.C. Office)
Cindy A. Yellen
Janet T. Yeung
John P. Ziaukas

For full biographical listings, see the Martindale-Hubbell Law Directory

WINDELS, MARX, DAVIES & IVES (AV)

156 West 56th Street, 10019
Telephone: 212-237-1000
Cable Address: "Winmarlaw"
Telex: 126959 WU; 66103 WUI
Telecopier: 212-262-1215
Word Processing Telecommunications: 212-315-1531
New Brunswick, New Jersey Office: 120 Albany Street Plaza.
Telephone: 908-846-7600.
Facsimile: 908-846-8877.

MEMBERS OF FIRM

Thomas A. Banahan
Eric W. Bruenner
James P. Conroy
Anthony R. Coscia
Anthony A. Dean
Daniel V. Duff, Jr.
Mitchell A. Gilbert
Walter F. X. Healy
Arthur E. Hoffmann, Jr.
Susan F. Jennison
R. Scott Johnston
John M. Kriz
Jeffrey S. Levin
Valerie S. Mason
John J. McDermott
Michael M. Moriarty
Thomas J. Mulligan
Craig P. Murphy
Edward P. Nolan
Clayton A. Prugh
James M. Shaughnessy
Edward E. Shea
Charles E. Simpson
John Yeatman Taggart
Robert D. Taisey
James J. Thomas
Edward G. Williams

COUNSEL

Paul Windels, Jr.
Roger I. Harris
Elizabeth King
Raymond T. Munsell

SPECIAL COUNSEL

Clifford H. Stein

Henry M. Marx (1908-1984)
Julien T. Davies (1895-1978)
Dermod Ives (1904-1992)

ASSOCIATES

David S. Broderick
Debra R. Cardinali
Iryna Lomaga Carey
Joseph G. Colbert
Daniel W. Dienst
Matthew C. Ferguson
Stephen C. Green
Darrell M. Joseph
Keelin A. Kavanagh
David B. Kostman
Leonard A. LaBarbiera
Dominic P. Morandi
Mark Allan Poole
Aimee F. Rapaport
Ann Ryan
Richard C. Rubinstein
Mark A. Slama
Bevan M. Watt
Deborah L. Wiacek
(Not admitted in NY)

For full biographical listings, see the Martindale-Hubbell Law Directory

WINSTON & STRAWN (AV)

175 Water Street, 10038
Telephone: 212-269-2500
Telecopier: 212-952-1474/5
Cable Address: "Coledeitz, NYK"
Telex: (RCA) 232459
Chicago, Illinois Office: 35 West Wacker Drive.
Telephone: 312-558-5600.
Cable Address: "Winston Chicago".
Facsimile: 312-558-5700.
Washington, D.C. Office: 1400 L Street, N.W.
Telephone: 202-371-5700.
Telecopier: 202-371-5950.
Telex: 440574 Intlaw UI.
Geneva, Switzerland Office: 43 Rue du Rhone, 1204.
Telephone: (4122) 7810506.
Fax: (4122) 7810361.

MEMBERS OF FIRM

Harold M. Cole (1905-1972)
Edward L. Levine
Robert W. Ericson
Herbert J. Deitz (1908-1992)
Donald L. Laufer
Richard B. Teiman
Anthony J. D'Auria
Edward N. Meyer
Jonathan Goldstein
Joseph A. DiBenedetto
Jeffrey H. Elkin
Michael Hirschfeld
Howard Seife
Robert Scott Edmonds
James J. Terry
Amy B. Siegel
Susan Berkwitt-Malefakis
Robert S. Fischler
John C. Phelan
Robert C. Satrom
Richard S. Talesnick
Paul B. Abramson
Kenneth C. H. Willig
Leonard Orkin
R. Evan Smith
Loren M. Dollet
Thomas J. Quigley
Norman Newman
Anthony F. LoFrisco
Ronald G. Caso
Thomas R. Bearrows
Rex L. Sessions
Douglas L. Wisner
Harry C. Bull
(Not admitted in NY)
Andrea L. Flink
Alex C. Lengyel
Marc C. Lewis
Derek G. P. Mackenzie
Lori J. Van Auken

SENIOR ATTORNEYS

Jane E. Croes
Barry L. Salkin

(See Next Column)

WINSTON & STRAWN—*Continued*

ASSOCIATES

Kenneth A. Adams
Marjorie A. Adams-Manson
Karen Bergreen
Anthony DiSarro
Lisa B. Dubrow
David Florendo
Jonathan H. Freiberger
Karen Geiss
Gregory P. Gulia
Douglas P. Hardy
Richard C. Harmon (Not admitted in NY)
Bradley D. Houser
William A. Kapell
Shana Kassoff
John H. Killeen
Gregory M. Kobrick
Carolyn A. Koven
Margot A. Leffler
Robert F. Mace
Farid R. Maluf
Caryn S. Mohan (Not admitted in NY)
Amy Moskowitz
Irma J. Nimetz
Elyse Pepper
Jeanette L. Pinard
Steven B. Rissman
Matthew C. Rueter
Howard Schiff
George J. Seeberger
Karen E. Sherman
Heidi Jan Sorvino
Tycho H. E. Stahl
Tracy M. Thomas

For full biographical listings, see the Martindale-Hubbell Law Directory

WINTHROP, STIMSON, PUTNAM & ROBERTS (AV)

One Battery Park Plaza, 10004-1490
Telephone: 212-858-1000
Telex: 62854 WINSTIM
Telefax: 212-858-1500
Stamford, Connecticut Office: Financial Centre, 695 East Main Street, P.O. Box 6760, 06904-6760.
Telephone: 203-348-2300.
Washington, D.C. Office: 1133 Connecticut Avenue, N.W., 20036.
Telephone: 202-775-9800.
Palm Beach, Florida Office: 125 Worth Avenue, 33480.
Telephone: 407-655-7297.
London Office: 2 Throgmorton Avenue, London EC2N 2AP, England.
Telephone: 011-4471-628-4931.
Brussels Office: Rue Du Taciturne 42, B-1040 Brussels, Belgium.
Telephone: 011-322-230-1392.
Tokyo, Japan Office: 608 Atagoyama Bengoshi Building 6-7, Atago 1-chome, Minato-ku, Tokyo 105 Japan.
Telephone: 011-813-3437-9740.
Hong Kong Office: 2505 Asia Pacific Finance Tower, Citibank Plaza, 3 Garden Road, Central.
Telephone: 011-852-530-3400.

Bronson Winthrop (1893-1944)
Henry L. Stimson (1893-1950)
Albert W. Putnam (1904-1955)
George Roberts (1914-1968)

MEMBERS OF FIRM

Kenneth E. Adelsberg
Takeo Akiyama
David W. Ambrosia
Mary Patricia Azevedo
William L. Burke
John H. Byington, Jr.
Francis Carling
James T. Chudy
Thomas F. Clauss, Jr.
Richard G. Cohen
C. Payson Coleman, Jr.
Leo T. Crowley
Michael F. Cusick
Hugh M. Dougan
Philip Le B. Douglas
Richard L. Epling
William M. Evarts, Jr.
David P. Falck
Barton D. Ford
Arthur H. Fredston
Max Friedman
Elizabeth H. W. Fry
Howard J. Goldman
A. Edward Grashof
Robert W. Gray
Philip G. Hull
Peter J. Hunt
Barton T. Jones
Sutton Keany
Howard S. Kelberg
David G. Keyko
Susan J. Kohlmann
William C. F. Kurz
Stephen Lefkowitz
David M. Lindley
Harold S. Nathan
Peter D. Nesgos
F. Joseph Owens, Jr.
J. Michael Parish
Jerry P. Peppers
John F. Pritchard
Stephen R. Rusmisel
Michael P. Schumaecker
Susan P. Serota
Glenn E. Siegel
James R. Silkenat
Robin L. Spear
Jane Wallison Stein
Michael V. Sterlacci
Charles H. Vejvoda
Mark J. Volow
Stephen K. Waite
Robert D. Webster
Stephen A. Weiner
Ruth Joseph Weinstein
Edwin J. Wesely
Jonathan B. Whitney
Douglas F. Williamson, Jr.

COUNSEL

Glen R. Cuccinello
Richard L. Harden
Mark R. Hellerer
Thomas D. Lee
John P. MacMaster
Daniel J. McSwiggan
Sheila AnnMarie Moeller
Joseph M. Silvestri
Charles S. Wassell

SENIOR COUNSEL

Allison Choate
Peter H. Kaminer
Merrell E. Clark, Jr.
John S. Russell, Jr.
John J. Boland
Robert Anthoine
J. Philip Bahn
William W. Karatz
John B. Daniels
George C. Leness
John B. Jessup
Donald L. Medlock

(See Next Column)

CONNECTICUT OFFICE
MEMBERS OF FIRM

Thomas F. Clauss, Jr.
Elizabeth H. W. Fry
Arthur W. Hooper, Jr.
Frode Jensen, III
G. William Sisley
Edward W. Wellman, Jr.

COUNSEL

Thomas R. Trowbridge, III

SENIOR COUNSEL

Endicott P. Davison
David M. Payne
Richard B. Tweedy

LONDON OFFICE
MEMBER OF FIRM

Peter S. Brown

BRUSSELS, BELGIUM OFFICE
MEMBER OF FIRM

Raymond S. Calamaro

FLORIDA OFFICE
MEMBERS OF FIRM

Philip G. Hull
Michael V. Sterlacci
Douglas F. Williamson, Jr.

FLORIDA OFFICE
COUNSEL

John C. Dotterrer

SENIOR COUNSEL

Howard J. Falcon, Jr. (Retired)

WASHINGTON, D.C. OFFICE
MEMBERS OF FIRM

Raymond S. Calamaro
Donald A. Carr
John E. Gillick
Jeffrey M. Lang
Gerald D. Morgan, Jr.
Christopher R. Wall
Roger D. Wiegley

WASHINGTON, D.C.
COUNSEL

Stuart N. Brotman
Robert Reed Gray
Louis H. Kurrelmeyer
Aileen Meyer
C. Christopher Parlin
Kenneth P. Quinn

TOKYO OFFICE
MEMBER OF FIRM

Jeffrey L. Pote

HONG KONG OFFICE
MEMBERS OF FIRM

William C. F. Kurz
Robert L. Lin
Yeow Ming Choo

ASSOCIATES

Robert T. Abramson
Mitchell Ash
Nancy M. Baxley
Robert K. Benjamin
Stephen R. Blacklocks
Matthew J. Borger
David M. Boyhan
Kerry Ann Brennan
L. Crawford Brickley, Jr.
Frederick A. Brodie
Shane Byrne
P. Joseph Campisi, Jr.
James Jeng-Yang Chen
John Michael Coleman
Robert Scott De Leon
Jeffrey J. Delaney
Katarina V. Dimich
Ella W. Dodson
Marie P. Donoghue
Dennis R. Dumas
Bryan R. Dunlap
Todd W. Eckland
Vitaly Fiks
Valerie L. Fitch
Edward Flanders
Ronald A. Fleming, Jr.
Susan K. Foster
Demetra V. Frawley
M. Lee White Galvis
Melissa Goldman
Cheryl Ann Gorman
Caroline A. Harcourt
Catherine A. Harrington
Erik W. Hepler
Lori S. Hoberman
Jennifer E. Hochberg
Meg Mataraso Hochman
Maria M. Homan
A. Elisabeth Hooykaas (Not Admitted in the United States)
David Hubelbank
Sophie Hager Hume
Michael A. Kalish
Rena W. Katz
Jonathan B. Kim
Yong Hyun Kim
Amelia M. Klein
Barry Langman
Helen F. R. Lawson
Michael A. Lehmann
Scott J. Lorinsky
Daniel A. Lowenthal, III
Ujwala Mahatme
Peter D. C. Mason
Christina D. McCloskey
Sarah L. McGill
Armen H. Merjian
Laurie E. Meyers
Antoinette A. Moro
Stacey E. Nadell
Dale G. Nissenbaum
Christine M. Pallares
J. Mark Pohl
Robert W. Putnam
Dona L. Radey
Stephanie L. Ray
Mark R. Rennie
Brian T. Robinson
Timothy Sander
Steven R. Schindler
Leslie E. Shigaki
Mara L. Shore
Bradley A. Siciliano
Shirley Staples
Mitchell J. Stier
Rachel D. Tanur
April P. Tash
Lucas F. Torres
Takemi Ueno
James D. Walsh
Carroll D. Welch
Mark M. Whitney
Renée S. Zylberberg

For full biographical listings, see the Martindale-Hubbell Law Directory

NIAGARA FALLS, Niagara Co. — (Refer to Buffalo)

*NORWICH,** Chenango Co. — (Refer to Binghamton)

NYACK, Rockland Co.

MacCartney, MacCartney, Kerrigan & MacCartney (AV)

MacCartney Building, 13 North Broadway, P.O. Box 350, 10960
Telephone: 914-358-0074
Fax: 914-358-0793

MEMBERS OF FIRM

Harold Y. MacCartney (1901-1988)
Harold Y. MacCartney, Jr.
John D. MacCartney
William K. Kerrigan

ASSOCIATES

Christopher J. Walsh
Stephen M. Honan
Brigitte M. Gulliver
Phyllis A. Ingram
David Castagna
Harold Y. MacCartney, III
Anthony J. Mamo
Reginald H. Rutishauser

Local Trial Counsel for: Associated Mutual Insurance Co.; The Andover Cos.; County of Orange; Government Employees Insurance Co.; Maryland Casualty Co.; North American Specialty Insurance Co.; Orange and Rockland Utilities, Inc.; Preferred Mutual Insurance Co.; Utica Fire Insurance Co.

For full biographical listings, see the Martindale-Hubbell Law Directory

ONEONTA, Otsego Co.

Frank W. Getman (AV)

16 Dietz Street, P.O. Box 613, 13820
Telephone: 607-432-3530
FAX: 607-432-3571

ASSOCIATES

Michael F. Getman

References: Key Bank, N.A.; Wilber National Bank Oneonta, N.Y.

For full biographical listings, see the Martindale-Hubbell Law Directory

OSSINING, Westchester Co.

Daly & Lavery (AV)

First National Bank Building, 13 Croton Avenue, 10562
Telephone: 914-941-7000

MEMBERS OF FIRM

Hugh A. Lavery (1906-1986)
Emanuel Lauterbach (1899-1989)
John E. Babchak Jr. (1925-1992)
William J. Daly
Hugh A. Lavery, Jr.

ASSOCIATES

Stella K. Lemmon

Representative Clients: Transamerica Insurance Group; Ossining Urban Renewal Agency.
Reference: The Bank of New York.

For full biographical listings, see the Martindale-Hubbell Law Directory

*OSWEGO,** Oswego Co.

Bond, Schoeneck & King (AV)

130 East Second Street, 13126-2625
Telephone: 315-343-9116
Fax: 315-343-1231
Syracuse, New York Office: 18th Floor, One Lincoln Center.
Telephone: 315-422-0121.
Fax: 315-422-3598.
Albany, New York Office: 111 Washington Avenue.
Telephone: 518-462-7421.
Fax: 518-462-7441.
Boca Raton, Florida Office: 5355 Town Center Road, Suite 1002.
Telephone: 407-368-1212.
Fax: 407-338-9955.
Naples, Florida Office: 1167 Third Street South.
Telephone: 813-262-6812.
Fax: 813-262-6908.
Overland Park, Kansas Office: 7500 College Boulevard, Suite 910.
Telephone: 913-345-8001.
Fax: 913-345-9017.

MEMBERS OF FIRM

John D. Allen
John G. McGowan

ASSOCIATES

Edward A. Mervine

For full biographical listings, see the Martindale-Hubbell Law Directory

*OWEGO,** Tioga Co. — (Refer to Endicott)

PATCHOGUE, Suffolk Co. — (Refer to Islandia)

PEARL RIVER, Rockland Co.

Dranoff & Johnson (AV)

Suite 900, One Blue Hill Plaza, P.O. Box 1629, 10965-8629
Telephone: 914-735-6200
Fax: 914-735-7585
Tarrytown, New York Office: 220 White Plains Road.
Telephone: 914-631-1900.
New York, N.Y. Office: 950 3rd Avenue.
Telephone: 212-643-5351.

MEMBERS OF FIRM

Sanford S. Dranoff
Martin T. Johnson
Veronica A. Shea
Daniel J. Block
Sylvia Goldschmidt
Mitchell Y. Cohen

Susan G. Yellen
Donna M. Genovese
Kenneth P. Silver

For full biographical listings, see the Martindale-Hubbell Law Directory

*PENN YAN,** Yates Co. — (Refer to Geneva)

PITTSFORD, Monroe Co.

Sutton, DeLeeuw, Clark & Darcy (AV)

40 Grove Street, 14534
Telephone: 716-586-8060

Rae A. Clark
John J. Darcy
Frank R. Monfredo
Robert L. Teamerson
Edward T. Hanley, Jr.
John J. Considine, Jr.
George H. Gray

*PLATTSBURGH,** Clinton Co.

Lewis & Rogers (AV)

53 Court Street, 12901-0515
Telephone: 518-561-3700
Fax No: 518-561-2080

MEMBERS OF FIRM

Clyde A. Lewis
Mark J. Rogers
Harold A. Jerry (1893-1990)
Robert A. Lyon (1924-1982)

ASSOCIATES

Christopher A. Lacombe
Larry A. Kudrle

Attorneys for: Graystone Materials, Inc.; Rosebud Creamery Inc.; Plattsburgh Motor Service Inc.; Town of Plattsburgh.
Local Counsel for: Imperial Paper Co.; Holiday Inn of Plattsburgh.

For full biographical listings, see the Martindale-Hubbell Law Directory

PORT CHESTER, Westchester Co.

Gioffre, Gioffre and Mascali, P.C. (AV)

220 Westchester Avenue, 10573-0391
Telephone: 914-939-2800
Telecopier: 914-939-0275

Lisa Gioffre Baird
Robert P. Mascali

Anthony B. Gioffre, III (Not admitted in NY)

OF COUNSEL

Bruno J. Gioffre
Anthony B. Gioffre

Representative Clients: Sound Federal Savings & Loan Assn.; New York State Society of Certified Public Accountants; Port Chester Public Library; Rye Town Hilton Inn; Shalom Nursing Home; Westchester Business Institute.

For full biographical listings, see the Martindale-Hubbell Law Directory

POTSDAM, St. Lawrence Co.

Ingram and Ingram (AV)

19 Market Street, 13676
Telephone: 315-265-8680

Verner M. Ingram
Verner M. Ingram, Jr.

ASSOCIATES

Deborah A. Bellomo

Representative Clients: Clarkson University Student Assn.; North Country Savings Bank; Renewal Housing Corp.; New Plan Realty Trust; Youth Educating Society (YES), Inc.

For full biographical listings, see the Martindale-Hubbell Law Directory

*POUGHKEEPSIE,** Dutchess Co.

CORBALLY, GARTLAND AND RAPPLEYEA (AV)

35 Market Street, 12601
Telephone: 914-454-1110
FAX: 914-454-4857
Millbrook, New York Office: Bank of Millbrook Building, Franklin Avenue.
Telephone: 914-677-5539.
Clearwater, Florida Office: Citizens Bank Building, Suite 250, 1130 Cleveland Street.
Telephone: 813-461-3144.

MEMBERS OF FIRM

John Hackett (Died 1916)
James L. Williams (Died 1908)
Charles J. Corbally (1888-1966)
John J. Gartland, Jr.
Allan E. Rappleyea
Daniel F. Curtin
Fred W. Schaeffer
Michael G. Gartland
Jon H. Adams
Vincent L. DeBiase
Paul O. Sullivan
William F. Bogle, Jr.

ASSOCIATES

Rena Muckenhoupt O'Connor
Allan B. Rappleyea, Jr.

OF COUNSEL

Joseph F. Hawkins (1916-1986)
Milton M. Haven
Edward J. Murtaugh

Representative Clients: Hudson Valley Farm Credit, A.C.A.; St. Francis Hospital; Marist College; Merritt-Meridian Construction Corp.
Counsel for: Poughkeepsie Savings Bank, F.S.B.; Bank of New York; Farm Credit Bank of Springfield; Equitable Life Assurance Society of the United States; McCann Foundation, Inc.
Reference: Bank of New York.

For full biographical listings, see the Martindale-Hubbell Law Directory

GUERNSEY BUTTS OSTERTAG & O'LEARY (AV)

75 Washington Street, P.O. Box G, 12602
Telephone: 914-452-1100
FAX: 914-452-0150
Boca Raton, Florida Office: 2424 North Federal Highway, Suite 314.
Telephone: 407-368-3400.

MEMBERS OF FIRM

Robert L. Ostertag
Robert R. Butts
Diane M. O'Leary

OF COUNSEL

Charles A. Butts
David B. Van Kleeck (Not admitted in NY; Resident, Roca Raton, Florida Office)

Representative Clients: Bank of New York Dutchess Division; Vassar College; International Business Machines Corp.
Local Counsel for: John Hancock Mutual Insurance Co.; Connecticut National Bank.

For full biographical listings, see the Martindale-Hubbell Law Directory

MCCABE & MACK (AV)

63 Washington Street, P.O. Box 509, 12602-0509
Telephone: 914-452-2800
FAX: 914-485-6971

MEMBERS OF FIRM

John E. Mack (1874-1958)
Joseph A. McCabe (1890-1973)
Joseph C. McCabe (1925-1981)
Phillip Shatz
J. Joseph McGowan
Michael A. Hayes, Jr.
Harold L. Mangold
Richard A. Mitchell
David L. Posner
Ellen L. Baker
Paul Caltagirone
Scott D. Bergin
Richard R. DuVall

OF COUNSEL

Edward J. Mack
John Howley
Martin P. Rutberg
Jay P. Rolison, Jr.

ASSOCIATES

Lance N. Portman
Jessica Lynn Vinall
Juliana Muyot
Arthur J. Doran, III
M. Randolf Belkin
Eric P. Darnauer

Representative Clients: Marine Midland Bank; Central Hudson Gas & Electric Corp.; Associates Commercial Corp.; Amica Mutual Insurance Co.; McDonald's Corp.; Hanover Insurance Co.; Liberty Mutual Insurance Co.; Manufacturers and Traders Trust Co.; Vassar College; County of Dutchess.

For full biographical listings, see the Martindale-Hubbell Law Directory

PURDYS, Westchester Co.

RALPH R. MACKIN (AV)

112 Titicus Road (Route 116), P.O. Box 409, 10578-0409
Telephone: 914-277-3993
Telecopier: 914-277-8663

(See Next Column)

LEGAL SUPPORT PERSONNEL

Lorraine Fragette Mackin (Paralegal)

For full biographical listings, see the Martindale-Hubbell Law Directory

*RIVERHEAD,** Suffolk Co.

SCHEINBERG, SCHNEPS, DE PETRIS & DE PETRIS (AV)

One Union Square (Aquebogue), P.O. Box 599, 11901
Telephone: 516-722-5100
Telecopier: 516-722-5093

MEMBERS OF FIRM

Isidore Scheinberg (1900-1985)
Shepard M. Scheinberg
Murray B. Schneps
Emil F. De Petris
Richard E. De Petris

General Counsel for: Relay Communications, Inc.; Village of Quogue; American Eagle Systems, Inc. V & V Noordland, Inc.
Special Counsel for: Town of East Hampton.

For full biographical listings, see the Martindale-Hubbell Law Directory

SMITH, FINKELSTEIN, LUNDBERG, ISLER AND YAKABOSKI (AV)

456 Griffing Avenue, P.O. Box 389, 11901
Telephone: 516-727-4100
Telecopier: 516-727-4130

Reginald C. Smith (1897-1983)

MEMBERS OF FIRM

Howard M. Finkelstein
Pierre G. Lundberg
Francis J. Yakaboski
Frank A. Isler
Susan Rogers Grun
Gair G. Betts

ASSOCIATES

Dawn C. Thomas
Matthew M. Finkelstein

General Counsel for: Suffolk County National Bank; Riverhead Central, Remsenburg; Montauk Union Free School Districts; Board of Cooperative Educational Services, 1st District; Leisure Village Assn.; Co-operative Extension Assn.
Local Counsel for: Village of Ocean Beach; Towns of Southhold, Riverhead and East Hampton; Pecomic Bay Broadcasting Corp.

For full biographical listings, see the Martindale-Hubbell Law Directory

*ROCHESTER,** Monroe Co.

BECKERMAN & BECKERMAN (AV)

1 West Main Street Four Corners Building, Suite 300, 14614
Telephone: 716-546-6010
Facsimile: 716-546-7035

MEMBERS OF FIRM

Gerald Beckerman
Steven M. Beckerman
David S. Beckerman

ASSOCIATES

Betsy L. Album

Reference: Marine Midland Bank, Rochester.

For full biographical listings, see the Martindale-Hubbell Law Directory

LAW OFFICES OF A. VINCENT BUZARD (AV)

The Granite Building, Suite 420, 130 East Main Street, 14604
Telephone: 716-454-3984
Fax: 716-454-2177

ASSOCIATES

Gail A. Donofrio
Adele M. Fine
Albert L. Parisi

Reference: Central Trust Co.

For full biographical listings, see the Martindale-Hubbell Law Directory

CHAMBERLAIN, D'AMANDA, OPPENHEIMER & GREENFIELD (AV)

1600 Crossroads Office Building, Two State Street, 14614
Telephone: 716-232-3730
Telecopier: 716-232-3882

MEMBERS OF FIRM

Robert Oppenheimer
Louis D'Amanda
Jerry R. Greenfield
Stanley M. Friedman
Henry R. Ippolito
Michael T. Harren
Anita C. Miller
Edward C. Radin, III
Richard B. Sullivan
Sheldon W. Boyce
Douglas Jones
Lewis J. Heisman
John F. D'Amanda
Roy Z. Rotenberg
Matthew J. Fusco
Steven J. Tranelli
Sanford J. Liebschutz

ASSOCIATES

James L. Bradley
Susan R. L. Bernis
Nancy Lynne Baker
Eugene M. O'Connor
Eileen M. Potash
E. Adam Leyens
Sandra W. Gelb
Michael R. Mendola

(See Next Column)

CHAMBERLAIN, D'AMANDA, OPPENHEIMER & GREENFIELD, *Rochester—Continued*

TRIAL COUNSEL

Jay M. Friedman

OF COUNSEL

Robert H. Antell
Thomas G. Collins

For full biographical listings, see the Martindale-Hubbell Law Directory

CONNORS & CORCORAN (AV)

4th Floor Times Square Building, 45 Exchange Street, 14614
Telephone: 716-232-5885
FAX: 716-546-3631

MEMBERS OF FIRM

Richard M. Brindisi
Herbert J. LePage
Roger W. Avery
Joseph G. Fritsch, Jr.
James E. Maslyn
Patrick E. Tydings
Eileen E. Buholtz
Cheryl Loria-Dinolfo

ASSOCIATES

Timothy J. Herbst
Gregg H. Redmond

Attorneys for: Aetna Life Insurance Co.; Agricultural Insurance Group; Allstate Insurance Co.; Continental National American Group; Criterion Insurance Co.; General Accident Group; Ideal Mutual Insurance Co.; Sentry Insurance; United States Fidelity & Guaranty Co.
Reference: Marine Midland Bank.

For full biographical listings, see the Martindale-Hubbell Law Directory

ERNSTROM & DRESTE (AV)

Court Exchange Building, 144 Exchange Boulevard, 14614
Telephone: 716-325-4203
FAX: 716-325-1262

MEMBERS OF FIRM

J. William Ernstrom
John W. Dreste

ASSOCIATES

Martha A. Connolly
Theodore M. B. Baum
Todd R. Braggins
Kevin F. Peartree

For full biographical listings, see the Martindale-Hubbell Law Directory

FIX, SPINDELMAN, BROVITZ, TURK, HIMELEIN & SHUKOFF (AV)

500 Crossroads Building, 2 State Street, 14614-1369
Telephone: 716-232-1660
Cable Address: "Meyerfix"
FAX: 716-232-4791

MEMBERS OF FIRM

Meyer Fix
Norman M. Spindelman
Ronald J. Turk
Igor Shukoff
Philip F. Spahn, Jr.
Richard S. Brovitz
Robert D. Schultz
Karl S. Essler
John F. LaFave
William L. Kreienberg
Stephen M. Kruk
Don H. Twietmeyer

ASSOCIATES

Joseph T. Coolican
Laurie A. Donofrio
Francis C. Affronti
James W. Campbell, Jr.
Betsy Davis Brugg

Reference: Central Trust Company of Rochester.

For full biographical listings, see the Martindale-Hubbell Law Directory

FORSYTH, HOWE, O'DWYER & KALB, P.C. (AV)

Suite 1600, Midtown Tower, 14604
Telephone: 716-325-7515
FAX: 716-325-6407
Getzville, New York Office: 2350 North Forest Road, 14068.
Telephone: 716-871-0758.
Fax: 716-871-0846.
Liverpool, New York Office: Granito & Sondej, Corporate Woods #1, 1035 Seventh North Street.
Telephone: 315-451-2387.
Fax: 315-451-3981.

Charles B. Forsyth (1890-1968)
C. Benn Forsyth
Gordon A. Howe, II
Duncan W. O'Dwyer
Robert J. Kalb

Gerald N. Murphy
Cathleen W. Smith
Caren M. Cook
Christopher J. Currier

OF COUNSEL

John F. Forsyth
Allan Wolk
Hoffman Stone
Debra A. Martin
Janice M. Iati
Valerie L. Barbic
Thad F. Sondej (Resident, Liverpool Office)
V. James Granito, Jr. (Resident, Liverpool Office)

(See Next Column)

References: Chase Manhattan Bank, N.A.; Fleet Bank.

For full biographical listings, see the Martindale-Hubbell Law Directory

HARTER, SECREST & EMERY (AV)

700 Midtown Tower, 14604-2070
Telephone: 716-232-6500
Telecopier: 716-232-2152
Naples, Florida Office: Suite 400, 800 Laurel Oak Drive.
Telephone: 813-598-4444.
Telecopier: 813-598-2781.
Albany, New York Office: One Steuben Place.
Telephone: 518-434-4377.
Telecopier: 518-449-4025.
Syracuse, New York Office: 431 East Fayette Street.
Telephone: 315-474-4000.
Telecopier: 315-474-7789.

MEMBERS OF FIRM

C. Vincent Wiser (1898-1979)
John G. Shaw (1903-1977)
Donald R. Harter (1917-1980)
Hyman B. Freeman (1904-1991)
Richard B. Secrest (1921-1993)
Nathan J. Robfogel
Thomas A. Solberg
Alan Illig
W. Reynolds Bowers
Peter M. Blauvelt
Lawrence R. Palvino
William D. Smith
Thomas B. Garlick (Resident Partner, Naples, Florida Office)
Alan F. Hilfiker (Resident Partner, Naples, Florida Office)
C. Richard Cole
Barry R. Whitman
James C. Moore
William M. Colby
Kenneth A. Payment
Stuart B. Meisenzahl
James P. Burns, 3rd (Resident Partner, Syracuse Office)
James A. Locke, III
Michael F. Buckley
William H. Helferich, III
Robert J. Hughes, Jr. (Resident Partner, Syracuse Office)
Neal D. Madden
Peter G. Smith
James B. Gray, Jr.
John R. Weider
H. Robert Herman
William N. La Forte
Thomas G. Smith
Jack D. Eisenberg
Frank S. Hagelberg
Eric A. Evans
Fred G. Aten, Jr.
Philip R. Fileri
Susan Mascette Brandt
T. Mary McDonald
Margaret Artale Catillaz
Jeffrey H. Bowen
David R. Ferris
Michael R. McEvoy
Donald S. Mazzullo
John C. Herbert
Kathleen C. Passidomo (Not admitted in NY; Resident Partner, Naples, Florida Office)
Timothy R. Parry (Not admitted in NY; Resident Partner, Naples, Florida Office)
Mary E. Ross
Gary L. Karl (Resident Partner, Syracuse Office)
Peter O. Brown
Ronald J. Mendrick
Maureen T. Alston
Edward F. Premo II
Richard E. Alexander

OF COUNSEL

Harry M. Grace
E. James Hickey
William A. Centner
R. Clinton Emery
D. Dyson Gay
John F. Mahon
Bruce E. Hansen
John E. Swett

COUNSEL

A. Paul Britton, Jr.
Bonnie A. Blenis

SENIOR ATTORNEYS

William W. Bell
William F. Brandes, Jr. (Resident Counsel, Naples, Florida Office)
M. Stephanie Zeller
Paul M. Hetland
Russell W. Roberts

ASSOCIATES

Cathy Kaman Ryan
Brian V. McAvoy
M. Kathleen Lynn (Resident Associate, Syracuse Office)
Carol O'Keefe
Ross P. Lanzafame
Martin W. O'Toole
Peter H. Abdella
Dorothy H. Ferguson
Peter T. Wlasuk (Resident Associate, Naples, Florida Office)
Kenneth A. Marvald
Jeffrey P. Stone
Jane A. Conrad
Susan A. Roberts
Barry S. Wisset
James M. Jenkins
Robert McDonough
Raymond P. Miller
C. Perry Peeples (Resident Associate, Naples, Florida Office)
Thomas James Kanaley, Jr
Jill M. Myers
Paul D. Sylvestri
Walter D. Bay
Sheila M. Rembert
Judith E. Christiansen
Amy Hartman Nichols
Paul W. Holloway
Michele Anne Mobley
Kathleen M. Beckman
Michelle R. Dennison
Craig S. Wittlin
Jean Anne McDonnell (Resident Associate, Albany Office)
Kelly M. Braun (Resident Associate, Naples, Florida Office)
Jon D. Parrish (Resident Associate, Naples, Florida Office)
Teresa M. Roney (Resident Associate, Syracuse Office)
Mia Hsu Burton
Robert L. Cholette
Jacqueline A. Phipps
Christopher M. Potash
Christopher W. Thome
Judy A. Romano (Resident Associate, Naples, Florida Office)

(See Next Column)

HARTER, SECREST & EMERY—*Continued*

LEGAL SUPPORT PERSONNEL

Eve M. Peck (Tax Accountant)
Thomas E. Cardillo (Health Care Consultant)
Richard E. Scanlan, Jr. (Government Affairs Specialist)

For full biographical listings, see the Martindale-Hubbell Law Directory

LACY, KATZEN, RYEN & MITTLEMAN (AV)

The Granite Building, 130 East Main Street, 14604
Telephone: 716-454-5650
FAX: 716-454-6525

MEMBERS OF FIRM

Burton J. Greene (1910-1976)
Robert H. Jones (1928-1979)
Herbert W. Lacy (1920-1989)
Leon Katzen
Louis A. Ryen
Ronald A. Mittleman
Michael S. Schnittman
Peter T. Rodgers
Sally A. Smith
Karen Schaefer
Richard G. Curtis
Stephen P. Mayka
Lawrence J. Schwind
David H. Walsh IV
David E. Anderson
Christina Potter Moraski
Craig R. Welch
Christopher B. Mumford

COUNSEL

George F. Frey, Jr.
Samuel L. Yaroslow

ASSOCIATES

David D. MacKnight
Nia J. Nichols
William A. Levine
Albert Kusak
Mark Annunziata
Leslie W. Kernan, Jr.
Terrance W. Emmens
Mark H. Stein
Denine K. Carr
Jacqueline M. Thomas

General Counsel for: Village of Bergen, Bergen, New York; Village of Hilton, Hilton, New York; Byron-Bergen Central School District No. 1, Bergen, New York; Dynalab Corp.
Reference: Chemical Bank, Rochester, N.Y.

For full biographical listings, see the Martindale-Hubbell Law Directory

OSBORN, REED, BURKE & TOBIN (AV)

Watts Building, Suite 300, 47 South Fitzhugh Street, 14614
Telephone: 716-454-6480
FAX: 716-232-4877
Clifton Springs, New York Office: 26 East Main Street,
Telephone: 315- 462-3010.
Fax: 315-462-5039.
Honeoye Falls, New York Office: 29 West Main Street.
Telephone: 716-624-3311.
Fax: 716-624-4167.
Pittsford, New York Office: 57 Monroe Avenue.
Telephone: 716-264-0570.
Fax: 716-264-0621.

MEMBERS OF FIRM

John C. Osborn
James A. Reed, Jr.
David S. Van de Vate (1932-1992)
Thomas C. Burke
Michael J. Tobin
Robert T. Di Giulio
John F. Riley
Jeffrey M. Wilkens
Jane B. Hopfinger
Paul M. Riordan
Jeffrey L. Turner

ASSOCIATES

John A. Ferr
Diane Love
Kathleen B. Benesh
Holly A. Adams
Frank G. Montemalo
Alice Lyons Messina

Representative Clients: General Electric Co.; GMA Development Corp.; Liberty Mutual Insurance Co.; Merchants Mutual Insurance Co.; Onbank; PNC Mortgage Corp. of America; The Chubb Group; Town and Village of Pittsford, N.Y.; Source One Mtg.

For full biographical listings, see the Martindale-Hubbell Law Directory

PHILLIPS, LYTLE, HITCHCOCK, BLAINE & HUBER (AV)

1400 First Federal Plaza, 14614
Telephone: 716-238-2000
Telecopier: 716-232-3141
Buffalo, New York Office: 3400 Marine Midland Center.
Telephone: 716-847-8400.
Telecopier: 716-852-6100.
Jamestown, New York Office: 307 Chase Bank Building, 8 E. Third Street.
Telephone: 716-664-3906.
Telecopier: 716-664-4230.
New York, New York Office: 437 Madison Avenue.
Telephone: 212-759-4888.
Telecopier: 212-308-9079.
Fredonia, New York Office: 11 East Main Street.
Telephone: 716-672-2164.
FAX: 716-672-7979.

(See Next Column)

RESIDENT PARTNERS

Thomas R. Burns
Alan R. Feldstein
Robert C. Johnson
Michael R. Law
Albert M. Mercury
Mark J. Moretti
Michael E. O'Neill
Gerald L. Paley
John T. Sullivan, Jr.
Paul A. Vick
Robert F. Zogas

ASSOCIATES

Richard M. Beers, Jr. (Resident)
Robert A. Colón
Donald L. Crumb, Jr.
Karen A. DiNardo
William P. Fletcher (Resident)
Kenneth W. Gordon
John B. Kaman
Bradley P. Kammholz
Glenn D. Leonardi
Raymond L. Ruff
Deborah Kall Schaal
Mark L. Suher
R. Vincent Taylor
Gregory M. Trusso (Resident)

For full biographical listings, see the Martindale-Hubbell Law Directory

UNDERBERG & KESSLER (AV)

1800 Chase Square, 14604
Telephone: 716-258-2800
Fax: 716-258-2821

MEMBERS OF FIRM

Alan J. Underberg
Irving L. Kessler
Michael J. Beyma
Frank T. Crego
Robert W. Croessmann
John W. Crowe
Michael C. Dwyer
Bernard A. Frank
Steven R. Gersz
John L. Goldman
Lawrence P. Keller
Gordon J. Lipson
Robert F. Mechur
Paul V. Nunes
Terry M. Richman
Sharon P. Stiller
Stephen H. Waite
Russell I. Zuckerman

OF COUNSEL

Richard G. Crawford
Andrew M. Greenstein

SENIOR ATTORNEY

Thomas P. Young

ASSOCIATES

Patrick L. Cusato
Sean E. Gleason
Katherine Howk Karl
Suzanne D. Nott
Linda Prestegaard

For full biographical listings, see the Martindale-Hubbell Law Directory

EUGENE VANVOORHIS (AV)

1820 East Avenue, 14610-1892
Telephone: 716-232-4221
Telecopier: 716-232-6752

Reference: Chase Lincoln First Bank of Rochester.

For full biographical listings, see the Martindale-Hubbell Law Directory

ROME, Oneida Co.

GRIFFITH LAW OFFICES (AV)

225 North Washington Street, 13440
Telephone: 315-336-6500
Fax: 315-336-6628

Emlyn I. Griffith
James R. Griffith

Representative Clients: Camroden Associates, Inc.; C & H Plastics, Inc.; D & H Asphalt Co., Inc.; H-P Farmers Cooperative; Knowledge Systems Concepts, Inc.; Pohl Feedway, Inc.; Statewide Funding Corp; Stonehedge Nursing Home.
Approved Attorneys for: The Title Guarantee Co.

For full biographical listings, see the Martindale-Hubbell Law Directory

MCMAHON, GROW & GETTY (AV)

301 North Washington Street, P.O. Box 4350, 13440
Telephone: 315-336-4700
Fax: 315-336-5851

MEMBERS OF FIRM

Johnson D. McMahon (1887-1963)
George B. Grow
Richard H. McMahon
David C. Grow
Charles R. Getty, Jr.

ASSOCIATES

Richard H. McMahon, Jr.

OF COUNSEL

Abraham H. Baker

Counsel for: Rome Savings Bank; Marine Midland Bank, N.A. (Rome Branch); Fleet Bank of New York; Rome Strip Steel Co.; Canterbury Press; Rome Sentinel Co.; M G S Manufacturing, Inc.; Engelberts Jewelers, Inc.; Resident Shoppers Service, Inc.

For full biographical listings, see the Martindale-Hubbell Law Directory

Rome—Continued

PAUL L. PILECKAS (AV)

Professional Building, 217 N. Washington Street, 13440
Telephone: 315-339-3020
Utica: 315-724-6381

Representative Clients: Don Davidson Motors, Inc.; Maple Lane Farms, Inc.; Cataldo Ready Mix, Inc.; Cataldo Bros., Inc.

For full biographical listings, see the Martindale-Hubbell Law Directory

ROSLYN HEIGHTS, Nassau Co.

BLODNICK ABRAMOWITZ & BLODNICK (AV)

Suite 200 Expressway Plaza Two, 11577-2032
Telephone: 516-621-7500
Telecopier: 516-621-7533

Arnold C. Abramowitz
Peter L. Blodnick
Edward K. Blodnick
Randy Scott Zelin

Donna M. Feinberg
Daniel R. Olivieri
Alison S. Gallub
Stuart Thalblum

OF COUNSEL

Samuel Gordon

For full biographical listings, see the Martindale-Hubbell Law Directory

NATISS & FERENZO, P.C. (AV)

277 Willis Avenue, 11577
Telephone: 516-621-0900
Telecopier: 516-621-1304

Marvin Natiss
André L. Ferenzo

James B. Fuccio
Stacey M. Natiss

For full biographical listings, see the Martindale-Hubbell Law Directory

SARANAC LAKE, Essex & Franklin Cos. — (Refer to Plattsburgh)

SARATOGA SPRINGS, Saratoga Co. — (Refer to Glens Falls)

*SCHENECTADY,** Schenectady Co.

HIGGINS, ROBERTS, BEYERL & COAN, P.C. (AV)

1430 Balltown Road, 12309-4332
Telephone: 518-374-3399
Fax: 518-374-9416

Richard E. Roberts
Michael R. Suprunowicz
Robert J. Coan
Charles J. Assini, Jr.
James H. Erceg
Michael E. Basile
John K. Sharkey
Amy J. Herter Robinson

Maura C. Mottolese
Gwenn B. Lee
Robert Patrick Coan
Heather Galligan Bennett

Representative Clients: Schenectady International, Inc.; Schenectady Board of Realtors, Inc.; Niskayuna Central School District; New York State Society of Anesthesiologists, Inc.; Union College of Schenectady, N.Y.; Sunnyview Hospital and Rehabilitation Center; Power Technologies, Inc.

For full biographical listings, see the Martindale-Hubbell Law Directory

WEMPLE & DALY (AV)

508 Union Street, 12305
Telephone: 518-374-9125

MEMBERS OF FIRM

William W. Wemple (1898-1972)
Charles W. Daly
James S. Daly

References: Trustco Bank; Norstar Bank of Upstate New York; Key Bank, NA; Northeast Savings.

For full biographical listings, see the Martindale-Hubbell Law Directory

*SCHOHARIE,** Schoharie Co. — (Refer to Schenectady)

SMITHTOWN, Suffolk Co.

GRESHIN, ZIEGLER & PRUZANSKY (AV)

199 East Main Street, P.O. Box 829, 11787
Telephone: 516-265-2550
Telecopier: 516-265-2832

Benjamin Greshin
Joel J. Ziegler
Joshua M. Pruzansky

ASSOCIATES

Joanne Skiadas

For full biographical listings, see the Martindale-Hubbell Law Directory

MEYER, MEYER & METLI (AV)

28 Manor Road, 11787
Telephone: 516-265-4500
Telecopier: 516-265-4534

Bernard K. Meyer
Richard Metli
Terence X. Meyer
Joseph Patrick Keneally

ASSOCIATES

James E. Robinson
Mitchel A. Hill
Kara Cheeseman-Bak

Representative Clients: Chemical Bank; Commack Fire District; The Chase Manhattan Bank; The Bank of New York; United Artists; ITT Commercial Finance Corp.; Fleet Bank; EAB; Long Island Savings Bank; Crossland Savings Bank.

For full biographical listings, see the Martindale-Hubbell Law Directory

SPRING VALLEY, Rockland Co.

GREENBERG, WANDERMAN & FROMSON (AV)

35 North Madison Avenue, 10977
Telephone: 914-356-3334
Fax: 914-356-7067

MEMBERS OF FIRM

David Greenberg
Carl L. Wanderman
Stephen M. Fromson

For full biographical listings, see the Martindale-Hubbell Law Directory

STANFORDVILLE, Dutchess Co.

WILLIAM E. STANTON (AV)

Village Centre, Route 82, P.O. Box 370, 12581
Telephone: 914-868-7514
FAX: 914-868-7761

Representative Clients: Dupont de Nemours & Co.; Millbrook School; Hanover Insurance Co.; New York Telephone Co.
Reference: Fishkill National Bank.

For full biographical listings, see the Martindale-Hubbell Law Directory

*STATEN ISLAND,** Richmond Co.

SIMONSON & COHEN, P.C. (AV)

4060 Amboy Road, 10308
Telephone: 718-948-2100
Telecopier: 718-356-2379

Sidney O. Simonson (1911-1986)
Robert M. Cohen
Daniel Cohen
James R. Cohen

Michael Adler
Lawrence J. Lorczak

For full biographical listings, see the Martindale-Hubbell Law Directory

STONY POINT, Rockland Co.

HURLEY, FOX, SELIG & KELLEHER (AV)

Liberty Building, Route 9 W, 10980
Telephone: 914-942-2222
Fax: 914-942-0378
New City, New York Office: 60 Pine Street.
Telephone: 914-634-2050.

MEMBERS OF FIRM

Benjamin E. Selig
Glenn W. Kelleher

ASSOCIATES

Jeanne Marie Hurley
Paul Anthony Hurley

LEGAL SUPPORT PERSONNEL

Eileen M. Kehnle

Representative Clients: Bradlees, Inc.; Amerisure Insurance Co.; Continental Insurance Cos.; Wausau Insurance Co.; Federal Insurance Co.; Chubb & Son; Commercial Union Group of Insurance Cos.; Empire Insurance Co.; Universal Underwriters Insurance Co.

For full biographical listings, see the Martindale-Hubbell Law Directory

SUFFERN, Rockland Co.

SICHOL & HICKS, P.C. (AV)

139 Lafayette Avenue, P.O. Box 359, 10901
Telephone: 914-357-4422
FAX: 914-357-0998

William R. Sichol (1908-1980)
William R. Sichol, Jr.
Stanley D. Hicks (1905-1986)
Brian A. Sichol

(See Next Column)

SICHOL & HICKS P.C.—*Continued*

J. O'Neil Kelly
John R. Lindstrom
Patricia H. Palumbo (Not admitted in NY)

Representative Clients: Plaza Materials Corp.; Continental American Group; Continental National American Group; Utica Mutual Insurance Co.; Millers Mutual Insurance Co.; Ohio Casualty Co.; Bakers Mutual Insurance Co.
References: Marine Midland Bank of Southeastern New York, N.A.; Bank of New York; Provident Savings, Haverstraw, N.Y.

For full biographical listings, see the Martindale-Hubbell Law Directory

SYOSSET, Nassau Co. — (Refer to Merrick)

*SYRACUSE,** Onondaga Co.

BOND, SCHOENECK & KING (AV)

18th Floor One Lincoln Center, 13202-1355
Telephone: 315-422-0121
Fax: 315-422-3598
Albany, New York Office: 111 Washington Avenue.
Telephone: 518-462-7421.
Fax: 518-462-7441.
Boca Raton, Florida Office: 5355 Town Center Road, Suite 1002.
Telephone: 407-368-1212.
Fax: 407-338-9955.
Naples, Florida Office: 1167 Third Street South.
Telephone: 813-262-6812.
Fax: 813-262-6908.
Oswego, New York Office: 130 East Second Street.
Telephone: 315-343-9116.
Fax: 315-343-1231.
Overland Park, Kansas Office: 7500 College Boulevard, Suite 910.
Telephone: 913-345-8001.
Fax: 913-345-9017.

MEMBERS OF FIRM

George H. Bond, Jr. (1909-1973)
Anton H. Zahm (1917-1984)
Charles A. Schoeneck, Jr. (1912-1989)
Howard H. Cannon (1903-1979)
Hubert C. Stratton (1901-1978)
William F. FitzPatrick (1902-1984)
Tracy H. Ferguson
Lyle W. Hornbeck
Chester H. King, Jr.
N. Earle Evans
John C. Kinney (1918-1974)
Francis D. Price
James E. Wilber (Resident, Boca Raton, Florida Office)
Henry R. McCarthy
Raymond W. Murray, Jr.
Joseph J. Lawton, Jr.
George C. Shattuck
John J. Dee
John A. Beach (Resident, Albany Office)
Charles T. Beeching, Jr.
William P. Burrows
John M. Freyer (Resident, Albany Office)
Robert W. Kopp
Charles T. Major, Jr.
John S. Ferguson
Arthur E. Bongiovanni
Robert E. Moses
William L. Bergan
Anthony R. Pittarelli
Francis E. Maloney, Jr.
Wallace J. McDonald
James D. FitzPatrick
Stephen L. Johnson
James E. Mackin
David N. Sexton (Resident, Naples, Florida Office)
Gary R. Germain
Thomas S. Evans
H. Dean Heberlig, Jr.
Thomas J. Grooms
Richard L. Smith (Resident, Albany Office)
James P. McDonald (Resident, Boca Raton, Florida Office)
Stephen J. Vollmer
S. Paul Battaglia
L. Lawrence Tully
Paul M. Sansoucy
Richard C. Heffern (Resident, Albany Office)
Richard D. Hole
George H. Lowe
John D. Allen
David M. Pellow
Thomas E. Myers
Louis P. DiLorenzo
Carl Rosenbloom (Resident, Albany Office)
M. Catherine Richardson
Barry R. Kogut
John Gaal
Thomas R. Smith
Joseph Zagraniczny
R. Daniel Bordoni
Ronald C. Berger
Robert C. Zundel, Jr. (Resident, Boca Raton, Florida Office)
David L. Dawson (Resident, Naples, Florida Office)
David R. Sheridan (Resident, Albany Office)
James N. Seeley
Thomas D. Keleher
Thaddeus J. Lewkowicz
Edwin J. Kelley, Jr.
Edward R. Conan
Henry H. Melchor
Larry P. Malfitano
John H. Callahan
John G. McGowan
D. Fred Garner (Resident, Naples, Florida Office)
Nicholas J. D'Ambrosio, Jr. (Resident, Albany Office)
George J. Getman
Robert A. LaBerge
Richard A. Reed (Resident, Albany Office)
Susan Phillips Read (Resident, Albany Office)
Michael S. Glazier (Resident, Overland Park, Kansas Office)
Joseph P. Van De Loo (Resident, Albany Office)
Louis A. Alexander (Resident, Albany Office)
Deborah H. Karalunas
Patrick J. Pedro
Robert S. McLaughlin
Margaret M. Cassady
Jonathan B. Fellows
Arthur J. Siegel (Resident, Albany Office)
Brian K. Haynes

(See Next Column)

ASSOCIATES

Raymond J. Pascucci
Virginia C. Robbins
James D. Dati
Thomas G. Eron
Stephen C. Daley
David M. Ferrara
Anne F. Sirota
Edward A. Mervine (Resident, Oswego Office)
William M. Burke
Robert H. Kirchner
Steven J. Ford
Thomas J. Collura (Resident, Albany Office)
John E. Higgins (Resident, Albany Office)
Peter V. White
Hermes A. Fernandez, III (Resident, Albany Office)
Kevin M. Bernstein
Jean A. Ryan (Resident, Naples, Florida Office)
Richard B. Crockett
Joseph C. Dole
William M. Buchan
Donald E. Budmen
Deborah L. Gray
Robert P. Lane, Jr.
Scott W. Tompsett
Michael J. Grygiel (Resident, Albany Office)
Cynthia K. Jones (Resident, Overland Park, Kansas Office)
Kevin G. Martin
Gregory J. Champion (Resident, Albany Office)
Ellen Gottmann Kulik
H. J. Hubert
Thomas M. Shephard
James R. Muldoon
Dennis P. Cronin (Resident, Naples, Florida Office)
Peter A. Jones
Anthony E. Koester
John G. Mc Donald
Thomas Patrick Mc Quade (Resident, Albany Office)
Patrick L. Seely, Jr. (Resident, Albany Office)
Philip J. Zaccheo
John P. Ramos
Richard J. Evrard (Resident, Overland Park, Kansas Office)
Mark R. McGrath
Dennis C. Brown
Robert R. Tyson
Darren J. Carroll
Rosemarie A. Perez
Robert P. Storch (Resident, Albany Office)
Scott R. Hatz
Michael P. McCarthy
Kathleen A. Drapeau
Paul W. Reichel
Kenneth E. Spahn (Resident, Boca Raton, Florida Office)

OF COUNSEL

Robert R. Snashall, III

General Counsel for: Syracuse University; Unity Mutual Life Insurance Co.; Manufacturers Association of Central New York.
Regional or Special Counsel for: Newhouse Broadcasting Corp. (WSYR, AM-FM); Syracuse Herald-Post Standard Newspapers.; Miller Brewing Co.; Allied Corp.; General Electric Co.; National Grange.

For full biographical listings, see the Martindale-Hubbell Law Directory

COSTELLO COONEY & FEARON (AV)

Salina Place, 205 South Salina Street, 13202
Telephone: 315-422-1152
Fax: 315-422-1139

MEMBERS OF FIRM

David F. Costello (1872-1934)
Charles E. Cooney (1873-1958)
George R. Fearon (1883-1976)
Vincent A. O'Neil
Richard D. Hillman
Donald L. Nicholas
Warren W. Bader
Raymond R. D'Agostino
Robert D. Essig
Kevin M. Gilligan
Frances A. Ciardullo
Robert J. Smith
Michael A. Tremont
Alicia S. Calagiovanni
James J. Gascon

ASSOCIATES

Michael Religa
Paul G. Ferrara
Maureen G. Fatcheric
Barbara DiPiazza
Michelle C. Lombino
Timothy J. Conan
John R. Langey
Joanne E. Michaels
Paul M. Gallagher
Daniel Fletcher
Iris J. Iler

General Counsel for: Auburn Memorial Hospital; Crouse-Irving Memorial Hospital; Health Services Association of Central New York; St. Joseph's Hospital Health Center.
Local Counsel for: Deere & Co.; New York Telephone Co.; Crum & Forster Insurance Co.; The Tavelers Insurance Companies; Caterpillar, Inc.; Otis Elevator.

For full biographical listings, see the Martindale-Hubbell Law Directory

COULTER, FRASER, BOLTON, BIRD & VENTRE (AV)

6th Floor, 499 South Warren Street, 13202-2690
Telephone: 315-475-8461
Phoenix, New York Office: 827 State Street.
Telephone: 315-695-6377.

MEMBERS OF FIRM

Sidney B. Coulter (1897-1968)
Donald V. Carr (1902-1972)
James E. Bird, III (1931-1992)
Robert F. Coulter
Robert D. Ventre
J. Mark McCarthy
P. David Twichell
Ralph E. Coleman

COUNSEL

Henry S. Fraser
David A. Fraser
Bruce Bolton

(See Next Column)

COULTER, FRASER, BOLTON, BIRD & VENTRE, *Syracuse—Continued*

ASSOCIATES

M. Joanne Van Dyke
Michael J. Hrab
Michael N. Livingston

Representative Clients: Aetna Life & Casualty Co.; Maryland Casualty Company of Baltimore, Maryland; The St. Paul Insurance Cos.; CIGNA Cos.; CNA Insurance Co.; Merchants Mutual Insurance Co.; Garlock, Inc.; Micro Glass Inc.; M.G.I. Systems; Town of Lysander.

For full biographical listings, see the Martindale-Hubbell Law Directory

GROSSMAN KINNEY DWYER & HARRIGAN, P.C. (AV)

5720 Commons Park, 13057
Telephone: 315-449-2131
Telecopier: 315-449-2905

Richard D. Grossman
John P. Kinney
James F. Dwyer
C. Frank Harrigan
Robert E. Hornik, Jr.
Harris N. Lindenfeld

Ruth Moors D'Eredita
Edward P. Dunn
Joseph G. Shields

Representative Clients: County of Onondaga; County of Tompkins; Therm, Incorporated, Ithaca, New York; Village of Marcellus; Smith Barney Shearson; The Mitsubishi Bank, Limited (New York Branch); C&S Engineers, Inc.; Town of Harrietstown, New York.

For full biographical listings, see the Martindale-Hubbell Law Directory

HANCOCK & ESTABROOK (AV)

Mony Tower 1, P.O. Box 4976, 13221-4976
Telephone: 315-471-3151
Telecopier: 315-471-3167
Albany, New York Office: Suite 505, 125 Wolf Road.
Telephone: 518-458-7660.
Telecopier: 518-458-7731.

Stewart F. Hancock (1883-1966)
Theodore M. Hancock (1913-1988)
Lewis C. Ryan (1891-1961)
Charles S. Estabrook (1879-1975)
Benjamin E. Shove (1892-1977)
Morris Berman (1906-1987)
Joseph H. Murphy (1916-1986)
A. Van W. Hancock (1909-1993)
Charles H. Bassett (1915-1994)

COUNSEL

Stewart F. Hancock, Jr.
Raymond A. Hust
John M. Hastings, Jr.
James J. Kaufman
Kevin E. McCormack

MEMBERS OF FIRM

W. Carroll Coyne
Donald P. McCarthy
Paul M. Hanrahan
Edward J. Pfohl
John R. Vaɪney
William L. Allen, Jr.
Charles H. Umbrecht, Jr.
Donald J. Kemple
Carl W. Peterson, Jr.
Clark A. Pitcher
James R. McVety
Robert A. Small
Walter L. Meagher, Jr.
Donald A. Denton
J. Thomas Bassett
Richard W. Cook
David S. Howe
Gregory R. Thornton
Doreen A. Simmons
David E. Peebles
James J. Canfield
Gerald F. Stack
James E. Hughes
Jeffrey B. Andrus
Janet D. Callahan
Thomas C. Buckel, Jr.
Michael L. Corp
Daniel B. Berman
John T. McCann
Steven R. Shaw
David T. Garvey (Resident, Albany Office)
John L. Murad, Jr.
Stephen A. Donato
Kenneth P. Holden
Mark J. Schulte
Alan J. Pierce
Nancy Friel Hornik
Martha L. Berry

ASSOCIATES

Neil M. Gingold
Marion Hancock Fish
R. John Clark
Renee L. James
David G. Linger
Patricia A. McGevna
Patrick M. Connors
Michael A. Oropallo
Elizabeth A. Salvagno
Camille Wolnik Hill
Timothy P. Murphy
Kathy R. Lamb
Cora A. Alsante
Douglas H. Zamelis
Debra Chini Sullivan
Edward J. Smith III
Sarah Grace Campbell
Eric C. Nordby
Charles J. Sullivan
John F. Corcoran
Michael C. Griffen

General Counsel for: Marine Midland Bank, (Mid-State Region); Deanco.
Representative Clients: Anheuser-Busch, Inc.; Bristol Laboratories, Division of Bristol-Meyers Squibb; Mutual Benefit Life Insurance Co.; Hartford Insurance Group; Metropolitan Life Insurance Co.; Foremost Insurance Co.

For full biographical listings, see the Martindale-Hubbell Law Directory

HARTNETT LAW OFFICE (AV)

The Syracuse Building, Suite 208, 224 Harrison Street, 13202
Telephone: 315-478-5791
FAX: 315-478-0106

Robert W. Hartnett
Peter M. Hartnett

Reference: Chase Manhattan.

For full biographical listings, see the Martindale-Hubbell Law Directory

MELVIN & MELVIN (AV)

220 South Warren Street, 13202
Telephone: 315-422-1311
Telefax: 315-479-7612

MEMBERS OF FIRM

Jonathan E. Fox
Roger W. Bradley
Robert S. Scalione
Ronald S. Carr
Louis Levine
Douglas H. Young
Richard M. Storto
Kenneth J. Bobrycki
Howard J. Woronov
Susan E. Otto

ASSOCIATES

Holly Salop Wallace
Mark N. Wladis

COUNSEL

Louis Young
Domenic A. Mazza
William C. Fox
Merle D. Melvin
Charles R. Greiner

Special Counsel for: OnBank & Trust Co.; The Equitable Life Assurance Society of the United States; Government Employees Insurance Co.
Reference: OnBank & Trust Co.

For full biographical listings, see the Martindale-Hubbell Law Directory

NOTTINGHAM, ENGEL, GORDON & KERR (AV)

Eighth Floor, One Lincoln Center, 13202
Telephone: 315-474-6046
Fax: 315-474-6065

MEMBERS OF FIRM

Richard L. Engel
Richard E. Gordon
J. Craig Kerr

For full biographical listings, see the Martindale-Hubbell Law Directory

O'HARA & HANLON (AV)

One Park Place, 13202
Telephone: 315-422-5177
Cazenovia, New York Office: Mitchell and O'Hara & Hanlon, 9 Albany Street.
Telephone: 315-655-8000.

MEMBERS OF FIRM

David Patrick O'Hara
Kerry J. Hanlon
Peter W. Knych

COUNSEL

Peter W. Mitchell (Resident, Mitchell and O'Hara and Hanlon, Cazenovia, N.Y.)

OF COUNSEL

Robert G. Ritz

ASSOCIATES

Alexander Pobedinsky

For full biographical listings, see the Martindale-Hubbell Law Directory

SUGARMAN, WALLACE, MANHEIM & SCHOENWALD (AV)

Marine Midland Bank Building, 360 South Warren Street, 13202
Telephone: 315-474-2943
FAX: 315-474-0235

MEMBERS OF FIRM

David B. Sugarman (1885-1968)
Milton Wallace (1917-1985)
Donald L. Schoenwald
Alan J. Goldberg
George E. DeMore
James G. Stevens, Jr.
Samuel Vulcano
Robert P. Dwyer
Paul M. Gonzalez
Timothy J. Perry

ASSOCIATES

Thomas E. O'Bryan
Stephen G. Pesarchick
Paul V. Mullin
David A. Kalabanka
Laura A. Alderman
Sherry R. Bruce
Kevin T. Hunt
Mary Keib Smith
Sam A. Elbadawi

OF COUNSEL

Charles M. Manheim

Representative Clients: Allstate Insurance Co.; Continental National American Insurance Co.; Chubb & Son; Liberty Mutual Insurance Co.; Carpenter Manufacturing Co., Inc.; General Accident Group; Hartford Accident & Indemnity Co.; Firemans Fund; New York Central Mutual.
Reference: Onbank.

For full biographical listings, see the Martindale-Hubbell Law Directory

*TROY,** Rensselaer Co.

E. STEWART JONES (AV)

28 Second Street, 12181
Telephone: 518-274-5820
Fax: 518-274-5875

E. Stewart Jones, Jr.
W. Farley Jones
Jeffrey K. Anderson
David J. Taffany
Peter J. Moschetti, Jr.

OF COUNSEL

E. Stewart Jones
Arthur L. Rosen
Abbott H. Jones (1873-1939)
Charles W. Marshall (1882-1945)

References: Key Bank and On Bank; Troy Savings Bank.

For full biographical listings, see the Martindale-Hubbell Law Directory

UNADILLA, Otsego Co. — (Refer to Cooperstown)

UNIONDALE, Nassau Co.

FARRELL, FRITZ, CAEMMERER, CLEARY, BARNOSKY & ARMENTANO, PROFESSIONAL CORPORATION (AV)

EAB Plaza, 11556-0120
Telephone: 516-227-0700
Facsimile: 516-227-0777

John D. Caemmerer (1928-1982)
Frank A. Fritz, Jr. (1924-1982)
John M. Armentano
John J. Barnosky
Igor Bilewich
John P. Cleary
John F. Coffey
George J. Farrell, Jr.
Dolores Fredrich
Robert V. Guido
Thomas J. Killeen
John R. Morken
Andrew J. Simons
Charles M. Strain
William D. Wall

COUNSEL

Thomas J. Doran
J. Kemp Hannon
Leonard Lazarus
Samuel S. Tripp
Eli Wager

Kenneth Auerbach
James A. Bradley
Ilene S. Cooper
Christopher P. Daly
Sally M. Donahue
Kelly A. Dunbar
Arthur K. Feldman
Steven G. Gaebler
Anthony S. Guardino
Joshua A. Hazelwood
Michael J. Healy
F. Judith Hepworth
Eric M. Kramer
Christopher J. Kutner
Scott L. Lanin
Susan W. Lawlor
Nora M. Link
Barbara Quinn McElroy
Stephen F. Melore
Diane K. Mendez
Willets S. Meyer
Dina Talmor Miller
Gerhardt M. Nielsen
Robert E. Sandler
Janice L. Snead
John V. Soderberg
Sanford Strenger
Karen J. Tenenbaum
A. Kathleen Tomlinson

For full biographical listings, see the Martindale-Hubbell Law Directory

RIVKIN, RADLER & KREMER (AV)

A Partnership including Professional Corporations
EAB Plaza (Long Island), 11556-0111
Telephone: 516-357-3000
Cable Address: "Atlaw"
Telex: 645-074
Telecopier: 516-357-3333
Chicago, Illinois Office: Suite 4300, 30 North LaSalle Street.
Telephone: 312-782-5680.
Telecopier: 312-782-3112.
New York, New York Office: 275 Madison Avenue.
Telephone: 212-455-9555.
Telecopier: 212-687-9044.
Santa Rosa, California Office: 100 B Street, Suite 300, P.O. Box 14609.
Telephone: 707-576-8033.
Telecopier: 707-576-7955.
Pasadena, California Office: 123 South Marengo Avenue, Suite 400.
Telephone: 818-795-1800.
Fax: 818-795-2255.
Newark, New Jersey Office: One Gateway Center, Suite 1226.
Telephone: 201-622-0900.
Fax: 201-622-7878.

MEMBERS OF FIRM

Warren S. Radler (Resident, Chicago, Illinois Office)
Arthur J. Kremer
Bruce D. Drucker (P.C.)
William M. Savino (P.C.)
Donald T. McMillan (Resident, Santa Rosa, California Office)
James P. Nunemaker, Jr.
Joseph J. Ortego
John L. Rivkin
Stephen J. Smirti, Jr., (P.C.)
Peter L. Curry
Richard S. Feldman
Barry R. Shapiro
Gary D. Centola
Anthony R. Gambardella
Peter C. Contino
Erica B. Garay
Daniel A. Bartoldus

(See Next Column)

MEMBERS OF FIRM (Continued)

Cheryl Blackwell Bryson (Resident, Chicago Office)
Alan S. Rutkin
Michael R. Brown (Resident, Pasadena Office)
Keith R. Abrams (Resident, Chicago Office)
Neil H. Ackerman
Elizabeth Adels
S. Timothy Ball
Charlotte Biblow
William J. Borman
Steven Brock
Kenneth L. Brown
William J. Candee, III
David M. Cassidy
Edward A. Christensen
George K. DeHaven
Janice J. DiGennaro
J. Douglas Durham (Resident, Santa Rosa Office)
Alan C. Eagle
Phillip England
Stewart C. Fink
Peter D. Finocchiaro (Resident, Chicago Office)
Glenn A. Friedman (Resident, Santa Rosa Office)
Daniel Gammerman
Judy L. Goodstein
M. Paul Gorfinkel
Walter J. Gumersell
Laurence S. Hughes
James J. Jennings
George D. Kappus
Josh H. Kardisch
Jay V. Krafsur (Resident, Chicago, Illinois Office)
Heather G. Kress
Evan H. Krinick
Lawrence A. Levy
P. Michael Loftus (Resident, Chicago Office)
Patrick J. McDonnell
Kevin McElroy
Peter P. McNamara
Steven R. Merican (Resident, Chicago Office)
Howard J. Newman
James F. Quinn
Charles H. Reinhardt, Jr.
Joyce Lipton Rogak
Eric L. Routman (Resident, Chicago Office)
Sally H. Saltzberg (Resident, Chicago Office)
Charles M. Schnepp, Jr.
Gerard Terry
George W. Williams, Jr. (Resident, Pasadena Office)

OF COUNSEL

Leonard L. Rivkin (P.C.)
Stanley Pierce
Herbert L. Stern, Jr. (Resident, Chicago Office)

ASSOCIATES

Joyce Onorato Abamont
Korri E. Abrams
Larry D. Aftel
Gina Marie Alvino
Michael J. Balch
Marvin J. Bellovin
Todd M. Belous
Bruce A. Bendix
Merril C. Biscone
David H. Blackwell (Resident, Santa Rosa Office)
Jonathan Bloom
Christopher J. Borders (Resident, Santa Rosa Office)
Michael E. Buckley
Celeste M. Butera
Barry R. Carus
Gerard S. Catalanello
Peter R. Chatzinoff
Steven M. Connolly
Pauline A. Constantino
Jeffrey M. Coyle
Christopher A. Crevasse (Resident, Santa Rosa Office)
Mario A. D'Aversa
Laura A. Endrizzi
Chris J. Fichtl
Richard C. Fitzmaurice
David A. Friedman
Geri A. Friedman
Barbara E. Frohnhofer
Sally N. Fryer (Resident, Santa Rosa Office)
Florence B. Gibbons
Frank J. Giliberti
Arthur J. Golder, III
Theodore F. Goralski, Jr.
Howard R. Greenwald
Anurag Gulati (Resident, Chicago Office)
Jeffrey D. Hayes (Resident, Santa Rosa Office)
Gary C. Hisiger
Christopher A. Jeffreys
Brian A. Kalman
George J. Keller (Resident, Santa Rosa Office)
Karen C. Keller
Jay D. Kenigsberg
Cameron Kirk, Jr. (Resident, Santa Rosa Office)
Abbe L. Koplitz
Cheryl Korman
Michael A. Kotula (Not admitted in NY)
John J. Kozlowski (Resident, Santa Rosa Office)
Joshua N. Krellen
Emily H. Levin
Shari C. Lewis
Leslie A. Evans Lynch
Michael C. Marsh
Joni F. Mason (Resident, Newark, New Jersey Office)
Karin M. McCarthy
Stephen E. McCarthy
Thomas J. McGowan
Christine M. Metzner
Andrew K. Miller (Resident, Chicago Office)
Joseph N. Mondello, Jr.
John F. Morrison
Anne M. Murray
Harold Neher
Gregory S. Nelson
Eric L. Nesbitt (Resident, Chicago Office)
Jill Rosen Nikoloff
Steven C. November
Kenneth A. Novikoff
Mitchell S. Nussbaum
Kevin D. O'Leary (Resident, Pasadena Office)
Peter Orthodoxou
John J. Panagopoulos
Anthony W. Paradiso
Rebecca Berman Phelps (Resident, Santa Rosa Office)
Velly B. Polycarpe
Donald V. Pupke, Jr.
Frank J. Raia
Veena A. Rao (Resident, Santa Rosa Office)
Lisa Ann Rathbun (Resident, Santa Rosa Office)
Pia Elena Riverso
Brian R. Sahn
Mark R. Salsberg
Jill R. Sands
John F. Schutta
D. Douglas Shureen (Resident, Santa Rosa Office)
Dina L. Shuster
Paul K. Sidorenko (Resident, Santa Rosa Office)
Jeffrey S. Siegel
Robyn D. Simon
Michael A. Sirignano
Jonathan J. Somerstein
Carol A. Stark (Resident, Chicago Office)
James F. Stewart
Ronald S. Stewart (Resident, Santa Rosa Office)
Howard M. Tollin
Patrick M. Tomovic

(See Next Column)

RIVKIN, RADLER & KREMER, *Uniondale—Continued*

ASSOCIATES (Continued)

David Vendler (Resident, Pasadena Office)
Michael P. Versichelli
Miriam E. Villani
Robert G. Vizza
Alyse Walker
Belinda Kittles Walker
Richard Weber
James W. Weller
Madeline F. Willi
Jon Zimring (Resident, Chicago Office)
Joel Zuckerberg

Representative Clients: Allstate Insurance Co.; Chase Manhattan Bank, N.A.; Chemical Bank; The DOW Chemical Co.; Government Employees Insurance Co.; Liquidation Bureau; New York Insurance Dept.; Prudential Property & Casualty Insurance Co.; The Dime Savings Bank of New York.

For full biographical listings, see the Martindale-Hubbell Law Directory

*UTICA,** Oneida Co.

DURR AND KEINZ (AV)

The Paul Building, 209 Elizabeth Street, 13501
Telephone: 315-735-6185
FAX: 315-797-5521

MEMBERS OF FIRM

Robert W. Durr (1927-1973)
Donald E. Keinz

Reference: Fleet Bank.

For full biographical listings, see the Martindale-Hubbell Law Directory

GORMAN, WASZKIEWICZ, GORMAN & SCHMITT (AV)

1508 Genesee Street, 13502-5178
Telephone: 315-724-2147
Fax: 315-724-1183

MEMBERS OF FIRM

Bartle Gorman (1897-1974)
Bartle J. Gorman
Lee Palmer Armstrong
William P. Schmitt

ASSOCIATES

Darryl B. Rahn

OF COUNSEL

Edwin A. Waszkiewicz

General Counsel for: Carton Foundation, Inc.; G & I Homes, Inc.; T. C. Peters Printing Co., Inc.
Local Counsel for: Utica Mutual Insurance Co.; Graphic Arts Mutual Insurance Co.; United National Insurance Co.;
References: Key Bank of N.Y.; Marine Midland Bank.

For full biographical listings, see the Martindale-Hubbell Law Directory

GROBEN, GILROY, OSTER & SAUNDERS (AV)

Formerly Groben, Liddy, Cardamone & Gilroy
Suite 1013-1027, 185 Genesee Street, 13503
Telephone: 315-724-4166
FAX: 315-797-1944

MEMBERS OF FIRM

Gilbert R. Hughes (1889-1977)
Joseph J. Cardamone, Jr. (1918-1979)
John M. Liddy (1910-1987)
Robert Groben
James H. Gilroy, Jr.
Stanley J. Kowal, Jr.
James C. Oster
Joseph E. F. Saunders

ASSOCIATES

Claudia Tenney Cleary
Nathan M. Hayes

Counsel for: Marine Midland Bank, N.A.; Norstar Bank of Upstate N.Y.; The Homestead Savings (FA); United Parcel Service, Inc.; Reliance Insurance Cos.; Prudential Insurance Co.

For full biographical listings, see the Martindale-Hubbell Law Directory

KERNAN AND KERNAN, P.C. (AV)

S-600, 258 Genesee Street, 13502
Telephone: 315-797-8300; Herkimer: 866-7497
Telecopier: 315-797-6467

James S. Kernan, Jr.
Leighton R. Burns
Gregory A. Hamlin
Mark W. McLane
Steven A. Smith
Matthew E. Hamlin
John E. Short

COUNSEL

Thomas Spratt Kernan

Counsel for: Stetson-Harza Architects and Engineers.
Local Counsel for: Key Bank of Central New York; U. S. Air, Inc.; General Electric Co.; Aetna Life & Casualty Cos.; Consolidated Rail Corp.; General Motors Corp.; Allstate Ins. Co.; Kemper Insurance Group.

For full biographical listings, see the Martindale-Hubbell Law Directory

ROSSI, MURNANE, BALZANO & HUGHES (AV)

Suite 300 Paul Building, 209 Elizabeth Street, P.O. Box 209, 13503-0209
Telephone: 315-733-4671
FAX: 315-733-4609

Vincent J. Rossi
Don P. Murnane
John S. Balzano
Vincent J. Rossi, Jr.
Thomas P. Hughes

General Counsel for: Utica Fire Insurance Co.
Reference: Chemical Bank, Utica, New York.

For full biographical listings, see the Martindale-Hubbell Law Directory

WALDEN, Orange Co.

BARTLETT AND BARTLETT (AV)

Bartlett Building, 11 Orchard Street, P.O. Box 153, 12586
Telephone: 914-778-5621; Goshen: 914-294-9014
FAX: 914-778-7020

George R. Bartlett (1923-1953)
George R. Bartlett, Jr.

Reference: Key Bank of New York.

For full biographical listings, see the Martindale-Hubbell Law Directory

WALTON, Delaware Co. — (Refer to Binghamton)

*WARSAW,** Wyoming Co.

SMALLWOOD-COOK & SCHMIEDER (AV)

140 North Main Street, 14569
Telephone: 716-786-2274
FAX: 716-786-2138

MEMBERS OF FIRM

Charlotte Smallwood-Cook
Jane A.C. Schmieder

Reference: Wyoming County Bank.

For full biographical listings, see the Martindale-Hubbell Law Directory

WARWICK, Orange Co. — (Refer to Middletown)

*WATERLOO,** Seneca Co. — (Refer to Seneca Falls)

*WATERTOWN,** Jefferson Co.

CONBOY, MCKAY, BACHMAN & KENDALL (AV)

407 Sherman Street, 13601
Telephone: 315-788-5100
Clayton, New York Office: 342 Riverside Drive.
Telephone: 315-686-3487.
Carthage, New York Office: 307 State Street.
Telephone: 315-493-0030.
Canton, New York Office: 24 Court Street, P.O. Box 650.
Telephone: 315-386-4539.

OF COUNSEL

Joanne M. Novak (Resident, Canton Office)

MEMBERS OF FIRM

Philip A. Maphey
George K. Myrus
Floyd J. Chandler
Lawrence D. Hasseler (Resident, Carthage Office)
Stephen W. Gebo
Arthur C. Stever, III
William F. Maginn, Jr. (Resident, Canton Office)
Joseph W. Russell (Resident, Clayton Office)

ASSOCIATES

Timothy A. Farley
Edward J. Sheats, Jr.
Peter L. Walton
David B. Geurtsen

Attorneys for: Conrail; Champion International Corp.; Travelers Indemnity Co.; St. Joe Minerals Corp.; Maryland Casualty Co.; Royal Insurance Co.; Niagara Mohawk Power Corp.; Marine Midland Bank, N.A.

For full biographical listings, see the Martindale-Hubbell Law Directory

*WHITE PLAINS,** Westchester Co.

BLEAKLEY PLATT & SCHMIDT (AV)

One North Lexington Avenue, 10601-1700
Telephone: 914-949-2700
Telecopier: 914-683-6956
Somers, New York Office: 272 Route 202.
Telephone: 914-277-3924.
Telecopier: 914-277-7133.
Greenwich, Connecticut Office: Sixty-Six Field Point Road.
Telephone: 203-661-5222.
Telecopier: 203-661-1197.

MEMBERS OF FIRM

Frederick J. Martin
William F. Harrington
Joseph B. Glatthaar
John J. Ferguson (Resident, Greenwich, Connecticut Office)
Donald J. Sullivan
Robert D. Meade
Hugh D. Fyfe, Jr.
Raymond M. Planell
William Hughes Mulligan, Jr.
James J. Sullivan
Janice H. Eiseman
Lester Berkelhamer

(See Next Column)

BLEAKLEY PLATT & SCHMIDT—*Continued*

MEMBERS OF FIRM (Continued)

John E. Meerbergen (Resident, Greenwich, Connecticut Office)
William P. Harrington
Mary Ellen Manley
Brian E. Lorenz
Timothy P. Coon

COUNSEL

Henry R. Barrett, III
Joseph A. Izzillo (Resident, Greenwich, Connecticut Office)
Nancy L. Long
Peter T. Gahagan
Joseph De Giuseppe, Jr.
Kimberlea Shaw Rea
J. Lincoln Hallowell (Resident, Greenwich, Connecticut Office)
Mary E. Quaranta Morrissey
William C. Fahey
John P. Hannigan
Timothy J. Joyce
Richard N. Pitassy
John I. O'Neill
Carl A. D'Angelo
John F. Tague, III (Resident, Greenwich, Connecticut Office)

James W. Glatthaar
Frank J. Ingrassia
Vincent W. Crowe
Veronica C. Staplefield (Resident, Greenwich, Connecticut Office)
Sheila T. Murphy
John F. Martin
Mark K. Malone
Leanne M. Freda
Bart R. McGowan
Matthew G. Parisi

Representative Clients: American Telephone & Telegraph Co.; The Bank of New York-County Trust Region; General Foods Corp.; The Guardian Life Insurance Co.; Mobil Oil Corp.; New York American Water Company, Inc-.(a subsidiary of American Water Works Co., Inc.); St. Joseph's Hospital, Yonkers; The Singer Co.; Yonkers Racing Corp.

For full biographical listings, see the Martindale-Hubbell Law Directory

CLARK, GAGLIARDI & MILLER, P.C. (AV)

Inns of Court Building, 99 Court Street, 10601
Telephone: 914-946-8900
Telecopier: 914-946-8960
New York, New York Office: Suite 2525, 230 Park Avenue.
Telephone: 914-926-8900.

Robert Y. Clark (1881-1961)
Frank M. Gagliardi (1886-1980)
Joseph F. Gagliardi (1911-1992)
Henry G. Miller
Lawrence T. D'Aloise, Jr.
Lucille A. Fontana
Robert J. Frisenda

Angela Morcone Giannini
Padraic D. Lee
Denise Liotta DeMarzo

OF COUNSEL

Morton B. Silberman

For full biographical listings, see the Martindale-Hubbell Law Directory

CUDDY & FEDER (AV)

90 Maple Avenue, 10601-5196
Telephone: 914-761-1300
Telecopier: 914-761-5372; 914-761-6405
New York, N.Y. Office: 60 East 42nd Street.
Telephone: 212-949-6280.
Telecopier: 212-949-6346.
Stamford, Connecticut Office: 707 Summer Street.
Telephone: 203-348-4780.
Norwalk, Connecticut Office: 4 Berkeley Street.
Telephone: 203-853-8001.
Telecopier: 203-831-8250.

MEMBERS OF FIRM

Thomas R. Beirne (Resident, New York, N.Y. Office)
Joseph P. Carlucci
Kenneth DuBroff
Robert Feder
Andrew A. Glickson (Resident, Stamford & Norwalk, Connecticut Offices)
Joshua J. Grauer
Kenneth F. Jurist
Richard A. Katzive
Dennis C. Krieger
Barry E. Long
William S. Null
Neil T. Rimsky
Ruth Schorr Roth
Kevin G. Ryan
Chauncey L. Walker
Robert L. Wolfe
Kathleen Donelli
Lawrence J. Reiss

ASSOCIATES

Suzanne Bogdanoff
Ann Farrissey Carlson
Erica Tukel Wax

OF COUNSEL

William V. Cuddy
Daniel M. Zane

Reference: The Bank of New York County Trust Region.

For full biographical listings, see the Martindale-Hubbell Law Directory

HOFFMAN, WACHTELL, KOSTER, MAIER & MANDEL (AV)

399 Knollwood Road, 10603
Telephone: 914-682-8000
FAX: 914-682-1512
New City, New York Office: 82 Maple Avenue, 10956.
Telephone: 914-634-8169.

MEMBERS OF FIRM

Lee A. Hoffman, Jr.
Marc J. Wachtell
Eric D. Koster
Lynn J. Maier
Richard G. Mandel

Representative Clients: Mount Hope Mines, Inc.; Eastern Educational Consortium; Westchester Community College; Prime Office Systems, Inc.; Gateway Management Corp.; Purchase Environmental Protection Association, Inc.; The Jay Coalition; The Town of Greenburgh; The Town of Mamaroneck.
Reference: Citibank, N.A. (White Plains Branch).

For full biographical listings, see the Martindale-Hubbell Law Directory

KEANE & BEANE, P.C. (AV)

One North Broadway, 10601
Telephone: 914-946-4777
Telecopier: 914-946-6868
Rye, New York Office: 49 Purchase Street.
Telephone: 914-967-3936.

Thomas F. Keane, Jr. (1932-1991)

Edward F. Beane
David Glasser
Ronald A. Longo
Richard L. O'Rourke
Lawrence Praga
Joel H. Sachs
Steven A. Schurkman
Judson K. Siebert

Debbie G. Jacobs
Lance H. Klein
Donna E. Frosco
Nicholas M. Ward-Willis

LEGAL SUPPORT PERSONNEL

Barbara S. Durkin
Toni Ann Huff

OF COUNSEL

Eric F. Jensen
Peter A. Borrok

For full biographical listings, see the Martindale-Hubbell Law Directory

KENT, HAZZARD, JAEGER, GREER, WILSON & FAY (AV)

50 Main Street, 10606
Telephone: 914-948-4700
Telecopier: 914-948-4721

MEMBERS OF FIRM

Ralph S. Kent (1878-1949)
Lawrence S. Hazzard (1900-1958)
William J. Greer (1920-1994)
Mizell Wilson, Jr.
Lawrence F. Fay
Robert D. Hazzard
Gregory C. Freeman
Robert G. O'Donnell
Katharine Wilson Conroy
John R. Dinin

OF COUNSEL

Malcolm Wilson
Edward J. Freeman
Otto C. Jaeger
George Beisheim, Jr.
Peter F. Blasi

Representative Clients: The Bank of New York.
References: Bank of New York; Peoples Westchester Savings Bank.

For full biographical listings, see the Martindale-Hubbell Law Directory

KURZMAN & EISENBERG (AV)

One North Broadway, 10601
Telephone: 914-285-9800
Fax: 914-285-9855
New York, N.Y. Office: 99 Park Avenue.
Telephone: 212-671-1322.
Hollywood, Florida Office: 2021 Tyler Street.
Telephone: 305-921-5500.

MEMBERS OF FIRM

Robert G. Kurzman
Sam Eisenberg
Lee Harrison Corbin
Robert L. Ecker
Joel S. Lever
Jack S. Older
Alan John Rein
Fred D. Weinstein

OF COUNSEL

Richard A. Danzig
R. Mark Goodman
Stephen R. Levy

For full biographical listings, see the Martindale-Hubbell Law Directory

MEAD, HECHT, CONKLIN & GALLAGHER (AV)

399 Knollwood Road, 10603
Telephone: 914-686-6200
Fax: 914-686-1007

(See Next Column)

MEAD, HECHT, CONKLIN & GALLAGHER, *White Plains—Continued*

MEMBERS OF FIRM

Donald A. Mead (Founder of Mead & Dore, P.C. and its' successors)
Elizabeth M. Hecht
Kevin Thomas Conklin
Eugene G. Gallagher

ASSOCIATES

Thomas L. Montagnino

OF COUNSEL

Kingdon P. Locker
Vincent Gurahian

For full biographical listings, see the Martindale-Hubbell Law Directory

O'CONNOR, MCGUINNESS, CONTE, DOYLE, OLESON & COLLINS (AV)

One Barker Avenue, 10601
Telephone: 914-948-4500
Telecopier: 914-948-0645

MEMBERS OF FIRM

Dennis L. O'Connor (1913-1989)
Rocco Conte
Dennis T. Doyle
William S. Oleson
J. Peter Collins
Richard C. Oleson
Dennis L. O'Connor, Jr.
William R. Watson
Kevin M. Loftus

ASSOCIATES

Craig P. Curcio
Louis K. Szarka
Mary Pat Burke
Patricia Lacy
Pamela R. Millian
Andrew F. Pisanelli
Montgomery Lee Effinger
Dara A. Ruderman
Philomena Basuk
Debora J. Dillon
Daniel M. Miller

OF COUNSEL

Eugene J. McGuinness
Russell J. Hauck

Attorneys for: Insurance Company of North America; Allstate Insurance Co.; Continental Insurance Group; Government Employers Insurance Co.; Merchants Mutual Insurance Co.; Prudential Insurance Co.; Consolidated Rail Corp.; Medical Liability Mutual Insurance Co.; Colonial Penn Insurance Co.

For full biographical listings, see the Martindale-Hubbell Law Directory

QUINN & SUHR (AV)

170 Hamilton Avenue, 10601
Telephone: 914-949-0800
Facsimile: 914-949-1094

MEMBERS OF FIRM

Timothy Charles Quinn, Jr.
J. Nicholas Suhr
Zachary Marantis
Craig M. Shields

OF COUNSEL

E. Martin Davidoff
Lars Forsberg
Bradford D. Conover

For full biographical listings, see the Martindale-Hubbell Law Directory

SMITH, RANSCHT, CONNORS, MUTINO, NORDELL & SIRIGNANO, P.C. (AV)

235 Main Street, 10601
Telephone: 914-946-8800
Telecopier: 914-946-8861
Cable Address: "Smiran" White Plains, New York
Greenwich, Connecticut Office: P.O. Box 4847, 06830-0605.
Telephone: 203-622-6660.

Peter T. Manos (1923-1991)
James P. Connors, Jr.
William F. Ranscht, Jr.
Peter J. Mutino
Michael Nordell
George A. Sirignano, Jr.

OF COUNSEL

Gary E. Bashian
James M. Pollock
Anthony J. Enea

Counsel for: The Corham Artificial Flower Co.; Universal Builders Supply, Inc.; Kalman Floor Co., Inc.; The Walter Karl Companies.

For full biographical listings, see the Martindale-Hubbell Law Directory

STEPHENS, BARONI, REILLY & LEWIS (AV)

Northcourt Building, 175 Main Street, 10601
Telephone: 914-761-0300; 683-5185
Telecopier: 914-761-0995; 683-1323
Cross River, New York Office: Northern Westchester Office, Old Post Road Professional Building, 10518.
Telephone: 914-763-3232.

MEMBERS OF FIRM

Gerald D. Reilly
Roland A. Baroni, Jr.
Stephen R. Lewis

ASSOCIATES

Claudia Guerrino

(See Next Column)

OF COUNSEL

Thomas J. Stephens
Michael Fuller Sirignano
James R. Caruso (1906-1994)

For full biographical listings, see the Martindale-Hubbell Law Directory

VOUTÉ, LOHRFINK, MAGRO & COLLINS (AV)

Formerly Mead, Dore & Vouté
170 Hamilton Avenue, 10601
Telephone: 914-946-1400
Facsimile: 914-946-8024

Arthur J. Vouté, Jr.
Richard L. Magro
Charles D. Lohrfink, Jr.
Charles A. Collins, Jr.

Elliot A. Cristantello
Stephen F. Fischer
Ralph F. Schoene
Stephen P. Falvey
Kathleen V. Gudmundsson
Dennis P. Glascott
Anthony R. Tirone
Kevin P. Fitzpatrick

Representative Clients: Allstate Insurance Co.; Crum & Forster Group; Electric Mutual Liability Insurance Co.; Commercial Union Group; General Accident Group; General Electric Co.; Liberty Mutual Insurance Co.; Medical Liability Mutual Insurance Co.

For full biographical listings, see the Martindale-Hubbell Law Directory

WILSON, BAVE, CONBOY, COZZA & COUZENS, P.C. (AV)

Two William Street, 10601
Telephone: 914-686-9010
Telecopier: 914-686-0873

William H. Bave (1919-1991)
Donald C. Wilson (1917-1994)
R. Kevin Conboy
William H. Bave, Jr.
Michael J. Cozza
John C. Couzens, Jr.
Michele A. Fournier
Joseph T. Jednak
Patricia Bave-Planell
Kevin D. Odell
Leo T. McGrath
Alexandra C. Karamitsos

LEGAL SUPPORT PERSONNEL

PARALEGAL

John R. Pearsall

Representative Clients: Royal Insurance; Kemper Insurance Co.; State Farm Mutual Automobile Insurance Co.; Continental National American Group; Utica Mutual Insurance Co.; Jefferson Insurance Co.; Nationwide Insurance Co.; Medical Liability Mutual Insurance Co.

For full biographical listings, see the Martindale-Hubbell Law Directory

NORTH CAROLINA

*ALBEMARLE,** Stanly Co.

BROWN, BROWN, BROWN AND STOKES (AV)

101 South Second Street, P.O. Drawer 400, 28002
Telephone: 704-982-2141
Telecopier: 704-982-0902

Richard L. Brown, Jr.
Richard Lane Brown III
Charles P. Brown
Fred Stokes
G. Crawford Rippy, III

Representative Clients: Allstate Insurance Co.; American Circuit Breaker Corp.; Norfolk Southern Railway; Nationwide Mutual Insurance Co.; State Farm Mutual Insurance Co.
Approved Attorneys for: Lawyers Title Insurance Corp.; Chicago Title Insurance Co.; First Union National Bank; Federal Land Bank of Columbia; Wachovia Bank & Trust Co.

For full biographical listings, see the Martindale-Hubbell Law Directory

*ASHEBORO,** Randolph Co.

O'BRIANT, O'BRIANT, BUNCH, WHATLEY & ROBINS (AV)

117 Sunset Avenue, 27203
Telephone: 910-629-2121
FAX: 910-626-5736

MEMBERS OF FIRM

Thomas L. O'Briant
Lillian B. O'Briant
W. Edward Bunch
L. McKay Whatley
Thomas D. Robins

Representative Clients: Duke Power Co.; First Southern Savings Bank; First National Bank & Trust Company; Klaussner Furniture Industries, Inc.; Branco Enterprises, Inc.; Triad Heating and Cooling, Inc.; Petroleum Sales, Inc.; Allen Precision Industries, Inc.; Laurven, Inc.; The Timken Company.

*ASHEVILLE,** Buncombe Co.

MCGUIRE, WOOD & BISSETTE, P.A. (AV)

Suite 705 First Union National Bank Building, 82 Patton Avenue, P.O. Box 3180, 28802
Telephone: 704-254-8806
Fax: 704-252-2438

Walter R. McGuire
Richard A. Wood, Jr.
W. Louis Bissette, Jr.
Douglas O. Thigpen
Joseph P. McGuire
Doris Phillips Loomis
M. Charles Cloninger
Thomas C. Grella
Grant B. Osborne
Richard A. Kort

OF COUNSEL

Frank M. Parker

Representative Clients: Asheville Citizen-Times Publishing Co.; Dave Steel Co., Inc. (Steel Fabricating); WLOS-TV; The Givens Estates, Inc. (Retirement Community); Hayes & Lunsford Electrical Contractors, Inc.; Wellco Enterprises, Inc.; BASF Corp.; First Union National Bank; St. Joseph's Hospital; Revco Scientific, Inc.

For full biographical listings, see the Martindale-Hubbell Law Directory

PATLA, STRAUS, ROBINSON & MOORE, P.A. (AV)

Suite 300, 29 North Market, P.O. Box 7625, 28802
Telephone: 704-255-7641
Fax: 704-258-9222

Joseph A. Patla (1881-1979)
Robert J. Robinson
William C. Moore (Retired, 1987)
Steven I. Goldstein
Victor W. Buchanan
Jones Pharr Byrd
Robert A. Freeman, III
Richard S. Daniels
Kerry A. Friedman
Virginia P. Litzenberger
Sharon Tracey Barrett
Carol Eubank
Eileen M. McMinn
Mark C. Martin
Clifford Paul Parson
Harris Miller Livingstain

OF COUNSEL

Karl H. Straus

Representative Clients: Asheville Regional Airport Authority; Asheville Waste Paper Co.; Giles Chemical Corp.; Matthews Ford, Inc.; Memorial Mission Hospital, Inc.; Pelle Automotive Group, Inc.; Price/McNabb Advertising Agency; H. Putsch & Co., a Division of H. Putsch & Co. (Germany); Royal Crown Cola Bottling Co.

For full biographical listings, see the Martindale-Hubbell Law Directory

AULANDER, Bertie Co.

JOHN R. JENKINS, JR. (AV)

111 West Main Street, P.O. Box 189, 27805
Telephone: 919-345-4631
Reference: Wachovia Bank & Trust Co., N.A., Aulander, N. C.

*BAYBORO,** Pamlico Co. — (Refer to New Bern)

*BEAUFORT,** Carteret Co.

WHEATLY, WHEATLY, NOBLES & WEEKS, P.A. (AV)

410 Front Street, P.O. Drawer 360, 28516
Telephone: 919-728-3158
FAX: 919-728-5282

Claud R. Wheatly, Jr.
Claud R. Wheatly, III
John E. Nobles, Jr.
Stevenson L. Weeks
J. Christy Maroules
Stephen M. Valentine

Reference: First Citizens Bank.

For full biographical listings, see the Martindale-Hubbell Law Directory

*BOONE,** Watauga Co.

CHARLES E. CLEMENT (AV)

756 West King Street, P.O. Drawer 32, 28607
Telephone: 704-264-6411
FAX: 704-264-5424

Representative Clients: First Union National Bank.
Approved Attorney for: Lawyers Title Insurance Corp.; Chicago Title Insurance Co.

For full biographical listings, see the Martindale-Hubbell Law Directory

EGGERS, EGGERS & EGGERS (AV)

737 West King Street, P.O. Box 248, 28607
Telephone: 704-264-3601
FAX: 704-262-5229

MEMBERS OF FIRM

Stacy C. Eggers, Jr.
Stacy C. Eggers, III (1948-1990)
Rebecca Eggers-Gryder

ASSOCIATES

Grier Hurley

Representative Clients: Watauga Savings and Loan Assn., Inc.; NCNB; First Union National Bank.
Approved Attorneys for: Lawyers Title Insurance Corp.; Farm Credit Assn.; Jefferson-Pilot Title Insurance Co.
References: Southern National Bank; First Union National Bank.

For full biographical listings, see the Martindale-Hubbell Law Directory

*BREVARD,** Transylvania Co. — (Refer to Hendersonville)

*BRYSON CITY,** Swain Co. — (Refer to Waynesville)

BURLINGTON, Alamance Co.

HOLT, LONGEST, WALL & LILES, P.L.L.C. (AV)

407 South Broad Street, P.O. Drawer 59, 27216
Telephone: 910-227-7461
FAX: 910-227-9716

W. Clary Holt
Frank A. Longest, Jr.
N. Madison Wall, II
G. Kemp Liles
Peter T. Blaetz

Counsel for: NationsBank of North Carolina; Burlington Industries; AT&T Technologies; Burlington Board of Realtors; Nationwide Mutual Insurance Co.; Security Insurance Group; United States Fidelity and Guaranty Co.

For full biographical listings, see the Martindale-Hubbell Law Directory

WISHART, NORRIS, HENNINGER & PITTMAN, P.A. (AV)

3120 South Church Street, P.O. Box 1998, 27216-1998
Telephone: 910-584-3388
FAX: 910-584-3994
Charlotte, North Carolina Office: 6832 Morrison Boulevard.
Telephone: 704-364-0010.
Telecopier: 704-365-5945; 364-0569.

Robert J. Wishart
Robert B. Norris (Resident, Charlotte, North Carolina Office)
Joseph B. Henninger, Jr. (Resident, Charlotte, North Carolina Office)
Dorn C. Pittman, Jr.
June K. Allison
Alan R. Krusch (Resident, Charlotte, North Carolina Office)
Gregory L. Kunkleman (Resident, Charlotte, North Carolina Office)
J. Wade Harrison

(See Next Column)

WISHART, NORRIS, HENNINGER & PITTMAN P.A., *Burlington—Continued*

Kenneth R. Raynor (Resident, Charlotte, North Carolina Office)
Thomas B. Templeton (Resident, Charlotte, North Carolina Office)
William H. Elam (Resident, Charlotte, North Carolina Office)
Brian P. Gavigan
C. Thomas Steele, Jr.
John B. Honeycutt, Jr.
G. Wayne Abernathy

Christine B. Simpson
Timothy B. Gavigan (Resident, Charlotte, North Carolina Office)
Pamela S. Duffy
Daniel C. Marks (Resident, Charlotte, North Carolina Office)
Maura K. Gavigan
James H. Culbreth, Jr.
Karl F. Edgar
Steven B. Long (Resident, Charlotte, North Carolina Office)
Christopher H. Roberts (Resident, Charlotte, North Carolina Office)
William Timothy Moreau (Resident, Charlotte, North Carolina Office)
W. Brien Lewis
Michael J. Rousseaux (Resident, Charlotte, North Carolina Office)
Laura Stephanie Buff

For full biographical listings, see the Martindale-Hubbell Law Directory

*CARTHAGE,** Moore Co. — (Refer to Pinehurst)

CHAPEL HILL, Orange Co.

BERNHOLZ & HERMAN (AV)

Suite 300, The Center, 1506 East Franklin Street, 27514
Telephone: 919-929-7151
Fax: 919-929-3892

MEMBERS OF FIRM

Steven A. Bernholz
Roger B. Bernholz
G. Nicholas Herman

OF COUNSEL

J. Austin Lybrand, IV

For full biographical listings, see the Martindale-Hubbell Law Directory

*CHARLOTTE,** Mecklenburg Co.

BLAKENEY & ALEXANDER (AV)

3700 NationsBank Plaza, 101 South Tryon Street, 28280
Telephone: 704-372-3680
Facsimile: 704-332-2611

MEMBERS OF FIRM

Whiteford S. Blakeney (1906-1991)
J. W. Alexander, Jr. (1919-1990)
John O. Pollard
W. T. Cranfill, Jr.
Richard F. Kane
David L. Terry
Michael V. Matthews

ASSOCIATES

Jay L. Grytdahl
Robert B. Meyer
Kevin V. Parsons

Representative Clients: Freightliner Corporation; Ingles Markets, Inc.; Lance, Inc.; NationsBank Corporation; Old Dominion Freight Line, Inc.; Overnite Transportation Co.; The Lane Company, Inc.; Trinity Industries, Inc.; U.S. Air; Vaughan Furniture Cos.

For full biographical listings, see the Martindale-Hubbell Law Directory

LOUIS A. BLEDSOE, JR. PROFESSIONAL ASSOCIATION (AV)

1057 East Morehead Street, P.O. Box 36779, 28236-6779
Telephone: 704-372-1676
Fax: 704-372-1862

Louis A. Bledsoe, Jr.

Margaret M. Bledsoe

General Counsel for: Milner Airco, Inc.; Rich Plan Piedmont, Inc.; R.T. Barbee Co., Inc.; Shrine Bowl of the Carolinas, Inc.; Grace Christian Center, Inc.; S & F Company; Rasberry Agency, Ltd.; Spinco, Inc.; Fesco Manufacturing Co.; Crawford International Corp.

For full biographical listings, see the Martindale-Hubbell Law Directory

R. CARTWRIGHT CARMICHAEL, JR. (AV)

Suite 106, 216 North McDowell Street, P.O. Box 32246, 28232
Telephone: 704-347-0992
FAX: 704-342-4971

Representative Clients: CIGNA Cos.; E. C. Griffith Co.; Frank H. Conner Co.; Jefferson Standard Life Ins. Co.; Johnson & Johnson; The St. Paul Companies; Lawyers Mutual Ins. Co.; Medical Mutual Ins. Co.; Home Ins. Co.; Canal Ins. Co.

For full biographical listings, see the Martindale-Hubbell Law Directory

CASSTEVENS, HANNER, GUNTER & GORDON, P.A. (AV)

602 East Morehead Street, P.O. Box 34607, 28234
Telephone: 704-372-2140
Fax: 704-372-1150

Nelson M. Casstevens, Jr.
Robert P. Hanner, II
Dorian H. Gunter
Marc R. Gordon

Teresa L. Conrad
Elizabeth J. M. Caldwell

Representative Clients: Overnite Transportation Co.; NationsBank; Overhead Door Company of the Piedmont.
Approved Attorneys for: Lawyers Title Insurance Corp.; Old Republic Title Company; Fidelity National Title Company; First American Title Co.; Investors Title Company; Stewart Title Company.
Reference: Central Carolina Bank.

For full biographical listings, see the Martindale-Hubbell Law Directory

CAUDLE & SPEARS, P.A. (AV)

2600 Interstate Tower, 121 West Trade Street, 28202
Telephone: 704-377-1200
Telecopier: 704-338-5858

Lloyd C. Caudle
Harold C. Spears
Thad A. Throneburg
Patrick Jenkins
L. Cameron Caudle, Jr.
Nancy E. Walker
Timothy T. Leach
John A. Folmar
Sean M. Phelan
Jeffrey L. Helms

Counsel for: Bituminous Casualty Corp.; Baumann Springs A.G.; The A. G. Boone Co.; Consolidated Freightways; Employers Mutual Casualty Co.; Metromont Materials; Otis Elevator Co.; N.C. Farm Bureau Mutual Insurance Co.; Toyoda Textile Machinery, Inc.; U. S. Bottlers Machinery Co.

For full biographical listings, see the Martindale-Hubbell Law Directory

JONES, HEWSON & WOOLARD (AV)

301 South McDowell Street Suite 320, 28204
Telephone: 704-372-6541

MEMBERS OF FIRM

Harry C. Hewson
Robert Gilroy Spratt, III
Kenneth H. Boyer

ASSOCIATES

Lawrence J. Goldman

OF COUNSEL

William L. Woolard

RETIRED

Hunter M. Jones

Representative Clients: Norfolk Southern Corp.; Norfolk Southern Railway Co. (Assistant Division Counsel); Cincinnati Insurance Co. of N.C.; CNA Insurance; Maryland Casualty Co.; Provident Life & Accident Insurance Co.; United States Fidelity & Guaranty Co.; Virginia Mutual Insurance Co.; City of Charlotte.

For full biographical listings, see the Martindale-Hubbell Law Directory

KENNEDY COVINGTON LOBDELL & HICKMAN, L.L.P. (AV)

NationsBank Corporate Center Suite 4200, 100 North Tryon Street, 28202-4006
Telephone: 704-331-7400
Fax: 704-331-7598
Rock Hill, South Carolina Office: First Union Center, 113 Main Street, 29730.
Telephone: 803-329-7600.
Fax: 803-329-7677.

RETIRED

William T. Covington, Jr.

SPECIAL COUNSEL

Robert R. Carpenter (Resident, Rock Hill, South Carolina Office)

MEMBERS OF FIRM

Frank H. Kennedy (1893-1975)
Hugh L. Lobdell (1908-1982)
Marcus T. Hickman
Clarence W. Walker
Henry C. Lomax
Edgar Love III
Charles V. Tompkins, Jr.
Glen B. Hardymon
J. Donnell Lassiter
Ross J. Smyth
A. Zachary Smith III
William F. Drew, Jr.
Charles O. DuBose
Raleigh A. Shoemaker
John M. Murchison, Jr.
Richard D. Stephens
F. Fincher Jarrell
Maynard E. Tipps
Wayne P. Huckel
J. Norfleet Pruden III
William C. Livingston
Lee West Movius
Joseph B. C. Kluttz
Jonathan A. Barrett
Eugene C. Pridgen
Stephen K. Rhyne
E. Allen Prichard
Raymond E. Owens, Jr.
Henry W. Flint
David H. Jones
James C. Hardin III (Resident, Rock Hill, South Carolina Office)
Peter McLean III
Myles E. Standish
Kiran H. Mehta
Michael S. Hawley
James P. Cooney III

(See Next Column)

KENNEDY COVINGTON LOBDELL & HICKMAN L.L.P.—*Continued*

MEMBERS OF FIRM (Continued)

Brian P. Evans
Jefferson W. Brown
Lynn Oliver Wenige
George C. Covington
Daniel L. Johnson, Jr.
Walter D. Fisher, Jr.
Stephen R. McCrae, Jr. (Resident, Rock Hill, South Carolina Office)
Alice Carmichael Richey
John H. Culver III
Herbert W. Hamilton (Resident, Rock Hill, South Carolina Office)
Dean A. Warren

ASSOCIATES

Dennard Lindsey Teague
W. Henry Sipe III (Resident, Rock Hill, South Carolina Office)
Beverly A. Carroll (Resident, Rock Hill, South Carolina Office)
Leslee K. Daugherty
Randall W. Lee
James L. Conner, II
Michael L. Flynn
William N. Harris
Warren P. Kean
Barbara R. Frith
A. Lee Hogewood III
Cory Hohnbaum
C. Corley Holt
Felicia A. Washington
David W. Brown, Jr.
Laura E. Cude (Resident, Rock Hill, South Carolina Office)
James E. Earle
Clifford R. Jarrett
Sean M. Jones
M. Paige Reece
Carol A. Jones Van Buren
A. Kimberly Raymer
Victoria S. Aiken (Resident, Rock Hill, South Carolina Office)
Daniel J. Ballou (Resident, Rock Hill, South Carolina Office)
Jennifer Campbell
Amy L. Pritchard
G. Lee Cory, Jr.
Lara E. Simmons
James T. Hedrick, Jr.
David P. Mitchell
Joseph W. Moss, Jr.
Eric S. Rohm
Kimberly Ann Short
Skottowe W. Smith, Jr.
Benjamin A. Yarbrough
Christopher J. Allabashi

Representative Clients: Allstate Insurance Co.; American Savio Corp.; Duke/Fluor Daniel; Duke Power Co.; First Union Corporation and Subsidiaries; General Motors Corp.; Lance, Inc.; Medical Mutual Insurance Co. of N.C.; NationsBank Corporation and Subsidiaries; Oakwood Homes Corp.

For full biographical listings, see the Martindale-Hubbell Law Directory

LINDSEY AND SCHRIMSHER, P.A. (AV)

2316 Randolph Road, 28207
Telephone: 704-333-2141
Fax: 704-376-2562

Robert L. Lindsey, Jr.
Frank L. Schrimsher
B. Scott Schrimsher

Representative Clients: American General Finance; C.I.T. Group/Sales Financing, Inc.; Crestar Bank; Crestar Mortgage; Wachovia Bank of North Carolina, N.A.; Central Carolina Bank & Trust Co.; NationsBanc Financial Services; Lawyers Title Insurance Corp.; First Union Home Equity Corp.; Sunshine Mortgage Corp.; ContiMortgage Corp.

For full biographical listings, see the Martindale-Hubbell Law Directory

MOORE & VAN ALLEN, PLLC (AV)

NationsBank Corporate Center, 100 North Tryon Street, Floor 47, 28202-4003
Telephone: 704-331-1000
FAX: 704-331-1159
Durham, North Carolina Office: Suite 800, 2200 West Main Street.
Telephone: 919-286-8000.
Fax: 919-286-8199.
Raleigh, North Carolina Office: One Hannover Square, Suite 1700, P.O. Box 26507.
Telephone: 919-828-4481.
FAX: 919-828-4254.

William Miller Abernethy, Jr.
A. Mark Adcock
H. Heath Alexander
Robert V. Baker
W. Doak Barnhardt
Mark E. Carpenter
R. Michael Childs
Dumont Clarke, IV
Daniel G. Clodfelter
Kenneth S. Coe
Aaron Dale Cowell, Jr.
Jeffrey J. Davis
Miriam Ann Dixon
David L. Eades
Robert J. Hahn (Not admitted in NC)
C. Wells Hall, III
George V. Hanna III
W. B. Hawfield, Jr.
Stephen D. Hope
James W. Hovis
H. Frasier Ives
Stephanie Lea Stromire Johnson
Christopher C. Kupec
Hal A. Levinson
Margaret Ann Behringer Maloney
Neill G. McBryde
Peter J. McGrath, Jr.
John V. McIntosh
James P. McLoughlin, Jr.
Randel E. Phillips
David J. Quattlebaum
T. Edmund Rast
Ernest W. Reigel
Barney Stewart III
David S. Walls

OF COUNSEL

Harry J. Grim
Donald J. Hodgens
William K. Van Allen

(See Next Column)

Michelle Monique Arruda
Jay S. Bilas
James Edward Dillon
Mary Elizabeth Erwin
William H. Fuller, III
John T. Gathings, Jr.
Granice Geyer-Smith
Grant Alan Harbrecht
Meredith West Shackelford Holler
Jacqueline Jarvis Jones
Todd Michael Kegler
Sarah Johnson Kromer
Karin Marie Rebescher McGinnis
John G. Mebane
Thomas Leo Mitchell
Gregory J. Murphy
John Webster Nurkin
Thomas C. O'Bannon
Jonathan D. Oechsle
Bradley E. Pearce
Robert C. Reed, III
Elizabeth L. Rippetoe
Susan Elizabeth Rowell
David H. Sampsell
Karen Stokes
Dirk P. Tischer
Victoria S. Windell
Jodi Pearson Zbinden

DURHAM, NORTH CAROLINA OFFICE

Brian R. Brown
James H. Clarke
Eugene F. Dauchert, Jr.
Edward L. Embree, III
Richard W. Evans
William E. Freeman
David A. Harlow
Charles R. Holton
Donna G. LeGrand
William L. London, III
Laura Bernstein Luger
Lisa James Mansfield
Neill G. McBryde
E. K. Powe
Richard Beverly Raney Webb
Mark H. Webbink
Reich L. Welborn

OF COUNSEL

Oliver W. Alphin
William G. Dosse

Gloria Cabada-Leman
Kevin M. Capalbo
Melanie Shelton Caudill
Andrew B. Cohen
Michael Johnston
Brian S. Kelly
Joseph H. Nanney, Jr.
Rita M.K. Purut
Agnes Maria Elizabeth Schipper
Randolph Lewis Stanford
Susan Elizabeth Wright

RALEIGH, NORTH CAROLINA OFFICE

Christopher J. Blake
Denise Smith Cline
Joseph W. Eason
David E. Fox
William H. Gammon
Douglas Ronald Ghidina
Dean M. Harris
Joseph D. Joyner, Jr.
C. Steven Mason
Isabel Worthy Mattox
John Spotswood Russell
Jonathan Drew Sasser
Hayden J. Silver, III
George M. Teague
Richard Beverly Raney Webb
William A. White (Not admitted in NC)

OF COUNSEL

Arch T. Allen, III
Leon M. Killian, III

Martin H. Brinkley
Robert Ashley Meynardie
Kelley Dixon Moye
Ann Marie Knops Nader
A. Bailey Nager
David S. Robinson
Beverly Lynn Rubin
Curtis J. Shipley
Joy Heath Thomas
Richard H. Vetter
Louis Samuel Watson, Jr.
Jeffrey Mark Young

For full biographical listings, see the Martindale-Hubbell Law Directory

PERRY, PATRICK, FARMER & MICHAUX, P.A. (AV)

2200 The Carillon, 227 West Trade Street, 28202
Telephone: 704-372-1120
Fax: 704-372-9635
Other Charlotte, North Carolina Office: South Park, 1901 Roxborough Road, Suite 100.
Telephone: 704-364-9695.
Fax: 704-364-9698.
Raleigh, North Carolina Office: 3716 National Drive, Suite 100.
Telephone: 919-787-8812.
Fax: 919-787-3312.

Robert E. Perry, Jr.
Bailey Patrick, Jr.
B. D. Farmer, III
Roy H. Michaux, Jr.
Richard W. Wilson
James G. Wallace
Carolyn Gilmer Hisley
Bryan W. Pittman
Laura L. Yaeger
Richard W. Moore (Resident, Raleigh Office)
J. Christopher Oates
W. Richard Jamison (Resident, Raleigh Office)
Leslie Miller Webb
David A. Raynes (Resident, Raleigh Office)
George S. Warren
David L. Huffstetler (Resident, Raleigh Office)
John H. Carmichael

Representative Clients: The Bissell Cos.; Centex Real Estate Corp.; Charlotte Pipe and Foundry Co.; The Crosland Group, Inc.; Crown Life Insurance Co.; C.D. Spangler Construction Co.; International Construction Equipment, Inc.; The Manufacturers Life Insurance Co.; M/I Schottenstein Cos., Inc.; The Ryland Group, Inc.

For full biographical listings, see the Martindale-Hubbell Law Directory

Charlotte—Continued

PETREE STOCKTON, L.L.P. (AV)

3500 One First Union Center, 301 South College Street, 28202-6001
Telephone: 704-338-5000
Telecopier: 704-338-5125
Winston-Salem, North Carolina Office: 1001 West Fourth Street, 27101-2400.
Telephone: 910-607-7300.
Telecopier: 910-607-7500.
Raleigh, North Carolina Office: 4101 Lake Boone Trail. 27607-6519.
Telephone: 919-420-1700.
Telecopier: 919-420-1800.

MEMBERS OF FIRM

David P. Underwood (1941-1982)
Ralph M. Stockton, Jr.
John T. Allred (Resident)
Ray S. Farris (Resident)
E. Lynwood Mallard (Resident)
Thomas E. Cummings (Resident)
J. Michael Booe (Resident)
Jackson N. Steele (Resident)
David B. Hamilton (Resident)
F. Joseph Treacy, Jr. (Resident)
Meg D. Goldstein (Resident)
William F. Potts, Jr. (Resident)
Elizabeth L. Moore
Charles E. Johnson (Resident)
Elizabeth G. Wren (Resident)
Bruce A. Buckley (Resident)
L. Elizabeth Henry (Resident)
J. Neil Robinson (Resident)
Eileen McDermott Taylor (Resident)
Rebecca S. Henderson
Richard C. Gaskins, Jr. (Resident)
Richard E. Fay (Resident)
Linda J. Sarazen (Resident)
Kimberlee Scott (Resident)

ASSOCIATES

Susan Ivy McCrory (Resident)
Dana Disque Hearn (Resident)
Anne E. Essaye (Resident)
B. David Carson (Resident)
David B. Whelpley, Jr. (Resident)
Richard E. Morton (Resident)
Charles H. Rabon, Jr. (Resident)
Jonathan P. Moss (Resident)
Noelle E. Lambert (Resident)
Keith J. Merritt (Resident)
Christopher J. Brady (Resident)
Lucy Vanderberry Fountain
Amy Yager Jenkins (Resident)
John C. Nicholls (Resident)
Shawn F. Sullivan (Resident)
Christine M. Schilling
Teresa DeLoatch
Rebecca K. Gatehouse
Cynthia A. Glasgow

Representative Clients: First Union National Bank; Sara Lee Corp.; Mobile Oil Corp.; CPC International, Inc.; Southern Bell Telephone and Telegraph Co.; Charlotte Hornets; Shelton Companies.

For full biographical listings, see the Martindale-Hubbell Law Directory

RAYBURN, MOON & SMITH, P.A. (AV)

The Carillon, 227 West Trade Street, Suite 1200, 28202
Telephone: 704-334-0891
FAX: 704-377-1897; 704-358-8866

Albert F. Durham
Travis W. Moon
C. Richard Rayburn, Jr.
James C. Smith
W. Scott Cooper
Matthew R. Joyner
James L. Bagwell
Cynthia D. Lewis
Patricia B. Edmondson
Paul R. Baynard
Laura D. Fennell
G. Kirkland Hardymon

For full biographical listings, see the Martindale-Hubbell Law Directory

ROBINSON, BRADSHAW & HINSON, P.A. (AV)

One Independence Center, 101 North Tryon Street, Suite 1900, 28246-1900
Telephone: 704-377-2536
Fax: 704-378-4000
Telex: 802046
Rock Hill, South Carolina Office: The Guardian Building, One Law Place, Suite 600, Post Office Drawer 12070.
Telephone: 803-325-2900.
FAX: 803-325-2929.

Russell M. Robinson, II
Robert W. Bradshaw, Jr.
Robin L. Hinson
David A. White (Resident, Rock Hill, South Carolina Office)
Robert C. Sink
A. Ward McKeithen
Gibson L. Smith, Jr.
Graham D. Holding, Jr.
Carroll M. Pitts, Jr. (Resident, Rock Hill, South Carolina Office)
Carl E. Johnson, Jr.
Richard A. Vinroot
Claude Q. Freeman, Jr.
William T. Graves
John R. Wester
Martin L. Brackett, Jr.
John R. Miller
Peter C. Buck
Robert M. Bryan
Christy Eve Reid
Robert G. Griffin
Edwin F. Lucas, III
Thomas B. Henson
Everett J. Bowman
Benjamin A. Johnson (Resident, Rock Hill, South Carolina Office)
Haynes P. Lea
Caroline Wannamaker Sink
Henry H. Ralston
Herman Spence, III
Brent A. Torstrick
Mark W. Merritt
Ken R. Bramlett, Jr.
Garland S. Cassada
Robert W. Fuller
Kent J. McCready
David C. Wright, III
Robert W. Simmons
Frank E. Emory, Jr.

(See Next Column)

Louis A. Bledsoe, III
Christopher W. Loeb
D. Blaine Sanders
Richard W. Gibson, Jr.
Stokely G. Caldwell, Jr.
Stephen M. Lynch
R. Steven DeGeorge
Jane S. Ratteree
Caroline T. Wilson
Allain C. Andry, IV
Benjamin W. Baldwin
David R. Wiles
John B. Garver, III
Edward F. Hennessey, IV
Richard L. Mack
Allen K. Robertson
James C. Reno, Jr. (Resident, Rock Hill, South Carolina Office)
Stuart H. Johnson
Karen A. Gledhill
Charlotte L. Offerdahl
Julie C. Chiu
J. Daniel Bishop
Charles C. Lucas, III
Mimi D. Lucas
Patrick S. Bryant
William W. Toole
J. Stephen Dockery, III
David M. Schilli
Tamille W. Bryant
Sarah B. Boucher (Not admitted in NC)
Brian S. McCoy (Not admitted in NC)
Frank H. Lancaster
Brett J. Denton
S. Graham Robinson
Keith A. Smith
Julian H. Wright, Jr.

OF COUNSEL

John M. Conley

For full biographical listings, see the Martindale-Hubbell Law Directory

RUFF, BOND, COBB, WADE & MCNAIR, L.L.P. (AV)

2100 Two First Union Center, 301 South Tryon Street, 28282-8283
Telephone: 704-377-1634
FAX: 704-342-3308

MEMBERS OF FIRM

Thomas C. Ruff
Lyn Bond, Jr.
James O. Cobb
Hamlin L. Wade
William H. McNair
Marvin A. Bethune
Moses Luski
Francis W. Sturges
Robert S. Adden, Jr.
James H. Pickard

ASSOCIATES

George R. Jurch, III
Stephen D. Koehler

For full biographical listings, see the Martindale-Hubbell Law Directory

SMITH HELMS MULLISS & MOORE, L.L.P. (AV)

227 North Tryon Street, P.O. Box 31247, 28231
Telephone: 704-343-2000
Telecopier: 704-334-8467
Telex: 572460
Greensboro, North Carolina Office: Smith Helms Mulliss & Moore, Suite 1400 First Union Tower, 300 North Greene Street, P.O. Box 21927.
Telephone: 910-378-5200.
Telecopier: 910-379-9558.
Raleigh, North Carolina Office: 316 West Edenton Street, P.O. Box 27525.
Telephone: 919-755-8700.
Telecopier: 919-828-7938.

COUNSEL

John W. Johnston
James H. Guterman

MEMBERS OF FIRM

William H. Bobbitt (1926-1968)
William F. Mulliss (1911-1987)
Larry J. Dagenhart
E. Osborne Ayscue, Jr.
Herbert H. Browne, Jr.
R. Malloy McKeithen
Robert B. Cordle
Kenneth C. Day
Boyd C. Campbell, Jr.
Jonathan E. Buchan, Jr.
Saxby M. Chaplin
Douglas W. Ey, Jr.
E. Graham McGoogan, Jr.
Peter J. Covington
J. Richard Hazlett
Catherine E. Thompson
Robert G. Brinkley (Also at Greensboro)
Robert H. Pryor
H. Landis Wade, Jr.
B. Palmer McArthur, Jr.
L. D. Simmons, II
Benne C. Hutson
R. Douglas Harmon
James G. Middlebrooks
Harrison L. Marshall, Jr.
Robert W. Cramer
Rolly L. Chambers
Charles F. Bowman
Manley W. Roberts
Stephen L. Cordell
Scott P. Vaughn
Elizabeth Whitener Goode

ASSOCIATES

Irving M. Brenner
Bradley R. Kutrow
Anne F. Team
Julie Zydron Griggs
Harry J. Stathopoulos
Eugene Steven Griggs
Gregory S. Hilderbran
Kathy L. Pilkington
Wendy J. Allen
Leigh F. Moran
Brian D. Barger
Melissa Garrett Burns
Katherine T. Lange
Stephen David Allred
Christopher S. Nesbit
Maurice O. Green
Wade M. Kennedy
Robert Scott Boatwright
Kevin M. Bringewatt
Robert S. McLean
David B. Fountain
Jeff T. Harris

For full biographical listings, see the Martindale-Hubbell Law Directory

Charlotte—Continued

UNDERWOOD KINSEY WARREN & TUCKER, P.A. (AV)

2020 Charlotte Plaza, 201 South College Street, 28244
Telephone: 704-333-1200
Telecopier: 704-377-9630

William E. Underwood, Jr.
C. Ralph Kinsey, Jr.
Joseph Warren, III
Robert B. Tucker, Jr.
John H. Northey III
Shirley J. Linn
Kenneth S. Cannaday
William L. Sitton, Jr.
Susan L. Sowell
Carlton A. Shannon, Jr.
Richard L. Farley
Russell M. Black
Francis Morris Pinckney, III
Kimberlye Fayssoux Cornelson

OF COUNSEL

Frank W. Snepp

Representative Clients: Aetna Casualty & Surety Co.; Bojangles' Restaurants Inc.; Charlotte/Douglas International Airport; Dick Keffer Pontiac-GMC Truck, Inc.; Cameron M. Harris & Co.; Kyle Petty Development Co.; Sabco Racing; Southeast Anesthesia Associates, P.A.; Thor-Lo, Inc.

For full biographical listings, see the Martindale-Hubbell Law Directory

WOMBLE CARLYLE SANDRIDGE & RICE (AV)

A Professional Limited Liability Company
3300 One First Union Center, 301 S. College Street, 28202-6025
Telephone: 704-331-4900
Telecopy: 704-331-4955
Telex: 853609
Winston-Salem, North Carolina Office: 1600 Southern National Financial Center.
Telephone: 919-721-3600.
Telecopy: 919-721-3660.
Telex: 806498.
Raleigh, North Carolina Office: 2100 First Union Capitol Center, 150 Fayetteville Street Mall, P.O. Box 831.
Telephone: 919-755-2100.
Telecopy: 919-755-2150.
Telex: 806498.
Atlanta, Georgia Office: One Ninety One Peachtree Tower, 191 Peachtree Street N.E., Suite 3250.
Telephone: 404-614-2580.
Fax: 404-614-2595.

MEMBERS OF FIRM

Garza Baldwin, III
Timothy G. Barber
G. Michael Barnhill
James R. Bryant, III
Gary D. Chamblee
Joe B. Cogdell, Jr.
Jim D. Cooley
James E. Daniel
J. Carlton Fleming
Deborah L. Fletcher
Debbie Weston Harden
Bobby D. Hinson
Cyrus M. Johnson, Jr.
James E. Johnson, Jr.
David E. Johnston
William C. Raper
J. Alexander Salisbury
F. Lane Williamson

RESIDENT ASSOCIATES

David W. Dabbs
Steven D. Gardner
W. Clark Goodman
Mark P. Henriques
Jane Jeffries Jones
Douglas A. Mays
William P. McMillan (Not admitted in NC)
Kenneth B. Oettinger, Jr.
Richard L. Rainey
Scott W. Stevenson

OF COUNSEL

Bradford A. DeVore

Representative Clients: Childress Klein Properties, Inc.; Food Lion, Inc.; Fieldcrest Cannon, Inc.; J.A. Jones Construction Company; Parkdale Mills, Inc.; Duke Power Company; Bowles Hollowell Conner & Company; ALLTEL Carolina, Inc.; Belk Store Services, Inc.; Philip Holzmann A.G.

For full biographical listings, see the Martindale-Hubbell Law Directory

CLAYTON, Johnston Co.

ALLEN R. TEW, P.A. (AV)

202 South Lombard Street, P.O. Box 145, 27520
Telephone: 919-553-6142; 553-2143
FAX: 919-553-8742

Allen R. Tew

For full biographical listings, see the Martindale-Hubbell Law Directory

*CONCORD,** Cabarrus Co.

HARTSELL, HARTSELL & MILLS, P.A. (AV)

77 McCachern Boulevard, S.E., P.O. Box 368, 28025
Telephone: 704-786-5161

(See Next Column)

Luther T. Hartsell (1870-1961)
Luther T. Hartsell, Jr. (1902-1961)
William Lee Mills, Jr. (1914-1980)
J. Maxton Elliott
W. Erwin Spainhour
Fletcher L. Hartsell, Jr.
Starkey Sharp, V

OF COUNSEL

John Sharpe Hartsell

Representative Clients: First Charter National Bank; Southern Railway Co.; Nationwide Insurance Co.; Travelers Indemnity Co.; The Shoe Show, Inc.; S & D Coffee, Inc.; Cabarrus County Board of Education; Cabarrus Memorial Hospital; Lawyers Title Insurance Corp.; Cabarrus County.

For full biographical listings, see the Martindale-Hubbell Law Directory

WILLIAMS, BOGER, GRADY, DAVIS & TUTTLE, P.A. (AV)

147 Union Street, South, P.O. Box 810, 28025
Telephone: 704-782-1173
FAX: 704-788-2215
Kannapolis, North Carolina Office: 708 McLain Road, P.O. Box 2.
Telephone: 704-932-3157.
FAX: 704-932-9597.

John R. Boger, Jr.
Thomas Myers Grady
Samuel F. Davis, Jr.
M. Slate Tuttle, Jr.
Randall R. Combs
Duane S. Miller

OF COUNSEL

John Hugh Williams

Representative Clients: Southtrust FSB; Cabarrus Savings Bank; Hilbish Motor Co.; Sabco Racing, Inc.; Schrader Racing, Inc.; Wallace Racing, Inc.; Kulwicki Racing, Inc.; Charlotte Motor Speedway, Inc.; Irvan Racing, Inc.; Cale Yarborough Motor Sports, Inc.

For full biographical listings, see the Martindale-Hubbell Law Directory

CONWAY, Northampton Co. — (Refer to Murfreesboro)

*CURRITUCK,** Currituck Co. — (Refer to Elizabeth City)

*DANBURY,** Stokes Co. — (Refer to Madison)

*DOBSON,** Surry Co. — (Refer to Mount Airy)

DUNN, Harnett Co. — (Refer to Lillington)

*DURHAM,** Durham Co.

FAISON & FLETCHER (AV)

Suite 1400 University Tower, 3100 Tower Boulevard Post Office Box 51729, 27717-1729
Telephone: 919-489-9001
FAX: 919-489-5774 WATS: 800-437-9001
Wilmington, North Carolina Office: 130 North Front Street, Suite 300.
Telephone: 919-251-9900.
FAX: 919-251-9667.

MEMBERS OF FIRM

O. William Faison
George L. Fletcher
Reginald B. Gillespie, Jr.
Gary R. Poole

ASSOCIATES

Michael R. Ortiz
Cynthia T. Shriner
Selina S. Nomeir
David L. Ray
Lisa L. Lanier
John T. Honeycutt
Catherine L. Clark
Keith D. Burns
Donna Miller-Slade

OF COUNSEL

Kathleen D.H. Pawlowski (Resident, Wilmington Office)

For full biographical listings, see the Martindale-Hubbell Law Directory

MOORE & VAN ALLEN, PLLC (AV)

Suite 800, 2200 West Main Street, 27705
Telephone: 919-286-8000
Fax: 919-286-8199
Charlotte, North Carolina Office: NationsBank Corporate Center, 100 North Tryon Street, Floor 47.
Telephone: 704-331-1000.
Fax: 704-331-1159.
Raleigh, North Carolina Office: One Hannover Square, Suite 1700, P.O. Box 26507.
Telephone: 919-828-4481.
Fax: 919-828-4254.

Brian R. Brown
Lewis A. Cheek
James H. Clarke
Eugene F. Dauchert, Jr.
Edward L. Embree, III
Richard W. Evans
William E. Freeman
David A. Harlow
Charles R. Holton
Donna G. LeGrand
William L. London, III
Laura Bernstein Luger
Lisa James Mansfield
Neill G. McBryde
E. K. Powe
Richard Beverly Raney Webb
Reich L. Welborn

(See Next Column)

MOORE & VAN ALLEN PLLC, *Durham—Continued*

OF COUNSEL

Oliver W. Alphin | William G. Dosse

Gloria Cabada-Leman
Kevin M. Capalbo
Melanie Shelton Caudill
Andrew B. Cohen
Michael Johnston
Joseph H. Nanney, Jr.
Rita M.K. Purut
Agnes Maria Elizabeth Schipper
Randolph Lewis Stanford
Mark H. Webbink
Susan Elizabeth Wright

For full biographical listings, see the Martindale-Hubbell Law Directory

NEWSOM, GRAHAM, HEDRICK & KENNON, P.A. (AV)

Suite 1200 University Tower, 3100 Tower Boulevard, P.O. Box 51579, 27717-1579
Telephone: 919-490-0500
Telecopier: 919-490-0873

James T. Hedrick
A. William Kennon
John L. Crill
John E. Markham, Jr.
Katherine McKee Holeman
William P. Daniell
Robert O. Belo
Joel M. Craig
John R. Long
David S. Kennett
G. Rhodes Craver

Dieter Mauch
Linda Imboden Ellington
Vedia Jones-Richardson
Henry A. Mitchell, III
Amy B. Quillen
Michelle Buerkle Beischer

OF COUNSEL

James L. Newsom
Alexander H. Graham, Jr.
Lynne Townsend Albert
Donald M. Etheridge, Jr.

Representative Clients: Wachovia Bank & Trust Co.; Duke Power Co.; Liggett Group, Inc.; General Telephone Company of the South; Exxon Corp.; Kemper Group of Insurance Cos.; Liberty Mutual Group.

For full biographical listings, see the Martindale-Hubbell Law Directory

EDEN, Rockingham Co.

HARRINGTON & STULTZ (AV)

708 West Washington Street, P.O. Box 989, 27289-0989
Telephone: 910-623-8436
Fax: 910-627-4243
Wentworth, North Carolina Office: 2 Courthouse Square.
Telephone: 910-349-2943.

MEMBERS OF FIRM

Thomas S. Harrington | J. Hoyte Stultz, Jr.

Representative Clients: Morgan Drive Away, Inc.; Jimmy Wright Pontiac-Buick-GMC, Inc.
Local Counsel: Duke Power Co.
Approved Attorneys for: Lawyers Title Insurance Corp.; United Title Insurance Co.; Chicago Title Insurance Co.; Jefferson Pilot Title Insurance Co.; First Title Insurance Co.

For full biographical listings, see the Martindale-Hubbell Law Directory

*ELIZABETH CITY,** Pasquotank Co.

HORNTHAL, RILEY, ELLIS & MALAND, L.L.P. (AV)

301 E. Main Street, P.O. Box 220, 27909
Telephone: 919-335-0871
Fax: 919-335-4223
Nags Head, North Carolina Office: 2502 South Croatan Highway, P.O. Box 310, 27959-0310.
Telephone: 919-441-0871.
Telefax: 919-441-8822.

L. P. Hornthal, Jr.
J. Fred Riley
M. H. Hood Ellis
Mark M. Maland
Donald C. Prentiss
Robert B. Hobbs, Jr. (Resident, Nags Head Office)
John D. Leidy

ASSOCIATES

Michael P. Sanders
Lee L. Leidy
Phillip K. Woods

Representative Clients: CIGNA Group; Elizabeth City-Pasquotank County Board of Education; Camden County Board of Education; Kemper Insurance Group; State Farm Mutual; Travelers Insurance Co.; Wachovia Bank of North Carolina, N.A.; Branch Banking & Trust Co.; College of the Albemarle; USF&G.

For full biographical listings, see the Martindale-Hubbell Law Directory

WHITE, HALL & DIXON (AV)

501 East Main Street, P.O. Box 304, 27907-0304
Telephone: 919-338-3906
Telecopier: 919-335-2456

(See Next Column)

MEMBERS OF FIRM

Gerald F. White
John H. Hall, Jr.
Samuel B. Dixon

Representative Clients: Shelby Mutual Insurance Co.; Lumbermen's Mutual Casualty Co.; Utica Mutual Insurance Co.; Kemper Insurance Group; Maryland Casualty Co.; Security Insurance Group; United States Automobile Assn.; Pennsylvania Manufacturers' Association Insurance Co.; Gates County Board of Education; Pasquotank County.

For full biographical listings, see the Martindale-Hubbell Law Directory

*ELIZABETHTOWN,** Bladen Co.

HESTER, GRADY, HESTER & GREENE (AV)

115 Courthouse Drive, P.O. Drawer 127, 28337
Telephone: 910-862-3191
FAX: 910-862-4802

MEMBERS OF FIRM

Worth H. Hester
Gary A. Grady
H. Clifton Hester
Paula Hobbs Greene

ASSOCIATES

W. White, III

OF COUNSEL

Frank T. Grady

For full biographical listings, see the Martindale-Hubbell Law Directory

ENFIELD, Halifax Co. — (Refer to Roanoke Rapids)

FARMVILLE, Pitt Co. — (Refer to Greenville)

*FAYETTEVILLE,** Cumberland Co.

McCOY, WEAVER, WIGGINS, CLEVELAND & RAPER (AV)

222 Maiden Lane, P.O. Box 2129, 28301
Telephone: 910-483-8104
FAX: 910-483-0094
West Fayetteville Office: 500 McPherson Church Road.
Fax: 910-867-6576.

MEMBERS OF FIRM

Donald W. McCoy
L. Stacy Weaver, Jr.
Richard M. Wiggins
Alfred E. Cleveland
John E. Raper, Jr.
Jeffrey Neill Surles
Anne Mayo Evans

ASSOCIATES

Rodney B. Davis
Jeff Dunham
Sandra Martin Clark

General Counsel for: North Carolina Natural Gas Corp.; United Carolina Bank; Mid-South Insurance Co.; Putt-Putt Golf Courses of America, Inc.; Fayetteville Technical Community College; Methodist College, Inc.
Representative Clients: United States Fidelity & Guaranty Co.; Ellis-Walker Builders, Inc.; Time-Warner, Inc.

For full biographical listings, see the Martindale-Hubbell Law Directory

ROSE, RAY, WINFREY, O'CONNOR & LESLIE, P.A. (AV)

214 Mason Street, P.O. Box 1239, 28302-1239
Telephone: 910-483-2101
FAX: 910-483-8444

George M. Rose (1846-1924)
Charles G. Rose (1880-1948)
Robert G. Ray
Ronald E. Winfrey
Steven J. O'Connor
Pamela S. Leslie

OF COUNSEL

Chas. G. Rose, Jr.

Brian K. Manning
Geraldine O. Spates
James A. Hadley, Jr.

Representative Clients: Home Federal Savings & Loan Assn.; Carolina Lithotripsy, Ltd.; Parker Marking Systems, Inc.; Modern Moving and Storage, Inc.; Fayetteville Diagnostic Center, Ltd.; Cross Creek Plaza, Inc.; Medical Arts Imaging Center Limited Partnership; Southern Peanut, Inc.; Riddle Commercial Properties, Inc.

For full biographical listings, see the Martindale-Hubbell Law Directory

SINGLETON, MURRAY, CRAVEN & INMAN (AV)

Highland Place, 2517 Raeford Road, P.O. Drawer 53007, 28305-3007
Telephone: 910-483-4990
FAX: 910-483-6822

MEMBERS OF FIRM

Rudolph G. Singleton, Jr.
Ocie F. Murray, Jr.
Richard T. Craven
Stephen G. Inman

Representative Clients: E. I. duPont de Nemours & Co.; First Union National Bank; State Farm Insurance Cos.; Bankers and Shippers Insurance Co.; Ford Motor Co.; Metropolitan Life Insurance Co.; Westinghouse Corp.; Amerisure Cos.; Southeastern Hospital Supply Co.; Lawyers Mutual Liability Insurance Company of North Carolina.

For full biographical listings, see the Martindale-Hubbell Law Directory

FOREST CITY, Rutherford Co.

ROBERT W. WOLF (AV)

12 South Broadway, 28043
Telephone: 704-245-7366
Fax: 704-245-7359

ASSOCIATES

Laura J. Bridges

Approved Attorney for: Lawyers Title Insurance Cos.; Chicago Title Insurance Co.; Commonwealth Title Insurance Co.; Investors Title Insurance Co.; Federal Land Bank, Columbia.
Representative Clients: Rutherford County Board of Education; Branch Banking & Trust Co.; Town of Alexander Mills.

For full biographical listings, see the Martindale-Hubbell Law Directory

*FRANKLIN,** Macon Co.

JONES, KEY, MELVIN & PATTON, P.A. (AV)

19 East Main Street, P.O. Box 108, 28734
Telephone: 704-524-4444
Fax: 704-369-7343
Highlands, North Carolina Office: 4th Street.
Telephone: 704-526-3762.

Richard S. Jones, Jr.
Bobby Joe Key
Richard Melvin
Lawrence M. Patton, Jr.
Gilbert R. Key, II
Chester M. Jones
E. Elizabeth Lefler
Fred Howell Jones

Representative Clients: Highlands County Club; Macon Savings & Loan Assn.; Wildcat Cliffs Country Club; County of Macon; First Union National Bank; Town of Franklin; Bank of Clayton.
Approved Attorneys for: Fidelity National Title Insurance Co.; Lawyers Title Insurance Corp.

For full biographical listings, see the Martindale-Hubbell Law Directory

*GASTONIA,** Gaston Co.

ALALA MULLEN HOLLAND & COOPER P.A. (AV)

301 South York Street, P.O. Box 488, 28053
Telephone: 704-864-6751
Facsimile: 704-861-8394

Langdon M. Cooper
Joseph B. Alala, Jr.
Raboteau T. Wilder, Jr.
H. Randolph Sumner
Nancy Borders Paschall
Mark E. Shelley
J. Mark Heavner
Jane Foy Painter
John H. Griffing
J. Reid McGraw, Jr.
James H. Price
Jesse V. Bone, Jr.
Blake W. Hassan

COUNSEL

James Mullen (Retired)
J. Mack Holland, Jr. (Retired)
Elizabeth Neisler Sumner

Representative Client: Belmont Abbey College.

For full biographical listings, see the Martindale-Hubbell Law Directory

TIM L. HARRIS AND ASSOCIATES (AV)

223 West Main Avenue, P.O. Box 249, 28053-0249
Telephone: 704-864-3409
Fax: 704-853-1040
Charlotte, North Carolina Office: 4000 Tuckaseegee Road.
Telephone: 704-392-4111.

MEMBERS OF FIRM

Tim L. Harris
Jerry Neil Ragan

ASSOCIATES

T. Scott White
Russell L. Needell
William K. Goldfarb
Stephen M. Coe

For full biographical listings, see the Martindale-Hubbell Law Directory

STOTT, HOLLOWELL, PALMER & WINDHAM (AV)

3rd Floor, Branch Banking & Trust Building, 110 West Main Avenue, P.O. Box 995, 28053-0995
Telephone: 704-864-3425
Fax: 704-864-0478

MEMBERS OF FIRM

L. B. Hollowell (1904-1981)
Grady B. Stott
Linwood Branton Hollowell, Jr.
James C. Windham, Jr.
H. William Palmer

ASSOCIATES

Aaron E. Bradshaw
Charles L. Graham, Jr.
Charlton K. Torrence, III
Martha R. Thompson
John M. Nunnally
Elizabeth A. Danziger

(See Next Column)

Representative Clients: Wix Corp.; Allstate Insurance Co.; State Farm Mutual Automobile Insurance Co.; United States Fidelity & Guaranty Co.; Travelers Insurance Co.; Nationwide Mutual Insurance Co.; The Hartford and Kemper Group; Aetna Insurance; Parkdale Mills, Inc.; Gaston County.

For full biographical listings, see the Martindale-Hubbell Law Directory

*GATESVILLE,** Gates Co. — (Refer to Elizabeth City)

*GOLDSBORO,** Wayne Co. — (Refer to Smithfield)

*GRAHAM,** Alamance Co.

RIDGE, HOLLEY & MORRIS (AV)

A Partnership including a Professional Association
114 South Maple Street, P.O. Drawer 148, 27253-0148
Telephone: 910-227-7411
Fax: 910-227-7415

Paul H. Ridge (P.A.)
David Kent Holley
Gary Sven Morris

Representative Clients: The Alamance County Board of Education; Duke Power Co.; L.I.V. Pritchett, Jr. Inc.; Wendy's of Burlington, Inc.
Trial Counsel for: Southern Railway Co. (Alamance and Orange Counties).

For full biographical listings, see the Martindale-Hubbell Law Directory

*GREENSBORO,** Guilford Co.

ADAMS KLEEMEIER HAGAN HANNAH & FOUTS (AV)

North Carolina Trust Center, 301 N. Elm Street, P.O. Box 3463, 27402
Telephone: 910-373-1600
Fax: 910-273-5357

MEMBERS OF FIRM

John A. Kleemeier, Jr. (1911-1973)
William J. Adams, Jr. (1908-1993)
Walter L. Hannah
Daniel W. Fouts
Robert G. Baynes
Joseph W. Moss
Clinton Eudy, Jr.
M. Jay DeVaney
Michael H. Godwin
W. Winburne King III
F. Cooper Brantley
Bruce H. Connors
Charles T. Hagan III
Larry I. Moore III
Elizabeth Dunn White
W. B. Rodman Davis
Thomas W. Brawner
Margaret Shea Burnham
Peter G. Pappas
William M. Wilcox IV
Katherine Bonan McDiarmid
David A. Senter
J. Alexander S. Barrett
Christine L. Myatt

OF COUNSEL

Charles T. Hagan, Jr.
Horace R. Kornegay

ASSOCIATES

Trudy A. Ennis
A. Scott Jackson
Amiel J. Rossabi
James W. Bryan
Betty Pincus Balcomb
Edward L. Bleynat, Jr.
Stephen A. Mayo
Louise Anderson Maultsby
R. Harper Heckman
Dena Beth Langley
David S. Pokela

Representative Clients: NationsBank of North Carolina, N.A.; Hafele America Co.; Duke Power Co.; U.S. Fidelity & Guaranty Co.; Dillard Paper Co.; Carolina Steel Corp.; Electrical South Inc.

For full biographical listings, see the Martindale-Hubbell Law Directory

BROOKS, PIERCE, MCLENDON, HUMPHREY & LEONARD, L.L.P. (AV)

2000 Renaissance Plaza, 230 North Elm Street, P.O. Box 26000, 27420-6000
Telephone: 910-373-8850
Telex: 574301
Facsimile: 910-378-1001
Raleigh, North Carolina Office: 1600 First Union Capitol Center, 150 Fayetteville Street Mall, P.O. Box 1800.
Telephone: 919-839-0300.
Facsimile: 919-839-0304.

MEMBERS OF FIRM

Aubrey L. Brooks (1872-1958)
William H. Holderness (1904-1965)
Lennox P. McLendon (1890-1968)
Kenneth M. Brim (1898-1974)
C. Theodore Leonard, Jr. (1929-1983)
Claude C. Pierce (1913-1988)
Thornton H. Brooks (1912-1988)
G. Neil Daniels (Of Counsel, 1973--)
Lennox P. McLendon, Jr.
Hubert Humphrey
Edgar B. Fisher, Jr.
W. Erwin Fuller, Jr.
James T. Williams, Jr.
Wade H. Hargrove
M. Daniel McGinn
Michael D. Meeker
William G. McNairy
Edward C. Winslow, III
Howard L. Williams
George W. House
William P. H. Cary
Reid L. Phillips
Robert A. Singer
John H. Small
Randall A. Underwood
S. Leigh Rodenbough, IV
William G. Ross, Jr.
Jill R. Wilson
Marc D. Bishop
Jim W. Phillips, Jr.

(See Next Column)

BROOKS, PIERCE, MCLENDON, HUMPHREY & LEONARD L.L.P., *Greensboro—Continued*

MEMBERS OF FIRM (Continued)

Mack Sperling
Jeffrey E. Oleynik
Mark Davidson
Melissa H. Weaver
James R. Saintsing
John W. Ormand, III
James H. Jeffries, IV
Robert J. King, III
V. Randall Tinsley
John R. Archambault
S. Kyle Woosley
Catherine Thomas McGee
William C. Scott
Mark J. Prak
William A. Davis, II
Marcus W. Trathen

ASSOCIATES

Anne C. Brennan
Daniel M. Sroka
Forrest W. Campbell, Jr.
Ellen P. Hamrick
Allison M. Grimm
Jean C. Brooks
James C. Adams, II
Elizabeth S. Brewington
John K. Eason
Wayne A. Logan
H. Arthur Bolick, II
Natasha Rath Marcus

General Counsel for: N.C. Alliance of Community Financial Institutions; W.H. Weaver Construction Co.
Division Counsel for: Norfolk Southern Railway Co.
Attorneys for: Burlington Industries, Inc.; Masco Corp.; Wachovia Bank of North Carolina, N.A.; Provident Life & Accident Insurance Co.; Pennsylvania & Southern Gas Co.; AMP Inc.
Labor Counsel for: Lorillard Tobacco Co.

For full biographical listings, see the Martindale-Hubbell Law Directory

CARRUTHERS & ROTH, P.A. (AV)

235 North Edgeworth Street, P.O. Box 540, 27402
Telephone: 910-379-8651
Telecopier: 910-273-7885

Joseph T. Carruthers, Jr. (1906-1992)
Charles E. Roth (1917-1992)
Walter Rand
Seldon E. Patty
Thomas E. Wagg, III
Kenneth M. Greene
Richard L. Vanore
William L. Tankersley, III
Kenneth R. Keller
L. Worth Holleman, Jr.
Arthur A. Vreeland
Thomas W. Sinks
Howard L. Borum
J. Scott Dillon
J. Stanley Atwell
Kenneth L. Jones
June L. Basden
Desmond G. Sheridan
Michael J. Allen

Pamela Sarsfield Fox
Barbara L Curry
Gregory S. Williams
Keith A. Wood
John M. Flynn
Robert R. Niccolini

Representative Clients: AC Corporation; The Bank of New York; Barclays Commercial Corp.; Chrysler Financial Corp.; First Union Commercial Corp.; Kay Chemical Company; Kemper Insurance Group; Marine Midland Business Loans, Inc.; Metropolitan Life Insurance Co.; Thompson-Arthur Paving Co.

For full biographical listings, see the Martindale-Hubbell Law Directory

CLARK WHARTON & BERRY (AV)

600 Dixie Building, 125 South Elm Street, P.O. Box 1349, 27402
Telephone: 910-275-7275
Fax: 910-275-0672

David M. Clark
Richard L. Wharton
Frederick L. Berry
Virginia Schabacker

Representative Clients: The Prudential Insurance Company of America (litigation); Johnson Controls, Inc.
Approved Attorneys for: Jefferson-Pilot Insurance Co.

For full biographical listings, see the Martindale-Hubbell Law Directory

COOKE & COOKE (AV)

Suite 301 First Citizens Bank Building, 100 South Elm Street, P.O. Box 187, 27402
Telephone: 910-272-4514
Facsimile: 910-272-4516

MEMBERS OF FIRM

Arthur O. Cooke (1916-1983)
William Owen Cooke
Barden W. Cooke
William O. Cooke, Jr.

Representative Clients: N. C. Grange Mutual Insurance Co.; Piedmont Triad Airport Authority; Brown-Gardiner Drug Co.; Engineered Plastics, Inc.; Strandberg Engineering Laboratories; Texwood, Inc.

For full biographical listings, see the Martindale-Hubbell Law Directory

ISAACSON ISAACSON & GRIMES (AV)

Suite 400 NationsBank Building, 101 West Friendly Avenue, P.O. Box 1888, 27402
Telephone: 910-275-7626
FAX: 910-273-7293

(See Next Column)

MEMBERS OF FIRM

Henry H. Isaacson
Marc L. Isaacson
L. Charles Grimes

ASSOCIATES

Thomas B. Kobrin

For full biographical listings, see the Martindale-Hubbell Law Directory

IVEY, IVEY, MCCLELLAN & GATTON, L.L.P. (AV)

121 South Elm Street, P.O. Box 3324, 27402
Telephone: 910-274-4658
TELEFAX: 910-274-4540

MEMBERS OF FIRM

Charles M. Ivey, Jr. (1914-1993)
Charles M. Ivey, III
Robert L. McClellan
Edwin R. Gatton
James K. Talcott
Lillian H. Pinto

ASSOCIATES

John M. Blust
Kevin W. Whiteheart
Marilyn H. Stout
Hugh A. Winters

Representative Clients: First Home Federal Savings and Loan Assoc.; First Citizens Bank & Trust Company; First National Bank of Randolph Co.; Wachovia Bank and Trust; Friendly Rubber & Seal Co.; Mercedes-Benz Credit Corp.; Norwest Financial, North Carolina.
Approved Attorneys for: Jefferson-Pilot Title Insurance Co.; Lawyers Title Insurance Corp.

For full biographical listings, see the Martindale-Hubbell Law Directory

NICHOLS, CAFFREY, HILL & EVANS, L.L.P. (AV)

1400 Renaissance Plaza, 230 North Elm Street, P.O. Box 989, 27402
Telephone: 910-379-1390
Fax: 910-379-1198

MEMBERS OF FIRM

Welch Jordan (1912-1976)
William D. Caffrey (1928-1991)
Karl N. Hill, Jr.
G. Marlin Evans
Thomas C. Duncan
William Welch Jordan
Lindsay Reeves Davis, Jr.
Joseph R. Beatty
Ronald P. Johnson
Fred T. Hamlet
R. Thompson Wright
Everett B. Saslow, Jr.
Dolores D. Follin
Richard J. Votta
Martha Taylor Peddrick
Douglas E. Wright

ASSOCIATES

Polly D. Sizemore
ToNola D. Brown
Gregory A. Stakias
Patricia P. Ridenhour
Michele G. Smith
Charles W. Coltrane

OF COUNSEL

Charles E. Nichols
Jonathan W. Yarbrough

Representative Clients: Ford Motor Credit Co.; Georgia-Pacific Corp.; Gilbarco, Inc.; Jefferson-Pilot Corp.; Nationwide Mutual Insurance Cos.; Rheem Manufacturing Company; Overnight Transportation Co.; Southern National Bank; The St. Paul Insurance Cos.

For full biographical listings, see the Martindale-Hubbell Law Directory

SCHELL BRAY AYCOCK ABEL & LIVINGSTON L.L.P. (AV)

1500 Renaissance Plaza, 230 North Elm Street, P.O. Box 21847, 27420
Telephone: 910-370-8800
Fax: 910-370-8830

MEMBERS OF FIRM

Braxton Schell
Doris R. Bray
William P. Aycock, II
Michael R. Abel
Paul H. Livingston, Jr.
Kenneth N. Shelton

ASSOCIATES

Barbara R. Christy
Mark Thomas Cain
Dan T. Barker, Jr.
Russell M. Robinson, III
Marshall Todd Jackson

COUNSEL

Pamela DeAngelis Duncan
Thomas C. Watkins

Representative Clients: The Breakers Palm Beach, Inc.; CBP Resources, Inc. (Carolina By-Products); Cone Mills Corp.; Cornwallis Development Co.; Kenan Transport Co.; Klaussner Furniture Industries, Inc.; North Carolina Trust Co.; Texfi Industries, Inc.; University of North Carolina at Chapel Hill Foundation, Inc.; Vanguard Cellular Systems, Inc.

For full biographical listings, see the Martindale-Hubbell Law Directory

SMITH HELMS MULLISS & MOORE, L.L.P. (AV)

Suite 1400 First Union Tower, 300 North Greene Street, P.O. Box 21927, 27420
Telephone: 910-378-5200
Telecopier: 910-379-9558
Charlotte, North Carolina Office: Smith Helms Mulliss & Moore, L.L.P., 227 North Tryon Street, P.O. Box 31247.
Telephone: 704-343-2000.
Telecopier: 704-334-8467.
Telex: 572460.

(See Next Column)

SMITH HELMS MULLISS & MOORE L.L.P.—*Continued*

Raleigh, North Carolina Office: Smith Helms Mulliss & Moore, L.L.P., 316 West Edenton Street, P.O. Box 27525.
Telephone: 919-755-8700.
Telecopier: 919-828-7938.

John J. Dortch (1930-1984)

OF COUNSEL

A. Harrell Pope | Jack L. Donnell

MEMBERS OF FIRM

McNeill Smith
Julius C. Smith, III
Bynum M. Hunter
Stephen Perry Millikin
Richmond G. Bernhardt, Jr.
Charles E. Melvin, Jr.
Herbert O. Davis
Larry B. Sitton
Martin N. Erwin
Harold N. Bynum
David M. Moore, II
Benjamin F. Davis, Jr.
James A. Medford
Richard A. Leippe
J. Donald Cowan, Jr.
Michael E. Kelly
Thomas S. Stukes
Gerard H. Davidson, Jr.
E. Garrett Walker
Stephen W. Earp
William L. Young
JoAnn T. Harllee
Carole Watkins Bruce
Jeri L. Whitfield
Alan W. Duncan
Maureen Demarest Murray
Allan L. Shackelford
Caroline Hudson Lock
Robert G. Brinkley (Also at Charlotte)
Timothy Peck
Evan Kent Auberry
Kathy E. Manning
William Sam Byassee
Jonathan A. Berkelhammer
Mack D. Pridgen, III
Ramona O. O'Bryant
Donald C. Lampe
Julianna C. Theall
Bruce P. Ashley

ASSOCIATES

Davis McDonald
George D. Kimberly, Jr.
Amy Smith Klass
W. Alexander Audilet
William K. Edwards
Marilyn Feuchs-Marker
Fran M. Shaver
Mark R. Smith
Andrew S. Chamberlin
Terrill Johnson Harris
D. Erik Albright
Lyn K. Broom
Lynette A. Barnes
Jeffrey G. Weber
Christine T. Nero
Alexander L. Maultsby
Gregory G. Holland
John J. Korzen
Dayna J. Kelly
Larissa J. Erkman
Joseph L. Anderson
Todd W. Cline
Richard A. Coughlin
William E. Burton, III
Stephen E. Klee
D. Marsh Prause
Robert R. Marcus
Amy Zakrajsheck Babb
Lisa Frye Garrison
Kara W. Edmunds

For full biographical listings, see the Martindale-Hubbell Law Directory

TUGGLE DUGGINS & MESCHAN, P.A. (AV)

228 West Market Street, P.O. Box 2888, 27402
Telephone: 910-378-1431
Telecopier: (910) 274-1148

Richard J. Tuggle
James N. Duggins, Jr.
David F. Meschan
Thomas S. Thornton, Jr.
Joseph F. Brotherton
Richard J. Tuggle, Jr.
Henry B. Mangum, Jr.
J. Reed Johnston, Jr.
William R. Sage
Paul M. Dennis, Jr.
Robert C. Cone
John R. Barlow, II
Barbara C. Ruby
Joseph F. McNulty, Jr.
H. Vaughn Ramsey
Harold A. Lloyd
William C. Connor
Bradley L. Jacobs
Michael J. Wenig
Denis Jacobson
Robert A. Ford
C. Scott Hester
William G. Burgin, III
Ryan Dyson
Elizabeth Glover Grimes
Jonathan S. Dills
Judy H. Urbania
Gerald L. Evans
Frank J. Chut, Jr.
Robert W. Franklin

Representative Clients: Adaron Group, Inc.; Byrd Food Stores, Inc.; Carolina Hosiery Mills, Inc.; First Union National Bank; Kingsdown, Incorporated; Highland Industries, Inc.; Newman Machine Co., Inc.; Triton Management Co.
Reference: First Union National Bank.

For full biographical listings, see the Martindale-Hubbell Law Directory

*GREENVILLE,** Pitt Co.

EVERETT, EVERETT, WARREN & HARPER (AV)

200 South Washington Street, P.O. Box 1220, 27834
Telephone: 919-758-4257
Telefax: 919-758-9282
Bethel, North Carolina Office: P.O. Box 609.
Telephone: 919-825-5691.
Telefax: 919-825-9259.

MEMBERS OF FIRM

C. W. Everett (1917-1989)
Clifton W. Everett, Jr.
Tyler B. Warren (Resident Partner at Bethel)
Edward J. Harper, II
Lewis H. Swindell, IV

(See Next Column)

Representative Client: F & D Motor Co.
General Counsel for: Town of Bethel; Home Federal Savings Bank of Eastern North Carolina.
References: NationsBank; Wachovia Bank & Trust Co.

For full biographical listings, see the Martindale-Hubbell Law Directory

GAYLORD, SINGLETON, MCNALLY, STRICKLAND AND SNYDER (AV)

206 S. Washington Street, P.O. Box 545, 27835-0545
Telephone: 919-758-3116

MEMBERS OF FIRM

Louis W. Gaylord, Jr.
A. Louis Singleton
Danny D. McNally
D. Michael Strickland
Vernon G. Snyder, III

Representative Clients: Wachovia Bank & Trust Co., N.A.; United States Fidelity and Guaranty Co.; The Daily Reflector, Inc.; Hastings Ford, Inc.; Overton's Sports Center, Inc.; A.B. Whitley, Inc.; Nationwide Mutual Insurance Co.; NCNB National Bank of North Carolina; Coldwell Banker Relocation Management Services, Inc.

For full biographical listings, see the Martindale-Hubbell Law Directory

*HAYESVILLE,** Clay Co. — (Refer to Franklin)

*HENDERSONVILLE,** Henderson Co.

HOWE, WATERS & CARPENTER, P.A. (AV)

134 South Main Street, P.O. Box 586, 28793
Telephone: 704-692-9636
Telefax: 704-692-2643

William B. W. Howe
R. Charles Waters
Walter C. Carpenter
Linda A. Moxley

General Counsel for: Hendersonville Housing Authority.
Representative Client: First Southern Savings Bank.
Approved Attorneys for: Lawyers Title Insurance Corp.; Chicago Title Insurance Co.; Investors Title Insurance Co.
References: Wachovia Bank & Trust Co.; First Union National Bank of North Carolina; First Citizens Bank & Trust Co.

For full biographical listings, see the Martindale-Hubbell Law Directory

PRINCE, YOUNGBLOOD & MASSAGEE (AV)

240 Third Avenue, West, 28739
Telephone: 704-692-2595
FAX: 704-693-0177

MEMBERS OF FIRM

L. B. Prince (1898-1982)
Kenneth R. Youngblood
Boyd B. Massagee, Jr.
B. B. Massagee, III
Sharon B. Alexander
Jennifer O. Jackson

Representative Clients: Margaret R. Pardee Memorial Hospital; E. I. DuPont DeNemours & Co.; NCNB National Bank of North Carolina; First Citizens Bank and Trust Co.; First Southern Savings Bank; Duke Power Co.; Blue Cross & Blue Shield of North Carolina; Blue Ridge Community College; Fletcher Motor Co., Inc.; Hunter Chevrolet-Volvo-Subaru Co., Inc.

For full biographical listings, see the Martindale-Hubbell Law Directory

*HERTFORD,** Perquimans Co. — (Refer to Elizabeth City)

HICKORY, Catawba Co.

PATRICK, HARPER AND DIXON (AV)

The Southern National Bank Building, P.O. Box 218, 28603
Telephone: 704-322-7741
Fax: 704-322-9340

MEMBERS OF FIRM

Bailey Patrick (1898-1989)
James T. Patrick (1936-1990)
Charles D. Dixon
Stephen Mason Thomas
Donald R. Fuller, Jr.
Gary F. Young
Kim Stafford Clarke
Eloise DeLaney Bradshaw
Robert Allen Ingram, Jr.

ASSOCIATES

David Wallace Hood
Robert Oren Eades
Kimberly A. Huffman
F. Gwyn Harper, Jr. (Retired, 1991)

General Counsel for: Century Furniture Co.; Shuford Mills, Inc.; First Savings Bank.
Special Counsel for: Norfolk-Southern Railway Co.
Local Counsel for: Ryder Truck Rental, Inc.; Duke Power Co.; Martin Marietta Corp.; The Lane Co.; Nationwide Insurance Co.

For full biographical listings, see the Martindale-Hubbell Law Directory

SIGMON, MACKIE & HUTTON, P.A. (AV)

Suite 508 First Union Bank Building, P.O. Drawer 1470, 28603
Telephone: 704-328-2596
FAX: 704-328-6876

(See Next Column)

SIGMON, MACKIE & HUTTON P.A., *Hickory—Continued*

William R. Sigmon
Jeffrey T. Mackie
Warren A. Hutton

J. Scott Hanvey
Mary F. Pyron

Representative Clients: First Union National Bank; McDermott, Canaday & Little Engineers; Cox Manufacturing Co.
Local Counsel for: Aetna Life & Casualty Co.; The Ohio Casualty Group of Insurance Cos.; United States Fidelity and Guaranty Insurance Co.

For full biographical listings, see the Martindale-Hubbell Law Directory

TATE, YOUNG, MORPHIS, BACH AND FARTHING (AV)

First Lawyers Building, 400 Second Avenue, N.W., P.O. Drawer 2428, 28601
Telephone: 704-322-4663
FAX: 704-322-2023

MEMBERS OF FIRM

E. Murray Tate, Jr.
Charles R. Young
Thomas C. Morphis
Wayne M. Bach
Edwin G. Farthing
Terry M. Taylor

ASSOCIATES

T. Dean Amos
Tiana Gibson Ayotte
Vanessa Barlow Hawkins
Paul E. Culpepper

Representative Clients: City of Hickory; First Citizens Bank & Trust Co.; Shuford Mills, Inc.; United States Hosiery Corp.; Graystone Ophthalmology Associates, P.A.; The Brian Center Corp.
Approved Attorneys for: Lawyers Title Insurance Corp.; NationsBank of North Carolina.

For full biographical listings, see the Martindale-Hubbell Law Directory

HIGHLANDS, Macon Co. — (Refer to Franklin)

HIGH POINT, Guilford Co.

FISHER FISHER GAYLE CLINARD & CRAIG, P.A. (AV)

Suite 800 First Factors Building, 101 S. Main Street, P.O. Drawer 1150, 27261
Telephone: 910-883-9156
Fax: 910-886-8593

Louis J. Fisher (1901-1981)
Louis J. Fisher, Jr.
Scott C. Gayle
Aaron N. Clinard
John O. Craig III
M. Bradley Harrold
Warren R. Lackey
Jennifer R. Lynch
Robert G. Griffin

Representative Clients: U.S. Furniture Industries, Inc.; First-Citizens Bank & Trust Co.; Southern National Bank; First Financial Bank, F.S.B.; High Point Surgical Associates, Inc.; Henley Paper Co.; Snow Lumber Co.; Dixie Container Corp.; International Textile & Design, Inc.

For full biographical listings, see the Martindale-Hubbell Law Directory

HAWORTH, RIGGS, KUHN & HAWORTH (AV)

Law Building, 212 East Green Drive, Suite 300, P.O. Box 109, 27261
Telephone: 910-883-0191
Telecopier: 910-883-6478

MEMBERS OF FIRM

John Haworth
John C. Riggs
William B. Haworth
Rick Cornwell

Representative Clients: Davis Furniture Industries, Inc.; Thayer Coggin, Inc.; High Point Medical Center, Inc.; High Point Elastic Corp.; Cloverleaf Super Market, Inc.; Kennedy Oil Co.; Oakhurst Textiles, Inc.

For full biographical listings, see the Martindale-Hubbell Law Directory

KEZIAH, GATES & SAMET, L.L.P. (AV)

Suite 400 High Point Bank & Trust Building, 300 North Main Street, P.O. Box 2608, 27261-2608
Telephone: 910-889-6900
Telecopier: 910-889-7055

MEMBERS OF FIRM

S. Perry Keziah
Gilbert L. Gates
Jan H. Samet
Charles E. Lynch, Jr.
Maurice S. S. Hull
Andrew S. Lasine
Judith C. Walker
Steven H. Bouldin

Counsel for: Furniture Manufacturers Credit Assn., Inc.; High Point Bank & Trust Co.; J. B. White Construction Co.; NationsBank of North Carolina, N.A.

For full biographical listings, see the Martindale-Hubbell Law Directory

POST & POST (AV)

516 North Wrenn, P.O. Box 2531, 27261
Telephone: 910-887-7566
Telecopier: 910-887-2133

(See Next Column)

MEMBERS OF FIRM

Edward N. Post
Alan N. Post

General Counsel for: Housing Authority of City of High Point.
Counsel For: North State Telephone Co.; Nations Bank.
Local Counsel for: Mortgage Loans: Federal National Mortgage Assn.; Federal Housing Administration; Northwestern Life Insurance Co.; Veterans Administration.

For full biographical listings, see the Martindale-Hubbell Law Directory

SCHOCH & WOODRUFF, L.L.P. (AV)

310 South Main Street, P.O. Box 1893, 27261
Telephone: 910-884-4151
Telecopier: 910-883-7151
Greensboro, North Carolina Office: 301 South Green Street, Suite 102, 27401.
Telephone: 910-272-91222.
Telecopier: 910-272-7991.

MEMBERS OF FIRM

Arch K. Schoch (1909-1980)
Louise Rodes Schoch
Arch K. Schoch, Jr.
Carolyn J. Woodruff

ASSOCIATES

Katherine Wiggins Goodson

Representative Clients: Archdale Oil Co.; Classic Gallery, Inc.; Cramer Wood Products, Inc.; The High Point Enterprise, Inc.; Jones & Peacock Insurance, Inc.; Lyon Collection Services, Inc.; Phillips Industries, Inc.; Piedmont Chemical Industries, Inc.; Ultraflex Corporation.

For full biographical listings, see the Martindale-Hubbell Law Directory

WYATT, EARLY, HARRIS, WHEELER & HAUSER, L.L.P. (AV)

Old Courthouse Building, 258 South Main Street, P.O. Drawer 2086, 27261
Telephone: 910-884-4444
FAX: 910-889-5232

MEMBERS OF FIRM

Frank Burkhead Wyatt
William P. Harris
A. Doyle Early, Jr.
William E. Wheeler
David B. Ashcraft
Kim W. Gallimore
Kim R. Bauman
Calvin B. Bryant
R. Bruce Laney
Charles A. Alt
Frederick G. Sawyer
James R. Hundley
Charles L. Cain
Thomas E. Terrell, Jr.
Lee M. Cecil
Kevin L. Rochford
Ann E. Hanks
John David Bryson

Representative Clients: Allstate Insurance Co.; Davis Furniture Industries; First Union National Bank; United States Fidelity and Guaranty Co.; Dar-Ran Furniture Industries; First Citizens Bank & Trust Co.; Ohio Casualty Insurance Co.; Mid-State Petroleum; Rite Industries; Branch Bank & Trust Co.

For full biographical listings, see the Martindale-Hubbell Law Directory

*HILLSBOROUGH,** Orange Co.

COLEMAN, GLEDHILL & HARGRAVE, P.C. (AV)

129 East Tryon Street, P.O. Drawer 1529, 27278
Telephone: 919-732-2196
FAX: 919-732-7997

Alonzo B. Coleman, Jr.
Geoffrey E. Gledhill
Douglas Hargrave

Kim K. Steffan
Janet B. Dutton
Douglas P. Thoren

For full biographical listings, see the Martindale-Hubbell Law Directory

*JACKSON,** Northampton Co. — (Refer to Roanoke Rapids)

*JACKSONVILLE,** Onslow Co.

ELLIS, HOOPER, WARLICK, MORGAN & HENRY (AV)

313 New Bridge Street, P.O. Drawer 1006, 28541-1006
Telephone: 910-455-3637
FAX: 910-455-4068

MEMBERS OF FIRM

John D. Warlick, Sr. (1890-1952)
Albert J. Ellis (1913-1969)
Glenn L. Hooper, Jr. (1927-1978)
John D. Warlick, Jr.
William J. Morgan
Charles H. Henry, Jr.

ASSOCIATES

Victor H.E. Morgan, Jr.
Stephen C. Baynard

For full biographical listings, see the Martindale-Hubbell Law Directory

Jacksonville—Continued

WARLICK MILSTED DOTSON & CARTER (AV)

320 New Bridge Street, P.O. Box 766, 28541-0766
Telephone: 910-455-1215
Fax: 910-455-4702

MEMBERS OF FIRM

Alex Warlick, Jr.
Marshall F. Dotson, Jr.
Carl S. Milsted
John T. Carter, Jr.

General Counsel for: Coastal Carolina Community College; City of Jacksonville; Padgett Motors; Rand Oil Co.; Major Furniture & Appliance.
Local Counsel for: Weyerhaeuser Co.; Westminster Co.
References: First Citizens Bank & Trust Co.; Centura Bank.

For full biographical listings, see the Martindale-Hubbell Law Directory

*JEFFERSON,** Ashe Co. — (Refer to Boone)

*KINSTON,** Lenoir Co.

WALLACE, MORRIS, BARWICK & ROCHELLE, P.A. (AV)

131 South Queen Street, P.O. Box 3557, 28502-3557
Telephone: 919-523-2000
FAX: 919-523-0408

Fitzhugh E. Wallace, Jr.
Thomas H. Morris
P. C. Barwick, Jr.
Vernon H. Rochelle
Richard F. Landis, II
Paul A. Rodgman
Edwin M. Braswell, Jr.
Elizabeth A. Heath
William E. Manning, Jr.
Stuart L. Stroud

Regional and Local Clients: Seaboard Coast Line Railroad.
Representative Clients: E.I. du Pont De Nemours & Co., Inc.; First Citizens Bank & Trust Co.; Branch Banking & Trust Co.; City of Kinston; Kinston Daily Free Press Co.
Insurance Clients: Aetna Casualty & Surety Co.; Nationwide Mutual Insurance Co.; State Farm Mutual Automobile Insurance Co.; Allstate Insurance Co.

For full biographical listings, see the Martindale-Hubbell Law Directory

WHITE & ALLEN, P.A. (AV)

106 South McLewean Street, P.O. Box 3169, 28501
Telephone: 919-527-8000
Telecopier: 919-527-8128

Thomas J. White (1903-1991)
William A. Allen, Jr.
John R. Hooten
John C. Archie
C. Gray Johnsey
Joseph Sidney Bower
David J. Fillippeli, Jr.
James B. Stephenson II
John P. Marshall
Jonathon L. Sargeant
Dale S. Davidson

Special Counsel for: Southern Railway Co.
Representative Clients: Lenoir Memorial Hospital; Carolina Power & Light Co.; First American Savings Bank; Kinston Housing Authority; First Citizens Bank & Trust Co.; Wachovia Bank of North Carolina, N.A.; NationsBank, N.A.; Kemper National Group; Hampton Industries, Inc.

For full biographical listings, see the Martindale-Hubbell Law Directory

*LAURINBURG,** Scotland Co.

ETHERIDGE, MOSER, GARNER AND BRUNER, P.A. (AV)

600 E. South Main Street, P.O. Box 1827, 28353
Telephone: 910-276-2631
FAX: 910-276-0326

Kennieth S. Etheridge
Terry R. Garner
William F. Moser
Jerry L. Bruner

Christopher Neil Heiskell

Representative Clients: Scotland Savings Bank; Southern Bell Telephone & Telegraph Co.; Carolina Power & Light Co.; Z. V. Pate, Inc.; Travelers Insurance Co.; Ohio Casualty Insurance Co.; First Scotland Bank; Dixie Guano Co.; LOF Glass, Inc.; The Morgan Co.

For full biographical listings, see the Martindale-Hubbell Law Directory

WILLIAMSON, DEAN, BROWN, WILLIAMSON & PURCELL, L.L.P. (AV)

213C East Cronly Street, P.O. Box 1627, 28353
Telephone: 910-276-8082
FAX: 910-276-1011

MEMBERS OF FIRM

Andrew G. Williamson
Andrew G. Williamson, Jr.
Daniel B. Dean
William R. Purcell, II
Richard T. Brown
Nickolas J. Sojka, Jr.

Counsel for: Scotland Memorial Hospital; St. Andrews Presbyterian College; Scotland County Board of Education; Charles Craft, Inc.; Waverly Mills, Inc.
Representative Clients: McCarter Electrical Company; LOF Glass, Inc.; Toastmaster, Inc.; Swink Quality Oil Co.; Integon Insurance Co.

(See Next Column)

For full biographical listings, see the Martindale-Hubbell Law Directory

*LENOIR,** Caldwell Co.

TODD, VANDERBLOEMEN, RESPESS AND BRADY, P.A. (AV)

214 Ridge Street, Northwest, P.O. Drawer 1320, 28645
Telephone: 704-758-0044
FAX: 704-758-8467

Folger L. Townsend (1899-1973)
Bruce W. Vanderbloemen
James R. Todd, Jr.
William W. Respess, Jr.
Charles A. Brady, III

Representative Clients: NationsBank; Furniture City Broadcasters, Inc.; Duke Power Co.; Southern Bell Telephone & Telegraph Co.; Norfolk-Southern Railway; Bush Oldsmobile, Inc.; Travelers Insurance Co.; Fireman's Fund Insurance Co.
Approved Attorneys for: Lawyers Title Insurance Corp.

For full biographical listings, see the Martindale-Hubbell Law Directory

*LEXINGTON,** Davidson Co. — (Refer to Salisbury)

*LILLINGTON,** Harnett Co.

BAIN & MCRAE (AV)

813 Main Street, P.O. Box 99, 27546
Telephone: 910-893-5111
Fax: 910-893-6342

MEMBERS OF FIRM

Edgar R. Bain
Alton D. Bain
David F. McRae

Representative Clients: Mid-South Bank & Trust Co.; Food Folks, Inc.; Shaw Construction Company, Inc.; Becker Mineral Company; Machine Welding Company; East Coast Signs, Inc.

For full biographical listings, see the Martindale-Hubbell Law Directory

JOHNSON AND JOHNSON, P.A. (AV)

31 East Harnett Street, P.O. Box 69, 27546
Telephone: 910-893-5107
Fax: 910-893-6049

W. A. Johnson
Sandra L. Johnson
W. Glenn Johnson
Rebecca J. Davidson

Representative Clients: NCNB National Bank; Campbell University; Canal Land Co.; Carolina Power & Light Co.
Approved Attorneys for: Lawyers Title Insurance Corp.; First Title Insurance Co.; Pilot Title Insurance Co.
References: Southern National Bank, Lillington, North Carolina; NCNB National Bank, Lillington, North Carolina.

For full biographical listings, see the Martindale-Hubbell Law Directory

*LINCOLNTON,** Lincoln Co.

PENDLETON & PENDLETON, P.A. (AV)

211 North Academy Street, P.O. Box 159, 28092
Telephone: 704-735-0483
FAX: 704-735-1541

Don M. Pendleton
Clay Pendleton
Jeffrey A. Taylor

Representative Clients: Boger City Sanitary District; Excel, Inc.; Wash Queen, Inc.; Gaston County Dyeing Machine Co.; Craig Realty & Development Co., Inc.; Dallas Pillow Co., Inc.; First Federal Savings & Loan Assn.
Attorney for: Lincoln County.
Reference: First Citizens Bank & Trust Co.
Approved Attorneys for: Lawyers Title Insurance Company; Federal Land Bank of Columbia.

For full biographical listings, see the Martindale-Hubbell Law Directory

*LOUISBURG,** Franklin Co.

DAVIS, STURGES & TOMLINSON (AV)

DSS Building, 101 North Church Street, P.O. Drawer 708, 27549
Telephone: 919-496-2137
Telecopier: 919-496-6291

MEMBERS OF FIRM

Charles M. Davis
Conrad B. Sturges, Jr.
Aubrey S. Tomlinson, Jr.

General Counsel for: National American Corp.
Representative Clients: Nationwide Insurance Co.; Kemper Insurance Co.; Union Camp Corp.
Approved Attorneys for: Lawyers Title Insurance Corp.; Fidelity National Insurance Co.; Federal Land Bank of Columbia; Farmers Home Administration.
References: First Citizens Bank & Trust Co.; United Carolina Bank.

For full biographical listings, see the Martindale-Hubbell Law Directory

*LUMBERTON,** Robeson Co.

LEE AND LEE (AV)

407 North Elm Street, P.O. Box 1067, 28359
Telephone: 910-738-6211

MEMBERS OF FIRM

W. Osborne Lee (1904-1972) W. Osborne Lee, Jr.

Representative Clients: Blackmon's Furniture Co.; T. R. Driscoll, Inc.; Eagle Distributing Co.; Lumberton Medical Clinic, P.A.; Lumberton Surgical Associates, P.A.; Lumberton Urology Clinic, P.A.; Trustees of F. McKay Smith.
Reference: Wachovia Bank & Trust Co.; First Union National Bank.

For full biographical listings, see the Martindale-Hubbell Law Directory

MADISON, Rockingham Co.

FOLGER, TUCKER & HOWE (AV)

117 East Murphy Street, 27025
Telephone: 910-548-2309
Fax: 910-548-1751

MEMBERS OF FIRM

Alonzo D. Folger, Jr. Benjamin F. Tucker
F. Curtis Howe

Representative Clients: Guaranteed Systems, Inc.; First Union National Bank; BB&T, Madison, N.C.; New Madison Warehouse, Inc.
Approved Attorneys for: Jefferson-Pilot Title Insurance Co.; Investors Title Insurance Co.
References: First Union National Bank, Madison, N. C.; Wachovia Bank and Trust Co., N.A.

For full biographical listings, see the Martindale-Hubbell Law Directory

*MANTEO,** Dare Co.

KELLOGG, WHITE, EVANS AND GRAY (AV)

201 Ananias Dare Street, P.O. Box 189, 27954
Telephone: 919-473-2171
Fax: 919-473-1214
Kill Devil Hills, North Carolina Office: 3120 North Croatan Highway, Suite 101.
Telephone: 919-441-4338.
Fax: 919-441-8414.
Corolla, North Carolina Office: 821 Ocean Trail, Suite 3.
Telephone: 919-453-8080.
Fax: 919-453-8082.

MEMBERS OF FIRM

Martin Kellogg, Jr.
Thomas L. White, Jr.
Charles D. Evans (Resident, Kill Devil Hills Office)
E. Crouse Gray, Jr. (Resident, Kill Devil Hills Office)
Ronald E. DeVeau
Benita A. Lloyd (Resident, Kill Devil Hills Office)
Angelea C. Norcross (Resident, Corolla Office)
Michael G. Stein (Resident, Kill Devil Hills Office)
William Spencer (Billy) Daniels

Representative Clients: Centura Bank; Town of Nags Head; Town of Southern Shores.
Approved Attorneys for: Lawyers Title Insurance Corp.; Chicago Title Insurance Co.; American Title Insurance Co.; First Title Insurance Co.; The Title Company of N.C., Inc.

For full biographical listings, see the Martindale-Hubbell Law Directory

*MARSHALL,** Madison Co.

HUFF & HUFF (AV)

108 E. Main Street, P.O. Box 8, 28753
Telephone: 704-649-2851

Joseph B. Huff Stephen E. Huff

Representative Clients: Southern Railway System; First Union National Bank of North Carolina; Asheville Federal Savings and Loan Assn.; Continental Trailways; Dickerson, Inc.; United States Fidelity and Guaranty Co.; Aetna Casualty and Surety Co.; Insurance Companies of North America; Clyde Savings and Loan Assn.

*MOCKSVILLE,** Davie Co. — (Refer to Statesville)

*MONROE,** Union Co.

GRIFFIN, CALDWELL, HELDER, LEE & HELMS, P.A. (AV)

314 North Hayne Street, P.O. Drawer 99, 28111-0099
Telephone: 704-289-4577
Toll Free from Charlotte: 704-372-4808
Fax: 704-289-4218

C. Frank Griffin Jake C. Helder
Thomas J. Caldwell W. David Lee
R. Kenneth Helms, Jr.

Representative Clients: United Carolina Bank; Travelers Insurance Co.; State Farm Mutual Insurance Co.; Monroe Hardware Co.

(See Next Column)

Approved Attorneys for: Lawyers Title Insurance Corp.
Reference: United Carolina Bank.

For full biographical listings, see the Martindale-Hubbell Law Directory

MOREHEAD CITY, Carteret Co.

BENNETT, MCCONKEY, THOMPSON & MARQUARDT, P.A. (AV)

1007 Shepard Street, P.O. Drawer 189, 28557
Telephone: 919-726-4114
FAX: 919-726-7975

Thomas S. Bennett James W. Thompson, III
Samuel A. McConkey, Jr. Dennis M. Marquardt

Approved Attorneys For: Lawyers Title Insurance Corp.
Reference: First Citizens Bank & Trust Co.

For full biographical listings, see the Martindale-Hubbell Law Directory

NELSON W. TAYLOR, III (AV)

610 Arendell Street, P.O. Drawer 3627, 28557
Telephone: 919-726-0001

Representative Clients: Town of Morehead City; Town of Newport; Carteret Craven Electric Membership Corp.; Down East Togs; Harborview Health Care Center; Chicago Title Insurance Co.; Vanity Fair, Inc.
Approved Attorneys for: Lawyers Title Insurance Corp.; Chicago Title Insurance Co.
Reference: Branch Banking & Trust Co.

For full biographical listings, see the Martindale-Hubbell Law Directory

*MORGANTON,** Burke Co.

BYRD, BYRD, ERVIN, WHISNANT, MCMAHON & ERVIN, P.A. (AV)

One Northsquare, P.O. Drawer 1269, 28655
Telephone: 704-437-4220
FAX: 704-438-4517

Joe K. Byrd (Retired)
Robert B. Byrd
John W. Ervin, Jr.
C. Scott Whisnant
Lawrence D. McMahon, Jr.
Sam J. Ervin, IV
Robert C. Ervin
Peggy McDaniel Saunders

Representative Clients: Breeden Holdings, Inc.; Burke Construction Co., Inc.; Great Lakes Carbon Corp.; Surety Federal Savings and Loan Assn.; Southern Bell Telephone and Telegraph Co.

For full biographical listings, see the Martindale-Hubbell Law Directory

PATTON, STARNES, THOMPSON, AYCOCK & TEELE, P.A. (AV)

118 North Sterling Street, 28655
Telephone: 704-437-3335
Fax: 704-438-4929

Frank C. Patton (1896-1980) Robert L. Thompson
Thomas M. Starnes Ellis L. Aycock
H. Dockery Teele, Jr.

Representative Clients: Duke Power Co.; Wachovia Bank of N.C.; Grace Hospital, Inc.; The Aetna Insurance Group; Nationwide Insurance Cos.; Kemper Insurance Group; State Farm Insurance Co.; North Carolina Farm Bureau Insurance Co.
Approved Attorneys for: Lawyers Title Insurance Corp.
Reference: Wachovia Bank of N.C.

For full biographical listings, see the Martindale-Hubbell Law Directory

SIMPSON AYCOCK, P.A. (AV)

204 East McDowell Street, P.O. Drawer 1329, 28655
Telephone: 704-437-9744
Fax: 704-433-7708

Dan R. Simpson James Reid Simpson, II
Samuel E. Aycock Louis E. Vinay, Jr.
Randolph M. Fletcher

Representative Clients: WSMP, Inc.; Town of Glen Alpine; Unigard Insurance Co.; Foothills Harley-Davidson, Inc.

For full biographical listings, see the Martindale-Hubbell Law Directory

MOUNT AIRY, Surry Co.

FAW, FOLGER, JOHNSON & BELL (AV)

Southern National Bank Building, 541 North Main Street, P.O. Drawer 512, 27030
Telephone: 910-786-2401
Fax: 910-786-1785
Other Mount Airy Office: 140 Franklin Street, P.O. Box 1355, 27030.
Telephone: 919-786-2139.
Fax: 919-786-2130.

(See Next Column)

FAW, FOLGER, JOHNSON & BELL—*Continued*

Dobson, North Carolina Office: 129-A West Atkins Street, P.O. Box 332, 27030.
Telephone: 919-386-8173.
Fax: 919-386-8298.

MEMBERS OF FIRM

Thomas M. Faw
Fredrick G. Johnson (Resident, Dobson, North Carolina Office)
Carl E. Bell
George Wilborn Rives (Resident, Dobson, North Carolina Office)

OF COUNSEL

Charles L. Folger (Retired)

ASSOCIATES

Hugh B. Campbell, III

Approved Attorneys for: Lawyers Title Insurance Co.

For full biographical listings, see the Martindale-Hubbell Law Directory

MURFREESBORO, Hertford Co.

REVELLE, BURLESON, LEE & REVELLE (AV)

201 East Main Street, P.O. Box 448, 27855
Telephone: 919-398-4171

MEMBERS OF FIRM

J. Guy Revelle, Jr.
L. Frank Burleson, Jr.
Robert Edward Lee, Jr.
Charles L. Revelle, III

ASSOCIATES

Terrence N. Evans

General Counsel for: Hertford County; Chowan College; Town of Murfreesboro.
Representative Clients: Georgia-Pacific Corp.; Union Camp Corp.; Meherrin Agricultural and Chemical Co.; Southern Bank and Trust Co.
Approved Attorneys for: Farmers Home Administration; Lawyers Title Insurance Corp.; Chicago Title Insurance Co.

For full biographical listings, see the Martindale-Hubbell Law Directory

*MURPHY,** Cherokee Co. — (Refer to Franklin)

*NASHVILLE,** Nash Co.

VALENTINE, ADAMS, LAMAR, ETHERIDGE, SYKES & BRITT, L.L.P. (AV)

203 South Barnes Street, P.O. Box 727, 27856
Telephone: 919-459-7141
FAX: 919-459-2996

MEMBERS OF FIRM

Itimous T. Valentine (1887-1970)
Franklin L. Adams, Jr.
L. Wardlaw Lamar
William D. Etheridge
Raymond M. Sykes, Jr.
Sharon R. Britt

Approved Attorneys for: Lawyers Title Insurance Corp.; Title Guarantee Co.; Farm Credit Service; Commonwealth Land Title Insurance Co.; Investors Title Insurance Co.
References: Centura Bank, First Citizens Bank and Southern Bank &Trust Company, Nashville, N.C.

For full biographical listings, see the Martindale-Hubbell Law Directory

*NEW BERN,** Craven Co.

WARD, WARD, WILLEY AND WARD (AV)

409 Pollock Street, P.O. Drawer 1428, 28560
Telephone: 919-633-1103
FAX: 919-633-9400
Other New Bern Office: Raleigh Federal Savings Building, 513 Pollock Street.
Fax: 919-633-5578.

MEMBERS OF FIRM

Alfred Decatur Ward
Alfred Decatur Ward, Jr.
Joshua W. Willey, Jr.
Thomas M. Ward

J. Michael Mills

Representative Clients: City of New Bern; Wachovia Bank & Trust Company; Raleigh Federal Savings Bank; Trent Olds-Cadillac-Buick, Inc.; Turner-Tolson, Inc.; R.A. Precision, Inc.; NationsBank; Case Equipment Co.; Chemical Residential Mortgage Corp.; AMRESCO Institutional, Inc.
Approved Attorneys for: Stewart Title Insurance Co.

For full biographical listings, see the Martindale-Hubbell Law Directory

*NEWTON,** Catawba Co. — (Refer to Hickory)

NORTH WILKESBORO, Wilkes Co.

VANNOY, COLVARD, TRIPLETT & McLEAN (AV)

922 "C" Street, P.O. Box 1388, 28659
Telephone: 910-667-7201
FAX: 910-838-7250

(See Next Column)

MEMBERS OF FIRM

J. Gary Vannoy
Howard C. Colvard, Jr.
Anthony R. Triplett
Mitchell L. McLean

ASSOCIATES

John G. (Jay) Vannoy, Jr.
Tonya L. Urps

Representative Clients: Southern National Bank; Carolina Mirror Co.
References: NCNB National Bank of North Carolina; 1st Citizens Bank & Trust Co.

For full biographical listings, see the Martindale-Hubbell Law Directory

*OXFORD,** Granville Co. — (Refer to Henderson)

PILOT MOUNTAIN, Surry Co. — (Refer to Mt. Airy)

PINEHURST, Moore Co.

VAN CAMP, WEST, HAYES & MEACHAM, A PROFESSIONAL ASSOCIATION (AV)

Third Floor Suite, The Theatre Building, P.O. Box 1389, 28374
Telephone: 910-295-2525
Fax: 910-295-2001
Carthage, North Carolina Office: The Courthouse Square, P.O. Drawer 429, 28327.
Telephone: 910-947-1711.
Fax: 910-947-3700.

James R. Van Camp
Stanley W. West
Lu Pendleton Hayes
Eddie H. Meacham
S. Kent Smith
Katharine McLeod
Michael J. Newman
Thomas M. Van Camp
Victoria P. Brenner
Donnell G. Adams, Jr.

For full biographical listings, see the Martindale-Hubbell Law Directory

*PLYMOUTH,** Washington Co. — (Refer to Washington)

*RAEFORD,** Hoke Co.

HOSTETLER & McNEILL (AV)

109 Campus Avenue, P.O. Box 277, 28376
Telephone: 910-875-2142
FAX: Available upon request

MEMBERS OF FIRM

Charles A. Hostetler (Retired)
Bobby Burns McNeill

Representative Clients: Progressive Savings and Loan; United Carolina Bank; Farmer Home Administration; J. H. Wright Realty Co.; Connell Realty; Cartler Realty; Southern National Bank.
Approved Attorneys for: Lawyers Title Insurance Corp.; Federal Land Bank of Columbia; Chicago Title, Commonwealth Title and Investors Title.

*RALEIGH,** Wake Co.

* indicates certain Bar Register subscribers whose principal office is located elsewhere in the state and who have arranged for representation as a part of the state capital listings that follow

BURNS, DAY & PRESNELL, P.A. (AV)

Suite 560, 2626 Glenwood Avenue, P.O. Box 10867, 27605
Telephone: 919-782-1441
Fax: 919-782-2311

David W. Boone
James M. Day
Daniel C. Higgins
Greg L. Hinshaw
Lacy M. Presnell III
Susan F. Vick

OF COUNSEL

F. Kent Burns

For full biographical listings, see the Martindale-Hubbell Law Directory

EVERETT, GASKINS, HANCOCK & STEVENS (AV)

The Professional Building, Suite 600, 127 West Hargett Street, P.O. Box 911, 27602
Telephone: 919-755-0025
Fax: 919-755-0009
Durham, North Carolina Office: Suite 300, 301 West Main Street, P.O. Box 586.
Telephone: 919-682-5691.
Fax: 919-682-5469.

MEMBERS OF FIRM

R.O. Everett (1878-1971)
Kathrine R. Everett (1893-1992)
Eura DuVal (Ed) Gaskins, Jr.
William G. (Gerry) Hancock, Jr.
Hugh Stevens

ASSOCIATES

Katherine R. White
Jeffrey B. Parsons
Robert (Bob) H. Gourley, Jr.

OF COUNSEL

Robinson O. Everett (Resident, Durham, North Carolina Office)
Hugh Cannon

(See Next Column)

EVERETT, GASKINS, HANCOCK & STEVENS, *Raleigh—Continued*

LEGAL SUPPORT PERSONNEL

Allyson S. McNeill
Alison R. Weigold

For full biographical listings, see the Martindale-Hubbell Law Directory

GULLEY KUHN & TAYLOR, L.L.P. (AV)

4601 Six Forks Road, 27609
Telephone: 919-782-6811
Facsimile: 919-782-7220

Jack P. Gulley
David J. Kuhn
Patricia Potter Taylor

OF COUNSEL

William O. Kuhn

For full biographical listings, see the Martindale-Hubbell Law Directory

HOWARD & GREEN, L.L.P. (AV)

4000 Westchase Boulevard Suite 200, P.O. Box 10305, 27605
Telephone: 919-833-2422
Fax: 919-833-2430

Robert E. Howard
Charles P. Green, Jr.

ASSOCIATES

Dori Casey McDarris

References: United Carolina Bank; NationsBank; First Citizens Bank & Trust, Wachovia.

For full biographical listings, see the Martindale-Hubbell Law Directory

HUNTER, WHARTON & STROUPE (AV)

2626 Glenwood Avenue, Suite 430, P.O. Drawer 10037, 27605
Telephone: 919-881-9110
FAX: 919-881-0296

MEMBERS OF FIRM

John V. Hunter III
Odes L. Stroupe, Jr.
V. Lane Wharton, Jr.

Representative Clients: Bobbitt & Associates, Inc.; Commissioner of Insurance, State of North Carolina; G. Heileman Brewing Co.; Lawyers Mutual Liability Insurance Company of North Carolina.

For full biographical listings, see the Martindale-Hubbell Law Directory

MANNING, FULTON & SKINNER, P.A. (AV)

UCB Plaza, 3605 Glenwood Avenue, P.O. Box 20389, 27619-0389
Telephone: 919-787-8880
Telecopier: 919-787-8902

Howard E. Manning
Charles L. Fulton
William P. Skinner, Jr.
John B. McMillan
W. Gerald Thornton
Howard E. Manning, Jr.
Charles B. Morris, Jr.
Michael T. Medford
Samuel T. Oliver, Jr.
John I. Mabe, Jr.
David D. Dahl
Charles E. Nichols, Jr.
Barry D. Mann
Linda K. Wood
John C. Dorsey
David J. Witheft
William C. Smith, Jr.
Deborah Lowder Hildebran
Stephen T. Byrd
H. Forest Horne, Jr.
Michael S. Harrell

Alison R. Cayton
Samuel W. Whitt
David T. Pryzwansky
Cary Elizabeth Close
Kristen Gardner Lingo

Counsel for: Raleigh Merchants Bureau; Carolantic Realty, Inc.; Troxler Electronic Laboratories, Inc.; General Parts, Inc.; Raleigh Federal Savings Bank.
Representative Clients: International Business Machines Corp.; Siemens-Allis, Inc.; Mallinckrodt, Inc.; Employers Reinsurance Corp.

For full biographical listings, see the Martindale-Hubbell Law Directory

MAUPIN TAYLOR ELLIS & ADAMS, P.A. (AV)

Suite 500, 3200 Beechleaf Court, P.O. Drawer 19764, 27619
Telephone: 919-981-4000
Telecopier: 919-981-4300
Rock Hill, South Carolina Office: 448 Lakeshore Parkway, Suite 200.
Telephone: 803-324-8118.
Telecopier: 803-324-2093.
Durham, North Carolina Office: 411 Andrews Road, Suite 150.
Telephone: 919-382-0188.
Telecopier: 919-383-9771.

Armistead J. Maupin
William W. Taylor, Jr. (Retired)
Thomas F. Ellis
Thomas F. Adams, Jr.
Charles B. Neely, Jr.
Thomas Willis Haywood Alexander
Robert A. Valois
John T. Williamson
Frank P. Ward, Jr.

(See Next Column)

Richard M. Lewis
Nancy S. Rendleman
R. Stephen Camp
Margie Toy Case
M. Keith Kapp
Mark S. Thomas
David R. Dorton
Steven D. Simpson
John C. Cooke
Thomas A. Farr
Holmes P. Harden
James A. Roberts, III
D. Royce Powell
William B. Gwyn, Jr.
James E. Gates
Amos C. Dawson, III
Steven M. Rudisill (Resident, Rock Hill, SC Office)
Gilbert C. Laite, III
Joseph Michael Lischwe
Sharon Hartman Spence
Robert L. Wilson, Jr.
Ronald R. Rogers
Timothy S. Riordan
Elizabeth Davenport Scott
Reuben G. Clark, III
Winston L. Page, Jr.
Jack Spain Holmes
Arlene J. Diosegy
John W. (Jack) Marin
Daniel K. Bryson
Gretchen W. Ewalt
Michael C. Lord
William J. Brian, Jr.
Frank H. Sheffield, Jr.
Karon B. Thornton
Richard N. Cook
Sean Callinicos
Robert J. Reeves (Not admitted in NC; Resident, Rock Hill, SC Office)
Theron McKean vanDusen
Linda F. Nelson
William P. Barrett
James C. Dever, III
Amy Shaw McEntee
Julie Ann Alagna
John D. Elvers
A. Graham Shirley
Craig D. Mills
Kurt L. Dixon
M. Reid Acree, Jr.
Dawn E. Ely
Jeffrey R. Gilbert (Resident, Rock Hill, SC Office)
R. Christopher Matton

OF COUNSEL

Robert B. Broughton

District Counsel for: CSX Transportation, Inc.
Representative Clients: American Airlines; Daniel International Corp.; E&J Gallo Winery; First Union National Bank of North Carolina; Glaxo, Inc.; The Grand Union Co.; Liberty Mutual Insurance Co.; Northern Telecom Inc.; United States Fidelity and Guaranty Co.

For full biographical listings, see the Martindale-Hubbell Law Directory

* MOORE & VAN ALLEN, PLLC (AV)

One Hannover Square, Suite 1700, P.O. Box 26507, 27611
Telephone: 919-828-4481
FAX: 919-828-4254
Charlotte, North Carolina Offices: NationsBank Corporate Center.
Telephone: 704-331-1000.
FAX: 704-331-1159.
Durham, North Carolina Office: Suite 800, 2200 West Main Street.
Telephone: 919-286-8000.
Fax: 919-286-8199.

Christopher J. Blake
Denise Smith Cline
Joseph W. Eason
David E. Fox
William H. Gammon
Douglas Ronald Ghidina
Dean M. Harris
Joseph D. Joyner, Jr.
C. Steven Mason
Isabel Worthy Mattox
John Spotswood Russell
Jonathan Drew Sasser
Hayden J. Silver, III
George M. Teague
Richard Beverly Raney Webb
William A. White (Not admitted in NC)

OF COUNSEL

Arch T. Allen, III
Leon M. Killian, III

Martin H. Brinkley
Robert Ashley Meynardie
Kelley Dixon Moye
Ann Marie Knops Nader
A. Bailey Nager
David S. Robinson
Beverly Lynn Rubin
Curtis J. Shipley
Joy Heath Thomas
Richard H. Vetter
Louis Samuel Watson, Jr.
Jeffrey Mark Young

For full biographical listings, see the Martindale-Hubbell Law Directory

PERRY, PATRICK, FARMER & MICHAUX, P.A. (AV)

3716 National Drive, Suite 100, 27612
Telephone: 919-787-8812
Fax: 919-787-3312
Charlotte, North Carolina Office: 2200 The Carillon, 227 West Trade Street.
Telephone: 704-372-1120.
Fax: 704-372-9635.
Other Charlotte, North Carolina Office: South Park, 1901 Roxborough Road, Suite 100.
Telephone: 704-364-9695.
Fax: 704-364-9698.

Richard W. Moore (Resident)
W. Richard Jamison (Resident)
David A. Raynes (Resident)
David L. Huffstetler (Resident)

Representative Clients: The Bissell Cos.; Centex Real Estate Corp.; Charlotte Pipe and Foundry Co.; The Crosland Group, Inc.; Crown Life Insurance Co.; C.D. Spangler Construction Co.; International Construction Equipment, Inc.; The Manufacturers Life Insurance Co.; M/I Schottenstein Cos., Inc.; The Ryland Group, Inc.

For full biographical listings, see the Martindale-Hubbell Law Directory

Raleigh—Continued

* PETREE STOCKTON, L.L.P. (AV)

4101 Lake Boone Trail, 27607-6519
Telephone: 919-420-1700
Telecopier: 919-420-1800
Winston-Salem, North Carolina Office: 1001 West Fourth Street, 27101-2400.
Telephone: 910-607-7300.
Telecopier: 910-607-7500.
Charlotte, North Carolina Office: 3500 One First Union Center, 301 South College Street, 28202-6001.
Telephone: 704-338-5000.
Telecopier: 704-338-5125.

MEMBERS OF FIRM

Ralph M. Stockton, Jr.
John L. Sarratt (Resident)
Fred D. Hutchison (Resident)
Noah H. Huffstetler, III (Resident)
James F. Verdonik (Resident)
J. Stephen Shi
Gary K. Joyner (Resident)
J. Anthony Penry (Resident)
Adam H. Broome (Resident)
Craig B. Wheaton (Resident)
Sarah Wesley Fox (Resident)
Kevin L. Miller (Resident)
James P. Cain (Resident)
Gerald A. "Jeb" Jeutter, Jr. (Resident)

ASSOCIATES

Merrill McCall Mason (Resident)
Robert H. Lesesne (Resident)
Donald J. Harris (Resident)
Barbara B. Garlock (Resident)
Sharon Moylan McConnell (Resident)
Lois Eileen Wagman (Resident)
Gary S. Qualls (Resident)
Cynthia Gail Smith (Resident)
M. Gray Styers, Jr. (Resident)
Moanica M. Caston
William L. Christopher (Resident)
David Charles Hall (Resident)
Helga Lura Leftwich (Resident)
Jeffrey A. Benson (Resident)
Dianne Smith (Resident)
Melissa P. Phipps
Margaret K. Winfield

Representative Clients: Howard Perry & Walston Realty, Inc.; Branch Banking & Trust; Integrated Silicon Systems, Inc.; Cardiovascular Diagnostics, Inc.; Pulte Home Corp.

For full biographical listings, see the Martindale-Hubbell Law Directory

PIPKIN & KNOTT, L.L.P. (AV)

100 East Six Forks Road, Suite 308, 27609-7752
Telephone: 919-783-5900
Telecopier: 919-783-9650

MEMBERS OF FIRM

Ashmead P. Pipkin
Joe T. Knott, III
Michael Wood Clark

For full biographical listings, see the Martindale-Hubbell Law Directory

SMITH DEBNAM HIBBERT & PAHL (AV)

Hedingham Oaks, 4700 New Bern Avenue, P.O. Box 26268, 27611-6268
Telephone: 919-250-2000
Facsimile: 919-250-2100

MEMBERS OF FIRM

Fred J. Smith, Jr.
W. Thurston Debnam, Jr.
Carl W. Hibbert
J. Larkin Pahl
John W. Narron
Bettie Kelley Sousa
Terri L. Gardner
Jerry T. Myers
Laura K. Howell
Elizabeth B. Godfrey
Rose H. Stout
Byron L. Saintsing
R. Jonathan Charleston
Franklin Drake

ASSOCIATES

Scott N. Johnson
Gerald H. Groon, Jr.
William G. Berggren
Terry M. Kilbride
R. Andrew Patty, II
Melanie J. Hogg
Caren Davis Enloe
Santiago M. Estrada
Jay P. Tobin
Clayton D. Morgan
Shannon Lowry Nagle
Michael D. Zetts, III
Martha L. Sewell
Philip R. Isley
Jeff D. Rogers
James Alan Flynt

For full biographical listings, see the Martindale-Hubbell Law Directory

* SMITH HELMS MULLISS & MOORE, L.L.P. (AV)

316 West Edenton Street, P.O. Box 27525, 27611-7525
Telephone: 919-755-8700
Telecopier: 919-828-7938
Charlotte, North Carolina Office: 227 North Tryon Street, P.O. Box 31247.
Telephone: 704-343-2000.
Telecopier: 704-334-8467.
Telex: 572460.
Greensboro, North Carolina Office: Smith Helms Mulliss & Moore, Suite 1400 First Union Tower, 300 North Greene Street, P.O. Box 21927.
Telephone: 910-378-5200.
Telecopier: 910-379-9558.

(See Next Column)

MEMBERS OF FIRM

Richard W. Ellis
James L. Gale
Samuel O. Southern
Brad S. Markoff
George J. Oliver
Michael G. Winters
Leslie C. O'Toole
Charles N. Anderson, Jr.
Elizabeth M. Powell

ASSOCIATES

Gary R. Govert
Donna Kaye Blumberg
R. L. Adams
J. Donald Hobart, Jr.
Paul K. Sun, Jr.
Matthew W. Sawchak
Robert H. Bergdolt
Charles R. Monroe, Jr.
Mary Margaret Dillon

For full biographical listings, see the Martindale-Hubbell Law Directory

JAMES R. TROTTER (AV)

150 Fayetteville Street Mall, Suite 2700, First Union Capitol Center, 27601
Telephone: 919-831-4782

For full biographical listings, see the Martindale-Hubbell Law Directory

* WOMBLE CARLYLE SANDRIDGE & RICE (AV)

A Professional Limited Liability Company
2100 First Union Capitol Center, 150 Fayetteville Street Mall, P.O. Box 831, 27602
Telephone: 919-755-2100
Telecopy: 919-755-2150
Telex: 806498
Charlotte, North Carolina Office: 3300 One First Union Center, 301 South College Street.
Telephone: 704-331-4900.
Telecopy: 704-331-4955.
Telex: 853609.
Winston-Salem, North Carolina Office: 1600 Southern National Financial Center.
Telephone: 919-721-3600.
Telecopy: 919-721-3660.
Telex: 806498.
Atlanta, Georgia Office: One Ninety One Peachtree Tower, 191 Peachtree Street N.E., Suite 3250.
Telephone: 404-614-2580.
Fax: 404-614-2595.

RESIDENT PARTNERS

M. Christopher Bolen
Gordon Eugene Boyce
E. Lawrence Davis, III
Donald A. Donadio
Charles A. Edwards
Robert E. Fields, III
Marilyn R. Forbes
Deborah Hylton Hartzog
Johnny M. Loper
William Camp Matthews, Jr.
Pressly M. Millen
Robert Harrison Sasser, III
Stephen A. Yeagy

RESIDENT ASSOCIATES

Yvonne C. Bailey
Susan D. Crooks
Mark Allen Davis
Andrea Harris Fox
Willie D. Gilbert, II
Christopher T. Graebe
Elizabeth Janeway Hallyburton
Willie H. Johnson, III
Susan Sawin McFarlane
Cindy G. Oliver
Jennifer E. Bennett Overton
Simmons I. Patrick, Jr.
Elizabeth LeVan Riley
Nicolas P. Robinson
Samuel M. Taylor
Maury M. Tepper, III
Nellie Shipley Tomlinson
Kathleen Nowack Worm

RESIDENT OF COUNSEL

Charles S. Carter
Jasper L. Cummings, Jr.
Paul A. Jones

Representative Clients: Aetna Casualty and Surety Co., Inc.; ALSCO/AmeriMark Building Products, Inc.; Aoki Corporation America, Inc.; Empire of Carolina, Inc.; Hackney Brothers, Inc.; Lawyers Mutual Liability Insurance Company of North Carolina; Meredith College; Monk-Austin, Inc.; Regency Park Corporation; Wachovia Bank of North Carolina, N.A.

For full biographical listings, see the Martindale-Hubbell Law Directory

WYCHE & STORY (AV)

Registered Limited Liability Partnership
225 Hillsborough Street, Suite 130, Hillsborough Place P.O. Drawer 1389, 27602-1389
Telephone: 919-821-7700
Telecopier: 919-821-7703

MEMBERS

N. Hunter Wyche, Jr.
Ashley H. Story
James B. Angell

ASSOCIATES

Colleen C. McCulloch
Carolyn E. Wilson
Claire Bruni Casey
Kevin L. Sink

For full biographical listings, see the Martindale-Hubbell Law Directory

Raleigh—Continued

YOUNG, MOORE, HENDERSON & ALVIS, P.A. (AV)

3201 Glenwood Avenue, P.O. Box 31627, 27622
Telephone: 919-782-6860
Telecopier: 919-782-6753

Charles H. Young, Jr. (1947-1992)
Joseph C. Moore, Jr. (1919-1988)
B. T. Henderson, II
Jerry S. Alvis
Henry S. Manning, Jr.
J. Clark Brewer
John N. Fountain
William M. Trott
R. Michael Strickland
Joseph C. Moore, III
John A. Michaels
Robert C. Paschal
Walter E. Brock, Jr.
Evelyn M. Coman
Joseph W. Williford
David P. Sousa
J. Aldean Webster, III
Marvin M. Spivey, Jr.
M. Lee Cheney
David M. Duke
Ralph W. Meekins

OF COUNSEL

Charles H. Young

Josephine R. Darden
E. Knox Proctor, V
J. D. Prather
Brian E. Clemmons
Rudy L. Ogburn
Terryn D. Owens
Joe E. Austin, Jr.
Dana H. Davis
R. Christopher Dillon
Carolyn S. Knaut
Glenn C. Raynor
Fred M. Wood, Jr.
J. Mark Langdon

General Counsel for: Joe P. Wyatt & Sons Co.; North Carolina Rate Bureau; North Carolina Reinsurance Facility; State Board of Examiners of Plumbing and Heating Contractors.
Legislative Counsel for: State Farm Insurance Companies; Nationwide Insurance Companies.
Counsel for: Bridgestone/Firestone, Inc.; International Paper Co.; General Motors Corp.; Overnite Transportation Company.

For full biographical listings, see the Martindale-Hubbell Law Directory

---

REIDSVILLE, Rockingham Co.

HOLT & WATT (AV)

211 Gilmer Street, P.O. Box 728, 27320
Telephone: 910-342-2997

Clark M. Holt
Robert L. Watt, III

Counsel for: King Construction Co.
Representative Clients: Mutual Savings & Loan Assn. of Reidsville, N.C.; First National Bank of Reidsville, N.C.; Rentz Oil Co.
Approved Attorneys for: Lawyers Title Insurance Corp.; Chicago Title Insurance Co.; First Title Insurance Co.

For full biographical listings, see the Martindale-Hubbell Law Directory

---

ROANOKE RAPIDS, Halifax Co.

WHITAKER & DICKENS (AV)

1107 Hamilton Street, P.O. Box 1129, 27870
Telephone: 919-537-8204
FAX: 919-537-3145

MEMBERS OF FIRM

Cary Whitaker
William F. Dickens, Jr.

Counsel for: Champion International Corp.; Champion Timberlands; Roanoke Rapids Housing Authority; Glover Construction Co.; AutoVerters, Inc.; Roanoke Rapids Graded School District; Enfield Cotton Gin, Inc.

For full biographical listings, see the Martindale-Hubbell Law Directory

---

*ROBBINSVILLE,** Graham Co. — (Refer to Franklin)

---

*ROCKINGHAM,** Richmond Co.

LEATH, BYNUM, KITCHIN & NEAL, P.A. (AV)

111 Washington Street, P.O. Box 1657, 28379
Telephone: 910-997-2206
FAX: Available upon request

Thomas H. Leath (1905-1978)
Fred W. Bynum, Jr. (Retired)
Henry L. Kitchin
F. Brent Neal
Stephan R. Futrell

Representative Clients: Lumbermens Mutual Casualty Co.; The American Insurance Co.; Carolina Power & Light Co.; Southern Bell Telephone & Telegraph Co.
Approved Attorneys for: Lawyers Title Insurance Corp.

For full biographical listings, see the Martindale-Hubbell Law Directory

---

*ROXBORO,** Person Co.

HUBBARD, CATES & LONG (AV)

36 Court Street, P.O. Box 679, 27573
Telephone: 910-597-2251; 599-2443
FAX: 910-597-3042

(See Next Column)

MEMBERS OF FIRM

Charles E. Hubbard
Walter Bradsher Cates
Daniel R. Long, Jr.

LEGAL SUPPORT PERSONNEL

Deborah L. Barker

Representative Clients: Person County Memorial Hospital; Person County Family Medical Center; Carolane Propane Gas, Inc.; Camp Chemical Corp.; Person-Caswell Lake Authority.
Approved Attorneys for: Branch Banking and Trust; First Union National Bank of North Carolina; Central Carolina Bank and Trust Co., N.A.
References: First Union National Bank of North Carolina; Roxboro Savings Bank, SSB.

For full biographical listings, see the Martindale-Hubbell Law Directory

---

JACKSON, HICKS & FITZGERALD (AV)

22 Court Street, P.O. Box 490, 27573
Telephone: 910-599-0211
Fax: 910-599-2672

MEMBERS OF FIRM

George W. Jackson
Alan S. Hicks
Thomas L. Fitzgerald

Representative Clients: Eanes Oil Co.; Winstead Builders, Inc.; Crowm Crafts, Inc.; Piedmont Community College; Mid Atlantic Chrysler-Plymouth Dealer Advertising Assn.; Tultex Yarn Group; Courier-Times, Inc.; Peoples Bank & Trust Co.; Camp Chemical Corp.; Irvin Industries, Inc.

For full biographical listings, see the Martindale-Hubbell Law Directory

---

*RUTHERFORDTON,** Rutherford Co.

HAMRICK, BOWEN, NANNEY & DALTON (AV)

301 West Court Street, P.O. Drawer 790, 28139
Telephone: 704-286-9152
FAX: 704-287-9101

MEMBERS OF FIRM

Fred Delmar Hamrick, Jr. (1908-1982)
James M. Bowen
Louis W. Nanney, Jr.
Walter H. Dalton
Robert L. Mebane
Bradley K. Greenway
Elizabeth T. Miller

For full biographical listings, see the Martindale-Hubbell Law Directory

---

*SALISBURY,** Rowan Co.

KLUTTZ, REAMER, BLANKENSHIP & HAYES, L.L.P. (AV)

131 N. Main Street, P.O. Drawer 1617, 28145-1617
Telephone: 704-636-7100
Telecopier: 704-636-2284

Wm. Clarence Kluttz (Retired)
Lewis P. Hamlin, Jr. (1919-1988)
Richard R. Reamer
Malcolm B. Blankenship, Jr.
William C. Kluttz, Jr.
Glenn S. Hayes
James D.K.F. Randolph
Edward P. Norvell

Representative Clients: Duke Power Co.; General Electric Co.; Cone Mills Corp.; Security Bank & Trust Co.; Nationwide Mutual Insurance Co.; Kemper Insurance Group; North Carolina Farm Bureau Mutual Insurance Co.; The Papco Group, Inc.; Parmz Corporation; Johnson Concrete, Inc.

For full biographical listings, see the Martindale-Hubbell Law Directory

---

SHUFORD & CADDELL (AV)

205 Wachovia Bank Building, P.O. Box 198, 28144
Telephone: 704-636-8050

MEMBERS OF FIRM

W. T. Shuford (1905-1990)
Thomas M. Caddell

Representative Clients: Wachovia Bank & Trust Co.; Taylor Clay Products; Rowan Corp.; BellSouth Telecommunications; Dominion Yarn Corp.; Rockwell Farms; Gardner Mirror, Inc.

For full biographical listings, see the Martindale-Hubbell Law Directory

---

WOODSON, FORD, SAYERS, LAWTHER, SHORT, PARROTT & HUDSON (AV)

201 West Council Street, P.O. Box 829, 28145-0829
Telephone: 704-633-5000
Fax: 704-637-2388

MEMBERS OF FIRM

Walter H. Woodson (1875-1964)
J. Giles Hudson (1890-1973)
James L. Woodson (1916-1992)
Larry G. Ford
Donald D. Sayers
Francis Rivers Lawther, Jr.
Carl Meredith Short, Jr.
S. Edward Parrott
John T. Hudson

OF COUNSEL

James G. Hudson, Jr.

Representative Clients: Rowan County Board of Education; American Mutual Fire Insurance Co.; First Union National Bank of North Carolina; Cincinnati Insurance Company; City of Salisbury; Catawba College.

(See Next Column)

WOODSON, FORD, SAYERS, LAWTHER, SHORT, PARROTT & HUDSON—*Continued*

Local Counsel for: Piedmont Farm Credit, ACA; Cincinnati Insurance Co.

For full biographical listings, see the Martindale-Hubbell Law Directory

*SANFORD,** Lee Co.

STATON, PERKINSON, DOSTER, POST, SILVERMAN & ADCOCK (AV)

205 Courtland Drive, P.O. Box 1320, 27331
Telephone: 919-775-5616
FAX: 919-774-7148

MEMBERS OF FIRM

J. C. Pittman (1900-1975)
Robert L. Gavin (1916-1981)
William Wayne Staton
Ronald L. Perkinson
W. Woods Doster
Norman C. Post, Jr.
Jonathan Silverman
Paul J. Adcock

ASSOCIATES

Elizabeth Myrick Boone
Beverly D. Basden

Representative Clients: Golden Corral Corp.; Federal Spinning Corp.; Cigar Supply, Inc.; Virginia-Carolina Tools of Sanford, Inc.; GC Development Corp.; Mid-South Holding Co.
Local Counsel for: Nationwide Insurance Co.; State Farm Mutual Insurance Co.; Aetna Casualty & Surety Co.; Allstate Insurance Co.

For full biographical listings, see the Martindale-Hubbell Law Directory

SCOTLAND NECK, Halifax Co. — (Refer to Roanoke Rapids)

SHALLOTTE, Brunswick Co.

FRINK, FOY, GAINEY & YOUNT, P.A. (AV)

P.O. Box 307, 28459
Telephone: 910-754-6934
Southport, North Carolina Office: 319 North Howe Street.
Telephone: 919-457-5284.

Stephen B. Yount

Local Counsel for: Seaboard Coast Line Railroad Co.
Representative Clients: United Carolina Bank; Pilot Life Insurance Co.; Jefferson Standard Life Insurance Co.; Reeves Telecom Corp.; Nationwide Insurance Co.
Approved Attorneys for: Lawyers Title Insurance Corp.; First Title Insurance Corp.
References: United Carolina Bank; Security Savings & Loan Assn.

*SHELBY,** Cleveland Co.

LACKEY & LACKEY (AV)

301 East Warren Street, Suite B, P.O. Box 2544, 28150-4650
Telephone: 704-487-4511
Fax: 704-482-2103

MEMBERS OF FIRM

N. Dixon Lackey, Jr.
Mark D. Lackey
Seth N. Lackey

Representative Clients: Shelby Federal Savings and Loan Assn.; United States Fidelity & Guaranty Co.; PPG Industries, Inc.; Celanese Corp.; J. P. Stevens Co.; Martin-Marietta Corp.; Duke Power Co.; NationsBank; N.C. State Employees Credit Union; Grover Industries, Inc.

For full biographical listings, see the Martindale-Hubbell Law Directory

*SMITHFIELD,** Johnston Co.

NARRON, O'HALE & WHITTINGTON, P.A. (AV)

Market & Third Street, P.O. Box 1567, 27577
Telephone: 919-934-6021
Fax: 919-934-6280
Benson, North Carolina Office: 207 East Main Street, P.O. Box 457.
Telephone: 919-894-8565.

James W. Narron
John P. O'Hale
O. Hampton Whittington, Jr. (Resident, Benson Office)

Jacquelyn L. Lee
Clint E. Massengill

Representative Clients: Georgia-Pacific Corp.; T. E. Johnson Lumber Co., Inc.; Carolina Telephone & Telegraph Co.; Coor Farm Supply Service, Inc.; NationsBank; Etheridge Oil Co.

For full biographical listings, see the Martindale-Hubbell Law Directory

*SNOW HILL,** Greene Co. — (Refer to Kinston)

SOUTHERN PINES, Moore Co. — (Refer to Pinehurst)

SOUTHPORT, Brunswick Co.

FRINK, FOY, GAINEY & YOUNT, P.A. (AV)

319 North Howe Street, 28461
Telephone: 910-457-5284
Shallotte, North Carolina Office: P.O. Box 307.
Telephone: 919-754-6934.

S. Bunn Frink (1899-1989)
Henry G. Foy
A. H. Gainey, Jr.
Stephen B. Yount

Local Counsel for: Seaboard Coast Line Railroad Co.
Representative Clients: United Carolina Bank; Pilot Life Insurance Co.; Jefferson Standard Life Insurance Co.; Reeves Telecom Corp.; Nationwide Insurance Co.
Approved Attorneys for: Lawyers Title Insurance Corp.; First Title Insurance Corp.
References: United Carolina Bank; Security Savings & Loan Assn.

For full biographical listings, see the Martindale-Hubbell Law Directory

SPINDALE, Rutherford Co. — (Refer to Rutherfordton)

*STATESVILLE,** Iredell Co.

POPE, McMILLAN, GOURLEY, KUTTEH & SIMON (AV)

113 North Center Street, Suite 200, P.O. Drawer 1776, 28687-1776
Telephone: 704-873-2131; 704-664-2254
Fax: 704-872-7629
Mooresville, North Carolina Office: 207 South Broad Street.
Telephone: 704-664-2254.

MEMBERS OF FIRM

William P. Pope
William H. McMillan
Robert H. Gourley
Constantine H. Kutteh, II
Pamela H. Simon

Representative Clients: Nationwide Insurance Co.; Aetna Life & Casualty Insurance Co.; NationsBank; Davis Community Hospital; Bank of Iredell; Piedmont Farm Credit Assn.; Allstate Insurance Co.; Travelers Ins. Co.
Approved Attorneys for: Lawyers Title Insurance Corp.; Farmers Home and Federal Land Bank Association.

For full biographical listings, see the Martindale-Hubbell Law Directory

*SYLVA,** Jackson Co. — (Refer to Waynesville)

TABOR CITY, Columbus Co.

McGOUGAN, WRIGHT, WORLEY AND HARPER (AV)

202 South Lewis Street, P.O. Box 457, 28463
Telephone: 910-653-3682; 653-2082
FAX: 910-653-5726
Whiteville, North Carolina Office: 130 Jefferson Street.
Telephone: 910-640-1485.
Fax: 910-640-3132.

MEMBERS OF FIRM

Duncan F. McGougan, Jr. (1921-1994)
O. Richard Wright, Jr.
Dennis T. Worley
Willis H. Harper, Jr.

General Counsel: The Brunswick Electric Membership Corp.; Town of Tabor City; Frank Horne Construction Co.; Atlantic Publishing & Paper Co.; Town of Bolton; Town of Boardman; Town of Brunswick; Town of Fair Bluff; Town of Cerro Gordo; The Gore Co.
Representative Clients: Cooperative Savings & Loan Assn.; Southern National Bank; Gore Trailer Manufacturing Co.; Tabor City Lumber Co.; Jones Stores; United Carolina Bank.

For full biographical listings, see the Martindale-Hubbell Law Directory

*TAYLORSVILLE,** Alexander Co. — (Refer to Statesville)

*TROY,** Montgomery Co. — (Refer to Albemarle)

TRYON, Polk Co.

McFARLAND & McFARLAND (AV)

125 South Trade Street, 28782
Telephone: 704-859-9131
FAX: 704-859-9132

MEMBERS OF FIRM

Wm. A. McFarland
William A. McFarland, Jr.

Local Counsel for: Norfolk & Southern Railroad.
Representative Clients: Tryon Federal Savings & Loan Assn.; Public Service of North Carolina; Town of Tryon ABC Board; McFarland Funeral Chapel.
Approved Attorneys for: Lawyer's Title Insurance Corp.; First Federal Savings Bank (Hendersonville); North Carolina National Bank; Lawyers Title Insurance Corp.

For full biographical listings, see the Martindale-Hubbell Law Directory

UNION GROVE, Iredell Co. — (Refer to Morganton)

VALDESE, Burke Co. — (Refer to Morganton)

*WADESBORO,** Anson Co. — (Refer to Rockingham)

WALLACE, Duplin Co.

WELLS & BLOSSOM (AV)

124 East Boney Street, 28466
Telephone: 910-285-3400

MEMBERS OF FIRM

Winifred T. Wells (1919-1982) William C. Blossom

Representative Clients: Branch Banking & Trust Co.; Carolina Power & Light (Local Counsel); Carolina Telephone (Local Counsel); Cooperative Bank for Savings, Inc.; Murphy Farms, Inc.
Approved Attorneys for: Lawyers Title Insurance of North Carolina, Inc.
Reference: Branch Banking and Trust Co.

For full biographical listings, see the Martindale-Hubbell Law Directory

*WARRENTON,** Warren Co.

BANZET, BANZET & THOMPSON (AV)

Court House Square, P.O. Box 535, 27589
Telephone: 919-257-3166; 257-2201
Fax: 919-257-2053

MEMBERS OF FIRM

Julius Banzet, III Lewis A. Thompson, III

OF COUNSEL

Frank Banzet

Representative Clients: Branch Banking & Trust Co.; Town of Norlina; The Peck Manufacturing Company of North Carolina, Inc.; Warren County Board of Education.
Approved Attorneys for: Federal Land Bank of Columbia; Lawyers Title Insurance Corp.; Chicago Title Insurance Co.; Commonwealth Land Title Insurance Co.; AMI Title Insurance Co.; Savings & Loan Assn.

For full biographical listings, see the Martindale-Hubbell Law Directory

WARSAW, Duplin Co.

E.C. THOMPSON III, P.A. (AV)

114 West Hill Street, P.O. Box 901, 29398-0901
Telephone: 919-293-3124
Facsimile: 919-293-7171

E. C. Thompson, III

For full biographical listings, see the Martindale-Hubbell Law Directory

*WASHINGTON,** Beaufort Co.

RODMAN, HOLSCHER, FRANCISCO & PECK, P.A. (AV)

130 East Second Street, P.O. Drawer 1747, 27889
Telephone: 919-946-3122
FAX: 919-946-3125

Edward N. Rodman David C. Francisco
Frederick Norman Holscher R. Brantley Peck, Jr.

Representative Clients: NationsBank of North Carolina; Metropolitan Life; Jefferson-Pilot; Travelers; Nationwide; Liberty Mutual; Southern Railway (Local Counsel); Hartford Indemnity.

For full biographical listings, see the Martindale-Hubbell Law Directory

*WAYNESVILLE,** Haywood Co.

BROWN, WARD, HAYNES, GRIFFIN & SEAGO, P.A. (AV)

Suite 300 Savings and Loan Building, 505 North Main Street, P.O. Drawer 928, 28786-0928
Telephone: 704-456-9436

David J. Haynes Woodrow H. Griffin
Randal Seago

General Counsel for: Haywood Savings & Loan Assn., Inc.; Haywood Builders Supply Co., Inc.; Southeastern Jurisdictional Administrative Council, Inc. (f/k/a Lake Junaluska Assembly); Haywood County Board of Realtors.
Local Counsel for: Haywood Elect. Membership Corporation.
Approved Attorneys for: Lawyers Title Insurance Corp.; Chicago Title Insurance Co.; Federal Land Bank of Columbia; Lawyers Title of North Carolina; Commonwealth Title Co.

For full biographical listings, see the Martindale-Hubbell Law Directory

*WENTWORTH,** Rockingham Co.

HARRINGTON & STULTZ (AV)

2 Courthouse Square, 27375
Telephone: 910-349-2943
Fax: 910-627-4243
Eden, North Carolina Office: 708 West Washington Street.
Telephone: 919-623-8436.

MEMBERS OF FIRM

Thomas S. Harrington J. Hoyte Stultz, Jr.

Representative Clients: Morgan Drive Away, Inc.; Jimmy Wright Pontiac-Buick-GMC, Inc.

(See Next Column)

Local Counsel: Duke Power Co.; NationsBank.
Approved Attorneys for: Lawyers Title Insurance Corp.

WEST JEFFERSON, Ashe Co.

VANNOY & REEVES (AV)

306 East Main Street, P.O. Drawer 67, 28694
Telephone: 910-246-7172
FAX: 910-246-5966

MEMBERS OF FIRM

Wade E. Vannoy, Jr. (1927-1991) Jimmy D. Reeves

ASSOCIATES

David A. Jolly

Approved Attorneys for: Lawyers Title Insurance Corp.; United Title Insurance Co.; AMI Title Insurance Co.; Ashe Federal Savings and Loan Assn., West Jefferson; Centura Bank; First Title Insurance Co.; Southern National Bank; Investors Title Insurance Co.; United States Farmers Home Administration; Yadkin Valley Bank.

*WHITEVILLE,** Columbus Co.

WILLIAMSON & WALTON (AV)

136 Washington Street, P.O. Box 1467, 28472
Telephone: 910-642-7151
FAX: 910-640-1234

OF COUNSEL

Edward L. Williamson

MEMBERS OF FIRM

Benton H. Walton, III C. Greg Williamson
Carlton F. Williamson

General Counsel for: Columbus National Bank and First Investors Savings Bank.
Representative Clients: Nationwide Mutual Insurance Co.; Farmers Home Administration; City of Whiteville; Lowes, Inc.; Southeastern Community College; North Carolina Farm Bureau Insurance Co.

For full biographical listings, see the Martindale-Hubbell Law Directory

*WILKESBORO,** Wilkes Co.

WILLARDSON, LIPSCOMB & BENDER (AV)

206 East Main Street, 28697
Telephone: 910-838-5129
FAX: 910-838-8959

MEMBERS OF FIRM

John S. Willardson William F. Lipscomb
David M. Bender

ASSOCIATES

Michael D. Beal

Representative Clients: Aetna Casualty & Surety Co.; Bankers & Shippers Insurance Co.; Seibels Bruce Insurance Co.; North Carolina Farm Bureau Mutual; Pennsylvania National Mutual Insurance; Pennsylvania Mutual Insurance Co.; Nationwide Mutual Insurance Co.; Wausau Insurance Co.

For full biographical listings, see the Martindale-Hubbell Law Directory

*WILLIAMSTON,** Martin Co. — (Refer to Washington)

*WILMINGTON,** New Hanover Co.

CLARK, NEWTON, HINSON & MCLEAN, L.L.P. (AV)

509 Princess Street, 28401
Telephone: 910-762-8743
Facsimile: 910-762-6206

George T. Clark, Jr. Reid G. Hinson
John Richard Newton J. Dickson McLean

Representative Clients: North Carolina Natural Gas; North Carolina Shipping Assn. P&I CLUBS: The Britannia Club; Liverpool & London P&I Club; London Steamship Mutual P&I; Standard Steamship P&I; Steamship Mutual P&I Club; The Swedish Club; The Gard; United Kingdom Club; West of England Shipowners Mutual Insurance Assn.

For full biographical listings, see the Martindale-Hubbell Law Directory

FAISON & FLETCHER (AV)

130 North Front Street, Suite 300, 28401
Telephone: 910-251-9900
FAX: 910-251-9667
Durham, North Carolina Office: Suite 1400 University Tower, 3100 Tower Boulevard, Post Office Box 51729.
Telephone: 919-489-9001.
Telecopier: 919-489-5774. WATS: 800-437-9001.

MEMBERS OF FIRM

O. William Faison Reginald B. Gillespie, Jr.
George L. Fletcher Gary R. Poole

(See Next Column)

FAISON & FLETCHER—*Continued*

ASSOCIATES

Catherine L. Clark
Cynthia T. Shriner
Michael R. Ortiz
Selina S. Nomeir
David L. Ray
Lisa L. Lanier
John T. Honeycutt
Keith D. Burns
Donna Miller-Slade

OF COUNSEL

Kathleen D.H. Pawlowski (Resident)

For full biographical listings, see the Martindale-Hubbell Law Directory

HOGUE, HILL, JONES, NASH AND LYNCH (AV)

101 S. Third Street, P.O. Drawer 2178, 28402
Telephone: 910-763-4565
Telecopier: 910-762-6687

OF COUNSEL

Cyrus D. Hogue, Jr.

MEMBERS OF FIRM

Cyrus D. Hogue (1888-1960)
William L. Hill, II
W. Talmage Jones
David A. Nash
William O. J. Lynch
James B. Snow, III
Wayne A. Bullard
Patricia Cramer Jenkins

Representative Clients: NationsBank of North Carolina, N.A.; Cooperative Bank for Savings; St. Paul Insurance Cos.; New Hanover County Board of Education; Lower Cape Fear Water and Sewer Authority; Cape Fear Memorial Hospital, Inc.; Royal Globe Insurance Co.; Kaiser Aluminum & Chemical Corp.; Wilmington Shipping Co.; Brunswick Hospital; International Paper Co.

For full biographical listings, see the Martindale-Hubbell Law Directory

MARSHALL, WILLIAMS & GORHAM, L.L.P. (AV)

14 South Fifth Street, P.O. Drawer 2088, 28402-2088
Telephone: 910-763-9891
Telecopier: 910-343-8604

MEMBERS OF FIRM

Alan A. Marshall (1908-1979)
Lonnie B. Williams
A. Dumay Gorham, Jr.
Jerry C. Woodell
William Robert Cherry, Jr.
Ronald H. Woodruff
Lonnie B. Williams, Jr.
John Dearman Martin
Charles D. Meier
John L. Coble

Representative Clients: Miller Building Corp.; Kemper Insurance Cos.; New Hanover Regional Medical Center; The Housing Authority of the City of Wilmington; Ryan-Walsh, Inc.; CIGNA Cos.; Aetna Casualty & Surety Co.; Bituminous Insurance Co.; Government Employers Insurance Co.

For full biographical listings, see the Martindale-Hubbell Law Directory

MURCHISON, TAYLOR, KENDRICK, GIBSON & DAVENPORT, L.L.P. (AV)

16 North Fifth Avenue, 28401-4593
Telephone: 910-763-2426
FAX: 910-763-6561

OF COUNSEL

Wallace C. Murchison

MEMBERS OF FIRM

Joseph O. Taylor, Jr.
Vaiden P. Kendrick
Frank B. Gibson, Jr.
Fred B. Davenport, Jr.
Michael Murchison
Nancy M. Guyton
W. Berry Trice

ASSOCIATES

G. Stephen Diab
Alan D. McInnes

Representative Clients: Branch Banking & Trust Co.; Southern National Bank; General Electric Co.; Landfall Assn.; Landmark Organization, Inc.; Nationwide Insurance Co.; Southern Bell; Telechron, Inc.; Trustees, Employers-ILA Pension, Welfare and Vacation Fund; Worsley Cos., Inc.

For full biographical listings, see the Martindale-Hubbell Law Directory

ROUNTREE & SEAGLE, L.L.P. (AV)

2419 Market Street, P.O. Box 1409, 28402-1409
Telephone: 910-763-3404
Telecopier: 910-763-0320

MEMBERS OF FIRM

George Rountree, Jr. (1904-1979)
George Rountree, III
J. Harold Seagle
Charles M. Lineberry, Jr.

OF COUNSEL

George K. Freeman, Jr.

ASSOCIATES

Geoffrey A. Losee

Representative Clients: American International Marine Agency; Fireman's Fund Insurance Cos.; The Japan Shipowners' Mutual Protection & Indemnity Assn., Ltd.

(See Next Column)

Approved Attorneys for: Chicago Title Insurance Co.; Commonwealth Land Insurance Co.; Investors Title Insurance Co.; Lawyers Title Insurance Corp.
References: Centura Bank; First Union National Bank of North Carolina; NationsBank of North Carolina, N.A.

For full biographical listings, see the Martindale-Hubbell Law Directory

RYALS, ROBINSON & SAFFO, P.C. (AV)

701 Market Street, P.O. Box 135, 28402
Telephone: 910-763-3374
Fax: 910-763-4004

Granville A. Ryals
Robin Wicks Robinson
Anthony A. Saffo

Representative Clients: J.O. Baldwin Construction Co.; Cape Industries; Classic Inns of America, Inc.; Developers Diversified Management Co.; First Wilmington Corp.; General Electric Mortgage Insurance Co.; Gulf Stream Foods, Inc.; M.J.B. Manufacturing Co.; OPTION Care of Wilmington.

For full biographical listings, see the Martindale-Hubbell Law Directory

*WILSON,** Wilson Co.

CONNOR, BUNN, ROGERSON & WOODARD, P.A. (AV)

P.O. Box 3299, 27895-3299
Telephone: 919-243-3136
FAX: 919-243-2558

David M. Connor
Turner B. Bunn, III
James F. Rogerson
David W. Woodard
Henry Groves Connor (1911-1989)
C. Timothy Williford
Julie M. Watson

Counsel for: The Firestone Tire & Rubber Co.; The Wilson Daily Times, Inc.; New Hope Development Corp.; Nash Realty Co; Bunn & Co.

For full biographical listings, see the Martindale-Hubbell Law Directory

ROSE, RAND, ORCUTT, CAULEY & BLAKE, P.A. (AV)

2500 West Nash Street, Unit C, P.O. Drawer 2367, 27894-2367
Telephone: 919-291-3848
Telecopier: 919-291-9555

William A. Lucas (1881-1967)
Oliver G. Rand (1895-1967)
Naomi E. Morris (1921-1986)
Z. Hardy Rose (Retired)
William R. Rand
David S. Orcutt
James P. Cauley, III
Paul N. Blake, III

Susan K. Ellis

Representative Clients: City of Wilson; Wilson County Board of Education; Region L Council of Governments; Barton College; Wilson County Properties, Inc.; Braswell Equipment Company, Inc.; Town of Black Creek; Wilson-Greene Mental Health Association; Wilson Landholding Corporation; James B. Batts Distributing Company.

For full biographical listings, see the Martindale-Hubbell Law Directory

*WINDSOR,** Bertie Co. — (Refer to Ahoskie)

*WINSTON-SALEM,** Forsyth Co.

ALLMAN SPRY HUMPHREYS & LEGGETT, P.A. (AV)

Suite 700, 380 Knollwood Street, P.O. Box 5129, 27113-5129
Telephone: 910-722-2300
Telecopier: 910-721-0414

C. Edwin Allman (1926-1991)
James E. Humphreys, Jr. (1938-1989)
W. Dennie Spry
R. Bradford Leggett
Donald M. VonCannon
C. Edwin Allman, III
Thomas T. Crumpler
W. Thomas White
David C. Smith
Catharine R. Carruthers
Edward E. Raymer, Jr.
M. Joseph Allman
D. Barrett Burge
Walter R. Hinnant
Linda L. Helms

Representative Clients: Brendles, Inc.; Murray Supply Co., Inc.; Mutual of Omaha Insurance Co.; Tyson Foods, Inc.; Dixie Insurance Agency, Inc.; Roadway Express, Inc.; Town of Walkertown; Town of Rural Hall; Lyndon Steel Company.

For full biographical listings, see the Martindale-Hubbell Law Directory

BELL, DAVIS & PITT, P.A. (AV)

635 West Fourth Street, P.O. Box 21029, 27120-1029
Telephone: 910-722-3700
Fax: 910-722-8153

Frank M. Bell, Jr.
William Kearns Davis
Walter W. Pitt, Jr.
Joseph T. Carruthers
James R. Fox
William D. Harper
Stephen M. Russell
D. Anderson Carmen
John W. Babcock
J. Dennis Bailey
Stephen D. Poe
Amy K. Smith
Charlot F. Wood
Thomas W. Waldrep, Jr.

(See Next Column)

BELL, DAVIS & PITT P.A., *Winston-Salem—Continued*

James D. Wall
Howell A. Burkhalter
Elizabeth M. Repetti
Alan M. Ruley
Mallory M. Oldham

Local Counsel for: Builders Transport, Inc.; Chrysler Credit Corp.; NationsBank of North Carolina, N.A.; Piedmont Natural Gas Co.; St. Paul Insurance Co.; Travelers Insurance Co.; Southern National Bank of North Carolina.
General Counsel for: Adele Knits, Inc.; Landmark Builders of The Triad, Inc.; Piedmont Farm Credit, ACA.

For full biographical listings, see the Martindale-Hubbell Law Directory

CRAIGE, BRAWLEY, LIIPFERT, WALKER & SEARCY (AV)

500 West Fourth Street, Suite 200, P.O. Box 1666, 27102-1666
Telephone: 910-725-0583
FAX: 910-725-4677
Kernersville, North Carolina Office: Suite E, 516 East Mountain Street.
Telephone: 919-993-6912.
Telecopy: 919-993-6908.

MEMBERS OF FIRM

Cowles Liipfert
William W. Walker
Philip E. Searcy
Diane Brock Oser
George Wilson Martin, Jr.
Warren E. Kasper
Ronald J. Short
Kimberly D. Speiden

ASSOCIATES

B. Bailey Liipfert, III

Approved Attorneys for: Lawyers Title Insurance Corp.; Chicago Title Insurance Co.; Commonwealth Land Title Insurance Co.; First American Title Insurance Co.; Jefferson-Pilot Title Insurance Co.

For full biographical listings, see the Martindale-Hubbell Law Directory

HUTCHINS, TYNDALL, DOUGHTON & MOORE (AV)

115 West Third Street, P.O. Drawer 20039, 27120-0039
Telephone: 910-725-8385
Telecopier: 910-723-8838

Fred S. Hutchins, Sr. (1893-1977)
John M. Minor (1917-1974)
Roy L. Deal (1889-1982)

MEMBERS OF FIRM

Fred S. Hutchins, Jr.
George E. Doughton, Jr.
Thomas W. Moore, Jr.
Richard Tyndall
Richmond W. Rucker
H. Lee Davis, Jr.
Kent L. Hamrick
Laurie Hutchins
Claude M. Hamrick

ASSOCIATES

Thomas J. Doughton
David L. Hall

General Counsel for: Wachovia Oil Co.; Crown Drugs of North Carolina, Inc.; W.R. Vernon Produce Co.
Local Counsel for: Travelers Insurance Co.; Maryland Casualty Co.; State Farm Insurance Co.; Liberty Mutual Insurance Co.; Shelby Mutual Insurance Co.; Transport Insurance Co.

For full biographical listings, see the Martindale-Hubbell Law Directory

PETREE STOCKTON, L.L.P. (AV)

1001 West Fourth Street, 27101-2400
Telephone: 910-607-7300
Telecopier: 910-607-7500
Charlotte, North Carolina Office: 3500 One First Union Center, 301 South College Street, 28202-6001.
Telephone: 704-338-5000.
Telecopier: 704-338-5125.
Raleigh, North Carolina Office: 4101 Lake Boone Trail.
Telephone: 919-420-1700.
Telecopier: 919-420-1800.

MEMBERS OF FIRM

William H. Petree
Ralph M. Stockton, Jr.
Robert C. Vaughn, Jr.
Richard E. Glaze
Dudley Humphrey
J. Robert Elster
E. Lynwood Mallard (Resident, Charlotte Office)
Robert L. Edwards
C. Penn Craver, Jr.
John M. Harrington
George L. Little, Jr.
James H. Kelly, Jr.
R. Frank Murphy, II
Richard B. Howington
Alfred G. Adams
Fred D. Hutchison (Resident, Raleigh Office)
Daniel R. Taylor, Jr.
Robert E. Esleeck
Penni Pearson Bradshaw
Jeffrey C. Howard
Rodrick J. Enns
Richard J. Keshian
J. Stephen Shi
William E. Wright
Peter S. Brunstetter
Lynn P. Burleson
Steve M. Pharr
Timothy J. Ehlinger
R. Rand Tucker
Jeffrey T. Lawyer
Stephen R. Berlin
J. David Mayberry
Thomas E. Graham
Barbara E. Ruark

(See Next Column)

ASSOCIATES

Celeste Beron
Maureen Tierney Orbock
Denise M. Jennings
Mark A. Stafford
Marcus L. Moxley
Edwin W. Bowden
Louis W. Doherty
Michael L. Drye
Donald M. Nielsen
Henry C. Roemer, III
Nancy C. Schneider
Julia C. Archer
Susan Hager Cooper
Susan Pauline Ellis
Suzanne Dale
Christopher C. Fox
Susan H. Boyles
Susan R. Rinne
Lorie D. Steinhagen
Kimberly H. Stogner
B. Gordon Watkins

OF COUNSEL

Robert Gray Stockton (Inactive)
William A. Brackney
Charles Y. Lackey
Ralph N. Strayhorn, Jr.

Representative Clients: Carolina Medicorp, Inc.; Bernhardt Industries, Inc.; Ladd Furniture; First Union National Bank; Sara Lee Corp.; Mobil Oil Corp.; CPC International, Inc.; Browning-Ferris Industries, Inc.

For full biographical listings, see the Martindale-Hubbell Law Directory

ROBINSON MAREADY LAWING & COMERFORD (AV)

Suite 300, 380 Knollwood Street, 27103
Telephone: 910-631-8500
Fax: 910-631-6999

MEMBERS OF FIRM

Norwood Robinson
William F. Maready
Robert J. Lawing
W. Thompson Comerford, Jr.
Michael L. Robinson
Jane C. Jackson
Gray Robinson
Clifford Britt
Jerry M. Smith

ASSOCIATES

C. Ray Grantham, Jr.
Jolinda J. Steinbacher
Stephen Robinson
John N. Taylor, Jr.
Howard Brent Helms

Representative Clients: American Furniture Manufacturers Assn.; Amoco Corp.; Bernhardt Furniture Industries; Brown & Williamson Tobacco Corp.; CNA Insurance Co.; Ohio Casualty Insurance Co.; Pine State Knitwear Co.; RJR Tobacco International; Salem Leasing Corp.; W.R. Grace & Co.

For full biographical listings, see the Martindale-Hubbell Law Directory

WOMBLE CARLYLE SANDRIDGE & RICE (AV)

A Professional Limited Liability Company
1600 Southern National Financial Center, P.O. Drawer 84, 27102
Telephone: 910-721-3600
Telecopy: 910-721-3660
Telex: 806498
Charlotte, North Carolina Office: 3300 One First Union Center, 301 South College Street.
Telephone: 704-331-4900.
Telecopy: 704-331-4955.
Telex: 853609.
Raleigh, North Carolina Office: 2100 First Union Capitol Center, 150 Fayetteville Street Mall, P.O. Box 831.
Telephone: 919-755-2100.
Telecopy: 919-755-2150.
Telex: 806498.
Atlanta, Georgia Office: One Ninety One Peachtree Tower, 191 Peachtree Street, N.E., Suite 3250.
Telephone: 404-614-2580.
Fax: 404-614-2595.

MEMBERS OF FIRM

B. S. Womble (1882-1976)
Irving E. Carlyle (1896-1971)
W. Pendleton Sandridge (1904-1982)
Leon L. Rice Jr. (1912-1987)
Reid C. Adams, Jr.
Conrad C. Baldwin, Jr.
Janice C. Baldwin
Zeb E. Barnhardt, Jr.
Henry Grady Barnhill, Jr.
Jimmy Hamilton Barnhill
Samuel Fraley Bost
Anthony H. Brett
Leslie E. Browder
Karen Estelle Carey
Kenneth G. Carroll
Keith Ashford Clinard
Clayton M. Custer
Tyrus V. Dahl, Jr.
Linwood Layfield Davis
William Allison Davis, II
Bonnie Kay Donahue
Ellis B. Drew, III
Guy F. Driver, Jr.
Gusti W. Frankel
John L. W. Garrou
Allan R. Gitter
Murray C. Greason, Jr.
R. Howard Grubbs
Michael D. Gunter
Hardin Graham Halsey
Hada de Varona Haulsee
Martin L. Holton, III
Jeffrey C. Howland
David A. Irvin
Gary W. Jackson
R. Michael Leonard
Roddey M. Ligon, Jr.
James E. Lilly (Resident, Atlanta, Georgia Office)
Dennis W. McNames
Kenneth Allen Moser
Alexander S. Nicholas
Erna A. Patrick
James K. Phillips
Robert S. Pierce
Mark N. Poovey
Elizabeth L. Quick
Robert Louis Quick
George A. Ragland
Michael E. Ray
Richard T. Rice
W. Pendleton Sandridge, Jr.
Thomas D. Schroeder

(See Next Column)

WOMBLE CARLYLE SANDRIDGE & RICE—*Continued*

MEMBERS OF FIRM (Continued)

Greg L. Smith
William B. Sullivan
James H. Thompson (Resident, Atlanta, Georgia Office)
Charles F. Vance, Jr.
Keith W. Vaughan
Dewey W. Wells
W. Preston White, Jr.
William Robert Whitehurst
Karen M. Wilson
G. Criston Windham
Calder W. Womble
William F. Womble
William F. Womble, Jr.

ASSOCIATES

Jean Taylor Adams
Patrick Martin Allen
Cari Lyn Beck
Charles A. Burke
Laura Edgerton Crowson (Not admitted in NC)
Steven D. Draper
Lawrence P. Egerton
Jeffrey L. Furr
Ellen M. Gregg
Randall A. Hanson
Robert A. Hartsoe
Ursula Marie Henninger
Lori Privette Hinnant
Martha L. James (Not admitted in NC)
Dawn Jordan
Heather A. King
Christopher Decker Lane
Joel M. Leander
Kimberly Kelly Mann
Jonathan B. Mason
Jeffrey R. McFadden
Elizabeth B. McGee
J. Daniel McNatt
Kenneth R. Michael (Not admitted in NC)
Dawn H. Morgan
James R. Morgan, Jr.
Celeste Elizabeth O'Keeffe
Mary Sheehan Pollard
David A. Shirlen
Kurt C. Stakeman
Kimberly C. Stevens
J. Keith Tart
Timothy A. Thelen
James E. Vaughan
Taylor D. Ward (Not admitted in NC)
Rory D. Whelehan
Charles Mark Wiley
F. Bruce Williams
Ranlet Shelden Willingham

OF COUNSEL

Ashley O. Thrift

LEGAL SUPPORT PERSONNEL

Hassel L. Parker (Executive Director)
Marvin E. Chavis (Director of Technology and Marketing)
Donald H. Adamick (Office Manager - Winston-Salem)
Jean Anglin (Personnel Manager)
John E. Turlington (Office Administrator - Raleigh)
Melonia H. Carroll (Librarian)
Particia A. Kight (Recruiting Administrator)
Charles R. Allison (Office Administrator - Charlotte)
Terry Michael Wiley (Director of Finance and Systems)

Representative Clients: Brad Ragan, Inc.; Brenner Companies; Food Lion, Inc.; Hanes Companies, Inc.; North Carolina Baptist Hospitals, Inc.; R.J. Reynolds Tobacco Company; Summit Communications Group, Inc.; Thomasville Furniture Industries, Inc.; Wachovia Corporation; Wake Forest University.

For full biographical listings, see the Martindale-Hubbell Law Directory

*YADKINVILLE,** Yadkin Co. — (Refer to Jonesville)

*YANCEYVILLE,** Caswell Co.

FARMER & WATLINGTON (AV)

109 West Main Street, P.O. Drawer B, 27379-0330
Telephone: 910-694-4361; 694-6549
Cable Address: "CASLAW"
FAX: 910-694-5985

MEMBERS OF FIRM

R. Lee Farmer
Stuart N. Watlington

ASSOCIATES

W. Richard Anderson, Jr.

General Counsel for: Watlington's Inc.; Ronco, Inc.; A. D. Swann Trucking Co., Inc.
Representative Clients: Wachovia Bank of North Carolina, N.A.; Duke Power Co.; First Virginia Bank Piedmont; YMK Investments Limited.
Approved Attorneys for: Lawyers Title Insurance Corp.; Farmers Home Administration, U.S.D.A.

For full biographical listings, see the Martindale-Hubbell Law Directory

NORTH DAKOTA

*BEACH,** Golden Valley Co. — (Refer to Dickinson)

*BISMARCK,** Burleigh Co.

FLECK, MATHER & STRUTZ, LTD. (AV)

Sixth Floor, Norwest Bank Building, 400 East Broadway, P.O. Box 2798, 58502
Telephone: 701-223-6585
Telecopier: 701-222-4853

Ernest R. Fleck
Russell R. Mather
William A. Strutz
Gary R. Wolberg
Paul W. Summers
Steven A. Storslee
Brian R. Bjella
John W. Morrison, Jr.
Robert J. Udland
Curtis L. Wike
Charles S. Miller, Jr.
Craig Cordell Smith
DeeNelle Louise Ruud

Representative Clients: Norwest Bank, N.A.; ITT Hartford; CNA; American International Group; W.R. Grace; Firemen's Fund; Crum and Forster; Union Oil Company of California; Shell Oil Co.; Chevron U.S.A.

For full biographical listings, see the Martindale-Hubbell Law Directory

PEARCE AND DURICK (AV)

314 East Thayer Avenue, P.O. Box 400, 58502
Telephone: 701-223-2890
Fax: 701-223-7865

MEMBERS OF FIRM

William R. Pearce (1910-1978)
William P. Pearce
Patrick W. Durick
B. Timothy Durick
Christine A. Hogan
Joel W. Gilbertson
Lawrence A. Dopson
Gary R. Thune
David E. Reich
Jerome C. Kettleson
Larry L. Boschee
Lawrence Bender

ASSOCIATES

Michael F. McMahon
Stephen D. Easton

OF COUNSEL

Harry J. Pearce

Representative Clients: American Insurance Assn.; Cigna-INA Insurance Co.; Deere & Co.; Federal Deposit Insurance Corp.; Ford Motor Co.; General Motors Corp.; MDU Resources Group, Inc.; Northwest Airlines; Royal Insurance Co.; Travelers Insurance Co.

For full biographical listings, see the Martindale-Hubbell Law Directory

PETERSON, SCHMITZ, MOENCH & SCHMIDT, A PROFESSIONAL CORPORATION (AV)

Second Floor, Suite 200, 116 North Fourth Street, P.O. Box 2076, 58502-2076
Telephone: 701-224-0400
Fax: 701-224-0399

David L. Peterson
Orell D. Schmitz
Dale W. Moench
William D. Schmidt

OF COUNSEL

Gerald Glaser

LEGAL SUPPORT PERSONNEL

Vicki J. Kunz
Traci L. Albers

For full biographical listings, see the Martindale-Hubbell Law Directory

ZUGER KIRMIS & SMITH (AV)

A Partnership including Professional Corporations
United Services Life Building, 316 North Fifth Street, P.O. Box 1695, 58502-1695
Telephone: 701-223-2711
Fax: 701-223-7387

John A. Zuger, P.C.
Lyle W. Kirmis
Thomas O. Smith, P.C.
Murray G. Sagsveen, P.C.
Lance D. Schreiner, P.C.
James S. Hill, P.C.
Patrick J. Ward
Rebecca S. Thiem, P.C.
Charles T. Edin, P.C.
Daniel S. Kuntz, P.C.
Brenda L. Blazer, P.C.
Jerry W. Evenson, P.C.

ASSOCIATES

Brent J. Edison
Patricia E. Garrity
Lawrence E. King

Representative Clients: Burlington Northern Railroad Co.; Continental National Bank & Trust Company of Chicago; First Bank, Bismarck; Mor-Gran-Sou Electric Cooperative, Inc.; North Dakota Medical Association; Quain & Ramstad Clinic; St. Paul Cos.; State Farm Insurance Co.; Sun Oil & Exploration Co.; Williston Basin Interstate Pipeline Company, a wholly-owned subsidiary of MDU Resources Group, Inc.

For full biographical listings, see the Martindale-Hubbell Law Directory

*BOTTINEAU,** Bottineau Co. — (Refer to Minot)

*BOWMAN,** Bowman Co. — (Refer to Dickinson)

*CANDO,** Towner Co. — (Refer to Devils Lake)

*CARRINGTON,** Foster Co. — (Refer to Bismarck)

*CAVALIER,** Pembina Co. — (Refer to Grand Forks)

*CROSBY,** Divide Co. — (Refer to Williston)

*DEVILS LAKE,** Ramsey Co.

TRAYNOR, RUTTEN & TRAYNOR (AV)

Traynor Building, 509 Fifth Street, P.O. Box 838, 58301
Telephone: 701-662-4077
Fax: 701-662-7537

MEMBERS OF FIRM

Mack V. Traynor (1892-1970)
Fred J. Traynor (1878-1956)
John T. Traynor
Thomas E. Rutten
J. Thomas Traynor, Jr.

Representative Clients: First National Bank; United States Fidelity & Guaranty Co.; NODAK Mutual Insurance Co.; Cimarron Insurance Co.; Dairy Land Insurance Co.; Horace Mann Insurance Co.; Federated Insurance Co.; Hartford Insurance Co.; Minnesota Insurance Guaranty Assn.; State Farm Mutual.

For full biographical listings, see the Martindale-Hubbell Law Directory

*DICKINSON,** Stark Co.

MACKOFF, KELLOGG, KIRBY & KLOSTER, P.C. (AV)

46 West Second Street, P.O. Box 1097, 58601
Telephone: 701-227-1841
Fax: 701-227-4739
Beach, North Dakota Office: 41 Central Avenue, South.
Telephone: 701-872-3731.
FAX: 701-872-4695.
Baker, Montana Office: 15 South Main, P.O. Box 1075. Telephone/*FAX:* 406-778-2808.

H. A. Mackoff (1888-1963)
Theodore Kellogg (1904-1990)
Ward M. Kirby (1922-1993)
Paul G. Kloster
John L. Sherman
Gordon W. Schnell
Paul F. Ebeltoft, Jr.
Charles J. Peterson (Beach, North Dakota and Baker, Montana Offices)
Timothy A. Priebe
Glen R. Bruhschwein
Michael C. Waller
Randall N. Sickler
Sandra K. Kuntz

Representative Clients: Liberty National Bank and Trust Co.; St. Paul Companies; State Farm Group; ITT Hartford; North Dakota Stockmen's Assn.; United Power Assn.; Trinity High School of Dickinson; Steffes ETC, Inc.; TMI Systems Design Corp.; WellPro, Inc.

For full biographical listings, see the Martindale-Hubbell Law Directory

*ELLENDALE,** Dickey Co. — (Refer to Bismarck)

*FARGO,** Cass Co.

CONMY, FESTE, BOSSART, HUBBARD & CORWIN, LTD. (AV)

400 Norwest Center, Fourth Street and Main Avenue, 58126
Telephone: 701-293-9911
Fax: 701-293-3133

Charles A. Feste
David R. Bossart
Paul M. Hubbard
Wickham Corwin
Kim E. Brust
Lauris N. Molbert
Michael M. Thomas
Robert J. Schultz
Nancy J. Morris
Jiming Zhu

OF COUNSEL

E. T. Conmy, Jr.

State Counsel for: Metropolitan Life Insurance Company.
Representative Clients: Ford Motor Credit Co.; Norwest Corporation Region VII Banks (North Dakota & Minnesota West); U.S. Gypsum Co.
Insurance: American Hardware Insurance Group; Great American Insurance Companies; The Maryland.

For full biographical listings, see the Martindale-Hubbell Law Directory

GUNHUS, GRINNELL, KLINGER, SWENSON & GUY, LTD. (AV)

514 Gate City Building, P.O. Box 2783, 58108-2783
Telephone: 701-235-2506
Telecopier: 701-235-9862
Moorhead, Minnesota Office: 512 Center Avenue, P.O. Box 1077.
Telephone: 218-236-6462.
Telecopier: 218-236-9873.

ATTORNEYS

Edward F. Klinger
Robert H. Swenson
William L. Guy, III
Craig R. Campbell
Jon E. Strinden
David M. Petrocchi

(See Next Column)

GUNHUS, GRINNELL, KLINGER, SWENSON & GUY LTD.—*Continued*

Insurance Clients: Aetna Life and Casualty Co.; Crum & Forster Group; Home Insurance Co.; Royal Insurance—USTU; St. Paul Cos.; United States Fidelity and Guaranty Co.
Representative Clients: Certainteed Corp.; Farm Credit Services; Heartland Medical Center; U.S. West Communications.

For full biographical listings, see the Martindale-Hubbell Law Directory

JEFFRIES, OLSON, FLOM, OPPEGARD & HOGAN, P.A. (AV)

1325 23rd Street S.W., 58103
Telephone: 701-280-2300
Moorhead, Minnesota Office: 403 Center Avenue, P.O. Box 9, 56561-0001.
Telephone: 218-233-3222.
Fax: 218-233-7065.

Richard N. Jeffries
Thomas R. Olson
Joel A. Flom
Paul R. Oppegard
Barry P. Hogan

James R. Bullis
Ronald James Knoll

Representative Clients: American International Adjustment Co.; American States/Western Insurance Co.; Farmers Insurance Group; Federated Mutual Insurance Co.; Fireman's Fund Insurance Co.; Hartford Insurance Co.; Midwest Medical Insurance Co.; St. Paul Fire & Marine Insurance Co.

For full biographical listings, see the Martindale-Hubbell Law Directory

NILLES, HANSEN & DAVIES, LTD. (AV)

1800 Radisson Tower, P.O. Box 2626, 58108
Telephone: 701-237-5544

J. Gerald Nilles (1922-1990)
Lyle W. Selbo (1926-1989)
Donald R. Hansen
Timothy Q. Davies
Duane H. Ilvedson
Robert L. Stroup, II
Russell F. Freeman
E. Thomas Conmy, III
Stephen W. Plambeck
Gregory B. Selbo
Leo F. J. Wilking
Richard Henderson
Daniel J. Crothers
William P. Harrie
Mark R. Hanson
Harry M. Pippin
Thomas A. Jacobson
Douglas W. Gigler
Andrew L. B. Noah
Adele Hedley Page

State Counsel: Burlington Northern, Inc.
General Counsel: First Bank of North Dakota (NA) Fargo; Metropolitan Federal Bank (fsb); Blue Cross and Blue Shield of North Dakota; Nodak Mutual Insurance Co.; Pioneer Mutual Life Insurance Co.

For full biographical listings, see the Martindale-Hubbell Law Directory

SERKLAND, LUNDBERG, ERICKSON, MARCIL & MCLEAN, LTD. (AV)

10 Roberts Street, P.O. Box 6017, 58108-6017
Telephone: 701-232-8957
Fax: 701-237-4049

Edmund Pierce (1863-1927)
B.G. Tenneson (1865-1944)
Arthur W. Cupler (1881-1963)
Lynn U. Stambaugh (1890-1971)
Norman G. Tenneson (1898-1982)
Chester J. Serkland (Retired)
Armond G. Erickson
Jack G. Marcil
Ronald H. McLean
Roger J. Minch
Paul F. Richard
Steven K. Aakre
Maureen Holman
Brad A. Sinclair
LaDonne R. Vik
Jane L. Dynes
Cary Stephenson

OF COUNSEL
Lowell W. Lundberg

Representative Clients: American International Group; St. Paul Bank for Cooperatives; Cit Group, Inc.; Citizens State Bank of Enderlin; Industrial Indemnity Company; State Bank of Fargo; CENEX/Land O'Lakes Agronomy Company; Farm Credit Services of Fargo, ACA; Community First National Bank of Fargo; Prudential Insurance Company of America.

For full biographical listings, see the Martindale-Hubbell Law Directory

VOGEL, BRANTNER, KELLY, KNUTSON, WEIR & BYE, LTD. (AV)

502 First Avenue North, P.O. Box 1389, 58107
Telephone: 701-237-6983
Facsimile: 701-237-0847

Jerry O. Brantner
John D. Kelly
David F. Knutson
H. Patrick Weir
Kermit Edward Bye
Carlton J. Hunke
C. Nicholas Vogel
Maurice G. McCormick
Mart Daniel Vogel
William A. Schlossman, Jr.
Douglas R. Herman
Jane C. Voglewede
Jon R. Brakke
Harlan G. Fuglesten
Pamela J. Hermes
W. Todd Haggart
Lori J. Beck
Frank G. Gokey

(See Next Column)

Steven A. Johnson
Bruce Douglas Quick
Wayne W. Carlson
Charles Alan Stock
Mart R. Vogel (Retired)

Representative Clients: Associated General Contractors of North Dakota; Clark Equipment Co.; Dakota Hospital; Forum Communications Company; MeritCare Medical Group; Northern Improvement Co.; Dakota Clinic; Gateway Chevrolet, Inc.; West Acres Development Company; Fargo Glass & Paint Company.

For full biographical listings, see the Martindale-Hubbell Law Directory

*FESSENDEN,** Wells Co. — (Refer to Devils Lake)

*GRAFTON,** Walsh Co. — (Refer to Grand Forks)

*GRAND FORKS,** Grand Forks Co.

MCCONN, FISHER, OLSON AND DALEY, LTD. (AV)

315 First Avenue North, P.O. Box 5788, 58206-5788
Telephone: 701-775-4688
Fax: 701-775-2440
Larimore, North Dakota Office: 200 Towner Avenue.
Telephone: 701-343-2920.

Patrick W. Fisher
Richard W. Olson
Michael F. Daley
Linda E. Bata

OF COUNSEL
Robert L. McConn

Representative Clients: First National Bank North Dakota; First American Bank Valley; University of North Dakota; Grand Forks School District; Travelers Insurance Co.; CNA Insurance Cos.; Grand Forks Clinic; CENEX; Sears, Roebuck & Co.; Discover Card.

For full biographical listings, see the Martindale-Hubbell Law Directory

MCELROY, CAMRUD, MADDOCK & OLSON, LTD. (AV)

5th Floor, First National Bank Building, P.O. Box 5849, 58206-5849
Telephone: 701-775-5595
Fax: 701-772-3743

Theodore M. Camrud
Patrick J. Maddock
Donald J. Olson
Gerald J. Haga
Gordon W. Myerchin
Darrell E. Larson
Scott D. Jensen
Timothy R. Dittus
Randall S. Hanson
Russ J. Melland
David M. Box

OF COUNSEL
James L. Lamb

RETIRED
Thomas L. Degnan
Thomas P. McElroy

Representative Clients: First National Bank, North Dakota; United Hospital; Community National Bank of Grand Forks; Peterson Construction Co.; Aetna Insurance Cos.; Hartford Accident and Indemnity Co.; St. Paul Cos.; Lamb's Bank, Michigan, North Dakota; Phico Insurance Co.; Grand Forks Clinic, Ltd.

For full biographical listings, see the Martindale-Hubbell Law Directory

SHAFT, REIS, SHAFT & SOGARD, LTD. (AV)

106 North Third Street, Suite 105, P.O. Box 5116, 58206-5116
Telephone: 701-772-8156
Fax: 701-775-8498

John G. Shaft
Sharon M. Reis
Grant H. Shaft
Patrick Oliver Sogard

Representative Clients: First American Bank Valley; Chicago Title Insurance Co.; University of North Dakota; First National Bank North Dakota; J.R. Simplot Co.; First Banks of North Dakota; Grand Forks Air Force Base School District; Gate City Savings Bank.
Reference: First American Bank Valley.

For full biographical listings, see the Martindale-Hubbell Law Directory

VAALER, WARCUP, WOUTAT, ZIMNEY & FOSTER, CHARTERED (AV)

Fifth Floor, Metropolitan Building, 600 Demers Avenue, P.O. Box 13417, 58208-3417
Telephone: 701-772-8111
Fax: 701-772-7328

Robert Vaaler
Alan B. Warcup
Paul G. Woutat
Thomas L. Zimney
John S. Foster
Carol E. Johnson
Sandra B. Dittus
Allen J. Flaten
Scott J. Landa

OF COUNSEL
Edward C. Gillig

Representative Clients: Metropolitan Federal Bank; Federal Deposit Insurance Co.; First Bank of North Dakota; Union Carbide Co.; Sioux Manufacturing Co.; The Boeing Co.

(See Next Column)

VAALER, WARCUP, WOUTAT, ZIMNEY & FOSTER CHARTERED, *Grand Forks—Continued*

Representative Insurance Clients: Fireman's Fund; CIGNA; State Farm Insurance Cos.; Allied Group Insurance Co.; Lawyers Title Insurance Co.

For full biographical listings, see the Martindale-Hubbell Law Directory

*HETTINGER,** Adams Co. — (Refer to Dickinson)

*LAKOTA,** Nelson Co. — (Refer to Devils Lake)

*LA MOURE,** La Moure Co. — (Refer to Bismarck)

*LANGDON,** Cavalier Co. — (Refer to Devils Lake)

*LINTON,** Emmons Co. — (Refer to Bismarck)

*LISBON,** Ransom Co. — (Refer to Fargo)

*MANDAN,** Morton Co.

BAIR, KAUTZMANN & BAIR (AV)

210 First Avenue, N.W., P.O. Box 100, 58554-0100
Telephone: 701-663-6568
Fax: 701-663-6951

MEMBERS OF FIRM

Bruce B. Bair
Dwight C. H. Kautzmann
Thomas B. Bair

Representative Clients: Diocese of Bismarck; First Southwest Bank-Mandan; University of Mary-Bismarck; KEM Rural Electric Cooperative, Inc.; Mandan Public School District #1; North Dakota Milk Stabilization Board.

For full biographical listings, see the Martindale-Hubbell Law Directory

KELSCH, KELSCH, RUFF & AUSTIN (AV)

Collins Avenue and Main Street, P.O. Box 785, 58554
Telephone: 701-663-9818; 258-1300
Fax: 701-663-9810

MEMBERS OF FIRM

C. F. Kelsch (1890-1987)
William C. Kelsch
Thomas F. Kelsch
Arlen M. Ruff
Timothy J. Austin
Thomas D. Kelsch
Todd Kranda

Representative Clients: Seven Seas Motor Inn; L & H Manufacturing Co.; Cloverdale Foods Co.; Microage Computer Store; Logan Hill Realty, Bismarck.

For full biographical listings, see the Martindale-Hubbell Law Directory

*MCCLUSKY,** Sheridan Co. — (Refer to Mandan)

*MINOT,** Ward Co.

MCGEE, HANKLA, BACKES & WHEELER, P.C. (AV)

Suite 305 Norwest Center, 15 Second Avenue Southwest, P.O. Box 998, 58702-0998
Telephone: 701-852-2544
Fax: 701-838-4724

Richard H. McGee (1918-1992)
Walfrid B. Hankla
Orlin W. Backes
Robert A. Wheeler
Donald L. Peterson
Richard H. McGee, II
Collin P. Dobrovolny
Brian W. Hankla
Robert J. Hovland
Jon W. Backes

LEGAL SUPPORT PERSONNEL

Janice M. Eslinger
Jane K. Hutchison
Ardella M. Burtman
Michelle Erdmann

For full biographical listings, see the Martindale-Hubbell Law Directory

ELLA VAN BERKOM LAW OFFICE (AV)

303 Union National Annex, 7-A East Central Avenue, 58701-3880
Telephone: 701-852-4191
Fax: 701-839-1876

ASSOCIATES

Steven C. Farhart

For full biographical listings, see the Martindale-Hubbell Law Directory

*MOTT,** Hettinger Co. — (Refer to Dickinson)

*NEW ROCKFORD,** Eddy Co. — (Refer to Devils Lake)

*RUGBY,** Pierce Co. — (Refer to Minot)

*STANLEY,** Mountrail Co. — (Refer to Minot)

*TOWNER,** McHenry Co. — (Refer to Minot)

*VALLEY CITY,** Barnes Co. — (Refer to Bismarck)

*WAHPETON,** Richland Co. — (Refer to Fargo)

WEST FARGO, Cass Co.

OHNSTAD TWICHELL, P.C. (AV)

901 13th Avenue East, P.O. Box 458, 58078-0458
Telephone: 701-282-3249
FAX: 701-282-0825
Hillsboro, North Dakota Office: West Caledonia Avenue, P.O. Box 220.
Telephone: 701-436-5700.
FAX: 701-436-4025.
Mayville, North Dakota Office: 12 Third Street, S.E., P.O. Box 547.
Telephone: 701-786-3251.
FAX: 701-786-4243.
Fargo, North Dakota Office: 15 Broadway, Suite 202.
Telephone: 701-280-5801.
Fax: 701-280-5803.

Manfred R. Ohnstad (1914-1987)
Daniel R. Twichell
Duane R. Breitling
Robert E. Rosenvold
David L. Wanner
Michael D. Nelson
Brian D. Neugebauer
John A. Juelson (Resident, Hillsboro Office)
Dean A. Rindy
S. Lee Vinje (Resident, Mayville Office)
Steven E. McCullough
Robert G. Hoy

Robert L. Stroup III
Ross V. Keller (Resident, Hillsboro Office)

Representative Clients: First National Bank North Dakota; Quality Boneless Beef; City of West Fargo; Bond Counsel for Cities of Fargo, Jamestown, West Fargo and Valley City; Insurance Company of North America; Reliance Insurance Co.; The Continental Insurance Cos.; Underwriters Adjusting Co.; Industrial Indemnity Co.; Integrity Insurance Co.

For full biographical listings, see the Martindale-Hubbell Law Directory

*WILLISTON,** Williams Co.

MCINTEE & WHISENAND, P.C. (AV)

113 East Broadway, P.O. Box 1307, 58802-1307
Telephone: 701-774-0024
Fax: 701-774-0579

Fred E. Whisenand
Thomas Glenn Holum

OF COUNSEL

Michael R. McIntee

Representative Clients: U.S. F.&G. Insurance; CNA Insurance; Great American Insurance; National Farmers Union Property and Casualty; Nodak Mutual Insurance; Mountain West Farm Bureau Insurance; First National Bank & Trust of Williston; Mercy Hospital; Black Hills Trucking, Inc.; Coca Cola Bottling Co.; American State Bank & Trust Co. of Williston.

For full biographical listings, see the Martindale-Hubbell Law Directory

WINKJER MCKENNETT STENEHJEM REIERSON & FORSBERG, P.C. (AV)

314 First Avenue East, P.O. Box 1366, 58801
Telephone: 701-572-6771
Fax: 701-572-2163
Watford City, North Dakota Office: 233 North Main Street, P.O. Box 1469, 58854.
Telephone: 701-842-2619.
FAX: 701-842-4135.

Dean Winkjer
Richard A. McKennett
Mark L. Stenehjem
Kent Reierson
Laurel J. Forsberg
Kevin J. Chapman

Representative Clients: Dakota Realty; Farm Credit Bank of St. Paul; First International Bank of Watford City and Williston; First National Bank and Trust Company of Williston; Fred and Clara Eckert Foundation for Children; Imperial Oil of North Dakota; Mill Mutuals Insurance Co.; Northwest Communications Cooperative; Western Dakota Medical Group P.C.; Williston Public and McKenzie County School District.

For full biographical listings, see the Martindale-Hubbell Law Directory

OHIO

*AKRON,** Summit Co.

NUKES, PERANTINIDES & NOLAN CO., L.P.A. (AV)

300 Courtyard Square, 80 South Summit Street, 44308-1719
Telephone: 216-253-5454
Telecopier: 216-253-6524

S. Samuel Nukes — Paul G. Perantinides
Chris T. Nolan

James J. Gutbrod — Christopher L. Parker
Peter P. Janos

References: First National Bank of Akron; National City Bank, Akron; Society Bank; Charter One Bank.

For full biographical listings, see the Martindale-Hubbell Law Directory

RODERICK, MYERS & LINTON (AV)

One Cascade Plaza, 15th Floor, 44308
Telephone: 216-434-3000
Telecopier: 216-434-9220

MEMBERS OF FIRM

George T. Roderick (1909-1994) — Kurt R. Weitendorf
Robert F. Linton — Robert L. Myers (Retired)
Howard C. Walker, Jr. — Timothy J. Truby
Robert F. Orth — Lawrence R. Bach
Frederick S. Corns — Paul E. Weimer
Michael A. Malyuk — James E. Davis
Matthew W. Oby

ASSOCIATES

Stephen J. Pruneski — Rebecca M. Weimer
John K. Riemenschneider — Kimberly A. Kmentt
David P. Weimer — Christopher J. Niekamp
Stephan C. Kremer

OF COUNSEL

Robert Petersilge

Counsel for: National City Bank, Northeast; Ohio Edison Co.; K-Mart; Westfield Cos.; The Prudential Insurance Co. of America; Maryland Casualty Co.; Summit County Medical Society.

For full biographical listings, see the Martindale-Hubbell Law Directory

SCANLON & GEARINGER CO., L.P.A. (AV)

1100 First National Tower, 106 South Main Street, 44308-1463
Telephone: 216-376-4558
Telecopier: 216-376-3550

Timothy F. Scanlon — Michael J. Del Medico
Bradford M. Gearinger — Mark Hilkert
James A. Rudgers — Patrick J. Hart
Robert A. Royer

Suzanne C. Porter — John F. Hill
Kevin P. Hardman — Gregory M. Scanlon
Maura E. Scanlon — Tamara A. O'Brien

For full biographical listings, see the Martindale-Hubbell Law Directory

THOMPSON, HINE AND FLORY (AV)

50 S. Main Street, Suite 502, 44308-1828
Telephone: 216-376-8090
Fax: 216-376-8386
Cincinnati, Ohio Office: 312 Walnut Street, 14th Floor, 45202-4029.
Telephone: 513-352-6700.
Fax: 513-241-4771.
Telex: 938003.
Cleveland, Ohio Office: 1100 National City Bank Building, 629 Euclid Avenue, 44114-3070.
Telephone: 216-566-5500.
Fax: 216-556-5583.
Telex: 980217.
Cable Address: "Thomflor".
Columbus, Ohio Office: One Columbus, 10 West Broad Street, 43215-3435.
Telephone: 614-469-3200.
Fax: 614-469-3361.
Dayton, Ohio Office: 2000 Courthouse Plaza, 45402-1706.
Telephone: 513-443-6600.
Fax: 513-443-6637; 443-6635.
Palm Beach, Florida Office: 125 Worth Avenue, 33480-4466.
Telephone: 407-833-5900.
Fax: 407-833-5951.
Washington, D.C. Office: 1920 N Street, N.W., 20036-1601.
Telephone: 202-331-8800.
Fax: 202-331-8330.
Telex: 904173.
Cable Address: "Caglaw".

(See Next Column)

Brussels, Belgium Office: Rue des Chevaliers / Ridderstraat 14 - B.10, B - 1050.
Telephone: 011(32-2) 511-9326.
Fax: 011(32-2) 513-9206.

MEMBERS OF FIRM

Richard E. Guster (Partner-in-Charge in Akron) — Joseph S. Ruggie, Jr.

For full biographical listings, see the Martindale-Hubbell Law Directory

A. WILLIAM ZAVARELLO CO., L.P.A. (AV)

313 South High Street, Corner South High and Buchtel, 44308-1532
Telephone: 216-762-9700
Fax: 216-762-1680

A. William Zavarello — Rhonda G. Davis

References: First National Bank of Ohio; National City Bank, Akron.

For full biographical listings, see the Martindale-Hubbell Law Directory

ARCHBOLD, Fulton Co.

PLASSMAN, RUPP, HENSAL & SHORT (AV)

302 North Defiance Street, P.O. Box 178, 43502-0178
Telephone: 419-445-8815
Fax: 419-445-1080

MEMBERS OF FIRM

Owen Rice (1900-1978) — David P. Rupp, Jr.
Harold H. Plassman — James E. Hensal

Peter D. Short

Counsel for: The Farmers & Merchants State Bank; Sauder Woodworking Co.; Sauder Manufacturing Co.; Bil-Jax, Inc.; Miller Bros. Const., Inc.; Lugbill Bros., Inc.; Archbold Medical Group, Inc.
Local Counsel for: Allstate Insurance Co.; United Ohio Insurance Co.

For full biographical listings, see the Martindale-Hubbell Law Directory

*ASHLAND,** Ashland Co.

TROTH, VAN TILBURG & HALLIGAN (AV)

245 Sandusky Street, P.O. Box 606, 44805-0606
Telephone: 419-289-1199
FAX: 419-289-2400

MEMBERS OF FIRM

Hugh I. Troth — William D. Van Tilburg
Brian J. Halligan

ASSOCIATES

Robert E. Dezort

General Counsel for: Coburn, Inc.; Dalton and Hannah Co.; Jay Plastics, Inc.; Landoll, Inc.; Mansfield Screw Machine Products Co.; Taylor Metal Products, Inc.; Universal Enterprises, Inc.; Whirlaway Textile Spindles, Inc.
Local Counsel for: Bank One, Mansfield; Hess & Clark, Inc.

For full biographical listings, see the Martindale-Hubbell Law Directory

ASHTABULA, Ashtabula Co.

WARREN AND YOUNG (AV)

134 West 46th Street, P.O. Box 2300, 44004-6951
Telephone: (216) 997-6175
Facsimile: (216) 992-9114

MEMBERS OF FIRM

Theodore E. Warren (1897-1969) — William E. Riedel
Myron H. Young (1910-1971) — Carl F. Muller
Stuart W. Cordell

ASSOCIATES

James D. Masur II — J. Adam Zangerle

OF COUNSEL

E. Terry Warren

For full biographical listings, see the Martindale-Hubbell Law Directory

*ATHENS,** Athens Co.

ROBE AND ROBE (AV)

14 West Washington Street, P.O. Box 727, 45701-0727
Telephone: 614-593-5576
Telefax: 614-592-5280

Scott M. Robe

Representative Clients: Athens Medical Building, Inc.; Celina Insurance Group; Messenger Publishing Co.; Columbia Gas Transmission Co. (Local).

For full biographical listings, see the Martindale-Hubbell Law Directory

Athens—Continued

JOSEPH BLAIR YANITY, JR. (AV)

18 South Court Street, P.O. Drawer 748, 45701-0748
Telephone: 614-593-3385
FAX: 614-593-3387

Representative Clients: Athens Honda Cars; Athens Building Materials Co.; Bank One Athens N.A.; Consortium for Health Education in Appalachia Ohio, Inc.; General Telephone Company of Ohio; Le-Ax Water District; O'-Bleness Memorial Hospital; Ohio University Foundation.

*BATAVIA,** Clermont Co.

ELY AND TRUE (AV)

322 Main Street, 45103
Telephone: 513-732-2140
FAX: 513-732-0692

MEMBERS OF FIRM

Forrest E. Ely (1901-1981)
John S. Moore (1914-1991)
Rex E. Ely
J. Robert True
Gary D. Ostendarp
James C. Henderson
Richard P. Ferenc

Counsel for: The Cincinnati Gas & Electric Company; American States Insurance Cos.; GRE Insurance Group; Heritage Mutual Insurance Co.; Motorists Mutual Insurance Co.; Nationwide Mutual Insurance Co.; The Ohio Casualty Group of Insurance Cos.; State Automobile Mutual Insurance Co.; Travelers Insurance Co.; United Ohio Insurance Co.

For full biographical listings, see the Martindale-Hubbell Law Directory

BELLAIRE, Belmont Co. — (Refer to Steubenville)

*BELLEFONTAINE,** Logan Co.

SMITH, SMITH & MONTGOMERY (AV)

Citizens Federal Building, 112 North Main Street, 43311
Telephone: 513-593-8510
Fax: 513-599-4228

J. Ewing Smith (1906-1993)

MEMBERS OF FIRM

J. MacAlpine Smith
William R. Montgomery

ASSOCIATES

Douglas M. Smith
J. Gregory Smith

General Counsel for: Patrons Mutual Insurance Association of Ohio; Logan County Co-operative Power & Light Assn.; Citizens Federal Savings & Loan Assn.
Local Counsel for: Nationwide Insurance Co.; State Automobile Mutual Insurance Co.; National City Bank; Cincinnati Ins. Co.; Farm Credit Services of Mid-America, ACA.
Agents for: Lawyers Title Insurance Co.; Ohio Bar Title Insurance Co.

For full biographical listings, see the Martindale-Hubbell Law Directory

*BOWLING GREEN,** Wood Co.

SPITLER, VOGTSBERGER & HUFFMAN (AV)

131 East Court Street, 43402-2495
Telephone: 419-352-2535
FAX: 419-353-8728
Rossford, Ohio Office: 932 Dixie Highway.
Telephone: 419-666-7130.

MEMBERS OF FIRM

Emmett V. Spitler
Daniel T. Spitler
Robert E. Spitler
Thomas H. Vogtsberger
Rex H. Huffman
Diane Rausch Huffman

Representative Clients: First Federal Savings & Loan Association of Wood County; Prudential Insurance Company of America; The Mutual Benefit Life Insurance Co.; John Hancock Mutual Life Insurance Co.; Equitable Life Assurance Society of the U.S.; Minnesota Mutual Life Insurance Co.

For full biographical listings, see the Martindale-Hubbell Law Directory

BRIDGEPORT, Belmont Co. — (Refer to St. Clairsville)

*BRYAN,** Williams Co.

NEWCOMER, SHAFFER, BIRD & SPANGLER (AV)

117 West Maple Street, 43506
Telephone: 419-636-3196
Fax: 419-636-0867
Montpelier, Ohio Office: 104 Empire Street.
Telephone: 419-485-3238.

MEMBERS OF FIRM

James A. Hutton (1939-1984)
Wayne E. Shaffer
David C. Newcomer
John S. Shaffer
Steven R. Bird
Michael W. Spangler

OF COUNSEL

Arthur S. Newcomer

(See Next Column)

ASSOCIATES

Michael A. Shaffer

Local Counsel for: Farmers & Merchants State Bank.

For full biographical listings, see the Martindale-Hubbell Law Directory

*BUCYRUS,** Crawford Co. — (Refer to Mansfield)

*CADIZ,** Harrison Co. — (Refer to Steubenville)

*CALDWELL,** Noble Co. — (Refer to Zanesville)

*CANTON,** Stark Co.

DAY, KETTERER, RALEY, WRIGHT & RYBOLT (AV)

800 William R. Day Building, 121 Cleveland Avenue, South, 44702-1921
Telephone: 216-455-0173
Telecopier: 216-455-2633
Columbus, Ohio Office: Suite 1602, 50 West Broad Street.
Telephone: 614-228-3611.
Telecopier: 614-228-3663

MEMBERS OF FIRM

David B. Day (1863-1947)
John G. Ketterer (1901-1973)
Donald W. Raley (1905-1986)
Clyde H. Wright (1909-1991)
Robert M. Rybolt (Retired)
Robert P. Eshelman (Retired)
Robert E. Levitt (Retired)
Louis A. Boettler
John R. Werren
William B. Badger
James K. Brooker
E. Lang D'Atri
J. Sean Keenan
Sheila M. Markley
Fred H. Zollinger, Jr.
James R. Blake
John H. Brannen
Richard A. Princic
Tim A. Powell
Richard E. Davis, II
Douglas J. Maser (Resident, Columbus Office)
Michael S. Gruber
Alicia M. Wyler
William S. Cline
Daniel A. Minkler
Matthew Yackshaw
Raymond T. Bules
John A. Murphy, Jr.
Merle D. Evans, III
Craig G. Pelini
Darrell N. Markijohn
Robert E. Roland
Jill Freshley Otto
Sara E. Lioi

ASSOCIATES

Mark F. Fischer
J. Curtis Werren
James F. Contini, II
Thomas E. Hartnett
Andrew M. McIlvaine
Cari Fusco Evans

OF COUNSEL

John F. Buchman
Stephen A. Reilly (Resident, Columbus Office)
David M. Thomas

Representative Clients: The Timken Co.; Bank One, Akron; National City Bank; Detroit Diesel Corp.; Canton Drop Forge.

For full biographical listings, see the Martindale-Hubbell Law Directory

KRUGLIAK, WILKINS, GRIFFITHS & DOUGHERTY CO., L.P.A. (AV)

4775 Munson Street, N.W., P.O. Box 36963, 44735-6963
Telephone: 216-497-0700
FAX: 216-497-4020
Alliance, Ohio Office: Society Square Building, 960 West State Street.
Telephone: 216-823-9262.
Additional Canton, Ohio Office: Central Plaza South, 526 Citizens Savings Building.
Telephone: 216-456-2422.

Samuel Krugliak
F. Stuart Wilkins
Raymond E. Griffiths
Ronald W. Dougherty
David L. Simiele
Fred J. Haupt
Daniel A. Pramuk
John Bogniard
Michael A. Thompson
Randall C. Hunt
Sam O. Simmerman
Terry A. Moore
John R. Slater
Joseph I. Perkovich
A. Edward Moss
Karen Soehnlen McQueen
Russ Kendig
Jacqueline Bollas Caldwell
David E. Butz
Edward J. Elum
Dianne Blocker Braun
Bernadette J. Bollas
Leslie Ann Iams
Thomas W. Winkhart
Linda M. Peshek
Mary Ann Esber
Susan Carson Rodgers
Edward D. Murray
Shelly L. Kennedy
Christina D'Eramo Evans
Janel M. Myers
Christopher T. Vonderau
Christopher C. Ehrman

Representative Clients: The Citizens Savings Bank of Canton; Alfred Nickles Bakery, Inc.
Counsel For: National Pro Football Hall of Fame.
References: The Citizens Savings Bank of Canton; Society National Bank.

For full biographical listings, see the Martindale-Hubbell Law Directory

Canton—Continued

LESH, CASNER & MILLER A LEGAL PROFESSIONAL ASSOCIATION (AV)

606 Belden-Whipple Building, 4150 Belden Village Street, N.W., 44718
Telephone: 216-493-0040
Fax: 216-493-4108

Kenneth L. Lesh (1913-1991)
James W. Casner
Rex W. Miller
Jacob F. Hess, Jr.
Thomas J. Lombardi
Dennis J. Fox
John S. McCall, Jr.
Timothy W. Watkins
John R. Frank

OF COUNSEL

Ronald G. Figler

For full biographical listings, see the Martindale-Hubbell Law Directory

*CARROLLTON,** Carroll Co. — (Refer to Canton)

*CELINA,** Mercer Co. — (Refer to Van Wert)

*CHILLICOTHE,** Ross Co.

CUTRIGHT & CUTRIGHT (AV)

72 West Second Street, 45601
Telephone: 614-772-5595
Fax: 614-773-9261

MEMBERS OF FIRM

James M. Cutright
James K. Cutright

Representative Clients: Citizens National Bank; Chivaho Federal Credit Union; Fifth Third Bank of Southern Ohio; Rockhold, Brown & Co. Bank; Litter Industries; Scioto Valley Mental Health Center; Paint Valley Adamms Board.
Approved Attorneys for: Lawyers Title Insurance Co.; Ohio Bar Title Insurance Co.; Chicago Title Insurance Co., Inc.

For full biographical listings, see the Martindale-Hubbell Law Directory

*CINCINNATI,** Hamilton Co.

JAMES J. CHALFIE CO., L.P.A. (AV)

36 East Seventh Street, Suite 1600, 45202
Telephone: 513-381-8616
FAX: 513-381-8619

James J. Chalfie

Katrina Z. Farley

For full biographical listings, see the Martindale-Hubbell Law Directory

CORS & BASSETT (AV)

1200 Carew Tower, 45202-2990
Telephone: 513-852-8200
FAX: 513-852-8222
Covington, Kentucky Office: 250 Grandview Drive, Suite 200, Ft. Mitchell, 41017.
Telephone: 606-341-4666.

MEMBERS OF FIRM

Kenneth B. Bassett
L. Barry Cors
Paul R. Moran
William G. Kohlhepp
Richard J. Valleau
Joseph H. Vahlsing
Robert J. Hollingsworth
David L. Barth
Frank M. Diedrichs
Stephen A. Kappers
Michael L. Gay
Elizabeth A. Horwitz
Jeffrey J. Harmon
Hal L. Franke
John D. Wilson
Michelle A. Mullee
H. David Wallace (Not admitted in OH; Resident at Covington, Kentucky Office)
Thomas W. Coffey
Stephen S. Holmes

ASSOCIATES

D. Lynn Spraetz
Katharine C. Weber
Monica A. Andrews
Sherry P. Porter (Not admitted in OH)
David J. Schmitt
Kevin R. Feazell
Lisa Ge Shang Han
Jennifer K. Kopp
Karl F. Colón
Curtis L. Cornett

OF COUNSEL

James J. Carroll
Kenneth L. Byrne
David P. Heidrich (Not admitted in OH; Resident, Covington, Kentucky Office)
James W. Halloran
David L. Huprich
Thomas J. Westerfield
Hal F. Franke
Robert L. Seaver

Representative Clients: Belcan Corporation; Dorman Products; Keco Industries, Inc.; Zonic Corporation; Commonwealth of Kentucky.

For full biographical listings, see the Martindale-Hubbell Law Directory

DINSMORE & SHOHL (AV)

1900 Chemed Center, 255 East Fifth Street, 45202-3172
Telephone: 513-977-8200
FAX: 513-977-8141
Florence, Kentucky Office: Turfway Ridge Office Park, 7300 Turfway Road, Suite 430 41042-1355.
Telephone: 606-283-0515.
FAX: 606-283-6017.
Dayton, Ohio Office: 500 Courthouse Plaza, S.W., 10 N. Ludlow Street, 45402-1834.
Telephone: 513-228-8012.
FAX: 513-461-2543.
Columbus, Ohio Office: NBD Bank Building, Suite 330, 175 South Third Street, 43215-5134.
Telephone: 614-224-7887.
FAX: 614-224-7882.

Frank F. Dinsmore (1891-1962)
Walter M. Shohl (1908-1970)

MEMBERS OF FIRM

John E. McDowell
Thomas S. Calder
Harold S. Freeman
Lawrence A. Kane, Jr.
John W. Beatty
Jerome H. Kearns
Wiley Dinsmore
Clifford A. Roe, Jr.
Lawrence R. Elleman
John M. Kunst, Jr.
Thomas J. Sherman
Vincent B. Stamp
Frank C. Woodside, III
Gordon C. Greene
Harry L. Riggs, Jr. (Resident, Florence, Kentucky Office)
Jay A. Rosenberg
Mark L. Silbersack
Gerald V. Weigle, Jr.
Michael W. Hawkins
Mark A. Vander Laan
Gary L. Herfel (Resident, Florence, Kentucky Office)
William M. Freedman
James H. Stethem
William H. Seall (Resident, Dayton, Ohio Office)
Paul R. Mattingly
J. Michael Cooney
Richard J. Beckmann (Resident, Dayton, Ohio Office)
Michael S. Glassman
John E. Schlosser
Nancy A. Lawson
Michael D. Eagen
Edward J. Buechel (Resident, Florence, Kentucky Office)
David H. Beaver
Paul A. Ose
S. Richard Arnold
Charles F. Hertlein, Jr.
Patrick D. Lane
Carl J. Stich, Jr. (On Leave of Absence)
Joseph E. Conley, Jr. (Resident, Florence, Kentucky Office)
Joanne M. Schreiner
John D. Luken
Deborah R. Lydon
George H. Vincent
Lynda E. Roesch
George B. Wilkinson
John E. Jevicky
Jerry S. Sallee
C. Christopher Muth
Ronald J. Snyder
James D. Liles
Nancy J. Gill
Stephen K. Shaw
Lawrence A. Flemer
Mark C. Bissinger
Joel S. Taylor (Resident, Columbus, Ohio Office)
Robert R. Furnier
Gary E. Becker
Neal D. Baker
Charles M. Roesch
K. C. Green
Philip J. Schworer
M. Gabrielle Hils
Stephen G. Schweller
Steven H. Schreiber
June Smith Tyler
Gregory A. Harrison
Calvin D. Buford

OF COUNSEL

H. Truxtun Emerson, Jr.
Harris K. Weston
William L. Blum
Nolan W. Carson
Robert T. McConaughy
Powell McHenry

ASSOCIATES

G. Franklin Miller
Christine L. McBroom
Jeffrey S. Shoskin
Andrew C. Osterbrock
David W. Gerbus
Charles H. Brown, III
Frederick M. Erny
Timothy A. Tepe
Harvey Jay Cohen
James A. Comodeca
Beverly Hayes Pace
Lynn Marmer
Steven H. Ray
Douglas W. Campbell
John R. Glankler (Resident, Dayton, Ohio Office)
Richard L. Schuster
Susan J. Luken
Stephen M. Rosenberger
Rita A. Miller Altimari
Deborah Price Rambo
Joseph L. Sallee, Jr.
Joan M. Verchot
Patricia B. Hogan
Colleen P. Lewis
David M. Zuckerman
Charles R. Dyas, Jr.
Brian S. Sullivan
John H. Wendeln
Mark S. Booher
Robert Heuck II
Randel S. Springer
David K. Mullen
John J. Hoffmann (Resident, Dayton, Ohio Office)
Christopher A. Benintendi
Richard J. Mitchell, Jr.
Ann L. Munson
Christopher Ragonesi
Sara Simrall Rorer
Susan B. Zaunbrecher
Michael L. Squillace (Resident, Columbus, Ohio Office)
Marlene M. Evans
Melissa A. Fetters
John A. Finley
Linda A. Cooper
Louis D. Proietti
Laurie H. Schwab
Mary-Jo Middelhoff
Robert A. Williams
Frances L. Figetakis
Thomas A. Prewitt (Resident, Florence, Kentucky Office)
M. Christine Hice
David S. Rosenthal
Debra Page Coleman
William A. Sherman, II

(See Next Column)

DINSMORE & SHOHL, *Cincinnati—Continued*

ASSOCIATES (Continued)

Kim Wilson Burke
William M. Mattes (Resident, Columbus, Ohio Office)
Scott R. Thomas
Frederick N. Hamilton
James C. Venizelos
Ernamarie Messenger
Michael J. Suffern
Theodore J. Schneider
Moira J. Squier
Wilton E. Blake, II
Jeffrey P. Hinebaugh
Michael H. Strong
Robert F. Benintendi
Patrick E. Beck
Jeffrey L. Stec
Nancy Korb Griffiths
Ann Collins Hindman
Michael E. Finucane
William A. Dickhaut
Christopher L. Riegler (Resident, Dayton, Ohio Office)
Gregory O. Long
Dianne Goss Paynter (Resident, Columbus, Ohio Office)
Gregory S. Lampert
Jeffrey R. Schaefer
Reuel D. Ash
Kent A. Shoemaker
Alan H. Abes
Gina M. Saelinger
Donna R. Purifoy
Robert J. Reid
Corey M. MacGillivray
Jon S. Robins
Phillip A. Rotman, II
Thomas M. Dixon
Jerry L. Maynard, II
Merideth A. Trott (Resident, Dayton, Ohio Office)
Bonnie G. Camden
John F. Meisenhelder
Clyde Bennett, II
Letitia E. Carvey
Molly M. Thompson (Not admitted in OH)

For full biographical listings, see the Martindale-Hubbell Law Directory

FROST & JACOBS (AV)

2500 PNC Center, 201 East Fifth Street, P.O. Box 5715, 45201-5715
Telephone: 513-651-6800
Cable Address: "Frostjac"
Telex: 21-4396 F & J CIN
Telecopier: 513-651-6981
Columbus, Ohio Office: One Columbus, 10 West Broad Street.
Telephone: 614-464-1211.
Telecopier: 614-464-1737.
Lexington, Kentucky Office: 1100 Vine Center Tower, 333 West Vine Street.
Telephone: 606-254-1100.
Telecopier: 606-253-2990.
Middletown, Ohio Office: 400 First National Bank Building, 2 North Main Street.
Telephone: 513-422-2001.
Telecopier: 513-422-3010.
Naples, Florida Office: 4001 Tamiami Trail North, Suite 220.
Telephone: 813-261-0582.
Telecopier: 813-261-2083.

MEMBERS OF FIRM

Henry G. Frost (1875-1951)
Carl M. Jacobs (1886-1967)
Dennis J. Barron
James S. Wachs
Ronald E. Heinlen
James R. Adams
William D. Baskett, III
John S. Stith
Pierce E. Cunningham
Edmund J. Adams
Albert E. Heekin, III
Lawrence H. Kyte, Jr.
T. Stephen Phillips
Thomas P. Mehnert
James K. L. Lawrence
Robert A. Dimling
Gerald L. Baldwin
Richard J. Erickson
Frederick J. McGavran
Neil Ganulin
John H. Appel
Michael F. Haverkamp
Joseph J. Dehner
Samuel McW. Scoggins
Susan Grogan Faller
Jeffery R. Rush
Dennis J. Murphy
Todd H. Bailey
Larry H. McMillin
Mark H. Longenecker, Jr.
George E. Yund
David C. Horn
William H. Hawkins, II
Myron L. Dale
E. Richard Oberschmidt
Martin E. Mooney
David C. Olson
Thomas D. Anthony
Kathleen W. Carr
Walter E. Haggerty
David T. Croall
Thomas E. Taylor
Elizabeth A. Lanier
Charles E. Schroer
Paul W. Casper, Jr.
Douglas E. Hart
Richard M. Goehler
Beth A. Myers
Deborah S. Adams
John E. Barnes
Patricia D. Laub
Joseph W. Plye
Gregory P. Adams
Stephen N. Haughey
William C. Strangfeld
Grant S. Cowan
Claudia L. Schaefer
Vincent E. Mauer
W. Russell Wilson
Beth Schneider Naylor
Kim Martin Lewis
P. Reid Lemasters
Frederick W. Kindel

SENIOR ATTORNEYS

Fern E. Goldman
Mark H. Klusmeier
Barbara F. Applegarth
William W. Ford, III
Raymond D. Neusch
Douglas D. Thomson
Robert S. Kaiser

(See Next Column)

ASSOCIATES

Carla Haunz Rusconi
Scott A. Meyer
Nancy Dirkse DeWitt
Kevin N. McMurray
John C. Krug
Karen Johannes Bowman
D. Scott Gurney
Ronald E. Gold
Mina T. Jones
Bruce G. Hopkins
David S. Bence
Daniel W. Scharff
Nancy Burke Rue
Adam P. Hall
Hilla M. Zerbst
Scott D. Phillips
John C. Cummings
Thomas P. Price III
Douglas Halpert (Not admitted in OH)
Wm. Bruce Davis (Not admitted in OH)
Matthew S. Massarelli
Christopher J. Wilson
Christa F. Nordlund
Susan Mechley Lucci
Jonathan A. Conte
J. Paul Allen
Elizabeth A. Stautberg
Laura A. Ryan
Patrice Baughman Borders
Bryan S. Blade (Not admitted in OH)
Jack B. Harrison
Stuart B. Frankel
Michele M. Bradley
Michael F. Marhofer
Caroline Boeh Baesler
Barry A. Spaeth
Bernard L. McKay
Ruth Anne Wolfe
Nancy A. Leser

SENIOR PARTNERS

Charles G. Puchta
Henry W. Hobson, Jr.
J. Leland Brewster, II
Jerry L. Cowan
John K. Rose
Donald McG. Rose
Daniel P. Dooley

OF COUNSEL

Thomas E. Crafton (Not admitted in OH)
George W. Taliaferro Jr.
Albert E. Strasser
Alan R. Vogeler
Joseph J. Connaughton
Verena Smith
Anthony W. Hobson
Kimberly K. Mauer

PATENT, TRADEMARK AND COPYRIGHT ATTORNEYS
MEMBERS OF FIRM

Gibson R. Yungblut
James H. Hayes
David E. Schmit
Kenneth B. Germain
Steven J. Goldstein
Edwin R. Acheson, Jr.

ASSOCIATES

Louis Keith Ebling (Not admitted in OH)
Frederick H. Gribbell
Martin J. Miller
Scott T. Piering (Not admitted in OH)
Jay R. Deshmukh

COLUMBUS, OHIO OFFICE
MEMBERS OF FIRM

Thomas V. Williams
John I. Cadwallader
Michael K. Yarbrough

ASSOCIATES

Jeffrey N. Lindemann

LEXINGTON, KENTUCKY OFFICE
MEMBERS OF FIRM

Gerald L. Baldwin (Lexington, Kentucky & Cincinnati, Ohio Offices)
Richard A. Getty
Denise H. McClelland
Greg E. Mitchell

LEXINGTON KENTUCKY OFFICE
ASSOCIATES

Maryellen Buxton Mynear
C. Thomas Ezzell
Danielle Harlan

OF COUNSEL

Jackson W. White
Lawrence E. Forgy, Jr.
Thomas E. Crafton

MIDDLETOWN OFFICE
MEMBERS OF FIRM

Thomas A. Swope
Donald L. Crain

SENIOR ATTORNEY

Daniel J. Picard

ASSOCIATES

William L. Sennett, III
Thomas B. Allen

OF COUNSEL

Barry J. Levey

NAPLES, FLORIDA OFFICE
PARTNER

Roi E. Baugher, II

Representative Clients: Armco Inc.; Champion International Corp.; Cincinnati Bell Inc.; Cincinnati Milacron, Inc.; Federated Department Stores; The Cincinnati, New Orleans & Texas Pacific Railway Co. (Norfolk Southern Corporation); PNC Bank, Ohio, National Association; Turner Construction Co.; The United States Shoe Corp.; University of Cincinnati.

For full biographical listings, see the Martindale-Hubbell Law Directory

Cincinnati—Continued

KATZ, TELLER, BRANT & HILD A LEGAL PROFESSIONAL ASSOCIATION (AV)

2400 Chemed Center, 255 East Fifth Street, 45202-4724
Telephone: 513-721-4532
Telecopier: 513-721-7120

Reuven J. Katz
Jerome S. Teller
Joseph A. Brant
Guy M. Hild
Robert A. Pitcairn, Jr.
Robert E. Brant
Ronald J. Goret
Stephen C. Kisling
Andrew R. Berger
Mark J. Jahnke
William F. Russo
John R. Gierl
Bruce A. Hunter
Gregory E. Land
Bradley G. Haas
Daniel P. Utt
Brent G. Houk
Cynthia Loren Gibson
Suzanne Prieur Land
Tedd H. Friedman

Representative Clients: Eagle Picher Industries, Inc.; F & C International, Inc.; Jewish Hospitals of Cincinnati; Johnny Bench; Texo Corporation; University of Cincinnati Medical Associates, Inc.

For full biographical listings, see the Martindale-Hubbell Law Directory

KEATING, MUETHING & KLEKAMP (AV)

1800 Provident Tower, One East Fourth Street, 45202
Telephone: 513-579-6400
Facsimile: 513-579-6457

MEMBERS OF FIRM

John L. Muething
Donald P. Klekamp
Timothy A. Garry
Gary P. Kreider
Don R. Gardner
Michael J. Burke
Louis F. Gilligan
Herbert B. Weiss
Joseph P. Rouse
Richard D. Siegel
Joseph L. Trauth, Jr.
James R. Whitaker
J. David Rosenberg
Robert W. Maxwell II
J. Neal Gardner
Richard L. Creighton, Jr.
Paul V. Muething
Jerome C. Randolph
James E. Burke
Kevin E. Irwin
Timothy B. Matthews
William J. Keating, Jr.
William A. Posey
Joseph P. Mellen
Mark J. Weber
Gregory M. Utter
Robert E. Coletti
Sheryl M. Linne
James M. Jansing
Patrick F. Fischer
Robert A. Klingler
David K. Montgomery
Steven R. Smith
James R. Matthews
Michael F. Bigler
Vivian M. Raby
Edward E. Steiner
Stephen M. Goodson

ASSOCIATES

Thomas A. Caneris
Donald A. Lane
Robert G. Sanker
Gregory J. Tassone
Gail Glassmeyer Pryse
Lisa Wintersheimer Michel
W. Keith Noel
Pamela Morgan Hodge
Laura L. Warren
Kenneth P. Kreider
Laura S. Petrie
Daniel E. Izenson
Gail King
Mary R. True
Daniel J. Donnellon
Mary Ellen Malas
Matthew J. Rumpke
Michael L. Scheier
Jody Klekamp Stachler
Paul D. Dorger
Mark A. Weiss
Brian M. Babb
Joseph M. Callow Jr.
Douglas L. Hensley
Darryl Mitchell

OF COUNSEL

William J. Keating
Joseph B. Conn

Representative Clients: American Financial Corporation; BP America Inc.; Chiquita Brands International, Inc.; The Cincinnati Enquirer; Cintas Corporation; Comair Holdings, Inc.; Duke Associates; LSI Industries Inc.; Mosler Inc.; Provident Bankcorp, Inc.

For full biographical listings, see the Martindale-Hubbell Law Directory

KLAINE, WILEY, HOFFMANN & MEURER A LEGAL PROFESSIONAL ASSOCIATION (AV)

Suite 1850, 105 East Fourth Street, 45202-4080
Telephone: 513-241-0202
Fax: 513-241-9322

Franklin A. Klaine, Jr.
Donald L. Wiley
Gary R. Hoffmann
Gregory J. Meurer
Donald E. Schneider
James P. Minutolo
Joyce Ann Campbell

For full biographical listings, see the Martindale-Hubbell Law Directory

LINDHORST & DREIDAME CO., L.P.A. (AV)

312 Walnut Street, Suite 2300, 45202-4091
Telephone: 513-421-6630
Telecopier: 513-421-0212

(See Next Column)

Robert F. Dreidame (1914-1978)
Leo J. Breslin
James L. O'Connell
William M. Cussen
Charles J. Kelly
John A. Goldberg
William N. Kirkham
James M. Moore
James H. Smith, III
Jay R. Langenbahn
Thomas E. Martin
James F. Brockman
Michael F. Lyon
Edward S. Dorsey
Harold L. Anness
Dale A. Stalf
Gary F. Franke

James C. Frooman
Peter C. Newberry
Charles G. Skidmore
Barry F. Fagel
Peter J. Stautberg
Robert G. Jutze
Margaret G. Kippley

SENIOR COUNSEL

Ambrose H. Lindhorst
William J. Walsh
John A. Spain

Representative Clients: CNA; CSX Corp.; Fireman's Fund-American Group; Medical Protective Co.; Norfolk Southern Corp.; Roadway Express, Inc.; Sibcy Cline, Inc.; Jewish Hospital; T.W. Smith Aircraft, Inc.; U.S.F.&G.

For full biographical listings, see the Martindale-Hubbell Law Directory

GENE MESH & ASSOCIATES (AV)

2605 Burnet Avenue, P.O. Box 198069, 45219
Telephone: 513-221-8800
Fax: 513-221-1097

Robert B. Matusoff

ASSOCIATES

R. Michael Phebus
Michael G. Brautigam (Not admitted in OH)

LEGAL SUPPORT PERSONNEL

Charles H. Short

Representative Clients: Dino's Inc. (Clothing Retailers); Liberty Sheet Metal Co.; Malibu, Inc. (Theaters); Mr. B. Greeting Card Company of Miami, Florida; Computer Data Services, Inc.
Reference: Central Trust Co.

For full biographical listings, see the Martindale-Hubbell Law Directory

PORTER, WRIGHT, MORRIS & ARTHUR (AV)

250 E. Fifth Street, 45202-4166
Telephone: 513-381-4700; (800-582-5813)
Fax: 513-421-0991
Telex: 6503213584 MCI
Columbus, Ohio Office: 41 South High Street, 43215-3406.
Telephones: 614-227-2000; (800-533-2794).
Telex: 6503213584 MCI.
Fax: 614-227-2100.
Dayton, Ohio Office: One Dayton Center, One South Main Street. 45402.
Telephones: 513-228-2411; (800-533-4434).
Fax: 513-449-6820.
Cleveland, Ohio Office: 925 Euclid Avenue, 44115-1405.
Telephones: 216-443-9000; (800-824-1980).
Fax: 216-443-9011.
Washington, D.C. Office: 1233 20th Street, N.W., 20036-2395.
Telephones: 202-778-3000; (800-456-7962).
Fax: 202-778-3063.
Naples, Florida Office: 4501 Tamiami Trail North, 33940-3060.
Telephones: 813-263-8898; (800-876-7962).
Fax: 813-436-2990.

RESIDENT MEMBERS

John J. Cruze
Mark E. Elsener
Steven F. Gay
James R. Marlow
Jerome J. Metz, Jr.
Wm. Cates Rambo
Michael G. Reed
David Reichert
Stephen David Strauss

RESIDENT ASSOCIATES

Duane A. Boggs
Christopher R. Heekin
Stephen P. Kenkel
Francine A. Wayman
Mark G. Whittenburg

OF COUNSEL

Louis J. Schneider, Jr.

Representative Clients: Bank One of Cincinnati, N.A.; FDIC/RTC; The Harper Co.; Institute of Scrap Recycle Industries; International Teleunion Association; KDI Corporation; Lincoln National Life Insurance Co.; St. Publications; Society National Bank.

For full biographical listings, see the Martindale-Hubbell Law Directory

RENDIGS, FRY, KIELY & DENNIS (AV)

900 Central Trust Tower, 45202
Telephone: 513-381-9200
FAX: 513-381-9206
Courtesy Office: Kentucky National Bank Tower, Suite 1610, 50 East Rivercenter Boulevard, Covington, Kentucky.

(See Next Column)

RENDIGS, FRY, KIELY & DENNIS, *Cincinnati—Continued*

MEMBERS OF FIRM

August A. Rendigs, Jr. (1895-1988)
Robert M. Dennis (1917-1973)
William H. Fry (1905-1975)
John A. Kiely (1899-1986)
William H. Hutcherson, Jr.
Ralph F. Mitchell
W. Roger Fry
Thomas S. Shore, Jr.
David Winchester Peck
J. Kenneth Meagher
D. Michael Poast
Paul F. Wenker
Edward R. Goldman
Joseph W. Gelwicks
Leonard A. Weakley, Jr.
Carolyn A. Taggart
Donald C. Adams, Jr.
Wilson G. Weisenfelder, Jr.
Steven D. Hengehold
Thomas M. Evans
B. Scott Boster
Felix J. Gora
John F. McLaughlin

OF COUNSEL

Robert L. McLaurin
John P. Kiely

ASSOCIATES

Jill T. O'Shea
Peter L. Ney
Terrence M. Garrigan
John M. Hands
Robert F. Brown
Paul W. McCartney
Jonathan P. Saxton
Jeffrey S. Routh
Jane E. Gerhardt
James J. Englert
Fern T. Schmitz
David S. Washington, Jr.
Michael P. Foley
Kenneth B. Flacks

Local Counsel for: Associated Aviation Underwriters; Commercial Union Assurance Co.; Continental National American Group; The Medical Protective Co.; St. Paul Insurance Co.; Sherwin-Williams; State Automobile Mutual Insurance Co.; U.S. Aviation Underwriters; Zurich Insurance Co.

For full biographical listings, see the Martindale-Hubbell Law Directory

---

SANTEN & HUGHES A LEGAL PROFESSIONAL ASSOCIATION (AV)

Suite 3100, 312 Walnut Street, 45202
Telephone: 513-721-4450
FAX: 513-721-7644; 721-0109

Kenneth R. Hughes (1925-1993)
William E. Santen
Harry H. Santen
Charles M. Meyer
Charles E. Reynolds
John D. Holschuh, Jr.
James P. Wersching
C. Gregory Schmidt
William E. Santen, Jr.
David M. Kothman
R. Mark Addy
Edward E. Santen
Charles J. Kubicki, Jr.

LEGAL SUPPORT PERSONNEL

Karen W. Crane (Corporate Paralegal)
Deborah M. McKinney (Trust/Estate Paralegal)
Karen L. Jansen (Litigation Paralegal)
Bobbie S. Ebbers (Paralegal)

For full biographical listings, see the Martindale-Hubbell Law Directory

---

SCHWARTZ, MANES & RUBY A LEGAL PROFESSIONAL ASSOCIATION (AV)

2900 Carew Tower, 441 Vine Street, 45202
Telephone: 513-579-1414
Telecopier: 513-579-1418

Richard M. Schwartz
Dennis L. Manes
Stanley L. Ruby
Thomas J. Breed
Scott M. Slovin
Arthur D. Weber, Jr.
Howard L. Richshafer
Donald B. Hordes
Harry S. Sudman
Debbe A. Levin
William S. Wyler
Stephen J. Patsfall
Thomas S. Sapinsley
Kenneth R. Thompson, II
Robert H. Siegel
William B. Singer
Stephen M. Yeager
Charles J. Davis
Peter M. Burrell
Donna M. Bergmann
Lauren Weiner Cohn
Joseph F. Pflum
Michael G. Schwartz
Jill M. Ruby

OF COUNSEL

John B. Armstrong
James J. McGraw, Jr.
Herbert Bass

For full biographical listings, see the Martindale-Hubbell Law Directory

---

STRAUSS & TROY A LEGAL PROFESSIONAL ASSOCIATION (AV)

2100 PNC Center, 201 East Fifth Street, 45202-4186
Telephone: 513-621-2120
Telecopier: 513-241-8259
Northern Kentucky Office: Suite 1400, 50 East Rivercenter Boulevard, Covington, Kentucky, 41011.
Telephone: 513-621-8900; 513-621-2120.
Telecopier: 513-629-9444.

(See Next Column)

Lucien G. Strauss (1900-1982)
Orville A. Troy (1896-1967)
Kenneth D. Troy (1918-1993)
Samuel M. Allen (Resident, Covington, Kentucky Office)
Mark H. Berliant
Gordon H. Hood (Resident, Covington, Kentucky Office)
Charles G. Atkins
William V. Strauss
Mitchell B. Goldberg
Larry A. Neuman
William S. Abernethy, Jr.
Alan Comstock Rosser
Thomas C. Rink
William R. Jacobs
Daniel H. Demmerle, II
James G. Heldman
Charles Jay Postow
Stuart C. Brinn
Martin C. Butler (Resident, Covington, Kentucky Office)
R. Guy Taft
Ann W. Gerwin
Richard S. Wayne
Paul B. Calico
Larry A. Temin
David A. Groenke
Andrew M. Shott
Claudia G. Allen
Timothy B. Theissen (Resident, Covington, Kentucky Office)
William K. Flynn
Charles C. Ashdown

Marilyn J. Maag
Shawn M. Young
Cynthia A. Fazio
Allan J. Fossett
Eric H. Kearney
Thomas L. Stachler
Anthony M. Barlow
Marshall K. Dosker (Resident, Covington, Kentucky Office)
Thomas H. Stewart
Steven F. Stuhlbarg
Maria A. Longi
Sigmund E. Huber
Pete A. Smith (Resident, Covington, Kentucky Office)
Alan R. Barnes

OF COUNSEL

Douglas G. Cole
Richard D. Heiser
George H. Palmer
Leon L. Wolf
Paul J. Theissen (Resident, Covington, Kentucky Office)
Diane Schneiderman
Charles H. Melville
Nell D. Surber

Representative Clients: PNC Bank, N.A. (Ohio and Kentucky); Corporex Companies, Inc.; Mercantile Stores Company, Inc.; Star Bank, N.A. (Ohio and Kentucky).

For full biographical listings, see the Martindale-Hubbell Law Directory

---

TAFT, STETTINIUS & HOLLISTER (AV)

1800 Star Bank Center, 425 Walnut Street, 45202-3957
Telephone: 513-381-2838
Facsimile: 513-381-0205
Cable Address: "Taftol"
Washington, D.C. Office: Suite 500, 625 Indiana Avenue, N.W.
Telephone: 202-628-2838.
Columbus, Ohio Office: Twelfth Floor, 21 East State Street.
Telephone: 614-221-2838.
Crestview Hills, Kentucky Office: Thomas More Centre, 2670 Chancellor Drive.
Telephone: 606-331-2838; 531-381-2838.

MEMBERS OF FIRM

Robert A. Taft (1889-1953)
John B. Hollister (1890-1979)
Charles D. Lindberg
Robert G. Stachler
Wilbur L. Collins
L. Clifford Craig
William K. Engeman
Jerold A. Fink
J. Alan Lips
Gerald J. Rapien
Henry C. Kasson
Robert E. Rich
R. Joseph Parker
Timothy E. Hoberg
Richard S. Roberts
David L. Johnson (Resident, Columbus, Ohio Office)
Thomas C. Hill
Thomas T. Terp
Roger A. Weber
Donald C. Hess
Timothy P. Nagy (Resident, Columbus, Ohio Office)
Timothy J. Quinn
Edward D. Diller
Timothy J. Hurley
Steven W. Weeks
William J. Seitz III
Thomas R. Schuck
Michael J. Zavatsky
Kim K. Burke
Mark J. Stepaniak
Gerald S. Greenberg
Margaret Avril Lawson
Robert B. Craig (Resident, Crestview Hills, Kentucky Office)
Robert S. Corker
John L. Stettinius (1882-1924)
Murray S. Monroe
James R. Bridgeland Jr.
Frank H. Stewart
James J. Ryan
Robert J. Townsend
Ronal R. Newbanks
Thomas D. Heekin
Melvin S. Shotten
Stephen M. Nechemias
G. David Schiering (Resident, Washington, D.C. Office)
James M. Anderson
G. Jack Donson Jr.
Richard D. Spoor (Resident, Crestview Hills, Kentucky Office)
Lawrence J. Barty
Lawrence D. Walker (Resident, Columbus, Ohio Office)
Ross E. Wales
James M. Hall Jr.
William Stuart Dornette
J. Thomas Crutcher
Daniel J. Hoffheimer
John J. McCoy
Timothy P. Reilly
James H. Brun
Donald M. Hemmer (Resident, Crestview Hills, Kentucky Office)
Charles Michael Stephan
Brenda M. Kloos
Toshio Nakao
Elizabeth A. Galloway
Stephen M. Griffith Jr.
Thomas E. Grossmann
Jeffrey S. Schloemer

(See Next Column)

TAFT, STETTINIUS & HOLLISTER—*Continued*

MEMBERS OF FIRM (Continued)

Brian P. Gillan
Patrick J. Mitchell
Timothy C. Sullivan
Philip F. Schultz
Stephen D. Lerner

OF COUNSEL

J. Mack Swigert
Robert T. Keeler
William V. Finn
Leonard A. Weakley
Sydnor I. Davis
Cynthia F. Blank

ASSOCIATES

Margaret C. Colloton
Michael A. Byers (Resident, Columbus, Ohio Office)
Patricia O. Lowry
Samuel M. Duran
David G. Krall
Robert A. Winter Jr. (Resident, Crestview Hills, Kentucky Office)
Ronald C. Christian
Mark J. Ruehlmann
T. Scott Bucey
Abram S. Gordon
Michael E. DeFrank
Jennifer Bush Olano
Gregory Parker Rogers
Mark A. Kobasuk
Elizabeth York Schiff
Gregory C. Luke
Charles H. Pangburn III
Stephen H. Jett
Russell S. Sayre
Patricia L. Herbold
Juliana M. Faris (Resident, Columbus, Ohio Office)
James J. Barresi
Jan-Michele Lemon
Susan M. Stockton
Troy A. Blackburn
W. Timothy Miller
Timothy L. Coyle (Resident, Crestview Hills, Kentucky Office)
Daniel E. Fausz
Susan Evans Cancelosi
Daniel R. Warncke
Timothy S. Hall
Jill A. Campbell
Daniel J. Brake (Resident, Columbus, Ohio Office)
Howard M. Ullman
James E. Britain
Raymond W. Lembke
Christine M. Zimmer
Laura A. Ringenbach
Jeffrey Marks
Susan E. Wheatley
Mark A. Ferguson (Resident, Columbus, Ohio Office)
John Harleston
Michael R. Rickman
Michael C. Lueder
M. Bradford Sanders
Doreen Canton
Joan A. Heffernan
Marcia Voorhis Andrew
Maria R. Schaefer
Tammy P. Hamzehpour
John H. Phillips
Patricia D. Braxton
Robert A. Bilott
William E. Nakasian (Resident, Columbus, Ohio Office)
Andrew L. Woods (Not admitted in OH; Resident, Washington, D.C. Office)
David E. Carter
Earl K. Messer
Thomas J. Sarakatsannis
Jane Guenther Parent
David. H. Peck
Keith W. Johnson
Michael A. Manzler
Stephen C. Mahon
Joseph A. Rectenwald (Not admitted in OH; Resident, Crestview Hills, Kentucky Office)
David T. Andrews
Jennifer L. Eschedor
John M. Stanton III
Scott E. Wiegand

Counsel for: BASF Corporation; Cincinnati Bengals, Inc.; Cincinnati Gas & Electric Co.; Gibson Greetings, Inc.; Great American Broadcasting Co.; Kimball International, Inc.; Morton Thiokol, Inc.; Sisters of Charity Healthcare Systems, Inc.; Star Banc Corporation; Warm Bros. Construction.

For full biographical listings, see the Martindale-Hubbell Law Directory

THOMPSON, HINE AND FLORY (AV)

312 Walnut Street, 14th Floor, 45202-4029
Telephone: 513-352-6700
Fax: 513-241-4771;
Telex: 938003
Akron, Ohio Office: 50 S. Main Street, Suite 502, 44308-1828.
Telephone: 216-376-8090.
Fax: 216-376-8386.
Cleveland, Ohio Office: 1100 National City Bank Building, 629 Euclid Avenue, 44114-3070.
Telephone: 216-566-5500.
Fax: 216-556-5583.
Telex: 980217.
Cable Address: "Thomflor".
Columbus, Ohio Office: One Columbus, 10 West Broad Street, 43215-3435.
Telephone: 614-469-3200.
Fax: 614-469-3361.
Dayton, Ohio Office: 2000 Courthouse Plaza, N.E., 45402-1706.
Telephone: 513-443-6600.
Fax: 513-443-6637; 443-6635.
Palm Beach, Florida Office: 125 Worth Avenue, 33480-4466.
Telephone: 407-833-5900.
Fax: 407-833-5951.
Washington, D.C. Office: 1920 N Street, N.W., 20036-1601.
Telephone: 202-331-8800.
Fax: 202-331-8330.
Telex: 904173.
Cable Address: "Caglaw".
Brussels, Belgium Office: Rue des Chevaliers / Ridderstraat 14 - B.10, B - 1050.
Telephone: 011(32-2) 511-9326.
Fax: 011(-32-2) 513-9206.

(See Next Column)

MEMBERS OF FIRM

William T. Bahlman, Jr.
Christopher M. Bechhold
Daniel O. Berger
Barbara Schwartz Bromberg
Stephen J. Butler
Ethna Bennert Cooper
William H. Cordes
Robert W. Crawford
C. Jackson Cromer
Scott B. Crooks
Deborah DeLong
Jack F. Fuchs
Jane E. Garfinkel
Mary J. Healy
Stephen M. King
Earle Jay Maiman
Melvin E. Marmer
Ted T. Martin
William L. Martin, Jr.
Jacqueline K. McManus
Leonard S. Meranus
Edward B. Mitchell
Michael H. Neumark
Peter K. Newman
Michael R. Oestreicher (Partner-in-Charge in Cincinnati; Brussels Office Liaison Partner)
Jeffrey F. Peck
Richard J. Ruebel
Edna V. Scheuer
Robert A. Selak
Julie Cohen Shifman
Gerald W. Simmons
Patricia Mann Smitson
Louis F. Solimine
Jacob K. Stein
Peter E. Tamborski
Richard B. Tranter
Jill A. Weller

ASSOCIATES

Paul Allaer
Philomena Saldanha Ashdown
Sarah A. Barlage
John H. Beasley
Timothy R. Brown
Frank D. Chaiken (Not admitted in OH)
Vicki Christian
Deepak K. Desai
Robert S. Dizenhuz
Renee S. Filiatraut
Howard B. Gee
Gary M. Glass
Robert P. Johnson
Sandra P. Kaltman
Jeffrey A. Lydenberg
Richard A. Paolo
Michelle L. Pensyl
Stacie A. Seiler
Michael Soto
Keith P. Spiller

For full biographical listings, see the Martindale-Hubbell Law Directory

VORYS, SATER, SEYMOUR AND PEASE (AV)

Suite 2100, 221 East Fourth Street, P.O. Box 0236, 45201-0236
Telephone: 513-723-4000
Telecopier: 513-723-4056
Columbus, Ohio Office: 52 East Gay Street, P.O. Box 1008, 43216-1008.
Telephone: 614-464-6400.
Telex: 241348.
Telecopier: 614-464-6350.
Cable Address: "Vorysater".
Cleveland, Ohio Office: 2100 One Cleveland Center, 1375 East Ninth Street, 44114-1724.
Telephone: 216-479-6100.
Telecopier: 216-479-6060.
Washington, D.C. Office: Suite 1111, 1828 L Street, N.W., 20036-5104.
Telephone: 202-467-8800.
Telex: 440693.
Telecopier: 202-467-8900.

RESIDENT MEMBERS

Roger A. Yurchuck
Frederick R. Reed
Donald J. Shuller
John C. Vorys
Eugene P. Ruehlmann
Daniel J. Buckley
Theodore D. Grosser
Mark A. Norman
Andrew M. Kaplan
Terri Reyering Abare
Charles C. Bissinger, Jr.

RESIDENT ASSOCIATES

Arthur E. Phelps, Jr.
Cynthia A. Shafer
Melvin A. Bedree
Michael E. Samuels (Not admitted in OH)
W. Breck Weigel
Lorene F. Schaefer
Marianne E. Roche
William D. Hayes
Victor A. Walton, Jr.
Nathaniel Lampley, Jr.
Laura H. Martin
David A. Skidmore, Jr.
Richard L. Moore
Stephen S. Eberly
Eliot N. Meyers (Not admitted in OH)
Phillip J. Smith

RESIDENT OF COUNSEL

Jacob E. Davis
Ruth R. Longenecker
Glenn V. Whitaker

For full biographical listings, see the Martindale-Hubbell Law Directory

WOOD & LAMPING (AV)

2500 Cincinnati Commerce Center, 600 Vine Street, 45202-2409
Telephone: 513-852-6000
Fax: 513-852-6087
Ft. Mitchell, Kentucky Office: Kentucky Executive Building, 2055 Dixie Highway, Suites 248-252.
Telephone: 606-344-4052; 344-4052.
Fax: 606-344-9631.

MEMBERS OF FIRM

Robert F. Reckman
Kenneth J. Schneider
William H. Eder, Jr.
Harold G. Korbee
Albert H. Neman
David A. Caldwell
Stephen Cohen
Eric C. Holzapfel
Paul R. Berninger
Robert P. Malloy

(See Next Column)

WOOD & LAMPING, *Cincinnati—Continued*

MEMBERS OF FIRM (Continued)

Jeffrey M. Rollman
Stanton H. Vollman
William R. Ellis
Thomas C. Korbee
Mark S. Reckman
Jan M. Frankel
Gary J. Davis
James B. Harrison
Jane A. McTaggart
Gerald G. Salmen
Henry E. Menninger, Jr.

COUNSEL

John Wood, II
Harry M. Hoffheimer
Robert O. Leming

ASSOCIATES

John H. Flessa
Thomas M. Woebkenberg
Mark R. Fitch
Carl J. Schmidt, III
Amy L. Tolnitch
Geraldine M. Johnson
Martin J. Kenworthy
William C. Price
Diana K. Falstrom
Ralph J. Conrad

For full biographical listings, see the Martindale-Hubbell Law Directory

*CIRCLEVILLE,** Pickaway Co.

HUFFER AND HUFFER CO., L.P.A. (AV)

203 South Scioto Street, P.O. Box 464, 43113
Telephone: 614-474-2179
Fax: 614-477-1778

Robert H. Huffer
Roy H. Huffer, Jr.

Representative Client: PPG Industries.

For full biographical listings, see the Martindale-Hubbell Law Directory

*CLEVELAND,** Cuyahoga Co.

ARTER & HADDEN (AV)

1100 Huntington Building, 925 Euclid Avenue, 44115-1475
Telephone: 216-696-1100
Telex: 98-5384
In Columbus, Ohio: 21st Floor, One Columbus, 10 West Broad Street. 43215-3422.
Telephone: 614-221-3155.
In Washington, D.C.: 1801 K Street, N.W., Suite 400K. 20006-3480.
Telephone: 202-775-7100.
In Dallas, Texas: 1717 Main Street, Suite 4100. 75201-4605.
Telephone: 214-761-2100.
In Los Angeles, California: 700 South Flower Street. 90017-4101.
Telephone: 213-629-9300.
In Irvine, California: Two Park Plaza, Suite 700, Jamboree Center.
Telephone: 714-252-7500.
In Austin, Texas: 100 Congress Avenue, Suite 1800.
Telephone: 512-479-6403.
In San Antonio, Texas: Suite 540, Harte-Hanks Tower, 7710 Jones Maltsberger Road.
Telephone: 210-805-8497.

MEMBERS OF FIRM

Charles K. Arter (1875-1957)
John A. Hadden (1886-1979)
Walter A. Bates
Edwin A. Kennedy
Carlton B. Schnell
Joseph A. Rotolo
David L. Genger
William W. Taft
Robert E. Glaser
Stanley A. Williams
Jerome D. Neifach
John P. Hall
George Gore
James A. Laurenson
Charles J. O'Toole
Edward F. Meyers, Jr.
M. Neal Rains
Hugh M. Stanley, Jr.
Thomas V. Chema
Harry D. Cornett, Jr.
Stephen C. Ellis
John B. Lewis
Gary L. Dinner
Frank R. Osborne
John T. Doheny
Ed E. Duncan
Brian W. FitzSimons
Robert B. Tomaro
Mark F. McCarthy
Robert C. Tucker
Michael F. Harris
Glenn E. Morrical
Thomas J. Onusko
Henry E. Billingsley, II
Anthony J. Damelio, Jr.
Michael E. Elliott
Dominic V. Perry
Rita Bartnik Maimbourg
Irene C. Keyse-Walker
Tom McDonald
James E. Phillips
Kathy P. Lazar
Victoria L. Vance
Beth Whitmore
Diana M. Thimmig
Barry J. Miller
George M. Moscarino
Susan E. Raabe
Michael J. O'Brien
Kris H. Treu
Anthony C. LaPlaca
Bernard J. Smith
Gregory V. Mersol
Robert J. Hanna
Janet H. Smith

RETIRED PARTNERS

Howard M. Kohn
R. Crawford Morris
Quentin Alexander
Robert G. McCreary
Byron D. Fair
Edward C. Crouch
Thomas A. Quintrell
Robert S. Burton
Charles W. Landefeld
James H. Wilkinson
Robert B. Preston
Clay Mock
Leslie L. Knowlton

(See Next Column)

OF COUNSEL

Donald W. Morrison
George M. Brown
Robert G. Boes
Jacob I. Rosenbaum
Morris G. Shanker
Stanley M. Fisher
John P. Reinartz
Bourne P. Dempsey
Richard H. Brown
Karen H. Bauernschmidt

ASSOCIATES

Ann H. Womer Benjamin
Michael J. Bertsch
Carter E. Strang
Sonali Bustamante Wilson
Cynthia C. Schafer
Thomas H. Allison
William H. Falin
Lisa Amato Reid
Joan M. Englund
Eugene M. Killeen
William J. Stavole
Susan L. Racey
John C. Tillman
James K. Warren
Patricia Casey Cuthbertson
Jean Kerr Korman
Daniel C. Rose
John T. Bulloch
Lois J. Cole
Jason M. Gibbons
Kristen L. Mayer
Susan B. Cavanagh
Jeffrey A. Healy
William J. Muniak
Susan Massey
Robert T. Wilson
Michael F. Cunningham

For full biographical listings, see the Martindale-Hubbell Law Directory

BAKER & HOSTETLER (AV)

3200 National City Center, 1900 East Ninth Street, 44114-3485
Telephone: 216-621-0200
Telecopier: 216-696-0740
TWX: 810 421 8375
RCA Telex: 215032
In Columbus, Ohio: Capitol Square, Suite 2100, 65 East State Street.
Telephone: 614-228-1541.
In Denver, Colorado: 303 East 17th Avenue, Suite 1100.
Telephone: 303-861-0600.
In Houston, Texas: 1000 Louisiana, Suite 2000.
Telephone: 713-751-1600.
In Long Beach, California: 300 Oceangate, Suite 620.
Telephone: 310-432-2827.
In Los Angeles, California: 600 Wilshire Boulevard.
Telephone: 213-624-2400.
In Orlando, Florida: SunBank Center, Suite 2300, 200 South Orange Avenue.
Telephone: 407-649-4000.
In Washington, D. C.: Washington Square, Suite 1100, 1050 Connecticut Avenue, N.W.
Telephone: 202-861-1500.
In College Park, Maryland: 9658 Baltimore Boulevard, Suite 206.
Telephone: 301-441-2781.
In Alexandria, Virginia: 437 North Lee Street.
Telephone: 703-549-1294.
In San Francisco, California: One Sansome Street, Suite 2000.
Telephone: 415-951-4705.

MEMBERS OF FIRM

Newton D. Baker (1871-1937)
Joseph C. Hostetler (1885-1958)
Thomas L. Sidlo (1888-1955)
John H. Burlingame (Executive Partner)
Gary L. Bryenton (Managing Partner)

PARTNERS

Albert T. Adams
Frank H. Andorka
Oakley V. Andrews
William Appleton
Elliot Stephen Azoff
Richard H. Bamberger
Bruce O. Baumgartner
Paul E. Bennett
Mary M. Bittence
Dale A. Bradford
Maureen A. Brennan
Arthur V.N. Brooks
Robert M. Brucken
Diane P. Chapman
Elaine A. Chotlos
Avery S. Cohen
Susan B. Collins
Louis A. Colombo
Wayne C. Dabb, Jr.
George Downing
John D. Drinko
Paul P. Eyre
William W. Falsgraf
Paul H. Feinberg
José C. Feliciano
John H. M. Fenix
Paula L. Friedman
John Mills Gherlein
Wendy J. Gibson
Edward S. Ginsburg
Matthew R. Goldman
James B. Griswold
Donald W. Gruettner
J. Richard Hamilton
David G. Holcombe
Richard R. Hollington, Jr.
John S. Hopkins, III
Charles E. Jarrett
Norman S. Jeavons
Patrick J. Jordan
R. Scott Keller
R. Steven Kestner
Calvin B. Kirchick
Charles Klaus
Albert J. Knopp
Robert K. Lease
Earl M. Leiken
Stephen A. Lenn
Richard H. Leukart, II
Lawrence V. Lindberg
Thomas R. Lucchesi
Raymond M. Malone
David L. Marburger
Robert G. Markey
Gary R. Martz
John J. McGowan, Jr.
Karen B. Newborn
John F. Novatney, Jr.
Patricia J. O'Donnell
Ronald S. Okada
W. James Ollinger
John D. Parker
Charles T. Price
Edward G. Ptaszek, Jr.
Kevin G. Robertson
Raymond Rundelli
Thomas M. Seger
Hewitt B. Shaw, Jr.

(See Next Column)

BAKER & HOSTETLER—*Continued*

PARTNERS (Continued)

Thomas H. Shunk
Kenneth F. Snyder
Randall L. Solomon
Robert G. Stinchcomb
David J. Strauss
Victor Strimbu, Jr.
John E. Sullivan
Christopher J. Swift
William M. Toomajian
Richard R. Turney
Ernest E. Vargo, Jr.
R. Byron Wallace
Robert A. Weible
Charles D. Weller
Douglas P. Whipple
Paul D. White
John H. Wilharm, Jr.
John A. Zangerle

ASSOCIATES

Alan D. Alford
Thomas L. Anastos
William L. Arnold
Jeffrey J. Baldassari
Diane D. Bausback
Jordan Berns
Beth Brandon
David A. Bruscino
Dennis P. Byrnes
Phillip M. Callesen
C. Antoinette Clarke
R. Timothy Coerdt
Kathryn Young Connors
Thomas F. Cooke, II
Melanie S. Corcoran
Anne M. Everson
Michael K. Farrell
Robert R. Galloway
Loretta H. Garrison
William J. Gelm
Jerome P. Grisko, Jr.
Suzanne K. Hanselman
David B. Hathaway
Jane T. Haylor
Scott D. Irwin
Suzanne M. Jambe
Lisa Hammond Johnson
Daniel M. Israel
Catherine M. Kilbane
Tom A. King
Mark R. Koberna
James A. Loeb
Joy M. Maciejewski
John H. Macrae
Ruth Ann Maloney
Kathleen S. Mara
Daniel P. Mascaro
Sean M. McAvoy
Candace C. McIntoch
Elizabeth A. McNellie
Wade A. Mitchell
Gerardo C. Orlando
Jeffrey H. Paravano
Robert C. Petrulis
Kathleen A. Pettingill
Patricia A. Poole
Hilary Whipple Rule
Orlando Smith
Stacey S. Staub
Ronald A. Stepanovic
Alexander J. Szilvas
Deborah A. Schaff Wilcox

OF COUNSEL

Theodore W. Jones
Lloyd F. Loux, Jr.

RETIRED PARTNERS

Charles R. Ault
William L. Calfee
Sherman Dye
David R. Fullmer
James P. Garner
H. Stephen Madsen

LEGAL SUPPORT PERSONNEL

Barbara Harrison Kaye (Firmwide Director of Marketing)
Alvin M. Podboy, Jr. (Firmwide Director of Libraries)
James E. Taylor (Firmwide Director of Information Services)
Charles B. Thomas (Firmwide Director of Finance)
Michelle C. Vanderlip (Firmwide Director of Human Resources)

For full biographical listings, see the Martindale-Hubbell Law Directory

---

BENESCH, FRIEDLANDER, COPLAN & ARONOFF (AV)

2300 BP America Building, 200 Public Square, 44114-2378
Telephone: 216-363-4500
Telecopier: 216-363-4588
Columbus, Ohio Office: 88 East Broad Street, 43215-3506.
Telephone: 614-223-9300.
Telecopier: 614-223-9330.
Cincinnati, Ohio Office: 2800 Cincinnati Commerce Center, 600 Vine Street, 45202-2409.
Telephone: 713-762-6200.
Telecopier: 513-762-6245.

MEMBERS OF FIRM

George N. Aronoff
Lawrence M. Bell
Irv Berliner
Gary B. Bilchik
Gregory G. Binford
Harry M. Brown
Maynard A. Buck, III
Benjamin Calkins
Alan Doris
Mark S. Edelman
James M. Friedman
Jeremy Gilman
Allan Goldner
Bernard D. Goodman
Norman W. Gutmacher
Douglas E. Haas
E. William Haffke, Jr.
Gregory L. Hilbrich
James M. Hill
Patricia Marcus Holland
Edward A. Hurtuk
David S. Inglis
Edward Kancler
Ira C. Kaplan
Margaret A. Kennedy
Allan D. Kleinman
Harold E. Leidner
Howard A. Levy
Richard D. Margolis
David R. Mayo
Michael J. Meaney
David W. Mellott
Richard L. Phillips
Wayne D. Porter, Jr.
Harry T. Quick
Charles M. Rosenberg
Alan E. Schabes
William E. Schonberg
H. Jeffrey Schwartz
Kurt J. Smidansky
Howard A. Steindler
Joseph G. Tegreene

(See Next Column)

MEMBERS OF FIRM (Continued)

Mark D. Thompson
Russell B. Turell
Bradley A. VanAuken
Jeffry L. Weiler
Stephen David Williger

ASSOCIATES

Dona L. Arnold
Michael A. Benoit
Steven B. Berger
Stephen V. Cheatham
David M. Coffey
Rachel Cowan
Walter C. Danison, Jr.
Charles Daroff II
Elizabeth A. Dellinger
Dominic A. DiPuccio
Leslie A. Drockton
Kyle B. Fleming (Not admitted in OH)
Joseph N. Gross
Richard S. Hawrylak
Carol A. Jones
William J. Kerner, Sr.
Jennifer A. Lesny
David M. Levine
Jeffrey M. Levinson
James W. Margulies (Not admitted in OH)
Laura C. Meagher
Jefferson L. Mitchell
Susan L. Mizer
Sandi R. Murphy
David W. Neel
Sheila M. Ninneman
Daniel F. Petticord
Mark A. Phillips
Ross H. Pollock
Mary E. Reid
Nick D. Shofar
Michael K. Swearengen
Ronald J. Teplitzky
Richard F. Tracanna
Barbara Friedman Yaksic
Eric L. Zalud

COUNSEL

Robert C. Coplan (Retired)
Marvin I. Kelner
Deanna Coe Kursh
Leslee W. Miraldi
Jeffrey A. Perlmuter
Eugenia M. Schmidley
Judith Schacter Tykocinski
Warren L. Udisky
Alfred A. Benesch (1879-1973)
Jerome M. Friedlander (1900-1993)
Morton M. Stotter (1909-1991)

COLUMBUS, OHIO
RESIDENT MEMBERS

Orla Ellis Collier, III
James F. DeLeone
Terrence M. Fay
James B. Feibel
Leon Friedberg
N. Victor Goodman
Mark D. Thompson
Sara L. Todd
Michael K. L. Wager

COLUMBUS, OHIO
RESIDENT ASSOCIATES

Thomas S. Counts
Janet K. Feldkamp
Heather E. Goodman
J. Gregg Haught
Ronald L. House
Michael Kranitz
Rex A. Littrell
Jeffrey D. Meyer
Roger L. Schantz
John F. Stock
Mark D. Tucker

COLUMBUS, OHIO
RESIDENT OF COUNSEL

Robert N. Shamansky

CINCINNATI, OHIO
RESIDENT MEMBERS

Richard Boydston
Anthony G. Covatta
Robin E. Harvey
Donald J. Mooney, Jr.
Stuart A. Schloss, Jr.
Frederic X. Shadley
Stuart R. Susskind

CINCINNATI, OHIO
RESIDENT ASSOCIATES

Elizabeth Conkin (Not admitted in OH)
Thomas A. Coz
John R. Ipsaro
Shelley B. Jones
Paula Davis Lampley
Linda E. Maichl
Joseph P. Thomas

CINCINNATI, OHIO
OF COUNSEL

Michael A. Marrero
Henry H. Chatfield (1917-1991)

For full biographical listings, see the Martindale-Hubbell Law Directory

---

BERICK, PEARLMAN & MILLS A LEGAL PROFESSIONAL ASSOCIATION (AV)

1350 Eaton Center, 1111 Superior Avenue, 44114-2569
Telephone: 216-861-4900
Automatic Telecopier: 216-861-4929

James H. Berick
Samuel S. Pearlman
Osborne Mills, Jr.
William M. Mills
Paul J. Singerman
Gary S. Desberg
Daniel G. Berick

COUNSEL

Joseph G. Berick
Joan M. Gross

Arthur J. Tassi
Edmund G. Kauntz
Laura D. Nemeth
Robert G. Marischen

Representative Clients: Cleveland Browns Football Company, Inc.; Cleveland Surgical Society; The Equitable Life Assurance Society of the United States; The Huntington National Bank; Realty ReFund Trust; A. Schulman, Inc.; Society National Bank; Third Federal Savings; The Town and Country Trust; The Tranzonic Companies.

For full biographical listings, see the Martindale-Hubbell Law Directory

CALFEE, HALTER & GRISWOLD (AV)

Suite 1800, 800 Superior Avenue, 44114-2688
Telephone: 216-622-8200
Telecopier: 216-241-0816
Telex: 980499
Columbus, Ohio Office: 88 East Broad Street, Suite 1500.
Telephone: 614-321-1500.
Telecopier: 614-621-0010.

MEMBERS OF FIRM

Edwin G. Halter (1906-1975)
Bruce Griswold (1916-1993)
Daniel L. Ekelman
Richard Cusick
F. Rush McKnight
Joseph D. Sullivan
Charles R. Emrick, Jr.
Wm. Tousley Smith
Richard N. Ogle
William A. Papenbrock
John D. Wheeler
C. Richard Brubaker
Michael L. Miller
John D. Leech
James F. Streicher
Donald Frederic Woodcock
Thomas A. Jorgensen
Dale C. LaPorte
Phillip J. Campanella
Timothy J. Nolan
Brian M. Eisenberg
Frederick W. Assini
David Lyle Carpenter
Ronald H. Neill
Charles B. Lyon
Philip M. Dawson
Thomas E. Wagner
P. Michael DeAngelo (Resident, Columbus Office)
William N. Hogg
David E. Bishop
Robert N. Rapp
Harold W. Babbit
William A. Boyd
Thomas A. Cicarella
Walter G. Harper
Walter A. Rodgers
Kenneth R. Schmeichel
Thomas F. McKee
Mark I. Wallach
John E. Miller, Jr. (Not admitted in OH)
Virginia D. Benjamin
Stephen P. Kresnye
James G. Dickinson
David S. Goodman
Richard J. Hauer, Jr.
Michael D. Phillips
Scott R. Wilson
James M. Lawniczak
Ronald C. Stansbury
Guy F. Guinn
John Paul Batt
Lawrence N. Schultz
Michael E. Brittain
Richard P. Goddard
Bruce J. L. Lowe
Darlene Evans McCoy
Marcia J. Wexberg
John J. Eklund
Thomas W. McCrystal
Marc L. Oberdorff
Mitchell G. Blair
Edward W. Moore
D. Timothy Pembridge
Mary M. Reil
Joseph A. Castrodale
William E. Coughlin
James C. Vanderwist
John T. Wiedemann (Not admitted in OH)
Joseph K. Juster
Kathleen Keogh
Brent D. Ballard
Peter J. Comodeca
Jeanne E. Longmuir
JoEllen M. Minchak
John M. Mino
Patrick Morris
Douglas A. Neary
Robert P. Rink
Robert A. Ross
M. Ann Harlan
Albert J. Lucas (Resident, Columbus Office)

RETIRED PARTNERS

John B. Calfee
John L. Naylor, Jr.
Thomas K. M. Victory
Hubbard C. Capes

OF COUNSEL

John E. Gotherman
Lawrence R. Oremland
Anthony C. Sinagra
Robert W. Boich (Resident, Columbus Office)

SENIOR ATTORNEYS

William L. S. Ross
Laura J. Gorretta
Frank C. Manak III
Stanley J. Dobrowski (Resident, Columbus Office)
Jonathan P. Beck
Sandra G. Rolitsky

ASSOCIATES

Thomas R. Coerdt
Mary E. Golrick
Andréa L. Caruso
John R. Cernelich
Kevin P. Hallquist
John J. Jenkins
Anthony J. LaCerva
Robert A. Miller
Anne Marie Reidy
Vanessa L. Whiting
James R. Chriszt
Lynn M. Gattozzi
Daniel J. McMullen
Thomas P. Pappas (Resident, Columbus Office)
John P. Susany
Shelly Gay Dedmon
Martin S. Gates
James L. Koewler, Jr.
Thomas I. Michals
Reneé Tramble Richard
Brian C. Salvagni
Mark S. Yacano
Andrew C. Alexander
David A. Basinski, Jr.
Linda McIntyre Black
David J. Carney
John S. Cipolla
Anthea R. Daniels
Margaret S. Callesen
Steven C. Lee
Cornelius J. Whitford
Stephen J. Knoop
Christopher S. Williams
Philip J. Carino
Mara E. Cushwa
Michael W. Gregory, Jr.
Ann Marie Intili

(See Next Column)

ASSOCIATES (Continued)

John A. Kastelic
John F. Kramer
Chrysso B. Sarkos
David J. Crandall
Jean M. Cullen
John A. Heer, II
Suzanne Y. Park
James C. Scott
Karl S. Beus
Richard E. Brooks
James F. Lang
Paul Mancino
Gerald A. Monroe
Jill C. Boland
Suzanne F. Day
Maura L. Hughes
Donald E. Longwell, Jr.
Sean T. Moorhead
Chancellor W. Patterson
Nicholas A. Rossi
Stephen L. McCauley
Dorothy Regas Richards

For full biographical listings, see the Martindale-Hubbell Law Directory

DAVIS AND YOUNG CO., L.P.A. (AV)

1700 Midland Building, 44115
Telephone: 216-348-1700
FAX: 216-621-0602
Cable: DANDY CLE
Akron, Ohio Office: 1015 Society Building, 159 South Main Street.
Telephone 216-376-1717.
Fax: 216-376-1797.

Rees H. Davis, Sr. (1892-1965)
Fred J. Young (1889-1946)
George W. Lutjen
Martin J. Murphy
C. Richard McDonald
Paul D. Eklund
Jan L. Roller
Thomas W. Wright
David J. Fagnilli

William Vance
Gregory H. Collins
Patrick F. Roche
Bonnie M. Gust
Dennis R. Fogarty

OF COUNSEL

R. Emmett Moran

Counsel for: Alliance Insurance Co.; Amerisure Companies; Avis Rent-A-Car System, Inc.; Black & Decker; Dana Corp.; Central Mutual Insurance Co.;Eagle Picher Industries, Inc.; First National Supermarkets Inc.; Cincinnati Insurance Co.; U.S. Fidelity & Guaranty Co.

For full biographical listings, see the Martindale-Hubbell Law Directory

FADEL & BEYER (AV)

(Formerly Wuliger, Fadel and Beyer)
The Brownell Building, 1340 Sumner Court, 44115
Telephone: 216-781-7777
FAX: 216-781-0621

MEMBERS OF FIRM

William I. Fadel
William D. Beyer
Kathleen M. Sasala
Steven D. Jones
Eric S. Bravo

OF COUNSEL

Stephen O. Walker
Edward F. Marek

Reference: National City Bank.

For full biographical listings, see the Martindale-Hubbell Law Directory

GOLD, ROTATORI & SCHWARTZ, L.P.A. (AV)

1500 Leader Building, 44114
Telephone: 216-696-6122
FAX: 216-696-3214

Gerald S. Gold
Robert J. Rotatori
Niki Z. Schwartz
John S. Pyle
Susan L. Gragel
Robert A. Ranallo

Orville E. Stifel, II
Richard L. Stoper, Jr.
Brian P. Downey

Reference: Society National Bank of Cleveland.

For full biographical listings, see the Martindale-Hubbell Law Directory

JANIK & DUNN (AV)

400 Park Plaza Building, 1111 Chester Avenue, 44114
Telephone: 216-781-9700
Fax: 216-781-1250
Brea, California Office: 2601 Saturn Street, Suite 300.
Telephone: 714-572-1101.
Fax: 714-572-1103.

MEMBERS OF FIRM

Steven G. Janik
Theodore M. Dunn, Jr.

ASSOCIATES

Myra Staresina
David L. Mast

For full biographical listings, see the Martindale-Hubbell Law Directory

Cleveland—Continued

JONES, DAY, REAVIS & POGUE (AV)

North Point, 901 Lakeside Avenue, 44114
Telephone: 216-586-3939
Cable Address: "Attorneys Cleveland"
Telex: 980389
Telecopier: 216-579-0212
In Columbus, Ohio: 1900 Huntington Center.
Telephone: 614-469-3939.
Cable Address: "Attorneys Columbus."
Telecopier: 614-461-4198.
In Atlanta, Georgia: 3500 One Peachtree Center, 303 Peachtree Street, N.E.
Telephone: 404-521-3939.
Cable Address: "Attorneys Atlanta".
Telex: 54-2711.
Telecopier: 404-581-8330.
In Brussels, Belgium: Avenue Louise 480, 7th Floor. B-1050 Brussels.
Telephone: 011-32-2-645-14-11.
Telecopier: 011-32-2-645-14-45.
In Chicago, Illinois: 77 West Wacker.
Telephone: 312-782-3939.
Telecopier: 312-782-8585.
In Dallas, Texas: 2300 Trammell Crow Center, 2001 Ross Avenue.
Telephone: 214-220-3939.
Cable Address: "Attorneys Dallas."
Telex: 730852.
Telecopier: 214-969-5100.
In Frankfurt, Germany: Triton Haus, Bockenheimer Landstrasse 42, 60323 Frankfurt am Main.
Telephone: 49-69-9726-3939.
Telecopier: 49-69-9726-3993.
In Geneva, Switzerland: 20, rue de Candolle.
Telephone: 011-41-22-320-2339.
Telecopier: 011-41-22-320-1232.
In Hong Kong: 1501 One Exchange Square, 8 Connaught Place.
Telephone: 011-852-2526-6895.
Telecopier: 011-852-2810-5787.
In Irvine, California: 2603 Main Street, Suite 900.
Telephone: 714-851-3939.
Telex: 194911 Lawyers LSA.
Telecopier: 714-553-7539.
In London, England: One Mount Street.
Telephone: 011-44-71-493-9361.
Cable Address: "Surgoe London WI."
Telecopier: 011-44-71-493-9666.
In Los Angeles, California: 555 West Fifth Street, Suite 4600.
Telephone: 213-489-3939.
Telex: 181439 UD.
Telecopier: 213-243-2539.
In New York, New York: 599 Lexington Avenue.
Telephone: 212-326-3939.
Cable Address: "JONESDAY NEWYORK."
Telex: 237013 JDRP UR.
Telecopier: 212-755-7306.
In Paris, France: 62, rue du Faubourg Saint-Honore.
Telephone: 011-33-1-44-71-3939.
Cable Address: "Surgoe Paris."
Telex: 290156 Surgoe.
Telecopier: 011-33-1-49-24-0471.
In Pittsburgh, Pennsylvania: 500 Grant Street, 31st Floor.
Telephone: 412-391-3939.
Cable Address: "Attorneys Pittsburgh".
Telecopier: 412-394-7959.
In Riyadh, Saudi Arabia: Law Offices of Saud M.A. Shawwaf, P.O. Box 2700.
Telephones: 011 (966-1) 465-6543, 011 (966-1) 464-8534 or 011 (966-1) 464-8540.
Telex: 401831 SAUCON SJ.
Telecopier: (966-1) 464-8480.
In Taipei, Taiwan: 8th Floor, Tun Hwa South Road, Section 2.
Telephone: 011 (886-2) 704-6808.
Telecopier: 011 (886-2) 704-6791.
In Tokyo, Japan: Toranomon MT Building, 4th Floor, 10-3, Toranomon 3-Chome, Minato-Ku, Tokyo 105, Japan.
Telephone: 011-81-3-3433-3939.
Telecopier: 011-81-3-5401-2725.
In Washington, D.C.: Metropolitan Square, 1450 G Street, N.W.
Telephone: 202-879-3939.
Cable Address: "Attorneys Washington."
Telex: 89-2410 ATTORNEYS WASH.
Telecopier: 202-737-2832.

MEMBERS OF FIRM

Patrick F. McCartan
George J. Moscarino
Robert B. Nelson
William A. Reale
Marc L. Swartzbaugh
Hal D. Cooper
John L. Strauch
Leigh B. Trevor
Gary W. Melsher
Barbara B. Kacir
Irvin A. Leonard
Dennis M. Kelly
Dennis W. LaBarre
Paul T. Ruxin
Barry L. Springel
John L. Sterling
John R. Cornell
Andrew M. Kramer
William S. Paddock
(Resident in Atlanta)

(See Next Column)

MEMBERS OF FIRM (Continued)

Brian F. Toohey
John M. Newman, Jr.
Richard H. Sayler
David G. Heiman
Michael A. Nims
William Thomas Plesec
Robert H. Rawson, Jr.
John W. Sager
David W. Sloan
Kenneth E. Updegraft, Jr.
John C. Duffy, Jr.
James A. Rydzel
James E. Young
Kathleen B. Burke
Kenneth G. Hochman
Jeffrey S. Leavitt
Joseph L. Liegl
Zachary T. Paris
Richard B. Whitney
Paul G. Crist
John P. Dunn
John W. Edwards II
Regan J. Fay
Ronald R. Janke
Michael G. Marting
Richard L. Reppert
Hugh R. Whiting
Kenneth R. Adamo
William Hollis Coquillette
Leslie D. Dunn
Theodore M. Grossman
Michael J. Horvitz
Robert Conley Kahrl
Barbara J. Leukart
Anthony R. Moore
William H. Roj
Louis Rorimer
Steven E. Sigalow
James L. Wamsley, III
Richard G. Stuhan
Robert C. Weber
John D. Currivan
Mary Lynn Durham
William K. Smith
Joseph F. Winterscheid
Thomas Demitrack
Stephen J. Kaczynski
Janet L. Miller
Stephen J. Squeri
Robert P. Ducatman
Stephen Q. Giblin
Daniel C. Hagen
David A. Kutik
Richard P. Layman
Jeanne M. Rickert
Frederick G. Stueber
Richard M. Cieri
David P. Porter
Kim F. Bixenstine
Carl M. Jenks
Michael W. Vary
Robert S. Walker
Mark Herrmann
Lyle G. Ganske
Timothy J. O'Hearn
Jeffery D. Ubersax
Richard I. Werder, Jr.
John C. McIlwraith

OF COUNSEL

Albert I. Borowitz
Katherine Bryan Jenks

SENIOR ATTORNEYS

H. Duane Switzer
Randall A. Cole
Martha L. Sjogreen
(Not admitted in OH)
Charles M. Steines
Mary Turk-Meena
Kathleen Hohler
Charles M. Kennedy
Marc Alan Silverstein
Leozino Agozzino
Ted S. Hiser
Robert S. Gilmore
Timothy M. Opsitnick
Mary D. Maloney

ASSOCIATES

Rebecca Holloway Dent
Linda Gebauer
Joseph R. Daprile
Joseph D. Pollack
Stephen Gold
Sanjiv K. Kapur
James A. Klenkar
William D. Manson
Deborah Somerville Rodewig
Mark A. Belasic
Robert L. Canala
Thomas C. Daniels
Sandra E. Gammie
Paul D. Koethe
John M. Majoras
Stephen C. Mixter
Samuel J. Najim
Karen Kazel Poulos
Shawn M. Riley
Richard J. Bedell, Jr.
Ellen E. Halfon
Charles W. Hardin, Jr.
William A. Herzberger
Cheryl Farine
Lisa B. Gates
Calvin P. Griffith
Thomas N. Littman
Bernadette Mihalic Mast
Lisa A. Roberts-Mamone
Asmita Shirali
(Not admitted in OH)
Michael L. Snyder
Michelle K. Fischer
Anne Owings Ford
Deborah Platt Herman
Kelly Montgomery Hoy
Matthew L. Kuryla
Charles B. Meyer
Pauline M. Moorman
Allen D. Moreland
(Not admitted in OH)
Michael A. Primrose
Elizabeth A. Shaver
Randal S. Baringer
Deborah R. Blumenthal
Jackie M. Kenyon
(Not admitted in OH)
Marjorie H. Kitchell
Patrick J. Leddy
Dennis M. Myers
William H. Oldach III
(Not admitted in OH)
Edward Purnell
Catherine Williams Smith
Dennis L. Murphy
Rachel L. Rawson
(Not admitted in OH)
Edward J. Sebold
Bradley S. Smith
Stephan I. Voudris
Thomas W. Adams
Rodrigo R. de Llano
Lawrence S. Drasner
Robert S. Faxon
Geoffrey S. Frankel
Heather Lennox
Benjamin G. Lombard
Neil F. Luria
Kevin Doyle O'Rear
(Not admitted in OH)
Rosalie B. Sigall
Mary E. Sweeney
Terese M. Tiburzio
Brian Troyer
Paul F. Wingenfeld
Thaddeus Bereday
Timothy P. Fraelich
Stephen P. Goldrup
Barbara-Ann C. Gustaferro
Arthur C. Hall, III
(Not admitted in OH)
Geoffrey J. Ritts
David E. Rogers
John M. Saada, Jr.
David H. Saltzman
Jeffrey J. Weber
Mark J. Andreini
Steven M. Auvil
Thomas A. Briggs

(See Next Column)

JONES, DAY, REAVIS & POGUE, *Cleveland—Continued*

ASSOCIATES (Continued)

Susanne H. Deegan (Not admitted in OH)
Kathleen D. Huryn
Denise Jackson
Lance A. Kawesch
Thomas J. Osborne, Jr.
Kim M. Sanchez
Kevin A. Smith
David D. Watson
Lizbeth London Wright

INSURANCE COUNSEL

Charles D. Hassell

For full biographical listings, see the Martindale-Hubbell Law Directory

KADISH & BENDER A LEGAL PROFESSIONAL ASSOCIATION (AV)

2112 East Ohio Building, 44114
Telephone: 216-696-3030
Telecopier: 216-696-3492

Stephen L. Kadish
J. Timothy Bender
Kevin M. Hinkel
David G. Weibel

Aaron H. Bulloff
Joseph P. Alexander
David G. Lambert
William A. Duncan
Mary Beth Duffy
James H. Rownd

For full biographical listings, see the Martindale-Hubbell Law Directory

KAHN, KLEINMAN, YANOWITZ & ARNSON CO., L.P.A. (AV)

The Tower at Erieview, Suite 2600, 44114-1824
Telephone: 216-696-3311
Telecopiers: 216-696-1009; 696-1524

Harold H. Kahn (1906-1970)
Armond D. Arnson
Sheldon Berns
Morlee A. Rothchild
Lawrence C. Sherman
Neil Kurit
Thomas L. Dettelbach
Richard A. Rosner
Michael H. Diamant
Marc H. Morgenstern
Robert J. Valerian
Richard S. Rivitz
Bruce E. Gaynor
Brian A. Bash
Neil W. Gurney
M. Colette Gibbons
Anne L. Meyers
Michael A. Ellis
Judith A. Lemke
Kevin D. Barnes
Frederick N. Widen
James J. Bartolozzi
William M. Phillips
Gail B. Mayland
Scott M. Lewis
Sharon G. Newman
Sean A. H. Bowen
Frederic P. Schwieg
Benjamin J. Ockner
Toni M. Trafas
Terri G. Amernick
Dorothea M. Polster
Theodore Eliot Deutch
Michael D. Stovsky
Ronald P. Friedberg
Douglas R. Krause
Krishna Rao
Matthew S. Friedman

SENIOR PRINCIPAL

Bennett Yanowitz

OF COUNSEL

Michael A. Lamanna
Gerald I. Arnson
Thomas I. Hausman

RETIRED

Bennet Kleinman

Reference: National City Bank.

For full biographical listings, see the Martindale-Hubbell Law Directory

KAUFMAN & CUMBERLAND CO., L.P.A. (AV)

Third Floor, 1404 East 9th Street, 44114-1779
Telephone: 216-861-0707
Telefax: 216-694-6883
TDD: 216-694-6891
Columbus, Ohio Office: 300 South Second Street, 43215.
Telephone: 614-224-0717.
Telefax: 614-229-4111.

Steven S. Kaufman
Frank J. Cumberland, Jr.
Frank R. DeSantis
Robert A. Blattner
Gail E. Sindell
William W. Jacobs
Mitchell Ehrenberg
Hollis A. Selvaggi

Susan L. Belman
Edda Sara Post
David P. Lodwick
Thomas L. Feher
Laura Hauser Pfahl (Resident, Columbus, Ohio Office)
David B. Webster
Christine Sommer Riley
Holly M. Cook
Mary E. Darcy

OF COUNSEL

Jack G. Day
James A. Scott
Anthony R. Troia

Representative Clients: CertainTeed Corp.; Teledyne Inc.

For full biographical listings, see the Martindale-Hubbell Law Directory

KELLER AND CURTIN CO., L.P.A. (AV)

Suite 330 The Hanna Building, 44115-1901
Telephone: 216-566-7100
Telecopier: 216-566-5430
Akron, Ohio Office: 2304 First National Tower, 44308-1419.
Telephone: 216-376-7245.
Telecopier: 216-376-8128.

Stanley S. Keller
G. Michael Curtin
Walter H. Krohngold
James M. Johnson

Joseph G. Ritzler
Phillip A. Kuri

Reference: Bank One, Cleveland.

For full biographical listings, see the Martindale-Hubbell Law Directory

KELLEY, MCCANN & LIVINGSTONE (AV)

35th Floor, BP America Building, 200 Public Square, 44114-2302
Telephone: 216-241-3141
FAX: 216-241-3707

MEMBERS OF FIRM

Fred J. Livingstone
Stephen M. O'Bryan
John D. Brown
Joel A. Makee
James P. Oliver
Margaret Anne Cannon
Michael D. Schenker
Mark J. Valponi
Thomas J. Lee
M. Patricia Oliver
Bruce L. Waterhouse, Jr.
Carl A. Murway
Steven A. Goldfarb
David H. Wallace

OF COUNSEL

Walter C. Kelley
David E. Burke

ASSOCIATES

Sandra K. Hunter
Joanne Gross
Kurt D. Weaver
Robert A. Brindza, II
Sylvester Summers, Jr.
Peter M. Poulos
Colleen G. Treml
Peter K. Shelton
Halle Fine Terrion
Lisa Marie Ruda

For full biographical listings, see the Martindale-Hubbell Law Directory

MCDONALD, HOPKINS, BURKE & HABER CO., L.P.A. (AV)

2100 Bank One Center, 600 Superior Avenue, E., 44114-2653
Telephone: 216-348-5400
Telecopier: 216-348-5474

Nelson E. Weiss (1927-1991)
W. Dean Hopkins (1909-1993)
H. Guy Hardy (Retired)
Alvin M. Kendis (Retired)
Dwight M. Allgood, Jr.
Jeffrey P. Consolo
Richard S. Cooper
Michelle B. Creger
Ralph J. DiLeone
Anthony J. DiVenere
Steven L. Gardner
Carl J. Grassi
James A. Griffith
Daniel J. Hughes
Jeffrey R. Huntsberger
David G. Johnson
Bernard L. Karr
Thomas W. Keen
Roger L. Kleinman
Joseph J. LoPresti, Jr.
Jules L. Markowitz
George L. McGaughey, Jr.
Thomas P. Meaney, Jr.
John T. Mulligan
Brian M. O'Neill
William J. O'Neill
Stephen T. Parisi
R. Jeffrey Pollock
Albert N. Salvatore
Thomas C. Schrader
Oliver E. Seikel
Roger L. Shumaker
Barbara J. Smith
James M. Stone
Robert S. Stone
Dale R. Vlasek
Kenneth J. Walsh
David E. Weiss

Richard J. Ambrose
Patrick J. Berry
Walter F. Ehrnfelt, III
Theodore J. Esborn
Erica L. Eversman
Patricia L. Fries
David S. Hoffmann
Mark D. Klimek
Pamela S. Landy
Maria T. Lombardi
Dan L. Makee
Joseph E. McGraw
Michael G. Riley
Michael R. Spreng
George Voinovich
Jane Marie Pine Wood
K. Ann Zimmerman

OF COUNSEL

Stanley I. Adelstein
Robert F. Longano
Ralph Vince

General Counsel for: Corrpro Companies, Inc.; The Dickey-Grabler Co.; Drs. Hill and Thomas Co.; U.S.S., Div. of USX Corp.; A. Schulman, Inc.; Summitville Tiles, Inc.; Medic Drug, Inc.; Bearings, Inc.

For full biographical listings, see the Martindale-Hubbell Law Directory

MEYERS, HENTEMANN, SCHNEIDER & REA CO., L.P.A. (AV)

21st Floor, Superior Building, 815 Superior Avenue, N.E., 44114
Telephone: 216-241-3435
Telecopier: 216-241-6568
Elyria, Ohio Office: 301 Fifth Street, 44035.
Telephone: 216-323-6920.

(See Next Column)

MEYERS, HENTEMANN, SCHNEIDER & REA CO. L.P.A.—*Continued*

Kent H. Meyers (1902-1970)
Richard F. Stevens (1915-1981)
David S. Meyers (1928-1983)
Eugene J. Gilroy (1926-1984)
John S. Rea
Joseph G. Schneider
Henry A. Hentemann
Richard C. Talbert
Thomas L. Brunn
Gerald L. Jeppe
Don P. Brown
Lynn A. Lazzaro
Joseph H. Wantz
Kirk E. Roman

James C. Cochran
Kathleen Carrabine Hopkins
J. Michael Creagan
Sean P. Allan
Keith David Thomas
John Peter O'Donnell

Representative Clients: State Farm Mutual Insurance Co.; Travelers Insurance Co.; J.C. Penney Insurance, formerly Educator & Executive Insurance Co.; Lloyds Underwriters, London, England; Preferred Risk Mutual Insurance Co.; American Suzuki Motor Corp.; Detroit Automobile Inter-Insurance Exchange; Electrical Mutual; Automation Plastics, Inc.; Environmental Structures, Inc.

For full biographical listings, see the Martindale-Hubbell Law Directory

NURENBERG, PLEVIN, HELLER & MCCARTHY CO., L.P.A. (AV)

1370 Ontario Street First Floor, 44113-1792
Telephone: 216-621-2300
FAX: 216-771-2242

A. H. Dudnik (1905-1963)
S. F. Komito (1902-1984)
Marshall I. Nurenberg
Leon M. Plevin
Maurice L. Heller
John J. McCarthy
Thomas Mester
Harlan M. Gordon
Andrew P. Krembs
Anne L. Kilbane
David M. Paris
Richard C. Alkire
Richard L. Demsey
Joel Levin
Jamie R. Lebovitz
William S. Jacobson

Dean C. Nieding
Jeffrey A. Leikin
Robin J. Peterson
Robert S. Zeller
James T. Schumacher
Ellen M. McCarthy
J. Charles Ruiz-Bueno
Sandra J. Rosenthal
Kathleen St. John
Jessica F. Kahn

Reference: Society Key Corp.

For full biographical listings, see the Martindale-Hubbell Law Directory

PORTER, WRIGHT, MORRIS & ARTHUR (AV)

925 Euclid Avenue, 44115-1483
Telephone: 216-443-9000; (800-824-1980)
Fax: 216-443-9011
Telex: 6503213584 MCI
Columbus, Ohio Office: 41 South High Street, 43215-6194.
Telephones: 614-227-2000; (800-533-2794).
Telex: 6503213584 MCI.
Fax: 614-227-2100.
Dayton, Ohio Office: One Dayton Centre, One South Main Street, 45402.
Telephones: 513-228-2411. (800-533-4434).
Fax: 513-449-6820.
Cincinnati, Ohio Office: 250 E. Fifth Street, 45202-4166.
Telephones: 513-381-4700; (800-582-5813).
Fax: 513-421-0991.
Washington, D.C. Office: 1233 20th Street, N.W. 20036-2395.
Telephones: 202-778-3000; (800-456-7962).
Fax: 202-778-3063.
Naples, Florida Office: 4501 Tamiami Trail North, 33940-3060.
Telephones: 813-263-8898; (800-876-7962).
Fax: 813-436-2990.

MEMBERS OF FIRM

Jeffrey Baddeley
Herbert L. Braverman
Anthony J. Celebrezze, Jr.
James P. Conroy
Donald J. Fisher
Daniel F. Gourash
Richard M. Markus
Hugh E. McKay
Craig S. Miller
Terrance L. Ryan
Patricia A. Screen
Ralph Streza
Thomas J. Talcott
Sophia Papandreas Tjotjos
Anthony J. Viola
John W. Waldeck, Jr.
William R. Weir
Alan D. Wright

RESIDENT ASSOCIATES

David A. Bell
David Cohen
Robert G. Cohn
Anne T. Corrigan
Sophia M. Deseran
Margaret M. Koesel
Ezio A. Listati
Joyce Metti Papandreas
David C. Tryon
Alan C. Yarcusko

RESIDENT OF COUNSEL

Robert E. Bingham
James J. Schiller
Robert Wavrek

Representative Clients: Allstate Life Insurance Co.; Bonne Belle, Inc.; Centerior Energy Corp.; Chubb Group of Insurance Cos.; City of Cleveland; Consolidated Rail Corp.; Ducks Unlimited, Inc.; Honda North America, Inc.; Pfizer, Inc.

(See Next Column)

For full biographical listings, see the Martindale-Hubbell Law Directory

QUANDT, GIFFELS & BUCK CO., L.P.A. (AV)

800 Leader Building, 526 Superior Avenue, N.E., 44114-1460
Telephone: 216-241-2025
Telecopier: 216-241-2080

Robert G. Quandt
Walter R. Matchinga
Joseph R. Tira
Beth A. Sebaugh
Laurence F. Buzzelli
Larry C. Greathouse

OF COUNSEL

Stephen D. Richman

Hunter S. Havens
Timothy G. Sweeney
Jeffrey A. Schenk
Timothy L. Kerwin
Nita Kay Smith
Edward J. Stoll, Jr.
Ernest C. Pisanelli

Representative Clients: Physicians Insurance Company of Ohio; Royal Insurance Company; Continental Insurance Company; Heritage Insurance Company; Reliance Insurance Co.; Safeco Insurance Co.; Fireman's Fund Insurance Company.

For full biographical listings, see the Martindale-Hubbell Law Directory

RAY, ROBINSON, CARLE, DAVIES & SNYDER (AV)

1650 The East Ohio Building, 1717 East 9th Street, 44114-2898
Telephone: 216-861-4533
Telex: 810-421-8402
Cable Address: Lakelaw-Cleveland
Facsimile: 216-861-4568
Chicago, Illinois Office: 850 West Jackson Blvd, Suite 310.
Telephone: 312-421-3110.
Cable Address: Lakelaw-Chicago.
Facsimile: 312-421-2808.

MEMBERS OF FIRM

William D. Carle, III
David G. Davies
Michael A. Snyder, Ltd. (Resident at Chicago, Illinois Office)
Douglas R. Denny
Gene B. George
Julia R. Brouhard

ASSOCIATES

Robert T. Coniam
Sandra Maurer Kelly
Richard F. Schultz
Richard A. Forster (Resident at Chicago, Illinois Office)
William P. Ryan (Resident at Chicago, Illinois Office)
Charles A. Rozhon (Resident at Chicago, Illinois Office)
Shanshan Zhou (Resident at Chicago, Illinois Office)
Thomas More Wynne

OF COUNSEL

Lucian Y. Ray (1903-1987)
Theodore C. Robinson (Resident at Chicago, Illinois Office)

Representative Clients: The Cleveland-Cliffs Iron Co.; U.S.S., Great Lakes Fleet, Inc.; Bethlehem Steel Corp., Great Lakes Steamship Division; Canada Steamship Lines, Ltd.; The M.A. Hanna Co.; Canadian Shipowners Assn.; Interlake Steamship Co.; Inland Steel Co.; Amoco Oil Co.; Steamship Mutual Underwriting Assn., Ltd.

For full biographical listings, see the Martindale-Hubbell Law Directory

ROSENZWEIG, SCHULZ & GILLOMBARDO CO., L.P.A. (AV)

700 Transohio Tower, 2000 East 9th Street, 44115-1301
Telephone: 216-589-9300
FAX: 216-589-9176

David L. Rosenzweig
Isaac Schulz
Carl F. Gillombardo, Jr.
Bill J. Gagliano
Richard D. Fiktus
Irene M. MacDougall

Dean M. Rooney
Adam L. Gross
Sue A. Urbanowicz

OF COUNSEL

Patricia S. Kleri

For full biographical listings, see the Martindale-Hubbell Law Directory

SEELEY, SAVIDGE AND AUSSEM A LEGAL PROFESSIONAL ASSOCIATION (AV)

800 Bank One Center, 600 Superior Avenue, East, 44114-2655
Telephone: 216-566-8200
Cable Address: "See Sau"
Fax-Telecopier: 216-566-0213
Elyria, Ohio Office: 538 Broad Street.
Telephone: 216-236-8158.

(See Next Column)

SEELEY, SAVIDGE AND AUSSEM A LEGAL PROFESSIONAL ASSOCIATION, *Cleveland—Continued*

Glenn J. Seeley
Gregory D. Seeley
Keith A. Savidge
James S. Aussem
Jane T. Seelie
Gary A. Ebert
Edward J. Flanagan

James M. McClain (Resident, Elyria Office)
Patrick J. McIntyre
Carter R. Dodge
William E. Blackie, III
Thomas E. Giffels
Thomas E. Sharpe
Robert C. White
Caroline K. Weingart

OF COUNSEL

John F. Seelie
William E. Blackie
Edmund W. Rothschild
William M. Fumich, Jr.

References: Society National Bank; AmeriTrust.

For full biographical listings, see the Martindale-Hubbell Law Directory

SPANGENBERG, SHIBLEY, TRACI, LANCIONE & LIBER (AV)

2400 National City Center, 1900 East Ninth Street, 44114-3400
Telephone: 216-696-3232
FAX: 216-696-3924

MEMBERS OF FIRM

Norman W. Shibley (1921-1992)
John G. Lancione
John D. Liber
Robert A. Marcis
Robert V. Traci
Peter H. Weinberger
William Hawal
Peter J. Brodhead
Ellen Simon Sacks
Dennis R. Lansdowne

OF COUNSEL

Donald P. Traci

RETIRED

Craig Spangenberg

ASSOCIATES

James A. Marx
John A. Lancione
John R. Liber, II
Michael T. Pearson
Cathleen M. Bolek
Justin F. Madden

For full biographical listings, see the Martindale-Hubbell Law Directory

SPIETH, BELL, MCCURDY & NEWELL CO., L.P.A. (AV)

2000 Huntington Building, 925 Euclid Avenue, 44115-1496
Telephone: 216-696-4700
Telecopier: 216-696-6569; 216-696-2706; 216-696-1052

Lawrence C. Spieth (1883-1963)
Everett D. McCurdy (1905-1986)
Harold K. Bell (1895-1987)
Clyde E. Williams, Jr.
Glen O. Smith, Jr.
Sterling Newell, Jr.
John J. Whitney
Ron Tonidandel
Lincoln Reavis
Richard T. Watson
Patrick J. Amer
Henry E. Seibert, IV
Lance B. Johnson
Frederick I. Taft
James M. Havach
Stanley Dan Pace
Bruce G. Hearey
Dianne Foley Hearey
James R. Bright
John M. Slivka
Kevin L. Starrett
Kristin L. Ubersax
Wade M. Fricke
Debra L. Kackley

Representative Clients: Cleveland Cavaliers; Nationwide Advertising Services, Inc.; Independent Steel Co.; Baldwin Wallace College; The Tool-Die Engineering Company.
Representative Labor Relations Clients (Management Only): Parker Hannifin Corp.; Reliance Electric Co.; Brush Wellman Co.

For full biographical listings, see the Martindale-Hubbell Law Directory

SQUIRE, SANDERS & DEMPSEY (AV)

4900 Society Center, 127 Public Square, 44114-1304
Telephone: 216-479-8500
Fax's: 216-479-8780, 216-479-8781
216-479-8787, 216-479 -8795
216-479-8793, 216-479-8776, 216-479-8788
Columbus, Ohio Offices: 1300 Huntington Center, 41 South High Street, Columbus, Ohio 43215.
Telephone: 614-365-2700.
Fax: 614-365-2499.
Jacksonville, Florida Office: One Enterprise Center, Suite 2100, 225 Water Street, Jacksonville, Florida 32202.
Telephone: 904-353-1264.
Fax: 904-356-2986.
Miami, Florida Office: 201 South Biscayne Boulevard, Suite 2900 Miami Center, Miami, Florida 33131.
Telephone: 305-577-8700.
Fax: 305-358-1425.
New York, New York Office: 520 Madison Avenue, 32nd Floor, New York, New York 10022.
Telephone: 212-872-9800.
Fax: 212-872-9814.

(See Next Column)

Phoenix, Arizona Office: Two Renaissance Square, 40 North Central Avenue, Suite 2700, Phoenix, Arizona 85004-4441.
Telephone: 602-528-4000.
Fax: 602-253-8129.
Washington, D.C. Office: 1201 Pennsylvania Avenue, N.W., P.O. Box 407, Washington, D.C. 20044.
Telephone: 202-626-6600.
Fax: 202-626-6780.
London, England Office: 1 Gunpowder Square, Printer Street, London EC4A 3DE.
Telephone: 011-44-071-830-0055.
Fax: 011-44-071-830-0056.
Brussels, Belgium Office: Avenue Louise, 165-Box 15, 1050 Brussels, Belgium.
Telephone: 011-322-648-1717.
Fax: 011-322-648-1064.
Prague Office: Adria Palace, Jungmannova 31/36, 11000 Prague 1, Czech Republic.
Telephone: 011-42-2-231-5661.
Fax: 011-42-2-231-5482.
Bratislava Office: Mudronova 37, 811 01 Bratislava, Slovak Republic.
Telephone: 011-42-7-313-362; 011-42-7-315-370.
Fax: 011-42-7-313-918.
Budapest, Hungary Office: Deak Ferenc Ut. 10, Office 304, H-1052 Budapest V., Hungary.
Telephone: 011-361-226-2024; 011-361-226-5038.
Fax: 011-361-226-2025.
Kiev, Ukraine Office: vul. Prorizna 9 KV 20, Kiev, Ukraine 25203.
Telephones: 011-7-044-244-3452, 011-7-044-244-3453, 011-7-044-228-8687.
Fax: 011-7-044-228-4938.

RESIDENT MEMBERS
CLEVELAND OFFICE

Andrew Squire (1850-1934)
William B. Sanders (1854-1929)
James H. Dempsey (1859-1920)
Stephen J. Alfred
Mitchel B. Axler
Mara L. Babin
Stacy D. Ballin
Geoffrey K. Barnes
George R. Barry
Dean L. Berry
Jeffrey A. Bomberger
Alan P. Buchmann
Jonathan F. Buchter
Carolyn J. Buller
J. Donald Cairns
Paul B. Campbell
Van Carson
Terence J. Clark
Charles F. Clarke
William H. Conner
Joseph R. Cortese
Carol F. Dakin
Ernie K. Demanelis
James H. Dempsey, Jr.
Jon E. Denney
Richard K. Desmond
Frank A. Di Piero
John C. Dowd
Carl A. Draucker
Robert J. Eidnier
Irwin M. Feldman
Mark S. Floyd
D. Bruce Gabriel
Frances Floriano Goins
Richard Gurbst
W. Michael Hanna
Pamela Iddings Hanover
Barbara L. Hawley
Thomas G. Hermann
Ronald J. James
Bruce P. Jones
Mary Ann Jorgenson
Gordon S. Kaiser, Jr.
F. Barry Keefe
Thomas S. Kilbane
Arthur E. Korkosz
Helen Kryshtalowych (Resident Member, Kiev, Ukraine Office)
John Sigvard Larson
John F. Lewis
John E. Lynch, Jr.
Damond R. Mace
Jeffrey J. Margulies
Charles R. McElwee, II
George M. von Mehren
Michael G. Meissner
Cecil R. Mellin
John T. Meredith
G. Christopher Meyer
David J. Millstone
Kenneth C. Moore
Frederick R. Nance
Howard J.C. Nicols
Daniel J. O'Loughlin
Ivan L. Otto
Terrence G. Perris
Frank M. Rasmussen
Walter J. Rekstis, III
David W. Rowan
Timothy J. Sheeran
John F. Shelley
R. Thomas Stanton
Dale E. Stephenson
Robin G. Weaver

RESIDENT COUNSEL
CLEVELAND OFFICE

John B. Brueckel
Sidney B. Hopps
William H. Ransom
James A. Smith

RESIDENT OF COUNSEL
CLEVELAND OFFICE

Daniel L. Brockett (Not admitted in OH)
John H. Distin
Bernard J. Jerlstrom (Not admitted in OH)
Henry T. King, Jr. (Not admitted in OH)
Katherine G. Petrey

RESIDENT ASSOCIATES
CLEVELAND OFFICE

Janet Alter
Lisa R. Battaglia
Onee Bergfeld-Lowe
Scott D. Blackhurst
David Anthony Brown
David W. Burchmore
Paula B. Christ
Timothy J. Cosgrove
Virginia Ann Davidson
Christian Droop (Not admitted in OH)
David C. Dysert

(See Next Column)

SQUIRE, SANDERS & DEMPSEY—*Continued*

RESIDENT ASSOCIATES
CLEVELAND OFFICE (Continued)

Bebe A. Fairchild
Harold E. Farling
Dane K. Fernandes
Valerie M. Fladung
Lisa Babish Forbes
Steven A. Friedman
Amy Scott Gilchrist
Roger Michael Gold
James Gray
Micah D. Green
D. Michael Grodhaus
Mark P. Gustaferro
Amanda E. Haiduc
Susan C. Hastings
Lawrence H. Hatch
Thomas G. Havener
Leslye A. Herrmann
(Not admitted in OH)
Lisa E. Hollander
Laura Kingsley Hong
Brenda M. Johnson
Joseph Kamer
Michael W. Kelly
J. Joseph Korpics
Thomas G. Kovach
Robert D. Labes
Hans L. Larsen
David Lavey
Wendlene M. Lavey
Richard D. Manoloff
Amanda Martinsek
Margaret H. Mazanec
Antoinette G. McDermott
M. Elizabeth Monihan
Timothy C. Nash
Michael F. O'Brien
Jill G. Okun
(Not admitted in OH)
James S. Oliphant
Brian A. Paton
Michael R. Peterson
Henry B. Pickens
John A. Rego
Michael J. Reidy
Brian T. Robinson
Daniel F. Roules
Lynn M. Rowe
John M. Rumpf
Elizabeth Sanborn
James W. Satola
Philip C. Schillawski
Sanford Schwimmer
John K. Stipancich
Timothy F. Sweeney
Taras G. Szmagala, Jr.
Dennis G. Terez
Dynda L. Thomas
Gregory J. Viviani
Kristopher Wahlers
Jeffrey J. Wedel
Louis Weinstein
Emily L. Won
(Not admitted in OH)
Daniel T. Young
Mary Yuen-Ng
David A. Zagore

For full biographical listings, see the Martindale-Hubbell Law Directory

THOMPSON, HINE AND FLORY (AV)

1100 National City Bank Building, 629 Euclid Avenue, 44114-3070
Telephone: 216-566-5500
Fax: 216-566-5583
Telex: 980217
Cable Address: "Thomflor"
Akron, Ohio Office: 50 S. Main Street, Suite 502, 44308-1828.
Telephone: 216-376-8090.
Fax: 216-376-8386.
Cincinnati, Ohio Office: 312 Walnut Street, 14th Floor, 45202-4029.
Telephone: 513-352-6700.
Fax: 513-241-4771.
Telex: 938003.
Columbus, Ohio Office: One Columbus, 10 West Broad Street, 43215-3435.
Telephone: 614-469-3200.
Fax: 614-469-3361.
Dayton, Ohio Office: 2000 Courthouse Plaza, N.E., 45402-1706.
Telephone: 513-443-6600.
Fax: 513-443-6637; 443-6635.
Palm Beach, Florida Office: 125 Worth Avenue, Suite 117, 33480-4466.
Telephone: 407-833-5900.
Fax: 407-833-5951.
Washington, D.C. Office: 1920 N Street, N.W., 20036-1601.
Telephone: 202-331-8800.
Fax: 202-331-8330.
Telex: 904173.
Cable Address: "Caglaw".
Brussels, Belgium Office: Rue des Chevaliers, Ridderstraat 14 - B.10, B - 1050.
Telephone: 011(32-2) 511-9326.
Fax: 011(32-2) 513-9206.

Amos Burt Thompson
(1871-1965)
Charles P. Hine (1877-1942)
Walter L. Flory (1880-1951)

MEMBERS OF FIRM

Thomas A. Aldrich
Thomas R. Allen
(In Columbus, Ohio)
Bruce M. Allman
(In Dayton, Ohio)
Charles Wm. Anness
(In Cincinnati, Ohio)
Jeffrey R. Appelbaum
Barbara J. Arison
James B. Aronoff
Roberta B. Aronson
(In Washington, D.C.)
Keith A. Ashmus
Brett K. Bacon
William T. Bahlman, Jr.
(In Cincinnati, Ohio)
Malvin E. Bank
Douglas N. Barr
Christopher M. Bechhold
(In Cincinnati, Ohio)
Daniel O. Berger
(In Cincinnati, Ohio)
Richard C. Binzley
J. Wray Blattner
(In Dayton, Ohio)
Barry M. Block
(In Dayton, Ohio)
Thomas J. Bonasera
(In Columbus, Ohio)
Barbara Schwartz Bromberg
(In Cincinnati, Ohio)
Hugh D. Brown
Robert J. Brown
(In Dayton, Ohio)
Troy R. Brown
Virginia S. Brown

(See Next Column)

MEMBERS OF FIRM (Continued)

Stephen L. Buescher
T. Merritt Bumpass, Jr.
Lawrence T. Burick
(In Dayton, Ohio)
Stephen J. Butler
(In Cincinnati, Ohio)
Nancy H. Canary (In Palm Beach, Florida and Cleveland, Ohio) (Partner-in-Charge in Palm Beach, Florida)
Richard F. Carlile
(In Dayton, Ohio)
James R. Carlson
Keith L. Carson
Betsey Brewster Case
William R. Case
(In Columbus, Ohio)
Thomas J. Collin
Douglas O. Cooper
Ethna Bennert Cooper
(In Cincinnati, Ohio)
William H. Cordes
(In Cincinnati, Ohio)
Dianne Smith Coscarelli
Timothy J. Coughlin
Robert W. Crawford
(In Cincinnati, Ohio)
C. Jackson Cromer
(In Cincinnati, Ohio)
Scott B. Crooks
(In Cincinnati, Ohio)
Steven D. Cundra
(In Washington, D.C.)
Robert M. Curry
(In Dayton, Ohio)
Michael A. Cyphert
John L. Dampeer
Stephen H. Daniels
Thomas E. DeBrosse
(In Dayton, Ohio)
Deborah DeLong
(In Cincinnati, Ohio)
Peter J. Donahue
(In Dayton, Ohio)
Gerald L. Draper
(In Columbus, Ohio)
S. Stuart Eilers
Andrew L. Fabens
William S. Fein
(In Columbus, Ohio)
Francesco A. Ferrante
(In Dayton, Ohio)
Robert B. Ford
Michael J. Frantz
Charles L. Freed
(In Washington, D.C.)
Stanley A. Freedman
(In Dayton, Ohio)
Jack F. Fuchs
(In Cincinnati, Ohio)
Sharen Swartz Gage
(In Dayton, Ohio)
Jane E. Garfinkel
(In Cincinnati, Ohio)
John H. Gherlein (Retired)
Frederick B. Gibbon
(In Washington, D.C.)
Stephen F. Gladstone
Alfred M. Goldberg
(In Washington, D.C.)
R. Benton Gray
Peter A. Greene
(Partner-in-Charge in Washington, D.C.)
Jon M. Grogan
(In Dayton, Ohio)
Richard E. Guster
(Partner-in-Charge in Akron, Ohio)
Timothy J. Hackert
(In Dayton, Ohio)
Robert J. Hadley
(In Dayton, Ohio)
Daniel W. Hammer
Harry A. Hanna
Michael L. Hardy
Mary J. Healy
(In Cincinnati, Ohio)
Thomas A. Heffernan
Harold W. Henderson
Oliver C. Henkel, Jr.
J. Michael Herr
(In Dayton, Ohio)
Ralph P. Higgins, Jr.
Joel R. Hlavaty
David J. Hooker
Daniel J. Hunter
(In Columbus, Ohio)
Alan L. Hyde
Leslie W. Jacobs
George F. Karch, Jr.
Stephen M. King
(In Cincinnati, Ohio)
Donald J. Kinlin
(In Dayton, Ohio)
Thomas J. Kirkwood
(In Dayton, Ohio)
Samuel R. Knezevic
Thomas A. Knoth
(In Dayton, Ohio)
Donald L. Korb (In Washington, D.C. and Cleveland, Ohio)
John F. Kostelnik, III
Kenton L. Kuehnle
(In Columbus, Ohio)
Robert L. Larson
William B. Leahy
Alan R. Lepene
Mark P. Levy (In Dayton, Ohio)
Theodore D. Lienesch
(In Dayton, Ohio)
Thomas E. Lodge
(In Columbus, Ohio)
Bruce R. Lowry
(In Dayton, Ohio)
Barry L. Lubow
(In Columbus, Ohio)
Crofford J. Macklin, Jr.
(In Dayton, Ohio)
Earle Jay Maiman
(In Cincinnati, Ohio)
Kent L. Mann
Melvin E. Marmer
(In Cincinnati, Ohio)
Craig R. Martahus
Ted T. Martin
(In Cincinnati, Ohio)
William L. Martin, Jr.
(In Cincinnati, Ohio)
Thomas A. Mason
John F. McClatchey (Retired)
George C. McConnaughey
(Retired) (In Columbus, Ohio)
Sue K. McDonnell
(In Dayton, Ohio)
Jacqueline K. McManus
(In Cincinnati, Ohio)
James A. Meaney
(In Columbus, Ohio)
Leonard S. Meranus
(In Cincinnati, Ohio)
Donald H. Messinger
(Partner-in-Charge)
Edward B. Mitchell
(In Cincinnati, Ohio)
Robert P. Mone
(In Columbus, Ohio)
Robert D. Monnin
William C. Moul
(In Columbus, Ohio)
William R. Naeher
(In Washington, D.C.)
David J. Naftzinger
David E. Nash
David A. Neuhardt
(In Dayton, Ohio)
Michael H. Neumark
(In Cincinnati, Ohio)
Peter K. Newman
(In Cincinnati, Ohio)
James B. Niehaus
Allen R. Norris
(In Dayton, Ohio)
Michael R. Oestreicher
(Partner-in-Charge in Cincinnati, Ohio)
David L. Parham
Jeffrey F. Peck
(In Cincinnati, Ohio)
Susan A. Petersen
(In Columbus, Ohio)
Ben L. Pfefferle, III
(In Columbus, Ohio)
Norman J. Philion, III
(In Washington, D.C.)

(See Next Column)

THOMPSON, HINE AND FLORY, *Cleveland—Continued*

MEMBERS OF FIRM (Continued)

Michael A. Poe (In Columbus, Ohio)
Louis Pohoryles (In Washington, D.C.)
Deborah Zider Read
David M. Rickert (In Dayton, Ohio)
Joseph M. Rigot (Partner-in-Charge in Dayton, Ohio)
James D. Robenalt
Janis B. Rosenthal (In Columbus, Ohio)
Richard J. Ruebel (In Cincinnati, Ohio)
Joseph S. Ruggie, Jr.
Michael Wm. Sacks (In Washington, D.C.)
David W. Salisbury
Mark Roy Sandstrom (In Washington, D.C.)
Raymond T. Sawyer
Edna V. Scheuer (In Cincinnati, Ohio)
Thomas C. Scott (Partner-in-Charge in Columbus, Ohio)
Robert A. Selak (In Cincinnati, Ohio)
Michael T. Shannon (In Columbus, Ohio)
William A. Shenk (In Columbus, Ohio)
Arik A. Sherk (In Dayton, Ohio)
Julie Cohen Shifman (In Cincinnati, Ohio)
Gerald W. Simmons (In Cincinnati, Ohio)
Patricia Mann Smitson (In Cincinnati, Ohio)
Louis F. Solimine (In Cincinnati, Ohio)
Robert V. Staton (In Washington, D.C.)
Jacob K. Stein (In Cincinnati, Ohio)
Thomas C. Stevens
William R. Stewart
Robert D. Storey
Richard E. Streeter
Linda A. Striefsky
John T. Sunderland (In Columbus, Ohio)
Peter E. Tamborski (In Cincinnati, Ohio)
Howard N. Thiele, Jr. (In Dayton, Ohio)
Richard B. Tranter (In Cincinnati, Ohio)
William C. Trier, Jr.
Roy L. Turnell
Thomas M. Turner
Jerry Vande Werken (In Columbus, Ohio)
Daniel A. Ward
Daniel R. Warren
Paul R. Webber, IV (In Washington, D.C.)
Jill A. Weller (In Cincinnati, Ohio)
Richard V. Whelan, Jr.
William C. Wilkinson (In Columbus, Ohio)
Elizabeth B. Wright
Karen Daykin Youngstrom
Thomas F. Zych

ASSOCIATES

Paul Allaer (In Cincinnati, Ohio)
Joyce Z. Anderson (In Dayton, Ohio)
Philomena Saldanha Ashdown (In Cincinnati, Ohio)
Sarah A. Barlage (In Cincinnati, Ohio)
Timothy A. Barry
Colleen P. Battle
John H. Beasley (In Cincinnati, Ohio)
Petra J. Bradbury
Katherine D. Brandt
Suzanne E. Bretz
Daniel A. Brown (In Dayton, Ohio)
Timothy R. Brown (In Cincinnati, Ohio)
Thomas J. Callahan
Margaret R. Carmany (In Columbus, Ohio)
Patricia C. Cecil (In Dayton, Ohio)
Frank D. Chaiken (In Cincinnati, Ohio Office)
Michael N. Chesney
Vicki Christian (In Cincinnati, Ohio)
R. Michael Clark (In Columbus, Ohio)
Nicolle M. Clessuras
Kenneth G. Cole
Mark A. Conway (In Dayton, Ohio)
Elizabeth Costigan
Timothy E. Cowans (In Columbus, Ohio)
Thomas J. Coyne
Luke L. Dauchot
Steven J. Davis (In Dayton, Ohio)
Deepak K. Desai (In Cincinnati, Ohio)
Richard A. DiLisi
Robert S. Dizenhuz (In Cincinnati, Ohio)
David M. Dumas
Anne E. Eckhart (In Columbus, Ohio)
Stephen M. Edwards
Renee S. Filiatraut (In Cincinnati, Ohio)
Patrick J. Flynn
Lisa Sullivan Franzen (In Washington, D.C.)
Dean D. Gamin
Mark A. Gamin
Howard B. Gee (In Cincinnati, Ohio)
Gary M. Glass (In Cincinnati, Ohio)
Carl H. Gluek
Adam H. Gordon (In Washington, D.C. Office)
Patrick F. Haggerty
Daniel M. Haymond
Robert M. Henry (In Dayton, Ohio)
Douglas L. Hertlein (In Columbus, Ohio)
Jennifer Rose Hilkert
Michael J. Holleran
Deborah D. Hunt (In Dayton, Ohio)
Molly M. Israel
Robert P. Johnson (In Cincinnati, Ohio)
Christopher Jones (In Columbus, Ohio)
Teresa D. Jones (In Dayton, Ohio)
Sandra P. Kaltman (In Cincinnati, Ohio)
Mauritia G. Kamer
Grace Park Kelly (Not admitted in OH)
Scott A. King (In Dayton, Ohio)
Dena M. Kobasic
Christopher C. Koehler
Ellen B. Krist
Brian J. Lamb
Diane S. Leung
Walt A. Linscott
Lisa A. Lomax (In Columbus, Ohio)
Jeffrey A. Lydenberg (In Cincinnati, Ohio)
Michele D. Lynch (In Washington, D.C.)

(See Next Column)

ASSOCIATES (Continued)

Helen Mac Murray (In Columbus, Ohio)
F. Howard Mandel
Ronda R. Mascaro
Michael W. McArdle (In Dayton, Ohio)
Elizabeth D. Mclean
H. Kevin McNeelege
Ellen K. Meehan
Peter J. Muñiz
Andrew J. Natale
Todd H. Neuman (In Columbus, Ohio)
Laurie Nicholson (In Dayton, Ohio)
Brian J. O'Connell (In Dayton, Ohio)
Bonnie Irvin O'Neil (In Columbus, Ohio)
José Oxholm-Uribe
Stephen Pampush
Richard A. Paolo (In Cincinnati, Ohio)
Shawn R. Pearson
Anne B. Pellot (In Dayton, Ohio)
Michelle L. Pensyl (In Cincinnati, Ohio)
Thomas M. Phillips (In Dayton, Ohio)
Thomas J. Piatak
Donald S. Plum
Michelle Lafond Potter
Philip A. Reid (In Dayton, Ohio)
Michael A. Renne (In Columbus, Ohio)
Susan L. Rhiel (In Columbus, Ohio)
Patrick M. Richart (In Dayton, Ohio)
Mark N. Rose
Karen E. Rubin
Alexander M. Sanchez
Kathleen A. Scibetta
Donald P. Screen
Stacie A. Seiler (In Cincinnati, Ohio)
Andrew J. Sloniewsky (In Washington, D.C. Office)
Gregory A. Smith
Michael E. Smith
Marilyn W. Sonnie
Michael Soto (In Cincinnati, Ohio)
Keith P. Spiller (In Cincinnati, Ohio)
Melisa D. Stone (In Columbus, Ohio)
Richard K. Stovall (In Columbus, Ohio)
Patrick J. Sweeney
Kristine C. Syrvalin
Patricia L. Taylor (In Washington, D.C.)
Charles E. Ticknor, III (In Columbus, Ohio)
Margaret P. VanBuskirk
Robert F. Ware Jr.
James W. Wiggin, III (In Columbus, Ohio)

OF COUNSEL

William E. Constable (In Washington, D.C.)
John J. Conway
William D. Ginn
Robert E. Hickey, Jr. (In Columbus and Dayton, Ohio)
Gregory A. Jacobs
Charles B. Mills, Jr. (In Columbus, Ohio)
Glenn D. Simpson (In Washington, D.C.)

EUROPEAN COUNSEL

Ludo Deklerck (In Brussels, Belgium)

SENIOR ATTORNEYS

Richard A. Ciambrone (In Dayton, Ohio)
Philip B. Cochran (In Columbus, Ohio)
Amy G. Davies (In Washington, D.C.)
Annette Tucker Sutherland
Judith M. Woo

STAFF ATTORNEYS

Laura C. Gockel
Byron J. Horn
Pamela Zarlingo

For full biographical listings, see the Martindale-Hubbell Law Directory

ULMER & BERNE (AV)

Ninth Floor, Bond Court Building, 1300 East Ninth Street, 44114-1583
Telephone: 216-621-8400
Telex: 201999 UBLAW
Telecopier: 216-621-7488
Columbus, Ohio Office: 88 East Broad Street, Suite 1980.
Telephone: 614-228-8400.
Telecopier: 614-228-8561.

MEMBERS OF FIRM

Robert L. Lewis (Retired)
Jordan C. Band (Retired)
Herbert B. Levine
Morton L. Stone
William A. Edwards
Marvin L. Karp
Alan S. Sims
Harold E. Friedman
Albert B. Glickman
Donald E. Heiser
Richard E. Rubinstein
Ronald H. Isroff (Chairman, Commercial Litigation Group)
Murray K. Lenson
Stuart A. Laven
Robert A. Fein
Ronald L. Kahn (Chairman, Employee Benefits Group)
Harold H. Reader, III
Bruce P. Mandel
Christopher C. McCracken
Richard G. Hardy
Stephen A. Markus
Richard D. Sweebe
Jeffrey W. Van Wagner
John C. Goheen
Steven D. Bell
James A. Goldsmith
Ruth Anna Carlson
Stephanie E. Trudeau
F. Thomas Vickers
Stephen Rowan
Peter A. Rome
Patricia A. Shlonsky
Michael N. Ungar
Roberto H. Rodriguez
Martin W. Elson
Dale A. Bernard
Ruth E. Martin
Jay W. Pearlman
Stanley T. Koenig
James S. Wertheim
Jeffrey S. Gray
Michael J. Russo
Richard G. Witkowski
Robert E. Chudakoff
Charles R. Olsavsky, Jr.
Deborah J. Michelson
Brian N. Ramm
Marsha I. Paley

(See Next Column)

ULMER & BERNE—*Continued*

MEMBERS OF FIRM (Continued)

Timothy J. Downing
Thomas R. Kelly
Jennifer Hays Gorman
James A. DeRoche
Lawrence F. Peskin
Eric E. Bell
Kimberly B. Schroeder
Michael B. Gardner
Richard M. Gibson
James A. Vollins
Michael J. Shapiro

OF COUNSEL

Elliot M. Kaufman
Kenneth A. Bravo
James S. Hogg

ATTORNEYS IN COLUMBUS, OHIO OFFICE (SEE LISTING)

H. Tim Merkle
Alexander M. Andrews
Thomas L. Rosenberg
Edwin J. Hollern
Timothy M. Fox
Benjamin S. Zacks

For full biographical listings, see the Martindale-Hubbell Law Directory

VORYS, SATER, SEYMOUR AND PEASE (AV)

2100 One Cleveland Center, 1375 East Ninth Street, 44114
Telephone: 216-479-6100
Telecopier: 216-479-6060
Columbus, Ohio Office: 52 East Gay Street, P.O. Box 1008, 43216-1008.
Telephone: 614-464-6400.
Telex: 241348.
Telecopier: 614-464-6350.
Cable Address: "Vorysater".
Cincinnati, Ohio Office: Suite 2100, 221 East Fourth Street, P.O. Box 0236, 45201-0236.
Telephone: 513-723-4000.
Telecopier: 513-723-4056.
Washington, D.C. Office: Suite 1111, 1828 L Street, N.W., 20036-5104.
Telephone: 202-467-8800.
Telex: 440693.
Telecopier: 202-467-8900.

MEMBERS OF FIRM

F. Daniel Balmert (Resident)
Matthew J. Hatchadorian
Stephen J. Petras, Jr.
John W. Read
Charles J. French, III
Drew T. Parobek

RESIDENT ASSOCIATES

Chris Bator
Sarah J. Cruise
Timothy G. Clancy
Julie M. Larson
Jerome C. Webbs
K. Ellen Toth
Richard L. Lewis
Wendy Asma Ling (Not admitted in OH)
Margaret D. Everett
Bruce P. Batista

For full biographical listings, see the Martindale-Hubbell Law Directory

WALTER & HAVERFIELD (AV)

1300 Terminal Tower, 44113-2253
Telephone: 216-781-1212
Telecopier: 216-575-0911
Columbus, Ohio Office: 88 East Broad Street.
Telephone: 614-221-7371.

MEMBERS OF FIRM

Paul W. Walter (1907-1992)
D. Rusk Haverfield (1907-1993)
Arthur P. Steinmetz
Robert T. Rosenfeld
Russell C. Shaw
Michael T. McMenamin
W. Mowry Connelly
Robert J. Crump
Charles R. Schaefer
Robert S. Horbaly
Charles T. Riehl, III
John H. Gibbon
David W. Welty
James E. Betts
Ralph E. Cascarilla
Christopher L. Gibbon
Marcia E. Hurt
Nancy A. Noall
Frederick W. Whatley
Carl E. Anderson
Ricky Lee Bertram
Kenneth A. Zirm

ASSOCIATES

Peter D. Brosse
Patricia F. Weisberg
Jonathan D. Greenberg
Michael P. Harvey
James D. Wilson
R. Todd Hunt
Debora S. Lasch
David B. Waxman
Daniel N. Steiger
Katherine A. Friedell

OF COUNSEL

William A. Welty
D. Michael Betts
F. Wilson Chockley, Jr.
John P. Rice, Jr.
Timothy C. Jochim
Henry B. Fischer
Craig A. Adams
Sheldon M. Young
Robert L. Musser
J. Robert Malloy
Mark D. Weller

LEGAL SUPPORT PERSONNEL

John B. Eldred

Representative Clients: AGA Gas Inc.; City of Cleveland Heights; Cooper Tire & Rubber Co.; Meridia Health System; Oberlin Farms Dairy, Inc.; TRW, Inc.; WJW-TV (Cleveland).

For full biographical listings, see the Martindale-Hubbell Law Directory

WESTON HURD FALLON PAISLEY & HOWLEY (AV)

2500 Terminal Tower, 50 Public Square, 44113-2241
Telephone: 216-241-6602;
Ohio Toll Free: 800-336-4952
FAX: 216-621-8369

Joseph Philip Sullivan (1916-1974)
Lee C. Howley (1910-1983)
Harold Fallon (1910-1989)
Frank Seth Hurd (1913-1990)
Lloyd O. Brown (1928-1993)

MEMBERS OF FIRM

S. Burns Weston (Retired)
Herbert Buckman
Louis Paisley
Mark O'Neill
Jason C. Blackford
John W. Jeffers
Robert D. Rosewater
John M. Baker
Lewis T. Barr
Ronald A. Rispo
Joseph B. Swartz
James Lincoln McCrystal, Jr.
David Arnold
Carolyn M. Cappel
Donald H. Switzer
Hilary Sheldon Taylor
Kenneth A. Torgerson
John S. Kluznik
Jeffrey D. Fincun
William H. Baughman, Jr.
Robert P. McManus
John Winthrop Ours
Stephen D. Walters
William R. Joseph
Gary W. Johnson
Deirdre G. Henry
Harry Sigmier
Warren Rosman
Connie M. Horrigan
David R. Posteraro
Timothy D. Johnson
William R. Fanos
Jerome W. Cook
Kathryn M. Murray
Dana A. Rose
Hernan N. Visani

OF COUNSEL

Norbert F. Werner
Andrew J. McLandrich
John K. Sullivan

ASSOCIATES

John G. Farnan
Cecil Marlowe
Scott C. Smith
Raymond S. Ling
David C. Lamb
Patrick M. Dukes
Lisa G. McComas
Katherine Vierkorn
Gregory E. O'Brien
Todd G. Jackson
Ronald K. Lembright
Glenn D. Southworth
Maria A. Kortau
Daniel A. Richards

For full biographical listings, see the Martindale-Hubbell Law Directory

ZIEGLER, METZGER & MILLER (AV)

2020 Huntington Building, 44115-1407
Telephone: 216-781-5470
FAX: 216-781-0714

MEMBERS OF FIRM

William L. Ziegler
Robert L. Metzger
William L. Spring
Stephen M. Darlington
Timothy M. Bittel
Mary Beth Ballard
Richard T. Spotz, Jr.

ASSOCIATES

Stephen M. Bales
John E. Redeker
Christopher W. Siemen
Jeffrey L. Koberg
Joseph W. Kampman
William E. Karnatz, Jr

OF COUNSEL

Ivan L. Miller

LEGAL SUPPORT PERSONNEL

P. Thomas Austin (Consultant)
Cynthia Moore (Tax Accountant)

For full biographical listings, see the Martindale-Hubbell Law Directory

CLINTON, Summit Co. — (Refer to Sandusky)

*COLUMBUS,** Franklin Co.

* indicates certain Bar Register subscribers whose principal office is located elsewhere in the state and who have arranged for representation as a part of the state capital listings that follow

*** ARTER & HADDEN (AV)**

21st Floor, One Columbus, 10 West Broad Street, 43215-3422
Telephone: 614-221-3155
In Cleveland, Ohio: 1100 Huntington Building, 925 Euclid Avenue. 44115-1475.
Telephone: 216-696-1100.
In Washington, D.C.: 1801 K Street, N.W., Suite 400K. 20006-3480.
Telephone: 202-775-7100.
In Dallas, Texas: 1717 Main Street, Suite 4100. 75201-4605.
Telephone: 214-761-2100.
In Los Angeles, California: 700 South Flower Street. 90017-4101.
Telephone: 213:629-9300.
In Irvine, California: Two Park Plaza, Suite 700, Jamboree Center.
Telephone: 714-252-7500.
In Austin, Texas: 100 Congress Avenue, Suite 1800.
Telephone: 512-479-6403.
In San Antonio, Texas: Suite 540, Harte-Hanks Tower, 7710 Jones Malstberger Road.
Telephone: 210-805-8497.

(See Next Column)

ARTER & HADDEN, *Columbus—Continued*

MEMBERS OF FIRM

Charles K. Arter (1875-1957)
John A. Hadden (1886-1979)
Andrew J. White, Jr. (1901-1970)
Stephen E. Auch
John A. Carnahan
R. Cliffton Gibbs
Donald A. Davies
Dennis D. Grant
Thomas E. O'Connor, Jr.
Douglas M. Bricker
Richard P. Fahey
Donald G. Paynter
Grady L. Pettigrew, Jr.
Richard D. Brooks, Jr.
Michael P. Mahoney
Nick V. Cavalieri
David C. Patterson
Geoffrey D. Fallon (Not admitted in OH)
Danny L. Cvetanovich
Dan A. Bailey
John P. Gartland
Martin H. Lewis
Yvette A. Cox
Michael W. Currie
John E. Hoffman, Jr.
Gary S. Batke
William A. Adams
A. Brian Dengler
Nancy Manougian

RETIRED PARTNER

William E. Knepper
Louis E. Gerber

OF COUNSEL

R. P. Cunningham
John A. Jenkins
Timothy J. Doney
Harley E. Rouda Jr.

ASSOCIATES

Dane Stinson
Michael L. Maxfield
Carla I. Struble
Timothy A. Riedel
Daniel R. Hackett
Peter D. Welin
R. Stacy Lane
Robert R. Dunn
J. Kenneth Russell

Representative Clients: American Municipal Power-Ohio, Inc.; Bank One, Columbus, N.A.; Basic Inc.; Combustion Engineering; The Federal Home Loan Bank; Health Care & Retirement Corporation of America; Huntington National Bank; Muskingum College; Rockwell International; The W.W. Williams Co.

For full biographical listings, see the Martindale-Hubbell Law Directory

* BAKER & HOSTETLER (AV)

Capitol Square, Suite 2100, 65 East State Street, 43215-4260
Telephone: 614-228-1541
Telecopier: 614-462-2616
In Cleveland, Ohio: 3200 National City Center, 1900 East Ninth Street.
Telephone: 216-621-0200.
In Denver, Colorado: 303 East 17th Avenue, Suite 1100.
Telephone: 202-861-1500.
In Houston, Texas: 1000 Louisiana, Suite 2000.
Telephone: 713-751-1600.
In Long Beach, California: 300 Oceangate, Suite 620.
Telephone: 310-432-2827.
In Los Angeles, California: 600 Wilshire.
Telephone: 213-624-2400.
In Orlando, Florida: SunBank Center, Suite 2300, 200 South Orange Avenue.
Telephone: 407-649-4000.
In Washington, D. C.: Washington Square, Suite 1100, 1050 Connecticut Avenue, N.W.
Telephone: 202-861-1500.
In College Park, Maryland: 9658 Baltimore Boulevard, Suite 301.
Telephone: 301-441-2781.
In Alexandria, Virginia: 437 North Lee Street.
Telephone: 703-549-1294.
In San Francisco, California: One Sansome Street, Suite 2000.
Telephone: 415-951-4705.

MEMBERS OF FIRM IN COLUMBUS, OHIO

George W. Hairston (Managing Partner-Columbus Office)

PARTNERS

M.J. Asensio, III
Edward J. Bernert
Richard L. Bibart
John H. Burtch
Steven P. Elliott
Daniel J. Gunsett
Stephen J. Habash
Charles H. Hire
Bradley Hummel
Kristin Hay Ives
Mark A. Johnson
Robert M. Kincaid, Jr.
Sherri Blank Lazear
Ronald G. Linville
Thomas L. Long
Robert B. McAlister
Michael E. Minister
Thomas E. Moloney
Henry P. Montgomery, IV
Michael E. Moritz
Georgeann G. Peters
Randall S. Rabe
W. Irl Reasoner, III
Barry R. Robinson
Robert K. Rupp
David M. Selcer
Mark D. Senff
Richard W. Siehl
Robert H. Taylor
A. Charles Tell
David A. Turano
J. Stephen Van Heyde
Gary A. Wadman
Alec Wightman
John F. Winkler

ASSOCIATES

Joseph P. Boeckman
George H. Boerger
Bruce R. Bullock
Kevin H. Connor
Russell N. Cunningham
Pamela A. DeDent
Michael D. Dortch
R. Christopher Doyle

(See Next Column)

ASSOCIATES (Continued)

Stephen T. Falk
Christopher D. Fidler
Winston M. Ford
Mary L. Gallagher
Ellen J. Garling
Paul G. Ghidotti
Lorri A. Gorno
Richard J. Helmreich
Sharon A. Jennings
David C. Levine
Janine M. Marks
Robert W. McAdams, Jr.
Carot Terpstra McClarnon
Boyd Moehring
Nicole Fares Norman
Michelle Pepin
Karen E. Sheffer
E. Spencer Stewart, Jr.
Jerri H. Stewart
Jeffrey T. Williams

RETIRED PARTNERS

Charles J. Chastang
John W. Christensen
Kiehner Johnson
John P. McMahon

For full biographical listings, see the Martindale-Hubbell Law Directory

* BENESCH, FRIEDLANDER, COPLAN & ARONOFF (AV)

88 East Broad Street, 43215-3506
Telephone: 614-223-9300
Telecopier: 614-223-9330
Cleveland, Ohio Office: 2300 BP American Building, 200 Public Square, 44114-2378.
Telephone: 216-363-4500.
Telecopier: 216-363-4588.
Cincinnati, Ohio Office: 2800 Cincinnati Commerce Center, 600 Vine Street, 45202-2409.
Telephone: 513-762-6200.
Telecopier: 513-762-6245.

MEMBERS OF FIRM

Orla Ellis Collier, III
James F. DeLeone
Terrence M. Fay
James B. Feibel
Leon Friedberg
N. Victor Goodman
Mark D. Thompson
Sara L. Todd
Michael K. L. Wager

ASSOCIATES

Thomas S. Counts
Janet K. Feldkamp
Heather E. Goodman
Jack Gregg Haught
Ronald L. House
Michael Kranitz
Rex A. Littrell
Jeffrey D. Meyer
Roger L. Schantz
John F. Stock
Mark D. Tucker

OF COUNSEL

Robert N. Shamansky

For full biographical listings, see the Martindale-Hubbell Law Directory

BRICKER & ECKLER (AV)

100 South Third Street, 43215-4291
Telephone: 614-227-2300
Telecopy: 614-227-2390
Cleveland, Ohio Office: 600 Superior Avenue East, Suite 800.
Telephone: 216-771-0720. Fax 216-771-7702.

John W. Bricker (1893-1986)
John Eckler (1913-1994)
Charles F. Glander
James J. Hughes
James S. Monahan
Elbert J. Kram
Richard D. Rogovin
Edward A. Matto
Michael F. Sullivan
Thomas E. Workman
Sally W. Bloomfield
Stephen K. Yoder
Nicholas A. Pittner
Richard F. Kane
John F. Birath, Jr.
Michael S. Holman
Richard C. Simpson
John P. Beavers (Managing Partner)
David G. Baker
Michael J. Renner
John C. Rosenberger
Jerry E. Nathan
Marshall L. Lerner
Randolph C. Wiseman
Donald R. Keller
Karen Mueller Moore
Steven R. Kerber
Charles H. Walker
Michael A. Mess
Gordon W. Johnston
David A. Rogers
Charles H. Waterman III
Michael K. Gire
James A. Rutledge
Randall Edwin Moore
John W. Cook, III
Charles H. McCreary, III
James P. Burnes
Elisabeth A. Squeglia
Kenneth C. Johnson
David K. Conrad
Richard S. Lovering, III
Diane M. Signoracci
Rebecca Coleman Princehorn
Percy Squire
Martha Post Baxter
Gretchen A. McBeath
Craig A. Haddox
Susan O. Scheutzow (Resident Partner, Cleveland Office)
Charles D. Smith
Mary W. Christensen
William T. Conard, II
Robert C. Rafferty
Timothy J. Owens
Anne Marie Sferra
L. Brent Miller
Scott W. Taebel
Sue Wyskiver Yount
Catherine M. Ballard
Gordon F. Litt
Cary W. Purcell
Mark A. Engel

Mark J. Palmer
Jerry O. Allen
Andrew A. Folkerth
Frank L. Merrill
Quintin F. Lindsmith
James J. Hughes, III
Betsy A. Swift
Joyce B. Link

(See Next Column)

BRICKER & ECKLER—*Continued*

Jack R. Rosati
Susan E. Geary
Sylvia L. Gillis
Diane R. Richards
Harry Wright, IV
James F. Flynn
Price D. Finley
Kara J. Trott
Peggy A. Scott
H. Randy Bank
Luther L. Liggett, Jr.
Wendi R. Huntley
Drew H. Campbell
Michael D. Smith
Sarah J. DeBruin
Martha E. Horvitz
Julie A. Glover
Robert S. Melson
Laralyn M. Sasaki
Shawn A. Trell
Stephen P. Hardwick
Cynthia Rayak (Resident, Cleveland Office)
Elizabeth A. Preston
Marianne K. Mitchell
David A. Martin

OF COUNSEL

Joseph S. Gill
Edgar L. Lindley
Christine T. Mesirow
Kurtis A. Tunnell

RETIRED

Bruce G. Lynn
Clayton C. Hoskins
Richard C. Pickett
William H. Leighner

For full biographical listings, see the Martindale-Hubbell Law Directory

---

CALFEE, HALTER & GRISWOLD (AV)

88 East Broad Street, Suite 1500, 43215
Telephone: 614-621-1500
Telecopier: 614-621-0010
Cleveland, Ohio Office: Suite 1800, 800 Superior Avenue.
Telephone: 216-622-8200.
Telecopier: 216-241-0816.

RESIDENT MEMBERS

P. Michael DeAngelo
Albert J. Lucas

RESIDENT OF COUNSEL

Robert W. Boich

RESIDENT SENIOR ATTORNEY

Stanley J. Dobrowski

RESIDENT ASSOCIATES

Thomas P. Pappas

For full biographical listings, see the Martindale-Hubbell Law Directory

---

CHESTER, WILLCOX AND SAXBE (AV)

17 South High Street, Suite 900, 43215-3413
Telephone: 614-221-4000
Fax: 614-221-4012

MEMBERS OF FIRM

John J. Chester
Roderick H. Willcox
Charles Rockwell Saxbe
John W. Bentine
J. Anthony Kington
Donald C. Brey
Eugene B. Lewis
Richard A. Talda

ASSOCIATES

James J. Chester
John J. Chester, Jr.
Andrew J. Art
Elizabeth Jean Watters
Maryellen Corna
Jeffrey L. Small

OF COUNSEL

William B. Saxbe
Bruce E. Johnson

Representative Clients: American Municipal Power-Ohio, Inc.; The Limited; Scioto Downs, Inc.; Tee Jaye's Country Place Restaurants.

For full biographical listings, see the Martindale-Hubbell Law Directory

---

MICHAEL F. COLLEY CO., L.P.A. (AV)

Hoster & High Building, 536 South High Street, 43215-5674
Telephone: 614-228-6453
Fax: 614-228-7122

Michael F. Colley

David I. Shroyer
Daniel N. Abraham
Elizabeth Schorpp Burkett
Jennifer K. Thivener
Thomas F. Martello, Jr.

OF COUNSEL

Marvin Sloin
David K. Frank

Reference: Bank One of Columbus, NA.

For full biographical listings, see the Martindale-Hubbell Law Directory

---

CRABBE, BROWN, JONES, POTTS & SCHMIDT (AV)

500 South Front Street, Suite 1200, 43215
Telephone: 614-228-5511
Telecopier: 614-229-4559
Cincinnati, Ohio Office: 30 Garfield Place, Suite 940, 45202.
Telephone: 513-784-1525.
Telecopier: 513-784-1250.

(See Next Column)

MEMBERS OF FIRM

J. Roth Crabbe (1906-1989)
Robert C. Potts (1913-1994)
William T. McCracken (1929-1993)
Charles E. Brown
Theodore D. Sawyer
William H. Jones
Vincent J. Lodico
Steven B. Ayers
Keith H. Jung
Jeffrey M. Brown
Larry H. James
Brian E. Hurley (Resident, Cincinnati Office)
Gilbert J. Gradisar
Robert J. Behal
Jeffrey M. Lewis
Richard D. Wetzel, Jr.
Jerry A. Eichenberger
James D. Gilbert
Karen A. Seawall
Luis M. Alcalde
John C. Albert
George R. McCue, III
Gregory J. Dunn

ASSOCIATES

Michael R. Henry
Robert C. Buchbinder
John A. Van Sickle
Francesca M. Tosi
Stephen L. McIntosh
Lynne K. Schoenling
Kathleen McGarvey Hidy (Resident, Cincinnati Office)
Steven A. Davis
David J. Demers
Nicholas C. York
Todd William Collis
James P. Dinsmore
Michael C. Mentel
Kristen H. Smith

OF COUNSEL

John P. Kennedy
Wilbur W. Jones
William L. Schmidt
William Page Lewis

Representative Clients: Allstate Insurance Co.; American States Insurance Co.; General Electric.

For full biographical listings, see the Martindale-Hubbell Law Directory

---

DENMEAD & MALONEY (AV)

37 West Broad Street, Suite 1150, 43215-4189
Telephone: 614-228-5271
Telecopier: 614-228-7624

Craig Denmead
Kevin M. Maloney
Deborah A. Bonarrigo

OF COUNSEL

Mark A. Hutson

Representative Clients: Bode-Finn Co.; Century Surety Co.; COP, Inc.; Emco Maier Corp.; Inland Products, Inc.; National Head Injury Foundation, Inc., of Washington D.C.; Ohio Head Injury Assn.; Stonhard, Inc.; Sammons Corporate Services, Inc.

For full biographical listings, see the Martindale-Hubbell Law Directory

---

EMENS, KEGLER, BROWN, HILL & RITTER (AV)

Capitol Square Suite 1800, 65 East State Street, 43215-4294
Telephone: 614-462-5400
Telecopier: 614-464-2634
Cable Address: "Law EKBHR"
Telex: 246671

John F. Allevato
Donald A. Antrim
Jack A. Bjerke
John P. Brody
William J. Brown
Larry K. Carnahan
Stephen E. Chappelear
J. Richard Emens
Lawrence F. Feheley
Donald W. Gregory
Allen L. Handlan
Edward C. Hertenstein
Thomas W. Hill
Robin Smith Hoke
Gene W. Holliker
Charles J. Kegler
R. Kevin Kerns
Ronald L. Mason
Larry J. McClatchey
Samuel C. Randazzo
Paul D. Ritter, Jr.
Richard P. Rosenberry
Steven R. Russi
O. Judson Scheaf, III
Theodore Scott, Jr.
S. Martijn Steger
Roger P. Sugarman
Kevin L. Sykes
John R. Thomas
John B. Tingley
Frank A. Titus
Melvin D. Weinstein
Beatrice E. Wolper
R. Douglas Wrightsel
Michael E. Zatezalo

COUNSEL

John C. Deal
John L. Gray
Robert D. Marotta
S. Noel Melvin
Joseph M. Millious
Chalmers P. Wylie

Denise Cleary Clayton
Robert Garrett Cohen
Holly Robinson Fischer
Michael J. Galeano
James M. Groner
Paul R. Hess
Daniel G. Hilson
David M. Johnson
Nancy L. Koerner
Gregory D. May
Shelley A. McBride
Thomas M. L. Metzger
Todd F. Palmer
Karl W. Schedler
Richard W. Schuermann, Jr.
Robert C. Schuler
Robert G. Schuler
Amy M. Shepherd
Mary Ten Eyck Taylor
Timothy T. Tullis
Christopher J. Weber
Anthony C. White
Shawnell Williams

(See Next Column)

EMENS, KEGLER, BROWN, HILL & RITTER, *Columbus—Continued*

Representative Clients: BancOhio National Bank; Borden, Inc.; Columbus Metropolitan Housing Authority; Farmers Insurance Group; National Ground Water Association; The Ohio State University; Owens-Corning Fiberglas Corp.; Patrick Petroleum Co.; State Savings Bank.

For full biographical listings, see the Martindale-Hubbell Law Directory

ENZ, JONES & LEGRAND (AV)

1000 Polaris Parkway, Suite 150, 43240
Telephone: 614-431-4900
Fax: 614-431-4911

MEMBERS OF FIRM

Stephen D. Enz
Grey W. Jones
David G. LeGrand
James P. Seguin
Belinda S. Barnes

ASSOCIATES

Mark E. Phillips
Franz A. Geiger
Jeffrey A. Dittmer
Frank William Carsonie
Susan G. Sheridan
Joel K. Elkin
Robert Gage

Reference: Society Bank.

ROBERT F. HOWARTH, JR. (AV)

Two Nationwide Plaza, 280 North High Street, Suite 800, 43215
Telephone: 614-221-0717
Telecopier: 614-221-1278

*** JONES, DAY, REAVIS & POGUE** (AV)

1900 Huntington Center, 43215
Telephone: 614-469-3939
Cable Address: "Attorneys Columbus"
Telecopier: 614-461-4198
In Cleveland, Ohio: North Point, 901 Lakeside Avenue.
Telephone: 216-586-3939.
Cable Address: "Attorneys Cleveland."
Telex: 980389.
Telecopier: 216-579-0212.
In Atlanta, Georgia: 3500 One Peachtree Center, 303 Peachtree Street, N.E.
Telephone: 404-521-3939.
Cable Address: "Attorneys Atlanta".
Telex: 54-2711.
Telecopier: 404-581-8330.
In Brussels, Belgium: Avenue Louise 480, 7th Floor, B-1050 Brussels.
Telephone: 011-32-2-645-14-11.
Telecopier: 011-32-2-645-14-45.
In Chicago, Illinois: 77 West Wacker.
Telephone: 312-782-3939.
Telecopier: 312-782-8585.
In Dallas, Texas: 2300 Trammell Crow Center, 2001 Ross Avenue.
Telephone: 214-220-3939.
Cable Address: "Attorneys Dallas."
Telex: 730852.
Telecopier: 214-969-5100.
In Frankfurt, Germany: Triton Haus, Bockenheimer Landstrasse 42, 60323 Frankfurt am Main.
Telephone: 49-69-9726-3939.
Telecopier: 49-69-9726-3993.
In Geneva, Switzerland: 20, rue de Candolle.
Telephone: 011-41-22-320-2339.
Telecopier: 011-41-22-320-1232.
In Hong Kong: 1501 One Exchange Square, 8 Connaught Place.
Telephone: 011-852-2526-6895.
Telecopier: 011-852-2810-5787. Irvine, California: 2603 Main Street, Suite 900.
Telephone: 714-851-3939.
Telex: 194911 Lawyers LSA.
Telecopier: 714-553-7539.
In London, England: One Mount Street.
Telephone: 011-44-71-493-9361.
Cable Address: "Surgoe London WI."
Telecopier: 011-44-71-493-9666.
In Los Angeles, California: 555 West Fifth Street, Suite 4600.
Telephone: 213-489-3939.
Telex: 181439 UD.
Telecopier: 213-243-2539.
In New York, New York: 599 Lexington Avenue.
Telephone: 212-326-3939.
Cable Address: "JONESDAY NEWYORK."
Telex: 237013 JDRP UR.
Telecopier: 212-755-7306.
In Paris, France: 62, rue du Faubourg Saint-Honore.
Telephone: 011-33-1-44-71-3939.
Cable Address: "Surgoe Paris."
Telex: 290156 Surgoe.
Telecopier: 011-33-1-49-24-0471.

(See Next Column)

In Pittsburgh, Pennsylvania: 500 Grant Street, 31st Floor.
Telephone: 412-391-3939.
Cable Address: "Attorneys Pittsburgh".
Telecopier: 412-394-7959.
In Riyadh, Saudi Arabia: Law Offices of Saud M.A. Shawwaf, P.O. Box 2700.
Telephones: 011 (966-1) 465-6543, 011 (966-1) 464-8534 or 011 (966-1) 464-8540.
Telex: 401831 SAUCON SJ.
Telecopier: (966-1) 464-8480.
In Taipei, Taiwan: 8th Floor, 2 Tun Hwa South Road, Section 2.
Telephone: 011 (886-2) 704-6808.
Telecopier: 011 (886-2) 704-6791.
In Tokyo, Japan: Toranomon MT Building, 4th Floor, 10-3, Toranomon 3-Chome, Minato-Ku, Tokyo 105, Japan.
Telephone: 011-81-3-3433-3939.
Telecopier: 011-81-3-5401-2725.
In Washington, D.C.: Metropolitan Square, 1450 G Street, N.W.
Telephone: 202-879-3939.
Cable Address: "Attorneys Washington."
Telex: 89-2410 ATTORNEYS WASH.
Telecopier: 202-737-2832.

MEMBERS OF FIRM IN COLUMBUS

Roger F. Day
Robert J. Gilker
Harry J. Lehman
Fordham E. Huffman
John W. Edwards
Todd Shawn Swatsler
H. Theodore Meyer
Marlene P. Frank
Maryann Baker Gall
Gary D. Begeman
G. Roger King
Thomas E. Dutton
John H. Lahey
Gayle E. Parkhill
Roger R. Stinehart
Robert W. Hamilton
James R. King
Richard Alan Chesley
J. Kevin Cogan
Jeffrey J. Jones
Steven T. Catlett

SENIOR ATTORNEYS

Helen L. Liebman
Margaret L. Gramann

ASSOCIATES

Matthew J. Toddy
Charles M. Oellermann
James M. Jones
George N. Nicholas
Kevin D. Lyles
Colleen A. Deep
Harlan W. Robins
Gregory J. Henchel (Not admitted in OH)
Michael Dubetz, Jr.
Matthew W. Lampe
Jeffrey L. Kapp
Shawn J. Organ
Elizabeth P. Kessler
Paul E. Harner
Marybeth Bosko Oquendo
Christopher Skorina
Jeffrey P. Taft
Jeffrey S. Sutton
Ronald A. Bell
Jeffrey B. Ellman
Stephen P. Carney
Matthew A. Kairis
Jennifer L. Klitch
Elizabeth A. McLaughlin (Not admitted in OH)
Douglas M. Mansfield
Joseph M. Witalec

For full biographical listings, see the Martindale-Hubbell Law Directory

MARTIN, PERGRAM & BROWNING CO., L.P.A. (AV)

69 East Wilson Bridge Road, P.O. Box 6017, 43085-6017
Telephone: 614-436-8000
Telecopier: 614-846-4691
Delaware, Ohio Office: Manos, Martin, Pergram & Browning, 40 North Sandusky Street.
Telephone: 614-363-1313; Columbus Direct Line: 614-548-4825.
Telecopier: 614-548-4156.

SENIOR COUNSEL

Peter J. Manos

Stephen D. Martin
Craig B. Paynter
Dennis L. Pergram
James M. Dietz
William J. Browning
Wade E. Harrison
Karen A. Visocan

For full biographical listings, see the Martindale-Hubbell Law Directory

PORTER, WRIGHT, MORRIS & ARTHUR (AV)

41 South High Street, 43215-6194
Telephone: 614-227-2000; (800-533-2794)
Telex: 6503213584 MCI
Fax: 614-227-2100
Dayton, Ohio Office: One Dayton Centre, One South Main Street, 45402.
Telephones: 513-228-2411; (800-533-4434).
Fax: 513-449-6820.
Cincinnati, Ohio Office: 250 E. Fifth Street, 45202-4166.
Telephones: 513-381-4700; (800-582-5813).
Fax: 513-421-0991.
Cleveland, Ohio Office: 925 Euclid Avenue, 44115-1483.
Telephones: 216-443-9000; (800-824-1980).
Fax: 216-443-9011.
Washington, D.C. Office: 1233 20th Street, N.W., 20036-2395.
Telephones: 202-778-3000; (800-456-7962).
Fax: 202-778-3063.

(See Next Column)

PORTER, WRIGHT, MORRIS & ARTHUR—*Continued*

Naples, Florida Office: 4501 Tamiami Trail North, 33940-3060.
Telephones: 813-263-8898;(800-876-7962).
Fax: 813-436-2990.

MEMBERS OF FIRM
COLUMBUS, OHIO OFFICE

Jon M. Anderson
Edwin M. Baranowski
Michael J. Barren
Phillip H. Barrett
John C. Beeler
Kenneth S. Blumenthal
James P. Botti
John E. Brady
Marjorie Crowder Briggs
Daniel A. Brown
Robert L. Brubaker
Cornelius Bulman, Jr.
Brian L. Buzby
Ann H. Casto
Thomas E. Cavendish
Anthony J. Celebrezze, Jr.
Richard A. Cheap
Mary Beth Moser Clary
Deborah S. Clifton
Thomas C. Coady
Daniel R. Conway
S. Ronald Cook, Jr.
Daniel W. Costello
James D. Curphey
Joyce D. Edelman
Joseph F. Elliott
Mason Evans, IV
R. Leland Evans
Lloyd E. Fisher, Jr.
Michael E. Flowers
Robert E. Fultz
Ronald W. Gabriel
Stuart M. Gordon
Diane K. Goulder
Timothy E. Grady
Brian D. Hall
Paul A. Hanke
Polly J. Harris
John C. Hartranft
George M. Hauswirth
Jeffrey T. Hayes
Harry L. Henning
Janet J. Henry
C. Andrew Ireton, Jr.
Donald W. Jordan
William J. Kelly, Jr.
Robert C. Kiger
Randall W. Knutti
Charles J. Kurtz, III
David A. Laing
Wayman C. Lawrence, III
Curtis A. Loveland
William G. Martin
Daniel J. Massey
Elizabeth B. Mayo
Alvin J. McKenna
J. Jeffrey McNealey
Mark K. Merkle, Jr.
D. Michael Miller
Dixon F. Miller
Terrance M. Miller
Jennifer T. Mills
Denise M. Mirman
Frank R. Morris, Jr.
Robert J. Nordstrom
Scott E. North
Adele Ellen O'Conner
James S. Oliphant
Jack R. Pigman
Marvin R. Pliskin
James E. Pohlman
Samuel H. Porter
Fred G. Pressley, Jr.
James H. Prior
Michael T. Radcliffe
Teri G. Rasmussen
Diane C. Reichwein
John B. Rohyans
Joseph W. Ryan, Jr.
Christopher R. Schraff
Edward M. Segelken
Martin S. Seltzer
Darrell R. Shepard
Bradd N. Siegel
Norman T. Smith
Patrick J. Smith
Mark S. Stemm
John M. Stephen
H. Grant Stephenson
Richard G. Terapak
Jean Yingling Teteris
Kathleen McManus Trafford
Robert W. Trafford
David A. Tumen
Michael J. Underwood
Charles C. Warner
Franck G. Wobst
Nancy Belville Young
Thomas A. Young

ASSOCIATES
COLUMBUS, OHIO OFFICE

Douglas L. Anderson
Daniel A. Bellman
Charles H. Cooper, Jr.
Peggy W. Corn
Pedro C. Dallarda
Lisa L. Eschleman
Nancy Engbers Falk
H. Macy Favor, Jr.
Theresa M. Finneran
Craig M. Fullen
Ralph F. Gildehaus
Kevin E. Griffith
Heather Lynn Guise
Curtis A. Hansen
Julia Harden Helmreich
Kirk A. Hilbrands
Diane M. Hockman
Joseph R. Irvine
Laurie N. Jacques
Megan V. Kent
Lori-Lou Kimm
James A. King
Amy D. Klaben
Benjamin Kwakye
Virginia E. Lohmann
James McArdle Mattimoe
Steven M. McCarty
Waymon B. McLeskey, II
Richard C. McQuown
Alaine Y. Miller
Janice Nelson
John B. Pisaris
Virginia E. Richards
Donna M. Ruscitti
Christopher C. Russell
Kimberly Callery Shumate
Michael D. Steffensmeier
Karl J. Sutter
Robert J. Tannous
Debra Ann Willet

OF COUNSEL
COLUMBUS, OHIO OFFICE

John M. Adams
William E. Arthur
John M. Bowsher
Daniel C. K. Chow (Not admitted in OH)
John A. Dunkel
Robert F. Ebinger
Howard P. Fink
Theodore G. Fisher
Robert D. Hays
John M. Latsko
James D. Miller
Warren H. Morse
W. John Pritchard
David P. Shouvlin (Not admitted in OH)
Harry Wright, III

(See Next Column)

DAYTON, OHIO OFFICE
RESIDENT MEMBERS

William G. Deas
Roland F. Eichner
Gary W. Gottschlich
Samuel L. Hagans, Jr.
John J. Heron
Jonathan Hollingsworth
Thomas A. Holton
C. Terry Johnson
Richard H. Packard
Robert E. Portune
Thomas H. Pyper
Walter Reynolds
R. Bruce Snyder

DAYTON, OHIO OFFICE
RESIDENT ASSOCIATES

Richard D. Anglin II
Linda S. Holmes
Charles Y. Kidwell, Jr.
Ronald J. Kozar
Joseph D. Smallwood
Lawrence S. Walter

DAYTON, OHIO OFFICE
RESIDENT OF COUNSEL

Thomas L. Czechowski
Chester E. Finn

CINCINNATI, OHIO OFFICE
RESIDENT MEMBERS

John J. Cruze
Mark E. Elsener
Steven F. Gay
James R. Marlow
Jerome J. Metz, Jr.
David Reichert
Wm. Cates Rambo
Michael G. Reed
Stephen David Strauss

CINCINNATI, OHIO OFFICE
RESIDENT ASSOCIATES

Duane A. Boggs
Christopher R. Heekin
Stephen P. Kenkel
Francine A. Wayman
Mark G. Whittenburg

CINCINNATI, OHIO OFFICE
RESIDENT OF COUNSEL

Louis J. Schneider, Jr.

CLEVELAND, OHIO OFFICE
RESIDENT MEMBERS

Jeffrey Baddeley
Herbert L. Braverman
Anthony J. Celebrezze, Jr.
James P. Conroy
Donald J. Fisher
Daniel F. Gourash
Richard M. Markus
Hugh E. McKay
Craig S. Miller
Terrance L. Ryan
Patricia A. Screen
Ralph Streza
Thomas J. Talcott
Sophia Papandreas Tjotjos
Anthony J. Viola
John W. Waldeck, Jr.
William R. Weir
Alan D. Wright

CLEVELAND, OHIO OFFICE
RESIDENT ASSOCIATES

David A. Bell
David Cohen
Robert G. Cohn
Anne T. Corrigan
Sophia M. Deseran
Margaret M. Koesel
Ezio A. Listati
Joyce Metti Papandreas
David C. Tryon
Alan C. Yarcusko

CLEVELAND, OHIO OFFICE
RESIDENT OF COUNSEL

Robert E. Bingham
James J. Schiller
Robert Wavrek

WASHINGTON, D.C. OFFICE
MEMBERS

Anthony J. Celebrezze
Michael G. Dowd
E. Jay Finkel
Leslie Alan Glick
Judd L. Kessler
Mark L. Lezell
Ronald S. Perlman
Robert E. Steinberg

WASHINGTON, D.C. OFFICE
RESIDENT ASSOCIATES

Matthew Steven Bergman
Richard J. Burke
Ellen F. Randel
Elizabeth C. Sandoval

WASHINGTON, D.C. OFFICE
RESIDENT OF COUNSEL

Hugh O'Neill
William G. Porter, Jr.
Donald P. Young
John Hardin Young

NAPLES, FLORIDA OFFICE
MEMBERS

Robert M. Buckel (Resident)
W. Jeffrey Cecil (Resident)
Jeffrey S. Kannensohn
James E. Willis (Resident)
Gary K. Wilson (Resident)
Mary Beth Moser Clary
Harry L. Henning
Richard M. Markus
Ronald S. Perlman

NAPLES, FLORIDA OFFICE
RESIDENT ASSOCIATES

Margaret Racaniello
Samara S. Holland
Stuart A. Thompson

NAPLES, FLORIDA OFFICE
RESIDENT COUNSEL

John D. Gast

Representative Clients: American Electric Power Service Corporation; Bank One, Columbus, N.A.; Battelle Memorial Institute; Columbia Gas; Huntington Bancshares Incorporated; Shearson Lehman Brothers; Southern Ohio Coal Co.; Sun TV & Appliance, Inc.; Tenneco Gas Pipeline Group; White Castle System, Inc.

For full biographical listings, see the Martindale-Hubbell Law Directory

SCHOTTENSTEIN, ZOX & DUNN A LEGAL PROFESSIONAL ASSOCIATION (AV)

The Huntington Center, 41 South High Street, 43215
Telephone: 614-221-3211
Telecopier: 614-464-1135
Telex: 650 24 444 365

Melvin L. Schottenstein (1932-1993)
Benjamin L. Zox
Harvey Dunn
Jay R. Dingledy
James M. L. Ferber
Herbert R. Godby
E. James Hopple
John Terakedis, Jr.
James R. Winfree
Robert D. Weisman
Fredrick L. Fisher
Felix C. Wade
Richard A. Barnhart
Randall S. Arndt
John P. Gilligan
Daniel J. Kayne
William F. Simpson
James E. Davidson
Leonard A. Carlson
Kevin R. McDermott
John D. Robinett
Peter A. Pavarini
Roger L. Sabo
John C. McDonald
David A. Kadela
Nora E. Jones
Michael Bennett Coleman
Daniel T. Swanson
Catherine T. Dunlay
Kris M. Dawley
Richard W. Holz
Francis A. Kovacs, Jr.
Martin S. Rosenthal
Susan Darnell Rector
Susan Porter
Diane M. Lease
Michael D. Tarullo
Michael P. Kennedy (Not admitted in OH)

Edwin L. Skeens
Bridgette C. Roman
Corey V. Crognale
William J. Barath
Robert M. Robenalt
Lori Anne Black
Susan K. Cliffel
Melissa L. Zox
Victoria E. Powers
Murray A. Davis
Robert R. Ouellette
Keith Wylie Gizzi
William P. Zox
Robert C. Roesch
Nancy A. Brigner
David Robert Eberhart
Robert H. Nichols
Julie Mann Brightwell
Lisa Wu Fate
Michael A. Womack
Marcus D. Dunn
Marie-Joëlle C. Khouzam

OF COUNSEL

Leigh Ann Wobst
John V. Barger
Patrick A. Devine

Reference: Bank One of Columbus, N.A.

For full biographical listings, see the Martindale-Hubbell Law Directory

SIMPSON THACHER & BARTLETT (AV)

A Partnership which includes Professional Corporations
One Riverside Plaza, 43215
Telephone: 614-461-7799
Telecopier: 614-461-0040
New York, NY Office: 425 Lexington Avenue, 10017-3954.
Telephone: 212-455-2000.
Telecopier: 212-455-2502. ESL 62928462.
London Office: 100 New Bridge Street, London EC4V 6JE, England.
Telephone: 011-44-71-246-8000.
Telecopier: 011-44-71-329-3883.
Tokyo Office: Ark Mori Building, 29th Floor, 12-32, Akasaka 1-Chome, Minato-Ku, Tokyo 107, Japan.
Telephone: 81-3-5562-8601.
Fax: 81-3-5562-8606. ESL 62765846.
Hong Kong Office: Asia Pacific Finance Tower - 32nd Floor, 3 Garden Road, Central, Hong Kong.
Telephone: 852-514-7600.
Telecopier: 852-869-7694.

RESIDENT PARTNER

Michael P. Graney

RESIDENT ASSOCIATES

Mark S. Tibberts
Susan L. Simms

For full biographical listings, see the Martindale-Hubbell Law Directory

*** SQUIRE, SANDERS & DEMPSEY** (AV)

1300 Huntington Center, 41 South High Street, 43215
Telephone: 614-365-2700
Fax: 614-365-2499
Cleveland, Ohio Office: 4900 Society Center, 127 Public Square, Cleveland, Ohio 44114-1304.
Telephone: 216-479-8500. Fax's: 216-479-8780, 216-479-8781, 216-479-8787, 216-479-8795, 216-479-8793, 216-479-8776, 216-479-8788.
Jacksonville, Florida Office: One Enterprise Center, Suite 2100, 225 Water Street, Jacksonville, Florida 32202.
Telephone: 904-353-1264.
Fax: 904-356-2986.

(See Next Column)

Miami, Florida Office: 201 South Biscayne Boulevard, Suite 2900 Miami Center, Miami, Florida 33131.
Telephone: 305-577-8700.
Fax: 305-358-1425.
New York, New York Office: 520 Madison Avenue, 32nd Floor, New York, New York 10022.
Telephone: 212-872-9800.
Fax: 212-872-9814.
Phoenix, Arizona Office: Two Renaissance Square, 40 North Central Avenue, Suite 2700, Phoenix, Arizona 85004-4441.
Telephone: 602-528-4000.
Fax: 602-253-8129.
Washington, D.C. Office: 1201 Pennsylvania Avenue, N.W., P.O. Box 407, Washington, D.C. 20044.
Telephone: 202-626-6600.
Fax: 202-626-6780.
London, England Office: 1 Gunpowder Square, Printers Street, London EC4A 3DE.
Telephone: 011-44-071-830-0055.
Fax: 011-44-071-830-0056.
Brussels, Belgium Office: Avenue Louise, 165-Box 15, 1050 Brussels, Belgium.
Telephone: 011-322-648-1717.
Fax: 011-322-648-1064.
Prague Office: Adria Palace, Jungmannova 31/36, 11000 Prague 1, Czech Republic.
Telephone: 011-42-2-231-5661.
Fax: 011-42-2-231-5482.
Bratislava Office: Mudronova 37, 811 01 Bratislava, Slovak Republic.
Telephone: 011-42-7-313-362; 011-42-7-315-370.
Fax: 011-42-7-313-918.
Budapest, Hungary Office: Deak Ferenc Ut. 10, Office 304, H-1052 Budapest V., Hungary.
Telephones: 011-361-226-2024; 011-361-226-5038.
Fax: 011-361-226-2025.
Kiev, Ukraine Office: vul. Prorizna 9 KV 20, Kiev, Ukraine 25203.
Telephones: 011-7-044-244-3452, 011-7-044-244-3453, 011-7-044-228-8687.
Fax: 011-7-044-228-4938.

RESIDENT MEMBERS

Catherine Adams
David W. Alexander
Janice McKimmie Bernard
Ted B. Clevenger
John J. Dilenschneider
Patrick J. Dugan
John R. Gall
David Grauer
William A. Klatt
Kenneth J. Krebs
Daniel M. Maher
Steven F. Mount
James P. Mulroy
Richard W. Rubenstein
Michael D. Saad
Gregory B. Scott
Paul F. Sefcovic
Alex Shumate
David S. Sidor
Fredric L. Smith
Gregory W. Stype
Kim L. Swanson
James M. Tobin
William M. Todd
William J. Wahoff
Scott B. West
Karen A. Winters
Donald W. Wiper, Jr.
C. Craig Woods
David J. Young

RESIDENT OF COUNSEL

Donald C. Scriven

RESIDENT COUNSEL

Richard R. Murphey, Jr.
Fred A. Summer

RESIDENT ASSOCIATES

Vincent Atriano
Pamela H. Bouwman
Roger D. Branigin
Rebecca S. Chaffin (Not admitted in OH)
David Cooper, Jr.
Philomena M. Dane
Richard Goldberg
Stephen P. Grassbaugh
Nathan C. Hamilton
Holly Hickman Heer
Jerome J. Joondeph, Jr.
Scott Christopher Lehman
Phillip D. Lehmkuhl
Steven M. Loewengart
Robert C. Maier
Scott D. Marrah
Julie C. Martin
David W. Mason
Laurie Beth McGovern
Peter H. Mihaly
William A. Nolan
Scott B. Pfahl
Mark E. Shere (Not admitted in OH)
Keith Shumate
Terri-Lynne B. Smiles
Margaret M. Stolar
James K. Stucko, Jr.
Anthony J. Sugar
James D. Thomas
Randi Malcolm Thomas
Pamela H. Thurston
Deon Vaughan
Susan Ann Warner
Kymberly A. Troup Wellons
Lee A. Wendel
Leslie A. Yovan

For full biographical listings, see the Martindale-Hubbell Law Directory

*** TAFT, STETTINIUS & HOLLISTER** (AV)

Twelfth Floor 21 East State Street, 43215-4221
Telephone: 614-221-2838
Facsimile: 614-221-2007
Cincinnati, Ohio Office: 1800 Star Bank Center, 425 Walnut Street.
Telephone: 513-381-2838
Washington, D.C. Office: Suite 500, 625 Indiana Avenue, N.W.
Telephone: 202-628-2838.
Crestview Hills, Kentucky Office: Thomas More Centre, 2670 Chancellor Drive.
Telephone: 606-331-2838; 531-381-2838.

(See Next Column)

TAFT, STETTINIUS & HOLLISTER—*Continued*

RESIDENT MEMBERS

David L. Johnson
Timothy P. Nagy
Lawrence D. Walker
Brian P. Gillan

RESIDENT ASSOCIATES

Michael A. Byers
William E. Nakasian
Mark A. Ferguson
Juliana M. Faris
Daniel J. Brake

Counsel for: Citizens Federal Bank; Culligan International Co.; Department of Surgery (Ohio State University) Corporation; General Motors; Great American Broadcasting Company (WTVN and WLVQ); Nissan Motor Acceptance Corp.; Pepsi-Cola Bottling of Columbus; Shearson Lehman Brothers; Society Bank; Willis Corroon of Ohio, Inc.

For full biographical listings, see the Martindale-Hubbell Law Directory

* THOMPSON, HINE AND FLORY (AV)

One Columbus, 10 West Broad Street, 43215-3435
Telephone: 614-469-3200
Fax: 614-469-3361
Akron, Ohio Office: 50 S. Main Street, Suite 502, 44308-1828.
Telephone: 216-376-8090.
Fax: 216-376-8386.
Cincinnati, Ohio Office: 312 Walnut Street, 14th Floor, 45202-4029.
Telephone: 513-352-6700.
Fax: 513-241-4771.
Telex: 938003.
Cleveland, Ohio Office: 1100 National City Bank Building, 629 Euclid Avenue, 44114-3070.
Telephone: 216-566-5500.
Fax: 216-556-5583.
Telex: 980217.
Cable Address: "Thomflor".
Dayton, Ohio Office: 2000 Courthouse Plaza, N.E., 45402-1706.
Telephone: 513-443-6600.
Fax: 513-443-6637; 443-6635.
Palm Beach, Florida Office: 125 Worth Avenue, 33480-4466.
Telephone: 407-833-5900.
Fax: 407-833-5951.
Washington, D.C. Office: 1920 N Street, N.W., 20036-1601.
Telephone: 202-331-8800.
Fax: 202-331-8330.
Telex: 904173.
Cable Address: "Caglaw".
Brussels, Belgium Office: Rue des Chevaliers / Ridderstraat 14 - B.10, B - 1050.
Telephone: 011(32-2) 511-9326.
Fax: 011(32-2) 513-9206.

MEMBERS OF FIRM

Thomas R. Allen
Thomas J. Bonasera
William R. Case
Gerald L. Draper
William S. Fein
Daniel J. Hunter
Kenton L. Kuehnle
Thomas E. Lodge
Barry L. Lubow
George C. McConnaughey (Retired)
James A. Meaney
Robert P. Mone
William C. Moul
Susan A. Petersen
Ben L. Pfefferle, III
Michael A. Poe
Janis B. Rosenthal
Raymond T. Sawyer (In Columbus and Cleveland, Ohio)
Thomas C. Scott (Partner-in-Charge in Columbus)
Michael T. Shannon
William A. Shenk
John T. Sunderland
Jerry Vande Werken
William C. Wilkinson

ASSOCIATES

Margaret R. Carmany
R. Michael Clark
Timothy E. Cowans
Anne E. Eckhart
Douglas L. Hertlein
Christopher Jones
Lisa A. Lomax
Helen Mac Murray
Todd H. Neuman
Bonnie Irvin O'Neil
Michael A. Renne
Susan L. Rhiel
Melisa D. Stone
Richard K. Stovall
Charles E. Ticknor, III
James W. Wiggin, III

SENIOR ATTORNEY

Philip B. Cochran

OF COUNSEL

Robert E. Hickey, Jr.
Charles B. Mills, Jr.

For full biographical listings, see the Martindale-Hubbell Law Directory

VORYS, SATER, SEYMOUR AND PEASE (AV)

52 East Gay Street, P.O. Box 1008, 43216-1008
Telephone: 614-464-6400
Telex: 241348
Telecopier: 614-464-6350
Cable Address: "Vorysater"
Washington, D.C. Office: Suite 1111, 1828 L Street, N.W., 20036-5104.
Telephone: 202-467-8800.
Telex: 440693.
Telecopier: 202-467-8900.
Cleveland, Ohio Office: 2100 One Cleveland Center, 1375 East Ninth Street, 44114-1724.
Telephone: 216-479-6100.
Telecopier: 216-479-6060.
Cincinnati, Ohio Office: Suite 2100, 221 East Fourth Street, P.O. Box 0236, 45201-0236.
Telephone: 513-723-4000.
Telecopier: 513-723-4056.

Arthur I. Vorys (1856-1933)
Lowry F. Sater (1867-1935)
Augustus T. Seymour (1873-1926)
Edward L. Pease (1873-1924)

MEMBERS OF FIRM

John C. Elam
Edgar A. Strause
James P. Kennedy
Edward A. Schrag, Jr.
Colborn M. Addison
Lester S. Lash
Roger A. Yurchuck (Resident, Cincinnati, Ohio Office)
Jacob E. Davis, II
Duke W. Thomas
Richard R. Stedman
Sheldon A. Taft
Thomas M. Taggart
James B. Cushman
Robert W. Werth
George L. Jenkins
James H. Gross
James R. Beatley, Jr.
Lawrence L. Fisher
Thomas B. Ridgley
John W. Hoberg
James P. Friedt
Philip C. Johnston
William D. Kloss
Michael G. Long
Thomas M. Tarpy
Kenneth M. Royalty
David S. Cupps
James H. Hedden
Daniel H. Schoedinger
Phillip L. Nunnally
Susan E. Brown
Joseph D. Lonardo
Michael W. Donaldson
Michael J. Canter
Leon M. McCorkle, Jr.
Russell M. Gertmenian
Alan T. Radnor
Mary Ellen Fairfield
C. William O'Neill
Robert E. Tait
Charles S. DeRousie
George N. Corey
Frederick R. Reed (Resident, Cincinnati, Ohio Office)
G. Ross Bridgman
W. Jonathan Airey
Steven J. McCoy
Philip A. Brown
Stephen R. Buchenroth
James M. Ball
John K. Keller
R. Guy Cole, Jr.
Robert A. Minor
Ronald L. Rowland
Suzanne K. Richards
Donald J. Shuller (Resident, Cincinnati, Ohio Office)
Gary E. Davis
F. Daniel Balmert (Resident, Cleveland, Ohio Office)
Jonathan M. Norman
John Timothy Young
Thomas R. Boland (Resident, Washington, D.C. Office)
Robin R. Obetz
Sandra J. Anderson
James A. Yano
Nanci L. Danison
Ivery D. Foreman
Bruce L. Ingram
Laura G. Kuykendall
Bruce R. Henke
Raymond D. Anderson
Gerald P. Ferguson
Roger E. Lautzenhiser
J. Scott Jamieson
James E. Phillips
Randal C. Teague (Resident, Washington, D.C. Office)
William S. Newcomb, Jr.
Robert J. Sidman
Norton R. Webster
John P. Wellner
Aaron P. Rosenfeld
John W. Wilmer, Jr. (Resident, Washington, D.C. Office)
Chris J. North
John C. Vorys (Resident, Cincinnati, Ohio Office)
Reginald W. Jackson
Carl D. Smallwood
Joseph A. Brunetto
John J. Kulewicz
Terry M. Miller
David W. Hardymon
Steven W. Mershon
Robert G. Dykes
Jonathan D. Iten
Ellen A. Efros (Resident, Washington, D.C. Office)
Anker M. Bell
Michael A. Cline
Douglas L. Rogers
F. James Foley
M. Howard Petricoff
Matthew J. Hatchadorian (Resident, Cleveland, Ohio Office)
Warren W. Glick (Resident, Washington, D.C. Office)
Benita A. Kahn
Elizabeth Turrell Farrar
Thomas E. Szykowny
Jonathan R. Vaughn
Thomas O. Ruby
Stephen J. Petras, Jr. (Resident, Cleveland, Ohio Office)
Robert H. Maynard
Eugene P. Ruehlmann (Resident, Cincinnati, Ohio Office)
John W. Read (Resident, Cleveland, Ohio Office)
Richard D. Schuster
Anthony C. Ciriaco
Daniel J. Buckley (Resident, Cincinnati, Ohio Office)
G. Robert Lucas, II
Carole A. Mitchell
Andrew C. Smith
Shawn M. Flahive
J. Thomas Mason
William G. Porter, II
Charles J. French, III (Resident, Cleveland, Ohio Office)
Daniel J. Minor
Theodore D. Grosser (Resident, Cincinnati, Ohio Office)
Richard Heer Oman
Robert J. Styduhar
James K. Alford (Resident, Washington, D.C. Office)

(See Next Column)

VORYS, SATER, SEYMOUR AND PEASE, *Columbus—Continued*

MEMBERS OF FIRM (Continued)

William Mack Webner (Resident, Washington, D.C. Office)
Michael A. Grow (Resident, Washington, D.C. Office)
Drew T. Parobek (Resident, Cleveland, Ohio Office)
Mark A. Norman (Resident, Cincinnati, Ohio Office)
Andrew M. Kaplan (Resident, Cincinnati, Ohio Office)
Algenon L. Marbley
Thomas R. Winters
Terri Reyering Abare (Resident, Cincinnati, Ohio Office)
Charles C. Bissinger, Jr. (Resident, Cincinnati, Ohio Office)
Dan L. Jaffe
David A. Swift
Elizabeth E. Tulman
Webb I. Vorys
Robert N. Webner
Gail C. Ford
Scott M. Doran
Kenneth A. Golonka, Jr.
James A. Wilson
Anthony J. O'Malley

David A. Gurwin
Stephen M. Howard
Linda A. Blair
Arthur E. Phelps, Jr. (Resident, Cincinnati, Ohio Office)
James E. Arnold
Bradley K. Sinnott
Cynthia A. Shafer (Resident, Cincinnati, Ohio Office)
Brian C. Harrison (Resident, Washington, D.C. Office)
Chris Bator (Resident, Cleveland, Ohio Office)
Sarah J. Cruise (Resident, Cleveland, Ohio Office)
Anthony L. Ehler
Randall D. LaTour
Russell R. Rosler
Mark E. Vannatta
Gregory J. Zelasko
Melvin A. Bedree (Resident, Cincinnati, Ohio Office)
Carol Mahaffey
Timothy G. Clancy (Resident, Cleveland, Ohio Office)
Michael E. Samuels (Resident, Cincinnati, Ohio Office)
Robert E. Bardwell, Jr.
Elizabeth M. Campbell
Amy Haynes Geis
Anthony J. Giuliani
William D. Kloss, Jr.
Brent C. Taggart
Donald A. Brown
John B. Weimer
Stephen H. Brown (Resident, Washington, D.C. Office)
Barbara A. Duncombe (Resident, Washington, D.C. Office)
Paul J. Coval
Julie M. Larson (Resident, Cleveland, Ohio Office)
Laurie A. Briggs
Joseph M. Brooker
John L. Landolfi
Eric A. Pierce
Katherine Spies Giumenti
Kristin L. Watt
David A. Westrup
Douglas R. Matthews
W. Breck Weigel (Resident, Cincinnati, Ohio Office)
Allen S. Kinzer
Ellen L. Seats
Theodore A. Boggs
Gary Saalman
Kevin M. Czerwonka
Herbert A. Hedden
Ajili Hodari
Randall W. Mikes
Megan L. Musgrave
Bradley A. Smith
Lorene F. Schaefer (Resident, Cincinnati, Ohio Office)
Jerome C. Webbs (Resident, Cleveland, Ohio Office)
Terren B. Magid
Marianne E. Roche (Resident, Cincinnati, Ohio Office)
Lawrence J. Stelzer, Jr.
William D. Hayes (Resident, Cincinnati, Ohio Office)
Timothy N. McGarey (Resident, Washington, D.C. Office)
Dale R. Harburg (Resident, Washington, D.C. Office)
Douglas R. Bush (Resident, Washington, D.C. Office)
Susan Marie Barrett
Robert A. Hager (Resident, Washington, D.C. Office)
Michael D. Martz
Theodore P. Mattis
Richard T. Miller
William Evan Price, II
K. Ellen Toth (Resident, Cleveland, Ohio Office)
Victor A. Walton, Jr. (Resident, Cincinnati, Ohio Office)
Keith W. Schneider
Ceda G. Ogada
Philip F. Downey
Virgil R. Montgomery
D. Scott Powell
Nathaniel Lampley, Jr. (Resident, Cincinnati, Ohio Office)
Christina A. Masdea
Matthew P. Murphy
Robert A. Harris
Timothy C. Hall
Gregory D. Russell
David V. Dilenschneider
Margaret D. Everett
Troy L. Grigsby, Jr.
David C. House
Charles W. Haubiel, II
Lisa Pierce Reisz
Mark C. Kuster
Laura H. Martin (Resident, Cincinnati, Ohio Office)
Claire L. Wudowsky (Resident, Washington, D.C. Office)
Laura Westfall Casey
George W. Swenson, Jr. (Resident, Washington, D.C. Office)
Susan A. Cohen
D. Michael Schira
Scott D. Balderston (Resident, Washington, D.C. Office)
Ronald A. Robins, Jr.
Jacklyn J. Ford
Richard L. Lewis (Resident, Cleveland, Ohio Office)
Donald B. Allegro
Wendy Asma Ling (Not admitted in OH; Resident, Cleveland, Ohio Office)
David A. Skidmore, Jr. (Resident, Cincinnati, Ohio Office)
Julie A. Schafer
Scott S.C. Thomas
Richard L. Moore (Resident, Cincinnati, Ohio Office)
Tamara Theis
Julie E. Manning
Stephen D. Browning
Paula J. Lloyd
Stephen S. Eberly (Resident, Cincinnati, Ohio Office)
Eliot N. Meyers (Resident, Cincinnati, Ohio Office)
Phillip J. Smith (Resident, Cincinnati, Ohio Office)
Richard M. Rolwing
Bruce P. Batista (Resident, Cleveland, Ohio Office)

(See Next Column)

OF COUNSEL

Arthur I. Vorys
Russell P. Herrold, Jr.
Charles D. Minor
William W. Ellis, Jr.
Richard G. Ison
Kenneth D. Beck
Robert W. Minor
Morgan E. Shipman
Anne C. Griffin
Jacob E. Davis (Resident, Cincinnati, Ohio Office)
Ruth R. Longenecker (Resident, Cincinnati, Ohio Office)
Michael R. Thomas
David F. Axelrod
Glenn V. Whitaker (Resident at Cincinnati, Ohio Office)
Charles A. Schneider
Martyn T. Brodnik
Benjamin F. Suffron, III
Douglas L. Williams
Elizabeth T. Smith
Julia A. Davis
Linda R. Mendel

Representative Client: Honda of America Mfg., Inc.
Local Counsel: Abbott Laboratories; Anheuser-Busch, Inc.; Connecticut General Life Insurance Co.; Exxon Company U.S.A.; General Motors Corp.; Navistar International Corporation; Ohio Manufacturers Assn.; Ranco Inc.; Wendy's International, Inc.

For full biographical listings, see the Martindale-Hubbell Law Directory

---

CONNEAUT, Ashtabula Co. — (Refer to Painesville)

---

*DAYTON,** Montgomery Co.

ALTICK & CORWIN (AV)

1700 One Dayton Centre, One South Main Street, 45402
Telephone: 513-223-1201
Fax: 513-223-5100

MEMBERS OF FIRM

Hugh H. Altick (1905-1990)
Robert N. Farquhar
Marshall D. Ruchman
R. Paul Perkins, Jr.
Thomas R. Noland
Thomas M. Baggott
Robert B. Berner
Dennis J. Adkins
Richard A. Boucher
Philip B. Herron
Deborah J. Adler

OF COUNSEL

Raymond J. Pikna, Jr.

ASSOCIATES

Stephen M. McHugh
Donald K. Scott
Gregory P. Garner
Scott Alan Liberman

RETIRED

Robert B. Brumbaugh
Robert K. Corwin
Ronald H. McDonnell, Jr.

Representative Clients: City of Beavercreek; City of Centerville; The Miami Conservancy District; Miami Valley Cable Council; Woodland Cemetery Assn.

For full biographical listings, see the Martindale-Hubbell Law Directory

---

BIESER, GREER & LANDIS (AV)

400 Gem Plaza, Third and Main Streets, 45402
Telephone: 513-223-3277
FAX: 513-223-6339

MEMBERS OF FIRM

Irvin G. Bieser (1902-1989)
Rowan A. Greer, Jr. (1907-1967)
Robert K. Landis (1915-1991)
Charles D. Shook
Edward L. Shank
David C. Greer
Irvin G. Bieser, Jr.
Leo F. Krebs
Howard Penn Krisher, II
Edward H. Siddens
Michael W. Krumholtz
Gregory P. Dunsky
John F. Haviland, Jr.
David P. Williamson

ASSOCIATES

James H. Greer
James P. Nolan, II
Sharon L. Ovington
Konrad Kircher
Charles F. Shane
David P. Pierce

OF COUNSEL

Gerald D. Rapp

Representative Clients: Dayton Power & Light Company; Miami Valley Regional Transit Authority; Kettering Medical Center; The Dayton Foundation; Greater Dayton Public Television, Inc.; Medical Protective Company; St. Paul Insurance Company; Mead Corporation; Continental Loss Adjusting Services; Motorists Insurance Company.

For full biographical listings, see the Martindale-Hubbell Law Directory

---

CONWAY & HALL A LEGAL PROFESSIONAL ASSOCIATION (AV)

900 Courthouse Plaza Southwest, 45402
Telephone: 513-228-1111
Facsimile: 513-228-9340

Dennis L. Hall
W. Michael Conway

Wayne E. Southward
Elizabeth O. M. Troxell

For full biographical listings, see the Martindale-Hubbell Law Directory

Dayton—Continued

CREW, BUCHANAN & LOWE (AV)

Formerly Cowden, Pfarrer, Crew & Becker
2580 Kettering Tower, 45423-2580
Telephone: 513-223-6211
Facsimile: 513-223-7631

MEMBERS OF FIRM

Charles A. Craighead (1857-1926)
Robert E. Cowden (1886-1954)
Robert E. Cowden, Jr. (1910-1968)
Charles P. Pfarrer (1905-1984)
Philip Rohrer Becker (1905-1989)
Robert B. Crew
Joseph P. Buchanan
Charles D. Lowe
Jeffrey A. Swillinger
Robert J. Davidek

ASSOCIATES

R. Anne Shale
Dana K. Cole
James R. Crump
James G. Neary
Edith Slafka Willcox

Representative Clients: Chrysler Corporation; General Motors Corporation; Grandview/Southview Hospitals; James River Corporation; Saturn of Dayton, Inc.

For full biographical listings, see the Martindale-Hubbell Law Directory

FLANAGAN, LIEBERMAN, HOFFMAN & SWAIM (AV)

318 West Fourth Street, 45402
Telephone: 513-223-5200
Fax: 513-223-3335

MEMBERS OF FIRM

Thomas Angelo III
Patrick A. Flanagan
Charles F. Geidner
Robert D. Goelz
David L. Hall
Louis I. Hoffman
Emerson R. Keck
Don Edmond Kovich
Dennis A. Lieberman
Charles W. Slicer, Jr.
Bradley C. Smith
Wayne P. Stephan
James E. Swaim
Steven E. Yuhas

Frederick B. Lutz
V. Ellen Graham
Richard Hempfling
R. Todd Smith
Ellen C. Weprin
J. Donald Mottley
Lu Ann Stanley
Bruce E. Loving

Clarence J. Stewart (1901-1981)
Charles W. Slicer, Sr. (1914-1922)

References: Bank One, Dayton, NA; Society Bank, N.A.; The First National Bank, Dayton Ohio.

For full biographical listings, see the Martindale-Hubbell Law Directory

LOUIS & FROELICH A LEGAL PROFESSIONAL ASSOCIATION (AV)

1812 Kettering Tower, 45423
Telephone: 513-226-1776
FAX: 513-226-1945
Trotwood, Ohio Office: 101 East Main Street.
Telephone: 513-226-1776.

Herbert M. Louis
Gary L. Froelich
Jeffrey E. Froelich
Jeffrey A. Winwood
Marybeth W. Rutledge

F. Ann Crossman
James I. Weprin

Reference: Society Bank, N.A. of Dayton, Ohio.

For full biographical listings, see the Martindale-Hubbell Law Directory

PICKREL, SCHAEFFER & EBELING CO., L.P.A. (AV)

2700 Kettering Tower, 45423-2700
Telephone: 513-223-1130
Facsimile: 513-223-0339

William G. Pickrel (1931-1966)
Virgil Schaeffer (1932-1958)
Philip C. Ebeling (1931-1963)
Bradley J. Schaeffer (1935-1992)
Donald G. Schweller
Harry G. Ebeling
Thomas J. Harrington
Paul J. Winterhalter
Paul E. Zimmer
Richard J. Holzer
Alan B. Schaeffer
Janet K. Cooper
John W. Slagle
Andrew C. Storar
Jon M. Rosemeyer
David C. Korte

Beth W. Schaeffer
James W. Kelleher
Mary M. Biagioli
Paul H. Spaeth
Diane L. Gentile
Jeffrey S. Senney
L. Michael Bly
Joseph C. Hoskins
Joseph W. Meyer

(See Next Column)

OF COUNSEL

Gordon H. Savage

Representative Clients: Hearst Broadcasting Corp. (WDTN-TV); Marathon Oil Co.; Citizens Federal Bank, F.S.B., of Dayton; Allstate Insurance Co.; American Mutual Liability Co.; Miami Valley Cardiologists; American Aggregates; Sinclair Community College; Roberds Inc.; Bridgestone/Firestone; Appleton Paper Co.; SOFCO Erectors, Inc.

For full biographical listings, see the Martindale-Hubbell Law Directory

PORTER, WRIGHT, MORRIS & ARTHUR (AV)

One Dayton Centre, One South Main Street, 45402
Telephone: 513-228-2411; (800-533-4434)
Fax: 513-449-6820
Telex: 6503213584 MCI
Columbus, Ohio Office: 41 South High Street, 43215-6194.
Telephones: 614-227-2000; (800-533-2794).
Telex: 6503213584 MCI.
Fax: 614-227-2100.
Cincinnati, Ohio Office: 250 E. Fifth Street, 45202-4166.
Telephones: 513-381-4700; (800-582-5813);
Fax: 513-421-0991.
Cleveland, Ohio Office: 925 Euclid Avenue, 44115-1483.
Telephones: 216-443-9000; (800-824-1980).
Fax: 216-443-9011.
Washington, D.C. Office: 1233 20th Street, N.W., 20036-2395.
Telephones: 202-778-3000; (800-456-7962).
Fax: 202-778-3063.
Telex: 6503844872 MCI.
Naples, Florida Office: 4501 Tamiami Trail North, 33940-3060.
Telephones: 813-263-8898; (800-876-7962).
Fax: 813-436-2990.

RESIDENT MEMBERS

William G. Deas
Roland F. Eichner
Gary W. Gottschlich
Samuel L. Hagans, Jr.
John J. Heron
Jonathan Hollingsworth
Thomas A. Holton
C. Terry Johnson
Richard H. Packard
Robert E. Portune
Thomas H. Pyper
Walter Reynolds
R. Bruce Snyder

RESIDENT ASSOCIATES

Richard D. Anglin II
Linda S. Holmes
Charles Y. Kidwell, Jr.
Ronald J. Kozar
Joseph D. Smallwood
Lawrence S. Walter

OF COUNSEL

Thomas L. Czechowski
Chester E. Finn

Representative Clients: First National Bank of Dayton-Subsidiary of National City Corp.; Huntington National Bank of Dayton; The Ohio Casualty Insurance Co.

For full biographical listings, see the Martindale-Hubbell Law Directory

ROGERS & GREENBERG (AV)

2160 Kettering Tower, 45423
Telephone: 513-223-8171
Fax: 513-223-1649

MEMBERS OF FIRM

William A. Rogers, Jr.
Stanley Z. Greenberg
John M. Cloud
Barry W. Mancz
Keith R. Kearney

Richard L. Carr, Jr.
James G. Kordik
Carl D. Sherrets
L. Anthony Lush
Dawn S. Garrett

General Counsel for: Heartland Federal Credit Union; National Management Association; Moraine Materials Co.; Techway Industries, Inc.; Washington Township Park Board.

For full biographical listings, see the Martindale-Hubbell Law Directory

RICHARD G. SNELL (AV)

1212 Hulman Building, 45402
Telephone: 513-224-5297
Fax: 513-224-9926

For full biographical listings, see the Martindale-Hubbell Law Directory

THOMPSON, HINE AND FLORY (AV)

2000 Courthouse Plaza, N.E., 45402-1706
Telephone: 513-443-6600
Fax: 513-443-6637; 443-6635
Akron, Ohio Office: 50 S. Main Street, Suite 502, 44308-1828.
Telephone: 216-376-8090.
Fax: 216-376-8386.
Cincinnati, Ohio Office: 312 Walnut Street, 14th Floor, 45202-4029.
Telephone: 513-352-6700.
Fax: 513-241-4771.
Telex: 938003.

(See Next Column)

THOMPSON, HINE AND FLORY, *Dayton—Continued*

Cleveland, Ohio Office: 1100 National City Bank Building, 629 Euclid Avenue, 44114-3070.
Telephone: 216-566-5500.
Fax: 216-556-5583.
Telex: 980217.
Cable Address: "Thomflor".
Columbus, Ohio Office: One Columbus, 10 West Broad Street, 43215-3435.
Telephone: 614-469-3200.
Fax: 614-469-3361.
Palm Beach, Florida Office: 125 Worth Avenue, 33480-4466.
Telephone: 407-833-5900.
Fax: 407-833-5951.
Washington, D.C. Office: 1920 N Street, N.W., 20036-1601.
Telephone: 202-331-8800.
Fax: 202-331-8330.
Telex: 904173.
Cable Address: "Caglaw".
Brussels, Belgium Office: Rue des Chevaliers / Ridderstraat 14 - B.10, B - 1050.
Telephone: 011(32-2) 511-9326.
Fax: 011(32-2) 513-9206.

MEMBERS OF FIRM

Bruce M. Allman
J. Wray Blattner
Barry M. Block
Robert J. Brown
Lawrence T. Burick
Richard F. Carlile
Robert M. Curry
Thomas E. DeBrosse
Peter J. Donahue
Francesco A. Ferrante
Stanley A. Freedman
Sharen Swartz Gage
Jon M. Grogan (Not admitted in OH)
Timothy J. Hackert
Robert J. Hadley
J. Michael Herr
Donald J. Kinlin
Thomas J. Kirkwood
Thomas A. Knoth
Mark P. Levy
Theodore D. Lienesch
Bruce R. Lowry
Crofford J. Macklin, Jr.
Sue K. McDonnell
David A. Neuhardt
Allen R. Norris
David M. Rickert
Joseph M. Rigot (Partner-in-Charge in Dayton)
Arik A. Sherk
Howard N. Thiele, Jr.

ASSOCIATES

Joyce Z. Anderson
Mark A. Conway
Steven J. Davis
Robert M. Henry
Deborah D. Hunt
Teresa D. Jones
Scott A. King
Michael W. McArdle
Laurie Nicholson
Patricia C. Cecil
Brian J. O'Connell
Anne B. Pellot
Thomas M. Phillips
Philip A. Reid
Patrick M. Richart

SENIOR ATTORNEYS

Richard A. Ciambrone

OF COUNSEL

Robert E. Hickey, Jr.

For full biographical listings, see the Martindale-Hubbell Law Directory

---

TURNER, GRANZOW & HOLLENKAMP (AV)

50 East Third Street, 45402
Telephone: 513-228-4184
Telecopier: 513-228-4708

MEMBERS OF FIRM

Wellmore B. Turner (1888-1980)
Nicholas C. Hollenkamp
Ames Gardner, Jr.
Wayne H. Dawson
Charles S. Goodwin
Joseph A. Koenig
Kathryn A. Lamme

William B. Fecher

RETIRED

Paul H. Granzow

For full biographical listings, see the Martindale-Hubbell Law Directory

---

TYE & TYE (AV)

Suite 120, 2600 Far Hills Avenue, 45419
Telephone: 513-298-7078
Telecopier: 513-298-3104

MEMBERS OF FIRM

Rose R. Tye
Timothy N. Tye

References: The First National Bank; Bank One, Dayton N.A.

For full biographical listings, see the Martindale-Hubbell Law Directory

---

YOUNG & ALEXANDER CO., L.P.A. (AV)

Suite 100, 367 West Second Street, 45402
Telephone: 513-224-9291
Telecopier: 513-224-9679
Cincinnati, Ohio Office: 110 Boggs Lane, Suite 350.
Telephone: 513-326-5555.
FAX: 513-326-5550.

(See Next Column)

Robert F. Young (1905-1978)
Robert C. Alexander (1912-1982)
James M. Brennan
Anthony R. Kidd
Mark R. Chilson
John A. Smalley
A. Mark Segreti, Jr.
Margaret R. Young
Steven O. Dean
Barbara A. Lahmann
Ronald E. Mount

James K. Hemenway
Kenneth J. Ignozzi
William J. Moran, Jr.

Counsel for: The Children's Medical Center, Dayton, Ohio; The Colonial Stair & Woodwork Co.; The Greater Dayton Area Hospital Assn.; Mike-Sell's Potato Chip Co.; Moorman Pontiac, Inc.
Local Counsel for: Colonial Penn Insurance Co.; John Hancock Mutual Life Insurance Co.; Hertz Corp.; State Farm Insurance Co.

For full biographical listings, see the Martindale-Hubbell Law Directory

---

*DELAWARE,** Delaware Co.

MANOS, MARTIN, PERGRAM & BROWNING (AV)

40 North Sandusky Street, 43015-1995
Telephone: 614-363-1313;
Columbus Direct Line: 614-548-4825
Telecopier: 614-548-4156
Columbus, Ohio Office: Martin, Pergram & Browning, L.P.A., 69 East Wilson Bridge Road, P.O. Box 6017.
Telephone: 614-436-8000.
Telecopier: 614-846-4691.

SENIOR COUNSEL

Peter J. Manos

Stephen D. Martin
Dennis L. Pergram
William J. Browning
Craig B. Paynter
James M. Dietz
Wade E. Harrison
Karen A. Visocan

For full biographical listings, see the Martindale-Hubbell Law Directory

---

DOVER, Tuscarawas Co.

MARIO D. CORSI (AV)

117 East Third Street, 44622
Telephone: 216-364-4414
Fax: 216-364-4472

References: The Huntington National Bank; Bank One of Dover.

EAST LIVERPOOL, Columbiana Co. — (Refer to Alliance)

EAST PALESTINE, Columbiana Co. — (Refer to Alliance)

*EATON,** Preble Co.

BENNETT & BENNETT (AV)

Bennett Law Building, 200 West Main Street, 45320
Telephone: 513-456-4100
Fax: 513-456-5100

MEMBERS OF FIRM

Lloyd B. Bennett (1909-1983)
Herd L. Bennett
Gray W. Bennett

LEGAL SUPPORT PERSONNEL

LEGAL ASSISTANTS

Sandra K. Shafer
Laura A. Toschlog
Debbie Bennett

Representative Clients: The National Hummel Foundation and Museum; Star Bank of Preble County, Ohio; Eaton National Bank & Trust Co.; First National Bank of Southwestern Ohio; Brookville National Bank; Farm Credit Services of Mid-America; Miller's Super Markets, Inc.; Northedge Shopping Center, Inc.; Herman M. Brubaker Registered Holstein Cattle; The Eaton Foundation.

For full biographical listings, see the Martindale-Hubbell Law Directory

---

*ELYRIA,** Lorain Co.

SPIKE & MECKLER (AV)

1551 West River Street North, 44035
Telephone: 216-324-5353
Fax: 216-324-6529

MEMBERS OF FIRM

Allen S. Spike
Stephen G. Meckler
Douglas M. Brill

Representative Clients: Orlean Co.; ABC Management.
Agents and Approved Attorneys for: The Ohio Bar Title Insurance Co.
References: Premier Bank; Northern Savings & Loan.

For full biographical listings, see the Martindale-Hubbell Law Directory

*FINDLAY,** Hancock Co.

Oxley, Malone, Fitzgerald & Hollister (AV)

301 East Main Cross Street, P.O. Box 1086, 45840
Telephone: 419-422-8713
Fax: 419-422-6495

COUNSEL
Garver Oxley

MEMBERS OF FIRM
Michael J. Malone — Dennis M. Fitzgerald
Robert B. Hollister

ASSOCIATES
Michael E. Gilb — Teresa S. Glover

OF COUNSEL
Julie A. Davenport

LEGAL SUPPORT PERSONNEL
Laura L. Nye — Ann M. Berry

Representative Clients: Buckeye Union Insurance Co.; Hancock-Wood Electric Cooperative, Inc.; American States Insurance Company; Allstate Insurance Company; Auto-Owners Insurance Company; Shelby Mutual Insurance Company; Western Reserve Group; Grange Mutual Insurance Company.

For full biographical listings, see the Martindale-Hubbell Law Directory

Rakestraw & Rakestraw (AV)

119 East Crawford Street, 45840
Telephone: 419-422-9455
Fax: 419-422-2482

MEMBERS OF FIRM
Russell E. Rakestraw — Gregory A. Rakestraw

ASSOCIATES
Robert L. Hunt — Joyce C. Hall-Yates

Representative Clients: Budd Co.; Ohio Power Co.

For full biographical listings, see the Martindale-Hubbell Law Directory

FOSTORIA, Seneca, Hancock & Wood Cos. — (Refer to Tiffin)

*FREMONT,** Sandusky Co. — (Refer to Tiffin)

GALION, Crawford Co. — (Refer to Mansfield)

*GEORGETOWN,** Brown Co. — (Refer to Batavia)

*GREENVILLE,** Darke Co.

Goubeaux & Goubeaux (AV)

100 Washington Avenue, P.O. Box 158, 45331
Telephone: 513-548-2211
FAX: Available Upon Request

MEMBERS OF FIRM
Edward A. Goubeaux, Jr. (1906-1964)
Jerome H. Goubeaux (1908-1978)
James J. Goubeaux
Robert L. Morris
Eric H. Brand

Representative Clients: Fifth Third Bank; Osgood State Bank; Second National Bank; United Telephone Company of Ohio.
Local Counsel for: Penn Central Co.; Corning Glass Works; The St. Henry Bank, St. Henry, Ohio; New Amsterdam Casualty Co.

For full biographical listings, see the Martindale-Hubbell Law Directory

*HILLSBORO,** Highland Co. — (Refer to Wilmington)

*IRONTON,** Lawrence Co.

Spears & Spears (AV)

122 South Fourth Street, 45638
Telephone: 614-532-5815; 614-532-6913

MEMBERS OF FIRM
Harold D. Spears — David R. Spears

References: Star Bank; National City Bank.

For full biographical listings, see the Martindale-Hubbell Law Directory

*JACKSON,** Jackson Co. — (Refer to Portsmouth)

*JEFFERSON,** Ashtabula Co. — (Refer to Painesville)

*KENTON,** Hardin Co. — (Refer to Lima)

*LANCASTER,** Fairfield Co.

Huddle and Rose Co., L.P.A. (AV)

309 East Main Street, 43130
Telephone: 614-687-0506
Fax: 614-653-9405

(See Next Column)

John T. Huddle — Martha A. Rose

Reference: Fairfield National, Division of the Park National Bank.

For full biographical listings, see the Martindale-Hubbell Law Directory

Miller, Barnes and Christian (AV)

309 East Main Street, 43130-3851
Telephone: 614-653-3281
Fax: 614-653-9405

MEMBERS OF FIRM
Donald C. Miller (1903-1984) — Kenneth M. Barnes
T. Michael Christian

Representative Clients: General Machine & Mould Co., Inc.; McGraw Oldsmobile, Inc.; Society Bank.
Approved Attorneys for: Ohio Bar Title; Lawyers Title Insurance Corp.; The Guarantee Title & Trust Co.

For full biographical listings, see the Martindale-Hubbell Law Directory

*LEBANON,** Warren Co.

Kaufman & Florence (AV)

144 East Mulberry Street, P.O. Box 280, 45036
Telephone: 513-932-1515; 423-1363; 421-6456
Fax: 513-932-9172

MEMBERS OF FIRM
William H. Kaufman — Mark T. Florence

Representative Clients: Miami Valley Trotting, Inc.; Farm Credit Services; Lebanon Raceway; Lebanon Citizens National Bank;
Local Counsel for: Cincinnati Gas & Electric Co.; Ohio Casualty Insurance Co.; Western Water Company.
Approved Agent and Attorneys for: Ohio Bar Title Insurance Co.; Old Republic Nat'l Title Ins. Co.; Farmers Home Administration.

For full biographical listings, see the Martindale-Hubbell Law Directory

Young and Hubbell (AV)

Suite 300 Lebanon Bank Building, 45036
Telephone: 513-932-6015
Fax: 513-932-5841

MEMBERS OF FIRM
Marvin E. Young — Fred C. Hubbell
Warren C. Young

Representative Clients: Lebanon Citizen's National Bank; Lebanon Production Credit Assn.; Agri-Urban, Inc.

For full biographical listings, see the Martindale-Hubbell Law Directory

*LIMA,** Allen Co.

Cory, Meredith, Witter, Roush & Cheney A Legal Professional Association (AV)

607 Savings Building, P.O. Box 1217, 45802-1217
Telephone: 419-228-6365
Fax: 419-228-5319

Frank B. Cory
James E. Meredith
Richard E. Meredith
Donald J. Witter
W. Thomas Roush
David A. Cheney
Michael P. Anderson
Robert J. Meredith

General Counsel for: Lima Broadcasting Co.; West Ohio Gas Co.; Bank One, Lima, N.A.
Local Counsel for: British Petroleum; State Farm Insurance Company (fire and auto); Auto Owners Insurance Co.; Cincinnati Insurance; GRE America.

For full biographical listings, see the Martindale-Hubbell Law Directory

Robenalt & Robenalt (AV)

211-215 North Elizabeth Street, 45801-4302
Telephone: 419-229-0054
Telecopier: 419-228-3631
Osprey, Florida Office: 650 North Tamiami Trail. P.O. Box 460. 34229.
Telephone: 813-966-7755.
Fax: 813-966-6678.

MEMBERS OF FIRM
John A. Robenalt — John F. Robenalt (Resident, Osprey, Florida Office)

Representative Clients: Dot Lines, Inc.; Top Line Express; Warehouse Associates, Inc.; The Green and Sawyer Co.; Gooding Gallery of Homes; Allen County Regional Transit Authority.
Reference: Bank One, Lima, Ohio.

For full biographical listings, see the Martindale-Hubbell Law Directory

LINDSEY, Washington Co. — (Refer to Alliance)

*LISBON,** Columbiana Co. — (Refer to Alliance)

*LOGAN,** Hocking Co. — (Refer to Lancaster)

*LONDON,** Madison Co. — (Refer to Columbus)

LORAIN, Lorain Co.

COOK AND BATISTA CO., L.P.A. (AV)

28 Professional Building, 209 6th Street, 44052
Telephone: 216-244-6224. Cleveland - 216-871-0828
Fax: 216-244-6368

D. A. Cook (1883-1968)
Dan K. Cook (1915-1976)
Daniel P. Batista
Daniel A. Cook
David C. Wiersma
James W. Moennich

D. Chris Cook

General Counsel for: The Lorain National Bank; The Lorain Telephone Co.; Lorain County Medical Society; St. Joseph Hospital; Joyce Buick-Pontiac, Inc.
Local Counsel for: Ohio Edison Co.; Greyhound Corp.; B.F. Goodrich Co.; Century Telephone Co.; Gross Plumbing, Inc.; Liberty Ford Lincoln-Mercury, Inc.; Lorain County Association of Realtors; Northeast Ohio Home Therapies, Inc.

For full biographical listings, see the Martindale-Hubbell Law Directory

WARHOLA, O'TOOLE, LOUGHMAN, ALDERMAN & STUMPHAUZER (AV)

502 Broadway, P.O. Box 528, 44052-0528
Telephone: 216-244-1212
Telecopier: 216-245-9035
Elyria, Ohio Office: 209 Robinson Building.
Telephone: 216-323-5478.
Amherst, Ohio Office: 238 Church Street.
Telephone: 216-984-2481.

MEMBERS OF FIRM

Austin W. O'Toole (1904-1976)
Andrew J. Warhola
Dennis M. O'Toole
Michael J. Loughman
Larry D. Alderman (Resident at Elyria Office)
Kenneth S. Stumphauzer

ASSOCIATES

Abraham Lieberman
David K. Smith
Sally Drews Brodbeck
Daniel D. Mason
Jay C. Marcie

OF COUNSEL

Robert J. Fetterman (Retired)

References: The Central Trust Company of Northern Ohio, N.A.; Lorain National Bank.

For full biographical listings, see the Martindale-Hubbell Law Directory

WICKENS, HERZER & PANZA A LEGAL PROFESSIONAL ASSOCIATION (AV)

1144 West Erie Avenue, P.O. Box 840, 44052-0840
Telephone: 216-246-5268;
Elyria: 216-236-3921
Telecopier: 216-244-4380
Cleveland Direct Line: 216-447-4418
Cleveland, Ohio Office: Corporate Plaza II, Suite 160, 6480 Rockside Woods Boulevard, South.
Telephone: 216-447-4418.
Telecopier: 216-447-0998.

William G. Wickens
David L. Herzer
Richard D. Panza
Robert P. Ellis, Jr.
Thomas Pillari
Richard A. Naegele
Marsha L. Nicoloff
William F. Kolis, Jr.
Patricia F. Jacobson
Charles J. Pawlukiewicz
Joseph G. Corsaro
Mark P. Altieri
Brian J. Jereb
Linda C. Ashar
John D. Rybarczyk
Matthew W. Nakon
Ralph R. Lustri
William P. Prescott
Mary J. Satava
Russell R. Aukerman
Ginger A. Fuller
William J. Koval, JR.

Representative Clients: The Lorain Journal; Norfolk & Western Railway; Lorain Community Hospital; Drs. Russell, Berkebile & Associates, Radiologists; Bob Morris Pontiac and GMC Truck, Inc.; Ross Environmental Services, Inc.

For full biographical listings, see the Martindale-Hubbell Law Directory

*MANSFIELD,** Richland Co.

BROWN, BEMILLER, MURRAY & MCINTYRE (AV)

70 Park Avenue West, P.O. Box 728, 44901-0728
Telephone: 419-525-1611
FAX: 419-525-3810

(See Next Column)

MEMBERS OF FIRM

John T. Brown
F. Loyal Bemiller
D. Kim Murray
William T. McIntyre
Jeffrey Molyet
Adam Vetter, Jr.
J. Jeffrey Heck
Arthur D. Brannan (Not admitted in OH)

Local Counsel for: Society Bank & Trust; Travelers Insurance Co.; United States Fidelity & Guaranty Co.; Ohio Edison Co.; Montgomery Ward & Co.; Shiloh Corp.; Westfield Ins. Co.; Commercial Union Ins. Co.; Mansfield News Journal; Peoples Federal Savings Bank.

For full biographical listings, see the Martindale-Hubbell Law Directory

WELDON, HUSTON & KEYSER (AV)

Ninth and Tenth Floors, Bank One Building, 28 Park Ave W, 44902-1695
Telephone: 419-524-9811
Fax: 419-522-5758

MEMBERS OF FIRM

William McE. Weldon (1868-1952)
C. H. Huston (1871-1957)
Henry P. Huston (1903-1984)
George Hall
Richard R. Fowler
John H. Siegenthaler
David D. Carto
John S. Hire
Richard H. Otto

ASSOCIATES

John Allen Holmes
Michael P. Morley

OF COUNSEL

George H. Keyser

Representative Clients: Bank One, Mansfield; Mansfield General Hospital, Corp.; The Medical Protective Co.; Mechanics Bank; Hi-Stat Manufacturing Co., Inc.; Motorists Insurance Companies; Whitey's Auto Mall; United Telephone Long Distance; Milliron Waste Management; Richland Nursing Homes, Inc.

For full biographical listings, see the Martindale-Hubbell Law Directory

MARTINS FERRY, Belmont Co. — (Refer to Steubenville)

*MARYSVILLE,** Union Co.

ALLEN, YURASEK & MERKLIN (AV)

233 West Fifth Street, P.O. Box 391, 43040-0391
Telephone: 513-642-4070
Telecopier: 513-644-4390

MEMBERS OF FIRM

Gwynn Sanders (1906-1989)
David F. Allen
Stephen J. Yurasek
Jeffrey A. Merklin

General Counsel for: Ohio Grain Co.; Conklin Dairy Farms, Inc.; Richwood Banking Co.; Dana W. Morey Community Services, Inc.
Local Counsel for: State Auto Mutual Insurance Co.; John Hancock Mutual Life Insurance Co.; BancOhio National Bank; Auto-Owners Mutual Insurance Co.; Nestle, Inc.; Cincinnati Insurance Co.

For full biographical listings, see the Martindale-Hubbell Law Directory

*MCARTHUR,** Vinton Co. — (Refer to Wellston)

*MCCONNELSVILLE,** Morgan Co. — (Refer to Zanesville)

*MEDINA,** Medina Co.

BROWN AND AMODIO A LEGAL PROFESSIONAL ASSOCIATION (AV)

109 West Liberty Street, P.O. Box 1117, 44258
Telephone: 216-725-8816
FAX: 216-723-5448

David N. Brown
James A. Amodio

Rochelle E. Boland

General Counsel for: The Old Phoenix National Bank.
Representative Clients: Aztec Imports, Inc.; Interstate Systems, Inc.

For full biographical listings, see the Martindale-Hubbell Law Directory

MARCO, MARCO & BAILEY (AV)

Gazette Building, 52 Public Square, 44256-2204
Telephone: 216-725-0030;
Cleveland Direct Line: 216-273-5696
Akron Direct Line: 216-336-0006
Fax: 216-722-4888

Richard J. Marco
Daniel J. Marco
Steve C. Bailey
Mary Beth Corrigan

For full biographical listings, see the Martindale-Hubbell Law Directory

MIDDLETOWN, Butler Co.

FROST & JACOBS (AV)

400 First National Bank Building, 2 North Main Street, 45042-1981
Telephone: 513-422-2001
Telecopier: 513-422-3010
Cincinnati, Ohio Office: 2500 PNC Center, 201 East Fifth Street.
Telephone: 513-651-6800.
Telecopier: 513-651-6981.
Columbus, Ohio Office: One Columbus, 10 West Broad Street.
Telephone: 614-464-1211.
Telecopier: 614-464-1737.
Lexington, Kentucky Office: 1100 Vine Center Tower, 333 West Vine Street.
Telephone: 606-524-1100.
Telecopier: 606-253-2990.
Naples, Florida Office: Northern Trust Building, 4001 Tamiami Trail North, Suite 220.
Telephone: 813-261-0582.
Telecopier: 813-261-2083.

RESIDENT MEMBERS

Thomas A. Swope | Donald L. Crain

SENIOR ATTORNEY

Daniel J. Picard

ASSOCIATES

William L. Sennett, III | Thomas B. Allen

OF COUNSEL

Barry J. Levey

Representative Clients: Armco Inc.; The Cincinnati Gas & Electric Company; First National Bank of Southwestern Ohio; McGraw Construction Co., Inc.; International Paper Co.; Square D Co.
Labor Relations Counsel for: Middletown Board of Education; Champion International; Butler County, Ohio; City of Hamilton, Ohio.

For full biographical listings, see the Martindale-Hubbell Law Directory

RATHMAN, COMBS, SCHAEFER & KAUP (AV)

First National Bank Building, 2 Main Street, 45042
Telephone: 513-424-1660
Fax: 513-424-7467

MEMBERS OF FIRM

William E. Rathman | Gene E. Schaefer
C. Edward Combs | Gary H. Kaup

For full biographical listings, see the Martindale-Hubbell Law Directory

WILMER & GREATHOUSE (AV)

200 Savings & Loan Building, 45044
Telephone: 513-423-5718; 423-5719

MEMBERS OF FIRM

G. W. A. Wilmer (1890-1976) | Richard A. Wilmer
C. Richard Greathouse, Jr.

Representative Clients: Armco, Inc.; Midfed Savings Bank; Middletown Area Development Enterprise, Inc.; The William Sebald Realty Co.; Guyler Buick, Inc.; Wilson-Schramm Memorial Homes; Dohn Hardware and Paint Co.
Approved Attorneys for: Ohio Bar Title Insurance Co.; Lawyers Title Insurance Corp.

For full biographical listings, see the Martindale-Hubbell Law Directory

*MILLERSBURG,** Holmes Co. — (Refer to Wooster)

MONTPELIER, Williams Co. — (Refer to Bryan)

*MT. GILEAD,** Morrow Co. — (Refer to Mansfield)

*NEWARK,** Licking Co.

JONES, NORPELL, LIST, MILLER & HOWARTH (AV)

2 North First Street, P.O. Box 4010, 43058-4010
Telephone: 614-345-9801
Telefax: 614-345-6031

MEMBERS OF FIRM

A. David List | J. Michael King
Jack Miller | C. Herbert Koehler, Jr.
Rodney L. Howarth | Joseph A. Robison
Dennis E. Dove

OF COUNSEL

Thomas E. Norpell

Representative Clients: Spencer-Walker Press, Inc.; P & F Trucking, Inc.

For full biographical listings, see the Martindale-Hubbell Law Directory

MORROW, GORDON & BYRD (AV)

33 West Main Street, P.O. Box 4190, 43058-4190
Telephone: 614-345-9611;
Columbus: 614-221-4810

(See Next Column)

MEMBERS OF FIRM

L. James Gordon | Steven T. Greene
Martin D. Altmaier | James R. Cooper
Glenn A. White | John W. Noecker
A. Terrance Treneff | Adam K. Vernau

ASSOCIATES

W. David Branstool

OF COUNSEL

E. Clark Morrow | Donald M. Byrd

General Counsel for: Denison University; Ohio State Grange Mutual Insurance Co.; Weakley Apartments, Inc.; Newark Asphalt Paving Co.; Licking Memorial Hospital.
Local Counsel for: Motorists Mutual Insurance Co.; The Ohio Casualty Insurance Co.; The Park National Bank, Granville, Ohio.

For full biographical listings, see the Martindale-Hubbell Law Directory

*NEW LEXINGTON,** Perry Co. — (Refer to Lancaster)

*NORWALK,** Huron Co.

CARPENTER, PAFFENBARGER & MCGIMPSEY (AV)

Citizens National Bank Building, P.O. Box 737, 44857-0737
Telephone: 419-668-4441
Fax: 419-663-3385

Lawrence S. Carpenter (1914-1986)

OF COUNSEL

Thomas L. Paffenbarger (Retired)

MEMBERS OF FIRM

Earl R. McGimpsey | Paul F. Meyerhoefer

Representative Clients: Norfolk and Western Railway Co.; Travelers Insurance Cos.; Nationwide Mutual Insurance Cos.; Motorists Insurance Cos.; Grange Mutual Cos.; Westfield Cos.; Auto-Owners Insurance Co.; Union Bank & Savings Co., Monroeville, Ohio.

OAK HARBOR, Ottawa Co. — (Refer to Sandusky)

*OTTAWA,** Putnam Co. — (Refer to Lima)

*PAINESVILLE,** Lake Co.

BAKER, HACKENBERG & COLLINS CO., L.P.A. (AV)

77 North St. Clair Street, 44077
Telephone: 216-354-4364;
Cleveland Direct Line: 216-951-3295
Fax: 216-354-0135

I. James Hackenberg | Richard L. Collins, Jr.

OF COUNSEL

Richard A. Hennig

Representative Clients: Cleveland Electric Illuminating Co.; City of Mentor; Motorists Mutual Insurance Co.; Nationwide Insurance Co.; State Automobile Insurance Co.; Ohio Bell Telephone Co.; Hartford Insurance Group; Classic Chevrolet.

For full biographical listings, see the Martindale-Hubbell Law Directory

*PAULDING,** Paulding Co. — (Refer to Defiance)

PAYNE, Paulding Co. — (Refer to Defiance)

PERRYSBURG, Wood Co.

LEATHERMAN, WITZLER, DOMBEY & HART (AV)

353 Elm Street, 43551
Telephone: 419-874-3536
Fax: 419-874-3899

MEMBERS OF FIRM

Wayne M. Leatherman | James H. Hart
Earl N. Witzler | Timothy J. Brown
Philip L. Dombey | T. Hamilton Noll
Kay L. Howard

Representative Clients: Cook Insurance Agency, Inc.; Craig Transportation Co.; Ed Schmidt Pontiac, Inc.; Perrysburg Board of Education; Perrysburg Township Trustees; Service Travel Co.; Toledo Impression Co. (Dies & Molds); Village of Holland; 577 Foundation.

For full biographical listings, see the Martindale-Hubbell Law Directory

PIKETON, Pike Co. — (Refer to Jackson)

*PORTSMOUTH,** Scioto Co.

C. CLAYTON JOHNSON CO. A LEGAL PROFESSIONAL ASSOCIATION (AV)

400 Bank One Plaza, P.O. Box 1505, 45662
Telephone: 614-354-4200
Telecopier: 614-353-2413

C. Clayton Johnson

(See Next Column)

C. CLAYTON JOHNSON CO. A LEGAL PROFESSIONAL ASSOCIATION, *Portsmouth—Continued*

Stephen L. Oliver

OF COUNSEL

Robert Kurt McCurdy

Representative Clients: Bank One, Portsmouth, N.A.; OSCO Industries, Inc.; Citizens Deposit Bank and Trust; First National Bank of Lewis County, Kentucky; Home Federal Savings and Loan; McDonalds Corp.; National Maintenance & Repair, Inc.; McGinnis, Inc.
Approved Attorney for: Lawyers Title Insurance Co.

For full biographical listings, see the Martindale-Hubbell Law Directory

*RAVENNA,** Portage Co.

KANE, SICURO & SIMON (AV)

101 East Main Street, P.O. Box 167, 44266
Telephone: 216-296-3868;
Akron Direct Line: 216-678-9572
Facsimile: 216-296-7100

MEMBERS OF FIRM

H. W. Kane
William G. Bangas (1923-1983)
Thomas J. Sicuro
Ronald J. Kane
Terry G. P. Kane
William G. Simon

General Counsel for: Camelot Inc.; Paradise Lakes Inc.; English Realty.
Local Counsel for: State Automobile Mutual Insurance Co.; Household Finance Corp.; The Kemper Group; Society Corp.; Fireman's Fund Insurance Co.; Shelby Mutual Insurance Group.; U.S. Truck Lines, Inc.; Ravenna Savings & Loan Assn.

For full biographical listings, see the Martindale-Hubbell Law Directory

*ST. CLAIRSVILLE,** Belmont Co. — (Refer to Steubenville)

*SANDUSKY,** Erie Co.

BUCKINGHAM, HOLZAPFEL, ZEIHER, WALDOCK & SCHELL CO., L.P.A. (AV)

414 Wayne Street, P.O. Box 929, 44870
Telephone: 419-627-0414
Fax: 419-627-0009
Vermilion, Ohio Office: 678 Main Street.
Telephone: 216-967-6136.
Fax: 216-967-8541.

F. H. Buckingham (1901-1971)
George C. Steinemann (Retired)
Richard D. Holzapfel (Retired)
Arthur W. Zeiher (Retired)
Thomas S. Buckingham
Frederick D. Waldock
Lawrence H. Schell *
Maurice L. McDermond, Jr.
Kevin J. Zeiher
John D. Frankel
W. Zack Dolyk *

John D. Latchney
Troy Wisehart

Local Counsel: Erie County Cablevision, Inc.
General Counsel: Sandusky Newspapers, Inc.; The Cooke Properties; Firelands Community Hospital.
*Sandusky and Vermilion, Ohio Offices

For full biographical listings, see the Martindale-Hubbell Law Directory

FLYNN, PY & KRUSE A LEGAL PROFESSIONAL ASSOCIATION (AV)

165 East Washington Row, 44870
Telephone: 419-625-8324
Fax: 419-625-9007
Port Clinton, Ohio Office: 2-D Jefferson Building, 130 Jefferson Street.
Telephone: 419-734-3174.
Fax: 419-734-3175.

James F. Flynn (1887-1963)
John R. Py (1908-1969)
Richard R. Kruse (Retired)
Raymond N. Watts (Retired)
Melvyn J. Stauffer
William C. Steuk
Charles W. Waterfield
John D. Py
John A. Coppeler
John E. Rosino
James W. Hart
Richard A. Cathey
Mary Jane Stauffer Hill
Christopher M. Marinko

Randolph E. Digges

Representative Clients: Allstate Insurance Co.; Delco Chassis Division of General Motors; First National Bank of Bellevue; National City Bank of Sandusky; Nationwide Mutual Insurance Co.; Norfolk and Southern Corp.; Ohio Edison Co.; State Farm Insurance Co.; United Ohio Insurance Co.; Westfield Insurance Co.

For full biographical listings, see the Martindale-Hubbell Law Directory

*SPRINGFIELD,** Clark Co.

COLE ACTON HARMON DUNN A LEGAL PROFESSIONAL ASSOCIATION (AV)

Riverbend Condominiums, 333 North Limestone Street, P.O. Box 1687, 45501
Telephone: 513-322-0891
Fax: 513-322-9931

John M. Cole (1879-1960)
Abe Gardner (1903-1964)
Fred M. Cole (1909-1975)
George W. Cole (1914-1982)
Robert C. Acton (1924-1987)
James A. Harmon
Edward W. Dunn
Charles P. Crabill
Barry P. Reich
William C. Hicks
Phyllis S. Nedelman
Joseph A. Dunn

Representative Clients: Society National Bank; National City Bank; Huntington National Bank; Navistar International; Springfield Newspapers, Inc.; Fulmer Supermarkets, Inc.; Chakeres Theatres Inc.; Springfield Metropolitan Housing Authority; Prudential Insurance Company of America; Springfield Area Chamber of Commerce.

For full biographical listings, see the Martindale-Hubbell Law Directory

MARTIN, BROWNE, HULL & HARPER (AV)

Credit Life Building, One South Limestone Street, 45501-1488
Telephone: 513-324-5541
Telecopier: 513-325-5432

MEMBERS OF FIRM

Oscar T. Martin (1848-1913)
Paul C. Martin (1876-1939)
Homer C. Corry (1887-1955)
John C. Durfey (1902-1960)
Anson E. Hull (1915-1983)
Robin R. Freeman
Hugh Barnett
Robert E. Harley
Glenn W. Collier
Walter A. Wildman
David A. Weaver
William R. Groves
Steven J. McCready
Daniel C. Harkins

OF COUNSEL

Bitner Browne
John O. Harper

RETIRED PARTNER

Oscar T. Martin

ASSOCIATES

Richard F. Heil, Jr.
Regina Watson

Counsel for: Ohio Masonic Home; Antioch University; Vernay Laboratories; Vining Industries.
Local Counsel for: BancOhio National Bank; Ohio Edison Co.; Robbins & Myers, Inc.; The Kissell Company; Travelers Insurance Co.; Buckeye Union Insurance Co.; The Rital Corporation.

For full biographical listings, see the Martindale-Hubbell Law Directory

*STEUBENVILLE,** Jefferson Co.

KINSEY, ALLEBAUGH & KING (AV)

200 Sinclair Building, P.O. Box 249, 43952
Telephone: 614-282-1900

MEMBERS OF FIRM

W. I. Kinsey (1876-1962)
Carl F. Allebaugh (1896-1970)
Robert P. King

ASSOCIATES

Robert C. Hargrave

OF COUNSEL

Adam E. Scurti
Otto A. Jack, Jr.

Solicitors for: Consolidated Rail Corporation/Penn Central Transportation Co.
Attorneys for: Ohio Power Co.; Columbia Gas Company of Ohio; Ohio Bell Telephone Co.; Ohio Edison Co.; Continental Casualty Co.; Allstate Insurance Co.; Westfield Cos.; Federal Insurance Co.; Unibank.

For full biographical listings, see the Martindale-Hubbell Law Directory

SWANTON, Fulton Co.

THE MCQUADES CO., L.P.A. (AV)

Lincoln at Broadway, P.O. Box 237, 43558
Telephone: 419-826-0055
Fax: 419-825-3871
Archbold, Ohio Office: 200 N. Defiance Street.
Telephone: 419-445-3755.
Whitehouse, Ohio Office: 6632 Providence Street.
Telephone: 419-877-0746.

Daniel P. McQuade
Colin J. McQuade

Alan J. Lehenbauer

OF COUNSEL

Richard B. McQuade

For full biographical listings, see the Martindale-Hubbell Law Directory

*TIFFIN,** Seneca Co.

Tomb & Hering (AV)

84-88 South Washington Street, P.O. Box 767, 44883-0767
Telephone: 419-447-2521
FAX: Available Upon Request

MEMBERS OF FIRM

Webb D. Tomb (1907-1977)
Charles D. Hering, Jr. (1927-1992)
James D. Supance
James S. Nordholt, Jr.
Brent T. Howard
Susan Hering Howard

Representative Clients: Continental Cablevision of Ohio, Inc.; North-Central Electric Cooperative, Inc.; Webster Industries, Inc.; Corbin Corp.; Old Fort Banking Co.; Heidelberg College; Superior Distributing Co., Inc.; Cincinnati Insurance Co.

For full biographical listings, see the Martindale-Hubbell Law Directory

*TOLEDO,** Lucas Co.

Brown, Schlageter, Craig & Shindler (AV)

1200 Edison Plaza, 300 Madison Avenue, 43604-1537
Telephone: 419-243-6281
Fax: 419-243-0129

MEMBERS OF FIRM

Earl F. Boxell (1894-1987)
John W. Bebout (1898-1986)
Robert Nelson Torbet (1902-1986)
Harald F. Craig
James V. Shindler, Jr.
Carter Neff
William R. Ahern
Martin J. Holmes
John J. Schlageter, Jr.
Charles K. Boxell
Daniel A. Worline
David J. Simko
John W. Rozic
James E. Morgan
Paul S. Goldberg
Mark E. Lupe
Catherine H. Noble
Jeffrey J. Perkins
Mary E. Smith
James A. Sulewski
Scott A. Winckowski
Louis J. Yoppolo

ASSOCIATES

Eric W. Slack
Richard L. Emery

OF COUNSEL

Charles Earl Brown
Bernard R. Baker, II
John J. Schlageter

Counsel for: Building Service Contractors Association, Inc.; Century Equipment, Inc.; Funeral Directors Association of Northwestern Ohio, Inc.; Gutter Suppliers, Inc.; Medical College of Ohio at Toledo; Metropolitan Distributing Co.; City of Oregon; Stanbery Homes, Inc.; Toledo Clutch & Brake Service; Turner Vault Co.

For full biographical listings, see the Martindale-Hubbell Law Directory

Doyle, Lewis & Warner (AV)

202 North Erie Street, P.O. Box 2168, 43603
Telephone: 419-248-1500
Fax: 419-248-2002

John H. Doyle (1844-1919)
Charles T. Lewis (1850-1918)
Milo J. Warner (1891-1968)
Melvin P. Lewis (1913-1994)

MEMBERS OF FIRM

Steven Timonere
Richard F. Ellenberger
Michael E. Hyrne
John A. Borell
Michael A. Bruno

ASSOCIATES

Kevin A. Pituch

OF COUNSEL

Harold A. James
John R. Wanick

Counsel for: Consolidated Rail Corp.; The Lakefront Dock & Railroad Terminal Co.; Prudential Insurance Co. of America; Equitable Life Assurance Society of the U.S.; Metropolitan Life Insurance Co.; Greyhound Lines; Fireman's Fund Insurance Cos.

For full biographical listings, see the Martindale-Hubbell Law Directory

Eastman & Smith (AV)

One Seagate, Twenty-Fourth Floor, 43604
Telephone: 419-241-6000
Telecopier: 419-247-1777
Columbus, Ohio Office: 65 East State Street, Suite 1000, 43215.
Telephone: 614-460-3556.
Telecopier: 614-228-5371.

MEMBERS OF FIRM

Richard E. Antonini
M. Donald Carmin
Frank D. Jacobs
Patrick J. Johnson
James F. Nooney
Bruce L. Smith
Morton Bobowick
David M. Jones
Henry N. Heuerman
John H. Boggs
John T. Landwehr
David L. Kuhl
Richard T. Sargeant
Kenneth C. Baker

(See Next Column)

MEMBERS OF FIRM (Continued)

Robert J. Gilmer, Jr.
Peter R. Casey, III
David F. Cooper
Rudolph A. Peckinpaugh, Jr.
Ronald J. Tice
Thomas A. Dixon
Gary M. Harden
Barry W. Fissel
John D. Willey, Jr.
Joseph A. Gregg
Roger Paul Klee
Mark C. Abramson
Stuart J. Goldberg
Thomas J. Gibney
Steven D. Reinbolt
Dirk P. Plessner

ASSOCIATES

James L. Rogers
David W. Nunn
Timothy C. Kuhlman
Marcus J. Brubaker
Bryan K. Prosek
Kimberly S. Stepleton
John M. Kirsner
Oksana M. Ludd
Beth J. Olson
Albin Bauer, II
Michael W. Regnier
Bryan M. Bach
Michael J. Niedzielski
Lori B. Hart
David A. Dennis
John H. Schaeffer
David C. Krock

OF COUNSEL

John R. Eastman
Jamille G. Jamra
Frank E. Kane
Howard M. Friedman
Ralph S. Boggs
Gerald P. Moran

Counsel for: Chrysler Corp.; Marathon Oil; Envirosafe Service of Ohio, Inc.; Glasstech, Inc.; Toledo-Lucas County Port Authority; Huntington National Bank; Capital Bank, N.A.; Riverside Hospital; The Travelers Group; The Hartford Insurance Group.

For full biographical listings, see the Martindale-Hubbell Law Directory

Fuller & Henry (AV)

One Seagate Suite 1700, P.O. Box 2088, 43603-2088
Telephone: 419-247-2500
Telecopier: 419-247-2665
Port Clinton, Ohio Office: 125 Jefferson.
Telephone: 419-734-2153.
Telecopier: 419-732-8246.
Columbus, Ohio Office: 2210 Huntington Center, 41 South High Street.
Telephone: 614-228-6611.
Telecopier: 614-228-6623.

MEMBERS OF FIRM

Fred E. Fuller (1901-1981)
Leslie Henry (1904-1976)
Donald M. Hawkins
Thomas L. Dalrymple
Charles R. Leech, Jr.
Raymond G. Esch
James M. Morton, Jr.
John W. Hilbert, II
Louis E. Tosi
Stephen J. Stanford
Ray A. Farris
Thomas M. George
Craig J. Van Horsten
Stephen B. Mosier
Thomas S. Zaremba
William L. Patberg
John J. Siciliano
Martin J. Witherell
Douglas G. Haynam
Glenn L. Rambo
Mary Ann Whipple
Sue A. Sikkema
David R. Bainbridge
Martin D. Carrigan
Dennis A. Lyle
Michael E. Born
Daniel T. Ellis

COUNSEL

James W. Baehren
Alan C. Boyd
Dwight H. Morehead
Theodore R. Vogt
David W. Kienzle
Warren D. Wolfe
Nirav D. Parikh

SENIOR ATTORNEY

Regina Reid Joseph

ASSOCIATES

John E. Mauntler
Andrew K. Ranazzi
Lance Michael Keiffer
Michael J. O'Callaghan
Joseph S. Simpson
Scott G. Deller
James B. Yates
Craig A. Sturtz
Keith H. Raker
Margaret G. Beck
Mark Shaw
Timothy A. Dismond
John Christian Everhardus
Linda S. Woggon
Linda J. Callahan-Brown
Robert E. Nagucki
Donna K. Pesin

Counsel for: Building Industry Association of Northwest Ohio, Inc.; Catawba-Cleveland Development Corp.; Chrysler Corp.; Chubb Group of Insurance Cos.; E. I. DuPont De Nemours & Co.; The Ohio Bell Telephone Co.; Owens-Illinois, Inc.; Phillips Petroleum Co.; The Toledo Edison Co.

For full biographical listings, see the Martindale-Hubbell Law Directory

Moran & Moran (AV)

626 Madison Avenue, Suite 300, 43604
Telephone: 419-241-8171
Fax: Available Upon Request

Wayne R. Peppers (1894-1978)
Peter L. Moran
Mary Beth Moran

Representative Clients: The Exchange Bank; Payak Insurance Agency; Monroe Pharmacy, Inc.

(See Next Column)

MORAN & MORAN, *Toledo—Continued*

References: Society Bank; The Fifth Third Bank, Toledo, Ohio.

For full biographical listings, see the Martindale-Hubbell Law Directory

RITTER, ROBINSON, MCCREADY & JAMES (AV)

1850 National City Bank Building, 405 Madison Avenue, 43624
Telephone: 419-241-3213
Detroit, Michigan: 313-422-1610
FAX: 419-241-4925

MEMBERS OF FIRM

George W. Ritter (1886-1979)
Milton C. Boesel, Sr. (1893-1993)
Ellis F. Robinson (Retired)
William S. McCready
Timothy C. James

ASSOCIATES

Mark P. Seitzinger
Erin B. Parr
Raymond H. Pittman, III

OF COUNSEL

Milton C. Boesel, Jr.

Counsel for: Chrysler Corp.; Rubini Motors, Inc.; Ohio Casualty Insurance Co.; National Mutual Insurance Co.; Celina Mutual Insurance Co.; Westfield Insurance Co.; Northwestern National Insurance Co.; Midwestern Insurance Co.; United Ohio Insurance Co.; Toledo Auto Electric Co.

For full biographical listings, see the Martindale-Hubbell Law Directory

ROBISON, CURPHEY & O'CONNELL (AV)

Ninth Floor Four Seagate, 43604
Telephone: 419-249-7900
Telecopier: 419-249-7911
Blissfield, Michigan Office: 8651 East U.S. 223, P.O. Box 59.
Telephone: 517-486-4333.
Telecopier: 517-486-4271.

James J. Robison (1922-1986)

MEMBERS OF FIRM

John M. Curphey
Maurice D. O'Connell
E. Thomas Maguire
Douglas E. Metz
Ronald S. Moening
Edwin A. Coy
David W. Stuckey
Jack Zouhary
Timothy D. Krugh
C. Philip Baither, III
James E. Brazeau
Timothy A. Konieczny
Michael S. Messenger
Julia Smith Wiley
Thomas A. Gibson
Jean Ann S. Sieler
Kathryn M. Mohr
Thomas J. Antonini
William V. Beach

ASSOCIATES

Jean M. O'Brien
D. Casey Talbott
Charles C. Butler
Matthew Harper
Evy M. Jarrett
John E. Kessler
James E. Knepp

OF COUNSEL

David A. Ward

Counsel for: Nationwide Insurance Cos.; St. Paul Insurance Cos.; Motorists Insurance Cos.; Physicians Insurance Company of Michigan.

For full biographical listings, see the Martindale-Hubbell Law Directory

SCHNORF & SCHNORF CO., L.P.A. A PROFESSIONAL CORPORATION (AV)

1400 National City Bank Building, 405 Madison Avenue, 43604
Telephone: 419-248-2646
Facsimile: 419-248-2889

Brandon G. Schnorf, Sr. (1904-1977)
David M. Schnorf
Christopher F. Parker
Johna M. Bella
Barry F. Hudgin

Local Counsel for: Universal Underwriters Group; Cincinnati Insurance Company; Blue Cross and Blue Shield Mutual of Ohio; Bankers Multiple Line Insurance Company; National City Bank, Northwest; Charter One Bank.
Representative Clients: American Federation of Teachers, AFL-CIO; Ohio Federation of Teachers, AFL-CIO; Toledo Federation of Teachers, AFL-CIO; Thomas R. Hart Associates, Inc.

For full biographical listings, see the Martindale-Hubbell Law Directory

SHUMAKER, LOOP & KENDRICK (AV)

North Courthouse Square, 1000 Jackson, 43624-1573
Telephone: 419-241-9000
Telecopier: 419-241-6894
Tampa, Florida Office: Barnett Plaza, Suite 2500, 101 East Kennedy Boulevard.
Telephone: 813-229-7600.
Telecopier: 813-229-1660.
Charlotte, North Carolina Office: Suite 2150, 227 West Trade Street.
Telephone: 704-377-0057.
Telecopier: 704-332-1197.

(See Next Column)

MEMBERS OF FIRM

Gregory G. Alexander
Robert G. Clayton, Jr.
Marc Gertner
James F. Duggan
Donald M. Mewhort, Jr.
Edwin G. Emerson
Barton L. Wagenman
Rolf H. Scheidel
John F. Hayward
John W. Puffer, III (Resident, Tampa, Florida Office)
Michael T. Trocke (Resident, Tampa, Florida Office)
William H. Gosline
William H. Heywood, III
Michael M. Briley
Steven G. Schember (Resident, Tampa, Florida Office)
H. Francis McDaniel, Jr.
Thomas G. Pletz
John H. Burson
Larry A. Becker
Mark C. Stewart
Jery E. Barton
E. Fred McPhail, Jr. (Resident, Charlotte, North Carolina Office)
Thomas I. Webb, Jr.
Bruce H. Gordon (Resident, Tampa, Florida Office)
Gregory S. Shumaker
C. Philip Campbell, Jr. (Resident, Tampa, Florida Office)
David W. Wicklund
W. Thompson Thorn, III (Resident, Tampa, Florida Office)
Gary R. Diesing
John N. MacKay
David F. Waterman
Vivian C. Folk
Joseph A. Rideout
William G. Fischer
Gregory C. Yadley (Resident, Tampa, Florida Office)
Dennis P. Witherell
Kevin H. Graham (Resident, Tampa, Florida Office)
Jack G. Fynes
Lyman F. Spitzer
John C. Barron
Timothy C. McCarthy
John S. Inglis (Resident, Tampa, Florida Office)
Aleta M. Bonini
Susan D. McClay
Jeffrey S. Creamer
Robert A. Donat (Resident, Charlotte, North Carolina Office)
Michael G. Sanderson
Darrell C. Smith (Resident, Tampa, Florida Office)
Peter R. Silverman
Michael S. McGowan
Philip S. Chubb (Resident, Charlotte, North Carolina Office)
Mary Ellen Pisanelli
Gregory T. Lodge
Jeffrey E. Fort
Robert A. Koenig
Diane Vulich Jennens
Cynthia L. Rerucha
Thomas M. Wood (Resident, Tampa, Florida Office)
Charles W. Hiller
Paul R. Lynch (Resident, Tampa, Florida Office)

ASSOCIATES

Judith Leb Udell
David J. Rectenwald
Kathryn J. Woodward
David J. Coyle
Marlene (Neema) M. Cottrill-Bell
Jeffrey H. Miller
Stephen A. Rothschild
Richard A. Mitchell
Terrance K. Davis
Craig P. Burns
Edward J. Richardson (Resident, Tampa, Florida Office)
Ernest J. Marquart (Resident, Tampa, Florida Office)
Eric D. Britton
Thomas P. Dillon (Not admitted in OH)
J. Todd Timmerman (Resident, Tampa, Florida Office)
Matthew J. Fischer
Kevin D. Devaney
Thomas A. Cotter (Resident, Tampa, Florida Office)
James I Rothschild
Dean E. Weaver
William E. Haberman
James G. Lewis (Resident, Tampa, Florida Office)
Mark A. Catchur (Resident, Tampa, Florida Office)

For full biographical listings, see the Martindale-Hubbell Law Directory

SPENGLER NATHANSON (AV)

608 Madison Avenue, Suite 1000, 43604-1169
Telephone: 419-241-2201
FAX: 419-241-8599

Otto H. Spengler (1890-1970)
John J. McCarthy (1909-1969)
J.H. Nathanson (1906-1992)

MEMBERS OF FIRM

David A. Katz
Frank T. Pizza
Ralph Bragg
James R. Jeffery
Norman J. Rubinoff
B. Gary McBride
David G. Wise
Louis J. Hattner
Theodore M. Rowen
Ward Summerville
Gary D. Sikkema
Michael J. Berebitsky
James D. Jensen
Truman A. Greenwood
Cheryl F. Wolff
Richard E. Wolff
James M. Sciarini
Byron S. Choka
James C. Anderson
Susan B. Nelson
Lisa E. Pizza
Joan C. Szuberla
Michael S. Katz
Teresa L. Grigsby
Michael W. Bragg
Peter N. Kanios

ASSOCIATES

Renisa A. Dorner
Thomas A. Lupica
Shane A. Farolino

OF COUNSEL

Joel A. Levine
Joseph S. Heyman
Benjamin B. Durfee
Andrew E. Anderson
Richard A. Entenmann

(See Next Column)

SPENGLER NATHANSON—*Continued*

Counsel for: Fifth-Third Bank of Northwestern Ohio, N.A.; Huntington Bank of Toledo; Society Bank & Trust; Seaway Food Town, Inc.; The University of Toledo; AP Parts; Toledo Lucas County Port Authority; Toledo Board of Education.

For full biographical listings, see the Martindale-Hubbell Law Directory

WATKINS, BATES & CAREY (AV)

1200 Fifth Third Center, 608 Madison Avenue, 43604-1157
Telephone: 419-241-2100
Telecopier: 419-241-1960

MEMBERS OF FIRM

Harley A. Watkins (1902-1979)
William F. Bates
John M. Carey
Gary O. Sommer
Thomas C. Gess

ASSOCIATES

Gabrielle Davis
Jennifer L. Morrison

OF COUNSEL

Richard H. Peters
Robert A. Kelb (1910-1992)

Counsel for: Flower Hospital; Fostoria Community Hospital; National City Bank; Heidtman Steel Products, Inc.; Nazar Rubber Co.

For full biographical listings, see the Martindale-Hubbell Law Directory

*TROY,** Miami Co.

FAUST, HARRELSON, FULKER, McCARTHY & SCHLEMMER (AV)

12 South Cherry Street, P.O. Box 8, 45373
Telephone: 513-335-8324
Fax: 513-339-7155

MEMBERS OF FIRM

Charles F. Faust (1875-1950)
William M. Harrelson (1921-1985)
J. Andrew Fulker (1953-1989)
Leo H. Faust
John E. Fulker
Robert A. McCarthy
Robert N. Schlemmer
William J. Fulker
Robert M. Harrelson

Counsel: Aetna Casualty & Surety Co.; Aetna Life Insurance Co.; Troy Lumber Co.; Insurance Company of North America Cos.; Land Title Guarantee and Trust Co.; Fifth-Third Bank of Western Ohio.

For full biographical listings, see the Martindale-Hubbell Law Directory

SHIPMAN, UTRECHT & DIXON CO., L.P.A. (AV)

215 West Water Street, P.O. Box 310, 45373
Telephone: 513-339-1500
Fax: 513-339-1519

Leonard H. Shipman (1874-1955)
Frank Leonard Shipman (1906-1973)
James C. Utrecht (1922-1985)
William M. Dixon
W. McGregor Dixon, Jr.
James D. Utrecht
Gary A. Nasal
Gary E. Zuhl

General Counsel for: Star Bank, N.A.; Milton Federal Savings and Loan Assn.; Troy Daily News Inc.; City of Troy and Troy Board of Education.
Local Counsel for: CSX Transportation, Inc.; The Dayton Power & Light Co.; Travelers Insurance Co.; Celina Group; Westfield Companies; Lawyers Title Insurance Corp.

For full biographical listings, see the Martindale-Hubbell Law Directory

*UPPER SANDUSKY,** Wyandot Co. — (Refer to Bucyrus)

*URBANA,** Champaign Co.

PAULIG AND SINGER (AV)

40 Monument Square Suite 300, 43078
Telephone: 513-653-5257
Facsimilie: 513-653-3027

Karl E. Paulig
Brad C. Singer

ASSOCIATES

William Grimes Creviston

Representative Clients: Nationwide Mutual Insurance Co.; Ohio Casualty Insurance Co.; Republic Franklin Insurance Co.; Bodey & Sons, Inc. (Building Contractor); Georgia, Inc.; Cincinnati Insurance Co.; Akins Printing, Inc.; The Stephen L. Bodey Co. (Contracting); Urbana City Board of Education; Champaign County Preservation Alliance.

For full biographical listings, see the Martindale-Hubbell Law Directory

*VAN WERT,** Van Wert Co. — (Refer to Lima)

*WAPAKONETA,** Auglaize Co. — (Refer to St. Marys)

*WARREN,** Trumbull Co.

HOPPE, FREY, HEWITT & MILLIGAN (AV)

500 Second National Tower, 44481
Telephone: 216-392-1541
Fax: 216-394-6890

Henry H. Hoppe (1894-1979)
John Q. T. Ford (1897-1971)
James W. Frey (1922-1985)
John T. Milligan (1929-1994)
William R. Hewitt
Robert S. McGeough
John L. Pogue
Ned C. Gold, Jr.
Michael G. Marando
William L. Hawley
Thomas G. Carey, Jr.
Kevin P. Murphy

ASSOCIATES

Dean E. Nielsen
Patrick K. Wilson

General Counsel for: Danieli Wear, Inc.; The Second National Bank of Warren; Trumbull Memorial Hospital; First Federal Savings & Loan Assn.; The Taylor-Winfield Corp.
Local Counsel for: Ohio Edison Co.; The Travelers Insurance Co.; Aetna Casualty & Surety Co.; General Electric Co.; McDonalds Co rp.

For full biographical listings, see the Martindale-Hubbell Law Directory

*WAUSEON,** Fulton Co. — (Refer to Archbold)

*WAVERLY,** Pike Co. — (Refer to Chillicothe)

*WEST UNION,** Adams Co. — (Refer to Portsmouth)

WILLOUGHBY, Lake Co. — (Refer to Painesville)

*WILMINGTON,** Clinton Co.

BUCKLEY, MILLER & WRIGHT (AV)

145 North South Street, P.O. Box 311, 45177
Telephone: 513-382-0946
Fax: 513-382-1361
Sabina, Ohio Office: 34 North Howard Street.
Telephone: 513-584-4663.

MEMBERS OF FIRM

Frederick J. Buckley
James P. Miller
Jeffrey L. Wright
Karen Buckley
John P. Miller

Representative Clients: The Wilmington Savings Bank; Wilmington College; Sabina Farmers Exchange; Nationwide Mutual Insurance Co.; State Automobile Mutual Insurance Co.; Grange Mutual Casualty Co.; Cincinnati Insurance Co.; The Sabina Bank; Community Improvement Corporation of Wilmington.
Approved Attorneys for: Lawyers Title Insurance Corp. (Title Agent); The Ohio Bar Title Insurance Co. (Title Agent).

For full biographical listings, see the Martindale-Hubbell Law Directory

*WOODSFIELD,** Monroe Co. — (Refer to Marietta)

*WOOSTER,** Wayne Co.

CRITCHFIELD, CRITCHFIELD & JOHNSTON (AV)

225 North Market Street, P.O. Box 599, 44691-0488
Telephone: 216-264-4444
Telecopier: 216-263-9278
Millersburg, Ohio Office: Schuler Law Firm, Critchfield, Critchfield & Johnston. Professional Building.
Telephone: 216-674-3055.

MEMBERS OF FIRM

Robert Critchfield (1903-1981)
Henry B. Critchfield (1905-1980)
John C. Johnston, Jr. (Retired)
Walter C. Grosjean
Lincoln P. Oviatt
John T. Wigham
John C. Johnston, III
Daniel H. Plumly
J. Douglas Drushal
Christopher M. Milliken
Peggy J. Schmitz

ASSOCIATES

Bonnie C. Drushal
Robert C. Berry
Susan Eileen Baker
David J. Wigham
Todd A. Bickel

Representative Clients: Rubbermaid Inc.; Wooster Brush Co.; The College of Wooster; Bank One of Wooster, N.A.; First Federal Savings & Loan Association of Wooster; Sandy Supply Co.; Buehler Food Markets, Inc.; Cofsco, Inc.; Wayne Dalton Corp.; Ohio Packaging Corporation.

For full biographical listings, see the Martindale-Hubbell Law Directory

*XENIA,** Greene Co. — (Refer to Dayton)

*YOUNGSTOWN,** Mahoning Co.

HARRINGTON HUXLEY SMITH MITCHELL & REED (AV)

1200 Mahoning Bank Building, 44503-1508
Telephone: 216-744-1111
Telecopier: 216-744-2029

(See Next Column)

HARRINGTON HUXLEY SMITH MITCHELL & REED, *Youngstown—Continued*

MEMBERS OF FIRM

James E. Mitchell
George B. Woodman
Eldon S. Wright
John C. Litty, Jr.
Robert A. Lenga
George J. Limbert
Jay Tims
Paul M. Dutton
James L. Blomstrom
Frederick S. Coombs, III
Ralph A. Beard
Alan D. Wenger
John T. Dellick
Kelly J. Morrison
Shirley J. Christian
Neil H. Maxwell
Patrick J. Coady
Martin J. Boetcher

ASSOCIATES

Mark R. Fortunato
Neil D. Schor
Charles J. Kay
John F. Petrony

John T. Harrington (1873-1932)
Jared P. Huxley (1874-1942)
Charles F. Smith (1877-1949)
Osborne Mitchell (1886-1973)

OF COUNSEL

Susan Stanton Katz

Counsel for: The Mahoning National Bank; WKBN Broadcasting Corp.; WYTV, Inc.
Representative Clients: Ohio Edison Co.; Ohio Bell Telephone Co.; Bank One Cleveland, N.A.

For full biographical listings, see the Martindale-Hubbell Law Directory

MANCHESTER, BENNETT, POWERS & ULLMAN A LEGAL PROFESSIONAL ASSOCIATION (AV)

Atrium Level Two, The Commerce Building, 44503-1641
Telephone: 216-743-1171
Fax: 216-743-1190

Curtis A. Manchester (1876-1951)
James Eugene Bennett (1889-1964)
Franklin B. Powers (1887-1960)
Myron E. Ullman (1889-1974)
W. Stephen Meloy
Robert N. Dineen
Stephen T. Bolton
John F. Zimmerman, Jr.
James W. Ehrman
Thomas J. Travers, Jr.
Timothy J. Jacob
Franklin S. Bennett, Jr.
Charles S. Lanz
Mark A. Beatrice
Joseph R. Young, Jr.
Joseph M. Houser
Jeffrey D. Heintz

Martha L. Bushey
Kyra M. Fleming

OF COUNSEL

James E. Bennett, Jr.

Counsel for: Aetna Casualty & Surety Co.; Bank One, Youngstown, N.A.; The Dollar Savings & Trust Co.; East Ohio Gas Co.; Equitable Life Assurance Society; General Motors Corp.; Vindicator Printing Co.

For full biographical listings, see the Martindale-Hubbell Law Directory

*ZANESVILLE,** Muskingum Co.

KINCAID, CULTICE & GEYER (AV)

50 North Fourth Street, P.O. Box 1030, 43702-1030
Telephone: 614-454-2591
Telecopier: 614-454-6975

C. Alfred Zinn (1903-1977)
J. Donald Kincaid (Retired)

MEMBERS OF FIRM

R. Donald Cultice
R. William Geyer
Eric D. Johnson
William J. Taylor
Susan Cultice Brown
Peter N. Cultice
James P. Brown
Scott D. Eickelberger
Jennifer L. Nischan
Joel Deutch

Attorneys for: The Ohio Power Company; Mutual Federal Savings Bank; Halliburton Services; Bethesda Hospital Association; The Oxford Oil Company; The Buckeye Company; McDonalds of Zanesville and Cambridge; Nicoff Enterprises; Muskingum College.
Reference: Mutual Federal Savings Bank.

For full biographical listings, see the Martindale-Hubbell Law Directory

OKLAHOMA

*ADA,** Pontotoc Co.

DEATON & DAVISON, INC. (AV)

300 South Rennie, P.O. Box 1219, 74820
Telephone: 405-332-1752
Fax: 405-332-0827

Austin R. Deaton, Jr. Denver N. Davison
C. Steven Kessinger

For full biographical listings, see the Martindale-Hubbell Law Directory

*ALVA,** Woods Co. — (Refer to Woodward)

*ANADARKO,** Caddo Co.

PAIN AND GARLAND (AV)

111 S.W. Second Street, P.O. Box 158, 73005
Telephone: 405-247-3365

MEMBERS OF FIRM

Leslie Pain John W. Garland

ASSOCIATES

Richard A. Williams

Representative Clients: First State Bank, Anadarko, Okla.; Caddo Electric Cooperative, Binger, Okla.; Town of Cyril, Okla.; Town of Cement, Okla.; Community Bank; Federal Land Bank of Wichita.

For full biographical listings, see the Martindale-Hubbell Law Directory

*ANTLERS,** Pushmataha Co.

STAMPER, BURRAGE & HADLEY (AV)

112 North High Street, P.O. Box 100, 74523
Telephone: 405-298-3153; 405-298-3332
Fax: 405-298-3263
Atoka, Oklahoma Office: P.O. Box 28.
Telephone: 405-889-7384.
Telecopier: 405-889-7387.

MEMBERS OF FIRM

Joe Stamper Thomas J. Hadley
Paula Gayle Burrage

Representative Clients: Farmers Exchange Bank, Antlers, Okla.; First National Bank at Antlers, Okla.; Town of Antlers; U. S. F. & G. Co.

For full biographical listings, see the Martindale-Hubbell Law Directory

*ARDMORE,** Carter Co.

BICKFORD, PASLEY & FARABOUGH (AV)

29 B Street, S.W., P.O. Box 1027, 73402
Telephone: 405-226-1893
FAX: 405-223-5566

MEMBERS OF FIRM

Harry L. Bickford Ted J. Pasley
Gary W. Farabough

General Counsel: City of Ardmore, Oklahoma.
Local Counsel: Alliance Insurance Co.; Total Petroleum Inc..; Uniroyal, Inc.; Michelin Tire Co.; Delta Mining, Inc.; Merdian Aggretates Company.
Reference: American National Bank of Ardmore; Exchange National Bank and Trust Company; Citizens National Bank of Ardmore.

For full biographical listings, see the Martindale-Hubbell Law Directory

FISCHL CULP MCMILLIN CHAFFIN BAHNER & BROWN (AV)

100 E Street, S.W., P.O. Box 1766, 73402
Telephone: 405-223-4321
FAX: 405-226-4795

MEMBERS OF FIRM

Louis A. Fischl (1898-1973) Donald J. Chaffin
Joseph M. Culp S. Brent Bahner
F. Lovell McMillin Phillip L. Brown

Representative Clients: First National Bank and Trust Co. of Ardmore; Allstate Insurance Co.; Chubb Group of Insurance Cos.; Employers Mutual Cos.; Atlantic Richfield Co.; Texaco, Inc.; Winn-Dixie, Inc.; Holden Energy Corporation.

For full biographical listings, see the Martindale-Hubbell Law Directory

*BARTLESVILLE,** Washington Co.

BREWER, WORTEN, ROBINETT, JOHNSON, WORTEN & KING (AV)

500 Professional Building, 5th Street and Keeler Avenue, P.O. Box 1066, 74005-1066
Telephone: 918-336-4132
Fax: 918-336-9009

(See Next Column)

MEMBERS OF FIRM

Jesse J. Worten (1920-1983) James R. Johnson
Bruce W. Robinett Jesse J. Worten, III
David B. King

OF COUNSEL

Chester A. Brewer (Retired) James Mullen
John M. Keefer

Representative Clients: Basinger Oil Co.; The Kansas Power & Light Co.; Oklahoma Land and Cattle Co.; The Prudential Insurance Company of America; Bank of Oklahoma; Municipal Assurance Group; Mullendore Cross Bell Ranch; Applied Automation, Inc.; Phillips Petroleum Company, WestStar Bank.

For full biographical listings, see the Martindale-Hubbell Law Directory

*BEAVER,** Beaver Co.

TRIPPET AND KEE (AV)

P.O. Box 728, 73932
Telephone: 405-625-3212, 625-4597
Fax: 405-625-3733

MEMBERS OF FIRM

Richard P. Trippet Robert J. Kee

LEGAL SUPPORT PERSONNEL

C. Todd Trippet (Certified Legal Assistant Real Estate Specialist)

Designated Attorneys for: First American Title Insurance Co.
Representative Clients: The Bank of Beaver City; The First Security Bank, Beaver; Beaver County Abstract Co., Beaver, Oklahoma.

For full biographical listings, see the Martindale-Hubbell Law Directory

BLACKWELL, Kay Co.

JAMES R. RODGERS (AV)

Security Bank Building, P.O. Box 514, 74631
Telephone: 405-363-3684
Fax: 405-363-1063

William W. Rodgers (1907-1979)

Attorney for: Security Bank and Trust Co., Blackwell, Oklahoma; Electron Corp.; Blackwell Board of Education.

For full biographical listings, see the Martindale-Hubbell Law Directory

*CHANDLER,** Lincoln Co.

BUTTS & LENORA (AV)

116 West Eighth Street, P.O. Box 337, 74834-0337
Telephone: 405-258-1334
Fax: 405-258-0249

MEMBERS OF FIRM

Benjamin E. Butts Larry K. Lenora

Representative Client: Union National Bank, Chandler, Okla.
Approved Title Examiners for: First American Title & Trust Co., Oklahoma City; Chicago Title & Trust Co.

For full biographical listings, see the Martindale-Hubbell Law Directory

*CHEROKEE,** Alfalfa Co. — (Refer to Enid)

*CHICKASHA,** Grady Co.

HAYS & DABNEY, P.C. (AV)

Third Floor, Oklahoma National Building, 228 W. Chickasha Avenue, 73018
Telephone: 405-224-1950
Fax: 405-222-1033

Robert J. Hays B. Wayne Dabney

Craig W. Roddy Gretchen L. Roddy

Representative Clients: Chickasha Bank & Trust Co.; Hermetic Switch, Inc.; Southern Plains Medical Center, P.C.; Bank of Union; Cement Bank.
Local Counsel: Farmers Home Administration; Ward Petroleum Corp.

For full biographical listings, see the Martindale-Hubbell Law Directory

*CLAREMORE,** Rogers Co. — (Refer to Tulsa)

CLINTON, Custer Co. — (Refer to Weatherford)

*CORDELL,** Washita Co. — (Refer to Weatherford)

CUSHING, Payne Co. — (Refer to Stillwater)

*DUNCAN,** Stephens Co.

BONNEY, WEAVER, CORLEY, BENEFIELD & GOSSETT (AV)

Suite 300 Security National Bank Building, 16 South 9th Street, 73533
Telephone: 405-255-5600
FAX: 405-255-5843

(See Next Column)

BONNEY, WEAVER, CORLEY, BENEFIELD & GOSSETT, *Duncan—Continued*

MEMBERS OF FIRM

Henry C. Bonney
Thomas Michael Weaver
Ronald E. Corley
David L. Benefield
William A. Gossett
Scott W. Stone
John E. Campbell, Jr.

OF COUNSEL

Harold T. Garvin

Representative Clients: Security National Bank and Trust Co.; Mack Oil Co.; Thomas Drilling Co.; M & M Supply Co.; Investors Trust Co.; Security Corp.; L. E. Jones Production Co.; Duncan Public Schools.

For full biographical listings, see the Martindale-Hubbell Law Directory

LEACH, SULLIVAN, SULLIVAN & WATKINS (AV)

921 Main Street, P.O. Box 160, 73534
Telephone: 405-255-8260
Telecopier: 405-255-5587

MEMBERS OF FIRM

William O. Leach (1919-1990)
Paul D. Sullivan
Patrick D. Sullivan
Michael P. Sullivan
Kent P. Sullivan
Jay B. Watkins
Scott P. Sullivan

Representative Clients: The Oklahoma National Bank; Citizens' Bank, Velma, Oklahoma; Universal Fidelity Life Insurance Co.; Duncan Regional Hospital, Inc.; Leffler Construction Co.

For full biographical listings, see the Martindale-Hubbell Law Directory

*DURANT,** Bryan Co.

CRISWELL & CRISWELL, INC. A PROFESSIONAL CORPORATION (AV)

Criswell Building, 122 North Third Avenue, P.O. Box 541, 74702-0541
Telephone: 405-924-2119
Fax: 405-924-6468

T. O. Criswell (1913-1969)
Tom Criswell, III

Approved Title Examiners for: Pioneer Title Insurance Co.; Lawyers Title Insurance Co.; Chicago Title Insurance Co.; American First Title & Trust Co.; Southwest Title & Trust Co.; Title Insurance Agent for American Security Title Insurance Company.
References: First National Bank, Durant; The Durant Bank & Trust Co.; First State Bank, Bokchito; American Bank, Denison, Texas; The Bank of Southern Oklahoma.

ELK CITY, Beckham Co. — (Refer to Weatherford)

*EL RENO,** Canadian Co.

FOGG, FOGG & HANDLEY (AV)

421 South Rock Island, P.O. Box 310, 73036
Telephone: 405-262-3502
Fax: 405-262-3531
Oklahoma City Office: 5909 N.W. Expressway, Suite 402.
Telephone: 405-722-0577.
Fax: 405-722-0583.

MEMBERS OF FIRM

Rupert M. Fogg (1914-1989)
Richard M. Fogg
Fletcher Dal Handley, Jr.
Ronald L. Brown

ASSOCIATES

Kelley L. Cornelius
Robert E. Grantham

Attorneys for: Oklahoma Gas & Electric Co.; El Reno School District; Calumet School District; Parkview Hospital Trust Authority; Union City School District.

For full biographical listings, see the Martindale-Hubbell Law Directory

*ENID,** Garfield Co.

MITCHELL & DECLERCK, P.C. (AV)

202 West Broadway, 73701-4018
Telephone: 405-234-5144
Facsimile: 405-234-8890
Pond Creek Office: 161 W. Broadway.
Telephone: 405-532-6514.
Facsimile: 405-234-8890.

E. B. Mitchell (1895-1976)
Earl B. Mitchell, Jr.
Edward A. DeClerck
Bill G. Halstead
Larry D. Lahman
E. W. (Bill) Shaw
Gary D. Martin
Tim E. DeClerck
Kevin D. Anderson

Counsel for: Cleo State Bank; Travelers Insurance Co.; Bank of Drummond; United Services Auto Assn.; Bank of Garber, Garber, Okla.; Maryland Casualty Co.; Fireman's Fund; Vocational-Technical School District; Heartland Federal Savings & Loan.; Equitable Life Assurance Society of the United States (Real Estate Department).

For full biographical listings, see the Martindale-Hubbell Law Directory

*GUTHRIE,** Logan Co. — (Refer to Stillwater)

*GUYMON,** Texas Co.

JOHN BOARD (AV)

220 North Main, P.O. Box 408, 73942
Telephone: 405-338-6546

Representative Clients: The First National Bank of Guymon; Guymon Independent School District; Wirtz Lumber and Supply, Inc.; Memorial Hospital of Texas County.

For full biographical listings, see the Martindale-Hubbell Law Directory

DAVID K. PETTY A PROFESSIONAL CORPORATION (AV)

301 West Fifth, P.O. Box 1187, 73942
Telephone: 405-338-5484
FAX: 405-338-0066

David K. Petty

Jon K. Parsley

Attorney for: First National Bank, Texhoma, Oklahoma; Goodner Livestock Commission; Dorchester Hugoton Ltd.; Town of Hardesty; Oxy USA; Perryton Equity Exchange; City of Guymon; First Security Bank of Beaver, Oklahoma; Town of Goodwell.

For full biographical listings, see the Martindale-Hubbell Law Directory

WRIGHT, DALE & JETT (AV)

Dale Building, 114 East 4th Street, P.O. Box 591, 73942
Telephone: 405-338-6591
Fax: 405-338-8244

MEMBERS OF FIRM

F. Hiner Dale (1881-1969)
Vincent Dale (1912-1977)
Bryan L. Wright
Douglas Don Dale
A. Clark Jett
Peggy L. Carter

OF COUNSEL

Don Dale

For full biographical listings, see the Martindale-Hubbell Law Directory

HENNESSEY, Kingfisher Co. — (Refer to Enid)

HENRYETTA, Okmulgee Co. — (Refer to Okmulgee)

*HOBART,** Kiowa Co.

PERRY, GENTRY, PERRY & MARSH (AV)

Abstract Building, 73651
Telephone: 405-726-2301; 726-5622
Fax: 405-726-5623
Sentinel, Oklahoma Office: 213 East Main Street. P.O. Box 234.
Telephone: 405-393-4499; 393-4329.

MEMBERS OF FIRM

Finis C. Gillespie (1910-1981)
Johnny M. Perry
William E. Gentry
Nellie Perry
Ricky A. Marsh

Representative Clients: Southwest State Bank, Sentinel, Oklahoma; First State Bank of Lone Wolf, Oklahoma; Farmers Cooperative Assn., Hobart, Oklahoma; Hobart Seed Co., Hobart, Oklahoma; Hobart Ag-Chemical Co., Hobart, Oklahoma; Highland Supply Corp.; Beckham County Rural Water District #1; Hobart Stockyards, Inc.; Hobart Redi-Mix, Inc.

For full biographical listings, see the Martindale-Hubbell Law Directory

*HOLDENVILLE,** Hughes Co. — (Refer to Mc Alester)

*HUGO,** Choctaw Co.

RABON, WOLF & RABON (AV)

402 East Jackson, P.O. Box 726, 74743
Telephone: 405-326-6427
Fax: 405-326-6032

MEMBERS OF FIRM

Lon Kile (1914-1988)
Bob Rabon
J. Frank Wolf, III
Robert Lee Rabon

Representative Clients: Lone Star Gas Co.; General Accident Group.
General Counsel for: Security First National Bank, Hugo; Choctaw Nation; Chickasaw Nation; Housing Authority of Choctaw Nation of Oklahoma; Hugo Municipal Authority; Hugo Airport Authority; Hugo Industrial Authority; Red River Farmers Cooperative; Hugo Public Schools.

For full biographical listings, see the Martindale-Hubbell Law Directory

*KINGFISHER,** Kingfisher Co.

BEALL & JOHNSON LAW OFFICE, INC. (AV)

215 North Main Street, P.O. Box 298, 73750-0298
Telephone: 405-375-3188
Fax: 405-375-3308

(See Next Column)

BEALL & JOHNSON LAW OFFICE INC.—*Continued*

James P. Beall
Cloise E. Johnson, Jr.

General Counsel for: Kingfisher Bank and Trust Co.; Kingfisher Bancorp, Incl
Representative Clients: Oppel Bros., Inc. (construction and farms); Boeckman Ford, Inc.; Kingfisher Newspapers, Inc.; Francis Trust (land development); Okarche Development, Inc.; G.E.B., Inc. (real estate); Felta Yost Trust; Kingfisher County Rural Water Districts; Farmers Cooperative Supply.

For full biographical listings, see the Martindale-Hubbell Law Directory

*LAWTON,** Comanche Co.

ASHTON, ASHTON, WISENER AND MUNKACSY, INC. (AV)

711 "C" Avenue, 73501
Telephone: 405-357-2010
FAX: 405-357-2017

Alfred J. Ashton, Jr.
Mark A. Ashton
Thomas W. Wisener
John Munkacsy

Representative Clients: Security Bank and Trust Co., Lawton, Oklahoma; Wichita National Life Insurance Co.; Felton-Dean Pontiac-Oldsmobile-GMC; Park View Nursing Home, Inc., Walters, Oklahoma; Park-Jones Realty Company; Leister & Stabler, Inc. (CPAs); Shiflett Transport Services, Inc.; Town of Medicine Park.

For full biographical listings, see the Martindale-Hubbell Law Directory

GODLOVE, JOYNER, MAYHALL, DZIALO, DUTCHER & ERWIN, A PROFESSIONAL CORPORATION (AV)

802 "C" Avenue, P.O. Box 29, 73502
Telephone: 405-353-6700
Fax: 405-353-2900

W. W. Godlove (1908-1982)
Ernest F. Godlove
Sam A. Joyner
Michael C. Mayhall
Edward W. Dzialo, Jr.
J. Blake Dutcher, Jr.
Shon T. Erwin

Representative Clients: Citizens Bank; First Commercial Bank; Security Bank's Trust Co.; Norwest Financial Oklahoma, Inc.; Southwest Abstract Co.; Lawton Industrial Foundation, Inc.; Lawton Chamber of Commerce; General Motors Acceptance Corp.; Ed Warmack and Co.; Goodyear Tire & Rubber Co.; Sears Roebuck & Co.

For full biographical listings, see the Martindale-Hubbell Law Directory

*MADILL,** Marshall Co.

LITTLE, LITTLE, LITTLE, WINDEL & COPPEDGE (AV)

Little Building, P.O. Box 618, 73446
Telephone: 405-795-3397
Telefax: 405-795-5072
Tishomingo, Oklahoma Office: 224 West Main Street.
Telephone: 405-371-3655.
Telefax: 405-371-9869

MEMBERS OF FIRM

Reuel W. Little (1901-1993)
Dan Little
Prudence Mae Little
Jerry Lynn Windel
Jack W. Coppedge, II (Resident, Tishomingo Office)

For full biographical listings, see the Martindale-Hubbell Law Directory

*MANGUM,** Greer Co. — (Refer to Weatherford)

*MARIETTA,** Love Co. — (Refer to Ardmore)

*MC ALESTER,** Pittsburg Co.

ALLFORD, ASHMORE, IVESTER, ZELLMER & GREEN (AV)

Professional Building, 10 East Washington Street, P.O. Box 130, 74502
Telephone: 918-423-3131
FAX: 918-423-3133

MEMBERS OF FIRM

Walter J. Arnote (1905-1965)
James B. Bratton (1914-1982)
John A. Allford
Robert L. Ivester
George Zellmer
Elaine Green

OF COUNSEL

Anthony D. Ashmore

Attorneys for: The First National Bank and Trust Company of McAlester; Western Casualty & Surety Co.; Government Employees Insurance Co.; Shelter Insurance Co.; Central Mutual Insurance Co.; Empire Insurance Co.; Great Falls Insurance Co.; Sentry Insurance Co.; Utica Mutual Insurance Co.; Scottsdale Ins. Co.

For full biographical listings, see the Martindale-Hubbell Law Directory

*MEDFORD,** Grant Co.

J. C. DRENNAN (AV)

Drennan Building, P.O. Box 148, 73759
Telephone: 405-395-2351

(See Next Column)

John C. Drennan (1902-1967)

Counsel for: Grant County Bank, Medford; First State Bank, Pond Creek; State Exchange Bank, Lamont.

For full biographical listings, see the Martindale-Hubbell Law Directory

*MIAMI,** Ottawa Co.

WALLACE, OWENS, LANDERS, GEE, MORROW, WILSON, WATSON & JAMES, A PROFESSIONAL CORPORATION (AV)

21 South Main Street, P.O. Box 1168, 74355
Telephone: 918-542-5501
Fax: 918-542-5400
Jay, Oklahoma Office: 5 Krause Street, P.O. Box 1018.
Telephone: 918-253-6208.
Fax: 918-253-6209.

A. C. Wallace (1882-1971)
John R. Wallace (1913-1992)
Ben T. Owens (1919-1991)
Melvin H. Landers
Robert S. Gee
Coy Dean Morrow
W. Neil Wilson
Dennis J. Watson
Richard D. James (Resident, Jay, Oklahoma Office)
Ryan G. Robertson

Representative Clients: Oklahoma Farmers Union Mutual, Ins. Co.; Security Bank & Trust Co.; Mid-Continent Casualty Co.; Miami Coop; Eagle-Picher Industries, Inc.; The B. F. Goodrich Co.; Miami Stone and Rustique Brick; Tera Miranda; U.S. Blitz, Inc.

For full biographical listings, see the Martindale-Hubbell Law Directory

*MUSKOGEE,** Muskogee Co.

ROBINSON, LOCKE, GAGE, FITE & WILLIAMS (AV)

530 Court Street, P.O. Box 87, 74401
Telephone: 918-687-5424
Fax: 918-687-0761

MEMBERS OF FIRM

A. Carl Robinson
Robert L. Locke, Jr.
Edwin L. Gage
Julian K. Fite
Betty Outhier Williams

Edith M. Gregory
Douglas S. Pewitt

Representative Clients: First National Bank & Trust Co. of Muskogee; United States Fidelity & Guaranty Co.; Bacone College; Utica Mutual Insurance Co.; Yaffe Iron & Metal Co., Inc.; Cimmaron Insurance Co.; Nationwide Insurance Co.; OML Municipal Assurance Group.

For full biographical listings, see the Martindale-Hubbell Law Directory

WRIGHT, STOUT & FITE (AV)

501 Bank IV Building, P.O. Box 707, 74402-0707
Telephone: 918-682-0091
Fax: 918-683-6340

MEMBERS OF FIRM

J. Ron Wright
Weldon W. Stout
C. Bart Fite
Paula A. Ranallo Wilburn

Counsel for: Commercial Bank & Trust Co.; Ft. Howard Paper Co.; Arkhoela Sand & Gravel Co.; Equity Mutual Insurance Co.; Chubb Group; Home Insurance Co.; United Services Auto Assn.; Carolina Casualty Insurance Co.; Equitable Life & Casualty; Universal Underwriters Insurance Co.

For full biographical listings, see the Martindale-Hubbell Law Directory

*NORMAN,** Cleveland Co.

PENCE & HOUSLEY (AV)

314 East Comanche, P.O. Box 1629, 73070
Telephone: 405-364-8272
Fax: 405-364-8486

MEMBERS OF FIRM

James E. Pence
Roger O. Housley

References: Liberty National Bank.

For full biographical listings, see the Martindale-Hubbell Law Directory

*NOWATA,** Nowata Co. — (Refer to Bartlesville)

*OKEMAH,** Okfuskee Co. — (Refer to Okmulgee)

*OKLAHOMA CITY,** Oklahoma Co.

ANDREWS DAVIS LEGG BIXLER MILSTEN & PRICE, A PROFESSIONAL CORPORATION (AV)

500 West Main, 73102
Telephone: 405-272-9241
FAX: 405-235-8786

(See Next Column)

ANDREWS DAVIS LEGG BIXLER MILSTEN & PRICE A PROFESSIONAL CORPORATION, *Oklahoma City—Continued*

L. Karlton Mosteller (1895-1966)
John C. Andrews
J. Edward Barth
C. Temple Bixler
John J. Breathwit
Charles C. Callaway, Jr.
Gary S. Chilton
Carolyn C. Cummins
James F. Davis
Alan C. Durbin
John F. Fischer, II
Don G. Holladay
Richard B. Kells, Jr.
Mona S. Lambird
Timothy M. Larason
William J. Legg
Robert B. Milsten
Robert D. Nelon
Babette Patton
Mark H. Price
D. Joe Rockett
Joseph G. Shannonhouse, IV
R. Brown Wallace
William D. Watts
William H. Whitehill, Jr.

Craig D. Carter
Timothy D. DeGiusti
Lynn O. Holloman
Michelle Johnson
Barry Christopher Rooker
Elaine Bizzell Thompson
Shelia Darling Tims

OF COUNSEL

Joseph A. Buckles, II
Keith T. Childers
Carolyn Gregg Hill
Leroy J. Patton
John P. Roberts
Robert J. Troester

Representative Clients: Browning-Ferris Industries, Inc.; The Chase Manhattan Bank, N.A.; Cooper Industries, Inc.; Dow Jones & Co.; Marathon Oil Co.; Oklahoma Dental Assn.; Griffin Television, Inc. (KWTV, CBS Affiliate).

For full biographical listings, see the Martindale-Hubbell Law Directory

CONNER & WINTERS, A PROFESSIONAL CORPORATION (AV)

204 North Robinson, Suite 950, 73102
Telephone: 405-232-7711
Facsimile: 405-232-2695
Tulsa, Oklahoma Office: 15 East 5th Street, Suite 2400, 74103.
Telephone: 918-586-5711.
Facsimile: 918-586-8982.

Peter B. Bradford
Raymond E. Tompkins
Timothy J. Bomhoff

For full biographical listings, see the Martindale-Hubbell Law Directory

CROWE & DUNLEVY, A PROFESSIONAL CORPORATION (AV)

1800 Mid-America Tower, 20 North Broadway, 73102-8273
Telephone: 405-235-7700
Fax: 405-239-6651
Tulsa, Oklahoma Office: Crowe & Dunlevy, 500 Kennedy Building, 321 South Boston.
Telephone: 918-592-9800.
Fax: 918-592-9801.
Norman, Oklahoma Office: Crowe & Dunlevy, Luttrell, Pendarvis & Rawlinson, 104 East Eufaula Street.
Telephone: 405-321-7317.
Fax: 405-360-4002.

Vincil Penny Crowe (1897-1974)
Gary W. Davis
L. E. Stringer
Henry Rheinberger
Andrew M. Coats
Allen D. Evans
James L. Hall, Jr.
D. Kent Meyers
Preston G. Gaddis II
Clyde A. Muchmore
Robert M. Johnson
Lon Foster, III
Arlen E. Fielden
James F. Hartmann, Jr.
Harry A. Woods, Jr.
Jimmy Goodman
Earl A. Skarky
James H. Holloman, Jr.
Richard C. Ford
John J. Griffin, Jr.
Brooke Smith Murphy
Michael M. Stewart
Leonard Court
Cynda C. Ottaway
Judy Hamilton Morse
Kenni B. Merritt
Kelley C. Callahan
Mark D. Christiansen
Michael S. Laird
Arthur F. Hoge III
Mack J. Morgan III
Anton J. Rupert
Karen S. Rieger
Patricia J. Hanson
Wesley C. Fredenburg
Marie Weston Evans
Harvey D. Ellis, Jr.
Gayle L. Barrett
L. Mark Walker
Stephen L. DeGiusti
Mark S. Grossman
Kevin D. Gordon
Reeder E. Ratliff
Todd Taylor
Roger A. Stong
Robin D. Jenson
Robert E. Bacharach
Randal A. Sengel
Robert G. McCampbell

Mark D. Spencer
LeAnne Burnett
Peggy L. Clay
Paul D. Trimble
Dana M. Tacker
Timila S. Rother
David Nunn
Mark B. McDaniel
Teresa A. Williams
Joel S. Allen
Randy D. Gordon
Timothy E. Foley
Tamela R. Hughlett
Joseph J. Ferretti
Rustin J. Strubhar
William L. Teague

(*See Next Column*)

Cynthia L. Andrews
Edward E. Lane, III
C. Robert Stell
Cori Hook Loomis

OF COUNSEL

John W. Swinford
C. Harold Thweatt
Bruce H. Johnson
Lawrence E. Walsh
George S. Guysi
Ben L. Burdick
Val R. Miller
James C. Gibbens
James A. Peabody
James W. George
Florine G. Crockett
Robert A. Reece
Terry R. Hanna
Candace M. Williams

For full biographical listings, see the Martindale-Hubbell Law Directory

DAY, EDWARDS, FEDERMAN, PROPESTER & CHRISTENSEN, P.C. (AV)

Suite 2900 First Oklahoma Tower, 210 Park Avenue, 73102-5605
Telephone: 405-239-2121
Telecopier: 405-236-1012

Bruce W. Day
Joe E. Edwards
William B. Federman
Richard P. Propester
D. Wade Christensen
J. Clay Christensen
Kent A. Gilliland
Rodney J. Heggy
Ricki Valerie Sonders
Thomas Pitchlynn Howell, IV
John C. Platt

David R. Widdoes
Lori R. Roberts
Carolyn A. Romberg

OF COUNSEL

Herbert F. (Jack) Hewett
Jeanette Cook Timmons
Joel Warren Harmon
Jane S. Eulberg
Mark A. Cohen

Representative Clients: Aetna Life Insurance Co.; Boatmen's First National Bank of Oklahoma; Borg-Warner Chemicals, Inc.; City Bank & Trust; Federal Deposit Insurance Corp.; Bank One, Oklahoma City; Haskell Lemon Construction Co.; Merrill Lynch, Pierce, Fenner & Smith, Inc.; Prudential Securities, Inc.

For full biographical listings, see the Martindale-Hubbell Law Directory

FELLERS, SNIDER, BLANKENSHIP, BAILEY & TIPPENS, A PROFESSIONAL CORPORATION (AV)

First National Center, 120 North Robinson, Suite 2400, 73102
Telephone: 405-232-0621
Fax: 405-232-9659
Edmond, Oklahoma Office: 3330 French Park Drive, 73034.
Telephone: 405-340-7988.
Fax: 405-340-7995.

Jap W. Blankenship
Burck Bailey
Terry W. Tippens
K. Nicholas Wilson
Harry H. Selph, II
Warren F. Bickford, IV
John B. Heatly
Michael R. Ford
Eric S. Eissenstat
Stephen R. Stephens
Doneen Douglas Jones
Thomas J. Enis
Barbara G. Bowersox
Joe C. Lewallen, Jr.
David L. Kearney
Dino E. Viera
Gregory A. Castro
Kevin R. Donelson
Andrew L. Walding
Todd A. Nelson
Nancy H. Pennell (Resident, Edmond, Oklahoma Office)

OF COUNSEL

James D. Fellers
John Joseph Snider
Paul W. Dudman
Douglas A. Branch
Eric R. King
Linda A. King
Bert L. Belanger

Representative Clients: General Electric Capital Corp.; Halliburton Co.; Hertz Corp.; Service Corporation Intl.; United Parcel Service; Kerr McGee Corp.; Oklahoma Municipal Assurance Group; Oklahoma Natural Gas Co.; ONEOK Inc.; Steinhardt Partners, L.P.

For full biographical listings, see the Martindale-Hubbell Law Directory

FENTON, FENTON, SMITH, RENEAU & MOON, A PROFESSIONAL CORPORATION (AV)

Suite 800 One Leadership Square, 211 North Robinson, 73102
Telephone: 405-235-4671
Telecopier: 405-235-5247

Edgar Fenton (1890-1977)
Milton R. Moon (1921-1988)
Wm. G. Smith (1919-1993)
Dale Reneau
Donald R. Wilson
Stephen Peterson
John A. McCaleb
C. William Threlkeld
Tom E. Mullen
Brenda K. Peterson
Mary A. Kelly
Sherry L. Smith
Laurie Walker Jones
Beverly S. Pearson
Michael D. Duncan

(*See Next Column*)

FENTON, FENTON, SMITH, RENEAU & MOON A PROFESSIONAL CORPORATION—*Continued*

Robin A. Wiens
Michael S. McMillin
Greg K. Ballard
R. Dale Kimsey
C. Todd Ward
John B. Vera
Kevin E. Hill
Roger Reneau

OF COUNSEL

Elliott C. Fenton
Glen D. Johnson, Jr.
Ann M. Threlkeld
James P. Kelley
Gerald E. Kelley

Representative Clients: The Alliance Insurance Cos.; American Fidelity Insurance Co.; Chrysler Corp.; The Hartford Insurance Group; Insurance Company of North America; Roadway Express Inc.; The St. Paul Insurance Cos.; The Travelers Insurance Cos.; United States Fidelity & Guaranty Co.

For full biographical listings, see the Martindale-Hubbell Law Directory

FOGG, FOGG & HANDLEY (AV)

5909 N.W. Expressway, Suite 402, 73132
Telephone: 405-722-0577
Fax: 405-722-0583
El Reno, Oklahoma Office: 421 South Rock Island, P.O. Box 310.
Telephone: 405-262-3502.
Fax: 405-262-3531.

MEMBERS OF FIRM

Rupert M. Fogg (1914-1989)
Richard M. Fogg
Fletcher Dal Handley, Jr.
Ronald L. Brown

ASSOCIATES

Kelley L. Cornelius
Robert E. Grantham

Attorneys for: The Globe Savings Bank SSB; Oklahoma Gas & Electric Co.; El Reno School District; Frisco Railroad; Calumet School District; Parkview Hospital Trust Authority; Union City School District.

For full biographical listings, see the Martindale-Hubbell Law Directory

FULLER, TUBB & POMEROY (AV)

800 Bank of Oklahoma Plaza, 201 Robert S. Kerr Avenue, 73102-4292
Telephone: 405-235-2575
Fax: 405-232-8384

MEMBERS OF FIRM

G. M. Fuller
Jerry Tubb
L. David Pomeroy
Joe Heaton
Michael A. Bickford
Terry Stokes

OF COUNSEL

Thomas J. Kenan

LEGAL SUPPORT PERSONNEL

Sherie S. Adams (Legal Assistant)

Representative Clients: French Petroleum Corp.; Independent Insurance Agents of Oklahoma, Inc.; LTV Energy Products Co.; Northwestern National Life Insurance Co.; Purina Mills, Inc.; Sequa Corp.; Halliburton Oil Producing Co.; Chemical Bank/Chemical Financial Corporation; Pitney Bowes, Inc.; Norwest Banks.

For full biographical listings, see the Martindale-Hubbell Law Directory

HARTZOG CONGER & CASON, A PROFESSIONAL CORPORATION (AV)

1600 Bank of Oklahoma Plaza, 73102
Telephone: 405-235-7000
Facsimile: 405-235-7329

Larry D. Hartzog
J. William Conger
Len Cason
James C. Prince
Alan Newman
Steven C. Davis
Valerie K. Couch
Mark D. Dickey
Joseph P. Hogsett
John D. Robertson
Kurt M. Rupert
Laura Haag McConnell

Susan B. Shields
Ryan S. Wilson
Melanie J. Jester
Armand Paliotta
Julia Watson
J. Leslie LaReau

OF COUNSEL

Kent F. Frates

For full biographical listings, see the Martindale-Hubbell Law Directory

HASTIE AND KIRSCHNER, A PROFESSIONAL CORPORATION (AV)

3000 Oklahoma Tower, 210 Park Avenue, 73102-5604
Telephone: 405-239-6404
Telecopier: 405-239-6403

(See Next Column)

Mark H. Bennett
Mitchell D. Blackburn
George W. Dahnke
John W. Funk
John D. Hastie
Michael Paul Kirschner
Ronald L. Matlock
Kieran D. Maye, Jr.
Robert D. McCutcheon
David D. Morgan
Kiran A. Phansalkar
Irwin H. Steinhorn
John W. Swinford, Jr.
Ruston C. Welch
Monica A. Wittrock

OF COUNSEL

William S. Price

For full biographical listings, see the Martindale-Hubbell Law Directory

HUGHES, WHITE, ADAMS & GRANT (AV)

The Paragon, 5801 North Broadway Extension, Suite 302, 73118-7438
Telephone: 405-848-0111
FAX: 405-848-3507

Carl D. Hughes
Joe E. White, Jr.
Richard S. Adams
Michael E. Grant
Allan E. Mitchell

For full biographical listings, see the Martindale-Hubbell Law Directory

KERR, IRVINE, RHODES & ABLES, A PROFESSIONAL CORPORATION (AV)

600 Bank of Oklahoma Plaza, 73102-4267
Telephone: 405-272-9221
Fax: 405-236-3121

Robert S. Kerr, Jr.
Horace G. Rhodes
Don J. Gutteridge, Jr.
Jo Angela Ables
James W. Rhodes
F. Andrew Fugitt

James W. Berry
Michael D. Coleman
Robert G. Shoemaker
James R. Barnett
R. Thomas Lay

OF COUNSEL

Francis S. Irvine
Henry B. Taliaferro, Jr.

For full biographical listings, see the Martindale-Hubbell Law Directory

LOONEY, NICHOLS, JOHNSON & HAYES (AV)

528 Northwest 12th, P.O. Box 468, 73103
Telephone: 405-235-7641
Fax: 405-239-2050; 239-2052

Ned Looney (1886-1965)
Clyde J. Watts (1907-1975)
Willard R. Bergstrasser (1922-1993)
Robert Dudley Looney
Henry W. Nichols, Jr.
Burton J. Johnson
John B. Hayes
Edwin F. Garrison
Robert D. Looney, Jr.
Charles J. Watts
Tenal S. Cooley, III
Timothy L. Martin
Robert L. Magrini

Brigid F. Kennedy
H. Grady Parker, Jr.
Katresa Jo Riffel
Evan Blake Gatewood
John McPherson Hayes
Bradley K. Donnell

Representative Clients: Kansas City Southern Railway Co.; United States Fidelity & Guaranty Co.; Hartford Insurance Group; Atena Casualty and Surety Co.; U.S. Aviation Insurance Underwriters; CNA Insurance Company; The Goodyear Tire & Rubber Co.; Travelers Insurance Group; Home Insurance Co.; Fireman's Fund Group.

For full biographical listings, see the Martindale-Hubbell Law Directory

LYTLE SOULÉ & CURLEE (AV)

1200 Robinson Renaissance, 119 North Robinson, 73102
Telephone: 405-235-7471
Telecopy: 405-232-3852

MEMBERS OF FIRM

Roy Cobb Lytle (1902-1982)
Edward E. Soulé (1924-1984)
William D. Curlee (1929-1992)
James C. Chandler
Peter T. Van Dyke
David E. Nichols
Donald K. Funnell
Gary C. Pierson
G. David Ross
Michael D. Carter
Tony G. Puckett

ASSOCIATES

Samuel R. Fulkerson
Nathan L. Whatley
Rochelle L. Huddleston
Deborah S. Block

OF COUNSEL

John W. Mee, Jr.
Gordon D. Ryan

Representative Clients: Twentieth Century-Fox Film Corp.; Firestone Tire & Rubber Co.; Scrivner, Inc.; NCR Corporation; Northrop Worldwide Aircraft Services, Inc.; Sears Savings Bank; The Travelers Indemnity Company; Farmers Insurance Group of Companies; Great Plains Coca-Cola Bottling Company.

For full biographical listings, see the Martindale-Hubbell Law Directory

Oklahoma City—Continued

McAFEE & TAFT, A PROFESSIONAL CORPORATION (AV)

Tenth Floor, Two Leadership Square, 73102
Telephone: 405-235-9621
Cable Address: "Oklaw"
TWX: 910-831-3294
Facsimile: (405) 235-0439 (405) 232-2404

Kenneth E. McAfee (1903-1986)
Joseph G. Rucks (1913-1988)
Reford Bond (1930-1989)
Stewart W. Mark (1915-1993)
Judson S. Woodruff (Retired)
Terry R. Barrett
Marion C. Bauman
Joseph H. Bocock
Kenneth L. Buettner
Steven W. Bugg
Mark E. Burget
Gary W. Catron
W. Chris Coleman
Richard D. Craig
C. Bruce Crum
Stanley L. Cunningham
Robert W. Dace
Theodore M. Elam
Gary F. Fuller
Robert H. Gilliland, Jr.
Lenore Templeton Graham
Philip D. Hart
John N. Hermes
Frank D. Hill
Henry D. Hoss
Laurence M. Huffman
James Dudley Hyde
Michael E. Joseph
John A. Kenney
Myrna Schack Latham
John M. Mee
Sally Mock
John R. Morris
Richard D. Nix
John Michael Nordin
John A. Papahronis
Louis J. Price
Dee A. Replogle, Jr.
Richard A. Riggs
Reid E. Robison
John E. Sargent, Jr.
John N. Schaefer
Scott W. Sewell
James W. Sharrock
Joel D. Stafford
Connie S. Stamets
C. David Stinson
Brice E. Tarzwell
Elizabeth Dalton Tyrrell
Joseph Walters
Jerry A. Warren
Drew D. Webb
Steven R. Welch
Elizabeth Scott Wood

Sheryl N. Barr
Robert L. Garbrecht
David J. Ketelsleger
Michael F. Lauderdale
Steven T. Ledgerwood
Mark Richard Mullins
Amy J. Sine

OF COUNSEL

Richard G. Taft
Eugene Kuntz
Frank L. Polk
Sidney P. Upsher

Representative Clients: Boatman's First National Bank of Oklahoma; New York Life Insurance Company; Emerson Electric Co.; Merrill Lynch, Pierce, Fenner & Smith Inc.; Arthur Andersen & Co.; Fleming Companies, Inc.; USX Corp.; Amoco Production Company; Ford Motor Company.

For full biographical listings, see the Martindale-Hubbell Law Directory

---

MOCK, SCHWABE, WALDO, ELDER, REEVES & BRYANT, A PROFESSIONAL CORPORATION (AV)

Fifteenth Floor, One Leadership Square, 211 North Robinson Avenue, 73102
Telephone: 405-235-5500
Telecopy: 405-235-2875

Randall D. Mock
G. Blaine Schwabe, III
James R. Waldo
James C. Elder
John R. Reeves
Gary A. Bryant
Steven L. Barghols
Mary S. Robertson
Jay C. Jimerson
Richard C. Labarthe
Steven P. Cole
Kevin M. Coffey
Rob F. Robertson
Sarah Alexander Hall
Jack Cameron Moore

OF COUNSEL

Michael J. Hunter

Representative Clients: Amoco Production Co.; Atlantic Richfield Co.; Bank of Oklahoma, N.A.; Farm Credit Bank of Wichita; Massachusetts Mutual Life Insurance Co.; Metropolitan Life Insurance Co.; Sun Exploration and Production Co.; Texaco, Inc.; Liberty Bank & Trust Company of Oklahoma City.

For full biographical listings, see the Martindale-Hubbell Law Directory

---

MONNET, HAYES, BULLIS, THOMPSON & EDWARDS (AV)

Suite 1719 First National Center, West, 73102
Telephone: 405-232-5481
Fax: 405-235-9159

MEMBERS OF FIRM

Claude Monnet (1899-1980)
Lynn J. Bullis, Jr. (1910-1984)
Coleman H. Hayes (1903-1985)
Russell F. Thompson (1920-1985)
John T. Edwards
James M. Peters
James S. Drennan
Randall A. Breshears
Sarah H. Stuhr
Gayle Freeman Cook
Robert C. Smith, Jr.
Steven K. McKinney

(See Next Column)

Shannon L. Edwards
Jonathan Eric Miller
Christopher James Perry
Michael Peters
Phillip Dickey
Robert A. French

Representative Clients: The First National Bank of Beaver; Natural Gas Pipeline Company of America; Grace Petroleum Corp.; Travelers Insurance Co.; Chevron USA, Inc.; Oryx Energy; Oxy, Energy; Normac Foods, Inc.; Toys R Us.

For full biographical listings, see the Martindale-Hubbell Law Directory

---

PHILLIPS McFALL McCAFFREY McVAY & MURRAH, P.C. (AV)

One Leadership Square, 12th Floor, 211 North Robinson, 73102
Telephone: 405-235-4100
Fax: 405-235-4133
Other Oklahoma City Office: 1001 N.W. 63rd Street, Suite 200, 73116.
Telephone: 405-840-5240;
Fax: 405-840-2136.

T. Ray Phillips, III
D. Keith McFall
James A. McCaffrey
Melvin R. McVay, Jr.
Alfred P. Murrah, Jr.
Robert N. Sheets
J. Mark Lovelace
Terry L. Hawkins
Mark E. Pruitt
Joseph K. Heselton, Jr.
Thomas G. Wolfe
Sandra Leah Schovanec
Elizabeth Kemp Brown
Raymond E. Zschiesche

Marc Edwards
A. V. Peoples, III
Heather L. Hintz
O. Dudley Gilbert
Tom L. Burroughs

OF COUNSEL

Robert L. Berry
Brian H. Upp
D. Craig Story
Donald A. Pape

For full biographical listings, see the Martindale-Hubbell Law Directory

---

PIERCE COUCH HENDRICKSON BAYSINGER & GREEN (AV)

1109 North Francis, P.O. Box 26350, 73126
Telephone: 405-235-1611
Fax: 405-235-2904
Tulsa, Oklahoma Office: Suite 6110, 5555 East 71St. Street, 74136.
Telephone: 918-493-4944.
Fax: 918-493-6196.

MEMBERS OF FIRM

Calvin W. Hendrickson
Melvin F. Pierce
Hugh A. Baysinger
Gerald P. Green
Stephen L. Olson
James B. Durant (Resident, Tulsa Office)
D. Lynn Babb
Scott M. Rhodes
Inona Jane Harness
Russell L. Hendrickson
John Roger Hurt
Frances E. Patton
Curtis L. Smith
Charles A. Brandt
Robert S. Lafferrandre

ASSOCIATES

Jerrold Abramowitz
Kathleen J. Adler
John Christopher Condren
Steven W. Daniels
Darren B. Derryberry
Susan A. Doke
Todd Estes
Bradey T. Holler
E. Marissa Lane
Scott A. Law
G. Calvin Sharpe
Paul G. Summars
Haven Tobias
Peter L. Wheeler

OF COUNSEL

Janet Childers Pope
Larry G. Cassil, Jr.
Kevin T. Gassaway (Resident, Tulsa Office)

Representative Clients: CNA/Insurance; American Fidelity Insurance Co.; Insurance Company of North America; Royal Insurance Co.; Lloyd's of London; Kemper Insurance Group; Physicians Liability Insurance Co.; Shelter Insurance Co.; Sears, Roebuck & Co.; Chubb Insurance Group.

For full biographical listings, see the Martindale-Hubbell Law Directory

---

PRINGLE & PRINGLE, A PROFESSIONAL CORPORATION (AV)

1601 N.W. Expressway, Suite 2100, 73118
Telephone: 405-848-4810
Fax: 405-848-4819

Lynn A. Pringle
Laura Nan Smith Pringle
Conni L. Allen
Stephen W. Elliott
James R. Martin, Jr.

OF COUNSEL

Alvin C. Harrell
Michael P. Sullivan

Representative Clients: Bankers Systems, Inc.; Central Oklahoma Clearing House Association; The Bankers Bank; Bank of Western Oklahoma, Elk City; The Farmers Bank, Carnegie; The First National Bank and Trust Co., Chickasha; The First National Bank of Texhoma; Oklahoma Home Based Business Association; First State Bank, Idabel; Great Western Drilling Co.

For full biographical listings, see the Martindale-Hubbell Law Directory

Oklahoma City—Continued

RAINEY, ROSS, RICE & BINNS (AV)
735 First National Center West, 73102-7405
Telephone: 405-235-1356
Telecopier: 405-235-2340

MEMBERS OF FIRM

Robert M. Rainey (1882-1971)
Streeter Blanton Flynn (1892-1971)
Gordon F. Rainey (1913-1975)
William J. Ross
Hugh D. Rice
H. D. Binns, Jr.
Rodney L. Cook
Robert J. Campbell, Jr.
Roberta Browning Fields
Peggy Horinek
Michael R. Perri
Douglas M. Todd

General Attorneys for Oklahoma: Santa Fe Pacific Corp.; Santa Fe Railway System.
Oklahoma Counsel for: Oklahoma Gas & Electric Co.
Attorneys for: Agristor Credit Corp.; AT&T Communications; Boatmen's First National Bank of Oklahoma; The Circle K Corp.; Continental Air Lines; Dover Elevator Co.; Dover Industries Acceptance, Inc.

For full biographical listings, see the Martindale-Hubbell Law Directory

ROBERTSON & WILLIAMS, INC. (AV)
Three Chopt Square 6108 North Western Avenue, 73118-1044
Telephone: 405-848-1944
Fax: 405-843-6707

Mark A. Robertson
Thomas C. Williams

OF COUNSEL

R. Pope Van Cleef, Jr.

For full biographical listings, see the Martindale-Hubbell Law Directory

RYAN, GEISTER & WHALEY, A PROFESSIONAL CORPORATION (AV)
120 North Robinson Suite 2520, 73102
Telephone: 405-239-6041
Telefax: 405-235-3090

Patrick M. Ryan
Charles E. Geister, III
Phillip G. Whaley

Representative Clients: Allstate Life Insurance Co.; American Chambers Life Insurance Co.; Eli Lilly and Company; Globe Life and Accident Insurance Co.; McDonald's Corp.; Oakland Oil Co.; The Travelers Insurance Co.; The Liberty National Bank and Trust Co. of Oklahoma City.

For full biographical listings, see the Martindale-Hubbell Law Directory

SHIRK, WORK, ROBINSON & WORK, A PROFESSIONAL CORPORATION (AV)
800 Colcord Building, 73102
Telephone: 405-236-3571
FAX: 405- 236-8028

John H. Shirk (1897-1942)
George H. Shirk (1913-1977)
James E. Work
William J. Robinson
J. Kelly Work
Stanley F. Carroll

Representative Clients: AMF Inc.; Oklahoma County Finance Authority; Pizza Hut, Inc.; Circle K Corp.; Weyerhaeuser Co.; Federal Corp.; Little Giant Corp.; Bank IV Oklahoma; Fred Jones Manufacturing Co.; McDonalds, Corporation.

For full biographical listings, see the Martindale-Hubbell Law Directory

WHITE, COFFEY, GALT & FITE, P.C. (AV)
6520 North Western, Suite 300, 73116
Telephone: 405-842-7545
Fax: 405-840-9890

John M. Coffey
Jack P. Fite
Jay M. Galt
James U. White, Jr.

Linda Gensler Kaufmann
Margorie McCullough

OF COUNSEL

Henry John Hood
Robert V. Varnum

For full biographical listings, see the Martindale-Hubbell Law Directory

*OKMULGEE,** Okmulgee Co.

RAINEY & BARKSDALE (AV)
310 East Seventh Street, P.O. Box 1366, 74447
Telephone: 918-756-0900
Fax: 918-756-0943

MEMBERS OF FIRM

Dale F. Rainey (1907-1987)
John H. W. Barksdale
Bill Barksdale

(See Next Column)

ASSOCIATES

Rod W. Wiemer

Representative Clients: Citizens Bank & Trust Co.; Okmulgee School District; Okmulgee Creek Conservancy District; Emergency Medical Service; Cane Creek Conservancy District; Rowe Energy; OMH Medical Center, Inc.; Rural Water District No. 2; Chamber of Commerce of Okmulgee; Morris State Bank.

For full biographical listings, see the Martindale-Hubbell Law Directory

*PAULS VALLEY,** Garvin Co. — (Refer to Ada)

*PAWHUSKA,** Osage Co.

KANE, KANE & KANE (AV)
Law Office Building, 120 East Sixth Street, P.O. Box 1019, 74056
Telephone: 918-287-3143
Fax: 918-287-2233
Skiatook, Oklahoma Office: 500 West Rogers Boulevard.
Telephone: 918-396-1237.

Matthew J. Kane (1910-1992)

MEMBERS OF FIRM

Matthew J. Kane, Jr.
M. John Kane, IV
Cynthia M. Klots

Representative Clients: Barnsdall State Bank, Barnsdall; Exchange Bank, Skiatook; Pawhuska Urban Renewal Authority; Arrowhead Ranches of Oklahoma.
Local Attorneys for: Phillips Petroleum Co.
Approved Attorneys for: American First Title & Trust Co.; Equitable Life Assurance Society of U.S.

For full biographical listings, see the Martindale-Hubbell Law Directory

*PAWNEE,** Pawnee Co. — (Refer to Stillwater)

PONCA CITY, Kay Co.

NORTHCUTT, CLARK, GARDNER, HRON & POWELL (AV)
Fourth Floor, Heartland Federal Savings and Loan Building, P.O. Drawer 1669, 74602
Telephone: 405-762-1655
Fax: 405-765-4142

MEMBERS OF FIRM

Clarence D. Northcutt
Paul E. Northcutt
Guy P. Clark
John J. Gardner, II
John W. Hron, Jr.
Cleve W. Powell
Stuart L. Tate
Lynne Ann Wilkins Dixon

For full biographical listings, see the Martindale-Hubbell Law Directory

*POTEAU,** Le Flore Co. — (Refer to McAlester)

*PURCELL,** McClain Co.

JOHN MANTOOTH (AV)
Suite E Professional Building, 310 West Washington Street, P.O. Box 667, 73080
Telephone: 405-527-2137; 527-6517
Fax: 405-527-3440

Representative Client: First American Bank and Trust Co., Purcell, Oklahoma.
References: McClain County National Bank, Purcell, Oklahoma; First American Bank and Trust Co., Purcell, Oklahoma.

For full biographical listings, see the Martindale-Hubbell Law Directory

*SALLISAW,** Sequoyah Co. — (Refer to Muskogee)

*SAYRE,** Beckham Co. — (Refer to Weatherford)

SEMINOLE, Seminole Co.

ELSENER & CADENHEAD (AV)
300 East Seminole, P.O. Box 2067, 74818-2067
Telephone: 405-382-6341; 257-2773
Fax: 405-382-5513

MEMBERS OF FIRM

G. Dale Elsener
Ed Cadenhead

References furnished upon request.

For full biographical listings, see the Martindale-Hubbell Law Directory

*SHAWNEE,** Pottawatomie Co.

DIAMOND, STUART & CLOVER (AV)
Formerly Miller, Peters, Diamond & Stuart
116 North Bell, P.O. Box 1925, 74802-1925
Telephone: 405-275-0700
Telecopy: 405-275-6805

(See Next Column)

DIAMOND, STUART & CLOVER, *Shawnee—Continued*

MEMBERS OF FIRM

H. Jeffrey Diamond
James T. Stuart
Michael D. Clover

OF COUNSEL

Lindsay Peters

Representative Clients: Oklahoma Gas & Electric Co.; Shawnee Urban Renewal Authority; TDK Ferrites Corp.; Mobil Chemical Co.
General Counsel: BancFirst, Shawnee; Central Plastics Co.
Approved Examining Attorneys for: Southwest Title & Trust Co., Oklahoma City; Lawyers Title Insurance Corp.; American First Title & Trust Co., Oklahoma City.

For full biographical listings, see the Martindale-Hubbell Law Directory

HENSON, HENSON, HENSON, MARSHALL & MILBURN (AV)

101 West Ninth, 74801
Telephone: 405-275-2550
Fax: 405-275-2588

MEMBERS OF FIRM

Almon E. Henson
Karen Ann Henson
J. Roger Henson
James R. Marshall
Kermit M. Milburn

General Counsel for: Oklahoma Baptist University; Canadian Valley Electric Cooperative, Inc.; Bell Federal Credit Union; Bison Federal Credit Union.
Representative Clients: American National Bank and Trust Company of Shawnee; Modern Oil Co.
Approved Attorneys for: Southwest Title & Trust Co.; American First Title & Trust Co.; Lawyers Title Insurance Corp.

For full biographical listings, see the Martindale-Hubbell Law Directory

*STILLWATER,** Payne Co.

HERT & BAKER, A PROFESSIONAL CORPORATION (AV)

222 East Seventh, P.O. Box 668, 74076
Telephone: 405-377-8644
FAX: 405-377-6363

Robert L. Hert, Jr.
William J. Baker
Tina Mooney Koemel

For full biographical listings, see the Martindale-Hubbell Law Directory

HOUSTON AND OSBORN, P.C. (AV)

Suite 200, 7th Avenue Center, 123 West 7th Avenue, P.O. Box 1118, 74076
Telephone: 405-377-7618; 377-8233
Telecopier: 405-377-8234

Winfrey D. Houston
Lynn R. Osborn

Representative Clients: Payne County Bank, Perkins, Okla.; Citizens State Bank of Morrison, Oklahoma; Stillwater National Bank, BancFirst; Sumpter-Barker Drilling Co.; Stillwater School District.
Approved Attorneys for: American First Title & Trust Co.; Southwest Title & Trust Co.

For full biographical listings, see the Martindale-Hubbell Law Directory

*SULPHUR,** Murray Co. — (Refer to Ada)

*TAHLEQUAH,** Cherokee Co. — (Refer to Muskogee)

*TISHOMINGO,** Johnston Co. — (Refer to Madill)

*TULSA,** Tulsa Co.

BOESCHE, MCDERMOTT & ESKRIDGE (AV)

Suite 800 Oneok Plaza, 100 West Fifth Street, 74103
Telephone: 918-583-1777
Fax: 918-592-5809
Muskogee, Oklahoma Office: 420 Broadway, 74101.
Telephone: 918-683-6100.

MEMBERS OF FIRM

Fenelon Boesche (1910-1993)
Richard B. McDermott (1905-1977)
Franklin D. Hettinger (1927-1991)
R. Casey Cooper
David B. McKinney
Bradley K. Beasley
Frank D. Spiegelberg
David A. Johnson

ASSOCIATES

R. Kevin Layton
Sheila M. Powers
Byron E. (Rusty) Brown
Bradley H. Mallett

OF COUNSEL

T. Hillis Eskridge
Lance Stockwell
Nik Jones
Clifford K. Cate, Jr. (Resident at Muskogee)
Jane La Gree Allingham

Representative Clients: Apache Corp.; Atlantic Richfield; Oxy USA, Inc.; Dillon, Reed Co., Inc.; Elf Atochem North America, Inc.; The Chase Manhattan Bank (N.A.); Transwestern Pipeline Co.

(See Next Column)

For full biographical listings, see the Martindale-Hubbell Law Directory

BOONE, SMITH, DAVIS, HURST & DICKMAN, A PROFESSIONAL CORPORATION (AV)

500 Oneok Plaza, 100 West 5th Street, 74103
Telephone: 918-587-0000
Fax: 918-599-9317

Byron V. Boone (1908-1988)
Royce H. Savage (1904-1993)
L. K. Smith
Reuben Davis
J. Jerry Dickman
Frederic N. (Nick) Schneider III
William C. Kellough
J Schaad Titus
John A. Burkhardt
Paul E. Swain III
Carol A. Grissom
Kimberly Lambert Love
Teresa Meinders Burkett
Paul J. Cleary

R. Tom Hillis
Barry G. Reynolds
Laura L. Gonsalves
Scott R. Rowland
Shane Egan
Nancy Lynn Davis

OF COUNSEL

Edwin S. Hurst
Lloyd G. Minter

Representative Clients: American Airlines; Chevron U.S.A., Inc.; The F & M Bank & Trust Co.; Hillcrest Medical Center; Boatmen's First National Bank of Oklahoma; Phillips Petroleum Co.; Rockwell International; Sears, Roebuck & Co.; Thrifty Rent-A-Car Systems, Inc.; World Publishing Co.

For full biographical listings, see the Martindale-Hubbell Law Directory

CLARK & WILLIAMS (AV)

Suite 600 Fox Plaza Office Center, 5416 South Yale Avenue, 74135
Telephone: 918-496-9200
Fax: 918-496-3851

MEMBERS OF FIRM

Wendell W. Clark
Darrell E. Williams

ASSOCIATES

Mark R. Reents
Michael DeCarlo
Kathryn A. Herwig

References: Bank of Oklahoma; Peoples State Bank.

For full biographical listings, see the Martindale-Hubbell Law Directory

CONNER & WINTERS, A PROFESSIONAL CORPORATION (AV)

15 East 5th Street, Suite 2400, 74103-4391
Telephone: 918-586-5711
Fax: 918-586-8982
Oklahoma City, Oklahoma Office: 204 North Robinson, Suite 950, 73102.
Telephone: 405-232-7711.
Facsimile: 405-232-2695.

John E. Barry
James R. Ryan
John S. Athens
Henry G. Will
Joseph J. McCain, Jr.
Russell H. Harbaugh, Jr.
Lynnwood R. Moore, Jr.
Robert A. Curry
Steven W. McGrath
John T. Schmidt
D. Richard Funk
Randolph L. Jones, Jr. (Not admitted in OK)
J. David Jorgenson
Martin R. Wing
John W. Ingraham
Andrew R. Turner
Judith A. McCoy
Douglas M. Rather
Gentra Abbey Sorem
R. Kevin Redwine
Deirdre O'Neil E. Dexter
Tony W. Haynie
Bruce W. Freeman
David R. Cordell
G. W. Turner, III
Paul E. Braden
Robert J. Melgaard
P. David Newsome, Jr.

OFFICE PERSONNEL
OKLAHOMA CITY, OKLAHOMA

Peter B. Bradford
Raymond E. Tompkins
Timothy J. Bomhoff

Katherine Gallagher Coyle
Anne B. Sublett
Rebecca Sellers Woodward
C. Kevin Morrison
Beverly K. Smith
Phillip L. Allbritten
Greg S. Scharlau
P. Scott Hathaway
John A. Bugg
Lawrence A. Hall
Sean H. McKee
R. Richard Love, III
Steven G. Heinen
John M. Matheson
Christopher S. Thrutchley

OF COUNSEL

William E. Rutledge
Robert L. McGowen
Charles C. Killin
David J. Hyman
R. Mark Solano
Debbie L. Blackwell

For full biographical listings, see the Martindale-Hubbell Law Directory

Tulsa—Continued

Crawford, Crowe & Bainbridge, P.A. (AV)

1714 First National Building, 74103
Telephone: 918-587-1128
Fax: 918-587-3975

B. Hayden Crawford
Harry M. Crowe, Jr.
Robert L. Bainbridge
Kyle B. Haskins
Eric B. Bolusky

For full biographical listings, see the Martindale-Hubbell Law Directory

Doerner, Stuart, Saunders, Daniel & Anderson (AV)

Suite 500, 320 South Boston Avenue, 74103-3725
Telephone: 918-582-1211
FAX: 918-591-5360

MEMBERS OF FIRM

C. B. Stuart (1857-1936)
Erwin J. Doerner (1897-1980)
Samuel P. Daniel
William C. Anderson
Varley H. Taylor, Jr.
G. Michael Lewis
William B. Morgan
Lawrence T. Chambers, Jr.
Dallas E. Ferguson
Sam G. Bratton, II
Gary M. McDonald
H. Wayne Cooper
Kevin C. Coutant
Richard P. Hix
Lynn Paul Mattson
William F. Riggs
Lewis N. Carter
Linda Crook Martin
James Patrick McCann
Richard H. Foster
Charles S. Plumb
Leonard I. Pataki
S. Douglas Dodd
Elise Dunitz Brennan
Kathy R. Neal
John J. Carwile
Jon E. Brightmire
L. Dru McQueen
Tom Q. Ferguson

ASSOCIATES

Richard J. Eagleton
Rebecca McCarthy Fowler
Kristen L. Brightmire
Michael C. Redman
Steven K. Metcalf
Benjamin J. Chapman
R. Michael Cole
David B. Auer
Shelly L. Dalrymple
Russell W. Kroll
John R. Pinkerton
Robert A. Burk

OF COUNSEL

Dickson M. Saunders
R. Robert Huff

Representative Clients: Public Service Company of Oklahoma; Oklahoma Ordnance Works Authority; Sand Springs Home Co.; St. John Medical Center, Inc.

For full biographical listings, see the Martindale-Hubbell Law Directory

Gable & Gotwals (AV)

2000 Bank IV Center, 15 West Sixth Street, 74119-5447
Telephone: 918-582-9201
Facsimile: 918-586-8383

Teresa B. Adwan
Pamela S. Anderson
John R. Barker
David L. Bryant
Gene C. Buzzard
Dennis Clarke Cameron
Timothy A. Carney
Renee DeMoss
Elsie C. Draper
Sidney G. Dunagan
Theodore Q. Eliot
Richard W. Gable
Jeffrey Don Hassell
Patricia Ledvina Himes
Oliver S. Howard
Richard D. Koljack, Jr.
J. Daniel Morgan
Joseph W. Morris
Elizabeth R. Muratet
Richard B. Noulles
Ronald N. Ricketts
John Henry Rule
M. Benjamin Singletary
James M. Sturdivant
Patrick O. Waddel
Michael D. Hall
David Edward Keglovits
Stephen W. Lake
Kari S. McKee
Terry D. Ragsdale
Jeffrey C. Rambach

OF COUNSEL

G. Ellis Gable
Charles P. Gotwals, Jr.

For full biographical listings, see the Martindale-Hubbell Law Directory

Hall, Estill, Hardwick, Gable, Golden & Nelson, A Professional Corporation (AV)

320 South Boston Avenue Suite 400, 74103
Telephone: 918-594-0400
Facsimile: 918-594-0505
Telex: ITT 49-79311 or WU 49-2421
Oklahoma City Office: 2900 Liberty Tower, 100, North Broadway. 73102-8804.
Telephone: 405-232-2828.
Facsimile: 405-232-8004.
Washington, D.C. Office: Suite 750, South Building, 1120 20th Street N.W. 20036-3406.
Telephone: 202-822-9100.
Facsimile: 202-293-6492.

(See Next Column)

Walter B. Hall (1923-1986)
Fred S. Nelson (1928-1987)
James C. T. Hardwick
Thomas D. Gable
Thomas F. Golden
Larry W. Sandel
Raymond B. Kelly
Andrew M. Wolov
Frank M. Hagedorn
J. Patrick Cremin
J. Kevin Hayes
Michael D. Graves
Claire V. Eagan
James D. Satrom
Richard A. Groenendyke, Jr.
Graydon D. Luthey, Jr.
Del L. Gustafson
Mark K. Blongewicz
Michael D. Cooke
Matthew G. Livingood
Kenneth L. Hunt
B. Kenneth Cox, Jr.
Donald L. Kahl
Thomas P. Schroedter
Richard T. McGonigle
Doris J. Astle
James J. Proszek
James M. Reed
Thomas A. Creekmore, III
Stephen W. Ray
Margaret A. Swimmer
Michael T. Keester
Susan L. Gates
William G. Bernhardt
Kenneth G. M. Mather
Ronald A. White
Michael L. Nemec
Joseph D. Fincher
R. Mark Petrich
Fred M. Buxton
Pamela H. Goldberg
Robert S. Rizley
Pamela A. Mattson
Judith A. Colbert
Michele T. Gehres
Mark Banner
Steven A. Broussard
Tod J. Barrett
Kevin Y. Litz
Steven W. Soulé
Robert P. Fitz-Patrick
J. Christopher Hastings
John A. Menchaca, II
Curtis Lewis, Jr.
Kelly Kibbie Webster
T. Lane Wilson

OF COUNSEL

John S. Estill, Jr.
Graydon D. Luthey
Ross O. Swimmer

OKLAHOMA CITY, OKLAHOMA OFFICE
PERSONNEL

H. B. Watson, Jr.
William R. Burkett
J. Fred Gist
Kirk D. Fredrickson
Douglas N. Gould
Phil G. Busey
Mary Johnson Tidholm
Donna Nix Blakley
Linda G. Scoggins
Kwame Telli Mumina
Sharon Taylor Thomas
Elizabeth A. Scott
Daniel J. Glover
Janis Wood Preslar
Jon A. Epstein
Tod J. Barrett
Elaine R. Turner
Patricia D. Horn
N. Janine Wheeler

WASHINGTON, D.C. OFFICE
PERSONNEL

John B. Rudolph
Kathryn J. Kuhlen
Vera C. Neinast
Joseph R. Membrino, Jr.
Lisa M. Tonery

Reference: Bank of Oklahoma.

For full biographical listings, see the Martindale-Hubbell Law Directory

Holliman, Langholz, Runnels, Holden, Forsman & Sellers, A Professional Corporation (AV)

Suite 500 Holarud Building, Ten East Third Street, 74103-3695
Telephone: 918-584-1471
FAX: 918-587-9652,
Telex: 251773 GRC UR
Oklahoma City, Oklahoma Office: Suite 160, Two Broadway Executive Park, 205 N.W. 63rd Street.
Telephone: 405-848-6999.
Fax: 405-840-3312.

Robert W. Langholz
Gail R. Runnels
David W. Holden
Michael S. Forsman
Keith F. Sellers
James D. Bryant

Matthew James Browne, III
Ann Nicholson Smith
Laurence Langholz

AFFILIATES

David L. Sobel
Roderick Oxford

OF COUNSEL

Joe M. Holliman
Ted P. Holshouser (Resident, Oklahoma City Office)

Representative Clients: The F & M Bank and Trust Company, Tulsa, Ok.; Transportation Leasing Co., Inc.; The Sterling Group, Inc.; Albert Investments; Bryan Industries, Inc.; Enserch Corp.; Kaiser-Francis Oil Co.; Family & Children's Service, Inc.; Junior League of Tulsa; Anadarko Bank and Trust Co.

For full biographical listings, see the Martindale-Hubbell Law Directory

Tulsa—Continued

HUFFMAN ARRINGTON KIHLE GABERINO & DUNN, A PROFESSIONAL CORPORATION (AV)

1000 ONEOK Plaza, 74103
Telephone: 918-585-8141
Telecopier: 918-588-7873
Oklahoma City Office: 2212 NW 50th Street, Suite 163.
Telephone: 405-840-4408.
Telecopier: 405-843-9090.

John L. Arrington, Jr.
Donald A. Kihle
John A. Gaberino, Jr.
C. Burnett Dunn
Michael V. Snyder
John M. Sharp
J. Clarke Kendall II
Curtis M. Long
Thomas J. Kirby
Robert A. Huffman, Jr.
Sheppard F. Miers, Jr.
Larry D. Henry
Sidney K. Swinson
Juley M. Roffers
Stuart D. Campbell
William T. Walker
Barry K. Beasley

Sue C. Mayhue
Jean Ann Hudson
Tammy D. Barrett
Vivian C. Hale
Ronald W. Little
Patrick W. Cipolla

OF COUNSEL

Cody B. Waddell (Resident, Oklahoma City Office)
Robert A. Huffman

General Counsel for: ONEOK Inc.; Oklahoma Natural Gas Co.; H W Allen Co.; ONEOK Exploration Co.; Woodland Bank; ONEOK Drilling Co.; ONEOK Resources Co.; Renberg's, Inc.

For full biographical listings, see the Martindale-Hubbell Law Directory

---

JONES, GIVENS, GOTCHER & BOGAN, A PROFESSIONAL CORPORATION (AV)

3800 First National Tower, 74103
Telephone: 918-581-8200
Fax: 918-583-1189 or 918-583-6652

Neil E. Bogan (1945-1990)
William B. Jones
Jack R. Givens
Roy C. Breedlove
David C. Cameron
Vaden F. Bales
James E. Weger
Thomas L. Vogt
Ronald O. Ray, Jr.
Ira L. Edwards, Jr.

C. Michael Copeland

OF COUNSEL

Deryl Lee Gotcher
Dan A. Rogers
Richard C. Honn
Judi E. Beaumont
Gregory G. Meier

Representative Clients: Financial Services: Boatmen's First National Bank of Oklahoma. Insurance: Aetna Insurance Co.; Oklahoma Bar Professional Liability Insurance Co.; Physicians Liability Insurance Co.; Travelers Insurance Co.; Employers Casualty Insurance Co.; Government Employees Insurance Co. Professional Services: KPMG, Peat Marwick. Manufacturing & Commerce: Ciba-Geigy Chemical Co.; Clear Channel Communications.

For full biographical listings, see the Martindale-Hubbell Law Directory

JOYCE AND POLLARD (AV)

Suite 300, 515 South Main Mall, 74103
Telephone: 918-585-2751
Fax: 918-582-9308

MEMBERS OF FIRM

J. C. Joyce
Dwayne C. Pollard

Ted J. Nelson
Sheila M. Bradley
John C. Joyce

A list of Representative Clients furnished upon request.

For full biographical listings, see the Martindale-Hubbell Law Directory

---

LIPE, GREEN, PASCHAL, TRUMP & BRAGG, A PROFESSIONAL CORPORATION (AV)

3700 First National Tower, 15 East Fifth Street, Suite 3700, 74103-4344
Telephone: 918-599-9400
Fax: 918-599-9404

Larry B. Lipe
James E. Green, Jr.
Richard A. Paschal
Timothy T. Trump
Patricia Dunmire Bragg

Melodie Freeman-Burney
Mark E. Dreyer
Constance L. Young
Leah Lowder Mills

For full biographical listings, see the Martindale-Hubbell Law Directory

MOYERS, MARTIN, SANTEE, IMEL & TETRICK (AV)

Formerly Moyers, Martin, Conway, Santee & Imel
Suite 920, 320 South Boston Building, 74103
Telephone: 918-582-5281
Fax: 918-585-8318
Bixby, Oklahoma Office: 113 West Dawes, Suite 100, 74408.
Telephone: 918-366-3935.
Fax: 918-366-3936.

MEMBERS OF FIRM

Villard Martin (1889-1965)
Garrett Logan (1901-1975)
Jack H. Santee
John M. Imel
Charles B. Tetrick
Ronald G. Raynolds
Steven A. Stecher
James H. Ferris
Robert Scott Savage
D. Stanley Tacker
Patrick D. O'Connor
John E. Rooney, Jr.
Terry M. Kollmorgen
Terry M. Thomas

ASSOCIATES

John W. Cannon
James E. Maupin

OF COUNSEL

Donald P. Moyers
Villard Martin, Jr.

For full biographical listings, see the Martindale-Hubbell Law Directory

---

PRAY, WALKER, JACKMAN, WILLIAMSON & MARLAR, A PROFESSIONAL CORPORATION (AV)

900 ONEOK Plaza, 100 West 5th Street, 74103-4218
Telephone: 918-581-5500
Fax: 918-581-5599
Oklahoma City, Oklahoma Office: One Leadership Square, 211 North Robinson.
Telephone: 405-236-8911.
Fax: 405-236-0011.

J. Warren Jackman
W. Bland Williamson, Jr.
Donald F. Marlar
Thomas G. Noulles
William D. Toney
Terry R. Doverspike
John F. McCormick, Jr.
S. Erickson Grimshaw
Jean Walpole Coulter
John L. Randolph, Jr.
William L. Eagleton, IV
Wm. Gregory James
Kevin M. Abel
Donald S. Smith
Randall G. Vaughan
Charles Bretton Crane
Rita J. Gassaway
Kevin Pierce Doyle
William A. Caldwell
Thomas M. Askew
Dee E. Dismukes
Michael W. Pierce
Mallie Marlene Lawrence
Terri S. Roberts

OF COUNSEL

Donald E. Pray
Floyd L. Walker
Charles A. Kothe

OKLAHOMA CITY OFFICE

Henry A. Meyer, III (Resident, Oklahoma City Office)
Steven J. Goetzinger (Resident, Oklahoma City Office)

For full biographical listings, see the Martindale-Hubbell Law Directory

ROSENSTEIN, FIST & RINGOLD, A PROFESSIONAL CORPORATION (AV)

Suite 300, 525 South Main, 74103
Telephone: 918-585-9211
Facsimile: 918-583-5617

David L. Fist
A. F. Ringold
Coleman L. Robison
Gene L. Mortensen
J. Douglas Mann
John G. Moyer, Jr.
John E. Howland
Jerry L. Zimmerman
Mark S. Rains
Frederick J. Hegenbart
Andrea R. Kunkel
Eric P. Nelson
Karen L. Long
Lucia A. Lockwood
Catharine M. Bashaw
Douglas B. Anderson

OF COUNSEL

Jerry A. Richardson

Representative Clients: Affiliated Food Stores, Inc.; Berexco, Inc.; Crane Carrier Company; Davis Bros; Hillcrest Medical Center; Med-X Corporation; Peoples State Bank; Tulsa Dental Products, Ltd.; Tulsa Public Schools; Utica Park Clinic, Inc.

For full biographical listings, see the Martindale-Hubbell Law Directory

---

STEPHEN A. SCHULLER INCORPORATED (AV)

1111 ParkCentre, 525 South Main Mall, 74103-4522
Telephone: 918-583-8205
Facsimile: 918-583-1226

Stephen A. Schuller

For full biographical listings, see the Martindale-Hubbell Law Directory

---

*WAGONER,** Wagoner Co. — (Refer to Muskogee)

---

*WATONGA,** Blaine Co. — (Refer to Weatherford)

*WAURIKA,** Jefferson Co. — (Refer to Madill)

WEATHERFORD, Custer Co.

STEPHEN D. BEAM (AV)

110 South Broadway, P.O. Box 31, 73096
Telephone: 405-772-2900
Telecopier: 405-772-6879

Representative Clients: BancFirst & First National Bank & Trust Company, Clinton, Oklahoma; Bank of Hydro, Hydro, Oklahoma; Hydro Cooperative Assn., Hydro, Oklahoma; Federal Deposit Insurance Corp.; ANR Pipeline Co.; Transok, Inc.; Southern Natural Gas; Resolution Trust Corp.; Texaco; United Auto Workers.

For full biographical listings, see the Martindale-Hubbell Law Directory

*WEWOKA,** Seminole Co. — (Refer to Seminole)

*WILBURTON,** Latimer Co. — (Refer to McAlester)

*WOODWARD,** Woodward Co.

HIERONYMUS, HODGDEN & HALLREN (AV)

1002 Ninth Street, P.O. Box 529, 73802
Telephone: 405-256-5517
Fax: 405-256-8459

Tom Hieronymus (1911-1994) Bryce Hodgden
Kathleen Lies Hallren

Approved Examining Attorneys for: Chicago Title Co.; Lawyers Title Insurance Co.; American First Title & Trust Co.; Farmers Home Administration; Federal Land Bank.
Attorneys for: American National Bank.
References: Bank IV of Woodward, N.A.; Stock Exchange Bank; American National Bank, Woodward, Okla.

For full biographical listings, see the Martindale-Hubbell Law Directory

SPARKS & COOK, P.C. (AV)

1715 Main Street, P.O. Box 968, 73802
Telephone: 405-256-8647
Telecopy: 405-256-1913

John O. Sparks Vickie L. Cook

Counsel for: Al Norman, Inc.; OG&E Electric Services Shareholders' Association; Carpet Direct, Limited.
Local Counsel For: Bank IV Oklahoma; Bank IV Mortgage Co.; OG&E Electric Services Co.; Oklahoma Department of Transporation; Pope Distributing Co.

For full biographical listings, see the Martindale-Hubbell Law Directory

OREGON

*ALBANY,** Linn Co. — (Refer to Corvallis)

*ASTORIA,** Clatsop Co. — (Refer to Tillamook)

*BAKER CITY,** Baker Co. — (Refer to Ontario)

*BEND,** Deschutes Co.

HURLEY, BRYANT, LOVLIEN, LYNCH, JARVIS AND RE (AV)

40 N.W. Greenwood, P.O. Box 1151, 97709-1151
Telephone: 503-382-4331
Fax: 503-389-3386

MEMBERS OF FIRM

James V. Hurley
Neil R. Bryant
Robert S. Lovlien
Gregory P. Lynch
Lynn F. Jarvis
Daniel C. Re
William J. Storie
John A. Berge
Sharon R. Smith
Kevin J. Keillor

ASSOCIATES

Lisa N. Bertalan
Stanley D. Austin

Representative Clients: Bend Research, Inc.; Central Oregon Irrigation District; Robberson Ford Sales; Bend Memorial Clinic; Deschutes County Intermediate Education District; St. Charles Medical Center; Travelers Insurance Co.; Bend-LaPine School District; Bend River Mall; Lumbermen's Insurance.

For full biographical listings, see the Martindale-Hubbell Law Directory

*CANYON CITY,** Grant Co. — (Refer to Mount Vernon)

*CONDON,** Gilliam Co. — (Refer to Mount Vernon)

COOS BAY, Coos Co.

FOSS, WHITTY, LITTLEFIELD & McDANIEL (AV)

444 North Fourth Street, P.O. Box 1120, 97420
Telephone: 503-267-2156
Fax: 503-269-0839

MEMBERS OF FIRM

John T. Foss
John W. Whitty
Jon R. Littlefield
William A. McDaniel
Michael N. Bodkin
Juli Point

ASSOCIATES

James M. Hillas

General Counsel for: Western Bank; Al Peirce Co.; Tower Motor Co.; Industrial Services, Inc.; Stamper's J & J Tire Co.; Bay Area Chamber of Commerce; Coos Bay Towboat Co.
Representative Clients: United States National Bank; International Paper Co.

For full biographical listings, see the Martindale-Hubbell Law Directory

*COQUILLE,** Coos Co. — (Refer to Coos Bay)

*CORVALLIS,** Benton Co.

RINGO & STUBER, P.C. (AV)

605 S.W. Jefferson Avenue, P.O. Box 1108, 97339
Telephone: 503-757-1414
FAX: 503-753-0884

Robert G. Ringo
Larry W. Stuber
Stephen R. Ensor
Patrick L. Hadlock

Reference: The First Interstate Bank of Oregon, Corvallis Branch.

For full biographical listings, see the Martindale-Hubbell Law Directory

*DALLAS,** Polk Co. — (Refer to Salem)

*EUGENE,** Lane Co.

CALKINS & CALKINS (AV)

1163 Olive Street, 97401
Telephone: 503-345-0371
FAX: 503-342-1220

MEMBERS OF FIRM

Windsor Calkins (1910-1989)
S. M. Calkins (1872-1969)
W. W. Calkins (1860-1945)
Win Calkins
Judy Ann Calkins

Josephine H. Mooney

General Counsel for: Eugene Water & Electric Board; Sacred Heart General Hospital; Lane County Medical Society.
Local Counsel for: Oregon Automobile Insurance Co.; North Pacific Insurance Co.; St. Paul Insurance Cos.; American States Insurance Co.; Northwest Physicians Mutual Insurance Co.; General Accident Insurance Co.; Farmers Insurance Group.

For full biographical listings, see the Martindale-Hubbell Law Directory

DOYLE, GARTLAND, NELSON & McCLEERY, P.C. (AV)

44 Club Road, Suite 200, P.O. Box 11230, 97440
Telephone: 503-344-2174
Fax: 503-344-0209

Michael W. Doyle
John C. Gartland
Douglas A. Nelson
P. Scott McCleery

Peggy Ann Bond
David Wade

Reference: Pacific Continental Bank.

For full biographical listings, see the Martindale-Hubbell Law Directory

GLEAVES SWEARINGEN LARSEN POTTER SCOTT & SMITH (AV)

Formerly
Gleaves Swearingen Larsen & Potter
and
Cass, Scott, Woods & Smith
8th Floor, 975 Oak Street, 97401
Telephone: 503-686-8833
Fax: 503-345-2034

MEMBERS OF FIRM

Frederick A. Batson
Melvin J. Beck
Jon V. Buerstatte
Ansel J. Giustina
Vernon D. Gleaves
Thomas P.E. Herrmann
Stephen O. Lane
Eric L. Larsen
Patricia E. Lockary
William H. Martin
Standlee G. Potter
Dale A. Riddle
Martha J. Rodman
Douglas R. Schultz
Malcolm H. Scott
Bruce E. Smith

ASSOCIATES

Michael E. Farthing
Karen Fiorentino
James V. Shepherd
David A. Stanley
Arlen C. Swearingen
Laura Tandy Zagorin

OF COUNSEL

Orlando John Hollis

LEGAL SUPPORT PERSONNEL

Jana R. Bauman, CLA
Merrily A. Coldren
Shirley A. Morrow, CLAS
E. Diane Robison

Representative Clients: American Pacific Title & Escrow Co.; Centennial Bank; Farwest Steel Corp.; Giustina Timber Co.; Guard Publishing Co.; Eugene Association of Realtors; Seneca Sawmill Co.; Springfield Quarry Rock Products, Inc.; University of Oregon Foundation, Valley River Center.

For full biographical listings, see the Martindale-Hubbell Law Directory

HARRANG LONG GARY RUDNICK P.C. (AV)

400 South Park Building, 101 East Broadway, P.O. Box 11620, 97440-3820
Telephone: 503-485-0220
Fax: 503-686-6564
Roseburg, Oregon Office: 548 S.E. Jackson Street, Suite 2. P.O. Box 1370.
Telephone: 503-672-2525.
Fax: 503-672-3255.
Salem, Oregon Office: 333 High Street, N.E.
Telephone: 503-371-3330.
Fax: 503-371-5336.

William F. Gary
James P. Harrang
Glenn Klein
Stanton F. Long
A. Keith Martin
James E. Mountain, Jr. (Resident, Salem Office)
Arden J. Olson
Sharon A. Rudnick
Jens Schmidt

Ellen D. Adler
James N. Call (Resident, Roseburg Office)
Yuanxing Chen (Resident, Salem Office)
Anne C. Davies
Antonia De Meo
Judith Giers
Mary A. Schnabel-Bray
Leslie S. Stevens
D. Dennis Waldrop

Representative Clients: HealthGuard Services, Inc. (SelectCare); Sacred Heart Health Systems; University of Oregon Book Store; Northwest Eye Center; Whittier Wood Products, Co.; Willamette Graystone, Inc.; Cities of Eugene, Roseburg, Florence and Oakridge; Eugene Water & Electric Board; Lane Regional Air Pollution Authority.

For full biographical listings, see the Martindale-Hubbell Law Directory

HERSHNER, HUNTER, MOULTON, ANDREWS & NEILL (AV)

180 E. 11th Avenue, P.O. Box 1475, 97440
Telephone: 503-686-8511
Telecopier: 503-344-2025
Florence, Oregon Office: 1441 7th Street.
Telephone: 503-997-1997.
Telecopier: 503-997-1817.

(See Next Column)

HERSHNER, HUNTER, MOULTON, ANDREWS & NEILL—*Continued*

MEMBERS OF FIRM

James L. Hershner
Robert E. Moulton
David N. Andrews
Robert S. Quinney
K. Patrick Neill
Craig A. Smith
Norman J. LeCompte, Jr.
Arthur J. Clark
William R. Potter
William R. Turnbow
Paul V. Vaughan
Michael C. Arola
Janice C. Goldberg
William D. Brewer
Everett R. Moreland

OF COUNSEL

Garland D. Hunter
Walter W. Miller (Not admitted in OR)

ASSOCIATES

William L. Philbrick
Ronald C. Becker
Nancy K. Cary
Andrew G. Lewis
John V. Helmick
Patrick W. Wade
Cindy S. Helmick
Timothy M. Parks
Michael W. Bortz

Representative Clients: Bank of America; Federal Deposit Insurance Corp.; United States National Bank of Oregon; Davidson Industries, Inc.; Oregon Cedar Products Co.; Superior Lumber Co.; Cascade Title Co.; Delta Sand & Gravel Co.; John Hyland Construction, Inc.; Spectra-Physics Scanning Systems, Inc.

For full biographical listings, see the Martindale-Hubbell Law Directory

LUVAAS, COBB, RICHARDS & FRASER, P.C. (AV)

300 Forum Building, 777 High Street, P.O. Box 10747, 97401
Telephone: 503-484-9292
Fax: 503-343-1206

John L. Luvaas
Ralph F. Cobb
Joe B. Richards
Robert H. Fraser
J. Dominic Monahan
Varner Jay Johns, III
Louis L. Kurtz
Joel S. DeVore
Donald E. Johnson
Rodney B. Carter
Gregory E. Skillman

James W. Kemper
P. Rebecca Kamitsuka
Lisa Frost Chernaik

Representative Clients: Farmers Insurance Group; Professional Liability Fund of the Oregon State Bar; Radio-One Broadcast Group; Sunbelt Broadcasting Co.; Eagle Broadcasting Co.
Local Counsel for: Bi-Mart Corp.
General Counsel for: Romania Enterprises, Inc.; Combined Communications, Inc. (KUGN AM/FM); Peterson Pacific, Inc.
Public Corporation Client: School District Eugene 4J.

For full biographical listings, see the Martindale-Hubbell Law Directory

WATKINSON LAIRD RUBENSTEIN LASHWAY & BALDWIN, P.C. (AV)

101 East Broadway, Suite 300, P.O. Box 10567, 97440
Telephone: 503-484-2277
FAX: 503-484-2282
Roseburg, Oregon Office: 2750 West Harvard Boulevard.
Telephone: 503-672-2755.
FAX: 503-672-6379.
Portland, Oregon Office: Lincoln Center Tower, 10260 S.W. Greenburg Road, Suite 400.
Telephone: 503-293-8484.
FAX: 503-293-8499.

Steve C. Baldwin
Donald R. Laird
J. Lee Lashway
Barry Rubenstein
John C. Watkinson

B. Kevin Burgess

Representative Clients: Lane Individual Practice Association; Whittaker Realty Group; Gateway Mall Shopping Center; Douglas County Independent Practice Association, Inc.; Women's Health Care Associates, P.C.; Abby's Pizza, Inc.; East Earth Herb, Inc.; Oregon Research Institute; Far West Fibers, Inc.

For full biographical listings, see the Martindale-Hubbell Law Directory

*FOSSIL,** Wheeler Co. — (Refer to Mount Vernon)

*GRANTS PASS,** Josephine Co.

MYRICK, SEAGRAVES, ADAMS & DAVIS (AV)

600 N.W. Fifth Street, 97526
Telephone: 503-476-6627
Fax: 503-476-7048

MEMBERS OF FIRM

Donald H. Coulter (Retired)
Charles H. Seagraves, Jr.
Lynn Michael Myrick
Richard D. Adams
John E. Davis
Holly A. Preslar

(See Next Column)

Reference: United States National Bank of Oregon.

For full biographical listings, see the Martindale-Hubbell Law Directory

SCHULTZ, SALISBURY, CAUBLE, VERSTEEG & DOLE (AV)

One Eleven Building, 111 S.E. 6th Street, P.O. Box 378, 97526
Telephone: 503-476-8825
FAX: 503-471-1704

MEMBERS OF FIRM

Niel R. Allen (1894-1959)
Louis F. Schultz, Jr.
Walter L. Cauble
Ronald B. Versteeg
James R. Dole

Representative Clients: Colonial Banking Co.; Grants Pass School District; Josephine-Crater Title Companies, Inc.; Grants Pass Clinic; Rough & Ready Lumber Co.; Valley of the Rogue Bank; Environmental Container Systems; Copeland Sand and Gravel; Copeland Paving, Grayback Forestry Contracting, Inc.

For full biographical listings, see the Martindale-Hubbell Law Directory

*HILLSBORO,** Washington Co. — (Refer to Portland)

*HOOD RIVER,** Hood River Co. — (Refer to The Dalles)

*KLAMATH FALLS,** Klamath Co.

BOIVIN, JONES, UERLINGS, DIIACONI & ODEN (AV)

110 N. Sixth Street, 97601-6028
Telephone: 503-884-8101
FAX: 503-884-8498

MEMBERS OF FIRM

Robert D. Boivin
Stanley C. Jones
James R. Uerlings
Barbara M. DiIaconi
Dennis Oden

RETIRED PARTNER

Harry D. Boivin

Representative Clients: Alexsis Risk Management Services, Inc.; Basin Transit Service Transportation District; Carolina Casualty Insurance Co.; City of Malin.

For full biographical listings, see the Martindale-Hubbell Law Directory

GIACOMINI & KNIEPS (AV)

A Partnership of Professional Corporations
706 Main Street, 97601
Telephone: 503-884-7728
Fax: 503-883-1759

J. Anthony Giacomini (P.C.)
Karla J. Knieps (P.C.)

ASSOCIATES

Shalas J. Hughes

Representative Agricultural and Business Clients: Tulelake Cold Storage Co.; Boise Cascade Corp.; United States National Bank of Oregon; LK Produce; Orem Ranch, Inc.; Clough Oil Company; Klamath Publishing Co.; Quail Mountain, Inc. (Pepsicola Distributor); Heaton Steel & Supply, Inc.
Representative Insurance Client: Foremost Insurance.

For full biographical listings, see the Martindale-Hubbell Law Directory

*LA GRANDE,** Union Co. — (Refer to Pendleton)

*LAKEVIEW,** Lake Co. — (Refer to Klamath Falls)

LEBANON, Linn Co. — (Refer to Salem)

*MADRAS,** Jefferson Co. — (Refer to Bend)

*MEDFORD,** Jackson Co.

BLACKHURST, HORNECKER, HASSEN & ERVIN B. HOGAN (AV)

Suite 1, 129 N. Oakdale, P.O. Box 670, 97501
Telephone: 503-779-8550
Fax: 503-773-2635

MEMBERS OF FIRM

B. Kent Blackhurst
Ervin B. Hogan
Gregory T. Hornecker
John R. Hassen

ASSOCIATES

Joseph E. Kellerman
Richard H. Berman

Attorneys for: Medford Steel; Cascade Wood Products, Inc.; Jackson County Title; Black Oak Village Shopping Center; Airport Chevrolet, Inc.; Medford Clinic, P.C.; Crystal Springs Packing Co.; Pinacle Orchards.

For full biographical listings, see the Martindale-Hubbell Law Directory

BROPHY, MILLS, SCHMOR, GERKING & BROPHY (AV)

A Partnership including a Professional Corporation
Park Place Building, Fifth Floor, 201 West Main Street, P.O. Box 128, 97501
Telephone: 503-772-7123
Fax: 503-772-7249

(See Next Column)

BROPHY, MILLS, SCHMOR, GERKING & BROPHY, *Medford—Continued*

MEMBERS OF FIRM

Carl M. Brophy (P.C.)
Lee A. Mills
Douglass H. Schmor
Timothy C. Gerking
Timothy E. Brophy

ASSOCIATES

David B. Paradis
Todd B. Maddox

OF COUNSEL

H. Dewey Wilson

General Counsel for: Bear Creek Valley Sanitary Authority; California Oregon Broadcasting, Inc.; Medford Moulding Co.; Scala Electronic Corp.; Southern Oregon Sales, Inc.
Local Counsel for: Farmers Ins. Group; State Farm Fire & Casualty Co.; Stone Forest Industries, Inc.

For full biographical listings, see the Martindale-Hubbell Law Directory

FOSTER, PURDY, ALLAN, PETERSON & DAHLIN (AV)

Suite 4A, 201 West Main Street, P.O. Box 1667, 97501
Telephone: 503-770-5466
Telecopier: 503-770-6502

MEMBERS OF FIRM

Stuart E. Foster
William G. Purdy
Karen C. Allan
Gary C. Peterson
Lewis W. Dahlin
Carl R. J. Sniffen
Gerald M. Shean, III

Reference: First Interstate Bank of Oregon (Medford Main Branch).

For full biographical listings, see the Martindale-Hubbell Law Directory

FROHNMAYER, DEATHERAGE, PRATT JAMIESON & CLARKE, P.C. (AV)

Larson Creek Professional Center, 2592 Barnett Road, 97504
Telephone: 503-779-2333
Fax: 503-779-6379

Otto J. Frohnmayer
William V. Deatherage
Steven H. Pratt
Stephen G. Jamieson
Mark D. Clarke

Larry B. Workman
Robert E. Bluth
William F. Schireman

Local Counsel for: Allstate Insurance Company; CNA; Farmers Insurance Group; Fireman's Fund Insurance Companies; Grocers Insurance Group; Health Future, Inc.; Northwest Physicians Mutual Insurance Company; Professional Liability Fund; Safeco Insurance Company.

For full biographical listings, see the Martindale-Hubbell Law Directory

MILWAUKIE, Clackamas Co.

JAMES E. REDMAN (AV)

10565 S.E. 23rd Avenue, 97222
Telephone: 503-659-5335
Fax: 503-659-5568

For full biographical listings, see the Martindale-Hubbell Law Directory

ONTARIO, Malheur Co.

YTURRI, ROSE, BURNHAM, BENTZ & HELFRICH (AV)

Yturri Building, 89 S.W. Third Avenue, 97914
Telephone: 503-889-5368
Telecopier: 503-889-2432

MEMBERS OF FIRM

Anthony Yturri
Carl Burnham, Jr.
Cliff S. Bentz
Timothy J. Helfrich

ASSOCIATES

Bruno J. Jagelski
Scott K. Warner
David B. Brownhill

OF COUNSEL

Gene C. Rose
Emil R. Berg

Attorneys for: United States National Bank of Oregon (Ontario Branch); Cascade Natural Gas Inc.; Idaho Power Co.; Liberty Mutual Insurance Corp.; Interstate Production Credit Assn.; State Farm Insurance Co.; Farmers Insurance Exchange; Professional Liability Fund of the Oregon State Bar Assn.; Mountain Bell Telephone; American Hardware Insurance Company.

For full biographical listings, see the Martindale-Hubbell Law Directory

*OREGON CITY,** Clackamas Co.

HIBBARD, CALDWELL & SCHULTZ, A PROFESSIONAL CORPORATION (AV)

Suite 200, 1001 Molalla Avenue, P.O. Box 667, 97045
Telephone: 503-656-5200
Fax: 503-656-0125

(See Next Column)

John C. Caldwell
Paul D. Schultz
Nancy S. Tauman
Nelson L. Walker
Edward A. Lanton
Renee G. Wenger

Sherrie A. Kaiser Goff
Steven M. Carpenter

Representative Clients: Oregon State Bar Professional Liability Fund; Farmers Ins. Group; Northwest Physicians Mutual Ins. Co.; PACC Health Plans; Oregon City School District; Clackamas Community College.

For full biographical listings, see the Martindale-Hubbell Law Directory

*PENDLETON,** Umatilla Co.

COREY, BYLER, REW, LORENZEN & HOJEM (AV)

222 Southeast Dorion Street, P.O. Box 218, 97801
Telephone: 503-276-3331
Facsimile: 503-276-3148

MEMBERS OF FIRM

Alex M. Byler
Lawrence B. Rew
Steven H. Corey
Henry C. Lorenzen
Douglas E. Hojem
David M. Blanc
Timothy P. O'Rourke
Steven N. Thomas

OF COUNSEL

George H. Corey

ASSOCIATES

Patricia Sullivan

Representative Clients: Port of Umatilla; Farmers Insurance Group; St. Anthony Hospital; Pendleton Grain Growers; Pendleton School District 16R; J. R. Simplot Company (Food Processing); East Oregonian Publishing Co.; McCormack Construction Co.
Local Counsel for: First Interstate Bank of Oregon; Connecticut General Life Insurance Co.

For full biographical listings, see the Martindale-Hubbell Law Directory

KOTTKAMP & O'ROURKE (AV)

331 S.E. 2nd Street, P.O. Box 490, 97801
Telephone: 503-276-2141
Fax: 503-276-6463

MEMBERS OF FIRM

John H. Kottkamp
Robert E. O'Rourke
Stephen M. Bloom

ASSOCIATES

Steven L. Hill

General Counsel for: Blue Mountain Community College; Westland Irrigation District.
Representative Clients: Continental Insurance Cos.; Oregon Mutual Insurance Co.; Safeco Insurance Co.; Allstate Insurance Co.; State Farm Mutual Automobile Insurance Co.; Professional Liability Fund; Mutual of Enumclow Insurance Co.; Royal Insurance Co.

For full biographical listings, see the Martindale-Hubbell Law Directory

*PORTLAND,** Multnomah Co.

ATER WYNNE HEWITT DODSON & SKERRITT (AV)

Suite 1800, 222 S.W. Columbia Street, 97201-6618
Telephone: 503-226-1191
Telecopier: 503-226-0079
San Francisco, California Office: One Embarcadero Center, Suite 2420, 94111.
Telephone: 415-421-4143.
Seattle, Washington Office: Ater Wynne Hewitt Dodson & Skerritt, P.C., Two Union Square, 601 Union Street, Suite 5450, 98101-2327.
Telephone: 206-623-4711.
Washington, D.C. Office: 1317 F Street, N.W., Suite 400, 20004.
Telephone: 202-628-3200.

MEMBERS OF FIRM

William P. Buren (1950-1991)
Carol A. Hewitt (1945-1993)
Michael Peter Alcantar
Jonathan A. Ater
Lori Irish Bauman
Steven K. Blackhurst
Arthur A. Butler (Resident Shareholder, Seattle, Washington Office)
William C. Campbell
Carey L. Critchlow
Mark S. Dodson
Valerie D. Fisher
Douglas E. Goe
Peter H. Haller (Resident Shareholder, Seattle, Washington Office)
Gregory R. Harris (Resident Shareholder, Seattle, Washington Office)
Gregg D. Johnson
Benjamin H. Kaminash
Paul J. Kaufman
Stephen J. Kennedy (Resident Shareholder, Seattle, Washington Office)
Thomas M. Kilbane, Jr. (Resident Shareholder, Seattle, Washington Office)
Frank V. Langfitt, III
Stacey E. Mark
Claudia Kay Powers
Howard A. Rankin
Ronald L. Saxton (Firm Chairman)
Jack W. Schifferdecker, Jr.
John Michael Schultz
Michael W. Shackelford
Ann L. Sherman
Julie Simon (Resident Member of Firm, Washington, D.C. Office)

(See Next Column)

ATER WYNNE HEWITT DODSON & SKERRITT—*Continued*

MEMBERS OF FIRM (Continued)

Daniel H. Skerritt
Steven D. Stadum
Gregory E. Struxness
Linda Triplett
Mark A. Turner
Steven E. Wynne

ASSOCIATES

Roberto E. Berry
Leslie G. Bottomly
Grant R. Chaput
Susan Corser Daigle
Michael S. Gadd
Mark L. Huglin
Townsend Hyatt
Susheela Jayapal (Not admitted in OR)
Linda R. Johannsen
Diane Kownacki (Resident, Seattle, Washington Office)
James C. Lancaster
Brenda L. Meltebeke
Michael J. Sandmire
Sara J. Siegler-Miller
Amy M. Wayson
Divan Williams Jr.

OF COUNSEL

Richard L. Biggs
John H. Draneas
Evelyn K. Elsesser (Not admitted in OR)
George J. Gregores
Cynthia Rutzick
Scott E. Schickli
David C. Streicher

LEGAL SUPPORT PERSONNEL

Carol W. Callaway (Public Finance Administrator)

For full biographical listings, see the Martindale-Hubbell Law Directory

BLACK HELTERLINE (AV)

1200 The Bank of California Tower, 707 S.W. Washington Street, 97205
Telephone: 503-224-5560
Telecopier: 503-224-6148

Borden F. Beck, Jr. (1923-1989)
Harvey N. Black (1895-1986)
Guy J. Rappleyea (1921-1993)

MEMBERS OF FIRM

Ronald T. Adams
Albert J. Bannon
Clarence H. Greenwood
Russell M. Helterline (Retired)
Paul R. Hribernick
John M. McGuigan
Michael O. Moran
Thomas K. O'Shaughnessy
Robert J. Preston
Gerald H. Robinson
Richard N. Roskie
David P. Roy
Steven R. Schell
Susan Jane Widder

ASSOCIATES

Stark Ackerman
Deneen M. Hubertin
James M. Baumgartner
Donald L. Krahmer, Jr.
Paul R. Rundle

OF COUNSEL

Robert E. Glasgow

COUNSEL

John D. Picco

For full biographical listings, see the Martindale-Hubbell Law Directory

BULLIVANT, HOUSER, BAILEY, PENDERGRASS & HOFFMAN, A PROFESSIONAL CORPORATION (AV)

300 Pioneer Tower, 888 S.W. Fifth Avenue, 97204-2089
Telephone: 503-228-6351
Telex: 5101010486 BULLIVANT
Facsimile: 503-295-0915
Seattle, Washington Office: 2400 Westlake Office Tower, 1601 Fifth Avenue, 98101-1618.
Telephone: 206-292-8930.
Facsimile: 206-386-5130.
Vancouver, Washington Office: 300 First Independence Place, 1220 Main Street, P.O. Box 61745, 98666-1745.
Telephones: 360-693-2424; 360-225-1100.
Facsimile: 206-695-8504.
Rancho Cordova, California Office: 10969 Trade Center Drive, 95670-6140.
Telephone: 916-852-9100.
Fax: 916-852-5777.

Walter H. Pendergrass
Douglas G. Houser
Ronald E. Bailey
Ronald G. Stephenson
Stanley E. Martinson
James L. Knoll
Stephen F. English
I. Franklin Hunsaker, III
James D. Hibbard
Robert F. Riede (Resident, Seattle, Washington Office)
E. Pennock Gheen (Resident, Seattle, Washington Office)
Donald E. Murray (Resident, Seattle, Washington Office)
James G. Driscoll (Resident, Rancho Cordova, California Office)
S. Joel Wilson
John W. Buehler
R. Erick Johnson, II
Douglas F. Foley (Resident, Vancouver, Washington Office)
Douglas R. Andres
Neil G. Dorfman (Resident, Seattle, Washington Office)
John A. Bennett
Chrys A. Martin
David R. Foster
Nickolas J. Dibert
John P. Ashworth
Dianne K. Dailey
Loren D. Prescott (Resident, Seattle, Washington Office)
Thomas R. Merrick (Resident, Seattle, Washington Office)
Michael R. Seidl

(See Next Column)

Scott M. Stickney (Resident, Seattle, Washington Office)
Richard J. Whittemore
Jeremy E. Zuck
Stuart D. Jones
R. Daniel Lindahl
Loren D. Podwill
Steven V. Rizzo
Jerret E. Sale (Resident, Seattle, Washington Office)
Roger Westendorf
David A. Ernst
Robert B. Lowry
Thomas D. Adams (Resident, Seattle, Washington Office)
Stephen F. Cook
Lori R. Metz
Gregory E. Price (Resident, Vancouver, Washington, Office)
M. Taylor Florence (Resident, Rancho Cordova, California Office)
Stephen B. Hill

Randy L. Arthur
Robert E. Asperger (Resident, Rancho Cordova, California Office)
Janet L. Atwill
Diane C. Babbitt (Resident at Seattle, Washington Office)
Philip G. Bardsley (Resident, Seattle, Washington Office)
Tamara L. Boeck (Resident, Rancho Cordova, California Office)
Linda M. Bolduan
Molly M. Burns
Kimberly S. Burroughs (Resident, Seattle, Washington Office)
Ronald J. Clark
Clay D. Creps
Darleen R. Darnall
James T. Derrig (Resident, Seattle, Washington Office)
Jeffrey S. Eden
Monica Joan Fernandez (Resident, Seattle, Washington Office)
Jeffrey G. Frank (Resident, Seattle, Washington Office)
Gail E. Gearin (Resident, Rancho Cordova, California Office)
Kelly D. Greenfield (Resident, Seattle, Washington Office)
Troy D. Greenfield (Resident, Seattle, Washington Office)
John T. Kaempf
Lisa Elayne Lear
Marilyn E. Litzenberger
Jeanne F. Loftis
Medora A. Marisseau (Resident, Seattle, Washington Office)
Richard G. Matson
Mari F. McBurney
Paul D. Migchelbrink
John R. Osburn
Karen J. Park
Russell W. Pike
Douglas C. Rasmussen (Resident, Seattle, Washington Office)
Heidi D. Robinson
Robert J. Roche (Resident, Seattle, Washington Office)
Christopher B. Rounds (Resident, Vancouver, Washington Office)
Donna R. Sandoval
Robert J. Schnack
Judith A. Selby
Beth Skillern
Margaret M. Van Valkenburg
Karen M. Vickers
Laurence R. Wagner (Resident, Vancouver, Washington Office)
Georges H.G. Yates (Resident, Seattle, Washington Office)

OF COUNSEL

William A. Masters

SENIOR COUNSEL

Charles S. Crookham
Jack L. Hoffman (Retired)
Darrel L. Johnson (Retired)
Robert A. Leedy (Retired)
Charles E. Wright (Retired)

Representative Clients: Blue Cross and Blue Shield of Oregon; Exxon Chemical Co., U.S.A.; NIKE, Inc.; Hitachi Ltd.; Pacific Northwest Generating Cooperative; Caterpillar, Inc.
Representative Insurance Clients: American International Group; The Chubb Group of Insurance Cos.; Fireman's Fund American Insurance Cos.; Gulf Insurance Co.

For full biographical listings, see the Martindale-Hubbell Law Directory

BURT & VETTERLEIN, P.C. (AV)

Suite 3600 U.S. BanCorp Tower, 111 S.W. Fifth Avenue, 97204-3639
Telephone: 503-223-3600
FAX: 503-274-0778

Robert G. Burt
Eric H. Vetterlein

For full biographical listings, see the Martindale-Hubbell Law Directory

COPELAND, LANDYE, BENNETT AND WOLF (AV)

3500 First Interstate Tower, 97201
Telephone: 503-224-4100
Telecopier: 503-224-4133
Anchorage, Alaska Office: 550 West Seventh Avenue, Suite 1350.
Telephone: 907-276-5152.
Telecopier: 907-276-8433.

MEMBERS OF FIRM

J. David Bennett
David L. Blount
David S. Case (Resident, Anchorage, Alaska Office)
Mitchel R. Cohen
Mark G. Copeland (Resident, Anchorage, Alaska Office)
James S. Crane
Randall L. Dunn
David N. Goulder
Robert B. Hopkins
Robert H. Hume, Jr. (Resident, Anchorage, Alaska Office)
Thomas M. Landye
P. Stephen Russell, III
Richard L. Sadler
Thane W. Tienson
David P. Wolf (Resident, Anchorage, Alaska Office)

(See Next Column)

COPELAND, LANDYE, BENNETT AND WOLF, *Portland—Continued*

ASSOCIATES

Robert P. Owens (Resident, Anchorage, Alaska Office)
Thomas R. Benke
Patrick S. Galvin

Reference: First Interstate Bank of Oregon, Portland, Oregon.

For full biographical listings, see the Martindale-Hubbell Law Directory

COSGRAVE, VERGEER & KESTER (AV)

Bank of America Financial Center, Suite 1300, 121 S.W. Morrison Street, 97204-3193
Telephone: 503-323-9000
Fax: 503-323-9019

MEMBERS OF FIRM

Duane Vergeer (Retired)
Randall B. Kester
Walter J. Cosgrave
Walter H. Sweek
Austin W. Crowe, Jr.
James H. Gidley
Frank H. Lagesen
Eugene H. Buckle
David P. Morrison
Thomas W. Brown
David H. Williams
Jeffrey A. Johnson
Robert E. Barton
Charles J. Huber
Timothy J. Coleman
Lisa Almasy Miller

ASSOCIATES

Michael C. Lewton
Norma S. Poitras
Andrew T. Burns
Kathleen J. Tesner
Wendi K. Weiss
Christine B. Miller

Counsel for: Boise Cascade Corp.; Farmers Insurance Co. of Oregon; Maryland Casualty Co.; North Pacific Insurance Co.; Professional Liability Fund; State Farm Fire and Casualty Co.; State Farm Mutual Insurance Co.; TIG Insurance Co.; Union Pacific Railroad Co.; Valley Insurance Co.

For full biographical listings, see the Martindale-Hubbell Law Directory

DUNN, CARNEY, ALLEN, HIGGINS & TONGUE (AV)

15th Floor, Pacific First Federal Building, 851 S.W. Sixth Avenue, 97204
Telephone: 503-224-6440
FAX: 503-224-7324
Bend, Oregon Office: 700 N.W. Hill Street, 97701.
Telephone: 503-382-9241.
FAX: 503-389-6907.

MEMBERS OF FIRM

Robert L. Allen
Bradley O. Baker
Jonathan A. Bennett
Robert F. Blackmore
John C. Cahalan
Robert R. Carney
George J. Cooper
Andrew S. Craig
Michael J. Francis
Bryan W. Gruetter (Resident, Bend, Oregon Office)
Jack D. Hoffman
Marsha Murray-Lusby
Robert L. Nash (Resident, Bend, Oregon Office)
Jeffrey F. Nudelman
Joan O'Neill
Gilbert E. Parker
Helle Rode
G. Kenneth Shiroishi
Donald E. Templeton
Thomas Healy Tongue
Daniel F. Vidas
Robert K. Winger

ASSOCIATES

Roger A. Alfred
J. William Ashbaugh
Ernest G. Bootsma
Richard T. Borst
William H. Caffee
I. Kenneth Davis
John C. DeVoe
Kitri C. Ford (Resident, Bend, Oregon Office)
Eric A. Kekel
Staci L. Sawyer
Paul A. Stamnes

Representative Clients: North Pacific Lumber Co.; Miller Brewing Co.; California Casualty Insurance; Mountain Fir Lumber Co.; Hong Kong & Shanghai Bank; Farmers Insurance Co.; St. Paul Fire & Marine Insurance Co.; Eastern Western Corp.

For full biographical listings, see the Martindale-Hubbell Law Directory

GARVEY, SCHUBERT & BARER (AV)

Eleventh Floor, 121 S.W. Morrison Street, 97204
Telephone: 503-228-3939
Telecopier: 503-226-0259
Seattle, Washington Office: 1191 Second Avenue, 18th Floor, 98101.
Telephone: 206-464-3939.
Cable Address: "Lex, Seattle."
Telex: 32-1037.
Telecopier: 206-464-0125.
Washington, D.C. Office: 5th Floor, 1000 Potomac Street, N.W., 20007.
Telephone: 202-965-7880.
Telecopier: 202-965-1729.

MEMBERS OF FIRM

A. Jeffery Bird (Not admitted in OR)
Jeffrey E. Boly
Christine P. Brown
David L. Canary
Stephen J. Connolly
John M. Cowden
Mark E. Friedman
John H. Gadon
Fred M. Granum
Robert R. Griffith
Richard M. Layne
Eric A. Lindenauer
Michael McArthur-Phillips
Robert C. Weaver, Jr.

(See Next Column)

ASSOCIATES

Richard Baroway
Christopher S. Byrne
Charles D. Davidson
Christopher P. Koback
Margaret M. Maguire
Renée E. Rothauge
Lance N. Wessell

OF COUNSEL

Edward J. Murphy, Jr.
Russell R. Niehaus

Representative Clients: Bank of California, N.A.; Blue Cross and Blue Shield of Oregon; Federal Deposit Insurance Corp.; In Focus Systems, Inc.; Land O'Lakes/Cenex Feeds, Inc.; Murphy Timber Co.; Ore-Ida Foods, Inc.; Rentrak Corporation; St. John's Medical Center; Tollycraft Yachts Corp.

For full biographical listings, see the Martindale-Hubbell Law Directory

LANE POWELL SPEARS LUBERSKY (AV)

520 S.W. Yamhill Street, Suite 800, 97204-1383
Telephone: 503-226-6151
Telecopier: 224-0388
Other Offices at: Seattle, Mount Vernon and Olympia, Washington; Los Angeles and San Francisco, California; Anchorage, Alaska; London, England.

MEMBERS OF FIRM

Herbert H. Anderson
Nelson D. Atkin II
Craig D. Bachman
Paula A. Barran
James E. Bartels
Jeffrey M. Batchelor
John P. Bledsoe
C. Akin Blitz
Trish M. Brown
James H. Clarke
John B. Crowell, Jr.
Jean M. DeFond
Samuel R. DeSimone, Jr.
John H. Durkheimer
Marvin D. Fjordbeck
John Folawn
Bert K. Fukumoto
John Wiley Gould
John D. Guinasso
Bruce C. Hamlin
Timothy R. Harmon
Edwin A. Harnden
James L. Hiller
Wayne Hilliard
Danny L. Hitt, Jr.
Michael G. Holmes
Lewis M. Horowitz
David Glenn Hosenpud
Charles F. Hudson
Richard C. Hunt
George L. Kirklin
Richard F. Liebman
Michael J. Lilly
Stanley R. Loeb
Mark M. Loomis
William F. Lubersky
Robert E. Maloney, Jr.
Scott P. Monfils
Frank M. Parisi
Robin B. Parisi
Milo Petranovich
Charles J. Pruitt
Donald H. Pyle
Lewis K. Scott
Vicki L. Smith
Vivian Raits Solomon
Thomas W. Sondag
Frank H. Spears
Leigh D. Stephenson
John C. Stevason
Richard N. Van Cleave
Ian K. Whitlock
Richard H. Williams
O. Meredith Wilson, Jr.
Jeffrey C. Wolfstone
Oglesby H. Young

OF COUNSEL

George B. Campbell

ASSOCIATES

Christopher C. Brand
Nancy J. Brown
Lawrence B. Burke
Robert L Carey
Mark E. Chasse
Robert C. Dougherty
Scott Joseph Fortmann
Gary W. Glisson
Jerold W. Hilary
W. Iain E. Levie
Peter Livingston
Jeffrey S. Love
Christopher J. Marshall
Cara Kimiko Masuda
Monique S. Matheson
Stephen P. McCarthy
Brendan R. McDonnell
Ann K. Monahan
Deanna D. Nebert
Bryan E. Powell (Not admitted in OR)
Tae J. Rhee
Dian Rubanoff Rogers
Robert W. Roley
Kathryn P. Salyer
Darsee R. Staley
John C. Walsh

For full biographical listings, see the Martindale-Hubbell Law Directory

LINDSAY, HART, NEIL & WEIGLER (AV)

Suite 3400, 1300 S.W. Fifth Avenue, 97201-5696
Telephone: 503-226-7677
Telecopier: 503-226-7697
Washington, D.C. Office: 1201 Pennsylvania Avenue, N.W., Suite 821, 20004.
Telephone: 202-467-8383.
Fax: 202-467-8581.

MEMBERS OF FIRM

Gunther F. Krause (1895-1967)
Carmie R. Dafoe, Jr. (1920-1975)
Donald G. Krause (1921-1986)
C. Allan Hart, Jr. (Retired)
Dennis J. Lindsay
Carl R. Neil
Jerard S. Weigler
James H. Bean
Glen P. McClendon
Robert W. Palmer
Thomas E. McDermott
William M. Tomlinson
David T. Douthwaite
James L. Dumas
Jay W. Beattie

(See Next Column)

LINDSAY, HART, NEIL & WEIGLER—*Continued*

ASSOCIATES

Leslie F. Darby
Lisa Rackner
Matthew D. Samwick
Gilion C. Ellis
Thomas H. Cutler
Susan L. Bigcraft
Robin A. Jones

OF COUNSEL

Paul S. Cosgrove
Peter A. Friedmann (Resident, Washington, D.C. Office)
James N. Gardner
Lynda Nelson Gardner
John C. Ramig

For full biographical listings, see the Martindale-Hubbell Law Directory

MILLER, NASH, WIENER, HAGER & CARLSEN (AV)

111 S.W. Fifth Avenue, 97204-3699
Telephone: 503-224-5858
Telex: 364462, Kingmar PTL
Facsimile: 503-224-0155, 503-224-2450
Seattle, Washington Office: 4400 Two Union Square, 601 Union Street, 98101-2322.
Telephone: 206-622-8484.
Facsimile: 206-622-7485.

PORTLAND, OREGON PARTNERS

Michael E. Arthur
Jeffrey D. Austin
John R. Bakkensen
Harvey C. Barragar
Joyce M. Bernheim
Rece Bly
David W. Brown
Donald A. Burns
John D. Burns
J. Franklin Cable
Donna M. Cameron
Richard A. Canaday
Clifford N. Carlsen, Jr.
Milt Christensen
William B. Crow
David C. Culpepper
Dean D. DeChaine
John J. DeMott
Brian B. Doherty
Jeffrey J. Druckman
James F. Dulcich
Richard A. Edwards
Mary Ann Frantz
Gerald A. Froebe
Jonathon L. Goodling
M. Christie Helmer
Louis G. Henry
Kenneth W. Hergenhan
Graham M. Hicks
Thomas E. Lindley
Louis B. Livingston
John A. Lusky
Linda L. Marshall
Mark C. McClanahan
Michael W. Meltzer
Erich W. Merrill, Jr.
Jeffrey B. Millner
John Casey Mills
Conrad L. Moore
John F. Neupert
G. Todd Norvell
John W. Osburn
John F. Purcell
Douglas M. Ragen
Dennis P. Rawlinson
Peter C. Richter
Steven O. Rosen
Bruce A. Rubin
James B. Ruyle
Thomas C. Sand
Ronald A. Shellan
Maureen R. Sloane
Jeffrey C. Thede
William H. Walters
James N. Westwood
Norman J. Wiener
R. Alan Wight

SEATTLE, WASHINGTON PARTNERS

Scott J. Borth
James R. Dickens
James P. Donohue
James D. Gradel
Brooks E. Harlow
David W. Hercher
James R. Hermsen
Clyde H. MacIver
Paul W. Oden
Andrew H. Salter
Francis L. Van Dusen, Jr.
John L. West

PORTLAND, OREGON SENIOR COUNSEL

Donald R. Holman

PORTLAND, OREGON OF COUNSEL

Clifford B. Olsen

PORTLAND, OREGON RETIRED

Maurice O. Georges
Orval O. Hager
John W. Hill
Frank E. Nash

PORTLAND, OREGON ASSOCIATES

Jonathan D. Allred
Craig R. Armstrong
Jean Ohman Back
Janine C. Blatt
David G. Bristol
William F. Buchanan
Brian T. Burton
Bruce L. Campbell
D. Gary Christensen
Elizabeth Clark
Eryn E. Forbes
Ning Fu
Tami L. Graham
John R. Heninger
Steven F. Hill
Jerry B. Hodson
William R. Knuths
Sabrina P. Loiselle
M. Read Moore
Lynne A. Perry
Victoria Lee Rudometkin
Stephen M. Seidel
Catherine A. Shaw
Carole L. Souvenir
Brian S. Thompson
Sharon L. Toncray
M. Max Williams II

SEATTLE, WASHINGTON ASSOCIATES

James W. Allen
Beth M. Andrus
Lance W. Bass
Heidi A. Beck
Daniel A. Brown
Michael R. Francis
David J. W. Hackett
Peter S. Holmes
James H. Jordan, Jr.
Bruce A. Kaser
Vollie S. Scott
Susan K. Stahlfeld

(See Next Column)

LEGAL SUPPORT PERSONNEL

Leslie M. Meserve (Director of Information and Library Services)
Bernard F. Stea (Director of Legal Systems)

For full biographical listings, see the Martindale-Hubbell Law Directory

SUSSMAN SHANK WAPNICK CAPLAN & STILES (AV)

1000 S.W. Broadway Suite 1400, 97205
Telephone: 503-227-1111
Telecopier: 503-248-0130

MEMBERS OF FIRM

Gilbert Sussman (1905-1985)
Norman Wapnick
Barry P. Caplan
William N. Stiles
John P. Davenport
Jeffrey R. Spere
Howard M. Levine
Stuart I. Teicher
Jeffrey C. Misley

ASSOCIATES

Ann Boss
Robert L. Carlton
Helen Tompkins Dziuba
Gary E. Enloe
Michael G. Halligan
William S. Manne
Wendy Beth Oliver
Thomas W. Stilley

OF COUNSEL

Jerome B. Shank

SPECIAL COUNSEL

Aaron Jay Besen
John E. McCormick

For full biographical listings, see the Martindale-Hubbell Law Directory

WOOD TATUM SANDERS & MURPHY (AV)

1001 S.W. Fifth Avenue, Suite 1300, 97204
Telephone: 503-224-5430
Cable Address: "Linwood"
Telex: 296522
Facsimile: 503-241-7235

Erskine Wood (1879-1983)
Paul N. Wonacott (1939-1991)
Erskine B. Wood (Retired)
John G. Holden (Retired)
Lofton L. Tatum (1918-1992)
John D. Mosser (Retired)

MEMBERS OF FIRM

Robert I. Sanders
John C. Mercer
Craig C. Murphy
Kim Jefferies
Todd A. Zilbert

ASSOCIATES

John H. Chambers

Representative Clients: Allstate Insurance Co.; Assuranceforeningen Skuld; Britannia Steam Ship Ins. Assn. Ltd.; Continental Casualty Insurance Co.; Insurance Corporation of America; Japan Ship Owners' Mutual P & I Assn.; Professional Liability Fund; Professional Medical Insurance Co.; Steamship Mutual Underwriting Assn. Ltd.; United Kingdom Mutual Steam Ship Assurance Assn.

For full biographical listings, see the Martindale-Hubbell Law Directory

*PRINEVILLE,** Crook Co. — (Refer to Bend)

*ROSEBURG,** Douglas Co.

DOLE, COALWELL, CLARK & WELLS, P.C. (AV)

810 S.E. Douglas Avenue, P.O. Box 1205, 97470
Telephone: 503-673-5541
Fax: 503-673-1156
ABA/net !ddole

George W. Neuner (1914-1985)
Donald A. Dole
Bruce R. Coalwell
Dan W. Clark
Inge Dortmund Wells
Stephen Mountainspring
Jeffrey A. Mornarich

Representative Clients: Douglas County Title Co.; C & D Lumber Co.; Herbert Lumber Co.; South Umpqua State Bank.

For full biographical listings, see the Martindale-Hubbell Law Directory

*ST. HELENS,** Columbia Co. — (Refer to Portland)

*SALEM,** Marion Co.

CLARK, LINDAUER, MCCLINTON, FETHERSTON, EDMONDS & LIPPOLD (AV)

880 Liberty Street, N.E., P.O. Box 2206, 97308-2206
Telephone: 503-581-1542
Fax: 503-585-3978

MEMBERS OF FIRM

Edward L. Clark, Jr.
Eric B. Lindauer
Michael C. McClinton
Ben C. Fetherston, Jr.
James C. Edmonds
Steven M. Lippold

(See Next Column)

CLARK, LINDAUER, MCCLINTON, FETHERSTON, EDMONDS & LIPPOLD, *Salem—Continued*

Representative Clients: St. Paul Insurance Co.; North Pacific Insurance Co.; State Farm Insurance Co.; Colonial Penn Insurance Co.; Oregon State Bar Professional Liability Fund; Albertson's Inc.; Volkswagen of America, Inc.; Fleetwood Enterprises, Inc.; Portland General Electric Co.

For full biographical listings, see the Martindale-Hubbell Law Directory

ENFIELD, GUIMOND, BROWN & COLLINS (AV)

214 Pioneer Trust Building, 97301
Telephone: 503-581-6870
Fax: 503-581-3090

MEMBERS OF FIRM

Myron L. Enfield (Retired)
Joseph C. Guimond
James M. Brown
Loren W. Collins

ASSOCIATES

Lonny D. Bauscher

Reference: Pioneer Trust National Bank.

For full biographical listings, see the Martindale-Hubbell Law Directory

SPRINGFIELD, Lane Co. — (Refer to Eugene)

*THE DALLES,** Wasco Co.

DICK & DICK (AV)

601 Washington Street, 97058
Telephone: 503-296-2152
FAX: 503-296-4220

William G. Dick
Roger L. Dick
William G. Dick, II
Bradley V. Timmons

References: United States National Bank of Oregon (The Dalles Branch); First Interstate Bank of Oregon.

WEST LINN, Clackamas Co. — (Refer to Oregon City)

PENNSYLVANIA

*ALLENTOWN,** Lehigh Co.

BLACK, MCCARTHY & ANEWALT, P.C. (AV)

740 Hamilton Mall, 18101
Telephone: 610-437-4455
FAX: 610-437-5670

Alan M. Black
Daniel K. McCarthy
Thomas C. Anewalt

Robert A. Alpert
Nancy S. Skalangya

OF COUNSEL

Howard S. Epstein

For full biographical listings, see the Martindale-Hubbell Law Directory

DUANE, MORRIS & HECKSCHER (AV)

968 Postal Road, Suite 200, 18103-9390
Telephone: 610-266-3650
Fax: 610-640-2619
Philadelphia, Pennsylvania Office: Suite 4200 One Liberty Place.
Telephone: 215-979-1000.
FAX: 215-979-1020.
Harrisburg, Pennsylvania Office: 305 North Front Street, 5th Floor, P.O. Box 1003.
Telephone: 717-237-5500.
Fax: 717-232-4015.
Wilmington, Delaware Office: Suite 1500, 1201 Market Street.
Telephone: 302-571-5550.
Fax: 302-571-5560.
New York, N.Y. Office: 112 E. 42nd Street, Suite 2125.
Telephone: 212-499-0410.
Fax: 212-499-0420.
Wayne, Pennsylvania Office: 735 Chesterbrook Boulevard, Suite 300.
Telephone: 610-647-3555.
Cherry Hill, New Jersey Office: 51 Haddonfield Road, Suite 340.
Telephone: 609-488-7300.
Fax: 609-488-7021.

RESIDENT PARTNERS

John S. Hayes
Maxwell E. Davison
Edward H. Feege

RESIDENT ASSOCIATES

Wallace B. Eldridge III
Jeffrey M. Zimskind
John K. Baker
Michele T. Cann

For full biographical listings, see the Martindale-Hubbell Law Directory

KING, MCCARDLE, HERMAN, FREUND & OLEXA (AV)

110-112 North Sixth Street, P.O. Box 449, 18105
Telephone: 610-432-4506
FAX: 610-432-6656

MEMBERS OF FIRM

E. Drummond King
Edward C. McCardle
Kent H. Herman
John E. Freund, III
Georgine A. Olexa
James F. Swartz, III
David L. Masenheimer

For full biographical listings, see the Martindale-Hubbell Law Directory

SCOBLIONKO, SCOBLIONKO, MUIR & BARTHOLOMEW, A PROFESSIONAL CORPORATION (AV)

40 South Fifth Street, P.O. Box 1998, 18105
Telephone: 610-434-7138
Fax: 610-434-0520

E. G. Scoblionko (1909-1975)
Mark H. Scoblionko
Anthony Moyer Muir
James A. Bartholomew
Marla J. Melman
Andrew Hermann

Representative Clients: Industrial Development Corporation of Lehigh County.
References: Merchants National Bank of Allentown; First Valley Bank.

For full biographical listings, see the Martindale-Hubbell Law Directory

STEVENS & JOHNSON (AV)

(Successors to Butz & Rupp)
740 Hamilton Mall, 18101
Telephone: 610-439-1451
Telecopier: 610-439-1733

MEMBERS OF FIRM

Richard F. Stevens
Richard W. Shaffer
Robert J. Johnson
James B. Martin
Robert F. Fortin
Howard S. Stevens

ASSOCIATES

Timothy T. Stevens
Dina M. Branco

(See Next Column)

OF COUNSEL

Herbert M. Rafner

General Counsel for: Lehigh Valley Hospital Center, Inc.
Representative Clients: Maryland Casualty Co.; U.G.I. Corp.; Underwriters Adjusting Co.

For full biographical listings, see the Martindale-Hubbell Law Directory

TALLMAN, HUDDERS & SORRENTINO, P.C. (AV)

Suite 301 The Paragon Centre, 1611 Pond Road, 18104
Telephone: 610-391-1800
Fax: 610-391-1805

Robert G. Tallman
John R. Hudders
William H. Fitzgerald
Thomas C. Sadler, Jr.
Oldrich Foucek, III
Matthew R. Sorrentino
Timothy J. Siegfried
Dolores A. Laputka
Scott B. Allinson

Sherri L. Palopoli
David Andrew Williams
Mary C. Crocker
Scott R. Lipson
Theodore J. Zeller, III

OF COUNSEL

Harold Caplan
Paul J. Schoff

For full biographical listings, see the Martindale-Hubbell Law Directory

WEAVER, MOSEBACH, PIOSA, HIXSON & MARLES (AV)

One Windsor Plaza, Suite 200, 7535 Windsor Drive, 18195-1014
Telephone: 610-366-8000
FAX: 610-366-8001

MEMBERS OF FIRM

Thomas E. Weaver, Jr.
Barry N. Mosebach
Michael J. Piosa
Boyd G. Hixson
Blake C. Marles
John F. Hacker
Donald E. Wieand, Jr.
Donald H. Lipson
William H. Dayton, Jr.
David G. Knerr
Thomas E. Reilly, Jr.

ASSOCIATES

Thomas F. Smida
Paul D. North, Jr.
Robert J. Hobaugh, Jr.
Thomas A. Capehart
Irene Chiavaroli Johns

OF COUNSEL

Thomas E. Weaver
William H. Eckensberger, Jr.
Murray Mackson

LEGAL SUPPORT PERSONNEL

Jacqui Petch
Francine H. Glazier

For full biographical listings, see the Martindale-Hubbell Law Directory

BANGOR, Northampton Co.

CASSEBAUM, MCFALL & LAYMAN, A PROFESSIONAL CORPORATION (AV)

134 Broadway, P.O. Box 147, 18013
Telephone: 610-588-0484
Fax: 610-588-3455

J. Lawrence Davis (1905-1974)
James F. Pritchard (1923-1976)
William C. Cassebaum
Alan B. McFall
Peter C. Layman
Kimberly A. Cicci
David J. Jordan, Jr.

For full biographical listings, see the Martindale-Hubbell Law Directory

*BEAVER,** Beaver Co.

REED, LUCE, TOSH, MCGREGOR & WOLFORD, A PROFESSIONAL CORPORATION (AV)

804 Turnpike Street, 15009
Telephone: 412-774-9220
Fax: 412-774-1363

Harold F. Reed, Jr.
Wayne S. Luce
James C. Tosh
James A. McGregor, Jr.
Kathryn L. Johnston
Dennis F. Wolford

Counsel for: Jones & Laughlin Steel Corp.; Beaver Trust Co.; Century National Bank & Trust Co.; Tuscarora Plastics, Inc.; Beaver Newspaper, Inc.; Pennsylvania Manufacturers Insurance Assn.; Liberty Mutual Insurance Co.; Medical Center of Beaver Co. Inc.; Motorist Insurance Co.; Beaver Area School District.

For full biographical listings, see the Martindale-Hubbell Law Directory

BEAVER FALLS, Beaver Co. — (Refer to Beaver)

*BEDFORD,** Bedford Co. — (Refer to Somerset)

*BELLEFONTE,** Centre Co.

LEE, MARTIN, GREEN & REITER, INC. (AV)

115 East High Street, Lock Drawer 179, 16823
Telephone: 814-355-4769
Fax: 814-355-5024
State College, Pennsylvania Office: 270 Walker Drive.
Telephone: 814-237-6291.
Fax: 814-237-5861.

Donald E. Lee — Dennis O. Reiter
Robert L. Martin — Robert A. Mix
Joseph P. Green — William T. Fleming

Representative Clients: Peoples National Bank of Central Pennsylvania; State College Borough Water Authority; First National Bank of Spring Mills; Erie Insurance Group; Centre Community Hospital; Liberty Mutual Insurance Co.; Centre Area Transportation Authority.

For full biographical listings, see the Martindale-Hubbell Law Directory

BERWICK, Columbia Co. — (Refer to Milton)

BETHLEHEM, Northampton Co.

LABRUM AND DOAK (AV)

561 East Market Street, P.O. Box 1306, 18016
Telephone: 610-865-2644
Telecopier: 610-865-2713
Philadelphia, Pennsylvania Office: Suite 2900, 1818 Market Street.
Telephone: 610-564-4400.
Telecopier: 610-587-5350.
Norristown, Pennsylvania Office: One Montgomery Plaza, Suite 700.
Telephone: 610-277-7997.
Telecopier: 610-277-2852.
New York, N.Y. Office: 17 Battery Place.
Telephone: 212-809-7870.
Telecopier: 212-785-9279.
Woodbury, New Jersey Office: 66 Euclid Street, P.O. Box 836.
Telephone: 609-845-8855.
Telecopier: 609-848-2694.

RESIDENT MEMBERS

Robertson B. Taylor — R. Michael Carr
Barbara L. Hollenbach — J. Stephen Kreglow

RESIDENT ASSOCIATES

Maureen A. Jordan — Steven E. Hoffman
Jill R. Snyder — Doreen L. Smith
Laura J. Herzog — Beverly J. Doneker
Peter F. Darling

For full biographical listings, see the Martindale-Hubbell Law Directory

O'HARE & HEITCZMAN (AV)

18 East Market Street, P.O. Box 1446, 18018
Telephone: 610-691-5500
FAX: 610-691-7866

MEMBERS OF FIRM

Bernard V. O'Hare, Jr. (1923-1990) — George A. Heitczman

References: First Valley Bank; Meridan Bank.

For full biographical listings, see the Martindale-Hubbell Law Directory

BLANDON, Berks Co. — (Refer to Milton)

*BLOOMSBURG,** Columbia Co. — (Refer to Milton)

BLUE BELL, Montgomery Co.

KELLEY & MURPHY (AV)

Suite 160 Union Meeting Corporate Center V, 925 Harvest Drive, 19422
Telephone: 215-643-6500
Fax: 215-643-8356
Philadelphia, Pennsylvania Office: Suite 1100, 1420 Walnut Street.
Telephone: 215-941-6050.
Cable Address: "Bigtime".
Fax: 215-941-6053.

Joseph T. Kelley, Jr. — Patrick G. Murphy

For full biographical listings, see the Martindale-Hubbell Law Directory

BRADFORD, McKean Co.

MCDOWELL, WICK, DALY, GALLUP, HAUSER AND HARTLE (AV)

50 Boylston Street, P.O. Box 361, 16701
Telephone: 814-362-5517
Fax: 814-368-3404

(See Next Column)

MEMBERS OF FIRM

T. L. McDowell (1911-1970) — Robert H. Wick
Daniel W. Daly (1917-1980) — Frederick W. Gallup
J. J. McDowell (1906-1982) — Christopher G. Hauser
William J. Kubiak (1952-1991) — Daniel J. Hartle

Counsel for: Integra National Bank/North; Northwest Savings Bank, P.A.; Bradford City Water Authority; Pennzoil Co.; Zippo Manufacturing Co.; Bradford Area School District; University of Pittsburgh, Bradford, Pennsylvania; Werzalit of America, Inc.

For full biographical listings, see the Martindale-Hubbell Law Directory

BRISTOL, Bucks Co.

BEGLEY, CARLIN & MANDIO (AV)

120 Mill Street, 19007
Telephone: 215-750-0110
Langhorne, Pennsylvania Office: 680 Middletown Boulevard, P.O. Box 308.
Telephone: 215-750-0110.

MEMBERS OF FIRM

William J. Carlin — John P. Koopman
Anthony A. Mandio — Jeffrey P. Garton
S. Richard Klinges, III — Thomas R. Hecker
Thomas J. Profy, III — James A. Downey, III
Richard M. Snyder — Joseph S. Britton
Charles F. Sampsel — Douglas C. Maloney

ASSOCIATES

Thomas J. Profy, IV — William L. Weiner
Karen L. Saraco

Representative Clients: Borough of Bristol; Bristol Borough School Board; Fidelity Savings & Loan Association of Bucks County; Lower Makefield Township; Philadelphia National Bank; Waste Management, Inc.

For full biographical listings, see the Martindale-Hubbell Law Directory

*BROOKVILLE,** Jefferson Co. — (Refer to Clarion)

BRYN MAWR, Montgomery Co.

MURPHY AND MURPHY (AV)

801 Old Lancaster Road, 19010
Telephone: 610-519-0400
Fax: 610-519-0104
Trenton, New Jersey Office: Suite A 311 White Horse Avenue.
Telephone: 609-581-8559.

L. Francis Murphy — Francis J. Murphy
Michael T. Murphy

For full biographical listings, see the Martindale-Hubbell Law Directory

*BUTLER,** Butler Co.

DILLON, MCCANDLESS & KING (AV)

128 West Cunningham Street, 16001
Telephone: 412-283-2200
Fax: 412-283-2298
Cranberry Township, Pennsylvania Office: Route 19, Cranberry Professional Park, Suite 3, 501 Smith Drive. (Evans City).
Telephone: 412-776-6644.
Fax: 412-776-6608.

MEMBERS OF FIRM

Charles E. Dillon — James P. Coulter
Richard L. McCandless — Donald P. Graham (Resident, Cranberry Township, Pennsylvania Office)
Thomas W. King, III

ASSOCIATES

Thomas J. May — Mary Jo Dillon
Michael D. Hnath

Representative Clients: Pennsylvania Manufacturers Association Insurance Co.; Amerikohl Mining, Inc.; City of Butler.

For full biographical listings, see the Martindale-Hubbell Law Directory

*CARLISLE,** Cumberland Co.

DOUGLAS, DOUGLAS & DOUGLAS (AV)

27 West High Street, 17013-0261
Telephone: 717-243-1790
Fax: 717-243-8955

MEMBERS OF FIRM

George F. Douglas, Jr. — William P. Douglas
George F. Douglas, III

Representative Client: State Farm Insurance Cos.

For full biographical listings, see the Martindale-Hubbell Law Directory

Carlisle—Continued

MARTSON, DEARDORFF, WILLIAMS & OTTO, A PROFESSIONAL CORPORATION (AV)

Ten East High Street, 17013-3093
Telephone: 717-243-3341
Fax: 717-243-1850

William F. Martson
Daniel K. Deardorff
Thomas J. Williams, III
Ivo V. Otto, III
Stephen Larkin Bloom
George B. Faller, Jr.

Scott A. Freeland
William D. Powell

LEGAL SUPPORT PERSONNEL

Corrine L. Myers (Estates Administration)
Tricia L. James (Real Estate)

Representative Clients: Aetna Casualty and Surety Co.; Liberty Mutual Insurance Co.; The Travelers Insurance Group; Northland Insurance Co.; Celina Insurance Group; Pennsylvania Manufacturers Association Insurance Co.; United States Fidelity & Guarantee.

For full biographical listings, see the Martindale-Hubbell Law Directory

*CHAMBERSBURG,** Franklin Co. — (Refer to Waynesboro)

CHESTER, Delaware Co. — (Refer to Media)

*CLARION,** Clarion Co.

LAW OFFICES OF RICHARD W. KOOMAN, II (AV)

Marianne Professional Center, P.O. Box 700, 16214
Telephone: 814-226-9100
Fax: 814-226-7361

ASSOCIATES

Terry R. Heeter

Representative Clients: Pennsylvania National Mutual Casualty Insurance Co.; Erie Insurance Exchange; Sorce, Inc.; Charles Tool & Supply, Inc.; Brookville Locomotive, Inc.; G&G Contracting, Inc.; Ti-Brook, Inc.; Alpha Environmental Mining Corp.; Exley Oil & Gas Co.; Clarion County Economic Development Authority.

For full biographical listings, see the Martindale-Hubbell Law Directory

POPE, POPE AND DRAYER (AV)

Ten Grant Street, 16214
Telephone: 814-226-5700
Fax: 814-226-9669

MEMBERS OF FIRM

H. Ray Pope
Henry R. Pope, III
Kent S. Pope
H. John Drayer

For full biographical listings, see the Martindale-Hubbell Law Directory

*COUDERSPORT,** Potter Co. — (Refer to Wellsboro)

*DANVILLE,** Montour Co. — (Refer to Sunbury)

*DOYLESTOWN,** Bucks Co.

GATHRIGHT AND LEONARD (AV)

Suite 102, Landmark Building, 105 Clinton Street, 18901
Telephone: 215-340-7900
Fax: 215-340-9307

MEMBERS OF FIRM

Howard T. Gathright
Nicholas A. Leonard

LEGAL SUPPORT PERSONNEL

Lynn A. Leonard (Paralegal)

Reference: Bank & Trust Company of Old York Road.

For full biographical listings, see the Martindale-Hubbell Law Directory

POWER, BOWEN & VALIMONT (AV)

102 North Main Street, 18901-0818
Telephone: 215-345-7500
Fax: 215-345-7507
Sellersville, Pennsylvania Office: 64 North Main Street.
Telephone: 215-257-3661.

MEMBERS OF FIRM

William M. Power (1917-1988)
Robert W. Valimont (1922-1990)
James C. Bowen (Retired)
William B. Moyer
Samuel G. Moyer (Resident, Sellersville Office)
John D. Trainer
William E. Benner
Gordon G. Erdenberger
John J. Hart
William T. Renz
Thomas L. Sumter
Michael S. Valimont
Herbert K. Sudfeld, Jr.
William H. Fuss (Resident, Sellersville Office)
Edward M. Wild

(See Next Column)

Randal S. White
Marguerite McGarvey Whitaker
Susan Jean Smith

Representative Clients: General Accident Group; U.S. Gauge Division of AMETEK; Nockamixon-Bucks Commercial and Industrial Development Assn.; First Savings Bank.

For full biographical listings, see the Martindale-Hubbell Law Directory

*EASTON,** Northampton Co.

FOX, OLDT & BROWN (AV)

Suite 508, First Fidelity Bank Building, Six South Third Street, Center Square, 18042
Telephone: 610-258-6111
Fax: 610-253-4532

MEMBERS OF FIRM

Charles L. Oldt
Robert C. Brown, Jr.

Counsel for: Merchants Bank, N.A.; Easton Cemetery; Travelers Insurance Co.

For full biographical listings, see the Martindale-Hubbell Law Directory

HERSTER, NEWTON & MURPHY (AV)

127 North Fourth Street, P.O. Box 1087, 18042
Telephone: 610-258-6219

MEMBERS OF FIRM

Andrew L. Herster, Jr.
Henry R. Newton
William K. Murphy

General Counsel For: Valley Federal Savings & Loan Assn.; Lafayette Bank; Easton Printing Co.; Northampton Community College; Eisenhardt Mills, Inc.; Delaware Wood Products, Inc.; Panuccio Construction, Inc.
References: Merchants Bank, N.A.; Lafayette Bank; Valley Federal Savings and Loan.

LAUER AND MONAHAN, P.C. (AV)

704 Washington Street, 18042
Telephone: 610-258-5329
Fax: 610-258-0155

Philip D. Lauer
Brian M. Monahan

Reference: Meridian Bank.

For full biographical listings, see the Martindale-Hubbell Law Directory

GUS MILIDES (AV)

654 Wolf Avenue, 18042
Telephone: 610-258-0433

ASSOCIATES

Beth Ann Milides

For full biographical listings, see the Martindale-Hubbell Law Directory

*EBENSBURG,** Cambria Co. — (Refer to Johnstown)

*EMPORIUM,** Cameron Co. — (Refer to St. Marys)

*ERIE,** Erie Co.

ELDERKIN, MARTIN, KELLY & MESSINA, P.C. (AV)

Jones School Square, 150 East Eighth Street, P.O. Box 1819, 16507-0819
Telephone: 814-456-4000
FAX: 814-454-7411

Vedder J. White
Harry D. Martin
William J. Kelly
Joseph T. Messina
Kenneth G. Vasil
James H. Richardson, Jr.
Ronald L. Slater
John B. Enders
Robert C. LeSuer
Craig A. Markham
Thomas J. Minarcik
Gery T. Nietupski
Elizabeth K. Kelly
Evan C. Rudert
Edward J. Betza
James F. Geronimo
Craig A. Zonna
Michael T. Reynolds
William J. Kelly, Jr.

OF COUNSEL

Vernon H. Elderkin, Jr.

Representative Clients: Commonwealth Land Title Insurance Co.; Times Publishing Co.; Integra Bank/North; Gannon University; Sears, Roebuck & Co.; Waste Management, Inc.; Allstate Insurance Co.; State Farm Fire and Casualty Co.; Autoclave Engineers, Inc.

For full biographical listings, see the Martindale-Hubbell Law Directory

KNOX MCLAUGHLIN GORNALL & SENNETT, P.C. (AV)

120 West Tenth Street, 16501-1461
Telephone: 814-459-2800
Fax: 814-453-4530

(See Next Column)

KNOX MCLAUGHLIN GORNALL & SENNETT P.C., *Erie—Continued*

Conrad A. Pearson (1917-1969)
Jackson D. Magenau (1907-1984)
Mortimer E. Graham (1901-1987)
John M. McLaughlin
M. Fletcher Gornall
Joseph F. MacKrell
William C. Sennett
John W. Beatty
Edwin L. R. McKean
Wallace J. Knox, II
Richard H. Zamboldi
Richard A. Levick
Jack M. Gornall
Harry K. Thomas
Michael Alan Fetzner
James T. Marnen
Donald E. Wright, Jr.
Richard W. Perhacs
Robert G. Dwyer
Mark E. Mioduszewski
Carl N. Moore
David M. Mosier
Thomas A. Tupitza
Guy C. Fustine
Richard E. Bordonaro
John O. Dodick
Timothy M. Sennett
William C. Wagner
Brian Glowacki

Patricia K. Smith
Mark T. Wassell
Richard A. Lanzillo
Matthew J. McLaughlin
Joanna K. Budde
Peter A. Pentz
Sue A. Beck
Mark G. Claypool
Albert W. Zenner
Dorothy D. Morgan
Thomas C. Hoffman, II
Mark J. Kuhar
Christopher J. Sinnott

For full biographical listings, see the Martindale-Hubbell Law Directory

MACDONALD, ILLIG, JONES & BRITTON (AV)
100 State Street, Suite 700, 16507-1498
Telephone: 814-870-7600
FAX: 814-454-4647

MEMBERS OF FIRM

Henry A. MacDonald (1928-1984)
William F. Illig (1946-1989)
Frederick F. Jones (1939-1977, retired)
John M. Wolford (1973-1988)
Robert W. Parker, Jr. (1973-1991)
John E. Britton
Peter G. Schaaf
John F. Potter
John D. Wilson
John J. Stroh, Jr.
Norman H. Stark
T. Warren Jones
Edward W. Goebel, Jr.
James D. Cullen
William R. Brown
Roger H. Taft
David E. Holland
Wm. Patrick Delaney
James M. Antoun
James R. Walczak
Russell S. Warner
Marcia H. Haller
James E. Spoden
Dale E. Huntley

ASSOCIATES

John W. Draskovic
Richard J. Parks
John J. Mehler
Matthew W. McCullough
Stephen R. Thelin
Susan Fuhrer Reiter
Sheila Tolgyesi Kocan
Mark J. Shaw
John F. Mizner
Craig R. F. Murphey
Daniel M. Miller
Brian W. Bolash
Shaun B. Adrian
Kimberly A. Oakes
Eric J. Purchase
Norman A. Stark
Lisa Lynn Smith
Steven C. Beckman
Thomas A. Pendleton
Laura Anastasia Popoff

OF COUNSEL

Irving Olds Murphy

Representative Clients: American Sterilizer Co.; Erie Insurance Exchange; General Electric Co.; Hamot Health Foundation; Integra Bank/North; International Paper Co.

For full biographical listings, see the Martindale-Hubbell Law Directory

MARSH, SPAEDER, BAUR, SPAEDER & SCHAAF (AV)
Suite 300, 300 State Street, 16507
Telephone: 814-456-5301
Fax: 814-456-1112

MEMBERS OF FIRM

James E. Marsh, Sr. (1908-1988)
Ritchie T. Marsh (1870-1947)
John A. Spaeder (1902-1994)
Robert N. Spaeder (1915-1993)
Will J. Schaaf
Ritchie T. Marsh
William J. Schaaf
James E. Marsh, Jr.
John P. Eppinger
John C. Brydon
Thomas E. Kuhn
Thomas M. Lent
Francis J. Klemensic
John B. Fessler
Eugene C. Sundberg, Jr.
James R. Fryling

Donald F. Fessler, Jr.
Kurt L. Sundberg

OF COUNSEL

Byron A. Baur

Representative Clients: Aetna Life & Casualty; Borough of Edinboro; Chase Lincoln First Bank, N.A.; Erie Parking Authority; Home Insurance Co.; Marquette Savings Assn.; Motorists Insurance Co.; Northwest Savings Bank, Pa., S.A.; Ohio Casualty Insurance Co.; Pennsylvania Medical Society Liability Insurance Co.

(See Next Column)

For full biographical listings, see the Martindale-Hubbell Law Directory

MCCLURE & MILLER (AV)
Suite 701, 717 State Street, 16501
Telephone: 814-453-3681
Fax: 814-454-1554

MEMBERS OF FIRM

Harvey D. McClure
Daniel L. R. Miller
Eugene J. Brew, Jr.
Edward P. Wittmann
Michael J. Visnosky
Christine Hall McClure

OF COUNSEL

Herbert J. Johnson, Jr.

ASSOCIATES

Jeffery J. Cole

For full biographical listings, see the Martindale-Hubbell Law Directory

THE MCDONALD GROUP, P.C. (AV)
456 West 6th Street, 16507-1216
Telephone: 814-456-5318
Fax: 814-456-3840

James D. McDonald, Jr.
Gary Eiben

Frank J. Scutella
Daniel J. Pastore
Thomas J. Buseck
Bryan K. Shreckengost

OF COUNSEL

John G. Gent

For full biographical listings, see the Martindale-Hubbell Law Directory

QUINN, BUSECK, LEEMHUIS, TOOHEY & KROTO, INC. (AV)
2222 West Grandview Boulevard, 16506-4508
Telephone: 814-833-2222
Cable Address: "Lawmen"
Fax: 814-833-6753

Frank B. Quinn (1889-1964)
Raymond P. Leemhuis (1896-1972)
Alban W. Curtze (1901-1976)
Bernard F. Quinn (Retired, 1973)
John M. Quinn, Sr.
Donald C. Buseck
John P. Leemhuis, Sr.
John R. Falcone
James F. Toohey
Frank L. Kroto, Jr.
I. John Dunn
Paul F. Burroughs
Lawrence C. Bolla
James K. McNamara
John Paul Garhart
John M. Quinn, Jr.
J. W. Alberstadt, Jr.
George Joseph
Natalie Dwyer Haller
Michael S. Jan Janin
Kenneth W. Wargo

John P. Leemhuis, Jr
Richard A. Blakely
Patricia J. Kennedy
Arthur D. Martinucci
John E. Gomolchak
Kathryn J. Kisak
David S. Rzepecki
Jennifer L. Johnston

Representative Clients: Chicago Title Insurance Agent; General Telephone of Pennsylvania; Hartford Accident and Indemnity Co.; Kemper Group; National Fuel Gas Distribution Corp.; Pennsylvania Electric Co.; PHICO Insurance; Saint Vincent Health Center; Spectrum Control, Inc.; Zurn Industries.

For full biographical listings, see the Martindale-Hubbell Law Directory

*FRANKLIN,** Venango Co.

GENT, GENT AND SNYDER (AV)
314 West Park Street, 16323
Telephone: 814-437-3754

MEMBERS OF FIRM

Henry W. Gent, Jr.
Henry W. Gent, III
Michael D. Snyder
Robert L. Boyer

For full biographical listings, see the Martindale-Hubbell Law Directory

FRAZER, Chester Co.

LENTZ, CANTOR, KILGORE & MASSEY, LTD. (AV)
49 East Lancaster Avenue, 19355
Telephone: 610-647-3310
Fax: 610-647-3318

Robert W. Lentz
Richard L. Cantor
R. Lamar Kilgore
Albert P. Massey, Jr.
Christopher J. Clark
John C. Snyder
Andrew H. Dohan
William J. Scott, Jr.
Sean A. O'Neill
Robert C. F. Willson
Wendy W. McLean
Duke Schneider
Scott E. Yaw
Kimberly Cline Gibney
Sean P. Melvin

(See Next Column)

LENTZ, CANTOR, KILGORE & MASSEY LTD.—*Continued*

LEGAL SUPPORT PERSONNEL

Patricia L. Sierzant (Administrator)

Representative Clients: Donegal Mutual Insurance Co.; Home Insurance Co.; Matthews Ford; Meridian Bank; Nursecare Health Centers, Inc.

For full biographical listings, see the Martindale-Hubbell Law Directory

*GETTYSBURG,** Adams Co. — (Refer to York)

*GREENSBURG,** Westmoreland Co.

BELDEN, BELDEN, PERSIN, JOHNSTON & ZUZIK (AV)

Belden Building, 117 North Main Street, 15601
Telephone: 412-834-0300
Fax: 412-834-1307

MEMBERS OF FIRM

H. Reginald Belden (1907-1993)
Dennis N. Persin
H. Reginald Belden, Jr.
Robert I. Johnston
Denis P. Zuzik

ASSOCIATES

John K. Greiner

Represent: GenCorp.; The Goodman Co.; Mellon Bank, N.A., Greensburg Offices; Employers Insurance of Wausau; Fireman's Fund American Insurance Cos.; Pennsylvania Manufacturers' Association Insurance Co.; United States Fidelity & Guaranty Co.

For full biographical listings, see the Martindale-Hubbell Law Directory

COSTELLO, MARSH & WARD (AV)

15 North Main Street, 15601-2471
Telephone: 412-834-2100
Facsimile: 412-834-3813

MEMBERS OF FIRM

B. Patrick Costello
Rabe F. Marsh III
John N. Ward

ASSOCIATES

Barbara J. Christner

Representative Clients: GEICO (Government Employees Insurance Company); Kemper Insurance Group; Liberty Mutual Insurance Co.; Motorists Mutual Insurance Company; Adam Eidemiller, Inc.; West Penn Power Co.; Westmoreland Health System; Boy Scouts of America, Westmoreland-Fayette Council; Seton Hill College; Westmoreland County Industrial Development Corp.

For full biographical listings, see the Martindale-Hubbell Law Directory

DAVID R. GOLD, P.C. (AV)

201 Integra Bank Building, 125 South Main Street, 15601
Telephone: 412-837-3433
Fax: 412-837-3450

David R. Gold

Representative Clients: John Gulisek Construction Co.; George Wilson & Company, Inc.; Photographics Supply, Inc.; F.E. Business Trust; Celio Auto & Equipment Salvage, Inc.; Schreiber Industrial Development Co.; The Fig Tree.
References: Mellon Bank N.A.; Southwest National Bank of Pennsylvania; Integra Bank.

For full biographical listings, see the Martindale-Hubbell Law Directory

DAVID J. MILLSTEIN (AV)

218 South Maple Avenue, 15601
Telephone: 412-837-3333
Fax: 412-837-8344

For full biographical listings, see the Martindale-Hubbell Law Directory

WALTHOUR AND GARLAND (AV)

Park Building, 121 North Main Street, 15601
Telephone: 412-834-4900

MEMBERS OF FIRM

Christ. C. Walthour, Jr.
Robert Wm. Garland
Holly G. Garland

Representative Clients: Peoples National Gas Co.; Baltimore & Ohio Railroad; Old Guard Insurance Company; Manor National Bank.
References: Manor National Bank; Southwest National Bank of Pennsylvania.

For full biographical listings, see the Martindale-Hubbell Law Directory

GREENVILLE, Mercer Co. — (Refer to Franklin)

GROVE CITY, Mercer Co.

MCBRIDE AND MCBRIDE, P.C. (AV)

211 South Center Street, 16127
Telephone: 412-458-6640

Milford L. McBride (1889-1962)
Brenda K. McBride
Milford L. McBride, Jr.
Milford L. McBride, III

Counsel for: Bashlin Industries; George J. Howe Co.; Tri-County Industries, Inc.; Clinch-Tite Corp.; C-B Grove City Federal Credit Union; Liberty and Worth Townships.

For full biographical listings, see the Martindale-Hubbell Law Directory

*HARRISBURG,** Dauphin Co.

* indicates certain Bar Register subscribers whose principal office is located elsewhere in the state and who have arranged for representation as a part of the state capital listings that follow

BARLEY, SNYDER, SENFT & COHEN (AV)

240 North Third Street, P.O. Box 1129, 17108
Telephone: 717-238-8263
Telecopier: 717-238-8278
Lancaster, Pennsylvania Office: 126 East King Street.
Telephone: 717-299-5201.
Telecopier: 717-291-4660.
York, Pennsylvania Office: 100 East Market Street.
Telephone: 717-846-8888.
Telecopier: 717-843-8492.

MEMBERS OF FIRM

Harry J. Rubin
H. Robert Lasday
Donald D. Geyer

Representative State Tax Clients: American Home Products Corporation; Akzo America, Inc.; Capital Cities/ABC, Inc.; Combustion Engineering, Inc.; Conoco, Inc.; Dean Witter Reynolds, Inc.; E.I. DuPont de Nemours and Company; Ford Motor Company; General Electric Company; General Public Utilities Corporation.

For full biographical listings, see the Martindale-Hubbell Law Directory

BUCHANAN INGERSOLL, PROFESSIONAL CORPORATION (AV)

Vartan Parc, 30 North Third Street, 17101
Telephone: 717-237-4800
Telecopier: 717-233-0852
Pittsburgh, Pennsylvania Office: 5800 USX Tower, 600 Grant Street.
Telephone: 412-562-8800.
Philadelphia, Pennsylvania Office: Two Logan Square, Twelfth Floor, 18th & Arch Streets.
Telephone: 215-665-8700.
Tampa, Florida Office: 101 East Kennedy Boulevard, Suite 1030.
Telephone: 813-222-8180.
North Miami Beach, Florida Office: 19495 Biscayne Boulevard.
Telephone: 305-933-5600.
Lexington, Kentucky Office: 1210 Vine Center Office Tower, 333 West Vine Street.
Telephone: 606-225-5333.
Princeton, New Jersey Office: Buchanan Ingersoll, A Partnership, College Centre, 500 College Road East.
Telephone: 609-452-2666.

Daniel E. Beren
John R. Johnson
Robert G. Devlin
Robert A. Johnson
Jeffrey A. Ernico
Mary Hannah Leavitt
Andrew S. Gordon
Michael T. McCarthy
Bradley J. Gunnison
Gerald K. Morrison
Jonathan Vipond III

COUNSEL

Evelyn S. Harris

SENIOR ATTORNEYS

Richard H. Friedman
Kathryn Speaker MacNett
William D. Lenahan
Michael L. Solomon

Elizabeth A. Arnold
Katherine Pandelidis Granbois
Sarah M. Bricknell
Judith P. Musselman
John B. Consevage
Paul S. Romano
Samuel M. First
Arbelyn Elizabeth Wolfe

For full biographical listings, see the Martindale-Hubbell Law Directory

*** DECHERT PRICE & RHOADS (AV)**

Thirty North Third Street, 17101
Telephone: 717-237-2000
Telefax: 717-237-2040
Philadelphia, Pennsylvania: 4000 Bell Atlantic Tower, 1717 Arch Street.
Telephone: 215-994-4000.
New York, N.Y.: 477 Madison Avenue.
Telephone: 212-326-3500.
Washington, D.C.: 1500 K Street, N. W.
Telephone: 202-626-3300.

(See Next Column)

DECHERT PRICE & RHOADS, *Harrisburg—Continued*

Princeton, New Jersey: Princeton Pike Corporate Center, P.O. Box 5218.
Telephone: 609-520-3200.
Boston, Massachusetts: Ten Post Office Square South.
Telephone: 617-728-7100.
London, England: 2 Serjeants' Inn, EC4Y 1LT.
Telephone: (071) 583-5353. (Also see Titmuss Sainer Dechert).
Brussels, Belgium: 65 Avenue Louise, 1050.
Telephone: (02) 535-5411.

RESIDENT PARTNERS

H. Craig Lewis — Francis Mazzola

RESIDENT COUNSEL

Bradley L. Mallory

RESIDENT ASSOCIATES

Richard C. Kariss — David J. Shipley
David R. Kraus — Lee A. Zoeller

For full biographical listings, see the Martindale-Hubbell Law Directory

*** DILWORTH, PAXSON, KALISH & KAUFFMAN** (AV)

305 North Front Street, Suite 403, 17101
Telephone: 717-236-4812
Fax: 717-236-7811
Philadelphia, Pennsylvania Office: 3200 Mellon Building, 1735 Market Street.
Telephone: 215-575-7000.
Fax: 215-575-7200.
Plymouth Meeting, Pennsylvania Office: 630 West Germantown Pike, Suite 160.
Telephone: 610-941-4444.
Fax: 610-941-9880.
Westmont, New Jersey Office: 222 Haddon Avenue.
Telephone: 609-854-5150.
Fax: 609-854-2316.
Media, Pennsylvania Office: 606 E. Baltimore Pike.
Telephone: 610-565-4322.
Fax: 610-565-4131.

MEMBER OF THE FIRM

Victor P. Stabile

For full biographical listings, see the Martindale-Hubbell Law Directory

DUANE, MORRIS & HECKSCHER (AV)

305 North Front Street, 5th Floor, P.O. Box 1003, 17108-1003
Telephone: 717-237-5500
Cable-Telegraph Address: TWX 710-670-1164
Telecopier: (717) 232-4015
Fax: 717-232-4015
Philadelphia, Pennsylvania Office: Suite 4200 One Liberty Place.
Telephone: 215-979-1000.
Wilmington, Delaware Office: Suite 1500, 1201 Market Street.
Telephone: 302-571-5550.
Fax: 302-571-5560.
New York, N.Y. Office: 112 E. 42nd Street, Suite 2125.
Telephone: 212-499-0410.
Fax: 212-499-0420.
Wayne, Pennsylvania Office: 735 Chesterbrook Boulevard, Suite 300.
Telephone: 610-647-3555.
Allentown, Pennsylvania Office: 968 Postal Road, Suite 200.
Telephone: 610-266-3650.
Fax: 610-640-2619.
Cherry Hill, New Jersey Office: 51 Haddonfield Road, Suite 340.
Telephone: 609-488-7300.
Fax: 609-488-7021.

RESIDENT PARTNERS

Donald A. Tortorice — Allen C. Warshaw
Robert E. Kelly, Jr. — Arthur K. Hoffman
Jack M. Mumford — Kenneth L. Sable
Scott C. Penwell — Shaun R. Eisenhauer

RESIDENT ASSOCIATES

Matthew Chabal, III — Cletus C. Hess
Mary Patricia Patterson — Martin A. Fritz
Thomas J. Weber — Brian William Bisignani
Bruce A. Gelting

RESIDENT OF COUNSEL

Harold W. Swope

SPECIAL COUNSEL

Ruth M. Siegel

For full biographical listings, see the Martindale-Hubbell Law Directory

*** ECKERT SEAMANS CHERIN & MELLOTT** (AV)

One South Market Square Building, 213 Market Street, 17101
Telephone: 717-237-6000
Facsimile: 717-237-6019
Pittsburgh, Pennsylvania Office: 600 Grant Street, 42nd Floor.
Telephone: 412-566-6000.
Telex: 866172.
Facsimile: 412-566-6099.
Allentown, Pennsylvania Office: Sovereign Building, 609 Hamilton Mall, 3rd Floor.
Telephone: 610-432-3000.
Facsimile: 610-432-8827.
Philadelphia, Pennsylvania Office: 1700 Market Street, Suite 3232.
Telephone: 215-575-6000.
Telex: 845226.
Facsimile: 215-575-6015.
Boston, Massachusetts Office: One International Place, 18th Floor.
Telephone: 617-342-6800.
Facsimile: 617-342-6899.
Buffalo, New York Office: 606 Liberty Building.
Telephone: 716-854-4100.
Facsimile: 716-854-4227.
Fort Lauderdale, Florida Office: First Fort Lauderdale Place, Suite 900, 100 Northeast Third Avenue.
Telephone: 305-523-0400.
Facsimile: 305-523-7002.
Boca Raton, Florida Office: Suite 902, The Plaza, 5355 Town Center Road.
Telephone: 407-394-7775.
Facsimile: 407-394-9998.
Miami, Florida Office: Barnett Tower, 18th Floor, 701 Brickell Avenue.
Telephone: 305-373-9100.
Facsimile: 305-372-9400.
Tallahassee, Florida Office: 206 South Adams Street.
Telephone: 904-222-2515.
Facsimile: 904-222-3452.
Washington, D.C. Office: 2100 Pennsylvania Avenue, N.W., Suite 600.
Telephone: 202-659-6600.
Telex: 62030761.
Facsimile: 202-659-6699.

MEMBERS OF FIRM

LeRoy S. Zimmerman — Peter J. Kramer
C. Peter Carlucci, Jr. — James J. Kutz
Christopher M. Cicconi — G. Thomas Roberts
Carol Porell Cocheres — R. Scott Shearer
George E. Cornelius — Jack M. Stover
Jack M. Hartman — Thomas B. York

RESIDENT OF COUNSEL

Walter W. Shearer

RESIDENT SPECIAL COUNSEL

Burton D. Morris

RESIDENT ASSOCIATES

Charles I. Artz — Timothy A. Hoy
Robin L. Barber — Richard D. Michael
Mark D. Bradshaw — George A. Michak
Deneice Covert — Robert L. Shuster
Douglas J. Davison — Bruce J. Warshawsky
Elizabeth J. Gant — James A. M. Zarrella

For full biographical listings, see the Martindale-Hubbell Law Directory

GOLDBERG, KATZMAN & SHIPMAN, P.C. (AV)

320 Market Street - Strawberry Square, P.O. Box 1268, 17108-1268
Telephone: 717-234-4161
Telecopier: 717-234-6808; 717-234-6810

Ronald M. Katzman — David C. Miller, Jr.
Harry B. Goldberg — James M. Sheehan
F. Lee Shipman — Michael A. Finio
Paul J. Esposito — John A. Statler
Neil Hendershot — April L. Strang-Kutay
Jesse Jay Cooper — Guy H. Brooks
Thomas E. Brenner — Jefferson J. Shipman

Arnold B. Kogan — Michael J. Crocenzi
Karen S. Feuchtenberger — Jerry J. Russo
Drew Gannon

OF COUNSEL

Arthur L. Goldberg

Representative Clients: Cincinnati Insurance Co.; Pennsylvania National Insurance Co.; The Atlantic Mutual Cos.; Erie Insurance Group; State Auto Insurance Co.; Dauphin County General Authority; Flight Systems, Inc.; Tressler Lutheran Services; Merchants & Businessman's Mutual Insurance Co.
Reference: Fulton Bank.

For full biographical listings, see the Martindale-Hubbell Law Directory

Harrisburg—Continued

HEPFORD, SWARTZ & MORGAN (AV)

111 North Front Street, P.O. Box 889, 17108-0889
Telephone: 717-234-4121
Fax: 717-232-6802
Lewistown, Pennsylvania Office: 12 South Main Street, P.O. Box 867.
Telephone: 717-248-3913.

MEMBERS OF FIRM

H. Joseph Hepford
Lee C. Swartz
James G. Morgan, Jr.
Sandra L. Meilton
Stephen M. Greecher, Jr.
Dennis R. Sheaffer

COUNSEL

Stanley H. Siegel (Resident, Lewistown Office)

ASSOCIATES

Richard A. Estacio
Michael H. Park
Andrew K. Stutzman

For full biographical listings, see the Martindale-Hubbell Law Directory

KEEFER, WOOD, ALLEN & RAHAL (AV)

210 Walnut Street, P.O. Box 11963, 17108-1963
Telephone: 717-255-8000
Telecopier: 717-255-8050

MEMBERS OF FIRM

Heath L. Allen
N. David Rahal
William E. Miller, Jr.
Charles W. Rubendall II
Robert L. Weldon
Eugene E. Pepinsky, Jr.
Thomas E. Wood
John H. Enos, III
Gary E. French
Donna S. Weldon
Bradford Dorrance
Jeffrey S. Stokes
Stephen L. Grose
Robert R. Church

OF COUNSEL

William H. Wood
Samuel C. Harry

ASSOCIATES

Jeffrey F. Smith
Donald M. Lewis, III
Bridget M. Whitley
Gretchen C. Hanrahan
Karen J. Brothers

Representative Clients: ALCOA; Arnold Industries, Inc.; Bethlehem Steel Co.; Caterpillar, Inc.; Care States Bank, N.A.; Mellon Bank, N.A.; Harrisburg Hospital; IBM Corp.; Nuclear Support Services, Inc.; Pennsylvania Blue Shield; Upper Allen Township.

For full biographical listings, see the Martindale-Hubbell Law Directory

MANCKE, WAGNER, HERSHEY AND TULLY (AV)

2233 North Front Street, 17110
Telephone: 717-234-7051
Fax: 717-234-7080

MEMBERS OF FIRM

John B. Mancke
P. Richard Wagner
David E. Hershey
William T. Tully

ASSOCIATES

David R. Breschi

For full biographical listings, see the Martindale-Hubbell Law Directory

McNEES, WALLACE & NURICK (AV)

100 Pine Street, P.O. Box 1166, 17108
Telephone: 717-232-8000
Fax: 717-237-5300

Sterling G. McNees (1887-1959)
David M. Wallace (1892-1967)
Gilbert Nurick (1906-1993)

OF COUNSEL

Robert H. Griswold
Samuel A. Schreckengaust, Jr.

MEMBERS OF FIRM

Bruce D. Bagley
Terry R. Bossert
Alan R. Boynton, Jr.
Eric L. Brossman
Robert M. Cherry
William A. Chesnutt
David B. Disney
Michael A. Doctrow
Elizabeth A. Dougherty
Harvey Freedenberg
James L. Fritz
Francis B. Haas, Jr.
W. Jeffry Jamouneau
Michael G. Jarman
David M. Kleppinger
Bernard A. Labuskes, Jr.
Delano M. Lantz
Richard R. Lefever
David E. Lehman
Clyde W. McIntyre
Franklin A. Miles, Jr.
Robert A. Mills
Stephen A. Moore
Herbert R. Nurick
John S. Oyler
Timothy J. Pfister
Gary A. Ritter
Edward W. Rothman
S. Berne Smith
Robert D. Stets
Richard W. Stevenson
Diane M. Tokarsky
David M. Watts, Jr.
Steven J. Weingarten
Neal S. West
Norman I. White
Lawrence R. Wieder
Gary F. Yenkowski
William M. Young, Jr.

(See Next Column)

ASSOCIATES

Eric N. Athey
David M. Baker
Jonathan C. Berry
Brett D. Davis
James P. DeAngelo
James P. Dougherty
Kathleen A. Dunst
Robert J. Goduto
Scott A. Gould
P. Nicholas Guarneschelli
Robert G. Haas
Brian F. Jackson
Donald B. Kaufman
Michael R. Kelley
Peter F. Kriete
James W. Kutz
Camille C. Marion
Patrick J. Murphy
Sharon R. Paxton
Chuong H. Pham
Jonathan H. Rudd
Bruce R. Spicer
Carol A. Steinour
Catherine E. Walters
Derrick P. Williamson

For full biographical listings, see the Martindale-Hubbell Law Directory

METTE, EVANS & WOODSIDE, A PROFESSIONAL CORPORATION (AV)

3401 North Front Street, P.O. Box 5950, 17110-0950
Telephone: 717-232-5000
Telecopier: 717-236-1816

Howell C. Mette
James W. Evans
Robert Moore
Charles B. Zwally
Peter J. Ressler
Lloyd R. Persun
Craig A. Stone
James A. Ulsh
Daniel L. Sullivan
Steven D. Snyder
Glen R. Grell
Christopher C. Conner
Elyse E. Rogers
Andrew H. Dowling
Michael D. Reed
Robert P. Haynes III
Paula J. Leicht

David A. Fitzsimons
Guy P. Beneventano
Michael D. Pipa
Karen N. Connelly
Robyn J. Katzman
Jayson R. Wolfgang
Scott D. Moore
Elizabeth M. Calcagno
Andrew J. Ostrowski
Emily Long Hoffman

Counsel for: The B. F. Goodrich Co.; Juniata Valley Financial Corp.; MCI Telecommunications Corp.; Monongahela Power Co.; The Procter and Gamble Paper Products Co.; United States Fidelity and Guaranty Co.; Community Banks; GTE Products Corp.; Commerce Bank.

For full biographical listings, see the Martindale-Hubbell Law Directory

METZGER, WICKERSHAM, KNAUSS & ERB (AV)

Mellon Bank Building, 111 Market Street, P.O. Box 93, 17108-0093
Telephone: 717-238-8187
Telefax: 717-234-9478
Other Harrisburg, Pennsylvania Office: 4813 Jonestown Road, P.O. Box 93, 17108.
Telephone: 717-652-7020.

MEMBERS OF FIRM

Maurice R. Metzger (1918-1980)
F. Brewster Wickersham (1918-1974)
Edward E. Knauss, III (Retired)
Christian S. Erb, Jr.
Robert E. Yetter
James F. Carl
Robert P. Reed
Edward E. Knauss, IV
Jered L. Hock
Karl R. Hildabrand

ASSOCIATES

Richard B. Druby
Steven P. Miner
Clark DeVere

Representative Clients: Allstate Insurance Co.; Chubb Group of Insurance Companies; Fireman's Fund American Insurance Group; Liberty Mutual Insurance Co.; Continental Insurance Co.; Crum & Forster.

For full biographical listings, see the Martindale-Hubbell Law Directory

NAUMAN, SMITH, SHISSLER & HALL (AV)

Eighteenth Floor, 200 North Third Street, P.O. Box 840, 17108-0840
Telephone: 717-236-3010
Telefax: 717-234-1925

MEMBERS OF FIRM

David C. Eaton
Spencer G. Nauman, Jr.
John C. Sullivan
J. Stephen Feinour
Craig J. Staudenmaier

ASSOCIATES

Benjamin Charles Dunlap, Jr.
Stephen J. Keene

OF COUNSEL

Ralph W. Boyles, Jr.

Representative Clients: Consolidated Rail Corp.; The W.O. Hickok Mfg. Co.; Delta Dental of Pennsylvania; Mellon Bank, N.A.; PNC Bank, N.A.; General Motors Acceptance Corp.; Enders Insurance Associates; Capital Region EMS; Millersburg Area Ambulance Assn.; Harrisburg Baseball Club, Inc.

For full biographical listings, see the Martindale-Hubbell Law Directory

Harrisburg—Continued

PEPPER, HAMILTON & SCHEETZ (AV)

200 One Keystone Plaza, North Front and Market Streets, P.O. Box 1181, 17108-1181
Telephone: 717-255-1155
Telecopy: 717-238-0575
Philadelphia, Pennsylvania Office: 3000 Two Logan Square, Eighteenth and Arch Streets, 19103-2799.
Telephone: 215-981-4000.
Fax: 215-981-4750.
Washington, D.C. Office: 1300 Nineteenth Street, N.W., 20036-1685.
Telephone: 202-828-1200.
Fax: 202-828-1665.
Detroit, Michigan Office: 100 Renaissance Center, 36th Floor, 48243-1157.
Telephone: 313-259-7110.
Fax: 313-259-7926.
Berwyn, Pennsylvania Office: 1235 Westlakes Drive, Suite 400, 19312-2401.
Telephone: 610-640-7800.
Fax: 610-640-7835.
New York, New York Office: 450 Lexington Avenue, Suite 1600, 10017-3904.
Telephone: 212-878-3800.
Fax: 212-878-3835.
Wilmington, Delaware Office: 1201 Market Street, Suite 1401, P.O. Box 1709, 19899-1709.
Telephone: 302-571-6555.
Fax: 302-656-8865.
Westmont, New Jersey Office: Sentry Office Plaza, Suite 321, 216 Haddon Avenue, 08108-2811.
Telephone: 609-869-9555.
Fax: 609-869-9595.
London, England Office: City Tower, 40 Basinghall Street, EC2V 5DE.
Telephone: 011-44-71-628-1122.
Fax: 011-44-71-628-6010.
Moscow, Russia Office: 19-27 Grokholsky Pereulok, 129010.
Telephone: 011-7-095-280-4493.
Fax: 011-7-095-280-5518.

PARTNERS

Thomas B. Schmidt, III (Managing Partner)
John W. Carroll
Donna L. Fisher
Lewis S. Kunkel, Jr.
Daniel J. Malpezzi
David W. Sweet

ASSOCIATES

Timothy B. Anderson
Michael R. Bramnick
Amy Griffith Daubert
Brian P. Downey
Eloise J. Weatherill

For full biographical listings, see the Martindale-Hubbell Law Directory

---

*** REED SMITH SHAW & MCCLAY** (AV)

213 Market Street, P.O. Box 11844, 17108-2132
Telephone: 717-234-5988
FAX: 717-236-3777
Pittsburgh, Pennsylvania Office: James H. Reed Building, Mellon Square, 435 Sixth Avenue, 15219-1886.
Telephone: 412-288-3131.
Washington, D.C. Office: Ring Building, 1200 18th Street, N.W., 20036-2506.
Telephone: 202-457-6100.
Philadelphia, Pennsylvania Office: 2500 One Liberty Place, 19103-7301.
Telephone: 215-851-8100.
McLean, Virginia Office: Suite 1100, 8251 Greensboro Drive, 22102-3844.
Telephone: 703-734-4600.
Princeton, New Jersey Office: 136 Main Street, 08540-5799.
Telephone: 609-987-0050.
FAX: 609-951-0824.

MEMBERS OF FIRM

John McN. Cramer
Mark A. Fontana
Robert B. Hoffman
Franklin L. Kury
Christopher Zettlemoyer

OF COUNSEL

Carl F. Chronister

ASSOCIATES

Paul S. Kline
Dino A. Ross

For full biographical listings, see the Martindale-Hubbell Law Directory

---

RHOADS & SINON (AV)

One South Market Square, 12th Floor, P.O. Box 1146, 17108-1146
Telephone: 717-233-5731
Fax: 717-232-1459
Boca Raton, Florida Affiliated Office: Suite 301, 299 West Camino Gardens Boulevard.
Telephone: 407-395-5595.
Fax: 407-395-9497.
Lancaster, Pennsylvania Office: 15 North Lime Street.
Telephone: 717-397-5127.
Fax: 717-397-5267.

(See Next Column)

OF COUNSEL

Frank A. Sinon
John C. Dowling

MEMBERS OF FIRM

Paul H. Rhoads (1907-1984)
John M. Musselman (1919-1980)
Clyle R. Hendershot (1922-1980)
Henry W. Rhoads
Robert H. Long, Jr.
Sherill T. Moyer
Jan P. Paden
Richard B. Wood
Lawrence B. Abrams III
J. Bruce Walter
John P. Manbeck
Frank J. Leber
R. Stephen Shibla
Paul A. Lundeen
Jack F. Hurley, Jr.
Nathan H. Waters, Jr.
David B. Dowling
David Francis O'Leary
David O. Twaddell
Charles J. Ferry
Stanley A. Smith
Jens H. Damgaard
Drake D. Nicholas
Thomas A. French
Dean H. Dusinberre
Donna M. J. Clark
Charles E. Gutshall
Lucy E. Kniseley
Paul F. Wessell

ASSOCIATES

Shawn D. Lochinger
Jesse Raymond Ruhl
Lori J. McElroy
Kimberly A. Noel
Virginia P. Henschel
Susan E. Schwab
Dean F. Piermattei
Todd J. Shill
Jennifer M. McHugh
Kenneth L. Joel

For full biographical listings, see the Martindale-Hubbell Law Directory

---

SWARTZ, CAMPBELL & DETWEILER (AV)

2040 Linglestown Road, Suite 107, 17110-9483
Telephone: 717-540-8671
Fax: 717-540-5481
Philadelphia, Pennsylvania Office: 1600 Land Title Building, 100 South Broad Street.
Telephone: 215-564-5190.
Telefax: 215-299-4301.
Media, Pennsylvania Office: One Veterans Square, Suite 106.
Telephone: 610-566-9222.
Fax: 610-892-0636.
Wilmington, Delaware Office: 300 Delaware Avenue, Suite 818, P.O. Box 330.
Telephone: 302-656-5935.
Fax: 302-656-1434.
Allentown, Pennsylvania Office: Suite 230. 5100 Tilghman Street.
Telephone: 610-395-5903.
Fax: 610-395-7097.
Mount Laurel, New Jersey Office: Bloom Court, Suite 314. 1300 Route 73.
Telephone: 609-727-4777.
Fax: 609-727-0464.

Gregory D. Geiss (Resident Associate)
Debra A. Matherne (Resident Associate)

For full biographical listings, see the Martindale-Hubbell Law Directory

---

TUCKER ARENSBERG, P.C. (AV)

116 Pine Street, 17101
Telephone: 717-238-2007
Fax: 717-238-2242
Pittsburgh, Pennsylvania Office: 1500 One PPG Place.
Telephone: 412-566-1212.
Telex: 902914.
Fax: 412-594-5619.
Pittsburhg Airport Area Office: Airport Professional Office Center, 1150 Thorn Run Road Ext., Moon Township, Pennsylvania, 15108.
Telephone: 412-262-3730.
Fax: 412-262-2576.

J. Kent Culley

John G. Di Leonardo

For full biographical listings, see the Martindale-Hubbell Law Directory

---

HATBORO, Montgomery Co. — (Refer to Norristown)

HAVERFORD, Montgomery & Delaware Cos.

BENJAMIN S. OHRENSTEIN (AV)

354 West Lancaster Avenue, Suite 212, 19041
Telephone: 610-649-1268; 215-473-6900
Fax: 610-642-6553

For full biographical listings, see the Martindale-Hubbell Law Directory

---

*HOLLIDAYSBURG,** Blair Co. — (Refer to Altoona)

---

*HUNTINGDON,** Huntingdon Co. — (Refer to Altoona)

*INDIANA,** Indiana Co.

Bonya and Douglass (AV)
134 South Sixth Street, 15701
Telephone: 412-465-5535
Fax: 412-465-9685

MEMBERS OF FIRM
John A. Bonya
Stanley P. DeGory
Robert D. Douglass
Beverly A. Gazza
Nicholas J. Mikesic
David M. Zimmerman

Reference: S & T Bank, of Indiana, Pennsylvania.

For full biographical listings, see the Martindale-Hubbell Law Directory

Simpson, Kablack & Bell (AV)
20 North Seventh Street, 15701
Telephone: 412-465-5559
Fax: 412-465-2046

MEMBERS OF FIRM
John S. Simpson
Wayne A. Kablack
Paul A. Bell, II

ASSOCIATES
Robert S. Muir

Attorneys for: S & T Bank, Indiana, PA; Pennsylvania Electric Co.

For full biographical listings, see the Martindale-Hubbell Law Directory

*JIM THORPE,** Carbon Co. — (Refer to Allentown)

JOHNSTOWN, Cambria Co.

Spence, Custer, Saylor, Wolfe & Rose (AV)
4th Floor, U.S. National Bank Building, P.O. Box 280, 15907-0280
Telephone: 814-536-0735
Fax: 814-539-1423

MEMBERS OF FIRM
George M. Spence (1897-1984)
Everett E. Custer (1893-1981)
John P. Saylor (1908-1973)
David C. Wolfe (1916-1962)
Tillman K. Saylor, Jr. (1917-1968)
Robert G. Rose
J. Phillips Saylor
Gary C. Horner
John J. Bagnato
James C. Munro, II
James R. Walsh

ASSOCIATES
Ralph J. Trofino
Thomas A. Aurandt
Ronald P. Carnevali, Jr.
Timothy J. Sloan
George P. Wolfe
David J. Novak
Karen Trotz

OF COUNSEL
Wayne G. Wolfe

Local Counsel for: Bethlehem Steel Corp.; The Manufacturers Water Co.; Pennsylvania Electric Co.; Employers Mutual Casualty Co.; General Telephone Co.

For full biographical listings, see the Martindale-Hubbell Law Directory

KENNETT SQUARE, Chester Co.

MacElree, Harvey, Gallagher, Featherman & Sebastian, Ltd. (AV)
211 E. State Street, P.O. Box 363, 19348
Telephone: 610-444-3180
West Chester Office: 17 West Miner Street, P.O. Box 660.
Telephone: 215-436-0100.
Fax: 215-430-7885.

William J. Gallagher

For full biographical listings, see the Martindale-Hubbell Law Directory

Prickett, Jones, Elliott, Kristol & Schnee (AV)
217 West State Street, 19348
Telephone: 610-444-1573
Wilmington, Delaware Office: 1310 King Street.
Telephone: 302-888-6500.
Dover, Delaware Office: 26 The Green.
Telephone: 302-674-3841.

MEMBERS OF FIRM
Richard I. G. Jones
Walter P. McEvilly, Jr.
Richard P. S. Hannum

For full biographical listings, see the Martindale-Hubbell Law Directory

*KITTANNING,** Armstrong Co.

Steiner and Steiner (AV)
160 North McKean Street, P.O. Box 789, 16201
Telephone: 412-543-1469
Fax: 412-545-1611

(See Next Column)

MEMBERS OF FIRM
Edward J. Steiner
Jack J. Steiner

ASSOCIATES
Lisa K. Gavran

General Counsel for: Armstrong County Building and Loan Assn.; Peoples Bank of Pa.; Middle Armstrong County Area Development Organization.
Local Counsel for: P. P. G., Industries, Inc.; Eljer Manufacturing.
Representative Clients: Zurich Insurance Co.; Commonwealth Land Title Insurance; Mellon Bank NA; Integra National Bank.

*LANCASTER,** Lancaster Co.

Barley, Snyder, Senft & Cohen (AV)
126 East King Street, 17602-2893
Telephone: 717-299-5201
Telecopier: 717-291-4660
Harrisburg, Pennsylvania Office: 240 North Third Street.
Telephone: 717-238-8263.
Telecopier: 717-238-8278.
York, Pennsylvania Office: 100 East Market Street.
Telephone: 717-846-8888.
Telecopier: 717-843-8492.

MEMBERS OF FIRM
Lavere C. Senft (Resident, York Office)
Donn I. Cohen (Resident, York Office)
Harry J. Rubin (Harrisburg and York Offices)
Robert J. Stewart (Resident, York Office)
H. Robert Lasday (Resident, Harrisburg Office)
John O. Shirk
Donald E. LeFever
W. Jeffrey Sidebottom
Christopher W. Mattson
Donald D. Geyer (Resident, Harrisburg Office)
Frederick S. Spangler (Resident, York Office)
Jesse C. Robinson
Rees Griffiths (Resident, York Office)
James A. Humphreys III
Paul M. Browning
Kathleen Ann Gray
Patricia A. Butler (Resident, York Office)
James R. Adams
George C. Werner, Jr.
David R. Keller
Jeffrey D. Lobach (Resident, York Office)
James W. Saxton
Caroline M. Hoffer
Robert W. Hallinger
Steven J. Koehler (Resident, York Office)
Val E. Winter (Resident, York Office)
Nedric L. Nissly
Elaine Pennington Stanko
Thomas J. Lovelass
Arthur E. Wilmarth, Jr.
Paul D. Clouser
Michael A. Moore
Christopher A. Stump
Kendra D. McGuire
Paul G. Mattaini (Not admitted in PA)

ASSOCIATES
Nancy Mayer Hughes
Eric L. Winkle
Michael S. Butler (Resident, York Office)
Michael W. Davis
Katherine Betz Kravitz
Timothy P. Brown
Hanna-Aurelia Dunlap
Ronald H. Pollock, Jr.
Anne E. Doliner
Melanie A. Zampini (Resident, York Office)
Barbara B. May
Richard L. Grubb
Beverly J. Points (Resident, York Office)
Jennifer A. Kline (Resident, York Office)
Kathleen M. Quarto
Jennifer L. Craighead
Scott F. Landis
Mary Ann Moscony Cooke
Christopher A. Hackman

COUNSEL
John T. Barber
Paul A. Mueller, Jr.

RETIRED
Ralph M. Barley
Charles R. Cooper, Jr.

Counsel for: Franklin & Marshall College; Fulton Bank/Fulton Financial Corp.; The Graham Cos.; Lancaster Chamber of Commerce and Industry; Lancaster General Hospital; Robert A. Kinsley, Inc.
Local Counsel for: Armstrong World Industries; Susquehanna Pfaltzgraff Co.
Insurance Defense Counsel for: Medical Protective Co.; The PMA Group.

For full biographical listings, see the Martindale-Hubbell Law Directory

Kegel, Chesters, Lapp & Miller (AV)
24 North Lime Street, 17602
Telephone: 717-392-1100
Fax: 717-392-4385

MEMBERS OF FIRM
Clarence C. Kegel, Jr.
Frank C. Chesters
Dale E. Lapp
John H. Miller, Jr.
Howard L. Kelin

ASSOCIATES
Kenneth J. Almy
James R. Clark
Rhonda F. Lord
Ruth A. Courtney
Robert W. Pontz
D. Mark Grimm, Jr.
Kay Mercein Mann

General Counsel for: Herr Foods Incorporated; Pennfield Corporation; Goodville Mutual Casualty Company; F & M Hat Company; Laser Communications, Inc.

(See Next Column)

KEGEL, CHESTERS, LAPP & MILLER, *Lancaster—Continued*

Counsel for: Burle Industries, Inc.; Dean Witter Reynolds, Inc.; Farmers First Bank; St. Joseph Hospital; WGAL-TV.

For full biographical listings, see the Martindale-Hubbell Law Directory

LANGHORNE, Bucks Co.

BEGLEY, CARLIN & MANDIO (AV)

680 Middletown Boulevard, P.O. Box 308, 19047
Telephone: 215-750-0110
Fax: 215-750-0954
Bristol, Pennsylvania Office: 120 Mill Street.
Telephone: 215-750-0110.

MEMBERS OF FIRM

William J. Carlin
Anthony A. Mandio
S. Richard Klinges, III
Thomas J. Profy, III
Richard M. Snyder
Charles F. Sampsel
John P. Koopman
Jeffrey P. Garton
Thomas R. Hecker
James A. Downey, III
Joseph S. Britton
Douglas C. Maloney

ASSOCIATES

Thomas J. Profy, IV
William L. Weiner
Karen L. Saraco
Michael G. Fitzpatrick

Representative Clients: Borough of Bristol; Bristol Borough School Board; Fidelity Savings & Loan Association of Bucks County; Lower Makefield Township; Philadelphia National Bank; Waste Management, Inc.

For full biographical listings, see the Martindale-Hubbell Law Directory

*LAPORTE,** Sullivan Co. — (Refer to Wilkes-Barre)

*LEBANON,** Lebanon Co.

HENRY & BEAVER (AV)

937 Willow Street, P.O. Box 1140, 17042-1140
Telephone: 717-274-3644
Facsimile: 717-274-6782

MEMBERS OF FIRM

Charles V. Henry, III
R. Hart Beaver
Frederick S. Wolf
Thomas P. Harlan
Wiley P. Parker
John H. Whitmoyer
Christopher J. Coyle
Kevin M. Richards

ASSOCIATES

Marc A. Hess

Representative Clients: Lebanon Valley National Bank; Cornwall Manor; Medical Protective Company of Fort Wayne; Nationwide Insurance Co.; Liberty Mutual Insurance Co.; Utica Mutual Insurance Co.; CIGNA Insurance Co.; The Pennsylvania Sports Hall of Fame; North Lebanon Township; United Way of Lebanon County, Inc.

For full biographical listings, see the Martindale-Hubbell Law Directory

*LEWISBURG,** Union Co.

FETTER, KESSLER AND PERSING (AV)

8 North 3rd Street, P.O. Box 512, 17837
Telephone: 717-524-2207
Fax: 717-524-0377

MEMBERS OF FIRM

W. Roger Fetter
Frederick D. Kessler
James E. Persing

Reference: Northern Central Bank.

For full biographical listings, see the Martindale-Hubbell Law Directory

*LEWISTOWN,** Mifflin Co. — (Refer to Sunbury)

*LOCK HAVEN,** Clinton Co.

SNOWISS, STEINBERG, FAULKNER AND RAE (AV)

333 North Vesper Street, 17745
Telephone: 717-748-2961

MEMBERS OF FIRM

Alvin L. Snowiss
Donald L. Faulkner
Lewis G. Steinberg
Donna L. Rae

ASSOCIATES

Wesley J. Rish

OF COUNSEL

Michael K. Hanna

Representative Clients: Mellon Bank, N.A.; County of Clinton; Lock Haven Hospital; Harleysville Insurance Co.; Commonwealth Bank; M.L. Claster & Sons, Inc.; Keystone Central School District; Pennsylvania Hospital Insurance Co.; The Princeton Insurance Co.
Reference: Mellon Bank.

For full biographical listings, see the Martindale-Hubbell Law Directory

MALVERN, Chester Co.

SAUL, EWING, REMICK & SAUL (AV)

Suite 200, Great Valley Corporate Center, 300 Chester Field Parkway, 19355
Telephone: 610-251-5050
Cable Address: "BIDSAL"
TWX: 83-4798
Telecopier: XEROX 720 610-651-5930
Philadelphia, Pennsylvania Office: 3800 Centre Square West.
Telephone: 215-972-7777.
Cable Address: "Bidsal".
TWX: 83-4798.
Telecopier: XEROX 7020 215-972-7725.
Wilmington, Delaware Office: 222 Delaware Avenue, P.O. Box 1266, 19899-1266. For Courier Delivery: 222 Delaware Avenue, Suite 1200, 19801.
Telephone: 302-421-6800.
Cable Address: "Bidsal."
TWX: 83-4798.
Telecopier: XEROX 7020 302-421-6813.
New York, New York Office: Twenty-first Floor, 237 Park Avenue.
Telephone: 212-551-3502.
TWX: 425170.
Telecopier: 212-697-8486.
Voorhees, New Jersey Office: Plaza 1000, Main Street, Suite 206, Evesham & Kresson Roads.
Telephone: 609-424-0098.
Telecopier: XEROX 7020 609-424-2204.
Harrisburg, Pennsylvania Office: 240 North 3rd Street, P.O. Box 1291, 17108-1291. For Courier Delivery: 240 N. 3rd Street, Suite 700, 17101.
Telephone: 717-238-8300.
Telecopier: 717-238-4622.
Trenton, New Jersey Office: Capital Center, 50 East State Street, 08608.
Telephone: 609-393-0057.
Fax: 609-393-5962.

MEMBERS OF FIRM

Stephen S. Aichele
David S. Antzis
Joseph Neff Ewing, Jr. (Resident)
Richard T. Frazier
Scott D. Patterson (Resident)
John F. Stoviak

ASSOCIATES

George Asimos, Jr. (Resident)
Carol R. Blackman
Mary G. March (Resident)
Libby A. White (Resident, Malvern, Pennsylvania Office)

SPECIAL COUNSEL

Michael S. Burg (Resident)
Patrick G. Oakes (Resident)
Sondra K. Slade (Resident)
Michael L. Strong (Resident)

For full biographical listings, see the Martindale-Hubbell Law Directory

*MC CONNELLSBURG,** Fulton Co. — (Refer to Waynesboro)

*MEADVILLE,** Crawford Co.

SHAFER, SWICK, BAILEY, IRWIN & STACK (AV)

360 Chestnut Street, 16335
Telephone: 814-724-4540
Fax: 814-724-4545

MEMBERS OF FIRM

Paul E. Thomas (1892-1972)
Paul D. Shafer, Jr.
Charles J. Swick
Robert S. Bailey
James R. Irwin
Louis J. Stack
Jeffrey K. Millin

ASSOCIATES

John C. Swick

OF COUNSEL

Raymond P. Shafer

Local Counsel: Pennsylvania Electric Co.; Pennsylvania Manufacturers Association Casualty Insurance Co.; Allegheny College; Motorists Mutual Insurance Co.; Mellon Bank, N.A.; Meadville Medical Center; Meadville Area Industrial Commission; Seco-Warwick Corp.; Pennwest Farm Credit; Wesbury United Methodist Community.

For full biographical listings, see the Martindale-Hubbell Law Directory

MECHANICSBURG, Cumberland Co.

SNELBAKER & BRENNEMAN, A PROFESSIONAL CORPORATION (AV)

44 West Main Street, P.O. Box 318, 17055
Telephone: 717-697-8528
Fax: 717-697-7681

Richard C. Snelbaker
Keith O. Brenneman
Philip H. Spare

Representative Clients: Cumberland Valley School District; Cumberland Valley Joint School Authority; The First Bank & Trust Co., Mechanicsburg, Pennsylvania; Mechanicsburg Area School District; South Middleton School District; Township of Middlesex; South Middleton Township Municipal

(See Next Column)

SNELBAKER & BRENNEMAN A PROFESSIONAL CORPORATION—*Continued*

Authority; Township of Hampden; South Middleton School District Authority; Middlesex Township Municipal Authority.

For full biographical listings, see the Martindale-Hubbell Law Directory

*MEDIA,** Delaware Co.

BEATTY, YOUNG, OTIS & LINCKE (AV)

300 West State Street, Suite 200, P.O. Box 901, 19063-0901
Telephone: 610-565-8800
Fax: 610-565-8127

MEMBERS OF FIRM

Lewis B. Beatty, Jr.
David J. Otis
William P. Lincke

ASSOCIATES

Natalie M. Habert
Peter W. Dicce
Carol E. Tucci
Katherine J. Dickinson (Not admitted in PA)

OF COUNSEL

Robert C. Grasberger
Joseph R. Young (1921-1993)

Representative Clients: Suburban Federal Savings Bank; Elwyn Inc.; Delaware County School Employees Health and Welfare Trust.

For full biographical listings, see the Martindale-Hubbell Law Directory

CRAMP, D'IORIO, MCCONCHIE AND FORBES, P.C. (AV)

215 North Olive Street, P.O. Box 568, 19063
Telephone: 610-565-1700
Fax: 610-566-0379

Ralph B. D'Iorio
George J. McConchie
Andrew J. Forbes
Joseph W. Kauffman
David G. Blake
Gary C. Bender
Guy N. Paolino

Alexander D. DiSanti
Frances Marie Piccoli

OF COUNSEL

John F. Cramp

Local Counsel for: Bell Atlantic.
Trial Counsel for: Insurance Company of North America (CIGNA); Commercial Union Insurance Co.; State Farm Insurance Co.; Continental Casualty Co.; Fireman's Fund American Insurance Group; Pennsylvania Manufacturers Assn. (PMA); U.S. Fidelity & Guaranty Co.; United Services Automobile Association.
General Counsel for: Williamson School.

For full biographical listings, see the Martindale-Hubbell Law Directory

DUNN, HAASE, SULLIVAN, MALLON, CHERNER & BROADT (AV)

Hillhurst, 216 South Orange Street, 19063
Telephone: 610-565-9600
Fax: 610-565-9639
Philadelphia, Pennsylvania Office: The Bourse Building, Suite 1002, 21 South 5th Street.
Telephone: 215-922-1234.
Fax: 215-922-0335.
Cherry Hill, New Jersey Office: 1435 Brace Road.
Telephone: 609-354-1305.
Telefax: 609-795-1242.

MEMBERS OF FIRM

Peter A. Dunn
Norman L. Haase
Timothy F. Sullivan
Joseph T. Mallon
Susan J. Cherner
Thomas H. Broadt
Nicholas S. Lippincott
Steven H. Eichler (Resident, Philadelphia Office)
Emily Morris Salmons

Frank S. Blatcher
Kathleen A. Farrell
F. Bryant Blevins
Thomas C. Abrahamsen (Resident, Philadelphia Office)
Sharon H. Powell
Sheryl L. Axelrod

For full biographical listings, see the Martindale-Hubbell Law Directory

FRONEFIELD AND DE FURIA (AV)

107 West Third Street, P.O. Box 647, 19063
Telephone: 610-565-3100
Fax: 610-565-2349

MEMBERS OF FIRM

Frank I. Ginsburg
Rosemary C. McMunigal
F. Martin Duus
Charles F. Knapp
John R. Larkin
J. Joseph Herring, Jr.
Bruce A. Irvine
Leo A. Hackett
Francis T. Sbandi

ASSOCIATES

David C. Corujo
Jane E. Mcnerney
Donna Lynn Coyne

(See Next Column)

OF COUNSEL

Albert E. Holl, Jr.

For full biographical listings, see the Martindale-Hubbell Law Directory

HARRIS & SMITH (AV)

211 West State Street, 19063
Telephone: 610-565-5300
Fax: 610-565-7292

MEMBERS OF FIRM

G. Guy Smith

ASSOCIATES

Susan E. Murray
Russell F. Daly

OF COUNSEL

Edgar Y. Harris
Theresa Hagenbach White

For full biographical listings, see the Martindale-Hubbell Law Directory

KASSAB ARCHBOLD JACKSON & O'BRIEN (AV)

Lawyers-Title Building, 214 North Jackson Street, P.O. Box 626, 19063
Telephone: 610-565-3800
Telecopier: 610-892-6888
Wilmington, Delaware Office: 1326 King Street.
Telephone: 302-656-3393.
Fax: 302-656-1993.
Wildwood, New Jersey Office: 5201 New Jersey Avenue.
Telephone: 609-522-6559.

MEMBERS OF FIRM

Edward Kassab
William C. Archbold, Jr.
Robert James Jackson
Joseph Patrick O'Brien
Richard A. Stanko
Roy T. J. Stegena

OF COUNSEL

Matthew J. Ryan
John W. Nilon, Jr.

ASSOCIATES

Kevin William Gibson
Cynthia Kassab Larosa
Marc S. Stein
Terrance A. Kline
George C. McFarland, Jr.
Jill E. Aversa
Pamela A. La Torre
Kenneth D. Kynett

Representative Clients furnished upon request.

For full biographical listings, see the Martindale-Hubbell Law Directory

PETRIKIN, WELLMAN, DAMICO, CARNEY & BROWN, A PROFESSIONAL CORPORATION (AV)

The William Penn Building, 109 Chesley Drive, 19063
Telephone: 610-565-2670
Fax: 610-565-0178

John W. Wellman
Joseph A. Damico, Jr.
Edward J. Carney, Jr.
Steven G. Brown
Donald T. Petrosa
Steven A. Cohen
Denis M. Dunn
Mary Rogers Auchincloss
Mark J. Connor
Susan E. Line

Representative Clients: Scott Paper Co.; Sun Oil Co.; Radnor Corp.; Toll Brothers; Wawa Food Markets; Employers Insurance of Wausau; Nationwide Mutual Insurance Co.; McDonald's; American Universal Insurance Co.

For full biographical listings, see the Martindale-Hubbell Law Directory

RICHARD, DISANTI, HAMILTON & GALLAGHER, A PROFESSIONAL CORPORATION (AV)

25 West Second Street, P.O. Box 900, 19063
Telephone: 610-565-4600
Fax: 610-566-8257

Howard Richard
Alexander A. DiSanti
John M. Gallagher, Jr.
Lyn B. Schoenfeld
Leonard V. Tenaglia
Joseph W. Chupein, Jr.

Kevin Robert Marciano

OF COUNSEL

Thomas P. Hamilton, Jr.
Ronald H. Surkin
Nancy DeMis

For full biographical listings, see the Martindale-Hubbell Law Directory

SWARTZ, CAMPBELL & DETWEILER (AV)

One Veterans Square, Suite 106, 19063
Telephone: 610-566-9222
Fax: 610-892-0636
Philadelphia, Pennsylvania Office: 1600 Land Title Building, 100 South Broad Street.
Telephone: 215-564-5190.
Telefax: 215-299-4301.
Harrisburg, Pennsylvania Office: 2040 Linglestown Road, Suite 107.
Telephone: 717-540-8671.
Fax: 717-540-5481.

(See Next Column)

SWARTZ, CAMPBELL & DETWEILER, *Media—Continued*

Allentown, Pennsylvania Office: Suite 230. 5100 Tilghman Street.
Telephone 610-395-5903.
Fax: 610-395-7097.
Wilmington, Delaware Office: 300 Delaware Avenue, Suite 818, P.O. Box 330.
Telephone: 302-656-5935.
Fax: 302-656-1434.
Mount Laurel, New Jersey Office: Bloom Court, Suite 314. 1300 Route 73.
Telephone: 609-727-4777.
Fax: 609-727-0464.

Andrew J. Reilly (Resident Associate)

ASSOCIATES

Michael A. Cognetti

For full biographical listings, see the Martindale-Hubbell Law Directory

*MERCER,** Mercer Co. — (Refer to Grove City or Sharon)

*MIDDLEBURG,** Snyder Co. — (Refer to Sunbury)

*MIFFLINTOWN,** Juniata Co. — (Refer to Carlisle)

*MILFORD,** Pike Co.

BEECHER, WAGNER, ROSE & KLEMEYER (AV)

402 Broad Street, 18337
Telephone: 717-296-6453; 296-8561
Fax: 717-296-2769

Sanford D. Beecher, Jr.
Karl A. Wagner, Jr.
Jay R. Rose
John H. Klemeyer

General Counsel for: First National Bank of Pike County; Milford and Matamoras Boroughs; Lackawaxen and Dingman Townships; Pike County Coroner; Pike County Sherrif; Milford Water Authority.
Representative Clients: Commonwealth Land Title Insurance Co.; Pike County Tax Claim Bureau; Rank-Ahnest, Inc.; Masthope Rapids Property Owners Council.

For full biographical listings, see the Martindale-Hubbell Law Directory

MILTON, Northumberland Co.

DAVIS, DAVIS & KAAR (AV)

37 Arch Street, P.O. Box 319, 17847
Telephone: 717-742-8777
Fax: 717-742-6155

MEMBERS OF FIRM

Preston B. Davis (1907-1990)
Preston L. Davis
R. Michael Kaar

Representative Clients: Watsontown Bank; Kepler Brothers, Inc.; Sun Home Health Services, Inc.; Milton Steel, Inc.
Local Counsel for: Pennsylvania Power & Light Co.; PA-American Water Co.; Motorists Insurance Cos.
Counsel for: Delaware Township.
Agents for: T/A Title Insurance Co.; Commonwealth Land Title Insurance Company of Pennsylvania.

For full biographical listings, see the Martindale-Hubbell Law Directory

*MONTROSE,** Susquehanna Co. — (Refer to Tunkhannock)

NARBERTH, Montgomery Co.

EDWARD M. MEZVINSKY (AV)

815 Woodbine Avenue, 19072
Telephone: 610-664-7115
Fax: 610-664-7225

For full biographical listings, see the Martindale-Hubbell Law Directory

*NEW BLOOMFIELD,** Perry Co. — (Refer to Carlisle)

*NEW CASTLE,** Lawrence Co.

ROUTMAN, MOORE, GOLDSTONE & VALENTINO (AV)

2656 Wilmington Road, 16105
Telephone: 412-658-6900
Sharon, Pennsylvania Office: 194 East State Street.
Telephone: 412-981-6800.

Joseph Paul Valentino
John C. Reed
Richard W. Epstein
Frank J. Matune

For full biographical listings, see the Martindale-Hubbell Law Directory

NEWTOWN, Bucks Co.

STUCKERT AND YATES (AV)

1 South State Street, P.O. Box 70, 18940
Telephone: 215-968-4700
Fax: 215-968-8875

(See Next Column)

MEMBERS OF FIRM

Wm. R. Stuckert (1902-1960)
Sidney T. Yates
John Philip Diefenderfer
John J. Kerrigan, Jr.
Richard Danese, Jr.
Don F. Marshall
Steven H. Sailer

ASSOCIATES

D. Keith Brown
Kathleen A. Kerrigan
Stephen L. Needles
Donna J. Wengiel

Representative Clients: First National Bank & Trust Company of Newtown; St. Mary Hospital, Langhorne, Pennsylvania; Newtown Borough; Dublin Borough; Newtown Bucks County Joint Municipal Authority; Centennial Joint School Board Authority.
Reference: First National Bank & Trust Company of Newtown.

For full biographical listings, see the Martindale-Hubbell Law Directory

*NORRISTOWN,** Montgomery Co.

GERBER & GERBER (AV)

Suite 500, One Montgomery Plaza, 19401
Telephone: 610-279-6700
Fax: 610-279-7126

MEMBERS OF FIRM

Morris Gerber
A. Richard Gerber

ASSOCIATES

Parke H. Ulrich

For full biographical listings, see the Martindale-Hubbell Law Directory

HIGH, SWARTZ, ROBERTS & SEIDEL (AV)

40 East Airy Street, 19404
Telephone: 610-275-0700
Fax: 610-275-5290

MEMBERS OF FIRM

Samuel H. High, Jr. (1931-1978)
Gilbert P. High (1935-1975)
Aaron S. Swartz, 3rd (1940-1982)
Victor Jamison Roberts (1938-1984)
Marlyn F. Smith (Mr.)
Stephen G. Yusem
Gilbert P. High, Jr.
Paul Baker Bartle
Robert B. Durham, Jr.
D. Barry Pritchard, Jr.
Thomas D. Rees
Kevin E. McLaughlin

OF COUNSEL

Raymond M. Seidel
George M. Aman, III

ASSOCIATES

John P. Gregg
Mary L. Buckman
Jeffrey L. Abrams
Lois A. Nafziger
Lori K. Comer

LEGAL SUPPORT PERSONNEL

Katharine J. Bennett
Jeanine Marie Peterson
Kimberly Schonauer
Kathleen E. Carter
Ann M. Bulger

Solicitors for: Bryner Chevrolet, Inc.; Lower Merion Township; Bryn Athyn School District; Upper Merion Township; Upper Gwynedd Twp. Authority.
Local Counsel for: Nationwide Mutual Insurance Co.; Philadelphia Electric Co.; Prudential Insurance Co.; Patriot Savings Bank; First Valley Bank.

For full biographical listings, see the Martindale-Hubbell Law Directory

LABRUM AND DOAK (AV)

One Montgomery Plaza, Suite 700, 19401
Telephone: 610-277-7997
Telecopier: 610-277-2852
Philadelphia, Pennsylvania Office: Suite 2900, 1818 Market Street.
Telephone: 610-561-4400.
Telecopier: 610-587-5350.
Bethlehem, Pennsylvania Office: 561 East Market Street, P.O. Box 1306.
Telephone: 610-865-2644.
Telecopier: 610-865-2713.
New York, N.Y. Office: 17 Battery Place.
Telephone: 610-809-7870.
Telecopier: 610-785-9279.
Woodbury, New Jersey Office: 66 Euclid Street, P.O. Box 836.
Telephone: 609-845-8855.
Telecopier: 609-848-2694.

RESIDENT MEMBERS

Gerard Bruderle
Robert F. Blanck
William J. McKee

RESIDENT ASSOCIATES

William D. Longo
Peter A. Callahan
Patrick J. Gibbons
Patrick J. Moran

OF COUNSEL

Joseph F. Keener, Jr. (Resident)

For full biographical listings, see the Martindale-Hubbell Law Directory

Norristown—Continued

MANNING, KINKEAD, BROOKS & BRADBURY, A PROFESSIONAL CORPORATION (AV)

412 DeKalb Street, 19404-0231
Telephone: 610-279-1800
Fax: 610-279-8682

Franklin L. Wright (1880-1965)
William Perry Manning, Jr.
William H. Kinkead, III
William H. Bradbury, III

Cheri D. Andrews

Counsel for: The Philadelphia National Bank; John Deere Co.; The Rouse Co.; Consolidated Rail Corp.; Bethlehem Steel Co.; Royal Globe Insurance Co.; Nationwide Mutual Insurance Co.

For full biographical listings, see the Martindale-Hubbell Law Directory

McTIGHE, WEISS, O'ROURKE & MILNER, P.C. (AV)

Eleven East Airy Street, P.O. Box 510, 19404
Telephone: 610-275-8800
Telecopier: 610-272-5325

Desmond J. McTighe (1902-1990)
Philip D. Weiss
John R. O'Rourke, Jr.
Kenneth P. Milner
Julia M. Going
Cynthia Weiss Stein

Joseph A. Ferry

Representative Clients: Colonial Penn Insurance Cos.; Reliance Insurance Cos.; Allied Nut and Bolt Co.; Penn Mutual Fire Insurance Co.

For full biographical listings, see the Martindale-Hubbell Law Directory

*PHILADELPHIA,** Philadelphia Co.

ASTOR WEISS KAPLAN & ROSENBLUM (AV)

The Bellevue, 6th Floor, Broad Street at Walnut, 19102
Telephone: 215-790-0100
Fax: 215-790-0509
Bala Cynwyd, Pennsylvania Office: Suite 100, Three Bala Plaza West, P.O. Box 1665.
Telephone: 610-667-8660.
Fax: 610-667-2783.
Cherry Hill, New Jersey Office: Woodland Falls Corporate Park, 210 Lake Drive East, Suite 201.
Telephone: 609-795-1113.
Fax: 609-795-7413.

MEMBERS OF FIRM

Paul C. Astor
Alvin M. Weiss (1936-1976)
G. David Rosenblum
Arthur H. Kaplan
Barbara Oaks Silver
Richard H. Martin
Allen B. Dubroff
David S. Workman
David S. Mandel
David Gutin (Resident at Bala Cynwyd Office)
Joseph B. Finlay, Jr.
Howard K. Goldstein
Steven W. Smith
Gerald J. Schorr
Jean M. Biesecker (Resident, Bala Cynwyd Office)

ASSOCIATES

Carol L. Vassallo
Thomas J. Maiorino
John R. Poeta
Bradley J. Begelman
Andrew S. Kessler
Marc S. Zamsky
Janet G. Felgoise (Resident, Bala Cynwyd Office)
Jacqueline G. Segal (Resident, Bala Cynwyd Office)

SPECIAL COUNSEL

Neil Hurowitz (Resident, Bala Cynwyd Office)

OF COUNSEL

Erwin L. Pincus
Edward W. Silver
Lloyd Zane Remick

For full biographical listings, see the Martindale-Hubbell Law Directory

BALLARD SPAHR ANDREWS & INGERSOLL (AV)

1735 Market Street, 51st Floor, 19103-7599
Telephone: 215-665-8500
Fax: 215-864-8999
Denver, Colorado Office: Seventeenth Street Plaza Building, Suite 2300, 1225 17th Street.
Telephone: 303-292-2400.
Fax: 303-296-3956.
Kaunas, Lithuania Office: Donelaicio g., 71-2, Kaunas 3000.
Telephone: (370-7) 20 56 66.
Fax: (370-7) 20 56 91.
Salt Lake City, Utah Office: One Utah Center, Suite 1200, 201 South Main Street.
Telephone: 801-531-3000.
Fax: 801-531-3001.
Washington, D.C. Office: Suite 900 East, 555 13th Street, N.W.
Telephone: 202-383-8800.
Fax: 202-383-8877; 383-8893.

(See Next Column)

Baltimore, Maryland Office: 300 East Lombard Street. 19th Floor.
Telephone: 410-528-5600.
Fax: 410-528-5650.
Camden, New Jersey Office: 800 Hudson Square, 5th Floor.
Telephone: 609-541-5577.
Fax: 609-541-8272.

John N. Ake
Lawrence D. Berger
John Marley Bernard
Robert McLaurin Boote
C. Baird Brown
Jeffrey T. Chappelle
Frederic W. Clark
James D. Coleman
Alan J. Davis
Thomas R. Eshelman
Dianne Coady Fisher
Michael P. Gallagher
Richard R. Goldberg (Not admitted in PA)
Carl W. Hittinger
Cathleen C. Judge
Justin P. Klein
John B. Langel
James A. Lebovitz
Charisse R. Lillie
Arthur Makadon
Vincent J. Marriott, III
Darryl J. May
Robert E. McQuiston
Benjamin R. Neilson
David H. Pittinsky
Maureen M. Rayborn
Louis W. Ricker
Carl G. Roberts
Andrew J. Rudolph
Michael Sklaroff
Edward D. Slevin
Wayne R. Strasbaugh
Richard L. Strouse
Jere G. Thompson
Glenn L. Unterberger
J. Brian Walsh
Lynn R. Axelroth
E. Carolan Berkley
Creed C. Black, Jr.
Richard J. Braemer
Bruce L. Castor
Morris Cheston, Jr.
Rhonda Resnick Cohen
Kevin R. Cunningham
Thomas Jay Ellis
Gardner A. Evans
Carl H. Fridy
Robert C. Gerlach
Martha J. Hays
Brian T. Hirai
Joel E. Horowitz
Geoffrey A. Kahn
Philip B. Korb
Mary G. Lawler
Michael Lehr
Joseph E. Lundy
David G. Mandelbaum
Peter M. Mattoon
Robert B. McKinstry, Jr.
Bart I. Mellits
Claire C. Obade
H. David Prior
William H. Rheiner
Alan S. Ritterband
J. Douglas Rollow, III
William P. Scott
William A. Slaughter
Mark S. Stewart
Matthew M. Strickler
Regina O'Brien Thomas
Suzanne E. Turner
Kent Walker
William Y. Webb

SPECIAL COUNSEL

Donald J. Goldberg

OF COUNSEL

Francis Ballard
Joseph P. Flanagan, Jr.
Susan Bass Levin
Frank L. Newburger, III
Lila G. Roomberg
Robert R. Batt
H. Ober Hess
J. Robertson MacIver
Richard S. Perelman
Deborah J. Zateeny

COUNSEL

Barbara R. Beckman
Rachel Kipnes
Jamie B. Bischoff
Edward Ira Leeds
Marilyn C. Sanborne

Kris Williams Aldridge
David J. Armstrong
Gilpin W. Bartels
Martin C. Bryce, Jr.
Brendan K. Collins
Mark S. DePillis
Jeanne J. Dworetzky
Mark R. Eskin
David S. Fryman
Michele Berman Golkow
Gerald J. Guarcini
Celia E. Henry
Anjali Jesseramsing
Stephen J. Kastenberg
Marie Keeley
Elizabeth J. Killackey
Debra E. Kohn
Michelle D. Koss
Peter W. Laberee
Jin Hwang Liu
Vanessa Albert Lowry
James F. Mannion
Maria R. McGarry
Heidi M. Nicholson
Richard J. Orr
Joanne Phillips
Raymond Adam Quaglia
Kathleen M. Ranalli
William C. Rhodes
Daniel Schoor-Rube (Not admitted in PA)
Sally P. Schreiber
Jeffrey L. Silberman
Leslie H. Smith
Nancy A. Strelau
Jane K. Anastasia
Robert R. Baron, Jr.
James H. Bocchinfuso
James Bucci
Susan Sudick Colton
Brian D. Doerner
Walter M. Einhorn, Jr.
Kendra S. Follett
Leah Gold Gindoff
Barry E. Gosin
Yvonne B. Haskins
Maya Singh Hyland
Leslie E. John
Alison D. Keel
Lori D. Kettering
Barry L. Klein
Michael J. Konowal
Bradley A. Krouse
Martha Louise Lhamon
Ann T. Loftus
Michael D. Mabry (Not admitted in PA)
Heather H. Moyer
David P. O'Connor
Brian D. Pedrow
Margaret M. Prendergast
Pedro A. Ramos
Michael F. Reilly
Edward D. Rogers (Not admitted in PA)
Patricia A. Schoor-Rube
Alex E. Seldin
Lisa M. Sloan
Laura N. Solomon
Cynthia J. Tidwell

(See Next Column)

BALLARD SPAHR ANDREWS & INGERSOLL, *Philadelphia—Continued*

Randall J. Towers
Esther L. von Laue
Harry R. Weiss
Courtney L. Yeakel
Scott P. Towers
Kelly A. Walenda
Robert J. Werner
John M. Zerr

For full biographical listings, see the Martindale-Hubbell Law Directory

BEASLEY, CASEY, COLLERAN, ERBSTEIN, THISTLE & KLINE (AV)

1125 Walnut Street, 19107-4997
Telephone: 215-592-1000
Telecopier: 215-592-8360
Mount Laurel, New Jersey Office: Suite 266, 3000 Atrium Way.
Telephone: 609-273-6966.

MEMBERS OF FIRM

James E. Beasley
Benedict A. Casey
James E. Colleran
Keith S. Erbstein
Daniel L. Thistle
Thomas R. Kline
Scott A. Bennett
Ellen Q. Suria
Nancy H. Fullam
Shanin Specter
Barbara Axelrod
Jayne A. Piarulli
Gerald F. Kaplan
Paul A. Lauricella
Andrew J. Stern
Michael A. Smerconish
David A. Yanoff
Marsha F. Santangelo
Keith S. Grube

OF COUNSEL

William C. Hewson

For full biographical listings, see the Martindale-Hubbell Law Directory

BERGER & MONTAGUE, P.C. (AV)

1622 Locust Street, 19103
Telephone: 215-875-3000
Telecopier: 215-875-4604; 875-4608

David Berger
Harold Berger
H. Laddie Montague, Jr.
Stanley R. Wolfe
Merrill G. Davidoff
Sherrie Raiken Savett
Daniel Berger
Jay Robert Stiefel
Gary E. Cantor
Howard I. Langer
Stephen A. Whinston
Martin I. Twersky
Todd S. Collins
Carole A. Broderick
Janice Siegel
Peter R. Kahana
Ruthanne Gordon
Alan M. Sandals
Stephen D. Ramos
Karen S. Orman
Jeanne A. Markey
Lawrence Deutsch
Jonathan D. Berger

Kenneth L. Fox
Lawrence J. Lederer
Peter B. Nordberg
Sheryl S. Levy
Patricia D. Gugin
Andrew J. Lapat
John R. Taylor
Thomas F. Hughes
Catherine Ann Sullivan
Andrew Brenner
Stuart J. Guber
Michael L. Block
Barbara Lowe
Jerome M. Marcus
Susan Jaffe Sarner
Bart D. Cohen
Michael T. Fantini
Jeffrey M. Krulik
David F. Sorensen
Arthur Stock
Jonathan Auerbach
Ivonia K. Slade
Patrick E. Bradley
Genna C. Driscoll
Bret P. Flaherty
Charles Pearsall Goodwin
Joel M. Sweet
Nina Amster
Audrey A. Kraus
Leah R. Stolker

Reference: Corestates Bank N.A.

For full biographical listings, see the Martindale-Hubbell Law Directory

BOLGER PICKER HANKIN & TANNENBAUM (AV)

12th Floor, 1800 Kennedy Boulevard, 19103
Telephone: 215-561-1000
Facsimile: 215-564-2127
Cherry Hill, New Jersey Office: One Cherry Hill, One Mall Drive, Suite 801.
Telephone: 609-482-7000.
FAX: 609-482-9410.

MEMBERS OF FIRM

Bennett G. Picker
Elliot S. Gerson
Arthur W. Hankin
Carl S. Tannenbaum
Mark S. Blaskey
Terri N. Gelberg
B. Christopher Lee
David N. Zeehandelaar
Ellen Rosen Rogoff
Julia B. Fisher
E. David Chanin

(See Next Column)

ASSOCIATES

Jonathan F. Bloom
Karen Schecter Dayno
Kurt E. Kramer
Adam M. Share
Elaine D. Solomon
Kathy E. Herman
Patricia R. Kalla
Eric J. Pritchard
Jeffrey S. Brenner (Resident, Cherry Hill, New Jersey Office)
Susan J. Khantzian
Michael J. Revness

COUNSEL

Robert V. Bolger, II

OF COUNSEL

Elwood S. Levy
Neal S. Grabell
William M. Marutani

For full biographical listings, see the Martindale-Hubbell Law Directory

BUCHANAN INGERSOLL, PROFESSIONAL CORPORATION (AV)

Two Logan Square Twelfth Floor, 18th & Arch Streets, 19103
Telephone: 215-665-8700
Telecopier: 215-569-2066
Pittsburgh, Pennsylvania Office: 5800 USX Tower, 600 Grant Street.
Telephone: 412-562-8800.
Harrisburg, Pennsylvania Office: Vartan Parc, 30 North Third Street.
Telephone: 717-237-4800.
Tampa, Florida Office: 101 East Kennedy Boulevard, Suite 1030.
Telephone: 813-222-8180.
North Miami Beach, Florida Office: 19495 Biscayne Boulevard.
Telephone: 305-933-5600.
Lexington, Kentucky Office: 1210 Vine Center Office Tower, 333 West Vine Street.
Telephone: 606-225-5333.
Princeton, New Jersey Office: Buchanan Ingersoll, A Partnership, College Centre, 500 College Road East.
Telephone: 609-452-2666.

Kenneth E. Aaron
Thomas J. Bender, Jr.
Stephen C. Braverman
Alan C. Kessler
Jerome N. Kline
Lawrence J. Lichtenstein
George F. Nagle
Antoinette R. Stone
Thomas L. VanKirk
Marguerite S. Walsh

COUNSEL

Richard W. Hayden
Nathaniel Metz

SENIOR ATTORNEYS

Ralph E. Arpajian
Mary Ellen Krober

Andrew W. Allison
Mary Kay Brown
Stuart M. Brown
Kristine Grady Derewicz
Robert Bruce Eyre
Nancy Sabol Frantz
Paul B. Halligan
Sherry Kajdan Vetterlein
Lawrence J. Kotler
Raymond McGarry
Fern L. McGovern
Mark Andrew Polemeni
Robert W. Scott
Sherman W. Smith III
Noreen M. Walsh
Thomas G. Wolpert
DonnaMarie Zotter

For full biographical listings, see the Martindale-Hubbell Law Directory

LESLIE J. CARSON, JR. (AV)

42 South 15th Street, Suite 1150, 19102
Telephone: 215-568-1980
Fax: 215-568-6882

For full biographical listings, see the Martindale-Hubbell Law Directory

LOUIS J. CARTER (AV)

7300 City Line Avenue, 19151-2291
Telephone: 215-879-8665
FAX: 215- 877-0955

For full biographical listings, see the Martindale-Hubbell Law Directory

CLARK, LADNER, FORTENBAUGH & YOUNG (AV)

One Commerce Square, 2005 Market Street, 19103
Telephone: 215-241-1800
Telex: 831462
Cable Address: "Clarklad"
Telecopier: 215-241-1857
Cherry Hill, New Jersey Office: Woodland Falls Corporate Park, 200 Lake Drive East, Suite 300.
Telephone: 609-779-0900.
Telecopier: 609-779-8720.
Conshohocken, Pennsylvania Office: Plymouth Corporate Center, 625 West Ridge Pike-Building E, Suite 300.
Telephone: 215-825-7000.
Fax: 215-825-1480.

(See Next Column)

CLARK, LADNER, FORTENBAUGH & YOUNG—*Continued*

Frederic L. Clark (1902-1970)
Grover C. Ladner (1952-1954)
Samuel B. Fortenbaugh, Jr. (1926-1985)
John Randolph Young (1931-1987)

OF COUNSEL

Joseph J. Duffy
W. Charles Hogg, Jr.
G. Selden Pitt
Benjamin F. Stahl, Jr.

MEMBERS OF FIRM

Alan E. Boroff (Resident, Conshohocken, Pennsylvania Office)
George Williams Braun
Edward V. Cattell, Jr. (Resident, Cherry Hill, New Jersey Office)
Peter O. Clauss
Stephen M. Cohen
William G. Downey
Walter H. Flamm, Jr.
W. Roderick Gagné
Michael J. Glasheen
Stuart M. Goldstein (Resident, Cherry Hill, New Jersey Office)
Vahan H. Gureghian
Michael R. Harris (Resident, Conshohocken, Pennsylvania Office)
Richard W. Hollstein
James W. Johnson
E. Michael Keating, III
Paul David Keenan
Paul J. Kennedy
George J. Kroculick (Resident, Cherry Hill, New Jersey Office)
Aloysius T. Lawn, IV
Peter W. Leibundgut (Resident, Cherry Hill, New Jersey Office)
Stephen Wilcox Miller
Jeffrey S. Moller
William L. Mueller (Resident, Cherry Hill, New Jersey Office)
Victor S. Perlman
M. Rust Sharp
Douglas J. Smillie
Edward C. Toole, Jr.
Thomas J. Tumola
Henry J. Tyler (Resident, Cherry Hill, New Jersey Office)
Mary F. Walrath
Robert E. Walton
Marvin L. Wilenzik (Resident, Conshohocken, Pennsylvania Office)
Bernard E. Zbrzeznj

COUNSEL

Pace Reich
Albert Barnes Zink

RESIDENT ASSOCIATES

Sara A. Begley
Patricia A. Bill
Susan R. Bogart
Jacqulynn M. Broughton
Jennifer Walters Brown
Nina L. Burnaford
James B. Burns
James O. Carpenter
Thomas J. Cole
Charles V. Curley
Janeen Olsen Dougherty
Nancy J. Ehrlich
Joseph P. Galda
Michael D. Greenberg
Dominic S. Liberi
Mark G. Lionetti
Todd E. Mason
Matthew T. D'Annunzio
Frances Elek McComb
Pauline K. Morgan
Marjorie Singer Ochroch
James H. Pickering, Jr.
Maryann Rogers Piper
Gwyn M. Simmons
Frank P. Spada, Jr.
Timothy J. Szuhaj
John E. Tyrrell
John L. Thomas
Michael J. Torchia

CHERRY HILL, NEW JERSEY RESIDENT ASSOCIATES

W. Steven Berman
Susan DeRitis Hanratty
Jane L. Lawrason
Lynne M. Parker
Stephen P. Pazan
Shannon S. Sanfilippo
Kevin P. Smith
Wayne Streibich

CONSHOHOCKEN, PENNSYLVANIA RESIDENT ASSOCIATES

Edmunds J. Brokans
William O. Krekstein
Gary R. Leadbetter
Kathleen McCardle
Carol L. Urban

Representative Clients: Commercial Union Insurance Company; C.H. Masland & Sons; Clark Equipment Company; Maritrans Operating Partners L.P.; Norfolk Southern Railroad Co.; UNUM Life Insurance Co.; VF Corporation; BP America Inc.; ETI Explosives Technologies International, Inc.

For full biographical listings, see the Martindale-Hubbell Law Directory

COZEN AND O'CONNOR, A PROFESSIONAL CORPORATION (AV)

1900 Market Street, 19103
Telephone: 215-665-2000
800-523-2900
Telecopier: 215-665-2013
Charlotte, North Carolina Office: One First Union Plaza, 28202.
Telephones: 704-376-3400; 800-762-3575.
Telecopier: 704-334-3351.
Columbia, South Carolina Office: Suite 200 The Palmetto Center, 1426 Main Street.
Telephones: 803-799-3900; 800-338-1117.
Telecopier: 803-254-7233.
Dallas, Texas Office: Suite 4100, NationsBank Plaza, 901 Main Street.
Telephones: 214-761-6700; 800-448-1207.
Telecopier: 214-761-6788.
New York, N.Y. Office: 45 Broadway Atrium.
Telephones: 212-509-9400; 800-437-9400.
Telecopier: 212-509-9492.

(See Next Column)

San Diego, California Office: Suite 1610, 501 West Broadway.
Telephones: 619-234-1700; 800-782-3366.
Telecopier: 619-234-7831.
Seattle, Washington Office: Suite 5200, Washington Mutual Tower, 1201 Third Avenue.
Telephones: 206-340-1000; 800-423-1950.
Telecopier: 206-621-8783.
Westmont, New Jersey Office: 316 Haddon Avenue.
Telephones: 609-854-4900; 800-523-2900.
Telecopier: 609-854-1782.

Sydney C. Orlofsky (1936-1968)
Charles A. Fisher, III (1947-1990)

FIRM MEMBERS IN PHILADELPHIA

Stephen A. Cozen
Patrick J. O'Connor
Joseph A. Gerber
Richard C. Glazer
Michael J. Izzo, Jr.
Robert R. Reeder
Christopher C. Fallon, Jr.
Miles A. Jellinek
David R. Strawbridge
Ronald H. Isenberg
Burton K. Stein
A. Richard Bailey
Ronald B. Hamilton
Gerard F. Belz, Jr.
Gerald J. Dugan
Michael F. Henry
John F. Brown, Jr.
David J. Groth
Joshua Wall
Thomas M. Regan
Elliott R. Feldman
John T. Thorn
Thomas C. Zielinski
Robert W. Hayes
Eugene J. Maginnis, Jr.
Anita B. Weinstein
John D. Brinkmann
Richard M. Mackowsky
Vincent R. McGuinness, Jr.
Gregory T. Magarity
William H. Howard
Daniel Q. Harrington
Elaine M. Rinaldi
John T. Salvucci
Thomas R. Harrington
Richard C. Bennett
Robert E. Meyer
Douglas B. Fox
Douglas B. Lang
Mark T. Mullen
Daniel C. Theveny
Thomas G. Wilkinson, Jr.
Laurence M. Levin
Denise Brinker Bense
Robert H. Hawn, Jr.
Deborah Melamut Minkoff
Jeffrey L. Nash
Joseph H. Riches
Lewis A. Grafman
Huey P. Cotton
Albert G. Dugan, Jr.
Ann Thornton Field
James H. Heller
Peter G. Rossi
Douglas R. Widin
Brian L. Lincicome
Paul R. Bartolacci
Eric D. Freed
Steven V. Turner
Jennifer Gallagher
Mitchell S. Goldberg
William G. Flint
Kevin J. Hughes
Mark E. Opalisky
Steven L. Smith
John Dwyer
Michael R. McCarty
Cecilia M. O'Connor
Kathie D. King
Marcy C. Panzer
Arnold C. Joseph (Resident, New York, N.Y. Office)
James C. O'Connor
Gregg F. Carpene
June E. Gilson
Josh M. Greenbaum
Dexter R. Hamilton
Robert A. Stutman
Donald A. Waltz

FIRM ASSOCIATES IN PHILADELPHIA

Marc L. Ackerman
Kevin M. Apollo
Dorothy T. Attwood
Drew R. Barth
Gaele McLaughlin Barthold (Mrs.)
Joseph J. Bellew
Barbara E. Brockman
James E. Brown
Lisa M. Calvo
Madeline Caprioli
Elizabeth J. Chambers
William N. Clark, Jr.
John K. Conner
James P. Cullen, Jr.
Frances K. Davis
Robert V. Dell'Osa
James D. Dendinger
James B. Dolan
Carolann Jackson Dougherty
Martin P. Duffey
Christa A. Fabiani
Dolores F. Faraldo
Joseph P. Fenlin
Jim H. Fields, Jr.
Lori Fox
Thomas F. Gallagher
Steven K. Gerber
James D. Golkow
Stephen M. Halbeisen
Michael A. Hamilton
Gerianne Hannibal
Denise H. Houghton
Melissa A. Kelley
Catherine A. Lindsey
Michael J. McCarrie
John Francis Mullen
Wendy L. Pew
Garland P. Pezzuolo
Stephen M. Rymal
Mark D. Simon
Cathi Cozen Snyder
William F. Stewart
Jeffrey R. Stoner
Scott M. Waldman
Charles Weiner
Eric H. Weitz
Samuel S. Woodhouse, III (Not admitted in PA)

Representative Clients: Available upon request.

For full biographical listings, see the Martindale-Hubbell Law Directory

D'ANGELO AND EURELL (AV)

Twenty-Second Floor, Land Title Building, 19110
Telephone: 215-564-5022
Fax: 215-557-7651

(See Next Column)

D'ANGELO AND EURELL, *Philadelphia—Continued*

MEMBERS OF FIRM

George A. D'Angelo
John B. Eurell
David S. D'Angelo

For full biographical listings, see the Martindale-Hubbell Law Directory

DECHERT PRICE & RHOADS (AV)

4000 Bell Atlantic Tower, 1717 Arch Street, 19103-2793
Telephone: 215-994-4000
Telefax: 215-994-2222
New York, N.Y.: 477 Madison Avenue.
Telephone: 212-326-3500.
Washington, D.C.: 1500 K Street, N.W.
Telephone: 202-626-3300.
Harrisburg, Pennsylvania: Thirty North Third Street.
Telephone: 717-237-2000.
Princeton, New Jersey: Princeton Pike Corporate Center, P.O. Box 5218.
Telephone: 609-520-3200.
Boston, Massachusetts: Ten Post Office Square South.
Telephone: 617-728-7100.
London, England: 2 Serjeants' Inn, EC4Y 1LT.
Telephone: (071) 583-5353. (Also see Titmuss Sainer Dechert).
Brussels, Belgium: 65 Avenue Louise 1050.
Telephone: (02) 535-5411.

MEMBERS OF FIRM IN PHILADELPHIA

Anthony L. Bartolini
Norbert F. Bergholtz
Richard L. Berkman
Alan D. Berkowitz
Stephanie R. Bess
Glenn D. Blumenfeld
Michael A. Bogdonoff
Stephen D. Brown
Stanhope S. Browne
Jennifer R. Clarke
Isaac H. Clothier, IV
Abbi L. Cohen
Neal D. Colton
Diane Siegel Danoff
C. VanLeer Davis, III
Norman E. Donoghue, II
Thomas E. Doran
Jonathan L. Drake
Steven B. Feirson
Aaron C. F. Finkbiner, III
Linda A. Fisher
John E. Flaherty, Jr.
Ethan D. Fogel
Robert L. Freedman
Arthur S. Gabinet
Frederick J. Gerhart
Kevin P. Gilboy
Amy B. Ginensky
Craig L. Godshall
Susan E. Goldy
Herbert F. Goodrich, Jr.
Gary L. Green
Glenn A. Gundersen
Robert C. Heim
Frederick G. Herold
Joseph K. Hetrick
Jerome A. Hoffman
William A. Humenuk
David F. Jones
Christopher G. Karras
Morris C. Kellett
William J. Kennedy
Paul S. Kimbol
H. Ronald Klasko
Samuel E. Klein
Henry Kolowrat
Seymour Kurland
William G. Lawlor
Thomas H. Lee, II
Judy L. Leone
H. Craig Lewis
Robert A. Limbacher
Wm. Scott Magargee, III
Fred T. Magaziner
Francis Mazzola
Mary A. McLaughlin
George J. Miller
Thomas B. Morris, Jr.
Henry N. Nassau
Arthur Newbold
G. Daniel O'Donnell
George W. Patrick
Paul Wm. Putney (Resident at New York, N. Y. Office)
David J. Rachofsky
Arthur H. Rainey
Thomas A. Ralph
Lois Reznick
Richard C. Rizzo
Carmen J. Romano
Richard R. Rulon
Stuart T. Saunders, Jr.
Richard G. Schneider
David E. Schulman
Richard S. Seltzer
Mari Gursky Shaw
James J. Spadaro, Jr.
Stephen A. Stack, Jr.
Joseph A. Tate
Judson J. Wambold
Jeffrey G. Weil
Richard P. Wild
Barton J. Winokur
Minturn T. Wright, III
Kathleen Ziga

OF COUNSEL IN PHILADELPHIA

Wm. Alan Baird
John Bishop, VI
William F. Bohlen
Christopher Branda, Jr.
John J. Brennan
Matthew J. Broderick
John R. Clark
H. Francis De Lone
Harry T. Devine
Kenneth W. Gemmill
Gordon W. Gerber
Albert W. Gilmer
F. Hastings Griffin, Jr.
George J. Hauptfuhrer, Jr.
Chester C. Hilinski
William A. Kelley, Jr.
Robert M. Landis
William H. Lowery
John P. Mason
Robert V. Massey, Jr.
Raymond W. Midgett, Jr.
Arthur E. Newbold, III
George B. Ross
Hardie Scott
Carroll Robbins Wetzel
Robert Deland Williams

COUNSEL IN PHILADELPHIA

Nancy J. Bregstein
Sharon R. Klein
Robert L. Roth
James M. Seif
John T. Subak

(See Next Column)

ASSOCIATES IN PHILADELPHIA

John C. Agner
Teri S. Appelson
Scott Applebaum
Lynne M. Baldwin
Elizabeth H. Baus
Alison M. Benders
Martin J. Black
Martin Joel Bolstein
Tecla J. Borick
Jennifer Caillier Boston (Not admitted in PA)
Bruce P. Bowen
Sheila A. Briggs-Steuteville
Eli R. Brill
Lynne Lee Chang
Robert C. Clothier, III
Sheryl J. Cohen
Kathryn L. Connelly
Peter D. Cripps
Daniel L. Damstra
Timothy E. Davis
David S. Denious
Ivan S. DeVoren
Stephen DiBonaventura
Adam J. Dickstein
Linda S. Dwoskin
Alison L. Ehrlich
Robert M. Elwood
Salvatore R. Faia
Jacquelyn J. Fatula
Teresa Fink
Andrew L. Fish
Brian J. Foley
Vernon L. Francis
Stephen E. Friedman
Ronni E. Fuchs
George G. Gordon
Ann E. Green
Jay M. Green
Jeffrey W. Gutchess
John J. Haggerty
Angela J. Hansen
Michael F. R. Harris
Carla J. Heil
Joseph B. Heil
Elizabeth T. Hey
Douglas A. Holmberg
Otto W. Immel
Andrew K. Janas
Michael L. Kichline
Katherine L. Koenig
Jill M. Kuntz
Thomas M. Kurke
Thomas J. Kuzma
John D. LaRocca
James J. Lawless, Jr.
David M. Lazarus
Brian D. Lepard
Christine C. Levin
Jan P. Levine
Christopher D. Loizides
David S. Lorry
Andrew S. Miller
Kathleen A. Milsark
Andrew J. Mottes
Frank J. O'Hara
Henry A. Olsen, III
Robert O. Pineda
Scott D. Price
Cynthia L. Randall
Melissa B. Rasman
Steven C. Robbins
Christopher M. Roe
Frances E. Ryan
M. Frances Ryan
Louise E. Schmoyer
Stephanie M. Schwartzberg
Hope M. Seidenberg-Freiwald
Jill L. Sigmund
Geraldine A. Sinatra
Paul D. Snitzer
Jeffrey W. Soderberg
Arthur R. G. Solmssen, Jr.
David A. Soltz
William A. Stock
Debra L. Subar
Stephanie E. Thier (Not admitted in PA)
Carol C. B. Trask
Marshall J. Walthew
Rachel B. Weil
Eve Strauss West
Lisa M. Whitcomb
Gerald D. Wixted
Geanne K. Zelkowitz

For full biographical listings, see the Martindale-Hubbell Law Directory

DILWORTH, PAXSON, KALISH & KAUFFMAN (AV)

3200 Mellon Bank Center, 1735 Market Street, 19103
Telephone: 215-575-7000
Fax: 215-575-7200
Harrisburg, Pennsylvania Office: 305 N. Front Street, Suite 403.
Telephone: 717-236-4812.
Fax: 717-236-7811.
Plymouth Meeting, Pennsylvania Office: 630 West Germantown Pike, Suite 160.
Telephone: 610-941-4444.
Fax: 610-941-9880.
Westmont, New Jersey Office: 222 Haddon Avenue.
Telephone: 609-854-5150.
Fax: 609-854-2316.
Media, Pennsylvania Office: 606 E. Baltimore Pike.
Telephone: 610-565-4322.
Fax: 610-565-4131.

MEMBERS OF FIRM

Richardson Dilworth (1898-1974)
Henry D. Paxson (1904-1975)
Bruce W. Kauffman
Stephen J. Korn
William J. Henrich, Jr.
Stephen J. Harmelin
Joseph H. Jacovini
Carl H. Hanzelik
Steven L. Friedman
Peter J. Picotte, II
Richard M. Segal
Ross J. Reese
John R. Latourette, Jr.
Roger F. Wood
James F. Monteith
Marc A. Feller
Mark J. Levin
Lawrence G. McMichael
John W. Schmehl
Karen Lee Turner
Paul W. Baskowsky
James J. Rodgers
Edward N. Barol
Joseph F. Kessler
Ralph J. Kelly
Lawrence F. Shay
Virginia Hinrichs Miller
Barbara Alden Krancer
Victor P. Stabile (Resident, Harrisburg Office)
Harriet J. Koren
J. Bradford McIlvain
Benjamin J. Berger
Mary T. Tomich
Camille S. Andrews

SPECIAL COUNSEL

Robert J. F. Brobyn (Plymouth Meeting Office)

(See Next Column)

DILWORTH, PAXSON, KALISH & KAUFFMAN—*Continued*

COUNSEL

Vincent J. Fumo
Sheryl L. Auerbach
Merritt A. Cole
J. Roger Williams, Jr.
Robert Forrest Stewart, Jr.
Ellen Covner Weiss
John Philip Crampton
Anthony Repici
Milton A. Feldman
Benjamin Lerner
J. Shane Creamer
Marcus Manoff
Nathaniel Budin
Harry A. Kalish
Jules I. Whitman

ASSOCIATES

Gregory F. Cirillo
Joel L. Frank
Marjorie McMahon Obod
Maura E. Fay
Virginia L. Flick
Richard L. Fox
Bruce E. Hartman
Martin J. Weis
Thomas E. Groshens
Lynn A. Rosner Rauch
Steven Roth
Penny Conly Ellison
John T. Mannato
Joseph P. Canuso
Gerald E. Burns, III
Laura Elizabeth Vendzules
Thomas Biemer
William J. Brennan, IV
Peter C. Hughes
Bradley J. Lucido
Kimberly A. McAndrew
Linda L. Parthemer
C. Lawrence Holmes
Phillip Greenberg
Daniel H. Wheeler
Mark W. Helwig
Rosemary Jean Loverdi
Steven B. Goodman

For full biographical listings, see the Martindale-Hubbell Law Directory

DRINKER BIDDLE & REATH (AV)

Philadelphia National Bank Building, 1345 Chestnut Street, 19107-3496
Telephone: 215-988-2700
Telefax: 215-988-2757
Cable Address: "Debemac"
Washington, D.C. Office: 901 15th Street, N.W., Suite 900.
Telephone: 202-842-8800.
Telefax: 202-842-8465.
Princeton, New Jersey Office: Suite 400, 47 Hulfish Street, P.O. Box 627.
Telephone: 609-921-6336.
Telefax: 609-921-2265.
Berwyn, Pennsylvania Office: Suite 300, 1000 Westlakes Drive.
Telephone: 215-993-2200.
Telefax: 215-993-8585.

MEMBERS OF FIRM

David F. Abernethy
Robert M. Adler (Resident Partner, Washington, D.C. Office)
Bonnie Allyn Barnett
Marsha W. Beidler (Resident Partner at Princeton, N. J. Office)
John C. Bennett, Jr.
Wilson M. Brown, III
Henry S. Bryans
Harry Sarkis Cherken, Jr.
Francis J. Connell, III
Jeffrey A. Dalke
Raymond K. Denworth, Jr.
James Eiseman, Jr.
Homer L. Elliott
John W. Fischer (Resident Partner at Berwyn, Pa. Office)
Michael O'S. Floyd
Christopher H. Gadsden
Richard S. Goldman (Resident Partner at Princeton, N. J. Office)
Rush T. Haines, II
Stephen D. D. Hamilton
Robert J. Hoelscher
James C. Ingram
Elizabeth Youse Jewett
Morgan R. Jones
Robert Mead Jones, Jr.
Marty M. Judge (Resident Partner at Princeton, N.J. Office)
Sharon L. Klingelsmith
Samuel W. Lambert, III (Resident Partner at Princeton, N. J. Office)
Kathryn H. Levering
Michael P. Malloy
Karen Fox Marriott
Joaquin A. Marquez (Resident Partner at Washington, D.C. Office)
David W. Maxey
W. Bruce McConnel, III
H. John Michel, Jr.
Walter J. Mostek, Jr.
Peter P. Ackourey (Resident Partner at Princeton, N. J. Office)
Gary D. Ammon
Gary R. Battistoni
Thomas A. Belton (Resident Partner at Princeton, N. J. Office)
Melvin C. Breaux
David P. Bruton
William C. Bullitt
John Chesney
T. Andrew Culbert
Amy Fogel Davis
Joe D. Edge (Resident Partner at Washington, D.C. Office)
Jonathan I. Epstein (Resident Partner at Princeton, N.J. Office)
Lawrence J. Fox
Michael L. Gassmann (Resident Partner at Washington, D.C. Office)
William M. Goldstein
Daniel G. Hale
Henry S. Hilles, Jr.
J. Freedley Hunsicker, Jr.
Joseph F. Johnston, Jr. (Resident Partner at Washington, D.C. Office)
Michael B. Jordan
Jonathan A. Kane (Resident Partner at Berwyn, Pa. Office)
Andrew C. Kassner
Mary E. Kohart
Stuart A. Law, Jr.
Thomas J. Leach
William J. Lehane
John P. Lloyd
John Markle, Jr. (Resident Partner at Berwyn, Pa. Office)
Philip J. Mause (Resident Partner at Washington, D.C. Office)
E. Morgan Maxwell, III
James A. Meyers (Resident Partner at Washington, D.C. Office)

(See Next Column)

MEMBERS OF FIRM (Continued)

John W. Pettit (Resident Partner at Washington, D.C. Office)
Alfred W. Putnam, Jr.
Ralph Rodak
Michael J. Rotko
Joseph N. Schmidt, Jr. (Resident Partner at Princeton, N.J. Office)
Richard M. Singer (Resident Partner at Washington, D.C. Office)
Vernon Stanton, Jr.
George V. Strong, III (Resident Partner at Berwyn, Pa. Office)
Clifford H. Swain
James M. Sweet
Barry S. Wildstein
W. Steven Woodward (Resident Partner at Berwyn, Pennsylvania Office)
Edward M. Posner
Warren T. Pratt
F. Douglas Raymond
Daniel R. Ross
Patrick T. Ryan
Pam H. Schneider
Robert E. Shields
Bruce D. Shuter
Robert A. Skitol (Resident Partner at Washington, D.C. Office)
R. Philip Steinberg
Robert H. Strouse (Resident Partner, Berwyn, Pennsylvania Office)
Mark M. Wilcox
Thomas E. Wood (Resident Partner at Berwyn, Pa. Office)

COUNSEL

Carol Glaubman Kroch
Christina T. Simmons

OF COUNSEL

Duffield Ashmead, III
Lewis H. Van Dusen, Jr.
A. C. Reeves Hicks (Resident Partner at Princeton, N. J. Office)
John P. Bankson, Jr. (Resident Of Counsel at Washington, D.C. Office)
Henry W. Sawyer, III
Robert L. Banse (Resident, Princeton, N.J. Office)

ASSOCIATES

Patricia J. Almony
Richard J. Arsenault (Resident Associate at Washington, D.C. Office)
Thomas J. Barton
Frances Ruml Beckley
James Biehl (Resident Associate at Princeton, N.J. Office)
Sue W. Bladek (Resident Associate at Washington, D.C. Office)
Leslie Gillin Bohner
Daniel J. Brennan
Keith B. Brooks (Resident Associate at Washington, D. C. Office)
Robert D. Carmignani
Christine Cartwright (Resident Associate, Princeton, N.J. Office)
Charles B. Congdon
Robert D. Denious
Mark F. Dever (Resident Associate at Washington, D.C. Office)
Franklin E. Fink
Paul R. Fitzmaurice
Andrew J. Flame
Andrew P. Foster
Jacqueline I. Glassman
Kevin M. Gross (Resident Associate at Washington, D. C.)
Lori K. Irwin
Mark E. Jakubik
Alan J. Joaquin (Resident Associate at Washington, D.C. Office)
Stephen Michael Kanovsky (Resident Associate at Princeton, N.J. Office)
Fredric J. Kinkler, Jr.
Robert A. Kosik (Resident Associate at Washington, D. C. Office)
Deborah M. Levy (Resident Associate at Washington, D.C. Office)
Gregory J. Manderlink (Not admitted in PA)
Julia Anne Matheson
Diana E. McCarthy
Michael W. McTigue, Jr.
Kent T. Miller
Brian S. Mudge
Lawrence A. Nathanson
James William O'Brien
John E. Parker
Thomas M. Pinney
Mary H. Anderson
John P. Bartholomay (Resident Associate at Washington, D.C. Office)
Erica Loren Bazzell
David J. Berson (Resident Associate at Washington, D.C. Office)
Scott Andrew Blank
David E. Bloom (Resident Associate at Princeton, N.J. Office)
Lisa M. Britchkow
Michael F. Brown
Paula T. Calhoun (Resident Associate at Berwyn, Pa. Office)
Ethan D. Civan
Kerin Bischoff Clapp
Susan G. Collings
David Forrester Connor
Christine R. Deutsch
David M. Doto
Seamus C. Duffy
Carol L. Ferren
Ellen M. Fisher (Resident Associate at Princeton, N.J. Office)
Tracey S. Ging
Kenneth L. Greenberg
Maureen L. Hogel
Brenda W. Holston
Michael J. Holston
Lori A. Jackson
Nadia Mykytiuk Jannetta
Ute A. Joas (Resident Associate at Washington, D.C. Office)
Robert C. Juelke
Susan Marie Kennedy
Lisa Klass Kent (Resident Associate at Princeton, N.J. Office)
David J. Larsson (Resident Associate at Berwyn, Pa. Office)
Penelope M. Lister-Farano (Resident Associate at Washington, D.C. Office)
Elizabeth A. Marshall (Resident Associate at Washington, D.C. Office)
John F. McGuiness, Jr.
Gregg Reardon Melinson
Elena J. Morrow-Spitzer
Carol Ann Mueller
Barbara A. Nugent
Peter S. Paine III
Michael T. Pellegrino
Nora E. Pomerantz

(See Next Column)

DRINKER BIDDLE & REATH, *Philadelphia—Continued*

ASSOCIATES (Continued)

Jeffrey A. Pott
Karl L. Prior
Patricia Proctor
Margaret E. Reford
Jean D. Renshaw
William V. Roeder
Richard E. Ruffee
Roberta J. Sampson
David M. Scolnic
John E. Stoddard, III (Resident Associate at Princeton, N. J. Office)
Joan Ohlbaum Swirsky
Kathleen L. Thren
Ivy Melissa Wafford
Jeffrey Paul Wallack
Charles H. Wampold, III
Lisa S. Presser (Resident Associate at Princeton, N.J. Office)
Judith Reich
E. Graham Robb, Jr.
Jonathan S. Rosan
Paul Hewit Saint-Antoine
John F. Schultz
David A. Searles
Michael K. Sullivan
Mark N. Suprenant (Resident Associate at Berwyn, Pa. Office)
Charles J. Vinicombe (Resident Associate at Princeton, N. J. Office)
Sandra L. Ykema
Sinclair A. Ziesing

For full biographical listings, see the Martindale-Hubbell Law Directory

DUANE, MORRIS & HECKSCHER (AV)

Suite 4200 One Liberty Place, 19103-7396
Telephone: 215-979-1000
FAX: 215-979-1020
Harrisburg, Pennsylvania Office: 305 North Front Street, 5th Floor, P.O. Box 1003.
Telephone: 717-237-5500.
Fax: 717-232-4015.
Wilmington, Delaware Office: Suite 1500, 1201 Market Street.
Telephone: 302-571-5550.
Fax: 302-571-5560.
New York, N.Y. Office: 112 E. 42nd Street, Suite 2125.
Telephone: 212-499-0410.
Fax: 212-499-0420.
Wayne, Pennsylvania Office 735 Chesterbrook Boulevard, Suite 300.
Telephone: 610-647-3555.
Allentown, Pennsylvania Office: 968 Postal Road, Suite 200.
Telephone: 610-266-3650.
Fax: 610-640-2619.
Cherry Hill, New Jersey Office: 51 Haddonfield Road, Suite 340.
Telephone: 609-488-7300.
Fax: 609-488-7021.

COUNSEL

Maurice Heckscher
Thomas R. Bevan
John B. Felton
John B. Martin
Henry T. Reath
John A. Clark
Thomas M. Hyndman, Jr.

MEMBERS OF FIRM

A. John May
Roland Morris
Reeder R. Fox
Seymour C. Wagner
Robert W. Denious
David C. Toomey
David T. Sykes
Michael M. Baylson
Jay J. Lambert
Frank G. Cooper
Donald A. Tortorice (Resident, Harrisburg Office)
John S. Hayes (Resident, Allentown Office)
Maxwell E. Davison (Resident, Allentown Office)
Stephen D. Teaford
Hugh M. Emory
Thomas P. Preston (Resident, Wilmington, Delaware Office)
David M. Flynn
Michael M. Mustokoff
Frederick A. Levy
Andrew J. Ruck
Daniel F. Lindley (Resident, Wilmington, Delaware Office)
Kathleen M. Shay
John J. Soroko
Steven K. Kudatzky (Resident, Cherry Hill, New Jersey Office)
Barbara Adams
Beatrice O'Donnell
Frank A. Luchak (Resident, Cherry Hill, New Jersey Office)
Bruce J. Kasten
Jack M. Mumford (Resident, Harrisburg Office)
James J. McCabe
Sheldon M. Bonovitz
Frank L. White, Jr. (Resident, Wayne Office)
Vincent F. Garrity, Jr.
Frederick W. Dreher
Ronald F. Kidd
Robert L. Pratter
Jane Leslie Dalton
Donald R. Auten
Marc D. Brookman
David S. Swayze (Not admitted in PA; Resident, Wilmington, Delaware Office)
Edward M. Feege (Resident, Allentown, Office)
Paul J. Schneider
Edward Griffith (Resident, Wayne Office)
Gene E. K. Pratter
John F. Horstmann, III
William E. Manning (Not admitted in PA; Resident, Wilmington, Delaware Office)
Ralph A. Mariani
James Kenneth Brengle (Resident, Wayne Office)
George E. Pierce, Jr.
Robert E. Kelly, Jr. (Resident, Harrisburg Office)
Richard C. Unger, Jr.
Thomas W. Ostrander
Lewis R. Olshin (Resident, Wayne Office)
David I. Haas
Cecelia L. Fanelli
J. Scott Kramer
Rudolph J. DiMassa, Jr.
Scott C. Penwell (Resident, Harrisburg Office)

(See Next Column)

Patricia Leon Pregmon

MEMBERS OF FIRM (Continued)

David E. Loder
Elise E. Singer
Judith Nichols Renzulli (Resident, Wilmington, Delaware Office)
Peter S. Clark, II
Margery N. Reed
Claudia Z. Springer
Nolan N. Atkinson, Jr.
Kenneth L. Sable (Resident, Harrisburg Office)
Neil H. Feinstein
Thomas G. Thompson (Resident, Wayne Office)
Steven P. Berman
Shaun R. Eisenhauer (Resident, Harrisburg Office)
Gerald F. McCormick (Resident, Wayne Office)
W. Mark Mullineaux (Resident, Wayne Office)
Mark J. Packel
Peter J. Cronk
Scott J. Fields
Teresa N. Cavenagh
Thomas G. Spencer
Teresa K. D. Currier
Allen C. Warshaw (Resident, Harrisburg Office)
Arthur K. Hoffman (Resident, Harrisburg Office)
Anthony J. Bilotti
Steven M. Janove
James S. Green (Resident, Wilmington, Delaware Office)
Robert L. Archie, Jr.
Robert J. Hasday * (Resident, New York, N.Y. Office)
Thomas J. Karl
Amy E. Wilkinson
Thomas B. K. Ringe, III
James L. Allison
Brian J. Siegel (Resident, Wayne Office)
Seth v.d.H. Cooley
Joseph A. Fillip, Jr. (Resident, Wilmington, Delaware Office)
Edward G. Biester, III
David C. Weiss (Resident, Wilmington, Delaware Office)
Michael H. Margulis * (Resident, New York, N.Y. Office)
Mark M. Lipowicz

RESIDENT OF COUNSEL HARRISBURG OFFICE

Harold W. Swope

ASSOCIATES

John L. Olsen (Not admitted in PA)
John W. Kauffman
Wayne A. Mack, Jr.
Diane E. Vuocolo
David C. Toner
Wallace B. Eldridge, III (Resident, Allentown Office)
J. Shane Creamer, Jr.
Thomas G. Servodidio
Mark B. Sheppard
Lisa M. Batastini
Andrew S. Ross
Larry D. Silver
Mary Patricia Patterson (Resident, Harrisburg Office)
David L. Frank
Jeffrey S. Henderson
Kathleen Parks Loughhead
Gerald J. Pappert
Joshua Sarner
Michael J. Willner
Jeffrey M. Zimskind (Resident, Allentown Office)
John K. Baker (Resident, Allentown, Pennsylvania Office)
Melissa H. Maxman
Judy L. Ziegler (Resident, Wayne, Pennsylvania Office)
Nancy Conrad
James M. Keating, Jr.
Mark A. Morton (Resident, Wilmington, Delaware Office)
Melissa McKee Hackney
Joanne M. Murray
Thomas J. Weber (Resident, Harrisburg Office)
Frank P. Tuplin
Kevin W. Goldstein (Resident, Wilmington, Delaware Office)
John L. Aris
Robert J. Bohner, Jr.
Cletus C. Hess (Resident, Harrisburg Office)
Daniel B. Rath (Resident, Wilmington, Delaware Office)
Timothy J. Holman
E. Lynne Hirsch
John F. "Jack" Daniels
Mary Catherine Biondi (Resident, Wilmington, Delaware Office)
Martin A. Fritz (Resident, Harrisburg, Pennsylvania Office)
Matthew E. Tashman
Lisa K. W. Crossland
Linda M. Zimmermann
James J. Ferrelli (Resident, Cherry Hill, New Jersey Office)
Frank E. Noyes, II
Dianne A. Meyer
Lisa Wolff
Wayne J. Martorelli
Christopher J. Pippett
Michael O'Hayer (Resident, Wayne Office)
Matthew Chabal, III (Resident, Harrisburg Office)
Kenneth M. Denti (Resident, Cherry Hill, New Jersey Office)
Richard A. Forsten (Resident, Wilmington, Delaware Office)
Wendy R. Hughes
Lori A. Mills
Richard W. Riley
Craig F. Turet
David R. Augustin
Michelle Shriro (Resident, Wilmington, Delaware Office)
Robert J. Valihura, Jr. (Resident, Wilmington, Delaware Office)
Michele T. Cann (Resident, Allentown Office)
Lisa W. Clark
James J. Holman
Mark B. Schoeller
William R. Kane
Patrick J. Loftus
Sandra Lee Morris
David B. Smith
Bonnie Lynne Wolfgang (Resident, Wilmington, Delaware Office)
Alan P. Garubba
Mary F. Caloway (Resident, Wilmington, Delaware Office)
Jody Anne G. Werner
Suzanne M. Mitchell
Deborah Tate Pecci
Emily H. Hoechst (Resident, Wayne Office)
Kathleen A. O'Malley (Resident, Cherry Hill, New Jersey Office)
Richard S. Cobb (Resident, Wilmington, Delaware Office)
Thomas Ermi
Caroline J. Hasson
David L. Kwass
Sheila McVey Mangan
Steven J. Udicious
Marc H. Perry
Susan L. Wilder

(See Next Column)

DUANE, MORRIS & HECKSCHER—*Continued*

ASSOCIATES (Continued)

Linda Joy Jennings (Resident, Wilmington, Delaware Office)
Judith E. Baylinson
Linda Marie Doyle
Andrew Hamilton
Andrew P. Hoppes
James C. King
Joseph E. Mayk (Resident, Wayne, Pennsylvania Office)
David Romine
Teri L. Thompson (Resident, Wilmington, Delaware Office)
Brian William Bisignani (Resident, Harrisburg, Pennsylvania Office)
Bruce A. Gelting (Resident, Harrisburg, Pennsylvania Office)
Jeffrey D. Lippert
J.B. Todd McCoy
Mary J. Mullany
Paula Terese Ryan
Tamara Lee Sesok
Clare Ann Fitzgerald

SPECIAL COUNSEL

Eugene Lowenstein
Jeffrey M. Navon

SPECIAL COUNSEL HARRISBURG OFFICE

Ruth M. Siegel

SPECIAL COUNSEL CHERRY HILL OFFICE

Alma L. Saravia (Not admitted in PA)

*Hasday & Margulis, A Professional Corporation

For full biographical listings, see the Martindale-Hubbell Law Directory

---

FELLHEIMER EICHEN BRAVERMAN & KASKEY, A PROFESSIONAL CORPORATION (AV)

21st Floor, One Liberty Place, 19103-7334
Telephone: 215-575-3800
FAX: 215-575-3801
Camden, New Jersey Office: 519 Federal Street, Suite 503 Parkade Building, 08103-1147.
Telephone: 609-541-5323.
Fax: 609-541-5370.

Alan S. Fellheimer
David L. Braverman
Judith Eichen Fellheimer
John E. Kaskey
Kenneth S. Goodkind
Anna Hom
Peter E. Meltzer

OF COUNSEL

Helen Mandel Braverman

Barbara Anisko
Maia R. Caplan
Jeffrey L. Eichen
Michael N. Feder
Jolie G. Kahn
George F. Newton
Matthew A. Nyman
David B. Spitofsky
W. Thomas Tither, Jr.
David J. Perlman

For full biographical listings, see the Martindale-Hubbell Law Directory

---

FINEMAN & BACH, P.C. (AV)

19th Floor, 1608 Walnut Street, 19103
Telephone: 215-893-9300
Fax: 215-893-8719
Cherry Hill, New Jersey Office: 905 North Kings Highway.
Telephone: 609-795-1118.

Norman S. Berson
Robert J. Klein
S. David Fineman
Bonnie Brigance Leadbetter
Mitchell L. Bach
Tyler E. Wren
Richard A. Rubin
J. Randolph Lawlace
Jay Barry Harris
Richard J. Tanker (Resident, Cherry Hill, New Jersey Office)

Lee Applebaum
Diane C. Bernoff
Scott H. Brandt
June J. Essis
John C. Falls
Illene G. Greenberg
Julie Pearlman Meyers
Stefanie Newman Rabinowitz
Michael S. Saltzman
Alan J. Tauber
Alexander B. Zolfaghari

For full biographical listings, see the Martindale-Hubbell Law Directory

---

F. EMMETT FITZPATRICK, P.C. (AV)

926 Public Ledger Building, 19106
Telephone: 215-925-5200
Fax: 215-925-5991

F. Emmett Fitzpatrick
F. Emmett Fitzpatrick, III

For full biographical listings, see the Martindale-Hubbell Law Directory

FOX, ROTHSCHILD, O'BRIEN & FRANKEL (AV)

10th Floor, 2000 Market Street, 19103-3291
Telephone: 215-299-2000
Cable Address: FROF
Telecopier: 215-299-2150
Exton, Pennsylvania Office: Eagleview Corporate Center, 717 Constitution Drive, Suite 111, P.O. Box 673, 19341-0673.
Telephone: 610-458-2100.
Telecopier: 610-458-2112.
Trenton (Lawrenceville), New Jersey Office: Princeton Pike Corporate Center, 997 Lenox Drive, Building 3, 08648-2311.
Telephone: 609-896-3600.
Telecopier: 609-896-1469.

MEMBERS OF FIRM

Alex Satinsky
Isadore A. Shrager
Robert Perry Frankel
William A. Whiteside, Jr.
Samuel E. Dennis
Ramon R. Obod
Jay G. Ochroch
Jerome E. Bogutz
Louis W. Fryman
Norman Leibovitz
Stanley S. Cohen
Herbert Bass
Victor Walcoff (Not admitted in PA; Resident, Trenton (Lawrenceville), New Jersey Office)
Richard M. Kohn (Not admitted in PA; Resident, Trenton (Lawrenceville), New Jersey Office)
Joseph Smukler
Owen A. Knopping
Martin G. Heckler
E. Gerald Donnelly, Jr.
Howell J. Reeves
Stephen P. Weiss
Jeffrey B. Albert
Jonathan D. Weiner (Not admitted in PA; Resident, Trenton (Lawrenceville), New Jersey Office)
Barnett Satinsky
Abraham C. Reich
Phillip E. Griffin (Not admitted in PA; Resident, Trenton (Lawrenceville), New Jersey Office)
Steven C. Levitt (Not admitted in PA; Resident, Trenton (Lawrenceville), New Jersey Office)
David S. Rasner
Aaron Jay Beyer
Theodore A. Young
Ira B. Silverstein
Ezra D. Rosenberg (Not admitted in PA; Resident, Trenton (Lawrenceville), New Jersey Office)
Albert J. Slap
Mitchell T. Morris
Albert R. Riviezzo (Resident, Exton, Pennsylvania Office)
Sanford K. Mozes
Edward J. Hayes
Mark L. Silow
Robin B. Matlin
Joseph V. Southern
Simon Kimmelman (Not admitted in PA; Resident, Trenton (Lawrenceville), New Jersey Office)
Elaine N. Moranz
Ronald J. Shaffer
Jay S. Ruder (Resident, Trenton (Lawrenceville), New Jersey Office)
Philip L. Hinerman
James F. X. Rudy (Not admitted in PA; Resident, Trenton (Lawrenceville), New Jersey Office)
Roberta DeAngelis (Not admitted in PA; Resident, Trenton (Lawrenceville), New Jersey Office)
Mary Ann Rossi (Resident, Exton, Pennsylvania Office)
Gerald M. Hatfield
Mark R. Ashton (Resident, Exton, Pennsylvania Office)
Marvin L. Weinberg
Mark L. Morris
Gregory Kleiber
Stephanie Resnick
Allison E. Accurso (Resident, Trenton (Lawrenceville), New Jersey Office)
June H. Millington (Not admitted in PA; Resident, Trenton (Lawrenceville), New Jersey Office)
Paul Jonathan Brenman
Robert F. Zielinski

ASSOCIATES

John A. Rothschild
Marjorie Stern Jacobs
Jon C. Martin (Not admitted in PA; Resident, Trenton (Lawrenceville), New Jersey Office)
Marc E. Needles
H. Lee Schwartzberg, Jr. (Resident, Trenton (Lawrenceville), New Jersey Office)
Michael C. McBratnie (Resident, Exton, Pennsylvania Office)
Steven K. Ludwig
D. Jeffry Benoliel
Janet R. Seligman
Kevin B. Scott
Kathleen K. Weston
Tristram R. Fall III
Robert W. Gundlach
Scott L. Vernick
Eric L. Settle (Resident, Exton, Pennsylvania Office)
Leslie M. Gerstein
Gerald E. Arth
David B. Snyder
Martha Baskett Chovanes
Jane E. Lessner
Thomas D. Paradise
Barbara Flacker Elimelech
Philip W. Fisher
David J. Stutman
Jeffrey P. Scarpello
Shari J. Odenheimer
Richard A. Silfen
Michael G. Menkowitz
R. James Kravitz (Resident, Trenton (Lawrenceville), New Jersey Office)
Caroline Wroth O'Leary
Andrea Dobin
Deborah R. Popky
Barry H. Kitain
Lauren P. McKenna
Samuel H. Israel
Paul T. Porrini
Theodore H. Jobes
Anne Marie Ciesla
Bradley S. Rodos
Lisa A. Carney
Douglas J. Zeltt (Resident, Trenton (Lawrenceville), New Jersey Office)
Thomas J. Heitzman (Resident, Trenton (Lawrenceville), New Jersey Office)

(See Next Column)

FOX, ROTHSCHILD, O'BRIEN & FRANKEL, *Philadelphia—Continued*

ASSOCIATES (Continued)

Sue A. Gambaccini (Resident, Trenton (Lawrenceville), New Jersey Office)
Cynthia M. Horn
Frank G. Murphy
Susan M. DiMaria
Lisa Washington
Ian D. Meklinsky
Susan Brillman Naftulin
Jennifer Molish
Lynn B. McDougall (Resident, Trenton (Lawrenceville), New Jersey Office)
Magdalena Schardt (Resident, Trenton (Lawrenceville), New Jersey Office)
Richard E. Wegryn (Resident, Trenton (Lawrenceville), New Jersey Office)

SPECIAL COUNSEL

George R. Burrell, Jr.
Brian J. O'Neill
Alan E. Casnoff
Elaine C. Britt (Not admitted in PA; Resident, Trenton (Lawrenceville), New Jersey Office)

SENIOR COUNSEL

Jerome B. Weinstein
Murray H. Shusterman

For full biographical listings, see the Martindale-Hubbell Law Directory

---

GALLAGHER, REILLY AND LACHAT, P.C. (AV)

Suite 1300, 2000 Market Street, 19103
Telephone: 215-299-3000
FAX: 215-299-3010
Pennsauken, New Jersey Office: Kevon Office Center, Suite 130, 2500 McClellan Boulevard, 08109.
Telephone: 609-663-8200.

Stanley S. Frazee, Jr.
Paul F. X. Gallagher
Thomas F. Reilly
Frederick T. Lachat, Jr.
Richard K. Hohn
James Emerson Egbert
Stephen A. Scheuerle
Elizabeth F. Walker

David Scott Morgan
Wilfred T. Mills, Jr.
Maureen Rowan
Charles L. McNabb
Thomas O'Neill
Laurence I. Gross
Sean F. Kennedy
Milica Novakovic
John A. Livingood, Jr.

SPECIAL COUNSEL

Dolores Rocco Kulp

For full biographical listings, see the Martindale-Hubbell Law Directory

---

GERMAN, GALLAGHER & MURTAGH, A PROFESSIONAL CORPORATION (AV)

Fifth Floor, The Bellevue, 200 South Broad Street, 19102
Telephone: 215-545-7700
Telecopier: 215-732-4182
Cherry Hill, New Jersey Office: Suite 643, 1040 North Kings Highway.
Telephone: 609-667-7676.
Lancaster, Pennsylvania Office: 40 East Grant Street.
Telephone: 717-293-8070.

Edward C. German
Michael D. Gallagher
Dean F. Murtagh
Philip A. Ryan
Robert P. Corbin
David P. Rovner
Kathryn A. Dux
Gary R. Gremminger
Kim Plouffe
Jeffrey N. German
John P. Shusted

Kathleen M. Carson
Kevin R. McNulty
Linda Porr Sweeney
Gary H. Hunter
Frank A. Gerolamo, III
Milan K. Mrkobrad
Thomas M. Going
Vincent J. Di Stefano, Jr.
Jack T. Ribble, Jr.
Kimberly J. Keiser
Bernard E. Jude Quinn
Gerald C. Montella
Lisa Beth Zucker
Shelby L. Mattioli
Daniel J. Divis
D. Selaine Belver
Christine L. Davis
Daniel L. Grill
Marta I. Sierra-Epperson
Paul G. Kirk
Aileen R. Thompson
Otis V. Maynard
Gregory S. Capps

For full biographical listings, see the Martindale-Hubbell Law Directory

---

HARVEY, PENNINGTON, HERTING & RENNEISEN, LTD. (AV)

11 Penn Center, 29th Floor, 1835 Market Street, 19103
Telephone: 215-563-4470
FAX: 215-568-1044
Cherry Hill, New Jersey Office: Pennington & Thompson, 135 Woodcrest Road.
Telephone: 609-795-0882.
FAX: 609-795-4907.
New York, N.Y. Office: Twenty-First Floor, 237 Park Avenue.
Telephone: 212-551-1416.
FAX: 212-697-8486.

(See Next Column)

Greenville, Delaware Office: 4001 Kennett Pike, Suite 222.
Telephone: 302-428-0719.
FAX: 302-428-0723.

Norman Paul Harvey (1911-1978)
Eugene H. Feldman (1909-1979)
E. Dyson Herting
David L. Pennington
G. Wayne Renneisen
Glenn C. Equi
Bruce D. Lombardo
David J. Griffith
Elizabeth McKenna
Robert D. Thompson (Resident, Cherry Hill, New Jersey Office)
Stephen J. Cabot
William G. Adamson
Charles M. Weisman
Joel D. Gusky
Roger B. Wood
John E. Smith
Susan McLaughlin
George A. Amacker, III (Resident, Cherry Hill, New Jersey Office)
Gary C. Chiumento (Resident, Cherry Hill, New Jersey Office)
Katherine M. Mezzanotte
Lawrence A. Borda
Howard M. Cyr, III
Neil P. Clain, Jr.
Frederick M. Walton, Jr.

Donald D. Bush (Not admitted in PA)
Andrew Fylypovych
Lori A. Stubits
Richard J. Davies
Ernest J. Bernabei, III
Louis G. Rubino (Resident, Cherry Hill, New Jersey Office)
Mark A. Lockett
James F. Lynn
Catherine Panchou Cox
Philip J. Espinosa (Resident, Cherry Hill, New Jersey Office)
Danell Palladine Dean
Michael A. McGinly (Resident, Cherry Hill, N.J. Office)
Marcella J. Schell
Stephen A. Sheinen
John A. Gallagher
Maria L. Petrillo
Timothy J. Bloh
Robert G. Hughes
Adam S. Levy
John J. Jacko III
Lauri A. Kavulich
Stephen V. Yarnell
Glen D. Kimball
Lisa A. Davis
Mark W. Voigt
Denis C. Dice
Reed J. Slogoff
Patrick R. Delaney (Resident, Cherry Hill, New Jersey Office)
Michele Daniele
Robert J. Lenahan
Brian P. Kirby
Jeffrey D. Laudenbach
Andrew K. Worek
Christian A. Davis
Elise N. Lazarus (Resident, Cherry Hill, New Jersey Office)

For full biographical listings, see the Martindale-Hubbell Law Directory

---

HEPBURN WILLCOX HAMILTON & PUTNAM (AV)

1100 One Penn Center, 19103
Telephone: 215-568-7500
Cable Address: "Norlex"
Telecopier: 215-751-9044

MEMBERS OF FIRM

E. Brooks Keffer, Jr.
Spencer Ervin
J. Richard Greenstein
Edward J. Kaier
T. Sergeant Pepper
Kenneth Evert Ahl
Christopher F. Stouffer
Jerome C. Murray
John J. Hubbert, III

ASSOCIATES

Robert S. Cohen
Paul D. Inglesby
Sandra Kaplan Slap
Maureen R. Brown
G. Thomas Williams
John Thomas Rogers
John F. Barrett

OF COUNSEL

Alfred W. Putnam
Perrin C. Hamilton
Daniel S. Greenstein
Charles C. Coyne
Philip R. Hepburn
Frederick L. Fuges
Mark Willcox, Jr.
A. J. Drexel Paul, Jr.

For full biographical listings, see the Martindale-Hubbell Law Directory

---

HOYLE, MORRIS & KERR (AV)

Suite 4900, One Liberty Place, 1650 Market Street, 19103
Telephone: 215-981-5700
Telecopier: 851-0436

MEMBERS OF FIRM

Lawrence T. Hoyle, Jr.
Alexander Kerr
Bernard J. Smolens
Susan K. Herschel
Arlene Fickler
Stephen J. Mathes
Charles B. Blakinger
Ralph A. Jacobs
Richard M. Bernstein
Jill A. Douthett
R. Nicholas Gimbel
Eric B. Henson
Wayne W. Suojanen
Bebe H. Kivitz
Debra G. Staples
William R. Herman
David E. Landau
Denise D. Colliers
Sean P. Wajert
Elizabeth W. Fox

OF COUNSEL

Samuel W. Morris, Jr.
Arthur R. Littleton

SENIOR ATTORNEYS

Lisa M. Salazar
Lloyd A. Gelwan

(See Next Column)

HOYLE, MORRIS & KERR—*Continued*

ASSOCIATES

Ellen M. Briggs
Mark H. Fisher
Marisa P. Marcin
Joseph A. Eagan, Jr.
Peter Konolige
R. David Walk, Jr.
Laurie Gottlieb
Robert J. Dougher
Michael T. Starczewski
Thomas M. Glavin
Jan Fink Call
Mary K. Miluski
Nancy Stuart
Shelly L. Urban
Barbara Jane Subkow
Andrew S. Abramson
Mark F. Bernstein
Patricia A. Brooks
Barbara Shelley Magers
Joann M. Lytle
George Stephen Bobnak
Andrew R. Gaddes
Stacey J. Sinclair
Kevin J. Kotch
Kevin A. Marks
Lauren S. Kellner
Caroline M. Kurz

For full biographical listings, see the Martindale-Hubbell Law Directory

ROGER A. JOHNSEN (AV)

50th Floor, 1650 Market Street, 19103
Telephone: 215-561-3400
Fax: 215-851-9759

Reference: Constitution Bank.

For full biographical listings, see the Martindale-Hubbell Law Directory

KLEHR, HARRISON, HARVEY, BRANZBURG & ELLERS (AV)

1401 Walnut Street, 19102
Telephone: 215-568-6060
Fax: 215-568-6603
Cherry Hill, New Jersey Office: Colwick-Suite 200, 51 Haddonfield Road.
Telephone: 609-486-7900.
Fax: 609-486-4875.
Allentown, Pennsylvania Office: Roma Corporate Center, Suite 501, 1605 North Cedar Crest Boulevard.
Telephone: 215-432-1803.
Fax: 215-433-4031.
Wilmington, Delaware Office: 222 Delaware Avenue, Suite 1101.
Telephone: 302-426-1189.
Fax: 302-426-9193.

MEMBERS OF FIRM

Edward S. Ellers
Morton R. Branzburg
William A. Harvey
Donald M. Harrison
Leonard M. Klehr
Lawrence J. Arem
Robert C. Seiger, Jr.
Joan R. Sheak (Resident, Allentown Office)
Rona J. Rosen
Rosetta B. Packer
Mark L. Alderman
John Spelman
Stephen T. Burdumy
Richard S. Roisman
Stuart K. Askot
Alan M. Rosen
Carol Ann Slocum (Resident, Cherry Hill, New Jersey Office)
William R. Thompson
Gary W. Levi (Resident, Cherry Hill, New Jersey Office)
Matthew H. Kamens
M. Norman Goldberger
Jason M. Shargel
Michael C. Forman
Jeffrey Kurtzman
Brian J. Sisko
Mark S. Kenney
Michael K. Coran
Jill E. Jachera
Francis M. Correll, Jr.
David J. Margules (Resident, Wilmington, Delaware Office)

OF COUNSEL

Arnold E. Cohen

ASSOCIATES

Marcy Newman Hart
Douglas F. Schleicher
John J. Winter
Wayne D. Bloch
Keith W. Kaplan
Paul G. Nofer
Stewart Paley
Gary A. Deutsch (Resident, Cherry Hill, New Jersey Office)
Abbe F. Fletman
Kevin W. Mahoney
Steven G. Winters
Denise M. Day
John Keenan Fiorillo
Nancy J. Flickstein (Resident, Cherry Hill, New Jersey Office)
Benjamin D. Jogodnik
Barry J. Siegel
Marjorie Ann Thomas
Richard M. Beck
Michael J. Cordone
Joseph G. Gibbons
Todd L. Silverberg
Frederick J. Fisher
Stephen P. Lieske
Joshua R. Slavitt
Mindy Friedman
Peter J. Norman
Gerald F. Stahlecker, III
Francis A. Carchio (Resident, Allentown, Pennsylvania Office)
Jeffrey H. Cohen
Livingstone J. Johnson
William W. Matthews, III
Daniel J. O'Rourke
Shahan G. Teberian
Nina L. Cohen
David S. Eagle (Not admitted in PA)
Richard Alan Bendit
Malcolm T. Brown

LEGAL SUPPORT PERSONNEL

Brian K. Ehmann
Margaret S. Fallon

For full biographical listings, see the Martindale-Hubbell Law Directory

KLEINBARD, BELL & BRECKER (AV)

Suite 700, 1900 Market Street, 19103
Telephone: 215-568-2000
Telecopier: 215-568-0140
TWX: 710-670-1345 KLEINBELBR
Cherry Hill, New Jersey Office: Building B, 102 Browning Lane, 08003.
Telephone: 609-783-4448.

Joseph S. Kleinbard (1905-1994)

MEMBERS OF FIRM

Arthur S. Keyser
Paul E. Bomze
Murray I. Blackman
Howard N. Greenberg
Fred D. Furman
Howard J. Davis
Steven R. Waxman
Imogene E. Hughes
John P. Hickey
Kevin M. McKenna

ASSOCIATES

Jay R. Goldstein
Ralph J. Mauro
Thomas H. Speranza

COUNSEL

Joseph Bell
Robert John Brecker

For full biographical listings, see the Martindale-Hubbell Law Directory

KLETT LIEBER ROONEY & SCHORLING, A PROFESSIONAL CORPORATION (AV)

28th Floor, One Logan Square, 19103
Telephone: 215-567-7500
FAX: 215-567-2737
Pittsburgh, Pennsylvania Office: 40th Floor, One Oxford Centre, 15219.
Telephone: 412-392-2000.
Harrisburg, Pennsylvania Office: 240 North third Street, Suite 600,
Telephone: 717-231-7700.
Fax: 717-231-7712.

SHAREHOLDERS

Alan K. Cotler
Thomas S. Giotto
Jan Z. Krasnowiecki
William H. Schorling
William A. K. Titelman
Joan A. Yue

ASSOCIATES

LB Kregenow

For full biographical listings, see the Martindale-Hubbell Law Directory

KRUSEN EVANS & BYRNE (AV)

Suite 1100, The Curtis Center, 601 Walnut Street, 19106-3393
Telephone: 215-923-4400
Cable Address: "Kesel"
Telex: 83-4201
Telecopier: 215-925-0218
Westmont, New Jersey Office: Sentry Office Plaza, 216 Haddon Avenue, Suite 500, 08108-2813.
Telephone: 609-858-3444.
Telecopier: 609-858-6707.

MEMBERS OF FIRM

Leslie C. Krusen (1930-1987)
Rowland C. Evans (1930-1978)
Thomas E. Byrne (1942-1990)
James F. Young
Joseph A. Barone
E. Alfred Smith
Thomas A. Bell
A. Robert Degen
James A. Yulman
Peter Hansen Bach (Resident, Westmont, New Jersey Office)
Robert S. Forster, Jr.
William C. Miller
Mary Elisa Reeves
Sandra L. Knapp

OF COUNSEL

Eugene R. Lippman
Quentin C. Sturm, Jr.

ASSOCIATES

Donna L. Adelsberger
Gabriel Dino Cieri
Yolanda A. Konopacka
Diana L. Moro-Bishop
Robert M. Kline
Susan J. Wiener
June A. Taima (Not admitted in PA)

For full biographical listings, see the Martindale-Hubbell Law Directory

LABRUM AND DOAK (AV)

Suite 2900, 1818 Market Street, 19103-3629
Telephone: 215-561-4400
Telecopier: 215-587-5350
Norristown, Pennsylvania Office: One Montgomery Plaza, Suite 700.
Telephone: 610-277-7997.
Telecopier: 610-277-2852.
Bethlehem, Pennsylvania Office: 561 East Market Street, P.O. Box 1306.
Telephone: 610-865-2644.
Telecopier: 610-865-2713.
New York, N.Y. Office: 17 Battery Place.
Telephone: 212-809-7870.
Telecopier: 212-785-9279.
Woodbury, New Jersey Office: 66 Euclid Street, P.O. Box 836.
Telephone: 609-845-8855.
Telecopier: 609-848-2694.

(See Next Column)

LaBrum and Doak, *Philadelphia—Continued*

MEMBERS OF FIRM

J. Harry LaBrum (1927-1970)
James B. Doak (1935-1975)
Daniel J. Ryan
Perry S. Bechtle
John L. White (Not admitted in PA; Resident, Woodbury, New Jersey Office)
John D. Lucey, Jr.
Merle A. Wolfson
Harry F. Brennan
Edwin F. McCoy
Robert J. Stern
Robert F. Blanck (Resident, Norristown, Pennsylvania Office)
Stephen J. Springer
Zachary R. Estrin
Kean K. McDonald
Thomas P. Grace
Robertson B. Taylor, Resident, Bethlehem, Pennsylvania Office)
Michael H. Krekstein
Jonathan D. Herbst
John E. Salmon
Gerard Bruderle (Resident, Norristown Office)
John F. Ledwith
Peter J. Neeson
Ronald J. Uzdavinis (Not admitted in PA; Resident, Woodbury, New Jersey Office)
James D. Hilly
James O. Hausch
James M. Neeley
Barbara L. Hollenbach (Resident, Bethlehem Office)
R. Michael Carr (Resident, Bethlehem Office)
Samuel J. Pace, Jr.
William J. McKee (Resident, Norristown, Pennsylvania Office)
Michael G. Brennan (Resident, Woodbury, New Jersey Office)
David J. Parsells
Paul M. Silver
Carl R. Fogelberg (Not admitted in PA; Resident Partner, New York, New York Office)
J. Stephen Kreglow (Resident, Bethlehem Office)
Douglas J. Kent
Patrick R. Vitullo
Scott H. Mustin
Leslie Martinelli Cyr
Mary M. Jacobs
Jan M. Ritchie
John H. Osorio (Not admitted in PA; Resident, Woodbury, New Jersey Office)
Thomas C. Kaczka (Resident, Woodbury, New Jersey Office)

ASSOCIATES

Michael D. Dankanich (Resident, Woodbury, New Jersey Office)
Phillip J. Meyer
Steven J. Blumenthal (Resident, Woodbury, New Jersey Office)
Laurie Z. Lane
Jacqueline M. Carolan
Karen M. Ashdale
Maureen A. Jordan (Resident, Bethlehem Office)
Jill R. Snyder (Resident, Bethlehem Office)
Clarissa Greenman Raspanti
Jonathan J. Greystone
Sally J. Garber
Michelle Hoffmann Young
John J. Daly
John P. Cookson (Not admitted in PA; Resident, New York, New York Office)
Robert M. Stroh
Jeffrey D. Hutton
Joseph J. Urban
Stewart R. Singer
Randy C. Greene
Bonnie Dougherty Anapol
Mitchell S. Berger
Laura J. Herzog (Resident, Bethlehem Office)
Eileen Warner Strulson (Not admitted in PA; Resident, Woodbury, New Jersey Office)
John R. Brown
Kenneth H. Kell (Resident, Woodbury, New Jersey Office)
Patrick J. Moran (Resident, Norristown, Pennsylvania Office)
Patrick J. Gibbons (Resident, Norristown, Pennsylvania Office)
Susan Silverman Riechelson
John P. Dragani
William D. Longo (Resident, Norristown, Pennsylvania Office)
Steven E. Hoffman (Resident, Bethlehem, Pennsylvania Office)
J. Mark Pecci, II
Teresa Gerlock Hanni (Resident, Woodbury, New Jersey Office)
Cynthia M. Long
Helene L. Parise
Mary Elizabeth Bogan
Craig A. Styer
Pamela M. Tobin
Gregory H. Melick (Resident, Woodbury, New Jersey Office)
Raymond M. LaSalle (Resident, Woodbury, New Jersey Office)
Sarannah L. McMurtry (Resident, Woodbury, New Jersey Office)
Joseph L. Turchi
Michelle T. Wirtner
Sandra M. Freney
Peter A. Callahan (Resident, Norristown, Pennsylvania Office)
Lisa J. Kandel
Gregg L. Zeff (Resident, Woodbury, New Jersey Office)
Lynne G. Secunda
Michael T. McDonnell, III
Sally Ann Farrell
Geoffrey H. Baskerville
Doreen L. Smith (Resident, Bethlehem, Pennsylvania Office)
Joseph A. Ricchezza
David R. White, Jr.
Harry T. Lamb
Robert J. Birch
A. Grant Phelan
Anna Belle Rokeach Cedar
Jacqueline S. Ware
Lisa C. Fogel
John W. Dornberger
Maria B. Mazzeo
Audrey P. Cohen
Tracy L. Burnley (Resident, Woodbury, New Jersey Office)
Steven Antonelli (Resident, Woodbury, New Jersey Office)
Denise Lynn Werner (Resident, Woodbury, New Jersey Office)
Cari N. Kohn
Kevin M. Bothwell (Resident, Woodbury, New Jersey Office)

(See Next Column)

COUNSEL

I. Jerome Stern
K. Charles Gudenas
Joseph F. Keener, Jr. (Resident, Norristown Office)
Jane A. Kenney
Beverly J. Doneker (Resident, Bethlehem, Pennsylvania Office)
Peter F. Darling (Resident, Bethlehem, Pennsylvania Office)
Danielle DiNenna

For full biographical listings, see the Martindale-Hubbell Law Directory

Alfred Marroletti and Associates (AV)

The Graham Building-Suite 1504, One Penn Square West 30 S. 15th Street, 19102
Telephone: 215-563-0400

ASSOCIATES

Jacob N. Snyder
Joseph A. Marroletti

For full biographical listings, see the Martindale-Hubbell Law Directory

Marshall, Dennehey, Warner, Coleman and Goggin (AV)

1845 Walnut Street, 19103-4717
Telephone: 215-575-2600
Cable Address: "Marshall"
Telecopier: 215-575-0856; 575-0857; 575-0858; 575-0859; 575-0860; 575-0861
Allentown Pennsylvania Office: 640 Hamilton Mall.
Telephone: 215-776-7500.
Telecopier: 215-776-7994.
Doylestown, Pennsylvania Office: Suite 300, 20 East Court Street.
Telephone: 215-348-1611.
Telecopier: 215-348-5439.
Harrisburg, Pennsylvania Office: 100 Pine Street, Suite 400.
Telephone: 717-232-1022.
Telecopier: 717-232-1849.
Lancaster, Pennsylvania Office: Cipher Building, Second Floor, 36 East King Street.
Telephone: 717-399-1845.
Telecopier: 717-399-1853.
Media, Pennsylvania Office: 200 East State Street.
Telephone: 215-892-8700.
Telecopier: 215-892-8730.
Norristown, Pennsylvania Office: Suite 1002, One Montgomery Plaza.
Telephone: 215-292-4440.
Telecopier: 215-292-0410.
Pittsburgh, Pennsylvania Office: 600 Grant Street, USX Tower, Suite 2900.
Telephone: 412-394-4090.
Telecopier: 412-394-4095.
Scranton, Pennsylvania Office: Scranton Electric Building, 507 Linden Street, Suite 800.
Telephone: 717-342-1999.
Telecopier: 717-342-4999.
West Chester, Pennsylvania Office: The Atrium Building, 17 West Gay Street.
Telephone: 215-431-4100.
Telecopier: 215-431-4522.
Williamsport, Pennsylvania Office: One Executive Plaza, 330 Pine Street.
Telephone: 717-326-5507.
Fax: 717-326-5507.
Marlton, New Jersey Office: Suite 304, Three Greentree Centre.
Telephone: 609-985-3900.
Telecopier: 609-985-3934.
Roseland, New Jersey Office: 5 Becker Farm Road, 280 Corporate Center.
Telephone: 201-994-0303.
Telecopier: 201994-1965.

MEMBERS OF FIRM

LISTED ALPHABETICALLY

Paul A. Bechtel, Jr.
Louis Bell
Ralph P. Bocchino
Thomas R. Bond
Wendy Johnston Bracaglia
Paul R. Brady, III
Thomas A. Brophy (Resident, Norristown Office)
Edward R. Carpenter, Jr.
John J. Coffey
Robert J. Coleman
Kevin J. Connors
Charles W. Craven
Michael P. Creedon
Joseph W. Cunningham (Resident, Doylestown Office)
Barbara A. DeAntonio (Resident, Allentown Office)
Thomas C. DeLorenzo
Lisa D. Eldridge
Thomas K. Ellixson (Resident, Norristown Office)
Joseph L. Feliciani (Resident, Allentown Office)
Dominick Fiorello (Resident, Marlton, New Jersey Office)
T. Kevin FitzPatrick (Resident, Norristown Office)
William L. Foley, Jr. (Resident, West Chester Office)
M. Scott Gemberling (Resident, Media and West Chester Offices)
Robert St. Leger Goggin
Mitchell I. Golding
Richard L. Goldstein (Resident, Marlton, New Jersey Office)
Robert G. Hanna, Jr. (Resident, Harrisburg Office)
P. Brennan Hart (Resident, Pittsburgh Office)
Keith D. Heinold
Hiliary H. Holloway
Niki T. Ingram
Audrey L. Jacobsen
John D. Kearney
Richard A. Kraemer
Kathleen M. Kramer

(See Next Column)

MARSHALL, DENNEHEY, WARNER, COLEMAN AND GOGGIN—*Continued*

MEMBERS OF FIRM
LISTED ALPHABETICALLY (Continued)

Michael J. McCadden
Edward J. McGinn, Jr.
Ralph A. Michetti (Resident, Doylestown Office)
Peter S. Miller
R. Bruce Morrison
John P. Penders
James E. Pocius (Resident, Scranton Office)
Vincent P. Reilly
John R. Riddell (Resident, Media Office)
Daniel J. Ryan, Jr.
Joseph J. Santarone, Jr. (Resident, Norristown Office)
Robert A. Seiferth (Resident, Williamsport Office)
Thomas E. Sennett
Daniel J. Sherry
Harry A. Short, Jr.
Paul A. Snyder (Resident, Marlton, New Jersey Office)
Lori Olitsky Strauss
Paul V. Tatlow
Steven C. Tolliver
Philip B. Toran
John S. Tucci, Jr.
Joseph McCabe Walker (Resident, Doylestown Office)
John R. Warner (Resident, Norristown Office)
Eric A. Weiss
Kimberley J. Woodie

ASSOCIATES
LISTED ALPHABETICALLY

Laura Lubow Altman
Madeline S. Baio
Jonathan F. Ball
William Lance Banton, Jr.
Thomas B. Bate, Jr. (Resident, Marlton, New Jersey Office)
Lawrence B. Berg (Not admitted in PA; Resident, Marlton, New Jersey Office)
Marcia E. Berry (Resident, Norristown Office)
Gary L. Black (Resident, Williamsport Office)
Sean Robert Blake (Resident, Norristown Office)
Christine Mooney Brenner
Jeffrey H. Browndorf (Resident, Norristown Office)
Candace Calhoun (Resident, Pittsburgh Office)
Jacqueline H. Canter
Joseph M. Caputo (Resident, Scranton Office)
Ross A. Carrozza (Resident, Scranton Office)
Jeffrey J. Chomko (Resident, Doylestown Office)
Maureen E. Cleary
James J. Comitale (Resident, Harrisburg Office)
Cathy Marie Cosgrove
Brian C. Darreff (Resident, Marlton, New Jersey Office)
Barbara J. Davis (Resident, Marlton, New Jersey Office)
Mary Gene McLaughlin Davis (Resident, Westchester Office)
Andrew W. Davitt
Steve Woodward Day, Jr. (Resident, Doylestown Office)
Daniel V. DiLoretto
John F. Doherty (Resident, Pittsburgh Office)
Christopher E. Dougherty (Resident, Norristown Office)
Jillian Zacks Duhl
Angela L. Dumm
Scott G. Dunlop (Resident, Pittsburgh Office)
Howard P. Dwoskin
Joseph A. Dych (Resident, Media Office)
Cheryl L. Esposito (Resident, Pittsburgh Office)
Valerie S. Faeth (Resident, Pittsburgh Office)
Kenneth S. Fair
Mary T. Fox
Derek T. Frickey
Elizabeth M. Gallagher (Resident, Marlton, New Jersey Office)
Matthew F. Golden (Resident, Williamsport Office)
John P. Gonzales (Resident, Norristown Office)
James F. Graham
Daniel A. Griffith (Resident, Marlton, New Jersey Office)
Suzanne H. Gross
Mark John Gulasarian (Resident, West Chester Office)
Jeffrey Hark (Resident, Marlton, New Jersey Office)
Daniel J. Hart
John N. Hernick
Michelle Tiger Heyman
John P. Hickey
Robert J. Hoffman
Craig S. Hudson
Walter J. Klekotka (Resident, Marlton, New Jersey Office)
Brian J. Kredo
Lauren Wiatrak Lavelle (Not admitted in PA; Resident, Roseland, New Jersey)
Paul G. Lees (Resident, Allentown Office)
Mary Bernadette Lipinski
Kevin J. Mangan
Howard Mankoff (Not admitted in PA; Resident, Roseland, New Jersey Office)
Joseph A. Manning (Resident, Roseland, New Jersey Office)
Victoria S. Maranzini
Louis M. Masucci, Jr. (Not admitted in PA)
Anne Matchulet
Deborah A. Mattei (Resident, Allentown Office)
Mary N. McCann
Thierry L. McEldowney
Kathleen S. McGrath (Resident, Norristown Office)
Kevin M. McKeon (Resident, Marlton, New Jersey Office)
Timothy J. McMahon (Resident, Harrisburg Office)
Jeffrey W. Meehan
Michelle Leigh Morgan (Resident, Norristown Office)
Lynne Nina Nahmani (Resident, Norristown Office)
Norman D. Namey (Resident, Scranton Office)
M. Elizabeth Naughton (Resident, Media Office)
Karen S. Norris
Renee Nunley (Resident, Marlton, New Jersey Office)
Thomas Joseph O'Malley
Gail L. O'Neal (Resident, Harrisburg Office)
Demetrius J. Parrish, Jr.
James F. Pearn, Jr.
Juliana Marie Petito
Rosemary M. Petrantoni (Resident, Pittsburgh Office)
Michele R. Punturi
Conrad J. J. Radcliffe
Bradley D. Remick
William H. Resch, Jr.
Lynn F. Reutelhuber (Resident, Harrisburg Office)
Mark T. Riley (Resident, Media Office)
Robin M. Romano
Jay S. Rothman

(*See Next Column*)

ASSOCIATES
LISTED ALPHABETICALLY (Continued)

David F. Ryan (Resident, Pittsburgh Office)
Joseph D. Sams (Resident, Marlton, New Jersey Office)
Mary C. Schemery (Resident, Williamsport Office)
Kathleen A. Smith
Timothy R. Smith (Resident, Pittsburgh Office)
Tyler Smith (Resident, Pittsburgh Office)
Robin B. Snyder (Resident, Scranton Office)
Mark B. Spivak (Resident, Marlton, New Jersey Office)
James W. Stevens
Walter H. Swayze, III
L. Rostaing Tharaud
Joseph L. Vender (Resident, Scranton Office)
Louise Ann Watson (Resident, Marlton, New Jersey Office)
Melody C. Watts
Elizabeth A. Weill
Elizabeth Weismann-Lorry (Resident, Media Office)
Leo T. White
Peter R. White, Jr. (Resident, Williamsport Office)
Francis X. Wickersham (Resident, Norristown Office)
Stacy L. Wilson (Resident, Lancaster Office)
Michael Blaine Wolfe (Resident, Harrisburg Office)
Michael J. Zicolello (Resident, Williamsport Office)

RETIRED PARTNERS
LISTED ALPHABETICALLY

Gerald A. Dennehey
Francis E. Marshall

For full biographical listings, see the Martindale-Hubbell Law Directory

MATTIONI, MATTIONI & MATTIONI, LTD. (AV)

399 Market Street, 2nd Floor, 19106
Telephone: 215-629-1600
Cable Address: "Mattioni"
TWX: 710-670-1373
Fax: 215-923-2 227
Westmont, New Jersey Office: Suite 502 Sentry Office Plaza, 216 Haddon Avenue, 08108.
Telephone: 609-772-0098.

Dante Mattioni
Faustino Mattioni
John Mattioni
Blasco Mattioni *
Eugene Mattioni
Kenneth M. Giannantonio
Francis X. Kelly
George R. Zacharkow
Andrew H. Quinn
Eva Helena Bleich
Robert W. Weidner, Jr.
Scott J. Schwarz
Stephen M. Martin
Robert R. Hyde
Bruce A. O'Neill
John J. Sellinger
Stephen J. Galati
Anthony Granato
Kristi L. Treadway
Philip J. Ford
Joseph F. Bouvier
Michael Mattioni
John E. Minihan
Alan Mattioni
Louis J. Apoldo
Joseph P. Corcoran III
Scott William Barton
Heather A. Cicalese
Frank Carano *

LEGAL SUPPORT PERSONNEL
PARALEGALS

Rosaria Tesauro
Carmela Valeno
Tracey L. Smith
Andrea L. D'Alessandro
Linda A. Morris
Karen L. Knauss

*Counsel to the Firm

For full biographical listings, see the Martindale-Hubbell Law Directory

MESIROV GELMAN JAFFE CRAMER & JAMIESON (AV)

1735 Market Street, 19103
Telephone: 215-994-1000
FAX: 215-994-1111
Haddonfield, New Jersey Office: 44 Tanner Street, P.O. Box 183.
Telephone: 609-795-4988.

Frank H. Gelman (1960-1985)
Josef Jaffe (1962-1992)
Marvin Joseph Levin (1960-1968)
Julius H. Tolson (1984-1987)

MEMBERS OF FIRM

Gina M. Ameci
Gary L. Azorsky
Robert B. Bodzin
Arthur N. Brandolph
Jeffrey Cooper
Marc S. Cornblatt
Anthony E. Creato, Sr.
Allan M. Dabrow
Albert S. Dandridge, III
Walter B. Ferst
Lois R. Fogg
Barry H. Frank
Kenneth R. Gilberg
Jeremy E. Goldstein
Edward Greer
Howard I. Grossman
Paul L. Jaffe
Richard P. Jaffe
D. Donald Jamieson
Bernard B. Kolodner
Robert P. Krauss
John J. Lamb
Joseph C. Lepanto
Robert H. Malis
Richard M. Meltzer
Arthur J. Momjian
Bradley K. Moss
Gerald Pomerantz
Carl S. Primavera
Mark R. Rosen
Kenneth I. Rosenberg
Allan B. Schneirov
Harvey N. Shapiro
Jules Silk
Anthony J. Watkins
David H. Wice
Steven R. Williams

(*See Next Column*)

MESIROV GELMAN JAFFE CRAMER & JAMIESON, *Philadelphia—Continued*

OF COUNSEL

Harold Cramer
Marvin Garfinkel
Martin M. Krimsky
Leon I. Mesirov

SPECIAL COUNSEL

Kevin J. Carey
Ronald R. Donatucci
Don P. Foster
Philip R. Voluck
Fredric B. Weinstein

ASSOCIATES

Barbara J. Backman
Michael A. Brown
Bradford Merrill Brush
Charles S. Cooper
Patricia Gail Cramer
Joseph J. Devine
Mitchell Feigenbaum
Beth Stern Fleming
Charles Edward (Ted) Galfand
Jeffrey O. Greenfield
Jeffrey D. Hofferman
Jodi B. Isenberg
Alex Katz
M. Sean Maravich
Edward W. Millstein
Debra N. Nathanson
Steven E. Ostrow
Molly Peckman
Karen M. Reabuck
Jonathan Mark Rome
Lisa A. Watkins

For full biographical listings, see the Martindale-Hubbell Law Directory

MONTGOMERY, MCCRACKEN, WALKER & RHOADS (AV)

20th Floor Three Parkway, 19102
Telephone: 215-665-7200
Facsimile: 215-636-9373
Telex: 62761536
Cable: "Romock"
Cherry Hill, New Jersey Office: 1010 Kings Highway South.
Telephone: 609-429-1010.
Facsimile: 609-429-3432.

MEMBERS OF FIRM

Stephen W. Armstrong
Larry R. Barron
Timothy J. Bergère
Bruce H. Bikin
Ralph W. Brenner
C. Suzanne Buechner
Carter R. Buller
Leonard A. Busby
Baldo M. Carnecchia, Jr.
John E. Caruso
Charles B. Casper
Robert Gordon Chambers
Christopher Scott D'Angelo
Doreen S. Davis
Frank S. Deming
William F. Drake, Jr.
Gary M. Edelson
Edward T. Ellis
S. Jonathan Emerson
John S. Estey
H. Thomas Felix, II
Gregory J. Fox
John W. Frazier, IV
Karl A. Fritton
John Francis Gough
David L. Grove
Suzanne M. Hanlon
Mervin J. Hartman
Kenneth M. Jarin
Donald W. Kramer
Susan P. LeGros
Jeffrey R. Lerman
Stephen A. Madva
David H. Marion
Samuel Mason
Michael D. Matteo (Managing Partner, Resident, Cherry Hill, New Jersey Office)
Frances A. McElhill
Jeremy D. Mishkin
Arthur H. Moss
Francis Patrick Newell
Kathleen O'Brien
Louis A. Petroni (Resident, Cherry Hill, New Jersey Office)
Richard G. Placey
Mary F. Platt
Mitchell J. Rabil (Resident, Cherry Hill, New Jersey Office)
Natalie D. Ramsey
Elizabeth A. Read
Patrick T. Ryan
Harry Carl Schaub
Richard L. Scheff
Howard D. Scher
David Shechtman
Virginia P. Sikes
Joseph T. Stapleton
Jennifer A. Stiller
Larry L. Turner
Anthony F. Visco, Jr.
Stephen L. Volpicelli
James A. Willhite, Jr.
John C. Wright, Jr.
Craig E. Ziegler

OF COUNSEL

Walter L. Bartholomew, Jr.
Joseph K. Gordon
Alan Reeve Hunt
Richard S. Hyland (Resident, Cherry Hill, New Jersey Office)
Arthur Gregg Jackson
Daniel W. Myers, 2nd (Resident, Cherry Hill, New Jersey Office)
Alexander N. Rubin, Jr.
Albert S. Shaw, Jr.

ASSOCIATES

Arlene J. Angelo
Rosemary L. Auth
Howard J. Bashman
Arline L. Bayó-Santiago
Marianne Bechtle
Mariellen Bello
Steven E. Bizar
Martin W. Bond
Peter Breslauer
D. Craig Callaghan
Ramiro M. Carbonell (Resident, Cherry Hill, New Jersey Office)
Julie Hofmann Chelius
Frank A. Chernak
Ralph H. Colflesh, Jr.
Floyd W. Cotlar
Stephan L. Cutler
John A. Di Nome
Richard M. Donaldson
John Ehmann
James J. Eisenhower, III
Mary Theresa Enyart
Michael Epstein
Charles A. Ercole
Patrick J. Farris
Sharon O'Neill Finnegan
Catherine H. Gillespie
Geoffrey P. Gilmore
Elizabeth C. Gutman

(See Next Column)

ASSOCIATES (Continued)

Patrick J. Harvey
Caridad Diego Hopkins
Alycia Horn
Kimberly H. Humes
Thomas F. Hurley
Ronald E. Hurst
Michael D. Jones
Sally Ackerman King
Gregory S. Kurey
Eileen Lampe
David D. Langfitt
Patricia J. Larson
Eric Lechtzin
John J. Levy (Resident, Cherry Hill, New Jersey Office)
Maureen D. Luke
David J. MacMain
Cynthia B. MacQueen
Kenneth Maiman
Steven Maniloff
Nathalie Martin
Gerard M. McCabe
John P. McLaughlin
Francis V. Mc Namara, III
Barbara A. McNeil
Mariette J. Mooyman
Ronald I. Nagel
Mary Elizabeth Nagy
Douglas L. Overtoom
Catherine E. Pappas
Thomas K. Pasch
Stephen G. Rhoads
Susan E. Rippey
Brad A. Rubens
Joseph C. Rudolf
Joanne Semeister
Richard M. Simins
Larissa Renshaw Whitman
David Zalesne
Geraldine D. Zidow

NEW JERSEY OFFICE
RESIDENT PARTNERS

Michael D. Matteo
Louis A. Petroni
Mitchell J. Rabil

OF COUNSEL

Richard S. Hyland
Daniel W. Myers, 2nd

RESIDENT ASSOCIATES

Ramiro M. Carbonell
John J. Levy

For full biographical listings, see the Martindale-Hubbell Law Directory

OBERMAYER, REBMANN, MAXWELL & HIPPEL (AV)

14th Floor, Packard Building, 19102-2688
Telephone: 215-665-3000
Cable Address: "Edmer"
FAX: 215-569-1586
Haddonfield, New Jersey Office: Two Kings Highway West.
Telephone: 609-795-3300, TWX 49609730
Harrisburg, Pennsylvania Office: 204 State Street.
Telephone: 717-234-9730.

OF COUNSEL

Frank E. Hahn, Jr.
Jonathan H. Newman
William G. Schwartz

MEMBERS OF FIRM

Franklin S. Edmonds (1886-1945)
Leon J. Obermayer (1886-1984)
G. Ruhland Rebmann, Jr. (1898-1983)
David F. Maxwell (1900-1985)
John F. E. Hippel (1901-1984)
George B. Clothier (1905-1992)
H. Clayton Louderback (1913-1980)
William J. Fuchs (1921-1979)
Richard W. Thorington (1898-1994)
Martin Weinberg
Paul C. Heintz
Peter M. Breitling
Hugh Charles Sutherland
Robert I. Whitelaw
Robert A. MacDonnell
E. Parry Warner
Jeffrey B. Rotwitt
James M. Penny, Jr.
Gregory D. Saputelli (Resident Managing Partner, Haddonfield, New Jersey Office)
Kenneth L. Oliver, Jr.
Thorley C. Mills, Jr.
John J. Ehlinger, Jr.
Warren W. Ayres
Mark A. Lublin
Charles M. Golden
James W. Baumbach
Thomas A. Leonard
Stephen D. Schrier (Resident, Haddonfield, New Jersey Office)
Louis B. Kupperman
Joseph J. McGovern
Joseph P. Dougher
Julius M. Steiner
Paul S. Diamond
Lawrence J. Tabas
Ann G. Verber
Jeffrey S. Batoff
W. Atlee Davis, III
Scott E. Denman
Paul N. Allen
Victor A. Young
Anastasius Efstratiades
Cathleen Curran Myers
Jerald S. Batoff
Charles S. K. Scudder
Daniel P. Finegan
William J. Leonard
John Elliot Ryan
J. Eric Rathburn
Ruth Rudbarg Wessel
Marjorie H. Gordon

ASSOCIATES

Allen Weinberg
Michael C. Richman
Larry Besnoff
Michael P. Weinstein
Claudia M. Becker
Richard P. Limburg
Ronnie L. Bloom
Jacqueline T. Shulman
Edmond M. George
Elizabeth D. Shevlin
James R. Thompson (Resident, Haddonfield, New Jersey Office)
Barbara Weinberg
Nicholas Poduslenko
Elizabeth A. Lloyd
Steven A. Haber
Roger P. Cameron
John F. Reilly
Kimberly D'Arrigo Sutton (Resident, Haddonfield, New Jersey Office)
Denise Hopkins Canuso
John V. O'Hara
Clare M. Diemer
D. Madelaine Miller

(See Next Column)

OBERMAYER, REBMANN, MAXWELL & HIPPEL—*Continued*

ASSOCIATES (Continued)

Susan Sygenda
John D. Benson
Catherine C. Pyune
Kirsten Weltge
Staci B. Walkes
Arnold W. Winter
Alan W. Lesso
David C. Shuter
Loran Beth Wasserstrom
Lori A. Andreosky (Resident, Haddonfield, New Jersey Office)
Cynthia A. Tedeschi (Resident, Haddonfield, New Jersey Office)
Michael B. Dubin
Stephen W.W. Ching, Jr.
Steven Philip Steinberg
William K. Pelosi
Peter J. Oberkircher
Jason Eric Reisman

For full biographical listings, see the Martindale-Hubbell Law Directory

OMINSKY, WELSH & STEINBERG, P.C. (AV)

1760 Market Street, 10th Floor, 19103-4129
Telephone: 215-568-4500
Fax: 215-751-9005
Bridgeport, Pennsylvania Office: 408 East Fourth Street.
Telephone: 215-270-9600.
FAX: 215-270-9990.

Albert Ominsky
Barney B. Welsh
Lennard B. Steinberg
David M. Giles
Joseph L. Messa, Jr.
Mark W. Tanner
Glenn F. Gilman

OF COUNSEL

Jack A. Meyerson
Joel I. Fishbein
Thomas W. Sheridan

PELINO & LENTZ, A PROFESSIONAL CORPORATION (AV)

32nd Floor, One Liberty Place, 19103-7393
Telephone: 215-665-1540
Fax: 215-665-1536

John W. Pelino
Martin R. Lentz
Steven J. Serling
Dennis A. Holtz
David A. Gradwohl
Barry E. Bressler
Richard W. Kessler
Salvatore M. DeBunda
James W. Patterson
Kenneth J. Levin
Jeanne Schubert Barnum
Howard A. Rosenthal
Victoria Page-Wooten
Gary D. Fry
Cristina G. Cavalieri
Scott H Schley
Edward L. Ciemniecki
Debra Csik Kern

Patrick J. Doran
John G. McCormick
James E. Miller
Michael S. Sherman

OF COUNSEL

Henry W. Maxmin (1914-1990)
Albert W. Schiffrin

For full biographical listings, see the Martindale-Hubbell Law Directory

PEPPER, HAMILTON & SCHEETZ (AV)

3000 Two Logan Square, Eighteenth and Arch Streets, 19103-2799
Telephone: 215-981-4000
Telecopy: 215-981-4750
Washington, D.C. Office: 1300 Nineteenth Street, N.W., 20036-1685.
Telephone: 202-828-1200.
Fax: 202-828-1665.
Detroit, Michigan Office: 100 Renaissance Center, 36th Floor, 48243-1157.
Telephone: 313-259-7110.
Fax: 313-259-7926.
Harrisburg, Pennsylvania Office: 200 One Keystone Plaza, North Front and Market Streets, P.O. Box 1181, 17108-1181.
Telephone: 717-255-1155.
Fax: 717-238-0575.
Berwyn, Pennsylvania Office: 1235 WestlakesDrive, Suite 400, 19312-2401.
Telephone: 610-640-7800.
Fax: 610-640-7835.
New York, New York Office: 450 Lexington Avenue, Suite 1600, 10017-3904.
Telephone: 212-878-3800.
Fax: 212-878-3835.
Wilmington, Delaware Office: 1201 Market Street, Suite 1401, P.O. Box 1709, 19899-1709.
Telephone: 302-571-6555.
Fax: 302-656-8865.
Westmont, New Jersey Office: Sentry Office Plaza, Suite 321, 216 Haddon Avenue, 08108-2811.
Telephone: 609-869-9555.
Fax: 609-869-9595.
London, England Office: City Tower, 40 Basinghall Street, EC2V 5DE.
Telephone: 011-44-71-628-1122.
Fax: 011-44-71-628-6010.
Moscow, Russia Office: 19-27 Grokholsky Pereulok, 129010.
Telephone: 011-7-095-280-4493.
Fax: 011-7-095-280-5518.

(See Next Column)

PARTNERS

Barbara W. Mather (Executive Partner)
Jon A. Baughman (Chairman, Firm Executive Committee)
James L. Murray (Vice-Chairman, Firm Executive Committee)
William R. Klaus (Firm Co-Chairman)
Edward W. Madeira, Jr. (Firm Co-Chairman)
Bennett L. Aaron
Barry M. Abelson (Member, Firm Executive Committee)
Matthew H. Adler
James M. Beck
Harold R. Berk
Norman B. Berlin
Charles R. Bruton
Mitchell E. Burack
Vincent V. Carissimi
Lawrence S. Coburn
Deborah Fuchs Cohen
Julia D. Corelli
Kenneth M. Cushman
Robert F. Cushman
Alfred J. D'Angelo, Jr.
L. Garrett Dutton, Jr.
James D. Epstein
Eleanor N. Ewing
Bruce W. Ficken
Richard W. Foltz, Jr.
David A. Franklin
Michael W. Freeland
Michael H. Friedman
Marc R. Garber
M. Duncan Grant
Nina M. Gussack
Joyce K. Hackenbrach
Anthony B. Haller
Robert S. Hawkins
Jeffery C. Hayes
Helen R. Haynes
Peter Hearn
Robert E. Heideck
Robert L. Hickok
Elam M. Hitchner, III
Susan Katz Hoffman
Franklin B. Holland
James D. Hollyday
John B. Huffaker
Lisa D. Kabnick
Philip J. Katauskas
Paul B. Kerrigan
William F. Kershner
Nicholas M. Kouletsis
Raymond A. Kresge
Robert D. Lane, Jr.
Francis J. Lawall
Philip H. Lebowitz
James R. Ledwith
Kenneth I. Levin
Murray S. Levin
Cary S. Levinson
Jeffrey P. Libson
Joseph L. Lincoln
A. John May, III
John W. McLamb, Jr.
J. Anthony Messina
J. Gregg Miller
Thomas J. O'Neill
Vincent J. Pentima
Lisa B. Petkun
Stephen S. Phillips
James J. Prendergast
Frank M. Rapoport
Michael H. Reed
David Richman
Andrew R. Rogoff
James D. Rosener
William A. Scari, Jr.
Ellen Kittredge Scott
Joseph J. Serritella
Laurence Z. Shiekman
James J. Sullivan, Jr.
Stephen J. Sundheim
Anthony Vale
Erik N. Videlock
Louis C. Washburn
Edward M. Watters, III
Robert J. Weinberg
Alfred H. Wilcox
Thomas E. Zemaitis
Kenneth H. Zucker

OF COUNSEL

Augustus S. Ballard
A. Michael Pratt
Richard C. Sorlien
Edmund B. Spaeth, Jr.
Anson W. H. Taylor, Jr.
Frederick C. Tecce

ASSOCIATES

Seth A. Abel (Not admitted in PA)
Samuel J.B. Angell
Carol S. Armen
Frederic A. Beckley
Noel C. Birle
J. Bradley Boericke
Kara M. Bruge-Holland
Michael A. Ceramella
Colleen F. Coonelly
Johanna L. Davis
Timothy E. DeMasi
Henry J. Dewerth-Jaffe (Not admitted in PA)
Thomas F. Doyle
Alicia E. Fenton
Bruce K. Fenton
L. Suzanne Forbis
Dori A. Fragin
Robert A. Friedel
Jill E. Garfinkle
Scott D. Godshall
Ari Goldberger
Cynthia Newsome Graham
Kurt F. Gwynne
T. Truxtun Hare
Charles E. Harris
Michael S. Hino
Joann Hyle
Lisa R. Jacobs
Andrew E. Kantra
Brian M. Katz
William G. Kiesling
James P. Kimmel, Jr.
Susan A. King
Julie L. Kitze
Steven R. Klammer
Aaron Krauss
James S. Lawlor
Susan K. Lessack
Robin L. Litwa
Maureen E. Lowry
M. Kelly Malone (Not admitted in PA)
Phyllis M. Mannix
Sean P. McDevitt
James W. McGarry
Doretta Massardo McGinnis
Anthony J. Merhige
Marian C. Miller
Brad A. Molotsky
Thomas J. Momjian
John P. Monaghan
Noreen Hibbard Onimus
Brian T. Ortelere
Frances P. Rayer
Sarah E. Ricks
Eric Jonathan Rothschild
John E. Royer, Jr.
Suzanne Ilene Schiller
Richard S. Schlegel
Karl F. Schmuck
Randi Engel Schnell (Not admitted in PA)
Kathleen A. Shea
Barbara T. Sicalides
Jessamyne M. Simon
Kathleen A. Stephenson
Jean Gallagher Stoyer
Karen McDonnell Suddath
Margaret A. Suender
Gerald B. Sullivan

(See Next Column)

PEPPER, HAMILTON & SCHEETZ, *Philadelphia—Continued*

ASSOCIATES (Continued)

Terri W. Teitelbaum
Cuyler H. Walker
Christopher F. Wright
David C. Ziccardi

For full biographical listings, see the Martindale-Hubbell Law Directory

RAWLE & HENDERSON (AV)

(Rawle Law Offices Founded 1783)
The Widener Building, One South Penn Square, 19107
Telephone: 215-575-4200
Cable Address: "Rawle" Philadelphia
Telex: 83-4286
Telecopier: 215-563-2583
Marlton, New Jersey Office: Suite 104, Ten Lake Center Executive Park, 401 Route 73 North.
Telephone: 609-596-4800.
Telecopier: 609-596-6164.

J. Grant McCabe
Henry C. Lucas, III
Carl D. Buchholz, III
Alan Greenberg
James C. Stroud
Patricia A. Mattern
Thomas P. Wagner
Michael Slotznick
Fred B. Buck
John H. McCarthy
Thomas A. Kuzmick
James J. Kozuch
Robert A. Klein

C. J. Lyford
David A. O'Brien
Lawrence D. Wright
Peter A. Lentini
Judith A. Schneider
Ann F. Kenney
Robert W. Thomas, Jr.
V.P. dePillis
JoAnne Eskin Sutkin
Michael P. Zipfel
Joseph J. Hamill, Jr.
Barbara H. Zurzolo
Lois DeAntonio
John P. Meyers
Lizabeth R. Brown
John T. Donovan
Timothy J. Duffy
Ann-Michele G. Higgins
Catherine Tanaka
Joshua Bachrach
Mark J. Dianno
Philip S. Goore
Wendy S. Laurento

For full biographical listings, see the Martindale-Hubbell Law Directory

REED SMITH SHAW & MCCLAY (AV)

2500 One Liberty Place, 19103-7301
Telephone: 215-851-8100
Cable Address: "Reedsmith Phl"
FAX: 215-851-1420
Pittsburgh, Pennsylvania Office: James H. Reed Building, Mellon Square, 435 Sixth Avenue, 15219-1886.
Telephone: 412-288-3131.
FAX: 412-288-3063.
Washington, D.C. Office: Ring Building, 1200 18th Street, N.W., 20036-2506.
Telephone: 202-457-6100.
FAX: 202-457-6133.
Harrisburg, Pennsylvania Office: 213 Market Street, 17101-2132.
Telephone: 717-234-5988.
McLean, Virginia Office: Suite 1100, 8251 Greensboro Drive, 22102-3844.
Telephone: 703-734-4600.
Princeton, New Jersey Office: 136 Main Street, 08540-5799.
Telephone: 609-987-0050.
FAX: 609-951-0824.

MEMBERS OF FIRM

David C. Auten
Robert L. Bast
Leonard A. Bernstein (Also at Princeton, New Jersey)
Michael L. Browne
Douglas Y. Christian
Carl E. Esser
Solomon Fisher
David S. Fortney
Richard H. Glanton
Michael P. Haney
Marilyn Heffley
Louis M. Heidelberger
Selwyn A. Horvitz
Ben Burke Howell
Wendi L. Kotzen
Lori Leigh Lasher
Ira S. Lefton
Norman M. Loev
Stephen M. Lyons, III
Thomas J. McGarrigle
Margery K. Miller
Robert A. Nicholas
Robert C. Podwil
Michael B. Pollack
John E. Quinn
S. William Richter
Michael T. Scott
Joseph M. Sedlack
Carolyn P. Short
John F. Smith, III
Andrew J. Trevelise
Christopher K. Walters
Bradford F. Whitman

COUNSEL

David W. Marston

ASSOCIATES

Deidre J. Attea
Donald P. Augustino
Barbara R. Binis
Lloyd C. Birnbaum
Suzanne M. Bohannon
Nina R. Booz
Christine C. Ciarrocchi
Jessica N. Cone
Tobey M. Daluz
Lisa G. DiPietro
Robert P. Frank
John W. Goldschmidt, Jr.

(See Next Column)

ASSOCIATES (Continued)

Kelley A. Grady
Suzanne M. Hecht
Don A. Innamorato
Martin H. Karo (Not admitted in PA)
Kenneth M. Kolaski
Bari Susan Krein
Gerard J. Lewis, Jr.
Theodore Marasciulo, Jr.
Luci Jankowski McClure
Barbara S. Mishkin
Philip W. Newcomer
Henry F. Reichner
J. Michael Russell
Ellen B. Seckar
Willard A. Stanback (Not admitted in PA)
Donna Travia
Peter J. Tucci
Maria Verducci-Florio (Not admitted in PA)
Michael J. Wilder
Kathleen V. Yurchak

For full biographical listings, see the Martindale-Hubbell Law Directory

SAUL, EWING, REMICK & SAUL (AV)

3800 Centre Square West, 19102
Telephone: 215-972-7777
Cable Address: "Bidsal"
TWX: 83-4798
Telecopier: XEROX 7020 215-972-7725
Wilmington, Delaware Office: 222 Delaware Avenue, P.O. Box 1266, 19899-1266. For Courier Delivery: 222 Delaware Avenue, Suite 1200, 19801.
Telephone: 302-421-6800.
Cable Address: "Bidsal."
TWX: 83-4798.
Telecopier: XEROX 7020 302-421-6813.
New York, N.Y. Office: Twenty-first Floor, 237 Park Avenue.
Telephone: 212-551-3502.
TWX: 425170.
Telecopier: 212-697-8486.
Malvern, Pennsylvania Office: Suite 200, Great Valley Corporate Center, 300 Chester Field Parkway.
Telephone: 215-251-5050.
Cable Address: "BIDSAL".
TWX: 83-4798.
Telecopier: 215-651-5930.
Voorhees, New Jersey Office: Plaza 1000, Main Street, Suite 206 Evesham & Kresson Roads.
Telephone: 609-424-0098.
Telecopier: XEROX 7020 609-424-2204.
Harrisburg, Pennsylvania Office: 240 North 3rd Street, P.O. Box 1291, 17108-1291. For Courier Delivery: 240 N. 3rd Street, Suite 700, 17101.
Telephone: 717-238-8300.
Telecopier: 717-238-4622.
Trenton, New Jersey Office: Capital Center, 50 East State Street, 08608.
Telephone: 609-393-0057.
Fax: 609-393-5962.

MEMBERS OF FIRM

Stephen S. Aichele
David S. Antzis (Resident, Malvern, Pennsylvania Office)
John J. Barrett, Jr.
Edward F. Beatty, Jr.
James M. Becker
Russell C. Bellavance
Gabriel L. I. Bevilacqua
Lawrence G. Braitman
Timothy W. Callahan, II
Thomas J. Capano (Not admitted in PA; Resident, Wilmington, Delaware Office)
Timothy J. Carson
Robert N. de Luca
Carl B. Everett
Joseph Neff Ewing, Jr. (Resident Malvern, Pennsylvania Office)
David M. Felder
Constance B. Foster (Resident, Harrisburg, Pennsylvania Office)
Spencer W. Franck, Jr.
Richard T. Frazier
Timothy A. Frey (Resident, Wilmington, Delaware Office)
Charles C. Freyer
Rudolph Garcia
William S. Gee (Resident, Wilmington, Delaware Office)
Pamela S. Goodwin (Managing Resident Partner, Trenton, New Jersey Office)
Alan R. Gordon
Scott A. Green (Not admitted in PA)
John L. Harrison, Jr.
Paul M. Hummer
Martha R. Hurt
Joan A. Johnson
Robert J. Jones
John T. Kelley (Resident, Voorhees, N.J. Office)
Sandra W. Kugler
Daniel H. Krapf (Not admitted in PA)
Michael R. Lastowski
Maurice D. Lee, III
Paul C. Madden
George T. Magnatta
John F. Meigs
Walter R. Milbourne
Scott D. Patterson (Resident, Malvern Office)
John P. Pierce
Richard J. A. Popper (Resident, Wilmington, Delaware Office)
John B. Reiss
Herbert S. Riband, Jr.
Gregory J. Rice
Linda Richenderfer
James G. Rosenberg
Robert N. Sandler
James W. Schwartz
Peter J. Shanley (Resident, Wilmington, Delaware Office)
Edward F. Shay
Miles H. Shore
John F. Stoviak
Frederick D. Strober
John R. Suria
Lowell S. Thomas, Jr.
J. Clayton Undercofler
David Unkovic
J. Scott Victor
Anthony F. Walsh
William E. Ward (Not admitted in PA)
Edward S. Wardell (Resident, Voorhees, N.J. Office)

(See Next Column)

SAUL, EWING, REMICK & SAUL—*Continued*

MEMBERS OF FIRM (Continued)

William W. Warren, Jr. (Resident, Harrisburg, Pennsylvania Office)
F. Michael Wysocki
Charles C. Zall
Mark R. Zehner

OF COUNSEL

William Buchanan Gold, Jr.
William R. Hudson
C. Walter Randall, Jr.
Robert W. Sayre
John A. Shrader
Arthur R. G. Solmssen
Frederick A. Van Denbergh, Jr.
Thomas S. Weary
William T. Windsor, Jr.

SPECIAL COUNSEL

Patrick T. Beaty (Resident, Harrisburg, Pennsylvania Office)
Donald Beckman
Michael S. Burg (Resident, Malvern Office)
Robert F. Conte
Patrick G. Oakes (Resident, Malvern, Pennsylvania Office)
Robert W. O'Donnell
Robert S. Price
Sondra K. Slade (Resident, Malvern, Pennsylvania Office)
Michael L. Strong (Resident, Malvern Office)

ASSOCIATES

Mark S. Arena
George Asimos, Jr. (Resident, Malvern, Pennsylvania Office)
Neil R. Bigioni
Lisa Galante Blackburn
Carol R. Blackman (Resident, Malvern, Pennsylvania Office)
Thomas S. Bott (Not admitted in PA)
Trina M. Bragdon
William J. Cluck (Resident, Harrisburg, Pennsylvania Office)
Robert L. Cooney, Jr.
Bradley H.K. Cooper
Jeffrey S. Craig
Edward J. DeMarco, Jr.
Cathleen M. Devlin
Martin J. Doyle
Todd A. Ewan
Anthony P. Forte
Ellen C. K. Giangiordano
Steven A. Goldfield
Robert M. Greenbaum
Bruce D. Greenblatt
Patricia A. Gritzan
Jeffrey C. Hampton
Tim J. Harrington, Jr. (Resident, Harrisburg, Pennsylvania Office)
Adam H. Isenberg
William Michael Janssen
Andrea M. Kahn-Kothmann
Edward J. Kelbon, Jr. (Resident, Voorhees, New Jersey Office)
Alan V. Klein
Jane Kozinski (Not admitted in PA; Resident, Trenton, New Jersey Office)
Gail Cummings Levan
Mark Carlisle Levy
Elizabeth A. Macones
Mary G. March (Resident, Malvern, Pennsylvania Office)
Suzanne Serianni Mayes
Michael Francis McCarthy
Bonnie S. Milavec
Mark Minuti (Resident, Wilmington, Delaware Office)
Maurice R. Mitts
David R. Moffitt
Laura Sunstein Murphy (Resident, Wilmington, Delaware Office)
Lawrence C. Norford
Jeffrey W. Norris
Lisa K. North
Joseph F. O'Dea Jr.
James O'Toole, Jr.
Barbara L. Pedersen
Jennifer K. Peterson
Sandi J. Porter
Frances R. Roggenbaum (Resident, Harrisburg, Pennsylvania Office)
Alan N. Rosenberg
Veronica W. Saltz
Paula D. Shaffner
Gary Arlen Smith
Jennifer M. Spotila
Enid R. Stebbins
Karl A. Thallner, Jr.
Roger Lea Truemper (Resident, Wilmington, Delaware Office)
Patricia Ann Trujillo
Lynanne B. Wescott
Libby A. White (Resident, Malvern, Pennsylvania Office)
Valerie L. Yoder

For full biographical listings, see the Martindale-Hubbell Law Directory

---

SCHNADER, HARRISON, SEGAL & LEWIS (AV)

Suite 3600, 1600 Market Street, 19103
Telephone: 215-751-2000
Cable Address: "Walew"
Fax: 215-751-2205; 215-751-2313
Washington, D.C. Office: Suite 600, 1913 Eye Street, N.W.
Telephone: 202-463-2900.
Cable Address: "Dejuribus, Washington."
Fax: 202-296-8930; 202-775-8741.
New York, N.Y. Office: 330 Madison Avenue.
Telephone: 212-973-8000.
Cable Address: "Dejuribus, New York."
Fax: 212-972-8798.
Harrisburg, Pennsylvania: Suite 700, 30 North Third Street.
Telephone: 717-231-4000.
Fax: 717-231-4012.
Norristown, Pennsylvania Office: Suite 901, One Montgomery Plaza.
Telephone: 215-277-7700.
Fax: 215-277-3211.
Pittsburgh, Pennsylvania Office: Suite 2700, Fifth Avenue Place, 120 Fifth Avenue.
Telephone: 412-577-5200.
Fax: 412-765-3858.
Scranton, Pennsylvania Office: Suite 700, 108 North Washington Avenue.
Telephone: 717-342-6100.
Fax: 717-342-6147.

(See Next Column)

Washington, Pennsylvania Office: 8 East Pine Street.
Telephone: 412-222-7378.
Fax: 412-222-0771.
Cherry Hill, New Jersey Office: Suite 200, Woodland Falls Corporate Park, 220 Lake Drive East.
Telephone: 609-482-5222.
Fax: 609-482-6980.
Atlanta, Georgia Office: Suite 2550 Marquis Two Tower, 285 Peachtree Center Avenue, N.E.
Telephone: 404-215-8100.
Fax: 404-223-5164.

MEMBERS OF THE FIRM

Edward L. Baxter
Rolin P. Bissell
William H. Brown III
Mark S. Cohen
J. Gordon Cooney
James D. Crawford
John J. Cunningham, III
Diana S. Donaldson
J. Allen Dougherty
Henry C. Fader
Robert D. Feder
Jerald M. Goodman
Peter S. Greenberg
Vincent P. Haley
Jake Hart
Mary P. Higgins
Charles M. Honart
John D. Iskrant
Peter Jason
M Richard Kalter
Ronald E. Karam
John T. Kehner
Robert L. Kendall, Jr.
David E. Kenty
Wilbur L. Kipnes
Philip G. Kircher
Robert A. Koons, Jr.
Marilyn Z. Kutler
Larry P. Laubach
William L. Leonard
Nicholas J. LePore, III
Saul Levit
Alan M. Lieberman
William J. Maffucci
Michael J. Mangan
John E. McKeever
Thomas J. McLean
Louis R. Moffa, Jr. (Resident, Cherry Hill, New Jersey Office)
Albert Momjian
Rachel R. Munafo
William H. Murray
Michael G. Neri
Robert P. Oberly
David S. Petkun
Nicholas N. Price
Janice V. Quimby-Fox
Yves Pierre Quintin (Not admitted in PA)
Bruce A. Rosenfield
Frank C. Sabatino
Gerard J. St. John
Thomas R. Schmuhl
Deena Jo Schneider
Steve D. Shadowen
Barry Simon
David Smith
Ralph S. Snyder
Carl A. Solano
J. Robert Stoltzfus
Clinton A. Stuntebeck
Dennis R. Suplee
Sherry A. Swirsky
Ira P. Tiger
Martin Wald
Ralph G. Wellington
Margaret S. Woodruff

SENIOR COUNSEL

George H. Nofer
Irving R. Segal
J. Pennington Straus

COUNSEL TO THE FIRM

Arlin M. Adams
Andrew Gowa
Brenda C. Kinney
Morey M. Myers
Lisa J. Savitt
Bernard G. Segal
Ward T. Williams

RETIRED MEMBERS OF THE FIRM

Frank H. Abbott
William M. Barnes
Samuel Jay Cooke
James A. Drobile
Louis F. Floge
Thomas P. Glassmoyer
Philip M. Hammett
Bancroft D. Haviland
Ronald E. Haydanek
Charles C. Hileman, III
Arthur H. Kahn
John H. Leddy
John E. Littleton
Herbert S. Mednick
Gilbert W. Oswald
Sanford M. Rosenbloom
Barry R. Spiegel
Kimber E. Vought
W. Bradley Ward

SENIOR ATTORNEYS

Kurt R. Anderson
Stephen C.F. Diamond

ASSOCIATES

Stephen J. Anderer
Laura Antonelli
John M. Armstrong
Michael J. Barry
Wendy Beetlestone
Marcia Berman
Joan Kreider Bradwell
Joan O. Brandeis
Charles A. Brawley, III
Jeannette M. Brian
Michael S. Burkhardt
Loren Gail Cooper
Johannes M. De Jong
R. Anthony Diehl
Pamela L. Duris
Ruth Anne Eisenberg
Edward W. Ferruggia
Jan Marie Festa
Elise A. Fialkowski
Natalie Finkelman
Elizabeth Forman
Diane K. Foxman
Harriet Franklin
Paul G. Gagne
Lois A. Gianneschi
John K. Gisleson
Raquel N. Guzmán
James M. Holston
Jennifer DuFault James
Axel J. Johnson, IV
N. Stephan Kinsella (Not admitted in PA)
Constance A. Kossally
Stacy J. Levitan
Alan H. Lieblich
Robin P. Lincoln
Theresa E. Loscalzo
Joseph T. Lukens
Jane A. Makransky
Kathy C. Mandelbaum
Mickey M. Mardirossian
Maureen Murphy McBride

(See Next Column)

SCHNADER, HARRISON, SEGAL & LEWIS, *Philadelphia—Continued*

ASSOCIATES (Continued)

Kevin C. McCullough
Julia H. McLaughlin
Steve Mendelsohn
Mark A. Momjian
Christopher J. Moran
John J. Pease III
Christina E. Rainville
Barry L. Refsin
Nicole M. Reimann
Robert E. Rosenthal
Roy S. Ross
Kathleen M. Sandone
Dale P. Schomer
Kaethe B. Schumacher
J. Denny Shupe
Richard J. Silpe
Samuel W. Silver
Lisa Shari Smith
Joseph A. Sullivan
Margaret Gallagher Thompson
Michael G. Tierce
Gary M. Tocci
Karen Lee Tomlinson
Stephen Weaver
Cynthia R. White
Nancy Winkelman
Carolyn Moran Zack
Deborah Guerra Zitomer

For full biographical listings, see the Martindale-Hubbell Law Directory

SWARTZ, CAMPBELL & DETWEILER (AV)

1600 Land Title Building, 100 South Broad Street, 19110
Telephone: 215-564-5190
Telefax: 215-299-4301
Media, Pennsylvania Office: One Veterans Square Suite 106.
Telephone: 610-566-9222.
Fax: 610-892-0636.
Harrisburg, Pennsylvania Office: 2040 Linglestown Road, Suite 107.
Telephone: 717-540-8671.
Fax: 717-540-5481.
Allentown, Pennsylvania Office: Suite 230, 5100 Tilghman Street.
Telephone: 610-395-5903.
Fax: 610-395-7097.
Wilmington, Delaware Office: 300 Delaware Avenue, Suite 818, P.O. Box 330.
Telephone: 302-656-5935.
Fax: 302-656-1434.
Mount Laurel, New Jersey Office: Bloom Court, Suite 314. 1300 Route 73.
Telephone: 609-727-4777.
Fax: 609-727-0464.

C. Donald Swartz (1893-1976)
William T. Campbell (1896-1975)
Lynn L. Detweiler (1906-1989)

PARTNERS

Richard D. Harburg
Curtis P. Cheyney, III
Richard L. Goerwitz, Jr.
Joseph T. Bodell, Jr.
Charles S. Katz, Jr.
Joseph F. Van Horn, Jr.
Ronald F. Bové
Martin J. Fallon, Jr.
Frederick C. Fletcher, II
Stephen J. Harlen
G. Daniel Bruch, Jr.
James C. Haggerty
John A. Wetzel
John T. Carroll, III
Kevin Canavan
Walter L. McDonough
Robert B. Mulhern, Jr.
J. Eric Stedje
Charles L. Powell
Bruce W. McCullough (Resident Partner, Wilmington, Delaware Office)
David A. Pennington (Resident Partner, Allentown, Pennsylvania Office)
Joseph A. Venuti, Jr. (Resident Partner, Mount Laurel, New Jersey Office)

Sue Ellen Albert

ASSOCIATES

Gregory D. Geiss (Resident Associate, Harrisburg, Pennsylvania Office)
Michael T. Dolan
William T. Salzer
Jane Ann Lombard
William M. Bendon
Vincent J. Iozzi
Sharolyn L. Murphy
Andrew J. Reilly (Resident Associate, Media, Pennsylvania, Office)
Jeffrey B. McCarron
Louis A. Bové
Thomas More Marrone
Andrew K. Touchstone
Michael A. Cognetti (Resident, Media, Pennsylvania Office)
Daniel L. McKenty (Resident Associate, Wilmington, Delaware Office)
Paul A. Pauciulo
John J. Muldowney
Neil T. Dombrowski
Melissa Lang
Scott J. Tredwell
James D. Cella
Keith E. Donovan (Resident Associate, Wilmington, Delaware Office)
Sheilah Anne Tone (Resident Associate, Allentown, Pennsylvania Office)
Matthew S. Wynn
Alfred J. Carlson
Nataly A. Harker
John P. Dogum
Jeffrey L. Goodman
Catherine B. Herrmann
Amy Lynne Penfil
Debra A. Matherne (Resident Associate, Harrisburg, Pennsylvania Office)
Stephen A. Seach
Susan F. Evans
Thomas E. Panzer
Sharon Simkiss Merhige
Nancy M. Harris (Resident, Allentown, Pennsylvania Office)
Robert M. Smolen (Resident, Mount Laurel, New Jersey Office)
Joseph J. Centeno

For full biographical listings, see the Martindale-Hubbell Law Directory

SWEENEY, SHEEHAN & SPENCER, A PROFESSIONAL CORPORATION (AV)

19th Floor, 1515 Market Street, 19102
Telephone: 215-563-9811
Fax: 215-557-0999
Voorhees, New Jersey Office: 120 Fairview Avenue.
Telephone: 609-428-8088.
Fax: 609-428-9765.

George D. Sheehan (1911-1985)
Donald J. P. Sweeney
M. Landon Spencer
George D. Sheehan, Jr.
Walter S. Jenkins
Thomas L. Delevie
Dennis L. Platt
Robert B. Goodyear
Warren E. Voter
Guy Mercogliano
Andrew Siegeltuch
Barbara A. O'Connell

Gregory J. Sharkey

Suzanne M. O'Brien
Bayard H. Graf
Racheal De Cicco
Harold E. Viletto
Robyn Farrell McGrath
J. David Outtrim
Robert Thompson Veon
J. Michael Kunsch

Victoria L. Rees

For full biographical listings, see the Martindale-Hubbell Law Directory

WOLF, BLOCK, SCHORR AND SOLIS-COHEN (AV)

Twelfth Floor, Packard Building, S.E. Corner 15th and Chestnut Streets, 19102-2678
Telephone: 215-977-2000
Cable Address: "WOLBLORR PHA"
TWX: 710-670-1927
Telecopiers: 977-2334; 977-2346
Malvern, Pennsylvania Office: 20 Valley Stream Parkway.
Telephone: 215-889-4900.
Fax: 215-889-4916.
Harrisburg, Pennsylvania Office: 305 North Front Street, Suite 401.
Telephone: 717-237-7160.
Fax: 717-237-7161.

MEMBERS OF FIRM

Jerome J. Shestack
Anthony S. Minisi
David J. Kaufman
Carl W. Schneider
Michael L. Temin
Robert M. Segal
Gerald Gornish
Leonard J. Cooper
Steven A. Arbittier
Henry F. Miller
Jay L. Goldberg
E. Gerald Riesenbach
H. Robert Fiebach
Gerald J. McConomy
William A. Rosoff
Ronald B. Glazer
Donald K. Joseph
James R. Redeker
Michael M. Sherman
Alan S. Kaplinsky
David Maris Doret
Laurance E. Baccini
Ian A. L. Strogatz
Herman C. Fala
Henry L. Shrager
Michael Allan Budin
Thomas P. Witt
Patrick H. McCarthy
Leonard P. Goldberger
Thomas J. Gallagher, III
Bernard Lee
Ralph W. Siskind
Sandra A. Bloch
Burt M. Rublin
William G. Frey
Robert I. Friedman
Joseph C. Crawford
Virginia M. Duffy
David Gitlin
Andrew A. Chirls
Francine Friedman Griesing
Patrick Matusky
David I. Bookspan
Raymond D. Agran
Steven N. Haas
Alan G. Rosenbloom
Richard J. Busis
Jeffrey A. Leonard
Clifford D. Schlesinger
Stanton S. Oswald
Alvin H. Dorsky
W. Thomas Berriman
Michael M. Dean
Charles G. Kopp
Mark K. Kessler
Marvin Krasny
Alan H. Molod
Edward M. Glickman
Lowell H. Dubrow
Harold Jacobs
Henry A. Gladstone
Ronald M. Wiener
William J. Morehouse
Ivan I. Light
James A. Rosenstein
John S. Roberts, Jr.
Louis Coffey
James S. Burns
Joseph C. Bright
Arthur A. Zatz
Dennis L. Cohen
David R. Glyn
Philip E. Garber
Alan Singer
Elizabeth H. Mai
Mark H. Gallant
Joseph S. Finkelstein
Robert C. Jacobs
Barry M. Klayman
Robert M. Goldich
Brian P. Flaherty
Jeffrey S. Saltz
Roma Skeen Young
John Langdon Culhane, Jr.
Jeremy T. Rosenblum
Bruce Grohsgal
Jay A. Dorsch
Robert A. Silverman
John H. Schapiro
Jonathan D. Wetchler
James R. Williams
Anthony R. Twardowski
William J. Taylor
Debra Klebanoff
Jerold J. Novick
Jay A. Dubow
Jonathan A. Segal
Warren Fusfeld

Diana C. Liu

(See Next Column)

WOLF, BLOCK, SCHORR AND SOLIS-COHEN—*Continued*

OF COUNSEL

Robert B. Wolf
Morris L. Forer
Mitchell E. Panzer
Franklin H. Spitzer
Leonard J. Bucki
Franklin Poul
George M. Brantz
Helen Spigel Sax
Donald Bean
Raymond J. Bradley
Daniel C. Cohen
Robert E. Wachs
Albert J. Feldman
Daniel Promislo
Bernard Chanin

ASSOCIATES

Albert C. Braslow
Christine S. Dutton
Charlene A. Braida
Dana B. Klinges
Jacob C. Cohn
Laura B. Sorscher
Steven H. Slutsky
Tami L. Bogutz
Matthew A. White
Stephen D. Galowitz
Rachel S. Lieberman
Jodi Trager Plavner
Carol A. Cannerelli-Van Poortvliet
Joanne R. Soslow
Hannah Perkins
Lillian E. Benedict
Michele K. Cabot
Mary R. Kohler
Diane E. McTigue
Adam G. Silverstein
Brent H. Gray
Amy B. Anderson
John J. Kenney
Jayne S. Ressler
Yvette Kane
Martha E. Johnston
Benjamin J. Naitove
Ruth S. Ruben
Frances B. McGinley
Zachary L. Grayson
Daniel P. O'Meara
Mark E. Felger
John Corenswet
Liza B. Leidner Wolf
Pamela A. Morone
Laurence Weilheimer
Lester E. Lipschutz
Shari M. Solomon
Andrew M. Tebbe (Not admitted in PA)
Howard A. Trachtman
Julie L. Friedberg
Erin E. Lynch
Richard P. Pasquier
L. Richard Winchester
Patricia Sons Biswanger
Lynne M. Helfand
Robert G. Marks
William C. Sheffield
S. Lance Silver

For full biographical listings, see the Martindale-Hubbell Law Directory

---

*PITTSBURGH,** Allegheny Co.

ANSTANDIG, LEVICOFF & McDYER, A PROFESSIONAL CORPORATION (AV)

600 Gulf Tower, 15219
Telephone: 412-765-3700
Fax: 412-765-3730
Beckley, West Virgina Office: Brown, Levicoff & McDyer. 311 Prince Street. P.O. Drawer M.
Telephone: 304-253-3700.

Louis Anstandig
Avrum Levicoff
Daniel P. McDyer
Timothy J. Burdette
Edward A. Yurcon
James Michael Brown (Resident, Beckley, West Virginia Office)
Alan T. Silko

Paul G. Mayer, Jr.
Philip M.P. Buttenfield
Stephen J. Poljak
Eileen Anstandig Ziemke
William M. Adams
Elizabeth E. Deemer
Bryan J. Smith
Tracey A. Jordan
Jane E. Harkins (Resident, Beckley, West Virginia Office)
Mark A. Serge
James D. Stacy (Resident, Beckley, West Virginia Office)
R. Bruce Carlson

For full biographical listings, see the Martindale-Hubbell Law Directory

BALZARINI, CAREY & WATSON (AV)

3303 Grant Building, 15219
Telephone: 412-471-1200
Fax: 412-471-8326

MEMBERS OF FIRM

Edward J. Balzarini
Francis J. Carey
Edward J. Balzarini, Jr.
David J. Watson
Michael Balzarini
Joseph S. Bielecki

For full biographical listings, see the Martindale-Hubbell Law Directory

BUCHANAN INGERSOLL, PROFESSIONAL CORPORATION (AV)

5800 USX Tower, 600 Grant Street, 15219
Telephone: 412-562-8800
Telecopier: 412-562-1041
Philadelphia, Pennsylvania Office: Two Logan Square, Twelfth Floor, 18th & Arch Streets.
Telephone: 215-665-8700.
Harrisburg, Pennsylvania Office: Vartan Parc, 30 North Third Street.
Telephone: 717-237-4800.
Tampa, Florida Office: 101 East Kennedy Boulevard, Suite 1030.
Telephone: 813-222-8180.
North Miami Beach, Florida Office: 19495 Biscayne Boulevard.
Telephone: 305-933-5600.

(See Next Column)

Lexington, Kentucky Office: 1210 Vine Center Office Tower, 333 West Vine Street.
Telephone: 606-225-5333.
Princeton, New Jersey Office: Buchanan Ingersoll, A Partnership, College Centre, 500 College Road East.
Telephone: 609-452-2666.

John Grier Buchanan (1888-1986)
Frank Bostwick Ingersoll (1893-1977)
Lynn J. Alstadt
Bruce A. Americus
Richard J. Antonelli
George P. Baier
Stewart B. Barmen
Joseph J. Barnes
Ronald Basso
Paul A. Beck
Bruce I. Booken
A. Bruce Bowden
Thomas E. Boyle
Samuel W. Braver
John S. Brendel
George L. Cass
Sheryl Atkinson Clark
Carl A. Cohen
Rosemary L. Corsetti
Ronald W. Crouch
R. Michael Daniel
Lewis U. Davis, Jr.
Vincent C. Deluzio
Michael L. Dever
Robert G. Devlin
Melanie DiPietro, S.C.
Christopher F. Farrell
David B. Fawcett III
Michael J. Flinn
Denise W. Ford
Stanley R. Geary
Carole C. Gori
Calvin R. Harvey
Mark Raymond Hornak
Henry McC. Ingram
Robert A. Johnson
Stephen W. Johnson
Jack J. Kessler
Charles G. Knox
Robert Y. Kopf, Jr.
Paul D. Kruper
Lawrence J. Kuremsky
Deborah A. Little
Rebecca L. Livingston
J. Jerome Mansmann
Patricia J. Marley
Leonard J. Marsico
Pamela A. McCallum
William J. McCormick
M. Bruce McCullough
John J. McLean, Jr.
R. Henry Moore
James D. Morton
Francis A. Muracca, II
Gary Philip Nelson
K. Sidney Neuman
William R. Newlin
Wendelynne J. Newton
James D. Obermanns
Donald T. O'Connor
Gregory A. Pearson
Larry E. Phillips
John R. Previs
Robert B. Ramsey III
Thomas C. Reed
P. Jerome Richey
Carl E. Rothenberger, Jr.
John M. Rumin
Jonathan M. Schmerling
Arthur J. Schwab
Michael A. Snyder
James R. Sweeny
Thomas M. Thompson
Hugh G. Van der Veer
Thomas L. VanKirk
Jacques M. Wood
Stanley Yorsz
Paula A. Zawadzki
R. Dell Ziegler
Sidney Zonn

COUNSEL

Margaret B. Angel

SENIOR ATTORNEYS

Elizabeth Kluger Cooper
Karen Shichman Crawford
Michael A. Donadee
Joan G. Dorgan
Cristopher Charles Hoel
S. Howard Kline
William H. Morrow
George Raynovich, Jr.
Gary R. Walker
Reginald J. Weatherly
Philip J. Weis

Paul Amato
James J. Barnes
Jeffrey P. Bauman
Allison W. Berman
Michael G. Bock
Jeffrey J. Bresch
Thomas G. Buchanan
Kevin R. Burns
John M. Cerilli
Paul J. Corrado
George H. Crompton
Virginia A. DeMarco
R. Douglas DeNardo
Rebecca J. Dick-Hurwitz
Sheila Smith DiNardo
Candice Komar Ewonce
Jill R. Fisher
James W. Forsyth
Thomas S. Galey
Daniel H. Glasser
Samuel J. Goncz
Anthony James Guida Jr.
Russell W. Hahn (Not admitted in PA)
Frank B. Harrington
Susan M. Hartman
Nathaniel Chandler Hunter
Douglas S. Johnson
Susan Kircher
Eric D. Kline
Carrie Kochenbach
Harrison S. Lauer
S. Bryan Lawrence III
Leo A. Little
JoEllen Lyons
Donald E. Malecki
Christine D. Marton
Gregory A. Miller
John E. Muolo
Daniel Alan O'Connor
Frances Magovern O'Connor
John P. O'Connor
John F. O'Rourke
Stanley Joel Parker
Mark T. Phillis
David J. Porter
Robert J. Pugh
Timothy J. Reynolds
Peter S. Russ
Ronald W. Schuler
Lisa G. Silverman
Joseph S. Sisca
Stephen C. Smith
Mark G. Stall
Deborah B. Walrath
Christine J. Wichers
Pamela K. Wiles
Patricia L. Wozniak
Heather A. Wyman
Michael G. Young

(See Next Column)

BUCHANAN INGERSOLL PROFESSIONAL CORPORATION, *Pittsburgh—Continued*

OF COUNSEL

Jack G. Armstrong
Alexander Black
Jordan F. Hite
(Not admitted in PA)
Edward H. Schoyer

For full biographical listings, see the Martindale-Hubbell Law Directory

ROBERT A. COHEN (AV)

819 Frick Building, 15219
Telephone: 412-261-9700

For full biographical listings, see the Martindale-Hubbell Law Directory

COHEN & GRIGSBY, P.C. (AV)

2900 CNG Tower, 625 Liberty Avenue, 15222
Telephone: 412-394-4900
Telecopier: 412-391-3382

Charles C. Cohen
Robert S. Grigsby

Ronald J. Andrykovitch
Mark I. Baseman
Charles R. Brodbeck
James B. Brown
Anthony Cillo
Henry C. Cohen
Robert W. Doty
Jack W. Elliott
Larry K. Elliott
Charles M. Greenberg
Wayne C. Holcombe
Gordon S. Johnston
David J. Kalson
E. Donald Ladov
Lawrence M. Lebowitz
Dennis J. Lewis
David J. Lowe
John E. Lyncheski
Thomas J. Madigan
Jeffrey B. Markel
Joseph M. McDermott
Laura A. Meaden
Richard R. Nelson, II
Hugh W. Nevin, Jr.
C. Eric Pfeil
Michael J. Reilly
Andrew M. Roman
Evans Rose, Jr.
Richard D. Rosen
Jerry H. Seidler
Neil F. Siegel
Laura Williams Stone
Frederick L. Tolhurst
Jeffrey A. Van Doren
Curt Vazquez
Jeffrey P. Ward
Daniel L. Wessels

James M. Catanzarite
V. Susanne Cook
M. Theresa Creagh
Lynn Ellenberger
Lauren Venezia Ellis
(Not admitted in PA)
Thomas J. Farrell
William E. Gallagher
Lisa L. Garrett
Lisa K. Gavlik
Kevin C. Harkins
Nancy L. Heilman
Cheryl A. Mueller
James D. Painter
Jeffery D. Peters
Christopher J. Rayl
Jean Rowley Robertson
Michael E. Silverman
Tammy Singleton-English
Mark R. Stabile
William R. Taxay
Scott R. Thistle
Kelly R. Vehec

SPECIAL COUNSEL

Jonathan L. Alder
Robert D. German

CONSULTANT ON THE LAWS OF CHINA

Heidi Haipeng Zhang

For full biographical listings, see the Martindale-Hubbell Law Directory

DAVIES MCFARLAND & CARROLL, P.C. (AV)

One Gateway Center, Tenth Floor, 15222
Telephone: 412-281-0737

Ralph A. Davies
Gregg P. Otto
Edward A. McFarland
Daniel P. Carroll
William D. Geiger
Francis Garger
Lynn E. Bell
David S. Smith
James M. Poerio

C. Robert Keenan, III
David E. Lamm
Donna M. Lowman
Christopher Pierson
William S. Evans
Keith M. Hoffman
Lisa M. Montarti
Robert P. Walter

Representative Clients: The BOC Group; Continental Insurance Co.; The Goodyear Tire & Rubber Co.; Hobart Brothers Company; LTV Steel Co.; Medical Protective Co.; Motorists Insurance Cos.; Teledyne, Inc.; The Travelers Insurance Co.

For full biographical listings, see the Martindale-Hubbell Law Directory

DICKIE, MCCAMEY & CHILCOTE, A PROFESSIONAL CORPORATION (AV)

Suite 400, Two PPG Place, 15222-5402
Telephone: 412-281-7272
Fax: 412-392-5367
Wheeling, West Virginia Office: Suite 2002, 1233 Main Street, 26003-2839.
Telephone: 304-233-1022.
Facsimile: 304-233-1026.

J. Roy Dickie (1884-1962)
Harold E. McCamey (1894-1967)
Sanford M. Chilcote (1905-1974)
David B. Fawcett
David J. Armstrong
Richard D. Klaber
Theodore O. Struk
Wilbur McCoy Otto
Clayton A. Sweeney
Herbert Bennett Conner
Richard S. Dorfzaun
Daniel P. Stefko
James F. Malone, III
M. Richard Dunlap
Eugene F. Scanlon, Jr.
Charles W. Kenrick
John Edward Wall
James R. Miller
Paul W. Roman, Jr.
Joseph S. D. Christof, II
Stewart M. Flam
Stuart W. Benson, III
Thomas P. Lutz
J. Lawson Johnston
Stephen R. Mlinac
David M. Neuhart
George Edward McGrann
Robert F. Wagner
Robert W. Hastings
Robert J. Marino
Stephen M. Houghton
Larry A. Silverman
Arthur L. Schwarzwaelder
Frank M. Gianola
Leonard A. Costa, Jr.
Kenneth S. Mroz
Steven B. Larchuk
James D. Strader
Ingrid Medzius Lundberg
Frederick W. Bode, III
Jeffrey T. Wiley
Richard C. Polley
Christine A. Ward
Stephen C. Kifer
Thomas M. Fallert
Gloria N. Fuehrer
William D. Clifford
Robert G. Del Greco, Jr.
Judith Ference Olson
Edmund L. Olszewski, Jr.
Dorothy A. Davis
Charles G. Brown
William Campbell Ries
Richard J. Federowicz
John C. Conti
L. John Argento
Lu Ann R. Datesh
David J. Obermeier
Leland P. Schermer
John W. Lewis, II
Peter T. Stinson
Thomas H. May
Ray F. Middleman
George Monroe Schumann
George Randal Fox, III
Terry C. Cavanaugh

Bernhard Schaffler
Jean McCree Simmonds
Nancy R. Winschel
Eugene G. Berry
David S. Horvitz
Anthony J. Williott
George P. Kachulis
John T. Pion
Hunter A. McGeary, Jr.
Michael J. Sweeney
William M. Conwell
Bonnie Pearce Webster
Gregory A. Gross
Joseph L. Luvara
Andrew G. Kimball
W. Alan Torrance, Jr.
Howard A. Chajson
Marcelle M. Theis
Brian T. Must
David S. Bloom
M. Suzanne McCartney
Alyson J. Kirleis
S. Jane Anderson
John C. Carlos
W. Scott Campbell
Barry I. Friedman
Paul S. Mazeski
Anthony J. Rash
Peter A. Santos
Christopher Passodelis, Jr.
Kimberly G. Roberts
Eugene A. Giotto
Vincent Scaglione, Jr.
James M. Girman
Pamela Lee Leyden
Maureen Kowalski
Richard E. Lafferty
Michael F. Nerone
Christopher A. Brodman
Craig M. Lee
Christopher T. Lee
Ann Michailenko Wilson
Steven W. Zoffer
Robert G. Voinchet, Jr.
Rodger L. Puz
Jennifer M. Kirschler
John N. Cox
Donald E. Evans
Edward A. Miller
Douglas C. Dorsey
Nathan D. Bailey
James Otis Perry, IV
Laurel A. Peters
Vincent Grieco
Ralph J. Saunders, Jr.
Gail W. Kahle
(Not admitted in PA)

OF COUNSEL

Herman C. Kimpel

For full biographical listings, see the Martindale-Hubbell Law Directory

ECKERT SEAMANS CHERIN & MELLOTT (AV)

600 Grant Street, 42nd Floor, 15219-2787
Telephone: 412-566-6000
Telex: 866172
Facsimile: 412-566-6099
Harrisburg, Pennsylvania Office: One South Market Square Building, 213 Market Street.
Telephone: 717-237-6000.
Facsimile: 717-237-6019.
Allentown, Pennsylvania Office: Sovereign Building, 609 Hamilton Mall, 3rd Floor.
Telephone: 610-432-3000.
Facsimile: 610-432-8827.

(See Next Column)

ECKERT SEAMANS CHERIN & MELLOTT—*Continued*

Philadelphia, Pennsylvania Office: 1700 Market Street, Suite 3232.
Telephone: 215-575-6000.
Telex: 845226.
Facsimile: 215-575-6015.
Boston, Massachusetts Office: One International Place, 18th Floor.
Telephone: 617-342-6800.
Facsimile: 617-342-6899.
Buffalo, New York Office: 606 Liberty Building.
Telephone: 716-854-4100.
Facsimile: 716-854-4227.
Fort Lauderdale, Florida Office: First Fort Lauderdale Place, Suite 900, 100 Northeast Third Avenue.
Telephone: 305-523-0400.
Facsimile: 305-523-7002.
Boca Raton, Florida Office: Suite 902, The Plaza, 5355 Town Center Road.
Telephone: 407-394-7775.
Facsimile: 407-394-9998.
Miami, Florida Office: Barnett Tower, 18th Floor, 701 Brickell Avenue.
Telephone: 305-373-9100.
Facsimile: 305-372-9400.
Tallahassee, Florida Office: 206 South Adams Street.
Telephone: 904-222-2515.
Facsimile: 904-222-3452.
Washington, D.C. Office: 2100 Pennsylvania Avenue, N.W., Suite 600.
Telephone: 202-659-6600.
Telex: 62030761.
Facsimile: 202-659-6699.

William Watson Smith (1871-1964)
William H. Eckert (1900-1981)
Frank L. Seamans (1914-1984)
Milton W. Lamproplos (1910-1990)
Donald C. Winson (1931-1990)
Carl F. Barger (1930-1992)
Robert M. Brown (1929-1993)
Carl Cherin (1917-1994)

MEMBERS OF FIRM

Mary K. Austin
Peter C. Baggerman
Michael R. Borasky
Laura A. Candris
Mark C. Coulson
Barton Z. Cowan
Ronald S. Cusano
Richard K. Dandrea
Daniel M. Darragh
Fred W. George
Richard W. Gladstone, II
Edward J. Greene
Marcia Lucidi Grimes
Richard I. Halpern
Jack M. Hartman
Jonathan K. Hergert
Dale Hershey
John J. Kearns, III
William E. Kelleher, Jr.
John R. Kenrick
W. Gregg Kerr
Joel L. Lennen
William B. Mallin
Michael A. Martin
C. Kent May (Managing Partner)
Dennis R. McEwen
Ellen Page Mercer
Louis J. Moraytis
John J. Myers
Edward R. Noonan
James H. Norris
Dennis J. O'Brien
Edward G. O'Connor
Christopher R. Opalinski
John R. Owen, III
Clifford A. Pastel
Joseph M. Ramirez
Dean F. Richardson
Richard F. Rinaldo
James H. Roberts
Bryan D. Rosenberger
Timothy P. Ryan
Willis A. Siegfried
Thomas L. Snyder
Michael R. Stabile, Jr.
Ray C. Stoner
Mark R. Sullivan
David E. Tungate
Dennis L. Veraldi
Richard S. Wiedman
Mark A. Willard
Dale E. Williams
Robert B. Williams
Stuart A. Williams
C. Arthur Wilson, Jr.
Thomas D. Wright
Paul M. Yenerall

PATENT AND TRADEMARK COUNSEL

David V. Radack
Arnold B. Silverman
Richard V. Westerhoff

SPECIAL COUNSEL

Ray W. Brown
Robert D. Hazlett
J. Paul Martha
Robert F. Pugliese
Robert A. Wiesemann

COUNSEL

Walter J. Blenko, Jr.
Leon E. Hickman
Robert C. McCartney
Cloyd R. Mellott
Joseph A. Richardson, Jr.
Sidney M. Ruffin

ASSOCIATES

William E. Adams
Sheila Anderson
Jolene W. Appleman
Daniel L. Bell
Barbara L. Bower
Tina Campo
Stacey L. Cardenas
Scott D. Cessar
Timothy S. Coon
Mary Jo Corsetti
Gregory D. Cribbs
Marjorie E. Crist
Patricia L. Dallacroce
Emily M. Dargatz
Lane D. Dively
Laurie S. Duchateau
Steven F. Faeth
John D. Faucher
Anne M. Foulkes
David P. Gaertner
Catherine L. Garfinkel
Amy J. Greer

(See Next Column)

ASSOCIATES (Continued)

Terry H. Han
Lynn Fisher Hill
Eric L. Horne
Kirk D. Houser
Daniel P. Johnson
Stuart R. Kaplan
Veronica M. Kelly
John William A. Kenawell
Patrick F. Kilker
Patrick R. Kingsley
Diane D. Krausert
Michael A. Labriola
Michael E. Lloyd
Sharon M. Loftus
Elizabeth L. Lynch
Barbara Fisfis Marzina
Thomas D. Maxson
Daniel P. Orie
Maureen F. O'Shaughnessy
Jay L. Panzarella
Raymond P. Parker
Heather E. Rennie
James G. Seaman
Joseph D. Shelby
Eileen R. Sisca
Jeffrey W. Spear
Denise Bablak Springer
George K. Stacey
Martin J. Stanek
Anthony M. Tedesco
Raymond C. Vogliano
Gregory A. Weingart
Jarrell D. Wright

For full biographical listings, see the Martindale-Hubbell Law Directory

---

GAITENS, TUCCERI & NICHOLAS, A PROFESSIONAL CORPORATION (AV)

519 Court Place, 15219
Telephone: 412-391-6920
Fax: 412-391-1189

Larry P. Gaitens
Vincent A. Tucceri
Romel L. Nicholas

Suzanne Bernard Merrick
Anthony T. Colangelo
Patricia A. Monahan
Gregory G. Schwab
Michele A. McPeak
Donald J. Garwood
Gregory Gleason

Reference: Pittsburgh National Bank.

For full biographical listings, see the Martindale-Hubbell Law Directory

---

GROGAN, GRAFFAM, MCGINLEY & LUCCHINO, P.C. (AV)

22nd Floor, Three Gateway Center, 15222
Telephone: 412-553-6300
Fax: 412-642-2601

Vincent J. Grogan
Stephen W. Graffam
John R. McGinley, Jr.
Frank J. Lucchino
Dennis A. Watson
Robert W. Murdoch
Joseph A. Macerelli
Dennis J. Roman
William Christopher Passodelis
Kathryn Lease Simpson
James A. Pellow, III
Diane Barr Quinlin
Leo Gerard Daly
Terrence F. McVerry
Joseph A. Fricker, Jr.
John W. Smart
Ronald J. Brown

John A. Bass
Anna M. Bamonte
Elaine S. Nace
Susan M. Bicket
Gregg A. Guthrie
Rosalie Pugliese
Korry Alden Greene
John W. Joyce
Steven Leindecker
Lori Ann Gala
D. Helen Ford
Marty Young Brown
Eric J. Zagrocki
Robert P. Boyer, Jr.
Charles A. Buechel, Jr.
Jodi K. Innocent
Richard D. Kalson
Michael A. Sosnowski

For full biographical listings, see the Martindale-Hubbell Law Directory

---

HOUSTON, HOUSTON & DONNELLY (AV)

2510 Centre City Tower, 650 Smithfield Street, 15222
Telephone: 412-471-5828
FAX: 412-471-0736

MEMBERS OF FIRM

Fred Chalmers Houston (1886-1971)
William McC. Houston
Fred Chalmers Houston, Jr.
Thomas J. Donnelly
John F. Meck

ASSOCIATES

Mario Santilli, Jr.
Theodore M. Hammer

Representative Clients: Federated Investors; Federated Investors Group of Mutual Funds; Iron City Sash & Door Co.; The Park Mansions; A. Stucki Co.; Sewickley Valley Hospital Authority.

For full biographical listings, see the Martindale-Hubbell Law Directory

Pittsburgh—Continued

JONES, DAY, REAVIS & POGUE (AV)

500 Grant Street 31st Floor, 15219
Telephone: 412-391-3939
Cable Address: "Attorneys Pittsburgh".
Telecopier: 412-394-7959
In Atlanta, Georgia: 3500 One Peachtree Center, 303 Peachtree Street, N.E.
Telephone: 404-521-3939.
Cable Address: "Attorneys Atlanta".
Telex: 54-2711.
Telecopier: 404-581-8330.
In Brussels, Belgium: Avenue Louise 480, 7th Floor, B-1050 Brussels.
Telephone: 011-32-2-645-14-11.
Telecopier: 011-32-2-645-14-45.
In Chicago, Illinois: 77 West Wacker.
Telephone: 312-782-3939.
Telecopier: 312-782-8585.
In Cleveland, Ohio: North Point, 901 Lakeside Avenue.
Telephone: 216-586-3939.
Cable Address: "Attorneys Cleveland."
Telex: 980389.
Telecopier: 216-579-0212.
In Columbus, Ohio: 1900 Huntington Center.
Telephone: 614-469-3939.
Cable Address: "Attorneys Columbus."
Telecopier: 614-461-4198.
In Dallas, Texas: 2300 Trammell Crow Center, 2001 Ross Avenue.
Telephone: 214-220-3939.
Cable Address: "Attorneys Dallas."
Telex: 730852.
Telecopier: 214-969-5100.
In Frankfurt, Germany: Triton Haus, Bockenheimer Landstrasse 42, 60323 Frankfurt am Main.
Telephone: 49-69-9726-3939.
Telecopier: 49-69-9726-3993.
In Geneva, Switzerland: 20, rue de Candolle.
Telephone: 011-41-22-320-2339.
Telecopier: 011-41-22-320-1232.
In Hong Kong: 1501 One Exchange Square, 8 Connaught Place.
Telephone: 011-852-2526-6895.
Telecopier: 011-852-2810-5787.
In Irvine, California: 2603 Main Street, Suite 900.
Telephone: 714-851-3939.
Telex: 194911 Lawyers LSA.
Telecopier: 714-553-7539.
In London, England: One Mount Street.
Telephone: 011-44-71-493-9361.
Cable Address: "Surgoe London WI."
Telecopier: 011-44-71-493-9666.
In Los Angeles, California: 555 West Fifth Street, Suite 4600.
Telephone: 213-489-3939.
Telex: 181439 UD.
Telecopier: 213-243-2539.
In New York, New York: 599 Lexington Avenue.
Telephone: 212-326-3939.
Cable Address: "JONESDAY NEWYORK."
Telex: 237013 JDRP UR.
Telecopier: 212-755-7306.
In Paris, France: 62, rue du Faubourg Saint-Honore.
Telephone: 011-33-1-44-71-3939.
Cable Address: "Surgoe Paris."
Telex: 290156 Surgoe.
Telecopier: 011-33-1-49-24-0471.
In Riyadh, Saudi Arabia: Law Offices of Saud M.A. Shawwaf, P.O. Box 2700.
Telephones: 011 (966-1) 465-6543, 011 (966-1) 464-8534 or 011 (966-1) 464-8540.
Telex: 401831 SAUCON SJ.
Telecopier: (966-1) 464-8480.
In Taipei, Taiwan: 8th Floor, 2 Tun Hwa South Road, Section 2.
Telephone: 011 (886-2) 704-6808.
Telecopier: 011 (886-2) 704-6791.
In Tokyo, Japan: Toranomon MT Building, 4th Floor, 10-3, Toranomon 3-Chome, Minato-Ku, Tokyo 105, Japan.
Telephone: 011-81-3-3433-3939.
Telecopier: 011-81-3-5401-2725.
In Washington, D.C.: Metropolitan Square, 1450 G Street, N.W.
Telephone: 202-879-3939.
Cable Address: "Attorneys Washington."
Telex: 89-2410 ATTORNEYS WASH.
Telecopier: 202-737-2832.

MEMBERS OF FIRM IN PITTSBURGH

William H. Powderly, III
James J. Erb
J. W. Montgomery, III
Edward C. Schmidt
John W. Ubinger, Jr.
Richard A. Clark
Paul Michael Pohl
Charles A. Schliebs
Carey M. Brennan
Charles H. Moellenberg, Jr.
Roy A. Powell
Laura E. Ellsworth
Christopher B. Carson
Michael H. Ginsberg

(See Next Column)

ASSOCIATES

Alan D. Chute
John J. Mead
John H. Wilson
Mary Beth Pfohl
John D. Goetz
John E. Iole
Scott J. Davido (Not admitted in PA)
Kevin P. Holewinski
Amy E. Dias
Brian C. Castello
Kathleen Clover
Louis W. Hensler
Bryan D. Kocher
Joan C. Zangrilli
Peter D. Laun
Ned L. Spells, Jr.
Matthew C. Flannery
Luke J. Bergstrom
Gretchen L. Jankowski
Jennifer Brinkman Kosubinsky

SENIOR STAFF ATTORNEY

Ira L. Podheiser

For full biographical listings, see the Martindale-Hubbell Law Directory

---

KABALA & GEESEMAN, A PROFESSIONAL CORPORATION (AV)

The Waterfront, 200 First Avenue, 15222
Telephone: 412-391-1334
Fax: 412-391-6984

Edward J. Kabala
Robert G. Geeseman
Michael A. Cassidy
Susan Foreman Jordan
Kenneth E. Lewis
Samuel A. Landman
Alan Z. Lefkowitz
Sylvia Bell
Stanley Koepke
William H. Maruca
Donna J. Naab
Michael G. Wiethorn
Patricia Power Wolfinger

OF COUNSEL

Stewart R. Snodgrass
Herbert G. Sheinberg

SPECIAL COUNSEL

John Michael Studeny

For full biographical listings, see the Martindale-Hubbell Law Directory

---

KIGER MESSER & ALPERN (AV)

1404 Grant Building, 15219
Telephone: 412-281-7200
Fax: 412-765-0440

MEMBERS OF FIRM

Jerome W. Kiger
Howard F. Messer
Charles H. Alpern

ASSOCIATES

Alice Warner Shumlas

PARALEGALS

Cheryl E. Diehl

For full biographical listings, see the Martindale-Hubbell Law Directory

---

KLETT LIEBER ROONEY & SCHORLING, A PROFESSIONAL CORPORATION (AV)

40th Floor, One Oxford Centre, 15219-6498
Telephone: 412-392-2000
FAX: 412-392-2128; 412-392-2129
Harrisburg, Pennsylvania Office: 240 North Third Street, Suite 600.
Telephone: 717-231-7700.
Philadelphia, Pennsylvania Office: 28th Floor, One Logan Square.
Telephone: 215-567-7500

SHAREHOLDERS

Marcus Aaron, II
John A. Barbour
Peter C. Blasier
Jeffrey S. Blum
Thomas P. Brogan
William H. Clark, Jr.
Andrew J. Cornelius
Alan K. Cotler
Mary Jo Howard Dively
Christine L. Donohue
Bernard Eisen
Alan A. Garfinkel
Charles B. Gibbons
Thomas S. Giotto
G. Richard Gold
Foster S. Goldman, Jr.
Robert T. Harper
Jules S. Henshell
Jane E. Hepner
Craig S. Heryford
Richard T. Kennedy
Edwin L. Klett
Jan Z. Krasnowiecki
Stanley J. Lehman
Kenneth R. Luttinger
Michael M. Lyons
Elizabeth A. Malloy
Michael J. Manzo
Francis X. Matt, III
Terrence H. Murphy
Joseph J. Palumbo
Arthur J. Rooney, II
William H. Schorling
Robert P. Simons
William A. K. Titelman
Howard J. Wein
Joan A. Yue

SENIOR COUNSEL

Robert Engel
Jerome B. Lieber
Julian Ruslander

OF COUNSEL

Alan Meisel

(See Next Column)

KLETT LIEBER ROONEY & SCHORLING A PROFESSIONAL CORPORATION—*Continued*

ASSOCIATES

Lisa Marie Stafford Anderson
David R. Berk
Deborah Mahbod Bradley
Sandra A. Brown
James R. Carlisle, II
Jerome Cochran
Mäny Emamzadeh
Adam S. Ennis
Suzanne Ewing
Bruce C. Fuchs
Maureen P. Gluntz
Alicia M. Hawkins
Barbara A. Fure Hollinshead
Alice Sacks Johnston
Gregg Mitchell Kander
LB Kregenow
Jacqui Fiske Lazo
Patricia Lindauer
James A. Mercolini
James D. Newell
Timothy J. Nieman
John C. Pekar
Donald S. Prophete
Joseph F. Quinn
W. Gregory Rhodes
Leonard C. Sherer
Paul A. Supowitz
Amy M. Tonti
Philip James Uher
Michael Yablonski

For full biographical listings, see the Martindale-Hubbell Law Directory

LITMAN LITMAN HARRIS & BROWN, P.C. (AV)

3600 One Oxford Centre, 15219
Telephone: 412-456-2000
Fax: 412-456-2020

S. David Litman, P.C.
Roslyn M. Litman
Stephen J. Harris
David R. Brown
Martha S. Helmreich
Lester G. Nauhaus
Daniel L. Chunko
Mark F. Flaherty
Joseph Leibowicz
Robert J. O'Hara, III

For full biographical listings, see the Martindale-Hubbell Law Directory

MARCUS & SHAPIRA (AV)

35th Floor, One Oxford Centre, 301 Grant Street, 15219-6401
Telephone: 412-471-3490
Telecopier: 412-391-8758

MEMBERS OF FIRM

Bernard D. Marcus
Daniel H. Shapira
George P. Slesinger
Robert L. Allman, II
Estelle F. Comay
Susan Gromis Flynn
Darlene M. Nowak
Glenn M. Olcerst
Elly Heller-Toig
Sylvester A. Beozzo

OF COUNSEL

John M. Burkoff

SPECIAL COUNSEL

Jane Campbell Moriarty

ASSOCIATES

Scott D. Livingston
Robert M. Barnes
Stephen S. Zubrow
David B. Rodes
Lori E. McMaster
Melody A. Pollock
James F. Rosenberg
Amy M. Gottlieb

For full biographical listings, see the Martindale-Hubbell Law Directory

MCCANN, GARLAND, RIDALL & BURKE (AV)

Suite 4000, 309 Smithfield Street, 15222
Telephone: 412-566-1818
Fax: 412-566-1817

MEMBERS OF FIRM

John A. McCann (1891-1972)
G. Gray Garland, Jr.
Edmund W. Ridall, Jr.
Edward C. Wachter, Jr.
Stephen J. Jurman
Michael J. Woodring

OF COUNSEL

Charles R. Burke
Ewing C. Bashor
Gretchen G. Donaldson

ASSOCIATES

Thea G. Evankovich
Bernard J. Bercik, Jr.
Terry J. Himes

For full biographical listings, see the Martindale-Hubbell Law Directory

MEYER, UNKOVIC & SCOTT (AV)

1300 Oliver Building, 15222
Telephone: 412-456-2800
Fax: 412-456-2864
Telex: 902402

PARTNERS

Alexander Unkovic (1915-1988)
Thomas A. Berret
Michael J. Boyle
Patricia L. Dodge
Frederick J. Francis
William P. Getty
P. Christian Hague
Kevin C. Hansen
Kenneth G. Judson
Richard G. Kotarba
W. Reid Lowe
James R. Mall
Robert Mauro
Kevin F. McKeegan
William A. Meyer, Jr.
Stephen E. Nash
Lawrence B. Niemann
Russell J. Ober, Jr.

(See Next Column)

PARTNERS (Continued)

Joel Pfeffer
John W. Powell
Thomas William Renwand
Frank G. Salpietro
Janet L. Sargert
Robert P. Struble
Dennis Unkovic
Joseph A. Vater, Jr.
William F. Ward

SPECIAL COUNSEL

John W. Fahnestock
Ronald D. Morelli
Leonard D. Silk

ASSOCIATES

Joseph E. Bartoszewicz
Robert E. Dauer, Jr.
J. Robert Hanlon, Jr.
David L. Harnish
Ronald L. Hicks, Jr.
Douglas M. Hottle
Joseph E. Linehan
Sherry D. Lowe
John Lucas
Joan E. Marshall
Hugh F. McGough
Kim Orlando
W. Grant Scott, II
Beth Ann Slagle
Tracey A. Wilson

SENIOR COUNSEL

Herman S. Harvey, Jr.
William A. Meyer
Howard I. Scott

For full biographical listings, see the Martindale-Hubbell Law Directory

MILLER & ENTWISLE (AV)

614 Oliver Building, 15222
Telephone: 412-391-3211

MEMBERS OF FIRM

Harbaugh Miller
Robert M. Entwisle
Robert M. Entwisle, III

OF COUNSEL

Watson C. Marshall
Elizabeth Bradbury Entwisle

For full biographical listings, see the Martindale-Hubbell Law Directory

NASH & COMPANY, A PROFESSIONAL CORPORATION (AV)

700 Westinghouse Building, 15222
Telephone: 412-392-2333
Fax: 412-392-2343

Stephen P. Nash
Melinda J. Roberts

Anne D. Mullaney
Charles G. O'Hara
Terrence J. O'Rourke
Paul J. Kegaly
David W. Thomas
Nicole A. Normansell

OF COUNSEL

Jacqueline O. Shogan
Domenic A. Bellisario

For full biographical listings, see the Martindale-Hubbell Law Directory

PIETRAGALLO, BOSICK & GORDON (AV)

The Thirty-Eighth Floor, One Oxford Centre, 15219
Telephone: 412-263-2000
Facsimile: 412-261-5295

MEMBERS OF FIRM

William Pietragallo, II
Joseph J. Bosick
Mark Gordon
John E. Hall
Spencer D. Hirshberg
Robert J. Behling
Lawrence J. Baldasare
William S. Smith
Francis E. Pipak, Jr.
LuAnn Haley
Paul K. Vey
Nora Barry Fischer
Thomas J. Sweeney, Jr.
Daniel D. Harshman
Robert E. Dapper, Jr.
David H. Dille

ASSOCIATES

Robert H. Gustine
Harry J. Klucher
Robert R. Leight
Christopher L. Wildfire
Heather S. Heidelbaugh
Eric K. Falk
James G. Orie
Stacey F. Vernallis
Mark F. Haak
Pamela G. Cochenour
William W. Schrimpf, Sr.
Michael P. Sosso
Vincent A Coppola
Clem C. Trischler, Jr.
Anthony G. Sanchez
Kenneth T. Newman
C. Peter Hitson
Raymond G. McLaughlin
David Paul Franklin
Brian S. Kane
Linda M. Gillen
Robert J. Colville
Brian K. Parker
Sean B. Epstein
Lisa P. McQuarrie

COUNSEL

Harold Gondelman
Alfred S. Pelaez

For full biographical listings, see the Martindale-Hubbell Law Directory

PLOWMAN, SPIEGEL & LEWIS, P.C. (AV)

Grant Building, Suite 925, 15219-2201
Telephone: 412-471-8521
Fax: 412-471-4481

(See Next Column)

PLOWMAN, SPIEGEL & LEWIS P.C., *Pittsburgh—Continued*

Jack W. Plowman
John L. Spiegel
James A. Lewis
Frank J. Kernan
Clifford L. Tuttle, Jr.
Kenneth W. Lee
Bruce M. Campbell
Amy E. Bentz
Edward C. Terreri

Marshall J. Conn
William A. Houston
David Raves

Reference: Pittsburgh National Bank.

For full biographical listings, see the Martindale-Hubbell Law Directory

REED SMITH SHAW & McCLAY (AV)

James H. Reed Building, Mellon Square, 435 Sixth Avenue, 15219-1886
Telephone: 412-288-3131
Cable Address: "Reedsmith Pgh"
TWX: 710-664-2083
FAX: 412-288-3063
Mailing Address: P.O. Box 2009, 15230
Washington, D.C. Office: Ring Building, 1200 18th Street, N.W., 20036-2506.
Telephone: 202-457-6100.
FAX: 202-457-6113.
Philadelphia, Pennsylvania Office: 2500 One Liberty Place, 19103-7301.
Telephone: 215-851-8100.
FAX: 215-851-1420.
Harrisburg, Pennsylvania Office: 213 Market Street, 17101-2132.
Telephone: 717-234-5988.
McLean, Virginia Office: Suite 1100, 8251 Greensboro Drive, 22102-3844.
Telephone: 703-734-4600.
Princeton, New Jersey Office: 136 Main Street, 08540-5799.
Telephone: 609-987-0050.
FAX: 609-951-0824.

MEMBERS OF FIRM

Joel P. Aaronson
Thomas L. Allen
Anthony J. Basinski
William Bevan, III
Edward A. Bittner, Jr.
Walter G. Bleil
Russell J. Boehner
Dennis R. Bonessa
Daniel I. Booker
Mark Bookman
Douglas E. Cameron
David I. Cohen
Frederick H. Colen
Kathy K. Condo
Eugene K. Connors
Ernest R. Dell
Lawrence A. Demase
David L. DeNinno
Debra H. Dermody
Thomas J. Duman
Carolyn D. Duronio
Bruce D. Evans
John P. Fernsler
John G. Ferreira
Lawrence E. Flatley
J. Tomlinson Fort
Steven P. Fulton
Daniel P. Gallagher, Jr.
Pasquale D. Gentile, Jr.
G. Donald Gerlach
Sam P. Gidas
Dodi Walker Gross
Frank T. Guadagnino
James R. Haggerty
James H. Hardie
John C. Harmon
Robert W. Hartland
Ronald G. Hartman
Jane E. Helppie
Leo N. Hitt
Edward Hoopes
Craig W. Jones
Gregory B. Jordan
Carole S. Katz
Kerry A. Kearney
Gretchen L. Kelly
Kenneth C. Kettering
Joseph W. Klein
Carl Krasik
Thomas P. Lawton III
John F. LeBlond
Frederick C. Leech
Alan E. London
Robert G. Lovett
Michael E. Lowenstein
Glenn R. Mahone
Jan A. Marks
David J. McAllister
W. Thomas McGough, Jr.
J. Sherman McLaughlin
Blair S. McMillin
Robert K. Morris
Martha Hartle Munsch
Regis D. Murrin
Philip H. Myers
(Not admitted in PA)
Louis A. Naugle
Gerald C. Paris
Ruth S. Perfido
David S. Pollock
Peter D. Post
Robert F. Prorok
W. Franklin Reed
Eric P. Reif
James J. Restivo, Jr.
Patrick W. Ritchey
William M. Robinson
Eric A. Schaffer
Leonard L. Scheinholtz
Edward W. Seifert
Nancy J. Shurlow
Paul M. Singer
William J. Smith
Arland T. Stein
Leonard L. Stewart
Edward N. Stoner, II
Arthur H. Stroyd, Jr.
Thomas Todd
Harley N. Trice, II
John C. Unkovic
John L. Vitsas
Harry H. Weil
Richard T. Wentley
John H. White
Roger C. Wiegand
Daniel E. Wille
Nelson W. Winter
Thomas R. Wright
Nelson P. Young
David Ziegler
Scott F. Zimmerman

COUNSEL

John H. Demmler
William P. Hackney
Dorothy A. Servis
Henry J. Wallace, Jr.

(See Next Column)

SPECIAL COUNSEL

J. S. Bhandari

OF COUNSEL

William D. Armour
Davis C. Burroughs, Jr.
John P. Davis, Jr.
Ralph H. Demmler
Robert J. Dodds, Jr.
Carl E. Glock, Jr.
John B. Gordon
Donald B. Heard
Gilbert J. Helwig
Henry P. Hoffstot, Jr.
Edward W. Marsh
Walter T. McGough
William E. Miller, Jr.
John L. Propst
John H. Scott, Jr.
Edmund K. Trent
Joseph Van Buskirk
Charles Holmes Wolfe, Jr.

ASSOCIATES

Amy Acheson
Robert D. Anderle
Jeffrey G. Aromatorio
Elizabeth S. Athol
Karen E. Baillie
J. Brooke Bashore Smith
Todd M. Begg
James W. Bentz
Reginald J. Bridges
Vanessa S. Browne-Barbour
Ann P. Cahouet
Sarah L. Church
Jack B. Cobetto, III
Robert B. Cottington
Debra McC. Coulson
William J. DiPaolo
Pamina Ewing
Rudy A. Fabian
Stanley D. Ference III
Kevin J. Garber
Mary Jo Hackett
Ted R. Heuston
Gary L. Kaplan
(Not admitted in PA)
Cynthia E. Kernick
Maxine S. Kisilinsky
Lisa C. Labriola
Dianne M. Lancaster
Daniel P. Lynch
George F. Magera
Mary K. McDonald
Mark S. Melodia
Leslie J. Messineo
Daniel M. Miller
Joseph T. Moran
Perry A. Napolitano
Arlie R. Nogay
William C. Nowak
Stephen P. Paschall
Douglas L. Rabuzzi
Carl R. Reisacher
Joseph F. Rodkey, Jr.
Kimberly L. Sachse
Patricia Shearer
Beth L. (Balzer) Silver
Marketa Sims
(Not admitted in PA)
Jennifer A. Smokelin
George L. Stewart, II
Gretchen P. Stubenvoll
Patrick E. Sweeney
Gene A. Tabachnick
(Not admitted in PA)
Brian C. Vertz
Roberta R. Wilson

For full biographical listings, see the Martindale-Hubbell Law Directory

RILEY, McNULTY & HEWITT, P.C. (AV)

460 Cochran Road, 15228
Telephone: 412-341-9300
Fax: 412-341-9177

Patrick R. Riley
Sibyl S. McNulty
Patrick A. Hewitt

David E. Sweitzer

For full biographical listings, see the Martindale-Hubbell Law Directory

ROSE, SCHMIDT, HASLEY & DISALLE, P.C. (AV)

900 Oliver Building, 15222-2310
Telephone: 412-434-8600
Fax: 412-263-2829
Washington, Pennsylvania Office: 7th Floor, Millcraft Center.
Telephone: 412-228-8883.

Don Rose (1881-1965)
John Evans Rose (1908-1972)
Robert M. DeBroff (1934-1974)
Harold R. Schmidt (1913-1989)
Richard DiSalle
Samuel L. Douglass
Edmund M. Carney
Brian W. Ashbaugh
Gail L. Gratton
Susan Hileman Malone
Carl Andrew McGhee
Keithley D. Mulvihill
Steven M. Petrikis
Kim D. Eaton
James W. Barson
R. Stanley Mitchel
Raymond N. Baum
Charles L. Potter, Jr.

Jeffrey P. Brahan
Philip E. Cook
Francis J. DiSalle
Kenneth D. Joseph
Mary J. Lynch
Mark E. Mazzei
Dianne S. Wainwright

COUNSEL

Raymond G. Hasley
Daniel B. Dixon
Cyril A. Fox, jr.
Andrew L. Weil
Edward Gerjuoy
Charles R. Reis

WASHINGTON, PENNSYLVANIA OFFICE PERSONNEL

Richard DiSalle

For full biographical listings, see the Martindale-Hubbell Law Directory

Pittsburgh—Continued

ROSENBERG, KIRSHNER P.A. (AV)

1500 Grant Building, 15219-2203
Telephone: 412-281-4256
Telefax: 412-642-2380
Robinson Township, Pennsylvania Office: 5996-F Steubenville Pike, 15136.
Telephone: 412-788-0600.
Fax: 412-788-1503.
Imperial, Pennsylvania Office: 223 Main Street, 15126.
Telephone: 412-695-7888.
North Palm Beach, Florida Office: 4th Floor, 712 U.S. Highway One, 33408.
Telephone: 407-844-6206.
Telefax: 407-842-4104.

A. H. Rosenberg (1890-1968)
H. N. Rosenberg
Charles Kirshner
William R. Haushalter
Arthur L. Bloom
Richard E. Bliss
Miles A. Kirshner

Gregory L. Fitzpatrick
Charles H. Saul
Tony D. Skees
Bernadette M. Staroschuck

OF COUNSEL

Donald E. Machen
James F. Manley

Representative Clients: Erie Insurance Co.; Keene Corporation; Liberty Mutual Insurance Co.; Kemper Insurance; Union Carbide; McDonald's Corp.; General Electric Capital Corp.; Equitable Lomas Leasing Corp.; Hyatt Legal Services; Rite Aid Corp.

For full biographical listings, see the Martindale-Hubbell Law Directory

ROTHMAN GORDON FOREMAN & GROUDINE, P.C. (AV)

Third Floor-Grant Building, 15219
Telephone: 412-338-1100
Telefax: 412-281-7304
Washington, D.C. Office: 1120 Connecticut Avenue, N.W. Suite 440.
Telephone: 202-338-3248.

Emil W. Herman
Louis B. Kushner
Mark L. Unatin
Thomas R. Solomich
Stephen H. Jordan
Frederick A. Polner
James R. Farley
Ronald G. Backer
Shelley W. Elovitz
Carl E. Harvison
June S. Schulberg
Martha A. Zatezalo

Sandra Reiter Kushner
Sara A. Mercer
Paul R. Yagelski
Christopher Rulis
Mark S. Weis
Alan Carlos Blanco
Bernadette L. Puzzuole
Kevin W. Lee
Sally L. Burke
Jeffrey J. Russell
Lori Ella Brenner
John R. Fielding
Patricia L. Haas
Clare M. Wuest
John P. Fedorko
Kim A. Bodnar

OF COUNSEL

Norman A. Groudine

For full biographical listings, see the Martindale-Hubbell Law Directory

SHARLOCK, REPCHECK & MAHLER (AV)

3280 USX Tower, 600 Grant Street, 15219
Telephone: 412-391-6171
Fax: 412-391-8804

MEMBERS OF FIRM

John J. Repcheck
Gary F. Sharlock
Aloysius F. Mahler
David P. Helwig

ASSOCIATES

Cynthia M. Hutchins
Michael E. Lang
Robert D. Leidigh

For full biographical listings, see the Martindale-Hubbell Law Directory

SPRINGER, BUSH & PERRY, A PROFESSIONAL CORPORATION (AV)

Two Gateway Center, Fifteenth Floor, 15222
Telephone: 412-281-4900
Fax: 412-261-1645
Moon Township, Pennsylvania Office: 500 Cherrington Parkway, Suite 420, Coraopolis, Pennsylvania, 15108.
Telephone: 412-269-4200.
Fax: 412-269-9638.

Edward L. Springer
Donald C. Bush
Joseph Friedman
James C. Kletter
W. Ronald Stout
Stephen F. Ban
Robert E. Harper (Resident, Moon Township, Coraopolis, Pennsylvania Office)
John F. Perry
James H. Webster
Thomas P. Peterson
Edward R. Lawrence, Jr. (Resident, Moon Township, Coraopolis, Pennsylvania Office)
Gerri L. Sperling
Michael J. Hennessy
Samuel R. A. Grego
Henry R. Johnston, III

Michelle L. Kopnski
Daniel J. McNulty
Frederick J. Wolfe
John S. Morrow, Jr. (Resident, Moon Township, Coraopolis, Pennsylvania Office)
Andrew T. Flowers
Laurel S. Gleason
Jeffrey T. Jochims
Cynthia Storer Simpson

COUNSEL

Malcolm Anderson
Paul G. Perry
John E. Perry
Edward J. Krug

For full biographical listings, see the Martindale-Hubbell Law Directory

STONECIPHER, CUNNINGHAM, BEARD & SCHMITT (AV)

125 First Avenue, 15222
Telephone: 412-391-8510
Telecopier: 412-391-8522

MEMBERS OF FIRM

Charles L. Cunningham (1889-1961)
C. W. Cunningham (1916-1962)
Philip E. Beard
Joseph E. Schmitt
Roger S. Cunningham
Norman E. Gilkey

ASSOCIATES

Paul R. Rennie
George T. Snyder
Philip E. Beard, II
Nathaniel Beaumont Beard

Reference: Integra Bank of Pittsburgh

For full biographical listings, see the Martindale-Hubbell Law Directory

TARASI & JOHNSON, P.C. (AV)

510 Third Avenue, 15219
Telephone: 412-391-7135
Fax: 412-471-2673

Louis M. Tarasi, Jr.
David E. Johnson

John A. Adamczyk
Elizabeth Tarasi Stevenson
Jean A. Kell
Matthew A. Hartley

For full biographical listings, see the Martindale-Hubbell Law Directory

THOMPSON CALKINS & SUTTER (AV)

1412 Frick Building, 15219
Telephone: 412-261-4050
Fax: 412-261-2280

MEMBERS OF FIRM

George H. Thompson
Scott R. Calkins
Paul E. Sutter
Orlando R. Sodini
Toni J. Minner

ASSOCIATES

Hilary Sue Zakowitz
Kimberly McDaniel
Ann M. Coholan
Phyllis T. Procopio

For full biographical listings, see the Martindale-Hubbell Law Directory

THOMSON, RHODES & COWIE, P.C. (AV)

Tenth Floor, Two Chatham Center, 15219
Telephone: 412-232-3400
Fax: 412-232-3498

Thomas D. Thomson
John David Rhodes
Norman J. Cowie
Richard E. Rush
James R. Hartline
Linton L. Moyer
John K. Heisey
David R. Johnson
Jerry R. Hogenmiller
David M. McQuiston
William James Rogers
Glenn H. Gillette
Templeton Smith, Jr.

SPECIAL COUNSEL

John H. Morgan

William M. Bernhart
G. Jay Habas
Mark William Furry
Donna J. Geary
Harry W. Rosensteel

For full biographical listings, see the Martindale-Hubbell Law Directory

THORP, REED & ARMSTRONG (AV)

One Riverfront Center, 15222
Telephone: 412-394-7711
Fax: 412-394-2555

(See Next Column)

THORP, REED & ARMSTRONG, *Pittsburgh—Continued*

MEMBERS OF FIRM

Charles Monroe Thorp (1863-1942)
Earl Frederick Reed (1894-1963)
Clyde Allman Armstrong (1898-1975)
Clyde W. Armstrong (1926-1985)
Kevin C. Abbott
John H. Bingler, Jr.
Joseph R. Brendel
Michael R. Bucci, Jr.
G. Daniel Carney
James D. Chiafullo
Thomas W. Corbett, Jr.
John W. Eichleay, Jr.
George P. Faines
Craig E. Frischman
Douglas E. Gilbert
James K. Goldberg
Edward B. Harmon
Scott E. Henderson
Melissa A. Jad
Sidney J. Kelly
Michael J. Kline
Clifford B. Levine
Thomas E. Lippard
Joseph Mack, III
Julie A. Maloney
Kurt A. Miller
Mark F. Nowak
Deborah P. Powell
David G. Ries
Richard D. Rose
Barbara K. Ross
Edmund S. Ruffin, III
Martin J. Saunders
Ralph F. Scalera
David A. Scott
Robert H. Shoop, Jr.
Joseph D. Shuman
Richard V. Sica
Timothy M. Slavish
Leonard F. Spagnolo
Randolph T. Struk
Richard I. Thomas
Michael J. Tomana
Peter Greig Veeder
Keith H. West
William M. Wycoff
C. James Zeszutek

ASSOCIATES

Carolyn H. Allen
Paul D. Bangor, Jr.
Craig A. Barr
Kimberly A. Brown
Noland Jin-Poh Cheung
Chad A. Cicconi
Charles G. Cochenour
Jeffrey J. Conn
Ronald C. Gahagan, Jr.
Bruce V. Hicks
Stacey L. Jarrell
Maureen P. Kelly
Donald M. Lund
Alice B. Mitinger
Philip J. Murray III
Elizabeth L. Rabenold
Kimberly L. Wakim
David E. White
Darren E. Wolf

SENIOR COUNSEL

Frank J. Gaffney
William W. Scott, Jr.
William D. Sutton

OF COUNSEL

J. Robert Maxwell
Stuart C. Gaul
Charles Weiss

For full biographical listings, see the Martindale-Hubbell Law Directory

---

TUCKER ARENSBERG, P.C. (AV)

1500 One PPG Place, 15222
Telephone: 412-566-1212
Telex: 902914
Fax: 412-594-5619
Harrisburg, Pennsylvania Office: 116 Pine Street.
Telephone: 717-238-2007.
Fax: 717-238-2242.
Pittsburgh Airport Area Office: Airport Professional Office Center, 1150 Thorn Run Road Ext., Moon Township, Pennsylvania, 15108.
Telephone: 412-262-3730.
Fax: 412-262-2576.

Charles F. C. Arensberg (1879-1974)
Frank R. S. Kaplan (1886-1957)
Donald L. Very (1933-1979)
Linda A. Acheson
W. Theodore Brooks
Matthew J. Carl
Richard W. Cramer
J. Kent Culley
Donald P. Eriksen
Paul F. Fagan
Gary J. Gushard
William T. Harvey
Joel M. Helmrich
Gary P. Hunt
Raymond M. Komichak
Jeffrey J. Leech
Beverly Weiss Manne
Garland H. McAdoo, Jr.
John M. McElroy
Robert L. McTiernan
John B. Montgomery
Stanley V. Ostrow
William A. Penrod
Daniel J. Perry
Henry S. Pool
Richard B. Tucker, III
Bradley S. Tupi
Charles J. Vater
Gary E. Wieczorek
G. Ashley Woolridge

Donald E. Ambrose
Robin K. Capozzi
Diane Hernon Chavis
Toni L. DiGiacobbe
Donna M. Donaher
John E. Graf
Mark L. Heleen
David P. Hvizdos
Timothy S. Johnson
Joni L. Landy
Jonathan S. McAnney
G. Ross Rhodes
Christopher J. Richardson
Eric M. Schumann
Steven H. Seel
Steven B. Silverman
Michael J. Tobak, III
Homer L. Walton

HARRISBURG OFFICE

J. Kent Culley

John G. Di Leonardo

(See Next Column)

SPECIAL COUNSEL

Richard S. Crone
Elliott W. Finkel
Michael J. Laffey
John P. Papuga
William J. Staley
Richard B. Tucker, Jr.

For full biographical listings, see the Martindale-Hubbell Law Directory

---

WITTLIN GOLDSTON & CAPUTO, P.C. (AV)

213 Smithfield Street, Suite 200, 15222
Telephone: 412-261-4200
Telecopier: 412-261-9137

Charles E. Wittlin
Linda Leebov Goldston
Louis E. Caputo
Robert Simcox Adams
William L. Stang
John H. Iannucci
Laurence R. Landis
Sharon W. Perelman
John J. Franciscus
Joseph Brian Landy

For full biographical listings, see the Martindale-Hubbell Law Directory

---

ZIMMER KUNZ, PROFESSIONAL CORPORATION (AV)

3300 USX Tower, 600 Grant Street, 15219
Telephone: 412-281-8000
Fax: 412-281-1765

Harry J. Zimmer
Thomas A. Lazaroff
John E. Kunz
Andrew J. Banyas, III
Raymond H. Conaway
Fred C. Trenor, II
George N. Stewart
Joni M. Mangino
Joseph W. Selep
Raymond J. Conlon
Edward K. Dixon

OF COUNSEL

John W. Thomas

Nancy DeCarlo Fabi
Dara A. DeCourcy
Alexander P. Bicket
John W. Zotter
Daniel E. Krauth
George R. Farneth, II
Anthony Carone
Glenn M. Campbell

For full biographical listings, see the Martindale-Hubbell Law Directory

---

POTTSTOWN, Montgomery Co.

O'DONNELL, WEISS & MATTEI, P.C. (AV)

41 High Street, 19464
Telephone: 610-323-2800
Fax: 610-323-2845

Wm. A. O'Donnell, Jr. (1914-1971)
Emidio J. Mattei (1924-1981)
Alvin L. Weiss
John A. Koury, Jr.
David S. Kaplan
Henry T. Zale
David A. Megay
Joseph A. Suchoza
George Gerasimowicz, Jr.
Kim Marie Covello

Representative Clients: Midlantic Bank; Pottstown Memorial Medical Center; Elverson National Bank.
Local Counsel for: Dana Corp.
Reference: Midlantic Bank.

For full biographical listings, see the Martindale-Hubbell Law Directory

---

*POTTSVILLE,** Schuylkill Co.

LIPKIN, MARSHALL, BOHORAD & THORNBURG, A PROFESSIONAL CORPORATION (AV)

Suite 200 One Norwegian Plaza, P.O. Box 1280, 17901
Telephone: 717-622-1811
Fax: 717-622-4850
Mahanoy City, Pennsylvania Office: 9 East Center Street.
Telephone: 717-773-3790.
Tower City, Pennsylvania Office: 708 East Grand Avenue.
Telephone: 717-647-9546.
Ashland, Pennsylvania Office: 1435 Arch Street.
Telephone: 717-875-2121.
Frackville, Pennsylvania Office: 44 N. Balliet Street.
Telephone: 717-874-4700.

Henry Houck (1892-1959)
James P. Bohorad (1905-1964)
H. G. Stutzman (1907-1977)
Leroy G. Adams (1946-1988)
Alexander E. Lipkin
Alvin B. Marshall
Robert N. Bohorad
Richard A. Thornburg

S. John Price, Jr.
Mark Semanchik
Kathleen M. Callaghan

For full biographical listings, see the Martindale-Hubbell Law Directory

---

ZIMMERMAN, LIEBERMAN & DERENZO (AV)

111 East Market Street, P.O. Box 238, 17901
Telephone: 717-622-1988, 622-1989
Fax: 717-622-3261

(See Next Column)

ZIMMERMAN, LIEBERMAN & DERENZO—*Continued*

MEMBERS OF FIRM

John B. Lieberman, III
Frank L. Tamulonis, Jr.
Ronald T. Derenzo
Paul J. Dufallo

ASSOCIATES

Joseph G. Zerbe
Wayne S. Fegley
Robert L. Goodman
James E. Crossen

Representative Clients: USF & G; Royal Insurance Co.; Old Republican Insurance Co.; Aetna Casualty & Surety Co.; Southern Carbon Corp. (General Counsel); Miners National Bank; Pennsylvania National Insurance Group; Pennsylvania Mfrs. Association Casualty Co.; American Mutual Liability Co.; Keystone Automobile Casualty Co.

For full biographical listings, see the Martindale-Hubbell Law Directory

*READING,** Berks Co.

BINGAMAN, HESS, COBLENTZ & BELL, A PROFESSIONAL CORPORATION (AV)

660 Penn Square Center, 601 Penn Street, P.O. Box 61, 19603-0061
Telephone: 610-374-8377
Fax: 610-376-3105
Bernville, Pennsylvania Office: 331 Main Street.
Telephone: 610-488-0656.
Camden, New Jersey Office: 411 Cooper Street.
Telephone: 609-966-0117.
Fax: 609-965-0796.

James F. Bell (1921-1988)

OF COUNSEL

Llewellyn R. Bingaman
J. Wendell Coblentz
Raymond K. Hess
Ralph J. Althouse, Jr.
Gerald P. Sigal

David E. Turner
Kurt Althouse
Clemson North Page, Jr.
Harry D. McMunigal
Mark G. Yoder
Karen Feryo Longenecker
Carl D. Cronrath, Jr.
Shawn J. Lau

Lynne K. Beust
Susan N. Denaro
Elizabethanne D. McMunigal
Daniel J. Poruban
Patrick T. Barrett
Jill M. Scheidt

LEGAL SUPPORT PERSONNEL

Eric A. Barr (Office Administrator)

PARALEGALS

JoAnn Ruchlewicz
Ruth Ann Sunderland
Laura I. Lehane
Kristine L. Krammes
Louise E. Miller
Peter L. Torres

General Counsel for: Meridian Bank; Berks Products Corp.; Leighton Industries, Inc.; Utilities Employees Credit Union.
Local Counsel for: Erie Insurance Exchange; Liberty Mutual Insurance Co.; Old Guard Mutual Insurance Co.

For full biographical listings, see the Martindale-Hubbell Law Directory

MOGEL, SPEIDEL, BOBB & KERSHNER, A PROFESSIONAL CORPORATION (AV)

520 Walnut Street, P.O. Box 8581, 19603-8581
Telephone: 610-376-1515
Telecopier: 610-372-8710

George B. Balmer (1902-1969)
Samuel R. Fry II
George A. Kershner (1907-1969)
Kathleen A. B. Kovach
Carl F. Mogel (1919-1994)
Michael L. Mixell
Donald K. Bobb
George M. Lutz
Edwin H. Kershner
Stephen H. Price
Frederick R. Mogel
Kathryn K. Harenza

OF COUNSEL

Harry W. Speidel
Henry A. Gass

Representative Clients: Great Valley Savings Bank; Clover Farms Dairy Co.; National Penn Bank; Meridian Leasing, Inc.; Ducharme, McMillen & Associates; Edwards Business Machines, Inc.; Greater Berks Development Fund; Union Township, Berks County, Pennsylvania.

For full biographical listings, see the Martindale-Hubbell Law Directory

RHODA, STOUDT & BRADLEY (AV)

Sixth Floor The Berkshire, 501 Washington Street, P.O. Box 877, 19603-0877
Telephone: 610-374-8293
Fax: 610-374-6061
Birdsboro Office: 341A West Main Street.
Telephone: 610-582-4307.
Fleetwood Office: 42 West Main Street.
Telephone: 610-944-6334.
Kutztown Office: Main & Noble Streets.
Telephone: 610-683-8677.

(See Next Column)

Oley Office: Main Street.
Telephone: 610-987-3277.

MEMBERS OF FIRM

John S. Rhoda (1906-1968)
John C. Bradley, Jr.
John C. Bradley (1919-1984)
Jerry R. Richwine
Robert H. Kauffman
George J. Shoop
D. Frederick Muth
Timothy G. Dietrich
Norman E. Dettra, Jr.
Jeffrey L. Schmehl
Geoffrey M. Stoudt
John J. Speicher
Francis M. Mulligan
Robert R. Kreitz

ASSOCIATES

Timothy J. Rowley
Eden R. Bucher
James A. Fry
James T. Weikel
Barrie B. Gehrlein
Joan E. London
David K. Te Selle

OF COUNSEL

Dawson H. Muth
James W. Stoudt

Representative Clients: Allstate Insurance Co.; Home Insurance; Corestates Hamilton Bank; Blue Ball National Bank; Pennsylvania National Bank; Arrow International, Inc.; Arrow Precision Products, Inc.; Metropolitan Edison Co.; Sweet Street Desserts, Inc.; County of Berks.

For full biographical listings, see the Martindale-Hubbell Law Directory

ROLAND & SCHLEGEL, P.C. (AV)

627 North Fourth Street, P.O. Box 902, 19603-0902
Telephone: 610-372-5588
Fax: 610-372-5957
Pottsville, Pennsylvania Office: Route 61 North, P.O. Box 149, 17901.
Telephone: 717-622-3355.
Fax: 717-622-5147.
Boyertown, Pennsylvania Office: 45 East Philadelphia Avenue, 19512.
Telephone: 610-367-4384.

David H. Roland
Gregory C. Hartman
Raymond C. Schlegel
Mary M. Bertolet
John W. Roland
Edwin L. Stock
Edward M. Collins, III

Margaret Kaiser Collins
Andrew N. Howe
Christopher J. Hartman
Andrew F. Fick

OF COUNSEL

John E. Jones, III

Representative Clients: Albright College; CoreStates; Graco Children's Products, Inc.; Insurance Company of North America; Meridian Bank; Muhlenberg School District; National Penn Bank; Reading Hospital and Medical Center; Reading Housing Authority; Western Berks Water Authority.

For full biographical listings, see the Martindale-Hubbell Law Directory

STEVENS & LEE, A PROFESSIONAL CORPORATION (AV)

111 North Sixth Street, P.O. Box 679, 19603
Telephone: 610-478-2000
Fax: 610-376-5610
Wayne, Pennsylvania Office: One Glenhardie Corporate Center, 1275 Drummers Lane, P. O. Box 236.
Telephone: 610-964-1480.
Fax: 610-687-1384.
Lancaster, Pennsylvania Office: One Penn Square, P.O. Box 1594.
Telephone: 717-291-1031.
Fax: 717-394-7726.
Allentown, Pennsylvania Office: 740 North Hamilton Mall, P. O. Box 8838.
Telephone: 610-439-4195.
Fax: 610-439-8415.
Harrisburg, Pennsylvania Office: 208 North Third Street. Suite 310. P.O. Box 12090. 17101.
Telephone: 717-234-1250.
Fax: 717-234-1939.
Philadelphia, Pennsylvania Office: Two Penn Center Plaza, Suite 200.
Telephone: 215-854-6370.
Fax: 215-569-0216.
Wilkes-Barre, Pennsylvania Office: 289 North Main Street.
Telephone: 717-823-6116.
Fax: 717-823-1149.

John B. Stevens (1880-1940)
John B. Nason, III (Resident, Wayne and Philadelphia Offices)
Harry W. Lee (1894-1964)
Joseph E. Lewis
John D. Glase (1913-1970)
Jon W. Tryon (Resident, Lancaster Office)
John G. Rothermel (1896-1988)
Edward A. Fedok (Resident, Allentown Office)
Charles H. Weidner (1899-1989)
Charles J. Bloom (Resident, Wayne and Philadelphia Offices)
Robert T. Miller (1927-1990)
Joseph M. Harenza
Daniel G. Rothermel (1901-1993)
Sidney D. Kline, Jr.
Donald D. McFadden (Resident, Wilkes-Barre Office)
Clinton J. Najarian

(See Next Column)

STEVENS & LEE A PROFESSIONAL CORPORATION, *Reading—Continued*

Paul R. Lewis (Resident, Wayne and Philadelphia Offices)
Joseph Potts, III (Resident, Lancaster Office)
James M. Snyder
William J. Payne (Resident, Wayne Office)
H. Richard Brooks
Joseph H. Huston, Jr. (Resident, Wayne Office)
Daniel B. Huyett
R. John MacKoul, Jr.
Kurt H. Decker
John W. Espenshade (Resident, Lancaster Office)
Susan R. Friedman (Resident, Lancaster Office)
Steven E. Speece (Resident, Wayne Office)
Clinton W. Kemp (Resident, Lancaster Office)
Larry J. Rappoport (Resident, Wayne Office)
C. Thomas Work
Ernest J. Choquette
Daniel E. P. Bausher
Timothy F. Demers
Richard E. Fehling
David A. Vind
J. William Widing III
G. Thompson Bell, III
Wesley R. Kelso (Resident, Lancaster Office)
Kenneth D. Kleinman (Resident, Wayne Office)
James M. White (Resident, Harrisburg Office)
Gary D. Melchionni (Resident, Lancaster Office)
Jeffrey P. Waldron (Resident, Wayne Office)
Kenneth R. Dugan
David W. Swartz
David R. Richie, II
Scott H. Spencer (Resident, Lancaster Office)
Charles F. Harenza
Michael A. Setley
Steven M. Tyminski (Resident, Wayne Office)
Joseph E. Wolfson
John A. Harenza
Ronald L. Williams

Michael E. Loomis (Resident, Allentown Office)
Robert J. Henry
Joseph P. Hofmann (Resident, Lancaster Office)
Kirk L. Wolgemuth (Resident, Lancaster Office)
Kenneth Zielonis (Resident, Harrisburg Office)
Mark N. Raezer
Suzanne Elizabeth Palmer
Steven D. Buck
Edward C. Hogan (Resident, Wayne Office)
David R. Beane
Peter T. Edelman
B. Tyler Lincoln
Steven J. Adams
Charles A. DiNardo (Resident, Wayne Office)
E. Thomas Henefer
John J. Miravich (Resident, Wayne Office)
Douglas P. Rauch
Cathy L. Codrea (Resident, Allentown Office)
Michael J. Medveckus
William J. Reynolds
William P. Thornton, Jr.
Gerard R. Bosch
Jay R. Wagner
Joseph G. Lewis
David McCanney
George W. Bodenger (Resident, Wayne Office)

COUNSEL

Paul H. Edelman

OF COUNSEL

William R. Lessig, Jr.

RETIRED

Richard A. Bausher
John H. Bertolet

For full biographical listings, see the Martindale-Hubbell Law Directory

*RIDGWAY,** Elk Co. — (Refer to St. Marys)

*SCRANTON,** Lackawanna Co.

HAGGERTY, MCDONNELL, O'BRIEN & WRIGHT (AV)

Jordan Building, 203 Franklin Avenue, 18503-1922
Telephone: 717-344-9845
Telecopier: 717-343-9731

MEMBERS OF FIRM

James J. Haggerty
Frank J. McDonnell
Joseph J. O'Brien
Joseph T. Wright, Jr.

ASSOCIATES

George V. Lynett
Robert P. Casey, Jr.
Lori-Ann Barrett

Representative Clients: First National Community Bank; The Scranton Times & Sunday Times; Radio Stations WEJL & WEZX of Scranton, Pa.; Shamrock Communications, Inc.
References: Northeastern National Bank of Pennsylvania, Scranton, Pennsylvania; First National Community Bank.

For full biographical listings, see the Martindale-Hubbell Law Directory

KREDER, BROOKS, HAILSTONE & LUDWIG (AV)

Suite 200, 220 Penn Avenue, 18503
Telephone: 717-346-7922
Telecopier: 717-346-3715

Cody H. Brooks
Andrew Hailstone
Lawrence M. Ludwig
Lucille Marsh
Michael J. Donohue
David K. Brown
J. Frederick Rohrbeck
James J. Wilson
Richard G. Reed
Stephen William Saunders

(See Next Column)

ASSOCIATES

Ann Lavelle Powell
Linda Dwyer Cleary
Barbara Sardella
Alyce Hailstone Farrell
Robert B. Farrell
David A. Aikens, Jr.

OF COUNSEL

Joseph C. Kreder
Willard M. Henkelman
James Edson O'Connell

Counsel for: Consolidated Rail Corp.; PNC Bank; U.S. Fidelity & Guaranty Co.; Nationwide Insurance Co.; Liberty Mutual Insurance Co.; Citizens Savings Assn.; NEP Supershooters, Inc.

For full biographical listings, see the Martindale-Hubbell Law Directory

LENAHAN & DEMPSEY, A PROFESSIONAL CORPORATION (AV)

116 North Washington Avenue, 18503-0234
Telephone: 717-346-2097
Fax: 717-346-1174
Mailing Address: P.O. Box 234, Scranton, Pennsylvania, 18501-0234

John R. Lenahan, Sr.
William J. Dempsey
John R. Lenahan, Jr.
Joseph P. Lenahan
Kathleen A. Lenahan
David E. Heisler
Timothy G. Lenahan
Matthew D. Dempsey

Marianne J. Gilmartin
Alan P. Schoen
Brian J. Lenahan
Diane Hepford Lenahan
George E. Mehalchick
Brian Yeager
Thomas R. Daniels
Myles P. McAliney
Terrence E. Dempsey
Carmina M. Rinkunas
Thomas R. Chesnick
William M. Blaum
Christine S. Mayernick
Patricia Corbett

Representative Insurance Clients: Allstate Insurance Co.; America Security Insurance Co.; Metropolitan Casualty Insurance Co.; Statesman Insurance Group; Foremost Insurance Co.; Aetna Insurance Co.; Pennsylvania National Insurance Group; Kemper Insurance Group; American Mutual Insurance Cos.; American States Insurance, Co.

For full biographical listings, see the Martindale-Hubbell Law Directory

LEVY & PREATE (AV)

507 Linden Street, Suite 600, 18503
Telephone: 717-346-3816
FAX: 717-346-5370

MEMBERS OF FIRM

J. Julius Levy (1891-1978)
Ernest D. Preate
Robert A. Preate
William T. Jones

ASSOCIATES

Howard C. Terreri

OF COUNSEL

David B. Miller
David J. Tomaine
Harold M. Kane
Tullio De Luca

For full biographical listings, see the Martindale-Hubbell Law Directory

O'MALLEY & HARRIS, P.C. (AV)

345 Wyoming Avenue, 18503
Telephone: 717-348-3711
Fax: 717-348-4092
Stroudsburg, Pennsylvania Office: 111 North Seventh Street.
Telephone: 717-421-2252.
Wilkes-Barre, Pennsylvania Office: Courthouse Square Towers, North River Street.
Telephone: 717-829-3232.
FAX: 717-829-4418.
Williamsport, Pennsylvania Office: 321 Pine Street, Suite 308.
Telephone: 717-323-4380.

Eugene Nogi (1905-1975)
Henry Nogi (1900-1976)
Russell O. O'Malley, Sr. (1904-1993)
William H. Amesbury (Resident, Wilkes-Barre Office)
Paul A. Barrett
J. Scott Brady
Bruce L. Coyer
John Q. Durkin
Gerald J. Hanchulak
Norman Harris
Richard K. Hodges
Timothy J. Holland (Resident, Wilkes-Barre Office)
Daniel Morgan
Michael Perry
Joseph R. Rydzewski
Jane M. Carlonas
James M. Tressler
Matthew P. Barrett

Representative Clients: Robert Packer Hospital; GSGS & B Architects & Engineers; Aetna Casualty & Surety Co.; Pennsylvania Hospital Insurance Co.; United States Fidelity & Guaranty Insurance Co.; Selective Insurance Co.; Maryland Casualty Insurance Co.; Robert Packer Hospital; United Gilsonite Laboratories; Electric Mutual Insurance Co.

For full biographical listings, see the Martindale-Hubbell Law Directory

SCANLON, HOWLEY, SCANLON & DOHERTY (AV)

321 Spruce Street, 10th Floor, 18503
Telephone: 717-346-7651

(See Next Column)

SCANLON, HOWLEY, SCANLON & DOHERTY—*Continued*

MEMBERS OF FIRM

James M. Howley
James M. Scanlon
James A. Doherty, Jr.
Thomas R. Nealon
Thomas B. Helbig
Patrick R. Casey

OF COUNSEL

James W. Scanlon

Counsel for: CNA Insurance Company; Selective Insurance Company of America; The Medical Protective Co.; Harleysville Insurance Co.; Mutual Benefit Insurance Co.; The Procter & Gamble Co.; Prudential-Bach Securities, Inc.; Zurich-American Insurance Co.; The Coca-Cola Bottling Co.; The Home Insurance Co.

For full biographical listings, see the Martindale-Hubbell Law Directory

WELLES & MCGRATH (AV)

Room 1000, 321 Spruce Street, 18503
Telephone: 717-346-7651
FAX: 717-344-1542

MEMBERS OF FIRM

Charles H. Welles, Jr. (1876-1962)
Matthew D. Mackie (1897-1965)
Charles H. Welles (Retired)
Henry C. McGrath
Charles H. Welles, IV

Counsel for: PNC Bank; Prudential Insurance Co.; Moore Products Co.; Gann-Dawson, Inc.; Massachusetts Mutual Life Insurance Co.; Metropolitan Life Insurance Co.; Bethlehem Steel Co.

For full biographical listings, see the Martindale-Hubbell Law Directory

SELINSGROVE, Snyder Co.

MOORE & CRAVITZ (AV)

719 North Market Street, 17870
Telephone: 717-374-8138
FAX: 717-374-7558

MEMBERS OF FIRM

John R. Moore
Robert M. Cravitz

ASSOCIATES

Jonathan A. Moore

For full biographical listings, see the Martindale-Hubbell Law Directory

SHAMOKIN, Northumberland Co.

LARK, MAKOWSKI, MARATECK & KONOPKA (AV)

Pennsylvania National Bank & Trust Company Building, P.O. Box L, 17872
Telephone: 717-644-0481
Fax: 717-648-4647

MEMBERS OF FIRM

Frederick E. Lark (1911-1984)
Vincent B. Makowski
Sanford S. Marateck
Frank J. Konopka
David B. Marateck

Representative Clients: Allen Clark Inc.; Marion Heights Borough; John F. Miles Co.; Shamokin Area Industrial Corp.; Shamokin-Coal Township Joint Sewer Authority; Cabinet Industries, Inc.; National Ticket Co.

For full biographical listings, see the Martindale-Hubbell Law Directory

JACK C. YOUNKIN (AV)

One West Sunbury Street, 17872
Telephone: 717-648-6821
Fax: 717-648-4732

LEGAL SUPPORT PERSONNEL

Patricia Janovich

For full biographical listings, see the Martindale-Hubbell Law Directory

SHARON, Mercer Co.

CUSICK, MADDEN, JOYCE AND MCKAY (AV)

First Western Bank Building, 16146
Telephone: 412-981-2000
Fax: 412-981-2007

Martin E. Cusick (1902-1985)

MEMBERS OF FIRM

Donald R. McKay
Henry M. Ekker
P. Raymond Bartholomew
William G. McConnell
Thomas W. Kuster
Peter C. Acker

ASSOCIATES

Kevin Feeney

(See Next Column)

OF COUNSEL

William J. Joyce

Agent for: Lawyers Title Insurance Corporation.
Approved Attorneys for: Penn Attorneys Title Insurance Co.

For full biographical listings, see the Martindale-Hubbell Law Directory

ROUTMAN, MOORE, GOLDSTONE & VALENTINO (AV)

194 East State Street, P.O. Box 690, 16146-0690
Telephone: 412-981-6800
Fax: 412-981-4400
New Castle, Pennsylvania Office: 2656 Wilmington Road, 16105.
Telephone: 412-658-6900.

MEMBERS OF FIRM

Nathan Routman (1904-1974)
Harvey E. Moore (1903-1976)
Bernard Goldstone
Joseph Paul Valentino
John C. Reed
Charles Frederick Gilchrest
Richard W. Epstein
Frank J. Matune

ASSOCIATES

Margaret T. Lucas
Ronald P. McCall
Michael A. Joanow
Mark A. Longietti

LEGAL SUPPORT PERSONNEL

Pamela Sue Swartz
Maureen A. English

Representative Client: T. Bruce Campbell Construction Co. (industrial manufacturer).

For full biographical listings, see the Martindale-Hubbell Law Directory

*SMETHPORT,** McKean Co. — (Refer to Bradford)

*SOMERSET,** Somerset Co.

BARBERA, CLAPPER, BEENER, RULLO & MELVIN (AV)

(Formerly Barbera & Barbera)
146 West Main Street, P.O. Box 775, 15501-0775
Telephone: 814-443-4681
Fax: 814-443-2422

MEMBERS OF FIRM

Nathaniel A. Barbera
John J. Barbera
Samuel D. Clapper
James F. Beener
Daniel W. Rullo
Vincent J. Barbera
Matthew G. Melvin

ASSOCIATES

Patrick P. Svonavec
Annette L. Barbera

OF COUNSEL

Melanie R. Barbera

Local Counsel for: Pennsylvania Electric Co.; General Telephone Corp.

For full biographical listings, see the Martindale-Hubbell Law Directory

FIKE, CASCIO & BOOSE (AV)

Scull Building, 124 North Center Street, P.O. Box 431, 15501
Telephone: 814-445-7948
Fax: 814-443-2255

MEMBERS OF FIRM

Paul E. C. Fike (1901-1963)
Joseph N. Cascio
Robert I. Boose
John J. Dirienzo, Jr.
James R. Cascio
Jeffrey L. Berkey
Lois Witt Geary

Representative Clients: The Berwind Corp.; Somerset Trust Co.; Somerset Area Schools; Somerset County Housing Authority; Windber Area Authority; PBS Coals, Inc.

For full biographical listings, see the Martindale-Hubbell Law Directory

STATE COLLEGE, Centre Co.

LEE, MARTIN, GREEN & REITER, INC. (AV)

270 Walker Drive, 16801
Telephone: 814-237-6291
Fax: 814-237-5861
Bellefonte, Pennsylvania Office: 115 East High Street, Lock Drawer 179.
Telephone: 814-355-4769.
Fax: 814-355-5024.

Donald E. Lee
Robert L. Martin
Joseph P. Green
Dennis O. Reiter
Robert A. Mix
William T. Fleming

Representative Clients: Peoples National Bank of Central Pennsylvania; State College Borough Water Authority; First National Bank of Spring Mills; Erie Insurance Group; Centre Community Hospital; Liberty Mutual Insurance Co.; Centre Area Transportation Authority.

For full biographical listings, see the Martindale-Hubbell Law Directory

State College—Continued

McQuaide, Blasko, Schwartz, Fleming & Faulkner, Inc. (AV)

811 University Drive, 16801-6699
Telephone: 814-238-4926
Fax: 814-234-5620

John G. Love (1893-1966)
Delbert J. McQuaide
John W. Blasko
Thomas E. Schwartz
Grant H. Fleming
David M. Weixel
R. Mark Faulkner
Steven S. Hurvitz
James M. Horne
Wendell V. Courtney
Patricia L. Roenigk
Darryl R. Slimak
Mark Righter
Daniel E. Bright
Michael E. Koll
Sallie A. Updyke
Paul J. Tomczuk
Janine C. Gismondi
Maureen A. Gallagher
John A. Snyder
Daniel B. Vukmer
April L. Chamberlain

OF COUNSEL

Roy Wilkinson, Jr.

Representative Clients: The Pennsylvania State University; Milton S. Hershey Medical Center; Mid-State Bank & Trust Co.; Pennsylvania Medical Society Liability Insurance Co.; Pennsylvania Manufacturers Insurance Assn.; State Farm Mutual Insurance Co.; Aetna Insurance Co.; Insurance Company of North America.

For full biographical listings, see the Martindale-Hubbell Law Directory

*SUNBURY,** Northumberland Co.

Apfelbaum, Apfelbaum & Apfelbaum (AV)

43 South Fifth Street, 17801
Telephone: 717-286-9421
Fax: 717-286-5349

MEMBERS OF FIRM

Sidney Apfelbaum
Jeffrey Apfelbaum
Michael Morris Apfelbaum

Counsel for: Weis Markets, Inc.; Sunbury Textile Mills, Inc.; Shikellamy School District; City of Sunbury.
Agents for: Commonwealth Land Title Insurance Co.
Reference: Snyder County Trust Co.

For full biographical listings, see the Martindale-Hubbell Law Directory

Wiest, Wiest, Saylor & Muolo (AV)

244 Market Street, P.O. Box 791, 17801
Telephone: 717-286-7777
Fax: 717-286-8075

MEMBERS OF FIRM

Roger V. Wiest
Wm. Harvey Wiest
Charles H. Saylor
Robert J. Muolo

ASSOCIATES

David D. Noon
William R. Swinehart

References: First National Trust Bank, Sunbury; State Farm Insurance Cos.; Employers Mutual Cos.; Sunbury Motor Co.; Mertz Ford, Inc.; Zartman Construction, Inc.; John Fogarty Custom Built Homes, Inc.; Fleetwood Motor Homes.

For full biographical listings, see the Martindale-Hubbell Law Directory

*TIONESTA,** Forest Co. — (Refer to Oil City)

*TOWANDA,** Bradford Co. — (Refer to Tunkhannock)

*TUNKHANNOCK,** Wyoming Co.

Farr, Davis & Fitze (AV)

7 Marion Street, P.O. Box H, 18657
Telephone: 717-836-3185
Facsimile: 717-836-4991

MEMBERS OF FIRM

John B. Farr
James E. Davis
Judd B. Fitze

Representative Clients: First National Bank of Nicholson; Proctor & Gamble Paper Products Company; Pennsylvania Electric Company.
Title Agents for: Commonwealth Land Title Insurance Co.
References: Mellon Bank, Tunkhannock, PA Office; Fidelity Bank N.A. (Tunkhannock, PA Office); Community Bank and Trust Co.; Grange National Bank of Wyoming County.

For full biographical listings, see the Martindale-Hubbell Law Directory

*UNIONTOWN,** Fayette Co.

Margolis, George & Port (AV)

92 East Main Street, 15401
Telephone: 412-438-2544
Fax: 412-438-8327

(See Next Column)

Herman M. Buck (1910-1973)
Paul V. Mahoney (1914-1984)

MEMBERS OF FIRM

Herbert Margolis
Joseph M. George
Wayne H. Port
Douglas S. Sepic

Local Attorneys for: Columbia Gas of Pennsylvania; Anchor Hocking Glass Corp. (Connellsville Plant); Eastern Gas & Fuel Associates; Texas Eastern Transmission Corp.; Prudential Insurance Company of America; Republic Steel Corp.; Bell Telephone Company of Pennsylvania; Nationwide Insurance Co.; North American Cos.; Liberty Mutual Insurance Co.

For full biographical listings, see the Martindale-Hubbell Law Directory

Webster & Webster, P.C. (AV)

51 East South Street, 15401
Telephone: 412-438-1131, 438-4549
Fax: 412-438-0602

Robert L. Webster
Robert L. Webster, Jr.
Daniel L. Webster

George L. Hallal
Anthony S. Dedola, Jr.

Representative Clients: Frank A. Bock Enterprises, Inc.; Uniontown Hospital and its subsidiaries; Utown Motor Club.
Reference: Gallatin National Bank.

For full biographical listings, see the Martindale-Hubbell Law Directory

*WARREN,** Warren Co. — (Refer to Ridgway)

*WASHINGTON,** Washington Co.

Marriner & Crumrine (AV)

8th Floor, Washington Trust Building, 15301
Telephone: 412-225-6600
Fax: 412-225-8861

MEMBERS OF FIRM

Stephen D. Marriner (1917-1993)
Clarence A. Crumrine (1945-1993)
Stephen D. Marriner, Jr.
Cary D. Jones
Colin E. Fitch

Representative Clients: PNC Bank, Washington Office; Security Insurance Co.; Observer Publishing Co.; PennWest Farm Credit, ACA; Pennsylvania National Insurance Group; West Penn Power Co.

For full biographical listings, see the Martindale-Hubbell Law Directory

Peacock, Keller, Yohe, Day & Ecker (AV)

East Beau Building, 70 East Beau Street, 15301
Telephone: 412-222-4520
Telefax: 412-222-3318 ABA/NET ABA 34517
Waynesburg, Pennsylvania Office: 102 East High Street.
Telephone: 412-627-8331.
Telefax: 412-627-8025.

MEMBERS OF FIRM

Ralph W. Peacock (1902-1972)
Charles C. Keller
Reed B. Day
Roger J. Ecker
Robert T. Crothers
Kenneth L. Baker
Wesley A. Cramer
Mary Drake Korsmeyer
Richard J. Amrhein
Barbara A. Rizzo
Douglas R. Nolin
Mary K. Pruss

ASSOCIATES

Jonathan G. Higie
Timothy P. Stranko
Peter John Daley, II

OF COUNSEL

William C. Porter (1915-1988)

SENIOR COUNSEL

Davis G. Yohe

Representative Clients: Consolidation Coal Co.; Washington School District; Monongahela Valley Hospital, Inc.; Nationwide Insurance Co.; Family Health Council, Inc.; Cal-Ed Federal Credit Union; Marianna & Scenery Hill Telephone Co.; Maternal & Family Health Services, Inc.; Pennsylvania Hospital Insurance Company.

For full biographical listings, see the Martindale-Hubbell Law Directory

WAYNE, Delaware Co.

Duane, Morris & Heckscher (AV)

735 Chesterbrook Boulevard, Suite 300, 19087
Telephone: 610-647-3555
FAX: 610-640-2619
Philadelphia, Pennsylvania Office: Suite 4200 One Liberty Place.
Telephone: 215-979-1000.
Harrisburg, Pennsylvania Office: 305 North Front Street, 5th Floor, P.O. Box 1003.
Telephone: 717-237-5500.
Fax: 717-232-4015.

(See Next Column)

DUANE, MORRIS & HECKSCHER—*Continued*

Wilmington, Delaware Office: Suite 1500, 1201 Market Street.
Telephone: 302-571-5550.
Fax: 302-571-5560.
New York, N.Y. Office 112 E. 42nd Street, Suite 2125. Telephone: 212-499-0410.
Fax: 212-499-0420.
Allentown, Pennsylvania Office: 968 Postal Road, Suite 200.
Telephone: 610-266-3650.
Fax: 610-640-2619.
Cherry Hill, New Jersey Office: 51 Haddonfield Road, Suite 340.
Telephone: 609-488-7300.
Fax: 609-488-7021.

RESIDENT PARTNERS

Frank L. White, Jr. — Thomas G. Thompson
Edward Griffith — Brian J. Siegel
James Kenneth Brengle — Gerald F. McCormick
Lewis R. Olshin — W. Mark Mullineaux

RESIDENT ASSOCIATES

Christopher J. Pippett — Judy L. Ziegler
Michael O'Hayer — Emily H. Hoechst
Joseph E. Mayk

For full biographical listings, see the Martindale-Hubbell Law Directory

WAYNESBORO, Franklin Co.

MAXWELL, MAXWELL, DICK, WALSH & LISKO (AV)

Wayne Building, 92 W. Main Street, 17268
Telephone: 717-762-2118
Fax: 717-762-3296
Greencastle, Pennsylvania Office: Franklin House, 11 N. Carlisle Street, 17225.
Telephone: 717-597-2124.
Fax: 717-597-7161.

MEMBERS OF FIRM

LeRoy S. Maxwell — William S. Dick
LeRoy S. Maxwell, Jr. — Richard J. Walsh
John M. Lisko

Representative Clients: First National Bank and Trust Co., Waynesboro, Pa.; Landis Tool Co., a Division of Litton Industrial Products Inc.; Citizens National Bank of Southern Pennsylvania; Home Federal Savings Assn.; U.S.F. & G. Insurance Co.

For full biographical listings, see the Martindale-Hubbell Law Directory

*WELLSBORO,** Tioga Co.

COX, COX & STOKES, P.C. (AV)

19 Central Avenue, 16901
Telephone: 717-724-1444
Telecopier: 717-724-6633
Westfield, Pennsylvania Office: 144 Church Street.
Telephone: 814-376-2203.

Robert F. Cox, Sr. — Robert F. Cox, Jr.
William R. Stokes, II

Annette Doleski Maza

Reference: Commonwealth Bank

OWLETT, LEWIS & GINN, P.C. (AV)

One Charles Street, P.O. Box 878, 16901
Telephone: 717-723-1000
Fax: 717-724-6822
Elkland, Pennsylvania Office: 102 East Main Street.
Telephone: 814-258-5148.
Knoxville, Pennsylvania Office: 106 East Main Street.
Telephone: 814-326-4161.

Edwin A. Glover — Edward H. Owlett, III
Edward H. Owlett — Raymond E. Ginn, Jr.
Thomas M. Owlett

Bruce L. Vickery — Judith DeMeester Nichols

OF COUNSEL

John Dean Lewis

Reference: Citizens and Northern Bank.

For full biographical listings, see the Martindale-Hubbell Law Directory

*WEST CHESTER,** Chester Co.

BUCKLEY, NAGLE, GENTRY, MCGUIRE & MORRIS (AV)

304 North High Street, P.O. Box 133, 19380
Telephone: 610-436-4400
Telecopier: 610-436-8305
Thorndale, Pennsylvania Office: 3532 East Lincoln Highway.
Telephone: 215-383-5666.

(See Next Column)

MEMBERS OF FIRM

C. Barry Buckley — Anthony Morris
Ronald C. Nagle — John J. Teti, Jr.
W. Richard Gentry — Jeffrey R. Sommer
Stephen P. McGuire — Isabel M. Albuquerque

OF COUNSEL

R. Curtis Schroder

For full biographical listings, see the Martindale-Hubbell Law Directory

CRAWFORD, WILSON, RYAN & AGULNICK, P.C. (AV)

220 West Gay Street, 19380
Telephone: 610-431-4500
Fax: 610-430-8718
Radnor, Pennsylvania Office: 252 Radnor-Chester Road, P. O. Box 8333, 19087.
Telephone: 215-688-1205.
Fax: 215-688-7802.

Ronald M. Agulnick — Thomas R. Wilson
Fronefield Crawford, Jr. — Kevin J. Ryan

John J. Mahoney — Patricia T. Brennan
Kim Denise Morton — Richard H. Morton
Steven L. Mutart — Patricia J. Kelly
Rita Kathryn Borzillo — Charles W. Tucker

Reference: First National Bank of West Chester.

For full biographical listings, see the Martindale-Hubbell Law Directory

DUFFY & GREEN (AV)

10 North Church Street, Suite 307, 19380
Telephone: 610-692-0500
FAX: 610-430-6668

MEMBERS OF FIRM

John J. Duffy — Joseph P. Green, Jr.

ASSOCIATES

Richard E. Meanix — P.J. Redmond

For full biographical listings, see the Martindale-Hubbell Law Directory

GAWTHROP, GREENWOOD & HALSTED, A PROFESSIONAL CORPORATION (AV)

119 North High Street, P.O. Box 562, 19381-0562
Telephone: 610-696-8225
FAX: 610-344-0922

John S. Halsted — Kevin Holleran
Robert F. Adams — George C. Zumbano
Mark L. Tunnell

COUNSEL

Robert S. Gawthrop, Jr.

Walter P. Eells — Lisa Comber Hall
John L. Hall — Andrew D.H. Rau

Counsel for: ConRail; Amtrak; The Davey Co.; Travelers Insurance Co.; Chester County Hospital; Tredyffrin Township Municipal Authority; Brandywine Hospital; Easttown Township; Amica Mutual Insurance Co.; Coatesville Area School District.

For full biographical listings, see the Martindale-Hubbell Law Directory

GOLDBERG, EVANS, MALCOLM, HERALD, DONATONI & ROHLFS (AV)

135 West Market Street, 19382
Telephone: 610-436-6220
Fax: 610-436-0628

Lawrence A. Goldberg — Bruce A. Herald
Eugene H. Evans — Robert J. Donatoni
Thomas O. Malcolm — Walter M. Rohlfs

For full biographical listings, see the Martindale-Hubbell Law Directory

LAMB, WINDLE & MCERLANE, P.C. (AV)

24 East Market Street, P.O. Box 565, 19381-0565
Telephone: 610-430-8000
Telecopier: 610-692-0877

COUNSEL

Theodore O. Rogers

William H. Lamb — John D. Snyder
Susan Windle Rogers — William P. Mahon
James E. McErlane — Guy A. Donatelli
E. Craig Kalemjian — Vincent M. Pompo
James C. Sargent, Jr. — James J. McEntee III

(See Next Column)

LAMB, WINDLE & MCERLANE P.C., *West Chester—Continued*

Tracy Blake DeVlieger
P. Andrew Schaum
Lawrence J. Persick
Thomas K. Schindler
Daniel A. Loewenstern
Thomas F. Oeste
John W. Pauciulo
Andrea B. Pettine
John J. Cunningham

Representative Clients: Chester County; First Financial Savings Bank, PaSA; Bank of Chester County; Jefferson Bank; Downingtown Area and Great Valley School Districts; Philadelphia Electric Company; Central and Western Chester County Industrial Development Authority; Valley Forge Sewer Authority; Manito Title Insurance Company.

For full biographical listings, see the Martindale-Hubbell Law Directory

MACELREE, HARVEY, GALLAGHER, FEATHERMAN & SEBASTIAN, LTD. (AV)

17 West Miner Street, P.O. Box 660, 19381-0660
Telephone: 610-436-0100
Fax: 610-430-7885
Kennett Square, Pennsylvania Office: 211 E. State Street, P. O. Box 363. Telephone 215-444-3180.
Fax: 215-444-3270.
Spring City, Pennsylvania Office: 3694 Schuylkill Road.
Telephone: 215-948-5700.

Lawrence E. MacElree
Dominic T. Marrone
William J. Gallagher
John A. Featherman, III
Randy L. Sebastian
Terry W. Knox
Michael G. Louis
Randall C. Schauer
Stacey W. McConnell
Frederick P. Kramer, II
John F. McKenna
C. Douglas Parvin
Harry J. DiDonato
Lance J. Nelson
Bernadette M. Walsh
Linda C. Tice
Joseph F. Harvey (1921-1985)
J. Barton Rettew, Jr. (1901-1981)
Richard Reifsnyder (1928-1974)

For full biographical listings, see the Martindale-Hubbell Law Directory

C. RICHARD MORTON (AV)

Atrium Building, Suite 100, 17 West Gay Street, P.O. Box 626, 19381
Telephone: 610-436-5200
1-800-272-8712

ASSOCIATES

Jeannine F. Notaro

For full biographical listings, see the Martindale-Hubbell Law Directory

*WILKES-BARRE,** Luzerne Co.

HOURIGAN, KLUGER, SPOHRER & QUINN, A PROFESSIONAL CORPORATION (AV)

700 Mellon Bank Center, 8 West Market Street, 18701-1867
Telephone: 717-825-9401
FAX: 717-829-3460
Scranton, Pennsylvania Office: Suite 200, 434 Lackawanna Avenue.
Telephone: 717-346-8414.
Allentown, Pennsylvania Office: Sovereign Building, 609 Hamilton Mall.
Telephone: 610-437-1584.
Hazelton, Pennsylvania Office: CAN DO Building, One South Church Street.
Telephone: 717-455-5141.

Allan M. Kluger
Joseph A. Quinn, Jr.
Richard M. Goldberg
Arthur L. Piccone
Joseph P. Mellody, Jr.
David W. Saba
Neil L. Conway (Resident, Allentown Office)
Joseph A. Lach (Managing Partner)
Richard S. Bishop (Resident, Scranton Office)
Ronald V. Santora
Eugene D. Sperazza
Terrence J. Herron (Resident, Hazelton Office)
Neil E. Wenner (Resident, Allentown Office)
Walter T. Grabowski
Jonathan A. Spohrer
Melissa A. Scartelli
Joseph E. Kluger
Sandra L. Namey-Richards
Shawn P. Phillips (Resident, Allentown Office)
Fred T. Howe
James T. Shoemaker
Mark T. Perry
David J. Selingo
Donald C. Ligorio
Alexia Kita Blake
Lara J. Endler
John R. Hill (Resident, Allentown Office)
Jacqueline Musto Carroll
Daniel J. Distasio, Jr.
Malachy E. Mannion (Resident, Scranton Office)
Joseph M. Campolieto (Resident, Scranton Office)
Kathleen Quinn DePillis (Resident, Allentown Office)
Christina A. Morrison
Michael J. Kowalski
Richard M. Williams

OF COUNSEL

George A. Spohrer
Joseph J. Musto

Representative Client: Aetna Casualty & Surety Co.

For full biographical listings, see the Martindale-Hubbell Law Directory

ROSENN, JENKINS & GREENWALD (AV)

15 South Franklin Street, 18711-0075
Telephone: 717-826-5600
Fax: 717-826-5640

Mitchell Jenkins (1896-1977)
Henry Greenwald (1908-1994)

OF COUNSEL

Harold Rosenn
Joseph J. Savitz

MEMBERS OF FIRM

Eugene Roth
Harry R. Hiscox
John J. Aponick, Jr.
Daniel G. Flannery
Marshall S. Jacobson
Murray Ufberg
Bruce C. Rosenthal
Donald H. Brobst
Joseph L. Persico
Howard M. Levinson
Alan S. Hollander
Garry S. Taroli
Richard A. Russo
James P. Valentine
Mark A. Van Loon
Lee S. Piatt
David B. Hiscox
William L. Higgs
Robert D. Schaub
Michael A. Shucosky
Lewis A. Sebia
Robert N. Gawlas, Jr.
Gerard M. Musto, Jr.

ASSOCIATES

Francis G. Wenzel, Jr.
Carolyn Carr Rhoden
Sandra L. Richelmy
Thomas F. Ford
James C. Oschal
Steven P. Roth
Joseph G. Ferguson
MaryJo Kishel
Mary Margaret Griffin
Patricia Ermel Lakhia
Maureen Monahan
Mark W. Drasnin
Lawrence W. Roth
Carl J. Guagliardo
Thomas B. Carpenter
Jennifer Glor Dressler
Sean P. Fahey
Joseph J. Schwerha, IV
Joseph F. Dietrick
Joseph J. Notarianni, Jr.

Representative Clients: Allstate Insurance Co.; C-TEC Corporation; Chicago Title Insurance Co.; Franklin First Savings Bank; The Geisinger Medical Center; Guard Insurance Group; The Mays Department Stores Company; Student LoanMarketing Association (Sallie Mae); Subaru of America, Inc.

For full biographical listings, see the Martindale-Hubbell Law Directory

*WILLIAMSPORT,** Lycoming Co.

CANDOR, YOUNGMAN, GIBSON AND GAULT (AV)

25 West Third Street, 8th Floor, 17701
Telephone: 717-322-6144
Fax: 717-322-8935

John G. Candor (1879-1971)

OF COUNSEL

John C. Youngman
Harry R. Gibson
John C. Gault

MEMBERS OF FIRM

John C. Youngman, Jr.

Local Counsel for: Bell Telephone Co. of Pa.; Allstate; Gulf Insurance Co.; Hartford Life Insurance Co.; Household Finance; Motorist Insurance Co.; National Grange Insurance Co.; Northwestern Life Insurance; Metropolitan Life Insurance Co.; Security Mutual Life Insurance.

For full biographical listings, see the Martindale-Hubbell Law Directory

MCCORMICK, REEDER, NICHOLS, BAHL, KNECHT & PERSON (AV)

(Formerly McCormick, Herdic & Furst).
835 West Fourth Street, 17701
Telephone: 717-326-5131
Fax: 717-326-5529

OF COUNSEL

Henry Clay McCormick

MEMBERS OF FIRM

S. Dale Furst, Jr. (1904-1969)
Robert J. Sarno (1941-1982)
Paul W. Reeder
William E. Nichols
David R. Bahl
William L. Knecht
John E. Person, III
J. David Smith
Robert A. Eckenrode
Cynthia Ranck Person

ASSOCIATES

Joanne C. Ludwikowski
R. Matthew Patch
Sean P. Roman
Kenneth B. Young

General Counsel for: Northern Central Bank; Jersey Shore Steel Co.
Representative Clients: Pennsylvania Power & Light Co.; Consolidated Rail Corp.; Royal Insurance Co.; State Automobile Insurance Association.

For full biographical listings, see the Martindale-Hubbell Law Directory

Williamsport—Continued

McNerney, Page, Vanderlin & Hall (AV)

433 Market Street, 17701
Telephone: 717-326-6555
Fax: 717-326-3170
Muncy, Pennsylvania Office: R.D. #6, Box 260-1.
Telephone: 717-546-5111.

MEMBERS OF FIRM

Joseph M. McNerney (1909-1967)
Allen P. Page, Jr. (1923-1975)
O. William Vanderlin
T. Max Hall
George V. Cohen
Charles J. McKelvey
E. Eugene Yaw
Michael H. Collins
Ann Pepperman
Brett O. Feese
Thomas A. Marino

ASSOCIATES

Robin A. Read
Thomas C. Marshall
Peter G. Facey
Joy Reynolds McCoy

Approved Agent for: American Title Insurance.
Representative Clients: Williamsport National Bank; Textron Lycoming; Underwriters Adjustment Co.; Continental Insurance Co.; Little League Baseball, Inc.; The West Co.; Shop Vac Corp.; Divine Providence Hospital; Pennsylvania College of Technology.

For full biographical listings, see the Martindale-Hubbell Law Directory

*YORK,** York Co.

Barley, Snyder, Senft & Cohen (AV)

100 East Market Street, P.O. Box 15012, 17405-7012
Telephone: 717-846-8888
Fax: 717-843-8492
Lancaster, Pennsylvania Office: 126 East King Street.
Telephone: 717-299-5201.
Telecopier: 717-291-4660.
Harrisburg, Pennsylvania Office: 240 North Third Street.
Telephone: 717-238-8263.
Telecopier: 717-238-8278.

MEMBERS OF FIRM

Lavere C. Senft
Donn I. Cohen
Harry J. Rubin
Robert J. Stewart
H. Robert Lasday (Resident, Harrisburg Office)
John O. Shirk (Resident, Lancaster Office)
Donald E. LeFever (Resident, Lancaster Office)
W. Jeffrey Sidebottom (Resident, Lancaster Office)
Christopher W. Mattson (Resident, Lancaster Office)
Donald D. Geyer (Resident, Harrisburg Office)
Frederick S. Spangler
Jesse C. Robinson (Resident, Lancaster Office)
Rees Griffiths
James A. Humphreys III (Resident, Lancaster Office)
Paul M. Browning (Resident, Lancaster Office)
Kathleen Ann Gray (Resident, Lancaster Office)
Patricia A. Butler
James R. Adams (Resident, Lancaster Office)
George C. Werner, Jr. (Resident, Lancaster Office)
David R. Keller (Resident, Lancaster Office)
Jeffrey D. Lobach
James W. Saxton (Resident, Lancaster Office)
Caroline M. Hoffer (Resident, Lancaster Office)
Robert W. Hallinger (Resident, Lancaster Office)
Steven J. Koehler
Val E. Winter
Nedric L. Nissly (Resident, Lancaster Office)
Elaine Pennington Stanko (Resident, Lancaster Office)
Thomas J. Lovelass (Resident, Lancaster Office)
Arthur E. Wilmarth, Jr. (Resident, Lancaster Office)
Paul D. Clouser (Resident, Lancaster Office)
Michael A. Moore (Resident, Lancaster Office)
Christopher A. Stump (Resident, Lancaster Office)
Kendra D. McGuire (Resident, Lancaster Office)
Paul G. Mattaini (Resident, Lancaster Office)

ASSOCIATES

Nancy Mayer Hughes (Resident, Lancaster Office)
Eric L. Winkle (Resident, Lancaster Office)
Michael S. Butler
Michael W. Davis (Resident, Lancaster Office)
Katherine Betz Kravitz (Resident, Lancaster Office)
Timothy P. Brown (Resident, Lancaster Office)
Hanna-Aurelia Dunlap (Resident, Lancaster Office)
Ronald H. Pollock, Jr. (Resident, Lancaster Office)
Anne E. Doliner (Resident, Lancaster Office)
Melanie A. Zampini
Barbara B. May (Resident, Lancaster Office)
Richard L. Grubb (Resident, Lancaster Office)
Beverly J. Points
Jennifer A. Kline
Kathleen M. Quarto
Jennifer L. Craighead
Scott F. Landis
Mary Ann Moscony Cooke
Christopher A. Hackman (Resident, Lancaster Office)

COUNSEL

John T. Barber (Resident, Lancaster Office)
Paul A. Mueller, Jr. (Resident, Lancaster Office)

(See Next Column)

RETIRED

Ralph M. Barley
Charles R. Cooper, Jr.

Counsel for: Franklin & Marshall College; Fulton Bank/Fulton Financial Corp.; The Graham Cos.; Lancaster Chamber of Commerce and Industry; Lancaster General Hospital; Robert A. Kinsley, Inc.
Local Counsel for: Armstrong World Industries; Susquehanna Pfaltzgraff Co.
Insurance Defense Counsel for: Medical Protective Co.; The PMA Group.

For full biographical listings, see the Martindale-Hubbell Law Directory

Stock and Leader (AV)

35 South Duke Street, P.O. Box 5167, 17401-5167
Telephone: 717-846-9800
Fax: 717-843-6134
Hallam, Pennsylvania Office: 450 West Market Street.
Telephone: 717-840-4491.
Stewartstown, Pennsylvania Office: 5 South Main Street.
Telephone: 717-993-2845.
Shrewsbury, Pennsylvania Office: 28 Northbrook Drive, Suite 2F.
Telephone: 717-235-3608.

MEMBERS OF FIRM

McClean Stock (1881-1962)
Henry B. Leader
J. Ross McGinnis
Raymond L. Hovis
William H. Neff, Jr.
D. Reed Anderson
William C. Gierasch, Jr.
W. Bruce Wallace
Byron H. LeCates
Michael W. King
Timothy P. Ruth
Richard A. Bramhall, Jr.
Marietta Harte Barbour
Emily J. Leader
Jane H. Schussler

ASSOCIATES

Robert R. Lloyd, Jr.
Steven M. Hovis
Craig T. Trebilcock
Amy L. Nelson
Jody N. Anderson

General Counsel: The Drovers & Mechanics Bank; Paradise Mutual Insurance Co.; Yorktowne Paper Mills, Inc.; York Electrical Supply Co.; Eisenhart Wallcoverings Co.; York Suburban School District; York Township; Central York School District.

For full biographical listings, see the Martindale-Hubbell Law Directory

RHODE ISLAND

*BRISTOL,** Bristol Co. — (Refer to Providence)

CRANSTON, Providence Co.

TAFT & MCSALLY (AV)

21 Garden City Drive, P.O. Box 20130, 02920
Telephone: 401-946-3800
Fax: 401-943-8859

MEMBERS OF FIRM

James L. Taft (1901-1959)
Bernard F. McSally (1928-1978)
James L. Taft, Jr.

ASSOCIATES

Sarah Taft-Carter
John V. McGreen
Robert D. Murray
David H. Ferrara
Eleanor W. Taft

LEGAL SUPPORT PERSONNEL

Mary T. Rochford

Representative Clients: General Motors Corp.; General Motors Acceptance Corp.; Chrysler Credit Corp.; Providence Gas Co.; Fleet National Bank; Fleet Mortgage; Citizens Savings Bank; Rhode Island Hospital Trust National Bank; Town of Narragansett, Rhode Island (Bond Counsel); Brown Broadcasting Service, Inc.

For full biographical listings, see the Martindale-Hubbell Law Directory

EAST PROVIDENCE, Providence Co.

HOGAN & HOGAN (AV)

201 Waterman Avenue, 02914-3591
Telephone: 401-421-3990
Telecopier: 401-438-3460
Peace Dale, Rhode Island Office: 23 North Road, 02883.
Telephone: 401-782-4488.
Fax: 401-782-4496.

MEMBERS OF FIRM

Edward T. Hogan (1924-1953)
Mary C. Hogan (1928-1981)
Laurence J. Hogan (1924-1984)
Edward T. Hogan
Thomas S. Hogan

Margaret L. Hogan

For full biographical listings, see the Martindale-Hubbell Law Directory

JAMESTOWN, Newport Co.

MORNEAU & MURPHY (AV)

77 Narragansett Avenue, 02835
Telephone: 401-423-0400
Telecopier: 401-423-7059
Providence, Rhode Island Office: 38 N. Court Street. 02903
Telephone: 401-453-0500.
Telecopier: 401-453-0505.

MEMBERS OF FIRM

John Austin Murphy
John B. Murphy (Resident at Providence Office)
Richard N. Morneau
Gloria C. Dahl

ASSOCIATES

Sheila M. Cooley
Stephen T. Morrissey
Anne Maxwell Livingston
Virginia Spaziano
Scott H. Moskol (Resident, Providence Office)

OF COUNSEL

Neale D. Murphy

For full biographical listings, see the Martindale-Hubbell Law Directory

*NEWPORT,** Newport Co.

CORCORAN, PECKHAM & HAYES, P.C. (AV)

31 America's Cup Avenue, P.O. Box 389, 02840
Telephone: 401-847-0872
Telecopier: 401-847-5810

William Augustus Peckham (1892-1963)
Edward John Corcoran
Patrick O'Neill Hayes
Edward B. Corcoran
William W. Corcoran
Joseph T. Houlihan
Kathleen Managhan
Patrick O'Neill Hayes, Jr.
Jeffrey Jonathan Teitz
William J. Corcoran
William C. O'Connell

Counsel for: Bank of Newport; National Lawn Tennis Hall of Fame and Tennis Museum; Newport Hospital; Preservation Society of Newport County, Inc.; Long Wharf Mall Associates; Fraternal Order of Police, Newport, R.I.; Trinity Church; Newport County Boys and Girls Club.

For full biographical listings, see the Martindale-Hubbell Law Directory

MOORE, VIRGADAMO & LYNCH, LTD. (AV)

112 Bellevue Avenue, 02840
Telephone: 401-846-0120
Telecopier: 401-848-0234

Cornelius C. Moore (1885-1970)
Salvatore L. Virgadamo (1914-1986)
Jeremiah C. Lynch, Jr. (1928-1987)
Laurent L. Rousseau
Stephen A. Haire
Marie Teresa Paiva Weed
Jeremiah C. Lynch, III

Counsel for: The People's Credit Union; The Portsmouth Abbey School; Salve Regina University; Newport Jai Alai Sports Theatre, Inc.

For full biographical listings, see the Martindale-Hubbell Law Directory

PAWTUCKET, Providence Co. — (Refer to Providence)

*PROVIDENCE,** Providence Co.

ASQUITH, MAHONEY & ROBINSON (AV)

Packet Building, 155 South Main Street, 02903-2963
Telephone: 401-331-9100
Telecopier: 401-331-6736

Edward W. Moses (1943-1993)

MEMBERS OF FIRM

Harry W. Asquith, Jr.
John R. Mahoney
Stephen M. Robinson
Elizabeth Peterson Santilli
Daniel J. Archetto
Patricia K. Shaw

OF COUNSEL

Harry W. Asquith

For full biographical listings, see the Martindale-Hubbell Law Directory

BLISH & CAVANAGH (AV)

Commerce Center, 30 Exchange Terrace, 02903
Telephone: 401-831-8900
Telecopier: 401-751-7542

MEMBERS OF FIRM

John H. Blish
Joseph V. Cavanagh, Jr.
William R. Landry
Michael DiBiase
Stephen J. Reid, Jr.

Karen A. Pelczarski
Raymond A. Marcaccio
Scott P. Tierney

Representative Clients: Providence Journal Co.; Fleet Financial Group; Rhode Island Hospital Trust National Bank; Allstate Insurance Co.; U-Haul International, Inc.; Delta Dental of Rhode Island; Gilbane Building Co.; Colony Communications; Providence Housing Authority.

For full biographical listings, see the Martindale-Hubbell Law Directory

BOYAJIAN, HARRINGTON & RICHARDSON (AV)

182 Waterman Street, 02906
Telephone: 401-273-9600
Telecopier: 401-273-9605

MEMBERS OF FIRM

John Boyajian
Alden C. Harrington
Andrew S. Richardson

Kathleen A. Ryan

For full biographical listings, see the Martindale-Hubbell Law Directory

CARROLL, KELLY & MURPHY (AV)

The Packet Building, 155 South Main Street, 02903
Telephone: 401-331-7272
Telecopier: 401-331-4404

MEMBERS OF FIRM

Joseph A. Kelly
James E. Murphy
C. Russell Bengtson
Ruth DiMeglio
William H. Jestings

ASSOCIATES

John P. McCoy
Patricia A. Buckley
Robert E. Hardman
Keith B. Kyle
Shannon Gilheeney
Michael T. Sullivan

OF COUNSEL

Bernard P. Campbell

Representative Clients: Hartford Accident and Indemnity Co.; Greater New York Insurance Co.; St. Paul's Insurance Co.; Joint Underwriter's Association; Premiere Alliance Insurance Co.; Professional Risk Management Services, Inc.; General Accident Insurance Company of America; Guaranty Fund Management Services; First State Insurance Co.
Reference: Fleet National Bank.

For full biographical listings, see the Martindale-Hubbell Law Directory

Providence—Continued

MARTIN K. DONOVAN (AV)

Second Floor, One Park Row, 02903
Telephone: 401-831-2500
Facsimile: 401-751-7830

Reference: Fleet National Bank.

For full biographical listings, see the Martindale-Hubbell Law Directory

EDWARDS & ANGELL (AV)

2700 Hospital Trust Tower, 02903
Telephone: 401-274-9200
Telecopier: 401-276-6611
Cable Address: "Edwangle Providence"
Telex: 952001 "E A PVD"
Boston, Massachusetts Office: 101 Federal Street, 02110.
Telephone: 617-439-444.
Telecopier: 617-439-4170.
New York, New York Office: 750 Lexington Avenue, 10022.
Telephone: 212-308-4411.
Telecopier: 212-308-4844.
Palm Beach, Florida Office: 250 Royal Palm Way, 33480.
Telephone: 407-833-7700.
Telecopier: 407-655-8719.
Newark, New Jersey Office: Gateway three, 07120.
Telephone: 201-623-7717.
Telecopier: 201-623-7717.
Hartford, Connecticut Office: 750 Main Street, 14th Floor, 06103.
Telephone: 203-525-5065.
Telecopier: 203-527-4198.
Newport, Rhode Island Office: 130 Bellevue Avenue, 02840.
Telephone: 401-849-7800.
Telecopier: 401-849-7887.

Bernard A. Heeke (1935-1994)
Bancroft Littlefield (1913-1994)

MEMBERS OF FIRM

James H. Barnett
Alan S. Flink
Alvin M. Glazerman (Not admitted in RI; Resident Boston, Massachusetts Office)
Martin A. Purcell (Resident, Palm Beach, Florida Office)
Benjamin P. Harris III
Richard M. Borod
Arthur W. Murphy (Resident, Newport, Rhode Island Office)
Bernard V. Buonanno, Jr.
Neil N. Glazer (Not admitted in RI; Resident, Boston, Massachusetts Office)
V. Duncan Johnson
James J. Skeffington
Edward J. Bertozzi, Jr.
James P. Kelly
Deming E. Sherman
John H. Reid III
S. Michael Levin
Richard M. C. Glenn III
Timothy T. More
Robert A. S. Silberman (Not admitted in RI; Resident, Boston, Massachusetts Office)
Jonathan E. Cole (Resident Palm Beach, Florida Office)
Alfred S. Lombardi
Kinnaird Howland
Richard A. Perras (Not admitted in RI; Resident Boston, Massachusetts Office)
David K. Duffell
Richard J. McCarthy (Not admitted in RI; Resident, Boston, Massachusetts Office)
Terrence M. Finn (Resident Boston, Massachusetts Office)
Martin S. Allen (Resident, Boston, Massachusetts Office)
Andrew J. Chlebus
Ira G. Greenberg (Resident, New York, New York Office)
Gerald P. Hendrick (Not admitted in RI; Resident, Boston, Massachusetts Office)
James R. McGuirk
William P. Robinson III
Joseph C. Maher, Jr. (Not admitted in RI; Resident, Boston, Massachusetts Office)
Charles F. Rogers, Jr.
Michael H. Miller (Not admitted in RI; Resident Boston, Massachusetts Office)
Susan S. Egan (Not admitted in RI; Resident New York, New York Office)
Mary Louise Kennedy
Philip B. Barr, Jr.
Christine M. Marx (Resident, Newark, New Jersey Office)
Philip D. O'Neill, Jr. (Resident Boston, Massachusetts Office)
Albert L. Sokol (Not admitted in RI; Resident Boston, Massachusetts Office)
James D. McGinley (Not admitted in RI; Resident, Boston, Massachusetts Office)
Walter G. D. Reed
Stephen O. Meredith (Resident Boston, Massachusetts Office)
Patricia A. Sullivan Zesk
Gail E. McCann
G. Scott Nebergall
Kurt J. von Boeselager
Sandra A. Riemer (Not admitted in RI; Resident, New York, New York Office)
Elizabeth H. Munnell (Not admitted in RI; Resident Boston, Massachusetts Office)
Lynn Wright (Not admitted in RI; New York, New York and Newark, New Jersey Office)
Robert W. Curry (Resident, Boston, Massachusetts Office)
John A. Houlihan (Resident Boston, Massachusetts Office; Partner-in-Charge, Boston, Massachusetts Office)
Christopher D. Graham
John G. Igoe (Resident Palm Beach, Florida Office; Partner-in Charge, Palm Beach, Florida Office)
Donald E. Frechette (Not admitted in RI; Resident, Hartford, Connecticut Office)
Walter C. Hunter
Mary P. Heffner
Lorne W. McDougall
Robert D. Gilbert (Not admitted in RI)

(See Next Column)

MEMBERS OF FIRM (Continued)

Alfred R. Paliani (Not admitted in RI; New York, New York and Newark, New Jersey Offices)
Karen G. DelPonte
Gary A. Woodfield (Not admitted in RI; Resident, Palm Beach, Florida Office)
Mark A. Pogue
Robin F. Price (Resident, Palm Beach, Florida Office)
Dana T. Pickard (Resident, Palm Beach, Florida Office)
Susan E. Siebert (Not admitted in RI; Resident Boston, Massachusetts Office)
Leonard Q. Slap (Resident Boston, Massachusetts Office)
John E. Ottaviani
Charles H. DeBevoise
Geoffrey Etherington III (Resident, New York, New York Office)
Pamela S. Robertson
Patricia L. Kantor (Not admitted in RI; Resident New York, New York Office)
Laura N. Wilkinson
David T. Miele
Theodore P. Augustinos (Not admitted in RI; Resident, Hartford Connecticut Office)
Justin M. Sullivan (Not admitted in RI; Resident, Hartford, Connecticut Office)
Stephen M. Prignano
Timothy P. Van Dyck (Not admitted in RI; Resident Boston, Massachusetts Office)
William E. Smith

COUNSEL

Max Schorr (Not admitted in RI; Resident, Palm Beach, Florida Office)
Edwin Fortune Russo (Resident, Palm Beach Office)
Calvert C. Groton
Edward W. Dence, Jr.
Winfield W. Major, Jr.
Norman E. Taplin (Resident, Palm Beach Office)
John B. Rosenquest III
Kenneth L. Levine
James I. Rubens (Resident, Boston, Massachusetts Office)
Nicholas S. Hodge (Resident, Boston, Massachusetts Office)
Carla J. L. Spacone
Laurie B. Kirby (Resident, Newport Office)
Madeleine A. Estabrook
John M. Wolfson (Resident, Hartford, Connecticut Office)
Alan J. Levin (Resident, Hartford, Connecticut Office)
David D. Wasserman (Resident, New York, New York Office)
Rosemary Healey
Colette O. de Labry (Resident, Palm Beach, Florida Office)

ASSOCIATES

Adele Geffen Eil
Alan J. Bouffard (Not admitted in RI; Resident Boston, Massachusetts Office)
Cheryl A. Green (Not admitted in RI)
Matthew T. Oliverio
Susan Stanton Rotman (Not admitted in RI; Resident Boston, Massachusetts Office)
Jonathan M. Lourie (Not admitted in RI; Resident, Boston, Massachusetts Office)
Susan A. Keller
Kenni F. Judd (Resident, Palm Beach, Florida Office)
Colin A. Coleman (Resident Boston, Massachusetts Office)
Mark W. Freel
James L. Sheridan
Regina A. Matejka (Not admitted in RI; Resident, New York, New York and Newark, New Jersey Offices)
David C. Ristaino
Lauren A. Mogensen
Jon M. Anderson
Joseph S. Larisa, Jr.
Andrew P. Fishkin (Not admitted in RI; Resident, New York, New York and Newark, New Jersey Offices)
Paul N. Gilmore (Not admitted in RI; Resident, Hartford, Connecticut Office)
Joseph A. Kuzneski, Jr.
Lincoln Douglas Almond
Alicia Murphy Milligan
Sarianna T. Honkola (Not admitted in RI; Resident, Boston, Massachusetts Office)
Steven M. Cowley (Not admitted in RI; Resident, Boston, Massachusetts Office)
Andrea J. Corcoran (Resident, Boston, Massachusetts Office)
Steven M. Kumins
Cathryn A. Neaves (Resident, Boston, Massachusetts Office)
Adam J. Morgan (Resident, Palm Beach, Florida Office)
Katherine V. G. Leff (Not admitted in RI; Resident, New York, New York Office)
Kate A. Frame (Resident, Boston, Massachusetts Office)
Renee Adelle Roberti
Stephen D. Zubiago
Jill Ann Tracy (Not admitted in RI; Resident, New York, New York and Newark, New Jersey Offices)
Maura C. Doherty (Resident, Boston, Massachusetts Office)
Lynne J. Urbanowicz (Resident, Newark, New Jersey Office)
Thomas E. Hone (Resident, New York, New York Office)
David B. Gorman (Resident, Hartford, Connecticut Office)
Gregory S. Kinoian (Not admitted in RI)
Jeannette M. MacLeod
Robert A. Arena
Terence M. Fracassa
Gregory F. Lang (Resident, Hartford, Connecticut Office)
Joshua L. Ditelberg (Resident, Boston, Massachusetts Office)
Andrea B. Adler (Resident, Boston, Massachusetts Office)
Marc A. Crisafulli
Melissa D. Famiglietti
Susan L. Fornaro
Susan M. Schiappa
Matthew C. Womble
Cynthia Hahn (Resident, Boston, Massachusetts Office)
Stephanie W. Raymond (Resident, Hartford, Connecticut Office)

OF COUNSEL

Edward Winsor
Gerald W. Harrington
John V. Kean
Edward F. Hindle
Beverly Glenn Long
Knight Edwards
Robert Spink Davis
James K. Edwards
Paul F. Greene

(See Next Column)

EDWARDS & ANGELL, *Providence—Continued*

OF COUNSEL (Continued)

George Michaels (Not admitted in RI; Resident Boston, Massachusetts Office)
Ernest N. Agresti
Roger V. Pugh, Jr. (Resident)
Barry G. Hittner
Stephen A. Fanning (Retired)

For full biographical listings, see the Martindale-Hubbell Law Directory

FLANDERS + MEDEIROS INC. (AV)

One Turks Head Place, Suite 700, 02903
Telephone: 401-831-0700
Telecopier: 401-274-2752

Matthew F. Medeiros
Robert G. Flanders, Jr.
Robert Karmen

Neal J. McNamara
Fausto C. Anguilla
Amelia E. Edwards
Stacey P. Nakasian

For full biographical listings, see the Martindale-Hubbell Law Directory

GIDLEY, SARLI & MARUSAK (AV)

Greater Providence Bank Building, 170 Westminster Street, 02903
Telephone: 401-274-6644
Telecopier: 401-331-9304

MEMBERS OF FIRM

Thomas D. Gidley
Michael G. Sarli
James P. Marusak
Mark C. Hadden

ASSOCIATES

Michael R. DeLuca
Linn Foster Freedman
Denise M. Lombardo
William L. Wheatley
Stuart D. Hallagan III

LEGAL SUPPORT PERSONNEL

Elaine M. Noren
Mary Repoza Caplette
Darlene E. Kotkofski

For full biographical listings, see the Martindale-Hubbell Law Directory

HANSON, CURRAN, PARKS & WHITMAN (AV)

146 Westminster Street, 02903-2218
Telephone: 401-421-2154
Telecopier: 401-521-7040

Kirk Hanson (1948-1991)

MEMBERS OF FIRM

A. Lauriston Parks
David P. Whitman
Michael T. F. Wallor
Robert D. Parrillo
Dennis J. McCarten
James T. Murphy
Seth E. Bowerman
Thomas R. Bender

ASSOCIATES

Amy Beretta
Mark W. Dana
Richard H. Burrows
Daniel P. McKiernan

OF COUNSEL

William A. Curran

General Counsel for: Medical Malpractice Joint Underwriting Association of Rhode Island.
Rhode Island Counsel for: Amica Mutual Insurance Co.; CIGNA; St. Paul Insurance Cos.; Occidental Life Insurance Co.; Exchange Mutual Insurance Co.; Aetna Casualty & Surety Co.

For full biographical listings, see the Martindale-Hubbell Law Directory

HIGGINS, CAVANAGH & COONEY (AV)

The Hay Building, Fourth Floor, 123 Dyer Street, 02903
Telephone: 401-272-3500; 800-274-5299
Telecopier: 401-273-8780

James H. Higgins, Jr. (1952-1975)
Joseph V. Cavanagh (1952-1985)
John P. Cooney, Jr. (1960-1981)
Kenneth P. Borden
Gerald C. DeMaria
John T. Walsh, Jr.
Charles A. Hambly, Jr.
Stephen B. Lang
Lawrence P. McCarthy, III
James A. Ruggieri
Madeline Quirk
Michael D. Lynch

ASSOCIATES

James T. Hornstein
John J. Hogan
John F. Kelleher
Rajaram Suryanarayan
Vivian B. Dogan
Patrick B. Landers
Paul S. Callaghan
Jodie Raccio Small
Brenda A. Doyle

For full biographical listings, see the Martindale-Hubbell Law Directory

HIGGINS & SLATTERY (AV)

Greater Providence Bank Building, 170 Westminster Street, Suite 1100, 02903
Telephone: 401-751-3600
Telecopier: 401-751-4648

MEMBERS OF FIRM

James A. Higgins (1902-1985)
John H. Slattery (1948-1962)
John A. Baglini
Robert J. Dumouchel
John A. McQueeney
Joseph W. Baglini

ASSOCIATES

Jessica L. Papazian-Ross

OF COUNSEL

Eugene V. Higgins

Representative Clients: General Accident Group; John Hancock Property & Casualty Insurance Co.; Prudential Property & Casualty Insurance Co.; Ryder Truck; USAA Rental,Inc.; Wausau Insurance Cos.
Reference: Fleet National Bank.

For full biographical listings, see the Martindale-Hubbell Law Directory

HINCKLEY, ALLEN & SNYDER (AV)

(Formerly Hinckley, Allen, Tobin & Silverstein and Snyder, Tepper & Comen)
1500 Fleet Center, 02903
Telephone: 401-274-2000
Boston, Massachusetts Office: One Financial Center.
Telephone: 617-345-9000.

MEMBERS OF FIRM

John R. Allen (Retired)
Richard W. Billings (Retired)
Thomas J. Hogan (Retired)
Robert F. Pickard (Retired)
Robert W. Shadd (Retired)
Richard F. Staples (Retired)
Edward M. Watson (Retired)
Susan H. Alexander (Not admitted in RI)
Paula K. Andrews (Not admitted in RI)
Richard C. Arrighi (Not admitted in RI)
E. Jerome Batty
Jonathan Bell
Edmund C. Bennett
Thomas C. Carey (Not admitted in RI)
Stephen J. Carlotti
Gordon A. Carpenter
Sean O. Coffey
Scott E. Cooper
Thomas Roberts Courage
Thomas S. Crane (Not admitted in RI)
Joseph P. Curran
Michael P. DeFanti
Kristin A. DeKuiper
Joseph M. Di Orio
Malcolm Farmer, III
Margaret D. Farrell
Noel M. Field, Jr.
Pasco Gasbarro Jr.
Alan P. Gottlieb (Not admitted in RI)
Gerard R. Goulet
William R. Grimm
Paul A. Hedstrom (Not admitted in RI)
Jacques V. Hopkins
James A. Jackson
James E. Keeley
Robert J. Kerwin (Not admitted in RI)
Joel Lewin (Not admitted in RI)
Doris Jami Licht
Sandra Matrone Mack
Matthew T. Marcello, III
Frederick P. McClure
Michael B. Nulman
H. Peter Olsen
John J. Pendergast, III
Gerald J. Petros
Richard H. Pierce
Debra G. Reece (Not admitted in RI)
Brian P. Richards
David J. Rubin
Dennis M. Ryan (Not admitted in RI)
Charles E. Schaub, Jr. (Not admitted in RI)
Frank A. Segall (Not admitted in RI)
Paul A. Silver
Michael A. Silverstein
Evan Slavitt (Not admitted in RI)
Richard G. Small
Herman Snyder (Not admitted in RI)
Robert F. Sylvia (Not admitted in RI)
Richard J. Tetrault (Not admitted in RI)
Edwin G. Torrance
Howard E. Walker
Richard D. Wayne (Not admitted in RI)
Joachim A. Weissfeld

ASSOCIATES

Jeffrey D. Abbey (Not admitted in RI)
John W. Bishop, Jr. (Not admitted in RI)
Joseph S. U. Bodoff (Not admitted in RI)
Leon C. Boghossian III
Sarah J. Bulger (Not admitted in RI)
Beth Ann Carlson
David Barry Connolly (Not admitted in RI)
Robin A. DeAugustinis (Not admitted in RI)
Lynne Barry Dolan
Susan F. Donahue (Not admitted in RI)
Bradley P. Dorman
Robert M. Duffy
Eric F. Eisenberg (Not admitted in RI)
Robert D. Emerson
Michael C. Fee (Not admitted in RI)
Joseph P. Ferrucci
Michelle A. Ruberto Fonseca
Hugh J. Gorman, III (Not admitted in RI)
Kim Herman Goslant (Not admitted in RI)
Gloria Maria Gutierrez (Not admitted in RI)
Richard L. E. Jocelyn
James S. Judd
Michael S. McSherry (Not admitted in RI)
Toni Ann Motta
Mary Powers Murray (Not admitted in RI)
Christopher W. Nelson
Christopher M. Neronha

(See Next Column)

HINCKLEY, ALLEN & SNYDER—*Continued*

ASSOCIATES (Continued)

Paul F. O'Donnell, III (Not admitted in RI)
Elena B. Olson (Not admitted in RI)
Gardner H. Palmer, Jr.
Julianne Palumbo (Not admitted in RI)
Susan E. Raitt (Not admitted in RI)
James O. Reavis
Steven A. Remsberg (Not admitted in RI)
Mark Resnick (Not admitted in RI)
Claire J.V. Richards
Jeremy Ritzenberg (Not admitted in RI)
Craig Michael Scott
Francis A. Shannon, III (Not admitted in RI)
Michael F. Sweeney
Susan B. Tuchman (Not admitted in RI)

OF COUNSEL

David D. Barricelli
Anthony J. Buccitelli (Not admitted in RI)
Willard Krasnow (Not admitted in RI)
Willard R. Pope (Not admitted in RI)
Edward W. Powers (Not admitted in RI)
Bentley Tobin

For full biographical listings, see the Martindale-Hubbell Law Directory

HODOSH, SPINELLA & ANGELONE (AV)

128 Dorrance Street, Shakespeare Hall, Suite 450, P.O. Box 1516, 02901-1516
Telephone: 401-274-0200
Fax: 401-274-7538

Thomas C. Angelone
Hugh L. Moore, Jr.
Paul J. Bogosian, Jr.
Kevin M. Cain

ASSOCIATES

Manuel Andrews
John R. Izzo

LEGAL SUPPORT PERSONNEL

Jody V. Harrison

Reference: Fleet National Bank.

For full biographical listings, see the Martindale-Hubbell Law Directory

LICHT & SEMONOFF (AV)

Fourth Floor, Historic Wayland Building, One Park Row, 02903
Telephone: 401-421-8030
Telecopier: 401-272-9408

MEMBERS OF FIRM

Frank Licht (1916-1987)
Ralph P. Semonoff (1918-1992)
Jeremiah J. Gorin
Melvin L. Zurier
Bruce R. Ruttenberg
Norman G. Orodenker
Nathan W. Chace
George E. Lieberman
Richard A. Licht
Robert N. Huseby, Sr.
Joseph De Angelis
Richard A. Boren
Robert B. Berkelhammer
Carl I. Freedman
Robert D. Fine
Susan Leach De Blasio
Susann G. Mark
Drew P. Kaplan
Lori Caron Silveira
Patrick A. Guida
Anthony J. Bucci, Jr.
Casby Harrison, III

ASSOCIATES

Susan M. Huntley
Glenn R. Friedemann
Paul J. Adler
Maureen L. Mallon
Jerry H. Elmer
Michael Prescott
Richard P. Bennett (Not admitted in RI)
Rosamond A. Talbot
Steven C. Sidel
Catherine Sammartino-Berg
Mary McLeod
Keith H. Fine

OF COUNSEL

Daniel J. Murray

For full biographical listings, see the Martindale-Hubbell Law Directory

MEROLLA & KANE (AV)

Packet Building, 155 South Main Street, 02903-2963
Telephone: 401-331-9100
Telecopier: 401-331-6736

Amedeo C. Merolla
Vincent F. Kane

Katherine A. Merolla
Steven B. Merolla

For full biographical listings, see the Martindale-Hubbell Law Directory

PUCCI & GOLDIN, INC. (AV)

The Hay Building Third Floor North, 123 Dyer Street, 02903
Telephone: 401-861-7400
Telecopier: 401-861-0954

Edward S. Goldin
Samuel A. Olevson
Joseph R. Tutalo
Stephen R. White
Sherry A. Goldin

(See Next Column)

OF COUNSEL

Thomas D. Pucci
William B. Gamble

LEGAL SUPPORT PERSONNEL

Kristine A. Turi

General Counsel for: Automobile Insurance Plans Service Office (AIPSO); Steingold Auto Sales, Ltd.; Bonanza Bus Line, Inc.

For full biographical listings, see the Martindale-Hubbell Law Directory

RICE, DOLAN & KERSHAW (AV)

Greater Providence Bank Building, 170 Westminster Street, Suite 900, 02903
Telephone: 401-272-8800
Telecopier: 401-421-7218

OF COUNSEL

H. Eliot Rice

MEMBERS OF FIRM

John F. Dolan
John W. Kershaw
Mark P. Dolan

ASSOCIATES

Charles Garganese, Jr.
Mark A. Fay
Elizabeth Flynn Sullivan

Local Counsel for: American International Adjustment Co.; Andover Cos.; Chubb Group of Insurance Cos.; CNA/Insurance; Government Employees Insurance; Holyoke Mutual Insurance Co.; Mutual of Omaha; Providence-Washington Insurance Group; Reliance Insurance Co.; Rhode Island Hospital.

For full biographical listings, see the Martindale-Hubbell Law Directory

TEMKIN & STONE LTD. (AV)

2500 Hospital Trust Tower, 02903
Telephone: 401-751-2400
Telecopier: 401-751-7180
Newport, Rhode Island Office: 14 Pelham Street.
Telephone: 401-847-7820.

Martin M. Temkin
Daniel Stone
Stephen H. Burke
Michael D. Mitchell

For full biographical listings, see the Martindale-Hubbell Law Directory

FRANK J. WILLIAMS, LTD. (AV)

2 Williams Street, (At South Main Street), 02903
Telephone: 401-331-2222
Cable Address: "LINCOLN"
Telecopier: 401-751-5257

Frank J. Williams

Michael A. Ursillo

References: Shawmut Bank of R.I.; Citizens Trust Co.

For full biographical listings, see the Martindale-Hubbell Law Directory

WESTERLY, Washington Co.

URSO, LIGUORI AND URSO (AV)

85 Beach Street, P.O. Box 1277, 02891
Telephone: 401-596-7751
Telecopier: 401-596-7963

MEMBERS OF FIRM

Natale Louis Urso
Thomas J. Liguori, Jr.
M. Linda Urso

General Counsel for: National Education Association Rhode Island; Westerly Broadcasting Co.
Approved Attorneys for: Lawyers Title Insurance Corporation of Richmond, Virginia.
Reference: Fleet National Bank.

For full biographical listings, see the Martindale-Hubbell Law Directory

SOUTH CAROLINA

*AIKEN,** Aiken Co.

BODENHEIMER, BUSBEE, HUNTER & GRIFFITH (AV)

147 Newberry Street, N.W., P.O. Drawer 2009, 29802
Telephone: 803-648-3255
Telefax: 803-648-3278

MEMBERS OF FIRM

John T. Bodenheimer
O. Dantzler Busbee, II
John M. Hunter, Jr.
M. Anderson Griffith

For full biographical listings, see the Martindale-Hubbell Law Directory

HENDERSON & SALLEY (AV)

111 Park Avenue, Southwest, P.O. Box 517, 29802-0517
Telephone: 803-648-4213
Fax: 803-648-2601

MEMBERS OF FIRM

Julian B. Salley, Jr.
Michael K. Farmer
William H. Tucker
James D. Nance

ASSOCIATES

Amy Patterson Shumpert

Attorneys for: NationsBank South Carolina (N.A.); South Carolina Electric & Gas Co.; The Graniteville Co.; Maryland Casualty Co.; Southern Bell Telephone & Telegraph Co.; Owens Corning Fiberglass Corp.; City of Aiken; United Merchants & Manufacturers, Inc.; Allstate Insurance Co.

For full biographical listings, see the Martindale-Hubbell Law Directory

JOHNSON, JOHNSON, WHITTLE, SNELGROVE & WEEKS, P.A. (AV)

117 Pendleton Street, N.W., P.O. Box 2619, 29802-2619
Telephone: 803-649-5338
FAX: 803-641-4517

B. Henderson Johnson, Jr.
Barry H. Johnson
James E. Whittle, Jr.
Vicki Johnson Snelgrove
John W. (Bill) Weeks
Paige Weeks Johnson
Todd J. Johnson

For full biographical listings, see the Martindale-Hubbell Law Directory

*ALLENDALE,** Allendale Co. — (Refer to Barnwell)

*ANDERSON,** Anderson Co.

MCINTOSH, SHERARD & SULLIVAN (AV)

138 North Main Street, P.O. Box 197, 29622
Telephone: 803-225-0001
Fax: 803-225-0004

MEMBERS OF FIRM

Jack F. McIntosh
Marshall P. Sherard, Jr.
Rivers Lawton McIntosh
George P. Sullivan

Representative Clients: Perpetual Bank, FSB, Anderson, South Carolina; NationsBank, Anderson, South Carolina; The Commercial Bank, Honea Path, South Carolina; People's Bank of Iva, Iva, South Carolina.

For full biographical listings, see the Martindale-Hubbell Law Directory

WATKINS, VANDIVER, KIRVEN, GABLE & GRAY (AV)

500 South McDuffie Street, P.O. Box 4086, 29621
Telephone: 803-225-2527

OF COUNSEL

Wm. L. Watkins

MEMBERS OF FIRM

T. Frank Watkins (1881-1973)
Robert E. Vandiver (1917-1977)
Wilburn C. Gable, Jr. (1930-1978)
H. Grady Kirven (1925-1994)
Wm. Douglas Gray
James W. Logan, Jr.
Steven C. Kirven
James D. Jolly, Jr.
Reginald M. Gay
Michael T. Smith

ASSOCIATES

Todd R. Davidson

Representative Clients: Southern National Bank of South Carolina; J. P. Stevens & Co., Inc.; LaFrance Division of Reigel Textiles; The Kendall Co.; Duke Power Co.; American Mutual Insurance Companies; Continental Insurance Companies; Employers Mutual of Wausau; Factory Mutual.

For full biographical listings, see the Martindale-Hubbell Law Directory

*BAMBERG,** Bamberg Co. — (Refer to Barnwell)

*BARNWELL,** Barnwell Co.

BROWN, JEFFERIES AND BOULWARE (AV)

Bankers Trust Building, P.O. Box 248, 29812
Telephone: 803-259-3532; 259-3533
Telefax: 803-259-7507

MEMBERS OF FIRM

Edgar A. Brown (1888-1975)
R. M. Jefferies, Jr. (1919-1985)
Herman I. Mazursky (1903-1970)
Thomas M. Boulware
Herman Edward Smith

Assistant Division Counsel: Southern Railway Co.
State Counsel: Kenan Transport Co.; Eagle Transport Corp.; Belue Trucking.
Local Counsel: NCNB South Carolina; Deering Milliken, Inc.; Chem-Nuclear Systems, Inc.

For full biographical listings, see the Martindale-Hubbell Law Directory

*BEAUFORT,** Beaufort Co.

DOWLING LAW FIRM, P.A. (AV)

1509 King Street, P.O. Drawer 1507, 29901-1507
Telephone: 803-521-8000
Fax: 803-521-8003

Joab M. Dowling (1917-1992)
G. G. Dowling
Joab M. Dowling, Jr.

References: South Carolina National Bank; South Carolina Federal Savings Bank; Nations Bank, Community Bank; Citizens and Southern National Bank.

For full biographical listings, see the Martindale-Hubbell Law Directory

HARVEY & BATTEY, P.A. (AV)

1001 Craven Street, P.O. Drawer 1107, 29902
Telephone: 803-521-1963
Telefax: 803-521-5005

W. Brantley Harvey (1893-1981)
W. Brantley Harvey, Jr.
Colden R. Battey, Jr.
Peter L. Fuge
Frederick M. Corley
William B. Harvey, III
John M. Tatum, III
Thomas C. Davis
H. Grady Brown, III
E. Carew Rice, III

OF COUNSEL

Noel M. Seeburg, Jr.

D. L. (Dirk) Aydlette, III

Approved Attorneys for: Lawyers Title Insurance Corp.; Chicago Title Insurance Corp.
Representative Clients: Nations Bank; Savings Bank of Beaufort County, F.S.B.; United Telephone of the Carolinas, Inc.; Berkeley Federal Savings Bank for Harbor Island ; Pleasant Point Plantation Associates; Century 21-Carolina Realty, Inc.; Lobeco Products, Inc.

For full biographical listings, see the Martindale-Hubbell Law Directory

LEVIN & FULP (AV)

811 Craven Street, P.O. Box 2358, 29901-2358
Telephone: 803-522-9000
Fax: 803-524-8248

Julian S. Levin
Kenneth E. Fulp, Jr.

Approved Attorneys for: Lawyers Title Insurance Co.; Old Republic National; Title Insurance Company.

For full biographical listings, see the Martindale-Hubbell Law Directory

SAMS AND SAMS (AV)

811 Craven Street, P.O. Box 849, 29901-0849
Telephone: 803-524-4189

MEMBERS OF FIRM

Talbird Reeve Sams
W. Toland Sams

Approved Attorneys for: Lawyers Title Insurance Co.

For full biographical listings, see the Martindale-Hubbell Law Directory

*BENNETTSVILLE,** Marlboro Co.

GOLDBERG & EASTERLING, P.A. (AV)

116 North Liberty Street, P.O. Box 655, 29512-0655
Telephone: 803-479-2878
Fax: 803-479-2879

William C. Goldberg (1917-1972)
Harry R. Easterling
Harry R. Easterling, Jr.

Local Counsel for: J. P. Stevens; Boise Cascade Corporation; Powell Manufacturing Company, Inc.; Travelers Insurance Company; Carolina Power and Light Company; Willamette Industries, Inc.; Delta Mills, Inc.; John Hancock Mutual Life Insurance Company.

(See Next Column)

GOLDBERG & EASTERLING P.A.—*Continued*

Approved Attorneys for: Lawyers Title Insurance Corp.
Reference: South Carolina National Bank, Bennettsville, S.C.

For full biographical listings, see the Martindale-Hubbell Law Directory

*CAMDEN,** Kershaw Co.

SAVAGE, ROYALL AND SHEHEEN (AV)

1111 Church Street, P.O. Drawer 10, 29020
Telephone: 803-432-4391
Telefax: 803-425-4816

MEMBERS OF FIRM

Edward M. Royall
Robert J. Sheheen
Moultrie B. Burns, Jr.
Dana A. Morris
John W. Rabb, Jr.
William F. Nettles IV

ASSOCIATES

William B. Cox, Jr.

Representative Clients: Nations Bank NBSC; First Palmetto Bank; Farmers Bureau Insurance Cos.; Georgia Pacific Corp.; Carolina Power & Light Co.; Cassatt Water Co.; Bowaters Southern Paper Corp.; Kershaw County Memorial Hospital.
Approved Attorneys for: Stewart Title Insurance; Ticor Title Insurance,

For full biographical listings, see the Martindale-Hubbell Law Directory

*CHARLESTON,** Charleston Co.

BARNWELL WHALEY PATTERSON & HELMS (AV)

134 Meeting Street, Suite 300, P.O. Drawer H, 29402
Telephone: 803-577-7700
Telecopier: 803-577-7708

MEMBERS OF FIRM

Nathaniel B. Barnwell
Ben Scott Whaley (1909-1987)
Robert A. Patterson
Samuel J. Corbin (1907-1976)
William C. Helms, III
Thomas J. Wills
M. Dawes Cooke, Jr.
Bruce E. Miller
B. C. Killough
Matthew H. Henrikson

ASSOCIATES

Aubrey R. Alvey
Eleanor D. Washburn
Warren William Ariail
Robert P. Gritton
Lori S. Dandridge
Thomas B. Pritchard
Heather K. Coleman
James E. Reeves

Representative Clients: The Citadel, The Military College of South Carolina; S.C. Insurance Reserve Fund; Bon Secours St. Francis Xavier Hospital; Brown & Root, Inc.; Continental Ins.; Medical University of South Carolina; Liberty Mutual Ins. Co.; Tiffin Motor Homes; Travelers Ins. Co.; United States Aviation Underwriters.

For full biographical listings, see the Martindale-Hubbell Law Directory

BROCKINTON, BROCKINTON & KERR, P.A. (AV)

51 State Street, P.O. Box 663, 29402-0663
Telephone: 803-722-8845
FAX: 803-722-3069

D. A. Brockinton (1890-1986)
D. A. Brockinton, Jr.
W. H. Brockinton
W. Harvey Brockinton, Jr.
John J. Kerr

Representative Clients: Equitable Life Assurance Society of the U.S.; The News & Courier Company; Evening Post Publishing Co.

For full biographical listings, see the Martindale-Hubbell Law Directory

BUIST, MOORE, SMYTHE & MCGEE, P.A. (AV)

Successors to Buist, Buist, Smythe and Smythe and Moore, Mouzon and McGee.
Five Exchange Street, P.O. Box 999, 29402
Telephone: 803-722-3400
Cable Address: "Conferees"
Telex: 57-6488
Telecopier: 803-723-7398
North Charleston, South Carolina Office: Atrium Northwood Office Building, 7301 Rivers Avenue, Suite 288. Zip: 29406-2859.
Telephone: 803-797-3000.
Telecopier: 803-863-5500.

Henry Buist (1895-1977)
B. Allston Moore (1900-1988)
Augustine T. Smythe (1918-1991)
Henry B. Smythe
Benj. Allston Moore, Jr.
Joseph H. McGee
Gordon D. Schreck
Henry B. Smythe, Jr.
Susan M. Smythe
W. Foster Gaillard
Kenneth F. Smith
David B. McCormack
C. Allen Gibson, Jr.
Morris A. Ellison
Charles P. Summerall, IV
James L. Parris

(See Next Column)

David M. Collins
Robert A. Kerr, Jr.
James D. Myrick
Douglas M. Muller
Elizabeth H. Warner
Jeffrey A. Winkler
David S. Yandle
Patricia L. Quentel
John Marshall Allen
Robert H. Mozingo
Catherine Pulley Ballard
Roger Edward George
Julius H. Hines
David S. Cox
Phillip E. Bryson
Christine E.W. Edenfield

OF COUNSEL

David H. Crawford

Counsel for: CSX Transportation; NationsBank; Metropolitan Life Insurance Co.; E. I. du Pont de Nemours & Co.; AIG Aviation, Inc.; Lamorte, Burns & Co., Inc.; Allstate Insurance Co.; General Dynamics Corp.; Independent Life & Accident Insurance Co.; Georgia-Pacific Corp.

For full biographical listings, see the Martindale-Hubbell Law Directory

GRIMBALL & CABANISS (AV)

The Franke Building, 171 Church Street, Suite 120, P.O. Box 816, 29402-0816
Telephone: 803-722-0311
Fax: 803-722-1374

MEMBERS OF FIRM

William H. Grimball
Joseph W. Cabaniss
Henry E. Grimball
Frank E. Grimball
Max G. Mahaffee
Eugene Patrick Corrigan, III
E. Warren Moise
Michael J. Ferri

ASSOCIATES

Kathryn S. Craven
Julie L. Weinheimer
E. Charles Grose, Jr.
Henry H. Cabaniss

Representative Clients: Chubb Group; CIGNA; CNA Insurance Cos.; Nationwide Mutual Insurance Co.; Prudential Insurance Co.; State Farm Insurance Cos.
Local Counsel for: Exxon Corp.; The Greyhound Corp.; Norfolk-Southern Corp.; Baker Hospital.

For full biographical listings, see the Martindale-Hubbell Law Directory

HAYNSWORTH, MARION, MCKAY & GUÉRARD, L.L.P (AV)

#2 Prioleau Street, P.O. Box 1119, 29402
Telephone: 803-722-7606
Telecopier: 803-723-5263
Columbia, South Carolina Office: Suite 2400 AT&T Building, 1201 Main Street, P.O. Drawer 7157, 29202.
Telephone: 803-765-1818.
Telecopier: 803-765-2399.
Greenville, South Carolina Office: Two Insignia Financial Plaza, 75 Beattie Place, P.O. Box 2048, 29602.
Telephone: 803-240-3200.
Telecopier: 803-240-3300.

OF COUNSEL

Theodore B. Guérard
Julius W. McKay

SPECIAL COUNSEL

Nancy Lark Schulze
Julian W. Walker, Jr.

MEMBERS OF FIRM

Henry J. Haynsworth (1859-1941)
Clement Furman Haynsworth (1886-1953)
James M. Perry (1894-1964)
Eugene Bryant (1902-1969)
W. E. Applegate, III
William C. Cleveland
J. Paul Trouche
James J. Hinchey, Jr. (Resident)
Samuel W. Howell, IV
Donald Bancroft Meyer
Carol L. Clark

ASSOCIATES

James E. Lady
Paul M. Lynch
Coleman Miller Legerton
J. Walker Coleman, IV
Meredith Grier Buyck
Robert M. Cook, II
Karen A. Wood (Not admitted in SC)

Counsel for: Bank of South Carolina; Baker Hospital; Healthsource of South Carolina; Allstate Insurance Co.; CSX Corporation; Lloyd's Underwriters; Coward-Hund Construction Co.; City of Hanahan; Duke Power Company; Anheuser Busch Company; Roper Hospital.

For full biographical listings, see the Martindale-Hubbell Law Directory

HOLMES & THOMSON, L.L.P. (AV)

A Registered Limited Liability Partnership
200 Meeting Street, Suite 202, P.O. Box 858, 29402
Telephone: 803-723-2000
Facsimile: 803-724-1338

(See Next Column)

HOLMES & THOMSON L.L.P., *Charleston—Continued*

Wade H. Logan, III
Thomas Waring
Keating L. Simons, III
Susan Taylor Wall
Scott Y. Barnes
Wm. Howell Morrison
Danny H. Mullis
David B. Wheeler
David C. Humphreys, Jr.
Charles J. Baker, III
Martha Dantzler Ballenger
Cody W. Smith, Jr.
Trent M. Kernodle
Thomas J. Keaveny, II
Mary Leigh Arnold

Mitzi Grove Ball
John A. Massalon
Lynn L. Crooks
Mia Lauren Maness
Kelley M. Braithwaite
Cynthia Jordan Lowery
Stanley C. Rodgers
Joseph R. Weston
John P. Seibels, Jr.
Trudy Y. Hartzog
A. Baron Holmes, III (1905-1991)
Bernard M. Thomson, Jr. (1913-1991)

Representative Clients: Chrysler Corp; CIGNA Cos.; CSX Transportation (Division Counsel); First Federal of Charleston (General Counsel); Ford Motor Corp.; General Motors Corp.; Home Insurance Co.; South Carolina Electric & Gas Co.: NationsBank of South Carolina, N.A.; Bon Secours St. Francis Xavier Hospital.

For full biographical listings, see the Martindale-Hubbell Law Directory

HOOD LAW FIRM (AV)

172 Meeting Street, P.O. Box 1508, 29402
Telephone: 803-577-4435
FAX: 803-722-1630

MEMBERS OF FIRM

Robert H. Hood
Louis P. Herns
G. Mark Phillips
Carl Everette Pierce, II
John K. Blincow, Jr.

James G. Kennedy
James Dowell Gandy, III
William R. Hearn, Jr.
Joseph C. Wilson, IV
Dixon F. Pearce, III
Margaret Allison Snead
Barbara Wynne Showers
Christine L. Companion
Hugh Willcox Buyck
Jerry A. Smith
Allan Poe Sloan, III
Todd W. Smyth

For full biographical listings, see the Martindale-Hubbell Law Directory

MCKAY & GUÉRARD, P.A.

(See Haynsworth, Marion, McKay & Guérard, L.L.P.)

ROSEN, ROSEN & HAGOOD, P.A. (AV)

134 Meeting Street, Suite 200, P.O. Box 893, 29402
Telephone: 803-577-6726

Morris D. Rosen
Robert N. Rosen
Richard S. Rosen
H. Brewton Hagood
Alice F. Paylor
Susan Corner Rosen
Donald B. Clark
Irvin G. Condon

Diane C. Current
Randy Horner
Peter Brandt Shelbourne
Alexander B. Cash
Daniel F. Blanchard, III

Reference: NationsBank of South Carolina, N.A.

For full biographical listings, see the Martindale-Hubbell Law Directory

SINKLER & BOYD, P.A. (AV)

160 East Bay Street, P.O. Box 340, 29402-0340
Telephone: 803-722-3366
FAX: 803-722-2266
Columbia, South Carolina Office: Suite 1200 The Palmetto Center, 1426 Main Street, P.O. Box 11889.
Telephone: 803-779-3080.
FAX: 803-765-1243.
Greenville, South Carolina Office: 15 South Main Street, Suite 500, Wachovia Building, P.O. Box 275.
Telephone: 803-467-1100.
FAX: 803-467-1521.

John C. Bruton (1907-1969)
W. C. Boyd (1904-1975)
Huger Sinkler (1908-1987)
Charles W. Knowlton (1923-1990)
Kirkman Finlay, Jr. (1936-1993)
Charles H. Gibbs (1915-1993)
H. Simmons Tate, Jr. (Resident, Columbia Office)
William C. Boyd (Resident, Columbia Office)
Francis P. Mood (Resident, Columbia Office)
J. Donald Dial, Jr. (Resident, Columbia Office)
Bachman S. Smith III
Manton M. Grier (Resident, Columbia Office)
George S. King, Jr. (Resident, Columbia Office)
Thomas R. Gottshall (Resident, Columbia Office)

(See Next Column)

Hamilton Osborne, Jr. (Resident, Columbia Office)
Stephen E. Darling
John P. Linton
Margaret Christian Pope (Resident, Columbia Office)
Harold E. Trask
Charlton deSaussure, Jr.
Marvin D. Infinger
Palmer Freeman, Jr. (Resident, Columbia Office)
Daryl L. Williams (Resident, Columbia Office)
John C. Bruton, Jr. (Resident, Columbia Office)
F. Mitchell Johnson, Jr.
Michael D. Jones
Elizabeth A. Carpentier (Resident, Columbia Office)
Benton D. Williamson (Resident, Columbia Office)
Sue C. Erwin (Resident, Columbia Office)
John B. McArthur (Resident, Columbia Office)
David M. Swanson
Robert S. Galloway, III (Resident, Greenville Office)
Clarke W. DuBose (Resident, Columbia Office)
Terri Morrill Lynch
Randolph B. Epting (Resident, Columbia Office)
Steve A. Matthews (Resident, Columbia Office)
Robert Y. Knowlton (Resident, Columbia Office)
Suzanne Hulst Clawson (Resident, Columbia Office)
William H. Short, Jr. (Resident, Columbia Office)
Theodore B. DuBose (Resident, Columbia Office)
Thomas C. Hildebrand, Jr.
John M. G. McLeod (Resident, Columbia Office)
Robert W. Buffington (Resident, Columbia Office)
S. Marshall Huey, Jr.
Frank W. Cureton (Resident, Columbia Office)
Bert Glenn Utsey III
Charles H. Gibbs, Jr.
Stanley H. McGuffin (Resident, Columbia Office)
John K. Van Duys (Resident, Columbia Office)
John H. Tiller
Roy A. Howell III
Virginia L. Vroegop (Resident Columbia Office)

Edward K. Pritchard III
David W. Whittington
Robert Wilson, III
Mark E. Rostick
Henry J. White (Resident, Columbia Office)
Joseph Hubert Wood, III
Tara Elizabeth Nauful (Resident, Columbia Office)
John F. Emerson (Resident, Columbia Office)
Deborah Paris Morgan (Resident, Columbia Office)
Perrin Q. Dargan, III
Joseph D. Thompson, III

OF COUNSEL

Albert Simons, Jr.
Martin C. McWilliams, Jr. (Resident, Columbia Office)
Katherine W. Hill (Resident, Columbia Office)

Attorneys for: The South Carolina National Bank; First Union National Bank; Westvaco; American Cyanamid Co.; Dean Witter Reynolds; Waste Management of North America, Inc.; Sonoco Products; Lawyers Title Insurance Corporation; Heater Utilities, Inc.

For full biographical listings, see the Martindale-Hubbell Law Directory

WARREN & SINKLER (AV)

Suite 340 171 Church Street, P.O. Box 1254, 29402
Telephone: 803-577-0660
Fax: 803-577-6843

MEMBERS OF FIRM

G. Dana Sinkler
John H. Warren, III
Henry B. Fishburne, Jr.
Mark S. Sharpe
Elizabeth W. Settle
Elizabeth T. Thomas

For full biographical listings, see the Martindale-Hubbell Law Directory

YOUNG, CLEMENT, RIVERS & TISDALE (AV)

28 Broad Street, P.O. Box 993, 29402
Telephone: 803-577-4000
Fax: 803-724-6600
Columbia, South Carolina Office: 1901 Assembly Street, Suite 300, P.O. Box 8476.
Telephone: 803-799-4000.
Fax: 803-799-7083.
North Charleston , South Carolina Office: 2170 Ashley Phosphate Road, Suite 700, P.O. Box 61509.
Telephone: 803-720-5400.
Fax: 803-724-7796.

MEMBERS OF FIRM

Thomas S. Tisdale, Jr.
William J. Bates
J. Rutledge Young, Jr.
Wallace G. Holland
Bradish J. Waring
W. Jefferson Leath, Jr.
John C. Von Lehe, Jr.
Timothy W. Bouch
William Bobo, Jr.
H. Michael Bowers
Carol Brittain Ervin
Joseph E. DaPore
Michael A. Molony
C. Michael Branham
Randell C. Stoney, Jr.
Stephen P. Groves
Shawn Daughtridge Wallace
John Hamilton Smith
Lawrence W. Johnson, Jr.

SPECIAL COUNSEL

B. Lindsay Crawford, III

(See Next Column)

YOUNG, CLEMENT, RIVERS & TISDALE—*Continued*

ASSOCIATES

Elizabeth B. Luzuriaga
Shawn M. Flanagan
Robert W. Pearce, Jr.
Sally H. Rhoad
E. Courtney Gruber
Jonathan L. Yates
F. Drake Rogers
Edward D. Buckley, Jr.
Duke R. Highfield
Amy Rogers Jordan
H. Bowen Woodruff
E. Ellen Howard
Stephen L. Brown
Wilbur E. Johnson

OF COUNSEL

Robert L. Clement, Jr.
G. L. Buist Rivers, Jr.

RETIRED

Joseph R. Young

Counsel for: Albright & Wilson; The Asten Group, Inc.; Charleston Metro Chambers of Commerce; Coburg Dairy, Inc.; Eastman Kodak Corp.; National Bank of South Carolina; Southern Dredging Company; Unisun; Wausau Insurance Company.

For full biographical listings, see the Martindale-Hubbell Law Directory

CHERAW, Chesterfield Co. — (Refer to Bennettsville)

*CHESTER,** Chester Co. — (Refer to York)

*CHESTERFIELD,** Chesterfield Co. — (Refer to Bennettsville)

*COLUMBIA,** Richland Co.

*** indicates certain Bar Register subscribers whose principal office is located elsewhere in the state and who have arranged for representation as a part of the state capital listings that follow**

WESTON ADAMS (AV)

1705 Richland Street, P.O. Box 291, 29202
Telephone: 803-254-1675
Fax: 803-799-3141

For full biographical listings, see the Martindale-Hubbell Law Directory

BARNES, ALFORD, STORK & JOHNSON, L.L.P. (AV)

1613 Main Street, P.O. Box 8448, 29202
Telephone: 803-799-1111
Telefax: 803-254-1335

Rudolph C. Barnes
James W. Alford
William C. Stork
Weldon R. Johnson
Robert E. Salane
David G. Wolff
Kay Gaffney Crowe
Richard C. Thomas
Thomas C. Cofield
Robert Thomas Strickland
R. Lewis Johnson
L. Elaine Mozingo

Curtis W. Dowling
Gregory G. Williams
Andrew E. Haselden
James R. Allen

OF COUNSEL

Rudolph C. Barnes, Jr.
Alan J. Reyner
Roger A. Way, Jr.

Representative Clients: First Union National Bank of South Carolina; Aetna Casualty and Surety Co.; Kline Iron & Steel Co.

For full biographical listings, see the Martindale-Hubbell Law Directory

BERRY, DUNBAR, DANIEL, O'CONNOR & JORDAN (AV)

A Partnership including Professional Associations
1200 Main Street, Eighth Floor, P.O. Box 11645, Capitol Station, 29211-1645
Telephone: 803-765-1030
Facsimile: 803-799-5536
Spartanburg, South Carolina Office: 112 West Daniel Morgan Avenue.
Telephone: 803-583-3975.
Atlanta, Georgia Office: 2400 Cain Tower, Peachtree Center.
Telephone: 404-588-0500.
Facsimile: 404-523-6714.

MEMBERS OF FIRM

Joe E. Berry, Jr.
James V. Dunbar, Jr.
J. Fitzgerald O'Connor, Jr. (P.A.)
Leonard R. Jordan, Jr. (P.A.)

ASSOCIATES

Preston R. Burch
William O. Higgins
Deborah R.J. Shupe
James A. Merritt, Jr.
John A. Hill
Jose F. Monge
Mary Katherine Sherman
William K. Witherspoon

SPECIAL COUNSEL

Edmund H. Monteith

(See Next Column)

OF COUNSEL

John W. Ragsdale, Jr. (Not admitted in SC)
Marcia R. Powell (Resident, Spartanburg Office)

Approved Attorneys for: Lawyers Title Insurance Corporation of Richmond.

For full biographical listings, see the Martindale-Hubbell Law Directory

COLLINS & LACY (AV)

1330 Lady Street, Suite 601, P.O. Box 12487, 29211
Telephone: 803-256-2660
Telefax: 803-771-4484

Joel W. Collins, Jr.
Stanford E. Lacy
Yolanda Coker Courie
Gray Thomas Culbreath
Arthur K. Aiken

Ellen A. Mercer
Eric G. Fosmire
Rebecca M. Monroy

LEGAL SUPPORT PERSONNEL

LEGAL ASSISTANTS

Jane A. Lo Cicero
Kelly L. Rabel
Jeanne S. Volin
Annette L. Horton
Susan S. Hornung

For full biographical listings, see the Martindale-Hubbell Law Directory

DANIEL & DANIEL (AV)

3100 Jefferson Executive Center, 1813 Main Street, P.O. Box 2085, 29202
Telephone: 803-771-8782
Fax: 803-771-9447
Litchfield, South Carolina Office: Litchfield Village Shopping Center.
Telephone: 803-237-4792.

MEMBERS OF FIRM

J. Reese Daniel
Michael R. Daniel

For full biographical listings, see the Martindale-Hubbell Law Directory

GLENN, IRVIN, MURPHY, GRAY & STEPP (AV)

Southern National Bank Building, Suite 390, 1901 Assembly Street, P.O. Box 1550, 29202-1550
Telephone: 803-765-1100
Telecopy: 803-765-0755

Terrell L. Glenn (1930-1993)

MEMBERS OF FIRM

Wilmot B. Irvin
Peter L. Murphy
Elizabeth Van Doren Gray
Robert E. Stepp
Elizabeth G. Howard

Blaney A. Coskrey, III
Robert A. Culpepper

Reference: Southern National.

For full biographical listings, see the Martindale-Hubbell Law Directory

*** HAYNSWORTH, MARION, MCKAY & GUÉRARD, L.L.P.** (AV)

Suite 2400 A T & T Building, 1201 Main Street, P.O. Drawer 7157, 29202
Telephone: 803-765-1818
Telecopier: 803-765-2399
Greenville, South Carolina Office: Two Insignia Financial Plaza, 75 Beattie Place, P.O. Box 2048, 29602.
Telephone: 803-240-3200.
Telecopier: 803-240-3300.
Charleston, South Carolina Office: #2 Prioleau Street, P.O. Box 1119, 29402.
Telephone: 803-722-7606.
Telecopier: 803-723-5263.

OF COUNSEL

Andrew B. Marion
Theodore B. Guérard
Julius W. McKay

SENIOR SPECIAL COUNSEL

Michael R. Daniel
Russell B. Shetterly

SPECIAL COUNSEL

Julian W. Walker, Jr.

MEMBERS OF FIRM

Henry J. Haynsworth (1859-1941)
Clement Furman Haynsworth (1886-1953)
James M. Perry (1894-1964)
Eugene Bryant (1902-1969)
William P. Simpson
Samuel W. Howell, IV
Gary W. Morris
Henry P. Wall
Steven Todd Moon

ASSOCIATES

Stephen F. McKinney
Edward G. Kluiters
Boyd B. Nicholson, Jr.
Jill R. Quattlebaum
Edward Wade Mullins, III

(See Next Column)

HAYNSWORTH, MARION, MCKAY & GUÉRARD L.L.P., *Columbia—Continued*

Counsel for: St. Paul Insurance Group; Allstate Insurance Co.; Fluor-Daniel Corp.; South Carolina Jobs - Economic Development Authority; Anheuser Busch Company; CSX Transportation; Ernst & Young, LLP; Willis Corroon of South Carolina, Inc.; Westinghouse Savannah River Co.; Wachovia Bank of South Carolina, N.A.

For full biographical listings, see the Martindale-Hubbell Law Directory

KING & VERNON, P.A. (AV)

1426 Richland Street, P.O. Box 7667, 29202
Telephone: 803-779-3090
Fax: 803-779-3396

Kermit S. King
W. Thomas Vernon

Rochelle Y. Williamson
B. Dean Pierce

For full biographical listings, see the Martindale-Hubbell Law Directory

MCCUTCHEN, BLANTON, RHODES & JOHNSON (AV)

1414 Lady Street, P.O. Drawer 11209, 29211
Telephone: 803-799-9791
Telecopier: 803-253-6084
Winnsboro, South Carolina Office: Courthouse Square, 29180.
Telephone: 803-635-6884.

MEMBERS OF FIRM

Thomas E. McCutchen
Hoover C. Blanton
Jeter E. Rhodes, Jr.
T. English McCutchen, III
Pope D. Johnson, III
William R. Taylor
Evans Taylor Barnette
G. D. Morgan, Jr.
John C. Bradley, Jr.

ASSOCIATES

Creighton B. Coleman
William E. Hopkins, Jr.

Representative Clients: Allstate Insurance Co.; Sears, Roebuck and Co.; J.B. White Co.; Anchor Continental Inc.; Western Fire Insurance Co.; Liberty Mutual Insurance Co.; Southeastern Freight Lines; American Mutual Fire Insurance Co.; Continental Life Insurance Co.; State Farm Fire & Casualty Co.

For full biographical listings, see the Martindale-Hubbell Law Directory

MCKAY & GUÉRARD, P.A.

(See Haynsworth, Marion, McKay & Guérard, L.L.P.)

MCKAY, MCKAY, HENRY & FOSTER, P.A. (AV)

1325 Laurel Street, P.O. Box 7217, 29202
Telephone: 803-256-4645
FAX: 803-765-1839

Douglas McKay, Jr.
Julius W. McKay, II
Angela L. Henry
Ruskin C. Foster

Daniel R. Settana, Jr.

Representative Clients: Americlaim Adjustment Corp.; Amoco Oil Company; Blue Cross & Blue Shield of South Carolina; Britanco Underwriters, Inc.; Browning-Ferris Industries, Inc.; Haverty's Furniture Company; Homestead Insurance Co.; Lincoln National Life Insurance Co.; Pennsylvania Manufacturers' Association Insurance Co. (PMA); Schneider National Carriers.

For full biographical listings, see the Martindale-Hubbell Law Directory

ERNEST J. NAUFUL, JR., P.C. (AV)

1330 Lady Street Suite 615, P.O. Box 5907, 29250
Telephone: 803-256-4045
Facsimile: 803-254-0776

Ernest J. Nauful, Jr.

For full biographical listings, see the Martindale-Hubbell Law Directory

NELSON MULLINS RILEY & SCARBOROUGH L.L.P. (AV)

A Registered Limited Liability Partnership including Professional Corporations
Third Floor, Keenan Building, 1330 Lady Street, P.O. Box 11070, 29211
Telephone: 803-799-2000
Telecopy: 803-256-7500; 733-9499
Atlanta, Georgia Office: 1201 Peachtree Street, N.E., P.O. Box 77707.
Telephone: 404-817-6000.
Telecopy: 404-817-6050.
Charleston, South Carolina Office: Suite 500, 151 Meeting Street, P.O. Box 1806.
Telephone: 803-853-5200.
Telecopy: 803-722-8700.

(See Next Column)

Florence, South Carolina Office: 600 W. Palmetto Street, Suite 200, P.O. Box 5955.
Telephone: 803-662-0019.
Telecopy: 803-662-0491.
Greenville, South Carolina Office: Twenty-Fourth Floor, BB&T Building, 301 North Main Street, P.O. Box 10084.
Telephone: 803-250-2300.
Telecopy: 803-232-2925.
Lexington, South Carolina Office: 334 Old Chapin Road, P.O. Box 729.
Telephone: 803-733-9494; 803-799-200.
Telecopy: 803-957-8226.
Myrtle Beach, South Carolina Office: 2411 N. Oak Street, Founders Centre, Suite 301. P.O. Box 3939.
Telephone: 803-448-3500.
Telecopy: 803-448-3437.

SPECIAL COUNSEL

David W. Harwell (Resident, Myrtle Beach, SC Office)

OF COUNSEL

Edward C. Brewer, III (Resident, Atlanta GA Office)
Daniel B. Hodgson (Resident, Atlanta, GA Office)
Edward P. Riley, Jr. (Resident, Greenville, SC Office)
Robert P. Wilkins (Resident, Lexington, SC Office)
Robert P. Wilkins, Jr. (Resident, Lexington, SC Office)
John S. Williams

MEMBERS OF FIRM

Patrick Henry Nelson (1856-1914)
William Shannon Nelson (1881-1939)
Patrick H. Nelson (1910-1964)
F. Barron Grier, Jr. (1907-1971)
Edward W. Mullins, Sr. (1893-1989)
Claude M. Scarborough, Jr.
Edward W. Mullins, Jr.
William S. Nelson, II
R. Bruce Shaw
John U. Bell, III
William S. Davies, Jr.
Donald H. Stubbs
Robert M. Erwin, Jr. (Resident, Greenville, SC Office)
James C. Blakely, Jr. (P.A.) (Resident, Greenville, SC Office)
Robert D. Pannell (Resident, Atlanta, GA Office)
Ralston B. Vanzant, II
Stephen G. Morrison
Edward E. Poliakoff
John C. Stewart, Jr. (Resident, Myrtle Beach, SC Office)
Thomas A. Hutcheson (Resident, Charleston, SC Office)
Robert E. Lee Garner (Resident, Atlanta, GA Office)
Brenton D. Jeffcoat
Sheryl Cudd Blenis
Thornwell F. Sowell
John T. Moore
George S. Bailey
John M. Campbell, Jr. (Resident, Greenville, SC Office)
Kenneth L. Millwood (Resident, Atlanta, GA Office)
Richard B. Watson (Resident, Charleston, SC Office)
William C. Hubbard
Dwight F. Drake
George B. Wolfe
George B. Cauthen
Henry S. Knight, Jr.
Kenneth E. Young (Resident, Greenville, SC Office)
James C. Gray, Jr.
John L. Latham (Resident, Atlanta, GA Office)
Jeffrey N. Plowman (Resident, Atlanta, GA Office)
Patrick G. Jones (Resident, Atlanta, GA Office)
Nina Nelson Smith
Charles R. Norris (Resident, Charleston, SC Office)
Jeffrey A. Allred (Resident, Atlanta, GA Office)
J. Douglas Nunn, Jr.
Richard H. Willis (Resident, Atlanta, GA Office)
Joel H. Smith
David G. Traylor, Jr.
Monteith P. Todd
Robert W. Foster, Jr. (Resident, Atlanta, GA Office)
S. Keith Hutto
Clarence Davis
Paul A. Quirós (Resident, Atlanta, GA Office)
Peter C. Quittmeyer (Resident, Atlanta, GA Office)
Rebecca Laffitte
Timothy D. Scrantom (Resident, Charleston, SC Office)
David E. Dukes
L. Walter Tollison, III
Sylvia King Kochler (Resident, Atlanta, GA Office)
Michael D. Bryan (Resident, Charleston, SC Office)
Stuart M. Andrews, Jr.
Carolyn Cason Matthews
Karen Aldridge Crawford
Glenn W. Sturm (Resident, Atlanta, GA Office)
Christopher J. Daniels
George K. Lyall (Resident, Greenville, SC Office)
Richard A. Farrier, Jr. (Resident, Charleston, SC Office)
Jane Thompson Davis (Resident, Charleston, SC Office)
Walter H. Hinton, II (Resident, Greenville, SC Office)
Trefor Thomas (Resident, Myrtle Beach, SC Office)
Lisa C. Heydinger (Resident, Charleston, SC Office)
W. Thomas Causby
Susan Pardue MacDonald (Resident, Myrtle Beach, SC Office)
John E. Schmidt, III
Kenneth A. Janik
Russell Z. Plowden (Resident, Greenville, SC Office)
John B. Hagerty (Resident, Charleston, SC Office)
Newman Jackson Smith (Resident, Charleston, SC Office)
Thomas E. Lydon (Resident, Charleston, SC Office)
David E. Hodge (Resident, Greenville, SC Office)
Robert O. Meriwether
Erroll Anne Yarbrough Hodges (Resident, Greenville, SC Office)
Howard A. VanDine, III
Grady L. Beard
Thomas F. Moran (Resident, Myrtle Beach, SC Office)
J. Calhoun Watson
J. Mark Jones
Neil E. Grayson (Resident, Atlanta, GA Office)

(See Next Column)

NELSON MULLINS RILEY & SCARBOROUGH L.L.P.—*Continued*

ASSOCIATES

Deborah Williamson Witt
Patrick F. O'Dea (Resident, Myrtle Beach, SC Office)
Phillip Luke Hughes (Resident, Myrtle Beach, SC Office)
Rose-Marie T. Carlisle
Cherie Wilson Blackburn (Resident, Charleston, SC. Office)
Joseph M. Melchers
Robert H. Brunson
Linda A. Wohlbruck
Karen Hudson Thomas
Augustus M. Dixon
Lynn Schutte Scott (Resident, Atlanta, GA Office)
Larry W. Shackelford (Resident, Atlanta, GA Office)
R. Jeneane Treace (Resident, Atlanta, GA Office)
William L. Hirata
Francis B. B. Knowlton
Julie Jeffords Moose (Resident, Florence, SC. Office)
Jeanne N. Guest (Resident, Myrtle Beach, SC Office)
A. Marvin Quattlebaum (Resident, Greenville, SC Office)
James F. Rogers
Benjamin Rush Smith, III
Amy C. Hendrix (Resident, Greenville, SC Office)
Elizabeth Scott Moise
Barbara E. Brunson
Daniel J. Westbrook
John F. Kuppens
C. Mitchell Brown
Darryl D. Smalls
Sarah Link Hardy (Resident, Atlanta, GA Office)
Daniel S. Sanders, Jr. (Resident, Atlanta, GA Office)
M. Clifton Scott, Jr.
Jeffrey A. Jacobs
Angus H. Macaulay, Jr.
Jane Harris Downey
Laura E. Zoole
Susan M. Glenn
Steven A. McKelvey, Jr.
James A. Shuchart (Resident, Atlanta, GA Office)
Bernard F. Hawkins, Jr.
William C. Wood, Jr.
N. Keith Emge, Jr. (Resident, Charleston, SC Office)
William R. Harbison
Anthony L. Harbin (Resident, Greenville, SC Office)
Carey T. Kilton
Christie Newman Barrett
Daniel J. Fritze
Marian L. Askins
Deirdre M. Shelton (Resident, Charleston, SC Office)
Christopher J. McCool (Resident, Charleston, SC Office)
Anne Frances Bleecker (Resident, Charleston, SC Office)
William Y. Klett, III
Denise C. Yarborough (Resident, Greenville, SC Office)
Susan E. Ziel
Frank T. Davis, III (Resident, Greenville, SC Office)
Alice Palmer Shaw
Michael W. Hogue
Stephen C. Petrovich (Resident, Atlanta, GA. Office)
William Stevens Brown
Jonathan P. Dyer
B. Shane Clanton (Resident, Atlanta, GA Office)
Don Lawrence Kristinik, III
Hannah M. Metcalf-Dodson
Lisa Woodbury Caldwell (Resident, Charleston, SC Office)
Craig E. Burgess (Resident, Charleston, SC Office)
William H. Latham
Kymric Y. Mahnke (Resident, Greenville, SC Office)
R. Len Rowe
Dodd M. Davis (Resident, Greenville, SC Office)
Joy Allred Rosati
John Aaron Ecton
Robert C. Calamari (Resident, Myrtle Beach, SC Office)
James Y. Becker
P. Mason Hogue, Jr.
James F. Mc Crackin (Resident, Myrtle Beach, SC Office)
Zoe Sanders Nettles
Rebecca Ann Dorman (Resident, Greenville, SC Office)
Allen J. Barnes
Robert E. Bogan
Timothy Mann, Jr. (Resident, Atlanta, GA Office)
Karen E. Blair
Brent M. Boyd
M. Catherin Cauthen
Alysia M. Loug
Tonya L. Lewis
Suzanne C. Massey
Kristie Porter
Rochelle Romosca
Dominic A. Starr (Resident, Myrtle Beach, SC Office)
Shannon Leigh Till
Christopher J. Weeks (Resident, Greenville, SC Office)
J. Andrew Williams (Resident, Greenville, SC Office)
Jennifer A. Gutek
Alice V. Harris
William A. Pusey, Jr. (Resident, Charleston, SC Office)
William H. Foster, III
Fredrick S. Pfeiffer (Resident, Greenville, SC Office)
Simpson Z. Fant

Representative Clients: Bi-Lo, Inc.; BMW, AG; E. I. DuPont de Nemours & Co.; General Motors Corp.; W. R. Grace & Company, Cryovac Division; Hoffmann-LaRoche; The National Bank of South Carolina; NationsBank; Owens-Illinois, Inc.; Southern Bell Telephone & Telegraph Co.; Union Camp Corp.

For full biographical listings, see the Martindale-Hubbell Law Directory

NEXSEN PRUET JACOBS & POLLARD, LLP (AV)

1441 Main Street, 15th Floor, P.O. Drawer 2426, 29202
Telephone: 803-771-8900
Facsimile: 803-253-8277
Charleston, South Carolina Office: 200 Meeting Street, Suite 301. P.O. Box 486.
Telephone: 803-577-9440.
Facsimile: 803-720-1777.

(*See Next Column*)

Greenville, South Carolina Office: 1000 East North Street, 2nd Floor, P.O. Box 10648.
Telephone: 803-370-2211.
Facsimile: 803-282-1177.

MEMBERS OF FIRM

T. Eugene Allen, III
Mark L. Bender
Henry W. Brown
Wilburn Brewer, Jr.
Russell T. Burke
Robert C. Byrd
Paul A. Dominick (Resident, Charleston Office)
Victoria L. Eslinger
Robert W. Hassold, Jr. (Resident, Greenville Office)
Leon C. Harmon
J. David Hawkins (Resident, Charleston Office)
Russell T. Infinger (Resident, Greenville Office)
Harold W. Jacobs
Fred L. Kingsmore, Jr.
G. Marcus Knight
W. Thomas Lavender, Jr.
Susan Batten Lipscomb
William Spencer McMaster
Susan Pedrick McWilliams
Julio E. Mendoza, Jr.
Edward G. Menzie
Samuel F. Painter
Thomas B. Pollard, Jr.
William A. Pollard
R. Kent Porth
Pamela J. Roberts
Neil C. Robinson, Jr. (Resident, Charleston Office)
John C. B. Smith, Jr.
John A. Sowards
Thomas L. Stephenson (Resident, Greenville Office)
Val H. Stieglitz, III
B. Joel Stoudenmire (Resident, Greenville Office)
David B. Summer, Jr.
M. Jeffrey Vinzani (Resident, Charleston Office)

COUNSEL

Robert D. Coble
David C. Eckstrom
Faye A. Flowers
David W. Gossett (Resident, Greenville Office)
Ernest R. (Ros) Huff, Jr.
Brian F. Kernaghan (Resident, Charleston Office)
Susan Lake
Joseph R. Lefft
Julian J. Nexsen
Gene V. Pruet
Jonathan Staebler (Resident, Charleston Office)

ASSOCIATES

Jennifer J. Aldrich
Ralph W. Barbier III
James C. Brice, III (Resident, Greenville Office)
Mark D. Cauthen
J. Michelle Childs
Edwin H. Cooper, III
Irene Rose Duggan
J. James Duggan (Resident, Charleston Office)
John G. Felder, Jr.
Hazel B. Fleshman
Hanna Casper George (Resident, Charleston Office)
Julian Hennig, III
Timothy L. Hewson
Elizabeth A. Holley (Resident, Greenville Office)
Cynthia Bankhead Hutto
Luther C. Kissam, IV
Thomas C. R. Legaré, Jr.
Alan M. Lipsitz
Reginald I. Lloyd
Elizabeth Ann Loadholt
James G. Long, III
W. Leighton Lord III
William G. Lyles III (Resident, Charleston Office)
Marcus A. Manos
Jeanne M. Mason
Jay S. Masty (Resident, Charleston Office)
Elizabeth M. McMillan (Resident, Greenville Office)
Rakel M. Meir
Matthew S. Moore, III
William G. Newsome, III
Matthew J. Norton (Resident, Charleston Office)
David J. Parrish (Resident, Charleston Office)
R. Morrison M. Payne
Angela D. Smith

For full biographical listings, see the Martindale-Hubbell Law Directory

QUINN, PATTERSON & WILLARD (AV)

2019 Park Street, P.O. Box 73, 29202
Telephone: 803-779-6365
Telefax: 803-779-6372

MEMBERS OF FIRM

Michael H. Quinn
Grady L. Patterson, III
Theodore DuBose Willard, Jr.

ASSOCIATES

Heidi Brown

Approved Attorneys for: Lawyers Title Insurance Corp.

For full biographical listings, see the Martindale-Hubbell Law Directory

RICHARDSON, PLOWDEN, GRIER AND HOWSER, P.A. (AV)

1600 Marion Street, P.O. Drawer 7788, 29202
Telephone: 803-771-4400
Telecopy: 803-779-0016
Myrtle Beach, South Carolina Office: Southern National Bank Building, Suite 202, 601 21st Avenue North, P.O. Box 3646, 29578.
Telephone: 803-448-1008.
FAX: 803-448-1533.

Donald V. Richardson, III
Charles N. Plowden, Jr.
F. Barron Grier, III
R. Davis Howser
Charles E. Carpenter, Jr.
Frank E. Robinson, II
Michael A. Pulliam
George C. Beighley
William H. Hensel
Frederick A. Crawford
Francis M. Mack
Samuel F. Crews, III

(*See Next Column*)

RICHARDSON, PLOWDEN, GRIER AND HOWSER P.A., *Columbia—Continued*

Franklin Jennings Smith, Jr.
Leslie A. Cotter, Jr.
James P. Newman, Jr.
Steven W. Hamm

Nina Reid Mack
Deborah Harrison Sheffield
Douglas C. Baxter
William G. Besley
S. Nelson Weston Jr.
Mary L. Sowell League
Benjamin D. McCoy
Jimmy Denning, Jr.
Anne Macon Flynn
Harley D. Ruff
Phillip Florence, Jr.
Williams Scalise Marian

Representative Clients: Insurance: CNA Insurance Co.; The Hartford; Kemper Insurance Co.; Pennsylvania National Mutual Casualty Insurance Co.; Wausau Insurance Cos.; The Reudlinger Cos. Real Estate, Corporate and Banking: Richland Memorial Hospital; First Union Bank; National Bank of South Carolina. Construction: S.C. Department of Transportation.

For full biographical listings, see the Martindale-Hubbell Law Directory

ROBINSON, MCFADDEN & MOORE, P.C. (AV)

Fifteen Hundred NationsBank Plaza, 1901 Main Street, P.O. Box 944, 29202
Telephone: 803-779-8900
Telecopier: 803-252-0724

David W. Robinson, Sr. (1869-1935)
R. Hoke Robinson (1916-1977)
J. Means McFadden (1901-1990)
David W. Robinson (1899-1989)
David W. Robinson, II
D. Reece Williams, III
John S. Taylor, Jr.
James M. Brailsford, III
Daniel T. Brailsford
Frank R. Ellerbe, III
Thomas W. Bunch, II
J. Kershaw Spong
D. Clay Robinson
Jacquelyn Lee Bartley
E. Meredith Manning
R. William Metzger, Jr.
Kevin K. Bell
Annemarie B. Mathews

OF COUNSEL

Thomas T. Moore

Representative Clients: NationsBank; Chemical Financial Corp.; Transcontinental Gas Pipe Line Corp.; The Equitable Life Insurance Society of the U.S.; Metropolitan Life Insurance Co.; Firestone Tire & Rubber Co.; Mutual Life Insurance Company of New York.; South Carolina Insurance Reserve Fund; South Carolina Insurance Co.

For full biographical listings, see the Martindale-Hubbell Law Directory

SHERRILL AND ROGERS, PC (AV)

1441 Main Street, 10th Floor, P.O. Box 100200, 29202-3200
Telephone: 803-771-7900
Fax: 803-254-6305

Mark Taylor Arden
Robert Bryan Barnes
B. Michael Brackett
Sherwood M. Cleveland
Arthur G. Fusco
Harry B. Gregory, Jr.
Carl L. Holloway, Jr.
Clifford O. Koon, Jr.
Franchelle Cole Millender
Albert L. Moses
Eugene F. Rogers
C. Joseph Roof
Henry F. Sherrill
John R. Tally
Robert J. Thomas
William H. Townsend
Joe W. Underwood
Samuel C. Waters
Robert P. Wood

Dean B. Bell
Cheryl H. Fisher
Kelly Jean Golden
Daniel B. Lott, Jr.
Stacey M. Lynch
Edward D. Sullivan
Kendall R. Walker
W. Alex Weatherly, Jr.
D. Randolph Whitt

OF COUNSEL

R. Larry Kight

LEGAL SUPPORT PERSONNEL

Carol A. Cummings

For full biographical listings, see the Martindale-Hubbell Law Directory

SINKLER & BOYD, P.A. (AV)

Suite 1200 The Palmetto Center, 1426 Main Street, P.O. Box 11889, 29211-1889
Telephone: 803-779-3080
FAX: 803-765-1243
Charleston, South Carolina Office: 160 East Bay Street, P.O. Box 340.
Telephone: 803-722-3366.
FAX: 803-722-2266.
Greenville, South Carolina Office: 15 South Main Street, Suite 500, Wachovia Building, P.O. Box 275.
Telephone: 803-467-1100.
FAX: 803-467-1521.

(See Next Column)

John C. Bruton (1907-1969)
W. C. Boyd (1904-1975)
Huger Sinkler (1908-1987)
Charles W. Knowlton (1923-1990)
Kirkman Finlay, Jr. (1936-1993)
Charles H. Gibbs (1915-1993)
H. Simmons Tate, Jr.
William C. Boyd
Francis P. Mood
J. Donald Dial, Jr.
Bachman S. Smith III (Resident, Charleston Office)
Manton M. Grier
George S. King, Jr.
Thomas R. Gottshall
Hamilton Osborne, Jr.
Stephen E. Darling (Resident, Charleston Office)
John P. Linton (Resident, Charleston Office)
Margaret Christian Pope
Harold E. Trask (Resident, Charleston Office)
Charlton deSaussure, Jr. (Resident, Charleston Office)
Marvin D. Infinger (Resident, Charleston Office)
Palmer Freeman, Jr.
Daryl L. Williams
John C. Bruton, Jr.
F. Mitchell Johnson, Jr. (Resident, Charleston Office)
Michael D. Jones (Resident, Charleston Office)
Elizabeth A. Carpentier
Benton D. Williamson
Sue C. Erwin
John B. McArthur
David M. Swanson (Resident, Charleston Office)
Robert S. Galloway, III (Resident, Greenville Office)
Clarke W. DuBose
Terri Morrill Lynch (Resident, Charleston Office)
Randolph B. Epting
Steve A. Matthews
Robert Y. Knowlton
Suzanne Hulst Clawson
William H. Short, Jr.
Theodore B. DuBose
Thomas C. Hildebrand, Jr. (Resident, Charleston Office)
John M. G. McLeod
Robert W. Buffington
S. Marshall Huey, Jr. (Resident, Charleston Office)
Frank W. Cureton
Bert Glenn Utsey III (Resident, Charleston Office)
Charles H. Gibbs, Jr. (Resident, Charleston Office)
Stanley H. McGuffin
John K. Van Duys
John H. Tiller (Resident, Charleston Office)
Roy A. Howell III (Resident, Charleston Office)
Virginia L. Vroegop

Edward K. Pritchard, III (Resident, Charleston Office)
David W. Whittington (Resident, Charleston Office)
Robert Wilson, III (Resident, Charleston Office)
Mark E. Rostick (Resident, Charleston Office)
Henry J. White
Joseph Hubert Wood, III (Resident, Charleston Office)
Tara Elizabeth Nauful
John F. Emerson
Deborah Paris Morgan
Perrin Q. Dargan, III (Resident, Charleston Office)
Joseph D. Thompson, III (Resident, Charleston Office)

OF COUNSEL

Albert Simons, Jr. (Resident, Charleston Office)
Martin C. McWilliams, Jr.
Katherine W. Hill

Attorneys for: The South Carolina National Bank; First Union National Bank; Westvaco; American Cyanamid Co.; Dean Witter Reynolds; Waste Management of North America, Inc.; Sonoco Products; Lawyers Title Insurance Corporation; Heater Utilities, Inc.

For full biographical listings, see the Martindale-Hubbell Law Directory

TOMPKINS AND MCMASTER (AV)

Palmetto Building, Fourth Floor, 1400 Main Street, P.O. Box 7337, 29202
Telephone: 803-799-4499
Telefax: 803-252-2240

MEMBERS OF FIRM

Frank G. Tompkins (1874-1956)
Frank G. Tompkins, Jr. (1908-1973)
Elizabeth Eldridge (1895-1976)
John Gregg McMaster
Henry Dargan McMaster
Frank Barnwell McMaster
Joseph Dargan McMaster

OF COUNSEL

George Hunter McMaster

For full biographical listings, see the Martindale-Hubbell Law Directory

TURNER, PADGET, GRAHAM & LANEY, P.A. (AV)

Seventeenth Floor, 1901 Main Street, P.O. Box 1473, 29202
Telephone: 803-254-2200
Telecopy: 803-799-3957
Florence, South Carolina Office: Fourth Floor, 1831 West Evans Street, P.O. Box 5478, 29501.
Telephone: 803-662-9008.
Telecopy: 803-667-0828.

Nathaniel A. Turner (1897-1959)
Edward W. Laney, III (1930-1980)
Harrell M. Graham (Retired)
George E. Lewis
Ronald E. Boston
Edwin P. Martin
Carl B. Epps, III
W. Duvall Spruill
Charles E. Hill
Thomas C. Salane
Elaine H. Fowler
Danny C. Crowe
R. Wayne Byrd (Resident, Florence, SC, Office)
W. Hugh McAngus
John S. Wilkerson, III (Resident, Florence, SC, Office)
Steven W. Ouzts
Michael S. Church
David G. Fawcett
Timothy D. St. Clair

(See Next Column)

TURNER, PADGET, GRAHAM & LANEY P.A.—*Continued*

Laura Callaway Hart
Lanneau William Lambert, Jr.
John E. Cuttino
Arthur E. Justice, Jr. (Resident, Florence, SC, Office)
Edward W. Laney, IV
Elbert S. Dorn
J. Russell Goudelock, II

OF COUNSEL

Henry Fletcher Padget, Jr.
Hugh M. Claytor (Resident, Florence, SC, Office)
James R. Courie

Franklin G. Shuler, Jr.
R. Todd Sherpy
J. Kenneth Carter, Jr.
Michael E. Chase
O. Carlisle Edwards, Jr.
Richard L. Hinson (Resident, Florence, SC, Office)
Jeffrey L. Payne (Resident, Florence, SC, Office)
Wilson S. Sheldon (Resident, Florence, SC, Office)
Walter H. Barefoot (Resident, Florence, SC, Office)
Elizabeth H. Philpot
Jessica C. Moe
Michael S. Hopewell (Resident, Florence, SC, Office)
Charles F. Turner, Jr. (Resident, Florence, SC, Office)
Teresa Arnold Clemenz
Curtis L. Ott
Michael C. Abbott (Resident, Florence, SC, Office)
Brian W. Bennett
David S. Cobb
Steven E. Williford
Scott B. Garrett
Tim F. Williams

Representative Clients: Independent Life & Accident Insurance Co.; Ford Motor Co.; Insurance Company of North America; Navistar International Corp.; Winn-Dixie Stores, Inc.; Allstate Insurance Co.; Continental Insurance Co.; Atlantic Soft Drink Co.; National Council on Compensation Insurance.

For full biographical listings, see the Martindale-Hubbell Law Directory

*CONWAY,** Horry Co.

McCUTCHEON, McCUTCHEON & BAXTER, P.A. (AV)

McCutcheon Building, 208 Elm Street, P.O. Box 1003, 29526
Telephone: 803-248-7225
Telecopier: 803-248-3568

John Betts McCutcheon
John Betts McCutcheon, Jr.
Mary Ruth M. Baxter

Clifford L. Welsh
M. Robin Morris
Arrigo P. Carotti

Representative Clients: The Travelers Insurance Group; State of South Carolina, Division of General Services, Insurance Reserve Fund; South Carolina Medical Malpractice Joint Underwriters Association; Virginia Professional Underwriters, Inc.; Companion Property and Casualty Company; Blue Cross and Blue Shield of South Carolina, Inc.; National Indemnity Company; American Continental Insurance Company.

For full biographical listings, see the Martindale-Hubbell Law Directory

THOMPSON, HENRY, GWIN, BRITTAIN & STEVENS, P.A. (AV)

1318 Third Avenue, P.O. Box 1533, 29526
Telephone: 803-248-5741
Fax: 803-248-5112
Myrtle Beach, South Carolina Office: 1601 North Oak Street, Suite 402. P.O. Box 1290.
Telephone: 803-448-7077.
Fax: 803-448-6923.

John C. Thompson
John P. Henry
Linda Weeks Gwin
Emma Ruth Brittain
Clay D. Brittain, III (Resident, Myrtle Beach Office)
Lynn Gatlin Stevens
G. Michael Smith
George E. McDowell, Jr.

Representative Clients: NationsBank; Burroughs & Chapin Company, Inc.; Canal Industries, Inc.; State Farm Mutual Automobile Insurance Company; State Farm Fire and Casualty Insurance Company; Horry County; Nationwide Insurance Company; United Carolina Bank; First Union National Bank.
Reference: NationsBank.

For full biographical listings, see the Martindale-Hubbell Law Directory

*DARLINGTON,** Darlington Co.

PAULLING & JAMES (AV)

112 Cashua Street, 29532
Telephone: 803-393-3881
Fax: 803-393-6089

MEMBERS OF FIRM

Treutlen Dudley Paulling (1896-1973)
Albert L. James, Jr.
Albert L. James, III
John Jay James, II

Counsel for: Carolina Power & Light Co.; Diamond Hill Plywood Co.; Darlington Veneer Co.; Wilson Clinic & Hospital, Inc.; R.E. Goodson Construction Co.

(See Next Column)

Local Counsel for: Southern Bell Telephone & Telegraph Co.; Employers Mutual Wausau; State Farm Insurance Co.; Nationwide Mutual Insurance Co.; Allstate Insurance Co.; NationsBank (Darlington); First Palmetto Savings Bank (Darlington).

For full biographical listings, see the Martindale-Hubbell Law Directory

*DILLON,** Dillon Co. — (Refer to Bennettsville)

EASLEY, Pickens Co. — (Refer to Greenville)

*EDGEFIELD,** Edgefield Co. — (Refer to Greenwood)

*FLORENCE,** Florence Co.

WRIGHT, POWERS AND McINTOSH (AV)

234 West Cheves Street, P.O. Box 1831, 29503
Telephone: 803-662-4328; 662-4329
Fax: 803-661-5183

MEMBERS OF FIRM

Jack J. Wright (1904-1991)
C. Dexter Powers (1921-1989)
D. Laurence McIntosh
Robert E. Lee

Attorneys for: Allstate; American States Insurance; Fireman's Fund American Co.; First Union National Bank of S.C.; Amerisure Cos.; Florence School District No. 1; McLeod Regional Medical Center; South Carolina Medical Malpractice Joint Underwriting Assoc.; Stone Container Corp.; S.C. Insurance Reserve Fund.

For full biographical listings, see the Martindale-Hubbell Law Directory

*GAFFNEY,** Cherokee Co.

WINTER & RHODEN (AV)

221 East Floyd Baker Boulevard, P.O. Box 1937, 29342
Telephone: 803-489-8128; 487-2289
Fax: 803-489-8806

William E. Winter, Jr.
William G. Rhoden

Representative Clients: NationsBank of South Carolina.
Approved Attorneys for: Chicago Title Insurance Co.; Lawyers Title Insurance Corp.; Chicago Title Insurance Co.

For full biographical listings, see the Martindale-Hubbell Law Directory

*GEORGETOWN,** Georgetown Co.

HINDS, COWAN, STRANGE, GEER & LUMPKIN (AV)

604 Front Street, P.O. Drawer 1410, 29442-1410
Telephone: 803-527-2441
Fax: 803-527-0065

MEMBERS OF FIRM

Douglas L. Hinds
William S. Cowan
Hal M. Strange
George R. Geer, Jr.
Peyre T. Lumpkin

Representative Client: General Fire and Casualty Insurance Co.
Approved Attorneys for: Lawyers Title Insurance Corp.
References: NationsBank; Anchor Bank.

For full biographical listings, see the Martindale-Hubbell Law Directory

*GREENVILLE,** Greenville Co.

FOSTER & SULLIVAN (AV)

117 Manly Street, P.O. Box 2146, 29602
Telephone: 803-232-5662
Fax: 803-370-1436

Richard J. Foster
Mark D. Sullivan, III
Sam L. Stephenson

For full biographical listings, see the Martindale-Hubbell Law Directory

HAYNSWORTH, MARION, McKAY & GUÉRARD, L.L.P. (AV)

Two Insignia Financial Plaza, 75 Beattie Place, P.O. Box 2048, 29602
Telephone: 803-240-3200
Telecopier: 803-240-3300
Columbia, South Carolina Office: Suite 2400 A T & T Building, 1201 Main Street, P.O. Drawer 7157, 29202
Telephone: 803-765-1818.
Telecopier: 803-765-2399.
Charleston, South Carolina Office: #2 Prioleau Street, P.O. Box 1119, 29402.
Telephone: 803-722-7606.
Telecopier: 803-723-5263.

OF COUNSEL

William Francis Marion
Andrew B. Marion
Theodore B. Guérard
Fred D. Cox, Jr.
Frances DeLoache Ellison
Julius W. McKay

SENIOR SPECIAL COUNSEL

Michael R. Daniel
Russell B. Shetterly

SPECIAL COUNSEL

Nancy Lark Schulze
Julian W. Walker, Jr.

(See Next Column)

HAYNSWORTH, MARION, MCKAY & GUÉRARD L.L.P., *Greenville—Continued*

MEMBERS OF FIRM

Henry J. Haynsworth (1859-1941)
Clement Furman Haynsworth (1886-1953)
James M. Perry (1894-1964)
Eugene Bryant (1902-1969)
Robert S. Galloway, Jr.
O. G. Calhoun, Jr.
Donald L. Ferguson
G. Dewey Oxner, Jr.
Jesse C. Belcher, Jr.
Maye R. Johnson, Jr.
W. E. Applegate, III
Charles E. McDonald, Jr.
William E. Shaughnessy
James B. Pressly, Jr.
H. Donald Sellers
Donald A. Harper
Andrew J. White, Jr.
Ellis M. Johnston, II
Joseph J. Blake, Jr.
William C. Cleveland
Thomas H. Coker, Jr.
J. Paul Trouche
William P. Simpson
W. Francis Marion, Jr.
John B. McLeod
David L. McMurray
Bryan Francis Hickey
Richard B. Kale, Jr.
Samuel W. Howell, IV
Gary W. Morris
Henry P. Wall
Anne S. Ellefson
Edwin Brown Parkinson, Jr.
H. Sam Mabry, III
David Hill Keller
Floyd Matlock Elliott
James J. Hinchey, Jr.
Knox H. White
Donald Bancroft Meyer
Moffatt Grier McDonald
Carol L. Clark
Steven Todd Moon

ASSOCIATES

Amy Miller Snyder
Stephen F. McKinney
Arthur Frazier McLean, III
Eric Keith Englebardt
Donna S. Kivett
James Derrick Quattlebaum
Melissa Miller Anderson
Norman Ward Lambert
James E. Lady
Brent O. Clinkscale
Sarah S. (Sally) McMillan
Karen Bruning Hipp
Harry L. Phillips, Jr.
Edward G. Kluiters
Paul M. Lynch
Julie Kaye Hackworth
Boyd B. Nicholson, Jr.
Jill R. Quattlebaum
Matthew P. Utecht
Coleman Miller Legerton
Harold J. Willson, Jr.
Jeffrey S. Jones
Cynthia Buck Brown
William David Conner
J. Walker Coleman, IV
Meredith Grier Buyck
Robert M. Cook, II
Karen A. Wood (Not admitted in SC)
Edward Wade Mullins, III
L. Elizabeth Patrick

Counsel for: Duke Power Co.; Liberty Mutual Insurance Co.; Equitable Life Assurance Society of the United States; St. Paul Insurance Group; Allstate Insurance Co.; Fluor-Daniel Corp.; Snyalloy Corporation; Greenville Hospital System.

For full biographical listings, see the Martindale-Hubbell Law Directory

HAYNSWORTH, PERRY, BRYANT, MARION & JOHNSTONE

(See Haynsworth, Marion, McKay & Guérard, L.L.P.)

LEATHERWOOD WALKER TODD & MANN, P.C. (AV)

100 East Coffee Street, P.O. Box 87, 29602
Telephone: 803-242-6440
FAX: 803-233-8461
Spartanburg, South Carolina Office: 1451 East Main Street, P.O. Box 3188.
Telephone: 803-582-4365.
Telefax: 803-583-8961.

D. B. Leatherwood (1896-1989)
James H. Watson
J. Brantley Phillips, Jr.
John E. Johnston
Harvey G. Sanders, Jr.
David A. Quattlebaum, III
O. Doyle Martin
Joseph E. Major
Duke K. McCall, Jr.
O. Jack Taylor, Jr.
Earle G. Prevost
J. Richard Kelly
H. Spencer King (Resident, Spartanburg Office)
A. Marvin Quattlebaum
Jack H. Tedards, Jr.
F. Marion Hughes
Michael J. Giese
Mark R. Holmes
William L. Dennis
Bradford Neal Martin
Natalma M. McKnew
Robert A. deHoll
Richard L. Few, Jr.
Steven E. Farrar
Nancy Hyder Robinson
Russell D. Ghent (Resident, Spartanburg Office)
Samuel Wright Outten
Eugene C. McCall, Jr.
Alexander Hray, Jr. (Resident, Spartanburg Office)
Harvey G. Sanders, III
Thomas W. Epting
James L. Rogers, Jr.

Tara H. Snyder
Sandra L. W. Miller
Frank C. Williams III
Susan A. Fretwell (Resident, Spartanburg Office)
Johanna B. Searle
Robert D. Moseley, Jr.
Randy E. Fisher
James T. Hewitt
Kurt M. Rozelsky
Karen B. Rollison
Thomas M. Sears, Jr.
Cathy H. Dunn (Resident, Spartanburg Office)

(See Next Column)

COUNSEL

Wesley M. Walker
J. D. Todd, Jr.
Fletcher C. Mann
Johnnie M. Walters

Counsel for: NationsBank; John D. Hollingsworth on Wheels, Inc.; Canal Insurance Co.; Platt Saco Lowell Corporation.
Representative Clients: Springs Industries, Inc.; American Federal Bank, F.S.B.; General Motors Acceptance Corp.; Ashland Oil, Inc.; Suitt Construction Co.

For full biographical listings, see the Martindale-Hubbell Law Directory

LOVE, THORNTON, ARNOLD & THOMASON, P.A. (AV)

410 East Washington Street, P.O. Box 10045, 29603
Telephone: 803-242-6360
Telefax: 803-271-7972

James L. Love (1892-1972)
Ben C. Thornton (1908-1968)
Belton O. Thomason, Jr. (1926-1993)
William M. Hagood, III
Donald R. McAlister
Theron G. Cochran
Mason A. Goldsmith
S. Gray Walsh
Carroll H. Roe, Jr.
Jennings L. Graves, Jr.
Jack D. Griffeth
William A. Coates
David L. Moore, Jr.
Ben Gibbs Leaphart
James H. Cassidy
V. Clark Price
John Robert Devlin, Jr.
Larry Lee Plumblee

Marion P. Sieffert
James A. Blair, III
Judith Ward Lineback

OF COUNSEL

W. Harold Arnold

Counsel for: Aetna Life & Casualty Insurance Co.; Kemper Insurance Group; Continental Insurance Companies Group; Government Employees Insurance Co.; Reliance Insurance Companies Group; American States Ins. Co.; First Citizens Bank & Trust Co.; American Federal Bank, F.S.B.; BP Oil, Inc.; Chrysler Corp.

For full biographical listings, see the Martindale-Hubbell Law Directory

NELSON MULLINS RILEY & SCARBOROUGH L.L.P. (AV)

A Registered Limited Liability Partnership including Professional Corporations
Twenty-Fourth Floor, BB&T Building, 301 North Main Street, P.O. Box 10084, 29603
Telephone: 803-250-2300
Telecopy: 803-232-2925
Atlanta, Georgia Office: 1201 Peachtree Street, N.E., P.O. Box 77707.
Telephone: 404-817-6000.
Telecopy: 404-817-6050.
Charleston, South Carolina Office: Suite 500, 151 Meeting Street, P.O. Box 1806.
Telephone: 803-853-5200.
Telecopy: 803-722-8700.
Columbia, South Carolina Office: Third Floor, Keenan Building, 1300 Lady Street, P.O. Box 11070.
Telephone: 803-799-2000.
Telecopy: 803-256-7500; 803-733-9499.
Florence, South Carolina Office: 600 W. Palmetto Street, Suite 200, P.O. Box 5955.
Telephone: 803-662-0019.
Telecopy: 803-662-0491.
Lexington, South Carolina Office: 334 Old Chapin Road, P.O. Box 729.
Telephone: 803-733-9494; 803-799-200.
Telecopy: 803-957-8226.
Myrtle Beach, South Carolina Office: 2411 N. Oak Street, Founders Centre, Suite 301, P.O. Box 3939.
Telephone: 803-448-3500.
Telecopy: 803-448-3437.

OF COUNSEL

Edward P. Riley, Jr.

MEMBERS OF FIRM

James C. Blakely, Jr. (P.A.)
Robert M. Erwin, Jr.
John M. Campbell, Jr.
Kenneth E. Young
George K. Lyall
Walter H. Hinton, II
Russell Z. Plowden
David E. Hodge
Erroll Anne Yarbrough Hodges

ASSOCIATES

A. Marvin Quattlebaum
Amy C. Hendrix
Anthony L. Harbin
Denise C. Yarborough
Frank T. Davis, III
Kymric Y. Mahnke
Dodd M. Davis
Rebecca Ann Dorman
Fredrick S. Pfeiffer
Christopher J. Weeks
J. Andrew Williams

Representative Clients: Bi-Lo, Inc.; BMW, AG; E. I. DuPont de Nemours & Co.; General Motors Corp.; NationsBank; W. R. Grace & Company, Cryovac Division; The National Bank of South Carolina; Owens-Illinois, Inc.; Southern Bell Telephone & Telegraph Co.; Union Camp Corp.

For full biographical listings, see the Martindale-Hubbell Law Directory

Greenville—Continued

Wyche, Burgess, Freeman & Parham, Professional Association (AV)

44 East Camperdown Way, P.O. Box 728, 29602-0728
Telephone: 803-242-8200
Telecopier: 803-235-8900

C. Thomas Wyche
David L. Freeman
James C. Parham, Jr.
James M. Shoemaker, Jr.
William W. Kehl
Charles W. Wofford
Larry D. Estridge
D. Allen Grumbine
Cary H. Hall, Jr.
Carl F. Muller
Henry L. Parr, Jr.
Bradford W. Wyche
Eric B. Amstutz
Marshall Winn
Wallace K. Lightsey
Lesley R. Moore
William D. Herlong
Jo Watson Hackl
William P. Crawford, Jr.
J. Theodore Gentry
Gregory J. English

STAFF ATTORNEY

Marion M. Goodyear

Counsel for: Multimedia, Inc.; Delta Woodside Industries, Inc.; Milliken & Company; Ryan's Family Steak Houses, Inc.; St. Francis Hospital; Span-America Medical Systems, Inc.; Carolina First Bank; KEMET Electronics Corp.; Builder Marts of America, Inc.; One Price Clothing, Inc.

For full biographical listings, see the Martindale-Hubbell Law Directory

*GREENWOOD,** Greenwood Co.

Burns, McDonald, Bradford, Patrick & Tinsley, L.L.P. (AV)

414 Main Street, P.O. Box 1547, 29648
Telephone: 803-229-2511
Fax: 803-229-5327

James E. McDonald
William B. Patrick, Jr.
William D. Tinsley, Jr.
Stephen D. Baggett
Kenneth W. Poston
William B. Watkins
Roy R. Hemphill

Peter J. Manning
W. Lee Roper, II
D. Welborn Adams
Steven M. Pruitt

OF COUNSEL

Howard Lamar Burns
J. William Bradford

Division Counsel: CSX Transportation, Inc. (Railroad).
Attorneys for: NationsBank; The Greenwood Mills; Geo. W. Park Seed Co.; Duke Power Co; State Farm Mutual Group; Allstate Insurance Co.; Liberty Mutual Insurance Co.; Nationwide Insurance Co.

For full biographical listings, see the Martindale-Hubbell Law Directory

*HAMPTON,** Hampton Co. — (Refer to Barnwell)

HARTSVILLE, Darlington Co.

Wilmeth Law Firm (AV)

119 West Home Avenue, P.O. Box 1139, 29551-1139
Telephone: 803-332-6551
FAX: 803-332-2182

MEMBERS OF FIRM

Philip Wilmeth
Harriet E. Wilmeth

General Counsel for: Hartsville Oil Mill; Coker College; SPC Cooperative Credit Union.
Representative Clients: Sonoco Products Co.; Trust Company of South Carolina; Mutual Savings & Loan Association.

For full biographical listings, see the Martindale-Hubbell Law Directory

HILTON HEAD ISLAND, Beaufort Co.

William M. Bowen, P.A. (AV)

Forty Pope Avenue, P.O. Drawer 6128, 29938
Telephone: 803-842-5000
Fax: 803-686-5990

William M. Bowen

Approved Attorneys for: Lawyers Title Insurance Corp.; Commonwealth Land Title Insurance Co.; Chicago Title Insurance Co.
References: Anchor Bank; NationsBank; South Carolina National Bank; Prudential Securities.

For full biographical listings, see the Martindale-Hubbell Law Directory

LAKE CITY, Florence Co. — (Refer to Florence)

*LANCASTER,** Lancaster Co.

Folks, Khoury & DeVenny (AV)

104 South Catawba Street, P.O. Box 1657, 29721-1657
Telephone: 803-286-6647
Real Estate Dept.: 803-286-4867
Telefax: 803-286-8528

MEMBERS OF FIRM

Robert K. Folks
Coreen B. Khoury
T. Alston DeVenny, Jr.

Representative Clients: Elliott White Springs Memorial Hospital, Inc.; Housing Authority of Lancaster; Kanawha Insurance Co.; First Citizens Bank and Trust Company; Morrison Textile Machinery Co.; Wachovia Bank of North Carolina, N.A.; Bowater Carolina Federal Credit Union.
Local Counsel for: Elliott White Springs Memorial Hospital, Inc.; Founders Federal Credit Union.

For full biographical listings, see the Martindale-Hubbell Law Directory

*LAURENS,** Laurens Co. — (Refer to Greenwood)

*LEXINGTON,** Lexington Co.

Nelson Mullins Riley & Scarborough L.L.P. (AV)

A Registered Limited Liability Partnership including Professional Corporations
334 Old Chapin Road, P.O. Box 729, 29072
Telephone: 803-733-9494; 799-2000
Telecopy: 803-957-8226
Atlanta, Georgia Office: 1201 Peachtree Street, N.E., P.O. Box 77707.
Telephone: 404-817-6000.
Telecopy: 404-817-6050.
Charleston, South Carolina Office: Suite 500, 151 Meeting Street, P.O. Box 1806.
Telephone: 803-853-5200.
Telecopy: 803-722-8700.
Columbia, South Carolina Office: Third Floor, Keenan Building. 1300 Lady Street. P.O. Box 11070.
Telephone: 803-799-2000.
Telecopy: 803-256-7500; 733-9499.
Florence, South Carolina Office: 600 W. Palmetto Street, Suite 200, P.O. Box 5955.
Telephone: 803-662-0019.
Telecopy: 803-662-0491.
Greenville, South Carolina Office: Twenty-Fourth Floor, BB&T Building, 301 North Main Street, P.O. Box 10084.
Telephone: 803-250-2300.
Telecopy: 803-232-2925.
Myrtle Beach, South Carolina Office: 2411 N. Oak Street, Founders Centre, Suite 301. P.O. Box 3939.
Telephone: 803-448-3500.
Telecopy: 803-448-3437.

OF COUNSEL

Robert P. Wilkins
Robert P. Wilkins, Jr.

For full biographical listings, see the Martindale-Hubbell Law Directory

*MANNING,** Clarendon Co. — (Refer to Sumter)

*MARION,** Marion Co. — (Refer to Florence)

*MCCORMICK,** McCormick Co. — (Refer to Greenwood)

MYRTLE BEACH, Horry Co.

Bellamy, Rutenberg, Copeland, Epps, Gravely & Bowers, P.A. (AV)

1000 29th Avenue North, P.O. Box 357, 29578
Telephone: 803-448-2400
Telecopier: 803-448-3022

Howell V. Bellamy, Jr.
John K. Rutenberg
John E. Copeland
Claude M. Epps, Jr.
David R. Gravely
Edward B. Bowers, Jr.
Bradley D. King
Henrietta U. Golding
R. Michael Munden
M. Edwin Hinds, Jr.
Jill F. Griffith
Kathryn M. Cook
David B. Miller
Deirdre M. Whisenant-Edmonds
Daniel J. MacDonald
C. Winfield Johnson, III
Janet L. Carter

Representative Clients: Dargan Construction Co.; Coastal Federal Savings Bank; Sands Investments; Wachovia Bank of South Carolina; AVX Corp.; NationsBank of South Carolina, N.A.; Parthenon Insurance Co.; Burroughs & Chapin Co.; International Paper Co.; Hospital Corporation of America.

For full biographical listings, see the Martindale-Hubbell Law Directory

Myrtle Beach—Continued

NELSON MULLINS RILEY & SCARBOROUGH L.L.P. (AV)

A Registered Limited Liability Partnership including Professional Corporations
Founders Centre, 2411 N. Oak Street, Suite 301, P.O. Box 3939, 29578-3939
Telephone: 803-448-3500
Telecopy: 803-448-3437
Atlanta, Georgia Office: 400 Colony Square, 1201 Peachtree Street, N.E., P.O. Box 77707.
Telephone: 404-817-6000.
Telecopy: 404-817-6050.
Charleston, South Carolina Office: 151 Meeting Street, Suite 400, P.O. Box 1806.
Telephone: 803-853-5200.
Telecopy: 803-722-8700.
Columbia, South Carolina Office: Third Floor, Keenan Building. 1330 Lady Street. P.O. Box 11070.
Telephone: 803-799-2000.
Telecopy: 803-256-7500; 733-9499.
Florence, South Carolina Office: 600 W. Palmetto Street, Suite 200, P.O. Box 5955.
Telephone: 803-662-0019.
Telecopy: 803-662-0491.
Greenville, South Carolina Office: Twenty-Fourth Floor, BB&T Building, 301 North Main Street.
Telephone: 803-250-2300.
Telecopy: 803-232-2925.
Lexington, South Carolina Office: 334 Old Chapin Road.
Telephone: 803-733-9494; 799-2000.
Telecopy: 803-957-8226

SPECIAL COUNSEL

David W. Harwell

MEMBERS OF FIRM

John C. Stewart, Jr.
Trefor Thomas
Susan Pardue MacDonald
Thomas F. Moran

ASSOCIATES

Patrick F. O'Dea
Phillip Luke Hughes
Jeanne N. Guest
Robert C. Calamari
James F. Mc Crackin
Dominic A. Starr

Representative Clients: Bi-Lo, Inc.; E. I. DuPont de Nemours & Co.; General Motors Corp.; W. R. Grace & Company, Cryovac Division; NationsBank; South Carolina Federal Savings Bank; Owens-Illinois, Inc.; Southern Bell Telephone & Telegraph Co.; Union Camp Corp.

For full biographical listings, see the Martindale-Hubbell Law Directory

*NEWBERRY,** Newberry Co.

POPE AND HUDGENS, P.A. (AV)

(Successor to Pope and Schumpert)
1508 College Street, P.O. Box 190, 29108
Telephone: 803-276-2532
FAX: 803-276-8684

Thomas H. Pope
Joseph W. Hudgens
Thomas H. Pope, III
Gary T. Pope

Samuel H. Jeffcoat

OF COUNSEL

Robert D. Schumpert

South Carolina Counsel: Champion International Corp.
Counsel for: Clinton Mills; The Citizens and Southern National Bank; NCNB; M.S. Bailey & Son, Bankers; Southern Railway Co.; Liberty Mutual Insurance Co.; Newberry County; Newberry Electric Cooperative, Inc.; Newberry County Water and Sewer Authority.

For full biographical listings, see the Martindale-Hubbell Law Directory

*ORANGEBURG,** Orangeburg Co.

HORGER, BARNWELL & REID (AV)

459 Amelia Street, P.O. Drawer 329, 29116-0329
Telephone: 803-531-3000
Facsimile: 803-531-3030

MEMBERS OF FIRM

Charlton B. Horger
Charles Brison Barnwell, Jr.
Robert R. Horger
Samuel F. Reid, Jr.
Robert F. McCurry, Jr.

General Counsel for: First National Bank, Orangeburg, S.C.; Farmers and Merchants Bank of S.C.; First National Bank of S.C., Holly Hill, S.C.; Orangeburg County; The Regional Medical Center of Orangeburg & Calhoun Counties.
Local Counsel for: South Carolina Electric & Gas Co.
Representative Clients: Maryland Casualty Co.; Nationwide Insurance Co.; Federated Mutual Insurance Co.

For full biographical listings, see the Martindale-Hubbell Law Directory

HORGER, HORGER & LANIER (AV)

160 Centre Street, N.E., P.O. Box 518, 29116-0518
Telephone: 803-531-1700
Fax: 803-531-0160

MEMBERS OF FIRM

William A. Horger
Michael P. Horger
Lewis C. Lanier

ASSOCIATES

Paul W. Owen, Jr.

Reference: First Union National Bank of South Carolina.

For full biographical listings, see the Martindale-Hubbell Law Directory

*PICKENS,** Pickens Co. — (Refer to Greenville)

*RIDGELAND,** Jasper Co. — (Refer to Beaufort)

ROCK HILL, York Co.

KENNEDY COVINGTON LOBDELL & HICKMAN, L.L.P. (AV)

First Union Center, 113 E. Main Street, 29730
Telephone: 803-329-7600
Fax: 803-329-7677
Charlotte, North Carolina Office: NationsBank Corporate Center, Suite 4200, 100 North Tryon Street, 28202-4006.
Telephone: 704-331-7400.
Fax: 704-331-7598.

SPECIAL COUNSEL

Robert R. Carpenter

RESIDENT PARTNERS

James C. Hardin III
Stephen R. McCrae, Jr.
Herbert W. Hamilton

RESIDENT ASSOCIATES

W. Henry Sipe III
Beverly A. Carroll
Laura E. Cude
Victoria S. Aiken
Daniel J. Ballou

For full biographical listings, see the Martindale-Hubbell Law Directory

ROBINSON, BRADSHAW & HINSON, P.A. (AV)

The Guardian Building, One Law Place, Suite 600 Post Office Drawer 12070, 29731
Telephone: 803-325-2900
FAX: 803-325-2929
Charlotte, North Carolina Office: One Independence Center, 101 North Tryon Street, Suite 1900, 28246-1900.
Telephone: 704-377-2536.
Fax: 704-378-4000.
Telex: 802046.

David A. White
Carroll M. Pitts, Jr.
Benjamin A. Johnson
James C. Reno, Jr.
Sarah B. Boucher
Brian S. McCoy

For full biographical listings, see the Martindale-Hubbell Law Directory

SPENCER & SPENCER, PROFESSIONAL ASSOCIATION (AV)

Suite 101 NationsBank Building, 245 East Main Street, P.O. Box 790, 29731-6790
Telephone: 803-327-7191
Telecopier: 803-327-3868

C. E. Spencer (1849-1921)
C. W. F. Spencer (1876-1956)
C. W. F. Spencer, Jr. (1911-1985)
William C. Spencer
William L. Ferguson
Emil W. Wald
James W. Sheedy
Paul W. Dillingham
W. Mark White

Counsel for: NationsBank; City of Rock Hill; Hartford Accident and Indemnity Co.; Great American Insurance Co.; York and Lancaster County Natural Gas Authorities; Maryland Casualty Co.; Lancaster County Water and Sewer District.

For full biographical listings, see the Martindale-Hubbell Law Directory

*ST. MATTHEWS,** Calhoun Co. — (Refer to Orangeburg)

*SALUDA,** Saluda Co. — (Refer to Newberry)

SENECA, Oconee Co. — (Refer to Anderson)

*SPARTANBURG,** Spartanburg Co.

HOLCOMBE, BOMAR, COTHRAN AND GUNN, P.A. (AV)

Flagstar Plaza, 203 East Main Street, P.O. Drawer 1897, 29304
Telephone: 803-585-4273
Telecopier: 803-585-3844

(See Next Column)

HOLCOMBE, BOMAR, COTHRAN AND GUNN P.A.—*Continued*

Neville Holcombe (1902-1983)
Horace L. Bomar (1912-1994)
William U. Gunn
James C. Cothran, Jr.
H. Leland Bomar
Reginald L. Foster
Paul B. Zion
Koger McIntosh Bradford
Perry D. Boulier

William B. Darwin, Jr.
Anthony H. Randall
S. Sterling Laney, III

Representative Clients: Flagstar Corporation; Denny's, Inc.; Wachovia Bank of South Carolina, N.A.; Community Cash Stores; Liberty Mutual Insurance Cos.; Kemper Insurance Group; Reliance Insurance Cos.; Mary Black Memorial Hospital, Inc.; Metromont Materials Corp.

For full biographical listings, see the Martindale-Hubbell Law Directory

LEATHERWOOD WALKER TODD & MANN, P.C. (AV)

1451 East Main Street, P.O. Box 3188, 29304-3188
Telephone: 803-582-4365
Telefax: 803-585-8961
Greenville, South Carolina Office: 100 East Coffee Street, P.O. Box 87.
Telephone: 803-242-6440.
FAX: 803-233-8461.

H. Spencer King
Russell D. Ghent
Alexander Hray, Jr.

Susan A. Fretwell
Cathy H. Dunn

For full biographical listings, see the Martindale-Hubbell Law Directory

LYLES, HAMMETT, DARR AND CLARK (AV)

240 Magnolia Street, 29306
Telephone: 803-585-4806
Telecopier: 803-585-4810
Mailing Address: P.O. Box 5726, 29304-5726,

William C. Lyles (Retired)
Frank A. Lyles
Herbert V. Hammett, Jr.
Terry F. Clark
Kenneth E. Darr, Jr.

Representative Clients: Triangle Ice Company of South Carolina, Inc. (ice manufacture and regional distributors of ice products and fuels); Hammond-Brown-Jennings Company (retail furniture stores); Converse College; Woodruff Federal Savings and Loan Assn.; L.P. Pitts Development Corp.; The Nutt Corp.; Cannon Roofing Co., Inc.; Cannon Supply, Inc.; Spartanburg County School Districts No. 4 and 7.

For full biographical listings, see the Martindale-Hubbell Law Directory

PERRIN, PERRIN, MANN & PATTERSON (AV)

200 Library Street, P.O. Box 1655, 29304
Telephone: 803-582-5461
Fax: 803-583-5235

L. W. Perrin (1918-1980)

OF COUNSEL

Edward P. Perrin

MEMBERS OF FIRM

Franklin M. Mann
Dwight F. Patterson, Jr.
Lawrence E. Flynn, Jr.
William O. Pressley, Jr.

General Counsel for: Carolina Cash Co.; Spartanburg Sanitary Sewer District.

For full biographical listings, see the Martindale-Hubbell Law Directory

THE WARD LAW FIRM, P.A. (AV)

233 South Pine Street, P.O. Box 5663, 29304
Telephone: 803-573-8500
Telefax: 803-585-3090

James G. Long, Jr.
James W. Hudgens
Gene Adams
Michael B. T. Wilkes
C. Roland Jones, Jr.
Stephen S. Wilson
Ladson F. Howell, Jr.
Rufus M. Ward (1908-1988)
L. Paul Barnes (1931-1986)

Representative Clients: Allstate Insurance Co.; American States Insurance Co.; CNA Insurance Co.; Cincinnati Insurance Co.; Crawford & Co.; General Accident Group; Harleysville Mutual Insurance Co.; Pennsylvania National Mutual Casualty Insurance Co.; St. Paul Insurance Cos.; State Farm Mutual Automobile Insurance Co.

For full biographical listings, see the Martindale-Hubbell Law Directory

*SUMTER,** Sumter Co.

LEE, WILSON & ERTER (AV)

126 North Main Street, P.O. Drawer 580, 29150
Telephone: 803-778-2471
Telecopier: 803-778-1643

(See Next Column)

MEMBERS OF FIRM

John Dozier Lee, Jr.
Jack W. Erter, Jr.
Harry C. Wilson, Jr.
David Cornwell Holler

OF COUNSEL

C. Douglas Lipscombe, Jr.

Representative Clients: South Carolina National Bank; Carolina Power and Light Co.; Peoples Natural Gas Company of South Carolina; First Federal Savings & Loan Assn.; Allstate Insurance Co.; American Surety Co.; Prudential Insurance Company of America; General Telephone; Korn Industries, Inc.; V-B William Furniture Company, Inc.

For full biographical listings, see the Martindale-Hubbell Law Directory

SURFSIDE BEACH, Horry Co.

THE FLOYD LAW FIRM PC (AV)

823 Surfside Drive, P.O. Drawer 14607, 29587-4607
Telephone: 803-238-5141
Fax: 803-238-9060
Lake City, South Carolina Office: 207 John Street, P.O. Box 1405.
Telephone: 803-394-2833.
Fax: 803-394-7207.

Dalton B. Floyd, Jr.

G. Derek Blanton
Frank J. Bryan

Representative Clients: THE PGA of America; Burroughs and Chapin Company; Conway National Bank; New York Carpet World; The Anchor Bank; NationsBank; County of Horry; Carolinas Section of the PGA; Halcyon, Inc.; Indigo Creek Resort Development Co. Inc.; Glenns Bay, Inc.; Wachesaw Development Co., Inc.

For full biographical listings, see the Martindale-Hubbell Law Directory

*UNION,** Union Co. — (Refer to Gaffney)

*WALHALLA,** Oconee Co.

LARRY C. BRANDT, P.A. (AV)

205 West Main Street, P.O. Drawer 738, 29691
Telephone: 803-638-5406
803-638-7873

Larry C. Brandt

D. Bradley Jordan
J. Bruce Schumpert

LEGAL SUPPORT PERSONNEL

Debra C. Miller

For full biographical listings, see the Martindale-Hubbell Law Directory

*WALTERBORO,** Colleton Co.

BOGOSLOW & JONES, P.A. (AV)

100 Commerce Drive, P.O. Box 1515, 29488
Telephone: 803-549-2502
Telefax: 803-549-2112

Isadore Bogoslow (1914-1993)
Marvin C. Jones

Robert J. Bonds
Christy S. Stephens
Jennifer E. Duty

Representative Clients: State Farm Insurance Companies; The Press & Standard (Newspaper).

For full biographical listings, see the Martindale-Hubbell Law Directory

*WINNSBORO,** Fairfield Co. — (Refer to Newberry)

*YORK,** York Co.

SPRATT, MCKEOWN & BRADFORD (AV)

26 West Liberty Street, P.O. Box 299, 29745
Telephone: 803-684-3559, 684-4851
Telecopier: 803-684-6682

MEMBERS OF FIRM

John M. Spratt (1907-1973)
Melvin B. McKeown, Jr.
Charles S. Bradford

Representative Clients: Governmental: County Attorneys, York County; Fort Mill School District No. 4; York School District No. 1; South Carolina Highway Dept. (Associate Counsel). Financial: Bank of York; Ford Motor Credit Co. Industrial: Springs Mills, Inc.; Cannon-Fieldcrest Mills.

For full biographical listings, see the Martindale-Hubbell Law Directory

SOUTH DAKOTA

*ARMOUR,** Douglas Co. — (Refer to Yankton)

*BELLE FOURCHE,** Butte Co.

BENNETT, MAIN & FREDERICKSON, A PROFESSIONAL CORPORATION (AV)

618 State Street, 57717-1489
Telephone: 605-892-2011
Fax: 605-892-4084

Max Main John R. Frederickson

Kevin S. Bailey

OF COUNSEL

Donn Bennett

Representative Clients: Atlantic Richfield Co.; Chevron USA, Inc.; Exxon U.S.A. Co.; Inland Oil & Gas Co.; Royal Bank of Canada; Bank of Montreal; Security Pacific National Bank; Timberline Oil & Gas Co.; Pioneer Bank and Trust; Norwest Bank South Dakota.

For full biographical listings, see the Martindale-Hubbell Law Directory

*BURKE,** Gregory Co. — (Refer to Winner)

*CANTON,** Lincoln Co. — (Refer to Parker)

*CHAMBERLAIN,** Brule Co. — (Refer to Huron)

*CLARK,** Clark Co. — (Refer to Watertown)

*CLEAR LAKE,** Deuel Co. — (Refer to Watertown)

*CUSTER,** Custer Co. — (Refer to Hot Springs)

*DEADWOOD,** Lawrence Co.

CHRISTENSEN LAW OFFICES (AV)

68 Sherman, Suite 311, P.O. Box 583, 57732
Telephone: 605-578-1953
FAX: 605-578-3078
Sturgis, South Dakota Office: 928 Lazelle, P.O. Box 785.
Telephone: 605-347-0052.
Fax: 605-347-0053.

Steven M. Christensen

For full biographical listings, see the Martindale-Hubbell Law Directory

DELL RAPIDS, Minnehaha Co. — (Refer to Sioux Falls)

*DE SMET,** Kingsbury Co. — (Refer to Huron)

*FAULKTON,** Faulk Co. — (Refer to Aberdeen)

*FLANDREAU,** Moody Co. — (Refer to Sioux Falls)

*FORT PIERRE,** Stanley Co. — (Refer to Pierre)

*GETTYSBURG,** Potter Co. — (Refer to Pierre)

GREGORY, Gregory Co. — (Refer to Winner)

*HAYTI,** Hamlin Co. — (Refer to Watertown)

*HIGHMORE,** Hyde Co. — (Refer to Huron)

*HOT SPRINGS,** Fall River Co.

FARRELL, FARRELL & GINSBACH (AV)

441 North River Street, 57747
Telephone: 605-745-5161
FAX: 605-745-3154

MEMBERS OF FIRM

Martin P. Farrell Jane M. Farrell
Patrick M. Ginsbach

Representative Clients: Blatchford's Inc.; Hot Springs Independent School District; Red Cloud Indian School.
References: Norwest Bank South Dakota, N.A.; Community First State Bank.

For full biographical listings, see the Martindale-Hubbell Law Directory

*HOWARD,** Miner Co. — (Refer to Sioux Falls)

*HURON,** Beadle Co.

CHURCHILL, MANOLIS, FREEMAN, KLUDT & KAUFMAN (AV)

201 Farmers & Merchants Bank Building, P.O. Box 176, 57350
Telephone: 605-352-8624
Fax: 605-352-2205

(See Next Column)

MEMBERS OF FIRM

Irwin A. Churchill (1882-1961) George N. Manolis
John P. Sauer (1901-1965) Rodney Freeman, Jr.
William S. Churchill (1911-1994) Douglas E. Kludt
Gerald L. Kaufman, Jr.

Kent A. Shelton

Representative Clients: Northwestern Public Service Co.; Mid-Continent Broadcasting Co.; American Mutual Liability Insurance Co.; National of Hartford Group; U.S. Fidelity & Guaranty Co.; Huron Publishing Co.; Travelers Insurance Co.; Dakota State Bank, Millbank, South Dakota; First Federal Savings & Loan Assn.; Farmers & Merchants Bank of Huron.

For full biographical listings, see the Martindale-Hubbell Law Directory

*IPSWICH,** Edmunds Co. — (Refer to Aberdeen)

*KENNEBEC,** Lyman Co. — (Refer to Pierre)

*LAKE ANDES,** Charles Mix Co. — (Refer to Yankton)

LEAD, Lawrence Co.

FULLER & TELLINGHUISEN (AV)

203 West Main Street, P.O. Box 898, 57754
Telephone: 605-584-2440
Fax: 605-584-1979
Spearfish, South Dakota Office: 132 East Illinois, P.O. Box 1087, 57783.
Telephone: 605-642-8080.
Fax: 605-642-1756.

MEMBERS OF FIRM

A. P. Fuller Roger A. Tellinghuisen

Bradley P. Gordon Jerome A. Eckrich

Representative Clients: Homestake Mining Co.; Hotel Franklin & Gaming; Black Hills Novelty/Automatic Vending, Inc.; Northern Hills General Hospital; Lantis Enterprises, Inc.; Norwest Bank South Dakota N.A.; Lead-Deadwood Independent School District # 40-1.

For full biographical listings, see the Martindale-Hubbell Law Directory

*LEOLA,** McPherson Co. — (Refer to Aberdeen)

*MADISON,** Lake Co.

LAMMERS, LAMMERS, KLEIBACKER & PARENT (AV)

108 North Egan, P.O. Box 45, 57042-0045
Telephone: 605-256-6677
FAX: 605-256-6679

MEMBERS OF FIRM

J. H. Lammers (1893-1983) Wilson M. Kleibacker, Jr.
Jerome B. Lammers Philip R Parent

ASSOCIATES

Ryker Lammers

Local Attorneys for: State Farm Mutual Automobile Insurance Co.; Northwestern Public Service Co., Huron, South Dakota.
Attorneys for: F & M Co-op Oil Co.; Madison Farmers Elevator Co.; Chester, Brant Lake, Lake Madison and Lake Poinsett Sanitary Districts; Madison Housing and Redevelopment Commission; Prostrollo Motor Co.; Norwest Bank; Green Thumb Commodities; Big Sioux and Minnehaha Rural Water Systems.
Reference: Norwest Bank.

*MILBANK,** Grant Co. — (Refer to Watertown)

*MILLER,** Hand Co.

HEIDEPRIEM, WIDMAYER, ZELL & JONES (AV)

103 West Third Street, P.O. Box 129, 57362
Telephone: 605-853-2456
Fax: 605-853-2457
Highmore, South Dakota Office: 209 Iowa Street, South.
Telephone: 605-852-2962.

Herbert A. Heidepriem (1922-1993) Ruben R. Widmayer
Bradley G. Zell
Brian W. Jones

ASSOCIATES

Samuel M. Goodhope

LEGAL SUPPORT PERSONNEL

Dennis W. Hochkammer

Representative Clients: Hand County State Bank, Miller, South Dakota; DeSmet Farm Mutual Ins. Co., DeSmet, South Dakota; Ree Electric Cooperative, Miller, South Dakota; Sheldon F. Reese Foundation, Sioux Falls, South Dakota.

For full biographical listings, see the Martindale-Hubbell Law Directory

*PARKER,** Turner Co.

ZIMMER AND DUNCAN (AV)

Law Building, 57053
Telephone: 605-297-4446
Fax: 605-297-4488

MEMBERS OF FIRM

John H. Zimmer
Dennis L. Duncan

ASSOCIATES

Jeffrey A. Cole

General Counsel for: South Dakota State Medical Holding Company (DakotaCare HMO); South Dakota State Board of Veterinary Medical Examiners; TM Rural Water District; Stern Oil Company, Inc.

For full biographical listings, see the Martindale-Hubbell Law Directory

*PHILIP,** Haakon Co. — (Refer to Rapid City)

*PIERRE,** Hughes Co.

MAY, ADAM, GERDES & THOMPSON (AV)

503 South Pierre Street, P.O. Box 160, 57501-0160
Telephone: 605-224-8803
Telecopier: 605-224-6289

MEMBERS OF FIRM

Glenn W. Martens (1881-1963)
Karl Goldsmith (1885-1966)
Warren W. May
Thomas C. Adam
David A. Gerdes
Charles M. Thompson
Robert B. Anderson
Brent A. Wilbur
Timothy M. Engel
Michael F. Shaw

General Counsel for: South Dakota Bankers Assn.; BankWest; South Dakota Medical Assn.; Dakota State Bank.
Representative Clients: Travelers Insurance Co.; Employers of Wausau; American States Insurance Co.; Montana-Dakota Utilities; Firemans Fund.

For full biographical listings, see the Martindale-Hubbell Law Directory

RITER, MAYER, HOFER, WATTIER & BROWN (AV)

Professional & Executive Building, 319 South Coteau Street, P.O. Box 280, 57501
Telephone: 605-224-5825
FAX: 605-224-7102

Ernest W. Stephens (1900-1989)
Robert C. Riter (1912-1994)

MEMBERS OF FIRM

Eugene D. Mayer
Robert D. Hofer
Robert C. Riter, Jr.
Jerry L. Wattier
John L. Brown

General Counsel for: First National Bank, Pierre, South Dakota.
State Counsel for: South Dakota Music & Vending Assn; United Parcel Service.
Local Attorneys for: United Services Automobile Assn.; Hartford Accident and Indemnity Co.; Continental Casualty Co.; Home Insurance Co.; The State Farms Insurance Cos.; National Farmers Union Insurance Co; Auto-Owners Insurance Co.

For full biographical listings, see the Martindale-Hubbell Law Directory

SCHMIDT, SCHROYER, COLWILL & MORENO, P.C. (AV)

Suite 201 Pierre Professional Plaza, 124 South Euclid, P.O. Box 1174, 57501-1174
Telephone: 605-224-0461
Fax: 605-224-1607

Ronald G. Schmidt
Charles P. Schroyer
Gary F. Colwill
Mark A. Moreno
Cheryl Schrempp Dupris
Ethan W. Schmidt

For full biographical listings, see the Martindale-Hubbell Law Directory

*PLANKINTON,** Aurora Co. — (Refer to Huron)

*RAPID CITY,** Pennington Co.

BANGS, McCULLEN, BUTLER, FOYE & SIMMONS (AV)

818 St. Joseph Street, P.O. Box 2670, 57709
Telephone: 605-343-1040
Telecopier: 605-343-1503

MEMBERS OF FIRM

George A. Bangs
W. A. McCullen (1907-1987)
Joseph M. Butler
Thomas H. Foye
Thomas E. Simmons
Charles L. Riter
Allen G. Nelson
James P. Hurley
Michael M. Hickey
Mark F. Marshall
Terry L. Hofer
Patrick Duffy

(See Next Column)

ASSOCIATES

Rodney W. Schlauger
Daniel F. Duffy
Jeffrey G. Hurd
Veronica L. Bowen

Representative Clients: Norwest Bank South Dakota, N.A., Rapid City, S.D.; Pete Lien & Sons; The Travelers Insurance Co.; Rapid City Regional Hospital; Dakota Steel & Supply Co.; Great American Insurance Co.; Fireman's Fund Insurance; United States Automobile Association; Moyle Petroleum; Rapid City Area School District 51-4.

For full biographical listings, see the Martindale-Hubbell Law Directory

COSTELLO, PORTER, HILL, HEISTERKAMP & BUSHNELL (AV)

200 Security Building, 704 St. Joseph Street, P.O. Box 290, 57709
Telephone: 605-343-2410
Telecopier: 605-343-4262

RETIRED

John M. Costello
William G. Porter

MEMBERS OF FIRM

Dennis H. Hill
Kenneth L. Heisterkamp
Gene R. Bushnell
Richard O. Sharpe
Edward C. Carpenter
Thomas H. Barnes
Donald A. Porter
Thomas W. Stanton
Robert L. Lewis
Lonnie R. Braun
David M. Dillon
Gregory G. Strommen
Patricia A. Meyers
William A. May

ASSOCIATES

Stephen C. Hoffman
Joseph R. Lux
Kenneth L. Chleborad

Representative Clients: Lutheran Hospital and Homes Society of America; American States Insurance Cos.; Southeastern Aviation Underwriters; Farmers Insurance Group; Equitable Life Assurance Society of the United States and Equitable Agri-Business, Inc.; John Hancock Mutual Life Insurance Company; Bowest Corp; St. Paul Insurance Company; Ford Motor Co.; Burlington Northern, Inc.

For full biographical listings, see the Martindale-Hubbell Law Directory

DEMERSSEMAN JENSEN (AV)

(Formerly, Gunderson, Farrar, Aldrich & DeMersseman)
516 Fifth Street, P.O. Box 1820, 57709-1820
Telephone: 605-342-2814
Fax: 605-342-0732

MEMBERS OF FIRM

Robert W. Gunderson (1915-1994)
John C. Farrar (1914-1982)
Ray J. Aldrich
Michael B. DeMersseman
Curtis S. Jensen
Frank Driscoll
James R. Wefso
Philip N. Hogen

References: Rushmore State Bank; Norwest Bank South Dakota, N.A.; First Bank of South Dakota.

For full biographical listings, see the Martindale-Hubbell Law Directory

GUNDERSON, PALMER, GOODSELL & NELSON (AV)

440 Mount Rushmore Road, 4th Floor, P.O. Box 8045, 57709-8045
Telephone: 605-342-1078
Fax: 605-342-9503

MEMBERS OF FIRM

Wynn A. Gunderson
J. Crisman Palmer
G. Verne Goodsell
James S. Nelson
Daniel E. Ashmore
Donald P. Knudsen
Patrick G. Goetzinger
Talbot J. Wieczorek
Paul S. Swedlund
Mark J. Connot

Representative Clients: Norwest Bank South Dakota, N.A.; Sodak Gaming, Inc.; Bally Gaming, Inc.; SEGA of America; United States Fidelity & Guaranty Co.; Aetna Life and Casualty Co.; Homestake Mining Company; Wal-Mart Stores, Inc.; Dain Bosworth, Inc.; Underwriters Counsel/Norwest Investment Services.

For full biographical listings, see the Martindale-Hubbell Law Directory

JOHNSON HUFFMAN A PROFESSIONAL CORPORATION OF LAWYERS (AV)

3202 West Main Street, P.O. Box 6100, 57709-6100
Telephone: 605-348-7300
FAX: 605-348-4757

Glen H. Johnson
Richard E. Huffman
Scott Sumner
Wayne F. Gilbert
Timothy J. Becker
John J. Delaney
Courtney R. Clayborne
Jay A. Alderman

LEGAL SUPPORT PERSONNEL
PARALEGALS

Cynthia J. Johnson
Renee Lehr
Dory M. Maks
Timothy Crawford

For full biographical listings, see the Martindale-Hubbell Law Directory

Rapid City—Continued

LA FLEUR, LA FLEUR & LA FLEUR, P.C. (AV)

815 St. Joe Street, Suite 203, P.O. Box 8147, 57709
Telephone: 605-343-4322
Fax: 605-343-2098

Robert F. La Fleur
Mitchell C. La Fleur
Jon J. La Fleur

References: American State Bank; Norwest Bank Black Hills, Rapid City, South Dakota.

For full biographical listings, see the Martindale-Hubbell Law Directory

LYNN, JACKSON, SHULTZ & LEBRUN, P.C. (AV)

Eighth Floor, Metropolitan Federal Bank Plaza, P.O. Box 8250, 57709
Telephone: 605-342-2592
Telecopier: 605-342-5185
Sioux Falls, South Dakota Office: First Bank Building, Sixth Floor, P.O. Box 1920.
Telephone. 605-332-5999.
Telecopier: 605-332-4249.

Kelton S. Lynn (1916-1974)
Horace R. Jackson (1907-1987)
Donald R. Shultz
William F. Day, Jr. (Resident, Sioux Falls Office)
Gene N. Lebrun
Thomas G. Fritz
Haven L. Stuck
Gary D. Jensen
Steven C. Beardsley
Lee A. Magnuson (Resident, Sioux Falls Office)
Steven J. Helmers
Jay C. Shultz
Larry M. VonWald
Jane Wipf Pfeifle
Jon C. Sogn (Resident, Sioux Falls Office)
Kurt E. Solay
R. Alan Peterson (Resident, Sioux Falls Office)
Leah J. Fjerstad
Craig A. Pfeifle
Steven J. Oberg
David L. Nadolski (Resident, Sioux Falls Office)
Mary A. Gubbrud
Steven J. Morgans

Representative Clients: First Bank of South Dakota; Employers Mutual of Wausau; South Dakota School Mines & Technology; CIGNA Insurance Co.; E.D. Jones & Co.; Prairie States Life Insurance Co.
General Counsel for: Rushmore Electric Power Cooperative; Black Hills Regional Eye Institute; Douglas School District.

For full biographical listings, see the Martindale-Hubbell Law Directory

MORRILL BROWN & THOMAS (AV)

625 9th Street, 8th Floor, P.O. Box 8108, 57709-8108
Telephone: 605-348-7516
Fax: 605-348-5852

MEMBERS OF FIRM

E. V. Morrill (1899-1974)
David E. Morrill
Portia K. Brown
Timothy L. Thomas
John Nooney

General Counsel for: Black Hills Corp.; Black Hills Power and Light Co.; Wyodak Resources Development Corp.; Western Production Co., Rapid City, South Dakota; Dakota Allied Business Corp., Rapid City, South Dakota.
Representative Clients: McKie Ford Inc.; Gold Key Oldsmobile, Cadillac; American Concept Insurance Company; GMAC Truck, Inc.
Reference: Norwest Bank South Dakota, N.A.

For full biographical listings, see the Martindale-Hubbell Law Directory

WALLAHAN, BANKS & EICHER, P.C. (AV)

Rushmore Professional Building, 731 St. Joseph Street, P.O. Box 328, 57709-0328
Telephone: 605-348-0456
Fax: 605-348-0458

Franklin J. Wallahan (1935-1994)
Ronald W. Banks
Benjamin J. Eicher
Samuel D. Kerr

Representative Clients: All Nations Insurance Company; Colonial Insurance Company of California; Dairyland Insurance Company; The Maryland Sentry Insurance Company; Union Insurance Company; U.S. Insurance Group.

For full biographical listings, see the Martindale-Hubbell Law Directory

WHITING, HAGG & HAGG (AV)

1220 Mt. Rushmore Road, P.O. Box 8008, 57701
Telephone: 605-348-1125
Fax: 605-348-9744

MEMBERS OF FIRM

Brian D. Hagg
Rexford A. Hagg
George E. Grassby
John Stanton Dorsey

ASSOCIATES

Terry L. Fredricks

(See Next Column)

LEGAL SUPPORT PERSONNEL

Beverly J. McCracken

For full biographical listings, see the Martindale-Hubbell Law Directory

*REDFIELD,** Spink Co. — (Refer to Huron)

*SALEM,** McCook Co. — (Refer to Sioux Falls)

*SELBY,** Walworth Co. — (Refer to Aberdeen)

*SIOUX FALLS,** Minnehaha Co.

BOYCE, MURPHY, MCDOWELL & GREENFIELD (AV)

Suite 600 Norwest Center, P.O. Box 5015, 57117
Telephone: 605-336-2424
Fax: 605-334-0618

OF COUNSEL

John R. McDowell

MEMBERS OF FIRM

Jesse W. Boyce (1860-1915)
John S. Murphy (1901-1966)
Jeremiah D. Murphy
Russell R. Greenfield
David J. Vickers
Gary J. Pashby
Vance R. C. Goldammer
Thomas J. Welk
Terry N. Prendergast
James E. McMahon
Douglas J. Hajek
Michael S. McKnight
Gregg S. Greenfield
Roger A. Sudbeck
Tamara A. Wilka

Representative Clients: John Morrell & Co., Packers; Federal Land Bank; Citibank South Dakota, N.A.; Sears Roebuck and Co.; General Electric Co.; Ford Motor Co.; Hartford Insurance Co.; Aetna Life and Casualty Co.; Automobile Club Insurance Co.; Design Professionals Insurance Co.

For full biographical listings, see the Martindale-Hubbell Law Directory

DAVENPORT, EVANS, HURWITZ & SMITH (AV)

513 South Main Avenue, P.O. Box 1030, 57101-1030
Telephone: 605-336-2880
Telecopier: 605-335-3639

OF COUNSEL

Ellsworth E. Evans
Louis R. Hurwitz
Deming Smith
Lyle J. Wirt

MEMBERS OF FIRM

Holton Davenport (1892-1966)
Michael F. Pieplow (1945-1987)
Richard A. Cutler
P. Daniel Donohue
David L. Knudson
Edwin E. Evans
Robert E. Hayes
Michael L. Luce
Charles D. Gullickson
Sarah Richardson Larson
Michael J. Schaffer
Monte R. Walz
Thomas M. Frankman
Rick W. Orr
Edward J. Leahy
Timothy M. Gebhart
Susan Jansa Brunick
Jonathan P. Brown
Catherine A. Tanck
Roberto A. Lange

ASSOCIATES

Michael A. Hauck
Marie Elizabeth Hovland
Cheryle M. Wiedmeier
Jean H. Bender
Lori Purcell Fossen
Scott Bradley Anderson
Sandra K. Hoglund
Mark W. Haigh

Counsel for: American Society of Composers, Authors and Publishers (A.S.C.A.P.); Burlington Northern, Inc.; Continental Insurance Cos.; The First National Bank in Sioux Falls; Ford Motor Credit Co.; General Motors Corp.; The St. Paul Cos.; The Travelers.

For full biographical listings, see the Martindale-Hubbell Law Directory

GALE FISHER, P.C. (AV)

First Bank of South Dakota, Suite 705, 141 North Main Avenue, P.O. Box 2206, 57101-2206
Telephone: 605-339-4242
FAX: 605-339-4545

Gale Fisher

For full biographical listings, see the Martindale-Hubbell Law Directory

MAY, JOHNSON, DOYLE & BECKER, P.C. (AV)

4804 South Minnesota Avenue, P.O. Box 88738, 57105-8738
Telephone: 605-336-2565
Telefax: 605-336-2604

Harold C. Doyle
James R. Becker
Derald W. Wiehl
Richard Moe
Lon J. Kouri
Jeffrey D. Brekke
Richard L. Travis
Martin Oyos

Terry G. Westergaard

OF COUNSEL

Robert G. May
George O. Johnson

General Counsel for: Trail King Industries, Inc.; United Parcel Service (North & South Dakota).

(See Next Column)

MAY, JOHNSON, DOYLE & BECKER P.C.—*Continued*

Representative Clients: Unisys Corporation; U.S. West Communications, Inc.; Cargill, Inc.; 3M Company; Underwriters at LLoyds of London; Northern Natural Gas Co.; Sears Roebuck & Co.; United Airlines, Inc.

For full biographical listings, see the Martindale-Hubbell Law Directory

*SISSETON,** Roberts Co. — (Refer to Aberdeen)

*STURGIS,** Meade Co.

MORMAN, SMIT, HUGHES, STRAIN, MOLSTAD & HAIVALA (AV)

1134 Main Street, P.O. Box 729, 57785-0729
Telephone: 605-347-3624
Fax: 605-347-2091
Buffalo, South Dakota Office: Harding County Abstract Building, Box 515.
Telephone: 605-375-3477.
Fax: 605-375-3318.

MEMBERS OF FIRM

Dale L. Morman
Keith R. Smit
John T. Hughes
Michael W. Strain
Russell C. Molstad, Jr.
Robert A. Haivala

Representative Clients: Farmers State Bank, Faith, S.D.; First Western Bank of Sturgis, S.D.; NAJA Shrine Temple; Bradley Sodding, Inc.; Harding County Hospital Association; Sky Ranch for Boys, Inc., Camp Crook, S.D.
References: Norwest Bank South Dakota, N.A., Sturgis, S.D.; First Western Bank of Sturgis, Sturgis, S.D.

For full biographical listings, see the Martindale-Hubbell Law Directory

*TYNDALL,** Bon Homme Co. — (Refer to Yankton)

*WATERTOWN,** Codington Co.

AUSTIN, HINDERAKER, HOPPER & STRAIT (AV)

25 First Avenue, S.W., P.O. Box 966, 57201-0023
Telephone: 605-886-5823
Fax: 605-886-7553

MEMBERS OF FIRM

J. Douglas Austin
Paul I. Hinderaker
Arthur M. Hopper
David R. Strait

ASSOCIATES

Scott R. Bratland

OF COUNSEL

Alan L. Austin
Irving A. Hinderaker

Representative Clients: Bank of South Dakota; Watertown Public Opinion; Human Service Agency; Persona, Inc.; American Family Insurance Group; Milwaukee Insurance Co.; Citizens Bank; Midcom, Inc.; American States Insurance; Watertown School District.

For full biographical listings, see the Martindale-Hubbell Law Directory

BARTRON, WILES, RYLANCE & HOLGERSON (AV)

A Partnership including Professional Corporations
3 East Kemp Avenue, 57201-0227
Telephone: 605-886-5881
Fax: 605-886-3934

MEMBERS OF FIRM

R. Greg Bartron (P.C.)
John C. Wiles (P.C.)
Raymond D. Rylance (P.C.)
Albert H. Holgerson (P.C.)

OF COUNSEL

Donald E. Osheim (P.C.)

Representative Clients: Allied Group Insurance Co.; Brown Clinic; Farmers and Merchants Bank and Trust of Watertown; Fireman's Fund Insurance Co.; Hartford Insurance Co.; Harvest Life Insurance Co.; Home Insurance Co.; Liberty Mutual Insurance Co.; National Farmers Union Insurance Co.; First Premier Bank, Watertown.

For full biographical listings, see the Martindale-Hubbell Law Directory

GREEN, SCHULZ, ROBY, OVIATT & CUMMINGS (AV)

A Partnership including Professional Corporations
816 South Broadway, P.O. Box 1600, 57201-6600
Telephone: 605-886-5812
Fax: 605-886-0934

Daniel K. Loucks (1916-1974)
Ross H. Oviatt (1918-1991)
Thomas J. Green (P.C.)
Ronald L. Schulz (P.C.)
James C. Roby (P.C.)
Nancy L. Oviatt
Timothy J. Cummings

Representative Clients: Prairie Lakes Health Care Systems, Inc. (Hospital); Farmers & Merchants Bank and Trust of Watertown; Norwest Bank South Dakota N.A. (Watertown); General Service Bureau (Commercial Collections); Cook's, Inc. (Office Equipment and Supplies); Watertown Board of Realtors, Inc.; Living Center, Inc. (Skilled Care Nursing Home); Enercept, Inc. (Building Products); Angus Industries, Inc.; Palm Industries, Inc. (Safety Equipment Manufacturers).

(See Next Column)

For full biographical listings, see the Martindale-Hubbell Law Directory

GRIBBIN, BURNS & EIDE (AV)

16 East Kemp Street, 57201
Telephone: 605-886-5885
FAX: 605-886-2899

MEMBERS OF FIRM

Edward P. Gribbin (1903-1958)
Francis C. Burns
Allen J. Eide
Thomas F. Burns

Representative Clients: The Prudential Insurance Company of America; Federated Mutual Insurance Co., Owatonna, Minnesota; Codington-Clark Rural Electric Cooperative; Northeast TV Cooperative, Inc.; Sioux Valley Coopratrive; Sioux Valley Federal Credit Union; Mother of God Monastery.

For full biographical listings, see the Martindale-Hubbell Law Directory

*WEBSTER,** Day Co. — (Refer to Watertown)

*WESSINGTON SPRINGS,** Jerauld Co. — (Refer to Huron)

*WINNER,** Tripp Co.

STANLEY E. WHITING (AV)

142 East Third Street, P.O. Box 48, 57580-0048
Telephone: 605-842-3373
Fax: 605-842-3375

Reference: Norwest Bank.

For full biographical listings, see the Martindale-Hubbell Law Directory

*WOONSOCKET,** Sanborn Co. — (Refer to Huron)

*YANKTON,** Yankton Co.

GOETZ, HIRSCH & KLIMISCH (AV)

311 West Third Street, P.O. Box 708, 57078-0708
Telephone: 605-665-9495
Fax: 605-665-0126

MEMBERS OF FIRM

James T. Goetz
Robert W. Hirsch
William J. Klimisch

Representative Clients: Lawyers Title Insurance Corp.; First Dakota National Bank; Gurney Seed and Nursery Co.; Valley State Bank; Stockmans Livestock Auction Co.; Wilson Trailer Co.

For full biographical listings, see the Martindale-Hubbell Law Directory

JOHNSON, HEIDEPRIEM, MINER & MARLOW (AV)

200 West Third Street, P.O. Box 667, 57078
Telephone: 605-665-5009
Fax: 605-665-4788
Sioux Falls, South Dakota Office: 1720 South Spring Avenue.
Telephone: 605-338-4304.
Fax: 605-338-4162.

MEMBERS OF FIRM

Steven M. Johnson
Celia Miner
Michael F. Marlow
Kevin L. Reiner

ASSOCIATES

Robert C. Brown

Representative Clients: First Dakota National Bank; Auto-Owners Ins. Co.; American States Ins. Co.; Home Ins. Co.; American Concept Ins. Co.; IMT Ins. Co.; North Star Mutual Ins. Co.; Stockmen's Livestock Market Co.; Mount Marty College; Welfl Construction Corp.

For full biographical listings, see the Martindale-Hubbell Law Directory

TENNESSEE

*ALAMO,** Crockett Co.

Emison and Emison, P.C. (AV)

116 West Main Street, P.O. Box 13, 38001
Telephone: 901-696-4597
Fax: 901-696-5980

Theophilus J. Emison
Theophilus J. Emison, Jr.

References: The Bank of Alamo; People's Bank; Bank of Friendship, Friendship, Tennessee.

For full biographical listings, see the Martindale-Hubbell Law Directory

*ASHLAND CITY,** Cheatham Co. — (Refer to Nashville)

*ATHENS,** McMinn Co.

Carter, Harrod & Cunningham (AV)

One Madison Avenue, P.O. Box 885, 37371-0885
Telephone: 615-745-7447
FAX: 615-745-6114

MEMBERS OF FIRM

Allen H. Carter (1938-1987)
David F. Harrod
Jeffrey L. Cunningham

ASSOCIATES

Jerri Saunders Bryant

Counsel for: Citizens National Bank; Athens Federal Savings & Loan Assn.; Athens Utilities Board; Bowaters Incorporated.
Representative Clients: Liberty Mutual Insurance Co.; Nationwide Insurance Cos.; State Farm Mutual Automobile Insurance Co.; United States Fidelity & Guaranty Insurance Co.

For full biographical listings, see the Martindale-Hubbell Law Directory

*BOLIVAR,** Hardeman Co.

Denton & Cary (AV)

118 Warren Street, P.O. Box 306, 38008
Telephone: 901-658-5170
Fax: 901-658-6806

MEMBERS OF FIRM

H. B. Denton (1910-1972)
Charles M. Cary
H. Morris Denton
William Boyette Denton

LEGAL SUPPORT PERSONNEL

Janice M. Bodiford

Counsel for: Merchants & Planters Bank; Hardeman County Board of Education; Town of Whiteville; City of Bolivar.

For full biographical listings, see the Martindale-Hubbell Law Directory

BRISTOL, Sullivan Co.

Massengill, Caldwell, Hyder & Bunn, P.C. (AV)

777 Anderson Street, P.O. Box 1745, 37621
Telephone: 615-764-1174
FAX: 615-764-1179

Joseph A. Caldwell (1884-1963)
Myers N. Massengill
Joseph K. Brown (1898-1968)
Craig H. Caldwell, Jr.
Thomas S. Curtin (1899-1970)
Jack W. Hyder, Jr.
David S. Bunn

OF COUNSEL

Craig H. Caldwell
Frank Winston

Representative Clients: United Inter-Mountain Telephone Co.; City of Bristol, Tennessee; Bristol Tennessee Electric System; First American National Bank; Twin City Federal Savings Bank; Nationwide Insurance Co.

For full biographical listings, see the Martindale-Hubbell Law Directory

*BROWNSVILLE,** Haywood Co. — (Refer to Jackson)

*CARTHAGE,** Smith Co. — (Refer to Nashville)

*CENTERVILLE,** Hickman Co. — (Refer to Hohenwald)

*CHATTANOOGA,** Hamilton Co.

Baker, Donelson, Bearman & Caldwell (AV)

1800 Republic Centre, 633 Chestnut Street, 37450-1800
Telephone: 615-752-4400
Telecopier: 615-752-4410
Memphis, Tennessee Office: 20th Floor, First Tennessee Building, 165 Madison, 38103.
Telephone: 901-526-2000.
Telecopier: 901-577-2303.

(See Next Column)

Nashville, Tennessee Office: 1700 Nashville City Center, 511 Union Street, 37219.
Telephone: 615-726-5600.
Telecopier: 615-726-0464.
Knoxville, Tennessee Office: 2200 Riverview Tower, 900 Gay Street, 37901.
Telephone: 615-549-7000.
Telecopier: 615-525-8569.
Huntsville, Tennessee Office: 3 Courthouse Square, 37756.
Telephone: 615-663-2321.
Telecopier: 615-663-2111.
Johnson City, Tennessee Office: Hamilton Bank Building, 207 Mockingbird Lane, 37604.
Telephone: 615-928-0181.
Telecopier: 615-928-5694; 615-928-3654; Kingsport: 615-246-6191.
Washington, D.C. Office: Market Square, 801 Pennsylvania Avenue, N.W., 20004.
Telephone: 202-508-3400.
Telecopier: 202-508-3402.

PARTNERS

Lewis R. Donelson, III
Virginia C. Love
Thomas A. Caldwell
Richard J. McAfee
John C. Mooney
James R. McKoon
Thomas O. Helton
Louann Prater Smith
Richard B. Gossett
Kenneth C. Beckman
David C. Burger
Randall L. Gibson
Carl E. Hartley
Joe A. Conner
Susan Elliott Rich
Julie Williams Watson
C. George Caudle
Jeffery A. Billings

OF COUNSEL

Hunter D. Heggie

ASSOCIATES

Deborah S. Humble
Mark D. Hackett
Timothy R. Simonds
Charles D. McDonald
Bob E. Lype
Matthew P. Huggins
Stephen L. Page

For full biographical listings, see the Martindale-Hubbell Law Directory

Chambliss & Bahner (AV)

1000 Tallan Building, Two Union Square, 37402-2500
Telephone: 615-756-3000
Fax: 615-265-9574

MEMBERS OF FIRM

John Alexander Chambliss (1887-1972)
Michael J. Mahn
Michael N. St. Charles
J. E. Gervin, Jr. (1946-1993)
Martin L. Pierce
T. Maxfield Bahner
David R. Evans
J. Nelson Irvine
Bruce C. Bailey
Kirk Snouffer
Jay A. Young
William P. Aiken, Jr.
Donald J. Aho
William H. Pickering
L. Andrew Clark
Gary D. Lander
Penelope W. Register
Dana B. Perry

ASSOCIATES

George H. Suzich
Anthony A. Jackson
K. Scott Graham
S. Mark Turner
Benjamin Younger Pitts
Timothy M. Gibbons
C. Caldwell H. Huckabay
R. Alston Hamilton
Collette R. Jones
Joseph A. San Filippo
J. Patrick Murphy
Lori L. Smith

OF COUNSEL

Jac Chambliss
Dudley Porter, Jr.
Charles N. Jolly
William Crutchfield, Jr.
Joe V. W. Gaston

Representative Clients: Hudson Construction Co.; McKee Foods Corp.; 3M Co.; NationsBank; North Park Hospital; Provident Life & Accident Insurance Co.; Porter Warner Indus., Inc.; SCT Yarns, Inc.; Stein Construction Co., Inc.; Valley Capital Corp.

For full biographical listings, see the Martindale-Hubbell Law Directory

Foster, Foster, Allen & Durrence (AV)

Formerly Hall, Haynes & Foster
Suite 515 Pioneer Bank Building, 37402
Telephone: 615-266-1141
Telecopier: 615-266-4618

MEMBERS OF FIRM

George Lane Foster
Craig R. Allen
William M. Foster
Phillip M. Durrence, Jr.

ASSOCIATES

David J. Ward
Clayton M. Whittaker
John M. Hull

LEGAL SUPPORT PERSONNEL

Peggy Sue Bates

Division Counsel for: Alabama Great Southern Railroad Co.; C.N.O. & T.P. Railway Co.

(See Next Column)

FOSTER, FOSTER, ALLEN & DURRENCE—*Continued*

Attorneys for: CNA/Insurance; U.S.P. & G. Co.; The Firestone Tire & Rubber Co.; Exxon, Corp.; Murphy Oil Corp.; Chicago Title Insurance Co.; City of East Ridge; Jim Walter Homes; Raymond James & Associates; Morgan Keegan & Co.

For full biographical listings, see the Martindale-Hubbell Law Directory

GEARHISER, PETERS & HORTON (AV)

320 McCallie Avenue, 37402-2007
Telephone: 615-756-5171
Fax: 615-266-1605

MEMBERS OF FIRM

Charles J. Gearhiser
R. Wayne Peters
William H. Horton
Roy C. Maddox, Jr.
Robert L. Lockaby, Jr.
Ralph E. Tallant, Jr.
Terry Atkin Cavett
Sam D. Elliott
Lane C. Avery
Michael A. Anderson
Wade K. Cannon

ASSOCIATES

Robin L. Miller

References: First Tennessee Bank; Pioneer Bank.

For full biographical listings, see the Martindale-Hubbell Law Directory

MILLER & MARTIN (AV)

Suite 1000 Volunteer Building, 832 Georgia Avenue, 37402
Telephone: 615-756-6600
FAX: 615-785-8480

Vaughn Miller (1892-1964)
Burkett Miller (1890-1977)
F. Linton Martin (1891-1979)
Jere T. Tipton (1904-1983)
James F. Waterhouse (1925-1986)
John L. Lenihan (1910-1990)

OF COUNSEL

H. James Hitching

MEMBERS OF FIRM

J. Guy Beatty, Jr.
Raymond R. Murphy, Jr.
Joel W. Richardson, Jr.
Howard I. Levine
Lowry F. Kline
Hal F. S. Clements
Whitney Durand
Ronald G. Ingham
Richard D. Crotteau
James G. Cate, Jr.
Edward N. Boehm
James R. Buckner
Roger W. Dickson
John B. Phillips, Jr.
James M. Haley, IV
W. Scott McGinness, Jr.
David F. Tugman
Alfred E. Smith, Jr.
Shelby R. Grubbs
William G. Trumpeter
E. Liston Bishop III
William Alan Nichols
Jeffrey W. Guild
A. Alexander Taylor, II
Allen L. McCallie
John C. Harrison
H. Allen Corey
Harry S. Mattice, Jr.
Marcia J. Meredith Eason
Shelley D. Rucker
William Randall Wilson
Douglas T. Johnson
Hugh F. Sharber
Christopher H. Steger
Virginia Anne Sharber
Jeffrey Scott Norwood
William E. Robinson
John R. Bode
Charles B. Lee
Ward W. Nelson
Robert C. Divine
Franklin Miller Williams
J. Porter Durham, Jr.
Jonathan F. Kent
Chester Crews Townsend
Brian E. Humphrey
Mark W. Degler

ASSOCIATES

Ansley T. Moses
Traci Shuster Umberger
Daniel B. Gilmore
Nicholas W. Whittenburg
William S. Parrish
Karen M. (Sutton) Smith
Clifford L. Beach, Jr.
R. Grant Dobson
Reuben Nisbet Pelot, IV
Kelly Lynn Weston
Theodore K. Whitfield, Jr.
Katharine McCallie Gardner
Charles W. Forlidas
Suzanne Noblit Forlidas
James T. Williams
Leah M. Gerbitz
Kevin B. Campbell

General Counsel for: American National Bank and Trust Company; Coca-Cola Enterprises, Inc.; The Krystal Company; Olan Mills, Inc.
Counsel for: Bowater Southern Paper Company; John Hancock Mutual Life Insurance Company; Chubb Life Insurance Company of America.

For full biographical listings, see the Martindale-Hubbell Law Directory

SHUMACKER & THOMPSON (AV)

Suite 500, First Tennessee Building, 701 Market Street, 37402-4800
Telephone: 615-265-2214
Telecopier: 615-266-1842
Branch Office: Suite 103, One Park Place, 6148 Lee Highway, Chattanooga, Tennessee, 37421-2900.
Telephone: 615-855-1814.
Telecopier: 615-899-1278.

(*See Next Column*)

MEMBERS OF FIRM

Ralph Shumacker
Frank M. Thompson
W. Neil Thomas, Jr.
Albert W. Secor
W. Neil Thomas, III
Ronald I. Feldman
Alan L. Cates
Ross I. Schram III
Stephen P. Parish
William Given Colvin
Harold L. North, Jr.
John K. Culpepper
Jeffery V. Curry
Everett L. Hixson, Jr.
Stanley W. Hildebrand
Phillip E. Fleenor
Donna S. Spurlock
James D. Henderson

ASSOCIATES

Char-La Cain Fowler
George G. Hixson
J. Christopher Hall
Jane M. Stahl

For full biographical listings, see the Martindale-Hubbell Law Directory

SPEARS, MOORE, REBMAN & WILLIAMS (AV)

8th Floor Blue Cross Building, 801 Pine Street, 37402
Telephone: 615-756-7000
Facsimile: 615-756-4801

MEMBERS OF FIRM

William Douglas Spears (1906-1992)
Alvin O'B. Moore
Andrew Frederick Rebman III (1917-1992)
Silas Williams, Jr.
William L. Taylor, Jr.
James W. Gentry, Jr.
Edward Blake Moore
Thomas S. Kale
Ford P. Mitchell (1930-1993)
Joseph C. Wilson, III
W. Ferber Tracy
Fred Henry Moore
Lynnwood Hale Hamilton
Michael W. Boehm
Robert J. Boehm
L. Marie Williams
Mark Allen Ramsey
F. Scott LeRoy
Harry L. Dadds, II
Randy Chennault
Joseph R. White
David E. Fowler

ASSOCIATES

Barry A. Steelman
Robert G. Norred Jr.
Rodney L. Umberger, Jr.
Howell Dean Clements
John B. Bennett
E. Brent Hill (Not admitted in TN)
Angela A. Ripper

OF COUNSEL

Buckner S. Morris
Micheline Kelly Johnson

Counsel for: Pioneer Bank; Chattanooga Gas Co.; South Central Bell Telephone Co.; Tennessee-American Water Co.; Blue Cross and Blue Shield of Tennessee; State Farm Mutual Automobile Insurance Cos.; Nationwide Insurance Co.; Siskin Steel & Supply Co., Inc.; CSX Transportation, Inc.; The McCallie School; Mueller Co.

For full biographical listings, see the Martindale-Hubbell Law Directory

STOPHEL & STOPHEL, P.C. (AV)

500 Tallan Building, Two Union Square, 37402-2571
Telephone: 615-756-2333
Fax: 615-266-5032

John C. Stophel
Glenn C. Stophel
Barton C. Burns
E. Stephen Jett
Wayne E. Thomas
Donald E. Morton
Richard W. Bethea, Jr.
Harry B. Ray
W. Lee Maddux
C. Douglas Williams
W. Jeffrey Hollingsworth
Arthur P. Brock

Brian L. Woodward
Ronald D. Gorsline
Stephen S. Duggins
James C. Heartfield
Tracy C. Wooden
William R. Dearing
Lisa A. Yacuzzo
Allison A. Cardwell
John W. Rose
Randall D. Van Dolson (Not admitted in TN)

Representative Clients: Astec Industries, Inc.; McKenzie Leasing Corporation; The National Group, Inc.; Tennessee Temple University; HCA Valley Psychiatric Hospital Corporation; Chattanooga Armature Works, Inc.; Graco Children's Products, Inc.; American Manufacturing Co.; The Maclellan Foundation, Inc.; Roy H. Pack Broadcasting of Tennessee, Inc. (WDEF AM, FM & TV).

For full biographical listings, see the Martindale-Hubbell Law Directory

STRANG, FLETCHER, CARRIGER, WALKER, HODGE & SMITH (AV)

400 Krystal Building, One Union Square, 37402
Telephone: 615-265-2000
Telecopier: 615-756-5861

S. Bartow Strang (1882-1954)
John Storrs Fletcher (1879-1961)
John S. Fletcher, Jr. (1911-1974)
John S. Carriger (1902-1989)

MEMBERS OF FIRM

Robert Kirk Walker
Carlos C. Smith
William C. Carriger
Richard T. Hudson
Frederick L. Hitchcock
Ewing Bradley Connell Strang
Larry Lee Cash
Christine Mabe Scott

(*See Next Column*)

STRANG, FLETCHER, CARRIGER, WALKER, HODGE & SMITH, *Chattanooga—Continued*

ASSOCIATES

Mary Craft Grambergs
J. Robin Rogers
James L. Catanzaro, Jr.
Gregory D. Willett
Mark W. Smith
Keila C. Tennent

OF COUNSEL

F. Thornton Strang
Albert L. Hodge

Representative Clients: Chattanooga-Hamilton County Hospital Authority; Distributors Insurance Co.; Electric Power Board of Chattanooga; First American National Bank; Liberty Mutual Insurance Co.; Rock-Tenn Mill Division; Tennessee Valley Public Power Assn.; Zurich-American Insurance Cos.

For full biographical listings, see the Martindale-Hubbell Law Directory

SUMMERS, MCCREA & WYATT, P.C. (AV)

500 Lindsay Street, 37402
Telephone: 615-265-2385
Fax: 615-266-5211

Jerry H. Summers
Sandra K. McCrea
Thomas L. Wyatt
Jeffrey W. Rufolo

For full biographical listings, see the Martindale-Hubbell Law Directory

WITT, GAITHER & WHITAKER, P.C. (AV)

1100 American National Bank Building, 37402-2608
Telephone: 615-265-8881
Telefax: 615-266-4138; 615-756-5612

John P. Gaither (1915-1994)
William P. Hutcheson (1923-1991)
Philip B. Whitaker
John W. Murrey, III
Hugh J. Moore, Jr.
Frank P. Pinchak
John F. Henry, Jr.
Harold Alan Schwartz, Jr.
K. Stephen Powers
Carter J. Lynch, III
Geoffrey G. Young
Ralph M. Killebrew, Jr.
Rosemarie Luise Bryan
Douglas E. Peck
Jonathan M. Minnen

Steven R. Barrett
Philip B. Whitaker, Jr.
Jane K. Ricci
Leigh Anne Battersby
Richard D. Faulkner, Jr.
Michael J. Mcsunas
Charles N. Whitaker

OF COUNSEL

Raymond Buckner Witt, Jr.
Shields Wilson
Gary M. Disheroon
Frank M. Groves, Jr.

Representative Clients: American National Bank & Trust Company; Chattanooga Cetropolitan Airport Authority; Chrysler Insurance Co.; Coca-Cola Bottling Co. Consolidated; Dean Witter Reynolds, Inc.; Dixie Yarns, Inc.; E.I. du Pont de Nemours & Company; Signal Apparel Company, Inc.; Southwest Motor Freight, Inc.; University of Chattanooga Foundation, Inc.

For full biographical listings, see the Martindale-Hubbell Law Directory

*CLARKSVILLE,** Montgomery Co.

DANIEL, HARVILL, BATSON & NOLAN (AV)

121 South Third Street, 37040
Telephone: 615-647-1501
Fax: 615-553-0153

MEMBERS OF FIRM

William M. Daniel (1837-1921)
William M. Daniel, Jr. (1875-1942)
William M. Daniel, III (1916-1991)
F. Evans Harvill
Richard H. Batson
Daniel L. Nolan, Jr.
John R. Brice
W. Timothy Harvey
Michael K. Williamson
Richard H. Batson, II

ASSOCIATES

Joel D. Ragland
Steven C. Girsky
Suzanne G. Marsh
D. Mark Nolan
Jill Bartee Nolan
Christopher J. Pittman

Representative Clients: Allstate Insurance Co.; CNA Insurance Companies; First Federal Savings Bank of Clarksville; Farmers & Merchants Bank; First American National Bank; South Central Bell; State Farm Mutual Automobile Insurance Co.
Approved Attorneys for: Lawyers Title Insurance Corp.; Minnesota Title Company; Ticor.

For full biographical listings, see the Martindale-Hubbell Law Directory

MARKS, SHELL, MANESS & MARKS (AV)

114 South Second Street, P.O. Box 1149, 37040
Telephone: 615-552-6000
Telecopier: 615-645-1890

(See Next Column)

MEMBERS OF FIRM

Robert L. McReynolds (1899-1951)
Dempsey H. Marks (1917-1990)
Albert P. Marks
Carmack C. Shell
Roger A. Maness
Robert C. Marks

ASSOCIATES

Christopher A. Smith

Representative Clients: First Union Bank; NationsBank; NationsBank Trust Co.; Illinois Central Railroad; Acme Boot Co.; Guaranty Federal Savings Bank; Cumberland Electric Membership Corp.
Approved Attorneys for: Lawyers Title Insurance Corp. (Agents); First American Title Insurance Co.; National Title Insurance of New York, Inc. (Agents).

For full biographical listings, see the Martindale-Hubbell Law Directory

*CLEVELAND,** Bradley Co.

BELL AND ASSOCIATES, P.C. (AV)

140 Ocoee Street, N.E., P.O. Box 1169, 37364-1169
Telephone: 615-476-8541
Facsimile: 615-339-3510

J. Hallman Bell (1896-1976)
Eddie L. Headrick (1949-1982)
L. Harlen Painter
Michael E. Callaway
John Edgar Brown, III
John F. Kimball
Marcia M. McMurray

Barrett T. Painter

OF COUNSEL

Robert L. McMurray

Local Attorneys for: Louisville & Nashville Railroad Co.; South Central Bell Telephone Co.
Representative Client: Estee Manufacturing Co., Inc.

For full biographical listings, see the Martindale-Hubbell Law Directory

JENNE, SCOTT & BRYANT (AV)

260 Ocoee Street, P.O. Box 161, 37364-0161
Telephone: 615-476-5506
Fax: 615-476-5058

MEMBERS OF FIRM

Roger E. Jenne
Robert A. Scott (1940-1984)
D. Mitchell Bryant

LEGAL SUPPORT PERSONNEL

Sharon A Wilson (Paralegal)

For full biographical listings, see the Martindale-Hubbell Law Directory

DENNY E. MOBBS (AV)

55 1/2 First Street, N.E., P.O. Box 192, 37364-0192
Telephone: 615-472-7181

Representative Clients: Liberty Mutual Ins. Co.; Shelby Mutual Insurance Co.; Carolina Casualty Co.; Maytag Corp. (Magic Chef, Inc.-Hardwick Stove Company); Industrial Development Board of Polk County; Polk County News-Citizen Advance; Ocoee Inn & Marina.

For full biographical listings, see the Martindale-Hubbell Law Directory

*COLUMBIA,** Maury Co.

LAWWELL, DALE & GRAHAM (AV)

610 North Garden Street, P.O. Box 1017, 38402-1017
Telephone: 615-388-2822
Fax: 615-381-3748

MEMBERS OF FIRM

T. Edward Lawwell
Frank K. Dale
William A. Graham

Counsel for: Tennessee National Bank of Columbia; CSX Transportation; Hall & Knox Mining Co.; Tennessee Farmers Mutual Insurance Co.
Representative Clients: NationsBank; Kemper Insurance Cos.; Morgan Brothers Electric Co., Inc.; Shapard Building Co.; L.D. Hill & Sons Realtors; Farm Credit Services.

TRABUE, STURDIVANT & DEWITT (AV)

100 West Sixth Street, P.O. Box 1004, 38402
Telephone: 615-388-7032
Fax: 615-388-7066
Nashville, Tennessee Office: 25th Floor, Nashville City Center, 511 Union Street.
Telephone: 615-244-9270.
Fax: 615-256-8197.

Edward C. Blank, II (1937-1988)
Robert L. Jones (Resident)
N. Houston Parks (Resident)
Edward K. Lancaster (Resident)

General Counsel for: Tennessee Farm Bureau Federation; Tennessee Farmers Life Insurance Companies.

(See Next Column)

TRABUE, STURDIVANT & DEWITT—*Continued*

For full biographical listings, see the Martindale-Hubbell Law Directory

WALLER LANSDEN DORTCH & DAVIS (AV)

809 S. Main Street, Suite 300, P.O. Box 1035, 38401
Telephone: 615-388-6031
Telecopier: 615-381-7317
Nashville, Tennessee Office: Nashville City Center, 511 Union Street, Suite 2100.
Telephone: 615-244-6380.
Telecopier: 615-244-5686; 615-244-6804.
Telex: 786535.

RESIDENT PARTNER

William M. Leech, Jr. — Charles A. Trost

RESIDENT OF COUNSEL

Robin S. Courtney

RESIDENT ASSOCIATES

Thomas H. Peebles IV

Representative Clients: Fedders Corporation; First Farmers and Merchants National Bank of Columbia (Branches in Centerville, Chapel Hill, Lawrenceburg, Lewisburg, Mt. Pleasant and Spring Hill); General Electric Company; Kasbar National Industries, Inc.; Monsanto Company; Saturn Corporation; Union Carbide Corporation.

For full biographical listings, see the Martindale-Hubbell Law Directory

*COOKEVILLE,** Putnam Co.

MADEWELL & JARED (AV)

Suite One, Fourth Floor, First Tennessee Bank Building, P.O. Box 721, 38503-0721
Telephone: 615-526-6101
FAX: 615-528-1909

MEMBERS OF FIRM

Eugene Jared — James D. Madewell
William E. Halfacre, III

ASSOCIATES

Kenneth S. Williams

Representative Clients: State of Tennessee; Trial Counsel as Special Assistant to Attorney General; Bank of Putnam County; First Tennessee Bank, N.A. at Cookeville; The Maryland; Transamerica Ins. Group; Home Insurance Co.; Auto Owners Ins. Co.; Insurance Company of North America; Fireman's Fund Insurance Co.

For full biographical listings, see the Martindale-Hubbell Law Directory

MOORE, RADER, CLIFT AND FITZPATRICK, P.C. (AV)

46 North Jefferson Avenue, P.O. Box 3347, 38501
Telephone: 615-526-3311
Fax: 615-526-3092

L. Dean Moore — Michael E. Clift
Daniel H. Rader, III — Walter S. Fitzpatrick, III

General Counsel for: First Tennessee Bank.
Local Counsel for: Heritage Ford-Lincoln-Mercury, Inc.
Representative Clients: Continental Insurance Co.; Kemper Group; U.S.F.&G.; Auto Owners Insurance Co.; Wausau Insurance Cos.

For full biographical listings, see the Martindale-Hubbell Law Directory

*COVINGTON,** Tipton Co.

J. HOUSTON GORDON (AV)

Suite 201 Lindo Hotel Building, 114 West Liberty Avenue, P.O. Box 846, 38019-0846
Telephone: 901-476-7100
Telecopier: 901-476-3537

ASSOCIATES

Molly A. Glover

For full biographical listings, see the Martindale-Hubbell Law Directory

*CROSSVILLE,** Cumberland Co. — (Refer to Oak Ridge)

*DAYTON,** Rhea Co. — (Refer to Chattanooga)

*DECATUR,** Meigs Co. — (Refer to Athens)

DICKSON, Dickson Co.

WHITE, REGEN & STUART (AV)

107 Professional Building, 110 North Mathis Drive, P.O. Box 190, 37055
Telephone: 615-446-2881
Fax: 615-446-4694

(See Next Column)

MEMBERS OF FIRM

Roger G. White (1935-1980) — Barney B. Regen
Marshall S. Stuart, Jr.

General Counsel: First Federal Savings Bank, Dickson; First Service Corporation of Dickson; Turnbull Utility District; Mid-Cumberland Title and Abstract Co.
Representative Clients: Farmers Home Administration; Veterans Administration; General Insurance Underwriters; Tennesco, Inc.; Farm Credit Services.

For full biographical listings, see the Martindale-Hubbell Law Directory

*DRESDEN,** Weakley Co.

THOMAS & NEESE (AV)

121 Main Street, P.O. Box 298, 38225
Telephone: 901-364-3111
Fax: 901-364-2664

MEMBERS OF FIRM

George C. Thomas — William R. Neese

ASSOCIATES

Colin Johnson — LeAnne Moore

For full biographical listings, see the Martindale-Hubbell Law Directory

*DYERSBURG,** Dyer Co.

ASHLEY, ASHLEY & ARNOLD (AV)

322 Church Avenue, P.O. Box H, 38024
Telephone: 901-285-5074
Telecopier: 901-285-5089

MEMBERS OF FIRM

Barret Ashley — Stephen D. Scofield
Randolph A. Ashley, Jr. — Marianna Williams
S. Leo Arnold — Carol Anne Austin
Anthony Lee Winchester

OF COUNSEL

Joree G. Brownlow

Representative Clients: Illinois Central Gulf Railroad; Bekeart Steel Wire Corp.; Fidelity and Deposit Company of Maryland; St. Paul Fire and Marine Insurance Company.
Construction Company Clients: Folk Construction Co.; Ford Construction Company; Luhr Brothers, Inc.; Pine Bluff Sand & Gravel; Valley Construction Co.

For full biographical listings, see the Martindale-Hubbell Law Directory

*ELIZABETHTON,** Carter Co.

ALLEN, NELSON & BOWERS (AV)

Bowers Building, 619 East Elk Avenue, 37643-3329
Telephone: 615-542-4154

MEMBERS OF FIRM

W. R. Allen (1863-1947) — John L. Bowers, Jr.
Roy C. Nelson (1904-1977) — John L. Bowers, III
Gregory H. Bowers

General Counsel for: Elizabethton Federal Savings Bank; Elizabethon Newspaper, Inc.
Local Counsel for: North American Rayon Corp.; State Farm Mutual Automobile Insurance Co.; Home Indemnity Co.; U. S. F. & G. Co.; State Automobile Mutual Insurance Co. of Ohio; Federated Implement and Hardware Insurance Co.
Approved Attorneys for: Lawyers Title Insurance Corp.

For full biographical listings, see the Martindale-Hubbell Law Directory

*FRANKLIN,** Williamson Co.

BERRY AND OGLESBY (AV)

Eaton House, 125 Third Avenue, North, 37064
Telephone: 615-794-4547

MEMBERS OF FIRM

C. Dewees Berry — James T. Oglesby

Representative Clients: Franklin Housing Authority; Walker Chevrolet-Olds, Inc.; The Industrial Development Board of the City of Franklin, TN; The Health and Educational Facilities Board of the City of Franklin, TN; Farm Credit Services of Mid-America, ASA; Mid-State Title & Escrow, Inc.; Claibourne Hughes Health Center; Harpeth Terrace Convalescent Center, Inc.

For full biographical listings, see the Martindale-Hubbell Law Directory

HARTZOG, SILVA & DAVIES (AV)

Trans Financial Building, 123 Fifth Avenue North, 37064
Telephone: 615-790-1500
Fax: 615-790-0091

(See Next Column)

HARTZOG, SILVA & DAVIES, *Franklin—Continued*

MEMBERS OF FIRM

H. Mark Hartzog
Edward P. Silva
Robert E. Lee Davies

For full biographical listings, see the Martindale-Hubbell Law Directory

*GREENEVILLE,** Greene Co.

KING & KING (AV)

124 South Main Street, 37743
Telephone: 615-639-6881

MEMBERS OF FIRM

Kyle K. King
K. Kidwell King, Jr.

For full biographical listings, see the Martindale-Hubbell Law Directory

ROGERS, LAUGHLIN, NUNNALLY, HOOD & CRUM (AV)

100 South Main Street Corner of Main & Depot Streets, 37743
Telephone: 615-639-5183
FAX: 615-639-6154

MEMBERS OF FIRM

John T. Milburn Rogers
William S. Nunnally
Jerry W. Laughlin
Kenneth C. Hood
Edward Grant Crum

ASSOCIATES

Jeffrey A. Powell

OF COUNSEL

Thomas W. Overall

Representative Clients: First Tennessee Bank; Andrew Johnson Bank; Marsh Petroleum Co.; Greeneville Insurance Agency, Inc.; Pet Credit Union; Bewley Motor Company & Olds-Subaru; Southern Packaging and Storage Co., Inc.
General Counsel for: Greene County Bank; Allen Petroleum Co., (Exxon); The Austin Co.

For full biographical listings, see the Martindale-Hubbell Law Directory

HARRIMAN, Roane Co. — (Refer to Knoxville)

*HARTSVILLE,** Trousdale Co. — (Refer to Lafayette)

*HENDERSON,** Chester Co. — (Refer to Jackson)

*HUNTINGDON,** Carroll Co. — (Refer to Milan)

*HUNTSVILLE,** Scott Co.

BAKER, DONELSON, BEARMAN & CALDWELL (AV)

3 Courthouse Square, 37756
Telephone: 615-663-2321
Telecopier: 615-663-2111
Memphis, Tennessee Office: 20th Floor, First Tennessee Building, 165 Madison, 38103.
Telephone: 901-526-2000.
Telecopier: 901-577-2303.
Nashville, Tennessee Office: 1700 Nashville City Center, 511 Union Street, 37219.
Telephone: 615-726-5600.
Telecopier: 615-726-0464.
Knoxville, Tennessee Office: 2200 Riverview Tower, 900 Gay Street, 37901.
Telephone: 615-549-7000.
Telecopier: 615-525-8569.
Chattanooga, Tennessee Office: 1800 Republic Centre, 633 Chestnut Street, 37450-1800.
Telephone: 615-752-4400.
Telecopier: 615-752-4410.
Johnson City, Tennessee Office: Hamilton Bank Building, 207 Mockingbird Lane, 37604.
Telephone: 615-928-0181.
Telecopier: 615-928-5694; 615-928-3654; Kingsport: 615-246-6191.
Washington, D.C. Office: Market Square, 801 Pennsylvania Avenue, N.W., 20004.
Telephone: 202-508-3400.
Telecopier: 202-508-3402.

PARTNERS

Lewis R. Donelson, III
Don C. Stansberry, Jr.
Howard H. Baker, Jr.
Ernest A. Petroff, III
Robert F. Worthington, Jr.
Stephen A. Marcum
P. Edward Pratt

ASSOCIATES

Mark E. Blakley

For full biographical listings, see the Martindale-Hubbell Law Directory

*JACKSON,** Madison Co.

MOSS, BENTON, WALLIS & PETTIGREW (AV)

325 North Parkway, P.O. Box 2103, 38302
Telephone: 901-668-5500
Telecopier: 901-664-2840

(See Next Column)

MEMBERS OF FIRM

William P. Moss (1897-1985)
Edwin E. Wallis, Jr.
George O. Benton
Charles R. Pettigrew
John R. Moss
W. Stanworth Harris

ASSOCIATES

Jon Mark Patey
C. Jerome Teel, Jr.

OF COUNSEL

William P. Moss, Jr.

Attorneys for: First American National Bank of Jackson; South Central Bell Telephone & Telegraph Co.; CSX Transportation, Inc.; The Equitable Life Assurance Society of the United States; Jackson Utility Division; Metropolitan Life Insurance Co.; United Services Automobile Assn.; Association of Tennessee Cola-Cola Bottlers; Central Distributors, Inc.; Combined Insurance Company of America.

For full biographical listings, see the Martindale-Hubbell Law Directory

RAINEY, KIZER, BUTLER, REVIERE & BELL (AV)

105 Highland Avenue South, P.O. Box 1147, 38302-1147
Telephone: 901-423-2414
Telecopier: 901-423-1386

MEMBERS OF FIRM

Thomas H. Rainey
John D. Burleson
Jerry D. Kizer, Jr.
Gregory D. Jordan
Clinton V. Butler, Jr.
Laura A. Williams
Russell E. Reviere
Clayton R. Sanders, Jr.
William C. Bell, Jr.
Robert O. Binkley, Jr.

ASSOCIATES

R. Dale Thomas
Marty R. Phillips
Deana C. Seymour
Stephen P. Miller
Mitchell Glenn Tollison
Clay M. McCormack
Charles C. Exum
Milton D. Conder, Jr.

Representative Clients: First Tennessee Bank, Jackson, Tennessee; CIGNA Insurance Co.; State Farm Mutual Automobile Insurance Co.; Auto-Owners Insurance Co.; USF&G; CNA Group; Royal Insurance Co.; Great American Insurance Co.; ITT-Hartford; Union Planters National Bank.

For full biographical listings, see the Martindale-Hubbell Law Directory

*JAMESTOWN,** Fentress Co.

NEAL, CRAVEN & ROMER (AV)

205 S. Norris Street, P.O. Box 797, 38556
Telephone: 615-879-8144
FAX: 615-879-8145

MEMBERS OF FIRM

Hollis A. Neal (Retired)
James P. Romer
William G. Craven
Stephen L. Rains

Representative Client: Fentress County Bank; Progressive Savings Bank, FSB; Estate of Bruno Gernt, Inc.
Approved Attorneys for: Lawyers Title Insurance Corp.; Fidelity National Title Insurance Co.; Farmers Home Administration; Plateau Title Services Inc.; First American Title Insurance Co.
References: Fentress County Bank; Progressive Savings Bank, FSB.

JEFFERSON CITY, Jefferson Co. — (Refer to Greeneville)

JOHNSON CITY, Washington Co.

BAKER, DONELSON, BEARMAN & CALDWELL (AV)

Hamilton Bank Building, 207 Mockingbird Lane, 37604
Telephone: 615-928-0181
Telecopier: 615-928-5694; 928-3654; Kingsport: 615-246-6191
Memphis, Tennessee Office: 20th Floor, First Tennessee Building, 165 Madison, 38103.
Telephone: 901-526-2000.
Telecopier: 901-577-2303.
Nashville, Tennessee Office: 1700 Nashville City Center, 511 Union Street, 37219.
Telephone: 615-726-5600.
Telecopier: 615-726-0464.
Knoxville, Tennessee Office: 2200 Riverview Tower, 900 Gay Street, 37901.
Telephone: 615-549-7000.
Telecopier: 615-525-8569.
Chattanooga, Tennessee Office: 1800 Republic Centre, 633 Chestnut Street, 37450-1800.
Telephone: 615-752-4400.
Telecopier: 615-752-4410.
Huntsville, Tennessee Office: 3 Courthouse Square, 37756.
Telephone: 615-663-2321.
Telecopier: 615-663-2111.
Washington, D.C. Office: Market Square, 801 Pennsylvania Avenue, N.W., 20004.
Telephone: 202-508-3400.
Telecopier: 202-508-3402.

(See Next Column)

BAKER, DONELSON, BEARMAN & CALDWELL—*Continued*

PARTNERS

Lewis R. Donelson, III
Howard H. Baker, Jr.
Robert F. Worthington, Jr.
Ed E. Williams, III
Gary C. Shockley
Melissa M. McGuire
Robert D. Van de Vuurst

ASSOCIATES

Ronald S. Range, Jr.
Van F. McClellan
Michael Merritt McKinney
Jack L. Mayfield
Steven H. Trent
Christopher J. Leonard

For full biographical listings, see the Martindale-Hubbell Law Directory

BRANDT & BEESON (AV)

206 Princeton Road, Suite 25, 37601
Telephone: 615-282-1981
Fax: 615-283-4778

MEMBERS OF FIRM

Frederic H. Brandt
D. R. Beeson, III

Representative Clients: Farm Credit Services; United Oil Marketers, Inc.; Johnson City Eye Clinic, P.C.; Medical Group, P.C.; Johnson City Housing Authority; Watauga Pathology, P.C.; Bolton Block, Inc.; Mountain Empire Radiology, P.C.; Thomas Construction Co.

For full biographical listings, see the Martindale-Hubbell Law Directory

LAW OFFICE OF EPPS AND EPPS (AV)

115 East Unaka Avenue, P.O. Drawer 2288, 37605-2288
Telephone: 615-928-7256
FAX: 615-928-0207

James H. Epps, III
James H. Epps, IV

For full biographical listings, see the Martindale-Hubbell Law Directory

HERNDON, COLEMAN, BRADING & MCKEE (AV)

104 East Main Street, P.O. Box 1160, 37605-1160
Telephone: 615-434-4700
Fax: 615-434-4738

MEMBERS OF FIRM

Charles T. Herndon III
J. Paul Coleman
James E. Brading II
Thomas C. McKee
Charles T. Herndon IV
Ronald W. Jenkins
H. Wayne Graves
J. Eddie Lauderback
Billie Jo Farthing

ASSOCIATES

James R. Wheeler

Assistant Division Counsel: Norfolk Southern Corporation.
Attorneys for: The Budd Co.; CNA Insurance; Travelers Insurance Co.; St. Paul Insurance Cos.; State Volunteer Mutual Insurance Co.; Aetna Life & Casualty; Kemper Insurance Group; Reliance Insurance Co.; CIGNA.

For full biographical listings, see the Martindale-Hubbell Law Directory

HERRIN & HERRIN (AV)

515 East Unaka Avenue, 37601
Telephone: 615-929-7113

MEMBERS OF FIRM

Kent Herrin
Erick Herrin

References: Home Federal Savings and Loan Association; Tri City Bank and Trust Co.

For full biographical listings, see the Martindale-Hubbell Law Directory

HUNTER, SMITH & DAVIS (AV)

Suite 500, First American Center, 208 Sunset Drive, 37604
Telephone: 615-283-6300
Telecopier: 615-283-6301
Kingsport, Tennessee Office: 1212 North Eastman Road, P. O. Box 3740.
Telephone: 615-378-8800.
Telecopier: 615-378-8801.

MEMBERS OF FIRM

George E. Penn, Jr. (1884-1954)
E. G. Hunter (1905-1957)
Ernest F. Smith (1897-1978)
Ben C. Davis (1911-1983)
Edwin O. Norris (1926-1994)
Edwin L. Treadway
S. Morris Hadden
T. Arthur Scott, Jr.
William C. Bovender
William T. Wray, Jr.
Douglas S. Tweed
William C. Argabrite
Jimmie Carpenter Miller
Mark S. Dessauer
Gregory K. Haden
Michael L. Forrester
T. Martin Browder, Jr.
Stephen M. Darden

ASSOCIATES

Edward Jennings Webb, Jr.
James N. L. Humphreys
Cynthia S. Kessler
Gary Dean Miller
John A. A. Bellamy
Rodney S. Klein
James E. Kaiser
K. Jeff Luethke
Julie Poe Bennett

(See Next Column)

COUNSEL

Shelburne Ferguson, Jr.
Thomas R. Wilson

LEGAL SUPPORT PERSONNEL

James R. Bowles (CPA; CFP)

Representative Clients: General Shale Products Corp.; Johnson City Medical Center; MiniFibers, Inc.; Land-o-Sun Dairies, Inc.; The Paty Co.; Moody Dunbar, Inc.; United Cities Gas Co.; First Tennessee Bank; Federated Insurance Companies.

For full biographical listings, see the Martindale-Hubbell Law Directory

JOHNSON, BOOZE & BURGESS (AV)

203 Broyles Drive, Suite 201, P.O. Box 3725 CRS, 37602
Telephone: 615-282-1781
Telecopier: 615-283-4139

MEMBERS OF FIRM

Dick L. Johnson
Earl R. Booze
Gwendolyn D. Burgess

Representative Clients: Harris-Tarkett, Inc.; Johnson City Chemical Co., Inc.; Dogwood Oil Co., Inc.; Elizabethan City Board of Education; Modern Forge of Tennessee; Kwick-Way Transportation Co.

For full biographical listings, see the Martindale-Hubbell Law Directory

RICHARD W. PECTOL, P.C. & ASSOCIATES (AV)

202 East Unaka Avenue, 37601
Telephone: 615-928-6106
Fax: 615-928-8802

Richard W. Pectol

Vincent A. Sikora

For full biographical listings, see the Martindale-Hubbell Law Directory

WELLER, MILLER, CARRIER, MILLER & HICKIE (AV)

160 West Springbrook Drive, P.O. Box 3217 Carroll Reece Station, 37601
Telephone: 615-282-1821
FAX: 615-283-4173

MEMBERS OF FIRM

Samuel B. Miller
Jack R. Carrier
Samuel B. Miller, II
Michael J. Hickie

Representative Clients: CNA Insurance Cos.; Coca-Cola Bottling Works; Columbus Electric Mfg. Co.; East Tennessee Natural Gas Co. (Pipeline); Hamilton Bank of Upper East Tennessee; Nationwide Insurance Co.; Pennsylvania National Mutual Insurance Cos.; TPI Corp.; USF & G Co.; Utica Mutual Insurance Co.

For full biographical listings, see the Martindale-Hubbell Law Directory

KINGSPORT, Sullivan Co.

HUNTER, SMITH & DAVIS (AV)

1212 North Eastman Road, P.O. Box 3740, 37664
Telephone: 615-378-8800;
Johnson City: 615-282-4186;
Bristol: 615-968-7604
Telecopier: 615-378-8801
Johnson City, Tennessee Office: Suite 500 First American Center, 208 Sunset Drive, 37604.
Telephone: 615-283-6300.
Telecopier: 615-283-6301.

MEMBERS OF FIRM

George E. Penn, Jr. (1884-1954)
E. G. Hunter (1905-1967)
Ernest F. Smith (1897-1978)
Ben C. Davis (1911-1983)
Edwin O. Norris (1926-1994)
Edwin L. Treadway
S. Morris Hadden
T. Arthur Scott, Jr.
William C. Bovender
William T. Wray, Jr.
Douglas S. Tweed
William C. Argabrite
Jimmie Carpenter Miller
Mark S. Dessauer
Gregory K. Haden
Michael L. Forrester
T. Martin Browder, Jr.
Stephen M. Darden

ASSOCIATES

Edward Jennings Webb, Jr.
James N. L. Humphreys
Cynthia S. Kessler
Gary Dean Miller
John A. A. Bellamy
Rodney S. Klein
James E. Kaiser
K. Jeff Luethke
Julie Poe Bennett

COUNSEL

Shelburne Ferguson, Jr.
Thomas R. Wilson

LEGAL SUPPORT PERSONNEL

James R. Bowles (CPA; CFP)

(See Next Column)

HUNTER, SMITH & DAVIS, *Kingsport—Continued*

PARALEGALS

Pam Talbott (Mineral Title Examiner-Paralegal)
Janet L. Snyder (Mineral Title Examiner-Paralegal)

Representative Clients: Kingsport Power Co. and Appalachian Power Co. (Subsidiaries of American Electric Power Co.); State Farm Insurance Co.; The Mead Corp.; United Telephone System-Southeast Group; Eastman Chemical Co.; Nationwide Insurance Co.; First American National Bank; Waste Management of North America; G.D. Searle & Co. (Searle Pharmaceuticals); Bristol Regional Medical Center.

For full biographical listings, see the Martindale-Hubbell Law Directory

MOORE, STOUT, WADDELL & LEDFORD (AV)

238 Broad Street, P.O. Box 1345, 37662
Telephone: 615-246-2344
Fax: 615-246-2210

MEMBERS OF FIRM

Frank K. Moore (1927-1987)
Dorman L. Stout
W. Gorman Waddell
J. Patrick Ledford
Robert Lane Arrington
William S. Lewis

ASSOCIATES

Douglas R. Pyne
Angela R. Kelley
Annette M. Konikiewicz

Representative Clients: Armstrong Construction Co., Inc.; Donihe Graphics, Inc.; First Tennessee Bank National Association; First Virginia Banks, Inc.; Kingsport Foundry & Manufacturing Corp.; Kingsport Housing Authority; Impact Plastics, Inc.; International Playing Card and Label Company Incorporated; State Farm Mutual Automobile Insurance Co.; The Industrial Development Board of the City of Kingsport, Tennessee.

For full biographical listings, see the Martindale-Hubbell Law Directory

SHINE & MASON LAW OFFICE (AV)

Suite 201, 433 East Center Street, 37660
Telephone: 615-246-8433
FAX: 615 247 2241
Washington, D.C. Office: Suite 200, 4427-A Wisconsin Avenue, N.W., 20016.
Telephone: 202-895-2699.

MEMBERS OF FIRM

D. Bruce Shine
Donald F. Mason, Jr.

Reference: Citizens Bank, Kingsport, TN.

For full biographical listings, see the Martindale-Hubbell Law Directory

WILSON, WORLEY, GAMBLE & WARD, P.C. (AV)

Fourth Floor Heritage Federal Building, 110 East Center Street, P.O. Box 1007, 37662-1007
Telephone: 615-246-8181
FAX: 615-246-2831

William T. Gamble
Donald G. Ward
Richard M. Currie, Jr.
Orren Taylor Pickard, Jr.
Frank A. Johnstone
Michael D. Stice
Katherine W. Singleton
Jo-Marie St. Martin
Russell W. Adkins
Cherie S. King
James W. Holmes

OF COUNSEL

Joe W. Worley

Assistant Division Counsel for: CSX Transportation, Inc.
Local Counsel for: Eastman Chemical Co.; General Motors Corp.; Holston Valley Hospital and Medical Center; United States Fidelity & Guaranty Co.; Eastman Credit Union; Heritage Federal Bank FSB; Vulcan Materials Co.; AFG Industries, Inc.; K mart Corporation.

For full biographical listings, see the Martindale-Hubbell Law Directory

*KINGSTON,** Roane Co. — (Refer to Knoxville)

*KNOXVILLE,** Knox Co.

ARNETT, DRAPER & HAGOOD (AV)

Suite 2300 Plaza Tower, 37929-2300
Telephone: 615-546-7000
Telecopier: 615-546-0423

MEMBERS OF FIRM

Foster D. Arnett
Jack B. Draper
Lewis R. Hagood
Thomas S. Scott, Jr.
William A. Simms
F. Michael Fitzpatrick
Rick L. Powers
Dan D. Rhea
Steven L. Hurdle
Thomas M. Cole
Johanna J. McGlothlin
Robert N. Townsend
R. Kim Burnette
John Steven Collins
Samuel C. Doak
Jeffrey L. Ingram
David Edward Long
W. Allen McDonald

(See Next Column)

Insurance Clients: Associated Aviation Underwriters; Crum & Forster Group; United States Aviation Underwriters; United States Fidelity & Guaranty Co.; General Accident Group.
Representative Clients: Blue Diamond Coal Co.; Fort Sanders Regional Medical Center; General Motors Corp.; Nissan Corp.; Phillips Petroleum Co.

For full biographical listings, see the Martindale-Hubbell Law Directory

BAKER, DONELSON, BEARMAN & CALDWELL (AV)

2200 Riverview Tower, 900 Gay Street, 37901
Telephone: 615-549-7000
Telecopier: 615-525-8569
Memphis, Tennessee Office: 20th Floor, First Tennessee Building, 165 Madison, 38103.
Telephone: 901-526-2000.
Telecopier: 901-577-2303.
Nashville, Tennessee Office: 1700 Nashville City Center, 511 Union Street, 37219.
Telephone: 615-726-5600.
Telecopier: 615-726-0464.
Chattanooga, Tennessee Office: 1800 Republic Centre, 633 Chestnut Street, 37450-1800.
Telephone: 615-752-4400.
Telecopier: 615-752-4410.
Huntsville, Tennessee Office: 3 Courthouse Square, 37756.
Telephone: 615-663-2321.
Telecopier: 615-663-2111.
Johnson City, Tennessee Office: Hamilton Bank Building, 207 Mockingbird Lane, 37604.
Telephone: 615-928-0181.
Telecopier: 615-928-5694; 615-928-3654; Kingsport: 615-246-6191.
Washington, D.C. Office: Market Square, 801 Pennsylvania Avenue, N.W., 20004.
Telephone: 202-508-3400.
Telecopier: 202-508-3402.

PARTNERS

Lewis R. Donelson, III
Howard H. Baker, Jr.
Robert F. Worthington, Jr.
Robert G. McCullough
Don C. Stansberry, Jr.
Nicholas A. Della Volpe
H. Wynne James, III
Courtney N. Pearre
James A. McIntosh
Stephen G. Anderson
John R. Barker (Not admitted in TN)
David E. Fielder
Edward A. Cox, Jr.
Daniel J. Moore
Stephen E. Roth

OF COUNSEL

Durward S. Jones
Frank Barnett
Paul T. Coleman

ASSOCIATES

Clarence Risin
Patti T. Cotten
Mary Dillard Miller
Nelwyn I. Rhodes
Melvin Joel Malone
Kelli L. Thompson
Melissa B. Isaacs
William Gregory Hall, Jr.

For full biographical listings, see the Martindale-Hubbell Law Directory

BAKER, MCREYNOLDS, BYRNE, BRACKETT, O'KANE & SHEA (AV)

11th Floor, 607 Market Street, P.O. Box 1708, 37901-1708
Telephone: 615-637-5600
Fax: 615-637-5608

MEMBERS OF FIRM

Harry T. Poore (1889-1956)
Taylor H. Cox (1903-1962)
J. W. Baker (1915-1991)
John W. Baker, Jr.
John A. McReynolds, Jr.
Arthur D. Byrne
Deke W. Brackett
James G. O'Kane, Jr.
James T. Shea, IV
Weldon E. Patterson
Elizabeth A. Townsend
Elizabeth M. Roy
Gerald L. Gulley, Jr.
Michael T. McClamroch

Representative Clients: CSX Transportation (Seaboard System Railroad); E.I. du Pont de Nemours & Co.; General Motors Corp.; Liberty Mutual Insurance Co.; Nationwide Mutual Insurance Co.; Amerisure Insurance Cos.; State Volunteer Insurance Co.; Kemper Insurance Group; Farmers Insurance Group; North American Van Lines.

For full biographical listings, see the Martindale-Hubbell Law Directory

BERNSTEIN, STAIR & MCADAMS (AV)

Suite 600, 530 South Gay Street, 37902
Telephone: 615-546-8030
Telecopier: 615-522-8879

MEMBERS OF FIRM

Bernard E. Bernstein
L. Caesar Stair III
Thomas N. McAdams
Doris C. Allen
J. Thomas Jones

ASSOCIATES

Celeste H. Herbert
James W. Parris
Robert Culver Schmid
Elizabeth K. Bacon Meadows
Kenneth M. Brown

(See Next Column)

BERNSTEIN, STAIR & MCADAMS—*Continued*

Representative Clients: Proffitt's Department Stores; Clayton Homes, Inc.; Whittle Communications L.P.; Plasti-Line, Inc.; ABB Flakt, Inc.; Modern Supply Co.; West Town Mall; Third National Bank of East Tennessee; First American National Bank; Union Planters National Bank.

For full biographical listings, see the Martindale-Hubbell Law Directory

BUTLER, VINES AND BABB (AV)

Suite 810, First American Center, P.O. Box 2649, 37901-2649
Telephone: 615-637-3531
Fax: 615-637-3385

MEMBERS OF FIRM

Warren Butler
William D. Vines, III
Dennis L. Babb
Martin L. Ellis
Ronald C. Koksal
James C. Wright
Bruce A. Anderson
Gregory Kevin Hardin
Steven Boyd Johnson
Edward U. Babb

ASSOCIATES

John W. Butler
Vonda M. Laughlin
Gregory F. Vines
Scarlett May

LEGAL SUPPORT PERSONNEL

PARALEGALS

Virginia H. Carver
Susie DeLozier
Dena K. Martin

Reference: First American Bank.

For full biographical listings, see the Martindale-Hubbell Law Directory

CARPENTER & O'CONNOR (AV)

1000 First American Center, P.O. Box 2485, 37901
Telephone: 615-546-1831
Fax: 615-546-0432

MEMBERS OF FIRM

Archie R. Carpenter
J. Gregory O'Connor
Robert A. Crawford
Charles F. Sterchi, III

ASSOCIATES

Louis A. McElroy, II
Christpher D. Heagerty

Representative Clients: Allstate Insurance Co.; CNA Insurance; St. Paul Fire & Marine Insurance Co.; State Farm Insurance Co.; Farmers Insurance Group; Coca Cola Co.; Food Lion; The Hyatt Corp.; The Kroger Co.; Levi Strauss & Co.

For full biographical listings, see the Martindale-Hubbell Law Directory

EGERTON, MCAFEE, ARMISTEAD & DAVIS, P.C. (AV)

500 First American National Bank Center, P.O. Box 2047, 37901
Telephone: 615-546-0500
Fax: 615-525-5293

M. W. Egerton (1897-1969)
Joseph A. McAfee (1903-1984)
William W. Davis
M. W. Egerton, Jr.
Joe M. McAfee
Lewis C. Foster, Jr.
William W. Davis, Jr.
Dan W. Holbrook
Herbert H. Slatery III
Barry K. Maxwell
Stephen A. McSween
William E. McClamroch, III

Jonathan D. Reed
Wesley L. Hatmaker

OF COUNSEL

John M. Armistead
Rockforde D. King

Representative Clients: First American National Bank of Knoxville; Home Federal Bank of Tennessee, F.S.B.; Bush Bros. & Co.; Johnson & Galyon Contractors; Baptist Hospital of East Tennessee; Revco D.S., Inc.; White Realty Corp.; Dick Broadcasting, Inc.

For full biographical listings, see the Martindale-Hubbell Law Directory

FRANTZ, MCCONNELL & SEYMOUR (AV)

Suite 500, 550 Main Avenue, 37902
Telephone: 615-546-9321
FAX: 615-637-5249

MEMBERS OF FIRM

John H. Frantz (1869-1933)
Charles M. Seymour (1882-1958)
Thomas G. McConnell (1883-1962)
Robert M. McConnell (1890-1971)
Harris M. Harton, Jr. (1906-1978)
John William Mills (1927-1977)
E. Bruce Foster (1910-1988)
Arthur G. Seymour
Fred H. Cagle, Jr.
Arthur G. Seymour, Jr.
Robert M. Bailey
Francis A. Cain
Robert L. Kahn
Reggie E. Keaton
Donald D. Howell
Charles M. Finn
Debra L. Fulton
Michael W. Ewell
Imogene Anderson King
John M. Lawhorn

(See Next Column)

ASSOCIATES

Jay E. Kohlbusch
N. David Roberts, Jr.
Lucy Dunn Hooper
James E. Wagner
Terrill L. Adkins

Counsel for: The Travelers Insurance Cos.; The Equitable Life Assurance Society of the United States; South Central Bell Telephone Co.; Palm Beach Co.; USX Corp.; ASARCO Incorporated; Coca Cola Bottlers Association; Texaco, Inc.; Aztex Energy Co.; Community Tectonics, Inc.; Norfolk Southern Corporation.

For full biographical listings, see the Martindale-Hubbell Law Directory

GENTRY, TIPTON, KIZER & LITTLE, P.C. (AV)

2610 Plaza Tower, 800 South Gay Street, 37929
Telephone: 615-525-5300
Telecopy: 615-523-7315

Mack A. Gentry
James S. Tipton, Jr.
W. Morris Kizer
Lawrence E. Little
Timothy M. McLemore
Mark Jendrek
Maurice K. Guinn
F. Scott Milligan

For full biographical listings, see the Martindale-Hubbell Law Directory

HODGES, DOUGHTY AND CARSON (AV)

617 Main Street, P.O. Box 869, 37901-0869
Telephone: 615-546-9611
Telecopier: 615-544-2014

MEMBERS OF FIRM

J. H. Hodges (1896-1983)
J. H. Doughty (1903-1987)
Richard L. Carson (1912-1980)
John P. Davis, Jr. (1923-1977)
Robert R. Campbell
David E. Smith
John W. Wheeler
Dalton L. Townsend
Douglas L. Dutton
William F. Alley, Jr.
Roy L. Aaron
Dean B. Farmer
David Wedekind
Julia Saunders Howard
Albert J. Harb
Edward G. White, II
Thomas H. Dickenson
J. William Coley
J. Michael Haynes
T. Kenan Smith
Wayne A. Kline

ASSOCIATES

James M. Cornelius, Jr.
W. Tyler Chastain

OF COUNSEL

Jonathan H. Burnett

Representative Clients: General Motors Corp.; Sears, Roebuck and Co.; Navistar International; Martin Marietta Energy Systems; Union Carbide Corp.; NationsBank of Tennessee; K-Mart Corporation; Aetna Life and Casualty Group; Fireman's Fund American Insurance Company; Safeco Insurance Group.

For full biographical listings, see the Martindale-Hubbell Law Directory

KENNERLY, MONTGOMERY & FINLEY, P.C. (AV)

Fourth Floor, NationsBank Center, 550 Main Avenue, P.O. Box 442, 37901-0442
Telephone: 615-546-7311
Fax: 615-524-1773

OF COUNSEL

Warren W. Kennerly

George D. Montgomery (1917-1985)
Robert A. Finley (1936-1990)
L. Anderson Galyon, III
Alexander M. Taylor
Jack M. Tallent, II
G. Wendell Thomas, Jr.
Ray J. Campbell, Jr. (1949-1986)
Steven E. Schmidt
Patti Jane Lay
Brian H. Trammell
C. Coulter Gilbert
Robert H. Green
William S. Lockett, Jr.
Rebecca Brake Murray
Robert Michael Shelor
James N. Gore, Jr.

SPECIAL COUNSEL

Jay Arthur Garrison

R. Hunter Cagle
Melody J. Bock
Rex A. Dale
Natasha K. Metcalf
Kenneth W. Ward
David Draper
James H. Price

Representative Clients: Knoxville Utilities Board; Aetna Casualty & Surety Co.; Allstate Insurance Co.; CNA Insurance Group; CIGNA Insurance; Nationwide Mutual Insurance Co.; Dow Chemical; Union Carbide; Westinghouse Electric Corp.; Mitsubishi International Corp.

For full biographical listings, see the Martindale-Hubbell Law Directory

Knoxville—Continued

Lewis, King, Krieg & Waldrop, P.C. (AV)

One Centre Square, 5th Floor, 620 Market Street, 37902
Telephone: 615-546-4646
Fax: 615-523-6529
Nashville, Tennessee Office: Third National Financial Center, 424 Church Street, Ninth Floor.
Telephone: 615-259-1366.
Fax: 615-259-1389.

Charles B. Lewis
John K. King
Richard W. Krieg
R. Loy Waldrop, Jr.
Ellis A. Sharp
Samuel W. Rutherford
Linda Jean Hamilton Mowles
Deborah C. Stevens
R. Dale Bay (Resident, Nashville Office)
M. Edward Owens, Jr.
H. Dennis Jarvis, Jr.
Harry P. Ogden
Reba Brown (Resident, Nashville Office)
Michael J. Mollenhour
Alan M. Parker
David L. Beck
Mary Jo Mann
Michael S. Pemberton
Leonard F. Pogue, III (Resident, Nashville Office)
David Nelson Garst

SPECIAL COUNSEL

Aaron Wyckoff (Resident, Nashville Office)
Lawrence F. Giordano
Tyree B. Harris IV (Resident, Nashville Office)

OF COUNSEL

Mary M. Farmer
Tyree B. Harris (Resident, Nashville Office)

Elma Elizabeth Rodgers
Patty K. Wheeler
R. Neal Mynatt (Resident, Nashville Office)
John R. Tarpley (Resident, Nashville Office)
Edwin H. Batts, III
Rodney A. Fields
David W. Tipton
Joseph Brent Nolan
Maria M. Salas (Resident, Nashville Office)
Lisa L. Ramsay
Charles W. Cagle (Resident, Nashville Office)
John J. Britton
J. Christopher Clem

Representative Clients: American International Group; Browning-Ferris Industries of Tennessee, Inc.; CMC Construction; Farmers Insurance Group; Federal Deposit Insurance Corporation; Hertz Corporation; Honda Motor Co., Ltd.; Interstate Mechanical Contractors; National Food Processors Association; Transamerica Insurance Group.

For full biographical listings, see the Martindale-Hubbell Law Directory

McCampbell & Young, A Professional Corporation (AV)

2021 Plaza Tower, P.O. Box 550, 37901-0550
Telephone: 615-637-1440
Telecopier: 615-546-9731

Herbert H. McCampbell, Jr. (1905-1974)
F. Graham Bartlett (1920-1982)
Robert S. Young
Lindsay Young
Robert S. Marquis
Robert S. Stone
J. Christopher Kirk
Mark K. Williams

Janie C. Porter
Gregory E. Erickson
R. Scott Elmore
Tammy Kaousias
Benét S. Theiss
Allen W. Blevins

For full biographical listings, see the Martindale-Hubbell Law Directory

Pryor, Flynn, Priest & Harber (AV)

Suite 600 Two Centre Square, 625 Gay Street, P.O. Box 870, 37901
Telephone: 615-522-4191
Telecopier: 615-522-0910

Robert E. Pryor
Frank L. Flynn, Jr.
Timothy A. Priest
John K. Harber

ASSOCIATES

Mark E. Floyd
Donald R. Coffey
M. Christopher Coffey

References: Third National Bank; First National Bank.

For full biographical listings, see the Martindale-Hubbell Law Directory

Wagner, Myers & Sanger, A Professional Corporation (AV)

1801 Plaza Tower, P.O. Box 1308, 37929
Telephone: 615-525-4600
Fax: 615-524-5731

Sam F. Fowler, Jr.
Herbert S. Sanger, Jr.
John R. Seymour
Charles W. Van Beke
Charles A. Wagner III
William C. Myers, Jr.
M. Douglas Campbell, Jr.

(See Next Column)

Joseph N. Clarke, Jr.
Ronald D. Garland
Robert E. Hyde
Barbara D. Boulton

Representative Clients: Carolina Power & Light Co.; Cullman Electric Cooperative; Diversified Energy, Inc.; Fort Sanders Health Systems; Gatliff Coal Company; Martin Marietta Energy Systems, Inc.; NorthAmerican Rayon Corp.; Regal Cinemas, Inc.; Roddy Vending; Skyline Coal Company.

For full biographical listings, see the Martindale-Hubbell Law Directory

Walker & Walker, P.C. (AV)

910 First American Center, P.O. Box 2774, 37901
Telephone: 615-523-0700
Telecopier: 615-523-4990

John A. Walker, Jr.
Mary C. Walker

For full biographical listings, see the Martindale-Hubbell Law Directory

*LAWRENCEBURG,** Lawrence Co. — (Refer to Columbia)

*LEBANON,** Wilson Co. — (Refer to Nashville)

*LEWISBURG,** Marshall Co. — (Refer to Shelbyville)

*LEXINGTON,** Henderson Co. — (Refer to Jackson)

*LIVINGSTON,** Overton Co. — (Refer to Oak Ridge)

*LOUDON,** Loudon Co. — (Refer to Madisonville)

*MADISONVILLE,** Monroe Co. — (Refer to Athens)

*MARYVILLE,** Blount Co.

Kizer and Black (AV)

329 Cates Street, 37801
Telephone: 615-982-7650
Fax: 615-982-5776

MEMBERS OF FIRM

David T. Black
Martha S. L. Black
Jerry G. Cunningham
John T. McArthur
J. Kevin Renfro
C. Edwin Shoemaker

For full biographical listings, see the Martindale-Hubbell Law Directory

*MCMINNVILLE,** Warren Co.

Galligan & Newman (AV)

308 West Main Street, P.O. Box 289, 37110
Telephone: 615-473-8405
Fax: 615-473-1888

MEMBERS OF FIRM

Michael D. Galligan
Robert W. Newman

Reference: City Bank & Trust Co.

For full biographical listings, see the Martindale-Hubbell Law Directory

*MEMPHIS,** Shelby Co.

Armstrong Allen Prewitt Gentry Johnston & Holmes (AV)

80 Monroe Avenue Suite 700, 38103
Telephone: 901-523-8211
Telecopier: 901-524-4936
Jackson, Missippi Office: 1350 One Jackson Place, 188 East Capitol Street.
Telephone: 601-948-8020.
Telecopier: 601-948-8389.

MEMBERS OF FIRM

Walter Preston Armstrong (1884-1949)
John Edward McCadden (1885-1964)
James Seddon Allen (1885-1970)
Emmett W. Braden (1901-1984)
Benjamin Goodman (1904-1994)
Newton P. Allen
Thomas R. Prewitt
Richard H. Allen
Gavin M. Gentry
Thomas F. Johnston
Elmore Holmes, III
Wm. Rowlett Scott
J. Edward Wise
Edward M. Kaplan
Carl H. Langschmidt, Jr.
Joseph Brent Walker
Thomas R. Prewitt, Jr.
Prince C. Chambliss, Jr.
Thomas W. Bell, Jr.
Paul A. Matthews
S. Russell Headrick
Randall D. Noel
William A. Carson, II
Mark S. Norris
James Rogers Hall, Jr.
Ellen Morris Davis (Resident, Jackson, Mississippi Office)
James B. McLaren, Jr.
Paul E. Prather
Teresa J. Sigmon
Charles R. Crawford
David A. Thornton
Stephen P. Hale
Lucian T. Pera
Nathaniel L. Prosser
John W. Simmons

COUNSEL

Walter P. Armstrong, Jr.

(See Next Column)

ARMSTRONG ALLEN PREWITT GENTRY JOHNSTON & HOLMES—*Continued*

Theodore E. Mackall, Jr.
Robertson M. Leatherman, Jr.
Cannon F. Allen
H. Tucker Dewey
Sidney W. Farnsworth, III
Steven W. Likens
Heber S. Simmons III (Resident, Jackson, Mississippi Office)
Renee Eva Mumford Greer
Richard R. Roberts
Martha M. Curley
John S. Golwen
Timothy G. Wehner
Kathy Laughter Laizure
R. Jeffery Kelsey
Stephanie L. Ganucheau (Resident Jackson, Mississippi Office)
Jennifer Ziegenhorn
J. Christopher Couch

For full biographical listings, see the Martindale-Hubbell Law Directory

BAKER, DONELSON, BEARMAN & CALDWELL (AV)

20th Floor, First Tennessee Building, 165 Madison, 38103
Telephone: 901-526-2000
Telecopier: 901-577-2303
Nashville, Tennessee Office: 1700 Nashville City Center, 511 Union Street, 37219.
Telephone: 615-726-5600.
Telecopier: 615-726-0464.
Knoxville, Tennessee Office: 2200 Riverview Tower, 900 Gay Street, 37901.
Telephone: 615-549-7000.
Telecopier: 615-525-8569.
Chattanooga, Tennessee Office: 1800 Republic Centre, 633 Chestnut Street, 37450-1800.
Telephone: 615-752-4400.
Telecopier: 615-752-4410.
Huntsville, Tennessee Office: 3 Courthouse Square, 37756.
Telephone: 615-663-2321.
Telecopier: 615-663-2111.
Johnson City, Tennessee Office: Hamilton Bank Building, 207 Mockingbird Lane, 37604.
Telephone: 615-928-0181.
Telecopier: 615-928-5694; 615-928-3654; Kingsport: 615-246-6191.
Washington, D.C. Office: Market Square, 801 Pennsylvania Avenue, N.W., 20004.
Telephone: 202-508-3400.
Telecopier: 202-508-3402.

PARTNERS

Lewis R. Donelson, III
Roy Keathley
David G. Williams
Donald A. Malmo
Leo Bearman, Jr.
Maurice Wexler
Stephen H. Biller
Michael F. Pleasants
Robert Walker
Boyd L. Rhodes, Jr.
John C. Speer
W. Michael Richards
Grady M. Garrison
Charles T. Tuggle, Jr.
Samuel H. Mays, Jr.
Larry E. Killebrew
Jerry Stauffer
Daniel B. Hatzenbuehler
Robert C. Liddon
William H.D. Fones, Jr.
William P. Kenworthy
Allan J. Wade
Henry P. Doggrell
Gregory G. Fletcher
Stephen D. Wakefield
Charles C. Harrell
Stephen D. Goodwin
Charles G. Walker
Robert Mark Glover
George T. Lewis, III
Harris Patton Quinn
Ben C. Adams, Jr.
G. Robert Morris
Eugene J. Podesta, Jr.
Sam B. Blair, Jr.
Carla Peacher-Ryan
Sheila Jordan Cunningham
John R. Branson
Mary Aronov
Linda M. Crouch
Jill M. Steinberg
Michael C. Patton
Scott K. Haight
David T. Popwell
John A. Good

OF COUNSEL

Robert M. Burton
Frierson M. Graves, Jr.
Ernest Williams, III

ASSOCIATES

Earl C. Buckles, Jr.
John R. Gregory
Ruth A. Hillis
Desiree M. Franklin
William B. Clemmons, Jr.
Janis M. Wild
Stephen William Ragland
Monique A. Nassar
Nora L. Liggett
Bradley E. Trammell
Elizabeth Einstman Chance
Charles F. Morrow
Edward M. Bearman
R. Alan Pritchard, Jr.
Robbin T. Sarrazin
Carl L. Sollee (Not admitted in TN)
Anthony N. Creasy
Sean M. Haynes
Hollie A. Smith
Paul V. Rost
W. Douglas Sweet
Anthony B. Norris
Robert J. DelPriore
Thad M. Barnes
Carrie Goldsby Tolbert
Robert B. Carter
James W. Curry, Jr.
William Scott Young

CHATTANOOGA OFFICE
PARTNERS

Lewis R. Donelson, III
Thomas A. Caldwell
John C. Mooney
Thomas O. Helton
Richard B. Gossett
David C. Burger
Carl E. Hartley
Susan Elliott Rich
C. George Caudle
Virginia C. Love

(See Next Column)

CHATTANOOGA OFFICE
PARTNERS (Continued)

Richard J. McAfee
James R. McKoon
Louann Prater Smith
Kenneth C. Beckman
Randall L. Gibson
Joe A. Conner
Julie Williams Watson
Jeffery A. Billings

OF COUNSEL

Hunter D. Heggie

ASSOCIATES

Deborah S. Humble
Timothy R. Simonds
Bob E. Lype
Mark D. Hackett
Charles D. McDonald
Matthew P. Huggins
Stephen L. Page

HUNTSVILLE OFFICE
PARTNERS

Lewis R. Donelson, III
Howard H. Baker, Jr.
Robert F. Worthington, Jr.
Don C. Stansberry, Jr.
Ernest A. Petroff, III
Stephen A. Marcum
P. Edward Pratt

ASSOCIATES

Mark E. Blakley

JOHNSON CITY OFFICE
PARTNERS

Lewis R. Donelson, III
Howard H. Baker, Jr.
Robert F. Worthington, Jr.
Ed E. Williams, III
Gary C. Shockley
Melissa M. McGuire
Robert D. Van de Vuurst

ASSOCIATES

Ronald S. Range, Jr.
Van F. McClellan
Michael Merritt McKinney
Jack L. Mayfield
Steven H. Trent
Christopher J. Leonard

KNOXVILLE OFFICE
PARTNERS

Lewis R. Donelson, III
Howard H. Baker, Jr.
Robert F. Worthington, Jr.
Robert G. McCullough
Don C. Stansberry, Jr.
Nicholas A. Della Volpe
H. Wynne James, III
Courtney N. Pearre
James A. McIntosh
Stephen G. Anderson
John R. Barker
David E. Fielder
Edward A. Cox, Jr.
Daniel J. Moore
Stephen E. Roth

OF COUNSEL

Durward S. Jones
Frank Barnett
Paul T. Coleman

ASSOCIATES

Clarence Risin
Patti T. Cotten
Mary Dillard Miller
Nelwyn I. Rhodes
Melvin Joel Malone
Kelli L. Thompson
Melissa B. Isaacs
William Gregory Hall, Jr.

NASHVILLE OFFICE
PARTNERS

Lewis R. Donelson, III
Howard H. Baker, Jr.
Maclin P. Davis, Jr.
Robert F. Worthington, Jr.
Robert G. McCullough
Richard D. Bird
Don C. Stansberry, Jr.
William Hume Barr
James T. O'Hare
Robert L. Baker
Robert G. McDowell
Rodger B. Kesley
James L. Beckner
Ed E. Williams, III
H. Wynne James, III
John A. Gupton, III
Claudia W. Dickerson
David C. Andrew
James A. DeLanis
Kenneth P. Ezell, Jr.
James L. McElroy
Douglas A. Walker
John Randolph Bibb, Jr.
H. Buckley Cole
Robert M. Steele
Anthony M. Iannacio
Gary C. Shockley
Randal S. Mashburn
Katherine A. Brown
Steven J. Eisen
Vance L. Broemel
Keith D. Frazier
David J. Hill

OF COUNSEL

Robert L. Crossley
L. H. (Bill) Armistead, III
Colman B. Hoffman
John S. Hicks

ASSOCIATES

Susan Duvier Bass
Matthew Thompson Harris
Peter T. Dirksen
Kelly R. Duggan
Barbara A. Rose
Fred Russell Harwell
James David Nave
Philip Stuart McSween
Frank A. Coyle
Clisby Hall Barrow
Jeffrey A. Calk
Scott D. Carey
Darwin A. Hindman III
Ann D. Jarvis
John W. McCullough

WASHINGTON, D.C. OFFICE
PARTNERS

Lewis R. Donelson, III
Howard H. Baker, Jr.
Robert F. Worthington, Jr.
Robert G. McCullough
Don C. Stansberry, Jr.
James W. McBride
Thomas L. Howard (Resident)
Ed E. Williams, III
George Cranwell Montgomery
Edward R. Hamberger (Resident)
David C. Andrew

(See Next Column)

BAKER, DONELSON, BEARMAN & CALDWELL, *Memphis—Continued*

WASHINGTON, D.C. OFFICE
PARTNERS (Continued)

W. Lee Rawls
Joan M. McEntee
Robert M. Steele
Anne M. Stolee
Charles Bradford Mathias

OF COUNSEL

William K. Coulter
Charles Richard Johnston, Jr.
Doreen M. Edelman

ASSOCIATES

Kevin Darrow Jones

For full biographical listings, see the Martindale-Hubbell Law Directory

BATEMAN & CHILDERS (AV)

Suite 1010 Cotton Exchange Building, 65 Union Avenue, P.O. Box 3351, 38173-0351
Telephone: 901-526-0412
Telecopier: (901) 525-8466

MEMBERS OF FIRM

William C. Bateman, Jr.
Jack Alford Childers, Jr.

ASSOCIATES

Ricky Dolan Click
Rhonda M. Bradley
David W. Hawkins

OF COUNSEL

J. Logan Sharp

For full biographical listings, see the Martindale-Hubbell Law Directory

EUGENE BERNSTEIN, SR. (AV)

5050 Poplar, Suite 2410, 38157
Telephone: 901-684-1652
Telecopier: 901-761-5505

For full biographical listings, see the Martindale-Hubbell Law Directory

THE BOGATIN LAW FIRM (AV)

A Partnership including Professional Corporations
(Formerly Bogatin Lawson & Chiapella)
860 Ridge Lake Boulevard, Suite 360, 38120
Telephone: 901-767-1234
Telecopier: 901-767-2803 & 901-767-4010

MEMBERS OF FIRM

G. Patrick Arnoult
Irvin Bogatin (P.C.)
H. Stephen Brown
Susan Callison (P.C.)
Tillman C. Carroll
Matthew P. Cavitch
John André Chiapella (P.C.)
David J. Cocke
Russell J. Hensley
Arlie C. Hooper
Charles M. Key
William H. Lawson, Jr., (P.C.)
David C. Porteous
Arthur E. Quinn
Thaddeus S. Rodda, Jr., (P.C.)

ASSOCIATES

Robert F. Beckmann
James Q. Carr, II
C. William Denton, Jr.
Thomas M. Federico (Not admitted in TN)
James S. King
John F. Murrah

For full biographical listings, see the Martindale-Hubbell Law Directory

BOROD & KRAMER, P.C. (AV)

Brinkley Plaza, 80 Monroe Avenue, 5th Floor, P.O. Box 3504, 38173-0504
Telephone: 901-524-0200
Telecopier: 901-524-0242

Marx J. Borod
Bruce S. Kramer

Sharon Lee Petty
Jeffery D. Parrish

For full biographical listings, see the Martindale-Hubbell Law Directory

BOURLAND, HEFLIN, ALVAREZ, HOLLEY & MINOR (AV)

Suite 100, 5400 Poplar Avenue, 38119
Telephone: 901-683-3526
Telecopier: 901-763-1037

MEMBERS OF FIRM

Donald E. Bourland
Robert K. Alvarez
John J. Heflin, III
R. Layne Holley
Lancelot Longstreet Minor, III

ASSOCIATES

Alex C. Elder
David M. Waldrop

OF COUNSEL

Albert C. Rickey
Aaron Shankman
George G. Leavell

For full biographical listings, see the Martindale-Hubbell Law Directory

BURCH, PORTER & JOHNSON (AV)

130 North Court Avenue, 38103
Telephone: 901-523-2311
Telecopy: 901-523-7140
Other Memphis, Tennessee Office: 50 North Front Street, Suite 650, 38103.
Telephone: 901-527-2311.

MEMBERS OF FIRM

Charles N. Burch (1868-1938)
H. D. Minor (1868-1947)
Clinton H. McKay (1889-1943)
Jesse E. Johnson, Jr. (1913-1980)
John S. Porter (1909-1990)
Lucius E. Burch, Jr.
Joel H. Porter
Charles Forrest Newman
W. J. Michael Cody
C. Thomas Cates
Joe M. Duncan
John A. Stemmler
J. Brook Lathram
Jef Feibelman
DeWitt M. Shy, Jr.
R. Michael Potter
John W. Chandler, Jr.
David J. Harris
Warner B. Rodda
David H. Lillard, Jr.
Holly K. Lillard
Sam L. Crain, Jr.
Nathan A. Bicks
Stephen D. Crawley
Laurel C. Williams

ASSOCIATES

Lisa A. Krupicka
LeeAnne M. Cox
Richard R. Spore, III
Beth Weems Bradley
Kathryn E. Story
William Lester Jones, Jr.
Ricky E. Wilkins
Melissa Ann Maravich
Reva M. Kriegel
Susan Clark Taylor
John W. Campbell
Roscoe Porter Feild
Douglas F. Halijan (Not admitted in TN)

For full biographical listings, see the Martindale-Hubbell Law Directory

CAUSEY, CAYWOOD, TAYLOR & MCMANUS (AV)

Suite 2400, 100 North Main Building, 38103
Telephone: 901-526-0206
Telecopier: 901-525-1540

MEMBERS OF FIRM

James D. Causey
David E. Caywood
Daniel Loyd Taylor
John E. McManus
Darrell D. Blanton
Craid B. Flood
Jean E. Markowitz
Amy R. Fulton
Marc E. Reisman
James H. Taylor III
David Shepherd Walker

For full biographical listings, see the Martindale-Hubbell Law Directory

CRISLIP, PHILIP & ASSOCIATES (AV)

Jefferson Plaza Building, Suite 300, 147 Jefferson Avenue, 38103
Telephone: 901-525-2427
Fax: 901-521-9306

MEMBERS OF FIRM

James A. Crislip
John B. Philip

ASSOCIATES

G. Gregory Voehringer

For full biographical listings, see the Martindale-Hubbell Law Directory

EVANS & PETREE (AV)

81 Monroe Avenue, 38103
Telephone: 901-525-6781
Telecopier: 901-521-0681; 526-0336

MEMBERS OF FIRM

Marion G. Evans (1877-1957)
Jack Petree (1921-1973)
Charles Pittman Cobb (Retired)
Elwood L. Edwards (Retired)
W. Lytle Nichol IV
John W. McQuiston II
Ernest G. Kelly, Jr.
Alan E. Glenn
Michael C. Williams
Joseph W. Barnwell, Jr.
David C. Scruggs
Leonard C. Dunavant, Jr.
E. Woods Weathersby
Henry C. Shelton III
C. Bradford Foster III
William L. Gibbons
Andrew H. Raines
Bruce M. Kahn
Frank N. Carney
P. Preston Wilson, Jr.
Paul F. T. Edwards
Patricia K. Horton
Percy H. Harvey
Katharine A. Jungkind
Michael R. Marshall
Caren Beth Fogelman

For full biographical listings, see the Martindale-Hubbell Law Directory

FARRIS, HANCOCK, GILMAN, BRANAN & HELLEN (AV)

50 North Front Street, Suite 1400, 38103
Telephone: 901-576-8200
Fax: 901-576-8250
East Memphis, Tennessee Office: Suite 400 United American Bank Building, 5384 Poplar Avenue.
Telephone: 901-763-4000.
Fax: 901-763-4095.

(See Next Column)

FARRIS, HANCOCK, GILMAN, BRANAN & HELLEN—*Continued*

MEMBERS OF FIRM

William W. Farris
Ronald Lee Gilman
Homer B. Branan, III
Tim Wade Hellen
Edwin Dean White, III
Charles B. Welch, Jr.
G. Ray Bratton
John M. Farris
O. Douglas Shipman, III
D. Edward Harvey
Rebecca P. Tuttle
Eugene Stone Forrester, Jr.

ASSOCIATES

G. Coble Caperton
Dedrick Brittenum, Jr.
Richard Stanfill Copeland
Barry F. White
Paul E. Perry
Bryan K. Smith
Gregory W. O'Neal
Steven Caines Brammer
Richard J. Myers

OF COUNSEL

Henry H. Hancock

For full biographical listings, see the Martindale-Hubbell Law Directory

GLANKLER BROWN (AV)

Suite 1700, One Commerce Square, 38103
Telephone: 901-525-1322
Telecopier: 901-525-2389
Other Memphis, Tennessee Office: Suite 200, 6000 Poplar Avenue.
Telephone: 901-685-1322.
Telecopier: 901-761-2454.

MEMBERS OF FIRM

Phil M. Canale (Deceased, February 2, 1952)
Frank Joseph Glankler (Deceased, January 3, 1954)
John William Loch (Deceased, March 6, 1963)
John Randolph Gilliland (Deceased, July 5, 1969)
Charles H. Davis (Deceased, September 22, 1976)
John M. Heiskell (Deceased, October 14, 1976)
Frank J. Glankler, Jr.
Robert Grattan Brown, Jr.
Lee James Chase, III
Michael A. Robinson
J. N. Raines
C. Barry Ward
Laurence D. Conn
John I. Houseal, Jr.
King W. Rogers
Oscar C. Carr, III
R. Hunter Humphreys
William Thomas Newton
J. Mark Griffee
George J. Nassar, Jr.
Steven H. McCleskey
Lynn Bledsoe Buhler
Randall B. Womack
J. William Pierce, Jr.
Michael E. Hewgley
William R. Bradley, Jr.
Lynn A. Gardner
Cecil C. Humphreys, Jr.
Donald E. Smart
Paul R. Lawler
William L. Hendricks, Jr.
Paul B. Billings, Jr.
Robert A. Udelsohn
John David Blaylock

OF COUNSEL

John S. Montedonico

ASSOCIATES

William L. Bomar
Jeffery A. Jarratt
Carolyn J. Chumney
Elizabeth Gardner Rudolph
James S. Strickland, Jr.
Tammy L. Irons
Sussan P. Harshbarger
Mindy Okeon Sorin
Paul J. Posey, Jr.
Robert Louis Hutton
Caldwell D. Lowrance, Jr.
Milton E. Magee, Jr.
Kenneth S. Schrupp
Elizabeth M. Cashman
Daniel F. Johnson
Stewart G. Austin, Jr.
Jason P. Hood

For full biographical listings, see the Martindale-Hubbell Law Directory

GOODMAN, GLAZER, GREENER & KREMER, P.C. (AV)

1500 First Tennessee Building, 165 Madison Avenue, 38103-0001
Telephone: 901-525-4466
Telecopier: 901-525-4714
Cable Address: "Goodman"
Marco Island, Florida Office: 950 North Collier Boulevard, Suite 400. 33937.
Telephone: 813-642-4500.
Fax: 813-642-0718.
Naples, Florida: Pelican Bay, 800 Laurel Oak Drive, Suite 200. 33963.
Telephone: 813-594-5159.
Fax: 813-642-0718.

William W. Goodman (1900-1981)
Morris L. Strauch (1909-Retired 1988)
Herbert Glazer
Eugene Greener, Jr.
Richard H. Kremer
Harriette R. Coleman

OF COUNSEL

B. Percy Magness

For full biographical listings, see the Martindale-Hubbell Law Directory

HANOVER, WALSH, JALENAK & BLAIR (AV)

Fifth Floor - Falls Building, 22 North Front Street, 38103-2109
Telephone: 901-526-0621
Telecopier: 901-521-9759

(See Next Column)

MEMBERS OF FIRM

Joseph Hanover (1888-1984)
David Hanover (1899-1963)
Jay Alan Hanover
William M. Walsh
James B. Jalenak
Allen S. Blair
Michael E. Goldstein
Edward J. McKenney, Jr.
James R. Newsom, III
John Kevin Walsh
James A. Johnson, Jr.
Donald S. Holm III
Barbara B. Lapides

Jennifer A. Sevier
Christina von Cannon Burdette
Jeffrey S. Rosenblum

OF COUNSEL

Helyn L. Keith

For full biographical listings, see the Martindale-Hubbell Law Directory

HARKAVY, SHAINBERG, KOSTEN & PINSTEIN (AV)

Oak Court Office Building, 530 Oak Court Drive, Suite 350, P.O. Box 241450, 38124-1450
Telephone: 901-761-1263
Telecopier: 901-763-3340

MEMBERS AND ASSOCIATES

Ronald M. Harkavy
Raymond M. Shainberg
Alan L. Kosten
Robert J. Pinstein
Michael D. Kaplan
Allen C. Dunstan
Neil Harkavy
Laurie A. Cooper
Jerome A. Broadhurst
Dixie White Ishee
Alan M. Harkavy

OF COUNSEL

Ira D. Pruitt, Jr.

For full biographical listings, see the Martindale-Hubbell Law Directory

HARRIS, SHELTON, DUNLAP AND COBB (AV)

Suite 2700, One Commerce Square, 38103
Telephone: 901-525-1455
Telecopier: 901-526-4084

MEMBERS OF FIRM

Walter Chandler (1887-1967)
John H. Harris, Jr.
Max Shelton
William W. Dunlap, Jr.
M. Anderson Cobb, Jr.
James L. Kirby
James R. Garts, Jr.
George T. Wheeler, Jr.
Charles C. Drennon, III
Michael F. Rafferty
James D. Wilson

ASSOCIATES

G. Rice Byars, Jr.
Barbara S. Gardner
Jonathan E. Scharff
W. Marshall Pearson
Thomas L. McAllister
Carol Johnson Magee

OF COUNSEL

A. J. Cook

For full biographical listings, see the Martindale-Hubbell Law Directory

HUMPHREYS DUNLAP WELLFORD ACUFF & STANTON, A PROFESSIONAL CORPORATION (AV)

Suite 2200 First Tennessee Building, 165 Madison Avenue, 38103
Telephone: 901-523-8088
Telecopier: 901-523-8261

J. Fraser Humphreys, Jr.
John R. Dunlap
Alexander W. Wellford, Jr.
Fred M. Acuff, Jr.
G. Russell Stanton, Jr.
Fred M. Ridolphi, Jr.
Thomas H. Fulton
Carole Jennings Freeburg
David M. Dunlap
J. Fraser Humphreys, III
Michael P. Coury
David L. Simpson, IV

COUNSEL

E. Brady Bartusch

For full biographical listings, see the Martindale-Hubbell Law Directory

JOHNSON, GRUSIN, KEE & SURPRISE, P.C. (AV)

780 Ridge Lake Boulevard, Suite 202, 38120
Telephone: 901-682-3450
Fax: 901-682-3590

David J. Johnson
Martin A. Grusin
James H. Kee
James W. Surprise
Robert A. Corrington

OF COUNSEL

Carl N. Stokes

For full biographical listings, see the Martindale-Hubbell Law Directory

KRIVCHER, MAGIDS, NEAL, COTTAM & CAMPBELL, P.C. (AV)

Suite 2929 Clark Tower, 5100 Poplar Avenue, 38137
Telephone: 901-682-6431
Telecopier: 901-682-6453

(See Next Column)

KRIVCHER, MAGIDS, NEAL, COTTAM & CAMPBELL P.C., *Memphis—Continued*

Robert R. Krivcher (1920-1991)
Jack Steven Magids
Michael B. Neal
Charles C. Cottam
L. Don Campbell, Jr.
Jennie D. Latta
Shawn Alexander Tidwell

For full biographical listings, see the Martindale-Hubbell Law Directory

MARTIN, TATE, MORROW & MARSTON, P.C. (AV)

The Falls Building, Suite 1100, 22 North Front Street, 38103-1182
Telephone: 901-522-9000
Telecopier: 901-527-3746

John D. Martin, Jr. (1910-1984)
George E. Morrow (1922-1982)
S. Shepherd Tate
W. Emmett Marston
James C. Warner
Lee L. Piovarcy
W. Thomas Hutton
David Wade
Lee Welch
Jeffrey E. Thompson
William Joseph Landers, II
Shepherd D. Tate
Clare Shields
Elizabeth Marston-Moore
Robert E. Orians
Harry J. Skefos
J. Philip Jones
Richard M. Carter
W. Price Morrison, Jr.
Ron W. McAfee

C. Lee Cagle
Scott Thomas Beall
David M. Rudolph
John Anthony Williamson
Christopher G. Lazarini
E. Cayce Wright
Eugene E. Tibbs, Jr.

For full biographical listings, see the Martindale-Hubbell Law Directory

McDONALD KUHN (AV)

80 Monroe Avenue, Suite 550, P.O. Box 3160, 38173-0160
Telephone: 901-526-0606
Fax: 901-521-8397

MEMBERS OF FIRM

W. Percy McDonald (1890-1969)
W. Percy McDonald, Jr. (1921-1967)
Braxton C. Gandy (1915-1979)
Edward W. Kuhn (1904-1983)
Henry T. V. Miller
J. Minor Tait, Jr.
Dale H. Tuttle
William A. Lucchesi
Carol A. Mills

ASSOCIATES

Richard H. Booth
Mariann Tait

OF COUNSEL

Edward P. A. Smith
Crawford McDonald

For full biographical listings, see the Martindale-Hubbell Law Directory

ROSSIE, BETHEA, LUCKETT, PARKER & LAUGHLIN, P.C. (AV)

675 Oakleaf Office Lane, Suite 200, 38117-4863
Telephone: 901-763-1800
Telecopier: 901-767-6514

J. Richard Rossie
Richard T. D. Bethea
William O. Luckett, Jr.
John H. Parker
Harry W. Laughlin, III

COUNSEL

Luckett Law Firm, P.A., , Clarksdale, Mississippi

For full biographical listings, see the Martindale-Hubbell Law Directory

THOMASON, HENDRIX, HARVEY, JOHNSON & MITCHELL (AV)

Twenty-Ninth Floor, One Commerce Square, 38103
Telephone: 901-525-8721
Telecopier: 901-525-6722

MEMBERS OF FIRM

John J. Thomason
Roy W. Hendrix, Jr.
Albert C. Harvey
J. Kimbrough Johnson
Jerry E. Mitchell
William H. Haltom, Jr.
James E. Conley, Jr.
Michael G. McLaren
Kemper B. Durand
Stephen W. Vescovo
Buckner Potts Wellford
Cheryl Rumage Estes
Robert L. Moore
Michael L. Robb
J. Martin Regan, Jr.

ASSOCIATES

Steven B. Crain
Lee Mitchell Glasgow
Elizabeth Tansil Collins
Stephen C. Barton
Christopher L. Vescovo
John W. Rodgers
Rebecca Adelman
John H. Dotson
Michael E. Keeney
Lara Butler Fonville
Warwick F. M. Spencer
Robert B. Gaia

Lloyd S. Adams, Jr. (Retired)
Jerred Blanchard (Retired)

For full biographical listings, see the Martindale-Hubbell Law Directory

WARING COX (AV)

Morgan Keegan Tower, 50 North Front Street, Suite 1300, 38103-1190
Telephone: 901-543-8000
Telecopy: 901-543-8030

MEMBERS OF FIRM

Roane Waring (1881-1958)
Sam P. Walker (1880-1957)
Allen Cox, Jr. (1902-1982)
Robert L. Cox
Jerald H. Sklar
Louis F. Allen
Frank L. Watson, Jr.
Samuel D. Chafetz
B. Douglas Earthman
John E. Kruger
Saul C. Belz
William E. Frulla
Robert S. Kirk, Jr.
Clayton D. Smith
James J. McMahon
Shellie G. McCain, Jr.
Ellen Bronaugh Vergos
Louis J. Miller
Charles W. Hill
Douglas P. Quay
Paul D. Amos
Earle J. Schwarz
Herbert B. Wolf, Jr.
David J. Sneed
William T. Mays, Jr.
Matthew S. Heiter

ASSOCIATES

Sara A. Benin
Laurie M. Maddox
Robert C. Starnes
Cynthia G. Bennett
Robert B.C. Hale
Michael B. Chance
Thomas L. Parker
Jay H. Lindy
Jennifer W. Sammons
Frank L. Watson, III
Cynthia J. Tobin
Dorothy Sanders Wells

SPECIAL COUNSEL

W. Clary Lunsford

OF COUNSEL

Roane Waring, Jr.
James M. Manire

Representative Clients: Federal Express Corp.; South Central Bell Telephone Co.; Delta Life and Annuity; Miles, Inc.; Underwriters at Lloyd's; United States Fidelity and Guaranty Co.; Vining-Sparks IBG; Flavorite Laboratories, Inc.; Perkins Family Restaurants.

For full biographical listings, see the Martindale-Hubbell Law Directory

WEINTRAUB, ROBINSON, WEINTRAUB, STOCK & BENNETT, P.C. (AV)

Suite 2560 One Commerce Square, 38103
Telephone: 901-526-0431
1-800-467-0435
Facsimile: 901-526-8183

Samuel J. Weintraub (1917-1993)
Earl W. DeHart (1933-1977)
Jay R. Robinson
Jeff Weintraub
James H. Stock, Jr.
Richard D. Bennett

Cindy Cole Ettingoff
J. Gregory Grisham
George H. Rieger, II
Elizabeth A. Holloway

For full biographical listings, see the Martindale-Hubbell Law Directory

WILSON, McRAE, IVY, SEVIER, McTYIER AND STRAIN (AV)

295 Washington Avenue, Suite Two, P.O. Box 3331, 38173
Telephone: 901-523-2364
Telecopier: 901-523-2366

MEMBERS OF FIRM

Fred P. Wilson
Albert T. McRae
Fred E. Ivy, Jr.
Charles A. Sevier
Douglas A. McTyier
Alan R. Strain

ASSOCIATES

Stuart A. Wilson
J. Whitten Gurkin
Mark L. Pittman
Charles A. Sevier, IV
Reid R. Phillips
David A. McLaughlin
Robert M. Nelson (1900-1967)

For full biographical listings, see the Martindale-Hubbell Law Directory

YOUNG & PERL, P.C. (AV)

Suite 2380, One Commerce Square, 38103
Telephone: 901-525-2761
FAX: 901-526-2702

Edward R. Young
Arnold E. Perl
Jay W. Kiesewetter
Jonathan E. Kaplan
Cary Schwimmer
W. Stephen Gardner

Karen W. Grochau (Resident)
James C. Holland
Leigh A. Hollingsworth
John Marshall Jones
Shawn R. Lillie
Todd L. Sarver (Not admitted in TN)
James M. Simpson
Mark Theodore (Not admitted in TN)

LEGAL SUPPORT PERSONNEL

Patrick T. Fleming (Labor Relations Specialist)

For full biographical listings, see the Martindale-Hubbell Law Directory

MILAN, Gibson Co.

FLIPPIN, COLLINS, HUEY & WEBB (AV)

1066 South Main Building, 38358
Telephone: 901-686-8355; 424-6079
Telecopier: 901-686-9094

MEMBERS OF FIRM

William Jerry Flippin — Benjamin M. Huey, II
Fred Collins — James Belew Webb

Representative Clients: First American National Bank of Milan; The Equitable Life Assurance Society of the United States; South Central Bell Telephone Company; Leader Federal Bank For Savings; Department of Public Utilities of the City of Milan; United States Fidelity & Guaranty Co.; City of Milan.

For full biographical listings, see the Martindale-Hubbell Law Directory

KIZER, BONDS, CROCKER & HUGHES (AV)

1026 College Street, Suite 201, P.O. Box 320, 38358
Telephone: 901-686-1198
Telecopier: 901-686-9868

MEMBERS OF FIRM

John F. Kizer — C. Timothy Crocker
W. Collins Bonds — Stephen L. Hughes

ASSOCIATES

Jeffrey A. Smith — Harold W. McLeary, Jr.

Reference: Volunteer Bank.

For full biographical listings, see the Martindale-Hubbell Law Directory

*MORRISTOWN,** Hamblen Co. — (Refer to Greeneville)

*MOUNTAIN CITY,** Johnson Co. — (Refer to Bristol)

*NASHVILLE,** Davidson Co.

BAKER, CAMPBELL & PARSONS (AV)

Suite 300, 303 Church Street, 37201-1786
Telephone: 615-255-7701
Fax: 615-255-7704

MEMBERS OF FIRM

Kenneth L. Campbell — David Bate Parsons

OF COUNSEL

Gary T. Baker

Representative Clients: Peterbilt of Nashville, Inc.; Great American Peterbilt, Inc.; Old South Peterbilt, Inc.; Cresent Enterprises, Inc.; Athens Paper Co.; Advantage Management, Inc.; Cool Springs Real Estate Associates, L.P.

For full biographical listings, see the Martindale-Hubbell Law Directory

BAKER, DONELSON, BEARMAN & CALDWELL (AV)

1700 Nashville City Center, 511 Union Street, 37219
Telephone: 615-726-5600
Telecopier: 615-726-0464
Memphis, Tennessee Office: 20th Floor, First Tennessee Building, 165 Madison, 38103.
Telephone: 901-526-2000.
Telecopier: 901-577-2303.
Knoxville, Tennessee Office: 2200 Riverview Tower, 900 Gay Street, 37901.
Telephone: 615-549-7000.
Telecopier: 615-525-8569.
Chattanooga, Tennessee Office: 1800 Republic Centre, 633 Chestnut Street, 37450-1800.
Telephone: 615-752-4400.
Telecopier: 615-752-4410.
Huntsville, Tennessee Office: 3 Courthouse Square, 37756.
Telephone: 615-663-2321.
Telecopier: 615-663-2111.
Johnson City, Tennessee Office: Hamilton Bank Building, 207 Mockingbird Lane, 37604.
Telephone: 615-928-0181.
Telecopier: 615-928-5694; 615-928-3654; Kingsport: 615-246-6191.
Washington, D.C. Office: Market Square, 801 Pennsylvania Avenue, N.W., 20004.
Telephone: 202-508-3400.
Telecopier: 202-508-3402.

PARTNERS

Lewis R. Donelson, III — James L. Beckner
Howard H. Baker, Jr. — Ed E. Williams, III
Maclin P. Davis, Jr. — H. Wynne James, III
Robert F. Worthington, Jr. — John A. Gupton, III
Robert G. McCullough — Claudia W. Dickerson
Richard D. Bird — David C. Andrew
Don C. Stansberry, Jr. — James A. DeLanis
William Hume Barr — Kenneth P. Ezell, Jr.
James T. O'Hare — James L. McElroy
Robert L. Baker — Douglas A. Walker
Robert G. McDowell — John Randolph Bibb, Jr.
Rodger B. Kesley — H. Buckley Cole

(See Next Column)

PARTNERS (Continued)

Robert M. Steele — Katherine A. Brown
Anthony M. Iannacio — Steven J. Eisen
Gary C. Shockley — Vance L. Broemel
Randal S. Mashburn — Keith D. Frazier
David J. Hill

OF COUNSEL

Robert L. Crossley — Colman B. Hoffman
L. H. (Bill) Armistead, III — John S. Hicks

ASSOCIATES

Susan Duvier Bass — Frank A. Coyle
Matthew Thompson Harris — Clisby Hall Barrow
Peter T. Dirksen — Jeffrey A. Calk
Kelly R. Duggan — Scott D. Carey
Barbara A. Rose — Darwin A. Hindman III
Fred Russell Harwell — Ann D. Jarvis
James David Nave — John W. McCullough
Philip Stuart McSween — Jonathan Cole

For full biographical listings, see the Martindale-Hubbell Law Directory

BOULT, CUMMINGS, CONNERS & BERRY (AV)

414 Union Street, Suite 1600, P.O. Box 198062, 37219
Telephone: 615-244-2582
Telecopy: 615-252-2380
Telex: 852980

William Hume (1888-1950) — Edwin F. Hunt (1902-1981)
Laurence B. Howard (1900-1959) — Joseph G. Cummings (1917-1988)
Lindsey M. Davis (1902-1960) — Reber Fielding Boult (1907—)

Patrick L. Alexander — Roger G. Jones
Paul A. Alexis — Kenneth H. King, Jr.
Andrea C. Barach — William D. Leader, Jr.
James I. Vance Berry — Samuel D. Lipshie
Jeffrey S. Bivins — Matthew C. Lonergan
Michael D. Brent — Charles W. McElroy
Karyn Crigler Bryant — Patricia Head Moskal
Eugene N. Bulso, Jr. — John E. Murdock III
Ann Peldo Cargile — Gordon Earle Nichols
Davis H. Carr — George H. Nolan
Lew Conner — William L. Norton III
John T. Conners, Jr. — James Craig Oliver
J. Greer Cummings, Jr. — Robert S. Patterson
Peter H. Curry — Jeffrey O. Powell
William N. Dearborn — David A. Rutter
William W. Earthman III — Charles S. Sanger
Douglas C. Franck — John M. Scannapieco
Joseph W. Gibbs — A. J. Sharenberger III
Steven L. Gill — Daniel P. Smith
John E. Gillmor — Kevin T. Sommers
Barry Goheen — Paul F. Soper
Joe M. Goodman, Jr. — David K. Taylor
Gail G. Greenfield — Robert P. Thomas
Michael J. Harbers — Larry T. Thrailkill
J. B. Hardcastle, Jr. — John W. Titus
Christopher Harris — J. Thomas Trent, Jr.
Jon E. Hastings — Thor Y. Urness
Deborah K. Hayes — John D. Vaughn
Larry G. Hayes, Jr. — Ralph C. Voltmer, Jr. (Not admitted in TN)
John R. Haynes — Henry M. Walker
Scott K. Haynes — Kellye L. Walker
E. Berry Holt III — Robert J. Warner, Jr.
H. Frederick Humbracht, Jr. — Richard F. Warren, Jr.
Philip N. Jett — Robert E. Wood
Christopher D.M. Jones — Steven K. Wood

Attorneys for: Community Health Systems, Inc.; First Union National Bank; Genesco Inc.; J.C. Bradford & Co.; Lincoln National Corporation; NationsBank of Tennessee; Opryland USA Inc.; Saint Thomas Hospital; State Industries, Inc.; Saturn Corporation.

For full biographical listings, see the Martindale-Hubbell Law Directory

CORNELIUS & COLLINS (AV)

Suite 2700 Nashville City Center, P.O. Box 190695, 37219-0695
Telephone: 615-244-1440
Facsimile: 615-254-9477

Charles L. Cornelius (1888-1968) — Richard L. Colbert
Charles L. Cornelius, Jr. — David A. King
William Ovid Collins, Jr. — Blakeley D. Matthews
Charles Hampton White — Joseph R. Wheeler
Thomas I. Carlton, Jr. — Kurtis J. Winstead
Charles G. Cornelius — Rebecca Wells-Demaree
Noel F. Stahl — Daniel P. Berexa
C. Bennett Harrison, Jr. — Jay Nelson Chamness
David L. Steed — Dana Davis Ballinger
Andrew Donelson Dunn

Representative Clients: General Motors Corp.; Tennessee Medical Assn; Tennessee Education Association; United Parcel Service; Hartford Insurance Group; State Volunteer Mutual Insurance Co.; Corroon & Black, Inc.; Bet-

(See Next Column)

CORNELIUS & COLLINS, *Nashville—Continued*

ter-Bilt Aluminum Products, Inc.; Johnson & Johnson Products, Inc.; Mercedes Benz of North American, Inc.

For full biographical listings, see the Martindale-Hubbell Law Directory

DAVIES, CANTRELL, HUMPHREYS & McCOY (AV)

150 Second Avenue North, Suite 225, P.O. Box 2726, 37219-0726
Telephone: 615-256-8125
FAX: 615-242-7853

MEMBERS OF FIRM

Ed Reynolds Davies
Luther E. Cantrell, Jr.
Jerry R. Humphreys
Carol L. McCoy
E. Reynolds Davies, Jr.
Robert R. Davies

For full biographical listings, see the Martindale-Hubbell Law Directory

EVANS, JONES & REYNOLDS, A PROFESSIONAL CORPORATION (AV)

1810 First Union Tower, 150 Fourth Avenue North, 37219-2424
Telephone: 615-259-4685
Telecopier: 615-256-4448

James Clarence Evans
Richard A. Jones
Winston S. Evans
J. Allen Reynolds III

Phillip Byron Jones

OF COUNSEL

Dennis J. Meaker

References: The Third National Bank in Nashville; First American National Bank.

For full biographical listings, see the Martindale-Hubbell Law Directory

FARRIS, WARFIELD & KANADAY (AV)

19th Floor, Third National Financial Center, 37219
Telephone: 615-244-5200
Fax: 615-726-3185

Frank M. Farris, Jr.
Charles H. Warfield
Thomas P. Kanaday, Jr. (Retired)
James G. Martin, III
W. Fred Williams, Jr.
Joseph N. Barker
Robert Norman Buchanan, III
Warren H. Wild, Jr.
Julian L. Bibb
A. Stuart Campbell
H. Naill Falls, Jr.
B. Riney Green
Bradley A. MacLean
Jeffrey R. King
Charles A. Grice
Michael Hinchion
Robert C. Goodrich, Jr.
Michael L. Dagley
Alden H. Smith, Jr.
Overton Thompson III
Katherine Simpson Allen
Pamela A. Taylor
Cynthia N. Sellers
Lea Wiggins Stouffer
Elizabeth M. Adams
C. Mark Carver
William L. Baggett, Jr.
Garry K. Grooms
Dianna Baker Shew
James S. Mathis
N. Sue Van Sant Palmer
Stephen H. Price
Linda C. Elam
W. Edward Ramage
G.A. Puryear IV

Representative Clients: Third National Bank in Nashville; Northern Telecom, Inc.; J.C. Bradford & Co.; Gaylord Entertainment Company; Kirby Building Systems; Edwin B. Raskin Co.; The Travelers Insurance; The Prudential Insurance Company of America; Rutherford County, Tennessee.

For full biographical listings, see the Martindale-Hubbell Law Directory

GRACEY, RUTH, HOWARD, TATE & SOWELL (AV)

Suite 201, 150 Second Avenue North, 37201
Telephone: 615-256-1125
FAX: 615-244-5467

MEMBERS OF FIRM

Hugh C. Gracey, Jr.
Patrick A. Ruth
Barry L. Howard
William H. Tate
Alan M. Sowell
Clifford Wilson
Katherine (Kitty) D. Boyte
Michael Lee Parsons
Raymond S. Leathers
Michael H. Johnson
Julia J. Tate

Representative Clients: Allstate Insurance Co.; APAC; Bridgestone, (U.S.A.),; CIGNA Corp.; Kroger Co.

For full biographical listings, see the Martindale-Hubbell Law Directory

KING & BALLOW (AV)

1200 Noel Place, 200 Fourth Avenue, North, 37219
Telephone: 615-259-3456
Fax: 615-254-7907
San Diego, California Office: 2700 Symphony Towers, 750 B Street, 92101.
Telephone: 619-236-9401.
Fax: 619-236-9437.

(See Next Column)

San Francisco, California Office: 100 First Street, Suite 2700, 94105.
Telephone: 415-541-7803.
Fax: 415-541-7805.

MEMBERS OF FIRM

Frank S. King, Jr.
Robert L. Ballow
Richard C. Lowe
R. Eddie Wayland
Larry D. Crabtree
Alan L. Marx
Paul H. Duvall (Resident, San Diego, California Office)
Steven C. Douse
Douglas R. Pierce
James P. Thompson
Howard M. Kastrinsky
Kenneth E. Douthat
Mark E. Hunt
Charles J. Mataya
Lynn Siegel (Resident, San Diego, California Office)
Nora T. Cannon
John J. Matchulat
M. Kim Vance

ASSOCIATES

Kevin M. Bagley (Resident, San Diego, California Office)
Katheryn M. Millwee
Christopher M. Kato (Not admitted in TN)
Dorothy L. Starnes
Patrick M. Thomas
R. Brent Ballow
Elizabeth B. Marney
Michael D. Oesterle
Lynn Morrow
Leslie E. Lewis (Resident, San Diego, California Office)
Paul H. Derrick
Richard S. Busch
Stephen F. Peluso
Mary M. Collier
Linda L. Stuessi (Resident, San Diego, California Office)
Brian K. Jordan (Not admitted in TN)
David S. Lionberger
John J. McCarthy, III (Not admitted in TN)
S. Kae Carpenter

Representative Clients: American Airlines, Nashville, Tennessee; Capital Cities/ABC, Inc., New York, New York; Denver Post, Denver, Colorado; Dollar General Corp.; Houston Post, Houston, Texas; Kansas City Star Co., Kansas City, Missouri; Northern Telecom, Inc.; Opryland USA, Inc.; NationsBank; Tribune Company, Chicago, Illinois; Union Tribune Publishing Company, San Diego, California.

For full biographical listings, see the Martindale-Hubbell Law Directory

LEWIS, KING, KRIEG & WALDROP, P.C. (AV)

Third National Financial Center, 424 Church Street, Ninth Floor, 37219
Telephone: 615-259-1366
FAX: 615-259-1389
Knoxville, Tennessee Office: One Centre Square, 5th Floor, 620 Market Street.
Telephone: 615-546-4646.

John K. King
R. Dale Bay (Resident)
Reba Brown (Resident)

SPECIAL COUNSEL

Aaron Wyckoff (Resident)
Tyree B. Harris IV

OF COUNSEL

Tyree B. Harris

Leonard F. Pogue, III (Resident)
R. Neal Mynatt (Resident)
John R. Tarpley (Resident)
Maria M. Salas (Resident)
Charles W. Cagle
David Nelson Garst

Representative Clients: The American Home Group; Central Mutual Insurance Co.; Cincinnati Insurance Co.; The Kemper Group; The Transamerica Group; Travelers Insurance Co.; Wausau Insurance Co.; CNA Ins. Co.; Pennsylvania National Mutual Casualty Insurance Co.

For full biographical listings, see the Martindale-Hubbell Law Directory

MANIER, HEROD, HOLLABAUGH & SMITH, A PROFESSIONAL CORPORATION (AV)

First Union Tower 2200 One Nashville Place, 150 Fourth Avenue North, 37219-2494
Telephone: 615-244-0030
Telecopier: 615-242-4203

Will R. Manier, Jr. (1885-1953)
Larkin E. Crouch (1882-1948)
Vincent L. Fuqua, Jr. (1930-1974)
J. Olin White (1907-1982)
Miller Manier (1897-1986)
William Edward Herod (1917-1992)
Lewis B. Hollabaugh
Don L. Smith
James M. Doran, Jr.
Stephen E. Cox
J. Michael Franks
Randall C. Ferguson
Terry L. Hill
James David Leckrone
Robert C. Evans
Tommy C. Estes
B. Gail Reese
Michael E. Evans
Laurence M. Papel
John M. Gillum
Gregory L. Cashion
Sam H. Poteet, Jr.
Samuel Arthur Butts III
David J. Deming
Mark S. LeVan
Richard McCallister Smith
Mary Paty Lynn Jetton
H. Rowan Leathers III
Jefferson C. Orr
William L. Penny

(See Next Column)

MANIER, HEROD, HOLLABAUGH & SMITH A PROFESSIONAL CORPORATION—*Continued*

Lawrence B. Hammet II
John H. Rowland
Susan C. West
John E. Quinn
John F. Floyd
Paul L. Sprader
Lela M. Hollabaugh
J. Steven Kirkham
T. Richard Travis
Stephanie M. Jennings
Jerry W. Taylor
C. Benton Patton
Kenneth A. Weber
Phillip Robert Newman
Brett A. Oeser

General Counsel for: McKinnon Bridge Co., Inc.

For full biographical listings, see the Martindale-Hubbell Law Directory

NEAL & HARWELL (AV)

Suite 2000, First Union Tower, 150 Fourth Avenue North, 37219
Telephone: 615-244-1713
Telecopier-FAX: 615-726-0573

MEMBERS OF FIRM

James F. Neal
Aubrey B. Harwell, Jr.
Jon D. Ross
James F. Sanders
Thomas H. Dundon
Robert L. Sullivan
Ronald G. Harris
Albert F. Moore
Philip N. Elbert
James G. Thomas
William T. Ramsey
James R. Kelley
Marc T. McNamee
Delta Anne Davis

Philip D. Irwin
George H. Cate, III
Edmund L. Carey, Jr.
John A. Coates
Pamela King
John C. Beiter
David P. Bohman
A. Scott Ross
Brian K. Frazier

Representative Clients: Johnny Cash; Channel Five Television Co. (WTVF); First American National Bank; General Motors Corp.; General Electric Capital Corp.; Hughes Aircraft Corp; Ingram Industries; NationsBank; Nissan Motor Corporation in U.S.A.; Tokio Marine & Fire Insurance Company, Ltd.

For full biographical listings, see the Martindale-Hubbell Law Directory

PARKER, LAWRENCE, CANTRELL & DEAN (AV)

Fifth Floor, 200 Fourth Avenue North, 37219
Telephone: 615-255-7500
Telecopy: 615-242-1515

MEMBERS OF FIRM

Robert E. Parker
Thomas W. Lawrence, Jr.
Rose Park Cantrell
George A. Dean
Richard K. Smith
Louis Marshall Albritton
M. Bradley Gilmore

ASSOCIATES

Michael K. Bassham
Garrett E. Asher

Representative Clients: Regions Bank; Sams Stores, Inc.; State Volunteer Mutual Ins. Co.; Harpeth Valley Utility District; Steinhouse Supply Co.

For full biographical listings, see the Martindale-Hubbell Law Directory

SCHULMAN, LEROY AND BENNETT, P.C. (AV)

7th Floor, 501 Union Building, 5th Avenue, North & Union Street, P.O. Box 190676, 37219-0676
Telephone: 615-244-6670
Fax: 615-254-5407

I. R. Schulman (1908-1986)
Theodore T. McCarley, Jr. (1918-1975)
Lewis D. Pride (1933-1978)
Seymour Samuels, Jr. (1912-1992)
W. Wayne LeRoy
H. Michael Bennett
Angus Gillis, III
Gary S. Rubenstein
Keene W. Bartley
Barbara Jones Perutelli
J. Anthony Arena

OF COUNSEL

J. Carson Stone, III

Representative Clients: Fruehauf Trailer Co.; Allstate Insurance Co.;
References: First American National Bank; Third National Bank; Commerce Union Bank; Nashville Bank & Trust.

For full biographical listings, see the Martindale-Hubbell Law Directory

STOKES & BARTHOLOMEW, P.A. (AV)

Third National Financial Center, 424 Church Street, 28th Floor, 37219
Telephone: 615-259-1450

Ogden Stokes
Samuel W. Bartholomew, Jr.
William R. Bruce
Thomas L. (Larry) Stewart
D. Reed Houk
Robert R. Campbell, Jr.
Cynthia Mitchell Barnett
Paul S. Davidson
Douglas J. Brown
D. Kirk Shaffer

(See Next Column)

William H. West
Carter R. Todd
Thomas T. Pennington
Rusty L. Moore
David T. Axford
Joshua F. Aylor
William H. Neely
Reber M. Boult
James H. Drescher

Darlene T. Marsh
Elizabeth E. Moore
Kim Harvey Looney
Lisa Ezell Peerman
Guilford F. Thornton, Jr.
Kevin Hunter Sharp
Christina A. Landeryou
Charles W. Cook, III
Martin Shallenberger Brown, Jr.
Nancy Adele Vincent

OF COUNSEL

John L. Chambers
Ruth M. Kinnard
Vaden M. Lackey, Jr.

For full biographical listings, see the Martindale-Hubbell Law Directory

TRABUE, STURDIVANT & DEWITT (AV)

25th Floor, Nashville City Center, 511 Union Street, 37219-1738
Telephone: 615-244-9270
Fax: 615-256-8197
Columbia, Tennessee Office: 100 West Sixth Street. P.O. Box 1004.
Telephone: 615-388-7032.
Fax: 615-388-7066.

Charles C. Trabue (1872-1942)
Robert W. Sturdivant (1914-1988)
Edward C. Blank, II (1937-1988)
Charles C. Trabue, Jr.
Ward DeWitt, Jr.
Hugh C. Howser
Alfred E. Abbey
Thomas H. Peebles, III
Russell H. Hippe, Jr.
Thomas C. Binkley
Charles C. Trabue, III
Robert L. Jones (Resident, Columbia Office)
Jack F. King, Jr.
Gayle Ingram Malone, Jr.
George E. Mudter, Jr.
Hugh C. Howser, Jr.
Lawrence C. Maxwell
William R. O'Bryan, Jr.
Dan H. Elrod
N. Houston Parks (Resident, Columbia Office)
Philip M. Richardson
Ellen Hobbs Lyle
Christopher M. Was
C. Eric Stevens
Donald P. Paul
Robert B. Littleton
Gerald G. Patterson
Mary Thomson LeMense
Edward K. Lancaster (Resident, Columbia Office)
C. Dale Allen
James H. Porter
Robert M. Holland, Jr.
Jeffrey Zager
Richard A. Johnson

ASSOCIATES

Anita L. Whisnant
Mary Ellen Morris
W. Neal McBrayer
Alexander S. Fuqua
James Charles Stanley II
Kathryn J. Ladd
G. Brian S. Jackson
Dwayne W. Barrett

OF COUNSEL

William H. Woods

General Counsel for: Werthan Industries, Inc.; Baptist Hospital, Inc., Nashville; Tennessee Farm Bureau Federation; Tennessee Trucking Association; The Shannon Group, Inc.
Attorneys for: Nashville Bank of Commerce; Federal Deposit Insurance Corporation; Resolution Trust Corporation; Capital Holding Corporation (Louisville, KY); Tennessee Farmer's Insurance Cos.

For full biographical listings, see the Martindale-Hubbell Law Directory

WALLER LANSDEN DORTCH & DAVIS (AV)

Nashville City Center, 511 Union Street, Suite 2100, 37219-1760
Telephone: 615-244-6380
Telecopier: 615-244-5686; 615-244-6804
Telex: 786535
Columbia, Tennessee Office: 809 S. Main Street, Suite 300, P.O. Box 1035.
Telephone: 615-388-6031.
Telecopier: 615-381-7317.

MEMBERS OF FIRM

William Waller, Jr.
Philip G. Davidson III
Charles A. Trost
William M. Leech, Jr.
James R. Chehire III
James J. Kendig
Ames Davis
Theodore W. Lenz
Justin P. Wilson
Walter H. Crouch
George W. Bishop III
William H. Farmer
Stephen C. Baker
J. Leigh Griffith
William E. Shofner
Alexander Blackman Buchanan
J. Chase Cole
Steve Cobb
Robert E. Boston
Joseph A. Sowell III
J. Reginald Hill
G. Scott Rayson
Kevin D. Norwood
William F. Carpenter III
Howard T. Wall III
Joseph A. Woodruff
W. Gregory Conway
Waverly D. Crenshaw, Jr.
E. Marlee Mitchell
Michael R. Paslay
Howard W. Herndon
David E. Lemke
James W. White

OF COUNSEL

Robin S. Courtney (Resident Of Counsel, Columbia Office)
Donald W. Fish

(See Next Column)

WALLER LANSDEN DORTCH & DAVIS, *Nashville—Continued*

ASSOCIATES

D. Billye Sanders
Neil B. Krugman
Nancy S. Jones
Michael D. Pearigen
Michael L. Silhol
Thomas H. Peebles IV (Resident Associate, Columbia Office)
Ralph W. Davis
Ben A. Burns
A. Beth Guest
Elizabeth Holcomb Lemke
Edward Andrew Norwood
James M. Weaver
John Dixon Claybrook
Deborah W. Larios
L. Hunter Rost, Jr.
Jon Michael Sundock
Angela R. Magill
Stephen W. Grace
Patricia Owen Powers
James Holt Walker
Hal Andrews
Carlyle McCulloch Urello
Edward Moye Callaway
Carla Fiddler Fenswick
Bradley A. Haneberg
Benjamin Cockrill Huddleston
Brian A. Lapps, Jr.
Dana Crosland McLendon, III
Donald Ray Moody
Beth Evans
Michael G. Stewart
Mary Ellen Sullivan

SENIOR COUNSEL

William Waller
D. L. Lansden

Representative Clients: J.C. Bradford & Co.; Equitable Securities Corp.; Healthtrust, Inc. - The Hospital Co.; Saturn Corporation; NationsBank of Tennessee; Worth, Inc.

For full biographical listings, see the Martindale-Hubbell Law Directory

WYATT, TARRANT & COMBS (AV)

1500 Nashville City Center, 511 Union Street, 37219
Telephone: 615-244-0020
Telecopier: 615-256-1726
Cable Address: "Nashlaw"
Music Row, Office: 29 Music Square East, Nashville, 37203.
Telephone: 615-255-6161.
Telecopier: 615-254-4490.
Louisville, Kentucky Office: Citizens Plaza.
Telephone: 502-589-5235.
Telecopier: 502-589-0309.
Lexington, Kentucky Office: 1700 Lexington Financial Center.
Telephone: 606-233-2012.
Telecopier: 606-259-0649.
Frankfort, Kentucky Office: The Taylor-Scott Building, 311 West Main Street.
Telephone: 502-223-2104.
Telecopier: 502-227-7681.
New Albany, Indiana Office: The Elsby Building, 117 East Spring Street,
Telephone: 812-945-3561.
Telecopier: 812-949-2524.
Hendersonville, Tennessee Office: 313 E. Main Street, Suite 1.
Telephone: 615-822-8822.
Telecopier: 615-824-4684.

MEMBERS OF FIRM

John M. Barksdale (1903-1983)
Ward Hudgins (1910-1966)
John Donelson Whalley (1921-1991)
Harris A. Gilbert
Parker W. Duncan, Jr.
Charles W. Bone
Sam J. McAllester III
W. Michael Milom (Resident, Music Row Office)
John W. Lewis
William R. Wright (Resident, Hendersonville Office)
C. Michael Norton
Christian A. Horsnell (Resident, Music Row Office)
William Warren Gibson
Marshall L. Hix
J. Graham Matherne

ASSOCIATES

Daniel B. Brown
Keith C. Dennen
Leah May Dennen
James C. Bradshaw III
Andrew B. Campbell

COUNSEL

Edwin S. Pyle
Jack F. Stringham II
Janet P. Medlin
Gail Smith Bradford
Robin Mitchell Joyce (Resident, Music Row Office)

Counsel for: Alley-Cassetty Coal Co.; Country Music Foundation; Country Radio Broadcasters; Emanuel Schatten Enterprises; General Trust Company; Gospel Music Association; H.G. Hill Company, Inc.; JRN, Inc.; Nashville Entertainment Association; Nashville Thermal Transfer Corporation.

For full biographical listings, see the Martindale-Hubbell Law Directory

OAK RIDGE, Anderson Co.

JOYCE, MEREDITH, FLITCROFT & NORMAND (AV)

Town Hall, 30 Kentucky Avenue, P.O. Box 6197, 37831-6197
Telephone: 615-482-2486
FAX: 615-482-5786
Nashville, Tennessee Office: 222 Second Avenue North, Suite 210.
Telephone: 615-726-0530.
Fax: 615-251-7094.
Knoxville, Tennessee Office: Old Courthouse, Room 302.
Telephone: 615-521-2617.

(See Next Column)

MEMBERS OF FIRM

Eugene L. Joyce
W. Clark Meredith
David L. Flitcroft
James T. Normand

ASSOCIATES

Josephine D. Clark
M. Lynn Rogers
Lars E. Schuller
Bruce C. Bryant

NASHVILLE ATTORNEYS

Lisa Cowan
Pamela G. Finch
W. Scott Rosenberg
Teresa P. Webb

Representative Clients: NationsBank of Tennessee, N.A.; South Central Bell; Heritage Federal Bank for Savings, FSB; Ridgeview Psychiatric Hospital and Center, Inc.; Y-12 Federal Credit Union; ORNL Employees Federal Credit Union; State of Tennessee Child Support Enforcement; Maximus, Inc.

For full biographical listings, see the Martindale-Hubbell Law Directory

*PARIS,** Henry Co. — (Refer to Union City)

PARSONS, Decatur Co. — (Refer to Jackson)

*RIPLEY,** Lauderdale Co.

LAW OFFICES OF J. THOMAS CALDWELL (AV)

114 Jefferson Street, 38063
Telephone: 901-635-9162
FAX: 901-635-0006

ASSOCIATES

Janice C. Craig

Representative Clients: Lauderdale County, Tennessee; Ohio Casualty Insurance Co.
References: Bank of Ripley; Lauderdale County Bank.

For full biographical listings, see the Martindale-Hubbell Law Directory

ROCKWOOD, Roane Co. — (Refer to Knoxville)

*ROGERSVILLE,** Hawkins Co.

ROGAN & WELCH (AV)

Rogan Building, P.O. Box 7, 37857
Telephone: 615-272-2142
Fax: 615-272-0214
Greeneville, Tennessee Office: 1104 Tusculum Boulevard, Suite 101. Phone: 615-787-0505.

Tom H. Rogan
Lawrence A. Welch, Jr.

For full biographical listings, see the Martindale-Hubbell Law Directory

*SAVANNAH,** Hardin Co.

HOPPER & PLUNK, P.C. (AV)

404 West Main Street, P.O. Box 220, 38372
Telephone: 901-925-8076

James A. Hopper
Dennis W. Plunk
Curtis F. Hopper

Representative Clients: United States Fidelity & Guaranty Co.; Tennessee Farmers Mutual Insurance Co.; Kemper Insurance Co.; Tennessee Municipal Insurance Pool; Savannah Electric.
References: Boatman's Bank, Savannah; The Hardin County Bank.

For full biographical listings, see the Martindale-Hubbell Law Directory

*SELMER,** McNairy Co. — (Refer to Savannah)

*SHELBYVILLE,** Bedford Co.

BOMAR, SHOFNER, IRION & RAMBO (AV)

104 Depot Street, P.O. Box 129, 37160
Telephone: 615-684-6213
Fax: 615-684-6227

MEMBERS OF FIRM

James L. Bomar, Jr.
John C. Shofner
Jack M. Irion
Andrew C. Rambo
John D. Templeton

Representative Clients: United Cities Gas Co.; Chattanooga Gas Co.; Petrolane, Partners L.P.; South Central Bell Telephone and Telegraph Co.; State Farm Mutual Automobile Insurance Co.; Empire Berol Corp.; Eaton Corp.; Tennessee-American Water Co.; Texas Eastern Transmission Corp.
Counsel for: First Community Bank of Bedford County.

For full biographical listings, see the Martindale-Hubbell Law Directory

*SMITHVILLE,** DeKalb Co.

J. Hilton Conger (AV)

200 South 3rd Street, 37166
Telephone: 615-597-4087
Fax: 615-597-7549

Representative Client: Citizens Bank.

*SPENCER,** Van Buren Co. — (Refer to Sparta)

*SPRINGFIELD,** Robertson Co. — (Refer to Clarksville)

*TAZEWELL,** Claiborne Co. — (Refer to Greeneville)

TULLAHOMA, Coffee Co.

Haynes, Hull & Rieder, P.A. (AV)

214 North Atlantic Street, P.O. Box 878, 37388
Telephone: 615-455-5478
Fax: 615-455-6148

Walter M. Haynes (1897-1967) William C. Rieder
Thomas M. Hull Gerald L. Ewell, Jr.
R. Cass Tinsley

Representative Clients: First National Bank of Tullahoma; The Board of Public Utilities of the City of Tullahoma, Tenn.; Elk River Public Utility District; SSI Services, Inc.; Sverdrup Technology, Inc.; State Farm Insurance Companies; United States Fidelity & Guaranty Company; Fireman's Fund Insurance Companies; State Volunteer Mutual Insurance Company; Nationwide Insurance Company.

For full biographical listings, see the Martindale-Hubbell Law Directory

Henry, McCord & Bean (AV)

300 North Jackson Street, 37388
Telephone: 615-455-9301
Telefax: 615-455-1621

MEMBERS OF FIRM

James H. Henry James H. Henry, II
John M. McCord Roger J. Bean
Clifton N. Miller

ASSOCIATES

Rick W. Gabriel

Representative Clients: Trans Financial Bank of Tennessee, FSB; South Central Bell Telephone Co.; CSX Transportation, Inc.; Coca-Cola Bottling Works, Tullahoma; Tennessee Apparel Corp.; Tennessee Dickel Distilling Co.; Wagner Division, Cooper Industries, Inc.; United Distillers, Inc.

For full biographical listings, see the Martindale-Hubbell Law Directory

*UNION CITY,** Obion Co.

Elam, Glasgow & Acree (AV)

NationsBank Building, 38261
Telephone: 901-885-2011, 885-2012

MEMBERS OF FIRM

Tom Elam William B. Acree, Jr.
James M. Glasgow James M. Glasgow, Jr.

Attorneys for: NationsBank, Union City; Illinois Central Gulf Railroad (Obion, Lake & Weakley Counties); Louisville & Nashville Railway; United States Fidelity & Guaranty Co.; Auto Owners Insurance Co.; C.N.A. Insurance, Union City; Travelers Insurance Co.; Goodyear Tire & Rubber Co.

For full biographical listings, see the Martindale-Hubbell Law Directory

*WAVERLY,** Humphreys Co. — (Refer to Dickson)

*WAYNESBORO,** Wayne Co. — (Refer to Savannah)

*WINCHESTER,** Franklin Co.

Lynch, Lynch & Lynch (AV)

North Side Court House Square, 37398
Telephone: 615-967-2228; 967-6718

MEMBERS OF FIRM

Frank L. Lynch (1873-1952) Ben P. Lynch
Pat B. Lynch (1917-1994) Mike P. Lynch
Frank C. Lynch

Representative Clients: Shelter Insurance Co.; American Fire & Casualty Co.; Liberty Mutual Insurance Co.; Rockwell Standard Corp.; Tennessee Farmers Mutual Insurance Co.; Continental National American Group; Citizens Community Bank; City of Decherd, Tennessee; Auto Owners Insurance Co.; Shelby Mutual Insurance Co.; Franklin County, Tennessee.

For full biographical listings, see the Martindale-Hubbell Law Directory

*WOODBURY,** Cannon Co. — (Refer to Murfreesboro)

TEXAS

*ABILENE,** Taylor Co.

Robert D. Batjer, Jr. (AV)

Suite 306, 104 Pine Street, P.O. Box 888, 79601
Telephone: 915-673-2597
Fax: 915-676-9329

Representative Clients: General Motors Corp.; International Harvester Co.; Freightliner Corp.; United States Fidelity and Guaranty Co.; Royal-Globe Insurance Cos.; Commercial Union Insurance Cos.; State Farm Mutual; USAA; Wausau Insurance Cos.; Union Standard Insurance.

For full biographical listings, see the Martindale-Hubbell Law Directory

McMahon, Surovik, Suttle, Buhrmann, Cobb & Hicks, A Professional Corporation (AV)

Suite 800 First National Bank Building, 400 Pine Street, P.O. Box 3679, 79604
Telephone: 915-676-9183
Fax: 915-676-8836

T. J. McMahon (1898-1979)
Bob J. Surovik
Stephen H. Suttle
David L. Buhrmann
David R. Cobb
William A. Hicks
Kelly Gill
Paul L. Cannon

Mark S. Zachary
Frank R. Stamey
J. McCord Wilson

OF COUNSEL

J. Neil Daniel
Stanley P. Wilson

Representative Clients: First National Bank of Abilene; Abilene Reporter News; West Central Texas Municipal Water District; CNA Insurance Cos.; Texas Medical Liability Trust.

For full biographical listings, see the Martindale-Hubbell Law Directory

Wagstaff, Alvis, Stubbeman, Seamster & Longacre, L.L.P. (AV)

290 Cedar, P.O. Box 360, 79604-0360
Telephone: 915-677-6291
Facsimile: 915-677-6313
Dallas, Texas Office: 750 North St. Paul Street, Suite 1290.
Telephone: 214-220-9171.
Facsimile: 214-871-9327.

MEMBERS OF FIRM

J. M. Wagstaff (1862-1952)
John H. Alvis (1896-1971)
R. M. Wagstaff (1892-1973)
Robert H. Alvis
David G. Stubbeman
Don N. Seamster
Roy B. Longacre
Russell C. (Rusty) Beard
Phillip J. Day
Darrell W. Moore
Charles L. Black
John R. Saringer
Kyle D. Tatom
Diann Waddill

ASSOCIATES

David M. Hurst
William P. Chesser
Michael S. Seamster
Vianei Lopez Robinson

Representative Clients: West Texas Utilities Co. (General Counsel); Abilene Independent School District; American International Group; CSW Energy, Inc.; Ford Motor Company; Hardin-Simmons University; Hondrick Medical Center; NationsBank of Texas, N.A.; Sears, Roebuck & Co.; United Services Automobile Assn.

For full biographical listings, see the Martindale-Hubbell Law Directory

*ALBANY,** Shackelford Co. — (Refer to Abilene)

*ALICE,** Jim Wells Co.

Warburton, Adami, McNeill, Paisley & McGuire, P.C. (AV)

Alice Bank of Texas Building, Fourth Floor, 601 East Main Street, P.O. Box 331, 78333-0331
Telephone: 512-668-8101
Fax: 512-668-8106

Lawrence H. Warburton, Jr.
John G. "Buster" Adami, Jr.
Wallis D. McNeill, Jr.
Mark R. Paisley
Robert J. McGuire

Representative Clients: Alice Bank of Texas; Bowden Ford Lincoln Mercury Co.; Brooks County Independent School District; Jim Wells County; Ponder Industries, Inc.; Lundells, Inc.; East Bros.; Brush County Bank.

For full biographical listings, see the Martindale-Hubbell Law Directory

*AMARILLO,** Potter Co.

Conant Whittenburg Whittenburg & Schachter, P.C. (AV)

1010 South Harrison, P.O. Box 31718, 79120
Telephone: 806-372-5700
Facsimile: 806-372-5757
Dallas, Texas Office: 2300 Plaza of the Americas, 600 North Pearl, LB 133,
Telephone: 214-999-5700.
Facsimile: 214-999-5747.

A. B. Conant, Jr.
George Whittenburg
Mack Whittenburg
Cary Ira Schachter
Susan Lynn Burnette
William B. Chaney
Charles G. White
Vikram K. D. Chandhok
J. Michael McBride

OF COUNSEL

Linda A. Hale

Karl L. Baumgardner
Raymond P. Harris, Jr.
Lewis Coppedge
Francis Hangarter, Jr.
Nanneska N. Magee
Stuart J. Ford
Shawn W. Phelan
Paul M. Saraceni

For full biographical listings, see the Martindale-Hubbell Law Directory

Underwood, Wilson, Berry, Stein & Johnson, P.C. (AV)

1500 Amarillo National Bank Building, P.O. Box 9158, 79105
Telephone: 806-376-5613
Telecopier: 806-379-0316

R. E. Underwood (1877-1966)
R. A. Wilson (1905-1986)
Hiram A. Berry (1907-1988)
Jerome W. Johnson
Jerry F. Lyons (Retired)
Edward H. Hill
James A. Besselman
E. T. Manning, Jr.
Don M. Dean
A. W. SoRelle III
Gerald G. Bybee
William A. Hoy, III
Richard F. Brown
Michael H. Loftin
R. Barrett Richards
Thomas R. Dixon, Jr.
Kelly Utsinger
Sharon E. White
Patrick B. Mosley
T. Alan Rhodes
James W. Wester
Michele Fortunato
D. Lynn Tate
Dan L. Schaap
Gregory M. Bednarz

OF COUNSEL

Clifford A. Stein
Winston R. Smith
Sally Holt Emerson

Michelle Eggleston
Nathan Paul Moore
Christopher K. Wrampelmeier
Delinda R. Johnson
R. Tracy Sprouls
Charles A. Mallard
Grant Adams

Representative Clients: Allstate Insurance Co.; Amarillo National Bank; Liberty Mutual Group; ASARCO Incorporated; Cal Farley's Boys Ranch; Amarillo Independent School District; Farmers Insurance Group; Maxus Energy Corp.; St. Anthony's Hospital; West Texas A & M University.

For full biographical listings, see the Martindale-Hubbell Law Directory

*ANSON,** Jones Co. — (Refer to Abilene)

*ARCHER CITY,** Archer Co. — (Refer to Wichita Falls)

ARLINGTON, Tarrant Co.

Cribbs & McFarland, A Professional Corporation (AV)

1000 West Abram, P.O. Box 13060, 76013
Telephone: 817-461-2000
Fax: 817-275-7810
Austin, Texas Office: 814 San Jacinto Boulevard, Suite 400.
Telephone: 512-478-1881.

James A. Cribbs
Bob McFarland
Paul F. Wieneskie
Paul Francis

John Paul Tomme

Representative Clients: Bank One Arlington; Bank One Euless; Bank One Mansfield; Security Bank of Arlington; Medical Technology, Inc.; Van Zandt Realtors; City of Euless, Texas; City of Richland Hills, Texas; American Title Ins. Co.

For full biographical listings, see the Martindale-Hubbell Law Directory

*ATHENS,** Henderson Co. — (Refer to Tyler)

ATLANTA, Cass Co. — (Refer to Texarkana)

*AUSTIN,** Travis Co.

* indicates certain Bar Register subscribers whose principal office is located elsewhere in the state and who have arranged for representation as a part of the state capital listings that follow

*** Akin, Gump, Strauss, Hauer & Feld, L.L.P.** (AV)

A Registered Limited Liability Partnership including Professional Corporations
Franklin Plaza, 111 Congress Avenue, Suite 2100, 78701
Telephone: 512-499-6200
Fax: 512-476-3866
Dallas, Texas Office: 1700 Pacific Avenue, Suite 4100.
Telephone: 214-969-2800.
Fax: 214-969-4343.
Houston, Texas Office: Pennzoil Place-South Tower, 711 Louisiana Street, Suite 1900.
Telephone: 713-220-5800.
Fax: 713-236-0822.
San Antonio, Texas Office: NationsBank Plaza, 300 Convent Street, Suite 1500.
Telephone: 210-270-0800.
Fax: 210-224-2035.
New York, New York Office: 65 East 55th Street, 33rd Floor.
Telephone: 212-872-1000.
Fax: 212-872-1002.
Washington, D.C. Office: 1333 New Hampshire Avenue. N.W., Suite 400.
Telephone: 202-887-4000.
Fax: 202-887-4288.
Brussels, Belgium Office: Akin, Gump, Strauss, Hauer, Feld & Dassesse, 65 Avenue Louise, P. B. #7.
Telephone: 011-322-535-29-11.
Fax: 011-322535-29-00.
Moscow, Russia Office: Bolshoi Sukharevsky, Pereulok 26, Building 1, 2nd Floor.
Telephone: 011 7 095 974 2411.
Fax: 011 7 095 974 2412.

MEMBERS

Thomas J. Bond (P.C.) — Daniel W. Nelson
James W. Cannon, Jr. — David W. Nelson
David B. Gross (P.C.) — Jody Richardson
Jack W. Gullahorn (P.C.) — Paul Seals
James W. Ingram (P.C.) — Robert N. Vedder
Kimberly A. Yelkin (P.C.)

ASSOCIATES

Nanette K. Beaird — Jonna Kay Hogeland
Jane R. Burruss — Susan Erickson Marin (Not admitted in TX)
Joe W. Christina, Jr. — Tracy Walters McCormack
Craig S. Comeaux — Demetrius McDaniel
Teresa I. Ford — Dewey Poteet
Patricia Fuller — Susan C. Scott
Elizabeth M. Galaway — Wallace H. Scott, III
John Greytok — Barry R. Senterfitt
Janet L. Hamilton

STAFF ATTORNEY

Lisa J. Bosman (Resident)

OF COUNSEL

Marianne Carroll — Ned Price, Sr.
Diana L. Granger — Diane E. Umstead
Frederick H. Young

For full biographical listings, see the Martindale-Hubbell Law Directory

Babb & Bradshaw, P.C. (AV)

905 Congress Avenue, P.O. Drawer 1963, 78767
Telephone: 512-473-8600
Facsimile: 512-322-9274

Charles M. Babb — Robert R. Bradshaw
Joseph S. Babb

Reference: Liberty National Bank.

For full biographical listings, see the Martindale-Hubbell Law Directory

Baker & Botts, L.L.P. (AV)

1600 San Jacinto Center, 98 San Jacinto Boulevard, 78701
Telephone: 512-322-2500
Fax: 512-322-2501
Houston, Texas Office: One Shell Plaza, 910 Louisiana.
Telephone: 713-229-1234.
Dallas, Texas Office: 2001 Ross Avenue.
Telephone: 214-953-6500.
Washington, D.C. Office: The Warner, 1299 Pennsylvania Avenue, N.W.
Telephone: 202-639-7700.
New York, New York Office: 885 Third Avenue, Suite 2000.
Telephone: 212-705-5000.
Moscow, Russian Federation Office: 10 ul. Pushkinskaya, 103031.
Telephone: 7095/921-5300 (Local); 7501/929-7070 (International).

(See Next Column)

MEMBERS OF FIRM

Shelley W. Austin — Robert W. Strauser
Pamela M. Giblin — William F. Stutts, Jr.
Robert I. Howell — Robb L. Voyles
William Noble Hulsey III — Mark J. White
Robert T. Stewart — Larry F. York

OF COUNSEL

Joe R. Greenhill — Bob E. Shannon
Robert D. Simpson

ASSOCIATES

Eric Anthony Allen — Joseph R. Knight
Dennis William Braswell — Ann Livingston
Catherine M. Del Castillo — Derek R. McDonald
Raman N. Dewan — Francesca Ortiz
Susan Denmon Gusky — Polly F. Powell
Aileen M. Hooks — Mark R. Robeck
Jennifer Keane — Kevin M. Sadler
Patrick O. Keel — R. Walton Shelton
Cynthia Cooke Smiley

For full biographical listings, see the Martindale-Hubbell Law Directory

Clark, Thomas & Winters, A Professional Corporation (AV)

12th Floor, Texas Commerce Bank Building, 700 Lavaca Street, P.O. Box 1148, 78767
Telephone: 512-472-8800
Fax: 512-474-1129
San Antonio, Texas Office: One Riverwalk Place, 700 North St. Mary's Street, Suite 600.
Telephone: 512-227-2691.

Edward A. Clark (1906-1992) — Jay A. Thompson
Donald S. Thomas — Leslie A. Benitez
J. Sam Winters — Casey Wren
Conrad P. Werkenthin — S. Meade Bauer
Mary Joe Carroll — Earl L. Yeakel, III
Mike Cotten — C. Joseph Cain
Barry K. Bishop — Mark T. Mitchell
Donald S. Thomas, Jr. — Rick Akin
Rhonda H. Brink — Joanne Summerhays
Burgain G. Hayes — Dan Ballard
Walter Demond — Ted Mishtal
Larry McNeill — Chris A. Pearson
James E. Mann — Phyllis B. Schunck
David C. Duggins — Kay L. Taylor
Kenneth J. Ferguson — Stephen C. Dickman
Daniel R. Renner — John J. Vay
L. G. Skip Smith — David H. Gilliland
Michael R. Klatt — Will Guerrant
James F. McNally, Jr.

A. Boone Almanza — David Lill
Terry Bassham — Tracy J. Mabry
Katherine E. Bell-Moss — Mark A. Mayfield
Louis D. Bonder — Kerry McGrath
Susan P. Burton — Christine M. Mullen
L. French Cadenhead — John D. Munn
Randall L. Christian — Laura Cerniglia O'Toole
Lisa McDaniel Crane — Kathryn Burnstein Peterson
Thomas G. Devine — Paul S. Ruiz
Anthony V.S. England — Roy Spezia
Amanda G. Foote — Mark P. Strain
Rogan B. Giles — Jan Steinour Thompson
Catherine M. Greaves — Susan E. Waelbroeck
Sarah H. Haynie — Valerie L. Wenger
Sam K. Hildebrand — John F. Williams
Evelyn N. Howard-Hand — Darrell D. Zurovec
Kelly R. Kimbrough (Not admitted in TX)

For full biographical listings, see the Martindale-Hubbell Law Directory

Law Office of David Cohen (AV)

1301 Nueces Suite 200, 78701
Telephone: 512-473-2111
FAX: 512-477-9569
Mailing Address: P.O. Box 163211, Austin, TX, 76716-3211

For full biographical listings, see the Martindale-Hubbell Law Directory

Davis & Davis, P.C. (AV)

Arboretum Plaza One, 9th Floor, 9442 Capitol of Texas Highway, P.O. Box 1588, 78767
Telephone: 512-343-6248
Fax: 512-343-0121

C. Dean Davis — Alexis J. Fuller, Jr.
Fred E. Davis — Francis A. (Tony) Bradley
Ruth Russell-Schafer

(See Next Column)

DAVIS & DAVIS P.C., *Austin—Continued*

Bill Cline, Jr.
Robert L. Hargett
Michael L. Neely
Brian Gregory Jackson
A. A. Jack Ross, IV
Kevin Wayde Morse
Mark Alan Keene
Kenda B. Dalrymple
Monte F. James
Marian Jeu

For full biographical listings, see the Martindale-Hubbell Law Directory

THOMAS A. FORBES (AV)

Suite 2300 515 Congress Avenue, 78701
Telephone: 512-480-5655
Fax: 512-478-1976

For full biographical listings, see the Martindale-Hubbell Law Directory

GRAVES, DOUGHERTY, HEARON & MOODY, A PROFESSIONAL CORPORATION (AV)

Suite 2300, 515 Congress Avenue, P.O. Box 98, 78767
Telephone: 512-480-5600
Kerrville, Texas Office: 222 Sidney Baker South.
Telephone: 210-257-7311.
Fax: 210-896-7273.

SHAREHOLDERS

Ireland Graves (1885-1969)
Karen J. Bartoletti
Lydia Wommack Barton
Eric G. Behrens
Wm. Terry Bray
Boyce C. Cabaniss
Patricia A. Campbell
Carol C. Clark
Michael Diehl
Richard S. Donoghue
Cliff Ernst
John M. Harmon
R. Alan Haywood
Robert J. Hearon, Jr.
R. Clarke Heidrick, Jr.
David G. Henry
Diane M. Henson
Thomas B. Hudson, Jr.
Glenn E. Johnson
James M. Laughead
Gary Michael Lawrence
John B. McFarland
John J. McKetta, III
Robin A. Melvin
Dan Moody, Jr.
MariBen Ramsey
Owen L. Roberts
Robert M. Roller
Steven D. Smit
Rick Triplett
Ann E. Vanderburg
Terry Lee Vanderburg
Selden Anne Wallace
James A. Williams

Rebecca A. Baird
Michelle Bourianoff Bray
Paul S. Crozier
G. Douglas Kilday
William W. Dibrell
Joseph P. Lally
Joan Dell Weaver Thompson (Resident, Kerrville Office)
Carey Steven Leva
Charles D. Moody
James Preston Randall
Michael J. Whellan

SENIOR COUNSEL

J. Chrys Dougherty

OF COUNSEL

David Herndon
Ben F. Vaughan, III, P.C.

For full biographical listings, see the Martindale-Hubbell Law Directory

*** HUGHES & LUCE, L.L.P. (AV)**

A Registered Limited Liability Partnership including Professional Corporations
111 Congress, Suite 900, 78701
Telephone: 512-482-6800
Fax: 512-482-6859
Dallas, Texas Office: 1717 Main Street, Suite 2800.
Telephone: 214-939-5500.
Fax: 214-939-6100.
Houston, Texas Office: Three Allen Center, 333 Clay Street, Suite 3800.
Telephone: 713-754-5200.
Fax: 713-754-5206.
Fort Worth, Texas Office: 2421 Westport Parkway, Suite 500A.
Telephone: 817-439-3000.
Fax: 817-439-4222.

MEMBERS OF FIRM

Linda J. Burgess
Jack Erskine
Arley D. Finley
Alexander J. Gonzales
Christopher A. Knepp
Sabrina L. Krakauer
Stephen A. Mitchell
H. Robert Powell
Grace Fisher Renbarger
Paul J. Van Osselaer

ASSOCIATES

Brenda E. Brockner
Brittan Lance Buchanan
Christopher H. Hahn
Vincent L. Hazen
Julie Caruthers Parsley
Ann Abrams Price
Rebecca L. Rosnack
Marc T. Shivers

SENIOR COUNSEL

Mack Wallace

For full biographical listings, see the Martindale-Hubbell Law Directory

MATTHEWS & BRANSCOMB, A PROFESSIONAL CORPORATION (AV)

301 Congress Avenue, Suite 2050, 78701
Telephone: 512-305-4400
Facsimile: 512-305-4413
San Antonio, Texas Office: One Alamo Center. 106 S. St. Mary's Street, Suite 800.
Telephone: 210-226-4211.
Facsimile: 210-226-0521.
Telex: 5106009283. Cable Code: MBLAW.
Corpus Christi, Texas Office: 802 N. Caranachua, Suite 1900.
Telephone: 512-888-9261.
Facsimile: 512-888-8504.
Eagle Pass, Texas Office: 675 Main Street.
Telephone: 210-773-6700.
Facsimile: 210-757-4045.
Uvalde, Texas Office: 200 E. Nopal # 208.
Telephone: 210-278-4597.
Facsimile: 210-278-4806.
(Associated with Hall, Quintanilla & Alarcon, L.C., Laredo, Texas, under the name of Hall, Quintanilla, Alarcon, Matthews & Branscomb, P.L.L.C.).

J. Tullos Wells
B. Lee Crawford, Jr.
Lacey L. Gourley
Holly Claghorn

For full biographical listings, see the Martindale-Hubbell Law Directory

MCGINNIS, LOCHRIDGE & KILGORE, L.L.P. (AV)

1300 Capitol Center, 919 Congress Avenue, 78701
Telephone: 512-495-6000
Houston, Texas Office: 3200 One Houston Center, 1221 McKinney Street.
Telephone: 713-615-8500.

OF COUNSEL

Robert W. Calvert (1905-1994)
Wade F. Spilman
Denny O. Ingram
W. James McAnelly, Jr.
Jack Ratliff

RETIRED PARTNER

Robert C. McGinnis (Retired)

RETIRED OF COUNSEL

Morgan Hunter

MEMBERS OF FIRM

Lloyd Lochridge
Joe M. Kilgore
B. D. St. Clair (1930-1991)
Bolivar C. Andrews (Resident, Houston Office)
Shannon H. Ratliff
C. Morris Davis
J. Gaylord Armstrong
Barry L. Wertz
John W. Stayton, Jr.
William H. Bingham
Robert Wilson
William H. Daniel
Thomas O. Barton
Julian Lockwood
Jeffrey A. Davis (Resident, Houston Office)
Brook Bennett Brown
Marc O. Knisely
Patton G. Lochridge
S. Jack Balagia, Jr.
Campbell McGinnis
James R. Raup
Theresa G. Eilers
W. Timothy George
Michael A. Wren
Scott Moore
David E. Jackson
William A. Rogers, Jr.
Edmond R. McCarthy, Jr.
Christine F. Miller
Jeff Bohm
John H. Spurgin, II
Richard Kelley
Paul J. Wataha
Gregory S. Chanon
John R. Breihan
Ashton G. Cumberbatch, Jr.
Don Henry Magee
Richard L. Whitley
Douglas D. Dodds
Lin Hughes
Thomas J. Forestier

SPECIAL COUNSEL

Frank Van Court

ASSOCIATES

Judy Frederick
Angela Chinn Woodbury
Andrew N. Barrett
Stuart Norman Whitlow
Cynthia L. Young
Clayton James Barton
David B. Young
Steve P. Turner
John Matthew Sjoberg
Karen Lynn Watkins
Penny Hobbs
John L. Wilson
Catherine Jean Webking
Shawn P. St. Clair
Karla H. Bell
D. Terrence McDonald
James R. Hines
Donald D. Jackson (Resident, Houston Office)
Michelle Gray Tobias
Margaret E. Baker
Travis Charles Barton

For full biographical listings, see the Martindale-Hubbell Law Directory

*** NAMAN, HOWELL, SMITH & LEE, A PROFESSIONAL CORPORATION (AV)**

221 West Sixth Street, 1900 Bank One Tower, 78701-3485
Telephone: 512-479-0300
FAX: 512-474-1901; ABA/Net ABA2117
Waco, Texas Office: Texas Center, Ninth & Washington, P.O Box 1470.
Telephone: 817-755-4100.
FAX: 817-754-6331.

(See Next Column)

NAMAN, HOWELL, SMITH & LEE A PROFESSIONAL CORPORATION—*Continued*

Temple, Texas Office: Bowmer, Courtney, Burleson, Normand & Moore, 6th Floor, First National Bank Building, P.O. Box 844.
Telephone: 817-778-1354.
FAX: 817-774-7254.

P. Clark Aspy
George M. Cowden
Allen H. King
Keith E. Gamel

William M. "Skip" King
Kelli A. Norris

Representative Client: Texas Municipal Power Agency.

For full biographical listings, see the Martindale-Hubbell Law Directory

STRASBURGER & PRICE, L.L.P. (AV)

A Partnership including Professional Corporations
2600, One American Center, 600 Congress Avenue, 78701
Telephone: 512-499-3600
Fax: 512-499-3660
Dallas, Texas Office: 901 Main Street, Suite 4300.
Telephone: 214-651-4300.
Fax: 214-651-4330.
Houston, Texas Office: Suite 2800, One Houston Center, 1221 McKinney.
Telephone: 713-951-5600.
Fax: 713-951-5660.
Mexico City Office: Edificio Hewlett-Packard, Monte Pelvoux No. 111, Piso 5, Lomas de Chapultepec, 11000 Mexico D.F.
Telephone: 525-202-8796.
Fax: 525-520-7671.
Mexico City Correspondent: Gonzalez, Calvillo y Forastieri, S.C. Edificio Hewlett-Packard, Monte Pelvoux No. 111, Piso 5, Lomas de Chapultepec, 11000 Mexico D.F.
Telephone: 525-202-7622.
Fax: 525-520-7671.

RESIDENT MEMBERS

David B. Armbrust
Frank B. Brown IV
Samuel D. Byars
Sharlene Neibauer Collins
Gary Ward Davis, Jr.
Lloyd E. Ferguson
Wayne S. Hollingsworth
Kenneth N. Jones
Sue Brooks Littlefield
Hal L. Sanders, Jr., (P.C.)
Richard T. Suttle, Jr.

Shireen I. Bacon
Robert D. Burton
John J. Carlton
Dirk M. Jordan
Gregg C. Krumme
Barry S. Read
Dawn Elise Reveley
J. Bruce Scrafford
Merritt N. Spencer
Scott A. Taylor

For full biographical listings, see the Martindale-Hubbell Law Directory

* THOMPSON & KNIGHT, A PROFESSIONAL CORPORATION (AV)

(Attorneys and Counselors)
1200 San Jacinto Center, 98 San Jacinto Boulevard, 78701
Telephone: 512-469-6100
Telecopy: 512-469-6180
Dallas, Texas Office: 1700 Pacific Avenue, Suite 3300, 75201.
Telephone: 214-969-1700.
Telecopy: 512-969-1751.
Cable Address: "Tomtex."
Telex: 732298.
Fort Worth, Texas Office: 801 Cherry Street, Suite 1600, 76102.
Telephone: 817-347-1700.
Telecopy: 817-347-1799.
Houston, Texas Office: 1700 Texas Commerce Tower, 600 Travis, 77002.
Telephone: 713-217-2800.
Telecopy: 713-217-2828; 713-217-2882.
Monterrey, Mexico Office: Edificio Losoles PD-4, Av. Lázaro Cárdenas No. 2400 Pte., San Pedro Garza Garcia, Nuevo Léon C.P. 66220.
Telephone: (52-8) 363-0096.
Telecopy: (52-8) 363-3067.

SHAREHOLDERS

Eugene W. Brees, II
James E. Cousar IV
Frank L. Hill
Debora Beck McWilliams
Carrie Parker Tiemann

ASSOCIATES

Jeffrey S. Boyd
Jane E. Fields
Becky L. Jolin
Caroline M. LeGette

SENIOR ATTORNEY

Elizabeth A. Webb

OF COUNSEL

Alexandra W. Albright
Richard J. Wieland

For full biographical listings, see the Martindale-Hubbell Law Directory

* VINSON & ELKINS L.L.P. (AV)

One American Center, 600 Congress Avenue, 78701-3200
Telephone: 512-495-8400
Fax: 512-495-8612
Houston, Texas Office: 1001 Fannin, Suite 2300.
Telephone: 713-758-2222.
Fax: 713-758-2346. International
Telex: 6868314.
Cable Address: Vinelkins.
Dallas, Texas Office: 3700 Trammell Crow Center, 2001 Ross Avenue.
Telephone: 214-220-7700.
Fax: 214-220-7716.
Washington, D.C. Office: The Willard Office Building, 1455 Pennsylvania Avenue, N.W.
Telephone: 202-639-6500.
Fax: 202-639-6604.
Cable Address: Vinelkins.
London, England Office: 47 Charles Street, Berkeley Square, London W1X 7PB, England.
Telephone: 011 (44-171) 491-7236.
Fax: 011 (44-171) 499-5320.
Cable Address: Vinelkins LondonW.1.
Moscow, Russian Federation Office: 16 Alezey Tolstoy Street, Second Floor, Moscow, 103001 Russian Federation.
Telephone: 011 (70-95) 956-1995.
Telecopy: 011 (70-95) 956-1996.
Mexico City, Mexico Office: Arisóteles 77, 5°Piso, Colonia Chapultepec Polanco, 11560 Mexico, D.F.
Telephone: (52-5) 280-7828.
Fax: (52-5) 280-9223.
Singapore Office: 50 Raffles Place, #19-05 Shell Tower, 0104. U.S. Voice Mailbox: 713-758-3500.
Telephone: (65) 536-8300.
Fax: (65) 536-8311.

RESIDENT PARTNERS

Kim Edward Brightwell
Molly Cagle
Harley R. Clark, Jr.
Susan G. Conway
Richard D. Milvenan
Roger P. Nevola
Jerry E. Turner
Joe Bill Watkins

OF COUNSEL

Amanda G. Birrell
Mary Barrow Nichols
Patrick Ford Thompson

RESIDENT ASSOCIATES

J. David Bickham, Jr.
Barry D. Burgdorf
Daniel R. Castro
Robbi B. Hull
Barbara Lovingfoss
Macy A. Melton
Donald W. Neal, Jr.
W. Glenn Opel
Mary Pape
R. Scott Placek
Eva C. Ramos
Beverly G. Reeves
Elizabeth P. Rippy
James W. Scarrow
Susan B. Snyder
Michael J. Tomsu
Alysia Wightman

For full biographical listings, see the Martindale-Hubbell Law Directory

WINSTEAD SECHREST & MINICK P.C. (AV)

Suite 800, 100 Congress Avenue, 78701
Telephone: 512-474-4330
Telex: 73-0051
Telecopier: 512-370-2850
Dallas, Texas Office: 5400 Renaissance Tower, 1201 Elm Street.
Telephone: 214-745-5400.
Telex: 73-0051.
Telecopier: 214-745-5390.
Houston, Texas Office: 1700 Bank One Center, 910 Travis Street.
Telephone: 713-655-0392.
Telex: 73-0051.
Telecopy: 713-951-3800.
Mexico, D.F., Mexico Office: Winstead Sechrest & Minick, S.A. de C.V., Galileo 20, P.H. - A, Col. Polanco, 11560 Mexico, D.F.
Telephone: 525-280-6766.
Telecopier: 525-280-0307.

Peter Winstead
Timothy E. Young
Berry D. Spears
Walter Earl Bissex
David R. Hewlett
Kent A. Caperton

James G. Ruiz
R. Eddie Dixon, Jr.
Kelly K. Kordzik
Michele Barbero Thompson
Glen A. Hodges
Mary E. Kragie

OF COUNSEL

George E. Clark
Mary B. Reagan
Robert C. Bass, Jr.

For full biographical listings, see the Martindale-Hubbell Law Directory

*BAIRD,** Callahan Co. — (Refer to Abilene)

BAYTOWN, Harris Co.

REID, STRICKLAND & GILLETTE, L.L.P. (AV)

A Partnership including Professional Corporations
407 Citizens Bank Tower, 1300 Rollingbrook at Garth, P.O. Box 809, 77522-0809
Telephone: 713-422-8166
Fax: 713-428-2962

Joe Reid (1887-1964)
Robert Strickland (1908-1982)
John R. Sandhop (P.C.)
Everett B. Williams (P.C.)
Jon C. Pfennig (P.C.)
Stephen H. DonCarlos

OF COUNSEL

Robert L. Gillette (P.C.)

Attorneys for: Citizens Bank & Trust Co. of Baytown, Texas; Harris County Water Control and Improvement District No. 1; The Baytown Sun.

For full biographical listings, see the Martindale-Hubbell Law Directory

*BEAUMONT,** Jefferson Co.

BENCKENSTEIN, NORVELL & NATHAN, L.L.P. (AV)

2615 Calder Avenue, Suite 600, P.O. Box 551, 77704
Telephone: 409-833-4309
Telecopier: 409-833-9558
Houston, Texas Office: One Riverway, Suite 100
Telephone: 713-871-8081.
FAX: 713-871-1509.

MEMBERS OF FIRM

Lipscomb Norvell, Jr.
Jerry J. Nathan
Gerald W. Riedmueller
Michael J. Reviere
Russell W. Heald
Donald Francis Lighty
Paul A. Scheurich

ASSOCIATES

Craig H. Clendenin
Kerry B. McKnight
Floyd F. McSpadden, Jr.
Elizabeth Ellen Brown
Wayne E. Revack
Stephen R. Whalen
Dennis S. Dresden
David A. Oubre
Jacqueline M. Stroh
Douglas C. Clark (Resident, Houston, Texas Office)

Representative Clients: Chubb/Pacific Indemnity Group; Mobil Oil Corp.; Aetna Casualty Insurance Co.; Hartford Insurance Group; The Home Insurance Company; Wausau; Cigna; Fina Oil & Chemical Company; Continental Insurance Group; Kemper Group Insurance.

For full biographical listings, see the Martindale-Hubbell Law Directory

BENCKENSTEIN & OXFORD, L.L.P. (AV)

First Interstate Bank Building, P.O. Box 150, 77704
Telephone: 409-833-9182
Cable Address: "Bmor"
Telex: 779485
Telefax: 409-833-8819
Austin, Texas Office: Suite 810, 400 West 15th Street, 78701.
Telephone: 512-474-8586.
Telefax: 512-478-3064.

MEMBERS OF FIRM

L. J. Benckenstein (1894-1966)
F. L. Benckenstein (1918-1987)
Hubert Oxford, III
Alan G. Sampson
Frank D. Calvert
Dana Timaeus
Mary Ellen Blade
William H. Yoes
William M. Tolin, III
Kip Kevin Lamb
Frances Blair Bethea
Robert J. Rose, Sr.

OF COUNSEL

James E. McNerney

ASSOCIATES

Susan J. Oliver
F. Blair Clarke
Keith A. Pardue (Resident, Austin, Texas Office)
Josiah Wheat, Jr.
Steve Johnson
Michael Keith Eaves
Nikki L. Redden
Mitchell W. Templeton

Representative Clients: Marine Office of American Corporation (MOAC); Moran Towing and Transportation Co., Inc.

For full biographical listings, see the Martindale-Hubbell Law Directory

MEHAFFY & WEBER, A PROFESSIONAL CORPORATION (AV)

2615 Calder Avenue, P.O. Box 16, 77704
Telephone: 409-835-5011
Fax: 409-835-5729; 835-5177
Orange, Texas Office: 1006 Green Avenue, P.O. Drawer 189.
Telephone: 409-886-7766.
Houston, Texas Office: One Allen Center, 500 Dallas, Suite 1200.
Telephone: 713-655-1200.

(See Next Column)

James W. Mehaffy (1914-1985)
Dewey J. Gonsoulin
Daniel V. Flatten
Roger S. McCabe
Jim I. Graves
John Cash Smith
Thomas L. Hanna
John J. Durkay
Arthur R. Almquist
Louis M. Scofield
Patricia Chamblin
Gene M. Williams
David B. Gaultney
Robert A. Black
Sandra F. Clark
M. C. Carrington
Kurt M. Andreason
Deborah A. Newman
Barbara J. Barron
Elizabeth Brandes Pratt
Joseph E. Broussard
John E. Haught

Elizabeth C. Lazenby
Keith W. Foley
Vickie R. Thompson
Cimron Campbell
Josephine Tennant-Hillegeist
Greg J. German
Ernest W. Boyd
Stephen H. Forman
Michele Y. Smith
Lynn M. Bencowitz
Charles S. Perry
James C. (Clay) Crawford
David W. Schultz
Deanne F. Rienstra
Paul R. Heyburn
Maria Artime
Douglas C. Monsour
Barrett F. Watson
David L. Red
Cecile E. Crabtree

OF COUNSEL

Otto J. Weber, Jr.

Representative Clients: E.I. du Pont de Nemours and Company; Bethlehem Steel Corp.; The Kansas City Southern Railway Co.; FMC Corp.; Eli Lilly & Company; Merrell Dow; Jefferson County Tax Appraisal District.
Approved Attorneys for: Stewart Title Guaranty Co.

For full biographical listings, see the Martindale-Hubbell Law Directory

ORGAIN, BELL & TUCKER, L.L.P. (AV)

470 Orleans Street, 77701
Telephone: 409-838-6412
FAX: 409-838-6959

Will E. Orgain (1883-1965)
Major T. Bell (1897-1969)

MEMBERS OF FIRM

James W. Hambright
Gilbert I. Low
Benny H. Hughes
J. Hoke Peacock, II
John Creighton, III
James H. Chesnutt, II
Jo Ben Whittenburg
Gary N. Reger
John W. Newton, III
D. Allan Jones
H. Hollis Horton, III
Lois Ann Stanton
Robert J. Hambright
Howard L. Close
Curry L. Cooksey
Charles K. Kebodeaux
Michael J. Truncale
Lance Fox
Leanne Johnson
David J. Fisher
John W. Johnson

ASSOCIATES

Jack P. Carroll
T. Lynn Walden
Stephanie D. Surratt
Dick LeMasters
Milli Alexander
Jonathan Campbell
Joel Reese
Jason Willett
David Allen

OF COUNSEL

John G. Tucker
B. D. Orgain
Stanley Plettman

General Counsel: Gulf States Utilities Co.; Texas Commerce Bank.
Local Counsel for: Mobil Oil Corp.; General Motors Corp.; City of Beaumont; Minnesota Mining & Manufacturing Co.; Wal-Mart Stores, Inc.
Representative Insurance Clients: Kemper Group; Hartford Insurance Group; Royal Insurance.

For full biographical listings, see the Martindale-Hubbell Law Directory

STRONG, PIPKIN, NELSON & BISSELL, L.L.P. (AV)

1400 San Jacinto Building, 77701-3255
Telephone: 409-835-4581
Facsimile: 409-835-0914

Ewell Strong (1905-1974)
Charles S. Pipkin (1896-1989)
John G. Bissell
David W. Ledyard
Michael L. Baker
Daniel C. Ducote
Philip Babin, III
Walter D. Snider
Richard L. Scheer
Thomas F. Mulvaney
Michael T. Bridwell
John W. Bridger
David W. Starnes
Mark D. Rayburn
David A. Oliver
Greg M. Dykeman

Julie Alyssa Richardson
G. Robert Sonnier
Judith A. Sachitano
Quentin D. Price
Theodore P. Ray
C. Patrick Waites
D. Ray Murphy
Andrea E. Treiber

OF COUNSEL

Louis V. Nelson

Representative Clients: The American General Cos.; The Travelers Insurance Co.; National Life and Accident Insurance Co.; Kemper Group; Bank One, Texas, N.A.; The Goodyear Tire & Rubber Co.

(See Next Column)

STRONG, PIPKIN, NELSON & BISSELL L.L.P.—*Continued*

For full biographical listings, see the Martindale-Hubbell Law Directory

WELLS, PEYTON, BEARD, GREENBERG, HUNT & CRAWFORD, L.L.P. (AV)

6th Floor, Petroleum Building, P.O. Box 3708, 77704-3708
Telephone: 409-838-2644
FAX: 409-838-4713

MEMBERS OF FIRM

Peter Wells (1915-1991)
George E. Duncan (1917-1979)
S. L. Greenberg
Tanner T. Hunt, Jr.
Walter J. Crawford, Jr.
John B. Quigley
Joseph Martin Green
Phil Dunlap
Peter Boyd Wells, III
Mark Freeman
Bruce M. Partain
Cheryl Olesen

ASSOCIATES

Randall D. Collins
Melody G. Thomas
J. Mitchell Smith

OF COUNSEL

Patrick T. Peyton
Louis H. Beard
Martin E. Broussard

For full biographical listings, see the Martindale-Hubbell Law Directory

*BELLVILLE,** Austin Co. — (Refer to Houston)

*BELTON,** Bell Co. — (Refer to Temple)

*BONHAM,** Fannin Co. — (Refer to Paris)

*BRADY,** McCulloch Co. — (Refer to Austin)

*BRECKENRIDGE,** Stephens Co. — (Refer to Eastland)

*BRENHAM,** Washington Co. — (Refer to Bryan)

*BROWNFIELD,** Terry Co. — (Refer to Tahoka)

*BROWNSVILLE,** Cameron Co.

RODRIGUEZ, COLVIN & CHANEY (AV)

1201 East Van Buren, P.O. Box 2155, 78520
Telephone: 210-542-7441
Fax: 210-541-2170

MEMBERS OF FIRM

Eduardo R. Rodriguez
Norton A. Colvin, Jr.
Mitchell C. Chaney
Marjory Colvin Batsell
Jaime A. Saenz

ASSOCIATES

Joseph A. (Tony) Rodriguez
Laura J. Urbis
Alison Kennamer
Lecia L. Chaney
Michael E. Rodriguez

OF COUNSEL

Benjamin S. Hardy
Neil E. Norquest
Chris A. Brisack

Division Attorneys for: Union Pacific Railroad.
Counsel for: Texas Commerce Bank-Rio Grande Valley, N.A.; Texas Commerce Bancshares, Inc.

For full biographical listings, see the Martindale-Hubbell Law Directory

ROYSTON, RAYZOR, VICKERY & WILLIAMS, L.L.P. (AV)

55 Cove Circle, 78521
Telephone: 210-542-4377
Cable Address: "Padre"
Telex: 767-817.
Telecopier: 210-542-4370
Mailing Address: P.O. Box 3509, Brownsville, Texas, 78523-3509
Houston, Texas Office: 2200 Texas Commerce Tower.
Telephone: 713-224-8380.
Cable Address: "Houport"
Telex: 6869017.
Telecopier: 713-225-9945.
Galveston, Texas Office: 205 Cotton Exchange Building. 2102 Mechanic Street.
Telephone: 409-763-1623.
Cable Address: "Royston"
Telex: 765-449.
Telecopier: 409-763-3853.
Corpus Christi, Texas Office: 1700 Wilson Plaza West, 606 North Carancahua.
Telephone: 512-884-8808.
Cable Address: "CC PORT"
Telex: 6866625.
Telecopier: 512-884-7261.

PARTNERS

Keith N. Uhles
Frank E. Perez

(See Next Column)

ASSOCIATES

Francisco J. Zabarte
Michael J. Urbis
James H. Hunter, Jr.
Rosemary J. Conrad

For full biographical listings, see the Martindale-Hubbell Law Directory

*BROWNWOOD,** Brown Co. — (Refer to Abilene)

*BRYAN,** Brazos Co.

THORNTON, PAYNE, WATSON & KLING, P.C. (AV)

308 East William J. Bryan Parkway, P.O. Drawer E, 77805
Telephone: 409-779-1444
Fax: 409-779-1447

William S. Thornton
Billy M. Payne
Jay Don Watson
Christopher J. Kling
Cindy L. Miller

H. Clinton Milner
Jerry M. Brown

OF COUNSEL

William T. Fleming, Jr.

Representative Clients: First American Bank, Bryan; First Bank of Snook, Snook; First Federal Savings & Loan; Lawyer's Title Company of Brazos County.

For full biographical listings, see the Martindale-Hubbell Law Directory

*BURNET,** Burnet Co. — (Refer to Austin)

*CALDWELL,** Burleson Co. — (Refer to Bryan)

*CAMERON,** Milam Co. — (Refer to Temple)

*CANADIAN,** Hemphill Co. — (Refer to Perryton)

*CANTON,** Van Zandt Co. — (Refer to Dallas)

*CARRIZO SPRINGS,** Dimmit Co.

PETRY & PETRY, P.C. (AV)

4th & Houston, Petry Building, P.O. Drawer 218, 78834
Telephone: 210-876-2431

Herbert C. Petry (1917-1992)
John W. Petry
August Linnartz, Jr.
Daniel Gonzalez

General Counsel: Union State Bank; Bear Motors Longhorn Pecan Ltd.
Local Counsel: Central Power & Light Co.; Carrizo Manufacturing Co., Inc.; Forest Oil Co.

For full biographical listings, see the Martindale-Hubbell Law Directory

*CENTER,** Shelby Co.

FAIRCHILD, PRICE, THOMAS & HALEY (AV)

413 Shelbyville Street, P.O. Drawer 1336, 75935
Telephone: 409-598-2981
Fax: 409-598-7712
Nacogdoches, Texas Office: 1801 North Street.
Telephone: 409-569-2327

MEMBERS OF FIRM

John L. Price
W. Miller Thomas
C. Victor Haley
Travis P. Clardy
David J. Fisher

OF COUNSEL

Robert L. Fairchild

ASSOCIATES

Thomas J. Harris
Clayton H. Haley
J. Ken Muckelroy
Russell R. Smith

For full biographical listings, see the Martindale-Hubbell Law Directory

*CHILDRESS,** Childress Co. — (Refer to Clarendon)

*CLARKSVILLE,** Red River Co. — (Refer to Paris)

*COLEMAN,** Coleman Co. — (Refer to Abilene)

*COLORADO CITY,** Mitchell Co. — (Refer to Sweetwater)

*COLUMBUS,** Colorado Co. — (Refer to Houston)

*COMANCHE,** Comanche Co. — (Refer to Eastland)

*COOPER,** Delta Co. — (Refer to Paris)

*CORPUS CHRISTI,** Nueces Co.

MATTHEWS & BRANSCOMB, A PROFESSIONAL CORPORATION (AV)

802 North Carancahua, Suite 1900, 78470-0700
Telephone: 512-888-9261
Facsimile: 512-888-8504
Austin, Texas Office: 301 Congress Avenue, Suite 2050.
Telephone: 512-305-4400.
Facsimile: 512-305-4413.
San Antonio, Texas Office: One Alamo Center, 106 S. St. Mary's Street, Suite 800.
Telephone: 210-226-4211.
Facsimile: 210-226-0521.
Telex: 51060009283. Cable Code: MBLAW.
Eagle Pass, Texas Office: 675 Main Street.
Telephone: 210-773-6700.
Facsimile: 210-757-4045.
Uvalde, Texas Office: 200 E. Nopal #208.
Telephone: 210-278-4597.
Facsimile: 210-278-4806.
(Associated with Hall, Quintanilla & Alarcon, L.C., Laredo, Texas, under the name of Hall, Quintanilla, Alarcon, Matthews & Branscomb, P.L.L.C.).

Harvie Branscomb, Jr.
G. Ray Miller, Jr.
Michael W. Stukenberg
Kenton E. McDonald
Craig L. Williams
Gerald E. Thornton, Jr.
Mark J. Hulings
J. A. (Andy) Carson
M. Colleen McHugh
James H. Robichaux
Robert S. Nichols
Keith B. Sieczkowski
Scott L. Sherman
W. Roger Durden
Jeffrey S. Dickerson
Beverly B. Swallows

OF COUNSEL

Douglas E. Mann

For full biographical listings, see the Martindale-Hubbell Law Directory

NICOLAS, MORRIS & BARROW (AV)

Suite 545, The Klee Square Building, 505 South Water Street, 78401
Telephone: 512-883-6341
Fax: 512-883-3923

MEMBERS OF FIRM

Alfred N. Nicolas (1924-1987)
Toufic Nicolas
Pat Morris
John D. Barrow
Mark B. Gilbreath
Robert C. Morris

ASSOCIATES

Bradley A. Smith

Representative Clients: Olson-Kessler Meat Company, Inc.; Warehouse Liquors, Inc.; Maverick Markets, Inc.; Zarsky Lumber Co.; Corpus, Inc.; Nolan Steakhouses; Navy-Army Federal Credit Union; San Jacinto Title Co.; Duke Control, Inc.
Reference: First City Bank of Corpus Christi.

For full biographical listings, see the Martindale-Hubbell Law Directory

REDFORD, WRAY, WOOLSEY & ANTHONY, L.L.P. (AV)

1000 North Tower, 500 North Water Street, 78471-0002
Telephone: 512-886-3200
Telecopier: 512-886-3299

Cecil D. Redford (1907-1990)
James W. Wray, Jr.
William N. Woolsey
James L. Anthony
Thomas M. Furlow
Scott D. Schmidt

OF COUNSEL

Ralph B. Weston

Representative Clients: Central and Southwest Corp.; United States Fidelity & Guaranty Company; Republic Insurance Company; National Indemnity Company; FMC Corporation; Great West Casualty Company; General Accident Insurance Company; United States Aviation Underwriters, Inc.

For full biographical listings, see the Martindale-Hubbell Law Directory

ROYSTON, RAYZOR, VICKERY & WILLIAMS, L.L.P. (AV)

1700 Wilson Plaza West, 606 North Carancahua, 78476
Telephone: 512-884-8808
Cable Address: "CC PORT"
Telex: 6866625.
Telecopier: 512-884 -7261.
Houston, Texas Office: 2200 Texas Commerce Tower.
Telephone: 713-224-8380.
Cable Address: "Houport"
Telex: 686-9017.
Telecopier: 713-225-9945.
Galveston, Texas Office: 205 Cotton Exchange Building, 2101 Mechanic Street.
Telephone: 409-763-1623.
Cable Address: "Royston"
Telex: 765-449.
Telecopier: 409-763-3853.

(See Next Column)

Brownsville, Texas Office: 55 Cove Circle, P.O. Box 3509.
Telephone: 210-542-4377.
Cable Address: "Padre"
Telex: 767-817.
Telecopier: 210-542-4370.

PARTNERS

Ralph F. Meyer
Will W. Pierson

ASSOCIATES

Timothy D. McMurtrie
Jack C. Partridge
Patrick M. Martinez
Myra K. Morris

For full biographical listings, see the Martindale-Hubbell Law Directory

*CORSICANA,** Navarro Co. — (Refer to Tyler)

*COTULLA,** LaSalle Co. — (Refer to Carrizo Springs)

*CROCKETT,** Houston Co. — (Refer to Jacksonville)

*CRYSTAL CITY,** Zavala Co. — (Refer to Carrizo Springs)

*CUERO,** De Witt Co. — (Refer to Victoria)

*DALHART,** Dallam Co. — (Refer to Amarillo)

*DALLAS,** Dallas Co.

AKIN, GUMP, STRAUSS, HAUER & FELD, L.L.P. (AV)

A Registered Limited Liability Partnership including Professional Corporations
1700 Pacific Avenue Suite 4100, 75201-4618
Telephone: 214-969-2800
Telex: 732324
FAX: 214-969-4343
Austin, Texas Office: Franklin Plaza, 111 Congress Avenue, Suite 2100.
Telephone: 512-499-6200.
Fax: 512-476-3866.
Houston, Texas Office: Pennzoil Place-South Tower, 711 Louisiana Street, Suite 1900.
Telephone: 713-220-5800.
Fax: 713-236-0822.
San Antonio, Texas Office: NationsBank Plaza, 300 Convent Street, Suite 1500.
Telephone: 210-270-0800.
Fax: 210-224-2035.
New York, New York Office: 65 East 55th Street, 33rd Floor.
Telephone: 212-872-1000.
Fax: 212-872-1002.
Washington, D.C. Office: 1333 New Hampshire Avenue, N.W., Suite 400.
Telephone: 202-887-4000.
Fax: 202-887-4288.
Brussels, Belgium Office: Akin, Gump, Strauss, Hauer, Feld & Dassesse, 65 Avenue Louise, B.P. #7.
Telephone: 011-322-535-29-11.
Fax: 011-322-535-29-00.
Moscow, Russia Office: Bolshoi Sukharevsky, Pereulok 26, Building 1, 2nd Floor.
Telephone: 011 7 095 974 2411.
Fax: 011 7 095 974 2412.

Gary A. Herman (1942-1987)
Herbert S. Kendrick (1934-1990)
Thomas J. Raleigh (1924-1993)

RETIRED

Henry D. Akin
Richard A. Gump, Sr.
John L. Hauer (P.C.)

MEMBERS OF FIRM

Dyke D. Bennett
Louis P. Bickel
John P. Buser (P.C.)
Michael Byrd (P.C.)
Edward A. Copley (P.C.)
Walter S. Cowger
G. Michael Curran
Clarice M. Davis (P.C.)
Michael E. Dillard (P.C.)
Diana C. Dutton (P.C.)
Alan D. Feld (P.C.)
N. Kathleen Friday (P.C.)
Paul E. Galvin
Kenneth R. Glaser
Christopher M. Gores (P.C.)
Dennis T. Griggs
J. Stephen Hatfield (P.C.)
Melinda G. Jayson (P.C.)
Edward S. Koppman (P.C.)
Randall R. Kucera (P.C.)
Ford Lacy (P.C.)
Kathleen M. LaValle (P.C.)
Alan L. Laves
Gary M. Lawrence (P.C.)
Carl B. Lee (P.C.)
George T. Lee, Jr., (P.C.)
Richard C. Levin (P.C.)
Michael Lowenberg (P.C.)
Richard K. Martin (P.C.)
J. Kenneth Menges, Jr., (P.C.)
Daniel J. Micciche (P.C.)
Allen P. Miller (P.C.)
Seth R. Molay (P.C.)
Steven M. Morgan (P.C.)
Gary S. Nash
Mary L. O'Connor
Randall M. Ratner (P.C.)
Hailey A. Roberts (P.C.)
Terry M. Schpok (P.C.)
Richard L. Schwartz
John Q. Stilwell (P.C.)
Robert S. Strauss (P.C.)
Timothy P. Tehan
Mark Weisbart

(See Next Column)

AKIN, GUMP, STRAUSS, HAUER & FELD L.L.P.—*Continued*

ASSOCIATES

Michael Brett Burns
Stephen L. Cohen (Not admitted in TX)
Diane Pearlstone Couchman
Dawn Davenport
Joseph F. DePumpo
Allison K. Exall
Lisa S. Gallerano
John Goldstone
John L. Hendricks
John R. Hulme
Laura Pence Johansen
Mark L. Johansen
Pamela Wildenthal Kernie
J. Christopher Kirk
Rodger I. Kohn
James R. Lancaster
Paul A. Ledbetter
George Terry Lee III
Lesley Lurie
Drew F. Nachowiak
Jonathan N. Quenzer
Khaled Rabbani (Not admitted in TX)
Eliot D. Raffkind
Patrick J. Respeliers
Lynn Brenner Roberts
Paul F. Schuster
Mark R. Shaw
David F. Staber
Daniel G. Strickfaden
J. Patrick Tielborg
Raymond P. Turner
Alan M. Utay

For full biographical listings, see the Martindale-Hubbell Law Directory

ANDREWS & KURTH L.L.P. (AV)

4400 Thanksgiving Tower, 75201
Telephone: 214-979-4400
Telex: 70-9669 Ankur Dal
Telecopier: 214-979-4401
Houston, Texas Office: 4200 Texas Commerce Tower.
Telephone: 713-220-4200.
Telecopier: 713-220-4285.
The Woodlands, Texas Office: Suite 150, 2170 Buckthorne Place, 77380.
Telephone: 713-364-9199.
Telecopier: 713-364-9538.
Washington, D.C. Office: Suite 200, 1701 Pennsylvania Avenue, N.W.
Telephone: 202-662-2700.
Telecopier: 202-662-2739.
Los Angeles, California Office: Suite 4200, 601 S. Figueroa Street.
Telephone: 213-896-3100.
Telecopier: 213-896-3137.
New York, N.Y. Office: 10th Floor, 425 Lexington Avenue.
Telephone: 212-850-2800.
Telecopier: 212-850-2929.

MEMBERS OF FIRM

David A. Allen
David A. Barbour
Alan W. Harris
Charles T. Marshall
J. Van Oliver
Joseph M. Osborne
Thomas R. Popplewell
Patrick C. Sargent
Michael B. Thimmig
Kathleen J. Wu

SENIOR COUNSEL

Robert F. Ritchie

OF COUNSEL

Lisa A. Barbour
Robert L. Trimble

ASSOCIATES

Muriel C. Brown
Andrew L. Campbell
Charles Carpenter
Mark W. Harris
J. Gregory Holloway
Patrick R. Kirby (Not admitted in TX)
Barbara B. Malin
Maura K. Reilly
Merri H. Royer

For full biographical listings, see the Martindale-Hubbell Law Directory

ARANSON & ASSOCIATES (AV)

Legal Arts Center, 600 Jackson Street, 75202
Telephone: 214-748-5100
Fax: 214-741-4540

Mike Aranson
Garry Philip Cantrell

For full biographical listings, see the Martindale-Hubbell Law Directory

JOSEPH E. ASHMORE, JR., P.C. (AV)

Regency Plaza, 3710 Rawlins, Suite 1210, LB 84, 75219-4217
Telephone: 214-559-7202
Fax: 214-520-1550

Joseph E. Ashmore, Jr.

C. Gregory Shamoun
W. Charles Campbell
L. James Ashmore
Howard J. Klatsky

OF COUNSEL

B. Garfield Haynes
Mark S. Michael
F. Bady Sassin

For full biographical listings, see the Martindale-Hubbell Law Directory

BAILEY AND WILLIAMS (AV)

717 North Harwood Street Suite 1650, 75201
Telephone: 214-777-6300

(See Next Column)

OF COUNSEL

Derol Todd

MEMBERS OF FIRM

R. T. Bailey (1900-1988)
James A. Williams
Glennis E. Sims
Douglas R. Lewis
Robert C. Brown
Suzanne Caldwell Ekvall
Sidney L. Murphy

ASSOCIATES

LeAnn Wainscott Cross
Robin Janene Hill
Katherine Lee Laws
Paula Shiroma-Bender

Representative Clients: American Physicians Insurance Exchange; Aetna Life & Casualty; Government Employees Insurance Co.; Vanliner Insurance Co.; Trans America Insurance Co.; Professional Risk Management; Montgomery Elevator; Akros Medico Enterprises; Childrens Medical Center of Dallas; St. Paul Medical Center of Dallas.

For full biographical listings, see the Martindale-Hubbell Law Directory

BAKER & BOTTS, L.L.P. (AV)

2001 Ross Avenue, 75201
Telephone: 214-953-6500
Fax: 214-953-6503
Houston, Texas Office: One Shell Plaza, 910 Louisiana.
Telephone: 713-229-1234.
Washington, D.C. Office: The Warner, 1299 Pennsylvania Avenue, N.W.
Telephone: 202-639-7700.
Austin, Texas Office: 1600 San Jacinto Center, 98 San Jacinto Boulevard.
Telephone: 512-322-2500.
New York, New York Office: 885 Third Avenue, Suite 2000.
Telephone: 212-705-5000.
Moscow, Russian Federation Office: 10 ul. Pushkinskaya, 103031.
Telephone: 7095/921-5300 (Local); 7095/929-7070.

MEMBERS OF FIRM

Richard C. Johnson
Ronald L. Palmer
Jerry W. Mills
Daniel J. Riley
Rod Phelan
Roderick A. Goyne
Robert W. Jordan
James A. Taylor
Jack L. Kinzie
Karen Leslye Wolf
Kerry C. L. North
Andrew M. Baker
Larry D. Carlson
Stan Hinton
George C. Lamb III
Bryant C. Boren, Jr.
Robert W. Kantner
Robb L. Voyles
Earl B. Austin
Jonathan W. Dunlay
Bobbie T. Shell
Patricia M. Stanton
Robert M. Chiaviello, Jr.
John W. Martin
Sarah R. Saldana
Carlos A. Fierro
Peter A. Moir
Edwin J. Tomko
Catharina J. H. D. Haynes
Stephen D. Marcus
Geoffrey L. Newton

OF COUNSEL

Richard S. Lombard

ASSOCIATES

Van H. Beckwith
Sylvia L. Braddom
Marvin S. Cash, IV
Amy E. Castle
Jeffrey Joseph Cox
Joseph M. Dencker
Timothy S. Durst
Thomas R. Felger
Charles S. Fish
David Norman Fogg, Sr.
David M. Genender
Thomas A. Gigliotti
Alison C. Glasstetter
Julie A. Gregory
Kenneth Arthur Hill
Susan Nethery Hogan
Harold Harvey Hunter
Wei Wei Jeang
B. Borden Johnson
Robert Hugh Johnston III
Samara Lackman Kline
Shelley LaGere
Tamara Gail Mattison
Margaret N. McGann
Paul E. McGreal
Kevin J. Meek
David G. Monk
Richard J. Moura (Not admitted in TX)
Joel Mendal Overton, Jr.
Eric Donovan Pearson
Anthony Ernest Peterman
Douglass Michael Rayburn
J. Gregory St. Clair
James Kemp Sawers
Mary L. Scott
Paul W. Searles
Barton Earl Showalter
Michelle White Suárez
Brenda Levine Sutherland
Lynn S. Switzer
Craig Tadlock
Jeffrey M. Tillotson
Kenneth B. Tomlinson
Craig Troyer
Kelly Mahon Tullier
Ariana Viroslav
Robert J. Ward
Eric N. Whitney
David Gerald Wille
Philip W. Woo
Elizabeth Wylie

For full biographical listings, see the Martindale-Hubbell Law Directory

Dallas—Continued

BAKER & McKENZIE (AV)

4500 Trammell Crow Center, 2001 Ross Avenue, 75201
Telephone: (214) 978-3000
Intn'l. Dialing: (1-214) 978-3000
Facsimiles: (1-214) 978-3099; 978-3096
Associated Offices of Baker & McKenzie in: Almaty, Amsterdam, Bangkok, Barcelona, Beijing, Berlin, Bogotá, Brasília, Brussels, Budapest, Buenos Aires, Cairo, Caracas, Chicago, Frankfurt, Geneva, Hanoi, Ho Chi Minh City, Hong Kong, Juárez, Kiev, London, Madrid, Manila, Melbourne, México City, Miami, Milan, Monterrey, Moscow, New York, Palo Alto, Paris, Prague, Rio de Janeiro, Riyadh, Rome, St. Petersburg, San Diego, San Francisco, São Paulo, Singapore, Stockholm, Sydney, Taipei, Tijuana, Tokyo, Toronto, Valencia, Warsaw, Washington, D.C. and Zürich.
Correspondent Law Firm: Hadiputranto, Hadinoto & Partners, Jakarta.

MEMBERS OF FIRM

Robert H. Albaral
Leo O. Bacher, Jr.
Dan S. Boyd
John D. Curtis
Dewey R. Hicks, Jr.
Lawrence J. Johnson
Clifford S. Jury
Daniel W. Rabun

LOCAL PARTNERS

John C. Fox
John J. Kendrick, Jr.
Joe W. (Chip) Pitts III
Mark D. Taylor

OF COUNSEL

Edward F. Sherman

ASSOCIATES

Amarnath Budarapu
Dana W. Easley
Michael F. Forrester
Beth Ann Godfrey
Alan G. Harvey
K. Janée Heizer
R. Edward Ishmael, Jr.
Lawrence R. Kemm
Cecilia A. Martin
Jonathan B. Newton
Gregory S. Porter
Jerald M. Rasansky
Michael E. Santa Maria
Terry L. Traveland

For full biographical listings, see the Martindale-Hubbell Law Directory

HAROLD B. BERMAN (AV)

8333 Douglas Avenue, Suite 1200, 75225
Telephone: 214-369-7779
Fax: 214-691-2691

For full biographical listings, see the Martindale-Hubbell Law Directory

BUTLER & BINION, L.L.P. (AV)

A Partnership including Professional Corporations
750 North St. Paul, Suite 1800, 75201
Telephone: 214-220-3100
Telecopiers: 214-969-7013; 214-954-4245
Houston, Texas Office: 1000 Louisiana, Suite 1600.
Telephone: 713-237-3111.
Telecopier: 713-237-3202.
San Antonio, Texas Office: 112 East Pecan Street, 27th Floor.
Telephone: 210-227-2200.
Telecopier: 210-223-6730.
Washington, D.C. Office: 1747 Pennsylvania Avenue, N.W.
Telephone: 202-446-6900.
Telecopier: 202-833-1274.

RESIDENT MEMBERS

Dan M. Cain (P.C.)
Brenda Turner Cubbage
Michael S. Forshey
James A. Stockard

OF COUNSEL

Dan D. Aaron

ASSOCIATES

Mark Louis Nastri

For full biographical listings, see the Martindale-Hubbell Law Directory

CALHOUN & STACY (AV)

5700 NationsBank Plaza, 901 Main Street, 75202-3747
Telephone: 214-748-5000
Telecopier: 214-748-1421
Telex: 211358 CALGUMP UR

Mark Alan Calhoun
David W. Elrod
Steven D. Goldston
Parker Nelson
Roy L. Stacy

ASSOCIATES

Shannon S. Barclay
Robert A. Bragalone
Dennis D. Conder
Jane Elizabeth Diseker
Lawrence I. Fleishman
Thomas C. Jones
Katherine Johnson Knight
V. Paige Pace
Veronika Willard
Michael C. Wright

LEGAL CONSULTANT

Rees T. Bowen, III

For full biographical listings, see the Martindale-Hubbell Law Directory

CANTEY & HANGER (AV)

A Registered Limited Liability Partnership
Suite 500 300 Crescent Court, 75201
Telephone: 214-978-4100
FAX: 214-978-4150
Fort Worth, Texas Office: 2100 Burnett Plaza, 801 Cherry Street.
Telephone: 817-877-2800, Metro Line: 429-3815.
Telex: 758631.
FAX: 877-2807.

MEMBERS OF FIRM

Thomas L. Kelly, Jr.
Jack L. Tickner
Randall K. Price
T. Lee Wilkins
Brenda Neel Hight
John C. Hart

ASSOCIATES

Ashley Ty Parrish
J. Wade Birdwell
M. Scott Stooksberry
O. Paul Dunagan

Represent: General Motors Corp.; Texas-New Mexico Power Co.; Miller Brewing Co.; The Medical Protective Co.; Union Oil Co.; Texas Utilities Electric Co.; NationsBank of Texas, N.A.; Union Pacific Resources; Kimbell Art Foundation.

For full biographical listings, see the Martindale-Hubbell Law Directory

CARRINGTON, COLEMAN, SLOMAN & BLUMENTHAL, L.L.P. (AV)

200 Crescent Court, Suite 1500, 75201
Telephone: 214-855-3000
Telecopy: 214-855-1333

MEMBERS OF FIRM

James E. Coleman, Jr.
Marvin S. Sloman
Robert L. Blumenthal
Fletcher L. Yarbrough
John Andrew Martin
James A. Ellis, Jr.
Peter Tierney
Earl F. Hale, Jr.
Lyman G. Hughes
Ronald M. Weiss
Corbet F. Bryant, Jr.
Don R. Hanmer
William B. Dawson
Barbara M. G. Lynn
Tyler A. Baker, III
Stephen A. Goodwin
Michael Prince
Mark S. Werbner
Charles C. Jordan
George M. Kryder, III
Michael A. Peterson
Robin Marie Gillespie
Tim Gavin
Michael T. Braden
Jane Makela
Bruce W. Collins
Rebecca Adams Cavner
David G. Drumm
Elizabeth D. Whitaker
Craig W. Weinlein
Rodney H. Lawson
Russell F. Nelms
Ken Carroll
Jeffrey S. Levinger
Sim Israeloff
Robert R. Ries
Richard A. Rohan
Karen L. Hirschman
John W. Wesley
Gordon K. Wright
Tod B. Edel
Barry R. Bell
Diane M. Sumoski
Lyndon F. Bittle
Ray D. Weston, Jr.

COUNSEL

Diane W. Bricker
William D. Underwood

ASSOCIATES

Allison Aranson
Christopher D. Atwell
Bonita Carol Barksdale
S. Todd Barton
Larry T. Bates
Mike Birrer
Robert H. Botts, Jr.
Barbara J. Brin
Dawn Ryan Budner
Cynthia S. Buhr
Gregg R. Cannady
David S. Coale
Monte M. Deere, Jr.
R. David Grant
Kenneth C. Greene, Jr.
David Michael Hugin
Daniel L. Jasica
Bradley J. Johnson (Not admitted in TX)
Gregory R. Knight
Jeffrey B. Lane
Monica Wiseman Latin
Leigh Logan
Sally A. Longroy
Jeffrey C. Mateer
Amy E. McKaig
Carol Collins Payne
Stephen J. Pierce, Jr.
William A. Reece, II
M. Fletcher Reynolds
Norton Rosenthal
Sharon J. Shumway
Daniel J. Smith
Michael A. Swartzendruber
Gregg L. Thorsen
J. Stuart Tonkinson
Alexandra D. Waddell

For full biographical listings, see the Martindale-Hubbell Law Directory

CONANT WHITTENBURG WHITTENBURG & SCHACHTER, P.C. (AV)

2300 Plaza of the Americas, 600 North Pearl, LB 133, 75201
Telephone: 214-999-5700
Facsimile: 214-999-5747
Amarillo, Texas Office: 1010 South Harrison.
Telephone: 806-372-5700.
Facsimile: 806-372-5757.

(See Next Column)

CONANT WHITTENBURG WHITTENBURG & SCHACHTER P.C.—*Continued*

A. B. Conant, Jr.
George Whittenburg
Mack Whittenburg
Cary Ira Schachter
Susan Lynn Burnette
William B. Chaney
Charles G. White
Vikram K. D. Chandhok
J. Michael McBride

OF COUNSEL

Linda A. Hale

Karl L. Baumgardner
Raymond P. Harris, Jr.
Lewis Coppedge
Francis Hangarter, Jr.
Nanneska N. Magee
Stuart J. Ford
Shawn W. Phelan
Paul M. Saraceni

For full biographical listings, see the Martindale-Hubbell Law Directory

FIGARI & DAVENPORT (AV)

A Registered Limited Liability Partnership including Professional Corporations
4800 NationsBank Plaza, 901 Main Street, 75202
Telephone: 214-939-2000

MEMBERS OF FIRM

Ernest E. Figari, Jr., (P.C.)
Mark T. Davenport
Thomas A. Graves
Alan S. Loewinsohn
A. Erin Dwyer
William J. Albright
Doug K. Butler
Donald Colleluori
Gary D. Eisenstat
Andrew G. Jubinsky
Parker D. Young

ASSOCIATES

Jill D. Bohannon
Michael G. Brown
Timothy A. Daniels
Bill E. Davidoff
Debi L. Davis
Jennifer Haltom Doan
Stephen D. Howen
Monica L. Luebker
Julie H. Roberson
Craig F. Simon
Keith R. Verges
Andrew C. Whitaker

For full biographical listings, see the Martindale-Hubbell Law Directory

GARDERE & WYNNE, L.L.P. (AV)

Thanksgiving Tower, 1601 Elm Street, Suite 3000, 75201
Telephone: 214-999-3000
Fax: 214-999-4667
Cable Address: "Garwyn Dallas"
Telex: 73-0197
Tulsa, Oklahoma Office: 401 South Boston, Mid-Continent Tower, Suite 2000.
Telephone: 918-560-2900.
Fax: 918-560-2929.
Houston, Texas Office: 600 Travis Street, Suite 5000.
Telephone: 713-547-3500.
Fax: 713-547-3535.
Mexico City, Mexico Office: Sèneca 245, Col. Chapultepec Polanco, 11560 Mèxico, D.F. Telèfonos: 011 (525) 282-0031; 011 (525) 282-0156; 011 (525) 282-0414; 011 (525) 282-0507; 011 (525) 282-1696.
FAX: 011 (525) 282-1821.

MEMBERS OF FIRM

Angus G. Wynne (1885-1974)
George P. Gardere (1899-1973)
Morris I. Jaffe (1912-1980)
G. Duffield Smith, Jr. (1930-1989)
Carl W. Wilson (1931-1989)
Richard F. Smith (1938-1990)
James F. Adams
Steven J. Adams (Resident, Tulsa, Oklahoma Office)
M. Douglas Adkins
Kelly Akins
Drew N. Bagot
Michael A. Barragan
Mark W. Bayer
Eric A. Blumrosen (Resident, Houston Office)
C. Robert Butterfield
Gregory W. Carr
John E. Castañeda
Gary B. Clark
Robert R. Cole, Jr.
Michael D. Craig
David M. Curtis
Daniel J. Davis
Calman L. Donsky
Barry D. Drees
W. Robert Dyer, Jr.
T. Mark Edwards
Suzan E. Fenner
Jane D. Fergason
Eduardo Fernández (Not admitted in TX; Resident, Mexico City, Mexico Office)
Felicia A. Finston
Brett B. Flagg
Curtis L. Frisbie, Jr.
Ronald M. Gaswirth
Stephen J. Gilles
Beverly B. Godbey
Lawrence B. Goldstein
Stephen D. Good
Susan M. Halpern
Douglas A. Harrison
Joe B. Harrison
Dan Hartsfield
Jack W. Hawkins
D. Steven Henry
Cynthia C. Hollingsworth
Kevin L. Kelley
John T. Kipp
Steven M. Ladik
Douglas S. Lang
Cym H. Lowell
M. Guillermina Magallón (Resident, Houston Office)
Neil Martin (Resident, Houston Office)
Stephen A. McCartin
Donald C. McCleary
William B. McClure, Jr.

(See Next Column)

MEMBERS OF FIRM (Continued)

Karen Kirkland McConnell (Resident, Houston Office)
David G. McLane
Fred J. Meier
Harold E. Meier
J. Randall Miller (Resident, Tulsa, Oklahoma Office)
Robert J. Miller
B. Prater Monning, III
John C. Nabors
Richard L. Nelson
Dan L. Nicewander
Kenneth M. Niesman
Julian D. Nihill
Keith V. Novick
Neil J. O'Brien
Michael A. O'Neil
David P. Page (Resident, Tulsa, Oklahoma Office)
Alan J. Perkins
Frances E. Phillips
Bruce D. Pingree
James S. Pleasant
James P. Reid
Edward E. Rhyne (Resident, Houston Office)
Richard M. Roberson
Martin E. Rose
Deirdre B. Ruckman
Deborah Cappozzo Ryan
Larry L. Schoenbrun
Katherine M. Seaborn
David H. Segrest
David R. Snodgrass
John K. Sterling
B. Jane Cantrell Taber
Richard A. Tulli
Peter S. Vogel
Richard L. Waggoner
Harold H. Walker, Jr. (Resident, Houston Office)
William G. Whitehill
Robert L. Wright
William D. Young
Keith C. Zagar

OF COUNSEL

Jeffrey M. Gaba
Harold Hoffman
Donald H. Mackaman
James S. Robertson, Jr.

SENIOR ATTORNEYS

Kalen M. Donnelly
Michael J. Donohue
Scott A. Flynn
William R. Keffer
Henry C. McFadyen, Jr.
Martin L. McGregor
Patrick A. Montgomery
Thomas R. Mylott III
Stacy R. Obenhaus
Robert W. Ruth
Joseph W. Spence
Nona B. Thomason (Resident, Houston Office)

ASSOCIATES

Joseph B. Alexander, Jr.
Michele T. Baird
Steven J. Berry
Stuart E. Blaugrund
Margaret E. Bond
Kenneth Chaim Broodo
Brent E. Bundick
Alexander C. Chae (Resident, Houston Office)
William J. Clay
Alan Condren
Dwayne Corbett
Mary C. Coulson (Resident, Tulsa, Oklahoma Office)
Madonna E. Cournoyer
Tamara Lynn DeGrazier Crouch
David C. D'Alessandro
Scott L. Davis
Elizabeth E. Drigotas (Not admitted in TX)
David R. Earhart
Joanne Early
T. Dawn Estes
Gwendolyn Feltis (Resident, Tulsa, Oklahoma Office)
Craig B. Florence
Patsy Sueko Fulton
Christopher L. Graff
Paul Grant
Douglas D. Haloftis
Lance M. Hardenburg
Gregory A. Harwell
Pedro V. Hernandez, Jr.
Carrie B. Hochfelder
Danlias F. Howe
Amy E. Hubbard
Marc Alan Hubbard
Jeffrey Jacobs
Edward Jorgenson
Robert J. Joyce (Resident, Tulsa, Oklahoma Office)
Jane M. Kessler
Carey Patrick Kinder
Brian A. King
Michael A. Krywucki
Lloyd W. Landreth (Resident, Tulsa, Oklahoma Office)
Keith M. Landry
Paul S. Leslie
Eric S. Levy
Carla S. Lindley
Dawn Phillips Loeliger
John Joseph Lopes
Julia S. Mandala
Nadine Mandel
Michael V. Marconi
Beth E. Maultsby
Carolyn McFatridge
Lori M. McNally
Stephanie Lynn McVay
Charles Edward Meacham (Resident, Mexico City, Mexico Office)
Jordan Carter Meyer
Lee Elizabeth Michaels
Todd R. Moore
Elaine A. Murphy
Holland Neff O'Neil
Shawn A. Orme
Larry B. Pascal
Virginia W. Pennington
Randall G. Ray
Michael D. Richardson
Patrick S. Richter
Russell N. Rippamonti
Kimberly M. Robinson
Mary K. Sahs
Phillip N. Sanov
Robert Sarfatis
Kristen A. Schonberg
Tracy A. Schrader
Matthew J. Schroeder
Kay Lyn Schwartz
Eric J. Senske
Lisa L. Shoemaker
Todd B. Siegler
Timothy Kent Skipworth
Pamela S. Smith
Erika G. Tyner
James E. Urmin
Stephen R. Ward (Resident, Tulsa, Oklahoma Office)
Margaret W. Weinkauf
Randy J. White
Paul T. Williamson
Janet B. Wright
Lisa S. Zamaludin
Randy Zipse

For full biographical listings, see the Martindale-Hubbell Law Directory

Dallas—Continued

GODWIN & CARLTON, A PROFESSIONAL CORPORATION (AV)

Suite 3300, 901 Main Street, 75202-3714
Telephone: 214-939-4400
Telecopier: 214-760-7332
Monterrey, Mexico Correspondent: Quintero y Quintero Abogodos. Martin De Zalva 840-3 Sur Esquinna Con Hidalgo.
Telephone: 44-07-74, 44-07-80, 44-06-56, 44-06-28.
Fax: 83-40-34-54.

Donald E. Godwin
George R. Carlton, Jr.
James G. Vetter, Jr.
David J. White
Bill R. Womble
Frank A. St. Claire
Thomas E. Rosen
John L. Hubble
Darrell G. Adkerson
Bob J. Shelton
William F. Pyne
Keith A. Glover
David L. Patterson
Frank P. Skipper, Jr.
Harvey M. Shapan
Danny C. Garner
Thomas L. Woodman
Marci L. Romick
Daniel P. Callahan
Maurice J. Bates
Thomas S. Hoekstra
Craig A. Harris

Franklin Blackstone, III (Not admitted in TX)
Rodney L. Hubbard
W. Blake Hyde
Robert R. Kincaid
James L. Kissire
Steven T. Polino

W. Darrell Armer
Micheal Wayne Bishop
Kathleen Weidinger Foster
Laura A. Frase
John M. Frick
Mark A. Girtz
Michael K. Hurst
Harvey Goldwater Joseph
Jeffrey M. Kershaw
Robert S. Luttrull
Levi G. McCathern, II
Susan Morris Mellow
Josephine H. Randall
Scott J. Scherr
Marlene D. Thomson
Julie I. Ungerman
Cynthia Jane Vadala
Patrick Alan Wadlington
Robert A. Womble

For full biographical listings, see the Martindale-Hubbell Law Directory

HOOVER LEGAL ASSOCIATES, A PROFESSIONAL CORPORATION (AV)

Two Galleria Tower, 13455 Noel Road, Suite 1000, 75240
Telephone: 214-991-2150
Telecopier: 214-490-1607

Dean S. Hoover

For full biographical listings, see the Martindale-Hubbell Law Directory

HUGHES & LUCE, L.L.P. (AV)

A Registered Limited Liability Partnership including Professional Corporations
1717 Main Street, Suite 2800, 75201
Telephone: 214-939-5500
Fax: 214-939-6100
Telex: 730836
Austin, Texas Office: 111 Congress, Suite 900.
Telephone: 512-482-6800.
Fax: 512-482-6859.
Houston, Texas Office: Three Allen Center, 333 Clay Street, Suite 3800.
Telephone: 713-754-5200.
Fax: 713-754-5206.
Fort Worth, Texas Office: 2421 Westport Parkway, Suite 500A.
Telephone: 817-439-3000.
Fax: 817-439-4222.

MEMBERS OF FIRM

Thomas B. Anderson, Jr.
Kim Juanita Askew
Terrence M. Babilla
Paul A. Berry
R. Doak Bishop
Alan J. Bogdanow
James C. Chadwick
Eric R. Cromartie
Allan B. Diamond
Jeff W. Dorrill
Scott C. Drablos
Zammurad Hyatt Feroze
William B. Finkelstein
David C. Godbey
David N. Guedry
Kenneth G. Hawari
Jay H. Hebert
Kathryn G. Henkel
Daniel K. Hennessy
Glen J. Hettinger
John B. Holden, Jr., (P.C.)
John E. Howell
Vester T. Hughes, Jr.
Clifton T. Hutchinson
Maryann Joerres
Darrell E. Jordan
David H. Judson
David C. Kent
Paul M. Koning
Thomas W. Luce, III
David G. Luther, Jr.
Larry A. Makel
Stanley O. Mayo
James D. McCarthy
William A. McCormack
R. Matthew Molash
James A. Moomaw
Robert H. Mow, Jr. (P.C.)
Ross Clayton Mulford
Dudley W. Murrey
David A. Newsom
Gary G. Null
Cynthia Morgan Ohlenforst
Walter G. Pettey, III
Jan M. Ramsay
Bobby M. Rubarts
Mark K. Sales
James W. Sargent

(See Next Column)

MEMBERS OF FIRM (Continued)

Charles M. Schwartz
Dwight A. Shupe
David L. Sinak
Karen K. Suhre
Michael W. Tankersley
J. Gregory Taylor
Kenneth Mark Vesledahl
David Weitman

ASSOCIATES

Bridgett C. Anderson
Danny S. Ashby
James H. Billingsley
Carol J. Biondo
Julie Edwards Blend
Thomas A. Bramlett
Craig W. Budner
James E. Cahill, III
Arthur T. Catterall
Robert Jeffery Cole
Joseph M. Cox
Ellen J. Curnes
Mark A. Damante
Deborah J. Eichner
Kimberly A. Elkjer
Sherry L. Evans
Walter E. Evans
David Lee Fields
Michael J. Forde
Robert D. Gage, Jr.
Stephen G. Gleboff
Kristin L. Goodin
Robert B. Hale
Elizabeth Sheen Helm
David C. Hernandez
James W. Hryekewicz
Laura M. Kalesnik
Jeffrey C. King
Leslie Klaassen
Ethan K. Knowlden
Bernard Lau
Timothy H. Law
David B. Lee
Jill B. Louis
Paulo B. McKeeby
H. Lynn Moore, Jr.
Jon L. Mosle III
Brett Lee Myers
Ann Marie Painter
Edward A. Razim, III
William T. Reid, IV
Tarek F.M. Saad
Holly A. Schymik
Bart Sloan
Daniel E. Smith
Anthony Gorham Soards
Mark W. Steirer
Theodore Stevenson, III
Elizabeth R. Turner
Corinna Ulrich
Brian D. Walker
Stacy L. Weiske
Barbara Whiten
Travis A. Willock
David A. Wood

STAFF ATTORNEY

Michael L. Kaufman

OF COUNSEL

Jill A. Kotvis

For full biographical listings, see the Martindale-Hubbell Law Directory

JACKSON & WALKER, L.L.P. (AV)

901 Main Street, Suite 6000, 75202-3797
Telephone: 214-953-6000
Fax: 214-953-5822
Fort Worth, Texas Office: 777 Main Street, Suite 1800.
Telephone: 817-334-7200.
Fax: 817-334-7290.
Houston, Texas Office: 1100 Louisiana, Suite 4200.
Telephone: 713-752-4200.
Fax: 713-752-4221.
San Antonio, Texas Office: 112 E. Pecan Street, Suite 2100.
Telephone: 210-978-7700.
Fax: 210-978-7790.

MEMBERS OF FIRM

John Paul Jackson (1902-1960)
Conan Cantwell (1907-1977)
W. B. Patterson (1915-1977)
Donald C. Fitch, Jr. (1918-1986)
A. W. Walker, Jr. (1901-1987)
Donald L. Case (1917-1993)
Susan S. Andrews
Charles L. Babcock
Roy Howard Baskin, III
Larry L. Bean
Rebecca R. Belcher
Bryan C. Birkeland
H. Dudley Chambers
Charles M. Cobbe
Bryan C. Collins
Gerald C. Conley
C. Wade Cooper
Richard F. Dahlson
D. Paul Dalton
Emily Stacy Donahue
Richard M. Dooley
George C. Dunlap
Celeste L. Frank
Michael C. French
Fred W. Fulton
James R. Griffin
R. Thomas Groves, Jr.
Michael Patrick Haggerty
Robert F. Henderson
Robert B. Holland, III
William H. Hornberger
Gary L. Ingram
Aaron Johnston, Jr.
William D. Jordan
Mark T. Josephs
John J. Klein
Michael L. Knapek
John B. Kyle
John L. Lancaster, III
Robert P. Latham
Charles D. Maguire, Jr.
Dena L. Mathis
Frank P. McEachern
Retta A. Miller
David T. Moran
Thomas J. Murphy
David C. Myers
Robert P. Palmer
Jack Pew, Jr.
Marla D. Price
Robert F. Ruckman
Dennis Neil Ryan
James S. Ryan, III
Gordon M. Shapiro
Jonathan L. Snare
Joan Sprince Sostek
Kenneth Stohner, Jr.
Frank C. Vecella
Robert B. Weathersby
Stephen Cass Weiland
Troy Michael Wilson
Allan C. Wisk

(See Next Column)

JACKSON & WALKER L.L.P.—*Continued*

OF COUNSEL

Bruce A. Cheatham
Ralph E. Hartman
Laura E. Hlavach
Phillip Ray Jones
Mary Emma Ackels Karam
J. Howard Lennon
W. Orrin Miller
John B. Nelson
Charles W. Pauly
John H. Peper
Harold M. Slaughter
Samuel G. Winstead

ASSOCIATES

Gabrielle M. Arrieh
Glenn E. Box
Carl C. Butzer
Colin P. Cahoon
E. Leon Carter
Sarah E. Clark
Linda E. Donohoe
Jennifer E. Dorn
Charles S. Gilbert
Alan N. Greenspan
Deborah Frome Hare
J. Colter Harris
Patricia Hartstern
Robert A. Hawkins
Kimberly Lynn Hilliard
Annabel Lugo Hoffman
William R. Jenkins, Jr.
Brian A. Kilpatrick
Patricia A. Logsdon
Bernard H. Masters
James M. McCown
Billy R. McGill
Fenita T. Morris
Earl S. Nesbitt
Elizabeth G. Palmer
Marilyn R. Post
Kimberlee Kline Rozman
Barbara K. Salyers
Thomas B. Shelton
Janice P. Stitziel
James D. Struble
Michael E. Taten
Timothy E. Taylor
Kimberly O'Dawn Thompson
David S. Vassar
Ann E. Ward
Sylvia Dalton Wells
Bradley L. Whitlock
Jeffrey A. Wier
Elizabeth L. Yingling

Representative Clients Furnished Upon Request.

For full biographical listings, see the Martindale-Hubbell Law Directory

JONES, DAY, REAVIS & POGUE (AV)

2300 Trammell Crow Center, 2001 Ross Avenue, 75201
Telephone: 214-220-3939
Cable Address: "Attorneys Dallas"
Telex: 730852
Telecopier: 214-969-5100
In Atlanta, Georgia: 3500 One Peachtree Center, 303 Peachtree Street, N.E.
Telephone: 404-521-3939.
Cable Address: "Attorneys Atlanta".
Telex: 54-2711.
Telecopier: 404-581-8330.
In Brussels, Belgium: Avenue Louise 480, 7th Floor, B-1050 Brussels.
Telephone: 011-32-2-645-14-11.
Telecopier: 011-32-2-645-14-45.
In Chicago, Illinois: 77 West Wacker.
Telephone: 312-782-3939.
Telecopier: 312-782-8585.
In Cleveland, Ohio: North Point, 901 Lakeside Avenue.
Telephone: 216-586-3939.
Cable Address: "Attorneys Cleveland."
Telex: 980389.
Telecopier: 216-579-0212.
In Columbus, Ohio: 1900 Huntington Center.
Telephone: 614-469-3939.
Cable Address: "Attorneys Columbus."
Telecopier: 614-461-4198.
In Frankfurt, Germany: Triton Haus, Bockenheimer Landstrasse 42, 60323 Frankfurt am Main.
Telephone: 49-69-9726-3939.
Telecopier: 49-69-9726-3993.
In Geneva, Switzerland: 20, rue de Candolle.
Telephone: 011-41-22-320-2339.
Telecopier: 011-41-22-320-1232.
In Hong Kong: 1501 One Exchange Square, 8 Connaught Place.
Telephone: 011-852-2526-6895.
Telecopier: 011-852-2810-5787.
In Irvine, California: 2603 Main Street, Suite 900.
Telephone: 714-851-3939.
Telex: 194911 Lawyers LSA.
Telecopier: 714-553-7539.
In London, England: One Mount Street.
Telephone: 011-44-71-493-9361.
Cable Address: "Surgoe London WI."
Telecopier: 011-44-71-493-9666.
In Los Angeles, California: 555 West Fifth Street, Suite 4600.
Telephone: 213-489-3939.
Telex: 181439 UD.
Telecopier: 213-243-2539.
In New York, New York: 599 Lexington Avenue.
Telephone: 212-326-3939.
Cable Address: "JONESDAY NEWYORK."
Telex: 237013 JDRP UR.
Telecopier: 212-755-7306.
In Paris, France: 62, rue du Faubourg Saint-Honore.
Telephone: 011-33-1-44-71-3939.
Cable Address: "Surgoe Paris."
Telex: 290156 Surgoe.
Telecopier: 011-33-1-49-24-0471.

(See Next Column)

In Pittsburgh, Pennsylvania: 500 Grant Street, 31st Floor.
Telephone: 412-391-3939.
Cable Address: "Attorneys Pittsburgh".
Telecopier: 412-394-7959.
In Riyadh, Saudi Arabia: Law Offices of Saud M.A. Shawwaf, P.O. Box 2700.
Telephones: 011 (966-1) 465-6543, 011 (966-1) 464-8534 or 011 (966-1) 464-8540.
Telex: 401831 SAUCON SJ.
Telecopier: (966-1) 464-8480.
In Taipei, Taiwan: 8th Floor, 2 Tun Hwa South Road, Section 2.
Telephone: 011 (886-2) 704-6808.
Telecopier: 011 (886-2) 704-6791.
In Tokyo, Japan: Toranomon MT Building, 4th Floor, 10-3, Toranomon, 3-Chome, Minato-Ku, Tokyo 105, Japan.
Telephone: 011-81-3-3433-3939.
Telecopier: 011-81-3-5401-2725.
In Washington, D.C.: Metropolitan Square, 1450 G Street, N.W.
Telephone: 202-879-3939.
Cable Address: "Attorneys Washington."
Telex: 89-2410 ATTORNEYS WASH.
Telecopier: 202-737-2832.

MEMBERS OF FIRM IN DALLAS

Robert L. Meyers, III
Robert W. Turner
Chester J. Hinshaw
Charles N. Warren
Francis P. Hubach, Jr.
Richard K. Kneipper
Terence M. Murphy
Gerry D. Osterland
Joseph L. McEntee
James F. Carey
Robert L. Estep
Keith C. McDole
Frederick J. Rerko
John T. McCafferty
Sydney Bosworth McDole
Dennis B. Drapkin
Thomas E. Fennell
David E. Cowling
Bradford G. Keithley (Not admitted in TX)
Kathleen Ryan McLaurin
Brett A. Ringle
Gary Stolbach
Steven Clark Wagner
Henry L. Gompf
Brian D. Lafving
David J. Lowery
Thomas R. Jackson
James P. Karen
Stanley Weiner
Jerome R. Doak
Stephen L. Fluckiger
Gregory M. Gordon
Michael K. Ording
Patricia Villareal
Ronald G. Weitz
Katie J. Colopy
Patrick K. Fox
Mark V. Minton
James S. Teater
Mark E. Betzen
Randy R. Jurgensmeyer

SENIOR COUNSEL

Thomas C. Nelson
Ian A. Boase

OF COUNSEL

John P. Pinkerton
Patricia Christ Naghshineh
James E. O'Bannon
Charles William Burton

SENIOR ATTORNEYS

Alfred E. Hall
William E. Marple
W. Paul Ditto, Jr.
Michael F. Albers
Mark R. Hall
Richard M. Moyed

ASSOCIATES

H. Tica Herns
Sheryl Smith Scovell
Jennifer R. Brandeis
Margaret I. Lyle
Teresa M. Cefalo
Deborah E. Bartlett
Sally L. Crawford
Todd Wallace
Lee L. Cameron, Jr.
Troy Blain Lewis
Edward H. Molter
Susan F. Monaco
Barbara Jean Oyer
Michael Lyn Rice
Michael Weinberg
Roy T. Atwood
Holly Elizabeth Stroud
Randy A. Bowman
Scott W. Burt
Scott E. Wolfe
Ronald A. Antush
Julia L. Armstrong
Dorothy Birnbryer
Stephen J. Gilhooly
Rose Marie Glazer
Jeffrey J. Joyce
Margaret S. C. Keliher
Stacy Malkin Overby
Mark N. Reiter
Reynaldo A. Valencia
Todd W. White
Catherine K. Faubion
Michael J. Newton (Not admitted in TX)
Charolette F. Noel
Chrysta L. Osborn
Rayne Rasty
W. Kelly Stewart
Gregory P. Wells
Gregory A. Willis
Karen J. Doswell (Not admitted in TX)
Deborah R. Eberts
Ross Spencer Garsson
Christine A. Hathaway
Diane Love Hill
Joan M. Hyde
Thomas C. Pavlik, Jr.
Donna C. Peavler
David M. Schwartz
Kacy J. Whitehead
Sara M. Allswede
Robert C. DeCarli
Cynthia J. Dollar
Jill E. Goldberger (Not admitted in TX)
Britt K. Latham
Amy N. Marlowe
Kathryn D. Musser (Not admitted in TX)
Shannon D. Norris
Matthew W. Ray
Donald W. Reid
Carl F. Schwenker
Katherine M. Warner
Greg L. Weselka
Stephen B. Yeager
Cynthia J. Bishop
James J. Boteler
Thomas M. Dooley

(See Next Column)

JONES, DAY, REAVIS & POGUE, *Dallas—Continued*

ASSOCIATES (Continued)

Clay A. Hartmann
April D. Henley
Michael C. Streiter
Martha Wach
Kristi J. Whiteside

For full biographical listings, see the Martindale-Hubbell Law Directory

KILGORE & KILGORE, A PROFESSIONAL CORPORATION (AV)

700 McKinney Place, 3131 McKinney Avenue - LB 103, 75204-2471
Telephone: 214-969-9099
Fax: 214-953-0133; 214-953-0242

Wilmer D. Masterson, III
W. Stephen Swayze
Robert M. Thornton
Roger F. Claxton
Theodore C. Anderson, III

Melissa A. Johnson
William G. Shaw, Jr.
Robert J. Hill
Daniel A. Weinstein
John H. Crouch

For full biographical listings, see the Martindale-Hubbell Law Directory

LOCKE PURNELL RAIN HARRELL, A PROFESSIONAL CORPORATION (AV)

2200 Ross Avenue, Suite 2200, 75201
Telephone: 214-740-8000
Telecopier: 214-740-8800
Telex: 73-0911 Locke Dal
New Orleans, Louisiana Office: 601 Poydras Street, Suite 2400.
Telephone: 504-558-5100.
Telecopier: 504-558-5200.
Austin, Texas Office: 515 Congress Avenue, Suite 2500.
Telephone: 512-305-4700.
Telecopier: 512-305-4800.

Morris Harrell
H. Gene Emery
John H. McElhaney
Barney T. Young
Peter J. Butler (Resident, New Orleans, Louisiana Office)
William D. White, Jr.
Larry M. Lesh
Stan McMurry
L. Money Adams, Jr.
Dan Busbee
Edward V. Smith, III
James L. Armour
Joe H. Staley, Jr.
William Andrew Barr
Maurice E. Purnell, Jr.
Robert F. See, Jr.
Robert E. Wilbur
Earl A. Berry, Jr.
Ronald R. Cresswell
H. Edward Dobroski
Royce Jay Hailey, Jr. (Resident, Austin, Texas Office)
Mark G. Magilow
Stuart M. Bumpas
Peter A. Franklin, III
Harriet E. Miers
Robert N. Rule, Jr.
Rutledge C. Clement, Jr. (Resident, New Orleans, Louisiana Office)
Bryan E. Bishop
D. Dale Gillette
William Mahomes, Jr.
Andrew D. Rooker
Larry V. Smith
George E. Bowles
Harlan P. Cohen
Jane A. Matheson (Resident, Austin, Texas Office)
Donna D. Fraiche (Resident, New Orleans, Louisiana Office)
M. Charles Jennings
Jerry M. Keys (Resident, Austin, Texas Office)
Elizabeth Lang-Miers
Robert R. Veach, Jr.
Michael V. Powell
Frederick W. Addison, III
Christopher F. Allison, Jr.
William John Bux
Michael H. Collins
Martin R. Griffin
Robert T. Mowrey
Michael K. Sanderson
Linda Albright Wilkins
Barbara McComas Anderson
E. Philip Bush
C. W. Flynn, IV
Aubrey B. Hirsch, Jr. (Resident, New Orleans, Louisiana Office)
Guy H. Kerr
Charles M. Moore
James A. Moseley
Charles C. Reeder
Mark T. Story
Danielle Lombardo Trostorff (Resident, New Orleans, Louisiana Office)
J. Robert Beatty
J. Mitchell Bell
Thomas A. Connop
Don M. Glendenning
Robert D. Graham
C. Ronald Kalteyer
Joyce G. Mazero
Timothy W. Mountz
William B. Steele, III
Frank E. Stevenson, II
Mark G. Johnson
Raymond E. LaDriere, II
Janis H. Loegering
Thomas D. Moore, Jr.
Molly Buck Richard
Jerry K. Warren
Jennifer Burr Altabef
David G. McCracken
Robb P. Stewart
Cynthia Keely Timms
Amelia Williams Koch (Resident, New Orleans, Louisiana Office)
Robert P. Taylor, III
Thomas P. Arnold
Michael P. Petersilia
William A. Broussard (Resident, Austin, Texas Office)
Russell F. Coleman
Karen Fry Gray
Susan L. Karamanian
John B. McKnight
Randall C. Brown
Laura Peterson Elkind
Dean W. Ferguson
Kent Jamison
Van M. Jolas
Bruce K. Packard
Gary Powell

(See Next Column)

Kevin L. Twining
Gregory A. Lowry
Brian J. Woram
Peter J. Butler, Jr. (Resident, New Orleans, Louisiana Office)
Henry M. Cutler III
Ann Hurwitz
Jack E. Jacobsen
Eugene F. Segrest
Bradley C. Weber

OF COUNSEL

W. D. White
Benjamin N. Boren
James J. Laney
Stanley E. Neely
Talbot Rain
Robert E. Rain, Jr.
Charles G. Purnell
Trevor Wm. Rees-Jones
Charles Rosen, II (Resident, New Orleans, Louisiana Office)
John L. Estes
Daniel N. Matheson, III (Resident, Austin, Texas Office)

SPECIAL COUNSEL

Jan R. Newsom

SENIOR ATTORNEYS

Robert M. Candee
James T. Rain
Elizabeth A. Howard

Michele Tobias Courtois
Loral R. Conrad
Elizabeth A. Cook (Resident, New Orleans, Louisiana Office)
Alicia Reggie Freysinger (Resident, New Orleans, Louisiana Office)
Matthew K. Brown (Resident, New Orleans, Louisiana Office)
Deborah M. Rhodus
Elaine W. Selle (Resident, New Orleans, Louisiana Office)
Margaret McAlister Silverstein (Resident, New Orleans, Louisiana Office)
Wallace A. W. Watkins
Jonetta Brooks
Angela Darby Dickerson
Margaret Donahue Hall
Vincent J. Hess
Thomas F. Loose
Elizabeth E. Mack
John P. McDonald
Richard D. Morrow
Steven L. Skov
Kevin C. Cabaniss
David H. Dahl
Henry Exall, IV
Jan S. Gilbert (Not admitted in TX)
R. Kevin Hardage
Mark H. Ralston
Scott C. Tankersley
Donald E. Uloth
George H. Barber
Lori E. Davidson
Brian R. Forbes
Mark B. Forseth
Bradley W. Foster
Thomas R. Greenwood
Heinz D. Grether (Resident, Austin, Texas Office)
Yasue Koezuka
Lendy Leggett Jones
Rodolfo (Rudy) Rodriguez, Jr.
Stacy Jordan Rodriguez
Michelle R. Allen
Cynthia L. Degitz (Resident, Austin, Texas Office)
Craig Donahue
Becky Rector McDaniel
Kim T. Phipps
Irma Carrillo Ramirez
Julia A. Simon
Michael J. Boydston
Karen L. Conway
David Peavler
Carleen A. Richards
Anna Bilhartz Roberts
Whit Roberts
T. Kathleen Vance
Thomas B. Walsh, IV
Thomas G. Yoxall
Cynthia B. Asensio
Indra S. Chalk
Elizabeth C. Jenkins
Alex D. Madrazo
Thomas H. Neuhoff, Jr.
James F. Struthers
Clarence B. Brown, III
Toby M. Galloway
Gavin M. Melmed
Khanh Nguyen
George E. Seay, III
Christopher D. Speer
Karen E. Sprole
Ona A. Steele
Phyllis R. Guin (Resident, New Orleans, Louisiana Office)
Robert W. Mouton (Resident, New Orleans, Louisiana Office)
Charles C. Bourque, Jr. (Resident, New Orleans, Louisiana Office)
Richard G. Passler (Resident, New Orleans, Louisiana Office)

For full biographical listings, see the Martindale-Hubbell Law Directory

MEADOWS, OWENS, COLLIER, REED, COUSINS & BLAU, L.L.P. (AV)

3700 NationsBank Plaza, 901 Main Street, 75202-3792
Telephone: 214-744-3700
Telecopier: 214-747-3732
Wats: 1-800-451-0093

MEMBERS OF FIRM

Charles M. Meadows, Jr.
Rodney J. Owens
Robert Don Collier
David N. Reed
Thomas G. Hineman
William R. Cousins, III
Charles W. Blau
George R. Bedell
Michael E. McCue
Lauren C. LaRue

ASSOCIATES

Joel N. Crouch
Alan K. Davis
Fielder F. Nelms
Patricia King Dorey
Jeffrey C. Adams
Frank E. Sheeder, III
Robert M. Bolton
Michael Todd Welty
Lisa R. Newman

For full biographical listings, see the Martindale-Hubbell Law Directory

Dallas—Continued

Novakov, Davidson & Flynn, A Professional Corporation (AV)

2000 St. Paul Place, 750 North St. Paul, 75201-3286
Telephone: 214-922-9221
Telecopy: 214-969-7557

Steven D. Davidson
Ronald R. Davis
James Kevin Flynn
Gary C. Morgan
Daniel P. Novakov
Charles N. Nye
Thomas M. Whelan
Steven D. Erdahl

OF COUNSEL

Marvin J. Wise

Representative Clients: BEI Management, Inc.; Bluebonnet Savings Bank FSB; Bonnet Resources Corporation; Colonial Storage Centers; Commercial Metals Company; Computer Language Research, Inc.; Custom Coils, Inc.

For full biographical listings, see the Martindale-Hubbell Law Directory

Payne & Blanchard, L.L.P. (AV)

Plaza of the Americas, 600 North Pearl Street 2500 South Tower, 75201
Telephone: 214-953-1313
Telecopier: 214-220-0439

MEMBERS OF FIRM

Arthur Blanchard (Retired)
James C. Allums, Jr.
John William Payne
Frank J. Betancourt
Charles A. Girand
Bobby D. Dyess
Kevin J. Cook
Gary W. Maxfield
James S. Wright
Jonathan A. Manning
Harold R. McKeever, Jr.

ASSOCIATES

Brian S. Hellberg
Mark B. Greenberg

Representative Clients: American Home Products; Liberty Mutual Insurance Co.; Merrill Lynch, Pierce, Fenner & Smith, Inc.; Mutual and United of Omaha Insurance Co.; State Farm Fire & Casualty Companies; Texas Association of Counties.

For full biographical listings, see the Martindale-Hubbell Law Directory

Prescott & Prescott (AV)

Fitzhugh Center, 4131 North Central Expressway, Suite 710, 75204
Telephone: 214-528-9510
Fax: 214-528-3154

J. Phillip Prescott
Byron C. Prescott

For full biographical listings, see the Martindale-Hubbell Law Directory

Smith & Smith (AV)

Two Turtle Creek Village, 3838 Oaklawn Avenue, Suite 224, 75219-4610
Telephone: 214-522-5571
Fax: 214-522-5009

Russell B. Smith
Robert B. Smith

For full biographical listings, see the Martindale-Hubbell Law Directory

Strasburger & Price, L.L.P. (AV)

A Partnership including Professional Corporations
901 Main Street, Suite 4300, 75202
Telephone: 214-651-4300
Fax: 214-651-4330
Austin, Texas Office: 2600 One American Center, 600 Congress Avenue.
Telephone: 512-499-3600.
Fax: 512-499-3660.
Houston, Texas Office: Suite 2800, One Houston Center, 1221 McKinney.
Telephone: 713-951-5600.
Fax: 713-951-5660.
Mexico City Office: Edificio Hewlett-Packard, Monte Pelvoux No. 111, Piso 5, Lomas de Chapultepec, 11000 Mexico D.F.
Telephone: 525-202-8796.
Fax: 525-520-7671.
Mexico City Correspondent: Gonzalez, Calvillo y Forastieri, S.C. Edificio Hewlett-Packard, Monte Pelvoux No. 111, Piso 5, Lomas de Chapultepec, 11000 Mexico D.F.
Telephone: 525-202-7622.
Fax: 525-520-7671.

MEMBERS OF FIRM

Henry W. Strasburger (1898-1972)
Hobert Price (1899-1965)
Ben H. Admire (P.C.)
M. Kelly Allbritton
Roland C. Anderson (P.C.)
Ron K. Barger
Jerry L. Beane (P.C.)
Diana Joseph Bearden
Royal H. Brin, Jr., (P.C.)
Michael R. Buchanan (P.C.)
Daniel L. Butcher
E. Paul Cauley, Jr.
Duncan L. Clore (P.C.)
Martha Crandall Coleman
John M. Cone
Deborah Cox
Colleen A. Coyne
Gary C. Crapster (P.C.)
W. Richard Davis (P.C.)
Mark M. Donheiser

(See Next Column)

MEMBERS OF FIRM (Continued)

William C. (Trey) Dowdy, III, (P.C.)
Robert Keith Drummond (P.C.)
Jack R. Dugan (P.C.)
Eric O. English
Jeffrey R. Fine
Rowland B. Foster (P.C.)
William L. Fouché, Jr.
Frederick J. Fowler (P.C.)
Paige H. Fugate
Carol Glendenning
Andrew G. Halpern
Brian G. Hamilton
Mary C. Harlan
R. Chris Harvey (P.C.)
Ernest R. Higginbotham (P.C.)
Leo J. Hoffman (P.C.)
Stuart C. Hollimon (P.C.)
Charles M. Hosch
Karen Gren Johnson
Mike Joplin (P.C.)
P. Michael Jung
Michael Keeley
Jack M. Kinnebrew (P.C.)
David N. Kitner (P.C.)
D. Bradley Kizzia
David J. LaBrec
Donald P. Lan, Jr.
Billy G. Leonard, Jr.
Bryan J. Maedgen (P.C.)
Wayne B. Mason
Randal Mathis
Sheree Lynn McCall (P.C.)
John H. McDowell, Jr.
Patrick F. McGowan (P.C.)
William M. Methenitis
David K. Meyercord (P.C.)
Alan S. Miller
James Hamilton Moody, III
Elmer Murphey, III
Jeffrey S. Osgood (P.C.)
Patrick Owens
David W. Parham
Angelo P. Parker (P.C.)
James K. Peden, III, (P.C.)
J. Mark Penley
John E. Phillips (P.C.)
W. Neil Rambin
John R. Riddle
William M. Rippey (P.C.)
John K. Round
Thomas G. Rundell (P.C.)
Kirk F. Sniff
Robert W. Strauss
Daniel F. Susie (P.C.)
Robert Hyer Thomas (P.C.)
John R. Tilly
Joseph A. Turano
Alan R. Vickery
W. Edward Walts, II, (P.C.)
Kevin L. Wentz
Karen Brown Willcutts
Greg K. Winslett

OF COUNSEL

John M. Vernon
Steven P. Watten

SENIOR COUNSEL

Kenneth S. Beat (P.C.)
Earl Jeffery Story
Camille R. Comeau

ASSOCIATES

Craig A. Albert (Not admitted in TX)
Gregory L. Allen
Mark B. Blackburn
George A. Boll
Melinda K. Bradley
W. Edward Carlton
Elizann Carroll
William L. Clayborn
Deborah S. Coldwell
Christine Van Vooren Cole
Kristi Cox
Jeffrey L. Crouch
JoAnn Dalrymple
James A. Deets
Sheri L. Deterling
Steven L. Dickerson
Carol E. Doonan
Hilda Contreras Galvan
Jonathan S. Gansell
Paul R. Genender
Jeffrey S. George
Jill S. Giroir
Gene C. Griffin
Bruce A. Griggs
Faith Stovall James
Karin S. Janick
Timothy N. Johnson
John W. Lanius, Jr.
Ernest W. Leonard
Wm. Lance Lewis
Kevin J. Maguire
Kurt W. Meaders
D. Randall Montgomery
Charles E. Moody
David G. Moore
Kimberly S. Moore
Paul L. Myers
Laura Reilly O'Hara
Kevin E. Oliver
Allyson L. Perkins
Marjorie L. Powell
Toni Scott Reed
David M. Reichert, Jr.
Jill M. Renfro
Christine M. Robinson
Ross T. Robinson
Dennis L. Roossien, Jr.
Jeff L. Rose
Lisa Schiffman
Thomas J. Schlesinger (Not admitted in TX)
Mark S. Scudder
Scott A. Shanes
Alfredo L. Silva
Elvin E. Smith, III
Katherine E. Smith
Mark T. Smith
Richard L. Smith, Jr.
Ashley E. Thomas
Elizabeth Lee Thompson
Beth Pace Tiggelaar
Wendy C. Tripodi
William M. Vcherek, II
Eugene C. Vallow
Robert E. Vinson, Jr.
David W. Whitehurst
J. Gregory Whitten
S. Vance Wittie
Bart M. Wyrick

STAFF ATTORNEY

Michael A. Walsh

For full biographical listings, see the Martindale-Hubbell Law Directory

Taylor Lohmeyer Corrigan, P.C. (AV)

2911 Turtle Creek Boulevard, Suite 1010, 75219
Telephone: 214-528-1590
Fax: 214-528-1591

Robert C. Taylor
Fred Lohmeyer
Bradford D. Corrigan, Jr.

For full biographical listings, see the Martindale-Hubbell Law Directory

Dallas—Continued

THOMPSON, COE, COUSINS & IRONS, L.L.P. (AV)

200 Crescent Court, Eleventh Floor, 75201-1840
Telephone: 214-871-8200 (Dallas)
512-480-8770 (Austin)
FAX: 214-871-8209

MEMBERS OF FIRM

Emory L. White, Jr.
Franklin H. Perry
Richard S. Geiger
Robert O. Lamb
Jack M. Cleaveland, Jr.
Randy A. Nelson
David M. Taylor
Leo John Jordan
Jon G. Petersen
Robert B. Wellenberger
Peter A. T. Sartin
Rhonda Johnson Byrd
Scott Patrick Stolley
Robert P. Franke
Rodney D. Bucker
Roger D. Higgins
John L. Ross
Ronald G. Houdyshell
Michael A. McClelland
Alison H. Moore
Belinda A. Vrielink
Richard M. Mosher
Newton J. Jones
Beth D. Bradley
Ronald D. Horner
Jennifer D. Aufricht
William N. Radford

ASSOCIATES

Michael W. Jones
John B. Kronenberger
James D. Cartier
Richard D. Boston
David F. Eriksen
Harrison H. Yoss
D. Jackson Chaney
Karl A. Vogeler
Thomas A. Culpepper
James Richard Harmon
Layne L. Anderson
James L. Sowder
Bradley D. Broberg
Kelley L. Heide
Kevin B. Brown
Pamela J. Touchstone
Gina D. Boone
Lisa Curtis Lochridge
Wade C. Grosnoe
Edwin Carl Olsen, IV
Donald R. Loving, II
Sheila O'Hare
Thomas E. Gavigan
Ana Kirk Thornton
David A. McFarland
Robert C. Wiegand

COUNSEL

R. B. Cousins
Will C. Thompson (1889-1980)
David B. Irons (1917-1991)
Vernon Coe (1909-1994)
Ira Lee Allen, III
Murray M. McColloch

Representative Clients: Hartford Insurance Group; Texas Automobile Insurance Service Office; Trinity Universal Insurance Company.

For full biographical listings, see the Martindale-Hubbell Law Directory

THOMPSON & KNIGHT, A PROFESSIONAL CORPORATION (AV)

(Attorneys and Counselors)
1700 Pacific Avenue Suite 3300, 75201
Telephone: 214-969-1700
Telecopy: 214-969-1751
Cable Address: "Tomtex"
Telex: 732298
Austin, Texas Office: 1200 San Jacinto Center, 98 San Jacinto Boulevard, 78701.
Telephone: 512-469-6100.
Telecopy: 512-469-6180.
Fort Worth, Texas Office: 801 Cherry Street, Suite 1600, 76102.
Telephone: 817-347-1700.
Telecopy: 817-347-1799.
Houston, Texas Office: 1700 Texas Commerce Tower, 600 Travis, 77002.
Telephone: 713-217-2800.
Telecopy: 713-217-2828.
Monterrey, Mexico Office: Edificio Losoles PD-4, Av. Lázaro Cárdenas No. 2400 Pte., San Pedro Garza Garcia, Nuevo Léon C.P. 66220.
Telephone: (52-8) 363-0096.
Telecopy: (52-8) 363-3067.

SHAREHOLDERS

Margaret S. Alford
Robert B. Allen
G. Luke Ashley
P. Jefferson Ballew
William L. Banowsky
Michael L. Bengtson
David M. Bennett
Buford P. Berry
Michael R. Berry
Dorothy H. Bjorck
Hugh T. Blevins, Jr.
Jane Politz Brandt
Sam P. Burford, Jr.
Frederick W. Burnett, Jr.
Robert D. Campbell
Bennett W. Cervin
George C. Chapman
Steven K. Cochran
O. Paul Corley, Jr.
Richard L. Covington
Joseph Dannenmaier
Gregg C. Davis
Scott D. Deatherage
Cheryl E. Diaz
Jeffery Paul Drummond
Barbara B. Ferguson
Stephen F. Fink
Frank Finn
Sharon M. Fountain
Howard L. Gilberg
Rachelle H. Glazer
Dennis J. Grindinger
Gerald H. Grissom
Russell G. Gully
Samuel D. Haas
Deborah G. Hankinson
William T. Hankinson
Thornton Hardie III
James B. Harris
Martha Harris
Craig A. Haynes
M. Lawrence Hicks, Jr.
John Michael Holt
Gregory S. C. Huffman
James L. Irish
Paul M. Johnston
Jerry P. Jones
Lou H. Jones

(See Next Column)

SHAREHOLDERS (Continued)

Robert W. Jones
Harold F. Kleinman
C. Neel Lemon III
Jack M. Little
Stephen S. Livingston
Peter A. Lodwick
Samuel E. Long, Jr.
Karen E. Lynch
John A. Mackintosh, Jr.
Schuyler B. Marshall, IV
John H. Martin
Timothy R. McCormick
P. Mike McCullough
Don J. McDermett, Jr.
James W. McKellar
Beth Eileen Metty
David E. Morrison
James C. Morriss III
Maureen Murry
Judy C. Norris
Geoffrey D. Osborn
Emily A. Parker
James R. Peacock III
Joseph S. Pevsner
John W. Rain
Stephen C. Rasch
Rust E. Reid
Peter J. Riley
James Y. Robb III
Harry M. Roberts, Jr.
Norman R. Rogers
James W. Rose
David M. Rosenberg
Judith W. Ross
Joe A. Rudberg
Stephen C. Schoettmer
William J. Schuerger
Clint Shouse
Steven W. Sloan
Bruce S. Sostek
Molly Steele
Arlene Switzer Steinfield
Peter J. Thoma
James M. Underwood
William R. Van Wagner
Kenn W. Webb
Ben B. West
William R. Wright
Jeffrey A. Zlotky

ASSOCIATES

Craig N. Adams
James T. Anderson
Steven R. Baggett
L. James Berglund, II
Ann Marie Bixby
Lisa K. Bork
Johnny R. Buckles
Beverly Ray Burlingame
Juliet N. Carter
John R. Cohn
Pamela Corrigan
Linda S. Crawley
Greg W. Curry
Lori L. Dalton
D'Lesli M. Davis
F. Barrett Davis
Priscilla Lynn Dunckel
David L. Emmons
Andrew P. Flint
Susan D. Gillette
G. Martin Green
Katherine Romeo Gregory
Michael G. Guajardo
Mark C. Gunnin
Philip N. Islip
Craig Naveen Kakarla
William M. Katz, Jr.
Karen L. Kendrick
Marc H. Klein
Jacob B. Marshall
Mia M. Martin
Leasa G. McCorkle
Mindy L. McNew
Mary A. McNulty
D'Ana Howard Mikeska
Kirkmichael T. Moore
Donna M. Morrow
William R. Mureiko
Bryan P. Neal
James Prince
Allison Roseman
A. Kay Roska
Elizabeth A. Schartz
Michael E. Schonberg
Lisa A. Schumacher
Mark M. Sloan
Pamela J. Smith
John F. Sterling
Jon Daniel Van Gorp
Debra J. Villarreal
Robert V. Vitanza
R. David Wheat
David S. White
Scott V. Williams
Amy K. Witherite
Shelly A. Youree

STAFF ATTORNEYS

Renee H. Tobias
Dawn Marie Wright

OF COUNSEL

J. W. Bullion
William E. Collins
Julia Patterson Forrester
Sol Goodell
Fred L. Hamric
Richard L. Jones
David S. Kidder
Malia A. Litman
Verne H. Maxwell
William D. Neary
Cynthia S. Pladziewicz
Daniel R. Rogers
John W. Rutland, Jr.
Terry L. Simmons

For full biographical listings, see the Martindale-Hubbell Law Directory

VIAL, HAMILTON, KOCH & KNOX (AV)

A Partnership of Professional Corporations
1717 Main Street, Suite 4400, 75201
Telephone: 214-712-4400
FAX: 214-712-4402

MEMBERS OF FIRM

Robert G. Vial (P.C.)
William N. Hamilton (P.C.)
Graham R. E. Koch (P.C.)
James A. Knox (P.C.)
Byron L. Falk (P.C.)
James H. Baumgartner, Jr., (P.C.)
George W. Fazakerly (P.C.)
Paul D. Schoonover (P.C.)
Walter L. Abbey (P.C.)
M. Leigh Bartlett (P.C.)
Stephen L. Baskind (P.C.)
James L. Deem (P.C.)
Perry Oswin Chrisman (P.C.)
Bruce W. Bowman, Jr., (P.C.)
Guy W. Anderson, Jr., (P.C.)
Baker R. Rector (P.C.)
J. Raymond Chesney (P.C.)
W. Bruce Monning
Richard G. Dafoe (P.C.)
Howard W. Key (P.C.)
Robert M. Hoffman (P.C.)
John W. Nassen (P.C.)
Charles D. Pulman (P.C.)
Jerry C. Gilmore (P.C.)
Gary L. Woolfolk (P.C.)
Paul E. Pesek (P.C.)
Stephen E. Friend (P.C.)
Steve Kardell, Jr., (P.C.)
Donald H. Flanary, Jr., (P.C.)
Kent S. Hofmeister (P.C.)
Richard D. Pullman (P.C.)
James M. Schendle (P.C.)
Kenneth M. Horwitz (P.C.)

(See Next Column)

VIAL, HAMILTON, KOCH & KNOX—*Continued*

MEMBERS OF FIRM (Continued)

Michael D. Farris (P.C.)
Bryan T. Pope (P.C.)
Mark A. Hendrix (P.C.)
Steven A. Hollis (P.C.)
Robert C. Wendland (P.C.)
Thomas B. Alleman (P.C.)
Rockney D. Pletcher (P.C.)
Micheal V. Winchester (P.C.)
J. Mark Hansen (P.C.)
Robert D. Allen (P.C.)
Elizabeth A. Imhoff (P.C.)
Terrence S. Welch (P.C.)
J. Michael Colpoys (P.C.)
D. Bradley Dickinson (P.C.)
James A. McCorquodale (P.C.)
Robert F. Middleton (P.C.)
Robert W. Coleman (P.C.)
John R. Henderson (P.C.)
John E. Richards (P.C.)
David Kleiman (P.C.)
Laird E. Lawrence (P.C.)
Robert F. Brown (P.C.)
Janice Z. Davis (P.C.)
Michael T. Tarski (P.C.)
Robert S. Rendell (P.C.)
William C. Fleming (P.C.)
Robert E. Thackston (P.C.)
David J. Schubert (P.C.)
Sharla H. Myers (P.C.)
Paula M. Romberg (P.C.)
William E. Reid (P.C.)
F. Gayle Keahey (P.C.)
Larry J. Bridgefarmer

ASSOCIATES

Blake Allen Bailey
James A. Ballard
Laura L. Beachman
Tracy W. Berry
Russell H. Birner
Mae Brudner
H. Michelle Caldwell
Hala Linda Carey
Thomas D. Caudle
Steven H. Clemons
Charles D. Coleman
Jordan W. Cowman
Allison Culver
William B. Curtis
Mary Payton Emery
Blake S. Evans
Karen Kohler Fitzgerald
Gillian Galbraith
Robert B. Gilbreath
Bonnie Lee Goldstein
J. Lee Grable, Jr.
Barry L. Hardin
Scott E. Hayes
Gary W. Hays
Cathy Hendrickson
Janie E. James
Amy Sanders Kerber
Tori Smith Levine
Connie Parks Lust
Robin S. Martin
Alexander G. McGeoch
Lucy Elizabeth Meyers
Aaron L. Mitchell
Marilyn S. Mollet
Kyle E. Moore
David T. Morice
Jamison D. Newberg
Kimberly A. Parkinson
John R. Rowlett
Judy Keller Shore
Lisa Schafroth Sooter
William W. Speed
Christine L. Stetson
Scott Randall Sweet
Ardita Vick
Mark Vincent
James M. Welch
Megan P. Whitten
Martha Waters Wise
Robbyn P. Wysocki

OF COUNSEL

Gerald R. Powell
Cecil L. Smith

LEGAL SUPPORT PERSONNEL

William L. Evans
Dianne C. George

For full biographical listings, see the Martindale-Hubbell Law Directory

VINSON & ELKINS L.L.P. (AV)

3700 Trammell Crow Center, 2001 Ross Avenue, 75201-2975
Telephone: 214-220-7700
Fax: 214-220-7716
Houston, Texas Office: 1001 Fannin, Suite 2300.
Telephone: 713-758-2222.
Fax: 713-758-2346. International
Telex: 6868314.
Cable Address: Vinelkins.
Austin, Texas Office: One American Center, 600 Congress Avenue.
Telephone: 512-495-8400.
Fax: 512-495-8612.
Washington, D.C. Office: The Willard Office Building, 1455 Pennsylvania Avenue, N.W.
Telephone: 202-639-6500.
Fax: 202-639-6604.
Cable Address: Vinelkins.
London, England Office: 47 Charles Street, Berkeley Square, London, W1X 7PB, England.
Telephone: 011 (44-71) 491-7236.
Fax: 011 (44-71) 499-5320.
Cable Address: Vinelkins LondonW.1.
Moscow, Russian Federation Office: 16 Alexey Tolstoy Street, Second Floor, Moscow, 103001 Russian Federation.
Telephone: 011 (70-95) 956-1995.
Telecopy: 011 (70-95) 956-1996.
Mexico City, Mexico Office: Aristóteles 77, 5°Piso, Colonia Chapultepec Polanco, 11560 Mexico City, Mexico, D.F.
Telephone: (52-5) 280-7828.
Fax: (52-5) 280-9223
Singapore Office: 50 Raffles Place, #19-05 Shell Tower, 0104. U.S. Vocie Mailbox: 713-758-3500.
Telephone: (65) 536-8300.
Fax: (65) 536-8311.

RESIDENT PARTNERS

David P. Blanke
Michael R. Boulden
John C. Brannan, Jr.
Bryant W. Burke
Jeffrey E. Eldredge
Orrin L. Harrison, III
Monty Humble
Kenneth E. Johns, Jr.

(See Next Column)

RESIDENT PARTNERS (Continued)

Stuart Brooks Johnston, Jr.
Thomas S. Leatherbury
Dale Gene Markland
Derek R. McClain
James S. Meyer
Michael J. Schimberg
Jerry R. Selinger
Gary G. Short
William D. Sims, Jr.
J. Michael Sutherland
Robert C. Walters
Philip D. Weller
Buck J. Wynne, III

OF COUNSEL

Rodney M. Anderson
V. Craig Cantrell
Sheryl L. Hopkins
Michael L. Malone
Ellen Smith Pryor
Norman D. Radford, Jr.

RESIDENT ASSOCIATES

Craig B. Anderson
Steven T. Baron
Steven F. Barrett
Eldrige A. Burns, Jr.
William H. Church, Jr.
Scott L. Cole
Mark A. Cover
Samuel Poage Dalton
James A. Krause
Z. Melissa Lawrence
W. David Lee
Stephen L. Levine
Alan W. Lintel
Sharon Maberry
Heidi Mahon Cook
Steven C. Malin
Lila Clark Marsh
Paul A. Martin
Theodore D. Matula
Lisa M. McGrath
Jonathan Samuel Perlman
Michael L. Raiff
Russell L. Reid, Jr.
Tara Hanley Reynolds
George G. Rodriguez
C. Gregory Rogers
Steven L. Russell
Steve Shackelford
Stacy Deanne Siegel
William S. Snyder
Cynthia A. Stephens
Mark M. Stetler
John C. Wander
Russell Yager
Jessica W. Young

For full biographical listings, see the Martindale-Hubbell Law Directory

JAMES A. WALTERS, P.C. (AV)

1950 Thanksgiving Tower, 1601 Elm Street, 75201
Telephone: 214-880-0366
Telefax: 214-880-0829

James A. Walters

For full biographical listings, see the Martindale-Hubbell Law Directory

WINSTEAD SECHREST & MINICK P.C. (AV)

5400 Renaissance Tower, 1201 Elm Street, 75270-2199
Telephone: 214-745-5400
Telex: 73-0051
Telecopy: 214-745-5390
Houston, Texas Office: 1700 Bank One Center, 910 Travis Street.
Telephone: 713-655-0392.
Telex: 73-0051.
Telecopy: 713-951-3800.
Austin, Texas Office: Suite 800, 100 Congress Avenue.
Telephone: 512-474-4330.
Telex: 73-0051.
Telecopier: 512-370-2850.
Mexico, D.F., Mexico Office: Winstead Sechrest & Minick S.A. de C.V., Galileo 20, P.H. - A, Col. Polanco, 11560 Mexico, D.F.
Telephone: 525-280-6766.
Telecopier: 525-280-0307.

William B. Sechrest
Thomas W. Oliver
Darrel A. Rice
W. Mike Baggett
Daniel Clark Stewart
Steven D. Nelson
John M. Nolan
T. Randall Matthews
James J. Lee
Thomas R. Helfand
Jeffrey A. Ford
John A. Price
Jeffrey A. Hage
J. Richard White
James David Brown
Randall E. Roberts
David W. Elmquist
Robert E. Crawford, Jr.
Lynda Zimmerman
J. Kenneth Kopf
Barry R. Knight
Stanley G. Harvey
J. Maxwell Tucker
Josiah M. Daniel, III
Stephen K. Yungblut
Kevin A. Sullivan
Terry L. Salazar
Edward A. Peterson
Mike C. McWilliams
Gary L. White
Tonya Powers Johannsen
R. Michael Farquhar
Nan B. Braley
John F. Bergner
Nancy Wyman Furney
Michelle Parsons Goolsby
Keith H. Mullen
David H. Tannenbaum
Thomas W. Hughes
Valinda Barrett Wolfert
Patrick J. Wielinski
William L. Wallander
Franklin Eastwood Wright
Paul V. Downey
Wayne W. Bost
Diane Lettelleir
Scot W. O'Brien
Michael B. Cline
Arthur Anderson
H. Martin Gibson
Kirk R. Williams
Charles T. Clark
Michael W. Hilliard
James A. Markus

(See Next Column)

WINSTEAD SECHREST & MINICK P.C., *Dallas—Continued*

Amanda J. Jensen
Beverly Scott Barragan
Kenneth L. Betts
Michael K. O'Neal
Bennee B. Jones
David L. Swanson
John P. Kincade
Paul Heath
Walter D. James III
Brian T. Morris
Michelle I. Rieger
Linda Sue Kennon
X. Lane Folsom
Paul N. Wageman
James J. Murphy
David L. Winston
David B. Koch
Jeanne G. Selzer
Lynne P. Clarke
T. Andrew Dow
Elmer A. Johnston
Lisa N. Tyson
James S. Brouner
Joel S. Reed
Kimberly Frisch-Winters
John S. Chinuntdet
Christopher M. Ashby
Robyn S. Gill
Wesly Carl Maness
Niles W. Holmes
Pamela B. Stein
Jana L. Catterall
Edward C. Griffith, Jr.
John T. Mockler
Ted S. Schweinfurth
Robert J. Witte
H. Dodd Crutcher
Dawn M. Douthit
Brian M. Hoffman (Not admitted in TX)

OF COUNSEL

Richard G. Hamon
Bill H. Brister
Rodney D. Moore
Joe T. Hyde
Marc I. Steinberg
Luis F. Visoso (Not admitted in United States; Also at Mexico, D.F., Mexico Office)

For full biographical listings, see the Martindale-Hubbell Law Directory

*DEL RIO,** Val Verde Co. — (Refer to Carrizo Springs)

*DENTON,** Denton Co.

PHILIPS AND HOPKINS, P.C. (AV)

P.O. Box 2027, 76202-2027
Telephone: 817-566-7010
Facsimile: 817-898-0502

Gerald W. Cobb
T. Miller Davidge, Jr.
Robert N. Eames
William P. Philips, Jr.
Gray W. Shelton
Randolph W. Stout

OF COUNSEL

George Hopkins

Chris Raesz
Leigh Hilton
Barry D. Irwin

Representative Clients: North Texas Savings & Loan Assn., Denton, Texas; First State Bank of Texas, Denton, Texas; Sanger Bank, Sanger, Texas; BankOne, Texas, N.A.; Texas Bank, Denton, Texas; Dentex Title Co., Denton, Texas.

For full biographical listings, see the Martindale-Hubbell Law Directory

*DIMMITT,** Castro Co.

BURKETT AND ROSS (AV)

114 South Broadway, P.O. Box 35, 79027
Telephone: 806-647-2131
Fax: 806-647-4535

Swain Burkett (1903-1991)

MEMBERS OF FIRM

Jimmy L. Ross

ASSOCIATES

James R. Horton

Representative Clients: The First State Bank of Dimmitt; Dimmitt Agri Industries, Inc.
Local Counsel: Lawyers Title Insurance Corp.

For full biographical listings, see the Martindale-Hubbell Law Directory

*DUMAS,** Moore Co. — (Refer to Borger)

*EAGLE PASS,** Maverick Co. — (Refer to Carrizo Springs)

*EASTLAND,** Eastland Co.

TURNER, SEABERRY & WARFORD (AV)

400 Exchange Building, 76448
Telephone: 817-629-1777

John Williams Turner (1886-1952)
Virgil Theodore Seaberry (1892-1960)
Virgil T. Seaberry, Jr.
Tommy G. Warford

Representative Clients: Texas Electric Service Co.; Eastland National Bank; Southwestern Bell Telephone Co.; Hardware Mutuals; Peoples State Bank of Clyde, Ranger Branch.

For full biographical listings, see the Martindale-Hubbell Law Directory

*EDNA,** Jackson Co. — (Refer to Victoria)

*EL PASO,** El Paso Co.

DIAMOND RASH GORDON & JACKSON, P.C. (AV)

300 East Main Drive, 7th Floor, 79901
Telephone: 915-533-2277
Fax: 915-545-4623

Tom Diamond
Alan V. Rash
Norman J. Gordon
Ronald L. Jackson
John R. Batoon
Robert J. Truhill

Russell D. Leachman

Representative Clients: City of El Paso; El Paso Housing Finance Corp.; City of El Paso Industrial Development Authority; Ysleta del sur Pueblo Indian Tribe; Alabama and Coushatta Indian Tribe of Texas; Metropolitan Life Insurance Company; De Bruyn, Cooper, Maldonada Advertising, Inc.

For full biographical listings, see the Martindale-Hubbell Law Directory

JOHNSON & BOWEN (AV)

Suite 1600 Texas Commerce Bank Building, 79901
Telephone: 915-532-1497
FAX: 915-532-5415

MEMBERS OF FIRM

Travis C. Johnson
Phillip C. Bowen

Representative Clients: El Paso County 911 District; Fischer Cordova Partners, Inc.; Hudspeth County Conservation and Reclamation District No. 1; Southwest Airlines Co.; Texas Commerce Bank-El Paso, N.A.

For full biographical listings, see the Martindale-Hubbell Law Directory

KEMP, SMITH, DUNCAN & HAMMOND, A PROFESSIONAL CORPORATION (AV)

2000 State National Bank Plaza, 79901, P.O. Drawer 2800, 79999
Telephone: 915-533-4424
Fax: 915-546-5360
Albuquerque, New Mexico Office: 500 Marquette, N.W., Suite 1200, P.O. Box 1276.
Telephone: 505-247-2315.
Fax: 505-764-5480.

Tad R. Smith
J. Leighton Green, Jr.
Robert B. Zaboroski
Christopher Allan Paul
Charles C. High, Jr.
Jim Curtis
Dane George
Larry C. Wood
Michael D. McQueen
Taffy D. Bagley
Darrell R. Windham
Roger D. Aksamit
Michael F. Ainsa
Yvonne K. Puig
Charles A. Beckham, Jr.
Margaret A. Christian
Barbara Anne Kazen
Kenneth R. Carr
Mark Mendel
Nancy C. Santana
Mitzi Turner
Allan M. Goldfarb
Raymond E. White
Susan F. Austin
John S. Howell
Mark R. Flora
Donna M. Christopherson
Elizabeth J. Vann
Kathleen Campbell Walker
John R. Boomer
Cynthia S. Anderson
Kevin E. Shannon

RETIRED PARTNER

William Duncan

OF COUNSEL

Joseph P. Hammond
Raymond H. Marshall
William J. Derrick

SENIOR ATTORNEY

Mark N. Osborn

Gregory G. Johnson
Kay Cargill Jenkins
James W. Brewer
Kathryn Halsell Anderson
Susan K. Pine
Angela Morrow
Tom Wicker, Jr.
John R. Jones
Clara B. Burns
John A. Kazen
Kyle Lasley
Matthew R. Henry
Gene Wolf
Robert L. Blumenfeld
Hunter W. Burkhalter
Leticia Nunez
Frank J. Guzmán
Scott S. Crocker
Roger Lee White

Attorneys for: State National Bank; Continental National Bank; Sunwest Bank; Rio Grande Bancshares; Atchison, Topeka & Santa Fe Railway Co.; Southern Pacific Transportation Co.; Circle K Corporation; Pet Inc.; The Leavell Company; Asarco.

For full biographical listings, see the Martindale-Hubbell Law Directory

El Paso—Continued

MAYFIELD AND PERRENOT, A PROFESSIONAL CORPORATION (AV)

Fifth Floor, First City National Bank Building, 79901
Telephone: 915-533-2468
Telecopier: 915-533-0620

Richard B. Perrenot
Steven Tredennick
Robert G. Gilbert
Robert V. Gibson
Victor F. Poulos
Roy R. Brandys
Jeffery W. McElroy
Harold Robert Hayes, III
Burton I. Cohen

OF COUNSEL

Ellis O. Mayfield
James B. McIntyre
Roy D. Jackson, Jr.

Susan Ramirez Stowe

For full biographical listings, see the Martindale-Hubbell Law Directory

LAW OFFICES OF MALCOLM MCGREGOR, INC. A PROFESSIONAL CORPORATION (AV)

1011 North Mesa Street, 79902
Telephone: 915-544-5230
FAX: 915-533-4368

Malcolm McGregor

John Schwambach

For full biographical listings, see the Martindale-Hubbell Law Directory

MOUNCE & GALATZAN, A PROFESSIONAL CORPORATION (AV)

7th Floor, Texas Commerce Bank Building, 79901-1334
Telephone: 915-532-3911
Fax: 915-541-1597

William J. Mounce
William T. Kirk
Wiley F. James, III
Merton B. Goldman
Sabre Anthony Safi
H. Keith Myers
Carl H. Green
Risher Smith Gilbert
Timothy V. Coffey
John Steven Birkelbach
Harrel L. Davis III
Corey W. Haugland
Barbara Wiederstein
Kurt G. Paxson
Michael J. Hutson
Mark C. Walker
Victor M. Firth
Steven L. Hughes
Bernard R. Given, II
Mark D. Dore

Clyde A. Pine, Jr.
Raymond C. Palmer, Jr.
James C. Jones
Marylee V. Warwick
Bill C. Anderson
Bruce A. Koehler
Carrie D. Helmcamp
Darryl S. Vereen
Lisa Anne Elizondo
Raul H. Loya

OF COUNSEL

Morris A. Galatzan

Attorneys for: El Paso Natural Gas Co.; Texas Commerce Bank National Association; El Paso Independent School District; Commercial Union Assurance Cos.; State Farm Mutual Automobile Insurance Co.; Employers Insurance of Texas; Greater El Paso Association of Realtors.

For full biographical listings, see the Martindale-Hubbell Law Directory

SCOTT, HULSE, MARSHALL, FEUILLE, FINGER & THURMOND, P.C. (AV)

11th Floor Texas Commerce Bank Building, 79901
Telephone: 915-533-2493
Telecopier: 915-546-8333

Louis A. Scott (1895-1974)
James F. Hulse (1905-1989)
Schuyler B. Marshall (1920-1993)
Richard H. Feuille
George W. Finger
Charles R. Jones
James L. Gallagher
Richard G. Munzinger
Stephen B. Tatem, Jr.
Frank Feuille, IV
James T. McNutt, Jr.
G. Russell Hill
Myron D. Brown
W. Dean Hester
David P. Hassler
W. David Bernard
Carl E. Ryan
Terry L. Johnson
Stuart R. Schwartz
Leila Safi Hobson
Robert R. Feuille
Milton C. Colia
Joseph L. Hood, Jr.
Jeffrey C. Brown
William V. Ballew, III
Bernard D. Felsen
David R. Pierce
Darren G. Woody
Jeffrey S. Alley
James R. Dennis
Scott A. Agthe

(See Next Column)

Patricia Ann Goeldner
Paul Gay
Michael D. Stell
Christine York Johnston
Michael G. McLean
J. L. Jay
Gary A. Norton
Amy Stewart Sanders
Eric M. Brittain
W. Scott McLellan
Hal J. Taylor
Benjamin A. Escobar, Jr.
Rachel Anne Ekery
Robert Eric Riojas
John Wesley Dorman, Jr.

Representative Clients: Chevron U.S.A.; Phelps Dodge Corp.; Southwestern Bell Telephone Co.; Dow Chemical Co.; Popular Dry Goods Co., Inc.; General Motors Corp.; Allstate Insurance Co.; Kemper Insurance Group; Liberty Mutual Insurance Co.; Zurich General Accident & Liability Insurance Co.

For full biographical listings, see the Martindale-Hubbell Law Directory

STUDDARD & MELBY, A PROFESSIONAL CORPORATION (AV)

Third Floor, Franklin Plaza, 415 North Mesa, 79901
Telephone: 915-533-5938
Fax: 915-533-6225
Van Horn, Texas Office: Van Horn State Bank Building.
Telephone: 915-283-2714.
Fax: 915-283-9227.

Don Studdard
John C. Melby (1939-1985)
Jonathan D. Schwartz, Jr.
Brainerd S. Parrish
Stephen L. Mitchell
Christopher R. Johnston
Jeffrey T. Weikert
Ernesto L. Cisneros
David L. Curl
Stephen H. Nickey

Representative Clients: Banes Construcciones, S.A. de C.V.; Gorman de Mexico, S.A. de C.V.; Grupo Industrial Matamoros, S.A., de C. V.; Brown, Alcantar & Brown (Custom Brokers); Farmers Ins. Co.; Mid-County Ins. Co.; Highlands Insurance Co.; Farmland Insurance Co.; John Deere Insurance Co.; Gallagher Bassett Service, Inc.

For full biographical listings, see the Martindale-Hubbell Law Directory

*FARWELL,** Parmer Co. — (Refer to Lubbock)

*FLOYDADA,** Floyd Co. — (Refer to Plainview)

*FORT WORTH,** Tarrant Co.

CANTEY & HANGER (AV)

A Registered Limited Liability Partnership
2100 Burnett Plaza, 801 Cherry Street, 76102-6899
Telephone: 817-877-2800, Metro Line: 429-3815
Telex: 758631 FAX: 877-2807
Dallas
Dallas, Texas Office: Suite 500, 300 Crescent Court.
Telephone: 214-978-4100.
FAX: 214-978-4150.

MEMBERS OF FIRM

Whitfield J. Collins
Sloan B. Blair
Edward L. Kemble
H. Carter Burdette
Ira Butler, Jr.
Estil A. Vance, Jr.
Allan Howeth
Richard L. Griffith
Robert S. Travis
Harry E. Bartel
Tolbert L. Greenwood
John Frank Taylor, II
S. G. Johndroe III
Kirk R. Manning
Stephen A. Madsen
John F. Gray
Evelyn R. Leopold
Donald K. Buckman
Rod Patterson
Lynette Guy Williamson
Ralph H. Duggins
Paul Boudloche
Robert E. Aldrich, Jr.
J. Robert Forshey
T. Pollard Rogers
David C. Bakutis
Mark D. Beatty
Rory Divin
Perry J. Cockerell
Ernest Reynolds, III
Bradley C. Poulos
Larry Hayes
Noel C. Ice
James A. Riddell
Barbara G. Heptig
Mark G. Creighton
Dean A. Tetirick
Jeff P. Prostok
J. Frank Kinsel, Jr.
Charles J. Mason, Jr.
John C. Stewart
Carol J. Traylor
Clay Dean Humphries
William L. Hughes, Jr.
Christine E. Holland
Mary Colchin Johndroe
Shayne D. Moses
Lonnie J. Copps
D. Mark Daniel
Walter E. Tate
Sarah Walls
Michael D. Moore
Sandra Cockran Liser

OF COUNSEL

W. Douglas Bailey
Cecil E. Munn
Warren W. Shipman, III
Diego O. Giordano

ASSOCIATES

R. Dyann McCully
David Bradley Dowell
Joel T. Sawyer
Melody McDonald Wilkinson
Shannon Gilbert
Rosemary Behan
Jordan M. Parker
Kevin Norton
Brian C. Newby
Kenneth C. Cunningham
Scott V. Allen
Robert M. Doby III
Thomas Patrick Gordon III
C. Matthew Terrell

(See Next Column)

CANTEY & HANGER, *Fort Worth—Continued*

ASSOCIATES (Continued)

Michael G. Appleman
Jeffrey S. McFall
Farolito Parco
(Not admitted in TX)
Deeia D. Beck
R. Jeffrey Layne

Represent: General Motors Corp.; Texas-New Mexico Power Co.; Miller Brewing Co.; The Medical Protective Co.; Union Oil Co.; Texas Utilities Electric Co.; NationsBank of Texas, N.A.; Union Pacific Resources; Kimbell Art Foundation; Texas Commerce Bank.

For full biographical listings, see the Martindale-Hubbell Law Directory

CHAPPELL & McGARTLAND, L.L.P. (AV)

1800 City Center Tower II, 301 Commerce Street, 76102-4118
Telephone: 817-332-1800
Telecopy: 817-332-1956

David F. Chappell
Michael P. McGartland
Robert A. Parmelee

Robert S. (Bob) Johnson
James L. Williams, Jr.
Mark Allan Anderson
Jason C.N. Smith

OF COUNSEL

R. David Jones
Cathy Csaky Hirt
(Not admitted in TX)

For full biographical listings, see the Martindale-Hubbell Law Directory

JOHN W. CRUMLEY, P.C. (AV)

210 University Centre 1, 1300 South University Drive, 76107-5734
Telephone: 817-334-0291
Fax: 817-334-0775

John W. Crumley

For full biographical listings, see the Martindale-Hubbell Law Directory

JACKSON & WALKER, L.L.P. (AV)

777 Main Street, Suite 1800, 76102-5322
Telephone: 817-334-7200
Fax: 817-334-7290
Dallas, Texas Office: 901 Main Street, Suite 6000.
Telephone: 214-953-6000.
Fax: 214-953-5822.
Houston, Texas Office: 1100 Louisiana, Suite 4200.
Telephone: 713-752-4200.
Fax: 713-752-4221.
San Antonio, Texas Office: 112 E. Pecan Street, Suite 2100.
Telephone: 210-978-7700.
Fax: 210-978-7790.

MEMBERS OF FIRM

Susan A. Halsey
Albon O. Head, Jr.
Bonnie Arnett Horinek
Gary L. Ingram
Catherine A. Lenox
Michael A. McConnell

ASSOCIATES

Kevin W. Haney
Jay K. Rutherford
Kent R. Smith
Jeffrey J. Wolf

For full biographical listings, see the Martindale-Hubbell Law Directory

KELLY, HART & HALLMAN, A PROFESSIONAL CORPORATION (AV)

201 Main Street, Suite 2500, 76102
Telephone: 817-332-2500
Telecopy: 817-878-9280
Austin, Texas Office: 301 Congress Avenue, Suite 2000, 78701.
Telephone: 512-495-6400.
Fax: 512-495-6401.

Dee J. Kelly
Mark L. Hart, Jr.
William P. Hallman, Jr.

Drew G. Alexandrou
F. Richard Bernasek
C. William Blair
Clive D. Bode
Brian D. Bowden
Thomas W. Briggs
David P. Derber
Billie J. Ellis, Jr.
Marc N. Epstein
Dirk E. Eshleman
John H. Fant
Robert C. Grable
Chester W. Grudzinski, Jr.
Wesley N. Harris
Alan D. Hegi
Donald E. Herrmann
Calvin M. Jackson
E. Glen Johnson
Dee J. Kelly, Jr.
Keith D. Kohlhepp
Kevin G. Levy
Daniel L. Lowry
David M. Mellina
Sharon S. Millians
Barbara P. Neely
Don C. Plattsmier
Patrick A. Reardon
Brad G. Repass
Henry H. Robinson
J. Andrew Rogers

(See Next Column)

Marshall M. Searcy
Dan Settle, Jr.
Dulaney G. "Dee" Steer
Wayne B. Whitham

Robert C. Beal
Scott R. Bernhart
Mark E. Bishop
Kimberly S. Bowers
Sean A. Bryan
Robert L. Chaiken
Hugh G. Connor, II
Cheryl L. Coon
Peter B. Dewar
Roger C. Diseker
Mary Nan Doran
Greg S. Gober
John R. Hunter
Elizabeth J. Kohn
Jack E. Larson
J. Curtis Linscott
L. Edward Martin, III
Kimberly R. McGartland
Tomi Kay Mills
Paula T. Perkins
Lisa A. Peterson
Bart A. Rue
Susan H. Sorrells
Todd E. Tyler
Corinne B. Viso
William N. Warren

OF COUNSEL

Patricia F. Meadows

For full biographical listings, see the Martindale-Hubbell Law Directory

McDONALD SANDERS, A PROFESSIONAL CORPORATION (AV)

1300 Continental Plaza, 777 Main Street, 76102
Telephone: 817-336-8651
Metro Telephone: 429-1150
Fax: 817-334-0271

Atwood McDonald (1899-1989)
Earnest E. Sanders (1906-1979)
Robert St. Claire Newkirk
Michael M. Gibson
James E. Webb
Rick G. Sorenson
Daniel W. Sykes
A. Gary Thompson
Karen Hutchinson Gordon
Greg S. Hargrove
Kevin D. Kuenzli
Robert L. Ginsburg
William F. Peters, Jr.
Thomas Nezworski
William L. Latham
Nicholas S. Pappas
George C. Haratsis
Randyl S. Meigs
Mark Barnett French
John W. Wright

OF COUNSEL

Marcus Ginsburg
Robert D. Maddox
J. Olcott Phillips

Stuart B. Lumpkins, Jr.
Catherine B. Whited
David W. Kirkman
Alan L. Bowling
Nicholas S. Bettinger
S. Patrick Woodson
Jennifer J. Last

Representative Clients: Bank One, Texas, N.A.; The Dunlap Co. (Stripling-Cox Department Stores); General Motors Acceptance Corp.; Hickman Investments, Inc.; Montgomery Ward & Co., Inc.; Overton Bancshares; Specific Cruise System, Inc.; Texas Christian University; Texas Commerce Bank.

For full biographical listings, see the Martindale-Hubbell Law Directory

THOMPSON & KNIGHT, A PROFESSIONAL CORPORATION (AV)

(Attorneys and Counselors)
801 Cherry Street, Suite 1600, 76102
Telephone: 817-347-1700
Telecopy: 817-347-1799
Dallas, Texas Office: 1700 Pacific Avenue, Suite 3300, 75201.
Telephone: 214-969-1700.
Telecopy: 214-969-1751.
Cable Address: "Tomtex."
Telex: 732298.
Austin, Texas Office: 1200 San Jacinto Center, 98 San Jacinto Boulevard, 78701.
Telephone: 512-469-6100.
Telecopy: 512-469-6180.
Houston, Texas Office: 1700 Texas Commerce Tower, 600 Travis, 77002.
Telephone: 713-217-2800.
Telecopy: 713-217-2828; 713-2882.
Monterrey, Mexico Office: Edificio Losoles PD-4, Av. Lázaro Cárdenas No. 2400 Pte., San Pedro Garza Garcia, Nuevo Léon C.P. 66220.
Telephone: (52-8) 363-0096.
Telecopy: (52-8) 363-3067.

SHAREHOLDERS

R Gordon Appleman
Stephen B. Norris
E. Michael Sheehan

ASSOCIATES

Susan E. Coleman
Jennifer Pettijohn Henry
Mary M. Penrose

For full biographical listings, see the Martindale-Hubbell Law Directory

*FREDERICKSBURG,** Gillespie Co. — (Refer to Boerne)

*GALVESTON,** Galveston Co.

McLeod, Alexander, Powel & Apffel, A Professional Corporation (AV)

802 Rosenberg, P.O. Box 629, 77553-0629
Telephone: 409-763-2481
Houston Line: 713-488-7150

V.W. McLeod (1914-1977)
Robert W. Alexander (Retired)
Benjamin R. Powel
Ervin A. Apffel, Jr.
Fredrick J. Bradford
James L. Ware
W. Daniel Vaughn
Douglas W. Poole
Michael B. Hughes
James B. Galbraith
J. D. Bashline
Anthony P. Brown
James R. Ansell
Kenneth J. Bower
David P. Salyer
Wm. Hulse Wagner
David E. Cowen

Patricia McGarvey Rosendahl
George P. Pappas
Genevieve Bacak McGarvey
Tod A. Phillips
Phillip W. Snyder
William R. Floyd
Andrew E. Steinberg
Michele B. Chimene
David K. Vallance
Bryan R. Lasswell
Sherri R. Malpass
Stephen Kuzmich
Laura B. Walters
Glynis L. Zavarelli
Mark S. La Spina
Melissa K. Cooney
Mark J. Oberti
Joseph Blizzard
Derek Phillips

Claims Attorneys: Santa Fe Lines in Texas and Louisiana.
Counsel for: Aetna Casualty and Surety Co.; Continental Insurance Cos.; Port of Galveston; Farmers Insurance Group.

For full biographical listings, see the Martindale-Hubbell Law Directory

Mills, Shirley, Eckel & Bassett, L.L.P. (AV)

400 Washington Building, 2228 Mechanic Street, P.O. Box 1943, 77553
Telephone: 409-763-2341; Houston Line: 713-488-8716
Facsimile: 409-763-2879
Houston
Houston, Texas Office: 6230 Texas Commerce Tower.
Telephone: 713-225-0547.
Facsimile: 713-225-0844.

MEMBERS OF FIRM

Preston Shirley (1912-1990)
Ballinger Mills, Jr. (1914-1992)
John Eckel
Roland L. Bassett
Jack C. Brock
Carla Cotropia
Fred D. Raschke
William E. Griffey
Robert A. Davee
Christopher S. Cahill
George W. Vie, III

ASSOCIATES

Carl J. Wilkerson
Christopher D. Bertini
Kathryn Ammerman Horner
Scott Lyford
Maureen Kuzik
Chris Reeder
Taylor Townsend Schwab

OF COUNSEL

Chas. G. Dibrell, Jr.

General Attorneys for: American Indemnity Group.
Counsel for: Continental-National-American Group; United States Fidelity & Guaranty Co.; Employers Insurance of Texas; CNA Insurance Group; INA Insurance Group.

For full biographical listings, see the Martindale-Hubbell Law Directory

Royston, Rayzor, Vickery & Williams, L.L.P. (AV)

205 Cotton Exchange Building, 2102 Mechanic Street, 77550-1692
Telephone: 409-763-1623
Cable Address: "Royston"
Telex: 765449
Telecopier: 713-763-3853
Houston, Texas Office: 2200 Texas Commerce Tower.
Telephone: 713-224-8380.
Cable Address: "Houport"
Telex: 686-9017.
Telecopier: 713-225-9945.
Brownsville, Texas Office: 55 Cove Circle, P.O. Box 3509.
Telephone: 210-542-4377.
Cable Address: "Padre"
Telex: 767-817.
Telecopier: 210-542-4370.
Corpus Christi, Texas Office: 1700 Wilson Plaza West, 606 North Carancahua.
Telephone: 512-884-8808.
Cable Address: "CC PORT"
Telex: 210-686-6625.
Telecopier: 512-884-7261.

PARTNERS

Bryan F. Williams, Jr. (1928-1980)
Robert S. DeLange
James R. Watkins
S. Mark Strawn

(See Next Column)

ASSOCIATES

William P. Glenn, Jr.

Counsel for: West Gulf Maritime Assn.; American International Underwriters Corp.; Galveston Cotton Exchange; Lykes Bros. Steamship Co.; Shipowners Claims Bureau, Inc.; The United Kingdom Mutual Steamship Assurance Assn., Ltd.

For full biographical listings, see the Martindale-Hubbell Law Directory

*GATESVILLE,** Coryell Co. — (Refer to Temple)

*GEORGETOWN,** Williamson Co.

William D. Bryce (AV)

511 Main Street, 78626
Telephone: 512-930-3725

ASSOCIATES

Douglas D. Bryce
David D. Bryce

For full biographical listings, see the Martindale-Hubbell Law Directory

*GEORGE WEST,** Live Oak Co.

Schneider & McWilliams, P.C. (AV)

301 Bowie Street, P.O. Box 550, 78022
Telephone: 512-449-1501
Fax: 512-449-2042

R. E. Schneider, Jr. (1906-1976)
J. R. Schneider
Dwayne L. McWilliams

Joseph Robert Schneider, Jr.

Counsel for: First National Bank in George West; San Patricio Electric Cooperative, Inc.

For full biographical listings, see the Martindale-Hubbell Law Directory

*GILMER,** Upshur Co. — (Refer to Tyler)

*GOLDTHWAITE,** Mills Co. — (Refer to Eastland)

*GOLIAD,** Goliad Co. — (Refer to Victoria)

*GONZALES,** Gonzales Co. — (Refer to Victoria)

*GREENVILLE,** Hunt Co.

Morgan and Gotcher (AV)

2610-A Stonewall Street, P.O. Box 556, 75403-0556
Telephone: 903-455-3183
Dallas Telephone: 214-226-1474
Fax: 903-454-4654

J. Harris Morgan
Holly H. Gotcher

Representative Clients: Huffines Enterprises; Greenville Independent School District; International Cassettes, Inc.; Universal Health Services, Inc.; Hunt County Appraisal District; Bank One Greenville; Citizens Bank of Royce City.

For full biographical listings, see the Martindale-Hubbell Law Directory

*GROESBECK,** Limestone Co. — (Refer to Waco)

*GROVETON,** Trinity Co. — (Refer to Bryan)

HARLINGEN, Cameron Co.

Adams and Graham, L.L.P. (AV)

222 East Van Buren, West Tower, 78550
Telephone: 210-428-7495
Fax: 210-428-2954

MEMBERS OF FIRM

John Q. Adams (1900-1968)
Marshall W. Graham (1924-1988)
James S. Graham, Jr. (1922-1990)
Ferriel C. Hamby, Jr.
Tom A. Lockhart
Jim Denison
Leo S. Salzman
Roger W. Hughes
Craig H. Vittitoe
William L. Pope
Patricia Kelly
Jaime Balli
Gina M. Benavides

ASSOCIATES

Charlie J. Cilfone
Juan A. Gonzalez
Barry Ray
Wilbert Hughes
Trinidad P. Galdean
Rafael Garcia, Jr.

Representative Clients: The Travelers Insurance Cos.; Employers Casualty Co.; CIGNA; AIAC; GAB; State Farm Insurance Co.; Valley Baptist Medical Center; Continental Loss Adjusting Services; McAllen Medical Center; Brownsville Medical Center.

For full biographical listings, see the Martindale-Hubbell Law Directory

Harlingen—Continued

JOHNSON & DAVIS (AV)

402 East Van Buren Street, 78550
Telephone: 210-423-0213
FAX: 210-425-7842

MEMBERS OF FIRM

Orrin W. Johnson
Richard D. Davis (1929-1994)
William C. Rountree, III
David E. Kithcart
Buddy R. Dossett
Andrew K. Rozell
Lisa Lynne Taylor

Representative Clients: NationsBank, Harlingen; San Benito Bank & Trust Co.; Boggus Motor Co.; Marine Military Academy, Inc.; Harbenito Broadcasting Co.; Harlingen Industrial Foundation, Inc.; KGBT-TV, L.P.; Valley Baptist Medical Center; San Benito Cameron County Drainage District No. 3; Harlingen Industrial Foundation, Inc.

For full biographical listings, see the Martindale-Hubbell Law Directory

*HASKELL,** Haskell Co. — (Refer to Abilene)

HEARNE, Robertson Co. — (Refer to Bryan)

*HENRIETTA,** Clay Co. — (Refer to Wichita Falls)

*HEREFORD,** Deaf Smith Co. — (Refer to Amarillo)

*HILLSBORO,** Hill Co.

MARTIN, SHOWERS, SMITH & McDONALD (AV)

62 West Elm Street, P.O. Box 257, 76645-0257
Telephone: 817-582-2536
Telecopier: 817-582-9561

MEMBERS OF FIRM

James A. Showers
Stephen N. Smith
Michael W. McDonald
Kirk Bryant

OF COUNSEL

William B. Martin

Representative Clients: Nations Bank Texas, Hillsboro; First National Bank, Whitney; First State Bank, Hubbard and Hillsboro Branch; City of Itasca; Hillsboro Abstract & Title Co.; Whitney Independent School Districts; First State Bank, Mt. Calm; Cercon, a Division of Howmet-Cercast (USA), Inc; Towne Square Furniture, Inc.; First National Bank, Henrietta.

For full biographical listings, see the Martindale-Hubbell Law Directory

SIMS MOORE HILL & GANNON, L.L.P. (AV)

211 East Franklin Street, P.O. Box 1096, 76645-1096
Telephone: 817-582-5346
Telecopier: 817-582-7667

Jack Sims
Henry Moore
Gregg Hill
Jack T. Gannon

Representative Clients: Hill County Appraisal District; Aquilla Water Supply District; Eastland Title Co.; The Enterprise Foundation, Inc.; The Dallas Affordable Housing Partnership, Inc.; BEG Enterprises, Inc.; Cornerstone Housing Corporation; Parker Water Supply Corporation; Hill College; Westside Motors-I-35, Inc.

For full biographical listings, see the Martindale-Hubbell Law Directory

*HONDO,** Medina Co. — (Refer to San Antonio)

*HOUSTON,** Harris Co.

AKIN, GUMP, STRAUSS, HAUER & FELD, L.L.P. (AV)

A Registered Limited Liability Partnership including Professional Corporations
Pennzoil Place-South Tower, 711 Louisiana Street, Suite 1900, 77002
Telephone: 713-220-5800
Fax: 713-236-0822
Dallas, Texas Office: 1700 Pacific Avenue, Suite 4100.
Telephone: 214-969-2800.
Fax: 214-969-4343.
Austin, Texas Office: Franklin Plaza, 111 Congress Avenue, Suite 1900.
Telephone: 512-499-6200.
Fax: 512-476-3866.
San Antonio, Texas Office: NationsBank Plaza, 300 Convent Street, Suite 1500.
Telephone: 210-270-0800.
Fax: 210-224-2035.
New York, New York Office: 65 East 55th Street, 33rd Floor.
Telephone: 212-872-1000.
Fax: 212-872-1002.
Washington, D.C. Office: 1333 New Hampshire Avenue, N.W., Suite 400.
Telephone: 202-887-4000.
Fax: 202-887-4288.
Brussels, Belgium Office: Akin, Gump, Strauss, Hauer, Feld & Dassesse, 65 Avenue Louise, P.B. #7.
Telephone: 011-322-535-29-11.
Fax: 011-322-535-29-00.

(See Next Column)

Moscow, Russia Office: Bolshoi Sukharevsky, Pereulok 26, Building 1, 2nd Floor.
Telephone: 011 7 095 974 2411.
Fax: 011 7 095 974 2412.

MEMBERS OF FIRM

Douglas C. Atnipp (P.C.)
Kenneth R. Barrett
Douglas Y. Bech
Rick L. Burdick (P.C.)
Richard O. Faulk
L. Todd Gremillion (P.C.)
Paula Weems Hinton
Randall K. Howard (P.C.)
Jack J. Langlois (P.C.)
Charles A. Moore (P.C.)
William D. Morris
David S. Peterman (P.C.)
Robert L. Smith
H. Rey Stroube, III, (P.C.)
Michael K. Swan (P.C.)
Fabené W. Talbot
José L. Valera (P.C.)
S. Margie Venus
Stephen A. Wakefield
Michael R. Waller
Sarah Bing Wolfe
Blaine Yamagata (Not admitted in TX)

ASSOCIATES

Edward E. Abels, Jr.
Robert S. Ballentine
K. B. Battaglini
James W. Bowen
Betty C. Bradley
Suzanne Reddell Chauvin
Kevin L. Colbert
Kate Gamble Courtney (Not admitted in TX)
Roseann M. Engeldorf
Kevin P. Erwin
Kimberly Ann Evans
Judith Gail Foster
Karen P. Freeman
Amy B. Hutson
J. Vincent Kendrick
Susan Cregor Mathews
Richard Marshall Parr
L. David Rabinowitz
Margaret G. Reed
Coralina Rivera-Mazziotta
Jacquelyne M. Rocan (Not admitted in TX)
Gregory S. Roden
David R. Roth
A. Haag Sherman
S. Shawn Stephens
Richard J. Wilkie
Roderick B. Williams
Mark T. Woolfolk
Tseliang Shane Yang

OF COUNSEL

James M. Lemond
Stephen R. Melton

For full biographical listings, see the Martindale-Hubbell Law Directory

ANDREWS & KURTH L.L.P. (AV)

4200 Texas Commerce Tower, 77002
Telephone: 713-220-4200
Telex: 79-1208 Ankur
Telecopier: 713-220-4285
Washington, D.C. Office: Suite 200, 1701 Pennsylvania Avenue, N.W.
Telephone: 202-662-2700.
Telecopier: 202-662-2739.
Dallas, Texas Office: 4400 Thanksgiving Tower.
Telephone: 214-979-4400.
Telecopier: 214-979-4401.
The Woodlands, Texas: Suite 150, 2170 Buckthorne Place, 77380.
Telephone: 713-364-9199.
Telecopier: 713-364-9538.
Los Angeles, California Office: Suite 4200, 601 S. Figueroa Street.
Telephone: 213-213-896-3100.
Telecopier: 213-896-3137.
New York, N.Y. Office: 10th Floor, 425 Lexington Avenue.
Telephone: 212-850-2800.
Telecopier: 212-850-2929.

MEMBERS OF FIRM

Frank Andrews (deceased)
Melvin E. Kurth (deceased)
Milton H. West, Jr.
Alfred H. Ebert, Jr.
Laurence D. Sikes, Jr.
James V. Carroll, III
P. Dexter Peacock
John T. Cabaniss
Frederick M. Knapp, Jr.
David G. Elkins
Marcus L. Thompson
Hugh M. Ray
William T. Miller
Taylor M. Hicks, Jr.
Barry R. Miller
Joel I. Shannon
O. Clayton Lilienstern
Lawrence L. Bellatti
Douglas E. Clarke
Denton N. Thomas
Timothy J. Unger
Thomas J. Perich
Michael D. Stuart
Bruce R. Coulombe
Patricia Greek Vederman
James E. Myers
John R. Williford
Richard T. Boone
Priscilla Richman Owen
Barksdale Hortenstine
James Vernon Baird
Jack E. Fields
Robert V. Jewell
Terri Lacy
Fraser A. McAlpine
Kent W. Robinson
Douglas J. Dillon
C. Thomas Biddle, Jr.
Christine Burlingame LaFollette
G. Michael O'Leary
Doris Rodriguez
Lawrence Bernard Schreve
A. Ross Rommel, Jr.
William Edward Junell, Jr.
William N. Finnegan, IV
Thomas P. Mason
Thomas W. Ford, Jr.
James M. Prince
Elizabeth Howard
Steven R. Biegel
Christopher S. Collins
Thomas G. Bateman, Jr.
Jan K. Holzinger
Linda Ingols Dole
David J. Graham
John Boyd (Not admitted in TX)
Gregg Laswell
Mark E. Schwartz
O'Banion Williams, III
Lori Meghan Gallagher
Darrell D. Hancock
Jay D. Kelley
John Lee

(See Next Column)

ANDREWS & KURTH L.L.P.—*Continued*

MEMBERS OF FIRM (Continued)

David R. Margrave
T. Deon Warner
Jeffrey R. Harder (Resident, The Woodlands, Texas Office)
Jack D. Ballard
Paul M. Bohannon
Janiece M. Longoria
James Donnell
Hal V. Haltom, Jr.
Paul J. Pipitone
David G. Runnels
Robin Russell
John B. Shely
Jeffrey E. Spiers
John B. Thomas
Holly Harvel Williamson
John Carlton Wynne
Howard T. Ayers, Jr.
Mark C. Hodges
Thomas W. Taylor
John F. Wombwell

SENIOR COUNSEL

Robert L. Bradley
Lee R. Larkin
Clinton F. Morse
William H. Tenison, Jr.
Bass C. Wallace
Robert S. Weatherall

OF COUNSEL

Robert J. Collins
John P. Courtney
Kathleen E. Fenwick
Jerry V. Kyle
Walter B. Loeffler, Jr.
William D. Noel
Diane Pappas
Larry B. Phillips, III
Joe H. Reynolds

ASSOCIATES

John Arbour (Not admitted in TX)
Michael C. Blaney (Not admitted in TX)
Michael A. Boyd
Louise W. Brollier
Melinda Held Brunger
David Clyde Buck
Edward A. Cavazos
Johanna S. Coulter
Maria D. Dickson
Rosemarie Donnelly
Laura Leigh Eastman
Katherine E. Flanagan (Not admitted in TX)
Eileen Marie Gaffney
Charles R. Gregg, Jr
Kenneth M. Hale
Jim S. Hart
Thomas M. Hart
Gary R. Huffman
Darren Scott Inoff
Kendrick A. James
Brian Keller
Suzanne S. Killian
James Alan Knight
Suzie Leggio
Scott Locher
Stephen M. Loftin
Allison Donnell Mantor
Melissa M. Martin
Chanse L. McLeod
William L. Moll, Jr.
Geddings C. Moorefield
Kelly Marie Noel
David P. Oelman
James (Jay) R. Old, Jr.
Tana LaDon Pool
Blake E. Rasmussen
Sarah Wimberly Ray
Steven R. Rech
Laura Rowe
Ronald G. Skloss
John J. Sparacino
Elisabeth Scott Stone
William P. Swenson
Darrell G. Thomas
Melanie Montague Trent
Craig M. Van De Mark
Jeffrey L. Wade
J. Dale Wainwright
Douglas G. Walter (Not admitted in TX)
Mark O. Webb
Wade H. Whilden, Jr.
Susan Y. Yang
David A. Zdunkewicz

SENIOR STAFF ATTORNEYS

Cynthia Aafedt
Victoria C. Blanks
Suzanne Byerly
Suzanne E. Goss
Mariann Sears
David J. Stone

STAFF ATTORNEYS

Cecelia J. Bentz
Peter K. Jameson

For full biographical listings, see the Martindale-Hubbell Law Directory

BAKER & BOTTS, L.L.P. (AV)

One Shell Plaza, 910 Louisiana, 77002
Telephone: 713-229-1234
Cable Address: "Boterlove"
Fax: 713-229-1522
Washington, D.C. Office: The Warner, 1299 Pennsylvania Avenue, N.W.
Telephone: 202-639-7700.
New York, New York Office: 885 Third Avenue, Suite 2000.
Telephone: 212-705-5000.
Austin, Texas Office: 1600 San Jacinto Center, 98 San Jacinto Boulevard.
Telephone: 512-322-2500.
Dallas, Texas Office: 2001 Ross Avenue.
Telephone: 214-953-6500.
Moscow, Russian Federation Office: 10 ul. Pushkinskaya, 103031.
Telephone: 7095/921-5300 (Local); 7095/929-7070 (International).

James A. Baker (1857-1941)
W. B. Botts (1836-1894)

MEMBERS OF FIRM

Finis E. Cowan
James Addison Baker, III
E. William Barnett
Moulton Goodrum, Jr.
William C. Griffith
Robert L. Stillwell
Robert J. Malinak
James D. Randall
Joseph D. Cheavens
John M. Huggins
Thad T. Hutcheson, Jr.
Harold L. Metts
F. Walter Conrad, Jr.
Michael S. Moehlman
Stanley C. Beyer
Larry B. Feldcamp
Frank W. R. Hubert, Jr.
Philip J. John, Jr.
Lewis Proctor Thomas, III
Wade H. Whilden

(See Next Column)

MEMBERS OF FIRM (Continued)

Richard R. Brann
James L. Leader
Roy L. Nolen
John P. Cogan, Jr.
J. Patrick Garrett
L. Chapman Smith
David Alan Burns
Fred H. Dunlop
I. Jay Golub
William C. Slusser
Benjamin G. Wells
Joseph A. Cialone, II
Jefferson Gregory Copeland
Richard L. Josephson
John Edward Neslage
Rufus W. Oliver, III
R. Joel Swanson
G. Irvin Terrell
Rufus Cormier, Jr.
Michael Paul Graham
Louis Lee Bagwell
S. Stacy Eastland
Scott F. Partridge
James R. Raborn
Walter J. Smith
Stephen Gillham Tipps
C. Michael Watson
James Edward Maloney
Stephen A. Massad
Scott E. Rozzell
Charles Szalkowski
George F. Goolsby
Gray Jennings
Allister M. Waldrop, Jr.
Robert P. Wright
J. Michael Baldwin
Lee Landa Kaplan
Marley Lott
Tony P. Rosenstein
Joe S. Poff
Ronald W. Kesterson
Gregory V. Nelson
Thomas H. Adolph
Pamela B. Ewen
Jay T. Kolb
Claudia W. Frost
Michael S. Goldberg
J. David Kirkland, Jr.
David R. Poage
Stuart F. Schaffer
Louise A. Shearer
George T. Shipley
Robert M. Weylandt
R. Paul Yetter
Paul B. Landen
Ronald C. Lewis
Gene J. Oshman
Margo S. Scholin
Gail Woodson Stewart
Mitchell D. Lukin
David D. Sterling
David F. Asmus
Gerard A. Desrochers
Darrell W. Taylor
Kenneth S. Culotta
Joshua Davidson
Tony M. Davis
Stephen Krebs
Paul L. Mitchell
Karen Kay Maston
John W. Porter

RETIRED PARTNERS

H. Malcolm Lovett
Joseph C. Hutcheson, III
John T. McCullough
John T. Maginnis
John F. Heard
Robert K. Jewett
James K. Nance
Garrett R. Tucker, Jr.
A. B. White
Frank B. Pugsley
William Rufus Choate
Ross Staine
James P. Lee
William C. Harvin
C. Brien Dillon
John B. Abercrombie
Alvin Owsley
R. D. Richards, Jr.
Frank G. Harmon
George H. Jewell
William G. Woodford
John S. Sellingsloh
James G. Ulmer
Ewell E. Murphy, Jr.
Sam G. Croom, Jr.
V. Reagan Burch
Walter E. Workman

ASSOCIATES

Thomas R. Ajamie
John Anaipakos
Marc A. Antonetti
Nancy K. Archer-Yanochik
Andres M. Arismendi, Jr.
Cesar Enrique Arreaza
Frederick William Backus
Richard A. Bales
James H. Barkley
Parker Bond Binion
Jane Nenninger Bland
Dorothy Fong Blefeld
Maria Wyckoff Boyce
Marian L. Brancaccio
Jennifer Breidenbach
Michael Lamar Brem
Michael P. Bresson
Richard A. Brooks
Elizabeth F. Brown
Margaret W. Brown
William C. Bullard
Charles Tynan Buthod
Katherine Butler
Karen Skeens Caldwell
William R. Caldwell
Michael L. Calhoon
T. Chuck Campbell
Bill Brannen Caraway
Janet Chambers
Ross E. Cockburn
Stephanie K. Copp
Cynthia Crawford
Robin Elizabeth Curtis
Shane Robert DeBeer
Jennifer J. De La Rosa
Laura K. Devitt
Sarah Sharlot Dietrich
Sashe D. Dimitroff
Victoria Donnenberg
Phillip L. Douglass
J. Kristine Dubiel
Stephen T. Dyer
Matthew P. Eastus
Louis B. Eble
Paul R. Elliott
Katherine P. Ellis
Nicolas J. Evanoff
Brian P. Fenske
Nancy E. Field
Jason D. Firth
Kevin S. Fiur
Roger J. Fulghum
John D. Geddes
Kristen Wigh Goodman
James M. Grace, Jr.
Mary Millwood Gregory
Elizabeth M. Guffy
Sten L. Gustafson
Lynne Harkel-Rumford
Bill Hart, Jr.
Christine Hurt Harvey
Henry Havre
J. Timothy Headley
Laura C. Higley
Marjorie A. Hirsch
Pamela Lunn Hohensee
Ronald E. Holmes
David Charles Hricik
Richard Allen Husseini
Silvia Iglesias
Linda K. Jackson
Laura Friedl Jones
M. Lamont Jones
J. Alison Juban
Alan F. Kansas
Myriam R. Klein

(See Next Column)

BAKER & BOTTS L.L.P., *Houston—Continued*

ASSOCIATES (Continued)

William Karl Kroger
Daniel Harris Kroll
Rosalind M. Lawton
Victoria V. Lazar
Michael P. Lennon, Jr.
Susan Davenport Letney
Tracee Kennedy Lewis
Maryanne Lyons
Danita J. M. Maseles
J. Bruce McDonald
Jennifer S. McGinty
Scott Joseph Miller
Elise Bauman Neal
Peter M. Oxman
John M. Padilla
Theodore William Paris
David G. Patent
Robert H. Pemberton
Kay M. Peterson
Sandra J. Pomerantz
Jeffrey A. Potts
James LeGrand Read
Macey Reasoner
John K. Rentz
Carol M. Reumont
Jayme Partridge Roden
Kelly Brunetti Rose
Richard S. Roth
Carol L. St. Clair
Travis James Sales
Jeffrey Alan Schlegel
Michael J. Schofield
W. Lance Schuler
Tim T. Shen
Nancy E. Siegal
Richard S. Siluk
Consuella D. Simmons
Brian A. E. Smith
Clayton L. Smith
Jennifer M. Smith
Michael H. Smith
Mark S. Snell
Carolyn Brostad Southerland
Howard L. Speight
Suzanne H. Stenson
Rebecca S. Stierna
Lori D. Stiffler
M. Virginia Stockbridge
Michael T. Swaim
J. David Tate
Timothy S. Taylor
Dahl C. Thompson
Lori McFarlin Troutman
C. Patrick Turley
Teresa Slowen Valderrama
Kathryn S. Vaughn
Cynthia D. Vreeland
Jennifer L. Walker-Elrod
Mark L. Walters
Diane T. Weber
Michelle L. Whipkey
Robert M. White
Michael E. Wilson
Shira R. Yoshor
Beverly A. Young

For full biographical listings, see the Martindale-Hubbell Law Directory

---

BAKER & HOSTETLER (AV)

1000 Louisiana, Suite 2000, 77002-5008
Telephone: 713-751-1600
FAX: 713-751-1717
In Cleveland, Ohio: 3200 National City Center, 1900 East Ninth Street.
Telephone: 216-621-0200.
In Columbus, Ohio: Capitol Square, Suite 2100, 65 East State Street.
Telephone: 614-228-1541.
In Denver, Colorado: 303 East 17th Avenue, Suite 1100.
Telephone: 303-861-0600.
In Long Beach, California: 300 Oceangate, Suite 620.
Telephone: 310-432-2827.
In Los Angeles, California: 600 Wilshire Boulevard.
Telephone: 213-624-2400.
In Orlando, Florida: SunBank Center, Suite 2300, 200 South Orange Avenue.
Telephone: 407-649-4000.
In Washington, D.C.: Washington Square, Suite 1100, 1050 Connecticut Avenue, N. W.
Telephone: 202-861-1500.
In College Park, Maryland: 9658 Baltimore Boulevard, Suite 206.
Telephone: 301-441-2781.
In Alexandria, Virginia: 437 North Lee Street.
Telephone: 703-549-1294.
In San Francisco, California: One Sansome Street, Suite 2000.
Telephone: 415-951-4705.

MEMBERS OF FIRM IN HOUSTON, TEXAS

Sheldon A. Gebb (Not admitted in TX; Managing Partner-Los Angeles and Long Beach, California and Houston, Texas Offices)

PARTNERS

Roger P. Balog
Scott G. Camp
Mark C. Joye
Lisa H. Pennington
Kenneth R. Valka (Partner in Charge-Houston Office)
James C. Winton
Robert M. Wolin
Ivan Wood, Jr.

ASSOCIATES

Todd F. Barth
Max L. Bouthillette
Claudia D. Christin
Hurlie H. Collier
Tonya A. Jacobs
Lindsay L. Lambert
Melanie Rosenthal Margolis
Gail E. Papermaster
Bryan J. Schillinger
Ricki J. Shoss
Staci F. Spalding
Lilly E. Thrower
Sandy H. Wotiz

OF COUNSEL

Jon David Ivey
Salvador E. Rodriguez

For full biographical listings, see the Martindale-Hubbell Law Directory

---

BEIRNE, MAYNARD & PARSONS, L.L.P. (AV)

First Interstate Tower 24th Floor, 1300 Post Oak Boulevard, 77056-3000
Telephone: 713-623-0887
Fax: 713-960-1527

(See Next Column)

MEMBERS OF FIRM

Martin D. Beirne
William L. Maynard
Jeffrey R. Parsons
Sawnie A. McEntire
Suzanne B. Baker
Gerald J. Brown
Jay W. Brown
Kay L. Burkhalter
Robert B. Dillon
David S. Gamble
Craig B. Glidden
J. Michael Jordan
Roger L. McCleary
John W. Odam
David A. Pluchinsky
James E. Smith
David K. Williams

OF COUNSEL

Cindy Ann Lopez Garcia
Robert E. Jones
Clarence E. Kendall, Jr.
Wallace T. Ward, III

PARTICIPATING ASSOCIATES

David A. Clark
Kyle L. Jennings
Philip A. Lionberger
Michael J. Stanley
Linda P. Wills

ASSOCIATES

Denise A. Acebo
Tamara L. Annalora
Mary Maydelle Bambace
Remsen H. Beitel, III
Danya W. Blair
John E. Carlson
Shelley Clarke
Kevin M. Feeney
Ron E. Frank
Jennifer A. Giaimo
Richard B. Graves, III
Gregory L. Griffith
Timothy J. Hill
Maria C. Jorik
Jeffrey A. Kaplan
Jeffrey B. Lucas
Scott D. Marrs
David T. McDowell
Mark W. Moran
Petula P. Palmer
Tracy A. Phillips
Lenora D. Post
Keith A. Rowley
Donald W. Towe
Gregory R. Travis
Patricia H. Webb
Jared R. Woodfill, V

For full biographical listings, see the Martindale-Hubbell Law Directory

---

BUTLER & BINION, L.L.P. (AV)

A Partnership including Professional Corporations
1000 Louisiana, Suite 1600, 77002-5093
Telephone: 713-237-3111
Telecopier: 713-237-3202
Dallas, Texas Office: 750 N. St. Paul, Suite 1800.
Telephone: 214-220-3100.
Telecopiers: 214-969-7013; 214-954-4245.
San Antonio, Texas Office: 112 East Pecan Street, 27th Floor.
Telephone: 210-227-2200.
Telecopier: 210-223-6730.
Washington, D.C. Office: 1747 Pennsylvania Avenue, N.W.
Telephone: 202-466-6900.
Telecopier: 202-833-1274.

MEMBERS OF FIRM

Richard W. Avery
Jonathan T. Bickham
Robert Hayden Burns
Rueben C. Cásarez
Philip B. Carson
Bernard F. Clark, Jr.
Steven J. Clausen
O. Don Crites
Robert C. Curfiss
James A. DeMent, Jr.
Jeffrey D. Dunn (P.C.)
Theresa A. Einhorn (P.C.)
John English
James M. Harbison, Jr.
Martha Susan Hardie
John R. Hohlt
Joe C. Holzer (P.C.)
Ronald H. Jacobe (P.C.)
David Mark Koogler
Phillip W. Lacy
Jack Lapin (P.C.)
Joel L. Laser (P.C.)
William G. Lawhon (P.C.)
Everett A. Marley, Jr. (P.C.)
Everard A. Marseglia, Jr.
Marion E. McDaniel, Jr.
Gail J. McDonald (P.C.)
Louis B. Paine, Jr.
Joseph H. Peck, Jr. (P.C.)
Paul E. Pryzant (P.C.)
Robert B. Reynolds (P.C.)
Louis H. Salinas, Jr.
Herbert D. Simons (P.C.)
Patricia A. Totten (P.C.)
Frederick J. Tuthill (P.C.)
William E. Wilson
Andrew Wooley
George G. Young, III (P.C.)

OF COUNSEL

Raymond D. McGrew
Robert H. Parsley
Dempsey J. Prappas
Claude C. Roberts
Sue Z. Shaper

SPECIAL COUNSEL

James I. Smith, Jr.

ASSOCIATES

Azalea Aleman
Linda A. Allen
Joseph D. Batson
Francis R. Bradley, III
Stephen W. Crawford
Gary I. Currier
Juliette E. Daniels
Gislar R. Donnenberg
Stephen D. Elison
Marsha Z. Gerber
Paula K. Gingrich
Sean R. D. Gorman
John R. Hawkins
Theresa Rohr Kelley
Judithe H. Linse
Jack H. Mayfield, III
John W. Menke
Stanley T. Proctor
Julie L. Rhoades
Nancy Talavera
Thomas Alan Zabel

For full biographical listings, see the Martindale-Hubbell Law Directory

Houston—Continued

GILPIN, PAXSON & BERSCH (AV)

A Registered Limited Liability Partnership
1900 West Loop South, Suite 2000, 77027-3259
Telephone: 713-623-8800
Telecopier: 713-993-8451

MEMBERS OF FIRM

Gary M. Alletag
Timothy R. Bersch
Deborah J. Bullion
James L. Cornell, Jr.
George R. Diaz-Arrastia
Frank W. Gerold
John D. Gilpin
William T. Little
Darryl W. Malone
Michael W. McCoy
Michael J. Pappert
Stephen Paxson
Lionel M. Schooler
Mary E. Wilson
Kevin F. Risley

ASSOCIATES

Russell T. Abney
N. Terry Adams, Jr.
John W. Burchfield
Evan N. Kramer
Dale R. Mellencamp
P. Wayne Pickering
Susan M. Schwager

OF COUNSEL

Harless R. Benthul
Thomas F. Aubry

Representative Clients: Bank of America, N.A.; Charter Bancshares, Inc.; First Interstate Bank of Texas, N.A.; Greater Houston Builders Association; ICM Mortgage Corporation; Pulte Home Corporation; Texas Association of Builders; U.S. West, Inc.; Weekley Homes, Inc.

For full biographical listings, see the Martindale-Hubbell Law Directory

GREGG & MIESZKUC, P.C. (AV)

17044 El Camino Real (Clear Lake City), 77058-2686
Telephone: 713-488-8680
Facsimile: 713-488-8531

Dick H. Gregg, Jr.
Marilyn Mieszkuc
Polly P. Lewis
Charles A. Daughtry

Elizabeth E. Scott
Dick H. Gregg, III

For full biographical listings, see the Martindale-Hubbell Law Directory

HILL & HILL ATTORNEYS AT LAW A PROFESSIONAL CORPORATION (AV)

2600 First City National Bank Building, 1021 Main Street, 77002
Telephone: 713-228-1451
Telecopier: 713-651-1712

J. Marcus Hill

OF COUNSEL

Jerry G. Hill
Winston E. Cochran, Jr.

For full biographical listings, see the Martindale-Hubbell Law Directory

HUGHES & LUCE, L.L.P. (AV)

A Registered Limited Liability Partnership including Professional Corporations
Three Allen Center, 333 Clay Street, Suite 3800, 77002
Telephone: 713-754-5200
Fax: 713-754-5206
Dallas, Texas Office: 1717 Main Street, Suite 2800.
Telephone: 214-939-5500.
Fax: 214-939-6100.
Austin, Texas Office: 111 Congress Avenue, Suite 900.
Telephone: 512-482-6800.
Fax: 512-482-6859.
Fort Worth, Texas Office: 2421 Westport Parkway, Suite 500A.
Telephone: 817-439-3000.
Fax: 817-439-4222.

MEMBERS OF FIRM

Paul A. Berry
Vidal Gregory Martinez
Allan B. Diamond
Robert M. Hardy, Jr, (P.C.)
Mont P. Hoyt

ASSOCIATES

Linnie A. Freeman
Neil D. Kelly
Rush A. Selden
Stephen B. Schulte

For full biographical listings, see the Martindale-Hubbell Law Directory

HUTCHESON & GRUNDY, L.L.P. (AV)

1200 Smith Street, Suite 3300, 77002-4579
Telephone: 713-951-2800
1-800-364-0007
Telex: 79-0255
Telecopy: 713-951-2925
Dallas, Texas Office: 901 Main Street, Suite 6200 75202-3714.
Telephone: 214-761-2800 or 1-800-443-0845.
Telecopy: 214-761-2805.
Austin, Texas Office: 111 Congress Avenue, Suite 2700, 78701-4043.
Telephone: 512-478-2800 or 1-800-648-7445.
Telecopy: 512-472-3173.

Palmer Hutcheson (1887-1966)
Palmer Hutcheson, Jr. (1913-1990)
Thad T. Hutcheson (1915-1986)

OF COUNSEL

Thad Grundy
J. O. Terrell Couch

MEMBERS OF FIRM

Elbert Hooper, Jr.
James L. Truitt
John D. Roady
Charles R. Gregg
Greg N. Martin
Thomas N. Crowell
Larry O. Littleton (Dallas Office)
Roland M. Chamberlin, Jr.
D. Michael Dalton
Rex Harding White, Jr.
J. Currie Bechtol
Allen B. Craig, III
Thomas R. Kelsey
Thomas T. Hutcheson
Robert G. Richardson
Jeffrey C. Londa
Benjamin G. Clark
Lynda Myska Irvine
Douglas K. Eyberg
Philip S. Haag
Bradley I. Raffle
James P. Grove IV
T. Michael Wall
W. David Tidholm
Michael L. Grove
Paul Strohl
John R. Eldridge
Laurie B. Easter
Linda Ottinger Headley
Lisa J. Mellencamp
J. Daniel McElroy
Daniel T. Torrez
G. Mark Jodon
James L. Baldwin, Jr.
Carla S. Doyne
E. Scott Lineberry

COUNSEL

Constance E. Courtney
Terence J. Hart
Arcelia Izquierdo Jordan

ASSOCIATES

Pamela C. Barksdale
Kendall Barrett
Mary Jo Cantu
Anthony S. Corbett
J. Todd Culwell
Stephen H. Dimlich, Jr.
Rudy A. England
Judy A. Echols
Douglas S. Griffith
Thomas D. Kennedy
Steven Kesten
K. Shawn Kirksey
Beverly E. Landis
Lori B. McCool
Kate McCormick
Scott Daniel McDonald
Martha F. McDugald
Steven C. Meisgeier
Michael D. Mitchell
Diane Christy Nichols
B. Scott Smith
Martha Lee Smith
James Alfred Southerland
Hunter H. White
Robin Rankin Willis

For full biographical listings, see the Martindale-Hubbell Law Directory

JACKSON & WALKER, L.L.P. (AV)

1100 Louisiana, Suite 4200, P.O. Box 4771, 77210-4771
Telephone: 713-752-4200
Fax: 713-752-4221
Dallas, Texas Office: 901 Main Street, Suite 6000.
Telephone: 214-953-6000.
Fax: 214-953-5822.
Fort Worth, Texas Office: 777 Main Street, Suite 1800.
Telephone: 817-334-7200.
Fax: 817-334-7290.
San Antonio, Texas Office: 112 E. Pecan Street, Suite 2100.
Telephone: 210-978-7700.
Fax: 210-978-7790.

MEMBERS OF FIRM

Charles L. Babcock
N. David Bleisch
Teresa G. Bushman
Michael J. Byrd
Janet Douvas Chafin
Ross Citti
Gregory P. Crinion
Wayne G. Dotson
David G. Dunlap
Anthony W. Hall, Jr.
Tracey Smith Lindeen
Charles D. Maguire, Jr.
Kurt D. Nondorf
William C. Norvell, Jr.
Michael P. Pearson
Sharon S. Rodgers
Bruce J. Ruzinsky
John B. Scofield
Donna Ng Shen
Robert O. Thomas
Robert H. Walls
Wayne A. Yaffee
J. Lanier Yeates

OF COUNSEL

William M. Schultz

(See Next Column)

JACKSON & WALKER L.L.P., *Houston—Continued*

ASSOCIATES

Leslie Garcia Ashby
Bill C. Boyd
Paul E. Comeaux
Michelle M. DeVoe
Lori L. Elam
Cory S. Fein
James W. Goolsby, Jr.
Cynthia S. Grady
Nancy Wells Hamilton
Michael A. Heilman
Mary Bowley Jenke
Lynn S. Johnson
Bruce C. Morris
Richard T. Nelson
Jo Ann Tower Rothfelder
Susan A. Stanton
Susan L. Weiss

For full biographical listings, see the Martindale-Hubbell Law Directory

MICHAEL A. MANESS (AV)

1900 North Loop West, Suite 500, 77018
Telephone: 713-680-9922
Fax: 713-680-0804

For full biographical listings, see the Martindale-Hubbell Law Directory

MAYER, BROWN & PLATT (AV)

700 Louisiana Street, Suite 3600, 77002-2730
Telephone: (713) 221-1651
Pitney Bowes: (713) 224-6410
Telex: 775809
Cable: LEMAYHOU
Chicago, Illinois Office: 190 South LaSalle Street, 60603-3441.
Telephone: (312) 782-0600. Pitney Bowes: (312) 701-7711.
Telex: 190404.
Cable: LEMAY.
Washington, D.C. Office: 2000 Pennsylvania Avenue, N.W., 20006-1882.
Telephone: (202) 463-2000. Pitney Bowes: (202) 861-0484, Pitney Bowes: (202) 861-0473.
Telex: 892603.
Cable: LEMAYDC.
New York, New York Office: 787 Seventh Avenue, Suite 2400, 10019-6018.
Telephone: (212) 554-3000. Pitney Bowes: (212) 262-1910.
Telex: 701842.
Cable: LEMAYEN.
Los Angeles, California Office: 350 South Grand Avenue, 25th Floor, 90071-1503.
Telephone: (213) 229-9500. Pitney Bowes: (213) 625-0248.
Telex: 188089.
Cable: LEMAYLA.
London, England Office: 162 Queen Victoria Street, EC4V 4DB.
Telephone: 011-44-71-248-1465.
Fax: 011-44-71-329-4465.
Telex: 8811095.
Cable: LEMAYLDN.
Tokyo, Japan Office: (Kawachi Gaikokuho Jimu Bengoshi Jimusho), Urbannet Otemachi Building 13F 2-2, Otemachi 2-chome, Chiyoda-ku, Tokyo 100.
Telephone: 011-81-3-5255-9700.
Facsimile: 011-81-3-5255-9797.
Berlin, Germany Office: Spreeufer 5, 10178.
Telephone: 011-49-30-240-7930.
Facsimile: 011-49-30-240-79344.
Brussels, Belgium Office: Square de Meeûs 19/20, Bte. 4, 1040.
Telephone: 011-32-2-512-9878.
Fax: 011-32-2-511-3305.
Telex: 20768 MBPBRU B.
Mexico City, Mexico, D.F., Mexico Correspondent: Jáuregui, Navarrete, Nader y Rojas, S.C., Abogados, Paseo de la Reforma 199, Pisos 15, 16 y 17, 06500, Mexico.
Telephone: 011-525-591-16-55.
Fax: 011-525-535-80-62; 011-525-703-22-47.
Cable: JANANE.

PARTNERS

Paul B. Clemenceau
Jeff C. Dodd
A. Duncan Gray, Jr.
Catherine W. Hoeg
M. Marvin Katz
William H. Knull, III
John H. Nash
Michael E. Niebruegge
Eddy J. Rogers, Jr.
George Ruhlen
James E. Tancula
James J. Tyler
Terry Otero Vilardo

ASSOCIATES

Patricia K. Brito
Kimberlee S. Cagle
Barbara A. Clark
Diana L. Davis
Timothy B. Ellwood
Carlos R. Escobar
Robert H. George
Terri T. Griffiths
Sally A. T. Hawkins
Judith Hession
Walter Keneally
Terry Kernell
Mary B. Lemuth
Travis C. McCullough
Michael C. Overman
Susan K. Pavlica
Vytas A. Petrulis
Ronald M. Shoss
David F. Sladic

For full biographical listings, see the Martindale-Hubbell Law Directory

MAYOR, DAY, CALDWELL & KEETON, L.L.P. (AV)

1900 NationsBank Center, 700 Louisiana, 77002
Telephone: 713-225-7000
Austin, Texas Office: 100 Congress, Suite 1500.
Telephone: 512-320-9200.
Fax: 512-320-9292.

Richard B. Mayor
Jonathan S. Day
Richard H. Caldwell
Richard P. Keeton
J. Kent Friedman
Michael O. Connelly
Robert M. Collie, Jr.
Dillon J. Ferguson
J. Gerald Martin
Geoffrey K. Walker
Gerald L. Bracht
Diana M. Hudson
Gary J. Winston
Roy E. Bertolatus
David W. Martin
Gail Merel
Jeffrey B. McClure
Roliff H. Purrington, Jr. (Resident, Austin Office)
Daniel E. McCormick
Cassie B. Stinson
L. Lee McMurtry III
Russell C. Shaw
Rex D. VanMiddlesworth (Resident, Austin Office)
Gary C. Miller
Kathleen M. Kopp
Thomas M. Farrell
Debra L. Baker
J. Mark Breeding
Robert S. Godlewski
Matthew L. Hoeg
Thomas A. Hagemann
Thomas A. Bres
Jesse J. Gelsomini
Rick A. Witte

Mark B. Arnold
Lorette Bauarschi
Janet R. Carl
Chris Cessac
David A. Chaumette
Thomas E. Clifford
John B. Clutterbuck
Mindy G. Davidson
Patricia A. DeLaney
Rebecca A. Doke
Robert B. Dubose
Arthur S. Feldman
Joseph A. Fischer, III
Irene E. (Nene) Foxhall
Alberto T. Garcia, III
David P. Griffith
E. Wayne Herndon
A. Colleen Hutchison
Frederick D. Junkin
Jeffrey B. King
Solace H. Kirkland
Ann E. Kitzmiller
Jeffrey T. Knebel (Resident, Austin Office)
Stephanie Anne Kroger (Resident, Austin Office)
Jeffrey D. Meyer
John Muir
Lori M. Muratta (Not admitted in TX)
Raina S. Newsome
Basil P. Nichols
Lizzette M. Palmer
Scott R. Peterson
Cheryl S. Phillips
Margaret Coullard Phillips
Karen K. Roberts
Cheryl K. Rosenberg
Catherine E. Stallworth
Alison McMorran Sulentic
W. Earl Touchstone
T. Griffin Vincent
Laura J. Ware
Phillip H. Watts
Helen E. Weidner
John T. S. Williams
Earnest W. Wotring
Michael J. Wynne

OF COUNSEL

Doreen Z. Bartlett
Gail A. Bartlett
Ronald J. Bigelow
Sylvia Matthews Egner
Kathryn V. Garner
Charles Manning Williams

For full biographical listings, see the Martindale-Hubbell Law Directory

MCFALL, SHERWOOD & SHEEHY, A PROFESSIONAL CORPORATION (AV)

2500 Two Houston Center, 909 Fannin Street, 77010-1003
Telephone: 713-951-1000
Telecopier: 713-951-1199

Donald B. McFall
Thomas P. Sartwelle
William A. Sherwood
Richard A. Sheehy
Kent C. Sullivan
David B. Weinstein
D. Wayne Clawater
John S. Serpe
Kenneth R. Breitbeil
Shelley Rogers
Joseph A. Garnett
R. Edward Perkins
Raymond A. Neuer

Caroline E. Baker
Lauren Beck
Marjorie C. Bell
David Brill
John M. Davidson
Robert R. Debes, Jr.
Eugene R. Egdorf
John H. Ferguson IV
Jeffrey R. Gilbert
M. Randall Jones
Christopher J. Lowman
James J. Maher
David J. McTaggart
David W. Medack
Catherine A. Mezick
Matthew G. Pletcher
Martin S. Schexnayder
David R. Tippetts
James W. K. Wilde

OF COUNSEL

Gay C. Brinson, Jr.
Edward S. Hubbard
Paul B. Radelat

Representative Clients: Dresser Industries, Inc.; The Procter & Gamble Co.; Channel Two Television; St. Paul Fire & Marine Insurance Co.; Texas Lawyers' Insurance Exchange; U.S. Aviation Underwriters; Dow Corning Corp.; Columbia Hospital Corp.; Farm & Home Savings Association.

For full biographical listings, see the Martindale-Hubbell Law Directory

Houston—Continued

McGinnis, Lochridge & Kilgore, L.L.P. (AV)

3200 One Houston Center, 1221 McKinney Street, 77010-2009
Telephone: 713-615-8500
Austin, Texas Office: 1300 Capitol Center, 919 Congress Avenue.
Telephone: 512-495-6000.

OF COUNSEL

W. James McAnelly, Jr.

MEMBERS OF FIRM

Bolivar C. Andrews
Shannon H. Ratliff
Barry L. Wertz
Jeffrey A. Davis
S. Jack Balagia, Jr.
Thomas J. Forestier

ASSOCIATES

Donald D. Jackson

For full biographical listings, see the Martindale-Hubbell Law Directory

Mills, Shirley, Eckel & Bassett, L.L.P. (AV)

6230 Texas Commerce Tower, 77002
Telephone: 713-225-0547
Facsimile: 713-225-0844
Galveston, Texas Office: 400 Washington Building, 2228 Mechanic Street, P.O. Box 1943.
Telephone: 409-763-2341; Houston Line: 713-488-8716.
Facsimile: 409-763-2879.

MEMBERS OF FIRM

Grant G. Gealy (Resident)
William E. Griffey
Finis E. Cowan III (Resident)

ASSOCIATES

John W. Teague (Resident)
Kelly Forester (Resident)

General Attorneys for: American Indemnity Group.
Counsel for: Royal-Globe Insurance Cos.; Continental-National-American Group; United States Fidelity & Guaranty Co.; Employers Insurance of Texas; CNA Insurance Group; INA Insurance Group.

For full biographical listings, see the Martindale-Hubbell Law Directory

James E. Ross & Associates (AV)

3209 Montrose Boulevard, 77006
Telephone: 713-523-8087
Telecopier: 713-523-8224

Edwin K. Nelson, IV

For full biographical listings, see the Martindale-Hubbell Law Directory

Royston, Rayzor, Vickery & Williams, L.L.P. (AV)

2200 Texas Commerce Tower, 77002-2913
Telephone: 713-224-8380
Cable Address: "Houport"
Telex: 6869017
Telecopier: 713-225-9945
Galveston, Texas Office: 205 Cotton Exchange Building, 2102 Mechanic Street.
Telephone: 409-763-1623.
Cable Address: "Royston"
Telex: 765-449.
Telecopier: 409-763-3853.
Brownsville, Texas Office: 55 Cove Circle, P.O. Box 3509.
Telephone: 210-542-4377.
Cable Address: "Padre"
Telex: 767-817.
Telecopier: 210-542-4370.
Corpus Christi, Texas Office: 1700 Wilson Plaza West, 606 North Carancahua.
Telephone: 512-884-8808.
Cable Address: "CC PORT"
Telex: 6866625.
Telecopier: 512-884-7261.

OF COUNSEL

Decatur J. Holcombe

PARTNERS

Mart H. Royston (1892-1948)
J. Newton Rayzor (1895-1970)
Bryan F. Williams, Jr. (1928-1980)
M. L. Cook (1908-1987)
Edward D. Vickery
Gus A. Schill, Jr.
Ben L. Reynolds
Kenneth D. Kuykendall
Ted C. Litton
William M. Jensen
W. Robins Brice
James P. Cooney
Bradley A. Jackson
Robert H. Etnyre, Jr.
James G. Blain, II
John M. Elsley
David R. Walker
Tobi A. Tabor
John F. Unger
Mark Cohen
William R. Towns
Marilyn Tanner Hebinck
Kim J. Fletcher

(See Next Column)

ASSOCIATES

Lisa J. Wesely
Marcus R. Tucker
C. Scott Kinzel
Mary A. Stevens
Christopher Lowrance
Kimberly D. McMath
Chester J. Makowski
Richard L. Gorman
Kevin D. King
Jeffrey J. Putnam
Frazor (Ty) Edmondson
Trevor R. Jefferies

Representative Clients: G & H Towing Co.; Lykes Bros. Steamship Co., Inc.; American International Underwriters Corp.; West of England Steam Ship Owners' Protection and Indemnity Assn., Ltd.; The United Kingdom Mutual Steam Ship Assurance Assn. Ltd.; Underwriter at Lloyds; Institute of London Underwriters.

For full biographical listings, see the Martindale-Hubbell Law Directory

Schlanger, Mills, Mayer & Grossberg, L.L.P. (AV)

A Limited Liability Partnership including Professional Corporations
Suite 1700, 5847 San Felipe, 77057
Telephone: 713-785-1700
Facsimile: 713-785-2091
Telex: 7409527 aba uc

Daniel Schlanger (1902-1973)
Joel W. Cook (1910-1986)
Lee D. Schlanger (P.C.)
Michael A. Mills (P.C.)
Clarence Mayer (P.C.)
Marc E. Grossberg (P.C.)
Stephen C. Paine (P.C.)
Irwin M. Barg (P.C.)
Steven D. Lerner (P.C.)
Louis E. Silver (P.C.)
Ellen S. Lain (P.C.)
Steven D. Grossman (P.C.)
Marcy Higbie (P.C.)
Jon D. Totz

Julia A. Cook
Catherine Graubart Wile
Kyle Longhofer
Marc L. Ellison
Lydia Kale Mason
Brett Lanier
John Schneller, IV
Michele E. Marquit
Jack Loftis

OF COUNSEL

Melvin S. Cohn (P.C.)
David R. Toomim

Representative Clients: Delta-Lloyds Insurance Co.; Proler International Corp.

For full biographical listings, see the Martindale-Hubbell Law Directory

Strasburger & Price, L.L.P. (AV)

A Partnership including Professional Corporations
Suite 2800, One Houston Center, 1221 McKinney, 77010
Telephone: 713-951-5600
Fax: 713-951-5660
Dallas, Texas Office: 901 Main Street, Suite 4300.
Telephone: 214-651-4300.
Fax: 214-651-4330.
Austin, Texas Office: 2600 One American Center, 600 Congress Avenue.
Telephone: 512-499-3600.
Fax: 512-499-3660.
Mexico City Office: Edificio Hewlett-Packard, Monte Pelvoux No. 111, Piso 5, Lomas de Chapultepec, 11000 Mexico D.F.
Telephone: 525-202-8796.
Fax: 525-520-7671.
Mexico City Correspondent: Gonzalez, Calvillo y Forastieri, S.C. Edificio Hewlett-Packard, Monte Pelvoux No. 111, Piso 5, Lomas de Chapultepec, 11000 Mexico D.F.
Telephone: 525-202-7622.
Fax: 525-520-7671.

RESIDENT MEMBERS

J. Wiley George
James J. Juneau
William A. Worthington

RESIDENT ASSOCIATES

Jonathan B. Clayton
J. Greg Dow
Pamela K. Estes
Tanyel Harrison-Bennett
John K. Spiller

Representative Clients: Chrysler Corp.; General Motors Corp.; GTE; K mart Corp.; Syndicates of Lloyd's of London; NationsBank of Texas, N.A.; Rolex Watch U.S.A.; The Travelers Insurance Co.

For full biographical listings, see the Martindale-Hubbell Law Directory

Thompson & Knight, A Professional Corporation (AV)

(Attorneys and Counselors)
1700 Texas Commerce Tower, 600 Travis, 77002
Telephone: 713-217-2800
Telecopy: 713-217-2828; 713-217-2882
Dallas, Texas Office: 1700 Pacific Avenue, Suite 3300, 75201.
Telephone: 214-969-1700.
Telecopy: 214-969-1751.
Cable Address: "Tomtex."
Telex: 732298.
Austin, Texas Office: 1200 San Jacinto Center, 98 San Jacinto Boulevard, 78701.
Telephone: 512-469-6100.
Telecopy: 512-469-6180.

(See Next Column)

THOMPSON & KNIGHT A PROFESSIONAL CORPORATION, *Houston—Continued*

Fort Worth, Texas Office: 801 Cherry Street, Suite 1600, 76102.
Telephone: 817-347-1700.
Telecopy: 817-347-1799.
Monterrey, Mexico Office: Edificio Losoles PD-4, Av. Lázaro Cárdenas No. 2400 PTE., San Pedro Garza Garcia, Nuevo Léon C.P. 66220.
Telephone: (52-8) 363-0096.
Telecopy: (52-8) 363-3067.

SHAREHOLDERS

Mary Margaret Bearden
Daniel J. Hayes
Debbi M. Johnstone
Gregory S. Meece
David R. Noteware
Michael K. Pierce

ASSOCIATES

Anne Marie Finch
Patricia A. Nolan
David P. Whittlesey

For full biographical listings, see the Martindale-Hubbell Law Directory

VINSON & ELKINS L.L.P. (AV)

2300 First City Tower, 1001 Fannin, 77002-6760
Telephone: 713-758-2222
Fax: 713-758-2346
International Telex: 6868314
Cable Address: Vinelkins
Austin, Texas Office: One American Center, 600 Congress Avenue.
Telephone: 512-495-8400.
Fax: 512-495-8612.
Dallas, Texas Office: 3700 Trammell Crow Center, 2001 Ross Avenue.
Telephone: 214-220-7700.
Fax: 214-220-7716.
Washington, D.C. Office: The Willard Office Building, 1455 Pennsylvania Avenue, N.W.
Telephone: 202-639-6500.
Fax: 202-639-6604.
Cable Address: Vinelkins.
London, England Office: 47 Charles Street, Berkeley Square, London, W1X 7PB, England.
Telephone: 011 (44-171) 491-7236.
Fax: 011 (44-71) 499-5320.
Cable Address: Vinelkins London W.1.
Moscow, Russian Federation Office: 16 Alexey Tolstoy Street, Second Floor, Moscow, 103001 Russian Federation.
Telephone: 011 (70-95) 956-1995.
Telecopy: 011 (70-95) 956-1996.
Mexico City, Mexico Office: Aristóteles 77, 5°Piso, Colonia Chapultepec Polanco, 11560 Mexico, D.F.
Telephone: (52-5) 280-7828.
Fax: (52-5) 280-9223.
Singapore Office: 50 Raffles Place, #19-05 Shell Tower, 0104. U.S. Voice Mailbox: 713-758-3500.
Telephone: (65) 536-8300.
Fax: (65) 536-8311.

MEMBERS OF FIRM

Wm. A. Vinson (1874-1951)
James A. Elkins (1879-1972)
Wharton E. Weems (1890-1961)
John C. Ale
Joe B. Allen
Charles L. Almond (Resident, Washington, D.C. Office)
Christopher B. Amandes
Gary P. Amaon
Milton H. Anders
Kenneth M. Anderson
David T. Andril (Resident, Washington, D.C. Office)
Robert A. Armitage (Resident, Washington, D.C. Office)
Ronald T. Astin (Resident, Washington, D.C. Office)
Alden L. Atkins (Resident, Washington, D.C. Office)
Scott J. Atlas
J. Evans Attwell
Page I. Austin
Marcia E. Backus
Alan P. Baden
Robert S. Baird
Larry G. Barbour
Robert F. Barrett
Dennis M. Barry (Resident, Washington, D.C. Office)
Walker W. Beavers
Roger L. Beebe
Mark Stephen Berg
Charles L. Berry
James R. Bertrand
Bruce R. Bilger
Douglas S. Bland
David T. Searls (1905-1972)
Harry M. Reasoner (Managing Partner)
David P. Blanke (Resident, Dallas, Texas Office)
Gary E. Block (Resident, Washington, D.C. Office)
Brian R. Bloom
David M. Bond
James A. Boone
Steven R. Borgman
Michael R. Boulden (Resident, Dallas, Texas Office)
John C. Brannan, Jr. (Resident, Dallas, Texas Office)
Kim Edward Brightwell (Resident, Austin, Texas Office)
Travis C. Broesche
David H. Brown
Bryant W. Burke (Resident, Dallas, Texas Office)
C. Michael Buxton (Resident, Washington, D.C. Office)
Christopher W. Byrd
Molly Cagle (Resident, Austin, Texas Office)
Bert L. Campbell
John L. Carter
John E. Chapoton (Resident, Washington, D.C. Office)
Harley R. Clark, Jr. (Resident, Austin, Texas Office)
Pat E. Clark
Fielding B. Cochran, III

(See Next Column)

MEMBERS OF FIRM (Continued)

David B. Cohen (Resident, Washington, D.C. Office)
Francis J. Coleman, Jr.
Susan G. Conway (Resident, Austin, Texas Office)
Morgan Lee Copeland, Jr.
Thomas Crichton, IV (Resident, Washington, D.C. Office)
James L. Cuclis (Resident, Moscow, Russian Federation Office)
Thad T. Dameris
Platt W. Davis, III
Stephen D. Davis (Resident, Singapore Office)
John C. Dawson, Jr.
Paul C. Deemer (Resident, London, England Office)
Elena-Faye DiIorio
Joseph C. Dilg
Theodore G. Dimitry
Carol E. Dinkins
William H. Drushel, Jr.
Sarah A. Duckers
Dennis C. Dunn
George Harvey Dunn, III
Phillip B. Dye, Jr.
Billy Coe Dyer
Gary W. Eiland
Jeffrey E. Eldredge (Resident, Dallas, Texas Office)
G. Edward Ellison
Jon David Epstein
A. H. Evans
Ky P. Ewing, Jr. (Resident, Washington, D.C. Office)
Harrell Feldt
Kenneth B. Fenelon
Michael P. Finch
Jeffery Burton Floyd
Timothy F. Foarde (Resident, Mexico City, Mexico Office)
Lawrence J. Fossi
Kevin A. Gaynor (Resident, Washington, D.C. Office)
George M. Gerachis (U.S. Liaison for Mexico City, Mexico Office)
Steven H. Gerdes
Douglas B. Glass
Alberto R. Gonzales
Celso M. Gonzalez-Falla
R. Todd Greenwalt
Douglas E. Hamel
C. Michael Harrington
Orrin L. Harrison, III (Resident, Dallas, Texas Office)
David T. Harvin
David T. Hedges, Jr.
Max Hendrick, III
Michael J. Henke (Resident, Washington, D.C. Office)
Ted A. Hodges
Patricia Hunt Holmes
John B. Holstead
Robert M. Hopson
Donald L. Howell
Monty Humble (Resident, Dallas, Texas Office)
Lynne B. Humphries
Barry Hunsaker, Jr.
Daniel A. Hyde
Neil W. Imus (Resident, Washington, D.C. Office)
Karen Jewell
Carol H. Jewett
Kenneth E. Johns, Jr. (Resident, Dallas, Texas Office)
Judith M. Johnson
Stuart Brooks Johnston, Jr. (Resident, Dallas, Texas Office)
William E. Joor III
W. Carl Jordan
Theodore W. Kassinger (Resident, Washington, D.C. Office)
T. Mark Kelly
Wm. Franklin Kelly, Jr.
John E. Kennedy
David R. Keyes
Yolanda Chávez Knull
Gary M. Kotara (Resident,
William L. LaFuze
Kathleen C. Lake
John C. LaMaster (Resident, London, England Office)
Thomas S. Leatherbury (Resident, Dallas, Texas Office)
William Gentry Lee
John W. Leggett
Cathy A. Lewis (Resident, Washington, D.C. Office)
Kevin P. Lewis (Resident, Singapore Office)
Guy S. Lipe
John E. Lynch
L. Price Manford
Thomas P. Marinis, Jr.
Dale Gene Markland (Resident, Dallas, Texas Office)
J. Clark Martin
Sharon M. Mattox
Henry S. May, Jr.
Louis E. McCarter
James W. McCartney
Derek R. McClain (Resident, Dallas, Texas Office)
Sidney S. McClendon, III
Andrew McCollam III
Frank E. McCreary, III
Jarrel D. McDaniel
Richard Kelly McGee
Terrence G. McGreevy
Hugh M. McIntosh (Resident, Washington, D.C. Office)
Thomas V. McMahan
D. Ferguson McNiel, III
Clara L. Meek
Michael W. Mengis
J. Mark Metts
James S. Meyer (Resident, Dallas, Texas Office)
Richard D. Milvenan (Resident, Austin, Texas Office)
Peter E. Mims
H. Dixon Montague
Darrell C. Morrow
William S. Moss, Jr.
John L. Murchison, Jr.
Arthur E. Murphy, III
Craig W. Murray
Larry W. Nettles
Roger P. Nevola (Resident, Austin, Texas Office)
Charles T. Newton, Jr.
Penelope E. Nicholson
D. Bobbitt Noel, Jr.
Knox D. Nunnally
Larry A. Oday (Resident, Washington, D.C. Office)
Edward C. Osterberg, Jr.
Glenn L. Pinkerton
Benjamin H. Powell, III
Barbara A. Radnofsky
Robert R. Randolph
Rush H. Record
Alan J. Robin
W. Ronald Robins
Glen A. Rosenbaum
James B. Rylander, Jr.
Robert M. Schick
Adam P. Schiffer
Michael J. Schimberg (Resident, Dallas, Texas Office)
Charles W. Schwartz
C. Boone Schwartzel
Robert A. Seale, Jr.
Jerry R. Selinger (Resident, Dallas, Texas Office)
Russell B. Serafin
Ben H. Sheppard, Jr.
Gary G. Short (Resident, Dallas, Texas Office)
August E. Shouse
Eugene J. Silva
William D. Sims, Jr. (Resident, Dallas, Texas Office)
Jeffery A. Smisek
Alison L. Smith
Frank F. Smith, Jr.
L. Boyd Smith, Jr.
John H. Smither
Craig Smyser

(See Next Column)

VINSON & ELKINS L.L.P.—*Continued*

Washington, D.C. Office)

MEMBERS OF FIRM (Continued)

J. Brian Sokolik (Resident, Moscow, Russian Federation Office)
Mark R. Spivak (Resident, Washington, D.C. Office)
Mark R. Spradling
Paul E. Stallings
Karl S. Stern
Edward T. Stockbridge
Brenda T. Strama
Mary Lou Strange
Walter B. Stuart IV
J. Michael Sutherland (Resident, Dallas, Texas Office)
Albert S. Tabor, Jr.
Stephen C. Tarry
John D. Taurman (Resident, Washington, D. C. Office)
Charles D. Tetrault (Resident, Washington, D.C. Office)
Kaaran E. Thomas
James D. Thompson III
Raybourne Thompson, Jr.
James "Rell" Tipton, Jr.
W. Dalton Tomlin
Carolyn Truesdell
Jerry E. Turner (Resident, Austin, Texas Office)
Allan Van Fleet
Christine L. Vaughn (Resident, Washington, D.C. Office)
Larry R. Veselka
Eric Viehman
Robert C. Walters (Resident, Dallas, Texas Office)
D. Gibson Walton
Joe Bill Watkins (Resident, Austin, Texas Office)
John S. Watson
William H. Weiland (Resident, Mexico City, Mexico Office)
Sanford A. Weiner
Philip D. Weller (Resident, Dallas, Texas Office)
H. Ronald Welsh
Robert H. Whilden, Jr.
Hugh C. Wilfong II
Margaret A. Wilson
Thomas H. Wilson
Donald F. Wood
Scott N. Wulfe
Buck J. Wynne, III (Resident, Dallas, Texas Office)
Terry A. Yates
Marie R. Yeates
Clifford W. Youngblood
J. Craig Youngblood

HOUSTON OF COUNSEL

Frank L. Heard, Jr.
Hollis A. Hubenak
Stanley M. Johanson
Philip M. Kinkaid
John H. Kyles
James D. Penny
Alan R. Thiele
Jack C. Wood

AUSTIN OF COUNSEL

Amanda G. Birrell
Mary Barrow Nichols
Patrick Ford Thompson

DALLAS OF COUNSEL

Rodney M. Anderson
V. Craig Cantrell (Resident, Dallas, Texas Office)
Sheryl L. Hopkins
Michael L. Malone
Ellen Smith Pryor
Norman D. Radford, Jr.

WASHINGTON, D.C. OF COUNSEL

Roderick Glen Ayers
Thomas R. Bartman
Samuel B. Sterrett
Thomas A. Stout, Jr.

ASSOCIATES

Dorene Aber
Ann Ainsworth
Anissa M. Albro
Fields Alexander
Craig B. Anderson (Resident, Dallas, Texas Office)
Paul I. Aronowitz
Ann Ashton
Lori Auray
Joël Elaine Baird
Pavel L. Bakulev (Resident, Moscow, Russian Federation Office)
Steven T. Baron (Resident, Dallas, Texas Office)
Steven F. Barrett (Resident, Dallas, Texas Office)
Sherie Potts Beckman
Rasmani Bhattacharya
J. David Bickham, Jr. (Resident, Austin, Texas Office)
Kirkland J. Bily
Henry Binder
Ernest J. Blansfield, Jr.
Bruce A. Blefeld
Judith M. Blissard
Mark A. Bodron
Barron P. Bogatto
Kathleen M. Bone
Timothy K. Borchers
Alex J. Bourelly (Resident, Washington, D.C. Office)
Valerie S. Boutwell
Carrie L. Brandon
James Mark Brazzil
David D. Brittain
W. Scott Brown
R. Michael Bryant, Jr.
Barry D. Burgdorf (Resident, Austin, Texas Office)
Dusty Burke
Jack F. Burleigh
Michael Lance Burnett
Eldrige A. Burns, Jr. (Resident, Dallas, Texas Office)
Sharon L. Burrell
Daniel S. Cahill
Charles F. Caldwell
Herman Mallory Caldwell
Ramon M. Cantu
Dale Carpenter
Edward A. Carr
Daniel R. Castro (Resident, Austin, Texas Office)
Trina Hill Chandler
William H. Church, Jr. (Resident, Dallas, Texas Office)
David T. Cindric
Donna Schmerin Clark
Leslie Jean Clark
J. Anne Bernard Clayton
Cristen Cline
Scott L. Cole
J. Barclay Collins, III (Resident, Washington, D.C. Office)
Alexey L. Condratchick (Resident, Moscow, Russian Federation Office)
Mark A. Cover (Resident, Dallas, Texas Office)
Robert H. Cox (Resident, Washington, D.C. Office)
Stephanie Crain
Christopher L. Crosswhite (Resident, Washington, D.C. Office)
Laura A. Crowe
Samuel Poage Dalton (Resident, Dallas, Texas Office)

(See Next Column)

ASSOCIATES (Continued)

Larry E. Davidson, Jr.
Oscar de la Rosa
John S. Decker (Resident, Washington, D.C. Office)
Sabrina L. DiMichele
Andrew DiNovo
Timothy J. Dorsey
Debra J. Duncan (Resident, Washington, D.C. Office)
Meredith Johnson Duncan
Karey Dubiel Dye
Mary E. Edmondson (Not admitted in TX; Resident, Washington, D.C. Office)
Susan M. Edwards
Matthew D. Eisele
Barry E. Engel
Joel N. Ephross
Jeffrey W. Ferguson (Resident, Washington, D.C. Office)
David T. Field
N. Scott Fletcher
Tegan M. Flynn (Resident, Washington, D. C. Office)
Joshua S. Force
Scott Mitchell Frederick (Resident, Washington, D.C. Office)
Robin S. Fredrickson
Valerie K. Friedrich
Keith R. Fullenweider
Kathleen A. Gallagher
Carlos Garcia
Roland Garcia, Jr.
Patricia Ann Gardner
Sandra R. Garza
Catherine Legro Gentry
Laura Van Os Gilchrist
Don C. Griffin, Jr.
Paul Steven Hacker
Sarah Elizabeth Hagy
Wallis M. Hampton
Kevin M. Hart
Robert K. Hatcher
Sondra Burling Hatcher
Lynn G. Haufrect
Sherrard L. Hayes, Jr.
Bruce C. Herzog
Cynthia L. Hill
Mary H. Hirth (Resident, Washington, D.C. Office)
Jon Scott Hollyfield
Scott A. Hooper
George C. Hopkins (Resident, Washington, D.C. Office)
Robert W. Horton
Tracy L. Howard
Wade T. Howard
Anne M. Huff
Robbi B. Hull (Resident, Austin, Texas Office)
Robert L. Ivey
Sheila R. Jones
Katherine D. Jordan
Tara Isa Koslov (Resident, Washington, D.C. Office)
Bruce E. Kosub (Resident, Washington, D.C. Office)
James A. Krause
Erica L. Krennerich
Jason Kuller
Z. Melissa Lawrence (Resident, Dallas, Texas Office)
L. DeWayne Layfield
Bryan W. Lee
W. David Lee (Resident, Dallas, Texas Office)
Dean H. Lefler
Nancy C. LeGros
Suzanne M. Lehman
William R. Leighton
Lisa Lynne Lepow
Kimberly Z. Lesniak
Stephen L. Levine (Resident, Dallas, Texas Office)
Deborah E. Lewis
Margaret Christina Ling
Alan W. Lintel (Resident, Dallas, Texas Office)
Barbara Popper Lipshultz
Dana C. Livingston
Tina Kyle Livingston
James Lloyd Loftis
Andrew James Logan
Daniel Lopez
Manuel Lopez
Barbara Lovingfoss (Resident, Austin, Texas Office)
Robert R. Luke
Holley Thomas Lutz (Resident, Washington, D.C. Office)
Jeffrey Scott Lynn
Jeffrey Scott Mūnoz
Sharon Maberry (Resident, Dallas, Texas Office)
A. Sam MacGibbon (Resident, London, England Office)
Heidi Mahon Cook (Resident, Dallas, Texas Office)
Steven C. Malin (Resident, Dallas, Texas Office)
James R. Markham (Resident, Washington, D.C. Office)
Paul A. Martin (Resident, Dallas, Texas Office)
D'Waine M. Massey
Theodore D. Matula (Resident, Dallas, Texas Office)
Jeanne H. McDonald
James M. McGee
Lisa M. McGrath (Resident, Dallas, Texas Office)
Christopher H. Meakin
Gil M. Melman
Macy A. Melton (Resident, Austin, Texas Office)
N. Alan Metni
Patrick W. Mizell
Vincent S. Moreland
Natalya (Natasha) Morozova (Resident, Moscow, Russian Federation Office)
Richard H. Mourglia
Michael J. Mucchetti
George Robertson Murphy, III
Joseph John Naples, III
Donald W. Neal, Jr. (Resident, Austin, Texas Office)
Thomas Nork
Kevin Michael O'Gorman
J. Cavanaugh O'Leary
Harold A. Odom III
Matthew S. Okin
W. Glenn Opel (Resident, Austin, Texas Office)
Betty R. Owens
Richard H. Page
Mary Pape (Resident, Austin, Texas Office)
Frank A. Parigi
Kirill Yurievich Parinov (Resident, Moscow, Russian Federation Office)
Paige C. Patton
James E. Payne
Larry J. Pechacek
Jonathan Samuel Perlman (Resident, Dallas, Texas Office)
Lori E. Peterson (Resident, Washington, D.C. Office)
Frederick Paul Phillips, IV
Anne M. Pike
R. Scott Placek (Resident, Austin, Texas Office)
Clayton A. Platt
Charles M. Preston, III
Robert René Rabalais
Dimitri P. Racklin (Resident, Washington, D.C. Office)
Michael L. Raiff (Resident, Dallas, Texas Office)
Jeffrey L. Raizner
Kelly Williams Raley
Eva C. Ramos (Resident, Austin, Texas Office)
Clifton S. Rankin
James Arthur Reeder, Jr.
Beverly G. Reeves (Resident, Austin, Texas Office)
Russell L. Reid, Jr. (Resident, Dallas, Texas Office)
Patricia F. Reilly
Tara Hanley Reynolds (Resident, Dallas, Texas Office)

(See Next Column)

VINSON & ELKINS L.L.P., *Houston—Continued*

ASSOCIATES (Continued)

Patrick Ragan Richard
R. Glen Rigby
Elizabeth P. Rippy (Resident, Austin, Texas Office)
George G. Rodriguez (Resident, Dallas, Texas Office)
Pamela L. Roger
C. Gregory Rogers (Resident, Dallas, Texas Office)
Steven L. Russell (Resident, Dallas, Texas Office)
Gwen J. Samora
Michael A. Sanzo (Resident, Washington, D.C. Office)
John Walter Van Schwartzenburg
Terrie L. Sechrist
James D. Seegers
Steve Shackelford (Resident, Dallas, Texas Office)
Darryl K. Shaper
Thomas Sheffield
Daniel B. Shilliday
Bryant Siddoway
Stacy Deanne Siegel (Resident, Dallas, Texas Office)
Carin J. Sigel (Resident, Washington, D.C. Office)
Shadow Sloan
Catherine Bukowski Smith
D. Virginia Smith
Paul W. Smith
Susan B. Snyder (Resident, Austin, Texas Office)
William S. Snyder (Resident, Dallas, Texas Office)
Carlos Soltero
Stephanie Sowell
Charles A. Spears, Jr.
Pamela Hays Stabler
Scott Statham
Annette Faubion Stephens
Cynthia A. Stephens (Resident, Dallas, Texas Office)
Mark M. Stetler (Resident, Dallas, Texas Office)
David Stone
Russell W. Sullivan (Resident, Washington, D.C. Office)
Lewis C. Sutherland
William Richard Thompson, II
Michael J. Tomsu
Fernando Tovar
Jeanne Klinefelter Trippon
David J. Tuckfield
Cliff W. Vrielink
Dirk P. Walker
John C. Wander (Resident, Dallas, Texas Office)
Karen A. Wardell
Ann E. Webb
Sara A. Welch
Paul S. Wells
John E. West
Karen Tucker White
Wayne Wiesen
Alysia Wightman (Resident, Austin, Texas Office)
George O. Wilkinson, Jr.
Richard C. Williams
Anita Rutkowski Wilson (Resident, Washington, D.C. Office)
James H. Wilson
Steven J Wright
Russell Yager (Resident, Dallas, Texas Office)
Michael J. Yanochik
Jessica W. Young (Resident, Dallas, Texas Office)
Jonathan M. Zeitler (Resident, Washington, D.C. Office)

For full biographical listings, see the Martindale-Hubbell Law Directory

WINSTEAD SECHREST & MINICK P.C. (AV)

1700 Bank One Center, 910 Travis Street, 77002-5895
Telephone: 713-655-0392
Telex: 73-0051
Telecopy: 713-951-3800
Dallas, Texas Office: 5400 Renaissance Tower, 1201 Elm Street.
Telephone: 214-745-5400.
Telex: 73-0051.
Telecopy: 214-745-5390.
Austin, Texas Office: Suite 800, 100 Congress Avenue.
Telephone: 512-474-4330.
Telex: 73-0051.
Telecopier: 512-370-2850.
Mexico, D.F., Mexico Office: Winstead Sechrest & Minick S.A. de C.V., Galileo 20, P.H. - A, Col. Polanco, 11560 Mexico, D.F.
Telephone: 525-280-6766.
Telecopier: 525-280-0307.

RESIDENT ATTORNEYS

W. Ted Minick
J. Robert Fisher
Jeffrey L. Joyce
Wesley W. Steen
Denis C. Braham
Ann Ryan Robertson
Jeffrey A. Shadwick
Kem Thompson Frost
Richard W. McDugald
Douglas S. Craig, Jr.
John D. White
David D. Knoll
Ross D. Margraves, Jr.
Stephen W. Schueler
James W. Doyle
Mark D. Goranson
Mark C. Guthrie
Arthur S. Berner
David M. Washburn
Benjamin C. Wilson
N. Elton Dry
William T. Johnson

Linda D. King
Todd B. Brewer
Charles M. Silverman
Vince Hannigan
William A. Wood, III
Teresa Letson
Brian F. Antweil
Yasmin Islam
Bridget L. O'Toole
Melissa Gayle Johnson
Joseph A. C. Fulcher
Jon L. Johnson
Gregory S. Mathews
Christopher L. Martin
Evelyn E. Terrell
Carl T. Wimberley
Elizabeth R. Hall
Philip T. Golden
John R. Bakht
Bruce K. Jamison

OF COUNSEL

John A. Sieger

For full biographical listings, see the Martindale-Hubbell Law Directory

WOODARD, HALL & PRIMM, A PROFESSIONAL CORPORATION (AV)

7100 Texas Commerce Tower, 600 Travis Street, 77002
Telephone: 713-221-3800
Cable Address: "Woodhall"
Telex: 79-2173

Tom C. Primm (1934-1981)
Roger R. Wright, Jr. (1936-1990)
Ripley E. Woodard, Jr.
Robert A. Hall
Stephen S. Andrews
Ralph Kenneth Miller, Jr.
Richard R. Cruse
Robert M. Corn
Mark C. Watler
Wilburn O. McDonald, Jr.
JoAnne Ray
Jonathan B. Shoebotham
Robert A. Jones
Phyllis J. Cohen
Larkin C. Eakin, Jr.
Edward M. Carstarphen
G. Joe Ellis
Elizabeth Bonvillain Kamin
Lawrence E. Goldenthal

OF COUNSEL

Janet Mortenson

Douglas B. Dougherty
John L. Meredith
Catherine L. Schnaubelt
Gregory M. Clark
Kimberly A. Willis
Craig M. Sico
David B. Mantor
Ricky A. Raven
Lisa A. Louck
Elizabeth H. Painter

For full biographical listings, see the Martindale-Hubbell Law Directory

*HUNTSVILLE,** Walker Co. — (Refer to Bryan)

*JACKSBORO,** Jack Co. — (Refer to Fort Worth)

JACKSONVILLE, Cherokee Co.

NORMAN, THRALL, ANGLE & GUY (AV)

215 East Commerce Street, P.O. Drawer 1870, 75766
Telephone: 903-586-2595
Fax: 903-586-0524
Rusk, Texas Office: 106 East Fifth Street, P.O. Box 350.
Telephone: 903-683-2226.
FAX: 903-683-5911.

MEMBERS OF FIRM

Wyatt T. Norman (1877-1945)
Summers A. Norman (1905-1986)
Steven R. Guy (Rusk Office)
Gordon F. Thrall
Marvin J. Angle

ASSOCIATES

Forrest K. Phifer (Rusk Office)
R. Christopher Day

For full biographical listings, see the Martindale-Hubbell Law Directory

*JASPER,** Jasper Co. — (Refer to Beaumont)

*JEFFERSON,** Marion Co. — (Refer to Texarkana)

*JUNCTION,** Kimble Co. — (Refer to Uvalde)

*KARNES CITY,** Karnes Co. — (Refer to San Antonio)

*KAUFMAN,** Kaufman Co. — (Refer to Dallas)

*KERMIT,** Winkler Co. — (Refer to Odessa)

*KERRVILLE,** Kerr Co. — (Refer to Boerne)

KILGORE, Gregg Co. — (Refer to Henderson)

KILLEEN, Bell Co. — (Refer to Temple)

*KINGSVILLE,** Kleberg Co.

SHARPE & KRUEGER (AV)

617 East Kleberg, P.O. Box 1538, 78364
Telephone: 512-592-9361
FAX: 512-592-6547

Nelson R. Sharpe (1930-1989)
Michael J. Krueger

Representative Clients: State Bank of Kingsville; Kleberg First National Bank; Greater South Texas, F.S.B.

For full biographical listings, see the Martindale-Hubbell Law Directory

*LAMPASAS,** Lampasas Co. — (Refer to Temple)

*LAREDO,** Webb Co.

JULIO A. GARCIA (AV)

2602 Arkansas Avenue, 78040
Telephone: 210-724-1123

ASSOCIATES

Leticia Garcia Mata

For full biographical listings, see the Martindale-Hubbell Law Directory

Laredo—Continued

MANN, TREVINO, HALE & GALLEGO (AV)

1116 Calle del Norte, P.O. Box 820, 78042-0820
Telephone: 210-723-5581
Fax: 210-725-8811

MEMBERS OF FIRM

G. C. Mann (1898-1969)
John E. Mann
J. C. Trevino, III
Shirley Hale Mathis
Paul D. Gallego

Representative Clients: Roberto Zuniga Compania S.C.; Yellow Freight Systems, Inc.; Southwestern Motor Transport, Inc.; American General Insurance; Fireman's Fund Insurance.

For full biographical listings, see the Martindale-Hubbell Law Directory

PERSON, WHITWORTH, RAMOS, BORCHERS & MORALES (AV)

602 East Calton Road, P.O. Box 6668, 78042-6668
Telephone: 210-727-4441
Fax: 210-727-2696

MEMBERS OF FIRM

George J. Person
Stephen A. Whitworth
Donato D. Ramos
Charles R. Borchers
Richard G. Morales, Jr.
Alejandro E. Villarreal, III
William E. Casey
Mark D. Willett
Pete Saenz, Jr.
Martha Louise Cigarroa Dellano
Anthony Treviño, Jr.
David E. Garcia
Blanca A. Pellegrin
Bruce John Werstak, III
Maria Cristina Gonzalez
Heberto Gonzalez, Jr.
Baldemar Garcia, Jr.

For full biographical listings, see the Martindale-Hubbell Law Directory

*LEVELLAND,** Hockley Co. — (Refer to Lubbock)

*LIBERTY,** Liberty Co. — (Refer to Baytown)

*LINDEN,** Cass Co. — (Refer to Texarkana)

*LITTLEFIELD,** Lamb Co. — (Refer to Lubbock)

*LIVINGSTON,** Polk Co. — (Refer to Beaumont)

*LLANO,** Llano Co. — (Refer to Austin)

*LOCKHART,** Caldwell Co. — (Refer to San Marcos)

*LONGVIEW,** Gregg Co. — (Refer to Henderson)

*LUBBOCK,** Lubbock Co.

CARR, FOUTS, HUNT, CRAIG, TERRILL & WOLFE, L.L.P. (AV)

1001 Texas Avenue, P.O. Box 2585, 79408
Telephone: 806-765-7491
Fax: 806-765-0553

MEMBERS OF FIRM

Marvin Warlick Carr
Aubrey Jan Fouts
Donald M. Hunt
Robert (Bob) L. Craig, Jr.
H. Grady Terrill
Billy R. Wolfe
Latrelle Bright Joy
Robert A. Doty
Tom H. Whiteside
Kent D. Hale (P.C.)
Hugh N. Lyle
Terry L. Grantham
Leslie F. Hatch

ASSOCIATES

Lex Herrington
James E. Joplin
Gary Michael Bellair
Leonard R. (Bud) Grossman

Representative Clients: Commercial Union Assurance Cos.; EXCEL Corp.; NCNB Texas National Bank, N.A.; The St. Paul Cos.; Utica Mutual Insurance Co.

For full biographical listings, see the Martindale-Hubbell Law Directory

CRENSHAW, DUPREE & MILAM, L.L.P. (AV)

Norwest Center, P.O. Box 1499, 79408-1499
Telephone: 806-762-5281
Fax: 806-762-3510

Chas. C. Crenshaw (1886-1964)
Geo. W. Dupree (1890-1973)
R. K. Harty (1911-1978)
J. Orville Smith (1912-1985)
James H. Milam (1911-1994)
William R. Moss
Cecil C. Kuhne
Joe H. Nagy
Brad Crawford, Jr.
John Crews
William F. Russell
William J. Wade
Jack McCutchin, Jr.
Philip W. Johnson
W C Bratcher
Layton Z. Woodul
Robert L. Duncan
W. Chris Boyer
Robert L. Jones
Mark W. Harmon
Mark O. Blankenship
Charlotte D. Bingham
John R. Parker
Jay K. Weatherby
Charles L. Carlson, Jr
James E. Freeman

(See Next Column)

OF COUNSEL

Tom S. Milam

For full biographical listings, see the Martindale-Hubbell Law Directory

HANKINS, MOODY & HAYS, L.L.P. (AV)

City Bank Building, 5211 Brownfield Highway, 79407
Telephone: 806-793-0776
Fax: 806-793-0779

MEMBERS OF FIRM

Mitchell D. Hankins
Bobby J. Moody
J. Phillip Hays

For full biographical listings, see the Martindale-Hubbell Law Directory

HARDING, BASS, FARGASON & BOOTH, L.L.P. (AV)

University Plaza Building, 1901 University, Suite 500, P.O. Box 5950, 79408
Telephone: 806-744-1100
Fax: 806-744-1170

MEMBERS OF FIRM

Derry D. Harding
Roy Byrn Bass, Jr.
Ray Fargason
Monti Rice Booth
Robert W. St. Clair

For full biographical listings, see the Martindale-Hubbell Law Directory

JONES, FLYGARE, GALEY, BROWN & WHARTON (AV)

1600 Civic Center Plaza, P.O. Box 2426, 79408
Telephone: 806-765-8851
Fax: 806-765-8829

Charles B. Jones (1928-1988)
John A. Flygare
Charles E. Galey
Harold P. (Bo) Brown, Jr.
James L. Wharton
Jeffrey B. Jones
Myrtle D. McDonald
John P. Levick
Michael P. Reed
Bradley M. Pettiet
Lois A. Wischkaemper
John D. Rosentreter

Representative Clients: The Aetna Casualty & Surety Co.; Archer Daniels Midland Company; Farmers Insurance Group; Furr's/Bishop Cafeterias; Furr's Supermarkets, Inc.; Lee Lewis Construction, Inc.; Lummus Industries; Penn General Service Corporation; Bain Hogg Robinson; St. Joseph Health System.

For full biographical listings, see the Martindale-Hubbell Law Directory

MCCLESKEY, HARRIGER, BRAZILL & GRAF, L.L.P. (AV)

A Partnership including Professional Corporations
Plains National Bank Building, 5010 University Avenue, P.O. Box 6170, 79493
Telephone: 806-796-7300
Fax: 806-796-7365

MEMBERS OF FIRM

R. Rex Aycock (P.C.)
William F. (Pete) Baker
Clarence P. Brazill (1919-1990)
Dennis R. Burrows (P.C.)
H. Alan Carmichael
Don Graf (P.C.)
Bill Harriger
Harold O. Harriger (P.C.)
Jim Hund
Stephen L. Johnson
Jerry M. Kolander, Jr., (P.C.)
George H. McCleskey (P.C.)
George D. McDonald, P.C.
Frank E. Murchison (P.C.)
Tommy J. Swann
Mike Worley (P.C.)
Dan G. Young

ASSOCIATES

Allen Lee Adkins
Donna L. Courville
Paula M. Johnson
William P. Lane
Terry L. Witter

OF COUNSEL

George W. McCleskey (Retired)

For full biographical listings, see the Martindale-Hubbell Law Directory

MCWHORTER, COBB & JOHNSON, L.L.P. (AV)

1722 Broadway, P.O. Box 2547, 79408
Telephone: 806-762-0214
Fax: 806-762-8014

Owen W. McWhorter (1897-1986)
Dale H. Johnson
D. Thomas Johnson
Jack P. Driskill
D. Murray Hensley
Don R. Richards
Dulan D. Elder
Ann Manning
Joseph F. Postnikoff

OF COUNSEL

Charles L. Cobb
J. R. Blumrosen
Owen W. McWhorter, Jr.

(See Next Column)

McWhorter, Cobb & Johnson L.L.P., *Lubbock—Continued*

ASSOCIATES

Sabra J. Srader
Timothy T. Pridmore
Jamey Laney Phillips
Gary R. McLaren

Representative Clients: American State Bank, Lubbock, Texas; The Atchison Topeka & Santa Fe Railway Co.; South Plains Electric Cooperative; Plains Cotton Cooperative Association; Plains Cooperative Oil Mill; Farmers Cooperative Compress; Lubbock Independent School District; Lubbock Avalanche Journal Newspaper; Texas Statewide Telephone Cooperatives Assn.; Liberty State Bank, Lubbock, Texas.

For full biographical listings, see the Martindale-Hubbell Law Directory

*MADISONVILLE,** Madison Co. — (Refer to Bryan)

*MARFA,** Presidio Co. — (Refer to Monahans)

*MARSHALL,** Harrison Co.

JONES, JONES & CURRY, INC., A PROFESSIONAL CORPORATION (AV)

201 West Houston Street, P.O. Drawer 1249, 75671-1249
Telephone: 903-938-4395
Fax: 903-938-3360

Franklin Jones
Franklin Jones, Jr.
Doyle W. Curry

Mike C. Miller
Rosemary T. Snider
Sam F. Baxter

References: Bank One Marshall; First National Bank.

For full biographical listings, see the Martindale-Hubbell Law Directory

MCALLEN, Hidalgo Co.

ATLAS & HALL, L.L.P. (AV)

Professional Arts Building, 818 Pecan Avenue, P.O. Box 3725, 78501
Telephone: 210-682-5501
Telecopier: 210-686-6109
Brownsville, Texas Office: 2334 Boca Chica Boulevard, Suite 500.
Telephone: 210-542-1850.

MEMBERS OF FIRM

Morris Atlas
Robert L. Schwarz
Gary R. Gurwitz
Edmon G. Hall
Travis Hiester
Charles C. Murray
A. Kirby Cavin
Mike Mills
Molly Thornberry
Charles W. Hury
Frederick J. Biel
Rex N. Leach
Lisa Powell
Stephen L. Crain
O. C. Hamilton, Jr.
Mario "Max" Yzaguirre
Randy Crane
Vicki M. Skaggs
Velma Garza
Stephen C. Haynes

OF COUNSEL

Scott Toothaker

ASSOCIATES

Karen J. Stevens-Minor
Kristen Goodson Clark
Valorie C. Glass
Dan K. Worthington
Daniel G. Gurwitz
Brian Keith Ingram
Patrick F. Madden
David E. Girault

Representative Clients: Texas Commerce Bank-McAllen; Commercial Union Insurance Co.; Hartford Accident & Indemnity Co.; Bentsen Development Co.

For full biographical listings, see the Martindale-Hubbell Law Directory

BARRON, ORENDAIN, MALANY & FLANAGAN (AV)

Suite 1400 Texas Commerce-Neuhaus Tower, 200 South 10th Street, 78501-4892
Telephone: 210-682-0111
Fax: 210-631-2653

MEMBERS OF FIRM

Russell R. Barron
Abel A. Orendain
Douglas S. Malany
Michael E. Flanagan
Ernesto J. Dominguez

ASSOCIATES

Fidel Luis Peña, III

For full biographical listings, see the Martindale-Hubbell Law Directory

CARDENAS, WHITIS & STEPHEN, L.L.P. (AV)

100 South Bicentennial, 78501
Telephone: 210-631-3381
Telecopier: 210-687-5542

(See Next Column)

MEMBERS OF FIRM

Ruben R. Cardenas
Robert W. Whitis
John Kurt Stephen

Representative Client: Texas Commerce Bank-McAllen, N.A.

For full biographical listings, see the Martindale-Hubbell Law Directory

FLORES, CASSO, ROMERO & PETTITT (AV)

321 South 12th Street, P.O. Box 2128, 78505-2128
Telephone: 210-686-9591
Telecopy: 210-686-9478

Rafael H. Flores
David Casso
Glenn D. Romero
B. Buck Pettitt

OF COUNSEL

J. Perry Jones

For full biographical listings, see the Martindale-Hubbell Law Directory

LEWIS, SKAGGS & REYNA, L.L.P. (AV)

710 Laurel, P.O. Box 2285, 78502-2285
Telephone: 210-687-8203
Fax: 210-630-6570

MEMBERS OF FIRM

John E. Lewis
John B. Skaggs
Rose Marie Guerra Reyna

Representative Clients: Farmers Insurance Group; Burlington Insurance Company; Horace Mann Insurance Company; Insurance Company of North America; The Travelers Insurance Co.; Texas Farm Bureau Insurance Cos.; Floyd West & Co.; The Home Insurance Co.; Aetna Casualty & Surety Co.; Firemen's Fund.

For full biographical listings, see the Martindale-Hubbell Law Directory

WILKINS & SLUSHER (AV)

800 First City Bank Tower, P.O. Box 3609, 78501
Telephone: 210-682-4551
Fax: 210-682-4554

MEMBERS OF FIRM

Tom Wilkins
Boone Slusher

ASSOCIATES

Brian Howell

Representative Clients: L.G. Community Exchange (Cattleman's Exchange); Romain Orchards, Inc.; Rio National Bank, McAllen, Texas; The Border Bank, Hidalgo, Texas; Beauregard Groves, Inc.; Rio Grande Railcar, Inc.; Skloss Farms, Inc.
References: First State Bank & Trust Company of Mission, Texas; Texas State Bank, McAllen, Texas.

For full biographical listings, see the Martindale-Hubbell Law Directory

*MEMPHIS,** Hall Co. — (Refer to Clarendon)

*MENARD,** Menard Co. — (Refer to San Angelo)

*MIDLAND,** Midland Co.

KERR, FITZ-GERALD & KERR, L.L.P. (AV)

Century Plaza Building, Suite 600, 310 West Wall Street, 79701
Telephone: 915-683-5291
FAX: 915-683-5257

William L. Kerr (1904-1978)
Gerald Fitz-Gerald (1906-1980)
Wm. Monroe Kerr
Theodore M. Kerr
Harris E. Kerr
William M. Kerr, Jr.

A. M. Nunley III
Brian T. McLaughlin
J. Devin Alsup

For full biographical listings, see the Martindale-Hubbell Law Directory

LYNCH, CHAPPELL & ALSUP, A PROFESSIONAL CORPORATION (AV)

The Summit, Suite 700, 300 North Marienfeld, 79701
Telephone: 915-683-3351
Fax: 915-683-2587

Raymond A. Lynch (1913-1971)
James M. Alsup
Wm. Randall Lundy
Robert A. Spears
David W. Childress
Thomas W. Ortloff
Steven C. Lindgren
Harper Estes
Steven C. Kiser
W. Scott Ryburn
William C. Morrow
James C. Brown
L. Shane Stokes

OF COUNSEL

Clovis G. Chappell

Representative Clients: Tom Brown, Inc.; NationsBank of Texas, N.A.; Parker & Parsley Development Company; Chevron U.S.A. Inc.; Texas National Bank of Midland; Wagner & Brown, Ltd.

For full biographical listings, see the Martindale-Hubbell Law Directory

LESLIE G. MCLAUGHLIN (AV)

1209 West Texas Avenue, 79701
Telephone: 915-687-1331
Fax: 915-687-1336

For full biographical listings, see the Martindale-Hubbell Law Directory

MINERAL WELLS, Palo Pinto Co. — (Refer to Fort Worth)

MISSION, Hidalgo Co. — (Refer to McAllen)

*MOUNT PLEASANT,** Titus Co. — (Refer to Greenville)

*NEW BRAUNFELS,** Comal Co. — (Refer to San Antonio)

*ODESSA,** Ector Co.

MCMAHON, TIDWELL, HANSEN, ATKINS & PEACOCK, P.C. (AV)

4001 East 42nd Street, Suite 200, P.O. Box 1311, 79760
Telephone: 915-367-7271
Fax: 915-363-9121

William B. Deaderick (1918-1966)
Q. B. McMahon (1918-1991)
Jack Q. Tidwell
Blake Hansen
Mike Atkins
Jimmy W. Peacock
J. T. Morgan
James M. Rush
Michael G. Kelly

Denis Dennis
Scott M. Tidwell
M. Michele Greene
Darrell Wayne Corzine

Representative Clients: Bank One, Odessa; Texas Bank, Odessa; Ector County Independent School District; Commercial Union Assurance Co.; The Hartford; State Farm Cos.; Members Insurance Cos.

For full biographical listings, see the Martindale-Hubbell Law Directory

SHAFER, DAVIS, ASHLEY, O'LEARY & STOKER, A PROFESSIONAL CORPORATION (AV)

Second Floor, Nations Bank Building, 700 North Grant Street, P.O. Drawer 1552, 79760
Telephone: 915-332-0893
Telecopier/Fax: 915-333-5002; 915-335-8329

W. O. Shafer (1917-1992)
Perry Davis, Jr.
Connell Ashley
James M. O'Leary
Ray C. Stoker, Jr.
Richard E. Buck
Joel B. Locke
Bruce Bangert
James E. Nelson
Randall L. Rouse
Kathleen McCollum McCulloch
Richard A. Bonner
W. Stacy Trotter
Stephen C. Ashley
Robert E. Motsenbocker
B. Calvin Hendrick, VII
Stephen M. Steen, Jr.

Representative Clients: The Continental Insurance Cos.; The Fireman's Fund Insurance Cos.; The Hartford; American General Cos.; Texas Employers' Insurance Assn.; The Aetna Life & Casualty Co.; Union-Pacific Railroad; NCNB Texas (formerly The First National Bank of Odessa, Texas)

For full biographical listings, see the Martindale-Hubbell Law Directory

*ORANGE,** Orange Co.

MEHAFFY & WEBER, A PROFESSIONAL CORPORATION (AV)

1006 Green Avenue, P.O. Drawer 189, 77630
Telephone: 409-886-7766
Fax: 409-886-7790
Beaumont, Texas Office: 2615 Calder Avenue, P.O. Box 16.
Telephone: 409-835-5011.
Houston Office: One Allen Center, 500 Dallas, Suite 1200.
Telephone: 713-655-1200.

John Cash Smith

Cimron Campbell

Representative Clients: Sabine River Authority of Texas; Orange Housing Authority; Orange Ship Building, Inc.; Equitable Bag Co., Southern Division; Farmers Insurance Group; Texas Farm Bureau; City of Orange.

For full biographical listings, see the Martindale-Hubbell Law Directory

*PALESTINE,** Anderson Co. — (Refer to Jacksonville)

*PAMPA,** Gray Co.

WATERS, HOLT & FIELDS (AV)

Formerly Smith, Teed, Wade & Waters
Combs-Worley Building, P.O. Box 662, 79066-0662
Telephone: 806-669-6851
FAX: 806-669-0440

MEMBERS OF FIRM

Wm. Jarrel Smith (1897-1974)
Arthur M. Teed (1904-1968)
Thos. L. Wade (1905-1972)
Bill W. Waters
David E. Holt
Kenneth W. Fields

Representative Clients: Celanese Corp.; First National Bank in Pampa; Brainard Cattle Co.; Equitable Life Assurance Society of the U.S.; American General Life Insurance Co.; Heaton Cattle Co., Inc.; Halliburton Co.; Beacon Insurance Group.

For full biographical listings, see the Martindale-Hubbell Law Directory

*PARIS,** Lamar Co.

LYLE H. JEANES, II, P.C. (AV)

805 Lamar Avenue, 75460
Telephone: 903-737-9100
Fax: 903-784-2651

Lyle H. Jeanes, II

For full biographical listings, see the Martindale-Hubbell Law Directory

*PEARSALL,** Frio Co. — (Refer to Carrizo Springs)

*PECOS,** Reeves Co. — (Refer to Odessa)

*PERRYTON,** Ochiltree Co.

LEMON, SHEARER, EHRLICH, PHILLIPS & GOOD, A PROFESSIONAL CORPORATION (AV)

311 South Main Street, P.O. Box 1066, 79070
Telephone: 806-435-6544
FAX: 806-435-4377
Booker, Texas Office: 122 South Main Street, P.O. Box 348.
Telephone: 806-658-4545.
FAX: 806-658-4524.

Robert D. Lemon
Otis C. Shearer
Mitchell Ehrlich
Randall M. Phillips
F. Keith Good

Representative Clients: The Perryton National Bank; The Perryton Equity Exchange; The North Plains Ground Water Conservation District; Natural Gas Anadarko Company; Courson Oil & Gas, Inc.; The City of Perryton; The Booker Equity Exchange; The Follett National Bank; Lyco Energy Corporation; Unit Petroleum Company.

For full biographical listings, see the Martindale-Hubbell Law Directory

*PITTSBURG,** Camp Co. — (Refer to Greenville)

*PLAINVIEW,** Hale Co.

OWEN, LYLE, VOSS & OWEN, P.C. (AV)

700 West Seventh Street, P.O. Box 328, 79073-0328
Telephone: 806-296-6304
Fax: 806-296-6829

Gene V. Owen
Paul Lyle
Lanny R. Voss
Rudd F. Owen

Kregg Hukill

Representative Clients: Plainview Independent School District; Plainview Production Credit Assn.; Wayland Baptist University; Farmers Home Administration; Kress National Bank; Funeral Directors Life Insurance Co.
References: Hale County State Bank; Norwest Bank of Plainview.

For full biographical listings, see the Martindale-Hubbell Law Directory

PORT ARTHUR, Jefferson Co.

BLACK & BLACK (AV)

3627 Professional Drive, P.O. Box 3286, 77642
Telephone: 409-982-9433

MEMBERS OF FIRM

Earl Black
James M. Black

For full biographical listings, see the Martindale-Hubbell Law Directory

*QUANAH,** Hardeman Co. — (Refer to Clarendon)

*REFUGIO,** Refugio Co. — (Refer to Beeville)

*ROBY,** Fisher Co. — (Refer to Sweetwater)

*ROCKWALL,** Rockwall Co.

THE HALL LAW OFFICE (AV)

207 East Rusk Street, 75087
Telephone: 214-771-5192

Donald R. Stodghill
Brett A. Hall
Blakeley Hall

For full biographical listings, see the Martindale-Hubbell Law Directory

*RUSK,** Cherokee Co.

NORMAN, THRALL, ANGLE & GUY (AV)

106 East Fifth Street, P.O. Box 350, 75785
Telephone: 903-683-2226
FAX: 903-683-5911
Jacksonville, Texas Office: 215 East Commerce Street, P.O. Drawer 1870.
Telephone: 903-586-2595.
FAX: 903-586-0524.

MEMBERS OF FIRM

Wyatt T. Norman (1877-1945)
Summers A. Norman (1905-1986)
Gordon F. Thrall (Jacksonville Office)
Marvin J. Angle (Jacksonville Office)
Steven R. Guy

ASSOCIATES

Forrest K. Phifer
R. Christopher Day (Jacksonville Office)

For full biographical listings, see the Martindale-Hubbell Law Directory

*SAN ANGELO,** Tom Green Co.

SMITH, CARTER, ROSE, FINLEY & GRIFFIS, A PROFESSIONAL CORPORATION (AV)

222 West Harris Avenue, P.O. Box 2540, 76902-2540
Telephone: 915-653-6721
FAX: 915-653-9580

William A. Griffis, Jr. (1913-1978)
W. Truett Smith
James A. Carter
Frank W. Rose
George S. Finley
Donald W. Griffis
Terri H. Motl
James H. Harp
Allen L. Price
Stephen W. Holt
Robert A. Junell
Samuel S. Allen

Dana Ehrlich
Ben Nolen
Kimberly Waterhouse
Dana Diane Quapaw

OF COUNSEL

Maroney, Crowley & Bankston, L.L.P., Austin, Texas

Representative Clients: Travelers Insurance Co.; Aetna Casualty & Surety Co.; Insurance Corporation of America.

For full biographical listings, see the Martindale-Hubbell Law Directory

*SAN ANTONIO,** Bexar Co.

AKIN, GUMP, STRAUSS, HAUER & FELD, L.L.P. (AV)

A Registered Limited Liability Partnership including Professional Corporations
NationsBank Plaza, 300 Convent Street, Suite 1500, 78205
Telephone: 210-270-0800
Fax: 210-224-2035
Dallas, Texas Office: 1700 Pacific Avenue, Suite 4100.
Telephone: 214-969-2800.
Fax: 214-969-4343.
Austin, Texas Office: Franklin Plaza, 111 Congress Avenue, Suite 2100.
Telephone: 512-499-6200.
Fax: 512-476-3866.
Houston, Texas Office: Pennzoil Place-South Tower, 711 Louisiana Street, Suite 1900.
Telephone: 713-220-5800.
Fax: 713-236-0822.
New York, New York Office: 65 East 55th Street, 33rd Floor.
Telephone: 212-872-1000.
Fax: 212-872-1002.
Washington, D.C. Office: 1333 New Hampshire Avenue, N.W., Suite 400.
Telephone: 202-887-4000.
Fax: 202-887-4288.
Brussels, Belgium Office: Akin, Gump, Strauss, Hauer, Feld & Dassesse, 65 Avenue Louise, P. B. #7.
Telephone: 011-322-535-29-11.
Fax: 011-322-535-29-00.
Moscow, Russia Office: Bolshoi Sukharevsky, Pereulok 26, Building 1, 2nd Floor.
Telephone: 011 7 095 974 2411.
Fax: 011 7 095 974 2412.

(See Next Column)

MEMBERS OF FIRM

Herbert M. Schenker (1913-1994)
Thomas H. Sharp, Jr. (1934-1989)
Robert E. Bettac
Kris J. Bird
Barry A. Chasnoff
J. Mark Craun
Michael C. Elrod
Stephen L. Golden
Charles W. Hanor (P.C.)
R. Laurence Macon (P.C.)
M. Paul Martin
Shelton E. Padgett
Kim E. Ramsey (P.C.)
Mitchell S. Rosenheim
J. Patrick Ryan (P.C.)
Cecil Schenker (P.C.)
Alan Schoenbaum (P.C.)
Andy A. Tschoepe II
Gilbert F. Vázquez
Jose Villarreal
W. Thomas Weir (P.C.)

ASSOCIATES

Matthew Royden Bair
Ruben Cantu
Toni I. Chamberlain
Cathleen L. Chapman
Dawn Ferrell Clements
Lee A. Collins
David L. Dawson
Mary Claire Fischer
Karen Kroesche Gulde
Benita Falls Harper
Ronald A. Kern
C. David Kinder
Daniel McNeel Lane, Jr.
Glenn D. Levy
Joseph C. Martin IV
Pamela Gregg Matthews
Stephen C. Mount
Kirt S. O'Neill
James Patrick Robinson III
Raul M. Rodriguez
Stephan Bruce Rogers
Ricky H. Rosenblum
David R. Stephens
Robert A. Stevenson
Sidney H. Swearingen

OF COUNSEL

Rebecca Simmons

For full biographical listings, see the Martindale-Hubbell Law Directory

BUTLER & BINION, L.L.P. (AV)

A Partnership including Professional Corporations
112 East Pecan Street, 27th Floor, 78205
Telephone: 210-227-2200
Telecopier: 210-223-6730
Houston, Texas Office: 1000 Louisiana, Suite 1600.
Telephone: 713-237-3111.
Telecopier: 713-237-3202.
Dallas, Texas Office: 750 N. St. Paul, Suite 1800.
Telephone: 214-220-3100.
Telecopiers: 214-969-7013; 214-954-4245.
Washington, D.C. Office: 1747 Pennsylvania Avenue, N.W.
Telephone: 202-466-6900.
Telecopier: 202-833-1274.

RESIDENT MEMBERS

James E. Ingram
Lawrence R. Linnartz

ASSOCIATES

Byrd L. Bonner
Dawna R. Carr
R. Rene Escobedo
James M. Hughes
Bridgette Sopper Oliva
James M. Parker, Jr.
Frederick D. Schraub

For full biographical listings, see the Martindale-Hubbell Law Directory

COX & SMITH INCORPORATED (AV)

112 East Pecan Street, Suite 1800, 78205
Telephone: 210-554-5500
Telecopier: 210-226-8395

John J. Cox (1905-1971)
J. Burleson Smith
Paul H. Smith
David C. Spoor
Dan G. Webster, III
Richard T. Brady
Keith E. Kaiser
William H. Lemons, III
Ward T. Blacklock, Jr.
Jon R. Ray
Gale R. Peterson
James B. Smith, Jr.
Diann M. Bartek
Barron W. Dowling
William H. Lester, Jr.
A. Michael Ferrill
Deborah D. Williamson
Cary Plotkin Kavy
Stephen D. Seidel
David B. West
Kevin M. Beiter
David L. Butler
Donna K. McElroy
James M. McDonough
J. Daniel Harkins
Steven R. Jacobs
Michael A. Morell
William J. McDonough, Jr.
John T. Reynolds
Gardner S. Kendrick
Lee S. Garsson
Patrick L. Huffstickler
Raymond E. Gallaway, Jr.
Elizabeth Johnson Keig
Robert W. Nelson
Steven A. Elder
Margaret Pedrick Sullivan
Peter R. Broderick
Stephen R. Pilcher
W. Bradley Haymond (Not admitted in TX)
Tobin E. Olson
Erika S. Carter
Devethia Nichols-Thompson (Not admitted in TX)
Britannia Hobbs Hardee
David D. Jones
Charles A. Japhet
John S. Beauchamp
Hamlet T. Newsom, Jr.

OF COUNSEL

Jack Guenther
Stephen M. Marceau
W. Bebb Francis, III
W. Al Schaich
Joe R. McFarlane

(See Next Column)

COX & SMITH INCORPORATED—*Continued*

Representative Clients: Abraxas Petroleum Corporation; Babbage's, Inc.; Cancer Therapy & Research Center; City of San Antonio; The Dee Howard Co.; International Bancshares Corporation; Kinetic Concepts, Inc.; OXY USA, Inc.; San Antonio Federal Credit Union; Solo Serve Corporation.

For full biographical listings, see the Martindale-Hubbell Law Directory

DAVIDSON & TROILO, A PROFESSIONAL CORPORATION (AV)

Suite 1000 Spectrum Building, 613 N.W. Loop 410, 78216
Telephone: 210-349-6484
Telecopier: 210-349-0041
Austin, Texas Office: 301 Congress Avenue, Suite 1400. 78701.
Telephone: 512-469-5445.
Telecopier: 512-473-2159.

John W. Davidson
Arthur C. Troilo
Terry Topham
Richard W. Wolf
Russell S. Johnson
Cheree Tull Kinzie
R. Gaines Griffin
Richard E. Hettinger
Ruben R. Barrera
Patrick W. Lindner
John T. Sanders, IV

Richard D. O'Neil
Donald D. Gavlick (Resident, Austin Office)
Mary Mishtal
L. Eric Friedland
Lea A. Ream
Michael P. Warren
James D. Rosenblatt

OF COUNSEL

Thomas H. Peterson

Representative Clients: San Antonio Water System; Bank One, Texas N.A.; Federal Deposit Insurance Corporation; Resolution Trust Corporation; Cities of Eagle Pass, McAllen, Pearsall and San Marcos; Public Utility Boards of Brownsville, Kerrville and Weatherford; Texas Municipal League Intergovernmental Risk Pool; Texas Association of Counties Risk Management Pool; United Parcel Services; Morrison-Knudsen Corporation.

For full biographical listings, see the Martindale-Hubbell Law Directory

FOSTER, LEWIS, LANGLEY, GARDNER & BANACK, INCORPORATED (AV)

112 East Pecan Street, Suite 1100, 78205-1533
Telephone: 210-226-3116
FAX: 210-226-1065

A. J. Lewis (1902-1981)
Ralph Langley
Emerson Banack, Jr.
Charles R. Roberts
Edward Kliewer, III
Richard L. Kerr
William T. Armstrong, III
Kenneth L. Malone
Ron Patterson
Scott E. Breen
John B. Stewart
Harry W. Wolff, Jr.
Michael R. Garatoni
Dale Wilson
Mark S. Helmke
Jamie M. Wilson
James K. Lowry, Jr.
Peter L. Kilpatrick
Thomas M. Pickford

Roger D. Kirstein
Robert C. Jones
Donald C. Wood
Jeffrey A. Rochelle

OF COUNSEL

A. J. Lewis, Jr.
Andrew J. Lewis, III
Ben F. Foster (Retired)
Pat H. Gardner (Retired)

Counsel for: Jefferson State Bank; Morton Cos.; Entex Construction Company; Vaughan & Sons; Northeast Independent School District.
Local/Special Counsel for: General Motors Corp.; Connecticut General Life Insurance Company.

For full biographical listings, see the Martindale-Hubbell Law Directory

GRESHAM, DAVIS, GREGORY, WORTHY & MOORE, A PROFESSIONAL CORPORATION (AV)

Formerly Boyle, Wheeler, Gresham, Davis & Gregory
112 East Pecan Street, Ninth Floor, 78205-1542
Telephone: 210-226-4157
Telecopier: 210-226-5154

Rupert Neely Gresham (1892-1973)
Richard T. Davis (1911-1991)
Claiborne B. Gregory
Bond Davis
Albert W. Worthy
Richard B. Moore
Joe R. Beard
Ben J. Chilcutt
Claiborne B. Gregory, Jr.
Moulton S. Dowler, Jr.
Marshall B. Miller, Jr.
John W. Harris
Nancy A. Norman
Peter E. Hosey
Samuel H. Bayless
Richard M. Taylor, III

R. Christopher Clark
Byron L. LeFlore, Jr.
Brad S. Akin
Matthew D. Bradley
James E. McCutcheon, III

For full biographical listings, see the Martindale-Hubbell Law Directory

GROCE, LOCKE & HEBDON, A PROFESSIONAL CORPORATION (AV)

1800 Frost Bank Tower, 100 West Houston, 78205-1497
Telephone: 210-246-5000
FAX: 210-246-5999

Marshall Eskridge (1877-1958)
Winchester Kelso (1895-1965)
Josh H. Groce (1901-1985)
John R. Locke, Jr.
Charles L. Smith
Robert P. Thomas, III
Marshall Groce
Norman L. Nevins
James D. Guess
Robert E. Wehmeyer, Jr.
John J. Franco, Jr.
Lisa A. Vance
Andrew L. Kerr
Paul A. Drummond
Gerry A. Lozano
Mark G. Sessions
Lawrence D. Smith
Thomas A. T. McRae
John Alex Huddleston
Cynthia Glass Bivins
Larry G. Berkman
Mary Quella Kelly

Melanie T. Hewell
Edward F. Valdespino
Brennan T. Holland
Beth S. Johnston
Deborah D. Di Filippo
Zachary B. Aoki
Abel Martinez
John D. Wittenberg, Jr.
Jeffrey G. House
Lisa R. Miller

OF COUNSEL

Jack Hebdon
Edward P. Fahey

For full biographical listings, see the Martindale-Hubbell Law Directory

MATTHEWS & BRANSCOMB, A PROFESSIONAL CORPORATION (AV)

One Alamo Center, 106 S. St. Mary's Street, Suite 800, 78205
Telephone: 210-226-4211
Facsimile: 210-226-0521
Telex: 5106009283
Cable Code: MBLAW
Austin, Texas Office: 301 Congress Avenue, Suite 2050.
Telephone: 512-305-4400.
Facsimile: 512-305-4413.
Corpus Christi, Texas Office: 802 N. Carancahua, Suite 1900.
Telephone: 512-888-9261.
Facsimile: 512-888-8504.
Eagle Pass, Texas Office: 675 Main Street.
Telephone: 210-773-6700.
Facsimile: 210-757-4045.
Uvalde, Texas Office: 200 E. Nopal #208.
Telephone: 210-278-4597.
Facsimile: 210-278-4806.
(Associated with Hall, Quintanilla & Alarcon, L.C., Laredo, Texas, under the name of Hall, Quintanilla, Alarcon, Matthews & Branscomb, P.L.L.C.)

William F. Nowlin (1902-1978)
Harper Macfarlane (1901-1980)
Lionel R. Fuller (1919-1984)
Grady Barrett (1895-1986)
William H. Nowlin (1934-1987)
Wilbur L. Matthews
Patrick H. Swearingen, Jr.
Lewis T. Tarver, Jr.
Richard E. Goldsmith
William H. Robison
John D. Fisch
Jon C. Wood
J. Joe Harris
George P. Parker, Jr.
James M. Doyle, Jr.
C. Michael Montgomery
W. Roger Wilson
Howard P. Newton
Charles J. Muller, III
John McPherson Pinckney, III
Richard C. Danysh
J. Tullos Wells
Charles J. Fitzpatrick
Marshall T. Steves, Jr.
Judith R. Blakeway
James H. Kizziar, Jr.
Frank Z. Ruttenberg
Leslie Selig Byrd
Patrick H. Autry
Farley P. Katz
Dawn Bruner Finlayson
John A. Ferguson, Jr.
Julie B. Adler Koppenheffer
Mary M. Potter
Annalyn G. Smith
Arthur G. Uhl, III
Nancy H. Stumberg
Howard D. Bye
Judy K. Jetelina
Mark A. Phariss
Merritt M. Clements
Robert Shaw-Meadow
Daniel M. Elder
Mark A. Jones
Kay L. Reamey
Timothy H. Bannwolf
Victoria M. García
Anthony E. Rebollo
Steven J. Pugh
Elizabeth H. Chumney
Craig A. Arnold
Inez M. McBride
Kathleen A. Devine
Raquel G. Perez
David L. Doggett
Roberta J. Sharp
Mary Helen Medina

OF COUNSEL

Francis W. Baker
Judson Wood, Jr.

Representative Clients: Coca Cola Bottling Company of the Southwest; Concord Oil Co.; Ellison Enterprises, Inc.; H. E. Butt Grocery Co.; Frank B. Hall & Co., Inc.; The Hearst Corp., San Antonio Light Division; San Antonio Gas & Electric Utilities (City Board); Southern Pacific Transportation Co.; Southwest Texas Methodist Hospital.

For full biographical listings, see the Martindale-Hubbell Law Directory

San Antonio—Continued

OPPENHEIMER, BLEND, HARRISON & TATE, INC. (AV)

711 Navarro, Sixth Floor, 78205-1796
Telephone: 210-224-2000
Telecopier: 210-224-7540
Telex: 3787504

Jesse H. Oppenheimer
Reese L. Harrison, Jr.
Stanley L. Blend
John H. Tate, II
Kenneth M. Gindy
J. David Oppenheimer
Richard N. Weinstein
Taylor S. Boone
Glen A. Yale
Raymond W. Battaglia
Craig A. Stokes
Bruce M. Mitchell
Cheryl K. Freed
Kirk L. James

R. Flint Bourgeois
Roberto G. Cantu
Jerome B. Cohen
Elizabeth A. Dawson
A. Ryland Howard, III
Julie Cobb Perez
Martin I. Roos
Brad L. Sklencar
David P. Stanush
Cathy Raba Turcotte

OF COUNSEL

Joseph B. C. Fitzsimons
Karen Vaughan

For full biographical listings, see the Martindale-Hubbell Law Directory

PLUNKETT, GIBSON & ALLEN, INC. (AV)

6243 IH - 10 West, Suite 600, P.O. Box BH002, 78201
Telephone: 210-734-7092
Fax: 210-734-0379

Lewin Plunkett
Jerry A. Gibson
Robert A. Allen
Mark R. Stein
Daniel Diaz, Jr.
Ronald Hornberger
Joseph C. Elliott
Tim T. Griesenbeck, Jr.
Keith B. O'Connell
William L. Powers
Harry S. Bates
Jennifer Gibbins Durbin
Richard N. Francis, Jr.
Ernest F. Avery
A. Dale Hicks
Richard W. Hunnicutt, III

Margaret Netemeyer
Jeffrey C. Manske
David P. Benjamin
Cathy J. Sheehan
Richard B. Copeland
John C. Howell
P. Brian Berryman
Isidro O. Castanon
Nina E. Henderson
Dan Vana
D. Ann Comerio
David L. Downs
Nancy L. Farrer
Deborah L. Klein
William J. Baine
Paul J. Janik
Tom L. Newton, Jr.
Karen H. Norris
Donald L. Crook
Peter B. Gostomski
William J. Maiberger, Jr.
Cynthia L. Beverage
Anthony A. Avey
Clayborne L. Nettleship

Representative Clients: Traveler's Insurance Co.; CIGNA; State Farm Mutual Automobile Insurance Co.; University of Texas Health Science Center at San Antonio; Commercial Union Insurance Cos.; Galen Health Care, Inc.; Ford Motor Co.; Allstate Insurance; Zurich American Insurance Group; Santa Rosa Medical Center.

For full biographical listings, see the Martindale-Hubbell Law Directory

SOULES & WALLACE ATTORNEYS AT LAW A PROFESSIONAL CORPORATION (AV)

Fifteenth Floor Frost Bank Tower, 100 W. Houston Street, 78205-1457
Telephone: 210-224-9144
Telecopier: 210-224-7073
Austin, Texas Office: Barton Oaks Plaza Two, Suite 315, 901 MoPac Expressway South.
Telephone: 512-328-5511.
Telecopier: 512-327-4105.
Houston, Texas Office: 1360 Post Oak Boulevard, Suite 1500.
Telephone: 713-297-0500.
Telecopier: 713-297-0555.

Luther H. Soules, III
James P. Wallace (Resident, Austin Office)
Susan Shank Patterson
Ronald J. Johnson
Wayne I. Fagan
Keith M. Baker
Marc J. Schnall
Herbert Gordon Davis
Richard M. Butler
Phil Steven Kosub
Ronald E. Tigner
Darryl K. Carter (Resident, Houston Office)
William S. Hart

Paul D. Andrews
Jeannette McAllister Baker (Resident Houston Office)
Nancy B. Mc Camish
Sara S. Murray
George C. Noyes
Barbara Hunt Paulissen (Resident, Houston Office)
Robinson C. Ramsey
Bruce K. Spindler
William T. Sullivan
Luis R. Garciá

(See Next Column)

Norman W. Peters, Jr. (Resident, Houston Office)
Jeffrey L. Diamond (Resident, Houston Office)
Stacy J. Williams (Resident, Houston Office)
Robert L. Eschenburg, II

For full biographical listings, see the Martindale-Hubbell Law Directory

WELMAKER & WELMAKER, P.C. (AV)

8151 Broadway, 78209
Telephone: 210-828-6033
FAX: 210-821-6358

Nolan Welmaker
Forrest N. Welmaker, Jr.

For full biographical listings, see the Martindale-Hubbell Law Directory

*SAN AUGUSTINE,** San Augustine Co. — (Refer to Center)

*SANDERSON,** Terrell Co. — (Refer to Monahans)

*SAN MARCOS,** Hays Co.

ANDREW GARY (AV)

108 East San Antonio, 78666
Telephone: 512-396-2541
Fax: 512-396-2870

Representative Clients: State Bank and Trust Co., San Marcos, Texas; Ingram Readymix, Inc., New Braunfels, Texas.

For full biographical listings, see the Martindale-Hubbell Law Directory

*SAN SABA,** San Saba Co. — (Refer to Austin)

*SEGUIN,** Guadalupe Co. — (Refer to San Marcos)

*SEYMOUR,** Baylor Co. — (Refer to Wichita Falls)

*SINTON,** San Patricio Co. — (Refer to Corpus Christi)

*SNYDER,** Scurry Co. — (Refer to Sweetwater)

*SONORA,** Sutton Co. — (Refer to San Angelo)

*SULPHUR SPRINGS,** Hopkins Co. — (Refer to Greenville)

*TAHOKA,** Lynn Co.

HUFFAKER, GREEN & HUFFAKER (AV)

1629 Avenue K, P.O. Box 419, 79373
Telephone: 806-998-4515
Fax: 806-998-4800

MEMBERS OF FIRM

Calloway Huffaker (1914-1988)
Harold Green
Gerald Huffaker

ASSOCIATES

W. Calloway Huffaker, Jr.

Representative Clients: The First National Bank, Tahoka; The Wilson State Bank, Wilson, Texas; Lyntegar Electric Cooperative, Inc.; Taylor Tractor & Equipment, Inc.

For full biographical listings, see the Martindale-Hubbell Law Directory

TEMPLE, Bell Co.

BOWMER, COURTNEY, BURLESON, NORMAND & MOORE (AV)

6th Floor, First National Bank Building, P.O. Box 844, 76503
Telephone: 817-778-1354
FAX: 817-774-7254
Waco, Texas Office: Naman, Howell, Smith & Lee, A Professional Corporation, Texas Center, Ninth and Washington, P.O. Box 1470.
Telephone: 817-755-4100.
FAX: 817-754-6331.
Austin, Texas Office: Naman, Howell, Smith & Lee, A Professional Corporation, 221 West Sixth Street, 1900 Bank One Tower.
Telephone: 512-479-0300.
FAX: 512-474-1901.

DeWitt Bowmer (1890-1940)
Walker Saulsbury (1895-1944)
Jim D. Bowmer
Bob Burleson
William R. Courtney
Jack M. Moore
Tom Normand

John P. Cunningham, Jr.
Lisa L. Havens-Cortes

Counsel for: State Farm Mutual Automobile Insurance Co. First National Bank of Temple; American Desk Mfg. Co.; Ralph Wilson Plastics Co.

For full biographical listings, see the Martindale-Hubbell Law Directory

TEXARKANA, Bowie Co.

ATCHLEY, RUSSELL, WALDROP & HLAVINKA, L.L.P. (AV)

1710 Moores Lane, P.O. Box 5517, 75505-5517
Telephone: 903-792-8246
Fax: 903-792-5801

(See Next Column)

ATCHLEY, RUSSELL, WALDROP & HLAVINKA L.L.P.—*Continued*

MEMBERS OF FIRM

Otto H. Atchley (1904-1989)
Norman C. Russell
Howard Waldrop
Charles J. Hlavinka
Victor F. Hlavinka
Stephen Oden
J. Dennis Chambers
Robert W. Weber
Alan D. Harrel
Josh R. Morriss, III
John R. Mercy
J. Michael Smith
Jeffrey C. Elliott
Kenneth Dale Edwards (1940-1976)
Robert W. Littrell (1953-1983)
William Howard Mowery
Louise E. Tausch

ASSOCIATES

Jeffery C. Lewis
Christy P. Paddock

Representative Clients: United States Fidelity & Guaranty Co.; Employer's Casualty Co.; Liberty Mutual Insurance Co.; The Home Co.; Missouri-Pacific Railway Co.; St. Louis Southwestern Railway Co.; State First National Bank in Texas; State Bank of DeKalb; St. Paul Insurance Co.; First-Bank.

For full biographical listings, see the Martindale-Hubbell Law Directory

PATTON, HALTOM, ROBERTS, MCWILLIAMS & GREER, L.L.P. (AV)

A Registered Limited Liability Partnership including Professional Corporations
700 Texarkana National Bank Building, P.O. Box 1928, 75504-1928
Telephone: 903-794-3341
Fax: 903-792-6542; 903-792-0448

Kirk Patton (P.C.)
James N. Haltom (P.C.)
William B. Roberts
George L. McWilliams (P.C.)
John B. Greer, III, (P.C.)
Donald W. Capshaw
Phillip N. Cockrell
William G. Bullock
Fred R. Norton, Jr.

ASSOCIATES

Kristi Ingold McCasland
Caroline Malone
Ralph K. Burgess
Johanna Elizabeth Haltom Salter (1960-1993)
Steven W. Caple
Keith A. Scott

Representative Clients: Allstate Insurance Co.; Aetna Casualty & Surety Co.; Royal Insurance Group; Continental Insurance Group; Ranger/Pan American Insurance Cos.; The Hanover Insurance Group; American Mutual Liability Insurance Co.; American Hardware Mutual Insurance Co.; Kemper Insurance Co.; Texarkana National Bancshares, Inc.

For full biographical listings, see the Martindale-Hubbell Law Directory

THREE RIVERS, Live Oak Co. — (Refer to George West)

*TULIA,** Swisher Co. — (Refer to Plainview)

*TYLER,** Smith Co.

BAIN FILES ALLEN AND WORTHEN, A PROFESSIONAL CORPORATION (AV)

109 West Ferguson Street, P.O. Box 2013, 75710
Telephone: 903-595-3573
Fax: 903-597-7322

Jerry E. Bain
F. R. (Buck) Files, Jr.
Michael D. Allen
James T. Worthen
Michael E. Jarrett

For full biographical listings, see the Martindale-Hubbell Law Directory

LASATER & KNIGHT (AV)

206 West Erwin, 75702
Telephone: 903-595-3526
FAX: 903-595-3528

MEMBERS OF FIRM

F. Wilbert Lasater
William A. Knight
W. Scott Knight

Representative Clients: Exxon Corp.; Amoco Production Co.; NationsBank of Texas, N.A.
Reference: NCNB Texas National Bank.

For full biographical listings, see the Martindale-Hubbell Law Directory

*UVALDE,** Uvalde Co.

CRAWFORD, CRAWFORD & HUGHES (AV)

218 North Getty Street, 78801
Telephone: 210-278-6271, 278-6272
Fax: 210-278-7643

MEMBERS OF FIRM

R. S. Crawford (1894-1977)
Robert S. Crawford, Jr.
Phillip M. Hughes

Representative Clients: Medina Electric Co-Operative, Inc.; White's Uvalde Mines.

(See Next Column)

For full biographical listings, see the Martindale-Hubbell Law Directory

KESSLER & KESSLER (AV)

Suite 200, First State Bank Building, P.O. Box 1040, 78802-1040
Telephone: 210-278-2515
Fax: 210-278-7037

MEMBERS OF FIRM

W. A. Kessler
William A. Kessler, Jr.

Attorneys for: First State Bank of Uvalde; Garner Abstract & Land Co.; Coastal Plains Production Credit Association; Leona Valley Gin Company, LLC.
Local Counsel: Central Power & Light Co.

For full biographical listings, see the Martindale-Hubbell Law Directory

*VICTORIA,** Victoria Co.

ANDERSON, SMITH, NULL, STOFER & MURPHREE, L.L.P. (AV)

7th Floor, One O'Connor Plaza, P.O. Box 1969, 77902
Telephone: 512-573-9191
Fax: 512-573-5288

Munson Smith
James N. Stofer
John D. Murphree
James H. Murray, Jr.
Richard T. Chapman, Jr.
Jerome A. Brown
Janis L. Scott

J. Milton Chapman
Darryl E. Atkinson
Alan L. Rucker
Duane G. Crocker

OF COUNSEL

Melvin L. Null

RETIRED PARTNERS

Conde N. Anderson

Representative Clients: Victoria Bankshares, Inc.; Victoria Bank & Trust Co.; Central Power & Light Co.; Missouri Pacific/Union Pacific Railroad; Union Carbide Corp.; Southern Pacific Transportation Co.; C.N.A. Insurance; Victoria Independent School District.

For full biographical listings, see the Martindale-Hubbell Law Directory

CULLEN, CARSNER, SEERDEN & CULLEN, L.L.P. (AV)

119 South Main Street, P.O. Box 2938, 77902
Telephone: 512-573-6318
Fax: 512-573-2603

MEMBERS OF FIRM

Richard D. Cullen
Charles C. Carsner, Jr. (1917-1993)
William F. Seerden
Kevin D. Cullen
Jean Smetana Cullen
Juergen Koetter
Mark C. Rains
Kemper Stephen Williams, III

ASSOCIATES

Michael A. Johnson
Garland Sandhop, Jr.
Wendy Atkinson

Representative Clients: American General Insurance Co.; Aetna Casualty & Surety Co.; Hartford Accident & Indemnity Co.; U.S.F.&G. Co.; Travelers Insurance Co.; Allstate Insurance Company; Formosa Plastics Corporation and its affiliated companies; Edna Independent School District; Victoria Independent School District; Victoria County, Texas (civil only)

For full biographical listings, see the Martindale-Hubbell Law Directory

*WACO,** McLennan Co.

CHERRY, DAVIS, HARRISON, MONTEZ, WILLIAMS & BAIRD, P.C. (AV)

801 Washington Avenue Seventh Floor, First National Bank Building, 76701-1291
Telephone: 817-756-5545
Fax: 817-757-0522

David E. Cherry
Billy H. Davis, Jr.
Stephen E. Harrison, II
John A. Montez
Aubrey R. Williams
Robin E. Baird

A List of Representative Clients will be furnished upon request.

For full biographical listings, see the Martindale-Hubbell Law Directory

DUNNAM & DUNNAM, L.L.P. (AV)

4125 West Waco Drive, P.O. Box 8418, 76714-8418
Telephone: 817-753-6437
Fax: 817-753-7434

MEMBERS OF FIRM

W. V. Dunnam (1891-1974)
W. V. Dunnam, Jr.
Vance Dunnam
Vance Dunnam, Jr.
Damon L. Reed
James R. Dunnam

(See Next Column)

DUNNAM & DUNNAM L.L.P., *Waco—Continued*

ASSOCIATES

Cathy Dunnam
Alan Stucky

For full biographical listings, see the Martindale-Hubbell Law Directory

NAMAN, HOWELL, SMITH & LEE, A PROFESSIONAL CORPORATION (AV)

Texas Center, Ninth and Washington, P.O. Box 1470, 76703-1470
Telephone: 817-755-4100
FAX: 817-754-6331 ABA/Net ABA2117
Austin, Texas Office: 221 West Sixth Street, 1900 Bank One Tower.
Telephone: 512-479-0300.
FAX: 512-474-1901.
Temple, Texas Office: Bowmer, Courtney, Burleson, Normand & Moore, 6th Floor, First National Bank Building, P.O. Box 844.
Telephone: 817-778-1354.
FAX: 817-774-7254.

Wilford W. Naman (1887-1978)
Hilton E. Howell (1897-1968)
Hilton H. Howell (1928-1986)
P. Clark Aspy (Resident, Austin Office)
Roy L. Barrett
Charles K. Barrow
Frederick deB. Bostwick, III
Jim D. Bowmer (Resident, Temple Office)
Larry O. Brady
Richard E. Brophy, Jr.
Bob Burleson (Resident, Temple Office)
Jerry P. Campbell
William R. Courtney (Resident, Temple Office)
George M. Cowden (Resident, Austin Office)
Wesley J. Filer
Keith E. Gamel (Resident, Austin Office)
Kerry L. Haliburton
Alexander M. Haw
John T. Hawkins
Paul H. Hubbard
Allen H. King (Resident, Austin Office)
J. Rodney Lee
Steve L. Moody
Jack M. Moore (Resident, Temple Office)
Tom Normand (Resident, Temple Office)
C. Patrick Nunley
Dan Pleitz
Michael L. Scanes
F. Ben Selman, Jr.
Cullen Smith
Stuart Smith
Thomas D. Swann
David G. Tekell
Rex S. Whitaker
Albert Witcher

Patrick O. Brady
Nick R. Bray
Keith C. Cameron
Cara M. Chase
John P. Cunningham, Jr. (Resident, Temple Office)
Lisa L. Havens-Cortes (Resident, Temple Office)
William M. "Skip" King
Nancy Napier Morrison
Kelli A. Norris (Resident, Austin Office)
John P. Palmer
Enid A. Wade

Representative Clients: Texas National Bank; Santa Fe Railway; St. Paul Insurance Cos.; Texas Municipal Power Agency.

For full biographical listings, see the Martindale-Hubbell Law Directory

SHEEHY, LOVELACE & MAYFIELD, P.C. A PROFESSIONAL CORPORATION (AV)

510 North Valley Mills Drive, Suite 500, 76710
Telephone: 817-772-8022
FAX: 817-772-9297

John F. Sheehy (1898-1979)
J. Henry Lovelace (1926-1992)
John F. Sheehy, Jr.
Dan E. Mayfield
Henry W. Fielder
Philip E. McCleery
Gary K. Jordan
G. Maynard Green
Robert A. Watson
L. Hayes Fuller, III
J. David Dickson
Peter K. Rusek
Jeffrey R. Cox
John O'Herren

J. Patrick Atkins

OF COUNSEL

Michael J. Gulig
Jerome Cartwright

General Attorneys for: First Title Company of Waco.
General Counsel for: American Amicable Life Insurance Co.; Central Freight Lines, Inc.
Local Counsel for: Fireman's Fund Insurance Group; Kemper Insurance Group; Floyd West & Co.; Aetna Life Insurance Co.

For full biographical listings, see the Martindale-Hubbell Law Directory

SMITH & BRATCHER, INC. (AV)

American Plaza, Suite 420, 200 West Highway 6, P.O. Box 21473, 76702-1473
Telephone: 817-751-0044
Fax: 817-751-0049

Kent Bratcher
Samuel T. Kinslow
D. Daryle Echols, Jr.

(See Next Column)

OF COUNSEL

Vernon L. Smith

For full biographical listings, see the Martindale-Hubbell Law Directory

*WAXAHACHIE,** Ellis Co.

JENKINS & JENKINS, P.C. (AV)

516 West Main Street, P.O. Box 557, 75165
Telephone: 214-937-5710; Dallas: 214-938-1234
FAX: 214-937-5758

Warwick H. Jenkins
Clay Lewis Jenkins

Representative Clients: TU Electric (Area); Ellis County Water Control and Improvement District No. 1; Waxahachie Daily Light (Newspaper); The First National Bank in Midlothian; Trego Industries.

For full biographical listings, see the Martindale-Hubbell Law Directory

*WEATHERFORD,** Parker Co. — (Refer to Fort Worth)

WESLACO, Hidalgo Co.

JONES, GALLIGAN & KEY, L.L.P. (AV)

615 International Avenue P.O. Drawer 1247, 78599-1247
Telephone: 210-968-5402
Fax: 210-968-6089

MEMBERS OF FIRM

Forrest L. Jones
Robert L. Galligan
Terry D. Key

Anita G. Lozano
Julie A. Crockett
David J. Guerrero
Todd A. Clark

For full biographical listings, see the Martindale-Hubbell Law Directory

*WICHITA FALLS,** Wichita Co.

BANNER, BRILEY & WHITE, L.L.P. (AV)

900 Eighth Street, Suite 1200, 76301-6899
Telephone: 817-723-6644
Fax: 817-322-1960

Jack G. Banner
Steve Briley
Harold White

OF COUNSEL

Ed McIntosh

Reference: American National Bank.

For full biographical listings, see the Martindale-Hubbell Law Directory

MORRISON & SHELTON, A PROFESSIONAL CORPORATION (AV)

City National Building, 807 Eighth Street, Suite 1010, 76301-3319
Telephone: 817-322-2929
Telecopier: 817-322-7463

Lonny D. Morrison
Stephen R. Shelton

For full biographical listings, see the Martindale-Hubbell Law Directory

SHERRILL, CROSNOE & GOFF, A PROFESSIONAL CORPORATION (AV)

900 Eighth Street, Suite 1100, P.O. Box 97511, 76307-7511
Telephone: 817-322-3145
Facsimile: 817-322-8324

Joseph N. Sherrill Jr.
R. Caven Crosnoe
Robert W. Goff, Jr.
R. Ken Hines
Richard K. Bowersock

William Frank Smith
Randy R. Martin

For full biographical listings, see the Martindale-Hubbell Law Directory

*WOODVILLE,** Tyler Co. — (Refer to Beaumont)
YOAKUM, Lavaca & De Witt Cos. — (Refer to Victoria)

UTAH

CEDAR CITY, Iron Co.

CHAMBERLAIN & HIGBEE (AV)

250 South Main Street, P.O. Box 726, 84720
Telephone: 801-586-4404
Fax: 801-586-1002
Kanab, Utah Office: 9 West Center.
Telephone: 801-644-8808.

Hans Q. Chamberlain
Thomas M. Higbee

R. Todd Macfarlane (Resident, Kanab Office)
Steven D. Burge
James W. Jensen

Representative Clients: Carter Enterprises, Inc.; Cedar Land Title, Inc.; First Security Bank of Utah, N.A.; Iron County School District; New Castle Water Co.; Quality Ready Mix Concrete, Inc.; Security Title Co.; State Bank of Southern Utah; Southern Utah Title Company of Cedar City, Inc.

For full biographical listings, see the Martindale-Hubbell Law Directory

*HEBER CITY,** Wasatch Co. — (Refer to Provo)

*MANTI,** Sanpete Co. — (Refer to Provo)

*NEPHI,** Juab Co. — (Refer to Provo)

*OGDEN,** Weber Co.

VAN COTT, BAGLEY, CORNWALL & MCCARTHY, A PROFESSIONAL CORPORATION (AV)

Suite 900, 2404 Washington Boulevard, 84401
Telephone: 801-394-5783
Telecopier: 801-627-2522
Salt Lake City, Utah Office: 50 South Main Street, Suite 1600.
Telephone: 801-532-3333.
Park City, Utah Office: 314 Main Street, Suite 205.
Telephone: 801-649-3889.
Reno, Nevada Office: Jeppson & Lee, 100 West Liberty, Suite 990.
Telephone: 702-333-6800.

Scott M. Hadley (Resident)
Timothy W. Blackburn (Resident)
Douglas A. Taggart (Resident)

OF COUNSEL

Marlin K. Jensen

Michael T. Roberts

Representative Clients: Standard Oil Company of California (and affiliated companies); FMC Corp.; Leucadia National Corp.; Key Bank of Utah; Southern Pacific Lines; Intermountain Health Care, Inc.; Huntsman Chemical Corp.; Iomega Corp.; Metropolitan Life Ins. Co.

For full biographical listings, see the Martindale-Hubbell Law Directory

PARK CITY, Summit Co.

PRINCE, YEATES & GELDZAHLER (AV)

614 Main Street, P.O. Box 38, 84060
Telephone: 801-524-1000; 649-7440.
Fax: 801-524-1099
Salt Lake City, Utah Office: City Centre I, Suite 900, 175 East 400 South.
Telephone: 801-524-1000.

Jon C. Heaton
Ronald E. Nehring
John P. Ashton
J. Randall Call
Geoffrey W. Mangum

Counsel for: Allstate Insurance; Bed & Breakfast Inns of Utah; CrossLand Savings FSB; Deer Valley Club; Ingersoll-Rand Co.; Marker Ski Bindings; ShopKo Stores; Park City Ski Resort; Labor Matters: Smith's Food and Drug Centers, Inc.

For full biographical listings, see the Martindale-Hubbell Law Directory

VAN COTT, BAGLEY, CORNWALL & MCCARTHY, A PROFESSIONAL CORPORATION (AV)

314 Main Street, Suite 205, P.O. Box 4611, 84060
Telephone: 801-649-3889
Telecopier: 801-649-3373
Salt Lake City, Utah Office: Suite 1600, 50 South Main Street, P.O. Box 45340.
Telephone: 801-532-3333.
Telex: 453149.
Telecopier: 801-534-0058.
Ogden, Utah Office: Suite 900, 2404 Washington Boulevard.
Telephone: 801-394-5783.
Reno, Nevada Office: Jeppson & Lee, 100 West Liberty, Suite 990.
Telephone: 702-333-6800.

(See Next Column)

M. Scott Woodland
Thomas T. Billings

Representative Clients: Standard Oil Company of California (and affiliated companies); FMC Corp.; Leucadia National Corp.; Key Bank of Utah; Southern Pacific Lines; Intermountain Health Care, Inc.; Huntsman Chemical Corp.; Iomega Corp.; Metropolitan Life Ins. Co.

For full biographical listings, see the Martindale-Hubbell Law Directory

*PROVO,** Utah Co.

HOWARD, LEWIS & PETERSEN, P.C. (AV)

Delphi Building, 120 East 300 North Street, P.O. Box 778, 84603
Telephone: 801-373-6345
Fax: 801-377-4991

Jackson Howard
Don R. Petersen
Craig M. Snyder
John L. Valentine
D. David Lambert
Fred D. Howard
Leslie W. Slaugh

Richard W. Daynes
Phillip E. Lowry
Kenneth Parkinson

OF COUNSEL

S. Rex Lewis

LEGAL SUPPORT PERSONNEL

Mary Jackson
John O. Sump
Ray Winger

For full biographical listings, see the Martindale-Hubbell Law Directory

JEFFS AND JEFFS, P.C. (AV)

90 North 100 East, P.O. Box 888, 84603
Telephone: 801-373-8848
Fax: 801-373-8878

M. Dayle Jeffs
A. Dean Jeffs
David D. Jeffs
Robert L. Jeffs
William M. Jeffs

Lorie D. Fowlke

Representative Clients: Farmers Insurance Group; American Service Life Insurance Co.; Central Reserve Life Insurance Co.; R.B.& G. Engineers, Inc.; Horrocks Engineers, Inc.; Duchesne County Upper Country Water Improvement District; Provo Postal Credit Union; Interwest Safety Supply, Inc.
References: Zion First National Bank; Bank of American Fork.

For full biographical listings, see the Martindale-Hubbell Law Directory

RAY, QUINNEY & NEBEKER, A PROFESSIONAL CORPORATION (AV)

210 First Security Bank Building, 92 North University Avenue, 84601-4420
Telephone: 801-226-7210
Telecopier: 801-375-8379
Salt Lake City, Utah Office: Suite 400 Deseret Building. 79 South Main Street, P.O. Box 45385.
Telephone: 801-532-1500.
Telecopier: 801-532-7543.

Don B. Allen
James L. Wilde (Resident)
Larry G. Moore
Dale M. Okerlund
Craig Carlile (Resident)

For full biographical listings, see the Martindale-Hubbell Law Directory

*ST. GEORGE,** Washington Co.

JONES, WALDO, HOLBROOK & MCDONOUGH, A PROFESSIONAL CORPORATION (AV)

The Tabernacle Tower Building, 249 East Tabernacle, 84770
Telephone: 801-628-1627
Telecopier: 801-628-5225
Salt Lake City, Utah Office: 1500 First Interstate Plaza, 170 South Main Street.
Telephone: 801-521-3200.
Telecopier: 801-328-0537.
Washington, D.C. Office: Suite 900, 2300 M Street, N.W.
Telephone: 202-296-5950.
Telecopier: 202-293-2509.

John W. Palmer (Resident)
Timothy B. Anderson (Resident)
G. Rand Beacham (Resident)
D. Williams Ronnow (P.C.) (Resident)
Michael R. Shaw (Resident)

John J. Walton (Resident)

(See Next Column)

Jones, Waldo, Holbrook & McDonough A Professional Corporation, *St. George—Continued*

OF COUNSEL

Calvin L. Rampton
Gary A. Terry (Not admitted in UT; Resident)

Representative Clients: First Interstate Bank; St. George Steel Fabrication; BrianHead Property Management Co.; Winchester Hills Home Owners Assn.; Ideal Waste Systems, Inc.; United Mortgage Co.; Skywest Airlines.
Reference: First Interstate Bank.

For full biographical listings, see the Martindale-Hubbell Law Directory

Snow, Nuffer, Engstrom, Drake, Wade & Smart, A Professional Corporation (AV)

90 East 200 North, 84771-0400
Telephone: 801-674-0400
Fax: 801-628-1610
Salt Lake City, Utah Office: 341 South Main, Suite 201.
Telephone: 801-538-0400.

Steven E. Snow
David Nuffer
Chris L. Engstrom
Lyle R. Drake
Terry L. Wade
Randall R. Smart

Jeffrey N. Starkey
E. Scott Awerkamp
Michael A. Day

Representative Clients: Sun Capital Bank; Washington City; L & L Mechanical Contractors, Inc.; J & J Mill & Lumber Co.; First Security Bank; Ence Construction.
Reference: First Security Bank.

For full biographical listings, see the Martindale-Hubbell Law Directory

*SALT LAKE CITY,** Salt Lake Co.

Callister, Nebeker & McCullough, A Professional Corporation (AV)

800 Kennecott Building, 84133
Telephone: 801-530-7300
Telecopier: 801-364-9127

Louis H. Callister, Sr. (1904-1983)
Louis H. Callister
Gary R. Howe
Leland S. McCullough
Fred W. Finlinson
Dorothy C. Pleshe
John A. Beckstead
Jeffrey N. Clayton
James R. Holbrook
Charles M. Bennett
W. Waldan Lloyd
James R. Black
H. Russell Hettinger
Jeffrey L. Shields
Steven E. Tyler
Craig F. McCullough
Randall D Benson
R. Willis Orton
George E. Harris, Jr.
T. Richard Davis
Damon E. Coombs
Brian W. Burnett
Cass C. Butler
Andrés Diaz
Lynda Cook
John H. Rees
Mark L. Callister
P. Bryan Fishburn
Jan M. Bergeson

John B. Lindsay
Douglas K. Cummings
Lucy Knight Andre
Kathryn Cook Knight
Zachary T. Shields
Penni Ann Johnson

OF COUNSEL

Wayne L. Black
Richard H. Nebeker
Fred L. Finlinson
Earl P. Staten

Representative Clients: Zions First National Bank; Western Farm Credit Bank; Chrysler Credit Corp.; Utah Automobile Dealers Association; Sinclair Oil (Little America); Keystone Communications; Central Valley Water Reclamation Facility Board; Citicorp; Intermountain Health Care; Children's Miracle Network (Osmond Foundation).

For full biographical listings, see the Martindale-Hubbell Law Directory

Campbell Maack & Sessions, A Professional Corporation (AV)

One Utah Center Thirteenth Floor, 201 South Main Street, 84111-2115
Telephone: 801-537-5555
Telecopier: 801-537-5199

Robert S. Campbell, Jr.
Robert D. Maack
Clark W. Sessions
E. Barney Gesas
Kevin Egan Anderson
Martin R. Denney
Tracy H. Fowler
Mark A. Larsen
Perrin R. Love

Dean C. Andreasen
Jay W. Butler
Stephen R. Cochell
Joann Shields
William H. Christensen

Representative Clients: American Honda Motor Co., Inc.; BMC West Corp.; Boise Cascade Corp.; Nucor Steel Co.; Town of Alta; Westinghouse Electric Co.

(See Next Column)

For full biographical listings, see the Martindale-Hubbell Law Directory

Chapman and Cutler (AV)

Suite 800, Key Bank Tower, 50 South Main Street, 84144
Telephone: 801-533-0066
Fax: 801-533-9595
Chicago, Illinois Office: 111 West Monroe Street.
Telephone: 312-845-3000.
TWX: 910-221-2103.
Fax: 312-701-2361.
Phoenix, Arizona Office: Suite 1100, One Renaissance Square, 2 North Central Avenue.
Telephone: 602-256-4060.
Fax: 602-256-4099.

James C. Burr
Darrell R. Larsen, Jr.
Richard J. Scott

Bradley D. Patterson
Donald B. Rohbock
David J. Stevens
Rodney G. Wendt

For full biographical listings, see the Martindale-Hubbell Law Directory

Giauque, Crockett, Bendinger & Peterson, A Professional Corporation (AV)

First Interstate Plaza, 170 South Main, Suite 400, 84101-1664
Telephone: 801-533-8383
Fax: 801-531-1486

Richard W. Giauque
Stephen G. Crockett
Gary F. Bendinger
Robert A. Peterson
Richard W. Casey
Stephen T. Hard
Milo Steven Marsden

OF COUNSEL

Roger D. Sandack
Robert D. Moore
Kevin M. McDonough

Steven E. McCowin
Douglas H. Patton
Stephen R. Waldron (Not admitted in UT)
Kathy A. Lavitt
Jeffery S. Williams
Catherine Agnoli
Catherine L. Brabson
Wesley D. Felix
Nanci Snow Bockelie

For full biographical listings, see the Martindale-Hubbell Law Directory

Hanson, Epperson & Smith, A Professional Corporation (AV)

4 Triad Center, Suite 500, P.O. Box 2970, 84110-2970
Telephone: 801-363-7611
Fax: 801-531-9747

Rex J. Hanson (1911-1980)
David H. Epperson
Lowell V. Smith
Robert R. Wallace
Scott W. Christensen
Terry M. Plant
Theodore E. Kanell
John N. Braithwaite
Richard K. Glauser
Mark J. Williams
Daniel Stoddar McConkie

Jaryl L. Rencher
Eric K. Davenport
Daniel Lee Steele
David S. Doty
Bradley R. Helsten
Bruce M. Pritchett, Jr.

Representative Clients: State Farm Ins. Co.; Continental Insurance Cos. (C.N.A.); St. Paul Fire & Marine; Kemper Insurance Group; Prudential Insurance; Transamerica Insurance Co.; Ranger Insurance; Guaranty National Ins. Co.; Utah Transit Authority; Western Surety.

For full biographical listings, see the Martindale-Hubbell Law Directory

Holme Roberts & Owen LLC (AV)

Suite 1100, 111 East Broadway, 84111
Telephone: 801-521-5800
Telecopier: 801-521-9639
Denver, Colorado Office: Suite 4100, 1700 Lincoln.
Telephone: 303-861-7000.
Telex: 45-4460.
Telecopier: 303-866-0200.
Boulder, Colorado Office: Suite 400, 1401 Pearl Street.
Telephone: 303-444-5955.
Telecopier: 303-444-1063.
Colorado Springs, Colorado Office: Suite 1300, 90 South Cascade Avenue.
Telephone: 719-473-3800.
Telecopier: 719-633-1518.
London, England Office: 4th Floor, Mellier House, 26a Albemarle Street.
Telephone: 44-171-499-8776.
Telecopier: 44-171-499-7769.
Moscow, Russia Office: 14 Krivokolenny Pr., Suite 30, 101000.
Telephone: 095-925-7816.
Telecopier: 095-923-2726.

(See Next Column)

HOLME ROBERTS & OWEN LLC—*Continued*

MEMBERS OF FIRM

Brent V. Manning
David K. Detton
R. Bruce Johnson
Mark K. Buchi (Managing Member)
McKay Marsden
LeGrand R. Curtis, Jr.
P. Christian Anderson
Alan C. Bradshaw
David Harold Little
Wm. Kelly Nash
Wm. Robert Wright
David J. Crapo

ASSOCIATES

Jensie L. Anderson
Steven C. Bednar
Diane D. Card
Mary C. Gordon
Pamela B. Hunsaker
Richard E. Malmgren
Sheri Ann Mower
Alan Romero
Gary R. Thorup
R. Gary Winger

For full biographical listings, see the Martindale-Hubbell Law Directory

JONES, WALDO, HOLBROOK & McDONOUGH, A PROFESSIONAL CORPORATION (AV)

1500 First Interstate Plaza, 170 South Main Street, 84101
Telephone: 801-521-3200
Telecopier: 801-328-0537
Mailing Address: P.O. Box 45444, 84145-0444
St. George, Utah Office: The Tabernacle Tower Building, 249 East Tabernacle.
Telephone: 801-628-1627.
Telecopier: 801-628-5225.
Washington, D.C. Office: Suite 900, 2300 M Street, N.W.
Telephone: 202-296-5950.
Telecopier: 202-293-2509.

Joseph S. Jones (1905-1988)
Harold R. Waldo, Jr. (1928-1975)
Donald B. Holbrook
Randon W. Wilson
K. S. Cornaby
James S. Lowrie
Ronny L. Cutshall
Christopher L. Burton
Harry E. McCoy, II
D. Miles Holman
John W. Palmer (Resident, St. George Office)
Craig R. Mariger
David B. Lee (Resident, Washington D.C. Office)
Barry D. Wood (Resident, Washington, D.C. Office)
Timothy B. Anderson (Resident, St. George Office)
Elizabeth M. Haslam
G. Rand Beacham (Resident, St. George Office)
Randall N. Skanchy
Steven D. Peterson
James E. Gleason
Bruce E. Babcock
George W. Pratt III
James W. Stewart
Timothy C. Houpt
Paul M. Harman
Robert G. Pruitt, III
Vincent C. Rampton
Thomas G. Bennett
Ronald S. Poelman
James W. Burch
Kay Allan Morrell (Resident, Washington, D.C. Office)
D. Williams Ronnow (P.C.) (Resident, St. George Office)
Keven M. Rowe
Michael Patrick O'Brien
Andrew H. Stone
James W. Peters
Jerome Romero
Michael R. Shaw (Resident, St. George Office)
Gregory Cropper

Barry G. Lawrence
Michael J. Kelley
Jeffrey N. Walker
Deno G. Himonas
Alice L. Whitacre
Lisa M. Rischer
Howard C. Young
D. James Morgan
Shannon Stewart
Scott D. Cheney
Daniel A. Kaplan
Rob M. Alston
Susan B. Peterson
David M. Milan
John J. Walton (Resident, St. George Office)
Lewis McKay Francis

OF COUNSEL

Hill, Harrison, Johnson & Schmutz, P.C., , Provo, Utah
Calvin L. Rampton
Sidney G. Baucom
Timothy D. Kelley (Not admitted in UT)
Roger J. McDonough
Gary A. Terry (Resident, St. George Office)
Alden B. Tueller

LEGAL SUPPORT PERSONNEL

Larry Jay Pearson, CPA (Director of Administration)

Counsel for: First Interstate Bank of Utah, N.A.; Questar Corp.; Newspaper Agency Corp.; American Stores Co.; Skaggs Telecommunications Service, Inc.; Lucky Stores, Inc.; Alpha Beta Co.; Intermountain Farmers Assn.; Design Professional Insurance Co.; Blue Cross and Blue Shield of Utah.

For full biographical listings, see the Martindale-Hubbell Law Directory

KIMBALL, PARR, WADDOUPS, BROWN & GEE, A PROFESSIONAL CORPORATION (AV)

Suite 1300, 185 South State Street, P.O. Box 11019, 84147
Telephone: 801-532-7840
Fax: 801-532-7750

(See Next Column)

Dale A. Kimball
Clayton J. Parr
Clark Waddoups
Richard G. Brown
David E. Gee
Scott W. Loveless
Patricia W. Christensen
David K. Redd
Robert G. Holt
James C. Swindler
Robert B. Lochhead
Gary A. Dodge
Robert S. Clark
Alan R. Andersen
Michael M. Later
Carolyn B. McHugh
Steven J. Christiansen
Scott F. Young
Victor A. Taylor
Ronald G. Russell
Roger D. Henriksen
Mark E. Wilkey
Matthew B. Durrant
Jill Niederhauser Parrish
Brian J. Romriell
Gregory D. Phillips
David G. Angerbauer
Heidi E. C. Leithead
John M. Burke
Stephen E. W. Hale
Daniel A. Jensen
Mark F. James
David B. Hancock
Brian G. Lloyd
David F. Crabtree
Scott R. Ryther
Gregory M. Hess
Terry E. Welch
Jeffery J. Hunt
Paul C. Drecksel
Clay W. Stucki
D. Matthew Dorny
Mark A. Wagner
Jeffrey M. Moss
Margaret E. Wilson
Robert A. McConnell
Bentley J. Tolk
Christian J. Rowley

OF COUNSEL

Charles L. Maak
Bruce A. Maak
Kent H. Collins

For full biographical listings, see the Martindale-Hubbell Law Directory

KIPP AND CHRISTIAN, P.C. (AV)

175 East 400 South 330 City Centre I, 84111
Telephone: 801-521-3773
Fax: 801-359-9004

Carman E. Kipp
D. Gary Christian
J. Anthony Eyre
William W. Barrett
Gregory J. Sanders
Heinz J. Mahler
Michael F. Skolnick
Shawn McGarry
Kirk G. Gibbs
Sandra L. Steinvoort

OF COUNSEL

Lawrence D. Buhler

LEGAL SUPPORT PERSONNEL

M. Korinne Ellsworth

Representative Clients: United States Fidelity & Guaranty Co.; Capital City Bank/BankOne; Utah State Bar; Home Ins. Co.; National Farmers Union Ins. Co.; Utah Medical Insurance Association (UMIA); Utah Paper Box; Skivations, Condominium & Land Developers; Montgomery Elevators; Tim Dahle Imports/Nissan.

For full biographical listings, see the Martindale-Hubbell Law Directory

KIRTON & McCONKIE, A PROFESSIONAL CORPORATION (AV)

1800 Eagle Gate Tower, 60 East South Temple, 84111
Telephone: 801-328-3600
Telecopier: 801-321-4893

Wilford W. Kirton, Jr.
Oscar W. McConkie, Jr.
Raymond W. Gee
Anthony I. Bentley, Jr.
J. Douglas Mitchell
Richard R. Neslen
Myron L. Sorensen
Robert W. Edwards
B. Lloyd Poelman
Raeburn G. Kennard
Jerry W. Dearinger
R. Bruce Findlay
Charles W. Dahlquist, II
M. Karlynn Hinman
Robert P. Lunt
Brinton R. Burbidge
Gregory S. Bell
Lee Ford Hunter
Larry R. White
William H. Wingo
David M. McConkie
Read R. Hellewell
Rolf H. Berger
Oscar W. McConkie, III
Marc Nick Mascaro
David A. Westerby
Lorin C. Barker
David M. Wahlquist
Robert S. Prince
Wallace O. Felsted
Merrill F. Nelson
Paul H. Matthews
Fred D. Essig
Clark B. Fetzer
Samuel D. McVey
Blake T. Ostler
Daniel Bay Gibbons
Gregory M. Simonsen
Von G. Keetch
Patrick Hendrickson
Stuart F. Weed
Thomas D. Walk
James E. Ellsworth
Daniel V. Goodsell
David J. Hardy
Val D. Ricks
Randy T. Austin

OF COUNSEL

Richard G. Johnson, Jr.

For full biographical listings, see the Martindale-Hubbell Law Directory

MORGAN & HANSEN (AV)

Kearns Building, Eighth Floor, 136 South Main Street, 84101
Telephone: 801-531-7888
Telefax: 801-531-9732

(See Next Column)

MORGAN & HANSEN, *Salt Lake City—Continued*

MEMBERS OF FIRM

Stephen G. Morgan
Darwin C. Hansen
John C. Hansen
Cynthia K.C. Meyer
Mitchel T. Rice
Joseph E. Minnock
Eric C. Singleton

OF COUNSEL

Dennis R. James

Representative Clients: Albertsons, Inc.; Smith's Food and Drug Center's Inc.; Colorado Casualty; Farmers Insurance Group; St. Paul Fire and Marine Insurance Co.; State Farm Fire and Casualty; State Farm Mutual Automobile Insurance Co.; Utah Farm Bureau Insurance Company.

For full biographical listings, see the Martindale-Hubbell Law Directory

PARRY MURRAY WARD & MOXLEY, A PROFESSIONAL CORPORATION (AV)

1270 Eagle Gate Tower, 60 East South Temple, 84111
Telephone: 801-521-3434
Fax: 801-521-3484

Douglas J. Parry
Kevin Reid Murray
Brent D. Ward
Paul T. Moxley

OF COUNSEL

Richard J. Lawrence
James E. Cannon

David M. McGrath
Robert E. Mansfield
James K. Tracy
Bret F. Randall
Brad W. Merrill
Cathleen Clark

Representative Clients: Zions First National Bank; Trammell Crow Co.; Monroc; Salt Lake County Water Conservancy District; Blaine Hudson Printing; Western Petroleum; Aloha Petroleum; Minit-Lube Franchisee Assoc.; Preferred Reductions Services.

For full biographical listings, see the Martindale-Hubbell Law Directory

PRINCE, YEATES & GELDZAHLER (AV)

City Centre I, Suite 900, 175 East 400 South, 84111
Telephone: 801-524-1000
Fax: 801-524-1099
Park City, Utah Office: 614 Main Street, P.O. Box 38.
Telephones: 801-524-1000; 649-7440.

MEMBERS OF FIRM

John K. Mangum (1930-1971)
F. Seaton Prince (1910-1991)
Ronald F. Sysak (1938-1993)
David S. Geldzahler (1932-1994)
Robert M. Yeates
Denis Roy Morrill
Jon C. Heaton
John P. Ashton
Richard L. Blanck
John M. Bradley
D. Jay Gamble
C. Craig Liljenquist
J. Randall Call
John S. Chindlund
Geoffrey W. Mangum
James A. Boevers
Ronald E. Nehring
David K. Broadbent
Thomas J. Erbin
M. David Eckersley
Robert G. Wing
Carl W. Barton
Gregory E. Lindley

ASSOCIATES

Sally Buck McMinimee
Roger J. McConkie
Michael D. McCully
Elizabeth M. Peck
Thomas R. Barton

OF COUNSEL

Lyle M. Ward
Kenneth A. Okazaki
Victor A. Pollak

For full biographical listings, see the Martindale-Hubbell Law Directory

RAY, QUINNEY & NEBEKER, A PROFESSIONAL CORPORATION (AV)

Suite 400 Deseret Building, 79 South Main Street, P.O. Box 45385, 84145-0385
Telephone: 801-532-1500
Telecopier: 801-532-7543
Provo, Utah Office: 210 First Security Bank Building, 92 North University Avenue.
Telephone: 801-226-7210.
Telecopier: 801-375-8379.

Paul H. Ray (1893-1967)
C. Preston Allen (1921-1971)
Marvin J. Bertoch (1915-1979)
A. H. Nebeker (1895-1980)
S. J. Quinney (1893-1983)
L. Ridd Larson (1935-1990)
Albert E. Bowen (1905-1993)
Alonzo W. Watson, Jr.
Stephen B. Nebeker
Herschel J. Saperstein
Mitchell Melich
Don B. Allen
Clark P. Giles
Robert M. Graham
Narrvel E. Hall
James L. Wilde (Resident at Provo)
Herbert C. Livsey
William A. Marshall
Paul S. Felt
D. Jay Curtis
Gerald T. Snow

(See Next Column)

Alan A. Enke
Weston L. Harris
Jonathan A. Dibble
Scott Hancock Clark
Steven H. Gunn
James S. Jardine
Allan T. Brinkerhoff
Janet Hugie Smith
Douglas Matsumori
Robert P. Hill
Richard G. Allen
Floyd Andrew Jensen
Allen L. Orr
Brad D. Hardy
A. Robert Thorup
John P. Harrington
Brent W. Todd
Larry G. Moore
Dale M. Okerlund
Bruce L. Olson
John A. Adams
Douglas M. Monson
Craig Carlile (Resident at Provo)
James M. Dester
Dee R. Chambers
Kevin G. Glade
Lester K. Essig
Ira B. Rubinfeld
Boyd A. Ferguson
Steven T. Waterman
Stephen C. Tingey
Kelly J. Flint
John R. Madsen
Steven J. Aeschbacher
Keith A. Kelly
Mark M. Bettilyon
Rick L. Rose
Rick B. Hoggard
Lisa A. Yerkovich
Brent D. Wride
Michael E. Blue
Scott A. Hagen
Steven W. Call

Cameron M. Hancock
Elaine A. Monson
Sylvia I. Iannucci
Katie A. Eccles
George S. Adondakis
David A. Cutt
Calvin Carl Curtis
Robert O. Rice
Dianna R. Woolsey
Frederick R. Thaler, Jr.
John W. Mackay

OF COUNSEL

M. John Ashton

Representative Clients: First Security Bank of Utah, N.A.; Borden, Inc.; Southern Pacific Transportation; Utah Power & Light Co.; Travelers Insurance Co.; Greyhound Leasing & Financial; Holy Cross Hospital and Health System; Amoco Production Co.

For full biographical listings, see the Martindale-Hubbell Law Directory

SNOW, CHRISTENSEN & MARTINEAU (AV)

Formerly Worsley, Snow & Christensen.
10 Exchange Place, Eleventh Floor, P.O. Box 45000, 84145
Telephone: 801-521-9000
Telecopier: 801-363-0400

MEMBERS OF FIRM

Wood R. Worsley (1913-1975)
John H. Snow (1917-1980)
Reed L. Martineau
Stuart L. Poelman
H. James Clegg
David W. Slagle
A. Dennis Norton
Allan L. Larson
John E. Gates
R. Brent Stephens
Kim R. Wilson
Michael R. Carlston
David G. Williams
Rex E. Madsen
Max D. Wheeler
Robert H. Henderson
Stephen J. Hill
David W. Slaughter
Stanley J. Preston
Joy L. Clegg
Shawn E. Draney
John R. Lund
Ryan E. Tibbitts
Anne Swensen
Rodney R. Parker
Richard A. Van Wagoner
Robert C. Keller
Scott Daniels
Andrew M. Morse

OF COUNSEL

Harold G. Christensen
Gordon R. Hall
Merlin R. Lybbert
Joseph Novak
Travis L. Bowen
Bryan A. Geurts

ASSOCIATES

Marc T. Wangsgard
Rick J. Hall
Camille Neddo Johnson
Randall D. Lund
Terence L. Rooney
Dennis V. Dahle
Korey D. Rasmussen
David L. Pinkston
David B. Dellenbach
Julianne Blanch
Brian P. Miller
Timothy Farrell

Representative Clients: General Motors Corp.; General Electric Co.; Ryder Systems, Inc.; Utah State Medical Assn.; Royal Insurance Co.; Novell, Inc.; The Hartford.

For full biographical listings, see the Martindale-Hubbell Law Directory

STRONG & HANNI, A PROFESSIONAL CORPORATION (AV)

Sixth Floor Boston Building, 9 Exchange Place, 84111
Telephone: 801-532-7080
Fax: 801-596-1508

Gordon R. Strong (1909-1969)
Glenn C. Hanni
Henry E. Heath
Philip R. Fishler
Roger H. Bullock
Robert A. Burton
R. Scott Williams
Dennis M. Astill (Managing Partner)
S. Baird Morgan
Stuart H. Schultz
Paul M. Belnap
Stephen J. Trayner
Joseph J. Joyce
Bradley Wm. Bowen

(See Next Column)

STRONG & HANNI A PROFESSIONAL CORPORATION—*Continued*

Robert L. Janicki
Elizabeth L. Willey
Peter H. Christensen
H. Burt Ringwood
David R. Nielson
Adam Trupp
Catherine M. Larson

Representative Clients: State Farm Mutual Automobile Insurance Co.; Standard Accident Insurance Co.; United Services Automobile Assn.; Western Casualty & Surety Co.; Government Employees Insurance Co.; Guaranty Mutual Life Co.

For full biographical listings, see the Martindale-Hubbell Law Directory

---

SUITTER AXLAND & HANSON, A PROFESSIONAL LAW CORPORATION (AV)

7th Floor, 175 South West Temple Street, 84101-1480
Telephone: 801-532-7300
Facsimile: 801-532-7355

Francis H. Suitter
LeRoy S. Axland (1941-1990)
William L. Prater
David R. Olsen
Bruce T. Jones
Jerold G. Oldroyd
Francis J. Carney
J. Michael Hansen
Carl F. Huefner
Andrew W. Buffmire
Michael W. Homer
Dan W. Egan
Michael L. Allen
Charles P. Sampson
Jesse C. Trentadue
Paul M. Simmons
Claudia F. Berry
Gary R. Henrie
H. Michael Drake
Mark R. Gaylord
Lorin E. Patterson
Jill L. Dunyon-Hansen
Dahnelle B. Burton

OF COUNSEL

Stewart M. Hanson, Jr.

Representative Clients: Aetna Insurance Cos.; Amoco Corp.; Evans & Sutherland Computer Corp.; Ernst & Young; Fleming Cos., Inc.; Dean Witter; Discover & Co.; State of Utah, Department of Financial Institutions; Suburban/Petrolane Propane; Title Insurance Co. of Minnesota.

For full biographical listings, see the Martindale-Hubbell Law Directory

---

VAN COTT, BAGLEY, CORNWALL & MCCARTHY, A PROFESSIONAL CORPORATION (AV)

Suite 1600, 50 South Main Street, P.O. Box 45340, 84145
Telephone: 801-532-3333
Telex: 453149
Telecopier: 801-534-0058
Ogden, Utah Office: Suite 900, 2404 Washington Boulevard.
Telephone: 801-394-5783.
Park City, Utah Office: 314 Main Street, Suite 205.
Telephone: 801-649-3889.
Reno, Nevada Office: Jeppson & Lee, 100 West Liberty, Suite 990.
Telephone: 702-333-6800.

David E. Salisbury
M. Scott Woodland
Norman S. Johnson
Stephen D. Swindle
Robert D. Merrill
William G. Fowler
Gregory P. Williams
Alan F. Mecham
Brent J. Giauque
E. Scott Savage
Kenneth W. Yeates
Rand L. Cook
John A. Snow
David A. Greenwood
Maxilian A. Farbman
Arthur B. Ralph
Alan L. Sullivan
J. Keith Adams
Thomas T. Billings
Richard C. Skeen
John T. Nielsen
Michael F. Richman
Danny C. Kelly
Steven D. Woodland
Richard H. Johnson, II
H. Michael Keller
Brent Christensen
Jeffrey E. Nelson
Patricia M. Leith
R. Stephen Marshall
Thomas Berggren
Ervin R. Holmes
Ronald G. Moffitt
Eric C. Olson
Patrick J. O'Hara
Matthew F. McNulty, III
S. Robert Bradley
Jon C. Christiansen
Guy P. Kroesche
John A. Anderson
Wayne D. Swan
Gregory N. Barrick
Scott M. Hadley (Resident, Ogden, Utah Office)
Timothy W. Blackburn (Resident, Ogden, Utah Office)
Donald L. Dalton
Gerald H. Suniville
David L. Arrington
Casey K. McGarvey
Douglas A. Taggart (Resident, Ogden, Utah Office)
Kathryn Holmes Snedaker
Phyllis J. Vetter
Jeremy M. Hoffman
Clark K. Taylor
Bryon J. Benevento
Roger W. Jeppson (Resident, Reno, Nevada)
Keith L. Lee (Resident, Reno, Nevada Office)

OF COUNSEL

Leonard J. Lewis
Clifford L. Ashton
Richard K. Sager
James P. Cowley
John Crawford, Jr.
Marlin K. Jensen
George M. McMillan
J. Holmes Armstead, Jr. (Resident, Reno, Nevada Office)

(See Next Column)

Susan Pierce Lawrence
Robert W. Payne
James D. Gilson
Nathan W. Jones
Elizabeth D. Winter
Jon E. Waddoups
David E. Sloan
Bradley R. Cahoon
David E. Allen
Melyssa D. Davidson
Craig W. Dallon
Sandra L. Crosland
Michele Ballantyne
Thomas W. Clawson
Daniel P. McCarthy
Pamela Martinson
Matthew M. Durham
S. Blake Parrish
Preston C. Regehr
A. Craig Hale
Michael T. Roberts (Resident, Ogden, Utah Office)
Todd M. Shaughnessy
Andrew S. Gabriel (Resident, Reno, Nevada Office)
Mark G. Simons (Resident, Reno, Nevada Office)
R. Blain Andrus (Resident, Reno, Nevada Office)

Representative Clients: Standard Oil Company of California (and affiliated companies); FMC Corp.; Leucadia National Corp.; Key Bank of Utah; Southern Pacific Lines; Intermountain Health Care, Inc.; Huntsman Chemical Corp.; Iomega Corp.; Metropolitan Life Ins. Co.

For full biographical listings, see the Martindale-Hubbell Law Directory

VERMONT

*BENNINGTON,** Bennington Co. — (Refer to Rutland)

BRATTLEBORO, Windham Co.

CRISPE & CRISPE (AV)

114 Main Street, P.O. Box 556, 05302
Telephone: 802-254-4441
Fax: 802-254-4482

A. Luke Crispe (1911-1992)
Lawrin P. Crispe

ASSOCIATES

Kristen Swartwout

Representative Clients: Mutual of New York; The Stratton Corp.; Liberty Mutual Insurance Co.; DeWitt Beverage Co.

For full biographical listings, see the Martindale-Hubbell Law Directory

KRISTENSEN, CUMMINGS & MURTHA, P.C. (AV)

5 Grove Street, P.O. Box 677, 05302-0677
Telephone: 802-254-8733
FAX: 802-254-8860

John G. Kristensen
Charles R. Cummings
J. Garvan Murtha

Stephen R. Phillips
Richard C. Carroll
Joseph C. Galanes

LEGAL SUPPORT PERSONNEL

Mary Louise Nelson (Paralegal)

For full biographical listings, see the Martindale-Hubbell Law Directory

WEBER, PERRA & WILSON, P.C. (AV)

16 Linden Street, P.O. Box 558, 05302
Telephone: 802-257-7161
Fax: 802-257-0572

E. Bruce Weber
Raymond P. Perra
Douglas U. Wilson
Richard H. Munzing
Lucy W. McVitty

For full biographical listings, see the Martindale-Hubbell Law Directory

*BURLINGTON,** Chittenden Co.

BURAK & ANDERSON (AV)

Executive Square, 346 Shelburne Street, P.O. Box 64700, 05406-4700
Telephone: 802-862-0500
Telecopier: 802-862-8176

MEMBERS OF FIRM

Michael L. Burak
Jon Anderson
Thomas R. Melloni
David M. Hyman

ASSOCIATES

Brian J. Sullivan
Robert I. Goetz
Andrew H. Montroll
Josephine L. Peyser
Julie D. M. Sovern

For full biographical listings, see the Martindale-Hubbell Law Directory

DINSE, ERDMANN & CLAPP (AV)

209 Battery Street, P.O. Box 988, 05402
Telephone: 802-864-5751
Telecopier: 802-864-1960

COUNSEL

John M. Dinse

MEMBERS OF FIRM

Robert H. Erdmann
Michael B. Clapp
Spencer R. Knapp
Karen McAndrew
Barbara E. Cory
Robert R. McKearin
James W. Spink
John D. Monahan, Jr.
Emily R. Morrow
Ritchie E. Berger
Austin D. Hart
Samuel Hoar, Jr.
Steven L. Knudson

ASSOCIATES

Noah Paley
Sandra Strempel
Molly K. Lebowitz
Pietro J. Lynn
Philip C. Woodward
Sarah Gentry Tischler
Susan J. Flynn
Jeffrey J. Nolan
Douglas D. Le Brun
Shapleigh Smith, Jr.
Robert A. Spencer

Representative Clients: Chittenden Trust Co.; Vermont Transit Co., Inc.; Sears, Roebuck & Co.; Ford Motor Co.; Medical Center Hospital of Vermont, Inc.; Middlebury College.

For full biographical listings, see the Martindale-Hubbell Law Directory

GRAVEL AND SHEA, A PROFESSIONAL CORPORATION (AV)

Corporate Plaza, 76 St. Paul Street, P.O. Box 369, 05402-0369
Telephone: 802-658-0220
Fax: 802-658-1456

Charles T. Shea
Stephen R. Crampton
Stewart H. McConaughy
Robert B. Hemley
William G. Post, Jr.
Craig Weatherly
James E. Knapp
John R. Ponsetto
Dennis R. Pearson
Peter S. Erly
Robert F. O'Neill
Margaret L. Montgomery

Lucy T. Brown
James L. Vana
Stephen P. Magowan
Karin J. Immergut (Not admitted in VT)

OF COUNSEL

Clarke A. Gravel

SPECIAL COUNSEL

Norman Williams

For full biographical listings, see the Martindale-Hubbell Law Directory

HOFF, CURTIS, PACHT, CASSIDY & FRAME, P.C. (AV)

100 Main Street, P.O. Box 1124, 05402-1124
Telephone: 802-864-4531
Fax: 802-860-1565

Richard T. Cassidy
Julie A. Frame
Philip H. Hoff
Jennifer E. Nelson
John L. Pacht
Robert W. Katims
Richard H. Thomas

OF COUNSEL

David W. Curtis

For full biographical listings, see the Martindale-Hubbell Law Directory

LISMAN & LISMAN, A PROFESSIONAL CORPORATION (AV)

84 Pine Street, P.O. Box 728, 05402-0728
Telephone: 802-864-5756
Fax: 802-864-3629

Carl H. Lisman
Allen D. Webster
Mary G. Kirkpatrick
E. William Leckerling, III
Douglas K. Riley

Judith Lillian Dillon
Richard W. Kozlowski

OF COUNSEL

Bernard Lisman
Louis Lisman

For full biographical listings, see the Martindale-Hubbell Law Directory

MANCHESTER LAW OFFICES, PROFESSIONAL CORPORATION (AV)

One Lawson Lane, P.O. Box 1459, 05402-1459
Telephone: 802-658-7444
Fax: 802-658-2078

Robert E. Manchester
Patricia S. Orr

LEGAL SUPPORT PERSONNEL

LEGAL NURSE CONSULTANTS

Tina L Mulvey
Rosemeryl S. Harple
Maureen P. Tremblay

For full biographical listings, see the Martindale-Hubbell Law Directory

MILLER, EGGLESTON & ROSENBERG, LTD. (AV)

150 South Champlain Street, P.O. Box 1489, 05402-1489
Telephone: 802-864-0880
Telecopier: 802-864-0328

Martin K. Miller
Jon R. Eggleston
Michael B. Rosenberg
Anne E. Cramer
Kathleen M. Boe

Mark A. Saunders
Victoria J. Brown
Peter F. Young
Frederick S. Lane III

OF COUNSEL

Catherine Kronk

For full biographical listings, see the Martindale-Hubbell Law Directory

SHEEHEY BRUE GRAY & FURLONG, PROFESSIONAL CORPORATION (AV)

119 South Winooski Avenue, P.O. Box 66, 05402
Telephone: 802-864-9891
Facsimile: 802-864-6815

(See Next Column)

SHEEHEY BRUE GRAY & FURLONG PROFESSIONAL CORPORATION—*Continued*

William B. Gray (1942-1994)
David T. Austin
R. Jeffrey Behm
Nordahl L. Brue
Michael G. Furlong
Ralphine Newlin O'Rourke
Donald J. Rendall, Jr.
Christina Schulz
Paul D. Sheehey
Peter H. Zamore

Rebecca L. Owen

Representative Client: Green Mountain Power Corp.

For full biographical listings, see the Martindale-Hubbell Law Directory

*CHELSEA,** Orange Co. — (Refer to Montpelier)

ESSEX JUNCTION, Chittenden Co.

KOLVOORD, OVERTON AND WILSON (AV)

3 Main Street, 05452
Telephone: 802-878-3346
FAX: 802-879-0964

Philip A. Kolvoord
Alan D. Overton
Gregg H. Wilson
Michael D. Danley

ASSOCIATES

Herbert J. Downing
Carol N. Angus
Daniel L. Overton

Representative Clients: The Howard Bank; Chittenden Bank; S. T. Griswold & Co., Inc. (Construction); Aquatec, Inc. (Environmental Studies); Burlington Savings Bank; Champlain Water District (Regional Water Municipality); Town of Essex School District; Town of Jericho; International Business Machines (IBM Corp.).

MANCHESTER CENTER, Bennington Co. — (Refer to Rutland)

*MIDDLEBURY,** Addison Co.

CONLEY & FOOTE (AV)

11 South Pleasant Street, P.O. Drawer 391, 05753
Telephone: 802-388-4061
Fax: 802-388-0210

MEMBERS OF FIRM

John T. Conley (1900-1971)
Ralph A. Foote
Charity A. Downs
D. Michael Mathes
Richard P. Foote
Janet P. Shaw

For full biographical listings, see the Martindale-Hubbell Law Directory

*MONTPELIER,** Washington Co.

THERIAULT & JOSLIN, P.C. (AV)

141 Main Street, P.O. Box 249, 05601-0249
Telephone: 802-223-2381
Fax: 802-223-1461

William N. Theriault (1877-1961)
Peter B. Joslin
Fletcher Brian (Ted) Joslin

Peter S. Cullen
John Davis Buckley
Robert S. Behrens

OF COUNSEL

Fletcher B. Joslin
Jeffry W. White

LEGAL SUPPORT PERSONNEL

Betsy A. LaFlame

Representative Clients: Allstate Insurance Co.; American International Cos.; Hartford Insurance Group; St. Paul Insurance Cos.; Nationwide Insurance Cos.; Metropolitan Insurance Co.; American Home Group; Commercial Union Insurance Cos.; Prudential Insurance Cos.; PHICO Insurance Co.

For full biographical listings, see the Martindale-Hubbell Law Directory

*NEWPORT,** Orleans Co. — (Refer to Montpelier)

*RUTLAND,** Rutland Co.

CARROLL, GEORGE & PRATT (AV)

64 & 66 North Main Street, P.O. Box 280, 05702-0280
Telephone: 802-775-7141
Telecopier: 802-775-6483
Woodstock, Vermont Office: The Mill - Route #4 E., P.O. Box 388, 05091.
Telephone: 802-457-1000.
Telecopier: 802-457-1874.

MEMBERS OF FIRM

Henry G. Smith (1938-1974)
James P. Carroll
Alan B. George
Robert S. Pratt
Neal C. Vreeland
Jon S. Readnour
Timothy U. Martin
Randall F. Mayhew (Resident Partner, Woodstock Office)
Richard S. Smith
Judy Godnick Barone
John J. Kennelly

(See Next Column)

ASSOCIATES

Thomas A. Zonay
Jeffrey P. White
Susan Boyle Ford (Resident, Woodstock Office)
Charles C. Humpstone

For full biographical listings, see the Martindale-Hubbell Law Directory

DAVID L. CLEARY ASSOCIATES A PROFESSIONAL CORPORATION (AV)

110 Merchants Row, P.O. Box 6740, 05702-6740
Telephone: 802-775-8800
Telefax: 802-775-8809

David L. Cleary

Kaveh S. Shahi
George A. Holoch, Jr.
Ellen J. Abbott
Thomas P. Aicher
Karen S. Heald

For full biographical listings, see the Martindale-Hubbell Law Directory

HULL, WEBBER & REIS (AV)

(Formerly Dick, Hackel & Hull)
60 North Main Street, P.O. Box 890, 05702-0890
Telephone: 802-775-2361
Fax: 802-775-0739

Donald H. Hackel (1925-1985)
John B. Webber
Robert K. Reis
John C. Holler
Lisa L. Chalidze

ASSOCIATES

Phyllis R. McCoy
Karen Abatiell Kalter

OF COUNSEL

Richard A. Hull (P.C.)
Steven D. Vogl

Representative Clients: Aetna Insurance Co.; Great American Insurance Cos.

For full biographical listings, see the Martindale-Hubbell Law Directory

MILLER & FAIGNANT, A PROFESSIONAL CORPORATION (AV)

36 Merchants Row, P.O. Box 6688, 05702-6688
Telephone: 802-775-2521
Fax: 802-775-8274

Lawrence Miller
John Paul Faignant

Barbara R. Blackman
Christopher J. Whelton

LEGAL SUPPORT PERSONNEL

Cynthia L. Bonvouloir
Marie T. Fabian

Representative Clients: Travelers Insurance Co.; Government Employees Insurance Co.; Utica Mutual Insurance Co.; Universal Underwriters Insurance Co.
Reference: Travelers Insurance Co.

For full biographical listings, see the Martindale-Hubbell Law Directory

RYAN SMITH & CARBINE, LTD. (AV)

Mead Building, 98 Merchants Row, P.O. Box 310, 05702-0310
Telephone: (802)-773-3344
Fax: (802)-773-1343

Charles F. Ryan (1901-1977)
R. Clarke Smith
Leonard F. Wing, Jr.
R. Joseph O'Rourke
Joseph H. Badgewick
John J. Zawistoski
Thomas M. Dowling
E. Patrick Burke
Allan R. Keyes
Harry R. Ryan, III
Glenn S. Morgan
Harold P. Berger
James B. Anderson
William A. O'Rourke, III
Elizabeth A. Glynn

Marion T. Ferguson
Ellen W. Burgess
Martha M. Smyrski
Joan Loring Wing
Andrew H. Maass
Karl C. Anderson
John A. Serafino
Aaron Peter Eaton
John William Valente
Kimberly K. Hayden

Representative Clients: Casella Waste Management, Inc.; Central Vermont Public Service Corp.; First Vermont Bank; Rutland City Schools; Rutland Regional Medical Center; SKI LTD.; STO Industries; Maine Bonding Co.; St. Paul Insurance Co.; United States Fidelity & Guaranty Co.

For full biographical listings, see the Martindale-Hubbell Law Directory

*ST. ALBANS,** Franklin Co.

JAMES L. LEVY A PROFESSIONAL CORPORATION (AV)

79 North Main Street, 05478
Telephone: 802-524-2108

(See Next Column)

JAMES L. LEVY A PROFESSIONAL CORPORATION, *St. Albans—Continued*

James L. Levy

For full biographical listings, see the Martindale-Hubbell Law Directory

SPRINGFIELD, Windsor Co.

DOUGLAS RICHARDS, P.C. (AV)

85 Main Street, P.O. Box 200, 05156-0200
Telephone: 802-885-5131
FAX: 802-885-4699

Douglas Richards John E. Brady

For full biographical listings, see the Martindale-Hubbell Law Directory

*WOODSTOCK,** Windsor Co. — (Refer to White River Junction)

VIRGINIA

*ABINGDON,** Washington Co.

Tate, Lowe & Rowlett, P.C. (AV)

205 West Main Street, 24210
Telephone: 703-628-5185
Telecopier: 703-628-5045

Mary Lynn Tate
C. Randall Lowe
Fredrick A. Rowlett
Terrence Shea Cook

Representative Clients: Island Creek Coal Co.; Jewell Resources, Inc.; Pikeville National Bank; Charter Federal Savings Bank; Rapoca Energy Co.
Approved Attorneys for: Lawyers Title Insurance Co.; Safeco Title Insurance Co.; Nations Bank; First Virginia Bank; Bank of Marion; Central Fidelity Bank.

For full biographical listings, see the Martindale-Hubbell Law Directory

Yeary & Associates, P.C. (AV)

161 East Main Street, P.O. Box 1685, 24210
Telephone: 703-628-9107
Telecopier: 703-628-1998

Emmitt F. Yeary

W. Hobart Robinson
Kathleen Calvert Yeary

LEGAL SUPPORT PERSONNEL

Michael A. Bragg (Legal Assistant)

Representative Clients: Abingdon Nursing Homes, Inc.; D.S. Buck, Inc.; Food Country U.S.A., Inc.; East Gate Drug Stores of Abingdon, Inc.; Abingdon Printing, Inc.; ERA Anderson & Associates; Southwest Virginia Research & Development Corp.
Approved Attorneys for: Lawyers Title Insurance Co.; Chicago Title Insurance Co.

For full biographical listings, see the Martindale-Hubbell Law Directory

*ACCOMAC,** Accomack Co.

Ayres & Hartnett, P.C. (AV)

Court Green, 23301
Telephone: 804-787-1341
Fax: 804-787-8803

B. Drummond Ayres (1896-1984)
Daniel Hartnett

Representative Clients: United Virginia Bank, Onancock, Va.; U. S. Fidelity & Guaranty Co.; Aetna Casualty and Surety Co.; State Farm Insurance Companies; The Travelers; Liberty Mutual Insurance Co.

For full biographical listings, see the Martindale-Hubbell Law Directory

ALEXANDRIA, (Independent City)

Gold & Stanley, P.C. Professional Corporation (AV)

Third Floor, King Street Station, 1800 Diagonal Road, 22314-2808
Telephone: 703-836-7004
Facsimile: 703-548-9430
Silver Spring, Maryland Office: 1010 Wayne Avenue, Suite 1440.
Telephone: 301-589-7800.
Washington, D.C. Office: Suite 300, 1155 Connecticut Avenue, N.W.
Telephone: 703-836-7004.

H. Jason Gold
Daniel C. Stanley, Jr.
Valerie P. Morrison
Alexander M. Laughlin
John O. Long, III

Loraine E. O'Hanlon
Howard I. Rubin
Jill T. Deutsch

OF COUNSEL

Steven A. Silverman (Not admitted in VA)
Thomas C. Schild (Not admitted in VA)

For full biographical listings, see the Martindale-Hubbell Law Directory

Hazel & Thomas, A Professional Corporation (AV)

Suite 200, 510 King Street, P.O. Box 820, 22313
Telephone: 703-836-8400
Fairfax County (Falls Church), Virginia Office: Suite 1400, 3110 Fairview Park Drive, P.O. Box 12001.
Telephone: 703-641-4200.
Leesburg, Virginia Office: 44084 Riverside Parkway, Suite 300.
Telephone: 703-729-8500. Metro: 703-478-1992.
Manassas, Virginia Office: 9324 West Street, Third Floor.
Telephone: 703-330-7400. Metro: 703-803-7474.
Richmond, Virginia Office: Suite 600, 411 East Franklin Street, P.O. Box 788.
Telephone: 804-344-3400.

(See Next Column)

Michael A. Banzhaf (Resident, Leesburg Office)
Duane W. Beckhorn (Resident, Falls Church Office)
Kirk D. Beckhorn (Resident, Falls Church Office)
Benton Burroughs, Jr. (Resident, Falls Church Office)
E. William Chapman (Resident, Leesburg Office)
Bruce L. Christman (Resident, Falls Church Office)
John E. Coffey
John Paul Corrado
David C. Culbert (Resident, Leesburg Office)
R. Mark Dare (Resident, Falls Church Office)
Steven D. Delaney (Resident, Richmond Office)
Robert M. Diamond (Resident, Falls Church Office)
Robert M. Dilling (Resident, Falls Church Office)
S. Miles Dumville (Resident, Richmond Office)
H. Bradley Evans, Jr.
Karen C. Fagelson (Resident, Leesburg Office)
Gail W. Feagles (Resident, Falls Church Office)
Thomas R. Folk (Resident, Falls Church Office)
John H. Foote (Resident, Manassas Office)
Grady C. Frank, Jr.
Donald N. Goldrosen (Resident, Falls Church Office)
Patrick O. Gottschalk (Resident, Richmond Office)
Robert E. Gregg (Resident, Falls Church Office)
Grayson P. Hanes (Resident, Falls Church Office)
Henry A. Hart
John T. Hazel, Jr. (Resident, Falls Church Office)
A. Everett Hoeg, III (Resident, Falls Church Office)
John P. Holman (Resident, Falls Church Office)
Carol C. Honigberg (Resident, Falls Church Office)
Thomas C. Junker
Julia Krebs-Markrich (Resident, Falls Church Office)
James S. Kurz (Resident, Falls Church Office)
D. Patrick Lacy, Jr. (Resident, Richmond Office)
Robert A. Lawrence (Resident, Falls Church Office)
Joseph S. Luchini (Resident, Church Falls Office)
Bran R. Marron (Resident, Richmond Office)
Walter A. Marston, Jr. (Resident, Richmond Office)
Charles F. B. McAleer, Jr. (Resident, Falls Church Office)
Kathleen S. Mehfoud (Resident, Richmond Office)
J. Howard Middleton, Jr.
J. Randall Minchew (Resident, Leesburg Office)
Lee W. Morris (Resident, Falls Church Office)
Thomas W. Nalls (Resident, Leesburg Office)
Steven W. Pearson (Resident, Richmond Office)
Donna M. Phillips (Resident, Falls Church Office)
Jonathan P. Rak (Resident, Falls Church Office)
Anne M. Richard
John J. Sabourin, Jr. (Resident, Falls Church Office)
Richard C. Sullivan, Jr.
William Griffith Thomas
Benjamin F. Tompkins (Resident, Falls Church Office)
Anthony J. Trenga
Garth M. Wainman (Resident, Manassas Office)
Mark W. Wasserman
Robert B. Webb, III (Resident, Falls Church Office)
Wiley R. Wright, Jr. (Resident, Falls Church Office)
Michael L. Zupan

COUNSEL

Robert C. Fitzgerald (Resident, Falls Church Office)
H. Lane Kneedler (Resident, Richmond Office)
Patrick A. O'Hare (Resident, Richmond Office)
W. Lawrence Wallace, Sr. (Resident, Falls Church Office)

OF COUNSEL

Thomas Moore Lawson (Also practicing individually at Winchester)
John O. Marsh, Jr. (Falls Church Office; Also practicing individually at Winchester)
Richard C. Riemenschneider (Resident, Leesburg Office)
Linda C. Stokely (Resident, Falls Church Office)
Henry A. Thomas

Philip F. Abraham (Resident, Richmond Office)
John A. Burlingame
Michael S. Dingmam (Resident, Falls Church Office)
Geoffrey C. Dodson (Resident, Falls Church Office)
Merrell B. Green (Resident, Falls Church Office)
Dee Ann Herring
Darryl P. Hobbs (Resident, Falls Church Office)
Lisa Marie Hughes (Resident, Falls Church Office)
Vernon E. Inge, Jr. (Resident, Richmond Office)
Otto W. Konrad (Resident, Richmond Office)
Jennifer L. W. Korjus (Resident, Falls Church Office)
George E. Kostel (Resident, Falls Church Office)
Jonathan E. Lyon (Resident, Falls Church Office)
John L. McBride (Resident, Manassas Office)
Jeffery Keith Mitchell (Resident, Richmond Office)
Pamela G. Parsons (Resident, Richmond Office)
Deborah K. Raines (Resident, Falls Church Office)
Frederick K. Roseman (Resident, Falls Church Office)
Steven L. Rosenberg (Resident, Falls Church Office)
Thomas W. Smith, III (Resident, Manassas Office)
Julia Beecher Strickland (Resident, Falls Church Office)
Alison R. Wright

CONTRACT ATTORNEYS

David P. O'Brien (Resident, Leesburg Office)

(See Next Column)

HAZEL & THOMAS A PROFESSIONAL CORPORATION, *Alexandria—Continued*

LEGAL SUPPORT PERSONNEL

Sally K. Montrey (Director of Finance/Treasurer; Resident, Falls Church Office)

For full biographical listings, see the Martindale-Hubbell Law Directory

HOWARD, LEINO & HOWARD, P.C. (AV)

128 North Pitt Street, 22314
Telephone: 703-549-1188
Facsimile: 703-549-1533

T. Brooke Howard (1902-1990)
Blair D. Howard
John Frank Leino

For full biographical listings, see the Martindale-Hubbell Law Directory

MCGUIRE, WOODS, BATTLE & BOOTHE (AV)

Transpotomac Plaza, Suite 1000, 1199 North Fairfax Street, 22314-1437
Telephone: 703-739-6200
Fax: 703-739-6270
Baltimore, Maryland Office: The Blaustein Building, One North Charles Street, 21201-3793.
Telephone: 410-659-4400.
Fax: 410-659-4599.
Charlottesville, Virginia Office: Court Square Building, P.O. Box 1288, 22902-1288.
Telephone: 804-977-2500.
Fax: 804-980-2222.
Jacksonville, Florida Office: Barnett Center, Suite 2750, 50 North Laura Street, 32202-3635.
Telephone: 904-798-3200.
Fax: 904-798-3207.
McLean (Tysons Corner), Virginia Office: 8280 Greensboro Drive, Suite 900, Tysons Corner, 22102-3892.
Telephone: 703-712-5000.
Fax: 703-712-5050.
Norfolk, Virginia Office: World Trade Center, Suite 9000, 101 West Main Street, 23510-1655.
Telephone: 804-640-3700.
Fax: 804-640-3701.
Richmond, Virginia Office: One James Center, 901 East Cary Street, 23219-4030.
Telephone: 804-775-1000.
Fax: 804-775-1061.
Washington, D.C. Office: The Army and Navy Club Building, 1627 Eye Street, N.W., 20006-4007.
Telephone: 202-857-1700.
Fax: 202-857-1737.
Brussels, Belgium Office: 250 Avenue Louise, Ste. 64, 1050.
Telephone: (32 2) 629 42 11.
Fax: (32 2) 629 42 22.
Zürich, Switzerland Office: P.O. Box 4930, Bahnhofstrasse 3, 8022.
Telephone: (41 1) 225 20 00.
Fax: (41 1) 225 20 20.

MEMBERS OF FIRM

Fred C. Alexander, Jr.
C. Torrence Armstrong
John Foster Anderson
Stephen M. Colangelo
Philip Tierney

RESIDENT ASSOCIATES

Adrienne K. Dwyer
Laurie A. Hand
Michael Joseph Klisch

For full biographical listings, see the Martindale-Hubbell Law Directory

SHAW, PITTMAN, POTTS & TROWBRIDGE (AV)

A Partnership including Professional Corporations
115 South Union Street, 22314-3361
Telephone: 703-739-6650
Fax: 703-739-6699
Washington, D.C. Office: 2300 N Street, N.W.
Telephone: 202-663-8000.
Cable Address: "Shawlaw".
Telex: 89-2693 (Shawlaw Wsh).
Telecopier: 202-663-8007.
McLean, Virginia Office 1501 Farm Credit Drive. Telephone: 703-790-7900.
Telecopier: 703-821-2397.
Leesburg, Virginia Office: 201 Liberty Street, S.W.
Telephone: 703-777-0004. Metro: 478-8989.
Facsimile: 703-777-9320.
New York, N.Y. Office: 900 Third Avenue, Suite 1800.
Telephone: 212-836-4200.
Facsimile: 212-836-4201.

RESIDENT MEMBERS

David G. Fiske
Philip J. Harvey (Not admitted in VA)

(See Next Column)

RESIDENT ASSOCIATES

Maureen Byrne Beahn
Lori L. Vaughn (Not admitted in VA)
Thomas W. Mitchell
Michael J. Wendorf

For full biographical listings, see the Martindale-Hubbell Law Directory

THOMAS, BALLENGER, VOGELMAN AND TURNER, P.C. (AV)

124 South Royal Street, 22314
Telephone: 703-836-3400
Fax: 703-836-3549

Earl G. Thomas
Jeffrey A. Vogelman
John M. Ballenger
James D. Turner

References: First Union National Bank of Virginia; Burke & Herbert Bank & Trust Co.

For full biographical listings, see the Martindale-Hubbell Law Directory

*AMHERST,** Amherst Co. — (Refer to Lynchburg)

*APPOMATTOX,** Appomattox Co. — (Refer to Buckingham)

ASHLAND, Hanover Co. — (Refer to Richmond)

*BEDFORD,** Bedford Co.

LAW OFFICES GARRETT & GARRETT A PROFESSIONAL CORPORATION (AV)

116 East Main Street, P.O. Box 534, 24523
Telephone: 703-586-1034
FAX: 703-586-0545

Harry W. Garrett, Jr.
Carter B. Garrett

Representative Clients: Bedford Federal Savings Bank; Morgan Development Corp.; Piedmont Label Company, Inc.; Scott & Bond, Inc.; Roanoke Farm Credit, ACA.
Approved Attorneys for: Lawyers Title Insurance Co.; Southern Title Insurance Co.
References: Bedford Federal Savings Bank; First Union Bank.

For full biographical listings, see the Martindale-Hubbell Law Directory

*BERRYVILLE,** Clarke Co. — (Refer to Winchester)

BIG STONE GAP, Wise Co.

KEULING-STOUT, P.C. (AV)

123 Wood Avenue East, P.O. Box 400, 24219
Telephone: 703-523-1676
FAX: 703-523-1608

Henry S. Keuling-Stout

For full biographical listings, see the Martindale-Hubbell Law Directory

BLACKSBURG, Montgomery Co.

GILMER, SADLER, INGRAM, SUTHERLAND & HUTTON (AV)

201 West Roanoke Street, P.O. Box 908, 24063-0908
Telephone: 703-552-1061
Telecopier: 703-552-8227
Pulaski, Virginia Office: Midtown Professional Building, 65 East Main Street, P.O. Box 878.
Telephone: 703-980-1360; 703-639-0027.
Telecopier: 703-980-5264.

MEMBERS OF FIRM

James L. Hutton
Todd G. Patrick
Howard C. Gilmer, Jr. (1906-1975)
Roby K. Sutherland (1909-1975)
Philip M. Sadler (1915-1994)
Robert J. Ingram
Thomas J. McCarthy, Jr.
John J. Gill
Gary C. Hancock
Jackson M. Bruce
Michael J. Barbour
Deborah Wood Dobbins
Debra Fitzgerald-O'Connell
Scott A. Rose
Timothy Edmond Kirtner

OF COUNSEL

James R. Montgomery

Representative Clients: Appalachian Power Co.; Magnox, Inc.; Liberty Mutual Insurance Co.; Norfolk Southern Railway Co.; Pulaski Furniture Corp.; NationsBank; Travelers Insurance Co.; Charles Lunsford Sons & Associates; Corning Glass Works.

For full biographical listings, see the Martindale-Hubbell Law Directory

*BOWLING GREEN,** Caroline Co. — (Refer to Warsaw)

*BOYDTON,** Mecklenburg Co. — (Refer to South Boston)

BRISTOL, (Independent City)

ELLIOTT LAWSON & POMRENKE (AV)

Sixth Floor, First Union Bank Building, P.O. Box 8400, 24203-8400
Telephone: 703-466-8400
Fax: 703-466-8161

(See Next Column)

ELLIOTT LAWSON & POMRENKE—*Continued*

James Wm. Elliott, Jr.
Mark M. Lawson
Kurt J. Pomrenke
Steven R. Minor
Kyle P. Macione
Lisa King Crockett

For full biographical listings, see the Martindale-Hubbell Law Directory

WOODWARD, MILES & FLANNAGAN, P.C. (AV)

Suite 200, Executive Plaza, 510 Cumberland Street, P.O. Box 789, 24203-0789
Telephone: 703-669-0161
Telecopier: 703-669-7376

S. Bruce Jones (1892-1966)
Jno. W. Flannagan, Jr. (1885-1955)
Waldo G. Miles (1911-1973)
Wm. H. Woodward (1907-1992)
Francis W. Flannagan
John E. Kieffer
Larry B. Kirksey
Elizabeth Smith Jones
Christen W. Burkholder
Beth Osborne Skinner

Representative Clients: CNA Companies; Cooper Tire and Rubber; First Union National Bank; Ford Motor Company; Lawyers Title Insurance Company; Nationwide Mutual; United Telephone-Southeast, Inc.; Universal Underwriters Group; Worldwide Insurance Group.

For full biographical listings, see the Martindale-Hubbell Law Directory

*BUCKINGHAM,** Buckingham Co.

WRIGHT AND DUNKUM (AV)

Courthouse Square, P.O. Box 200, 23921
Telephone: 804-969-4809
FAX: 804-969-1597

E. M. Wright, Jr.
Marvin H. Dunkum, Jr.

Approved Attorneys for: Lawyer's Title Insurance Corp.; Southern Title Insurance Corp.
Representative Clients: NationsBank, Dillwyn, Virginia; Central Virginia Health Services, Inc.; Kyanite Mining Corp.
Reference: NationsBank, Dillwyn, Virginia.

For full biographical listings, see the Martindale-Hubbell Law Directory

*CHARLOTTE COURT HOUSE,** Charlotte Co. — (Refer to South Boston)

*CHARLOTTESVILLE,** (Ind. City; Seat of Albemarle Co.)

BARRICK & MCKAY (AV)

408 Park Street, P.O. Box 2018, 22902-2018
Telephone: 804-979-0077
Telecopier: 804-979-8550

MEMBERS OF FIRM

Richard Hamilton Barrick
John D. McKay

ASSOCIATES

Jennifer Hall McKay
David C. Wagoner

For full biographical listings, see the Martindale-Hubbell Law Directory

MCGUIRE, WOODS, BATTLE & BOOTHE (AV)

Court Square Building, P.O. Box 1288, 22902-1288
Telephone: 804-977-2500
Fax: 804-980-2222
Alexandria, Virginia Office: Transpotomac Plaza, Suite 1000, 1199 North Fairfax Street, 22314-1437.
Telephone: 703-739-6200.
Fax: 703-739-6270.
Baltimore, Maryland Office: The Blaustein Building, One North Charles Street, 21201-3793.
Telephone: 410-659-4400.
Fax: 410-659-4599.
Jacksonville, Florida Office: Barnett Center, Suite 2750, 50 North Laura Street, 32202-3635.
Telephone: 904-798-3200.
Fax: 904-798-3207.
McLean (Tysons Corner), Virginia Office: 8280 Greensboro Drive, Suite 900, Tysons Corner, 22102-3892.
Telephone: 703-712-5000.
Fax: 703-712-5050.
Norfolk, Virginia Office: World Trade Center, Suite 9000, 101 West Main Street, 23510-1655.
Telephone: 804-640-3700.
Fax: 804-640-3701.
Richmond, Virginia Office: One James Center, 901 East Cary Street, 23219-4030.
Telephone: 804-775-1000.
Fax: 804-775-1061.
Washington, D.C. Office: The Army and Navy Club Building, 1627 Eye Street, N.W., 20006-4007.
Telephone: 202-857-1700.
Fax: 202-857-1737.

(See Next Column)

Brussels, Belgium Office: 250 Avenue Louise, Ste. 64, 1050.
Telephone: (32 2) 629 42 11.
Fax: (32 2) 629 42 22.
Zürich, Switzerland Office: P.O. Box 4930, Bahnhofstrasse 3, 8022.
Telephone: (41 1) 225 20 00.
Fax: (41 1) 225 20 20.

RESIDENT MEMBERS

Steven W. Blaine
Lucius H. Bracey, Jr.
J. Robert Brame III
Dennis W. Good, Jr.
Kurt J. Krueger
Fred S. Landess
Gary C. McGee
Leigh B. Middleditch, Jr.
Frederick L. Russell
D. French Slaughter III
Robert E. Stroud
R. Craig Wood

OF COUNSEL

Jean Bilger Arnold
William C. Battle

RESIDENT ASSOCIATES

Michael Holt Cole
Robert T. Danforth
J. Brian Jackson
Patricia Merrill
Kristen E. Smith
Bruce M. Steen

For full biographical listings, see the Martindale-Hubbell Law Directory

MICHIE, HAMLETT, LOWRY, RASMUSSEN AND TWEEL, P.C. (AV)

Suite 300, 500 Court Square Building, P.O. Box 298, 22902-0298
Telephone: 804-977-3390
Facsimile: 804-295-0681

Thomas J. Michie, Jr.
Leroy R. Hamlett, Jr.
Edward B. Lowry
Bruce D. Rasmussen
Ronald R. Tweel
Gary W. Kendall
John V. Little
Kevin W. Ryan
Elizabeth P. Coughter
James P. Cox, III
Robert W. Jackson

Peter McIntosh
Edmund R. Michie
Denise Yvette Lunsford
David S. Randle
B. Stephanie Commander
Garrett M. Smith
April Russell Fletcher

Representative Clients: NationsBank of Virginia, N.A.; Central Telephone Company of Virginia; Virginia Power; Ohio Casualty Co.; Sears Roebuck & Co.; Muhammad Ali; The Mitchie Co.; General Electric Capital Corp.; Bourne Leisure Group, Ltd.; Edgcomb Metals Co.

For full biographical listings, see the Martindale-Hubbell Law Directory

RICHMOND AND FISHBURNE (AV)

Queen Charlotte Square, 214 East High Street, P.O. Box 559, 22902
Telephone: 804-977-8590
Telefax: 804-296-9861

MEMBERS OF FIRM

Joseph W. Richmond (1916-1986)
Junius R. Fishburne (1915-1991)
Joseph W. Richmond, Jr.
Matthew B. Murray
Wendall L. Winn, Jr.
Thomas G. Nolan

ASSOCIATES

Joseph M. Cochran
Sharon G. Portwood
Mark J. Nelson

LEGAL SUPPORT PERSONNEL

Gibson W. Gahan

Representative Clients: Budget-Rent-A-Car; Charlottesville Area Association of Realtors; Fireman's Fund; Horace Mann Insurance Co.; Martha Jefferson Hospital; Nationwide Insurance Co.; Norfolk-Southern Corp.; State Farm Insurance Co.; USAA; Virginia Farm Bureau Insurance Services.

For full biographical listings, see the Martindale-Hubbell Law Directory

TAYLOR, ZUNKA, MILNOR & CARTER, LTD. (AV)

414 Park Street, P.O. Box 1567, 22902
Telephone: 804-977-0191
FAX: 804-977-0198

Robert Edward Taylor (Retired)
John W. Zunka
Richard H. Milnor
Richard E. Carter

H. Robert Yates, III

Representative Clients: State Farm Insurance Companies; Allstate Insurance Company; The Travelers Insurance Companies; The Harleysville Insurance Companies; Kemper National Insurance Company; Commercial Union Insurance Co.; Selective Insurance Co.; Blue Cross and Blue Shield of Virginia; Crestar Bank.

For full biographical listings, see the Martindale-Hubbell Law Directory

TREMBLAY & SMITH (AV)

105-109 East High Street, P.O. Box 1585, 22902
Telephone: 804-977-4455
Fax: 804-979-1221

(See Next Column)

TREMBLAY & SMITH, *Charlottesville—Continued*

MEMBERS OF FIRM

John K. Taggart, III
Melvin E. Gibson, Jr.
Thomas E. Albro
Christine Thomson
Patricia D. McGraw

OF COUNSEL

E. Gerald Tremblay
Lloyd T. Smith, Jr.

ASSOCIATES

R. Lee Livingston
Christopher L. McLean

Representative Clients: Commonwealth of Virginia, Department of Transportation; First Virginia Bank—Central; Sieg Distributing Co. (Anheuser-Busch Distributors); Kloeckner Pentaplast of America, Inc.; Virginia Broadcasting Corp.; Farmington Country Club; Management Services Corporation of Charlottesville; InterTrans Carrier Co.; Sprint Cellular Company; Wade Apartments.

For full biographical listings, see the Martindale-Hubbell Law Directory

*CHATHAM,** Pittsylvania Co. — (Refer to Danville)

CHESAPEAKE, (Independent City) — (Refer to Virginia Beach)

*CHESTERFIELD,** Chesterfield Co. — (Refer to Richmond)

*CHRISTIANSBURG,** Montgomery Co.

CRAFT & McGHEE, P.C. (AV)

3 North Franklin Street, 24073
Telephone: 703-382-6176

William R. L. Craft, Jr.
William J. McGhee

Of Counsel: Federal Land Bank of Baltimore.
Counsel for: Central Fidelity Bank (local); Town of Christiansburg; Montgomery County Development Corp.; Christiansburg Industrial Corp.; Montgomery County Public Service Authority; Industrial Development Authorities of Floyd County.

For full biographical listings, see the Martindale-Hubbell Law Directory

*CLINTWOOD,** Dickenson Co. — (Refer to Norton)

*COURTLAND,** Southampton Co. — (Refer to Franklin)

*COVINGTON,** Allegheny Co. — (Refer to Lexington)

DANVILLE, (Independent City)

CLEMENT & WHEATLEY, A PROFESSIONAL CORPORATION (AV)

549 Main Street, P.O. Box 8200, 24543-8200
Telephone: 804-793-8200
Fax: 804-793-8436

Rutledge C. Clement (1906-1979)
C. Stuart Wheatley (1905-1982)
Joseph M. Winston, Jr.
Glenn W. Pulley
Whittington W. Clement
R. Lee Yancey
Patrick H. Musick
Luis A. Abreu
Harry P. Sakellaris

Ronald Lee (R.J.) Lackey
Mark B. Holland
Kevin W. Tydings

General Counsel for: American National Bank & Trust Co.; Danville Redevelopment & Housing Authority; Danville Regional Medical Center; Piedmont Broadcasting Corp.; Danville Area Chamber of Commerce; Danville Development Council.
Representative Clients: Charter Federal Savings & Loan Assn. (Danville); Corning, Inc.; USF&G; Goodyear Tire & Rubber Co.; Dan River, Inc.

For full biographical listings, see the Martindale-Hubbell Law Directory

LAW OFFICES OF MICHAEL P. REGAN, P.C. (AV)

703 Patton Street, 24541
Telephone: 804-793-9670; 793-1622
Telecopier: 804-793-6647

Michael P. Regan

LEGAL SUPPORT PERSONNEL

Janet E. Armstrong (Legal Assistant)

References: Sovran Bank, N.A.; Signet Bank.

For full biographical listings, see the Martindale-Hubbell Law Directory

*EASTVILLE,** Northampton Co.

TANKARD AND GORDON (AV)

Court Green, P.O. Box 5, 23347-0005
Telephone: 804-678-5117
Fax: 804-678-7664

(See Next Column)

MEMBERS OF FIRM

Baxley T. Tankard
Croxton Gordon

Representative Clients: Chesapeake Bay Bridge and Tunnel District; A & N Electric Cooperative; First Virginia Bank-Tidewater, Exmore, Virginia; Town of Exmore.
Approved Attorneys for: Lawyers Title Insurance Corp.; Ticor Title Insurance Co.

For full biographical listings, see the Martindale-Hubbell Law Directory

*EMPORIA,** Greensville Co.

OUTTEN, BARRETT, BURR & SHARRETT, P.C. (AV)

314 South Main Street, P.O. Box 232, 23847
Telephone: 804-634-2167
Fax: 804-634-3798
Lawrenceville, Virginia Office: 214 Court Street.
Telephone: 804-848-3184.
Fax: 804-848-0116.

W. Curtis Outten, Jr. (Resident, Lawrenceville Office)
C. Butler Barrett
Theodore J. Burr, Jr.
W. Allan Sharrett

Local Condemnation Attorneys for: Virginia Department of Highways and Transportation.
Representative Clients: Travelers Insurance Co.; Virginia Farm Bureau Mutual Insurance Co.; The Town of Lawrenceville; City of Emporia; Town of Courtland; Georgia Pacific Corp.; Union Camp Corp.; CSX Corp.; NationsBank.

For full biographical listings, see the Martindale-Hubbell Law Directory

*FAIRFAX,** (Ind. City; Seat of Fairfax Co.)

BRAULT, PALMER, GROVE, ZIMMERMAN, WHITE & MIMS (AV)

10533 Main Street, P.O. Box 1010, 22030-1010
Telephone: 703-273-6400
Fax: 703-273-3514
Manassas, Virginia Office: 8567-D Sudley Road. P.O. Box 534.
Telephone: 703-369-7500; 631-9727.
Fax: 703-369-2285.

MEMBERS OF FIRM

Adelard L. Brault (Emeritus)
Thomas C. Palmer, Jr. (Resident, Manassas Office)
Edward H. Grove, III
Michael L. Zimmerman
Bruce D. White
Gary B. Mims
August W. Steinhilber, III

ASSOCIATES

Nancy J. Goodiel
Andrew M. Adams (Resident, Manassas Office)
Jack A. Robbins, Jr. (Resident, Manassas Office)
Benjamin M. Smith, III
Lisa Kent Duley

Representative Clients: CIGNA Cos.; CNA Insurance Cos.; Commerical Union Insurance Co.; Erie Insurance Group; Harleysville Insurance Co.; Home Insurance Co.; Kemper Insurance Group; Selective Insurance Co.; State Farm Insurance Cos.; U.S.F. & G.

For full biographical listings, see the Martindale-Hubbell Law Directory

MILES & STOCKBRIDGE, A PROFESSIONAL CORPORATION (AV)

Fair Oaks Plaza, 11350 Random Hills Road, 22030-7429
Telephone: 703-273-2440
Telecopier: 273-4446
Baltimore, Maryland Office: 10 Light Street.
Telephone: 410-727-6464.
Telecopier: 385-3700.
Towson, Maryland Office: 600 Washington Avenue, Suite 300.
Telephone: 410-821-6565.
Telecopier: 823-8123.
Easton, Maryland Office: 101 B0y Street.
Telephone: 410-822-5280.
Telecopier: 822-5450.
Cambridge, Maryland Office: 300 Academy Street.
Telephone: 410-228-4545.
Telecopier: 228-5652.
Rockville, Maryland Office: 22 West Jefferson Street.
Telephone: 301-762-1600.
Telecopier: 762-0363.
Frederick, Maryland Office: 30 West Patrick Street.
Telephone: 301-662-5155.
Telecopier: 662-3647.
Washington, D.C. Office: 1450 G. Street, N.W., Suite 445.
Telephone: 202-737-9600.
Telecopier: 737-0097.

Jesse B. Wilson, III
Peter A. Arntson
Marc E. Bettius
Gary W. Brown
Randolph A. Sutliff
Robert H. J. Loftus
Barent L. Fake
Stephen K. Fox
Douglas J. Sanderson
R. Peyton Mahaffey
Margaret Ann Brown
Peter Lipresti
William L. Carey
R. Kevin Kennedy

(See Next Column)

MILES & STOCKBRIDGE A PROFESSIONAL CORPORATION—*Continued*

Edward J. Longosz, II (Not admitted in VA)
Wm. Quinton Robinson
Brian F. Kenney
Richard M. Pollak
Celeste E. Burns

Amy Sanborn Owen
Eric J. Berghold
Randall K. Bowen
Laura L. Ratchford
Adam W. Smith
Deborah Donick Cochran
Daniel P. Lyon
Patrick M. Pickett
Susan L. Bozorth
Rodney B. Boddie

STAFF ATTORNEY

Marian L. Beckett

For full biographical listings, see the Martindale-Hubbell Law Directory

MONTEDONICO, HAMILTON & ALTMAN, P.C. (AV)

Suite 500, 10306 Eaton Place, 22030
Telephone: 703-591-9700
FAX: 703-591-0023
Washington, D.C., Office: 5301 Wisconsin Avenue, N.W., Suite 400.
Telephone: 202-364-1434.
FAX: 202-364-1544.
Richmond, Virginia Office: 700 East Main Street, Suite 1633.
Telephone: 804-780-2898.
Frederick, Maryland Office: 220 North Market Street.
Telephone: 301-695-7004.
FAX: 301-695-0055.
Rockville, Maryland Office: Suite 201, 600 East Jefferson Street.
Telephone: 301-424-3900.
FAX: 301-217-0409.

Stephen L. Altman
Kenneth G. Roth (Resident)
Joseph C. Veith, III
Dennis R. Carluzzo (Resident)

Bruce A. Levine
Brendy B. Esmond
Kathryn A.K. Untiedt
Leah Hadad

For full biographical listings, see the Martindale-Hubbell Law Directory

MOSHOS, HADEN & DE DEO, P.C. (AV)

Suite 201, 10521 Judicial Drive, 22030
Telephone: 703-352-5770
Fax: 703-352-0190

Arthur L. Moshos
Fred M. Haden
James F. De Deo

Mark R. Machen

References: Community Bank; Fairfax Bank & Trust; Nations Bank.

For full biographical listings, see the Martindale-Hubbell Law Directory

ODIN, FELDMAN & PITTLEMAN, P.C. (AV)

9302 Lee Highway, Suite 1100, 22031
Telephone: 703-218-2100
Facsimile: 703-218-2160

Dexter S. Odin
David E. Feldman
James B. Pittleman
John S. Wisiackas
David J. Brewer
Robert K. Richardson
J. Patrick McConnell
Thomas J. Shaughnessy
David A. Lawrence
Nelson Blitz
Donald F. King
Sally Ann Hostetler
Robert A. Hickey
F. Douglas Ross
Harry N. Lowe, III
Bruce M. Blanchard
Leslye S. Fenton
Frances P. Dwornik
Robert G. Nath
John P. Dedon
Edward W. Cameron
George A. Zaphiriou
John W. Farrell
Elizabeth L. Salans
James W. Reynolds
Lawrence A. Schultis
Kevin Thomas Oliveira

OF COUNSEL

Hugh A. M. Shafer, Jr.
Thomas E. Chilcott
Stephen J. O'Brien (Not admitted in VA)
Thomas R. Daly

For full biographical listings, see the Martindale-Hubbell Law Directory

TYDINGS, BRYAN & ADAMS, P.C. (AV)

Suite 420 The Fairfax Bank & Trust Building, 4117 Chain Bridge Road, P.O. Box 250, 22030-0250
Telephone: 703-359-9100
Fax: 703-352-8913

Roy A. Swayze (1919-1987)
Ronald W. Tydings
Kennon W. Bryan
Robert C. Adams

Stuart L. Crenshaw, III
Corinne N. Lockett

(See Next Column)

LEGAL SUPPORT PERSONNEL

James F. Robinson

For full biographical listings, see the Martindale-Hubbell Law Directory

FALLS CHURCH, (Independent City)

BASKIN, JACKSON & HANSBARGER, A PROFESSIONAL CORPORATION (AV)

301 Park Avenue, 22046
Telephone: 703-534-3610
Fax: 703-536-7315

William M. Baskin
William M. Baskin, Jr.
John G. Jackson
William H. Hansbarger
Southy E. Walton

For full biographical listings, see the Martindale-Hubbell Law Directory

HAZEL & THOMAS, A PROFESSIONAL CORPORATION (AV)

Fairfax County Office Suite 1400, 3110 Fairview Park Drive, P.O. Box 12001, 22042
Telephone: 703-641-4200
Alexandria, Virginia Office: Suite 200, 510 King Street, P.O. Box 820.
Telephone: 703-836-8400.
Leesburg, Virginia Office: 44084 Riverside Parkway, Suite 300.
Telephone: 703-729-8500. Metro: 703-478-1992.
Manassas, Virginia Office: 9324 West Street, Third Floor.
Telephone: 703-330-7400. Metro: 703-803-7474.
Richmond, Virginia Office: Suite 600, 411 East Franklin Street, P.O. Box 788.
Telephone: 804-344-3400.

Michael A. Banzhaf (Resident, Leesburg Office)
Duane W. Beckhorn
Kirk D. Beckhorn
Benton Burroughs, Jr.
E. William Chapman (Resident, Leesburg Office)
Bruce L. Christman
John E. Coffey (Resident, Alexandria Office)
John Paul Corrado (Resident, Alexandria Office)
David C. Culbert (Resident, Leesburg Office)
R. Mark Dare
Steven D. Delaney (Resident, Richmond Office)
Robert M. Diamond
Robert M. Dilling
S. Miles Dumville (Resident, Richmond Office)
H. Bradley Evans, Jr. (Resident, Alexandria Office)
Karen C. Fagelson (Resident, Leesburg Office)
Gail W. Feagles
Thomas R. Folk
John H. Foote (Resident, Manassas Office)
Grady C. Frank, Jr. (Resident, Alexandria Office)
Donald N. Goldrosen
Patrick O. Gottschalk (Resident, Richmond Office)
Robert E. Gregg
Grayson P. Hanes
Henry A. Hart (Resident, Alexandria Office)
John T. Hazel, Jr.
A. Everett Hoeg, III
John P. Holman
Carol C. Honigberg
Thomas C. Junker (Resident, Alexandria Office)
Julia Krebs-Markrich
James S. Kurz
D. Patrick Lacy, Jr. (Resident, Richmond Office)
Robert A. Lawrence
Joseph S. Luchini
Brian R. Marron (Resident, Richmond Office)
Walter A. Marston, Jr. (Resident, Richmond Office)
Charles F. B. McAleer, Jr.
Kathleen S. Mehfoud (Resident, Richmond Office)
J. Howard Middleton, Jr. (Resident, Alexandria Office)
J. Randall Minchew (Resident, Leesburg Office)
Lee W. Morris
Thomas W. Nalls (Resident, Leesburg Office)
Steven W. Pearson (Resident, Richmond Office)
Donna M. Phillips
Jonathan P. Rak
Anne M. Richard (Resident, Alexandria Office)
John J. Sabourin, Jr.
Richard C. Sullivan, Jr. (Resident, Alexandria Office)
William Griffith Thomas (Resident, Alexandria Office)
Benjamin F. Tompkins
Anthony J. Trenga (Resident, Alexandria Office)
Garth M. Wainman (Resident, Manassas Office)
Mark W. Wasserman (Resident, Alexandria Office)
Robert B. Webb, III
Wiley R. Wright, Jr.
Michael L. Zupan (Resident, Alexandria Office)

COUNSEL

Robert C. Fitzgerald
H. Lane Kneedler (Resident, Richmond Office)
Patrick A. O'Hare (Resident, Richmond Office)
W. Lawrence Wallace, Sr. (Not admitted in VA)

OF COUNSEL

Thomas Moore Lawson (Also practicing individually at Winchester)
John O. Marsh, Jr. (Also practicing individually at Winchester)
Richard C. Riemenschneider (Resident, Leesburg Office)
Linda C. Stokely
Henry A. Thomas (Resident, Alexandria Office)

(See Next Column)

HAZEL & THOMAS A PROFESSIONAL CORPORATION, *Falls Church—Continued*

Philip F. Abraham (Resident, Richmond Office)	George E. Kostel
John A. Burlingame (Resident, Alexandria Office)	Jonathan E. Lyon
Michael S. Dingman	John L. McBride (Resident, Manassas Office)
Geoffrey C. Dodson	Jeffery Keith Mitchell (Resident, Richmond Office)
Merrell B. Green	Pamela G. Parsons (Resident, Richmond Office)
Dee Ann Herring (Resident, Alexandria Office)	Deborah K. Raines
Darryl P. Hobbs	Frederick K. Roseman
Lisa Marie Hughes	Steven L. Rosenberg
Vernon E. Inge, Jr. (Resident, Richmond Office)	Thomas W. Smith, III (Resident, Manassas Office)
Otto W. Konrad (Resident, Richmond Office)	Julia Beecher Strickland
Jennifer L. W. Korjus	Alison R. Wright (Resident, Alexandria Office)

CONTRACT ATTORNEYS

David P. O'Brien (Resident, Leesburg Office)

LEGAL SUPPORT PERSONNEL

Sally K. Montrey (Director of Finance/Treasurer)

For full biographical listings, see the Martindale-Hubbell Law Directory

*FARMVILLE,** Prince Edward Co. — (Refer to Lynchburg)

FRANKLIN, Southampton Co.

MOYLER, MOYLER, RAINEY & COBB (AV)

506 North Main Street, P.O. Box 775, 23851
Telephone: 804-562-5133
FAX: 804-562-7628

MEMBERS OF FIRM

J. Edward Moyler (1894-1982)	James E. Rainey
J. Edward Moyler, Jr.	G. Elliott Cobb, Jr.

Representative Clients: Union Camp Corp.; Nations Bank; Crestar Bank; Hercules, Inc.; Southampton Memorial Hospital; Appollo Plastics; Insight Communications Co.; Virginia Carolina Peanut Farmers Cooperative Assn; The Village at Woods Edge; Cable Associates.

For full biographical listings, see the Martindale-Hubbell Law Directory

FREDERICKSBURG, (Independent City)

ROBERTS, SOKOL, ASHBY & JONES (AV)

(Member of the Commonwealth Law Group, Ltd.)
701 Kenmore Avenue, 22404-7166
Telephone: 703-373-3500
Telex: 151274389
Telecopier: 703-899-6394
Mailing Address: P.O. Box 7166, 22404-7166

MEMBERS OF FIRM

William M. Sokol	James Ashby, III
Russell H. Roberts	William E. Glover
Kevin S. Jones	Jeannie P. Dahnk

ASSOCIATES

Jennifer Lee Parrish	Tracy A. Houck

OF COUNSEL

Kenneth T. Whitescarver

General Counsel for: Mary Washington Hospital; The Free Lance-Star; Massaponax Building Components, Inc.; Pohanka Datsun Cadillac Oldsmobile; First Virginia Bank (Trust).

For full biographical listings, see the Martindale-Hubbell Law Directory

*FRONT ROYAL,** Warren Co. — (Refer to Winchester)

*GATE CITY,** Scott Co. — (Refer to Bristol)

*GLOUCESTER,** Gloucester Co.

MARTIN, INGLES & INGLES, LTD. (AV)

Court Circle, P.O. Box 708, 23061
Telephone: 804-693-2500; 877-7371
Fax: 804-693-0122

G.P. De Hardit (1921-1958)	McClanahan Ingles
James B. Martin (1907-1992)	Breckenridge Ingles

For full biographical listings, see the Martindale-Hubbell Law Directory

*GRUNDY,** Buchanan Co.

STREET, STREET, STREET, SCOTT & BOWMAN (AV)

339 West Main Street, P.O. Box 2100, 24614
Telephone: 703-935-2128
Telecopier: 703-935-4162

Eugene K. Street (1943-1990)

(See Next Column)

OF COUNSEL

H. A. Street

MEMBERS OF FIRM

N. D. Street	Robert J. Breimann
Thomas R. Scott, Jr.	Russell M. Large
Joseph W. Bowman	S. T. Mullins
Fay Hibbitts	James H. Street

ASSOCIATES

Russell Vern Presley, II	Lucy G. Williams

Representative Clients: Norfolk & Western Railroad Co.; Dominion Bank, N.A.; United Coal Cos.; Jewell Coal & Coke Co.; Old Republic Insurance Co.; Appalachian Power Co.; Georgia Pacific Corp.
Approved Attorneys for: Lawyers Title Insurance Corp.

For full biographical listings, see the Martindale-Hubbell Law Directory

*HALIFAX,** Halifax Co.

HARRY L. MAPP, JR. (AV)

Courthouse Square, P.O. Box 1146, 24558
Telephone: 804-476-2161
FAX: 804-476-2162

References: South Boston Bank; Crestar Bank, South Boston, Va.

For full biographical listings, see the Martindale-Hubbell Law Directory

HAMPTON, (Independent City)

CUMMING, HATCHETT, MOSCHEL, PATRICK & CLANCY, A PROFESSIONAL CORPORATION (AV)

2236 Cunningham Drive, 23666
Telephone: 804-827-9207
FAX: 804-826-5029

Kenneth G. Cumming (1912-1991)	Frederic L. Moschel
Gorin F. Hatchett (1916-1994)	Albert W. Patrick, III
Lawrence G. Cumming	Philip L. Hatchett
	Timothy G. Clancy

Representative Clients: B & F Contracting Company, Inc.; Hampton Roads Educators Credit Union; Crestar Bank; Hampton Roads Manufacturing Corp.; Investors Savings Bank; Lincoln National Life Insurance; Martin and Richardson Seafood Co., Inc.; Riverdale Plaza Shopping Center; Sentara Hampton General Hospital; SpaceTec Ventures, Inc.

For full biographical listings, see the Martindale-Hubbell Law Directory

*HARRISONBURG,** (Ind. City; Seat of Rockingham Co.)

LITTEN & SIPE (AV)

410 Neff Avenue, 22801
Telephone: 703-434-5353
Fax: 703-434-6069
Woodstock, Virginia Office: 140 South Main Street, 22664.
Telephone: 703-459-5909.
Fax: 703-434-6069.

MEMBERS OF FIRM

Donald D. Litten	Stephen T. Heitz
James R. Sipe	Jonathan J. Litten
James V. Lane	William H. Ralston, Jr.

ASSOCIATES

Lorrie A. Bradley	Susan R. Mackniak
Stephanie R. Sipe	John C. Wirth

General Counsel for: Rockingham Mutual Insurance Co.; Rockingham Casualty Co.; Nielsen Construction Company; Shenandoah's Pride; Towns of Bridgewater and Dayton.

For full biographical listings, see the Martindale-Hubbell Law Directory

WHARTON, ALDHIZER & WEAVER, P.L.C. (AV)

100 South Mason Street, 22801
Telephone: 703-434-0316
Fax: 703-434-5502

W. W. Wharton (1907-1985)	Roger D. Williams
George S. Aldhizer, II (1907-1986)	Charles F. Hilton
	Daniel L. Fitch
Russell M. Weaver (1901-1985)	Jeffrey G. Lenhart
George R. Aldhizer, Jr.	Mark D. Obenshain
Donald E. Showalter	Thomas E. Ullrich
Glenn M. Hodge	George W. Barlow, III
M. Bruce Wallinger	Carolyn Madden Perry
Ronald D. Hodges	Marshall H. Ross
William E. Shmidheiser, III	G. Chris Brown
Douglas L. Guynn	Jeffrey S. Zurbuch
John W. Flora	Jennifer E. Kirkland
Roy W. Ferguson, Jr.	Phillip C. Stone, Jr.
Gregory T. St. Ours	Cathleen P. Welsh

(See Next Column)

WHARTON, ALDHIZER & WEAVER P.L.C.—*Continued*

G. Rodney Young, II
Mark W. Botkin
Kevin M. Rose
David A. Temeles, Jr.
A. Gene Hart, Jr.

Representative Clients: First Union National Bank of Virginia; Rockingham Memorial Hospital; Rockingham County; Bridgewater College; The Travelers; Norfolk-Southern; Rocco Enterprises, Inc.; WLR Food, Inc.; State Farm Insurance Cos.; The Virginia Insurance Reciprocal; Transprints, USA, Inc.

For full biographical listings, see the Martindale-Hubbell Law Directory

*HILLSVILLE,** Carroll Co. — (Refer to Galax)

*INDEPENDENCE,** Grayson Co. — (Refer to Galax)

IRVINGTON, Lancaster Co.

BREEDEN, HUBBARD, TERRY & BREEDEN, A PROFESSIONAL CORPORATION (AV)

Irvington Professional Offices, Steamboat Road, P.O. Box 340, 22480
Telephone: 804-438-5522
Telecopier: 804-438-5003

James C. Breeden
B. H. B. Hubbard, III
Matson C. Terry, II
Barbara H. Breeden

OF COUNSEL

William J. Kopcsak

General Counsel for: Rappahannock General Hospital; Chesapeake Anesthesia, Ltd.; Simons Hauling Co., Inc.; F. H. Jett's Seafood, Inc.; Treakle Foundation; Davis Dodge, Inc.; Kilmarnock-Lancaster Rescue Squad, Inc.; Russell Pontiac GMC, Inc.; Rappahannock Orthopedics, Ltd.; Rappahannock Seafood, Inc.

For full biographical listings, see the Martindale-Hubbell Law Directory

RUMSEY & BUGG, A PROFESSIONAL CORPORATION (AV)

P.O. Box 720, 22480
Telephone: 804-438-5588
Telecopier: 804-438-5599

Dexter C. Rumsey, III
A. Davis Bugg, Jr.

General Counsel for: WKNI-AM/FM Radio; Atkins Petroleum Products, Inc.; Town of White Stone; White Stone Volunteer Fire Department; Northern Neck Coca Cola Bottling Co., Inc.; Classic Vending Services, Inc.
Local Counsel for: Signet Bank; Litton Industrial Products, Inc.
Special Counsel for: Zapata Haynie Corp.

For full biographical listings, see the Martindale-Hubbell Law Directory

*JONESVILLE,** Lee Co. — (Refer to Norton)

*KING GEORGE,** King George Co. — (Refer to Fredericksburg)

*LAWRENCEVILLE,** Brunswick Co.

OUTTEN, BARRETT, BURR & SHARRETT, P.C. (AV)

214 Court Street, 23868
Telephone: 804-848-3184
Fax: 804-848-0116
Emporia, Virginia Office: 314 South Main Street, P.O. Box 232.
Telephone: 804-634-2167.
Fax: 804-634-3798.

W. Curtis Outten, Jr.

Local Condemnation Attorneys for: Virginia Department of Highways and Transportation.
Representative Clients: Travelers Insurance Co.; Virginia Farm Bureau Mutual Insurance Co.; The Town of Lawrenceville; City of Emporia; Town of Courtland; Georgia Pacific Corp.; Union Camp Corp.; CSX Corp.; NationsBank.

For full biographical listings, see the Martindale-Hubbell Law Directory

*LEBANON,** Russell Co. — (Refer to Abingdon)

*LEESBURG,** Loudoun Co.

HALL, MONAHAN, ENGLE, MAHAN & MITCHELL (AV)

3 East Market Street, P.O. Box 390, 22075
Telephone: 703-777-1050
Fax: 703-771-4113
Winchester, Virginia Office: 9 East Boscawen Street. P.O. Box 848.
Telephone: 703-662-3200.
Fax: 703-662-4304.

MEMBERS OF FIRM

Wilbur C. Hall (1892-1972)
Thomas V. Monahan
Samuel D. Engle
O. Leland Mahan

Local Counsel for: United States Fidelity & Guaranty Co.; Hartford Accident & Indemnity Co.; Loudoun Mutual Insurance Company; Fidelity and Casualty Co. of New York; Washington Gas and Light Co.
Counsel for: Sovran Bank, Leesburg, Branch.

For full biographical listings, see the Martindale-Hubbell Law Directory

HANES, SEVILA, SAUNDERS & MCCAHILL, A PROFESSIONAL CORPORATION (AV)

30 North King Street, P.O. Box 678, 22075
Telephone: 703-777-5700
Metro: 471-9800; Fax: 703-771-4161

William B. Hanes
Robert E. Sevila
Richard R. Saunders, Jr.
Burke F. McCahill
Douglas L. Fleming, Jr.
Jon D. Huddleston
Craig E. White

For full biographical listings, see the Martindale-Hubbell Law Directory

HAZEL & THOMAS, A PROFESSIONAL CORPORATION (AV)

44084 Riverside Parkway, Suite 300, 22075
Telephone: 703-729-8500; Metro: 703-478-1992
Alexandria, Virginia Office: Suite 200, 510 King Street, P.O. Box 820.
Telephone: 703-836-8400.
Fairfax County (Falls Church), Virginia Office: Suite 1400, 3110 Fairview Park Drive, P.O. Box 12001.
Telephone: 703-641-4200.
Manassas, Virginia Office: 9324 West Street, Third Floor.
Telephone: 703-330-7400. Metro: 703-803-7474.
Richmond, Virginia Office: Suite 600, 411 East Franklin Street, P.O. Box 788.
Telephone: 804-344-3400.

RESIDENT ATTORNEYS

Michael A. Banzhaf
E. William Chapman
David C. Culbert
Karen C. Fagelson
J. Randall Minchew
Thomas W. Nalls

OF COUNSEL

Richard C. Riemenschneider

CONTRACT ATTORNEY

David P. O'Brien

For full biographical listings, see the Martindale-Hubbell Law Directory

*LOVINGSTON,** Nelson Co. — (Refer to Buckingham)

LYNCHBURG, (Independent City)

CASKIE & FROST, A PROFESSIONAL CORPORATION (AV)

2306 Atherholt Road, P.O. Box 6360, 24505
Telephone: 804-846-2731
Fax: 804-845-1191

James Randolph Caskie (1909-1969)
E. Marshall Frost (1920-1988)
S. Bolling Hobbs (Retired)
S. J. Thompson, Jr. (1936-1994)
Joseph C. Knakal, Jr.
John R. Alford
Leighton S. Houck
Theodore J. Craddock
Gregory P. Cochran
George L. Mason
John T. Cook
Joy Lee Price
Mark J. Peake
John R. Alford, Jr.

General Counsel: Leggett Stores; Elderberry Nursing Homes, Inc.; First Federal Savings Bank of Lynchburg.
Local Counsel: Cincinnati Insurance Co.; General Accident Fire & Life Assurance; Nationwide Insurance Co.; NationsBank, N.A.; Crestar Bank.

For full biographical listings, see the Martindale-Hubbell Law Directory

EDMUNDS & WILLIAMS, P.C. (AV)

800 Main Street, P.O. Box 958, 24505-0958
Telephone: 804-846-9000
Telecopier: 804-846-0337

Edmund Schaefer, III (Retired)
B. C. Baldwin, Jr. (Retired)
Samuel H. Williams (1890-1970)
J. Easley Edmunds, Jr. (1889-1977)
Douglas A. Robertson (1900-1982)
Edward S. Graves (1909-1985)
Henry M. Sackett, Jr. (1911-1989)
Robert D. Richards (1928-1994)
Paul H. Coffey, Jr.
Kenneth S. White
Robert C. Wood, III
Henry M. Sackett, III
Rayner V. Snead, Jr.
Bernard C. Baldwin, III
Wm. Tracey Shaw
R. Edwin Burnette, Jr.
William E. Phillips

Kevin L. Cash
James O. Watts, IV
Kristine H. Smith

Representative Clients: Appalachian Power Company; Central Fidelity Bank C. B. Fleet Company, Inc.; Harris Trucking; Lynchburg Foundry Co.; Norfolk Southern Corporation; Smithfield Companies; State Farm Mutual Auto. Ins. Co.; Sweet Briar College; Centra Health, Inc.

For full biographical listings, see the Martindale-Hubbell Law Directory

*MADISON,** Madison Co. — (Refer to Charlottesville)

*MANASSAS,** Prince William Co.

HAZEL & THOMAS, A PROFESSIONAL CORPORATION (AV)

9324 West Street, Third Floor, 22110
Telephone: 703-330-7400
Metro: 703-803-7474
Alexandria, Virginia Office: Suite 200, 510 King Street, P.O. Box 820.
Telephone: 703-836-8400.
Fairfax County (Falls Church), Virginia Office: Suite 1400, 3110 Fairview Park Drive, P.O. Box 12001.
Telephone: 703-641-4200.
Leesburg, Virginia Office: 44084 Riverside Parkway, Suite 300.
Telephone: 703-729-8500. Metro: 703-478-1992.
Richmond, Virginia Office: Suite 600, 411 East Franklin Street, P.O. Box 788.
Telephone: 804-344-3400.

RESIDENT ATTORNEYS

John H. Foote — Garth M. Wainman

John L. McBride — Thomas W. Smith, III

For full biographical listings, see the Martindale-Hubbell Law Directory

*MARION,** Smyth Co. — (Refer to Pulaski)

*MARTINSVILLE,** (Ind. City; Seat of Henry Co.)

YOUNG, HASKINS, MANN & GREGORY, A PROFESSIONAL CORPORATION (AV)

400 Starling Avenue, P.O. Box 72, 24114
Telephone: 703-638-2367
Telefax: 703-638-1214

R. R. (Jim) Young, Jr.
James W. Haskins
Robert W. Mann
John L. Gregory, III
Kelli A. Krumenacker
G. Carter Greer
James R. McGarry

Representative Clients: E.I. Dupont deNemours; Conoco, Inc.; Fieldcrest Cannon, Inc.; Appalachian Power Co.; American Furniture Co.; Hooker Furniture Co.; Central Telephone Co.; Liberty Mutual Insurance Co.

For full biographical listings, see the Martindale-Hubbell Law Directory

MCLEAN, Fairfax Co.

H. CLAYTON COOK, JR. (AV)

1011 Langley Hill Drive, 22101
Telephone: 703-821-2468
Rapifax: 703-821-2469
Washington, D.C. Office: 2828 Pennsylvania Avenue, N.W. 20007.
Telephone: 202-338-8088.
Rapifax: 202-338-1843.
(Not admitted in VA)

For full biographical listings, see the Martindale-Hubbell Law Directory

MAGRUDER & ASSOCIATES, P.C. (AV)

6756 Old McLean Village Drive, 22101
Telephone: 703-448-0900
FAX: 703-448-0813

Anne-Marie Magruder

Barbara L. Portman
Kent A. Bieberich
Cynthia R. Cook
Aimee N. Richardson
James Donald Sadowski (Not admitted in VA)

For full biographical listings, see the Martindale-Hubbell Law Directory

MCGUIRE, WOODS, BATTLE & BOOTHE (AV)

8280 Greensboro Drive, Suite 900, Tysons Corner, 22102-3892
Telephone: 703-712-5000
Fax: 703-712-5050
Alexandria, Virginia Office: Transpotomac Plaza, Suite 1000, 1199 North Fairfax Street, 22314-1437.
Telephone: 703-739-6200.
Fax: 703-739-6270.
Baltimore, Maryland Office: The Blaustein Building, One North Charles Street, 21201-3793.
Telephone: 410-659-4400.
Fax: 410-659-4599.
Charlottesville, Virginia Office: Court Square Building, P.O. Box 1288, 22902-1288.
Telephone: 804-977-2500.
Fax: 804-980-2222.
Jacksonville, Florida Office: Barnett Center, Suite 2750, 50 North Laura Street, 32202-3635.
Telephone: 904-798-3200.
Fax: 904-798-3207.

(See Next Column)

Norfolk, Virginia Office: World Trade Center, Suite 9000, 101 West Main Street, 23510-1655.
Telephone: 804-640-3700.
Fax: 804-640-3701.
Richmond, Virginia Office: One James Center, 901 East Cary Street, 23219-4030.
Telephone: 804-775-1000.
Fax: 804-775-1061.
Washington, D.C. Office: The Army and Navy Club Building, 1627 Eye Street, N.W., 20006-4007.
Telephone: 202-857-1700.
Fax: 202-857-1737.
Brussels, Belgium Office: 250 Avenue Louise, Ste. 64, 1050.
Telephone: (32 2) 629 42 11.
Fax: (32 2) 629 42 22.
Zürich, Switzerland Office: P.O. Box 4930, Bahnhofstrasse 3, 8022.
Telephone: (41 1) 225 20 00.
Fax: (41 1) 225 20 20.

MEMBERS OF FIRM

Thomas L. Appler
Michael T. Bradshaw
James C. Brashares
Jocelyn West Brittin
Thomas C. Brown, Jr.
Thomas E. Cabaniss
Antonio J. Calabrese
J. Jay Corson IV
Curtis M. Coward
Ann-Mac Cox
Mark Charles Dorigan
Waller T. Dudley
James Webster Dyke, Jr.
K. Stewart Evans, Jr.
Carson Lee Fifer, Jr.
Michael D. Flemming
Stanley M. Franklin
Michael J. Giguere
Jacqueline M. Gordon
William C. Haney
Anne Hurst Hardock
Richard R. G. Hobson
David S. Houston
James M. Lewis
R. Dennis McArver
Sean F. Murphy
R. Terrence Ney
Edward F. Rodriguez, Jr.
Arthur P. Scibelli
John S. Stump
Courtland L. Traver, Jr.
Gerald B. Treacy, Jr. (Not admitted in VA)
Haynie Seay Trotter
Robert R. Vieth
Edward E. Zughaib

RETIRED OF COUNSEL

Minerva Wilson Andrews
Edgar Allen Prichard
Carrington Williams

OF COUNSEL

Russell E. Dougherty (Not admitted in VA)
Edmund D. Harllee
Elizabeth Land Lewis
Stephen P. Robin
John H. Toole

ASSOCIATES

Vincent Badolato
John J. Bellaschi
Marianne G. Bundren
M. Melissa Glassman
James Allen Hoffman
Christopher L. Keefer
John G. Lavoie
M. Elizabeth Leverage
Francis X. Mellon
Arlene Paul
Melanie Miller Reilly
Lawrence Eric Rifken
Nathan B. Smith
Karen L. Turner
Peter J. Willsey
Joseph W. Wright III

For full biographical listings, see the Martindale-Hubbell Law Directory

REED SMITH SHAW & MCCLAY (AV)

Suite 1100, 8251 Greensboro Drive, 22102-3844
Telephone: 703-734-4600
Pittsburgh, Pennsylvania Office: James H. Reed Building, Mellon Square, 435 Sixth Avenue, 15219-1886.
Telephone: 412-288-3131.
Philadelphia, Pennsylvania Office: 2500 One Liberty Place, 19103-7301.
Telephone: 215-851-8100.
Harrisburg, Pennsylvania Office: 213 Market Street, 17101-2132.
Telephone: 717-234-5988.
Washington, D.C. Office: Ring Building, 1200 18th Street, N.W., 20036-2506.
Telephone: 202-457-6100.
Princeton, New Jersey Office: 136 Main Street, 08540-5799.
Telephone: 609-987-0050.
FAX: 609-951-0824.

MEMBERS OF FIRM

Paul R. Dean, Jr.
Michael F. Marino
Thomas P. Murphy
W. Scott Railton (Not admitted in VA)
Lee A. Rau

COUNSEL

Frederic Freilicher (Not admitted in VA)
David Machanic

ASSOCIATES

Marjorie P. Alloy (Not admitted in VA)
Jill M. Lashay
Mark B. Peabody
Eric A. Welter (Not admitted in VA)

For full biographical listings, see the Martindale-Hubbell Law Directory

McLean—Continued

SHAW, PITTMAN, POTTS & TROWBRIDGE (AV)

A Partnership including Professional Corporations
1501 Farm Credit Drive, 22102
Telephone: 703-790-7900
Telecopier: 703-821-2397
Washington, D.C. Office: 2300 N Street, N.W.
Telephone: 202-663-8000.
Cable Address: "Shawlaw".
Telex: 89-2693 (Shawlaw Wsh.)
Telecopier: 202-663-8007.
Leesburg, Virginia Office: 201 Liberty Street, S.W.
Telephone: 703-777-0004. Metro: 478-8989.
Facsimile: 703-777-9320.
Alexandria, Virginia Office: 115 South Union Street.
Telephone: 703-739-6650.
Fax: 703-739-6699.
New York, N.Y. Office: 900 Third Avenue, Suite 1800.
Telephone: 212-836-4200.
Facsimile: 212-836-4201.

MEMBERS OF FIRM

George F. Albright, Jr.
Frank J. Baltz (P.C.) (Resident)
Alan B. Croft (Resident)
John Engel (P.C.)
Robert M. Gordon
C. Thomas Hicks, III (P.C.) (Resident)

COUNSEL

Scott E. Barat (Resident)

ASSOCIATES

Charis R. Keitelman (Resident)
Jackson H. Sherrill III (Not admitted in VA; Resident)
Hala M. Sibay (Resident)
Danielle O. Stieger (Resident)

For full biographical listings, see the Martindale-Hubbell Law Directory

STEPHENS LAW FIRM (AV)

1800 Old Meadow Road, P.O. Box 1096, 22101
Telephone: 703-821-8700
Facsimile: 703-827-7761
Washington, D.C. Office: 1029 Vermont Avenue, N.W., Suite 400, 20005.
Telephone: 202-331-8200.

MEMBER OF FIRM

William T. Stephens

ASSOCIATES

Michael A. Williams

COUNSEL

Sean C. Connors

For full biographical listings, see the Martindale-Hubbell Law Directory

VENABLE, BAETJER AND HOWARD (AV)

A Partnership including Professional Corporations
Suite 400, 2010 Corporate Ridge, 22102
Telephone: 703-760-1600
FAX: 703-821-8949
Baltimore, Maryland Office: 1800 Mercantile Bank & Trust Building, 2 Hopkins Plaza.
Telephone: 410-244-7400.
Washington, D.C. Office: Venable, Baetjer, Howard & Civiletti, Suite 1000, 1201 New York Avenue, N.W.
Telephone: 202-962-4800.
Rockville, Maryland Office: Suite 500, One Church Street, P.O. Box 1906.
Telephone: 301-217-5600.
Towson, Maryland Office: 210 Allegheny Avenue, P. O. Box 5517.
Telephone: 410-494-6200.

MEMBERS OF FIRM

William L. Walsh, Jr. (P.C.)
David T. Stitt
Robert E. Madden (Also at Washington, D.C. and Baltimore, Maryland Offices)
Kenneth C. Bass, III (Also at Washington, D.C. Office)
Lars E. Anderson
John G. Milliken (Also at Washington, D.C. Office)
Bruce E. Titus
William D. Dolan, III (P.C.)
David G. Lane
Ellen F. Dyke
Joel J. Goldberg (Also at Washington, D.C. Office)
Herbert G. Smith, II

OF COUNSEL

Richard H. Mays (Not admitted in VA; Also at Baltimore, Maryland and Washington, D.C. Offices)
Mary T. Flynn

ASSOCIATES

Julian Sylvester Brown
Wm. Craig Dubishar
David R. Hodnett
J. Scott Hommer, III
Jon M. Lippard
Christine M. McAnney
Michael W. Robinson

For full biographical listings, see the Martindale-Hubbell Law Directory

WATT, TIEDER & HOFFAR (AV)

7929 Westpark Drive, Suite 400, 22102
Telephone: 703-749-1000
Telecopier: 703-893-8029
Washington, D.C. Office: 601 Pennsylvania Ave, N.W., Suite 900.
Telephone: 202-462-4697.
Irvine California Office: 3 Park Plaza, Suite 1530.
Telephone: 714-852-6700.

MEMBERS OF FIRM

John B. Tieder, Jr.
Robert G. Watt
Julian F. Hoffar
Robert M. Fitzgerald
Robert K. Cox
William R. Chambers
David C. Romm
Charles E. Raley (Not admitted in VA)
Francis X. McCullough
Barbara G. Werther (Not admitted in VA)
Garry R. Boehlert
Thomas B. Newell
Lewis J. Baker
Benjamin T. Riddles, II
Timothy F. Brown
Richard G. Mann, Jr.
David C. Mancini
David C. Haas
Henry D. Danforth
Carter B. Reid
Donna S. McCaffrey
Mark J. Groff (Not admitted in VA)
Mark A. Sgarlata
Daniel E. Cohen
Michael G. Long (Resident, Irvine, California Office)

OF COUNSEL

Avv. Roberto Tassi
Clyde Harold Slease (Not admitted in VA)

ASSOCIATES

Thomas J. Powell
Douglas C. Proxmire
Tara L. Vautin
Edward Parrott
Steven G. Schassler
Joseph H. Bucci
Steven J. Weber
Paul A. Varela
Vivian Katsantonis
Charlie Lee
Kathleen A. Olden
Christopher P. Pappas (Resident, Irvine, California Office)
Shelly L. Ewald
Christopher J. Brasco
Jean V. Misterek
Charles W. Durant
Susan Latham Timoner
Fred A. Mendicino
Susan G. Sisskind
Robert G. Barbour
Keith C. Phillips
Marybeth Zientek Gaul
Timothy E. Heffernan (Not admitted in VA)
William Drew Mallender
James Moore Donahue
Heidi Brown Hering
Kerrin Maureen McCormick (Not admitted in VA)
Gretal J. Toker

For full biographical listings, see the Martindale-Hubbell Law Directory

NARROWS, Giles Co.

WARREN & SCHEID, P.C. (AV)

225 Main Street, P.O. Box 392, 24124
Telephone: 703-726-2357
FAX: 703-726-2549

James L. Warren
Brian T. Scheid

LEGAL SUPPORT PERSONNEL

Diana Lynn Johnson
Lisa Boone

Representative Clients: First Virginia Bank-Southwest; McKenzie Lumber Co.; Celco Federal Credit Union; Giles County School Board; Pembroke Telephone Coop, Inc.; Bland County Medical Clinic, Inc.; VA Department of Highways and Transportation; Bland County Board of Supervisors; Muncy Electric, Inc.

For full biographical listings, see the Martindale-Hubbell Law Directory

NEWPORT NEWS, (Independent City)

WILLIAM V. HOYLE, JR. (AV)

10401 Warwick Boulevard, 23601
Telephone: 804-596-1850
Fax: 804-596-1925

JONES, BLECHMAN, WOLTZ & KELLY, P.C. (AV)

600 Thimble Shoals Boulevard, P.O. Box 12888, 23612-2888
Telephone: 804-873-8000
Fax: 804-873-8103

Allan D. Jones (1875-1954)
Daniel Schlosser (1915-1977)
Franklin O. Blechman (1905-1986)
Arthur W. Woltz (1905-1993)
Herbert V. Kelly
Raymond H. Suttle
B. M. Millner
Ralph M. Goldstein
John T. Tompkins, III
Conway H. Sheild, III
Edward D. David
Svein J. Lassen
Kenneth B. Murov
Herbert V. Kelly, Jr.
Richard B. Donaldson, Jr.
Robert L. Freeman, Jr.
Michael B. Ware
Robyn Hylton Hansen
James C. Smith, Jr.
Charles Peter Tench

(See Next Column)

JONES, BLECHMAN, WOLTZ & KELLY P.C., *Newport News—Continued*

Raymond H. Suttle, Jr.
Gary Andrew Mills
Blanche M. Garber
Kevin W. Grierson

Representative Clients: NationsBank of Virginia; Crestar Bank; Hampton Roads Sanitation District Commission; Peninsula Airport Commission; Ferguson Enterprises; Maida Development Co.; The Bionetics Corporation; Bell Atlantic; Great Atlantic Management Co.; City of Newport News Industrial Development Authority.

For full biographical listings, see the Martindale-Hubbell Law Directory

KAUFMAN & CANOLES, A PROFESSIONAL CORPORATION (AV)

Suite 408, 11817 Canon Boulevard, 23606
Telephone: 804-873-6300
Fax: 804-873-6359
Norfolk, Virginia Office: One Commercial Place, P.O. Box 3037, 23514-3037.
Telephone: 804-624-3000.
Virginia Beach, Virginia Office: 700 Pavilion Center, P.O. Box 626, 23451.
Telephone: 804-491-4000.

RESIDENT PERSONNEL

H. Vincent Conway, Jr.
Arthur J. Kamp
Barbara Hays Kamp
James L. Windsor

Elizabeth L. White

OF COUNSEL

Thomas N. Downing

Representative Clients: American Property Services; Casey Auto Group, Inc.; CENIT Bancorp, Inc.; Crestar Bank; Daily Press, Inc.; NationsBank, N.A.; Newport News Municipal Employees Credit Union, Inc.; Noland, Inc.; NView Corporation; Olympia Development Co.; Victor Management.

For full biographical listings, see the Martindale-Hubbell Law Directory

PATTEN, WORNOM & WATKINS, L.C. (AV)

Patrick Henry Corporate Center Suite 360, 12350 Jefferson Avenue, 23602
Telephone: 804-249-1881
Facsimile: 804-249-3242; 804-249-1627

Neal J. Patten
I. Leake Wornom, Jr.
Thomas R. Watkins
Donald N. Patten
Robert R. Hatten
Joseph H. Latchum, Jr.
Benjamin A. Williams, III
William M. Martin, III
Avery Tillinghast Waterman, Jr.
Joseph M. DuRant
Jonathan A. Smith-George

Gary R. West
South Trimble Patterson
James H. Shoemaker, Jr.
Rachel M. Gluckman
Hugh B. McCormick, III
Steven A. Meade
Deborah W. Smith-George

Representative Clients: Mary Immaculate Hospital Inc.; Cochran Construction Co.; Modern Machine & Tool Co., Inc.; NationsBank of Virginia, N.A.; Virginia Power; Coliseum Mall Shopping Center; D & P Embroidery, Inc.; Cannon Virginia, Inc.; Noland Co.; Blessings Corp.

For full biographical listings, see the Martindale-Hubbell Law Directory

NORFOLK, (Independent City)

BREEDEN, MACMILLAN & GREEN, P.L.C. (AV)

1700 First Virginia Tower, 555 Main Street, 23510-2230
Telephone: 804-622-1111
Telecopier: 804-622-4049

Edward L. Breeden (1905-1990)
Robert R. MacMillan (1923-1990)
Berryman Green, IV (Retired)

OF COUNSEL

Edward L. Breeden, III
T. Jeffrey Salb
S. Lawrence Dumville
Michael T. Zugelder
Allen W. Beasley
James B. Covington

Darlene P. Bradberry

Representative Clients: First Virginia Bank of Tidewater; A.S.C.A.P.; Aetna Life and Casualty Co.; Allstate Insurance Co..

For full biographical listings, see the Martindale-Hubbell Law Directory

CRENSHAW, WARE AND MARTIN, P.L.C. (AV)

Suite 1200 NationsBank Center, One Commercial Place, 23510-2111
Telephone: 804-623-3000
FAX: 804-623-5735

(See Next Column)

Francis N. Crenshaw
Guilford D. Ware
Howard W. Martin, Jr.
Timothy A. Coyle
Ann K. Sullivan
James L. Chapman, IV
John T. Midgett
Martha M. Poindexter

Melanie Fix
David H. Sump
Donald C. Schultz
Kristen L. Hodeen

Representative Clients: Crestar Bank; Contel Cellular, Inc.; Exxon Co., U.S.A.; First Virginia Bank of Tidewater; Ghent Square Community Association; Norfolk Dredging Co.; Norfolk Redevelopment and Housing Authority; Norfolk Warehouse Distribution Centers, Inc.; Southern States Cooperative; Westinghouse Electric Co.

For full biographical listings, see the Martindale-Hubbell Law Directory

THOMAS J. HARLAN, JR., P.C. (AV)

1200 Dominion Tower, 999 Waterside Drive, 23510
Telephone: 804-625-8300
FAX: 804-625-3714

Thomas J. Harlan, Jr.

John M. Flora
Kevin M. Thompson (Not admitted in VA)

LEGAL SUPPORT PERSONNEL

Mary Hayse Grant Wareing (Paralegal)
Barry Wade Vanderhoof (Paralegal)

Reference: Commerce Bank.

For full biographical listings, see the Martindale-Hubbell Law Directory

HOFHEIMER, NUSBAUM, MCPHAUL & SAMUELS, A PROFESSIONAL CORPORATION (AV)

1700 Dominion Tower, 999 Waterside Drive, 23510
Telephone: 804-622-3366
Telecopier: 804-629-0660

Alan J. Hofheimer (1902-1992)
Robert C. Nusbaum
Thomas F. McPhaul
Stanley L. Samuels
Robert C. Miller
Howard E. Gordon
H. David Embree
Linda S. Laibstain
Joseph R. Lassiter, Jr.
William L. Nusbaum
William A. Old, Jr.
Patrick C. Devine, Jr.
John L. Deal
David A. Greer
William F. Devine
E. Diane Thompson
Beth Hirsch Berman
Amy G. Pesesky

Maria Stefanis
Jeffrey Lance Stredler
John M. McGowan
John S. Mitchell, Jr.
Tasos A. Galiotos

OF COUNSEL

Jack Rephan

LEGAL SUPPORT PERSONNEL

Timothy J. Fallon (Director of Administration)

Representative Clients: Barr Construction Co., Inc.; Colonial Auto Group; Colonial Coast Girl Scout Council; The Hall Auto Group; MMM Design Group; S.L. Nusbaum Realty Co.; Only One Dollar; Sandler Foods; Sentara Hospitals; Ticor Title Insurance Co.

For full biographical listings, see the Martindale-Hubbell Law Directory

KAUFMAN & CANOLES, A PROFESSIONAL CORPORATION (AV)

One Commercial Place, P.O. Box 3037, 23514-3037
Telephone: 804-624-3000
Fax: 804-624-3169
Virginia Beach, Virginia Office: 700 Pavilion Center, P.O. Box 626, 23451.
Telephone: 804-491-4000.
Newport News, Virginia Office: Suite 408, 11817 Canon Boulevard.
Telephone: 804-873-6300.

Michael E. Barney
Stanley G. Barr, Jr.
Robert J. Barry
R. Barrow Blackwell
Paul K. Campsen
Leroy T. Canoles, Jr.
George L. Consolvo
H. Vincent Conway, Jr. (Resident, Newport News Office)
John R. Crumpler, Jr.
David M. Delpierre
Robert E. Farmer, III
Paul W. Gerhardt
Robert C. Goodman, Jr.
R. Braxton Hill, III (Resident, Virginia Beach Office)
Barry W. Hunter
Gus J. James, II
Arthur J. Kamp (Resident, Newport News Office)
Barbara Hays Kamp (Resident, Newport News Office)
Charles L. Kaufman (1896-1985)
Kirkland M. Kelley
Charles E. Land
Dennis T. Lewandowski
Joseph L. Lyle, Jr. (Resident, Virginia Beach Office)
Richard C. Mapp, III
Vincent J. Mastracco, Jr.
T. Braxton McKee
Charles V. McPhillips
Terence Murphy
Stephen E. Noona

(See Next Column)

KAUFMAN & CANOLES A PROFESSIONAL CORPORATION—*Continued*

Michael H. Nuckols (Resident, Virginia Beach Office)
John M. Paris, Jr.
David J. Pierce
C. Edward Russell, Jr.
Winthrop A. Short, Jr.
Hunter W. Sims, Jr.
Robert E. Smartschan
J. Douglas Sorensen
W. Edgar Spivey
Jeffrey M. Stedfast
James G. Steiger
Stephen E. Story
Guy K. Tower
Winship C. Tower (Resident, Virginia Beach Office)
William R. Van Buren, III
Jody M. Wagner
Lewis W. Webb, III
Burt H. Whitt
James L. Windsor (Resident, Newport News Office)

COUNSEL

Thomas C. Broyles (Resident, Virginia Beach Office)
Ann S. Dodson
Thomas N. Downing (Resident, Newport News Office)
Harry H. Mansbach

David Neal Anthony
Megan E. Burns
Ellen C. Carlson
Jennifer V. Dragas
Richard M. Feathers
Joseph Gardner Fiveash III
Ann Mayhew Golski
Laura Geringer Gross
John W. Hamilton
Scott W. Kezman
Arlene F. Klinedinst
T. Richard Litton, Jr.
Patrick H. O'Donnell
David J. Owens
L. Allan Parrott, Jr.
Pamela J. Piscatelli
Alfred M. Randolph, Jr.
Jonathan L. Thornton
Elizabeth L. White (Resident, Newport News Office)

Representative Clients: Crestar Bank; Farm Fresh, Inc.; Goodman-Segar-Hogan Hoffler, Inc.; Hofheimer's, Inc.; NationsBank, N.A.; Telecable Corporation; Virginia Insurance Reciprocal; Federal Deposit Insurance Corp.; International Family Entertainment, Inc. (Family Channel); The Daily Press, Inc.

For full biographical listings, see the Martindale-Hubbell Law Directory

KNIGHT, DUDLEY, DEZERN & CLARKE, P.L.L.C. (AV)

Smithfield Building, Suite 101A, 6160 Kempsville Circle, P.O. Box 13109, 23506
Telephone: 804-466-0464
Telecopier: 804-466-8242

Montgomery Knight, Jr.
William L. Dudley, Jr.
Harry Pincus, Jr. (Retired)
Ray W. Dezern, Jr.
H. H. Hunter Clarke
William M. Sexton
Cyrus A. Dolph, IV
Robert W. Hardy
Robert A. Rapaport
Sarah S. Hull
Andrew A. Protogyrou

Lawrence A. Dunn
Robert B. Rigney
Jimese L. Pendergraft
Timothy S. Brunick

Representative Clients: Liberty Mutual Insurance Co.; St. Paul Insurance Cos.; Cornhill Insurance Co.; Commonwealth of Virginia, Department of Highways; Union Camp Corp.; K-Mart Corp.; Central Fidelity Bank.
References: NationsBank of Virginia, N.A.; Crestar Bank.

For full biographical listings, see the Martindale-Hubbell Law Directory

MCGUIRE, WOODS, BATTLE & BOOTHE (AV)

World Trade Center, Suite 9000, 101 West Main Street, 23210-1655
Telephone: 804-640-3700
Fax: 804-640-3701
Alexandria, Virginia Office: Transpotomac Plaza, Suite 1000, 1199 North Fairfax Street, 22314-1437.
Telephone: 703-739-6200.
Fax: 703-739-6270.
Baltimore, Maryland Office: The Blaustein Building, One North Charles Street, 21201-3793.
Telephone: 410-659-4400.
Fax: 410-659-4599.
Charlottesville, Virginia Office: Court Square Building, P.O. Box 1288, 22902-1288.
Telephone: 804-977-2500.
Fax: 804-980-2222.
Jacksonville, Florida Office: Barnett Center, Suite 2750, 50 North Laura Street, 32202-3635.
Telephone: 904-798-3200.
Fax: 904-798-3207.
McLean, (Tysons Corner) Virginia Office: Suite 900, 8280 Greensboro Drive, Tysons Corner, 22102-3892.
Telephone: 703-712-5000.
Fax: 703-712-5050.
Richmond, Virginia Office: One James Center, 901 East Cary Street, 23219-4030.
Telephone: 804-775-1000.
Fax: 804-775-1061.
Washington, D.C. Office: The Army and Navy Club Building, 1627 Eye Street, N.W., 20006-4007.
Telephone: 202-857-1700.
Fax: 202-857-1737.

(See Next Column)

Brussels, Belgium Office: 250 Avenue Louise, Bte. 64, 1050.
Telephone: (32 2) 629 42 11.
Fax: (32 2) 629 42 22.
Zürich, Switzerland Office: P.O. Box 4930, Bahnhofstrasse 3, 8022.
Telephone: (41 1) 225 20 00.
Fax: (41 1) 225 20 20.

RESIDENT MEMBERS

Waverley Lee Berkley, III
Jerry L. Bowman
Thomas E. Cabaniss
Page D. Cranford
Glenn W. Hampton
R. Arthur Jett, Jr.
Vann H. Lefcoe
Laura R. Lucas
Robert W. McFarland
John D. Padgett
F. Bradford Stillman
Mark D. Williamson

OF COUNSEL

Carter B. S. Furr

RESIDENT ASSOCIATES

Lisa Ann Bertini
John C. Bilzor
Richard Joshua Cromwell
Mark S. Davis
Douglas M. Foley
Carol W. Hahn
Patrick L. Hayden
Ute Heidenreich
Andrew T. Shilling
J. Randolph Stokes
David M. Young

For full biographical listings, see the Martindale-Hubbell Law Directory

SACKS, SACKS & IMPREVENTO (AV)

Suite 501 Town Point Center, 150 Boush Street, P.O. Box 3874, 23514
Telephone: 804-623-2753
FAX: 804-640-7170

Herman A. Sacks (1886-1983)
Stanley E. Sacks
Andrew M. Sacks
Michael F. Imprevento

For full biographical listings, see the Martindale-Hubbell Law Directory

STACKHOUSE, SMITH & NEXSEN (AV)

1600 First Virginia Tower, 555 Main Street, P.O. Box 3640, 23514
Telephone: 804-623-3555
FAX: 804-624-9245

MEMBERS OF FIRM

Robert C. Stackhouse
Peter W. Smith, IV
William W. Nexsen
R. Clinton Stackhouse, Jr.
Janice McPherson Doxey

ASSOCIATES

Mary Painter Opitz
Timothy P. Murphy
Carl J. Khalil

Representative Clients: Heritage Bank & Trust; The Atlantic Group, Inc.; Roughton Pontiac Corp; Federal National Mortgage Association; Kemper National Insurance Cos.; Shearson/American Express Mortgage Corp.; Harleysville Mutual Insurance Co.; Heritage Bankshares, Inc.; Presbyterian League of the Presbytery of Eastern Virginia, Inc.; Oakwood Acceptance Corp.

For full biographical listings, see the Martindale-Hubbell Law Directory

TAVSS, FLETCHER, EARLEY & KING, P.C. (AV)

Suite 100, Two Commercial Place, 23510
Telephone: 804-625-1214
Fax: 804-622-7295
Mailing Address: P.O. Box 3747, 23514

Richard J. Tavss
John R. Fletcher
Mark L. Earley
Ray W. King
Besianne Tavss Shilling

LEGAL SUPPORT PERSONNEL

Maurice J. O'Connor

Reference: Bank of the Commonwealth.

For full biographical listings, see the Martindale-Hubbell Law Directory

VANDEVENTER, BLACK, MEREDITH & MARTIN (AV)

500 World Trade Center, 23510
Telephone: 804-446-8600
Cable Address: "Hughsvan"
Telex: 823-671
Telecopier: 446-8670
North Carolina, Kitty Hawk Office: 6 Juniper Trail.
Telephone: 919-261-5055.
Fax: 919-261-8444.
London, England Office: Suite 692, Level 6, Lloyd's, 1 Lime Street.
Telephone: (071) 623-2081.
Facsimile: (071) 929-0043.
Telex: 987321.

OF COUNSEL

Braden Vandeventer

(See Next Column)

VANDEVENTER, BLACK, MEREDITH & MARTIN, *Norfolk—Continued*

MEMBERS OF FIRM

Braden Vandeventer (1878-1943)
Barron F. Black (1893-1974)
Walter B. Martin, Jr.
Charles F. Tucker
Joseph A. Gawrys
Morton H. Clark
John M. Ryan
George William Birkhead
James S. Mathews
Geoffrey F. Birkhead
Norman W. Shearin, Jr. (Not admitted in VA; Resident, Kitty Hawk, North Carolina Office)
Anita O. Poston
Robert L. O'Donnell
Carter T. Gunn
Daniel R. Weckstein
Mark T. Coberly
F. Nash Bilisoly
Michael P. Cotter
Henry P. Bouffard
R. John Barrett
Patrick W. Herman
William E. Franczek
Thomas M. Lucas
Dean T. Buckius
Michael L. Sterling
Bryant C. McGann
Deborah Mancoll Casey

ASSOCIATES

William M. Dozier
Patrick A. Genzler
Susan B. Potter
Jane D. Tucker
Robert V. Timms, Jr.
Howard W. Roth, III
Kimberley Herson Timms
William V. Power
Neil S. Lowenstein
Valerie J. Brodsky
Edward J. Powers
Price M. Shapiro
Arthur Serratelli
Mary Chapman Hamilton
Tammy J. Gatchell
Christopher R. Hedrick (Resident, Kitty Hawk, North Carolina Office)

For full biographical listings, see the Martindale-Hubbell Law Directory

WILLCOX & SAVAGE, P.C. (AV)

1800 NationsBank Center, 23510-2197
Telephone: 804-628-5500
Telecopy: 804-628-5566

Toy D. Savage, Jr.
Palmer S. Rutherford, Jr.
Joseph A. Leafe
Hugh L. Patterson
William E. Rachels, Jr.
Allan G. Donn
Conrad M. Shumadine
Thomas G. Johnson, Jr.
John Y. Pearson, Jr.
James C. Howell
Ross C. Reeves
James R. Warner, Jr.
Thomas A. Rucker
Anthony M. Thiel
Guy R. Friddell, III
Bruce T. Bishop
Peter M. Huber
William W. Harrison, Jr.
Keith C. Cuthrell, Jr.
Stephen W. Brewer
James S. McNider, III
Walter D. Kelley, Jr.
Jeffrey H. Gray
Marshall B. Martin
Robert L. Dewey
Kenneth B. Tillou
Warren L. Tisdale
Peter G. Zemanian
Sheila Ryan Horne
James J. Wheaton
Randy D. Singer
S. Bernard Goodwyn
David C. Bowen
Stephen R. Davis
Gary A. Bryant

Joyce Jackson Wood
Jeffrey W. Breeser
Stephen R. Jackson
John S. Wilson
William M. Furr
Susan Shaw Hulbert
David A. Snouffer
Mark D. Stiles
John F. Faber, Jr.
Kevin L. Keller
Peter Vincent Chiusano
Amy Moss Levy
Rebecca L. Deloria
Frank A. Edgar, Jr.
John D. McIntyre
Thomas Corbett Inglima
John Emery Buehner
Thomas Scott McGraw

OF COUNSEL

Frederic A. Nicholson

Representative Clients: NationsBank of Virginia, N.A.; Landmark Communications, Inc.; Southeastern Public Service Authority of Virginia; Superfos a/s; Metro Machine Corporation; Sentara Health System; Norfolk & Portsmouth Belt Line Railroad; Virginia Farm Bureau Insurance Services; Massachusetts Mutual Life Insurance Company.

For full biographical listings, see the Martindale-Hubbell Law Directory

WILLIAMS KELLY & GREER, A PROFESSIONAL CORPORATION (AV)

600 Crestar Bank Building, P.O. Box 3416, 23514
Telephone: 804-624-2600
Fax: 804-624-2511

William Leigh Williams (1859-1936)
W. H. T. Loyall (1869-1951)
Robert B. Tunstall (1880-1956)
Leigh D. Williams (1893-1967)
William Ruffin Coleman Cocke (1884-1967)
William C. Worthington (1917-1973)
Lawson Worrell, Jr. (1909-1988)
Joseph L. Kelly (Retired)
Jack E. Greer
Edward L. Oast, Jr.
James L. Miller
Kenneth H. Lambert, Jr.
Richard M. Swope
Robert H. Powell III
J. Anderson Stalnaker
Samuel J. Webster
Daniel R. Warman
John Y. Richardson, Jr.
Wilson B. Dodson III

(See Next Column)

M. Wayne Ringer
Joan F. Martin
Mark F. Williams
Mark H. Mapp
Richard B. Baker
Neal P. Brodsky
Heather A. Mullen

Raymond L. Hogge, Jr.
Christopher R. Papile
David N. Payne
Daniel Kent Brady
Martha E. Drum

Counsel for: Bell Atlantic-Virginia, Inc.; Virginia Power Co.; Crestar Bank; Norfolk Southern Corporation; CSX Transportation, Inc.; DePaul Medical Center; City of Norfolk.

For full biographical listings, see the Martindale-Hubbell Law Directory

NORTON, Wise Co.

MULLINS, THOMASON & HARRIS, A PROFESSIONAL CORPORATION (AV)

The Law Building, 30 Seventh Street, P.O. Box 1200, 24273
Telephone: 703-679-3110
Telecopier: 703-679-3113

Fred Bonham Greear (1899-1960)
William Thomas Bowen (1908-1964)
Leslie Morris Mullins (Retired)
Ronald G. Thomason
Elsey A. Harris, III

W. Shawn McDaniel
Roy M. Jessee
Herndon P. Jeffreys III

Counsel for: Old Dominion Power Co.
Local Counsel for: Penn Virginia Resources Corp.; Allstate Insurance Company; United States Fidelity & Guaranty Co.; Norfolk-Southern Corp.; Westmoreland Coal Co.; Blue Diamond Coal Co.; Seaboard System Railroad; Paramount Mining Corporation; Virginia Iron, Coal & Coke Co.

For full biographical listings, see the Martindale-Hubbell Law Directory

ONANCOCK, Accomack Co.

AMES & AMES (AV)

Ames Building, 71 Market Street, P.O. Box 177, 23417
Telephone: 804-787-3535
FAX: 804-787-3536

MEMBERS OF FIRM

E. Almer Ames, Jr. (1903-1987)
Edward A. Ames, III

General Counsel for: Town of Onancock.
Local Counsel for: First Virginia Bank of Tidewater.

For full biographical listings, see the Martindale-Hubbell Law Directory

*ORANGE,** Orange Co.

SHACKELFORD, HONENBERGER, THOMAS & WILLIS, P.L.C. (AV)

One Perry Plaza, P.O. Box 871, 22960
Telephone: 703-672-2711
Fax: 703-672-2714
Culpeper, Virginia Office: 147 West Davis Street, P.O. Box 1002.
Telephone: 703-825-0305.

OF COUNSEL

Virginius R. Shackelford, Jr.
Virginius R. Shackelford, III
Christopher J. Honenberger
Frank A. Thomas, III
Jere M. H. Willis, III (Resident, Culpeper, Virginia Office)
Sarah Collins Honenberger

Sean D. Gregg

Counsel for: Woodberry Forest School; County of Madison; Rapidan Service Authority.
Assistant Division Counsel for: Norfolk Southern Corp.
Approved Attorneys for: Lawyers Title Insurance Corp.; Southern Title Insurance Co.; Chicago Title Insurance Co.; Federal Land Bank of Baltimore; Farmers Home Administration.

For full biographical listings, see the Martindale-Hubbell Law Directory

*PEARISBURG,** Giles Co. — (Refer to Narrows)

PETERSBURG, (Independent City)

WHITE, HAMILTON, WYCHE & SHELL, P.C. (AV)

20 East Tabb Street, 23803
Telephone: 804-733-9010
FAX: 804-796-5163
Prince George, Virginia Office: Route 106.
Telephone: 804-732-4019.

(See Next Column)

WHITE, HAMILTON, WYCHE & SHELL P.C.—*Continued*

Wm. Earle White (1898-1988)
Alex. Hamilton, Jr. (Retired)
Francis L. Wyche (1905-1991)
Louis C. Shell
Stephen G. White
Jerry H. Jones
F. Lewis Wyche, Jr.
Samuel P. Johnson, III
Marcus D. Minton
John E. Griswold
Pamela Shell Baskervill
Charles T. Baskervill
M. Duncan Minton, Jr.

Counsel for: The Hospital Authority of the City of Petersburg; First Federal Savings and Loan Assn.

For full biographical listings, see the Martindale-Hubbell Law Directory

PORTSMOUTH, (Independent City)

COOPER, SPONG & DAVIS, P.C. (AV)

Central Fidelity Bank Building, High & Crawford Streets, P.O. Box 1475, 23705
Telephone: 804-397-3481
Fax: 804-397-8167
Other Portsmouth Office: 3300 Tyre Neck Road, Suite Two, Churchland/ Portsmouth, Virginia, 23703.
Telephone: 804-483-9215.
Fax: 804-483-6998.

Clyde W. Cooper (1893-1980)
Vincent L. Parker (1920-1989)
Robert C. Barclay, III
Louis Brenner
H. Thomas Fennell, Jr. (1937-1981)
Albert J. Taylor, Jr.
Ralph W. Buxton
Branch H. Daniels, Jr.
Joseph P. Massey
David R. Tynch
Gregory M. Pomije
James H. Flippen, III
Susan Taylor Hansen
Robert C. Barclay IV
Katherine S. Cross

OF COUNSEL

William B. Spong, Jr.
Richard J. Davis
Arnold H. Leon

General Counsel: Portsmouth Redevelopment and Housing Authority; Maryview Hospital; Virga Pizza Crust of Virginia, Inc.; Tidewater Area Central Hospital Laundry, Inc.; Action Oldsmobile-Cadillac-GMC Trucks, Inc.; Don Comer Ford.
Local Counsel: Central Fidelity Bank; Bell Atlantic.

For full biographical listings, see the Martindale-Hubbell Law Directory

DONALD C. KILGORE (AV)

Suite 302 Central Fidelity Bank Building, P.O. Box 1051, 23705
Telephone: 804-397-7955
Fax: 804-393-3647

Reference: Central Fidelity Bank.

For full biographical listings, see the Martindale-Hubbell Law Directory

*PRINCE GEORGE,** Prince George Co. — (Refer to Petersburg)

*PULASKI,** Pulaski Co.

GILMER, SADLER, INGRAM, SUTHERLAND & HUTTON (AV)

Midtown Professional Building, 65 East Main Street, P.O. Box 878, 24301
Telephone: 703-980-1360; 703-639-0027
Telecopier: 703-980-5264
Blacksburg (Montgomery County), Virginia Office: 201 West Roanoke Street, P.O. Box 908.
Telephone: 703-552-1061.
Telecopier: 703-552-8227.

MEMBERS OF FIRM

Howard C. Gilmer, Jr. (1906-1975)
Roby K. Sutherland (1909-1975)
Philip M. Sadler (1915-1994)
Robert J. Ingram
James L. Hutton (Resident, Blacksburg Office)
Thomas J. McCarthy, Jr.
John J. Gill
Gary C. Hancock
Jackson M. Bruce
Michael J. Barbour
Deborah Wood Dobbins
Todd G. Patrick (Resident, Blacksburg Office)
Debra Fitzgerald-O'Connell
Scott A. Rose
Timothy Edmond Kirtner

OF COUNSEL

James R. Montgomery

Representative Clients: Appalachian Power Co.; Chevron; Liberty Mutual Insurance Co.; Norfolk Southern Railway Co.; Pulaski Furniture Corp.; NationsBank; Travelers Insurance Group; Renfro, Inc.; Magnox, Inc.; Corning Glass Works.

For full biographical listings, see the Martindale-Hubbell Law Directory

RADFORD, (Independent City)

SPIERS AND SPIERS (AV)

Spiers Building, 1206 Norwood Street, P.O. Box 1052, 24141-0052
Telephone: 703-639-1601
Telecopier: 703-639-6802

(See Next Column)

John B. Spiers (1897-1956)
John B. Spiers, Jr.

For full biographical listings, see the Martindale-Hubbell Law Directory

STONE, HARRISON, TURK & SHOWALTER, P.C. (AV)

Tyler Office Plaza, 1902 Downey Street, P.O. Box 2968, 24143-2968
Telephone: 703-639-9056
Telecopier: 703-731-4665

Edwin C. Stone
Clifford L. Harrison
James C. Turk, Jr.
Josiah T. Showalter, Jr.
Margaret E. Stone

Representative Clients: St. Albans Psychiatric Hospital; Radford Community Hospital; Inland Motor Corp.; The K-C Corp.; Meadowgold Dairies; Lynchburg Foundry; Hartford Accident and Indemnity Co.; Cigna Insurance Cos.; Hercules, Inc.; Norfolk Southern Corp.

For full biographical listings, see the Martindale-Hubbell Law Directory

RESTON, Fairfax Co.

GLENNON, GOODMAN & LUBELEY (AV)

11480 Sunset Hills Road, 22090
Telephone: 703-689-2100
Telecopier: 703-471-6496

MEMBERS OF FIRM

Elizabeth Q. Glennon
Andrew H. Goodman
Richard A. Lubeley

OF COUNSEL

Robert Lee Vaughn, Jr.

Approved Attorneys for: Chicago Title Insurance Co.; Lawyers Title Insurance Co.; Commonwealth Title Insurance Co.; Stewart Title Insurance Co.; First American Title Insurance Co.
References: Suburban Bank, N.A.; Crestar Bank; George Mason Bank.

For full biographical listings, see the Martindale-Hubbell Law Directory

*RICHMOND,** (Ind. City; Seat of Henrico Co.)

HAZEL & THOMAS, A PROFESSIONAL CORPORATION (AV)

Suite 600, 411 East Franklin Street, P.O. Box 788, 23206
Telephone: 804-344-3400
Alexandria, Virginia Office: Suite 200, 510 King Street, P.O. Box 820.
Telephone: 703-836-8400.
Fairfax County (Falls Church), Virginia Office: Suite 1400, 3110 Fairview Park Drive. P.O. Box 12001.
Telephone: 703-641-4200.
Leesburg, Virginia Office: 44084 Riverside Parkway, Suite 300.
Telephone: 703-729-8500. Metro: 703-478-1992.
Manassas, Virginia Office: 9324 West Street, Third Floor.
Telephone: 703-330-7400. Metro: 703-803-7474.

RESIDENT ATTORNEYS

Steven D. Delaney
S. Miles Dumville
Patrick O. Gottschalk
D. Patrick Lacy, Jr.
Brian R. Marron
Walter A. Marston, Jr.
Kathleen S. Mehfoud
Steven W. Pearson

COUNSEL

H. Lane Kneedler
Patrick A. O'Hare

Philip F. Abraham
Vernon E. Inge, Jr.
Otto W. Konrad
Jeffery Keith Mitchell
Pamela G. Parsons

For full biographical listings, see the Martindale-Hubbell Law Directory

MCGUIRE, WOODS, BATTLE & BOOTHE (AV)

One James Center, 901 East Cary Street, 23219-4030
Telephone: 804-775-1000
Fax: 804-775-1061
Alexandria, Virginia Office: Transpotomac Plaza, Suite 1000, 1199 North Fairfax Street, 22314-1437.
Telephone: 703-739-6200.
Fax: 703-739-6270.
Baltimore, Maryland Office: The Blaustein Building, One North Charles Street, 21201-3793.
Telephone: 410-659-4400.
Fax: 410-659-4599.
Charlottesville, Virginia Office: Court Square Building, P.O. Box 1288, 22902-1288.
Telephone: 804-977-2500.
Fax: 804-980-2222.
Jacksonville, Florida Office: Barnett Center, Suite 2750, 50 North Laura Street, 32202-3635.
Telephone: 904-798-3200.
Fax: 904-798-3207.
McLean, (Tysons Corner) Virginia Office: 8280 Greensboro Drive, Suite 900, Tysons Corner, 22102-3892.
Telephone: 703-712-5000.
Fax: 703-712-5050.

(See Next Column)

McGuire, Woods, Battle & Boothe, *Richmond—Continued*

Norfolk, Virginia Office: World Trade Center, Suite 9000, 101 West Main Street, 23510-1655.
Telephone: 804-640-3700.
Fax: 804-640-3701.
Washington, D.C. Office: The Army and Navy Club Building, 1627 Eye Street, N.W., 20006-4007.
Telephone: 202-857-1700.
Fax: 202-857-1737.
Brussels, Belgium Office: 250 Avenue Louise, Ste. 64, 1050.
Telephone: (32 2) 629 42 11.
Fax: (32 2) 629 42 22.
Zürich, Switzerland Office: P.O. Box 4930, Bahnhofstrasse 3, 8022.
Telephone: (41 1) 225 20 00.
Fax: (41 1) 225 20 20.

MEMBERS OF FIRM

Robert T. Adams
Fred C. Alexander, Jr. (Resident, Alexandria Office)
W. Allen Ames, Jr.
Arthur E. Anderson II
Donald D. Anderson
John Foster Anderson (Resident, Alexandria Office)
Thomas L. Appler (Resident, McLean (Tysons Corner) Office)
C. Torrence Armstrong (Resident, Alexandria Office)
Terrence Mitchell Bagley
James E. Ballowe, Jr. (Resident, Washington, D.C. Office)
John W. Bates III
Dennis I. Belcher
Ann Ramsey Bergan (Resident, Baltimore, Maryland Office)
Waverley Lee Berkley, III (Resident, Norfolk Office)
Steven W. Blaine (Resident, Charlottesville Office)
J. William Boland
Jerry L. Bowman (Resident, Norfolk Office)
Lucius H. Bracey, Jr. (Resident, Charlottesville Office)
Michael T. Bradshaw (Resident, McLean (Tysons Corner) Office)
J. Robert Brame III
James C. Brashares (Resident, McLean (Tysons Corner) Office)
James D. Bridgeman (Resident, Washington, D.C. Office)
Robert K. Briskin (Resident, Baltimore, Maryland Office)
Jocelyn West Brittin (Resident, McLean (Tysons Corner) Office)
William G. Broaddus
Brickford Y. Brown
Thomas C. Brown, Jr. (Resident, McLean (Tysons Corner) Office)
Donald F. Burke (Resident, Baltimore, Maryland Office)
John W. Burke III
Evan A. Burkholder
Robert L. Burrus, Jr.
Stephen D. Busch
Thomas E. Cabaniss (Norfolk and McLean (Tysons Corner) Offices)
Scott S. Cairns
Antonio J. Calabrese (Resident, McLean (Tysons Corner) Office)
Joseph C. Carter III
Alan C. Cason (Resident, Baltimore, Maryland Office)
John V. Cogbill III
Stephen M. Colangelo (Resident, Alexandria, Virginia Office)
J. Jay Corson IV (Resident, McLean (Tysons Corner) Office)
Curtis M. Coward (Resident, McLean, (Tysons Corner) Office)
Ann-Mac Cox (Resident, McLean (Tysons Corner) Office)
Page D. Cranford (Resident, Norfolk Office)
Thomas L. Crowe (Resident, Baltimore, Maryland Office)
Richard Cullen
H. Slayton Dabney, Jr.
John W. Daniel II
Michael F. Dawes (Resident, Jacksonville, Florida Office)
Thomas F. Dean
Grace R. den Hartog
Mark Charles Dorigan (Resident, McLean (Tysons Corner) Office)
W. Birch Douglass III
Waller T. Dudley (Resident, McLean (Tysons Corner) Office)
James Webster Dyke, Jr. (McLean (Tysons Corner) and Richmond Offices)
Marshall H. Earl, Jr.
Elizabeth Flannagan Edwards
David E. Evans
K. Stewart Evans, Jr. (Resident, McLean (Tysons Corner) Office)
Thomas F. Farrell II
Howard Feller
Carson Lee Fifer, Jr. (Resident, McLean (Tysons Corner) Office)
Michael D. Flemming (Resident, McLean (Tysons Corner) Office)
Bonnie M. France
Stanley M. Franklin (Resident, McLean (Tysons Corner) Office)
John L. Fugh (Resident, Washington, D.C. Office)
Sam Young Garrett, Jr.
Ernest K. Geisler, Jr.
Earle Duncan Getchell, Jr.
William F. Gieg
Michael J. Giguere (Resident, McLean (Tysons Corner) Office)
Nathan D. Goldman (Resident, Jacksonville, Florida Office)
Dennis W. Good, Jr. (Resident, Charlottesville Office)
Larry M. Goodall
Jacqueline M. Gordon (Resident, McLean (Tysons Corner) Office)
John S. Graham III (Richmond and Baltimore, Maryland Offices)
Leslie A. Grandis
Larry B. Grimes (Resident, Washington, D.C. Office)
Glenn W. Hampton (Resident, Norfolk Office)
William C. Haney (Resident McLean (Tysons Corner) Office)
Anne Hurst Hardock (Resident, McLean (Tysons Corner) Office)
T. Craig Harmon
J. Waller Harrison
Richard R. G. Hobson (Resident, McLean (Tysons Corner) Office)

(See Next Column)

MEMBERS OF FIRM (Continued)

David S. Houston (Resident, McLean (Tysons Corner) Office)
R. Arthur Jett, Jr. (Resident, Norfolk Office)
Donald E. King (Resident, Brussels, Belgium Office)
William H. King, Jr.
Steven D. Kittrell (Resident, Washington, D.C. Office)
Kurt J. Krueger (Resident, Charlottesville Office)
Fred S. Landess (Resident, Charlottesville Office)
David Craig Landin
Vann H. Lefcoe (Resident, Norfolk Office)
James M. Lewis (Resident, McLean (Tysons Corner) Office)
Nancy Ruth Little
Laura R. Lucas (Resident, Norfolk Office)
Gary S. Marshall
George Keith Martin
R. Dennis McArver (McLean (Tysons Corner) and Baltimore, Maryland Offices)
Steven C. McCallum
John E. McCann (Resident, Baltimore, Maryland Office)
James P. McElligott, Jr.
Robert W. McFarland (Resident, Norfolk Office)
Gary C. McGee (Resident, Charlottesville Office)
Thomas J. McGonigle (Resident, Washington, D.C. Office)
Joseph P. McMenamin
Henry H. McVey III
David E. Melson (Resident, Baltimore, Maryland Office)
Charles L. Menges
R. Marshall Merriman, Jr.
Leigh B. Middleditch, Jr. (Resident, Charlottesville Office)
Kenneth J. Moran
Brian D. Murphy
Sean F. Murphy (McLean (Tysons Corner) and Richmond Offices)
Thomas L. Newton, Jr.
R. Terrence Ney (Resident, McLean (Tysons Corner) Office)
David N. Oakey
John M. Oakey, Jr.
Clive R. G. O'Grady (Resident, Washington, D.C. Office)
John Brad O'Grady
John D. Padgett (Resident, Norfolk Office)
Rosewell Page III
David H. Pankey (Resident, Washington, D.C. Office)
Charles E. Partridge, Jr. (Resident, Baltimore, Maryland Office)
John W. Patterson
Robert H. Patterson, Jr.
Maria L. Payne
James H. Price III
David L. Richardson II
David W. Robertson
Stephen W. Robinson (Resident, Washington, D.C. Office)
Edward F. Rodriguez, Jr. (Resident, McLean (Tysons Corner) Office)
Thomas P. Rohman
Charlotte Rothenberg Rosen (Resident, Washington, D.C. Office)
Deborah Moreland Russell
Frederick L. Russell (Resident, Charlottesville Office)
Dana L. Rust
Morton A. Sacks (Resident, Baltimore, Maryland Office)
Joseph L. S. St. Amant
James L. Sanderlin
Wellford L. Sanders, Jr.
Raymond F. Scannell
Michael J. Schewel
Gilbert E. Schill, Jr.
Arthur P. Scibelli (Resident, McLean (Tysons Corner) Office)
George L. Scruggs, Jr.
Jane Whitt Sellers
Larry D. Sharp (Resident, Washington, D.C. Office)
Alexander H. Slaughter
D. French Slaughter III (Resident, Charlottesville Office)
Daniel K. Slone
R. Gordon Smith
Robert S. Smith (Resident, Washington, D.C. Office)
Kathleen Taylor Sooy
Thomas E. Spahn
Christopher C. Spencer
F. Bradford Stillman (Resident, Norfolk Office)
Jacquelyn E. Stone
Gresham R. Stoneburner (Resident, Jacksonville, Florida Office)
William J. Strickland
Robert E. Stroud (Resident, Charlottesville Office)
John S. Stump (Resident, McLean (Tysons Corner) Office)
James F. Stutts
Charles R. Swartz
Eva S. Tashjian-Brown
George J. Terwilliger III (Resident, Washington, D.C. Office)
Philip Tierney (Resident, Alexandria Office)
Wallace L. Timmeny (Resident, Washington, D.C. Office)
Courtland L. Traver, Jr. (Resident, McLean (Tysons Corner) Office)
Gerald B. Treacy, Jr. (Resident, McLean (Tysons Corner) Office)
Haynie Seay Trotter (Resident, McLean (Tysons Corner) Office)
Thomas H. Tullidge, Jr.
William E. Twomey, Jr.
Daniel Urech (Also Member, Hurlimann, Urech & Uhlmann, Zurich, Switzerland) (Resident, Zurich, Switzerland Office)
Robert R. Vieth (Resident, McLean (Tysons Corner) Office)
William R. Waddell
James H. Walsh
Stephen H. Watts II
Craig H. Weber
John M. Weisner
Anne Marie Whittemore
Mark D. Williamson (Resident, Norfolk Office)
Ernest G. Wilson (Resident, Baltimore, Maryland Office)
J. Christopher Wiltshire
John J. Woloszyn (Resident, Baltimore, Maryland Office)
R. Craig Wood (Resident, Charlottesville Office)
Thomas S. Word, Jr.
David H. Worrell, Jr.
W. Carter Younger
Mims Maynard Zabriskie
Warren E. Zirkle
Edward E. Zughaib (Resident, McLean (Tysons Corner) Office)

(See Next Column)

McGuire, Woods, Battle & Boothe—*Continued*

RETIRED OF COUNSEL

Minerva Wilson Andrews (Resident, McLean (Tysons Corner) Office)
John S. Battle, Jr.
Calhoun Bond (Resident, Baltimore, Maryland Office)
C. Keating Bowie (Resident, Baltimore, Maryland Office)
Richard H. Catlett, Jr.
Carle E. Davis
W. Gibson Harris
Alexander W. Neal, Jr.
Edgar Allen Prichard (Resident, McLean (Tysons Corner) Office)
Carrington Williams (Resident, McLean (Tysons Corner) Office)

OF COUNSEL

William A. Agee (Resident, Baltimore, Maryland Office)
Jean Bilger Arnold (Resident, Charlottesville Office)
William C. Battle (Resident, Charlottesville Office)
Russell E. Dougherty (Not admitted in VA; Resident, McLean (Tysons Corner) Office)
Carter B. S. Furr (Resident, Norfolk Office)
Edmund D. Harllee (Resident, McLean (Tysons Corner) Office)
Mary S. Head (Resident, Washington, D.C. Office)
Kemper K. Hyers
Lawrence A. Kaufman (Resident, Baltimore, Maryland Office)
Elizabeth Land Lewis (Resident, McLean (Tysons Corner) Office)
Michele A. W. McKinnon
John V. Murray
Clifford R. Oviatt, Jr. (Resident, Washington, D.C. Office)
Mary Moffett Hutcheson Priddy
Joseph C. Reid (Resident, Baltimore, Maryland Office)
Martin B. Richards
Stephen P. Robin (Resident, McLean (Tysons Corner) Office)
John H. Toole (Resident, McLean (Tysons Corner) Office)
Jeffrey P. White (Not admitted in VA)

ASSOCIATES

Hugh E. Aaron
Russell Taylor Aaronson III
Michael A. Abel
Mary Ellen Albin (Resident, Washington, D.C. Office)
T. William Alvey III
Vincent Badolato (Resident, McLean (Tysons Corner) Office)
Mary Dalton Baril
John J. Bellaschi (Resident, McLean (Tysons Corner) Office)
William W. Belt, Jr.
Lisa Ann Bertini (Resident, Norfolk Office)
John C. Bilzor (Resident, Norfolk Office)
Olivia Norman Biss
Kelly M. Boehringer
William J. Bradley III
Robert M. Buell
Marianne G. Bundren (Resident, McLean (Tysons Corner) Office)
Elizabeth L. Butterworth
F. Paul Calamita III
Jeffrey R. Capwell
Brian K. Cary
Michael Holt Cole (Resident, Charlottesville Office)
James B. Comey
Martha Saine Condyles
Jeffrey G. Cook (Resident, Baltimore, Maryland Office)
Richard Joshua Cromwell (Resident, Norfolk Office)
Kenneth D. Crowder
David F. Dabbs
Robert T. Danforth (Resident Charlottesville Office)
Mark S. Davis (Resident, Norfolk Office)
Adrienne K. Dwyer (Resident, Alexandria Office)
William R. Elliott, Jr. (Not admitted in VA)
Christopher G. Emsley
Valerie A. Fant (Resident, Washington, D.C. Office)
Michael J. Farley
Dana J. Finberg
Jonathan M. Fine
Douglas M. Foley (Resident, Norfolk Office)
Melissa K. Force (Resident, Baltimore, Maryland Office)
Gloria L. Freye
Joy C. Fuhr
Wendy B. Gayle
Mark E. Gebauer
Paul G. Gill
Montia O. Givens
M. Melissa Glassman (Resident, McLean (Tysons Corner) Office)
F. Brawner Greer
Carol W. Hahn (Resident, Norfolk Office)
Stephanie L. Hamlett
Laurie A. Hand (Resident, Alexandria Office)
Patrick L. Hayden (Resident, Norfolk Office)
Dion W. Hayes
Ute Heidenreich (Resident, Norfolk Office)
J. Randal Hervey
Robert L. Hodges
James Allen Hoffman (Resident, McLean (Tysons Corner) Office)
Sandra Morris Holleran
Amy Tredway Holt
Marcia Morales Howard (Resident, Jacksonville, Florida Office)
Cynthia E. Hudson
Michael P. Huecker (Resident, Baltimore, Maryland Office)
Kimberly S. Hugo
Karen Suzanne Iezzi
J. Brian Jackson (Resident, Charlottesville Office)
Michael L. Jennings (Resident, Baltimore, Maryland Office)
K. Roger Johnson, Jr.
Theresa W. Johnson
Joanne Katsantonis (Resident, Brussels, Belgium Office)
Stephen Michael Kayan
Christopher L. Keefer (Resident, McLean (Tysons Corner) Office)
Michael Joseph Klisch (Resident, Alexandria Office)
Mark J. La Fratta
John M. Lain
Lisa M. Landry
Frank G. La Prade

(*See Next Column*)

ASSOCIATES (Continued)

John G. Lavoie (Resident, McLean (Tysons Corner) Office)
M. Elizabeth Leverage (Resident, McLean (Tysons Corner) Office)
Darryl S. Lew (Not admitted in VA)
Joshua N. Lief
Michael J. Marino
A. Carter Marshall
J. Michael Martinez (Not admitted in VA)
Silvia N. Martínez Cazón
Eugene Edward Mathews III
Michael P. McGovern
Charles W. McIntyre, Jr.
Emery B. McRill (Resident, Baltimore, Maryland Office)
Francis X. Mellon (Resident, McLean (Tysons Corner) Office)
Patricia Merrill (Resident, Charlottesville Office)
Charles G. Meyer III
John J. Michels, Jr.
R. Lisa Mojiri-Azad (Resident, Washington, D.C. Office)
John S. Morris III
Roberta Marie Mowery
Keith D. Munson (Resident, Jacksonville, Florida Office)
James A. Murphy
Kevin M. O'Hagan (Not admitted in VA)
James P. O'Hare (Resident, Baltimore, Maryland Office)
Susan Morley Olson (Resident, Washington, D.C. Office)
Scott C. Oostdyk
Jaemin Park (Resident, Baltimore, Maryland Office)
Arlene Paul (Resident, McLean (Tysons Corner) Office)
Edmund S. Pittman
Mary C. Powell
H. Carter Redd
Robert F. Redmond, Jr.
Joseph K. Reid III
Melanie Miller Reilly (Resident, McLean (Tysons Corner) Office)
Lloyd M. Richardson
Lawrence Eric Rifken (Resident, McLean (Tysons Corner) Office)
Brian C. Riopelle
Victoria J. Roberson (Not admitted in VA)
Robert C. Ross
Deanna L. Ruddock
Christopher John Sabec
Robert N. Saffelle
Rodney A. Satterwhite
Christine M. Schwab
Gregg A. Scoggins
Richard H. Sedgley
Andrew T. Shilling (Resident, Norfolk Office)
Charles M. Sims
Shannon E. Sinclair
Kristen E. Smith (Resident, Charlottesville Office)
Nathan B. Smith (Resident, McLean (Tysons Corner) Office)
Ann Lisa Spletzer (Not admitted in VA)
Thomas J. Stallings
Bruce M. Steen (Resident, Charlottesville Office)
J. Randolph Stokes (Resident, Norfolk Office)
Samuel L. Tarry, Jr.
Lynn Lewis Tavenner
James A. Thornhill
B. Scott Tilley
Joseph J. Traficanti
Jane M. Troutman
Karen L. Turner (Resident, McLean (Tysons Corner) Office)
Jonathan R. Tuttle (Resident, Washington, D.C. Office)
Anthony F. Vittone
Natalie Kaye Wargo
Stephan J. Willen
Steven R. Williams
Peter J. Willsey (Resident, McLean (Tysons Corner) Office)
Harrison B. Wilson III
David A. Woodmansee
Joseph W. Wright III (Resident, McLean (Tysons Corner) Office)
Andrea Pierce Yalof (Resident, Baltimore, Maryland Office)
David M. Young (Resident, Norfolk Office)
Dorothy C. Young
Ann W. Zedd (Resident, Washington, D.C. Office)
Christiane Zuñiga (Resident, Brussels, Belgium Office)

For full biographical listings, see the Martindale-Hubbell Law Directory

Montedonico, Hamilton & Altman, P.C. (AV)

700 East Main Street, Suite 1633, 23219
Telephone: 804-780-2898
Fairfax, Virginia Office: 10306 Eaton Place, Suite 500.
Telephone: 703-591-9700.
FAX: 703-591-0023.
Washington D.C. Office: 5301 Wisconsin Avenue, N.W., Suite 400.
Telephone: 202-364-1434.
FAX: 202-364-1544.
Frederick, Maryland Office: 220 North Market Street.
Telephone: 301-695-7004.
FAX: 301-695-0055.
Rockville, Maryland Office: Suite 201, 600 East Jefferson Street.
Telephone: 301-424-3900.

Stephen L. Altman
Joseph C. Veith, III

For full biographical listings, see the Martindale-Hubbell Law Directory

Morris and Morris, A Professional Corporation (AV)

1200 Ross Building, 801 East Main Street, 23201-0030
Telephone: 804-344-8300
FAX: 804-344-8359

John B. Browder (1910-1989)
Rufus G. Coldwell, Jr. (1934-1987)
James W. Morris, III
Philip B. Morris
Robert M. White
R. Hunter Manson
Thomas D. Stokes, III
Ann Adams Webster
Jacqueline G. Epps

(*See Next Column*)

MORRIS AND MORRIS A PROFESSIONAL CORPORATION, *Richmond—Continued*

Lynne Jones Blain
Kirk D. McQuiddy
Michelle Preston Wiltshire
John P. Driscoll
James W. Walker
Lori Morris Whitten
William B. Tiller

For full biographical listings, see the Martindale-Hubbell Law Directory

WILLIAMS, MULLEN, CHRISTIAN & DOBBINS, A PROFESSIONAL CORPORATION (AV)

Two James Center, 1021 East Cary Street, P.O. Box 1320, 23210-1320
Telephone: 804-643-1991
Fax: 804-783-6456
Glen Allen, Virginia Office: 4401 Waterfront Drive, Suite 140.
Telephone: 804-965-9168.
Fax: 804-965-0955.
Washington, D.C. Office: 1575 Eye Street, N.W.
Telephone: 202-289-6200.
Fax: 202-289-4126.

Lewis C. Williams (1875-1959)
James Mullen (1876-1967)
Stuart G. Christian (1883-1967)
Morton L. Wallerstein (1890-1980)
Virgil R. Goode (1897-1972)
David D. Addison
Ralph L. Axselle, Jr.
David George Ball (Resident, Washington, D.C. Office)
R. Brian Ball
Stephen E. Baril
William D. Bayliss
Paul S. Bliley, Jr.
A. Peter Brodell
James J. Burns
Michael C. Buseck
Charles L. Cabell
Theodore L. Chandler, Jr.
C. Richard Davis
Louis Armand Dejoie (Resident, Washington, D.C. Office)
Howard W. Dobbins
Robert E. Eicher
Siran S. Faulders
Sarah Hopkins Finley
Byron E. Fox
W. F. Drewry Gallalee
Alexander C. Graham, Jr.
Hugh T. Harrison, II
Timothy G. Hayes
Samuel W. Hixon, III
A. Brooks Hock
Lynn F. Jacob
David R. Johnson
Reginald N. Jones
R. Hart Lee
Randolph H. Lickey
Channing J. Martin
William R. Mauck, Jr.
Dana D. McDaniel
Thomas B. McVey (Not admitted in VA; Resident, Washington, D.C. Office)
James V. Meath
John M. Mercer
Robert L. Musick, Jr.
Douglas M. Nabhan
G. Andrew Nea, Jr.
Warren E. Nowlin (Washington, D.C. Office)
Robert D. Perrow
Craig L. Rascoe
Malcolm E. Ritsch, Jr.
Philip deB. Rome
Walter H. Ryland
Paul G. Saunders, II
William H. Schwarzschild, III
Derek L. Smith
Julious P. Smith, Jr.
Robert E. Spicer, Jr.
Robin Robertson Starr
Andrea Rowse Stiles
W. Scott Street, III
Sandy T. Tucker
C. William Waechter, Jr.
Clayton L. Walton
B. Randolph Wellford, Jr.
Wayne A. Whitham, Jr.
Fielding L. Williams, Jr.
Russell Alton Wright

OF COUNSEL

Fred G. Pollard

Heidi Wilson Abbott
Naila Townes Ahmed
Wyatt S. Beazley, IV
William J. Benos
David C. Burton
Andrew M. Condlin
David L. Dallas, Jr.
David L. Delk, Jr.
Theodore J. Edlich, IV
Calvin W. Fowler, Jr.
Brian J. Goodman
Curtis M. Hairston, Jr.
M. Peebles Harrison
Kelly Harrington Johnson
A. Brent King
Glen Andrew Lea
George W. Marget, III
Robert Temple Mayo
Tara A. McGee
Sherri M. Mearns
William L. Pitman
Charles B. Scher
Mark S. Shepard
Karen L. Starke
Henry C. Su
Ian D. Titley
John L. Walker, III
Charles E. Wall

LEGAL SUPPORT PERSONNEL

Danny W. Jackson (Director of Administration)

For full biographical listings, see the Martindale-Hubbell Law Directory

ROANOKE, (Independent City)

GLENN, FLIPPIN, FELDMANN & DARBY, A PROFESSIONAL CORPORATION (AV)

200 First Campbell Square, P.O. Box 2887, 24001
Telephone: 703-224-8000
Telecopier: 703-224-8050

(See Next Column)

Robert E. Glenn
G. Franklin Flippin
Mark E. Feldmann
Harwell M. Darby, Jr.
Maryellen F. Goodlatte
Claude M. Lauck
Robert A. Ziogas
Charles E. Troland, Jr.
David E. Perry
Paul G. Beers
Phillip R. Lingafelt
James Peyton Cargill
Sarah Elizabeth Powell

Representative Clients: Liberty Mutual Insurance Co.; Grand Piano & Furniture Co.; Sears, Roebuck and Co.
References: NationsBank; Crestar Bank.

For full biographical listings, see the Martindale-Hubbell Law Directory

JOHNSON, AYERS & MATTHEWS (AV)

Southwest Virginia Savings Bank Building Second Floor, 302 Second Street, S.W., P.O. Box 2200, 24009
Telephone: 703-982-3666
Fax: 703-982-1552

MEMBERS OF FIRM

James F. Johnson
Ronald M. Ayers
Joseph A. Matthews, Jr.
John D. Eure
William P. Wallace, Jr.
Kenneth J. Ries
Jonnie L. Speight
David B. Carson

ASSOCIATES

Robert S. Ballou
Philip O. Garland
L. Johnson Sarber, III

Representative Clients: Bell Atlantic-Virginia, Inc.; Blue Cross and Blue Shield of Virginia (Trigon); Federated Mutual Insurance Co.; General Motors Corp.; Nationwide Mutual Insurance Company; Norfolk and Western Railway Co.; Progressive Insurance Cos.; Royal Insurance Co.; State Farm Insurance Cos.; The Travelers Cos.

For full biographical listings, see the Martindale-Hubbell Law Directory

*ROCKY MOUNT,** Franklin Co. — (Refer to Roanoke)

*RUSTBURG,** Campbell Co.

OVERBEY, HAWKINS & SELZ (AV)

Court House Square, P.O. Box 38, 24588
Telephone: 804-332-5155
FAX: 804-332-5143

W. Hutchings Overbey (1906-1991)
W. Hutchings Overbey, Jr.
A. David Hawkins
Bryan K. Selz

Local Counsel for: First Virginia Bank, Piedmont; Central Fidelity Bank; WESTVACO; Truck Body Corp.; Falwell Aviation, Inc.; Federal Land Bank of Baltimore; Campbell County School Board; Industrial Development Authority of the County of Campbell; Virginia State Department of Highways and Transportation.

For full biographical listings, see the Martindale-Hubbell Law Directory

*SALEM,** (Ind. City; Seat of Roanoke Co.) — (Refer to Roanoke)

SOUTH BOSTON, Halifax Co.

VAUGHAN & SLAYTON (AV)

Security Building, 554 Main Street, P.O. Box 446, 24592
Telephone: 804-572-4983
Fax: 804-572-4900

Franklin M. Slayton

ASSOCIATES

Charles A. Butler, Jr.

OF COUNSEL

Robert T. Vaughan

District Counsel for: Virginia Power Co.
Local Attorneys for: Virginia Farm Bureau Mutual Insurance Co.; NationsBank, N.A.; U.S.F.&G. Co.; Sentry Claims Service; Aetna Insurance Co.

For full biographical listings, see the Martindale-Hubbell Law Directory

SOUTH HILL, Mecklenburg Co. — (Refer to South Boston)

SPERRYVILLE, Rappahannock Co. — (Refer to Luray)

*SPOTSYLVANIA,** Spotsylvania Co.

JARRELL, HICKS & SASSER (AV)

Spottswood Inn Building, P.O. Box 127, 22553
Telephone: 703-582-5300
Fax: 703-582-5993

MEMBERS OF FIRM

James E. Jarrell, Jr.
Ronald L. Hicks
Phillip Sasser, Jr
James E. Jarrell III

Representative Clients: Union Bank & Trust Co.; Chicago Title Insurance Corp.; Rappahannock Forge, Inc.; Sun Asphalt, Inc.; Joy Construction Co.; Universal Land & Development Corp.; Pitts Foundation; Rappahannock Wire Co.; Breezewood, Inc.; MITCO.

(See Next Column)

JARRELL, HICKS & SASSER—*Continued*

For full biographical listings, see the Martindale-Hubbell Law Directory

*STANARDSVILLE,** Greene Co. — (Refer to Culpeper)

*STAUNTON,** (Ind. City; Seat of Augusta Co.)

BLACK, NOLAND & READ (AV)

One Barristers Row, P.O. Box 1206, 24402-1206
Telephone: 703-885-0888
FAX: 703-885-0890

Peyton Cochran (1880-1969) Philip Lee Lotz (1913-1986)

MEMBERS OF FIRM

Benham M. Black
N. Douglas Noland, Jr.
Susan B. Read

ASSOCIATES

Deborah Gartzke Goolsby

Division Counsel for: CSX Transportation, Inc.
General Counsel for: Planters Bank & Trust Co.
Representative Clients: Norfolk Southern Corporation; Utica.

For full biographical listings, see the Martindale-Hubbell Law Directory

TIMBERLAKE, SMITH, THOMAS & MOSES, P.C. (AV)

The Virginia Building, P.O. Box 108, 24402-0108
Telephone: 703-885-1517
FAX: 703-885-4537

Wayt B. Timberlake, Jr. (1908-1989)
Colin J. S. Thomas, Jr.
Preston Donald Moses
John W. Sills, III
James G. Welsh
Thomas G. Bell, Jr.
B. E. Brannock
J. Ross Newell, III
C. J. Steuart Thomas, III

Jayne Kelley

OF COUNSEL

Richard W. Smith

Local Counsel for: General Motors Corp.; Commonwealth of Virginia, Division of Risk Management; Montgomery Ward & Co.; Augusta Hospital Corporation; First Virginia Bank of Augusta; State Farm Insurance.

For full biographical listings, see the Martindale-Hubbell Law Directory

*STUART,** Patrick Co. — (Refer to Martinsville)

SUFFOLK, (Independent City)

GLASSCOCK, GARDY AND SAVAGE (AV)

4th Floor National Bank Building, P.O. Box 1876, 23434
Telephone: 804-539-3474
FAX: 804-925-1419

MEMBERS OF FIRM

J. Samuel Glasscock
Jeffrey L. Gardy
William R. Savage, III

Representative Clients: Seaboard Railway System; Planters Peanuts (Division of Nabisco); Norfolk Southern Railway Co.; Nationwide Mutual Insurance Co.; State Farm Mutual Automobile Insurance Co.; Virginia Power Co.; Virginia Farm Bureau Mutual Insurance Co.; Suffolk Redevelopment and Housing Authority.
Approved Attorneys for: Lawyers Title Insurance Corp.

*TAPPAHANNOCK,** Essex Co.

DILLARD AND KATONA (AV)

Ritchie House Prince and Cross Streets, P.O. Box 356, 22560
Telephone: 804-443-3368
FAX: 804-443-2219

A. Fleet Dillard (1912-1990)
Alexander F. Dillard, Jr.
Scot A. Katona

Reference: Bank of Essex.

For full biographical listings, see the Martindale-Hubbell Law Directory

*TAZEWELL,** Tazewell Co.

GILLESPIE, HART, ALTIZER & WHITESELL, P.C. (AV)

Main Street, P.O. Box 718, 24651
Telephone: 703-988-5525; 988-5526
Fax: 988-6427

Carl C. Gillespie (Semi-Retired)
Carl C. Gillespie, Jr.
Harris Hart, II
Robert B. Altizer
Eric D. Whitesell
Jack S. Hurley, Jr.
F. Bradley Pyott
Thomas C. Givens, Jr.

(See Next Column)

Approved Attorneys for: Lawyers Title Insurance Corp.
Representative Clients: Nationwide Insurance Co.; State Farm Insurance Co.; The Travelers Insurance Co.; Allstate Insurance Co.; Virginia Farm Bureau Insurance Co.; Town of Tazewell, Virginia; Bank of Tazewell County; Humana, Inc.; Southern State Cooperative, Inc.

For full biographical listings, see the Martindale-Hubbell Law Directory

VIRGINIA BEACH, (Independent City)

CLARK & STANT, P.C. (AV)

One Columbus Center, 23462
Telephone: 804-499-8800
Telecopier: 804-473-0395
Internet: Info @ CLRKNSTNT, COM

Jo Ann Blair-Davis
Stephen W. Burke
Donald H. Clark
Joseph A. DiJulio
Thomas R. Frantz
Eric A. Hauser
Robert M. Reed
Robert L. Samuel, Jr.
C. Grigsby Scifres
Lawrence R. Siegel
Thomas E. Snyder
Frederick T. Stant, III
Stephen C. Swain
Stephen G. Test
Abram W. VanderMeer, Jr.

OF COUNSEL

Frederick T. Stant, Jr.

Clifford A. Coppola
Shannon Knight Dashiell
Robert J. Eveleigh
Michael J. Gardner
S. Geoffrey Glick
Samuel M. Kroll
James T. Lloyd, Jr.
Charles E. Malone
Frances W. Russell
Wayne G. Souza
Carol E. Summers
Jack Louis Young

Counsel for: Tidewater Regional Transit; Virginia Beach General Hospital; Portsmouth General Hospital.
Representative Clients: Central Fidelity Bank; Crestar Bank; Miller Oil Company, Inc.; City of Virginia Beach; Hillenbrand Industries, Inc.; Abbott Laboratories; Pet, Inc.; Denny's TW/Services, Inc.

For full biographical listings, see the Martindale-Hubbell Law Directory

KAUFMAN & CANOLES, A PROFESSIONAL CORPORATION (AV)

700 Pavilion Center, P.O. Box 626, 23451
Telephone: 804-491-4000
Fax: 804-491-4020
Norfolk, Virginia Office: One Commercial Place, P.O. Box 3037, 23514-3037.
Telephone: 804-624-3000.
Newport News, Virginia Office: Suite 408, 11817 Canon Boulevard.
Telephone: 804-873-6300.

RESIDENT PERSONNEL

R. Braxton Hill, III
Joseph L. Lyle, Jr.
Winship C. Tower
Michael H. Nuckols

OF COUNSEL

Thomas C. Broyles

Representative Clients: Bank of Tidewater; C.E. Thurston and Sons, Inc.; Commerce Bank; Crestar Bank; Hermes Abrasives, Inc.; Lillian Vernon Corp.; NationsBank, N.A.; Virginia Beach Federal Savings Bank.

For full biographical listings, see the Martindale-Hubbell Law Directory

*WARRENTON,** Fauquier Co.

O'CONNELL & MAYHUGH, P.C. (AV)

82 Main Street, 22186-3390
Telephone: 703-347-2424
Metro: 471-0528
Fax: 703-349-1705

Daniel M. O'Connell, Jr.
George M. Mayhugh
Elizabeth V. Munro

General Counsel for: The Consumers Group Title Insurance Agency, Inc.; USA Remediation Services, Inc.
Representative Clients: Commonwealth of Virginia; Blue Ridge Orthopedic Associates, P.C.; First Virginia Bank; Warrenton Heating & Air Conditioning, Inc.; Opal Industrial Park.
Approved Attorneys for: First American Title Insurance Co.; Lawyers Title Insurance Corp.; Commonwealth Land Title Insurance Co.

For full biographical listings, see the Martindale-Hubbell Law Directory

WALKER, JONES, LAWRENCE, PAYNE & DUGGAN, P.C. (AV)

Carter Hall, 31 Winchester Street, 22186
Telephone: 703-347-9223
(Metro) 591-4378
Fax: 703-349-1715

Howard P. Walker
H. Ben Jones, Jr.
Robert deT. Lawrence, IV
H. Dudley Payne, Jr.
Powell L. Duggan
Julia S. Savage

(See Next Column)

WALKER, JONES, LAWRENCE, PAYNE & DUGGAN P.C., *Warrenton—Continued*

Susan F. Pierce James K. Bounds

General Counsel: Fauquier Hospital, Inc.; Fauquier County Industrial Development Authority; Fauquier Association of Realtors; Greater Piedmont Area Association of Realtors, Inc.
Representative Clients: Metropolitan Life Insurance Co.; Jefferson Savings & Loan; Hagerstown Block Co.; Colonial Pipeline Co.; Virginia Power Co.; The Artery Organization, Inc.

For full biographical listings, see the Martindale-Hubbell Law Directory

*WARSAW,** Richmond Co.

RYLAND AND DAVIS, A PROFESSIONAL CORPORATION (AV)

26 West Richmond Road, P.O. Box 185, 22572
Telephone: 804-333-3661
FAX: 804-333-0185

Charles H. Ryland J. Maston Davis

General Counsel for: Northern Neck State Bank; Northern Neck Electric Cooperative; Frederick Northup, Inc.; Richmond County School Board.
Approved Attorneys for: Lawyers Title Insurance Corp.; American Title Insurance Co.; Colonial Farm Credit; ACA; Farmers Home Administration.

For full biographical listings, see the Martindale-Hubbell Law Directory

*WASHINGTON,** Rappahannock Co. — (Refer to Luray)

WAYNESBORO, (Independent City)

ALLEN & CARWILE, P.C. (AV)

Suite 200 Lambert, Barger & Branaman Building, 109 South Wayne Avenue, P.O. Box 1558, 22980-1415
Telephone: 703-943-8200
Fax: 703-943-9708

Carter R. Allen G. William Watkins
R. Toms Dalton, Jr. Timothy C. Carwile
Charles L. Ricketts, III

Representative Clients: Virginia Metalcrafters, Inc.; Waynesboro Community Hospital; Virginia Federal Savings & Loan Assn.; First American Bank; Wayn-Tex, Inc.
Approved Attorneys for: Lawyers Title Insurance Corp.

For full biographical listings, see the Martindale-Hubbell Law Directory

WHITE STONE, Lancaster Co.

DUNTON, SIMMONS & DUNTON (AV)

P.O. Box 5, 22578
Telephone: 804-435-1611
Telecopier: 804-435-1614

MEMBERS OF FIRM

Ammon G. Dunton Craig H. Smith
C. Jackson Simmons William R. Curdts
Ammon G. Dunton, Jr. John S. Martin
J. Rawleigh Simmons

General Counsel: Bank of Lancaster; Northern Neck Insurance Co.; Virginia Health and Accident Assn.; Zapata Haynie Corp.; Brown Oil Corp.
Local Counsel: Zapata Corp.; Litton Industrial Products, Inc.

For full biographical listings, see the Martindale-Hubbell Law Directory

*WINCHESTER,** (Ind. City; Seat of Frederick Co.)

HARRISON & JOHNSTON (AV)

21 South Loudoun Street, 22601
Telephone: 703-667-1266
FAX: 703-667-1312
Mailing Address: P.O. Box 809, 22604,

MEMBERS OF FIRM

Burr P. Harrison (1904-1973) Billy Joe Tisinger
William A. Johnston Thomas A. Schultz, Jr.
Harry K. Benham, III Ian R. D. Williams

ASSOCIATES

Bruce E. Downing

For full biographical listings, see the Martindale-Hubbell Law Directory

KUYKENDALL, JOHNSTON & KUYKENDALL, P.C. (AV)

208 South Loudoun Street, P.O. Box 2760, 22604
Telephone: 703-667-4644
FAX: 703-667-2769

J. Sloan Kuykendall George W. Johnston, III
J. Sloan Kuykendall, III

(See Next Column)

Phillip S. Griffin, II

Counsel for: The Potomac Edison Co.; Winchester Medical Center; O'Sullivan Corporation; The Henkel-Harris Company, Inc.; Valley Health Services, Inc.; Surgi-Center of Winchester, Inc.
Local Counsel for: Travelers Insurance Co.; Shenandoah Mutual Fire Insurance Company; USAA; Selective Insurance Companies.

For full biographical listings, see the Martindale-Hubbell Law Directory

*WISE,** Wise Co. — (Refer to Norton)

WOODBRIDGE, Prince William Co.

COMPTON & DULING, L.C. (AV)

14914 Jefferson Davis Highway, 22191
Telephone: 703-690-6800
FAX: 703-690-3546

C. Lacey Compton, Jr. Geary H. Rogers
Thomas D. Duling Jay du Von

Katherine M. Waters H. Jan Roltsch-Anoll
Raymond J. Gallagher David B. Wilks

Representative Clients: The Hylton Group; Potomac Hospital Corp. of Prince William; Taco Bell Corporation; Thomas P. Harkins, Inc.; National Birchwood; B econ Services Corp.; Resolution Trust Corporation; Hechinger Company; Town of Occoquan, Virginia.

For full biographical listings, see the Martindale-Hubbell Law Directory

*WOODSTOCK,** Shenandoah Co. — (Refer to Luray)

*WYTHEVILLE,** Wythe Co. — (Refer to Pulaski)

*YORKTOWN,** York Co. — (Refer to Hampton)

WASHINGTON

BELLEVUE, King Co.

Davis Wright Tremaine (AV)

10500 N.E. 8th Street, 1800 Bellevue Place, 98004
Telephone: 206-646-6100
Fax: 206-646-6199
Anchorage, Alaska Office: Suite 1450, 550 W. Seventh Avenue. 99501.
Telephone: 907-257-5300.
FAX: 907-257-5399.
Boise, Idaho Office: Suite 911, 999 Main Street, 83702-9010.
Telephone: 208-338-8200.
FAX: 208-338-8299.
Honolulu, Hawaii Office: 1360 Pauahi Tower, 1001 Bishop Street, 96813.
Telephone: 808-538-3360.
FAX: 808-526-0101.
Los Angeles, California Office: Suite 600, 1000 Wilshire Boulevard. 90017.
Telephone: 213-229-9600.
FAX: 213-627-4874.
Portland, Oregon Office: 2300 First Interstate Tower, 1300 SW Fifth Avenue. 97201.
Telephone: 503-241-2300.
FAX: 503-778-5299.
Richland, Washington Office: Suite 260, 1100 Jadwin Avenue. 99352.
Telephone: 509-946-5369.
FAX: 509-946-4211.
San Francisco, California Office: Suite 1500, 235 Pine Street, 94104.
Telephone: 415-765-5333.
FAX: 415-421-6619.
Seattle, Washington Office: 2600 Century Square, 1501 Fourth Avenue. 98101.
Telephone: 206-622-3150.
FAX: 206-628-7040.
Washington, D.C. Office: Suite 700, 1155 Connecticut Avenue N.W. 20036.
Telephone: 202-508-6600.
FAX: 202-508-6699.
Shanghai, China Office: Suite 1008/1009, Jin Jiang Hotel, 59 Mao Ming Road (S), 200020.
Telephones: 011-8621-472-3344; 011-8621-415-3002.
FAX: 011-8621-415-3003.

PARTNERS

Jeff Belfiglio
Mark W. Berry
Allen D. Clark
Richard W. Elliott
Michael R. Green
Larry E. Halvorson
Steven J. Hopp
Richard A. Klobucher
Warren E. Koons
David V. Marshall
Nick S. Verwolf

RESIDENT ASSOCIATES

Linda White Atkins
Crissa Cugini
Rhys Matthew Farren
Delwen A. Jones
Jin H. Kim
Cassandra Lynn Kinkead
Lynn T. Manolopoulos
James E. Pruitt III
Kerry G. Robinson
Michael B. Saunders

COUNSEL

Lisle R. Guernsey (Retired)

Representative Clients: Bank of Tokyo, Ltd.; ELDEC Corp.; Pay 'N Pak Stores, Inc.; Pope Resources; Seattle Times Co.; Seattle-First National Bank; Virginia Mason Medical Center; Washington Bankers Assn.

For full biographical listings, see the Martindale-Hubbell Law Directory

Donald D. Fleming, P.S. (AV)

800 Bellevue Way, N.E., Suite 300, 98004
Telephone: 206-637-3001
FAX: 206-453-9062

Donald D. Fleming

For full biographical listings, see the Martindale-Hubbell Law Directory

Inslee, Best, Doezie & Ryder, P.S. (AV)

777-108th Avenue, N.E., Suite 1900, P.O. Box C-90016, 98009-9016
Telephone: 206-455-1234
FAX: 206-635-7720

Evan E. Inslee
David A. Best
Michael Doezie
William C. Irvine
Milan Gail Ryder
Jerome D. Carpenter
William J. Lindberg, Jr.
Henry R. Hanssen, Jr.
Thomas H. Grimm
Don E. Dascenzo
Patricia Ann Murray
Thomas H. De Buys
Joe E. Wishcamper
James S. Turner
Stephen D. Rose
John W. Milne
John F. Rodda
Michael P. Ruark
Rod P. Kaseguma
Richard U. Chapin
Peter A. Deming
John F. Sullivan

(See Next Column)

David J. Lawyer
Douglas L. Phillips
Andrew L. Symons
Richard G. Birinyi

Deborah S. Berg
Rosemary A. Larson
Carey L. Caldwell
Eric C. Frimodt
Dan S. Lossing
John W. Miller

For full biographical listings, see the Martindale-Hubbell Law Directory

Perkins Coie (AV)

A Law Partnership including Professional Corporations
Strategic Alliance with Russell & DuMoulin
Suite 1800, One Bellevue Center, 411 - 108th Avenue N.E., 98004
Telephone: 206-453-6980
Facsimile: 206-453-7350
Telex: 32-0319 PERKINS SEA
Seattle, Washington Office: 1201 Third Avenue, 40th Floor.
Telephone: 206-583-8888.
Facsimile: 206-583-8500.
Cable Address: "Perkins Seattle".
Telex: 32-0319 PERKINS SEA.
Spokane, Washington Office: North 221 Wall Street, Suite 600.
Telephone: 509-458-3399.
Facsimile: 509-458-3399.
Telex: 32-0319 PERKINS SEA.
Anchorage, Alaska Office: 1029 West Third Avenue, Suite 300.
Telephone: 907-279-8561.
Facsimile: 907-276-3108.
Telex: 32-0319 PERKINS SEA.
Los Angeles, California Office: 1000 Avenue of the Stars, Ninth Floor.
Telephone: 310-788-9900.
Telex: 32-0319 PERKINS SEA.
Facsimile: 310-788-3399.
Washington, D.C. Office: 607 Fourteenth Street, N.W.
Telephone: 202-628-6600.
Facsimile: 202-434-1690.
Telex: 44-0277 PCSO.
Portland, Oregon Office: U.S. Bancorp Tower, Suite 2500, 111 S.W. Fifth Avenue.
Telephone: 503-295-4400.
Facsimile: 503-295-6793.
Telex: 32-0319 PERKINS SEA.
Olympia, Washington Office: 1110 Capitol Way South, Suite 405.
Telephone: 206-956-3300.
Strategic Alliance with Russell & DuMoulin, 1700-1075 West Georgia Street, Vancouver, B.C. V6E 3G2. Telephone: 604-631-3131.
Hong Kong Office: 23rd Floor Asia Pacific Finance Tower, Citibank Plaza, 3 Garden Road.
Telephone: 852-2878-1177.
Facsimile: 852-2524-9988. DX-9230.
London, England Office: 36/38 Cornhill, EC3V 3ND.
Telephone: 0171-369-9966.
Facsimile: 0171-369-9968.
Taipei, Taiwan Office: 8/F, TFIT Tower, 85 Jen Ai Road, Sec 4, Taipei 106, R.O.C.
Telephone: 886-2-778-1177.
Facsimile: 086-2-777-9898.

RESIDENT PARTNERS/SHAREHOLDERS

Joan C. Clarke
Bruce E. Dick
Charles N. Eberhardt
Lawrence B. Hannah, Jr.
Valerie L. Hughes
Donald G. Kari (P.S.)
Steven C. Marshall (P.S.)
Sherilyn Peterson
Steven E. Pope
Markham A. Quehrn
Richard R. Rohde
James P. Savitt
Craig E. Shank
James M. Van Nostrand

COUNSEL

F. Theodore Thomsen

RESIDENT ASSOCIATES

Ruth Todd Chattin
Aniruddha (Rudy) Garde
Suzanne M. Larsen
R. Gerard Lutz
Susan C. Lybeck
Greg P. Mackay
Mark E. McCulley
Robert M. McKenna
Pamela H. Salgado
Neal M. Suggs
Paul E. Smith
Lisa J. Tanzi

For full biographical listings, see the Martindale-Hubbell Law Directory

Williams, Kastner & Gibbs (AV)

2000 Skyline Tower, 10900 N.E. Fourth Street, P.O. Box 1800, 98004-5841
Telephone: 206-462-4700
Telecopier: 206-451-0714
Seattle, Washington Office: 4100 Two Union Square, 601 Union Street, P.O. Box 21926, 98111-3926.
Telephone: 206-628-6600.
Fax: 206-628-6611.
Tacoma, Washington Office: 1000 Financial Center, 1145 Broadway, 98402-3502.
Telephone: 206-593-5620; Seattle: 628-2420.
Fax: 206-593-5625.

(See Next Column)

WILLIAMS, KASTNER & GIBBS, *Bellevue—Continued*

Vancouver, Washington Office: First Independent Place, 1220 Main Street, Suite 510.
Telephone: 206-696-0248.
Fax: 206-696-2051.

RESIDENT PARTNERS

Peter E. Peterson
Josephine B. Vestal
Judd H. Lees
Bruce T. Thurston
Christopher K. Shank
Gregory L. Russell
Joseph C. Calmes
David W. Wiley
John F. Boespflug, Jr.

RESIDENT ASSOCIATES

Carmen L. Cook
Darren A. Feider
Betsy A. Gillaspy
Hollis C. Holman
Patrick Moran
Lisa T. Oratz

OF COUNSEL

Mark D. Schedler

For full biographical listings, see the Martindale-Hubbell Law Directory

---

*BELLINGHAM,** Whatcom Co.

BRETT & DAUGERT (AV)

300 North Commercial, P.O. Box 5008, 98227
Telephone: 360-733-0212
FAX: 360-647-1902

MEMBERS OF FIRM

Dean R. Brett
Larry Daugert
Timothy C. Farris
Cynthia Lee Pope
J. Bruce Smith

ASSOCIATES

Breean Lawrence Beggs
Rand Jack
Shon C. Ramey
Stanley E. Soper

References: Security Pacific Bank Washington (Bellingham Branch); Key Bank.

For full biographical listings, see the Martindale-Hubbell Law Directory

---

LUDWIGSON, THOMPSON, HAYES & BELL (AV)

119 North Commercial, P.O. Box 399, 98227
Telephone: 206-734-2000
Fax: 206-734-2019

MEMBERS OF FIRM

John S. Ludwigson
James P. (Casey) Thompson
Craig P. Hayes
James G. Bell
George W. McCush (1902-1994)

Representative Clients: Horizon Bank; Whatcom Medical Bureau; Allstate Insurance; Farmers Insurance Group; Bornstein Seafoods, Inc.

For full biographical listings, see the Martindale-Hubbell Law Directory

---

*COLFAX,** Whitman Co. — (Refer to Pullman)

---

*COLVILLE,** Stevens Co. — (Refer to Spokane)

---

*DAYTON,** Columbia Co. — (Refer to Walla Walla)

---

*EVERETT,** Snohomish Co.

NEWTON - KIGHT (AV)

1820 32nd Street, P.O. Box 79, 98206
Telephone: 206-259-5106
FAX: 206-339-4145

MEMBERS OF FIRM

Henry T. Newton
R. Michael Kight
Thomas D. Adams
Lorna S. Corrigan
Bruce E. Jones
Thomas A. Hulten

ASSOCIATES

M. Geoffrey G. Jones

Representative Clients: Everett Mutual Savings Bank; Frontier Bank; First Interstate Bank, Snohomish County Branches; Principal Mutual Life Insurance Co.; Erickson Furniture Co.; Judd & Black Electric, Inc.; K & H Printers, Inc.; Pay-Less Food Stores, Inc.; Everett Housing Authority.
Reference: Everett Mutual Savings Bank.

For full biographical listings, see the Martindale-Hubbell Law Directory

---

HOQUIAM, Grays Harbor Co.

PARKER, JOHNSON & PARKER, P.S. (AV)

813 Levee Street, P.O. Box 700, 98550
Telephone: 206-532-5780
FAX: 206-532-5788

Omar S. Parker
Arlis W. Johnson
Jon C. Parker

Representative Clients: Public Utility District No. I of Grays Harbor County; Lamb-Grays Harbor Co.; Timberland Savings Bank.

(See Next Column)

For full biographical listings, see the Martindale-Hubbell Law Directory

---

*KELSO,** Cowlitz Co. — (Refer to Longview)

KENNEWICK, Benton Co.

LEAVY, SCHULTZ, DAVIS & FEARING, P.S. (AV)

2415 West Falls Avenue, 99336
Telephone: 509-736-1330
Fax: 509-736-1580

James Leavy (1915-1987)
John G. Schultz
William E. Davis
George B. Fearing
Robert G. Schultz

Timothy M. Coleman

Representative Client: Franklin County Irrigation District.
Insurance Clients: Nationwide Insurance Co.; Safeco Insurance Co.; Grange Insurance Co.; State Farm Mutual Insurance Cos.

For full biographical listings, see the Martindale-Hubbell Law Directory

---

RAEKES, RETTIG, OSBORNE, FORGETTE & O'DONNELL (AV)

6725 West Clearwater Avenue, 99336
Telephone: 509-783-6154
Fax: 509-783-0858

MEMBERS OF FIRM

Philip M. Raekes
Diehl R. Rettig
Stephen T. Osborne
Francois X. Forgette
Michael L. O'Donnell
Brian J. Iller

ASSOCIATES

Cheryl R.G. Adamson
Albert Coke Roth

Representative Clients: Columbia School District; Kennewick General Hospital; Chevron Pipeline Co.; Federal Land Bank.
Insurance Clients: Farmers Insurance Group; American States Insurance Co.; Continental Insurance Co.; Cigna Insurance Co.; Mutual of Enumclaw.

For full biographical listings, see the Martindale-Hubbell Law Directory

---

*MONTESANO,** Grays Harbor Co.

STEWART & STEWART LAW OFFICES, INC., P.S. A PROFESSIONAL SERVICE CORPORATION (AV)

101 First Street, South, 98563
Telephone: 206-249-4342
Fax: 206-249-6068

James M. Stewart
William J. Stewart

David S. Hatch

References: Key Bank; First Interstate Bank of Washington; Timberland Savings Bank.

For full biographical listings, see the Martindale-Hubbell Law Directory

---

MOSES LAKE, Grant Co.

DANO * MILLER * RIES (AV)

100 East Broadway, P.O. Box 1159, 98837
Telephone: 509-765-9285
FAX: 509-766-0087
Othello, Washington Office: 705 East Hemlock, P.O. Box 494.
Telephone: 509-488-2601.
Fax: 509-488-2703.

OF COUNSEL

Harrison K. Dano

MEMBERS OF FIRM

Brian J. Dano
Garth L. Dano
Brian H. Miller (Resident at Othello Office)
Harry E. Ries
Christopher F. Ries

Representative Clients: El Oro Cattle Co.; Sunfresh Potato; Irrigators, Inc.; Quincy Livestock Market; Nexus Ag Chemical, Inc.; Evergreen Implement, Inc.

For full biographical listings, see the Martindale-Hubbell Law Directory

---

*NEWPORT,** Pend Oreille Co. — (Refer to Spokane)

---

*OKANOGAN,** Okanogan Co. — (Refer to Wenatchee)

---

*OLYMPIA,** Thurston Co.

OWENS DAVIES MACKIE A PROFESSIONAL SERVICES CORPORATION (AV)

926 - 24th Way S.W., Courthouse Square, P.O. Box 187, 98507-0187
Telephone: 206-943-8320
FAX: 206-943-6150

(See Next Column)

OWENS DAVIES MACKIE A PROFESSIONAL SERVICES CORPORATION—*Continued*

Frank J. Owens
Burton R. Johnson (1935-1970)
Arthur L. Davies
Alexander W. Mackie, Jr.
John V. Lyman
Richard G. Phillips, Jr.
Brian L. Budsberg
Michael W. Mayberry
Robert F. Hauth
Kirk M. Veis

Cynthia Dale Turner
Matthew B. Edwards
James H. Blundell, Jr.

Representative Clients: Heritage Bank, FSB; Washington State Employees Credit Union; Port of Olympia; Republic Leasing; Lakeside Industries (Local Counsel); Pabst Brewing Company; Columbia Beverage Company.

For full biographical listings, see the Martindale-Hubbell Law Directory

*POMEROY,** Garfield Co. — (Refer to Pullman)

*PORT ORCHARD,** Kitsap Co. — (Refer to Seattle)

*PORT TOWNSEND,** Jefferson Co. — (Refer to Bellingham)

PRESTON, King Co. — (Refer to Kennewick)

*PROSSER,** Benton Co. — (Refer to Kennewick)

PULLMAN, Whitman Co.

AITKEN, SCHAUBLE, PATRICK, NEILL & RUFF (AV)

210 Downtown Professional Building, P.O. Box 307, 99163
Telephone: 509-334-3505
Fax: 509-334-5367
Colfax, Washington Office: North 209 Main Street.
Telephone: 509-397-3091.
St. John, Washington Office: Inland Empire Milling Co. Building, North 4th Park Street.
Telephone: 509-648-3346.

MEMBERS OF FIRM

Bruce A. Charawell (1952-1989)
Hugh J. Aitken
Albert J. Schauble
Robert F. Patrick
Howard M. Neill
Linda Schauble-Ruff

OF COUNSEL

James D. McMannis
Donald L. McMannis

Representative Clients: Johnson Union Warehouse Co.; Bank of Pullman; Uniontown Coop.; St. John Grain Growers; Lamont Bank of St. John; Inland Empire Milling Co.
References: Seattle-First National Bank, Pullman Branch; Bank of Pullman; The U.S. Bank of Washington.

For full biographical listings, see the Martindale-Hubbell Law Directory

*SEATTLE,** King Co.

CARNEY BADLEY SMITH & SPELLMAN A PROFESSIONAL SERVICES CORPORATION (AV)

Suite 2200 Columbia Center, 701 Fifth Avenue, 98104
Telephone: 206-622-8020
Cable Address: "Interlex"
Telex: 321270
Telecopier: 206-467-8215

Elvin P. Carney (1904-1984)
Milton C. Smith
Nicholas P. Scarpelli, Jr.
Timothy J. Parker
Richard J. Padden
Palmer Robinson
Charles N. Evans
Stephen C. Sieberson
Daniel W. Unti
Stephen L. Nourse
Clifford A. Webster
Frederick M. Robinson
Ruth Nielsen
James E. Lobsenz
Catherine A. Johnson
William M. Wood
Ted R. Katterheinrich
P. Douglas House
Mark E. Cavanagh
Thomas G. Morton
C. Scott Penner

A. Reid Allison, III
David W. Bever
Elena L. Garella
Patrick R. Lamb
Gail M. Taylor
Barbara J. Van Ess

OF COUNSEL

Basil Badley
John D. Spellman
John Huston
B. Shana Saichek

Insurance Clients: AIG Transport; American Insurance Assn.; American Star Insurance Co.; Transamerica Insurance Co.
Representative Clients: Albertsons, Inc.; Carpenters Trusts of Western Washington; Chrysler Credit; Manson Construction & Engineering Co.

For full biographical listings, see the Martindale-Hubbell Law Directory

CULP, GUTERSON & GRADER (AV)

27th Floor, One Union Square, 600 University Street, 98101-3143
Telephone: 206-624-7141
Facsimile: 206-624-5128

(See Next Column)

MEMBERS OF FIRM

Louis F. Nawrot, Jr.
Jerry R. McNaul
John S. Ebel
Richard C. Yarmuth
Peter M. Vial
Bradley D. Stam
Michele Coad
Robert D. Stewart
Egil Krogh
James E. Hadley
Kathleen L. Albrecht
Earle J. Hereford, Jr.
Tyler B. Ellrodt
Michael D. Helgren
David J. Lenci
Diane G. Fitz-Gerald
Barbara Hallowell
Timothy K. Thorson
Anthony L. Rafel
Robert M. Sulkin
Cyrus R. Vance, Jr.

OF COUNSEL

Lewis L. Ellsworth
Ronald J. English
Murray B. Guterson
Susan L. Guthrie
Bruce W. Hilyer
Robert N. Meals
J. Thomas McCully
Lawrence R. Ream
Robert A. Wright

RETIRED

Gordon C. Culp
George L. Grader

ASSOCIATES

Deborah T. Boylston
Shaya Calvo
Kristin A. Henderson
John J. Lapham, III
Mark W. Loschky
Matthew N. Menzer
Kerry M. Regan
Barbara H. Schuknecht
Jane A. Shapira
Amy L. Sommers
Nancy G. Stephenson
Kristi M. Wallis
Elaine B. Weinstein
Michael C. Williams
Scott T. Wilsdon
Marc O. Winters

Representative Clients: Washington State Convention and Trade Center; Warner Bros., Inc.; Washington Public Power Supply System; Kennedy Associates Real Estate Counsel, Inc.; Pacific Northwest Utilities Conference Committee; Tele-Communications, Inc.; Cornerstone Columbia Development Co.; Sealaska Corporation.

For full biographical listings, see the Martindale-Hubbell Law Directory

DAVIS WRIGHT TREMAINE (AV)

2600 Century Square, 1501 Fourth Avenue, 98101
Telephone: 206-622-3150
FAX: 206-628-7040
Anchorage, Alaska Office: Suite 1450, 550 W. Seventh Avenue. 99501.
Telephone: 907-257-5300.
FAX: 907-257-5399.
Bellevue, Washington Office: 1800 Bellevue Place, 10500 NE 8th Street. 98004.
Telephone: 206-646-6100.
FAX: 206-646-6199.
Boise, Idaho Office: Suite 911, 999 Main Street, 83702-9010.
Telephone: 208-338-8200.
FAX: 208-338-8299.
Honolulu, Hawaii Office: 1360 Pauahi Tower, 1001 Bishop Street, 96813.
Telephone: 808-538-3360.
FAX: 808-526-0101.
Los Angeles, California Office: Suite 600, 1000 Wilshire Boulevard. 90017.
Telephone: 213-229-9600.
FAX: 213-627-4874.
Portland, Oregon Office: 2300 First Interstate Tower, 1300 SW Fifth Avenue. 97201.
Telephone: 503-241-2300.
FAX: 503-778-5299.
Richland, Washington Office: Suite 260, 1100 Jadwin Avenue. 99352.
Telephone: 509-946-5369.
FAX: 509-946-4211.
San Francisco, California Office: Suite 1500, 235 Pine Street, 94104.
Telephone: 415-765-5333.
FAX: 415-421-6619.
Washington, D.C. Office: Suite 700, 1155 Connecticut Avenue N.W. 20036.
Telephone: 202-508-6600.
FAX: 202-508-6699.
Shanghai, China Office: Suite 1008/1009, Jin Jiang Hotel, 59 Mao Ming Road (S), 200020.
Telephones: 011-8621-472-3344; 011-8621-415-3002.
FAX: 011-8621-415-3003.

MEMBERS OF FIRM

Greg F. Adams
C. Keith Allred
Kathleen A. Anamosa
Steven W. Andreasen
Hall Baetz
Robert A. Baskerville
Jeff Belfiglio (Resident, Bellevue, Washington Office)
Mark W. Berry (Resident, Bellevue, Washington Office)
Robert A. Blackstone
Lynda L. Brothers
Lynne A. Chafetz
Allen D. Clark (Resident, Bellevue, Washington Office)
Richard A. Derham
P. Cameron DeVore
Bradley C. Diggs
Mary Elizabeth Drobka
Susan G. Duffy
Stuart R. Dunwoody
Richard W. Elliott (Bellevue and Richland, Washington Offices)
Dirk J. Giseburt
Thomas A. Goeltz
Marvin L. Gray, Jr.
Michael R. Green (Resident, Bellevue, Washington Office)
Larry E. Halvorson (Resident, Bellevue, Washington Office)

(See Next Column)

DAVIS WRIGHT TREMAINE, *Seattle—Continued*

MEMBERS OF FIRM (Continued)

Richard L. Hames
Ralph L. Hawkins
Jayanne A. Hino
Robert G. Homchick
Steven J. Hopp (Resident, Bellevue, Washington Office)
Mark A. Hutcheson
Thomas S. James
Bruce E. H. Johnson
C. James Judson
Francis A. Kareken
John E. Keegan
Michael J. Killeen
Richard A. Klobucher (Resident, Bellevue, Washington Office)
Warren E. Koons (Resident, Bellevue, Washington Office)
Donald S. Kunze
Bruce Lamka
Edward N. Lange
Ladd B. Leavens
Thomas A. Lemly
David V. Marshall (Resident, Bellevue, Washington Office)
Dennis E. McLean
Craig Miller
Malcolm A. Moore
Marshall J. Nelson
Anne L. Northrup
Norman B. Page
A. Peter Parsons
Donna M. Peck-Gaines
William G. Pusch
Amy L. Ragen
Richard M. Rawson
John Alan Reed
Carrie J. Rehrl
Michael Reiss
Daniel B. Ritter
William D. Rives
Mark W. Roberts
Douglas C. Ross
Stephen M. Rummage
Samuel F. Saracino
Margaret L. Schaaf
Richard J. Schroeder
Payton Smith
William R. Squires III
Howard Stambor
Mary E. Steele
David C. Tarshes
Thomas G. Thorbeck
David W. Thorne
Jeffrey B. Van Duzer
Nick S. Verwolf (Resident, Bellevue, Washington Office)
Daniel Waggoner
Joseph D. Weinstein
LaVerne Woods
James E. Wreggelsworth
Richard S. Wyde
John H. Zobel

ASSOCIATES

Erich D. Andersen
Linda White Atkins (Resident, Bellevue, Washington Office)
Glenn J. Blumstein
Jeanne Bumpus
Ward E. Buringrud
Philip W. Clements
John Creahan
Crissa Cugini (Resident, Bellevue, Washington Office)
Frank E. Cuthbertson
Marco de Sa e Silva
Eric A. DeJong (Not admitted in WA)
Jason A. Farber (Not admitted in WA)
Rhys Matthew Farren (Resident, Bellevue, Washington Office)
James A. Flaggert
Jennifer M. Follette
Randy Gainer
Camille E. Gearhart
Carolyn J. Glenn
Jessica L. Goldman
Nathaniel B. Green, Jr.
Lawton Henry Hansell
Nicholas D. Hyslop
David Jennings
Delwen A. Jones (Resident, Bellevue, Washington Office)
Jin H. Kim (Resident, Bellevue, Washington Office)
Cassandra Lynn Kinkead (Resident, Bellevue, Washington Office)
Gregory J. Kopta
Debora K. Kristensen
Katherine Kramer Laird
Kara A. Larsen
Lynn T. Manolopoulos (Resident, Bellevue, Washington Office)
Laura E. Matsuda
Christine A. McCabe
Jonathan M. Michaels
Alan S. Middleton
Jeff C. Minzel
Janet E. Murphy
S. Hossein Nowbar
John H. Parnass
James E. Pruitt III (Resident, Bellevue, Washington Office)
William K. Rasmussen
Rosemary Reeve
Janine V. Roberts
Kerry G. Robinson (Resident, Bellevue, Washington Office)
Michael B. Saunders (Resident, Bellevue Washington Office)
John M. Sharp
Erin M. Sheridan
Bergitta K. Trelstad
Alan G. Waldbaum
Jeffrey S. Weber
William L. Weigand, III
Gina M. Zadra

COUNSEL

John M. Davis
Clifton L. Elliott
Henry E. Farber
Garry G. Fujita
Robert S. Gruhn
Lisle R. Guernsey (Retired)
Bradley T. Jones (Retired)
Shelly C. Shapiro
Kimbrough Street
Charles H. Todd (Retired)
Willard J. Wright

Representative Clients: Alexander & Alexander, Inc.; AT&T Communications, Inc.; Axa-Midi Assurances; Battelle Pacific Northwest Division; Buckner News Alliance; C. Itoh & Co., Ltd.; Cable News Network CNN; Children's Hospital & Medical Center; Chrysler Capital Corporation; City of Seattle.

For full biographical listings, see the Martindale-Hubbell Law Directory

FAULKNER, BANFIELD, DOOGAN & HOLMES, A PROFESSIONAL CORPORATION (AV⓪)

999 Third Avenue, Suite 2600, 98104
Telephone: 206-292-8008
Telecopier: 206-340-0289
Juneau, Alaska Office: 302 Gold Street.
Telephone: 907-586-2210.
Telecopier: 907-586-8090.
Anchorage, Alaska Office: 550 West Seventh Avenue, Suite 1000.
Telephone: 907-274-0666.
Telecopier: 907-277-4657.

Michael M. Holmes (Resident)
Michael A. Barcott (Resident)
John E. Casperson (Resident)

OF COUNSEL

Dwight L. Guy (Resident)
James F. Whitehead (Resident)
Lawrence T. Feeney (Retired)
Norman C. Banfield (Retired)

William D. DeVoe (Resident)
Raymond H. Warns, Jr. (Resident)
Philip W. Sanford (Resident)
Alec W. Brindle, Jr. (Resident)

For full biographical listings, see the Martindale-Hubbell Law Directory

FOSTER PEPPER & SHEFELMAN (AV)

A Partnership including Professional Service Corporations
34th Floor, 1111 Third Avenue, 98101
Telephone: 206-447-4400
Facsimile: 206-447-9700
Bellevue, Washington Office: Security Pacific Plaza, 15th Floor, 777 108th Avenue N.E.
Telephone: 206-451-0500.
Facsimile: 206-455-5487.
Portland, Oregon Office: One Main Place, 15th Floor, 101 S.W. Main Street.
Telephone: 503-221-0607.
Facsimile: 503-221-1510.

James P. Weter (1877-1959)
F. M. Roberts (1880-1973)
W. V. Tanner (1881-1953)
John P. Garvin (1888-1972)
Paul P. Ashley (1896-1979)
Harold S. Shefelman (1898-1984)
James C. Harper (1915-1993)
Robert F. Buck (Retired)
James Gay (Retired)
Victor D. Lawrence (Retired)
Arthur S. Quigley (Retired)

MEMBERS OF FIRM

Gary N. Ackerman (P.S.)
Thomas F. Ahearne
Paul L. Ahern, Jr. (Resident, Bellevue Office)
Bradley J. Berg
Michael D. Bohannon
Dean V. Butler
Fay L. Chapman
Beth A. Clark
Edward R. Coulson
Jack J. Cullen
Robert J. Diercks
P. Stephen DiJulio
Thomas E. Dixon
Dwight J. Drake (Resident, Bellevue Office)
Peter S. Ehrlichman
Timothy J. Filer
Gary E. Fluhrer
Linda L. Foreman
Joseph M. Gaffney (P.S.)
Curt B. Gleaves (Resident, Portland, Oregon Office)
Lynne E. Graybeal
Camden M. Hall
Willard Hatch
John L. Hendrickson (Resident, Bellevue Office)
G. Richard Hill
David B. Howorth (Resident, Portland, Oregon Office)
Brian D. Hulse
Allen D. Israel
Diane M. Istvan
Dillon E. Jackson
Richard E. Keefe (P.S.)
Stellman K. Keehnel
Patrick F. Kennedy
Catharine E. Killien
Michael D. Kuntz
Laurie Neilson Lee (Resident, Portland, Oregon Office)
Lynn J. Loacker
George M. Mack
Jon W. MacLeod
Marco J. Magnano, Jr.
Larry C. Martin (Resident, Bellevue Office)
Bennet A. McConaughy (Resident, Bellevue Office)
Robert A. Medved
Roger D. Mellem
Andrew J. Morrow, Jr. (Resident, Portland, Oregon Office)
Jonathan B. Noll
Charles P. Nomellini
Douglas S. Palmer, Jr. (P.S.)
Jennifer L. Palmquist (Resident, Portland, Oregon Office)
Jane Pearson
Douglas R. Prince
Warren J. Rheaume
Paul V. Rieke
Daniel J. Riviera
Kenneth E. Roberts, Jr. (Resident, Portland, Oregon Office)
Judith M. Runstad
Bernard L. Russell
Michael D. Sandler
Laurin S. Schweet
Robert C. Seidel
Bonnie P. Serkin (Resident, Portland, Oregon Office)
Michael R. Silvey (Resident, Portland Oregon Office)
George L. Smith (Resident, Bellevue Office)
Hugh D. Spitzer
V. Rafael Stone
David B. Sweeney
Daniel L. Thieme
William G. Tonkin
David Utevsky
Michael K. Vaska
Lee Voorhees
Thomas M. Walsh
J. Tayloe Washburn
Judee A. Wells
Kent Whiteley (Resident, Bellevue Office)

(See Next Column)

FOSTER PEPPER & SHEFELMAN—*Continued*

MEMBERS OF FIRM (Continued)

Joseph P. Whitford
Alan K. Willert
David R. Wilson
Phillip B. Winberry
Deborah S. Winter
Steven H. Winterbauer
Christopher W. Wright

RESIDENT OF COUNSEL
AT SEATTLE, WASHINGTON OFFICE

Dan D. Dixon (Not admitted in WA)
Thomas B. Foster
Robert G. Moch
Stuart T. Rolfe
Richard L. Settle
Carl J. West III, (P.S.)

RESIDENT OF COUNSEL
AT PORTLAND, OREGON OFFICE

Phillip E. Grillo

ASSOCIATES

Cynthia F. Adkins
Aliza C. Allen
Christopher M. Alston
Mary L. Beyer
Lynn E. Blough (Resident Associate, Portland, Oregon Office)
Karen J. Boyle
Laura J. Brackett
James B. Bristol
Marque C. Chambliss
Grover E. Cleveland
Polly Kim Close
Bruce A. Coffey
Shannon M. Connelly (Resident Associate, Portland, Oregon Office)
Gordon E. Crim (Resident Associate, Portland, Oregon Office)
Clifford M. Curry
David J. Dadoun
Rebecca Dean (Resident Associate, Portland, Oregon Office)
Joseph E. Delaney
Cynthia L. Doll
J. Scott Emery
John A. Fandel
Fara E. Faubus
Cynthia R. First
Elizabeth L. Foster-Nolan (Not admitted in WA)
Anne W. Glazer
Bradley W. Hoff
Brian L. Holtzclaw
Steven G. Jones
Xiaoming Ke
Alan D. Koslow
Marc T. Kretschmer
Cynthia A. Kuno
Robert Kunold, Jr.
Jeremy R. (Jake) Larson
Richard E. Leigh, Jr.
C. Christine Maloney
Marsha L. Martin (Resident Associate, Bellevue Office)
Annette M. Mouton
Lori Nomura
Batur H. Oktay
Roger A. Pearce
Nancy L. Peterson (Resident Associate, Portland, Oregon Office)
Thomas M. Pors
Robert J. Riley
Sharon Seung
Matthew M. Smith
Carolann O'Brien Storli
Philip N. Tanaka
Susan R. Taylor
Douglas V. Van Dyk (Resident Associate, Portland, Oregon Office)
Tamara J. Warren (Resident Associate, Bellevue Office)
Lauren E. Winters (Resident Associate, Portland, Oregon Office)
Timothy M. Woodland

For full biographical listings, see the Martindale-Hubbell Law Directory

---

GAITÁN & CUSACK (AV)

30th Floor Two Union Square, 601 Union Street, 98101-2324
Telephone: 206-521-3000
Facsimile: 206-386-5259
Anchorage, Alaska Office: 425 G Street, Suite 760.
Telephone: 907-278-3001.
Facsimile: 907-278-6068.
San Francisco, California Office: 275 Battery Street, 20th Floor.
Telephone: 415-398-5562.
Fax: 415-398-4033.
Washington, D.C. Office: 2000 L Street, Suite 200.
Telephone: 202-296-4637.
Fax: 202-296-4650.

MEMBERS OF FIRM

José E. Gaitán
Kenneth J. Cusack (Resident, Anchorage, Alaska Office)
William F. Knowles
Ronald L. Bozarth

OF COUNSEL

Howard K. Todd
Gary D. Gayton
Michel P. Stern (Also practicing alone, Bellevue, Washington)
Christopher A. Byrne
Patricia D. Ryan

ASSOCIATES

Mary F. O'Boyle
Bruce H. Williams
David J. Onsager
Diana T. Jimenez
Robert T. Mimbu
Cristina C. Kapela
Camilla M. Hedberg
John E. Lenker
Kathleen C. Healy

Representative Clients: The Chubb Group of Insurance Companies; Commercial Union Insurance Companies; Elscint, Inc.; Transamerica Insurance Companies; Federal Deposit Insurance Corporation; Resolution Trust Corporation; Chemical Bank; Toshi Products; Hosho America, Inc.; Northshore Utility District.

For full biographical listings, see the Martindale-Hubbell Law Directory

GARVEY, SCHUBERT & BARER (AV)

1191 Second Avenue, 18th Floor, 98101
Telephone: 206-464-3939
Cable Address: "Lex, Seattle"
Telex: 32-1037
Telecopier: 206-464-0125
Washington, D.C. Office: 5th Floor, 1000 Potomac Street, N.W., 20007.
Telephone: 202-965-7880.
Telecopier: 202-965-1729.
Portland, Oregon Office: Eleventh Floor, 121 S.W. Morrison Street, 97204.
Telephone: 503-228-3939.
Telecopier: 503-226-0259.

MEMBERS OF FIRM

Rodney B. Carman
Susan L. Coskey
Keven J. Davis
Steven M. Dickinson
Jan L. Essenburg
David J. Grant
John K. Hoerster
Barbara L. Holland
Stephen B. Johnson
James G. Kibble
Jonathan A. Kroman
Donald L. Logerwell
Bruce A. McDermott
Brian A. Morrison
Bruce A. Robertson
Charles C. Robinson
E. Charles Routh
Mark A. Rowley
Lori Salzarulo
Sara P. Sandford
Kenneth L. Schubert, Jr.
Alan P. Sherbrooke
Robert B. Spitzer
R. Jack Stephenson
Gary J. Strauss
Donald P. Swisher
David R. West

RESIDENT ASSOCIATES

Joanne Thomas Blackburn
Christopher J. Breunig
Timothy C. Burkart
Michael R. Gotham
Lisa R. Hanna
Annalisa Clar Johnson
C. Andrew McCarthy
Pegeen Mulhern
Anne F. Preston
Kevin Demone Rainge
Carol L. Saboda
Donald B. Scaramastra
Michael A. Skinner
Gary D. Swearingen
Clay F. West
Susan Richardson Willert

OF COUNSEL

Stanley H. Barer
M. John Bundy
Gregory R. Dallaire
Lucinda D. Fernald
Michael D. Garvey
Stephen C. Kelly
John L. Mericle
Kerry E. Radcliffe

Representative Clients: Foss Maritime Co.; K-2 Corp.; National Bank of Canada; Nissho Iwai American Corp.; PeaceHealth; Sun Transport, Inc.; The Commerce Bank of Washington; Western Star Trucks.

For full biographical listings, see the Martindale-Hubbell Law Directory

---

GRAHAM & DUNN A PROFESSIONAL SERVICE CORPORATION (AV)

33rd Floor, 1420 Fifth Avenue, 98101-2390
Telephone: 206-624-8300
Telecopier (Panafax UF-400 AD): 206-340-9599
Tacoma, Washington Office: 1300 Tacoma Financial Center, 1145 Broadway Plaza, 98402-3517.
Telephone: 206-572-9294.

Donald G. Graham (1894-1972)
Bryant R. Dunn (1909-1992)
Timothy L. Austin
W. George Bassett
Douglas C. Berry
Keith C. Cochran
Stephen A. Crary
Gary R. Duvall
K. Michael Fandel
Mark A. Finkelstein
James C. Fowler
Frederick O. Frederickson
Ben J. Gantt, Jr.
Alice F. Gustafson
John T. John
Michael E. Kipling
Stephen M. Klein
Mark C. Lewington (Resident, Tacoma Office)
James L. Magee
Peter S. McCormick
Martin R. Morfeld
Frank R. Morrison, Jr.
Charles S. Mullen
Noreen M. Nearn
Mark D. Northrup
Scott B. Osborne
Edward W. Pettigrew
James D. Rolfe
Irvin W. Sandman
Carmen L. Smith
Larry J. Smith
Jack G. Strother
Michael J. Swofford

COUNSEL

Stephen H. Goodman
George Hunter
James W. Johnston
V. Lee Okarma Rees

Estera F. Gordon

Robert G. Bergquist
Maren K. Gaylor
John J. Hansell
Marisa L. Lindell
Sharon L. Rosse
Donald J. Verfurth
Ye-Ting Woo

Representative Clients: West One Bancorp; West One Bank, Washington; Ackerley Communications; Safeco; Fisher Mills; KOMO-AM, KOMO-TV and KATU-TV; Atlantic Richfield; Icicle Seafoods; The Equitable Life Assurance Society of the U.S.; Westin Hotel; American Insurance Group.

For full biographical listings, see the Martindale-Hubbell Law Directory

Seattle—Continued

HELSELL, FETTERMAN, MARTIN, TODD & HOKANSON (AV)

1500 Puget Sound Plaza, 1325 Fourth Avenue, P.O. Box 21846, 98111
Telephone: 206-292-1144
Telecopier: 206-340-0902
Bellevue, Washington Office: 2233 Skyline Tower, 10900 N.E. 4th Street.
Telephone: 206-292-1144.
Telecopier: 206-455-3713.

MEMBERS OF FIRM

Paul Fetterman (Retired)
Thomas Todd (Retired)
Lloyd Shorett (Retired)
Richard S. White
Gary F. Linden
John Edward Ederer (Bellevue Office)
Phillip D. Noble
David F. Jurca
Lish Whitson
John G. Bergmann
R. Broh Landsman
Danferd W. Henke
Karen J. Vanderlaan
Pauline V. Smetka
David S. Gross
Bruce H. Benson
Ragan L. Powers
Bradley H. Bagshaw
Andrew J. Kinstler
Fredrick D. Huebner
Mark F. Rising
Kevin L. Stock
Llewelyn G. Pritchard
Mark C. Dean
C. James Frush
Robert N. Gellatly
Jerry E. Thonn
Watson B. Blair
Dirk A. Bartram
Deborah L. Martin
Linda D. Walton
George A. Nicoud III
Patricia E. Anderson
Scott E. Collins

COUNSEL

William A. Helsell
Russell V. Hokanson
Roger L. Decker (Bellevue Office)
Lynn Bahrych Squires
Thomas W. Huber
Linda J. Cochran
Harold R. Rooks
Peter J. Eglick

ASSOCIATES

Polly K. Becker
Scott W. Campbell
B. Jeffrey Carl
David T. Cluxton
Jennifer S. Divine
Jacki L. Kirklin
Jonathan P. Meier
Tom Montgomery
Laura F. Pasik
Susan L. Peterson
Erik D. Price
Peter G. Ramels
Steven J. Samario
Richard E. Spoonemore
Bradley S. Shannon
William R. Spurr
Bob C. Sterbank

LEGAL SUPPORT PERSONNEL

Jane S. Kiker (Land Use Analyst)

Representative Clients: Bethlehem Steel Corp.; Chevron Corp.; Chiyoda International Corp.; Farmers Insurance Group; Holland America Line-Westours Inc.; Nicholson Industries, Inc.; Star Industries, Inc.

For full biographical listings, see the Martindale-Hubbell Law Directory

HILLIS CLARK MARTIN & PETERSON A PROFESSIONAL SERVICE CORPORATION (AV)

500 Galland Building, 1221 Second Avenue, 98101-2925
Telephone: 206-623-1745
Facsimile: 206-623-7789

Joel N. Bodansky
Laurie Lootens Chyz
Mark S. Clark
Sally H. Clarke
Lynne M. Cohee
T. Ryan Durkan
Thomas J. Ehrlichman
Gary M. Fallon
Douglas M. Garrou
Richard E. Gifford
Steven C. Gonzalez
Ann M. Gygi
Jane W. Harvey
Jerome L. Hillis
Irene M. Ibarra
George A. Kresovich
Eric D. Lansverk
Sarah E. Mack
George W. Martin, Jr.
Melody B. McCutcheon
Mark C. McPherson
Louis D. Peterson
Richard M. Peterson
Steven R. Rovig
Michael F. Schumacher
Michael R. Scott
Matthew P. Smith
Robert B. Van Cleve
Richard R. Wilson

Representative Clients: Continental, Inc.; Continental Savings Bank; Horizon Air; JAMCO AMERICA, Inc.; Merrill Lynch, Pierce, Fenner & Smith Inc.; Mitsubishi International Corporation; Port of Seattle; The Quadrant Corporation; Weyerhaeuser Company and subsidiaries.

For full biographical listings, see the Martindale-Hubbell Law Directory

KELLER ROHRBACK (AV)

1201 Third Avenue, Suite 3200, 98101-3052
Telephone: 206-623-1900
FAX: 206-623-3384
Bremerton, Washington Office: 400 Warren Avenue.
Telephone: 360-479-5151.
Fax: 360-479-7403.

(See Next Column)

MEMBERS OF FIRM

Robert K. Keller (1916-1992)
Pinckney M. Rohrback (1923-1994)
Fred R. Butterworth
Harold Fardal
Glen P. Garrison
Laurence Ross Weatherly
Lynn Lincoln Sarko (Mr.)
John H. Bright
William C. Smart
Lawrence B. Linville
Irene M. Hecht
Kirk S. Portmann
Kathleen Kim Coghlan
David R. Major
Benson D. Wong
Nikki L. Anderson (Ms.)
John T. Mellen
Karen E. Boxx
Thomas A. Heller
Stephen J. Henderson
Michael Woerner

ASSOCIATES

T. David Copley
Rob J. Crichton
Juli E. Farris
Mark A. Griffin
William A. Linton
Paulette Peterson
Stella L. Pitts
Roberta N. Riley
Britt L. Tinglum
David J. Russell
John H. Wiegenstein

OF COUNSEL

Burton C. Waldo
Melvin F. Buol

Attorneys For: Allstate Insurance Company; American Honda Motor Co., Inc.; American States Insurance Co.; America Suzuki Motor Corp.; Bell Helmets, Inc.; Pacific Northwest Bank; Ticor Title; United Services Automobile Association; National Bank of Bremerton; Pend Oreille Bank.

For full biographical listings, see the Martindale-Hubbell Law Directory

LANE POWELL SPEARS LUBERSKY (AV)

A Partnership including Professional Corporations
1420 Fifth Avenue, Suite 4100, 98101-2338
Telephone: 206-223-7000
Cable Address: "Embe"
Telex: 32-8808
Telecopier: 206-223-7107
Other Offices at: Mount Vernon and Olympia, Washington; Los Angeles and San Francisco, California; Anchorage, Alaska; Portland, Oregon; London, England.

MEMBERS OF FIRM

Frank W. Draper
D. Wayne Gittinger
Richard F. Allen
Dale E. Kremer
Hartley Paul
Robert R. Davis, Jr.
Wayne W. Hansen
Robert L. Israel (P.S.)
Michael L. Cohen (P.S.)
Charles R. Ekberg (P.S.)
Kenyon P. Kellogg
Richard C. Siefert
Michael D. Dwyer
Mark Edwin Johnson
James L. Robart
C. William Bailey
Christopher B. Wells
Michael E. Morgan
Timothy J. Pauley
James B. Stoetzer
Larry S. Gangnes (P.S.)
Michael H. Runyan
Rudy A. Englund
David G. Johansen
H. Peter Sorg, Jr.
Michael D. McKay
Gary P. Tober
Jeffrey L. Gingold
W. L. Rivers Black, III
Barry N. Mesher
Douglas J. Shaeffer
Kenneth B. Kaplan
Glenn J. Amster
Thomas F. Grohman
D. Joseph Hurson
Scott F. Campbell
Reed P. Schifferman
William A. Pelandini
Ralph C. Pond
Mark G. Beard
David T. Hunter
Joseph E. Lynam
John J. Mitchell
Craig L. McIvor
Paul D. Swanson
Matthew E. Swaya
Randall P. Beighle
David M. Schoeggl
Bruce W. Leaverton
Gail E. Mautner (P.S.)
Warren E. Babb, Jr.
Tim D. Wackerbarth
Bruce Winchell
Christian N. Oldham
D. Michael Reilly
Douglas E. Wheeler
Suzanne Kelly Michael
Michael B. King
Cathy A. Spicer
Stephen C. Smith
Grant S. Degginger
Jane Rakay Nelson
Stanton Phillip Beck
John R. Neeleman
Jeffrey D. Laveson
Mark P. Scheer
Douglas E. Smith
Timothy J. Tompkins

COUNSEL

Wilbur J. Lawrence
Meade Emory
Mary Jo Heston

OF COUNSEL

W. Byron Lane (1905-1989)
Pendleton Miller (1910-1988)
George V. Powell
William J. Walsh, Jr. (1919-1994)
Gordon W. Moss
G. Keith Grim
Raymond W. Haman
John R. Tomlinson
Barry H. Biggs
Robert W. Thomas
David C. Lycette
Deborah D. Wright

ASSOCIATES

John J. Albrecht
Gregory L. Anderson
Nancy Watkins Anderson
Geri Ann Baptista
Rehman H. Bashey
Ronald E. Beard
Jennifer Milestone Bishop
Louise D. Bush

(See Next Column)

LANE POWELL SPEARS LUBERSKY—*Continued*

ASSOCIATES (Continued)

John B. Chafee, Jr.
Arthur R. Chapman
Samuel S. Chung
James D. Clack
Linda Blohm Clapham
Grant E. Courtney
Ellen M. Davis
John R. Dawson
Stephania Camp Denton
John S. Devlin, III
Barbara J. Duffy
J.C. Ditzler
Gregory J. Duff
Elizabeth Fitzhugh
Joseph D. Hampton
Joseph I. Hochman
Charles C. Huber
Jim D. Johnston
Teena M. Killian
Gary M. Kirk
Joyce C. Kling
Charlene A. Launer
Tammy L. Lewis
Katie Belinda Smith Matison
Jodi A. McDougall
Stephen P. McGrath
David A. Miller
James D. Mitchell
Michael A. Nesteroff
James E. Niemer
Todd L. Nunn
Thomas J. Owens
Charles W. Riley, Jr.
Katherine Riffle Roper
David C. Spellman
Maria E. Sotirhos
N. Claire Stack
Elizabeth A. Sullivan
Emilia L. Sweeney
W. Michael Targett
Thomas W. Top
Paul I. Tyler
Raymond S. Weber
Patricia Hunt Welch
Lucy Keenan Williams

Representative Clients: AT&T; Dow Corning Corp.; Fred Hutchinson Cancer Research Center; The Home Depot; Key Bank of Washington; Mitsui & Co., Ltd.; Nordstrom, Inc.; Simpson Investment Co. and Affiliates; Texaco, Inc.; Underwriters at Lloyds, London.

For full biographical listings, see the Martindale-Hubbell Law Directory

OLES, MORRISON & RINKER (AV)

3300 Columbia Center, 701 Fifth Avenue, 98104-7082
Telephone: 206-623-3427
Telecopier: 206-682-6234

MEMBERS OF FIRM

Seth W. Morrison
David C. Stewart
Sam E. Baker, Jr.
Arthur D. McGarry
B. Michael Schestopol
Theodore L. Preg
Robert J. Burke
David H. Karlen
Bradley L. Powell
Douglas S. Oles
Peter N. Ralston
Mark F. O'Donnell
John Lukjanowicz
James F. Nagle
Glenn R. Nelson
J. Craig Rusk
T. Daniel Heffernan
Harlan M. Hatfield
Robert W. Sargeant

ASSOCIATES

Todd M. Nelson
Traeger Machetanz
Richard T. Black
Evalyn K. Hodges
William D Garcia (Not admitted in WA)
George T. Schroth

OF COUNSEL

Stuart G. Oles

For full biographical listings, see the Martindale-Hubbell Law Directory

PERKINS COIE (AV)

A Law Partnership including Professional Corporations
Strategic Alliance with Russell & DuMoulin
1201 Third Avenue, 40th Floor, 98101-3099
Telephone: 206-583-8888
Facsimile: 206-583-8500
Cable Address: "Perki ns Seattle."
Telex: 32-0319 PERKINS SEA
Anchorage, Alaska Office: 1029 West Third Avenue, Suite 300.
Telephone: 907-279-8561.
Facsimile: 907-276-3108.
Telex: 32-0319 PERKINS SEA.
Los Angeles, California Office: 1999 Avenue of the Stars, Ninth Floor.
Telephone: 310-788-9900.
Telex: 32-0319 PERKINS SEA.
Facsimile: 310-788-3399.
Washington, D.C. Office: 607 Fourteenth Street, N.W.
Telephone: 202-628-6600.
Facsimile: 202-434-1690.
Telex: 44-0277 PCSO.
Portland, Oregon Office: U.S. Bancorp Tower, Suite 2500, 111 S.W. Fifth Avenue.
Telephone: 503-295-4400.
Facsimile: 503-295-6793.
Telex: 32-0319 PERKINS SEA.
Bellevue, Washington Office: Suite 1800, One Bellevue Center, 411 - 108th Avenue N.E.
Telephone: 206-453-6980.
Facsimile: 206-453-7350.
Telex: 32-0319 PERKINS SEA.

(See Next Column)

Spokane, Washington Office: North 221 Wall Street, Suite 600.
Telephone: 509-624-2212.
Facsimile: 509-458-3399.
Telex: 32-0319 PERKINS SEA.
Olympia, Washington Office: 1110 Capitol Way South, Suite 405.
Telephone: 206-956-3300.
Strategic Alliance with Russell & DuMoulin, 1700-1075 West Georgia Street, Vancouver, B.C. V6E 3G2. Telephone: 604-631-3131.
Hong Kong Office: 23rd Floor Asia Pacific Finance Tower, Citibank Plaza, 3 Garden Road.
Telephone: 852-2878-1177.
Facsimile: 852-2524-9988. DX-9230-IC.
London, England Office: 36/38 Cornhill, ECV3 3ND.
Telephone: 071-369-9966.
Facsimile: 071-369-9968.
Taipei, Taiwan Office: 8/F TFIT Tower, 85 Jen AiRoad, Sec. 4,Taipei 106, Taiwan, R.O.C.
Telephone: 886-2-778-1177.
Facsimile: 086-2-777-9898.

PARTNERS/SHAREHOLDERS

John D. Alkire
J. David Andrews, P.S.
John F. Aslin
John Daniel Ballbach
Richard L. Baum
George M. Beal II
Kurt Becker
Dennis L. Bekemeyer, P.S.
Steven Scott Bell
Thomas C. Bell
Ronald L. Berenstain
Thomas L. Boeder
Marc A. Boman
Andrew Bor (Resident, London, England Office)
Dori E. Lee Brewer
Bruce M. Brooks
Rex C. Browning
David J. Burman
Bruce D. Campbell
Joan C. Clarke (Resident, Bellevue, Washington Office)
J. Paul Coie
Bruce D. Corker
Richard C. Coyle
Bruce Michael Cross
Janis A. Cunningham
Ellen Conedera Dial
Bruce E. Dick (Resident, Bellevue, Washington Office)
Calhoun Dickinson
John D. Dillow
Charles N. Eberhardt (Resident, Bellevue, Washington Office)
Paul J. Ehlenbach
Graham H. Fernald
Bruce P. Flynn
H. Weston Foss, P.S.
Susan E. Foster
Keith Gerrard
Albert Gidari, Jr.
Robert Edward Giles (Managing Partner)
Gregory Gorder
Charles C. Gordon
Ronald M. Gould
William A. Gould
Stephen M. Graham
William L. Green
Kevin J. Hamilton
Michael L. Hall
Lawrence B. Hannah, Jr. (Resident, Bellevue, Washington Office)
Steven M. Hedberg
James M. Hilton (P.S.)
Jeffrey A. Hollingsworth
Ramer B. Holtan, Jr.
Valerie L. Hughes (Resident, Bellevue, Washington Office)
Barry M. Kaplan
Donald G. Kari (P.S.) (Resident, Bellevue, Washington Office)
Charles J. Katz, Jr.
Heng-Pin Kiang
Reginald S. Koehler III
Edward W. Kuhrau (P.C.)
Stewart M. Landefeld
James R. Lisbakken
Douglas S. Little
Douglas S. MacBain
Steven C. Marshall (P.S.)
Richard E. McCann
Stephen A. McKeon
M. Margaret McKeown
Thomas J. McLaughlin
J. Christian Moller
James R. Moore
Philip S. Morse
Richard L. Mull
J. Shan Mullin
Clark Reed Nichols
Richard W. Oehler
Omar S. Parker, Jr.
Russell L. Perisho
Vicki M. Pierce
Sherilyn Peterson (Resident, Bellevue, Washington Office)
Thomas E. Platt
Steven E. Pope (Resident, Bellevue, Washington Office)
Richard Ottesen Prentke
Markham A. Quehrn (Resident, Bellevue, Washington Office)
Michael T. Reynvaan
Catherine B. Roach
Richard R. Rohde (Resident, Bellevue, Washington Office)
James P. Savitt (Resident, Bellevue, Washington Office)
Harry H. Schneider, Jr.
Mark W. Schneider
Mark D. Schultz
Scott F. Seablom
Craig E. Shank (Resident, Bellevue, Washington Office)
Evelyn Cruz Sroufe
Michael E. Stansbury
Jeffrey I. Tilden
James M. Van Nostrand (Resident, Bellevue, Washington Office)
David E. Wagoner
Bart Waldman
David R. Walton
Richard A. White
Nancy Williams
L. Michelle Wilson
V. L. Woolston
Colleen S. Yamaguchi

COUNSEL

Walter W. Eyer
Lowell P. Mickelwait
Harold F. Olsen
Richard E. Walker
Andrew M. Williams

OF COUNSEL

Gene S. Anderson
Wayne C. Booth, Jr.
Joseph E. Bringman
Robert L. Capizzi
Michael J. Havers
Roland L. Hjorth
Gregory K. McCall
Thomas P. McCormick
J. Sue Morgan
Deborah J. Phillips
John R. Price
Kevin W. Quigley
Charles B. Roe, Jr.
Heidi L. Sachs

(See Next Column)

PERKINS COIE, *Seattle—Continued*

OF COUNSEL (Continued)

Damian C. Smith
Conrad Teitell
(Not admitted in WA)
Philip T. Temple
(Not admitted in WA)

RESIDENT ASSOCIATES

Elizabeth A. Alaniz
Thomas A. Barkewitz
Daniel R. Barnhart
Gretchen F. Baumgardner
John Randolph Beck
Ted D. Billbe
Michael D. Broaddus
Jack L. Brown
Jay S. Brown
Zane A. Brown, Jr.
Aaron H. Caplan
Karen P. Clark
David C. Clarke
J. Thomas Cristy
Shelly Crocker
Robert C. Cumbow
David Dabroski
Stephanie Gayle Daley-Watson
Kristina M. Dalman
John P. Deery-Schmitt
Wendi J. Delmendo
John L. Dentler
David L. Dieter
Katerina I. Drakos
Lorri A. Dunsmore
David Eber
Melisa D. Evangelos
Susan Fahringer
Bradley L. Fisher
Karin L. Foster
Michael D. Gallagher
Nicholas P. Gellert
Claire S. Grace
Douglas W. Greene
Sandra Blair Hernshaw
Michael Himes
Rebecca J. Huss
John Stuart Kaplin
Thomas More Kellenberg
Yuriko Kotani
Alice D. Leiner
Mark H. Lough
Erik G. Marks
Michael D. Martin
Matthew B. McCutchen
William Kenneth McGraw
Kathleen N. McKereghan
Gaye L. McNutt
David F. McShea
(Not admitted in WA)
Yukio Morikubo
Kevin C. Osborn
Julia L. Parsons
Elizabeth K. Peck
Alesia L. Pinney-Hawkins
Alicia Z. Ramos
James R. Rasband
Traci A. Sammeth
Linda A. Schoemaker
Jack L. Siemering
Grant Josiah Silvernale, III
Kari Anne Smith
Richard Chongsoo Sohn
Philip D. Song
Erika Jongejan Starrs
Mitchell D. Stocks
Ben D. Straughan
James W. Talbot
Jeffrey M. Thomas
Thomas C. Tsai
Kathryn L. Tucker
Alison T. Wachterman
Elizabeth Blomberg Weigand
Laura N. Whitaker
John D. White
Stephen C. Willey
James Fitzgerald Williams
Vickie J. Williams
David Williamson
Jeffrey A. Wool
Gregory J. Wrenn
Steven R. Yentzer

Counsel for: Alaska Airlines, Inc.; The Boeing Company; Children's Hospital and Medical Center; Commerce Bank, N.A.; General Motors Corporation; Lloyd's of London (Aviation); Puget Sound Power & Light Company; Seattle School District.; Shurgard Capital Group; Weyerhaeuser Company.

For full biographical listings, see the Martindale-Hubbell Law Directory

REED MCCLURE (AV)

3600 Columbia Center, 701 Fifth Avenue, 98104-7081
Telephone: 206-292-4900
Telecopier: 206-223-0152
AB A/Net 1429

SHAREHOLDERS

Lori Nelson Adams
Stuart C. Allen
Keith Gormley Baldwin
Katharine Witter Brindley
Mary R. DeYoung
Kathryn L. Feldman
Bradley D. Grisham
William R. Hickman
William L. Holder
Mark M. Hough
D. Bradley Hudson
Robert D. Johns
Mark B. Kantor
C. Dean Little
Christopher Marsh
Joseph P. McCarthy
Darrell S. Mitsunaga
Michael P. Monroe
Pamela A. Okano
R. Thomas Olson
Mary S. Petersen
John W. Rankin, Jr.
Charles A. Robinson
Michael S. Rogers
Roger L. Stouder
Waller Taylor, III
Stephen M. Todd
Guy Towle
Scott Channing Wakefield
Robert J. Walerius

OF COUNSEL

Charles P. Moriarty, Jr.

PRINCIPALS

Brad Britzmann
Bruce E. Heller
Earl M. Sutherland
Deborah J. Youngblood

ASSOCIATES

Steven L. Burgon
Marilee C. Erickson
Peter M. Fabish
Robin A. Gower
Danielle A. Hess
Kimberly A. Johnston
Kurt M. Langkow
Beth Mattler Picardo
Petrea Knudsen Reilly
Peter M. Ruffatto
George S. Treperinas
Mark William Weakley

Representative Clients: Intercommunity Housing; McCormick Land Company; Northwest Hospital; Seattle University; State Farm Insurance Companies; The Procter and Gamble Company; W & H Pacific, Inc.; Wards Cove

(See Next Column)

Packing Company; Washington Federal Savings; Washington Casualty Company.

For full biographical listings, see the Martindale-Hubbell Law Directory

SAYRE LAW OFFICES (AV)

1016 Jefferson Street, 98104
Telephone: 206-625-0092
Fax available upon request

Matt Sayre
Jeffrey M. Sayre

References: Seattle-First National Bank; Security Pacific Bank Washington.

For full biographical listings, see the Martindale-Hubbell Law Directory

SHORT CRESSMAN & BURGESS (AV)

A Partnership including Professional Service Corporations
3000 First Interstate Center, 999 Third Avenue, 98104-4088
Telephone: 206-682-3333
Fax: 206-340-8856

MEMBERS OF FIRM

Paul R. Cressman, Sr. (P.S.)
John O. Burgess
Douglas R. Hartwich
Brian L. Comstock
Robert E. Heaton
John H. Strasburger
James A. Oliver
David R. Koopmans
Kenneth L. Myer
Robert J. Shaw
Paul R. Cressman, Jr.
Andrew W. Maron
Christopher J. Soelling
Paul J. Dayton
Bryan P. Coluccio
Robert E. Hibbs (P.S.)
Christopher R. Osborn
Michael R. Garner
Paul S. Bishop
David E. Breskin
Scott A. Smith
Thomas W. Read
Stephen P. Connor
Susan Thorbrogger
Lisa A. Wolfard
Jeffrey S. Myers
Stephan J. Francks
Kerry S. Bucklin
Ann T. Wilson
William A. Burge
Chris L. Farias
Karen A. Gruen
Claudia L. Crawford
Walter H. Olsen, Jr.

OF COUNSEL

Kenneth P. Short
Josef Diamond
Scott M. Missall

Counsel for: West One Bank; The Farmers Bank of China; U.S. Bank; National Electrical Contractors Assn.; Westin Hotels.
Representative Construction Clients: Cochran Electric Co., Inc.; Tri-State Construction, Inc.; Lakeside Industries.

For full biographical listings, see the Martindale-Hubbell Law Directory

TOUSLEY BRAIN (AV)

A Partnership
56th Floor, AT&T Gateway Tower, 700 Fifth Avenue, 98104-5056
Telephone: 206-682-5600
Facsimile: 206-682-2992

Russell F. Tousley
Christopher I. Brain
Kim D. Stephens (Mr.)
Cynthia Thomas
Mary Foster Vrbanac
Vincent B. DePillis
Stephan E. Todd
Rebecca A. McIntyre
Susan A. Shyne
Brian P. Ward
Stephan O. Fjelstad
Deborah A. Knapp

Kimberly J. Kernan
Barbara E. Barnhart
Albert H, Hughes, Jr.

Representative Clients: Chicago Title Insurance Company & Affiliates; Brookfield Development, Inc.; Evergreen State Construction; Hart Crowser, Inc.; Intrawest Companies; Lone Star Northwest; Murray Franklin Companies; PACCAR Automotive, Inc.; Trammell Crow Company; University Savings Bank.

For full biographical listings, see the Martindale-Hubbell Law Directory

WILLIAMS, KASTNER & GIBBS (AV)

4100 Two Union Square, 601 Union Street, P.O. Box 21926, 98111-3926
Telephone: 206-628-6600
Fax: 206-628-6611
Bellevue, Washington Office: 2000 Skyline Tower, 10900 N.E. Fourth Street, P.O. Box 1800, 98004-5841.
Telephone: 206-462-4700.
Fax: 206-451-0714.
Tacoma, Washington Office: 1000 Financial Center, 1145 Broadway, 98402-3502.
Telephone: 206-593-5620; Seattle: 628-2420.
Fax: 206-593-5625.
Vancouver, Washington Office: First Independent Place, 1220 Main Street, Suite 510.
Telephone: 206-696-0248.
Fax: 206-696-2051.

(See Next Column)

WILLIAMS, KASTNER & GIBBS—*Continued*

MEMBERS OF FIRM

Robert H. Lorentzen
Daniel E. Tolfree
Peter E. Peterson (Resident Partner, Bellevue Office)
Gerald A. Palm
J. Kenneth McMullin (1940-1987)
Don T. Mohlman
P. Arley Harrel
William J. Leedom
Joel D. Cunningham
Jerry B. Edmonds
Douglas A. Hofmann
Thomas H. Fain
Mark S. Davidson
William H. Mays (Resident Partner, Tacoma Office)
Dwayne E. Copple
Thomas O. McLaughlin
Kenneth E. Petty
William H. Robertson (1953-1989)
Franklin L. Dennis
Jeffrey R. Johnson
Richard M. Slagle
John A. Rosendahl (Resident Partner, Tacoma Office)
Randy J. Aliment
Josephine B. Vestal (Resident Partner, Bellevue Office)
Sheryl J. Willert
Mary H. Spillane
Judd H. Lees (Resident Partner, Bellevue Office)
Patrick M. O'Loughlin
Timothy D. Blue
John P. Evans
Bruce T. Thurston (Resident Partner, Bellevue Office)
Dennis D. Reynolds
Scott B. Henrie
John A. Knox
Christopher K. Shank (Resident Partner, Bellevue Office)
Harold D. Johnson
Jerry A. Creim
David C. Kelly
Frankie Adams Crain
James W. Minorchio
David H. Smith
Patrick C. Sheldon
Elizabeth A. Christianson
Robert C. Manlowe
Philip J. VanDerhoef
Margaret A. Sundberg
Michael Jay Brown
Stephen G. Leatham (Resident Partner, Vancouver Office)
Mark M. Myers
Ronald J. Knox
Gregory L. Russell (Resident Partner, Bellevue Office)
Daniel W. Ferm
Randall B. Printz (Resident Senior Attorney, Vancouver Office)
Joseph C. Calmes (Resident Partner, Bellevue Office)
David W. Wiley (Resident Partner, Bellevue Office)
Sheena Ramona Aebig
John F. Boespflug, Jr. (Resident, Partner, Bellevue Office)
Joseph A. Just (Resident Associate, Tacoma Office)
Joan L.G. Morgan

ASSOCIATES

Matthew S. Adams
Christopher H. Anderson
Mark D. Bensen
Pamela A Cairns
June K. Campbell
Stuart C. Campbell
Eric S. (Rick) Carlson
Carmen L. Cook (Resident Associate, Bellevue Office)
Colleen M. Cook
Robert W. Denomy, Jr. (Resident Associate, Tacoma Office)
Marcia P. Ellsworth
Darren A. Feider (Resident Associate, Bellevue Office)
Harriet J. Flo
Catherine Troy Franklin
John E. Gagliardi
Betsy A. Gillaspy (Resident Associate, Bellevue Office)
Matthew D. Green
Nancy Harriss
Bonnie Bakeman Harrison
Joanne R. Hicken
Hollis C. Holman (Resident Associate, Bellevue Office)
Carol Sue Hunting
Jan C. Kirkwood
Margaret "Maggie" J. Lucas
Stephanie E. Marshall
Elizabeth K. Maurer
Baldwin F. Minton
Patrick Moran (Resident Associate, Bellevue Office)
Karin M. Nelsen
Michael R. O'Clair
Lisa T. Oratz (Resident Associate, Bellevue Office)
David B. Petrich (Resident Associate, Tacoma Office)
David L. Ribble
Rebekah R. Ross
Curtis R. Smelser
Matthew L. Sweeney (Resident Associate, Tacoma Office)
Rebecca D. Warnock (Not admitted in WA)

OF COUNSEL

DeWitt Williams
Henry E. Kastner
Paul C. Gibbs
John D. Barline (Tacoma Office)
Mark D. Schedler (Bellevue Office)
John W. Dayhoff (Tacoma Office)

Representative Clients: Aetna Casulaty & Surety Co.; Atlantic-Richfield Co.; CIGNA; CNA Insurance; Continental Can Company, Inc.; Cushman & Wakefield of Washington, Inc.; General Motors Acceptance Corp.; Loomis Armored, Inc.; Mayne Nickless Incorporated; UNICO Properties, Inc.

For full biographical listings, see the Martindale-Hubbell Law Directory

*SHELTON,** Mason Co. — (Refer to Olympia)

*SOUTH BEND,** Pacific Co. — (Refer to Aberdeen or Hoquiam)

*SPOKANE,** Spokane Co.

CHASE, HAYES & KALAMON, P.S. (AV)

1000 Seafirst Financial Center, 99201
Telephone: 509-456-0333
FAX: 509-838-9826

(See Next Column)

Roger F. Chase
Richard E. Hayes
James M. Kalamon
Gregory J. Arpin
Andrew C. Smythe
Hedley W. Greene

Gervais Ward McAuliffe III
Nancy A. Pohlman
Timothy O'Brien
Susan W. Troppmann
Brent T. Stanyer
Christine M. Weaver
Gerald Kobluk
Michael B. Love

OF COUNSEL

W. Kenneth Jones
Bruce Bischof (Not admitted in WA)

Representative Clients: Albertson's Inc.; Key Tronic Corp.; Volvo of America, Inc.; Security Management; Familian Northwest; Tidyman's Inc.; Farmers Insurance Group; Sacred Heart Medical Center; Farm Credit Bank of Spokane.

For full biographical listings, see the Martindale-Hubbell Law Directory

TURNER, STOEVE, GAGLIARDI & GOSS, P.S. (AV)

West 301 Indiana, P.O. Box 5210, 99205
Telephone: 509-326-1552
FAX: 509-325-1425

Clare E. Turner (1909-1983)
Robert E. Stoeve (1917-1990)
William W. Goss, Jr.
Joseph P. Gagliardi
Michael C. Geraghty
Ernest D. Greco
Everett B. Coulter, Jr.

Representative Clients: John Deere Co.; Safeway, Inc.; U.S. West; Associated Aviation Underwriters; Fireman's Fund Insurance Cos.; State Farm Fire and Casualty Co.; Travelers Insurance Co.; United States Fidelity & Guaranty Co.; Sedgwick James; ITT Hartford.

For full biographical listings, see the Martindale-Hubbell Law Directory

UNDERWOOD, CAMPBELL, BROCK & CERUTTI, P.S. (AV)

1100 Seafirst Financial Center, West 601 Riverside, 99201
Telephone: 509-455-8500
FAX: 509-838-1005
Davenport, Washington Office: 529 Morgan Street.
Telephone: 509-725-3101.
Fax: 509-725-5854.
Odessa, Washington Office: 9 East First Street.
Telephone: 509-982-2672.
Fax: 509-982-2808.
Ritzville, Washington Office: West 601 Main.
Telephone: 509-659-0425.
Fax: 509-659-0529.
Sprague, Washington Office: Costello Building.
Telephone: 509-257-2301.
St. John, Washington Office: E 21 Front Street.
Telephone: 509-648-3900.

Floyd J. Underwood (1906-1980)
Fred G. Campbell (Davenport Office; Retired)
Roger H. Underwood (Spokane, Davenport and Sprague Offices)
Norman D. Brock (Davenport, Odessa, Ritzville, Spokane and St. John Offices)
Patrick B. Cerutti (Resident)
Kenneth D. Carpenter (Davenport, Odessa and Ritzville Offices)
Jay E. Leipham (Resident)
Dan J. Cadagan, III (Spokane, Sprague & St. John Offices)
Gary R. Stenzel (Resident)
Daniel M. Danforth (Resident)
L. Diane Emmons (Resident)

L. R. "Rusty" McGuire, Jr. (Davenport, Odessa, Ritzville, Sprague and St. John Offices)
Michelle K. Wolkey (Resident)
Mark W. DeWulf (Davenport and Odessa Offices)
Corey F. Brock (Spokane and Davenport Offices)

OF COUNSEL

Laurence Libsack

Representative Clients: U.R.M. Stores, Inc. (Spokane); Yoke's Foods, Inc. (Spokane); Appleway Chevrolet and Appleway Leasing (Spokane); CXT Incorporated (Spokane); Great American Insurance Co.; Central Life Assurance Co.; West One Bank (Spokane); The Wheatland Bank (Davenport); Spokane Association of Realtors; Lawton Printing, Inc. and File-Ez Folders, Inc. (Spokane).
References: West One Bank, Spokane, Washington; The Wheatland Bank, Davenport, Washington.

For full biographical listings, see the Martindale-Hubbell Law Directory

WINSTON & CASHATT, LAWYERS A PROFESSIONAL SERVICE CORPORATION (AV)

1900 Seafirst Financial Center, 99201-0695
Telephone: 509-838-6131
Facsimile: 509-838-1416
Coeur d'Alene, Idaho Office: 250 Northwest Boulevard, Suite 107A.
Telephone: 208-667-2103.
Facsimile: 208-765-2121.

(See Next Column)

WINSTON & CASHATT, LAWYERS A PROFESSIONAL SERVICE CORPORATION, *Spokane—Continued*

Leo N. Cashatt (1910-1977)
Patrick A. Sullivan
Robert P. Beschel
Stanley D. Moore
Tim M. Higgins
Lynden O. Rasmussen
Maris Baltins
Patricia C. Williams
Lawrence H. Vance, Jr.
Lucinda S. Whaley
Meriwether D. (Mike) Williams
F. J. Dullanty, Jr.
C. Matthew Andersen
Richard W. Relyea
Fred C. Pflanz
Carl E. Hueber
Stephen L. Farnell
Dennis A. Dellwo
Beverly L. Anderson
Richard L. Cease
Thomas M. McBride
Brian T. McGinn

OF COUNSEL

Michael J. Cronin
James A. Fish
Joseph J. Rekofke
Patrick H. Winston

Representative Clients: City of Spokane; General Motors Acceptance Corporation; General Motors Corporation; J.I. Case Company; Kaiser Aluminum & Chemical Corporation; Pacific Gas Transmission Company; Royal Insurance Companies; Seattle-First National Bank; U.S. West Direct; UNOCAL.

For full biographical listings, see the Martindale-Hubbell Law Directory

WITHERSPOON, KELLEY, DAVENPORT & TOOLE, P.S. (AV)

1100 U.S. Bank Building, 422 West Riverside, 99201
Telephone: 509-624-5265
Fax: 509-458-2728
Coeur d'Alene, Idaho Office: 608 Northwest Boulevard, Suite 301.
Telephone: 208-667-4000.

Robert L. Magnuson
Ned M. Barnes
William D. Symmes
Robert H. Lamp
K. Thomas Connolly
Thomas D. Cochran
Duane M. Swinton
Joseph H. Wessman
Jeffrey L. Supinger
Donald J. Lukes
Leslie R. Weatherhead
Michael D. Currin
Brian T. Rekofke
R. Max Etter, Jr.
Stanley R. Schultz
Michael F. Nienstedt
John M. Riley, III
Daniel B. DeRuyter

Daniel E Finney
Mary R. Giannini
Timothy M. Lawlor
Spencer A.W. Stromberg
Kathleen D. Jensen
Theodore S. O'Neal
William M. Symmes

OF COUNSEL

William A. Davenport
John E. Heath, Jr.
William V. Kelley
Allan H. Toole
Karl K Krogue

Representative Clients: Aetna Casualty & Insurance Co.; Boeing Commerical Airplanes; Cowles Publishing Co. (The Spokesman-Review); First Security Bank of Idaho; Inland Empire Paper Co.; Shopko Stores, Inc.; Sterling Savings Assn.; Travelers Insurance Co.; U.S. Bank of Washington, N.A.; Western Union Telegraph Co.

For full biographical listings, see the Martindale-Hubbell Law Directory

*TACOMA,** Pierce Co.

THE DOLACK HANSLER FIRM A PROFESSIONAL SERVICES CORPORATION (AV)

Seafirst Center, Suite 800, 950 Pacific Avenue, 98402-4410
Telephone: 206-383-7123; Seattle: 838-9061
Fax: 206-572-1435

Richard J. Dolack
John F. Hansler
Joseph J. Loran
Robert H. Rowan
Michael E. Ritchie

Representative Clients: Westop Credit Union; McChord Credit Union; Cheney Trusts; Ben B. Cheney Foundation, Inc.; Korum Ford, Inc.; Jesse Engineering (steel fabricator); Bosnick Roofing, Inc.; Tacoma Plumbing and Heating; Barkshire Construction Co.; Burr Lawrence Rising Architects, P.S.

For full biographical listings, see the Martindale-Hubbell Law Directory

EISENHOWER & CARLSON (AV)

1201 Pacific Avenue, First Interstate Plaza - Suite 1200, 98402
Telephone: 206-572-4500
Fax: 206-272-5732
Seattle, Washington Office: 601 Union Street, 2830 Two Union Square, 98101.
Telephone: 206-382-1830.
FAX: 206-382-1920.

MEMBERS OF FIRM

Ronald A. Roberts
S. Alan Weaver
Richard D. Turner
Richard A. Jessup (Resident, Seattle, Washington Office)
Robert Baronsky (Resident, Seattle, Washington Office)
Donald L. Anderson
James M. Hushagen
Kathryn J. Nelson

(See Next Column)

MEMBERS OF FIRM (Continued)

Charles K. Douthwaite
Robert G. Casey
Mark J. Rosenblum (Resident, Seattle, Washington Office)
Terrence J. Donahue
Rebecca D. Craig
Gibby M. Stratton (Resident, Seattle, Washington Office)
Gregory J. Murphy
Guy J. Sternal

OF COUNSEL

C. John Newlands (Retired)
James F. Henriot
H. Eugene Quinn

ASSOCIATES

P. Craig Beetham
Charles D. Broderick (Resident, Seattle, Washington Office)
Carl R. Peterson
Barry Alan Johnsrud
Bernadette Pratt Sadler
Bradley D. Fresia (Resident, Seattle, Washington Office)
Amy C. Lewis
Jason M. Whalen

Counsel for: Cammarano Bros. Inc.; J.M. Martinac Shipbuilding Corp.; Kelly Television Co. (KCPQ, Channel 13); Parker Paint Mfg. Co., Inc.; University of Puget Sound.
Local Counsel for: E.I. DuPont deNemours & Co.

For full biographical listings, see the Martindale-Hubbell Law Directory

VANDEBERG JOHNSON & GANDARA (AV)

A Partnership of Professional Service Corporations
1900 First Interstate Plaza, 1201 Pacific Avenue, 98402-4391
Telephone: 206-383-3791
Fax: 206-383-6377
Seattle, Washington Office: 3200 Columbia SeaFirst Center, 701 5th Avenue.
Telephone: 206-464-0404.

Darrel B. Addington
John H. Binns, Jr.
John H. Breckenridge
Kerry E. Brink
James H. Bush
William A. Coats
George T. Cowan (Resident, Seattle Office; See Biographical Card at Seattle Washington)
H. Frank Crawford
Richard A. Finnigan
Clifford D. Foster, Jr.
Daniel Gandara (Resident, Seattle Office; See Biographical Card at Seattle, Washington)
Harold T. Hartinger
Kinne F. Hawes (Resident, Seattle Office: See Biographical Card at Seattle, Washington)
Joanne Henry
John A. Holmes (Resident, Seattle Office; See Biographical Card at Seattle, Washington)
Mark A. Hood
W. Roger Johnson
Joni R. Kerr
James A. Krueger (P.S.)
John L. Nichols
Mark R. Patterson
Joseph F. Quinn
H. Andrew Saller, Jr.
Andrew L. Seiple (Resident, Seattle Office; See Biographical Card at Seattle Washington)
Jamie L. Siegel
Mary J. Urback
Elvin J. Vandeberg
G. Perrin Walker

For full biographical listings, see the Martindale-Hubbell Law Directory

*VANCOUVER,** Clark Co.

BLAIR, SCHAEFER, HUTCHISON & WOLFE (AV)

1014 Franklin Street, P.O. Box 1148, 98666-1148
Telephone: 206-693-5883; Portland: 503-285-4103
Telecopier Only: 206-693-1777

MEMBERS OF FIRM

John F. Wynne (1920-1988)
Robert M. Schaefer
Brian H. Wolfe
Hugh J. Potter
James D. Horton
James D. Mullins
Donald Russo
Michael C. Simon
David W. Christel
Steven N. Bogdon

RETIRED

Donald C. Blair

OF COUNSEL

David C. Hutchison
Terrance D. Hannan

For full biographical listings, see the Martindale-Hubbell Law Directory

MORSE & BRATT (AV)

Sixth Floor, Main Place, 1111 Main Street, P.O. Box 61566, 98666
Telephone: 360-699-4780
Portland, Oregon 503-286-2520
Fax: 360-699-4839

John E. Morse
Douglas J. Bratt
John David Morse
Ben Shafton
J. D. Nellor
William D. Robison
Larry E. Juday
Gideon D. Caron
Diane Marie Woolard
Don Thacker
Gimi D. Page
Nancy A. Nellor
Bruce R. Colven
Katherine Y. Chang

(See Next Column)

MORSE & BRATT—*Continued*

Barbara G. Deurwaarder
Scott Shipplett
Michael W. Brace
Dean K. Langsdorf

OF COUNSEL

Mark A. Erikson

Reference: First Interstate Bank of Washington.

For full biographical listings, see the Martindale-Hubbell Law Directory

*WENATCHEE,** Chelan Co.

DAVIS, ARNEIL, DORSEY, KIGHT & PARLETTE (AV)

617 Washington Street, P.O. Box 2136, 98801
Telephone: 509-662-3551
FAX: 509-662-9074

Harvey F. Davis (1906-1988)

OF COUNSEL

James Arneil

MEMBERS OF FIRM

David J. Dorsey
Milburn D. Kight
Robert L. Parlette
Robert L. White
Jay A. Johnson
Roger A. Braden
Thomas F. O'Connell
Julie A. Anderson

ASSOCIATES

Brian J. Dorsey
John R. San Fellipo
Malcolm C. McLellan
Glen Howard Utzman

Representative Clients: Trout, Inc. (Fruit Warehouse); Eastmont School District; Central Washington Health Services Assn. (Hospital); Wilbur Ellis Co. (Agricultural Supplies); Public Utility District No. 1 of Chelan County, Wash.; Pangborn Memorial Airport; Reliance Insurance Co.; Skookum, Inc. (Fruit Warehouse); Chelan County Fire Protection District, No. 1; State Farm Mutual.

For full biographical listings, see the Martindale-Hubbell Law Directory

JEFFERS, DANIELSON, SONN & AYLWARD, P.S. (AV)

317 North Mission, P.O. Box 1688, 98807
Telephone: 509-662-3685
Fax: 509-662-8972
Moses Lake, Washington Office: 515 N. Stratford Road.
Telephone: 509-765-9705.
Fax: 509-765-5060.

Garfield R. Jeffers
James M. Danielson
David E. Sonn
J. Patrick Aylward
J. Kirk Bromiley
Gregory A. Lair
Susan Cawley
Douglas J. Takasugi
Peter A. Spadoni
Robert C. Nelson
Donald L. Dimmitt
Steven W. Woods
Robert R. Siderius, Jr.
Stanley A. Bastian
Mitchell P. Delabarre
Theodore A. Finegold
Joseph L. Hughes (1905-1982)
Richard G. Jeffers (1910-1976)

Attorneys for: Public Utility District No. 1 of Douglas County; Wells Hydroelectric Project; Eye and Ear Clinic of Wenatchee, Inc.; Kemper Insurance Group; Auvil Fruit Co.; Wenatchee Reclamation District.

For full biographical listings, see the Martindale-Hubbell Law Directory

*YAKIMA,** Yakima Co.

HALVERSON & APPLEGATE, P.S. (AV)

311 North Fourth Street, P.O. Box 22730, 98907-2715
Telephone: 509-575-6611
Telecopier: 509-457-2419

Frederick N. Halverson
Donald H. Bond
Thomas B. Grahn
Terry C. Schmalz
J. Lawrence Wright
Don W. Schussler
Gerard L. Sandersen
Timothy J. Carlson
James S. Berg
Donald A. Boyd
Lawrence E. Martin

Linda A. Sellers
Gregory S. Lighty
Christopher E. Tucker
Brad L Englund
Ryan M. Edgley
Erin L. Anderson
Michael F. Shinn

OF COUNSEL

C. W. Halverson
J. S. Applegate
Richard L. Wiehl

Representative Clients: Farmers Insurance Group; Seafirst; Pacific Power & Light Co. (local counsel); Tree Top, Inc.; Snokist Growers; Hogue Cellars Winery; S.S. Steiner (Hop Dealer/Broker); Holtzinger Fruit, Inc.; Inland Fruit & Produce Co.; S. Martinez Livestock, Inc.

For full biographical listings, see the Martindale-Hubbell Law Directory

LYON, WEIGAND, SUKO & GUSTAFSON, P.S. (AV)

222 North Third Street, P.O. Box 1689, 98901
Telephone: 509-248-7220
Fax: 509-575-1883
Mailing Address: P.O. Box 1689, Yakima, Washington, 98907-1689

Charles R. Lyon
William L. Weigand, Jr.
Lonny R. Suko
J. Eric Gustafson
Robert M. Boggs

Jeanie R. Zimmerman
Jeff Cutter

Representative Clients: Equitable Life Assurance Society; First Interstate Bank of Washington; J. R. Simplot Co.; Hop Growers of Washington; West Valley School District No. 208; Yakima Credit Bureau; Pepsi-Cola Bottling Company of Yakima, Inc.

For full biographical listings, see the Martindale-Hubbell Law Directory

MEYER, FLUEGGE AND TENNEY, P.S. (AV)

230 South Second Street, P.O. Box 22680, 98907
Telephone: 509-575-8500
Fax: 509-575-4676

Walter G. Meyer
Dennis L. Fluegge
Robert C. Tenney
Mark D. Watson
Jerome R. Aiken

John A. Maxwell, Jr.
Kirk A. Ehlis
Donald A. Treat

Representative Clients: Albertson's, Inc.; Caterpillar Tractor Co.; FMC Corp.; Hyster Co.; J.R. Simplot Co.; Farmers Insurance Group; Fireman's Fund Insurance; The St. Paul Companies; Safeco Insurance Co.; Washington Casualty Company.

For full biographical listings, see the Martindale-Hubbell Law Directory

VELIKANJE, MOORE & SHORE, INC., P.S. (AV)

405 East Lincoln Avenue, 98901
Telephone: 509-248-6030
Fax: 509-453-6880

E. Frederick Velikanje
John S. Moore
Morris G. Shore
George F. Velikanje
C. James Lust
James P. Hutton
Alan D. Campbell
Patrick F. Hussey
James C. Carmody
Carter L. Fjeld
J. Jay Carroll
Mark E. Fickes
Matthew J. Anderton
Douglas L. Federspiel
Sarah Geary Ottem
Brendan Victor Monahan
Robert G. Velikanje
Julia A. Dooris
Brian Nagle

Representative Clients: Washington Fruit & Produce Co.; Layman Lumber Co.; Farm Credit Services; Michelsen Packaging Co., Inc.; Klickitat Valley Bank; Yakima Herald-Republic; Pioneer National Bank.
Local Counsel for: U.S. Bank of Washington.

For full biographical listings, see the Martindale-Hubbell Law Directory

WEST VIRGINIA

*BECKLEY,** Raleigh Co.

ABRAMS, BYRON, HENDERSON & RICHMOND (AV)

Commonwealth Building, 108 Main Street, P.O. Drawer W, 25802-2820
Telephone: 304-253-1500
Fax: 304-252-0601

MEMBERS OF FIRM

A. David Abrams, Jr.
C. Elton Byron, Jr.
James M. Henderson, II
William F. Richmond, Jr.

General Counsel for: Bank One, WV, Beckley, N.A.; Ranger Fuel; USF&G; First Empire Federal Savings & Loan Association.
Reference: Bank One, WV, Beckley, N.A.

For full biographical listings, see the Martindale-Hubbell Law Directory

FILE, PAYNE, SCHERER & FILE (AV)

Law Building, 130 Main Street, P.O. Drawer L, 25801
Telephone: 304-253-3358
Fax: 304-255-5136

MEMBERS OF FIRM

Edward M. Payne, III
John Payne Scherer
Robert N. File
William H. File, III

ASSOCIATES

C. Michael Griffith

OF COUNSEL

William Henry File, Jr.

Representative Clients: Bank of Raleigh; Norfolk and Western Railway Co.; A. T. Massey Coal Co.; Raleigh General Hospital; State Automobile Mutual Insurance Co.; Liberty Mutual Insurance Co.; Continental Insurance Group; Professional Medical Insurance Co.

For full biographical listings, see the Martindale-Hubbell Law Directory

LYNCH, MANN, SMITH & MANN (AV)

108 1/2 South Heber Street, P.O. Box 1600, 25802-1600
Telephone: 304-253-3349

MEMBERS OF FIRM

Jack A. Mann
Clyde A. Smith, Jr.
Kimberly G. Mann

Representative Clients: State Farm Insurance Companies; Horace Mann Insurance Co.; Erie Insurance Company; Sears, Roebuck and Co.; Dairyland Insurance Company; Allstate Insurance Co.; U.S.F.&G. Insurance Company; American States Insurance Company; Atlantic Mutual Insurance Company; Transamerica Corporation.

For full biographical listings, see the Martindale-Hubbell Law Directory

BLUEFIELD, Mercer Co.

BREWSTER, MORHOUS & CAMERON (AV)

418 Bland Street, P.O. Box 529, 24701
Telephone: 304-325-9177
Fax: 304-327-9317
Peterstown, West Virginia Office: 113 1/2 Market Street, P.O. Box 429.
Telephone: 1-800-325-9177.

RETIRED

Paul S. Hudgins
Louis Roberdeau Coulling, Jr.

MEMBERS OF FIRM

Harold D. Brewster, Jr.
Lawrence E. Morhous
Jerry J. Cameron
Donald T. Caruth
Kermit J. Moore
David M. Kersey

ASSOCIATES

William P. Stafford, II

Representative Clients: Chubb Group; First Community Bank, Inc.; GTE South; The First National Bank of Bluefield; One Valley Bank of Mercer County, Inc.; Allstate Insurance Company; Carter Machinery Company, Inc.; Kemper Group; Erie Group; Truck World, Inc.

For full biographical listings, see the Martindale-Hubbell Law Directory

KATZ, KANTOR & PERKINS (AV)

Suite 502-17 Law & Commerce Building, P.O. Box 727, 24701
Telephone: 304-327-3551
Fax: 304-325-7495

MEMBERS OF FIRM

Norris Kantor
Guy W. Perkins

ASSOCIATES

Wayne L. Evans
Wayne S. Stonestreet
Phillip A. Scantlebury
David L. Harmon
Gregory S. Matney
Hobert F. Muncey, Jr.
Robert H. Miller, II
Edward L. Pauley
LeRoy H. Katz (1917-1994)

(See Next Column)

General Counsel for: Bluefield Regional Medical Center, Inc.; Bluefield Municipal Building Commission; Mercer County Building Commission; Bluefield Health Systems, Inc.; Mountaineer Resources, Inc.; Cumberland Care Center, Inc.; Bluefield Regional Medical Center Foundation, Inc.; Sanitary Board of Bluefield.
References: First National Bank of Bluefield; Flat Top National Bank of Bluefield, West Virginia.

For full biographical listings, see the Martindale-Hubbell Law Directory

*BUCKHANNON,** Upshur Co.

HYMES AND COONTS (AV)

Hymco Building, 23 West Main Street, P.O. Box 310, 26201-0310
Telephone: 304-472-1565
Fax: 304-472-1615

MEMBERS OF FIRM

Myron B. Hymes (1897-1988)
Gilbert Gray Coonts
Terry D. Reed

ASSOCIATES

Kelley Haught Wilmoth

For full biographical listings, see the Martindale-Hubbell Law Directory

*CHARLESTON,** Kanawha Co.

BOWLES RICE MCDAVID GRAFF & LOVE (AV)

16th Floor Commerce Square, P.O. Box 1386, 25325-1386
Telephone: 304-347-1100
Fax: 304-343-2867
Martinsburg, West Virginia Office: (Serves Berkeley Springs and Charles Town, West Virginia). 105 West Burke Street, P.O. Drawer 1419.
Telephone: 304-263-0836.
Fax: 304-267-3822.
Morgantown, West Virginia Office: 206 Spruce Street.
Telephone: 304-296-2500.
Fax: 304-296-2513.
Parkersburg, West Virginia Office: 601 Avery Street, P.O. Box 48.
Telephone: 304-485-8500.
Fax: 304-485-7973.
Lexington, Kentucky Office: Bowles Rice McDavid Graff Love & Getty, 12th Floor Vine Center Tower, 333 West Vine Street.
Telephone: 606-225-8700.
Fax: 606-225-8418.

MEMBERS OF FIRM

Paul N. Bowles (1921-1986)
F. Thomas Graff, Jr. (Firm Managing Partner)
Charles M. Love, III
P. Michael Pleska
Gary G. Markham
David C. Hardesty, Jr.
Carl D. Andrews
Edward D. McDevitt
Ricklin Brown
J. Thomas Lane
Gerard R. Stowers
P. Nathan Bowles, Jr.
Thomas B. Bennett
Sarah E. Smith
Richard M. Francis
George A. Patterson, III
Roger D. Hunter
Thomas E. Scarr
Phyllis M. Potterfield
Deborah A. Sink
Gordon C. Lane
John W. Woods, III
Thomas A. Heywood
Camden P. Siegrist
Benjamin L. Bailey
Sandra M. Murphy
Julia A. Chincheck
Anthony P. Tokarz
Leonard Knee
Marc A. Monteleone
Lesley Hiscoe Russo
Ellen Maxwell-Hoffman

ASSOCIATES

Lynn Photiadis
Fazal A. Shere
Charles B. Dollison
Kenneth E. Webb, Jr.
Michael J. Schessler
Robert G. Lilly
John R. Teare, Jr.
Elizabeth D. Harter
Douglas L. Davis
Robert V. Leydon
Elizabeth Benston Elmore
Gina E. Mazzei
Ronda L. Harvey
Stuart A. McMillan
Betsy Ennis Dulin

EXECUTIVE DIRECTOR

James N. Rogers

SPECIAL COUNSEL

Giles D. H. Snyder

OF COUNSEL

William R. McDavid

For full biographical listings, see the Martindale-Hubbell Law Directory

CAMPBELL, WOODS, BAGLEY, EMERSON, MCNEER & HERNDON (AV)

Bank One Center, Suite 1400, 707 Virginia Street East, P.O. Box 2393, 25328-2393
Telephone: 304-346-2391
Fax: 304-346-2433
Huntington, West Virginia Office: 14th Floor, Coal Exchange Building, P.O. Box 1835, 25719.
Telephone: 304-529-2391.
Fax: 304-529-1832.

(See Next Column)

CAMPBELL, WOODS, BAGLEY, EMERSON, MCNEER & HERNDON—*Continued*

Ashland, Kentucky Office: 1608 Carter Avenue, P.O. Box 1862, 41105-1832.
Telephone: 606-329-1974
Fax: 606-324-2025

MEMBERS OF FIRM

Milton T. Herndon (Resident) | John D. Hoffman (Resident)
David A. Mohler (Resident) | John F. McCuskey (Resident)
Charles I. Jones, Jr. | James W. Gabehart (Resident)

ASSOCIATES

William J. Hanna | John F. Hussell, IV

OF COUNSEL

James Hornor Davis, III (Resident)

Representative Clients: Corporate: Federal Deposit Insurance Corp. (FDIC); Resolution Trust Corp. (RTC); Prestera Center for Mental Health Services, Inc.; Valley Health Systems, Inc.; Dingess-Rum Coal Co.; Cole & Crane Real Estate Trust. Insurance: State Farm Mutual Automobile Insurance Co.; Continental Casualty Co.; Liberty Mutual Insurance Co.

For full biographical listings, see the Martindale-Hubbell Law Directory

JOHN B. CARRICO (AV)

606 Virginia Street, East, 25301
Telephone: 304-345-2280

For full biographical listings, see the Martindale-Hubbell Law Directory

GOODWIN & GOODWIN (AV)

1500 One Valley Square, 25301
Telephone: 304-346-7000
Fax: 304-344-9692
Ripley, West Virginia Office: 500 Church Street, P.O. Box 349.
Telephone: 304-372-2651.
Parkersburg, West Virginia Office: 201 Third Street, Town Square.
Telephone: 304-485-2345.
Fax: 304-485-3459.

Robert B. Goodwin (1909-1955)

OF COUNSEL

C. E. Goodwin

MEMBERS OF FIRM

Thomas R. Goodwin | Carrie L. Newton
Joseph R. Goodwin | Leonard S. Coleman
Stephen P. Goodwin | Susan C. Wittemeier
Michael I. Spiker | Robert W. Full (Resident at Parkersburg Office)
Steven F. White | Richard D. Owen
Richard E. Rowe | Tammy J. Owen
Robert Q. Sayre, Jr.

ASSOCIATES

Suzanne Jett Trowbridge | J. David Fenwick
Debra C. Price | Alexander Macia
William K. Bragg, Jr. | James Edward White, Jr.
Jeffry H. Hall | Lisa A. Tackett
George M. Smith | Rebecca L. Stafford
John N. Ellem (Resident, Parkersburg Office)

Representative Clients: Bucyrus-Erie Co.; CSX Corp.; Eastern American Energy Corp.; The Eureka Pipe Line Company.

For full biographical listings, see the Martindale-Hubbell Law Directory

HAMB & POFFENBARGER (AV)

Bank One Center, Suite 515, P.O. Box 1671, 25301-1671
Telephone: 304-343-4128
Telecopier: 304-344-1974

MEMBERS OF FIRM

William E. Hamb | John T. Poffenbarger

ASSOCIATES

Robert W. Kiefer, Jr.

Representative Clients: Old Colony Co.; Simonton Building Products, Inc.; Storck Baking Company; Fisher-Brison Properties, Incorporated; First Empire Federal Savings & Loan Assn.; Eagle Bancorp.; SBR, Inc.; Travelers Insurance Companies; Yorel Development Co.; Bays, Inc.

For full biographical listings, see the Martindale-Hubbell Law Directory

HEREFORD & HEREFORD (AV)

Suite 306, 405 Capitol Street, 25301
Telephone: 304-342-5127
Fax: 304-342-5106

MEMBERS OF FIRM

Joe C. Hereford | Philip B. Hereford

Reference: One Valley Bank, N.A.

For full biographical listings, see the Martindale-Hubbell Law Directory

HUDDLESTON, BOLEN, BEATTY, PORTER & COPEN (AV)

One Bridge Place, 10 Hale Street, P.O. Box 3786, 25337
Telephone: 304-344-9869
Telecopier: 304-344-4309
Huntington, West Virginia Office: 611 Third Avenue, P.O. Box 2185.
Telephone: 304-529-6181
Telecopier: 304-522-4312.
Ashland, Kentucky Office: 1422 Winchester Avenue, P.O. Box 770.
Telephone: 606-329-8771
Telecopier: 606-324-4651.

MEMBERS OF FIRM

William C. Beatty (1925-1994) | Fred B. Westfall, Jr.
Noel P. Copen | Christopher J. Plybon
R. Kemp Morton | Mary H. Sanders (Resident)
Richard J. Bolen | Janice P. Epperly
Fred Adkins | Marc E. Williams
John R. Fowler (Resident) | R. Russell Alexander
Thomas H. Gilpin | Daniel J. Konrad
Thomas J. Murray | Scott K. Sheets
Andrew S. Zettle | Luke A. Lafferre
Bruce L. Stout | David H. Lunsford

ASSOCIATES

Janet Smith Holbrook | Deirdre M. MacCarthy
James Wade Turner | Daniel A. Earl
Mark A. Bramble (Resident) | Macel E. Rhodes (Resident)
Angela Wynn Konrad | John K. McHugh
Colin M. Cline | M. Margaret Evans
Troy N. Giatras (Resident) | Shawn M. Cox
Mark H. Hayes | Melissa G. Foster
Robert L. Massie | Margaret M. Singleton
Blake Benton | James C. Stebbins

For full biographical listings, see the Martindale-Hubbell Law Directory

HUNT, LEES, FARRELL & KESSLER (AV)

7 Players Club Drive, P.O. Box 2506, 25329-2506
Telephone: 304-344-9651
Telecopier: 304-343-1916
Huntington, West Virginia Office: Prichard Building, 601 Ninth Street, P.O. Box 2191, 25722.
Telephone: 304-529-1999.
Martinsburg, West Virginia Office: 1012 B Winchester Avenue. P.O. Box 579. 25401.
Telephone: 304-267-3100.

MEMBERS OF FIRM

James B. Lees, Jr. | John A. Kessler
Joseph M. Farrell, Jr. (Resident, Huntington Office)

ASSOCIATES

James A. McKowen | Meikka A. Cutlip (Resident, Huntington Office)
Jeffrey T. Jones | Sharon M. Fedorochko
Marion Eugene Ray
Mark Jenkinson (Resident, Martinsburg Office)

OF COUNSEL

L. Alvin Hunt

For full biographical listings, see the Martindale-Hubbell Law Directory

JACKSON & KELLY (AV)

1600 Laidley Tower, P.O. Box 553, 25322
Telephone: 304-340-1000
Fax: 304-340-1130
Martinsburg, West Virginia Office: 300 Foxcroft Avenue, P.O. Box 1068.
Telephone: 304-263-8800.
Morgantown, West Virginia Office: 6000 Hampton Center, P.O. Box 619.
Telephone: 304-599-3000.
New Martinsville, West Virginia Office: 256 Russell Avenue, P.O. Box 68.
Telephone: 304-455-1751.
Charles Town, West Virginia Office: 700 East Washington Street, P.O. Box 983.
Telephone: 304-728-6088.
Clarksburg, West Virginia Office: 203 Main Street, P.O. Box 1587.
Telephone: 304-623-3002.
Lexington, Kentucky Office: 175 East Main Street, Suite 500, P.O. Box 2150.
Telephone: 606-255-9500.
Washington, D. C. Office: 2401 Pennsylvania Avenue, N.W., Suite 400.
Telephone: 202-973-0200.
Denver, Colorado Office: Suite 2710, 1660 Lincoln Street.
Telephone: 303-837-0003.

MEMBERS OF FIRM

Thomas B. Jackson (1892-1966) | Winfield T. Shaffer
Robert G. Kelly (1898-1979) | Edward W. Rugeley, Jr.
Homer A. Holt (1898-1975) | John L. McClaugherty
William T. O'Farrell (1906-1983) | Thomas E. Potter
J. S. Francis (New Martinsville, West Virginia Office) | George R. Farmer, Jr. (Resident, Morgantown, West Virginia Office)
James Knight Brown

(See Next Column)

JACKSON & KELLY, *Charleston—Continued*

MEMBERS OF FIRM (Continued)

Lee O. Hill
John R. Lukens
W. Warren Upton
Louis S. Southworth, II
James L. Gay (Resident Lexington, Kentucky Office)
John M. Slack, III
Charles Q. Gage
Michael A. Albert
William K. Bodell, II (Resident, Lexington, Kentucky Office)
Stephen R. Crislip
William F. Dobbs, Jr.
Thomas G. Freeman, II
Roger A. Wolfe
Harvey Alan Siler
Wm. Richard McCune, Jr. (Martinsburg and Charles Town, West Virginia Offices)
W. Henry Jernigan, Jr. (Resident, Lexington, Kentucky Office)
Michael D. Foster
Henry Chajet (Resident, Washington, D.C. Office)
Mark N. Savit (Resident, Washington, D.C. Office)
Alvin L. Emch
William A. Hoskins, III (Resident, Lexington, Kentucky Office)
Barry S. Settles (Resident Lexington, Kentucky Office)
Taunja Willis Miller
Charles M. Surber, Jr.
Robert J. Busse
James R. Snyder
Thomas N. McJunkin
David Allen Barnette
Barbara D. Little
Laura E. Beverage (Resident, Denver, Colorado Office)
Ellen S. Cappellanti
Allen R. Prunty
Cheryl Harris Wolfe
Dennis C. Sauter
James W. Thomas
Larry W. Blalock (Administrative Manager, New Martinsville, West Virginia Office)
Mary Clare Eros (Martinsburg and Charles Town, West Virginia Offices)
Gary W. Hart
Robert G. McLusky
George E. Roeder, III (Resident, Morgantown, West Virginia Office)
Douglas A. Smoot
Jeff Chandler Woods
Jeffrey J. Yost (Resident, Lexington, Kentucky Office)
Daniel L. Stickler
A. Stuart Bennett (Lexington, Kentucky Office)
Samme L. Gee
Thomas J. Hurney, Jr.
John Philip Melick
Lynn Oliver Frye
Gale Reddie Lea
William E. Doll, Jr. (Resident, Lexington, Kentucky Office)
Stephen M. LaCagnin (Resident, Morgantown, West Virginia Office)
James I. Manion (Martinsburg and Charles Town, West Virginia Offices)
Charles D. Dunbar
Thad S. Huffman (Resident, Washington, D.C. Office)
Martin E. Hall (Resident, Lexington, Kentucky Office)
Kevin M. McGuire (Resident, Lexington, Kentucky Office)
W. Rodes Brown (Resident, Lexington, Kentucky Office)
Timothy E. Huffman
Charles W. Loeb, Jr.
G. Lindsay Simmons (Resident, Washington, D.C. Office)
L. Poe Leggette (Resident, Washington, D.C. Office)
Natalie D. Brown (Resident, Lexington, Kentucky Office)
L. Anthony George
William J. Powell
Wendel B. Turner
Albert F. Sebok
William S. Mattingly (Resident, Morgantown, West Virginia Office)
David Layva (Martinsburg and Charles Town, West Virginia Offices)
Ann Brannon Rembrandt
Dean K. Hunt (Resident, Lexington, Kentucky Office)
Mark B. D'Antoni
David J. Hardy

ASSOCIATES

Brooks K. Barkwill (New Martinsville, West Virginia Office)
John A. Mairs
Gene W. Bailey, II
Jennifer Z. Cain (New Martinsville, West Virginia Office)
Mary Jane Brown
Jacqueline Syers Duncan (Resident, Lexington, Kentucky Office)
Eric H. London (Resident, Morgantown Office)
Mary Rich Lewis Maloy
Stanton L. Cave (Resident, Lexington, Kentucky Office)
Bradley A. Crouser
Robert K. Parsons
Robert L. Johns
Dennis N. Broglio
Anthony J. Majestro
Elizabeth Osenton Lord
Timothy Ray Coleman (Not admitted in WV; Resident, Lexington, Kentucky Office)
J. Rudy Martin
Lucinda Fluharty Fitch (New Martinsville, West Virginia Office)
William Prentice Young (Martinsburg and Charles Town, West Virginia Offices)
Stephen R. Kershner (Martinsburg and Charles Town, West Virginia Offices)
Patrick W. Pearlman
Maris E. McCambley
Tammy A. Mitchell-Bittorf (Martinsburg and Charles Town, West Virginia Offices)
Jeffery L. Robinette (Resident, Morgantown, West Virginia Office)
Pamela Wray Blackshire
James Zissler (Resident, Washington, D.C. Office)
Julia M. Chico (Resident, Morgantown, West Virginia Office)
Anthony J. Ferrise
Melissa Mize Robinson
John G. Byrd
Patience A. Alexander
Christopher L. Callas (Resident, Morgantown Office)
Donald P. Cookman (Charles Town and Martinsburg Offices)
Rebecca Graves Payne (Resident, Denver, Colorado Office)
Vincent Tad Greene (Resident, New Martinsville Office)
Erin E. Magee

(See Next Column)

ASSOCIATES (Continued)

Christopher Kenneth Robertson (Charles Town and Martinsburg Offices)
Mychal S. Schulz
R. Scott Summers (Resident, Morgantown Office)
Kathy L. Snyder (Resident, Morgantown Office)
Shannon Upton Johnson (Resident, Lexington, Kentucky Office)
Linden R. Evans
Katherine Shand Larkin (Resident, Denver, Colorado Office)
William C. Miller, II
Mary L. Galan (Resident, Clarksburg, West Virginia Office)
Michael T. Cimino
Nancy L. Ford (Charles Town and Martinsburg Offices)
George Anthony Halkias
Michelle Tulane Mensore
Sannie Overly (Resident, Lexington, Kentucky Office)
James Eric Whytsell (Charles Town and Martinsburg Offices)
Kelly S. Crites (Not admitted in WV)
Robert G. Tweel (Not admitted in WV)
William D. Esbenshade
Katherine Venti
Lee Van Egmond (Not admitted in WV)
Whitney G. Clegg (New Martinsville, West Virginia Office)
M. Shane Harvey
James V. Kelsh
Kelley L. Mount
Barry T. Wetzel (Lexington, Kentucky Office)

OF COUNSEL

Andrew L. Blair (Retired)
David D. Johnson (Retired)
John S. Palmore (Frankfort and Lexington, Kentucky Offices) (Retired)
Robert L. Elkins

LEGAL SUPPORT PERSONNEL

Donald W. Rayment
James A Lowen
Richard Earl Boaz (Not admitted in WV)
Robin Smith Claudio
Betty S. Ireland
Deanna L. Luxbacher
Donna A. Harper
Charlene T. Caldwell
Mary Ann Baker
Janet R. Robin
Laura B. Hackney

Representative Clients: Consol Inc.; Go-Mart, Inc.; Monongahela Power Co.; One Valley Bancorp of West Virginia, Inc.; Pittston Coal Co.; Rhone-Poulenc AG Co.; Thomas Memorial Hospital; Union Carbide Corp.; United Parcel Service; West Virginia-American Water Co.

For full biographical listings, see the Martindale-Hubbell Law Directory

KAY, CASTO, CHANEY, LOVE & WISE (AV)

1600 Bank One Center, P.O. Box 2031, 25327
Telephone: 304-345-8900
Telefax: 304-345-8909; 304-343-9833
Morgantown, West Virginia Office: Suite C, 3000 Hampton Center.
Telephone: 304-599-8900.
Telefax: 304-599-8901.
Abingdon, Virginia Office: 329 West Main Street.
Telephone: 703-628-9211.
Telefax: 703-628-9334.

OF COUNSEL

Vincent V. Chaney
John O. Kizer
Dale George Casto (1900-1958)
Charles M. Love (1902-1987)
Charles C. Wise, Jr. (1911-1982)
Robert H. C. Kay (1896-1994)
Robert E. Magnuson

MEMBERS OF FIRM

Robert L. Brandfass
Charles E. Barnett
William W. Booker
Michael T. Chaney
Ralph C. Dusic, Jr.
Barney W. Frazier, Jr.
George W. S. Grove, Jr.
Ann L. Haight
John S. Haight
Steven C. Hanley
Elliot G. Hicks
John R. Hoblitzell
John T. Kay, Jr.
Craig M. Kay
John R. McGhee, Jr.
Dina M. Mohler
W. Michael Moore
Kevin A. Nelson
Jonathan Nicol
Harry M. Rubenstein (Morgantown, West Virginia Office)
Howard G. Salisbury, Jr. (Abingdon, Virginia Office)
Mark A. Swartz (Abingdon, Virginia Office)
Steven L. Thomas
Stephen A. Weber

ASSOCIATES

Bethann Regina Lloyd
Patricia Jo Loehr
Elma M. Reed (Morgantown, West Virginia Office)
F. Thomas Rubenstein (Morgantown, West Virginia Office)
Joseph E. Starkey, Jr.
Crystal S. Stump

Attorneys for: Allegheny & Western Energy Corp.; Ford Motor Co.; Bank One, West Virginia; Chrysler Corp.; Aetna Insurance Co.; Wausau Insurance Cos,; West Virginia Contractors Bargaining Assn.

For full biographical listings, see the Martindale-Hubbell Law Directory

PAYNE, LOEB & RAY (AV)

1210 One Valley Square, 25301
Telephone: 304-342-1141
Fax: 304-342-0691

(See Next Column)

PAYNE, LOEB & RAY—*Continued*

MEMBERS OF FIRM

John V. Ray (1893-1974)
Walter C. Price, Jr. (1910-1976)
Charles W. Loeb
John L. Ray
Christopher J. Winton
William H. Scharf

ASSOCIATES

Mark W. Kelley

Counsel for: One Valley Bank, N.A.; Outdoor Advertising Association of West Virginia; Trojan Steel Co.; Thomas, Field & Co.; Kanawha Village Apartments, Inc.; Guyan Machinery Co.

For full biographical listings, see the Martindale-Hubbell Law Directory

SHUMAN, ANNAND & POE (AV)

Suite 1007, 405 Capitol Street, P.O. Box 3953, 25339
Telephone: 304-345-1400
Telecopier: 304-343-1826
Wheeling, West Virginia Office: Suite 3002, 1233 Main Street, 26003.
Telephone: 304-233-3100.
Telecopier: 304-233-0201.

MEMBERS OF FIRM

David L. Shuman
Stephen Darley Annand
Edgar A. Poe, Jr.
Charles R. Bailey
Richard L. Earles
David L. Wyant (Resident, Wheeling Office)
R. Ford Francis
David E. Schumacher
David Venable Moore
H. Gerard Kelley
Mark William Browning
William R. Slicer

ASSOCIATES

Jon L. Brown (Resident, Wheeling Office)
Jay W. Craig
Desireé Halkias Haden
Paul L. Weber
David F. Nelson
Belinda Bartley Neal
G. Kenneth Robertson
Elizabeth Summers Lawton
W. Christopher Wickham
George J. Joseph
Roberta F. Green
Shaun L. Peck

COUNSEL

Harry P. Henshaw, III

Representative Clients: CNA Insurance Companies; Insurance Corporation of America; Metropolitan Property & Liability Ins. Co.; MMI Companies, Inc.; Motorists Insurance Cos.; Travelers Insurance Cos.; Westfield Companies.
Reference: One Valley Bank.

For full biographical listings, see the Martindale-Hubbell Law Directory

SPILMAN, THOMAS & BATTLE (AV)

Spilman Center, 300 Kanawha Boulevard, East, P.O. Box 273, 25321-0273
Telephone: 304-340-3800
Fax: 304-340-3801
Morgantown, West Virginia Office: 990 Elmer Price Drive, Suite 205, P.O. Box 4474, 26504-4474.
Telephone: 304-599-8175.
Fax: 304-599-8229.
Parkersburg, West Virginia Office: PM Center, 417 Grand Park Drive, Suite 203, P.O. Box 1468, 26102-1468.
Telephone: 304-422-6700.
Fax: 304-422-6733.

MEMBERS OF FIRM

Hawthorne D. Battle (1901-1984)
Howard R. Klostermeyer (1904-1983)
W. Victor Ross (1913-1992)
James P. Robinson (1914-1993)
Charles B. Stacy
G. Thomas Battle
John H. Tinney
Larry A. Winter
Lee F. Feinberg
Charles L. Woody
K. Paul Davis
Ward D. Stone, Jr. (Resident, Morgantown, West Virginia Office)
F. Richard Hall (Resident, Parkersburg, West Virginia Office)
John J. Nesius
David B. Shapiro
William T. Brotherton, III
Joyce Fleming Ofsa
Carl L. Fletcher, Jr.
David B. Thomas
David D. Johnson, III
Robert J. O'Neil
T. Randolph Cox, Jr.
William A. Trainer (Resident, Parkersburg, West Virginia Office)
William M. Herlihy
Carl H. Cather, III (Resident, Morgantown, West Virginia Office)
Paul E. Parker, III (Resident, Morgantown, West Virginia Office)
Richard A. Hudson (Resident, Parkersburg, West Virginia Office)
J. Michael Weber (Resident, Parkersburg, West Virginia Office)
Lynn S. Clarke
Heather Heiskell Jones
David G. Hammond
Eric M. James
B. Judd Hartman
Neva G. Lusk

ASSOCIATES

Trina L. Leone
Nancy A. Green (Resident, Morgantown, West Virginia Office)
Robert A. Lockhart
Kimberley R. Fields
Niall A. Paul
Allyn G. Turner

(See Next Column)

ASSOCIATES (Continued)

Virginia A. Conley (Resident, Parkersburg, West Virginia Office)
Paula Durst Gillis
Linda M. Gutsell (Resident, Morgantown, West Virginia Office)
Brett J. Preston
Dean A. Furner (Resident, Parkersburg, West Virginia)
Mark A. Sadd
H. Dill Battle, III
Bruce M. Jacobs
Eric W. Iskra
Stephen C. Musilli

OF COUNSEL

William B. Maxwell, III
Frederick L. Thomas, Jr.
Thomas W. Bayley (Resident, Parkersburg, West Virginia Office)

Representative Clients: Allied-Signal, Inc.; Anker Group, Inc.; Berwind Land Company; Charleston Area Medical Center, Inc.; E.I. du Pont de Nemours and Company; Ernst & Young LLP; Liggett Group, Inc.; State Farm Insurance Companies; United National Bank; Weirton Steel Corporation.

For full biographical listings, see the Martindale-Hubbell Law Directory

STEPTOE & JOHNSON (AV)

Seventh Floor, Bank One Center, P.O. Box 1588, 25326-1588
Telephone: 304-353-8000
Fax: 304-353-8180
Clarksburg, West Virginia Office: Bank One Center, P.O. Box 2190, 26302-2190.
Telephone: 304-624-8000.
Fax: 304-624-8183.
Morgantown, West Virginia Office: 1000 Hampton Center, P.O. Box 1616, 26507-1616.
Telephone: 304-598-8000.
Fax: 304-598-8116.
Martinsburg, West Virginia Office: 126 East Burke Street, P.O. Box 2629, 25401-5429.
Telephone: 304-263-6991.
Fax: 304-263-4785.
Charles Town, West Virginia Office: 104 West Congress Street, P.O. Box 100, 25414-0100.
Telephone: 304-725-1414.
Fax: 304-725-1913.
Hagerstown, Maryland Office: The Bryan Centre, 82 West Washington Street, Fourth Floor, P.O. Box 570, 21740-0570.
Telephone: 301-739-8600.
Fax: 301-739-8742.
Wheeling, West Virginia Office: The Riley Building, Suite 400, 14th & Chapline Streets, P.O. Box 150, 26008-0020.
Telephone: 304-233-0000.
Fax: 304-233-0014.

MEMBERS OF FIRM

Otis L. O'Connor
James R. Watson
Daniel R. Schuda
Harry P. Waddell
Steven P. McGowan
Bryan R. Cokeley
W. Randolph Fife
Martin R. Smith, Jr.
George E. Carenbauer
Arthur M. Standish
Patrick D. Kelly

ASSOCIATES

Cynthia R. Cokeley
Susan Osenton Phillips
Robert D. Pollitt
Luci R. Wellborn
Susan L. Basile
Joanna I. Tabit
Janet N. Kawash
Jeffrey K. Phillips
Richard J. Wolf
Wendy D. Young
Michael J. Funk
Marc B. Lazenby
Jan L. Fox
John W. Alderman, III
John C. Stump
Sarah Lovejoy Brack
Keith A. Jones
Denese Venza
Frank W. Volk
Christopher Kroger
Kelly R. Reed

Representative Clients: Ameribank; ARCO Chemical Co.; City National Bank of Charleston; Federal Kemper Insurance Co.; Goodyear Tire & Rubber Co.; The Hartford Group; Hope Gas, Inc.; Olin Corp.; South Charleston Stamping & Manufacturing Co.; State Farm Insurance Cos.

For full biographical listings, see the Martindale-Hubbell Law Directory

*CHARLES TOWN,** Jefferson Co.

JACKSON & KELLY (AV)

700 East Washington Street, P.O. Box 983, 25414
Telephone: 304-728-6088
Fax: 304-728-6029
Charleston, West Virginia Office: 1600 Laidley Tower, P.O. Box 553.
Telephone: 304-340-1000.
Morgantown, West Virginia Office: 6000 Hampton Center, P.O. Box 619.
Telephone: 304-599-3000.
Martinsburg, West Virginia Office: 300 Foxcroft Avenue, P.O. Box 1068.
Telephone: 304-263-8800.
Clarksburg, West Virginia Office: 203 Main Street, P.O. Box 1587.
Telephone: 304-623-3002.
New Martinsville, West Virginia Office: 256 Russell Avenue, P.O. Box 68.
Telephone: 304-455-1751.

(See Next Column)

JACKSON & KELLY, *Charles Town—Continued*

Lexington, Kentucky Office: 175 East Main Street, Suite 500, P.O. Box 2150.
Telephone: 606-255-9500.
Washington, D. C. Office: 2401 Pennsylvania Avenue, N.W., Suite 400.
Telephone: 202-973-0200.
Denver, Colorado Office: Suite 2710, 1660 Lincoln Street.
Telephone: 303-837-0003.

MEMBERS OF FIRM

Wm. Richard McCune, Jr.
James I. Manion
Mary Clare Eros
David Layva

ASSOCIATES

William Prentice Young
Donald P. Cookman
Stephen R. Kershner
Christopher Kenneth Robertson
Tammy A. Mitchell-Bittorf
Nancy L. Ford
James Eric Whytsell

LEGAL SUPPORT PERSONNEL

Charlene T. Caldwell

Representative Clients: Peoples Bank of Charles Town; Tuscawilla Utilities, Inc.; Ye Olde Sweet Shoppe, Inc.; Shenandoah Federal Savings Bank; One Valley Bank of Martinsburg, N.A.; Bonded Carriers, Inc.; Cress Creek Golf & Country Club, Inc.; Home Hill Corp.; Aetna Casualty and Surety Corp.; State Automobile Mutual Ins.

For full biographical listings, see the Martindale-Hubbell Law Directory

STEPTOE & JOHNSON (AV)

104 West Congress Street, P.O. Box 100, 25414-0100
Telephone: 304-725-1414
Fax: 304-725-1913
Clarksburg, West Virginia Office: Bank One Center, P.O. Box 2190, 26302-2190.
Telephone: 304-624-8000.
Fax: 304-624-8183.
Charleston, West Virginia Office: Seventh Floor, Bank One Center, P.O. Box 1588, 25326-1588.
Telephone: 304-353-8000.
Fax: 304-353-8180.
Morgantown, West Virginia Office: 1000 Hampton Center, P.O. Box 1616, 26507-1616.
Telephone: 304-598-8000.
Fax: 304-598-8116.
Martinsburg, West Virginia Office: 126 East Burke Street, P.O. Box 2629, 25401-5429.
Telephone: 304-263-6991.
Fax: 304-263-4785.
Hagerstown, Maryland Office: The Bryan Centre, 82 West Washington Street, Fourth Floor, P.O. Box 570, 21740-0570.
Telephone: 301-739-8600.
Fax: 301-739-8742.
Wheeling, West Virginia Office: The Riley Building, Suite 400, 14th & Chapline Streets, P.O. Box 150, 26003-0020.
Telephone: 304-233-0000.
Fax: 304-233-0014.

MEMBER OF FIRM

Douglas S. Rockwell

Representative Clients: Blakeley Bank and Trust Co.; Blue Ridge Acres; Great American Insurance Cos.; Inwood Quarry, Inc.; Jefferson County Development Authority; Keyes Ferry Acres; Nationwide Mutual Insurance Cos.; Peoples Bank of Charles Town; State Farm Mutual Insurance Cos.; Virginia Mutual Insurance Co.

For full biographical listings, see the Martindale-Hubbell Law Directory

*CLARKSBURG,** Harrison Co.

JACKSON & KELLY (AV)

203 Main Street, P.O. Box 1587, 26302
Telephone: 304-623-3002
Fax: 304-623-3027
Charleston, West Virginia Office: 1600 Laidley Tower, P.O. Box 553.
Telephone: 304-340-1000.
Martinsburg, West Virginia Office: 300 Foxcroft Avenue, P.O. Box 1068.
Telephone: 304-263-8800.
Morgantown, West Virginia Office: 6000 Hampton Center, P.O. Box 619.
Telephone: 304-599-3000.
New Martinsville, West Virginia Office: 256 Russell Avenue, P.O. Box 68.
Telephone: 304-455-1751.
Charles Town, West Virginia Office: 700 East Washington Street, P.O. Box 983.
Telephone: 304-728-6088. 304-623-3002.
Lexington, Kentucky Office: 175 East Main Street, Suite 500, P.O. Box 2150.
Telephone: 606-255-9500.
Washington, D. C. Office: 2401 Pennsylvania Avenue, N.W., Suite 400.
Telephone: 202-973-0200.
Denver, Colorado Office: Suite 2710, 1660 Lincoln Street.
Telephone: 303-837-0003.

(See Next Column)

ASSOCIATES

Mary L. Galan

For full biographical listings, see the Martindale-Hubbell Law Directory

JOHNSON, SIMMERMAN & BROUGHTON, L.C. (AV)

Suite 210, Goff Building, P.O. Box 150, 26301
Telephone: 304-624-6555
Telecopier: 304-623-4933

Charles G. Johnson
Frank E. Simmerman, Jr.
Marcia Allen Broughton

For full biographical listings, see the Martindale-Hubbell Law Directory

MCNEER, HIGHLAND & MCMUNN (AV)

Empire Building, P.O. Drawer 2040, 26301
Telephone: 304-623-6636
Facsimile: 304-623-3035
Morgantown Office: McNeer, Highland & McMunn, Baker & Armistead, 168 Chancery Row. P.O. Box 1615.
Telephone: 304-292-8473.
Fax: 304-292-1528.
Martinsburg, Office: 1446-1 Edwin Miller Boulevard. P.O. Box 2509.
Telephone: 304-264-4621.
Fax: 304-264-8623.

MEMBERS OF FIRM

C. David McMunn
Harold M. Sklar
J. Cecil Jarvis
Jeffrey S. Bolyard
James A. Varner
Steven R. Bratke
Lisa Stout Rogers
Michael J. Novotny (Resident, Martinsburg Office)
George B. Armistead (Resident, Morgantown Office)
Rhonda L. Miller (Resident at Morgantown Office)
Catherine D. Munster
Nancy Kennedy Quinn
Robert W. Trumble (Resident, Martinsburg Office)
William F. Rohrbaugh (Resident, Martinsburg Office)
James N. Riley
Larry West Chafin
Dennis M. Shreve
Tracey A. Rohrbaugh
Geraldine S. Roberts
D. Kevin Moffatt

OF COUNSEL

James E. McNeer
William L. Fury
Cecil B. Highland, Jr.
Charles S. Armistead (Resident, Morgantown Office)

Representative Clients: One Valley Bank of Clarksburg, National Association; Bruceton Bank; Harrison County Bank; Nationwide Mutual Insurance Cos.; Clarksburg Publishing Co.; C.I.T. Financial Services; State Automobile Mutual Insurance Co.; United Hospital Center, Inc.; West Virginia Coals, Inc.; Swanson Plating Company.

For full biographical listings, see the Martindale-Hubbell Law Directory

STEPTOE & JOHNSON (AV)

Bank One Center, P.O. Box 2190, 26302-2190
Telephone: 304-624-8000
Fax: 304-624-8183
Mailing Address: P.O. Box 2190, 26302-2190
Charleston, West Virginia Office: Seventh Floor, Bank One Center, P.O. Box 1588, 25326-1588.
Telephone: 304-353-8000
Fax: 304-353-8180.
Morgantown, West Virginia Office: 1000 Hampton Center, P.O. Box 1616, 26507-1616.
Telephone: 304-598-8000.
Fax: 304-598-8116.
Martinsburg, West Virginia Office: 126 East Burke Street, P.O. Box 2629, 25401-5429.
Telephone: 304-263-6991.
Fax: 304-263-4785.
Charles Town, West Virginia Office: 104 West Congress Street, P.O. Box 100, 25414-0100.
Telephone: 304-725-1414.
Fax: 304-725-1913.
Hagerstown, Maryland Office: The Bryan Centre, 82 West Washington Street, Fourth Floor, P.O. Box 570, 21740-0570.
Telephone: 301-739-8600.
Fax: 301-739-8742.
Wheeling, West Virginia Office: The Riley Building, Suite 400, 14th & Chapline Streets, P.O. Box 150, 26003-0020.
Telephone: 304-233-0000.
Fax: 304-233-0014.

MEMBERS OF FIRM

Herbert G. Underwood
J. Greg Goodykoontz
Robert G. Steele
Evans L. King, Jr.
James M. Wilson
Walter L. Williams
Patrick D. Deem
Ronald H. Hanlan
Robert M. Steptoe, Jr.
C. David Morrison
James D. Gray
Clement D. Carter, III
Vincent A. Collins
W. Henry Lawrence IV
William T. Belcher
Gordon H. Copland

(See Next Column)

STEPTOE & JOHNSON—*Continued*

MEMBERS OF FIRM (Continued)

Randall C. Light
Richard M. Yurko, Jr.
Gary W. Nickerson
Louis E. Enderle, Jr.
Charles F. Johns

OF COUNSEL

Jackson L. Anderson
Anne R. Williams
Frank K. Abruzzino

ASSOCIATES

Francesca Tan
Matthew J. Mullaney
Michael Kozakewich, Jr.
Carolyn A. Wade
Daniel C. Cooper
Douglas G. Lee
Sherri S. Johns
Timothy R. Miley
Jacqueline A. Wilson
John R. Merinar, Jr.
Nancy W. Brown
Michael J. Florio
Larry J. Rector
Gregory J. Plizga
Stephen D. Williams
Jill Oliverio Florio
Amy M. Smith
Robert E. Gifford
Nicholas A. Wininsky
Pamela E. Hepp
Rodney L. Bean
John C. Lynch
Janis P. White

EXECUTIVE DIRECTOR

Edward M. Mockler (Executive Director)

CHIEF FINANCIAL OFFICER

Frederick W. Siegrist (Chief Financial Officer)

Representative Clients: Consolidated Gas Transmission Corp.; Consolidated Coal Co.; CNA; E.I. DuPont de Nemours & Co.; Equitable Resources, Inc.; The Hartford Group; Peabody Coal Co.; PPG Industries; Union National Bank of West Virginia; Ogden Newspapers, Inc.

For full biographical listings, see the Martindale-Hubbell Law Directory

WATERS, WARNER & HARRIS (AV)

Formerly Stathers & Cantrall
701 Goff Building, P.O. Box 1716, 26301
Telephone: 304-624-5571
Fax: 304-624-7228

Birk S. Stathers (1884-1945)
W. G. Stathers (1889-1970)
Arch M. Cantrall (1896-1967)
Stuart R. Waters
Boyd L. Warner
James A. Harris
Scott E. Wilson
James C. Turner
Francis L. Warder, Jr.
G. Thomas Smith
Thomas G. Dyer

ASSOCIATES

Michael J. Folio
Katherine M. Carpenter
Ernest Glen Hentschel, II
Katrina L. Gallagher

Representative Clients: Bethlehem Steel Corp.; United States Fidelity and Guaranty Co.; State Farm Insurance Companies; Davis-Weaver Funeral Home, Inc.; Dowell Schlumberger, Inc.; Fuel Resources Production and Development Company, Inc.; Grafton Coal Company; Harry Green Chevrolet, Inc.; Emax Oil Co.; Southern Steel Products Co.

For full biographical listings, see the Martindale-Hubbell Law Directory

WEST & JONES (AV)

360 Washington Avenue, P.O. Box 2348, 26302
Telephone: 304-624-5501
FAX: 304-624-4454

MEMBERS OF FIRM

James C. West, Jr.
Jerald E. Jones
Dean C. Ramsey
John S. Kaull
Lewis A. Clark

ASSOCIATES

Kathryn K. Allen
Norman T. Farley

OF COUNSEL

W. Lyle Jones

Reference: The Union National Bank of West Virginia.

For full biographical listings, see the Martindale-Hubbell Law Directory

*CLAY,** Clay Co. — (Refer to Charleston)

*ELKINS,** Randolph Co.

BUSCH & TALBOTT, L.C. (AV)

Court and High Streets, P.O. Box 1397, 26241
Telephone: 304-636-3560
Fax: 304-636-2290

John E. Busch
Richard H. Talbott, Jr.

Cynthia Santoro Gustke
Peter G. Zurbuch
David Thompson
Bridgette Rhoden Wilson

(See Next Column)

LEGAL SUPPORT PERSONNEL

Cheryl J. Given

Representative Clients: Monongahela Power Co.; Davis Trust Co.; Community Bank & Trust Company of Randolph County; Coastal Lumber Co.; USF&G; Nationwide Insurance Co.; State Farm Insurance Companies; Nissan Motor Corporation in USA; Chrysler Corp.; General Motors.

For full biographical listings, see the Martindale-Hubbell Law Directory

*FAIRMONT,** Marion Co.

FURBEE, AMOS, WEBB & CRITCHFIELD (AV)

132 Adams Street, P.O. Box 1189, 26555
Telephone: 304-363-8800
Telecopier: 304-366-3783
Morgantown, West Virginia Office: 5000 Hampton Center, Suite 4.
Telephone: 304-598-0900.
Telecopier: 304-598-2712.

MEMBERS OF FIRM

Russell L. Furbee (1898-1978)
John D. Amos
Benjamin Hays Webb
Charles Vincent Critchfield
Alfred J. Lemley
Billy Atkins
Kenneth R. Miller
Stephen R. Brooks
Russell M. Clawges, Jr.
William T. Holmes
Mary H. Davis
Debra Hodges Scudiere (Resident at Morgantown Office)
Rebecca J. Zuleski
Tamara J. DeFazio

ASSOCIATES

Susan Yurko
Timothy N. Logan (Resident at Morgantown Office)
Carol Ann Marunich
Michael W. Barill

Attorneys for: Consolidation Coal Co.; Westinghouse Electric Co.; Monongahela Power Co.; Eastern Associated Coal Corp.; West Virginia Community Television Association; Continental Casualty Co.; State Farm Insurance Co.; Nationwide Insurance Co.; City National Bank of Fairmont; Community Bank & Trust, N.A.

For full biographical listings, see the Martindale-Hubbell Law Directory

ROSE PADDEN & PETTY, L.C. (AV)

612 WesBanco Building, 26555
Telephone: 304-363-4260
Fax: 304-363-4284
Morgantown, West Virginia Office: 201 Walnut Street, P.O. Box 1618.
Telephone: 304-292-5036.
Fax: 304-296-0846.

Herschel Rose (1912-1992)
Timothy J. Padden
Philip C. Petty
Elisabeth H. Rose
Bruce A. Kayuha
Charles J. Crooks

Jeffery D. Taylor

Representative Clients: Chessie System; Consolidated Gas Supply Corp.; General Motors Corp.; Aetna Life & Casualty; Hartford Insurance Group; Insurance Company, North America; First National Bank in Fairmont; Travelers Insurance Co.; United States Fidelity & Guaranty Insurance Co.
Reference: WesBanco Bank, Fairmont.

For full biographical listings, see the Martindale-Hubbell Law Directory

THARP, LIOTTA & JANES (AV)

WesBanco Building, P.O. Box 1509, 26554
Telephone: 304-363-1123
FAX: 304-366-1386

MEMBERS OF FIRM

J. Scott Tharp
James A. Liotta
David R. Janes
Karen M. Yokum

Representative Clients: WesBanco Bank Fairmont, N.A.; Industrial Contracting of Fairmont, Inc.; Town of Barrackville; Funk Oil and Gas Co.; Farmers Mutual Fire Association of West Virginia.
Approved Attorneys for: Lawyers Title Insurance Corp.
Reference: WesBanco Bank Fairmont, N.A.

For full biographical listings, see the Martindale-Hubbell Law Directory

*FAYETTEVILLE,** Fayette Co. — (Refer to Beckley)

*GRAFTON,** Taylor Co. — (Refer to Clarksburg)

*GRANTSVILLE,** Calhoun Co. — (Refer to Ripley)

*HARRISVILLE,** Ritchie Co. — (Refer to Parkersburg)

*HINTON,** Summers Co. — (Refer to Beckley)

*HUNTINGTON,** Cabell & Wayne Cos.

CAMPBELL, WOODS, BAGLEY, EMERSON, McNEER & HERNDON (AV)

14th Floor, Coal Exchange Building, P.O. Box 1835, 25719-1835
Telephone: 304-529-2391
Fax: 304-529-1832
Charleston, West Virginia Office: Bank One Center, Suite 1400, 707 Virginia Street East, P.O. Box 2393, 25328-2393.
Telephone: 304-346-2391.
Fax: 304-346-2433.
Ashland, Kentucky Office: 1608 Carter Avenue, P.O. Box 1862, 41105-1862.
Telephone: 606-329-1974
Fax: 606-324-2025

MEMBERS OF FIRM

Rolla D. Campbell (1895-1987)
Selden S. McNeer (1894-1963)
Robert K. Emerson (1922-1991)
Luther E. Woods (Retired)
Charles F. Bagley, Jr.
Selden S. McNeer, Jr.
Milton T. Herndon (Resident, Charleston, West Virginia Office)
Richard Gregory McNeer
James R. Bailes
Howard Ross Crews, Jr.
Charles F. Bagley, III
Edward M. Kowal, Jr.
James H. Moore, III (Resident, Ashland, Kentucky Office)
J. Patrick Jones
W. Nicholas Reynolds
R. Carter Elkins
Cheryl Lynne Connelly
J. Grant McGuire
David C. Ray
David A. Mohler (Resident, Charleston, West Virginia Office)
Charles I. Jones, Jr. (Resident, Charleston, West Virginia Office)
John D. Hoffman (Resident, Charleston, West Virginia Office)
John F. McCuskey (Resident, Charleston, West Virginia Office)
James W. Gabehart (Resident, Charleston, West Virginia Office)
Christopher A. Conley (Resident, Ashland, Kentucky Office)

ASSOCIATES

Laura L. Gray
William J. Hanna (Resident, Charleston West Virginia Office)
Philip Q. Ratliff (Resident, Ashland, Kentucky Office)
Daniel T. Yon
W. Joseph Bronosky
Raymond A. Nolan
Robert A. Wilson, Jr.
John F. Hussell, IV (Resident at Charleston, West Virginia Office)

OF COUNSEL

James Hornor Davis, III (Resident at Charleston, West Virginia Office)

Representative Clients: Corporate: Federal Deposit Insurance Corp. (FDIC); Resolution Trust Corp. (RTC); Ashland Oil, Inc. and Subsidiaries; Commerce Bank N.A. Huntington; The Matewan National Bank; Valley Health Systems, Inc.; Huntington Internal Medicine Group, Inc. Insurance; State Farm Mutual Automobile Insurance Co.; Continental Casualty Co.; Liberty Mutual Insurance Co.

For full biographical listings, see the Martindale-Hubbell Law Directory

HUDDLESTON, BOLEN, BEATTY, PORTER & COPEN (AV)

611 Third Avenue, P.O. Box 2185, 25722
Telephone: 304-529-6181
Telecopier: 304-522-4312
Ashland, Kentucky Office: 1422 Winchester Avenue, P.O. Box 770.
Telephone: 606-329-8771.
Telecopier: 606-324-4651.
Charleston, West Virginia Office: One Bridge Place, 10 Hale Street, P.O. Box 3786.
Telephone: 304-344-9869.
Telecopier: 304-344-4309.

MEMBERS OF FIRM

Jackson N. Huddleston (1908-1977)
William C. Beatty (1925-1994)
Noel P. Copen
R. Kemp Morton
Richard J. Bolen
Fred Adkins
John R. Fowler (Resident at Charleston Office)
Thomas H. Gilpin
James E. Cleveland, III (Not admitted in WV; Resident at Ashland, Kentucky Office)
Thomas J. Murray
Andrew S. Zettle
Bruce L. Stout
Fred B. Westfall, Jr.
Christopher J. Plybon
David L. Bole (Resident at Ashland, Kentucky Office)
Mary H. Sanders (Resident at Charleston Office)
Janice P. Epperly
Marc E. Williams
R. Russell Alexander
Daniel J. Konrad
T. Scott Sennett (Not admitted in WV; Resident at Ashland, Kentucky Office)
Scott K. Sheets
Luke A. Lafferre
David H. Lunsford

ASSOCIATES

Janet Smith Holbrook
James Wade Turner
Mark A. Bramble (Resident at Charleston Office)
Angela Wynn Konrad
Colin M. Cline
Troy N. Giatras (Resident at Charleston Office)
Mark H. Hayes
Robert L. Massie

(See Next Column)

ASSOCIATES (Continued)

Blake Benton (Resident at Charleston Office)
Deirdre M. MacCarthy
Daniel A. Earl
Macel E. Rhodes (Resident at Charleston Office)
John K. McHugh (Resident at Charleston Office)
M. Margaret Evans
Shawn M. Cox
Melissa G. Foster
Margaret M. Singleton
James C. Stebbins

OF COUNSEL

Amos A. Bolen
Paul C. Hobbs (Resident at Ashland, Kentucky Office)
James O. Porter

Representative Clients: CSX Transportation Inc.; Norfolk and Western Railway Company; Banc One West Virginia Corporation; The Herald-Dispatch, Huntington, WV; Ashland Oil, Inc.; Cabell Huntington Hospital; Metropolitan Life Insurance Co.; Insurance Company of North America.

For full biographical listings, see the Martindale-Hubbell Law Directory

JENKINS, FENSTERMAKER, KRIEGER, KAYES, FARRELL & AGEE (AV)

Eleventh Floor Coal Exchange Building, P.O. Drawer 2688, 25726
Telephone: 304-523-2100
Charleston, WV 304-345-3100
Facsimile: 304-523-2347; 304-523-9279

MEMBERS OF FIRM

John E. Jenkins (1897-1961)
P. Thomas Krieger
Henry M. Kayes
Michael J. Farrell
Wesley F. Agee
Barry M. Taylor

ASSOCIATES

Suzanne McGinnis Oxley
Charlotte A. Hoffman
Robert H. Sweeney, Jr.
Patricia A. Jennings
Stephen J. Golder
William J. McGee, Jr.
Anne Maxwell McGee
Tamela J. White
Lee Murray Hall
Thomas J. Obrokta

OF COUNSEL

John E. Jenkins, Jr.
Susan B. Saxe

For full biographical listings, see the Martindale-Hubbell Law Directory

*KEYSER,** Mineral Co. — (Refer to Elkins)

*KINGWOOD,** Preston Co. — (Refer to Morgantown)

*LEWISBURG,** Greenbrier Co.

HAYNES, FORD AND ROWE (AV)

203 West Randolph Street, 24901
Telephone: 304-645-1858; 645-1859

MEMBERS OF FIRM

Richard E. Ford
James J. Rowe
Richard E. Ford, Jr.

ASSOCIATES

Jeffrey S. Rodgers

OF COUNSEL

Sheldon E. Haynes

Representative Clients: Humana Hospital-Greenbrier Valley; First National Bank in Ronceverte; Aetna Casualty Co.; Greenbrier Valley National Bank; Federal Land Bank of Baltimore; U.S.F. and G. Co.; America Fore Loyalty Group.

For full biographical listings, see the Martindale-Hubbell Law Directory

*LOGAN,** Logan Co.

EILAND & BENNETT (AV)

200 Bank One Building, P.O. Box 899, 25601
Telephone: 304-752-2275
Fax: 304-752-2281

MEMBERS OF FIRM

Edward I. Eiland
John W. Bennett

Attorneys for: Don C. Elkins Music, Inc.; Ferrell Excavating Co.; Logan Concrete, Inc.; Man Clothing & Jewelry Company; Buffalo Creek Public Service District.
Local Counsel for: Island Creek Coal Company; Metropolitan Insurance Company; National Mines Corp.; Sharples Coal Corp.; The Horace Mann Cos.; ANPAC.

For full biographical listings, see the Martindale-Hubbell Law Directory

JOHN C. VALENTINE (AV)

National Bank Building, 229 Stratton Street, Suite 301, P.O. Box 840, 25601
Telephone: 304-752-7600
Fax: 304-752-7601

Representative Clients: BankOne, West Virginia, Logan, N.A.; Appalachian Power Co.; Mingo Wyoming Coal Land Co.

(See Next Column)

JOHN C. VALENTINE—*Continued*

Reference: The National Bank of Logan.

For full biographical listings, see the Martindale-Hubbell Law Directory

*MADISON,** Boone Co.

SHAFFER AND SHAFFER (AV)

330 State Street, P.O. Box 38, 25130
Telephone: 304-369-0511
Fax: 304-369-5431
Charleston, West Virginia Office: 1710 Bank One Center, P.O. Box 3973.
Telephone: 304-344-8716.
Fax: 304-342-1105.

MEMBERS OF FIRM

Harry G. Shaffer (1885-1971)
Harry G. Shaffer, Jr. (Retired)
Richard L. Theibert
James J. MacCallum
George D. Blizzard, II
Charles S. Piccirillo
Harry G. Shaffer, III (Resident, Charleston Office)
Anthony J. Cicconi (Resident, Charleston Office)
Norman W. White

ASSOCIATES

Edward L. Bullman
Timothy L. Mayo
L. Lee Javins, II

Representative Clients: Bank One, West Virginia, N.A., Boone; Armco Inc.; Westmoreland Coal Co.; State Farm Mutual Insurance Cos.; Nationwide Insurance Co.

For full biographical listings, see the Martindale-Hubbell Law Directory

*MARLINTON,** Pocahontas Co. — (Refer to Lewisburg)

*MARTINSBURG,** Berkeley Co.

BOWLES RICE MCDAVID GRAFF & LOVE (AV)

(Formerly Rice, Douglas & Shingleton)
105 West Burke Street, P.O. Drawer 1419, 25401
Telephone: 304-263-0836
Fax: 304-267-3822
Charleston, West Virginia Office: 16th Floor Commerce Square, P.O. Box 1386.
Telephone: 304-347-1100.
Fax: 304-343-2867.
Morgantown, West Virginia Office: 206 Spruce Street.
Telephone: 304-296-2500.
Fax: 304-296-2513.
Parkersburg, West Virginia Office: 601 Avery Street, P.O. Box 48.
Telephone: 304-485-7973.
Lexington, Kentucky Office: Bowles Rice McDavid Graff Love & Getty, 12th Floor Vine Center Tower, 333 West Vine Street.
Telephone: 606-225-8700.
Fax: 606-225-8418.

MEMBERS OF FIRM

Lacy I. Rice (1901-1974)
Lacy I. Rice, Jr.
Richard L. Douglas
Hoy G. Shingleton, Jr.
J. Oakley Seibert
Michael B. Keller
Michael E. Caryl
Charles F. Printz, Jr.
Michael D. Lorensen
Joan L. Casale
M. Shannon Brown
Norwood Bentley

ASSOCIATES

Stephen McDowell Mathias
Claudia W. Bentley
David A. DeJarnett
Amy R. Lamp

For full biographical listings, see the Martindale-Hubbell Law Directory

JACKSON & KELLY (AV)

300 Foxcroft Avenue, P.O. Box 1068, 25401
Telephone: 304-263-8800
Fax: 304-263-7110
Charleston, West Virginia Office: 1600 Laidley Tower, P.O. Box 553.
Telephone: 304-340-1000.
Morgantown, West Virginia Office: 6000 Hampton Center, P.O. Box 619.
Telephone: 304-599-3000.
Charles Town, West Virginia Office: 700 East Washington Street, P.O. Box 983.
Telephone: 304-728-6088.
Clarksburg, West Virginia Office: 203 Main Street, P.O. Box 1587.
Telephone: 304-623-3002.
New Martinsville, West Virginia Office: 256 Russell Avenue, P.O. Box 68.
Telephone: 304-455-1751.
Lexington, Kentucky Office: 175 East Main Street, Suite 500, P.O. Box 2150.
Telephone: 606-255-9500.
Washington, D. C. Office: 2401 Pennsylvania Avenue, N.W., Suite 400.
Telephone: 202-973-0200.
Denver, Colorado Office: Suite 2710, 1660 Lincoln Street.
Telephone: 303-837-0003.

MEMBERS OF FIRM

Wm. Richard McCune, Jr.
Mary Clare Eros
James I. Manion
David Layva

(See Next Column)

ASSOCIATES

William Prentice Young
Stephen R. Kershner
Tammy A. Mitchell-Bittorf
Donald P. Cookman
Christopher Kenneth Robertson
Nancy L. Ford
James Eric Whytsell

LEGAL SUPPORT PERSONNEL

Charlene T. Caldwell

Representative Clients: Anthem Personal Ins. Co.; Blue Ridge Bank; Continental Ins. Co.; GEICO; The Home Ins. Co.; Huntington Bank of Martinsburg, N.A.; One Valley Bank - East, N.A.; State Automobile Mutual Ins. Co.; Davis Memorial Hospital; First Empire Federal Savings & Loan Associates.

For full biographical listings, see the Martindale-Hubbell Law Directory

MCNEER, HIGHLAND & MCMUNN (AV)

1446-1 Edwin Miller Boulevard, P.O. Box 2509, 25401-2509
Telephone: 304-264-4621
Facsimile: 304-264-8623
Morgantown Office: McNeer, Highland & McMunn, Baker & Armistead, 168 Chancery Row. P.O. Box 1615.
Telephone: 304-292-8473.
Fax: 304-292-1528.
Clarksburg Office: Empire Building. P.O. Drawer 2040.
Telephone: 304-623-6636.
Facsimile: 304-623-3035.

Robert W. Trumble
Michael J. Novotny
William F. Rohrbaugh

Representative Clients: Westfield Companies; West Virginia Fire & Casualty; Home Insurance Co.; Bruceton Bank; Celina Insurance Company.

For full biographical listings, see the Martindale-Hubbell Law Directory

STEPTOE & JOHNSON (AV)

126 East Burke Street, P.O. Box 2629, 25401-5429
Telephone: 304-263-6991
Fax: 304-263-4785
Clarksburg, West Virginia Office: Bank One Center, P.O. Box 2190, 26302-2190.
Telephone: 304-624-8000.
Fax: 304-624-8183.
Charleston, West Virginia Office: Seventh Floor, Bank One Center, P.O. Box 1588, 25326-1588.
Telephone: 304-353-8000.
Fax: 304-353-8180.
Morgantown, West Virginia Office: 1000 Hampton Center, P.O. Box 1616, 26507-1616.
Telephone: 304-598-8000.
Fax: 304-598-8116.
Charles Town, West Virginia Office: 104 West Congress Street, P.O. Box 100, 25414-0100.
Telephone: 304-725-1414.
Fax: 304-725-1913.
Hagerstown, Maryland Office: The Bryan Centre, 82 West Washington Street, Fourth Floor, P.O. Box 570, 21740-0570.
Telephone: 301-739-8600.
Fax: 301-739-8742.
Wheeling, West Virginia Office: The Riley Building, Suite 400, 14th & Chapline Streets, P.O. Box 150, 26003-0020.
Telephone: 304-233-0000.
Fax: 304-233-0014.

MEMBERS OF FIRM

J. Lee Van Metre, Jr.
Lucien G. Lewin
James D. Steptoe
Curtis G. Power III
Kathy M. McCarty

ASSOCIATES

Michael S. Santa Barbara
Melissa L. Flowers

Representative Clients: Active Industries, Inc.; Blue Ridge Acres; Farmer and Mechanics Mutual Fire Insurance Co. of West Virginia; Great American Insurance Cos.; Insurance Corporation of America; Keyes Ferry Acres; Nationwide Mutual Insurance Cos.; One Valley Bank of Martinsburg; Peoples National Bank of Martinsburg; State Farm Mutual Insurance Cos.

For full biographical listings, see the Martindale-Hubbell Law Directory

*MOOREFIELD,** Hardy Co. — (Refer to Martinsburg)

*MORGANTOWN,** Monongalia Co.

BOWLES RICE MCDAVID GRAFF & LOVE (AV)

206 Spruce Street, 26505
Telephone: 304-296-2500
Fax: 304-296-2513
Charleston, West Virginia Office: 16th Floor Commerce Square, P.O. Box 1386.
Telephone: 304-347-1100.
Fax: 304-343-2867.

(See Next Column)

BOWLES RICE McDAVID GRAFF & LOVE, *Morgantown—Continued*

Martinsburg, West Virginia Office: (Serves Berkeley Springs and Charles Town, West Virginia). 105 West Burke Street, P.O. Drawer 1419.
Telephone: 304-263-0836.
Fax: 304-267-3822.
Parkersburg, West Virginia Office: 601 Avery Street, P.O. Box 48.
Telephone: 304-485-8500.
Fax: 304-485-7973.
Lexington, Kentucky Office: Bowles Rice McDavid Graff Love & Getty, 12th Floor Vine Center Tower, 333 West Vine Street.
Telephone: 606-225-8700.
Fax: 606-225-8418.

MEMBERS OF FIRM

Robert W. Dinsmore
Paul E. Frampton

ASSOCIATES

Charles C. Wise, III
Beth Kraus Haley
Kimberly S. Croyle

For full biographical listings, see the Martindale-Hubbell Law Directory

FURBEE, AMOS, WEBB & CRITCHFIELD (AV)

5000 Hampton Center, Suite 4, 26505
Telephone: 304-598-0900
Telecopier: 304-598-2712
Fairmont, West Virginia Office: 132 Adams Street, P.O. Box 1189.
Telephone: 304-363-8800.

MEMBERS OF FIRM

Billy Atkins
Russell M. Clawges, Jr.
Mary H. Davis
Debra Hodges Scudiere (Resident)
Rebecca J. Zuleski

ASSOCIATES

Timothy N. Logan (Resident at Morgantown Office)

Attorneys for: Consolidation Coal Co.; Westinghouse Electric Co.; Monongahela Power Co.; C & P Telephone Co.; Eastern Associated Coal Corp.; Continental Casualty Co.; State Farm Insurance Co.; Nationwide Insurance Co.; Aetna Life & Casualty.

For full biographical listings, see the Martindale-Hubbell Law Directory

FUSCO & NEWBRAUGH (AV)

2400 Cranberry Square, 26505-9209
Telephone: 304-594-1000
Telecopier: 304-594-1181

Andrew G. Fusco
Thomas H. Newbraugh

ASSOCIATES

Margaret A. Droppleman
Steven M. Prunty
Jeffrey A. Ray
Debra A. Bowers

OF COUNSEL

Vincent P. Cardi

Representative Clients: Mylan Pharmaceuticals, Inc.
Reference: One Valley Bank.

For full biographical listings, see the Martindale-Hubbell Law Directory

JACKSON & KELLY (AV)

6000 Hampton Center, P.O. Box 619, 26507
Telephone: 304-599-3000
Fax: 304-599-3166
Charleston, West Virginia Office: 1600 Laidley Tower, P.O. Box 553.
Telephone: 304-340-1000.
Martinsburg, West Virginia Office: 300 Foxcroft Avenue. P.O. Box 1068.
Telephone: 304-263-8800.
Charles Town, West Virginia Office: 700 East Washington Street, P.O. Box 983.
Telephone: 304-728-6088.
Clarksburg, West Virginia Office: 203 Main Street, P.O. Box 1587.
Telephone: 304-623-3002.
New Martinsville, West Virginia Office: 256 Russell Avenue, P.O. Box 68.
Telephone: 304-455-1751.
Lexington, Kentucky Office: 175 East Main Street, Suite 500, P.O. Box 2150.
Telephone: 606-255-9500.
Washington, D. C. Office: 2401 Pennsylvania Avenue, N.W. Suite 400.
Telephone: 202-973-0200.
Denver, Colorado Office: Suite 27100, 1660 Lincoln Street.
Telephone: 303-837-0003.

MEMBERS OF FIRM

George R. Farmer, Jr.
George E. Roeder, III
Stephen M. LaCagnin
William S. Mattingly

ASSOCIATES

Eric H. London
Jeffery L. Robinette
Julia M. Chico
Christopher L. Callas
R. Scott Summers
Kathy L. Snyder

(See Next Column)

LEGAL SUPPORT PERSONNEL

Donna A. Harper

Representative Clients: One Valley Bank of Morgantown; West Virginia University Hospitals, Inc.; Monongalia General Hospital; Chico Dairy; Superior Hydraulics Industries, Inc.; Swanson Plating Co.; Integra Bank; Fed One Savings Bank FSB; T & T Pump Inc.; Asplundh Tree Expert Co.

For full biographical listings, see the Martindale-Hubbell Law Directory

McNEER, HIGHLAND & McMUNN, BAKER & ARMISTEAD (AV)

168 Chancery Row, P.O. Box 1615, 26507-1615
Telephone: 304-292-8473
Fax: 304-292-1528
Clarksburg Office: McNeer, Highland & McMunn, Empire Building, P.O. Drawer 2040.
Telephone: 304-623-6636.
Facsimile: 304-623-3035.
Martinsburg Office: McNeer, Highland & McMunn, 1446-1 Edwin Miller Boulevard, P.O. Box 2509.
Telephone: 304-264-4621.
Facsimile: 304-264-8623.

George B. Armistead (Resident)
Rhonda L. Miller (Resident)

OF COUNSEL

Charles S. Armistead

Representative Clients: The Chesapeake and Potomac Telephone Company of West Virginia; Federal Kemper Insurance Co.; Home Insurance Co.

For full biographical listings, see the Martindale-Hubbell Law Directory

ROSE PADDEN & PETTY, L.C. (AV)

201 Walnut Street, P.O. Box 1618, 26507
Telephone: 304-292-5036
Fax: 304-296-0846
Fairmont, West Virginia Office: 612 WesBanco Building.
Telephone: 304-363-4260.
Fax: 304-363-4284.

Timothy J. Padden
Bruce A. Kayuha
Charles J. Crooks

For full biographical listings, see the Martindale-Hubbell Law Directory

STEPTOE & JOHNSON (AV)

1000 Hampton Center, P.O. Box 1616, 26507-1616
Telephone: 304-598-8000
Fax: 304-598-8116
Clarksburg, West Virginia Office: Bank One Center, P.O. Box 2190, 26302-2190.
Telephone: 304-624-8000.
Fax: 304-624-8183.
Charleston, West Virginia Office: Seventh Floor, Bank One Center, P.O. Box 1588, 25326-1588.
Telephone: 304-353-8000.
Fax: 304-353-8180.
Martinsburg, West Virginia Office: 126 East Burke Street, P.O. Box 2629, 25401-5429.
Telephone: 304-263-6991.
Fax: 304-263-4785.
Charles Town, West Virginia Office: 104 West Congress Street, P.O. Box 100, 25414-0100.
Telephone: 304-725-1414.
Fax: 304-725-1913.
Hagerstown, Maryland Office: The Bryan Centre, 82 West Washington Street, Fourth Floor, P.O. Box 570, 21740-0570.
Telephone: 301-739-8600.
Fax: 301-739-8742.
Wheeling, West Virginia Office: The Riley Building, Suite 400, 14th & Chapline Streets, P.O. Box 150, 26003-0020.
Telephone: 304-233-0000.
Fax: 304-233-0014.

MEMBERS OF FIRM

James A. Russell
Susan Slenker Brewer
William E. Galeota

OF COUNSEL

Thomas A. Vorbach

ASSOCIATES

Cynthia B. Jones (Not admitted in WV)
Laurie L. Crytser
P. Gregory Haddad
David E. Dick
Beth A. Raffle
William H. Smith
Brian D. Gallagher

Representative Clients: American Electric Power; Consolidaton Coal Co.; Ford Motor Co.; The Hartford Group; State Farm Mutual; WVU Hospitals, Inc.; West Virginia Medical Corp.; W.Va. Publishing Co.

For full biographical listings, see the Martindale-Hubbell Law Directory

*NEW MARTINSVILLE,** Wetzel Co.

JACKSON & KELLY (AV)

256 Russell Avenue, P.O. Box 68, 26155
Telephone: 304-455-1751
Fax: 304-455-6314
Charleston, West Virginia Office: 1600 Laidley Tower, P.O. Box 553.
Telephone: 304-340-1000.
Clarksburg, West Virginia Office: 203 Main Street, P.O. Box 1587.
Telephone: 304-623-3002.
Martinsburg, West Virginia Office: 300 Foxcroft Avenue, P.O. Box 1068.
Telephone: 304-263-8800.
Morgantown, West Virginia Office: 6000 Hampton Center, P.O. Box 619.
Telephone: 304-599-3000.
Charles Town, West Virginia Office: 700 East Washington Street, P.O. Box 983.
Telephone: 304-728-6088.
Lexington, Kentucky Office: 175 East Main Street, Suite 500, P.O. Box 2150.
Telephone: 606-255-9500.
Washington, D. C. Office: 2401 Pennsylvania Avenue, N.W., Suite 400.
Telephone: 202-973-0200.
Denver, Colorado Office: Suite 2700, 1660 Lincoln Street.
Telephone: 303-837-0003.

MEMBERS OF FIRM

J. S. Francis
Larry W. Blalock (Administrative Manager)

ASSOCIATES

Brooks K. Barkwill
Jennifer Z. Cain
Lucinda Fluharty Fitch
Vincent Tad Greene
Whitney G. Clegg

LEGAL SUPPORT PERSONNEL

Mary Ann Baker

Representative Clients: Miles Inc.; PPG Industries, Inc.; Wetzel County Hospital; Olin Corp.; Allstate Insurance Co.; State Farm Insurance Co.; The Hartford Insurance Co.; Physicians Insurance Co. of Ohio; Huntington National Bank; Crum & Forster Insurance Co.

For full biographical listings, see the Martindale-Hubbell Law Directory

*PARKERSBURG,** Wood Co.

BOWLES RICE MCDAVID GRAFF & LOVE (AV)

(Formerly Davis, Bailey, Pfalzgraf & Hall)
601 Avery Street, P.O. Box 48, 26102-0048
Telephone: 304-485-8500
Fax: 304-485-7973
Charleston, West Virginia Office: 16th Floor Commerce Square, P.O. Box 1386.
Telephone: 304-347-1100.
Fax: 304-343-2867.
Martinsburg, West Virginia Office (Serves Berkeley Springs and Charles Town, West Virginia): 105 West Burke Street, P.O. Drawer 1419.
Telephone: 304-263-0836.
Fax: 304-267-3822.
Morgantown, West Virginia Office: 206 Spruce Street.
Telephone: 304-296-2500.
Fax: 304-296-2513.
Lexington, Kentucky Office: Bowles Rice McDavid Graff Love & Getty, 12th Floor Vine Center Tower, 333 West Vine Street.
Telephone: 606-225-8700.
Fax: 606-225-8418.

MEMBERS OF FIRM

John S. Bailey, Jr.
Howard E. Seufer, Jr.
Robert J. Kent
Steven R. Hardman
Robert L. Bays

ASSOCIATES

Spencer D. Conard
Ellen T. Medaglio

For full biographical listings, see the Martindale-Hubbell Law Directory

GOODWIN & GOODWIN (AV)

201 Third Street, Town Square, 26101
Telephone: 304-485-2345
Fax: 304-485-3459
Charleston, West Virginia Office: 1500 One Valley Square.
Telephone: 304-346-7000
Fax: 304-344-9692
Ripley, West Virginia Office: 500 Church Street, P.O. Box 349.
Telephone: 304-372-2651.

RESIDENT PARTNER

Robert W. Full

RESIDENT ASSOCIATES

John N. Ellem

For full biographical listings, see the Martindale-Hubbell Law Directory

RULEY & EVERETT (AV)

The PMC Building, Suite 101, 417 Grand Park Drive, P.O. Box 628, 26102
Telephone: 304-422-6463
FAX: 304-422-6462

Charles V. Renner (1913-1994)

MEMBERS OF FIRM

Daniel Avery Ruley, Jr.
Diana Everett

Representative Clients: Camden-Clark Memorial Hospital; Cabot Corp.; United National Bank; Gatewood Products, Inc.; Aetna Casualty Co.; Commercial Union.

For full biographical listings, see the Martindale-Hubbell Law Directory

*PARSONS,** Tucker Co. — (Refer to Elkins)

*PETERSBURG,** Grant Co.

DUKE A. MCDANIEL (AV)

304 Virginia Avenue, P.O. Box 417, 26847
Telephone: 304-257-4377
Telefax: 304-257-4033

Reference: Potomac Valley Bank, Petersburg, W. Va.

For full biographical listings, see the Martindale-Hubbell Law Directory

*PHILIPPI,** Barbour Co. — (Refer to Clarksburg)

*PINEVILLE,** Wyoming Co.

BAILEY, WORRELL, VIERS & BROWNING (AV)

Lyons Building, 24874
Telephone: 304-732-6100
FAX: 304-732-6109

MEMBERS OF FIRM

R. D. Bailey (1883-1961)
C. S. Worrell (1910-1980)
Paul A. Viers (1922-1985)
Robert Bailey (1912-1994)
Robert Browning, Jr.

Representative Clients: The Norfolk and Western Railway Co.; Appalachian Power Co.; Pocahontas Land Corp.; The Peoples Bank of Mullens; Pineville Land Co., Inc.

For full biographical listings, see the Martindale-Hubbell Law Directory

*POINT PLEASANT,** Mason Co. — (Refer to Ripley)

*PRINCETON,** Mercer Co.

JOHNSTON, HOLROYD & ASSOCIATES (AV)

1438 Main Street, 24740
Telephone: 304-425-2103

MEMBERS OF FIRM

W. Broughton Johnston (1905-1978)
Robert E. Holroyd
David C. Smith
John E. (Jay) Williams, Jr.
Thomas Leonard Berry

Representative Clients: McDowell-Pocahontas Coal Co.; One Valley Bank; Maidenform, Inc.; Princeton Community Hospital.

For full biographical listings, see the Martindale-Hubbell Law Directory

*RIPLEY,** Jackson Co.

GOODWIN & GOODWIN (AV)

500 Church Street, P.O. Box 349, 25271
Telephone: 304-372-2651
Charleston, West Virginia Office: 1500 One Valley Square.
Telephone: 304-346-7000.
Fax: 304-344-9692
Parkersburg, West Virginia Office: 201 Third Street, Town Square.
Telephone: 304-485-2345.
Fax: 304-485-3459.

Robert B. Goodwin (1909-1955)

OF COUNSEL

C. E. Goodwin

MEMBERS OF FIRM

Joseph R. Goodwin
Stephen P. Goodwin
Michael I. Spiker
Steven F. White
Richard E. Rowe
Robert Q. Sayre, Jr.
Carrie L. Newton

For full biographical listings, see the Martindale-Hubbell Law Directory

*ROMNEY,** Hampshire Co. — (Refer to Martinsburg)

*SPENCER,** Roane Co. — (Refer to Ripley)

*SUMMERSVILLE,** Nicholas Co.

CALLAGHAN & RUCKMAN (AV)

600 Main Street, 26651
Telephone: 304-872-6050

Brooks B. Callaghan (1906-1983) Dan O. Callaghan
Timothy R. Ruckman

ASSOCIATES

Eric A. Collins Stephen O. Callaghan
Julia R. Wise

For full biographical listings, see the Martindale-Hubbell Law Directory

*SUTTON,** Braxton Co. — (Refer to Charleston)

WEIRTON, Hancock & Brooke Cos.

FRANKOVITCH & ANETAKIS (AV)

337 Penco Road, 26062
Telephone: 304-723-4400
Fax: 304-723-5892
Wheeling, West Virginia Office: 1233 Main Street.
Telephone: 304-233-1212.
Fax: 304-233-1251.
Pittsburgh, Pennsylvania Office: 411 Seventh Avenue, Suite 1402 A.
Telephone: 412-391-5281.
Fax: 412-281-1249.
Chester, West Virginia Office: 529 Carolina Avenue, 26034.
Telephone: 304-387-4400.
Fax: 304-387-4412.

MEMBERS OF FIRM

George J. Anetakis M. Eric Frankovitch
Carl N. Frankovitch Mark A. Colantonio
John J. Anetakis Michael G. Simon

ASSOCIATES

Deborah Ross Mulhall James Mulhall

OF COUNSEL

Carl Frankovitch John H. Kamlowsky

For full biographical listings, see the Martindale-Hubbell Law Directory

*WELCH,** McDowell Co. — (Refer to Princeton)

*WELLSBURG,** Brooke Co.

WILLIAM E. WATSON & ASSOCIATES (AV)

800 Main Street, P.O. Box 111, 26070
Telephone: 304-737-0881; 527-3220

Marc B. Chernenko Joyce D. Chernenko
Christine Machel

General Counsel for: Advance Financial Savings Bank, F.S.B.
Local Counsel for: Scott Lumber Co.; First Federal Savings and Loan Assn. of Greene County, Waynesburg, Pa. and Uniontown, Pa.; Follansbee Steel Corp.

For full biographical listings, see the Martindale-Hubbell Law Directory

*WESTON,** Lewis Co. — (Refer to Clarksburg)

*WHEELING,** Ohio Co.

BACHMANN, HESS, BACHMANN & GARDEN (AV)

1226 Chapline Street, P.O. Box 351, 26003
Telephone: 304-233-3511
Fax: 304-233-3199

MEMBERS OF FIRM

Carl G. Bachmann (1890-1980) R. Noel Foreman
Lester C. Hess (1903-1971) Paul T. Tucker
John B. Garden (1925-1994) George E. McLaughlin
Gilbert S. Bachmann Jeffrey R. Miller
Lester C. Hess, Jr. Suzanne Quinn
John L. Allen Anthony Ira Werner

ASSOCIATES

Rhonda L. Wade Elizabeth A. Abraham
Jeffrey A. Grove Samuel H. Foreman

Representative Clients: American Electric Power; Mercantile Bank; Ohio Power Co.; United National Bank; Wheeling Housing Authority; Wheeling Power Co.; Windsor Coal Co.

For full biographical listings, see the Martindale-Hubbell Law Directory

GOMPERS, BUCH, MCCARTHY & MCCLURE (AV)

Suite 302, Board of Trade Building, 26003
Telephone: 304-233-2450
Fax: 304-233-3656

(See Next Column)

MEMBERS OF FIRM

William J. Gompers (1887-1957) T. Carroll McCarthy, Jr.
Joseph A. Gompers James T. McClure
Harry L. Buch John E. Gompers

For full biographical listings, see the Martindale-Hubbell Law Directory

PHILLIPS, GARDILL, KAISER & ALTMEYER (AV)

61 Fourteenth Street, 26003
Telephone: 304-232-6810
Fax: 304-232-4918

OF COUNSEL

John D. Phillips

MEMBERS OF FIRM

James C. Gardill Joseph M. Palmer
Charles J. Kaiser, Jr. William A. Kolibash
H. Brann Altmeyer Ronald M. Musser

ASSOCIATES

Edward M. George III Robin Capehart (Mr.)
W. Elgine Heceta McArdle

General Counsel for: WesBanco Bank Wheeling; M. Marsh & Son; Centre Foundry & Machine Co.; Mull Industries, Inc.; Dalzell Corp.
Local Counsel for: Consolidation Coal Co.; Fidelity & Deposit Company of Maryland.

For full biographical listings, see the Martindale-Hubbell Law Directory

SCHRADER, RECHT, BYRD, COMPANION & GURLEY (AV)

1000 Hawley Building, 1025 Main Street, P.O. Box 6336, 26003
Telephone: 304-233-3390
Fax: 304-233-2769
Martins Ferry, Ohio Office: 205 North Fifth Street, P.O. Box 309.
Telephone: 614-633-8976.
Fax: 614-633-0400.

PARTNERS

Henry S. Schrader (Retired) Teresa Rieman-Camilletti
Arthur M. Recht Yolonda G. Lambert
Ray A. Byrd Patrick S. Casey
James F. Companion Sandra M. Chapman
Terence M. Gurley Daniel P. Fry (Resident, Martins Ferry, Ohio Office)
Frank X. Duff
James P. Mazzone

ASSOCIATES

Sandra K. Law Edythe A. Nash
D. Kevin Coleman Robert G. McCoid
Denise A. Jebbia Denise D. Klug
Thomas E. Johnston

OF COUNSEL

James A. Byrum, Jr.

General Counsel: WesBanco Bank-Elm Grove.
Representative Clients: CIGNA Property and Casualty Cos.; Columbia Gas Transmission Corp.; Commercial Union Assurance Co.; Hazlett, Burt & Watson, Inc.; Stone & Thomas Department Stores; Transamerica Commercial Finance Corp.; Wheeling-Pittsburgh Steel Corp.

For full biographical listings, see the Martindale-Hubbell Law Directory

SEIBERT, KASSERMAN, FARNSWORTH, GILLENWATER, GLAUSER, RICHARDSON & CURTIS, L.C. (AV)

1217 Chapline Street, P.O. Box 311, 26003
Telephone: 304-233-1220
Fax: 304-233-4813

Carl B. Galbraith (1903-1972) Elba Gillenwater, Jr.
George H. Seibert, Jr. (1913-1986) M. Jane Glauser
Randolf E. Richardson
Ronald W. Kasserman Ronald William Kasserman
Sue Seibert Farnsworth Linda Weatherholt Curtis
James E. Seibert Donald A. Nickerson, Jr.

Representative Clients: Ohio Valley Medical Center, Inc.; Ohio Valley Window Co.; The Travelers Cos.
Reference: United National Bank - Wheeling, W. Va.

For full biographical listings, see the Martindale-Hubbell Law Directory

WISCONSIN

*ANTIGO,** Langlade Co. — (Refer to Wausau)

*ASHLAND,** Ashland Co. — (Refer to Superior)

*BALSAM LAKE,** Polk Co. — (Refer to Eau Claire)

*BARABOO,** Sauk Co.

CROSS, JENKS, MERCER AND MAFFEI (AV)

221 Third Avenue, P.O. Box 556, 53913
Telephone: 608-356-3981
Fax: 608-356-1179
Lake Delton, Wisconsin Office: 220 South Wisconsin Dells Parkway, P.O. Box 237.
Telephone: 608-254-2000.
Fax: 608-254-8581.

MEMBERS OF FIRM

Clyde C. Cross (1918-1994)
Richard S. Jenks
Jerome P. Mercer
Wayne L. Maffei
Richard W. Cross
Beth Roney Drennan
Robert K. Ginther
Jean M. Wilson

ASSOCIATES

Sandra Sweeney

Representative Clients: Baraboo National Bank; Flambeau Corp.; American Family Insurance Co.; Ohio Casualty Co.; General Casualty Company of Wisconsin; Baraboo Federal Bank.

For full biographical listings, see the Martindale-Hubbell Law Directory

QUALE, HARTMANN, BOHL, REYNOLDS & PULSFUS (AV)

619 Oak Street, P.O. Box 443, 53913-0443
Telephone: 608-356-3977
Facsimile: 608-356-3110
Sauk City, Wisconsin Office: 635 Water Street, P.O. Box 564.
Telephone: 608-643-8579.

MEMBERS OF FIRM

Forrest D. Hartmann
James C. Bohl
Guy D. Reynolds
Dwight W. Pulsfus (Resident, Sauk City Office)
Thomas C. Groeneweg
Brian F. Glynn (Resident, Sauk City Office)
Mark R. Reitz
Dale E. Hughes
Maro R. Soderbloom
Bradley L. Hutter

OF COUNSEL

Glenn R. Quale
Barbara M. Mattei

Representative Clients: First National Bank & Trust Company of Baraboo.

For full biographical listings, see the Martindale-Hubbell Law Directory

*BARRON,** Barron Co. — (Refer to Eau Claire)

*BLACK RIVER FALLS,** Jackson Co.

SHERMAN, OLSHER & SHERMAN (AV)

104 Main Street, P.O. Box 487, 54615
Telephone: 715-284-5381
FAX: 715-284-5453

MEMBERS OF FIRM

Berton D. Sherman
Robert A. Olsher
Jonathan D. Sherman

ASSOCIATES

Anna L. Nemec

For full biographical listings, see the Martindale-Hubbell Law Directory

BURLINGTON, Racine Co. — (Refer to Racine)

*CHIPPEWA FALLS,** Chippewa Co. — (Refer to Eau Claire)

*CRANDON,** Forest Co. — (Refer to Rhinelander)

*DODGEVILLE,** Iowa Co. — (Refer to Madison)

*EAGLE RIVER,** Vilas Co.

DRAGER, O'BRIEN, ANDERSON, BURGY & GARBOWICZ (AV)

Arbutus Court, P.O. Box 639, 54521
Telephone: 715-479-6444
FAX: 715-479-3021
Boulder Junction, Wisconsin Office: County Highway M, 54512.
Telephone: 715-385-2047.
Fax: 715-385-2344.

Edmund H. Drager (1894-1988)

MEMBERS OF FIRM

John L. O'Brien
William W. Anderson
Dennis M. Burgy
Steven C. Garbowicz

(See Next Column)

ASSOCIATES

Alexander E. Brown

Representative Clients: First National Bank; Eagle River Memorial Hospital; Valley First National Bank, Three Lakes, Wisconsin; Lakeland State Bank, Woodruff, Wisconsin; M&I Bank of Eagle River; Northern Title Corp., Eagle River, Wisconsin; Cranberry Products, Inc.
Reference: First National Bank.

For full biographical listings, see the Martindale-Hubbell Law Directory

*EAU CLAIRE,** Eau Claire Co.

CARROLL, POSTLEWAITE, GRAHAM & PENDERGAST, S.C. (AV)

419 South Barstow Street, P.O. Box 1207, 54702
Telephone: 715-834-7774
Fax: 715-834-1298

Bailey E. Ramsdell (1890-1963)
George Y. King (1892-1966)
George M. Carroll
Jack A. Postlewaite
Thomas J. Graham, Jr.
Raymond K. Hughes
Rick L. Pendergast

Attorneys for: Metropolitan Life Insurance Co.; The Continental Insurance Cos.; Indemnity Insurance Company of N.A.; Travelers Insurance Co.; Sentry Insurance Company; CNA Insurance Companies; State Farm Insurance Companies.

For full biographical listings, see the Martindale-Hubbell Law Directory

GARVEY, ANDERSON, JOHNSON, GABLER & GERACI, S.C. (AV)

402 Graham Avenue, P.O. Box 187, 54702-0187
Telephone: 715-834-3425
FAX: 715-834-9240

Frank L. Morrow (1905-1969)
James E. Garvey
David G. Anderson
Douglas M. Johnson
William M. Gabler
Sebastian J. Geraci
Joseph R. Mirr
Carol S. Dittmar
Jane E. Lokken
Linda M. Danielson
Randi L. Osberg
John D. Leary
Steven T. Dzibinski
Steven V. Schlitz

Representative Clients: Aetna Life & Casualty Co.; Eau Claire-Chippewa Board of Realtors; Employer's Insurance of Wausau; Great American Insurance Co.; Lyman Lumber, Inc.; Northern States Power Co.; Pope & Talbot.

For full biographical listings, see the Martindale-Hubbell Law Directory

WILCOX, WILCOX, DUPLESSIE, WESTERLUND & ENRIGHT (AV)

1030 Regis Court, P.O. Box 128, 54701
Telephone: 715-832-6645
Fax: 715-832-8438

MEMBERS OF FIRM

Roy P. Wilcox (1873-1946)
Francis J. Wilcox
Roy S. Wilcox
Richard D. Duplessie
William J. Westerlund
Daniel A. Enright
John F. Wilcox

Attorneys for: Aetna Insurance Group; Medical Protective Assn.; American Surety Co.; Viking Insurance Co.; American Mutual Liability Ins. Co.; Continental Cas. Co.; Farmers Insurance Group.

For full biographical listings, see the Martindale-Hubbell Law Directory

*ELKHORN,** Walworth Co.

GODFREY, NESHEK, WORTH & LEIBSLE, S.C. (AV)

The Godfrey Building, 11 North Wisconsin Street, P.O. Box 260, 53121-0291
Telephone: 414-723-3220
Fax: 414-723-5091; 414-723-5121

Alfred L. Godfrey (1888-1970)
Thomas G. Godfrey
Milton E. Neshek
Harry F. Worth, Jr.
Robert C. Leibsle
Robert V. Conover
Kim A. Howarth
Lisle W. Blackbourn
Larry D. Steen
Dale L. Thorpe
Theodore N. Johnson

Scott T. Christian
Joanne M. McCormack (Not admitted in WI)
Holly L. Mattick
Robyn A. Nefstead

Attorneys for: Banc One Wisconsin Corporation; General Casualty Companies; American Family Insurance Company; Country Mutual Insurance Company; Kikkoman Foods, Inc.; Allstate Insurance Company.

For full biographical listings, see the Martindale-Hubbell Law Directory

SWEET & REDDY, S.C. (AV)

Inns of Court Building, 114 North Church Street, 53121
Telephone: 414-723-5480
Fax: 414-723-2180

(See Next Column)

SWEET & REDDY S.C., *Elkhorn—Continued*

Lowell E. Sweet David M Reddy

For full biographical listings, see the Martindale-Hubbell Law Directory

*ELLSWORTH,** Pierce Co. — (Refer to Eau Claire)

*FOND DU LAC,** Fond du Lac Co.

EDGARTON, ST. PETER, PETAK, MASSEY & BULLON (AV)

A Partnership including Service Corporations
10 Forest Avenue, P.O. Box 1276, 54936-1276
Telephone: 414-922-0470
Fax: 414-922-9091

MEMBERS OF FIRM

Allan L. Edgarton (1908-1994)
Neil Hobbs (Retired)
George M. St. Peter
A. D. Edgarton
Thomas L. Massey
Robert V. Edgarton
Ronald L. Petak
John A. St. Peter
Kathryn M. Bullon

ASSOCIATES

Paul W. Rosenfeldt

Representative Clients: Firstar Bank Fond du Lac, N.A.; Waterford Food Products, Inc.; The Combination Door Co.; Ready Mix Concrete, Inc.; Mayville Engineering Co., Inc.; J. F. Aherm Co.; Giddings & Lewis; Associated Milk Producers, Inc.; Moraine Park Technical College; Fond du Lac School District.

For full biographical listings, see the Martindale-Hubbell Law Directory

SAGER, PAVLICK & WIRTZ, S.C. (AV)

Suite 708, 104 South Main, 54935
Telephone: 414-921-1320
Fax: 414-921-0262

John J. Schneider (1913-1971)
Kenneth E. Worthing (1905-1982)
Steven P. Sager
Elizabeth V. Pavlick
Robert J. Wirtz

Jonathan Cermele

References: Insurance: Fireman's Fund Group; Kemper Group; Rural Mutual Insurance Co.; Wausau Insurance; The Medical Protective Co.; Wisconsin Health Care Liability Insurance Plan; Physicians Insurance Co. of Wisconsin; Corporate: American Bank of Fond Du Lac; State Bank of St. Cloud; Wisconsin Adjusting Service, Inc.

For full biographical listings, see the Martindale-Hubbell Law Directory

FORT ATKINSON, Jefferson Co. — (Refer to Janesville)

GRAFTON, Ozaukee Co.

HOUSEMAN, FEIND, GALLO & MALLOY (AV)

1214 13th Avenue, 53024-0104
Telephone: 414-377-0600
Fax: 414-377-6080

Ralph E. Houseman
Robert L. Feind, Jr.
John M. Gallo
Paul V. Malloy

ASSOCIATES

Michael P. Herbrand

Representative Clients: Dickmann Mfg. Co., Inc.; Town of Fredonia; Village of Fredonia; Grafton State Bank; Village of Grafton; Village of Thiensville.

For full biographical listings, see the Martindale-Hubbell Law Directory

*GREEN BAY,** Brown Co.

EVERSON, WHITNEY, EVERSON & BREHM, S.C. (AV)

Suite 106, 125 South Jefferson Street, P.O. Box 22248, 54305-2248
Telephone: 414-435-3734
Fax: 414-435-0126

John C. Whitney (1915-1994)
Philip R. Brehm
John E. Herald
Rodney A. Charnholm
George F. Savage
Peter J. Hickey
Susan J. Reigel
Bruce B. Deadman
John M. Thompson, IV
Jeffrey T. DeMeuse
John H. Heide

OF COUNSEL

James L. Everson

LEGAL SUPPORT PERSONNEL

Cheryl Lynn Morin

Counsel for: American Family Insurance; Valley Bank; Kemper Insurance Group; Bank One; U.S. Fidelity & Guaranty Co.; Employers Insurance of Wausau; State Farm Mutual Cos.; Travelers Insurance Co.; Farmers Insurance Group; Liberty Mutual Insurance Co.

For full biographical listings, see the Martindale-Hubbell Law Directory

GODFREY & KAHN, S.C. (AV)

333 Main Street, 54301
Telephone: 414-432-9300
Telecopier: 414-436-7988
Milwaukee, Wisconsin Office: 780 North Water Street.
Telephone: 414-273-3500.
Madison, Wisconsin Office: Suite 202, 131 West Wilson Street.
Telephone: 608-251-4670. Oshkosh, Wisconsin Office: 219 Washington Avenue.
Telephone: 414-233-6050.
Sheboygan, Wisconsin Office: 605 North Eighth.
Telephone: 414-451-8340.

Benjamin W. Laird
Ronald T. Pfeifer
Joseph M. Nicks
Winston A. Ostrow
Robert W. Burns
Dennis W. Rader
William J. Plummer
Kelly Bogart Servais
Angela M. Samsa
Eric R. von Estorff

OF COUNSEL

Mark Andrew Green

For full biographical listings, see the Martindale-Hubbell Law Directory

*HAYWARD,** Sawyer Co. — (Refer to Superior)

*HURLEY,** Iron Co. — (Refer to Eagle River)

*JANESVILLE,** Rock Co.

BRENNAN, STEIL, BASTING & MACDOUGALL, S.C. (AV)

One East Milwaukee Street, P.O. Box 1148, 53547
Telephone: 608-756-4141
Facsimile: 608-756-9000
Madison, Wisconsin Office: 433 West Washington Avenue, P.O. Box 990.
Telephone: 608-251-7770.
Facsimile: 608-251-6626.
Monroe, Wisconsin Office: 1628 11th Street, P.O. Box 739.
Telephone: 608-325-2131.
Facsimile: 608-325-9546.
Delavan, Wisconsin Office: 512 East Walworth Avenue.
Telephone: 414-728-5591.
Facsimile: 414-728-1780.

Glen R. Campbell (1927-1972)
Paul M. Ryan (1931-1986)
James E. Brennan
George K. Steil, Sr.
Thomas J. Basting, Sr.
David J. MacDougall
Thomas S. Hornig
James E. Hartwig
George K. Steil, Jr.
John R. Steil
William B. Vogt
Michael E. Grubb
Dennis M. White (Resident, Madison Office)
Edward A. Corcoran (Resident, Madison Office)
Peter B. Kelly (Resident, Monroe Office)
Michael R. Fitzpatrick
Clarence F. Asmus (Resident, Monroe Office)
Marc T. McCrory

Bryan D. Woods (Resident, Madison Office)
Howard Goldberg (Resident, Madison Office)
Frank W. Hammett (Resident, Delavan Office)
David B. Williams (Resident, Delavan Office)
D. Schuyler Davies (Resident at Delavan Office)
Leslie L. Johnson (Resident at Delavan Office)
Margery Mebane Tibbetts
Kevin C. Potter
Patrick J. Anderson
Jonathan W. Groessl
Barbara W. McCrory
Gordon R. Ladwig (Resident at Monroe Office)
Nancy B. Johnson
James F. Loebl
Terry J. Finman
Dennis E. Robertson (Resident at Madison Office)

OF COUNSEL

Robert M. Berg
Richard A. Miller (Resident at Delavan, Wisconsin Office)

Counsel for: Rock County National Bank; Blain Supply, Inc.; Farm and Fleet Stores.
Local Counsel for: Fireman's Fund Insurance Co.; Insurance Company of North America; Heritage Mutual Insurance Co.; PICW; CIVMIC; Capitol Indemnity Corp.

For full biographical listings, see the Martindale-Hubbell Law Directory

*JEFFERSON,** Jefferson Co. — (Refer to Watertown)

*JUNEAU,** Dodge Co. — (Refer to Watertown)

*KENOSHA,** Kenosha Co.

ROSE & ROSE (AV)

5529 Sixth Avenue, 53140
Telephone: 414-658-8550, 657-7556

William S. Rose (1914-1994) Terry W. Rose

For full biographical listings, see the Martindale-Hubbell Law Directory

*KEWAUNEE,** Kewaunee Co. — (Refer to Green Bay)

*LA CROSSE,** La Crosse Co.

HALE, SKEMP, HANSON & SKEMP (AV)

505 King Street, King on 5th Building, Suite 300, P.O. Box 1927, 54602
Telephone: 608-784-3540
Fax: 608-784-7414

MEMBERS OF FIRM

Quincy H. Hale (1893-1987)
Thomas H. Skemp (1896-1977)
Ernest O. Hanson
Robert C. Skemp
William A. Kirkpatrick
Roger L. Imes
Thomas S. Sleik
James G. Curtis, Jr.
Charles E. Hanson
David B. Russell
Michael W. Gill
Thomas L. Horvath
Richard W. Schroeder

ASSOCIATES

Margaret M. Ahne
Shannon B. Hart
Donald L. Mabry
Kevin James Roop

Representative Clients: State Bank of La Crosse; First Federal Savings and Loan Assn.; Century Telephone Co.; Western Wisconsin Technical College; Credit Bureau of La Crosse, Inc.; La Crosse Lutheran Hospital; Skemp Clinic, Ltd.

For full biographical listings, see the Martindale-Hubbell Law Directory

JOHNS & FLAHERTY, S.C. (AV)

621 Exchange Building, P.O. Box 1626, 54602-1626
Telephone: 608-784-5678
Fax: 608-784-0557

Daniel T. Flaherty
Robert D. Johns, Jr.
Maureen L. Kinney
Janet A. Jenkins
Brent P. Smith
Peder G. Arneson
James P. Gokey
Ellen M. Frantz
Gregory S. Bonney
Jeffrey C. Mochalski
Michael L. Stoker

Maureen C. Roberts

Representative Clients: Aetna Casualty & Surety Co.; Allstate Insurance Co.; CNA; INA; Norwest Bank, La Crosse, N.A.; St. Paul Cos.; U.S.F. & G. Co.; Gundersen Clinic, Ltd.; Altec International, Inc.; Franciscan Health Systems.

For full biographical listings, see the Martindale-Hubbell Law Directory

KLOS, FLYNN & PAPENFUSS, CHARTERED (AV)

Formerly Steele, Klos & Flynn, Chartered
8th Floor, Lynne Tower, 318 Main Street, 54601
Telephone: 608-784-8600
Fax: 608-784-8606
West Salem, Wisconsin Office: 147 South Leonard Street.
Telephone: 608-786-0520.

Fred E. Steele (1895-1972)
Jerome Klos
John E. Flynn
Francis D. Papenfuss
Bryant H. Klos

Kristen D. Goedert

OF COUNSEL

Merwin A. Mellor

Representative Clients: Lutheran Hospital Foundation; Union State Bank; Head Start, Inc.; Farmers Insurance Group; Farmers State Bank; La Crosse Lutheran Hospital; Westby-Coon Valley State Bank; American Family Life Insurance Co.

For full biographical listings, see the Martindale-Hubbell Law Directory

MOEN, SHEEHAN, MEYER, LTD. (AV)

Suite 700, First Bank Place, 201 Main Street, P.O. Box 0786, 54602-0786
Telephone: 608-784-8310
FAX: 608-782-6611

William E. Meyer
Leon E. Sheehan
Paul W. Henke, Jr.
Michael S. Moen
Michael E. Ehrsam
James Naugler
G. Jeffrey George
David F. Stickler
James L. Kroner, Jr.
Joseph J. Skemp, Jr.

OF COUNSEL

Richard S. Moen

Representative Clients: Allstate Ins. Co.; First Bank, N.A.; Mathy Construction Co.; St. Paul Insurance Cos; State Farm Insurance Co.
References: First Bank, N.A.; First Wisconsin Trust Co. (Milwaukee); La Crosse Trust Co.; Marshall & Ilsley Bank (Milwaukee).

For full biographical listings, see the Martindale-Hubbell Law Directory

*LADYSMITH,** Rusk Co. — (Refer to Eau Claire)

*LANCASTER,** Grant Co. — (Refer to Madison)

*MADISON,** Dane Co.

* indicates certain Bar Register subscribers whose principal office is located elsewhere in the state and who have arranged for representation as a part of the state capital listings that follow

AXLEY BRYNELSON (AV)

(Formerly Brynelson, Herrick, Bucaida, Dorschel & Armstrong Including the former Easton & Assoc., S.C.)
2 East Mifflin Street, P.O. Box 1767, 53701-1767
Telephone: 608-257-5661
Fax: 608-257-5444

MEMBERS OF FIRM

Frank J. Bucaida
Bradley D. Armstrong
John H. Schmid, Jr.
Timothy D. Fenner
John C. Mitby
Daniel T. Hardy
John Walsh
Bruce L. Harms
David Easton
Peter Weisenberger (1946-1992)
Curtis C. Swanson
Michael S. Anderson
Patricia M. Gibeault
Michael J. Westcott
Larry K. Libman
Richard E. Petershack
Steven A. Brezinski
Steven M. Streck
Joy L. O'Grosky

ASSOCIATES

Arthur E. Kurtz
Edith F. Merila
Michael J. Modl
Sabin S. Peterson
Guy J. DuBeau
Ritchie J. Sturgeon
Beverly A. Seagraves
Mark Hazelbaker
Gregory C. Collins
Paul Voelker
Marcia MacKenzie
Amelia McCarthy
Amy B.F. Tutwiler
Darold J. Londo
Grant B. Spellmeyer

OF COUNSEL

Ralph E. Axley
Floyd A. Brynelson
James C. Herrick
Griffin G. Dorschel

For full biographical listings, see the Martindale-Hubbell Law Directory

BELL, METZNER, GIERHART & MOORE, S.C. (AV)

44 East Mifflin Street, P.O. Box 1807, 53701
Telephone: 608-257-3764
FAX: 608-257-3757

Glen H. Bell (1902-1988)
Carroll E. Metzner
Roger L. Gierhart
John M. Moore
Hugh H. Bell
Steven J. Caulum
Ward I. Richter
William A. Abbott
Barrett J. Corneille
John W. Markson
Stephen O. Murray
Robert J. Kasieta
Stephen J. Nording
William C. Williams
Mary L. McDaniel

W. Scott McAndrew
David J. Pliner
Teresa Ann Mueller
Stephen E. Ehlke
Suzanne E. Williams
Jeanne M. Armstrong

Counsel for: American Family Mutual Insurance Group; Superior Water, Light & Power Co.; North-West Telecommunications, Inc.; Wisconsin Southern Gas Co., Inc.; St. Paul Fire and Marine Insurance Cos.; Allstate Insurance Co.; Fireman's Fund Insurance Co.

For full biographical listings, see the Martindale-Hubbell Law Directory

BOARDMAN, SUHR, CURRY & FIELD (AV)

One South Pinckney Street, Suite 410, P.O. Box 927, 53701-0927
Telephone: 608-257-9521
FAX: 608-283-1709

W. Wade Boardman (1905-1983)

OF COUNSEL

Frederick C. Suhr

MEMBERS OF FIRM

Henry A. Field, Jr.
Kenneth T. McCormick, Jr.
Thomas J. Sobota
Bradway A. Liddle, Jr.
Paul A. Hahn
John E. Knight
James F. Lorimer
Claude J. Covelli
Rebecca A. Erhardt
Paul R. Norman
Mark W. Pernitz
Walter Kuhlmann
Michael P. May
Michael G. Stuart
Richard J. Delacenserie
Richard A. Lehmann
John S. Robison
James E. Bartzen
Carl J. Rasmussen
Steven C. Zach
Gail V. Perry
Amanda J. Kaiser
Catherine M. Rottier
Lawrie J. Kobza
Jon C. Nordenberg
Bonnie A. Wendorff
Susan J. Erickson
Mark J. Steichen
Madelyn D. Leopold

(See Next Column)

BOARDMAN, SUHR, CURRY & FIELD, *Madison—Continued*

ASSOCIATES

Richard L. Schmidt
Anita T. Gallucci
Paul M. Schmidt
Dane E. Allen
Elizabeth A. Heiner

Representative Clients: BancInsure, Inc.; CUNA Mutual Insurance Group; Liberty Mutual Insurance Co.; Madison Newspapers, Inc.; Oscar Mayer Foods Corp.; Physicians Plus Medical Group; State Farm Insurance Co.; Wausau Insurance Cos.; Wisconsin Bankers Assn.; Wisconsin Public Power, Inc. SYSTEM.

For full biographical listings, see the Martindale-Hubbell Law Directory

DEWITT ROSS & STEVENS, S.C. (AV)

Manchester Place, 2 East Mifflin Street, Suite 600, 53703
Telephone: 608-255-8891
Facsimile: 608-252-9243
West Madison Office: 8000 Excelsior Drive, Suite 401, Madison, WI 53717.
Telephone: 608-831-2100.
Telecopier: 608-831-2106.

Jack R. DeWitt
Charles P. Seibold
Duane P. Schumacher
Thomas D. Zilavy
Peter R. Dohr
Daniel W. Hildebrand
John Rashke
John Koeppl
Jon P. Axelrod
Peter A. Peshek
John Duncan Varda
Henry J. Handzel, Jr.
Eli H. Schmukler
Ronald W. Kuehn
Jayne K. Kuehn
Anne Taylor Wadsack
Paul A. Croake
Denis P. Bartell
Michael R. Davis
Wrede H. Smith, Jr.
Frederic J. Brouner
Donald Leo Bach
Stuart C. Herro
Anthony R. Varda
Ronald R. Ragatz
Gregory E. Scallon
Eric A. Farnsworth
Richard J. Lewandowski
J. Thomas McDermott
Joseph A. Ranney
Stephen E. Bablitch
Steven J. Kirschner
Patience D. Roggensack
Paul G. Kent
William E. McCardell
Jeffery Mandell
Charles S. Sara (Resident)
Dennis P. Birke
Christopher D. Daniels
Timm Speerschneider
Bradley W. Hauck
Robert E. Shumaker

OF COUNSEL

Philip H. Porter (1891-1976)
James W. Morgan (1932-1988)
A.J. McAndrews (1903-1990)
Frank A. Ross (1901-1990)
Donald R. Huggett (1933-1993)
Myron Stevens (1902-1994)
Norman C. Herro
Jean G. Setterholm
William F. Nelson
James G. Derouin
John H. Lederer
David W. Kruger

Karen K. Gruenisen
David E. Fowler
Troy A. Mayne
Don M. Millis
Warren J. Day
Todd E. Palmer
John W. Stoneman
Colleen A. Breister
Stephen A. DiTullio
Jeanette C. Lytle
Craig A. Fieschko

Representative Clients: American Family Insurance Group; Dean Foundation for Health, Research and Education, Inc.; Firstar Bank Madison, N.A.; Independent Insurance Agents; Kennecott Corporation; Northern Engraving Corp.; Perry Printing Corporation; Promega Corp.; Wisconsin Assn. of Manufacturers and Commerce Transportation, Mining and Environmental Advisory Committees; Wisconsin Alumni Research Foundation.

For full biographical listings, see the Martindale-Hubbell Law Directory

* FOLEY & LARDNER (AV)

One South Pinckney Street, P.O. Box 1497, 53701-1497
Telephone: 608-257-5035
Facsimile: 608-258-4258
Milwaukee, Wisconsin Office: Firstar Center, 777 East Wisconsin Avenue.
Telephone: 414-271-2400.
Telex: 26-819 (Foley Lard Mil).
Facsimile: 414-297-4900.
Chicago, Illinois Office: Suite 3300, One IBM Plaza, 330 N. Wabash Avenue.
Telephone: 312-755-1900.
Facsimile: 312-755-1925.
Washington, D.C. Office: Washington Harbour, Suite 500, 3000 K Street, N.W.
Telephone: 202-672-5300.
Telex: 904136 (Foley Lard Wash).
Facsimile: 202-672-5399.
Annapolis, Maryland Office: Suite 102, 175 Admiral Cochrane Drive.
Telephone: 301-266-8077.
Telex: 899149 (Oldtownpat).
Facsimile: 301-266-8664.
Jacksonville, Florida Office: The Greenleaf Building, 200 Laura Street, P.O. Box 240.
Telephone: 904-359-2000.
Facsimile: 904-359-8700.

(See Next Column)

Orlando, Florida Office: Suite 1800, 111 North Orange Avenue, P.O. Box 2193.
Telephone: 407-423-7656.
Telex: 441781 (HQ ORL).
Facsimile: 407-648-1743.
Tallahassee, Florida Office: Suite 450, 215 South Monroe Street, P.O. Box 508.
Telephone: 904-222-6100.
Facsimile: 904-224-0496.
Tampa, Florida Offices: Suite 2700, 100 North Tampa Street, P.O. Box 3391.
Telephones: 813-229-2300; Pinellas County: 813-442-3296.
Facsimile: 813-221-4210.
West Palm Beach, Florida Office: Suite 200, Phillips Point East Tower, 777 South Flagler Drive.
Telephone: 407-655-5050.
Facsimile: 407-655-6925.
New Address Effective Spring, 1995: 150 East Gilman Street, P.O. Box 1497, Madison, Wisconsin. Telephone: 608-257-5035. Facsimile: 608-258-4258.

PARTNERS

Michael H. Auen
Christopher S. Berry
Lawrence J. Bugge
William M. Conley
Charles G. Curtis, Jr.
Gordon Davenport III
Harry C. Engstrom
Michael P. Erhard
Henry A. Gempeler
David J. Harth
S. Richard Heymann
Joseph P. Hildebrandt
Allan R. Koritzinsky
Michael G. Laskis
Wayman C. Lawrence, IV
Timothy J. Radelet
Thomas G. Ragatz
David W. Reinecke
Anne Elizabeth Ross
William J. Scanlon
John S. Skilton
Leonard S. Sosnowski
Steven R. Suleski (Resident)
Harvey L. Temkin
Michael B. Van Sicklen
David G. Walsh (Partner-in-Charge, Madison Office)
Robert M. Whitney

RESIDENT OF COUNSEL

John J. Walsh

RESIDENT SPECIAL COUNSEL

James R. Conohan
Michael S. Heffernan
Mark L. Langenfeld

ASSOCIATES

Allen A. Arntsen
John A. Chosy
Douglas B. Clark (Resident)
Douglas John Cropsey (Resident)
Amy E. Dombrowski
Joan L. Eads (Resident)
Julie Genovese (Resident)
Tamara S. Grant
Nancy Y. Hanewicz
Wayne Omar Hanewicz
Thomas W. Henshue (Resident)
Roberta F. Howell (Resident)
Bradley D. Jackson (Resident)
Arthur W. Jorgensen III
Mark A. Kassel
Katherine M. Lunsford
Marta T. Meyers
Gregory F. Monday
Blaine Renfert (Resident)
Anita M. Sorensen
Lynn J. Splitek (Resident)
Gisèle M. Sutherland

For full biographical listings, see the Martindale-Hubbell Law Directory

GODFREY & KAHN, S.C. (AV)

Suite 202, 131 West Wilson Street, P.O. Box 1110, 53701-1110
Telephone: 608-251-4670
Telecopier: 608-251-2983
Milwaukee, Wisconsin Office: 780 North Water Street.
Telephone: 414-273-3500.
Green Bay, Wisconsin Office: 333 Main Street.
Telephone: 414-432-9300.
Oshkosh, Wisconsin Office: 219 Washington Avenue.
Telephone: 414-233-6050.
Sheboygan, Wisconsin Office: 605 North Eighth.
Telephone: 414-451-8340.

Jon E. Anderson
Kirk D. Strang
Peter L. Albrecht

OF COUNSEL

Robert I. Fassbender

For full biographical listings, see the Martindale-Hubbell Law Directory

KAY & ANDERSEN, S.C. (AV)

One Point Place, Suite 201, 53719
Telephone: 608-833-0077
Fax: 608-833-3901

Robert J. Kay
Randall J. Andersen

Edith M. Petersen

OF COUNSEL

James C. Geisler

Representative Clients: Ameritech; AT&T Co.; Wisconsin Knife Works; Chicago Title Insurance Co.; Bankers' Bank of Wisconsin, Inc.; Dean Foods; Thorstad Chevrolet, Inc.

For full biographical listings, see the Martindale-Hubbell Law Directory

LAFOLLETTE & SINYKIN (AV)

One East Main, Suite 500, 53703
Telephone: 608-257-3911
Fax: 608-257-0609
Mailing Address: P.O. Box 2719, 53701-2719
Sauk City, Wisconsin Office: 603 Water Street.
Telephone: 608-643-2408.
Stoughton, Wisconsin Office: 113 East Main Street, P.O. Box 191.
Telephone: 608-873-9464.
Fax: 608-873-0781.

MEMBERS OF FIRM

Philip F. LaFollette (1897-1965)
Gordon Sinykin (1910-1991)
James E. Doyle (1915-1987)
Earl H. Munson
Christopher J. Wilcox
Howard A. Sweet
Thomas A. Hoffner
David E. McFarlane
Brady C. Williamson
Robert E. Chritton
Timothy J. Muldowney
Michael E. Skindrud
Teresa M. Elguézabal
Linda M. Clifford
Lawrence Bensky
Jonathan C. Aked
Brett A. Thompson
Richard M. Burnham
Robert J. Dreps
Jeffrey J. Kassel
Noreen J. Parrett
Eugenia G. Carter

ASSOCIATES

Timothy F. Nixon
Joanne R. Whiting
Melanie E. Cohen
Linda M. Zech
James Alan Friedman
Robert V. Petershack
Stephen R. White

OF COUNSEL

William E. Chritton (Resident, Stoughton Office)
Daniel Sinykin
Frank M. Tuerkheimer

Reference: M&I Madison Bank.

For full biographical listings, see the Martindale-Hubbell Law Directory

LATHROP & CLARK (AV)

Suite 1000, 122 West Washington Avenue, P.O. Box 1507, 53701-1507
Telephone: 608-257-7766
Fax: 608-257-1507
Poynette, Wisconsin Office: 111 North Main Street, P.O. Box 128.
Telephone: 608-635-4324.
FAX: 608-635-4690.
Lodi, Wisconsin Office: 108 Lodi Street, P.O. Box 256.
Telephone: 608-592-3877.
FAX: 608-592-5844.
Belleville, Wisconsin Office: 27 West Main.
Telephone: 608-424-3404.

MEMBERS OF FIRM

G. Burgess Ela (1904-1976)
Leon E. Isaksen (1903-1979)
San W. Orr (1906-1991)
James F. Clark
Donald L. Heaney
Theodore J. Long
Ronald J. Kotnik
Jerry E. McAdow
David S. Uphoff
James A. Kemmeter
John C. Frank
Michael J. Lawton
William L. Fahey
Michael J. Julka
Shelley J. Safer
Jeffrey P. Clark
Kenneth B. Axe
David E. Rohrer
Marjorie H. Schuett
Jill Weber Dean
David R. J. Stiennon

OF COUNSEL

John H. Esch
Edmund J. Hart
Donald M. Ryan (Resident, Lodi, Wisconsin Office)
Trayton L. Lathrop

ASSOCIATES

Heidi S. Tepp
Patrick J. G. Stiennon
Peter A. Martin
Daniel L. Dooge
Malina R. Piontek Fischer
Frank C. Sutherland
Paul A. Johnson

Representative Clients: Research Products Corp.; Olin Corp.; Murphy Oil Corp.; The Richard & David Jacobs Group; Wickes Companies, Inc.; Kayser Ford, Inc.; Hopkins Agricultural Chemical Co.; Metropolitan Life Insurance Co.; Wisconsin Association of School Boards, Inc.; American Family Mutual Insurance Co.

For full biographical listings, see the Martindale-Hubbell Law Directory

MELLI, WALKER, PEASE & RUHLY, S.C. (AV)

Suite 600, 119 Martin Luther King, Jr. Boulevard, P.O. Box 1664, 53701
Telephone: 608-257-4812
Telefax: 608-258-7470

(See Next Column)

Joseph A. Melli
Jack D. Walker
James K. Pease, Jr.
James K. Ruhly
Thomas R. Crone
John R. Sweeney
Philip J. Bradbury
JoAnn M. Hart
Susan C. Sheeran
Douglas E. Witte
Dana J. Erlandsen
Lora H. Woods
Christopher B. Hughes
Lisa A. Polinske
Devon R. Baumbach

OF COUNSEL

John H. Shiels

Representative Clients: Oshkosh Truck Corp.; Coca-Cola Bottling Company of Madison; Wisconsin Road Builders Assn.; Associated Builders & Contractors of Wisconsin, Inc.; Marshall Erdman & Associates, Inc.; Research Products Corp.; Wells Manufacturing Corp.; JJ Security, Inc.; Perry Printing Co.; Racine Unified School District.

For full biographical listings, see the Martindale-Hubbell Law Directory

*** MICHAEL, BEST & FRIEDRICH** (AV)

One South Pinckney Street, Firstar Plaza, P.O. Box 1806, 53701-1806
Telephone: 608-257-3501
Telecopier: 608-283-2275
Milwaukee, Wisconsin Office: 100 East Wisconsin Avenue. 53202-4108.
Telephone: 414-271-6560.
Telecopier: 414-277-0656.
Chicago, Illinois Office: 135 South LaSalle Street, Suite 1610, 60603-4391.
Telephone: 312-845-5800.
Telecopier: 312-845-5828.
Affiliated Law Firm: Edward D. Heffernan, Penthouse One, 1019 19th Street, N.W., Washington, D.C. 20036.
Telephone: 202-331-7444.
Telecopier: 202-331-4976.

RESIDENT PARTNERS

Arvid A. Sather
David J. Hanson
Tod B. Linstroth
Nelson D. Flynn
Thomas E. Klancnik
Thomas P. Godar
William F. White
Jesse S. Ishikawa
James R. Troupis
Ann Ustad Smith
Richard J. Langer
Linda H. Bochert
Charles V. Sweeney
Richard C. Glesner
Robert W. Cleveland (Not admitted in WI)

RESIDENT ASSOCIATES

Christiane M. Loidl
Raymond P. Taffora
Steven P. Means
Lynda R. Templen
David A. Crass
Richard A. Latta
Jon G. Furlow
Randall J. Ney
Kimberly A. Reinecke
Kimberly Cash Tate
Lisa S. Keyes
Paul J. Dombrowski
Troy A. Hilliard
Eric M. McLeod
Amy O. Bruchs
Steven L. Ritt
Thomas Patrick Heneghan
Lauren L. Azar
J. Donald Best

For full biographical listings, see the Martindale-Hubbell Law Directory

MURPHY & DESMOND, S.C. (AV)

Manchester Place, Suite 800, 2 East Mifflin Street, P.O. Box 2038, 53701-2038
Telephone: 608-257-7181
Telecopier: 608-257-2508
Mailing Address: P.O. Box 2038,

Robert B. L. Murphy
William F. Mundt
Michael R. Vaughan
Richard W. Pitzner
William J. Rameker
James D. Sweet
Stephen L. Morgan
Robert A. Pasch
Tim R. Valentyn
Debbie Garten
William Smoler
Alan E. Korpady
Stephen C. Beilke
Edward S. Marion
Catherine J. Furay
Stephen R. Tumbush
Lawrence E. Bechler

Leslie D. Shear
Jane F. (Ginger) Zimmerman
Pamela J Schmelzer
Diane M. Pica
Gregory P. Seibold
David A. McLean

OF COUNSEL

John P. Desmond
Gordon Brewster Baldwin

Representative Clients: Anheuser-Busch Comp.; Bank of Sun Prairie; Gross Common Carrier; M.B.C., Inc. (Hotel Division); Mapco Gas Products, Inc.; R.J. Reynolds Tobacco Company; Samuels Recycling Comp.; Shockley Communications Corp.; The Company Store; Wisconsin Bankers Association.

For full biographical listings, see the Martindale-Hubbell Law Directory

STROUD, STROUD, WILLINK, THOMPSON & HOWARD (AV)

25 West Main Street, Suite 300, P.O. Box 2236, 53701
Telephone: 608-257-2281
FAX: 608-257-7643

(See Next Column)

STROUD, STROUD, WILLINK, THOMPSON & HOWARD, *Madison—Continued*

MEMBERS OF FIRM

Ray M. Stroud (1885-1972)
Seward Ritchey Stroud
C. Vernon Howard
Ronald W. Todd
Robert R. Stroud
H. Dale Peterson
Robert J. Schwab
Carolyn A. Hegge
Mark S. Zimmer
James F. Gebhart
Teresa J. Welch
Grady J. Frenchick

OF COUNSEL

Donald R. Stroud
Donald D. Willink
Dale R. Thompson
Carl E. Gulbrandsen

ASSOCIATES

Margaret M. Liss
Joseph P. Bartol

General Counsel for: Appleton Mills; University of Wisconsin Foundation; Temperature Systems, Inc.; Wisconsin Farm Bureau Federation; Anchor Savings and Loan Assn.; The Wisconsin Cheeseman, Inc.; J.H. Findorff & Son, Inc.; Edward Kraemer & Sons, Inc.; Hilldale Shopping Center; American T.V. & Appliance of Madison, Inc.

For full biographical listings, see the Martindale-Hubbell Law Directory

*MANITOWOC,** Manitowoc Co.

NASH, SPINDLER, DEAN & GRIMSTAD (AV)

(Firm Founded in 1872 as Nash and Nash).
201 East Waldo Boulevard, 54220
Telephone: 414-684-3321
Fax: 414-684-0544

MEMBERS OF FIRM

D. William Dean
Paul H. Grimstad
Robert L. McCracken
Peter W. Deschler
William R. Wick
Thomas B. Rusboldt
Arden A. Muchin

John F. Mayer
Katherine M. Reynolds
Timothy A. Burkard
Steven D. Hitzeman

Counsel for: Lakeside Foods, Inc.; Eck Industries, Inc.; Hamilton Industries, Inc.; Paragon Electric Co.; Manitowoc Clinic, S.C.; Cher-Make Sausage Co.; Medical Protective Co.; Wausau Insurance Co.; State Farm Insurance Cos.; General Casualty Insurance Cos.

For full biographical listings, see the Martindale-Hubbell Law Directory

*MAUSTON,** Juneau Co. — (Refer to Baraboo)

*MEDFORD,** Taylor Co. — (Refer to Wausau)

MENOMONEE FALLS, Waukesha Co.

NIEBLER, PYZYK & WAGNER (AV)

River Court Center, N95 W16975 Richfield Way, P.O. Box 444, 53052-0444
Telephone: 414-251-5330
Fax: 414-251-1823

MEMBERS OF FIRM

John H. Niebler
Robert G. Pyzyk
Robert F. Klaver, Jr.
Roy E. Wagner

ASSOCIATES

Jynine A. Strand

OF COUNSEL

Chester J. Niebler

For full biographical listings, see the Martindale-Hubbell Law Directory

*MENOMONIE,** Dunn Co. — (Refer to Eau Claire)

*MERRILL,** Lincoln Co. — (Refer to Wausau)

*MILWAUKEE,** Milwaukee Co.

BIRD, MARTIN & SALOMON S.C. (AV)

735 North Water Street, Suite 1600, 53202-4104
Telephone: 414-276-7290
Facsimile: 414-276-7291

John D. Bird, Jr.
Frances H. Martin
Allen M. Salomon

References: Firstar Bank; Biltmore Investors Bank.

For full biographical listings, see the Martindale-Hubbell Law Directory

COOK & FRANKE S.C. (AV)

660 East Mason Street, 53202
Telephone: 414-271-5900
Facsimile: 414-271-2002

(See Next Column)

Robert E. Cook
Harry F. Franke
Thomas J. Drought
Francis R. Croak
L. William Staudenmaier
Robert F. Johnson
Kevin J. Lyons
Joseph E. Tierney, Jr.
William A. Jennaro
Margaret T. Lund
Thomas N. Harrington
Charles I. Henderson
Brian R. Wanasek
Pamela H. Schaefer
John M. Swietlik, Jr.
Kathy L. Nusslock
Victor J. Schultz
Philip C. Reid
Sandra J. Janssen
Lawrence Clancy
John G. Gehringer
Michael J. Lund
David J. Hase
Kaye K. Vance
Paul J. Hinkfuss
Ann M. Rieger
Thomas J. Lonzo
Alexander T. Pendleton
Heidi L. Vogt
Laura E. Schuett
Mark C. Veldey
Steven L. Nelson
Mark J. Maichel
Christopher J. Jaekels
Stacy Gerber Ward
Pamela Ann Johnson
LeeAnne Neumann
Ellen Steinnafel-Lappe

OF COUNSEL

Ben G. Slater

Representative Clients: Kenosha Beef Inc.; Bradley Center Corp.; CH2M Hill; Coca Cola; Safeco Insurance Co.; General Casualty Co. of Wisconsin; Payne & Dolan, Inc.

For full biographical listings, see the Martindale-Hubbell Law Directory

FIORENZA & HAYES, S.C. (AV)

Kildeer Court, 3900 West Brown Deer Road, 53209
Telephone: 414-355-3600
Fax: 414-355-8080

John A. Fiorenza
Clare L. Fiorenza
Richard D. Moake
Daniel J. Miske
William J. Mantyh
Lawrence G. Wickert
Jeffrey M. Leggett
Lisa A. Dziadulewicz
Timothy M. Hughes

Representative Clients: M & I Marshall & Ilsley Bank, Silver Spring Division; Valley Bank; Miller-Bradford & Risberg, Inc.; Magnetek, Inc.; Litton Industries, Inc.; Centel Communications, Inc.; FJA Christiansen Roofing Co.; North American Van Lines; Kendor Corp.; Todd Equipment, Inc.

For full biographical listings, see the Martindale-Hubbell Law Directory

FOLEY & LARDNER (AV)

Firstar Center, 777 East Wisconsin Avenue, 53202-5367
Telephone: 414-271-2400
Telex: 26-819 (Foley Lard Mil)
Facsimile: 414-297-4900
Madison, Wisconsin Office: 150 E. Gilman Street, P.O. Box 1497.
Telephone: 608-257-5035.
Facsimile: 608-258-4258.
Chicago, Illinois Office: Suite 3300, One IBM Plaza, 330 N. Wabash Avenue.
Telephone: 312-755-1900.
Facsimile: 312-755-1925.
Washington, D.C. Office: Washington Harbour, Suite 500, 3000 K Street, N.W.
Telephone: 202-672-5300.
Telex: 904136 (Foley Lard Wash).
Facsimile: 202-672-5399.
Annapolis, Maryland Office: Suite 102, 175 Admiral Cochrane Drive.
Telephone: 301-266-8077.
Telex: 899149 (Oldtownpat).
Facsimile: 301-266-8664.
Jacksonville, Florida Office: The Greenleaf Building, 200 Laura Street. P.O. Box 240.
Telephone: 904-359-2000.
Facsimile: 904-359-8700.
Orlando, Florida Office: Suite 1800, 111 North Orange Avenue, P.O. Box 2193.
Telephone: 407-423-7656.
Telex: 441781 (HQ ORL).
Facsimile: 407-648-1743.
Tallahassee, Florida Office: Suite 450, 215 South Monroe Street, P.O. Box 508.
Telephone: 904-222-6100.
Facsimile: 904-224-0496.
Tampa, Florida Offices: Suite 2700, One Hundred Tampa Street, P.O. Box 3391.
Telephones: 813-229-2300; Pinellas County: 813-442-3296.
Facsimile: 813-221-4210.
West Palm Beach, Florida Office: Suite 200, Phillips Point East Tower, 777 South Flagler Drive.
Telephone: 407-655-5050.
Facsimile: 407-655-6925.

(See Next Column)

FOLEY & LARDNER—*Continued*

PARTNERS

Leon F. Foley (1894-1978)
Lynford Lardner, Jr. (1915-1973)
William J. Abraham, Jr.
Benjamin J. Abrohams
Russell T. Alba (Tampa, Florida Office)
Kevin D. Anderson
J. Gordon Arkin (Orlando, Florida Office)
Michael H. Auen (Madison, Wisconsin Office)
Russell J. Barron
Steven R. Barth
Edmund T. Baxa, Jr. (Orlando, Florida Office)
Wesley N. Becker (Chicago, Illinois Office)
David E. Beckwith
Linda E. Benfield
Charles A. Benner
Stephen A. Bent (Washington, D.C. Office)
Christopher S. Berry (Madison, Wisconsin Office)
Kenneth A. Beytin (Tampa, Florida Office)
Michael M. Biehl
James N. Bierman (Washington, D.C. Office)
Robert L. Binder
David A. Blumenthal (Washington, D.C. Office)
Ralf-Reinhard Böer
Robert J. Bonner
Michael A. Bowen
Robert B. Bradley
John W. Brahm
Joseph C. Branch
Mary Kathryn Braza
Lawrence J. Bugge (Madison, Wisconsin Office)
Robert A. Burka (Washington, D.C. Office)
Carolyn C. Burrell
Daniel N. Burton (Tampa, Florida Office)
John F. Callan
Harry V. Carlson, Jr.
Richard H. Casper
Steven B. Chameides (Washington, D.C. Office)
Harrison K. Chauncey, Jr. (West Palm Beach, Florida Office)
Robert A. Christensen
Jon P. Christiansen
Keith A. Christiansen
James R. Clark
Charles E. Commander, III (Jacksonville, Florida, Office)
William M. Conley (Madison, Wisconsin Office)
James P. Connelly
Paul E. Cooney (Washington, D.C. Office)
John C. Cooper, III
Stephen A. Crane (Tampa, Florida Office)
George D. Cunningham
Charles G. Curtis, Jr. (Madison, Wisconsin Office)
Gordon Davenport III (Madison, Wisconsin Office)
Gardner F. Davis (Jacksonville, Florida Office)
John R. Dawson
Terence J. Delahunty, Jr. (Orlando, Florida Office)
Lloyd J. Dickinson
George A. Dionisopoulos
Benn S. DiPasquale
Gregg H. Dooge
Rodney H. Dow
Robert K. Drummond
Robert A. DuPuy
Richard A. DuRose (Orlando, Florida Office)
Scott E. Early (Chicago, Illinois Office)
Harry C. Engstrom (Madison, Wisconsin Office)
Michael P. Erhard (Madison, Wisconsin Office)
Richard M. Esenberg
Thomas C. Ewing
Mark C. Extein (Orlando, Florida Office)
Guy O. Farmer, II (Jacksonville, Florida Office)
James A. Farrell (West Palm Beach, Florida Office)
John J. Feldhaus (Washington, D.C. Office)
Wendy L. Fields (Washington, D.C. Office)
Michael Fischer
Stephen M. Fisher
Michael D. Flanagan
David H. Fleck
Richard S. Florsheim
Howard W. Fogt, Jr. (Washington, D.C. Office)
Mark F. Foley
Timothy C. Frautschi
Richard S. Gallagher
Benjamin F. Garmer, III
Michael A. Gehl
C. Frederick Geilfuss, II
Henry A. Gempeler (Madison, Wisconsin Office)
Patrick N. Giordano (Chicago, Illinois Office)
Ilene Knable Gotts (Washington, DC Office)
Michael W. Grebe
James S. Grodin (Orlando, Florida Office)
Reed Groethe
Edward J. Hammond
Phillip J. Hanrahan
David J. Harth (Madison, Wisconsin Office)
Michael W. Hatch
Charles V. Hedrick (Jacksonville, Florida Office)
Richard A. Heinle (Orlando, Florida Office)
John R. Heitkamp, Jr.
Keith James Hesse (Orlando, Florida Office)
S. Richard Heymann (Madison, Wisconsin Office)
Joseph P. Hildebrandt (Madison, Wisconsin Office)
Lewis H. Hill, III (Tampa, Florida Office)
John P. Horan (Orlando, Florida Office)
Michael A. Hornreich (Orlando, Florida Office)
James O. Huber
Marsha E. Huff
James L. Huston
Emory Ireland
Joseph W. Jacobs (Tallahassee, Florida Office)
Stanley S. Jaspan
Donald D. Jeffery (Washington, D.C. Office)
Sarah O. Jelencic
Jeffrey J. Jones
Christopher K. Kay (Orlando, Florida Office)
Michael J. Kelly
Linda Y. Kelso (Jacksonville, Florida Office)
Joan F. Kessler
William D. King (Jacksonville, Florida Office)
W. David Knox, II
Joan M. Kubalanza (Chicago, Illinois Office)
Bernard S. Kubale
Harvey A. Kurtz
Jack L. Lahr (Washington, D.C. Office)
James M. Landis (Tampa, Florida Office)
Jeffrey H. Lane
Thomas E. Lange (Tampa, Florida Office)

PARTNERS (Continued)

(See Next Column)

Michael G. Laskis (Madison, Wisconsin Office)
Peter G. Latham (Orlando, Florida Office)
Wayman C. Lawrence, IV (Madison, Wisconsin Office)
Mitchell W. Legler (Jacksonville, Florida Office)
Chauncey W. Lever, Jr. (Jacksonville, Florida Office)
John D. Lien (Chicago, Illinois Office)
Peter C. Linzmeyer (Washington, D.C. Office)
J. Craig Long (Chicago, Illinois Office)
David S. Lott (Chicago, Illinois Office)
Emerson M. Lotzia (Jacksonville, Florida Office)
David Lucey
Wayne R. Lueders
Lawrence T. Lynch
Peter G. Mack (Washington, D.C. Office)
F. Anthony Maio
Susan R. Maisa
Jean M. Mangu (Jacksonville, Florida Office)
Martin D. Mann
Robert P. Marschall (West Palm Beach, Florida Office)
Edwin D. Mason (Chicago, Illinois Office)
Thomas K. Maurer (Orlando, Florida Office)
K. Rodney May (Orlando, Florida Office)
Michael G. McCarty
Jere D. McGaffey
Maureen A. McGinnity
Brian W. McGrath
James T. McKeown
Brian J. McNamara (Washington, D.C. and Annapolis, Maryland Offices)
Maurice J. McSweeney
E. Robert Meek (Jacksonville, Florida Office)
Sybil Meloy (Jacksonville, Orlando, Tampa, West Palm Beach, Florida and Washington, D.C. Offices)
Philip G. Meyers
Chris J. Mollet (Chicago, Illinois Office)
Donald D. Mondul (Not admitted in WI)
Paul R. Monsees (Washington, D.C., Office)
Thomas F. Munro, II (West Palm Beach, Florida Office)
Gerald J. Neal (Chicago, Illinois Office)
Paul G. Neilan (Chicago, Illinois Office)
Michael S. Nolan
James P. O'Shaughnessy
Michael E. Olsen (Chicago, Illinois Office)
John M. Olson
Andrew A. Ostrow (West Palm Beach, Florida Office)
Nehad S. Othman (Chicago, Illinois Office)
Joseph R. Panzl (Orlando, Florida Office)
Jamshed J. Patel
Thomas C. Pence
Jack A. Porter (West Palm Beach, Florida Office)
Mark L. Prager (Chicago, Illinois Office)
Lyman A. Precourt
Patrick G. Quick
George E. Quillin (Washington, D.C. Office)
Timothy J. Radelet (Madison, Wisconsin Office)
Thomas G. Ragatz (Madison, Wisconsin Office)
Randall S. Rapp (Chicago, Illinois Office)
Michael D. Regenfuss
David M. Reicher
David W. Reinecke (Madison, Wisconsin Office)
Greg W. Renz
David M. Rieth (Tampa, Florida Office)
David L. Robbins (Tampa, Florida Office)
R. Andrew Rock (Tampa, Florida Office)
Christopher D. Rolle (Orlando, Florida Office)
Paul E. Rosenthal (Orlando, Florida Office)
Anne Elizabeth Ross (Madison, Wisconsin Office)
Jay O. Rothman
Amy S. Rubin (West Palm Beach, Florida Office)
David B. Ryan
David A. Sacks (Washington, D.C. Office)
Luther F. Sadler, Jr. (Jacksonville, Florida Office)
Colin G. Sandercock (Washington, D.C. Office)
John A. Sanders (Orlando, Florida Office)
Jacqueline Marie Saue (Washington, D.C. Office)
Bernhard D. Saxe (Washington, D.C. Office)
William J. Scanlon (Madison, Wisconsin Office)
Ronald M. Schirtzer (Orlando, Florida Office)
Richard L. Schwaab (Washington, D.C. Office)
Arthur Schwartz (Washington, D.C. and Annapolis, Maryland Offices)
John T. Sefton (Jacksonville, Florida Office)
Hoken S. Seki (Chicago, Illinois Office)
Nancy J. Sennett
Timothy J. Sheehan
Thomas L. Shriner, Jr.
George T. Simon (Chicago, Illinois Office)
Luke E. Sims
Christopher C. Skambis, Jr. (Orlando, Florida Office)
John S. Skilton (Madison, Wisconsin Office)
William P. Sklar (West Palm Beach, Florida Office)
Stephen M. Slavin (Chicago, Illinois Office)
David W. Slook
Leonard S. Sosnowski (Madison, Wisconsin Office)
Charles J. Steele (Washington, D.C. Office)
Christian G. Steinmetz
Peter J. Stone
Steven R. Suleski (Madison, Wisconsin Office)
Pierre C. Talbert, Jr. (Chicago, Illinois Office)
Stanley A. Tarkow (Tampa, Florida Office)
Richard L. Teigen
Harvey L. Temkin (Madison, Wisconsin Office)
Mark A. Thimke
Martin A. Traber (Tampa, Florida Office)
Ronald D. Tym
James T. Tynion III (Not admitted in WI)
Joseph B. Tyson, Jr.
Egerton K. van den Berg (Orlando, Florida Office)
Michael B. Van Sicklen (Madison, Wisconsin Office)
Jay N. Varon (Washington, D.C. Office)
Harry L. Wallace
David G. Walsh (Madison, Wisconsin Office)
Ronald L. Walter

PARTNERS (Continued)

(See Next Column)

FOLEY & LARDNER, *Milwaukee—Continued*

Ronald M. Wawrzyn
Robert G. Weber
Richard A. Weiss
Samuel H. Weissbard (Washington, D.C. Office)
John M. Welch, Jr. (Jacksonville, Florida Office)
Steven A. Werber (Jacksonville, Florida Office)
Robert M. Whitney (Madison, Wisconsin Office)
Edwin P. Wiley
Trevor J. Will
Allen W. Williams, Jr.
Jon M. Wilson (Orlando, Florida Office)
James A. Winkler (Chicago, Illinois Office)
Mark J. Wolfson (Tampa, Florida Office)
Ira C. Wolpert (Washington, D.C. Office)
R. Duke Woodson (Orlando, Florida Office)
Patrick M. Zabrowski
Robert J. Zimmerman (Chicago, Illinois Office)

RETIRED PARTNERS

Paul M. Barnes
James P. Brody
Norman F. Burke (Orlando, Florida Office)
George M. Chester
Eugene C. Daly
Edwin Jason Dryer (Washington, D.C. Office)
Francis V. Gay (Orlando, Florida Office)
Richard L. Harrington
William J. Kiernan, Jr.
Marvin E. Klitsner
Richard H. Miller
Orin Purintun
Thomas B. Slade, III (Jacksonville, Florida Office)
Allen M. Taylor
Edwin Fitch Walmer
Herbert P. Wiedemann
William J. Willis

OF COUNSEL

Thomas F. Clasen
Linda Heller Kamm (Washington, D.C. Office)
David C. Latham (Orlando, Florida Office)
Barbara Ann McDowell (Washington, D.C. Office)

SPECIAL COUNSEL

Ronald E. Barry
Melvin Blecher (Washington, D.C. Office)
Edward W. Brown (Not admitted in WI)
James R. Conohan (Madison, Wisconsin Office)
Michael S. Heffernan (Madison, Wisconsin Office)
Ralph H. Lane
Mark L. Langenfeld (Madison, Wisconsin Office)
Lisa A. Smith (Washington, D.C. Office)
Robert J. Walter (Orlando, Florida Office)
Harold C. Wegner (Washington, D.C. Office)

ASSOCIATES

Brian P. Akers
Laura Henry Allen (Jacksonville, Florida Office)
Bradley K. Alley (Orlando, Florida Office)
Michael J. Aprahamian
Lisa M. Arent
Evelyn C. Arkebauer (Chicago, Illinois Office)
Allen A. Arntsen (Madison, Wisconsin Office)
Phillip John Articola (Washington, D.C., Office)
Karen A. Balistreri
Anita L. Barber (Orlando, Florida Office)
Paul Bargren
David P. Barker (Orlando, Florida Office)
Michael J. Beaudine (Orlando, Florida Office)
Ann C. Becker
Robert S. Bernstein
Bradley S. Block (Chicago, Illinois Office)
Elizabeth S. Blutstein
Bernard J. Bobber
Larry J. Bonney
Wendy Reed Bosworth
Jeffrey M. Bowersock
Michael B. Brennan
Deanna S. Brocker (Chicago, Illinois Office)
Christopher W. Brownell (Chicago, Illinois Office)
Adam J. Buss (Jacksonville, Florida Office)
Christian G. Cabou
James M. Caragher
Tracy S. Carlin (Jacksonville, Florida Office)
John A. Chosy (Madison, Wisconsin Office)
Douglas B. Clark (Madison, Wisconsin Office)
John P. Cole (West Palm Beach, Florida Office)
Susan Conwell
David C. Cook (Jacksonville, Florida Office)
George R. Corrigan
Deborah A. Corsico (Washington, D.C. Office)
Jeffrey N. Costakos
Karen Kaechele Costantino (Washington, D.C., Office)
Douglas John Cropsey (Madison, Wisconsin Office)
Paul Damm
Donald A. Daugherty, Jr.
Larry J. Davis, Jr. (Tampa, Florida Office)
W. Bruce DelValle (Orlando, Florida Office)
Judith L. Dennison (Chicago, Illinois Office)
Amy E. Dombrowski (Madison, Wisconsin Office)
Patrick A. Doody (Washington, D.C. Office)
Mary A. Doty (Orlando, Florida Office)
Gary Ray Driver, Jr. (Jacksonville, Florida Office)
Joan L. Eads (Madison, Wisconsin Office)
Joseph D. Edmondson (Washington, DC Office)
William E. Eshelman (Washington, D.C. Office)
Bruce M. Essen (Chicago, Illinois Office)
Lloyd N. Fantroy (Washington, D.C. Office)
Mark R. Farris
Patrick P. Fee
Deborah L. Bundy Ferry
Kevin G. Fitzgerald (Tallahassee, Florida Office)

(See Next Column)

ASSOCIATES (Continued)

Martha Hunter Formella (Orlando, Florida Office)
Carl D. Fortner
Laura J. Gage
Julie Genovese (Madison, Wisconsin Office)
Allison C. George (Washington, D.C. Office)
Doralice M. Graff
Patricia D. Granados (Washington, D.C. Office)
Tamara S. Grant (Madison, Wisconsin Office)
Vitauts M. Gulbis (Tampa, Florida Office)
Douglas M. Hagerman
G. Michael Halfenger
Scott R. Halloin (Not admitted in WI)
John R. Hamilton (Orlando, Florida Office)
Sherri Carl Hampel
Nancy Y. Hanewicz (Madison, Wisconsin Office)
Wayne Omar Hanewicz (Madison, Wisconsin Office)
Rachelle R. Hart
Thomas E. Hartman
Steven J. Hartung
Richard W. Hawthorne (Jacksonville, Florida Office)
Thomas W. Henshue (Madison, Wisconsin Office)
Bryan B. House
Chanley T. Howell (Jacksonville, Florida Office)
Roberta F. Howell (Madison, Wisconsin Office)
Kevin E. Hyde (Jacksonville, Florida Office)
John P. Isacson, Jr. (Washington, D.C. Office)
Bradley D. Jackson (Madison, Wisconsin Office)
Mary Cynthia Atchley Jester (Washington, D.C. Office)
Mark A. Johnson
Phillip B. C. Jones (Washington, D.C. Office)
Edward P. Jordan, II (Orlando, Florida Office)
Arthur W. Jorgensen III (Madison, Wisconsin Office)
Jennifer Gugel Karron
Mark A. Kassel (Madison, Wisconsin Office)
Patricia F. Kaufman (Washington, D.C. Office)
Joongi Kim (Washington, D.C. Office)
Maria E. Gonzalez Knavel
Deborah L. Koconis
Edward M. Krishok
Mark D. Kunkel
Susan A. La Budde
Glenn Law (Washington, D.C. Office)
Kevin P. Leasure (Jacksonville, Florida Office)
Eugene M. Lee (Washington, D.C. Office)
Charles C. Lemley (Jacksonville, Florida Office)
Donna J. Lenz
Benjamin D. Levin
Melinda F. Levitt (Washington, D.C. Office)
Keith Lindenbaum
Amy Wright Littrell (Jacksonville, Florida Office)
Cindy L. LoCicero (Tampa, Florida Office)
Randall W. Lord (Tampa, Florida Office)
Karen A. Lorenzen (Orlando, Florida Office)
Katherine M. Lunsford (Madison, Wisconsin Office)
Stephen B. Maebius (Washington, D.C. Office)
Kathleen L. Maloney (Orlando, Florida Office)
Lucy Johnson Mangan (Orlando, Florida Office)
Lisa S. Mankofsky (Washington, D.C. Office)
Marc J. Marotta
Alice O. Martin (Chicago, Illinois Office)
Susan Ham Martin
Kurt S. Meckstroth
Kenneth J. Meister (Tampa, Florida Office)
Ann I. Mennell
Lili C. Metcalf (Orlando, Florida Office)
Marta T. Meyers (Madison, Wisconsin Office)
J. Hugh Middlebrooks (Jacksonville, Florida Office)
Donald A. Mihokovich (Tampa, Florida Office)
Jerry K. Miles, Jr. (Not admitted in WI)
William D. Miller (Washington, D.C. Office)
Gregory F. Monday (Madison, Wisconsin Office)
Marilyn A. Moore (West Palm Beach, Florida Office)
Michael Lynn Moore (Orlando, Florida Office)
James G. Morrow
Nancy A. Needlman (Chicago, Illinois Office)
Eric C. Nelson
Lisa Stephens Neubauer
Cynthia K. Nicholson (Washington, D.C. Office)
Jeffery S. Norman (Chicago, Illinois Office)
Hugh J. O'Halloran
Laura R. Oleck (Orlando, Florida Office)
Richard C. Peet (Washington, D.C. Office)
Don J. Pelto (Washington, D.C. Office)
Todd B. Pfister (West Palm Beach, Florida Office)
John G. Rauch (Chicago, Illinois Office)
Kelly B. Reilly
Blaine Renfert (Madison, Wisconsin Office)
Michael D. Rosenberg
David T. Rusoff (Chicago, Illinois Office)
Russell E. Ryba
Susan M. Seigle (West Palm Beach, Florida Office)
Becky B. Serafini (Chicago, Illinois Office)
Gary L. Shaffer (Washington, D.C. Office)
Andrew V. Showen (Orlando, Florida Office)
Arthur D. Sims, II (Orlando, Florida Office)
Patricia J. Slater
Anita M. Sorensen (Madison, Wisconsin Office)
J. Walter Spiva (Orlando, Florida Office)
Lynn J. Splitek (Madison, Wisconsin Office)
Ann St. Laurent (Washington, D.C. Office)
James F. Stern
Samuel B. Sterrett, Jr. (Washington, D.C. Office)
Thomas L. Stricker, Jr.
Gisèle M. Sutherland
Mark E. Toth
Xuan T. Tran
Timothy M. Truel
Terri Gillis Tucker (Tampa, Florida Office)
Christi L. Underwood (Orlando, Florida Office)
Robert A. Van Someren
John P. Veschi (Washington, D.C. and Annapolis, Maryland Office)

(See Next Column)

FOLEY & LARDNER—*Continued*

ASSOCIATES (Continued)

Scott A. Westfahl (Washington, D.C. Office)
Kevin P. Whaley
Michael C. Wieber
Adam J. Wiensch
Anne J. Williams (Tampa, Florida Office)
Marcus P. Williams (Washington, D.C. Office)
R. Mark Williamson
Edward B. Witte
David Warren Woodward (Washington, D.C. Office)
Andrew J. Wronski
Patrick S. Yoder
Steven W. Zelkowitz (Orlando, Florida Office)
Joseph N. Ziebert
Lynette M. Zigman
Walter E. Zimmerman
Gary M. Zinkgraf (Washington, D.C. Office)

For full biographical listings, see the Martindale-Hubbell Law Directory

GIBBS, ROPER, LOOTS & WILLIAMS, S.C. (AV)

735 North Water Street, 53202
Telephone: 414-273-7000
Fax: 414-273-7897

Leroy J. Burlingame (1896-1961)
Wayne J. Roper
Robert J. Loots
Clay R. Williams
John W. Hein
William J. French
George A. Evans, Jr.
Thomas P. Guszkowski
Brent E. Gregory
Terry E. Nilles
Charles P. Magyera
Stephen L. Knowles
Thomas R. Streifender
Robert L. Gegios
David J. Edquist
Beth J. Kushner
Catherine Mode Eastham

OF COUNSEL

Richard S. Gibbs
Thomas B. Fifield

William R. West
Douglas S. Knott
Kenneth A. Hoogstra
Mark S. Diestelmeier
Glen E. Lavy
Deanna C. Kress

Representative Clients: Dairyland Greyhound Park, Inc.; David White, Inc.; Family Health Plan Cooperative; Froedtert Memorial Lutheran Hospital, Inc.; Greater Milwaukee Synod of the Evangelical Lutheran Church in America; Green Bay Packaging Inc.; Kemper Clearing Corp.; Simon Aerials Inc.; Twin Disc, Incorporated; Waupaca Foundry, Inc.

For full biographical listings, see the Martindale-Hubbell Law Directory

GODFREY & KAHN, S.C. (AV)

780 North Water Street, 53202-3590
Telephone: 414-273-3500
Telecopier: 414-273-5198
Green Bay, Wisconsin Office: 333 Main Street.
Telephone: 414-432-9300.
Madison, Wisconsin Office: Suite 202, 131 West Wilson Street.
Telephone: 608-251-4670.
Oshkosh, Wisconsin Office: 219 Washington Avenue.
Telephone: 414-233-6050.
Sheboygan, Wisconsin Office: 605 North Eighth.
Telephone: 414-451-8340.

Dudley J. Godfrey, Jr.
Gerald J. Kahn
John M. Byers
Joseph M. Bernstein
William H. Alverson
Andrew R. Lauritzen
William H. Levit, Jr.
Peter M. Sommerhauser
Henry E. Fuldner
Terrence K. Knudsen
Michael Ash
Stephen L. Chernof
Charles G. Vogel
Howard A. Pollack
Richard S. Marcus
Richard J. Bliss
Kenneth C. Hunt
Howard A. Schoenfeld
Arthur J. Harrington
James G. Schweitzer
Michael J. Dwyer
Mark E. Sostarich
Robert L. Kamholz, Jr.
Stephen R. Lundeen
Debra Sadow Koenig
Thomas A. Myers
James N. Phillips
Pamela Barker
James A. Sheriff
John A. Dickens
Bradden C. Backer
John R. Peterson
Michael B. Apfeld
John F. Gaebler
Thomas E. Griggs
Kristi E. Leswing
Jane C. Schlicht
Christopher B. Noyes
Randall J. Erickson
Linda R. Olson
Elizabeth Gamsky Rich
John C. Vitek
Kevin S. Dittmar
Mark T. Ehrmann
George G. Grigel
Larry D. Lieberman
Paul A. Lucey
Patricia L. Leiker
John L. Kirtley
Robert C. Risch, Jr.
Daniel D. Seibel
J. Gardner Govan
William E. Duffin
Karen M. Schapiro
Sally R. Bentley
Carol A. Gehl
Joseph E. Dannecker
Scott A. Moehrke
Mark J. Backe
Kristin A. Roeper
Brian L. Fielkow
Anna M. Geyso
Thomas P. DeMuth
Kim E. Patterson
Steven S. Bartelt
Raymond J. Manista
Diane M. Marchik
Nicholas P. Wahl

(See Next Column)

Jeffrey S. Sokol
Daniel B. Geraghty
John L. Clancy
Timothy K. Oleszczuk
Kelley Kimmel Falkner
David G. Peterson
Joan D. Klimpel
Tonit M. Cole
Michael J. Pendleton, Jr.
Scott C. Frandle
Daniel A. Ryan
Thomas O. Rabenn
Michael D. Atella
Pamela M. Krill
Timothy A. Otto
Peter J. Faust
Jacqueline L. Emanuel
Joseph R. Cincotta
Susan J. Cray
Mark C. Witt
Ruth E. Booher
Roger T. Lambert

OF COUNSEL

Michael P. Waxman

For full biographical listings, see the Martindale-Hubbell Law Directory

MICHAEL, BEST & FRIEDRICH (AV)

100 East Wisconsin Avenue, 53202-4108
Telephone: 414-271-6560
Telecopier: 414-277-0656
Cable Address: "Mibef"
Madison, Wisconsin Office: One South Pinckney Street, Firstar Plaza, P.O. Box 1806, 53701-1806.
Telephone: 608-257-3501.
Telecopier: 283-2275.
Chicago, Illinois Office: 135 South LaSalle Street, Suite 1610, 60603-4391.
Telephone: 312-845-5800.
Telecopier: 312-845-5828.
Affiliated Law Firm: Edward D. Heffernan, Penthouse One, 1019 19th Street, N.W., Washington, D.C. 20036.
Telephone: 202-331-7444.

PARTNERS

Roy C. LaBudde
John K. MacIver
Frank J. Pelisek
James S. Levin
Joseph A. Gemignani
Robert E. Clemency
Thomas G. A. Herz
Robert A. Teper
Andrew O. Riteris
Marshall R. Berkoff
John J. McHugh (Resident Partner, Chicago, Illinois Office)
Jacob L. Bernheim
David R. Olson
Rickard T. O'Neil
F. William Haberman
Robert A. Schnur
David W. Croysdale
Lee J. Geronime
Jerome H. Kringel
David J. Cannon
Scott H. Engroff
Thomas E. Obenberger
Arvid A. Sather (Resident Partner, Madison, Wisconsin Office)
David J. Hanson (Resident Partner, Madison, Wisconsin Office)
David E. Leichtfuss
Glenn A. Busé
John R. Sapp
Paul E. Prentiss
Jeffrey L. Abraham
W. Charles Jackson
Tod B. Linstroth (Resident Partner, Madison, Wisconsin Office)
Gordon K. Miller
Donald A. Schoenfeld
David B. Smith
John A. Busch
Gregory G. Johnson
John C. Lapinski
Charles P. Graupner
Robert J. Johannes
Michael E. Husmann
Thomas W. Scrivner
Toni Lee Bonney
Nelson D. Flynn (Resident Partner, Madison, Wisconsin Office)
Hal Karas
Peggy E. Brever
Nancy Leary Haggerty
Bartlett C. Petersen
Charles G. Crosse IV
Paul S. Medved
Thomas E. Klancnik (Resident Partner, Madison, Wisconsin Office)
Thomas P. Godar (Resident Partner, Madison, Wisconsin Office)
William F. White (Resident Partner, Madison, Wisconsin Office)
Richard J. Canter
J. Lewis Perlson
Fred Wiviott
Lorna J. Granger
Gary A. Ahrens
David R. Price
David V. Meany
Nathaniel A. Hoffman
José A. Olivieri
Charles A. Brizzolara (Resident Partner, Chicago, Illinois Office)
William E. Snyder (Resident Partner, Chicago, Illinois Office)
Jesse S. Ishikawa (Resident Partner, Madison, Wisconsin Office)
James R. Troupis (Resident Partner, Madison, Wisconsin Office)
Robert W. Mulcahy
Peter L. Coffey
Chris J. Trebatoski
Robert D. Rothacker, Jr.
Tracey L. Klein
Ann Ustad Smith (Resident Partner, Madison, Wisconsin Office)
Richard J. Langer (Resident Partner, Madison, Wisconsin Office)
Paul Jordan Cherner (Resident Partner, Chicago, Illinois Office)
Robert S. Beiser (Resident Partner, Chicago, Illinois Office)
Linda H. Bochert (Resident Partner, Madison, Wisconsin Office)
Raymond R. Krueger
Geoffrey R. Morgan
Timothy G. Schally
Eric E. Hobbs
Paul G. Hoffman
Sean Lanphier
John E. Flanagan
Kristine H. Cleary
Paul F. Linn

(See Next Column)

MICHAEL, BEST & FRIEDRICH, *Milwaukee—Continued*

PARTNERS (Continued)

Charles V. Sweeney (Resident Partner, Madison, Wisconsin Office)
Robyn S. Shapiro
Saul N. Winsten
Bret A. Roge
Donald P. Gallo
Donovan W. Riley (Resident Partner, Chicago, Illinois Office)
Richard C. Glesner (Resident Partner, Madison, Wisconsin Office)
Thomas C. Judge (Resident Partner, Chicago, Illinois Office)
John E. Noel (Resident Partner, Chicago, Illinois Office)
Robert W. Cleveland (Resident Partner, Madison, Wisconsin Office)
Kate M. Fleming
Joshua L. Gimbel
Kimberly A. Kunz
Donald F. Kiesling
Michael A. Gral
JoAnne M. Denison (Resident Partner, Chicago, Illinois Office)
Casimir F. Laska

OF COUNSEL

Joseph R. Filachek
James C. Mallatt
Thomas C. Hynes (Not admitted in WI)
Bayard H. Michael

ASSOCIATES

Julie Gorens-Winston
David J. Winkler
David B. Kennedy
Jonathan O. Levine
Dyann L. Bumpke
Scott C. Beightol
Christiane M. Loidl (Resident Associate, Madison, Wisconsin Office)
Timothy M. Kelley
Eric H. Rumbaugh
Paul D. Windsor
Peter R. Reckmeyer
Grant C. Killoran
Kenneth D. Wahlin
Joseph A. Pickart
Mitchell W. Quick
Paul E. Benson
Steven P. Means (Resident Associate, Madison, Wisconsin Office)
Raymond P. Taffora (Resident Associate, Madison, Wisconsin Office)
Jonathan D. Kron
Lynda R. Templen (Resident Associate, Madison, Wisconsin Office)
David A. Crass (Resident Associate, Madison, Wisconsin Office)
Paul J. Dombrowski (Resident Associate, Madison, Wisconsin Office)
Douglas P. Dehler
David A. Krutz
Jonathan H. Margolies
Daniel A. Kaufman (Resident Associate, Chicago, Illinois Office)
Roger D. Strode, Jr.
Richard A. Latta (Resident Associate, Madison, Wisconsin Office)
Jon G. Furlow (Resident Associate, Madison, Wisconsin Office)
Thomas J. Basting, Jr.
Teresa M. Levy
Thomas A. Miller
Peter K. Richardson
Billie Jean Strandt
Randall J. Ney (Resident Associate, Madison, Wisconsin Office)
Kimberly A. Reinecke (Resident Associate, Madison, Wisconsin Office)
Kimberly Cash Tate (Resident Associate, Madison, Wisconsin Office)
Lisa S. Keyes (Resident Associate, Madison, Wisconsin Office)
Jeffrey D. Hunt
Sara M. Berman
Kurt T. Oosterhouse
David W. Runke
Robin M. Sheridan
Cynthia E. Smith
James Patrick Thomas
Lisa M. Toussaint
Troy A. Hilliard (Resident Associate, Madison, Wisconsin Office)
Eric M. McLeod (Resident Associate, Madison, Wisconsin Office)
Amy O. Bruchs (Resident Associate, Madison, Wisconsin Office)
Steven L. Ritt (Resident Associate, Madison, Wisconsin Office)
Thomas Patrick Heneghan (Resident Associate, Madison, Wisconsin Office)
David K. Hoover
Lauren L. Azar (Resident, Associate, Madison, Wisconsin Office)
J. Donald Best (Resident Associate, Madison, Wisconsin Office)
Scott J. Campbell
Karen G. Esser
Alexander P. Fraser
John J. Kalter
Christy Brown Leflore
John R. Mills (Not admitted in WI)
Mark S. Poker
Linda J. Sauser
Paul R. Seifert
William D Talbert
Mark C. Treter
Julie A. Zavoral

For full biographical listings, see the Martindale-Hubbell Law Directory

QUARLES & BRADY (AV)

411 East Wisconsin Avenue, 53202-4497
Telephone: 414-277-5000
Cable Address: "Lawdock"
Fax: 414-271-3552.
TWX: 910-262-3426
Madison, Wisconsin Office: Firstar Plaza, One South Pinckney Street, P.O. Box 2113.
Telephone: 608-251-5000.
Fax: 608-251-9166.

(See Next Column)

West Palm Beach, Florida Office: 222 Lakeview Avenue, 4th Floor.
Telephone: 407-653-5000.
Fax: 407-653-5333.
Naples, Florida Office: Barnett Center, 4501 Tamiami Trail North.
Telephone: 813-262-5959.
Fax: 813-434-4999.
Phoenix, Arizona Office: One Camelback Building, One East Camelback Road, Suite 400.
Telephone: 602-230-5500.
Fax: 602-230-5598.

Louis Quarles (1883-1972)
Bernard V. Brady (1891-1977)

MEMBERS OF FIRM

(ALPHABETICALLY BY YEAR OF ADMISSION TO BAR)

Arthur H. Laun, Jr.
John S. Sammond (Resident, West Palm Beach, Florida Office)
David L. MacGregor
James Urdan
Jackson M. Bruce, Jr.
Allan W. Leiser
Roger P. Paulsen
Harry G. Holz
Robert J. Kalupa
Thad F. Kryshak
Charles Q. Kamps
Thomas W. Ehrmann
Anthony S. Earl (Resident, Madison Office)
Fred G. Groiss
Thomas O. Kloehn
Richard C. Ninneman
Samuel J. Recht
Jeremy C. Shea (Resident, Madison Office)
James A. McSwigan (Resident, West Palm Beach, Florida Office)
Donald S. Taitelman
P. Robert Fannin (Resident, Phoenix, Arizona Office)
John A. Hazelwood
Ross R. Kinney
John S. Holbrook, Jr. (Resident, Madison Office)
Peter J. Lettenberger
Arthur B. Harris
Henry J. Loos
Michael J. Spector
George K. Whyte, Jr.
Robert H. Diaz, Jr.
David L. Kinnamon
J. Rodman Steele, Jr. (Resident, West Palm Beach, Florida Office)
Michael L. Zaleski (Resident, Madison Office)
Anthony W. Asmuth, III
Wayne E. Babler, Jr.
Thomas E. Maloney (Resident, Naples, Florida Office)
Thomas W. O'Brien
W. Stuart Parsons
Jeffrey B. Bartell (Resident, Madison Office)
Frank J. Daily
Charles W. Herf (Resident, Phoenix, Arizona Office)
David E. Jarvis
Larry J. Martin
David L. Petersen (Resident, West Palm Beach, Florida Office)
James R. Cole (Resident, Madison Office)
Steven R. Duback
Conrad G. Goodkind
Lawrence J. Jost
Patrick M. Ryan
Barry E. Sammons
Ronald L. Wallenfang
Michael S. Weiden (Resident, Madison Office)
Theodore F. Zimmer
John A. Casey
Bruce C. Davidson
P. Robert Moya (Resident, Phoenix, Arizona Office)
Stephen E. Richman
Gerald E. Connolly
Anthony H. Driessen
James D. Friedman
J. Paul Jacobson
Peter C. Karegeannes
John R. Maynard
William M. Shattuck (Resident, Phoenix, Arizona Office)
James H. Baxter III
Quinn W. Martin
Michael J. McGovern
F. Joseph McMackin, III (Resident, Naples, Florida Office)
Ned R. Nashban (Resident, West Palm Beach, Florida Office)
Robert L. Titley
Thomas J. Phillips
Robert T. Bailes (Resident, Phoenix, Arizona Office)
Bruce R. Bauer
Darryl S. Bell
Michael J. Conlan
James F. Daly
John W. Daniels, Jr.
George E. Haas
Timothy G. Hains (Resident, Naples, Florida Office)
Alyce C. Katayama
John H. Lhost
Charles W. Littell (Resident, West Palm Beach, Florida Office)
Michael L. Roshar
Paul R. Schilling
O. Thomas Armstrong
Judith M. Bailey (Resident, Phoenix, Arizona Office)
Andrew M. Barnes
Robert E. Doyle, Jr. (Resident, Naples, Florida Office)
Matthew J. Flynn
Roy L. Prange, Jr. (Resident, Madison Office)
Michael H. Schaalman
Patrick W. Schmidt
John T. Bannen
Fred Gants (Resident, Madison Office)
Mary Pat Ninneman
Jon E. Pettibone (Resident, Phoenix, Arizona Office)
Phillip E. Recht
Roger K. Spencer (Resident, Phoenix, Arizona Office)
Eric J. Van Vugt
Warren S. Blumenthal
Peter C. Christianson
Patrick J. Goebel
Molly K. Martin (Resident, Madison Office)
Michael S. McCauley
Patricia K. McDowell
Nicholas J. Seay (Resident, Madison Office)
John T. Whiting (Resident, Madison Office)
Carolyn A. Gnaedinger
Joseph D. Masterson
William D. McEachern (Resident, West Palm Beach, Florida Office)
Carl R. Schwartz
Peter A. Terry (Resident, Phoenix, Arizona Office)
Paul J. Tilleman
David B. Kern
Ely A. Leichtling
Jeffrey Morris
Ann M. Murphy
John A. Rothstein
Arthur A. Vogel, Jr.
Kenneth V. Hallett

(See Next Column)

QUARLES & BRADY—*Continued*

MEMBERS OF FIRM
(ALPHABETICALLY BY YEAR OF ADMISSION TO BAR) (Continued)

William H. Harbeck
Charles H. McMullen
Paul M. Platte (Resident, West Palm Beach, Florida Office)
Elizabeth A. Orelup
Leo J. Salvatori (Resident, Naples, Florida Office)
Donald K. Schott (Resident, Madison Office)
Ralph V. Topinka (Resident, Madison Office)
David B. Bartel
David G. Beauchamp (Resident, Phoenix, Arizona Office)
David R. Cross
Julianna Ebert
Mary N. Fertl
Glenn Spencer Bacal (Resident, Phoenix, Arizona Office)
Kimberly Leach Johnson (Resident, Naples, Florida Office)
Nancy Meissner Kennedy
Brian G. Lanser
Daniel L. Muchow (Resident, Phoenix, Arizona Office)
Thomas A. Simonis
David D. Wilmoth
Paul M. Gales (Resident, Phoenix, Arizona Office)
Michael J. Gonring
Kathleen A. Gray
Michael A. Levey
Lauri D. Morris (Resident, Madison Office)
Elizabeth G. Nowakowski
William J. Toman (Resident, Madison Office)
Michael K. Bresson
John D. Franzini
Marta S. Levine
Thomas P. McElligott
Gregory A. Nelson (Resident, West Palm Beach, Florida Office)
Nancy K. Peterson
Robert H. Duffy
Steven P. Emerick (Resident, Phoenix, Arizona Office)
Michael D. Zeka
Mark A. Kircher
Fredrick G. Lautz
David P. Olson
Sheila M. Reynolds
Gerald L. Shelley (Resident, Phoenix, Arizona Office)
Daniel E. Conley

OF COUNSEL

Roger C. Minahan
Richard R. Teschner
Paul Noelke
Patrick W. Cotter
A. William Asmuth, Jr.
Richard W. Cutler
James C. Mallien
Michael E. Crane (Not admitted in WI)
John T. Harrington
Laurence E. Gooding, Jr.
Elwin J. Zarwell
Neal E. Madisen
Dale L. Sorden
Laurence C. Hammond, Jr.
William A. Stearns

ASSOCIATES

Neil E. Hamilton
Lynn Frances Chandler (Resident, Naples, Florida Office)
Patrick J. Schoen
Lindy P. Funkhouser (Mr.) (Resident, Phoenix, Arizona Office)
William G. Shofstall (Resident, West Palm Beach, Florida Office)
Waltraud A. Arts (Resident, Madison Office)
Sally C. Merrell
Erica M. Eisinger (Resident, Madison Office)
Ann K. Comer
Keith M. Baxter
Jane F. Clokey
Jerome R. Kerkman
Dana L. O'Brien
Cynthia L. Jewett (Resident, Phoenix, Arizona Office)
Robert S. Bornhoft (Resident, Phoenix, Arizona Office)
James Brennan
Kathryn M. Coates
Kevin A. Delorey (Resident, Madison Office)
Jeffrey L. Elverman
Mary Z. Horton (Not admitted in WI; Resident, Phoenix, Arizona Office)
John D. Humphreville (Resident, Naples, Florida Office)
Scott L. Langlois
Francis H. LoCoco
Jeffrey O. Davis
Chris K. Gawart
Kenneth J. Hansen (Resident, Madison Office)
Stuart S. Mermelstein (Resident, West Palm Beach, Florida Office)
Michelle M. Thorpe (Resident, Phoenix, Arizona Office)
Sharon S. Moyer (Resident, Phoenix, Arizona Office)
Benjamin R. Norris (Resident, Phoenix, Arizona Office)
Jennifer Vogel Powers
Joseph E. Puchner
David L. Bourne
Nancy Berz Colman (Resident, West Palm Beach, Florida Office)
N. (Norrie) Daroga
Louis D. D'Agostino (Resident, Naples, Florida Office)
Christopher H. Kallaher
Lorraine J. Koeper
Anthony A. Tomaselli (Resident, Madison Office)
Fran C. Windsor (Resident, Phoenix, Arizona Office)
Susan A. Cerbins
Kevin A. Denti (Resident, Naples, Florida Office)
John E. Dunn
Margaret C. Kelsey
Andra J. Palmer (Resident, Madison Office)
Colleen A. Scherkenbach (Resident, Phoenix, Arizona Office)
Jeffrey K. Spoerk
Charles M. Weber
Patricia M. Anania (Resident, Phoenix, Arizona Office)
Joseph W. Bain (Resident, West Palm Beach, Florida Office)
Jean C. Baker
Laurene M. Brooks
Mark A. Dotson
Gregg M. Formella
Carmella A. Huser
George J. Marek
Jose L. Martinez (Resident, Phoenix, Arizona Office)
Michael J. Ostermeyer
Robert J. Sacco (Resident, West Palm Beach, Florida Office)
Walter J. Skipper
Deborah L. Skurulsky
Rebecca A. Speckhard

(See Next Column)

ASSOCIATES (Continued)

Sandra L. Tarver (Resident, Madison Office)
Valerie L. Bailey-Rihn (Resident, Madison Office)
Elizabeth A. Dougherty (Resident, West Palm Beach, Florida Office)
Wendy L. Gerlach (Resident, Phoenix, Arizona Office)
Kurt A. Johnson (Resident, Phoenix, Arizona Office)
Mitchell S. Moser
Mark Hubert Muller (Resident, Naples, FLorida Office)
Tracy D. Taylor (Resident, Phoenix, Arizona Office)
Bennett Berson (Resident, Madison, Wisconsin Office)
Kevin P. Crooks
Rosanne M. Duane (Not admitted in WI)
Sean D. Garrison (Resident, Phoenix, Arizona Office)
Amy M. Hindman
Michael A. Jaskolski
Letha Joseph
Lisa A. Lyons
Jennifer N. MacLennan (Resident, Phoenix, Arizona Office)
Gregory L. Mayback (Resident, West Palm Beach, Florida Office)
Nora M. Platt
Harold O.M. Rocha
David G. Ryser
Guri Ademi
Gregory A. Baxley
Ronni M. Flannery
Katherine H. Grebe
Michael M. Grebe
Daniel M. Janssen
Cheryl A. Johnson
Colin M. Lancaster
Michael Lappin
Amy O'Melia-Endres (Resident, Phoenix, Arizona Office)
Pamela M. Ploor
Mark A. Sanders
Tia Tartaglione
James M. Brennan
Kathleen P. Browe
Bonnie J. Buhrow
Elizabeth L.R. Donley (Resident, Madison, Wisconsin Office)
Juan Carlos Ferrucho (Resident, West Palm Beach, Florida Office)
Patricia A. Hintz
James R. Hoy
Virginia H. Jones
Linda E. Jorge (Resident, Naples, Florida Office)
Joan Phillips

LEGAL SUPPORT PERSONNEL

LEGAL ASSISTANTS

Gayle L Adrian
Susan T. Barker
Tracy A. Berrones
Ronald J. Burtch
Richard P. Carney
Teresa M. Como
Laura Dutscheck
Philip M. Gatewood
Diane C. Haase
Barbara A. Henes
Mary Ann Hutchinson
Cynthia Z. Jorgensen
Barbara A. Juran
Kaye E. Kern
Carolyn P. Kinney
Patricia M. Murphy
Susan M. Nygren
Jean Rakers
A. R. Schulz
Kenneth M. Smith
Lola Surwille
Deborah A. Thomson
Cynthia Vick
Corrine L. Weber
Susan M. Weber
Jane A. Welch
Kristine G. Wilson

BUSINESS MANAGEMENT SUPPORT GROUP

John J. Peterburs (Executive Director)
Linda J. Hornbeck
Robert H. Klein (Director, Communications)
Mary V. Oelstrom (Director, Human Resources)
Thomas R. Schoewe
Jack H. Washow

For full biographical listings, see the Martindale-Hubbell Law Directory

REINHART, BOERNER, VAN DEUREN, NORRIS & RIESELBACH, S.C. (AV)

1000 North Water Street, P.O. Box 92900, 53202-0900
Telephone: 414-298-1000
Facsimile: 414-298-8097
Denver, Colorado Office: One Norwest Center, 1700 Lincoln Street, Suite 3725.
Telephone: 303-831-0909.
Fax: 303-831-4805.
Madison, Wisconsin Office: 7617 Mineral Point Road, 53701-2020.
Telephone: 608-283-7900.
Fax: 608-283-7919.
Washington, D.C. Office: 601 Pennsylvania Avenue, N.W., North Building, Suite 750.
Telephone: 202-393-3636.
Fax: 202-393-0796.

John M. Reinhart (1923-1982)
Roger L. Boerner
Richard A. Van Deuren
Richard H. Norris III
Allen N. Rieselbach
Paul V. Lucke
Robert E. Meldman
Arthur F. Lubke, Jr.
Donald J. Christl
Thomas E. Funk
David A. Erne
Robert E. Bellin
William R. Steinmetz
Burton A. Wagner (Resident, Madison Office)
Gary A. Hollman
John A. Erich
Jeffrey R. Fuller
Frederic G. Friedman
Delos N. Lutton
Robert E. Dallman
Mary A. Brauer (Resident, Denver, Colorado Office)
Stephen T. Jacobs
Chester P. Schwartz (Resident, Denver, Colorado Office)
Scott W. Hansen
Joseph Semo (Resident, Washington, D.C. Office)
Michael H. Simpson

(See Next Column)

REINHART, BOERNER, VAN DEUREN, NORRIS & RIESELBACH S.C.,
Milwaukee—Continued

John L. Schliesmann
Steven D. Huff
William F. Flynn
Peter C. Blain
Bruce T. Block
Jeffrey P. Clark
Daniel J. Brink
Michael T. Pepke
John H. Zawadsky (Resident, Madison, Wisconsin Office)
Peter L. Gardon (Resident, Madison, Wisconsin Office)
Michael D. Rechtin
Richard P. Carr
Robert F. Henkle, Jr.
Richard W. Graber
Anne Willis Reed
Robert K. Sholl
Kristin M. Bergstrom
Lawrence J. Burnett
John A. Herbers
Francis W. Deisinger
Jerome M. Janzer
Ulice Payne, Jr.
Philip P. Mann
Kevin J. Howley
Anthony J. Handzlik
Mark L. Metz
Steven P. Bogart
Joseph J. Balistreri
Timothy G. Atkinson (Resident, Denver, Colorado Office)
Timothy A. Nettesheim
John M. Van Lieshout
James M. Bedore
Michael R. Smith
Robert J. Heath
Arnold R. Kaplan (Resident, Denver, Colorado Office)
Herbert A. Delap (Resident, Denver, Colorado Office)
Donald Alford Weadon, Jr. (Resident, Washington, D.C. Office)
Denise P. Goergen
Stephen C. Peters (Resident, Denver, Colorado Office)
Mary H. Michal (Resident, Madison, Wisconsin Office)

OF COUNSEL

Thomas M. Stanton (Resident, Neenah Office)

Jill M. Koch
Albert S. Orr
R. Timothy Muth
Steven J. Cottingham
William T. Shroyer
Thomas J. Nolte
Anne Morgan Hlavacka
Kathleen S. Donius
David D. Pavek (Resident, Denver, Colorado Office)
Martin J. McLaughlin
Larri J. Broomfield
Timothy P. Reardon
Christine L. Thierfelder
Michael D. Jankowski
William P. Scott
Carleen T. Clark (Resident, Denver, Colorado Office)
David R. Krosner
William R. Cummings
Bennett E. Choice
David M. Sanders
Rodney D. DeKruif
R. Bruce Phillips (Resident, Denver, Colorado Office)
Susan A. Turner (Resident, Washington, D.C. Office)
John R. Austin
Catherine L. Davies
David J. Sisson
Patrick J. Hodan
John E. Mossberg
Martin G. Flyke
Margaret M. Derus
Paul L. Winter (Not admitted in WI)
Katherine McConahay Nealon
Carolyn A. Sullivan
Vincent J. Beres
Peter W. Becker
Colleen D. Ball
Dean E. Mabie
John E. Schembari
Gerald L. Fellows
Geri Krupp-Gordon
Daniel J. La Fave
David G. Hanson
Matthew J. Flanary
Thomas A. Cabush
Steven S. Gensler
Peggy E. McCloud
Robert A. Kukuljan
Jennifer R. D'Amato
Michael R. Miller
Jeffrey S. Rheeling
Eric S. Tower (Resident, Madison, Wisconsin Office)
Deborah C. Tomczyk
Patricia S. Novacheck
Wendy J. Keith (Not admitted in WI)
John N. Kurowski
James L. Frasher
Susan B. Stein
Robert Arendell

LEGAL SUPPORT PERSONNEL

Karen Ambelang
Sheryl Deer
Ellen Heib
Colleen Held-Messana
Dwayne Krager
Richard Laswell
Kellene Marzhal
Cindy Miilu
Kathy Minter
Dianne Ostrowski
Donna Paulsen
Mary Ellen Raney
Eileen Revers
Deborah Russell
Jeanne Scherkenbach
Colleen McGuire Schmitz
Deanna Shimko-Herman
Ruth Smith
Bradley Snyder

For full biographical listings, see the Martindale-Hubbell Law Directory

---

*MONROE,** Green Co.

KITTELSEN, BARRY, ROSS, WELLINGTON AND THOMPSON (AV)

916 17th Avenue, 53566
Telephone: 608-325-2191
Fax: 608-325-7968
Argyle, Wisconsin Office: Rossing Building.
Telephone: 608-543-3636.
Albany, Wisconsin Office: 205 East Main Street.
Telephone: 608-862-3271.
Monticello, Wisconsin Office: 139 North Main Street, P.O. Box 436.
Telephone: 608-938-4381.

(See Next Column)

MEMBERS OF FIRM

Rodney O. Kittelsen
R. Finley Barry
Carl W. Ross
Charles R. Wellington
Scott Thompson

ASSOCIATES

Joseph Pecora

Representative Clients: American Family Insurance Co.; Heritage Insurance; Bank One Monroe; Knight Manufacturing Corp.; The Monroe Clinic; Darlington Dairy Supply Co., Inc.; Lugano Cheese Co., Inc.; Monroe Board of Education; Green County Broadcasting Corp.

For full biographical listings, see the Martindale-Hubbell Law Directory

---

*MONTELLO,** Marquette Co. — (Refer to Fond du Lac)

NEENAH, Winnebago Co.

DI RENZO AND BOMIER (AV)

231 East Wisconsin Avenue, P.O. Box 788, 54957-0788
Telephone: 414-725-8464
Fax: 414-725-8568

MEMBERS OF FIRM

Robert C. Di Renzo
Jerome T. Bomier
Dennis L. Simon
Philip A. Munroe
Howard T. Healy
Roy N. Fine
Samuel J. Bomier

ASSOCIATES

Ross A. Sharkey
R. Valjon Anderson

Representative Clients: Kimberly-Clark Corporation, Neenah, WI; Banta Publishing Co., Inc., Menasha, WI; Phillips Plastics Corp., Phillips, WI; Kennedy Center for the Hip and Knee, S.C., Neenah, Wi.; Great Northern Corporation, Appleton, WI; Bank One, Neenah, WI; Geo. A. Whiting Paper Co., Menasha, WI; Bergstrom Chevrolet-Buick-Cadillac, Inc., Neenah and Appleton, WI; Paper Valley Hotel and Conference Center, Inc., Appleton, WI.

For full biographical listings, see the Martindale-Hubbell Law Directory

---

*NEILLSVILLE,** Clark Co. — (Refer to Eau Claire)

*OCONTO,** Oconto Co. — (Refer to Marinette)

*OSHKOSH,** Winnebago Co.

GODFREY & KAHN, S.C. (AV)

219 Washington Avenue, P.O. Box 1278, 54902-1278
Telephone: 414-233-6050
Telecopier: 414-233-8528
Milwaukee, Wisconsin Office: 780 North Water Street.
Telephone: 414-273-3500.
Green Bay, Wisconsin Office: 333 Main Street.
Telephone: 414-432-9300.
Madison, Wisconsin Office: Suite 202, 131 West Wilson Street.
Telephone: 608-251-4670.
Sheboygan, Wisconsin Office: 605 North Eighth.
Telephone: 414-451-8340.

Edward J. Williams
James R. Macy
John E. Thiel
Timothy M. Whiting

For full biographical listings, see the Martindale-Hubbell Law Directory

---

PARK FALLS, Price Co. — (Refer to Rhinelander)

*PHILLIPS,** Price Co. — (Refer to Rhinelander)

*PORT WASHINGTON,** Ozaukee Co. — (Refer to West Bend)

*PRAIRIE DU CHIEN,** Crawford Co. — (Refer to Madison)

*RACINE,** Racine Co.

CAPWELL AND BERTHELSEN (AV)

601 Lake Avenue, P.O. Box 247, 53401
Telephone: 414-637-1266
Facsimile: 414-637-1831
Brookfield, Wisconsin Office: 400 North Executive Drive, Suite 472.
Telephone: 414-789-2735.
Fax: 414-785-4184.

Rex Capwell
Gilbert J. Berthelsen
David J. Nolden
John V. Casanova
Terrance L. Kallenbach
John E. Grahovac

Philip Lehner
Camela M. Meyer
Linda S. Isnard
Roxanne Felizmena

Representative Clients: Bank One (Racine, Kenosha and Milwaukee Counties); Racine Unified School District; Merril Area Public Schools; Racine County Business Development Corporation; General Casualty Cos.; Kemper Insurance Group; Hanover Insurance Co.; GRE Insurance Co.; Economy Fire and Casualty; American States Insurance.

For full biographical listings, see the Martindale-Hubbell Law Directory

Racine—Continued

HOSTAK, HENZL & BICHLER, S.C. (AV)

840 Lake Avenue, P.O. Box 516, 53401-0516
Telephone: 414-632-7541
Milwaukee: 933-6866
Fax: 414-632-1256

Kenneth F. Hostak
Robert R. Henzl
Robert H. Bichler
James W. Hill
Stephen J. Smith
Thomas M. Devine
Roy J. Josten
Timothy J. Pruitt
Susan M. Perry
Barbara A. Kuhl
David A. Wolfe
JoAnne Breese-Jaeck
Brenda J. Stugelmeyer

Representative Clients: Advance Mechanical Contractors, Inc.; Andis Co.; Christ Iron Works, Inc.; Marino Construction Co., Inc.; Warren Industries, Inc.; M & I Bank of Racine; American Family Mutual Insurance Co.; Wisconsin Health Care Liability Plan; Bud Orth & Associates, Inc.; St. Luke's Memorial Hospital, Inc.

For full biographical listings, see the Martindale-Hubbell Law Directory

PAULSON, HANKEL, BRUNER & NICHOLS, S.C. (AV)

6921 Mariner Drive, 53406
Telephone: 414-886-0206
Fax: 414-886-6748
Union Grove, Wisconsin Office: 1222 Main Street.
Telephone: 414-878-3749.

David W. Paulson
Robert E. Hankel
Edward J. Bruner, Jr.
Harrison W. Nichols (Resident, Union Grove Office)
W Richard Chiapete

For full biographical listings, see the Martindale-Hubbell Law Directory

*RHINELANDER,** Oneida Co.

ECKERT & STINGL (AV)

158 South Anderson Street, P.O. Box 1247, 54501-1247
Telephone: 715-369-1624
FAX: 715-369-1273

MEMBERS OF FIRM

Michael L. Eckert
Michael J. Stingl
James O. Moermond, III
Timothy B. Melms

OF COUNSEL

John R. Lund

Reference: M & I Merchants Bank.

For full biographical listings, see the Martindale-Hubbell Law Directory

JOHNSON, HOULIHAN, PAULSON & PRIEBE, S.C. (AV)

28 North Stevens Street, P.O. Box 1148, 54501
Telephone: 715-369-5060
FAX: 715-369-1017
Minocqua, Wisconsin Office: Professional & Financial Plaza, Highway 51 and 70, PO Box 630.
Telephone: 715-356-1422.
FAX: 715-356-1446.

James A. Johnson
John C. Houlihan
C. Gordon Paulson
John H. Priebe

For full biographical listings, see the Martindale-Hubbell Law Directory

O'MELIA, SCHIEK & MCELDOWNEY, S.C. (AV)

O'Melia Building, 4 South Stevens Street, P.O. Box 797, 54501
Telephone: 715-369-2456
Fax: 715-369-1126
Crandon, Wisconsin Office: 503 South Lake Avenue, P.O. Box 36.
Telephone: 715-478-3636.

A. J. O'Melia (1889-1964)
Walter F. Kaye (1897-1969)
Clarence J. Simon (1911-1974)
William A. Melby (1938-1982)
Donald C. O'Melia (1917-1991)
John H. Schiek
John F. O'Melia
John F. O'Melia, II
Todd R. McEldowney
Michael F. Roe
Jeffrey T. Jackomino
Lawrence J. Wiesneske
Leon D. Stenz

Attorneys for: USAA Casualty Insurance; American Family Insurance; General Casualty Co.; Heritage Mutual Insurance Co.; Chicago Title Insurance Co.; Security Savings and Loan Association; School District of Wabeno; Rhinelander Telephone Co.; Dairymen's Country Club.

For full biographical listings, see the Martindale-Hubbell Law Directory

*RICHLAND CENTER,** Richland Co. — (Refer to La Crosse)

*SHAWANO,** Shawano Co. — (Refer to Wausau)

*SHEBOYGAN,** Sheboygan Co.

GODFREY & KAHN, S.C. (AV)

605 North Eighth, P.O. Box 1287, 53082-1287
Telephone: 414-451-8340
Telecopier: 414-451-8344
Milwaukee, Wisconsin Office: 780 North Water Street.
Telephone: 414-273-3500.
Green Bay, Wisconsin Office: 333 Main Street.
Telephone: 414-432-9300.
Madison, Wisconsin Office: Suite 202, 131 West Wilson Street.
Telephone: 608-251-4670.
Oshkosh, Wisconsin Office: 219 Washington Avenue.
Telephone: 414-233-6050.

Paul C. Hemmer

For full biographical listings, see the Martindale-Hubbell Law Directory

ROHDE, DALES, MELZER, TE WINKLE & GASS (AV)

607 North Eighth Street, 7th Floor, 53081-4556
Telephone: 414-458-5501
Telecopier: 414-458-5874
Branch Offices: Sheboygan Falls and Plymouth, Wisconsin.

MEMBERS OF FIRM

Ronald P. Dales
Robert T. Melzer
William P. Te Winkle
David O. Gass
Richard L. Binder
K. Allan Voss
Peter R. Mayer

ASSOCIATES

Michael J. Vowinkel (Resident, Sheboygan Falls Office)
Melvin H. Blanke (Resident, Plymouth Office)
Beth A. Froelich
E. Anthony Fessler

Representative Clients: Norwest Bank of Wisconsin; Hartford Accident & Indemnity Company; H. C. Prange Co.; Polar Ware Co.; Hayssen Manufacturing Co.; Optenburg Inc.; Brillion Iron Works; Bemis Manufacturing Co.; Gabe's Construction Co., Inc.

For full biographical listings, see the Martindale-Hubbell Law Directory

*SHELL LAKE,** Washburn Co. — (Refer to Superior)

SHERWOOD, Calumet Co. — (Refer to Superior)

*SPARTA,** Monroe Co.

GLEISS, LOCANTE & GLEISS (AV)

111 South Court Street, P.O. Box 379, 54656
Telephone: 608-269-2171
FAX: 608-269-7907

MEMBERS OF FIRM

William M. Gleiss (1890-1961)
William J. Gleiss
Shari LePage Locante
Elizabeth J. Gleiss

ASSOCIATES

Andrew C. Kaftan

Attorneys for: First Bank of Sparta; Union National Bank & Trust, Sparta; Valley Bank Western, F.S.B.; Sparta Manufacturing Co.; American Family Insurance Co.; Highlight, Inc.; Hamburg Mutual Insurance.

For full biographical listings, see the Martindale-Hubbell Law Directory

SPOONER, Washburn Co. — (Refer to Superior)

*STEVENS POINT,** Portage Co.

ANDERSON, SHANNON, O'BRIEN, RICE & BERTZ (AV)

1257 Main Street, P.O. Box 228, 54481
Telephone: 715-344-0890
Fax: 715-344-1012
Plover, Wisconsin Office: 2840 Post Road, 54467.
Telephone: 715-341-2560.
Fax: 715-341-2676.

OF COUNSEL

Hiram D. Anderson, Jr.
John E. Shannon, Jr.

PARTNERS

Gerald M. O'Brien
Maurice G. Rice, Jr.
Thomas W. Bertz
Daniel G. Golden (Resident at Plover Office)
Ronald T. Skrenes
Russell T. Golla
Robert F. Konkol (Resident at Plover Office)
Torren K. Pies
David G. Keefe
Nadine I. Davy
Rick A. Flugaur

ASSOCIATES

Robert J. Shannon
Daniel J. Rupar

General Attorneys for: Allstate Insurance; Mid-State Bank, N.A.; F & M Bank - Portage County; Delta Dental Plan of Wisconsin, Inc.; Joerns Healthcare, Inc.; Rice Clinic, S.C.; Stevens Point Journal; The Copps Corp.; Wisconsin Interscholastic Athletic Assn.; American Potato.

For full biographical listings, see the Martindale-Hubbell Law Directory

GLINSKI, HAFERMAN, ILTEN & KLEIN, S.C. (AV)

Professional Building, 1025 Clark Street, 54481
Telephone: 715-341-3323
Fax: 715-341-2466

Herman J. Glinski
James T. Haferman
Mark O. Ilten
James M. Klein

David J. Glinski
Paul A. Anderson

For full biographical listings, see the Martindale-Hubbell Law Directory

TERWILLIGER, WAKEEN, PIEHLER & CONWAY, S.C. (AV)

1045 Clark Street, P.O. Box 1060, 54481-8260
Telephone: 715-341-7855
Fax: 715-341-7255
Wausau, Wisconsin Office: 555 Scott Street, P.O. Box 8063.
Telephone: 715-845-2121.

E. John Buzza (Resident)
Mark S. Henkel (Resident)
Gary L. Dreier (Resident)
David A. Ray (Resident)
Kelly S. Benjamin (Resident)
Virginia L. Erdman (Resident)

For full biographical listings, see the Martindale-Hubbell Law Directory

*STURGEON BAY,** Door Co. — (Refer to Green Bay)

*VIROQUA,** Vernon Co. — (Refer to Sparta)

*WASHBURN,** Bayfield Co. — (Refer to Superior)

WATERLOO, Jefferson Co. — (Refer to Watertown)

WATERTOWN, Jefferson & Dodge Cos.

BENDER, LEVI & BUSS, S.C. (AV)

117 North Second Street, P.O. Box 16, 53094-0016
Telephone: 414-261-7626
Fax: 414-261-1249

Robert A. Bender
Thomas J. Levi

Todd C. Buss

For full biographical listings, see the Martindale-Hubbell Law Directory

*WAUKESHA,** Waukesha Co.

CRAMER, MULTHAUF & HAMMES (AV)

1601 East Racine Avenue, P.O. Box 558, 53187
Telephone: 414-542-4278
Telecopier: 414-542-4270

MEMBERS OF FIRM

Clayton A. Cramer (1913-1993)
John E. Multhauf
James W. Hammes
Richard R. Kobriger
Peter J. Plaushines
John M. Remmers

ASSOCIATES

Kathryn Sawyer Gutenkunst
Timothy J. Andringa
Brian S. Miller
Dean P. Delforge
Suzanne Lorenz Fischer

Representative Clients: Waukesha State Bank; First Federal Savings Bank of Waukesha; Pillar Technologies, Inc.; Payco American Corp.; Badger Exposition Service, Inc.; Bielinski Bros. Builders, Inc.; Dorner Manufacturing Corp.; Waukesha Foundry; Towns of Waukesha, Lisbon, Brookfield and Wales.

For full biographical listings, see the Martindale-Hubbell Law Directory

HUNTER & SOMMERS (AV)

259 South Street, P.O. Box 1136, 53186
Telephone: 414-547-7788
Telecopier: 414-548-1055

MEMBERS OF FIRM

Richard N. Hunter
James R. Sommers
Jeffrey Wm. Bartelt

ASSOCIATES

Richard P. Bourne

Representative Clients: First Financial Savings Association; The Aeroshade Co.; Carroll College; Southeastern Wisconsin Regional Planning Commission; American Family Insurance Group; General Casualty Cos. of Wisconsin; Link Associates, Inc.; Beloit Beverage Co.; Golden Guernsey Dairy Cooperative; Delzer Lithograph Co.

For full biographical listings, see the Martindale-Hubbell Law Directory

*WAUPACA,** Waupaca Co.

JOHNSON, HANSEN, SHAMBEAU, MARONEY & ANDERSON, S.C. (AV)

204 South Main Street, P.O. Box 111, 54981
Telephone: 715-258-4000
FAX: 715-258-4015
Toll Free: 800-675-4013

Stephen F. Hansen
Steven D. Shambeau
Thomas A. Maroney
Kaye E. Anderson

OF COUNSEL

Richard E. Johnson

Representative Clients: American Family Insurance; Waupaca Family Medicine Associates, S.C.; First National Bank of Waupaca, Wisconsin.

For full biographical listings, see the Martindale-Hubbell Law Directory

*WAUSAU,** Marathon Co.

PATTERSON, RICHARDS, HESSERT, WENDORFF & ELLISON (AV)

630 Fourth Street, P.O. Box 1144, 54402-1144
Telephone: 715-845-1151
Fax: 715-845-1167

MEMBERS OF FIRM

Richard P. Tinkham (1917-1978)
John E. Bliss (Retired)
Charles F. Smith, Jr. (Retired)
C. Duane Patterson
George A. Richards
Peter L. Hessert
Mark P. Wendorff
Keith F. Ellison

ASSOCIATES

David J. Eckert
Paul E. David

Representative Clients: M&I First American National Bank of Wausau; Allstate Insurance Co.; American Bankers Insurance Co.; American Family Mutual Insurance Co.; American Hardware Insurance Group; Auto Owners Insurance Co.; Badger Mutual Insurance Co.; Badger State Mutual Casualty Co.; CIGNA.
Reference: M&I First American National Bank.

For full biographical listings, see the Martindale-Hubbell Law Directory

RUDER, WARE & MICHLER, S.C. (AV)

500 Third Street Suite 700, P.O. Box 8050, 54402-8050
Telephone: 715-845-4336
Facsimile: 715-845-2718

George L. Ruder (1920-1970)
G. Lane Ware
John F. Michler
Lon E. Roberts
Douglas J. Klingberg
Thomas P. Macken
Arnold J. Kiburz III
Stewart L. Etten
William R. Tehan
Russell W. Wilson
Kevin E. Wolf
Keith I. Johnston
Mark J. Bradley
Ronald J. Rutlin
Dean R. Dietrich
James F. Harrington
Jeffrey T. Jones
David B. Welles
Paul C. Schlindwein II

Robin L. Bentley
Jay M. Wiedenman
Steven M. Anderson
Mary Ellen Schill
Dorothy L. Bain
Matthew E. Yde
Joseph M. Mella
Christopher T. Starkey
Dale M. Eaton
Alvin Q. Liu
Cari L. Hoida
Karen L. Trzinski

For full biographical listings, see the Martindale-Hubbell Law Directory

TERWILLIGER, WAKEEN, PIEHLER & CONWAY, S.C. (AV)

555 Scott Street, P.O. Box 8063, 54402-8063
Telephone: 715-845-2121
Fax: 715-845-3538
Stevens Point, Wisconsin Office: 1045 Clark Street, P.O. Box 1060.
Telephone: 715-341-7855.
Fax: 715-341-7255.

Herbert L. Terwilliger (1914-1990)
W. Thomas Terwilliger
E. John Buzza (Resident, Stevens Point Office)
Mark S. Henkel (Resident, Stevens Point Office)
Walter Gene Lew
D. G. Graff
David A. Piehler
Richard W. Zalewski
Robert D. Reid
Randall J. Sandfort
Gary L. Dreier (Resident, Stevens Point Office)
Cassandra Brown Westgate
John P. Runde
Jeffrey J. Strande
David A. Ray (Resident, Stevens Point Office)
Mark A. Klinner
Gregory J. Strasser
Kathleen E. Grant
Kelly S. Benjamin (Resident, Stevens Point Office)
Virginia L. Erdman (Resident, Stevens Point Office)

(See Next Column)

TERWILLIGER, WAKEEN, PIEHLER & CONWAY S.C.—*Continued*

OF COUNSEL

Emil A. Wakeen | Walter H. Piehler
Neil M. Conway

Representative Clients: Bank One, Stevens Point, NA; LB Trucking Co., Inc.; Land O' Lakes, Inc.; Marathon Savings Bank; Marshfield Clinic; Midstate Contracting, Inc.; Urban Steel Building, Inc.; Wausau Medical Center; Wausau Supply Co.; Wisconsin Public Service Corp.

For full biographical listings, see the Martindale-Hubbell Law Directory

*WEST BEND,** Washington Co.

O'MEARA, ECKERT, POUROS & GONRING (AV)

622 Elm Street, P.O. Box 348, 53095
Telephone: 414-334-2331
Telecopier: 414-334-8042

MEMBERS OF FIRM

Phillip J. Eckert | Andrew T. Gonring
James G. Pouros | Karen M. Christianson
Louis R. Briska

ASSOCIATES

Timothy J. Algiers | James O'Meara

Representative Clients: Bank One West Bend; Amity Leather Products; West Bend Mutual Insurance Co.; Rural Mutual Insurance Co.; B. C. Ziegler & Co.; Valley Bank Corp.; Farm Credit Services; West Bend Co.

For full biographical listings, see the Martindale-Hubbell Law Directory

*WHITEHALL,** Trempealeau Co. — (Refer to Eau Claire)

WYOMING

*BASIN,** Big Horn Co. — (Refer to Cody)

*BUFFALO,** Johnson Co.

KIRVEN & KIRVEN, P.C. (AV)

104 Fort Street, P.O. Box 640, 82834
Telephone: 307-684-2248
Fax: 307-684-2242

William J. Kirven (Retired) | Dennis M. Kirven
Timothy J. Kirven

Nancy Zerr

Representative Clients: Texaco Inc.; Wyoming Bank and Trust Co.; Buffalo Federal Savings & Loan Assn.; Reeves Concrete Products; Gordon Ranch; Independent Insurance Agents of Wyoming; Powder River Corporation Reservoir.

For full biographical listings, see the Martindale-Hubbell Law Directory

OMOHUNDRO, PALMERLEE AND DURRANT (AV)

An Association of Attorneys
130 South Main Street, 82834
Telephone: 307-684-2207
Telecopier: 307-684-9364
Gillette, Wyoming Office: East Entrance, Suite 700, 201 West Lakeway Road.
Telephone: 307-682-7826.

William D. Omohundro (P.C.) | David F. Palmerlee
Sean P. Durrant

For full biographical listings, see the Martindale-Hubbell Law Directory

*CASPER,** Natrona Co.

BROWN & DREW (AV)

Casper Business Center, Suite 800, 123 West First Street, 82601-2486
Telephone: 307-234-1000
800-877-6755
Telefax: 307-265-8025

MEMBERS OF FIRM

William H. Brown (1913-1991)
Morris R. Massey
Harry B. Durham, III
W. Thomas Sullins, II
Donn J. McCall
John A. Warnick
Thomas F. Reese
Russell M. Blood
J. Kenneth Barbe
Jeffrey C. Brinkerhoff

ASSOCIATES

Jon B. Huss
Carol Warnick
P. Jaye Rippley
Courtney Robert Kepler
Drew A. Perkins

OF COUNSEL

B. J. Baker
Bruce N. Willoughby

RETIRED

William F. Drew
George M. Apostolos

Attorneys for: First Interstate Bank of Wyoming, N.A.; Norwest Bank Wyoming, N.A.; The CIT Group/Industrial Financing; The Doctor's Co.; MEDMARC; WOTCO, Inc.; Chevron USA; Kerr-McGee Corp.; Wold Trona Co., Inc.; Chicago and NorthWestern Transportation Company.

For full biographical listings, see the Martindale-Hubbell Law Directory

VLASTOS, BROOKS & HENLEY, P.C. (AV)

Suite 320, Key Bank Building, 300 South Wolcott, P.O. Box 10, 82602
Telephone: 307-235-6613
Fax: 307-235-6645

J. E. Vlastos
John C. Brooks
John I. Henley
David A. Drell

OF COUNSEL

Wendy S. Eberle

Representative Clients: BKP, real estate developers; St. Paul Insurance Cos.; State Farm Mutual Auto Insurance Co.; Travelers Insurance Cos.; New Mexico Physicians Mutual Liability Co.; State Farm Fire & Casualty Co.; Crum & Forster Commercial Insurance; Golden Rule Insurance Co.; Fortis Benefits Insurance Co.; The Doctors' Company.

For full biographical listings, see the Martindale-Hubbell Law Directory

WILLIAMS, PORTER, DAY & NEVILLE, P.C. (AV)

Suite 300 Durbin Center, 145 South Durbin Street, 82601
Telephone: 307-265-0700
Fax: 307-266-2306

(See Next Column)

Houston G. Williams
Geo. M. Porter (1915-1990)
Richard E. Day
Frank D. Neville
Barry G. Williams
Patrick J. Murphy
Stuart R. Day
Ann M. Rochelle
Mark L. Carman
William H. Everett
Stephenson D. Emery
Scott E. Ortiz

Representative Clients: Wyoming Medical Center; Casper College; ITT Hartford Insurance Cos.; Pacific Power & Light Co.; Amoco Corp.; Texaco Inc.; Conoco Inc.; True Industries; Marathon Oil Co.; Frontier Certified Development Company; Attorneys Liability Protection Society; USX Corporation.

For full biographical listings, see the Martindale-Hubbell Law Directory

*CHEYENNE,** Laramie Co.

DAVIS AND CANNON (AV)

2710 Thomes Avenue, P.O. Box 43, 82003
Telephone: 307-634-3210
Fax: 307-778-7118
Gillette, Wyoming Office: Suite 701, First Interstate Bank Tower, 222 South Gillette,
Telephone: 307-686-6316.
Sheridan, Wyoming Office: 40 South Main Street, P.O. Box 728.
Telephone: 307-672-7491.
Fax: 307-672-8955.

MEMBERS OF FIRM

Richard M. Davis, Jr.
Kim D. Cannon
Hayden F. Heaphy, Jr.
Anthony T. Wendtland
Kate M. Fox

John C. McKinley

For full biographical listings, see the Martindale-Hubbell Law Directory

HATHAWAY, SPEIGHT & KUNZ (AV)

Suite 402, 2424 Pioneer Avenue, P.O. Box 1208, 82003-1208
Telephone: 307-634-7723
Fax: 307-634-0985

MEMBERS OF FIRM

Stanley K. Hathaway
John B. "Jack" Speight
Brent R. Kunz
Rick A. Thompson
Michael B. Rosenthal
Robert T. McCue
Dominique D.Y. Cone

Representative Clients: Pacificorp; Exxon; Key Bank of Wyoming; Little America Refining Co.; Sinclair Oil Corp.; Wyoming Refining Co.; Blue Cross-Blue Shield; Black Hills Bentonite; Rhone Poulenc of Wyoming.

For full biographical listings, see the Martindale-Hubbell Law Directory

HICKEY, MACKEY, EVANS, WALKER & STEWART (AV)

1712 Carey Avenue, P.O. Drawer 467, 82003
Telephone: 307-634-1525
Telecopier: 307-638-7335

MEMBERS OF FIRM

Paul J. Hickey
Terry W. Mackey
David F. Evans
John M. Walker
Mark R. Stewart III
Richard D. Tim Bush

A List of Representative Clients will be furnished upon request.
Reference: Norwest Bank, Cheyenne, N.A.

For full biographical listings, see the Martindale-Hubbell Law Directory

HIRST & APPLEGATE, A PROFESSIONAL CORPORATION (AV)

200 Boyd Building, P.O. Box 1083, 82003-1083
Telephone: 307-632-0541
Telefax: 307-632-4999

James L. Applegate
Thomas G. Gorman
Thomas A. Nicholas III
Gary R. Scott
John J. Metzke

Mark E. Macy
Dale W. Cottam

Representative Clients: Transamerica Insurance Group (TIG); Aetna Life & Casualty; Allied Group; Royal Insurance Co.; Wyoming Stock Growers Assn.; General Motors Corp.; Coastal Corp.; Fassett-Nickel, Inc.
Reference: Norwest Bank Wyoming Cheyenne, N.A.

For full biographical listings, see the Martindale-Hubbell Law Directory

Cheyenne—Continued

HOLLAND & HART (AV)

A Partnership including Professional Corporations
Suite 500, 2020 Carey Avenue, P.O. Box 1347, 82003-1347
Telephone: 307-778-4200
Telecopier: 307-778-8175
Denver, Colorado Office: Holland & Hart, Suite 2900, 555 Seventeenth Street. P.O. Box 8749.
Telephone: 303-295-8000.
Cable Address: "Holhart Denver."
Telecopier: 303-295-8261.
TWX: 910-931-0568.
Southeast Denver, Colorado Office: Holland & Hart, Suite 1050, 4601 DTC Boulevard.
Telephone: 303-290-1600.
Telecopier: 303-290-1606.
Aspen, Colorado Office: Holland & Hart, 600 East Main Street.
Telephone: 303-925-3476.
Telecopier: 303-925-9367.
Boulder, Colorado Office: Suite 500, 1050 Walnut.
Telephone: 303-473-2700.
Telecopier: 303-473-2720.
Colorado Springs, Colorado Office: Holland & Hart, Suite 1000, 90 S. Cascade Avenue.
Telephone: 719-475-7730.
Telex: 820770 SHHTLX.
Telecopier: 719-634-2461.
Washington, D.C. Office: Holland & Hart, Suite 310, 1001 Pennsylvania Avenue, N.W.
Telephone: 202-638-5500.
Telecopier: 202-737-8998.
Boise, Idaho Office: Holland & Hart, Suite 1400, West One Plaza, 101 South Capitol Boulevard, P.O. Box 2527.
Telephone: 208-342-5000.
Telecopier: 208-343-8869.
Billings, Montana Office: Holland & Hart, Suite 1500, First Interstate Center, 401 North 31st Street, P.O. Box 639.
Telephone: 406-252-2166.
Telecopier: 406-252-1669.
Jackson, Wyoming Office: Suite 2, 175 South King Street, P.O. Box 68.
Telephone: 307-739-9741.
Telecopier: 307-739-9744.
Salt Lake City, Utah Office: Suite 880, 111 East Broadway.
Telephone: 801-578-6000.
FAX: 801-578-6010.

PARTNERS

Ronald M. Martin
Jack D. Palma, II (P.C.) (Resident)
Donald I. Schultz (P.C.) (Resident)
Patrick R. Day (P.C.) (Resident)
Edward W. Harris (Resident)
Joe M. Teig (P.C.) (Resident)
Lawrence J. Wolfe (P.C.) (Resident)

OF COUNSEL

Teresa Burkett Buffington
Thomas L. Sansonetti

RESIDENT ASSOCIATES

James R. Belcher
Lynnette J. Boomgaarden
Bradley T. Cave
William R. Dabney
Catherine W. Hansen
Susan E. Laser-Bair
Edward E. Risha
Richard Schneebeck

For full biographical listings, see the Martindale-Hubbell Law Directory

LATHROP & RUTLEDGE, A PROFESSIONAL CORPORATION (AV)

Suite 500 City Center Building, 1920 Thomes Avenue, P.O. Box 4068, 82003-4068
Telephone: 307-632-0554
Telecopier: 307-635-4502

Carl L. Lathrop
J. Kent Rutledge
Corinne E. Rutledge
Loyd E. Smith

Roger E. Cockerille
James T. Dinneen

OF COUNSEL

Arthur Kline
Byron Hirst

General Counsel for: Cheyenne Internal Medicine and Neurology, P.C.; Laramie County School District No. 2; Cheyenne Newspapers, Inc.; Wyoming Hospital Assn.
Insurance Clients: Omaha Property Casualty Insurance Co.; National Chiropractic Insurance Co.; Underwriters at Lloyds; Omaha Property Casualty; Underwriters at Lloyds; CIGNA Insurance Group.

For full biographical listings, see the Martindale-Hubbell Law Directory

*CODY,** Park Co.

SIMPSON, KEPLER & EDWARDS (AV)

1135 14th Street, P.O. Box 490, 82414
Telephone: 307-527-7891
FAX: 307-527-7897

(See Next Column)

MEMBERS OF FIRM

Milward L. Simpson (1897-1993)
Charles G. Kepler
William L. Simpson
Colin M. Simpson
Chris D. Edwards

References: Key Bank-Cody; Shoshone-First National Bank; Jackson State Bank.

For full biographical listings, see the Martindale-Hubbell Law Directory

*DOUGLAS,** Converse Co. — (Refer to Casper)

*EVANSTON,** Uinta Co. — (Refer to Riverton)

*GILLETTE,** Campbell Co.

OMOHUNDRO, PALMERLEE AND DURRANT (AV)

An Association of Attorneys
East Entrance, Suite 700, 201 West Lakeway Road, 82716
Telephone: 307-682-7826
Buffalo, Wyoming Office: 130 South Main Street.
Telephone: 307-684-2207.
Telecopier: 307-684-9364.

William D. Omohundro (P.C.)
Sean P. Durrant

*GREEN RIVER,** Sweetwater Co. — (Refer to Riverton)

*JACKSON,** Teton Co.

HOLLAND & HART (AV)

A Partnership including Professional Corporations
Suite 2, 175 South King Street, P.O. Box 68, 83001
Telephone: 307-739-9741
Telecopier: 307-739-9744
Denver, Colorado Office: Holland & Hart, Suite 2900, 555 Seventeenth Street. P.O. Box 8749.
Telephone: 303-295-8000.
Cable Address: "Holhart Denver."
Telecopier: 303-295-8261.
TWX: 910-931-0568.
Southeast Denver, Colorado Office: Holland & Hart, Suite 1050, 4601 DTC Boulevard.
Telephone: 303-290-1600.
Telecopier: 303-290-1606.
Aspen, Colorado Office: Holland & Hart, 600 East Main Street.
Telephone: 303-925-3476.
Telecopier: 303-925-9367.
Boulder, Colorado Office: Suite 500, 1050 Walnut.
Telephone: 303-473-2700.
Telecopier: 303-473-2720.
Colorado Springs, Colorado Office: Holland & Hart, Suite 1000, 90 S. Cascade Avenue.
Telephone: 719-475-7730.
Telex: 820770 SHHTLX.
Telecopier: 719-634-2461.
Washington, D.C. Office: Holland & Hart, Suite 310, 1001 Pennsylvania Avenue, N.W.
Telephone: 202-638-5500.
Telecopier: 202-737-8998.
Boise, Idaho Office: Holland & Hart, Suite 1400, West One Plaza, 101 South Capitol Boulevard, P.O. Box 2527.
Telephone: 208-342-5000.
Telecopier: 208-343-8869.
Billings, Montana Office: Holland & Hart, Suite 1500, First Interstate Center, 401 North 31st Street, P.O. Box 639.
Telephone: 406-252-2166.
Telecopier: 406-252-1669.
Cheyenne, Wyoming Office: Suite 500, 2020 Carey Avenue, P.O. Box 1347.
Telephone: 307-778-4200.
Telecopier: 307-778-8175.
Salt Lake City, Utah Office: Suite 880, 111 East Broadway.
Telephone: 801-578-6000.
FAX: 801-578-6010.

RESIDENT PARTNERS

John L. Gallinger (P.C.)
Marilyn S. Kite (P.C.)

OF COUNSEL

Stephen R. Duerr

For full biographical listings, see the Martindale-Hubbell Law Directory

SPENCE, MORIARITY & SCHUSTER (AV)

15 South Jackson Street, P.O. Box 548, 83001
Telephone: 307-733-7290
Fax: 307-733-5248
Cheyenne, Wyoming Office: Suite 302 Pioneer Center, 2424 Pioneer Avenue, P.O. Box 1006.
Telephone: 307-635-1533.
Fax: 307-635-1539.

MEMBERS OF FIRM

Gerry L. Spence
Edward P. Moriarity
Robert P. Schuster
Gary L. Shockey
J. Douglas McCalla
Roy A. Jacobson, Jr.

(See Next Column)

SPENCE, MORIARITY & SCHUSTER, *Jackson—Continued*

ASSOCIATES

Glen G. Debroder
Kent W. Spence
Robert A. Krause
Heather Noble
Christopher H. Hawks

Reference: First Interstate Bank, Casper, Wyoming.

For full biographical listings, see the Martindale-Hubbell Law Directory

*LANDER,** Fremont Co. — (Refer to Riverton)

*LUSK,** Niobrara Co. — (Refer to Torrington)

*NEWCASTLE,** Weston Co. — (Refer to Buffalo)

*RAWLINS,** Carbon Co. — (Refer to Laramie)

RIVERTON, Fremont Co.

HETTINGER & LEEDY (AV)

Suite 214 Masonic Temple Building, 107 South Broadway, 82501-4380
Telephone: 307-856-2239; 856-2231
Fax: 307-856-2230

MEMBERS OF FIRM

James L. Hettinger
Richard I. Leedy

ASSOCIATES

Bob Nicholas

Representative Clients: Masonic Temple Assn.; Wagon Box Ranch; First Interstate Bank of Riverton, N.A.; Gilpatrick Construction Co., Inc.; Riverton Fire Protection District.

For full biographical listings, see the Martindale-Hubbell Law Directory

ROCK SPRINGS, Sweetwater Co.

BUSSART, WEST, ROSSETTI, PIAIA & TYLER, P.C. (AV)

Suite A, 409 Broadway, P.O. Box 1020, 82902-1020
Telephone: 307-362-3300; 307-875-4080
Telecopier: 307-362-3309

Ford T. Bussart
L. Galen West
John D. Rossetti
Marvin L. Tyler
David M. Piaia
Michael J. Finn

Representative Clients: City of Green River, Wyoming; Farmers Insurance Co.; Memorial Hospital of Sweetwater County; Rock Springs-Casper Coca-Cola Bottling Co., Inc.; The Rock Springs National Bank; Sweetwater County School District No. 1; Sweetwater County School District No. 2; Western Wyoming Community College; University of Wyoming.
Reference: Rock Springs National Bank, Rock Springs, Wyoming.

For full biographical listings, see the Martindale-Hubbell Law Directory

*SHERIDAN,** Sheridan Co.

DAVIS AND CANNON (AV)

Formerly Burgess, Davis & Cannon
40 South Main Street, P.O. Box 728, 82801
Telephone: 307-672-7491
Fax: 307-672-8955
Cheyenne, Wyoming Office: 2710 Thomes Avenue, P.O. Box 43, 82003.
Telephone: 307-634-3210.
Fax: 307-778-7118.

MEMBERS OF FIRM

Henry A. Burgess (Retired)
Richard M. Davis, Jr.
Kim D. Cannon
Hayden F. Heaphy, Jr.
Anthony T. Wendtland
Kate M. Fox

John C. McKinley

Representative Clients: Consol, Inc.; Hesston Corporation; Mutual of New York; Peter Kiewit Sons, Inc.; Wichita River Oil Corporation; Phillips Petroleum; First Interstate Bank of Commerce; Merrell Dow Pharmaceuticals, Inc.; Philip Morris, Inc.; Range Telephone Cooperative.

For full biographical listings, see the Martindale-Hubbell Law Directory

YONKEE & TONER (AV)

319 West Dow Street, P.O. Box 6288, 82801
Telephone: 307-674-7451
Fax: 307-672-6250

MEMBERS OF FIRM

Lawrence A. Yonkee
Tom C. Toner
Michael K. Davis
John F. Araas

ASSOCIATES

Lynne Ann Collins
John G. Fenn

Representative Clients: Equitable Life Assurance Society of the United States; Travelers Insurance Co.; Hartford Accident & Indemnity Co.; Western Casualty & Surety Co.; The Employers Group; Prudential Insurance Co. of America; State Farm Insurance Co.; Metropolitan Insurance Co.; Ohio Hospital Insurance Co.; Lexington Insurance Company.

(See Next Column)

For full biographical listings, see the Martindale-Hubbell Law Directory

*SUNDANCE,** Crook Co. — (Refer to Buffalo)

*THERMOPOLIS,** Hot Springs Co. — (Refer to Riverton)

*WHEATLAND,** Platte Co.

JONES, JONES, VINES & HUNKINS (AV)

An Association of Lawyers
Ninth and Maple, P.O. Drawer 189, 82201
Telephone: 307-322-2882
FAX: 307-322-4827

W. B. Jones (1896-1964)
William R. Jones
Raymond B. Hunkins
William H. Vines

Bruce A. Hellbaum

Representative Clients: Wyoming Realty; John Hancock Life Insurance Co.; Metropolitan Life Insurance Co.; Connecticut Mutual Life Ins. Co.
Counsel for: Platte County School Districts #1 and #2; Wheatland Irrigation District; Banner and Associates (Architects and Engineers).

For full biographical listings, see the Martindale-Hubbell Law Directory

SHERARD, SHERARD AND JOHNSON (AV)

602 10th Street, P.O. Drawer 69, 82201
Telephone: 307-322-2102, 322-5555, 322-5050
Fax: 307-322-4822

MEMBERS OF FIRM

D. N. Sherard
Stephen N. Sherard
Rex E. Johnson

Corporate Counsel: Western Fuels Assn.; Western Fuel-Illinois; Western Fuels-Utah.
Representative Clients: Wheatland Rural Electric Assn.; Springfield Ranch, Inc.; Basin Electric Power Co-op; Wyoming Machinery Co.
Wyoming Counsel: Missouri Basin Power Project.
Reference: First State Bank of Wheatland.

For full biographical listings, see the Martindale-Hubbell Law Directory

GUAM

AGANA, Agana Dist.

CARLSMITH BALL WICHMAN MURRAY CASE & ICHIKI

A Partnership including Law Corporations
4th Floor Bank of Hawaii Building, P.O. Box BF, 96910-5027
Telephone: 671-472-6813
Telex: 721-6445 CWCMI GM
Telecopier: 671-477-4375
Honolulu, Hawaii Office: Suite 2200, Pacific Tower, 1001 Bishop Street. P.O. Box 656.
Telephone: 808-523-2500.
Los Angeles, California Office: 555 South Flower Street, 25th Floor.
Telephone: 213-955-1200.
Long Beach, California Office: 301 East Ocean Boulevard, 7th Floor.
Telephone: 310-435-5631.
Washington, D.C. Office: 700 14th Street, N.W., 9th Floor.
Telephone: 202-508-1025.
Mexico City, Mexico Office: Monte Pelvoux 111, Piso 1, Col. Lomas de Chapultepec, 11000 Mexico, D.F.
Telephone: (011-52-5) 520-8514.
Fax: (011-52-5) 540-1545.
Mexico, D.F. Office of Carlsmith Ball Garcia Cacho y Asociados, S.C. (Authorized to practice Mexican Law): Monte Pelvoux 111, Piso 1, Col. Lomas de Chapultepec, 11000 Mexico, D.F.
Telephone: (011-52-5) 520-8514.
Fax: (011-52-5) 540-1545.
Saipan, Commonwealth of the Northern Mariana Islands Office: Carlsmith Building, Capitol Hill, P.O. Box 5241.
Telephone: 670-322-3455.
Wailuku, Maui, Hawaii Office: One Main Plaza, Suite 400, 2200 Main Street, P.O. Box 1086.
Telephone: 808-242-4535.
Kailua-Kona, Hawaii Office: Second Floor, Bank of Hawaii Annex Building, P.O. Box 1720.
Telephone: 808-329-6464.
Hilo, Hawaii Office: 121 Waianuenue Avenue, P.O. Box 686.
Telephone: 808-935-6644.
Kapolei, Hawaii Office: Kapolei Building, Suite 318, 1001 Kamokila Boulevard.
Telephone: 808-674-0850.

MEMBERS OF FIRM

Ruth D. Davis
Philip D. Isaac
Garry W. Morse
William C. Williams, Jr.

RESIDENT ASSOCIATES

Kristen S. Armstrong
Lisanne M. Butterfield
Meredith M. Sayre
Sinforoso M. Tolentino

OF COUNSEL

Roger P. Crouthamel

For full biographical listings, see the Martindale-Hubbell Law Directory

PUERTO RICO

BAYAMON, Bayamon Dist. — (Refer to San Juan)

MAYAGUEZ, Mayaguez Dist. — (Refer to Ponce)

PONCE, Ponce Dist.

Parra, Del Valle, Frau & Limeres

Second Floor, Banco Popular Building, P.O. Box 1429, 00733-1429
Telephone: 809-848-4900
Cable Address: "Parratoro"
Telecopier: 809-840-2022

MEMBERS OF FIRM

Francisco J. Parra-Toro (1904-1985)
Waldemar Del Valle-López
Waldemar Del Valle-Armstrong
Manuel A. Frau-Pietri
Miguel Limeres-Grau
Ramon I. Ortiz-Palmieri
Maria M. Del Valle-Armstrong

Representative Clients: Banco Popular de Puerto Rico; Integrand Assurance Co.; Damas Foundation; National Insurance Co.; Puerto Rican Cement Co., Inc.; Ferré Development Co., Inc.; Bonnin & Cía., Inc.; Cine Foto, Inc.; Hospital de Damas.

For full biographical listings, see the Martindale-Hubbell Law Directory

SAN JUAN, San Juan Dist.

Del Toro & Santana

Suite 807 Royal Bank Center (Hato Rey), 00917
Telephone: 809-754-8722
Telecopier: 809-756-6677

MEMBERS OF FIRM

Russell A. Del Toro
Roberto Santana Aparicio

For full biographical listings, see the Martindale-Hubbell Law Directory

Fiddler, González & Rodríguez

Chase Manhattan Bank Building (Hato Rey), P.O. Box 363507, 00936-3507
Telephone: 809-753-3113
Telecopier: 809-759-3123

OF COUNSEL

Eduardo Negrón-Rodríguez
Julio M. Rodriguez
Ileana Fernandez-Buitrago

MEMBERS OF FIRM

Earle T. Fiddler (1887-1962)
José G. González (1905-1982)
Harold Toro-Toro (1938-1983)
Federico Tilén (1913-1988)
Richard J. González (1928-1988)
Rubén Rodríguez-Antongiorgi (1913-1992)
Salvador E. Casellas
Rafael R. Vizcarrondo
Salvador Antonetti-Zequeira
Pedro Pumarada
Rafael Cortés-Dapena
Julio L. Aguirre
Aurelio Emanuelli-Belaval
Antonio R. Sifre
Jay A. Garcia-Gregory
Roberto B. Suárez
Leopoldo J. Cabassa-Sauri
Juan Carlos Pérez-Otero
Eduardo R. Estrella
Tristán Reyes-Gilestra
Eduardo M. Negrón-Navas
José A. Silva-Cofresí
Pedro J. Polanco
José A. Acosta-Grubb
Teodoro Peña-Garcia
Mario Arroyo-Dávila
Arturo Bauermeister-Baldrich
Diego A. Ramos
Manuel López-Zambrana
Raúl J. Vilá-Sellés
Clara E. Lopez-Baralt
Rafael E. Dávila-Thomas
José E. González-Borgos
Maria del Carmen Taboas
José Julián Alvarez-Maldonado
José Luis Verdiales Morales
José J. Santiago
Humberto Guzmán-Rodríguez
Jose R. Jimenez del Valle
Carlos V. J. Dávila
Pedro A. Cantero-Frau
Ricardo F. Casellas
Lolita J. Semidey Garcia

JUNIOR PARTNERS

Juan Carlos Gómez Escarce
Fernando Van Derdys
Charles Bimbela-Quiñones
Armando Martínez-Fernández
Fernando J. Bonilla Ortiz
Rosa M. Méndez-Santoni
César Gómez Negrón
Arline V. Bauzá-Figueroa
Yldefonso López-Morales
Heriberto J. Burgos-Pérez
Eddie López Alonso

SENIOR ASSOCIATES

Federico Tilén
Pedro I. Vidal-Cordero
Juan Carlos Fierres
Cesar T. Alcover-Acosta
María Luisa González-Hernández
Pedro J. Reyes-Bibiloni
Zoraida Cruz
Myrna I. Lozada-Guzmán
Juan Carlos Guzmán Rodriguez
Alberto Luis Toro-Suarez
Ricardo L. Ortiz-Colón
German Ojeda Bracero

(See Next Column)

ASSOCIATES

Pedro J. Manzano-Yates
Juan A. Santos-Berríos
JoséAlberto Sosa-Lloréns
Manuel E. Elías-Rivera
Miglisa L. Capo-Suria
Javier A. Feliciano Guzmán
LeRoy Lewis
Carmen Rosa Juarbe
Juan C. Benitez Colon
Luis A. Oliver
Maria Teresa Szendrey
Raul M. Arias
Miguel Agustín Blanco Fuertes
Alicia Figueroa Llinds
Juan C. Salichs Pou

Representative Clients: The Chase Manhattan Bank, N.A.; The Equitable Life Assurance Society of the U.S.; Westinghouse Electric Corp.; Pfizer, Inc.; Merck & Co., Inc.; American Cyanamid Co.; Metropolitan Life Insurance Co.; Bacardi Corp.

For full biographical listings, see the Martindale-Hubbell Law Directory

Goldman Antonetti & Córdova

American International Plaza Fourteenth & Fifteenth Floors, 250 Muñoz Rivera Avenue (Hato Rey), P.O. Box 70364, 00936-0364
Telephone: 809-759-8000
Telecopiers: 809-767-9333 (Main)
809-767-9177 (Litigation Department)
809-767-8660 (Labor & Corporate Law Departments)
809-767-9325 (Tax & Environmental Law Departments)

MEMBERS OF FIRM

Vicente J. Antonetti
José A. Cepeda-Rodriguez
Roberto Montalvo Carbia
Luis F. Antonetti
Jorge Souss
Luis D. Ortiz-Abreu
Gregory T. Usera
Edgar Cartagena-Santiago
Pedro Morell Losada
Ramón E. Dapena
Francis Torres-Fernández
Jorge L. Martinez
Carlos A. Rodríguez-Vidal
Raymond E. Morales
Thelma Rivera-Miranda
Jorge Segurola
Francisco J. García-García
Edgardo Colón Arrarás
Jesús E. Cuza
Howard Pravda
Braulio García Jiménez
Karín G. Díaz-Toro

OF COUNSEL

Max Goldman
Enrique Córdova Díaz
Francisco de Jesús-Schuck
Charles P. Adams

ASSOCIATES

Jorge R. Rodriguez-Micheo
José M. Lorié Velasco
Ivonne Palerm Cruz
Eli Matos-Alicea
Mildred Cabán
Wilda Rodriguez Plaza
John A. Uphoff-Figueroa
Edwin J. Seda-Fernández
Carlos E. Colón-Franceschi
Carlos Rodriguez Cintron
Marta Figueroa-Torres
Carlos A. García-Pérez
Iván R. Fernández-Vallejo
Georgiana S. Colón
Mercedes M. Barreras Soler
Migdalia Davila-Garcia
Manuel E. Lopez-Fernandez
Roberto Ariel Fernández
Josefina Cruz-Melendez
Gretchen M. Mendez-Vilella
María Patricia Lake
Orlando Cabrera-Rodriguez
Jose E. Franco
Ruben Colon-Morales
Jose J. Ledesma Rodriguez
Lora J. Espada-Medina
Aileen M. Navas-Auger
Ina M. Berlingeri Vincenty
Artemio Rivera Rivera

Representative Clients: Borden, Inc.; Crown Cork de Puerto Rico, Inc.; Maidenform, Inc.; Philip Morris, Inc.; Seven Up Flavors Mfg. Co.; Xerox Corp.

For full biographical listings, see the Martindale-Hubbell Law Directory

Gonzalez & Bennazar

Capital Center Building South Tower - 9th Floor, Arterial Hostos Avenue (Hato Rey), 00918
Telephone: 809-754-9191
Fax: 809-754-9325

MEMBERS OF FIRM

Raul E. González Díaz
A. J. Bennazar-Zequeira

OF COUNSEL

Luis F. Negrón-Garcia
Ruth De Leon

ASSOCIATES

José R. García Pérez
Jorge E. Velez-Velez
Elowina Torres-Cancel

Representative Clients: American Express Travel Related Services Co., Inc.; Mars, Inc.; Amway Corp.; Federal Deposit Insurance Corp.; GIGNA Insurance Group; BWAC International; M & M Mars; G-Tech Corporation; First Financial Caribbean Corp.

For full biographical listings, see the Martindale-Hubbell Law Directory

Jiménez, Graffam & Lausell

Formerly Jiménez & Fusté
Suite 505, Midtown Building, 421 Muñoz Rivera Avenue, Hato Rey, P.O. Box 366104, 00936-6104
Telephone: 809-767-1030; 767-1000; 767-1061; 767-1064
Telefax: 809-751-4068;
Cable: "Nezte"; RCA
Telex: 325-2730

(See Next Column)

JIMÉNEZ, GRAFFAM & LAUSELL—*Continued*

MEMBERS OF FIRM

Nicolás Jiménez
William A. Graffam
Steven C. Lausell
J. Ramón Rivera-Morales
José Juan Torres-Escalera
Raquel M. Dulzaides
Manuel San Juan

ASSOCIATES

Manolo T. Rodríguez-Bird
Patricia Garrity
Carlos E. Bayrón
Isabel J. Vélez-Serrano
Edgardo A. Vega-López
Alexandra M. Serracante-Cadilla
Luis Saldaña-Roman

Representative Clients: Sea-Land Service, Inc.; McAllister Brothers; Crowley Maritime Corp.; General Motors Overseas Distribution Corp.; Sphere Drake Underwriting Management, Ltd.; University of Puerto Rico.

For full biographical listings, see the Martindale-Hubbell Law Directory

MÁRTINEZ ODELL & CALABRIA

Banco Popular Center, 16th Floor, (Hato Rey), P.O. Box 190998, 00919-0998
Telephone: 809-753-8914
Facsimile: 809-753-8402; 809-759-9075; 809-764-5664

MEMBERS OF FIRM

Fred H. Martínez
Lawrence Odell
Jose L. Calabria
Jose B. Diaz Asencio
Juan Ramón Cancio-Ortiz
Francisco M. Ramirez-Rivera
Luis E. Lopez Correa
Patrick D. O'Neill
Graciela J. Belaval
Luis Morales-Steinmann
Fernando A. Pérez-Colon
Alberto Rodríguez-Ramos
Fanny Auz-Patiño
Donald J. Reiser (Not admitted in PR)
Angel S. Ruiz-Rodriguez
Benjamín Hernández-Nieves
Anabelle Rodriguez-Rodriguez
Roberto E. Vega Pacheco
Francisco L. Acevedo-Nogueras
Carlos Berreteaga

OF COUNSEL

Jose R. Cestero
Jose Luis Vila-Perez
Dominic T. Longo
Hernan R. Franco
Eugenio C. Romero

ASSOCIATES

Brunilda Rodríguez-Vélez
Rafael Kodesh-Baragaño
Javier E. Ferrer-Canals
Maria del Carmen Garriga
Lucé Vela Gutiérrez
Amelia Fortuño-Ruiz
Gary L. Leonard
Eric Perez Ochoa
Jose David Medina-Rivera
Ramón Eugenio-Meléndez
Luis R. Perez-Giusti
Jose Antonio Fernandez-Jaquete
Victor Armando Lago
Jose G. Fagot-Diaz
Arnaldo A. Mignucci-Giannoni
Gloria M. Sierra-Enriquez
Eileen Landrón-Guardiola
Guillermo A. Somoza-Colombani
Lourdes M. Defendini-Rodriguez
Maria Teresa Rigau-Escudero
Brunilda R. Santiago-Acevedo
M. Georgina Carrion-Christiansen
Luis J. Acevedo-Bengochea
Waldemar Fabery-Villaespesa
Juan C. Consuegra-Barquin

Representative Clients: A.T. & T. Corp.; Pepsi-Cola P.R. Bottling Co.; Banco Popular de Puerto Rico; I.T.T. Financial Corp.; John H. Harland Company of Puerto Rico, Inc.; Lutron Electronics Co., Inc.; Paine Webber, Inc.; Lotus Development Corp.; Western Digital.

For full biographical listings, see the Martindale-Hubbell Law Directory

MCCONNELL VALDÉS

270 Muñoz Rivera Avenue, 9th Floor (Hato Rey), 00918
Telephone: 809-759-9292
Cable Address: "Macval"
Telex (ITT): 345-0067 (Easylink 6243678)
Telecopier: 809-759-9225 or 809-759-8282
Mailing Address: P.O. Box 364225, San Juan, Puerto Rico, 00936-4225

MEMBERS OF FIRM

Herbert S. McConnell (1905-1971)
Robert W. Van Kirk
Walter G. McConnell
Samuel T. Céspedes
Antonio Escudero-Viera
Jorge R. González
Aurelio Torres Ponsa
Radamés (Rudy) A. Torruella
Carlos O. Souffront
Manuel A. Guzmán-Rodríguez
Antonio J. Rodríguez
Rafael Pérez-Bachs
Francisco G. Bruno
Aníbal Irizarry-Rivera
Frederick E. Hulser
José Rafael González-Irizarry
Donald E. Hull
Ana Matilde Nin-Torregrosa
Néstor Durán-González
Harry O. Cook
Rafael A. Carazo-Hernández
Manuel Moreda-Toledo
Mario L. Paniagua
Arturo J. García-Solá
Xenia Vélez-Silva
Odette Portuondo-Díaz
Julio Pietrantoni-Arce
Maggie Correa-Avilés
Esteban F. Bird
Esteban R. Bengoa
John F. Malley III
José Antonio Tulla
Rafael Fernández-Suárez
Rossell Barrios-Amy
Juan C. Galanes-Valldejuli
Carl Schuster
Francisco Chévere
Ramón Coto-Ojeda
Roberto L. Cabañas
Nereida Meléndez-Rivera
Richard M. Graffam-Rodríguez

(See Next Column)

MEMBERS OF FIRM (Continued)

Paul R. Cortés-Rexach
William A. Power
Ernesto N. Mayoral-Megwinoff
Angel Rafael Marrero
Arturo Pérez-Figaredo
Jaime E. Toro-Monserrate
Ramón J. Abarca-Schwartz
Antonio A. Arias-Larcada
Manuel Fernández-Bared
Maria Santiago De Vidal
Dora M. Peñagarícano-Suárez
Salvador F. Casellas
Alfredo M. Hopgood-Jovet
Luisa Wert-Serrano
Eduardo Tamargo
Jorge L. San Miguel
José Ricardo Toro
Rosa María Cruz-Niemiec

SPECIAL COUNSEL

Robert S. Griggs
Joseph T. Wynne
Donald M. Hall
Víctor M. Comolli
Isis Carballo

OF COUNSEL

Adolfo Valdés
Gonzalo Sifre
Fernando Ruiz-Suria
Abelardo Ruiz-Suria
Daniel F. Kelley, Jr.

ASSOCIATES

David Muñoz-Ocasio
Leonor M. Aguilar-Guerrero
Víctor R. Rodríguez
Maria de los Angeles Diez-Fulladosa
Patricia G. Cara
Mari Carmen Bosch
Lilia R. Rodríquez-Ruiz
Joan Mulet (Not admitted in PR)
María Isabel Castañer
Aurelio Emanuelli Freese
Laura González-Bothwell
Carmencita Velázquez-Márquez
Nerylú Figueroa-Estasie
Vivian Nuñez
Giselle Colon De Ferenczi
Laura T. Rozas
Antonio J. Sifre-Sein
Anita Montaner-Sevillano
Rafael J. Vázquez González
Eduardo A. Bhatia
Samuel T. Céspedes Jr.
Desirée Laborde-Sanfiorenzo
Edna Laura Pérez
Pedro E. Ruiz-Meléndez
Rafael Mullet Sánchez
Frank E. Guerra Pujol
Cristina M. Fernandez Neumann
Ana T. Miranda
Gloria M. De Corral-Hernández
José A. B. Nolla-Mayoral
Gilberto J. Marxuach-Torrós
Juan Carlos Albors
Mônica Vega-Quintana
Raul E. Bandas-Del Pilar
Marîa T. Juan-Urrutia

Representative Clients: American Home Products Corp.; Chrysler Corp.; Citibank, N.A.; Eli Lilly & Co.; ITT; The Shell Company; Union Carbide Corp.

For full biographical listings, see the Martindale-Hubbell Law Directory

MELLADO & MELLADO-VILLARREAL

Suite 202, 165 Ponce de Leon Avenue, 00918
Telephone: 809-767-2600
Telecopier: 809-767-2645

Ramon Mellado-Gonzalez
Jairo Mellado-Villarreal

Vanessa I. Raffucci-Vázquez
Maria S. Jiménez-Meléndez

Representative Clients: Advanced Cellular Systems; Meyers Parking System, Inc.; San Juan Gas Company; Procesadora de Granos de Puerto Rico, Inc.; Banesco Internacional Bank; Progreso Internacional Bank; Caribe Federal Credit; Coulter Biochemical; Coulter Electronics Sales, Inc.; P.E.D. Food Distributors; Magla Products, Inc.; San Juan Realty, Inc.

For full biographical listings, see the Martindale-Hubbell Law Directory

O'NEILL & BORGES

10th Floor, Chase Manhattan Bank Building (Hato Rey), 254 Muñoz Rivera Avenue, 00918-1995
Telephone: 809-764-8181
Telecopier: 809-753-8944

MEMBERS OF FIRM

Raymond C. O'Neill
Edward M. Borges
Eduardo E. Franklin
Juan Agustín Rivero
Walter F. Chow
David P. Freedman
Carlos M. Maldonado-Casillas
Irwin H. Flashman
Mario J. Pabón
Pedro J. Santa-Sánchez
Jorge L. Capó-Matos
Jaime J. Aponte-Parsi
José R. Cacho
Rosa M. Lázaro-San Miguel
Rosa M. González-Lugo
Luis A. Nuñez-Salgado
Luis Edwin González-Ortiz
Pablo Rodríguez-Solá

ASSOCIATES

Estela I. Vallés-Acosta
Christian M. Echavarri-Junco
Alfredo F. Ramirez-MacDonald
María de Lourdes Medina
Eduardo J. Negrón
Néstor R. Nadal-López
Ramón L. Velasco
Jacabed Rodriguez-Coss
Carlos A. Valldejuly-Sastre
Ana M. Leal-Gamba
María del Carmen Betancourt
Gilberto Maymí
David Rivé-Power
Jorge Izquierdo-San Miguel
Sila M. González
Sylvia M. Arizmendi
David W. Román-Vargas
Carlos M. Sánchez

Representative Clients: Bankers Trust Co.; The First Boston Corp.; Ford Motor Co.; H.H. Brown Shoe Company, Inc.; Interpublic Group of Companies; Manpower, Inc.; The Procter & Gamble Commercial Co.; Sara Lee Corp.; Sealand Corp.; Wang Laboratories, Inc.; Westinghouse Electric Corp.

For full biographical listings, see the Martindale-Hubbell Law Directory

UNITED STATES PACIFIC TERRITORY

SAIPAN, Mariana Islands

CARLSMITH BALL WICHMAN MURRAY CASE & ICHIKI

A Partnership including Law Corporations
Carlsmith Building, Capitol Hill, P.O. Box 5241, 96950
Telephone: 670-322-3455
Telecopier: 670-322-3368
Honolulu, Hawaii Office: Suite 2200, Pacific Tower, 1001 Bishop Street. P.O. Box 656.
Telephone: 808-523-2500.
Los Angeles, California Office: 555 South Flower Street, 25th Floor.
Telephone: 213-955-1200.
Long Beach, California Office: 301 East Ocean Boulevard, 7th Floor.
Telephone: 310-435-5631.
Washington, D.C. Office: 700 14th Street, N.W., 9th Floor.
Telephone: 202-508-1025.
Mexico City, Mexico Office: Monte Pelvoux 111, Piso 1, Col. Lomas de Chapultepec, 11000 Mexico, D.F.
Telephone: (011-52-5) 520-8514.
Fax: (011-52-5) 540 1545.
Mexico, D.F. Office of Carlsmith Ball Garcia Cacho y Asociados, S.C. (Authorized to practice Mexican Law): Monte Pelvoux 111, Piso 1, Col. Lomas de Chapultepec, 11000 Mexico, D.F.
Telephone: (011-52-5) 520-8514.
Fax: (011-52-5) 540-1545.
Agana, Guam Office: 4th Floor, Bank of Hawaii Building, P.O. Box BF.
Telephone: 671-472-6813.
Wailuku, Maui, Hawaii Office: One Main Plaza, Suite 400, 2200 Main Street, P.O. Box 1086.
Telephone: 808-242-4535.
Kailua-Kona, Hawaii Office: Second Floor, Bank of Hawaii Annex Building, P.O. Box 1720.
Telephone: 808-329-6464.
Hilo, Hawaii Office: 121 Waianuenue Avenue, P.O. Box 686.
Telephone: 808-935-6644.
Kapolei, Hawaii Office: Kapolei Building, Suite 318, 1001 Kamokila Boulevard.
Telephone: 808-674-0850.

RESIDENT PARTNERS

John F. Biehl
David R. Nevitt
John D. Osborn
Marcia K. Schultz

For full biographical listings, see the Martindale-Hubbell Law Directory

VIRGIN ISLANDS

*CHRISTIANSTED, ST. CROIX,** St. Croix

JEAN-ROBERT ALFRED

46B-47 King Street, 00820
Telephone: 809-773-2156
Telecopier: 809-773-4301

COUNSEL

Jane Wells Kleeger

For full biographical listings, see the Martindale-Hubbell Law Directory

PATTIE & DALEY

1104 Strand Street, Suite 204, Caravelle Arcade, 00820-5005
Telephone: 809-773-6650
Fax: 809-773-5479

MEMBERS OF FIRM

Bernard C. Pattie — Richard E. Daley, II

For full biographical listings, see the Martindale-Hubbell Law Directory

*CHARLOTTE AMALIE, ST. THOMAS,** St. Thomas

BIRCH, DE JONGH & HINDELS

Poinsettia House at Bluebeards Castle, P.O. Box 1197, 00804
Telephone: 809-774-1100
Telefax: 809-774-7300
Other St. Thomas Office: Palm Passage, Charlotte Amalie, 00802.

MEMBERS OF FIRM

Everett B. Birch (1922-1987) — James H. Hindels
John P. de Jongh — Samuel H. Hall, Jr.

ASSOCIATES

Stanley L. de Jongh — T. Lee Mason

OF COUNSEL

Richard P. Farrelly

Representative Clients: Barclays Bank PLC; The Chase Manhattan Bank, N.A.; Citibank, N.A.; Ernst & Young; Corestates First Pennsylvania Bank; FNMA/FHLMC (Regional Counsel); Westinghouse Foreign Sales Corp.; Hess Oil Virgin Islands Corp.; Peat, Marwick, V.I.

For full biographical listings, see the Martindale-Hubbell Law Directory

BORNN BORNN HANDY

No. 8 Norre Gade, P.O. Box 1500, 00804
Telephone: 809-774-1400
Fax: 809-774-9607

SENIOR PARTNER

Edith L. Bornn

PARTNERS

David A. Bornn — Veronica J. Handy

ASSOCIATES

Tregenza A. Roach — Seshigiri R. Alla

OF COUNSEL

Joseph M. Erwin (Not admitted in VI)

References: Bank of Nova Scotia; Banco Popular de P.R., St. Thomas, U.S. Virgin Islands.

For full biographical listings, see the Martindale-Hubbell Law Directory

GRUNERT STOUT BRUCH & MOORE

24-25 Kongensgade, P.O. Box 1030, 00804
Telephone: 809-774-1320
Fax: 809-774-7839

MEMBERS OF FIRM

John E. Stout — Susan Bruch Moorehead
Treston E. Moore

ASSOCIATES

Maryleen Thomas — H. Kevin Mart (Not admitted in VI)
Richard F. Taylor

OF COUNSEL

William L. Blum

For full biographical listings, see the Martindale-Hubbell Law Directory

CANADA
ALBERTA

*CALGARY,** Calgary Jud. Dist.

ATKINSON MILVAIN (AV)

1900 First Canadian Centre, 350 - 7th Avenue S.W., T2P 3N9
Telephone: 403-260-8500
Telecopier: 403-264-7084

MEMBERS OF FIRM

William T. Corbett, Q.C.
Michael F. Casey, Q.C.
Roy D. Boettger, Q.C.
John F. Costello
Peter M. Clark, Q.C.
G. Sean Dunnigan
Stuart F. Blyth
Jean C. Van der Lee
Janice B. Odegaard
Peter L. Collins
Lisa J. P. Gaunt

ASSOCIATES

Brian A. Yaworski
Graham G. Baugh
Faralee A. Chanin
Kelly R. Palmer
Anne Wallis
Graham M. Law
Doreen M. Saunderson
Thomas P. Kehler
Todd W. Kathol
Joanne J. Ruitenschild
Barbara J. Kimmitt

COUNSEL

Miles G. Atkinson, Q.C.

For full biographical listings, see the Martindale-Hubbell Law Directory

BENNETT JONES VERCHERE (AV)

4500 Bankers Hall East, 855-2nd Street S.W., T2P 4K7
Telephone: (403) 298-3100
Facsimile: (403) 265-7219
Edmonton, Alberta Office: 1000, 10035-105 Street.
Telephone: (403) 421-8133.
Facsimile: (403) 421-7951.
Toronto, Ontario Office: 3400 1 First Canadian Place. P.O. Box 130.
Telephone: (416) 863-1200.
Facsimile: (416) 863-1716.
Ottawa, Ontario Office: Suite 1800. 350 Alberta Street, Box 25, K1R 1A4.
Telephone: (613) 230-4935.
Facsimile: (613) 230-3836.
Montreal, Quebec Office: Suite 1600, 1 Place Ville Marie.
Telephone: (514) 871-1200.
Facsimile: (514) 871-8115.

MEMBERS OF FIRM

Rt. Hon. R. B. Bennett, P.C., K.C. (1870-1947)
Donnel O. Sabey, Q.C.
W. Gordon Brown, Q.C.
Garry C. Johnson, Q.C.
William L. Britton, Q.C.
John F. Curran, Q.C.
David H. McDermid
Lenard M. Sali, Q.C.
John G. Martland, Q.C.
H. Martin Kay
Richard B. Low
J. D. Bruce McDonald
William S. Rice
Douglas A. Ast
Alan W. Rubin
Garnet M. Schulhauser
Philip D. Backman
Bradley G. Nemetz
Daniel T. Gallagher
John Richels
Frank R. Dearlove
Stephen P. Sibold
R. Vance Milligan
Lawrence E. Smith
Donald E. Greenfield
William F. Quigley
Lorne W. Carson
Jo'Anne Strekaf
D. Alan Ross
J. Douglas Foster
Neil H. Stevenson
C. Perry Spitznagel
Robert R. Rooney
Michael J. Hopkins
Patrick J. Brennan
Herbert D. Wyman, Q.C.
Hon. E. Peter Lougheed, P.C., C.C., Q.C.
Walter B. O'Donoghue, Q.C.
Clifton D. O'Brien, Q.C.
John C. Armstrong, Q.C.
Lawrence A. Johnson
John S. Burns, Q.C.
Robert J. Pitt
Donald G. Anderson
Derek Y. Urban
Sal J. LoVecchio
Ronald B. Sirkis
Wayne R. Whitlock
Brian K. O'Ferrall
C. Michael Ryer
Robert P. Desbarats
Anthony L. Friend
John F. Cordeau
Robert T. Booth
David M. Lennox
Grant N. Stapon
Tim D. Kerrigan
Martin A. Lambert
Robert W. Thompson
Paul M. Farion
Margaret G. Lemay
James G. Smeltzer
Karen M. Horner
Loyola G. Keough
James A. D'Andrea
Blair C. Yorke-Slader
Henry W. Sykes
Kim D. Nixon
Hugh L. Mackinnon
J. David D. Steele
John W. Gulak

Heather I. Forester
David J. Corry
John L. Townley
Stuart G. O'Connor
Peter R. S. Leveque
Keith W. Templeton
Martin P. J. Kratz
John E. E. Lowe
Renée M. Ratke
John N. Craig
Nicholas M. Gretener
Darcy D. Moch

(See Next Column)

Donald M. Boykiw
Shawn H. T. Denstedt
Stanley R. Ebel
Ronald M. Barron
Patricia C. A. Irwin
Sherri L. Fountain
Karen J. Middleton
Al Meghji (Not admitted in AB)
Donald G. MacDiarmid
Deborah L. Petriuk
Brent J. Walter
Andrea H. Palmer
E. Bruce Mellett
Philip B. Hodge
George C. Tai
Catherine J. Valestuk
Heather J. Smith
Myron A. Tétreault
Janet L. McCready
Daniel K. Halyk
Peter A. Piliounis
Eamon J.B. Hurley
Susan M. Anderson
K. Louise Redmond
John D. Macneil (Not admitted in AB)
David J. Macaulay
Valerie R. Prather
Nick P. Fader
Richard H. Peters
L. Jeffrey J. Murray
Carsten Jensen
John Kousinioris
Belinda B. Moore
Noralee M. Gibson
Brenda J. Johnson
Glenn Solomon
Scott H.D. Bower
Patrick T. Maguire
Kenneth T. Lenz
Cynthia L. Mintz
Paul A. Beke
Patricia H. Sutherland
William E. Cascadden
Christopher A. Brown
Shawn M. Munro
Kevin L. Zemp
John R. Gilmore

OF COUNSEL

Maclean E. Jones, Q.C.
W. R. Jackett, O.C., Q.C. (Not admitted in AB)

For full biographical listings, see the Martindale-Hubbell Law Directory

BLAKE, CASSELS & GRAYDON (AV)

Bankers Hall East, Suite 3500, 855-2nd Street S.W., T2P 4J8
Telephone: 403-260-9600
Telecopier: 403-263-9895
Internet: calgary@blakes.ca
Toronto, Ontario Office: Box 25, Commerce Court West, M5L 1A9.
Telephone: 416-863-2400.
Facsimile: 416-863-2653. Internet: toronto@blakes.ca.
Telex: 06-219687.
Ottawa, Ontario Office: World Exchange Plaza, 20th Floor, 45 O'Connor Street, K1P 1A4.
Telephone: 613-788-2200.
Facsimile: 613-594-3965. Internet: ottawa@blakes.ca.
Vancouver, British Columbia Office: 1700-1030 West Georgia Street, V6E 2Y3.
Telephone: 604-631-3300.
Telecopier: 604-631-3309 - 16th Floor; 604-631-3305 - 17th Floor.
Internet: vancouver@blakes.ca.
European Office-London, England: 27 Austin Friars, EC2N 2QQ.
Telephone: 0171-374-2334.
Facsimile: 0171-638-3342.

PARTNERS

Leslie R. Duncan
Richard L. Dawson
A. Robert Anderson
Daniel P.E. Fournier
Patrick C. Finnerty
Brock W. Gibson
Kenneth B. Mills
Aleck H. Trawick
Gerald M. Deyell
Dallas L. Droppo
Wally Y. Shaw
Martin G. Abbott
Anthony F.W. Grenon
Joni R. Paulus
Dale Rathgeber

ASSOCIATES

B.J. Clapp
M.W. McCachen
R.A. Deyholos
D.W. McGrath
C. Hunka
C. Nicholson
B.C. Duguid
G.D. Holub
D.D. Bright
M. Hardwicke-Brown
L.A. O'Donoghue
P. Keohane
B.E. Munroe
J.S. Moore
W.E.B. Code
C.M. Good
L.E. Moore
L.D. Wilson

For full biographical listings, see the Martindale-Hubbell Law Directory

CODE HUNTER WITTMANN (AV)

Barristers & Solicitors
1200, 700 2nd Street, S.W., T2P 4V5
Telephone: 403-298-1000
Telecopier: 403-263-9193

MEMBERS OF FIRM

William E. Code, Q.C. *
Alan D. Hunter, Q.C.
Neil C. Wittmann, Q.C.
Joseph B. Katchen, Q.C. *
C. Scott Brooker, Q.C. *
John N. Iredale *
Alan S. Hollingsworth
Ronald G. Stevens
Anthony J. Jordan, Q.C.
Eric R. Holden
Mark N. Woolstencroft *
Richard W. Myers
James S. Peacock
Eric P. Groody
Andrew L. Oppenheim
Denis A. Hickey
Deborah B. Neale *
Brian G. Kapusianyk
Gregory G. Turnbull
Peter Pastewka
Eric L. Semmens
James R. Ferguson
Linda A. Taylor
Kevin W. Keyes

(See Next Column)

CODE HUNTER WITTMANN—*Continued*

MEMBERS OF FIRM (Continued)

Joan S. Saunders
Kenneth J. Warren
James T. Eamon
Gary B. Laviolette
Edith M. Gillespie
Paul J. Stein
Alan Jochelson
Locklynn T. Craig

ASSOCIATES

H. Vincent O'Connor
Marlis M. Schoenemann
Brian W. Mainwaring
Robert R. Hagerman
Robert L. Culton
Robert D. McCue
John Kingman Phillips
Christian J. Popowich
Bradley S. Dobbin
Jeffrey E. Dyck
Gordon E. Desautels
Thomas P. O'Leary
Sherrilynn J. Kelly
Thomas N. Cotter
Deirdre A. Mullan
Scott E. Cozens
Gary R. Bugeaud
Randall B. Schai
David C. Bishop
Stuart M. Olley
David M. Pick
Barbara L. Hearn
Daniel R. Horner
Heather D. Clarke
Michael E. Mestinsek
Glen M. Hickerson
Jeffrey R. Piercy
Philip W. Nykyforuk
Ronald J. Robinson

Reference: Bank of Nova Scotia.
*Denotes Lawyer Whose Professional Corporation is a Member of the Partnership.

For full biographical listings, see the Martindale-Hubbell Law Directory

FIELD & FIELD PERRATON (AV)

4000 Canterra Tower, 400-3 Avenue S.W., T2P 4H2
Telephone: 403-290-0990
Telecopier: 403-266-4466
Edmonton, Alberta Office: 2000 Oxford Tower, Edmonton Centre, 10235-101 Street.
Telephone: 403-423-3003.
Telecopier: 403-428-9329.

MEMBERS OF FIRM

John (Jack) R. Perraton, Q.C.
Daniel P. Carroll
Gerald R. Albert
Ian R. MacDonald
Douglas E. Roberts

ASSOCIATES

Gordon R. Meurin
Peter Varsanyi
Carol A. Neale
Judith Shriar
A.M. Lydia Lytwyn
Levente Frank Molnar
Craig L. Bentham
Leslie G. Morris

For full biographical listings, see the Martindale-Hubbell Law Directory

HOWARD, MACKIE (AV)

Barristers, Solicitors, Notaries
1000 Canterra Tower, 400 Third Avenue, S.W., T2P 4H2
Telephone: 403-232-9500
Telecopier: 403-266-1395

William Arnold Howard, C.M.M., C.D., Q.C.
Douglas H. Mitchell, Q.C.
Gerard C. Hawco
Hugh D. Williamson, Q.C.
George E. Anderson
Frank R. Foran, Q.C.
Allan D. Nielsen
John P. Petch *
Ross A. Reaburn
Patrick T. McCarthy
James W. Surbey
Frederick W. T. Somerville *
Brian E. Roberts *
John L. Ircandia
Ross D. Freeman *
Larry M. Kwinter
Andrew K. Maciag
John Poetker
David R. Wright
William C. Guinan
Jeffery D. Vallis
Stephen W. Wilson
Frank P. J. Cahill
Katherine L. Milani
David O. C. Elder
David C. Whelan
Peter T. Farkas
Randall W. Block
Brad J. Pierce

ASSOCIATES

William R. Blain, Q.C.
Terence G. Lidster
Donald F. Mackie
Colin P. MacDonald
Gregory L. Wells
Dean T. Allatt
Jean E. Blacklock
David T. Madsen
David M. Kohlenberg
M. Scott Wilson
Daniel G. Kolibar
C. Bryce Code
Marilyn D. Paterson
Marnie B. Rusen
Murray T. Brown
Colleen T. Legge
Linda C. French
Kelly E. Kimbley
Michael G. Massicotte
Amy K. Murphy
David G.L. McKenzie
Jonathan M. Liteplo

COUNSEL

T. John Hopwood, Q.C.
Edward M. Bredin, Q.C.
William D. Dickie, Q.C.

Reference: The Royal Bank of Canada, Main Branch, Calgary.
*Denotes Lawyer Whose Professional Corporation is a Member of the Partnership.

For full biographical listings, see the Martindale-Hubbell Law Directory

*DRUMHELLER,** Drumheller Jud. Dist. — (Refer to Calgary)

*EDMONTON,** Edmonton Jud. Dist.

BENNETT JONES VERCHERE (AV)

1000, 10035-105 Street, T5J 3T2
Telephone: (403) 421-8133
Facsimile: (403) 421-7951
Calgary, Alberta Office: 4500 Bankers Hall East. 855-2nd Street S.W.
Telephone: (403) 298-3100.
Facsimile: (403) 265-7219.
Toronto, Ontario Office: 3400 1 First Canadian Place. P.O. Box 130.
Telephone: (416) 863-1200.
Facsimile: (416) 863-1716.
Ottawa, Ontario Office: Suite 1800, 350 Alberta Street, Box 25, K1R 1A4.
Telephone: (613) 230-4935.
Facsimile: (613) 230-3836.
Montreal, Quebec Office: Suite 1600, 1 Place Ville Marie.
Telephone: (514) 871-1200.
Facsimile: (514) 871-8115.

MEMBERS OF FIRM

Glyn K. Edwards, Q.C.
Walter S. McKall
Paul M. Farion
Enzo J. Barichello

Martin P. J. Kratz
Rose M. Carter
Mark P. Kortbeek
David K. Wong
Edward R. Feehan
James J. Heelan
Jennifer A. Miller

For full biographical listings, see the Martindale-Hubbell Law Directory

DUNCAN & CRAIG (AV)

2800 Scotia Place, 10060 Jasper Avenue, T5J 3V9
Telephone: 403-428-6036
Fax: 403-428-9683
West End Office: 17731 - 103 Avenue, Edmonton, Alberta.
Telephone: 403-428-6036.
Fax: 403-489-8044.
Vegreville Office: 4925-50th Street, Box 700, T0B 4L0.
Telephone: 403-632-2877.
Fax: 403-632-2898.

PARTNERS

J. William D. Craig, Q.C. *
John M. Hope, Q.C. *
Solomon J. Rolingher *
Ronald W. Dutchak *
Ferne E.L. Onusko
Douglas P. Gahn *
Eric F. Macklin *
Stephen D. Laird
Philip J. Renaud
I. Thomas Colquhoun *
W. Scott Schlosser
James L. Bowen *
Dawn L. Pentelechuk
Denis J. Horne
Donald H. Heighington *
Brewster H.P. Kwan *
W. Gordon Plewes *
Thomas G. Cooke, Q.C.
John P. Poirier
Stephen L. Livergant
David C. Romaniuk
Percival E. Odynak
Debra J. Poon (On Leave)
John A. Kosolowski *
Darcy G. Readman
Patrick J. Feehan
Paul Pidde

SENIOR MEMBERS

Joseph H. Shoctor, O.C., Q.C., LL.D.
Joseph A. Blonsky (Resident, Vegreville Office)
D'Arcy D. Duncan, Q.C.
Hyman I. Shandling, Q.C.

ASSOCIATES

Douglas A. Lynass *
F. David Cook
Andrea O. Blonsky (Resident, Vegreville Office)
Helen R. Ward
Louis M.H. Belzil
Paul J.D. Alpern
Roberto Noce
Teresa (Terry) M. DeMarco
Dennis K.H. Wong
David M. Hawreluk
Richard G. Ferguson *
Marshall Shoctor
Gary I. Biasini
William W. Shores
Deborah M. Howes (On Leave)
Peter J. Dobbie (Resident, Vegreville Office)
Tracy L. Hanson
Joe D. Spelliscy
Jennifer L. Madsen
Janet L. Hutchison

RETIRED

The Hon. Peter Greschuk, Q.C.

LEGAL SUPPORT PERSONNEL

Wiggert Hessels

*Denotes Lawyer Whose Professional Corporation is a Member of the Partnership.

For full biographical listings, see the Martindale-Hubbell Law Directory

EMERY JAMIESON (AV)

1700 Oxford Tower, Edmonton Centre, 10235 - 101 Street, T5J 3G1
Telephone: 403-426-5220
Telecopier: 403-420-6277

(See Next Column)

EMERY JAMIESON, *Edmonton—Continued*

MEMBERS OF FIRM

Howard T. Emery, Q.C. (1899-1990)
Sydney A. Bercov, Q.C.
Henry B. Martin, Q.C.
W. Paul Sharek
Phyllis A. Smith, Q.C.
Gordon D. Sustrik
Michael J. Penny
Rex M. Nielsen
Susan L. Bercov
Terrence N. Kuharchuk
Murray F. Tait
John H. Jamieson, Q.C. (Retired)
L. Wayne Drewry, Q.C.
Richard B. Drewry
Robert W. Thompson
Andrew R. Hudson
Shirley A. McNeilly
G. Bruce Comba
Donna Carson Read
Bruce F. Hughson
Helen Garwasiuk
Robert D. McDonald

ASSOCIATES

Ellen S. Ticoll
Jeffrey K. Friesen
Blair E. Maxston
Frederica L. Schutz
Donald V. Tomkins
Earl J. Evaniew
Edward T. Yoo
Janet N. Alexander-Smith
Claire M. Klassen
Jennifer Kaufman-Shaw
Regina M. Corrigan

Reference: Canadian Imperial Bank of Commerce.

For full biographical listings, see the Martindale-Hubbell Law Directory

FIELD & FIELD PERRATON (AV)

2000 Oxford Tower, Edmonton Centre, 10235-101 Street, T5J 3G1
Telephone: 403-423-3003
Telecopier: 403-428-9329;
Cable Address: "Fieldman"
Calgary, Alberta Office: 4000 Canterra Tower, 400-3 Avenue, S.W.
Telephone: 403-290-0990.
Telecopier: 403-266-4466.

MEMBERS OF FIRM

Sem Wissler Field, Q.C. (1886-1976)
Louis D. Hyndman, Sr., Q.C. (1904-1993)
Harris G. Field, Q.C. (Semi-Active)
Harvey A. Bodner, Q.C.
Thomas S. Millman, Q.C. (Semi-Active)
Pierre J. Mousseau
Louis D. Hyndman, Q.C.
William M. Wintermute, Q.C.
C. Philip Clarke, Q.C.
Gary V. Frohlich
Robert H. Teskey, Q.C.
Michael C. J. Elias, Q.C.
Stephen D. Hillier, Q.C.
Christine G. Rapp
Donald K. Neeland
Barbara C. Howell
J. David McInnes
Deborah A. Miller
P. Jonathan Faulds
Jennifer J. Oakes
James W. Rea
Douglas S. Murray
Brian A. Vail
Adrian R. Currie
Greg A. Harding
Lorna E. Melnyk
Chereda L. Bodner
Brent F. Windwick
Donald M. McLaughlin
Wendy C. Rollins
Jay M. Guthrie
Warren T. Brown
James T. Casey
Heinrich (Rick) H. Pabst
Raylene Y. Palichuk
Sharon R. Stefanyk

ASSOCIATES

Carolyn J. Hutniak
Sandra J. Wagenseil
Anna Maria Moscardelli
Derek G. Alty
Leah D. Wintermute
Sandra M. Anderson
Kevin S. Feth
Thomas K. O'Reilly
Teresa A. Crotty-Wong
Garett A. Eisenbraun
Peter D. Gibson
John D. Toogood

COUNSEL

Peter M. Owen, Q.C.

For full biographical listings, see the Martindale-Hubbell Law Directory

LUCAS BOWKER & WHITE (AV)

Esso Tower - Scotia Place, 1201-10060 Jasper Avenue, T5J 4E5
Telephone: 403-426-5330
Telecopier: 403-428-1066

MEMBERS OF FIRM

Gerald A. I. Lucas, Q.C.
George E. Bowker, Q.C.
Robert B. White, Q.C.
David J. Stratton, Q.C.
Cecilia I. Johnstone, Q.C.
John Reginald Day, Q.C.
E. James Kindrake
Elizabeth A. Johnson
Norman J. Pollock
Robert C. Dunseith
Douglas H. Shell
Kent H. Davidson
Alan R. Gray
Robert A. Seidel
Robert P. Bruce
David J. Stam
Donald J. Wilson

ASSOCIATES

Kevin J. Smith
Gordon V. Garside
Deborah L. Hughes
Annette E. Koski
Douglas A. Bodner
Michael Alexander Kirk
Mark E. Lesniak
Eric C. Lund
Linda A. Maj
Dusten E. Stewart
Debbie E. Bryden
Kathleen Audrey Scott

(See Next Column)

COUNSEL

H. Neil Bowker
Joan C. Copp
Linda R. Flynn

Reference: Canadian Imperial Bank of Commerce.

For full biographical listings, see the Martindale-Hubbell Law Directory

MCLENNAN ROSS (AV)

600 West Chambers, 12220 Stony Plain Road, P.O. Box 12040, T5J 3L2
Telephone: 403-482-9200
Telecopier: 403-482-9100; 403-482-9101; 403-482-9102
INTERNET: mross@supernet.ab.ca

Roderick A. McLennan, Q.C. *
John Sterk, Q.C. *
Philip G. Ponting, Q.C.
Havelock B. Madill, Q.C.
Brian R. Burrows, Q.C.
Johanne L. Amonson, Q.C. *
Kevin J. Anderson *
Douglas G. Gorman
Glenn D. Tait
Yolanda S. Van Wachem
Michelle G. Crighton
Walter J. Pavlic
Donald J. McGarvey
Donald W. Dear
Scott A. Watson
Stephen J. Livingstone
Doreen C. Mueller
Douglas J. Boyer
John K. Gormley
Timothy C. Mavko
Timothy F. Garvin
David J. Ross, Q.C.
Peter P. Taschuk, Q.C.
D. Mark Gunderson *
Darren Becker *
Frederick A. Day, Q.C. *
Hugh J. D. McPhail
Jonathan P. Rossall *
R. Graham McLennan *
William S. Rosser *
Ronald M. Kruhlak
Gerhard J. Seifner
Rodney R. Neys
Damon S. Bailey
Christopher J. Lane
Clay K. Hamdon
Sandra J. Weber
Steven J. Ferner
Karen J.A. Metcalfe
Katharine L. Hurlburt
Lucien R. Lamoureux
Renée Craig

*Denotes Lawyer Whose Professional Corporation is a Member of the Partnership.

For full biographical listings, see the Martindale-Hubbell Law Directory

PARLEE MCLAWS (AV)

15th Floor Manulife Place, 10180 101st Street, T5J 4K1
Telephone: 403-423-8500
Telecopier: 403-423-2870
Calgary, Alberta Office: 3400, Western Canadian Place, 707 - 8th Avenue, S.W.
Telephone: 403-294-7000.
Telecopier: 403-265-8263.

MEMBERS OF FIRM

C. H. Kerr, Q.C.
M. D. MacDonald
K. F. Bailey, Q.C.
R. B. Davison, Q.C.
F. R. Haldane
P. E. J. Curran
D. G. Finlay
J. K. McFadyen
R. C. Secord
D. L. Kennedy
D. C. Rolf
D. F. Pawlowski
A. A. Garber
R. P. James
D. C. Wintermute
J. L. Cairns
R. A. Newton, Q.C.
T. A. Cockrall, Q.C.
H. D. Montemurro
F. J. Niziol
R. W. Wilson
I. L. MacLachlan
R. O. Langley
R. G. McBean
J. T. Neilson
E. G. Rice
J. F. McGinnis
J. H. H. Hockin
G. W. Jaycock
M. J. K. Nikel
B. J. Curial
S. L. May
M. S. Poretti

ASSOCIATES

C. R. Head
A.W. Slemko
L. H. Hamdon
K.A. Smith
K. D. Fallis-Howell
D. S. Tam
J.W. McClure
F.H. Belzil
R.A. Renz
J.G. Paulson
K. E. Buss
B. L. Andriachuk
P. E. S. J. Kennedy
R. Feraco
R.J. Billingsley
N.B.R. Thompson
P. A. Shenher
I. C. Johnson
K.G. Koshman
D.D. Dubrule
G. T. Lund
W.D. Johnston
G. E. Flemming
K. P. Nayyer

For full biographical listings, see the Martindale-Hubbell Law Directory

*GRANDE PRAIRIE,** Grande Prairie Jud. Dist. — (Refer to Edmonton)

*HANNA,** Hanna Jud. Dist. — (Refer to Calgary)

*LETHBRIDGE,** Lethbridge Jud. Dist. — (Refer to Calgary)

*MEDICINE HAT,** Medicine Hat Jud. Dist. — (Refer to Calgary)

*PEACE RIVER,** Peace River Jud. Dist. — (Refer to Edmonton)

*RED DEER,** Red Deer Jud. Dist. — (Refer to Edmonton)

BRITISH COLUMBIA

*KAMLOOPS,** Yale Co. — (Refer to Vancouver)

NANAIMO, Vancouver Island Co. — (Refer to Vancouver)

*NELSON,** Kootenay Co. — (Refer to Vancouver)

*PRINCE GEORGE,** Cariboo Co. — (Refer to Vancouver)

*PRINCE RUPERT,** Prince Rupert Co. — (Refer to Vancouver)

*VANCOUVER,** Vancouver Co.

ALEXANDER, HOLBURN, BEAUDIN & LANG (AV)

P.O. Box 10057 2700 Toronto Dominion Bank Tower, 700 West Georgia Street, V7Y 1B8
Telephone: 604-688-1351
Fax: 604-669-7642
Hong Kong, In Association with Lawrence Ong & Chung: 8th Floor, Chekiang First Bank Centre, 1 Duddell Street. Central.
Telephone: (852-2) 526-1171.
Fax: (852-2) 845-0686.
Taipei, Taiwan Office, In Association with Perennial Law Office: c/o 7F-2, No. 9, Roosevelt Road, Section 2.
Telephone: (886-2) 395-6989.
Fax: (886-2) 391-4235.

PARTNERS

Ernest A. Alexander, Q.C. (1918-1983)
William M. Holburn, Q.C.
Michael P. Ragona, Q.C.
F. Stuart Lang
Lawrance J. Gwozd
Thomas A. Roper
David A. Gooderham
James A. Dowler
Michael C. Scholz
Robert G. Payne
Robert B. Kennedy
Roger M. Bourbonnais
Michael V. Roche
R. Patrick Saul
James A. Henshall
William P. Work
Gregory J. Nash
J.J. McIntyre
Jo Ann Carmichael
Bruno De Vita
David B. Wende
Terry C. Vos
Frances R. Watters
Gary M. Nijman
Judith P. Kennedy
Ross Shamenski
George F. T. Gregory
J. Dale Stewart
Michel E. Giasson
Patrick M. Gilligan-Hackett
Kenneth H. Crook

PARTNER IN HONG KONG

Calvin Kam-Wing Chung

ASSOCIATES

Sharon M. Urquhart
Darcie A. Laurient
Andrew S. MacKay
Glen A. McEachran
Matthew Cooperwilliams
Delayne M. Sartison
Sharleen L. Dumont
Vivien M. W. Own
Barbara L. Devlin
Peggy M. Tugwood
Eileen E. Vanderburgh
Richard P. Harnetty (Resident, Taipei, Taiwan)
Janet L. Winteringham
Renee T. E. Goult
Susan Grattan-Doyle
Dana G. Graves
Banafsheh Sokhansanj
Yee-Wah Erika Tse
D. Christopher Fong
David T. McKnight
Todd R. Davies
Parrish Kang-Kwan Kwan
Andrea A. Rayment
Cheryl E. Shizgal
Jean-Marc F. Hébert

Reference: The Toronto-Dominion Bank.
A list of Representative Clients will be furnished on request.

For full biographical listings, see the Martindale-Hubbell Law Directory

BLAKE, CASSELS & GRAYDON (AV)

1700-1030 West Georgia Street, V6E 2Y3
Telephone: 604-631-3300
Telecopier: 604-631-3309 - 16th Floor
604-631-3305 - 17th Floor
Internet: vancouvr@blakes.ca
Toronto, Ontario Office: Box 25, Commerce Court West, M5L 1A9.
Telephone: 416-863-2400.
Facsimile: 416-863-2653. Internet: toronto@blakes.ca.
Telex: 06-219687.
Ottawa, Ontario Office: World Exchange Plaza, 20th Floor, 45 O'Connor Street, K1P 1A4.
Telephone: 613-788-2200.
Facsimile: 613-594-3965. Internet: ottawa@blakes.ca.
Calgary, Alberta Office: Bankers Hall East, Suite 3500, 855-2nd Street S.W., T2P 4J8.
Telephone: 403-260-9600.
Telecopier: 403-263-9895. Internet: calgary@blakes.ca.
European Office - London England: 27 Austin Friars, EC2N 2QQ.
Telephone: 0171-374-2334.
Facsimile: 0171-638-3342.

PARTNERS

Marvin R.V. Storrow, Q.C.
Roger G. Howay
Anne M. Stewart, Q.C.
William C. Kaplan
James P. Taylor, Q.C.
Donald J. Jordan, Q.C.
Peter C. Kalbfleisch (Not admitted in BC)

(See Next Column)

Israel Chafetz
Jocelyn M. Kelley

PARTNERS (Continued)

Maria A. Morellato
Randy J. Kaardal
Bill S. MacLagan
Joanne R. Lysyk

ASSOCIATE COUNSEL

Peter T. Burns, Q.C.

ASSOCIATES

Joanne B. Payne
Scott A. Turner
Jeffrey Merrick
Gayle Hunter
Geoffrey S. Belsher
Darryl M. Chambers
Nicole L. Hunter
Darrell W. Podowski
Francis L. Lamer
Jennifer J. Lynch
Kelly E. Stark-Anderson
Wendy S. Morrison
Ian M. Brindle
Roslyn Goldner
Laura L. Jessome
Sheila M. Tucker
Curt D. Bernardi

For full biographical listings, see the Martindale-Hubbell Law Directory

BULL, HOUSSER & TUPPER (AV)

Patent and Trade Mark Agents
A Member of McMillan Bull Casgrain
Suite 3000, 1055 West Georgia Street, P.O. Box 11130, V6E 3R3
Telephone: 604-687-6575
Cable Address: "Tursid"
Telex: 04-53395; 04-55121
Fax: 604-641-4949
Surrey, British Columbia Office: Suite 201, 9648 - 128th Street, V3T 2X9.
Telephone: 604-581-4677.
Fax: 604-581-5947.
Hong Kong Office: McMillan Bull Casgrain, 17th Floor, 9 Queen's Road, Central.
Telephone: 852-843-7333.
Fax: 852-845-5566.
Taipei, Taiwan Office: McMillan Bull Casgrain, 5F-1, No. 415, Sec. 4, Hsinyi Road.
Telephone: (02) 720-0192.
Fax: (02) 720-0219.

MEMBERS OF FIRM

Harvey R. Bowering
Frank Low-Beer
Barry O'N. Dryvynsyde, Q.C.
Daniel A. Webster, Q.C.
Philip B. Webber
R. Eric P. Maurice
Nils E. Daugulis
Robert J. Bauman
Alan N. Robertson
Grant K. Weaver
Douglas G. Morrison
Robert W. Hunter
William J. McFetridge
C. Decatur Howe
James B. Stewart (Resident, Surrey Office)
John S. Haythorne
Ann Gourley
George D. Burke
N. Victoria Gray
Howard L. Ehrlich
Simon B. Margolis
Lynda C. Darling
Brian E. Taylor
Herbert B. Regehr
Peter J. O'Callaghan
R.S. Jindy Bhalla
Carole E. Hickey (Resident, Surrey Office)
Shelley F. O'Callaghan
Penny A. Washington
Daniel R. Bennett
Harbans Dhillon
Gregory D. Lewis
Norine MacDonald
Elliott Myers
Don H. Holubitsky
Hamish C. Cameron
William C. Bice
J.D. Lach Morrison
William G. Gooderham
William M. Burris
D. Larry Page
R. Brian Wallace
Brian C. Duncan (Resident, Surrey Office)
George D. Mucalov
John G. Dives
Trevor C. Armstrong (Resident, Surrey Office)
R. John Kearns
Judith B. Downes
J. Christopher Grauer
Christopher G. Speakman
Robin J. Harper
Brian McLaughlin
John D. Ankenman
David R. Bain
Kerry A. Short
E. Jane Milton
Catherine L. Woods
Karen Martin
Angela T.F. Mong
Mark R. Slay (Resident, Surrey Office)
Herbert J. Isherwood
Margaret H. Mason
Mark Sachs
David A. Garner
Jennifer McCarron
Marion Shaw
David Bursey
Andrew Konnert
Rodney A. Chorneyko (Resident, Surrey Office)

ASSOCIATES

Clive M. Ansley (Resident, Taipei, Taiwan Office)
Linda Sum
Lyle E. Braaten
Andrew P. Jackson (Resident, Surrey Office)
Stephen Hayward
T. Ryan Darby
Katherine S. Camp
Matthew D. Howard
Ronald P. Labossiere (Resident, Surrey Office)
Michael B. Hetherington
David R. Reid
William S. Garton
Robert P. Pirooz
Catherine J. G. Ryan
Jean Billing
Ivy Loree Young
Janet P. Grove
James H. Goulden
Michael G. Martin
Randy E. Lonsdale (Resident, Surrey Office)

(See Next Column)

BULL, HOUSSER & TUPPER—*Continued*

A. Daniel Conn
Sandra Carter

ASSOCIATES (Continued)

Todd J. Wetmore
Catherine D. Thompson
Helen E. Allard
Randal J.C. Barker
Jean Yuen

ASSOCIATE COUNSEL

David W.H. Tupper, Q.C.
Ivan B. Quinn
Wilfred J. Wallace, Q.C.

LEGAL SUPPORT PERSONNEL

PATENT/TRADEMARK AGENTS

John W. Knox
Jane S. Baggott
Brian J. Wood

For full biographical listings, see the Martindale-Hubbell Law Directory

CAMPNEY & MURPHY (AV)

2100-1111 West Georgia Street, P.O. Box 48800, V7X 1K9
Telephone: 604-688-8022
Cable Address: "Omur"
Telex: 04-53320.
Facsimile: 604-688-0829

MEMBERS OF FIRM

Marshall M. Soule
David P. R. Roberts, Q.C.
John D. Montgomery
Robert F. Hungerford
Peter G. Bernard
David A. Zacks
Henning W. Wiebach
Robert J. MacRae
Robert D. Standerwick
Murray A. Clemens, Q.C.
Timothy J. Nichols
W. Bruce Tattrie
Christopher K. Haines
John W. Marquardt
Douglas R. Garrod
Colin M. Emslie
Deborah D. Anderson
Howie A. Caldwell
Paul C. MacNeill
Robert E. Breivik
Lynn C. Waterman
Ian M. Lawrenson
Shelley C. Fitzpatrick
Heather M. B. Ferris
Nevin L. Fishman
Andrew G. Kadler
David J. Raffa
Murray L. Smith
W. Gary Wharton
Paula M. Palyga
Elaine E. Reynolds
James P. Shumka

ASSOCIATES

Arthur M. Grant
H. Peter Swanson
Thomas S. Hawkins
Mary P. Collyer
Mark W. Hilton
Rupert M. Shore
Bryan C. Gibbons
Michael R. Axford
Peter E. Norell
Silvana M. Facchin
Neville J. McClure
Iain R. Mant
Melinda G. Voros
Adele L. Burchart
Kent G. Burnham
Gregg E. Rafter
Peeyush K. Varshney

ASSOCIATE COUNSEL

Denis W. H. Creighton (Retired)
John R. Cunningham, Q.C. (Retired)
W. Donald C. Tuck (Retired)
R. I. A. Smith (Retired)

Reference: Bank of Montreal.

For full biographical listings, see the Martindale-Hubbell Law Directory

CONNELL LIGHTBODY (AV)

Royal Centre, 1900 - 1055 West Georgia Street, P.O. Box 11161, V6E 4J2
Telephone: 604-684-1181
Telex: 51-94070493
Fax: 604-641-3916

MEMBERS OF FIRM

Walley P. Lightbody, Q.C.
J. Gavin Connell, Q.C.
John J. Reynolds
Michael H. Heller
Philip G. Ferber
Thomas E. Baillie
S. Harry Lipetz
Francis Y. Hanano
J. Stephen Cheng
Mark R. Steven
R. Michael Young
Kerry-Lynne D. Findlay
John W. A. Bromley

ASSOCIATE COUNSEL

Arthur Fouks, Q.C.
Benjamin J. McConnell (Retired)
Terence E. Wolfe (On Leave)

ASSOCIATES

James D. Burns
E. Ajit S. Saran
Hugh H. Claxton
Robert A. Margolis
Peter A. Eccles
Richard K. Uhrle
J. Geoffrey Howard
Brian D. Rhodes
Shelley A. Chapelski
John D. Whyte
Kathleen H. Walker
C.M. Paulina Lee

For full biographical listings, see the Martindale-Hubbell Law Directory

DAVIS & COMPANY (AV)

Trade Mark Agents
2800 Park Place, 666 Burrard Street, V6C 2Z7
Telephone: 604-687-9444
Facsimile: 604-687-1612
Whitehorse, Yukon Territory Office: Suite 101, 307 Jarvis Street, Y1A 2H3.
Telephone: 403-668-6444.
Facsimile: 403-667-2669.
Yellowknife, Northwest Territories Office: Suite 802 Northwest Tower, 5201 50th Avenue, X1A 3S9.
Telephone: 403-873-6455.
Facsimile: 403-873-6456.

MEMBERS OF FIRM

D. S. D. Hossie
A. C. Robertson, Q.C.
Patrick J. Furlong
Robert T. Banno
R. B. D. Swift
Grant D. Burnyeat, Q.C.
Wolfgang Schwegler
W. Ross Ellison
Vincent Morgan
Dale G. Sanderson
James I. Reynolds
John I. McLean
A. G. Henderson, Q.C.
Rodney A. Snow
Lewis F. Harvey
Frank S. Borowicz
D. W. Cooper
Robert T. Groves
Arnold M. Abramson
Jodie F. Werier
Rolf N. Kaplun
Rhys Davies
Walter G. Rilkoff
S. Scott Dunlop
Stanley Wong
Garry E. P. Mancell
Robert A. Fashler
Mary L. Ruhl
Kathryn I. Denhoff
Brian D. MacKay
David C. Davenport
Peter W. Bogardus
Joseph M. Pelrine
Robert E. Marriott
Rowland K. McLeod
D. Ross Clark
Jacqueline A. Kelly
Douglas C. Morley
Michael P. Carroll
John J. L. Hunter
Warren H. Downs
David H. Searle, Q.C.
Peter C. Lee
Glenn Morgan
Paul R. Albi
Stuart B. Morrow
M. Patricia Gallivan
Robert D. C. Malcolm
P. John Landry
Peter G. Voith
Malcolm O. Maclean
Douglas Blair Buchanan
John Saunders
Cynthia A. Millar
R. C. Strother
P. Anthony McArthur
Allen A. Soltan
P. D. Lailey
Blair Shaw
Lenore R. Rowntree

ASSOCIATES

Albert J. Hudec
Michael J. Todd
Paul R. Cassidy
Mary Hamilton
Brian F. Hiebert
Franco E. Trasolini
W. P. Kiang
Keith E. W. Mitchell
M. Bingham
Robert A. Sider
Tamara L. Hunter
Laura Ingrid Cabott
Catherine J. Branch
Clare W. Cheah
Ben Singer
Hilton W.C. Sue
Alanna Yvette Lee
Hamish Cumming
James G. Matkin
Roger Douglas Lee
Richard I. Hardy
Monika Gehlen
Caroline K. H. Findlay
James M. Sullivan
Kim G. Thorne
D. Lawrence Munn
Mark A. Schmidt
Geoffrey A. Dabbs
Debra M. Hanuse
Diana L. Dorey
Douglas G. Shields
Gordon J. Haskins
Catherine A. Boddez
Grace G.Y. Choi
Corrie L. Stepan
Elaine P. Hassell
Simon Robert Wells
Michael Logie
Donald R.M. Bell
Douglas Arthur Scullion
Robert B. Hunter

COUNSEL

L. Allan Williams, Q.C.
D. H. C. Paterson
David M. Johnston

FOREIGN LEGAL CONSULTANT

Peter P.L. Li (Not admitted in BC)

RETIRED ASSOCIATE COUNSEL

A. W. Fisher, Q.C.
A. J. F. Johnson, Q.C.

Representative Clients: Canadian Imperial Bank of Commerce; Mitsubishi Canada Limited; Scott Paper Ltd.; The Canadian Fishing Company Limited; B.C. Central Credit Union; General Foods, Limited; Hudson's Bay Co.; Vancouver City Savings Credit Union.

For full biographical listings, see the Martindale-Hubbell Law Directory

FARRIS, VAUGHAN, WILLS & MURPHY (AV)

P.O. Box 10026, Pacific Centre South Toronto Dominion Bank Tower, 700 West Georgia Street, V7Y 1B3
Telephone: 604-684-9151
Telex: 04-507819
Telecopier: 604-661-9349
Cable Address: "Farem"

Hon. John Wallace deBeque Farris, Q.C. (1903-1970)

(See Next Column)

FARRIS, VAUGHAN, WILLS & MURPHY, *Vancouver—Continued*

COUNSEL

C. Francis Murphy, Q.C.

MEMBERS OF FIRM

Peter Woods Butler, Q.C.
Jack M. Giles, Q.C.
R. Christopher Holmes
A. Keith Mitchell, Q.C.
Elizabeth J. Harrison, Q.C.
Alan J. Hamilton
George K. Macintosh, Q.C.
Hugh M. Matthews
John J. Swift
Barry T. Gibson
Charles G. Pearson
Herbert D. Dodd
R. Hector MacKay-Dunn
Peter F. Parsons
Paul S. Richardson
Jeffrey J. Kay
Robert S. Anderson
Judy Jansen
Robert P. Sloman
Robert J. McDonell
Brock R. Rowland
Geoffrey N. M. Lewis
David I. McBride
Rupert A. Legge
James P. Hatton
Dean A. O'Leary

ASSOCIATES

Donald L. Richards
J. Kenneth McEwan
Gordon A. Love
Karen Shirley-Paterson
R. Christopher Boulton
Michael Gianacopoulos
Brian R. Canfield
Derek J. May
Charmaine H. Hung
Lisa A. Warren
Stacey S. Silber
Nancy E. Fish
David A. Goult
Catherine M. McEachern
Carolyn L. Berardino
Ronald A. Chin
Heather Lynne Jones
Douglas A. Holl
J.D. Taggart
David Thomas Woodfield

Reference: The Toronto-Dominion Bank.

For full biographical listings, see the Martindale-Hubbell Law Directory

FRASER & BEATTY (AV)

15th Floor, The Grosvenor Building, 1040 West Georgia Street, V6E 4H8
Telephone: 604-687-4460
Telecopier: 604-683-5214
Toronto, Ontario Office: 1 First Canadian Place, P.O. Box 100, M5X 1B2.
Telephone: 416-863-4511.
Telecopier: 416-863-4592.
North York, Ontario Office: The Madison Centre, 4950 Yonge Street, Suite 2300, M2N 6K1.
Telephone: 416-733-3300.
Telecopier: 416-221-5254.
Ottawa, Ontario Office: 180 Elgin Street, Suite 1200, K2P 2K7.
Telephone: 613-238-6294.
Telecopier: 613-563-7800.
Montreal, Quebec Affiliated Office: McMaster Meighen. 7th Floor, 630 René-Lévesque Boulevard West, H3B 4H7.
Telephone: 514-879-1212.
Telecopier: 514-878-0605.
Cable Address: "Camerall".
Telex: "Camerall MTL" 05-268637.

PARTNERS, CONSULTANTS AND ASSOCIATES

J. Donald Mawhinney, Q.C.
Howard J. Kellough, Q.C.
John G. R. Third
Gordon S. Funt
Colin J. McIver
Joel A. Nitikman
Ernest A. Hee
Laura Penelope Ettinger
Robert G. Nikelski
Kelly L. Geddes
G. Lisa Heddema
Juliet D.W. Smith
Robin A. Gokey
J. T. English
Douglas I. Knowles
Gordon W. Esau
Deborah E. Nesbitt
Clayton W. Caverly
Jeffrey A. Read
K. Gregory Senda
Tim T. Bezeredi
Gary R. Menzies
Benjamin J. Ingram
Marie-France Leroi
Neal S. Steinman
Lee-Ann McGuire

For full biographical listings, see the Martindale-Hubbell Law Directory

HARPER GREY EASTON (AV)

3100 Vancouver Centre, 650 West Georgia Street, P.O. Box 11504, V6B 4P7
Telephone: 604-687-0411
Telex: 04-55448
Telecopier: 604-669-9385

MEMBERS OF FIRM

Harvey J. Grey, Q.C.
M. Donald Easton
L. N. Matheson
Terrence C. O'Brien
Isidor M. Wolfe
Terrence L. Robertson, Q.C.
W. J. McJannet
James M. Lepp
Bryan G. Baynham
John B. Brown
C. E. Hinkson, Q.C.
Howard A. Barends
Gordon G. Hilliker
M. M. Skorah
Kathryn E. Neilson, Q.C.
G. Bruce Butler
Paul T. McGivern
Scott W. Fleming
Larry H. Koo
Stephen P. Grey
Peter M. Willcock
James A. Doyle
Maureen L. A. Lundell
Victor P. Harwardt
Laura B. Gerow
Barbara J. Norell

(See Next Column)

MEMBERS OF FIRM (Continued)

David A. Gagnon
Guy Patrick Brown
Bernard S. Buettner
Loreen M. Williams

ASSOCIATES

Robert J. Rose
Kieron G. Grady
Juliet A. Donnici
Geoffrey L. K. Yeung
Cheryl L. Talbot
William S. Clark
M. Lynn McBride
Douglas L. Long
David W. Pilley
Anu K. Khanna
Bena Wendy Stock
Katherine E. Armstrong

Anne F. Cameron
Janet E. Currie
Andrea Finch
Marion (Mara) E. Stickland

RETIRED PARTNERS

Arthur M. Harper, Q.C. (Retired)
David Sigler, Q.C. (Retired)

Solicitors for: Commercial Union Assurance Company of Canada; Lumbermens Mutual Casualty Co.; State Farm Fire and Casualty Co.

For full biographical listings, see the Martindale-Hubbell Law Directory

LADNER DOWNS (AV)

900 Waterfront Centre, 200 Burrard Street, P.O. Box 48600, V7X 1T2
Telephone: 604-687-5744
Fax: 604-687-1415
Telex: 04-507553

MEMBERS OF FIRM AND ASSOCIATES

Stephen Antle
Kenneth M. Bagshaw, Q.C.
Clive S. Bird
Debra L. Browning
Mary Jo E. Campbell
Edward C. Chiasson, Q.C., F.C.I.Arb.,C.Arb.
Celia M. Courchene
Neil de Gelder
J. Kelly Edmison
Bradley J. Freedman
Gerald W. J. Ghikas
Larry R. Jackie
Edwin G. Kroft
Paul J. Lowry
P. Donald MacDonald
Roger D. McConchie
William K. McNaughton
Stephen J. Mulhall
Otto Hans Nowak
Vincent R. K. Orchard
George P. Reilly
John L. Sampson
Deborah A. Satanove
Robert R. Shouldice
G. Ross Switzer
Geoffrey Thompson
Ian A. Webb
Warren T. Wilson, Q.C.
Peter M. Archibald, Q.C.
D. Gregory Batcheller
Ron L. Bozzer
David K. Camp
Barry D. Chase
Michael A. Coady
Douglas G. Copland
G. Sidney Cross
Martin D. Donner
Patrick G. Foy
David C. Frydenlund
Stein K. Gudmundseth
Gordon R. Johnson
Richard E. Lester
Russell W. Lusk, Q.C.
Peter A. Manson, Q.C.
Daniel B. McIntyre
William R. Miles
David P. L. Mydske
Christopher J. O'Connor
C. R. Laurence Peers
J. Donald Rose
Larry R. Sandrin
Timothy R. Sehmer
William F. Sirett
Brian W. Thom
Shelley M. Tratch
Gary J. Wilson
Rosanna Wong

Cameron G. Belsher
Nigel P.H. Cave
Alixe B. Cormick
Debashis Dey
Bradley W. Dixon
John P. Ferber
Leonard A. Glass
Carl C. Januszczak
Sandra D. Lloyd
Lori A. Lothian
D. Ross McGowan
Shelley-Mae Mitchell
Heather Northrup
Robert G. Owen
Candace J. Pinter
Oren Samuel
Robert D. Shaw
Michael A. Skene
Peter W. Spicker
Graham Walker
Donald G. Bird
Joan C. Chambers
Marylee A. Davies
Adrian G. Dirassar
Douglas R. Eyford
Bruce E.B. Gailey
Do-Ellen S. Hansen
Sharon Kearney
David C.S. Longcroft
Michelle A. MacPhee
David L. Miachika
Shawn C. D. Neylan
Deborah H. Overholt
Sudhir K. Padmanabhan
Fred R. Pletcher
C. Bruce Scott
Key-Yong Shin
F. Randolph Smith
Jeffrey S. Thomas
Matthew G. Watson
Irene K. Winel

ASSOCIATE COUNSEL

Maurice D. Copithorne, Q.C.
Charles C. Locke, Q.C.

For full biographical listings, see the Martindale-Hubbell Law Directory

Vancouver—Continued

McCarthy Tétrault (AV)

P.O. Box 10424, Pacific Centre, Suite 1300, 777 Dunsmuir Street, V7Y 1K2
Telephone: 604-643-7100
Fax: 604-643-7900
Surrey, British Columbia Office: Suite 1300, Station Tower, Gateway, 13401 108th Avenue, Surrey, British Columbia V3T 5T3.
Telephone: 604-583-9100.
Fax: 604-583-9150.
London, Ontario Office: Suite 2000, 1 London Place, 255 Queens Avenue, London, Ontario N6A 5R8.
Telephone: 519-660-3587.
Facsimile: 519-660-3599.
Toronto, Ontario Office: Suite 4700, Toronto Dominion Bank Tower, Toronto Dominion Centre, Toronto, Ontario M5K 1E6.
Telephone: 416-362-1812.
Facsimile: 416-868-0673.
Ottawa, Ontario Office: Suite 1000, 275 Sparks Street, Ottawa, Ontario, K1R 7X9.
Telephone: 613-238-2000.
Facsimile: 613-563-9386.
Montréal, Québec Office: "Le Windsor" 1170 rue Peel, Montréal Québec H3B 4S8.
Telephone: 514-397-4100.
Facsimile: 514-875-6246.
Québec, Québec Office: 112 rue Dalhousie, Québec, Québec G1K 4C1.
Telephone: 418-692-1532.
Facsimile: 418-692-4354.
United Kingdom Office: 1 Pemberton Row, Fetter Lane, London, England EC4A 3EX.
Telephone: 011-44-71-353-2355.
Facsimile: 011-44-71-583-5644.

MEMBERS AND ASSOCIATES

Sholto Hebenton, Q.C.
Winton Derby, Q.C.
John W. Lutes
John W. Pearson
Theodor A. Zacks
Rosemarie Wertschek
Ashley F. Hilliard
D. Anthony Knox
A. Brent Kerr
Michael E. Mitchell
Peter Pagnan
Donna Cooke
Gabriel M. Somjen
Brian Vick
Elaine J. Adair
Elizabeth M. Vogt
Shael H. I. Wilder
Karen M. Gilmore
Sally Dennis
Alan Schapiro
Ted I. Koffman
Bronson Toy
Kevin Wright
George W. Holloway
Ariel DeJong (Resident, Surrey Office)
Nancy A. Trott
Annelle Wilkins
Maureen S. Boyd
Beverly G. Ellingson
Naomi M. Youngson
K. Beth Macdonald
H. William Veenstra
Thomas D. Ciz
Elizabeth H. Yip
Joanne K. Glover
Kathleen M. Doyle
Warren B. Milman
R. Paul Beckmann, Q.C.
Mitchell H. Gropper, Q.C.
Robert J. Sewell
Byran Gibson
Trevor W. Bell
James A. Titerle
Keith E. Burrell
Derek Winnett (Resident, Surrey Office)
R. Barry Fraser
Earl G. Phillips
Peter D. Fairey
Alan H. Brown
Richard J. Balfour
Peter Kenward
Robin Sirett
Robert W. Cooper
Herman Van Ommen
Scott A. Griffin
John A. Doolan
Linda G. Parker
Timothy P. McCafferty
Dawn P. Whittaker
Russell G. Benson
B. Glenn Leung
Noreen V. Brox
Timothy S. Kwan
Colin S. McIvor
Nicholas Hughes
Michael T. Scott
Shauna Tucker
Richard P. Attisha
François LeTourneux
Lesley M. Midzain
Randall N. Rae
Julie L. Owen
Lisa Martz
Mark E.W. East
Charles C. Gagnon

COUNSEL

Leonard T. Doust, Q.C.
Nicolaas A. Blom
John B. Zaozirny, Q.C.
Owen C. Dolan, Q.C.

For full biographical listings, see the Martindale-Hubbell Law Directory

Paine Edmonds (AV)

Suite 1100 Montreal Trust Centre, 510 Burrard Street, V6C 3A8
Telephone: 604-683-1211
Facsimile: 604-681-5084
Abbotsford, British Columbia Office: 31205 Old Yale Road. V2T 5E5.
Telephone: (604) 864-2880.
Fax: (604) 864-8445.

(See Next Column)

W. H. Kemp Edmonds, Q.C. (1916-1986)

MEMBERS OF FIRM

Leonard C. Dudley
J. Lyle Woodley, Q.C.
James C. Taylor
Elmer A. Yusep
Owen G. Jones
Henry D.M. Edmonds
Steven H. Heringa
John J. Hyde

ASSOCIATES

Eric B. Heringa
John Bancroft-Jones
Bradford D.S. Garside
Anthony E. Thomas
P. L. (Lee) Quinton
Robert D. Kirkham
Kirsten J. Madsen
Clay Bruce Williams

Reference: Toronto Dominion Bank.

For full biographical listings, see the Martindale-Hubbell Law Directory

Russell & DuMoulin (AV)

2100-1075 West Georgia Street, V6E 3G2
Telephone: 604-631-3131
Fax: 604-631-3232
A Member of the national association of Borden DuMoulin Howard Gervais, comprising Russell & DuMoulin, Vancouver, British Columbia; Howard Mackie, Calgary, Alberta; Borden & Elliot, Toronto, Ontario; Mackenzie Gervais, Montreal, Quebec and Borden DuMoulin Howard Gervais, London, England.
Strategic Alliance with Perkins Coie with offices in Seattle, Spokane and Bellevue, Washington; Portland, Oregon; Anchorage, Alaska; Los Angeles, California; Washington, D.C.; Hong Kong and Taipei, Taiwan.
Represented in Hong Kong by Vincent T.K. Cheung, Yap & Co.

MEMBERS OF FIRM

Henri C. Alvarez
Mark D. Andrews
W. S. Berardino, Q.C.
Murray B. Blok
Holly A. Brinton
James G. Carphin
Gary Catherwood
Donald M. Dalik
Bryce A. Dyer
Peter H. Finley
B. W. F. Fodchuk
Robert A. Goodrich
Bruce R. Grist
Norah J. Hall
Charles G. Harrison
Gavin H. G. Hume, Q.C.
Patricia L. Janzen
C. B. Johnson
Anne L. B. Kober
Elizabeth B. Lyall
James H. MacMaster
W. Stanley Martin
John S. McKercher
Robert A. Millar
Richard J. Olson
Gary W. Ott
Marcel J. Peerson
P. Geoffrey Plant
Douglas G. S. Rae
Allan P. Seckel
L. Barry Sheppard
Peter H. Stafford
Benjamin B. Trevino, Q.C.
Donald J. Weaver
Paul C. Wilson
Leopold Amighetti, Q.C.
Arthur J. Bensler
Richard J. Berrow
Frances K. Boyle
H. Laing Brown
W. Ian Cassie
D. Geoffrey G. Cowper
D. Jane Dardi
Lauri Ann Fenlon
Michael A. Fitch
George W. Forster
John F. Grieve
R. H. Guile, Q.C.
David C. Harris
Christopher Harvey, Q.C.
Michael W. Hunter
Helmut K. Johannsen
David W. Kington
Allison R. Kuchta
Gordon C. Lyall
Thomas Manson
J. M. McCormick
Avon M. Mersey
William T. Morley
Kevin P. O'Neill
Susan I. Paish
James D. Piers
Marina A. Pratchett
William A. Randall, Jr.
Merrill W. Shepard
Gary R. Sollis
Norman K. Trerise
Barbara Vanderburgh
Charles F. Willms
Alan D. Winter

ASSOCIATES

Aiyaz A. Alibhai
Stephen C. Best
Ward K. Branch
Shaun C. Cathcart
Lynne M. Charbonneau
Brian L. Child
Simon R. Coval
Jennifer L. Harry
Mark Peter Hicken
Clark B. Ledingham
Robert M. Lonergan
Edmond C. C. Luke
J. Geoffrey Lyster
Joyce A. Mitchell
W. Simon Patey
Thomas J. Prescott
Gregory S. Pun
Marianne Sue Shannon
Michael J. Sobkin
Janine A. S. Thomas
Teresa A. White
David Wotherspoon
Katherine Anne Arnold
Andrew O. Borrell
Gillian Case
Linda G. Chan
Lesley R. Charkow
Tracey M. Cohen
J. Gregory Diamond
Gregory J. Heywood
Theresa T. Johannsen
Brent J. Lewis
Helen H. Low
E. Jane Luke
William S. McLean
Lorene A. Novakowski
Scott Lewis Perrin
Kevin I. Price
Frank S. Schober
Thora A. Sigurdson
Keith E. Spencer
William Westeringh
Darrell J. Wickstrom
Wei Zhang

COUNSEL

William R. McIntyre, C.C., Q.C.
Nathan T. Nemetz, C.C., Q.C.

(See Next Column)

RUSSELL & DUMOULIN, *Vancouver—Continued*

ASSOCIATE COUNSEL

C. Edward Barnes

Representative Clients: Alcan Smelters & Chemicals Ltd.; The Bank of Nova Scotia; Canada Trust Co.; The Canada Life Assurance Co.; Forest Industrial Relations Ltd.; Honda Canada Inc.; IBM Canada Ltd.; Macmillan Bloedel Ltd.; Nissho Iwai Canada Ltd.; The Toronto-Dominion Bank.

For full biographical listings, see the Martindale-Hubbell Law Directory

SINGLETON URQUHART MACDONALD (AV)

1200 - 1125 Howe Street, V6Z 2K8
Telephone: 604-682-7474
Fax: 604-682-1283
Calgary, Alberta Office: 203 - 200 Barclay Parade, S.W., T2P 0J1.
Telephone: 403-261-9043.
Fax: 403-265-4632.

Glenn A. Urquhart
A. Webster Macdonald, Jr., Q.C. (Resident, Calgary Office)
Bonita J. Thompson, Q.C.
Dale B. Pope
Nathan H. Smith
John R. Singleton
Lorne W. Scott, Q.C. (Resident, Calgary Office)
Linda A. Loo, Q.C.
Derek A. Brindle
James G. Hanley (Resident, Calgary Office)
David G. Butcher

ASSOCIATE COUNSEL

Rolf Weddigen

ASSOCIATES

J.M. (Tim) Mackenzie
V.A. (Bud) MacDonald (Resident, Calgary Office)
Marsha C. Erb (Resident, Calgary Office)
Mindy A. Jong
Jane Ingman-Baker
Mark D. Nordman
Jeffery A. Hand
Robin E. Elliott (Resident, Calgary Office)
Michael J. Hewitt
Terence C. Semenuk (Resident, Calgary Office)
Craig R. Thomson
Janet E. Russell (Resident, Calgary Office)
Gail H. Forsythe
Stephan M. Reinhold (Resident, Calgary Office)
John C. Zang (Resident, Calgary Office)
C.L. (Kate) Mclean
Andrew N. Epstein

Representative Clients: Agra Industries Ltd.; Architectural Institute of B.C.; Attorney General of B.C.; Attorney General of Canada; B.C. Hydro & Power Authority; B.C. Railway; College of Dental Surgeons of B.C.; Deloitte & Touche; Department of Indian and Northern Affairs Canada; Discipline Committee, College of Chiropractors of Alberta.

For full biographical listings, see the Martindale-Hubbell Law Directory

STIKEMAN, ELLIOTT (AV)

666 Burrard Street, Suite 1700, Park Place, V6C 2X8
Telephone: 604-631-1300
Fax: 604-681-1825
Montreal, Quebec Office: 1155 René-Lévesque Boulevard West, 40th Floor, H3B 3V2.
Telephone: 514-397-3000.
Fax: 514-397-3222.
Toronto, Ontario Office: Commerce Court West, 53rd Floor, M5L 1B9.
Telephone: 416-869-5500.
Fax: 416-947-0866.
Ottawa, Ontario Office: 50 O'Connor Street, Suite 914, K1P 6L2.
Telephone: 613-234-4555.
Fax: 613-230-8877.
Calgary, Alberta Office: 855 - 2nd Street S.W., 1500 Bankers Hall, T2P 4J7.
Telephone: 403-266-9000.
Fax: 403-266-9034.
New York, New York Office: 126 East 56th Street, 11th Floor, Tower 56, 10022.
Telephone: 212-371-8855.
Fax: 212-371-7087.
Washington, D.C. Office: 1300 I Street, N.W., Suite 1210 West, 20005-3314.
Telephone: 202-326-7555.
Fax: 202-326-7557.
London, England Office: Cottons Centre, Cottons Lane, SE1 2QL.
Telephone: 71-378-0880.
Fax: 71-378-0344.
Paris, France Office: In Association with Société Juridique Internationale, 39, rue François Ier, 75008.
Telephone: 33-1-40-73-82-00.
Fax: 33-1-40-73-82-10.
Budapest, Hungary Office: Andrássy út 100, II Floor, H-1062.
Telephone: 36-1-269-1790.
Fax: 36-1-269-0655.
Hong Kong Office: 29 Queen's Road Central, Suite 1506, China Building.
Telephone: 852-2868-9903.
Fax: 852-2868-9912.

(See Next Column)

Hong Kong: In Association with Shum & Co., 29 Queen's Road Central, Suite 1103, China Building.
Telephone: 852-2526-5531.
Fax: 852-2845-9076.
Taipei, Taiwan Office: 117 Sec. 3 Min Sheng East Road, 8th Floor.
Telephone: 886-2-719-9573.
Fax: 886-2-719-4540.

RESIDENTS IN VANCOUVER

Michael S. Allen
John F. Anderson
Clint A. Calder
Jonathan S. Drance
Cameron R. W. Duff
Deborah A. Fahy
David E. Gillanders
Chantal L. Goodmanson
Richard J. Jackson
Eugene H. Kwan
Susan E. Lloyd
Ralph J. Lutes
Ross A. MacDonald
Maria McKenzie
Clifford S. M. Ng
Nicholas Paczkowski
John N. Paton
Alan W. Pinkney
L. Greg Plater
Vicky Wong
Bruce D. Woolley

For full biographical listings, see the Martindale-Hubbell Law Directory

*VICTORIA,** Vancouver Island Co.

COX, TAYLOR (AV)

Third Floor, Burnes House, 26 Bastion Square, V8W 1H9
Telephone: 604-388-4457
Fax: 604-382-4236

MEMBERS OF FIRM

Allan L. Cox, Q.C.
Rodney J. E. Taylor, Q.C.
Murray J. Holmes
R. T. Johnston, Q.C.
C. Edward Hanman
S. Frank B. Carson
L. John Alexander
William Murphy-Dyson
John Van Driesum
Melissa R. Clarke

For full biographical listings, see the Martindale-Hubbell Law Directory

MANITOBA

*BRANDON,** Western Jud. Dist. — (Refer to Winnipeg)

*DAUPHIN,** Dauphin Jud. Dist. — (Refer to Winnipeg)

*PORTAGE LA PRAIRIE,** Central Jud. Dist. — (Refer to Winnipeg)

*WINNIPEG,** Eastern Jud. Dist.

AIKINS, MACAULAY & THORVALDSON (AV)

Thirtieth Floor, Commodity Exchange Tower, 360 Main Street, R3C 4G1
Telephone: 204-957-0050
Fax: 204-957-0840

MEMBERS OF FIRM

Sir James Aikins, K.B., K.C., LL.D. (1879-1929)
John A. MacAulay, C.C., Q.C., LL.D. (1919-1978)
A. Lorne Campbell, O.C., C.D., Q.C., LL.D.
Michael J. Mercury, Q.C.
Martin H. Freedman, Q.C.
James E. Foran, Q.C.
Robert G. Smellie, Q.C.
Raymond H.G. Flett, Q.C.
Cyril G. Labman
Bryan D. Klein
Charles L. Chappell
Thomas P. Dooley
Gerald D. Parkinson
E. Bruce Parker
Judith M. Blair
Barbara M. Hamilton, Q.C.
Marc M. Monnin
G. Bruce Taylor
Robert G. Siddall
Herbert J. Peters
J. Milton Christiansen
David M. Carrick
Betty A. Johnstone
L. William Bowles
Jonathan B. Kroft
J. Douglas Sigurdson
Catherine E. Carlson
William K.A. Emslie
Thor J. Hansell
James C.R. Ludlow
Michael E. Guttormson
Robert L. Tyler
Keith Ferbers
Lori A. Lavoie
Jacqueline N. Freedman
Francis J. St.Hilaire
Jonathan G. Penner
Nigel J. Thompson
G.H. Aikins, D.S.O., Q.C., LL.D. (1910-1954)
Hon. G.S. Thorvaldson, Q.C., LL.D. (1925-1969)
John S. Lamont, Q.C.
Roger J. Hansell, Q.C.
A.J. Mercury, Q.C.
Andrew C. Tough
Knox B. Foster, Q.C.
Leon N. Mercury, Q.C.
J. Timothy Samson
Larry R. Crane, Q.C.
Roland B. Dias
Colin R. MacArthur, Q.C.
Rod E. Stephenson, Q.C.
Joel A. Weinstein
S. Jane Evans, Q.C.
Eleanor R. Dawson, Q.C.
David L. Voechting
Daryl J. Rosin
Richard L. Yaffe
Frank Lavitt
G. Todd Campbell
Lori T. Spivak
Lisa M. Collins
Fay-Lynn Katz
Barbara R. Hochman
Kristin L. Lercher
John R. Braun
Kathleen M.T. Craton
J. Guy Joubert
Brian D. Lerner
Anita R. Wortzman
Carmele N. Peter
D. Salin Guttormsson
Theodor E. Bock
Helga D. Van Iderstine
Barbara S. MacDonald
Georgina A. Garrett
Philip T. Samyn
Harley C. Boles
Lorna L. McConnell

Counsel for: Air Canada; Bank of Montreal; Boeing of Canada; Canada Safeway Limited; Canadian Medical Protective Association; Federal Industries Ltd.; The Great West Life Assurance Company; John Labatt Limited; Winnipeg Free Press; Winnipeg Jets.

For full biographical listings, see the Martindale-Hubbell Law Directory

MONK, GOODWIN (AV)

800 Centra Gas Building, 444 St. Mary Avenue, R3C 3T1
Telephone: 204-956-1060
Telecopier: 204-957-0423

Henry B. Monk, Q.C. (Retired)
Richd. R. Goodwin, Q.C. (1903-1984)
Max Wolinsky, Q.C. (1907-1989)
Robert Hucal
David Wolinsky
Herbert Liffmann
Richard N. Hoeschen
Charles J. Phelan, Q.C.
Laurent J. Roy, Q.C.
Ernest M. Shewchuk
James H. Dixon
Barry L. Gorlick, Q.C.
Mark T. O'Neill
Benjamin R. Hecht
Randall A. Horton
Remo Paolo De Sordi
Michel J. Chartier
Randall Fleisher

For full biographical listings, see the Martindale-Hubbell Law Directory

PITBLADO & HOSKIN (AV)

1900-360 Main Street Winnipeg Square, R3C 3Z3
Telephone: 204-942-0391
Facsimile: 204-957-1790, 204-957-0272, 204-957-5181
Cable Address: "Camfords"
Telex: 07-55175

(See Next Column)

PARTNERS

Gary T. Brazzell, Q.C.
James B. Fraser
David G. Newman
Peter J. Falk
Robert A. Dewar, Q.C.
George E. Van Den Bosch
E. Wells Peever
Kevin R. Bolt
Robert P. Sokalski
John T. McGoey
Bruce H. King
Roger W. Wight
Lionel J. Martens
Robert A. Watchman
Peter M. Ramsay
William C. Kushneryk, Q.C.
Duncan D. Jessiman
Edward L. Warkentin
John R. Toone
Walter Thiessen
Richard J. Handlon
James A. Ferguson
William S. Gardner
Walter S. Saranchuk, Q.C.
Robert M. Jessiman
Robert F. Peters
David R.M. Jackson
Thomas W. Turner

SENIOR ASSOCIATES

William C. Gardner, Q.C.
Duncan J. Jessiman, Q.C.
Michael Skwark, Q.C.

ASSOCIATES

Joseph D. Barnsley
Todd W. Hewett
Robert D. Brazzell
Elizabeth E.I. Beaupré
Jeff A. Baigrie
Douglas J. Forbes
Philip P. Pauls
Christopher P. Besko
Richard D. Buchwald
Tina Giesbrecht
Jennifer A. Cooper
Glen W. Agar
Joe R. Gallagher
Marianne Rivoalen
Tracey Lynn Epp
Murray Froese
Daron Werthman
James A. Dolynchuk
Karen M. Dunlop
Michelle R. Redekopp

Representative Clients: Prudential Insurance Company of America; Canadian Imperial Bank of Commerce; The Canada Trust Co.; James Richardson & Sons, Ltd.; Ford Motor Company of Canada Ltd.; Petro Canada Inc.; Health Sciences Centre; AMCA International Ltd.

For full biographical listings, see the Martindale-Hubbell Law Directory

NEW BRUNSWICK

*BATHURST,** Gloucester Co. — (Refer to Fredericton)

*EDMUNDSTON,** Madawaska Co. — (Refer to Fredericton)

*FREDERICTON,** York Co.

ALLEN, DIXON & BELL (AV)

Frederick Square, Suite 340, 77 Westmorland Street Frederick Square, P.O. Box 1418, E3B 5E3
Telephone: 506-453-0900
Telefax: 506-453-0907

MEMBERS OF FIRM

G. Keith Allen, Q.C.
Ray W. Dixon, Q.C.
B. Richard Bell
Charles A. Sargeant, Q.C.
Lorraine C. King, Q.C.
Patrick E. Hurley
Richard J. Scott
Gale L. MacDonald
Patrick B. Gorman

Reference: Bank of Montreal.

For full biographical listings, see the Martindale-Hubbell Law Directory

HANSON, HASHEY (AV)

Suite 400 Phoenix Square, Queen Street, P.O. Box 310, E3B 4Y9
Telephone: 506-453-7771
Telecopier: 506-453-9600
Saint John, New Brunswick Office: One Brunswick Square, Suite 1212.
Telephone: 506-652-7771.
Telecopier: 506-632-9600.

MEMBERS OF FIRM

H. A. Hanson, Q.C. (1909-1985)
David T. Hashey, Q.C.
David M. Norman, Q.C.
J. Ian M. Whitcomb, Q.C. (Resident, Saint John Office)
John M. Hanson, Q.C.
Walter D. Vail
Michael E. Bowlin
Bruce D. Hatfield
Julian A. G. Dickson
Anne D. Wooder
Terrence J. Morrison
J. Charles Foster
Lucie Richard

ASSOCIATES

Catherine M. Bowlen
J. Marc Richard
Amanda J. Frenette
Monika M. L. Zauhar
Leslie F. Matchim
Bruce M. Logan (Resident, Saint John Office)
Frank E. Hughes
Ann Marie Leeuw

For full biographical listings, see the Martindale-Hubbell Law Directory

*MONCTON,** Westmorland Co.

STEWART MCKELVEY STIRLING SCALES (AV)

Formerly McKelvey, Macaulay, Machum
Suite 601, 644 Main Street, P.O. Box 20070, E1C 9M1
Telephone: 506-853-1970
Telecopier: 506-858-8454
Halifax, Nova Scotia Office: Suite 900, Purdy's Wharf Tower One, 1959 Upper Water Street, P.O. Box 997.
Telephone: 902-420-3200.
Telecopier: 902-420-1417.
Telex: 019-22593.
Sydney, Nova Scotia Office: 50 Dorchester Street, P.O. Box 820.
Telephone: 902-539-5135.
Telecopier: 902-539-8256.
Saint John, New Brunswick Office: Suite 1000, 10th Floor, Brunswick House, 44 Chipman Hill, P.O. Box 7289 Station "A".
Telephone: 506-632-1970.
Telecopier: 506-652-1989.
St. John's, Newfoundland Office: Cabot Place, 100 New Gower Street, P.O. Box 5038.
Telephone: 709-722-4270.
Telex: 016-4733.
Telecopier: 709-722-4565.
Charlottetown, Prince Edward Island Office: 65 Grafton Street, P.O. Box 2140.
Telephone: 902-892-2485.
Telecopier: 902-566-5283.

MEMBERS OF FIRM

Levi E. Clain, Q.C.
André G. Richard
John E. Pöllabauer

ASSOCIATES

Micheline T. Doiron
Marie-Claude Bélanger-Richard
Guy A. Belliveau

For full biographical listings, see the Martindale-Hubbell Law Directory

*NEWCASTLE,** Northumberland Co. — (Refer to Moncton)

*SAINT JOHN,** Saint John Co.

CLARK, DRUMMIE & COMPANY (AV)

40 Wellington Row, P.O. Box 6850 Station "A", E2L 4S3
Telephone: 506-633-3800
Telecopier (Automatic): 506-633-3811

MEMBERS OF FIRM

Thomas B. Drummie, Q.C.
Donald F. MacGowan, Q.C.
M. Robert Jette
Terrence W. Hutchinson
W. Andrew LeMesurier
Patrick J. P. Ervin
Frederick A. Welsford
Donald J. Higgins
Timothy M. Hopkins
Deno P. Pappas, Q.C.
Willard M. Jenkins
Barry R. Morrison, Q.C.
Norman J. Bossé
John M. McNair
William B. Richards
Sherrie R. Boyd
Karen M. Colpitts
John C. Warner
Peter H. MacPhail

OF COUNSEL

Richard W. Bird, Q.C.
L. Paul Zed, M.P.

Reference: Royal Bank of Canada.

For full biographical listings, see the Martindale-Hubbell Law Directory

GILBERT, MCGLOAN, GILLIS (AV)

Suite 710, Mercantile Centre, 55 Union Street P.O. Box 7174, Station "A", E2L 4S6
Telephone: 506-634-3600
Telecopier: 506-634-3612

T. Louis McGloan, Q.C. (1896-1986)
Adrian B. Gilbert, Q.C. (1895-1986)

MEMBERS OF FIRM

Donald M. Gillis, Q.C.
Thomas L. McGloan, Q.C.
A. G. Warwick Gilbert, Q.C.
Rodney J. Gillis, Q.C.
Douglas A. M. Evans, Q.C.
Brenda J. Lutz
David N. Rogers

ASSOCIATES

Paulette C. Garnett, Q.C.
Edward Veitch
Hugh J. Flemming, Q.C.
Anne F. MacNeill
Nancy E. Forbes
Marie T. Bérubé
Guy C. Spavold
Claire B.N. Porter
Michael J. Murphy
Mark A. Canty

Representative Clients: Bank of Montreal; Canada Packers Ltd.; McCain Foods Ltd.; The Sunderland Steamship Protecting & Indemnity Association; Steamship Mutual Underwriting Association (Bermuda) Limited; Royal Insurance Co.; Wawanesa Mutual Insurance Co.; Dominion of Canada General Insurance Co.; Canadian General Insurance Co.

For full biographical listings, see the Martindale-Hubbell Law Directory

PALMER, O'CONNELL, LEGER, RODERICK, GLENNIE (AV)

Suite 1600, One Brunswick Square, P.O. Box 1324, E2L 4H8
Telephone: 506-632-8900
Telecopier: 506-632-8809
Moncton, New Brunswick Office: Suite 220, Blue Cross Centre, 644 Main Street, E1C 1E2.
Telephone: 506-856-9800.
Telecopier: 506-856-8150.

MEMBERS OF FIRM

John P. Palmer, Q.C. (1916-1979)
Peter S. Glennie, Q.C.
R. Gary Faloon
Peter M. Wright
William H. Teed, Q.C.
Cedric B. Allaby
Colette M. d'Entremont
John B. D. Logan
Franklin O. Leger, Q.C.
M. Barry Roderick
Raymond F. Glennie, Q.C.
William F. O'Connell
Peter R. Forestell
Charles D. Whelly
James K. O'Connell
John D. Laidlaw
E. Ann Mowatt
Raymond T. French

ASSOCIATE COUNSEL

Gerald W. O'Brien, C.A.

COUNSEL

George F. O'Connell, Q.C.

ASSOCIATES

Karen L. Rogers
Edward W. Keyes
Rick F. T. Nesbitt
Kathryn L. Stratton
Ellen C. Desmond

Reference: The Bank of Nova Scotia.

For full biographical listings, see the Martindale-Hubbell Law Directory

Saint John—Continued

STEWART MCKELVEY STIRLING SCALES (AV)

Formerly McKelvey, Macaulay, Machum
Suite 1000, 10th Floor, Brunswick House, 44 Chipman Hill, P.O. Box 7289 Station "A", E2L 4S6
Telephone: 506-632-1970
Telecopier: 506-652-1989
Halifax, Nova Scotia Office: Suite 900, Purdy's Wharf Tower One, 1959 Upper Water Street, P.O. Box 997.
Telephone: 902-420-3200.
Telecopier: 902-420-1417.
Telex: 019-22593.
Sydney, Nova Scotia Office: 50 Dorchester Street, P.O. Box 820.
Telephone: 902-539-5135.
Telecopier: 902-539-8256.
Moncton, New Brunswick Office: Suite 601, 644 Main Street, P.O. Box 20070.
Telephone: 506-853-1970.
Telecopier: 506-858-8454.
St. John's, Newfoundland Office: Cabot Place, 100 New Gower Street, P.O. Box 5038.
Telephone: 709-722-4270.
Telex: 016-4733.
Telecopier: 709-722-4565.
Charlottetown, Prince Edward Island Office: 65 Grafton Street, P.O. Box 2140.
Telephone: 902-892-2485.
Telecopier: 902-566-5283.

MEMBERS OF FIRM

Lawrence M. Machum, Q.C.
Ronald G. Lister, Q.C.
Donald L. Cullinan, Q.C.
Wayne R. Chapman, Q.C.
D. Hayward Aiton
Frederick D. Toole
Gerald S. McMackin
Robert G. Vincent, Q.C.
Kenneth B. McCullogh
Lynne M. Burnham
Michael D. Wennberg
Barbara E. Stanley
Gregory S. Sinclair
James F. LeMesurier
Charles A. LeBlond
Stephen J. Hutchison
Peter M. Klohn
Rodney D. Gould
Darrell J. Stephenson
C. Paul W. Smith

ASSOCIATES

James D. Murphy
Randall A. Hatfield
Christopher J. Stewart
J. Paul M. Harquail
Cynthia J. Benson
Catherine A. Lahey
William C. Kean
Mark J. Doucet

COUNSEL

E. Neil McKelvey, O.C., Q.C.

For full biographical listings, see the Martindale-Hubbell Law Directory

ST. STEPHEN, Charlotte Co.

NICHOLSON, TURNER, WALKER & WHITE (AV)

46 Milltown Boulevard, P.O. Box 218, E3L 2X1
Telephone: 506-466-2338
Telecopier: 506-466-1299
St. Andrews, New Brunswick Office: 177 Water Street. P.O. Box 569.
Telephone: 506-529-8831.
Telecopier: 506-529-3066.

G. Fred Nicholson, Q.C.
G. Melvin Turner, Q.C.
David C. Walker (Resident, St. Andrews Office)
Randall S. White

Representative Clients: Bank of Nova Scotia; Bank of Montreal; Royal Bank of Canada; Central Guaranty Trust Co.; Georgia-Pacific Corp.; Town of St. Stephen; Town of St. Andrews; Village of Blacks Harbour; Maritime Supermarket Ltd.

For full biographical listings, see the Martindale-Hubbell Law Directory

*WOODSTOCK,** Carleton Co. — (Refer to Fredericton)

NEWFOUNDLAND

*ST. JOHN'S,**

O'REILLY, NOSEWORTHY (AV)

Suite 401, Scotia Centre 235 Water Street, A1C 1B6
Telephone: 709-726-3321
Telecopier: 709-726-2992

MEMBERS OF FIRM

Thomas J. O'Reilly, Q.C.
Ronald S. Noseworthy, Q.C.
John F. Roil, Q.C.
Reginald H. Brown
Roland C. Snelgrove
Robert E. Simmonds
D. Richard Robbins
Randall W. Smith
Robert P. Stack
Paul M. McDonald
Sandra R. Chaytor
Philip J. Buckingham
Jorge P. Segovia
F. Richard Gosse

Reference: Royal Bank of Canada.

For full biographical listings, see the Martindale-Hubbell Law Directory

STEWART MCKELVEY STIRLING SCALES (AV)

Formerly Stirling, Ryan
Cabot Place, 100 New Gower Street, P.O. Box 5038, A1C 5V3
Telephone: 709-722-4270
Telex: 016-4733
Telecopier: 709-722-4565
Halifax, Nova Scotia Office: Suite 900, Purdy's Wharf Tower One, 1959 Upper Water Street, P.O. Box 997.
Telephone: 902-420-3200.
Telecopier: 902-420-1417.
Telex: 019-22593.
Sydney, Nova Scotia Office: 50 Dorchester Street, P.O. Box 820.
Telephone: 902-539-5135.
Telecopier: 902-539-8256.
Moncton, New Brunswick Office: Suite 601, 644 Main Street, P.O. Box 20070.
Telephone: 506-853-1970.
Telecopier: 506-858-8454.
Saint John, New Brunswick Office: Suite 1000, 10th Floor, Brunswick House, 44 Chipman Hill, P.O. Box 7289 Station "A".
Telephone: 506-632-1970.
Telecopier: 506-652-1989.
Charlottetown, Prince Edward Island Office: 65 Grafton Street, P.O. Box 2140.
Telephone: 902-892-2485.
Telecopier: 902-566-5283.

MEMBERS OF FIRM

Gordon M. Stirling, C.M., Q.C., LL.D. (1907-1985)
Francis J. Ryan, Q.C.
Ernest G. Reid, Q.C.
Michael F. Harrington, Q.C.
Lewis B. Andrews, Q.C.
Augustus G. Lilly
Harold M. Smith
Geoffrey E. J. Brown
Janet M. Henley Andrews
Kenneth A. Templeton
Bruce C. Grant
William H. Goodridge
Colm St. R. Seviour
Dennis J. Ryan
Neil L. Jacobs
Ian C. Wallace
Daniel M. Boone

ASSOCIATES

R. Wayne Bruce
Maureen E. Ryan
Paul L. Coxworthy
Cecily Y. Strickland
Anne F. Murphy
Erroll G. Treslan
Rodney J. Zdebiak
Michael J. McNicholas

For full biographical listings, see the Martindale-Hubbell Law Directory

NOVA SCOTIA

*AMHERST,** Cumberland Co. — (Refer to Truro)

*ANNAPOLIS ROYAL,** Annapolis Co. — (Refer to Yarmouth)

*HALIFAX,** Halifax Co.

COX DOWNIE (AV)

1100 Purdy's Wharf Tower One, 1959 Upper Water Street, P.O. Box 2380 Stn Central RPO, B3J 3E5
Telephone: 902-421-6262 and Fax: 902-421-3130

MEMBERS OF FIRM

Ronald J. Downie, Q.C.
David McD. Mann, Q.C.
Michael S. Ryan, Q.C.
John Arnold
Douglas C. Campbell, Q.C.
Peter W. Gurnham
Frederick P. Crooks
Anthony L. Chapman
J. Craig McCrea
Brian W. Downie
Robert W. Carmichael
A. James Musgrave
Jan McKenzie
Jocelyn M. Campbell
Brian A. Tabor
George M. Mitchell, Q.C.
Robert G. MacKeigan, Q.C.
Daniel M. Campbell, Q.C.
Gregory I. North, Q.C.
Daniel F. Gallivan
Thomas P. Donovan
Terry L. Roane
Michael E. Dunphy
Leslie J. Dellapinna
Jamie S. Campbell
Alan J. Dickson
Lorraine P. Lafferty
D. Kevin Latimer
Jonathan R. Gale
John H. (Jack) Graham

ASSOCIATES

Karen A. Fitzner
Marc J. Belliveau
Colin J. Clarke
Sandra Olga Arab
Daniel W. Ingersoll
James L. Chipman
A. Margaret Wadden
D. Kevin Burke
George A. Monroe

OF COUNSEL

A. William Cox, Q.C.

Representative Clients: Air Canada; Association of Professional Engineers of N.S.; Canadian Imperial Bank of Commerce; Camp Hill Medical Centre; Canadian Medical Protective Association; Canadian Surety Co.; Coca Cola Ltd.; Institute of Chartered Accountants of N.S.; Maritime Telegraph & Telephone Co., Ltd.; Metropolitan Authority of Halifax-Dartmouth.

For full biographical listings, see the Martindale-Hubbell Law Directory

DALEY, BLACK & MOREIRA (AV)

400-The TD Centre, 1791 Barrington Street, P.O. Box 355, B3J 2N7
Telephone: 902-423-7211
Fax: 902-420-1744

MEMBERS OF FIRM

John W. Alward, Q.C.
Edwin C. Harris, Q.C.
James M. MacGowan, Q.C.
Richard W. Cregan, Q.C.
Robert W. Wright, Q.C.
B. William Piercey, Q.C.
Peter J. MacKeigan, Q.C.
Alexander S. Beveridge
M. Jill Hamilton, Q.C.
M. Gerard Tompkins
A. William Moreira
Robert L. Mellish
Wayne R. Marryatt
Marjorie A. Hickey
Gregory H. Cooper

ASSOCIATES

David A. Cameron
Diana M. Musgrave
Kelly L. Greenwood
Kate D. Harris
R. Daren Baxter

COUNSEL

Arthur R. Moreira, Q.C.

Representative Clients: Canadian Imperial Bank of Commerce; L. E. Shaw Limited; Irving Oil Limited; The Manufacturers Life Insurance Co.

For full biographical listings, see the Martindale-Hubbell Law Directory

FLINN MERRICK (AV)

1801 Hollis Street, Suite 2100, P.O. Box 1054, B3J 2X6
Telephone: 902-429-4111
Fax: 902-429-8215; 429-5645

MEMBERS OF FIRM

E. J. Flinn, Q.C.
John P. Merrick, Q.C.
Robin N. Calder
John W. Chandler, Q.C.
Brian MacLellan
R. J. Ross Stinson
Michael M. Kennedy
Geoffrey Saunders
Roy F. Redgrave
James P. Boudreau

James B. Isnor
Kenzie MacKinnon
J. George Byrne
Darlene Jamieson
C. Scott Sterns
Dufferin Roy Harper
Jay Washington
Robert J. Aske
Lloyd J. MacNeil

Representative Clients: The Toronto-Dominion Bank; I.M.P. Group Ltd.; Atlantic Television System Ltd.; Barclays Bank of Canada; Pratt & Whitney Canada Ltd.; Lasmo Nova Scotia Limited; La Farge Canada Limited; The

(See Next Column)

Great West Life Assurance Company; Victoria General Hospital; Volvo Canada Limited.

For full biographical listings, see the Martindale-Hubbell Law Directory

MCINNES COOPER & ROBERTSON (AV)

1601 Lower Water Street, P.O. Box 730, B3J 2V1
Telephone: 902-425-6500
Fax: 902-425-6350
St. John's, Newfoundland Office: Suite 602, Scotia Centre, 235 Water Street, P.O. Box 547. A1C, 5K8.
Telephone: 709-726-9500.
Fax: 709-726-9550.

Reginald A. Cluney, Q.C.
Stewart McInnes, P.C., Q.C.
Alan J. Stern, Q.C.
George T. H. Cooper, Q.C.
Peter J. E. McDonough, Q.C.
David H. Reardon, Q.C.
Eric Durnford, Q.C.
Lawrence A. Freeman
Wylie Spicer
Linda Lee Oland
Christopher C. Robinson
Thomas E. Hart
David A. Graves
Marcia L. Brennan
Deborah K. Smith
Fae J. Shaw
Stephen J. Kingston
Harry E. Wrathall, Q.C.
Lawrence J. Hayes, Q.C.
Joseph A. F. Macdonald, Q.C.
David B. Ritcey, Q.C.
James E. Gould, Q.C.
George W. MacDonald, Q.C.
Robert G. Belliveau, Q.C.
Peter McLellan, Q.C.
F. V. W. Penick
John D. Stringer
Harvey L. Morrison
Brian G. Johnston
Peter M. S. Bryson
Scott C. Norton
Maureen E. Reid
Karen Oldfield
Eric LeDrew
Malcolm D. Boyle

ASSOCIATES

John Kulik
Bernard F. Miller
Aidan J. Meade
Noella Martin
Brenda L. Rice
David S. Mac Dougall
J. David Connolly
Michelle C. Awad
Hugh Wright

COUNSEL

Harold F. Jackson, Q.C.
Hector McInnes, Q.C.

Attorneys for: Bank of Nova Scotia; Imperial Oil, Limited; Frank B. Hall & Co., Inc. (New York); American Steamship Owners Protection & Indemnity Association, Inc.; Coca-Cola, Ltd.; Scott Worldwide Inc.; Hong Kong Bank of Canada.

For full biographical listings, see the Martindale-Hubbell Law Directory

STEWART MCKELVEY STIRLING SCALES (AV)

Suite 900, Purdy's Wharf Tower One, 1959 Upper Water Street, P.O. Box 997, B3J 2X2
Telephone: 902-420-3200
Telecopier: 902-420-1417
Telex: 019-22593
Sydney, Nova Scotia Office: 50 Dorchester Street, P.O. Box 820.
Telephone: 902-539-5135.
Telecopier: 902-539-8256.
Moncton, New Brunswick Office: Suite 601, 644 Main Street, P.O. Box 20070.
Telephone: 506-853-1970.
Telecopier: 506-858-8454.
Saint John, New Brunswick Office: Suite 1000, 10th Floor, Brunswick House, 44 Chipman Hill, P.O. Box 7289 Station "A".
Telephone: 506-632-1970.
Telecopier: 506-652-1989.
St. John's, Newfoundland Office: Cabot Place, 100 New Gower Street, P.O. Box 5038.
Telephone: 709-722-4270.
Telex: 016-4733.
Telecopier: 709-722-4565.
Charlottetown, Prince Edward Island Office: 65 Grafton Street, P.O. Box 2140.
Telephone: 902-892-2485.
Telecopier: 902-566-5283.

MEMBERS OF FIRM

J. William E. Mingo, Q.C.
J. Thomas MacQuarrie, Q.C.
George A. Caines, Q.C.
James S. Cowan, Q.C.
J. Gerald Godsoe, Q.C.
William L. Ryan, Q.C.
Carman G. McCormick, Q.C.
G. Wayne Beaton, Q.C. (Resident, Sydney Office)
Guy LaFosse, Q.C. (Resident, Sydney Office)
Robert P. Dexter
J. Michael MacDonald (Resident, Sydney Office)
Mark E. MacDonald
Michael T. Pugsley
Glen V. Dexter
Charles S. Reagh
John D. Moore, Q.C.
David A. Stewart, Q.C.
G. David N. Covert, Q.C.
Donald H. McDougall, Q.C.
John S. McFarlane, Q.C.
Richard K. Jones, Q.C.
David Miller, Q.C.
Douglas J. Mathews, Q.C.
John D. Murphy, Q.C.
John D. Plowman
Jonathan C. K. Stobie
Timothy C. Matthews
Karin A. McCaskill
Robert G. Grant
Patrick J. Murray (Resident, Sydney Office)
Nancy I. Murray
Elizabeth M. Haldane

(See Next Column)

STEWART MCKELVEY STIRLING SCALES, *Halifax—Continued*

MEMBERS OF FIRM (Continued)

T. Arthur Barry
John MacL. Rogers
Richard A. Hirsch
James M. Dickson
Paul W. Festeryga
D. Geoffrey Machum
Lawrence J. Stordy
R. Blois Colpitts
David P. S. Farrar
D. Fraser MacFadyen

ASSOCIATES

Dawn A. Russell
Maurice P. Chiasson
Mark S. Bursey
Roderick H. Rogers
Ann E. Smith
Nancy G. Rubin
Elizabeth Jollimore
Virve Sandstrom
Meinhard Doelle
Claire E. Milton
Andrew V. Burke
James K. Cruickshank
Richard F. Southcott

COUNSEL

Donald A. Kerr, Q.C.
Sir Graham Day
Hugh K. Smith, Q.C.

Representative Clients: The Royal Bank of Canada; Canadian General Insurance; Prudential Insurance; Guardian Insurance; Allstate Insurance; Sun Life Assurance Company of Canada; Royal Insurance; Victoria Insurance; Bowater Mersey Paper Company; Eastern Telephone and Telegraph Co.

For full biographical listings, see the Martindale-Hubbell Law Directory

*KENTVILLE,** Kings Co. — (Refer to Halifax)

*LIVERPOOL,** Queens Co. — (Refer to Halifax)

*PICTOU,** Pictou Co. — (Refer to Truro)

*SYDNEY,** Cape Breton Co. — (Refer to Halifax)

STEWART MCKELVEY STIRLING SCALES (AV)

50 Dorchester Street, P.O. Box 820, B1P 6J1
Telephone: 902-539-5135
Telecopier: 902-539-8256
Halifax, Nova Scotia Office: Suite 900, Purdy's Wharf Tower One, 1959 Upper Water Street, P.O. Box 997.
Telephone: 902-420-3200.
Telecopier: 902-420-1417.
Telex: 019-22593.
Moncton, New Brunswick Office: Suite 601, 644 Main Street, P.O. Box 20070.
Telephone: 506-853-1970.
Telecopier: 506-858-8454.
Saint John, New Brunswick Office: Suite 1000, 10th Floor, Brunswick House, 44 Chipman Hill, P.O. Box 7289 Station "A".
Telephone: 506-632-1970.
Telecopier: 506-652-1989.
St. John's, Newfoundland Office: Cabot Place, 100 New Gower Street, P.O. Box 5038.
Telephone: 709-722-4270.
Telex: 016-4733.
Telecopier: 709-722-4565.
Charlottetown, Prince Edward Island Office: 65 Grafton Street, P.O. Box 2140.
Telephone: 902-892-2485.
Telecopier: 902-566-5283.

MEMBERS OF FIRM

G. Wayne Beaton, Q.C.
Guy LaFosse, Q.C.
J. Michael MacDonald
Patrick J. Murray

ASSOCIATES

Glenn F. Gouthro
Lee Anne MacLeod
Dwight J. W. Rudderham

For full biographical listings, see the Martindale-Hubbell Law Directory

*TRURO,** Colchester Co.

BURCHELL MACDOUGALL (AV)

710 Prince Street, P.O. Box 1128, B2N 5H1
Telephone: 902-895-1561
Telecopier: 902-895-7709
Halifax, Nova Scotia Office: Sovereign Place, 5121 Sackville Street, Suite 400.
Telephone: 902-421-1536.
FAX: 902-425-0085.

R. Lorne MacDougall, Q.C.
Robert B. MacLellan
James W. Stonehouse
Brian W. Stilwell
John T. Rafferty
Michael R. Brooker (Resident Partner, Halifax Office)
Cameron S. McKinnon
Stephen J. Topshee
Dianne Elizabeth Daguet
John R. M. Akerman, Q.C.
Michael W. Stokoe, Q.C.
M. Heather Robertson (Resident Partner, Halifax Office)
Gerald R. P. Moir, Q.C.
James W. Stanley
Vernon B. Hearn
Gary A. Richard
Peggy Power

(See Next Column)

COUNSEL

J. Robert Winters, Q.C.

Representative Clients: Royal Bank of Canada; Company; Town of Truro; Montreal Trust; Lafarge Canada, Inc.; Truro Industrial Commission; Federal Business Development Bank; Nova Scotia Farm Loan Board; National Bank of Canada.

WOLFVILLE, Kings Co. — (Refer to Halifax)

ONTARIO

*BARRIE,** Simcoe Co.

Carroll, Heyd (AV)
77 Mary Street, P.O. Box 548, L4M 4T7
Telephone: 705-722-4400
Fax: 705-722-0704

D. Kevin Carroll, Q.C. | Richard A.N. Heyd
Roger H. Chown

*BELLEVILLE,** Hastings Co. — (Refer to Kingston)

*BRAMPTON,** Regional Munic. of Peel — (Refer to Toronto)

*BRANTFORD,** Brant Co. — (Refer to Hamilton)

*BROCKVILLE,** Leeds Co. — (Refer to Kingston)

*CHATHAM,** Kent Co. — (Refer to Windsor)

*CORNWALL,** Stormont Co. — (Refer to Ottawa)

*GODERICH,** Huron Co. — (Refer to London)

*GUELPH,** Wellington Co. — (Refer to Kitchener)

*HAMILTON,** Regional Munic. of Hamilton-Wentworth

John F. Evans, Q.C. (AV)
1201 One King Street West, L8P 1A4
Telephone: 905-523-5666
Fax: 905-523-8098

ASSOCIATES

Elizabeth C. Sheard | Paul Richard Sweeny

For full biographical listings, see the Martindale-Hubbell Law Directory

Simpson, Wigle (AV)
Standard Life Centre, Suite 1030 - 120 King Street West, P.O. Box 990, L8N 3R1
Telephone: 416-528-8411
Facsimile: 416-528-9008
Burlington, Ontario Office: Suite 501, Sims Square, 390 Brant Street, L7R4S4.
Telephone: 416-639-1052.
Facsimile: 416-333-3960.

MEMBERS OF FIRM AND ASSOCIATES

Francis E. Wigle, Q.C.
J. Benjamin Simpson, Q.C.
George A. C. Simpson, Q.C.
Richard T. Hamel
Paul D. Milne
Larry W. Matthews (Resident, Burlington Office)
Clark V. Craig (Resident, Burlington Office)
Jay N. Rosenblatt
Gerald B. Aggus
David J. Jackson
John M. Wigle (Resident, Burlington Office)
Timothy Bullock
Derek A. Schmuck
Ronald S. Danks
Joseph C. Monaco
Michael G. Emery (Resident, Burlington Office)
Kathrine E. Lemmon
Frank D'Alessandro
Kathryn I. Osborne
Rosemary Fisher-Cobb (Resident, Burlington Office)
Shelley Stanzlik

COUNSEL

William N. Callaghan, Q.C. | Halliwell Soule, Q.C.
John S. Marshall, Q.C. | Grant W. Howell, Q.C.

Thoman Soule Gage (AV)
46 Jackson Street East, P.O. Box 187, L8N 3C5
Telephone: 416-529-8195
Fax: 416-529-7906

J. Douglas Thoman, Q.C.
George S. Gage
S. Stuart Aird
Lesley G. Matthewson
John A. Soule
Joseph Fred Arsenault, Q.C.
George Gligoric
William F. Bastien

For full biographical listings, see the Martindale-Hubbell Law Directory

*KINGSTON,** Frontenac Co.

Hickey & Hickey (AV)
93 Clarence Street, P.O. Box 110, K7L 4V6
Telephone: 613-548-3191
FAX: 613-548-8195

Michael G. Hickey, Q.C. | J. Michael Hickey

*LINDSAY,** Victoria Co. — (Refer to Toronto)

*LONDON,** Middlesex Co.

McCarthy Tétrault (AV)
Suite 2000, One London Place, 255 Queens Avenue, N6A 5R8
Telephone: 519-660-3587
Facsimile: 519-660-3599
Vancouver, British Columbia Office: Suite 1300, 777 Dunsmuir Street, P.O. Box 10424, Vancouver, British Columbia V7Y 1K2.
Telephone: 604-643-7100.
Facsimile: 604-643-7900.
Surrey, British Columbia Office: Suite 1300, Station Tower, Gateway 13401-108th Avenue, Surrey, British Columbia V3T 5T3.
Telephone: 604-583-9100.
Fax: 604-583-9150.
Toronto, Ontario Office: Suite 4700, Toronto Dominion Bank Tower, Toronto-Dominion Centre, Toronto, Ontario M5K 1E6.
Telephone: 416-362-1812.
Facsimile: 416-868-0673.
Ottawa, Ontario Office: Suite 1000, 275 Sparks Street, Ottawa, Ontario K1R 7X9.
Telephone: 613-238-2000.
Facsimile: 613-563-9386.
Montréal, Québec Office: "le Windsor", 1170 rue Peel, Montréal, Québec H3B 4S8.
Telephone: 514-397-4100.
Facsimile: 514-875-6246.
Québec, Québec Office: Le Complexe St-Amable 1150, rue Claire Fontaine 7e Étage, Québec, Québec G1R 5G4.
Telephone: 418-521-3000.
Facsimile: 418-521-3099.
United Kingdom and European Office: 1 Pemberton Row, Fetter Lane, London, England EC4A 3BA.
Telephone: 011-44-171-353-2355.
Facsimile: 011-44-171-583-5644.

MEMBERS OF FIRM AND ASSOCIATES

Gordon B. Carmichael
F. Glenn Jones
David I.W. Hamer
Jeffrey S. Kafka
W. Duncan Leggett
Christopher C. White
Anthony G.J. Van Klink
Lawrence H. Crossan
Jane E. Ferguson
David J. Thompson
Daniel R. Ross
Peter C. Johnson
A. Duncan Grace
Marie-France Menc
Kelly L. Schlemmer
Alec S. Bildy
Gregory K.G. Clark
Thomas J. Corbett
Victoria McInnis
Alissa K. Mitchell

COUNSEL

T. David Little | R. Gregory Hatt
Barry R. Card | Alan W. Bryant

For full biographical listings, see the Martindale-Hubbell Law Directory

Siskind, Cromarty, Ivey & Dowler (AV)
680 Waterloo Street, P.O. Box 2520, N6A 3V8
Telephone: 519-672-2121
Fax: 519-672-6065

Paul E. Knill
Fausto Boniferro
Grant R. C. Barker, Q.C.
J. Richard Lockwood
Ronald J. Kelly
John D. Hiscock
Heather-Anne Hubbell
Joaquim Balles
Nicholas W. Fursman
Kathryn L. McKerlie
Patricia A. Conlon
Ian S. Wright
Paul C. Strickland
Charles W. Walters
James R. Caskey, Q.C.
David S. Thompson
James J. Mays
Terrence R. Shillington
André I. G. Michael
Rosanne M. Kyle
Eelco H. (Ed) Jager
Keith Gordon
C. Scott Ritchie, Q.C.
Hilda Cukavac
Michael A. Eizenga
Michael J. Peerless
Charles Wright
John S. M. Mitchell
Denise M. Korpan
James D. Virtue
Renato M. Gasparotto
Nancy J. Courtney
Robert A. Blackburn
Wayne A. Petrie
Donald A. S. Cromarty, Q.C.
Arlene D. L. Gavloski
Paul M. Siskind, Q.C.
Gerald H. Kleiman
Ottavio Colosimo
Gerald A. Richardson
R. K. Wayne Goldstein
Jennifer E. Cairns
J. Wayne McLeish
Raymond F. Leach
Mark P. Macdonald
Barbara F. Fischer

For full biographical listings, see the Martindale-Hubbell Law Directory

MARKHAM, Regional Munic. of York

MILLER THOMSON (AV)

60 Columbia Way Suite 600, L3R 0C9
Telephone: 905-415-6700
Fax: 905-415-6777
Toronto, Ontario Office: 20 Queen Street West, Box 27, Suite 2700, M5H 3S1.
Telephone: 416-595-8500.
Fax: 416-595-8695.

PARTNERS

Eric M. Lane
Roderick M. McLeod, Q.C.
David J. Moxon, Q.C.
Judson D. Whiteside

PARTNERS (Continued)

Eduardo M. Barradas
Peter F. Kiborn
Wayne D. Gray
Michael L. Shell
John R. Tidball

ASSOCIATES

Allan P. Webster

CONSULTANTS

Paul E. Brace

For full biographical listings, see the Martindale-Hubbell Law Directory

*MILTON,** Regional Munic. of Halton — (Refer to Hamilton)

MISSISSAUGA, Regional Munic. of Peel

KEYSER MASON BALL (AV)

Suite 701, 201 City Centre Drive, L5B 2T4
Telephone: 905-276-9111
Fax: 905-276-2298

MEMBERS OF FIRM

Colin I. Mason, Q.C.
John B. Keyser, Q.C.
John J. Ball
Garth D. Walkden
Eugene J. A. Gierczak
Silja S. Seppi
James D. Henderson
Richard A. B. Devenney
Wendy D. Templeton
W. Grant Buchan-Terrell
Richard A. Hanesiak
Brian M. Jenkins
Marc S. Tannenbaum
M. Lee Stratton
Ruben R. Goulart
Garth Manning, Q.C.
Ian J. Wick
John M. Gray
Manfred S. Schneider
Ken Bousfield

COUNSEL

The Honourable B. Barry Shapiro, Q.C.

For full biographical listings, see the Martindale-Hubbell Law Directory

McMILLAN BINCH (AV)

A Member of McMillan Bull Casgrain
Mississauga Executive Centre, 3 Robert Speck Parkway, Suite 800, L4Z 2G5
Telephone: 905-896-1850
Fax: 905-566-2029
Internet: @ Mcbinch. COM
Toronto, Ontario Office: Royal Bank Plaza, Suite 3800, South Tower.
Telephone: 416-865-7000.
Fax: 416-865-7048 CBANET MC.BINCH.

MEMBERS OF FIRM AND ASSOCIATES

C. David Macdonald, Q.C.
David G. Butler
David G. Woolford
Bruce N. McWilliam
Earl Stuart
John G. Armstrong
Peter E. Milligan
David H. Stewart
David R. Dunlop
Peter A. Willis

For full biographical listings, see the Martindale-Hubbell Law Directory

WEIR & FOULDS (AV)

50 Burnhamthorpe Road, West, Suite 902, L5B 3C2
Telephone: 905-896-1110
Telecopier: 905-896-0803
Toronto, Ontario Office: Suite 1600 Exchange Tower, 2 First Canadian Place, P.O. Box 480.
Telephone: 416-365-1110.
Telecopier: 416-365-1876.

PARTNERS

Daniel P. Ferguson
Allen V. Craig
Ronald S. Sleightholm

ASSOCIATES

Peter M. Daigle
Joe Conte

For full biographical listings, see the Martindale-Hubbell Law Directory

NIAGARA FALLS, Regional Munic. of Niagara — (Refer to St. Catharines)

NORTH YORK, Regional Munic. of York

FRASER & BEATTY (AV)

4950 Yonge Street, Suite 2300, The Madison Centre, M2N 6K1
Telephone: 416-733-3300
Telecopier: 416-221-5254
Toronto, Ontario Office: 1 First Canadian Place, P.O. Box 100, M5X 1B2.
Telephone: 416-863-4511.
Telecopier: 416-863-4592.
Ottawa, Ontario Office: 180 Elgin Street, Suite 1200, K2P 2K7.
Telephone: 613-238-6294.
Telecopier: 613-563-7800.
Vancouver, British Columbia Office: 15th Floor, The Grosvenor Building, 1040 West Georgia Street.
Telephone: 604-687-4460.
Telecopier: 604-683-5214.
Montreal, Quebec Affiliated Office: McMaster Meighen. 7th Floor, 630 René-Lévesque Boulevard West, H3B 4H7.
Telephone: 514-879-1212.
Telecopier: 514-878-0605.
Cable Address: "Camerall".
Telex: "Camerall MTL" 05-268637.

PARTNERS AND CONSULTANTS

Albert Page, Q.C.
Frank E. P. Bowman
P. Martin Emmons
Roy D. R. Stewart
Gale W. Robertson
Jules L. Lewy
Leslie A. White
Richard C. Hoffman

For full biographical listings, see the Martindale-Hubbell Law Directory

OSHAWA, Regional Munic. of Durham — (Refer to Toronto)

*OTTAWA,** Regional Munic. of Ottawa-Carleton

BENNETT JONES VERCHERE (AV)

Suite 1800, 350 Alberta Street, P.O. Box 25, K1R 1A4
Telephone: (613) 230-4935
Facsimile: (613) 230-3836
Calgary, Alberta Office: 4500 Bankers Hall East. 855-2nd Street S.W.
Telephone: (403) 298-3100.
Facsimile: (403) 265-7219.
Edmonton, Alberta Office: 1000, 10035-105 Street.
Telephone: (403) 421-8133.
Facsimile: (403) 421-7951.
Toronto, Ontario Office: 3400 1 First Canadian Place, P.O. Box 130.
Telephone: (416) 863-1200.
Facsimile: (416) 863-1716.
Montreal, Quebec Office: Suite 1600, 1 Place Ville Marie.
Telephone: (514) 871-1200.
Facsimile: (514) 871-8115.

RESIDENT MEMBERS OF FIRM

George Edward Fisk

Jeffrey M. Measures

OF COUNSEL

W. R. Jackett, O.C., Q.C.

For full biographical listings, see the Martindale-Hubbell Law Directory

BLAKE, CASSELS & GRAYDON (AV)

World Exchange Plaza, 20th Floor, 45 O'Connor Street, K1P 1A4
Telephone: 613-788-2200
Facsimile: 613-594-3965
Internet: ottawa@blakes.ca
Toronto, Ontario Office: Box 25, Commerce Court West, M5L 1A9.
Telephone: 416-863-2400.
Facsimile: 416-863-2653. Internet: toronto@blakes.ca.
Telex: 06-219687.
Calgary, Alberta Office: Bankers Hall Heast, Suite 3500, 855 2nd Street, S.W., T2P 4J8.
Telephone: 403-260-9600.
Facsimile: 403-263-9895. Internet: calgary@blakes.ca.
Vancouver, British Columbia Office: 1700-1030 West Georgia Street, V6E 2Y3.
Telephone: 604-631-3300.
Telecopier: 604-631-3309 - 16th Floor; 604-631-3305 - 17th Floor.
Internet: vancouver@blakes.ca.
European Office, London, England: 27 Austin Friars, EC2N 2QQ.
Telephone: 0171-374-2334.
Facsimile: 0171-638-3342.

PARTNERS

Paul C. LaBarge
Matthew J. Halpin
Deborah L. Weinstein
Gordon K. Cameron

ASSOCIATES

J.E.M. Lawrence, Q.C. (Not admitted in ON)
D.A. Liston
G. Jessop
M.Z. Black
D. Greenfield
N.R. Boyle
C.L. McGann
R.L. Taylor

For full biographical listings, see the Martindale-Hubbell Law Directory

Ottawa—Continued

Fraser & Beatty (AV)

Suite 1200, 180 Elgin Street, K2P 2K7
Telephone: 613-238-6294
Telecopier: 613-563-7800
Toronto, Ontario Office: 1 First Canadian Place, P.O. Box 100, M5X 1B2.
Telephone: 416-863-4511.
Telecopier: 416-863-4592.
North York, Ontario Office: The Madison Centre, 4950 Yonge Street, Suite 2300, M2N 6K1.
Telephone: 416-733-3300.
Telecopier: 416-221-5254.
Vancouver, British Columbia Office: 15th Floor, The Grosvenor Building, 1040 West Georgia Street.
Telephone: 604-687-4460.
Telecopier: 604-683-5214.
Montreal, Quebec Affiliated Office: McMaster Meighen. 7th Floor, 630 René-Lévesque Boulevard West, H3B 4H7.
Telephone: 514-879-1212.
Telecopier: 514-878-0605.
Cable Address: "Camerall".
Telex: "Camerall MTL" 05-268637.

PARTNERS, CONSULTANTS AND COUNSEL

Roger Tassé, O.C. Q.C.
John N. McFarlane
Nikol J. Schultz
Philip M. Rimer
Karen D. Zypchen
William T. Houston
John F. Blakney
Thomas A. Houston
Jennifer J. Smith
Richard J. Mahoney

For full biographical listings, see the Martindale-Hubbell Law Directory

Lang Michener (AV)

Suite 300, 50 O'Connor Street, K1P 6L2
Telephone: 613-232-7171
Telecopier: 613-231-3191
Toronto, Ontario Office: BCE Place, Suite 2500, 181 Bay Street, P.O. Box 747, M5J 2T7.
Telephone: 416-360-8600.
Mississauga, Ontario Office: Suite 1001, 1290 Central Parkway West. L5C 4R3.
Telephone: 905-566-1000.
Telecopier: 905-566-1015.
Vancouver, British Columbia Office: 2500 Three Bentall Centre, P.O. Box 49200, 595 Burrard Street, V7X 1L1.
Telephone: 604-232-7171.
Telecopier: 604-685-7084.
Calgary, Alberta Office: Suite 1900, 355 4th Avenue, S.W., T2P 0J1.
Telephone: 403-237-5858.
Fax: 403-266-5272.

RESIDENT MEMBERS

John G.M. Hooper, Q.C.
Edward L. Gladu, Q.C.
John M. Connolly
Terry W. Peterman
Pierre Richard, Q.C.
Jennifer Lynch, Q.C.
Eugene Meehan
Richard O. Gasparini
Norman M. Fera
Emanuel Montenegrino
Charles Saikaley
Michael S. Rankin
James M. Canapini

RESIDENT ASSOCIATES

Jennifer Ward
Jeffrey W. Beedell
Morris M. Kertzer
Andrea R. Camacho
Barbara J. Sinclair
Joseph H. Konst
Allan T. Hirsch
Edward A. Pundyk
Daniel J. Leduc
Robert J. Phillips

COUNSEL

Ronald Martland

For full biographical listings, see the Martindale-Hubbell Law Directory

McCarthy Tétrault (AV)

Suite 1000, 275 Sparks Street, K1R 7X9
Telephone: 613-238-2000
Facsimile: 613-563-9386
Vancouver, British Columbia Office: Suite 1300, 777 Dunsmuir Street, P.O. Box 10424, Vancouver, British Columbia V7Y 1K2.
Telephone: 604-643-7100.
Facsimile: 604-643-7900.
Surrey, British Columbia Office: Suite 1300, Station Tower, Gateway 13401-108th Avenue, Surrey, British Columbia V3T 5T3.
Telephone: 604-583-9100.
Fax: 604-583-9150.
London, Ontario Office: Suite 2000, One London Place, 255 Queens Avenue, London, Ontario N6A 5R8.
Telephone: 519-660-3587.
Facsimile: 519-660-3599.

(See Next Column)

Toronto, Ontario Office: Suite 4700, Toronto Dominion Bank Tower, Toronto-Dominion Centre, Toronto, Ontario M5K 1E6.
Telephone: 416-362-1812.
Facsimile: 416-868-0673.
Montréal, Québec Office: "le Windsor", 1170 rue Peel, Montréal, Québec H3B 4S8.
Telephone: 514-397-4100.
Facsimile: 514-875-6246.
Québec, Québec Office: Le Complexe St-Amable 1150, rue Claire Fontaine 7e Étage, Québec, Québec G1R 5G4.
Telephone: 418-521-3000.
Facsimile: 418-521-3099.
United Kingdom and European Office: 1 Pemberton Row, Fetter Lane, London, England EC4A 3BA.
Telephone: 011-44-171-353-2355.
Facsimile: 011-44-171-583-5644.

MEMBERS OF FIRM AND ASSOCIATES

Robert D. Chapman
Michael S. Polowin
David O. Cox
Anthony H.A. Keenleyside
Anna M. Tosto
Colin Baxter
Lance B. Curtis

OF COUNSEL

William H. Jarvis, P.C., Q.C.
Barbara A. McIsaac, Q.C.

For full biographical listings, see the Martindale-Hubbell Law Directory

Ogilvy Renault (AV)

Suite 1600, 45 O'Connor Street, K1P 1A4
Telephone: 613-780-8661
Telex: 053-3379
Fax: 613-230-5459
Montréal, Québec Office: Suite 1100, 1981 McGill College Avenue, H3A 3C1.
Telephone: 514-847-4747.
Cable Address: "Jonhall" Montreal.
Telex: 05-25362.
Fax: 514-286-5474.
Québec, Québec Office: Suite 520, 500 Grande-Allée Est, G1R 2J7.
Telephone: 418-640-5000.
Fax: 418-640-1500.
Osler Renault, an international partnership of Osler, Hoskin & Harcourt, and Ogilvy Renault, has offices at:
London, England Office: 20 Little Britain, EC1A 7DH.
Telephone: 071-606-0777.
Fax: 071-606-0222.
Paris, France Office: (Correspondent Office) 4, rue Bayard, 75008.
Telephone: (1)42.89.00.54.
Fax: (1)42.89.51.60.
Hong Kong Office: Suite 1708, One Pacific Place, 88 Queensway.
Telephone: (852) 8773933.
Fax: (852) 8770866.
New York, New York Office: Suite 3217, 200 Park Avenue, 10166-0193.
Telephone: 212-867-5800.
Fax: 212-867-5802.
Singapore Office: Suite No. 40-05, OCBC Centre, 65 Chulia Street, Singapore 0104.
Telephone: (65) 538-2077.
Fax: (65) 538-2977.

Catherine L. Auchinleck
Lise M. Chassé
I. H. Fraser
Mary J. Gleason
Norman B. Lieff
Heidi S. Levenson Polowin
Gregory Sanders
C. Ross Carson
Brian C. Elkin
David C. Gavsie
Nancy (Tin Gee) Hong
Deen C. Olsen
Renato M. Pontello-Concina
Peter J. Stanford

For full biographical listings, see the Martindale-Hubbell Law Directory

Osler, Hoskin & Harcourt (AV)

Barristers & Solicitors
Patent and Trade-Mark Agents
Suite 1500, 50 O'Connor Street, K1P 6L2
Telephone: 613-235-7234
FAX: 613-235-2867
Toronto, Ontario Office: 1 First Canadian Place, P.O. Box 50, M5X 1B8.
Telephone: 416-362-2111.
FAX: 416-862-6666.
New York, N.Y. Office: Osler Renault* - Suite 3217, 200 Park Avenue, 10166-0193.
Telephone: 212-867-5800.
Fax: 212-867-5802.
London, England Office: Osler Renault* - 20 Little Britain, London, EC1A 7DH.
Telephone: 071-606-0777.
FAX: 071-606-0222.
Paris, France Office: Osler Renault* - 4 rue Bayard, 75008.
Telephone: 33-1.42.89.00.54.
Fax: 33-1.42.89.51.60.

(See Next Column)

OSLER, HOSKIN & HARCOURT, *Ottawa—Continued*

Hong Kong Office: Osler Renault* - Suite 1708, One Pacific Place. 88 Queensway.
Telephone: 011-852-2877-3933.
Fax: 011-852-2877-0866.
Singapore Office: Osler Renault* - 65 Chulia Street, #40-05 OCBC Centre, Singapore 0104.
Telephone: (65) 538-2077.
Fax: (65) 538-2977.
* *Osler Renault is an international partnership of Osler, Hoskin & Harcourt and Ogilvy Renault.*

MEMBERS OF FIRM

Ronald G. Belfoi, Q.C.
Kent H.E. Plumley
Francois Lemieux
Rodolph W. Groulx
Kenneth L. W. Boland
Michael L. Phelan
James H. Smellie
Ronald C. Cheng
K. Scott McLean
Glen A. Bloom
Carol Tennenhouse Diamond (On Leave)
Lorne H. Abugov
J. Andrew Pritchard
Stephen G. Blair
David W. Aitken
Donna G. White
Patricia J. Wilson
David K. Wilson
Heather P. Griffiths
Gregory O. Somers

ASSOCIATES

R. Alan Young
Michal E. Minkowski
Diane E. Cornish
Cheryl D.M. Emberley
Martha A. Healey
Melanie A. Polowin
M. Lynn Starchuk
Jonathan A. Blakey
Christine E. Hicks
Derek S. Keay

RETIRED PARTNERS

John R. Tolmie, Q.C.
John M. Coyne, Q.C.
James G. Fogo

PATENT AGENT

James R. Keneford

TRADE-MARK LAW CLERK

Marion Bailey

For full biographical listings, see the Martindale-Hubbell Law Directory

STIKEMAN, ELLIOTT (AV)

50 O'Connor Street, Suite 914, K1P 6L2
Telephone: 613-234-4555
Telex: 053-3646
FAX: 613-230-8877
Cable Address: "Stike Ott"
Montreal, Quebec Office: 1155 René-Lévesque Boulevard West, 40th Floor, H3B 3V2.
Telephone: 514-397-3000.
Telex: 05-267316.
Cable Address: "TAXMONT MTL".
Telecopier: 514-397-3222.
Toronto, Ontario Office: Commerce Court West, Suite 5300, M5L 1B9.
Telephone: 416-869-5500.
Telex: 06-22536.
FAX: 416-947-0866.
Cable Address: "STIKETOR".
Calgary, Alberta Office: 1500 Bankers Hall, 855 - 2nd Street S.W., T2P 4J7.
Telephone: 403-266-9000.
FAX: 403-266-9034.
Vancouver, British Columbia Office: Suite 1700, Park Place, 666 Burrard Street, V6C 2X8.
Telephone: 604-631-1300.
Telecopier: 604-681-1825.
New York, N.Y. Office: Tower 56, 126 East 56th Street, 11th Floor, 10022.
Telephone: 212-371-8855.
Fax: 212-371-7087.
Washington, D.C. Office: 1300 I Street, N.W., Suite 1210 West, 20005-3314.
Telephone: 202-326-7555.
Fax: 202-326-7557.
London, England Office: Cottons Centre, Cottons Lane, SE1 2QL.
Telephone: 071-378-0880.
Telecopier: 71-378-0344; 71-865-0226.
Paris, France Office: 39, rue Francois Ier, 75008.
Telephone: 33-1-40-73-82-00.
Fax: 31-1-40-73-82-10.
Budapest, Hungary Office: Andrássy út 100 II Floor, H-1062.
Telephone: 36-1-269-1790.
Fax: 36-1-269-0655.
Hong Kong Office: China Building, Suite 1506, 29 Queen's Road Central.
Telephone: 852-868-9903.
Telecopier: 852-868-9912.
Hong Kong: In Association with Shum & Co., China Building, Suite 1102, 29 Queen's Road Centre.
Telephone: 852-526-5531.
Telecopier: 852-845-9076.
Taipei, Taiwan Office: 117 Sec. 3 Min Sheng East Road, 8th Floor.
Telephone: 886-2-719-9573.
FAX: 886-2-719-4540.

(See Next Column)

RESIDENTS IN OTTAWA

Martine M. N. Band
Bruce Clarke Caughill
Lawson A. W. Hunter, Q.C.
T. Gregory Kane, Q.C.
Stuart C. McCormack
Mirko Bibic
Michel Coderre
Susan M. Hutton
Donald A. Kubesh
Thurlow Bradbrooke Smith, Q.C.

For full biographical listings, see the Martindale-Hubbell Law Directory

*OWEN SOUND,** Grey Co. — (Refer to London)

*PARRY SOUND,** Parry Sound Dist. — (Refer to London)

*PEMBROKE,** Renfrew Co. — (Refer to Ottawa)

*PERTH,** Lanark Co. — (Refer to Ottawa)

*PICTON,** Prince Edward Co. — (Refer to Kingston)

*ST. CATHARINES,** Regional Munic. of Niagara

SULLIVAN, MAHONEY (AV)

40 Queen Street, P.O. Box 1360, L2R 6Z2
Telephone: 905-688-6655
Facsimile: 905-688-5814

MEMBERS OF FIRM

P. H. Sullivan (1909-1988)
C. H. Mahoney, Q.C.
Barry H. Matheson, Q.C.
Victor F. Muratori, Q.C.
Peter B. Bedard
Gordon A. Wiggins
Peter T. Banwell, Q.C.
Thomas A. Richardson
Philip M. Sheehan
Woodward B. McKaig
Linda M. McKaig
Joseph Dallal
Catherine Anne Bain
Joseph M. Gottli
J. Rodney Bush
Robert B. Culliton
Peter A. Mahoney
Bruce A. MacDonald
Michael J. Bonomi

ASSOCIATES

Glen W. McCann
Michael G. Kyne
Sara J. Preni

OF COUNSEL

Marvin D. Kriluck

For full biographical listings, see the Martindale-Hubbell Law Directory

*SARNIA,** Lambton Co. — (Refer to London)

*SIMCOE,** Regional Munic. of Haldimand-Norfolk — (Refer to Hamilton)

*STRATFORD,** Perth Co. — (Refer to London)

*TORONTO,** Regional Munic. of York

AIRD & BERLIS (AV)

Suite 1800 BCE Place, North Tower, 181 Bay Street, P.O. Box 754, M5J 2T9
Telephone: 416-364-1241
Cable Address: "Maxims"
Telex: 06-22702
Telecopier: 416-364-4916

MEMBERS OF FIRM

Carl T. Grant, Q.C.
David I. Matheson, Q.C.
Harold R. Berry, Q.C.
W. Stearns Vaughan
Ralph D. Dalgarno
John Swan
Peter Y. Atkinson
N. Jane Pepino, Q.C.
William G. VanderBurgh
Harry M. Fogul
Martin E. Kovnats
Richard R. Arblaster
Diane Harris
Eldon J. Bennett
Leo F. Longo
Frederick D. Cass
Bernard McGarva
Christopher J. Williams
K. J. Harild
David Malach
Lindsay Ann Histrop
Jay A. Lefton
R. Grant Cansfield
Barbara J. Worndl
Michael J. Bourassa
Karl F. Leppmann
Margaret T. Nelligan
Kim M. Kovar
Timothy J. Hill
Barbra H. Miller
John W. Torrey
Thomas R. Whitby
J. Paul Terry
Mortimer S. Bistrisky
James D. Sharples
Joseph Philip Dawson
James G. Matthews
Michael W. Bader, Q.C.
Albert J. Milstein
Edmund C. D. Smith
Garry W. Dawson
Robert J. Howe
Donald L. West
Jack Bernstein
Paul V. McCallen
Grant H. Doak
S. Michael Brooks
Lloyd F. Cornett
Douglas A. Palmateer
Brian G. Wright
Barbara J. Lawrie
Michael D. Smith
Marilyn G. Lee
S. Brian Levett
Nick Torchetti
Andy Ayotte
Steven P. Kelman
Cecilia M. Moffat
Harold S. Springer
Allan S. Bronstein
Ronald M. Kosonic
S. Steve Popoff
Andrew R.C. Webster
Randy T. Hooke

(See Next Column)

AIRD & BERLIS—*Continued*

John J. Longo | Eric M. Carmona

MEMBERS OF FIRM (Continued)

Michael T. Garvey | Kevin G. Rooney
Louise R. Summerhill | Steven L. Graff
Steven A. Zakem

ASSOCIATES

Grace Kim-Cho | William B. McDiarmid
Jamie Mason | David T. Takenaka
Andrew M. Kain | Julie Tricarico
John A. McAndrew | Sonia M. Yung

OF COUNSEL

The Honourable John Black | Douglas A. Berlis, Q.C.

For full biographical listings, see the Martindale-Hubbell Law Directory

BAKER & MCKENZIE (AV)

BCE Place, 181 Bay Street, Suite 2100, P.O. Box 874, M5J 2T3
Telephone: (416) 863-1221
Intn'l. Dialing: (1-416) 863-1221
Facsimile: (1-416) 863-6275
Associated Offices of Baker & McKenzie in: Almaty, Amsterdam, Bangkok, Barcelona, Beijing, Berlin, Bogotá, Brasília, Brussels, Budapest, Buenos Aires, Cairo, Caracas, Chicago, Dallas, Frankfurt, Geneva, Hanoi, Ho Chi Minh City, Hong Kong, Juárez, Kiev, London, Madrid, Manila, Melbourne, México City, Miami, Milan, Monterrey, Moscow, New York, Palo Alto, Paris, Prague, Rio de Janeiro, Riyadh, Rome, St. Petersburg, San Diego, San Francisco, São Paulo, Singapore, Stockholm, Sydney, Taipei, Tijuana, Tokyo, Valencia, Warsaw, Washington, D.C. and Zürich.
Correspondent Law Firm: Hadiputranto, Hadinoto & Partners, Jakarta.

PARTNERS

Salvador M. Borraccia | Paul D. Burns
Joseph F. Caruso | David T. A. Côté
Cheryl J. Elliott | Mary C. Hall
Caleb J. Hayhoe | Edward J. Kowal, Q.C.
Roy K. Kusano | Harold Margles
S. Janice McAuley | Elaine S. Peritz
Stewart D. Saxe | Brian D. Segal
Schuyler M. Sigel, Q.C. | Hubert J. Stitt, Q.C.
Allan H. Turnbull | William R. Watson

ASSOCIATES

Christopher Aide | M. Marlene Atlas
Dawn C. Benson | Blair W. M. Bowen
Kevin B. Coon | Dean M. Dolan
Sharona M. Freudmann | James J. Holloway
Lisa Kirby | Mitchell E. Kowalski
Theodore C. Ling | Charles M. Magerman
Brian C. McLean | Kathleen M. Orysiuk
Carol S. Osmond | Gabriela Ramó
Susan G. Seller | James R. Sennema
David C. Turner | Kanta L. Wadhwan
Barbara G. Wohl

For full biographical listings, see the Martindale-Hubbell Law Directory

BASTEDO SHELDON MCGIVNEY & PECK (AV)

180 Dundas Street West, Suite 1800, M5G 1Z8
Telephone: 416-595-5151
Facsimile: 416-596-7538

MEMBERS OF FIRM

Thomas G. Bastedo, Q.C. | Donald A. R. Sheldon
Robert D. Peck | Bradley J.C. Huxtable
Evlyn L. McGivney | Joanne H. Stewart

ASSOCIATES

Robert E. Salisbury | Bryan R. G. Smith
Nadim Wakeam | Ari B. Kulidjian
Evelyn tenCate

OF COUNSEL

Henry J. Knowles, Q.C.

For full biographical listings, see the Martindale-Hubbell Law Directory

BENNETT JONES VERCHERE (AV)

3400 1 First Canadian Place, M5X 1A4
Telephone: 416-863-1200
Facsimile: 416-863-1716
Calgary, Alberta Office: 4500 Bankers Hall East. 855-2nd Street S.W.
Telephone: (403) 298-3100.
Facsimile: (403) 265-7219.
Telex: 038-24524.
Cable Address: "Benford".
Edmonton, Alberta Office: 1000, 10035-105 Street.
Telephone: (403) 421-8133.
Facsimile: (403) 421-7951.
Telex: 037-2050.
Ottawa, Ontario Office: Suite 1800, 350 Alberta Street, Box 25, K1R 1A4.
Telephone: (613) 230-4935.
Facsimile: (613) 230-3836.

(See Next Column)

Montreal, Quebec Office: Suite 1600 1 Place Ville Marie.
Telephone: (514) 871-1200.
Facsimile: (514) 871-8115.

MEMBERS OF FIRM

Ross B. Eddy | Adrian A. Phillips
D. Bernard Morris | Janice A. McCart
Roderick M. Wilkinson | R. Geoffrey Walker

Stephen Paddon | Peter R. Welsh
Renate D. Herbst | Peter B. Budd
Russell D. Laishley | Roger O. MacLeod
Steve Suarez | Mark S. Laugesen
Michael Marcovitz

OF COUNSEL

W. R. Jackett, O.C., Q.C.

For full biographical listings, see the Martindale-Hubbell Law Directory

BLAKE, CASSELS & GRAYDON (AV)

Box 25, Commerce Court West, M5L 1A9
Telephone: 416-863-2400
Cable Address: "Blakes" Toronto
Facsimile: 416-863-2653
Internet: toronto@blakes.ca
Telex: 06-219687
Ottawa, Ontario Office: World Exchange Plaza, 20th Floor, 45 O'Connor Street, K1P 1A4.
Telephone: 613-788-2200.
Facsimile: 613-594-3965. Internet: ottawa@blakes.ca.
Calgary, Alberta Office: Bankers Hall East, Suite 3500, 855-2nd Street S.W., T2P 4J8.
Telephone: 403-260-9600.
Facsimile: 403-263-9895. Internet: calgary@blakes.ca.
Vancouver, British Columbia Office: 1700-1030 West Georgia Street, V6E 2Y3.
Telephone: 604-631-3300.
Telecopier: 604-631-3309 - 16th Floor; 604-631-3305 - 17th Floor.
Internet: vancouvr@blakes.ca.
European Office - London, England: 27 Austin Friars, EC2N 2QQ.
Telephone: 0171-374-2334.
Facsimile: 0171-638-3342.

PARTNERS

George W. Hately, Q.C. | Ronald C. Brown, Q.C.
John W. Brown, Q.C. | J. Roy Weir, Q.C.
Burton H. Kellock, Q.C. | John D. Brownlie, Q.C.
James W. Garrow, Q.C. | Edward L. Donegan, Q.C.
Desmond M. O'Rorke | Warren M.H. Grover, Q.C.
James S. Hausman | Donald J.M. Brown, Q.C.
G. Robert W. Gale, Q.C. | Brian C. Westlake
David J. Kee | Timothy N. Unwin
James P. Dube | Joseph W. Mik
John M. Stewart | Robert A. Bondy
Edwin S. Langdon | Robert E.H. Macdonald
Richard M. Ross (Not admitted in ON) | John M. Solursh
| J. Anthony Doyle
Martin Fingerhut | J. Rob Collins
James A. Hodgson | Elizabeth L. McNaughton
Joel Shafer | Peter W. Gilchrist
Robert S. Bruser | John D. DeSipio
J. David A. Jackson | Glenn F. Leslie
Alan Bell | Richard C. McIvor
Derek L. Rogers | David J. Sharpless
John W. Teolis | Harry Freedman
Greg M. Frenette | James S. Hilton
Barry G. McGee | Robin J. McGillis
Paul K. Tamaki | Dorothy Wahl
James R. Christie | Eric R. Elvidge
Brian W. Gray | Joan C. G. Kennedy
Peter A. Love | Leslie J. Morgan
Brian MacLeod Rogers | Edward (Ted) M. Perlmutter
Gary R. Shiff | Philip W. Slayton
Gerald S. Swinkin | Sheldon Burshtein
Susan M. Grundy | Gail D. Lilley
Joel Richler | Bonnie A. Tough
Alan F. Brown | T. Nigel M. Campbell
Daniel A. Kennedy | Deborah H. Rowat
Timothy W. Bermingham | Neil Finkelstein
Ben A. Jetten | C. Dawn Jetten
Kevin P. McElcheran | Thomas A. McKee
Samuel J. Principi | Mark J. Selick
Mary Jane Stitt | John M. Tuzyk
Randy V. Bauslaugh | Shirley A. Brown
Robert M. Granatstein | David B. Maclachlan
W. Ross F. McKee | Daniel J. Shields
Alison B. Woodbury | J. Alan Aucoin
Geoffrey S. Belsher | Kathryn M. Bush
Michael R. Harquail | Susan J. Heakes
Jeffrey Kerbel | John J. Lucki
Sheila A. Murray | M. Connie Reeve
Andrea D. Vabalis | David D. Valentine
E. Mitchell Wigdor | Gordon A. M. Currie
Robert M. Fishlock | Jeremy J. Forgie

(See Next Column)

BLAKE, CASSELS & GRAYDON, *Toronto—Continued*

PARTNERS (Continued)

Christopher A. Huband
William D. Mugford
Michael W. Sharp
Henry Bertossi
Hugh M. Des Brisay
Robert E. Kwinter
John J. Quinn
Nathan Cheifetz
Christopher A. Hewat
Dale P. Philp
Craig C. Thorburn
J. Paul Belanger
Jeffrey W. Galway
Anna I. MacMillan
Ernest McNee
Sharon S. Wong
Robert B. F. Barr, Q.C. (1903-1974)
B. Bruce Lockwood, Q.C. (1930-1987)
Douglas W. Blackburn, Q.C. (1916-1989)
Alexander J. MacIntosh, Q.C. (1921-1993)
Anne C. McNeely
James J. Shanks
Bliss A. White
Gwen Chamberlain
Frank D. Guarascio
David R. McCarthy
Paul B. Schabas
Caroline L. Helbronner
Pamela L.J. Huff
J.A. Prestage
Thomas P.B. von Hahn
Michael E. Burke
Jonathan W. Kahn
S. Gordon McKee
Julie A. O'Donnell
Allan Graydon, Q.C. (1898-1973)
Francis J. Hamill, Q.C. (1923-1980)
Peter S. Osler, Q.C. (1916-1988)
William P. DeRoche, Q.C. (1907-1990)

ASSOCIATE COUNSEL

V. Richard E. Perry, Q.C.

COUNSEL

Britton B. Osler, Q.C.
Robert A. Kingston, Q.C.
Norman M. Simpson, Q.C.
John M. Hodgson, Q.C.
John F. Howard, Q.C.
William E. Brown, Q.C.
Peter M. Harvie, Q.C.
John B. Tinker, Q.C.
James F. Heal
Walter H. C. Boyd, Q.C.
Theodore A. King, Q.C.
James F. McCallum, Q.C.
W. O. Chris Miller, Q.C.
Robert W. Stevens, Q.C.
Arthur L. Davies, Q.C.
Strachan Heighington, Q.C.
Lionel J. Goffart, Q.C.
David G. Guest, Q.C. (Retired)

ASSOCIATES

S.M. Séguin
S.E. Slattery
K.M. Richardson
M.G. Manocchio
J. Canvin
R.N. Shukla
A. Thomas
G.T. Daniel
C.C. Hale
K.V. Penny
R.S.M. Woods
L.F. Christofolakos
G. Kanargelidis
H.M. Lendon
A.M. Prenol
D.J. Toswell
S.R. Ashbourne
S.M. D'Alimonte
J.S. Elliott
M.C. Kowal
A. Muto
J. Trossman
S.J. Weisz
E.H. Boyd
J.S. Hamilton
E. Jelich
K.E. Lovell
K.A. McGrath
D.E. Reuter
B.A. Stokes
M.I.A. Buttery
R.J. Crook
G.G. D'Alessandro
J.A. Lee
S.G. Thompson
T.P. Bernard
M. Chow
F.M. Davis
M.A. Emerson
J.M. Hatherly
C.A. MacCready
D.K. Orida
T.W. Pollen
G.B. Rome
S.D. Booley
M.M. Cusimano
R.G. Maisey
B.D. O'Brien
A.J. Gelkopf
C.E. Wade
C.N. Marchessault
L.S. Corne
M.A. Soyland
S.L. Walker
E.M. Gearing
M.C. Katz
M.R. Stephenson
F.P. Arnone
L.A. Fung
B.M. Lehmann
M.J. Nicholson
A. Svoboda
E.J. Warren (Not admitted in ON)
A.M. Diamond
J. Glass
L.A. MacFarlane
M.A. Stone
G.C. Vegh
L.P. Bosschart
J.I. Galloway
T.L. Howarth
J.A. Kolada
P.S. MacGowan
J.C. Moss
A. Stevenson-Lee
J.R. Brookes
M.H. Cooper
C.A. Cusinato
J.M. Lawrie
A.J. Nicholls
I.M. Aitken
C.L. Carson
E.J. Cormack
L.A. Eckel
I.M. Goldberg
R.J. Ingram
K. Murphy
K. Podrebarac
D.M. Rodgers
C.A. Beckett
S.M. Colman
B.L. Harden
B.D.G. Reay
R.R. Strathdee

For full biographical listings, see the Martindale-Hubbell Law Directory

BLANEY, MCMURTRY, STAPELLS (AV)

Suite 1400, 20 Queen Street West, M5H 2V3
Telephone: 416-593-1221
Telecopier: 416-593-5437
Cable Address: "BLANLAW"
Telex: 06-22326

MEMBERS AND ASSOCIATES OF FIRM

James W. Blaney, Q.C. *
William R. McMurtry, Q.C. *
Stephen H. Aarons, Q.C. *
Phillip Spencer, Q.C. *
Glenn J. Cooper *
Robert Cohen, Q.C. *
Robert J. Potts *
Roderick S. W. Winsor *
Wayne S. Gray *
Joan H. Garson *
Gary Steinhart *
Howard L. Fox *
Mark E. Geiger *
Stephen R. Moore *
Timothy P. Alexander *
Roger J. Horst *
Mirilyn R. Selznick *
Brett Tkatch *
Stanley Kugelmass *
H. Todd Greenbloom *
Mona R. Taylor
Robert Muir
William D. Anderson
Karen A. Henein
Elizabeth J. Forster
Katherine L. Higginson
Derwin Wong
Eugene G. Mazzuca
Giovanna Asaro
Murray A. Thompson, Q.C.
Richard H. Krempulec, Q.C. *
Alex A. Mesbur, Q.C. *
Rodney L. K. Smith, Q.C. *
Barry T. Grant *
John S. Kelly *
Jeffrey L. Freelan *
Geza R. Banfai *
Crawford W. Spratt *
David S. Wilson
Michael J. Bennett *
Mary L. MacGregor *
Ian S. Epstein *
Jess C. Bush *
Sean Dewart *
Jeffrey P. Friedman *
Suzanne Bailey
Barry D. Fisher *
Stephen I. Selznick *
Maria Scarfo
Jacqueline C. Maarse
Craig R. Anderson
Chris J. Clapperton
Thomas W. Ward
D. Barry Prentice
Warren M. Bongard
Simon Thomas Newton Cridland
Tim Farrell
Elizabeth A. Hyde
Jennifer McKenzie

*Denotes Member of Firm

For full biographical listings, see the Martindale-Hubbell Law Directory

BORDEN & ELLIOT (AV)

Barristers & Solicitors
Scotia Plaza, 40 King Street West, M5H 3Y4
Telephone: 416-367-6000
Telecopier: 416-367-6749
Internet: @ borden.com

A Member of the national association of Borden DuMoulin Howard Gervais, comprising Borden & Elliot in Toronto, Ontario, Russell & DuMoulin in Vancouver, British Columbia, Howard, Mackie in Calgary, Alberta and Mackenzie Gervais in Montréal, Québec. Borden DuMoulin Howard Gervais also operates an office in London, England.

MEMBERS AND ASSOCIATES

Beverley V. Elliot, Q.C.
Kenneth W. Scott, Q.C.
John D. Holding, Q.C.
Rino A. Stradiotto, Q.C.
J. D'Arcy P. Brooks, Q.C.
Jordan Dimoff, Q.C.
R. Lee Woods
Terrance A. Sweeney
Barry W. Earle, Q.C.
John F. T. Warren
Gordon E. Thompson
Frank J. C. Newbould, Q.C.
William P. McCarten
Edward A. Ayers, Q.C.
Gordon A. Park
Edmund F. Merringer
William T. Pashby
Richard A. Applebaum
William J. McNeill
Martin Sclisizzi
Steven N. Iczkovitz
Robert P. Hutchison
J. Fraser Mann
William D. T. Carter
Stanley B. Bush
Evelyn Goldfarb
Eva M. Krasa
Michael J. Lang
Murray B. Shopiro
Todd L. Archibald
Geoffrey B. Morawetz
Marguerite P. Mooney
W. Douglas R. Beamish
Thomas G. Andrews
James D. G. Douglas
Paul A. D. Mingay
Larissa V. Tkachenko
Robert N. Black
Selma M. Lussenburg
David A. L. Britnell, Q.C.
David M. Harley, Q.C.
W. Ross Murray, Q.C.
John D. Hylton, Q.C.
James H. McC. McNair
Dennis R. O'Connor, Q.C.
Simon B. Scott, Q.C.
Morton G. Gross, Q.C.
Donald L. Macdonald, Q.C.
Hans J. B. A. Dickie, Q.C.
A. Winn Oughtred
Brent J. Lisowski
Peter R. Braund
Donna C. Cappon
William S. Robertson
L. (Lou) Kozak, Q.C.
Meta M. Tory
John R. Wood
Thomas W. Ouchterlony
Brian C. Keith
Timothy P. Bates
Stanley M. Makuch
Randall S. Echlin
M. Jeffrey Dermer
John D. Marshall
Robert W. Kitchen
Stephen F. Waqué
Paul G. Findlay
Andrew J. Skinner
Barry H. Bresner
Robert B. Bell
Michael K. McKelvey
Randy M. Shiff
Anne C. Corbett
Mary Margaret Fox
Brian D. Mulroney
Sean Weir
Frank S. Callaghan
James W. Mathers

(See Next Column)

BORDEN & ELLIOT—*Continued*

MEMBERS AND ASSOCIATES (Continued)

Ilsa J. Shore
Timothy O. Buckley
John J. Morris
John W. Woon
Mark A. Davis
Sean L. Gosnell
Winnie C. W. Tse
Doris L. Baughan
L. A. (Lex) Bullock
Scott E. Pilkey
Richard H. Shaban
Carol E. Derk
Daphne G. Jarvis
Shelley L. Timms
James R. Elder
Mary Lynn Gleason
Luke C. Mullin
Eric M. Roher
Alan M. Cornwall
Ian F. Gavaghan
Steven H. Leitl
Noella M. Milne
Neil C. Saxe
James D. Skippen
R. Andrew G. Harrison
Paul T. Knudsen
Darcy J. LeNeveu
Malcolm J. MacKillop
William A. McClelland
Christine A. Philp
Margaret J. M. Atkinson
Rudy V. Buller
Kimberley M. Graham
Carole A. Lindsay
Shawn L. Murphy
Anne E. Spafford
Barry L. Glaspell
Carole E. Hoglund
John W. Montgomery
Edward R. Smith
Elaine Victoria Wilson
Denise L. Tulk
Patrick J. Hawkins
Gabrielle K. Kramer
May J. Sproat
Carolyn L. Tate
Barbara J. Caplan
Michael P. Fitzgibbon
John A. Matheson
Craig J. Webster
Scott D. Bates
Tess Di Ponio
Robert L. Love
François P. Paroyan
Gordon J. Zimmerman
Joanne E. Foot
R. Bruce Reynolds
Christopher D. Bredt
Wendy J. Earle
Rosalind Morrow
David R. Woods
Catherine E. Bray
Julie K. Hannaford
Robert S. Russell
Robert W. Traves
Clare M. Gaudet
John K. Rodgers
Jonathan F. B. Barker
Ronald Foerster
Andrew W. Kingsmill
Joanne M. Poljanowski
Doreen M. Wong
Bruce E. Fowler
David A. Huctwith
William R. Middleton
James D. Patterson
Paul B. Scargall
M. Christine Fotopoulos
Sheila M. Holmes
Freya J. Kristjanson
Norman G. Letalik
Robert B. MacLellan
John J. Tobin
Douglas M. Worndl
Keith N. Batten
F.F. (Rick) Coburn
Ian J. Houston
Lynn M. McGrade
Robert B. Pattison
Melany V. Franklin
Craig J. Hill
Kevin A. McGivney
Howard S. Silverman
Harvey S. Stone
Rebecca A. Clements
Louis A. Frapporti
Michael J. Killeen
Joel M. Scoler
David L. Sterns
Prema K. R. Thiele
Daniel J. Dochylo
Benjamin T. Glustein
Sharon C. Vogel
Hilda W. Wong
Dolores Di Felice
Eric R. Hoaken
Laleh Moshiri
Julia S. Shin

OF COUNSEL

Carl H. Morawetz, Q.C.
M. E. (Libby) Burnham, Q.C.
Richard C. Meech, Q.C.
Charles Simon
Norman MacL. Rogers, Q.C.
William L. N. Somerville, Q.C.
George Cihra, Q.C.
Alfred L. J. Page

PATENT AND TRADEMARK COUNSEL

G. James M. Shearn

For full biographical listings, see the Martindale-Hubbell Law Directory

CASSELS BROCK & BLACKWELL (AV)

Suite 2100 Scotia Plaza, 40 King Street, West, M5H 3C2
Telephone: 416-869-5300
Cable Address: "Cassels"
Fax: 416-360-8 877
Internet: Casselsbrock.com

MEMBERS OF FIRM AND ASSOCIATES

H. Donald Guthrie, Q.C.
Gordon G. Dickson
Walter M. Bowen, Q.C.
Vernol I. Rogers
David R. Peterson, Q.C.
Ian A. Blue, Q.C.
Peter E. Steinmetz, Q.C.
Harvey J. Kirsh
Lorne H. Saltman
Kenneth C. Cancellara, Q.C.
Bruce T. McNeely
William Johnson Burden
Lanning J. Abramson
Phillip G. Bevans
Sheldon Plener
Robert D. Kligman
Mark G. Lichty
Timothy Pinos
Robert Law, Q.C.
Bruce Alexander Thomas, Q.C.
Crawford R. Spencer, Q.C.
M. Virginia MacLean, Q.C.
Donald Robert Arthurs
E. Bruce Leonard
John H. Craig
Ralph E. Lean, Q.C.
D. Rick Angelson
John W. R. Day
James M. Parks
John S. McKeown
Maxwell Gotlieb
Frank P. Monteleone
Alison R. Manzer
Stephen R. Le Drew
S. John Page
Cameron D. Stewart

(See Next Column)

MEMBERS OF FIRM AND ASSOCIATES (Continued)

Mark I. Young
W. Bruce Clark
Rui M. Fernandes
A. Peter Trebuss
Mark Vincent Ellis
Richard A. Row
Gregory J. Peebles
Paul M. Stein
Glenn M. Zakaib
Dennis M. O'Leary
Christopher W. Besant
Ian H. Gold
Sheldon Teicher
Howard Barry Kohn
John P. McGowan
Geoffrey B. Shaw
M. Gordon Hearn
M. Janine Kovach
David A. Redmond
Lawrence G. Theall
Peter A. Dunne
William H. Steele
Ramon V. Andal
Lori A. Prokopich
Robyn Collver
Marcus B. Snowden
Julie A. Thorburn
Keith G. Fairbairn
John R. Sandrelli
D'Arcy D. Mc Goey
David S. Ward
Marie Elizabeth Beyette
Gregory B.A. Greatrex
Thomas A. J. Harley
Bruce C. Bell
Leilah Edroos
Roberta McGill
Karen K. H. Bell
J. Brian Reeve
Christopher B. Norton
Lori A. Roth
Grace A. Westcott
Donald G. Gray
Lorne S. Silver
Ian R. Dick
B. Robin Moodie
Anne-Marie Widner
Peter Marrone
Cathy L. Mercer
Patricia M. Vakil
Diane E. Klukach
Lori A. McBurney
L. Michael Shannon
David R. Bugaresti
Ian A. Mair
Ani M. Abdalyan
Michael V. MacKay
Ann L. Watterworth
Stevan Novoselac
Sari Springer
Robert Cohen
Gordon P. Goodman
Joan C. Takahashi
Alexander David Pettingill
Christine Duerden
Tracey L. Durand
Catherine Christine Grant
Michael P. J. Mc Kendry
Christopher John Schnarr

COUNSEL

John W. Graham, Q.C.
Sanford World, Q.C.
Ian L. McCulloch, Q.C.
W. Hamilton Grass, Q.C.
Aubrey A. Russell, Q.C.
C. John Stubbs
Albert Abramson, Q.C.

ASSOCIATE COUNSEL

The Hon. Richard J. Stanbury,
Lawrence L. Herman

For full biographical listings, see the Martindale-Hubbell Law Directory

DAVIES, WARD & BECK (AV)

44th Floor, 1 First Canadian Place, P.O. Box 63, M5X 1B1
Telephone: 416-863-0900
Fax: 416-863-0871

PARTNERS AND ASSOCIATES

Robert A. Davies, Q.C. (1924-1975)
David A. Brown, Q.C.
Derek J. Watchorn
Nicholas J. Leblovic
Martin J. Rochwerg
Jay A. Swartz
Calvin S. Goldman, Q.C.
I. Berl Nadler
Jean-Paul Bisnaire
John A. Zinn
Douglas G. Hatch
Steven Sharpe
Timothy G. Youdan
Gregory J. Howard
William M. Ainley
Colin Campbell
A. Gerold Goldlist
Andrew A. L. Blair
Edward C. Hannah
Catherine G. Ross
Jeremy M. Freedman
D. Shawn McReynolds
Geoffrey P. Cornish
K. A. Siobhan Monaghan
Joel T. Kissack
John D. Bodrug
James J. Lawson
Robyn M. Bell
R. Ian Crosbie
James Jeremy Dorr
Vincent A. Mercier
Nigel S. Wright
Carol A. Hansell
Ian R. McBride
Matthew P. Gottlieb
D. John Purcell
Maureen Y. Berry
David A. Dell
Sandra A. Forbes
David A. Ward, Q.C.
Charles K. E. Overland, Q.C.
David W. Smith, Q.C.
Maurice Cullity, Q.C.
Donald C. Stanbury
Brian R. Carr
Robert T. Bauer
Gavin MacKenzie
Arthur S. Shiff
Ronald S. Wilson
William Gula
Grant R. M. Haynen
Gray E. Taylor
Michael Disney
John M. Ulmer
Carol D. Pennycook
Stephen I. Erlichman
Brian K. Grasmuck
Mark Q. Connelly
Jeffrey O. Palmer
Neal H. Armstrong
Paul M. Kennedy
Kevin J. Thomson
Michael Creery
Ian D. Johnson
Christina H. Medland
David G. F. Ellins
Thomas A. Smee
I. Kevin Coutts
Edward M. Morgan
Rahul Suri
Cameron M. Rusaw
Paul S. Crampton
Michael W. Clifford
Jeremy J. De Melo
Timothy H. Moran
Crystal L. Witterick
Richard F. D. Corley
James W. E. Doris
Fiona J. Kelly

(See Next Column)

DAVIES, WARD & BECK, *Toronto—Continued*

PARTNERS AND ASSOCIATES (Continued)

Ian D. MacDonald
J. Hugh Macdonnell
Mark Wilson
T. Scott Henderson
Sarbjit S. Basra
Margot L. Chapman
Linda P. Mantia
Christine J. Prudham
Patrick G. Barry
Geoffrey S. Turner
Cynthia L. Giagnocavo
Janet A. Holmes
Kent F. Beattie
Jacqueline M. Y. Clements
Paul D. Paton
Gilian R. Stacey
Andrew L. Welsh

COUNSEL

Thomas I. A. Allen, Q.C.

For full biographical listings, see the Martindale-Hubbell Law Directory

FASKEN CAMPBELL GODFREY (AV)

Toronto-Dominion Centre Toronto-Dominion Bank Tower, P.O. Box 20, M5K 1N6
Telephone: 416-366-8381
Toll Free: 1-800-268-8424 (Ontario & Quebec)
Facsimile: 416-364-7813
The partners and associates of Fasken Campbell Godfrey are also partners and associates of the national and international firm of Fasken Martineau which has offices in Toronto, Montreal, Quebec, Vancouver (Affiliated), London and Brussels.
Montreal, Quebec Office: Martineau Walker, Stock Exchange Tower, Suite 3400, P.O. Box 242. 800 Place-Victoria H4Z 1E9.
Telephone: 514-397-7400. Toll-Free: 1-800-361-6266 (Ontario & Quebec).
Facsimile: 514-397-7600.
Telex: 05-24610 BUOY MTL.
Quebec City, Quebec Office: Martineau Walker, Immeuble Le Saint-Patrick, 140, rue Grande Allée est, bureau 800, G1R 5M8.
Telephone: 418-640-2000. Toll Free: 1-800-463-2827 (Ontario & Quebec).
Facsimile: 418-647-2455.
Vancouver (Affiliated): Davis & Co., 2800 Park Place, 666 Burrard Street, V6C 2Z7.
Telephone: 604-687-9444.
Fax: 604-687-1612.
London, England Office: Fasken Martineau, 10 Arthur Street, 5th Floor, EC4R 9AY.
Telephone: 71-929-2894.
Facsimile: 71-929-3634.
Brussels, Belgium Office: Fasken Martineau, Avenue Franklin D. Roosevelt, 96 A, 1050, Brussels.
Telephone: 2-640-9796.
Facsimile: 2-640-2779.

MEMBERS

Robert M. Sutherland, Q.C.
James A. Bradshaw, Q.C.
Ronald J. Rolls, Q.C.
Claude R. Thomson, Q.C.
Roger D. Wilson, Q.C.
Rudolph W. Gardner, Q.C.
Donald J. Steadman
J. Michael Robinson, Q.C.
Arthur R. Kitamura
David M. Doubilet
Stephen T. P. Risk
Robert E. Smolkin
Roger R. Elliott, Q.C.
George C. Glover, Jr.
Stephen S. Ruby
John A. Campion
Robert S. Harrison
Kenneth C. Morlock
Esther L. Lenkinski
Walter J. Palmer
Samuel R. Rickett
Donald E. Short
Douglas C. New
Peter L. Roy
D. George Kelly
David G. Stinson
Craig R. Carter
Beryl B. Green
Jeffrey S. Leon
Edward W. Purdy
Peter W. Vair
Colleen Spring Zimmerman
Douglas E. Grundy
Elizabeth J. Johnson
Douglas A. Cannon
Michael N. Melanson
Donald E. Milner
J. David Vincent
Paul R. King
Roxanne E. McCormick
Sheryl E. Seigel
John D. Abraham
Ronald D. Collins
Ronald N. Robertson, Q.C.
Roger G. Doe, Q.C.
Robert L. Shirriff, Q.C.
Robert B. Tuer, Q.C.
George Tiviluk, Q.C.
Ian MacGregor
John H. Hough, Q.C.
Benjamin J. Hutzel
Richard B. Potter, Q.C.
John T. Morin, Q.C.
Alan M. Schwartz, Q.C. (Managing Partner)
David W. Salomon
Robert W. McDowell
Douglas R. Scott
Robert W. Cosman
Douglas C. Hunt, Q.C.
S. Bruce Blain
Jonathan A. Levin
Mark A. Richardson
Leslie H. Rose
William J. Bies
Brian A. T. O'Byrne
Eleanore A. Cronk
Rand A. Lomas
Joan M. H. Weppler
David N. Corbett
Lorri Kushnir
Ronald J. McCloskey
Constance L. Sugiyama
Philip J. Wolfenden
Anthony F. Baldanza
M. Elena Hoffstein
Allan G. Beach
Jon J. Holmstrom
Barbara Miller
Neal J. Smitheman
Jeffrey A. Kaufman
C. Ian Kyer
Bruce Salvatore
Ronald J. Walker
W. Thomas Barlow
E. Stuart Griffith

(See Next Column)

MEMBERS (Continued)

Richard E. Johnston
J. Mark Stinson
Gregory D. Gubitz
Mark S. Hayes
Paul J. Martin
Eric C. Belli-Bivar
Gary S. Fogler
Heather A. Laidlaw
Liana L. Turrin
Peter S. Ascherl
Michael J. MacNaughton
Cathy Singer
John G. Lorito
Robert W. Staley
Norman F. Findlay
Belinda J. James
Wayne P. J. McArdle
J. Steven Follett
S. Ronald Haber
Nigel P. J. Johnston
Gerald L. R. Ranking
Scott D. Conover
Bryan E. Kelling
David C. Rosenbaum
David G. Allsebrook
Peter A. Downard
Michael J. W. Round
Ruth M. Foster
David Koichi Moritsugu
Steven K. D'Arcy
Ralph J. Glass
Katherine M. Pollock

ASSOCIATES

Ronald W. McInnes
Daniel R. Law
Alan L. W. D'Silva
John M. Elias
Stephen M. Fitterman
Peter J. Pliszka
Neil M. Smiley
Linda S. Beairsto
Janne M. Duncan
Kathryn L. Knight
Ralph N. Nero
Christopher J. Staples
John S. Zimmer
Ruby E. Barber
Stephanie Anne Brown
Peter K. Czegledy
David Hausman
Kevin D. Lee
Grant B. Moffat
Richard B. Swan
T. Anthony Ball
Garth J. Foster
C. William Hourigan
Edmond F.B. Lamek
Andrew D. Burns
Gloria J. Geddes
Louise J.A. Greig
Darrell T. Kent
George J. Ahtipis
David J. Coultice
James L. Craven
Christopher E. Erickson
Gregory A. McElheran
Mitchell D. New
Bruce C. Treichel
Hugh G. Laurence
A. Thomas Little
Brian P. Dominique
Mark J. Fecenko
B. Lynne Golding
Peter J. Roberts
John S. M. Turner (Resident, London, England)
Jane E. Kelly
Kelley M. McKinnon
W. David Rance
Heidi Visser
Michael Balter
Joel E. Binder
Rosalind H. Cooper
Ed Esposto
Nina N. Hoque
Laura Lundie
Rahul Erik Saxena
J. Michael Armstrong
Martin K. Denyes
R. Craig Hoskins
Norm D. Kribs
David F. O'Connor
Brian A. Facey
Lisa A. Goldschleger
Cynthia L. Heinz
Jonathan F. Lancaster
Elizabeth G. Beattie
Laura F. Cooper
Kathryn J. Daniels
A.B. Laidlaw
Andrea L. Nauf
William K. Russell
Kerry F. Wood
Brian D. Wylynko

COUNSEL

Hon. John M. Godfrey, Q.C.
D. G. C. Menzel, Q.C.
Jack W. Huckle, Q.C.
Alexander D. T. Givens, Q.C.
Lucien Lamoureux, P.C., Q.C. (Resident, Brussels, Belgium)
Karl J. C. Harries, Q.C.
Fraser M. Fell, Q.C.

For full biographical listings, see the Martindale-Hubbell Law Directory

FRASER & BEATTY (AV)

1 First Canadian Place, P.O. Box 100, M5X 1B2
Telephone: 416-863-4511
Telecopier: 416-863-4592
North York, Ontario Office: The Madison Centre, 4950 Yonge Street, Suite 2300, M2N 6K1.
Telephone: 416-733-3300.
Telecopier: 416-221-5254.
Ottawa, Ontario Office: 180 Elgin Street, Suite 1200, K2P 2K7.
Telephone: 613-238-6294.
Telecopier: 613-563-7800.
Vancouver, British Columbia Office: 15th Floor, The Grosvenor Building, 1040 West Georgia Street, V6E 4H8.
Telephone: 604-687-4460.
Telecopier: 604-683-5214.
Montreal, Quebec Affiliated Office: McMaster Meighen. 7th Floor, 630 René-Lévesque Boulevard West, H3B 4H7.
Telephone: 514-879-1212.
Telecopier: 514-878-0605.
Cable Address: "Camerall".
Telex: "Camerall MTL" 05-268637.

PARTNERS AND CONSULTANTS

Stanley E. Edwards, Q.C.
D.B. Horsley, Q.C.
David I. Bristow, Q.C.
C. Michael McKeown, Q.C.
Robert G. Thomson, Q.C.
John S. Elder, Q.C.
J. Michael Bradley
Harry Sutherland, Q.C.
Robin W. W. Fraser, Q.C.
William A. Corbett, Q.C.
William Owen Francis
Donald F. Pounsett
Jeremy G. N. Johnston
Colin H. H. McNairn

(See Next Column)

FRASER & BEATTY—*Continued*

PARTNERS AND CONSULTANTS (Continued)

Michael I. Jeffery, Q.C.
Ian C. B. Currie, Q.C.
Michael B. Vaughan, Q.C.
J.H. (Jack) Whiteside
Terrence H. Young
David J. T. Mungovan
Raymond P. Quinlan
Ronald A. Goldenberg
Peter W. Hand
Michael J. Penman
Paul F. Baston
P. David McCutcheon
Patricia J. Williams
David Hunter
H. Alec Zimmerman
Paul D. Shantz
Michael L. McGowan
Peter A. Shiroky
Rick H. Kesler
Graham Turner
H. Stewart Ash
Marc Duguay
Susan J. Guttman
Michael N. Kaplan
Christopher E. Pinnington
Clare A. Sullivan
Maureen Farson
Robert E. Dickson
Victor Y. Hum
Howard M. Wise
Lisa G. Davis
Michèle D. McCarthy
Mary M. Picard
Richard A. M. Scott
David L. Miller
Joseph Debono
William D. Chambers
John L. McDougall, Q.C.
David G. Fuller
John W. Adams, Q.C.
John M. Langs
Paul P. Ginou
Hon. David P. Smith, P.C., Q.C.
A. Benson Lorriman
Gregory R. Hiseler
Jeffery A. Barnes
William H. Gravely
Ross W. Walker
J. Blair MacAulay
Ian V. B. Nordheimer
Robb C. Heintzman
Ronald J. Matheson
Peter E. Murphy
Barbara L. Grossman
Nancy M. Riley
Christopher D. Woodbury
Patrick J. Boyle
James A. S. Dunbar
Randal T. Hughes
N. Anneli Legault
Karen V. Ray
Peter J. Cavanagh
Susan E. Paul
Ronald H. Marshall
Dennis R. Wiebe
Riccardo C. Trecroce
Michael G. Horan
James G. Knight
M. Catherine Osborne
Christopher J. Matthews
Russel Z. Kowalyk
Raymond H. Mikkola

For full biographical listings, see the Martindale-Hubbell Law Directory

GARDINER, ROBERTS (AV)

31st Floor, 40 King Street West, Scotia Plaza, M5H 3Y2
Telephone: 416-865-6600
Telecopier: 416-865-6636

MEMBERS OF FIRM

John B. Conlin, Q.C.
John G. Parkinson, Q.C.
Barrie W. Webb, Q.C.
Ray G. Goodwin
C. Barry Tarshis
J. Brian Casey
J. Gordon McMehen
Jonathan H. Wigley
Evert Van Woudenberg
Jane E.B. Thompson
Robert D. Muncaster
Paul J. Stoyan
J. J. Robert Picard
Lori D. Mark
Holly E. Nicholson
Robert A. Maxwell
Milton J. Mowbray, Q.C.
Peter Webb, Q.C.
Roderick R. MacDougall
Robert C. Rossow
David E. Fine
Robert G. Doumani
Robert C. Taylor
David C. Poynton
Carol A. Albert
Paul E. Hawa
William E. Taberner
Ann C. Dinnert
Josephine A. Matera
Jeffrey Paul Hoffman
Jay Z. Josefo
Douglas M. Cunningham

ASSOCIATES

William S. O'Hara
Janet E. Kirby
Gavin J. Tighe
Judith G. Goldring
Lisa Douglas
John Atchison

COUNSEL

Richard J. Hassard, Q.C.
George A. Bassin
J. Douglas Crane, Q.C.
John F. Collins

For full biographical listings, see the Martindale-Hubbell Law Directory

KEYSER MASON BALL

(See Mississauga)

LAFLEUR BROWN (AV)

Suite 920, 1, First Canadian Place, P.O. Box 359, M5X 1E1
Telephone: 416-869-0994
Telecopier: 416-362-5818
Montreal, Quebec Office: 37th Floor, 1 Place Ville Marie.
Telephone: 514-878-9641.
Cable Address: "Mankin".
Telex: 05-25610.
Telecopier: 514-878-1450.
Brussels, Belgium Office: Av. Louise 386, 1050.
Telephone: 011 322 647 1112; 647 7158.
Telecopier: 011 322-648-7519.

(See Next Column)

L.-P. de Grandpré, C.C., Q.C.
Donald E. MacKenzie
Richard A. Thompson
Donald B. Johnston
D. Gordon Bent
Gina S. Brannan
David B. Kierans
M. Steven Alizadeh
David Zarek
Barbara Muir
Terry P. Mocherniak
Eric K. Grossman
John C. Papadakis
Danielle K. LiChong

For full biographical listings, see the Martindale-Hubbell Law Directory

LANG MICHENER (AV)

BCE Place Suite 2500, 181 Bay Street, P.O. Box 747, M5J 2T7
Telephone: 416-360-8600
Telecopier: 416-365-1719
Vancouver, British Columbia Office: 2500 Three Bentall Centre, P.O. Box 49200, 595 Burrard Street, V7X 1L1.
Telephone: 604-689-9111.
Telecopier: 604-685-7084.
Mississauga, Ontario Office: Suite 1001, 1290 Central Parkway West. L5C 4R3.
Telephone: 905-566-1000.
Telecopier: 905-566-1015.
Ottawa, Ontario Office: Suite 300, 50 O'Connor Street, K1P 6L2.
Telephone: 613-232-7171.
Telecopier: 613-231-3191.
Calgary, Alberta Office: Suite 1900, 355 4th Avenue, S.W., T2P 0J1.
Telephone: 403-237-5858.
Fax: 403-266-5272.

RESIDENT MEMBERS

Gordon M. Farquharson, Q.C.
Arnold Englander
Gerhard K. Selzer, Q.C.
Warren S.R. Seyffert, Q.C.
Donald H. MacOdrum
Wayne F. Carney
William J.V. Sheridan
J. Douglas Wilson
David W. Pamenter
Martin D. Rabinovitch
Robert R. Cranston
Daniel R. Dowdall
Bruce A. McKenna
Peter E.J. Wells
Gerald D. Courage
Robert E. Glass
Geofrey Myers
Thomas J. Hunter
David E. Thring
H. Scott Fairley
David A. Knight
Patrick J. Phelan
Carol V.E. Hitchman
William A. Rowlands
F. Paul Collins
Gerald F. Hayden, Jr.
James B. Musgrove
D. Paul Tackaberry
Mark S. Mitchell
Frank H. Herbert
A. Burke Doran, Q.C.
Robert M. McDerment, Q.C.
Donald N. Plumley, Q.C.
Albert Gnat, Q.C.
Kalle Soomer, Q.C.
Michael R. Gray
C. Robert Vernon
John L. Dillman
R. Nairn Waterman
Marni M.K. Whitaker
David Hager
David M.W. Young
Frank Palmay
Mark E.P. Cavanaugh
Bruce W. Cameron
Alexandra Hoy
Jeffrey B. Simpson
Gordon A. Meiklejohn
Howard M. Drabinsky
Nancy M. Johnston
Elise Orenstein
Duncan Cornell Card
William P. Lambert
David Burstein
William C. Cortis
Jacqueline M. Mills
J. Mark Richardson
Carl A. De Vuono
Philippe Tardif
Joseph C. D'Angelo
Carol Virginia Lyons

RESIDENT ASSOCIATES

Jack H.O. Peppler, Q.C.
E. Llana Nakonechny
R. Shayne Kukulowicz
Daniel G. Edmondstone
Helen Sava
John H. Currie
Michael Adrian Smith
Bernd S. Christmas
Clive Elkin
Alex Ilchenko
Sylvia L. Tint
William B. Henderson
Eric B. Friedman
John S. Contini
D. Scott Lamb
Hellen L. Siwanowicz
Sara A. Morton
Warren N. Sprigings
Edna A. Chu
Sudha Berry
Ranald I. Sinclair
Stephanie Chong

COUNSEL

Robert A. Cranston, Q.C.
Geoffrey I. Pringle, Q.C.
Hon. Daniel A. Lang, Q.C.
Donald J. Wright, Q.C.
John B. Clements, Q.C.

For full biographical listings, see the Martindale-Hubbell Law Directory

McCARTHY TÉTRAULT (AV)

Suite 4700 Toronto Dominion Bank Tower, Toronto Dominion Centre, M5K 1E6
Telephone: 416-362-1812
Facsimile: 416-868-0673
Vancouver, British Columbia Office: Pacific Centre, P.O. Box 10424, Suite 1300, 777 Dunsmuir Street, Vancouver, British Columbia V7Y 1K2.
Telephone: 604-643-7100.
Facsimile: 604-643-7900.

(See Next Column)

McCarthy Tétrault, *Toronto—Continued*

Surrey, British Columbia Office: Suite 1300, Station Tower, Gateway 13401-108th Avenue, Surrey, British Columbia V3T 5T3.
Telephone: 604-583-9100.
Fax: 604-583-9150.
London, Ontario Office: Suite 2000, One London Place, 255 Queens Avenue, London, Ontario N6A 5R8.
Telephone: 519-660-3587.
Facsimile: 519-660-3599.
Ottawa, Ontario Office: Suite 1000, 275 Sparks Street, Ottawa, Ontario K1R 7X9.
Telephone: 613-238-2000.
Facsimile: 613-563-9386.
Montréal, Québec Office: "le Windsor", 1170 rue Peel, Montréal, Québec H3B 4S8.
Telephone: 514-397-4100.
Facsimile: 514-875-6246.
Québec, Québec Office: Le Complexe St-Amable 1150, rue Claire Fontaine 73 Étage, Québec, Québec G1R 5G4.
Telephone: 418-521-3000.
Facsimile: 418-521-3099.
United Kingdom and European Office: 1 Pemberton Row, Fetter Lane, London, England EC4A 3BA.
Telephone: 011-44-171-353-2355.
Facsimile: 011-44-171-583-5644.

MEMBERS OF FIRM AND ASSOCIATES

Basil R. Cheeseman, Q.C.
H. J. Michael Croghan, Q.C.
John H. Francis, Q.C.
W. Ian C. Binnie, Q.C.
Bradley Crawford, Q.C.
Donald E. Smith, Q.C., P.Eng.
Arthur R. A. Scace, Q.C.
William J. Cornwall, Q.C.
Thomas G. Heintzman, Q.C.
Terence M. Dolan
Peter S. Grant, Q.C.
Daryl E. McLean
Donald G. Gibson
Dale L. Robinette
Dennis H. Wood
Glen G. MacArthur
M. Patricia Richardson
R. B. (Biff) Matthews
Christopher S. L. Hoffmann
Henry J. P. Wiercinski
David M. Harley
F. David Rounthwaite
Judith M. Woods
Eric Gertner
Eric F. Spindler
Stephen D. A. Clark
Garth M. Girvan
Gerald P. Sadvari
René R. Sorell
Elizabeth M. Stewart
Thomas B. Akin
Christopher A. Montague
Iain W. Scott
Gordon F. Willcocks
Susan A. Bisset
Michael G. Quigley
Kirby Chown
Owen A. Johnson
A. Brad Teichman
Michael E. Barrack
Abraham Costin
Brian C. Kelsall
Conor D. M. McCourt
Michael C. Nicholas
Gabrielle M. R. Richards
R. Paul Steep
Michael Weizman
John P. Brown
Philip C. Moore
David M. Porter
William G. Scott
Mary M. Thomson
Jane A. Ford
Malcolm M. Mercer
David B. Tennant
Martin Felsky
C. Roderick MacKenzie
Godyne N. L. Sibay
Ian W. Arellano
Bernard Crotty
Nancy A. Eber
Cynthia A. MacDougall
Fred M. Rubinoff
A. S. Peter Kingsmill, Q.C.
Peter G. Beattie, Q.C.
C. Edward Walden
L. Thomas Forbes, Q.C.
James C. McCartney, Q.C.
Colin L. Campbell, Q.C.
Burton Tait, Q.C.
David H. Gordon
E. Alan Peters
George D. Elliott, Q.C.
Peter H. Harris, Q.C.
Thomas H. Bjarnason
James B. Noonan
D. Murray Paton
Edward P. Kerwin
W. Niels F. Ortved
G. Blair Cowper-Smith
Peter D. Quinn
Lorne P. Salzman
James R. Wilson
Henry G. Intven
Adam D. Vereshack
Robert E. Forbes
F. Paul Morrison
James H. Archer
Joseph J. Colangelo
Shanon O. N. Grauer
Phillip L. Sanford
Robert W. F. Stephenson
Frances B. Wright
Linda J. Betts
Gordon S. Sato
J. Stephen Stohn
David M. Armstrong
Richard B. Miner
Charles J. Birchall
Brian D. Edmonds
Robert A. Macpherson
Harry C. G. Underwood
Susan J. Biggar
Graham P. C. Gow
Jacqueline H. R. Le Saux
Kevin C. McLoughlin
Richard J. Nixon
Barry Sookman
Doug R. Thomson
Wendy G. Bellack-Viner
Heather A. Howe
S. Richard Orzy
Barry J. Ryan
F. Gordon Thompson
Riyaz Dattu
William D. McCullough
Steven F. Rosenhek
Mary Beth Currie
Mark J. Freiman
Dean T. Palmer
George S. Takach
Nancy J. Carroll
Thomas J. Curry
Michael B. Fraleigh
William H. Richardson
Leslie A. Sigurdson

(See Next Column)

MEMBERS OF FIRM AND ASSOCIATES (Continued)

Donald M. Sugg
Christa C. Wessel
Suzanne M. Duncan
Douglas J. Klaassen
Marta O. Lewycky
Susan E. Opler
Brian C. Pel
John L. Walker
Mary K. Bull
Delee A. Fromm
Hilary E. Laidlaw
Sheena J. MacAskill
Scott L. Perkin
Gregory J. Winfield
Karen F. Douglas
Marsha P. Gerhart
Glen F. Ireland
Jacqueline E.H. Lord
Iain R. Morton
Sean D. Sadler
Neil E. Bass
Danielle M. Bush
Julie Garner-Smith
David Judson
Marc J. MacMullin
Frank Mclaughlin
Tracey-Anne Pearce
Paul Peterson
Caroline R. Zayid
Darryl R. Ferguson
Simon D. Johnson
Andrew P. Werbowski
Jerald M. Wortsman
Susan L. Gratton
Darryl Alexander Cruz
Stephanie L. Leaist
Jonathan Lisus
Janet Becker
Carla J. Brewer
Eileen E. Clarke
James D. Gage
Tanneke Heersche
Sarah V. Powell
Catherine M. Poyen
Monique Smith
Anthony Bond
Jeremy Devereux
J. Stephen Furlan
Navin Khanna
Michele J. Lund
Judy Naiberg
Stephen Shantz
Robert Richardson
M. Philip Tunley
Barbara J. Boake
Jay M. Hoffman
David A. N. Lever
Lori J. Nicholls-Car
Catherine M. Patterson
Ronald R. Schwass
Jillian M. Welch
Bernadette Dietrich
John R. Jason
Jeremy A. Oliver
William C. McDowell
Jenny P. Stephenson
William D. Black
Cindy J. Findlay
Daniel C. Grandilli
C. Elizabeth Koester
James G. Morand
Steven J. Rapkin
Leneo E. Sdao
Steven Baum
Timothy Foster Civil
Lloyd M. Hoffer
Lorenzo Lisi
Robert D. Minnes
Rodney V. Northey
Dana M. Peebles
Andrew J. Reddon
Gordon D. Baird
Jonathan R. Grant
Bernard C. Leblanc
David E. Woollcombe
M. Stephen Blimkie
Lisa A. Clarkson
Robert J. M. Janes
Linda Pieterson
Kevin Zych
Robert J. Brant
Glynnis P. Burt
Sacha C. Fraser
Geoff R. Hall
Soraya Kim
Stephen Scholtz
Gregory B. Shepherd
Anthony Mark C. Alexander
Lisa Constantine
Robert Fenton
Leanne Hewlin
David Leonard
Steven Mason
Stuart D. Waugh
Mary Kirwan
Gina Papageorgiou

COUNSEL

Willard Z. Estey, Q.C.
John H. C. Clarry, Q.C.
Harry W. Macdonell, Q.C.
Michael Gee, Q.C.
Duncan J. McRae
Douglas G. Milne, Q.C.
Donald S. Macdonald, P.C.
Thomas E. (Tim) Armstrong
James W. McCutcheon, Q.C.
John A. Keefe
Brian P. Smeenk

ASSOCIATE COUNSEL

Beverley Matthews, Q.C.
John W. Blain, Q.C.
Philip H. G. Walker, Q.C.
G. Patrick H. Vernon, Q.C.
James W. Walker, Q.C.
Ian Douglas, Q.C.
John B. Lawson, Q.C.
Donald J. Donahue, Q.C.

PATENT AND TRADE-MARK AGENTS

Peter A. Brown
Omar A. Nassif
Pamela Feldman
David A. Ruston
Robert P. Stratton

For full biographical listings, see the Martindale-Hubbell Law Directory

McMillan Binch (AV)

A Member of McMillan Bull Casgrain
Royal Bank Plaza Suite 3800 South Tower, M5J 2J7
Telephone: 416-865-7000
Fax: 416-865-7048
Internet: @ Mcbinch. COM
Missisauga, Ontario Office: Mississauga Executive Centre, 3 Robert Speck Parkway, Suite 800.
Telephone: 905-896-1850.
Fax: 905-566-2029 CBANET MC.BINCH.

MEMBERS OF FIRM AND ASSOCIATES

Malcolm C. Kronby, Q.C.
Peter G. Cathcart, Q.C.
Robert K. McDermott
W. David McCordic
John W. Craig
Richard B. Thomas
Stanley G. Fisher, Q.C.
John A. Paterson
Graham W. S. Scott, Q.C.
William Woloshyn
Robert N. Gilmore
Michael M. Peterson

(See Next Column)

McMillan Binch—*Continued*

MEMBERS OF FIRM AND ASSOCIATES (Continued)

J. William F. Rowley, Q.C.
J. Christopher Osborne
Alice-Anne Morlock
William G. Horton
Bruce C. Barker
George K.S. Payne
Sarah E. Pepall
Andrew J. F. Kent
David S. McLean
Francis A. Archibald
Thomas E. Scott
Stephen W. Bowman
Leonard Ricchetti
David N. Ross
Vernon V. Kakoschke
Michael D. Templeton
David G. Wentzell
Jeffrey B. Gollob
Daniel V. MacDonald
James D. Scarlett
Teresa M. Dufort
Marlene J. Kane
Hilary E. Clarke
Margaret C. McNee
Hollis R. S. Brent
Gary K. Ostoich
Michael P. Whitcombe
Diana Cafazzo
Nancy J. Iadeluca
John F. Clifford
Scott A. Horner
Fred S. Maxim
D. Lisa Goldstein
Richard T. Higa
A. Neil Campbell
Martha A. McCarthy
Stephen C. E. Rigby
John D. Davis
Amanda K. Worley
Denise A. Denomme
Sean M. Farrell
Scott R. Hyman
Sean S. McNamee
Melanie A. Yach
W.G.Tad Brown
Andrew D. Green
Ronald G. Hay
John B.V. Kelly
Mark D. Pratt
William V. Sasso
Terrence J. O'Sullivan
Anne E. P. Armstrong
John A. Kazanjian
Douglas Barrett
Mickey M. Yaksich
Harold P. Rolph
Luigi Macchione
Patricia L. Olasker
Heather R. Douglas
Jean E. Anderson
Daniel F. Hirsh
Holly A. Robertson
R. Simon G. Chester
Catherine F. Nixon
Dennis A. Trinaistich
David S. Elenbaas
David W. Kent
Paul G. F. Macdonald
Dalton J. Albrecht
Kathleen S.M. Hanly
Samuel C. Billard
Mary-Ann E. Haney
John M. Sibley
Carmen S. Theriault
Robert M. Scavone
Jennifer K. Badley
Chris N. Germanakos
Markus Koehnen
Diane L. Evans
J. Scott Maidment
E. Jane Richardson
Elizabeth J. Herrema
Richard J. B. Price
L. Jane Luck
David M. McIntyre
Shirley G. Casola
Ray R. Rubin
Brian K. Barron
Mark O. Dickerson
Michelle M. Gage
Tracey A. Lazareth
Pierre F. Michaud
Candace M. Barrett
Nancy C. Coté
W. Brad Hanna
Glen R. Johnson
Kathy M. O'Brien
R.D. Jeffrey Rogers
Cyndee B. Todgham

For full biographical listings, see the Martindale-Hubbell Law Directory

Meighen Demers (AV)

Suite 1100, Merrill Lynch Canada Tower, 200 King Street West, M5H 3T4
Telephone: 416-977-8400
Telecopier: 416-977-5239

MEMBERS OF FIRM

Honourable Michael A. Meighen, Q.C.
John D. Pennal
Nigel H. Frawley
Peter E. Lockie
John D. Stirling
James R. Cade
James B. Love, Q.C.
Richard S. Sutin
W. Jacques Demers
Mary J. Braun
Alan Whiteley
Robert L. Armstrong
Dana B. Fuller
Derrick C. Tay
Peter S. Newell
Robert A. Kozlov
Ian A. Ness
John T. Porter
Mark A. Convery
Patrick G. Egan
William L. Dimitroff
Kevin J. Morley
Marlin J. Horst
Richard P. Uldall
Ross V. Whalen
Nicholas C. Williams
Jeff Burtt
Merie-Anne E. Beavis
Philip I. Lieberman
Elizabeth J. Sanderson
Rahul K. Bhardwaj
M. Lynne O'Brien
Christopher J. Steeves
Heather L. Evans

For full biographical listings, see the Martindale-Hubbell Law Directory

Miller Thomson (AV)

20 Queen Street West, Box 27, Suite 2700, M5H 3S1
Telephone: 416-595-8500
Fax: 416-595-8695
York Region Office: 60 Columbia Way, Suite 600, Markham, Ontario, L3R 0C9.
Telephone. 905-415-6700.
Fax: 905-415-6777.

(See Next Column)

PARTNERS

David Churchill-Smith, Q.C.
John N. Turner, P.C. Q.C. *
Gerald C. Hollyer, Q.C.
Ralph Brown, Q.C.
Wylie B. Ivany, Q.C.
Eric B. Russell, Q.C.
Arthur D. Angus
David J. Moxon, Q.C. (Resident, Markham Office)
John S. Buchan
T. Keith Billings
Lawrence A. Bertuzzi
Judson D. Whiteside (Resident, Markham Office)
Eduardo M. Barradas (Resident, Markham Office)
Michael J. Pace
Wayne D. Gray (Resident, Markham Office)
John R. Sproat
Michael W. Kerr
Martin J. Addario
Peter F. Kiborn (Resident, Markham Office)
Charles R. Robertson
Peter K. Foulds
Constance M. Brothers
John J. Chapman
John R. Tidball (Resident, Markham Office)
Peter F. Chauvin
Susan M. Manwaring
James A. Proskurniak
K. Duncan Finlayson, Q.C.
Eric M. Lane (Resident, Markham Office)
James J. Murphy, Q.C.
Lawrence H. Iron, Q.C.
Douglas C. McTavish, Q.C.
Andrew M. Robinson
Robert J. Fuller, Q.C.
Roderick M. McLeod, Q.C. (Resident, Markham Office)
Andrew J. Roman
James T. Beamish
James D.M. Fraser
F. Max E. Maréchaux
Peter A. Daley
Harold W.D. Cares
Rosanne T. Rocchi
D. Bruce McCartney
Jane A. Roffey
Lawrence M. Foy
David W. Croft
John L. Martin
Michael L. Shell (Resident, Markham Office)
Susan J. Robins
Jennifer E. Babe
John M. Campbell
Robert W. England
Douglas F. Best
Jeffrey C. Carhart
Hugh R. Dyer
Mark J. Fuller
Steven L. Wesfield
Chris T.J. Blom

ASSOCIATES

A. Catherina Spoel
Les D. Manley
Sheila C. MacKinnon
Douglas J.R. Moodie
Kenneth J. Coulson
Drazen J. Bulat
Clifford J. Hart
M. Jasmine Sweatman
J. Kelly Hermant
M. Christine O'Donohue
Michael K. Walter
Gregory T. Callahan
R. Peter A. Macdonald
Gita Anand
J. Bruce McMeekin
Wendy G. Hulton
Novalea M.A. Jarvis
Derek J. Ferris
Allan P. Webster (Resident, Markham Office)
Dirk L. Van de Kamer
Andrew C. Hancharyk
Nishan Swais

CONSULTANTS

William R. B. Herridge, Q.C.
Glenn A. MacPherson, Q.C.
Peter H. Smith
John R. Varley
M. Stephen Georgas
Brian H. Wheatley, Q.C.
Ward R. Passi
Norman S. Rankin
Paul E. Brace (Resident, Markham Office)
Barbara R.C. Doherty

*Denotes Professional Corporation

For full biographical listings, see the Martindale-Hubbell Law Directory

O'Donohue & O'Donohue (AV)

Suite 1600, 390 Bay Street, M5H 2Y2
Telephone: 416-361-3231
Fax: 416-361-3472

MEMBERS OF FIRM

Melville O'Donohue, Q.C.
Stephen O'Donohue

ASSOCIATES

Mary-Jo O'Donohue
Allan J. Lyons

For full biographical listings, see the Martindale-Hubbell Law Directory

Osler, Hoskin & Harcourt (AV)

Barristers & Solicitors
Patent and Trade-Mark Agents
1 First Canadian Place, P.O. Box 50, M5X 1B8
Telephone: 416-362-2111
FAX: 416-862-6666
Ottawa, Ontario Office: Suite 1500, 50 O'Connor Street, K1P 6L2.
Telephone: 613-235-7234.
FAX: 613-235-2867.
New York, N.Y. Office: Osler Renault* - Suite 3217, 200 Park Avenue, 10166-0193.
Telephone: 212-867-5800.
Fax: 212-867-5802.
London, England Office: Osler Renault* - 20 Little Britain, London EC1A 7DH.
Telephone: 071-606-0777.
FAX: 071-606-0222.
Paris, France Office: Osler Renault* - 4, rue Bayard, 75008.
Telephone: 33-1.42.89.00.54.
Fax: 33-1.42.89.51.60.

(See Next Column)

OSLER, HOSKIN & HARCOURT, *Toronto—Continued*

Hong Kong Office: Osler Renault* - Suite 1708, One Pacific Place. 88 Queensway.
Telephone: 011-852-2877-3933.
Fax: 011-852-2877-0866.
Singapore Office: Osler Renault* - 65 Chulia Street, #40-05 OCBC Centre, Singapore 0104.
Telephone: (65) 538-2077.
Fax: (65) 538-2977.
**Osler Renault is an international partnership of Osler, Hoskin & Harcourt and Ogilvy Renault.*

MEMBERS OF FIRM

John G. Goodwin, Q.C.
Laurence D. Hebb, Q.C. (Managing Partner)
J. Edgar Sexton, Q.C. (Chair of the Firm)
John F. Petch, Q.C.
Peter White
John T. Evans
Francois Lemieux (Resident in Ottawa, Ontario)
Stephen V. Arnold
Rodolph W. Groulx (Resident in Ottawa, Ontario)
Maurice J. Coombs
Michael J. Gough
John F. Layton
Stanley B. Stein
Lyndon A. J. Barnes
Brian D. Bucknall
Michael L. Phelan (Resident in Ottawa, Ontario)
Rupert H. Chartrand
Barbara J. McGregor
Nancy D. Chaplick
Blake M. Murray
James H. Smellie (Resident in Ottawa, Ontario)
Jean M. De Marco
Deborah M. Alexander
Ronald C. Cheng (Resident in Ottawa, Ontario)
Richard A. Lococo
Joseph M. Steiner
James H. Lisson
J. Brett G. Ledger
Linda D. Robinson
Francis R. Allen
Penelope S. Bonner
Marilyn M.M. Field-Marsham
Stephen W. Luff
Ian J. F. McSweeney
Arthur J. Peltomaa
Scott L. Scheuermann
Lorne H. Abugov (Resident in Ottawa, Ontario)
Linda G. Currie
Valerie A. E. Dyer
C. W. Daniel Kirby
Heather R. McKean
J. Andrew Pritchard (Resident in Ottawa, Ontario)
Stephen G. Blair (Resident in Ottawa, Ontario)
J. Mark DesLauriers
Terence D. Hall
Larry P. Lowenstein
David W. Aitken (Resident in Ottawa, Ontario)
Adrian P. Hartog
James E. Kofman
David T. Tetreault
Donna G. White (Resident in Ottawa, Ontario)
Donald G. Gilchrist
P. Mark Meredith
Christopher S. Murray
Timothy P. Schumacher
David K. Wilson (Resident in Ottawa, Ontario)
S. Firoz Ahmed
Terence S. Dobbin
Douglas T. Hamilton
John A. MacDonald
Stephen P. Sigurdson
Heather P. Griffiths (Resident in Ottawa, Ontario)
Ruth I. Wahl
Gregory O. Somers (Resident in Ottawa, Ontario)
James F. Kennedy, Q.C.
R. Gordon Marantz, Q.C.
Ronald G. Belfoi, Q.C. (Resident in Ottawa, Ontario)
Donald E. Wakefield
Kent H.E. Plumley (Resident in Ottawa, Ontario)
J. Timothy Kennish
A. David G. Purdy
John M.M. Roland, Q.C.
Ronald G. Atkey, P.C., Q.C.
Edward T. McDermott
Kenneth L. W. Boland (Resident in Ottawa, Ontario)
Stephen B. Smart
Christopher Portner
Terrence J. Tone
Arthur Birnbaum
Donald L. Marston
John F. Rook
Frank Zaid
Norman C. Loveland
William R. Rauenbusch
James E. Fordyce
Donald C. Ross
David R. Allgood
Robert J. Clayton
James R. Hassell
Brian R. Bawden
Michael J. Davies
Jean M. Fraser
K. Scott McLean (Resident in Ottawa, Ontario)
J. George Vesely
Brian G. Morgan
Richard G. Tremblay
Glen A. Bloom (Resident in Ottawa, Ontario)
Julie Y. Lee
Carol Tennenhouse Diamond (Resident in Ottawa, Ontario) (On Leave)
W. Lee Webster
Laurie E. Barrett
Richard J. Coleman
D. Aleck Dadson
W. Jason M. Hanson
Stanley Magidson
Dale R. Ponder
Janet E. Sim
Steven W. Smith
Michael H. D. Bowman
Terrence R. Burgoyne
Steven G. Golick
Philip J. B. Heath
Randy A. Pepper
John M. Bishop
Peter H. G. Franklyn
Andrew H. Kingissepp
David S. Morritt
George M. Valentini
Patricia J. Wilson (Resident in Ottawa, Ontario)
Barry I. Goldberg
G. Lee Muirhead
Shelley W. Obal
John W. Stevens (Resident in New York, N.Y.)
Thane P. Woodside
D. Robert Beaumont
Peter L. Glossop
H. B. Clay Horner
Frederick L. Myers
Karen J. Weinstein
Allyson C. Landy
Andrew S. McGuffin
J. Craig Wright (On secondment)
David W. Stratas

(See Next Column)

ASSOCIATES

Anthony J. Devir
R. Alan Young (Resident in Ottawa, Ontario)
Sean C. Aylward
Irene P. Christie
Linne M. North
Geoffrey K. Taber
Andrew W. Aziz
John C. Cotter
Jolie Lin
Paul J. Morassutti
Brian M. Blugerman
Douglas R. Marshall
Lawrence E. Ritchie (On secondment)
Mark A. Trachuk
Elizabeth M. Walker
Cheryl D.M. Emberley (Resident in Ottawa, Ontario)
Deborah A. Glendinning
Sushma Jobanputra
Paul W. Litner
Kelly Anne Thomson
Ahab Abdel-Aziz
Christian B.L. Erickson
Paula B. Hurwitz
Robert C. Lando
John H. Macfarlane
Susan L. Nicholas
Jeffrey A. Rubinoff
Russell W. Watson
Michael Bennett
Michael A. Burns
Clara M. González-Martin (Resident in London, England)
John M. Hovland
Stephen Lamont
J. Scott Martyn
Frank W.B. Morison
Randall W. Pratt
Robert T. Stuart
Irene L. Wolfe
Felicia B. Bortolussi
Jennifer J. Fong
Karen E. Galpern
Joy L. Hulton
Andrew D. Little
Laura J. Nield
Laurie A. Reiner
Neil M. Selfe
Francis J. Turner
David H. Zemans
John A. Black
Eugene A.G. Cipparone
Jocelyn A. Cornforth
Christine E. Hicks (Resident in Ottawa, Ontario)
Derek S. Keay (Resident in Ottawa, Ontario)
Bruce R. Latimer
Laura P. Nichols
Douglas J. Rienzo
Michael D. Wilhelmson
Robert D. Wortzman
Richard M. Borins
Monica Creery
Angie Karna
Jacqueline G. Lawrence
John C. Menear
Nancy J. Stitt
Eden M. Oliver
Monica E. Biringer
Michal E. Minkowski (Resident in Ottawa, Ontario)
Mark A. Gelowitz
Robert A. Roberts
Caroline L.M. Thomas
Diane E. Cornish (Resident in Ottawa, Ontario)
David S. McFarlane
Jack A. Silverson
Tristram J. Mallett
Richard J. Nathan
M. Janet Salter
Edward A. Sellers (Resident in New York, N.Y.)
William A. Charnetski (On leave)
David R. Forster
Kenneth Herlin
Amy C. Lewtas
Heidi A. Rees
David J. Wenger
Jennifer Dolman
Laurie A. Galway
Alvin S. Lampert
Toby C.D. Lennox
Rodger Madden
Hugh M.B. O'Reilly
Tracy C. Sandler
Robert M. Yalden
S. Andrew Brown
Edith P. Dover
Donald D. Hanna
Martha A. Healey (Resident in Ottawa, Ontario)
A. Michelle Lally
Jimmy Y. Levy
Kelly L. Moffatt
Jodi M. Nieman
David A. Stamp
Edward Weidberg
Gregory R. Wylie
Peter J. Chapin
Melissa G. Fox-Revett
Tanya M. Goldberg
Abhimanyu Julan
Andrew J. MacDougall
Melanie A. Polowin (Resident in Ottawa, Ontario)
M. Lynn Starchuk (Resident in Ottawa, Ontario)
David J. Bannon
Jonathan A. Blakey (Resident in Ottawa, Ontario)
Robert I. Frank
Peter S. Janicki
John T. Kalm
Kenneth A. Krupat
Bernard J. Kwasniewski (on leave)
Katherine E. Petcher
Rocco M. Sebastiano
Henry J. Wolfond
Ian D. Bock
Patrick J. Callaghan
Natalie M. Jenner
Jeffrey E. Koch
Laurie S. May
Cameron G. Negraiff
Carla R. Swansburg
David W. Tucker

RETIRED PARTNERS

Stuart Thom, Q.C.
Peter White, Q.C.
John M. Coyne, Q.C.
William P. Rogers, Q.C.
Bradshaw M. W. Paulin, Q.C.
Edward J. M. Huycke, Q.C.
James G. Fogo
Thomas R. Judge
Mills Mraz
John R. Tolmie, Q.C.
W. Stewart Rogers, Q.C.
Campbell R. Osler, Q.C.
William M. Bryden, Q.C.
Frederick A. M. Huycke, Q.C.
Harold K. Boylan, Q.C.
James K. Doran, Q.C.
Donald F. Pattison, Q.C.
Anthony O. Hendrie
Robert F. Lindsay, Q.C.

DEPARTMENT OF LEGAL EDUCATION

John E. Claydon
Mara L. Nickerson

PATENT AGENT

James R. Keneford (Resident in Ottawa, Ontario)

(See Next Column)

OSLER, HOSKIN & HARCOURT—*Continued*

TRADE-MARK LAW CLERK

Marion Bailey
(Resident in Ottawa, Ontario)

For full biographical listings, see the Martindale-Hubbell Law Directory

SHIBLEY RIGHTON (AV)

Suite 1800 The Simpson Tower, 401 Bay Street, P.O. Box 32, M5H 2Z1
Telephone: 416-363-9381 Telecopier: 416-365-1717
Voicemail: 416-363-3425
Affiliated Offices:
Swinton & Company, 1000-840 Hume Street, Vancouver, British Columbia, Canada.
Multilaw (international affiliation of law firms).
Great Lakes Law Association (Canada-U.S. regional affiliation of law firms).
Attorneys' Joint Office No. 32, Mr. Przemyslaw Helsztynski, Jerozolimskie 11/19, 00-508 Warszawa, Polska.
Legal Office No. 140, Dr. Istvan Gellerthegyi, H-1054 Budapest, Republic of Hungary.

MEMBERS AND ASSOCIATES

Richard E. Shibley, Q.C.
Rupert F. Righton, Q.C.
Harold H. Elliott, Q.C.
Dennis C. Hefferon
Donald K. Robinson, Q.C.
Richard E. Anka, Q.C.
Barry S. Wortzman, Q.C.
Leslie S. Mason
Dez Windischmann
John P. Bell
Michael M. K. Fitzpatrick, Q.C.
George J. Corn
V. Ross Morrison
Linda S. Bohnen
John C. Spearn
Michael C. Birley
Peter C. Williams
Paul E. McInnis
Peter G. Neilson
Clifford I. Cole
Jonathan H. Flanders
Charles Simco
Thomas A. Stefanik
William L. Northcote
James Rossiter
Helder M. Travassos
Peter V. Raytek
J. Jay Rudolph
Cynthia J. Gunn
Martin J. Henderson
Nicholas T. Macos
Warren S. Rapoport
Richard E. Coles
Martin Peters
Alexander P. Torgov
Charles Gastle
Philip P. Healey
Charles Wiebe
Wade D. Jamieson
Leonard D. Rodness
Sandra E. Dawe
Linda J. Godel
Janis E. Ingram
Christine M. Silversides
Salvatore Frisina
Thomas McRae
James W. Bussin
Karen I. McMaster
Jennifer L. Perry
Craig A. Lewis
William A. Chalmers
Elizabeth G. Martin

COUNSEL

Barry D. Lipson, Q.C.
Martin L. O'Brien, Q.C.

For full biographical listings, see the Martindale-Hubbell Law Directory

SMITH, LYONS, TORRANCE, STEVENSON & MAYER (AV)

Suite 6200 Scotia Plaza, 40 King Street West, M5H 3Z7
Telephone: 416-369-7200
Facsimile: 416-369-7250
Ottawa, Ontario Office: Suite 1700, 45 O'Connor Street.
Telephone: 613-230-3988.
Facsimile: 613-230-7085.
Vancouver, British Columbia Office: World Trade Centre, 550-999 Canada Place.
Telephone: 604-662-8082.
Facsimile: 604-685-8542.
Kiev, Ukraine Office: Suite 175, 5th Floor, Predslavynska Street, 38.
Telephone: 7-044-268-4181.
Facsimile: 7-044-268-3171.
Hong Kong: In Association with Fred Kan & Co., 31st Floor, Central Plaza, 18 Harbour Road, Wanchai, Hong Kong.
Telephone: 011 852 598 1318.
Facsimile: 011 852 588 1318.
Taipei, Taiwan: In Association with Formosa Transnational, 15th Floor, Lotus Building, 136 Jen Ai Road, Section 3.
Telephone: 011 886 755-7366.
Facsimile: 011 886 755-6486.
Member of Smith Lyons, Langlois Robert, Bryan, González Vargas: Toronto, Ottawa, Vancouver, Hong Kong, Taipei, Kiev, Montréal, Québec, New York, México City, Ciudad Juárez, Chihuahua, Matamoros, Tijuana, Mexicali.

MEMBERS OF FIRM AND ASSOCIATES

H. Bernard Mayer, Q.C.
James G. Torrance, Q.C.
Frederick W. Benn
John R. Finley, Q.C.
Paul A. Carroll, Q.C.
D. William Mutch, Q.C.
Bohdan S. Onyschuk, Q.C.
Janet S. Brown
Fred K. C. Kan
(Resident, Hong Kong)
Brian G. Armstrong, Q.C.
John D. Stevenson, Q.C.
Robert Alexander Smith, Q.C.
Thomas G. Deacon, Q.C.
Robert W. Comish, Q.C.
Robert G. Witterick, Q.C.
Thomas R. Hawkins
John G. Myers
Michael J. Anderson
Jerry H. Farrell
Harold N. Little
Robert E. Milnes

(See Next Column)

MEMBERS OF FIRM AND ASSOCIATES (Continued)

M. John Fingret
Arthur P. Tarasuk
Rodney W. J. Seyffert
J. Robert Boxma
Robert J. Hamilton
Leslie T. Gord
Hein Poulus (Resident, Vancouver, British Columbia Office)
Glenn A. Hainey
Donald J. Haslam (Resident, Vancouver, British Columbia Office)
Alan P.C. Dean
Nicholas E. J. Dietrich
Sharon E. Dowdall
Mark K. Levitz (Resident, Vancouver, British Columbia Office)
Kathryn M. Tamaki
Robert G. S. Hull
Andrew D. Brands
Daniel G. Kostiuk (Resident, Vancouver, British Columbia Office)
Grant W. Gold
Christopher J. Bardsley
Mark A. McHughan
Carolyn J. Horkins
Jacques J. M. Shore (Resident, Ottawa, Ontario Office)
Donald K. Charter
Hugh A. Christie
R. Brock Johnston (Resident, Vancouver, British Columbia Office)
Helen T. Soudek
Christopher J. Theodoropoulos (Resident, Vancouver, British Columbia Office)
Christine M. Dixon (Resident, Vancouver, British Columbia Office)
Phillip P. Macdonald
Stephen A. Pike
Frank D. Wheatley (Resident, Vancouver, British Columbia Office)
Timothy S. Wach
Russell D. Cheeseman
Martha L. McKinnon
Steven I. Sofer
Graeme Mew
Michael S. Koch
Pamela D. Horton
Charles L. Halam-Andres
Brian A. Ward (Resident, Ottawa, Ontario Office)
Paul K. Lepsoe (Resident, Ottawa, Ontario Office)
Daniel R. Hayhurst
Darryl J. Brown
Tina M. Woodside
David J. Goodman
Barry D. Horne
Karine Krieger
Shawn H. Patey
David F. W. Cohen
Elizabeth A. King
John Paul Barry
Robert K. Allen
Myron B. Dzulynsky
G. Grant Machum
Kathryn Th. Seymour
M. Catherine Smallman
Karen W. Tamaki (Resident, Vancouver, British Columbia Office)
Shannon J. Sadler
Jane M. Waechter
Seanna L. Dumbrell
Robert D. Finlayson
Arthur O. Jacques
David J. McFadden, Q.C.
Frank N. Marrocco, Q.C.
Robert J. Carew
R. Stuart Angus (Resident, Vancouver, British Columbia Office)
Ronald M. Richler
Fran P. Kiteley
Serafino P. Mantini
Bruce M. Graham
Michael S. F. Watson
Peter A. Magnus (Resident, Ottawa, Ontario Office)
Margaret A. Brady
David F. Bell
Paul H. Harricks
Evelyn P. Moskowitz
R. Bruce Smith
James D. Tomlinson
David B. Light
Louis G. Montpellier (Resident, Vancouver, British Columbia Office)
Lilly A. Wong
Cameron A. Mingay
Franklin L. Davis
Merle D. Rosenhek
Terence A. McNally
Gordon D. Phillips (Resident, Vancouver, British Columbia Office)
Dean J. Blain
Katherine M. van Rensburg
Mark S. Brennan
Roderick C. McKeen (Resident, Vancouver, British Columbia Office)
Elizabeth E. Bates
James M. Ayres
Daniel W. Sooley
Kristina S. Dragaitis
Michael C. Varabioff (Resident, Vancouver, British Columbia Office)
Graham B. Smith
Hugh E. Gillespie (Resident, Hong Kong)
Lawrence W.E. Talbot (Resident, Vancouver, British Columbia Office)
Jay C. Kellerman
K. Lynn Mahoney
Kevan B. Cowan
John S.C. Mao (Resident, Vancouver, British Columbia Office)
John E. Callaghan
Richard C. Owens
Mark Y. Kowalsky (Resident, Kiev, Ukraine Office)
Peter E. Manderville
Diana S. Galassi
John W. Petrykanyn
Joseph P. Giuffre (Resident, Vancouver, British Columbia Office)
David E. Liblong
Maxine M. Kerr
Verlee L. Webb (Resident, Vancouver, British Columbia Office)
Elizabeth L. (Waterson) Fanjoy
Jacqueline A. Jones
Valliammai Chettiar (Resident, Vancouver, British Columbia Office)
Barbara Jo Caruso
Joel A. Heard
Laurie K. Murphy

COUNSEL

J. Chisholm Lyons, Q.C.
(Resident, Hong Kong)

TRADEMARK AGENTS

Dr. C.B. Barlow (Patent Agent)
J.M. Baigent

For full biographical listings, see the Martindale-Hubbell Law Directory

Toronto—Continued

STIKEMAN, ELLIOTT (AV)

Commerce Court West, Suite 5300, M5L 1B9
Telephone: 416-869-5500
Telex: 06-22536
FAX: 416-947-0866
Cable Address: "STIKETOR"
Montreal, Quebec Office: 1155 René-Lévesque Boulevard West, 40th Floor, H3B 3V2.
Telephone: 514-397-3000.
Telex: 05-267316.
Cable Address: "TAXMONT MTL".
Telecopier: 514-397-3222.
Ottawa, Ontario Office: 50 O'Connor Street, Suite 914, K1P 6L2.
Telephone: 613-234-4555.
Telex: 053-3646.
FAX: 613-230-8877.
Cable Address: "Stike Ott".
Calgary, Alberta Office: 1500 Bankers Hall, 855 - 2nd Street S.W., T2P 4J7.
Telephone: 403-266-9000.
FAX: 403-266-9034.
Vancouver, British Columbia Office: Suite 1700, Park Place, 666 Burrard Street, V6C 2X8.
Telephone: 604-631-1300.
Telecopier: 604-681-1825.
New York, N.Y. Office: Tower 56, 126 East 56th Street, 11th Floor, 10022.
Telephone: 212-371-8855.
Fax: 212-371-7087.
Washington, D.C. Office: 1300 I Street, N.W., Suite 1210 West, 20005-3314.
Telephone: 202-326-7555.
Fax: 202-326-7557.
London, England Office: Cottons Centre, Cottons Lane, SE1 2QL.
Telephone: 071-378-0880.
Telecopier: 71-378-0344; 71-865-0226.
Paris, France Office: 39, rue Francois Ier, 75008.
Telephone: 33-1-40-73-82-00.
Fax: 31-1-40-73-82-10.
Budapest, Hungary Office: Andrássy út 100 II Floor, H-1062.
Telephone: 36-1-269-1790.
Fax: 36-1-269-0655.
Hong Kong Office: China Building, Suite 1506, 29 Queen's Road Central.
Telephone: 852-868-9903.
Telecopier: 852-868-9912.
Hong Kong: In Association with Shum & Co., China Building, Suite 1102, 29 Queen's Road Centre.
Telephone: 852-526-5531.
Telecopier: 852-845-9076.
Taipei, Taiwan Office: 117 Sec. 3 Min Sheng East Road, 8th Floor.
Telephone: 886-2-719-9573.
FAX: 886-2-719-4540.

MEMBERS OF FIRM AND ASSOCIATES LISTED IN ALPHABETICAL ORDER

Patricia Kim Alletson
Roderick F. Barrett
Neil Berlad
William J. Braithwaite
David M. Brown
Mark Edward Burton
Michael R. Carman
Bruce Clarke Caughill (Resident, Ottawa Office)
Michel Coderre (Resident, Ottawa Office)
Joel T. Cuperfain
Rocco M. Delfino
John R. Dow
Ronald K. Durand
David N. Finkelstein
C. Keith Ham
James W. Harbell
Brenda Hebert
L. Milton Hess, Q.C.
Ruth A. C. Horn
Donald B. Houston
John T. Hunt
Susan M. Hutton (Resident, Ottawa Office)
John A. M. Judge
Katherine L. Kay
Kevin B. Kelly
Marianne Kennedy
Rosemin Keshvani
Maryanne E. Kramer
Jennifer G. Legge
Derek N. Linfield
Daphne J. MacKenzie
Michael Matheson
Stuart C. McCormack (Resident, Ottawa Office)
E. Lianne Miller
Martine M. N. Band (Resident, Ottawa Office)
Mirko Bibic (Resident, Ottawa Office)
K. A. Milisa Burns
David R. Byers
John R. Cattanach
Kathryn I. Chalmers
Richard E. Clark
Paul Collins
Christopher J. Cosgriffe
James C. Davis
Ian M. Douglas
Sean F. Dunphy
R. Fraser Elliott, C.M., Q.C.
Margaret E. Grottenthaler
Peter E. Hamilton
Douglas F. Harrison
Philip J. Henderson
Tamra Hopkins
Samantha G. Horn
Peter F.C. Howard
Lawson A. W. Hunter, Q.C. (Resident, Ottawa Office)
Thomas Johnson
T. Gregory Kane, Q.C. (Resident, Ottawa Office)
Mary E. Kelly
Heather I. Kerr
Geoffrey K. Ketcheson
Donald A. Kubesh (Resident, Ottawa Office)
Brent J. Ludwig
Darren J. MacLennan
Steven J. McCormack
Catherine S. McKendry
Heather M. McMaster
Shawna M. Miller

(See Next Column)

Peter George William Miscevich
Edgar D. Moss

MEMBERS OF FIRM AND ASSOCIATES LISTED IN ALPHABETICAL ORDER (Continued)

Carolyn Musselman
Jennifer L. Northcote
Margaret R. O'Sullivan
Carmine M. Paura
Sharon C. Polan
R. Bruce Pollock
Brian M. Pukier
James A. Riley
Simon A. Romano
Michael D. Rumball
Ronald J. Schlumpf
Wayne E. Shaw
Thurlow Bradbrooke Smith, Q.C. (Resident, Ottawa Office)
Johanna M. E. Superina
Hemant K. S. Tilak
Frederick R. von Veh, Q.C.
Thomas Vowinckel
Kathleen G. Ward
David G. Weekes
David Wex
F. Derek Woods
Robert W. A. Nicholls
Patrick J. O'Kelly
John A. Paterson, Jr.
Elizabeth Pillon
Andra M. Pollak
Dana Porter
John Rider
Anne L. Ristic
W. Brian Rose
David S. Sanderson
Michael D. Shadbolt
Jacqueline D. Shinfield
H. Heward Stikeman, Q.C., O.C.
John M. Stransman
Melissa E. Taylor
Elizabeth Turner
Mihkel E. Voore
John E. Walker
Michael John Waterston
Mark D. Welton
J. Scott Wilkie
Marvin Yontef
Alison J. Youngman

For full biographical listings, see the Martindale-Hubbell Law Directory

THOMSON, ROGERS (AV)

Suite 3100 390 Bay Street, M5H 1W2
Telephone: 416-868-3100
Telecopier: 416-868-3134

PARTNERS

Kenneth E. Howie, Q.C.
Ralph O. Howie, Q.C.
Hillel David
Desmond H. Dixon
Stephen J. MacDonald
Jeffrey Wm. Strype
James R. Howie
Richard M. Bogoroch
Richard C. Halpern
Leonard H. Kunka
Douglas W. Goudie, Q.C.
Lawrence H. Mandel, Q.C.
Roger T. Beaman
David R. Neill
Patrick D. Schmidt
L. Craig Brown
Alan A. Farrer
Stephen J. D'Agostino
Robert S. Cash
Vangel Krkachovski

ASSOCIATES

Sharon E. Ramsden
Linda J. Wolanski
Michael J. Henry
Harry F. Steinmetz
G. Joseph Falconeri
Jordan S. Solway
Reine E. Reynolds
Maria Louise Z. McDonald
David R. Tenszen
Jeffrey J. Wilker
P. H. Auberbach
Lisa D. Trabucco

For full biographical listings, see the Martindale-Hubbell Law Directory

TORY TORY DESLAURIERS & BINNINGTON (AV)

Suite 3000, Aetna Tower, Toronto-Dominion Centre, P.O. Box 270, M5K 1N2
Telephone: 416-865-0040
Facsimile: 416-865-7380
Office in:
London: 44/45 Chancery Lane, London WC2A 1JB England.
Telephone: 071-831 8155.
Facsimile: 071-831 1812.
Hong Kong: Suite 1705 One Exchange Square, 8 Connaught Place, Central Hong Kong.
Telephone: (852) 868-3099.
Facsimile: (852) 523-8140.
Affiliated With:
Desjardins Ducharme Stein Monast-Montreal, Quebec City, Quebec.
Lawson Lundell Lawson & McIntosh-Vancouver, Yellowknife, British Columbia.

PARTNERS AND ASSOCIATES

James M. Tory, Q.C.
Anne R. Dubin, Q.C.
Arthur A. Kennedy, Q.C.
David E. Baird, Q.C.
Ross L. Kennedy
Gordon Coleman, Q.C.
J. Garnet Pink, Q.C.
Paul M. Moore, Q.C.
Sidney P. H. Robinson
Richard R. Neville
Brian M. Flood
Gabor G. S. Takach
Peter E. S. Jewett
Charles F. Scott
Laurence A. Pattillo
Barry A. Leon
Geoffrey J. R. Dyer
John H. Loosemore
Barry J. Reiter
William J. DesLauriers, Q.C.
Douglas Andison, Q.C.
Brian W. Shields, Q.C.
Desmond J. Mackey, Q.C.
James C. Baillie, Q.C.
Michael G. Thorley, Q.C.
Robert W. Torrens, Q.C.
Robert P. Armstrong, Q.C.
Robin D. Walker, Q.C.
Peter D. Maddaugh, Q.C.
Victor Peters
Sheila R. Block
Patricia J. Myhal
Wilfred M. Estey
Stephen R. Richardson
James E. A. Turner
Thomas J. Matz
Herman J. Wilton-Siegel
Michael B. Rotsztain

(See Next Column)

TORY TORY DESLAURIERS & BINNINGTON—*Continued*

PARTNERS AND ASSOCIATES (Continued)

Douglas C. Betts
Marlene J. Davidge
Richard C. van Banning
Ann D. Dillon
John W. McIninch
Donald B. Roger
John Unger
Thomas A. Bogart
Kathleen L. Keller-Hobson (Resident, London, England Office)
Geoffrey D. Creighton
Karen A. Malatest
Cosimo Racco
Robin A. Campbell
Rebecca A. Cowdery
James C. Tory
James W. Welkoff
Brian A. Davis
Michael K. Feldman
Judith E. Harris
Stephen O. Marshall
Michael A. Penny
Kent E. Thomson
Peter D. Ballantyne
Paul D. Blundy
R. Jay Holsten
Philip Mohtadi
Linda A. Telgarsky
Donald P. Wright
Lisa Tucker Boulton
Sheryl Fischer
Robert Mansell
Richard L. Pivnick
Edward J. Babin
David A. Chaikof
Debbie De Girolamo
Ellen L. Hayes
Alison Lacy
Patrick Kuehner Lewtas
Mary H. Mullens
Richard G. Willoughby
Sharon C. Geraghty
Cheryl L.C. Lewis
Tony Reyes
Jenifer E. Aitken
Tony DeMarinis
Blair W. Keefe
Lillian Y. Pan
Rose T. Bailey
Rosemary Chan
Larry Cobb
E. Richard Gold
Tallat Hussain
J.G. Michel Ouellet
M. J. Stewart
Melissa Thomas
Clare E. Burns
Lewis Dubrofsky
Blair F. Morrison
David M. Rosenberg
Ilene R. Shiller
S. Gregory Warren
J. James Duffield
D. Scott Howson
Ronald K. Lepin
Gordon R. Pansegrau
William L. Thompson
Jonathan B. Weisz
Lisa H. Kerbel Caplan
Patrick D. Flaherty
Miriam Kagan
Michael S. McDonald
Kathryn E. Moore
Kyong W. Nahm
David P. Roney
David A. Steele
Patrice S. Walch-Watson
Janice L. Wright
George Begic
Sarah Cohen
Andrew E. Iacobucci
Michael A. Kelly
Naomi Margo
Stephen Pitel
Lorraine Stillaway
Michael C. Ward
John H. Butler
Patricia D. S. Jackson
John B. Laskin
David S. Ehrlich
Stephen J. Donovan
John H. Tory, Q.C.
Richard J. Balfour
Heather G. Hisey
Jacqueline R. Bryers
Richard A. Conway
Roger Cotton
Sandra J. Geddes
W. Kenneth McCarter
Cheryl L. Waldrum
Corrado Cardarelli
Patricia A. Koval
Les M. Viner
R. John Cameron
Beth DeMerchant
Mark Gannage
Robert H. Karp
Sharon C. Pel
Dawn V. Scott
Robert M. Aziz
Ernest W. Belyea
Leonard J. Griffiths
Mary T. McConkey
Gary S. A. Solway
Lucia M. ten Kortenaar
W. Geoffrey Beattie
Philip J. Brown
Peter K. Fritze
Christopher C. Nicholls
Candy L. Saga
David W. Binet
David L. Corbett
Mario J. Forte
Jane C. Helmstadter
R. Gregory Laing
Anita E. Mackey
Susan M. Silma
Linda S. Abrams
Timothy G. Leishman
Wendy M. Matheson
Valerie B. Seager
Heather G. Crawford
Daniel R. Donnelly
Bradley P. Martin
Helen T. Aston
Stephen P. Billion
Alison M. Chilcott
Adam E. Delean
Clarence T. Hay
Jennifer M. Le Dain
David F. Sheridan
Philip D.A. Symmonds
Peter B. Birkness
S. Wendy Del Mul
Kenneth D. Kraft
Donna L. Parish
Agostino E. Russo
Richard M. Tory
Julia L. Deans
Julia E. Holland
Wendy A. Kelley
Shelley L. Munro
Steve J. Tenai
Michael A. Weinczok
Peter A. Aziz
David P. Chernos
Teresa K. Y. Hung
John P. Koch
Elizabeth C. Messud
Kevin M. Morris
Katarina T. Premovic
John C. Sheedy
Susan Valencia
Presley L. Warner
Anita Anand
Graeme Coffin
A. Douglas Harris
Mary Jackson
John C. Knowlton
Antoinette Mongillo
Nicholas A. Richter
John Frederick Tuer
Eric Jonathan Yolles

(See Next Column)

COUNSEL

Hon. William G. Davis, P.C.
H. Lorne Morphy, Q.C.

For full biographical listings, see the Martindale-Hubbell Law Directory

WEIR & FOULDS (AV)

Suite 1600 Exchange Tower, 2 First Canadian Place, P.O. Box 480, M5X 1J5
Telephone: 416-365-1110
Telecopier: 416-365-1876
Mississauga, Ontario Office: 50 Burnhamthorpe Road, West, Suite 902.
Telephone: 905-896-1110.
Telecopier: 905-896-0803.

PARTNERS

John P. Hamilton
John D. McKellar, Q.C.
N. William C. Ross
Bryan Finlay, Q.C.
Gordon Roy Baker, Q.C.
Leslie J. O'Connor
Richard R. Wozenilek
Ronald S. Sleightholm (Resident, Mississauga Office)
Jeffrey G. Cowan
Christopher J. Tzekas
John D. Campbell
J. Gregory Richards
Gary M. Caplan
Lori M. Duffy
Ian J. Lord
George H. Rust-D'Eye
Ralph H. Kroman
John Rosolak
Albert G. Formosa
Alec K. Clute
John B. A. Wilkinson
John C. O'Sullivan
Malcolm S. Archibald, Q.C.
Michael J. McQuaid, Q.C.
W. Thomas R. Wilson
R. Wayne Rosenman
William J. McNaughton
W. A. Derry Millar
Lynda C. E. Tanaka
Paul M. Perell
Kenneth Prehogan
Jerry S. Prypasniak
Bradley N. McLellan
John M. Buhlman
Lisa A. Borsook
Deborah R. Rogers
Debbie S. Tarshis
Robert B. Warren
Richard J. Lachcik
Daniel P. Ferguson (Resident, Mississauga Office)
D. Keith Laushway
Jill Dougherty
Allen V. Craig (Resident, Mississauga)
David R. Wingfield

ASSOCIATES

Hugh S. O. Morris, Q.C.
John L. Pandell
Glenn W. Ackerley
David S. Brown
Gary M. Freedman
Marilyn L. Sparrow
Joe Conte (Resident, Mississauga Office)
Barnet H. Kussner
Terry D. Hancock
Geoffrey G. Farr
A. Samuel Wakim, Q.C.
Peter M. Daigle (Resident, Mississauga Office)
Bruce H. Engell
Wendy Kady
Milton M. Chambers
Warren Coughlin
Wayne T. Egan
Sue A. Metcalfe
John A. Keith
Carole McAfee Wallace
Steven Rukavina

For full biographical listings, see the Martindale-Hubbell Law Directory

*WALKERTON,** Bruce Co. — (Refer to London)

*WATERLOO,** Regional Munic. of Waterloo — (Refer to Kitchener)

*WELLAND,** Regional Munic. of Niagara — (Refer to St. Catharines)

*WHITBY,** Regional Munic. of Durham — (Refer to Toronto)

*WINDSOR,** Essex Co.

BARTLET & RICHARDES (AV)

1000 Canada Building, 374 Ouellette Avenue, N9A 1A9
Telephone: 519-253-7461
Detroit, Michigan: 313-963-8238
Telecopier: 519-253-2321

MEMBERS OF FIRM

James N. Bartlet, Q.C.
Frederick W. Knight, Q.C.
Frederick D. Wilson, Q.C.
Milton H. Grant
Richard C. Gates, Q.C.
Colin F. Dodd
D. Stephen Jovanovic
Lawrence R. McRae
Daniel L. G. Bornais
Jean Leslie Marentette
Gerald E. Skillings
Karol F. Dycha

ASSOCIATES

Charles F. Clark
Robert R. Istl
John T. Clark
Gerald E. Trottier
Ruth Stewart
Elizabeth J. Musyj

For full biographical listings, see the Martindale-Hubbell Law Directory

GIGNAC, SUTTS (AV)

600 Westcourt Place, 251 Goyeau Street, P.O. Box 670, N9A 6V4
Telephone: 519-258-9333
Detroit Michigan: 313-962-0137
Facsimile: Windsor 519-258-9527
Detroit 313-962-0139

(See Next Column)

GIGNAC, SUTTS, *Windsor—Continued*

MEMBERS OF FIRM

Achille F. Gignac, Q.C. (1902-1984)
Robert E. Barnes, Q.C.
Clifford N. Sutts, Q.C.
Harvey T. Strosberg, Q.C.
Gary V. Wortley
James K. Ball
John C. Holland
William C. Chapman
Mary M. S. Fox
Donald M. Gordon
Sharman Sharkey Bondy
Paul C. Nesseth
Heather Rumble Peterson
Patricia A. Speight
Edward W. Ducharme
Michelle A. Gagnon
Craig J. Allen
Werner H. Keller
Francine A. Herlehy
Paul Simard

COUNSEL FOR CRIMINAL MATTERS

Patrick J. Ducharme

For full biographical listings, see the Martindale-Hubbell Law Directory

McTAGUE LAW FIRM (AV)

455 Pelissier Street, N9A 6Z9
Telephone: 519-255-4300
Detroit, Michigan Telephone: 313-965-1332
Fax: 519-255-4360(Corporate/Labor)
Fax: 519-255-4384 (Litigation/Real Estate)

MEMBERS OF FIRM

H. M. McTague, Miss, Q.C. (1900-1986)
Alexander R. Szalkai, Q.C.
Michael K. Coughlin
Jerry B. Udell
Josephine Stark
J. Douglas Lawson, Q.C.
Roger A. Skinner
George W. King
Peter J. Kuker
Theodore Crljenica
Gerri L. Wong
R. Paul Layfield

ASSOCIATES

John D. Leslie
Tom Serafimovski
Marilee Marcotte

For full biographical listings, see the Martindale-Hubbell Law Directory

*WOODSTOCK,** Oxford Co. — (Refer to London)

PRINCE EDWARD ISLAND

*CHARLOTTETOWN,** Queen's Co.

CAMPBELL, LEA, MICHAEL, MCCONNELL & PIGOT (AV)

15 Queen Street, P.O. Box 429, C1A 7K7
Telephone: 902-566-3400
Telecopier: 902-566-9266

MEMBERS OF FIRM

William G. Lea, Q.C.
Paul D. Michael, Q.C.
Robert A. McConnell
Ross D. Pigot
M. Jane Ralling
Kenneth L. Godfrey

ASSOCIATES

Karolyn M. Godfrey

General Counsel in Prince Edward Island for: Canadian Imperial Bank of Commerce; Maritime Electric Co., Ltd.; Michelin Tires (Canada) Ltd.; Newsco Investments Ltd. (Dundas Farms); Queen Elizabeth Hospital Inc.; Imperial Oil Limited; General Motors of Canada; Co-op Atlantic; Liberty Mutual; Employers Reinsurance Group.

For full biographical listings, see the Martindale-Hubbell Law Directory

STEWART MCKELVEY STIRLING SCALES (AV)

Formerly Scales, Jenkins & McQuaid
65 Grafton Street, P.O. Box 2140, C1A 8B9
Telephone: 902-892-2485
Telecopier: 902-566-5283
Halifax, Nova Scotia Office: Suite 900, Purdy's Wharf Tower One, 1959 Upper Water Street, P.O. Box 997.
Telephone: 902-420-3200.
Telecopier: 902-420-1417.
Telex: 019-22593.
Sydney, Nova Scotia Office: 50 Dorchester Street. P.O. Box 820.
Telephone: 902-539-5135.
Telecopier: 902-539-8256.
Moncton, New Brunswick Office: Suite 601, 644 Main Street, P.O. Box 20070.
Telephone: 506-853-1970.
Telecopier: 506-858-8454.
Saint John, New Brunswick Office: Suite 1000, 10th Floor, Brunswick House, 44 Chipman Hill, P.O. Box 7289 Station "A".
Telephone: 506-632-1970.
Telecopier: 506-652-1989.
St. John's, Newfoundland Office: Cabot Place, 100 New Gower Street, P.O. Box 5038.
Telephone: 709-722-4270.
Telex: 016-4733.
Telecopier: 709-722-4565.

Alan K. Scales, Q.C.
John K. Mitchell
Shawn A. Murphy
J. Scott MacKenzie
Eugene P. Rossiter, Q.C.
Brian L. Waddell
Rosemary Scott
Ronald J. Keefe
James C. Travers
A. Brendan Curley
Gordon L. Campbell
Sean Casey
Keith M. Boswell

ASSOCIATES

James W. Gormley
Barbara E. Smith
Geoffrey D. Connolly

For full biographical listings, see the Martindale-Hubbell Law Directory

QUEBEC

*ARTHABASKA,** Arthabaska Dist. — (Refer to Quebec)

*CHICOUTIMI,** Chicoutimi Dist. — (Refer to Quebec)

*DRUMMONDVILLE,** Drummond Dist. — (Refer to Montreal)

*HULL,** Hull Dist. — (Refer to Montreal)

*JOLIETTE,** Joliette Dist. — (Refer to Montreal)

*MONTMAGNY,** Montmagny Dist. — (Refer to Quebec)

*MONTREAL,** Montreal Dist.

BÉLANGER, SAUVÉ (AV)

1 Place Ville Marie, Suite 1700, H3B 2C1
Telephone: 514-878-3081
Telecopier: 514-878-3053

Paul Adam
Ronald Adam
André Asselin
Dominique Aubry
Jean-Pierre Baldassare
Pascale Bédard
Sylvain Bélair
Christiane Béland
Marcel Bélanger, Q.C.
Véronique Bélanger
Yves Bélanger
Alain Bergeron
Alexandre Boileau
Bernard Boucher
Richard Burgos
Pierre Cadotte
Gérard Caisse
Michel Cantin
Richard Coutu
Conrad Delisle
Michel Delorme
Alain-Claude Desforges
Sylvie Devito
Pierre Dozois
Robert Dupaul
Claude J. E. Dupont
Michel Dupuy
Denis Durocher
Jean-Yves Fortin
Jean Fréchette
Rita-Rose Gagné
Michel Gilbert
Jacques Hurlet
Sophie Jean
Pierre Journet
Pierre Labrie
Marie-Michelle Lavigne
Natalie Le Cavalier
Yvon Leclerc
Luc Lefebvre
Jean-Paul Legault
Jean-François Lemay
Daniel Mandron
Joanne Marchand
Michèle Monast
Pierre Moreau
Claude Nadeau
Richard Nadeau
Eric Paul-Hus
René Piotte
Rosa Riolo-Vaccaro
Yves Rodillard
André Roulean
Pierre-Georges Roy
Pierre Sauvé
Hubert Sibre
Marc Simard
Francine St Onge
Josee Talbot

For full biographical listings, see the Martindale-Hubbell Law Directory

BENNETT JONES VERCHERE

Suite 1600, 1 Place Ville Marie, H3B 2B6
Telephone: (514) 871-1200
Facsimile: (514) 871-8115
Calgary, Alberta Office: 4500 Bankers Hall East. 855-2nd Street S.W.
Telephone: (403) 298-3100.
Facsimile: (403) 265-7219.
Edmonton, Alberta Office: 1000, 10035-105 Street.
Telephone: (403) 421-8133.
Facsimile: (403) 421-7951.
Toronto, Ontario Office: 3400 1 First Canadian Place.
Telephone: 416-863-1200.
Facsimile: 416-863-1716.
Ottawa, Ontario Office: Suite 1800, 350 Alberta Street, Box 25, K1R 1A4.
Telephone: (613) 230-4935.
Facsimile: (613) 230-3836.

MEMBERS OF FIRM

Geoffrey Lawson
Simon J. Tardif
Jacques Bernier

Claude Nadeau
Ginette Gaulin Lachance
Deborah Duncan
Sébastien Rheault
Paul Somma

OF COUNSEL

W. R. Jackett, O.C., Q.C.
(Not admitted in QU)

For full biographical listings, see the Martindale-Hubbell Law Directory

BYERS CASGRAIN (AV)

A Member of McMillan Bull Casgrain
Suite 3900, 1 Place Ville-Marie, H3B 4M7
Telephone: 514-878-8800
Telecopier: 514-866-2241
Cable Address: "Magee"
Telex: 05-24195

(See Next Column)

Philippe Casgrain, Q.C.
Herbert B. McNally, Q.C.
Paul F. Dingle, Q.C.
Marc Bourgeois
Claude E. Leduc
Robert S. Carswell
Hon. Jean Bazin, Q.C.
Ray E. Lawson
Pierre Langlois
Jean-Pierre Dépelteau
Luc Giroux
Claire Richer
John F. Lemieux
Allan A. Mass
Céline April
Michel A. Brunet
William S. Grodinsky
Michel Towner
John Hurley
David McAusland
Pierre A. Lessard
Gérard Dugré
Louis Dumont
Denis Manzo
Nicolas Beaudin
Martin Bernard
Alain Rondeau
Guy Lavoie
Alain Roberge
Guy A. Gagnon
Christian J. Brossard
André Racine
Jean Lefrançois
André Morrissette
Laurent Nahmiash
Caroline A. Pratte
Hélène Bourque
Daniel Garant
Francine Mercure
Charles R. Spector
Stéphane Dansereau
Richard B. Epstein
Sophie Latraverse
Nicole Sirois
Yves Turgeon
Jean-Pierre Huard
Constantine Kyres
Ronald Audette
Jean M. Gagnon
Pierre Grenier
Christian Létourneau
Pascale Nolin
Patrice Beaudin
Julie Desrochers
Claude Morency
Natali Boulva
Josée Dumoulin
Stéphane Lemay
Christine Rudolph
Serge Tousignant
Susan Clarke
Stéphane W. Miron
Sébastien Grammond
Stephen Lloyd
Joseph Mastrogiuseppe
Marie-Claude St-Gelais

OF COUNSEL

J. Arclen Blakely, Q.C.
Gil Rémillard

For full biographical listings, see the Martindale-Hubbell Law Directory

CHAIT AMYOT (AV)

Suite 1900, 1 Place Ville-Marie, H3B 2C3
Telephone: 514-879-1353
Fax: 514-879-1460

MEMBERS OF FIRM

Samuel Chait, Q.C. (1904-1982)
Nathaniel H. Salomon
Nahum Gelber, Q.C.
Arthur I. Bronstein
Bernard Reis
Gordon L. Echenberg
C. Ralph Lipper
Sandor J. Klein
David H. Kauffman
Normand Amyot
Daniel Lessard
André A. Lévesque
Ronald H. Levy
David G. Masse
Ronald L. Stein
Marc J. Rubin
Carol Cohen
Louis Samuel
André Giroux
Jeffrey F. Edwards
Virginia K. H. Lam
Eric Lalanne
Pierre Brossoit
Frederica Jacobs
Benoît Larose
Martin Tétreault
Martin Joyal
Jacynthe Charpentier
Martin Langelier
Anne Milot

Representative Clients: Barclays Bank; Canada Life; National Bank of Canada; Metropolitan Trust; Desourdy Construction; Royal Bank; ICN Canada; Mortgage Insurance Company of Canada; Club Mediteranne; Banque Nationale de Paris.

For full biographical listings, see the Martindale-Hubbell Law Directory

COLBY, MONET, DEMERS, DELAGE & CREVIER (AV)

McGill College Tower, 1501 McGill College Avenue Suite 2900, H3A 3M8
Telephone: 514-284-3663
Telecopier: 514-284-1961

PARTNERS AND ASSOCIATES

Jean Monet, Q.C.
Paul Michael Demers
Jean Delage
Monique Dionne
David Crevier
Michael C. Martin
Marek Nitoslawski
Katherine M. Peacocke
Campbell J. Stuart
Valérie A. Miglia
Lyne Carrier
Martin D. Boily
Brian J. Stammer
Nancy Fancott
Christian R. Leblanc

For full biographical listings, see the Martindale-Hubbell Law Directory

DE GRANDPRÉ, GODIN (AV)

1000 de la Gauchetière Street West Suite 2900, H3B 4W5
Telephone: 514-878-4311
Telecopier: 514-878-4333

(See Next Column)

DE GRANDPRÉ, GODIN—*Continued*

Pierre de Grandpré, Q.C.
René-C. Alary, Q.C.
Jean-Jacques Gagnon
Richard David
J. Lucien Perron
André P. Asselin
Alain Robichaud
Marie-Christine LaBerge
Jacques L. Archambault
Paul Trudel
Pierre Labelle
Jean-Pierre Desmarais
Micheline Bouchard
Jean Benoît
Daniel Courteau
Diane Lajeunesse
Hélène Mondoux
Marc Beauchemin
Louis Charron
Daniel L'Africain
Jasmin Lefebvre
Gilles Godin, Q.C.
André Paquette, Q.C.
Olivier Prat
Gilles Fafard
Gabriel Kordovi
Pierre Mercille
Bernard Corbeil
Mario Proulx
Pierre Chesnay
Yves Poirier
François Beauchamp
Jean-François Ménard
Daniel Séguin
Andrée Gosselin
Pierre Hamel
Christiane Alary
Guy Gilain
Anne Bélanger
Lucie Guimond
Benoît Pelchat
Mylène C. Forget

For full biographical listings, see the Martindale-Hubbell Law Directory

DESJARDINS DUCHARME STEIN MONAST (AV)

600 de La Gauchetière Street West, Suite 2400, H3B 4L8
Telephone: 514-878-9411
Telecopier: 878-9092
Quebec, Quebec Office: Suite 300, 1150 Claire Fontaine Street, G1R 5G4.
Telephone: 418-529-6531.
Telecopier: 418-523-5391.
Affiliated Offices:
Tory Tory DesLauriers & Binnington.
Toronto, Suite 3000, Aetna Tower, Toronto-Dominion Centre, P.O. Box 270, Toronto (Ontario) M5K 1N2. Telephone: 416-865-0040.
Telecopier: 416-865-7398.
London, England, 44/45 Chancery Lane, London WC2A 1JB England.
Telephone: 071-831-8155.
Telecopier: 071-831-1812.
Hong Kong, Suite 1705, Exchange Square, 8 Cannought Place Central, Hong Kong. Telephone: 852-868-3099.
Telecopier: 852-523-8140.
Lawson Lundell Lawson & McIntosh.
Vancouver, 1600 Cathedral Place, 925 West Georgia Street, Vancouver, (British Columbia). Telephone: 604-685-3456.
Telecopier: 604-669-1620.
Yellowknife, North West Territories, Suite 204, 4817- 49th Street, X1A 3S7.
Telephone: 403-669-9990.
Telecopier: 403-669-9991.

PARTNERS AND ASSOCIATES OF FIRM

Pierre Bourque, Q.C.
Alain Lortie
Guy Lord
Daniel Bellemare, Q.C.
Denis St-Onge
Jacques Paquin
Gérard Coulombe, Q.C.
Marc Rochefort
Michel Benoit
André Wery
Luc Bigaouette
Serge Gloutnay
Jean-Réne Gauthier
Michel McMillan
Odette Nadon
Paul Marcotte
François Garneau
Michel Legendre
Marie St-Pierre
Marcel Racicot
Joanne Biron
Suzanne Courteau
Claire Brassard
André Vautour
Johanne Bérubé
Lucia Bourbonnais
Dominique Fortin
François Renaud
Stéphane F. PréFontaine
Nicole Nobert
Joëlle Boisvert
Chantal Roy
Pierre M. Lajoie
Sonia Paradis
Jocelyne Gagné
Patrice Benoit
Jean Yoon
Mark Hounsell
Julie Faucher
Jean-Paul Zigby
Michel Roy
Claude Bédard
Réjean Lizotte
C. François Couture
Marc A. Léonard
Jean-Maurice Saulnier
Louis Payette
Roger Page, Q.C.
Robert J. Phénix
Paul R. Granda
Maurice Mongrain
Pierre-Yves Châtillon
Pierre Legault
Armando Aznar
Danièle Mayrand
Sylvain Lussier
Louise Lalonde
Gilles LeClerc
Benoit Emery
Eugène Czolij
Michel G. Beaudin
Daniel Majeau
Michèle Beauchamp
Bruno Deslauriers
Marc Beauchemin
Dominique Bélisle
Nicolas Dion
Mason Poplaw
Richard Comtois
Julie Bergeron
Lucie Letendre
Sophie Picard
Paule Hamelin
Paule Tardif
Line Lacasse
Martin Cloutier
Frédéric Lesage
Jean Boucher

(See Next Column)

PARTNERS AND ASSOCIATES OF FIRM (Continued)

Sylvie Champagne
Tiziana Di Donato
Sylvain Joannisse
Normand Daignault
Nancy Paquet

COUNSEL

Adrien Bordua
Claude Ducharme, Q.C.
Georges Emery, Q.C.
Guy Desjardins, Q.C.
Charles J. Gélinas, Q.C.
André E. Gadbois, Q.C.
Richard Mineau

For full biographical listings, see the Martindale-Hubbell Law Directory

DUNTON, RAINVILLE, TOUPIN, PERRAULT (AV)

Suite 4300, 800 Square Victoria, P.O. Box 303, H4Z 1H1
Telephone: 514-866-6743
Fax: 514-866-8854

MEMBERS OF FIRM AND ASSOCIATES

Jaime W. Dunton
Pierre J. Perrault
Jean-Pierre Rémillard
Louis-Philippe Bourgeois
André Leduc
Sophie Beauchemin
Michel J. Lanctôt
Paul André Martel
Marie Corriveau
Alain Chevrier
Claude Paquet
Pierre Lefebvre
Marie-Claude Jarry
Jacques Des Marais
Catherine Papineau
Louis A. Toupin
Jean-Jacques Rainville
Gérald Bélanger
Jean Rochette
Guy Lauzon
Brigitte Charron
Louis-Denis Laberge
Mario St-Pierre
Martine Trudeau
Louise Marchand
Geneviève Paquette
Charles Caza
Philippe Marcoux
Antonio Manuel Hortas
Marie-Josée Richard

LEGAL SUPPORT PERSONNEL

Réal W. LaFontaine

For full biographical listings, see the Martindale-Hubbell Law Directory

GOODMAN PHILLIPS & VINEBERG (AV)

5 Place Ville Marie, 17th Floor, H3B 2G2
Telephone: 514-866-8541
Facsimile Communications: 514-875-0344
Toronto Office: 250 Yonge Street, Suite 2400, P.O. Box 24, Toronto, Ontario, Canada M5B 2M6.
Telephone: 416-979-2211. Facsimile communications: 416-979-1234.
New York, New York Office: 430 Park Avenue, 10th Floor, New York, New York, 10022.
Telephone: 212-308-8866. Facsimile Communications: 212-308-0132.
Hong Kong Office: 30/F, Peregrine Tower, Lippo Centre, 89 Queensway Road, G.P.O. 953, Hong Kong.
Telephone: (852) 5221061. Facsimile Communications: (852) 8459089.

MEMBERS AND ASSOCIATES

The Hon. Lazarus Phillips, O.B.E., Q.C., LL.D. (1895-1986)
Neil Franklin Phillips, Q.C. (Resident at New York, New York)
Douglas C. Robertson
Robert S. Vineberg
Michael D. Vineberg
George R. Hendy
Guy Du Pont
Paul Harris
William Brock
Michel Pelletier
Maryse Bertrand
Sylvain Cossette
Robert B. Issenman
François Barette
Pierre Nollet
Basile Angelopoulos
Benoît Lapointe
Hillel W. Rosen
Elias Benhamou
Shahir Guindi
Mark D. Brender
Ariane Bourque
Stephen Klar
Evelyn Jerassy
Robert Fabes
Philip F. Vineberg, O.C., Q.C., LL.D. (1914-1987)
Alan B. Gold
Mitchell H. Klein
Daniel S. Miller
Alan Z. Golden
Nathan Boidman
Peter Mendell
Robert Mongeon
Samuel Minzberg
Pierre-André Themens
Sidney M. Horn
Robert J. Abrams
Alan J. Shragie
Rita Lc de Santis
Richard Cherney
Johane Thibodeau
Louise Patry
Marie-Andrée Latreille
Leon P. Garfinkle
Claude E. Jodoin
David J. Shapiro
Daniel Belleau
Silvana Conte
Michael T. McGuinty (Resident in Paris)
Scott D. Miller
Martine Vanasse
Arielle Meloul
Anie Perrault

For full biographical listings, see the Martindale-Hubbell Law Directory

Montreal—Continued

GUY & GILBERT (AV)

770 Sherbrooke Street West, Suite 2300, H3A 1G1
Telephone: 514-281-1766
Telecopier: 514-281-1059
Paris, France Office: 77 Rue Boissière, 75116.
Telephone: 1-44-17-48-00.
Telecopier: 1-45-01-86-41.
Telex: Raffin 620565 F.

MEMBERS & ASSOCIATES

Guy Gilbert, Q.C.
Jean Guy
Francois Boisclair
Jean-Jacques L'Heureux, Q.C.
Gilles Bertrand
Guy Marcotte
Yvon Brizard
André Simard
Jacques Laurent, Q.C.
Guy Duranleau
Michel Robin
Pierre Gariépy
Jean Tremblay
Pierre Donati
Yvon Brisson
Pierre-Marc Johnson
François Tremblay
Michel Richer
Paul Bédard
Robert Tessier
Michel Fleury
Claude J. Melançon
Richard J. Roy
Paul Paradis
Louise Baillargeon
Pierre Brosseau
Jacques Bourque
Robert Dorion
Mark E. Turcot
Jean Y. Nadeau
Pierre R. Sicotte
Gilles Thibault
Roger Maisonneuve
Martin Hébert
Benoit Roussy
Raymond L'Abbé
Michel Villeneuve
David I. Johnston
Marc Paquet
Louis Coallier
Pierre G. Hébert
Maurice Régnier
Marc Laperrière
Claude I. Savoie
Robert Y. Girard
Lyne Burelle
Sylvie Lefebvre
Gilles Séguin
Jean M. Leclerc
Hubert Camirand
Paul Dupéré
Nicole Chouinard
André Goyer
Line Poirier
Marie Charest
Marie Marmet
Monique Therrien
Simon Grégoire
Rachel Brûlé
Normand Laurendeau
Julie Bourduas
Jean-Francois Dagenais
Sylvie Girard
Pierre D. Saint-Aubin
Isabelle Synnott
Pierre-Stephane Poitras
Lydia Brown
Joël Gauthier
Catherine Frigon
Louise Doré
Mireille Fontaine
Mark Phillips

For full biographical listings, see the Martindale-Hubbell Law Directory

HEENAN BLAIKIE (AV)

Suite 2500, 1250, René-Lévesque Boulevard West, H3B 4Y1
Telephone: 514-846-1212
Telecopier: 514-846-3427
Toronto, Ontario Office: Suite 3350 P.O. Box 185, 200 Bay Street, South Tower, Royal Bank Plaza, M5J 2J4.
Telephone: 416-360-6336.
Telecopier: 416-360-8425.
Vancouver, British Columbia Office: Suite 600, 1199 West Hastings, V6E 3T5.
Telephone: 604-669-0011.
Telecopier: 604-669-5101.
Trois-Rivières Office: Suite 360, 1500 Royale Street, G9A 6E6.
Telephone: 819-373-7000.
Telecopier: 819-373-0943.
Affiliated Office: Beverly Hills, California, Suite 1100, 9401 Wilshire Boulevard, 90210-2924.
Telephone: 310-275-3600.
Telecopier: 310-724-8340.

COUNSEL

The Right Honourable Pierre Elliott Trudeau, P.C., Q.C.
André Bureau
The Honourable Donald J. Johnston, P.C., Q.C.
Peter M. Blaikie, Q.C.
James W. Hemens, Q.C.

MEMBERS

Kenneth S. Atlas
Sam Berliner
Yvan M. Bolduc
Jean Boulet (Resident Partner, Trois-Riviéres Office)
Guy Dufort
Michel J. Duranleau
Clément Gascon
Yves Hébert
Louise Houle
Danny Jack Kaufer
Pierre C. Lemoine
Claude Martin
Auguste Masson
M. Bruce McNiven
Sylvain Poirier
Claudette Bellemare
Max R. Bernard
Robert Bonhomme
Benoit G. Bourgon
Nicola Di Iorio
Robert Dupont
Ralph D. Farley
Joel H. Goldberg
Roy L. Heenan
Manon Jolicoeur
Louis Leclerc
Richard Lewin, C.A. (Not admitted in QU)
Patrick McClemens (On Leave of Absence)
Jean Potvin

(See Next Column)

MEMBERS (Continued)

Michael Prupas
Guy Sarault
Suzanne Thibaudeau, Q.C.
Guy Tremblay
Jean Trudel
André Roy (Resident Partner, Trois-Rivières Office)
Manon Thivierge
Pierre Trépanier
Neil Wiener

ASSOCIATES

Linda Adams (On Leave of Absence)
Andrew M. Cohen
Dominique Coindre
J. Brian Cornish
Corrado De Stefano
Andre D'Orsonnens
Sophie Emond
Claire Fournier
Marie-Josée Hogue
Allan Joli-Coeur
Bernard Jolin
Chantal Lamarche
Elizabeth Laroche
Laurent Lesage
Pascale Mongrain
Sylvi Plante
Normand Quesnel
Michael Reha
Howard J. Rosenoff
Shari L. Segal
Ronald W. Silverson
Daniel Urbas
Patrice Vachon
Christopher Atchison
Thomas E.F. Brady (Not admitted in QU)
Elisabeth Colson
Martine Desjardins
Norman A. Dionne
Louise Dubé
Keith C. Flavell
Marie-Joseée Hétu (Resident, Associate, Trois-Riviéres Office)
Patricia Kosseim
Louise Larivière
Francine Legault
Robert Michelin
Lise Morissette
Dean M. Proctor
François A. Raymond
Karen M. Rogers
Victor Salvaggio
Ann Shaw
Philippe Tremblay (Resident, Associate, Trois-Rivières Office)
Keith D. Wilson

For full biographical listings, see the Martindale-Hubbell Law Directory

LAFLEUR BROWN (AV)

1 Place Ville Marie, 37th Floor, H3B 3P4
Telephone: 514-878-9641
Cable Address: "Mankin"
Telex: 05-25610
Telecopier: 514-878-1450
Brussels, Belgium Office: Av. Louise 386, 1050.
Telephone: 011 322 647 1112.
Telecopier: 011-322-648-7519.
Toronto, Ontario Office: Suite 920 P.O. Box 359 1, First Canadian Place.
Telephone: 416-869-0994.
Telecopier: 416-362-5818.

MEMBERS OF FIRM

L.-P. de Grandpré, C.C., Q.C.
John Brooke Claxton, Q.C.
Michael P. J. Rusko, Q.C.
A. Keith Ham
Arnold B. Sharp
Ronald Montcalm
Leonard Serafini
Benoit Groleau
Pierre Boyer
Marzia Frascadore
Philippe Ferland
Mark Bantey
Daniel Lacelle
Olivier Fraticelli
Marc Laflèche
Barbara Muir
Julie-Martine Loranger
Marc-André Blanchard
F. Susan Singer
André Rivest
Alain Lalonde
Charles Roy
Leonardo Giampa
Nicolas Plourde
Hunter Wilson, Q.C.
Charles S. Bradeen, Q.C.
Jean M. Tardif
Donald B. Wilkie
John A. Penhale
Henri Lanctôt
Marc De Wever
Helene Deslauriers
Jean-Guy Campeau
Yves Ouellette
Luc Lissoir
David B. Kierans
Pierre-Denis Leroux
Robert A. Fyfe
Raymond DeWaele
Richard LaRue
Bernard Amyot
Luc Deshaies
Pierre Lissoir
Gascon Benoit
Francine Martel
Guy Poitras
Ann-Marie Ryan
Stephanie Beauregard
Eve Poirier

For full biographical listings, see the Martindale-Hubbell Law Directory

LANGLOIS ROBERT (AV)

1002 Sherbrooke Street West, 28th Floor, H3A 3L6
Telephone: 514-842-9512
Cable Address: "Lamer MTL"
Telex: 055-61452
Telecopier: 514-845-6573
Quebec, Quebec Office: 801 Chemin St. Louis, Suite 160, G1S 1C1.
Telephone: 418-682-1212.
Telex: 055-61452.
Fax: 418-682-2272.

MEMBERS OF FIRM

Pierre Bélanger
Jacques Bellemarre
Johanne Boilard
Sylvie Bourdeau
Nathalie Beauregard
Suzanne Benoit
Jean-R. Boivin
Louise Cadieux

(See Next Column)

LANGLOIS ROBERT—*Continued*

MEMBERS OF FIRM (Continued)

Marc Cantin
Alexandre Ciocilteu
Nathalie Drouin
Louis Gagnon
Siri C. Genik
William D. Hart
Daniel Lafortune
Yves Lauzon
Jacques Lemieux
Jean-François Longtin
Luc Martineau
John Mavridis
David E. Platts
Le Bâtonnier J.J. Michel Robert, P.C., Q.C.
Ève-Stéphanie Sauvé
Pierre Tourigny
Suzanne Chartier
Maria De Michèle
Véronique Dubois
Céline Garneau
Helene Hallak
Luc Huppé
Raynold Langlois, Q.C.
Pierre-Yves Leduc
Catherine Lemonde
Carmelle Marchessault
Guy Matte
Dominique Pion
Nicole Riendeau
Lyne Robichaud
André Sasseville
France Simard
Guy Turner
Marise Viger

LEGAL SUPPORT PERSONNEL

Lise Desharnais

For full biographical listings, see the Martindale-Hubbell Law Directory

LAVERY, DE BILLY (AV)

1 Place Ville Marie, 40th Floor, H3B 4M4
Telephone: 514-871-1522
Facsimile: 514-871-8977
Quebec City, Quebec Office: 925 Chemin St-Louis, Suite 500, Quebec, Quebec G1S 1C1.
Telephone: 418-688-5000.
Facsimile: 418-688-3458.
Ottawa, Ontario Office: 45 O'Connor, 20th Floor, Ottawa, Ontario K1P 1A4.
Telephone: 613-594-4936.
Facsimile: 613-594-8783.

MEMBERS OF FIRM AND ASSOCIATES

A. Jean de Grandpré, C.C., Q.C.
Jerome C. Smyth, Q.C.
M. Kevin Smyth
Georges Dubé
Robert W. Mason
Michel Blouin
Guy Lemay
Jacques Nols
Edouard Baudry
Pierre Caron
J.-François de Grandpré
Paul Cartier
Monique Lagacé
Ian Rose
Jean Hébert
Michel Yergeau
Pierre Daviault
Richard A. Hinse
Pierre L. Baribeau
Jacques Paul-Hus
Jacques Audette
Dionigi M. Fiorita
Serge Benoît
Gary D.D. Morrison
Donald R. McCarty
Richard Wagner
Jocelyne Forget
Odette Jobin-Laberge
Marie Gaudreau
Jean Beauregard
Jean-Pierre Colpron
Francois Duprat
René Branchaud
Suzanne Daigle
Elise Paul-Hus
Marie-Andrée Gravel
Yvan Biron
Yves Jobin
Christian Drapeau
Élise Poisson
Geneviève Marcotte
Yves St-Cyr
Dominique Vézina
Jean-Yves Simard
Jean-Francois Michaud
Nicolas Gagnon
Alessandra Massobrio
Nathalie Bélanger
Martin Dupras
Pascale Chapdelaine
Anne-Marie Papineau
Erik Sabbatini
Marie-Claude Armstrong
M. Carlyle Johnston, Q.C.
J. Vincent O'Donnell, Q.C.
Serge Bourque
Douglas S. Pryde
Jean Bélanger
Jean Turgeon
Paul A. R. Townsend
André René
Allan Lutfy, Q.C.
André Laurin (Managing Partner)
Jean Pomminville
Jean-Piere Casavant
Claude Baillargeon
Michel Caron
Denis Charest
Réal Favreau
Jacques M. Saint-Denis
Louis André Leclerc
Hélène Langlois
Alain Gascon
Michel Gélinas
David M. Eramian
Daniel Alain Dagenais
Richard F. Dolan
Louise Cérat
Jean Saint-Onge
Jean-Francois Hotte
Michel Desrosiers
Raymond Doray
Pierre Denis
Pamela McGovern
Jacques A. Nadeau
Philippe Frère
Dominique Benoît
Denis Ferland
Hélène Lauzon
Pascale Mercier
Antoine St-Germain
Julie Veilleux
Monique Brassard
Francois Lavallée
Carl Lessard
Louis Clément
Philip Nolan
Marie-Claude Cantin
Marie-Claude Perreault
Francois Charette
Patrick Buchholz
Antoine Dore
Patrice Picard
Christina Cusano
Andrew G. Deere

(See Next Column)

David Heurtel
Marc Lussier

MEMBERS OF FIRM AND ASSOCIATES (Continued)

Catherine H. Maheu
Louis G. Véronneau
Suzanne Moquin
Michel Servant

For full biographical listings, see the Martindale-Hubbell Law Directory

MACKENZIE GERVAIS S.E.N.C. (AV)

Trademark Agents
Place Mercantile, Suite 1300, 770 Sherbrooke Street West, H3A 1G1
Telephone: 514-842-9831
Fax: 514-288-7389

David Mackenzie, Q.C.
Tass G. Grivakes, Q.C.
Raymond Darley LeMoyne
Peter C. Casey
Ian B. Taylor
Peter Richardson
Robert E. Charbonneau
Jean-René Ranger
Johanne Thomas
Roger P. Simard
André Dufour
Sylvie Bouvette
Hélène Mireault
Bruno Duguay
Michael Bantey
Alain Vauclair
Christine Duchaine
Lise Fortier
François Ouellette
Nathalie-Anne Béliveau
Louis Mousseau
Jack Greenstein, Q.C.
P. André Gervais, Q.C.
Lionel J. Blanshay
Luc LaRochelle
Georges R. Thibaudeau
Ghislain Brossard
Louis Lemire
Virgile A. Buffoni
Michael Patry
Carl LaRoche
Élise Dubé
Rosaire S. Houde
Mathilde Carrière
Joel Heft
François Longpré
Stéphane Garon
Alain-François Meunier
Smaranda Ghibu
Alain N. Tardif
Alexandra Gillespie
Mark Vinet

COUNSEL

Daniel O'Connel Doheny, Q.C.
Charles M. Bédard
Albert H. Malouf, Q.C.
Nicolas Mateesco Matte, O.C., Q.C., F.R.S.C.

For full biographical listings, see the Martindale-Hubbell Law Directory

MARTINEAU WALKER (AV)

Stock Exchange Tower, Suite 3400, 800 Place-Victoria, P.O. Box 242, H4Z 1E9
Telephone: 514-397-7400
Toll Free: 1-800-361-6266 (Ontario & Quebec)
Facsimile: 514-397-7600.
Telex: 05-24610 BUOY MTL
The partners and associates of Martineau Walker are also partners and associates of the national and international firm of Fasken Martineau which has offices in Montreal, Quebec City, Toronto, Vancouver (Affiliated), London and Brussels.
Quebec City, Quebec Office: Immeuble Le Saint-Patrick, 140, rue Grande Allée est, bureau 800, G1R 5M8.
Telephone: 418-640-2000. Toll Free: 1-800-463-2827 (Ontario & Quebec).
Facsimile: 418-647-2455.
Toronto, Ontario Office: Fasken Campbell Godfrey, Toronto-Dominion Centre, Toronto Dominion Bank Tower, P.O. Box 20, M5K 1N6.
Telephone: 416-366-8381. Toll Free: 1-800-268-8424 (Ontario & Quebec).
Facsimile: 416-364-7813.
Vancouver (Affiliated): Davis & Company, 2800 Park Place, 666 Burrard Street, V6C 2Z7.
Telephone: 604-687-9444.
Fax: 604-687-1612.
London, England Office: Fasken Martineau, 10 Arthur Street, 5th Floor, EC4R 9AY.
Telephone: 71-929-2894.
Facsimile: 71-929-3634.
Brussels, Belgium Office: Fasken Martineau, Avenue Franklin D. Roosevelt, 96 A, 1050.
Telephone: 2-640-9796.
Facsimile: 2-640-2779.

MEMBERS OF FIRM

André J. Clermont, Q.C.
Jean H. Lafleur, Q.C.
C. Stephen Cheasley
Pierre B. Meunier
James G. Wright
Richard Martel
Rolland Forget
Lawrence P. Yelin
Claude Brunet
Paul Martel
Louis Bernier
Wilbrod Claude Décarie
Claude Désy
Francois Rolland
André Durocher
Denis Lachance
Marie Giguère
Xenophon C. Martis
J. Lambert Toupin, Q.C.
Robert J. Stocks
Francis Fox, P.C., Q.C.
Robert M. Skelly
Maurice A. Forget
Stephen S. Heller
Pierrette Rayle
Yvon Martineau
Réal A. Forest
Serge Guérette
Jean-Francois Buffoni
Donald M. Hendy
Dennis P. Griffin
Jean Masson
Gilles Carli
Richard J. Clare
Eric M. Maldoff
Ronald J. McRobie

(See Next Column)

MARTINEAU WALKER, *Montreal—Continued*

MEMBERS OF FIRM (Continued)

David Powell
Richard Lacoursière
Daniel Picotte
Karl Delwaide
Mark D. Walker
R. Andrew Ford
Louis H. Séguin
Pierre Lefebvre
Robert Paré
Pierre Deslauriers
Jacques Rajotte
Daniel Rochefort
George Artinian
Marc-André Fabien
Marc Généreux
Alain Ranger
Claude Auger

ASSOCIATES

Louise Béchamp
Claudette Allard
Edith Bonnot
Dominique Monet
Paul Mayer
Stéphane Gilker
Marie-Jose Roux-Fauteux
Pierre Setlakwe
Suzanne Anfousse
Nathalie Faucher
Michel Lalande
Natalie Pouliot
Charles Kazaz
Antoine Turmel
Guy Dionne
Dominique Gibbens
Linda Facchin
Marie Lafleur
Marilyn Piccini-Roy
Jacques Dalpé
Benoit Turmel
Sharon Druker
Alain Riendeau
Claude Marseille
Jean G. Lamothe
Eric Ménard
Michel Boislard
Marc Novello
Rene Cadieux
Dimitri G. Mastrocola
Julie Desrosiers
Martin Sheehan
Angela Onesi
David Lemieux

COUNSEL

George A. Allison, Q.C.
Bâtonnier Marcel Cinq-Mars, Q.C.
Hon. Alan A. Macnaughton, P.C., Q.C.
Peter R. D. MacKell, Q.C.
Guy Gagnon, Q.C.

For full biographical listings, see the Martindale-Hubbell Law Directory

MCCARTHY TÉTRAULT (AV)

"Le Windsor", 1170 rue Peel, H3B 4S8
Telephone: 514-397-4100
Facsimile: 514-875-6246 or 514-397-4187
Vancouver, British Columbia Office: Suite 1300, 777 Dunsmuir Street, P.O. Box 10424, Vancouver, British Columbia V7Y 1K2.
Telephone: 604-643-7100.
Facsimile: 604-643-7900.
Surrey, British Columbia Office: Suite 1300, Station Tower, Gateway 13401-108th Avenue, Surrey, British Columbia V3T 5T3.
Telephone: 604-583-9100.
Fax: 604-583-9150.
London, Ontario Office: Suite 2000, One London Place, 255 Queens Avenue, London, Ontario N6A 5R8.
Telephone: 519-660-3587.
Facsimile: 519-660-3599.
Toronto, Ontario Office: Suite 4700, Toronto Dominion Bank Tower, Toronto-Dominion Centre, Toronto, Ontario M5K 1E6.
Telephone: 416-362-1812.
Facsimile: 416-868-0673.
Ottawa, Ontario Office: Suite 1000, 275 Sparks Street, Ottawa, Ontario, K1R 7X9.
Telephone: 613-238-2000.
Facsimile: 613-563-9386.
Québec, Québec Office: Le Complexe St-Amable 1150, rue Claire Fontaine 7e Étage, Québec, Québec G1R 5G4.
Telephone: 418-521-3000.
Facsimile: 418-521-3099.
United Kingdom and European Office: 1 Pemberton Row, Fetter Lane, London, England EC4A 3BA.
Telephone: 011-44-171-353-2355.
Facsimile: 011-44-171-583-5644.

MEMBERS OF FIRM AND ASSOCIATES

Jacques Tétrault, Q.C.
Michael Dennis
Guy P. Dancosse, Q.C.
Richard A. Beaulieu
Gérald R. Tremblay, Q.C.
J. Michel Deschamps
André P. Gauthier
Guy Dubé
Jean-François Giroux
Thomas R.M. Davis
Ann M. Bigué
Allan R. Hilton
Carol Anne Laramée
André Prévost
Julien Lanctôt
Dominique Têtu
Hubert T. Lacroix
Maurice Régnier, Q.C.
Graham Nesbitt
Claude P. Desaulniers
Yves Bériault
Paul Dupuy Leblanc
Michael D. Levinson
André J. Payeur
Michel Racicot
Jacques Béland
Lazar Sarna
Robert-Jean Chénier
Louis Lacoursière
Peter S. Martin
Robert B. Schubert
Pierre Lepage
Daniel Bénay
J. Robert Doyle

(See Next Column)

MEMBERS OF FIRM AND ASSOCIATES (Continued)

Lorna Jean Telfer
Pierre J. Dalphond
Louis Terriault
Jacques Jeansonne
Sylvie Lachapelle
Jean-François Lehoux
Benjamin H. Silver
Laurent M. Themens
Jean-Pierre Bertrand
Sylvain A. Vauclair
Michel Pierre Arseneau
Paul A. Venne
Louis Brousseau
Marc H. Dufour
Michel Laplante
Carole Tremblay
Martine Kaigle
Madeleine Renaud
Lonnie J. Brodkin-Schneider
Michel Gagné
Christiane Larouche
Angelina Argento
Janie C. Béique
Laurent L. Debrun
Catherine D. Mandeville
Anne-Marie Sheahan
Cindy Morantz
Jacques S. Vézina
Daniel E. Torsher
Pierre Rousseau
Michel Bergeron
Martine Cohen
Ilan Dunsky
Nathalie Gagnon
Hélène LeBlanc
Franziska Ruf
Michel A. Brisebois
Hubert Graton
Warren M. Goodman
R. Timothé Huot
Daniel W. Payette
Jacques Rousse
John T. Sullivan
Marc Benoit
Cherine Cheftechi
Jeanne Wojas
Christiane Jodoin
Robert Metcalfe
Julie Chenette
Louise Houle
Elaine Marchand
Sarah Kathryn Dougherty
Marc Lemieux
Sonia Jacqueline Struthers
Vivian Paraskevi Cyriacopoulos
Guylaine Bachand
Stephen G. Schenke
André L. Baril
Philippe H. Belanger
G. Scot Diamond
Sally Gomery
Cristian Gagnon
Nina V. Fernandez
Georgina P. Hunter
Chloé Archambault
Philippe Trudel (Not admitted in QU)
Marie-Hélène Côté
Jean Farley
Peter Hoffmann
Jean Lortie
Isabelle Viger

COUNSEL

Paul E. Bisaillon, Q.C.
Raymond E. Parsons, Q.C.
Paul E. Hurtubise

For full biographical listings, see the Martindale-Hubbell Law Directory

MCMASTER MEIGHEN (AV)

A General Partnership
7th Floor, 630 René-Lévesque Boulevard West, H3B 4H7
Telephone: 514-879-1212
Telecopier: 514-878-0605
Cable Address: "Cammerall"
Telex: "Cammerall MTL" 05-268637
Affiliated with Fraser & Beatty in Toronto, North York, Ottawa and Vancouver.

MEMBERS OF FIRM

Thomas C. Camp, Q.C.
Richard J. Riendeau, Q.C.
William E. Stavert
Jacques Brien
Hubert Senécal
Paul R. Marchand
Sean J. Harrington
Brian M. Schneiderman
Pierre Flageole
Richard W. Shannon
Elizabeth A. Mitchell
P. Jeremy Bolger
Philippe C. Vachon
Marc Duchesne
Yves A. Dubois
Nancy G. Cleman
Richard R. Provost
Janet Casey
Pierre B. Côté
Jacques Gauthier
Francois Morin
D. James Papadimitriou
Yvan Houle
John G. Murphy
Luc Béliveau
Catherine Rakush
Darren E. Graham McGuire
Bruce W. Johnston
Nathalie E. Duguay
Alex K. Paterson, O.C., O.Q., Q.C.
R. Jamie Plant
Colin K. Irving
Timothy R. Carsley
Alexis P. Bergeron
Norman A. Saibil
Daniel Ayotte
Jon H. Scott
Michel A. Pinsonnault
Diane Quenneville
Benoît M. Provost
Thomas M. Davis
Michael S. McAuley
Nicholas J. Spillane
Charles P. Marquette
Robert J. Torralbo
Pierre Trudeau
Jean Daigle
André Royer
Peter G. Pamel
H. John Godber
Douglas C. Mitchell
Chantal Béique
Valérie Beaudin
Kurt A. Johnson
Marc L. Weinstein
J. Anthony Penhale
Tina Hobday
Elana Weissbach

COUNSEL

A. Stuart Hyndman, Q.C.
Pierre Gattuso
Maurice D. Godbout, Q.C.
Bartha M. Knoppers

For full biographical listings, see the Martindale-Hubbell Law Directory

Montreal—Continued

MENDELSOHN ROSENTZVEIG SHACTER (AV)

1000 Sherbrooke Street West, 27th Floor, H3A 3G4
Telephone: 514-987-5000
Telex: 05-27284 Colorlaw
Telecopier: 514-987-1213

MEMBERS OF FIRM AND ASSOCIATES

S. Leon Mendelsohn, Q.C.
Leo Rosentzveig, Q.C.
Manuel Shacter, Q.C.
Jack C. Shayne
William Levitt
Arthur A. Garvis
Max Mendelsohn
Edward E. Aronoff
L. Michael Blumenstein
Monroe A. Charlap
Earl S. Cohen
William Fraiberg
Michael Garonce
Philip S. Garonce, Q.C.
Donald M. Devine
Richard S. Uditsky
Boris P. Stein
Joel Weitzman
Ian R. Rudnikoff
Marc I. Leiter
L. B. Erdle
Frank Zylberberg
Fredric L. Carsley
David L. Rosentzveig
Jules Brossard
Michael Ludwick
Catherine Muraz
Judith G. Shenker
Judie K. Jokinen
Gilles Seguin
Martin Desrosiers
Jean Carrière

ASSOCIATES

Alain Breault
Joelle Sebag
Sharyn W. Gore
Louis Frédérick Côté
Hillel D. Frankel
Sandra Abitan
Dominique Lafleur
Linda Schachter
Roberto Buffone
Emmanuelle Saucier
Arnold Cohen
Isabelle Papillon
Lorne Beiles
Aaron Makovka
Céline Tessier

For full biographical listings, see the Martindale-Hubbell Law Directory

OGILVY RENAULT (AV)

Suite 1100, 1981 McGill College Avenue, H3A 3C1
Telephone: 514-847-4747
Cable Address: "Jonhall" Montreal
Telex: 05-25362
Fax: 514-286-5474
Ottawa, Ontario Office: Suite 1600, 45 O'Connor Street, K1P 1A4.
Telephone: 613-780-8661.
Telex: 053-3379.
Fax: 613-230-5459.
Québec, Québec Office: Suite 520, 500 Grande-Allée Est, G1R 2J7.
Telephone: 418-640-5000.
Fax: 418-640-1500.
Osler Renault, an international partnership of Osler, Hoskin & Harcourt, and Ogilvy Renault, has offices at:
London, England Office: 20 Little Britain, EC1A 7DH.
Telephone: 071-606-0777.
Fax: 071-606-0222.
Paris, France Office: (Correspondent Office) 4, rue Bayard, 75008.
Telephone: (1)42.89.00.54.
Fax: (1)42.89.51.60.
Hong Kong Office: Suite 1708, One Pacific Place, 88 Queensway.
Telephone: (852) 8773933.
Fax: (852) 8770866.
New York, N.Y. Office: Suite 3217, 200 Park Avenue, 10166-0193.
Telephone: 212-867-5800.
Fax: 212-867-5802.
Singapore Office: Suite No. 40-05, OCBC Centre, 65 Chulia Street, Singapore 0104.
Telephone: (65) 538-2077.
Fax: (65) 538-2977.

Jean R. Allard
Christian J. Beaudry
R. Luc Beaulieu
Jean G. Bertrand
Casper M. Bloom, Q.C.
Charles J. Boivin
Robert G. Borduas
Danièle Boutet
Katherine R. Britt
(Not admitted in QU)
Isabelle Cantin
Mario M. Caron
Christine A. Carron
Jules Charette
Olivier P.A. Chouc
Lysiane Clément-Major
David R. Collier
Donald F. Cope
Pierre G. Côté
Robert J. Cowling
Louis-Paul Cullen
Nathalie David
Claude Demers
Richard L. Desgagnés
Paul M. Amos
Chantal C. Beaulieu
Lise Bergeron
Pierre Bienvenu
Jane Bogaty
Gregory B. Bordan
Martine S. Boucher
Richard J. F. Bowie
Yves W. Brunet, Q.C.
Donald H. Bunker
Michel G. Carle
Sandra E. Carr
Brigitte K. Catellier
Robert P. Charlton
Joan Clark, Q.C.
John A. Coleman
Françoise Colpron
François B. Côté
Renaud Coulombe
Raymond Crevier, Q.C.
Brian R. Daley
Philippe L. David
Claudia Déry
Emmanuelle J. Doyon

(See Next Column)

Daniel S. Drapeau
Pierre-André Dubois
Eric Dunberry
Marc Duquette
Hélène Floch
François Fontaine
Guy Fortin
Michel A. Gagnon
Denis Gascon
Thomas S. Gillespie
Claire M. Gohier
Louis J. Gouin
Manon Guesthier
Sylvie Hébert
Marianne Ignacz
Olivier F. Kott
Pierre Laflamme
Pierre Y. Lamarre
Louise Laplante
Amar Leclair-Ghosh
Hélène Lefebvre
Francis R. Legault
Pierre Legrand, Q.C.
Patrick Lemieux
Miguel F. Manzano
Patrice Marceau
Philip R. Matthews
Malcolm E. McLeod
Sophie Melchers
The Rt. Hon. Brian Mulroney, P.C., LL.D.
Josée Noiseux
Franco Pacetti
Sophie Perreault
Caroline Pillon
Marc Prévost
Paul Prosterman
Paul Raymond
Donald A. Riendeau
Judith M. Robinson
Gérard Rochon
Bernard A. Roy, Q.C.
Lucie J. Roy
Jean A. Savard, Q.C.
Manon Savard
Martine St-Louis
Michel G. Sylvestre
Bogdan A. Teofilovici
John L. Treleaven
(Not admitted in QU)
Peter D. Walsh, Q.C.
Stephen L. Drymer
Jacques Dufresne
François Dupuis
Andrew Fleming
Claude Fontaine, Q.C.
L. Yves Fortier, C.C., Q.C.
Kathleen Joan Gagné
Rémi Gagnon
Johanne Gauthier
André C. Giroux
Michel Goudreau
Sylvie Graton
Pierre Hébert
William Hesler, Q.C.
Patrick E. Kierans
Daniel I. Lack
Anne-Louise Lamarre
J. Nelson Landry
Yan-Wen Le
Ginette Leclerc
Wilfrid Lefebvre, Q.C.
André Legrand
Stéphane P. Lemay
George R. Locke
(Not admitted in QU)
Christine M. Marsan
G. B. Maughan, Q.C.
William W. McNamara
Robert Monette
Peter S. Noble
Angelo Noce
John J. O'Connor
André Papillon
Frank L. Picciola
Simon V. Potter
Pierre Pronovost
Bernard P. Quinn
Jean-Charles René
Sylvain Rigaud
Martin Rochette
Sylvie Rodrigue
Claudine Roy
Solomon Sananes
Johanne Savard
Diane C. Skiejka
Norman M. Steinberg
Douglas H. Tees
Gilles Touchette
Marc Tremblay
Anouk Violette
Margriet Zwarts

COUNSEL

Julian C. C. Chipman, Q.C.
Robert L. Munro
Kenneth S. Howard, Q.C.
John A. Ogilvy, Q.C.

For full biographical listings, see the Martindale-Hubbell Law Directory

POULIOT, MERCURE (AV)

31st Floor, C1BC Tower, 1155 Rene Levesque Boulevard, West, H3B 3S6
Telephone: 514-875-5210
Cable Address: "Justice"
Telecopier: 515-875-4308

MEMBERS OF FIRM

Georges A. Pouliot, Q.C.
Jacques LeBel, Q.C.
Serge Desrochers
Pierre Sébastien, Q.C.
Alain Nadon
Gilles Brunelle
C. Keenan LaPierre
Jean Larivière
Jean H. Gagnon
Luc Gratton
Ronald M. Auclair
Alain Bond
Louis-Michel Tremblay
Claude Lapierre
Daniel Gagné
Normand Royal
Stéphane Rivard
Lilia Pouliot
Pierre Paquet
Maxime B. Rhéaume
Jacques St-Louis
André C. Lavigne
Louise Tremblay
Stéphane Hébert
Beatrice Arronis
Chantal Joubert
Linda Mercier
Marie Cartier
Normand D'Amour
Brent J. Muir
Dany Barbeau
Johanne Gagnon
Claude Bérard
Richard Fontaine
Micheline Perrault
Christian Vaillancourt
Caroline Lemoine

COUNSEL

Marcel Piché, O.C., Q.C.

For full biographical listings, see the Martindale-Hubbell Law Directory

ROBINSON SHEPPARD SHAPIRO, G.P. (AV)

800 Place Victoria Suite 4700, H4Z 1H6
Telephone: 514-878-2631
Telecopier: 514-878-1865

(See Next Column)

ROBINSON SHEPPARD SHAPIRO G.P., *Montreal—Continued*

PARTNERS AND ASSOCIATES

Jonathan J. Robinson
Barry H. Shapiro
Michel J. Green
Yves Cousineau
Eric Boulva
Claude-Henri Grignon
Karen Kear-Jodoin
Jacques Bouchard, Jr.
Andrey Hollinger
Brigitte Nadeau
Nicholas John Krnjevic
Maria R. Battaglia
Brigitte Roy
Louis Guay
Richard J. Rosensweig
Claude-Armand Sheppard
Charles E. Flam
Herbert Z. Pinchuk
Patrick Henry
Lynne Kassie
Robert Scalesse
Edward D. Bridge
Steve McInnes
Martin Lord
Jean-Pierre Sheppard
Dominique Poulin
Mariella De Stefano
Rhona Luger
Caroline Biron
Brigitte B. Garceau

PARTNERS AND ASSOCIATES (Continued)

Kim Lachapelle
Catherine Chaput
Michael Wolfe
Marie-Pierre Grignon
André Ryan

COUNSEL

Samuel Greenblatt, Q.C.
Jules Allard

For full biographical listings, see the Martindale-Hubbell Law Directory

STIKEMAN, ELLIOTT (AV)

1155 René-Lévesque Boulevard West, 40th Floor, H3B 3V2
Telephone: 514-397-3000
Telex: 05-267316
Cable Address: "TAXMONT MTL"
Fax: 514-397-3222
Toronto, Ontario Office: Commerce Court West, 53rd Floor, M5L 1B9.
Telephone: 416-869-5500.
Fax: 416-947-0866.
Ottawa, Ontario Office: 50 O'Connor Street, Suite 914, K1P 6L2.
Telephone: 613-234-4555.
Fax: 613-230-8877.
Calgary, Alberta Office: 855 - 2nd Street S.W., 1500 Bankers Hall, T2P 4J7.
Telephone: 403-266-9000.
Fax: 403-266-9034.
Vancouver, British Columbia Office: 666 Burrard Street, Suite 1700, Park Place, V6C 2X8.
Telephone: 604-631-1300.
Fax: 604-681-1825.
New York, New York Office: 126 East 56th Street, 11th Floor, Tower 56, 10022.
Telephone: 212-371-8855.
Fax: 212-371-7087.
Washington, D.C. Office: 1300 I Street, N.W., Suite 1210 West, 20005-3314.
Telephone: 202-326-7555.
Fax: 202-326-7557.
London, England Office: Cottons Centre, Cottons Lane, SE1 2QL.
Telephone: 71-378-0880.
Fax: 71-378-0344.
Paris, France Office: In Association with Société Juridique Internationale, 39, rue François Ier, 75008.
Telephone: 33-1-40-73-82-00.
Fax: 33-1-40-73-82-10.
Budapest, Hungary Office: Andrássy út 100, II Floor, H-1062.
Telephone: 36-1-269-1790.
Fax: 36-1-269-0655.
Hong Kong Office: 29 Queen's Road Central, Suite 1506, China Building.
Telephone: 852-2868-9903.
Fax: 852-2868-9912.
Hong Kong: In Association with Shum & Co., 29 Queen's Road Central, Suite 1103, China Building.
Telephone: 852-2526-5531.
Fax: 852-2845-9076.
Taipei, Taiwan Office: 117 Sec. 3 Min Sheng East Road, 8th Floor.
Telephone: 886-2-719-9573.
Fax: (852) 2845-9076; 2868-9912.

PARTNERS AND ASSOCIATES

Hon. W. David Angus, Q.C.
Bruno Arnould
Frédéric Beauvais
Jean-Pierre Belhumeur
Hélène Blanchet
Hélène Bussières
Lise D. Chamberland
David A. Chemla
Edward B. Claxton
Suzanne Côté
Glenn A. Cranker
Christine Desaulniers
Bruno ÉTienne Duguay
F. Pearl Eliadis
David N. Finkelstein
Laurent Fortier
Helen Antonio
A. Edward Aust
Louis P. Bélanger
Patrick L. Benaroche
Martin Bourgeault
Marc Casavant
Lyse Charette
Viateur Chénard
Stuart H. (Kip) Cobbett
Marc-André Coulombe
Peter J. Cullen
Sterling Harrison Dietze
Lyne Duhaime
R. Fraser Elliott, C.M., Q.C.
Jean Fontaine
Donald Francoeur

(See Next Column)

PARTNERS AND ASSOCIATES (Continued)

Mortimer G. Freiheit
Michel GéLinas
Jean Boris Grayson
Stephen W. Hamilton
Jean Marc Huot
Pierre Jauvin
Donna Soble Kaufman
Kevin Kyte
Marc Laurin
Jean Lemoine
Martin Claude Lepage
Pierre Martel
Alain Massicotte
Guy Masson
Bertrand P. Ménard
Eric Mongeau
Angelo Nikolakakis
Jean Pierre Ouellet
Bernard Pageau
Claudette Picard
Jocelyn Poirier
Vincent M. Prager
Stephen M. Raicek
Pierre Raymond
Elinore J. Richardson
James A. Robb, Q.C.
William B. Rosenberg
Pierre-Georges Roy
Martin H. Scheim
David F. Skinner
Mireille A. Tabib
Anik Trudel
François Gaudet
James A. Grant, Q.C.
Tadeusz Gruchalla-Wesierski
Robert Hogan
Sydney J. Isaacs
Catherine A. Jenner
Ingi Khouzam
Hon. Marc Lalonde, P.C., O.C., Q.C.
John W. Leopold
Monique Lussier
Yves Martineau
Etienne Massicotte
Clemens Mayr
François Mercier, O.C., Q.C.
Gary F. Nachshen
Peter R. O'Brien
François H. Ouimet
Isabelle Paquet
Frederic Pierrestiger
Richard W. Pound, O.C., O.Q., Q.C.
Robert Raizenne
Michael L. Richards
Erik Richer La Fleche
Steeve Robitaille
André Roy
Richard J. Rusk
Paul J. Setlakwe
H. Heward Stikeman, Q.C., O.C.
Louise Touchette
Eric Vallières
Michel Vennat, Q.C.

COUNSEL

Hon. Maurice Riel, P.C., Q.C.
E. Jacques Courtois, P.C., Q.C.

For full biographical listings, see the Martindale-Hubbell Law Directory

WOODS & PARTNERS (AV)

2000 McGill College Avenue, Suite 1100, H3A 3H3
Telephone: 514-982-4545
Telecopier: 514-284-0472

MEMBERS OF FIRM

James A. Woods
Chantal Corriveau
Normand Perreault
Monique Ryan
Marc-André Blanchard
Christian Immer
Mathieu Savaris

For full biographical listings, see the Martindale-Hubbell Law Directory

*QUEBEC,** Quebec Dist.

DESJARDINS DUCHARME STEIN MONAST (AV)

Formerly Stein Monast Pratte & Marseille
Suite 300, 1150 Claire Fontaine Street, G1R 5G4
Telephone: 418-529-6531
Telecopier: 418-523-5391
Montreal, Quebec Office: 600 de la Gauchetiere Street West, Suite 2400, H3B 4L8.
Telephone: 514-878-9411.
Telecopier: 514-878-9092.
Toronto, Ontario Affiliated Office: Tory, Tory DesLauriers & Binnington. Suite 3000, Aetna Tower, Toronto-Dominion Centre, P.O. Box 270, M5K 1N2.
Telephone: 416-865-0040; 7394
Telecopier: 416-865-7398.
London, England Office: Tory Tory Deslauriers & Binnington: 44/45 Chancery Lane, London WC2A 1JB England.
Telephone: 071-831-8155.
Telecopier: 071-831-1812.
Hong Kong Office: Tory Tory Deslauriers & Binnington, Suite 1705, One Exchange Square, 8 Connaught Place Central, Hong Kong.
Telephone: 852-868-3099.
Telecopier: 852-523-8140.
Vancouver, British Columbia Affiliated Office: Lawson, Lundell, Lawson & McIntosh. 1600 Cathedral Place, 925 West Georgia Place, Vancouver, British Columbia, V6C 3L2.
Telephone: 604-685-3456.
Telecopier: 604-669-1620.
Yellowknife, Northwest Territories Office: Suite 204, 4817 49th Street, X1A 3S7.
Telephone: 403-669-9990.
Facsimile: 403-669-9991.
Desjardins Ducharme Stein Monast is a member of the international partnership Tory Ducharme Lawson Lundell.

(See Next Column)

DESJARDINS DUCHARME STEIN MONAST—*Continued*

MEMBERS OF FIRM

André Monast, Q.C.
Pierre LaRue, Q.C.
Pierre Lesage
Hon. Paule Gauthier, P.C., O.C., Q.C.
Jean F. Keable
Luc L. Lamarre
Jean Houle
Henri-Louis Fortin
Jean Brunet
Serge Baribeau
Eric Lemay
Élise Poulin
Sophie Sénéchal
Jacques Boulanger
Marie Vezina
Raymond Lacroix
Pierre Marseille, Q.C.
Jean Marier
Roger Vallières
Louis Huot
Pierre Pelletier
Claude Girard
Michel Dupont
Michel Demers
Claude Rochon
André Johnson
René Delorme
Charles G. Gagnon
Martin Roy
Anne Caron
Julie-Suzanne Doyon
Louise Boulianne
Suzy Guillemette
Sylvie Godbout

COUNSEL

Charles Stein, Q.C., LL.D.

For full biographical listings, see the Martindale-Hubbell Law Directory

LAFLEUR BROWN

(See Montreal)

MARTINEAU WALKER (AV)

Immeuble Le Saint-Patrick, 140, rue Grande Allée est Bureau 800, G1R 5M8
Telephone: 418-640-2000
Toll Free: 1-800-463-2827 (Ontario & Quebec)
Facsimile: 418-647-2455
The partners and associates of Martineau Walker are also partners and associates of the national and international firm of Fasken Martineau which has offices in Quebec City, Montreal, Toronto, Vancouver (Affiliated), London and Brussels.
Montreal, Quebec Office: Tour De La Bourse, Suite 800 Place Victoria Suite 3400, P.O. Box 242 , Montreal (Quebec) Canada, H4Z 1E9.
Telephone: 514-397-7400. Toll Free: 1-800-361-6266 (Ontario & Quebec).
Facsimile: 514-397-7600.
Telex: 05-24610 BUOY MTL.
Toronto, Ontario Office: Fasken Campbell Godfrey, Toronto-Dominion Centre, Toronto Dominion Bank Tower, P.O. Box 20, M5K 1N6.
Telephone: 416-366-8381. Toll Free: 1-800-268-8424 (Ontario & Quebec).
Facsimile: 416-364-7813.
Vancouver (Affiliated): Davis & Company, 2800 Park Place, 666 Burrard Street, V6C 2Z7.
Telephone: 604-687-9444.
Fax: 604-687-1612.
London, England Office: Fasken Martineau, 10 Arthur Street, 5th Floor, EC4R 9AY.
Telephone: 71-929-2894.
Facsimile: 71-929-3634.
Brussels, Belgium Office: Fasken Martineau, Avenue Franklin D. Roosevelt, 96 A, 1050.
Telephone: 2-640-9796.
Facsimile: 2-640-2779.

MEMBERS OF FIRM

Roger Duval
Yves Le May
Jean Lemelin
Jean G. Morency
Claude Paré

ASSOCIATES

Guy Leblanc
Claudette Tessier-Couture
Guy C. Dion
Julien Reid
Louis Roy
Ingrid Stefancic
Carl Tremblay
Sylvie Harbour

For full biographical listings, see the Martindale-Hubbell Law Directory

McCARTHY TÉTRAULT (AV)

Le Complexe St-Amable, 1150, rue Claire Fontaine 7e Étage, G1R 5G4
Telephone: 418-521-3000
Facsimile: 418-521-3099
Vancouver, British Columbia Office: Suite 1300, 777 Dunsmuir Street, P.O. Box 10424, Vancouver, British Columbia V7Y 1K2.
Telephone: 604-643-7100.
Facsimile: 604-643-7900.
Surrey, British Columbia Office: Suite 1300, Station Tower, Gateway 13401-108th Avenue, Surrey, British Columbia V3T 5T3.
Telephone: 604-583-9100.
Fax: 604-583-9150.

(See Next Column)

London, Ontario Office: Suite 2000, One London Place, 255 Queens Avenue, London, Ontario N6A 5R8.
Telephone: 519-660-3587.
Facsimile: 519-660-3599.
Toronto, Ontario Office: Suite 4700, Toronto Dominion Bank Tower, Toronto-Dominion Centre, Toronto, Ontario M5K 1E6.
Telephone: 416-362-1812.
Facsimile: 416- 868-0673.
Ottawa, Ontario Office: Suite 1000, 275 Spark Street, Ottawa, Ontario, K1R 7X9.
Telephone: 613-238-2000.
Facsimile: 613-563-9386.
Montréal, Québec Office: "le Windsor" 1170 rue Peel, Montréal, Québec H3B 4S8.
Telephone: 514-397-4100.
Facsimile: 514-875-6246.
United Kingdom and European Office: 1 Pemberton Row, Fetter Lane, London, England EC4A 3BA.
Telephone: 011-44-171-353-2355.
Facsimile: 011-44-171-583-5644.

MEMBERS OF FIRM AND ASSOCIATES

William J. Atkinson
Marc N. Dorion, Q.C.
François Amyot
France Bonsaint
Bernard M. Tremblay
Christine Caouette
François Grondin
Philippe Leclerc
Marie-Paule Gagnon
Marc Germain
Jean Martel
Robert Baker
Georges P. Racine
Denis Roy
Chantal Masse
Manon DesLauriers
Nathalie Leroux
Kimberley Okell

For full biographical listings, see the Martindale-Hubbell Law Directory

OGILVY RENAULT (AV)

Suite 520, 500 Grande-Allée Est, G1R 2J7
Telephone: 418-640-5000
Fax: 418-640-1500
Montréal, Québec Office: Suite 1100, 1981 McGill College Avenue, H3A 3C1.
Telephone: 514-847-4747.
Cable Address: "Jonhall" Montréal.
Telex: 05-25362.
Fax: 514-286-5474.
Ottawa, Ontario Office: Suite 1600, 45 O'Connor Street, K1P 1A4.
Telephone: 613-780-8661.
Telex: 053-3379.
Fax: 613-230-5459.
Osler Renault, an international partnership of Osler, Hoskin & Harcourt, and Ogilvy Renault, has offices at:
London, England Office: 20 Little Britain, EC1A 7DH.
Telephone: 071-606-0777.
Fax: 071-606-0222.
Paris, France Office: (Correspondent Office) 4, rue Bayard, 75008.
Telephone: (1)42.89.00.54.
Fax: (1)42.89.51.60.
Hong Kong Office: Suite 1708, One Pacific Place, 88 Queensway.
Telephone: (852) 8773933.
Fax: (852) 8770866.
New York, N.Y. Office: Suite 3217, 200 Park Avenue, 10166-0193.
Telephone: 212-867-5800.
Fax: 212-867-5802.
Singapore Office: Suite No. 40-05, OCBC Centre, 65 Chulia Street, Singapore 0104.
Telephone: (65) 538- 2077.
Fax: (65) 538-2977.

Jean-Sébastien Bernatchez
Louis-M. Cossette
Isabelle Fournier
Ian Gosselin
Marie-Pierre Lamarche
Lucie Pariseau
Jocelyn F. Rancourt
Pierre Cimon
Pierre Déry
Yves Gonthier
Éric Hardy
Marc Paradis
Jean Piette
Martin Rochette
Louis Vaillancourt

For full biographical listings, see the Martindale-Hubbell Law Directory

*RIMOUSKI,** Rimouski Dist. — (Refer to Quebec)

*RIVIERE DU LOUP,** Kamouraska Dist. — (Refer to Quebec)

*ST. HYACINTHE,** St. Hyacinthe Dist. — (Refer to Montreal)

*ST-JEAN-SUR-RICHELIEU,** Iberville Dist. — (Refer to Montreal)

*ST. JEROME,** Terrebonne Dist. — (Refer to Montreal)

*SOREL,** Richelieu Dist. — (Refer to Montreal)

*TROIS-RIVIERES,** Trois-Rivieres Dist. — (Refer to Quebec)

*VALLEYFIELD,** Beauharnois Dist. — (Refer to Montreal)

SASKATCHEWAN

*ASSINIBOIA,** Assiniboia Jud. Centre — (Refer to Regina)

*ESTEVAN,** Estevan Jud. Centre — (Refer to Regina)

*GRAVELBOURG,** Gravelbourg Jud. Centre — (Refer to Moose Jaw)

*HUMBOLDT,** Humboldt Jud. Centre — (Refer to Saskatoon)

*KERROBERT,** Kerrobert Jud. Centre — (Refer to Saskatoon)

*MELFORT,** Melfort Jud. Centre — (Refer to Saskatoon)

*MOOSOMIN,** Moosomin Jud. Centre — (Refer to Regina)

*PRINCE ALBERT,** Prince Albert Jud. Centre — (Refer to Saskatoon)

*REGINA,** Regina Jud. Centre

BALFOUR MOSS (AV)

Bank of Montreal Building, 700-2103 11th Avenue, S4P 4G1
Telephone: 306-347-8300
Fax: 306-569-2321
Saskatoon, Saskatchewan Office: 850-410 22nd Street East.
Telephone: 306-665-7844.
Fax: 306-652-1586.

PARTNERS

A. John Beke, Q.C.
Fredrick C. McBeth
Brian J. Scherman
(Resident Saskatoon)
D.E. Wayne McIntyre
Jennifer L. Garvie Pritchard
Roger J.F. Lepage
Reginald A. Watson
David C. Knoll
(Resident Saskatoon)
Glen S. Lekach
Rick M. Van Beselaere
George E. Nystrom
Jeff N. Grubb

COUNSEL

E. John Moss, Q.C.
Hon. R. James Balfour, Q.C.
Robert A. Milliken, Q.C.
Roy B. Laschuk, Q.C.

ASSOCIATES

Elke Churchman
(Resident Saskatoon)
Gordon D. McKenzie
(Resident Saskatoon)
Karen M. Bolstad
(Resident Saskatoon)
James L. Nugent
Randy R. Semenchuck
Douglas R. Sanders
(Resident Saskatoon)
David G. Gerecke
(Resident Saskatoon)
W. Kevin Rogers
Phyllis L. Norrie
Michele Klebuc-Simes
W. Andrew Donovan
Isa Gros-Louis Ahenakew
(Resident, Saskatoon)
Susan Engel
Gil A. Malfair

Representative Clients: Bank of Montreal; Saskatchewan Wheat Pool; London Life Assurance Co.

For full biographical listings, see the Martindale-Hubbell Law Directory

MACPHERSON LESLIE & TYERMAN (AV)

1500-1874 Scarth Street, S4P 4E9
Telephone: 306-347-8000
Telecopier: 306-352-5250
Saskatoon, Saskatchewan Office: 1500-410 22nd Street East, S7K 5T6.
Telephone: 306-975-7100.
Telecopier: 306-975-7145.

MEMBERS OF FIRM

Harold H. MacKay, Q.C.
Stephen A. Arsenych
Robert B. Pletch, Q.C.
Frederick J. Kovach
Maurice O. Laprairie
Larry B. LeBlanc
Leonard D. Andrychuk
Bruce W. Wirth
(Resident, Saskatoon Office)
Alain J. Gaucher
(Resident Saskatoon Office)
Brian J. Kenny
Douglas C. Hodson
(Resident, Saskatoon Office)
James S. Kerby
(Resident, Saskatoon Office)
Carl A. P. Wagner
Dennis P. Ball, Q.C.
A. Robson Garden, Q.C.
(Resident, Saskatoon Office)
Donald K. Wilson
R. Neil MacKay
(Resident, Saskatoon Office)
John T. Nilson
Garret J. Oledzki
Robert G. Richards
Douglas A. Ballou
Danny R. Anderson
(Resident, Saskatoon Office)
Robert W. Leurer

ASSOCIATES

Melissa A. Brunsdon
(Resident, Saskatoon Office)
John A. Dipple
Jeffrey M. Lee
(Resident, Saskatoon Office)
Susan D. McGillivray
Larry M. Korchinski
Maureen L. Douglas
(Resident, Saskatoon Office)
Eileen V. Libby
Jeffrey D. Scott
Wally D. Leis
(Resident, Saskatoon Office)
Kevin C. Wilson
(Resident, Saskatoon Office)
Conrad D. Hadubiak
Curtis R. Stewart
(Resident, Saskatoon Office)
Brad D. Markel
Scott A. Exner

(See Next Column)

ASSOCIATES (Continued)

Nathalie Ruel
(Resident, Saskatoon Office)
Dave J. Bramwell
Lyle S. Yuzdepski
Vanessa Monar Enweani
(Resident, Saskatoon Office)
Linda A. Christensen
Elizabeth J. Siemens
(Resident, Saskatoon Office)
David J. Smith

COUNSEL

David M. Tyerman, Q.C.
W. Thomas Molloy, Q.C.
(Resident, Saskatoon Office)
William M. Elliott, Q.C.

For full biographical listings, see the Martindale-Hubbell Law Directory

MCDOUGALL, READY (AV)

700 Royal Bank Building, 2010-11th Avenue, S4P 0J3
Telephone: 306-757-1641
Telecopier: 306-359-0785
Saskatoon, Saskatchewan, Canada Office: 301 - 111 2nd Avenue South.
Telephone: 306-653-1641.
Telecopier: 306-665-8511.

J. Lorn McDougall, Q.C. (1919-1981)

MEMBERS OF FIRM

William F. Ready, Q.C.
Elmer Youck
Gordon J. Kuski, Q.C.
Robert N. Millar
Lynn A. Smith
R. Shawn Smith
Kenneth A. Ready
Michael W. Milani
W. Randall Rooke
(Resident, Saskatoon Office)
Aaron A. Fox
Philip J. Gallet
Wayne L. Bernakevitch
Ronald L. Miller
(Resident, Saskatoon Office)
Merri-Ellen Wright
(Resident, Saskatoon Office)
Brian M. Banilevic
Pamela J. Lothian
Murray R. Sawatzky
Walter J. Matkowski
(Resident, Saskatoon Office)
Susan B. Barber

Kevin A. Lang
Brent D. Barilla
(Resident, Saskatoon Office)
Catherine M. Wall
Erin M.S. Kleisinger
James Nelson Korpan
Penny Overby
(Resident, Saskatoon Office)

Representative Clients: Royal Bank of Canada; Imperial Oil, Ltd.; John Deere Limited; Ford Motor Company of Canada, Ltd.; Chrysler Canada Ltd.; General Motors of Canada Limited; Phoenix of London Group; University of Regina.

For full biographical listings, see the Martindale-Hubbell Law Directory

*SASKATOON,** Saskatoon Jud. Centre

GAULEY & CO. (AV)

701 Broadway Avenue, P.O. Box 638, S7K 3L7
Telephone: 306-653-1212
Telecopier: 306-652-1323
Regina, Saskatchewan Office: Suite 400, 2201 11th Avenue S4P 0J8.
Telephone: 306-352-1643.
Telecopier: 306-525-8499.

MEMBERS OF FIRM

David E. "Tom" Gauley, Q.C.
Harry H. Dahlem, Q.C.
Peter Foley, Q.C.
J. J. (Joe) Dierker, Q.C.
Larry F. Seiferling, Q.C.
David J. McKeague, Q.C.
William J. Shaw
Robert G. Kennedy
Rex M. Beaton
Nancy E. Hopkins, Q.C.
James E. Seibel
Gary A. Zabos
James Russell
William A. Grieve
Ian Sutherland

ASSOCIATES

Brenda R. Hildebrandt
Scott R. Spencer
Michael J. Brannen
Christopher C. Boychuk
Stephanie L. Tynan
Roger V. De Corby
Raymond Wiebe
Paul A. Day

Reference: Royal Bank of Canada.

For full biographical listings, see the Martindale-Hubbell Law Directory

MCDOUGALL, READY (AV)

301-111 2nd Avenue, South, S7K 1K6
Telephone: 306-653-1641
Telecopier: 306-665-8511
Regina, Saskatchewan Office: 700 Royal Bank Building, 2010 - 11th Avenue.
Telephone: 306-757-1641.
Telecopier: 306-359-0785.

MEMBERS OF FIRM

W. Randall Rooke
Ronald L. Miller
Merri-Ellen Wright
Walter J. Matkowski

(See Next Column)

McDougall, Ready—*Continued*

Brent D. Barilla
Penny Overby

Representative Clients: Royal Bank of Canada; The Prudential Insurance Company of America; Imperial Oil, Ltd.; Navistar International Corporation Canada; Deutz-Allis Corporation Canada; Ford Motor Company of Canada, Ltd.

For full biographical listings, see the Martindale-Hubbell Law Directory

McKercher, McKercher & Whitmore (AV)
374 Third Avenue, South, S7K 1M5
Telephone: 306-653-2000
Fax: 306-244-7335
Regina, Saskatchewan Office: 1000 - 1783 Hamilton Street.
Telephone: 306-352-7661.
Fax: 306-781-7113.

MEMBERS OF FIRM

Hon. Stewart McKercher, Q.C. (1893-1977)
J.A. Stack (1937-1987)
D. S. McKercher, Q.C.
Robert H. McKercher, Q.C.
Neil G. Gabrielson, Q.C.
Peter A. Whitmore, Q.C. (Resident, Regina Office)
Brian W. Wilkinson
Lorne Larson
John R. Beckman, Q.C.
Leslie J. Dick Batten
J. D. Denis Pelletier
Thomas G. (Casey) Davis
Daniel B. Konkin
Douglas B. Richardson
Richard W. Elson
C.J. Glazer
Paul D. Grant
Joel A. Hesje
Gregory A. Thompson

ASSOCIATES

L. J. Korchin
Caroline M. K. Gorsalitz
Gordon S. Wyant
Shaunt Parthev
David E. Thera
Humphrey Tam
Deric B. Karolat
Catherine A. Sloan
J. Denis Bonthoux
Pat Loran
Catherine J. Hearn
Sandra J. Schnell
Michelle J. Ouellette
Shannon L. Potter
James T. Sproule

Representative Clients: The Royal Bank of Canada; Cominco Ltd.; Saskatoon City Hospital; London Life Insurance Co.; The University of Saskatchewan; Gulf Oil Canada, Ltd.; Chicago Title Insurance Co.

For full biographical listings, see the Martindale-Hubbell Law Directory

*SHAUNAVON,** Shaunavon Jud. Centre — (Refer to Moose Jaw)

*SWIFT CURRENT,** Swift Current Jud. Centre — (Refer to Moose Jaw)

*WEYBURN,** Weyburn Jud. Centre — (Refer to Regina)

*WYNYARD,** Wynyard Jud. Centre — (Refer to Regina)

*YORKTON,** Yorkton Jud. Centre — (Refer to Regina)

ARGENTINA

*BUENOS AIRES,**

American Lawyers In Buenos Aires

BAKER & MCKENZIE

Avenida Leandro N. Alem 1110, Piso 13, 1001 Buenos Aires
Telephone: 311-5412
Intn'l. Dialing: (54-1) 311- 5412
Facsimiles: (54-1) 11-1873; 311-6435
Associated Offices of Baker & McKenzie in: Almaty, Amsterdam, Bangkok, Barcelona, Beijing, Berlin, Bogotá, Brasília, Brussels, Budapest, Cairo, Caracas, Chicago, Dallas, Frankfurt, Geneva, Hanoi, Ho Chi Minh City, Hong Kong, Juárez, Kiev, London, Madrid, Manila, Melbourne, México City, Miami, Milan, Monterrey, Moscow, New York, Palo Alto, Paris, Prague, Rio de Janeiro, Riyadh, Rome, St. Petersburg, San Diego, San Francisco, São Paulo, Singapore, Stockholm, Sydney, Taipei, Tijuana, Tokyo, Toronto, Valencia, Warsaw, Washington, D.C. and Zürich.
Correspondent Law Firm: Hadiputranto, Hadinoto & Partners, Jakarta.

PARTNERS

Gonzalo Enrique Cáceres
Pablo Dukarevich
Miguel Menegazzo Cané
Horacio César Soares

LOCAL PARTNERS

Alejandro J. Olivera
Avelino Rolón, Jr.

ASSOCIATES

Pedro Julio Agote
Juan Martín Alchouron
Ana María Aufiero
Martín José Barreiro
Marcos Jorge Basso
Gustavo Boruchowicz
María Alejandra Bouquet
Martín Román Bourel
Carolina Valeria Correa Crovetto
Carlos Andres A. Dodds
Adolfo Duraňona
Eduardo Enrici
María Patricia González Presedo
María Gabriela Hahan
Alexis Kook Weskott
Gabriela López Cremaschi
Bernard William Malone
Eduardo Esteban Mariscotti
Jorge Daniel Orlansky
María Julia Palamara
Julio Alberto Pueyrredon
Xavier Ruiz (Not admitted in Argentina)
Marcelo Slonimsky
Pablo Augusto Van Thienen
Diego Fernando Wartjes
Augusto Zampini Davies
Rafael J. Zemborain

For full biographical listings, see the Martindale-Hubbell Law Directory

AUSTRALIA

MELBOURNE, VICTORIA,

BAKER & MCKENZIE

Level 39 Rialto, 525 Collins Street, Melbourne, Victoria 3000
Telephone: (03) 617-4200
Intn'l. Dialing: (61-3) 617-4200
Telex: AA21618
Answer Back: ABOGADO AA21618
Facsimile: (61-3) 614-2103
Associated Offices of Baker & McKenzie in: Almaty, Amsterdam, Bangkok, Barcelona, Beijing, Berlin, Bogotá, Brasília, Brussels, Budapest, Buenos Aires, Cairo, Caracas, Chicago, Dallas, Frankfurt, Geneva, Hanoi, Ho Chi Minh City, Hong Kong, Juárez, Kiev, London, Madrid, Manila, México City, Miami, Milan, Monterrey, Moscow, New York, Palo Alto, Paris, Prague, Rio de Janeiro, Riyadh, Rome, St. Petersburg, San Diego, San Francisco, São Paulo, Singapore, Stockholm, Sydney, Taipei, Tijuana, Tokyo, Toronto, Valencia, Warsaw, Washington, D.C. and Zürich.
Correspondent Law Firm: Hadiputranto, Hadinoto & Partners, Jakarta.
Postal Address: P.O. Box 2119T, G.P.O., Melbourne, Victoria 3001

MEMBERS OF FIRM

Timothy C. Garrood
Paul D. McSweeney
Christopher B. Penman
Graham V. Sherry

LOCAL PARTNERS

Ian M. Dixon
Leigh W. Duthie
Theo Kindynis
Bruce C. Webb

ASSOCIATES

Gillad Dalal
Danielle T. Galvin
Darren S. Olney
Michael J. Pabst
Donna O. Pelka
Simon Phillipson
G. Matthew Sheridan
Julian Speed
Peter G. Vitale
Antony J. Wyatt

For full biographical listings, see the Martindale-Hubbell Law Directory

SULLIVAN & CROMWELL

101 Collins Street, Melbourne, Victoria 3000
Telephone: (011)(613)654-1500
Telecopier: (011)(613)654-2422
New York City Offices: 125 Broad Street, 10004-2498; Midtown Office: 250 Park Avenue, 10177-0021.
Telephone: 212-558-4000.
Telex: 62694 (International); 12-7816 (Domestic).
Cable Address: "Ladycourt, New York".
Telecopier: 125 Broad Street 212-558-3588; 250 Park Avenue 212-558-3792.
Washington, D.C. Office: 1701 Pennsylvania Avenue, N.W., 20006-5805.
Telephone: 202-956-7500.
Telex: 89625.
Telecopier: 202-293-6330.
Los Angeles, California Office: 444 South Flower Street, 90071-2901.
Telephone: 213-955-8000.
Telecopier: 213-683-0457.
Paris Office: 8, Place Vendôme, Paris 75001, France.
Telephone: (011)(331)4450-6000.
Telex: 240654.
Telecopier: (011)(331)4450-6060.
London Office: St. Olave's House, 9a Ironmonger Lane, London EC2V 8EY, England.
Telephone: (011)(44171)710-6500.
Telecopier: (011)(44171)710-6565.
Tokyo Office: Gaikokuho Jimu Bengoshi Office of Robert G. DeLaMater, a member of the firm of Sullivan & Cromwell, Tokio Kaijo Building Shinkan, 2-1, Marunouchi, 1-chome Chiyoda-ku, Tokyo 100, Japan.
Telephone: (011)(813)3213-6140.
Telecopier: (011)(813)3213-6470.
Hong Kong Office: 28th Floor, Nine Queen's Road, Central, Hong Kong.
Telephone: (011)(852)826-8688.
Telecopier: (011)(852)522-2280.

PARTNERS IN MELBOURNE

Jeffrey F. Browne
Duncan C. McCurrach (Not admitted in Australia)

ASSOCIATES IN MELBOURNE

Gary W. Cobbledick (Not admitted in Australia)
Michael D. Schecter (Not admitted in Australia)
Richard H. Siegel (Not admitted in Australia)

For full biographical listings, see the Martindale-Hubbell Law Directory

SYDNEY, NEW SOUTH WALES,

BAKER & MCKENZIE

A.M.P. Centre, 50 Bridge Street, Sydney, New South Wales 2000
Telephone: (02) 225-0200
Intn'l. Dialing: (61-2) 225-0200
Cable Address: ABOGADO
Telex: AA21618
Answer Back: ABOGADO AA21618
Facsimile: (61-2) 223-7711
Associated Offices of Baker & McKenzie in: Almaty, Amsterdam, Bangkok, Barcelona, Beijing, Berlin, Bogotá, Brasília, Brussels, Budapest, Buenos Aires, Cairo, Caracas, Chicago, Dallas, Frankfurt, Geneva, Hanoi, Ho Chi Minh City, Hong Kong, Juárez, Kiev, London, Madrid, Manila, Melbourne, México City, Miami, Milan, Monterrey, Moscow, New York, Palo Alto, Paris, Prague, Rio de Janeiro, Riyadh, Rome, St. Petersburg, San Diego, San Francisco, São Paulo, Singapore, Stockholm, Taipei, Tijuana, Tokyo, Toronto, Valencia, Warsaw, Washington, D.C. and Zürich.
Correspondent Law Firm: Hadiputranto, Hadinoto & Partners, Jakarta.
Postal Address: Box R126, Royal Exchange P.O.

MEMBERS OF FIRM

Michael C. Ahrens
Frank Cahill
Mark D. Chapple
John A. Connors
Graeme J. Dickson
Peter T. Dwight
Steven M. Glanz
Richard T. Gough
George C. Harris
David L. Jacobs
Michael J. Kunstler
Ross G. McLean
Roy E. Melick
Timothy P. O'Doherty
Ralph B. Pliner
Robert I. Richards
Andrew M. Salgo
Christopher J. Saxon
Rodney Stone
Timothy A. Woodhouse
Edwin J. Zemancheff

LOCAL PARTNERS

Frank J. Castiglia
Christopher J. Connor
John R. Fabbro
Joan T. Fitzhenry
Anthony J. Foley
James A. Hamilton
Fiona J. Inverarity
Carolyn D. Mall
Benjamin T. McLaughlin
Michael J. Reed
Timothy J. Reed
Geoffrey J. Short
Penelope J. Ward
Timothy H. Weekes

(See Next Column)

BAKER & MCKENZIE—*Continued*

ASSOCIATES

Anne-Marie L. Allgrove
Susan P. Baines
Andrew J. D. Barclay
Libbie J. Biggin
Stephanie M. Bronk
Paul G. Brown
Dora S. Y. Chan (Not admitted in Australia)
Leslie J. Christy
Julieanne E. Cox
John A. Ellis
Prisca Shing Lan Fai
Howard H. Fraser
Sandra K. Gibbons
Michael G. Gibson
Steven M. Goodman
Christine E. Gray
Philip G. Gray
Pauline J. Gulleford (Not admitted in Australia)
Michael R. Hall
Karen Hanigan
Sally A. Hanson
William Hara
Diane E. Houghton
Teresa M. Lentile
Bronwyn M. James
Andrew W. Jones
Frances A. Kyrikos
Scott Laycock
Cindy J. Lazarus
Rhonda Lee Quan
Kelli S. Longworth
Sarah A. L. Madew
Jonathan M. Marquard
David C. McCredie
Anna L. McHugh
Kerry E. Medd
Derek A. Neve
C. Mary Nixon
Nicholas J. O'Day
Nicholas B. Pappas
Steven M. Pateman
Jeffrey V. Rodwell
Mark A. Russell
Lynne M. Saunder
Cheryl L. Slusarchuk
Roger D. Soo
Chiaki Sugishita-Mahnken
Annette Teckemeier
Martyn P. Tier
Thomas D. Wait (Not admitted in Australia)
Lesley A. Waters
Stephen J. Watts
Robert J. Wilcher
D. Jason Williams

For full biographical listings, see the Martindale-Hubbell Law Directory

BELGIUM

*BRUSSELS,**

AKIN, GUMP, STRAUSS, HAUER, FELD & DASSESSE

(Brussels office of Akin, Gump, Strauss, Hauer & Feld, L.L.P.)
65 Avenue Louise P.B.7, 1050 Brussels
Telephone: 011-322-535-29-11
Telefax: (+32 2) 535 29 00
Telex: 20125 ECAKIN B
Dallas, Texas Office: Akin, Gump, Strauss, Hauer & Feld, L.L.P., 1700 Pacific Avenue, Suite 4100, 75201-4618.
Telephone: 214-969-2800.
Austin, Texas Office: Akin, Gump, Strauss, Hauer & Feld, L.L.P., 2100 Franklin Plaza, 111 Congress Avenue, Suite 2100, 78701.
Telephone: 512-499-6200.
Houston, Texas Office: Akin, Gump, Strauss, Hauer & Feld, L.L.P., 1900 Pennzoil Place-South Tower, 711 Louisiana Street, 77002.
Telephone: 713-220-5800.
San Antonio, Texas Office: Akin, Gump, Strauss, Hauer & Feld, L.L.P., Nationsbank Plaza, 300 Convent Street, Suite 1500, 78205.
Telephone: 210-270-0800.
New York, New York Office: Akin, Gump, Strauss, Hauer & Feld, L.L.P., 65 East 55th Street, 33rd Floor.
Telephone: 212-872-1000.
Fax: 212-872-1002.
Washington, D.C. Office: Akin, Gump, Strauss, Hauer & Feld, L.L.P., 1333 New Hampshire Avenue, N.W., Suite 400, 20036.
Telephone: 202-887-4000.
Moscow, Russia Office: Akin, Gump, Strauss, Hauer & Feld, L.L.P., Bolshoi Sukharevsky Pereulok 26, 103051 Moscow, Russia.
Telephone: 011-7095-974-2411 or (202) 887-4545.
Fax: 011-7095-974-2412 or (202) 887-4544.

PARTNERS

Jay D. Zeiler
Marc Dassesse
Edwin Vermulst
Richard M. Gittleman
Martine De Witte
Peter Verhaeghe
Paul Waer

SPECIAL COUNSEL

Steven E. Brummel
Annabelle J. Ewing

OF COUNSEL

Jan Van Besien
Kenneth E. Natale

ASSOCIATES

Ann Rose Stouthuysen
Ian Roxan
Stanley Stewart
Christoph Zeyen
Darren S. Trigonoplos
Folkert Graafsma
Alain De Jonge
Ellen L. Marx
John C. Lepore
Tom Nelson
Pilar De La Cal
Bart Driessen

For full biographical listings, see the Martindale-Hubbell Law Directory

BAKER & MCKENZIE

40 Boulevard du Régent-Regentlaan 40, Fifth Floor, 1000 Brussels
Telephone: (02) 506-36-11
Intn'l. Dialing: (32-2) 506-36-11
Cable Address: ABOGADO
Telex: 23880
Answer Back: 23880 ABOGAD B
Facsimile: (32-2) 511-62-80
Associated Offices of Baker & McKenzie in: Almaty, Amsterdam, Bangkok, Barcelona, Beijing, Berlin, Bogotá, Brasília, Budapest, Buenos Aires, Cairo, Caracas, Chicago, Dallas, Frankfurt, Geneva, Hanoi, Ho Chi Minh City, Hong Kong, Juárez, Kiev, London, Madrid, Manila, Melbourne, México City, Miami, Milan, Monterrey, Moscow, New York, Palo Alto, Paris, Prague, Rio de Janeiro, Riyadh, Rome, St. Petersburg, San Diego, San Francisco, São Paulo, Singapore, Stockholm, Sydney, Taipei, Tijuana, Tokyo, Toronto, Valencia, Warsaw, Washington, D.C. and Zürich.
Correspondent Law Firm: Hadiputranto, Hadinoto & Partners, Jakarta.

Jacques H. J. Bourgeois
François Gabriel
Jacques Ghysbrecht
Otto J. Grolig
Paul G. Herten
Luc Hinnekens
Alain Huyghe
Anne Laurent
Dominique Lechien
Ignace Maes
Pierre Sculier
Jozef Slootmans
Peter J. Sturtevant
Koen Vanhaerents

Pierre Bové
Mia Declercq
Antoine D. R. M. De Raeve
Yves J. J. M. de Voghel
Daniel D. Fesler
Joanna R. Goyder
Catherine I. Grisart
Arne K. E. Gutermann
Peter E. Leys
Xavier Michel
Jean-François Vandenberghe
Annick Van Hoorebeke
Johan L. Ysewyn

For full biographical listings, see the Martindale-Hubbell Law Directory

American Lawyers In Brussels

CLEARY, GOTTLIEB, STEEN & HAMILTON

Rue de la Loi 23, Bte 5, 1040 Brussels
Telephone: 32/2/287.20.00
Telex: 22635
Fax: 32/2/231.16.61
New York, New York Office: One Liberty Plaza, New York, N.Y. 10006.
Telephone: 212-225-2000.
Washington, D.C. Office: 1752 N Street, N.W., Washington, D.C. 20036.
Telephone: 202-728-2700.
Paris, France Office: 41, Avenue de Friedland, 75008 Paris, France.
Telephone: 33-1-4074-6800.
London, England Office: City Place House, 55 Basinghall Street, London EC2V 5EH England.
Telephone: 44-71-614-2200.
Hong Kong Office: 56th Floor, Bank of China Tower, One Garden Road, Hong Kong.
Telephone: 852-521-4122.
Tokyo, Japan Office: Morgan Carroll Terai Gaikokuho Jimubengoshi Jimusho, 20th Floor, Shin Kasumigaseki Building, 3-2, Kasumigaseki 3-Chome, Chiyoda-Ku, Tokyo 100, Japan.
Telephone: 81-3-3595-3911.
Frankfurt, Germany Office: Ulmenstrasse 37-39, 60325 Frankfurt am Main, Germany.
Telephone: 49-69-971-03-0.

RESIDENT PARTNERS

Walter W. Oberreit
Mario Siragusa
Wolfgang Knapp
John S. Magney
George L. Bustin
Jean-Louis Joris
David G. Sabel
Jan Meyers
Dirk Vandermeersch
Jacques Reding
Yoichi Shibasaki
Antoine Winckler
Maurits J.F.M. Dolmans

RESIDENT ASSOCIATES

Thijs Alexander
Barbara Brandtner
Randall Costa
Aline Daufresne
Laurent A. Garzaniti
Michael A. Gerstenzang
Reinhard Hermes
Jan W. Hoevers
Caroline Y. Levi
Nicholas Levy
Patrick J. McDermott
Filip J. Moerman
Francesca M. Moretti
Till Müller-Ibold
Catherine Noirfalisse
Miguel Odriozola
Stephen E. Pomper (Not admitted in Belgium)
Giulio Cesare Rizza
Giuseppe Scassellati-Sforzolini
Annette Luise Schild
Robbert Snelders
Romano Francesco Subiotto
Karen Vandekerckhove
Jan Van Gysegem
Amaryllis Verhoeven
Sabien Vermeulen

For full biographical listings, see the Martindale-Hubbell Law Directory

COUDERT BROTHERS

Tour Louise, 149 Avenue Louise, Box 8, B-1050 Brussels
Telephone: 542.18.11
Telecopier: (32) (2) 542.18.88; 539.28.88
Cable Address: "Treduoc"
Telex: 24284 "Couder B"
New York, New York 10036-7794: 1114 Avenue of Americas.
Washington, D.C.20006: 1627 I Street, N.W.
Los Angeles, California 90017: 1055 West Seventh Street, Twentieth Floor.
San Francisco, California 94111: 4 Embarcadero Center, Suite 3300.
San Jose, California 95113: Suite 1250, Ten Almaden Boulevard.
Paris 75008, France: Coudert Frères, 52, Avenue des Champs-Elysées, 75008.
London, EC4M 7JP England: 20 Old Bailey.
Beijing, People's Republic of China 100020: Suite 2708-09 Jing Guang Centre Hu Jia Lou, Chao Yang Qu.
Shanghai, People's Republic of China 200002: c/o Suite1804, Union Building, 100 Yanan Road East.
Hong Kong: 25th Floor, Nine Queen's Road Central.
Singapore, 0104: Tung Centre, 20 Collyer Quay.
Sydney N.S.W. 2000, Australia: Suite 2202, State Bank Centre, 52 Martin Place.
Tokyo 107, Japan: 1355 West Tower, Aoyama Twin Towers, 1-1-1 Minami-Aoyama, Minato-ku.
Moscow, Russia: Ulitsa Staraya Basmannaya 14.
01301 Sao Paulo, SP, Brazil: Machado, Meyer, Sendacz, e Opice, Advogados, Rua da Consolacao, 247, 8 Andar.
Bangkok 10500, Thailand: Bubhajit Building, 20 North Sathorn Road, 10th Floor.
Ho Chi Minh City, Vietnam: c/o Saigon Business Centre, 49-57 Dong Du Street, District 1.

PARTNERS

Jacques Buhart
Stephen O. Spinks
Paulette Vander Schueren

ASSOCIATES

Peter Alexiadis (Not admitted in Belgium)
Jean-Yves Art
Kent Karlsson
David Chijner
Hervé F. Cogels
Anthony Laurence Gardner
Nathalie Gilson
Roland P. Montfort
Dr. Karl H. Pilny (Not admitted in Belgium)
Olivier Prost (Not admitted in Belgium)
Dirk Van Liedekerke

SPECIAL CONSULTANT

Prof. Valentine Korah (Not admitted in Belgium)

(Not admitted to practice in Belgian courts)

For full biographical listings, see the Martindale-Hubbell Law Directory

CRUMMY, DEL DEO, DOLAN, GRIFFINGER & VECCHIONE

Avenue Louise 475, BTE. 8, B-1050 Brussels
Telephone: 011-322-646-0019
Telecopier: 011-322-646-0152
Newark, New Jersey Office: Crummy, Del Deo, Dolan, Griffinger & Vecchione, A Professional Corporation. One Riverfront Plaza, 07102.
Telephone: 201-596-4500.
Telecopier: 201-596-0545.
Cable-Telex: 138154.

RESIDENT PARTNER

Terry R. Broderick (Not admitted in Belgium)

(Not admitted to practice in Belgian courts)

For full biographical listings, see the Martindale-Hubbell Law Directory

DECHERT PRICE & RHOADS

65 Avenue Louise, 1050 Brussels
Telephone: (02) 535-5411
Telefax: (02) 535-5400
Philadelphia, Pennsylvania: 4000 Bell Atlantic Tower, 1717 Arch Street, 19103-2793.
Telephone: 215-994-4000.
New York, N.Y.: 477 Madison Avenue, 10022.
Telephone: 212-326-3500.
Washington, D.C.: 1500 K Street, N.W., 20005.
Telephone: 202-626-3300.
Harrisburg, Pennsylvania: Thirty North Third Street, 17101.
Telephone: 717-237-2000.
Princeton, N.J.: Princeton Pike Corporate Center, P.O. Box 5218, 08543-5218.
Telephone: 609-520-3200.
Boston, Massachusetts: Ten Post Office Square South, 02109.
Telephone: 617-728-7100.
London, England: 2 Serjeants' Inn, EC4Y 1LT.
Telephone: (0171) 583-5353. (Also see Titmuss Sainer Dechert).

RESIDENT PARTNERS

Bernard E. Amory
Richard J. Temko

RESIDENT ASSOCIATES

Pierre Philippe Berthe
Stanislas De Peuter
Jean-Pierre Lenaerts
Isabelle Mahnaz Rahman
Ursula Schliessner
Alexandre Verheyden

(See Next Column)

(Not admitted to practice in Belgian courts)

For full biographical listings, see the Martindale-Hubbell Law Directory

JONES, DAY, REAVIS & POGUE

Avenue Louise 480, bte 7 Louizalaan 480, bus 7, B-1050 Brussels
Telephone: 32-2-645-14-11
Telecopier: 32-2-645-14-45
In Atlanta, Georgia: 3500 One Peachtree Center, 303 Peachtree Street, N.E. .
Telephone: 404-521-3939.
Cable Address: "Attorneys Atlanta".
Telex: 54-2711.
Telecopier: 404-581-8330.
In Chicago, Illinois: 77 West Wacker.
Telephone: 312-782-3939.
Telecopier: 312-782-8585.
In Cleveland, Ohio: North Point, 901 Lakeside Avenue.
Telephone: 216-586-3939.
Cable Address: "Attorneys Cleveland."
Telex: 980389.
Telecopier: 216-579-0212.
In Columbus, Ohio: 1900 Huntington Center.
Telephone: 614-469-3939.
Cable Address: "Attorneys Columbus."
Telecopier: 614-461-4198.
In Dallas, Texas: 2300 Trammell Crow Center, 2001 Ross Avenue.
Telephone: 214-220-3939.
Cable Address: "Attorneys Dallas."
Telex: 730852.
Telecopier: 214-969-5100.
In Frankfurt, Germany: Triton Haus, Bockenheimer Landstrasse 42, 60323 Frankfurt am Main.
Telephone: 49-69-9726-3939.
Telecopier: 49-69-9726-3993.
In Geneva, Switzerland: 20, rue de Candolle.
Telephone: 41-22-320-2339.
Telecopier: 41-22-320-1232.
In Hong Kong: 1501 One Exchange Square, 8 Connaught Place.
Telephone: 852-2526-6895.
Telecopier: 852-2810-5787.
In Irvine, California: 2603 Main Street, Suite 900.
Telephone: 714-851-3939.
Telex: 194911 Lawyers LSA.
Telecopier: 714-553-7539.
In London, England: One Mount Street.
Telephone: 44-71-493-9361.
Cable Address: "Surgoe London WI."
Telecopier: 44-71-493-9666.
In Los Angeles, California: 555 West Fifth Street, Suite 4600.
Telephone: 213-489-3939.
Telex: 181439 UD.
Telecopier: 213-243-2539.
In New York, New York: 599 Lexington Avenue.
Telephone: 212-326-3939.
Cable Address: "JONESDAY NEWYORK."
Telex: 237013 JDRP UR.
Telecopier: 212-755-7306.
In Paris, France: 62, rue du Faubourg Saint-Honore.
Telephone: 33-1-44-71-3939.
Cable Address: "Surgoe Paris."
Telex: 290156 Surgoe.
Telecopier: 33-1-49-24-0471.
In Pittsburgh, Pennsylvania: 500 Grant Street, 31st Floor.
Telephone: 412-391-3939.
Cable Address: "Attorneys Pittsburgh".
Telecopier: 412-394-7959.
In Riyadh, Saudi Arabia: Law Offices of Saud M.A. Shawwaf, P.O. Box 2700.
Telephones: (966-1) 465-6543, (966-1) 464-8534 or (966-1) 464-8540.
Telex: 401831 SAUCON SJ.
Telecopier: (966-1) 464-8480.
In Taipei, Taiwan: 8th Floor, 2 Tun Hwa South Road, Section 2.
Telephone: (886-2) 704-6808.
Telecopier: (886-2) 704-6791.
In Tokyo, Japan: Toranomon MT Building, 4th Floor, 10-3, Toranomon 3-Chome, Minato-Ku, Tokyo 105, Japan.
Telephone: 81-3-3433-3939.
Telecopier: 81-3-5401-2725.
In Washington, D.C.: Metropolitan Square, 1450 G Street, N.W.
Telephone: 202-879-3939.
Cable Address: "Attorneys Washington."
Telex: 89-2410 ATTORNEYS WASH.
Telecopier: 202-737-2832.

MEMBERS OF FIRM IN BRUSSELS

Norbert Koch (Not admitted in Belgium)
Ghislain Joseph (Not admitted in Belgium)
Luc G. Houben (Not admitted in Belgium)

(See Next Column)

JONES, DAY, REAVIS & POGUE—*Continued*

ASSOCIATES

James E. Thompson (Not admitted in Belgium)
Anand S. Pathak (Not admitted in Belgium)
Marc N. Bombeeck (Not admitted in Belgium)
Bart A. Servaes

(Not admitted to practice in Belgian courts)

For full biographical listings, see the Martindale-Hubbell Law Directory

MAYER, BROWN & PLATT

Square de Meeûs 19/20, Bte. 4, 1040 Brussels
Telephone: 011-32-2-512-9878
Fax: 011-32-2-511-3305
Telex: 20768 MBPBRU B
Chicago, Illinois Office: 190 South LaSalle Street, 60603-3441.
Telephone: (312) 782-0600. Pitney Bowes: (312) 701-7711.
Telex: 190404.
Cable: LEMAY.
Washington, D.C. Office: 2000 Pennsylvania Avenue, N.W., 20006-1882.
Telephone: (202) 463-2000. Pitney Bowes: (202) 861-0484, Pitney Bowes: (202) 861-0473.
Telex: 892603.
Cable: LEMAYDC.
New York, New York Office: 787 Seventh Avenue, Suite 2400, 10019-6018.
Telephone: (212) 554-3000. Pitney Bowes: (212) 262-1910.
Telex: 701842.
Cable: LEMAYEN.
Houston, Texas Office: 700 Louisiana Street, Suite 3600, 77002-2730.
Telephone: (713) 221-1651. Pitney Bowes: (713) 224-6410.
Telex: 775809.
Cable: LEMAYHOU.
Los Angeles, California Office: 350 South Grand Avenue, 25th Floor, 90071-1503.
Telephone: (213) 229-9500. Pitney Bowes: (213) 625-0248.
Telex: 188089.
Cable: LEMAYLA.
London, England Office: 162 Queen Victoria Street, EC4V 4DB.
Telephone: 011-44-71-248-1465.
Fax: 011-44-71-329-4465.
Telex: 8811095.
Cable: LEMAYLDN.
Tokyo, Japan Office: (Kawachi Gaikokuho Jimu Bengoshi Jimusho). Urbannet Otemachi Building 13F 2-2, Otemachi 2-chome, Chiyoda-ku, Tokyo 100.
Telephone: 011-81-3-5255-9700.
Facsimile: 011-81-3-5255-9797.
Berlin, Germany Office: Spreeufer 5, 10178.
Telephone: 011-49-30-240-7930.
Facsimile: 011-49-30-240-79344.
Mexico City, Mexico, D.F., Mexico Correspondent: Jáuregui, Navarrete, Nader y Rojas, S.C. Abogados, Paseo de la Reforma 199, Pisos 15, 16 y 17, 06500.
Telephone: 011-525-591-16-55.
Facsimile: 011-525-535-80-62, 011-525-703-22-47.
Cable: JANANE.

PARTNERS

Thierry G. F. Buytaert
S. Alan Hamburger (Not admitted in Belgium)

ASSOCIATES

Susan J. Launi
Caroline Neyrinck

For full biographical listings, see the Martindale-Hubbell Law Directory

SQUIRE, SANDERS & DEMPSEY

Avenue Louise, 165, Box 15, 1050 Brussels
Telephone: 011-32-2-648-1717
Cable Address: "Coxsquire"
TLX: 61961 Brussels Squire B
Fax: 011-32-2-648-1064
Cleveland, Ohio Office: 4900 Society Center, 127 Public Square, Cleveland, Ohio 44114-1304.
Telephone: 216-479-8500. Fax's: 216-479-8780, 216-479-8781, 216-479-8787, 216-479-8795, 216-479-8793, 216-479-8776, 216-479-8788.
Columbus, Ohio Offices: 1300 Huntington Center, 41 South High Street, Columbus, Ohio 43215.
Telephone: 614-365-2700.
Fax: 614-365-2499.
Jacksonville, Florida Office: One Enterprise Center, Suite 2100, 225 Water Street, Jacksonville, Florida 32202.
Telephone: 904-353-1264.
Fax: 904-356-2986.
Miami, Florida Office: 201 South Biscayne Boulevard, Suite 2900 Miami Center, Miami, Florida 33131.
Telephone: 305-577-8700.
Fax: 305-358-1425.
New York, New York Office: 520 Madison Avenue, 32nd Floor, New York, New York 10022.
Telephone: 212-872-9800.
Fax: 212-872-9814.

(See Next Column)

Phoenix, Arizona Office: Two Renaissance Square, 40 North Central Avenue, Suite 2700, Phoenix, Arizona 85004-4441.
Telephone: 602-528-4000.
Fax: 602-253-8129.
Washington, D.C. Office: 1201 Pennsylvania Avenue, N.W., P.O. Box 407, Washington, D.C. 20044.
Telephone: 202-626-6600.
Fax: 202-626-6780.
London, England Office: 1 Gunpowder Square, Printer Street, London EC4A 3DE.
Telephone: 011-44-71-830-0055.
Fax: 011-44-71-830-0056.
Prague Office: Adria Palace, Jungmannova 31/36, 11000 Prague 1, Czech Republic.
Telephone: 011-42-2-231-5661.
Fax: 011-42-2-231-5482.
Bratislava Office: Mudronova 37, 811 01 Bratislava, Slovak Republic.
Telephone: 011-42-7-313-362; 011-42-7-315-370.
Fax: 011-42-7-313-918.
Budapest, Hungary Office: Deak Ferenc Ut. 10, Office 304, H-1052 Budapest V., Hungary.
Telephone: 011-36-1-266-2024.
Fax: 011-36-1-226-2025.
Kiev, Ukraine Office: vul. Prorizna 9, Suite 20, Kiev 252035, Ukraine.
Telephones: 011-7-044-244-3452, 011-7-044-244-3453, 011-7-044-228-8687.
Fax: 011-7-044-228-4938.

RESIDENT PARTNERS

Thomas J. Ramsey (Not admitted in Belgium)
Brian Hartnett (Not admitted in Belgium)

RESIDENT OF COUNSEL

Guy J. Pevtchin

RESIDENT ASSOCIATES

Rebecca O'Donnell
Peter Alexiadas
Hartmut Seibel

(Not admitted to practice in Belgian courts)

For full biographical listings, see the Martindale-Hubbell Law Directory

THOMPSON, HINE AND FLORY

Rue des Chevaliers × Ridderstraat 14 - B.10, B-1050 Brussels
Telephone: 011(32-2) 511-9326
Fax: 011(32-2) 513-9206
Akron, Ohio Office: 50 S. Main Street, Suite 502, 44308-1828.
Telephone: 216-376-8090.
Fax: 216-376-8386.
Cincinnati, Ohio Office: 312 Walnut Street, 14th Floor, 45202-4029.
Telephone: 513-352-6700.
Fax: 513-241-4771.
Telex: 938003.
Cleveland, Ohio Office: 1100 National City Bank Building, 629 Euclid Avenue, 44114-3070.
Telephone: 216-566-5500.
Fax: 216-556-5583.
Telex: 980217. Cable Address "Thomflor".
Columbus, Ohio Office: One Columbus, 10 West Broad Street, 43215-3435.
Telephone: 614-469-3200.
Fax: 614-469-3361.
Dayton, Ohio Office: 2000 Courthouse Plaza, 45402-1706.
Telephone: 513-443-6600.
Fax: 513-443-6637; 443-6635.
Palm Beach, Florida Office: 125 Worth Avenue, 33480-4466.
Telephone: 407-833-5900.
Fax: 407-833-5951.
Washington, D.C. Office: 1920 N Street, N.W., 20036-1601.
Telephone: 202-331-8800.
Fax: 202-331-8330.
Telex: 904173.
Cable Address: "Caglaw".

RESIDENT COUNSEL

Ludo Deklerck

For full biographical listings, see the Martindale-Hubbell Law Directory

WILMER, CUTLER & PICKERING

Rue de la Loi 15 Wetstraat, B-1040 Brussels
Telephone: (32 2) 231-0903
Facsimile: (32 2) 230-4322
Washington, D.C. Office: 2445 M Street, N.W., 20037-1420.
Telephone: 202-663-6000.
Facsimile: 202-663-6363. Internet: Law@Wilmer.Com.
London, England Office: 4 Carlton Gardens, London, SW1Y 5AA.
Telephone: (44 71) 839-4466.
Facsimile: (44 71) 839-3537.
Berlin, Germany Office: Friedrichstrasse 95, D-10117.
Telephone: (49 30) 2643-3601.
Facsimile: (49 30) 2643-3630.

(See Next Column)

WILMER, CUTLER & PICKERING, *Brussels—Continued*

RESIDENT PARTNERS AND COUNSEL

W. Scott Blackmer (Not admitted in Belgium)
Dr. Andreas Weitbrecht (Not admitted in Belgium)
Paul A. von Hehn (Not admitted in Belgium)
Marc C. Hansen (Not admitted in Belgium)
James S. Venit (Not admitted in Belgium)

ASSOCIATES

Christian L. Duvernoy
Dr. Constantin Von Alvensleben
Sarah Waywell

For full biographical listings, see the Martindale-Hubbell Law Directory

WINTHROP, STIMSON, PUTNAM & ROBERTS

Rue Du Taciturne 42, Brussels B-1040
Telephone: 011-322-230-1392
Telefax: 011-322-230-9288
New York Main Office: One Battery Park Plaza. New York, N.Y., 10004-1490.
Telephone: 212-858-1000.
Stamford, Connecticut Office: Financial Centre, 695 East Main Street, P.O. Box 6760, 06904-6760.
Telephone: 203-348-2300.
Washington, D.C. Office: 1133 Connecticut Avenue, N.W., 20036.
Telephone: 202-775-9800.
Palm Beach, Florida Office: 125 Worth Avenue, 33480.
Telephone: 407-655-7297.
London Office: 2 Throgmorton Avenue, London EC2N 2AP, England.
Telephone: 011-4471-628-4931.
Toyko, Japan Office: 608 Atagoyama Bengoshi Building 6-7, Atago 1-chome, Minato-ku, Tokyo 105 Japan.
Telephone: 011-813-3437-9740.
Hong Kong Office: 2505 Asia Pacific Finance Tower, Citibank Plaza, 3 Garden Road Central.
Telephone: 011-852-530-3400.

MEMBER OF FIRM

Raymond S. Calamaro (Not admitted in Belgium)

RESIDENT ASSOCIATES

Jon G. Filipek (Not admitted in Belgium)
Rita Rique-Pearson

For full biographical listings, see the Martindale-Hubbell Law Directory

Canadian Lawyers In Brussels

FASKEN MARTINEAU

Avenue Franklin D. Roosevelt, 96 A, 1050 Brussels
Telephone: 2-640-9796
Facsimile: 2-640-2779
Fasken Martineau is a national and international firm composed of the partners and associates of Martineau Walker (Montreal and Quebec City, Quebec) and Fasken Campbell Godfrey (Toronto, Ontario). Fasken Martineau also has an office in London, England.
Montreal, Quebec, Canada Office: Martineau Walker, Stock Exchange Tower, Suite 3400. P.O. Box 242, 800 Place-Victoria, H4Z 1E9.
Telephone: 514-397-7400. Toll Free: 1-800-361-6266 (Ontario & Quebec).
Facsimile: 514-397-7600.
Telex: 05-24610 BUOY MTL.
Quebec City, Quebec, Canada Office: Martineau Walker, Immeuble Le Saint-Patrick, 140 rue Grande Allée est, bureau 800, G1R 5M8.
Telephone: 418-640-2000. Toll Free: 1-800-463-2827 (Ontario & Quebec).
Facsimile: 418-647-2455.
Toronto, Ontario, Canada: Fasken Campbell Godfrey, Toronto-Dominion Centre, Toronto Dominion Bank Tower, P.O. Box 20, M5K 1N6.
Telephones: 416-366-8381. Toll Free: 1-800-268-8424 (Ontario & Quebec).
Facsimile: 416-364-7813.
Vancouver (Affiliated): Davis & Company, 2800 Park Place, 666 Burrard Street, V6C 2Z7.
Telephone: 604-687-9444.
Fax: 604-687-1612.
London, England Office: Fasken Martineau, 10 Arthur Street, 5th Floor, EC4R 9AY.
Telephone: 71-929-2894.
Facsimile: 71-929-3634.

RESIDENT COUNSEL

Lucien Lamoureux, P.C., Q.C. (Resident)
(Not admitted to practice in Belgian courts)

For full biographical listings, see the Martindale-Hubbell Law Directory

LAFLEUR BROWN

Av. Louise 386, 1050 Brussels
Telephone: 011 322 647 1112; 647 7158
Telecopier: 011-322-648-7519
Montreal, Quebec Office: 1 Place Ville Marie, 37th Floor.
Telephone: 514-878-9641.
Telecopier: 514-878-1450.
Cable Address: "Mankin".
Telex: 05-25610.
Toronto, Ontario Office: Suite 920, 1 First Canadian Place.
Telephone: 416-869-0994.
Telecopier: 416-362-5818.

RESIDENT PARTNERS

Helene Deslauriers
Richard LaRue
(Not admitted to practice in Belgian courts)

For full biographical listings, see the Martindale-Hubbell Law Directory

BRAZIL

*BRASÍLIA,** Distrito Federal

EGITO COELHO, TRENCH E VEIRANO ADVOGADOS

(Associated Office of Baker & McKenzie)
SCS - Ed. Oscar Niemeyer, Conj. 601, 70316-900 Brasília
Telephone: (061) 224-4377
Intn'l Dialing: (55-61) 224-4377
Facsimile: (55-61) 226-6743
Associated Offices of Baker & McKenzie in: Almaty, Amsterdam, Bangkok, Barcelona, Beijing, Berlin, Bogotá, Brussels, Budapest, Buenos Aires, Cairo, Caracas, Chicago, Dallas, Frankfurt, Geneva, Hanoi, Ho Chi Minh City, Hong Kong, Juárez, Kiev, London, Madrid, Manila, Melbourne, México City, Miami, Milan, Monterrey, Moscow, New York, Palo Alto, Paris, Prague, Rio de Janeiro, Riyadh, Rome, St. Petersburg, San Diego, San Francisco, São Paulo, Singapore, Stockholm, Sydney, Taipei, Tijuana, Tokyo, Toronto, Valencia, Warsaw, Washington, D.C. and Zürich.
Correspondent Law Firm: Hadiputranto, Hadinoto & Partners, Jakarta.

LOCAL PARTNERS

Tulio Freitas do Egito Coelho
Fábio de Sousa Coutinho

ASSOCIATES

Julio Lopa Sélles Da Silva
Gisela Guimarães Farah

For full biographical listings, see the Martindale-Hubbell Law Directory

RIO DE JANEIRO, Rio de Janeiro, RJ

VEIRANO E ADVOGADOS ASSOCIADOS

(Associated Office of Baker & McKenzie)
Av. Nilo Peçanha, 50 - 17th Floor Edificio Rodolpho de Paoli, 20044-900 Rio de Janeiro
Telephone: (021) 282-1232
Intn'l. Dialing: (55-21) 282-1232
Cable Address: ABOGADO-RIO
Telex: 2130413
Answerback: 2130413 ABOG BR
Facsimile: (55-21) 262-4247
Postal Address: Caixa Postal 2748, RJ, Rio de Janeiro
Associated Offices of Baker & McKenzie in: Almaty, Amsterdam, Bangkok, Barcelona, Beijing, Berlin, Bogotá, Brasília, Brussels, Budapest, Buenos Aires, Cairo, Caracas, Chicago, Dallas, Frankfurt, Geneva, Hanoi, Ho Chi Minh City, Hong Kong, Juárez, Kiev, London, Madrid, Manila, Melbourne, México City, Miami, Milan, Monterrey, Moscow, New York, Palo Alto, Paris, Prague, Riyadh, Rome, St. Petersburg, San Diego, San Francisco, São Paulo, Singapore, Stockholm, Sydney, Taipei, Tijuana, Tokyo, Toronto, Valencia, Warsaw, Washington, D.C. and Zürich.
Correspondent Law Firm: Hadiputranto, Hadinoto & Partners, Jakarta.

PARTNERS

Robson Goulart Barreto
Carlos Americo Ferraz e Castro
Gabriel Araujo de Lacerda
Kevin L. Mundie (Not admitted in Brazil)
Ricardo Coelho Salles
Paulo Cesar Gonçalves Simões
Ronaldo Camargo Veirano

OF COUNSEL

Jorge Ibrain Salluh

LOCAL PARTNERS

Ligia Ciancaglini
Fábio Amaral Figueira
Luiz Guilherme Moraes Rego Migliora
Valdir de Oliveira Rocha Filho

RESIDENT ASSOCIATES

Mario Neder de Araujo
Luiz Fernando Fraga
Mônica Maria Moreira Carneiro Kurtz
Claudio D. Lampert
Marcelo Ribeiro Mattos
Nilo Cunha Furtado de Mendonça
Luis Fernando Ayres de Mello Pacheco

(See Next Column)

VEIRANO E ADVOGADOS ASSOCIADOS—*Continued*

RESIDENT ASSOCIATES (Continued)

Paula Monnerat de Araujo Penna Porto
Rodolpho de Oliveira Franco Protásio
Guilherme Guerra d'Arriaga Schmidt
Bruno C. Soter Da Silveira
Eduardo M. Zobaran

For full biographical listings, see the Martindale-Hubbell Law Directory

SÃO PAULO, São Paulo

TRENCH, ROSSI E WATANABE

(Associated Office of Baker & McKenzie)
Rua Martiniano de Carvalho, 1049, Paraiso, CEP 01321 - 905, São Paulo SP
Telephone: (011) 253-7999
Intn'l. Dialing: (55-11) 253-7999
Cable Address: ABOGADO
Telex: 1132393
Answer Back: 1132393 ABOG BR
Facsimiles: (55-11) 287-6967; 287-6256
Postal Address: Caixa Postal 2673, CEP 01060-970
Associated Offices of Baker & McKenzie in: Almaty, Amsterdam, Bangkok, Barcelona, Beijing, Berlin, Bogotá, Brasília, Brussels, Budapest, Buenos Aires, Cairo, Caracas, Chicago, Dallas, Frankfurt, Geneva, Hanoi, Ho Chi Minh City, Hong Kong, Juárez, Kiev, London, Madrid, Manila, Melbourne, México City, Miami, Milan, Monterrey, Moscow, New York, Palo Alto, Paris, Prague, Rio de Janeiro, Riyadh, Rome, St. Petersburg, San Diego, San Francisco, Singapore, Stockholm, Sydney, Taipei, Tijuana, Tokyo, Toronto, Valencia, Warsaw, Washington, D.C. and Zürich.
Correspondent Law Firm: Hadiputranto, Hadinoto & Partners, Jakarta.

PARTNERS

Sérgio Paula Souza Caiuby
Virgílio Garcia Cassemunha
Augusto Marianno Dias Netto
Antonio Carlos S. Farroco, Jr.
Eduardo de Cerqueira Leite
Dagmar da Silva Lisboa
Claudia Farkouh Prado
Carlos Alberto de Souza Rossi
Luiz Antonio D'Arace Vergueiro
Juliana Laura Bruna Viegas
Kazuo Watanabe

ASSOCIATES

Silvana Benincasa Campos
Fátima Aparecida Carr
Zélia Cunha Castro
Hércules Celescuekci
Isabel R. De Sio Perez (Not admitted in Brazil)
Esther Miriam Flesch
José Roberto Baldoini Martins
Antonio Carlos C. Mazzuco
Gilberto de Castro Moreira
Alberto Mori
Francisco Toshio Ohno
Débora Marcondes Fernandez Pecucci
Marcelo Vilas Bôas Pegoraro
Antonio Urbino Penna, Jr.
Mary H. Swanson (Not admitted in Brazil)
Caterina Tancredi

For full biographical listings, see the Martindale-Hubbell Law Directory

PEOPLE'S REPUBLIC OF CHINA

*BEIJING (PEKING),**

American Lawyers In Beijing (Peking)

BAKER & MCKENZIE

Suite 2526 China World Tower China World Trade Center, 1 Jianguomenwai Dajie, 100004 Beijing (Peking)
Telephone: 505-0591; 505-0592; 505-4867; 505-4967; 505-4969; 505-2288, Ext. 2596
Intn'l. Dialing: (86-1) 505-0591; 505-0592; 505-4867; 505-4967; 505-4969; *505-2288, Ext. 2526*
Cable: ABOGADO BEIJING
Telex: 22907
Answer Back: 22907 ABOGA CN
Facsimiles: (86-1) 505-2309; 505-0378
Associated Offices of Baker & McKenzie in: Almaty, Amsterdam, Bangkok, Barcelona, Berlin, Bogotá, Brasília, Brussels, Budapest, Buenos Aires, Cairo, Caracas, Chicago, Dallas, Frankfurt, Geneva, Hanoi, Ho Chi Minh City, Hong Kong, Juárez, Kiev, London, Madrid, Manila, Melbourne, México City, Miami, Milan, Monterrey, Moscow, New York, Palo Alto, Paris, Prague, Rio de Janeiro, Riyadh, Rome, St. Petersburg, San Diego, San Francisco, São Paulo, Singapore, Stockholm, Sydney, Taipei, Tijuana, Tokyo, Toronto, Valencia, Warsaw, Washington, D.C. and Zürich.
Correspondent Law Firm: Hadiputranto, Hadinoto & Partners, Jakarta.

PARTNER

Michael J. Moser (Not admitted in People's Republic of China)

LOCAL PARTNER

Yuehua Liu

(See Next Column)

ASSOCIATES

Michael A. Aldrich (Not admitted in People's Republic of China)
Jon S. Eichelberger (Not admitted in People's Republic of China)
Allan K. A. Marson (Not admitted in People's Republic of China)
Paul D. McKenzie (Not admitted in People's Republic of China)
John W. Sullivan, III (Not admitted in People's Republic of China)

CONSULTANT

Xiangyang Ge

For full biographical listings, see the Martindale-Hubbell Law Directory

KAYE, SCHOLER, FIERMAN, HAYS & HANDLER

Scite Tower, Suite 708, 22 Jianguomenwai Dajie, 100004 Beijing (Peking)
Telephone: 861-5124755
Telex: 222540 KAY CN
Facsimile: 861-5124760
New York, N.Y.: 425 Park Avenue, 10022.
Telephone: 212-836-8000.
Telex: 234860 KAY UR.
Facsimile: 212-836-8689.
Washington, D.C.: McPherson Building, 901 Fifteenth Street, N.W., Suite 1100, 20005.
Telephone: 202-682-3500.
Telex: 897458 KAYSCHOL WSH.
Facsimile: 202-682-3580.
Los Angeles, California: 1999 Avenue of the Stars, Suite 1600, 90067.
Telephone: 213-788-1000.
Facsimile: 213-788-1200.
Hong Kong: 9 Queen Road Centre, 18th Floor.
Telephone: 852-8458989.
Telex: 62816 KAY HX.
Facsimile: 852-8453682; 852-8452389.

PARTNERS

Franklin D. Chu (Not admitted in People's Republic of China)

For full biographical listings, see the Martindale-Hubbell Law Directory

SHEARMAN & STERLING

Suite #2205, Capital Mansion, No. 6, Xin Yuan Nan Road Chao Yang District, Beijing (Peking) 100004
Telephone: (861) 465-4574
Fax: (861) 465-4578
New York, N.Y. Office: 599 Lexington Avenue, New York, New York 10022-6069 and Citicorp Center, 153 East 53rd Street, New York, New York 10022-4676.
Telephone: (212) 848-4000.
Telex: 667290 Num Lau.
Fax: 599 Lexington Avenue: (212) 848-7179. Citicorp Center: (212) 848-5252.
Abu Dhabi, United Arab Emirates Office: P.O. Box 2948.
Telephone: (971-2) 324477.
Fax: (971-2) 774533.
Budapest, Hungary Office: Szerb utca 17-19, 1056 Budapest.
Telephone: (36-1) 266-3522.
Fax: (36-1) 266-3523.
Düsseldorf, Federal Republic of Germany Office: Königsallee 46, D-40212 Düsseldorf.
Telephone: (49-211) 13 62 80.
Telex: 8 588 294 NYLO.
Fax: (49-211) 13 33 09.
Frankfurt, Federal Republic of Germany Office: Bockenheimer Landstrasse 55, D-60325 Frankfurt am Main.
Telephone: (49-69) 97-10-70.
Fax: (49-69) 97-10-71-00.
Hong Kong, Hong Kong Office: Standard Chartered Bank Building, 4 Des Voeux Road Central, Hong Kong.
Telephone: (852) 2978-8000.
Fax: (852) 2978-8099.
London, England Office: 199 Bishopsgate, London EC2M 3TY.
Telephone: (44-71) 920-9000.
Fax: (44-71) 920-9020.
Los Angeles, California Office: 725 South Figueroa Street, 21st Floor, 90017-5421.
Telephone: (213) 239-0300.
Fax: (213) 239-0381, 614-0936.
Paris, France Office: 12 rue d'Astorg, 75008.
Telephone: (33-1) 44-71-17-17.
Telex: 282964 Royale.
Fax: (33-1) 44-71-01-01.
San Francisco, California Office: 555 California Street, 94104-1522.
Telephone: (415) 616-1100.
Fax: (415) 616-1199.
Taipei, Taiwan Office: 7th Floor, Hung Kuo Building, 167 Tun Hwa North Road.
Telephone: (886-2) 545-3300.
Fax: (866-2) 545-3322.

(See Next Column)

SHEARMAN & STERLING, *Beijing (Peking)—Continued*

Tokyo, Japan Office: Shearman & Sterling (Thomas Wilner Gaikokuho-Jimu-Bengoshi Jimusho), Fukoku Seimei Building, 5th Fl. 2-2-2, Uchisaiwaicho, Chiyoda-ku, Tokyo 100, Japan.
Telephone: (81 3) 5251-1601.
Fax: (81 3) 5251-1602.
Toronto, Ontario, Canada Office: Commerce Court West, Suite 4405, P.O. Box 247, M5L 1E8.
Telephone: (416) 360-8484.
Fax: (416) 360-2958.
Washington, D.C. Office: 801 Pennsylvania Avenue, N.W., Suite 900, 20004-2604.
Telephone: (202) 508-8000.
Fax: (202) 508-8100.

RESIDENT ASSOCIATES

Hong Liu (Not admitted in People's Republic of China)

For full biographical listings, see the Martindale-Hubbell Law Directory

COLOMBIA

*BOGOTÁ,**

RAISBECK, LARA, RODRIGUEZ & RUEDA

(Associated Office of Baker & McKenzie)
Calle 35 No. 7-25, 4th Floor, Bogotá D.C.
Telephone: 285-1400
Intn'l. Dialing: (57-1) 285-1400
Telex: 43282
Answer Back: 43282 ABOGA CO
Facsimile: (57-1) 285-6908
Associated Offices of Baker & McKenzie in: Almaty, Amsterdam, Bangkok, Barcelona, Beijing, Berlin, Brasília, Brussels, Budapest, Buenos Aires, Cairo, Caracas, Chicago, Dallas, Frankfurt, Geneva, Hanoi, Ho Chi Minh City, Hong Kong, Juárez, Kiev, London, Madrid, Manila, Melbourne, México City, Miami, Milan, Monterrey, Moscow, New York, Palo Alto, Paris, Prague, Rio de Janeiro, Riyadh, Rome, St. Petersburg, San Diego, San Francisco, São Paulo, Singapore, Stockholm, Sydney, Taipei, Tijuana, Tokyo, Toronto, Valencia, Warsaw, Washington, D.C. and Zürich.
Correspondent Law Firm: Hadiputranto, Hadinoto & Partners, Jakarta.
Postal Address: Apartado Aereo No. 3746

Alvaro Correa O.
Antonio Duarte-Amezquita
Jorge Lara-Urbaneja
James W. F. Raisbeck
Robert B. Raisbeck
Jorge Rodríguez Rojas
Sergio Rueda
Eduardo Zuleta

OF COUNSEL

Carlos Del Castillo

Michael Anderson-Gómez
William J. Araque-Jaimes
Maria F. Carvajal Navia
Martha Tatiana Garces-Carvajal
Juan Manuel Garrido-Diaz
Hugo A. Gonzalez Castellanos
Mark Laskay (Not admitted in Colombia)
Maria Clara López
Graciela Melo Sarmiento
Carlos A. Olarte-Garcia (Not admitted in Colombia)
Juan Carlos Restrepo
Maria Consuelo Rozo-Caro
Maria Claudia Rueda
Sylvia Rueda Iglesias
Maria Mercedes Samudio
Jaime H. Tobar Ordoñez
Jaime E. Trujillo Caiceda
Luz Helena Villamil-Jiménez

For full biographical listings, see the Martindale-Hubbell Law Directory

CZECH REPUBLIC

PRAGUE,

American Lawyers In Prague

BAKER & MCKENZIE

Čelakovského Sady, No. 4
Telephone: Telephone: (02) 24 22 7330; 24 22 5687; 265 492; 268 536; 262 792; 262 391
Int'l Dialing: (42-2) 24 22 7330; 24 22 5687; 265 492; 268 536; 262 792; 262 391
Facsimile: (42-2) 24 22 2124; 26 75 26
Chgo., IL
Associated Offices of Baker & McKenzie in: Almaty, Amsterdam, Bangkok, Barcelona, Beijing, Berlin, Bogotá, Brasília, Brussels, Budapest, Buenos Aires, Cairo, Caracas, Chicago, Dallas, Frankfurt, Geneva, Hanoi, Ho Chi Minh City, Hong Kong, Juárez, Kiev, London, Madrid, Manila, Melbourne, México City, Miami, Milan, Monterrey, Moscow, New York, Palo Alto, Paris, Rio de Janeiro, Riyadh, Rome, St. Petersburg, San Diego, San Francisco, São Paulo, Singapore, Stockholm, Sydney, Taipei, Tijuana, Tokyo, Toronto, Valencia, Warsaw, Washington, D.C. and Zürich.

(See Next Column)

Correspondent Law Firm: Hadiputranto, Hadinoto & Partners, Jakarta.

PARTNERS

Dr. Martin Radvan

ASSOCIATES

Dr. Andrea Bednaříková
Edmund J. Gemmell (Not admitted in Czech Republic)
Romain Nacu
Dr. František Schulmann
Marek J. Svoboda (Not admitted in Czech Republic)

For full biographical listings, see the Martindale-Hubbell Law Directory

SQUIRE, SANDERS & DEMPSEY

Adria Palace, Jungmannova 31/36, CSFR 11000 Prague
Telephone: 011-42-2-231-5661; 011-42-2-231-5678; 011-42-2-231-5698
Fax: 011-42-2-231-5482
Cleveland, Ohio Office: 4900 Society Center, 127 Public Square, Cleveland, Ohio 44114-1304.
Telephone: 216-479-8500. Fax's: 216-479-8780, 216-479-8781, 216-479-8787, 216-479-8795, 216-479-8777, 216-479-8793, 216-479-8776, 216-479-8788.
Columbus, Ohio Offices: 1300 Huntington Center, 41 South High Street, Columbus, Ohio 43215.
Telephone: 614-365-2700.
Fax: 614-365-2499.
Jacksonville, Florida Office: One Enterprise Center, Suite 2100, 225 Water Street, Jacksonville, Florida 32202.
Telephone: 904-353-1264.
Fax: 904-356-2986.
Miami, Florida Office: 201 South Biscayne Boulevard, Suite 2900 Miami Center, Miami, Florida 33131.
Telephone: 305-577-8700.
Fax: 305-358-1425.
New York, New York Office: 520 Madison Avenue, 32nd Floor, New York, New York 10022.
Telephone: 212-715-4990.
Fax: 212-715-4915.
Phoenix, Arizona Office: Two Renaissance Square, 40 North Central Avenue, Suite 2700, Phoenix, Arizona 85004-4441.
Telephone: 602-528-4000.
Fax: 602-253-8129.
Washington, D.C. Office: 1201 Pennsylvania Avenue, N.W., P.O. Box 407, Washington, D.C. 20044.
Telephone: 202-626-6600.
Fax: 202-626-6780.
London, England Office: 1 Gunpowder Square, Printer Street, London EC4A 3DE.
Telephone: 011-44-71-830-0055.
Fax: 011-44-71-830-0056.
Brussels, Belgium Office: Avenue Louise, 165-Box 15, 1050 Brussels, Belgium.
Telephone: 011-32-2-648-1717.
Fax: 011-32-2-648-1064.
Bratislava Office: Mudronova 37, 811 01 Bratislava, Slovak Republic.
Telephone: 011-42-7-313-362; 011-42-7-315-370.
Fax: 011-42-7-313-918.
Budapest, Hungary Office: Deak Ferenc Ut. 10, Office 304, H-1052 Budapest V., Hungary.
Telephones: 011-36-1-266-2024.
Fax: 011-36-1-226-2025.
Kiev, Ukraine Office: vul. Prorizna 9, Suite 20, Kiev 252035, Ukraine.
Telephones: 011-7-044-244-3452, 011-7-044-244-3453, 011-7-044-228-8687.
Fax: 011-7-044-228-4938.

PARTNERS

James F. Allen (Not admitted in Czech Republic)
Jan Matejcek (Not admitted in Czech Republic)
Richard S. Surrey (Not admitted in Czech Republic)
Carol M. Welu (Not admitted in Czech Republic)

OF COUNSEL

John M. Clapp (Not admitted in Czech Republic)
Julian Juhasz (Not admitted in Czech Republic)
Jaromir Ruzicka

COUNSEL

Ivan Cestr
Rudolf Kožušník
Lubos Tichy

RESIDENT ASSOCIATES

John G. Loughrey (Not admitted in Czech Republic)
Kevin T. Connor (Not admitted in Czech Republic)
Roland J. Behm (Not admitted in Czech Republic)
Oliver C. Brahmst (Not admitted in Czech Republic)
Evan Z. Lazar (Not admitted in Czech Republic)
Heidi Pemberton (Not admitted in Czech Republic)
Janet Levine Nahirny (Not admitted in Czech Republic)
Sasha S. Stepan (Not admitted in Czech Republic)

(Not admitted to practice in Czech courts)

For full biographical listings, see the Martindale-Hubbell Law Directory

EGYPT

*CAIRO,**

BAKER & MCKENZIE

Twentieth Floor, 56 Gamyat El Dowal El Arabeya Street Mohandessin, Giza, Cairo
Telephone: 360-0071; 360-0072; 360-9571; 360-9572
Intn'l Dialing: (20-2) 360-0071; 360-0072; 360-9571; 360-9572
Telex: 21847
Answer Back: 21847 ABOGA UN
Facsimile: (20-2) 360-0073
Associated Offices of Baker & McKenzie in: Almaty, Amsterdam, Bangkok, Barcelona, Beijing, Berlin, Bogotá, Brasília, Brussels, Budapest, Buenos Aires, Caracas, Chicago, Dallas, Frankfurt, Geneva, Hanoi, Ho Chi Minh City, Hong Kong, Juárez, Kiev, London, Madrid, Manila, Melbourne, México City, Miami, Milan, Monterrey, Moscow, New York, Palo Alto, Paris, Prague, Rio de Janeiro, Riyadh, Rome, St. Petersburg, San Diego, San Francisco, São Paulo, Singapore, Stockholm, Sydney, Taipei, Tijuana, Tokyo, Toronto, Valencia, Warsaw, Washington, D.C. and Zürich.
Correspondent Law Firm: Hadiputranto, Hadinoto & Partners, Jakarta.

PARTNERS

Samir M. Hamza
M. Taher Helmy

LOCAL PARTNER

Mohammad B. Samih Talaat

ASSOCIATES

Karim Ali Azmi
Hatem Sayed Badr (Not admitted in Egypt)
Sherif Ali Khalil El Atfy
Mohamed Adel Ghannam
Mohamed Adel Nour

For full biographical listings, see the Martindale-Hubbell Law Directory

EIRE

— (See Ireland)

ENGLAND

*LONDON,**

American Lawyers In London

BIGHAM ENGLAR JONES & HOUSTON

Lloyds Suite 699, 1 Lime Street, London EC3M 7DQ
Telephone: 71-283-9541
Cable: "Kedge"
Telex: 893323 BEJH G
Telefax: 016262382 GR I II III
New York, N.Y. Office: 14 Wall Street, 10005-2140.
Telephone: 212-732-4646.
Cable: "Kedge."
Telex: RCA 235332 BEJHUR.
Telefax: 2126190781 GR I II III; 2122279491 GR I II III.
Newark, New Jersey Office: One Gateway Center, 07102-5311.
Telephone: 201-643-1303.
Telecopier: 201-643-1124.

RESIDENT ASSOCIATES

Christopher J. Keegan (Resident Associate, London, England)
Michelle L. Wilson (Resident Associate, London, England)

(Not admitted to practice in English courts)

For full biographical listings, see the Martindale-Hubbell Law Directory

BINGHAM, DANA & GOULD

39 Victoria Street, London SWIH 0EE
Telephone: 011-44-71-799-2646
Telecopy: 011-44-71-799-2654
Boston, Massachusetts Office: 150 Federal Street.
Telephone: 617-951-8000.
Telecopy: 617-951-8736.
Hartford, Connecticut Office: 100 Pearl Street.
Telephone: 203-244-3770.
Telefax: 203-527-5188.
Washington, D.C. Office: 1550 M Street, N.W.
Telephone: 202-822-9320.
Telecopy: 202-833-1506.

RESIDENT PARTNERS

Jay S. Zimmerman (Not admitted in England)
Mark A. Andrew (Not admitted in England)

RESIDENT ASSOCIATES

T. Malcolm Sandilands (Not admitted in England)
Loraine de Jong (Not admitted in England)
Susan Spring

(See Next Column)

(Not admitted to practice in English courts)

For full biographical listings, see the Martindale-Hubbell Law Directory

CHADBOURNE & PARKE

86 Jermyn Street, SW1 6JD London
Telephone: 44-171-925-7400
Facsimile: 44-171-839-3393
New York, N.Y. Office: 30 Rockefeller Plaza, 10112.
Telephone: 212-408-5100.
Telecopier: 212-541-5369.
Washington, D.C. Office: Suite 900, 1101 Vermont Avenue, N.W., 20005.
Telephone: 202-289-3000.
Telecopier: 202-289-3002.
Los Angeles, California Office: 601 South Figueroa Street, 90017.
Telephone: 213-892-1000.
Telecopier: 213-622-9865.
Moscow, Russia Office: 38 Maxim Gorky Naberezhnaya, 113035.
Telephone: 7095-974-2424.
Telecopier: 7095-974-2425, International satellite lines via U.S.:
Telephone: 212-408-1190.
Telecopier: 212-408-1199.
Hong Kong Office: Suite 3704, Peregrine Tower, Lippo Centre, 89 Queensway.
Telephone: (852) 2842-5400.
Telecopier: (852) 2521-7527.
New Delhi, India Office: Chadbourne & Parke Associates, A16-B Anand Niketan, 110 021.
Telephone: 91-11-301-7568/7581/7582.
Telecopier: 91-11-301-7351.

RESIDENT PARTNER

Paul A. Randour (Not admitted in England)

RESIDENT COUNSEL

Peter K. Eck (Not admitted in England)

For full biographical listings, see the Martindale-Hubbell Law Directory

CLEARY, GOTTLIEB, STEEN & HAMILTON

City Place House, 55 Basinghall Street, London EC2V 5EH
Telephone: 44-71-614-2200
Cable Address: "Cleargolaw London"
Telex: 887659.
Facsimile: Gps. 3 44-71-600-1698; 44-71-588-5163
New York, New York Office: One Liberty Plaza, New York, N.Y. 10006.
Telephone: 212-225-2000.
Washington, D.C. Office: 1752 N Street, N.W., Washington, D.C. 20036.
Telephone: 202-728-2700.
Paris, France Office: 41, Avenue de Friedland, 75008 Paris, France.
Telephone: 33-1-4074-6800.
Brussels, Belgium Office: Rue de la Loi 23, Bte 5, 1040 Brussels, Belgium.
Telephone: 32-2-287-2000.
Hong Kong Office: 56th Floor, Bank of China Tower, One Garden Road, Hong Kong.
Telephone: 852-521-4122.
Tokyo, Japan Office: Morgan Carroll Terai Gaikokuho Jimubengoshi Jimusho, 20th Floor, Shin Kasumigaseki Building, 3-2, Kasumigaseki 3-Chome, Chiyoda-Ku, Tokyo 100, Japan.
Telephone: 81-3-3595-3911.
Frankfurt, Germany Office: Ulmenstrasse 37-39, 60325 Frankfurt am Main, Germany.
Telephone: 49-69-971-03-0.

RESIDENT PARTNERS

Manley O. Hudson, Jr. (Not admitted in England)
James A. Duncan (Not admitted in England)
Edward F. Greene (Not admitted in England)
Daniel A. Braverman (Not admitted in England)
Glen M. Scarcliffe

ASSOCIATES

Sebastian R. Sperber (Not admitted in England)
Clinton H. Elliott (Not admitted in England)
Ann K. Laemmle (Not admitted in England)
Elena L. Daly (Not admitted in England)
Jennifer M. Schneck (Not admitted in England)
Michael T. Prior (Not admitted in England)
Phoebe B. McKinnell (Not admitted in England)
Jacqueline Duval-Major (Not admitted in England)
Christopher J. Walton (Not admitted in England)
John L. Farry (Not admitted in England)
Robert T. Bradford (Not admitted in England)
David A. Christman (Not admitted in England)
Ashar Qureshi (Not admitted in England)

(Not admitted to practice in English courts)

For full biographical listings, see the Martindale-Hubbell Law Directory

COUDERT BROTHERS

A Partnership of English Solicitors
and Registered Foreign Lawyers
20 Old Bailey, London EC4M 7JP
Telephone: (44) (71) 248-3000
Telex: 887071 Couder G
Cable Address: "Treduoc" London
Telecopier: (44) (71) 248-3001, 248-3002
New York, New York 10036-7794: 1114 Avenue of the Americas.
Washington, D.C. 20006: 1627 I Street, N.W.
Los Angeles, California 90017: 1055 West Seventh Street, Twentieth Floor.
San Francisco, California 94111: 4 Embarcadero Center, Suite 3330.
San Jose, California 95113: Suite 1250, Ten Almaden Boulevard.
Paris 75008, France: Coudert Frères, 52 Avenue des Champs-Elysées.
Brussels B-1050, Belgium: Tour Louise. 149 Avenue Louise-Box 8.
Beijing, People's Republic of China 100020: Suite 2708-09 Jing Guang Centre Hu Jia Lou, Chao Yang Qu.
Shanghai, People's Republic of China 200002: c/o Suite 1804, Union Building, 100 Yanan Road East.
Hong Kong: 25th Floor, Nine Queen's Road Central.
Singapore 0104: Tung Centre, 20 Collyer Quay.
Sydney N.S.W. 2000, Australia: Suite 2202, State Bank Centre, 52 Martin Place.
Tokyo 107, Japan: 1355 West Tower, Aoyama Twin Towers, 1-1-1 Minami-Aoyama, Minato-ku.
Moscow, Russia: Ulitsa Staraya Basmannaya 14.
01301 Sao Paulo, SP, Brazil: Machado, Meyer, Sendacz, e Opice, Advogados, Rua da Consolacao, 247, 8 Andar.
Bangkok 10500, Thailand: Bubhajit Building, 20 North Sathorn Road, 10th Floor. Ho Chi Minh City, Vietnam: c/o Saigon Business Centre, 49-57 Dong Du Street, District 1.

RESIDENT PARTNERS

Barry Metzger (Not admitted in England)
Steven R. Beharrell
Philip Anthony Burroughs
Hugh E. Thompson
Julian D.M. Lew (Resident)
Colin D. Long
Jeremy McCallum
Peter F. Simpson

RESIDENT ASSOCIATES

Stuart Blythe
Sara Bond
Jonathan Bor
Michael P. Chissick
Samantha Crowfoot
Richard Kennedy Guelff (Not admitted in England)
Julian E. James
Dean Poster
Julian Stait
Kim Hoa To

(Not admitted to practice in English courts)

For full biographical listings, see the Martindale-Hubbell Law Directory

CRAVATH, SWAINE & MOORE

33 King William Street, 10th Floor, London EC4R 9DU
Telephone: 071-606-1421
Facsimile: 071-860-1150
New York City Office: Worldwide Plaza, 825 Eighth Avenue, 10019.
Telephone: 212-474-1000.
Facsimile: 212-474-3700.
Cable Address: "Cravath, New York".
Telex: 1-25547.
Hong Kong Office: Suite 2609, Asia Pacific Finance Tower, Citibank Plaza, 3 Garden Road, Central, Hong Kong.
Telephone: 852-509-7200.
Facsimile: 852-509-8282.

RESIDENT PARTNER

John E. Young (Not admitted in England)

EUROPEAN COUNSEL

Sarah C. Murphy (Not admitted in England)

(Not admitted to practice in English courts)

For full biographical listings, see the Martindale-Hubbell Law Directory

CROWELL & MORING

Denning House 90 Chancery Lane, London WC2A 1ED
Telephone: 011-44-71-413-0011
Fax: 011-44-71-413-0333
Washington, D.C. Office: 1001 Pennsylvania Avenue, N.W., 20004-2595.
Telephone: 202-624-2500.
Telex: W.U.I. (International) 64344; W.U. (Domestic) 89-2448.
Cable Address: "Cromor."
Fax: (202) 628-5116.
Irvine, California Office: 2010 Main Street, Suite 1200, 92714-7217.
Telephone: 714-263-8400.
Fax: 714-263-8414.

OF COUNSEL

Anthony J. Coleby
Peter A. D. Teare

ASSOCIATES

Susan E. McLaughlin
Sarah E. Lambie

For full biographical listings, see the Martindale-Hubbell Law Directory

CURTIS, MALLET-PREVOST, COLT & MOSLE

Two Throgmorton Avenue, London EC2N 2DL
Telephone: 71-638-7957
Telecopier: 71-638-5512
New York, New York Office: 101 Park Avenue, 10178-0061.
Telephone: 212-696-6000.
Telecopier: 212-697-1559.
Cable Address: "Migniard New York".
Telex: 12-6811 Migniard; ITT 422127 MGND.
Newark, New Jersey Office: One Gateway Center, Suite 403.
Telephone: 201-622-0605.
Telecopier: 201-622-5646.
Washington, D.C. 20006 Office: Suite 1205L, 1801 K Street, N.W.
Telephone: 202-452-7373.
Telecopier: 202-452-7333.
Telex: ITT 440379 CMPUI.
Houston, Texas Office: 2 Houston Center, 909 Fannin Street, Suite 3725.
Telephone: 713-759-9555.
Telecopier: 713-759-0712.
Mexico City, D.F., Mexico Office: Torre Chapultepec, Ruben Dario 281, Col. Bosques de Chapultepec, 11530 Mexico, D.F.
Telephone: 525-282-0444.
Telecopier: 525-282-0637.
Paris, France Office: 8 Avenue Victor Hugo, 75116 Paris.
Telephone: 45-00-99-68.
Telecopier: 45-00-84-06.
Frankfurt am Main 1 Office: Staufenstrasse 42.
Telephone: 069-971-4420.
Telecopier: 69-17 33 99.

RESIDENT PARTNER

Bruce B. Palmer (Not admitted in England)

RESIDENT ASSOCIATES

Robert N. Dawbarn
Robert E. Stemmons (Not admitted in England)

(Not admitted to practice in English courts)

For full biographical listings, see the Martindale-Hubbell Law Directory

DAVIS POLK & WARDWELL

1 Frederick's Place, London EC2R 8AB
Telephone: 011-44-71-418-1300
Telex: 888238
Telecopier: 011-44-71-418-1400
New York, N.Y. Office: 450 Lexington Avenue, 10017.
Telephone: 212-450-4000.
Cable Address: "Davispolk New York".
Telex: ITT-421341; ITT-423356.
Telecopier: 212-450-4800.
Washington, D.C. Office: 1300 I Street, N.W., 20005.
Telephone: 202-962-7000.
Telecopier: 202-962-7111.
Paris, France Office: 4, Place de la Concorde, 75008.
Telephone: 011-331-4017-3600.
Telecopier: 011-331-42.65.22.34.
Cable Address: "Davispolk Paris".
Tokyo, Japan Office: In Tokyo practicing as Reid Gaikokuho-Jimu-Bengoshi Jimusho. Tokio Kaijo Building Annex, 2-1, Marunouchi 1-Chome, Chiyoda-Ku, Tokyo 100, Japan.
Telephone: 011-81-3-201-8421.
Telecopier: 011-81-3-201-8444.
Telex: 2224472 DPWTOK.
Frankfurt, Germany Office: MesseTurm, 60308 Frankfurt am Main, Federal Republic of Germany.
Telephone: 011-49-69-97-57-03-0.
Telecopier: 011-49-69-74-77-44.
Hong Kong Office: The Hong Kong Club Building, 3A Chater Road.
Telephone: 852 533 3300.
Fax: 852 533 3388.

SENIOR COUNSEL

Joseph Chubb (Not admitted in England)

RESIDENT PARTNERS

Paul Kumleben
David M. Wells (Not admitted in England)

COUNSEL

John D. Paton

SENIOR ATTORNEY

Jeffrey M. Oakes (Not admitted in England)

ASSOCIATES

Julia K. Cowles (Not admitted in England)
Lisa F. Firenze (Not admitted in England)
Miriam Haber (Not admitted in England)
Marcelle R. Joseph (Not admitted in England)
Stowell R. R. Kelner (Not admitted in England)
Deanna L. Kirkpatrick (Not admitted in England)
Reinhard B. Koester (Not admitted in England)
Nicholas Adams Kronfeld (Not admitted in England)
Michael T. Mollerus (Not admitted in England)

(See Next Column)

DAVIS POLK & WARDWELL—*Continued*

(Not admitted to practice in English courts)

For full biographical listings, see the Martindale-Hubbell Law Directory

DEBEVOISE & PLIMPTON

1 Creed Court, 5 Ludgate Hill, London EC4M 7AA
Telephone: (44-171) 329-0779
Telecopier: (44-171) 329-0860
New York Office: 875 Third Avenue, 10022.
Telephone: 212-909-6000.
Telex: (Domestic) 148377 DEBSTEVE NYK.
Telecopier: (212) 909-6836.
Washington, D.C. Office: 555 13th Street, N.W., 20004.
Telephone: 202-383-8000.
Telex: 405586 DPDC WUUD.
Telecopier: (202) 383-8118.
Los Angeles, California Office: 601 South Figueroa Street, Suite 3700, 90017.
Telephone: 213-680-8000.
Telecopier: 213-680-8100.
Paris, France Office: 21 Avenue George V, 75008.
Telephone: (33-1) 40 73 12 12.
Telecopier: (33-1) 47 2050 82.
Telex: 648141F DPPAR.
Budapest, Hungary Office: 1065 Budapest, Révay Köz 2.III/2.
Telephone: (36-1) 112-8067.
Telecopier: (36-1) 132-7995.
Hong Kong Office: 13/F Entertainment Building, 30 Queen's Road Central.
Telephone: (852) 2810-7918.
Fax: (852) 2810-9828.

RESIDENT PARTNERS

George B. Adams (Not admitted in England)
Robert R. Bruce (Not admitted in England)
Hugh Rowland, Jr. (Not admitted in England)

RESIDENT COUNSEL

Raymond G. Wells (Not admitted in England)

RESIDENT ASSOCIATES

Katherine Ashton (Not admitted in England)
Edmund H. Price (Not admitted in England)
David Brewster (Not admitted in England)
Christine A. Worrell

(Not admitted to practice in English courts)

For full biographical listings, see the Martindale-Hubbell Law Directory

DECHERT PRICE & RHOADS

(also see Titmuss Sainer Dechert)
2 Serjeants' Inn, London EC4Y 1LT
Telephone: (0171) 583-5353
Telefax: (0171) 353-3683
Philadelphia, Pennsylvania: 4000 Bell Atlantic Tower, 1717 Arch Street, 19103-2793.
Telephone: 215-994-4000.
Telefax: 215-994-2222.
New York, N.Y.: 477 Madison Avenue, 10022.
Telephone: 212-326-3500.
Washington, D.C.: 1500 K Street, N.W., 20005.
Telephone: 202-626-3300.
Harrisburg, Pennsylvania: Thirty North Third Street, 17101.
Telephone: 717-237-2000.
Princeton, New Jersey: Princeton Pike Corporate Center, P.O. Box 5218, 08543-5218.
Telephone: 609-520-3200.
Boston, Massachusetts: Ten Post Office Square South, 02109.
Telephone: 617-728-7100.
Brussels, Belgium: 65 Avenue Louise, 1050.
Telephone: (02) 535-5411.

RESIDENT PARTNERS

Edward L. Kling
Peter Draper

(Not admitted to practice in English courts)

For full biographical listings, see the Martindale-Hubbell Law Directory

FAEGRE & BENSON

Professional Limited Liability Partnership
10 Eastcheap, London EC3M 1ET
Telephone: 44-71-623-6163
Facsimile: 44-71-623-3227
Minneapolis, Minnesota Office: 2200 Norwest Center, 90 South Seventh Street, 55402-3901.
Telephone: 612-336-3000.
Facsimile: 612-336-3026.

(See Next Column)

Denver, Colorado Office: 2500 Republic Plaza, 370 Seventeenth Street, 80202-4004.
Telephone: 303-592-5900.
Facsimile: 303-592-5693.
Des Moines: Iowa Office: 400 Capital Square, 400 Locust Street, 50309-2335.
Telephone: 55-248-9000.
Facsimile: 515-248-9010.
Washington, D. C. Office: The Homer Building, Suite 450 North, 601 Thirteenth Street, N.W.
Telephone: 202-783-3880.
Facsimile: 202-783-3899.
Frankfurt, Germany Office: Westendstrasse 24, 6000 Frankfurt am Main 1.
Telephone: 49-69-1743 43.
Facsimile: 49-69-1743 49.

RESIDENT MEMBERS

Thomas E. Johnson (Not admitted in England)
Scott M. James (Not admitted in England)

RESIDENT ASSOCIATE

Tracey Chippendale-Holmes

EUROPEAN COMMUNITY COUNSEL

Paul Egerton-Vernon

(Not admitted to practice in English courts)

For full biographical listings, see the Martindale-Hubbell Law Directory

FRIED, FRANK, HARRIS, SHRIVER & JACOBSON

4 Chiswell Street, London EC1Y 4UP
Telephone: 011-44-71-972-9600
Fax: 011-44-171-972-9602
Telex: 011-44-171-972-9602
New York, New York Office: One New York Plaza, 10004.
Telephone: 212-859-8000.
Cable Address: "Steric New York." W.U. Int.
Telex: 620223. W.U. Int.
Telex: 662119. W.U. Domestic: 128173.
Telecopier: 212-859-4000 (Dex 6200).
Washington, D.C. Office: Suite 800, 1001 Pennsylvania Avenue, N.W., 20004-2505.
Telephone: 202-639-7000.
Los Angeles, California Office: 725 South Figueroa Street, 90017.
Telephone: 213-689-5800.
Paris, France Office: 7, Rue Royale, 75008.
Telephone: (+331) 40 17 04 04.
Fax: (+331) 40 17 08 30.

PARTNERS

Jerry L. Smith (Not admitted in England)
Robert P. Mollen (Not admitted in England)

RESIDENT ASSOCIATES

Louis Cammarosano (Not admitted in England)
Amory B. Schwartz (Not admitted in England)

(Not admitted to practice in English courts)

For full biographical listings, see the Martindale-Hubbell Law Directory

HOLME ROBERTS & OWEN LLC

U.S. Counsellors at Law
4th Floor, Mellier House, 26a Albemarle Street, London W1X 3FA
Telephone: 44-171-499-8776
Telecopier: 44-171-499-7769
Denver, Colorado Office: Suite 4100, 1700 Lincoln, 80203.
Telephone: 303-861-7000.
Telex: 45-4460.
Telecopier: 303-866-0200.
Boulder, Colorado Office: Suite 400, 1401 Pearl Street, 80302.
Telephone: 303-444-5955.
Telecopier: 303-444-1063.
Colorado Springs, Colorado Office: Suite 1300, 90 South Cascade Avenue, 80903.
Telephone: 719-473-3800.
Telecopier: 719-633-1518.
Salt Lake City, Utah Office: Suite 1100, 111 East Broadway, 84111.
Telephone: 801-521-5800.
Telecopier: 801-521-9639.
Moscow, Russia Office: 14 Krivokolenny Pr., Suite 30, 101000.
Telephone: 095-925-7816.
Telecopier: 095-923-2726.

MEMBERS OF FIRM

Bruce R. Kohler (Not admitted in England; Managing Resident Member; Co-Director, Moscow Office)
Judith L. L. Roberts (Not admitted in England; Co-Director, Moscow Office; London Office)

SPECIAL COUNSEL

Lawrence A. Leporte (Not admitted in England)
David K. Schollenberger (Not admitted in England)

(See Next Column)

HOLME ROBERTS & OWEN LLC, *London—Continued*

ASSOCIATES

Paul G. Thompson (Not admitted in England)

(Not admitted to practice in English courts)

For full biographical listings, see the Martindale-Hubbell Law Directory

JONES, DAY, REAVIS & POGUE

One Mount Street, London WIY 5AA
Telephone: 44-71-493-9361
Cable Address: "Surgoe London W1"
Telecopier: 44-71-493-9666
In Atlanta, Georgia: 3500 One Peachtree Center, 303 Peachtree Street, N.E.
Telephone: 404-521-3939.
Cable Address: "Attorneys Atlanta".
Telex: 54-2711.
Telecopier: 404-581-8330.
In Brussels, Belgium: Avenue Louise 480, 7th Floor. B-1050 Brussels.
Telephone: 32-2-645-14-11.
Telecopier: 32-2-645-14-45.
In Chicago, Illinois: 77 West Wacker.
Telephone: 312-782-3939.
Telecopier: 312-782-8585.
In Cleveland, Ohio: North Point, 901 Lakeside Avenue.
Telephone: 216-586-3939.
Cable Address: "Attorneys Cleveland."
Telex: 980389.
Telecopier: 216-579-0212.
In Columbus, Ohio: 1900 Huntington Center.
Telephone: 614-469-3939.
Cable Address: "Attorneys Columbus."
Telecopier: 614-461-4198.
In Dallas, Texas: 2300 Trammell Crow Center, 2001 Ross Avenue.
Telephone: 214-220-3939.
Cable Address: "Attorneys Dallas."
Telex: 730852.
Telecopier: 214-969-5100.
In Frankfurt, Germany: Triton Haus, Bockenheimer Landstrasse 42, 60323 Frankfurt am Main.
Telephone: 49-69-9726-3939.
Telecopier: 49-69-9726-3993.
In Geneva, Switzerland: 20, rue de Candolle.
Telephone: 41-22-320-2339.
Telecopier: 41-22-320-1232.
In Hong Kong: 1501 One Exchange Square, 8 Connaught Place.
Telephone: 852-2526-6895.
Telecopier: 852-2810-5787.
In Irvine, California: 2603 Main Street, Suite 900.
Telephone: 714-851-3939.
Telex: 194911 Lawyers LSA.
Telecopier: 714-553-7539.
In Los Angeles, California: 555 West Fifth Street, Suite 4600.
Telephone: 213-489-3939.
Telex: 181439 UD.
Telecopier: 213-243-2539.
In New York, New York: 599 Lexington Avenue.
Telephone: 212-326-3939.
Cable Address: "JONESDAY NEWYORK."
Telex: 237013 JDRP UR.
Telecopier: 212-755-7306.
In Paris, France: 62, rue du Faubourg Saint-Honore.
Telephone: 33-1-44-71-3939.
Cable Address: "Surgoe Paris."
Telex: 290156 Surgoe.
Telecopier: 33-1-49-24-0471.
In Pittsburgh, Pennsylvania: 500 Grant Street, 31st Floor.
Telephone: 412-391-3939.
Cable Address: "Attorneys Pittsburgh".
Telecopier: 412-394-7959.
In Riyadh, Saudi Arabia: Law Offices of Saud M.A. Shawwaf, P.O. Box 2700.
Telephones: (966-1) 465-6543, (966-1) 464-8534 or (966-1) 464-8540.
Telex: 401831 SAUCON SJ.
Telecopier: (966-1) 464-8480.
In Taipei, Taiwan: 8th Floor, 2 Tun Hwa South Road, Section 2.
Telephone: (886-2) 704-6808.
Telecopier: (886-2) 704-6791.
In Tokyo, Japan: Toranomon MT Building, 4th Floor, 10-3, Toranomon 3-Chome, Minato-Ku, Tokyo 105, Japan.
Telephone: 81-3-3433-3939.
Telecopier: 81-3-5401-2725.
In Washington, D.C.: Metropolitan Square, 1450 G Street, N.W.
Telephone: 202-879-3939.
Cable Address: "Attorneys Washington."
Telex: 89-2410 ATTORNEYS WASH.
Telecopier: 202-737-2832.

MEMBERS OF FIRM IN LONDON

Hugh W. Chapman
Jere Rogers Thomson
(Not admitted in England)
Stephen E. Fiamma
(Not admitted in England)
Jai S. Pathak
(Not admitted in England)

(See Next Column)

ASSOCIATES

David P. Curtin
(Not admitted in England)
Elizabeth A. Oberle-Robertson
(Not admitted in England)
Jane D. Wessel
(Not admitted in England)

(Not admitted to practice in English courts)

For full biographical listings, see the Martindale-Hubbell Law Directory

MAYER, BROWN & PLATT

(Mayer, Friedlich, Spiess, Tierney, Brown & Platt)
162 Queen Victoria Street, London EC4V 4DB
Telephone: 011-44-71-248-1465
Fax: 011-44-71-329-4465
Telex: 8811095
Cable: LEMAYLDN
Chicago, Illinois Office: 190 South LaSalle Street, 60603-3441.
Telephone: (312) 782-0600. Pitney Bowes: (312) 701-7711.
Telex: 190404.
Cable: LEMAY.
Washington, D.C. Office: 2000 Pennsylvania Avenue, N.W., 20006-1882.
Telephone: (202) 463-2000. Pitney Bowes: (202) 861-0484, Pitney Bowes: (202) 861-0473.
Telex: 892603.
Cable: LEMAYDC.
New York, New York Office: 787 Seventh Avenue, Suite 2400, 10019-6018.
Telephone: (212) 554-3000. Pitney Bowes: (212) 262-1910.
Telex: 701842.
Cable: LEMAYEN.
Houston, Texas Office: 700 Louisiana Street, Suite 3600, 77002-2730.
Telephone: (713) 221-1651. Pitney Bowes: (713) 224-6410.
Telex: 775809.
Cable: LEMAYHOU.
Los Angeles, California Office: 350 South Grand Avenue, 25th Floor, 90071-1503.
Telephone: (213) 229-9500. Pitney Bowes: (213) 625-0248.
Telex: 188089.
Cable: LEMAYLA.
Tokyo, Japan Office: (Kawachi Gaikokuho Jimu Bengoshi Jimusho). Urbannet Otemachi Building 13F 2-2, Otemachi 2-chome, Chiyoda-ku, Tokyo 100.
Telephone: 011-81-3-5255-9700.
Facsimile: 011-81-3-5255-9797.
Berlin, Germany Office: Spreeifer 5, 10178.
Telephone: 011-49-30-240-7930.
Facsimile: 011-49-30-240-79344.
Brussels, Belgium Office: Square de Meeûs 19/20, Bte. 4, 1040.
Telephone: 011-32-2-512-9878.
Fax: 011-32-2-511-3305.
Telex: 20768 MBPBRU B.
Mexico City, Mexico, D.F., Mexico Correspondent: Jáuregui, Navarrete, Nader y Rojas, S.C., Abogados, Paseo de la Reforma 199, Pisos 15, 16 y 17, 06500.
Telephone: 011-525-591-16-55.
Fax: 011-525-535-80-62; 011-525-703-22-47.
Cable: JANANE.

PARTNERS

Richard A. Cole
(Not admitted in England)
Ian R. Coles
Peter M. Gaines
(Not admitted in England)
Douglas M. Rutherford
(Not admitted in England)

ASSOCIATES

Marwan Al-Turki
Catherine M. Collins
(Not admitted in England)
Manzer Ijaz
Nabil L. Khodadad
(Not admitted in England)
Stefan H. Sarles
(Not admitted in England)
Mark R. Uhrynuk
(Not admitted in England)
Thomas C. Wexler
(Not admitted in England)
Nigel A. Wright
Karen L. Young
(Not admitted in England)

(Not admitted to practice in English courts)

For full biographical listings, see the Martindale-Hubbell Law Directory

MILBANK, TWEED, HADLEY & MCCLOY

Ropemaker Place, 25 Ropemaker Street, London EC2Y 9AS
Telephone: 44-171-374-0423
Cable Address: "MILTUK G"
Fax: 44-171-374-0912
Offices of an Affiliated Partnership:
New York, New York Office: 1 Chase Manhattan Plaza, 10005.
Telephone: 212-530-5000.
Cable Address: "Miltweed NYK" ITT: 422962; 423893.
Fax: 212- 530-5219. ABA/net: Milbank NY. MCI Mail: Milbank Tweed.
Midtown Office: 50 Rockefeller Plaza, 10020.
Telephone: 212-530-5800.
Fax: 212-530-0158.

(See Next Column)

MILBANK, TWEED, HADLEY & MCCLOY—*Continued*

Los Angeles, California Office: 601 South Figueroa Street, 30th Floor, 90017.
Telephone: 213-892-4000.
Fax: 213-629-5063.
Telex: 678754. ABA Net: Milbank LA.
Washington, D.C. Office: Suite 1100, 1825 Eye Street, N.W., 20006.
Telephone: 202-835-7500.
Cable Address: "Miltweed Wsh". ITT 440667.
Fax: 202-835-7586. ABA/net: Milbank DC.
Tokyo, Japan Office: Nippon Press Center Building, 2-1, Uchisaiwai-cho 2-chome, Chiyoda-ku, Tokyo 100.
Telephone: 81-3-3504-1050.
Fax: 81-3-3595-2790; 81-3-3502-5192.
Hong Kong Office: 3007 Alexandra House, 16 Chater Road.
Telephone: 852-2526-5281.
Fax: 852-2840-0792; 852-2845-9046. ABA/net: Milbank HK.
Singapore Office: 14-02 Caltex House, 30Raffles Place, 0104.
Telephone: 65-534-1700.
Fax: 65-534-2733.
Moscow, Russia Office: 24/27 Sadovaya-Samotyochnaya, Moscow, 103051.
Telephone: 7-502-258-5015.
Fax: 7-502-258-5014.
Jakarta, Indonesia Correspondent Office: Makarim & Taira S., 17th Floor, Summitmas Tower, Jl, Jend. Sudirman 61, Jakarta.
Telephone: 62-21252-1272 or 2460.
Fax: 62-21-252-2750 or 2751.

RESIDENT PARTNERS

Nicholas Buckworth
Phillip D. Fletcher
(Not admitted in England)
Kenneth MacRitchie

RESIDENT ASSOCIATES

John Dewar
Edmund Glentworth
Dominic J.F. Gregory
David M. Hudanish
(Not admitted in England)
Helfried J. Schwarz
(Not admitted in England)
Nigel Thompson

(Not admitted to practice in English courts)

For full biographical listings, see the Martindale-Hubbell Law Directory

O'MELVENY & MYERS

10 Finsbury Square, London EC2A 1LA
Telephone: 011-44-171-256-8451
Facsimile: 011-44-171-638-8205
Los Angeles, California Office: 400 South Hope Street.
Telephone: 213-669-6000.
Cable Address: "Moms."
Facsimile: 213-669-6407.
Century City, California Office: 1999 Avenue of the Stars, 7th Floor, 90067-6035.
Telephone: 310-553-6700.
Facsimile: 310-246-6779.
Newport Beach, California Office: 610 Newport Center Drive, Suite 1700.
Telephone: 714-760-9600.
Cable Address: "Moms."
Facsimile: 714-669-6994.
San Francisco, California Office: Three Embarcadero Center West Tower, 275 Battery Street, Suite 2600.
Telephone: 415-984-8700.
Facsimile: 415-984-8701.
New York, N.Y. Office: Citicorp Center. 153 East 53rd Street, 54th Floor.
Telephone: 212-326-2000.
Facsimile: 212-326-2061.
Washington, D.C. Office: 555 13th Street, N.W., Suite 500 West.
Telephone: 202-383-5300.
Cable Address: "Moms."
Facsimile: 202-383-5414.
Newark, New Jersey Office: One Gateway Center, 7th Floor, 07102.
Telephone: 201-639-8600.
Facsimile: 201-639-8630.
Tokyo, Japan Office: Sanbancho KB-6 Building, 6 Sanbancho, Chiyoda-ku, Tokyo 102, Japan.
Telephone: 011-81-3-3239-2800.
Facsimile: 011-81-3-3239-2432.
Hong Kong Office: 1104 Lippo Tower, Lippo Centre, 89 Queensway, Central Hong Kong.
Telephone: 011-852-523-8266.
Facsimile: 011-852-522-1760.

RESIDENT PARTNER

Christopher D. Hall

SPECIAL COUNSEL

Christopher N. Kandel
(Not admitted in England)
Mary Molyneux

For full biographical listings, see the Martindale-Hubbell Law Directory

ROGERS & WELLS

58 Coleman Street, London EC2R 5BE
Telephone: 44-71-628-0101
Facsimile: 44-71-638-2008
Telex: 884964 USLAW G
New York, New York Office: Two Hundred Park Avenue, New York, N.Y., 10166-0153.
Telephone: 212-878-8000.
Facsimile: 212-878-8375.
Telex: 234493 RKWUR.
Washington, D.C. Office: 607 Fourteenth Street, N.W., Washington, D.C. 20005-2011.
Telephone: 202-434-0700.
Facsimile: 202-434-0800.
Los Angeles, California Office: 444 South Flower Street, Los Angeles, California 90071-2901.
Telephone: 213-689-2999.
Facsimile: 213-689-2900.
Paris, France Office: 47, Avenue Hoche, 75008-Paris, France.
Telephone: 33-1-44-09-46-00.
Facsimile: 33-1-42-67-50-81.
Telex: 651617.
Frankfurt, Germany Office: Lindenstrasse 37, 60325 Frankfurt/Main, Federal Republic of Germany. Telephone 49-69-97-57-11-0.
Facsimile: 49-69-97-57-11-33.

PARTNERS

Eric C. Bettelheim
Daniel Bushner
(Not admitted in England)
Sidney Charles Kurth
(Not admitted in England)

CONSULTANT

Hugh Dykes

ASSOCIATES

Edward B. Black
Rossano Y. Mansoori-Dara
(Not admitted in England)

(Not admitted to practice in English courts)

For full biographical listings, see the Martindale-Hubbell Law Directory

SHEARMAN & STERLING

199 Bishopsgate, London EC2M 3TY
Telephone: (44-71) 920-9000
Fax: (44-71) 920-9020
New York, N.Y. Office: 599 Lexington Avenue, New York, New York 10022-6069 and Citicorp Center, 153 East 53rd Street, New York, New York 10022-4676.
Telephone: (212) 848-4000.
Telex: 667290 Num Lau.
Fax: 599 Lexington Avenue: (212) 848-7179. Citicorp Center: (212) 848-5252.
Abu Dhabi, United Arab Emirates Office: P.O. Box 2948.
Telephone: (971-2) 324477.
Fax: (971-2) 774533.
Beijing, People's Republic of China Office: Suite #2205, Capital Mansion, No. 6, Xin Yuan Nan Road. Chao Yang District Beijing, 100004.
Telephone: (861) 465-4574.
Fax: (861) 465-4578.
Budapest, Hungary Office: Szerb utca 17-19, 1056 Budapest.
Telephone: (36-1) 266-3522.
Fax: (36-1) 266-3523.
Düsseldorf, Federal Republic of Germany Office: Königsallee 46, D-40212 Düsseldorf.
Telephone: (49-211) 13 62 80.
Telex: 8 588 294 NYLO.
Fax: (49-211) 13 33 09.
Frankfurt, Federal Republic of Germany Office: Bockenheimer Landstrasse 55, D-60325 Frankfurt am Main.
Telephone: (49-69) 97-10-70.
Fax: (49-69) 97-10-71-00.
Hong Kong, Hong Kong Office: Standard Chartered Bank Building, 4 Des Voeux Road Central, Hong Kong.
Telephone: (852) 2978-8000.
Fax: (852) 2978-8099.
Los Angeles, California Office: 725 South Figueroa Street, 21st Floor, 90017-5421.
Telephone: (213) 239-0300.
Fax: (213) 239-0381, 614-0936.
Paris, France Office: 12 rue d'Astorg, 75008.
Telephone: (33-1) 44-71-17-17.
Telex: 282964 Royale.
Fax: (33-1) 44-71-01-01.
San Francisco, California Office: 555 California Street, 94104-1522.
Telephone: (415) 616-1100.
Fax: (415) 616-1199.
Taipei, Taiwan Office: 7th Floor, Hung Kuo Building, 167 Tun Hwa North Road.
Telephone: (886-2) 545-3300.
Fax: (866-2) 545-3322.

(See Next Column)

SHEARMAN & STERLING, *London—Continued*

Tokyo, Japan Office: Shearman & Sterling (Thomas Wilner Gaikokuho-Jimu-Bengoshi Jimusho), Fukoku Seimei Building, 5th Fl. 2-2-2, Uchisaiwaicho, Chiyoda-ku, Tokyo 100, Japan.
Telephone: (81 3) 5251-1601.
Fax: (81 3) 5251-1602.
Toronto, Ontario, Canada Office: Commerce Court West, Suite 4405, P.O. Box 247, M5L 1E8.
Telephone: (416) 360-8484.
Fax: (416) 360-2958.
Washington, D.C. Office: 801 Pennsylvania Avenue, N.W., Suite 900, 20004-2604.
Telephone: (202) 508-8000.
Fax: (202) 508-8100.

RESIDENT PARTNERS

Thomas Joyce (Not admitted in England; Managing Partner)
John A. Marzulli, Jr. (Not admitted in England)

EUROPEAN COUNSEL

James M. Bartos (Not admitted in England)

INTERNATIONAL FINANCIAL COUNSEL

John G. Stewart (Not admitted in England)

RESIDENT ASSOCIATES

D. Max Aaron (Not admitted in England)
Thomas D. Abbondante (Not admitted in England)
Aaron M. Brown (Not admitted in England)
Andrew J. Foley (Not admitted in England)
Kenneth A.K. Martin (Not admitted in England)
Mark W. Mancinelli (Not admitted in England)
Laura S. Miller (Not admitted in England)
Kenneth Schneider (Not admitted in England)

(Not admitted to practice in English courts)

For full biographical listings, see the Martindale-Hubbell Law Directory

SIDLEY & AUSTIN

A Partnership including Professional Corporations
Broadwalk House, 5 Appold Street, London EC2A 2AA
Telephone: 011-44-71-621-1616
Telecopier: 011-44-71-626-7937
Chicago, Illinois Office: One First National Plaza, 60603.
Telephone: 312-853-7000.
Telecopier: 312-853-7036.
Los Angeles, California Office: 555 W. Fifth Street, 40th Flr., 90013-1010.
Telephone: 213-896-6000.
Telecopier: 213-896-6600.
New York, New York Office: 875 Third Avenue, 10022.
Telephone: 212-906-2000.
Telecopier: 212-906-2021.
Washington, D.C. Office: 1722 Eye Street, N.W., 20006.
Telephone: 202-736-8000.
Telecopier: 202-736-8711.
Tokyo, Japan Office: Taisho Seimei Hibiya Building, 7th Floor, 9-1, Yurakucho, 1 Chome, Chiyoda-ku, 100.
Telephone: 011-81-3-3218-5900.
Facsimile: 011-81-3-3218-5922.
Singapore Office: 36 Robinson Road, #18-01 City House, Singapore 0106.
Telephone: 011-65-224-5000.
Telecopier: 011-65-224-0530.

RESIDENT PARTNER

Mark A. Angelson (Not admitted in England)

ASSOCIATES

Jean A.Y. du Pont (Not admitted in England)
Robert M. Plehn (Not admitted in England)

(Not admitted to practice in English courts)

For full biographical listings, see the Martindale-Hubbell Law Directory

SIMPSON THACHER & BARTLETT

A Partnership which includes Professional Corporations
100 New Bridge Street, London EC4V 6JE
Telephone: 0171 246 8000
Telecopier: 0171 329 3883
New York, NY Office: 425 Lexington Avenue, 10017-3954.
Telephone: 212-455-2000.
Telecopier: 212-455-2502. ESL 62928462.
Columbus, Ohio Office: One Riverside Plaza, 43215.
Telephone: 614-461-7799.
Telecopier: 614-461-0040.
Tokyo Office: Ark Mori Building, 29th Floor, 12-32, Akasaka 1-Chome, Minato-Ku, Tokyo 107, Japan.
Telephone: 81-3-5562-8601.
Telecopier: 81-3-5562-8606. ESL 62765846.
Hong Kong Office: Asia Pacific Finance Tower - 32nd Floor, 3 Garden Road, Central, Hong Kong.
Telephone: 852-2514-7600.
Telecopier: 852-2869-7694.

RESIDENT PARTNERS

D. Rhett Brandon (Not admitted in England)
Alan M. Klein (Not admitted in England)
John D. Lobrano (Not admitted in England)

RESIDENT ASSOCIATES

A. Danzey Burnham (Not admitted in England)
Gordon R. Caplan (Not admitted in England)
James T. Duncan, Jr. (Not admitted in England)
Michael J. Nooney (Not admitted in England)
Gregory J. Ruffa (Not admitted in England)
Christina Lynn Scobey (Not admitted in England)
Ryerson Symons (Not admitted in England)

(Not admitted to practice in English courts)

For full biographical listings, see the Martindale-Hubbell Law Directory

SQUIRE, SANDERS & DEMPSEY

1 Gunpowder Square, Printer Street, London EC4A 3DE
Telephone: 011-44-71-830-0055
Fax: 011-44-71-830-0056
Cleveland, Ohio Office: 4900 Society Center, 127 Public Square, Cleveland, Ohio 44114-1304.
Telephone: 216-479-8500. Fax's: 216-479-8780, 216-479-8781, 216-479-8787, 216-479-8795, 216-479-8777. 216-479-8793, 216-479-8776, 216-479-8788.
Columbus, Ohio Offices: 1300 Huntington Center, 41 South High Street, Columbus, Ohio 43215.
Telephone: 614-365-2700.
Fax: 614-365-2499.
Jacksonville, Florida Office: One Enterprise Center, Suite 2100, 225 Water Street, Jacksonville, Florida 32202.
Telephone: 904-353-1264.
Fax: 904-356-2986.
Miami, Florida Office: 201 South Biscayne Boulevard, Suite 2900 Miami Center, Miami, Florida 33131.
Telephone: 305-577-8700.
Fax: 305-358-1425.
New York, New York Office: 520 Madison Avenue, 32nd Floor, New York, New York 10022.
Telephone: 212-715-4990.
Fax: 212-715-4915.
Phoenix, Arizona Office: Two Renaissance Square, 40 North Central Avenue, Suite 2700, Phoenix, Arizona 85004-4441.
Telephone: 602-528-4000.
Fax: opier: 602-253-8129.
Washington, D.C. Office: 1201 Pennsylvania Avenue, N.W., P.O. Box 407, Washington, D.C. 20044.
Telephone: 202-626-6600.
Fax: 202-626-6780.
Brussels, Belgium Office: Avenue Louise, 165-Box 15, 1050 Brussels, Belgium.
Telephone: 011-32-2-648-1717.
Fax: 011-32-2-648-1064.
Prague Office: Adria Palace, Jungmannova 31/36, 11000 Prague 1, Czech Republic.
Telephone: 011-42-2-231-5661.
Fax: 011-42-2-231-5482.
Bratislava Office: Mudronova 37, 811 01 Bratislava, Slovak Republic.
Telephone: 011-42-7-313-362; 011-42-7-315-370.
Fax: 011-42-7-313-918.
Budapest, Hungary Office: Deak Ferenc Ut. 10, Office 304, H-1052 Budapest V., Hungary.
Telephone: 011-36-1-266-2024.
Fax: 011-36-1-226-2025.
Kiev, Ukraine Office: vul. Prorizna 9, Suite 20, Kiev 252035, Ukraine.
Telephones: 011-7-044-244-3452, 011-7-044-244-3453, 011-7-044-228-8687.
Fax: 011-7-044-228-4938.

RESIDENT PARTNER

Mark A. Cusick

For full biographical listings, see the Martindale-Hubbell Law Directory

SULLIVAN & CROMWELL

St. Olave's House, 9a Ironmonger Lane, London EC2V 8EY
Telephone: (011)(44171)710-6500
Telecopier: (011)(44171)710-6565
New York City Offices: 125 Broad Street, 10004-2498; Midtown Office: 250 Park Avenue, 10177-0021.
Telephone: 212-558-4000.
Telex: 62694 (International); 12-7816 (Domestic).
Cable Address: "Ladycourt, New York".
Telecopier: 125 Broad Street 212-558-3588; 250 Park Avenue 212-558-3792.
Washington, D.C. Office: 1701 Pennsylvania Avenue, N.W., 20006-5805.
Telephone: 202-956-7500.
Telex: 89625.
Telecopier: 202-293-6330.

(See Next Column)

SULLIVAN & CROMWELL—*Continued*

Los Angeles, California Office: 444 South Flower Street, 90071-2901.
Telephone: 213-955-8000.
Telecopier: 213-683-0457.
Paris Office: 8, Place Vendôme, Paris 75001, France.
Telephone: (011)(331)4450-6000.
Telex: 240654.
Telecopier: (011)(331)4450-6060.
Melbourne, Australia Office: 101 Collins Street, Melbourne, Victoria 3000.
Telephone: (011)(613)654-1500.
Telecopier: (011)(613)654-2422.
Tokyo Office: Gaikokuho Jimu Bengoshi Office of Robert G. DeLaMater, a member of the firm of Sullivan & Cromwell, Tokio Kaijo Building Shinkan, 2-1, Marunouchi, 1-chome Chiyoda-ku, Tokyo 100, Japan.
Telephone: (011)(813)3213-6140.
Telecopier: (011)(813)3213-6470.
Hong Kong Office: 28th Floor, Nine Queen's Road, Central, Hong Kong.
Telephone: (011)(852)826-8688.
Telecopier: (011)(852)522-2280.

PARTNERS IN LONDON

John W. Dickey (Not admitted in England)
Robert M. Osgood (Not admitted in England)
William A. Plapinger (Not admitted in England)
George H. White, III (Not admitted in England)
Richard C. Morrissey (Not admitted in England)
Scott D. Miller (Not admitted in England)

EUROPEAN COUNSEL IN LONDON

Kathryn Ann Campbell (Not admitted in England)

ASSOCIATES IN LONDON

Mark D. Alexander (Not admitted in England)
Barbara A. Bayliss (Not admitted in England)
Corey R. Chivers (Not admitted in England)
Francis P. Crispino (Not admitted in England)
Richard A. Ely (Not admitted in England)
Laura Ayn Holleman (Not admitted in England)
Douglas E. Holtz (Not admitted in England)
Christopher L. Mann (Not admitted in England)
Michael B. Miller (Not admitted in England)
Steven J. P. Miller (Not admitted in England)
Nicolas A. Paglietti (Not admitted in England)
David B. Rockwell (Not admitted in England)
Adam S. Rubinson (Not admitted in England)

For full biographical listings, see the Martindale-Hubbell Law Directory

VINSON & ELKINS

Registered Foreign Lawyers and Solicitors
47 Charles Street, Berkeley Square, London W1X 7PB
Telephone: (44-171)491-7236
Fax: (44-171)499-5320
Moscow, Russian Federation Office: 16 Alexey Tolstoy Street, Second Floor, Moscow, 103001 Russian Federation.
Telephone: (70-95) 956-1995.
Telecopy: (70-95) 956-1996.
Mexico City, Mexico Office: Aristóteles 77, 5°Piso, Colonia Chapultepec Polanco, 11560 Mexico, D.F.
Telephone: (52-5) 280-7828.
Fax: (52-5) 280-9223.
Singapore Office: 50 Raffles Place, #19-05 Shell Tower, Singapore, 0104.
U.S. Voice Mailbox: 713-758-3500.
Telephone: (65) 536-8300.
Fax: (65) 536-8311.
Houston, Texas Office: 1001 Fannin, Suite 2300, 77002-6760.
Telephone: 713-758-2222.
Fax: 713-758-2346.
Cable Address: "Vinelkins". International
Telex: 6868314.
Washington, D.C. Office: The Willard Office Building, 1455 Pennsylvania Avenue, N.W., 20004-1008.
Telephone: 202-639-6500.
Fax: 202-639-6604. Cable Adress: "Vinelkins".
Dallas, Texas Office: 3700 Trammell Crow Center, 2001 Ross Avenue, 75201-2975.
Telephone: 214-220-7700.
Fax: 214-220-7716.
Austin, Texas Office: One American Center, 600 Congress Avenue, 78701-3200.
Telephone: 512-495-8400.
Fax: 512-495-8612.

RESIDENT PARTNERS

Paul C. Deemer (Not admitted in England)
John C. LaMaster (Not admitted in England)
A. Sam MacGibbon

For full biographical listings, see the Martindale-Hubbell Law Directory

WHITE & CASE

7-11 Moorgate, London EC2R 6HH
Telephone: (44-171) 726-6361
Facsimile: (44-171) 726-4314; 726-8558
New York, New York:
Telephone: 212-819-8200.
Facsimile: 212-354-8113.
Washington, D.C.:
Telephone: 202-872-0013.
Facsimile: 202-872-0210.
Los Angeles, California:
Telephone: 213-620-7700.
Facsimile: 213-687-0758; 213-617-2205.
Miami, Florida:
Telephone: 305-371-2700.
Facsimile: 305-358-5744.
Mexico City, Mexico:
Telephone: (52-5) 207-9717.
Facsimile: (52-5) 208-3628.
Tokyo, Japan:
Telephone: (81-3) 3239-4300.
Facsimile: (81-3) 3239-4330.
Hong Kong:
Telephone: (852) 2822-8700.
Facsimile: (852) 2845-9070; Grice & Co., Solicitors,
Telephone: (852) 2826-0333.
Facsimile: (852) 2526-7166.
Singapore, Republic of Singapore:
Telephone: (65) 225-6000.
Facsimile: (65) 225-6009.
Bangkok, Thailand: Pacific Legal Group Ltd., In Association With White & Case,
Telephone: (662) 236-6154/7.
Facsimile: (662) 237-6771.
Hanoi, Viet Nam: Representative Office,
Telephone: (84-4) 227-575/6/7.
Facsimile: (84-4) 227-297.
Bombay, India:
Telephone: (91-22) 282-6300.
Facsimile: (91-22) 282-6305.
Paris, France:
Telephone: (33-1) 42-60-34-05.
Facsimile: (33-1) 42-60-82-46.
Brussels, Belgium:
Telephone: (32-2) 647-05-89.
Facsimile: (32-2) 647-16-75.
Stockholm, Sweden:
Telephone: (46-8) 679-80-30.
Facsimile: (46-8) 611-21-22.
Helsinki, Finland:
Telephone: (358-0) 631-100.
Facsimile: (358-0) 179-477.
Moscow, Russia:
Telephone: (7-095) 201-9292/3/4/5.
Facsimile: (7-095) 201-9284.
Budapest, Hungary:
Telephone: (36-1) 269-0550; (36-1) 131-0933.
Facsimile: (36-1) 269-1199.
Prague, Czech Republic:
Telephone: (42-2) 2481-1796.
Facsimile: (42-2) 232-5522.
Warsaw, Poland: Telephone/
Facsimile: (48-22) 26-80-53; (48-22) 27-84-86. International Telephone/
Facsimile: (48-39) 12-19-06.
Istanbul, Turkey:
Telephone: (90-212) 275-68-98; (90-212) 275-75-33.
Facsimile: (90-212) 275-75-43.
Ankara, Turkey:
Telephone: (90-312) 446-2180.
Facsimile: (90-312) 437-9677.
Jeddah, Saudi Arabia: Law Office of Hassan Mahassni,
Telephone: (966-2) 651-3535.
Facsimile: (966-2) 651-3636.
Riyadh, Saudi Arabia: Law Office of Hassan Mahassni,
Telephone: (966-1) 476-7099.
Facsimile: (966-1) 479-0110.
Almaty, Kazakhstan:
Telephone: (7-3272) 50-7491/2.
Facsimile: (7-3272) 61-0842.

RESIDENT PARTNERS

John M. H. Bellhouse
William E. Butler (Not admitted in England)
Peter Finlay
Francis Fitzherbert-Brockholes
Bernard E. Nelson
H. Philip T. Stopford

(See Next Column)

WHITE & CASE, *London—Continued*

RESIDENT ASSOCIATES

Ruth Ambrose
Carolyn M. Brzezinski (Not admitted in England)
Jonathan M. Clark, Jr. (Not admitted in England)
Gerard N. Cranley
Gregory J. Hammond
Thomas A. Hartnett (Not admitted in England)
Kaya H. Proudian (Not admitted in England)
Jeffrey A. Washenko (Not admitted in England)

For full biographical listings, see the Martindale-Hubbell Law Directory

WHITMAN BREED ABBOTT & MORGAN

11 Waterloo Place, London SW1Y 4AU
Telephone: 01-839-3226
Cable Address: "Whitsom London SW1"
Telex: 917881
Telecopier: 01-839-6741
New York, N.Y. Offices: 200 Park Avenue, 10166.
Telephone: 212-351-3000.
Los Angeles, California Office: 633 West Fifth Street, 90071.
Telephone: 213-896-2400.
Sacramento, California Office: Senator Hotel Building, 1121 L Street, 95814.
Telephone: 916-441-4242.
Washington, D.C. Offices: 1215 17th Street, N.W. Telephone 202-887-0353; 1818 N Street, N.W.
Telephone: 202-466-1100.
Greenwich, Connecticut Office: 2 Greenwich Plaza, 06830.
Telephone: 203-869-3800.
Newark, New Jersey Office: One Gateway Center, 07102-5398.
Telephone: 201-621-2230.
Palm Beach, Florida Office: 220 Sunrise Avenue.
Telephone: 407-832-5458.
Tokyo, Japan Office: Suite 450, New Otemachi Building, 2-2-1 Otemachi, Chiyoda-Ku, Tokyo 100.
Telephone: 81-3-3242-1289.
Associated with: Tyan & Associes, 22, La Sagesse Street, Beirut, Lebanon.
Telephone: 337968.
Fax: 200969.
Telex: 43928.

RESIDENT PARTNERS

Gordon L. Jaynes (Not admitted in England)
Michael J. McNulty (Not admitted in England)
Elwood A. Rickless (Not admitted in England)
Elton Shane

RESIDENT ASSOCIATE

Lucinda M. Williams

(Not admitted to practice in English courts)

For full biographical listings, see the Martindale-Hubbell Law Directory

WILLKIE FARR & GALLAGHER

3rd Floor, 35 Wilson Street, London EC2M 25J
Telephone: 011-44-71-696-9060
Fax: 011-44-71-417-9191
New York City Office: One Citicorp Center, 153 East 53rd Street, 10022-4669.
Telephone: 212-821-8000.
Fax: 212-821-8111.
Telex: RCA 233780-WFGUR; RCA 238805-WFGUR.
Washington, D.C. Office: Three Lafayette Centre, 1155 21st Street, N.W., 6th Floor, 20036-3384.
Telephone: 202-328-8000.
Fax: 202-887-8979; 202-331-8187.
Telex: RCA 229800-WFGIG; WU 89-2762.
Paris, France Office: 6, Avenue Velasquez 75008.
Telephone: 011-33-1-44-35-44-35.
Fax: 011-33-1-42-89-87-01.
Telex: 652740 WFG Paris.

PARTNER

Christopher E. Manno (Not admitted in England)

RESIDENT ASSOCIATES

William H. Gump (Not admitted in England)
Jeffrey R. Poss (Not admitted in England)

(Not admitted to practice in English courts)

For full biographical listings, see the Martindale-Hubbell Law Directory

WILMER, CUTLER & PICKERING

Registered Foreign Lawyers and Solicitors
4 Carlton Gardens, London SW1Y 5AA
Telephone: (44 71) 839-4466
Facsimile: (44 71) 839-3537
Washington, D.C. Office: 2445 M Street, N.W., 20037-1420.
Telephone: 202-663-6000.
Facsimile: 202-663-6363. Internet: Law@Wilmer.Com.

(See Next Column)

Brussels, Belgium Office: Rue de la Loi 15 Wetstraat. B-1040.
Telephone: (32 2) 231-0903.
Facsimile: (32 2) 230-4322.
Berlin, Germany Office: Friedrichstrasse 95, D-10117.
Telephone: (49 30) 2643-3601.
Facsimile: (49 30) 2643-3630.

RESIDENT PARTNERS

Gary B. Born (Not admitted in England)
Dieter G. F. Lange (Not admitted in England)
Arthur L. Marriott
Andrew K. Parnell

SPECIAL COUNSEL

John J. Kallaugher (Not admitted in England)

ASSOCIATES

Angela Bedford
Michael R. Holter
Neil D. Midgley (Resident, European Office, London, England)

For full biographical listings, see the Martindale-Hubbell Law Directory

WINTHROP, STIMSON, PUTNAM & ROBERTS

2 Throgmorton Avenue, London EC2N 2AP
Telephone: 011-4471-628-4931
Telefax: 011-4471-638-0443
Cable Address: "Winstim, London EC2"
Telex: 8950511 ONEONE G BOX 24723001
New York Main Office: One Battery Park Plaza, New York, N.Y., 10004-1490.
Telephone: 212-858-1000.
Stamford, Connecticut Office: Financial Centre, 695 East Main Street, P.O. Box 6760, 06904-6760.
Telephone: 203-348-2300.
Washington, D.C. Office: 1133 Connecticut Avenue, N.W., 20036.
Telephone: 202-775-9800.
Palm Beach, Florida Office: 125 Worth Avenue, 33480.
Telephone: 407-655-7297.
Brussels Office: Rue Du Taciturne 42, B-1040 Brussels, Belgium.
Telephone: 011-322-230-1392.
Tokyo, Japan Office: 608 Atagoyama Bengoshi Building 6-7, Atago 1-chome, Minato-ku, Tokyo 105 Japan.
Telephone: 011-813-3437-9740.
Hong Kong Office: 2505 Asia Pacific Finance Tower, Citibank Plaza, 3 Garden Road, Central.
Telephone: 011-852-530-3400.

RESIDENT PARTNERS

Peter S. Brown (Not admitted in England)

RESIDENT ASSOCIATES

Stefanie L. Roth (Not admitted in England)

(Not admitted to practice in English courts)

For full biographical listings, see the Martindale-Hubbell Law Directory

Canadian Lawyers In London

BLAKE, CASSELS & GRAYDON

27 Austin Friars, London EC2N 2QQ
Telephone: 0171-374-2334
Facsimile: 0171-638-3342
Toronto, Ontario Office: Box 25, Commerce Court West, M5L 1A9.
Telephone: 416-863-2400.
Facsimile: 416-863-2653.
Telex: 06-219687. Internet: toronto@blakes.ca.
Ottawa, Ontario Office: World Exchange Plaza, 20th Floor, 45 O'Connor Street, K1P 1A4.
Telephone: 613-788-2200.
Facsimile: 613-594-3965. Internet: ottawa@blakes,ca.
Calgary, Alberta Office: Bankers Hall East, Suite 3500, 855-2nd Street S.W., T2P 4J8.
Telephone: 403-260-9600.
Facsimile: 403-263-9895. Internet: calgary@blakes.ca.
Vancouver, British Columbia Office: 1700-1030 West Georgia Street, V6E 2Y3.
Telephone: 604-631-3300.
Telecopier: 604-631-3309 - 16th Floor; 604-631-3305 - 17th Floor.
Internet: vancouvr@blakes.ca.

PARTNERS

David G. Glennie (Not admitted in England)

ASSOCIATES

Jeffrey R. Lloyd (Not admitted in England)

(Not admitted to practice in English courts)

For full biographical listings, see the Martindale-Hubbell Law Directory

FASKEN MARTINEAU

10 Arthur Street, 5th Floor, London EC4R 9AY
Telephone: 71-929-2894
Facsimile: 71-929-3634
Fasken Martineau is a national and international firm composed of the partners and associates of Fasken Campbell Godfrey (Toronto, Ontario) and Martineau Walker (Montreal and Quebec City, Quebec). Fasken Martineau also has an office in Brussels and Belgium.
Toronto, Ontario, Canada Office: Fasken Campbell Godfrey, Toronto-Dominion Bank Tower, Toronto-Dominion Centre, P.O. Box 20, M5K 1N6.
Telephones: 416- 366-8381. Toll Free: 1-800-268-8424 (Ontario & Quebec)
Facsimile: 416-364-7813.
Montreal, Quebec, Canada Office: Martineau Walker, Stock Exchange Tower, Suite 3400. P.O. Box 242, 800 Place-Victoria, H4Z 1E9.
Telephone: 514-397-7400. Toll Free: 1-800-361-6266 (Ontario & Quebec).
Facsimile: 514-397-7600.
Telex: 05-24610 BUOY MTL.
Quebec City, Quebec, Canada Office: Martineau Walker, Immeuble Le Saint-Patrick, 140, rue Grande Allée est, bureau 800 G1R 5M8.
Telephone: 418-640-2000. Toll Free: 1-800-463-2827 (Ontario & Quebec)
Facsimile: 418-647-2455.
Vancouver (Affiliated): Davis & Company, 2800 Park Place, 666 Burrard Street, V6C 2Z7.
Telephone: 604-687-9444.
Fax: 604-687-1612.
Brussels, Belgium Office: Fasken Martineau, Avenue Franklin D. Roosevelt, 96 A, 1050 Brussels, Belgium.
Telephone: 2-640-9796.
Facsimile: 2-640-2779.

RESIDENT PARTNERS

John S. M. Turner (Not admitted in England; Resident)
Mark D. Walker (Not admitted in England; Resident)

(Not admitted to practice in English courts)

For full biographical listings, see the Martindale-Hubbell Law Directory

MCCARTHY TÉTRAULT

1 Pemberton Row, Fetter Lane, London EC4A 3BA
Telephone: 011-44-171-353-2355
Facsimile: 011-44-171-583-5644
Vancouver, British Columbia Office: Suite 1300, 777 Dunsmuir Street, P.O. Box 10424, Vancouver, British Columbia V7Y 1K2.
Telephone: 604-643-7100.
Facsimile: 604-643-7900.
Surrey, British Columbia Office: Suite 1300, Station Tower, Gateway 13401-108th Avenue, Surrey, British Columbia V3T 5T3.
Telephone: 604-583-9100.
Fax: 604-583-9150.
Calgary, Alberta Office: Suite 3200, 421-7 Avenue, S.W., Calgary, Alberta T2P 4K9.
Telephone: 403-260-3500.
Facsimile: 403-260-3501.
London, Ontario Office: Suite 2000, One London Place, 255 Queens Avenue, London, Ontario N6A 5R8.
Telephone: 519-660-3587.
Facsimile: 519-660-3599.
Toronto, Ontario Office: Suite 4700, Toronto Dominion Bank Tower, Toronto-Dominion Centre, Toronto, Ontario M5K 1E6.
Telephone: 416-362-1812.
Facsimile: 416-868-0673.
Ottawa, Ontario Office: Suite 1000, 275 Spark Street, Ottawa, Ontario K1R 7X9.
Telephone: 613-238-2000.
Facsimile: 613-563-9386.
Montréal, Québec Office: "le Windsor" 1170 rue Peel, Montréal, Québec H3B 4S8.
Telephone: 514-397-4100.
Facsimile: 514-875-6246.
Québec, Québec Office: Le Complexe St-Amable 1150, rue Claire Fontaine 7e Étage, Québec, Québec G1R 5G4.
Telephone: 418-521-3000.
Facsimile: 418-521-3099.

Oliver J. Borgers (Not admitted in England)
Harry W. Macdonell, Q.C. (Not admitted in England)

(Not admitted to practice in English courts)

For full biographical listings, see the Martindale-Hubbell Law Directory

OSLER RENAULT

Canadian Barristers and Solicitors
20 Little Britain, London EC1A 7DH
Telephone: 071-606-0777
Fax: 071-606-0222
Paris, France Office: 4, rue Bayard, 75008.
Telephone: 1.42.89.00.54.
Fax: 1.42.89.51.60.
New York, N.Y. Office: 200 Park Avenue, Suite 3217, 10166-0193.
Telephone: 212-867-5800.
Fax: 212-867-5802.

(See Next Column)

Hong Kong Office: Suite 1708, One Pacific Place, 88 Queensway.
Telephone: 011-852-2877-3933.
Fax: 011-852-2877-0866.
Singapore Office: 65 Chulia Street, #40-05 OCBC Centre, Singapore 0104.
Telephone: (65) 538-2077.
Fax: (65) 538-2977.
Osler Renault is an international partnership of Osler, Hoskin & Harcourt and Ogilvy Renault.
Osler, Hoskin & Harcourt has offices at: P.O. Box 50, 1 First Canadian Place, Toronto, Ontario, Canada M5X 1B8.
Telephone: 416-362-2111.
Fax: 416-862-6666 and 50 O'Connor Street, Suite 1500, Ottawa, Ontario, Canada K1P 6L2.
Telephone: 613-235-7234.
Fax: 613-235-2867.
Ogilvy Renault has offices at: 1981 McGill College Avenue, Suite 1100, Montreal, Quebec, Canada H3A 3C1.
Telephone: 514-847-4747.
Fax: 514-286-5474 and Suite 1600, 45 O'Connor Street, Ottawa, Ontario, Canada K1P 1A4.
Telephone: 613-780-8661; 613-230-5459 and 500 Grande-Allée Est, Suite 520, Quebec, Quebec, G1R 2J7.
Telephone: 418-640-5000.
Fax: 418-640-1500.

RESIDENT IN LONDON

David W. Drinkwater
Michael M. Fortier
Clara M. González-Martin (Not admitted in England)

(Not admitted to practice in English courts).

For full biographical listings, see the Martindale-Hubbell Law Directory

STIKEMAN, ELLIOTT

Cottons Centre, Cottons Lane, London SE1 2QL
Telephone: 71-378-0880
Fax: 71-378-0344
Montreal, Quebec Office: 1155 René-Lévesque Boulevard West, 40th Floor, H3B 3V2.
Telephone: 514-397-3000.
Fax: 514-397-3222.
Toronto, Ontario Office: Commerce Court West, 53rd Floor, M5L 1B9.
Telephone: 416-869-5500.
Fax: 416-947-0866.
Ottawa, Ontario Office: 50 O'Connor Street, Suite 914, K1P 6L2.
Telephone: 613-234-4555.
Fax: 613-230-8877.
Calgary, Alberta Office: 855 - 2nd Street S.W., 1500 Bankers Hall, T2P 4J7.
Telephone: 403-266-9000.
Fax: 403-266-9034.
Vancouver, British Columbia Office: 666 Burrard Street, Suite 1700, Park Place, V6C 2X8.
Telephone: 604-631-1300.
Fax: 604-681-1825.
New York, New York Office: 126 East 56th Street, 11th Floor, Tower 56, 10022.
Telephone: 212-371-8855.
Fax: 212-371-7087.
Washington, D.C. Office: 1300 I Street, N.W., Suite 1210 West, 20005-3314.
Telephone: 202-326-7555.
Fax: 202-326-7557.
Paris, France Office: In Association with Société Juridique Internationale, 39, rue François Ier, 75008.
Telephone: 33-1-40-73-82-00.
Fax: 33-1-40-73-82-10.
Budapest, Hungary Office: Andrássy út 100, II Floor, H-1062.
Telephone: 36-1-269-1790.
Fax: 36-1-269-0655.
Hong Kong Office: 29 Queen's Road Central, Suite 1506, China Building.
Telephone: 852-2868-9903.
Fax: 852-2868-9912.
Hong Kong: In Association with Shum & Co., 29 Queen's Road Central, Suite 1103, China Building.
Telephone: 852-2526-5531.
Fax: 852-2845-9076.
Taipei, Taiwan Office: 117 Sec. 3 Min Sheng East Road, 8th Floor.
Telephone: 886-2-719-9573.
Fax: 886-2-719-4540.

RESIDENTS IN LONDON

Marc Barbeau (Not admitted in England)
Michele J. Buchignani (Not admitted in England)
Richard J. Hay (Not admitted in England)
Calin Rovinescu (Not admitted in England)
William A. Scott (Not admitted in England)
Marianne Sussex (Not admitted in England)

(Not admitted to practice in English courts)

For full biographical listings, see the Martindale-Hubbell Law Directory

TORY TORY DESLAURIERS & BINNINGTON

Canadian Barristers and Solicitors
44/45 Chancery Lane, London WC2A 1JB
Telephone: 071-831 8155
Facsimile: 071-831 1812
Toronto, Ontario Office: Suite 3000, Aetna Tower, Toronto-Dominion Centre, P.O. Box 270, Toronto, Canada M5K 1N2.
Telephone: 416-865-0040.
Facsimile: 416-865-7380.
Hong Kong Office: Suite 1705, One Exchange Square, 8 Connaught Place, Central, Hong Kong.
Telephone: (852) 868-3099.
Facsimile: (852) 523-8140.
Affiliated with:
Desjardins Ducharme Stein Monast:
Montreal, Quebec Office: Bureau 2400, 600 rue de la Gauchetière West, H3B 4L8.
Telephone: (514) 878-9411.
Facsimile: (514) 878-9092.
Quebec City, Quebec Office: 1150, rue de Claire-Fontaine Bureau 300, G1R 5G4.
Telephone: (418) 529-6531.
Facsimile: (418) 523-5391.
Lawson Lundell Lawson & McIntosh:
Vancouver, British Columbia Office: 1600 Cathedral Place, 925 West Georgia Street, V6C 3L2.
Telephone: (604) 685-3456.
Facsimile: (604) 669-1620.
Yellowknife, Northwest Territories Office: Suite 204, 4817 - 49th Street, X1A 3S7.
Telephone: (403) 669-9990.
Facsimile: (403) 669-9991.

RESIDENT IN LONDON

Kathleen L. Keller-Hobson

For full biographical listings, see the Martindale-Hubbell Law Directory

FORMOSA
— (See Taiwan)

FRANCE

*PARIS,**

PROSKAUER ROSE GOETZ & MENDELSOHN LLP

9 rue Le Tasse, 75116 Paris
Telephone: (33-1) 45 27 43 01
FAX: (33-1) 40.50.36.71
New York, New York Office: 1585 Broadway.
Telephone: 212-969-3000.
Washington, D.C. Office: 1233 Twentieth Street, N.W., Suite 800.
Telephone: 202-416-6800.
Los Angeles, California Office: 2121 Avenue of the Stars, Suite 2700.
Telephone: 310-557-2900.
San Francisco, California Office: 555 California Street, Suite 4604.
Telephone: 415-956-2218.
Boca Raton, Florida Office: One Boca Place, Suite 340 West, 2255 Glades Road.
Telephone: 407-241-7400.
Clifton, New Jersey Office: 1373 Broad Street. P.O. Box 4444.
Telephone: 201-779-6300.

William E. Krisel
Delia Spitzer

For full biographical listings, see the Martindale-Hubbell Law Directory

American Lawyers In Paris

BAKER & MCKENZIE

32 Avenue Kleber, 75116 Paris
Telephone: 44 17 53 00
Intn'l. Dialing: (33-1) 44 17 53 00
Cable Address: ABOGADOFRANCE
Telex: 643914F
Answer Back: ABOGA A643914F
Facsimiles: (33-1) 44 17 45 75
Associated Offices of Baker & McKenzie in: Almaty, Amsterdam, Bangkok, Barcelona, Beijing, Berlin, Bogotá, Brasília, Brussels, Budapest, Buenos Aires, Cairo, Caracas, Chicago, Dallas, Frankfurt, Geneva, Hanoi, Ho Chi Minh City, Hong Kong, Juárez, Kiev, London, Madrid, Manila, Melbourne, México City, Miami, Milan, Monterrey, Moscow, New York, Palo Alto, Prague, Rio de Janeiro, Riyadh, Rome, St. Petersburg, San Diego, San Francisco, São Paulo, Singapore, Stockholm, Sydney, Taipei, Tijuana, Tokyo, Toronto, Valencia, Warsaw, Washington, D.C. and Zürich.

(See Next Column)

Correspondent Law Firm: Hadiputranto, Hadinoto & Partners, Jakarta.

RESIDENT ATTORNEYS

Wallace R. Baker
Pierre-Yves Bourtourault
Jean-François Bretonnière
Rémy Bricard
Jean-Francois Buisson
Jean-Claude Demoulin
Alex Dowding
Laurent Epstein
Christine Lagarde
Monique Petit Nion
Pierre A. Ray
Henry de Suremain

LOCAL PARTNER

Reida S. Guenfoud

OF COUNSEL

François Meunier
Michel Peridier

Laurent Barbara
Marie-Françoise Bréchignac
Denise Broussal
Vanessa Carpano
Dominique Clouet d'Orval
Catherine Daoud
Jeanne DuBard
David F. Freedman
Sappho S. Garelli
Claudia M. Heins (Not admitted in France)
Gilles Jolivet
Delphine F. Laisney-Dreux
Denise Lebeau-Marianna
Mathieu Lescot
Corinne E. Mathez
William C. Phillips (Not admitted in France)
Eric Pomonti
Anne-Laure Reveilhac
Jean-Dominique Touraille
Frédéric Vallet
Olivier Vasset

(Firm registered as Conseils Juridiques, not admitted to practice in French Courts reserved for Avocats)

For full biographical listings, see the Martindale-Hubbell Law Directory

CAHILL GORDON & REINDEL

A Partnership including a Professional Corporation
19 rue François 1er, 75008 Paris
Telephone: 33.1-47.20.10.50
Facsimile: 33.1-47.23.06.38
Telex: 842-642331; CGR 642331F
Cable Address: "Cottofrank Paris"
New York City Office: 80 Pine Street, 10005.
Telephone: 212-701-3000.
District of Columbia Office: 1990 K Street, N.W., Washington, D.C., 20006.
Telephone: 202-862-8900.

EUROPEAN COUNSEL

Freddy Dressen

ASSOCIATES

François Bonnin

(Firm admitted to practice in French Courts reserved for Avocats)

For full biographical listings, see the Martindale-Hubbell Law Directory

CLEARY, GOTTLIEB, STEEN & HAMILTON

41, Avenue de Friedland, 75008 Paris
Telephone: 33-1-4074-6800
Telex: 650021
Facsimile/Infotec: 33-1-45-63-35-09
Facsimile/Infotec: 33-1-45-63-66-37
New York, New York Office: One Liberty Plaza, New York, N.Y. 10006.
Telephone: 212-225-2000.
Washington, D.C. Office: 1752 N Street, N.W., Washington, D.C. 20036.
Telephone: 202-728-2700.
Brussels, Belgium Office: Rue de la Loi 23, Bte 5, 1040 Brussels, Belgium.
Telephone: 32-2-287-2000.
London, England Office: City Place House, 55 Basinghall Street, London EC2V 5EH England.
Telephone: 44-71-614-2200.
Hong Kong Office: 56th Floor, Bank of China Tower, One Garden Road, Hong Kong.
Telephone: 852-521-4122.
Tokyo, Japan Office: Morgan Carroll Terai Gaikokuho Jimubengoshi Jimusho, 20th Floor, Shin Kasumigaseki Building, 3-2, Kasumigaseki 3-Chome, Chiyoda-Ku, Tokyo 100, Japan.
Telephone: 81-3-3595-3911.
Frankfurt, Germany Office: Ulmenstrasse 37-39, 60325 Frankfurt am Main, Germany.
Telephone: 49-69-971-03-0.

COUNSEL

Richard H. Moore
Jean L. Blondeel
Hubert de Grandcourt
Donald L. Holley

RESIDENT PARTNERS

Roger J. Benrubi
Sydney M. Cone, III
Bernard Josien
Jean-Michel Tron
Jean-Pierre Vignaud
Gilles Entraygues
William B. McGurn, III
Robert Bordeaux-Groult
François Jonemann
Jean-Marcel Cheyron
Daniel S. Sternberg
Laurent Cohen-Tanugi
Arnaud de Brosses
Jean-Marie Ambrosi

(See Next Column)

CLEARY, GOTTLIEB, STEEN & HAMILTON—*Continued*

ASSOCIATES

Karine Audouze
Caroline Bertin
Nathalie Biderman
Pierre-Marie Boury
John D. Brinitzer
(Not admitted in France)
Pierre-Yves Chabert
Anne Chrun
Serge Cohen
Francois Funck-Brentano
Jean-Yves Garaud
Raymond Gianno
(Not admitted in France)
Antoine Kirry
Frédéric LaLance
Marguerite A. Lampley
(Not admitted in France)
Carine L'Hote
Carl L. Liederman
(Not admitted in France)
Carine Perrier
Xavier Renard
Alan M. Rifkin
(Not admitted in France)
Isabelle B. Roux
Christophe A. Salamon
Fabienne Schaller
Yvette P. Teofan
(Not admitted in France)
Marie-Laurence Tibi
Pascale Trager-Lewis

For full biographical listings, see the Martindale-Hubbell Law Directory

COUDERT FRÈRES

Avocats à la Cour
52, Avenue des Champs Elysées, 75008 Paris
Telephone: (33) 1 43590160
Cable Address: "Treduf"
Telex: 650164
Telecopier: (33) 1 43596655
New York, New York 10036-7794: 1114 Avenue of the Americas.
Washington, D.C. 20006: 1627 I Street, N.W.
Los Angeles, California Office 90017: 1055 West Seventh Street, Twentieth Floor.
San Francisco, California 94111: 4 Embarcadero Center, Suite 3300.
San Jose, California 95113: Suite 1250, Ten Almaden Boulevard.
London, EC4M 7JP, England: 20 Old Bailey.
Brussels B-1050, Belgium: Tour Louise. 149 Avenue Louise-Box 8.
Beijing, People's Republic of China 100020: Suite 2708-29 Jing Guang Centre, Hu Jia Lou, Choa Yang Qu.
Shanghai, People's Republic of China 200002: Suite 1804, Union Building, 100 Yanan Road East.
Hong Kong: 25th Floor, Nine Queen's Road Central.
Singapore, 0104: Tung Centre, 20 Collyer Quay.
Sydney N.S.W. 2000, Australia: Suite 2202, State Bank Centre, 52 Martin Place.
Tokyo, 107 Japan: 1355 West Tower, Aoyama Twin Towers, 1-1-1 Minami-Aoyama, Minato-ku.
Moscow, Russia: Ulitsa Staraya Basmannaya 14.
01301 Sao Paulo, SP, Brazil: Machado, Meyer, Sendacz, e Opice, Advogados, Rua da Consolacao, 247, 8 Andar.
Bangkok 10500, Thailand: Chandler and Thong-Ek, Southeast Insurance Building, 315 Silom Road, 10th Floor.
Ho Chi Minh City, Vietnam: c/o Saigon Business Centre, 49-57 Dong Du Street, District 1.

PARTNERS

Jacques Buhart
Catherine Charpentier
William Laurence Craig
Jean-Patrice de la Laurencie
Charles Kaplan
Eric Laplante
Van Kirk Reeves
Robin Trevor Tait
Jonathan M. Wohl
George T. Yates, III

OF COUNSEL

Hubert de Mahuet
Didier Nedjar
(European Counsel)
Jean-Claude Petilon

ASSOCIATES

Delphine Abellard
Monique R. Beguiachvili
Jean-Mathieu Cot
Olivier de Précigout
Laure Givry
Aline Gladiline
(Not admitted in France)
Arnaud Guérin
(Not admitted in France)
Hélène Lepetit
Michael Polkinghorne
Pascale Rouast-Bertier
Catherine Santoul
Philippe Shin
Elisabeth Terron

(Firm registered as Conseils Juridiques, not admitted to practice in French Courts reserved for Avocats)

For full biographical listings, see the Martindale-Hubbell Law Directory

CURTIS, MALLET-PREVOST, COLT & MOSLE

8 Avenue Victor Hugo, 75116 Paris
Telephone: 45-00-99-68
Telecopier: 45-00-84-06.
New York, New York Office: 101 Park Avenue, 10178.
Telephone: 212-696-6000.
Telecopier: 212-697-1559.
Cable Address: " Migniard New York".
Telex: 12-6811 Migniard; ITT 422127 MGND.
Newark, New Jersey Office: One Gateway Center, Suite 403.
Telephone: 201-622-0605.
Telecopier: 201-622-5646.

(See Next Column)

Washington, D.C. Office: Suite 1205L, 1801 K Street, N.W., 20006.
Telephone: 202-452-7373.
Telecopier: 202-452-7333.
Telex: ITT 440379 CMPUI.
Houston, Texas Office: 2 Houston Center, 909 Fannin Street, Suite 3725.
Telephone: 713-759-9555.
Telecopier: 713-759-0712.
Mexico City, D.F., Mexico Office: Torre Chapultepec, Ruben Dario 281, Col. Bosques de Chapultepec, 11530 Mexico, D.F.
Telephone: 525-282-0444.
Telecopier: 525-282-0637.
London, England Office: Two Throgmorton Avenue, EC2N 2DL.
Telephone: 71-638-7957.
Telecopier: 71-638-5512.
Frankfurt am Main 1 Office: Staufenstrasse 42.
Telephone: 069-971-4420.
Telecopier: 69-17 33 99.

PARTNER

Peter M. Wolrich

COUNSEL

John M. Cochran, III

RESIDENT ASSOCIATES

Geoffroy P. Lyonnet
Leila S. Anglade

For full biographical listings, see the Martindale-Hubbell Law Directory

DAVIS POLK & WARDWELL

4, Place de la Concorde, 75008 Paris
Telephone: 011-331-40.17.36.00
Telecopier: 011-331-42.65.22.34
Cable Address: "Davispolk Paris"
New York, N.Y. Office: 450 Lexington Avenue, 10017.
Telephone: 212-450-4000.
Cable Address: "Davispolk New York".
Telex: ITT-421341; ITT 423356.
Telecopier: 212-450-4800.
Washington, D.C. Office: 1300 I Street, N.W., 20005.
Telephone: 202-962-7000.
Telecopier: 202-962-7111.
London, England Office: 1 Frederick's Place, EC2R 8AB.
Telephone: 011-44-71-418-1300.
Telex: 888238.
Telecopier: 011-44-71-418-1400.
Tokyo, Japan Office: In Tokyo practicing as Reid Gaikokuho-Jimu-Bengoshi Jimusho. Tokio Kaijo Building Annex, 2-1, Marunouchi 1-Chome, Chiyoda-Ku, Tokyo 100, Japan.
Telephone: 011-81-3-201-8421.
Telecopier: 011-81-3-201-8444.
Telex: 2224472 DPWTOK.
Frankfurt, Germany Office: MesseTurm, 60308 Frankfurt am Main, Federal Republic of Germany.
Telephone: 011-49-69-97-57-03-0.
Telecopier: 011-49-69-74-77-44.
Hong Kong Office: The Hong Kong Club Building, 3A Chater Road.
Telephone: 852 533 3300.
Fax: 852 533 3388.

RESIDENT PARTNER

Marlene J. Alva

ASSOCIATES

Kathleen de Carbuccia
Arthur P. Morin
M. Elizabeth Pauchet
Joseph S. Roslanowick
(Not admitted in France)
Deborah Frank Shabecoff
(Not admitted in France)
Craig E. Sherman
(Not admitted in France)
Laurence Yansouni
(Not admitted in France)

(Firm not admitted to practice in French Courts reserved for Avocats)

For full biographical listings, see the Martindale-Hubbell Law Directory

DEBEVOISE & PLIMPTON

21 Avenue George V, 75008 Paris
Telephone: (33-1) 40 73 12 12
Telecopier: (33-1) 47 20 50 82.
Telex: 648141F DPPAR
New York Office: 875 Third Avenue, 10022.
Telephone: 212-909-6000.
Telex: (Domestic) 148377 DEBSTEVE NYK.
Telecopier: (212) 909-6836.
Washington, D.C. Office: 555 13th Street, N.W., 20004.
Telephone: 202-383-8000.
Telex: 405586 DPDC WUUD.
Telecopier: (202) 383-8118.
Los Angeles, California Office: 601 South Figueroa Street, Suite 3700, 90017.
Telephone: 213-680-8000.
Telex: 401527 DPLA.
Telecopier: 213-680-8100.

(See Next Column)

DEBEVOISE & PLIMPTON, *Paris—Continued*

London, England Office: 1 Creed Court, 5 Ludgate Hill, EC4M 7AA.
Telephone: (44-171) 329-0779.
Telex: 884569 DPLON G
Facsimile: (44-171) 329-0860.
Budapest, Hungary Office: 1065 Budapest, Révay Köz 2.III/2.
Telephone: (36-1) 131-0845.
Telecopier: (36-1)132-7995.
Hong Kong Office: 13/F Entertainment Building, 30 Queen's Road Central.
Telephone: (852) 2810-7918.
Fax: (852) 2810-9828.

James A. Kiernan III	Deborah Frank
Gerald M. Shea	Valérie Gaillard
James Cecil Swank	Gerard Lacroix
Susan H. Abramovitch (Not admitted in France)	Emmanuel Lulin
	Jean-Louis Martin
Ann G. Baker	Sylvie DeParis-Maze
E. Raman Bet-Mansour (Not admitted in France)	Antoine d'Ornano
	Peter Shabecoff (Not admitted in France)
Cécile Boyer	

Claude Vuillieme

For full biographical listings, see the Martindale-Hubbell Law Directory

DONOVAN LEISURE NEWTON & IRVINE

130 rue du Faubourg Saint-Honoré, 75008 Paris
Telephone: 1-42-25-47-10
Telecopier: 011-33-1-42-56-08-06
NewYork, New York Office: 30 Rockefeller Plaza, 10112.
Telephone: 212-632-3000.
Cable Address: "Donlard, N.Y."
Telecopiers: 212-632-3315; 212-632-3321; 212-632-3322.
Washington, D.C. Office: 1250 Twenty-Fourth Street, N.W., 20037-1124.
Telephone: 202-467-8300.
Telecopier: 202-467-8484.
Los Angeles, California Office: 333 South Grand Avenue, 90071.
Telephone: 213-253-4000.
Cable Address: "Donlard, L.A."
Telecopier: 213-617-2368; 213-617-3246.
Palm Beach, Florida Office: 450 Royal Palm Way.
Telephone: 407-833-1040.
Telecopier: 407-835-8511.

PARTNERS

William J. T. Brown	René de Monseignat

COUNSEL

Reid L. Feldman

ASSOCIATES

Sandrine M. Bonnet

For full biographical listings, see the Martindale-Hubbell Law Directory

FRIED, FRANK, HARRIS, SHRIVER & JACOBSON

Correspondance Organique
7, Rue Royale, Paris 75008
Telephone: (+331) 40 17 04 04
Fax: (+331) 40 17 08 30
New York, New York Office: One New York Plaza, 10004.
Telephone: 212-859-8000.
Cable Address: "Steric New York." W.U. Int.
Telex: 620223. W.U. Int.
Telex: 662119. W.U. Domestic: 128173.
Telecopier: 212-859-4000 (Dex 6200).
Washington, D.C. Office: Suite 800, 1001 Pennsylvania Avenue, N.W., 20004-2505.
Telephone: 202-639-7000.
Los Angeles, California Office: 725 South Figueroa Street, 90017.
Telephone: 213-689-5800.
London, England Office: 4 Chiswell Street, London EC1Y 4UP.
Telephone: 011-44-171-972-9600.
Fax: 011-44-171-972-9602.

PARTNER

Eric M. Cafritz

ASSOCIATES

Jean-Philippe Lambert	Jean-Pierre Hyun Lee

Sylvie A. Mongelous

For full biographical listings, see the Martindale-Hubbell Law Directory

HUGHES HUBBARD & REED

47, Avenue Georges Mandel, 75116 Paris
Telephone: 33.1.44.05.80.00
Cable Address: "Hughreed, Paris"
Telex: 645440
Telecopier: 33.1.45.53.15.04.
New York, New York Office: One Battery Park Plaza, 10004.
Telephone: 212-837-6000.
Cable Address: "Hughreed, New York."
Telex: 427120.
Telecopier: 212-422-4726.
Los Angeles, California Office: 350 S. Grand Avenue, Suite 3600, 90071-3442.
Telephone: 213-613-2800.
Telecopier: 213-613-2950.
Miami, Florida Office: 801 Brickell Avenue, 33131.
Telephone: 305-358-1666.
Telex: 51-8785.
Telecopier: 305-371-8759.
Washington, D.C. Office: 1300 I Street, N.W., Suite 900 West, 20005.
Telephone: 202-408-3600.
Telex: 89-2674.
Telecopier: 202-408-3636.
Berlin, Germany Office: Kurfürstendamm 44, D-1000 Berlin 15.
Telephone: 030-880008-0.
Telefax: 030-880008-65.
Telex: 185803 KNAPA D.

RESIDENT PARTNERS

Joël Alquezar (Partner)	Dominique Mendy (Partner)
Claire S. Ayer (Partner)	Jonathan A. Schur (Partner)
Axel H. Baum (Partner)	Vincent Sol (Partner)
James J. Lightburn (Partner)	Thomas Henry Webster (Partner)

OF COUNSEL

George W. Balkind	Claude Suleyman

RESIDENT ASSOCIATES

Eveline Beltzung	John G. Heard
Bouziane Behillil	Joelle Herschtel
Laure Colli-Patel	Theodor W. Krauss
Laurence Dumure-Lambert	Winston J. Maxwell
Alexandre De Goüyon Matignon	Laure Mottet

Bertrand Thouny

(Firm authorized to appear before the French Courts reserved for Avocats)

For full biographical listings, see the Martindale-Hubbell Law Directory

JONES, DAY, REAVIS & POGUE

62, rue du Faubourg Saint-Honore, 75008 Paris
Telephone: 33-1-44-71-3939
Cable Address: "Surgoe Paris"
Telex: 290156 Surgoe
Telecopier: 33-1-49-24-0471
In Atlanta, Georgia: 3500 One Peachtree Center, 303 Peachtree Street, N.E.
Telephone: 404-521-3939.
Cable Address: "Attorneys Atlanta".
Telex: 54-2711.
Telecopier: 404-581-8330.
In Brussels, Belgium: Avenue Louise 480, 7th Floor. B-1050 Brussels.
Telephone: 32-2-645-14-11.
Telecopier: 32-2-645-14-45.
In Chicago, Illinois: 77 West Wacker.
Telephone: 312-782-3939.
Telecopier: 312-782-8585.
In Cleveland, Ohio: North Point, 901 Lakeside Avenue.
Telephone: 216-586-3939.
Cable Address: "Attorneys Cleveland."
Telex: 980389.
Telecopier: 216-579-0212.
In Columbus, Ohio: 1900 Huntington Center.
Telephone: 614-469-3939.
Cable Address: "Attorneys Columbus."
Telecopier: 614-461-4198.
In Dallas, Texas: 2300 Trammell Crow Center, 2001 Ross Avenue.
Telephone: 214-220-3939.
Cable Address: "Attorneys Dallas."
Telex: 730852.
Telecopier: 214-969-5100.
In Frankfurt, Germany: Triton Haus, Bockenheimer Landstrasse 42, 60323 Frankfurt am Main.
Telephone: 49-69-9726-3939.
Telecopier: 49-69-9726-3993
Geneva, Switzerland: 20, rue de Candolle.
Telephone: 41-22-320-2339.
Telecopier: 41-22-1232.
In Hong Kong: 1501 One Exchange Square, 8 Connaught Place.
Telephone: 852-2526-6895.
Telecopier: 852-2810-5787.

(See Next Column)

JONES, DAY, REAVIS & POGUE—*Continued*

In Irvine, California: 2603 Main Street, Suite 900.
Telephone: 714-851-3939.
Telex: 194911 Lawyers LSA.
Telecopier: 714-553-7539.
In London, England: One Mount Street.
Telephone: 44-71-493-9361.
Cable Address: "Surgoe London WI."
Telecopier: 44-71-493-9666.
In Los Angeles, California: 555 West Fifth Street, Suite 4600.
Telephone: 213-489-3939.
Telex: 181439 UD.
Telecopier: 213-243-2539.
In New York, New York: 599 Lexington Avenue.
Telephone: 212-326-3939.
Cable Address: "JONESDAY NEWYORK."
Telex: 237013 JDRP UR.
Telecopier: 212-755-7306.
In Pittsburgh, Pennsylvania: 500 Grant Street, 31st Floor.
Telephone: 412-391-3939.
Cable Address: "Attorneys Pittsburgh".
Telecopier: 412-394-7959.
In Riyadh, Saudi Arabia: Law Offices of Saud M.A. Shawwaf, P.O. Box 2700.
Telephones: (966-1) 465-6543, (966-1) 464-8534 or (966-1) 464-8540.
Telex: 401831 SAUCON SJ.
Telecopier: (966-1) 464-8480.
In Taipei, Taiwan: 8th Floor, 2 Tun Hwa South Road, Section 2.
Telephone: (886-2) 704-6808.
Telecopier: (886-2) 704-6791.
In Tokyo, Japan: Toranomon MT Building, 4th Floor, 10-3, Toranomon 3-Chome, Minato-Ku, Tokyo 105 Japan.
Telephone: 81-3-3433-3939.
Telecopier: 81-3-5401-2725.
In Washington, D.C.: Metropolitan Square, 1450 G Street, N.W.
Telephone: 202-879-3939.
Cable Address: "Attorneys Washington."
Telex: 89-2410 ATTORNEYS WASH.
Telecopier: 202-737-2832.

MEMBERS OF FIRM IN PARIS

John F. Crawford
David F. Clossey
(Not admitted in France)
Pierre Ullmann
Philippe Billot
Anne C. Boileau
Wesley R. Johnson, Jr.
Laurent Faugérolas
Gael P. Saint Olive
Peter R. Sternberg

SENIOR ATTORNEY

Marie-Laure Larget-Bozonnet

ASSOCIATES

Nathalie Garnier
Sophie Hagège
Agnès L. Férey
Etienne Mouthon
Arnaud G. Vanbremeersch
Pierre-Nicolas Ferrand
François R. Bonteil
Antoine Echard

For full biographical listings, see the Martindale-Hubbell Law Directory

MUDGE ROSE GUTHRIE ALEXANDER & FERDON

(Mudge, Stern, Baldwin & Todd)
(Caldwell, Trimble & Mitchell)
12, Rue de la Paix, 75002 Paris
Telephone: 42.61.57.71
Cable Address: "Baltuchins, Paris"
Telecopier: 42.61.79.21
New York City Office: 180 Maiden Lane, New York, N.Y., 10038.
Telephone: 212-510-7000.
Telecopier: 212-248-2655/57.
Los Angeles, California Office: 21st Floor, 333 South Grand Avenue, 90071.
Telephone: 213-613-1112.
Telecopier: 213-680-1358.
Washington, D.C. Office: 2121 K Street, N.W., 20037.
Telephone: 202-429-9355.
Telecopier: 202-429-9367.
West Palm Beach, Florida Office: Suite 900, 515 North Flagler Drive, 33401.
Telephone: 407-650-8100.
Telecopier: 407-833-1722.
Parsippany, New Jersey Office: Morris Corporate Center Two, Building D, 1 Upper Pond Road, 07054-1075.
Telephone: 201-335-0004.
Telecopier: 201-402-1593.
Tokyo, Japan Office: Infini Akasaka, 8-7-15 Akasaka, Minato-Ku, Tokyo 107, Japan.
Telephone: (03) 3423-3970.
Fax: (03) 3423-3971.

RESIDENT PARTNERS

Alan F. Cariddi
Bruce C. Mee
Fabrice Rué

INTERNATIONAL COUNSEL

Vuong Van Bac

(See Next Column)

ASSOCIATES

Christine Bougis
Michael S. Carter
Hervé De Kervasdoué
Bijan-Emmanuel Eghbal
Carol A. Umhoefer
(Not admitted in France)

(Advocats à la Cour admitted to appear before French Courts)

For full biographical listings, see the Martindale-Hubbell Law Directory

PAUL, WEISS, RIFKIND, WHARTON & GARRISON

199, Boulevard Saint-Germain, 75007 Paris
Telephone: (33-1) 45.49.33.85
Telex: 269940F
Facsimile: (33-1) 42-22-64-38
New York, N.Y. Office: 1285 Avenue of the Americas, 10019-6064.
Telephones: (212) 373-3000, TDD 212-373-2000.
Cable Address: "Longsight, New York".
Telex: WUI 666-843.
Facsimile: 212-757-3990.
Washington, D.C. Office: 1615 L Street, N.W., Suite 1300, 20036-5694.
Telephones: 202-223-7300, TDD 202-223-7490.
Telex: 248237 PWA UR.
Facsimile: 202-223-7420.
Cable Address: "Longsight, Washington".
Tokyo, Japan Office: 11th Floor, Main Tower, Akasaka Twin Tower, 17-22 Akasaka 2-chome, Minato-Ku. 107.
Telephone: (81-3) 3505-0291.
Facsimile: (81-3) 3505-4540.
Telex: 02428120 PWRWGT.
Beijing, People's Republic of China Office: Suite 1910, Scite Tower, 22 Jianguomenwai Dajie, 10004.
Telephones: (86-1) 5123628-30, (86-1) 5122288X.1910.
Telex: 210169 PWRWG CN.
Facsimile: (86-1) 5123631.
Hong Kong Office: 13th Floor, Hong Kong Club Building, 3A Chater Road, Central Hong Kong.
Telephone: (011-852) 2536-9933.
Facsimile: 011 (852) 2536-9622.

RESIDENT PARTNERS

Dominique Fargue
Steven E. Landers

COUNSEL

Richard Dehé
Joseph S. Iseman
Philippe Jambrun
Pierre E. Petit

EEC LAW COUNSEL

Anthony McClellan

RESIDENT ASSOCIATES

Katia Chéron
Henri Glaser
Valérie Masset-Branche
Dominique M. Ryder

(Firm registered as Conseils Juridiques, not admitted to practice in French Courts reserved for Avocats)

For full biographical listings, see the Martindale-Hubbell Law Directory

ROGERS & WELLS

47, Avenue Hoche, 75008 Paris
Telephone: 33-1-44-09-46-00
Facsimile: 33-1-42-67-50-81
Telex: 651617 EURLAW
New York, New York Office: Two Hundred Park Avenue, New York, N.Y., 10166-0153.
Telephone: 212-878-8000.
Facsimile: 212-878-8375.
Telex: 234493 RKWUR.
Washington, D.C. Office: 607 Fourteenth Street, N.W., Washington, D.C. 20005-2011.
Telephone: 202-434-0700.
Facsimile: 202-434-0800.
Los Angeles, California Office: 444 South Flower Street, Los Angeles, California 90071-2901.
Telephone: 213-689-2900.
Facsimile: 213-689-2999.
London, England Office: 58 Coleman Street, London EC2R 5BE, England.
Telephone: 44-71-628-0101.
Facsimile: 44-71-638-2008.
Telex: 884964 USLAW G.
Frankfurt, Germany Office: Lindenstrasse 37, 60325 Frankfurt/Main, Federal Republic of Germany. Telephone 49-69-97-57-11-0.
Facsimile: 49-69-97-57-11-33.

PARTNERS

Philippe X. Ledoux
Alexander Marquardt
Christian Orengo
Antoine Paszkiewicz

CONSULTANT

Souham El Harati

(See Next Column)

ROGERS & WELLS, *Paris—Continued*

ASSOCIATES

Servane Bonnet	Géraldine Maspetiol-Lunven
Ellen H Clark	Pascaline Neveu
Marie-Christine Fournier-Gille	Odile I. Renner
Corinne Hershkovitch	Wadie Sanbar
Geraldine Kantor-Lerner	John A. Stevenson
Marika Tourres	

(Licensed as Avocats in France and authorized to appear before the French Courts)

For full biographical listings, see the Martindale-Hubbell Law Directory

SHEARMAN & STERLING

12 rue d'Astorg, 75008 Paris
Telephone: (33-1) 44-71-17-17
Telex: 282964 Royale
Fax: (33-1) 44-71-01-01
New York, N.Y. Office: 599 Lexington Avenue, New York, New York 10022-6069 and Citicorp Center, 153 East 53rd Street, New York, New York 10022-4676.
Telephone: (212) 848-4000.
Telex: 667290 Num Lau.
Fax: 599 Lexington Avenue: (212) 848-7179. Citicorp Center: (212) 848-5252.
Abu Dhabi, United Arab Emirates Office: P.O. Box 2948.
Telephone: (971-2) 324477.
Fax: (971-2) 774533.
Beijing, People's Republic of China Office: Suite #2205, Capital Mansion, No. 6, Xin Yuan Nan Road. Chao Yang District Beijing, 100004.
Telephone: (861) 465-4574.
Fax: (861) 465-4578.
Budapest, Hungary Office: Szerb utca 17-19, 1056 Budapest.
Telephone: (36-1) 266-3522.
Fax: (36-1) 266-3523.
Düsseldorf, Federal Republic of Germany Office: Königsallee 46, D-40212 Düsseldorf.
Telephone: (49-211) 13 62 80.
Telex: 8 588 294 NYLO.
Fax: (49-211) 13 33 09.
Frankfurt, Federal Republic of Germany Office: Bockenheimer Landstrasse 55, D-60325 Frankfurt am Main.
Telephone: (49-69) 97-10-70.
Fax: (49-69) 97-10-71-00.
Hong Kong, Hong Kong Office: Standard Chartered Bank Building, 4 Des Voeux Road Central, Hong Kong.
Telephone: (852) 2978-8000.
Fax: (852) 2978-8099.
London, England Office: 199Bishopsgate, London EC2M 3TY.
Telephone: (44-71) 920-9000.
Fax: (44-71) 920-9020.
Los Angeles, California Office: 725 South Figueroa Street, 21st Floor, 90017-5421.
Telephone: (213) 239-0300.
Fax: (213) 239-0381, 614-0936.
San Francisco, California Office: 555 California Street, 94104-1522.
Telephone: (415) 616-1100.
Fax: (415) 616-1199.
Taipei, Taiwan Office: 7th Floor, Hung Kuo Building, 167 Tun Hwa North Road.
Telephone: (886-2) 545-3300.
Fax: (866-2) 545-3322.
Tokyo, Japan Office: Shearman & Sterling (Thomas Wilner Gaikokuho-Jimu-Bengoshi Jimusho), Fukoku Seimei Building, 5th Fl. 2-2-2,Uchisaiwaicho, Chiyoda-ku, Tokyo 100, Japan.
Telephone: (81 3) 5251-1601.
Fax: (81 3) 5251-1602.
Toronto, Ontario, Canada Office: Commerce Court West, Suite 4405, P.O. Box 247, M5L 1E8.
Telephone: (416) 360-8484.
Fax: (416) 360-2958.
Washington, D.C. Office: 801 Pennsylvania Avenue, N.W., Suite 900, 20004-2604.
Telephone: (202) 508-8000.
Fax: (202) 508-8100.

RESIDENT PARTNERS

Hubertus V. Sulkowski (Managing Partner)	John J. Madden (Not admitted in France; Managing Partner, Europe)

OF COUNSEL

Robert A. MacCrindle	David T. McGovern

EUROPEAN COUNSEL

Norbert Andreae	Andrea K. Muller
Emmanuel Gaillard	Robert C. Treuhold

FRENCH COUNSEL

Hervé Letréguilly

CONSULTANT

Dominique Carreau (Not admitted in France)

(See Next Column)

RESIDENT ASSOCIATES

Christopher Armeniades	Michèle F. Moss
Isabelle Chauvet	Lee D. Neumann (Not admitted in France)
Michael J. Coleman (Not admitted in France)	Philippe Pinsolle
Alessandro C. De Giorgis	Philippe Rosenpick
Christophe Dugué	John Savage (Not admitted in France)
Peter Griffin (Not admitted in France)	Lesley Simmons
Michèle Hulin	Eric Teynier
Nitsch Marianna	Sami L. Toutounji (Not admitted in France)

For full biographical listings, see the Martindale-Hubbell Law Directory

SULLIVAN & CROMWELL

8, Place Vendôme, 75001 Paris
Telephone: (011)(331)4450-6000
Telex: 240654
Telecopier: (011)(331)4450-6060
New York City Offices: 125 Broad Street, 10004-2498; Midtown Office: 250 Park Avenue, 10177-0021.
Telephone: 212-558-4000.
Telex: 62694 (International); 12-7816 (Domestic).
Cable Address: "Ladycourt, New York".
Telecopier: 125 Broad Street 212-558-3588; 250 Park Avenue 212-558-3792.
Washington, D.C. Office: 1701 Pennsylvania Avenue, N.W., 20006-5805.
Telephone: 202-956-7500.
Telex: 89625.
Telecopier: 202-293-6330.
Los Angeles, California Office: 444 South Flower Street, 90071-2901.
Telephone: 213-955-8000.
Telecopier: 213-683-0457.
London Office: St. Olave's House, 9a Ironmonger Lane, London EC2V 8EY, England.
Telephone: (011)(44171)710-6500.
Telecopier: (011)(44171)710-6565.
Melbourne, Australia Office: 101 Collins Street, Melbourne, Victoria 300.
Telephone: (011)(613)654-1500.
Telecopier: (011)(613)654-2422.
Tokyo Office: Gaikokuho Jimu Bengoshi Office of Robert G. DeLaMater, a member of the firm of Sullivan & Cromwell, Tokio Kaijo Building Shinkan, 2-1 Marunouchi, 1-chome Chiyoda-ku, Tokyo 100, Japan.
Telephone: (011)(813)3213-6140.
Telecopier: (011)(813)3213-6470.
Hong Kong Office: 28th Floor, Nine Queen's Road, Central, Hong Kong.
Telephone: (011)(852)826-8688.
Telecopier: (011)(852)522-2280.

PARTNERS IN PARIS

Richard G. Asthalter	David F. Morrison

EUROPEAN COUNSEL IN PARIS

Pierre Servan-Schreiber

ASSOCIATES IN PARIS

Ari Assayag	Mathias Turck
Michal Dlouhy (Not admitted in France)	Dimitri Nikolakakos (Not admitted in France)
Nancy C. Jackson	Jean Raby (Not admitted in France)
Susan Silverman Liautaud (Not admitted in France)	

(Firm not admitted to practice in French Courts reserved for Avocats)

For full biographical listings, see the Martindale-Hubbell Law Directory

WHITE & CASE

11, Boulevard de la Madeleine, 75001 Paris
Telephone: (33-1) 42-60-34-05
Facsimile: (33-1) 42-60-82-46
New York, New York:
Telephone: 212-819-8200.
Facsimile: 212-354-8113.
Washington, D.C.:
Telephone: 202-872-0013.
Facsimile: 202-872-0210.
Los Angeles, California:
Telephone: 213-620-7700.
Facsimile: 213-687-0758; 213-617-2205.
Miami, Florida:
Telephone: 305-371-2700.
Facsimile: 305-358-5744.
Mexico City, Mexico:
Telephone: (52-5) 207-9717.
Facsimile: (52-5) 208-3628.
Tokyo, Japan:
Telephone: (81-3) 3239-4300.
Facsimile: (81-3) 3239-4330.
Hong Kong:
Telephone: (852) 2822-8700.
Facsimile: (852) 2845-9070; Grice & Co., Solicitors,
Telephone: (852) 2826-0333.
Facsimile: (852) 2526-7166.

(See Next Column)

WHITE & CASE—*Continued*

Singapore, Republic of Singapore:
Telephone: (65) 225-6000.
Facsimile: (65) 225-6009.
Bangkok, Thailand: Pacific Legal Group Ltd., In Association With White & Case,
Telephone: (662) 236-6154/7.
Facsimile: (662) 237-6771.
Hanoi, Viet Nam: Representative Office,
Telephone: (84-4) 227-575/6/7.
Facsimile: (84-4) 227-297.
Bombay, India:
Telephone: (91-22) 282-6300.
Facsimile: (91-22) 282-6305.
London, England:
Telephone: (44-171) 726-6361.
Facsimile: (44-171) 726-4314; (44-171) 726-8558.
Brussels, Belgium:
Telephone: (32-2) 647-05-89.
Facsimile: (32-2) 647-16-75.
Stockholm, Sweden:
Telephone: (46-8) 679-80-30.
Facsimile: (46-8) 611-21-22.
Helsinki, Finland:
Telephone: (358-0) 631-100.
Facsimile: (358-0) 179-477.
Moscow, Russia:
Telephone: (7-095) 201-9292/3/4/5.
Facsimile: (7-095) 201-9284.
Budapest, Hungary:
Telephone: (36-1) 269-0550; (36-1) 131-0933.
Facsimile: (36-1) 269-1199.
Prague, Czech Republic:
Telephone: (42-2) 2481-1796.
Facsimile: (42-2) 232-5522.
Warsaw, Poland: Telephone/
Facsimile: (48-22) 26-80-53; (48-22) 27-84-86. International Telephone/
Facsimile: (48-39) 12-19-06.
Istanbul, Turkey:
Telephone: (90-212) 275-68-98; (90-212) 275-75-33.
Facsimile: (90-212) 275-75-43.
Ankara, Turkey:
Telephone: (90-312) 446-2180.
Facsimile: (90-312) 437-9677.
Jeddah, Saudi Arabia: Law Office of Hassan Mahassni,
Telephone: (966-2) 651-3535.
Facsimile: (966-2) 651-3636.
Riyadh, Saudi Arabia: Law Office of Hassan Mahassni,
Telephone: (966-1) 476-7099.
Facsimile: (966-1) 479-0110.
Almaty, Kazakhstan:
Telephone: (7-3272) 50-7491/2.
Facsimile: (7-3272) 61-0842.

RESIDENT PARTNERS

Stephen R. Bond
Jean-Luc Boussard
Anthony Giustini
Rosine Lorotte
Gilles Peigney
John H. Riggs, Jr.
Christopher R. Seppala

RESIDENT COUNSEL

Nicholas Budd
Pierre-Yves Corrieu

RESIDENT ASSOCIATES

Paule Biensan
Robert Brada, Jr. (Not admitted in France)
Bertrand Caradet
Rémy Cottage-Stone
Dr. Reinhard Dammann
Jean-Charles De Daruvar
Philippe Deneux
Carroll S. Dorgan
Suzanne Durdevic
François Farmine
Pierre Forget
Eric Gastinel
Ronald E. M. Goodman
Clifford J. Hendel (Not admitted in France)
Caroline Kahn
Jean-Francois LeCorre
Anne-France Marmot
Philippe Metais
Mark G. Milford (Not admitted in France)
Vincent Morin
Marie-Helene Peres
Laura Restelli (Not admitted in France)
Mark B. Richards (Not admitted in France)
Peter Rosher
Stewart Robert Shackleton

For full biographical listings, see the Martindale-Hubbell Law Directory

---

WILLKIE FARR & GALLAGHER

6, Avenue Velasquez, 75008 Paris
Telephone: 011-33-1-44-35-44-35
Fax: 011-33-1-42-89-87-01
Telex: 652740-WFG Paris
New York City Office: One Citicorp Center, 153 East 53rd Street, 10022-4669.
Telephone: 212-821-8000.
Fax: 212-821-8111.
Telex: RCA 233780-WFGUR; RCA 238805-WFGUR.

(See Next Column)

Washington, D.C. Office: Three Lafayette Centre, 1155 21st Street, N.W., 6th Floor, 20036-3384.
Telephone: 202-328-8000.
Fax: 202-887-8979; 331-8787.
Telex: RCA 229800-WFGIG; WU 89-2762.
London, England Office: 35 Wilson Street, 3rd Floor. EC2M 2SJ.
Telephone: 011-44-71-696-9060.
Fax: 011-44-71-417-9191.

RESIDENT PARTNERS

Jean-Luc Cuadrado
Eric J. Fleury
Michel Frieh
Jay F. Leary
Bernard Le-Pezron
Daniel Payan
Emmanuel Rosenfeld
Kristen van Riel

SPECIAL COUNSEL

Anna De Nerciat-Lascar

ASSOCIATES

Thomas W. Bark
Guy Benda
Alexandra Bigot
Adrien Cadieux (Not admitted in France)
Jean-Christophe Castera
Pascal Chadenet
Franck Courmont
Allard De Waal
Renaud DuBois
Claire Duval
John R. Flanigan
Jeffrey W. Fouts
Catherine Jeancolas
Jonathan E. Marsh (Not admitted in France)
Didier Penot
Muriel Serre-Prevost
Christophe Garaud

(Firm registered as Conseils Juridiques, not admitted to practice in French Courts reserved for Avocats)

For full biographical listings, see the Martindale-Hubbell Law Directory

Canadian Lawyers In Paris

OSLER RENAULT

4, rue Bayard, 75008 Paris
Telephone: 1.42.89.00.54
Fax: 1.42.89.51.60
London, England Office: 20 Little Britain, London, EC1A 7DH.
Telephone: 071-606-0777.
Fax: 071-606-0222.
New York, N.Y. Office: 200 Park Avenue, Suite 3217, 10166-0193.
Telephone: 212-867-5800.
Fax: 212-867-5802.
Hong Kong Office: Suite 1708, One Pacific Place, 88 Queensway.
Telephone: 011-852-2877-3933.
Fax: 011-852-2877-0866.
Singapore Office: 65 Chulia Street, #40-05 OCBC Centre, Singapore 0104.
Telephone: (65) 538-2077.
Fax: (65) 538-2977.
Osler Renault is an international partnership of Osler, Hoskin & Harcourt and Ogilvy Renault.
Osler, Hoskin & Harcourt has offices at: P.O. Box: 50, 1 First Canadian Place, Toronto, Ontario, Canada M5X 1B8.
Telephone: 416-362-2111.
Fax: 416-862-6666 and 50 O'Connor Street, Suite 1500, Ottawa, Ontario, Canada K1P 6L2.
Telephone: 613-235-7234.
Fax: 613-235-2867.
Ogilvy Renault has offices at: 1981 McGill College Avenue, Suite 1100, Montreal, Quebec, Canada H3A 3C1.
Telephone: 514-847-4747.
Fax: 514-286-5474 and Suite 1600, 45 O'Connor Street, Ottawa, Ontario, Canada K1P 1A4.
Telephone: 613-780-8661.
Fax: 613-230-5459 and 500 Grande-Allée Est, Suite 520, Quebec, Quebec G1R 2J7.
Telephone: 418-640-5000. Fax 418-640-1500.

RESIDENT IN PARIS

Serge Gravel

For full biographical listings, see the Martindale-Hubbell Law Directory

GERMANY

BERLIN,

DÖSER AMERELLER NOACK

(Baker & McKenzie)
Kleiststrasse 23-26, D-10787 Berlin
Telephone: (030) 214990-0
Intn'l Dialing: (49-30) 214990-0
Facsimile: (49-30) 214990-99
Frankfurt/Main, Germany Office: Bethmannstrasse 50-54, D-60311 Frankfurt/Main.
Telephone: (069) 299080.
Facsimile: (069) 29908108.

(See Next Column)

DÖSER AMERELLER NOACK, *Berlin—Continued*

Carl H. Andres * Wilhelm B. Hebing *
Ulrich Hennings *

OF COUNSEL

Reinhard Pöllath

ASSOCIATES

Gregor Frank
Max B. Gutbrod
Andre Sayatz
Andres Schollmeier
Frank-Rainer Töpfer
Frank Vogel
Heidemarie Wagner
Hubertus Welsch
Peter Wessels

*Also Partner of Baker & McKenzie, Chicago, Illinois, U.S.A.

For full biographical listings, see the Martindale-Hubbell Law Directory

MAYER, BROWN & PLATT

Spreeufer 5, Berlin 10178
Telephone: 011-49-30-240-7930
Facsimile: 011-49-30-240-79344
Chicago, Illinois Office: 190 South LaSalle Street, 60603-3441.
Telephone: (312) -782-0600. Pitney Bowes: (312) 701-7711.
Telex: 190404.
Cable: LEMAY.
Washington, D.C. Office: 2000 Pennsylvania Avenue, N.W., 20006-1882.
Telephone: (202) 463-2000. Pitney Bowes: (202) 861-0484, Pitney Bowes: (202) 861-0473.
Telex: 892603.
Cable: LEMAYDC
New York, New York Office: 787 Seventh Avenue, Suite 2400, 10019-6018.
Telephone: (212) 554-3000. Pitney Bowes: (212) 262-1910.
Telex: 701842.
Cable: LEMAYEN.
Houston, Texas Office: 700 Louisiana Street, Suite 3600, 77002-2730.
Telephone: (713) 221-1651. Pitney Bowes: (713) 224-6410.
Telex: 775809.
Cable: LEMAYHOU.
Los Angeles, California Office: 350 South Grand Avenue, 25th Floor, 90071-1503.
Telephone: (213) 229-9500. Pitney Bowes: (213) 625-0248.
Telex: 188089.
Cable: LEMAYLA.
London, England Office: 162 Queen Victoria Street, EC4V 4DB.
Telephone: 011-44-71-248-1465.
Fax: 011-44-71-329-4465.
Telex: 8811095.
Cable: LEMAYLDN.
Tokyo, Japan Office: (Kawachi Gaikokuho Jimu Bengoshi Jimusho) Urbannet Otemachi Building 13F 2-2, Otemachi 2-chome, Chiyoda-ku, Tokyo 100.
Telephone: 011-81-3-5255-9700.
Facsimile: 011-81-3-5255-9797.
Brussels, Belgium Office: Square de Meeûs 19/20, Bte. 4, 1040.
Telephone: 011-32-2-512-9878.
Fax: 011-32-2-511-3305.
Telex: 20768 MBPBRU B.
Mexico City, Mexico, D.F., Mexico Correspondent: Jáuregui, Navarrete, Nader y Rojas, S.C., Abogados, Paseo de la Reforma 199, Pisos 15, 16 & 17, 06500.
Telephone: 011-525-591-16-55.
Fax: 011-525-535-80-62, 011-525-703-22-47.
Cable: JANANE.

PARTNER

C. Mark Nicolaides (Not admitted in Germany)

ASSOCIATE

Richard L. Bjelde (Not admitted in Germany)

For full biographical listings, see the Martindale-Hubbell Law Directory

WILMER, CUTLER & PICKERING

Friedrichstrasse 95, D-10117 Berlin
Telephone: (49 30) 2643-3601
Facsimile: (49 30) 2643-3630
Washington, D.C. Office: 2445 M Street, N.W., 20037-1420.
Telephone: 202-663-6000.
Facsimile: 202-663-6363. Internet: Law@Wilmer.Com.
London, England Office: 4 Carlton Gardens, London, SW1Y 5AA.
Telephone: (44 71) 839-4466.
Facsimile: (44 71) 839-3537.
Brussels, Belgium Office: Rue de la Loi 15 Wetstraat, B-1040.
Telephone: (32 2) 231-0903.
Facsimile: (32 2) 230-4322.

RESIDENT PARTNERS

Dr. Manfred Balz
Bryan Slone (Not admitted in Germany)

ASSOCIATES

Dr. Natalie Lübben
Jutta Von Falkenhausen
Henning Mennenoeh

For full biographical listings, see the Martindale-Hubbell Law Directory

DÜSSELDORF,

American Lawyers In Düsseldorf

SHEARMAN & STERLING

Königsallee 46, D-40212 Düsseldorf
Telephone: (49-211) 13 62 80
Telex: 8 588 294 NYLO
Fax: (49-211) 13 33 09
New York, N.Y. Office: 599 Lexington Avenue, New York, New York 10022-6069 and Citicorp Center, 153 East 53rd Street, New York, New York 10022-4676.
Telephone: (212) 848-4000.
Telex: 667290 Num Lau.
Fax: 599 Lexington Avenue: (212) 848-7179. Citicorp Center: (212) 848-5252.
Abu Dhabi, United Arab Emirates Office: P.O. Box 2948.
Telephone: (971-2) 324477.
Fax: (971-2) 774533.
Beijing, People's Republic of China Office: Suite #2205, Capital Mansion, No. 6, Xin Yuan Nan Road. Chao Yang District Beijing, 100004.
Telephone: (861) 465-4574.
Fax: (861) 465-4578.
Budapest, Hungary Office: Szerb utca 17-19, 1056 Budapest.
Telephone: (36-1) 266-3522.
Fax: (36-1) 266-3523.
Frankfurt, Federal Republic of Germany Office: Bockenheimer Landstrasse 55, D-60325 Frankfurt am Main.
Telephone: (49-69) 97-10-70.
Fax: (49-69) 97-10-71-00.
Hong Kong, Hong Kong Office: Standard Chartered Bank Building, 4 Des Voeux Road Central, Hong Kong.
Telephone: (852) 2978-8000.
Fax: (852) 2978-8099.
London, England Office: 199 Bishopsgate, London EC2M 3TY.
Telephone: (44-71) 920-9000.
Fax: (44-71) 920-9020.
Los Angeles, California Office: 725 South Figueroa Street, 21st Floor, 90017-5421.
Telephone: (213) 239-0300.
Fax: (213) 239-0381, 614-0936.
Paris, France Office: 12 rue d'Astorg, 75008.
Telephone: (33-1) 44-71-17-17.
Telex: 282964 Royale.
Fax: (33-1) 44-71-01-01.
San Francisco, California Office: 555 California Street, 94104-1522.
Telephone: (415) 616-1100.
Fax: (415) 616-1199.
Taipei, Taiwan Office: 7th Floor, Hung Kuo Building, 167 Tun Hwa North Road.
Telephone: (886-2) 545-3300.
Fax: (866-2) 545-3322.
Tokyo, Japan Office: Shearman & Sterling (Thomas Wilner Gaikokuho-Jimu-Bengoshi Jimusho), Fukoku Seimei Building, 5th Fl. 2-2-2, Uchisaiwaicho, Chiyoda-ku, Tokyo 100, Japan.
Telephone: (81 3) 5251-1601.
Fax: (81 3) 5251-1602.
Toronto, Ontario, Canada Office: Commerce Court West, Suite 4405, P.O. Box 247, M5L 1E8.
Telephone: (416) 360-8484.
Fax: (416) 360-2958.
Washington, D.C. Office: 801 Pennsylvania Avenue, N.W., Suite 900, 20004-2604.
Telephone: (202) 508-8000.
Fax: (202) 508-8100.

RESIDENT PARTNERS

Georg F. Thoma (Managing Partner, Dusseldorf and Frankfurt)
Michael Gruson (Not admitted in Germany)

RESIDENT ASSOCIATES

Dr. Anton Klösters
Dr. Alfred L. Kossmann
Dr. Henning H. Krauss
Dr. Hans Jürgen Meyer-Lindemann
Wanda Kim (Not admitted in Germany)

For full biographical listings, see the Martindale-Hubbell Law Directory

FRANKFURT/MAIN,

CLEARY, GOTTLIEB, STEEN & HAMILTON

Ulmenstrasse 37-39, 60325 Frankfurt/Main
Telephone: 49-69-971 03-0
Facsimile: 49-69-971 03 199
New York, New York Office: One Liberty Plaza, New York, N.Y. 10006.
Telephone: 212-225-2000.
Washington, D.C. Office: 1752 N Street, N.W., Washington, D.C. 20036.
Telephone: 202-728-2700.
Paris, France Office: 41, Avenue de Friedland, 75008 Paris, France.
Telephone: 33-1-4074-6800.
Brussels, Belgium Office: Rue de la Loi 23, Bte 5, 1040 Brussels, Belgium.
Telephone: 32-2-287-2000.

(See Next Column)

CLEARY, GOTTLIEB, STEEN & HAMILTON—*Continued*

London, England Office: City Place House, 55 Basinghall Street, London EC2V 5EH England.
Telephone: 44-71-614-2200.
Hong Kong Office: 56th Floor, Bank of China Tower, One Garden Road, Hong Kong.
Telephone: 852-521-4122.
Tokyo, Japan Office: Morgan Carroll Terai Gaikokuho Jimubengoshi Jimusho, 20th Floor, Shin Kasumigaseki Building, 3-2, Kasumigaseki 3-Chome, Chiyoda-Ku, Tokyo 100, Japan.
Telephone: 81-3-3595-3911.

RESIDENT PARTNERS

Russell H. Pollack (Not admitted in Germany)
Christof von Dryander
Thomas M. Buhl

ASSOCIATES

Gabriele Apfelbacher
Stephan Barthelmess
Ward A. Greenberg (Not admitted in Germany)
Susanne Halstrick
Reinhard Hermes
Werner Meier
Francesca M. Moretti (Not admitted in Germany)
Ralf M. Nitschke
Brendan J. Ross (Not admitted in Germany)
Christian Oscar Zschocke

For full biographical listings, see the Martindale-Hubbell Law Directory

DÖSER AMERELLER NOACK

(Baker & McKenzie)
Bethmannstrasse 50-54, D-60311 Frankfurt/Main
Telephone: (069) 299080
Intn'l Dialing: (49-69) 299080
Cable Address: ABOGADO
Telex: 414239
Answer back: 414239a BM D
Facsimile: (49-69) 29908108
Berlin, Germany Office: Kleiststrasse 23-26, D-10787 Berlin.
Telephone: (030) 214990-0.
Facsimile: (030) 214990-99.

PARTNERS

Horst Amereller *
Christian Brodersen *
Wulf H. Döser *
Hans-Georg Feick *
Peter Ficht *
Wolfgang Fritzemeyer *
Günther Heckelmann *
Walter Henle *
Matthias G. Jaletzke *
Karl-Ludwig Koenen *
Rainer A. Magold *
Werner Müller *
Hilmar Noack *
Ulrich Ränsch *
Andreas Rodin *
Joachim Scherer *
Rainer Stachels *
Joachim Treeck *
Franz J. Waltermann *

ASSOCIATES

Michael A. Fammler
Bernd J. Götze
Sebastian Gronstedt
Axel Hamm
Andreas Hoffmann
Ingrid M. Kalisch
Markus O. Kappenhagen
Jörg K. Kirchner
Michael Mack
Jürgen Mark
Grace Nacimiento
Sibilla Nagel
Hansjörg Piehl
Thilo Räpple
Achim Schäfer
Matthias P. Scholz
Jörg-Martin Schultze
Peter Sigel
Stephan J. Spehl
Leokadia Szalkiewicz-Zaradzka
Constanze Ulmer-Eilfort
Ulf Wauschkuhn

*Also Partner of Baker & McKenzie, Chicago, Illinois, U.S.A.

For full biographical listings, see the Martindale-Hubbell Law Directory

American Lawyers In Frankfurt/Main

JONES, DAY, REAVIS & POGUE

Triton Haus, Bockenheimer Landstrasse 42, 60323 Frankfurt/Main
Telephone: 49-69-9726-3939
Telecopier: 49-69-9726-3993.
In Atlanta, Georgia: 3500 One Peachtree Center, 303 Peachtree Street, N.E.
Telephone: 404-521-3939.
Cable Address: "Attorneys Atlanta".
Telex: 54-2711.
Telecopier: 404-581-8330.
In Brussels, Belgium: Avenue Louise 480, 7th Floor. B-1050 Brussels.
Telephone: 32-2-645-14-11.
Telecopier: 32-2-645-14-45.
In Chicago, Illinois: 77 West Wacker.
Telephone: 312-782-3939.
Telecopier: 312-782-8585.
In Cleveland, Ohio: North Point, 901 Lakeside Avenue.
Telephone: 216-586-3939.
Cable Address: "Attorneys Cleveland."
Telex: 980389.
Telecopier: 216-579-0212.

(See Next Column)

In Columbus, Ohio: 1900 Huntington Center.
Telephone: 614-469-3939.
Cable Address: "Attorneys Columbus."
Telecopier: 614-461-4198.
In Dallas, Texas: 2300 Trammell Crow Center, 2001 Ross Avenue.
Telephone: 214-220-3939.
Cable Address: "Attorneys Dallas."
Telex: 730852.
Telecopier: 214-969-5100.
In Geneva, Switzerland: 20, rue de Candolle.
Telephone: 41-22-320-2339.
Telecopier: 41-22-320-1232.
In Hong Kong: 1501 One Exchange Square, 8 Connaught Place.
Telephone: 852-2526-6895.
Telecopier: 852-2810-5787.
In Irvine, California: 2603 Main Street, Suite 900.
Telephone: 714-851-3939.
Telex: 194911 Lawyers LSA.
Telecopier: 714-553-7539.
In London, England: One Mount Street.
Telephone: 44-71-493-9361.
Cable Address: "Surgoe London WI."
Telecopier: 44-71-493-9666.
In Los Angeles, California: 555 West Fifth Street, Suite 4600.
Telephone: 213-489-3939.
Telex: 181439 UD.
Telecopier: 213-243-2539.
In New York, New York: 599 Lexington Avenue.
Telephone: 212-326-3939.
Cable Address: "JONESDAY NEWYORK."
Telex: 237013 JDRP UR.
Telecopier: 212-755-7306.
In Paris, France: 62, rue du Faubourg Saint-Honore.
Telephone: 33-1-44-71-3939.
Cable Address: "Surgoe Paris."
Telex: 290156 Surgoe.
Telecopier: 33-1-49-24-0471.
In Pittsburgh, Pennsylvania: 500 Grant Street, 31st Floor.
Telephone: 412-391-3939.
Cable Address: "Attorneys Pittsburgh".
Telecopier: 412-394-7959.
In Riyadh, Saudi Arabia: Law Offices of Saud M.A. Shawwaf, P.O. Box 2700.
Telephones: (966-1) 465-6543, (966-1) 464-8534 or (966-1) 464-8540.
Telex: 401831 SAUCON SJ.
Telecopier: (966-1) 464-8480.
In Taipei, Taiwan: 8th Floor, 2 Tun Hwa South Road, Section 2.
Telephone: (886-2) 704-6808.
Telecopier: (886-2) 704-6791.
In Tokyo, Japan: Toranomon MT Building, 4th Floor, 10-3, Toranomon 3-Chome, Minato-Ku, Tokyo 105, Japan.
Telephone: 81-3-3433-3939.
Telecopier: 81-3-5401-2725.
In Washington, D.C.: Metropolitan Square, 1450 G Street, N.W.
Telephone: 202-879-3939.
Cable Address: "Attorneys Washington."
Telex: 89-2410 ATTORNEYS WASH.
Telecopier: 202-737-2832.

MEMBERS OF FIRM IN FRANKFURT

Karl G. Herold
Dr. Norbert Koch (Resident, Brussels, Belgium)
Richard H. Kreindler

OF COUNSEL

Dr. Helga Elizabeth Kroeger

ASSOCIATES

Oliver Passavant (Not admitted in Germany)
Ansgar C. Rempp
Douglas J. Whipple (Not admitted in Germany)
Phillip H. Schmandt (Not admitted in Germany)
Antje Westphal (Not admitted in Germany)

For full biographical listings, see the Martindale-Hubbell Law Directory

SHEARMAN & STERLING

Bockenheimer Landstrasse 55, D-60325 Frankfurt/Main
Telephone: (49-69) 97-10-70
Fax: (49-69) 97-10-71-00
New York, N.Y. Office: 599 Lexington Avenue, New York, New York 10022-6069 and Citicorp Center, 153 East 53rd Street, New York, New York 10022-4676.
Telephone: (212) 848-4000.
Telex: 667290 Num Lau.
Fax: 599 Lexington Avenue: (212) 848-7179. Citicorp Center: (212) 848-5252.
Abu Dhabi, United Arab Emirates Office: P.O. Box 2948.
Telephone: (971-2) 324477.
Fax: (971-2) 774533.
Beijing, People's Republic of China Office: Suite #2205, Capital Mansion, No. 6, Xin Yuan Nan Road. Chao Yang District Beijing, 100004.
Telephone: (861) 465-4574.
Fax: (861) 465-4578.

(See Next Column)

SHEARMAN & STERLING, *Frankfurt/Main—Continued*

Budapest, Hungary Office: Szerb utca 17-19, 1056 Budapest.
Telephone: (36-1) 266-3522.
Fax: (36-1) 266-3523.
Düsseldorf, Federal Republic of Germany Office: Königsallee 46, D-40212 Düsseldorf.
Telephone: (49-211) 13 62 80.
Telex: 8 588 294 NYLO.
Fax: (49-211) 13 33 09.
Hong Kong, Hong Kong Office: Standard Chartered Bank Building, 4 Des Voeux Road Central, Hong Kong.
Telephone: (852) 2978-8000.
Fax: (852) 2978-8099.
London, England Office: 199 Bishopsgate, London EC2M 3TY.
Telephone: (44-71) 920-9000.
Fax: (44-71) 920-9020.
Los Angeles, California Office: 725 South Figueroa Street, 21st Floor, 90017-5421.
Telephone: (213) 239-0300.
Fax: (213) 239-0381, 614-0936.
Paris, France Office: 12 rue d'Astorg, 75008.
Telephone: (33-1) 44-71-17-17.
Telex: 282964 Royale.
Fax: (33-1) 44-71-01-01.
San Francisco, California Office: 555 California Street, 94104-1522.
Telephone: (415) 616-1100.
Fax: (415) 616-1199.
Taipei, Taiwan Office: 7th Floor, Hung Kuo Building, 167 Tun Hwa North Road.
Telephone: (886-2) 545-3300.
Fax: (866-2) 545-3322.
Tokyo, Japan Office: Shearman & Sterling (Thomas Wilner Gaikokuho-Jimu-Bengoshi Jimusho), Fukoku Seimei Building, 5th Fl. 2-2-2, Uchisaiwaicho, Chiyoda-ku, Tokyo 100, Japan.
Telephone: (81 3) 5251-1601.
Fax: (81 3) 5251-1602.
Toronto, Ontario, Canada Office: Commerce Court West, Suite 4405, P.O. Box 247, M5L 1E8.
Telephone: (416) 360-8484.
Fax: (416) 360-2958.
Washington, D.C. Office: 801 Pennsylvania Avenue, N.W., Suite 900, 20004-2604.
Telephone: (202) 508-8000.
Fax: (202) 508-8100.

RESIDENT PARTNERS

William J. Wiegmann (Not admitted in Germany)
Michael Gruson (Not admitted in Germany)

RESIDENT ASSOCIATES

Jonathan S. Berck (Not admitted in Germany)
Dr. Herbert Harrer
Dr. Stephan Hutter (Not admitted in Germany)
Dr. Thomas N. König
Michael A. Leppert
Johann Georg Mühlmann
Petra J. Pellicano (Not admitted in Germany)
Titus J. Weinheimer
Dr. Johannes Weisser

For full biographical listings, see the Martindale-Hubbell Law Directory

HONG KONG (BRITISH CROWN COLONY)

HONG KONG,

BAKER & MCKENZIE

14th Floor, Hutchison House, 10 Harcourt Road, Hong Kong
Telephone: 2846-1888
Intn'l. Dialing: (852) 2846-1888
Cable Address: ABOGADO
Telex: 76416
Answer Back: 76416 ABOG HX
Facsimiles: (852) 2845-0476; 2845-0487; 2845-0490
Associated Offices of Baker & McKenzie in: Almaty, Amsterdam, Bangkok, Barcelona, Beijing, Berlin, Bogotá, Brasília, Brussels, Budapest, Buenos Aires, Cairo, Caracas, Chicago, Dallas, Frankfurt, Geneva, Hanoi, Ho Chi Minh City, Juárez, Kiev, London, Madrid, Manila, Melbourne, México City, Miami, Milan, Monterrey, Moscow, New York, Palo Alto, Paris, Prague, Rio de Janeiro, Riyadh, Rome, St. Petersburg, San Diego, San Francisco, São Paulo, Singapore, Stockholm, Sydney, Taipei, Tijuana, Tokyo, Toronto, Valencia, Warsaw, Washington, D.C. and Zürich.
Correspondent Law Firm: Hadiputranto, Hadinoto & Partners, Jakarta.

Robert A. Arnold
John C. Atkinson
Pius K. W. Cheng
Yuk Tong Cheung
Paul S. Elliott
Stephen R. Eno
Patrick B. Fontaine
George Forrai
Mark S. Goetze
Graeme Ross Halford
William Kuo
Angela W. Y. Lee
Lawrence K. H. Lee
Cheuk-Yan Leung
David R. Martin
John M. Morgans
Graham D. Morrison
Michael A. Olesnicky

(See Next Column)

David R. Shannon
Paul Chuen Yan Tan
Poh Lee Tan
Christopher J. Wilson

Cole R. Capener (Not admitted in Hong Kong)
Mitchell M. Gitin (Not admitted in Hong Kong)
Michael J. Moser (Not admitted in Hong Kong)
Richard L. Weisman (Not admitted in Hong Kong)
Winston K. T. Zee (Not admitted in Hong Kong)

LOCAL PARTNERS

Paul John Carolan
Barry Wai-Man Cheng
Betty Man Yee Choi
Neil M. Donoghue
David J. Fleming
Junri Konii
Alan H. Linning
Fiona Loughrey
Rodney J. McNeil
F. Jeannie Smith
Ernest Kam Too Wong

Frederick R. Burke (Not admitted in Hong Kong)
Stephen M. Nelson (Not admitted in Hong Kong)

ASSOCIATES

Andrew J. L. Aglionby
Angela C. S. Ang
Judy Brown
Edmond Lap Yan Chan
Edward P. Chan
Elsa S. C. Chan
Rico W. K. Chan
Anne Wai Yui Chen
Gerami King Hoi Cheng
Milton W. M. Cheng
Debbie Fong Cheung
Anna Chong
Lisa K. F. Chu
Ying Woo Chung
Sally A. Durant
Mark G. Fairbairn
Dow P. Famulak
Veronica K. S. Fok
Wendy W. T. Fung
Joyce K. W. Ho
Thomas K. H. Ho
William K. K. Ho
Frederick J. Horsey
James T. O. Huang
Mark C. Innis
Graeme S. M. Johnston
Molly Kiat
Joseph Kwan
Vinnie Lam
Harvey Lau
Vivian W. W. Lau
Benny Lee
Anita P. F. Leung
Florence C. H. Leung
Karen L. Linker
Elaine Y. L. Liu
Jackie F. K. Lo
Andrew W. Lockhart
Thessa Mac
John M. Maguire
Allan J. McCay
Elizabeth Wai Yin Mo
Jennifer Ng
Hilary M. Ng-Cordell
Gary A. Seib
Susan Shyu
Douglas C. T. So
Cindy Synn-Chee Tam
Loke Khoon Tan
Cynthia Y. S. Tang
Renouka Tucker
Philip A. Walden
Sin Yee Wong
Steve S. Woo
Sharon P. Yau
Chlorophyll W. Y. Yip
Ricky C. W. Yiu
Christina S. Y. Yu
Priscilla H. S. Yu
Lap Yan Yung

Sara Yang Bosco (Not admitted in Hong Kong)
Christopher M. Buchan (Not admitted in Hong Kong)
Andrew S. Case (Not admitted in Hong Kong)
H. Theodore Chang (Not admitted in Hong Kong)
Annie A. Y. Chen (Not admitted in Hong Kong)
Lance C. H. Chen (Not admitted in Hong Kong)
Maggie C. F. Cheng (Not admitted in Hong Kong)
Elizabeth A. Chippindale (Not admitted in Hong Kong)
Alexander G. Christie (Not admitted in Hong Kong)
Wei Han Chung (Not admitted in Hong Kong)
Thao H. Cung (Not admitted in Hong Kong)
Linda A. De Silva (Not admitted in Hong Kong)
John V. Grobowski (Not admitted in Hong Kong)
Victor Ho (Not admitted in Hong Kong)
Stanley D. Jia (Not admitted in Hong Kong)
Andreas W. Lauffs (Not admitted in Hong Kong)
Hanh Le Young (Not admitted in Hong Kong)
Robert D. Lewis (Not admitted in Hong Kong)
Chiang Ling Li (Not admitted in Hong Kong)
Mei Yin Lim (Not admitted in Hong Kong)
Seok Hui Lim (Not admitted in Hong Kong)
Shih Yann Loo (Not admitted in Hong Kong)
Chun Fai Lui (Not admitted in Hong Kong)
David E. Neuville (Not admitted in Hong Kong)
Andrew W. Petry (Not admitted in Hong Kong)
Philana Wai-Yin Poon (Not admitted in Hong Kong)
Iain C. L. Seow (Not admitted in Hong Kong)
Jeffrey R. Sims (Not admitted in Hong Kong)
Christopher W. Smith (Not admitted in Hong Kong)
Peter J. Stirling (Not admitted in Hong Kong)
Richard Y. Sung (Not admitted in Hong Kong)
Andrew C. K. Tan (Not admitted in Hong Kong)
Gregory Woo Hin Tan (Not admitted in Hong Kong)
Huey S. Tan (Not admitted in Hong Kong)
Jefferson P. VanderWolk (Not admitted in Hong Kong)
Danchi Wang (Not admitted in Hong Kong)
Corinna M. Wong (Not admitted in Hong Kong)
Helen H. Yee (Not admitted in Hong Kong)

(See Next Column)

BAKER & MCKENZIE—*Continued*

Danian Zhang (Not admitted in Hong Kong)
Yulin Zhang (Not admitted in Hong Kong)

For full biographical listings, see the Martindale-Hubbell Law Directory

O'MELVENY & MYERS

1104 Lippo Tower, Lippo Centre 89 Queensway, Central, Hong Kong
Telephone: 011-852-523-8266
Facsimile: 011-852-522-1760
Los Angeles, California Office: 400 South Hope Street.
Telephone: 213-669-6000.
Cable Address: "Moms."
Facsimile: 213-669-6407.
Century City, California Office: 1999 Avenue of the Stars, 7th Floor.
Telephone: 310-553-6700.
Facsimile: 310-246-6779.
Newport Beach, California Office: 610 Newport Center Drive, Suite 1700.
Telephone: 714-760-9600.
Cable Address: "Moms."
Facsimile: 714-669-6994.
San Francisco, California Office: Embarcadero Center West Tower, 275 Battery Street, Suite 2600.
Telephone: 415-984-8700.
Facsimile: 415-984-8701.
New York, N.Y. Office: Citicorp Center. 153 53rd Street, 54th Floor.
Telephone: 212-326-2000.
Facsimile: 212-326-2061.
Washington, D.C. Office: 555 13th Street, N.W., Suite 500 West.
Telephone: 202-383-5300.
Cable Address: "Moms."
Facsimile: 202-383-5414.
Newark, New Jersey Office: One Gateway Center, 7th Floor, 07102.
Telephone: 201-639-8600.
Facsimile: 201-639-8630.
London, England Office: 10 Finsbury Square, London, EC2A 1LA.
Telephone: 011-44-171-256-8451.
Facsimile: 011-44-171-638-8205.
Tokyo, Japan Office: Sanbancho KB-6 Building, 6 Sanbancho, Chiyoda-Ku.
Telephone: 011-81-3-3239-2800.
Facsimile: 011-81-3-3239-2432.
Hong Kong Office: 1104 Lippo Tower, Lippo Centre, 89 Queensway, Central Hong Kong.
Telephone: 011-852-523-8266.
Facsimile: 011-852-522-1760.

PARTNER

Howard Chao

SPECIAL COUNSEL

Fiona M. Connell

For full biographical listings, see the Martindale-Hubbell Law Directory

SULLIVAN & CROMWELL (AV)

28th Floor, Nine Queen's Road, Central, Hong Kong
Telephone: (011)(852)826-8688
Telecopier: (011)(852)522-2280
New York City Offices: 125 Broad Street. 10004-2498; Midtown Office: 250 Park Avenue, 10177-0021.
Telephone: 212-558-4000.
Telex: 62694 (International); 12-7816 (Domestic).
Cable Address: "Ladycourt, New York".
Telecopier: 125 Broad Street 212-558-3588; 250 Park Avenue 212-558-3792.
Washington, D.C. Office: 1701 Pennsylvania Avenue, N.W., 20006-5805.
Telephone: 202-956-7500.
Telex: 89625.
Telecopier: 202-293-6330.
Los Angeles, California Office: 444 South Flower Street, 90071-2901.
Telephone: 213-955-8000.
Telecopier: 213-683-0457.
Paris Office: 8, Place Vendôme, Paris 75001, France.
Telephone: (011)(331)4450-6000.
Telex: 240654.
Telecopier: (011)(331)4450-6060.
London Office: St. Olave's House, 9a Ironmonger Lane, London EC2V 8EY, England.
Telephone: (011)(44171)710-6500.
Telecopier: (011)(44171)710-6565.
Melbourne, Australia Office: 101 Collins Street, Melbourne, Victoria 3000.
Telephone: (011)(613)654-1500.
Telecopier: (011)(613)654-2422.
Tokyo Office: Gaikokuho Jimu Bengoshi Office of Robert G. DeLaMater, a member of the firm of Sullivan & Cromwell, Tokio Kaijo Building Shinkan, 2-1, Marunouchi, 1-chome Chiyoda-ku, Tokyo 100, Japan.
Telephone: (011)(813)3213-6140.
Telecopier: (011)(813)3213-6470.

PARTNERS IN HONG KONG

Donald C. Walkovik
John Evangelakos

(See Next Column)

ASSOCIATES IN HONG KONG

John Nelson Chrisman
Peter P.H. Lin
Scott D. Clemens
Yoichiro Taniguchi
Sung Jin Hwang
Chun Wei
John D. Young, Jr.

(Not admitted to practice in Hong Kong courts)

For full biographical listings, see the Martindale-Hubbell Law Directory

American Lawyers In Hong Kong

CHADBOURNE & PARKE

Suite 3704 Peregrine Tower Lippo Centre, 89 Queensway, Hong Kong
Telephone: (852) 2842-5400
Telecopier: (852) 2521-7527
New York, N.Y. Office: 30 Rockefeller Plaza, 10112.
Telephone: 212-408-5100.
Telecopier: 212-541-5369.
Washington, D.C. Office: Suite 900, 1101 Vermont Avenue, N.W., 20005.
Telephone: 202-289-3000.
Telecopier: 202-289-3002.
Los Angeles, California Office: 601 South Figueroa Street, 90017.
Telephone: 213-892-1000.
Telecopier: 213-622-9865.
London, England Office: 86 Jermyn Street, SW1 6JD.
Telephone: 44-171-925-7400.
Facsimile: 44-171-839-3393.
Moscow, Russia Office: 38 Maxim Gorky Naberezhnaya, 113035.
Telephone: 7095-974-2424.
Telecopier: 7095-974-2425. International satellite lines via U.S.:
Telephone: 212-408-1190.
Telecopier: 212-408-1199.
New Delhi, India Office: Chadbourne & Parke Associates, A16-B Anand Niketan, 110 021.
Telephone: 91-11-301-7568/7581/7582.
Telecopier: 91-11-301-7351.

RESIDENT PARTNERS

Peter D. Cleary (Not admitted in Hong Kong)
Robert J. Bohme (Not admitted in Hong Kong)

RESIDENT COUNSEL

Martin C.M. Bashall (Not admitted in Hong Kong)

RESIDENT ASSOCIATES

Kerin Cantwell (Not admitted in Hong Kong)
George He Zhu (Not admitted in Hong Kong)
Mitchell A. Silk (Not admitted in Hong Kong)

For full biographical listings, see the Martindale-Hubbell Law Directory

CLEARY, GOTTLIEB, STEEN & HAMILTON

56th Floor Bank of China Tower, One Garden Road, Hong Kong
Telephone: 852-521-4122
Cable Address: "Cleargolaw, Hong Kong"
Telex: 60401 Clear HX
Fax: 852-845-9026
New York, New York Office: One Liberty Plaza, New York, N.Y. 10006.
Telephone: 212-225-2000.
Washington, D.C. Office: 1752 N Street, N.W., Washington, D.C. 20036.
Telephone: 202-728-2700.
Paris, France Office: 41, Avenue de Friedland, 75008 Paris, France.
Telephone: 33-1-4074-6800.
Brussels, Belgium Office: Rue de la Loi 23, Bte 5, 1040 Brussels, Belgium.
Telephone: 32-2-287-2000.
London, England Office: City Place House, 55 Basinghall Street, London, EC2V 5EH, England.
Telephone: 44-71-614-2200.
Tokyo, Japan Office: Morgan Carroll Terai Gaikokuho Jimu Bengoshi Jimusho, 20th Floor, Shin Kasumigaseki Building, 3-2, Kasumigaseki 3-Chome, Chiyoda-Ku, Tokyo 100, Japan.
Telephone: 81-3-3595-3911.
Frankfurt, Germany Office: Ulmenstrasse 37-39, 60325 Frankfurt am Main, Germany.
Telephone: 49-69-971-03-0.

RESIDENT PARTNERS

Robert P. Davis (Not admitted in Hong Kong)
Christopher E. Austin (Not admitted in Hong Kong)

SPECIAL COUNSEL

Michael M. Hickman (Not admitted in Hong Kong)

ASSOCIATES

Jinduk Han (Not admitted in Hong Kong)
David F. Johnson (Not admitted in Hong Kong)
David W. Hirsch (Not admitted in Hong Kong)
Fabrice Baumgartner (Not admitted in Hong Kong)
Laurie A. Smiley (Not admitted in Hong Kong)
Yong G. Lee (Not admitted in Hong Kong)

(Not admitted to practice in Hong Kong courts)

For full biographical listings, see the Martindale-Hubbell Law Directory

COUDERT BROTHERS

American Attorneys at Law
25th Floor, Nine Queen's Road Central, Hong Kong
Telephone: (852) 2810-4111
Cable Address: "Treduoc"
Telecopier: (852) 2845-9021
Telex: HX74073 "Amlaw"
New York, N.Y. 10036-7794: 1114 Avenue of the Americas.
Washington, D.C. 20006: 1627 I Street, N.W.
Los Angeles, California 90017: 1055 West Seventh Street, Twentieth Floor.
San Francisco, California 94111: 4 Embarcadero Center, Suite 3300.
San Jose, California 95113: Suite 1250, Ten Almaden Boulevard.
Paris 75008, France: Coudert Frères, 52, Avenue des Champs-Elysees.
London, EC4V 5AA, England: 4 Dean's Court.
Brussels B-1050, Belgium: Tour Louise. 149 Avenue Louise-Box 8.
Beijing 100020, People's Republic of China: Suite 2708-09 Jing Guang Centre Hu Jia Lou, Chao Yang Qu.
Shanghai 200002, People's Republic of China: c/o Suite 1804, Union Building, 100 Yanan Road East.
Singapore 0104: Tung Centre, 20 Collyer Quay.
Sydney N.S.W. 2000, Australia: Suite 2202, State Bank Centre, 52 Martin Place.
Tokyo 107, Japan: 1355 West Tower, Aoyama Twin Towers, 1-1-1 Minami-Aoyama, Minato-ku.
Moscow, Russia: Ulitsa Staraya Basmannaya 14.
01301 Sao Paulo, SP, Brazil: Machado, Meyer, Sendacz, e Opice, Advogados, Rua da Consolacao, 247, 8 Andar.
Bangkok 10500, Thailand: Bubhajit Building, 20 North Sathorn Road, 10th Floor.
Ho Chi Minh City, Vietnam: c/o Saigon Business Centre, 49-57 Dong Du Street, District 1.

RESIDENT PARTNERS

Vivienne Bath (Not admitted in Hong Kong)
David Richard Halperin (Not admitted in Hong Kong)
W. Gage McAfee (Not admitted in Hong Kong)
Owen D. Nee, Jr. (Not admitted in Hong Kong; Managing Partner)
Henry J. Uscinski
Sook Young Yeu (Not admitted in Hong Kong)

RESIDENT ASSOCIATES

Elizabeth A. Bowler (Not admitted in Hong Kong)
John C. Cole, Jr. (Not admitted in Hong Kong)
Cornelia S. Edelman (Not admitted in Hong Kong)
Jong-Dae Lee (Not admitted in Hong Kong)
Rupert X. Li (Not admitted in Hong Kong)
Jeffrey J. Miller (Not admitted in Hong Kong)
Steven L. Toronto (Not admitted in Hong Kong)

(Not admitted to practice in Hong Kong courts)

For full biographical listings, see the Martindale-Hubbell Law Directory

CRAVATH, SWAINE & MOORE

Suite 2609 Asia Pacific Finance Tower Citibank Plaza, 3 Garden Road, Central, Hong Kong
Telephone: 852-509-7200
Facsimile: 852-509-7272
New York City Office: Worldwide Plaza, 825 Eighth Avenue, 10019.
Telephone: 212-474-1000.
Facsimile: 212-474-3700.
Cable Address: "Cravath, New York".
Telex: 1-25547.
London, England Office: 33 King William Street, 10th Floor, London, EC4R 9DU.
Telephone: 071-606-1421.
Facsimile: 071-860-1150.

RESIDENT PARTNERS

Richard M. Allen (Not admitted in Hong Kong)
W. Clayton Johnson (Not admitted in Hong Kong)

SPECIALIST ATTORNEY-HONG KONG

Su Lin Han (Not admitted in Hong Kong)

For full biographical listings, see the Martindale-Hubbell Law Directory

DEBEVOISE & PLIMPTON

13/F Entertainment Building, 30 Queen's Road Central, Hong Kong
Telephone: 852-2810-7918
Fax: 852-2810-9828
New York, N.Y. Office: 875 Third Avenue, 10022.
Telephone: 212-909-6000,
Telex: (Domestic) 148377 DEBSTEVE NYK.
Telecopier: 210-909-68363
Los Angeles, California Office: 601 South Figueroa Street, Suite 3700, 90017.
Telephone: 213-680-8000.
Telex: 401527 DPLA.
Telecopier: 213-680-8100.

(See Next Column)

Washington, D.C. Office: 555 13th Street, N.W., 20004.
Telephone: 202-383-8000.
Telex: 405586 DPDC WUUD.
Telecopier: (202) 383-8118.
Paris, France Office: 21 Avenue George V 75008.
Telephone: (33-1) 40 73 12 12.
Telecopier: (33-1) 47 20 50 82.
Telex: 648141F DPPAR.
London, England Office: 1 Creed Court, 5 Ludgate Hill, EC4M 7AA.
Telephone: (44-171) 329-0779.
Telex: 88 4569 DPLON G.
Facsimile: (44-171) 329-0860.
Budapest, Hungary Office: 1065 Budapest, Révay Köz 2.III/2.
Telephone: (36-1) 131-0845.
Telecopier: (36-1) 132-7995.

RESIDENT PARTNER

Jeffrey S. Wood (Not admitted in Hong Kong)

SPECIAL COUNSEL

Neil Kaplan (Not admitted in Hong Kong)

ASSOCIATES

Gregory V. Gooding (Not admitted in Hong Kong)
Xiaoming Li (Not admitted in Hong Kong)

For full biographical listings, see the Martindale-Hubbell Law Directory

JONES, DAY, REAVIS & POGUE

1501 One Exchange Square, 8 Connaught Place, Hong Kong
Telephone: 852-2526-6895
Telecopier: 852-2810-5787 or 852-2868-5871
In Atlanta, Georgia: 3500 One Peachtree Center, 303 Peachtree Street, N.E.
Telephone: 404-521-3939.
Cable Address: "Attorneys Atlanta".
Telex: 54-2711.
Telecopier: 404-581-8330.
In Brussels, Belgium: Avenue Louise 480, 7th Floor. B-1050 Brussels.
Telephone: 32-2-645-14-11.
Telecopier: 32-2-645-14-45.
In Chicago, Illinois: 77 West Wacker.
Telephone: 312-782-3939.
Telecopier: 312-782-8585.
In Cleveland, Ohio: North Point, 901 Lakeside Avenue.
Telephone: 216-586-3939.
Cable Address: "Attorneys Cleveland."
Telex: 980389.
Telecopier: 216-579-0212.
In Columbus, Ohio: 1900 Huntington Center.
Telephone: 614-469-3939.
Cable Address: "Attorneys Columbus."
Telecopier: 614-461-4198.
In Dallas, Texas: 2300 Trammell Crow Center, 2001 Ross Avenue.
Telephone: 214-220-3939.
Cable Address: "Attorneys Dallas."
Telex: 730852.
Telecopier: 214-969-5100.
In Frankfurt, Germany: Triton Haus, Bockenheimer Landstrasse 42, 60323 Frankfurt am Main.
Telephone: 49-69-9726-3939.
Telecopier: 49-69-9726-3993.
In Geneva, Switzerland: 20, rue de Candolle.
Telephone: 41-22-320-2339.
Telecopier: 41-22-320-1232.
In Irvine, California: 2603 Main Street, Suite 900.
Telephone: 714-851-3939.
Telex: 194911 Lawyers LSA.
Telecopier: 714-553-7539.
In London, England: One Mount Street.
Telephone: 44-71-493-9361.
Cable Address: "Surgoe London WI."
Telecopier: 44-71-493-9666.
In Los Angeles, California: 555 West Fifth Street, Suite 4600.
Telephone: 213-489-3939.
Telex: 181439 UD.
Telecopier: 213-243-2539.
In New York, New York: 599 Lexington Avenue.
Telephone: 212-326-3939.
Cable Address: "JONESDAY NEWYORK."
Telex: 237013 JDRP UR.
Telecopier: 212-755-7306.
In Paris, France: 62, rue du Faubourg Saint-Honore.
Telephone: 33-1-44-71-3939.
Cable Address: "Surgoe Paris."
Telex: 290156 Surgoe.
Telecopier: 33-1-49-24-0471.
In Pittsburgh, Pennsylvania: 500 Grant Street, 31st Floor.
Telephone: 412-391-3939.
Cable Address: "Attorneys Pittsburgh".
Telecopier: 412-394-7959.

(See Next Column)

JONES, DAY, REAVIS & POGUE—*Continued*

In Riyadh, Saudi Arabia: Law Office of Saud M.A. Shawwaf, P.O. Box 2700.
Telephones: (966-1) 465-6543, (966-1) 464-8534 or (966-1) 464-8540.
Telex: 401831 SAUCON SJ.
Telecopier: (966-1) 464-8480.
In Taipei, Taiwan: 8th Floor, 2 Tun Hwa South Road, Section 2.
Telephone: (886-2) 704-6808.
Telecopier: (886-2) 704-6791.
In Tokyo, Japan: Toranomon MT Building, 4th Floor, 10-3, Toranomon 3-Chome, Minato-Ku, Tokyo 105, Japan.
Telephone: 81-3-3433-3939.
Telecopier: 81-3-5401-2725.
In Washington, D.C.: Metropolitan Square, 1450 G Street, N.W.
Telephone: 202-879-3939.
Cable Address: "Attorneys Washington."
Telex: 89-2410 ATTORNEYS WASH.
Telecopier: 202-737-2832.

MEMBER OF FIRM IN HONG KONG

William Anthony Stewart (Not admitted in Hong Kong)

ASSOCIATES

Mitchell David Dudek (Not admitted in Hong Kong)
Xiangyuan Y. Jiang (Not admitted in Hong Kong)

For full biographical listings, see the Martindale-Hubbell Law Directory

KAYE, SCHOLER, FIERMAN, HAYS & HANDLER

9 Queen Road Centre, 18th Floor, Hong Kong
Telephone: 852-8458989
Telex: 62816 KAY HX
Facsimile: 852-8453682; 852-8452389
New York, N.Y.: 425 Park Avenue, 10022.
Telephone: 212-836-8000.
Telex: 234860 KAY UR.
Facsimile: 212-836-8689.
Washington, D.C.: McPherson Building, 901 Fifteenth Street, N.W., Suite 1100, 20005.
Telephone: 202-682-3500.
Telex: 897458 KAYSCHOL WSH.
Facsimile: 202-682-3580.
Los Angeles, California: 1999 Avenue of the Stars, Suite 1600, 90067.
Telephone: 213-788-1000.
Facsimile: 213-788-1200.
Beijing (Peking), People's Republic of China: Scite Tower, Suite 708, 22 Jianguomenwai Dajie, 100004.
Telephone: 861-5124755.
Telex: 222540 KAY CN.
Facsimile: 861-5124760.

RESIDENT PARTNERS

Franklin D. Chu (Not admitted in Hong Kong)

HONG KONG COUNSEL

Frank L. Gniffke

RESIDENT ASSOCIATES

Rongwei Cai (Not admitted in Hong Kong)
Bridget Chi (Not admitted in Hong Kong)
Neil L. Meyers
Juan E. Zuniga (Not admitted in Hong Kong)

(Not admitted to practice in Hong Kong courts)

For full biographical listings, see the Martindale-Hubbell Law Directory

MILBANK, TWEED, HADLEY & MCCLOY

3007 Alexandra House, 16 Chater Road, Hong Kong
Telephone: 852-2526-5281
Fax: 852-2840-0792, 852-2845-9046 ABA/net Milbank HK
New York, New York Office: 1 Chase Manhattan Plaza, 10005.
Telephone: 212-530-5000.
Cable Address: "Miltweed NYK" ITT: 422962; 423893.
Fax: 212- 530-5219. ABA/net: Milbank NY; MCI Mail: Milbank Tweed.
Midtown Office: 50 Rockefeller Plaza, 10020.
Telephone: 212-530-5800.
Fax: 212-530-0158.
Los Angeles, California Office: 601 South Figueroa Street, 30th Floor, 90017.
Telephone: 213-892-400.
Fax: 213-629-5063.
Telex: 678754. ABA/net: Milbank LA.
Washington, D.C. Office: Suite 1100, 1825 Eye Street, N.W., 20006.
Telephone: 202-835-7500.
Cable Address: "Miltweed Wsh". ITT 440667.
Fax: 202-835-7586.
Tokyo, Japan Office: Nippon Press Center Building, 2-1, Uchisaiwai-cho 2-chome, Chiyoda-ku, Tokyo 100.
Telephone: 81-3-3504-1050.
Fax: 81-3-3595-2790, 81-3-3502-5192.
London, England Office: Ropemaker Place, 25 Ropemaker Street, EC2Y 9AS.
Telephone: 44-171-374-0423.
Cable Address: "Miltuk G."
Fax: 44-171-374-0912.

(See Next Column)

Singapore Office: 14-02 Caltex House, 30 Raffles Place, 0104.
Telephone: 65-534-1700.
Fax: 65-534-2733. ABA/net: EDNANG.
Moscow, Russia Office: 24/27 Sadovaya-Samotyochnaya, Moscow, 103051.
Telephone: 7-502-258-5015.
Fax: 7-502-258-5014.
Jakarta, Indonesia Correspondent Office: Makarim & Taira S., 17th Floor, Summitmas Tower, Jl, Jend. Sudirman 61, Jakarta.
Telephone: 62-211252-1272 or 2460.
Fax: 62-21-252-2750 or 2751.

PARTNERS

Glenn S. Gerstell (Not admitted in Hong Kong; Partner in Charge at Singapore Office)
Douglas A. Tanner (Not admitted in Hong Kong)

OF COUNSEL

Young Joon Kim (Not admitted in Hong Kong)
Peter James Thompson

ASSOCIATES

J. Nixon Fox III (Not admitted in Hong Kong)
Jacqueline Seen-Man Leung (Not admitted in Hong Kong)
Yibing Mao (Not admitted in Hong Kong)
Brent Vardeman Woods (Not admitted in Hong Kong)
Anthony Chan Wing Yuen

(Not admitted to practice in Hong Kong courts)

For full biographical listings, see the Martindale-Hubbell Law Directory

SHEARMAN & STERLING

Standard Chartered Bank Building, 4 Des Voeux Road Central, Hong Kong
Telephone: (852) 2978-8000
Fax: (852) 2978-8099
New York, N.Y. Office: 599 Lexington Avenue, New York, New York 10022-6069 and Citicorp Center, 153 East 53rd Street, New York, New York 10022-4676.
Telephone: (212) 848-4000.
Telex: 667290 Num Lau.
Fax: 599 Lexington Avenue: (212) 848-7179. Citicorp Center: (212) 848-5252.
Abu Dhabi, United Arab Emirates Office: P.O. Box 2948.
Telephone: (971-2) 324477.
Fax: (971-2) 774533.
Beijing, People's Republic of China Office: Suite #2205, Capital Mansion, No. 6, Xin Yuan Nan Road. Chao Yang District Beijing, 100004.
Telephone: (861) 465-4574.
Fax: (861) 465-4578.
Budapest, Hungary Office: Szerb utca 17-19, 1056 Budapest.
Telephone: (36-1) 266-3522.
Fax: (36-1) 266-3523.
Düsseldorf, Federal Republic of Germany Office: Königsallee 46, D-40212 Düsseldorf.
Telephone: (49-211) 13 62 80.
Telex: 8 588 294 NYLO.
Fax: (49-211) 13 33 09.
Frankfurt, Federal Republic of Germany Office: Bockenheimer Landstrasse 55, D-60325 Frankfurt am Main.
Telephone: (49-69) 97-10-70.
Fax: (49-69) 97-10-71-00.
London, England Office: 199 Bishopsgate, London EC2M 3TY.
Telephone: (44-71) 920-9000.
Fax: (44-71) 920-9020.
Los Angeles, California Office: 725 South Figueroa Street, 21st Floor, 90017-5421.
Telephone: (213) 239-0300.
Fax: (213) 239-0381, 614-0936.
Paris, France Office: 12 rue d'Astorg, 75008.
Telephone: (33-1) 44-71-17-17.
Telex: 282964 Royale.
Fax: (33-1) 44-71-01-01.
San Francisco, California Office: 555 California Street, 94104-1522.
Telephone: (415) 616-1100.
Fax: (415) 616-1199.
Taipei, Taiwan Office: 7th Floor, Hung Kuo Building, 167 Tun Hwa North Road.
Telephone: (886-2) 545-3300.
Fax: (866-2) 545-3322.
Tokyo, Japan Office: Shearman & Sterling (Thomas Wilner Gaikokuho-Jimu-Bengoshi Jimusho), Fukoku Seimei Building, 5th Fl. 2-2-2,Uchisaiwaicho, Chiyoda-ku, Tokyo 100, Japan.
Telephone: (81 3) 5251-1601.
Fax: (81 3) 5251-1602.
Toronto, Ontario, Canada Office: Commerce Court West, Suite 4405, P.O. Box 247, M5L 1E8.
Telephone: (416) 360-8484.
Fax: (416) 360-2958.
Washington, D.C. Office: 801 Pennsylvania Avenue, N.W., Suite 900, 20004-2604.
Telephone: (202) 508-8000.
Fax: (202) 508-8100.

(See Next Column)

SHEARMAN & STERLING, *Hong Kong—Continued*

RESIDENT PARTNERS

Albert Theodore Powers (Not admitted in Hong Kong; Managing Partner)
Alan F. Denenberg (Not admitted in Hong Kong)
Clark T. Randt, Jr. (Not admitted in Hong Kong)
Edward L. Turner III (Not admitted in Hong Kong; Managing Partner, Asia)

RESIDENT ASSOCIATES

Scott B. Bollinger (Not admitted in Hong Kong)
Marcelo A. Cosma (Not admitted in Hong Kong)
R. Lee Edwards (Not admitted in Hong Kong)
Stephanie S. L. Wong (Not admitted in Hong Kong)
Jia Jonathan Zhu (Not admitted in Hong Kong)

For full biographical listings, see the Martindale-Hubbell Law Directory

SIMPSON THACHER & BARTLETT

A Partnership which includes Professional Corporations
Asia Pacific Finance Tower - 32nd Floor, 3 Garden Road, Central, Hong Kong
Telephone: 852-2514-7600
Telecopier: 852-2869-7694
New York, NY Office: 425 Lexington Avenue, 10017-3954.
Telephone: 212-455-2000.
Telecopier: 212-455-2502. ESL 62928462.
Columbus, Ohio Office: One Riverside Plaza, 43215.
Telephone: 614-461-7799.
Telecopier: 614-461-0040.
London Office: 100 New Bridge Street, London EC4V 6JE, England.
Telephone: 0171 246 8000.
Telecopier: 0171 329 3883.
Tokyo Office: Ark Mori Building, 29th Floor, 12-32, Akasaka 1-Chome, Minato-Ku, Tokyo 107, Japan.
Telephone: 81-3-5562-8601.
Telecopier: 81-3-5562-8606. ESL 62765846.

PARTNERS

Walter A. Looney, Jr. (Not admitted in Hong Kong)
George Keith Miller (Not admitted in Hong Kong)

RESIDENT ASSOCIATES

Alan G. Brenner (Not admitted in Hong Kong)
Philip M. J. Culhane (Not admitted in Hong Kong)
Kuang-Hsiang (Chris) Lin (Not admitted in Hong Kong)
Karen Mieko Sakanashi (Not admitted in Hong Kong)
Elizabeth A. Shaghalian (Not admitted in Hong Kong)
Anuradha M. Shastri (Not admitted in Hong Kong)
Benedict Tai (Not admitted in Hong Kong)
Lawrence A. Vranka, Jr. (Not admitted in Hong Kong)

For full biographical listings, see the Martindale-Hubbell Law Directory

WHITE & CASE

3503 Edinburgh Tower, 15 Queen's Road Central, Hong Kong
Telephone: (852) 822-8700
Facsimile: (852) 845-9070
New York, New York:
Telephone: 212-819-8200.
Facsimile: 212-354-8113.
Washington, D.C.:
Telephone: 202-872-0013.
Facsimile: 202-872-0210.
Los Angeles, California:
Telephone: 213-620-7700.
Facsimile: 213-687-0758; 213-617-2205.
Miami, Florida:
Telephone: 305-371-2700.
Facsimile: 305-358-5744.
Mexico City, Mexico:
Telephone: (52-5) 207-9717.
Facsimile: (52-5) 208-3628.
Tokyo, Japan:
Telephone: (81-3) 3239-4300.
Facsimile: (81-3) 3239-4330.
Singapore, Republic of Singapore:
Telephone: (65) 225-6000.
Facsimile: (65) 225-6009.
Bangkok, Thailand: Pacific Legal Group Ltd., In Association With White & Case,
Telephone: (662) 236-6154/7.
Facsimile: (662) 237-6771.
Hanoi, Viet Nam: Representative Office,
Telephone: (84-4) 227-575/6/7.
Facsimile: (84-4) 227-297.
Bombay, India:
Telephone: (91-22) 282-6300.
Facsimile: (91-22) 282-6305.
London, England:
Telephone: (44-171) 726-6361.
Facsimile: (44-171) 726-4314; (44-171) 726-8558.

(See Next Column)

Paris, France:
Telephone: (33-1) 42-60-34-05.
Facsimile: (33-1) 42-60-82-46.
Brussels, Belgium:
Telephone: (32-2) 647-05-89.
Facsimile: (32-2) 647-16-75.
Stockholm, Sweden:
Telephone: (46-8) 679-80-30.
Facsimile: (46-8) 611-21-22.
Helsinki, Finland:
Telephone: (358-0) 631-100.
Facsimile: (358-0) 179-477.
Moscow, Russia:
Telephone: (7-095) 201-9292/3/4/5.
Facsimile: (7-095) 201-9284.
Budapest, Hungary:
Telephone: (36-1) 269-0550; (36-1) 131-0933.
Facsimile: (36-1) 269-1199.
Prague, Czech Republic:
Telephone: (42-2) 2481-1796.
Facsimile: (42-2) 232-5522.
Warsaw, Poland: Telephone/
Facsimile: (48-22) 26-80-53; (48-22) 27-84-86. International Telephone/
Facsimile: (48-39) 12-19-06.
Istanbul, Turkey:
Telephone: (90-212) 275-68-98; (90-212) 275-75-33.
Facsimile: (90-212) 275-75-43.
Ankara, Turkey:
Telephone: (90-312) 446-2180.
Facsimile: (90-312) 437-9677.
Jeddah, Saudi Arabia: Law Office of Hassan Mahassni,
Telephone: (966-2) 651-3535.
Facsimile: (966-2) 651-3636.
Riyadh, Saudi Arabia: Law Office of Hassan Mahassni,
Telephone: (966-1) 476-7099.
Facsimile: (966-1) 479-0110.
Almaty, Kazakhstan:
Telephone: (7-3272) 50-7491/2.
Facsimile: (7-3272) 61-0842.

RESIDENT PARTNERS

George K. Crozer, IV (Not admitted in Hong Kong)
Lawrence S. Yee (Not admitted in Hong Kong)

RESIDENT ASSOCIATES

Steven P. Allen (Not admitted in Hong Kong)
Andrew Hin Chi Chan
Isabella de la Houssaye (Not admitted in Hong Kong)
Mei-Ying Hao (Not admitted in Hong Kong)
Sharon E. Hartline (Not admitted in Hong Kong)
Andrew P. McLean
Jack H. Su (Not admitted in Hong Kong)
Alex Y. Wong

(Not admitted to practice in Hong Kong courts)

For full biographical listings, see the Martindale-Hubbell Law Directory

WINTHROP, STIMSON, PUTNAM & ROBERTS

2505 Asia Pacific Finance Tower Citibank Plaza, 3 Garden Road, Central, Hong Kong
Telephone: 011-852-530-3400
Telefax: 011-852-530-3355
New York Main Office: One Battery Park Plaza, New York, N.Y. 10004-1490.
Telephone: 212-858-1000.
Stamford, Connecticut Office: Financial Centre, 695 East Main Street, P.O. Box 6760, 06904-6760.
Telephone: 203-348-2300.
Washington, D.C. Office: 1133 Connecticut Avenue, N.W., 20036.
Telephone: 202-775-9800.
Palm Beach, Florida Office: 125 Worth Avenue, 33480.
Telephone: 407-655-7297.
London Office: 2 Throgmorton Avenue, London EC2N 2AP, England.
Telephone: 011-4471-628-4931.
Brussels Office: Rue du Taciturne 42, B-1040 Brussels, Belgium.
Telephone: 011-322-230-1392.
Tokyo, Japan Office: 608 Atagoyama Bengoshi Building 6-7, Atago 1-chome, Minato-ku, Tokyo 105 Japan.
Telephone: 011-813-3437-9740.

RESIDENT PARTNERS

William C. F. Kurz (Not admitted in Hong Kong)
Yeow Ming Choo (Not admitted in Hong Kong)
Robert L. Lin (Not admitted in Hong Kong)

RESIDENT ASSOCIATES

Jeng-Yang Chen (Not admitted in Hong Kong)
Richard R. J. Ding (Not admitted in Hong Kong)
Li Li (Not admitted in Hong Kong)
Jeffrey M. Maddox (Not admitted in Hong Kong)
David T. I. Vong (Not admitted in Hong Kong)
Ella Betsy Wong (Not admitted in Hong Kong)

For full biographical listings, see the Martindale-Hubbell Law Directory

Canadian Lawyers In Hong Kong

GOODMAN PHILLIPS & VINEBERG

30/F, Peregrine Tower, Lippo Centre, 89 Queensway Road, G.P.O. 953, Hong Kong
Telephone: 852-522-1061
Facsimile Communications: 852-845-9089
Montreal Office: 5 Place Ville Marie, 17th Floor, Montreal, Quebec, Canada H3B 2G2.
Telephone: 514-866-8541. Facsimile Communications: 514-875-0344.
Toronto Office: 250 Yonge Street, Suite 2400, P.O. Box 24, Toronto, Ontario, Canada M5H 2M6.
Telephone: 416-979-2211. Facsimile Communications: 416-979-1234.
New York, New York Office: 430 Park Avenue, 10th Floor, New York, New York, 10022.
Telephone: 212-308-8866. Facsimile Communications: 212-308-0132.

RESIDENTS

Ermanno Pascutto (Not admitted in Hong Kong)
Marie-Josée Trépanier (Not admitted in Hong Kong)
Cally Jordan (Not admitted in Hong Kong)

For full biographical listings, see the Martindale-Hubbell Law Directory

OSLER RENAULT

Canadian Barristers and Solicitors
Suite 1708, One Pacific Place, 88 Queensway, Hong Kong
Telephone: 011-852-2877-3933
Fax: 011-852-2877-0866
London, England Office: Osler Renault* - 20 Little Britain, London, EC1A 7DH.
Telephone: 071-606-0777.
Fax: 071-606-0222.
Paris, France Office: Osler Renault* - 4, rue Bayard, 75008 Paris.
Telephone: 33-1.42.89.00.54.
Fax: 33-1.42.89.51.60.
New York, N.Y. Office: Osler Renault* - 200 Park Avenue, Suite 3217, 10166-0193.
Telephone: 212-867-5800.
Fax: 212-867-5802.
Singapore Office: Osler Renault* - 65 Chulia Street, #40-05 OCBC Centre, Singapore 0104.
Telephone: (65) 538-2077.
Fax: (65) 538-2977.
**Osler Renault is an international partnership of Osler, Hoskin & Harcourt and Ogilvy Renault.*
Osler, Hoskin & Harcourt has offices at: P.O. Box 50, 1 First Canadian Place, Toronto, Ontario, Canada M5X 1B8.
Telephone: 416-362-2111.
Fax: 416-862-6666 and 50 O'Connor Street, Suite 1500, Ottawa, Ontario, Canada K1P 6L2.
Telephone: 613-235-7234.
Fax: 613-235-2867.
Ogilvy Renault has offices at: 1981 McGill College Avenue, Suite 1100, Montreal, Quebec, Canada H3A 3C1.
Telephone: 514-847-4747.
Fax: 514-286-5474 and Suite 1600, 45 O'Connor Street, Ottawa, Ontario, Canada K1P 1A4.
Telephone: 613-780-8661.
Fax: 613-230-5459 and 500 Grande-Allée Est, Suite 520, Quebec, Quebec G1R 2J7.
Telephone: 418-640-5000.
Fax: 418-640-1500.

RESIDENT IN HONG KONG

Steven J. Trumper (Not admitted in Hong Kong)
Hartland J. A. Paterson (Not admitted in Hong Kong)
P. Dougal MacDonald (Not admitted in Hong Kong)
Olivia S. M. Lee

For full biographical listings, see the Martindale-Hubbell Law Directory

STIKEMAN, ELLIOTT

29 Queen's Road Central, Suite 1506, China Building, Hong Kong
Telephone: 852-2868-9903
Fax: 852-2868-9912
Montreal, Quebec Office: 1155 René-Lévesque Boulevard West, 40th Floor, H3B 3V2.
Telephone: 514-397-3000.
Fax: 514-397-3222.
Toronto, Ontario Office: Commerce Court West, 53rd Floor, M5L 1B9.
Telephone: 416-869-5500.
Fax: 416-947-0866.
Ottawa, Ontario Office: 50 O'Connor Street, Suite 914, K1P 6L2.
Telephone: 613-234-4555.
Fax: 613-230-8877.
Calgary, Alberta Office: 855 - 2nd Street S.W., 1500 Bankers Hall, T2P 4J7.
Telephone: 403-266-9000.
Fax: 403-266-9034.

(See Next Column)

Vancouver, British Columbia Office: 666 Burrard Street, Suite 1700, Park Place, V6C 2X8.
Telephone: 604-631-1300.
Fax: 604-681-1825.
New York, New York Office: 126 East 56th Street, 11th Floor, Tower 56, 10022.
Telephone: 212-371-8855.
Fax: 212-371-7087.
Washington, D.C. Office: 1300 I Street, N.W., Suite 1210 West, 20005-3314.
Telephone: 202-326-7555.
Fax: 202-326-7557.
London, England Office: Cottons Centre, Cottons Lane, SE1 2QL.
Telephone: 71-378-0880.
Fax: 71-378-0344.
Paris, France Office: In Association with Société Juridique Internationale, 39, rue François Ier, 75008.
Telephone: 33-1-40-73-82-00.
Fax: 33-1-40-73-82-10.
Budapest, Hungary Office: Andrássy út 100, II Floor, H-1062.
Telephone: 36-1-269-1790.
Fax: 36-1-269-0655.
Hong Kong: In Association with Shum & Co., 29 Queen's Road Central, Suite 1103, China Building.
Telephone: 852-2526-5531.
Fax: 852-2845-9076.
Taipei, Taiwan Office: 117 Sec. 3 Min Sheng East Road, 8th Floor.
Telephone: 886-2-719-9573.
Fax: 886-2-719-4540.

RESIDENTS IN HONG KONG

Brian G. Hansen (Not admitted in Hong Kong)
Andes Fu-Min Lin (Not admitted in Hong Kong)
(Not admitted to practice in Hong Kong courts)

For full biographical listings, see the Martindale-Hubbell Law Directory

HUNGARY

BUDAPEST,

DEBEVOISE & PLIMPTON

1065 Budapest, Révay Köz 2.III/2., Budapest
Telephone: (36-1) 112-8067
Telecopier: (36-1) 132-7995
New York Office: 875 Third Avenue, 10022.
Telephone: 212-909-6000.
Telex: (Domestic) 148377 DEBSTEVE NYK.
Telecopier: (212) 909-6836.
Washington, D.C. Office: 555 13th Street, N.W., 20004.
Telephone: 202-383-8000.
Telex: 405586 DPDC WUUD.
Telecopier: (202) 383-8118.
Los Angeles, California Office: 601 South Figueroa Street, Suite 3700, 90017.
Telephone: 213-680-8000.
Telex: 401527 DPLA.
Telecopier: 213-680-8100.
Paris, France Office: 21 Avenue George V 75008.
Telephone: (33-1) 40 73 12 12.
Telecopier: (33-1) 47 20 50 82.
Telex: 648141F DPPAR.
London, England Office: 1 Creed Court, 5 Ludgate Hill.
Telephone: (44-171) 329-0779.
Telex: 884569 DPLON G.
Telecopier: (44-171) 329-0860.
Hong Kong Office: 13/F Entertainment Building, 30 Queen's Road Central.
Telephone: (852) 2810-7918.
Fax: (852) 2810-9828.

RESIDENT COUNSEL

David F. Hickok (Not admitted in Hungary)

RESIDENT ATTORNEY

Vera Losonci (Not admitted in Hungary)

HUNGARIAN COUNSEL

Dr. Zsuzsa Kovács
Dr. Zsuzsanna Nagy

For full biographical listings, see the Martindale-Hubbell Law Directory

American Lawyers in Budapest

Baker & McKenzie

Andrássy-út 125, H-1062 Budapest
Telephone: (1) 251-5777; 268-0422
Intn'l Dialing: (36-1) 251-5777; 268-0422
Telex: 22 3554
Answer Back: BMCK H
Facsimile: (36-1) 342-0513
Associated Offices of Baker & McKenzie in: Almaty, Amsterdam, Bangkok, Barcelona, Beijing, Berlin, Bogotá, Brasília, Brussels, Buenos Aires, Cairo, Caracas, Chicago, Dallas, Frankfurt, Geneva, Hanoi, Ho Chi Minh City, Hong Kong, Juárez, Kiev, London, Madrid, Manila, Melbourne, México City, Miami, Milan, Monterrey, Moscow, New York, Palo Alto, Paris, Prague, Rio de Janeiro, Riyadh, Rome, St. Petersburg, San Diego, San Francisco, São Paulo, Singapore, Stockholm, Sydney, Taipei, Tijuana, Tokyo, Toronto, Valencia, Warsaw, Washington, D.C. and Zürich.
Correspondent Law Firm: Hadiputranto, Hadinoto & Partners, Jakarta.

PARTNERS

Robert C. Knuepfer, Jr. (Not admitted in Hungary)
Peter Pásint Magyar (Not admitted in Hungary)
Dr. János Martonyi

LOCAL PARTNER

Dr. Géza Kajtár

SENIOR COUNSEL

Dr. Kálmán Gyárfás

ASSOCIATES

John F. Langan (Not admitted in Hungary)
Ines K. Radmilovic (Not admitted in Hungary)
Nathalie Pigeon (Not admitted in Hungary)

AFFILIATED HUNGARIAN ATTORNEYS

Dr. Zita Fekete
Dr. Éva Hegedüs
Dr. Anna Halustyik
Dr. Tünde Hegyi
Dr. Konrád Siegler

For full biographical listings, see the Martindale-Hubbell Law Directory

Shearman & Sterling

Szerb utca 17-19, 1056 Budapest
Telephone: (36-1) 266-3522
Fax: (36-1) 266-3523
New York, N.Y. Office: 599 Lexington Avenue, New York, New York 10022-6069 and Citicorp Center, 153 East 53rd Street, New York, New York 10022-4676.
Telephone: (212) 848-4000.
Telex: 667290 Num Lau.
Fax: 599 Lexington Avenue: (212) 848-7179. Citicorp Center: (212) 848-5252.
Abu Dhabi, United Arab Emirates Office: P.O. Box 2948.
Telephone: (971-2) 324477.
Fax: (971-2) 774533.
Beijing, People's Republic of China Office: Suite #2205, Capital Mansion, No. 6, Xin Yuan Nan Road. Chao Yang District Beijing, 100004.
Telephone: (861) 465-4574.
Fax: (861) 465-4578.
Düsseldorf, Federal Republic of Germany Office: Königsallee 46, D-40212 Düsseldorf.
Telephone: (49-211) 13 62 80.
Telex: 8 588 294 NYLO.
Fax: (49-211) 13 33 09.
Frankfurt, Federal Republic of Germany Office: Bockenheimer Landstrasse 55, D-60325 Frankfurt am Main.
Telephone: (49-69) 97-10-70.
Fax: (49-69) 97-10-71-00.
Hong Kong, Hong Kong Office: Standard Chartered Bank Building, 4 Des Voeux Road Central, Hong Kong.
Telephone: (852) 2978-8000.
Fax: (852) 2978-8099.
London, England Office: 199 Bishopsgate, London EC2M 3TY.
Telephone: (44-71) 920-9000.
Fax: (44-71) 920-9020.
Los Angeles, California Office: 725 South Figueroa Street, 21st Floor, 90017-5421.
Telephone: (213) 239-0300.
Fax: (213) 239-0381, 614-0936.
Paris, France Office: 12 rue d'Astorg, 75008.
Telephone: (33-1) 44-71-17-17.
Telex: 282964 Royale.
Fax: (33-1) 44-71-01-01.
San Francisco, California Office: 555 California Street, 94104-1522.
Telephone: (415) 616-1100.
Fax: (415) 616-1199.
Taipei, Taiwan Office: 7th Floor, Hung Kuo Building, 167 Tun Hwa North Road.
Telephone: (886-2) 545-3300.
Fax: (866-2) 545-3322.

(See Next Column)

Tokyo, Japan Office: Shearman & Sterling (Thomas Wilner Gaikokuho-Jimu-Bengoshi Jimusho), Fukoku Seimei Building, 5th Fl. 2-2-2, Uchisaiwaicho, Chiyoda-ku, Tokyo 100, Japan.
Telephone: (81 3) 5251-1601.
Fax: (81 3) 5251-1602.
Toronto, Ontario, Canada Office: Commerce Court West, Suite 4405, P.O. Box 247, M5L 1E8.
Telephone: (416) 360-8484.
Fax: (416) 360-2958.
Washington, D.C. Office: 801 Pennsylvania Avenue, N.W., Suite 900, 20004-2604.
Telephone: (202) 508-8000.
Fax: (202) 508-8100.

MANAGING PARTNER

Hubertus V. Sulkowski (Not admitted in Hungary)

RESIDENT EUROPEAN COUNSEL

John E. Baltay (Not admitted in Hungary)

RESIDENT ASSOCIATES

Dr. Chrysta Bán
Dr. Andrea Gyurácz

For full biographical listings, see the Martindale-Hubbell Law Directory

Squire, Sanders & Dempsey

Deak Ferenc Ut. 10 Office 304, H-1052 Budapest V.
Telephone: 011-36-1-266-2024
Fax: 011-36-1-266-2025
Cleveland, Ohio Office: 4900 Society Center, 127 Public Square, Cleveland, Ohio 44114-1304.
Telephone: 216-479-8500. Fax's: 216-479-8780, 216-479-8781, 216-479-8787, 216-479-8795, 216-479-8777, 216-479-8783, 216-479-8776, 216-479-8788.
Columbus, Ohio Offices: 1300 Huntington Center, 41 South High Street, Columbus, Ohio 43215.
Telephone: 614-365-2700.
Fax: 614-365-2499.
Jacksonville, Florida Office: One Enterprise Center, Suite 2100, 225 Water Street, Jacksonville, Florida 32202.
Telephone: 904-353-1264.
Fax: 904-356-2986.
Miami, Florida Office: 201 South Biscayne Boulevard, Suite 2900 Miami Center, Miami, Florida 33131.
Telephone: 305-577-8700.
Fax: 305-358-1425.
New York, New York Office: 520 Madison Avenue, 32nd Floor, New York, New York 10022.
Telephone: 212-872-9800.
Fax: 212-872-9814.
Phoenix, Arizona Office: Two Renaissance Square, 40 North Central Avenue, Suite 2700, Phoenix, Arizona 85004-4441.
Telephone: 602-528-4000.
Fax: 602-253-8129.
Washington, D.C. Office: 1201 Pennsylvania Avenue, N.W., P.O. Box 407, Washington, D.C. 20044.
Telephone: 202-626-6600.
Fax: 202-626-6780.
London, England Office: 1 Gunpowder Square, Printer Street, London EC4A 3DE.
Telephone: 011-44-71-830-0055.
Fax: 011-44-71-830-0056.
Brussels, Belgium Office: Avenue Louise, 165, Box 15, 1050 Brussels, Belgium.
Telephone: 011-32-2-648-1717.
Fax: 011-32-2-648-1064.
Prague Office: Adria Palace, Jungmannova 31/36, 11000 Prague 1, Czech Republic.
Telephone: 011-42-2-231-5661.
Fax: 011-42-2-231-5482.
Bratislava Office: Mudronova 37, 811 01 Bratislava, Slovak Republic.
Telephone: 011-42-7-313-362; 011-42-7-315-370.
Fax: 011-42-7-313-918.
Kiev, Ukraine Office: vul. Prorizna 9, Suite 20, Kiev 252035, Ukraine.
Telephones: 011-7-044-244-3452, 011-7-044-244-3453, 011-7-044-228-8687.
Fax: 011-7-044-228-4938.

RESIDENT ASSOCIATES

Andras I. Hanak (Not admitted in Hungary)
Andrea Kozma

For full biographical listings, see the Martindale-Hubbell Law Directory

INDIA

*NEW DELHI,**

American Lawyers in New Delhi

Chadbourne & Parke Associates

A16-B Anand Niketan, 110 021 New Delhi
Telephone: 91-11-301-7568/7581/7582
Telecopier: 91-11-301-7351
New York, N.Y. Office: Chadbourne & Parke, 30 Rockefeller Plaza, 10112.
Telephone: 212-408-5100.
Telecopier: 212-541-5369.
Washington, D.C. Office: Chadbourne & Parke, Suite 900, 1101 Vermont Avenue, N.W., 20005.
Telephone: 202-289-3000.
Telecopier: 202-289-3002.
Los Angeles, California Office: Chadbourne & Parke, 601 South Figueroa Street, 90017.
Telephone: 213-892-1000.
Telecopier: 213-622-9865.
London, England Office: Chadbourne & Parke, 86 Jermyn Street, SW1 6JD.
Telephone: 44-171-925-7400.
Facsimile: 44-171-839-3393.
Moscow, Russia Office: Chadbourne & Parke, 38 Maxim Gorky Naberezhnaya, 113035.
Telephone: 7095-974-2424.
Telecopier: 7095-974-2425. International satellite lines via U.S.:
Telephone: 212-408-1190.
Telecopier: 212-408-1199.
Hong Kong Office: Chadbourne & Parke, Suite 3704, Peregrine Tower, Lippo Centre, 89 Queensway.
Telephone: (852) 2842-5400.
Telecopier: (852) 2521-7527.

RESIDENT PARTNER

Gregory N. Ullman (Not admitted in India)

RESIDENT ASSOCIATES

Anand S. Dayal (Not admitted in India)
Sadhana Kaul (Not admitted in India)
Meaghan McGrath (Not admitted in India)
Jeffrey B.L. Meller (Not admitted in India)

For full biographical listings, see the Martindale-Hubbell Law Directory

INDONESIA

*JAKARTA,**

Hadiputranto, Hadinoto & Partners

The Landmark Centre I, 24th Floor, Jalan Jenderal Sudirman No. 1, Jakarta 12910
Telephone: (21) 570-0396, 520-9424, 520-2444
Intn'l. Dialing: (62-21) 570-0396, 520-9424, 520-2444
Telex: 65347
Answer Back: 65347 ABOGAD IA
Facsimile: (62-21) 570-0399; 520-9434

MEMBERS OF FIRM

Sri Indrastuti Hadiputranto
Tuti Dewi Hadinoto
Erna Letty Kusoy
Enny Melanita
Timur Sukirno
Ike Andriani
Salomo Rahmatuah Damanik
Sarina Sutadisastra Danuningrat
Dwi Daru Herdani
Daniel Ginting
Indri P. Guritno
Yandri Hendarta
Sri Wahyu Karini
Teguh Maramis
Parmagita Moerad
Siendy Katirachmadiah Musmar
Mohamad Kadri Nizaroeddin
Erika Chiko Noveni
Indri Pramitaswari
Grace P. Pranata
Agusdin Tri Rachmanto
Harun Admana Reksodiputro
Indah N. Respati
Nia K. Harimatara Sujani
Sri Irmiati Sumaryo
Zoraida Syarfuan
Christian Budianto Teo
Ilya Utama
Alex Rasi Wangge
Budi Unggul W.
Wimbanu Widyatmoko
Dorothea Nawang Wulan

FOREIGN LEGAL CONSULTANT

Charles Gaylord Watkins (Not admitted in Indonesia)

For full biographical listings, see the Martindale-Hubbell Law Directory

ITALY

MILAN,

Baker & McKenzie

3 Piazza Meda, 20121 Milan
Telephone: (02) 76 01 39 21
Intn'l. Dialing: (39-2) 76 01 39 21
Cable Address: ABOGADO MILANO
Telex: 311655
Answer Back: 311655 ABOMIL I
Facsimiles: (39-2) 76 00 83 22; 76 00 81 65; 76 00 70 74; 76 00 75 17; 78 42 57
Associated Offices of Baker & McKenzie in: Almaty, Amsterdam, Bangkok, Barcelona, Beijing, Berlin, Bogotá, Brasília, Brussels, Budapest, Buenos Aires, Cairo, Caracas, Chicago, Dallas, Frankfurt, Geneva, Hanoi, Ho Chi Minh City, Hong Kong, Juárez, Kiev, London, Madrid, Manila, Melbourne, México City, Miami, Monterrey, Moscow, New York, Palo Alto, Paris, Prague, Rio de Janeiro, Riyadh, Rome, St. Petersburg, San Diego, San Francisco, São Paulo, Singapore, Stockholm, Sydney, Taipei, Tijuana, Tokyo, Toronto, Valencia, Warsaw, Washington, D.C. and Zürich.
Correspondent Law Firm: Hadiputranto, Hadinoto & Partners, Jakarta.

PARTNERS

Corrado Bartoli
Gerardo M. Boniello
Claudio Camilli
Alberto de Libero
Gianfranco Di Garbo
Pierfrancesco Federici
Alberto Semeria

ASSOCIATES

Francesco Adami
Pietro Bernasconi
Giovanni Buccirossi
Roberto Camilli
Raffaele Cavani
Andrea Cicala
Giulia Comparini
Anna Deiana
Lorenzo De Martinis
Alberto Maria Fornari
Elise Edith Lehoczky
Marco Mazzeschi
Tiziano Membri
Giovanni Marco Mileni Munari
Uberto Percivalle
Silvia Picchetti
Gaetano Pizzitola
Giuliana Polacco
Domenico Vacca

For full biographical listings, see the Martindale-Hubbell Law Directory

American Lawyers In Milan

Graham & James

12, Montenapoleone, 20121 Milan
Telephone: (02) 76006839, (02) 76006484
Telex: 843-314157 GJ MIL I
Telecopier: (02) 783091
Other offices located in: San Francisco, Los Angeles, Newport Beach, Palo Alto, Sacramento and Fresno, California; Washington, D.C.; New York, New York; Beijing, China; Tokyo, Japan; London, England; Dusseldorf, Germany; Taipei, Taiwan.
Associated Offices: Deacons in Association with Graham & James, Hong Kong; Sly and Weigall, Sydney, Melbourne, Brisbane, Perth and Canberra, Australia.
Affiliated Offices: Graham & James in Affiliation with Taylor Joynson Garrett, London, England, Bucharest, Romania and Brussels, Belgium; Hanafiah Soeharto Ponggawa, Jakarta, Indonesia; Deacons and Graham & James, Bangkok, Thailand; Haarmann, Hemmelrath & Partner, Berlin, Munich, Leipzig, Frankfurt and Dusseldorf, Germany; Mishare M. Al-Ghazali & Partners, Kuwait; Sly & Weigall Deacons in Association with Graham & James, Hanoi, Vietnam and Guangzhou, China; Gallastegui y Lozano, S.C., Mexico City, Mexico; Law Firm of Salah Al-Hejailan, Jeddah and Riyadh, Saudi Arabia.

RESIDENT PARTNERS

Gabriele Bernascone
Filippo Disertori
Gianfranco Negri Clementi
Gabriella Agliati
Paolo Montironi
Rossella Adamo
Barnaba Ricci

RESIDENT ASSOCIATES

David Donald (Not admitted in Italy)
Massimo Mantovani
Fabrizia Maurici
Silvia Re
Priscilla Serena

For full biographical listings, see the Martindale-Hubbell Law Directory

*ROME,**

Baker & McKenzie

Via Degli Scipioni, 288, 00192 Rome
Telephone: (06) 3225162
Intn'l. Dialing: (39-6) 3225162
Cable Address: ABOGADO ROMA
Telex: 611087
Answer Back: 611087 ABOROM I
Facsimile: (39-6) 3203502
Associated Offices of Baker & McKenzie in: Almaty, Amsterdam, Bangkok, Barcelona, Beijing, Berlin, Bogotá, Brasília, Brussels, Budapest, Buenos Aires, Cairo, Caracas, Chicago, Dallas, Frankfurt, Geneva, Hanoi, Ho Chi Minh City, Hong Kong, Juárez, Kiev, London, Madrid, Manila, Melbourne, México City, Miami, Milan, Monterrey, Moscow, New York, Palo Alto, Paris, Prague, Rio de Janeiro, Riyadh, St. Petersburg, San Diego, San Francisco, São Paulo, Singapore, Stockholm, Sydney, Taipei, Tijuana, Tokyo, Toronto, Valencia, Warsaw, Washington, D.C. and Zürich.
Correspondent Law Firm: Hadiputranto, Hadinoto & Partners, Jakarta.

RESIDENT PARTNERS

Fabio M. Brembati
Aurelio Giovannelli
G. Franco Macconi

ASSOCIATES

Claudia Barsotti
Guido Brocchieri
Giulio Brunelli
Antonella Centra
Stefano Ciullo
Giada Cortesi
Giorgio Gallenzi
Raffaele Giarda
Federico Limiti
Angelica Lodigiani
Alfredo Lucente
Anna Sofia N. Mauro
Francesco Portolano
Raffaele G. Rizzi

For full biographical listings, see the Martindale-Hubbell Law Directory

American Lawyers In Rome

Loeb and Loeb

A Partnership including Professional Corporations
Piazza Digione 1, Rome 00197
Telephone: 011-396-808-8456
Telecopier: 011-396-674-8223
Los Angeles, California Office: Suite 1800, 1000 Wilshire Boulevard, 90017-2475.
Telephone: 213-688-3400.
Cable Address: "Loband LSA".
Telecopier: 213-688-3460; 688-3461.
Century City (Los Angeles), California Office: Suite 2200, 10100 Santa Monica Boulevard, Los Angeles, 90067-4164.
Telephone: 310-282-2000.
Telecopier: 310-282-2191; 282-2192.
New York, N.Y. Office: 345 Park Avenue, 10154-0037.
Telephone: 212-407-4000.
Facsimile: 212-407-4990.
Nashville, Tennessee Office: 45 Music Square West, 37203-3205.
Telephone: 615-749-8300.
Facsimile: 615-749-8308.

MEMBERS OF FIRM

John J. Dellaverson
(Not admitted in Italy)
Lorenzo De Sanctis
Guendalina Ponti

ASSOCIATES

Giovanni A. Pedde
(Not admitted in Italy)
Paola Amelia Massardi
Riccardo Siciliani

For full biographical listings, see the Martindale-Hubbell Law Directory

JAPAN

*TOKYO,**

Tokyo Aoyama Law Office

(Associated Office of Baker & McKenzie)
410 Aoyama Building, 2-3, Kita Aoyama 1 Chome, Tokyo 107
Telephone: (03) 3403-5281
Intn'l. Dialing: (81-3) 3403-5281
Cable Address: ABOGADO TOKYO
Telex: 28249
Answer Back: ABOGADO J28249
Facsimiles: (81-3) 3470-3152; 3470-3658; 3479-4224; 3479-4386
Associated Offices of Baker & McKenzie in: Almaty, Amsterdam, Bangkok, Barcelona, Beijing, Berlin, Bogotá, Brasília, Brussels, Budapest, Buenos Aires, Cairo, Caracas, Chicago, Dallas, Frankfurt, Geneva, Hanoi, Ho Chi Minh City, Hong Kong, Juárez, Kiev, London, Madrid, Manila, Melbourne, México City, Miami, Milan, Monterrey, Moscow, New York, Palo Alto, Paris, Prague, Rio de Janeiro, Riyadh, Rome, St. Petersburg, San Diego, San Francisco, São Paulo, Singapore, Stockholm, Sydney, Taipei, Tijuana, Toronto, Valencia, Warsaw, Washington, D.C. and Zürich.
Correspondent Law Firm: Hadiputranto, Hadinoto & Partners, Jakarta.
Postal Address: C.P.O Box 1576, Tokyo, 100-91, Japan

Mikako Fujiki
Morihiro Murata
Kiyoshi Odaka
Hideo Ohta
Shinichi Saito
Hidetaka Sekine
Masatsugu Suzuki
Yukinori Watanabe

LOCAL PARTNERS

Hiroshi Kondo
Nobuko Narita

OF COUNSEL

Kohji Mori

ATTORNEYS AT FOREIGN LAW

John Kakinuki
Jeremy D. Pitts

ASSOCIATES

Naoaki Eguchi
Yasuyoshi Goto
Yoshiya Ishimura
Masa Matsushita
Shoji Mizushima
Yoshiaki Muto
Miho Niunoya
Takeshi Takahashi
Shinji Toyohara
Hideyuki Yamamoto

Anne Ka Tse Hung
W. Temple Jorden
(Not admitted in Japan)
Bruce W. MacLennan
(Not admitted in Japan)
Jean-Denis Marx
(Not admitted in Japan)
Bernhard Steves
(Not admitted in Japan)

Paul A. Davis

For full biographical listings, see the Martindale-Hubbell Law Directory

American Lawyers In Tokyo

Cleary, Gottlieb, Steen & Hamilton

(Morgan Carroll Terai Gaikokuho Jimubengoshi Jimusho)
Shin Kasumigaseki Building, 20th Floor, 3-2, Kasumigaseki 3-Chome, Chiyoda-ku, Tokyo 100
Telephone: 81-3-3595-3911
Cable Address: "Cleargolaw, Tokyo"
Telex: 28546 CGSHTYO
Facsimile: (81) (3) 3595-3910
New York, New York Office: One Liberty Plaza, New York, N.Y. 10006.
Telephone: 212-225-2000.
Washington, D.C. Office: 1752 N Street, N.W., Washington, D.C. 20036.
Telephone: 202-728-2700.
Paris, France Office: 41, Avenue de Friedland, 75008 Paris, France.
Telephone: 33-1-4074-6800.
Brussels, Belgium Office: Rue de la Loi 23, Bte 5, 1040 Brussels, Belgium.
Telephone: 32-2-287-2000.
London, England Office: City Place House, 55 Basinghall Street, London EC2V 5EH England.
Telephone: 44-71-614-2200.
Hong Kong Office: 56th Floor, Bank of China Tower, One Garden Road, Hong Kong.
Telephone: 852-521-4122.
Frankfurt, Germany Office: Ulmenstrasse 37-39, 60325 Frankfurt am Main, Germany.
Telephone: 49-69-971-03-0.

RESIDENT PARTNERS

Tsunemasa Terai
Donald L. Morgan

(See Next Column)

CLEARY, GOTTLIEB, STEEN & HAMILTON—*Continued*

ASSOCIATES

Thomas M. Doyle II (Not admitted in Japan)
Peter A. E. Swanger (Not admitted in Japan)
Joseph M. Titlebaum (Not admitted in Japan)

For full biographical listings, see the Martindale-Hubbell Law Directory

COUDERT BROTHERS

(Pickrell Gaikokuho-Jimu-Bengoshi Jimusho)
1355 West Tower, Aoyama Twin Towers, 1-1-1 Minami-Aoyama, Minato-Ku, Tokyo 107
Telephone: (81) (3) 3423-0337
Facsimile: (81) (3) 3423-3550; 3423-0929
New York, New York 10036-7794: 1114 Avenue of the Americas.
Washington, D.C. 20006: 1627 I Street, N.W., 12th Floor.
Los Angeles, California 90017: 1055 West Seventh Street, Twentieth Floor.
San Francisco, California 94111: 4 Embarcadero Center, Suite 3300.
San Jose, California 95113: Suite 1250, Ten Almaden Boulevard.
Paris 75008, France: Coudert Frères, 52, Avenue des Champs-Elysées.
London, EC4M 7JP, England: 20 Old Bailey.
Brussels B-1050, Belgium: Tour Louise. 149 Avenue Louise-Box 8.
Beijing, People's Republic of China 100020: Suite 2708-09, Jing Guang Centre, Hu Jia Lou, Chao Yang Qu.
Shanghai, People's Republic of China 200002: c/o Suite 1804, Union Building, 100 Yanan Road East.
Hong Kong: Nine Queen's Road, 25th Floor.
Singapore 0104: Tung Centre, 20 Collyer Quay.
Sydney N.S.W. 2000, Australia: Suite 2202, State Bank Centre, 52 Martin Place.
01301 Sao Paulo, SP, Brazil: Machado, Meyer, Sendacz, e Opice, Advogados, Rua da Consolacao, 247, 8 Andar.
Moscow, Russia: Ulitsa Staraya Basmannaya 14.
Bangkok 10500, Thailand: Bubhajit Building, 20 North Sathorn Road, 10th Floor.
Ho Chi Minh City, Vietnam: c/o Saigon Business Centre, 49-57 Dong Du Street, District 1.

RESIDENT PARTNERS

Greg L. Pickrell (Resident)

RESIDENT ASSOCIATES

Julie N. Mack (Not admitted in Japan)
Marilyn Selby Okoshi (Not admitted in Japan)

For full biographical listings, see the Martindale-Hubbell Law Directory

JONES, DAY, REAVIS & POGUE

(DeMarchi Gaikokuho Jimu Bengoshi Jimusho)
Toranomon MT Building, 4th Floor, 10-3, Toranomon 3-Chome, Tokyo 105
Telephone: 81-3-3433-3939
Telecopier: 81-3-5401-2725
In Atlanta, Georgia: 3500 One Peachtree Center, 303 Peachtree Street, N.E.
Telephone: 404-521-3939.
Cable Address: "Attorneys Atlanta".
Telex: 54-2711.
Telecopier: 404-581-8330.
In Brussels, Belgium: Avenue Louise 480, 7th Floor. B-1050 Brussels.
Telephone: 32-2-645-14-11.
Telecopier: 32-2-645-14-45.
In Chicago, Illinois: 77 West Wacker.
Telephone: 312-782-3939.
Telecopier: 312-782-8585.
In Cleveland, Ohio: North Point, 901 Lakeside Avenue.
Telephone: 216-586-3939.
Cable Address: "Attorneys Cleveland."
Telex: 980389.
Telecopier: 216-579-0212.
In Columbus, Ohio: 1900 Huntington Center.
Telephone: 614-469-3939.
Cable Address: "Attorneys Columbus."
Telecopier: 614-461-4198.
In Dallas, Texas: 2300 Trammell Crow Center, 2001 Ross Avenue.
Telephone: 214-220-3939.
Cable Address: "Attorneys Dallas."
Telex: 730852.
Telecopier: 214-969-5100.
In Frankfurt, Germany: Triton Haus, Bockenheimer Landstrasse 42, 60323 Frankfurt am Main.
Telephone: 49-69-9726-3939.
Telecopier: 49-69-9726-3993.
In Geneva, Switzerland: 20, rue de Candolle.
Telephone: 41-22-320-2339.
Telecopier: 49-22-320-1232.
In Hong Kong: 1501 One Exchange Square, 8 Connaught Place.
Telephone: 852-2526-6895.
Telecopier: 852-2810-5787.

(See Next Column)

In Irvine, California: 2603 Main Street, Suite 900.
Telephone: 714-851-3939.
Telex: 194911 Lawyers LSA.
Telecopier: 714-553-7539.
In London, England: One Mount Street.
Telephone: 44-71-493-9361.
Cable Address: "Surgoe London WI."
Telecopier: 44-71-493-9666.
In Los Angeles, California: 555 West Fifth Street, Suite 4600.
Telephone: 213-489-3939.
Telex: 181439 UD.
Telecopier: 213-243-2539.
In New York, New York: 599 Lexington Avenue.
Telephone: 212-326-3939.
Cable Address: "JONESDAY NEWYORK."
Telex: 237013 JDRP UR.
Telecopier: 212-755-7306.
In Paris, France: 62, rue du Faubourg Saint-Honore.
Telephone: 33-1-44-71-3939.
Cable Address: "Surgoe Paris."
Telex: 290156 Surgoe.
Telecopier: 33-1-49-24-0471.
In Pittsburgh, Pennsylvania: 500 Grant Street, 31st Floor.
Telephone: 412-391-3939.
Cable Address: "Attorneys Pittsburgh".
Telecopier: 412-394-7959.
In Riyadh, Saudi Arabia: Law Offices of Saud M.A. Shawwaf, P.O. Box 2700.
Telephones: (966-1) 465-6543, (966-1) 464-8534 or (966-1) 464-8540.
Telex: 401831 SAUCON SJ.
Telecopier: (966-1) 464-8480.
In Taipei, Taiwan: 8th Floor, 2 Tun Hwa South Road, Section 2.
Telephone: (886-2) 704-6808.
Telecopier: (886-2) 704-6791.
In Washington, D.C.: Metropolitan Square, 1450 G Street, N.W.
Telephone: 202-879-3939.
Cable Address: "Attorneys Washington."
Telex: 89-2410 ATTORNEYS WASH.
Telecopier: 202-737-2832.

PARTNERS

Darvin DeMarchi, Jr.

ASSOCIATES

David R. Nelson (Not admitted in Japan)

For full biographical listings, see the Martindale-Hubbell Law Directory

MAYER, BROWN & PLATT

(Kawachi Gaikokuho Jimu Bengoshi Jimusho)
Urbannet Otemachi Building 13F, 2-2, Otemachi 2-chome, Chiyoda-ku, Tokyo 100
Telephone: 011-81-3-5255-9700
Facsimile: 011-81-3-5255-9797
Chicago, Illinois Office: 190 South LaSalle Street, 60603-3441.
Telephone: (312) 782-0600. Pitney Bowes: (312) 701-7711.
Telex: 190404.
Cable: LEMAY.
Washington, D.C. Office: 2000 Pennsylvania Avenue, N.W., 20006-1882.
Telephone: (202) 463-2000. Pitney Bowes: (202) 861-0484, Pitney Bowes: (202) 861-0473.
Telex: 892603.
Cable: LEMAYDC.
New York, New York Office: 787 Seventh Avenue, Suite 2400, 10019-6018.
Telephone: (212) 554-3000. Pitney Bowes: (212) 262-1910.
Telex: 701842.
Cable: LEMAYEN.
Houston, Texas Office: 700 Louisiana Street, Suite 3600, 77002-2730.
Telephone: (713) 221-1651. Pitney Bowes: (713) 224-6410.
Telex: 775809.
Cable: LEMAYHOU.
Los Angeles, California Office: 350 South Grand Avenue, 25th Floor, 90071-1503.
Telephone: (213) 229-9500. Pitney Bowes: (213) 625-0248.
Telex: 188089.
Cable: LEMAYLA.
London, England Office: 162 Queen Victoria Street, EC4V 4DB.
Telephone: 011-44-71-248-1465.
Fax: 011-44-71-329-4465.
Telex: 8811095.
Cable: LEMAYLDN.
Berlin, Germany Office: Spreeufer 5, 10178.
Telephone: 011-49-30-240-7930.
Facsimile: 011-49-30-240-79344.
Brussels, Belgium Office: Square de Meeûs 19/20, Bte. 4, 1040.
Telephone: 011-32-2-512-9878.
Fax: 011-32-2-511-3305.
Telex: 20768 MBPBRU B.
Mexico City, Mexico, D.F. Correspondent: Jáuregui, Navarrete, Nader y Rojas, S.C., Abogados, Paseo de la Reforma 199, Pisos 15, 16 y 17, 06500.
Telephone: 011-525-591-16-55.
Fax: 011-525-535-80-62; 011-525-703-22-47.
Cable: JANANE.

(See Next Column)

MAYER, BROWN & PLATT, *Tokyo—Continued*

PARTNERS

Michael T. Kawachi
John C. Roebuck
(Not admitted in Japan)
Andrew G. Haring
(Not admitted in Japan)

For full biographical listings, see the Martindale-Hubbell Law Directory

MILBANK, TWEED, HADLEY & MCCLOY

(Watanabe Tsugumichi Gaikokuho Jimu Bengoshi Jimusho)
Nippon Press Center Building, 2-1, Uchisaiwai-Cho 2 Chome, Chiyoda-Ku, Tokyo 100
Telephone: 81-3-3504-1050
Fax: 81-3-3595-2790; 81-3-3502-5192
New York, New York Office: 1 Chase Manhattan Plaza, 10005.
Telephone: 212-530-5000.
Cable Address: "Miltweed NYK" ITT: 422962; 423893.
Fax: 212-530-5219. ABA/net: Milbank NY. MCI Mail: Milbank Tweed.
Midtown Office: 50 Rockefeller Plaza, 10020.
Telephone: 212-530-5800.
Fax: 212-530-0158.
Los Angeles, California Office: 601 South Figueroa Street, 30th Floor, 90017.
Telephone: 213-892-4000.
Fax: 213-629-5063.
Telex: 678754. ABA/net: Milbank LA.
Washington, D.C. Office: Suite 1100, 1825 Eye Street, N.W., 20006.
Telephone: 202-835-7500.
Cable Address: "Miltweed Wsh". ITT 440667.
Fax: 202-835-7586. ABA/net: Milbank DC.
London, England Office: Ropemaker Place, 25 Ropemaker Street, EC2Y 9AS.
Telephone: 44-171-374-0423.
Cable Address: "Miltuk G."
Fax: 44-171-374-0912.
Hong Kong Office: 3007 Alexandra House, 16Chater Road.
Telephone: 852-2526-5281.
Fax: 852-2840-0792, 852-2845-9046. ABA/net: Milbank HK.
Singapore Office: 14-02 Caltex House, 30 Raffles Place, 0104.
Telephone: 65-534-1700.
Fax: 65-534-2733. ABA/net: EDNANG.
Moscow, Russia Office: 24/27 Sadivaya-Samotyochnaya, 103051.
Telephone: 7-502-258-5015.
Fax: 7-502-258-5014.
Jakarta, Indonesia Correspondent Office: Makarim & Taira S., 17th Floor, Summitmas Tower, Jl, Jend. Sudirman 61, Jakarta.
Telephone: 62-211252-1272 or 2460.
Fax: 62-21-252-2750 or 2751.

PARTNER

Jay D. Grushkin

OF COUNSEL

Hisayo Yasuda

RESIDENT ASSOCIATES

Chieko Eda
(Not admitted in Japan)
Dao Nguyen
(Not admitted in Japan)
David J. Impastato
(Not admitted in Japan)

(Not admitted to practice in Japanese courts)

For full biographical listings, see the Martindale-Hubbell Law Directory

O'MELVENY & MYERS

Sanbancho KB-6 Building, 6 Sanbancho, Chiyoda-ku, Tokyo 102
Telephone: 011-81-3-3239-2800
Facsimile: 011-81-3-3239-2432
Los Angeles, California Office: 400 South Hope Street.
Telephone: 213-669-6000.
Cable Address: "Moms."
Facsimile: 213-669-6407.
Century City, California Office: 1999 Avenue of the Stars, 7th Floor.
Telephone: 310-553-6700.
Facsimile: 310-246-6779.
Newport Beach, California Office: 610 Newport Center Drive, Suite 1700.
Telephone: 714-760-9600.
Cable Address: "Moms."
Facsimile: 714-669-6994.
San Francisco, California Office: Embarcadero Center West Tower, 275 Battery Street, Suite 2600.
Telephone: 415-984-8700.
Facsimile: 415-984-8701.
New York, N.Y. Office: Citicorp Center. 153 53rd Street, 54th Floor.
Telephone: 212-326-2000.
Facsimile: 212-326-2061.
Washington, D.C. Office: 555 13th Street, N.W., Suite 500 West.
Telephone: 202-383-5300.
Cable Address: "Moms."
Facsimile: 202-383-5414.
Newark, New Jersey Office: One Gateway Center, 7th Floor, 07102.
Telephone: 201-639-8600.
Facsimile: 201-639-8630.

(See Next Column)

London, England Office: 10 Finsbury Square, London, EC2A 1LA.
Telephone: 011-44-171-256-8451.
Facsimile: 011-44-171-638-8205.
Hong Kong Office: 1104 Lippo Tower, Lippo Centre, 89 Queensway, Central Hong Kong.
Telephone: 011-852-523-8266.
Facsimile: 011-852-522-1760.

SPECIAL COUNSEL

Dale M. Araki

ASSOCIATES

David G. Litt

For full biographical listings, see the Martindale-Hubbell Law Directory

PAUL, HASTINGS, JANOFSKY & WALKER

A Partnership including Professional Corporations
(Futami Gaikokuho-Jimu-Bengoshi Jimusho)
Firm Established in 1951; Office in 1988
Toranomon Ohtori Building, Eighth Floor, 4-3 Toranomon 1-Chome, Minato-Ku, Tokyo 105
Telephone: (03) 3507-0730
Facsimile: (03) 3507-0734
Los Angeles, California Office: Twenty-Third Floor, 555 South Flower Street, 90071-2371.
Telephone: 213-683-6000.
Cable Address: "Paulhast."
Twx: 910-321-4065.
Orange County, California Office: Seventeenth Floor, 695 Town Center Drive, Costa Mesa, 92626-1924.
Telephone: 714-668-6200.
Washington, D.C. Office: Tenth Floor, 1299 Pennsylvania Avenue, N.W., 20036-5331.
Telephone: 202-508-9500.
Atlanta, Georgia Office: 42nd Floor, Georgia Pacific Center, 133 Peachtree Street, N.E., 30303-1840.
Telephone: 404-588-9900.
Santa Monica, California Office: Fifth Floor, 1299 Ocean Avenue, 90401-1078.
Telephone: 310-319-3300.
Stamford, Connecticut Office: Ninth Floor, 1055 Washington Boulevard, 06901-2217.
Telephone: 203-961-7400.
New York, New York Office: 31st Floor, 399 Park Avenue, 10022-4697.
Telephone: 212-318-6000.

MEMBERS OF FIRM

Norman A. Futami
Kaoruhiko Suzuki
(Not admitted in Japan)

ASSOCIATES

Stephen A. Yamaguchi (Not admitted in Japan)

For full biographical listings, see the Martindale-Hubbell Law Directory

SHEARMAN & STERLING

(Thomas Wilner Gaikokuho-Jimu-Bengoshi Jimusho)
Fukoku Seimei Building, 5th Floor, 2-2-2, Uchisaiwaicho, Tokyo 100
Telephone: (81-3) 5251-1601
Fax: (81-3) 5251-1602
New York, N.Y. Office: 599 Lexington Avenue, New York, New York 10022-6069 and Citicorp Center, 153 East 53rd Street, New York, New York 10022-4676.
Telephone: (212) 848-4000.
Telex: 667290 Num Lau.
Fax: 599 Lexington Avenue: (212) 848-7179. Citicorp Center: (212) 848-5252.
Abu Dhabi, United Arab Emirates Office: P.O. Box 2948.
Telephone: (971-2) 324477.
Fax: (971-2) 774533.
Beijing, People's Republic of China Office: Suite #2205, Capital Mansion, No. 6, Xin Yuan Nan Road. Chao Yang District Beijing, 100004.
Telephone: (861) 465-4574.
Fax: (861) 465-4578.
Budapest, Hungary Office: Szerb utca 17-19, 1056 Budapest.
Telephone: (36-1) 266-3522.
Fax: (36-1) 266-3523.
Düsseldorf, Federal Republic of Germany Office: Königsallee 46, D-40212 Düsseldorf.
Telephone: (49-211) 13 62 80.
Telex: 8 588 294 NYLO.
Fax: (49-211) 13 33 09.
Frankfurt, Federal Republic of Germany Office: Bockenheimer Landstrasse 55, D-60325 Frankfurt am Main.
Telephone: (49-69) 97-10-70.
Fax: (49-69) 97-10-71-00.
Hong Kong, Hong Kong Office: Standard Chartered Bank Building, 4 Des Voeux Road Central, Hong Kong.
Telephone: (852) 2978-8000.
Fax: (852) 2978-8099.
London, England Office: 199Bishopsgate, London EC2M 3TY.
Telephone: (44-71) 920-9000.
Fax: (44-71) 920-9020.

(See Next Column)

SHEARMAN & STERLING—*Continued*

Los Angeles, California Office: 725 South Figueroa Street, 21st Floor, 90017-5421.
Telephone: (213) 239-0300.
Fax: (213) 239-0381, 614-0936.
Paris, France Office: 12 rue d'Astorg, 75008.
Telephone: (33-1) 44-71-17-17.
Telex: 282964 Royale.
Fax: (33-1) 44-71-01-01.
San Francisco, California Office: 555 California Street, 94104-1522.
Telephone: (415) 616-1100.
Fax: (415) 616-1199.
Taipei, Taiwan Office: 7th Floor, Hung Kuo Building, 167 Tun Hwa North Road.
Telephone: (886-2) 545-3300.
Fax: (866-2) 545-3322.
Toronto, Ontario, Canada Office: Commerce Court West, Suite 4405, P.O. Box 247, M5L 1E8.
Telephone: (416) 360-8484.
Fax: (416) 360-2958.
Washington, D.C. Office: 801 Pennsylvania Avenue, N.W., Suite 900, 20004-2604.
Telephone: (202) 508-8000.
Fax: (202) 508-8100.

MANAGING PARTNER

Thomas B. Wilner

For full biographical listings, see the Martindale-Hubbell Law Directory

SIDLEY & AUSTIN

A Partnership including Professional Corporations
(John R. Box Gaikokuho-Jimu-Bengoshi)
Taisho Seimei Hibiya Building, 7th Floor, 9-1 Yurakucho, 1 Chome Chiyoda-Ku, 100 Tokyo
Telephone: 011-81-3-3218-5900
Facsimile: 011-81-3-3218-5922
Chicago, Illinois Office: One First National Plaza 60603.
Telephone: 312-853-7000.
Telecopier: 312-853-7036.
Los Angeles, California Office: 555 W. 5th Street, 40th Floor. 90013-1010.
Telephone: 213-896-6000.
Telecopier: 213-896-6600.
Washington, D.C. Office: 1722 Eye Street, N.W. 20006.
Telephone: 202-736-8000.
Telecopier: 202-736-8711.
New York, N.Y. Office: 875 Third Avenue 10022.
Telephone: 212-906-2000.
Telecopier: 212-906-2021.
London, England Office: Broadwalk House, 5 Appold Street, EC2A 2AA.
Telephone: 011-44-71-621-1616.
Telecopier: 011-44-71-626-7937.
Singapore Office: 36 Robinson Road, #18-01 City House, Singapore 0106.
Telephone: 011-65-224-5000.
Telecopier: 011-65-224-0530.

RESIDENT PARTNER

John R. Box

For full biographical listings, see the Martindale-Hubbell Law Directory

SIMPSON THACHER & BARTLETT

A Partnership which includes Professional Corporations
David Sneider Gaikokuho Jimu Bengoshi Jimusho
Ark Mori Building, 29th Floor, 12-32, Akasaka 1-Chome, Minato-Ku, Tokyo 107
Telephone: 81-3-5562-8601
Telecopier: 81-3-5562-8606
ESL 62765846
New York, NY Office: 425 Lexington Avenue, 10017-3954.
Telephone: 212-455-2000.
Telecopier: 212-455-2502. ESL 62928462.
Columbus, Ohio Office: One Riverside Plaza, 43215.
Telephone: 614-461-7799.
Telecopier: 614-461-0040.
London Office: 100 New Bridge Street, London EC4V 6JE, England.
Telephone: 0171 246 8000.
Telecopier: 0171 329 3883.
Hong Kong Office: Asia Pacific Finance Tower - 32nd Floor, 3 Garden Road, Central, Hong Kong.
Telephone: 852-2514-7600.
Telecopier: 852-2869-7694.

PARTNER

David A. Sneider

RESIDENT ASSOCIATES

Michael S. Bennett (Not admitted in Japan)
Jay M. Ptashek (Not admitted in Japan)

For full biographical listings, see the Martindale-Hubbell Law Directory

SULLIVAN & CROMWELL

(Gaikokuho Jimu Bengoshi Office of Robert G. DeLaMater)
Tokio Kaijo Building Shinkan, 2-1, Marunouchi, 1-Chome Chiyoda-Ku, Tokyo 100
Telephone: (011)(813)3213-6140
Telecopier: (011)(813)3213-6470
New York City Offices: 125 Broad Street, 10004-2498; Midtown Office: 250 Park Avenue, 10177-0021.
Telephone: 212-558-4000.
Telex: 62694 (International); 12-7816 (Domestic).
Cable Address: "Ladycourt, New York".
Telecopier: 125 Broad Street 212-558-3588; 250 Park Avenue 212-558-3792.
Washington, D.C. Office: 1701 Pennsylvania Avenue, N.W., 20006-5805.
Telephone: 202-956-7500.
Telex: 89625.
Telecopier: 202-293-6330.
Los Angeles, California Office: 444 South Flower Street, 90071-2901.
Telephone: 213-955-8000.
Telecopier: 213-683-0457.
Paris Office: 8, Place Vendôme, Paris 75001, France.
Telephone: (011)(331)4450-6000.
Telex: 240654.
Telecopier: (011)(331)4450-6060.
London Office: St. Olave's House, 9a Ironmonger Lane, London EC2V 8EY, England.
Telephone: (011)(44171)710-6500.
Telecopier: (011)(44171)710-6565.
Melbourne, Australia Office: 101 Collins Street, Melbourne, Victoria 3000.
Telephone: (011)(613)654-1500.
Telecopier: (011)(613)654-2422.
Hong Kong Office: 28th Floor, Nine Queen's Road, Central, Hong Kong.
Telephone: (011)(852)826-8688.
Telecopier: (011)(852)522-2280.

PARTNER IN TOKYO

Robert G. DeLaMater

SPECIAL COUNSEL IN TOKYO

Osamu Watanabe (Not admitted in Japan)

ASSOCIATE IN TOKYO

Taneki Ono (Not admitted in Japan)

For full biographical listings, see the Martindale-Hubbell Law Directory

WHITE & CASE

American International Building, 20-5, Ichibancho, Chiyoda-Ku, Tokyo 102
Telephone: (81-3) 3239-4300
Facsimile: (81-3) 3239-4330
New York, New York:
Telephone: 212-819-8200.
Facsimile: 212-354-8113.
Washington, D.C.:
Telephone: 202-872-0013.
Facsimile: 202-872-0210.
Los Angeles, California:
Telephone: 213-620-7700.
Facsimile: 213-687-0758; 213-617-2205.
Miami, Florida:
Telephone: 305-371-2700.
Facsimile: 305-358-5744.
Mexico City, Mexico:
Telephone: (52-5) 207-9717.
Facsimile: (52-5) 208-3628.
Hong Kong:
Telephone: (852) 2822-8700.
Facsimile: (852) 2845-9070; Grice & Co., Solicitors,
Telephone: (852) 2826-0333.
Facsimile: (852) 2526-7166.
Singapore, Republic of Singapore:
Telephone: (65) 225-6000.
Facsimile: (65) 225-6009.
Bangkok, Thailand: Pacific Legal Group Ltd., In Association With White & Case,
Telephone: (662) 236-6154/7.
Facsimile: (662) 237-6771.
Hanoi, Viet Nam: Representative Office,
Telephone: (84-4) 227-575/6/7.
Facsimile: (84-4) 227-297.
Bombay, India:
Telephone: (91-22) 282-6300.
Facsimile: (91-22) 282-6305.
London, England:
Telephone: (44-171) 726-6361.
Facsimile: (44-171) 726-4314; (44-171) 726-8558.
Paris, France:
Telephone: (33-1) 42-60-34-05.
Facsimile: (33-1) 42-60-82-46.
Brussels, Belgium:
Telephone: (32-2) 647-05-89.
Facsimile: (32-2) 647-16-75.

(See Next Column)

WHITE & CASE, *Tokyo—Continued*

Stockholm, Sweden:
Telephone: (46-8) 679-80-30.
Facsimile: (46-8) 611-21-22.
Helsinki, Finland:
Telephone: (358-0) 631-100.
Facsimile: (358-0) 179-477.
Moscow, Russia:
Telephone: (7-095) 201-9292/3/4/5.
Facsimile: (7-095) 201-9284.
Budapest, Hungary:
Telephone: (36-1) 269-0550; (36-1) 131-0933.
Facsimile: (36-1) 269-1199.
Prague, Czech Republic:
Telephone: (42-2) 2481-1796.
Facsimile: (42-2) 232-5522.
Warsaw, Poland: Telephone/
Facsimile: (48-22) 26-80-53; (48-22) 27-84-86. International Telephone/
Facsimile: (48-39) 12-19-06.
Istanbul, Turkey:
Telephone: (90-212) 275-68-98; (90-212) 275-75-33.
Facsimile: (90-212) 275-75-43.
Ankara, Turkey:
Telephone: (90-312) 446-2180.
Facsimile: (90-312) 437-9677.
Jeddah, Saudi Arabia: Law Office of Hassan Mahassni,
Telephone: (966-2) 651-3535.
Facsimile: (966-2) 651-3636.
Riyadh, Saudi Arabia: Law Office of Hassan Mahassni,
Telephone: (966-1) 476-7099.
Facsimile: (966-1) 479-0110.
Almaty, Kazakhstan:
Telephone: (7-3272) 50-7491/2.
Facsimile: (7-3272) 61-0842.

RESIDENT PARTNERS

Robert F. Grondine (Not admitted in Japan)
Gary M. Thomas
Christopher P. Wells

RESIDENT ASSOCIATES

Jonathan M. Heimer (Not admitted in Japan)
Glen Sugimoto
Osamu Umejima (Not admitted in Japan)

For full biographical listings, see the Martindale-Hubbell Law Directory

WINTHROP, STIMSON, PUTNAM & ROBERTS

(Nathan-Pote Gaikokuho Jimu Bengoshi Jimusho)
608 Atagoyama Bengoshi Building, 6-7, Atago 1-Chome, Minato-Ku, Tokyo 105
Telephone: 011-813-3437-9740
Telefax: 011-813-3437-9261
New York Main Office: One Battery Park Plaza, New York, N.Y. 10004-1490.
Telephone: 212-858-1000.
Stamford, Connecticut Office: Financial Centre, 695 East Main Street, P.O. Box 6760, 06904-6760.
Telephone: 203-348-2300.
Washington, D.C. Office: 1133 Connecticut Avenue, N.W., 20036.
Telephone: 202-775-9800.
Palm Beach, Florida Office: 125 Worth Avenue, 33480.
Telephone: 407-655-7297.
London Office: 2 Throgmorton Avenue, London EC2N 2AP, England.
Telephone: 011-4471-628-4931.
Brussels Office: Rue du Taciturne 42, B-1040 Brussels, Belgium.
Telephone: 011-322-230-1392.
Hong Kong Office: 2505 Asia Pacific Finance Tower, Citibank Plaza, 3 Garden Road, Central.
Telephone: 011-852-530-3400.

RESIDENT PARTNER

Jeffrey L. Pote

RESIDENT ASSOCIATES

Daniel A. Schlesinger (Not admitted in Japan)

For full biographical listings, see the Martindale-Hubbell Law Directory

KAZAKHSTAN

ALMATY,

American Lawyers In Almaty

BAKER & MCKENZIE - CIS LIMITED

155 Abai Avenue #29/30
Telephone: (3272) 50-99-45
Intn'l. Dialing: (7-3272) 50-99-45
Facsimile: (7-3272) 50-95-79
Associated Offices of Baker & McKenzie in: Amsterdam, Bangkok, Barcelona, Beijing, Berlin, Bogotá, Brasília, Brussels, Budapest, Buenos Aires, Cairo, Caracas, Chicago, Dallas, Frankfurt, Geneva, Hanoi, Ho Chi Minh City, Hong Kong, Juárez, Kiev, London, Madrid, Manila, Melbourne, México City, Miami, Milan, Monterrey, Moscow, New York, Palo Alto, Paris, Prague, Rio de Janeiro, Riyadh, Rome, St. Petersburg, San Diego, San Francisco, São Paulo, Singapore, Stockholm, Sydney, Taipei, Tijuana, Tokyo, Toronto, Valencia, Warsaw, Washington, D.C. and Zürich.
Correspondent Law Firm: Hadiputranto, Hadinoto & Partners, Jakarta.

PARTNER

Michael E. Wilson (Not admitted in Kazakhstan)

ASSOCIATES

Marat Ibragimov
Igor A. Novikov
Phillip Rosenblatt (Not admitted in Kazakhstan)

For full biographical listings, see the Martindale-Hubbell Law Directory

LEBANON

*BEIRUT,** (Beyrouth)

TYAN & ASSOCIES

22, La Sagesse Street, Beirut
Telephone: 337968
Fax: 200969
Telex: 43928 LEX
Paris, France Office: Law Offices of Nady Tyan, 12, Avenue Pierre ler de Serbie, 75116 Paris.
Telephone: 4.720.18.50.
Fax: 47200628.
Associated with Whitman Breed Abbott & Morgan, 200 Park Avenue, New York, N.Y. Telephone: 212-351-3000. 212-351-3022.
Fax: 212-351-3131. 212-351-3003.

MEMBERS OF FIRM

Nady Tyan
Bechara Tarabay (Resident, Paris, France Office)
Chamel Bassil
Maurice Absi
Souheil Elias
Mireille Richa
Graziella Saliba
Ghada Yazbeck

OF COUNSEL

Antoine Basile
Berge Setrakian

For full biographical listings, see the Martindale-Hubbell Law Directory

MEXICO

CIUDAD JUAREZ, CHIHUAHUA,

BAKER & MCKENZIE ABOGADOS, S.C.

P.T. de la Republica 3304, Piso 2
Telephone: (16) 29-1300
Intn'l. Dialing: (52-16) 29-1300
Facsimile: (52-16) 29-1399
Mailing Address: P.O. Box 9338, El Paso, Texas, 79984
Associated Offices of Baker & McKenzie in: Almaty, Amsterdam, Bangkok, Barcelona, Beijing, Berlin, Bogotá, Brasília, Brussels, Budapest, Buenos Aires, Cairo, Caracas, Chicago, Dallas, Frankfurt, Geneva, Hanoi, Ho Chi Minh City, Hong Kong, Kiev, London, Madrid, Manila, Melbourne, México City, Miami, Milan, Monterrey, Moscow, New York, Palo Alto, Paris, Prague, Rio de Janeiro, Riyadh, Rome, St. Petersburg, San Diego, San Francisco, São Paulo, Singapore, Stockholm, Sydney, Taipei, Tijuana, Tokyo, Toronto, Valencia, Warsaw, Washington, D.C. and Zürich.
Correspondent Law Firm: Hadiputranto, Hadinoto & Partners, Jakarta.

PARTNERS

Carlos Angulo-Parra
Jaime González Bendiksen
Raul Jaquez-Madrid
Andrés Ochoa-Bünsow
Eduardo Romero-Ramos

(See Next Column)

BAKER & MCKENZIE ABOGADOS, S.C.—*Continued*

LOCAL PARTNERS

Oscar Becerra-Tucker
Edmundo Elías-Fernandez
Francisco Javier Legarreta Martinez
Fidencio Raul Martinez-Buenrostro
Jorge Luis Ruiz-Martínez

ASSOCIATES

Roberto Anaya
Graciela M. Diedrich
Sergio Ferrer M.
Hector Mario Granados-Hernandez
Cesar Humberto Lara-Godina
Juan Eleuterio Muñoz-Rivera
Arturo Muñoz-Vázquez
Manuel Padrón-Castillo
Rafael Piñones-Romero
Virginia Portugal-Ceniceros
Gilberto Alonso Ramirez Romero
Rocío Rodríguez-Saro
Max Enrique Salazar-Quintana
Claudia Ivonne Tabuenca-Orozco
Maria Velez-Perez
Victor Gerardo Yanar-Rios

For full biographical listings, see the Martindale-Hubbell Law Directory

*MEXICO, D.F.,**

BAKER & MCKENZIE

(Bufete Sepúlveda, S.C.)
Edificio Plaza Comermex Blvd. M. Avila Camacho No. 1-12o., Col. Lomas de Chapultepec, 11000 Mexico, D.F.
Telephone: (5) 557-8844; 580-0701
Intn'l. Dialing: (52-5) 557-8844; 580-0701
Facsimiles: (52-5) 557-8829; 557-8841; 557-8615; 580-1668; 580-4042; 557-8812; 580-4418; 580-1795; 557-8627
Associated Offices of Baker & McKenzie in: Almaty, Amsterdam, Bangkok, Barcelona, Beijing, Berlin, Bogotá, Brasília, Brussels, Budapest, Buenos Aires, Cairo, Caracas, Chicago, Dallas, Frankfurt, Geneva, Hanoi, Ho Chi Minh City, Hong Kong, Juárez, Kiev, London, Madrid, Manila, Melbourne, Miami, Milan, Monterrey, Moscow, New York, Palo Alto, Paris, Prague, Rio de Janeiro, Riyadh, Rome, St. Petersburg, San Diego, San Francisco, São Paulo, Singapore, Stockholm, Sydney, Taipei, Tijuana, Tokyo, Toronto, Valencia, Warsaw, Washington, D.C. and Zürich.
Correspondent Law Firm: Hadiputranto, Hadinoto & Partners, Jakarta.

Abraham G. Alegría Martínez
Jorge A. de Regil
Raymundo E. Enriquez
Carlos R. Grimm
Manuel Limón Aguirre-Berlanga
Jaime F. Malagón
Ricardo Martinez-Rojas
Genaro Martinez-Siller
Jorge Pelaez-Bolaños
Jorge M. Sánchez-DeVanny

LOCAL PARTNERS

Perla D. Arreola Carbajal
Hedwig Adelheid Lindner López
Jorge Narváez-Hasfura
Juan Carlos Quintana Serur
Gerardo F. Saavedra Silva

José A. Ambrosi
María Casas Lopez
Jacinto Cruz-Galvan
José Antonio Garduño
Robert Heinrich Polycarp Lenz Braun
Liliana C. Hernández Suárez
Maria del Rosario Lombera
Ana Laura Méndez Burkart
Luis Eduardo Meurinne Martinez
Luis J. Pérez-Eguiarte
Guillermo Ramirez Victoria
Monica Romo Heredia
Miguel Angel Ruggeri Correa
Ivonne Sáenz Padilla
Armando Sañudo Trueba
Jorge Arturo Tenorio Coronado

For full biographical listings, see the Martindale-Hubbell Law Directory

CARLSMITH BALL WICHMAN MURRAY CASE & ICHIKI

A Partnership including Law Corporations
Monte Pelvoux 111, Piso 1, Col. Lomas de Chapultepec, 11000 Mexico, D.F.
Telephone: (011-52-5) 520-8514
Fax: (011-52-5) 540-1545
Honolulu, Hawaii Office: Suite 2200, Pacific Tower, 1001 Bishop Street, P.O. Box 656.
Telephone: 808-523-2500.
Hilo, Hawaii Office: 121 Waianuenue Avenue. P.O. Box 686.
Telephone: 808-935-6444.
Kailua-Kona, Hawaii Office: Second Floor, Bank of Hawaii Annex Building, P.O. Box 1720.
Telephone: 808-329-6464.
Agana, Guam Office: 4th Floor, Bank of Hawaii Building, P.O. Box BF.
Telephone: 671-472-6813.
Wailuku, Mau, Hawaii Office: One Main Plaza, Suite 400, 2200 Main Street, P.O. Box 1086.
Telephone: 808-242-4535.
Los Angeles, California Office: 555 South Flower Street, 25th Floor.
Telephone: 213-955-1200.
Long Beach, California Office: 301 East Ocean Boulevard 7th Floor.
Telephone: 310-435-5631.
Mexico City, Mexico Office: Campos Eliseos 385, Torre "B" Col. Chapultepec Polanco.
Telephone: (011-52-5) 281-2428.
Saipan, Commonwealth of the Northern Mariana Islands Office: Carlsmith Building, Capitol Hill, P.O. Box 5241 CHRB.
Telephone: 670-322-3455.

(See Next Column)

Washington, D.C. Office: 700 14th Street, N.W., 9th Floor.
Telephone: 202-508-1025.
Kapolei, Hawaii Office: Kapolei Building, Suite 318, 1001 Kamokila Boulevard.
Telephone: 808-674-0850.

RESIDENT PARTNER

John E. Rogers (Not admitted in Mexico)

For full biographical listings, see the Martindale-Hubbell Law Directory

STRASBURGER & PRICE, L.L.P.

A Partnership including Professional Corporations
Edifico Hewlett-Packard Monte Pelvoux No. 111, Piso 5, Lomas de Chapultepec, 11000 Mexico, D.F.
Telephone: 525-202-8796
Fax: 525-520-7671
Dallas, Texas Office: 901 Main Street, Suite 4300.
Telephone: 214-651-4300.
Fax: 214-651-4330.
Austin, Texas Office: 2600 One American Center, 600 Congress Avenue.
Telephone: 512-499-3600.
Fax: 512-499-3660.
Houston, Texas Office: Suite 2800, One Houston Center, 1221 McKinney.
Telephone: 713-951-5600.
Fax: 713-951-5660.

Holly Sherman Peña (Not admitted in Mexico)

For full biographical listings, see the Martindale-Hubbell Law Directory

MONTERREY, NUEVO LEÓN,

Monterrey, Nuevo León

BAKER & MCKENZIE ABOGADOS, S.C.

Oficinas en el Parque- piso 10, Blvd. Constitución 1884 Pte., 64650 Monterrey, Nuevo León
Telephone: (8) 399-1300
Intn'l Dialing: (52-8) 399-1300
Facsimile: (52-8) 399-1399
Associated Offices of Baker & McKenzie in: Almaty, Amsterdam, Bangkok, Barcelona, Beijing, Berlin, Bogotá, Brasília, Brussels, Budapest, Buenos Aires, Cairo, Caracas, Chicago, Dallas, Frankfurt, Geneva, Hanoi, Ho Chi Minh City, Hong Kong, Juárez, Kiev, London, Madrid, Manila, Melbourne, México City, Miami, Milan, Moscow, New York, Palo Alto, Paris, Prague, Rio de Janeiro, Riyadh, Rome, St. Petersburg, San Diego, San Francisco, São Paulo, Singapore, Stockholm, Sydney, Taipei, Tijuana, Tokyo, Toronto, Valencia, Warsaw, Washington, D.C. and Zürich.
Correspondent Law Firm: Hadiputranto, Hadinoto & Partners, Jakarta.

PARTNER

Andrés Ochoa-Bünsow

LOCAL PARTNER

Maria Teresa Fuentes

ASSOCIATES

Ricardo Castro-Garza
Barbara N. Cazares-Treviño
Juan Carlos Gastelum-Treviño
José María González-Elizondo
Ma. Elena Mayer-Garza
Nancy L. Paine (Not admitted in Mexico)
Gerardo Prado-Hernández

For full biographical listings, see the Martindale-Hubbell Law Directory

THOMPSON & KNIGHT, A PROFESSIONAL CORPORATION

(Attorneys and Counselors)
Edificio Losoles PD-4, Av. Lázaro Cárdenas No. 2400 PTE San Pedro Garza Garcia, Monterrey, Nuevo León 66220
Telephone: (52-8) 363-0096
Telecopy: (52-8) 363-3067
Dallas, Texas Office: 1700 Pacific Avenue, Suite 3300, 75201.
Telephone: 214-969-1700.
Telecopy: 214-969-1751.
Cable Address: "Tomtex."
Telex: 732298.
Austin, Texas Office: 1200 San Jacinto Center, 98 San Jacinto Boulevard, 78701.
Telephone: 512-469-6100.
Telecopy: 512-469-6180.
Fort Worth, Texas Office: 801 Cherry Street, Suite 1600, 76102.
Telephone: 817-347-1700.
Telecopy: 817-347-1799.
Houston, Texas Office: 1700 Texas Commerce Tower, 600 Travis, 77002.
Telephone: 713-217-2800.
Telecopy: 713-217-2828; 713-217-2882.

SHAREHOLDERS

Joe A. Rudberg
Michael C. Titens

For full biographical listings, see the Martindale-Hubbell Law Directory

TIJUANA, BAJA CALIFORNIA,

BAKER & MCKENZIE ABOGADOS, S.C.

Blvd. Agua Caliente no. 4558-1005, 22420 Tijuana, Baja California
Telephone: (66) 81-7740
Intn'l. Dialing: (52-66) 81-7740
Facsimile: (52-66) 81-7745
Associated Offices of Baker & McKenzie in: Almaty, Amsterdam, Bangkok, Barcelona, Beijing, Berlin, Bogotá, Brasília, Brussels, Budapest, Buenos Aires, Cairo, Caracas, Chicago, Dallas, Frankfurt, Geneva, Hanoi, Ho Chi Minh City, Hong Kong, Juárez, Kiev, London, Madrid, Manila, Melbourne, México City, Miami, Milan, Monterrey, Moscow, New York, Palo Alto, Paris, Prague, Rio de Janeiro, Riyadh, Rome, St. Petersburg, San Diego, San Francisco, São Paulo, Singapore, Stockholm, Sydney, Taipei, Tokyo, Toronto, Valencia, Warsaw, Washington, D.C. and Zürich.
Correspondent Law Firm: Hadiputranto, Hadinoto & Partners, Jakarta.
Postal Address: P.O. Box 1205, Chula Vista, California 91912.

PARTNER

Gaspar Gutiérrez-Centeno

LOCAL PARTNERS

Jose Larroque de la Cruz
René Xavier Pérez-Ruiz

ASSOCIATES

Rodrigo Armada-Osorio
Ma. Ofelia Guajardo Calvillo
Francisco Toshiro Lam Ishino
Federico M. Ruanova Guinea
Juan J. Thomas-Moreno

For full biographical listings, see the Martindale-Hubbell Law Directory

THE NETHERLANDS

*AMSTERDAM,**

CARON & STEVENS

(Associated Office of Baker & McKenzie)
Leidseplein 29, 1017 PS Amsterdam
Telephone: (020) 5517555
Intn'l. Dialing: (31-20) 5517555
Cable Address: ABOGADO
Telex: 16474
Answer Back: 16474 ABOG NL
Facsimiles: (31-20) 6267949; 6232884
Mailing Address: P.O. Box 19720, 1000, GS Amsterdam,

Jacobus J. J. Blocks
Mark P. Bongard
M. H. Frank van Buuren
Peter Dekker
Eduard J. Ferman
Carla Hamburger
Albert van Herk
Fredericus C. de Hosson
Norbert R. Jansen
Maarten L. B. van der Lande
Gijsbert Loos
Hendrikus M. N. Schonis
Piet L. A. M. Schroeder
Willem F. C. Stevens
Joseph F. van Vlijmen
Willem C. B. Van Wettum
A. Jurriaan Zoetmulder

LOCAL PARTNERS

Theo L. van Maaren
Hélène A. M. Stuijt
Wil van Willigen
Henk van Wilsum

Boris M. van Beek
Mirjam A. de Blécourt-Wouterse
Karin W. M. Bodewes
J. Arnaud Booij
Caroline A. Bun
Jan Louis Burggraaf
Paul W. J. Coenen
Ernst W. J. Ferdinandusse
Jan-Willem Gerritsen
Lucas P. L. Habets
René M. M. Haerkens
Anne C. J. G. van der Henst
Peter C. Hilders
Carel R. F. Hilferink
Jeroen O. Hoekstra
Roelof O. N. van Holthe tot Echten
Anita A. de Jong
Bart Lb. H. J. Jonkman
G. Christine Koelman
Antal Steven van der Laken
Lenet T. Leusink
Robertus M. van Meerwijk
Loes M. de Moor
Arnoud J. Noordam
Wendela P. van Oosterom
Hans V. van Ophem
Tjeerd F. W. Overdijk
Wouter A. Paardekooper
Leonie C. V. Pels Rijcken
Charles G. A. van Rijckevorsel
Carlo P. M. Roelofs
Peter Roos
Françoise A. Roosenboom-de Vries
Eric T. Scheer
Karin J. T. Smit
Justine A. Takx
Klaas-Jan Visser
Patrick H. de Waal
Marco Wallart
Redmar A. Wolf
Gerard D. J. Zaalberg
Barend W. J. M. de Roy van Zuidewijn

For full biographical listings, see the Martindale-Hubbell Law Directory

REPUBLIC OF THE PHILIPPINES

*METRO MANILA,**

QUISUMBING TORRES & EVANGELISTA

(Associated with Baker & McKenzie)
11th Floor, Pacific Star Building, Makati Ave. corner Sen Gil. J. Puyat Ave. Makati 1200, Metro Manila
Telephone: 817-3016 to 20; 817-0940 to 42; 817-1292; 817-1275
Intn'l. Dialing: (63-2) 817-3016 to 20; 817-0940 to 42; 817-1292; 817-1275
Cable Address: ABOGADO MANILA
Telex: 63726; 66848
Answer Back: 63726 JCL PN; 66848 JCL PN
Facsimiles: (63-2) 817-4432; 817-5416
Mailing Address: MCPO Box 327, Makati 1299, Metro Manila, Philippines,
Associated Offices of Baker & McKenzie in: Almaty, Amsterdam, Bangkok, Barcelona, Beijing, Berlin, Bogotá, Brasília, Brussels, Budapest, Buenos Aires, Cairo, Caracas, Chicago, Dallas, Frankfurt, Geneva, Hanoi, Ho Chi Minh City, Hong Kong, Juárez, Kiev, London, Madrid, Melbourne, México City, Miami, Milan, Monterrey, Moscow, New York, Palo Alto, Paris, Prague, Rio de Janeiro, Riyadh, Rome, St. Petersburg, San Diego, San Francisco, São Paulo, Singapore, Stockholm, Sydney, Taipei, Tijuana, Tokyo, Toronto, Valencia, Warsaw, Washington, D.C. and Zürich.
Correspondent Law Firm: Hadiputranto, Hadinoto & Partners, Jakarta.

Leo G. Dominguez
Rafael E. Evangelista, Jr.
Natividad B. Kwan
Lucas M. Nunag
Ramon J. Quisumbing
Francisco E. Rodrigo, Jr.
Romeo L. Salonga
Jose R. Sandejas

OF COUNSEL

Vicente A. Torres

LOCAL PARTNERS

Ricardo P. C. Castro, Jr.
Edgardo M. de Vera
Christopher L. Lim
Pearl T. Liu

Cornelio B. Abuda
Arthur P. Autea
Anthony D. Bengzon
André Philippe G. Betita
Emmanuel S. Buenaventura
Solomon Ricardo B. Castro
Douglas P. Defensor
Benjamin B. del Rosario
George Gilbert G. Dela Cuesta
Angel M. Esguerra, III
Manuel C. Fausto, Jr.
Rachel P. Follosco
Virgilio C. Herce
Rene K. Limcaoco
Narciso A. Manantan
Ma. Ruby Sarah S. Nitorreda
Eduardo M. Pañgan
Anna Regina Legaspi Pantaleon
Marivic K. Punzalan-Espiritu
Rodrigo Lope S. Quimbo
Kennedy B. Sarmiento
Ulfredo A. Tuyac
Ceazar Lorenzo T. Veneracion, III
Josephine V. Tañada Yam-Narciso
Gil Roberto L. Zerrudo

For full biographical listings, see the Martindale-Hubbell Law Directory

POLAND

WARSAW,

American Lawyers in Warsaw

BAKER & MCKENZIE JUR GRUSZCZYSKI LAW OFFICE

ul. Dluga 26/28, 00-238 Warsaw
Telephone: (02) 635 3521; 635 4111; 635 0521; 635 8611; 635 9611; 39121203 (Komertel/satellite)
Intn'l Dialing: (48-2) 635 3521; 635 4111; 635 0521; 635 8611; *635 9611; (48) 39121203 (Komertel/satellite)*
Facsimiles: (48-2) 635 9447; (48) 39121213 (Komertel/satellite)
Associated Offices of Baker & McKenzie in: Almaty, Amsterdam, Bangkok, Barcelona, Beijing, Berlin, Bogotá, Brasília, Brussels, Budapest, Buenos Aires, Cairo, Caracas, Chicago, Dallas, Frankfurt, Geneva, Hanoi, Ho Chi Minh City, Hong Kong, Juárez, Kiev, London, Madrid, Manila, Melbourne, México City, Miami, Milan, Monterrey, Moscow, New York, Palo Alto, Paris, Prague, Rio de Janeiro, Riyadh, Rome, St. Petersburg, San Diego, San Francisco, São Paulo, Singapore, Stockholm, Sydney, Taipei, Tijuana, Tokyo, Toronto, Valencia, Washington, D.C. and Zürich.
Correspondent Law Firm: Hadiputranto, Hadinoto & Partners, Jakarta.

RESIDENT PARTNERS

Jur Gruszczyński
Tomasz Z. H. Ujejski (Not admitted in Poland)

RESIDENT ASSOCIATES

Wojciech T. Bialik
Krzysztof Korzeniewski
Nicholas H. Richardson (Not admitted in Poland)
Jerzy Skrzypowski
Andrzej Tynel
Joseph Zuromski

For full biographical listings, see the Martindale-Hubbell Law Directory

RUSSIA

MOSCOW,

American Lawyers in Moscow

Baker & McKenzie

Bolshoi Strochenovsky Pereulok, 22/25, 113054 Moscow
Telephone: Telephone: (095) 230-60-36
Intn'l Dialing: (1-212) 891-3799* (7-095) 230-60-36
Telex: 413671
Answer Back: 413671 BAKER SU
Facsimile: (7-095) 230-60-47
**This number is available as a telephone line from 9:* 00 a.m. to 9:00 p.m. Moscow time. After 9:00 p.m. Moscow time, the number is switched to serve as a facsimile line.
Associated Offices of Baker & McKenzie in: Almaty, Amsterdam, Bangkok, Barcelona, Beijing, Berlin, Bogotá, Brasília, Brussels, Budapest, Buenos Aires, Cairo, Caracas, Chicago, Dallas, Frankfurt, Geneva, Hanoi, Ho Chi Minh City, Hong Kong, Juárez, Kiev, London, Madrid, Manila, Melbourne, México City, Miami, Milan, Monterrey, New York, Palo Alto, Paris, Prague, Rio de Janeiro, Riyadh, Rome, St. Petersburg, San Diego, San Francisco, São Paulo, Singapore, Stockholm, Sydney, Taipei, Tijuana, Tokyo, Toronto, Valencia, Warsaw, Washington, D.C. and Zürich.
Correspondent Law Firm: Hadiputranto, Hadinoto & Partners, Jakarta.

PARTNERS

William F. Atkin (Not admitted in Russia)
Paul J. Melling (Not admitted in Russia)
Carol A. M. Patterson (Not admitted in Russia)

OF COUNSEL

Alexander I. Feinstein

ASSOCIATES

Marsha W. Blitzer (Not admitted in Russia)
Mark W. Borghesani (Not admitted in Russia)
Jean A. Brough (Not admitted in Russia)
Alexander A. Bychkov
Alexander Chmelev (Not admitted in Russia)
Marina Drel
Karen M. Handelsman (Not admitted in Russia)
Igor S. Martinov
Vladimir V. Mironov
Graham J. Nicholson (Not admitted in Russia)
Maxim D. Smyslov
Mark C. Swords (Not admitted in Russia)
Benedikt M.M. Weiffenbach (Not admitted in Russia)
Corinna M. Wissels (Not admitted in Russia)

For full biographical listings, see the Martindale-Hubbell Law Directory

Chadbourne & Parke

38 Maxim Gorky Naberezhnaya, 113035
Telephone: 7095-974-2424 Telecopier: 7095-974-2425
International satellite lines via U.S.: Telephone: 212-408-1190. Telecopier: 212-408-1199
New York, N.Y. Office: 30 Rockefeller Plaza, 10112.
Telephone: 212-408-5100.
Telecopier: 212-541-5369.
Los Angeles, California Office: 601 South Figueroa Street, 90017.
Telephone: 213-892-1000.
Telecopier: 213-622-9865.
Washington, D.C. Office: Suite 900, 1101 Vermont Avenue, N.W., 20005.
Telephone: 202-289-3000.
Telecopier: 202-289-3002.
London, England Office: 86 Jermyn Street, SW1 6JD.
Telephone: 44-171-925-7400.
Facsimile: 44-171-839-3393.
Hong Kong Office: Suite 3704, Peregrine Tower, Lippo Centre, 89 Queensway.
Telephone: (852) 2842-5400.
Telecopier: (852) 2521-7527.
New Delhi, India Office: Chadbourne & Parke Associates, A16-B Anand Niketan, 110 021.
Telephone: 91-11-301-7568/7581/7582.
Telecopier: 91-11-301-7351.

PARTNER

William E. Holland (Not admitted in Russia)

GENERAL DIRECTOR

Genrikh P. Padva

RESIDENT COUNSEL

John T. Connor, Jr. (Not admitted in Russia)
Robert E. Langer (Not admitted in Russia)

RESIDENT ASSOCIATES

Alexander J. Buyevitch
Mikhail A. Rozenberg
Melissa J. Schwartz (Not admitted in Russia)
Natalie Menshikova Whitman

For full biographical listings, see the Martindale-Hubbell Law Directory

Milbank, Tweed, Hadley & McCloy

24/27 Sadovaya-Samotyochnaya, Moscow 103051
Telephone: 7-502-258-5015
Fax: 7-502-258-5014
New York, New York Office: 1 Chase Manhattan Plaza, 10005.
Telephone: 212-530-5000.
Cable Address: "Miltweed NYK" ITT: 422962; 423893.
Fax: 212- 530-5219. ABA/net: Milbank NY.
Midtown Office: 50 Rockefeller Plaza, 10020.
Telephone: 212-530-5800.
Fax: 212-530-0158.
Los Angeles, California Office: 601 South Figueroa Street, 30th Floor, 90017.
Telephone: 213-892-4000.
Fax: 213-629-5063.
Telex: 678754. ABA/net: Milbank LA.
Washington, D.C. Office: Suite 1100, 1825 Eye Street, N.W., 20006.
Telephone: 202-835-7500.
Cable Address: "Miltweed Wsh". ITT 440667.
Fax: 202-835-7586. ABA/net: Milbank DC.
Tokyo, Japan Office: Nippon Press Center Building, 2-1, Uchisaiwai-cho 2-chome, Chiyoda-ku, Tokyo 100.
Telephone: 81-3-3504-1050.
Fax: 81-3-3595-2790, 81-3-3502-5192.
London, England Office: Ropemaker Place, 25 Ropemaker Street, EC2Y 9AS.
Telephone: 44-171-374-0423.
Cable Address: "Miltuk G."
Fax: 44-171-374-0912.
Hong Kong Office: 3007 Alexandra House, 16 Chater Road.
Telephone: 852-2526-5281.
Fax: 852-2840-0792, 852-2845-9046. ABA/net: Milbank HK.
Singapore Office: 14-02 Caltex House, 30 Raffles Place, 0104.
Telephone: 65-534-1700.
Fax: 65-534-2733. ABA/net: Milbank EDNANG.
Jakarta, Indonesia Correspondent Office: Makarim & Taira S., 17th Floor, Jl, Jend. Sudirman 61, Jakarta.
Telephone: 62-211252-1272 or 2460.
Fax: 62-21-252-2750 or 2751.

RESIDENT ASSOCIATE

Irina Mashlenko
(Not admitted to practice in Russian courts)

For full biographical listings, see the Martindale-Hubbell Law Directory

ST. PETERSBURG,

American Lawyers in St. Petersburg

Baker & McKenzie

Bolshaya Morskaya, 57, 19000 St. Petersburg
Telephone: Telephone: (812) 310-54-46; 310-55-44; 310-01-71;
Int'l Dialing: (7- 812) 310-54-46; 310-55-44; 310-01-71;
(7-812) 850-14-25 (Satellite)
Telex: 612151
Answer Back: 612151 BMSTP
Facsimile: (7-812) 310-59-44 (7-812) 119-60-13 (Satellite)
Associated Offices of Baker & McKenzie in: Almaty, Amsterdam, Bangkok, Barcelona, Beijing, Berlin, Bogotá, Brasília, Brussels, Budapest, Buenos Aires, Cairo, Caracas, Chicago, Dallas, Frankfurt, Geneva, Hanoi, Ho Chi Minh City, Hong Kong, Juárez, Kiev, London, Madrid, Manila, Melbourne, México City, Miami, Milan, Monterrey, Moscow, New York, Palo Alto, Paris, Prague, Rio de Janeiro, Riyadh, Rome, San Diego, San Francisco, São Paulo, Singapore, Stockholm, Sydney, Taipei, Tijuana, Tokyo, Toronto, Valencia, Warsaw, Washington, D.C. and Zürich.
Correspondent Law Firm: Hadiputranto, Hadinoto & Partners, Jakarta.

PARTNERS

Arthur L. George (Not admitted in Russia)

ASSOCIATES

Evgeny V. Astakhov
Maxim V. Kalinin
Nicholas M.N. Rumin (Not admitted in Russia)
David I. Scott (Not admitted in Russia)

For full biographical listings, see the Martindale-Hubbell Law Directory

SAUDI ARABIA

JEDDAH,

LAW OFFICE OF HASSAN MAHASSNI

(In Association with White and Case)
Al Hada Building, 2013 Wali Al-Ahd Street, P.O. Box 2256, Jeddah 21451
Telephone: (966-2) 651-3535
Facsimile: (966-2) 651-3636
Telex: 604750 LIBRA SJ
New York, New York:
Telephone: 212-819-8200.
Facsimile: 212-354-8113.
Washington, D.C.:
Telephone: 202-872-0013.
Facsimile: 202-872-0210.
Los Angeles, California:
Telephone: 213-620-7700.
Facsimile: 213-687-0758; 213-617-2205.
Miami, Florida:
Telephone: 305-371-2700.
Facsimile: 305-358-5744.
Mexico City, Mexico:
Telephone: (52-5) 207-9717.
Facsimile: (52-5) 208-3628.
Tokyo, Japan:
Telephone: (81-3) 3239-4300.
Facsimile: (81-3) 3239-4330.
Hong Kong:
Telephone: (852) 2822-8700.
Facsimile: (852) 2845-9070; Grice & Co., Solicitors,
Telephone: (852) 2826-0333.
Facsimile: (852) 2526-7166.
Singapore, Republic of Singapore:
Telephone: (65) 225-6000.
Facsimile: (65) 225-6009.
Bangkok, Thailand: Pacific Legal Group Ltd., In Association With White & Case,
Telephone: (662) 236-6154/7.
Facsimile: (662) 237-6771.
Hanoi, Viet Nam: Representative Office,
Telephone: (84-4) 227-575/6/7.
Facsimile: (84-4) 227-297.
Bombay, India:
Telephone: (91-22) 282-6300.
Facsimile: (91-22) 282-6305.
London, England:
Telephone: (44-171) 726-6361.
Facsimile: (44-171) 726-4314; (44-171) 726-8558.
Paris, France:
Telephone: (33-1) 42-60-34-05.
Facsimile: (33-1) 42-60-82-46.
Brussels, Belgium:
Telephone: (32-2) 647-05-89.
Facsimile: (32-2) 647-16-75.
Stockholm, Sweden:
Telephone: (46-8) 679-80-30.
Facsimile: (46-8) 611-21-22.
Helsinki, Finland:
Telephone: (358-0) 631-100.
Facsimile: (358-0) 179-477.
Moscow, Russia:
Telephone: (7-095) 201-9292/3/4/5.
Facsimile: (7-095) 201-9284.
Budapest, Hungary:
Telephone: (36-1) 269-0550; (36-1) 131-0933.
Facsimile: (36-1) 269-1199.
Prague, Czech Republic:
Telephone: (42-2) 2481-1796.
Facsimile: (42-2) 232-5522.
Warsaw, Poland: Telephone/
Facsimile: (48-22) 26-80-53; (48-22) 27-84-86. International Telephone/
Facsimile: (48-39) 12-19-06.
Istanbul, Turkey:
Telephone: (90-212) 275-68-98; (90-212) 275-75-33.
Facsimile: (90-212) 275-75-43.
Ankara, Turkey:
Telephone: (90-312) 446-2180.
Facsimile: (90-312) 437-9677.
Riyadh, Saudi Arabia: Law Office of Hassan Mahassni,
Telephone: (966-1) 476-7099.
Facsimile: (966-1) 479-0110.
Almaty, Kazakhstan:
Telephone: (7-3272) 50-7491/2.
Facsimile: (7-3272) 61-0842.

Hassan Mahassni (Partner, White & Case, New York, New York).

(See Next Column)

Alexander S. Kritzalis (Not admitted in Saudi Arabia; Partner, White & Case, New York, New York).

RESIDENT ASSOCIATES

E. William Cattan, Jr. (Not admitted in Saudi Arabia)
Imad Ai-Dine Ghazi (Not admitted in Saudi Arabia)
Anas Kailani (Not admitted in Saudi Arabia; Legal Consultant)
Farouk Kouatli (Not admitted in Saudi Arabia; Legal Consultant)
Walid Labadi (Not admitted in Saudi Arabia)
Amin Munajed (Not admitted in Saudi Arabia)
Gassim Zanoon (Not admitted in Saudi Arabia)

For full biographical listings, see the Martindale-Hubbell Law Directory

RIYADH,

LEGAL ADVISORS DR. MOSAAD M. AL-AIBAN

License No. 188
(In Association with Baker & Mckenzie)
King Faisal Foundation Building, King Fahad Road, P.O. Box 4288, Riyadh 11491
Telephone: (01) 462-9886
Intn'l. Dialing: (966-1) 462-9886
Facsimile: (966-1) 463-2657
In Association with Baker & McKenzie with offices in:
Chicago, Illinois: One Prudential Plaza, 130 East Randolph Drive, 60601.
Dallas, Texas: 4500 Trammell Crow Center, 2001 Ross Avenue, 75201.
Miami, Florida: Barnett Tower, 701 Brickell Avenue, Suite 1600, 33131-2827.
New York, New York: 805 Third Avenue, 10022.
Palo Alto, California: 660 Hansen Way, P.O. Box 60309, 94304-0309.
San Diego, California: The Wells Fargo Plaza, Twelfth Floor, 101 West Broadway, 92101.
San Francisco, California: Two Embarcadero Center, 24th Floor, 94111-3909.
Washington, D.C.: 815 Connecticut Avenue, N.W., 20006-4078.

SECONDED PERSONNEL

John E. Xefos (Not admitted in Saudi Arabia)

Brian D. Earp (Not admitted in Saudi Arabia)
Nadim Kyriakos-Saad (Not admitted in Saudi Arabia)
Hazim Abd El-Ghafar Rizkana (Not admitted in Saudi Arabia)
George Sayen (Not admitted in Saudi Arabia)

For full biographical listings, see the Martindale-Hubbell Law Directory

LAW OFFICE OF SAUD M.A. SHAWWAF

(In Association with Jones, Day, Reavis & Pogue)
P.O. Box 2700, Riyadh 11461
Telephone: (966-1) 465-6543, (966-1) 464-8534 or (966-1) 464-8540
Telex: 401831 SAUCON SJ
Telecopier: (966-1) 464-8480
In Atlanta, Georgia: 3500 One Peachtree Center. 303 Peachtree Street, N.E.
Telephone: 404-521-3939.
Cable Address: "Attorneys Atlanta".
Telex: 54-2711.
Telecopier: 404-581-8330.
In Brussels, Belgium: Avenue Louise 480, 7th Floor. B-1050 Brussels.
Telephone: 32-2-645-14-11.
Telecopier: 32-2-645-14-45.
In Chicago, Illinois: 77 West Wacker.
Telephone: 312-782-3939.
Telecopier: 312-782-8585.
In Cleveland, Ohio: North Point, 901 Lakeside Avenue.
Telephone: 216-586-3939.
Cable Address: "Attorneys Cleveland."
Telex: 980389.
Telecopier: 216-579-0212.
In Columbus, Ohio: 1900 Huntington Center.
Telephone: 614-469-3939.
Cable Address: "Attorneys Columbus."
Telecopier: 614-461-4198.
In Dallas, Texas: 2300 Trammell Crow Center, 2001 Ross Avenue.
Telephone: 214-220-3939.
Cable Address: "Attorneys Dallas."
Telex: 730852.
Telecopier: 214-969-5100.
In Frankfurt, Germany: Triton Haus, Bockenheimer Landstrasse 42, 60323 Frankfurt am Main.
Telephone: 49-69-9726-3939.
Telecopier: 49-69-9726-3993.
In Geneva, Switzerland: 20, rue de Candolle.
Telephone: 41-22-320-2339.
Telecopier: 41-22-320-1232.

(See Next Column)

LAW OFFICE OF SAUD M.A. SHAWWAF—*Continued*

In Hong Kong: 1501 One Exchange Square, 8 Connaught Place.
Telephone: 852-2526-6895.
Telecopier: 852-2810-5787.
In Irvine, California: 2603 Main Street, Suite 900.
Telephone: 714-851-3939.
Telex: 194911 Lawyers LSA.
Telecopier: 714-553-7539.
In London, England: One Mount Street.
Telephone: 44-71-493-9361.
Cable Address: "Surgoe London WI."
Telecopier: 44-71-493-9666.
In Los Angeles, California: 555 West Fifth Street, Suite 4600.
Telephone: 213-489-3939.
Telex: 181439 UD.
Telecopier: 213-243-2539.
In New York, New York: 599 Lexington Avenue.
Telephone: 212-326-3939.
Cable Address: "JONESDAY NEWYORK."
Telex: 237013 JDRP UR.
Telecopier: 212-755-7306.
In Paris, France: 62, rue du Faubourg Saint-Honore.
Telephone: 33-1-44-71-3939.
Cable Address: "Surgoe Paris."
Telex: 290156 Surgoe.
Telecopier: 33-1-49-24-0471.
In Pittsburgh, Pennsylvania: 500 Grant Street, 31st Floor.
Telephone: 412-391-3939.
Cable Address: "Attorneys Pittsburgh".
Telecopier: 412-394-7959.
In Taipei, Taiwan: 8th Floor, 2 Tun Hwa South Road, Section 2.
Telephone: (886-2) 704-6808.
Telecopier: (886-2) 704-6791.
In Tokyo, Japan: Toranomon MT Building, 4th Floor, 10-3, Toranomon 3-chome, Minato-Ku.
Telephone: 81-3-3433-3939.
Telecopier: 81-3-5401-2725.
In Washington, D.C.: Metropolitan Square, 1450 G Street, N.W.
Telephone: 202-879-3939.
Cable Address: "Attorneys Washington."
Telex: 89-2410 ATTORNEYS WASH.
Telecopier: 202-737-2832.

RESIDENT LAWYERS

Saud M.A. Shawwaf, Saudi national
Vernon Cassin, Jr. (Not admitted in Saudi Arabia)
Martin L. Camp (Not admitted in Saudi Arabia)
Hassan M. Hammad, Sudanese national (Not admitted in Saudi Arabia)
Saleh Salman Al Amin (Not admitted in Saudi Arabia)
Walid M. Ayache, American national (Not admitted in Saudi Arabia)

For full biographical listings, see the Martindale-Hubbell Law Directory

SINGAPORE

SINGAPORE,

American Lawyers In Singapore

BAKER & MCKENZIE

21 Collyer Quay #16-01, Hongkong Bank Building, Singapore 0104
Telephone: 2248066
Intn'l. Dialing: (65) 2248066
Cable Address: ABOGADO
Telex: 20852
Answer Back: ABOSIN RS20852
Facsimile: (65) 2243872; 2241038
Associated Offices of Baker & McKenzie in: Almaty, Amsterdam, Bangkok, Barcelona, Beijing, Berlin, Bogotá, Brasília, Brussels, Budapest, Buenos Aires, Cairo, Caracas, Chicago, Dallas, Frankfurt, Geneva, Hanoi, Ho Chi Minh City, Hong Kong, Juárez, Kiev, London, Madrid, Manila, Melbourne, México City, Miami, Milan, Monterrey, Moscow, New York, Palo Alto, Paris, Prague, Rio de Janeiro, Riyadh, Rome, St. Petersburg, San Diego, San Francisco, São Paulo, Stockholm, Sydney, Taipei, Tijuana, Tokyo, Toronto, Valencia, Warsaw, Washington, D.C. and Zürich.
Correspondent Law Firm: Hadiputranto, Hadinoto & Partners, Jakarta.

David J. Howell (Not Admitted in Singapore)
Kien Keong Wong

LOCAL PARTNER

Deborah L. Blum (Not admitted in Singapore)

OF COUNSEL

John K. Connor (Not admitted in Singapore)

(See Next Column)

Neal A. Bieker (Not admitted in Singapore)
Edmund H. M. Leow (Not admitted in Singapore)
Chiu-ing Ngooi (Not admitted in Singapore)
Angus T. S. Phang
Rachel S. H. Tan (Not admitted in Singapore)
Michael G. Velten (Not admitted in Singapore)
Adeline M. K. Wong (Not admitted in Singapore)

(Not authorized to appear before the Singapore courts)

For full biographical listings, see the Martindale-Hubbell Law Directory

COUDERT BROTHERS

Tung Centre, 20 Collyer Quay, Singapore 0104
Telephone: (65) 2229973
Telex: 21466 Coudert RS
Telecopier: (65) 2241756
Cable Address: "Treduoc"
New York, New York 10036-7794: 1114 Avenue of the Americas.
Washington, D.C. 20006: 1627 I Street, N.W.
Los Angeles, California 90017: 1055 West Seventh Street, Twentieth Floor.
San Francisco, California 94111: 4 Embarcadero Center, Suite 3300.
San Jose, California 95113: Suite 1250, Ten Almaden Boulevard.
Paris 75008, France: Coudert Frères, 52, Avenue des Champs-Elysees.
London, EC4M 7JP, England: 20 Old Bailey.
Brussels B-1050, Belgium: Tour Louise. 149 Avenue Louise-Box 8.
Beijing, People's Republic of China 100020: Suite 2708-09 Jing Guang Centre, Hu Jia Lou Chao Yang Qu.
Shanghai, People's Republic of China 200002: c/o Suite 1804, Union Building, 100 Yanan Road East.
Hong Kong: 25th Floor, Nine Queen's Road Central.
Sydney N.S.W. 2000, Australia: Suite 2202, State Bank Centre, 52 Martin Place.
Tokyo 107, Japan: 1355 West Tower, Aoyama Twin Towers, 1-1-1 Minami-Aoyama, Minato-ku.
Moscow, Russia: Ulitsa Staraya Basmannaya 14.
01301 Sao Paulo, SP, Brazil: Machado, Meyer, Sendacz, e Opice, Advogados, Rua da Consolacao, 8 Andar.
Bangkok 10500, Thailand: Bubhajit Building, 20 North Sathorn Road, 10th Floor.
Ho Chi Minh City, Vietnam: c/o Saigon Business Centre, 49-57 Dong Du Street, District 1.

RESIDENT PARTNERS

Irwin L. Gubman
Jeffrey Leow (Not admitted in Singapore)

SENIOR ATTORNEY

Richard L. Cassin, Jr. (Not admitted in Singapore)

RESIDENT ASSOCIATES

M. Tamara Box (Not admitted in Singapore)
Michael S. Horn (Not admitted in Singapore)
Efi Kremetis (Not admitted in Singapore)
Mark A. Nelson (Not admitted in Singapore)
Eleanor Siew-Yin Wong

(Not authorized to appear before the Singapore courts)

For full biographical listings, see the Martindale-Hubbell Law Directory

MILBANK, TWEED, HADLEY & MCCLOY

14-02 Caltex House, 30 Raffles Place, Singapore 0104
Telephone: 65-534-1700
Fax: 65-534-2733
ABA/net: EDNANG
New York, New York Office: 1 Chase Manhattan Plaza, 10005.
Telephone: 212-530-5000.
Cable Address: "Miltweed NYK" ITT: 422962; 423893.
Fax: 212- 530-5219. ABA/net: Milbank NY.
Midtown Office: 50 Rockefeller Plaza, 10020.
Telephone: 212-530-5800.
Fax: 212-530-0158.
Los Angeles, California Office: 601 South Figueroa Street, 30th Floor, 90017.
Telephone: 213-892-4000.
Fax: 213-629-5063.
Telex: 678754. ABA/net: Milbank LA.
Washington, D.C. Office: Suite 1100, 1825 Eye Street, N.W., 20006.
Telephone: 202-835-7500.
Cable Address: "Miltweed Wsh". ITT 440667.
Fax: 202-835-7586. ABA/net: Milbank DC.
Tokyo, Japan Office: Nippon Press Center Building, 2-1 Uchisaiwai-cho 2-chome, Chiyoda-ku, Tokyo 100.
Telephone: 81-3-3504-1050.
Fax: 81-3-3595-2790, 81-3-3502-5192.
London, England Office: Ropemaker Place, 25 Ropemaker Street, EC2Y 9AS.
Telephone: 44-171-374-0423.
Cable Address: Miltuk G."
Fax: 44-171-374-0912.
Hong Kong Office: 3007 Alexandra House, 16 Chater Road.
Telephone: 8522-526-5281.
Fax: 852-2840-0792, 852-2845-9046. ABA/net: Milbank HK.

(See Next Column)

MILBANK, TWEED, HADLEY & MCCLOY, *Singapore—Continued*

Moscow, Russia Office: 28 Pokrovka Street, 1st Floor, Moscow, 103062. International
Telephone: 7-502-220-4776. International
Fax: 7-502-220-4617. Local
Telephone: 7-095-956-37507. Local Telephone/
Fax: 7-095-956-3991.
Jakarta, Indonesia Correspondent Office: Makarim & Tiara S., 17th Floor, Summitmas Tower, Jl, Jend. Sudirman 61, Jakarta.
Telephone: 62-211252-1272 or 2460.
Fax: 62-21-252-2750 or 2751.

PARTNERS

Glenn S. Gerstell (Not admitted in Singapore; Resident in Hong Kong Office)
Thomas B. Siebens (Not admitted in Singapore)
Gary S. Wigmore (Not admitted in Singapore)

ASSOCIATES

Caroline G. Angoorly (Not admitted in Singapore)
Renisha Bharvani
Saburabi Nila Ibrahim (Not admitted in Singapore)

(Not authorized to appear before the Singapore courts)

For full biographical listings, see the Martindale-Hubbell Law Directory

WHITE & CASE

50 Raffles Place #22-01, Shell Tower, Singapore 0104
Telephone: (65) 225-6000
Facsimile: (65) 225-6009
New York, New York:
Telephone: 212-819-8200.
Facsimile: 212-354-8113.
Washington, D.C.:
Telephone: 202-872-0013.
Facsimile: 202-872-0210.
Los Angeles, California:
Telephone: 213-620-7700.
Facsimile: 213-687-0758; 213-617-2205.
Miami, Florida:
Telephone: 305-371-2700.
Facsimile: 305-358-5744.
Mexico City, Mexico:
Telephone: (52-5) 207-9717.
Facsimile: (52-5) 208-3628.
Tokyo, Japan:
Telephone: (81-3) 3239-4300.
Facsimile: (81-3) 3239-4330.
Hong Kong:
Telephone: (852) 2822-8700.
Facsimile: (852) 2845-9070; Grice & Co., Solicitors,
Telephone: (852) 2826-0333.
Facsimile: (852) 2526-7166.
Bangkok, Thailand: Pacific Legal Group Ltd., In Association With White & Case,
Telephone: (662) 236-6154/7.
Facsimile: (662) 237-6771.
Hanoi, Viet Nam: Representative Office,
Telephone: (84-4) 227-575/6/7.
Facsimile: (84-4) 227-297.
Bombay, India:
Telephone: (91-22) 282-6300.
Facsimile: (91-22) 282-6305.
London, England:
Telephone: (44-171) 726-6361.
Facsimile: (44-171) 726-4314; (44-171) 726-8558.
Paris, France:
Telephone: (33-1) 42-60-34-05.
Facsimile: (33-1) 42-60-82-46.
Brussels, Belgium:
Telephone: (32-2) 647-05-89.
Facsimile: (32-2) 647-16-75.
Stockholm, Sweden:
Telephone: (46-8) 679-80-30.
Facsimile: (46-8) 611-21-22.
Helsinki, Finland:
Telephone: (358-0) 631-100.
Facsimile: (358-0) 179-477.
Moscow, Russia:
Telephone: (7-095) 201-9292/3/4/5.
Facsimile: (7-095) 201-9284.
Budapest, Hungary:
Telephone: (36-1) 269-0550; (36-1) 131-0933.
Facsimile: (36-1) 269-1199.
Prague, Czech Republic:
Telephone: (42-2) 2481-1796.
Facsimile: (42-2) 232-5522.
Warsaw, Poland: Telephone/
Facsimile: (48-22) 26-80-53; (48-22) 27-84-86. International Telephone/
Facsimile: (48-39) 12-19-06.
Istanbul, Turkey:
Telephone: (90-212) 275-68-98; (90-212) 275-75-33.
Facsimile: (90-212) 275-75-43.

(See Next Column)

Ankara, Turkey:
Telephone: (90-312) 446-2180.
Facsimile: (90-312) 437-9677.
Jeddah, Saudi Arabia: Law Office of Hassan Mahassni,
Telephone: (966-2) 651-3535.
Facsimile: (966-2) 651-3636.
Riyadh, Saudi Arabia: Law Office of Hassan Mahassni,
Telephone: (966-1) 476-7099.
Facsimile: (966-1) 479-0110.
Almaty, Kazakhstan:
Telephone: (7-3272) 50-7491/2.
Facsimile: (7-3272) 61-0842.

RESIDENT PARTNERS

J. Haywood Blakemore, IV (Not admitted in Singapore)
Kenneth C. Ellis (Not admitted in Singapore)
Wendell C. Maddrey (Not admitted in Singapore)

RESIDENT COUNSEL

Kimberley R. Landon (Not admitted in Singapore)

RESIDENT ASSOCIATES

Michael R. Barz (Not admitted in Singapore)
Alistair A. Duffield (Not admitted in Singapore)
John-Michael Lind (Not admitted in Singapore)
Brian M. Miller (Not admitted in Singapore)
Kevin J. Murphy (Not admitted in Singapore)
Madhurani Powar Garg (Not admitted in Singapore)
Neela Ramanathan (Not admitted in Singapore)
Michael R. Reading (Not admitted in Singapore)
S. M. Edwin Tham (Not admitted in Singapore)
Brian J. Wesol (Not admitted in Singapore)

(Not authorized to appear before the Singapore courts)

For full biographical listings, see the Martindale-Hubbell Law Directory

SLOVAKIA

BRATISLAVA,

American Lawyers in Bratislava

SQUIRE, SANDERS & DEMPSEY

Mudronova 37, 811 01 Bratislava
Telephone: 011-42-7-315-370
Fax: 011-42-7-313-918
Cleveland, Ohio Office: 4900 Society Center, 127 Public Square, Cleveland, Ohio 44114-1304.
Telephone: 216-479-8500. Fax's: 216-479-8780, 216-479-8781, 216-479-8787, 216-479-8795, 216-479-8793, 216-479-8776, 216-479-8788.
Columbus, Ohio Offices: 1300 Huntington Center, 41 South High Street, Columbus, Ohio 43215.
Telephone: 614-365-2700.
Fax: 614-365-2499.
Jacksonville, Florida Office: One Enterprise Center, Suite 2100, 225 Water Street, Jacksonville, Florida 32202.
Telephone: 904-353-1264.
Fax: 904-356-2986.
Miami, Florida Office: 201 South Biscayne Boulevard, Suite 2900 Miami Center, Miami, Florida 33131.
Telephone: 305-577-8700.
Fax: 305-358-1425.
New York, New York Office: 520 Madison Avenue, 32nd Floor, New York, New York 10022.
Telephone: 212-872-9800.
Fax: 212-872-9814.
Phoenix, Arizona Office: Two Renaissance Square, 40 North Central Avenue, Suite 2700, Phoenix, Arizona 85004-4441.
Telephone: 602-528-4000.
Fax: 602-253-8129.
Washington, D.C. Office: 1201 Pennsylvania Avenue, N.W., P.O. Box 407, Washington, D.C. 20044.
Telephone: 202-626-6600.
Fax: 202-626-6780.
London, England Office: 1 Gunpowder Square, Printer Street, London EC4A 3DE.
Telephone: 011-44-71-830-0055.
Fax: 011-44-71-830-0056.
Brussels, Belgium Office: Avenue Louise, 165-Box 15, 1050 Brussels, Belgium.
Telephone: 011-32-2-648-1717.
Fax: 011-32-2-648-1064.
Prague Office: Adria Palace, Jungmannova 31/36, 11000 Prague 1, Czech Republic.
Telephone: 011-42-2-231-5661.
Fax: 011-42-2-231-5482.
Budapest, Hungary Office: Deak Ferenc Ut. 10, Office 304, H-1052 Budapest V., Hungary.
Telephones: 011-36-1-226-2024.
Fax: 011-36-1-226-2025.

(See Next Column)

SQUIRE, SANDERS & DEMPSEY—*Continued*

Kiev, Ukraine Office: vul. Prorizna 9, Suite 20, Kiev 252035, Ukraine.
Telephones: 011-7-044-244-3452, 011-7-044-244-3453, 011-7-044-228-8687.
Fax: 011-7-044-228-4938.

Richard S. Surrey (Not admitted in Slovakia)

For full biographical listings, see the Martindale-Hubbell Law Directory

SPAIN

BARCELONA,

BAKER & MCKENZIE

Passeig De Gràcia 11, Esc. B, 2°-1°, 08007 Barcelona
Telephone: (93) 302 27 28
Intn'l. Dialing: (34-3) 302 27 28
Facsimile: (34-3) 318 93 88
AssociatedOffices of Baker & McKenzie in: Almaty, Amsterdam, Bangkok, Beijing, Berlin, Bogotá, Brasília, Brussels, Budapest, Buenos Aires, Cairo, Caracas, Chicago, Dallas, Frankfurt, Geneva, Hanoi, Ho Chi Minh City, Hong Kong, Juárez, Kiev, London, Madrid, Manila, Melbourne, México City, Miami, Milan, Monterrey, Moscow, New York, Palo Alto, Paris, Prague, Rio de Janeiro, Riyadh, Rome, St. Petersburg, San Diego, San Francisco, São Paulo, Singapore, Stockholm, Sydney, Taipei, Tijuana, Tokyo, Toronto, Valencia, Warsaw, Washington, D.C. and Zürich.
Correspondent Law Firm: Hadiputranto, Hadinoto & Partners, Jakarta.

PARTNERS

Pedro Aguarón
Jesús M. de Alfonso
Alvaro Espinós
Alejandro Valls

ASSOCIATES

Josep Maria Balcells
Francisco A. Baygual
Cristina Calvo
Miguel Canals
Margarita Doménech Viñas
José Ramón Fernández-Castellanos
Ma. Del Pilar T. Garcia
Rafael Jiménez-Gusi
Xavier Junquera
Jose Maria Llull
Fe L. Lopez
Andrés Millán
Ma. Mercè Pujadas
Eusebio Pujol
Esteban Raventos
Alexandre Solsona
José-Luis Stampa
Rosana Velasco Masó
Ma. Teresa R. Vidal

For full biographical listings, see the Martindale-Hubbell Law Directory

*MADRID,**

American Lawyers In Madrid

BAKER & MCKENZIE

Pinar 18, Madrid 28006
Telephone: (91) 411-3062
Intn'l. Dialing: (34-1) 411-3062
Facisimiles: (34-1) 562-2425; 564-6035
Associated Offices of Baker & McKenzie in: Almaty, Amsterdam, Bangkok, Barcelona, Beijing, Berlin, Bogotá, Brasília, Brussels, Budapest, Buenos Aires, Cairo, Caracas, Chicago, Dallas, Frankfurt, Geneva, Hanoi, Ho Chi Minh City, Hong Kong, Juárez, Kiev, London, Manila, Melbourne, México City, Miami, Milan, Monterrey, Moscow, New York, Palo Alto, Paris, Prague, Rio de Janeiro, Riyadh, Rome, St. Petersburg, San Diego, San Francisco, São Paulo, Singapore, Stockholm, Sydney, Taipei, Tijuana, Tokyo, Toronto, Valencia, Warsaw, Washington, D.C. and Zürich.
Correspondent Law Firm: Hadiputranto, Hadinoto & Partners, Jakarta.

José A. Arcila
James A. Baker
Cristina Bustillo Munoz
Eduardo García Calleja
Antonio López Barrio
Alberto Pérez-Fontán Estefania
Fernando Pérez-Fontán Estefania
Carlos E. Rubio
Antonio Selas Lopez

OF COUNSEL

José Maria Delgado Cobos

ASSOCIATES

Carmen Araujo
María Barragán
José Antonio Cainzos
Juan Manuel De Castro
Leticia Díez De La Lastra
Maite Díez Vergara
Isabel Fernández
Beatriz Garcia Cienfuegos
Carlos Iribarren
Adela Lario
Concepción Martín
Javier Morera
Cecilia Pastor Caballero
Luis Peinado Mataix
Elizabeth A. Powers
Iñigo Rodriguez Sastre
Enrique Valera

For full biographical listings, see the Martindale-Hubbell Law Directory

SWEDEN

*STOCKHOLM,**

BAKER & MCKENZIE ADVOKATBYRA

Eriksbergsgatan 46, P.O. Box 26163, 100 41 Stockholm
Telephone: (08) 676 77 00
Intn'l Dialing: (46-8) 676 77 00
Facsimile: (46-8) 24 89 20
Associated Offices of Baker & McKenzie in: Almaty, Amsterdam, Bangkok, Barcelona, Beijing, Berlin, Bogotá, Brasília, Brussels, Budapest, Buenos Aires, Cairo, Caracas, Chicago, Dallas, Frankfurt, Geneva, Hanoi, Ho Chi Minh City, Hong Kong, Juárez, Kiev, London, Madrid, Manila, Melbourne, México City, Miami, Milan, Monterrey, Moscow, New York, Palo Alto, Paris, Prague, Rio de Janeiro, Riyadh, Rome, St. Petersburg, San Diego, San Francisco, São Paulo, Singapore, Sydney, Taipei, Tijuana, Tokyo, Toronto, Valencia, Warsaw, Washington, D.C. and Zürich.
Correspondent Law Firm: Hadiputranto, Hadinoto & Partners, Jakarta.

MEMBERS OF FIRM

Jonas Benedictsson
Claes Cronstedt
Robert Fröman
Leif G. Gustafsson
Bo Lindqvist
Mauritz Silfverstolpe

LOCAL PARTNER

Sten Bauer

COUNSEL

Sven Harald Bauer
Bengt Bergendal
Carl Göran Risberg

ASSOCIATES

Jeanette Almsätter
Rikard Bentelius
Agneta Gustafsson
Fredrik Niklasson
Michael Nyman
Anna-Karin Olsson
Tomas Rudenstam
Carl M. Svernlöv

For full biographical listings, see the Martindale-Hubbell Law Directory

WHITE & CASE ADVOKAT AB

Birger Jarlsgatan 14, Box 5573, S-114 85 Stockholm
Telephone: (46-8) 679-80-30
Facsimile: (46-8) 611-21-22
New York, New York:
Telephone: 212-819-8200.
Facsimile: 212-354-8113.
Washington, D.C.:
Telephone: 202-872-0013.
Facsimile: 202-872-0210.
Los Angeles, California:
Telephone: 213-620-7700.
Facsimile: 213-687-0758; 213-617-2205.
Miami, Florida:
Telephone: 305-371-2700.
Facsimile: 305-358-5744.
Mexico City, Mexico:
Telephone: (52-5) 207-9717.
Facsimile: (52-5) 208-3628.
Tokyo, Japan:
Telephone: (81-3) 3239-4300.
Facsimile: (81-3) 3239-4330.
Hong Kong:
Telephone: (852) 2822-8700.
Facsimile: (852) 2845-9070; Grice & Co., Solicitors,
Telephone: (852) 2826-0333.
Facsimile: (852) 2526-7166.
Singapore, Republic of Singapore:
Telephone: (65) 225-6000.
Facsimile: (65) 225-6009.
Bangkok, Thailand: Pacific Legal Group Ltd., In Association With White & Case,
Telephone: (662) 236-6154/7.
Facsimile: (662) 237-6771.
Hanoi, Viet Nam: Representative Office,
Telephone: (84-4) 227-575/6/7.
Facsimile: (84-4) 227-297.
Bombay, India:
Telephone: (91-22) 282-6300.
Facsimile: (91-22) 282-6305.
London, England:
Telephone: (44-171) 726-6361.
Facsimile: (44-171) 726-4314; (44-171) 726-8558.
Paris, France:
Telephone: (33-1) 42-60-34-05.
Facsimile: (33-1) 42-60-82-46.
Brussels, Belgium:
Telephone: (32-2) 647-05-89.
Facsimile: (32-2) 647-16-75.
Helsinki, Finland:
Telephone: (358-0) 631-100.
Facsimile: (358-0) 179-477.

(See Next Column)

WHITE & CASE ADVOKAT AB, *Stockholm—Continued*

Moscow, Russia:
Telephone: (7-095) 201-9292/3/4/5.
Facsimile: (7-095) 201-9284.
Budapest, Hungary:
Telephone: (36-1) 269-0550; (36-1) 131-0933.
Facsimile: (36-1) 269-1199.
Prague, Czech Republic:
Telephone: (42-2) 2481-1796.
Facsimile: (42-2) 232-5522.
Warsaw, Poland: Telephone/
Facsimile: (48-22) 26-80-53; (48-22) 27-84-86. International Telephone/
Facsimile: (48-39) 12-19-06.
Istanbul, Turkey:
Telephone: (90-212) 275-68-98; (90-212) 275-75-33.
Facsimile: (90-212) 275-75-43.
Ankara, Turkey:
Telephone: (90-312) 446-2180.
Facsimile: (90-312) 437-9677.
Jeddah, Saudi Arabia: Law Office of Hassan Mahassni,
Telephone: (966-2) 651-3535.
Facsimile: (966-2) 651-3636.
Riyadh, Saudi Arabia: Law Office of Hassan Mahassni,
Telephone: (966-1) 476-7099.
Facsimile: (966-1) 479-0110.
Almaty, Kazakhstan:
Telephone: (7-3272) 50-7491/2.
Facsimile: (7-3272) 61-0842.

RESIDENT PARTNERS

Göran Åseborn — Rolf Olofsson
Claes Zettermarck

COUNSEL

Jan Gregorsson — Lars G. Kjellman

RESIDENT ASSOCIATES

Cecilia Ahrbom
Penelope E. Codrington (Not admitted in Sweden)
Thomas Engwall
Jan Gustavsson (Not admitted in Sweden)
Ulf Johansson
André Lindekrantz
Fredrik Schultz

For full biographical listings, see the Martindale-Hubbell Law Directory

SWITZERLAND

GENEVA, (Genève)

ETUDE ETIENNE, BLUM, STEHLÉ, MANFRINI ET ASSOCIÉS

(Associated Office of Baker & McKenzie)
Rue Bellot 6, 1206 Geneva
Telephone: (022) 346 76 08; 346 70 70
Intn'l. Dialing: (41-22) 346 76 08; 346 70 70
Facsimile: (41-22) 347 02 84

MEMBERS OF FIRM

Denis Berdoz
François Blum
Donald Etienne
Louis Gaillard
Gabrielle Kaufmann
Pierre Louis Manfrini
Daniel Antonio Peregrina
Alain Stehlé

LOCAL PARTNERS

Quentin Byrne-Sutton — Sylvie M. A. Gurry-Veit
Joëlle Zumoffen

RESIDENT ASSOCIATES

Martin S. Anderson
François Bellanger
Yves Bonnard
Christophe C. Zellweger

For full biographical listings, see the Martindale-Hubbell Law Directory

American Lawyers In Geneva

JONES, DAY, REAVIS & POGUE

20, rue de Candolle, CH-1205 Geneva
Telephone: 011-41-22-320-2339
Telecopier: 011-41-22-320-1232
In Atlanta, Georgia: 3500 One Peachtree Center, 303 Peachtree Street, N.E.
Telephone: 404-521-3939.
Cable Address: "Attorneys Atlanta".
Telex: 54-2711.
Telecopier: 404-581-8330.
In Brussels, Belgium: Avenue Louise 480, 7th Floor. B-1050 Brussels.
Telephone: 32-2-645-14-11.
Telecopier: 32-2-645-14-45.
In Chicago, Illinois: 77 West Wacker.
Telephone: 312-782-3939.
Telecopier: 312-782-8585.

(See Next Column)

In Cleveland, Ohio: North Point, 901 Lakeside Avenue.
Telephone: 216-586-3939.
Cable Address: "Attorneys Cleveland."
Telex: 980389.
Telecopier: 216-579-0212.
In Columbus, Ohio: 1900 Huntington Center.
Telephone: 614-469-3939.
Cable Address: "Attorneys Columbus."
Telecopier: 614-461-4198.
In Dallas, Texas: 2300 Trammell Crow Center, 2001 Ross Avenue.
Telephone: 214-220-3939.
Cable Address: "Attorneys Dallas."
Telex: 730852.
Telecopier: 214-969-5100.
In Frankfurt, Germany: Triton Haus, Bockenheimer Landstrasse 42, 60323 Frankfurt am Main.
Telephone: 49-69-9726-3939.
Telecopier: 49-69-9726-3993.
In Hong Kong: 1501 One Exchange Square, 8 Connaught Place.
Telephone: 852-2526-6895.
Telecopier: 852-2810-5787.
In Irvine, California: 2603 Main Street, Suite 900.
Telephone: 714-851-3939.
Telex: 194911 Lawyers LSA.
Telecopier: 714-553-7539.
In London, England: One Mount Street.
Telephone: 44-71-493-9361.
Cable Address: "Surgoe London WI."
Telecopier: 44-71-493-9666.
In Los Angeles, California: 555 West Fifth Street, Suite 4600.
Telephone: 213-489-3939.
Telex: 181439 UD.
Telecopier: 213-243-2539.
In New York, New York: 599 Lexington Avenue.
Telephone: 212-326-3939.
Cable Address: "JONESDAY NEWYORK."
Telex: 237013 JDRP UR.
Telecopier: 212-755-7306.
In Paris, France: 62, rue du Faubourg Saint-Honore.
Telephone: 33-1-44-71-3939.
Cable Address: "Surgoe Paris."
Telex: 290156 Surgoe.
Telecopier: 33-1-49-24-0471.
In Pittsburgh, Pennsylvania: 500 Grant Street, 31st Floor.
Telephone: 412-391-3939.
Cable Address: "Attorneys Pittsburgh".
Telecopier: 412-394-7959.
In Riyadh, Saudi Arabia: Law Offices of Saud M.A. Shawwaf, P.O. Box 2700.
Telephones: (966-1) 465-6543, (966-1) 464-8534 or (966-1) 464-8540.
Telex: 401831 SAUCON SJ.
Telecopier: (966-1) 464-8480.
In Taipei, Taiwan: 8th Floor, 2 Tun Hwa South Road, Section 2.
Telephone: (886-2) 704-6808.
Telecopier: (886-2) 704-6791.
In Tokyo, Japan: Toranomon MT Building, 4th Floor, 10-3, Toranomon 3-Chome, Minato-Ku, Tokyo 105, Japan.
Telephone: 81-3-3433-3939.
Telecopier: 81-3-5401-2725.
In Washington, D.C.: Metropolitan Square, 1450 G Street, N.W.
Telephone: 202-879-3939.
Cable Address: "Attorneys Washington."
Telex: 89-2410 ATTORNEYS WASH.
Telecopier: 202-737-2832.

MEMBER OF FIRM IN GENEVA

Roy F. Ryan, III (Not admitted in Switzerland)

OF COUNSEL

Mohamed Amersi (Not admitted in Switzerland)

For full biographical listings, see the Martindale-Hubbell Law Directory

ZÜRICH,

BAKER & MCKENZIE

(Achermann, Müller, Heini & Wehrli)
Zollikerstrasse 225, 8034 Zürich
Telephone: (01) 384 14 14
Intn'l. Dialing: (41-1) 384 14 14
Facsimile: (41-1) 384 12 84
Postal Address: P.O. Box 57

PARTNERS

Lic. iur. Peter Achermann
Prof. Dr. Anton C. Heini
Philip Marcovici (Not admitted in Switzerland)
Dr. Johannes J. Müller
Dr. Franz W. Schenker
Dr. Urs Schenker
Dr. Max Wehrli

OF COUNSEL

Prof. Dr. Oscar Vogel

(See Next Column)

BAKER & MCKENZIE—*Continued*

ASSOCIATES

Dr. Markus Affentranger	Dr. Peter Urs Paul Reinert
Dr. Markus H. Berni	Dr. Rolf C. Schmid
Fürsprecher Martin Frey	Dr. Thomas Stäheli
Dr. Joachim G. Frick	Dr. Michael Treis
Dr. Marcel Giger	(Not admitted in Switzerland)
Lic. Iur. Kilian Perroulaz	Dr. Urs Zenhäusern

For full biographical listings, see the Martindale-Hubbell Law Directory

TAIWAN

*TAIPEI,**

BAKER & MCKENZIE

15th Floor, Hung Tai Center, No. 168, Tun Hwa North Road, Taipei 105
Telephone: (02) 712-6151
Intn'l. Dialing: (886-2) 712-6151
Facsimiles: (886-2) 716-9250; 712-8292
Associated Offices of Baker & McKenzie in: Almaty, Amsterdam, Bangkok, Barcelona, Beijing, Berlin, Bogotá, Brasília, Brussels, Budapest, Buenos Aires, Cairo, Caracas, Chicago, Dallas, Frankfurt, Geneva, Hanoi, Ho Chi Minh City, Hong Kong, Juárez, Kiev, London, Madrid, Manila, Melbourne, México City, Miami, Milan, Monterrey, Moscow, New York, Palo Alto, Paris, Prague, Rio de Janeiro, Riyadh, Rome, St. Petersburg, San Diego, San Francisco, São Paulo, Singapore, Stockholm, Sydney, Tijuana, Tokyo, Toronto, Valencia, Warsaw, Washington, D.C. and Zürich.
Correspondent Law Firm: Hadiputranto, Hadinoto & Partners, Jakarta.

Lindy L. Y. Chern	John S. Lee
Remington Huang	James T. T. Tseng
David H. J. Yang	

Kenneth W. Gray	Dolly Tai-lan Lo

Tiffany T. F. Huang	Keye S. Wu

William E. Bryson, Jr.	Michelle Ya-Ling Gon
Michael Wong	

Nancy Nai-Wen Chang	Justin C. Liang
Victor C. M. Chang	Ivan Lee-En Liu
Justin Shi-Jeng Ding	Vita Wei-chi Liu
Erion Ya-Li Lee	Seraphim G. R. Mar
Stacey Guemin Lee	Grace Shao
Vincent Li-Cheng Shih	

H. Henry Chang	Yuan-San Lu
Ting-Ting Chu	Kevin Yueh-Hsien Wang
Wai B. Zee	

For full biographical listings, see the Martindale-Hubbell Law Directory

JONES, DAY, REAVIS & POGUE

8th Floor, 2 Tun Hwa South Road Section 2, Taipei 10654
Telephone: (886-2) 704-6808
Telecopier: (886-2) 704-6791
In Atlanta, Georgia: 3500 One Peachtree Center, 303 Peachtree Street, N.E.
Telephone: 404-521-3939.
Cable Address: "Attorneys Atlanta".
Telex: 54-2711.
Telecopier: 404-581-8330.
In Brussels, Belgium: Avenue Louise 480, 7th Floor, B-1050 Brussels.
Telephone: 32-2-645-14-11.
Telecopier: 32-2-645-14-45.
In Chicago, Illinois: 77 West Wacker.
Telephone: 312-782-3939.
Telecopier: 312-782-8585.
In Cleveland, Ohio: North Point, 901 Lakeside Avenue.
Telephone: 216-586-3939.
Cable Address: "Attorneys Cleveland."
Telex: 980389.
Telecopier: 216-579-0212.
In Columbus, Ohio: 1900 Huntington Center.
Telephone: 614-469-3939.
Cable Address: "Attorneys Columbus."
Telecopier: 614-461-4198.
In Dallas, Texas: 2300 Trammell Crow Center, 2001 Ross Avenue.
Telephone: 214-220-3939.
Cable Address: "Attorneys Dallas."
Telex: 730852.
Telecopier: 214-969-5100.

(See Next Column)

In Frankfurt, Germany: Triton Haus, Bockenheimer Landstrasse 42, 60323. Frankfurt am Main.
Telephone: 49-69-9726-3939.
Telecopier: 49-69-9726-3993.
In Geneva, Switzerland: 20, rue de Candolle.
Telephone: 41-22-320-2339.
Telecopier: 41-22-320-1232.
In Hong Kong: 1501 One Exchange Square, 8 Connaught Place.
Telephone: 852-2526-3939.
Telecopier: 852-2810-5787.
In Irvine, California: 2603 Main Street, Suite 900.
Telephone: 714-851-3939.
Telex: 194911 Lawyers LSA.
Telecopier: 714-553-7539.
In London, England: One Mount Street.
Telephone: 44-71-493-9361.
Cable Address: "Surgoe London WI".
Telecopier: 44-71-493-9666.
In Los Angeles, California: 555 West Fifth Street, Suite 4600.
Telephone: 213-489-3939.
Telex: 181439 UD.
Telecopier: 213-243-2539.
In New York, New York: 599 Lexington Avenue.
Telephone: 212-326-3939.
Cable Address: "JONESDAY NEWYORK."
Telex: 237013 JDRP UR.
Telecopier: 212-755-7306.
In Paris, France: 62, rue du Faubourg Saint-Honore.
Telephone: 33-1-44-71-3939.
Cable Address: "Surgoe Paris."
Telex: 290156 Surgoe.
Telecopier: 33-1-49-24-0471.
In Pittsburgh, Pennsylvania: 500 Grant Street, 31st Floor.
Telephone: 412-391-3939.
Cable Address: "Attorneys Pittsburgh".
Telecopier: 412-394-7959.
In Riyadh, Saudi Arabia: Law Offices of Saud M.A. Shawwaf, P.O. Box 2700.
Telephones: (966-1) 465-6543, (966-1) 464-8534 or (966-1) 464-8540.
Telex: 401831 SAUCON SJ.
Telecopier: (966-1) 464-8480.
In Tokyo, Japan: Toranomon MT Building, 4th Floor, 10-3, Toranomon 3-Chome, Minato-Ku, Tokyo 105, Japan.
Telephone: 81-3-3433-3939.
Telecopier: 81-3-5401-2725.
In Washington, D.C.: Metropolitan Square, 1450 G Street, N.W.
Telephone: 202-879-3939.
Cable Address: "Attorneys Washington."
Telex: 89-2410 ATTORNEYS WASH.
Telecopier: 202-737-2832.

MEMBER OF FIRM IN TAIPEI

Jack Jih-Tsan Huang

ASSOCIATES

Ke-Wei William Hsu	Michael E. Mangelson
(Not admitted in Taiwan)	(Not admitted in Taiwan)
Jeffrey H. Chen	Louis Fang-Lin Meng
(Not admitted in Taiwan)	Andrew D. Ruff

STAFF ATTORNEYS

Thomas Tai-Ming Chen	Eric C.A. Tsai
(Not admitted in Taiwan)	Saria Hsin-Hsien Tseng
	(Not admitted in Taiwan)

For full biographical listings, see the Martindale-Hubbell Law Directory

MCCUTCHEN, DOYLE, BROWN & ENERSEN

International Trade Building, Tenth Floor, 333 Keelung Road, Section 1, Taipei 110
Telephone: 886-2-723-5000
Facsimile: 886-2-757-6070
San Francisco, California Office: Three Embarcadero Center, 94111-4066.
Telephone: 415-393-2000.
Facsimile: 415-393-2286.
Telex: 340817 MACPAG SFO.
Los Angeles, California Office: 355 South Grand Avenue, Suite 4400, 90071-1560.
Telephone: 213-680-6400.
Facsimile: 213-680-6499.
San Jose, California Office: Market Post Tower, Suite 1500, 55 South Market Street, 95113-2327.
Telephone: 408-947-8400.
Facsimile: 408-947-4750.
Telex: 9102502931 MACPAG SJ.
Walnut Creek, California Office: 1331 North California Boulevard. Post Office Box V, 94596-4502.
Telephone: 510-937-8000.
Facsimile: 510-975-5390.
Menlo Park, California Office: 2740 Sand Hill Road, 94025-7020.
Telephone: 415-233-4000.
Facsimile: 415-233-4086.

(See Next Column)

McCUTCHEN, DOYLE, BROWN & ENERSEN, *Taipei—Continued*

Washington, D.C. Office: The Evening Star Building, Suite 800, 1101 Pennsylvania Avenue, N.W., 20004-2514.
Telephone: 202-628-4900.
Facsimile: 202-628-4912.
Affiliated Offices In: Bangkok, Thailand; Beijing, China; Shanghai, China.

Robert P. Parker
Robert E. Cox
Joan C. Y. Chen
Jacqueline C. Fu
David C. Getzinger
(Not admitted in Taiwan)
Keating H.S. Hsu
Flora M. Hsu
Julie H. Shu

For full biographical listings, see the Martindale-Hubbell Law Directory

American Lawyers in Taipei

SHEARMAN & STERLING

7th Floor, Hung Kuo Building, 167 Tun Hwa North Road, Taipei
Telephone: (886-2) 545-3300
Fax: (886-2) 545-3322
New York, N.Y. Office: 599 Lexington Avenue, New York, New York 10022-6069 and Citicorp Center, 153 East 53rd Street, New York, New York 10022-4676.
Telephone: (212) 848-4000.
Telex: 667290 Num Lau.
Fax: 599 Lexington Avenue: (212) 848-7179. Citicorp Center: (212) 848-5252.
Abu Dhabi, United Arab Emirates Office: P.O. Box 2948.
Telephone: (971-2) 324477.
Fax: (971-2) 774533.
Beijing, People's Republic of China Office: Suite #2205, Capital Mansion, No. 6, Xin Yuan Nan Road. Chao Yang District Beijing, 100004.
Telephone: (861) 465-4574.
Fax: (861) 465-4578.
Budapest, Hungary Office: Szerb utca 17-19, 1056 Budapest.
Telephone: (36-1) 266-3522.
Fax: (36-1) 266-3523.
Düsseldorf, Federal Republic of Germany Office: Königsallee 46, D-40212 Düsseldorf.
Telephone: (49-211) 13 62 80.
Telex: 8 588 294 NYLO.
Fax: (49-211) 13 33 09.
Frankfurt, Federal Republic of Germany Office: Bockenheimer Landstrasse 55, D-60325 Frankfurt am Main.
Telephone: (49-69) 97-10-70.
Fax: (49-69) 97-10-71-00.
Hong Kong, Hong Kong Office: Standard Chartered Bank Building, 4 Des Voeux Road Central, Hong Kong.
Telephone: (852) 2978-8000.
Fax: (852) 2978-8099.
London, England Office: 199Bishopsgate, London EC2M 3TY.
Telephone: (44-71) 920-9000.
Fax: (44-71) 920-9020.
Los Angeles, California Office: 725 South Figueroa Street, 21st Floor, 90017-5421.
Telephone: (213) 239-0300.
Fax: (213) 239-0381, 614-0936.
Paris, France Office: 12 rue d'Astorg, 75008.
Telephone: (33-1) 44-71-17-17.
Telex: 282964 Royale.
Fax: (33-1) 44-71-01-01.
San Francisco, California Office: 555 California Street, 94104-1522.
Telephone: (415) 616-1100.
Fax: (415) 616-1199.
Tokyo, Japan Office: Shearman & Sterling (Thomas Wilner Gaikokuho-Jimu-Bengoshi Jimusho), Fukoku Seimei Building, 5th Fl. 2-2-2, Uchisaiwaicho, Chiyoda-ku, Tokyo 100, Japan.
Telephone: (81 3) 5251-1601.
Fax: (81 3) 5251-1602.
Toronto, Ontario, Canada Office: Commerce Court West, Suite 4405, P.O. Box 247, M5L 1E8.
Telephone: (416) 360-8484.
Fax: (416) 360-2958.
Washington, D.C. Office: 801 Pennsylvania Avenue, N.W., Suite 900, 20004-2604.
Telephone: (202) 508-8000.
Fax: (202) 508-8100.

ASIAN COUNSEL

Mark J. Harty (Not admitted in Taiwan)

For full biographical listings, see the Martindale-Hubbell Law Directory

Canadian Lawyers in Taipei

STIKEMAN, ELLIOTT

117 Sec. 3 Min Sheng East Road, 8th Floor, Taipei
Telephone: 886-2-719-9573
Fax: 886-2-719-4540
Montreal, Quebec Office: 1155 René-Lévesque Boulevard West, 40th Floor, H3B 3V2.
Telephone: 514-397-3000.
Fax: 514-397-3222.
Toronto, Ontario Office: Commerce Court West, 53rd Floor, M5L 1B9.
Telephone: 416-869-5500.
Fax: 416-947-0866.
Ottawa, Ontario Office: 50 O'Connor Street, Suite 914, K1P 6L2.
Telephone: 613-234-4555.
Fax: 613-230-8877.
Calgary, Alberta Office: 855 - 2nd Street S.W., 1500 Bankers Hall, T2P 4J7.
Telephone: 403-266-9000.
Fax: 403-266-9034.
Vancouver, British Columbia Office: 666 Burrard Street, Suite 1700, Park Place, V6C 2X8.
Telephone: 604-631-1300.
Fax: 604-681-1825.
New York, New York Office: 126 East 56th Street, 11th Floor, Tower 56, 10022.
Telephone: 212-371-8855.
Fax: 212-371-7087.
Washington, D.C. Office: 1300 I Street, N.W., Suite 1210 West, 20005-3314.
Telephone: 202-326-7555.
Fax: 202-326-7557.
London, England Office: Cottons Centre, Cottons Lane, SE1 2QL.
Telephone: 71-378-0880.
Fax: 71-378-0344.
Paris, France Office: In Association with Société Juridique Internationale, 39, rue François Ier, 75008.
Telephone: 33-1-40-73-82-00.
Fax: 33-1-40-73-82-10.
Budapest, Hungary Office: Andrássy út 100, II Floor, H-1062.
Telephone: 36-1-269-1790.
Fax: 36-1-269-0655.
Hong Kong Office: 29 Queen's Road Central, Suite 1506, China Building.
Telephone: 852-2868-9903.
Fax: 852-2868-9912.
Hong Kong: In Association with Shum & Co., 29 Queen's Road Central, Suite 1103, China Building.
Telephone: 852-2526-5531.
Fax: 852-2845-9076.

Ching-Wo Ng
(Not admitted in Taiwan)
Andes Fu-Min Lin
(Not admitted in Taiwan)

(Not authorized to appear before the Taiwan courts)

For full biographical listings, see the Martindale-Hubbell Law Directory

THAILAND

*BANGKOK,**

BAKER & McKENZIE

Sathorn Thani II Building, 19th Floor, 92/54-57 North Sathorn Road, Bangrak, Bangkok 10500
Telephone: 236-6060; 266-8282; 266-8490; 267-5800
Intn'l. Dialing: (66-2) 236-6060; 266-8282; 266-8490; 267-5800
Cable Address: ABOGADO
Telex: 82129
Answer Back: 82129 ABOGADO TH
Facsimiles: (66-2) 236-6071 to 73
Postal Address: G.P.O. Box 2815, Bangkok 10501, Thailand
Associated Offices of Baker & McKenzie in: Almaty, Amsterdam, Barcelona, Beijing, Berlin, Bogotá, Brasília, Brussels, Budapest, Buenos Aires, Cairo, Caracas, Chicago, Dallas, Frankfurt, Geneva, Hanoi, Ho Chi Minh City, Hong Kong, Juárez, Kiev, London, Madrid, Manila, Melbourne, México City, Miami, Milan, Monterrey, Moscow, New York, Palo Alto, Paris, Prague, Rio de Janeiro, Riyadh, Rome, St. Petersburg, San Diego, San Francisco, São Paulo, Singapore, Stockholm, Sydney, Taipei, Tijuana, Tokyo, Toronto, Valencia, Warsaw, Washington, D.C. and Zürich.
Correspondent Law Firm: Hadiputranto, Hadinoto & Partners, Jakarta.

MEMBERS OF FIRM

Athueck Asvanund
Suchint Chaimungkalanont
John W. Hancock
(Not admitted in Thailand)
Pornapa Luengwattanakit
Hatasakdi Na Pombejra
Sawanee Amoradhat Sethsathira
Siripong Silpakul
Anurat Tiyaphorn
Kitipong Urapeepatanapong

(See Next Column)

BAKER & MCKENZIE—*Continued*

LOCAL PARTNERS

Weerawong Chittmittrapap	Wirot Poonsuwan
Chaipat Kamchadduskorn	Dhiraphol Suwanprateep
Chirachai Okanurak	Suriyong Tungsuwan

Kanit Vallayapet

Supparut Allapach	Pravith Mangklatanakul
Somchitt Attapich	Pilaipan Mekaratana
Jakkarin Bantathong	Angela Nobthai
Mananya Benjakul	Duangjai Sae-Ung
Lakkanasiri Bhusathong	Asawin Sangchay
Thinawat Bukhamana	Taj Singusaha
Montien Bunjarnondha	Surachai Suksriwong
Choopun Chaiprabha	Sunpasiri Sunpa-a-sa
Pattarasupang Chalermnon	Nattaya Techarochanarit
Manoon Changchumni	Ornanong Tesabamroong
Thanasak Chanyapoon	Tang Thongpakdee
Pichitphon Eammongkolchai	Prachern Tiyapunjanit
Prechaya Ebrahim	Peerapan Tungsuwan
Wisit Kanjanopas	Vit Vatanayothin
Sasiwimol Kasemsri	Piphob Veraphong
Kulkanist Khamsirivatchara	Wanee Visitvudhikul
Suttiphat Khamsirivatchara	Nitat Wattanakul
Thiti Kumnerddee	Yoh Wiwatthanopas
Wittaya Luengsukcharoen	Wanchai Yiamsamatha

For full biographical listings, see the Martindale-Hubbell Law Directory

TURKEY

*ANKARA,**

American Lawyers In Ankara

WHITE & CASE

Ziya Ur Rahman Caddesi 17/5 06700 Gaziosmanpaşa, Ankara
Telephone: (90-312) 446-2180
Facsimile: (90-312) 437-9677
New York, New York:
Telephone: 212-819-8200.
Facsimile: 212-354-8113.
Washington, D.C.:
Telephone: 202-872-0013.
Facsimile: 202-872-0210.
Los Angeles, California:
Telephone: 213-620-7700.
Facsimile: 213-687-0758; 213-617-2205.
Miami, Florida:
Telephone: 305-371-2700.
Facsimile: 305-358-5744.
Mexico City, Mexico:
Telephone: (52-5) 207-9717.
Facsimile: (52-5) 208-3628.
Tokyo, Japan:
Telephone: (81-3) 3239-4300.
Facsimile: (81-3) 3239-4330.
Hong Kong:
Telephone: (852) 2822-8700.
Facsimile: (852) 2845-9070; Grice & Co., Solicitors,
Telephone: (852) 2826-0333.
Facsimile: (852) 2526-7166.
Singapore, Republic of Singapore:
Telephone: (65) 225-6000.
Facsimile: (65) 225-6009.
Bangkok, Thailand: Pacific Legal Group Ltd., In Association With White & Case,
Telephone: (662) 236-6154/7.
Facsimile: (662) 237-6771.
Hanoi, Viet Nam: Representative Office,
Telephone: (84-4) 227-575/6/7.
Facsimile: (84-4) 227-297.
Bombay, India:
Telephone: (91-22) 282-6300.
Facsimile: (91-22) 282-6305.
London, England:
Telephone: (44-171) 726-6361.
Facsimile: (44-171) 726-4314; (44-171) 726-8558.
Paris, France:
Telephone: (33-1) 42-60-34-05.
Facsimile: (33-1) 42-60-82-46.
Brussels, Belgium:
Telephone: (32-2) 647-05-89.
Facsimile: (32-2) 647-16-75.
Stockholm, Sweden:
Telephone: (46-8) 679-80-30.
Facsimile: (46-8) 611-21-22.

(See Next Column)

Helsinki, Finland:
Telephone: (358-0) 631-100.
Facsimile: (358-0) 179-477.
Moscow, Russia:
Telephone: (7-095) 201-9292/3/4/5.
Facsimile: (7-095) 201-9284.
Budapest, Hungary:
Telephone: (36-1) 269-0550; (36-1) 131-0933.
Facsimile: (36-1) 269-1199.
Prague, Czech Republic:
Telephone: (42-2) 2481-1796.
Facsimile: (42-2) 232-5522.
Warsaw, Poland: Telephone/
Facsimile: (48-22) 26-80-53; (48-22) 27-84-86. International Telephone/
Facsimile: (48-39) 12-19-06.
Istanbul, Turkey:
Telephone: (90-212) 275-68-98; (90-212) 275-75-33.
Facsimile: (90-212) 275-75-43.
Jeddah, Saudi Arabia: Law Office of Hassan Mahassni,
Telephone: (966-2) 651-3535.
Facsimile: (966-2) 651-3636.
Riyadh, Saudi Arabia: Law Office of Hassan Mahassni,
Telephone: (966-1) 476-7099.
Facsimile: (966-1) 479-0110.
Almaty, Kazakhstan:
Telephone: (7-3272) 50-7491/2.
Facsimile: (7-3272) 61-0842.

RESIDENT PARTNER

Hugh Verrier (Not admitted in Turkey)

RESIDENT ASSOCIATES

Mesut Cakmak	Zeynep Onalan
Anne E. Lederer (Not admitted in Turkey)	

For full biographical listings, see the Martindale-Hubbell Law Directory

ISTANBUL,

WHITE & CASE

Maya Akar Center, Buyukdere Caddesi 101-102 B Blok, Kat 17 80280 Esentepe, Istanbul
Telephone: (90-212) 275-75-33; (90-212) 275-68-98
Facsimile: (90-212) 275-75-43
New York, New York:
Telephone: 212-819-8200.
Facsimile: 212-354-8113.
Washington, D.C.:
Telephone: 202-872-0013.
Facsimile: 202-872-0210.
Los Angeles, California:
Telephone: 213-620-7700.
Facsimile: 213-687-0758; 213-617-2205.
Miami, Florida:
Telephone: 305-371-2700.
Facsimile: 305-358-5744.
Mexico City, Mexico:
Telephone: (52-5) 207-9717.
Facsimile: (52-5) 208-3628.
Tokyo, Japan:
Telephone: (81-3) 3239-4300.
Facsimile: (81-3) 3239-4330.
Hong Kong:
Telephone: (852) 2822-8700.
Facsimile: (852) 2845-9070; Grice & Co., Solicitors,
Telephone: (852) 2826-0333.
Facsimile: (852) 2526-7166.
Singapore, Republic of Singapore:
Telephone: (65) 225-6000.
Facsimile: (65) 225-6009.
Bangkok, Thailand: Pacific Legal Group Ltd., In Association With White & Case,
Telephone: (662) 236-6154/7.
Facsimile: (662) 237-6771.
Hanoi, Viet Nam: Representative Office,
Telephone: (84-4) 227-575/6/7.
Facsimile: (84-4) 227-297.
Bombay, India:
Telephone: (91-22) 282-6300.
Facsimile: (91-22) 282-6305.
London, England:
Telephone: (44-171) 726-6361.
Facsimile: (44-171) 726-4314; (44-171) 726-8558.
Paris, France:
Telephone: (33-1) 42-60-34-05.
Facsimile: (33-1) 42-60-82-46.
Brussels, Belgium:
Telephone: (32-2) 647-05-89.
Facsimile: (32-2) 647-16-75.
Stockholm, Sweden:
Telephone: (46-8) 679-80-30.
Facsimile: (46-8) 611-21-22.

(See Next Column)

WHITE & CASE, *Istanbul—Continued*

Helsinki, Finland:
Telephone: (358-0) 631-100.
Facsimile: (358-0) 179-477.
Moscow, Russia:
Telephone: (7-095) 201-9292/3/4/5.
Facsimile: (7-095) 201-9284.
Budapest, Hungary:
Telephone: (36-1) 269-0550; (36-1) 131-0933.
Facsimile: (36-1) 269-1199.
Prague, Czech Republic:
Telephone: (42-2) 2481-1796.
Facsimile: (42-2) 232-5522.
Warsaw, Poland: Telephone/
Facsimile: (48-22) 26-80-53; (48-22) 27-84-86. International Telephone/
Facsimile: (48-39) 12-19-06.
Ankara, Turkey:
Telephone: (90-312) 446-2180.
Facsimile: (90-312) 437-9677.
Jeddah, Saudi Arabia: Law Office of Hassan Mahassni,
Telephone: (966-2) 651-3535.
Facsimile: (966-2) 651-3636.
Riyadh, Saudi Arabia: Law Office of Hassan Mahassni,
Telephone: (966-1) 476-7099.
Facsimile: (966-1) 479-0110.
Almaty, Kazakhstan:
Telephone: (7-3272) 50-7491/2.
Facsimile: (7-3272) 61-0842.

RESIDENT PARTNER

Asli F. Basgoz (Not admitted in Turkey)

RESIDENT COUNSEL

Prof. Dr. M. Fadlullah Cerrahoğlu

RESIDENT ASSOCIATES

Sebnem Isik Kaplanoglu
Refika Tulay Tuzun
Aldoru Uluatam (Not admitted in Turkey)
Deniz Ulusoy
Meltem Usluakol
Can Verdi
Christopher G. Wilkinson (Not admitted in Turkey)
Serap Zuvin

For full biographical listings, see the Martindale-Hubbell Law Directory

UKRAINE

KIEV,*

American Lawyers in Kiev

BAKER & MCKENZIE

Pankivska 5, Fifth Floor, Kiev
Telephone: Telephone: (044) 244-2964; 223-5531
Int'l Dialing: (7-044) 244-2964; 223-5531
Facsimile: (7-044) 223-6184
Associated Offices of Baker & McKenzie in: Almaty, Amsterdam, Bangkok, Barcelona, Beijing, Berlin, Bogotá, Brasília, Brussels, Budapest, Buenos Aires, Cairo, Caracas, Chicago, Dallas, Frankfurt, Geneva, Hanoi, Ho Chi Minh City, Hong Kong, Juárez, London, Madrid, Manila, Melbourne, México City, Miami, Milan, Monterrey, Moscow, New York, Palo Alto, Paris, Prague, Rio de Janeiro, Riyadh, Rome, St. Petersburg, San Diego, San Francisco, São Paulo, Singapore, Stockholm, Sydney, Taipei, Tijuana, Tokyo, Toronto, Valencia, Warsaw, Washington, D.C. and Zürich.
Correspondent Law Firm: Hadiputranto, Hadinoto & Partners, Jakarta.

PARTNER

John P. Hewko (Not admitted in Ukraine)

LOCAL PARTNER

Borys Y. Dackiw (Not admitted in Ukraine)

ASSOCIATES

Serhiy V. Chorny
Oleksi V. Levenets
Alexander Martinenko
Peter Z. Teluk (Not admitted in Ukraine)

For full biographical listings, see the Martindale-Hubbell Law Directory

UNION OF SOVIET SOCIALIST REPUBLICS — (See Russia)

UNITED ARAB EMIRATES

ABU DHABI,

American Lawyers In Abu Dhabi

SHEARMAN & STERLING

P.O. Box 2948, Abu Dhabi
Telephone: (971-2) 324477
Fax: (971-2) 774533
New York, N.Y. Office: 599 Lexington Avenue, New York, New York 10022-6069 and Citicorp Center, 153 East 53rd Street, New York, New York 10022-4676.
Telephone: (212) 848-4000.
Telex: 667290 Num Lau.
Fax: 599 Lexington Avenue: (212) 848-7179. Citicorp Center: (212) 848-5252.
Beijing, People's Republic of China Office: Suite #2205, Capital Mansion, No. 6, Xin Yuan Nan Road. Chao Yang District Beijing, 100004.
Telephone: (861) 465-4574.
Fax: (861) 465-4578.
Budapest, Hungary Office: Szerb utca 17-19, 1056 Budapest.
Telephone: (36-1) 266-3522.
Fax: (36-1) 266-3523.
Düsseldorf, Federal Republic of Germany Office: Königsallee 46, D-40212 Düsseldorf.
Telephone: (49-211) 13 62 80.
Telex: 8 588 294 NYLO.
Fax: (49-211) 13 33 09.
Frankfurt, Federal Republic of Germany Office: Bockenheimer Landstrasse 55, D-60325 Frankfurt am Main.
Telephone: (49-69) 97-10-70.
Fax: (49-69) 97-10-71-00.
Hong Kong, Hong Kong Office: Standard Chartered Bank Building, 4 Des Voeux Road Central, Hong Kong.
Telephone: (852) 2978-8000.
Fax: (852) 2978-8099.
London, England Office: 199 Bishopsgate, London EC2M 3TY.
Telephone: (44-71) 920-9000.
Fax: (44-71) 920-9020.
Los Angeles, California Office: 725 South Figueroa Street, 21st Floor, 90017-5421.
Telephone: (213) 239-0300.
Fax: (213) 239-0381, 614-0936.
Paris, France Office: 12 rue d'Astorg, 75008.
Telephone: (33-1) 44-71-17-17.
Telex: 282964 Royale.
Fax: (33-1) 44-71-01-01.
San Francisco, California Office: 555 California Street, 94104-1522.
Telephone: (415) 616-1100.
Fax: (415) 616-1199.
Taipei, Taiwan Office: 7th Floor, Hung Kuo Building, 167 Tun Hwa North Road.
Telephone: (886-2) 545-3300.
Fax: (866-2) 545-3322.
Tokyo, Japan Office: Shearman & Sterling (Thomas Wilner Gaikokuho-Jimu-Bengoshi Jimusho), Fukoku Seimei Building, 5th Fl. 2-2-2, Uchisaiwaicho, Chiyoda-ku, Tokyo 100, Japan.
Telephone: (81 3) 5251-1601.
Fax: (81 3) 5251-1602.
Toronto, Ontario, Canada Office: Commerce Court West, Suite 4405, P.O. Box 247, M5L 1E8.
Telephone: (416) 360-8484.
Fax: (416) 360-2958.
Washington, D.C. Office: 801 Pennsylvania Avenue, N.W., Suite 900, 20004-2604.
Telephone: (202) 508-8000.
Fax: (202) 508-8100.

MANAGING PARTNER

Philip B. Dundas, Jr. (Not admitted in United Arab Emirates)

RESIDENT ASSOCIATE

William F. Ranieri (Not admitted in United Arab Emirates)

OF COUNSEL

Michael W. Smith
(Not admitted to practice in United Arab Emirates courts)

For full biographical listings, see the Martindale-Hubbell Law Directory

VENEZUELA

*CARACAS,**

BAKER & MCKENZIE

Edificio Aldemo, Avenida Venezuela, Urb. El Rosal, Caracas
Telephone: (02) 9530833; 9531333
Intn'l. Dialing: (58-2) 9530833; 9531333
Cable Address: ABOGAD0-CARACAS
Telex: 23133
Answer Back: 23133 ABOGA VC
Facsimiles: (58-2) 9537094; 9533642
U.S. Mailing Address: Baker & McKenzie, M-287, Jet Cargo International, P.O. Box 020010, Miami, Florida 33102-0010, U.S.A.
Associated Offices of Baker & McKenzie in: Almaty, Amsterdam, Bangkok, Barcelona, Beijing, Berlin, Bogotá, Brasília, Brussels, Budapest, Buenos Aires, Cairo, Chicago, Dallas, Frankfurt, Geneva, Hanoi, Ho Chi Minh City, Hong Kong, Juárez, Kiev, London, Madrid, Manila, Melbourne, México City, Miami, Milan, Monterrey, Moscow, New York, Palo Alto, Paris, Prague, Rio de Janeiro, Riyadh, Rome, St. Petersburg, San Diego, San Francisco, São Paulo, Singapore, Stockholm, Sydney, Taipei, Tijuana, Tokyo, Toronto, Valencia, Warsaw, Washington, D.C. and Zürich.
Correspondent Law Firm: Hadiputranto, Hadinoto & Partners, Jakarta.
Postal Address: P.O. Box 1286, Caracas 1010-A, Venezuela

PARTNERS

Alejandro Alfonzo-Larrain R.
Pedro Pablo Benedetti H.
Diego Bustillos B.
Malcolm Caplan
(Not admitted in Venezuela)
Raúl Curiel Carías
Manuel Diaz Mujica
Gilberto Haiek-Wülff
Eduardo Machado Iturbe
Roberto J. Mendoza Dávila
Francisco Palma Carrillo
Freddy Paván V.
Carlos Plaza Anselmi
Emilio José Roche
Henry Torrealba Ledesma
Luis Miguel Vicentini
Miguel Zaldívar Zaydin

LOCAL PARTNERS

Nedo Boccardo Miranda
Humberto J. Briceño
José Henrique D'Apollo
Carlos E. Delgado
Fernando M. Fernández
José Alfredo Giral
Eugenio Hernández-Bretón R.
Alejandro Lares Díaz
Maritza Mészáros Reyes
Leopoldo E. Ustáriz C.

Orlando E. Abinazar
Delfina María Alonso Briceño
Ramón J. Alvins Santi
Mario Calosso
Norma V. Cigala
Clementina M. de Castro
Maria Antonieta Di Gianluca
Rossanna D'Onza
Elisabeth E. Eljuri
Ronald E. Evans
Carlos A. Felce
Adriana C. García
Joaquín Gonçalves
José Ignacio Gutiérrez
Luis E. Homes
Marcel Imery
Carolina Lanao
Anibal Latuff
Martha C. Luchsinger
Leopoldo E. Olavarría
Erasmo A. Pérez Fernández
Alvaro J. Posada
Juan Carlos Pro Rísquez
María Eugenia Reyes Feo
Marisela Sanfeliz
Antonella D. Sciubba
Moisés Vallenilla Tolosa
María C. Torres
Juan C. Varela

For full biographical listings, see the Martindale-Hubbell Law Directory

VALENCIA,

BAKER & MCKENZIE

Edificio Torre 'H', Piso 3, Calle 139 Con Avenida 101, Urb. El Viñedo, Valencia
Telephone: (41) 22-85-15; 22-29-19
Intn'l. Dialing: (58-41) 22-85-15; 22-29-19
Facsimile: (58-41) 22-85-54
Associated Offices of Baker & McKenzie in: Almaty, Amsterdam, Bangkok, Barcelona, Beijing, Berlin, Bogotá, Brasília, Brussels, Budapest, Buenos Aires, Cairo, Caracas, Chicago, Dallas, Frankfurt, Geneva, Hanoi, Ho Chi Minh City, Hong Kong, Juárez, Kiev, London, Madrid, Manila, Melbourne, México City, Miami, Milan, Monterrey, Moscow, New York, Palo Alto, Paris, Prague, Rio de Janeiro, Riyadh, Rome, St. Petersburg, San Diego, San Francisco, São Paulo, Singapore, Stockholm, Sydney, Taipei, Tijuana, Tokyo, Toronto, Warsaw, Washington, D.C. and Zürich.
Correspondent Law Firm: Hadiputranto, Hadinoto & Partners, Jakarta.
Postal Address: P.O. Box 1155 Valencia, Estado Carabobo, Venezuela

RESIDENT PARTNER

Omar Benitez Ramírez

RESIDENT ASSOCIATES

Carlos Enrique Lüdart L.
Francisco J. Velasquez Arcay

For full biographical listings, see the Martindale-Hubbell Law Directory

VIETNAM

HANOI,

BAKER & MCKENZIE

Hanoi Representative Office
41 Ly Thai To Street Hoan Kiem District, Hanoi
Telephone: (4) 251428; 251429; 251430
Intn'l Dialing: (84-4) 251428; 251429; 251430
Facsimile: (84-4) 251432
Associated Offices of Baker & McKenzie in: Almaty, Amsterdam, Bangkok, Barcelona, Beijing, Berlin, Bogotá, Brasília, Brussels, Budapest, Buenos Aires, Cairo, Caracas, Chicago, Dallas, Frankfurt, Geneva, Ho Chi Minh City, Hong Kong, Juárez, Kiev, London, Madrid, Manila, Melbourne, México City, Miami, Milan, Monterrey, Moscow, New York, Palo Alto, Paris, Prague, Rio de Janeiro, Riyadh, Rome, St. Petersburg, San Diego, San Francisco, São Paulo, Singapore, Stockholm, Sydney, Taipei, Tijuana, Tokyo, Toronto, Valencia, Warsaw, Washington, D.C. and Zürich.
Correspondent Law Firm: Hadiputranto, Hadinoto & Partners, Jakarta.

LOCAL PARTNERS

Nguyen Tan Hai
Mark Andrew Lockwood
(Not admitted in Vietnam)

For full biographical listings, see the Martindale-Hubbell Law Directory

HO CHI MINH CITY,

BAKER & MCKENZIE

Ho Chi Minh City Branch Representative Office
4th Floor, 58 Dong Khoi Street District 1, Ho Chi Minh City
Telephone: (8) 295 585; 295 601; 295 602; 295 613
Intn'l Dialing: (84-8) 295-585; 295 601; 295 602; 295 613
Facsimile: (84-8) 295 618
Associated Offices of Baker & McKenzie in: Almaty, Amsterdam, Bangkok, Barcelona, Beijing, Berlin, Bogotá, Brasília, Brussels, Budapest, Buenos Aires, Cairo, Caracas, Chicago, Dallas, Frankfurt, Geneva, Hanoi, Hong Kong, Juárez, Kiev, London, Madrid, Manila, Melbourne, México City, Miami, Milan, Monterrey, Moscow, New York, Palo Alto, Paris, Prague, Rio de Janeiro, Riyadh, Rome, St. Petersburg, San Diego, San Francisco, São Paulo, Singapore, Stockholm, Sydney, Taipei, Tijuana, Tokyo, Toronto, Valencia, Warsaw, Washington, D.C. and Zürich.
Correspondent Law Firm: Hadiputranto, Hadinoto & Partners, Jakarta.

LOCAL PARTNERS

Mark Andrew Lockwood
(Not admitted in Vietnam)
Nguyen Tan Hai

For full biographical listings, see the Martindale-Hubbell Law Directory

HEALTH CARE LAW

ALABAMA

*BIRMINGHAM,** Jefferson Co.

BALCH & BINGHAM (AV)

1710 Sixth Avenue North, P.O. Box 306, 35201
Telephone: 205-251-8100
Facsimile: 205-226-8798
Other Birmingham, Alabama Office: 1901 Sixth Avenue North, 35203.
Telephone: 205-251-8100.
Facsimile: 205-226-8799.
Montgomery, Alabama Office: The Winter Building, 2 Dexter Avenue, 36101.
Telephone: 205-834-6500.
Facsimile: 205-269-3115.
Huntsville, Alabama Office: Suite 810, 200 West Court Square, 35801.
Telephone: 205-551-0171.
Facsimile: 205-551-0174.
Washington, D.C. Office: Suite 800, 1101 Connecticut Avenue, N.W., 20036.
Telephone: 202-296-0387.
Facsimile: 202-452-8180.

MEMBERS OF FIRM

James F. Hughey, Jr. | Cavender Crosby Kimble

ASSOCIATE

Colin H. Luke

Counsel for: Alabama Power Co.; Blue Cross and Blue Shield of Alabama; The Boeing Company; Brasfield & Gorrie, Inc.; Compass Bancshares, Inc.; Harbert Corp.; Kimberly-Clark Corp.; Southern Company Services, Inc.; Southern Research Institute; Vesta Insurance Group, Inc.

For Complete List of Firm Personnel, See General Section

For full biographical listings, see the Martindale-Hubbell Law Directory

BERKOWITZ, LEFKOVITS, ISOM & KUSHNER, A PROFESSIONAL CORPORATION (AV)

1600 SouthTrust Tower, 420 North Twentieth Street, 35203
Telephone: 205-328-0480
Telecopier: 205-322-8007

Harold B. Kushner | David A. Larsen
B. G. Minisman, Jr. | Ronald A. Levitt
Thomas O. Kolb

Walton E. Williams III | Robin L. Tucker

Representative Clients: AlaTenn Resources, Inc.; AMI Brookwood Medical Centers; The Baptist Medical Centers; B.A.S.S., Inc.; Hanna Steel Co., Inc.; McDonald's Corp.; Parisian, Inc.; Outpatient Services East, Ltd.; Southeast Health Plan, Inc.

For Complete List of Firm Personnel, See General Section

For full biographical listings, see the Martindale-Hubbell Law Directory

BRADLEY, ARANT, ROSE & WHITE (AV)

1400 Park Place Tower, 2001 Park Place, 35203
Telephone: 205-521-8000
Telex: 494-1324
Facsimile: 205-251-8611, 251-8665, 252-0264
Facsimile (Southtrust Office): 205-251-9915
Huntsville, Alabama Office: 200 Clinton Avenue West, Suite 900.
Telephone: 205-517-5100.
Facsimile: 205-533-5069.

MEMBERS OF FIRM

John K. Molen | Lant B. Davis
Joan Crowder Ragsdale

ASSOCIATES

Deane K. Corliss | K. Wood Herren
Richard L. Sharff, Jr.

For Complete List of Firm Personnel, See General Section

For full biographical listings, see the Martindale-Hubbell Law Directory

HASKELL SLAUGHTER YOUNG & JOHNSTON, PROFESSIONAL ASSOCIATION (AV)

1200 AmSouth/Harbert Plaza, 1901 Sixth Avenue North, 35203
Telephone: 205-251-1000
Facsimile: 205-324-1133
Montgomery, Alabama Office: Haskell Slaughter Young Johnston & Gallion. Bailey Building, Suite 375, 400 South Union Street, P.O. Box 4660. 36104
Telephone: 205-265-8573.
Facsimile: 205-264-7945.

William M. Slaughter | E. Alston Ray
J. Brooke Johnston, Jr. | Ross N. Cohen

Representative Clients: American Dental Plan of Alabama; Baxter Healthcare Corporation; The Bradford Group, Inc.; The Coalition for Employee Health-care, Inc.; HEALTHSOUTH Rehabilitation Corporation/HEALTHSOUTH Medical Centers; High Field NMR Systems, Inc.; MedPartners, Inc.; Northeast Alabama Regional Medical Center; Pickens County (Alabama) Medical Center; Psychiatric Healthcare Corporation.

For Complete List of Firm Personnel, See General Section

For full biographical listings, see the Martindale-Hubbell Law Directory

SIROTE & PERMUTT, P.C. (AV)

2222 Arlington Avenue, South, P.O. Box 55727, 35255
Telephone: 205-933-7111
Facsimile: 205-930-5301
Huntsville, Alabama Office: 200 Clinton Avenue, N.W., Suite 1000.
Telephone: 205-536-1711.
Facsimile: 205-534-9650.
Mobile, Alabama Office: One St. Louis Centre, Suite 1000.
Telephone: 205-432-1671.
Facsimile: 205-434-0196.
Montgomery, Alabama Office: Colonial Commerce Center, Suite 305 One Commerce Street.
Telephone: 205-261-3400.
Facsimile: 205-261-3434.
Tuscaloosa, Alabama Office: 2216 14th Street.
Telephone: 205-752-2089.

George M. (Jack) Neal, Jr. | Thomas G. Tutten, Jr.
Greggory M. Deitsch | W. McCollum Halcomb
Rodney E. Nolen | C. Randal Johnson
Jeffrey H. Wertheim

Representative Clients: International Business Machines (IBM); General Motors Corp.; Colonial Bank; Bruno's, Inc.; University of Alabama Hospitals; Westinghouse Electric Corp.; First Alabama Bank; Monsanto Chemical Company; South Central Bell; Prudential Insurance Company; American Home Products, Inc.; Minnesota Mining and Manufacturing, Inc. (3M).

For Complete List of Firm Personnel, See General Section

For full biographical listings, see the Martindale-Hubbell Law Directory

*HUNTSVILLE,** Madison Co.

SIROTE & PERMUTT, P.C. (AV)

Suite 1000, 200 Clinton Avenue, N.W., 35801
Telephone: 205-536-1711
Facsimile: 205-534-9650
Birmingham, Alabama Office: 2222 Arlington Avenue, South, P.O. Box 55727.
Telephone: 205-933-7111.
Facsimile: 205-930-5301.
Mobile, Alabama Office: One St. Louis Centre, Suite 1000.
Telephone: 205-432-1671.
Facsimile: 205-434-0196.
Montgomery, Alabama Office: Colonial Commerce Center, Suite 305, One Commerce Street.
Telephone: 205-261-3400.
Facsimile: 205-261-3434.
Tuscaloosa, Alabama Office: 2216 14th Street.
Telephone: 205-752-2089.

George W. Royer, Jr. | June Wang
Fred L. Coffey, Jr.

For Complete List of Firm Personnel, See General Section

For full biographical listings, see the Martindale-Hubbell Law Directory

*MOBILE,** Mobile Co.

HAND, ARENDALL, BEDSOLE, GREAVES & JOHNSTON (AV)

3000 First National Bank Building, P.O. Box 123, Drawer C, 36601
Telephone: 334-432-5511
Fax: 334-694-6375
Washington, D.C. Office: 410 First Street, S.E., Suite 300. 20003.
Telephone: 202-863-0053.
Fax: 202-863-0096.

(See Next Column)

HAND, ARENDALL, BEDSOLE, GREAVES & JOHNSTON, *Mobile—Continued*

MEMBERS OF FIRM

Edward S. Sledge, III
Judith L. McMillin
R. Preston Bolt, Jr.
Walter T. Gilmer, Jr.

General Counsel for: The Bank of Mobile; Delchamps, Inc.; The Mobile Press Register, Inc.; Mobile Asphalt Company; Gulf Telephone Company; Folmar & Associates; Mobile Community Foundation; Gulf Lumber Company; Scotch Lumber Company; Mobile Pulley & Machine Works, Inc.; Pennsylvania Shipbuilding Co.

For Complete List of Firm Personnel, See General Section

For full biographical listings, see the Martindale-Hubbell Law Directory

JOHNSTONE, ADAMS, BAILEY, GORDON AND HARRIS (AV)

Royal St. Francis Building, 104 St. Francis Street, P.O. Box 1988, 36633
Telephone: 334-432-7682
Facsimile: 334-432-2800
Telex: 782040

MEMBERS OF FIRM

E. Watson Smith
Gregory C. Buffalow
Wade B. Perry, Jr.
R. Gregory Watts

General Counsel for: First Alabama Bank, Mobile; Infirmary Health System/Mobile Infirmary Medical Center/Rotary Rehabilitation Hospital (Multi-Hospital System).
Counsel for: Oil and Gas: Exxon Corp. Business and Corporate: Bell South Telecommunications, Inc.; Aluminum Co. of America; Michelin Tire Corp.; Metropolitan Life Insurance Co.; The Travelers Insurance Cos. Marine: The West of England Ship Owners Mutual Protection and Indemnity Association (Luxembourg); The Standard Steamship Owners' Protection and Indemnity Association (Bermuda) Ltd.

For Complete List of Firm Personnel, See General Section

For full biographical listings, see the Martindale-Hubbell Law Directory

SIROTE & PERMUTT, P.C. (AV)

One St. Louis Centre, Suite 1000, P.O. Drawer 2025, 36652-2025
Telephone: 334-432-1671
Facsimile: 334-434-0196
Birmingham, Alabama Office: 2222 Arlington Avenue, South, P.O. Box 55727.
Telephone: 205-933-7111.
Facsimile: 205-930-5301.
Huntsville, Alabama Office: 200 Clinton Avenue, N.W., Suite 1000.
Telephone: 205-536-1711.
Facsimile: 205-534-9650.
Montgomery, Alabama Office: Colonial Commerce Center, Suite 305, One Commerce Street.
Telephone: 205-261-3400.
Facsimile: 205-261-3434.
Tuscaloosa, Alabama Office: 2216 14th Street.
Telephone: 205-752-2089.

Shirley Mahan Justice

For Complete List of Firm Personnel, See General Section

For full biographical listings, see the Martindale-Hubbell Law Directory

*MONTGOMERY,** Montgomery Co.

PARKER, BRANTLEY & WILKERSON, P.C. (AV)

323 Adams Avenue, P.O. Box 4992, 36103-4992
Telephone: 334-265-1500
Fax: 334-265-0319

Edward B. Parker, II
Mark D. Wilkerson
Paul A. Brantley
Leah Snell Stephens
Darla T. Furman

Representative Clients: Alabama Board of Nursing; State Health Planning and Development Agency (Hearing Officer); Unicor Medical, Inc.; Alabama Emergency Room Administrative Services, P.C.
Reference: South Trust Bank, N.A.

For full biographical listings, see the Martindale-Hubbell Law Directory

ARIZONA

*PHOENIX,** Maricopa Co.

BONN, LUSCHER, PADDEN & WILKINS, CHARTERED (AV)

805 North Second Street, 85004
Telephone: 602-254-5557
Fax: 602-254-0656

Brian A. Luscher
Jeff C. Padden

For full biographical listings, see the Martindale-Hubbell Law Directory

FENNEMORE CRAIG, A PROFESSIONAL CORPORATION (AV)

Two North Central, Suite 2200, 85004
Telephone: 602-257-8700
Fax: 602-257-8527
Scottsdale, Arizona Office: 6263 North Scottsdale Road, Suite 290, 85250.
Telephone: 602-257-5400.
Fax: 602-945-4932.
Tucson, Arizona Office: One South Church Avenue, Suite 1030, 85701.
Telephone: 602-624-9312.
Fax: 602-882-7383.

Michael Preston Green
Andrew M. Federhar

Jean Marie Sullivan

Representative Clients: ASARCO Incorporated; AT&T Communications; Bridgestone/Firestone, Inc.; Catellus Development Corp.; Citibank (Arizona); First Interstate Bank of Arizona; GIANT Industries; Phelps Dodge Corporation; The Atchison, Topeka & Santa Fe Railway, Co.; US WEST Communications.

For Complete List of Firm Personnel, See General Section

For full biographical listings, see the Martindale-Hubbell Law Directory

GAMMAGE & BURNHAM (AV)

One Renaissance Square, Two North Central Avenue, Suite 1800, 85004
Telephone: 602-256-0566
Fax: 602-256-4475

MEMBERS OF FIRM

Richard B. Burnham
Curtis A. Ullman
Susan L. Watchman

Representative Clients: St. Joseph's Hospital; Samaritan Health System; St. Mary's Hospital & Health Center; Holy Cross Hospital & Health Center; John C. Lincoln Hospital & Health Center; Southwest Catholic Health Network Corp.; Yuma Regional Medical Center; St. Joseph's Hospital of Tucson.

For Complete List of Firm Personnel, See General Section

For full biographical listings, see the Martindale-Hubbell Law Directory

JENNINGS, STROUSS AND SALMON, P.L.C. (AV)

A Professional Limited Liability Company
One Renaissance Square, Two North Central, 85004-2393
Telephone: 602-262-5911
Fax: 602-253-3255

John B. Weldon, Jr.
John A. Micheaels
Rita A. Meiser
Robert J. Werner
Lisa M. McKnight

For Complete List of Firm Personnel, See General Section

For full biographical listings, see the Martindale-Hubbell Law Directory

LEWIS AND ROCA (AV)

A Partnership including Professional Corporations
40 North Central Avenue, 85004-4429
Telephone: 602-262-5311
Fax: 602-262-5747
Tucson, Arizona Office: One South Church Avenue, Suite 700.
Telephone: 602-622-2090.
Fax: 602-622-3088.

MEMBERS OF FIRM

Merton E. Marks (P.C.)
Foster Robberson
Beth J. Schermer
David M. Bixby
Karen Carter Owens

ASSOCIATES

J. Tyler Haahr
Barbara A. Anstey

Representative Clients: Arizona Hospital Association; Blood Systems, Inc.; Marcus J. Lawrence Medical Center; Mutual Insurance Company of Arizona; Phoenix Memorial Hospital; Private Healthcare Systems, Ltd.; Samaritan Health System.

For Complete List of Firm Personnel, See General Section

For full biographical listings, see the Martindale-Hubbell Law Directory

O'CONNOR, CAVANAGH, ANDERSON, WESTOVER, KILLINGSWORTH & BESHEARS, A PROFESSIONAL ASSOCIATION (AV)

One East Camelback Road, Suite 1100, 85012-1656
Telephone: 602-263-2400
FAX: 602-263-2900
Sun City, Arizona Office: 13250 North Del Webb Boulevard, Suite B, 85351.
Telephone: 602-263-2808.
FAX: 602-933-3100.

(See Next Column)

O'CONNOR, CAVANAGH, ANDERSON, WESTOVER, KILLINGSWORTH & BESHEARS A PROFESSIONAL ASSOCIATION—*Continued*

Tucson, Arizona Office: Suite 2200, One South Church Avenue, 85701.
Telephone: 602-882-8912.
FAX: 602-624-9564.
Nogales, Arizona Office: 1827 North Mastick Way, 85621.
Telephone: 602-761-4215.
FAX: 602-761-3505.

Ralph E. Hunsaker
George H. Mitchell
Harding B. Cure
Richard C. Smith
Philip C. Gerard
John B. Furman
Paul J. Roshka, Jr.
John E. DeWulf
Stephen E. Richman
David A. Van Engelhoven
Paul J. Giancola
Donald R. Greene (Not admitted in AZ)
Janice H. Moore

Janet E. Kornblatt
Leigh A. Kaylor

Representative Clients: Good Samaritan Health Systems; MICA; St. Paul Insurance Co.; Podiatry Insurance Company of America; United Health Care; MediMax; Golden Rule Insurance Company; Samsung Electronics Corp.

For Complete List of Firm Personnel, See General Section

For full biographical listings, see the Martindale-Hubbell Law Directory

SNELL & WILMER (AV)

One Arizona Center, 85004-0001
Telephone: 602-382-6000
Fax: 602-382-6070
Tucson, Arizona Office: 1500 Norwest Tower, One South Church Avenue 85701-1612.
Telephone: 602-882-1200.
Fax: 602-884-1294.
Orange County Office: 1920 Main Street, Suite 1200, P.O. Box 19601, Irvine, California, 92714.
Telephone: 714-253-2700.
Fax: 714-955-2507.
Salt Lake City, Utah Office: Broadway Centre, 111 East Broadway, Suite 900, 84111.
Telephone: 801-237-1900.
Fax: 801-237-1950.

OF COUNSEL

Edward Jacobson

MEMBERS OF FIRM

Gerard Morales
Barry D. Halpern
Richard W. Sheffield

ASSOCIATE

Thea Foglietta Silverstein

Representative Clients: Arizona Public Service Co.; Bank One, Arizona, NA.; First Security Bank of Utah, N.A.; Ford Motor Co.; Chrysler Motors Corp.; Toyota Motor Sales U.S.A.; Magma Copper Co.; U.S. Home Corp.; Pinnacle West Capital Corp.; Safeway, Inc.

For Complete List of Firm Personnel, See General Section

For full biographical listings, see the Martindale-Hubbell Law Directory

ULRICH, THOMPSON & KESSLER, P.C. (AV)

Suite 1000, 3030 North Central Avenue, 85012-2717
Telephone: 602-248-9465
Fax: 602-248-0165

Paul G. Ulrich
Nancy C. Thompson
Donn G. Kessler

For full biographical listings, see the Martindale-Hubbell Law Directory

*TUCSON,** Pima Co.

O'CONNOR, CAVANAGH, ANDERSON, WESTOVER, KILLINGSWORTH & BESHEARS, A PROFESSIONAL ASSOCIATION (AV)

Suite 2200 One South Church Avenue, 85701-1621
Telephone: 602-882-8912
FAX: 602-624-9564
Phoenix, Arizona Office: One East Camelback Road, Suite 1100, 85012.
Telephone: 602-263-2400.
FAX: 602-263-2900.
Sun City, Arizona Office: 13250 North Del Webb Boulevard, Suite B, 85351.
Telephone: 602-263-2808.
FAX: 602-933-3100.
Nogales, Arizona Office: 1827 North Mastick Way, 85621.
Telephone: 602-761-4215.
FAX: 602-761-3505.

(See Next Column)

Thomas M. Pace

Representative Client: Jeffco, Inc.
Reference: Citibank.

For Complete List of Firm Personnel, See General Section

For full biographical listings, see the Martindale-Hubbell Law Directory

RAVEN, KIRSCHNER & NORELL, P.C. (AV)

Suite 1600, One South Church Avenue, 85701-1612
Telephone: 602-628-8700
Telefax: 602-798-5200

Bradley G.A. Cloud
Andrew Oldland Norell
Mark B. Raven

Representative Clients: Pace American Bonding Company; Citibank (Arizona); Continental Medical Systems, Inc.; El Paso Natural Gas Co.; Norwest Bank Arizona; El Rio-Santa Cruz Neighborhood Health Center, Inc.; Resolution Trust Corp.; Sierra Vista Community Hospital; Southern Arizona Rehabilitation Hospital; Ford Motor Credit.

For Complete List of Firm Personnel, See General Section

For full biographical listings, see the Martindale-Hubbell Law Directory

ARKANSAS

*LITTLE ROCK,** Pulaski Co.

BARBER, MCCASKILL, AMSLER, JONES & HALE, P.A. (AV)

2700 First Commercial Building, 400 West Capitol Avenue, 72201-3414
Telephone: 501-372-6175
Telecopier: 501-375-2802

Azro L. Barber (1885-1979)
Elbert A. Henry (1889-1966)
John B. Thurman (1912-1971)
Austin McCaskill, Sr.
Guy Amsler, Jr.
Glenn W. Jones, Jr.
Michael E. Hale
John S. Cherry, Jr.
Robert L. Henry, III
Micheal L. Alexander
William H. Edwards, Jr.
Richard C. Kalkbrenner
G. Spence Fricke
M. Stephen Bingham
Gail Ponder Gaines
Michael J. Emerson
R. Kenny McCulloch
Tim A. Cheatham
Joseph F. Kolb
Scott Michael Strauss
Karen Hart McKinney

Attorneys for: Associated Aviation Underwriters; Canal Insurance Co.; Fireman's Fund Insurance Co.; General Motors Corp.; General Motors Acceptance Corp.; Hanover Insurance Co.; Home Insurance Co.; Royal Insurance; United States Fidelity & Guaranty Co.; Universal Underwriters Insurance Co.

For full biographical listings, see the Martindale-Hubbell Law Directory

CALIFORNIA

*FRESNO,** Fresno Co.

DOWLING, MAGARIAN, AARON & HEYMAN, INCORPORATED (AV)

Suite 200, 6051 North Fresno Street, 93710
Telephone: 209-432-4500
Fax: 209-432-4590

Michael D. Dowling
Richard M. Aaron
John C. Ganahl

Reference: Wells Fargo Bank (Main).

For Complete List of Firm Personnel, See General Section

For full biographical listings, see the Martindale-Hubbell Law Directory

JACKSON EMERICH PEDREIRA & NAHIGIAN, A PROFESSIONAL CORPORATION (AV)

7108 North Fresno Street, Suite 400, 93720-2938
Telephone: 209-261-0200
Facsimile: 209-261-0910

Donald A. Jackson
David R. Emerich
Thomas A. Pedreira
Eliot S. Nahigian
David A. Fike

John W. Phillips
John M. Cardot
Nicholas A. Tarjoman
Jeffrey B. Pape
David G. Hansen

(See Next Column)

JACKSON EMERICH PEDREIRA & NAHIGIAN A PROFESSIONAL CORPORATION, *Fresno—Continued*

Reference: Bank of California.

For full biographical listings, see the Martindale-Hubbell Law Directory

KIMBLE, MACMICHAEL & UPTON, A PROFESSIONAL CORPORATION (AV)

Fig Garden Financial Center, 5260 North Palm Avenue, Suite 221, P.O. Box 9489, 93792-9489
Telephone: 209-435-5500
Telecopier: 209-435-1500

Joseph C. Kimble (1910-1972)
Thomas A. MacMichael (1920-1990)
Jon Wallace Upton
Robert E. Bergin
Jeffrey G. Boswell
Steven D. McGee
Robert E. Ward
John P. Eleazarian
Robert H. Scribner
Michael E. Moss
David D. Doyle
Mark D. Miller
Michael F. Tatham
W. Richard Lee
D. Tyler Tharpe
Sylvia Halkousis Coyle

Michael J. Jurkovich
S. Brett Sutton
Douglas V. Thornton
Robert William Branch
Brian N. Folland
Christopher L. Wanger
Elise M. Krause
Donald J. Pool
Susan King Hatmaker

For full biographical listings, see the Martindale-Hubbell Law Directory

STAMMER, MCKNIGHT, BARNUM & BAILEY (AV)

2540 West Shaw Lane, Suite 110, P.O. Box 9789, 93794-9789
Telephone: 209-449-0571
Fax: 209-432-2619

W. H. Stammer (1891-1969)
James K. Barnum (1918-1987)
Dean A. Bailey (Retired)
Galen McKnight (1904-1991)
James N. Hays
Carey H. Johnson
Jan M. Biggs
Frank D. Maul
Daniel O. Jamison
Craig M. Mortensen
Jerry D. Jones
Michael P. Mallery
M. Bruce Smith

ASSOCIATES

A. John Witkowski
Thomas J. Georgouses
Steven R. Stoker
M. Jaqueline Yates
Bruce J. Berger

OF COUNSEL

Donald D. Pogoloff

Representative Clients: Community Hospital of Central California; Memorial Hospital of Modesto; Madera Community Hospital; Valley Medical Center; Truck Insurance Exchange.
Reference: Bank of America National Trust & Savings Assn. (Fresno Main Office).

For full biographical listings, see the Martindale-Hubbell Law Directory

*LOS ANGELES,** Los Angeles Co.

GALTON & HELM (AV)

500 South Grand Avenue, Suite 1200, 90071
Telephone: 213-629-8800
Telecopier: 213-629-0037

MEMBERS OF FIRM

Stephen H. Galton
Hugh H. Helm
Michael F. Bell
Daniel W. Maguire
David A. Lingenbrink

ASSOCIATES

Nancy A. Jerian
Keith A. Jacoby
Michael Hoffman
Cori Gayle Stockman
Susan G. Wells
Chris D. Olsen

For full biographical listings, see the Martindale-Hubbell Law Directory

HOOPER, LUNDY & BOOKMAN, INC. (AV)

Watt Plaza, Suite 1600, 1875 Century Park East, 90067-2517
Telephone: 310-551-8111
Telecopier: 310-551-8181
Sacramento, California Office: 400 Capitol Mall, Suite 2400.
Telephone: 916-447-0203.
Telecopier: 916-447-0502.

Robert W. Lundy, Jr.
Patric Hooper
Lloyd A. Bookman
W. Bradley Tully
John R. Hellow
Angela A. Mickelson
Laurence D. Getzoff
Douglas S. Cumming (Resident, Sacramento Office)
Jay N. Hartz
Byron J. Gross
Todd E. Swanson
Patricia H. Wirth
Gina Reese
David P. Henninger
Rebecca Lambeth
Rina J. Pakula
Jonathan P. Neustadter
Jonathan F. Atzen

Representative Clients: American Medical International, Inc.; National Medical Enterprises, Inc.; Kaiser Foundation Health Plan; City of Hope National Medical Center; Orthopedic Hospital; County of Los Angeles Hospitals and Health Systems; National Association of Psychiatric Treatment Centers for Children; Physicians and Surgeons Laboratories, Inc.
Reference: City National Bank.

For full biographical listings, see the Martindale-Hubbell Law Directory

HORVITZ & LEVY (AV)

A Partnership including Professional Corporations
18th Floor, 15760 Ventura Boulevard (Encino), 91436
Telephone: 818-995-0800; 213-872-0802
FAX: 818-995-3157

Ellis J. Horvitz (A P.C.)
Barry R. Levy (A P.C.)
Peter Abrahams
David M. Axelrad
Frederic D. Cohen
S. Thomas Todd
David S. Ettinger
Daniel J. Gonzalez
Mitchell C. Tilner
Christina J. Imre
Lisa Perrochet
Stephen E. Norris
Sandra J. Smith

Mary F. Dant
Ari R. Kleiman
Lisa R. Jaskol
Julie L. Woods
Holly R. Paul
H. Thomas Watson
John A. Taylor, Jr.
Annette E. Davis
Andrea M. Gauthier
Elizabeth Skorcz Anthony
Christine A. Pagac (Not admitted in CA)
Gary T. Gleb
Bruce Adelstein

Representative Clients: California Medical Association; California Association of Hospitals and Health Systems; Truck Insurance Exchange; Cedars-Sinai Medical Center; Southern California Physicians Insurance Exchange; Truck Insurance Exchange; Physicians & Surgeons Division of Fremont Indemnity; NORCAL Mutual Insurance Company; Kaiser Foundation Health Plan, Inc.; CHD Insurance Services.

For full biographical listings, see the Martindale-Hubbell Law Directory

LAW OFFICES OF MICHAEL DUNDON ROTH (AV)

The Wilshire Landmark Building, 11755 Wilshire Boulevard, Suite 1400, 90025-1520
Telephone: 310-477-5455
Facsimile: 310-477-1979

Sharon F. Roth

Reference: Marathon National Bank.

For full biographical listings, see the Martindale-Hubbell Law Directory

VEATCH, CARLSON, GROGAN & NELSON (AV)

A Partnership including a Professional Corporation
3926 Wilshire Boulevard, 90010
Telephone: 213-381-2861
Telefax: 213-383-6370

MEMBERS OF FIRM

Wayne Veatch
Henry R. Thomas (1905-1963)
James R. Nelson (1925-1987)
James C. Galloway, Jr. (A Professional Corporation)
C. Snyder Patin
Anthony D. Seine
Mark A. Weinstein
John A. Peterson

ASSOCIATES

Michael Eric Wasserman
Richard A. Wood
Michael A. Kramer
Mark M. Rudy
André S. Goodchild
Lyn A. Woodward
Kevin L. Henderson
Betty Rubin-Elbaz
John B. Loomis
Judith Randel Cooper
Karen J. Travis
Amy W. Lyons
Wayne Rozenberg
Gilbert A. Garcia
Judy Lew
James A. Jinks

OF COUNSEL

Robert C. Carlson (A Professional Corporation)
Stephen J. Grogan
David J. Aisenson

For full biographical listings, see the Martindale-Hubbell Law Directory

WEISSBURG AND ARONSON, INC. (AV)

32nd Floor, Two Century Plaza, 2049 Century Park East (Century City), 90067-3271
Telephone: 310-277-2223
Facsimile: 310-557-8475
Sacramento, California Office: Suite 1050, 770 L Street.
Telephone: 916-443-8005.
Facsimile: 916-443-2240.

(See Next Column)

WEISSBURG AND ARONSON INC.—*Continued*

San Diego, California Office: 402 West Broadway, 23rd. Floor.
Telephone: 619-234-6655.
Facsimile: 619-234-3510.
San Francisco, California Office: Suite 2400, 555 California Street.
Telephone: 415-434-4484.
Facsimile: 415-434-4507.

Robert A. Klein
Peter Aronson
Carl Weissburg
Richard A. Blacker
Mark S. Windisch
J. Mark Waxman
Carl H. Hitchner (Resident at San Francisco Office)
Robert D. Sevell
Richard F. Seiden
Gregory W. McClune (Resident at San Francisco Office)
George L. Root, Jr. (Resident at San Diego Office)
James R. Kalyvas
Margaret Mary Manning
Richard M. Albert
Ralph B. Kostant
Laurence R. Arnold (Resident at San Francisco Office)
Anita D. Lee
Samuel F. Hoffman (Resident at San Diego Office)
Thomas L. Driscoll (San Francisco and Sacramento Offices)
Jonathan M. Lindeke (Resident at San Francisco Office)
C. Darryl Cordero
Wayne J. Miller
Denise Rodriguez
Stephen W. Parrish (Resident at San Francisco Office)
R. Michael Scarano, Jr. (Resident at San Diego Office)
Lowell C. Brown
Gregory V. Moser (Resident at San Diego Office)
Robert E. Goldstein
Tami S. Smason
Lawrence C. Conn
Mark T. Schieble (Resident at San Francisco Office)
Robert C. Leventhal
Ralph T. Ferguson (Resident, Sacramento Office)
Larry L. Marshall (Resident, San Diego Office)
Clare Richardson
Carol Isackson (Resident at San Diego Office)
Dorothy J. Stephens (Resident at San Francisco Office)

OF COUNSEL

Robert J. Gerst
Judith E. Solomon (Resident at San Diego Office)
Robert J. Enders
James N. Godes
Ingeborg E. Penner (Resident at San Francisco Office)

Paul Gustav Neumann (Resident at San Francisco Office)
Gary D. Koch
Mark E. Reagan (Resident, San Francisco Office)
Elizabeth R. Ison (Resident at Sacramento Office)
Shirley J. Paine
M. Lee Dickinson
Rebecca J. Kurland (At San Francisco and Sacramento Offices)
Thomas A. Bolan
Howard W. Cohen
John Michael Hogan (Resident at San Diego Office)
Jonathon E. Cohn
Steven J. Simerlein (Resident at San Diego Office)
Charles B. Oppenheim
Amy Blumberg Hafey
Rex J. Beaber
Diane Ung
Sandra L. Bierman
Eva Giordano (Resident, San Francisco Office)
Christopher E. Love
Terri L. Wagner
Leila Nourani-Sadjadi
Edwin N. Sasaki
Bret J. Davis
Shana T. Toren
David A. Renas

For full biographical listings, see the Martindale-Hubbell Law Directory

*OAKLAND,** Alameda Co.

HAIMS, JOHNSON, MACGOWAN & MCINERNEY (AV)

490 Grand Avenue, 94610
Telephone: 510-835-0500
Facsimile: 510-835-2833

MEMBERS OF FIRM

Arnold B. Haims
Gary R. Johnson
Clyde L. MacGowan
Thomas McInerney
Lawrence A. Baker
Randy M. Marmor
John K. Kirby
Robert J. Frassetto
Caroline N. Valentino

ASSOCIATES

Joseph Y. Ahn
Edward D. Baldwin
Kathleen B. Boehm
Marc P. Bouret
Anne M. Michaels
Dianne D. Peebles
Michelle D. Perry
Edward C. Schroeder, Jr.

For full biographical listings, see the Martindale-Hubbell Law Directory

PEZZOLA & REINKE, A PROFESSIONAL CORPORATION (AV)

Suite 1300, Lake Merritt Plaza, 1999 Harrison Street, 94612
Telephone: 510-839-1350
Telecopier: 510-834-7440
San Francisco, California Office: 50 California Street, Suite 470. 94111.
Telephone: 415-989-9710.

Stephen P. Pezzola
Donald C. Reinke
Thomas A. Maier
Thomas C. Armstrong
Bruce D. Whitley

(See Next Column)

OF COUNSEL

Robert E. Krebs

LEGAL SUPPORT PERSONNEL

Loretta H. Hintz
Mary A. Fitzpatrick

For full biographical listings, see the Martindale-Hubbell Law Directory

*SACRAMENTO,** Sacramento Co.

MCKINLEY & SMITH (AV)

3425 American River Drive, Suite B, 95864
Telephone: 916-972-1333
Fax: 916-972-1335

William C. McKinley
Timothy M. Smith

For full biographical listings, see the Martindale-Hubbell Law Directory

RICHARD K. TURNER (AV)

555 Capitol Mall, Suite 1500, 95814
Telephone: 916-557-1111

For full biographical listings, see the Martindale-Hubbell Law Directory

WILKE, FLEURY, HOFFELT, GOULD & BIRNEY (AV)

A Partnership including Professional Corporations
400 Capitol Mall, Suite 2200, 95814-4408
Telephone: 916-441-2430
Telefax: 916-442-6664
Mailing Address: P.O. Box 15559, 95852-0559

MEMBERS OF FIRM

Richard H. Hoffelt (Inc.)
William A. Gould, Jr., (Inc.)
Philip R. Birney (Inc.)
Thomas G. Redmon (Inc.)
Scott L. Gassaway
Donald Rex Heckman II (Inc.)
Alan G. Perkins
Bradley N. Webb
Ernest James Krtil
Robert R. Mirkin
Matthew W. Powell
Mark L. Andrews
Stephen K. Marmaduke
David A. Frenznick
John R. Valencia
Angus M. MacLeod

ASSOCIATES

Paul A. Dorris
Kelli M. Kennaday
Tracy S. Hendrickson
Joseph G. De Angelis
Jennifer L. Kennedy
Anthony J. DeCristoforo
Rachel N. Kook
Alicia F. From
Michael Polis
Matthew J. Smith
Wayne L. Ordos

OF COUNSEL

Sherman C. Wilke
Anita Seipp Marmaduke
Benjamin G. Davidian

Representative Clients: NOR-CAL Mutual Insurance Co.; California Optometric Assn.; KPMG Peat Marwick; Glaxo, Inc.

For full biographical listings, see the Martindale-Hubbell Law Directory

*SAN BERNARDINO,** San Bernardino Co.

KASSEL & KASSEL (AV)

A Group of Independent Law Offices
Suite 207, Wells Fargo Bank Building, 334 West Third Street, 92401
Telephone: 909-884-6455
Fax: 909-884-8032

Philip Kassel
Gregory H. Kassel

References: Wells Fargo Bank; Bank of America; Bank of San Bernardino.

For full biographical listings, see the Martindale-Hubbell Law Directory

*SAN DIEGO,** San Diego Co.

LINDLEY, LAZAR & SCALES, A PROFESSIONAL CORPORATION (AV)

One America Plaza, 600 West Broadway, Suite 1400, 92101-3302
Telephone: 619-234-9181
Fax: 619-234-8475

Robert M. McLeod
William E. Johns
Stephen F. Treadgold

Representative Clients: San Diego Hospital Association; San Diego Blood Bank; Donald N. Sharp Memorial Hospital; Sharp Cabrillo Hospital; Sharp Knollwood Convalescent Hospital.

For Complete List of Firm Personnel, See General Section

For full biographical listings, see the Martindale-Hubbell Law Directory

*SAN FRANCISCO,** San Francisco Co.

ERLACH & ERLACH (AV)

4 Embarcadero Center, Seventeenth Floor, 94111
Telephone: 415-788-3322
FAX: 415-788-8613

(See Next Column)

ERLACH & ERLACH, *San Francisco—Continued*

Raymond N. Erlach
Gregory J. Erlach
Stephen Peter U. Erlach

For full biographical listings, see the Martindale-Hubbell Law Directory

FLEISCHMANN & FLEISCHMANN (AV)

650 California Street, Suite 2550, 94108-2606
Telephone: 415-981-0140
FAX: 415-788-6234

MEMBERS OF FIRM

Hartly Fleischmann
Roger Justice Fleischmann
Stella J. Kim
Mark S. Molina

OF COUNSEL

Grace C. Shohet

LEGAL SUPPORT PERSONNEL

Lissa Dirrim

For full biographical listings, see the Martindale-Hubbell Law Directory

STUBBS, HITTIG & LEONE, A PROFESSIONAL CORPORATION (AV)

Suite 818, Fox Plaza, 1390 Market Street, 94102-5399
Telephone: 415-861-8200
Telecopier: 415-861-6700

Gregory E. Stubbs
H. Christopher Hittig
Louis A. Leone

For full biographical listings, see the Martindale-Hubbell Law Directory

*SAN JOSE,** Santa Clara Co.

FERRARI, ALVAREZ, OLSEN & OTTOBONI, A PROFESSIONAL CORPORATION (AV)

333 West Santa Clara Street, Suite 700, 95113
Telephone: 408-280-0535
Fax: 408-280-0151
Palo Alto, California Office: 550 Hamilton Avenue.
Telephone: 415-327-3233.

Clarence J. Ferrari, Jr.
Kent E. Olsen
John M. Ottoboni
Richard S. Bebb
James J. Eller
Robert C. Danneskiold
Terence M. Kane
Emma Peña Madrid
John P. Thurau
Roger D. Wintle
Christopher E. Cobey

Michael D. Brayton
Lisa Intrieri Caputo
Jil Dalesandro
Gregory R. Dietrich
J. Timothy Maximoff
Joseph W. Mell, Jr.
George P. Mulcaire
Eleanor C. Schuermann
Melva M. Vollersen

OF COUNSEL

Edward M. Alvarez

For full biographical listings, see the Martindale-Hubbell Law Directory

COLORADO

*DENVER,** Denver Co.

HOLME ROBERTS & OWEN LLC (AV)

Suite 4100, 1700 Lincoln, 80203
Telephone: 303-861-7000
Telex: 45-4460
Telecopier: 303-866-0200
Boulder, Colorado Office: Suite 400, 1401 Pearl Street.
Telephone: 303-444-5955.
Telecopier: 303-444-1063.
Colorado Springs, Colorado Office: Suite 1300, 90 South Cascade Avenue.
Telephone: 719-473-3800.
Telecopier: 719-633-1518.
Salt Lake City, Utah Office: Suite 1100, 111 East Broadway.
Telephone: 801-521-5800.
Telecopier: 801-521-9639.
London, England Office: 4th Floor, Mellier House, 26a Albemarle Street.
Telephone: 44-171-499-8776.
Telecopier: 44-171-499-7769.
Moscow, Russia Office: 14 Krivokolenny Pr., Suite 30, 101000.
Telephone: 095-925-7816.
Telecopier: 095-923-2726.

(See Next Column)

MEMBERS OF FIRM

Donald J. Hopkins
Richard L. Nagl (Colorado Springs Office)
Nick Nimmo
Steve L. Gaines (Colorado Springs Office)
Robert Craig Ewing
Bruce F. Black
Susan E. Duffey Campbell (Colorado Springs Office)
John R. Wylie (Colorado Springs Office)
Mary L. Groves
Wm. Kelly Nash (Salt Lake City Office)
Thomas M. James (Colorado Springs Office)

OF COUNSEL

Richard L. Schrepferman

SPECIAL COUNSEL

Diane S. Barrett

SENIOR COUNSEL

Mary Hurley Stuart
Kathryn B. Stoker

ASSOCIATES

Timothy G. Pfeifer (Not admitted in CO; Colorado Springs Office)
Gary R. Thorup (Salt Lake City Office)

For Complete List of Firm Personnel, See General Section

For full biographical listings, see the Martindale-Hubbell Law Directory

CONNECTICUT

*HARTFORD,** Hartford Co.

O'BRIEN, TANSKI, TANZER & YOUNG (AV)

Cityplace, 06103-3402
Telephone: 203-525-2700

MEMBERS OF FIRM

Donald W. O'Brien
James M. Tanski
Lois B. Tanzer
Roland F. Young, III
Thomas O. Anderson
Robert E. Kiley
Nancy Phillips Maxwell

ASSOCIATES

Caroline Schnog
Robert D. Silva
Albert G. Danker, Jr.
Kathleen Morrison Grover
P. Jo Anne Burgh
Jennifer L. Cox
Mary R. Knack

References: United Bank & Trust Co.; Connecticut National Bank & Trust Co.

For full biographical listings, see the Martindale-Hubbell Law Directory

*NEW HAVEN,** New Haven Co.

WIGGIN & DANA (AV)

One Century Tower, 06508-1832
Telephone: 203-498-4400
Telefax: 203-782-2889
Hartford, Connecticut Office: One CityPlace.
Telephone: 203-297-3700.
FAX: 203-525-9380.
Stamford, Connecticut Office: Three Stamford Plaza, 301 Tresser Boulevard.
Telephone: 203-363-7600.
Telefax: 203-363-7676.

MEMBERS OF FIRM

John Q. Tilson
J. Michael Eisner
Melinda A. Agsten
Jeanette Carpenter Schreiber
Maureen Weaver

ASSOCIATES

John E. Buerkert, Jr. (Not admitted in CT)
Tanya F. Clark
Michelle Wilcox DeBarge
Alison K. Gilligan (Resident at Hartford)
Merton G. Gollaher
Eric P. Neff (Resident at Hartford)
Susan M. Neilson

For Complete List of Firm Personnel, See General Section

For full biographical listings, see the Martindale-Hubbell Law Directory

STAMFORD, Fairfield Co.

ROSENBLUM & FILAN (AV⊤)

One Landmark Square, 06901
Telephone: 203-358-9200
Fax: 203-969-6140
White Plains, New York Office: 50 Main Street. 10606.
Telephone: 914-686-6100.
Fax: 914-686-6140.

(See Next Column)

ROSENBLUM & FILAN—*Continued*

New York, New York Office: 400 Madison Avenue. 10017.
Telephone: 212-888-8001.
Fax: 212-888-3331.

MEMBERS OF FIRM

Patrick J. Filan
James B. Rosenblum

Jeannine M. Foran
James F. Walsh
Kate E. Maguire
M. Karen Noble
James Newfield

OF COUNSEL

Lee Judy Johnson (Not admitted in CT)
Katherine Benesch (Not admitted in CT)
Theodore J. Greene
Jack L. Most
Richard M. Schwartz (Not admitted in CT)

For full biographical listings, see the Martindale-Hubbell Law Directory

DISTRICT OF COLUMBIA

WASHINGTON, D.C. Co.

* indicates certain Bar Register subscribers, in cities of comparable size and importance, who maintain an additional office in Washington, D.C. and who have arranged for representation as a part of the Washington, D.C. listings that follow

THE FALK LAW FIRM A PROFESSIONAL LIMITED COMPANY (AV)

Suite 260 One Westin Center, 2445 M Street, N.W., 20037
Telephone: 202-833-8700
Telecopier: 202-872-1725

James H. Falk, Sr.
James H. Falk, Jr.
John M. Falk
Rose Burks Emery (Not admitted in DC)
Robert K. Tompkins (Not admitted in DC)

OF COUNSEL

Pierre E. Murphy

For full biographical listings, see the Martindale-Hubbell Law Directory

POWERS, PYLES, SUTTER & VERVILLE, P.C. (AV)

Third Floor, 1275 Pennsylvania Avenue, N.W., 20004
Telephone: 202-466-6550; 296-9243
Fax: 202-785-1756

Galen D. Powers
James C. Pyles
Ronald N. Sutter
Richard E. Verville
Mary Susan Philp
Mark R. Fitzgerald
Thomas K. Hyatt
Robert J. Saner, II
Stanley A. Freeman
Barbara E. Straub

Douglas Benson Tesdahl
Peter W. Thomas
Christopher L. Keough
Ivan J. Wasserman

OF COUNSEL

Bruce R. Hopkins
Jenny Ann Brody
Rebecca L. Burke
Donald W. Aaronson
William G. Beyer (Not admitted in DC)
Joe R. G. Fulcher

For full biographical listings, see the Martindale-Hubbell Law Directory

* **THOMPSON, HINE AND FLORY** (AV)

1920 N Street, N.W., 20036-1601
Telephone: 202-331-8800
Fax: 202-331-8330
Telex: 904173
Cable Address: "Caglaw"
Akron, Ohio Office: 50 S. Main Street, Suite 502, 44308-1828.
Telephone: 216-376-8090.
Fax: 216-376-8386.
Cincinnati, Ohio Office: 312 Walnut Street, 14th Floor, 45202-4029.
Telephone: 513-352-6700.
Fax: 513-241-4771.
Telex: 938003.
Cleveland, Ohio Office: 1100 National City Bank Building, 629 Euclid Avenue, 44114.
Telephone: 216-566-5500.
Fax: 216-566-5583.
Telex: 980217. Cable Address "Thomflor".
Columbus, Ohio Office: One Columbus, 10 West Broad Street, 43215-34353.
Telephone: 614-469-3200.
Fax: 614-469-3361.

(See Next Column)

Dayton, Ohio Office: 2000 Courthouse Plaza, N.E., 45402-1706.
Telephone: 513-443-6600.
Fax: 513-443-6637, 513-443-6635.
Palm Beach, Florida Office: 125 Worth Avenue, 33480-4466.
Telephone: 407-833-5900.
Fax: 407-833-5951.
Brussels, Belgium Office: Rue Des Chevaliers, Ridderstraat 14 - B.10, B-1050.
Telephone: 011-32-2-511-9326.
Fax: 011-32-2-513-9206.

MEMBERS OF FIRM

Steven D. Cundra
Norman J. Philion, III

For Complete List of Firm Personnel, See General Section

For full biographical listings, see the Martindale-Hubbell Law Directory

* **VENABLE, BAETJER, HOWARD & CIVILETTI** (AV)

A Partnership including Professional Corporations
Suite 1000, 1201 New York Avenue, N.W., 20005
Telephone: 202-962-4800
Fax: 202-962-8300
Baltimore, Maryland Office: Venable, Baetjer and Howard, 1800 Mercantile Bank & Trust Building, 2 Hopkins Plaza.
Telephone: 410-244-7400.
McLean, Virginia Office: Venable, Baetjer and Howard, Suite 400, 2010 Corporate Ridge.
Telephone: 703-760-1600.
Rockville, Maryland Office: Venable, Baetjer and Howard, Suite 500, One Church Street, P. O. Box 1906.
Telephone: 301-217-5600.
Towson, Maryland Office: Venable, Baetjer and Howard, 210 Allegheny Avenue, P. O. Box 5517.
Telephone: 410-494-6200.

MEMBERS OF FIRM

Benjamin R. Civiletti (P.C.) (Also at Baltimore and Towson, Maryland Offices)
Thomas J. Kenney, Jr. (P.C.) (Not admitted in DC)
Kenneth C. Bass, III (Also at McLean, Virginia Office)
Robert G. Ames (Also at Baltimore, Maryland Office)
James K. Archibald (Also at Baltimore and Towson, Maryland Offices)
Jeffrey A. Dunn (Also at Baltimore, Maryland Office)
George F. Pappas (Also at Baltimore, Maryland Office)
James L. Shea (Not admitted in DC; also at Baltimore, Maryland Office)
Amy Berman Jackson
William D. Quarles (Also at Towson, Maryland Office)
James A. Dunbar (Also at Baltimore, Maryland Office)
Mary E. Pivec (Not admitted in DC; Also at Baltimore, Maryland Office)

OF COUNSEL

Geoffrey R. Garinther (Not admitted in DC; Also at Baltimore, Maryland Office)

ASSOCIATE

David W. Goewey

For Complete List of Firm Personnel, See General Section

For full biographical listings, see the Martindale-Hubbell Law Directory

FLORIDA

*MIAMI,** Dade Co.

SPARBER, KOSNITZKY, TRUXTON, DE LA GUARDIA SPRATT & BROOKS, P.A. (AV)

1401 Brickell Avenue Suite 700, 33131
Telephone: Dade: 305-379-7200; Broward: 305-760-9133
Fax: 305-379-0800

Michael Kosnitzky
William J. Spratt, Jr.
Marc H. Auerbach
Louise T. Jeroslow

Martin B. Kofsky

For Complete List of Firm Personnel, See General Section

For full biographical listings, see the Martindale-Hubbell Law Directory

*ORLANDO,** Orange Co.

BOBO, SPICER, CIOTOLI, FULFORD, BOCCHINO, DEBEVOISE & LE CLAINCHE, P.A. (AV)

Landmark Center One, Suite 510, 315 East Robinson Street, 32801-1949
Telephone: 407-849-1060
Fax: 407-843-4751
West Palm Beach, Florida Office: Esperante, Sixth Floor, 222 Lakeview Avenue, 33401.
Telephone: 407-684-6600.
FAX: 407-684-3828.

John W. Bocchino
D. Andrew DeBevoise

Christopher C. Curry
Robert R. Saunders
Keith A. Scott
J. Clancey Bounds
Sharon A. Chapman
Sophia B. Ehringer
Tyler S. McClay

For full biographical listings, see the Martindale-Hubbell Law Directory

*TALLAHASSEE,** Leon Co.

MCFARLAIN, WILEY, CASSEDY & JONES, PROFESSIONAL ASSOCIATION (AV)

215 South Monroe Street, Suite 600, P.O. Box 2174, 32316-2174
Telephone: 904-222-2107
Telecopier: 904-222-8475

Richard C. McFarlain
William B. Wiley
Marshall R. Cassedy
Douglas P. Jones
Charles A. Stampelos
Linda McMullen
H. Darrell White, Jr.
Christopher Barkas

Harold R. Mardenborough, Jr.
Katherine Hairston LaRosa
J. Robert Griffin

OF COUNSEL

Betty J. Steffens

For full biographical listings, see the Martindale-Hubbell Law Directory

RADEY HINKLE THOMAS & MCARTHUR (AV)

Suite 1000 Monroe-Park Tower, 101 North Monroe Street, P.O. Drawer 11307, 32302
Telephone: 904-681-7766
Telecopier: 904-681-0506

John Radey
Robert L. Hinkle
Harry O. Thomas
Elizabeth Waas McArthur
Jeffrey L. Frehn

Representative Clients: Johnson & Johnson; Columbia/HCA Healthcare Corp.; Tallahassee Community Hospital; Tampa General Hospital; Central Florida Regional Hospital; Lawnwood Regional Medical Center; Anesthesiology Associates of Tallahassee.

For Complete List of Firm Personnel, See General Section

For full biographical listings, see the Martindale-Hubbell Law Directory

ROSE, SUNDSTROM & BENTLEY (AV)

A Partnership including Professional Associations
2548 Blairstone Pines Drive, P.O. Box 1567, 32302-1567
Telephone: 904-877-6555
Telecopier: 904-656-4029

MEMBERS OF FIRM

Chris H. Bentley (P.A.)
Diane D. Tremor (P.A.)
John L. Wharton

Representative Clients: Arbor Health Care Co.; Bethesda Memorial Hospital; Skilled Health Facilities, Ltd.
Reference: Barnett Bank, Tallahassee.

For full biographical listings, see the Martindale-Hubbell Law Directory

*TAMPA,** Hillsborough Co.

BUCHANAN INGERSOLL, PROFESSIONAL CORPORATION (AV)

Suite 1030, 101 East Kennedy Boulevard, 33602
Telephone: 813-222-8180
Telecopier: 813-222-8189
Pittsburgh, Pennsylvania Office: 5800 USX Tower, 600 Grant Street.
Telephone: 412-562-8800.
Philadelphia, Pennsylvania Office: Two Logan Square, Twelfth Floor, 18th & Arch Streets.
Telephone: 215-665-8700.
Harrisburg, Pennsylvania Office: Vartan Parc, 30 North Third Street.
Telephone: 717-237-4800.
North Miami Beach, Florida Office: 19495 Biscayne Boulevard.
Telephone: 305-933-5600.

(See Next Column)

Princeton, New Jersey Office: Buchanan Ingersoll, A Partnership, College Centre, 500 College Road East.
Telephone: 609-452-2666.
Lexington, Kentucky Office: Suite 600, PNC Bank Plaza, 200 West Vine Street.
Telephone: 606-225-5333.

James J. Kennedy III

For Complete List of Firm Personnel, See General Section

For full biographical listings, see the Martindale-Hubbell Law Directory

*WEST PALM BEACH,** Palm Beach Co.

BOBO, SPICER, CIOTOLI, FULFORD, BOCCHINO, DEBEVOISE & LE CLAINCHE, P.A. (AV)

Esperante, Sixth Floor, 222 Lakeview Avenue, 33401
Telephone: 407-684-6600
Fax: 407-684-3828
Orlando, Florida Office: Landmark Center One, Suite 510, 315 East Robinson Street, 32801-1949.
Telephone: 407-849-1060.
Fax: 407-843-4751.

A. Russell Bobo
David W. Spicer
Eugene L. Ciotoli
Jeffrey C. Fulford
John W. Bocchino (Resident, Orlando Office)
D. Andrew DeBevoise (Resident, Orlando Office)
Stephan A. Le Clainche

Christopher C. Curry (Resident, Orlando Office)
Patti A. Haber
Paul A. Nugent
Joseph A. Osborne
Richard B. Schwamm
Michael S. Smith
Paul M. Adams
Robert A. Zimmerman
Neil A. Deleon
Sharon A. Chapman (Resident, Orlando Office)
J. Clancey Bounds (Resident, Orlando Office)
Robert R. Saunders (Resident, Orlando Office)
Keith A. Scott (Resident, Orlando Office)
Sophia B. Ehringer (Resident, Orlando Office)
Tyler S. McClay (Resident, Orlando Office)
Michael D. Burt
Dominic John "Jack" Scalera, III
Casey D. Shomo
Armando T. Lauritano

For full biographical listings, see the Martindale-Hubbell Law Directory

WINTER PARK, Orange Co.

KENNETH E. BROOTEN, JR. CHARTERED (AV)

631 West Fairbanks Avenue, 32789
Telephone: 407-645-4447
Fax: 407-628-2220

Kenneth E. Brooten, Jr.

For full biographical listings, see the Martindale-Hubbell Law Directory

GEORGIA

*ATLANTA,** Fulton Co.

GOLDNER, SOMMERS, SCRUDDER & BASS (AV)

2839 Paces Ferry Road, Suite 800, 30339-3774
Telephone: 404-436-4777
Facsimile: 404-436-8777

Stephen L. Goldner
Susan V. Sommers

For Complete List of Firm Personnel, See General Section

For full biographical listings, see the Martindale-Hubbell Law Directory

HOLT, NEY, ZATCOFF & WASSERMAN (AV)

A Partnership including Professional Corporations
100 Galleria Parkway, Suite 600, 30339
Telephone: 404-956-9600
Facsimile Number: 404-956-1490

MEMBERS OF FIRM

Michael G. Wasserman (P.C.)
Charles D. Vaughn

Representative Clients: AmeriHealth, Inc.; Pathology Institute of Middle Georgia, P.C.

For Complete List of Firm Personnel, See General Section

For full biographical listings, see the Martindale-Hubbell Law Directory

Atlanta—Continued

JAMES P. KELLY & ASSOCIATES, P.C. (AV)
200 Galleria Parkway, Suite 1510, 30339
Telephone: 404-955-2770
Telecopier: 404-859-0831

James P. Kelly
Robert E. DeWitt
H. Carol Saul

For full biographical listings, see the Martindale-Hubbell Law Directory

LONG ALDRIDGE & NORMAN (AV)
A Partnership including Professional Corporations
One Peachtree Center, Suite 5300, 303 Peachtree Street, 30308
Telephone: 404-527-4000
Telecopier: 404-527-4198
Washington, D.C. Office: Suite 950, 1615 L Street, 20036.
Telephone: 202-223-7033.
Telecopier: 202-223-7013.

MEMBERS OF FIRM

Stanley S. Jones, Jr.
Mark S. Lange
Philip H. Moise
John E. Ramsey
Russell N. Sewell, Jr.

ASSOCIATE

John Warner Ray, Jr.

OF COUNSEL

Martin R. Tilson, Jr.

For Complete List of Firm Personnel, See General Section
For full biographical listings, see the Martindale-Hubbell Law Directory

PARKER, HUDSON, RAINER & DOBBS (AV)
1500 Marquis Two Tower, 285 Peachtree Center Avenue, N.E., 30303
Telephone: 404-523-5300
FAX: 404-522-8409
Tallahassee, Florida Office: The Perkins House, 118 North Gadsden Street, 32301.
Telephone: 904-681-0191.
FAX: 904-681-9493.

MEMBERS OF FIRM

John H. Parker, Jr.
Paul L. Hudson, Jr.
Robert A. Weiss (Not admitted in GA; Resident, Tallahassee, Florida Office)
Jonathan L. Rue
David G. Cleveland
Theodore N. McDowell, Jr.

For full biographical listings, see the Martindale-Hubbell Law Directory

LAW OFFICES OF J. WAYNE PIERCE, P.A. (AV)
Two Paces West, Suite 1700 4000 Cumberland Parkway, 30339
Telephone: 404-435-0500
Telecopier: 404-435-0362

J. Wayne Pierce

Dargan Scott Cole
Thomas L. Schaefer

For full biographical listings, see the Martindale-Hubbell Law Directory

SULLIVAN, HALL, BOOTH & SMITH, A PROFESSIONAL CORPORATION (AV)
One Midtown Plaza, 1360 Peachtree Street, N.E., Suite 800, 30309
Telephone: 404-870-8000
FAX: 404-870-8020

Terrance C. Sullivan
John E. Hall, Jr.
Alexander H. Booth
Rush S. Smith, Jr.
Henry D. Green, Jr.
Jack G. Slover, Jr.
Timothy H. Bendin
Michael A. Pannier
Brynda Sue Rodriguez
Roger S. Sumrall

David V. Johnson
Jeffrey T. Wise
Eleanor L. Martel
A. Spencer McManes, Jr.
David G. Goodchild, Jr.
Robert L. Shannon, Jr.
T. Andrew Graham
Earnest Redwine
Melanie P. Simon (Not admitted in GA)

Reference: Wachovia Bank of Georgia.

For full biographical listings, see the Martindale-Hubbell Law Directory

SUMNER & HEWES (AV)
Suite 700, The Hurt Building, 50 Hurt Plaza, 30303
Telephone: 404-588-9000

PARTNERS

William E. Sumner
Nancy Becker Hewes
Stephen J. Anderson
David A. Webster

(See Next Column)

ASSOCIATES

Rosemary Smith
Andrew A. Davenport
Marguerite Patrick Bryan
Michelle Harris Jordan
Edith M. Shine

For full biographical listings, see the Martindale-Hubbell Law Directory

SUTHERLAND, ASBILL & BRENNAN (AV)
999 Peachtree Street, N.E., 30309-3996
Telephone: 404-853-8000
Facsimile: 404-853-8806
Washington, D.C. Office: 1275 Pennsylvania Avenue, N.W., 20004-2404.
Telephone: 202-383-0100.
New York, N.Y. Office: 1270 Avenue of the Americas, 10020-1700.
Telephone: 212-332-3000.
Austin, Texas Office: 111 Congress Avenue, 23rd Floor, 78701-4079.
Telephone: 512-469-3350.

Katherine Meyers Cohen
James K. Hasson, Jr.
James R. McGibbon
Richard L. Robbins

For Complete List of Firm Personnel, See General Section
For full biographical listings, see the Martindale-Hubbell Law Directory

*CARROLLTON,** Carroll Co.

TISINGER, TISINGER, VANCE & GREER, A PROFESSIONAL CORPORATION (AV)
100 Wagon Yard Plaza, P.O. Box 2069, 30117
Telephone: 404-834-4467
FAX: 404-834-5426

J. Thomas Vance
Steven T. Minor

Representative Clients: Tanner Medical Center, Inc.; Carroll City-County Hospital Authority; Heard County Hospital Authority.

For Complete List of Firm Personnel, See General Section
For full biographical listings, see the Martindale-Hubbell Law Directory

*MACON,** Bibb Co.

SELL & MELTON (AV)
A Partnership including a Professional Corporation
14th Floor, Charter Medical Building, P.O. Box 229, 31297-2899
Telephone: 912-746-8521
Telecopier: 912-745-6426

John D. Comer

ASSOCIATE

Jeffrey B. Hanson

General Counsel for: Macon Telegraph Publishing Co. (The Macon Telegraph); Macon-Bibb County Hospital Authority; County of Bibb; County of Twiggs; Smith & Sons Foods, Inc. (S & S Cafeterias); Macon Bibb County Industrial Authority; Burgess Pigment Co.

For Complete List of Firm Personnel, See General Section
For full biographical listings, see the Martindale-Hubbell Law Directory

HAWAII

*HONOLULU,** Honolulu Co.

DWYER IMANAKA SCHRAFF KUDO MEYER & FUJIMOTO ATTORNEYS AT LAW, A LAW CORPORATION (AV)
1800 Pioneer Plaza, 900 Fort Street Mall, 96813
Telephone: 808-524-8000
Telecopier: 808-526-1419
Mailing Address: P.O. Box 2727, 96803

John R. Dwyer, Jr.
Mitchell A. Imanaka
Paul A. Schraff
Benjamin A. Kudo (Atty. at Law, A Law Corp.)
William G. Meyer, III
Wesley M. Fujimoto
Ronald Van Grant
Jon M. H. Pang
Blake W. Bushnell
Kenn N. Kojima

Adelbert Green
Richard T. Asato, Jr.
Scott W. Settle
Darcie S. Yoshinaga
Tracy Timothy Woo
Lawrence I. Kawasaki
Douglas H. Inouye
Christine A. Low

OF COUNSEL

Randall Y. Iwase

For full biographical listings, see the Martindale-Hubbell Law Directory

Honolulu—Continued

Law Office of Kenneth S. Robbins Attorney at Law, A Law Corporation (AV)

Suite 2220 Davies Pacific Center, 841 Bishop Street, 96813
Telephone: 808-524-2355
Fax: 808-526-0290

Kenneth S. Robbins

Vincent A. Rhodes
Shinken Naitoh

For full biographical listings, see the Martindale-Hubbell Law Directory

IDAHO

*BOISE,** Ada Co.

Hall, Farley, Oberrecht & Blanton (AV)

Key Financial Center, 702 West Idaho Street, Suite 700, P.O. Box 1271, 83701-1271
Telephone: 208-336-0404
Facsimile: 208-336-5193

Richard E. Hall
Donald J. Farley
Phillip S. Oberrecht
Raymond D. Powers
Candy Wagahoff Dale
Robert B. Luce
J. Kevin West
Bart W. Harwood

J. Charles Blanton
John J. Burke
Steven J. Hippler
Thorpe P. Orton
Ronald S. Best (Not admitted in ID)

References: Boise State University; Farm Bureau Mutual Insurance Company of Idaho; Medical Insurance Exchange of California; The St. Paul Cos.

For full biographical listings, see the Martindale-Hubbell Law Directory

*POCATELLO,** Bannock Co.

Merrill & Merrill, Chartered (AV)

Key Bank Building, P.O. Box 991, 83204
Telephone: 208-232-2286
Fax: 208-232-2499

D. Russell Wight

Representative Clients: Bannock Regional Medical Center.

For Complete List of Firm Personnel, See General Section

For full biographical listings, see the Martindale-Hubbell Law Directory

ILLINOIS

*CHICAGO,** Cook Co.

Bell, Boyd & Lloyd (AV)

Three First National Plaza Suite 3300, 70 West Madison Street, 60602
Telephone: 312-372-1121
FAX: 312-372-2098
Washington, D.C. Office: 1615 L Street, N.W.
Telephone: 202-466-6300.
FAX: 202-463-0678.

MEMBERS OF FIRM

Lee A. Daniels
Raymond H. Drymalski
Thomas C. Shields

For Complete List of Firm Personnel, See General Section

For full biographical listings, see the Martindale-Hubbell Law Directory

Chuhak & Tecson, P.C. (AV)

225 West Washington Street, Suite 1300, 60606
Telephone: 312-444-9300
FAX: 312-444-9027

Thomas S. Chuhak
Joseph A. Tecson
John Laurence Kienlen
Barry A. Feinberg
Albert L. Grasso
Andrew P. Tecson
Donald J. Russ, Jr.
Edwin I. Josephson
Cary S. Fleischer
Stephen M. Margolin
John P. Fadden
Dennis A. Ferraro
Ricky L. Hammond
Arnold E. Karolewski
James W. Naisbitt
Alan R. Dolinko
Don M. Sowers, Jr.

(See Next Column)

John P. Adams
Thomas F. Bennington, Jr.
Barbara Chuhak Bernau
Barbara A. Cronin
John M. Foley
Stephen A. Glickman
Jeffrey A. Kerensky
Karen S. Kogachi
Raymond S. Makowski
John F. Mahoney
Michael B. McVickar
Laurie A. Pegler
Shawn P. Ryan
Stacy E. Singer
Mitchell D. Weinstein
Michael D. Weis

OF COUNSEL

Lawrence E. Glick
Joseph O. Rubinelli

LEGAL SUPPORT PERSONNEL

William J. Kreft

For full biographical listings, see the Martindale-Hubbell Law Directory

Douglas L. Elden & Associates (AV)

150 North Michigan Avenue, 30th Floor, 60601-7567
Telephone: 312-781-3600
FAX: 312-781-3601

ASSOCIATE

Robbin C. Elden

OF COUNSEL

Charles M. Jacobs
Susan Weagly

For full biographical listings, see the Martindale-Hubbell Law Directory

Pretzel & Stouffer, Chartered (AV)

One South Wacker Drive Suite 2500, 60606-4673
Telephone: 312-346-1973
FAX: 312-346-8242; 346-8060

Richard L. Berdelle
Paula Meyer Besler
William B. Bower
Michael G. Bruton
Maryanne H. Capron
Robert Marc Chemers
Elizabeth Conkin
Jeffery W. Davis
Marilyn Brock Doig
Joseph M. Dooley, III
Matthew J. Egan
Sally Oxley Hagerty
Brian T. Henry
William E. Kenny
James A. LaBarge
Steven M. Laduzinsky
Donald B. Lenderman
David J. Loughnane
Patrick Foran Lustig
Daniel B. Mills
Edward H. Nielsen
Donald J. O'Meara, Jr.
Molly M. O'Reilly
Gary Arthur Peters
Paul L. Price
Neil K. Quinn
Charles F. Redden
Lynn M. Reid
Catherine Coyne Reiter
Mark D. Roth
Edward B. Ruff, III
Betty-Jane Schrum
Alan J. Schumacher
Peter G. Skiko
John V. Smith, II
Christine Hough Speranza
Mark P. Standa
Leo M. Tarpey, Jr.
Anthony J. Tunney
Stephen C. Veltman
John J. Walsh, III
Richard M. Waris
Timothy A. Weaver

Representative Clients: Allstate Insurance Co.; St. Paul Insurance Companies.

For Complete List of Firm Personnel, See General Section

For full biographical listings, see the Martindale-Hubbell Law Directory

EVANSTON, Cook Co.

Atkinson & Atkinson (AV)

1603 Orrington Avenue, Suite 2080, 60201
Telephone: 708-864-0070
Facsimile: 708-864-0588

MEMBERS OF FIRM

John F. Atkinson
Dale J. Atkinson

ASSOCIATE

David C. Thollander

A list of Representative Clients will be furnished upon request.

For full biographical listings, see the Martindale-Hubbell Law Directory

*KANKAKEE,** Kankakee Co.

Blanke, Norden, Barmann, Kramer & Bohlen, P.C. (AV)

Suite 502, 200 East Court Street, P.O. Box 1787, 60901
Telephone: 815-939-1133
FAX: 815-939-0994

Armen R. Blanke (Deceased)
Paul F. Blanke (Retired)
Dennis A. Norden
Glen R. Barmann
Christopher W. Bohlen
Michael D. Kramer

For full biographical listings, see the Martindale-Hubbell Law Directory

INDIANA

*BLOOMINGTON,** Monroe Co.

BUNGER & ROBERTSON (AV)

226 South College Square, P.O. Box 910, 47402-0910
Telephone: 812-332-9295
Fax: 812-331-8808

MEMBERS OF FIRM

Len E. Bunger, Jr. (1921-1993)
Don M. Robertson
Thomas Bunger
Joseph D. O'Connor III
James L. Whitlatch
Samuel R. Ardery

ASSOCIATES

Margaret M. Frisbie
William J. Beggs
John W. Richards

OF COUNSEL

Philip C. Hill

Representative Clients: Bloomington Hospital, Inc.; Bloomington Convalescent Center; Nurse Call Plus; Hospice of Bloomington; Phico Insurance, Co.; Medical Protective Insurance Co.; Children's Organ Transplant Association.

For full biographical listings, see the Martindale-Hubbell Law Directory

*COLUMBUS,** Bartholomew Co.

JONES PATTERSON BOLL & TUCKER, PROFESSIONAL CORPORATION (AV)

330 Franklin Street, P.O. Box 67, 47202
Telephone: 812-376-8266
Fax: 812-376-0981

Harold V. Jones, Jr.
Cynthia A. Boll

For Complete List of Firm Personnel, See General Section

For full biographical listings, see the Martindale-Hubbell Law Directory

*EVANSVILLE,** Vanderburgh Co.

FINE & HATFIELD (AV)

520 N.W. Second Street, P.O. Box 779, 47705-0779
Telephone: 812-425-3592
Telecopier: 812-421-4269

MEMBERS OF FIRM

Thomas R. Fitzsimmons
Stephen S. Lavallo

ASSOCIATE

Shannon Scholz Frank

For Complete List of Firm Personnel, See General Section

For full biographical listings, see the Martindale-Hubbell Law Directory

KAHN, DEES, DONOVAN & KAHN (AV)

P.O. Box 3646, 47735-3646
Telephone: 812-423-3183
Fax: 812-423-3841

MEMBERS OF FIRM

Alan N. Shovers
Thomas O. Magan
Larry R. Downs
G. Michael Schopmeyer
John E. Hegeman
Jeffrey K. Helfrich

ASSOCIATE

Kent A. Brasseale, II

Counsel for: Deaconess Hospital, Inc.; Wabash General Hospital; Welborn Baptist Hospital; St. Mary's Medical Center of Evansville, Inc.; St. Anthony's Medical Center; The Rehabilitation Center.

For Complete List of Firm Personnel, See General Section

For full biographical listings, see the Martindale-Hubbell Law Directory

STATHAM, JOHNSON & MCCRAY (AV)

215 North West Martin Luther King Jr. Boulevard, P.O. Box 3567, 47734-3567
Telephone: 812-425-5223
Facsimile: 812-421-4238

MEMBERS OF FIRM

William E. Statham
Thomas J. Kimpel

ASSOCIATES

Thomas P. Norton
Keith E. Rounder

Representative Clients: Welborn Memorial Baptist Hospital, Inc.; Medical Center of Southern Indiana; Tri-State Rehabilitation Hospital; Visiting Nurse Association of Southwestern Indiana, Inc.

For Complete List of Firm Personnel, See General Section

For full biographical listings, see the Martindale-Hubbell Law Directory

ZIEMER, STAYMAN, WEITZEL & SHOULDERS (AV)

(Formerly Early, Arnold & Ziemer)
1507 Old National Bank Building, P.O. Box 916, 47706
Telephone: 812-424-7575
Telecopier: 812-421-5089

MEMBERS OF FIRM

Ted C. Ziemer, Jr.
Patrick A. Shoulders
Gregory G. Meyer

ASSOCIATES

Rebecca T. Kasha
Gary K. Price
Robert L. Burkart

Reference: Old National Bank in Evansville.

For full biographical listings, see the Martindale-Hubbell Law Directory

GREENWOOD, Johnson Co.

VAN VALER WILLIAMS & HEWITT (AV)

Suite 400 National City Bank Building, 300 South Madison Avenue, P.O. Box 405, 46142
Telephone: 317-888-1121
Fax: 317-887-4069

MEMBERS OF FIRM

Joe N. Van Valer
Jon E. Williams
Brian C. Hewitt

ASSOCIATES

J. Lee Robbins
William M. Waltz
John M. White
Kim Van Valer Shilts
Mark E. Need

For full biographical listings, see the Martindale-Hubbell Law Directory

HAMMOND, Lake Co.

GALVIN, GALVIN & LEENEY (AV)

5231 Hohman Avenue, 46320
Telephone: 219-933-0380
Fax: 219-933-0471

MEMBERS OF FIRM

Edmond J. Leeney (1897-1978)
Timothy P. Galvin, Sr. (1894-1993)
Francis J. Galvin, Sr. (Retired)
Carl N. Carpenter
John E. Chevigny
Timothy P. Galvin, Jr.
Patrick J. Galvin
W. Patrick Downes

Brian L. Goins
William G. Crabtree II
John H. Lloyd, IV

Attorneys for: Mercantile National Bank of Indiana; Citizens Financial Services, F.S.B.; State Farm Insurance Co.; Auto Owners Insurance Co.; CIGNA; Armco, Inc.; St. Margaret Mercy Healthcare Centers, Inc.; St. Anthony Hospital and Health Centers (Michigan City); Calumet Council, Inc., Boy Scouts of America; Chicago Title Insurance Company.

For full biographical listings, see the Martindale-Hubbell Law Directory

*INDIANAPOLIS,** Marion Co.

HALL, RENDER, KILLIAN, HEATH & LYMAN, PROFESSIONAL CORPORATION (AV)

Suite 2000, One American Square Box 82064, 46282
Telephone: 317-633-4884
Telecopier: 317-633-4878
North Office: Suite 820, 8402 Harcourt Road, 46260.
Telephone: 317-871-6222.

William S. Hall
John C. Render
Rex P. Killian
R. Terry Heath
Stephen W. Lyman
L. Richard Gohman
Jeffrey Peek
Clifford A. Beyler
Joseph R. Impicciche
Timothy C. Lawson
Douglas P. Long
William H. Thompson
Timothy W. Kennedy
Steven H. Pratt
N. Kent Smith
Maureen O'Brien Griffin
Robert A. Hicks
Mary C. Gaughan
Fred J. Bachmann
Kevin P. Speer
Greta E. Gerberding
Doreen Denega
Jeffrey W. Short
Gregory W. Moore
John C. Meade
Jill Workman Martin
Clifton E. Johnson
Christine B. Zoccola
Martha B. Wentworth
Richard W. McMinn
Rebekah N. Murphy
Michael B. McMains
Todd J. Selby
Gregg M. Wallander
J. Scott Waters, IV
James B. Hogan
Donald R. Russell

Representative Clients: St. Vincent Hospital and Health Care Center, Inc.; Indiana Hospital Association; Indiana University Medical Center; St. Joseph Medical Center of Fort Wayne; Methodist Hospitals-Gary, Indiana; Caremet, Inc.; Sagamore Health Network; Memorial Hospital of South Bend; Good Samaritan Hospital.

For full biographical listings, see the Martindale-Hubbell Law Directory

ICE MILLER DONADIO & RYAN (AV)

One American Square Box 82001, 46282-0002
Telephone: 317-236-2100
Fax: 317-236-2219

MEMBERS OF FIRM

Gregory L. Pemberton
L. Alan Whaley

ASSOCIATE

Sherry A. Fabina-Abney

For Complete List of Firm Personnel, See General Section

For full biographical listings, see the Martindale-Hubbell Law Directory

JOHNSON, SMITH, DENSBORN, WRIGHT & HEATH (AV)

One Indiana Square Suite 1800, 46204
Telephone: 317-634-9777
Telecopier: 317-636-9061

MEMBERS OF FIRM

John F. Joyce (1948-1994)
Wayne O. Adams, III
Robert M. Baker, III
Thomas A. Barnard
David J. Carr
Peter D. Cleveland
David R. Day
Donald K. Densborn
Thomas N. Eckerle
Mark W. Ford
G. Ronald Heath
Robert B. Hebert
John David Hoover
Andrew W. Hull
Dennis A. Johnson
Richard L. Johnson
Michael J. Kaye
John R. Kirkwood
David Williams Russell
James T. Smith
Martha Taylor Starkey
David E. Wright

ASSOCIATES

Robert C. Wolf (1949-1993)
Carolyn H. Andretti
Maureen F. Barnard
David G. Blachly
Robert T. Buday
Sean Michael Clapp
Jeffrey S. Cohen
Charles M. Freeland
David W. Givens, Jr.
Gary P. Goodin
Patricia L. Marshall
Bradley C. Morris
Steven J. Moss
Padric K. J. O'Brien
Cathleen J. Perry
David D. Robinson
Ronald G. Sentman
David A. Tucker
Sally Franklin Zweig

OF COUNSEL

Earl Auberry (1923-1989)
Larry A. Conrad (1935-1990)
Bruce W. Claycombe
Laura S. Cohen
Paul D. Gresk
William T. Lawrence
Mark A. Palmer
Lawrence W. Schmits
Catherine A. Singleton

For full biographical listings, see the Martindale-Hubbell Law Directory

LOCKE REYNOLDS BOYD & WEISELL (AV)

1000 Capital Center South, 201 North Illinois Street, 46204
Telephone: 317-237-3800
Telecopier: 317-237-3900

Glenn T. Troyer
Michael T. Bindner
David E. Jose
Thomas W. Farlow

Peter H. Pogue
James O. Waanders

Representative Clients: Carmel Health Care Management, Inc.; Caylor-Nickel, P.C.; Evergreen Healthcare, Ltd.; G.U. Surgeons of Indiana, Inc.; Memorial Hospital of Michigan City; Michiana Community Hospital; St. Francis Hospital Center; St. Joseph Hospital of Huntingburg; Southern Indiana Radiological Associates, Inc.; Tri-County Community Mental Health Center.

For Complete List of Firm Personnel, See General Section

For full biographical listings, see the Martindale-Hubbell Law Directory

MCCLURE, MCCLURE & KAMMEN (AV)

235 North Delaware, 46204
Telephone: 317-236-0400
Telecopier: 317-236-0404

MEMBERS OF FIRM

Richard Kammen
Susan W. Brooks

Reference: Indiana National Bank.

For full biographical listings, see the Martindale-Hubbell Law Directory

MCNAMAR, FEARNOW & MCSHARAR, P.C. (AV)

Bank One Center Tower, 111 Monument Circle, Suite 4500, 46204-5145
Telephone: 317-630-4500
Fax: 317-630-4501

(See Next Column)

David F. McNamar
Randall R. Fearnow
Janet A. McSharar
Alastair J. Warr

For full biographical listings, see the Martindale-Hubbell Law Directory

MERRILLVILLE, Lake Co.

HODGES & DAVIS, P.C. (AV)

5525 Broadway, 46410
Telephone: 219-981-2557
Fax: 219-980-7090
Portage, Indiana Office: 6508 U.S. Highway 6.
Telephone: 219-762-9129.
Fax: 219-762-2826.

Clyde D. Compton
William B. Davis
Earle F. Hites
R. Lawrence Steele
Gregory A. Sobkowski
Bonnie C. Coleman
Jill M. Madajczyk
Laura B. Brown
David H. Kreider

OF COUNSEL

Edward J. Hussey

Representative Clients: The Methodist Hospitals, Inc.; Clinipath Laboratories, Inc.; Lincolnshire Health Center; The Lutheran Retirement Home of Northwest Indiana; Geminus Corp.; Porter-Starke Services, Inc.; Visiting Nurse Association of Northwest Indiana, Inc.; Visiting Nurse Association of Porter County, Indiana, Inc.

For Complete List of Firm Personnel, See General Section

For full biographical listings, see the Martindale-Hubbell Law Directory

PORTAGE, Porter Co.

HODGES & DAVIS, P.C. (AV)

6508 U.S. Highway 6, 46368
Telephone: 219-762-9129
Fax: 219-762-2826
Merrillville, Indiana Office: 5525 Broadway.
Telephone: 219-981-2557.
Fax: 219-980-7090.

Clyde D. Compton
Earle F. Hites
R. Lawrence Steele
Gregory A. Sobkowski
Bonnie C. Coleman

Representative Clients: The Methodist Hospitals, Inc.; Clinipath Laboratories, Inc.; Lincolnshire Health Center; The Lutheran Retirement Home of Northwest, Indiana; Geminus Corp.; Porter-Starke Services, Inc.; Visiting Nurse Association of Northwest Indiana, Inc.; Visiting Nurse Association of Porter County, Indiana, Inc.

For full biographical listings, see the Martindale-Hubbell Law Directory

*SOUTH BEND,** St. Joseph Co.

JONES, OBENCHAIN, FORD, PANKOW, LEWIS & WOODS (AV)

1800 Valley American Bank Building, P.O. Box 4577, 46634
Telephone: 219-233-1194
Fax: 233-8957; 233-9675

Vitus G. Jones (1879-1951)
Roland Obenchain (1890-1961)
Francis Jones (1907-1988)
Roland Obenchain (Retired)
Milton A. Johnson (Retired)

MEMBERS OF FIRM

James H. Pankow
Thomas F. Lewis, Jr.
Timothy W. Woods
John R. Obenchain
Robert W. Mysliwiec
Robert M. Edwards, Jr.
John B. Ford
Mark J. Phillipoff
John W. Van Laere

ASSOCIATES

Patrick D. Murphy
Edward P. Benchik
Wendell G. Davis, Jr.

OF COUNSEL

G. Burt Ford

Representative Clients: Saint Joseph's Medical Center; Holy Cross Health Systems; Healthwin Hospital; St. Joseph's Care Group.

For full biographical listings, see the Martindale-Hubbell Law Directory

*TERRE HAUTE,** Vigo Co.

WILKINSON, GOELLER, MODESITT, WILKINSON & DRUMMY (AV)

333 Ohio Street, P.O. Box 800, 47808-0800
Telephone: 812-232-4311
Fax: 812-235-5107

(See Next Column)

WILKINSON, GOELLER, MODESITT, WILKINSON & DRUMMY—*Continued*

MEMBERS OF FIRM

Myrl O. Wilkinson
David H. Goeller
Raymond H. Modesitt
B. Curtis Wilkinson
William W. Drummy
Kelvin L. Roots
John C. Wall
William M. Olah
Craig M. McKee
Scott M. Kyrouac
Jeffrey A. Boyll

ASSOCIATES

David P. Friedrich
Anthony R. Jost

Representative Corporate Clients: Merchants National Bank; Owens Corning Fiberglass; CSX, Inc.; General Housewares Corp.; MAB Paints; Chicago Title Insurance Co.; Terre Haute Board of Realtors; Union Hospital; Associated Physicians and Surgeons Clinic, Inc.; PSI Energy, Inc.

For full biographical listings, see the Martindale-Hubbell Law Directory

IOWA

*DES MOINES,** Polk Co.

FINLEY, ALT, SMITH, SCHARNBERG, MAY & CRAIG, P.C. (AV)

Fourth Floor Equitable Building, 50309
Telephone: 515-288-0145
Telecopier: 515-288-2724

Thomas A. Finley

Representative Clients: Aetna Casualty & Surety Co.; Aetna Life Insurance Co.; ALAS; American Society of Composers, Authors and Publishers; Equitable Life Assurance Society of the U.S.; Federated Insurance Co.; Meredith Corp.; Catholic Health Corp.
Iowa Attorneys for: Midwest Medical Insurance Co.

For Complete List of Firm Personnel, See General Section

For full biographical listings, see the Martindale-Hubbell Law Directory

KANSAS

*WICHITA,** Sedgwick Co.

FOULSTON & SIEFKIN (AV)

(Formerly Foulston, Siefkin, Powers & Eberhardt)
700 Fourth Financial Center, Broadway at Douglas, 67202
Telephone: 316-267-6371
Facsimile: 316-267-6345
Topeka, Kansas Office: 1515 Bank IV Tower, 534 Kansas Avenue. 66603.
Telephone: 913-233-3600.
FAX: 913-233-1610.
Member: Lex Mundi, A Global Association of Independent Firms

MEMBERS OF FIRM

Stanley G. Andeel
Gary E. Knight

SPECIAL COUNSEL

Robert L. Heath
Matthew C. Hesse

For Complete List of Firm Personnel, See General Section

For full biographical listings, see the Martindale-Hubbell Law Directory

KENTUCKY

*BOWLING GREEN,** Warren Co.

CAMPBELL, KERRICK & GRISE (AV)

1025 State Street, P.O. Box 9547, 42102-9547
Telephone: 502-782-8160
FAX: 502-782-5856

MEMBERS OF FIRM

Joe Bill Campbell
Thomas N. Kerrick
John R. Grise
Gregory N. Stivers
H. Brent Brennenstuhl
Deborah Tomes Wilkins

ASSOCIATES

H. Harris Pepper, Jr.
Lanna Martin Kilgore
Laura Hagan

Representative Clients: Greenview Hospital; Riverdell Hospital; Hospital Corporation of America; Russell County Hospital; Wayne County Hospital; Hardin Memorial Hospital; Kentucky Hospital Association Trust.

For full biographical listings, see the Martindale-Hubbell Law Directory

CATRON, KILGORE & BEGLEY (AV)

918 State Street, P.O. Box 280, 42102-0280
Telephone: 502-842-1050
Fax: 502-842-4720

Stephen B. Catron
J. Patrick Kilgore
Ernest Edward Begley, II

Representative Client: Bowling Green Orthopaedic Associates.

For full biographical listings, see the Martindale-Hubbell Law Directory

COVINGTON, Kenton Co.

GREENEBAUM DOLL & MCDONALD (AV)

A Partnership including Professional Service Corporations
50 East Rivercenter Boulevard, P.O. Box 2050, 41012-2050
Telephone: 606-655-4200
Telecopier: 606-655-4239
Louisville, Kentucky Office: 3300 National City Tower.
Telephone: 502-589-4200.
Fax: 502-587-3695.
Lexington, Kentucky Office: 1400 Vine Center Tower.
Telephone: 606-231-8500.
Fax: 606-255-2742.
Cincinnati, Ohio Office: 832 Main Street.
Telephone: 513-421-8087.
Fax: 513-421-8089.

MEMBERS OF FIRM

Wm. T. Robinson, III
Phillip D. Scott
Roger N. Braden (Resident)

Representative Clients: Aetna Life Insurance Co.; ANDALEX Resources, Inc.; Ashland Oil, Inc.; A T & T Communications, Inc.; Bethlehem Steel Corp.; Brown-Forman Corp.; Citizens Fidelity Bank & Trust Co.; Humana, Inc.; KFC National Cooperative Advertising Program, Inc.

For Complete List of Firm Personnel, See General Section

For full biographical listings, see the Martindale-Hubbell Law Directory

CRESTVIEW HILLS, Kenton Co.

THE LAW OFFICE OF JOHN C. GILLILAND, II (AV)

Chancellor Commons/Thomas More Centre, 2670 Chancellor Drive, Suite 290, 41017
Telephone: 606-344-8515
Fax: 606-344-8516

Elizabeth A. Zink-Pearson

For full biographical listings, see the Martindale-Hubbell Law Directory

*LEXINGTON,** Fayette Co.

GREENEBAUM DOLL & MCDONALD (AV)

A Partnership including Professional Service Corporations
1400 Vine Center Tower, 40508
Telephone: 606-231-8500
Telecopier: 606-255-2742
Telex: 213029
Louisville, Kentucky Office: 3300 National City Tower.
Telephone: 502-589-4200.
Fax: 502-587-3695.
Covington, Kentucky Office: 50 East River Center Boulevard, P.O. Box 2050.
Telephone: 606-655-4200.
Fax: 606-655-4239.
Cincinnati, Ohio Office: 832 Main Street.
Telephone: 513-421-8087.
Fax: 513-421-8089.

MEMBERS OF FIRM

Phillip D. Scott
Wm. T. Robinson, III
John R. Cummins
James G. LeMaster (Resident)
Deborah H. Tudor (Resident)
Mark T. Hayden (Resident)

ASSOCIATE

Benjamin D. Crocker

Representative Clients: Aetna Life Insurance Co.; ANDALEX Resources, Inc.; Ashland Oil, Inc.; AT&T Communications, Inc.; Bethlehem Steel Corp.; Brown-Forman Corp.; Columbia Gas & Transmission Co.; Columbia/HCA Healthcare Corp.; Commonwealth Aluminum Corp.; Consolidation Coal Co.; Costain Coal, Inc.

For Complete List of Firm Personnel, See General Section

For full biographical listings, see the Martindale-Hubbell Law Directory

Lexington—Continued

PIPER, WELLMAN & BOWERS (AV)

200 North Upper Street, 40507
Telephone: 606-231-1012
FAX: 606-231-7367

MEMBERS OF FIRM

George C. Piper
Dean T. Wellman
Barbara J. Bowers

ASSOCIATE

Johann F. Herklotz

Representative Clients: Kentucky Hospital Assn. Trust; Woodford Hospital; Garrard Memorial Hospital; Century American Insurance Co.; Guaranty National Ins. Co.; Rhone Pharmaceuticals; Glaxo; Hillhaven Corp.; Sisters of Charity of Nazareth Health System, Inc.; Ky. River Medical Center; St. Josephs Hospital.

For Complete List of Firm Personnel, See General Section

For full biographical listings, see the Martindale-Hubbell Law Directory

STOLL, KEENON & PARK (AV)

201 E. Main Street, Suite 1000, 40507-1380
Telephone: 606-231-3000
Telecopier: 606-253-1093; 606-253-1027
Frankfort, Kentucky Office: 326 West Main Street.
Telephone: 502-875-6000.
Telecopier: 502-875-6008.
Louisville, Kentucky Office: 400 West Market Street, Suite 2650, 40202.
Telephone: 502-568-9100.
Telecopier: 502-568-6340.

MEMBERS OF FIRM

Samuel D. Hinkle, IV
R. David Lester
Dan M. Rose
J. Guthrie True

Representative Clients: Bank One, Lexington, NA; Farmers Capital Bank Corp.; The Tokai Bank Ltd.; Link Belt Construction Equipment Co.; General Motors Corp.; International Business Machines Corp.; Ohbayashi Corp.; R. J. Reynolds Tobacco Co.; Rockwell International Corp.; Square D Co.

For Complete List of Firm Personnel, See General Section

For full biographical listings, see the Martindale-Hubbell Law Directory

*LOUISVILLE,** Jefferson Co.

GREENEBAUM DOLL & McDONALD (AV)

A Partnership including Professional Service Corporations
3300 National City Tower, 40202
Telephone: 502-589-4200
Fax: 502-587-3695
Lexington, Kentucky Office: 1400 Vine Center Tower.
Telephone: 606-231-8500.
Fax: 606-255-2742.
Covington, Kentucky Office: 50 East River Center Boulevard, P.O. Box 2050.
Telephone: 606-655-4200.
Fax: 606-655-4239.
Cincinnati, Ohio Office: 832 Main Street.
Telephone: 513-421-8087.
Fax: 513-421-8089.

Phillip D. Scott (Covington and Lexington, Kentucky)
Wm. T. Robinson, III
John R. Cummins
James G. LeMaster (Resident at Lexington, Kentucky)
Roger N. Braden (Resident at Covington, Kentucky)
Patrick J. Welsh
Deborah H. Tudor (Resident at Lexington, Kentucky)
Mark T. Hayden (Resident at Lexington, Kentucky)

ASSOCIATE

Benjamin D. Crocker (Resident, Lexington Office)

Representative Clients: Aetna Life Insurance Co.; ANDALEX Resources, Inc.; Ashland Oil, Inc.; A T & T Communications, Inc.; Bethlehem Steel Corp.; Brown-Forman Corp.; Columbia/HCA Healthcare Corp.; Humana, Inc.; Kentucky Kingdom, Inc.; KFC National Cooperative Advertising Program, Inc.

For Complete List of Firm Personnel, See General Section

For full biographical listings, see the Martindale-Hubbell Law Directory

OGDEN NEWELL & WELCH (AV)

1200 One Riverfront Plaza, 40202-2973
Telephone: 502-582-1601
Fax: 502-581-9564

MEMBERS OF FIRM

John T. Ballantine
Joseph C. Oldham
Gregory J. Bubalo
W. Gregory King
Robert E. Thieman
James B. Martin, Jr.

(See Next Column)

ASSOCIATES

John Wade Hendricks
James G. Campbell
Tracy S. Prewitt
Sharon A. Mattingly

Counsel for: KU Energy Corp.; Kentucky Utilities Co.; Brown-Forman Corp.; B. F. Goodrich Co.; J.J.B. Hilliard, W.L. Lyons, Inc.; Interlock Industries, Inc.; Akzo Coatings, Inc.; United Medical Corp.; Bank of Louisville.

For Complete List of Firm Personnel, See General Section

For full biographical listings, see the Martindale-Hubbell Law Directory

WOODWARD, HOBSON & FULTON (AV)

2500 National City Tower, 101 South Fifth Street, 40202
Telephone: 502-581-8000
Fax: 502-581-8111
Lexington, Kentucky Office: National City Plaza, 301 East Main Street, Suite 650.
Telephone: 606-244-7100.
Telecopier: 606-244-7111.

MEMBERS OF FIRM

David R. Monohan
Bradley R. Hume
Thomas A. Hoy
Mary Jo Wetzel
Jann B. Logsdon

ASSOCIATES

Susan B. Booker
T. Kevin Flanery (Resident, Lexington, Kentucky Office)

Representative Clients: Sisters of St. Francis Health Services Inc.; Sisters of Charity of Nazareth Health System.

For Complete List of Firm Personnel, See General Section

For full biographical listings, see the Martindale-Hubbell Law Directory

LOUISIANA

*BATON ROUGE,** East Baton Rouge Parish

WATSON, BLANCHE, WILSON & POSNER (AV)

505 North Boulevard, P.O. Drawer 2995, 70821-2995
Telephone: 504-387-5511
Fax: 504-387-5972
Other Baton Rouge, Louisiana Office: 4000 South Sherwood Forest Boulevard, Suite 504.
Telephone: 504-291-5280.
Fax: 504-293-8075.

Robert L. Roland
Peter T. Dazzio
Felix R. Weill
William E. Scott, III
Mary H. Thompson
Michael M. Remson
P. Chauvin Wilkinson, Jr.
Randall L. Champagne
René J. Pfefferle

ASSOCIATES

P. Scott Jolly
Raymond A. Daigle, Jr.

Representative Clients: Baton Rouge General Medical Center; General Health System, Inc.; Louisiana Hospital Association Trust Fund; Woman's Hospital Foundation.

For Complete List of Firm Personnel, See General Section

For full biographical listings, see the Martindale-Hubbell Law Directory

*MONROE,** Ouachita Parish

McLEOD, VERLANDER, EADE & VERLANDER (AV)

A Partnership including Professional Law Corporations
1900 North 18th Street, Suite 610, P.O. Box 2270, 71207-2270
Telephone: 318-325-7000
Telecopier: 318-324-0580

MEMBERS OF FIRM

Robert P. McLeod (P.L.C.)
David E. Verlander, III (P.L.C.)
Ellen R. Eade
Paul J. Verlander
Rick W. Duplissey
Pamela G. Nathan

Representative Clients: HCA North Monroe Hospital; Hospital Corporation of America; The Orthopaedic Clinic of Monroe, Inc.; Louisiana Medical Mutual Insurance Co.; Extracorporeal Technologies, Inc.; Morehouse Parish General Hospital.

For full biographical listings, see the Martindale-Hubbell Law Directory

*NEW ORLEANS,** Orleans Parish

BOGGS, LOEHN & RODRIGUE (AV)

A Partnership including Law Corporations
Suite 1800 Lykes Center, 300 Poydras Street, 70130-3597
Telephone: 504-523-7090
Fax: 504-581-6822

Charles A. Boggs (A Law Corporation)
Thomas E. Loehn (A Law Corporation)
Edward A. Rodrigue, Jr., (A Law Corporation)
Chester A. Fleming, III
Thomas W. Lewis
Terry B. Deffes
Robert I. Baudouin
Samuel M. Rosamond, III
Betty P. Westbrook
Ralph T Rabalais

Reference: First National Bank of Commerce, New Orleans, La.

For full biographical listings, see the Martindale-Hubbell Law Directory

MAINE

*AUGUSTA,** Kennebec Co.

* indicates certain Bar Register subscribers whose principal office is located elsewhere in the state and who have arranged for representation as a part of the state capital listings that follow

*** PIERCE, ATWOOD, SCRIBNER, ALLEN, SMITH & LANCASTER (AV)**

77 Winthrop Street, 04330
Telephone: 207-622-6311
Fax: 207-623-9367
Portland, Maine Office: One Monument Square.
Telephone: 207-773-6411.
Camden, Maine Office: 36 Chestnut Street, P.O. Box 780.
Telephone: 207-236-4333.

MEMBER OF FIRM
Joseph M. Kozak
ASSOCIATE
Benjamin P. Townsend

For Complete List of Firm Personnel, See General Section

For full biographical listings, see the Martindale-Hubbell Law Directory

*BANGOR,** Penobscot Co.

EATON, PEABODY, BRADFORD & VEAGUE, P.A. (AV)

Fleet Center-Exchange Street, P.O. Box 1210, 04402-1210
Telephone: 207-947-0111
Telecopier: 207-942-3040
Augusta, Maine Office: 2 Central Plaza.
Telephone: 207-622-3747.
Telecopier: 207-622-9732.
Brunswick, Maine Office: 167 Park Row.
Telephone: 207-729-1144.
Telecopier: 207-729-1140.
Camden, Maine Office: 7-9 Washington Street.
Telephone: 207-236-3325.
Telecopier: 207-236-8611.
Dover-Foxcroft, Maine Office: 30 East Main Street.
Telephone: 207-564-8378.
Telecopier: 207-564-7059.

Malcolm E. Morrell, Jr.
Daniel G. McKay
Gregory A. Brodek

A List of Representative Clients available upon request.

For Complete List of Firm Personnel, See General Section

For full biographical listings, see the Martindale-Hubbell Law Directory

*PORTLAND,** Cumberland Co.

PIERCE, ATWOOD, SCRIBNER, ALLEN, SMITH & LANCASTER (AV)

One Monument Square, 04101
Telephone: 207-773-6411
Fax: 207-773-3419
Augusta, Maine Office: 77 Winthrop Street.
Telephone: 207-622-6311.
Camden, Maine Office: 36 Chestnut Street, P.O. Box 780.
Telephone: 207-236-4333.

MEMBERS OF FIRM
Joseph M. Kozak (Resident, Augusta Office)
Gordon K. Gayer
Wayne R. Douglas
ASSOCIATE
Benjamin P. Townsend

For Complete List of Firm Personnel, See General Section

For full biographical listings, see the Martindale-Hubbell Law Directory

PRETI, FLAHERTY, BELIVEAU & PACHIOS (AV)

443 Congress Street, P.O. Box 11410, 04104-7410
Telephone: 207-791-3000
Telecopier: 207-791-3111
Augusta, Maine Office: 45 Memorial Circle, P.O. Box 1058, 04332-1058.
Telephone: 207-623-5300.
Telecopier: 207-623-2914.
Rumford, Maine Office: 150 Congress Street, P.O. Drawer L, 04276-2035.
Telephone: 207-364-4593.
Telecopier: 207-369-9421.

MEMBERS OF FIRM
Christopher D. Nyhan
Eric P. Stauffer
John P. Doyle, Jr.
Michael G. Messerschmidt
Susan E. LoGiudice
ASSOCIATES
James E. Phipps
Charles F. Dingman (Augusta Office)

Representative Clients: Jackson Brook Institute; Mid-Maine Medical Center; Eastern Maine Medical Center; Southern Maine Medical Center; Franklin Memorial Hospital; Maine Hospital Assn.; Stephens Memorial Hospital; Rumford Community Hospital; Mt. Desert Island Hospital; Maine Health Care Assn.

For Complete List of Firm Personnel, See General Section

For full biographical listings, see the Martindale-Hubbell Law Directory

SOUTH PORTLAND, Cumberland Co.

VAN MEER & BELANGER, P.A. (AV)

25 Long Creek Drive, 04106
Telephone: 207-871-7500
Fax: 207-871-7505

Thomas J. Van Meer
Norman R. Belanger
D. Kelley Young
Richard N. Bryant

Betts J. Gorsky

For full biographical listings, see the Martindale-Hubbell Law Directory

MARYLAND

*BALTIMORE,** (Independent City)

GORDON, FEINBLATT, ROTHMAN, HOFFBERGER & HOLLANDER (AV)

The Garrett Building, 233 East Redwood Street, 21202
Telephone: 410-576-4000
Telex: 908041 BAL

MEMBERS OF FIRM
Barry F. Rosen (Chairman)
Henry E. Schwartz
OF COUNSEL
Eugene M. Feinblatt
ASSOCIATE
Charles A. Borek

For Complete List of Firm Personnel, See General Section

For full biographical listings, see the Martindale-Hubbell Law Directory

VENABLE, BAETJER AND HOWARD (AV)

A Partnership including Professional Corporations
1800 Mercantile Bank & Trust Building, 2 Hopkins Plaza, 21201
Telephone: 410-244-7400
Washington, D.C. Office: Venable, Baetjer, Howard & Civiletti. Suite 1000, 1201 New York Avenue, N.W.
Telephone: 202-962-4800.
McLean, Virginia Office: Suite 400, 2010 Corporate Ridge.
Telephone: 703-760-1600.
Rockville, Maryland Office: Suite 500, One Church Street, P. O. Box 1906.
Telephone: 301-217-5600.
Towson, Maryland Office: 210 Allegheny Avenue, P. O. Box 5517.
Telephone: 410-494-6200.

MEMBERS OF FIRM
Benjamin R. Civiletti (P.C.) (Also at Washington, D.C. and Towson, Maryland Offices)
Robert A. Shelton
Thomas J. Kenney, Jr. (P.C.) (Also at Washington, D.C. Office)
Kenneth C. Bass, III (Not admitted in MD; Also at Washington, D.C. and McLean, Virginia Offices)
Paul F. Strain (P.C.)
William D. Dolan, III (P.C.) (Not admitted in MD; Resident, McLean, Virginia Office)
Joseph C. Wich, Jr. (Resident, Towson, Maryland Office)
Robert G. Ames (Also at Washington, D.C. Office)
Nell B. Strachan
Barbara E. Schlaff
L. Paige Marvel

(See Next Column)

VENABLE, BAETJER AND HOWARD, *Baltimore—Continued*

MEMBERS OF FIRM (Continued)

Susan K. Gauvey (Also at Towson, Maryland Office)
James K. Archibald (Also at Washington, D.C. and Towson, Maryland Offices)
G. Stewart Webb, Jr.
George W. Johnston (P.C.)
Constance H. Baker
Edward L. Wender (P.C.)
David M. Fleishman
Jana Howard Carey (P.C.)
Jeffrey A. Dunn (also at Washington, D.C. Office)
George F. Pappas (Also at Washington, D.C. Office)
Peter P. Parvis
James L. Shea (Also at Washington, D.C. Office)
Amy Berman Jackson (Not admitted in MD; Resident, Washington, D.C. Office)
William D. Quarles (Also at Washington, D.C. and Towson, Maryland Offices)
Kathleen Gallogly Cox (Resident, Towson, Maryland Office)
W. Robert Zinkham
M. King Hill, III (Resident, Towson, Maryland Office)
James A. Dunbar (Also at Washington, D.C. Office)
Robert L. Waldman
Mary E. Pivec (Also at Washington, D.C. Office)
David J. Heubeck

OF COUNSEL

A. Samuel Cook (P.C.) (Resident, Towson, Maryland Office)
Herbert R. O'Conor, Jr. (Resident, Towson, Maryland Office)
Geoffrey R. Garinther (Also at Washington, D.C. Office)

ASSOCIATES

David W. Goewey (Not admitted in MD; Resident, Washington, D.C. Office)
Todd J. Horn
Vicki Margolis
John T. Prisbe
Michael W. Robinson (Not admitted in MD; Resident, McLean, Virginia Office)
John Peter Sarbanes
Davis V. R. Sherman
Terri L. Turner

For Complete List of Firm Personnel, See General Section

For full biographical listings, see the Martindale-Hubbell Law Directory

MASSACHUSETTS

*SPRINGFIELD,** Hampden Co.

ANNINO, DRAPER & MOORE, P.C. (AV)

Suite 1818 BayBank Tower, 1500 Main Street, P.O. Box 15428, 01115
Telephone: 413-732-6400
Fax: 413-732-3339
Westfield, Massachusetts Office: 52 Court Street.
Telephone: 413-562-9829.

Calvin W. Annino, Jr.
Mark E. Draper
Louis S. Moore
Michael R. Siddall

For full biographical listings, see the Martindale-Hubbell Law Directory

*WORCESTER,** Worcester Co.

CHRISTOPHER & LEDOUX (AV)

370 Main Street, 01608
Telephone: 508-792-2800
FAX: 508-792-6224

MEMBERS OF FIRM

William J. LeDoux
William W. Hays
David A. Wojcik
John A. Mavricos

OF COUNSEL

Christopher Christopher

Reference: Mechanics Bank.

For full biographical listings, see the Martindale-Hubbell Law Directory

MICHIGAN

BIRMINGHAM, Oakland Co.

GOREN & GOREN, P.C. (AV)

Suite 470, 30400 Telegraph Road, 48025
Telephone: 810-540-3100

(See Next Column)

Robert Goren
Steven E. Goren

Reference: Michigan National Bank-Oakland.

BLOOMFIELD HILLS, Oakland Co.

HOWARD & HOWARD ATTORNEYS, P.C. (AV)

The Pinehurst Office Center, Suite 101, 1400 North Woodward Avenue, 48304-2856
Telephone: 810-645-1483
Telecopier: 810-645-1568
Kalamazoo, Michigan Office: The Kalamazoo Building, Suite 400, 107 West Michigan Avenue.
Telephone: 616-382-1483.
Telecopier: 616-382-1568.
Lansing, Michigan Office: The Phoenix Building, Suite 500, 222 Washington Square, North.
Telephone: 517-485-1483.
Telecopier: 517-485-1568.
Peoria, Illinois Office: Howard & Howard, P.C., The Creve Coeur Building, Suite 200, 321 Liberty Street.
Telephone: 309-672-1483.
Telecopier: 309-672-1568.

Timothy M. Wittebort
John E. Young

Representative Clients: For Representative Client list, see General Practice, Bloomfield Hills, MI.

For Complete List of Firm Personnel, See General Section

For full biographical listings, see the Martindale-Hubbell Law Directory

PORTNOY, PIDGEON & ROTH, P.C. (AV)

3883 Telegraph, Suite 103, 48302
Telephone: 810-647-4242
Fax: 810-647-8251

Bernard N. Portnoy
James M. Pidgeon
Robert P. Roth
Marc S. Berlin
Berton K. May

Representative Clients: North Oakland Medical Center, Pontiac General Hospital Division; Hurly Medical Center, Flint, Michigan; McLaren Regional Medical Center, Flint, Michigan; William Beaumont Hospital, Royal Oak, Michigan; Detroit Osteopathic Hospital; Horizon Health Systems; Bi-County Community Hospital; Riverside Osteopathic; Crittenton Hospital, Rochester, Michigan.

For full biographical listings, see the Martindale-Hubbell Law Directory

*DETROIT,** Wayne Co.

BUTZEL LONG, A PROFESSIONAL CORPORATION (AV)

Suite 900, 150 West Jefferson, 48226
Telephone: 313-225-7000
Telecopier: 313-225-7080
Birmingham, Michigan Office: Suite 200, 32270 Telegraph Road.
Telephone: 810-258-1616.
Telecopier: 810-258-1439.
Lansing, Michigan Office: 118 West Ottawa Street.
Telephone: 517-372-6622.
Telecopier: 517-372-6672.
Ann Arbor, Michigan Office: Suite 400, 121 West Washington.
Telephone: 313-995-3110.
Telecopier: 313-995-1777.
Grosse Pointe Farms, Michigan Office: Suite 260, 21 Kercheval.
Telephone: 313-886-5446.
Telecopier: 313-886-2114.

Robert M. Vercruysse
Philip J. Kessler
Thomas E. Sizemore
John P. Hancock, Jr.
D. Stewart Green (Birmingham)
Gregory V. Murray
Keefe A. Brooks
Barbara S. Kendzierski
Raymond J. Carey
Mark R. Lezotte
Gordon J. Walker (Birmingham)
James L. Hughes
E. William S. Shipman
Andrea Roumell Dickson

Clara DeMatteis Mager
Joshua A. Sherbin

Representative Clients: William Beaumont Hospital; Mercy Health Services; University of Michigan; Providence Hospital; Michigan Health Care Corp.; Blue Cross and Blue Shield of Michigan; The Blue Care Network.

For Complete List of Firm Personnel, See General Section

For full biographical listings, see the Martindale-Hubbell Law Directory

Detroit—Continued

DYKEMA GOSSETT (AV)

400 Renaissance Center, 48243-1668
Telephone: 313-568-6800
Cable Address: "Dyke-Detroit"
Telex: 23-0121
Fax: 313-568-6594
Ann Arbor, Michigan Office: 315 East Eisenhower Parkway, Suite 100, 48108-3306.
Telephone: 313-747-7660.
Fax: 313-747-7696.
Bloomfield Hills, Michigan Office: 1577 North Woodward Avenue, Suite 300, 48304-2820.
Telephone: 810-540-0700.
Fax: 810-540-0763.
Grand Rapids, Michigan Office: 200 Oldtown Riverfront Building, 248 Louis Campau Promenade, N.W., 49503-2668.
Telephone: 616-776-7500.
Fax: 616-776-7573.
Lansing, Michigan Office: 800 Michigan National Tower, 48933-1707.
Telephone: 517-374-9100.
Fax: 517-374-9191.
Washington, D.C. Office: Franklin Square, Suite 300 West Tower, 1300 I Street, N.W., 20005-3306.
Telephone: 202-522-8600.
Fax: 202-522-8669.
Chicago, Illinois Office: Three First National Plaza, Suite 1400, 70 W. Madison, 60602-4270.
Telephone: 312-214-3380.
Fax: 312-214-3441.

MEMBERS OF FIRM

Maria B. Abrahamsen
Teresa A. Brooks (Resident at Washington, D.C. Office)
Bettye S. Elkins (Resident at Ann Arbor Office)
J. Kay Felt
Jane Forbes
Kathrin E. Kudner
Seth M. Lloyd
Thomas J. McGraw

ASSOCIATES

Phyllis G. Donaldson
Joanne R. Lax
Kathleen A. Reed (Resident at Ann Arbor Office)

For Complete List of Firm Personnel, See General Section

For full biographical listings, see the Martindale-Hubbell Law Directory

FEIKENS, VANDER MALE, STEVENS, BELLAMY & GILCHRIST, P.C. (AV)

One Detroit Center Suite 3400, 500 Woodward Avenue, 48226-3406
Telephone: 313-962-5909
Fax: 313-962-3125

Jack E. Vander Male
Frederick B. Bellamy
L. Neal Kennedy

Richard G. Koefod
Joseph E. Kozely, Jr.
Jeffrey Feikens
Keith J. Soltis
Michael B. Barey
Gary T. Tandberg
Susan Tillotson Mills

For Complete List of Firm Personnel, See General Section

For full biographical listings, see the Martindale-Hubbell Law Directory

HONIGMAN MILLER SCHWARTZ AND COHN (AV)

A Partnership including Professional Corporations
2290 First National Building, 48226
Telephone: 313-256-7800
Telecopier: 313-962-0176
Telex: 235705
Lansing, Michigan Office: Phoenix Building, 222 North Washington Square, Suite 400.
Telephone: 517-484-8282.
West Palm Beach, Florida Office: Suite 800 Esperante Building, 222 Lakeview Avenue.
Telephone: 407-838-4500.
Tampa, Florida Office: 2700 Landmark Centre, 401 E. Jackson Street.
Telephone: 813-221-6600.
Orlando, Florida Office: 390 North Orange Avenue, Suite 1300.
Telephone: 407-648-0300.
Houston, Texas Office: 3100 First Interstate Bank Plaza, 1000 Louisiana.
Telephone: 713-650-2600.
Los Angeles, California Office: McNeill Plaza, Suite 820, 15260 Ventura Boulevard, 91403.
Telephone: 818-784-2900.

MEMBERS OF FIRM

Joseph T. Aoun
William M. Cassetta
Gerald M. Griffith
William O. Hochkammer
Linn A. Hynds
Stuart M. Lockman
Kenneth R. Marcus
Joseph G. Nuyen, Jr.
Linda S. Ross
Chris E. Rossman
Margaret Shannon

(See Next Column)

ASSOCIATES

Melissa Leigh Markey
Tracy E. Silverman
Julie E. Robertson
Roy H. Wyman, Jr.

OF COUNSEL

Milton J. Miller
Rodman N. Myers
Jason L. Honigman (1904-1990)
Irwin I. Cohn (1896-1984)

RESIDENT IN WEST PALM BEACH, FLORIDA OFFICE

MEMBER

Mark Nussbaum (P.A.)

ASSOCIATES

Jose O. Diaz
Gina Greeson Hyland

RESIDENT IN TAMPA, FLORIDA OFFICE

MEMBERS

Maria Maistrellis
Barbara R. Pankau
Brad M. Tomtishen (P.A.)

GeneraL Counsel: Children's Hospital of Michigan; The Detroit Medical Center; Mercy Health Services; Michigan Hospital Association.
Local or Special Counsel: St. Mary's Hospital (West Palm Beach); Holy Cross Hospital (Ft. Lauderdale); Northern Michigan Hospital; Bronson Healthcare Group, Inc.

For Complete List of Firm Personnel, See General Section

For full biographical listings, see the Martindale-Hubbell Law Directory

JAFFE, RAITT, HEUER & WEISS, PROFESSIONAL CORPORATION (AV)

One Woodward Avenue, Suite 2400, 48226
Telephone: 313-961-8380
Telecopier: 313-961-8358
Cable Address: "Jafsni"
Southfield,Michigan Office: Travelers Tower, Suite 1520.
Telephone: 313-961-8380.
Monroe, Michigan Office: 212 East Front Street, Suite 3.
Telephone: 313-241-6470.
Telefacsimile: 313-241-3849.

Alexander B. Bragdon
Linda C. Scheuerman
Arthur A. Weiss

See General Practice Section for List of Representative Clients.

For Complete List of Firm Personnel, See General Section

For full biographical listings, see the Martindale-Hubbell Law Directory

KERR, RUSSELL AND WEBER (AV)

One Detroit Center, 500 Woodward Avenue, Suite 2500, 48226-3406
Telephone: 313-961-0200
Telecopier: 313-961-0388
Bloomfield Hills, Michigan Office: 3883 Telegraph Road.
Telephone: 810-649-5990.
East Lansing, Michigan Office: 1301 North Hagadorn Road.
Telephone: 517-336-6767.

Richard D. Weber
Monte D. Jahnke
Patrick McLain
Paul M. Shirilla
Stephen D. McGraw
Mark J. Stasa
Joanne Geha Swanson
Catherine Bonczak Edwards
Christopher A. Cornwall
Patrick J. Haddad
Susan I Chae

For Complete List of Firm Personnel, See General Section

For full biographical listings, see the Martindale-Hubbell Law Directory

KITCH, DRUTCHAS, WAGNER & KENNEY, P.C. (AV)

One Woodward, Tenth Floor, 48226-3412
Telephone: 313-965-7900
Fax: 313-965-7403
Lansing, Michigan Office: 120 Washington Square, North, Suite 805, One Michigan Avenue, 48933-1609.
Telephone: 517-372-6430.
Fax: 517-372-0441.
Macomb County Office: Towne Square Development, 10 South Main Street, Suite 301, Mount Clemens, 48043-7903.
Telephone: 810-463-9770.
Fax: 810-463-8994.
Toledo, Ohio Office: 405 Madison Avenue, Suite 1500, 43604-1235.
Telephone: 419-243-4006.
Fax: 419-243-7333.
Troy, Michigan Office: 3001 West Big Beaver Road, Suite 200, 48084-3103.
Telephone: 810-637-3500.
Fax: 810-637-6630.
Ann Arbor, Michigan Office: 303 Detroit Street, Suite 400, P.O. Box 8610, 48107-8610.
Telephone: 313-994-7600.
Fax: 313-994-7626.

(See Next Column)

KITCH, DRUTCHAS, WAGNER & KENNEY P.C., *Detroit—Continued*

Richard A. Kitch
Gregory G. Drutchas (Principal, Troy Office)
Mark D. Willmarth (Principal)
David L. Kaser (Principal, Troy Office)
Karen Bernard Berkery (Associate Principal)
Brian R. Garves
John M. Sier (Associate Principal)
Philip Cwagenberg (Troy Office)
Roselyn R. Parmenter (Resident, Ann Arbor Office)
Carol Ann Tarnowsky (Troy Office)
Kenneth G. Frantz (Troy Office)
Bridget Kerry Quinn (Resident, Ann Arbor Office)
Julia S. Hoffert-Rosen (Troy Office)

For Complete List of Firm Personnel, See General Section

For full biographical listings, see the Martindale-Hubbell Law Directory

LEWIS, WHITE & CLAY, A PROFESSIONAL CORPORATION (AV)

1300 First National Building, 660 Woodward Avenue, 48226-3531
Telephone: 313-961-2550
Washington, D.C. Office: 1250 Connecticut Avenue, N.W., Suite 630, 20036.
Telephone: 202-835-0616.
Fax: 202-833-3316.

David Baker Lewis
Richard Thomas White
Eric Lee Clay
Reuben A. Munday
Ulysses Whittaker Boykin
S. Allen Early, III
Carl F. Stafford
Helen Francine Strong
Derrick P. Mayes
Frank E. Barbee
Camille Stearns Miller
Melvin J. Hollowell, Jr.
Michael T. Raymond
Jacqueline H. Sellers
Thomas R. Paxton
Kathleen Miles (Resident, Washington, D.C. Office)
David N. Zacks

Karen Kendrick Brown (Resident, Washington, D.C. Office)
J. Taylor Teasdale
Wade Harper McCree
Tyrone A. Powell
Blair A. Person
Susan D. Hoffman
Stephon E. Johnson
John J. Walsh
Andrea L. Powell
Teresa N. Gueyser
Hans J. Massaquoi, Jr.
Werten F. W. Bellamy, Jr. (Resident, Washington, D.C. Office)
Akin O. Akindele
Regina P. Freelon-Solomon
Calita L. Elston
Nancy C. Borland
Terrence Randall Haugabook
Lynn R. Westfall
Lance W. Mason

OF COUNSEL

Otis M. Smith (1922-1994)
Inez Smith Reid (Resident, Washington, D.C. Office)

Representative Clients: Omnicare Health Plan; Aetna Life & Casualty Co.; Chrysler Motors Corp.; Chrysler Financial Corp.; MCI Communications Corp.; City of Detroit; City of Detroit Building Authority; City of Detroit Downtown Development Authority; Consolidated Rail Corp. (Conrail); Equitable Life Assurance Society of the United States.

For full biographical listings, see the Martindale-Hubbell Law Directory

TIMMIS & INMAN (AV)

300 Talon Centre, 48207
Telephone: 313-396-4200
Telecopier: 313-396-4228

MEMBERS OF FIRM

Wayne C. Inman
Charles W. Royer
Richard L. Levin

OF COUNSEL

William B. Fitzgerald

Representative Client: Mt. Clemens General Hospital.

For Complete List of Firm Personnel, See General Section
For full biographical listings, see the Martindale-Hubbell Law Directory

WACHLER & KOPSON, PROFESSIONAL CORPORATION (AV)

1028 Buhl Building, 48226
Telephone: 313-963-1700
Fax: 313-963-8598

Andrew B. Wachler
Mark S. Kopson

Vicki Sherman Myckowiak
Phyllis A. Avery

Representative Clients: United Dental Associates, Inc.

For full biographical listings, see the Martindale-Hubbell Law Directory

EAST LANSING, Ingham Co.

FARHAT, STORY & KRAUS, P.C. (AV)

Beacon Place, 4572 South Hagadorn Road, Suite 3, 48823
Telephone: 517-351-3700
Fax: 517-332-4122

Leo A. Farhat
James E. Burns (1925-1979)
Monte R. Story
Richard C. Kraus
Max R. Hoffman Jr.
Chris A. Bergstrom
Kitty L. Groh
Charles R. Toy
David M. Platt

Lawrence P. Schweitzer
Jeffrey J. Short
Kathy A. Breedlove
Thomas L. Sparks

Representative Clients: National Association of Rural Health Clinics; Cedar Springs Medical Clinic; Borgess Hospital; Michigan Association of Physician Assistants; Michigan Non-Profit Homes Association; Physical Therapy Associates; Pinconning Medical Care; Saginaw General Hospital; Muskegon General Hospital; Saratoga Community Hospital.
Reference: Capitol National Bank.

For full biographical listings, see the Martindale-Hubbell Law Directory

*GRAND RAPIDS,** Kent Co.

GRUEL, MILLS, NIMS AND PYLMAN (AV)

50 Monroe Place, Suite 700 West, 49503
Telephone: 616-235-5500
Fax: 616-235-5550

MEMBERS OF FIRM

Grant J. Gruel
William F. Mills
J. Clarke Nims
Norman H. Pylman, II
Scott R. Melton
Brion J. Brooks
Thomas R. Behm
J. Paul Janes

Representative Clients: Aquinas College; Bell Helmet Co.; Blodgett Memorial Medical Center; Butterworth Hospital; Chem Central, Inc.; Cook Pump Co.; Grove, Inc.; NBDC; Heim Corp.

For full biographical listings, see the Martindale-Hubbell Law Directory

WARNER, NORCROSS & JUDD (AV)

900 Old Kent Building, 111 Lyon Street, N.W., 49503-2489
Telephone: 616-752-2000
Fax: 616-752-2500
Muskegon, Michigan Office: 400 Terrace Plaza, P.O. Box 900.
Telephone: 616-727-2600.
Fax: 616-727-2699.
Holland, Michigan Office: Curtis Center, Suite 300, 170 College Avenue.
Telephone: 616-396-9800.
Fax: 616-396-3656.

MEMBERS OF FIRM

John H. Logie
Cameron S. DeLong
Richard L. Bouma

ASSOCIATE

Susan Gell Meyers

Representative Clients: Blodgett Memorial Medical Center; Ferguson Healthcare System; Holland Communications.

For Complete List of Firm Personnel, See General Section
For full biographical listings, see the Martindale-Hubbell Law Directory

*KALAMAZOO,** Kalamazoo Co.

HOWARD & HOWARD ATTORNEYS, P.C. (AV)

The Kalamazoo Building, Suite 400, 107 West Michigan Avenue, 49007-3956
Telephone: 616-382-1483
Telecopier: 616-382-1568
Bloomfield Hills, Michigan Office: The Pinehurst Office Center, Suite 101, 1400 North Woodward Avenue.
Telephone: 810-645-1483.
Telecopier: 810-645-1568.
Lansing, Michigan Office: The Phoenix Building, Suite 500, 222 Washington Square North.
Telephone: 517-485-1483.
Telecopier: 517-485-1568.
Peoria, Illinois Office: Howard & Howard, P.C., The Creve Coeur Building, Suite 200, 321 Liberty Street.
Telephone: 309-672-1483.
Telecopier: 309-672-1568.

William A. Dornbos
Peter J. Livingston

Representative Clients: First of America Bank Corp.; Simpson Paper Company; W.R. Grace & Co.; Stryker Corp.; Kalamazoo Valley Community College.
Local Counsel for: Chrysler Motors Corp.
International Counsel for: Sony Corp.

(See Next Column)

HOWARD & HOWARD ATTORNEYS P.C.—*Continued*

For Complete List of Firm Personnel, See General Section

For full biographical listings, see the Martindale-Hubbell Law Directory

KREIS, ENDERLE, CALLANDER & HUDGINS, A PROFESSIONAL CORPORATION (AV)

One Moorsbridge, 49002
Telephone: 616-324-3000
Telecopier: 616-324-3010

Alan G. Enderle
C. Reid Hudgins III
Daniel P. Mc Glinn

For Complete List of Firm Personnel, See General Section

For full biographical listings, see the Martindale-Hubbell Law Directory

LANSING, Ingham Co.

FOSTER, SWIFT, COLLINS & SMITH, P.C. (AV)

313 South Washington Square, 48933-2193
Telephone: 517-371-8100
Telecopier: 517-371-8200
Farmington Hills, Michigan Office: 32300 Northwestern Highway, Suite 230.
Telephone: 810-851-7500.
Fax: 810-851-7504.

Gary J. McRay
David VanderHaagen
Stephen I. Jurmu
James B. Jensen, Jr.
Brian A. Kaser
Louis K. Nigg
Jean G. Schtokal
Eric E. Doster

General Counsel for: First American Bank-Central; Story, Inc.; Michigan Milk Producers Assn.; Edward W. Sparrow Hospital; St. Lawrence Hospital; Demmer Corp.; Michigan Financial Corp.
Local Counsel for: Shell Oil Co.; Michigan-Mutual Insurance Co.; Century Cellunet.

For Complete List of Firm Personnel, See General Section

For full biographical listings, see the Martindale-Hubbell Law Directory

FRASER TREBILCOCK DAVIS & FOSTER, P.C. (AV)

1000 Michigan National Tower, 48933
Telephone: 517-482-5800
Fax: 517-482-0887
Okemos, Michigan Office: 2188 Commons Parkway.
Telephone: 517-349-1300.
Fax: 517-349-0922.

Peter L. Dunlap
Robert W. Stocker, II
Stephen L. Burlingame

Michael C. Levine

Counsel for: Beverly Enterprises; Health Management Services; Michigan Center Medical Center; Michigan Non-Profit Homes Association; Tendercare Corp.; The Nursing Home Group.

For Complete List of Firm Personnel, See General Section

For full biographical listings, see the Martindale-Hubbell Law Directory

SOUTHFIELD, Oakland Co.

FRIMET & MICHALSEN, P.C. (AV)

2000 Town Center, Suite 2700, 48075-1108
Telephone: 810-358-0080
Telecopier: 810-354-3106

Gilbert M. Frimet
John A. Michalsen

Alan T. Rogalski

OF COUNSEL

Bruce C. Blanton
Jason T. Range
Southfield, Michigan Rubenstein Plotkin, P.C.

Representative Clients: Michigan Psychoanalytic Society; Michigan Association of Independent Laboratories; Michigan Dermatological Society; Northern Michigan Medical Care Assn.; Upper Peninsula Corporation for Medical Care; Professional Review Organization-GLSC; Associated Physicians of Southeast Michigan Inc.; Woodland Medical Clinic, P.C.; Associated Physicians, P.C.; American Health Resources, Inc.

For full biographical listings, see the Martindale-Hubbell Law Directory

SOMMERS, SCHWARTZ, SILVER & SCHWARTZ, P.C. (AV)

2000 Town Center, Suite 900, 48075
Telephone: 810-355-0300
Telecopier: 810-746-4001
Plymouth, Michigan Office: 747 South Main Street.
Telephone: 313-455-4250.

(See Next Column)

Steven J. Schwartz
James J. Vlasic

General Counsel for: City of Taylor; Foodland Distributors; C.A. Muer Corporation; Vlasic & Company; Nederlander Corporation; Woodland Physicians; Midwest Health Centers, P.C.
Representative Clients: Crum & Forster Insurance Company; City of Pontiac; Michigan National Bank; Perry Drugs.

For Complete List of Firm Personnel, See General Section

For full biographical listings, see the Martindale-Hubbell Law Directory

TROY, Oakland Co.

BARLOW & LANGE, P.C. (AV)

3290 West Big Beaver Road Suite 310, 48084
Telephone: 810-649-3150
Facsimile: 810-649-3175

Thomas W. H. Barlow
Craig W. Lange
Paul W. Coughenour
Craig S. Schwartz
Donna A. Lavoie
Matthew S. Derby
Julie Benson Valice
John K. Ausdemore

For full biographical listings, see the Martindale-Hubbell Law Directory

MISSISSIPPI

*JACKSON,** Hinds Co.

WISE CARTER CHILD & CARAWAY, PROFESSIONAL ASSOCIATION (AV)

600 Heritage Building, 401 East Capitol Street, P.O. Box 651, 39205
Telephone: 601-968-5500
FAX: 601-968-5519

George Q. Evans
Margaret H. Williams
Douglas E. Levanway
Barbara Childs Wallace
Mark P. Caraway
George H. Ritter
Betty Toon Collins
Charles E. Ross

Ronald J. Artigues, Jr.
Rachael Hetherington Lenoir

Representative Clients: Mississippi Hospital Assn.; EPIC Healthcare Group; Southwest Mississippi Regional Medical Center; Greenwood Leflore Hospital; Garden Park Community Hospital; Charter Hospital of Jackson; Biloxi Regional Medical Center; Tulane Medical Center; Mississippi Emergency Assn.

For Complete List of Firm Personnel, See General Section

For full biographical listings, see the Martindale-Hubbell Law Directory

MISSOURI

ST. LOUIS, (Independent City)

PEPER, MARTIN, JENSEN, MAICHEL AND HETLAGE (AV)

720 Olive Street, Twenty-Fourth Floor, 63101
Telephone: 314-421-3850
Fax: 314-621-4834
Fort Myers, Florida Office: 2080 McGregor Boulevard, Third Floor.
Telephone: 813-337-3850.
Fax: 813-337-0970.
Punta Gorda, Florida Office: 1625 West Marion Avenue, Suite 2.
Telephone: 813-637-1955.
Fax: 813-637-8485.
Naples, Florida Office: 850 Park Shore Drive, Suite 202.
Telephone: 813-261-6525.
Fax: 813-649-1805.
Belleville, Illinois Office: 720 West Main Street, Suite 140.
Telephone: 618-234-9574.
Fax: 618-234-9846.

MEMBERS OF FIRM

Kathleen S. Schoene
Gary D. McConnell
Raymond S. Kreienkamp
Peter H. Ruger

ASSOCIATE

Thomas A. A. Cook

For Complete List of Firm Personnel, See General Section

For full biographical listings, see the Martindale-Hubbell Law Directory

MONTANA

*BILLINGS,** Yellowstone Co.

CROWLEY, HAUGHEY, HANSON, TOOLE & DIETRICH (AV)

500 Transwestern II, 490 North 31st Street, P.O. Box 2529, 59103
Telephone: 406-252-3441
Fax: 406-259-4159
Helena, Montana Office: IBM Building, 100 North Park Avenue, Suite 300, 59601.
Telephone: 406-449-4165.
Fax: 406-449-5149.

MEMBERS OF FIRM

John M. Dietrich
Gareld F. Krieg
Herbert I. Pierce, III
Lawrence B. Cozzens
Steven J. Lehman
Laura A. Mitchell
Daniel N. McLean
John R. Alexander
Michael S. Dockery
Mary Scrim

Representative Clients: Deaconess Medical Center of Billings; Deaconess Care Corporation; Deaconess Research Institute; The Billings Clinic; Trinity Hospital Association.

For Complete List of Firm Personnel, See General Section

For full biographical listings, see the Martindale-Hubbell Law Directory

NEBRASKA

*OMAHA,** Douglas Co.

DWYER, POHREN, WOOD, HEAVEY, GRIMM, GOODALL & LAZER (AV)

A Partnership including Professional Corporations
Suite 400, 8712 West Dodge Road, 68114
Telephone: 402-392-0101
Telefax: 402-392-1011

MEMBERS OF FIRM

Robert V. Dwyer, Jr.
Andrew E. Grimm
Mark L. Goodall

Representative Clients: Bishop Clarkson Memorial Hospital, Omaha, Nebraska; Nebraska Hospital Association, Lincoln, Nebraska; National Medical Enterprises, Inc.; Community Hospital Association, McCook, Nebraska; Lutheran Community Hospital, Norfolk, Nebraska; Cheyenne County Hospital Association, Sidney, Nebraska.

For Complete List of Firm Personnel, See General Section

For full biographical listings, see the Martindale-Hubbell Law Directory

MCGILL, GOTSDINER, WORKMAN & LEPP, P.C. (AV)

Suite 500 - First National Plaza, 11404 West Dodge Road, 68154
Telephone: 402-492-9200
Telecopier: 402-492-9222

Robert Lepp
Paul D. Kratz

Representative Clients: Vetter Health Services, Inc.; Aksarben Nursing Centers, Inc.; Bethesda Care Centers; Jones Eye Clinic; Community Care Nebraska.

For Complete List of Firm Personnel, See General Section

For full biographical listings, see the Martindale-Hubbell Law Directory

NEW HAMPSHIRE

*CONCORD,** Merrimack Co.

ORR & RENO, PROFESSIONAL ASSOCIATION (AV)

One Eagle Square, P.O. Box 3550, 03302-3550
Telephone: 603-224-2381
Fax: 603-224-2318

Neil F. Castaldo

Representative Clients: Beach Aircraft Corporation; Chubb Life America; Fleet Bank; Dartmouth-Hitchcock Medical Center; EnergyNorth, Inc.; National Grange Mutual Co.; New England College; New England Electric System Co.; Newspapers of New England, Inc.; St. Paul's School.

For Complete List of Firm Personnel, See General Section

For full biographical listings, see the Martindale-Hubbell Law Directory

NEW JERSEY

CLIFTON, Passaic Co.

CELENTANO, STADTMAUER & WALENTOWICZ (AV)

1035 Route 46 East, P.O. Box 2594, 07015-2594
Telephone: 201-778-1771
Telecopier: 201-778-4136

MEMBERS OF FIRM

John A. Celentano, Jr.
Arnold L. Stadtmauer
Henry Walentowicz

Ellen M. Seigerman

Representative Clients: Jefferson National Bank (N.A.); Clifton Savings Bank, S.L.A.; The General Hospital Center at Passaic (commercial); Passaic Boys Club; Smith Sondy Asphalt Construction Co., Inc.; Boro Lumber Co., Inc.; Castle Arms Condominium; ADX Copy Corp.; Country Club Towers.
References: Jefferson National Bank (N.A.), Passaic, New Jersey; Commonwealth Land Title Insurance Co., Paterson, New Jersey.

For full biographical listings, see the Martindale-Hubbell Law Directory

DENVILLE, Morris Co.

EINHORN, HARRIS, ASCHER & BARBARITO, A PROFESSIONAL CORPORATION (AV)

165 East Main Street, P.O. Box 541, 07834-0541
Telephone: 201-627-7300
FAX: 201-627-5847

Theodore E. B. Einhorn
Peter T. Harris
Michael R. Ascher
Patricia M. Barbarito
Victor B. Matthews
Robert A. Scirocco
Bonnie C. Frost

Michael J. Rowland
David H. Ironson
Ann T. Scucci
Janet Block
Lee Ann McCabe
Brett R. Fielo
Jodi F. Tish

Representative Client: Saint Clare's/Riverside Medical Center, Inc.

For full biographical listings, see the Martindale-Hubbell Law Directory

LIVINGSTON, Essex Co.

GENOVA, BURNS, TRIMBOLI & VERNOIA (AV)

Eisenhower Plaza II, 354 Eisenhower Parkway, 07039
Telephone: 201-533-0777
Facsimile: 201-533-1112
Trenton, New Jersey Office: Suite One, 160 West State Street.
Telephone: 609-393-1131.

MEMBERS OF FIRM

Angelo J. Genova
James M. Burns
Stephen E. Trimboli
Francis J. Vernoia

ASSOCIATES

Meryl G. Nadler
John C. Petrella
James J. McGovern, III
Kathleen M. Connelly
Joseph Licata
Elaine M. Reyes
Lynn S. Degen
James J. Gillespie
T. Sean Jackson

For full biographical listings, see the Martindale-Hubbell Law Directory

*NEWARK,** Essex Co.

MCCARTER & ENGLISH (AV)

Four Gateway Center, 100 Mulberry Street, P.O. Box 652, 07101-0652
Telephone: 201-622-4444
Telecopier: 201-624-7070
Cable Address: "McCarter" Newark
Cherry Hill, New Jersey Office: 1810 Chapel Avenue West.
Telephone: 609-662-8444.
Telecopier: 609-662-6203.
New York, New York Office: Suite 1519, One World Trade Center.
Telephone: 212-466-9018.
Telecopier: 212-432-6568.
Boca Raton, Florida Office: 2255 Glades Road, Suite 319-A.
Telephone: 407-994-6262.
Telecopier: 407-241-0798.
Wilmington, Delaware Office: Mellon Bank Center, 919 Market Street.
Telephone: 302-654-8010.
Telecopier: 302-654-0795.

MEMBERS OF FIRM

Charles R. Merrill
Frederick B. Lehlbach
Richard J. Webb
Scott A. Kobler
George H. Kendall

COUNSEL

Beth Yingling

(See Next Column)

McCarter & English—*Continued*

ASSOCIATES

Malke Borow
Robin L. Goldfischer
David W. Opderbeck
Dror Futter
Audrey A. Hale

For Complete List of Firm Personnel, See General Section

For full biographical listings, see the Martindale-Hubbell Law Directory

Sills Cummis Zuckerman Radin Tischman Epstein & Gross, A Professional Corporation (AV)

One Riverfront Plaza, 07102-5400
Telephone: 201-643-7000
Fax: 201-643-6500
Telex: 820630 Sillsbeck Nwk
Atlantic City, New Jersey Office: 17 Gordon's Alley.
Telephone: 609-344-2800.
New York, N.Y. Office: 250 Park Avenue.
Telephone: 212-643-7000.

Clive S. Cummis
Steven S. Radin
Michael B. Tischman
Barry M. Epstein
Charles J. Walsh
Stephen J. Moses
Steven M. Goldman
William M. Russell

Glenn E. Davis
Eileen O'Donnell
Richard S. Schkolnick

Representative Clients: Blue Cross/Blue Shield of New Jersey; Bristol-Myers Squibb Corporation; Jersey City Medical Center; Englewood Hospital; Ciba Geigy Pharmaceuticals; Becton Dickinson & Company; Johnson & Johnson; First Action Health Care.

For Complete List of Firm Personnel, See General Section

For full biographical listings, see the Martindale-Hubbell Law Directory

ROSELAND, Essex Co.

Brach, Eichler, Rosenberg, Silver, Bernstein, Hammer & Gladstone, A Professional Corporation (AV)

101 Eisenhower Parkway, 07068
Telephone: 201-228-5700
Telecopier: 201-228-7852

Todd C. Brower
Burton L. Eichler
John D. Fanburg
Joseph M. Gorrell

Georgette J. Siegel
Gary W. Herschman
Kevin M. Lastorino
Michael A. Weiss
Heidi M. Zaslow
Jill A. Cohen
Simone E. Handler Hutchinson

Representative Clients: Union Hospital; Radiological Society of New Jersey; New Jersey Academy of Ophthalmology; Saint Barnabas Medical Center; Mercer Medical Center; Emergency Medical Associates; The Axiom Group; New Jersey Pathology Society.

For Complete List of Firm Personnel, See General Section

For full biographical listings, see the Martindale-Hubbell Law Directory

*TRENTON,** Mercer Co.

Backes & Hill (AV)

(Originally Backes & Backes)
(Formerly Backes, Waldron & Hill)
15 West Front Street, 08608-2098
Telephone: 609-396-8257
Telefax: 609-989-7323

Peter Backes (1858-1941)
Herbert W. Backes (1891-1970)
William Wright Backes (1904-1980)
Michael J. Nizolek (1950-1994)

OF COUNSEL

Robert Maddock Backes

PARTNERS

Harry R. Hill, Jr.
Robert C. Billmeier
Brenda Farr Engel

ASSOCIATES

Susan E. Bacso
Michele N. Siekerka
Henry A. Carpenter II
Lawrence A. Reisman

Representative Clients: New Jersey National Bank; Mercer Medical Center; Catholic Diocese of Trenton; Roller Bearing Company of America; New Jersey Manufacturers Insurance Co.; St. Francis Medical Center; The Trenton Savings Bank; Richie & Page Distributing Co., Inc.; Hill Refrigeration Corporation; General Sullivan Group, Inc.; A-1 Collections, Inc.

For full biographical listings, see the Martindale-Hubbell Law Directory

WESTFIELD, Union Co.

Dwyer & Canellis, P.A. (AV)

150 Elm Street, 07090
Telephone: 908-233-2000
Fax: 908-233-2041

George W. Canellis

Brian M. Adams
Barbara Ann Canellis

OF COUNSEL

Thomas F. Dwyer

Reference: Summit Bank; Midlantic Bank.

For full biographical listings, see the Martindale-Hubbell Law Directory

Lindabury, McCormick & Estabrook, A Professional Corporation (AV)

53 Cardinal Drive, P.O. Box 2369, 07091
Telephone: 908-233-6800
Fax: 908-233-5078

Richard R. Width
Peter A. Somers
William R. Watkins
J. Ferd Convery III
Bruce P. Ogden
Robert S. Burney

Representative Clients: Bayonne Hospital; Central New Jersey Medical Group; Central New Jersey Maternal and Child Health Consortium; Chilton Memorial Hospital; Elizabeth General Medical Center; Helene Fuld Medical Center; HIP/Rutgers Health Plan; Kessler Institute for Rehabilitation; Memorial Hospital of Burlington County; Riverview Medical Center.

For Complete List of Firm Personnel, See General Section

For full biographical listings, see the Martindale-Hubbell Law Directory

NEW MEXICO

*ALBUQUERQUE,** Bernalillo Co.

Hinkle, Cox, Eaton, Coffield & Hensley (AV)

Suite 800, 500 Marquette, N.W., P.O. Box 2043, 87103
Telephone: 505-768-1500
FAX: 505-768-1529
Roswell, New Mexico Office: Suite 700, United Bank Plaza, P.O. Box 10, 88202.
Telephone: 505-622-6510.
FAX: 505-623-9332.
Midland, Texas Office: 6 Desta Drive, Suite 2800, P.O. Box 3580, 79705.
Telephone: 915-683-4691.
FAX: 915-683-6518.
Amarillo, Texas Office: 1700 Bank One Center. P.O. Box 9238, 79105-9238.
Telephone: 806-372-5569.
FAX: 806-372-9761.
Santa Fe, New Mexico Office: 218 Montezuma, P.O. Box 2068, 87504.
Telephone: 505-982-4554.
FAX: 505-982-8623.
Austin, Texas Office: 401 West 15th Street, Suite 800, 78701.
Telephone: 512-476-7137.
FAX: 512-476-5431.
Associated Office: Hoffman & Stephens, P.C., 401 West 15th Street, Suite 800, 78701.
Telephone: 512-476-5434.
Fax: 512-476-5431.

Marshall G. Martin
Nicholas J. Noeding
Jeffrey S. Baird (Amarillo Office)
Thomas E. Hood (Amarillo Office)
Diane Fisher

ASSOCIATE

Lisa K. Smith (Amarillo Office)

Representative Clients: Anadarko Petroleum Corp.; Atlantic Richfield Co.; Bass Enterprises Production Co.; BHP Petroleum; Caroon & Black Management, Inc.; Chevron, USA, Inc.; CIGNA; City of Albuquerque; Coastal Oil & Gas Corp. Co.; Dallam Hartley County Hospital District; Harrington Regional Medical Center at Amarillo, Inc.; NM Medical Group; Presbyterian Healthcare Services;

For Complete List of Firm Personnel, See General Section

For full biographical listings, see the Martindale-Hubbell Law Directory

Kelly, Rammelkamp, Muehlenweg, Lucero & León, A Professional Association (AV)

Simms Tower, 400 Gold Avenue S.W., Suite 500, P.O. Box 25127, 87125-5127
Telephone: 505-247-8860
Fax: 505-247-8881

(See Next Column)

KELLY, RAMMELKAMP, MUEHLENWEG, LUCERO & LEÓN A PROFESSIONAL ASSOCIATION, *Albuquerque—Continued*

Henry A. Kelly | David A. Rammelkamp

Paige G. Leslie

Representative Clients: John L. Rust Co. (Caterpillar); Ponderosa Products, Inc.; Rehobeth-McKinley Christian Healthcare Services; Kinney Agency, Inc.; Basis International, Ltd.; Bridgers & Paxton Consulting Engineers, Inc.; Jezlaine, Ltd.; D.W.B.H., Inc. (Nissan, Mitsubishi and Hyundai); Envirco Corporation; Sun Crest Hospital.

For Complete List of Firm Personnel, See General Section

For full biographical listings, see the Martindale-Hubbell Law Directory

RODEY, DICKASON, SLOAN, AKIN & ROBB, P.A. (AV)

Albuquerque Plaza, Suite 2200, 201 Third Street, N.W., P.O. Box 1888, 87103-1888
Telephone: 505-765-5900
Fax: 505-768-7395
Santa Fe, New Mexico Office: Suite 101 Marcy Plaza, 123 East Marcy Street, P.O. Box 1357, 87504-1357.
Telephone: 505-984-0100.
Fax: 505-989-9542.

W. Robert Lasater, Jr. | Angela M. Martinez
Edward Ricco | Patricia M. Taylor
Ellen G. Thorne | Theresa W. Parrish

Sheryl S. Mahaney

For Complete List of Firm Personnel, See General Section

For full biographical listings, see the Martindale-Hubbell Law Directory

*SANTA FE,** Santa Fe Co.

HUFFAKER & BARNES, A PROFESSIONAL CORPORATION (AV)

155 Grant Avenue, P.O. Box 1868, 87504-1868
Telephone: 505-988-8921
Fax: 505-983-3927

Gregory D. Huffaker, Jr. | Bradley C. Barron
Julia Hosford Barnes | Sharon A. Higgins (Not admitted in NM)

Representative Client: New Mexico Monitored Treatment Program.

For full biographical listings, see the Martindale-Hubbell Law Directory

NEW YORK

*ALBANY,** Albany Co.

ISEMAN, CUNNINGHAM, RIESTER & HYDE (AV)

9 Thurlow Terrace, 12203
Telephone: 518-462-3000
Telecopier: 518-462-4199

MEMBERS OF FIRM

Frederick C. Riester | Robert Hall Iseman
Michael J. Cunningham | Carol Ann Hyde
Michael J. McNeil

Brian M. Culnan | Linda J. Clark

For full biographical listings, see the Martindale-Hubbell Law Directory

O'CONNELL AND ARONOWITZ, P.C. (AV)

100 State Street, 12207-1885
Telephone: 518-462-5601
Telecopier: 518-462-2670
Plattsburgh, New York Office: Grand Plaza Building, Suite 204, 159 Margaret Street.
Telephone: 518-562-0600.
Fax: 518-562-0657.
Saratoga Springs, New York Office: Suite 202, 358 Broadway.
Telephone: 518-587-0425.
Fax: 518-587-0565.

Cornelius D. Murray | Sarah Walker Birn

James L. Coffin | Pamela A. Nichols

New York State Health Facilities Association; Foster Medical Supply, Inc.

For Complete List of Firm Personnel, See General Section

For full biographical listings, see the Martindale-Hubbell Law Directory

TOBIN AND DEMPF (AV)

33 Elk Street, 12207
Telephone: 518-463-1177
Telecopier: 518-463-7489

MEMBERS OF FIRM

Charles J. Tobin (1882-1954) | John W. Clark
Charles J. Tobin, Jr. (1915-1987) | John T. Mitchell
James W. Sanderson (1937-1992) | David A. Ruffo
Louis Dempf, Jr. | Kevin A. Luibrand
Michael L. Costello | R. Christopher Dempf

ASSOCIATES

Mark A. Mainello | William H. Reynolds
Gayle E. Hartz | Raul A. Tabora, Jr.

General and/or Health Counsel for: Teresian House Nursing Home Co.; Mohawk Valley Nursing Home; Isabella Geriatric Center; Lutheran Home of Central New York; Baptist Retirement Center; Baptist Home of Brooklyn, New York; Sephardic Home; Eddy Memorial Geriatric Center; Wesley Health Care Center; Mt. Loretto Nursing Home.

For full biographical listings, see the Martindale-Hubbell Law Directory

*BUFFALO,** Erie Co.

HURWITZ & FINE, P.C. (AV)

1300 Liberty Building, 14202-3613
Telephone: 716-849-8900
Telecopier: 716-855-0874

Sheldon Hurwitz | Ann E. Evanko
Robert P. Fine | Paul J. Suozzi
Lawrence C. Franco | Roger L. Ross
Dan D. Kohane | Christopher J. Hurley
Lawrence M. Ross

For Complete List of Firm Personnel, See General Section

For full biographical listings, see the Martindale-Hubbell Law Directory

*NEW YORK,** New York Co.

FINKELSTEIN BRUCKMAN WOHL MOST & ROTHMAN (AV)

575 Lexington Avenue, 10022-6102
Telephone: 212-754-3100
Telecopier: 212-371-2980
Stamford, Connecticut Office: 1 Landmark Square.
Telephone: 203-358-9200.
Telecopier: 203-969-6140.
Hackensack, New Jersey Office: 20 Court Street.
Telephone: 201-525-1800.
Telecopier: 201-489-4509.

MEMBERS OF FIRM

Allen L. Finkelstein | Bernard Ferster
George T. Bruckman | Samuel R. Dolgow
Ronald Gene Wohl | Joel A. Fruchter
Jack L. Most | David T. Harmon
Bernard Rothman | Joan Levin
Richard M. Schwartz | Joseph Milano
Harold A. Horowitz | Sidney Orenstein
T. Lawrence Tabak

ASSOCIATES

Michael R. Fleishman | Gavin C. Grusd
Marlene Zarfes | David B. Bruckman
David W. Wankoff | Maurice L. Miller

OF COUNSEL

Stuart Abrams | James B. Rosenblum
Eugenia M. Ballesteros | Patrick J. Filan
Sylvan J. Schaffer | Jacob H. Zamansky
Robert S. Barnett | Earle R. Tockman

SENIOR COUNSEL

Arthur S. Bruckman

For full biographical listings, see the Martindale-Hubbell Law Directory

MCALOON & FRIEDMAN, P.C. (AV)

116 John Street, 10038
Telephone: 212-732-8700

Edward H. McAloon (1908-1986) | Theodore B. Rosenzweig
Stanley D. Friedman | Gary A. Greenfield
Gunther H. Kilsch | Brendan J. Lantier
| Lawrence W. Mumm
Laura R. Shapiro

(See Next Column)

McALOON & FRIEDMAN P.C.—*Continued*

Rose Candeloro
Regina E. Schneller
Lisa B. Goldstein
John Langell
Barbara A. Dalton
Michelle E. Just
Eleanor M. Kanzler
Paul Nasta
Kim R. Kleppel
Kenneth Gordon Ellison
Evette E. Harrison
Thomas Medardo Oliva
Adam R. Goldsmith
Christopher B. O'Malley
Arlene Bergman

For full biographical listings, see the Martindale-Hubbell Law Directory

PARKER CHAPIN FLATTAU & KLIMPL, L.L.P. (AV)

1211 Avenue of the Americas, 10036
Telephone: 212-704-6000
Telecopier: 212-704-6288
Cable Address: "Lawpark"
Telex: 640347
Great Neck, New York Office: 175 Great Neck Road.
Telephone: 516-482-4422.
Telecopier: 516-482-4469.

MEMBERS OF FIRM

Karen F. Lederer
Kevin D. Porter

ASSOCIATE

Carolyn S. Reinach

For Complete List of Firm Personnel, See General Section

For full biographical listings, see the Martindale-Hubbell Law Directory

SCHILLER & ASSOCIATES, P.C. (AV)

598 Madison Avenue, 15th Floor, 10022
Telephone: 212-688-4100
Telecopier: 212-753-8940

Craig Schiller

OF COUNSEL

Lizabeth Rosenrauch
Richard J. Weiss

For full biographical listings, see the Martindale-Hubbell Law Directory

*ROCHESTER,** Monroe Co.

HARTER, SECREST & EMERY (AV)

700 Midtown Tower, 14604-2070
Telephone: 716-232-6500
Telecopier: 716-232-2152
Naples, Florida Office: Suite 400, 800 Laurel Oak Drive.
Telephone: 813-598-4444.
Telecopier: 813-598-2781.
Albany, New York Office: One Steuben Place.
Telephone: 518-434-4377.
Telecopier: 518-449-4025.
Syracuse, New York Office: 431 East Fayette Street.
Telephone: 315-474-4000.
Telecopier: 315-474-7789.

MEMBERS OF FIRM

Thomas B. Garlick (Resident Partner, Naples, Florida Office)
Kenneth A. Payment
James P. Burns, 3rd (Resident Partner, Syracuse Office)
Peter G. Smith
Thomas G. Smith
Eric A. Evans
Philip R. Fileri
Donald S. Mazzullo
John C. Herbert
Timothy R. Parry (Not admitted in NY; Resident Partner, Naples, Florida Office)
Mary E. Ross
Ronald J. Mendrick

ASSOCIATES

Carol O'Keefe
Ross P. Lanzafame
Susan A. Roberts
Sheila M. Rembert
Mia Hsu Burton

LEGAL SUPPORT PERSONNEL

Thomas E. Cardillo (Health Care Consultant)

For Complete List of Firm Personnel, See General Section

For full biographical listings, see the Martindale-Hubbell Law Directory

NORTH CAROLINA

*CHARLOTTE,** Mecklenburg Co.

SMITH HELMS MULLISS & MOORE, L.L.P. (AV)

227 North Tryon Street, P.O. Box 31247, 28231
Telephone: 704-343-2000
Telecopier: 704-334-8467
Telex: 572460
Greensboro, North Carolina Office: Smith Helms Mulliss & Moore, Suite 1400 First Union Tower, 300 North Greene Street, P.O. Box 21927.
Telephone: 910-378-5200.
Telecopier: 910-379-9558.
Raleigh, North Carolina Office: 316 West Edenton Street, P.O. Box 27525.
Telephone: 919-755-8700.
Telecopier: 919-828-7938.

COUNSEL

James H. Guterman

MEMBERS OF FIRM

Herbert H. Browne, Jr.
R. Malloy McKeithen
Douglas W. Ey, Jr.

For Complete List of Firm Personnel, See General Section

For full biographical listings, see the Martindale-Hubbell Law Directory

VAN HOY, REUTLINGER & TAYLOR (AV)

737 East Boulevard, 28203
Telephone: 704-375-6022
Fax: 704-375-6024

MEMBERS OF FIRM

Philip M. Van Hoy
Craig A. Reutlinger
Paul B. Taylor

Representative Clients: McDowell Hospital; Medical Review of North Carolina; National Health Labs, Inc.; Beverly Enterprises; Cannon Memorial Hospital; Carolina Medical Review; Southeast Radiation Oncology Group; University Medical Associates; Total Care Home Health; Cabarrus Nursing Center.

For full biographical listings, see the Martindale-Hubbell Law Directory

*GREENSBORO,** Guilford Co.

SMITH HELMS MULLISS & MOORE, L.L.P. (AV)

Suite 1400 First Union Tower, 300 North Greene Street, P.O. Box 21927, 27420
Telephone: 910-378-5200
Telecopier: 910-379-9558
Charlotte, North Carolina Office: Smith Helms Mulliss & Moore, L.L.P., 227 North Tryon Street, P.O. Box 31247.
Telephone: 704-343-2000.
Telecopier: 704-334-8467.
Telex: 572460.
Raleigh, North Carolina Office: Smith Helms Mulliss & Moore, L.L.P., 316 West Edenton Street, P.O. Box 27525.
Telephone: 919-755-8700.
Telecopier: 919-828-7938.

MEMBERS OF FIRM

Thomas S. Stukes
Alan W. Duncan
Maureen Demarest Murray

ASSOCIATES

William K. Edwards
Christine T. Nero

For Complete List of Firm Personnel, See General Section

For full biographical listings, see the Martindale-Hubbell Law Directory

*RALEIGH,** Wake Co.

* indicates certain Bar Register subscribers whose principal office is located elsewhere in the state and who have arranged for representation as a part of the state capital listings that follow

*** SMITH HELMS MULLISS & MOORE, L.L.P. (AV)**

316 West Edenton Street, P.O. Box 27525, 27611-7525
Telephone: 919-755-8700
Telecopier: 919-828-7938
Charlotte, North Carolina Office: 227 North Tryon Street, P.O. Box 31247.
Telephone: 704-343-2000.
Telecopier: 704-334-8467.
Telex: 572460.
Greensboro, North Carolina Office: Smith Helms Mulliss & Moore, Suite 1400 First Union Tower, 300 North Greene Street, P.O. Box 21927.
Telephone: 910-378-5200.
Telecopier: 910-379-9558.

(See Next Column)

SMITH HELMS MULLISS & MOORE L.L.P., *Raleigh—Continued*

MEMBERS OF FIRM

Richard W. Ellis
Leslie C. O'Toole

For Complete List of Firm Personnel, See General Section

For full biographical listings, see the Martindale-Hubbell Law Directory

*WINSTON-SALEM,** Forsyth Co.

WOMBLE CARLYLE SANDRIDGE & RICE (AV)

A Professional Limited Liability Company
1600 Southern National Financial Center, P.O. Drawer 84, 27102
Telephone: 910-721-3600
Telecopy: 910-721-3660
Telex: 806498
Charlotte, North Carolina Office: 3300 One First Union Center, 301 South College Street.
Telephone: 704-331-4900.
Telecopy: 704-331-4955.
Telex: 853609.
Raleigh, North Carolina Office: 2100 First Union Capitol Center, 150 Fayetteville Street Mall, P.O. Box 831.
Telephone: 919-755-2100.
Telecopy: 919-755-2150.
Telex: 806498.
Atlanta, Georgia Office: One Ninety One Peachtree Tower, 191 Peachtree Street, N.E., Suite 3250.
Telephone: 404-614-2580.
Fax: 404-614-2595.

MEMBERS OF FIRM

Anthony H. Brett
Roddey M. Ligon, Jr.

ASSOCIATE

Joel M. Leander

Representative Clients: Brad Ragan, Inc.; Brenner Companies; Food Lion, Inc.; Hanes Companies, Inc.; North Carolina Baptist Hospitals, Inc.; R.J. Reynolds Tobacco Company; Summit Communications Group, Inc.; Thomasville Furniture Industries, Inc.; Wachovia Corporation; Wake Forest University.

For Complete List of Firm Personnel, See General Section

For full biographical listings, see the Martindale-Hubbell Law Directory

NORTH DAKOTA

*MINOT,** Ward Co.

McGEE, HANKLA, BACKES & WHEELER, P.C. (AV)

Suite 305 Norwest Center, 15 Second Avenue Southwest, P.O. Box 998, 58702-0998
Telephone: 701-852-2544
Fax: 701-838-4724

Richard H. McGee (1918-1992)
Walfrid B. Hankla
Orlin W. Backes
Robert A. Wheeler
Donald L. Peterson
Richard H. McGee, II
Collin P. Dobrovolny
Brian W. Hankla
Robert J. Hovland
Jon W. Backes

LEGAL SUPPORT PERSONNEL

Janice M. Eslinger
Jane K. Hutchison
Ardella M. Burtman
Michelle Erdmann

For full biographical listings, see the Martindale-Hubbell Law Directory

OHIO

*CINCINNATI,** Hamilton Co.

BROWN, CUMMINS & BROWN CO., L.P.A. (AV)

3500 Carew Tower, 441 Vine Street, 45202
Telephone: 513-381-2121
Fax: 513-381-2125

J. W. Brown (Retired)
Robert S Brown
James R. Cummins
Donald S. Mendelsohn
Lynne Skilken
Amy G. Applegate
Kathryn Knue Przywara
Jeffrey R. Teeters

OF COUNSEL

Gilbert Bettman

Counsel for: The University of Cincinnati.
Reference: Star Bank of Cincinnati.

For full biographical listings, see the Martindale-Hubbell Law Directory

DINSMORE & SHOHL (AV)

1900 Chemed Center, 255 East Fifth Street, 45202-3172
Telephone: 513-977-8200
FAX: 513-977-8141
Florence, Kentucky Office: Turfway Ridge Office Park, 7300 Turfway Road, Suite 430 41042-1355.
Telephone: 606-283-0515.
FAX: 606-283-6017.
Dayton, Ohio Office: 500 Courthouse Plaza, S.W., 10 N. Ludlow Street, 45402-1834.
Telephone: 513-228-8012.
FAX: 513-461-2543.
Columbus, Ohio Office: NBD Bank Building, Suite 330, 175 South Third Street, 43215-5134.
Telephone: 614-224-7887.
FAX: 614-224-7882.

MEMBERS OF FIRM

Clifford A. Roe, Jr.
Frank C. Woodside, III
William M. Freedman
Nancy A. Lawson
Deborah R. Lydon
Stephen K. Shaw
K. C. Green
June Smith Tyler

ASSOCIATES

James A. Comodeca
Steven H. Ray
Richard L. Schuster
Joseph L. Sallee, Jr.
John J. Hoffmann (Resident, Dayton, Ohio Office)
Richard J. Mitchell, Jr.
Sara Simrall Rorer
Melissa A. Fetters
Laurie H. Schwab
Mary-Jo Middelhoff
David S. Rosenthal
William M. Mattes (Resident, Columbus, Ohio Office)
Frederick N. Hamilton
Jeffrey P. Hinebaugh
Ann Collins Hindman
Christopher L. Riegler (Resident, Dayton, Ohio Office)

For Complete List of Firm Personnel, See General Section

For full biographical listings, see the Martindale-Hubbell Law Directory

GOODMAN & GOODMAN A LEGAL PROFESSIONAL ASSOCIATION (AV)

123 East Fourth Street, 45202
Telephone: 513-621-1505; 1-800-494-4529
FAX: 513-621-6900

Stanley Goodman
Ronald J. Goodman

For full biographical listings, see the Martindale-Hubbell Law Directory

KATZ, TELLER, BRANT & HILD A LEGAL PROFESSIONAL ASSOCIATION (AV)

2400 Chemed Center, 255 East Fifth Street, 45202-4724
Telephone: 513-721-4532
Telecopier: 513-721-7120

Reuven J. Katz
Jerome S. Teller
Joseph A. Brant
Guy M. Hild
Robert A. Pitcairn, Jr.
Robert E. Brant
Ronald J. Goret
Stephen C. Kisling
Andrew R. Berger
Mark J. Jahnke
William F. Russo
John R. Gierl
Bruce A. Hunter
Gregory E. Land
Bradley G. Haas
Daniel P. Utt
Brent G. Houk
Cynthia Loren Gibson
Suzanne Prieur Land
Tedd H. Friedman

Representative Clients: Eagle Picher Industries, Inc.; F & C International, Inc.; Jewish Hospitals of Cincinnati; Johnny Bench; Texo Corporation; University of Cincinnati Medical Associates, Inc.

For full biographical listings, see the Martindale-Hubbell Law Directory

THOMPSON, HINE AND FLORY (AV)

312 Walnut Street, 14th Floor, 45202-4029
Telephone: 513-352-6700
Fax: 513-241-4771;
Telex: 938003
Akron, Ohio Office: 50 S. Main Street, Suite 502, 44308-1828.
Telephone: 216-376-8090.
Fax: 216-376-8386.
Cleveland, Ohio Office: 1100 National City Bank Building, 629 Euclid Avenue, 44114-3070.
Telephone: 216-566-5500.
Fax: 216-556-5583.
Telex: 980217.
Cable Address: "Thomflor".
Columbus, Ohio Office: One Columbus, 10 West Broad Street, 43215-3435.
Telephone: 614-469-3200.
Fax: 614-469-3361.
Dayton, Ohio Office: 2000 Courthouse Plaza, N.E., 45402-1706.
Telephone: 513-443-6600.
Fax: 513-443-6637; 443-6635.

(See Next Column)

THOMPSON, HINE AND FLORY—*Continued*

Palm Beach, Florida Office: 125 Worth Avenue, 33480-4466.
Telephone: 407-833-5900.
Fax: 407-833-5951.
Washington, D.C. Office: 1920 N Street, N.W., 20036-1601.
Telephone: 202-331-8800.
Fax: 202-331-8330.
Telex: 904173.
Cable Address: "Caglaw".
Brussels, Belgium Office: Rue des Chevaliers / Ridderstraat 14 - B.10, B - 1050.
Telephone: 011(32-2) 511-9326.
Fax: 011(-32-2) 513-9206.

MEMBERS OF FIRM

Scott B. Crooks
Melvin E. Marmer

For Complete List of Firm Personnel, See General Section

For full biographical listings, see the Martindale-Hubbell Law Directory

*CLEVELAND,** Cuyahoga Co.

THOMPSON, HINE AND FLORY (AV)

1100 National City Bank Building, 629 Euclid Avenue, 44114-3070
Telephone: 216-566-5500
Fax: 216-566-5583
Telex: 980217
Cable Address: "Thomflor"
Akron, Ohio Office: 50 S. Main Street, Suite 502, 44308-1828.
Telephone: 216-376-8090.
Fax: 216-376-8386.
Cincinnati, Ohio Office: 312 Walnut Street, 14th Floor, 45202-4029.
Telephone: 513-352-6700.
Fax: 513-241-4771.
Telex: 938003.
Columbus, Ohio Office: One Columbus, 10 West Broad Street, 43215-3435.
Telephone: 614-469-3200.
Fax: 614-469-3361.
Dayton, Ohio Office: 2000 Courthouse Plaza, N.E., 45402-1706.
Telephone: 513-443-6600.
Fax: 513-443-6637; 443-6635.
Palm Beach, Florida Office: 125 Worth Avenue, Suite 117, 33480-4466.
Telephone: 407-833-5900.
Fax: 407-833-5951.
Washington, D.C. Office: 1920 N Street, N.W., 20036-1601.
Telephone: 202-331-8800.
Fax: 202-331-8330.
Telex: 904173.
Cable Address: "Caglaw".
Brussels, Belgium Office: Rue des Chevaliers, Ridderstraat 14 - B.10, B - 1050.
Telephone: 011(32-2) 511-9326.
Fax: 011(32-2) 513-9206.

MEMBERS OF FIRM

Barbara J. Arison
Malvin E. Bank
Thomas A. Heffernan
Donald L. Korb (In Washington, D.C. and Cleveland, Ohio)
Donald H. Messinger (Partner-in-Charge)
Deborah Zider Read
Richard E. Streeter
William C. Trier, Jr.
Roy L. Turnell
Richard V. Whelan, Jr.

For Complete List of Firm Personnel, See General Section

For full biographical listings, see the Martindale-Hubbell Law Directory

*COLUMBUS,** Franklin Co.

* indicates certain Bar Register subscribers whose principal office is located elsewhere in the state and who have arranged for representation as a part of the state capital listings that follow

EMENS, KEGLER, BROWN, HILL & RITTER (AV)

Capitol Square Suite 1800, 65 East State Street, 43215-4294
Telephone: 614-462-5400
Telecopier: 614-464-2634
Cable Address: "Law EKBHR"
Telex: 246671

Donald A. Antrim
William J. Brown
R. Kevin Kerns
R. Douglas Wrightsel

Thomas M. L. Metzger
Karl W. Schedler

Representative Clients: Arbor Health Care Company; Charter Medical Corporation; Medco Containment Services, Inc.; Meridia Health System; National Medical Enterprises, Inc.; Nursing Care Management.

For Complete List of Firm Personnel, See General Section

For full biographical listings, see the Martindale-Hubbell Law Directory

SCHOTTENSTEIN, ZOX & DUNN A LEGAL PROFESSIONAL ASSOCIATION (AV)

The Huntington Center, 41 South High Street, 43215
Telephone: 614-221-3211
Telecopier: 614-464-1135
Telex: 650 24 444 365

Benjamin L. Zox
Fredrick L. Fisher
Peter A. Pavarini
Catherine T. Dunlay
Susan Darnell Rector
Susan Porter
Michael P. Kennedy (Not admitted in OH)

Nancy A. Brigner
Julie Mann Brightwell

Reference: Bank One of Columbus, N.A.

For Complete List of Firm Personnel, See General Section

For full biographical listings, see the Martindale-Hubbell Law Directory

* THOMPSON, HINE AND FLORY (AV)

One Columbus, 10 West Broad Street, 43215-3435
Telephone: 614-469-3200
Fax: 614-469-3361
Akron, Ohio Office: 50 S. Main Street, Suite 502, 44308-1828.
Telephone: 216-376-8090.
Fax: 216-376-8386.
Cincinnati, Ohio Office: 312 Walnut Street, 14th Floor, 45202-4029.
Telephone: 513-352-6700.
Fax: 513-241-4771.
Telex: 938003.
Cleveland, Ohio Office: 1100 National City Bank Building, 629 Euclid Avenue, 44114-3070.
Telephone: 216-566-5500.
Fax: 216-556-5583.
Telex: 980217.
Cable Address: "Thomflor".
Dayton, Ohio Office: 2000 Courthouse Plaza, N.E., 45402-1706.
Telephone: 513-443-6600.
Fax: 513-443-6637; 443-6635.
Palm Beach, Florida Office: 125 Worth Avenue, 33480-4466.
Telephone: 407-833-5900.
Fax: 407-833-5951.
Washington, D.C. Office: 1920 N Street, N.W., 20036-1601.
Telephone: 202-331-8800.
Fax: 202-331-8330.
Telex: 904173.
Cable Address: "Caglaw".
Brussels, Belgium Office: Rue des Chevaliers / Ridderstraat 14 - B.10, B - 1050.
Telephone: 011(32-2) 511-9326.
Fax: 011(32-2) 513-9206.

MEMBERS OF FIRM

Thomas J. Bonasera
Gerald L. Draper
William S. Fein
Susan A. Petersen
Jerry Vande Werken

ASSOCIATE

Michael A. Renne

For Complete List of Firm Personnel, See General Section

For full biographical listings, see the Martindale-Hubbell Law Directory

*DAYTON,** Montgomery Co.

SEBALY, SHILLITO & DYER (AV)

1300 Courthouse Plaza, NE, P.O. Box 220, 45402-0220
Telephone: 513-222-2500
Telefax: 513-222-6554; 222-8279
Springfield, Ohio Office: National City Bank Building, 4 West Main Street, Suite 530, P.O. Box 1346, 45501-1346.
Telephone: 513-325-7878.
Telefax: 513-325-6151.

MEMBERS OF FIRM

James A. Dyer
Gale S. Finley
William W. Lambert
Michael P. Moloney
Mary Lynn Readey
Jon M. Sebaly
Beverly F. Shillito
Jeffrey B. Shulman
Karl R. Ulrich
Robert A. Vaughn (Resident, Springfield Office)

Martin A. Beyer
Daniel A. Brown
Anne L. Rhoades
Orly R. Rumberg
Juliana M. Spaeth
Kendra F. Thompson

Representative Clients: Children's Medical Center; The Dartmouth Hospital; Imaging Physicians, Inc.; Anesthesia Associates of Cincinnati, Inc.; Ohio Psychiatric Institute.

For full biographical listings, see the Martindale-Hubbell Law Directory

Dayton—Continued

THOMPSON, HINE AND FLORY (AV)

2000 Courthouse Plaza, N.E., 45402-1706
Telephone: 513-443-6600
Fax: 513-443-6637; 443-6635
Akron, Ohio Office: 50 S. Main Street, Suite 502, 44308-1828.
Telephone: 216-376-8090.
Fax: 216-376-8386.
Cincinnati, Ohio Office: 312 Walnut Street, 14th Floor, 45202-4029.
Telephone: 513-352-6700.
Fax: 513-241-4771.
Telex: 938003.
Cleveland, Ohio Office: 1100 National City Bank Building, 629 Euclid Avenue, 44114-3070.
Telephone: 216-566-5500.
Fax: 216-556-5583.
Telex: 980217.
Cable Address: "Thomflor".
Columbus, Ohio Office: One Columbus, 10 West Broad Street, 43215-3435.
Telephone: 614-469-3200.
Fax: 614-469-3361.
Palm Beach, Florida Office: 125 Worth Avenue, 33480-4466.
Telephone: 407-833-5900.
Fax: 407-833-5951.
Washington, D.C. Office: 1920 N Street, N.W., 20036-1601.
Telephone: 202-331-8800.
Fax: 202-331-8330.
Telex: 904173.
Cable Address: "Caglaw".
Brussels, Belgium Office: Rue des Chevaliers / Ridderstraat 14 - B.10, B - 1050.
Telephone: 011(32-2) 511-9326.
Fax: 011(32-2) 513-9206.

MEMBERS OF FIRM

Richard F. Carlile
Robert M. Curry
Peter J. Donahue
Robert J. Hadley
Thomas A. Knoth
David M. Rickert

For Complete List of Firm Personnel, See General Section

For full biographical listings, see the Martindale-Hubbell Law Directory

*TOLEDO,** Lucas Co.

EASTMAN & SMITH (AV)

One Seagate, Twenty-Fourth Floor, 43604
Telephone: 419-241-6000
Telecopier: 419-247-1777
Columbus, Ohio Office: 65 East State Street, Suite 1000, 43215.
Telephone: 614-460-3556.
Telecopier: 614-228-5371.

MEMBERS OF FIRM

Bruce L. Smith
David L. Kuhl
Gary M. Harden

ASSOCIATE

John M. Kirsner

Counsel for: Riverside Hospital; Memorial Hospital (Fremont); The Toledo Clinic, Inc.; Medicare Equipment Supply Co.; Medical Protective Co.; The PM Group, Inc.; Magruder Hospital; Van Wert County Hospital.

For Complete List of Firm Personnel, See General Section

For full biographical listings, see the Martindale-Hubbell Law Directory

FULLER & HENRY (AV)

One Seagate Suite 1700, P.O. Box 2088, 43603-2088
Telephone: 419-247-2500
Telecopier: 419-247-2665
Port Clinton, Ohio Office: 125 Jefferson.
Telephone: 419-734-2153.
Telecopier: 419-732-8246.
Columbus, Ohio Office: 2210 Huntington Center, 41 South High Street.
Telephone: 614-228-6611.
Telecopier: 614-228-6623.

MEMBERS OF FIRM

Raymond G. Esch
Thomas M. George
Stephen B. Mosier

SENIOR ATTORNEY

Regina Reid Joseph

ASSOCIATE

Robert E. Nagucki

Representative Clients: First InterHealth Network, Inc.; Health Care & Retirement Corporation; OhioCare Health Systems, Inc.; Mercy Acute Care Services, Inc.; Northwest Ohio Emergency Services, Inc.; Professional Emergency Services, Inc.; St. Luke's Hospital.

For Complete List of Firm Personnel, See General Section

For full biographical listings, see the Martindale-Hubbell Law Directory

WATKINS, BATES & CAREY (AV)

1200 Fifth Third Center, 608 Madison Avenue, 43604-1157
Telephone: 419-241-2100
Telecopier: 419-241-1960

MEMBERS OF FIRM

William F. Bates
Gary O. Sommer

ASSOCIATE

Gabrielle Davis

Counsel for: Flower Hospital; Fostoria Community Hospital; Lake Park Hospital and Nursing Care Center; Crestview Club Apartments.

For Complete List of Firm Personnel, See General Section

For full biographical listings, see the Martindale-Hubbell Law Directory

OKLAHOMA

*OKLAHOMA CITY,** Oklahoma Co.

ANDREWS DAVIS LEGG BIXLER MILSTEN & PRICE, A PROFESSIONAL CORPORATION (AV)

500 West Main, 73102
Telephone: 405-272-9241
FAX: 405-235-8786

John C. Andrews
J. Edward Barth
Carolyn C. Cummins
Alan C. Durbin
John F. Fischer, II
Mona S. Lambird
Timothy M. Larason
Robert D. Nelon
Mark H. Price
D. Joe Rockett
R. Brown Wallace

Representative Clients: Oklahoma Dental Assn.; Bethany General Hospital; Oklahoma State Medical Assn.; Medical Arts Laboratories; Oklahoma Orthapedics, Inc.; Oklahoma Physicians Network-IPA, Inc.

For Complete List of Firm Personnel, See General Section

For full biographical listings, see the Martindale-Hubbell Law Directory

DAY, EDWARDS, FEDERMAN, PROPESTER & CHRISTENSEN, P.C. (AV)

Suite 2900 First Oklahoma Tower, 210 Park Avenue, 73102-5605
Telephone: 405-239-2121
Telecopier: 405-236-1012

Bruce W. Day
Joe E. Edwards
William B. Federman
Richard P. Propester
D. Wade Christensen
J. Clay Christensen
Kent A. Gilliland
Rodney J. Heggy
Ricki Valerie Sonders
Thomas Pitchlynn Howell, IV
John C. Platt

David R. Widdoes
Lori R. Roberts
Carolyn A. Romberg

OF COUNSEL

Herbert F. (Jack) Hewett
Jeanette Cook Timmons
Joel Warren Harmon
Jane S. Eulberg
Mark A. Cohen

Representative Clients: Aetna Life Insurance Co.; Boatmen's First National Bank of Oklahoma; Borg-Warner Chemicals, Inc.; City Bank & Trust; Federal Deposit Insurance Corp.; Bank One, Oklahoma City; Haskell Lemon Construction Co.; Merrill Lynch, Pierce, Fenner & Smith, Inc.; Prudential Securities, Inc.

For full biographical listings, see the Martindale-Hubbell Law Directory

HARTZOG CONGER & CASON, A PROFESSIONAL CORPORATION (AV)

1600 Bank of Oklahoma Plaza, 73102
Telephone: 405-235-7000
Facsimile: 405-235-7329

Larry D. Hartzog
J. William Conger
Len Cason
James C. Prince
Alan Newman
Steven C. Davis
Valerie K. Couch
Mark D. Dickey
Joseph P. Hogsett
John D. Robertson
Kurt M. Rupert
Laura Haag McConnell

Susan B. Shields
Ryan S. Wilson
Melanie J. Jester
Armand Paliotta
Julia Watson
J. Leslie LaReau

OF COUNSEL

Kent F. Frates

For full biographical listings, see the Martindale-Hubbell Law Directory

*TULSA,** Tulsa Co.

BOONE, SMITH, DAVIS, HURST & DICKMAN, A PROFESSIONAL CORPORATION (AV)

500 Oneok Plaza, 100 West 5th Street, 74103
Telephone: 918-587-0000
Fax: 918-599-9317

Byron V. Boone (1908-1988)
Royce H. Savage (1904-1993)
L. K. Smith
Reuben Davis
J. Jerry Dickman
Frederic N. (Nick) Schneider III
William C. Kellough
J Schaad Titus
John A. Burkhardt
Paul E. Swain III
Carol A. Grissom
Kimberly Lambert Love
Teresa Meinders Burkett
Paul J. Cleary

R. Tom Hillis
Barry G. Reynolds
Laura L. Gonsalves
Scott R. Rowland
Shane Egan
Nancy Lynn Davis

OF COUNSEL

Edwin S. Hurst
Lloyd G. Minter

Representative Clients: American Airlines; Chevron U.S.A., Inc.; The F & M Bank & Trust Co.; Hillcrest Medical Center; Boatmen's First National Bank of Oklahoma; Phillips Petroleum Co.; Rockwell International; Sears, Roebuck & Co.; Thrifty Rent-A-Car Systems, Inc.; World Publishing Co.

For full biographical listings, see the Martindale-Hubbell Law Directory

JOHNSON, ALLEN, JONES & DORNBLASER (AV)

900 Petroleum Club Building, 601 South Boulder, 74119
Telephone: 918-584-6644
FAX: 918-584-6645

MEMBERS OF FIRM

Mark H. Allen
W. Thomas Coffman
Kenneth E. Dornblaser
John B. Johnson, Jr.
C. Robert Jones
Richard D. Jones
Randy R. Shorb

ASSOCIATE

Frances F. Hillsman

For full biographical listings, see the Martindale-Hubbell Law Directory

OREGON

*PORTLAND,** Multnomah Co.

COONEY & CREW, P.C. (AV)

Pioneer Tower, Suite 890, 888 S.W. Fifth Avenue, 97204
Telephone: 503-224-7600
FAX: 503-224-6740

Paul A. Cooney
Thomas E. Cooney
Thomas M. Cooney
Brent M. Crew
Michael D. Crew
Kelly T. Hagan
Raymond F. Mensing, Jr.
Robert S. Perkins

LEGAL SUPPORT PERSONNEL

Alma Weber (Paralegal)

For full biographical listings, see the Martindale-Hubbell Law Directory

PENNSYLVANIA

BALA CYNWYD, Montgomery Co.

FURMAN & HALPERN, P.C. (AV)

Suite 612, 401 City Avenue, 19004
Telephone: 610-668-5454
Fax: 610-668-5455
Cherry Hill, New Jersey Office: Suite 245, 411 Route 70 East, 08034.
Telephone: 609-795-4440.
Fax: 609-428-5485.

Barry A. Furman
Mark S. Halpern
Robert S. Levy
Georgeann R. Fusco
Lisanne L. Mikula
Caryn M. DePiano

For full biographical listings, see the Martindale-Hubbell Law Directory

*HARRISBURG,** Dauphin Co.

BUCHANAN INGERSOLL, PROFESSIONAL CORPORATION (AV)

Vartan Parc, 30 North Third Street, 17101
Telephone: 717-237-4800
Telecopier: 717-233-0852
Pittsburgh, Pennsylvania Office: 5800 USX Tower, 600 Grant Street.
Telephone: 412-562-8800.
Philadelphia, Pennsylvania Office: Two Logan Square, Twelfth Floor, 18th & Arch Streets.
Telephone: 215-665-8700.
Tampa, Florida Office: 101 East Kennedy Boulevard, Suite 1030.
Telephone: 813-222-8180.
North Miami Beach, Florida Office: 19495 Biscayne Boulevard.
Telephone: 305-933-5600.
Lexington, Kentucky Office: 1210 Vine Center Office Tower, 333 West Vine Street.
Telephone: 606-225-5333.
Princeton, New Jersey Office: Buchanan Ingersoll, A Partnership, College Centre, 500 College Road East.
Telephone: 609-452-2666.

Jonathan Vipond III

SENIOR ATTORNEY

William D. Lenahan

Judith P. Musselman

For Complete List of Firm Personnel, See General Section

For full biographical listings, see the Martindale-Hubbell Law Directory

KEEFER, WOOD, ALLEN & RAHAL (AV)

210 Walnut Street, P.O. Box 11963, 17108-1963
Telephone: 717-255-8000
Telecopier: 717-255-8050

MEMBERS OF FIRM

William E. Miller, Jr.
Thomas E. Wood
Bradford Dorrance

OF COUNSEL

William H. Wood

ASSOCIATES

Donald M. Lewis, III
Gretchen C. Hanrahan
Karen J. Brothers

Representative Clients: Central Pennsylvania Blood Bank; Harrisburg Hospita l; Harrisburg Medical Management, Inc.; Homeland Center; Keystone Health Plan Central; Pennsylvania Blue Shield; Susquehanna Center for Nursing and Rehabilitation.

For Complete List of Firm Personnel, See General Section

For full biographical listings, see the Martindale-Hubbell Law Directory

MCNEES, WALLACE & NURICK (AV)

100 Pine Street, P.O. Box 1166, 17108
Telephone: 717-232-8000
Fax: 717-237-5300

MEMBERS OF FIRM

David B. Disney
Elizabeth A. Dougherty
Michael G. Jarman
Richard W. Stevenson

For Complete List of Firm Personnel, See General Section

For full biographical listings, see the Martindale-Hubbell Law Directory

THOMAS, THOMAS & HAFER (AV)

305 North Front Street, 6th Floor, P.O. Box 999, 17108
Telephone: 717-237-7100
Fax: 717-237-7105
Verify: 717-255-7642

MEMBERS OF FIRM

Joseph P. Hafer
James K. Thomas, II
Jeffrey B. Rettig
Peter J. Curry
R. Burke McLemore, Jr.
Edward H. Jordan, Jr.
C. Kent Price
Randall G. Gale
David L. Schwalm
Kevin E. Osborne
Douglas B. Marcello
Peter J. Speaker
Paul J. Dellasega

OF COUNSEL

James K. Thomas

Daniel J. Gallagher
Robert A. Taylor
Sarah W. Arosell
Eugene N. McHugh
Richard C. Seneca
Stephen E. Geduldig
Paula Gayle Sanders
Karen S. Coates
Ann F. DePaulis
Margaret A. Scheaffer
Todd R. Narvol

(See Next Column)

THOMAS, THOMAS & HAFER, *Harrisburg—Continued*

Representative Clients: Aetna Casualty & Surety Co.; Commercial Union Insurance Companies; Geisinger Medical Center; Hartford Insurance Group; Liberty Mutual Insurance Co.; Medical Inter-Insurance Exchange; Medical Protective Co.; Pennsylvania Hospital Insurance Co.; Pennsylvania Medical Society Liability Insurance Co.; Weis Markets, Inc.

For full biographical listings, see the Martindale-Hubbell Law Directory

*PHILADELPHIA,** Philadelphia Co.

BALLARD SPAHR ANDREWS & INGERSOLL (AV)

1735 Market Street, 51st Floor, 19103-7599
Telephone: 215-665-8500
Fax: 215-864-8999
Denver, Colorado Office: Seventeenth Street Plaza Building, Suite 2300, 1225 17th Street.
Telephone: 303-292-2400.
Fax: 303-296-3956.
Kaunas, Lithuania Office: Donelaicio g., 71-2, Kaunas 3000.
Telephone: (370-7) 20 56 66.
Fax: (370-7) 20 56 91.
Salt Lake City, Utah Office: One Utah Center, Suite 1200, 201 South Main Street.
Telephone: 801-531-3000.
Fax: 801-531-3001.
Washington, D.C. Office: Suite 900 East, 555 13th Street, N.W.
Telephone: 202-383-8800.
Fax: 202-383-8877; 383-8893.
Baltimore, Maryland Office: 300 East Lombard Street. 19th Floor.
Telephone: 410-528-5600.
Fax: 410-528-5650.
Camden, New Jersey Office: 800 Hudson Square, 5th Floor.
Telephone: 609-541-5577.
Fax: 609-541-8272.

Brian T. Hirai
Joseph E. Lundy
William P. Scott
John B. Langel
Peter M. Mattoon
Matthew M. Strickler

OF COUNSEL

Joseph P. Flanagan, Jr.

For Complete List of Firm Personnel, See General Section

For full biographical listings, see the Martindale-Hubbell Law Directory

DUANE, MORRIS & HECKSCHER (AV)

Suite 4200 One Liberty Place, 19103-7396
Telephone: 215-979-1000
FAX: 215-979-1020
Harrisburg, Pennsylvania Office: 305 North Front Street, 5th Floor, P.O. Box 1003.
Telephone: 717-237-5500.
Fax: 717-232-4015.
Wilmington, Delaware Office: Suite 1500, 1201 Market Street.
Telephone: 302-571-5550.
Fax: 302-571-5560.
New York, N.Y. Office: 112 E. 42nd Street, Suite 2125.
Telephone: 212-499-0410.
Fax: 212-499-0420.
Wayne, Pennsylvania Office 735 Chesterbrook Boulevard, Suite 300.
Telephone: 610-647-3555.
Allentown, Pennsylvania Office: 968 Postal Road, Suite 200.
Telephone: 610-266-3650.
Fax: 610-640-2619.
Cherry Hill, New Jersey Office: 51 Haddonfield Road, Suite 340.
Telephone: 609-488-7300.
Fax: 609-488-7021.

MEMBERS OF FIRM

Roland Morris
David E. Loder

ASSOCIATES

Dianne A. Meyer
Deborah Tate Pecci
Lisa W. Clark
Sheila McVey Mangan

SPECIAL COUNSEL CHERRY HILL OFFICE

Alma L. Saravia
(Not admitted in PA)

For Complete List of Firm Personnel, See General Section

For full biographical listings, see the Martindale-Hubbell Law Directory

MCKISSOCK & HOFFMAN, P.C. (AV)

1700 Market Street, Suite 3000, 19103
Telephone: 215-246-2100
Fax: 215-246-2144
Mount Holly, New Jersey Office: 211 High Street.
Telephone: 609-267-1006.
Doylestown, Pennsylvania Office: 77 North Broad Street, Second Floor.
Telephone: 215-345-4501.

(See Next Column)

Harrisburg, Pennsylvania Office: 127 State Street.
Telephone: 717-234-0103.

J. Bruce McKissock
Peter J. Hoffman
Richard L. McMonigle
Jill Baratz Clarke
Marybeth Stanton Christiansen
Catherine Hill Kunda
Bryant Craig Black
(Resident, Harrisburg, Office)
John M. Willis
John J. McGrath
Debra Schwaderer Dunne
Donald J. Brooks, Jr.
William J. Mundy
Elizabeth E. Davies
Christopher Thomson
Kathleen M. Kenna
K. Reed Haywood
Sara J. Thomson
Maureen P. Fitzgerald
Veronica E. Noonan
Kathleen M. Sholette
Patricia D. Shippee

For full biographical listings, see the Martindale-Hubbell Law Directory

MCWILLIAMS AND MINTZER, P.C. (AV)

Eight Penn Center, 20th Floor, 1628 John F. Kennedy Boulevard, 19103-2708
Telephone: 215-981-1060
Fax: 215-981-0133

Edward C. Mintzer, Jr.
Anthony F. Zabicki, Jr.
Kenneth D. Powell, Jr.

OF COUNSEL

Daniel T. McWilliams

Patrick S. Mintzer
John Michael Skrocki
Patricia A. Powell
Regina Spause McGraw

LEGAL SUPPORT PERSONNEL

Frances Kelly McCaffery

Representative Clients: Pennsylvania Hospital Insurance Co.; Frankford Hospital & Health Care Systems; Thomas Jefferson University Hospital; Princeton Insurance Co.; Pawtucket Insurance Co.; Medical Inter-Insurance Exchange; Medical Protective Co.; ITT Hartford; Common of Pennsylvania Medical Professional Liability Catastrophe Loss Fund.

For full biographical listings, see the Martindale-Hubbell Law Directory

*PITTSBURGH,** Allegheny Co.

BUCHANAN INGERSOLL, PROFESSIONAL CORPORATION (AV)

5800 USX Tower, 600 Grant Street, 15219
Telephone: 412-562-8800
Telecopier: 412-562-1041
Philadelphia, Pennsylvania Office: Two Logan Square, Twelfth Floor, 18th & Arch Streets.
Telephone: 215-665-8700.
Harrisburg, Pennsylvania Office: Vartan Parc, 30 North Third Street.
Telephone: 717-237-4800.
Tampa, Florida Office: 101 East Kennedy Boulevard, Suite 1030.
Telephone: 813-222-8180.
North Miami Beach, Florida Office: 19495 Biscayne Boulevard.
Telephone: 305-933-5600.
Lexington, Kentucky Office: 1210 Vine Center Office Tower, 333 West Vine Street.
Telephone: 606-225-5333.
Princeton, New Jersey Office: Buchanan Ingersoll, A Partnership, College Centre, 500 College Road East.
Telephone: 609-452-2666.

Thomas E. Boyle
Rosemary L. Corsetti
Melanie DiPietro, S.C.
J. Jerome Mansmann
Patricia J. Marley
William J. McCormick
James D. Obermanns
Robert B. Ramsey III

Douglas S. Johnson

For Complete List of Firm Personnel, See General Section

For full biographical listings, see the Martindale-Hubbell Law Directory

FELDSTEIN GRINBERG STEIN & MCKEE, A PROFESSIONAL CORPORATION (AV)

428 Boulevard of the Allies, 15219
Telephone: 412-471-0677
Fax: 412-263-6129
Elizabeth, Pennsylvania Office: 400 Second Street.
Telephone: 412-384-6111.
Wexford, Pennsylvania Office: 12300 Perry Highway.
Telephone: 412-935-5540.

Edwin I. Grinberg
Stanley M. Stein
Robert E. McKee, Jr.
Joan Singh

For full biographical listings, see the Martindale-Hubbell Law Directory

Pittsburgh—Continued

GACA, MATIS & HAMILTON, A PROFESSIONAL CORPORATION (AV)

300 Four PPG Place, 15222-5404
Telephone: 412-338-4750
Fax: 412-338-4742

Giles J. Gaca
Thomas A. Matis
Mark R. Hamilton
John W. Jordan, IV
Alan S. Baum
Thomas P. McGinnis
Bernard R. Rizza
Jeffrey A. Ramaley
Stephen J. Dalesio
John Timothy Hinton, Jr.
Shawn Lynne Reed

LEGAL SUPPORT PERSONNEL

PARALEGALS

Tina M. Shanafelt
Jill M. Peterson

For full biographical listings, see the Martindale-Hubbell Law Directory

HORTY, SPRINGER & MATTERN, P.C. (AV)

4614 5th Avenue, 15213
Telephone: 412-687-7677
Fax: 412-687-7692

John Horty
Eric W. Springer
Clara L. Mattern (1931-1981)
Barbara A. Blackmond
Linda Haddad
Daniel M. Mulholland III
Charlotte S. Jefferies
Henry M. Casale
Paul A. Verardi
Alan J. Steinberg
Susan M. Lapenta

Lauren M. Massucci

For full biographical listings, see the Martindale-Hubbell Law Directory

NASH & COMPANY, A PROFESSIONAL CORPORATION (AV)

700 Westinghouse Building, 15222
Telephone: 412-392-2333
Fax: 412-392-2343

Stephen P. Nash
Melinda J. Roberts

Anne D. Mullaney
Charles G. O'Hara
Terrence J. O'Rourke
Paul J. Kegaly
David W. Thomas
Nicole A. Normansell

OF COUNSEL

Jacqueline O. Shogan
Domenic A. Bellisario

For full biographical listings, see the Martindale-Hubbell Law Directory

THORP, REED & ARMSTRONG (AV)

One Riverfront Center, 15222
Telephone: 412-394-7711
Fax: 412-394-2555

MEMBERS OF FIRM

Sidney J. Kelly
Edmund S. Ruffin, III
David A. Scott

For Complete List of Firm Personnel, See General Section

For full biographical listings, see the Martindale-Hubbell Law Directory

RHODE ISLAND

*PROVIDENCE,** Providence Co.

GIDLEY, SARLI & MARUSAK (AV)

Greater Providence Bank Building, 170 Westminster Street, 02903
Telephone: 401-274-6644
Telecopier: 401-331-9304

MEMBERS OF FIRM

Thomas D. Gidley
Michael G. Sarli
James P. Marusak
Mark C. Hadden

ASSOCIATES

Michael R. DeLuca
Linn Foster Freedman
Denise M. Lombardo
William L. Wheatley
Stuart D. Hallagan III

LEGAL SUPPORT PERSONNEL

Elaine M. Noren
Mary Repoza Caplette
Darlene E. Kotkofski

For full biographical listings, see the Martindale-Hubbell Law Directory

SOUTH CAROLINA

*CHARLESTON,** Charleston Co.

HAYNSWORTH, MARION, MCKAY & GUÉRARD, L.L.P (AV)

#2 Prioleau Street, P.O. Box 1119, 29402
Telephone: 803-722-7606
Telecopier: 803-723-5263
Columbia, South Carolina Office: Suite 2400 AT&T Building, 1201 Main Street, P.O. Drawer 7157, 29202.
Telephone: 803-765-1818.
Telecopier: 803-765-2399.
Greenville, South Carolina Office: Two Insignia Financial Plaza, 75 Beattie Place, P.O. Box 2048, 29602.
Telephone: 803-240-3200.
Telecopier: 803-240-3300.

MEMBERS OF FIRM

J. Paul Trouche
James J. Hinchey, Jr. (Resident)
Donald Bancroft Meyer

ASSOCIATES

Paul M. Lynch
Coleman Miller Legerton
Meredith Grier Buyck
Karen A. Wood (Not admitted in SC)

Representative Clients: Greenville Hospital System; Baker Hospital; Roper Hospital; Oconee; Memorial Hospital; Beauford Memorial Hospital; Cooper Hall Nursing Home; Clemson Health Center; Medical Society Health Systems, Inc.; HealthSource of South Carolina.

For Complete List of Firm Personnel, See General Section

For full biographical listings, see the Martindale-Hubbell Law Directory

*COLUMBIA,** Richland Co.

RICHARDSON, PLOWDEN, GRIER AND HOWSER, P.A. (AV)

1600 Marion Street, P.O. Drawer 7788, 29202
Telephone: 803-771-4400
Telecopy: 803-779-0016
Myrtle Beach, South Carolina Office: Southern National Bank Building, Suite 202, 601 21st Avenue North, P.O. Box 3646, 29578.
Telephone: 803-448-1008.
FAX: 803-448-1533.

Donald V. Richardson, III
George C. Beighley
Frederick A. Crawford
Samuel F. Crews, III

Representative Clients: Richland Memorial Hospital; Anesthesiologist of Columbia, P.A.; Cardiovascular Associates, P.A.; MedCorp Health Systems, Inc.; Midland Internal Medicine, P.A.; Department of Internal Medicine, RMH; Palmetto Pathology Associates; Carolina Health Choice Network.

For Complete List of Firm Personnel, See General Section

For full biographical listings, see the Martindale-Hubbell Law Directory

*GREENVILLE,** Greenville Co.

HAYNSWORTH, MARION, MCKAY & GUÉRARD, L.L.P. (AV)

Two Insignia Financial Plaza, 75 Beattie Place, P.O. Box 2048, 29602
Telephone: 803-240-3200
Telecopier: 803-240-3300
Columbia, South Carolina Office: Suite 2400 A T & T Building, 1201 Main Street, P.O. Drawer 7157, 29202
Telephone: 803-765-1818.
Telecopier: 803-765-2399.
Charleston, South Carolina Office: #2 Prioleau Street, P.O. Box 1119, 29402.
Telephone: 803-722-7606.
Telecopier: 803-723-5263.

OF COUNSEL

Frances DeLoache Ellison

SPECIAL COUNSEL

Nancy Lark Schulze

MEMBERS OF FIRM

G. Dewey Oxner, Jr.
Joseph J. Blake, Jr.
David L. McMurray
Edwin Brown Parkinson, Jr.

ASSOCIATES

Arthur Frazier McLean, III
Donna S. Kivett
Sarah S. (Sally) McMillan
L. Elizabeth Patrick

Representative Clients: Greenville Hospital System; Baker Hospital; Roper Hospital; Oconee; Memorial Hospital; Beauford Memorial Hospital; Cooper Hall Nursing Home; Clemson Health Center; Medical Society Health Systems, Inc.; HealthSource of South Carolina.

For Complete List of Firm Personnel, See General Section

For full biographical listings, see the Martindale-Hubbell Law Directory

Greenville—Continued

WYCHE, BURGESS, FREEMAN & PARHAM, PROFESSIONAL ASSOCIATION (AV)

44 East Camperdown Way, P.O. Box 728, 29602-0728
Telephone: 803-242-8200
Telecopier: 803-235-8900

William W. Kehl — Henry L. Parr, Jr.

Counsel for: Multimedia, Inc.; Delta Woodside Industries, Inc.; Milliken & Company; Ryan's Family Steak Houses, Inc.; St. Francis Hospital; Span-America Medical Systems, Inc.; Carolina First Bank; KEMET Electronics Corp.; Builder Marts of America, Inc.; One Price Clothing, Inc.

For Complete List of Firm Personnel, See General Section

For full biographical listings, see the Martindale-Hubbell Law Directory

TENNESSEE

*CHATTANOOGA,** Hamilton Co.

BAKER, DONELSON, BEARMAN & CALDWELL (AV)

1800 Republic Centre, 633 Chestnut Street, 37450-1800
Telephone: 615-752-4400
Telecopier: 615-752-4410
Memphis, Tennessee Office: 20th Floor, First Tennessee Building, 165 Madison, 38103.
Telephone: 901-526-2000.
Telecopier: 901-577-2303.
Nashville, Tennessee Office: 1700 Nashville City Center, 511 Union Street, 37219.
Telephone: 615-726-5600.
Telecopier: 615-726-0464.
Knoxville, Tennessee Office: 2200 Riverview Tower, 900 Gay Street, 37901.
Telephone: 615-549-7000.
Telecopier: 615-525-8569.
Huntsville, Tennessee Office: 3 Courthouse Square, 37756.
Telephone: 615-663-2321.
Telecopier: 615-663-2111.
Johnson City, Tennessee Office: Hamilton Bank Building, 207 Mockingbird Lane, 37604.
Telephone: 615-928-0181.
Telecopier: 615-928-5694; 615-928-3654; Kingsport: 615-246-6191.
Washington, D.C. Office: Market Square, 801 Pennsylvania Avenue, N.W., 20004.
Telephone: 202-508-3400.
Telecopier: 202-508-3402.

PARTNERS

David C. Burger — Julie Williams Watson

For Complete List of Firm Personnel, See General Section

For full biographical listings, see the Martindale-Hubbell Law Directory

STOPHEL & STOPHEL, P.C. (AV)

500 Tallan Building, Two Union Square, 37402-2571
Telephone: 615-756-2333
Fax: 615-266-5032

E. Stephen Jett — Richard W. Bethea, Jr.
C. Douglas Williams

Representative Clients: HCA Valley Psychiatric Hospital Corporation; Anesthesiology Consultants Exchange, Inc.; Chattanooga Family Practice; Chattanooga Internal Medicine Group, Inc.; Chattanooga Women's Specialists, P.C.; Cumberland Radiological Group, Inc.; Oak Ridge Radiological Group, P.C.; Health Care Solutions, Inc.; Kimsey/Knight Radiology, P.C.; Anesthesiology Group, Inc.

For Complete List of Firm Personnel, See General Section

For full biographical listings, see the Martindale-Hubbell Law Directory

*KNOXVILLE,** Knox Co.

WAGNER, MYERS & SANGER, A PROFESSIONAL CORPORATION (AV)

1801 Plaza Tower, P.O. Box 1308, 37929
Telephone: 615-525-4600
Fax: 615-524-5731

John R. Seymour — William C. Myers, Jr.
M. Douglas Campbell, Jr.

Robert E. Hyde

Representative Clients: Fort Sanders Health System; Orthopedic Associates of Knoxville, P.C.; Blount Orthopedics Associates, P.C.; Allergy Associates, P.A.; Fort Sanders Regional Medical Center; Fort Sanders Parkwest Medical Center; Fort Sanders Sevier Medical Center; Fort Sanders London Medical Center; Fort Sanders West Outpatient Surgery Center.

(See Next Column)

For Complete List of Firm Personnel, See General Section

For full biographical listings, see the Martindale-Hubbell Law Directory

*NASHVILLE,** Davidson Co.

BAKER, DONELSON, BEARMAN & CALDWELL (AV)

1700 Nashville City Center, 511 Union Street, 37219
Telephone: 615-726-5600
Telecopier: 615-726-0464
Memphis, Tennessee Office: 20th Floor, First Tennessee Building, 165 Madison, 38103.
Telephone: 901-526-2000.
Telecopier: 901-577-2303.
Knoxville, Tennessee Office: 2200 Riverview Tower, 900 Gay Street, 37901.
Telephone: 615-549-7000.
Telecopier: 615-525-8569.
Chattanooga, Tennessee Office: 1800 Republic Centre, 633 Chestnut Street, 37450-1800.
Telephone: 615-752-4400.
Telecopier: 615-752-4410.
Huntsville, Tennessee Office: 3 Courthouse Square, 37756.
Telephone: 615-663-2321.
Telecopier: 615-663-2111.
Johnson City, Tennessee Office: Hamilton Bank Building, 207 Mockingbird Lane, 37604.
Telephone: 615-928-0181.
Telecopier: 615-928-5694; 615-928-3654; Kingsport: 615-246-6191.
Washington, D.C. Office: Market Square, 801 Pennsylvania Avenue, N.W., 20004.
Telephone: 202-508-3400.
Telecopier: 202-508-3402.

PARTNER

Claudia W. Dickerson

For Complete List of Firm Personnel, See General Section

For full biographical listings, see the Martindale-Hubbell Law Directory

BASS, BERRY & SIMS (AV)

2700 First American Center, 37238-2700
Telephone: 615-742-6200
Telecopy: 615-742-6293
Knoxville, Tennessee Office: 1700 Riverview Tower, 900 S. Gay Street, P.O. Box 1509, 37901-1509.
Telephone: 615-521-6200.
Telecopy: 615-521-6234.

MEMBERS OF FIRM

Charles K. Wray
John S. Bryant
H. Lee Barfield, II
Bob F. Thompson
Richard Lodge
Leigh Walton
E. Clifton Knowles
Samuel Lanier Felker
R. Dale Grimes
George P. McGinn, Jr.
Patricia Townsend Meador
G. Mark Mamantov (Resident, Knoxville, Tennessee Office)
Cynthia Y. Reisz
Kay Templeton Lang
W. Keith Ransdell

Representative Clients: American Healthcorp, Inc.; Coventry Corporation; Dialysis Clinic, Inc.; Geriatric Medical Care, Inc.; Health Source, Inc.; Med-Alliance, Inc.; Quorum Health Resources Group; Texas Oncology, P.A.; Tourchstone Companies; Vanderbilt University Medical Center.

For full biographical listings, see the Martindale-Hubbell Law Directory

TEXAS

*AUSTIN,** Travis Co.

* indicates certain Bar Register subscribers whose principal office is located elsewhere in the state and who have arranged for representation as a part of the state capital listings that follow

DAVIS & DAVIS, P.C. (AV)

Arboretum Plaza One, 9th Floor, 9442 Capitol of Texas Highway, P.O. Box 1588, 78767
Telephone: 512-343-6248
Fax: 512-343-0121

C. Dean Davis
Fred E. Davis
Alexis J. Fuller, Jr.
Francis A. (Tony) Bradley
Ruth Russell-Schafer

Bill Cline, Jr.
Robert L. Hargett
Michael L. Neely
Brian Gregory Jackson
A. A. Jack Ross, IV
Kevin Wayde Morse
Mark Alan Keene
Kenda B. Dalrymple

For Complete List of Firm Personnel, See General Section

For full biographical listings, see the Martindale-Hubbell Law Directory

Austin—Continued

DAVIS & WILKERSON, P.C. (AV)

200 One American Center, Six Hundred Congress Avenue, P.O. Box 2283, 78768-2283
Telephone: 512-482-0614
Fax: 512-482-0342
Alpine, Texas Office: 1110 East Holland. P.O. Box 777. 79831-0777.
Telephone: 915-837-5547.

David M. Davis
Steven R. Welch
Jeff D. Otto
Glen Wilkerson
David A. Wright
Leonard W. Woods
Kevin A. Reed
J. Mark Holbrook
Brian E. Riewe

Fletcher H. Brown
Deborah G. Clark
Frances W. Hamermesh
Kelly Ann McDonald
Brian McElroy
Michael Wilson
Stephen G. Wohleb
Stephen A. Wood

OF COUNSEL

Pete P. Gallego
Regina C. Williams

For full biographical listings, see the Martindale-Hubbell Law Directory

FORD & FERRARO, L.L.P. (AV)

A Registered Limited Liability Partnership
98 San Jacinto Boulevard, Suite 2000, 78701-4286
Telephone: 512-476-2020
Telecopy: 512-477-5267

Joseph M. Ford (P.C.)
Peter E. Ferraro (P.C.)
Thomas D. Fritz
Daniel H. Byrne (P.C.)
William S. Rhea, IV
Lisa C. Fancher
Clint Hackney (P.C.)
John D. Head
Robert O. Renbarger

ASSOCIATES

Patricia A. Becker
Linda Cangelosi
Bruce Perkins
James A. Rodman
James V. Sylvester
Cari S. Young

SPECIAL COUNSEL

Clark Watts

OF COUNSEL

Salvatore F. Fiscina (Not admitted in TX)
Lawrence H. Brenner (Not admitted in TX)

For full biographical listings, see the Martindale-Hubbell Law Directory

MICHAEL R. SHARP (AV)

1820 One American Center, 600 Congress Avenue, 78701
Telephone: 512-473-2265

LEGAL SUPPORT PERSONNEL

Kimberly Stamper (Legal Assistant)

For full biographical listings, see the Martindale-Hubbell Law Directory

*** THOMPSON & KNIGHT, A PROFESSIONAL CORPORATION** (AV)

(Attorneys and Counselors)
1200 San Jacinto Center, 98 San Jacinto Boulevard, 78701
Telephone: 512-469-6100
Telecopy: 512-469-6180
Dallas, Texas Office: 1700 Pacific Avenue, Suite 3300, 75201.
Telephone: 214-969-1700.
Telecopy: 512-969-1751.
Cable Address: "Tomtex."
Telex: 732298.
Fort Worth, Texas Office: 801 Cherry Street, Suite 1600, 76102.
Telephone: 817-347-1700.
Telecopy: 817-347-1799.
Houston, Texas Office: 1700 Texas Commerce Tower, 600 Travis, 77002.
Telephone: 713-217-2800.
Telecopy: 713-217-2828; 713-217-2882.
Monterrey, Mexico Office: Edificio Losoles PD-4, Av. Lázaro Cárdenas No. 2400 Pte., San Pedro Garza Garcia, Nuevo Léon C.P. 66220.
Telephone: (52-8) 363-0096.
Telecopy: (52-8) 363-3067.

SHAREHOLDERS

Eugene W. Brees, II
James E. Cousar IV

ASSOCIATE

Becky L. Jolin

For Complete List of Firm Personnel, See General Section

For full biographical listings, see the Martindale-Hubbell Law Directory

*DALLAS,** Dallas Co.

JOSEPH E. ASHMORE, JR., P.C. (AV)

Regency Plaza, 3710 Rawlins, Suite 1210, LB 84, 75219-4217
Telephone: 214-559-7202
Fax: 214-520-1550

Joseph E. Ashmore, Jr.

C. Gregory Shamoun
W. Charles Campbell
L. James Ashmore
Howard J. Klatsky

OF COUNSEL

B. Garfield Haynes
Mark S. Michael

For Complete List of Firm Personnel, See General Section

For full biographical listings, see the Martindale-Hubbell Law Directory

CALHOUN & STACY (AV)

5700 NationsBank Plaza, 901 Main Street, 75202-3747
Telephone: 214-748-5000
Telecopier: 214-748-1421
Telex: 211358 CALGUMP UR

Mark Alan Calhoun
David W. Elrod
Steven D. Goldston
Parker Nelson
Roy L. Stacy

ASSOCIATES

Shannon S. Barclay
Robert A. Bragalone
Dennis D. Conder
Jane Elizabeth Diseker
Lawrence I. Fleishman
Thomas C. Jones
Katherine Johnson Knight
V. Paige Pace
Veronika Willard
Michael C. Wright

LEGAL CONSULTANT

Rees T. Bowen, III

For full biographical listings, see the Martindale-Hubbell Law Directory

THOMPSON & KNIGHT, A PROFESSIONAL CORPORATION (AV)

(Attorneys and Counselors)
1700 Pacific Avenue Suite 3300, 75201
Telephone: 214-969-1700
Telecopy: 214-969-1751
Cable Address: "Tomtex"
Telex: 732298
Austin, Texas Office: 1200 San Jacinto Center, 98 San Jacinto Boulevard, 78701.
Telephone: 512-469-6100.
Telecopy: 512-469-6180.
Fort Worth, Texas Office: 801 Cherry Street, Suite 1600, 76102.
Telephone: 817-347-1700.
Telecopy: 817-347-1799.
Houston, Texas Office: 1700 Texas Commerce Tower, 600 Travis, 77002.
Telephone: 713-217-2800.
Telecopy: 713-217-2828.
Monterrey, Mexico Office: Edificio Losoles PD-4, Av. Lázaro Cárdenas No. 2400 Pte., San Pedro Garza Garcia, Nuevo Léon C.P. 66220.
Telephone: (52-8) 363-0096.
Telecopy: (52-8) 363-3067.

SHAREHOLDERS

Margaret S. Alford
Hugh T. Blevins, Jr.
Sam P. Burford, Jr.
Bennett W. Cervin
George C. Chapman
Richard L. Covington
Stephen F. Fink
Howard L. Gilberg
James B. Harris
Gregory S. C. Huffman
Samuel E. Long, Jr.
John H. Martin
Timothy R. McCormick
P. Mike McCullough
Beth Eileen Metty
Maureen Murry
Geoffrey D. Osborn
James R. Peacock III
Rust E. Reid
Peter J. Riley
Norman R. Rogers
James W. Rose
David M. Rosenberg
Bruce S. Sostek
Molly Steele
Arlene Switzer Steinfield

ASSOCIATES

A. Kay Roska
Elizabeth A. Schartz

OF COUNSEL

Terry L. Simmons

For Complete List of Firm Personnel, See General Section

For full biographical listings, see the Martindale-Hubbell Law Directory

*FORT WORTH,** Tarrant Co.

THOMPSON & KNIGHT, A PROFESSIONAL CORPORATION (AV)

(Attorneys and Counselors)
801 Cherry Street, Suite 1600, 76102
Telephone: 817-347-1700
Telecopy: 817-347-1799
Dallas, Texas Office: 1700 Pacific Avenue, Suite 3300, 75201.
Telephone: 214-969-1700.
Telecopy: 214-969-1751.
Cable Address: "Tomtex."
Telex: 732298.
Austin, Texas Office: 1200 San Jacinto Center, 98 San Jacinto Boulevard, 78701.
Telephone: 512-469-6100.
Telecopy: 512-469-6180.
Houston, Texas Office: 1700 Texas Commerce Tower, 600 Travis, 77002.
Telephone: 713-217-2800.
Telecopy: 713-217-2828; 713-2882.
Monterrey, Mexico Office: Edificio Losoles PD-4, Av. Lázaro Cárdenas No. 2400 Pte., San Pedro Garza Garcia, Nuevo Léon C.P. 66220.
Telephone: (52-8) 363-0096.
Telecopy: (52-8) 363-3067.

SHAREHOLDERS

R Gordon Appleman
E. Michael Sheehan

For Complete List of Firm Personnel, See General Section

For full biographical listings, see the Martindale-Hubbell Law Directory

*HOUSTON,** Harris Co.

THOMPSON & KNIGHT, A PROFESSIONAL CORPORATION (AV)

(Attorneys and Counselors)
1700 Texas Commerce Tower, 600 Travis, 77002
Telephone: 713-217-2800
Telecopy: 713-217-2828; 713-217-2882
Dallas, Texas Office: 1700 Pacific Avenue, Suite 3300, 75201.
Telephone: 214-969-1700.
Telecopy: 214-969-1751.
Cable Address: "Tomtex."
Telex: 732298.
Austin, Texas Office: 1200 San Jacinto Center, 98 San Jacinto Boulevard, 78701.
Telephone: 512-469-6100.
Telecopy: 512-469-6180.
Fort Worth, Texas Office: 801 Cherry Street, Suite 1600, 76102.
Telephone: 817-347-1700.
Telecopy: 817-347-1799.
Monterrey, Mexico Office: Edificio Losoles PD-4, Av. Lázaro Cárdenas No. 2400 PTE., San Pedro Garza Garcia, Nuevo Léon C.P. 66220.
Telephone: (52-8) 363-0096.
Telecopy: (52-8) 363-3067.

SHAREHOLDERS

Mary Margaret Bearden
Daniel J. Hayes
Debbi M. Johnstone

For Complete List of Firm Personnel, See General Section

For full biographical listings, see the Martindale-Hubbell Law Directory

*LUBBOCK,** Lubbock Co.

JONES, FLYGARE, GALEY, BROWN & WHARTON (AV)

1600 Civic Center Plaza, P.O. Box 2426, 79408
Telephone: 806-765-8851
Fax: 806-765-8829

Charles E. Galey
Michael P. Reed
Lois A. Wischkaemper

Representative Clients: St. Mary of the Plains Hospital; University Medical Center.

For Complete List of Firm Personnel, See General Section

For full biographical listings, see the Martindale-Hubbell Law Directory

UTAH

*SALT LAKE CITY,** Salt Lake Co.

PARSONS BEHLE & LATIMER, A PROFESSIONAL CORPORATION (AV)

One Utah Center, 201 South Main Street, Suite 1800, P.O. Box 45898, 84145-0898
Telephone: 801-532-1234
Telecopy: 801-536-6111

(See Next Column)

F. Robert Reeder
J. Gordon Hansen
Raymond J. Etcheverry
Richard M. Marsh
William J. Stilling

For full biographical listings, see the Martindale-Hubbell Law Directory

VAN COTT, BAGLEY, CORNWALL & MCCARTHY, A PROFESSIONAL CORPORATION (AV)

Suite 1600, 50 South Main Street, P.O. Box 45340, 84145
Telephone: 801-532-3333
Telex: 453149
Telecopier: 801-534-0058
Ogden, Utah Office: Suite 900, 2404 Washington Boulevard.
Telephone: 801-394-5783.
Park City, Utah Office: 314 Main Street, Suite 205.
Telephone: 801-649-3889.
Reno, Nevada Office: Jeppson & Lee, 100 West Liberty, Suite 990.
Telephone: 702-333-6800.

David E. Salisbury
Kenneth W. Yeates
Alan L. Sullivan
R. Stephen Marshall
Ronald G. Moffitt
John A. Anderson
David L. Arrington

For Complete List of Firm Personnel, See General Section

For full biographical listings, see the Martindale-Hubbell Law Directory

VERMONT

*BURLINGTON,** Chittenden Co.

MILLER, EGGLESTON & ROSENBERG, LTD. (AV)

150 South Champlain Street, P.O. Box 1489, 05402-1489
Telephone: 802-864-0880
Telecopier: 802-864-0328

Martin K. Miller
Anne E. Cramer

For Complete List of Firm Personnel, See General Section

For full biographical listings, see the Martindale-Hubbell Law Directory

SHEEHEY BRUE GRAY & FURLONG, PROFESSIONAL CORPORATION (AV)

119 South Winooski Avenue, P.O. Box 66, 05402
Telephone: 802-864-9891
Facsimile: 802-864-6815

William B. Gray (1942-1994)
David T. Austin
R. Jeffrey Behm
Nordahl L. Brue
Michael G. Furlong
Ralphine Newlin O'Rourke
Donald J. Rendall, Jr.
Christina Schulz
Paul D. Sheehey
Peter H. Zamore

Rebecca L. Owen

Representative Client: Green Mountain Power Corp.

For full biographical listings, see the Martindale-Hubbell Law Directory

*RUTLAND,** Rutland Co.

CARROLL, GEORGE & PRATT (AV)

64 & 66 North Main Street, P.O. Box 280, 05702-0280
Telephone: 802-775-7141
Telecopier: 802-775-6483
Woodstock, Vermont Office: The Mill - Route #4 E., P.O. Box 388, 05091.
Telephone: 802-457-1000.
Telecopier: 802-457-1874.

MEMBERS OF FIRM

Henry G. Smith (1938-1974)
James P. Carroll
Alan B. George
Robert S. Pratt
Neal C. Vreeland
Jon S. Readnour
Timothy U. Martin
Randall F. Mayhew (Resident Partner, Woodstock Office)
Richard S. Smith
Judy Godnick Barone
John J. Kennelly

ASSOCIATES

Thomas A. Zonay
Jeffrey P. White
Susan Boyle Ford (Resident, Woodstock Office)
Charles C. Humpstone

For full biographical listings, see the Martindale-Hubbell Law Directory

VIRGINIA

ALEXANDRIA, (Independent City)

GRAD, LOGAN & KLEWANS, P.C. (AV)

112 North Columbus Street, P.O. Box 1417-A44, 22313
Telephone: 703-548-8400
Facsimile: 703-836-6289

John D. Grad
Michael P. Logan
Samuel N. Klewans

Sean C. E. McDonough
Claire R. Pettrone
David A. Damiani

OF COUNSEL

Jeanne F. Franklin

For full biographical listings, see the Martindale-Hubbell Law Directory

*RICHMOND,** (Ind. City; Seat of Henrico Co.)

WILLIAMS, MULLEN, CHRISTIAN & DOBBINS, A PROFESSIONAL CORPORATION (AV)

Two James Center, 1021 East Cary Street, P.O. Box 1320, 23210-1320
Telephone: 804-643-1991
Fax: 804-783-6456
Glen Allen, Virginia Office: 4401 Waterfront Drive, Suite 140.
Telephone: 804-965-9168.
Fax: 804-965-0955.
Washington, D.C. Office: 1575 Eye Street, N.W.
Telephone: 202-289-6200.
Fax: 202-289-4126.

Ralph L. Axselle, Jr.
Reginald N. Jones
David George Ball (Resident, Washington, D.C. Office)
Malcolm E. Ritsch, Jr.

Wyatt S. Beazley, IV
Ian D. Titley
Charles E. Wall

For Complete List of Firm Personnel, See General Section

For full biographical listings, see the Martindale-Hubbell Law Directory

WASHINGTON

*SEATTLE,** King Co.

GERALD R. TARUTIS, INC., P.S. (AV)

Norton Building, Suite 1515, 801 Second Avenue, 98104
Telephone: 206-223-1515
Fax: 206-223-1325

Gerald R. Tarutis

Kathryn R. Barron

For full biographical listings, see the Martindale-Hubbell Law Directory

*SPOKANE,** Spokane Co.

CHASE, HAYES & KALAMON, P.S. (AV)

1000 Seafirst Financial Center, 99201
Telephone: 509-456-0333
FAX: 509-838-9826

Roger F. Chase
James M. Kalamon
Richard E. Hayes
Hedley W. Greene

Gervais Ward McAuliffe III
Susan W. Troppmann
Nancy A. Pohlman
Brent T. Stanyer
Timothy O'Brien
Gerald Kobluk

Representative Clients: Albertson's Inc.; Key Tronic Corp.; Volvo of America, Inc.; Security Management; Familian Northwest; Tidyman's Inc.; Farmers Insurance Group; Sacred Heart Medical Center; Farm Credit Bank of Spokane.

For Complete List of Firm Personnel, See General Section

For full biographical listings, see the Martindale-Hubbell Law Directory

*TACOMA,** Pierce Co.

ROSENOW, JOHNSON, GRAFFE, KEAY, POMEROY & MONIZ (AV)

Suite 101, 2115 North 30th Street, 98403
Telephone: 206-572-5323; Seattle: 838-1767
Fax: 206-572-5413
Seattle
Seattle, Washington Office: 1111 Third Avenue, Suite 3000.
Telephone: 206-223-4770.
Fax: 206-386-7344.

MEMBERS OF FIRM

Jack G. Rosenow
Clifford L. Peterson
A. Clarke Johnson
Marilyn W. Schultheis
Christopher W. Keay
Cheryl A. Asche

OF COUNSEL

Jeffrey F. Hale
W. Ben Blackett

Representative Clients: American States Insurance Company; Continental Casualty Company; Group Health Cooperative of Puget Sound; Johnson & Johnson; National General Insurance Company; Physicians Insurance Exchange; The Doctors' Company; Transamerica Insurance Group; Washington Casualty Company.

For full biographical listings, see the Martindale-Hubbell Law Directory

WEST VIRGINIA

*CHARLESTON,** Kanawha Co.

JACKSON & KELLY (AV)

1600 Laidley Tower, P.O. Box 553, 25322
Telephone: 304-340-1000
Fax: 304-340-1130
Martinsburg, West Virginia Office: 300 Foxcroft Avenue, P.O. Box 1068.
Telephone: 304-263-8800.
Morgantown, West Virginia Office: 6000 Hampton Center, P.O. Box 619.
Telephone: 304-599-3000.
New Martinsville, West Virginia Office: 256 Russell Avenue, P.O. Box 68.
Telephone: 304-455-1751.
Charles Town, West Virginia Office: 700 East Washington Street, P.O. Box 983.
Telephone: 304-728-6088.
Clarksburg, West Virginia Office: 203 Main Street, P.O. Box 1587.
Telephone: 304-623-3002.
Lexington, Kentucky Office: 175 East Main Street, Suite 500, P.O. Box 2150.
Telephone: 606-255-9500.
Washington, D. C. Office: 2401 Pennsylvania Avenue, N.W., Suite 400.
Telephone: 202-973-0200.
Denver, Colorado Office: Suite 2710, 1660 Lincoln Street.
Telephone: 303-837-0003.

MEMBERS OF FIRM

W. Warren Upton
William A. Hoskins, III (Resident, Lexington, Kentucky Office)
Taunja Willis Miller
James W. Thomas
Larry W. Blalock (Administrative Manager, New Martinsville, West Virginia Office)
Thomas J. Hurney, Jr.
William E. Doll, Jr. (Resident, Lexington, Kentucky Office)

ASSOCIATES

Jacqueline Syers Duncan (Resident, Lexington, Kentucky Office)
Timothy Ray Coleman (Not admitted in WV; Resident, Lexington, Kentucky Office)
Tammy A. Mitchell-Bittorf (Martinsburg and Charles Town, West Virginia Offices)

Representative Clients: Thomas Memorial Hospital; Camden-Clark Memorial Hospital; Wetzel County Hospital; Preston Memorial Hospital; St. Luke's Hospital; Chestnut Ridge Hospital; Shawnee Hills Mental Health Center; Valley Mental Health Center; Abraxas Foundation; Res-Care.

For Complete List of Firm Personnel, See General Section

For full biographical listings, see the Martindale-Hubbell Law Directory

STEPTOE & JOHNSON (AV)

Seventh Floor, Bank One Center, P.O. Box 1588, 25326-1588
Telephone: 304-353-8000
Fax: 304-353-8180
Clarksburg, West Virginia Office: Bank One Center, P.O. Box 2190, 26302-2190.
Telephone: 304-624-8000.
Fax: 304-624-8183.

(See Next Column)

STEPTOE & JOHNSON, *Charleston—Continued*

Morgantown, West Virginia Office: 1000 Hampton Center, P.O. Box 1616, 26507-1616.
Telephone: 304-598-8000.
Fax: 304-598-8116.
Martinsburg, West Virginia Office: 126 East Burke Street, P.O. Box 2629, 25401-5429.
Telephone: 304-263-6991.
Fax: 304-263-4785.
Charles Town, West Virginia Office: 104 West Congress Street, P.O. Box 100, 25414-0100.
Telephone: 304-725-1414.
Fax: 304-725-1913.
Hagerstown, Maryland Office: The Bryan Centre, 82 West Washington Street, Fourth Floor, P.O. Box 570, 21740-0570.
Telephone: 301-739-8600.
Fax: 301-739-8742.
Wheeling, West Virginia Office: The Riley Building, Suite 400, 14th & Chapline Streets, P.O. Box 150, 26008-0020.
Telephone: 304-233-0000.
Fax: 304-233-0014.

MEMBERS OF FIRM

Otis L. O'Connor
James R. Watson
Daniel R. Schuda
Harry P. Waddell
Steven P. McGowan
Bryan R. Cokeley
W. Randolph Fife
Martin R. Smith, Jr.
George E. Carenbauer
Arthur M. Standish
Patrick D. Kelly

ASSOCIATES

Cynthia R. Cokeley
Susan Osenton Phillips
Robert D. Pollitt
Luci R. Wellborn
Susan L. Basile
Joanna I. Tabit
Janet N. Kawash
Jeffrey K. Phillips
Richard J. Wolf
Wendy D. Young
Michael J. Funk
Marc B. Lazenby
Jan L. Fox
John W. Alderman, III
John C. Stump
Sarah Lovejoy Brack
Keith A. Jones
Denese Venza
Frank W. Volk
Christopher Kroger
Kelly R. Reed

Representative Clients: Ameribank; ARCO Chemical Co.; City National Bank of Charleston; Federal Kemper Insurance Co.; Goodyear Tire & Rubber Co.; The Hartford Group; Hope Gas, Inc.; Olin Corp.; South Charleston Stamping & Manufacturing Co.; State Farm Insurance Cos.

For full biographical listings, see the Martindale-Hubbell Law Directory

*CLARKSBURG,** Harrison Co.

STEPTOE & JOHNSON (AV)

Bank One Center, P.O. Box 2190, 26302-2190
Telephone: 304-624-8000
Fax: 304-624-8183
Mailing Address: P.O. Box 2190, 26302-2190
Charleston, West Virginia Office: Seventh Floor, Bank One Center, P.O. Box 1588, 25326-1588.
Telephone: 304-353-8000
Fax: 304-353-8180.
Morgantown, West Virginia Office: 1000 Hampton Center, P.O. Box 1616, 26507-1616.
Telephone: 304-598-8000.
Fax: 304-598-8116.
Martinsburg, West Virginia Office: 126 East Burke Street, P.O. Box 2629, 25401-5429.
Telephone: 304-263-6991.
Fax: 304-263-4785.
Charles Town, West Virginia Office: 104 West Congress Street, P.O. Box 100, 25414-0100.
Telephone: 304-725-1414.
Fax: 304-725-1913.
Hagerstown, Maryland Office: The Bryan Centre, 82 West Washington Street, Fourth Floor, P.O. Box 570, 21740-0570.
Telephone: 301-739-8600.
Fax: 301-739-8742.
Wheeling, West Virginia Office: The Riley Building, Suite 400, 14th & Chapline Streets, P.O. Box 150, 26003-0020.
Telephone: 304-233-0000.
Fax: 304-233-0014.

MEMBERS OF FIRM

Walter L. Williams
Gordon H. Copland

Representative Clients: Consolidated Gas Transmission Corp.; Consolidated Coal Co.; CNA; E.I. DuPont de Nemours & Co.; Equitable Resources, Inc.; The Hartford Group; Peabody Coal Co.; PPG Industries; Union National Bank of West Virginia; Ogden Newspapers, Inc.

For Complete List of Firm Personnel, See General Section

For full biographical listings, see the Martindale-Hubbell Law Directory

WISCONSIN

*MILWAUKEE,** Milwaukee Co.

EHLINGER & KRILL, S.C. (AV)

316 North Milwaukee Street, Suite 410, 53202-5803
Telephone: 414-272-8085
Facsimile: 414-272-8290

Ralph J. Ehlinger
R. Jeffrey Krill

For full biographical listings, see the Martindale-Hubbell Law Directory

QUARLES & BRADY (AV)

411 East Wisconsin Avenue, 53202-4497
Telephone: 414-277-5000
Cable Address: "Lawdock"
Fax: 414-271-3552.
TWX: 910-262-3426
Madison, Wisconsin Office: Firstar Plaza, One South Pinckney Street, P.O. Box 2113.
Telephone: 608-251-5000.
Fax: 608-251-9166.
West Palm Beach, Florida Office: 222 Lakeview Avenue, 4th Floor.
Telephone: 407-653-5000.
Fax: 407-653-5333.
Naples, Florida Office: Barnett Center, 4501 Tamiami Trail North.
Telephone: 813-262-5959.
Fax: 813-434-4999.
Phoenix, Arizona Office: One Camelback Building, One East Camelback Road, Suite 400.
Telephone: 602-230-5500.
Fax: 602-230-5598.

MEMBERS OF FIRM
(ALPHABETICALLY BY YEAR OF ADMISSION TO BAR)

Thad F. Kryshak
Thomas W. O'Brien
Michael S. Weiden (Resident, Madison Office)
James D. Friedman
Alyce C. Katayama
Michael L. Roshar
Paul R. Schilling
Judith M. Bailey (Resident, Phoenix, Arizona Office)
Matthew J. Flynn
Ralph V. Topinka (Resident, Madison Office)
Brian G. Lanser
Michael A. Levey
Sheila M. Reynolds

OF COUNSEL

Richard W. Cutler

ASSOCIATES

Lindy P. Funkhouser (Mr.) (Resident, Phoenix, Arizona Office)
Andra J. Palmer (Resident, Madison Office)
Lisa A. Lyons

For Complete List of Firm Personnel, See General Section

For full biographical listings, see the Martindale-Hubbell Law Directory

CANADA
ALBERTA

*CALGARY,** Calgary Jud. Dist.

BENNETT JONES VERCHERE (AV)

4500 Bankers Hall East, 855-2nd Street S.W., T2P 4K7
Telephone: (403) 298-3100
Facsimile: (403) 265-7219
Edmonton, Alberta Office: 1000, 10035-105 Street.
Telephone: (403) 421-8133.
Facsimile: (403) 421-7951.
Toronto, Ontario Office: 3400 1 First Canadian Place. P.O. Box 130.
Telephone: (416) 863-1200.
Facsimile: (416) 863-1716.
Ottawa, Ontario Office: Suite 1800. 350 Alberta Street, Box 25, K1R 1A4.
Telephone: (613) 230-4935.
Facsimile: (613) 230-3836.
Montreal, Quebec Office: Suite 1600, 1 Place Ville Marie.
Telephone: (514) 871-1200.
Facsimile: (514) 871-8115.

MEMBER OF FIRM

John G. Martland, Q.C.

For Complete List of Firm Personnel, See General Section

For full biographical listings, see the Martindale-Hubbell Law Directory

CANADA
NOVA SCOTIA

*HALIFAX,** Halifax Co.

McInnes Cooper & Robertson (AV)

1601 Lower Water Street, P.O. Box 730, B3J 2V1
Telephone: 902-425-6500
Fax: 902-425-6350
St. John's, Newfoundland Office: Suite 602, Scotia Centre, 235 Water Street, P.O. Box 547. A1C, 5K8.
Telephone: 709-726-9500.
Fax: 709-726-9550.

David A. Graves
Maureen E. Reid
Deborah K. Smith
Eric LeDrew

Attorneys for: Bank of Nova Scotia; Imperial Oil, Limited; Frank B. Hall & Co., Inc. (New York); American Steamship Owners Protection & Indemnity Association, Inc.; Coca-Cola, Ltd.; Scott Worldwide Inc.; Hong Kong Bank of Canada.

For Complete List of Firm Personnel, See General Section

For full biographical listings, see the Martindale-Hubbell Law Directory

CANADA
ONTARIO

*TORONTO,** Regional Munic. of York

Borden & Elliot (AV)

Barristers & Solicitors
Scotia Plaza, 40 King Street West, M5H 3Y4
Telephone: 416-367-6000
Telecopier: 416-367-6749
Internet: @ borden.com
A Member of the national association of Borden DuMoulin Howard Gervais, comprising Borden & Elliot in Toronto, Ontario, Russell & DuMoulin in Vancouver, British Columbia, Howard, Mackie in Calgary, Alberta and Mackenzie Gervais in Montréal, Québec. Borden DuMoulin Howard Gervais also operates an office in London, England.

MEMBER AND ASSOCIATES

Rino A. Stradiotto, Q.C.

For Complete List of Firm Personnel, See General Section

For full biographical listings, see the Martindale-Hubbell Law Directory

IMMIGRATION AND NATURALIZATION LAW

ALABAMA

*HUNTSVILLE,** Madison Co.

SIROTE & PERMUTT, P.C. (AV)

Suite 1000, 200 Clinton Avenue, N.W., 35801
Telephone: 205-536-1711
Facsimile: 205-534-9650
Birmingham, Alabama Office: 2222 Arlington Avenue, South, P.O. Box 55727.
Telephone: 205-933-7111.
Facsimile: 205-930-5301.
Mobile, Alabama Office: One St. Louis Centre, Suite 1000.
Telephone: 205-432-1671.
Facsimile: 205-434-0196.
Montgomery, Alabama Office: Colonial Commerce Center, Suite 305, One Commerce Street.
Telephone: 205-261-3400.
Facsimile: 205-261-3434.
Tuscaloosa, Alabama Office: 2216 14th Street.
Telephone: 205-752-2089.

George W. Royer, Jr. June Wang

For Complete List of Firm Personnel, See General Section

For full biographical listings, see the Martindale-Hubbell Law Directory

CALIFORNIA

*LOS ANGELES,** Los Angeles Co.

BONAPARTE & MIYAMOTO, A PROFESSIONAL LAW CORPORATION (AV)

11911 San Vicente Boulevard, Suite 355, 90049
Telephone: 310-471-3481
FAX: 310-471-2862; 310-471-1686
Los Angeles, California Office: 919 South Grand Avenue, Suite 208E.
Telephone: 213-688-8872.
FAX: 213-688-8887.
Newport Beach, California Office: 5030 Campus Drive.
Telephone: 714-955-2012.
FAX: 714-833-1423.

Ronald H. Bonaparte Lynn Miyamoto

Thomas E. Cummings Gerard Hekker

For full biographical listings, see the Martindale-Hubbell Law Directory

RALPH EHRENPREIS A PROFESSIONAL LAW CORPORATION (AV)

Suite 450, 1801 Century Park East, 90067
Telephone: 310-553-6600
Telefax: 310-553-2616
Cable Address: "Immlaw"

Ralph Ehrenpreis

Bernard J. Lurie

References: City National Bank (Beverly Hills Office, Beverly Hills, California); Great American Bank (Century City Office, Los Angeles, California).

For full biographical listings, see the Martindale-Hubbell Law Directory

MARK A. IVENER A LAW CORPORATION (AV)

11601 Wilshire Boulevard, Suite 2350, 90025
Telephone: 310-477-3000
FAX: 310-477-2652
Canadian Associate Office: 1300-808 Nelson Street, Vancouver, British Columbia V6Z 2H2.
Telephone: 604-688-0558.
Telex: 04507865 MGE VCR.
FAX: 604-685-8972.

(See Next Column)

Japanese Associate Office: 13th Floor Urbannet Otemachi Building, 2-2-2 Otemachi, Chiyoda-Ku, Tokyo 100, Japan.
Telephone: 813-3231-8888.
Fax: 813-3231-8881.

Mark A. Ivener

OF COUNSEL

Alice M. Yardum-Hunter

LEGAL SUPPORT PERSONNEL

Dina S. Hairapetian Deborah Wai Juen Ma
Sonya M. Varela-Valdez

For full biographical listings, see the Martindale-Hubbell Law Directory

JONES, DAY, REAVIS & POGUE (AV)

555 West Fifth Street Suite 4600, 90013-1025
Telephone: 213-489-3939
Telex: 181439 UD
Telecopier: 213-243-2539
In Irvine, California: 2603 Main Street, Suite 900.
Telephone: 714-851-3939.
Telex: 194911 Lawyers LSA.
Telecopier: 714-553-7539.
In Atlanta, Georgia: 3500 One Peachtree Center, 303 Peachtree Street, N.E.
Telephone: 404-521-3939.
Cable Address: "Attorneys Atlanta".
Telex: 54-2711.
Telecopier: 404-581-8330.
In Brussels, Belgium: Avenue Louise 480, 7th Floor, B-1050 Brussels.
Telephone: 011-32-2-645-14-11.
Telecopier: 011-32-2-645-14-45.
In Chicago, Illinois: 77 West Wacker.
Telephone: 312-782-3939.
Telecopier: 312-782-8585.
In Cleveland, Ohio: North Point, 901 Lakeside Avenue.
Telephone: 216-586-3939.
Cable Address: "Attorneys Cleveland."
Telex: 980389.
Telecopier: 216-579-0212.
In Columbus, Ohio: 1900 Huntington Center.
Telephone: 614-469-3939.
Cable Address: "Attorneys Columbus."
Telecopier: 614-461-4198.
In Dallas, Texas: 2300 Trammell Crow Center, 2001 Ross Avenue.
Telephone: 214-220-3939.
Cable Address: "Attorneys Dallas."
Telex: 730852.
Telecopier: 214-969-5100.
In Frankfurt, Germany: Triton Haus, Bockenheimer Landstrasse 42, 60323 Frankfurt am Main.
Telephone: 49-69-9726-3939.
Telecopier: 49-69-9726-3993.
In Geneva, Switzerland: 20, rue de Candolle.
Telephone: 011-41-22-320-2339.
Telecopier: 011-41-22-320-1232.
In Hong Kong: 1501 One Exchange Square, 8 Connaught Place.
Telephone: 011-852-2526-6895.
Telecopier: 011-852-2810-5787.
In London England: One Mount Street.
Telephone: 011-44-71-493-9361.
Cable Address: "Surgoe London WI."
Telecopier: 011-44-71-493-9666.
In New York, New York: 599 Lexington Avenue.
Telephone: 212-326-3939.
Cable Address: "JONESDAY NEWYORK."
Telex: 237013 JDRP UR.
Telecopier: 212-755-7306.
In Paris, France: 62, rue du Faubourg Saint-Honore.
Telephone: 011-33-1-44-71-3939.
Cable Address: "Surgoe Paris."
Telex: 290156 Surgoe.
Telecopier: 011-33-1-49-24-0471.
In Pittsburgh, Pennsylvania: 500 Grant Street, 31st Floor.
Telephone: 412-391-3939.
Cable Address: "Attorneys Pittsburgh".
Telecopier: 412-394-7959.
In Riyadh, Saudi Arabia: Law Offices of Saud M.A. Shawwaf, P.O. Box 2700.
Telephones: 011 (966-1) 465-6543, 011 (966-1) 464-8534 or 011 (966-1) 464-8540.
Telex: 401831 SAUCON SJ.
Telecopier: (966-1) 464-8480.
In Taipei, Taiwan: 8th Floor, 2 Tun Hwa South Road, Section 2.
Telephone: 011 (886-2) 704-6808.
Telecopier: 011 (886-2) 704-6791.
In Tokyo, Japan: Toranomon MT Building, 4th Floor, 10-3, Toranomon 3-Chome, Minato-Ku, Tokyo 105, Japan.
Telephone: 011-81-3-3433-3939.
Telecopier: 011-81-3-5401-2725.

(See Next Column)

JONES, DAY, REAVIS & POGUE, *Los Angeles—Continued*

In Washington, D.C.: Metropolitan Square, 1450 G Street, N.W.
Telephone: 202-879-3939.
Cable Address: "Attorneys Washington."
Telex: 89-2410 ATTORNEYS WASH.
Telecopier: 202-737-2832.

OF COUNSEL

Jerald B. Serviss

For Complete List of Firm Personnel, See General Section

For full biographical listings, see the Martindale-Hubbell Law Directory

BERNARD P. WOLFSDORF A PROFESSIONAL CORPORATION (AV)

17383 Sunset Boulevard, Suite 120 (Pacific Palisades), 90272
Telephone: 310-573-4242
FAX: 310-573-5093

Bernard P. Wolfsdorf

Kathleen L. Grzegorek
Michele A. Buchanan
Stephen M. Dewar (Not admitted in CA)
Christopher M. Wright (Not admitted in CA)
Janet Renée Braun

For full biographical listings, see the Martindale-Hubbell Law Directory

PASADENA, Los Angeles Co.

MARGARET ANN REDMOND (AV)

Suite 726, 301 East Colorado Boulevard, 91101
Telephone: 818-584-9050
FAX: 818-584-6463

For full biographical listings, see the Martindale-Hubbell Law Directory

*SAN DIEGO,** San Diego Co.

KING & BALLOW (AV)

2700 Symphony Towers, 750 B Street, 92101
Telephone: 619-236-9401
Fax: 619-236-9437
Nashville, Tennessee Office: 1200 Noel Place, 200 Fourth Avenue, North.
Telephone: 615-259-3456.
Fax: 615-254-7907.
San Francisco, California Office: 100 First Street Suite 2700, 94105.
Telephone: 415-541-7803.
Fax: 415-541-7805.

MEMBERS OF FIRM

Frank S. King, Jr. (Not admitted in CA)
Robert L. Ballow (Not admitted in CA)
Richard C. Lowe (Not admitted in CA)
R. Eddie Wayland (Not admitted in CA)
Paul H. Duvall (Resident)
Mark E. Hunt (Not admitted in CA)
Lynn Siegel

ASSOCIATES

Kevin M. Bagley
Leslie E. Lewis
Linda L. Stuessi

Representative Clients: Gen Probe, Inc., San Diego, California; Rohr Industries, Inc., Chula Vista, California; Solar Turbines, Inc., San Diego, California.

For full biographical listings, see the Martindale-Hubbell Law Directory

*SAN FRANCISCO,** San Francisco Co.

LAW OFFICES JACK I. KAISER (AV)

633 Battery Street, Sixth Floor, 94111
Telephone: 415-986-4444
Facsimile: 415-986-7224

For full biographical listings, see the Martindale-Hubbell Law Directory

STUDIO CITY, Los Angeles Co.

THE MILLER LAW OFFICES (AV)

12441 Ventura Boulevard, 91604
Telephone: 818-508-9005
Fax: 818-508-9458

Charles M. Miller
Terri Senesac Miller

John M. Levant

For full biographical listings, see the Martindale-Hubbell Law Directory

COLORADO

*DENVER,** Denver Co.

ALLOTT, ENGINEER & MAKAR, A PROFESSIONAL CORPORATION (AV)

Suite 260, 2305 East Arapahoe Road (Littleton), 80122
Telephone: 303-797-8055
Fax: 303-797-6136
Miami, Florida Affiliated Office: Corrigan, Zelman & Bander, Suite 300, 444 Brickell Avenue.
Telephone: 305-358-5800.
Fax: 305-374-6593.
Cambridge, Massachusetts Affiliated Office: Flynn & Clark, One Main Street.
Telephones: 617-354-1550;
Fax: 617- 661-2576.
Detroit, Michigan Affiliated Office: English & Van Horne, 4472 Penobscot Building, Suite 2900.
Telephone: 313-961-5100.
Fax: 313-961-1169.
Chicago, Illinois Affiliated Office: Terry Feiertag, 120 N. LaSalle Street, Suite 3900.
Telephones: 312-236-7080;
Fax: 312-236-0781.
Dallas, Texas Affiliated Office: Eugene Flynn, 1511 Villars Street.
Telephone: 214-821-1661;
Fax: 214-821-1668.
Minneapolis, Minnesota Affiliated Office: Ingber & Aronson, 1221 Nicollett Mall, Suite 225.
Telephone: 612-339-0517.
Fax: 612-349-6059.
Los Angeles, California Affiliated Office: Mark A. Ivener, Suite 2350, 11601 Wilshire Boulevard.
Telephone: 310-477-3000.
Fax: 310-477-2652.
New York, N.Y. Affiliated Office: Law Office of Allen E. Kaye, 11 Park Place.
Telephones: 212-964-5858;
Fax: 212- 608-3734.
San Francisco, California Affiliated Office: Lawler & Lawler, 275 Battery Street, Suite 2920.
Telephone: 415-391-2010.
Fax: 415-781-6181.
Philadelphia, Pennsylvania Affiliated Office: Orlow & Orlow, 1154 Public Ledger Building, 6th & Chestnut Streets.
Telephone: 215-922-1183.
Fax: 215-922-0516.
Washington, D.C. Affiliated Office: Law Offices of Jan M. Pederson, Lion Building, Suite 401, 1233 Twentieth Street, N.W.
Telephone: 202-785-1960.
Fax: 202-785-3815.
Atlanta, Georgia Affiliated Office: Jay I. Solomon, Suite 1350, 900 Circle 75 Parkway.
Telephone: 404-955-1055.
Fax: 404-955-9303.
Houston, Texas Affiliated Office: Peter D. Williamson Law Office, 1111 Fannin Street.
Telephone: 713-751-0222.
Fax: 713-650-1231.

Ann Allott
Rumi Engineer
Margaret C. Makar

For full biographical listings, see the Martindale-Hubbell Law Directory

C. JAMES COOPER, JR. (AV)

12075 East 45th Avenue, Suite 315, 80239-3128
Telephone: 303-371-1822
Fax: 303-373-1822

References: First Interstate Bank of Denver; City Wide Bank of Denver.

For full biographical listings, see the Martindale-Hubbell Law Directory

ROBERT G. HEISERMAN, P.C. (AV)

Suite 2280, Bank Western Tower, 1675 Broadway, 80202
Telephone: 303-629-1065
Fax: 303-623-1710

Robert G. Heiserman

David N. Simmons
Timothy R. Bakken

Reference: Norwest Bank, Denver, N.A.

For full biographical listings, see the Martindale-Hubbell Law Directory

CONNECTICUT

WESTPORT, Fairfield Co.

William L. Scheffler (AV®)

315 Post Road West, 06880
Telephone: 203-226-6600; 212-795-7800
Telecopier: 203-227-1873

For full biographical listings, see the Martindale-Hubbell Law Directory

DISTRICT OF COLUMBIA

WASHINGTON, D.C. Co.

* indicates certain Bar Register subscribers, in cities of comparable size and importance, who maintain an additional office in Washington, D.C. and who have arranged for representation as a part of the Washington, D.C. listings that follow

*** Jones, Day, Reavis & Pogue** (AV)

Metropolitan Square, 1450 G Street, N.W., 20005-2088
Telephone: 202-879-3939
Cable Address: "Attorneys Washington"
Telex: W.U. (Domestic) 89-2410 ATTORNEYS WASH (International) 64363 ATTORNEYS WASH
Telecopier: 202-737-2832
In Atlanta, Georgia: 3500 One Peachtree Center, 303 Peachtree Street, N.E .
Telephone: 404-521-3939.
Cable Address: "Attorneys Atlanta".
Telex: 54-2711.
Telecopier: 404-581-8330.
In Brussels, Belgium: Avenue Louise 480, 7th Floor, B-1050 Brussels.
Telephone: 011-32-2-645-14-11.
Telecopier: 011-32-2-645-14-45.
In Chicago, Illinois: 77 West Wacker.
Telephone: 312-782-3939.
Telecopier: 312-782-8585.
In Cleveland, Ohio: North Point, 901 Lakeside Avenue.
Telephone: 216-586-3939.
Cable Address: "Attorneys Cleveland."
Telex: 980389.
Telecopier: 216-579-0212.
In Columbus, Ohio: 1900 Huntington Center.
Telephone: 614-469-3939.
Cable Address: "Attorneys Columbus."
Telecopier: 614-461-4198.
In Dallas, Texas: 2300 Trammell Crow Center, 2001 Ross Avenue.
Telephone: 214-220-3939.
Cable Address: "Attorneys Dallas."
Telex: 730852.
Telecopier: 214-969-5100.
In Frankfurt, Germany: Triton Haus, Bockenheimer Landstrasse 42, 60323 Frankfurt am Main.
Telephone: 49-69-9726-3939.
Telecopier: 49-69-9726-3993.
In Geneva, Switzerland: 20, rue de Candolle.
Telephone: 011-41-22-320-2339.
Telecopier: 011-41-22-320-1232.
In Hong Kong: 1501 One Exchange Square, 8 Connaught Place.
Telephone: 011-852-2526-6895.
Telecopier: 011-852-2810-5787.
In Irvine, California: 2603 Main Street, Suite 900 .
Telephone: 714-851-3939.
Telex: 194911 Lawyers LSA.
Telecopier: 714-553-7539.
In London, England: One Mount Street.
Telephone: 011-44-71-493-9361.
Cable Address: "Surgoe London WI."
Telecopier: 011-44-71-493-9666.
In Los Angeles, California: 555 West Fifth Street, Suite 4600.
Telephone: 213-489-3939.
Telex: 181439 UD.
Telecopier: 213-243-2539.
In New York, New York: 599 Lexington Avenue.
Telephone: 212-326-3939.
Cable Address: "JONESDAY NEWYORK."
Telex: 237013 JDRP UR.
Telecopier: 212-755-7306.
In Paris, France: 62, rue du Faubourg Saint-Honore.
Telephone: 011-33-1-44-71-3939.
Cable Address: "Surgoe Paris."
Telex: 290156 Surgoe.
Telecopier: 011-33-1-49-24-0471.

(See Next Column)

In Pittsburgh, Pennsylvania: 500 Grant Street, 31st Floor.
Telephone: 412-391-3939.
Cable Address: "Attorneys Pittsburgh".
Telecopier: 412-394-7959.
In Riyadh, Saudi Arabia: Law Offices of Saud M.A. Shawwaf, P.O. Box 2700.
Telephones: 011 (966-1) 465-6543, 011 (966-1) 464-8534 or 011 (966-1) 464-8540.
Telex: 401831 SAUCON SJ.
Telecopier: (966-1) 464-8480.
In Taipai, Taiwan: 8th Floor, 2 Tun Hwa South Road, Section 2.
Telephone: 011 (886-2) 704-6808.
Telecopier: 011 (886-2) 704-6791.
In Tokyo, Japan: Toranomon MT Building, 4th Floor, 10-3, Toranomon 3-Chome, Minato-Ku, Tokyo 105, Japan.
Telephone: 011-81-3-3433-3939.
Telecopier: 011-81-3-5401-2725.

SENIOR ATTORNEY

Mary Dobson McDonald

For Complete List of Firm Personnel, See General Section

For full biographical listings, see the Martindale-Hubbell Law Directory

Maggio & Kattar (AV)

Eleven Dupont Circle, N.W., Suite 775, 20036
Telephone: 202-483-0053
FAX: 202-483-6801

MEMBERS OF FIRM

Michael Maggio
Candace A. Kattar

Alison J. Brown (Not admitted in DC)
Phillip T. Williams
Elizabeth A. Quinn (Not admitted in DC)

For full biographical listings, see the Martindale-Hubbell Law Directory

FLORIDA

*MIAMI,** Dade Co.

Brauwerman & Brauwerman, P.A. (AV)

Suite 300, 2800 Biscayne Boulevard, 33137
Telephone: 305-758-1234
Telecopier: 305-576-6251
Fort Lauderdale, Florida Office: Executive Pavilion, Suite 502, 300 N.W. 82 Avenue (Plantation).
Telephone: 305-527-1234.
Telecopier: 305-424-8935.

Jeffrey N. Brauwerman
Suzan C. Brauwerman

Bradley O. June

For full biographical listings, see the Martindale-Hubbell Law Directory

*ORLANDO,** Orange Co.

Maguire, Voorhis & Wells, P.A. (AV)

Two South Orange Plaza, P.O. Box 633, 32802
Telephone: 407-244-1100
Telecopier: 407-423-8796
Melbourne, Florida Office: 1499 South Harbor City Boulevard.
Telephone: 407-951-1776.
Fax: 407-951-1849.
Tavares, Florida Office: 131 West Main Street, Post Office Box 39.
Telephone: 904-343-5900.
Fax: 904-343-3524.

A. Guy Neff

Catherine R. Henin-Clark

Representative Clients: Chefs de France (EPCOT); Kastel Venture, Ltd.; EVV Florida Investments, Ltd.; ABB, B.V.

For full biographical listings, see the Martindale-Hubbell Law Directory

GEORGIA

*ATLANTA,** Fulton Co.

ALSTON & BIRD (AV)

A Partnership including Professional Corporations
One Atlantic Center, 1201 West Peachtree Street, 30309-3424
Telephone: 404-881-7000
Telecopier: 404-881-7777
Cable Address: AMGRAM GA
Telex: 54-2996
Easylink: 62985848
Washington, D.C. Office: 700 Thirteenth Street, Suite 350 20005-3960.
Telephone: 202-508-3300.
Telecopier: 202-508-3333.

MEMBER OF FIRM
Bernard L. Greer, Jr.

ASSOCIATE
Eileen M. G. Scofield

Representative Client: Suntory Water Group, Inc.

For Complete List of Firm Personnel, See General Section

For full biographical listings, see the Martindale-Hubbell Law Directory

GLASS, MCCULLOUGH, SHERRILL & HARROLD (AV)

1409 Peachtree Street, N.E., 30309
Telephone: 404-885-1500
Telecopier: 404-892-1801
Buckhead Office: Monarch Plaza, 3414 Peachtree Road, N.E., Suite 450, Atlanta, Georgia, 30326-1162.
Telephone: 404-885-1500.
Telecopier: 404-231-1978.
Washington, D.C. Office: 1155 15th Street, N.W., Suite 400, Washington, D.C., 20005.
Telephone: 202-785-8118.
Telecopier: 202-785-0128.

MEMBERS OF FIRM
Peter B. Glass
Kenneth R. McCullough
James W. King

For Complete List of Firm Personnel, See General Section

For full biographical listings, see the Martindale-Hubbell Law Directory

KILPATRICK & CODY (AV)

Suite 2800, 1100 Peachtree Street, 30309-4530
Telephone: 404-815-6500
Telephone Copier: 404-815-6555
Telex: 54-2307
Washington, D.C. Office: Suite 800, 700 13th Street, N.W., 20005.
Telephone: 202-508-5800. Telephone Copier: 202-508-5858.
Brussels, Belgium Office: Avenue Louise 65, BTE 3, 1050 Brussels.
Telephone: (32) (2) 533-03-00.
Telecopier: (32) (2) 534-86-38.
London, England Office: 68 Pall Mall, London, SW1Y 5ES, England.
Telephone: (44) (71) 321 0477.
Telecopier: (44) (71) 930 9733.
Augusta, Georgia Office: Suite 1400 First Union Bank Building, P.O. Box 2043, 30903. Telephone (706) 724-2622. Telecopier (706) 722-0219.

MEMBER OF FIRM
Robert E. Banta

Representative Clients: Southern Bell Telephone and Telegraph Co.; Lockheed Aeronautical Systems Co.; Frito-Lay, Inc.; Scientific-Atlanta, Inc.; Scripto-Tokai, Inc.; Coronet Industries, Inc.; Bank South Corporation; PepsiCo.

For Complete List of Firm Personnel, See General Section

For full biographical listings, see the Martindale-Hubbell Law Directory

LONG ALDRIDGE & NORMAN (AV)

A Partnership including Professional Corporations
One Peachtree Center, Suite 5300, 303 Peachtree Street, 30308
Telephone: 404-527-4000
Telecopier: 404-527-4198
Washington, D.C. Office: Suite 950, 1615 L Street, 20036.
Telephone: 202-223-7033.
Telecopier: 202-223-7013.

MEMBER OF FIRM
Gordon D. Giffin

ASSOCIATE
Kathleen Griffin

For Complete List of Firm Personnel, See General Section

For full biographical listings, see the Martindale-Hubbell Law Directory

POWELL, GOLDSTEIN, FRAZER & MURPHY (AV)

191 Peachtree Street, N.E., Sixteenth Floor, 30303
Telephone: 404-572-6600
Telex: 542864
Telecopier: 404-572-6999
Cable Address: "Pgfm"
Washington, D.C. Office: Sixth Floor, 1001 Pennsylvania Avenue, N.W., 20004.
Telephone: 202-347-0066.

MEMBER OF FIRM
Bruce R. Larson

ASSOCIATE
Charles H. Kuck (Not admitted in GA)

Representative Clients: Nedlloyd Lines (USA), Inc.; CSR America, Inc.; Miescor (USA), Inc.; The Fuji Bank-Atlanta, Limited; Kubota Manufacturing Corporation of America, Inc.

For Complete List of Firm Personnel, See General Section

For full biographical listings, see the Martindale-Hubbell Law Directory

JAY I. SOLOMON (AV)

Suite 1350 900 Circle 75 Parkway, 30339-3095
Telephone: 404-955-1055
Facsimile: 404-955-9303
EMAIL (Compuserve) 73411,10

For full biographical listings, see the Martindale-Hubbell Law Directory

SUTHERLAND, ASBILL & BRENNAN (AV)

999 Peachtree Street, N.E., 30309-3996
Telephone: 404-853-8000
Facsimile: 404-853-8806
Washington, D.C. Office: 1275 Pennsylvania Avenue, N.W., 20004-2404.
Telephone: 202-383-0100.
New York, N.Y. Office: 1270 Avenue of the Americas, 10020-1700.
Telephone: 212-332-3000.
Austin, Texas Office: 111 Congress Avenue, 23rd Floor, 78701-4079.
Telephone: 512-469-3350.

COUNSEL OF THE FIRM
IN ATLANTA, GEORGIA
Joycelyn L. Fleming

For Complete List of Firm Personnel, See General Section

For full biographical listings, see the Martindale-Hubbell Law Directory

DAN E. WHITE (AV)

The Peachtree Building, 1355 Peachtree Street N.W., Suite 2000, 30309
Telephone: 404-892-3114
Fax: 404-892-3309

For full biographical listings, see the Martindale-Hubbell Law Directory

HAWAII

*HONOLULU,** Honolulu Co.

DAMON KEY BOCKEN LEONG KUPCHAK ATTORNEYS AT LAW, A LAW CORPORATION (AV)

1600 Pauahi Tower, 1001 Bishop Street, 96813-3480
Telephone: 808-531-8031
Cable Address: ADVOCATES
Facsimile: 808-533-2242

Gerhard Frohlich
X. Ben Tao

OF COUNSEL
William F. Thompson, III

Representative Client: American Express; BHP Petroleum Americas (Hawaii); C. Brewer & Co., Ltd.; The Daiei (USA), Inc.; Federal Deposit Insurance Corporation; Fletcher Challenge, Ltd.; Molokai Ranch, Ltd.

For Complete List of Firm Personnel, See General Section

For full biographical listings, see the Martindale-Hubbell Law Directory

FOLEY MAEHARA NIP & CHANG (AV)

2700 Grosvenor Center, 737 Bishop Street, 96813
Telephone: 808-526-3011
Telecopier: 808-523-1171, 808-526-0121, 808-533-4814

MEMBERS OF FIRM

Thomas M. Foley
Eric T. Maehara
Renton L. K. Nip
Wesley Y. S. Chang
Carl Tom
Edward R. Brooks
Arlene S. Kishi
Susan M. Ichinose
Robert F. Miller
Christian P. Porter

(See Next Column)

FOLEY MAEHARA NIP & CHANG—*Continued*

ASSOCIATES

Paula W. Chong
Lenore H. Lee
Leanne A. N. Nikaido
Jordan D. Wagner
Donna H. Yamamoto
Mark J. Bernardin
Jenny K. T. Wakayama

OF COUNSEL

Elizabeth A. Ivey

References: First Hawaiian Bank; Bank of Honolulu; Bank of Hawaii.

For full biographical listings, see the Martindale-Hubbell Law Directory

ILLINOIS

*CHICAGO,** Cook Co.

GESSLER, FLYNN, FLEISCHMANN, HUGHES & SOCOL, LTD. (AV)

Three First National Plaza, Suite 2200, 60602
Telephone: 312-580-0100
Telecopy: 312-580-1994

Mark S. Dym
Michael J. Flaherty
Thomas J. Fleischmann
Terence E. Flynn
George W. Gessler
John K. Hughes
William P. Jones
Peter M. Katsaros
Mark A. LaRose
Terence J. Moran
Matthew J. Piers
David J. Pritchard
Kalman D. Resnick
Jonathan A. Rothstein
Donna Kaner Socol

Eric Berg
Benjamin P. Beringer
Anjali Dayal
Ruth M. Dunning
Jennifer Fischer
Charles J. Holley
Laura C. Liu
Kimberley Marsh
Alex W. Miller
Paul A. Reasoner
Michael P. Simkus
Marci S. Sperling
Maria L. Venturo
Vanessa J. Weathersby
Mark B. Weiner
Charles H. Winterstein

OF COUNSEL

James T. Derico, Jr.
Susan R. Gzesh
Foster Marshall, Jr.

For full biographical listings, see the Martindale-Hubbell Law Directory

MANDEL, LIPTON AND STEVENSON LIMITED (AV)

Suite 2900, 120 North La Salle Street, 60602
Telephone: 312-236-7080
Facsimile: 312-236-0781

Terry Yale Feiertag

Goldie C. Domingue

References: Northern Trust Co.; American National Bank of Chicago.

For Complete List of Firm Personnel, See General Section

For full biographical listings, see the Martindale-Hubbell Law Directory

MINSKY, MCCORMICK & HALLAGAN, P.C. (AV)

122 South Michigan Avenue, Suite 1800, 60603
Telephone: 312-427-6163
Telefax: 312-427-6513

Joseph Minsky (1925-1992)
Margaret H. McCormick
James E. Hallagan
Deborah J. Kartje
Carlina Tapia-Ruano

Veronica Maya Jeffers
Timothy G. Payne

For full biographical listings, see the Martindale-Hubbell Law Directory

INDIANA

*INDIANAPOLIS,** Marion Co.

ICE MILLER DONADIO & RYAN (AV)

One American Square Box 82001, 46282-0002
Telephone: 317-236-2100
Fax: 317-236-2219

MEMBERS OF FIRM

Donald G. Sutherland
Richard E. Parker
Thomas H. Ristine

(See Next Column)

ASSOCIATE

Dale E. Stackhouse

Representative Clients: Thomson Consumer Electronics; Haynes International, Inc.; Aisin Seiki, Ltd.; Butler University; Toyoda Automatic Looms Works, Ltd.; Onkyo Corp.; Biomet Inc.; Haka, Inc.; Southam Publishing; INTAT Precision, Inc.

For Complete List of Firm Personnel, See General Section

For full biographical listings, see the Martindale-Hubbell Law Directory

KENTUCKY

*BOWLING GREEN,** Warren Co.

ENGLISH, LUCAS, PRIEST & OWSLEY (AV)

1101 College Street, P.O. Box 770, 42102-0770
Telephone: 502-781-6500
Telecopier: 502-782-7782

MEMBER OF FIRM

Wade T. Markham, II

For Complete List of Firm Personnel, See General Section

For full biographical listings, see the Martindale-Hubbell Law Directory

*LOUISVILLE,** Jefferson Co.

MOSLEY, CLARE & TOWNES (AV)

Fifth Floor, Hart Block Building, 730 West Main Street, 40202
Telephone: 502-583-7400
Telecopier: 502-589-4997

MEMBERS OF FIRM

Eugene L. Mosley
W. Waverley Townes
Larry C. Ethridge
Victor L. Baltzell, Jr.
William J. Nold
Judith E. McDonald-Burkman

ASSOCIATE

E. Jeffrey Mosley

For full biographical listings, see the Martindale-Hubbell Law Directory

LOUISIANA

METAIRIE, Jefferson Parish

DAVID A. M. WARE & ASSOCIATES (AV)

Two Lakeway Center, 3850 North Causeway Boulevard, Suite 1525, 70002
Telephone: 504-830-5900
Toll Free: 1-800-537-0179
Local: (504) 830-5900
After hours: 504-893-3943
Telefax: 504-830-5909
Baton Rouge, Louisiana Office: Suite C, 11750 Bricksome Avenue.
Telephone: 504-292-9091.
Telefax: 504-296-5401.

Representative Clients: Ford, Bacon & Davis Engineers; Dover Elevator.

For full biographical listings, see the Martindale-Hubbell Law Directory

*NEW ORLEANS,** Orleans Parish

ALLAIN & LIBERTO, R.L.L.P. (AV)

228 St. Charles Avenue, Suite 1128, 70130-2611
Telephone: 504-529-7860
Telecopier: 504-523-2221

J. Francois Allain

For full biographical listings, see the Martindale-Hubbell Law Directory

MUROV & WARD, A PROFESSIONAL LAW CORPORATION (AV)

615 Baronne Street Suite 150, 70113
Telephone: 504-523-6100
Fax: 504-524-5240

Mark G. Murov
Rita K. Ward

Allyson C. Martin

Reference: Whitney National Bank, New Orleans, La.

For full biographical listings, see the Martindale-Hubbell Law Directory

MAINE

*PORTLAND,** Cumberland Co.

PIERCE, ATWOOD, SCRIBNER, ALLEN, SMITH & LANCASTER (AV)

One Monument Square, 04101
Telephone: 207-773-6411
Fax: 207-773-3419
Augusta, Maine Office: 77 Winthrop Street.
Telephone: 207-622-6311.
Camden, Maine Office: 36 Chestnut Street, P.O. Box 780.
Telephone: 207-236-4333.

MEMBER OF FIRM

Charles S. Einsiedler, Jr.

ASSOCIATE

Anthony R. Derosby

For Complete List of Firm Personnel, See General Section

For full biographical listings, see the Martindale-Hubbell Law Directory

MARYLAND

*BALTIMORE,** (Independent City)

VENABLE, BAETJER AND HOWARD (AV)

A Partnership including Professional Corporations
1800 Mercantile Bank & Trust Building, 2 Hopkins Plaza, 21201
Telephone: 410-244-7400
Washington, D.C. Office: Venable, Baetjer, Howard & Civiletti. Suite 1000, 1201 New York Avenue, N.W.
Telephone: 202-962-4800.
McLean, Virginia Office: Suite 400, 2010 Corporate Ridge.
Telephone: 703-760-1600.
Rockville, Maryland Office: Suite 500, One Church Street, P. O. Box 1906.
Telephone: 301-217-5600.
Towson, Maryland Office: 210 Allegheny Avenue, P. O. Box 5517.
Telephone: 410-494-6200.

MEMBERS OF FIRM

Alexander I. Lewis, III (P.C.) (Also at Towson, Maryland Office)
Jana Howard Carey (P.C.)
Maurice Baskin (Resident, Washington, D.C. Office)
Mary E. Pivec (Also at Washington, D.C. Office)
John M. Gurley (Not admitted in MD; Resident, Washington, D.C. Office)

For Complete List of Firm Personnel, See General Section

For full biographical listings, see the Martindale-Hubbell Law Directory

SILVER SPRING, Montgomery Co.

ALEXANDER, GEBHARDT, APONTE & MARKS, L.L.C. (AV)

Lee Plaza-Suite 805, 8601 Georgia Avenue, 20910
Telephone: 301-589-2222
Facsimile: 301-589-2523
Washington, D.C. Office: 1314 Nineteenth Street, N.W., 20036.
Telephone: 202-835-1555.
New York, New York Office: 330 Madison Avenue, 36th Floor.
Telephone: 212-808-0008.
Fax: 212-599-1028.

Koteles Alexander (Not admitted in MD)
Mari Carmen Aponte (Not admitted in MD; Resident Washington, D.C. Office)

Eleanor Pelta (Not admitted in MD)

Reference: Riggs National Bank of Washington, D.C.

For full biographical listings, see the Martindale-Hubbell Law Directory

MASSACHUSETTS

*BOSTON,** Suffolk Co.

PALMER & DODGE (AV)

(Storey Thorndike Palmer & Dodge)
One Beacon Street, 02108
Telephone: 617-573-0100
Telecopier: 617-227-4420
Telex: 951104
Cable Address: "Storeydike," Boston

(See Next Column)

MEMBERS OF FIRM

F. Kingston Berlew
Craig E. Stewart

COUNSEL

Kevin R. McNamara
Alan S. Musgrave
Russell B. Swapp

For Complete List of Firm Personnel, See General Section

For full biographical listings, see the Martindale-Hubbell Law Directory

MICHIGAN

BLOOMFIELD HILLS, Oakland Co.

HOWARD & HOWARD ATTORNEYS, P.C. (AV)

The Pinehurst Office Center, Suite 101, 1400 North Woodward Avenue, 48304-2856
Telephone: 810-645-1483
Telecopier: 810-645-1568
Kalamazoo, Michigan Office: The Kalamazoo Building, Suite 400, 107 West Michigan Avenue.
Telephone: 616-382-1483.
Telecopier: 616-382-1568.
Lansing, Michigan Office: The Phoenix Building, Suite 500, 222 Washington Square, North.
Telephone: 517-485-1483.
Telecopier: 517-485-1568.
Peoria, Illinois Office: Howard & Howard, P.C., The Creve Coeur Building, Suite 200, 321 Liberty Street.
Telephone: 309-672-1483.
Telecopier: 309-672-1568.

Gustaf R. Andreasen

Representative Clients: For Representative Client list, see General Practice, Bloomfield Hills, MI.

For Complete List of Firm Personnel, See General Section

For full biographical listings, see the Martindale-Hubbell Law Directory

*DETROIT,** Wayne Co.

BUTZEL LONG, A PROFESSIONAL CORPORATION (AV)

Suite 900, 150 West Jefferson, 48226
Telephone: 313-225-7000
Telecopier: 313-225-7080
Birmingham, Michigan Office: Suite 200, 32270 Telegraph Road.
Telephone: 810-258-1616.
Telecopier: 810-258-1439.
Lansing, Michigan Office: 118 West Ottawa Street.
Telephone: 517-372-6622.
Telecopier: 517-372-6672.
Ann Arbor, Michigan Office: Suite 400, 121 West Washington.
Telephone: 313-995-3110.
Telecopier: 313-995-1777.
Grosse Pointe Farms, Michigan Office: Suite 260, 21 Kercheval.
Telephone: 313-886-5446.
Telecopier: 313-886-2114.

James C. Bruno

Clara DeMatteis Mager
Guglielmo A. Pezza
Nicholas J. Stasevich
Debra Auerbach Clephane
Caridad Pastor-Klucens

Representative Clients: Bridgestone/Firestone, Inc.; The Detroit News, Inc.; Detroit Diesel Corp.; Kelly Services; Kelsey Hayes Co.; Merrill Lynch & Co., Inc.; Stroh Brewery Co.; Takata Corp.; United Parcel Services of America, Inc.; The University of Michigan.

For Complete List of Firm Personnel, See General Section

For full biographical listings, see the Martindale-Hubbell Law Directory

CLARK, KLEIN & BEAUMONT (AV)

1600 First Federal Building, 1001 Woodward Avenue, 48226
Telephone: 313-965-8300
Facsimile: 313-962-4348
Bloomfield Hills Office: 1533 North Woodward Avenue, Suite 220, 48304.
Telephone: 810-258-2900.
Facsimile: 810-258-2949.

MEMBERS OF FIRM

David H. Paruch
Dorothy Hanigan Basmaji

Representative Clients: American Rehabilitation Network, Inc.; BASF Corporation; The Budd Company; Detroit Center Tool, Inc.; Euclid-Hitachi Heavy Equipment, Inc.; Hayes Wheels International, Inc./Kelsey-Hayes Co.; Pontifical Institute for Foreign Missions (P.I.M.E.) Inc.; R.P. Scheret Corporation; UNISYS Corporation; Zeidler-Roberts Partnership/Architects.

(See Next Column)

CLARK, KLEIN & BEAUMONT—*Continued*

For Complete List of Firm Personnel, See General Section

For full biographical listings, see the Martindale-Hubbell Law Directory

DICKINSON, WRIGHT, MOON, VAN DUSEN & FREEMAN (AV)

500 Woodward Avenue, Suite 4000, 48226-3425
Telephone: 313-223-3500
Facsimile: 313-223-3598
Bloomfield Hills, Michigan Office: 525 North Woodward Avenue, Suite 2000.
Telephone: 810-433-7200.
Facsimile: 810-433-7274.
Grand Rapids, Michigan Office: 200 Ottawa Avenue, N.W., Suite 900.
Telephone: 616-458-1300.
Facsimile: 616-458-6753.
Lansing, Michigan Office: Suite 200, 215 South Washington Square.
Telephone: 517-371-1730.
Facsimile: 517-487-4700.
Washington, D.C. Office: Suite 800, 1901 L Street, N.W.
Telephone: 202-457-0160.
Facsimile: 202-659-1559.
Chicago, Illinois Office: 225 West Washington, Suite 400.
Telephone: 312-220-0300.
Facsimile: 312-220-0021.
Warsaw, Poland Office: 46 Wilcza Street, 4th Floor, 00-679.
Telephone: (48-22) 299-241.
Facsimile: (48-2) 628-4107. Komertel Satellite Phone: (48-39) 121-510.

MEMBERS OF FIRM

Roger H. Cummings
Henry M. Grix
Bruce C. Thelen
Larry J. Stringer
Tomoaki Ikenaga

ASSOCIATES

Mark Alan Densmore
Robert B. Hotchkiss (Bloomfield Hills Office)
Linda J. Truitt

For Complete List of Firm Personnel, See General Section

For full biographical listings, see the Martindale-Hubbell Law Directory

ENGLISH & VAN HORNE, P.C. (AV)

4472 Penobscot Building, 48226
Telephone: 313-961-5100

John E. English
Pieter H. van Horne (Retired)
Meghan E. Kennedy

OF COUNSEL

Richard W. Pierce, P.C.

Reference: First of America Bank (Main Office Branch), Detroit.

For full biographical listings, see the Martindale-Hubbell Law Directory

FARMINGTON HILLS, Oakland Co.

KAUFMAN AND PAYTON (AV)

200 Northwestern Financial Center, 30833 Northwestern Highway, 48334
Telephone: 810-626-5000
Telefacsimile: 810-626-2843
Grand Rapids, Michigan Office: 420 Trust Building.
Telephone: 616-459-4200.
Fax: 616-459-4929.
Traverse City, Michigan Office: 122 West State Street.
Telephone: 616-947-4050.
Fax: 616-947-7321.

Alan Jay Kaufman
Donald L. Payton
Kenneth C. Letherwood
Stephen R. Levine
Thomas L. Vitu
Ralph C. Chapa, Jr.
Raymond I. Foley, II
Jeffrey K. Van Hattum
Leo D. Neville

For full biographical listings, see the Martindale-Hubbell Law Directory

*GRAND RAPIDS,** Kent Co.

WARNER, NORCROSS & JUDD (AV)

900 Old Kent Building, 111 Lyon Street, N.W., 49503-2489
Telephone: 616-752-2000
Fax: 616-752-2500
Muskegon, Michigan Office: 400 Terrace Plaza, P.O. Box 900.
Telephone: 616-727-2600.
Fax: 616-727-2699.
Holland, Michigan Office: Curtis Center, Suite 300, 170 College Avenue.
Telephone: 616-396-9800.
Fax: 616-396-3656.

MEMBERS OF FIRM

Charles E. McCallum
Janet Percy Knaus

For Complete List of Firm Personnel, See General Section

For full biographical listings, see the Martindale-Hubbell Law Directory

LANSING, Ingham Co.

FOSTER, SWIFT, COLLINS & SMITH, P.C. (AV)

313 South Washington Square, 48933-2193
Telephone: 517-371-8100
Telecopier: 517-371-8200
Farmington Hills, Michigan Office: 32300 Northwestern Highway, Suite 230.
Telephone: 810-851-7500.
Fax: 810-851-7504.

Gary J. McRay
Jean G. Schtokal
Robert L. Knechtel

General Counsel for: First American Bank-Central; Story, Inc.; Michigan Milk Producers Assn.; Edward W. Sparrow Hospital; St. Lawrence Hospital; Demmer Corp.; Michigan Financial Corp.
Local Counsel for: Shell Oil Co.; Michigan-Mutual Insurance Co.; Century Cellunet.

For Complete List of Firm Personnel, See General Section

For full biographical listings, see the Martindale-Hubbell Law Directory

MISSOURI

KANSAS CITY, Jackson, Clay & Platte Cos.

SWANSON, MIDGLEY, GANGWERE, KITCHIN & MCLARNEY, L.L.C. (AV)

1500 Commerce Trust Building, 922 Walnut, 64106-1848
Telephone: 816-842-6100
Overland Park, Kansas Office: The NCAA Building, Suite 350, 6201 College Boulevard.
Telephone: 816-842-6100.

Robert W. McKinley

Counsel for: General Electric Co.; Chrysler Corp.; Conoco, Inc.; Yellow Freight System, Inc.; The Prudential Insurance Co. of America; Metropolitan Life Insurance Co.; National Collegiate Athletic Assn.; Land Title Insurance Co.; Safeway Stores, Inc.; The Lee Apparel Co.

For Complete List of Firm Personnel, See General Section

For full biographical listings, see the Martindale-Hubbell Law Directory

MONTANA

*BILLINGS,** Yellowstone Co.

CROWLEY, HAUGHEY, HANSON, TOOLE & DIETRICH (AV)

500 Transwestern II, 490 North 31st Street, P.O. Box 2529, 59103
Telephone: 406-252-3441
Fax: 406-259-4159
Helena, Montana Office: IBM Building, 100 North Park Avenue, Suite 300, 59601.
Telephone: 406-449-4165.
Fax: 406-449-5149.

MEMBER OF FIRM

James P. Sites

Representative Clients: Norfolk Energy, Inc.; Billings Clinic; Billings Cardiology Associates, P.C.; Dutch Brothers Bakery.

For Complete List of Firm Personnel, See General Section

For full biographical listings, see the Martindale-Hubbell Law Directory

NEBRASKA

*OMAHA,** Douglas Co.

KRIEGER & KRIEGER (AV)

Suite 302, 9290 West Dodge Road, 68114
Telephone: 402-392-1280
E MAIL: 73411.32@compuserve.com.
Fax: 402-392-1563

MEMBERS OF FIRM

Stanley A. Krieger
M. Angela Krieger

Reference: Norwest Bank Omaha, N.A.

For full biographical listings, see the Martindale-Hubbell Law Directory

NEW JERSEY

*NEWARK,** Essex Co.

CARPENTER, BENNETT & MORRISSEY (AV)

(Formerly Carpenter, Gilmour & Dwyer)
Three Gateway Center, 17th Floor, 100 Mulberry Street, 07102-4079
Telephone: 201-622-7711
New York City: 212-943-6530
Telex: 139405
Telecopier: 201-622-5314
EasyLink: 62827845
ABA/net: CARPENTERB

MEMBERS OF FIRM

Edward F. Ryan
Patrick G. Brady
James E. Patterson

Representative Clients: General Motors Corp.; E. I. du Pont de Nemours and Company; Texaco Inc.; AT&T; Litton Industries; ITT Corp.; International Flavors & Fragrances Inc.; New Jersey Hospital Association; Prudential Insurance Company of America; United Jersey Bank.

For Complete List of Firm Personnel, See General Section

For full biographical listings, see the Martindale-Hubbell Law Directory

MEYNER AND LANDIS (AV)

One Gateway Center, Suite 2500, 07102-5311
Telephone: 201-624-2800
Fax: 201-624-0356

MEMBERS OF FIRM

Edwin C. Landis, Jr.
Jeffrey L. Reiner
John N. Malyska
William J. Fiore
Anthony F. Siliato
Francis R. Perkins
Geralyn A. Boccher
Howard O. Thompson
Robert B. Meyner (1908-1990)

ASSOCIATES

Kathryn Schatz Koles
Linda Townley Snyder
William H. Schmidt, Jr.
Scott T. McCleary
Maureen K Higgins
Richard A. Haws
Michael J. Palumbo
Theodore E. Lorenz

For full biographical listings, see the Martindale-Hubbell Law Directory

RUBIN & DORNBAUM (AV)

Suite 1300, 744 Broad Street, 07102
Telephone: 201-623-4444
Fax: 201-623-6839

MEMBERS

Edwin R. Rubin
Neil S. Dornbaum

For full biographical listings, see the Martindale-Hubbell Law Directory

PRINCETON, Mercer Co.

JOHN KUHN BLEIMAIER (AV)

15 Witherspoon Street, 08542
Telephone: 609-924-7273
Fax: 609-924-7030

For full biographical listings, see the Martindale-Hubbell Law Directory

NEW YORK

*AUBURN,** Cayuga Co.

BOYLE & ANDERSON, P.C. (AV)

120 Genesee Street, 13021
Telephone: 315-253-0326
Fax: 315-253-4968

Robert K. Bergan

Representative Clients: Columbian Foundation, Inc.; Cayuga Savings Bank; Wells College, Aurora, New York; O. Mustad & Son (U.S.A.), Inc.; W. E. Bouley Co., Inc.; Cooperative Feed Dealers, Inc.; R.P.M. Industries, Inc.; Port Byron Telephone Co.; The Stanley W. Metcalf Foundation; Welch Allyn.

For Complete List of Firm Personnel, See General Section

For full biographical listings, see the Martindale-Hubbell Law Directory

*BUFFALO,** Erie Co.

HODGSON, RUSS, ANDREWS, WOODS & GOODYEAR (AV)

A Partnership including Professional Associations
Suite 1800, One M & T Plaza, 14203
Telephone: 716-856-4000
Cable Address: "Magna Carta" Buffalo, N.Y.
Telecopier: 716-849-0349
Albany, New York Office: Three City Square.
Telephone: 518-465-2333.
Telecopier: 518-465-1567.
Rochester, New York Office: 400 East Avenue.
Telephone: 716-454-6950.
Telecopier: 716-454-4698.
Boca Raton, Florida Office: Suite 400, Nations Bank Building, 2000 Glades Road.
Telephone: 407-394-0500.
Telecopier: 305-427-4303.
Mississauga, Ontario, Canada Office: Suite 880, 3 Robert Speck Parkway.
Telephone: 905-566-5061.
Telecopier: 905-566-2049.
New York, New York Office: 330 Madison Avenue, 11th Floor. Telephone 212-297-3370.
Telecopier: 212-972-6521.

MEMBER OF FIRM
(ALPHABETICALLY BY YEAR OF ADMISSION TO BAR)

Lance J. Madden

ASSOCIATE
(ALPHABETICALLY BY YEAR OF ADMISSION TO BAR)

Margot L. Watt

Counsel for: Manufacturers and Traders Trust Company; Computer Task Group, Inc.; Fisher-Price; The Children's Hospital of Buffalo; Moog Controls; Corning Glass Works; Alcan Rolled Products Co.; Domtar, Inc.

For Complete List of Firm Personnel, See General Section

For full biographical listings, see the Martindale-Hubbell Law Directory

*NEW YORK,** New York Co.

LAW OFFICES OF RICHARD S. GOLDSTEIN (AV)

145 West 57th Street, 10019
Telephone: 212-957-0502
London, England Office: 50 Stratton Street, Suite 432, London W1X 5FL, England.
Telephone: 071-491-6675.
FAX: 071-629-7900.
San Francisco California Office: Law Offices of Goldstein and Fanning, Bank of America Center, Suite 2950, 555 California Street. 94104-1605.
Telephone: 415-981-7000.
Facsimile: 415-981-8579.

Kimberly D. Fanning (Resident, San Francisco, California Office)

ASSOCIATES

Kelly J. Clifford
Stephen M. Hader

For full biographical listings, see the Martindale-Hubbell Law Directory

ALLEN E. KAYE, P.C. (AV)

11 Park Place, 10007
Telephone: 212-964-5858
Telex: VISALAW 429433
FAX: 212-608-3734

Allen E. Kaye

Gunnar A. Sievert

OF COUNSEL

Ira Fieldsteel
Sandi DiMola (Not admitted in NY)

For full biographical listings, see the Martindale-Hubbell Law Directory

SATTERLEE STEPHENS BURKE & BURKE (AV)

230 Park Avenue, 10169-0079
Telephone: 212-818-9200
Cable Address: "Saterfield," New York
Telex: 233437
Telecopy or Facsimile: (212) 818-9606 or 818-9607
Summit, New Jersey Office: 47 Maple Street.
Telephone: 908-277-2221.
Westfield, New Jersey Office: 105 Elm Street.
Telephone: 908-654-4200.

MEMBERS OF FIRM

Stanley Mailman
Kenneth A. Schultz

(See Next Column)

SATTERLEE STEPHENS BURKE & BURKE—*Continued*

ASSOCIATES

Careen Brett Shannon   Ted J. Chiappari

For Complete List of Firm Personnel, See General Section

For full biographical listings, see the Martindale-Hubbell Law Directory

*ROCHESTER,** Monroe Co.

HARTER, SECREST & EMERY (AV)

700 Midtown Tower, 14604-2070
Telephone: 716-232-6500
Telecopier: 716-232-2152
Naples, Florida Office: Suite 400, 800 Laurel Oak Drive.
Telephone: 813-598-4444.
Telecopier: 813-598-2781.
Albany, New York Office: One Steuben Place.
Telephone: 518-434-4377.
Telecopier: 518-449-4025.
Syracuse, New York Office: 431 East Fayette Street.
Telephone: 315-474-4000.
Telecopier: 315-474-7789.

MEMBER OF FIRM

Margaret Artale Catillaz

ASSOCIATES

Amy Hartman Nichols   Kathleen M. Beckman

For Complete List of Firm Personnel, See General Section

For full biographical listings, see the Martindale-Hubbell Law Directory

NORTH CAROLINA

*CHARLOTTE,** Mecklenburg Co.

SMITH HELMS MULLISS & MOORE, L.L.P. (AV)

227 North Tryon Street, P.O. Box 31247, 28231
Telephone: 704-343-2000
Telecopier: 704-334-8467
Telex: 572460
Greensboro, North Carolina Office: Smith Helms Mulliss & Moore, Suite 1400 First Union Tower, 300 North Greene Street, P.O. Box 21927.
Telephone: 910-378-5200.
Telecopier: 910-379-9558.
Raleigh, North Carolina Office: 316 West Edenton Street, P.O. Box 27525.
Telephone: 919-755-8700.
Telecopier: 919-828-7938.

MEMBER OF FIRM

Larry J. Dagenhart

For Complete List of Firm Personnel, See General Section

For full biographical listings, see the Martindale-Hubbell Law Directory

*FAYETTEVILLE,** Cumberland Co.

ROSE, RAY, WINFREY, O'CONNOR & LESLIE, P.A. (AV)

214 Mason Street, P.O. Box 1239, 28302-1239
Telephone: 910-483-2101
FAX: 910-483-8444

George M. Rose (1846-1924)   Ronald E. Winfrey
Charles G. Rose (1880-1948)   Steven J. O'Connor
Robert G. Ray   Pamela S. Leslie

OF COUNSEL

Chas. G. Rose, Jr.

Brian K. Manning   Geraldine O. Spates
James A. Hadley, Jr.

Representative Clients: Home Federal Savings & Loan Assn.; Carolina Lithotrips, Ltd.; Parker Marking Systems, Inc.; Dixie Yarns, Inc.; Modern Moving and Storage, Inc.; Fayetteville Diagnostic Center, Ltd.; Cross Creek Plaza, Inc.; Medical Arts Imaging Center Limited Partnership; Southern Peanut, Inc.

For full biographical listings, see the Martindale-Hubbell Law Directory

*GREENSBORO,** Guilford Co.

SMITH HELMS MULLISS & MOORE, L.L.P. (AV)

Suite 1400 First Union Tower, 300 North Greene Street, P.O. Box 21927, 27420
Telephone: 910-378-5200
Telecopier: 910-379-9558
Charlotte, North Carolina Office: Smith Helms Mulliss & Moore, L.L.P., 227 North Tryon Street, P.O. Box 31247.
Telephone: 704-343-2000.
Telecopier: 704-334-8467.
Telex: 572460.
Raleigh, North Carolina Office: Smith Helms Mulliss & Moore, L.L.P., 316 West Edenton Street, P.O. Box 27525.
Telephone: 919-755-8700.
Telecopier: 919-828-7938.

MEMBER OF FIRM

Kathy E. Manning

ASSOCIATE

Fran M. Shaver

For Complete List of Firm Personnel, See General Section

For full biographical listings, see the Martindale-Hubbell Law Directory

*RALEIGH,** Wake Co.

* indicates certain Bar Register subscribers whose principal office is located elsewhere in the state and who have arranged for representation as a part of the state capital listings that follow

ALLEN AND PINNIX (AV)

20 Market Plaza, Suite 200, P.O. Drawer 1270, 27602
Telephone: 919-755-0505
Telecopier: 919-829-8098
Woodlawn Green, Charlotte, North Carolina Telephone: 704-522-8069

MEMBERS OF FIRM

John L. Pinnix   C. Lynn Calder

General Counsel for: North Carolina State Board of CPA Examiners; North Carolina Board of Architecture.

For full biographical listings, see the Martindale-Hubbell Law Directory

* **SMITH HELMS MULLISS & MOORE, L.L.P.** (AV)

316 West Edenton Street, P.O. Box 27525, 27611-7525
Telephone: 919-755-8700
Telecopier: 919-828-7938
Charlotte, North Carolina Office: 227 North Tryon Street, P.O. Box 31247.
Telephone: 704-343-2000.
Telecopier: 704-334-8467.
Telex: 572460.
Greensboro, North Carolina Office: Smith Helms Mulliss & Moore, Suite 1400 First Union Tower, 300 North Greene Street, P.O. Box 21927.
Telephone: 910-378-5200.
Telecopier: 910-379-9558.

ASSOCIATE

Matthew W. Sawchak

For Complete List of Firm Personnel, See General Section

For full biographical listings, see the Martindale-Hubbell Law Directory

OHIO

*CINCINNATI,** Hamilton Co.

DINSMORE & SHOHL (AV)

1900 Chemed Center, 255 East Fifth Street, 45202-3172
Telephone: 513-977-8200
FAX: 513-977-8141
Florence, Kentucky Office: Turfway Ridge Office Park, 7300 Turfway Road, Suite 430 41042-1355.
Telephone: 606-283-0515.
FAX: 606-283-6017.
Dayton, Ohio Office: 500 Courthouse Plaza, S.W., 10 N. Ludlow Street, 45402-1834.
Telephone: 513-228-8012.
FAX: 513-461-2543.
Columbus, Ohio Office: NBD Bank Building, Suite 330, 175 South Third Street, 43215-5134.
Telephone: 614-224-7887.
FAX: 614-224-7882.

(See Next Column)

DINSMORE & SHOHL, *Cincinnati—Continued*

MEMBER OF FIRM

John E. Schlosser

For Complete List of Firm Personnel, See General Section

For full biographical listings, see the Martindale-Hubbell Law Directory

KATZ, GREENBERGER & NORTON (AV)

105 East Fourth Street, 9th Floor, 45202-4011
Telephone: 513-721-5151
FAX: 513-621-9285

Leonard H. Freiberg (1885-1954)
Alfred B. Katz
Mark Alan Greenberger
Louis H. Katz
Richard L. Norton
Steven M. Rothstein
Robert Gray Edmiston
Ellen Essig

ASSOCIATES

Scott P. Kadish
Stephen E. Imm
Stephen L. Robison
Jeffrey J. Greenberger

OF COUNSEL

Charles Weiner

For full biographical listings, see the Martindale-Hubbell Law Directory

THOMPSON, HINE AND FLORY (AV)

312 Walnut Street, 14th Floor, 45202-4029
Telephone: 513-352-6700
Fax: 513-241-4771;
Telex: 938003
Akron, Ohio Office: 50 S. Main Street, Suite 502, 44308-1828.
Telephone: 216-376-8090.
Fax: 216-376-8386.
Cleveland, Ohio Office: 1100 National City Bank Building, 629 Euclid Avenue, 44114-3070.
Telephone: 216-566-5500.
Fax: 216-556-5583.
Telex: 980217.
Cable Address: "Thomflor".
Columbus, Ohio Office: One Columbus, 10 West Broad Street, 43215-3435.
Telephone: 614-469-3200.
Fax: 614-469-3361.
Dayton, Ohio Office: 2000 Courthouse Plaza, N.E., 45402-1706.
Telephone: 513-443-6600.
Fax: 513-443-6637; 443-6635.
Palm Beach, Florida Office: 125 Worth Avenue, 33480-4466.
Telephone: 407-833-5900.
Fax: 407-833-5951.
Washington, D.C. Office: 1920 N Street, N.W., 20036-1601.
Telephone: 202-331-8800.
Fax: 202-331-8330.
Telex: 904173.
Cable Address: "Caglaw".
Brussels, Belgium Office: Rue des Chevaliers / Ridderstraat 14 - B.10, B - 1050.
Telephone: 011(32-2) 511-9326.
Fax: 011(-32-2) 513-9206.

ASSOCIATE

Stacie A. Seiler

For Complete List of Firm Personnel, See General Section

For full biographical listings, see the Martindale-Hubbell Law Directory

*CLEVELAND,** Cuyahoga Co.

BAKER & HOSTETLER (AV)

3200 National City Center, 1900 East Ninth Street, 44114-3485
Telephone: 216-621-0200
Telecopier: 216-696-0740
TWX: 810 421 8375
RCA Telex: 215032
In Columbus, Ohio: Capitol Square, Suite 2100, 65 East State Street.
Telephone: 614-228-1541.
In Denver, Colorado: 303 East 17th Avenue, Suite 1100.
Telephone: 303-861-0600.
In Houston, Texas: 1000 Louisiana, Suite 2000.
Telephone: 713-751-1600.
In Long Beach, California: 300 Oceangate, Suite 620.
Telephone: 310-432-2827.
In Los Angeles, California: 600 Wilshire Boulevard.
Telephone: 213-624-2400.
In Orlando, Florida: SunBank Center, Suite 2300, 200 South Orange Avenue.
Telephone: 407-649-4000.
In Washington, D. C.: Washington Square, Suite 1100, 1050 Connecticut Avenue, N.W.
Telephone: 202-861-1500.
In College Park, Maryland: 9658 Baltimore Boulevard, Suite 206.
Telephone: 301-441-2781.
In Alexandria, Virginia: 437 North Lee Street.
Telephone: 703-549-1294.

(See Next Column)

In San Francisco, California: One Sansome Street, Suite 2000.
Telephone: 415-951-4705.

PARTNERS

John H. M. Fenix
John H. Wilharm, Jr.

For Complete List of Firm Personnel, See General Section

For full biographical listings, see the Martindale-Hubbell Law Directory

THOMPSON, HINE AND FLORY (AV)

1100 National City Bank Building, 629 Euclid Avenue, 44114-3070
Telephone: 216-566-5500
Fax: 216-566-5583
Telex: 980217
Cable Address: "Thomflor"
Akron, Ohio Office: 50 S. Main Street, Suite 502, 44308-1828.
Telephone: 216-376-8090.
Fax: 216-376-8386.
Cincinnati, Ohio Office: 312 Walnut Street, 14th Floor, 45202-4029.
Telephone: 513-352-6700.
Fax: 513-241-4771.
Telex: 938003.
Columbus, Ohio Office: One Columbus, 10 West Broad Street, 43215-3435.
Telephone: 614-469-3200.
Fax: 614-469-3361.
Dayton, Ohio Office: 2000 Courthouse Plaza, N.E., 45402-1706.
Telephone: 513-443-6600.
Fax: 513-443-6637; 443-6635.
Palm Beach, Florida Office: 125 Worth Avenue, Suite 117, 33480-4466.
Telephone: 407-833-5900.
Fax: 407-833-5951.
Washington, D.C. Office: 1920 N Street, N.W., 20036-1601.
Telephone: 202-331-8800.
Fax: 202-331-8330.
Telex: 904173.
Cable Address: "Caglaw".
Brussels, Belgium Office: Rue des Chevaliers, Ridderstraat 14 - B.10, B - 1050.
Telephone: 011(32-2) 511-9326.
Fax: 011(32-2) 513-9206.

MEMBER OF FIRM

T. Merritt Bumpass, Jr.

SENIOR ATTORNEY

Judith M. Woo

For Complete List of Firm Personnel, See General Section

For full biographical listings, see the Martindale-Hubbell Law Directory

MARGARET W. WONG & ASSOCIATES (AV)

1128 Standard Building, 44113
Telephone: 216-566-9908
FAX: 216-566-1125

ASSOCIATES

Michael H. Sharon
William J. Nickerson, Jr.
(Not admitted in OH)
Aniko T. Kalnoki-kis
Michelle A. Stefanski

Reference: National City Bank.

For full biographical listings, see the Martindale-Hubbell Law Directory

*COLUMBUS,** Franklin Co.

EMENS, KEGLER, BROWN, HILL & RITTER (AV)

Capitol Square Suite 1800, 65 East State Street, 43215-4294
Telephone: 614-462-5400
Telecopier: 614-464-2634
Cable Address: "Law EKBHR"
Telex: 246671

S. Martijn Steger

Michael J. Galeano

For Complete List of Firm Personnel, See General Section

For full biographical listings, see the Martindale-Hubbell Law Directory

*DAYTON,** Montgomery Co.

LOUIS & FROELICH A LEGAL PROFESSIONAL ASSOCIATION (AV)

1812 Kettering Tower, 45423
Telephone: 513-226-1776
FAX: 513-226-1945
Trotwood, Ohio Office: 101 East Main Street.
Telephone: 513-226-1776.

Herbert M. Louis
Gary L. Froelich
Jeffrey E. Froelich
Jeffrey A. Winwood
Marybeth W. Rutledge

(See Next Column)

LOUIS & FROELICH A LEGAL PROFESSIONAL ASSOCIATION—*Continued*

F. Ann Crossman James I. Weprin

Reference: Society Bank, N.A. of Dayton, Ohio.

For full biographical listings, see the Martindale-Hubbell Law Directory

*TOLEDO,** Lucas Co.

AUBRY, MEYER, WALSH & POMMERANZ (AV)

(An Association of Independent Attorneys)
Lawyers Building, 329-10th Street, P.O. Box 2068, 43603-2068
Telephone: 419-241-4288
FAX: 419-241-5764

Jude T. Aubry
William G. Meyer
Joseph M. Walsh
Melvin R. Pommeranz
Thomas R. Stebbins
Colleen M. Dooley
M. Susan Swanson

For full biographical listings, see the Martindale-Hubbell Law Directory

OREGON

*PORTLAND,** Multnomah Co.

BLACK HELTERLINE (AV)

1200 The Bank of California Tower, 707 S.W. Washington Street, 97205
Telephone: 503-224-5560
Telecopier: 503-224-6148

MEMBERS OF FIRM

Paul R. Hribernick Gerald H. Robinson

OF COUNSEL

Robert E. Glasgow

Representative Clients: C H 2 M Hill; ESCO Corp.; Molecular Probes, Inc.; NIKE, Inc.; Overseas Merchandise Inspection Co.; Planar Systems, Inc.; S.E.H. America, Inc.; Siltec Corp.; Skies America Publishing Co.; Step Technology.

For Complete List of Firm Personnel, See General Section

For full biographical listings, see the Martindale-Hubbell Law Directory

PENNSYLVANIA

*PHILADELPHIA,** Philadelphia Co.

CORSON, GETSON & SCHATZ (AV)

Suite 300 The Carlton Business Center, 1819 John F. Kennedy Boulevard, 19103
Telephone: 215-564-3030; 568-2525
Fax: 215-564-5477

MEMBERS OF FIRM

Lawrence Corson
Allan Getson
Robert B. B. Schatz

For full biographical listings, see the Martindale-Hubbell Law Directory

ORLOW AND ORLOW, P.C. (AV)

1154 Public Ledger Building, Sixth and Chestnut Streets, 19106
Telephone: 215-922-1183
Telecopier: 215-922-0516

Abram Orlow (1900-1950) James J. Orlow

OF COUNSEL

Lena Orlow Ginsburg (Retired)

Joan Katz Betesh

For full biographical listings, see the Martindale-Hubbell Law Directory

STEEL, RUDNICK & RUBEN (AV)

Suite 936 Public Ledger Building, Sixth and Chestnut Streets, 19106
Telephone: 215-922-1181
Fax: 215-922-0219
Pittsburgh, Pennsylvania Office: Law & Finance Building, 429 Fourth Avenue.
Telephone: 412-391-4719.

MEMBERS OF FIRM

Richard D. Steel
Lawrence H. Rudnick
Ann A. Ruben

(See Next Column)

ASSOCIATE

Christina Aborlleile

For full biographical listings, see the Martindale-Hubbell Law Directory

*PITTSBURGH,** Allegheny Co.

BUCHANAN INGERSOLL, PROFESSIONAL CORPORATION (AV)

5800 USX Tower, 600 Grant Street, 15219
Telephone: 412-562-8800
Telecopier: 412-562-1041
Philadelphia, Pennsylvania Office: Two Logan Square, Twelfth Floor, 18th & Arch Streets.
Telephone: 215-665-8700.
Harrisburg, Pennsylvania Office: Vartan Parc, 30 North Third Street.
Telephone: 717-237-4800.
Tampa, Florida Office: 101 East Kennedy Boulevard, Suite 1030.
Telephone: 813-222-8180.
North Miami Beach, Florida Office: 19495 Biscayne Boulevard.
Telephone: 305-933-5600.
Lexington, Kentucky Office: 1210 Vine Center Office Tower, 333 West Vine Street.
Telephone: 606-225-5333.
Princeton, New Jersey Office: Buchanan Ingersoll, A Partnership, College Centre, 500 College Road East.
Telephone: 609-452-2666.

John S. Brendel

For Complete List of Firm Personnel, See General Section

For full biographical listings, see the Martindale-Hubbell Law Directory

SOUTH CAROLINA

*COLUMBIA,** Richland Co.

BERRY, DUNBAR, DANIEL, O'CONNOR & JORDAN (AV)

A Partnership including Professional Associations
1200 Main Street, Eighth Floor, P.O. Box 11645, Capitol Station, 29211-1645
Telephone: 803-765-1030
Facsimile: 803-799-5536
Spartanburg, South Carolina Office: 112 West Daniel Morgan Avenue.
Telephone: 803-583-3975.
Atlanta, Georgia Office: 2400 Cain Tower, Peachtree Center.
Telephone: 404-588-0500.
Facsimile: 404-523-6714.

MEMBER OF FIRM

James V. Dunbar, Jr.

ASSOCIATE

John A. Hill

Approved Attorneys for: Lawyers Title Insurance Corporation of Richmond.

For Complete List of Firm Personnel, See General Section

For full biographical listings, see the Martindale-Hubbell Law Directory

TENNESSEE

*MEMPHIS,** Shelby Co.

HANOVER, WALSH, JALENAK & BLAIR (AV)

Fifth Floor - Falls Building, 22 North Front Street, 38103-2109
Telephone: 901-526-0621
Telecopier: 901-521-9759

MEMBERS OF FIRM

Joseph Hanover (1888-1984)
David Hanover (1899-1963)
Jay Alan Hanover
William M. Walsh
James B. Jalenak
Allen S. Blair
Michael E. Goldstein
Edward J. McKenney, Jr.
James R. Newsom, III
John Kevin Walsh
James A. Johnson, Jr.
Donald S. Holm III
Barbara B. Lapides

Jennifer A. Sevier
Christina von Cannon Burdette
Jeffrey S. Rosenblum

OF COUNSEL

Helyn L. Keith

For full biographical listings, see the Martindale-Hubbell Law Directory

TEXAS

*HOUSTON,** Harris Co.

TINDALL & FOSTER, P.C. (AV)

2800 Texas Commerce Tower, 77002-3094
Telephone: 713-229-8733
Fax: 713-228-1303

Harry L. Tindall
Charles C. Foster
Lydia G. Tamez
Gary E. Endelman
Donna S. Anderson
Milenia I. Soto
Robert F. Loughran
Blanche V. Stovall

Reference: Texas Commerce Bank, N.A., Houston, Texas.

For full biographical listings, see the Martindale-Hubbell Law Directory

UTAH

*SALT LAKE CITY,** Salt Lake Co.

PARSONS BEHLE & LATIMER, A PROFESSIONAL CORPORATION (AV)

One Utah Center, 201 South Main Street, Suite 1800, P.O. Box 45898, 84145-0898
Telephone: 801-532-1234
Telecopy: 801-536-6111

James M. Elegante
Lorna Rogers Burgess

Representative Clients: American Barrick Resources Corporation; Kennecott Corporation; TheraTech, Inc.; University of Utah Medical Center.

For full biographical listings, see the Martindale-Hubbell Law Directory

VIRGINIA

*ARLINGTON,** Arlington Co.

SAMUEL JAY LEVINE, P.C. (AV)

4001 North 9th Street, Suite 224, 22203
Telephone: 703-524-8500
703-524-9009 (Spanish)
Telecopier: 703-527-4473

Samuel Jay Levine (Not admitted in VA)

Charles A. Mosher (Not admitted in VA)

For full biographical listings, see the Martindale-Hubbell Law Directory

NORFOLK, (Independent City)

VANDEVENTER, BLACK, MEREDITH & MARTIN (AV)

500 World Trade Center, 23510
Telephone: 804-446-8600
Cable Address: "Hughsvan"
Telex: 823-671
Telecopier: 446-8670
North Carolina, Kitty Hawk Office: 6 Juniper Trail.
Telephone: 919-261-5055.
Fax: 919-261-8444.
London, England Office: Suite 692, Level 6, Lloyd's, 1 Lime Street.
Telephone: (071) 623-2081.
Facsimile: (071) 929-0043.
Telex: 987321.

MEMBERS OF FIRM

Walter B. Martin, Jr.
Mark T. Coberly

For Complete List of Firm Personnel, See General Section

For full biographical listings, see the Martindale-Hubbell Law Directory

*RICHMOND,** (Ind. City; Seat of Henrico Co.)

WILLIAMS, MULLEN, CHRISTIAN & DOBBINS, A PROFESSIONAL CORPORATION (AV)

Two James Center, 1021 East Cary Street, P.O. Box 1320, 23210-1320
Telephone: 804-643-1991
Fax: 804-783-6456
Glen Allen, Virginia Office: 4401 Waterfront Drive, Suite 140.
Telephone: 804-965-9168.
Fax: 804-965-0955.

(See Next Column)

Washington, D.C. Office: 1575 Eye Street, N.W.
Telephone: 202-289-6200.
Fax: 202-289-4126.

William J. Benos

For Complete List of Firm Personnel, See General Section

For full biographical listings, see the Martindale-Hubbell Law Directory

WASHINGTON

*SEATTLE,** King Co.

GAITÁN & CUSACK (AV)

30th Floor Two Union Square, 601 Union Street, 98101-2324
Telephone: 206-521-3000
Facsimile: 206-386-5259
Anchorage, Alaska Office: 425 G Street, Suite 760.
Telephone: 907-278-3001.
Facsimile: 907-278-6068.
San Francisco, California Office: 275 Battery Street, 20th Floor.
Telephone: 415-398-5562.
Fax: 415-398-4033.
Washington, D.C. Office: 2000 L Street, Suite 200.
Telephone: 202-296-4637.
Fax: 202-296-4650.

MEMBERS OF FIRM

José E. Gaitán
Kenneth J. Cusack (Resident, Anchorage, Alaska Office)
William F. Knowles
Ronald L. Bozarth

OF COUNSEL

Howard K. Todd
Gary D. Gayton
Michel P. Stern (Also practicing alone, Bellevue, Washington)
Christopher A. Byrne
Patricia D. Ryan

ASSOCIATES

Mary F. O'Boyle
Bruce H. Williams
David J. Onsager
Diana T. Jimenez
Robert T. Mimbu
Cristina C. Kapela
Camilla M. Hedberg
John E. Lenker
Kathleen C. Healy

Representative Clients: Hosho America; HFI Foods.

For full biographical listings, see the Martindale-Hubbell Law Directory

WISCONSIN

*MILWAUKEE,** Milwaukee Co.

QUARLES & BRADY (AV)

411 East Wisconsin Avenue, 53202-4497
Telephone: 414-277-5000
Cable Address: "Lawdock"
Fax: 414-271-3552.
TWX: 910-262-3426
Madison, Wisconsin Office: Firstar Plaza, One South Pinckney Street, P.O. Box 2113.
Telephone: 608-251-5000.
Fax: 608-251-9166.
West Palm Beach, Florida Office: 222 Lakeview Avenue, 4th Floor.
Telephone: 407-653-5000.
Fax: 407-653-5333.
Naples, Florida Office: Barnett Center, 4501 Tamiami Trail North.
Telephone: 813-262-5959.
Fax: 813-434-4999.
Phoenix, Arizona Office: One Camelback Building, One East Camelback Road, Suite 400.
Telephone: 602-230-5500.
Fax: 602-230-5598.

MEMBER OF FIRM
(ALPHABETICALLY BY YEAR OF ADMISSION TO BAR)

Alyce C. Katayama

ASSOCIATES

Joseph E. Puchner
Jose L. Martinez (Resident, Phoenix, Arizona Office)
Harold O.M. Rocha

For Complete List of Firm Personnel, See General Section

For full biographical listings, see the Martindale-Hubbell Law Directory

PUERTO RICO

SAN JUAN, San Juan Dist.

FIDDLER, GONZÁLEZ & RODRÍGUEZ

Chase Manhattan Bank Building (Hato Rey), P.O. Box 363507, 00936-3507
Telephone: 809-753-3113
Telecopier: 809-759-3123

MEMBER OF FIRM

Lolita J. Semidey Garcia

For Complete List of Firm Personnel, See General Section

For full biographical listings, see the Martindale-Hubbell Law Directory

O'NEILL & BORGES

10th Floor, Chase Manhattan Bank Building (Hato Rey), 254 Muñoz Rivera Avenue, 00918-1995
Telephone: 809-764-8181
Telecopier: 809-753-8944

MEMBER OF FIRM

Jorge L. Capó-Matos

ASSOCIATE

Ramón L. Velasco

Representative Clients: Ballet Concierto de Puerto Rico; Elizabeth Arden Interamerica; Corporacion Ford; Kumagai Caribbean, Inc.; McCann-Erickson Corp.; The Procter & Gamble Commercial Co.

For Complete List of Firm Personnel, See General Section

For full biographical listings, see the Martindale-Hubbell Law Directory

CANADA ALBERTA

*EDMONTON,** Edmonton Jud. Dist.

PARLEE MCLAWS (AV)

15th Floor Manulife Place, 10180 101st Street, T5J 4K1
Telephone: 403-423-8500
Telecopier: 403-423-2870
Calgary, Alberta Office: 3400, Western Canadian Place, 707 - 8th Avenue, S.W.
Telephone: 403-294-7000.
Telecopier: 403-265-8263.

MEMBERS OF FIRM

C. H. Kerr, Q.C.
M. D. MacDonald
K. F. Bailey, Q.C.
R. B. Davison, Q.C.
F. R. Haldane
P. E. J. Curran
D. G. Finlay
J. K. McFadyen
R. C. Secord
D. L. Kennedy
D. C. Rolf
D. F. Pawlowski
A. A. Garber
R. P. James
D. C. Wintermute
J. L. Cairns
R. A. Newton, Q.C.
T. A. Cockrall, Q.C.
H. D. Montemurro
F. J. Niziol
R. W. Wilson
I. L. MacLachlan
R. O. Langley
R. G. McBean
J. T. Neilson
E. G. Rice
J. F. McGinnis
J. H. H. Hockin
G. W. Jaycock
M. J. K. Nikel
B. J. Curial
S. L. May
M. S. Poretti

ASSOCIATES

C. R. Head
A.W. Slemko
L. H. Hamdon
K.A. Smith
K. D. Fallis-Howell
D. S. Tam
J.W. McClure
F.H. Belzil
R.A. Renz
J.G. Paulson
K. E. Buss
B. L. Andriachuk
P. E. S. J. Kennedy
R. Feraco
R.J. Billingsley
N.B.R. Thompson
P. A. Shenher
I. C. Johnson
K.G. Koshman
D.D. Dubrule
G. T. Lund
W.D. Johnston
G. E. Flemming
K. P. Nayyer

For full biographical listings, see the Martindale-Hubbell Law Directory

CANADA BRITISH COLUMBIA

*VANCOUVER,** Vancouver Co.

RUSSELL & DUMOULIN (AV)

2100-1075 West Georgia Street, V6E 3G2
Telephone: 604-631-3131
Fax: 604-631-3232
A Member of the national association of Borden DuMoulin Howard Gervais, comprising Russell & DuMoulin, Vancouver, British Columbia; Howard Mackie, Calgary, Alberta; Borden & Elliot, Toronto, Ontario; Mackenzie Gervais, Montreal, Quebec and Borden DuMoulin Howard Gervais, London, England.
Strategic Alliance with Perkins Coie with offices in Seattle, Spokane and Bellevue, Washington; Portland, Oregon; Anchorage, Alaska; Los Angeles, California; Washington, D.C.; Hong Kong and Taipei, Taiwan.
Represented in Hong Kong by Vincent T.K. Cheung, Yap & Co.

ASSOCIATE

E. Jane Luke

Representative Clients: Alcan Smelters & Chemicals Ltd.; The Bank of Nova Scotia; Canada Trust Co.; The Canada Life Assurance Co.; Forest Industrial Relations Ltd.; Honda Canada Inc.; IBM Canada Ltd.; Macmillan Bloedel Ltd.; Nissho Iwai Canada Ltd.; The Toronto-Dominion Bank.

For Complete List of Firm Personnel, See General Section

For full biographical listings, see the Martindale-Hubbell Law Directory

CANADA ONTARIO

*TORONTO,** Regional Munic. of York

BORDEN & ELLIOT (AV)

Barristers & Solicitors
Scotia Plaza, 40 King Street West, M5H 3Y4
Telephone: 416-367-6000
Telecopier: 416-367-6749
Internet: @ borden.com
A Member of the national association of Borden DuMoulin Howard Gervais, comprising Borden & Elliot in Toronto, Ontario, Russell & DuMoulin in Vancouver, British Columbia, Howard, Mackie in Calgary, Alberta and Mackenzie Gervais in Montréal, Québec. Borden DuMoulin Howard Gervais also operates an office in London, England.

MEMBER AND ASSOCIATES

Stanley B. Bush

For Complete List of Firm Personnel, See General Section

For full biographical listings, see the Martindale-Hubbell Law Directory

CANADA SASKATCHEWAN

*REGINA,** Regina Jud. Centre

MACPHERSON LESLIE & TYERMAN (AV)

1500-1874 Scarth Street, S4P 4E9
Telephone: 306-347-8000
Telecopier: 306-352-5250
Saskatoon, Saskatchewan Office: 1500-410 22nd Street East, S7K 5T6.
Telephone: 306-975-7100.
Telecopier: 306-975-7145.

MEMBER OF FIRM

Robert B. Pletch, Q.C.

For Complete List of Firm Personnel, See General Section

For full biographical listings, see the Martindale-Hubbell Law Directory

INSURANCE DEFENSE LAW

ALABAMA

*ATHENS,** Limestone Co.

PATTON, LATHAM, LEGGE & COLE (AV)

Professional Building, 315 West Market Street, P.O. Box 470, 35611
Telephone: 205-232-2010
Fax: 205-230-0610

MEMBERS OF FIRM

Roy B. Patton (1885-1954)
David U. Patton (Retired)
Byrd R. Latham
Winston V. Legge, Jr.
P. Michael Cole

Local Counsel for: Auto-Owners Insurance Co.; Avis; Blue Cross and Blue Shield of Alabama; CIGNA Insurance Cos.; Gold Kist, Inc.; State Farm Life Insurance Co.; State Farm Mutual Automobile Insurance Co.; Travelers Insurance Co.; United States Fidelity and Guaranty Co.; Wausau Insurance Company.

For full biographical listings, see the Martindale-Hubbell Law Directory

*BIRMINGHAM,** Jefferson Co.

BALCH & BINGHAM (AV)

1710 Sixth Avenue North, P.O. Box 306, 35201
Telephone: 205-251-8100
Facsimile: 205-226-8798
Other Birmingham, Alabama Office: 1901 Sixth Avenue North, 35203.
Telephone: 205-251-8100.
Facsimile: 205-226-8799.
Montgomery, Alabama Office: The Winter Building, 2 Dexter Avenue, 36101.
Telephone: 205-834-6500.
Facsimile: 205-269-3115.
Huntsville, Alabama Office: Suite 810, 200 West Court Square, 35801.
Telephone: 205-551-0171.
Facsimile: 205-551-0174.
Washington, D.C. Office: Suite 800, 1101 Connecticut Avenue, N.W., 20036.
Telephone: 202-296-0387.
Facsimile: 202-452-8180.

MEMBERS OF FIRM

Michael L. Edwards
S. Allen Baker, Jr.
James A. Bradford
Alan T. Rogers
Cavender Crosby Kimble

Counsel for: Alabama Power Co.; Blue Cross and Blue Shield of Alabama; The Boeing Company; Brasfield & Gorrie, Inc.; Compass Bancshares, Inc.; Harbert Corp.; Kimberly-Clark Corp.; Southern Company Services, Inc.; Southern Research Institute; Vesta Insurance Group, Inc.

For Complete List of Firm Personnel, See General Section
For full biographical listings, see the Martindale-Hubbell Law Directory

BRADLEY, ARANT, ROSE & WHITE (AV)

1400 Park Place Tower, 2001 Park Place, 35203
Telephone: 205-521-8000
Telex: 494-1324
Facsimile: 205-251-8611, 251-8665, 252-0264
Facsimile (Southtrust Office): 205-251-9915
Huntsville, Alabama Office: 200 Clinton Avenue West, Suite 900.
Telephone: 205-517-5100.
Facsimile: 205-533-5069.

MEMBERS OF FIRM

John H. Morrow
Hobart A. McWhorter, Jr.
James W. Gewin
Brittin Turner Coleman
Scott M. Phelps
Norman Jetmundsen, Jr.
Joseph S. Bird, III
John D. Watson, III
Michael R. Pennington

ASSOCIATES

Philip J. Carroll III
Amy K. Myers

For Complete List of Firm Personnel, See General Section
For full biographical listings, see the Martindale-Hubbell Law Directory

HARRIS, EVANS, BERG & ROGERS, P.C. (AV)

Historic 2007 Building, 2007 Third Avenue North, 35203-2366
Telephone: 205-328-2366
Telecopier: 205-328-0013

Lyman H. Harris
Judy Whalen Evans
Lonette Lamb Berg
Susan Rogers

Matthew J. Dougherty
David L. Selby, II
Jeffrey K. Hollis
Stephen J. Bumgarner

For full biographical listings, see the Martindale-Hubbell Law Directory

LLOYD, SCHREIBER & GRAY, P.C. (AV)

Two Perimeter Park South Suite 100, 35243
Telephone: 205-967-8822
Telecopier: 205-967-2380

James S. Lloyd
Joseph Allen Schreiber
James C. Gray, III
Ralph D. Gaines, III
Mark C. Peterson

John A. Gant
Gerald Alan Templeton
Daniel S. Wolter
Stephen Errol Whitehead
Kyle L. Kinney
Legrand H. Amberson, Jr.
Thomas J. Skinner IV
Laura C. Nettles
Catherine L. Hogewood

For full biographical listings, see the Martindale-Hubbell Law Directory

LONDON, YANCEY, ELLIOTT & BURGESS (AV)

1000 Park Place Tower, 2001 Park Place, 35203
Telephone: 205-251-2531
FAX: 205-251-8929

MEMBERS OF FIRM

Thomas R. Elliott, Jr.
J. Thomas Burgess
Richard W. Lewis

ASSOCIATES

Allen R. Trippeer, Jr.
J. Flint, Liddon, III
Kelli A. Clayton

For full biographical listings, see the Martindale-Hubbell Law Directory

SPAIN, GILLON, GROOMS, BLAN & NETTLES (AV)

The Zinszer Building, 2117 2nd Avenue North, 35203
Telephone: 205-328-4100
Telecopier: 205-324-8866

MEMBERS OF FIRM

H. Hobart Grooms, Jr.
Ollie L. Blan, Jr.
Bert S. Nettles
Allwin E. Horn, III
Eugene P. Stutts
Charles D. Stewart
Thomas M. Eden, III
James A. Kee, Jr.

General Counsel for: Liberty National Life Insurance Co.; United States Fidelity & Guaranty Co.; Piggly Wiggly Alabama Distributing Co.; AmSouth Mortgage Co., Inc.; Alabama Insurance Guaranty Association; Alabama Life and Disability Insurance Guaranty Association; Alabama Insurance Underwriters Association.
Counsel for: The Prudential Insurance Company of America; Government Employees Insurance Co.; Massachusetts Mutual Life Insurance Co.

For Complete List of Firm Personnel, See General Section
For full biographical listings, see the Martindale-Hubbell Law Directory

STARNES & ATCHISON (AV)

100 Brookwood Place, P.O. Box 598512, 35259-8512
Telephone: 205-868-6000
Telecopier: 205-868-6099

MEMBERS OF FIRM

W. Stancil Starnes
W. Michael Atchison
William Anthony Davis, III
L. Graves Stiff, III
Carol A. Smith
E. Martin Bloom
Michael K. Beard
Robert P. Mackenzie, III
Jeffrey E. Friedman

ASSOCIATES

Steven T. McMeekin
Joe L. Leak
Mark W. Macoy
Barbara J. Bugg

Representative Clients: Mutual Assurance, Inc.; CNA Insurance Co.; United States Fidelity & Guaranty Co.; Zurich Insurance Company; AIG Adjustment Aviation; Travelers Ins. Co.; Aetna Casualty & Surety Co.; Hartford Insurance Company; State Farm Mutual Auto Co.; American Medical International.

For full biographical listings, see the Martindale-Hubbell Law Directory

*DECATUR,** Morgan Co.

EYSTER, KEY, TUBB, WEAVER & ROTH (AV)

Eyster Building, 402 East Moulton Street, S.E., P.O. Box 1607, 35602
Telephone: 205-353-6761
Fax: 205-353-6767

John C. Eyster (1863-1926)
Charles H. Eyster, Sr. (1888-1964)

(See Next Column)

EYSTER, KEY, TUBB, WEAVER & ROTH, *Decatur—Continued*

OF COUNSEL

Wm. B. Eyster

MEMBERS OF FIRM

John S. Key
J. Glynn Tubb
Larry C. Weaver
Nicholas B. Roth
J. Witty Allen
William L. Middleton, III
James G. Adams, Jr.

ASSOCIATES

Gina M. Fichter
Jenny L. Mcleroy

General Counsel for: Alabama Farmers Cooperative.
Regional Counsel for: AmSouth Bank.
Local Counsel for: Allstate Insurance Co.; Liberty Mutual Insurance Co.; Maryland Casualty Co.; Saginaw Steering Gear Division, General Motors Corp.; State Farm Mutual Automobile Insurance Co.; The Travelers.

For full biographical listings, see the Martindale-Hubbell Law Directory

*FLORENCE,** Lauderdale Co.

JONES, TROUSDALE & THOMPSON (AV)

115 Helton Court, Suite B, 35630
Telephone: 205-767-0333
Telefax: 205-767-0331

MEMBERS OF FIRM

Robert E. Jones, III
Preston S. Trousdale, Jr.
R. Waylon Thompson

For full biographical listings, see the Martindale-Hubbell Law Directory

KELLER & PITTS (AV)

212 South Cedar Street, P.O. Box 933, 35631
Telephone: 205-764-5822
Fax: 205-767-6360

MEMBERS OF FIRM

Jesse A. Keller
Conrad C. Pitts
Peter L. Paine

Counsel for: The American Road Insurance Co.; Lambert Transfer Co.

For full biographical listings, see the Martindale-Hubbell Law Directory

O'BANNON & O'BANNON (AV)

402 South Pine Street, P.O. Box 1428, 35631
Telephone: 205-767-6731

MEMBERS OF FIRM

A. Stewart O'Bannon, Jr.
A. Stewart O'Bannon, III
Christopher E. Connolly

For full biographical listings, see the Martindale-Hubbell Law Directory

*FORT PAYNE,** De Kalb Co.

KELLETT, GILLIS & KELLETT, P.A. (AV)

Black Building, P.O. Box 715, 35967
Telephone: 205-845-4541

Joseph C. Kellett
Terry D. Gillis
Patricia Kellett

Attorneys for: V.I. Prewett & Son, Inc.; AmSouth Bank, N.A.; St. Paul Insurance Cos.; Employers of Wausau Insurance Co.; DeKalb-Cherokee Counties Gas District; Williamson Oil Co.; Home Insurance Co.; Bank of Fyffe; Johnson Hosiery Mills, Inc.; Cherokee Hosiery Mills, Inc.

For full biographical listings, see the Martindale-Hubbell Law Directory

SCRUGGS, JORDAN & DODD, P.A. (AV)

207 Alabama Avenue, South, P.O. Box 1109, 35967
Telephone: 205-845-5932
Fax: 205-845-4325

William D. Scruggs, Jr.
Robert K. Jordan
David Dodd
E. Allen Dodd, Jr.

Representative Clients: State Farm Insurance Company; Allstate Insurance Co., Inc.; USF&G Insurance Co.; Nucor, Inc.; Ladd Engineering, Inc.; ALABAMA Band; First Federal Savings & Loan Association of Dekalb County; Fritz Structural Steel, Inc.; Williamson Oil Co., Inc.

For full biographical listings, see the Martindale-Hubbell Law Directory

*GADSDEN,** Etowah Co.

FORD & HUNTER, P.C. (AV)

The Lancaster Building, 645 Walnut Street, Suite 5, P.O. Box 388, 35902
Telephone: 205-546-5432
Fax: 205-546-5435

George P. Ford
J. Gullatte Hunter, III

(See Next Column)

Richard M. Blythe

References: General Motors Acceptance Corp.; AmSouth Bank, N.A.

For Complete List of Firm Personnel, See General Section

For full biographical listings, see the Martindale-Hubbell Law Directory

SIMMONS, BRUNSON, SASSER AND CALLIS, ATTORNEYS, P.A. (AV)

1411 Rainbow Drive, P.O. Box 1189, 35902
Telephone: 205-546-9206
Telecopier: 205-546-8091

Clarence Simmons, Jr.
Steve P. Brunson
James T. Sasser
Clifford Louis Callis, Jr.

Rebecca A. Walker
Jeffrey A. Brown

Attorneys for: Preferred Risk Mutual Insurance Co.; ALFA Mutual Insurance Co.; Royal Insurance Cos.
Approved Attorneys for: Lawyers Title Insurance Corp.; Mississippi Valley Title Insurance Co.

For full biographical listings, see the Martindale-Hubbell Law Directory

*GUNTERSVILLE,** Marshall Co.

LUSK & LUSK (AV)

452 Gunter Avenue, P.O. Box 609, 35976
Telephone: 205-582-3248

MEMBERS OF FIRM

Marion F. Lusk (1896-1986)
Louis B. Lusk

Representative Clients: AmSouth Bank, N.A., Guntersville; United States Fidelity & Guaranty Co.; The Travelers Insurance Co.; St. Paul Cos.; ALFA Mutual Insurance Cos.; Hartford Group; Liberty Mutual Insurance Co.; Allstate Insurance Co.; Home of New York Group.

For full biographical listings, see the Martindale-Hubbell Law Directory

HALEYVILLE, Winston Co.

JAMES, LOWE & MOBLEY (AV)

1210-21st Street, P.O. Box 576, 35565
Telephone: 205-486-5296
Fax: 205-486-4531

MEMBERS OF FIRM

Walter Joe James, Jr. (1923-1990)
John W. Lowe
Jeffery A. Mobley
Robert B. Aderholt

Representative Clients: Traders & Farmers Bank; Burdick-West Memorial Hospital.
Approved Attorneys for: Lawyers Title Insurance Corp.

For full biographical listings, see the Martindale-Hubbell Law Directory

*HUNTSVILLE,** Madison Co.

BRADLEY, ARANT, ROSE & WHITE (AV)

200 Clinton Avenue West, Suite 900, 35801
Telephone: 205-517-5100
Facsimile: 205-533-5069
Birmingham, Alabama Office: 1400 Park Place Tower, 2001 Park Place.
Telephone: 205-521-8000.
Telex: 494-1324.
Facsimile: 205-251-8611, 251-8665, 252-0264. Facsimile (Southtrust Office): 205-251-9915.

RESIDENT PARTNERS

Gary C. Huckaby
E. Cutter Hughes, Jr.
Patrick H. Graves, Jr.
G. Rick Hall

RESIDENT ASSOCIATES

Warne S. Heath
H. Knox McMillan
Frank M. Caprio

For Complete List of Firm Personnel, See General Section

For full biographical listings, see the Martindale-Hubbell Law Directory

SPURRIER, RICE, WOOD & HALL (AV)

3226 Bob Wallace Avenue, 35805
Telephone: 205-533-5015
Fax: 205-536-0105

MEMBERS OF FIRM

Donald N. Spurrier
Benjamin R. Rice
Robert V. Wood, Jr.
Ruth Ann Hall

(See Next Column)

SPURRIER, RICE, WOOD & HALL—*Continued*

ASSOCIATES

Clint W. Butler
Anthony B. Johnson

Representative Clients: Alabama Hospital Association Trust Fund; Alfa Insurance Co.; Allstate Insurance Co.; Atlanta Casualty; Auto-Owners Insurance Co.; Balboa Property & Casualty Co.; Bruno's; Casualty Indemnity Exchange; Chubb Group of Insurance Cos.; CIGNA Insurance Cos.

For full biographical listings, see the Martindale-Hubbell Law Directory

*MOBILE,** Mobile Co.

ARMBRECHT, JACKSON, DEMOUY, CROWE, HOLMES & REEVES (AV)

1300 AmSouth Center, P.O. Box 290, 36601
Telephone: 334-432-6751
Facsimile: 334-432-6843; 433-3821

MEMBERS OF FIRM

Wm. H. Armbrecht (1908-1991)
Theodore K. Jackson (1910-1981)
Marshall J. DeMouy
Wm. H. Armbrecht, III
Rae M. Crowe
Broox G. Holmes
W. Boyd Reeves
E. B. Peebles III
William B. Harvey
Kirk C. Shaw
Norman E. Waldrop, Jr.
Conrad P. Armbrecht
Edward G. Hawkins
Grover E. Asmus II
David A. Bagwell
Douglas L. Brown
Donald C. Radcliff
Christopher I. Gruenewald
James Donald Hughes
M. Kathleen Miller
Dabney Bragg Foshee
Edward A. Dean
David E. Hudgens
Ray Morgan Thompson
James Dale Smith
Duane A. Graham
Robert J. Mullican
Wm. Steele Holman, II
Coleman F. Meador
Broox G. Holmes, Jr.

ASSOCIATES

James E. Robertson, Jr.
Scott G. Brown
Clifford C. Brady
Richard W. Franklin
Stephen Russell Copeland
Tara T. Bostick
Rodney R. Cate
James F. Watkins

Representative Clients: AmSouth Bank N.A. (Regional Counsel); Burlington Northern Railroad Co. (District Counsel); Ryan-Walsh, Inc.; Scott Paper Co.; Travelers Insurance Co.

For Complete List of Firm Personnel, See General Section

For full biographical listings, see the Martindale-Hubbell Law Directory

BRISKMAN & BINION, P.C. (AV)

205 Church Street, P.O. Box 43, 36601
Telephone: 334-433-7600
Fax: 334-433-4485

Donald M. Briskman
Mack B. Binion

Donna Ward Black
Alex F. Lankford, IV
Christ N. Coumanis

A List of Representative Clients will be furnished upon request.
References: First Alabama Bank; AmSouth Bank, N.A.; Southtrust Bank of Mobile.

For full biographical listings, see the Martindale-Hubbell Law Directory

GARDNER, MIDDLEBROOKS & FLEMING, P.C. (AV)

64 North Royal Street, P.O. Drawer 3103, 36652
Telephone: 334-433-8100
Telecopier: 334-433-8181

J. Cecil Gardner
Sherwood C. Middlebrooks, III
Charles J. Fleming
W. Michael Hamilton (Not admitted in AL)

John D. Gibbons
Christopher E. Krafchak
William H. Reece

The Continental Insurance Cos.; The Fidelity and Casualty Co. of N.Y.; Canal Insurance Co.; Safeway Insurance Company of Alabama; Honda Motor Co.; Toyota Motor Co., U.S.A.; Bay Equipment Co.; Lyon Properties, Inc.

For full biographical listings, see the Martindale-Hubbell Law Directory

HAND, ARENDALL, BEDSOLE, GREAVES & JOHNSTON (AV)

3000 First National Bank Building, P.O. Box 123, Drawer C, 36601
Telephone: 334-432-5511
Fax: 334-694-6375
Washington, D.C. Office: 410 First Street, S.E., Suite 300. 20003.
Telephone: 202-863-0053.
Fax: 202-863-0096.

(See Next Column)

MEMBERS OF FIRM

Paul W. Brock
Alexander F. Lankford, III
Louis E. Braswell
Jerry A. McDowell
Michael D. Knight
G. Hamp Uzzelle, III
William C. Roedder, Jr.
Edward S. Sledge, III
Joseph Hodge Alves, III
Caine O'Rear, III
William Alexander Moseley
Joe E. Basenberg
George M. Walker
M. Mallory Mantiply
Orrin K. Ames, III
Henry A. Callaway, III
Blane H. Crutchfield
Forrest C. Wilson, III
Brian P. McCarthy
Walter T. Gilmer, Jr.
Archibald T. Reeves, IV

OF COUNSEL

Thomas G. Greaves, Jr.

General Counsel for: The Bank of Mobile; Delchamps, Inc.; The Mobile Press Register, Inc.; Mobile Asphalt Company; Gulf Telephone Company; Folmar & Associates; Mobile Community Foundation; Gulf Lumber Company; Scotch Lumber Company; Mobile Pulley & Machine Works, Inc.; Pennsylvania Shipbuilding Co.

For Complete List of Firm Personnel, See General Section

For full biographical listings, see the Martindale-Hubbell Law Directory

HELMSING, LYONS, SIMS & LEACH, P.C. (AV)

The Laclede Building, 150 Government Street, P.O. Box 2767, 36652
Telephone: 334-432-5521
Telecopy: 334-432-0633

Larry U. Sims
Champ Lyons, Jr.
Frederick G. Helmsing
John N. Leach, Jr.
Warren C. Herlong, Jr.
James B. Newman
Robert H. Rouse
Charles H. Dodson, Jr.
Sandy Grisham Robinson
Richard E. Davis
Joseph P. H. Babington
John J. Crowley, Jr.
Joseph D. Steadman

Todd S. Strohmeyer
William R. Lancaster
Robin Kilpatrick Fincher

For full biographical listings, see the Martindale-Hubbell Law Directory

JANECKY, NEWELL, POTTS, HARE & WELLS, P.C. (AV)

3300 First National Bank Building, P.O. Box 2987, 36652
Telephone: 334-432-8786
FAX: 334-432-5900
Birmingham, Alabama Office: Suite 3120, AmSouth-Harbert Plaza, 1901 Sixth Avenue North.
Telephone: 205-252-4441.
FAX: 205-252-0320.
Pensacola, Florida Office: Suite 280, 316 South Baylen Street.
Telephone: 904-432-6066.

J. F. (Jack) Janecky
Mark A. Newell
Charles J. Potts
Lynn Etheridge Hare (Resident, Birmingham Office)
Judson W. Wells

Desmond V. Tobias
Susan Gunnells
Daniel R. Klasing
Kevin F. Masterson
Edward B. Strong

Representative Clients: Alexis, Inc.; Associate Self Insurance Services, Inc.; Associated Group Services/Alabama Home Builders Self Insurers Fund; Auto-Owners Ins. Co.; Blue Cross and Blue Shield of Alabama; Canal Ins. Co.; Crum & Forster Ins. Co./U.S. Ins. Group; Electric Mutual Ins. Co.; Fireman's Fund Ins. Cos.; Nationwide Ins. Co.; Principal Mutual Life Ins. Co.

For full biographical listings, see the Martindale-Hubbell Law Directory

JOHNSTONE, ADAMS, BAILEY, GORDON AND HARRIS (AV)

Royal St. Francis Building, 104 St. Francis Street, P.O. Box 1988, 36633
Telephone: 334-432-7682
Facsimile: 334-432-2800
Telex: 782040

MEMBERS OF FIRM

Ben H. Harris, Jr.
William H. Hardie, Jr.
Joseph M. Allen, Jr.
I. David Cherniak
David C. Hannan
Wade B. Perry, Jr.
Celia J. Collins

ASSOCIATES

Tracy P. Turner
Lawrence J. Seiter

General Counsel for: First Alabama Bank, Mobile; Infirmary Health System/Mobile Infirmary Medical Center/Rotary Rehabilitation Hospital (Multi-Hospital System).
Counsel for: Oil and Gas: Exxon Corp. Business and Corporate: Bell South Telecommunications, Inc.; Aluminum Co. of America; Michelin Tire Corp.; Metropolitan Life Insurance Co.; The Travelers Insurance Cos. Marine: The West of England Ship Owners Mutual Protection and Indemnity Association (Luxembourg); The Standard Steamship Owners' Protection and Indemnity Association (Bermuda) Ltd.

(See Next Column)

JOHNSTONE, ADAMS, BAILEY, GORDON AND HARRIS, *Mobile—Continued*

For Complete List of Firm Personnel, See General Section

For full biographical listings, see the Martindale-Hubbell Law Directory

*MONTGOMERY,** Montgomery Co.

NIX, HOLTSFORD & VERCELLI, P.C. (AV)

A Water Street, Suite 300, P.O. Box 4128, 36103
Telephone: 334-262-2006
Fax: 334-834-3616

H. E. Nix, Jr.
Alex L. Holtsford, Jr.
Charles E. Vercelli, Jr.

Floyd R. Gilliland
Marianne T. Cosse
T. Randall Lyons
Dwayne R. Snyder
Steven A. Higgins

Representative Clients: Auto-Owners Insurance Co.; Alfa Insurance Companies; Crum & Forster; Gay & Taylor; Kemper Group; Ranger Insurance Co.; State Farm Mutual Insurance Companies; United States Fidelity & Guaranty Co.; Wal-Mart Stores; Wausau Insurance Co.

For full biographical listings, see the Martindale-Hubbell Law Directory

PARKER, BRANTLEY & WILKERSON, P.C. (AV)

323 Adams Avenue, P.O. Box 4992, 36103-4992
Telephone: 334-265-1500
Fax: 334-265-0319

Edward B. Parker, II
Mark D. Wilkerson
Paul A. Brantley
Leah Snell Stephens
Darla T. Furman

Representative Clients: ALLTEL; Construction Claims Management, Inc.; Federated Rural Electric Insurance Corp.; Alabama Emergency Room Administrative Services, P.C.
Reference: South Trust Bank, N.A.

For full biographical listings, see the Martindale-Hubbell Law Directory

PELL CITY, St. Clair Co.

BLAIR, HOLLADAY AND PARSONS (AV)

St. Clair Land Title Building, 1711 Cogswell Avenue, 35125
Telephone: 205-884-3440
Fax: 205-884-3442

MEMBERS OF FIRM

A. Dwight Blair
Hugh E. Holladay
Elizabeth S. Parsons

Representative Clients: Colonial Bank; Metro Bank; St. Clair Federal Savings Bank; State Farm Mutual Insurance Cos; ALFA Mutual Insurance Co.; Allstate Insurance Co.; St. Paul Insurance Cos.; Auto Owners Insurance Co.; Reliance Insurance Cos.; St. Clair Land Title Co., Inc.

For full biographical listings, see the Martindale-Hubbell Law Directory

*RUSSELLVILLE,** Franklin Co.

FINE & McDOWELL (AV)

507 North Jackson, P.O. Box 818, 35653
Telephone: 205-332-1660
Fax: 205-332-0318

Joe Fine
Daniel G. McDowell

ASSOCIATES

Eddie Beason
John F. Pilati

Representative Clients: Citizens Bank & Savings Co. of Russellville; Citigroup; City of Phil Campbell; Russellville City Board of Education; Franklin County Board of Education; Mutual Savings Life Insurance Co.; State Farm Fire & Casualty Co.; State Farm Mutual Automobile Ins. Co.; Franklin County Board of Commissioners; Marshall Durbin Co.

For full biographical listings, see the Martindale-Hubbell Law Directory

*SCOTTSBORO,** Jackson Co.

LIVINGSTON, PORTER & PAULK, P.C. (AV)

123 East Laurel Street, P.O. Box 1108, 35768
Telephone: 205-259-1919
Telecopier: 205-259-1189

Jack Livingston
John F. Porter, III
Gerald R. Paulk

Counsel for: Jackson County, Alabama; Jackson County Board of Education; Jackson County Health Care Authority; Scottsboro Electric Power Board; First National Bank of Stevenson, Alabama; Jacobs Bank.
Local Counsel for: State Farm Insurance Cos.; The Travelers Insurance Cos.; Liberty Mutual Insurance Co.; The Hartford Insurance Co.

For full biographical listings, see the Martindale-Hubbell Law Directory

*TUSCALOOSA,** Tuscaloosa Co.

DAVIDSON, WIGGINS & CROWDER, P.C. (AV)

2625 Eighth Street, P.O. Box 1939, 35403
Telephone: 205-759-5771
Fax: 205-752-8259

M. McCoy Davidson
Courtney Crowder
G. Stephen Wiggins
David Ryan

OF COUNSEL

Hugh W. Roberts, Jr.

Attorneys for: Aetna Life & Casualty Co.; Canal Insurance Co.; Government Employees Insurance Co.; The Travelers Group; Auto-Owners Insurance Co.; Continental National American Group; Federated Insurance; Lynn Insurance Group; The Trinity Cos.; The PMA Group.

For full biographical listings, see the Martindale-Hubbell Law Directory

PHELPS, JENKINS, GIBSON & FOWLER (AV)

1201 Greensboro Avenue, P.O. Box 020848, 35402-0848
Telephone: 205-345-5100
Fax: 205-758-4394
Fax: 205-391-6658

MEMBERS OF FIRM

Sam M. Phelps
Randolph M. Fowler
James J. Jenkins
Michael S. Burroughs
Johnson Russell Gibson, III
C. Barton Adcox
Farley A. Poellnitz

ASSOCIATES

K. Scott Stapp
Sandra C. Guin
Karen C. Welborn
Kimberly B. Glass
Stephen E. Snow

Attorneys for: Aetna Insurance Co.; Allstate Insurance Co.; Carolina Casualty Insurance Co.; Continental Insurance Cos.; Fireman's Fund-American Insurance Cos.; Great American Insurance Co.; Hanover Insurance Co.

For full biographical listings, see the Martindale-Hubbell Law Directory

ZEANAH, HUST, SUMMERFORD & DAVIS, L.L.C. (AV)

Seventh Floor, AmSouth Bank Building, P.O. Box 1310, 35403
Telephone: 205-349-1383
Fax: 205-391-1319

MEMBERS OF FIRM

Olin W. Zeanah (1922-1987)
Kenneth D. Davis
Wilbor J. Hust, Jr.
Christopher H. Jones
E. Clark Summerford
Beverly A. Smith

OF COUNSEL

Marvin T. Ormond

Representative Clients: Alfa Insurance Cos.; Hartford Insurance Group; Home Insurance Co.; Nationwide Insurance Co.; Alabama Power Co.; Liberty Mutual Ins. Co.; The Uniroyal Goodrich Tire Co.

For full biographical listings, see the Martindale-Hubbell Law Directory

ARIZONA

*FLAGSTAFF,** Coconino Co.

ASPEY, WATKINS & DIESEL (AV)

123 North San Francisco, 86001
Telephone: 602-774-1478
Facsimile: 602-774-1043
Sedona, Arizona Office: 120 Soldier Pass Road.
Telephone: 602-282-5955.
Facsimile: 602-282-5962.
Page, Arizona Office: 904 North Navajo.
Telephone: 602-645-9694.
Winslow, Arizona Office: 205 North Williamson.
Telephone: 602-289-5963.
Cottonwood, Arizona Office: 905 Cove Parkway, Unite 201.
Telephone: 602-639-1881.

MEMBERS OF FIRM

Frederick M. Fritz Aspey
Bruce S. Griffen
Harold L. Watkins
Donald H. Bayles, Jr.
Louis M. Diesel
Kaign N. Christy
John J. Dempsey

Zachary Markham
Whitney Cunningham
James E. Ledbetter
Holly S. Karris

(See Next Column)

ASPEY, WATKINS & DIESEL—*Continued*

LEGAL SUPPORT PERSONNEL

Deborah D. Roberts (Legal Assistant)
C. Denece Pruett (Legal Assistant)
Dominic M. Marino, Jr, (Paralegal Assistant)

Representative Clients: Farmer's Insurance Company of Arizona; Kelley-Moore Paint Co.; Pepsi-Cola Bottling Company of Northern Arizona; Bill Luke's Chrysler-Plymouth, Inc.; First American Title Insurance Company ; Transamerica Title Insurance Co.; Page Electric Utility; Comprehensive Access Health Plan, Inc.
Reference: First Interstate Bank-Arizona, N.A., Flagstaff, Arizona.

For full biographical listings, see the Martindale-Hubbell Law Directory

MANGUM, WALL, STOOPS & WARDEN, P.L.L.C. (AV)

222 East Birch Avenue, P.O. Box 10, 86002
Telephone: 602-779-6951
Fax: 602-773-1312

H. Karl Mangum (1908-1993)

OF COUNSEL

Douglas J. Wall
Robert W. Warden

MEMBERS OF FIRM

Daniel J. Stoops
A. Dean Pickett
Stephen K. Smith
Melinda L. Garrahan
Jon W. Thompson

ASSOCIATES

Kathleen O'Brien
David W. Rozema
Corbin Vandemoer

Representative Clients: Northern Arizona University; Flagstaff Unified School District; Museum of Northern Arizona; City of Sedona; Arizona School Board Association.
Local Counsel for: Bank of America-Arizona; Arizona Public Service; U.S-.A.A.; State Farm Fire & Casualty Ins. Co.; Hartford Ins. Co.

For Complete List of Firm Personnel, See General Section

For full biographical listings, see the Martindale-Hubbell Law Directory

*PHOENIX,** Maricopa Co.

BESS & DYSART, P.C. (AV)

7210 North 16th Street, 82020-5201
Telephone: 602-331-4600
Telecopier: 602-331-8600

Leon D. Bess
Robert L. Dysart
Donald R. Kunz
Timothy R. Hyland
William M. Demlong
Connie Totorica Gould

LEGAL SUPPORT PERSONNEL

Cynthia S. Felton

For full biographical listings, see the Martindale-Hubbell Law Directory

BONNETT, FAIRBOURN, FRIEDMAN, HIENTON, MINER & FRY, P.C. (AV)

4041 North Central Avenue Suite 1100, 85012
Telephone: 602-274-1100
Fax: 602-274-1199

William G. Fairbourn
Robert J. Spurlock
C. Kevin Dykstra

For full biographical listings, see the Martindale-Hubbell Law Directory

BROENING, OBERG & WOODS, P.C. (AV)

1122 East Jefferson Street, P.O. Box 20527, 85036
Telephone: 602-271-7700
Telecopier: 602-258-7785

James R. Broening
Terrence P. Woods
John W. Oberg
Donald Wilson, Jr.
Vincent A. Cass
Kenneth C. Miller
Neal B. Thomas
Wesley S. Loy
Gregg A. Thurston
Michael M. Haran
Jerry T. Collen
Cynthia van R. Cheney
Bruce M. Preston
Robert M. Moore
James G. McElwee, Jr.
Deborah E. Solliday
Martha Masteller Burns
Gary A. Fadell
R. Jeffrey Woodburn
Kathleen Fawcett Collins
David S. Shughart, II
David C. Donohue
Barbara A. Hamner
Joel P. Borowiec
Marilyn D. Cage

Representative Clients: Farmers Insurance Group; Home Insurance Co.; Chubb Group of Insurance Cos.; St. Paul Fire and Marine Insurance Cos.; Ohio Casualty Insurance Group.

For full biographical listings, see the Martindale-Hubbell Law Directory

BURCH & CRACCHIOLO, P.A. (AV)

702 East Osborn Road, Suite 200, 85014
Telephone: 602-274-7611
Fax: 602-234-0341
Mailing Address: P.O. Box 16882, Phoenix, AZ, 85011

Brian Kaven
F. Michael Carroll
Daniel R. Malinski

Theodore (Todd) Julian

Representative Clients: Bashas' Inc.; Farmers Insurance Group; U-Haul International, Inc.

For Complete List of Firm Personnel, See General Section

For full biographical listings, see the Martindale-Hubbell Law Directory

COHEN MCGOVERN SHORALL & STEVENS, P.C. (AV)

2828 North Central Avenue, Suite 1210, 85004
Telephone: 602-230-5400
Fax: 602-230-5432

Larry J. Cohen
Thomas P. McGovern
Thomas J. Shorall, Jr.
Don C. Stevens, II

Penny Taylor Moore
Walter Grochowski

Representative Clients: Aetna; Atlantic Mutual; Allstate; Northbrook; Great American; Travelers; Transamerica; State of Arizona.

For full biographical listings, see the Martindale-Hubbell Law Directory

CRONIN & STANEWICH (AV)

One Columbus Plaza, 3636 North Central Avenue, Suite 560, 85012
Telephone: 602-222-4646

MEMBERS OF FIRM

Robert S. Cronin, Jr.
Robert B. Stanewich

For full biographical listings, see the Martindale-Hubbell Law Directory

FENNEMORE CRAIG, A PROFESSIONAL CORPORATION (AV)

Two North Central, Suite 2200, 85004
Telephone: 602-257-8700
Fax: 602-257-8527
Scottsdale, Arizona Office: 6263 North Scottsdale Road, Suite 290, 85250.
Telephone: 602-257-5400.
Fax: 602-945-4932.
Tucson, Arizona Office: One South Church Avenue, Suite 1030, 85701.
Telephone: 602-624-9312.
Fax: 602-882-7383.

John D. Everroad
Phillip F. Fargotstein

Debra L. Runbeck
Jean Marie Sullivan
Marc H. Lamber

Representative Clients: ASARCO Incorporated; AT&T Communications; Bridgestone/Firestone, Inc.; Catellus Development Corp.; Citibank (Arizona); First Interstate Bank of Arizona; GIANT Industries; Phelps Dodge Corporation; The Atchison, Topeka & Santa Fe Railway, Co.; US WEST Communications.

For Complete List of Firm Personnel, See General Section

For full biographical listings, see the Martindale-Hubbell Law Directory

HOLLOWAY ODEGARD & SWEENEY, P.C. (AV)

3101 North Central Avenue, Suite 1200, 85012
Telephone: 602-240-6670
Telefax: 602-240-6677

Paul W. Holloway
Sally A. Odegard
Kevin B. Sweeney

Ruth Franklin
Frank B. Jancarole
Peter C. Kelly
Sarah D. Jarrett
Valerie Fasolo
Mark Carl Brachtl

OF COUNSEL

Joseph C. Dolan
Charles M. Callahan

For full biographical listings, see the Martindale-Hubbell Law Directory

JENNINGS, STROUSS AND SALMON, P.L.C. (AV)

A Professional Limited Liability Company
One Renaissance Square, Two North Central, 85004-2393
Telephone: 602-262-5911
Fax: 602-253-3255

(See Next Column)

JENNINGS, STROUSS AND SALMON P.L.C., *Phoenix—Continued*

William T. Birmingham
T. Patrick Flood
W. Michael Flood
Gary L. Stuart
Michael A. Beale
John A. Micheaels
Barry E. Lewin
Jay A. Fradkin
H. Christian Bode
Jon D. Schneider
Frederick M. Cummings
Michael J. O'Connor
Katherine M. Cooper
Matthew D. Kleifield

Charles D. Onofry
Jennifer M. Bligh
K. Thomas Slack
Kim D. Steinmetz
Cody M. Hall
Elizabeth C. Painter
Thomas B. Dixon
Brian D. Wallace
Lisa A. Frey
Martin A. Tetreault

For Complete List of Firm Personnel, See General Section

For full biographical listings, see the Martindale-Hubbell Law Directory

JONES, SKELTON & HOCHULI (AV)

2901 North Central, Suite 800, 85012
Telephone: 602-263-1700
Telefax: 602-263-1784

MEMBERS OF FIRM

William R. Jones, Jr.
Edward G. Hochuli
Peter G. Kline
Donald L. Myles, Jr.
William D. Holm
Ronald W. Collett
Mark D. Zukowski
Bruce D. Crawford
Jeffrey Boyd Miller
Georgia A. Staton
William J. Schrank
Gary H. Burger
Kathleen L. Wieneke
Kevin D. Neal

ASSOCIATES

Daniel P. Struck
Lori A. Shipley
Robert R. Berk
John T. Masterson
Brian W. LaCorte

For full biographical listings, see the Martindale-Hubbell Law Directory

MARK & PEARLSTEIN, P.A. (AV)

Suite 150 The Brookstone, 2025 North Third Street, 85004
Telephone: 602-257-0200

Leonard J. Mark
Lynn M. Pearlstein, Mr.

OF COUNSEL

Stephen G. Campbell

For full biographical listings, see the Martindale-Hubbell Law Directory

MEYER, HENDRICKS, VICTOR, OSBORN & MALEDON, A PROFESSIONAL ASSOCIATION (AV)

2929 North Central Avenue Suite 2100, 85012-2794
Telephone: 602-640-9000
Facsimile: (24 Hrs.) 602-640-9050
Mailing Address: P.O. Box 33449, 85067-3449,

Ed Hendricks
William J. Maledon
Larry A. Hammond
Robert L. Palmer
R. Douglas Dalton
Don Bivens
Ron Kilgard
Donald M. Peters
David G. Campbell
David B. Rosenbaum
Diane M. Johnsen
Mark D. Samson
Shane R. Swindle
G. Murray Snow
Mark Andrew Fuller
Debra A. Hill

Reference: Bank One Arizona, NA.

For Complete List of Firm Personnel, See General Section

For full biographical listings, see the Martindale-Hubbell Law Directory

O'CONNOR, CAVANAGH, ANDERSON, WESTOVER, KILLINGSWORTH & BESHEARS, A PROFESSIONAL ASSOCIATION (AV)

One East Camelback Road, Suite 1100, 85012-1656
Telephone: 602-263-2400
FAX: 602-263-2900
Sun City, Arizona Office: 13250 North Del Webb Boulevard, Suite B, 85351.
Telephone: 602-263-2808.
FAX: 602-933-3100.
Tucson, Arizona Office: Suite 2200, One South Church Avenue, 85701.
Telephone: 602-882-8912.
FAX: 602-624-9564.
Nogales, Arizona Office: 1827 North Mastick Way, 85621.
Telephone: 602-761-4215.
FAX: 602-761-3505.

(See Next Column)

Harry J. Cavanagh
John H. Westover
Robert G. Beshears
Ralph E. Hunsaker
Thomas A. McGuire, Jr.
George H. Mitchell
Richard J. Woods
Lawrence H. Lieberman
J. Victor Stoffa
David W. Earl
Carol N. Cure
Scott A. Salmon
David L. Kurtz
Paul J. Giancola
Pamela M. Overton
Frank M. Fox
Lisa M. Sommer
William H. Westover

Michael R. Altaffer
Lucas J. Narducci
Janet E. Kornblatt
Steven M. Rudner

Jeffrey R. Hovik
Robert L. Ehmann
R. Corey Hill
Troy B. Froderman
John A. Felix
Ashley D. Adams
Carla A. Wortley
Carl O. Wortley, III
Janet M. Walsh
Mark D. Dillon
Frank W. Moskowitz
Eric A. Mark
Kent S. Berk
Jamal F. Allen
Steven J. German
Peter C. Prynkiewicz

Representative Clients: State Farm; Liberty Mutual; The Home; The Hartford; CNA; TIG (formerly Transamerica); Reliances; Mutual Insurance Company of Arizona.

For Complete List of Firm Personnel, See General Section

For full biographical listings, see the Martindale-Hubbell Law Directory

RIDENOUR, SWENSON, CLEERE & EVANS, P.C. (AV)

302 North First Avenue, Suite 900, 85003
Telephone: 602-254-2143
Fax: 602-254-8670

Harold H. Swenson
James W. Evans
Robert R. Beltz
Lloyd J. Andrews
Michael J. Frazelle
John W. Storer, III
Richard H. Oplinger
Joseph A. Kendhammer
Peter S. Spaw

Robert R. Byrne

Representative Clients: State Farm Insurance Co.; ; Cincinnati Insurance Co.; Travelers Insurance Co.; American National Insurance Co.; Allstate Insurance Co.; Geico; Transamerica Insurance Co.; St. Paul Fire & Marine Insurance Co.; G.A.B. Business Systems; Economy Insurance Co.

For full biographical listings, see the Martindale-Hubbell Law Directory

ROBBINS & GREEN, A PROFESSIONAL ASSOCIATION (AV)

1800 CitiBank Tower, 3300 North Central Avenue, 85012-9826
Telephone: 602-248-7600
Fax: 602-266-5369

Philip A. Robbins
Richard W. Abbuhl
Wayne A. Smith
Joe M. Romley
Edmund F. Richardson
William H. Sandweg III
Jack N. Rudel
Jeffrey P. Boshes
Brian Imbornoni
Janet B. Hutchison
Bradley J. Stevens
Ronald G. Wilson
Dwayne Ross
Alfred W. Ricciardi
K. Leonard Judson
Dorothy Baran
Austin D. Potenza, II
Sarah McGiffert
Michael S. Green
Kenneth A. Hodson
Daniel L. Brown

For full biographical listings, see the Martindale-Hubbell Law Directory

SHIMMEL, HILL, BISHOP & GRUENDER, P.C. (AV)

3700 North 24th Street, 85016
Telephone: 602-224-9500
Telecopier: 602-955-6176

Scott J. Richardson

OF COUNSEL

Charles A. Finch

Representative Clients: AZ Property & Casualty Guaranty Fund; GAB Business Services; Liberty Mutual Insurance Co.; Merchants Mutual Bonding Co.

For Complete List of Firm Personnel, See General Section

For full biographical listings, see the Martindale-Hubbell Law Directory

*PRESCOTT,** Yavapai Co.

FAVOUR, MOORE, WILHELMSEN & SCHUYLER, A PROFESSIONAL ASSOCIATION (AV)

1580 Plaza West Drive, P.O. Box 1391, 86302
Telephone: 602-445-2444
Fax: 602-771-0450

(See Next Column)

FAVOUR, MOORE, WILHELMSEN & SCHUYLER A PROFESSIONAL ASSOCIATION—*Continued*

John B. Schuyler, Jr.
David K. Wilhelmsen
Mark M. Moore
Lance B. Payette
Clifford G. Cozier

OF COUNSEL

John M. Favour
Richard G. Kleindienst

Representative Clients: Employers Mutual Co.; Lawyers Title Insurance Co.; Farmers Insurance Group; Equity General Insurance Co.; Central Life Assurance Co.; Equity Fire and Casualty Co.; Economy Fire & Casualty Co.

For full biographical listings, see the Martindale-Hubbell Law Directory

SCOTTSDALE, Maricopa Co.

JEFFREY A. MATZ A PROFESSIONAL CORPORATION (AV(T))

6711 East Camelback Road, Suite 8, 85251
Telephone: 602-955-0900
Fax: 602-955-1885

Jeffrey A. Matz (Not admitted in AZ)

*TUCSON,** Pima Co.

CHANDLER, TULLAR, UDALL & REDHAIR (AV)

1700 Bank of America Plaza, 33 North Stone Avenue, 85701
Telephone: 602-623-4353
Telefax: 602-792-3426

MEMBERS OF FIRM

Thomas Chandler
D. B. Udall
Jack Redhair
Joe F. Tarver, Jr.
Steven Weatherspoon
S. Jon Trachta
Edwin M. Gaines, Jr.
Dwight M. Whitley, Jr.
E. Hardy Smith
John J. Brady
Christopher J. Smith
Charles V. Harrington
Bruce G. MacDonald

ASSOCIATES

Margaret A. Barton
Joel T. Ireland
Mark Fredenberg
Mariann T. Shinoskie
Kurt Kroese

Representative Clients: Arizona Electric Power Cooperative, Inc.; CNA Insurance; Farmers Insurance Exchange; Mutual Insurance Company of Arizona; The Travelers Insurance Co.; Transamerica Insurance Co.; Chubb Group of Insurance Co.; National Aviation Underwriters; St. Paul Insurance Co.; State Farm Mutual Insurance Cos.

For full biographical listings, see the Martindale-Hubbell Law Directory

HAZLETT & WILKES (AV)

310 South Williams Boulevard, Suite 305, 85711
Telephone: 602-790-9663
Fax: 602-790-9616

MEMBERS OF FIRM

Carl E. Hazlett
James M. Wilkes

ASSOCIATE

Thomas M. Bayham

For full biographical listings, see the Martindale-Hubbell Law Directory

KIMBLE, GOTHREAU & NELSON, P.C. (AV)

5285 East Williams Circle, Suite 3500, 85711-7411
Telephone: 602-748-2440
Fax: 602-748-2469

Darwin J. Nelson
Daryl A. Audilett
Stephen E. Kimble
Lawrence McDonough
David F. Toone
Michael P. Morrison
Michelle T. Lopez
Negatu Molla
Carroll E. Mizelle

OF COUNSEL

William Kimble

Representative Clients: State of Arizona; General Motors Corp.; Procter & Gamble Co.; St. Paul Fire and Marine Insurance Co.; City of Tucson; Tucson Electric Power Co.; United States Fidelity & Guaranty Co.; Industrial Indemnity Insurance Co.; Allstate Insurance Co.

For Complete List of Firm Personnel, See General Section

For full biographical listings, see the Martindale-Hubbell Law Directory

MURPHY, GOERING, ROBERTS & BERKMAN, P.C. (AV)

Suite 302, 1840 East River Road, 85718
Telephone: 602-577-9300
FAX: 602-577-0848

(See Next Column)

James M. Murphy
Thomas M. Murphy
Scott Goering
Howard T. Roberts, Jr.
David L. Berkman
William L. Rubin
Carmine A. Brogna

Representative Clients: Roman Catholic Church Diocese of Tucson; Fireman's Fund Insurance; Safeco Insurance; Royal Insurance; Sentry Insurance; INA; Carondelet Health Services, Inc.; County of Pima; State Farm Insurance.
Reference: Bank One.

For full biographical listings, see the Martindale-Hubbell Law Directory

O'CONNOR, CAVANAGH, ANDERSON, WESTOVER, KILLINGSWORTH & BESHEARS, A PROFESSIONAL ASSOCIATION (AV)

Suite 2200 One South Church Avenue, 85701-1621
Telephone: 602-882-8912
FAX: 602-624-9564
Phoenix, Arizona Office: One East Camelback Road, Suite 1100, 85012.
Telephone: 602-263-2400.
FAX: 602-263-2900.
Sun City, Arizona Office: 13250 North Del Webb Boulevard, Suite B, 85351.
Telephone: 602-263-2808.
FAX: 602-933-3100.
Nogales, Arizona Office: 1827 North Mastick Way, 85621.
Telephone: 602-761-4215.
FAX: 602-761-3505.

Ted A. Schmidt
Peter Akmajian
Drue A. Morgan-Birch
Amy M. Samberg
James D. Campbell

Representative Client: Jeffco, Inc.
Reference: Citibank.

For Complete List of Firm Personnel, See General Section

For full biographical listings, see the Martindale-Hubbell Law Directory

SLUTES, SAKRISON, EVEN, GRANT & PELANDER, P.C. (AV)

33 North Stone Avenue, Suite 1100, 85701-1489
Telephone: 602-624-6691
Fax: 602-791-9632

Tom Slutes
Philip H. Grant
A. John Pelander
David E. Hill
Christopher C. Browning
Michael B. Smith
Mary Beth Joublanc

Representative Clients: Aetna Casualty and Surety Co.; Allstate Insurance Co.; Northbrook Insurance Co.; CNA Insurance Co.; Colonial Penn Insurance Co.; Employers Mutual; Farmers Insurance Group; St. Paul Insurance; 20th Century Insurance; USAA.

For Complete List of Firm Personnel, See General Section

For full biographical listings, see the Martindale-Hubbell Law Directory

ARKANSAS

*BENTON,** Saline Co.

ELLIS LAW FIRM (AV)

126 North Main Street, P.O. Box 1259, 72015
Telephone: 501-776-3916; Little Rock: 375-5210
FAX: 501-776-2278

MEMBER OF FIRM

George D. Ellis

LEGAL SUPPORT PERSONNEL

Rhonda Beck Malone (Legal Assistant and Office Manager)

References: The Union Bank of Benton; Benton State Bank.

For full biographical listings, see the Martindale-Hubbell Law Directory

*FAYETTEVILLE,** Washington Co.

JONES & JONES (AV)

112 South East Street, 72701
Telephone: 501-443-4313, 443-2021
Fax: 501-575-0528

MEMBERS OF FIRM

Lewis D. Jones
Gregory D. Jones

(See Next Column)

JONES & JONES, *Fayetteville—Continued*

J. Scott Hardin

Representative Clients: Allstate Insurance Co.; The Home Insurance Co.; Horace Mann Insurance Co.; Miller's Mutual Fire Insurance Co.; The Firemen's Insurance Companies; Countrywide Insurance Group; AM Family Ins. Co.; Worthen National Bank of Northwest Arkansas.
Approved Attorney for: Lawyers Title Insurance Co.
Reference: Worthen National Bank of Northwest Arkansas.

For full biographical listings, see the Martindale-Hubbell Law Directory

*FORT SMITH,** Sebastian Co.

DAILY, WEST, CORE, COFFMAN & CANFIELD (AV)

Stephens Office Building, 623 Garrison Avenue, P.O. Box 1446, 72902
Telephone: 501-782-0361
Fax: 501-782-6160

MEMBERS OF FIRM

Ben Core
Eldon F. Coffman
Jerry L. Canfield
Thomas A. Daily
Wyman R. Wade, Jr.
Stanley A. Leasure
Douglas M. Carson
Michael C. Carter
Robert W. Bishop

OF COUNSEL

James E. West

Counsel for: Claims Management, Inc. (Wal-Mart); Arkla, Inc.; City of Fort Smith; Commercial Union Insurance Cos.; Pennzoil Exploration and Production Co.; Silvey Cos., Inc.; CIGNA; Metropolitan Life Insurance Co.; Chevron U.S.A., Inc.

For full biographical listings, see the Martindale-Hubbell Law Directory

HARDIN, JESSON, DAWSON & TERRY (AV)

Suite 500, Superior Federal Tower, 5000 Rogers Avenue, P.O. Box 10127, 72917-0127
Telephone: 501-452-2200
FAX: 501-452-9097

MEMBERS OF FIRM

G. C. Hardin (1884-1964)
P. H. Hardin
Bradley D. Jesson
Robert T. Dawson
Rex M. Terry
Robert M. Honea
J. Leslie Evitts III
James Rodney Mills
Kirkman T. Dougherty
J. Gregory Magness

Counsel for: Superior Federal Bank, FSB; The Kansas City Southern Railway Co.; KFSM-TV; Johnson & Johnson; Ortho Pharmaceutical Corp; ASARCO Inc.; Allstate Insurance Co.; Southern Farm Bureau Insurance Co.; Dodson Insurance Group.

For full biographical listings, see the Martindale-Hubbell Law Directory

JONES, GILBREATH, JACKSON & MOLL (AV)

401 North Seventh Street, P.O. Box 2023, 72902
Telephone: 501-782-7203
Fax: 501-782-9460

MEMBERS OF FIRM

Robert L. Jones, Jr.
E. C. Gilbreath
Robert L. Jones, III
Randolph C. Jackson
Kendall B. Jones
Mark A. Moll

ASSOCIATES

Charles R. Garner, Jr.
Daniel W. Gilbreath
Lynn M. Flynn
Christina Dawn Ferguson

Insurance Counsel for: Argonaut Insurance Cos.; Farmers Insurance Group; Maryland-American General Insurance Cos.; Shelter Insurance Cos.; Travelers Insurance Co.; Continental Insurance Cos.
Counsel for: Merchants National Bank, Fort Smith, Ar.; Ryder Truck Rental, Inc.; Whirlpool Corp.

For full biographical listings, see the Martindale-Hubbell Law Directory

SHAW, LEDBETTER, HORNBERGER, COGBILL & ARNOLD (AV)

South Seventh and Parker, P.O. Box 185, 72902-0185
Telephone: 501-782-7294
FAX: 501-782-1493

Bruce H. Shaw (1904-1990)
Richard B. Shaw (1927-1988)

MEMBERS OF FIRM

Charles R. Ledbetter
Robert E. Hornberger
J. Michael Cogbill
James A. Arnold, II
Ronald D. Harrison

ASSOCIATES

E. Diane Graham
R. Ray Fulmer, II
Gill A. Rogers

OF COUNSEL

J. Michael Shaw

Representative Clients: First National Bank of Fort Smith; Bank of Mansfield; Commercial Bank at Alma; Mid-South Dredging Co.

(See Next Column)

Local Attorneys for: Liberty Mutual Insurance Co.; St. Paul Insurance Cos.; Fireman's Fund Ins. Co.; American Physicians Insurance Exchange; CIGNA Ins. Co.; Canal Insurance Co.

For full biographical listings, see the Martindale-Hubbell Law Directory

*JONESBORO,** Craighead Co.

BARRETT & DEACON (AV)

Mercantile Bank Building, 300 South Church Street, P.O. Box 1700, 72403
Telephone: 501-931-1700
FAX: 501-931-1800

MEMBERS OF FIRM

Joe C. Barrett (1897-1980)
John C. Deacon
J. Barry Deacon
David W. Cahoon
Ralph W. Waddell
Paul D. Waddell

ASSOCIATES

D. Price Marshall, Jr.
James D. Bradbury (Not admitted in AR)
Kevin W. Cole

For full biographical listings, see the Martindale-Hubbell Law Directory

WOMACK, LANDIS, PHELPS, MCNEILL & MCDANIEL, A PROFESSIONAL ASSOCIATION (AV)

Century Center, Washington at Madison, P.O. Box 3077, 72403
Telephone: 501-932-0900
Fax: 501-932-2553

Tom D. Womack
Carl David Landis
John V. Phelps
Paul D. McNeill
Lucinda McDaniel

Brant Perkins
Jeffrey W. Puryear
Mark Alan Mayfield

Representative Clients: Arkansas State University; Bank of Trumann; E.C. Barton & Co.; Kraft General Foods Corp.; Home Indemnity Company of N.Y.; St. Paul Insurance Cos.; Shelter Insurance Co.; United States Fidelity & Guaranty Co.

For full biographical listings, see the Martindale-Hubbell Law Directory

*LITTLE ROCK,** Pulaski Co.

ALLEN LAW FIRM, A PROFESSIONAL CORPORATION (AV)

950 Centre Place, 212 Center Street, 72201
Telephone: 501-374-7100
Telecopier: 501-374-1611

H. William Allen

Sandra E. Jackson

Representative Clients: Colonia Insurance Company; Shoney's, Inc.

For full biographical listings, see the Martindale-Hubbell Law Directory

ANDERSON & KILPATRICK (AV)

The First Commercial Building, 400 West Capitol Avenue, Suite 2640, 72201
Telephone: 501-372-1887
Fax: 501-372-7706

MEMBERS OF FIRM

Overton S. Anderson, II
Joseph E. Kilpatrick, Jr.
Michael E. Aud
Aylmer Gene Williams
Randy P. Murphy
Frances E. Scroggins

ASSOCIATES

Mariam T. Hopkins
Michael P. Vanderford

For full biographical listings, see the Martindale-Hubbell Law Directory

BARBER, MCCASKILL, AMSLER, JONES & HALE, P.A. (AV)

2700 First Commercial Building, 400 West Capitol Avenue, 72201-3414
Telephone: 501-372-6175
Telecopier: 501-375-2802

Azro L. Barber (1885-1979)
Elbert A. Henry (1889-1966)
John B. Thurman (1912-1971)
Austin McCaskill, Sr.
Guy Amsler, Jr.
Glenn W. Jones, Jr.
Michael E. Hale
John S. Cherry, Jr.
Robert L. Henry, III
Micheal L. Alexander
William H. Edwards, Jr.
Richard C. Kalkbrenner
G. Spence Fricke
M. Stephen Bingham
Gail Ponder Gaines
Michael J. Emerson
R. Kenny McCulloch
Tim A. Cheatham
Joseph F. Kolb
Scott Michael Strauss
Karen Hart McKinney

Attorneys for: Associated Aviation Underwriters; Canal Insurance Co.; Fireman's Fund Insurance Co.; General Motors Corp.; General Motors Acceptance Corp.; Hanover Insurance Co.; Home Insurance Co.; Royal Insurance;

(See Next Column)

BARBER, MCCASKILL, AMSLER, JONES & HALE P.A.—*Continued*

United States Fidelity & Guaranty Co.; Universal Underwriters Insurance Co.

For full biographical listings, see the Martindale-Hubbell Law Directory

FRIDAY, ELDREDGE & CLARK (AV)

A Partnership including Professional Associations
Formerly, Smith, Williams, Friday, Eldredge & Clark
2000 First Commercial Building, 400 West Capitol, 72201-3493
Telephone: 501-376-2011
Telecopier: 501-376-2147; 376-6369

MEMBERS OF FIRM

Robert V. Light (P.A.)
William H. Sutton (P.A.)
Frederick S. Ursery (P.A.)
John Dewey Watson (P.A.)
J. Phillip Malcom (P.A.)
James M. Simpson, Jr., (P.A.)
Donald H. Bacon (P.A.)
Barry E. Coplin (P.A.)
Elizabeth J. Robben (P.A.)
Laura Hensley Smith (P.A.)
William Mell Griffin III, (P.A.)
Kevin A. Crass (P.A.)
William A. Waddell, Jr., (P.A.)
Tab Turner (P.A.)
Calvin J. Hall (P.A.)
Scott J. Lancaster (P.A.)
James C. Baker (P.A.)
H. Charles Gschwend, Jr., (P.A.)
Scott H. Tucker (P.A.)
Guy Alton Wade (P.A.)

ASSOCIATES

J. Michael Pickens
Tonia P. Jones
David D. Wilson
Gregory D. Taylor
Fran C. Hickman
Betty J. Demory

Counsel for: Union Pacific System; St. Paul Insurance Co.; Liberty Mutual Insurance Co.; Cigna Property & Casualty Co.; Arkansas Power & Light Co.; Dillard Department Stores, Inc.; First Commercial Corp.; Browning Arms Co.; Phillips Petroleum Co.; Aetna Casualty & Surety Co.

For Complete List of Firm Personnel, See General Section

For full biographical listings, see the Martindale-Hubbell Law Directory

HUCKABAY, MUNSON, ROWLETT & TILLEY, P.A. (AV)

First Commercial Building, Suite 1900, 400 West Capitol, 72201
Telephone: 501-374-6535
FAX: 501-374-5906

Mike Huckabay
Bruce E. Munson
Beverly A. Rowlett
James W. Tilley
John E. Moore
Tim Boone
Rick Runnells
Sarah Ann Presson

Lizabeth Lookadoo
Valerie Denton
Edward T. Oglesby
D. Michael Huckabay, Jr.
Carol Lockard Worley
Mark S. Breeding
Elizabeth Fletcher Rogers
Jeffrey A. Weber

Representative Clients: Allstate Insurance Company; American International Group; American Medical International; Farmers Insurance Group; General Electric Company; Nationwide Insurance Company; Safeco Insurance Company; State Farm Mutual Automobile Insurance Company; State Farm Fire and Casualty Company; United States Fidelity and Guaranty Company.

For full biographical listings, see the Martindale-Hubbell Law Directory

LASER, SHARP, WILSON, BUFFORD & WATTS, P.A. (AV)

101 S. Spring Street, Suite 300, 72201-2488
Telephone: 501-376-2981
Telecopier: 501-376-2417

Sam Laser
Jacob Sharp, Jr.
Richard N. Watts
Kevin J. Staten
Alfred F. Angulo, Jr.
David M. Donovan
Walter A. Kendel, Jr.
Brian A. Brown
Karen J. Hughes
Gena Gregory
Keith Martin McPherson

Representative Clients: Allstate Insurance Co.; American International Insurance Group; Continental Insurance Cos.; Farm Bureau Insurance Cos. (Casualty & Fire); Farmers Insurance Group; GAB Business Services, Inc.; St. Paul Insurance Cos.; Scottsdale Insurance Co.; State Farm Auto (Fire) Insurance Cos.

For Complete List of Firm Personnel, See General Section

For full biographical listings, see the Martindale-Hubbell Law Directory

ROSE LAW FIRM, A PROFESSIONAL ASSOCIATION (AV)

120 East Fourth Street, 72201
Telephone: 501-375-9131
Telecopy: 501-375-1309

Phillip Carroll
Kenneth Robert Shemin
Jerry C. Jones
David L. Williams
Richard T. Donovan
James H. Druff
Jess Askew, III
Amy Lee Stewart

(See Next Column)

Representative Clients: The Equitable Life Assurance Society of the United States; Bridgestone/Firestone, Inc.; Georgia-Pacific Corp.; General Motors Corp.; John Hancock Mutual Life Insurance Co.; Kemper Insurance Group; New York Life Insurance Co.; The Prudential Insurance Company of America; USX Corp.

For Complete List of Firm Personnel, See General Section

For full biographical listings, see the Martindale-Hubbell Law Directory

WEST MEMPHIS, Crittenden Co.

RIEVES & MAYTON (AV)

304 East Broadway, P.O. Box 1359, 72303
Telephone: 501-735-3420
Telecopier: 501-735-4678

MEMBERS OF FIRM

Elton A. Rieves, Jr. (1909-1984)
Elton A. Rieves, III
Michael R. Mayton
Elton A. Rieves, IV

ASSOCIATES

Martin W. Bowen
William J. Stanley

For full biographical listings, see the Martindale-Hubbell Law Directory

CALIFORNIA

*BAKERSFIELD,** Kern Co.

ROBINSON, PALMER & LOGAN (AV)

Suite 150, 3434 Truxtun Avenue, 93301
Telephone: 805-323-8277
Fax: 805-323-4205

MEMBERS OF FIRM

Oliver U. Robinson
William D. Palmer
Gary L. Logan

ASSOCIATES

Luke A. Foster
Jeffrey B. Held

For full biographical listings, see the Martindale-Hubbell Law Directory

BERKELEY, Alameda Co.

BURESH, KAPLAN, JANG, FELLER & AUSTIN (AV)

2298 Durant Avenue, 94704
Telephone: 510-548-7474
Fax: 510-548-7488

Scott Buresh
Ann S. Kaplan
Alan J. Jang
Fred M. Feller
Steven K. Austin
Gina Dashman Boer
Peggy Chang
Daniel L. Cook
Noël Sidney Plummer

For full biographical listings, see the Martindale-Hubbell Law Directory

BURLINGAME, San Mateo Co.

NAGLE, KRUG & WINTERS (AV)

345 Lorton Avenue, Suite 204, 94010-4116
Telephone: 415-579-1422
Fax: 415-579-1852

MEMBERS OF FIRM

William L. Nagle
John S. Krug
Daniel W. Winters
David A. Delbon
Jeffrey W. Owen
Jerry E. Nastari
David F. Zucca

Representative Clients: State Farm Mutual Automobile Insurance Co.; State Farm Fire & Casualty Co.; Fireman's Fund Insurance Cos.; Tokio Marine Management Co.; California State Automobile Assn.; Chubb Group of Insurance Cos.; Argonaut Insurance Co.; Aviation Office of America; Cities of: Burlingame, Half Moon Bay, South San Francisco and San Carlos; Towns of Hillsborough and Woodside.

For full biographical listings, see the Martindale-Hubbell Law Directory

COSTA MESA, Orange Co.

MURTAUGH, MILLER, MEYER & NELSON (AV)

A Partnership including Professional Corporations
3200 Park Center Drive, 9th Floor, P.O. Box 5023, 92628-5023
Telephone: 714-513-6800
Facsimile: 714-513-6899

(See Next Column)

MURTAUGH, MILLER, MEYER & NELSON, *Costa Mesa—Continued*

Michael J. Murtaugh (A Professional Corporation)
Bradford H. Miller (A Professional Corporation)
Richard E. Meyer
Michael J. Nelson
Robert T. Lemen
Mark S. Himmelstein
Harry A. Halkowich
Madelyn A. Enright
James A. Murphy, IV
Lawrence A. Treglia, Jr.

Roberta A. Evans
Debra Lynn Braasch
Thomas J. Skane
Lydia R. Bouzaglou
David C. Holt
Robin L. More
Lawrence J. DiPinto
Debra L. Reilly
Susan Westover
Lawrence D. Marks
Carrie E. Phelan
Robert A. Fisher, II
John R. Browning
Eric J. Dubin
Stacey Sarowatz
Daniel E. Roston

OF COUNSEL

Susan W. Menkes
Gary M. Pohlson

Representative Clients: Continental Insurance Cos. (Continental Loss Adjusting Services); Design Professionals Insurance Co.
Reference: Wells Fargo Bank.

For full biographical listings, see the Martindale-Hubbell Law Directory

ENCINO, Los Angeles Co.

KRIVIS, PASSOVOY & SPILE (AV)

16501 Ventura Boulevard, Suite 301, 91436
Telephone: 818-784-6899
Facsimile: 818-784-0176

Jeffrey L. Krivis
Paul S. Passovoy
Steven D. Spile

ASSOCIATES

Andrew L. Leff
Gina M. Weihert
Mark C. Carlson
Michael P West
Fiona M. Connell

OF COUNSEL

Floyd J. Siegal

For full biographical listings, see the Martindale-Hubbell Law Directory

*EUREKA,** Humboldt Co.

MITCHELL, BRISSO, DELANEY, REINHOLTSEN & VRIEZE (AV)

814 Seventh Street, P.O. Drawer 1008, 95502
Telephone: 707-443-5643
Fax: 707-444-9586

MEMBERS OF FIRM

Clifford B. Mitchell
Dale A. Reinholtsen
Nancy K. Delaney
Paul A. Brisso
John M. Vrieze

ASSOCIATES

C. Todd Endres
William F. Mitchell

RETIRED PARTNER

Robert C. Dedekam

Representative Clients: California Automobile Assn.; State Farm; Allstate; Fireman's Fund; Hartford; Travelers; Wausau; Viking; Nationwide; Redwood Empire Municipal Insurance Fund.

For full biographical listings, see the Martindale-Hubbell Law Directory

*FRESNO,** Fresno Co.

DOWLING, MAGARIAN, AARON & HEYMAN, INCORPORATED (AV)

Suite 200, 6051 North Fresno Street, 93710
Telephone: 209-432-4500
Fax: 209-432-4590

Philip David Kopp

Francine Marie Kanne
Richard E. Heatter
James C. Sherwood

Reference: Wells Fargo Bank (Main).

For Complete List of Firm Personnel, See General Section

For full biographical listings, see the Martindale-Hubbell Law Directory

MCCORMICK, BARSTOW, SHEPPARD, WAYTE & CARRUTH (AV)

Five River Park Place East, 93720-1501
Telephone: 209-433-1300
Mailing Address: P.O. Box 28912, 93729-8912

(See Next Column)

MEMBERS OF FIRM

Lawrence E. Wayte
Lowell T. Carruth
Stephen R. Cornwell
Mario Louis Beltramo, Jr.
Michael G. Woods
James P. Wagoner
Gordon M. Park
Wade M. Hansard
Justus C. Spillner
Daniel P. Lyons
John A. Drolshagen
Brian M. Arax
Michael F. Ball
James H. Wilkins
Kevin D. Hansen
Philip M. Flanigan
Matthew K. Hawkins
Wendy S. Lloyd
Michael J. Czeshinski

ASSOCIATES

René L. Sample
Gregory S. Mason
Mart B. Oller, IV
Todd W. Baxter
Paul J. O'Rourke, Jr.
Roger A. Johnson
Ted A. Smith
Michael J. Ryan
James D. Garriott

OF COUNSEL

James H. Barstow
Dudley W. Sheppard
Deborah A. Byron

Counsel for: Aetna Life & Casualty Co.; California State Automobile Assn.; Firemen's Fund Insurance Co.; Bank of Fresno; Kings River State Bank; Glendale Federal Bank; Hartford Accident & Indemnity Co.; Kemper Insurance Group; The Travelers Insurance Co.; United Pacific/Reliance Insurance Co.

For Complete List of Firm Personnel, See General Section

For full biographical listings, see the Martindale-Hubbell Law Directory

PARICHAN, RENBERG, CROSSMAN & HARVEY, LAW CORPORATION (AV)

Suite 130, 2350 West Shaw Avenue, P.O. Box 9950, 93794-0950
Telephone: 209-431-6300
FAX: 209-432-1018

Harold A. Parichan
Charles L. Renberg
Richard C. Crossman
Ima Jean Harvey
Stephen T. Knudsen
Larry C. Gollmer
Robert G. Eliason
Steven M. McQuillan
Peter S. Bradley

Deborah A. Coe
Maureen P. Holford
Karen L. Lynch
Michael L. Renberg
Brady Kyle McGuinness

Reference: Bank of America, Commercial Banking Office, Fresno, California.

For full biographical listings, see the Martindale-Hubbell Law Directory

STAMMER, MCKNIGHT, BARNUM & BAILEY (AV)

2540 West Shaw Lane, Suite 110, P.O. Box 9789, 93794-9789
Telephone: 209-449-0571
Fax: 209-432-2619

W. H. Stammer (1891-1969)
James K. Barnum (1918-1987)
Dean A. Bailey (Retired)
Galen McKnight (1904-1991)
James N. Hays
Carey H. Johnson
Jan M. Biggs
Frank D. Maul
Daniel O. Jamison
Craig M. Mortensen
Jerry D. Jones
Michael P. Mallery
M. Bruce Smith

ASSOCIATES

A. John Witkowski
Thomas J. Georgouses
Steven R. Stoker
M. Jaqueline Yates
Bruce J. Berger

OF COUNSEL

Donald D. Pogoloff

Representative Clients: The Travelers Insurance Group; State Farm Insurance Cos.; Farmers Insurance Group; Grocers Insurance Company; Golden Eagle Insurance Company.
Reference: Bank of America Trust & Savings Assn. (Fresno Main Office).

For full biographical listings, see the Martindale-Hubbell Law Directory

GLENDALE, Los Angeles Co.

KANE & WHELAN (AV)

Suite 100, 330 Arden Avenue, P.O. Box 29009, 91209-9009
Telephone: 818-241-1919
Fax: 818-547-0325

Mark C. Kane
Allan C. Whelan
Michael J. Ciccozzi
Adam A. Wright
Nicholas Paulos

Representative Clients: Farmers Home Group; Deans & Homer; Western General Agency; Michigan Millers Insurance Co.; Liberty Mutual Insurance Co.; Worldwide Insurance Group; The Vons Companies Inc.; Vulcan Materials Co.; Huffy Corp.

For full biographical listings, see the Martindale-Hubbell Law Directory

IRVINE, Orange Co.

ANDRADE & ASSOCIATES (AV)

Marine National Bank Building, 18401 Von Karman, Suite 350, 92715
Telephone: 714-553-1951
Telecopier: 714-553-0655

Richard B. Andrade

ASSOCIATES

Jack W. Fleming
Andrew C. Muzi
Steven S. Hanagami

OF COUNSEL

Kurt Kupferman

Representative Clients: American International Cos.; American Home Assurance; Insurance Company of North America (INA); National Union Fire Insurance of Pittsburgh, PA; Aetna Insurance Co.; Fremont Insurance Co.; Maryland Casualty; Commercial Union Insurance Co.; Superior National Insurance Co.

For full biographical listings, see the Martindale-Hubbell Law Directory

PIVO & HALBREICH (AV)

1920 Main Street, Suite 800, 92714
Telephone: 714-253-2000; 213-688-7311

Kenneth R. Pivo
Eva S. Halbreich
Douglas A. Amo
Richard O. Schwartz

ASSOCIATES

Mona Z. Hanna
Karin H. Ota

Representative Clients: Physicians and Surgeons Underwriters Corp.; Fremont Indemnity; American Continental Insurance Co.; AKROS Medico Enterprises; Kaiser Foundation Healthplan, Inc.; Caronia Corp.; The Doctor's Company; Harbor Regional Center; Developmental Disabilities Regional Center; South Central Los Angeles Regional Center.

For full biographical listings, see the Martindale-Hubbell Law Directory

LA JOLLA, San Diego Co.

LAW OFFICES OF MAURILE C. TREMBLAY A PROFESSIONAL CORPORATION (AV)

4180 La Jolla Village Drive, Suite 210, 92037
Telephone: 619-558-3030
FAX: 619-558-2502

Maurile C. Tremblay

Mark D. Estle
Ted A. Connor

OF COUNSEL

David R. Endres

For full biographical listings, see the Martindale-Hubbell Law Directory

LARKSPUR, Marin Co.

WEINBERG, HOFFMAN & CASEY (AV)

A Partnership including a Professional Corporation
700 Larkspur Landing Circle, Suite 280, 94939
Telephone: 415-461-9666
Fax: 415-461-9681

Ivan Weinberg
Joseph Hoffman
A. Michael Casey

For full biographical listings, see the Martindale-Hubbell Law Directory

LONG BEACH, Los Angeles Co.

BENNETT & KISTNER (AV)

301 East Ocean Boulevard, Suite 800, 90802
Telephone: 310-435-6675
Fax: 310-437-8375
Riverside, California Office: 3403 Tenth Street, Suite 605. 92501-3676.
Telephone: 909-341-9360.
Fax: 909-341-9362.

Charles J. Bennett
Wayne T. Kistner

ASSOCIATES

Richard R. Bradbury
Mary A. Estante (Resident, Riverside Office)
Todd R. Becker
Karen H. Beckman (Resident, Riverside Office)

Representative Clients: The Hertz Corporation; Thrifty Oil Co.; Golden West Refining Co.; Standard Brands Paint Co.; Mattel, Inc.; Di Salvo Trucking Co.; County of Riverside; Southern California Rapid Transit District.
Reference: First Interstate Bank of California, The Market Place Office, Long Beach, California.

For full biographical listings, see the Martindale-Hubbell Law Directory

BURNS, AMMIRATO, PALUMBO, MILAM & BARONIAN, A PROFESSIONAL LAW CORPORATION (AV)

One World Trade Center, Suite 1200, 90831-1200
Telephone: 310-436-8338; 714-952-1047
Fax: 310-432-6049
Pasadena, California Office: 65 North Raymond Avenue, 2nd Floor.
Telephone: 818-796-5053; 213-258-8282.
Fax: 818-792-3078.

Vincent A. Ammirato

Thomas L. Halliwell
Robert Gary Mendoza
Joseph F. O'Hara
Michael P. Vicencia
Michael E. Wenzel

For full biographical listings, see the Martindale-Hubbell Law Directory

FLYNN, DELICH & WISE (AV)

One World Trade Center, Suite 1800, 90831-1800
Telephone: 310-435-2626
Fax: 310-437-7555
San Francisco, California Office: Suite 1750, 580 California Street.
Telephone: 415-693-5566.
Fax: 415-693-0410.

Erich P. Wise
Nicholas S. Politis

Representative Clients: American Hawaii Cruises; Holland America Line; Through Transport Mutual Insurance Association, Ltd.; The Britannia Steam Ship Insurance Association Limited; The Steamship Mutual Underwriting Association (Bermuda) Ltd.; General Steamship Corp., Ltd.; Commodore Cruise Line, Ltd.; Interocean Steamship Corporation; Sea-Land Service, Inc.; Hatteras Yachts.

For full biographical listings, see the Martindale-Hubbell Law Directory

FORD, WALKER, HAGGERTY & BEHAR, PROFESSIONAL LAW CORPORATION (AV)

One World Trade Center, Twenty Seventh Floor, 90831
Telephone: 310-983-2500
Telecopier: 310-983-2555

G. Richard Ford
Timothy L. Walker
William C. Haggerty
Jeffrey S. Behar
Mark Steven Hennings
Donna Rogers Kirby
Tina Ivankovic Mangarpan
Jamiel G. Dave
Susan D. Berger
Joseph A. Heath
Robert J. Chavez
J. Michael McClure

Arthur W. Schultz
Jon T. Moseley
Maxine J. Lebowitz
Timothy P. McDonald
K. Michele Williams
Kevin P. Bateman
Stephen Ward Moore
James D. Savage
Todd D. Pearl
Patrick J. Gibbs
James O. Miller
David Huchel
Sheila Anne Alexander
Heidi M. Yoshioka
Robert Reisinger
Theodore A. Clapp
Stanley L. Scarlett
Scott A. Ritsema
Michael Guy Martin
Colleen A. Strong
Kristin L. Jervis
Thomas L. Gourde
Patrick J. Stark
Shayne L. Wulterin

OF COUNSEL

Theodore P. Shield, P.L.C.

For full biographical listings, see the Martindale-Hubbell Law Directory

*LOS ANGELES,** Los Angeles Co.

ADAMS, DUQUE & HAZELTINE (AV)

A Partnership including Professional Corporations
777 South Figueroa Street, Tenth Floor, 90017
Telephone: 213-620-1240
FAX: 213-896-5500
San Francisco, California Office: 500 Washington Street.
Telephone: 415-982-1240.
FAX: 415-982-0130.

MEMBERS OF FIRM

Bruce A. Beckman
Lonnie E. Woolverton (P.C.)
David L. Bacon
Richard T. Davis, Jr.
Margaret Levy
Jeffrey P. Smith
James J. Moak
John L. Viola
Lesley C. Green

OF COUNSEL

Sidney W. Bishop

For Complete List of Firm Personnel, See General Section

For full biographical listings, see the Martindale-Hubbell Law Directory

Los Angeles—Continued

ALLEN, RHODES & SOBELSOHN (AV)

10866 Wilshire Boulevard, Suite 200, 90024
Telephone: 310-475-0875; 213-879-9660
Ontario, California Office: One Lakeshore Centre, 3281 Guasti Road, Suite 800.
Telephone: 909-395-0356.
Santa Barbara, California Office: 125 East De La Guerra.
Telephone: 805-965-5236.
Santa Ana, California Office: 200 West Santa Ana Boulevard, Suite 950.
Telephone: 714-558-7566.
Palm Desert, California Office: 73-710 Fred Waring Drive, Suite 210.
Telephone: 619-776-6830.

MEMBERS OF FIRM

Bernard Sobelsohn
Robert S. Goldberg
Jeffrey M. Wilson (Resident, Palm Springs Office)
Michael E. Johnson (Resident, Santa Barbara Office)
Peter G. Karikas (Resident, Ontario Office)
Richard D. Pesota
James C. Shipley (Resident, Santa Barbara Office)
James P. Ruiz
James C. Callas (Resident, Ontario Office)
Jamie Beth Fox
Lori A. Wenderoff
Juan S. M. Pichardo (Resident, Santa Ana Office)

OF COUNSEL

David B. Allen (Ontario Office)
J. Richard Rhodes (Resident, Ontario Office)

Tracy (Uran) Sturtevant (Resident, Santa Barbara Office)
Howard Lemberg (Resident, Santa Ana Office)
Eduardo Lopez (Resident, Ontario Office)
W. Steven Heise (Resident, Ontario Office)
Kenneth A. Wong (Resident, Santa Ana Office)
Cris M. Holbrook (Resident, Palm Desert Office)
Gordon J. Harrison
Michael G. Glover (Resident, Santa Ana Office)
Edward G. Samaha (Resident, Ontario Office)
Rosanne Wong
Randall B. Schwartz

Reference: Bank of America.

For full biographical listings, see the Martindale-Hubbell Law Directory

ANDERSON, MCPHARLIN & CONNERS (AV)

A Partnership including Professional Corporations
Nineteenth Floor, One Wilshire Building, 624 South Grand Avenue, 90017-3320
Telephone: 213-688-0080; 714-669-1609
Telecopier: 213-622-7594
Riverside, California Office: 3750 University Avenue, Suite 260.
Telephone: 909-787-1900.
Telecopier: 909-787-6749.

Newton E. Anderson (1897-1967)
William J. Conners (1911-1986)
Kenneth E. Lewis (1919-1990)

MEMBERS OF FIRM

G. Wayne Murphy (P.C.)
Michael C. Phillips (P.C.)
Thomas J. Casamassima
David T. DiBiase
David F. Wood
Eric A. Schneider
Kevin D. Smith
Gary J. Valeriano
Noreen Spencer Lewin
Jesse S. Hernandez
Joel A. Osman
Paul F. Schimley
Mark E. Aronson
David A. Borchert
Michael S. Robinson
Ann Graupmann Zuckerman
Jane Ellen Randolph
Brian S. Mizell (Resident, Riverside Office)

ASSOCIATES

Wayne B. Ducharme
Michael D. O'Shea
Alan A. Toki
Nicholas M. Gedo
Carleton R. Burch
Stephen J. Henning
Marci L. Bolter
Jeanette E. Jerles
Ernest J. Bartlett
Dennis L. Althouse
Daniel A. Berman
Adam Lincoln Rollins (Resident, Riverside Office)
Roger M. Franks
Cindy M. Strom
Arnold W. Holaday
Reid L. Denham
John J. Immordino
Lisa Marie Le Nay
Robert H. Beadel
Walter Y. Kim
Michael S. Barrett
Peter G. Szczepanski
Christine Y. Le Bel
Erin E. Martens
Gregory P. Arakawa

OF COUNSEL

Eldon V. McPharlin
Nelson P. Steitz

Representative Clients: American Reinsurance Co.; Employers Reinsurance Corp.; Fireman's Fund Insurance Co.; Ohio Casualty Insurance Co.; Globe Indemnity Co.; Royal Indemnity Co.; U.S. Fire Insurance Co.; Maryland Casualty Co.; U.S. Fidelity & Guaranty Co.

For full biographical listings, see the Martindale-Hubbell Law Directory

BOOTH, MITCHEL & STRANGE (AV)

30th Floor-Equitable Plaza, 3435 Wilshire Boulevard, 90010-2050
Telephone: 213-738-0100
Fax: 213-380-3308
Costa Mesa, California Office: 3080 Bristol Street, Suite 550.
Telephone: 714-641-0217.
Fax: 714-957-0411.

MEMBERS OF FIRM

Bates Booth (1903-1967)
Norman R. Willian (1917-1968)
George C. Mitchel
Owen W. Strange
William F. Rummler
Michael T. Lowe (Resident, Costa Mesa Office)
David S. Aikenhead
Michael D. Kellogg
Andrew P. Cipes
Joseph A. Burrow
Seth W. Whitaker
Walter B. Hill, Jr. (Resident, Costa Mesa Office)
Dennis M. Supanich
Robert H. Briggs (Resident, Costa Mesa Office)
David R. Kipper (Resident, Costa Mesa Office)
Marla Lamedman Kelley (Resident, Costa Mesa Office)
Kevin K. Callahan
Robert F. Keehn
Paul R. Howell (Resident, Costa Mesa Office)
Craig E. Guenther (Resident, Costa Mesa Office)
David L. Hughes (Resident, Costa Mesa Office)
Daniel M. Crowley
Steven M. Mitchel
Robert C. Niesley

ASSOCIATES

Richard W. Davis
Thomas M. Ferlauto
Michael D. Germain
Thomas T. Johnson
John J. Malley
Robert H. Shaffer, Jr.
Eldon S. Edson
Charles R. Gossage
Elizabeth Pepper
Roshi Rahnama
Raymond M. Williams
A. Brooks Gresham
Robert W. Huston
Janice S. Lucas
Michael L. Mengoli
Michael L. Horner
Robin S. Vialla

RESIDENT ASSOCIATES COSTA MESA OFFICE

Elizabeth Currin Bonn
Stacie L. Brandt
Lisa M. Dyson
Joseph C. Gebara
Attillio J. Giovanatto
Howard E. Hamann
Jeffrie R. Jimenez
Christopher A. Kall
Gregory H. King
Niccol D. Kording
Scott S. Mizen
Laila L. Morcos
James G. Stanley
Myron S. Steeves
Christopher A. White

Representative Clients: The Flintkote Co.; Southern California Gas Co.; Southern Counties Title Insurance Co.

For full biographical listings, see the Martindale-Hubbell Law Directory

BUCHALTER, NEMER, FIELDS & YOUNGER, A PROFESSIONAL CORPORATION (AV)

24th Floor, 601 South Figueroa Street, 90017
Telephone: 213-891-0700
Fax: 213-896-0400
Cable Address: "Buchnem"
Telex: 68-7485
New York, New York Office: 19th Floor, 237 Park Avenue.
Telephone: 212-490-8600.
Fax: 212-490-6022.
San Francisco, California Office: 29th Floor, 333 Market Street.
Telephone: 415-227-0900.
Fax: 415-227-0770.
San Jose, California Office: 12th Floor, 50 West San Fernando Street.
Telephone: 408-298-0350.
Fax: 408-298-7683.
Newport Beach, California Office: Suite 300, 620 Newport Center Drive.
Telephone: 714-760-1121.
Fax: 714-720-0182.
Century City, California Office: Suite 2400, 1801 Century Park East.
Telephone: 213-891-0700.
Fax: 310-551-0233.

Murray M. Fields
Sol Rosenthal
Richard Jay Goldstein
Michael L. Wachtell
Harvey H. Rosen
Robert C. Colton
Arthur Chinski
Jay R. Ziegler
Michael J. Cereseto
Bernard E. Le Sage
Terence S. Nunan
Philip J. Wolman
Mark A. Bonenfant
David S. Kyman
Kevin M. Brandt
Jeffrey S. Wruble
Pamela Kohlman Webster
Matthew W. Kavanaugh
Richard S. Angel
Bryan Mashian

OF COUNSEL

Ronald E. Gordon
Stuart D. Buchalter
Holly J. Fujie

(See Next Column)

BUCHALTER, NEMER, FIELDS & YOUNGER A PROFESSIONAL CORPORATION—*Continued*

Geoffrey Forsythe Bogeaus	Cheryl Croteau Orr
Raymond H. Aver	Kenneth W. Swenson
Jonathan D. Fink	Paul S. Arrow
Robert J. Davidson	William S. Brody
Stephen K. Lubega	Amy L. Rubinfeld
Bernard D. Bollinger, Jr.	Dean Stackel

J. Karren Baker

References: City National Bank; Wells Fargo Bank; Metrobank.

For Complete List of Firm Personnel, See General Section

For full biographical listings, see the Martindale-Hubbell Law Directory

CLARK & TREVITHICK, A PROFESSIONAL CORPORATION (AV)

800 Wilshire Boulevard, 12th Floor, 90017
Telephone: 213-629-5700
Telecopier: 213-624-9441

Philip W. Bartenetti	Leonard Brazil
Dolores Cordell	Arturo Santana Jr.
Vincent Tricarico	Kerry T. Ryan

References: Wells Fargo Bank (Los Angeles Main Office); National Bank of California.

For Complete List of Firm Personnel, See General Section

For full biographical listings, see the Martindale-Hubbell Law Directory

DANIELS, BARATTA & FINE (AV)

A Partnership including a Professional Corporation
1801 Century Park East, 9th Floor, 90067
Telephone: 310-556-7900
Telecopier: 310-556-2807

MEMBERS OF FIRM

John P. Daniels (Inc.)	Mary Hulett
James M. Baratta	Michael B. Geibel
Paul R. Fine	James I. Montgomery, Jr.
Nathan B. Hoffman	Lance D. Orloff

Mark R. Israel

ASSOCIATES

Deborah Kaplan Galer	Scott Ashford Brooks
Ilene Wendy Nebenzahl	Craig A. Laidig
Heidi Susan Hart	Paul E. Blevins
Janet Sacks	Joan T. Lind
Michael N. Schonbuch	Rodi F. Rispone
Linda A. Schweitz	Stephanie J. Berman
Christine S. Chu	Michelle C. Hopkins
Glenn T. Rosenblatt	Robin A. Webb
Scott M. Leavitt	Ronda Lynn Crowley
Karen Ann Holloway	Scott A. Spungin
Mark A. Vega	Theodore L. Wilson
Patricio Esquivel	Daniel Joseph Kolodziej
Robert B. Gibson	Craig Momita
Brett S. Markson	Spencer A. Schneider
Michelle R. Press	Angelo A. DuPlantier, III

OF COUNSEL

Timothy J. Hughes	Drew T. Hanker

For full biographical listings, see the Martindale-Hubbell Law Directory

GALTON & HELM (AV)

500 South Grand Avenue, Suite 1200, 90071
Telephone: 213-629-8800
Telecopier: 213-629-0037

MEMBERS OF FIRM

Stephen H. Galton	Michael F. Bell
Hugh H. Helm	Daniel W. Maguire

David A. Lingenbrink

ASSOCIATES

Nancy A. Jerian	Cori Gayle Stockman
Keith A. Jacoby	Susan G. Wells
Michael Hoffman	Chris D. Olsen

For full biographical listings, see the Martindale-Hubbell Law Directory

HAWKINS, SCHNABEL, LINDAHL & BECK (AV)

660 South Figueroa Street, Suite 1500, 90017
Telephone: 213-488-3900
Telecopier: 213-486-9883
Cable Address: "Haslin"

MEMBERS OF FIRM

Roger E. Hawkins	Jon P. Kardassakis
Laurence H. Schnabel	William E. Keitel
George M. Lindahl	R. Timothy Stone

For full biographical listings, see the Martindale-Hubbell Law Directory

HORNBERGER & CRISWELL (AV)

444 South Flower, 31st Floor, 90071
Telephone: 213-488-1655
Facsimile: 213-488-1255

MEMBERS OF FIRM

Nicholas W. Hornberger	Carla J. Feldman
Leslie E. Criswell	Ann M. Ghazarians

Michael A. Brewer

ASSOCIATES

Scott Alan Freedman	John Shaffery
Marlin E. Howes	Charles I. Karlin
Christopher T. Olsen	K. Christopher Branch
Scott B. Cloud	David F. Berry
Celeste S. Makuta	James M. Slominski

Gina T. Sponzilli

For full biographical listings, see the Martindale-Hubbell Law Directory

HORVITZ & LEVY (AV)

A Partnership including Professional Corporations
18th Floor, 15760 Ventura Boulevard (Encino), 91436
Telephone: 818-995-0800; 213-872-0802
FAX: 818-995-3157

Ellis J. Horvitz (A P.C.)	David S. Ettinger
Barry R. Levy (A P.C.)	Daniel J. Gonzalez
Peter Abrahams	Mitchell C. Tilner
David M. Axelrad	Christina J. Imre
Frederic D. Cohen	Lisa Perrochet
S. Thomas Todd	Stephen E. Norris

Sandra J. Smith

Mary F. Dant	Annette E. Davis
Ari R. Kleiman	Andrea M. Gauthier
Lisa R. Jaskol	Elizabeth Skorcz Anthony
Julie L. Woods	Christine A. Pagac (Not admitted in CA)
Holly R. Paul	Gary T. Gleb
H. Thomas Watson	Bruce Adelstein
John A. Taylor, Jr.	

Representative Clients: State Farm Insurance Company; Farmers Insurance Group of Companies; AIG Risk Management; Industrial Indemnity Insurance; CNA Insurance; Home Insurance Company; Allstate Insurance Company; Transamerica Insurance Company; California Insurance Guarantee Association; 20th Century Insurance Company.

For full biographical listings, see the Martindale-Hubbell Law Directory

KOSLOV & CADY (AV)

Suite 650 Roosevelt Building, 727 West Seventh Street, 90017
Telephone: 213-629-2647
FAX: 213-689-9628

MEMBERS OF FIRM

John Koslov	Eurus Cady

ASSOCIATES

Judy L. McKelvey	Melina J. Burns

William P. Medlen

For full biographical listings, see the Martindale-Hubbell Law Directory

LA FOLLETTE, JOHNSON, DE HAAS, FESLER & AMES, A PROFESSIONAL CORPORATION (AV)

865 South Figueroa Street, Suite 3100, 90017-5443
Telephone: 213-426-3600
Fax: 213-426-3650
San Francisco, California Office: 50 California Street, Suite 3350.
Telephone: 415-433-7610.
Telecopier: 415-392-7541.
Santa Ana, California Office: 2677 North Main Street, Suite 901.
Telephone: 714-558-7008.
Telecopier: 714-972-0379.
Riverside, California Office: 3403 Tenth Street, Suite 820.
Telephone: 714-275-9192.
Fax: 714-275-9249.

John T. La Follette (1922-1990)	Dennis J. Sinclitico
Daren T. Johnson	Christopher C. Cannon (Resident, Santa Ana Office)
Louis H. De Haas	Dorothy B. Reyes
Donald C. Fesler	Steven R. Odell (Santa Ana and Riverside Offices)
Dennis K. Ames (Resident, Santa Ana Office)	Christopher L. Thomas (Santa Ana and Riverside Offices)
Alfred W. Gerisch, Jr.	Robert K. Warford (Resident, Riverside Office)
Brian W. Birnie	John L. Supple (Resident, San Francisco Office)
Peter J. Zomber	Vincent D. Lapointe
Robert E. Kelly, Jr.	
Leon A. Zallen	
G. Kelley Reid, Jr. (Resident, San Francisco Office)	

(See Next Column)

LA FOLLETTE, JOHNSON, DE HAAS, FESLER & AMES A PROFESSIONAL CORPORATION, *Los Angeles—Continued*

Steven J. Joffe
Mark M. Stewart
Bradley J. McGirr (Resident, Santa Ana Office)
Sydney La Branche Merritt

Peter R. Bing
Larry P. Nathenson
Donald R. Beck (Resident, Santa Ana Office)
Donna R. Evans
David J. Ozeran
Mark B. Guterman
Terry A. Woodward (Resident, Santa Ana Office)
Stephen C. Dreher (Resident, Santa Ana Office)
Tatiana M. Schultz (Resident, San Francisco Office)
Peter E. Theophilos (Resident, San Francisco Office)
Deborah A. Cowley
Thomas S. Alch
Kenton E. Moore
Kent T. Brandmeyer
Garry O. Moses
Jeffery R. Erickson (Resident, Riverside Office)
Michael J. O'Connor
Elizabeth Anne Scherer (Resident, Santa Ana Office)
Hugh R. Burns
Stephen K. Hiura
James G. Wold
Eileen S. Lemmon (Resident, Riverside, Office)
David M. Wright
Larry E. White (Resident, Riverside Office)
Laurie Miyamoto Johnson
David James Reinard
Michelle Louise McCoy
Duane A. Newton (Resident, Riverside Office)
Adriaan F. van der Capellen (Resident, Santa Ana Office)
William T. Gray (Resident, Santa Ana Office)
Thomas J. Lo (Resident, Santa Ana Office)
Daniel D. Sorenson (Resident, Riverside Office)
Joanne Rosendin (Resident, San Francisco Office)
Henry P. Canvel (Resident, San Francisco Office)
Peter D. Busciglio (Resident, Santa Ana Office)
Mark S. Rader (Resident, Riverside Office)
Jay B. Lake
Erin L. Muellenberg (Resident, Riverside Office)
Phyllis M. Winston (Resident, Riverside Office)
John Calfee Mulvana (Resident, Santa Ana Office)
David L. Bell
Brian T. Chu (Resident, Santa Ana Office)
John Hammond
Laurent C. Vonderweidt
David Peim
Daniel V. Kohls (Resident, San Francisco Office)
Joel E. D. Odou
Robert T. Bergsten
Marcelo A. D'Asero
Natasha M. Riggs
Henry M. Su
Richard K. Kay
Annette A. Apperson

A list of References will be furnished upon request.

For full biographical listings, see the Martindale-Hubbell Law Directory

NEUMEYER & BOYD (AV)

2029 Century Park East, Suite 1100, 90067
Telephone: 310-553-9393
Fax: 310-553-8437

MEMBERS OF FIRM

Richard A. Neumeyer
Carol Boyd

ASSOCIATES

Lydia E. Hachmeister
Katherine Tatikian
Jeffrey B. Lehrman
Susie J. Kater
Daniel F. Sanchez

OF COUNSEL

Steven A. Freeman

For full biographical listings, see the Martindale-Hubbell Law Directory

O'MELVENY & MYERS (AV)

400 South Hope Street, 90071-2899
Telephone: 213-669-6000
Cable Address: "Moms"
Facsimile: 213-669-6407
Century City, California Office: 1999 Avenue of the Stars, 7th Floor, 90067-6035.
Telephone: 310-553-6700.
Facsimile: 310-246-6779.
Newport Beach, California Office: 610 Newport Center Drive, Suite 1700, 92660.
Telephone: 714-760-9600.
Cable Address: "Moms".
Facsimile: 714-669-6994.
San Francisco, California Office: Embarcadero Center West Tower, 275 Battery Street, Suite 2600, 94111.
Telephone: 415-984-8700.
Facsimile: 415-984-8701.
New York, N.Y. Office: Citicorp Center, 153 East 53rd Street, 54th Floor, 10022-4611.
Telephone: 212-326-2000.
Facsimile: 212-326-2061.
Washington, D.C. Office: 555 13th Street, N.W., Suite 500 West, 20004-1109.
Telephone: 202-383-5300.
Cable Address: "Moms".
Facsimile: 202-383-5414.

(See Next Column)

Newark, New Jersey Office: One Gateway Center, 7th Floor, 07102.
Telephone: 201-639-8600.
Facsimile: 201-639-8630.
London, England Office: 10 Finsbury Square, London, EC2A 1LA.
Telephone: 011-44-171-256 8451.
Facsimile: 011-44-171-638-8205.
Tokyo, Japan Office: Sanbancho KB-6 Building, 6 Sanbancho, Chiyoda-ku, Tokyo 102, Japan.
Telephone: 011-81-3-3239-2800.
Facsimile: 011-81-3-3239-2432.
Hong Kong Office: 1104 Lippo Tower, Lippo Centre, 89 Queensway, Central Hong Kong.
Telephone: 011-852-523-8266.
Facsimile: 011-852-522-1760.

MEMBERS OF FIRM

John L. Altieri, Jr. (New York, N.Y. Office)
Martin S. Checov (San Francisco Office)
Bertrand M. Cooper
Brian S. Currey
Ralph W. Dau
John F. Daum (Washington, D.C. Office)
Robert S. Draper
Andrew J. Frackman (Not admitted in CA; New York, N.Y. Office)
Martin Glenn (New York, N.Y. Office)
Richard B. Goetz
Stephen J. Harburg (Not admitted in CA; Washington, D.C. Office)
B. Boyd Hight
Phillip R. Kaplan (Newport Beach Office)
Holly E. Kendig
Louis B. Kimmelman (Not admitted in CA; New York, N.Y. Office)
Paul R. Koepff (New York, N.Y. Office)
Joseph M. Malkin (San Francisco Office)
Julie A. McMillan (San Francisco Office)
Paul G. McNamara
John G. Niles
Richard G. Parker (Washington, D.C. Office)
Mark A. Samuels
Carl R. Schenker, Jr. (Washington, D.C. Office)
John W. Stamper
Kim McLane Wardlaw
W. Mark Wood

SPECIAL COUNSEL

Peter B. Ackerman
Rosemary B. Boller (New York, N.Y. Office)
Joseph E. Boury (Newark, N.J. Office)
Richard W. Buckner
Cormac J. Carney (Newport Beach Office)
Thomas G. Carruthers (New York, N.Y. Office)
Charles W. Fournier (New York, N.Y. Office)
Kathleen A. Gallagher (New York, N.Y. Office)
H. Douglas Galt
Karen R. Growdon
Abigail A. Jones
Daniel M. Mansueto
Diane E. Pritchard

ASSOCIATES

Paul M. Alfieri (New York, N.Y. Office)
Mary Amilea Anderson (Washington, D.C. Office)
James D. Arbogast (New York, N.Y. Office)
Linda A. Bagley (San Francisco Office)
Patrick J. Bannon (San Francisco Office)
Alec M. Barinholtz
Bernard C. Barmann, Jr.
Kathleen L. Beiermeister (Newark, N.J. Office)
Michael G. Bosko (Newport Beach Office)
John M. Bowers
Laura C. Bremer (San Francisco Office)
William R. Burford (San Francisco Office)
John R. Call
Ralph P. DeSanto (New York, N.Y. Office)
Thomas J. Di Resta (New York, N.Y. Office)
Erica K. Doran (Not admitted in CA; New York, N.Y. Office)
Marcia A. Fay (Washington, D.C. Office)
Aaron F. Fishbein (New York, N.Y. Office)
James H. Gianninoto (Newark, N.J. Office)
Lawrence M. Hadley
Jennifer L. Isenberg (San Francisco Office)
Bruce Gen Iwasaki
Gloria Ching-hua Jan (New York, N.Y. Office)
Jeffrey M. Judd (San Francisco Office)
Kevin M. Kelcourse (Not admitted in CA; Washington, D.C. Office)
Jeffrey W. Kilduff (Not admitted in CA; Washington, D.C. Office)
Stephen V. Kovarik (New York, N.Y. Office)
Robert F. Kramer (Not admitted in CA; New York, N.Y. Office)
Paul A. Leodori (Newark, N.J. Office)
Lisa Litwiller (Newport Beach Office)
Michael M. Maddigan
Maria Rose Mazur (Washington, D.C. Office)
Darren S. McNally (Newark, N.J. Office)
Susan M. McNeill (New York, N.Y. Office)
Karen M. Mendalka (Newark, N.J. Office)
Kathleen A. Mishkin (Newark, N.J. Office)
M. Catherine Powell
Katherine W. Pownell
Claudia E. Ray (New York, N.Y. Office)
James Gerard Rizzo (New York, N.Y. Office)
Gregory Roer (Newark, N.J. Office)
Edward A. Rosic, Jr. (Not admitted in CA; Washington, D.C. Office)
Tancred V. Schiavoni, III (New York, N.Y. Office)

(See Next Column)

O'MELVENY & MYERS—*Continued*

ASSOCIATES (Continued)

Scott Schrader (New York Office)
Darrel M. Seife (New York, N.Y. Office)
Darin W. Snyder (San Francisco Office)
Frieda A. Taylor
Gloria Trattles (New York, N.Y. Office)
Scott Treanor (San Francisco Office)
Mary Catherine Wirth
Scott N. Yamaguchi

For Complete List of Firm Personnel, See General Section

For full biographical listings, see the Martindale-Hubbell Law Directory

STOCKWELL, HARRIS, ANDERSON & WIDOM, A PROFESSIONAL CORPORATION (AV)

6222 Wilshire Boulevard, Sixth Floor, P.O. Box 48917, 90048-0917
Telephone: 213-935-6669; 818-784-6222; 310-277-6669
Fax: 213-935-0198
Santa Ana, California Office: Suite 500, 1551 N. Tustin Avenue, P.O. Box 11979.
Telephone: 714-479-1180.
Fax: 714-479-1190.
Pomona, California Office: Suite 200, 363 South Park Avenue.
Telephone: 909-623-1459; 213-622-7427.
Fax: 909-623-5554.
Ventura, California Office: Suite 270, 2151 Alessandro Drive.
Telephone: 805-653-2710; 213-617-7290.
Fax: 805-653-2731.
San Bernardino, California Office: Suite 303, 215 North "D" Street.
Telephone: 909-381-5553.
Fax: 909-384-9981.
San Diego, California Office: Suite 400, 402 West Broadway.
Telephone: 619-235-6054.
Fax: 619-231-0129.
Grover Beach, California Office: Suite 307, 200 South 13th Street.
Telephone: 805-473-0720.
Fax: 805-473-0635.

Steven I. Harris (Managing Attorney)
Patricia A. Olive
David L. Slucter (Resident, San Bernardino Office)
Richard M. Widom (Managing Attorney)
Jeffrey T. Landres (Resident, Ventura Office)
Linda S. Freeman (Santa Ana and San Diego Offices)
Michael L. Terry (Resident, Grover Beach Office)
William M. Carero
Brian R. Horan
David F. Grant (Resident, Pomona Office)
Ian D. Paige
Edward S. Muehl (Resident, Pomona Office)
Lawrence S. Mendelsohn
Edwin H. McKnight, Jr. (Resident, Santa Ana Office)
Steven A. Meline (Resident, Santa Ana Office)
Michael K. McKibbin (Resident, San Bernardino Office)
Ted L. Hirschberger
Lawrence B. Madans
Jeffrey M. Williams (Resident, Ventura Office)
Lester D. Marshall
Jeffery M. Klein (Resident, Santa Ana Office)
John R. Payne

For full biographical listings, see the Martindale-Hubbell Law Directory

VEATCH, CARLSON, GROGAN & NELSON (AV)

A Partnership including a Professional Corporation
3926 Wilshire Boulevard, 90010
Telephone: 213-381-2861
Telefax: 213-383-6370

MEMBERS OF FIRM

Wayne Veatch
Henry R. Thomas (1905-1963)
James R. Nelson (1925-1987)
James C. Galloway, Jr. (A Professional Corporation)
C. Snyder Patin
Anthony D. Seine
Mark A. Weinstein
John A. Peterson

ASSOCIATES

Michael Eric Wasserman
Richard A. Wood
Michael A. Kramer
Mark M. Rudy
André S. Goodchild
Lyn A. Woodward
Kevin L. Henderson
Betty Rubin-Elbaz
John B. Loomis
Judith Randel Cooper
Karen J. Travis
Amy W. Lyons
Wayne Rozenberg
Gilbert A. Garcia
Judy Lew
James A. Jinks

OF COUNSEL

Robert C. Carlson (A Professional Corporation)
Stephen J. Grogan
David J. Aisenson

For full biographical listings, see the Martindale-Hubbell Law Directory

MARINA DEL REY, Los Angeles Co.

DONALD HUGH MOORE (AV)

Suite 429 - Marina Towers, 4640 Admiralty Way, 90292
Telephone: 310-305-8338
Facsimile: 310-827-5440

For full biographical listings, see the Martindale-Hubbell Law Directory

*MODESTO,** Stanislaus Co.

BRUNN & FLYNN, A PROFESSIONAL CORPORATION (AV)

928 12th Street, P.O. Box 3366, 95353
Telephone: 209-521-2133
Fax: 209-521-7584

Charles K. Brunn
Timothy T. Flynn
Gerald E. Brunn
Roger S. Matzkind

Reference: Pacific Valley Bank.

For full biographical listings, see the Martindale-Hubbell Law Directory

MONTEREY, Monterey Co.

HARRAY, PIERCE & MASUDA (AV)

80 Garden Court, Suite 260, 93940
Telephone: 408-373-3101
Fax: 408-373-6712

Richard K. Harray
Jacqueline M. Pierce
Michael P. Masuda

ASSOCIATE

Stan L. Linker

For full biographical listings, see the Martindale-Hubbell Law Directory

*OAKLAND,** Alameda Co.

BENNETT, SAMUELSEN, REYNOLDS AND ALLARD, A PROFESSIONAL CORPORATION (AV)

Suite 200, 1951 Webster Street, 94612
Telephone: 510-444-7688
Fax: 510-444-5849

Bryant M. Bennett
David J. Samuelsen
Richard L. Reynolds
Anthony J. Allard
John G. Cowperthwaite

Roger Blake Hohnsbeen
Don Henry Schaefer
Thomas S. Gelini
Kimberley A. Robbins
Angela M. Fiorentino

OF COUNSEL

Frederick W. Gatt

Representative Clients: Allstate Insurance Co.; California State Automobile Assn.; The Continental Insurance Cos.; Trinity Universal Insurance Co.; County of Alameda.

For full biographical listings, see the Martindale-Hubbell Law Directory

HAIMS, JOHNSON, MACGOWAN & MCINERNEY (AV)

490 Grand Avenue, 94610
Telephone: 510-835-0500
Facsimile: 510-835-2833

MEMBERS OF FIRM

Arnold B. Haims
Gary R. Johnson
Clyde L. MacGowan
Thomas McInerney
Lawrence A. Baker
Randy M. Marmor
John K. Kirby
Robert J. Frassetto
Caroline N. Valentino

ASSOCIATES

Joseph Y. Ahn
Edward D. Baldwin
Kathleen B. Boehm
Marc P. Bouret
Anne M. Michaels
Dianne D. Peebles
Michelle D. Perry
Edward C. Schroeder, Jr.

For full biographical listings, see the Martindale-Hubbell Law Directory

HARDIN, COOK, LOPER, ENGEL & BERGEZ (AV)

1999 Harrison Street, 18th Floor, 94612-3541
Telephone: 510-444-3131
Telecopier: 510-839-7940

MEMBERS OF FIRM

Raymond J. Bergez
Ralph A. Lombardi
Willard L. Alloway
Gennaro A. Filice, III
Bruce P. Loper
Bruce E. McLeod
Eugene Brown, Jr.
Matthew S. Conant
Chris P. Lavdiotis
Robert D. Eassa
Peter O. Glaessner

(See Next Column)

HARDIN, COOK, LOPER, ENGEL & BERGEZ, *Oakland—Continued*

Amber L. Kelly
Owen T. Rooney
John A. De Pasquale
Nicholas D. Kayhan
William H. Curtis
Elsa M. Baldwin
Rodney Ian Headington
Marshall A. Johnson
Diane R. Stanton
Jennifer M. Walker
Margaret L. Kotzebue
Amee A. Mikacich
Peter A. Strotz
Timothy J. McCaffery
Stephen J. Valen
Troy D. McMahan
Lisa L. Hillegas
GayLynn Renee Kirn
Richard V. Normington III
Kevin J. Chechak

Representative Clients: Firemans Fund Insurance Cos.; City of Piedmont; The Dow Chemical Co.; Nissan Motor Corp.; Subaru of America; Weyerhauser Co.; Bay Area Rapid Transit District; Diamond Shamrock; Home Indemnity Co.; Rhone-Poulenc.

For Complete List of Firm Personnel, See General Section

For full biographical listings, see the Martindale-Hubbell Law Directory

KINCAID, GIANUNZIO, CAUDLE & HUBERT, A PROFESSIONAL CORPORATION (AV)

200 Webster Street, P.O. Box 1828, 94604-0828
Telephone: 510-465-5212
Telecopier: 510-465-0362
Walnut Creek, California Office: Suite 400, 500 Ygnacio Valley Road.
Telephone: 510-930-9111.
Telecopier: 510-930-9346.
San Francisco, California Office: 221 Main Street, Suite 1300.
Telephone: 415-543-6212.
Telecopier: 415-543-1134.

Victor J. Gianunzio
Patrick J. Hagan
Eliot R. Hudson
Michael R. Welch
Gregory Michael Doyle
E. Jane Wells
William K. Bissell
Scott A. Bovée
Berta Helbing Schweinberger
Edward E. Hartley
M. David DeSantis

OF COUNSEL

Donald H. Kincaid

Irene Takahashi
Gene B. Eacret
Kirk E. Wallace
Kelly Ann Kilkenny
Andrew A. Goode
Owen E. Baylis
Jack C. Henning
S. Lynn Appleton
Amy C. Hirschkron
Brad C. Westlye
Matthew S. Cole
Joanna L. Shuttleworth
Mark A. Love
Sam Ferdows
Laura P. Yee
Joanne M. Chan
Kevin W. Kirsch
Eric S. Clarke
Jeffrey P. Mooney
Mark R. Goodale

Representative Clients: Farmers Insurance Exchange; Geico; Maryland Casualty Co.; State Farm Mutual Automobile Insurance Co.; Utica Insurance Co.

For full biographical listings, see the Martindale-Hubbell Law Directory

MARTIN, RYAN & ANDRADA, A PROFESSIONAL CORPORATION (AV)

Twenty-Second Floor, Ordway Building, One Kaiser Plaza, 94612
Telephone: 510-763-6510
Fax: 510-763-3921

Gerald P. Martin, Jr.
Joseph D. Ryan, Jr.
J. Randall Andrada
Jill J. Lifter
Jolie Krakauer
Glenn Gould
Michael J. Daley
Charles E. Kallgren
Rhonda D. Shelton
Betty J. Jones
Lora N. Vail
Vikki L. Barron-Jennings

Representative Clients: Alameda Contra Costa County Transit District; Continental Insurance Cos.; Commercial Union Insurance Group; Liberty Mutual Insurance Co.; Safeway Stores, Inc.

For full biographical listings, see the Martindale-Hubbell Law Directory

RANKIN, SPROAT & POLLACK (AV)

An Association including Professional Corporations
Suite 1616, 1800 Harrison Street, 94612
Telephone: 510-465-3922
Fax: 510-452-3006
San Francisco, California Office: 369 Pine Street, Suite 400.
Telephone: 415-392-4346.

Joseph F. Rankin (-1977)
Patrick T. Rankin (1943-1990)
Ronald G. Sproat (Member of Rankin & Sproat, Professional Corporation)
Thomas A. Trapani
Edward Vail Pollack (A Professional Corporation) (Resident, San Francisco Office)
Geoffrey A. Mires
Michael J. Reiser

(See Next Column)

Gregory P. Menzel (Resident, San Francisco)
Lynne P. McGhee
David T. Shuey
G. Trent Morrow
Eugene Ashley

LEGAL SUPPORT PERSONNEL

Jennifer L. Rankin
Betty E. Evans (Nurse Paralegal)
Sue Perata (Medical Paralegal)
Erika K. Ambacher (Paralegal)

Reference: Security Pacific Bank.

For full biographical listings, see the Martindale-Hubbell Law Directory

ONTARIO, San Bernardino Co.

ALLEN, RHODES & SOBELSOHN (AV)

One Lakeshore Centre, 3281 Guasti Road, Suite 800, 91761
Telephone: 909-395-0356
Los Angeles, California Office: 10866 Wilshire Boulevard, Suite 200.
Telephone: 310-475-0875; 213-879-9660.
Santa Barbara, California Office: 125 East De La Guerra.
Telephone: 805-965-5236.
Santa Ana, California Office: 200 West Santa Ana Boulevard, Suite 950
Telephone: 714-558-7566.
Palm Springs, California Office: 73-710 Fred Waring Drive, Suite 210.
Telephone: 619-776-6830.

MEMBERS OF FIRM

Peter G. Karikas
James C. Callas

OF COUNSEL

David B. Allen
J. Richard Rhodes

Eduardo Lopez
W. Steven Heise
Edward G. Samaha

Reference: Bank of America.

For full biographical listings, see the Martindale-Hubbell Law Directory

ORANGE, Orange Co.

WALSWORTH, FRANKLIN & BEVINS (AV)

1 City Boulevard West, Suite 308, 92668
Telephone: 714-634-2522
LAW-FAX: 714-634-0686
San Francisco, California Office: 580 California Street, Suite 1335.
Telephone: 415-781-7072.
Fax: 415-391-6258.

Jeffrey P. Walsworth
Ferdie F. Franklin
Ronald H. Bevins, Jr.
Michael T. McCall
Noel Edlin (Resident, San Francisco Office)
Lawrence E. Duffy, Jr.
Sheldon J. Fleming
J. Wayne Allen
James A. Anton
Ingrid K. Campagne (Resident, San Francisco Office)
Robert M. Channel (Resident, San Francisco Office)
Nicholas A. Cipiti
Sharon L. Clisham (Resident, San Francisco Office)
David W. Epps (Resident, San Francisco Office)
Richard M. Hills (Resident, San Francisco Office)
Sandra G. Kennedy
Randall J. Lee (Resident, San Francisco Office)
Kimberly K. Mays
Bruce A. Nelson (Resident, San Francisco Office)
Kevin Pegan
Allan W. Ruggles
Jonathan M. Slipp
Cyrian B. Tabuena (Resident, San Francisco Office)
John L. Trunko
Houston M. Watson, II
Mary A. Watson

For full biographical listings, see the Martindale-Hubbell Law Directory

PALM DESERT, Riverside Co.

ALLEN, RHODES & SOBELSOHN (AV)

73-710 Fred Waring Drive, Suite 210, 92260
Telephone: 619-776-6830
Los Angeles, California Office: 10866 Wilshire Boulevard, Suite 200.
Telephone: 310-475-0875; 213-879-9660.
Ontario, California Office: One Lakeshore Centre, 3281 Guasti Road, Suite 800.
Telephone: 909-395-0356.
Santa Barbara, California Office: 125 East De La Guerra.
Telephone: 805-965-5236.
Santa Ana, California Office: 200 West Santa Ana Boulevard, Suite 950.
Telephone: 714-558-7566.

Jeffrey M. Wilson

(See Next Column)

ALLEN, RHODES & SOBELSOHN—*Continued*

Cris M. Holbrook

Reference: Bank of America.

For full biographical listings, see the Martindale-Hubbell Law Directory

PASADENA, Los Angeles Co.

BURNS, AMMIRATO, PALUMBO, MILAM & BARONIAN, A PROFESSIONAL LAW CORPORATION (AV)

65 North Raymond Avenue, 2nd Floor, 91103-3919
Telephone: 818-796-5053; 213-258-8282
Fax: 818-792-3078
Long Beach, California Office: One World Trade Center, Suite 1200.
Telephone: 310-436-8338; 714-952-1047.
Fax: 310-432-6049.

Michael A. Burns
Bruce Palumbo
Jeffrey L. Milam
Robert H. Baronian
Steven J. Banner

Normand A. Ayotte
Colleen Clark
Vincent F. De Marzo
William D. Dodson
Valerie Julien-Peto
Susan E. Luhring
Grace C. Mori

Reference: First Los Angeles Bank.

For full biographical listings, see the Martindale-Hubbell Law Directory

CAIRNS, DOYLE, LANS, NICHOLAS & SONI, A LAW CORPORATION (AV)

Ninth Floor, 225 South Lake Avenue, 91101
Telephone: 818-683-3111
Telecopier: 818-683-4999

Rohini Soni (1956-1994)
John D. Cairns
John C. Doyle
Stephen M. Lans
Francisco J. Nicholas

David M. Phillips

Representative Clients: Allstate Insurance Companies; Burger King Corporation; California Insurance Guarantee Association; California United Bank; CIGNA Insurance Companies; City of Pasadena; Cumis Insurance Society, Inc.; Employer's Mutual Insurance Companies; State Farm Insurance Companies; Tokio Marine Insurance.

For full biographical listings, see the Martindale-Hubbell Law Directory

COLLINS, COLLINS, MUIR & TRAVER (AV)

Successor to Collins & Collins
Suite 300, 265 North Euclid, 91101
Telephone: 818-793-1163
Los Angeles: 213-681-2773
FAX: 818-793-5982

MEMBERS OF FIRM

James E. Collins (1910-1987)
John J. Collins
Samuel J. Muir
Robert J. Traver

ASSOCIATES

John B. Foss
Frank J. D'Oro
Paul L. Rupard
Brian K. Stewart
Robert H. Stellwagen, Jr.
Tomas A. Guterres
Karen B. Sharp
Amina R. Merritt
Christine E. Drage

For full biographical listings, see the Martindale-Hubbell Law Directory

FREEBURG, JUDY, MACCHIAGODENA & NETTELS (AV)

600 South Lake Avenue, 91106
Telephone: 818-585-4150
FAX: 818-585-0718
Santa Ana, California Office: Xerox Centre. 1851 East First Street, Suite 120. 92705-4017.
Telephone: 714-569-0950.
Facsimile: 714-569-0955.

Steven J. Freeburg
J. Lawrence Judy
Marina A. Macchiagodena
Charles F. Nettels

ASSOCIATES

Ingall W. Bull, Jr.
Richard B. Castle
Cynthia B. Schaldenbrand (Resident, Santa Ana Office)
Robert S. Brody
Sheral A. Hyde
Holly A. McNulty
Karen S. Freeburg
Jennifer D. Helsel
James P. Habel
Marianne L. Offermans

For full biographical listings, see the Martindale-Hubbell Law Directory

*REDDING,** Shasta Co.

HALKIDES & MORGAN, A PROFESSIONAL CORPORATION (AV)

833 Mistletoe Lane, P.O. Drawer 492170, 96049-2170
Telephone: 916-221-8150
Fax: 916-221-7963

G. Dennis Halkides
Arthur L. Morgan, Jr.

William D. Ayres
John P. Kelley
Mary Catherine Pearl

Representative Clients: American Hardware Mutual Insurance Company; Design Professionals Insurance Co.; Farmers Insurance Group; Gallagher Bassett Insurance Service; Great American Insurance Co.; National Insurance Co.; Safeco Insurance Co.; State Farm Mutual Insurance Co.

For full biographical listings, see the Martindale-Hubbell Law Directory

DOUGLAS H. NEWLAN (AV)

434 Redcliff Drive, Suite B, P.O. Box 491736, 96049-1736
Telephone: 916-221-0184
FAX: 916-221-8744

For full biographical listings, see the Martindale-Hubbell Law Directory

*REDWOOD CITY,** San Mateo Co.

OWEN & MELBYE, A PROFESSIONAL CORPORATION (AV)

700 Jefferson Street, 94063
Telephone: 415-364-6500
Fax: 415-365-7036
Tahoe City, California Office: P.O. Box 1524.
Telephone: 916-546-2473.

William H. Owen
Richard B. Melbye
Norman J. Roger
Edmund M. Scott
Pamela J. Helmer
John S. Posthauer
Paul R. Mangiantini

Albert P. Blake, Jr.
Dawn M. Patterson
Conor A. Meyers

Representative Clients: Aetna Cravens Dargan Co.; Avco Lycoming; Beech Aircraft Corp.; California Casualty Indemnity Exchange; K & K Claims Service; Kemper Insurance Cos.; Mutual Service Insurance Co.; State Farm Mutual Insurance Cos.; Underwriters at Lloyds; United States Aviation Insurance Group.

For full biographical listings, see the Martindale-Hubbell Law Directory

*SACRAMENTO,** Sacramento Co.

CAULFIELD, DAVIES & DONAHUE (AV)

3500 American River Drive, 1st Floor, 95864
Telephone: 916-487-7700
Fairfield, California Office: Fairfield West Plaza, 1455 Oliver Road, Suite 130.
Telephone: 707-426-0223.

MEMBERS OF FIRM

Richard Hyland Caulfield
Robert E. Davies
James R. Donahue
Bruce E. Leonard
Michael M. McKone
Douglas L. Smith

ASSOCIATES

David N. Tedesco
Matthew Paul Donahue
Brian C. Haydon
Paul R. Ramsey

For full biographical listings, see the Martindale-Hubbell Law Directory

DIEPENBROCK & COSTA (AV)

455 University Avenue, Suite 300, 95825
Telephone: 916-565-6222
Fax: 916-565-6220

MEMBERS OF FIRM

Anthony C. Diepenbrock
Daniel P. Costa
John D. Broghammer
Maria R. Vail
Karen L. Kovalsky

Representative Clients: American Nuclear Insurer; CIGNA; Century Surety Co.; Colonia Penn.; Connecticut Specialty Insurance Co.; Federated Mutual; Forum Insurance Co.; Great American Insurance Companies; National Continental Insurance Co.; Progressive Insurance Co.; Reliance Insurance Co.; Safeco Insurance Co.; Sedgwick James; Unigard Insurance Group; Central State of Omaha.

For full biographical listings, see the Martindale-Hubbell Law Directory

Sacramento—Continued

HANSEN, BOYD, CULHANE & WATSON (AV)

A Partnership including Professional Corporations
Central City Centre, 1331 Twenty-First Street, 95814
Telephone: 916-444-2550
Telecopier: 916-444-2358

Hartley T. Hansen (Inc.)
Kevin R. Culhane (Inc.)
David E. Boyd
Lawrence R. Watson
John J. Rueda
James J. Banks

OF COUNSEL

Betsy S. Kimball

Lorraine M. Pavlovich
Thomas L. Riordan
D. Jeffery Grimes
Joseph Zuber
James O. Moses

For full biographical listings, see the Martindale-Hubbell Law Directory

JOHNSON, SCHACHTER, LEWIS & COLLINS, A PROFESSIONAL CORPORATION (AV)

701 University Avenue, Suite 150, 95825
Telephone: 916-921-5800
Telecopier: 916-921-0247
Walnut Creek, California Office: 500 Ygnacio Valley Road #490.
Telephone: 510-947-0100.
Fax: 510-947-0111.
Chico, California Office: 515 Wall Street.
Telephone: 916-895-1623.

Robert H. Johnson
Alesa M. Schachter
Luther R. Lewis
Kim H. Collins

George W. Holt
Timothy P. Dailey
James B. Walker
R. James Miller

OF COUNSEL

Ford R. Smith
Carolyn M. Wood
Susanne M. Shelley
James W. Rushford

Representative Clients: Fireman's Fund Insurance Cos; GAB Business Services; Jonsson Communications Corp.; McClatchy Newspapers and Broadcasting; State Farm Fire & Casualty Co.; State Farm Mutual Automobile Insurance Co.
Reference: Business & Professional Bank, Sacramento.

For full biographical listings, see the Martindale-Hubbell Law Directory

LEWIS & BACON, A PROFESSIONAL CORPORATION (AV)

Ramona Hotel Office Building, 1001 Sixth Street, Suite 203, 95814
Telephone: 916-444-7340
Fax: 916-444-7411

Steven A. Lewis
Kenneth E. Bacon

Sharon B. Futerman
Heidi S. Cordeiro

For full biographical listings, see the Martindale-Hubbell Law Directory

MASON & THOMAS (AV)

2151 River Plaza Drive, Suite 100, P.O. Box 868, 95812-0868
Telephone: 916-567-8211
Fax: 916-567-8212

MEMBERS OF FIRM

Stephen A. Mason
Bradley S. Thomas
Robert L. Moore

ASSOCIATES

Douglas W. Brown
Robert G. Kruse
David S. Yost
Patrick J. Hehir
Kevin L. Elder
Tina L. Izen

OF COUNSEL

John D. Stumbos, Jr.

For full biographical listings, see the Martindale-Hubbell Law Directory

MATHENY, POIDMORE & SEARS (AV)

2100 Northrop Avenue, Building 1200, P.O. Box 13711, 95853-4711
Telephone: 916-929-9271
Fax: 916-929-2458

MEMBERS OF FIRM

Henry G. Matheny (1933-1984)
Anthony J. Poidmore
Douglas A. Sears
Richard S. Linkert
James C. Damir
Michael A. Bishop
Ernest A. Long
Joann Georgallis
Kent M. Luckey

(See Next Column)

ASSOCIATES

Matthew C. Jaime
Jill P. Telfer
Robert B. Berrigan
Daryl M. Thomas
Ronald E. Enabnit
Cathy A. Reynolds
Byron D. Damiani, Jr.
Catherine Kennedy

OF COUNSEL

A. Laurel Bennett

LEGAL SUPPORT PERSONNEL

PARALEGALS

Karen D. Fisher
Fran Studer
Lynell Rae Steed
Jennifer Bachman
David Austin Boucher

For full biographical listings, see the Martindale-Hubbell Law Directory

MCDONALD, SAELTZER, MORRIS, CREEGGAN & WADDOCK (AV)

555 Capitol Mall, Suite 700, 95814
Telephone: 916-444-5706
Fax: 916-444-8529

MEMBERS OF FIRM

Eugene W. Saeltzer
William O. Morris
Richard C. Creeggan
Thomas P. Waddock
Gregory R. Madsen

ASSOCIATES

Paul J. Wagstaffe
Ronald Craig Schwarzkopf
Hank G. Greenblatt
Jon S. Allin
Scott W. DePeel
Jonathan M. Cohen
Robert S. Brunelli
Gretchen K. Mello

OF COUNSEL

Douglas B. McDonald

Reference: Wells Fargo Bank.

For full biographical listings, see the Martindale-Hubbell Law Directory

SCHUERING ZIMMERMAN SCULLY & NOLEN (AV)

400 University Avenue, 95825
Telephone: 916-567-0400
Fax: 916-568-0400

MEMBERS OF FIRM

Leo H. Schuering, Jr.
Robert H. Zimmerman
Steven T. Scully
Rhudolph Nolen, Jr.
Thomas J. Doyle
Lawrence S. Giardina
Anthony D. Lauria

Keith D. Chidlaw
Regina A. Favors
Raymond R. Gates
Scott A. Linn
Donna W. Low
Dominique A. Pollara
Theodore D. Poppinga
Janet Marie Richmond
John J. Sillis

For full biographical listings, see the Martindale-Hubbell Law Directory

*SAN BERNARDINO,** San Bernardino Co.

FURNESS, MIDDLEBROOK, KAISER & HIGGINS, A PROFESSIONAL CORPORATION (AV)

1411 North "D" Street, P.O. Box 1319, 92402-1319
Telephone: 909-888-5751
Fax: 909-888-7360
Palm Springs, California Office: 3001 East Tahquitz Canyon Way, Suite 109.
Telephone: 619-322-0806.
Fax: 619-322-8979.

John W. Furness
Greg C. Middlebrook
Michael R. Kaiser (Resident, Palm Springs Office)
James A. Higgins

Floyd F. Fishell
Thomas J. Mullen
Jeffrey A. Weaver (Resident, Palm Springs Office)
Jeffrey Mark Yoss (Resident, Palm Springs Office)
Robert F. Wilson
Cheryl A. Shaw (Resident, Palm Springs Office)

References: First Interstate Bank; Dun & Bradstreet.

For full biographical listings, see the Martindale-Hubbell Law Directory

MAC LACHLAN, BURFORD & ARIAS, A LAW CORPORATION (AV)

560 East Hospitality Lane, Fourth Floor, 92408
Telephone: 909-885-4491
Fax: 909-888-6866
Rancho Cucamonga, California Office: 8280 Utica Avenue, Suite 200. 909-989-4481.
Palm Springs, California Office: 255 North El Cielo Road, Suite 470. 619-320-5761.
Victorville, California Office: 14011 Park Avenue, Suite 410. 619-243-7933.

(See Next Column)

MAC LACHLAN, BURFORD & ARIAS A LAW CORPORATION—*Continued*

Bruce D. Mac Lachlan
Ronald A. Burford
Joseph Arias
Michael W. Mugg
Dennis G. Popka
Leigh O. Harper (Resident, Palm Springs Office)
Clifford R. Cunningham (Resident, Rancho Cucamonga Office)
Dennis R. Stout
Sharon K. Burchett (Resident, Rancho Cucamonga Office)
Christopher D. Lockwood
Vernon C. Lauridsen (Resident, Rancho Cucamonga Office)
John G. Evans (Resident, Palm Springs Office)
Richard R. Hegner (Resident, Victorville Office)
Dennis J. Mahoney
Kathleen M. Keefe
Toni R. Fullerton
Mark R. Harris
Diana J. Carloni (Resident, Victorville Office)
Jean M. Landry
Frank M. Loo

Representative Clients: Aetna Life & Casualty; Automobile Club of Southern California; California State Automobile Association; City of San Bernardino; Reliance Insurance; Republic Insurance; Southern Pacific Transportation Co.; State Farm Fire and Casualty Co.; State Farm Mutual Automobile Insurance Co.; County of San Bernardino.

For full biographical listings, see the Martindale-Hubbell Law Directory

WILSON, BORROR, DUNN, SCOTT & DAVIS (AV)

Suite 307, The Bank of California Building, 255 North D Street, P.O. Box 540, 92401
Telephone: 909-884-8855
Fax: 909-884-5161

MEMBERS OF FIRM

Fred A. Wilson (1886-1973)
Wm. H. Wilson (1915-1981)
Caywood J. Borror
James R. Dunn
Richard L. Scott
Thomas M. Davis
Keith D. Davis

ASSOCIATES

Timothy P. Prince
Sarah L. Overton

Representative Clients: Travelers Insurance Co.; Rockwell International; Westinghouse Air Brake Co.; Goodyear Tire and Rubber Co.; Home Insurance Co.; Cities of: Redlands, Chino, Colton, San Bernardino and Upland; The Canadian Insurance Co.

For full biographical listings, see the Martindale-Hubbell Law Directory

*SAN DIEGO,** San Diego Co.

BELSKY & ASSOCIATES (AV)

610 West Ash Street, Suite 700, 92101
Telephone: 619-232-8300
Fax: 619-338-0066

Daniel S. Belsky

Gabriel M. Benrubi
Cynthia Brack McGrew
Vincent J. Iuliano
Laura L. Waterman

References: First National Bank; Kaiser Foundation Health Plan, Inc.; Norcal Mutual Insurance Company; Sharp Rees-Stealy Medical Group; Sharp Mission Park Medical Group; Southern California Physician Insurance Exchange.

For full biographical listings, see the Martindale-Hubbell Law Directory

CHAPIN, FLEMING & WINET, A PROFESSIONAL CORPORATION (AV)

1320 Columbia Street, 92101
Telephone: 619-232-4261
Telefax: 619-232-4840
Vista, California Office: 410 South Melrose Drive, Suite 101.
Telephone: 619-758-4261.
Telefax: 619-758-6420.
Los Angeles, California Office: 12121 Wilshire Boulevard, Suite 401.
Telephone: 310-826-4834.
Telefax: 310-207-4236.

Edward D. Chapin
George E. Fleming
Randall L. Winet (Resident, Vista Office)
Peter C. Ward
Roger L. Popeney
Lawrence W. Shea, II
Gregory S. Tavill
Aaron H. Katz
Maria C. Roberts
Shirley A. Gauvin
Kennett L. Patrick (Resident, Vista Office)
Terence L. Greene
Amy B. Vandeveld
Victor M. Barr, Jr.
Elizabeth J. Koumas
Leslie A. Greathouse
Kelli Jean Brooks
John F. Sahhar (Resident, Vista Office)
Andrew Nicholas Kohn
Frank L. Tobin
Shawn M. Robinson
Katherine M. Green
Dean G. Chandler (Resident, Vista Office)
Joseph A. Solomon
Victoria Chen
Jane Mobaldi
Dean A. Gonsonski
Daniel P. Murphy
Steven S. Richter
Gregory Kevin Hansen

(See Next Column)

OF COUNSEL

James Michael Zimmerman

For full biographical listings, see the Martindale-Hubbell Law Directory

FERRIS & BRITTON, A PROFESSIONAL CORPORATION (AV)

1600 First National Bank Center, 401 West A Street, 92101
Telephone: 619-233-3131
Fax: 619-232-9316

Christopher Q. Britton
Steven J. Pynes
Michael R. Weinstein

OF COUNSEL

Allan J. Reniche

Representative Clients: Allstate Insurance Co.; Cox Communications, Inc.; Enterprise Rent-a-Car; Exxon; Immuno Pharmaceutics, Inc.; Invitrogen Corporation; Maryland Casualty Co.; Teleport Communications Group; Southwest Airlines; Times-Mirror Cable Television.

For Complete List of Firm Personnel, See General Section

For full biographical listings, see the Martindale-Hubbell Law Directory

FRANCO BRADLEY & MARTORELLA (AV)

A Partnership of Professional Corporations
8880 Rio San Diego Drive, Suite 800, 92108
Telephone: 619-688-0080
Fax: 619-688-0081
Oakland, California Office: Suite 600, 1300 Clay Street.
Telephone: 510-466-6310.

MEMBERS OF THE FIRM

Elizabeth Franco Bradley (APC)
Daniel A. Martorella (APC)

OF COUNSEL

Charles A. Viviano (APC)

ASSOCIATES

Kerry Don Alexander
Elizabeth Leigh Bradley (Resident, Oakland, California)
Kathryn S. Clenney
Madeline Moriyama Clogston
Zoë G. Gruber
Kim Karels Resnick
Kenneth D. Richard
Daniel L. Rodriguez
Mary Crenshaw Tyler

For full biographical listings, see the Martindale-Hubbell Law Directory

HAASIS, POPE & CORRELL, A PROFESSIONAL CORPORATION (AV)

550 West "C" Street, 9th Floor, 92101-3509
Telephone: 619-236-9933
Fax: 619-236-8961
Voice Mail: 619-236-8955

Steven R. Haasis
A. Mark Pope
Thomas M. Correll
Harvey C. Berger
Kenneth E. Goates
William A. Calders
Robert V. Closson
Denis Long

Michael J. Wijas
Michelle M. Clark
Janelle Fike Garchie
A. David Mongan
Susan J. Gill
Mark R. VonderHaar
Nelson J. Goodin
Joan Creigh. Little
Wayne D. Thomas
Steven B. Bitter
David A. McMahon, Jr.
Terrell A. Quealy
Daniel C. Gallant

For full biographical listings, see the Martindale-Hubbell Law Directory

HILLYER & IRWIN, A PROFESSIONAL CORPORATION (AV)

550 West C Street, 16th Floor, 92101
Telephone: 619-234-6121
Telecopier: 619-595-1313

Howard A. Allen
Murray T. S. Lewis
Michael F. Millerick
Steven M. Hill

For full biographical listings, see the Martindale-Hubbell Law Directory

NEIL, DYMOTT, PERKINS, BROWN & FRANK, A PROFESSIONAL CORPORATION (AV)

1010 Second Avenue, Suite 2500, 92101-4959
Telephone: 619-238-1712
Fax: 619-238-1562

Michael I. Neil
Thomas M. Dymott
Roger G. Perkins
David G. Brown
Robert W. Frank
Gina L. Lacagnina
Robert W. Harrison

Reference: 1st Interstate Bank - San Diego.

For full biographical listings, see the Martindale-Hubbell Law Directory

San Diego—Continued

RICE FOWLER BOOTH & BANNING (AV)

Emerald - Shapery Center, 402 W. Broadway, Suite 850, 92101
Telephone: 619-230-0030
Telecopier: 619-230-1350
New Orleans, Louisiana Office: 36th Floor, Place St. Charles, 201 St. Charles Avenue, 70130
Telephone: 504-523-2600.
Telecopier: 504-523-2705.
Telex: 9102507910. ELN: 62548910.
London, England Office: Suite 692, Level 6 Lloyd's, 1 Lime Street, London EC3M 7DQ England.
Telephone: 071-327-4222.
Telecopier: 071-929-0043.
San Francisco, California Office: Embarcadero Center West, 275 Battery Street, 27th Floor, 94111.
Telephone: 415-399-9191.
Telecopier: 415-399-9192.
Telex: 451981.
Beijing, China Office: Beijing International Convention Centre, Suite 7024, No. 8 Beichendong Road, Chaoyang District, 100101, P.R.C.
Telephone: (861) 493-4250.
Telecopier: (861) 493-4251.
Bogota, Colombia Office: Avenida Jimenez #4-03 Officina 10-05.
Telephone: (571) 342-1062.
Telecopier: (571) 342-1062.

PARTNERS

William L. Banning
Keith Zakarin
Robert B. Krueger, Jr.

ASSOCIATE

Juan Carlos Dominguez

For full biographical listings, see the Martindale-Hubbell Law Directory

ROYCE, GRIMM, VRANJES, MCCORMICK & GRAHAM (AV)

A Partnership including Professional Corporations
185 West "F" Street, Suite 200, 92101-6098
Telephone: 619-231-8802
Fax: 619-233-6039
Temecula, California Office: 41877 Enterprise Circle North, Suite 100. 92590.
Telephone: 909-695-3220.

MEMBERS OF FIRM

Gene E. Royce (Professional Corporation)
W. Patrick Grimm (Professional Corporation)
Mark Vranjes (Professional Corporation)
Kathleen McCormick
Kevin R. Graham
A. Carl Yaeckel
Jeffrey Y. Greer

Charles A. Phillips
Stephen M. Hogan
Lisa F. Butler
Gregory D. Stephan
Brian L. Frary
Leslie H. Roe
Michael B. Martin
Larry D. Letofsky
Laurel L. Barry
Michael B Schaefer

For full biographical listings, see the Martindale-Hubbell Law Directory

WINGERT, GREBING, ANELLO & BRUBAKER (AV)

A Partnership including Professional Corporations
One America Plaza, Seventh Floor, 600 West Broadway, 92101-3370
Telephone: 619-232-8151
Facsimile: 619-232-4665

MEMBERS OF FIRM

John R. Wingert (A Professional Corporation)
Charles R. Grebing (A Professional Corporation)
Michael M. Anello (A Professional Corporation)
Alan K. Brubaker (A Professional Corporation)
Norman A. Ryan
James Goodwin
Robert M. Caietti
Eileen Mulligan Marks
Christopher W. Todd
Robert L. Johnson
Douglas J. Simpson
Shawn D. Morris
Robert M. Juskie

ASSOCIATES

Julie E. Saake
Michael Sullivan
John S. Addams
Carolyn P. Gallinghouse
Michael S. Burke
Kimberly I. Cary
Terie M. Theis
James P. Broder
James J. Brown, Jr.
Sara A. Henry
Sarah F. Burke
Beverly A. Kalasky
Craig Gross

OF COUNSEL

William L. Todd, Jr.

Representative Clients: California Casualty Insurance Co.; Farmers Insurance Group; The Ohio Casualty Group; United Services Automobile Assn.; Transamerica Insurance Group; United States Fidelity & Guaranty Co.

For full biographical listings, see the Martindale-Hubbell Law Directory

*SAN FRANCISCO,** San Francisco Co.

ADAMS, DUQUE & HAZELTINE (AV)

A Partnership including Professional Corporations
500 Washington Street, 94111
Telephone: 415-982-1240
FAX: 415-982-0130
Los Angeles, California Office: 777 South Figueroa Street, Tenth Floor.
Telephone: 213-620-1240.
FAX: 213-896-5500.

MEMBERS OF FIRM

James R. Willcox
George G. Weickhardt
Joseph M. Rimac, Jr.
David R. Shane

ASSOCIATES

Ann Sparkman
Marilyn A. Rogers
Anna Maria Martin
John C. Barker
Robert J. Taitz

For Complete List of Firm Personnel, See General Section

For full biographical listings, see the Martindale-Hubbell Law Directory

BOUGHEY, GARVIE & BUSHNER (AV)

One Post Street, 24th Floor, 94104-5228
Telephone: 415-398-4500
Telex: WU 408661
FAX: 415-398-2455

MEMBERS OF FIRM

James D. Boughey
Robert C. Garvie
Ronald S. Bushner

Donald A. Velez, Jr.
Eileen R. Ridley
Christine M. Renne
Nicholas R. Mack
Lawrence D. Goldberg
Todd Holcomb
Jeffrey George Benz
Ginger M. English

For full biographical listings, see the Martindale-Hubbell Law Directory

FLYNN, DELICH & WISE (AV)

Suite 1750, 580 California Street, 94104
Telephone: 415-693-5566
Fax: 415-693-0410
Long Beach, California Office: 1 World Trade Center, Suite 1800.
Telephone: 310-435-2626.
Fax: 310-437-7555.

John Allen Flynn
Sam D. Delich
James B. Nebel

Representative Clients: American Hawaii Cruises; Holland America Line; Through Transport Mutual Insurance Association, Ltd.; The Britannia Steam Ship Insurance Association Limited; The Steamship Mutual Underwriting Association (Bermuda) Ltd.; General Steamship Corp., Ltd.; Commodore Cruise Line, Ltd.; Interocean Steamship Corporation; Sea-Land Service, Inc.; Hatteras Yachts.

For full biographical listings, see the Martindale-Hubbell Law Directory

GUDMUNDSON, SIGGINS, STONE & SKINNER (AV)

One Embarcadero Center, Suite 1350, 94111
Telephone: 415-391-4200
FAX: 415-989-4739

MEMBERS OF FIRM

Richard J. Siggins
Harold A. Stone
Jeffrey A. Skinner
Francis M. McKeown

ASSOCIATES

Mark A. Hagopian
Paul F. Sherman
Eve M. Felitti

OF COUNSEL

W. W. Gudmundson

For full biographical listings, see the Martindale-Hubbell Law Directory

HARDIMAN, HA & OLSON, A LAW PARTNERSHIP (AV)

Spear Street Tower, Forty First Floor, One Market Street, 94105
Telephone: 415-267-7200
Fax: 415-512-9136
Torrance, California Office: Union Bank Tower, 21515 Hawthorne, Suite 590.
Telephone: 310-792-5200.

Michael F. Hardiman
Gloria Sung-Yun Ha

For full biographical listings, see the Martindale-Hubbell Law Directory

San Francisco—Continued

ROBERT A. HARLEM, INC. & ASSOCIATES A PROFESSIONAL CORPORATION (AV)

120 Montgomery Street, Suite 2410, 94104
Telephone: 415-981-1801
Fax: 415-981-5815

Robert A. Harlem

B. Mark Fong

OF COUNSEL

Patricia Knight
Jack Miller

For full biographical listings, see the Martindale-Hubbell Law Directory

KINCAID, GIANUNZIO, CAUDLE & HUBERT, A PROFESSIONAL CORPORATION (AV)

221 Main Street, Suite 1300, 94105
Telephone: 415-543-6212
Telecopier: 415-543-1134
Oakland, California Office: 200 Webster Street, P.O. Box 1828.
Telephone: 510-465-5212.
Telecopier: 510-465-0362.
Walnut Creek, California Office: Suite 400, 500 Ygnacio Valley Road.
Telephone: 510-930-9111.
Telecopier: 510-930-9346.

Garry J. D. Hubert
Shawn M. Throwe

Steven E. McDonald
Darrel K. Yasutake
Jean M. Curtis
Leilani F. Battiste

Representative Clients: Farmers Insurance Exchange; Geico; Maryland Casualty Co.; State Farm Mutual Automobile Insurance Co.; Utica Insurance Co.

For full biographical listings, see the Martindale-Hubbell Law Directory

LEACH, MCGREEVY, BAUTISTA & BRASS (AV)

1735 Pacific Avenue, 94109
Telephone: 415-775-4455
Telefax: 415-775-7435
Southern California Office: 13643 Fifth Street, Chino, 91710.
Telephone: 909-590-2224.

Theodore Tamba (1900-1973)
David G. Leach
John T. Harmon (1928-1993)
Richard E. McGreevy
M. Francis Brass

A. Marquez Bautista
J. Curtis Cox
Teresa A. Cunningham
Paul David Katerndahl

OF COUNSEL

Roger G. Eliassen
Lloyd F. Postel
Robert W. Shinnick

For full biographical listings, see the Martindale-Hubbell Law Directory

MORTON & LACY (AV)

Suite 2280, Three Embarcadero Center, 94111-3614
Telephone: 415-296-9000
Facsimile: 415-398-3295

Thomas E. Morton
Alan E. Lacy

ASSOCIATES

Jeremy Sugerman
David H. Bennett
Deborah M. Hall

For full biographical listings, see the Martindale-Hubbell Law Directory

RICE FOWLER BOOTH & BANNING (AV)

Embarcadero Center West, 275 Battery Street, 27th Floor, 94111
Telephone: 415-399-9191
Telecopier: 415-399-9192
Telex: 451981
New Orleans, Louisiana Office: Place St. Charles, 36th Floor, 201 St. Charles Avenue, 70130.
Telephone: 504-523-2600.
Telecopier: 504-523-2705.
Telex: 9102507910. ELN 62548910.
San Diego, California Office: Emerald-Shapery Center, 402 W. Broadway, Suite 850, 92101.
Telephone: 619-230-0030.
Telecopier: 619-230-1350.
London, England Office: Suite 692, Level 6 Lloyd's, 1 Lime Street, London EC3M 7DQ England.
Telephone: 071-327-4222.
Telecopier: 071-929-0043.
Beijing, China Office: Beijing International Convention Centre, Suite 7024, No. 8 Beichendong Road, Chaoyang District, 100101, P.R.C.
Telephone: (861) 493-4250.
Telecopier: (861) 493-4251.

(See Next Column)

Bogota, Colombia Office: Avenida Jimenez #4-03 Oficina 10-05, Bogota, Colombia.
Telephone: (571) 342-1062.
Telecopier: (571) 342-1062.

MEMBERS OF FIRM

Forrest Booth
Kurt L. Micklow
Norman J. Ronneberg, Jr.

ASSOCIATES

Cynthia L. Mitchell
Kim O. Dincel
Lynn Haggerty King
Amy Jo Poor
Edward M. Bull, III
Janice Amenta-Jones
Heidi Loken Benas

For full biographical listings, see the Martindale-Hubbell Law Directory

ST. CLAIR, MCFETRIDGE, GRIFFIN & LEGERNES, A PROFESSIONAL CORPORATION (AV)

Suite 1400 Telesis Tower, One Montgomery Street, 94104
Telephone: 415-421-2462
Fax: 415-397-1526

Edward J. McFetridge (1931-1991)
Bruce Legernes
Curtis R. Ponzi
Anthony Griffin
Michael M. Ierulli

Birgit A. Dachtera
Gayle L. Gough
Stefanie T. Sharp
Joyce A. Winters

OF COUNSEL

John D. St. Clair
C. D. Zappettini

Representative Clients: Firemen's Fund; Atlantic Mutual Insurance Co.; Proctor & Gamble; General Motors Corp.; Hertz Corp.; Royal Globe Insurance Group; Industrial Indemnity Co.; Navistar.

For full biographical listings, see the Martindale-Hubbell Law Directory

SARRAIL, LYNCH & HALL (AV)

44 Montgomery Street, 34th Floor, 94104
Telephone: 415-398-2404
Fax: 415-391-9076

Stephen W. Hall (1955-1993)
Linda J. Lynch
James A. Sarrail
Bruce C. F. McArthur

Michael J. Ruggles
Jonathan S. Larsen
David Y. Wong
Susan A. Byron
Todd M. Barnett
Ernest D. Faitos
Frances H. Yoshimura

LEGAL SUPPORT PERSONNEL

Cynthia R. Benzerara

For full biographical listings, see the Martindale-Hubbell Law Directory

SCADDEN, HAMILTON & RYAN (AV)

580 California Street, Suite 1400, 94104
Telephone: 415-362-5116
Facsimile: 415-362-4214

James G. Scadden
Robert P. Hamilton
Robert J. Ryan

James P. Cunningham
Julie M. Sinclair
James F. Hetherington
Charles O. Thompson
Eileen Santana Wright

For full biographical listings, see the Martindale-Hubbell Law Directory

STUBBS, HITTIG & LEONE, A PROFESSIONAL CORPORATION (AV)

Suite 818, Fox Plaza, 1390 Market Street, 94102-5399
Telephone: 415-861-8200
Telecopier: 415-861-6700

Gregory E. Stubbs
H. Christopher Hittig
Louis A. Leone

For full biographical listings, see the Martindale-Hubbell Law Directory

THORNTON, TAYLOR, DOWNS, BECKER, TOLSON & DOHERTY (AV)

A Partnership including Professional Corporations
16th Floor, 505 Sansome Street, 94111
Telephone: 415-421-8890
Fax: 415-421-0688

MEMBERS OF FIRM

H.A. Thornton (1887-1953)
Pamela Wilson Levin
Evans M. Taylor (1903-1991)
Clarke B. Holland
Otto F. Becker
Jonathan H. Erb
Greg S. Tolson (P.C.)
Phillip F. Shinn
Francis X. Doherty (P.C.)
Patrick J. Bailey

(See Next Column)

THORNTON, TAYLOR, DOWNS, BECKER, TOLSON & DOHERTY, *San Francisco—Continued*

ASSOCIATES

David B. A. Demo
Mary M. Drinan
Brendan J. Fogarty
Stephen F. Henry
Mark S. Julius
Elizabeth A. Tosaris
Marna A. Mitchell
Michael A. Papuc
Cindy L. Seeley
Stephan T. Pastis
Sandra E. Stone
Stephan L. Eberle
Fiel D. Tigno

OF COUNSEL

Jerome F. Downs
Michael F. Scully

For full biographical listings, see the Martindale-Hubbell Law Directory

VOGL & MEREDITH (AV)

456 Montgomery Street, 20th Floor, 94104
Telephone: 415-398-0200
Facsimile: 415-398-2820

Samuel E. Meredith
David R. Vogl
Bryan A. Marmesh
John P. Walovich
Jean N. Yeh
Janet Brayer
Thomas S. Clifton (Resident)

George C. Leal

For full biographical listings, see the Martindale-Hubbell Law Directory

*SAN JOSE,** Santa Clara Co.

CAMPBELL, WARBURTON, BRITTON, FITZSIMMONS & SMITH, A PROFESSIONAL CORPORATION (AV)

Suite 1200, 101 Park Center Plaza, P.O. Box 1867, 95113
Telephone: 408-295-7701
Fax: 408-295-1423

Austen D. Warburton
Willard R. Campbell
John R. Fitzsimmons, Jr.
C. Michael Smith
Ralph E. Mendell
Nicholas Pastore
J. Michael Fitzsimmons

William R. Colucci
Carolyn M. Rose

Representative Corporate Clients: Marriott Corp.; Swenson Builders; Helene Curtis, Inc.; Viking Freight Systems.
Representative Insurance Clients: California State Automobile Assn.; Farmers Insurance Group; Travelers Insurance Co.; Westfield Insurance Cos.; Michelin Tire Corp. (Self Insured).

For Complete List of Firm Personnel, See General Section

For full biographical listings, see the Martindale-Hubbell Law Directory

COLLINS & SCHLOTHAUER (AV)

An Association of Attorneys including a Professional Corporation
60 South Market Street, Suite 1100, 95113-2369
Telephone: 408-298-5161
Fax: 408-297-5766

Mark Scott Collins (Inc.)
Steven J. Plas
David N. Poll
Linda L. Duiven
Michael P. Dunn
Jovita Prestoza

Representative Clients: Unigard Insurance; Farmers Insurance Co.; Fire Insurance Exchange; National American Insurance Co.; American Hardware Mutual Insurance; ABAG (Association of Bay Area Governmental Entities).

For full biographical listings, see the Martindale-Hubbell Law Directory

HINSHAW, WINKLER, DRAA, MARSH & STILL (AV)

152 North Third Street, Suite 300, P.O. Box 15030, 95115-0030
Telephone: 408-293-5959
Fax: 408-280-0966

MEMBERS OF FIRM

Edward A. Hinshaw
Tyler G. Draa
Gerhard O. Winkler
Barry C. Marsh
Thomas E. Still

ASSOCIATES

Lynne Thaxter Brown
Bradford J. Hinshaw
Jennifer H. Still
Megan A. Smith

For full biographical listings, see the Martindale-Hubbell Law Directory

ROBINSON & WOOD, INC. (AV)

227 North First Street, 95113
Telephone: 408-298-7120

(See Next Column)

Archie S. Robinson
Weldon S. Wood
Thomas R. Fellows
David S. Henningsen
Hugh F. Lennon
Jesse F. Ruiz
Christian B. Nielsen
Jonathan L. Lee
Roberta M. Knapp
Jon B. Zimmerman
Mark B. Schellerup
Andrew W. Olsson
Erica R. Yew
Arthur J. Casey
Joseph C. Balestrieri

John L. Winchester, III
Chadney C. Ankele
Robert A. Nakamae
Kathleen M. Malone
Rebecca L. Moon
Wendy R. Flockhart
Gregory J. Antoniono
Wendy Woolpert
Daniel K. Janish

For full biographical listings, see the Martindale-Hubbell Law Directory

ROHLFF, HOWIE & FRISCHHOLZ (AV)

150 Almaden Boulevard Suite 400, 95113
Telephone: 408-286-1100
Fax: 408-286-5285

MEMBERS OF FIRM

Yale W. Rohlff
Robert G. Howie
Barbara J. Frischholz
Nancy L. Peterson
Michael A. Penfield
James S. Gottesman
Donn Waslif

For full biographical listings, see the Martindale-Hubbell Law Directory

VAN LOUCKS & HANLEY (AV)

First American Building, 160 West Santa Clara Street, Suite 1050, 95113
Telephone: 408-287-2773
Fax: 408-297-5480

Geoffrey Van Loucks
Anthony L. Hanley

Michael K. Budra
Laura Uddenberg

Reference: San Jose National Bank.

For full biographical listings, see the Martindale-Hubbell Law Directory

*SAN LUIS OBISPO,** San Luis Obispo Co.

SMITH, HELENIUS & HAYES, A LAW CORPORATION (AV)

Railroad Square, P.O. Box 1446, 93406
Telephone: 805-544-8100
Facsimile: 805-544-4381

J. Edmund Smith
Christopher A. Helenius
Carl E. Hayes
Linda D. Hurst
A. David Medeiros
Kevin J. Smith
Christopher J. Duenow
Shae Kolby

For full biographical listings, see the Martindale-Hubbell Law Directory

*SANTA ANA,** Orange Co.

ALLEN, RHODES & SOBELSOHN (AV)

200 West Santa Ana Boulevard, Suite 950, 92701
Telephone: 714-558-7566
Los Angeles, California Office: 10866 Wilshire Boulevard, Suite 200.
Telephone: 310-475-0875; 213-879-9660.
Ontario, California Office: One Lakeshore Centre, 3282 Guasti Road, Suite 800.
Telephone: 909-395-0356.
Santa Barbara, California Office: 125 East De La Guerra.
Telephone: 805-965-5236.
Palm Springs, California Office: 73-710 Fred Waring Drive, Suite 210.
Telephone: 619-776-6830.

MEMBERS OF FIRM

Richard D. Pesota
Juan S. M. Pichardo

ASSOCIATES

Howard Lemberg
Kenneth A. Wong
Michael G. Glover

Reference: Bank of America.

For full biographical listings, see the Martindale-Hubbell Law Directory

CASSIDY, WARNER, BROWN, COMBS & THURBER, A PROFESSIONAL CORPORATION (AV)

600 West Santa Ana Boulevard, Suite 700, 92701
Telephone: 714-835-9431
Fax: 714-835-5264

Alvin M. Cassidy
B. Kent Warner
Joe R. Brown
A. Bennett Combs
David K. Thurber
Timothy X. Lane
Bruce A. Winstead

(See Next Column)

CASSIDY, WARNER, BROWN, COMBS & THURBER A PROFESSIONAL CORPORATION—*Continued*

Lloyd W. Felver
John A. Monkvic
David C. Olson
Dale L. Pomerantz
Glen A. Stebens
Robert E. Tarozzi

For full biographical listings, see the Martindale-Hubbell Law Directory

GARRETT & JENSEN (AV)

433 Civic Center Drive, West, P.O. Box 22002, 92702-2002
Telephone: 714-550-0100
Fax: 714-550-0471
Riverside, California Office: 3403 10th Street, Suite 700.
Telephone: 714-781-0222.

MEMBERS OF FIRM

Boyd F. Jensen, II
Betty Fracisco
Mark S. Armijo
Jennifer Malone

OF COUNSEL

Kenneth R. Garrett

Representative Clients: Allstate Insurance Co.; Automobile Club of Southern California; Fireman's Fund American Insurance Co.; Government Employees Insurance Co.

For full biographical listings, see the Martindale-Hubbell Law Directory

HAIGHT, BROWN & BONESTEEL (AV)

A Partnership including Professional Corporations
Suite 900, 5 Hutton Centre Drive, 92707
Telephone: 714-754-1100
Telecopier: 714-754-0826
Santa Monica, California Office: 1620 26th Street, Suite 4000 North, P.O. Box 680.
Telephone: 310-449-6000.
Telecopier: 310-829-5117.
Telex: 705837.
Riverside, California Office: 3750 University Avenue, Suite 650.
Telephone: 909-341-8300.
Fax: 909-341-8309.

RESIDENT MEMBERS

Ronald C. Kline (A Professional Corporation)
Bruce L. Cleeland
Jay T. Thompson

ASSOCIATES

Paul N. Jacobs
Laura M. Knox (Resident)
Jeffrey S. Gerardo (Resident)

Counsel for: Orange County: Aetna Casualty and Surety Co.; Zurich-American Insurance Cos.; Industrial Indemnity Co.; Professional Liability Claims Managers; Maryland Casualty Insurance Co.; Royal Insurance Company of America.

For Complete List of Firm Personnel, See General Section

For full biographical listings, see the Martindale-Hubbell Law Directory

HOWARD, MOSS, LOVEDER, STRICKROTH & WALKER (AV)

A Partnership including Professional Corporations
2677 North Main Street, Suite 800, 92701-1226
Telephone: 714-542-6300
Telecopier: 714-542-6987
Riverside, California Office: 4505 Allstate Drive, Suite 3.
Telephone: 909-341-8353.
Telecopier: 909-275-9637.
San Diego, California Office: 12526 High Bluff Drive, Suite 290.
Telephone: 916-792-3450.

PARTNERS

Theodore R. Howard (A Professional Corporation)
Robert J. Moss (A Professional Corporation)
James E. Loveder
Michael J. Strickroth
Robert A. Walker (Resident, Riverside, California Office)
Margaret M. Parker
Michael F. Moran

ASSOCIATES

Eugene Edward Keller II
Anthony J. Dunne
Mitchell L. Leverett (Resident, Riverside Office)

For full biographical listings, see the Martindale-Hubbell Law Directory

LANCASTER & ASSOCIATES (AV)

313 North Birch Street, P.O. Box 22021, 92701-2021
Telephone: 714-836-1411
Fax: 714-836-9930

Michael J. Lancaster

ASSOCIATE

Dieter Zacher

For full biographical listings, see the Martindale-Hubbell Law Directory

*SANTA BARBARA,** Santa Barbara Co.

ALLEN, RHODES & SOBELSOHN (AV)

125 East De La Guerra, 93101
Telephone: 805-965-5236
Los Angeles, California Office: 10866 Wilshire Boulevard, Suite 200.
Telephone: 310-475-0875; 213-879-9660.
Ontario, California Office: One Lakeshore Centre, 3281 Guasti Road, Suite 800.
Telephone: 909-395-0356.
Santa Ana, California Office: 200 West Santa Ana Boulevard, Suite 950.
Telephone: 714-558-7566.
Palm Springs, California Office: 73-710 Fred Waring Drive, Suite 210.
Telephone: 619-776-6830.

MEMBERS OF FIRM

Michael E. Johnson
James C. Shipley

Tracy (Uran) Sturtevant

Reference: Bank of America.

For full biographical listings, see the Martindale-Hubbell Law Directory

*SANTA CRUZ,** Santa Cruz Co.

ATCHISON, ANDERSON, HURLEY & BARISONE, A PROFESSIONAL CORPORATION (AV)

333 Church Street, 95060
Telephone: 408-423-8383
Fax: 408-423-9401
Salinas, California Office: 137 Central Avenue, Suite 6. 93901.
Telephone: 408-755-7833.
Fax: 408-753-0293.

Rodney R. Atchison
Neal R. Anderson (1947-1986)
Vincent P. Hurley
John G. Barisone

Justin B. Lighty
Mitchell A. Jackman
David Y. Imai
Anthony P. Condotti
Mary C. Logan

Counsel for: City of Santa Cruz.

For full biographical listings, see the Martindale-Hubbell Law Directory

SANTA MONICA, Los Angeles Co.

DICKSON, CARLSON & CAMPILLO (AV)

120 Broadway, Suite 300, P.O. Box 2122, 90407-2122
Telephone: 310-451-2273
Telecopier: 310-451-9071

Robert L. Dickson
Jeffery J. Carlson
Ralph A. Campillo
William B. Fitzgerald
Hall R. Marston
Roxanne M. Wilson

For Complete List of Firm Personnel, See General Section

For full biographical listings, see the Martindale-Hubbell Law Directory

HAIGHT, BROWN & BONESTEEL (AV)

A Partnership including Professional Corporations
1620 26th Street, Suite 4000 North, P.O. Box 680, 90404
Telephone: 310-449-6000
Telecopier: 310-829-5117
Telex: 705837
Santa Ana, California Office: Suite 900, 5 Hutton Centre Drive.
Telephone: 714-754-1100.
Telecopier: 714-754-0826.
Riverside, California Office: 3750 University Avenue, Suite 650.
Telephone: 909-341-8300.
Fax: 909-341-8309.
San Francisco, California Office: Suite 300, 201 Sansome Street.
Telephone: 415-986-7700.
Fax: 415-986-6945.

MEMBERS OF FIRM

William K. Koska (A Professional Corporation)
Peter Q. Ezzell (A Professional Corporation)
William G. Baumgaertner (A Professional Corporation)
Peter A. Dubrawski
J. R. Seashore
Kevin R. Crisp
Lee Marshall
Steven E. Moyer
Frank Kendo Berfield (Resident, San Francisco Office)
Kenneth G. Anderson
William O. Martin, Jr.

ASSOCIATES

Ted J. Duffy
David C. McGovern
Lisa K. Sepe
Alicia E. Taylor
Elizabeth A. Livesay
S. Christian Stouder
Michael J. Sipos
Nancy W. Carman
Michael H. Gottschlich
Stacey R. Konkoff

(See Next Column)

HAIGHT, BROWN & BONESTEEL, *Santa Monica—Continued*

For Complete List of Firm Personnel, See General Section

For full biographical listings, see the Martindale-Hubbell Law Directory

KOHRS & FISKE (AV)

3250 Ocean Park Boulevard, 90405
Telephone: 310-452-5524
Telecopier: 310-452-6115

MEMBERS OF FIRM

Conrad Kohrs
J. Peter Fiske
Chad M. Steur
Michelle R. Williams

LEGAL SUPPORT PERSONNEL

Sarah Elizabeth Robbins

Reference: Bank of America.

For full biographical listings, see the Martindale-Hubbell Law Directory

SANTA ROSA, * Sonoma Co.

BELDEN, ABBEY, WEITZENBERG & KELLY, A PROFESSIONAL CORPORATION (AV)

1105 North Dutton Avenue, P.O. Box 1566, 95402
Telephone: 707-542-5050
Telecopier: 707-542-2589

Thomas P. Kelly, Jr.
Candace H. Shirley

Representative Clients: Exchange Bank of Santa Rosa; Westamerica Bank; North Bay Title Co.; Northwestern Title Security Co.; Geyser Peak Winery; Arrowood Vineyards & Winery; Hansel Ford; Santa Rosa City School District.

For Complete List of Firm Personnel, See General Section

For full biographical listings, see the Martindale-Hubbell Law Directory

THE LAW OFFICES OF CAMPBELL, ANDERSON, CASEY, SINK & JOHNSON A PROFESSIONAL CORPORATION (AV)

Suite 202, 3333 Mendocino Avenue, 95403
Telephone: 707-525-8200
Fax: 707-525-0435

Thomas A. Campbell
William D. Anderson
Michael J. Casey
Thomas Reed Sink
John E. Johnson

OF COUNSEL

Ellen D. Vogt

For full biographical listings, see the Martindale-Hubbell Law Directory

TARZANA, Los Angeles Co.

WASSERMAN, COMDEN & CASSELMAN (AV)

5567 Reseda Boulevard, Suite 330, P.O. Box 7033, 91357-7033
Telephone: 818-705-6800; 213-872-0995
Fax: 818-345-0162; 818-996-8266

MEMBERS OF FIRM

Steve K. Wasserman
Leonard J. Comden
David B. Casselman
Clifford H. Pearson
Mark S. Roth
Rebecca J. Schroer
Jay N. Rosenwald
Daniel E. Lewis
Crystal A. Zarpas
Gary S. Soter

ASSOCIATES

Joel Fischman
Jeffrey K. Jayson
Catherine Stevenson Garcia
Glenn A. Brown, Jr.
Robin F. Genchel
Lloyd S. Mann
J. Christopher Bennington
Paul H. Lasky
Norman L. Pearl
Todd A. Chamberlain
Howard S. Blum
Ted G. Schwartz
Richard A. Brownstein
Albert G. Turner, Jr.
Kenneth M. Jones
Sharon Zemel
Robert T. Leonard
Stephen D. Adler
Keith Nussbaum
L. Stephen Albright
John A. Raymond
Penny L. Wheat
Caroline S. Manankichian

OF COUNSEL

Cecilia S. Wu
John P. Doyle

Representative Clients: Toplis & Harding; Appalachian Insurance; Lumbermens Mutual Insurance Co.; State Farm Fire and Casualty Co.; Factory Mutual Engineering; Cravens, Dargan & Co.; Lloyd's of London.

For full biographical listings, see the Martindale-Hubbell Law Directory

TORRANCE, Los Angeles Co.

HARDIMAN, HA & OLSON, A LAW PARTNERSHIP (AV)

Union Bank Tower, 21515 Hawthorne, Suite 590, 90503
Telephone: 310-792-5200
San Francisco, California Office: Spear Street Tower, Forty First Floor, One Market Street.
Telephone: 415-267-7200.
Fax: 415-512-9136.

Glen R. Olson

For full biographical listings, see the Martindale-Hubbell Law Directory

VENTURA, * Ventura Co.

ENGLE & BRIDE (AV)

353 San Jon Road, 93001
Telephone: 805-643-2200
Fax: 805-643-3062

MEMBERS OF FIRM

Benjamin J. Engle
Robert F. Bride

ASSOCIATES

Walter M. Leighton
Daniel J. Carobine
Gary M. Schumacher
Matthew P. Guasco

For full biographical listings, see the Martindale-Hubbell Law Directory

WALNUT CREEK, Contra Costa Co.

ANDERSON, GALLOWAY & LUCCHESE, A PROFESSIONAL CORPORATION (AV)

1676 North California Boulevard, Suite 500, 94596-4183
Telephone: 510-943-6383
Facsimile: 510-943-7542

Robert L. Anderson
George Patrick Galloway
David R. Lucchese
Martin J. Everson
Thomas J. Donnelly
Ralph J. Smith
James M. Nelson
Scott E. Murray
Henry E. Needham
Stephen F. Lucey
David A. Depolo
Karen A. Sparks
Stephen J. Brooks
James J. Zenere
Joseph S. Picchi
Coleen L. Welch
Deborah C. Moritz-Farr
Marc G. Cowden
Lauren E. Tate
Erin C. Ruddy
Lea K. McMahan

For full biographical listings, see the Martindale-Hubbell Law Directory

KINCAID, GIANUNZIO, CAUDLE & HUBERT, A PROFESSIONAL CORPORATION (AV)

Suite 400, 500 Ygnacio Valley Road, 94596
Telephone: 510-930-9111
Telecopier: 510-930-9346
Oakland, California Office: 200 Webster Street, P.O. Box 1828.
Telephone: 510-465-5212.
Telecopier: 510-465-0362.
San Francisco, California Office: 221 Main Street, Suite 1300.
Telephone: 415-543-6212.
Telecopier: 415-543-1134.

John P. Caudle
John F. Van De Poel, Jr.
Deanne B. Politeo
Marjorie J. Heinrich

Marilyn E. Siegel
Daniel L. Dees
Roger Kent Miles
Gareth J. Umipeg
André Robert Hill
Judith Ann Pemberton
Steven L. Jawgiel
Sharon L. Ceasar
Gregory H. McCormick
Elizabeth S. Kim

Representative Clients: Farmers Insurance Exchange; Geico; Maryland Casualty Co.; State Farm Mutual Automobile Insurance Co.; Utica Insurance Co.

For full biographical listings, see the Martindale-Hubbell Law Directory

McNAMARA, HOUSTON, DODGE, McCLURE & NEY (AV)

1211 Newell Avenue, Second Floor, P.O. Box 5288, 94596-1288
Telephone: 510-939-5330
Facsimile: 510-939-0203
Fairfield, California Office: 639 Kentucky Street, Suite 110.
Telephone: 707-427-3998.
Fax: 707-427-0268.

MEMBERS OF FIRM

William K. Houston, Jr.
Richard E. Dodge
Douglas C. McClure
Michael J. Ney
Thomas G. Beatty
Robert M. Slattery
Thomas E. Pfalzer
William J. Diffenderfer (Resident, Fairfield Office)
Linda J. Seifert
Guy D. Borges (Resident at Fairfield Office)
Raymond L. MacKay
Roger J. Brothers

(See Next Column)

McNamara, Houston, Dodge, McClure & Ney—*Continued*

ASSOCIATES

Dianne Kremen Colville
Stuart C. Gilliam
Ricardo A. Martinez
R. Dewey Wheeler
Ellen H. Nolting
Kim E. McBride
Jane Luciano
Lisa R. Roberts
Martin J. Ambacher
Janet Sirlin Roberts (Resident, Fairfield Office)
Denise Billups-Slone
Natalie A. Meyer
Kathleen A. Nelson (Resident at Fairfield Office)
Jeffrey D. Hosking
Todd M. Green
Brendan J. Dooley
Jon A. Turigliatto
Brett M. Witter
Joseph E. Finkel
Edward M. Callaghan
Michael K. Walton (Resident, Fairfield Office)
John Wesley Smith
Donald A. Odell
Jenifer Kuhn

OF COUNSEL

Daniel J. McNamara

Representative Clients: Allstate Insurance Co.; Canadian Indemnity Co.; Chubb Group of Insurance Cos.; Kaiser-Permanente Medical Group; Medical Insurance Exchange of California; California State Automobile Assn.; Farmers Insurance Group.

For full biographical listings, see the Martindale-Hubbell Law Directory

WESTLAKE VILLAGE, Ventura Co.

Michaelis, Montanari & Johnson, A Professional Law Corporation (AV)

2829 Townsgate Road, Suite 150, 91361
Telephone: 805-371-4611
Fax: 805-371-4617

James I. Michaelis
James P. Johnson
Garry L. Montanari

Gary J. LaPook
Michael D. Pilla
Miriam Piwoz Goodman
Wesley S. Wenig

For full biographical listings, see the Martindale-Hubbell Law Directory

COLORADO

*COLORADO SPRINGS,** El Paso Co.

Kane, Donley & Shaffer (AV)

90 South Cascade Avenue, Suite 1100, P.O. Box 1119, 80901
Telephone: 719-471-1650
Fax: 719-471-1663

MEMBERS OF FIRM

Jerry A. Donley
E. William Shaffer, Jr.
Thomas Kelly Kane
Mark H. Kane
Jack E. Donley

ASSOCIATES

William A. Palmer
Hayden W. Kane, II

OF COUNSEL

Hayden W. Kane

Representative Clients: American States Insurance Co.; Hawkeye-Security Insurance Co.
Reference: Norwest Bank of Colorado Springs.

For full biographical listings, see the Martindale-Hubbell Law Directory

Retherford, Mullen, Johnson & Bruce (AV)

A Partnership including Professional Corporations
415 South Sahwatch, P.O. Box 1580, 80901
Telephone: 719-475-2014
Fax: 719-630-1267
Pueblo, Colorado Office: Suite 510, 201 West 8th Street, 81003.
Telephone: 719-543-7181.
Fax: 719-543-5650.

MEMBERS OF FIRM

Jerry A. Retherford
J. Stephen Mullen (P.C.)
Anthony A. Johnson (P.C.)
Neil C. Bruce
Thomas J. Barton (P.C.)
Patrick R. Salt
J. Ronald Voss

ASSOCIATES

Lori M. Moore
Amelia L. Klemme
Chad J. Hessel
M. James Zendejas

Representative Clients: State Farm Mutual Auto Insurance; USAA; Farmers Insurance; Travelers Insurance; AllState Insurance; Merastar Insurance; GEICO; Home Insurance; Case Corporation; The Hartford; Maryland Casualty Co.

For full biographical listings, see the Martindale-Hubbell Law Directory

*DENVER,** Denver Co.

Alexander Law Firm, P.C. (AV)

216 16th Street, Suite 1300, 80202
Telephone: 303-825-7307
Fax: 303-595-3202

Hugh Alexander

C. Scott Crabtree

For full biographical listings, see the Martindale-Hubbell Law Directory

Burg & Eldredge, P.C. (AV)

Suite 900 Regency Plaza One, 4643 South Ulster, 80237-2866
Telephone: 303-779-5595
Fax: 303-779-0527
Albuquerque, New Mexico Office: 20 First Plaza, Suite 508, 87102.
Telephone: 505-242-7020.
Fax: 505-242-7247.

Michael S. Burg
Peter W. Burg
Scott J. Eldredge
David P. Hersh
David M. Houliston
R. Hunter Ellington

Thomas Willard Henderson, IV
Janet R. Spies
Tom Van Buskirk
Matthew R. Giacomini
Kerry N. Jardine
Andrew M. Ominsky
Ashley Rea Kilroy
Brendan O'Rourke Powers
Jack D. Robinson
Kirstin G. Lindberg
Willie E. Shepherd, Jr.
John J. Mattey
Bradley W. Howard (Resident, Albuquerque, New Mexico Office)
Christian C. Doherty (Resident, Albuquerque, New Mexico Office)
Gillian Cooley Morrison
Christina Gratke Nason (Resident, Albuquerque, New Mexico Office)
Rosemary Orsini
Kathleen H. Bridges

OF COUNSEL

Gregory E. Bunker
Dale J. Coplan

Representative Clients: CNA Insurance Companies; Continental Divide Insurance Co.; Crum & Forster Commercial Insurance Co.; Fireman's Fund Insurance; Hartford Insurance Cos.; Progressive Insurance Co.; St. Paul Insurance Co.; State Farm Fire & Casualty Insurance; The Travelers Insurance Co.

For full biographical listings, see the Martindale-Hubbell Law Directory

Long & Jaudon, P.C. (AV)

The Bailey Mansion, 1600 Ogden Street, 80218-1414
Telephone: 303-832-1122
FAX: 303-832-1348

Lawrence A. Long (1908-1992)
Joseph C. Jaudon, Jr.
David B. Higgins
Frederick W. Long
Gary B. Blum
Michael T. McConnell
Stephen P. Hopkins
Robert M. Baldwin
Dennis Woodfin Brown
Alan D. Avery
Cecelia A. Fleischner
Walter N. Houghtaling
Ellen Rubright Ivy
Christine Anne Craigmile
Carla M. LaRosa
Sheri Lyn Hood
Thomas C. Kearns, Jr.
Michael Shaefer Drew
Margaret J. Walton
David H. Yun

OF COUNSEL

Michael T. DePinto

Representative Clients: Aetna Life & Casualty Company; The Doctors Company; Home Insurance Company; Baxter Healthcare; CNA.

For Complete List of Firm Personnel, See General Section

For full biographical listings, see the Martindale-Hubbell Law Directory

Montgomery, Green, Jarvis, Kolodny and Markusson, A Professional Corporation (AV)

Suite 2300, 1050 Seventeenth Street, 80265
Telephone: 303-534-4800
Fax: 303-595-3780
Fort Collins Office: 323 South College Avenue, Suite 2.
Telephone: 303-221-2800.
FAX: 303-221-0271.

C. Michael Montgomery
James K. Green
H. Keith Jarvis
Joel A. Kolodny
Dennis H. Markusson
John W. Grund
John T. Van Voorhis
Kevin F. Amatuzio
Scott A. McGath
Peter S. Dusbabek (Resident, Fort Collins Office)

(See Next Column)

MONTGOMERY, GREEN, JARVIS, KOLODNY AND MARKUSSON A PROFESSIONAL CORPORATION, *Denver—Continued*

Joyce L. Jenkins
Christopher J. Roberts
Jeffrey S. Greenblatt
Thomas E. Napp
Marc G. Lassman
James L. Gillies
Christopher J. Kuelling
Robert N. Clark (Resident, Fort Collins Office)
Lorraine E. Parker

Representative Clients: CIGNA Cos.; Commercial Union Insurance Companies; Farmers Insurance Group; Medmarc; Ohio Casualty Group; Reliance Insurance Co.; Republic Insurance Co.; Traveler's Insurance Companies; United Pacific Insurance Co.; Utah Home Fire Insurance Co.

For full biographical listings, see the Martindale-Hubbell Law Directory

PRYOR, CARNEY AND JOHNSON, A PROFESSIONAL CORPORATION (AV)

Carrara Place, Suite 400, 6200 South Syracuse Way (Englewood), P.O. Box 22003, 80222-0003
Telephone: 303-771-6200
Facsimile: 303-779-0740

Peter W. Pryor
Robert W. Carney
Irving G. Johnson
W. Randolph Barnhart
Thomas L. Roberts
Rodney R. Patula
David D. Karr
Christopher N. Mammel
Edward D. Bronfin
John L. Wheeler
Scott S. Nixon
Bruce A. Montoya
Arlene V. Dykstra
JoAnne M. Zboyan
Peggy S. Ball
Marilee E. Langhoff
Michael J. McNally
Elizabeth C. Moran
C. Gregory Tiemeier
Todd E. Kastetter
Daniel M. Hubbard
Steven G. York
Nick S. Kaluk, Jr.
Teresa L. Thraikill

Representative Clients: Aetna Life and Casualty; Hartford Accident and Indemnity Co.; CNA Insurance Group; Sentry Insurance Co.; MMI Companies, Inc.; The Doctors' Co.; Reliance Insurance Co.; Kaiser Foundation Health Plan of Colorado; Great West Life Assurance Co.; COPIC (Colorado Physicians Insurance Co.).

For Complete List of Firm Personnel, See General Section

For full biographical listings, see the Martindale-Hubbell Law Directory

REINHART, BOERNER, VAN DEUREN, NORRIS & RIESELBACH, P.C. (AV)

One Norwest Center, 1700 Lincoln Street, Suite 3725, 80203
Telephone: 303-831-0909
Fax: 303-831-4805
Milwaukee, Wisconsin Office: 1000 North Water Street.
Telephone: 414-298-1000.
Facsimile: 414-298-8097.
Madison, Wisconsin Office: 7617 Mineral Point Road, 53701-2020.
Telephone: 608-283-7900.
Fax: 608-283-7919.
Washington, D.C. Office: 601 Pennsylvania Avenue, N.W., North Building, Suite 750.
Telephone: 202-393-3636.
Fax: 202-393-0796.

Timothy G. Atkinson
Herbert A. Delap
Stephen C. Peters

David D. Pavek

Representative Clients: OnGuard Systems, Inc.; Club Sports International, Inc.; Gerophy & Miller, Inc.

For full biographical listings, see the Martindale-Hubbell Law Directory

WELLER FRIEDRICH, LLC (AV)

One Civic Center, Suite 2000, 1560 Broadway, P.O. Box 989, 80201-0989
Telephone: 303-812-1200
FAX: 303-812-1212

Geoffrey S. Race
David K. Kerr
Andrew J. Friedrich
Mary A. Wells
James C. Tienken
Sheryl Lynn Anderson
Jerome M. Joseph
Dennis J. Bartlett

OF COUNSEL

W. Robert Ward
Martin J. Andrew

Suanne Marie Dell
Gregory E. Sopkin
Kelly Koepp Robinson
Karen Martinson Girard
Fermin G. Montoya

Representative Clients: Allied Insurance Group; Commercial Union Insurance Companies; Farm Credit Corporation of America; Fidelity & Deposit Company of Maryland; Fireman's Fund/American Insurance Companies; Hartford Insurance Group; Transamerica Insurance Co.; Underwriters Adjusting Co.; United States Fire and Casualty Co.; United States Fidelity & Guaranty Co.

(See Next Column)

For full biographical listings, see the Martindale-Hubbell Law Directory

WHITE AND STEELE, PROFESSIONAL CORPORATION (AV)

1225 17th Street, Suite 2800, 80202
Telephone: 303-296-2828
Telecopier: 303-296-3131
Cheyenne, Wyoming Office: 1912 Capital Avenue, Suite 404, 82003.
Telephone: 307-778-4160.

Lowell White (1897-1983)
Walter A. Steele
R. Eric Peterson
Stephen K. Gerdes
Michael W. Anderson
James M. Dieterich
Glendon L. Laird
John M. Lebsack
Stephen G. Sparr
John P. Craver
David J. Nowak
Sandra Spencer
John M. Palmeri
Frederick W. Klann
William F. Campbell, Jr.
Richard M. Kaudy
Peter W. Rietz
Kurt A. Horton
Stewart J. Rourke
Allan Singer
Michael J. Daugherty
Robert R. Carlson
Ted A. Krumreich

Thomas B. Quinn
Michael A. Perales
George A. Codding, III
Christopher P. Kenney
Regina Marie Walsh
June Baker
Peter H. McGuire
Robert H. D. Coate
Michelle R. Magruder
Monty L. Barnett
Joseph R. King

Colorado Tort Counsel for: Goodyear Tire and Rubber Co.; The Dow Chemical Co.; Celotex.
Insurance Clients: Allied Insurance Co.; CNA; Kemper Insurance Group; Massachusetts Mutual Life Insurance Co.; Underwriters at Lloyds; U.S-.A.A.; Farmers Insurance Group.

For Complete List of Firm Personnel, See General Section

For full biographical listings, see the Martindale-Hubbell Law Directory

WOOD, RIS & HAMES, PROFESSIONAL CORPORATION (AV)

1775 Sherman Street, Suite 1600, 80203-4317
Telephone: 303-863-7700
Telecopier: 303-830-8772

Edward L. Wood (1899-1974)
Stephen E. Connor
F. Michael Ludwig
Charles E. Weaver
Clayton B. Russell
Christopher M. Brandt
Mark R. Davis
Colin C. Campbell
Christian M. Lind
Jeffrey Clay Ruebel
Clifton J. Latiolais, Jr.
Mary E. Kanan
William H. Short
Dennis A. Hanson
Jennifer L. Veiga
Michel P. Williams
William A. Rogers, III

OF COUNSEL

William K. Ris
Eugene S. Hames

SPECIAL COUNSEL

E. Gregory Martin
Donald B. Gentry

Counsel for: American Family Insurance Company; American International Companies; Continental Insurance Companies; Equitable Life Assurance Society of the United States; Fireman's Fund Insurance Company; Home Insurance Company; Maryland Casualty Company; Metropolitan Life Insurance Company; Prudential Insurance Co. of America; Safeco Insurance Company.

For Complete List of Firm Personnel, See General Section

For full biographical listings, see the Martindale-Hubbell Law Directory

*DURANGO,** La Plata Co.

SHAND, MCLACHLAN & NEWBOLD, P.C. (AV)

124 East Ninth Street, P.O. Drawer I, 81302-2790
Telephone: 303-247-3091
Fax: 303-247-3100

E. Bentley Hamilton (1918-1981)
J. Douglas Shand
Michael E. McLachlan
Keith Newbold

David A. Bode
A. Michael Chapman (Resident)
Sheryl Rogers

For full biographical listings, see the Martindale-Hubbell Law Directory

CONNECTICUT

*BRIDGEPORT,** Fairfield Co.

WILLIAMS, COONEY & SHEEHY (AV)

One Lafayette Circle, 06604
Telephone: 203-331-0888
Telecopier: 203-331-0896

MEMBERS OF FIRM

Ronald D. Williams
Robert J. Cooney
Edward Maum Sheehy
Peter D. Clark
Peter J. Dauk
Dion W. Moore
Ronald D. Williams, Jr.
Francis A. Smith, Jr. (1951-1989)

Lawrence F. Reilly
Michael P. Bowler
Michael Cuff Deakin

Representative Clients: Aetna Life & Casualty Co.; Nationwide Insurance Co.; Connecticut Medical Insurance Co.; The Travelers; Utica Mutual Insurance Co.; Pennsylvania National Insurance; Podiatry Insurance Company of America; Preferred Physicians Mutual; Medical Liability Mutual Insurance Company; General Star Indemnity Company.

For full biographical listings, see the Martindale-Hubbell Law Directory

*HARTFORD,** Hartford Co.

COONEY, SCULLY AND DOWLING (AV)

Hartford Square North, Ten Columbus Boulevard, 06106
Telephone: 203-527-1141
Fax: 203-247-5215

MEMBERS OF FIRM

Joseph P. Cooney (1906-1984)
John F. Scully
Vincent J. Dowling
Patrick J. Flaherty
Louis B. Blumenfeld
John W. Sitarz
Eugene A. Cooney
John T. Scully
Richard A. Ferris
Karen Jansen Casey
Jeffrey C. Pingpank
Paul T. Nowosadko
Herbert J. Shepardson
David A. Haught
Joseph A. La Bella
James T. Scully
William J. Scully

ASSOCIATES

Lorinda S. Coon
Jeffrey V. Phelon
Elizabeth D. Fairbanks
Robert G. Clemente
Eileen Mohan Flaherty
Sharone G. Kornman
Rodd J. Mantell
Arthur J. Hudon
Anthony J. Pantuso
Robb J. Canning
Matthew J. Scott

Reference: Fleet Bank.

For full biographical listings, see the Martindale-Hubbell Law Directory

GORDON, MUIR AND FOLEY (AV)

Hartford Square North, Ten Columbus Boulevard, 06106-1944
Telephone: 203-525-5361
Telecopier: 203-525-4849

MEMBERS OF FIRM

William S. Gordon, Jr. (1946-1956)
George Muir (1939-1976)
Edward J. Foley (1955-1983)
Peter C. Schwartz
John J. Reid
John H. Goodrich, Jr.
R. Bradley Wolfe
Jon Stephen Berk
William J. Gallitto
Gerald R. Swirsky
Robert J. O'Brien
Philip J. O'Connor
Kenneth G. Williams
Chester J. Bukowski
Mary Ann Santacroce

ASSOCIATES

J. Lawrence Price
Mary Anne Alicia Charron
James G. Kelly
Kevin F. Morin
Claudia A. Baio
Patrick T. Treacy
Andrew J. Hern
Eileen Geel
Christopher L. Slack
Renee W. Dwyer
David B. Heintz

OF COUNSEL

Stephen M. Riley

Reference: Fleet Bank.

For full biographical listings, see the Martindale-Hubbell Law Directory

HOWD & LUDORF (AV)

65 Wethersfield Avenue, 06114
Telephone: 203-249-1361
Telecopier: 203-543-7155

(See Next Column)

MEMBERS OF FIRM

John R. Lilliendahl, III
John J. Bogdanski
Philip T. Newbury, Jr.
Thomas R. Gerarde
Mark J. Claflin
William F. Corrigan
Christopher M. Vossler
Deborah Etlinger
Linda Gray MacDonald
Peter J. Casey
John P. Majewski
Sean C. Connors
Kimberly B. McCarthy
Michael T. McCormack
Emmet Michael Murphy

OF COUNSEL

Hadleigh H. Howd
Edward S. Ludorf

Representative Clients: CIGNA; Reliance; Ford Motors; Chrysler; Toyota; Harsco; Ladder Management; Baxter International; Black & Decker; Texaco.

For full biographical listings, see the Martindale-Hubbell Law Directory

JACKSON, O'KEEFE AND PHELAN (AV)

36 Russ Street, 06106-1571
Telephone: 203-278-4040
Fax: 203-527-2500
West Hartford, Connecticut Office: 62 LaSalle Road.
Telephone: 203-521-7500.
Fax: 203-561-5399.
Bethlehem, Connecticut Office: 423 Munger Lane.
Telephone: 203-266-5255.

MEMBERS OF FIRM

Jay W. Jackson
Andrew J. O'Keefe
Denise Martino Phelan
Matthew J. O'Keefe
Peter K. O'Keefe
Philip R. Dunn, Jr.
Michael J. Walsh
Anna M. Carbonaro
Denise Rodosevich

OF COUNSEL

Maureen Sullivan Dinnan

Representative Clients: Aetna Casualty & Surety Co.; ITT Hartford; Liberty Mutual Insurance Co.; Connecticut Medical Insurance Co.

For full biographical listings, see the Martindale-Hubbell Law Directory

KENNY, BRIMMER, MELLEY & MAHONEY (AV)

5 Grand Street, 06106
Telephone: 203-527-4226
FAX: 203-527-0214

Joseph P. Kenny (1920-1993)

MEMBERS OF FIRM

Leslie R. Brimmer
William J. Melley, III
Richard C. Mahoney

ASSOCIATES

Anita M. Varunes
Dennis F. McCarthy
Maurice M. O'Shea
Beverly Johns

Representative Clients: Allstate Insurance Co.; Peerless Insurance Co.; Berkshire Mutual Fire Insurance Co.; Dorchester Mutual Fire Insurance Co.; Abington Mutual Fire Insurance Co.

For full biographical listings, see the Martindale-Hubbell Law Directory

MOLLER, HORTON & SHIELDS, P.C. (AV)

90 Gillett Street, 06105
Telephone: 203-522-8338

William R. Moller
Wesley W. Horton
Robert M. Shields, Jr.
Susan M. Cormier
Kimberly A. Knox
Karen L. Murdoch

Christy Scott

For full biographical listings, see the Martindale-Hubbell Law Directory

REGNIER, TAYLOR, CURRAN & EDDY (AV)

CityPlace, 06103-4402
Telephone: 203-249-9121
FAX: 203-527-4343

MEMBERS OF FIRM

J. Ronald Regnier (1906-1987)
Robert F. Taylor (1930-1994)
Edmund T. Curran
Ralph G. Eddy
Jack D. Miller

ASSOCIATES

Lawrence L. Connelli
A. Patrick Alcarez
Robert B. McLaughlin
Sandra L. Connelli
A. Alan Sheffy
Robert A. Byers
Jay F. Huntington
John D. Palermo
Frederick M. O'Brien
Keith Mccabe
Margaret H. Ralphs

Representative Clients: Atlantic Mutual Insurance Co.; Government Employees Insurance Co.; Hartford Accident & Indemnity Co.; Hartford Fire Insurance Co.; Pioneer Co-operative Fire; United Services Automobile Assn.

For full biographical listings, see the Martindale-Hubbell Law Directory

Hartford—Continued

SKELLEY ROTTNER P.C. (AV)

P.O. Box 340890, 06134-0890
Telephone: 203-561-7077
Telecopier: 203-561-7088

Joseph F. Skelley, Jr.
Joel J. Rottner
Susan L. Miller
James G. Geanuracos
Randall M. Hayes
Elizabeth M. Cristofaro
Kirby G. Huget

OF COUNSEL

Susan E. Malliet
Barbara S. Levison

Edward W. Gasser
Laura Ondrush
Matthew Dallas Gordon
Robyn Sondak
Alys Portman Smith
Brad N. Mondschein
Jonathan Kline

LEGAL SUPPORT PERSONNEL

Karen L. Sonnie

References: Connecticut National Bank & Trust Co.; Society for Savings.

For full biographical listings, see the Martindale-Hubbell Law Directory

---

SOROKIN SOROKIN GROSS HYDE & WILLIAMS P.C. (AV)

One Corporate Center, 06103
Telephone: 203-525-6645
Fax: 203-522-1781
Simsbury, Connecticut Office: 730 Hopmeadow Street.
Telephone: 203-651-9348.
Rocky Hill, Connecticut Office: 2360 Main Street.
Telephone: 203-563-9305.
Fax: 203-529-6931.
Glastonbury, Connecticut Office: 124 Hebron Avenue.
Telephone: 203-659-8801.

John J. Bracken III
Clifford J. Grandjean
Jeffrey R. Martin
Richard C. Robinson

Jeffery P. Apuzzo

For Complete List of Firm Personnel, See General Section

For full biographical listings, see the Martindale-Hubbell Law Directory

---

*NEW HAVEN,** New Haven Co.

PAUL A. SCHOLDER ATTORNEY AT LAW, P.C. (AV)

2 Whitney Avenue, P.O. Box 1722, 06507
Telephone: 203-777-7218
Fax: 203-772-2672

Paul A. Scholder

John J. Morgan

References: Peoples Bank; Lafayette American Bank.

For full biographical listings, see the Martindale-Hubbell Law Directory

---

SHAY, SLOCUM & DEWEY (AV)

234 Church Street, P.O. Box 1921, 06509
Telephone: 203-772-3600
Fax: 203-787-4581

MEMBERS OF FIRM

Edward N. Shay
Shaun M. Slocum
Earl F. Dewey, II

ASSOCIATE

Kathryn J. Coassin

Representative Clients: Hartford Accident and Indemnity Co.; United Services Automobile Association; Commercial Union Insurance Co.; Atlantic Mutual Insurance Co.; Northbrook Insurance Co.; Safeco Insurance Co.; Andover Insurance Co.; National Interstate Transportation Insurance Specialists; First Financial Insurance Co.; Burlington Insurance Group.

For full biographical listings, see the Martindale-Hubbell Law Directory

---

*NORWICH,** New London Co.

BROWN, JACOBSON, TILLINGHAST, LAHAN & KING, P.C. (AV)

Uncas-Merchants National Bank Building, 22 Courthouse Square, 06360
Telephone: 203-889-3321
Fax: 203-886-0673
Groton, Connecticut Office: 4 Fort Hill Road.
Telephone: 203-449-8765.
Fax: 203-445-7634.

(See Next Column)

Allyn L. Brown, Jr.
Milton L. Jacobson
Charles W. Jewett
Vincent A. Laudone
James J. Dutton, Jr.
Wayne G. Tillinghast
P. Michael Lahan
Michael E. Driscoll
Timothy D. Bates
Deborah J. Tedford
David S. Williams
Robert A. Avena
Michael A. Blanchard
John C. Wirzbicki
Michael D. Colonese
Peter A. Anderson
Karl-Erik Sternlof
Michael P. Carey
Jeffrey R. Godley
Michael E. Kennedy
Doreen A. West
Elizabeth Conway
John F. Duggan
Gerald M. Smith, Jr.
Valerie G. Bataille-Ferry
Jeffrey F. Buebendorf

OF COUNSEL

Jackson T. King, Jr.

Representative Clients: Nationwide Insurance Co.; Aetna Casualty & Surety Co.; Chelsea-Groton Savings Bank; Norwich Community Development Corp.

For full biographical listings, see the Martindale-Hubbell Law Directory

---

WALLINGFORD, New Haven Co.

CHARLES J. WOOD, JR. (AV)

Elm Professional Center, 105 South Elm Street, P.O. Box 805, 06492
Telephone: 203-284-9988
Fax: 203-294-1516

ASSOCIATE

Helen M. Doherty

Representative Clients: Carolina Freight Carriers Corp.; Central National Insurance Co.; Jefferson Insurance Co. of New York/American Underwriting Managers; Lumber Insurance Companies; National Indemnity Co.; Norfolk & Dedham Mutual Fire Insurance Co.; Transport Insurance Co.; Van-Line Insurance Co.; Olympus Construction Co.

For full biographical listings, see the Martindale-Hubbell Law Directory

---

DELAWARE

*WILMINGTON,** New Castle Co.

BURT & BURT (AV)

Suite 1700 Mellon Bank Center, 919 Market Street, 19801
Telephone: 302-429-9430
Fax: 302-429-9427

Warren B. Burt
Richard D. Abrams
David H. Burt
Michael F. Duggan

For full biographical listings, see the Martindale-Hubbell Law Directory

CASARINO, CHRISTMAN & SHALK (AV)

Suite 1220, 222 Delaware Avenue, P.O. Box 1276, 19899
Telephone: 302-594-4500
Telecopier: 302-594-4509

MEMBERS OF FIRM

Stephen P. Casarino
Colin M. Shalk
Beth H. Christman

Donald M. Ransom
Kenneth M. Doss

For full biographical listings, see the Martindale-Hubbell Law Directory

PRICKETT, JONES, ELLIOTT, KRISTOL & SCHNEE (AV)

1310 King Street, P.O. Box 1328, 19899-1328
Telephone: 302-888-6500
Telecopier: 302-658-8111; 658-7257
Dover, Delaware Office: 26 The Green.
Telephone: 302-674-3841.
Kennett Square, Pennsylvania Office: 217 West State Street.
Telephone: 610-444-1573.

MEMBERS OF FIRM

Carl Schnee
Mason E. Turner, Jr.
Richard P. S. Hannum
David E. Brand
Timothy A. Casey
Paul M. Lukoff
Kevin M. Howard
(Resident at Dover Office)
Ralph K. ("Dirk") Durstein, III
W. Wade W. Scott

ASSOCIATES

Gary F. Traynor
(Resident at Dover Office)
Mark F. Dunkle
(Resident at Dover Office)
Chandlee Johnson Kuhn
Janet K. Stickles
Michael P. Freebery
Gretchen Ann Bender
John E. Tracey

(See Next Column)

PRICKETT, JONES, ELLIOTT, KRISTOL & SCHNEE—*Continued*

Representative Clients: Browning-Ferris Industries; Computer Associates International; Delmarva Power & Light; Nationwide.

For Complete List of Firm Personnel, See General Section

For full biographical listings, see the Martindale-Hubbell Law Directory

SMITH, KATZENSTEIN & FURLOW (AV)

1220 Market Building, P.O. Box 410, 19899
Telephone: 302-652-8400
FAX: 302-652-8405

MEMBERS OF FIRM

Robert J. Katzenstein
Susan L. Parker
Vicki A. Hagel
Laurence V. Cronin

Brett D. Fallon
Stephen M. Miller
Michele C. Gott
Patricia A. Garthwaite

For Complete List of Firm Personnel, See General Section

For full biographical listings, see the Martindale-Hubbell Law Directory

TRZUSKOWSKI, KIPP, KELLEHER & PEARCE, P.A. (AV)

1020 North Bancroft Parkway, P.O. Box 429, 19899-0429
Telephone: 302-571-1782
Fax: 302-571-1638

Francis J. Trzuskowski
James F. Kipp
Daniel F. Kelleher
Robert K. Pearce
Edward F. Kafader
Francis J. Schanne

For full biographical listings, see the Martindale-Hubbell Law Directory

TYBOUT, REDFEARN & PELL (AV)

Suite 1100, PNC Bank Building, 300 Delaware Avenue, P.O. Box 2092, 19899
Telephone: 302-658-6901
FAX: 658-4018

F. Alton Tybout
B. Wilson Redfearn
Richard W. Pell
Anne L. Naczi
Nancy E. Chrissinger
David G. Culley

ASSOCIATES

Sherry Ruggiero Fallon
Sean A. Dolan
Elizabeth Daniello Maron
Francis X. Nardo
Michael I. Silverman
Bernadette M. Plaza
Joel R. Brown
John J. Klusman, Jr.
Todd M. Finchler

Representative Clients: CIGNA Ins., Co.; Liberty Mutual Ins., Co.; Hartford Ins., Co.; Universal Underwriters; PHICO; State of Delaware; GAB Business Services Inc.; State Farm Ins., Co.; Alliance of American Insurers; Insurance Guarantee Assn.

For full biographical listings, see the Martindale-Hubbell Law Directory

DISTRICT OF COLUMBIA

WASHINGTON, D.C. Co.

***** indicates certain Bar Register subscribers, in cities of comparable size and importance, who maintain an additional office in Washington, D.C. and who have arranged for representation as a part of the Washington, D.C. listings that follow

ANDERSON & QUINN (AV)

1220 L Street, N.W., Suite 540, 20005
Telephone: 202-371-1245
Rockville, Maryland Office: Adams Law Center, 25 Wood Lane.
Telephone: 301-762-3303.
FAX: 301-762-3776.

MEMBERS OF FIRM

Charles C. Collins (1900-1973)
Robert E. Anderson (Retired)
Francis X. Quinn
William Ray Scanlin
Donald P. Maiberger

ASSOCIATE

Richard L. Butler

Representative Clients: C & P Telephone; Commercial Union Insurance Cos.; Allstate Insurance Co.; State Farm Mutual Automobile Insurance Co.; Northbrook Insurance Cos.; Travelers Insurance Co.; National General Insurance Co.; American International Adjustment Co.; Marriott Corp.

For Complete List of Firm Personnel, See General Section

For full biographical listings, see the Martindale-Hubbell Law Directory

CARR, GOODSON & LEE, P.C. (AV)

1301 K Street, N.W., Suite 400, East Tower, 20005-3300
Telephone: 202-310-5500
Telecopier: 202-310-5555
Fairfax, Virginia Office: 3923 Old Lee Highway, Suite 62-B, 22030.
Telephone: 703-691-8818.
Baltimore, Maryland Office: Suite 2700, 111 South Calvert Street, 21202.
Telephone: 410-752-1570.
Rockville, Maryland Office: 31 Wood Lane, 20850.
Telephone: 301-424-7024.

William M. Cusmano
Robert W. Goodson
James F. Lee, Jr.
Paul J. Maloney
Thomas L. McCally
Kevin M. Murphy
Walter J. Murphy, Jr.
Brian H. Rhatigan
James A. Welch

Janette M. Blee (Not admitted in DC)
Louis S. Bonanni
Lawrence Eiser
Karen E. Evans
Teresa Grace Fay
Jan E. Fieldsteel
Shadonna E. Hale
David H. Jacobs (Not admitted in DC)
Terrence M. McShane
Timothy J. Mulreany (Not admitted in DC)
Mary C. Nevius
Alexander D. Shoaibi
John A. Taylor
Clifton B. Welch

For Complete List of Firm Personnel, See General Section

For full biographical listings, see the Martindale-Hubbell Law Directory

KENNETH R. FEINBERG & ASSOCIATES (AV)

1120 20th Street, N.W. Suite 740 South, 20036
Telephone: 202-371-1110
Fax: 202-962-9290
New York, N.Y. Office: 780 3rd Avenue, Suite 2202.
Telephone: 212-527-9600.
Fax: 212-527-9611.

ASSOCIATES

Deborah E. Greenspan
Michael K. Rozen (Not admitted in DC)
Peter H. Woodin (Not admitted in DC)

For full biographical listings, see the Martindale-Hubbell Law Directory

JORDAN COYNE & SAVITS (AV)

1030 15th Street, N.W., 20005
Telephone: 202-371-1800
Telecopier: 202-842-2587
Rockville, Maryland Office: 33 Wood Lane.
Telephone: 301-424-4161.
Baltimore, Maryland Office: 400 E. Pratt Street, Suite 830.
Telephone: 410-625-5080.
Telecopier: 202-842-2587.
Fairfax, Virginia Office: 10486 Armstrong Street.
Telephone: 703-246-0900.
Telecopier: 703-591-3673.
Leesburg, Virginia Office: 105 Loudoun Street, S.E.
Telephones: 703-777-6084; 202-478-1895.
Telecopier: 703-771-6383.

MEMBERS OF FIRM

James F. Jordan
Joel M. Savits
Dwight D. Murray
John O. Easton
David P. Durbin
Carol Thomas Stone
John Tremain May
D. Stephenson Schwinn
David B. Stratton
John H. Carstens

ASSOCIATES

William Ward Nooter
William F. Pugh (Not admitted in DC)
Catherine M. O'Rourke
Terry L. Lazaron (Not admitted in DC)
Deborah Murrell Whelihan
Michael E. Reheuser
Clifton Merritt Mount
James P. Fisher (Not admitted in DC)
Deborah A. Farson
Ellen Giblin Draper

OF COUNSEL

Daniel D. Smith (P.C.)

Representative Clients: Aetna Casualty & Surety Co.; American International Group; Budget Car Rental; Design Professionals Insurance Co.; Giant Food; The Home Insurance Co.; Marriott Corp.; Minnesota Mining & Manufacturing; Scottsdale Insurance Co.; Washington Adventist Hospital.

For full biographical listings, see the Martindale-Hubbell Law Directory

SUTHERLAND, ASBILL & BRENNAN (AV)

1275 Pennsylvania Avenue, N.W., 20004-2404
Telephone: 202-383-0100
Cable Address: "Sutab Wash"
Telex: 89-501
Facsimile: 202-637-3593
Atlanta, Georgia Office: 999 Peachtree Street, N. E., 30309-3996.
Telephone: 404-853-8000.

(See Next Column)

SUTHERLAND, ASBILL & BRENNAN, *Washington—Continued*

New York, N.Y. Office: 1270 Avenue of the Americas, 10020-1700.
Telephone: 212-332-3000.
Austin, Texas Office: 111 Congress Avenue, 23rd Floor, 78701-4079.
Telephone: 512-469-3350.

Sheila J. Carpenter
Nicholas T. Christakos
Steuart H. Thomsen

For Complete List of Firm Personnel, See General Section

For full biographical listings, see the Martindale-Hubbell Law Directory

*** VENABLE, BAETJER, HOWARD & CIVILETTI** (AV)

A Partnership including Professional Corporations
Suite 1000, 1201 New York Avenue, N.W., 20005
Telephone: 202-962-4800
Fax: 202-962-8300
Baltimore, Maryland Office: Venable, Baetjer and Howard, 1800 Mercantile Bank & Trust Building, 2 Hopkins Plaza.
Telephone: 410-244-7400.
McLean, Virginia Office: Venable, Baetjer and Howard, Suite 400, 2010 Corporate Ridge.
Telephone: 703-760-1600.
Rockville, Maryland Office: Venable, Baetjer and Howard, Suite 500, One Church Street, P. O. Box 1906.
Telephone: 301-217-5600.
Towson, Maryland Office: Venable, Baetjer and Howard, 210 Allegheny Avenue, P. O. Box 5517.
Telephone: 410-494-6200.

MEMBERS OF FIRM

Benjamin R. Civiletti (P.C.) (Also at Baltimore and Towson, Maryland Offices)
Ronald R. Glancz
Douglas D. Connah, Jr. (P.C.) (Also at Baltimore, Maryland Office)
Joel Z. Silver
James K. Archibald (Also at Baltimore and Towson, Maryland Offices)
Jeffrey A. Dunn (Also at Baltimore, Maryland Office)
George F. Pappas (Also at Baltimore, Maryland Office)
James L. Shea (Not admitted in DC; also at Baltimore, Maryland Office)
Mary E. Pivec (Not admitted in DC; Also at Baltimore, Maryland Office)

For Complete List of Firm Personnel, See General Section

For full biographical listings, see the Martindale-Hubbell Law Directory

WILMER, CUTLER & PICKERING (AV)

2445 M Street, N.W., 20037-1420
Telephone: 202-663-6000
Facsimile: 202-663-6363
Internet: Law@Wilmer.Com
European Offices:
4 Carlton Gardens, London, SW1Y 5AA, England. Telephone: 011 (4471) 839-4466.
Facsimile: 011 (4471) 839-3537.
Rue de la Loi 15 Wetstraat, B-1040 Brussels, Belgium. Telephone: 011 (322) 231-0903.
Facsimile: 011 (322) 230-4322.
Friedrichstrasse 95, D-10117 Berlin, Germany. Telephone: 011 (4930) 2643-3601.
Facsimile: 011 (4930) 2643-3630.

MEMBERS OF FIRM

Dennis M. Flannery
James Robertson
A. Stephen Hut, Jr.
Lynn Bregman
John Payton
Thomas F. Connell
W. Scott Blackmer (Resident, European Office, Brussels, Belgium)
Philip D. Anker
Joseph K. Brenner
David P. Donovan
Roger W. Yoerges

COUNSEL

Carol H. Fishman

For Complete List of Firm Personnel, See General Section

For full biographical listings, see the Martindale-Hubbell Law Directory

FLORIDA

DAYTONA BEACH, Volusia Co.

EUBANK, HASSELL & LEWIS (AV)

Suite 301, 149 South Ridgewood Avenue, P.O. Box 2229, 32015-2229
Telephone: 904-238-1357
Telecopier: 904-258-7406

(See Next Column)

MEMBERS OF FIRM

James O. Eubank, II
F. Bradley Hassell
Lester A. Lewis

ASSOCIATES

Jennifer M. Dehn
Alfred Truesdell
Timothy A. Traster
Joseph D. Tessitore

For full biographical listings, see the Martindale-Hubbell Law Directory

*FORT LAUDERDALE,** Broward Co.

CONRAD, SCHERER, JAMES & JENNE (AV)

A Partnership of Professional Associations
Eighth Floor, 633 South Federal Highway, P.O. Box 14723, 33302
Telephone: 305-462-5500
Facsimile: 305-463-9244
Miami, Florida Office: 2180 Southwest 12th Avenue, P.O. Box 450888, 33245-0888.
Telephone: 305-856-9920.
Facsimile: 305-856-4546.

MEMBERS OF FIRM

William R. Scherer, Jr., (P.A.)
Gordon James, III, (P.A.)
Kenneth C. Jenne, II (P.A.)
Gary S. Genovese (P.A.)
Valerie Shea (P.A.)
William V. Carcioppolo (P.A.)

OF COUNSEL

Rex Conrad

ASSOCIATES

Linda Rae Spaulding
Lynn Futch Cooney
Kimberly A. Kisslan
Reid A. Cocalis
Albert L. Frevola, Jr.

Local Counsel for: American Home Assurance Group; Caterpillar Tractor Co.; Division of Risk Management, State of Florida; Florida East Coast Railway; Fort Motor Co.; Liberty Mutual Insurance Co.; Ryder Truck Lines; Unigard Insurance Group.
Approved Attorneys for: Attorneys' Title Insurance Fund.
Reference: Barnett Bank of Fort Lauderdale.

For Complete List of Firm Personnel, See General Section

For full biographical listings, see the Martindale-Hubbell Law Directory

ESLER PETRIE & SALKIN, P.A. (AV)

Suite 300 The Advocate Building, 315 S.E. Seventh Street, 33301
Telephone: 305-764-5400
FAX: 305-764-5408

Gary A. Esler
C. Daniel Petrie, Jr.
Sonya L. Salkin

Laurie S. Moss

Representative Clients: The Chubb Group of Insurance Cos.; Fireman's Fund Insurance Co.; Infinity Insurance Co.; Fortune Insurance Co.; State of Florida-Department of Risk Management; Crum and Forster Commercial Insurance Co.; Colonial Penn Insurance Co.; American Vehicle Insurance Co.
References: Capital Bank.

For full biographical listings, see the Martindale-Hubbell Law Directory

PETERSON, BERNARD, VANDENBERG, ZEI, GEISLER & MARTIN (AV)

707 Southeast Third Avenue, P.O. Drawer 14126, 33302
Telephone: 305-763-3200
Fax: 305-728-9019
West Palm Beach, Florida Office: 1550 Southern Boulevard.
Telephone: 407-686-5005.
Fax: 407-471-5603.
Stuart, Florida Office: 2100 E. Ocean Boulevard, Suite 202.
Telephone: 407-286-9881.
Naples, Florida Office: 3400 Bailey Lane, Suite 190.
Telephone: 813-263-6444.

William M. Martin
Eric A. Peterson
William Zei

Alexander Clark
Clifford Gorman
Michael A. Acker
Kindy K. Coogler

OF COUNSEL

Leonard M. Bernard, Jr.

For full biographical listings, see the Martindale-Hubbell Law Directory

*FORT MYERS,** Lee Co.

HENDERSON, FRANKLIN, STARNES & HOLT, PROFESSIONAL ASSOCIATION (AV)

1715 Monroe Street, P.O. Box 280, 33902-0280
Telephone: 813-334-4121
Telecopier: 813-332-4494

(See Next Column)

HENDERSON, FRANKLIN, STARNES & HOLT PROFESSIONAL ASSOCIATION—*Continued*

Albert M. Frierson
Stephen L. Helgemo
John A. Noland
Gerald W. Pierce
J. Terrence Porter
Michael J. Corso
Vicki L. Sproat
John W. Lewis
Craig Ferrante
James L. Nulman
Harold N. Hume, Jr.
Bruce M. Stanley
Daniel W. Sheppard
Chad J. Motes
Jack E. Lundy
Steven G. Koeppel
Douglas B. Szabo
Randal H. Thomas
Andrew L. Ringers, Jr.
John F. Potanovic, Jr.
Robert C. Shearman
Paula F. Kelley
Joseph R. North
Timothy J. Jesaitis
Kevin D. Cooper
Jeffrey D. Kottkamp
J. Eric Stiffler
Gregory D. Whitworth

Representative Clients: Aetna Life & Casualty Group; CIGNA Group; CSX Transportation, Inc.; Fireman's Fund Insurance Cos.; Barnett Bank of Lee County, N.A.; Northern Trust Bank of Florida, N.A.; The Hartford Insurance Group; Travelers Group; United Telephone Company of Florida.

For Complete List of Firm Personnel, See General Section

For full biographical listings, see the Martindale-Hubbell Law Directory

SMOOT ADAMS EDWARDS & GREEN, P.A. (AV)

One University Park Suite 600, 12800 University Drive, P.O. Box 60259, 33906-6259
Telephone: 813-489-1776
(800) 226-1777 (in Florida)
Fax: 813-489-2444

J. Tom Smoot, Jr.
Hal Adams
Bruce D. Green
Steven I. Winer
Mark R. Komray
Thomas P. Clark

Lynne E. Denneler
Clayton W. Crevasse
M. Brian Cheffer
Robert S. Forman
Thomas M. Howell
Plutarco M. Villalobos
Kathleen W. McBride

For Complete List of Firm Personnel, See General Section

For full biographical listings, see the Martindale-Hubbell Law Directory

*JACKSONVILLE,** Duval Co.

RUMRELL & JOHNSON, P.A. (AV)

One Harbert Center, 7077 Bonneval Road, Suite 200, 32216
Telephone: 904-296-3200
Telecopier: 904-296-3204

Richard G. Rumrell
Gregory W. Johnson
Lindsey C. Brock III
Joanne Reed Day
Ross Logan Bilbrey
W. David Vaughn

For full biographical listings, see the Martindale-Hubbell Law Directory

TYGART AND SCHULER, P.A. (AV)

103 Barnett Regency Tower, 9550 Regency Square Boulevard, 32225-8164
Telephone: 904-721-0744
Facsimile: 904-721-5080

S. Thompson Tygart, Jr.
Carl Scott Schuler

Representative Client: Allstate Insurance Co.
Reference: Barnett Bank of Regency.

For full biographical listings, see the Martindale-Hubbell Law Directory

*MIAMI,** Dade Co.

ANGONES, HUNTER, MCCLURE, LYNCH & WILLIAMS, P.A. (AV)

Ninth Floor-Concord Building, 66 West Flagler Street, 33130
Telephone: 305-371-5000
Fort Lauderdale: 305-728-9112
FAX: 305-371-3948

Frank R. Angones
Steven Kent Hunter
John McClure
Christopher J. Lynch
Stewart D. Williams
B. Scott Hunter

Leopoldo Garcia, Jr.
Thomas W. Paradise
Donna Joy Hunter
Lourdes Alfonsin Ruiz
Matthew K. Mitchell
Kara D. Phinney
C. David Durkee

Insurance Clients: Allstate Insurance Co.; Prudential Property & Casualty Insurance Company; State Farm Fire & Casualty Insurance Company; Rollins Hudig Hall Healthcare Risk, Inc.

For full biographical listings, see the Martindale-Hubbell Law Directory

CLARK, SPARKMAN, ROBB, NELSON & MASON (AV)

Suite 1003 Biscayne Building, 19 West Flagler Street, 33130
Telephone: 305-374-0033
Broward: 305-522-0045
Fax: 305-539-0767
Fort Lauderdale, Florida Office: Suite 1210, 110 Tower, 110 S.E. Sixth Street.
Telephones: 305-463-3590; Dade: 305-945-4461.
West Palm Beach, Florida Office: 324 Datura Street, Suite 303. Telephone 407-659-6933.
Fax: 407-659-4328.

MEMBERS OF FIRM

James K. Clark
James T. Sparkman
Michael A. Robb
Richard M. Nelson
Donald Edward Mason
Marc S. Buschman
Paul S. Ginsburg
Frances Fernandez Guasch
Dan Kaufman
Valerie Kiffin Lewis

For full biographical listings, see the Martindale-Hubbell Law Directory

DANIELS, KASHTAN & FORNARIS, P.A. (AV)

Two Alhambra Plaza, Suite 810 (Coral Gables), 33134
Telephone: 305-448-7988
Telecopier: 305-448-7978

Richard G. Daniels
Michael F. Kashtan
Martha D. Fornaris

Jannea S. Rogers
Angel Garcia
Kathleen A. Flynn
John E. Oramas
Ana M. Latour

Reference: Barnett Bank.

For full biographical listings, see the Martindale-Hubbell Law Directory

GEORGE, HARTZ, LUNDEEN, FLAGG & FULMER (AV)

4800 LeJeune Road (Coral Gables), 33146
Telephone: 305-662-4800
FAX: 305-667-8015
Fort Lauderdale, Florida Office: Suite 333 Justice Building East, 524 South Andrews Avenue.
Telephone: 305-462-1620. Palm Beach County
Telephone: 407-736-3620.
Fort Myers, Florida Office: Sun Bank Financial Center, Suite 403, 12730 New Brittany Boulevard.
Telephone: 813-939-3006.

Charles K. George
Charles Michael Hartz
Mitchell L. Lundeen
Clinton D. Flagg
Liana C. Silsby (Resident, Fort Lauderdale Office)
C. Richard Fulmer, Jr. (Resident, Fort Lauderdale Office)
A. Scott Lundeen
David V. King (Resident, Fort Lauderdale Office)
Stanley V. Buky (Resident, Fort Lauderdale Office)
Crane A. Johnstone (Resident, Fort Lauderdale Office)
Tracy E. Tomlin
Douglas W. Barnes

ASSOCIATES

John R. Buchholz
Maria A. Santoro
Esther E. Galicia
Matthew F. Minno
Craig R. Stevens (Resident at Ft. Myers Office)
Michael A. Petruccelli (Resident, Fort Lauderdale Office)
Keith J. Lambdin (Resident, Fort Lauderdale Office)
Mitchell H. Katler (Resident, Fort Lauderdale Office)
Michael H. Imber (Resident, Fort Lauderdale Office)
Peter K. Spillis
Loren Sonesen
Frederick W. Hoethke (Resident, Ft. Myers Office)
Michael T. Tomlin
Susan D. Bernhardt (Resident at Ft. Lauderdale Office)
Timonty Bunbrack (Resident at Ft. Lauderdale Office)

For full biographical listings, see the Martindale-Hubbell Law Directory

HADDAD, JOSEPHS, JACK, GAEBE & MARKARIAN (AV)

1493 Sunset Drive (Coral Gables), P.O. Box 345118, 33114
Telephone: Dade County: 305-666-6006
Broward County: 305-463-6699
Telecopier: 305-662-9931

MEMBERS OF FIRM

Gil Haddad
Michael R. Josephs
Lewis N. Jack, Jr.
John S. Gaebe
David K. Markarian

ASSOCIATES

Amarillys E. Garcia-Perez
Elisabeth M. McClosky

For full biographical listings, see the Martindale-Hubbell Law Directory

Miami—Continued

HAYDEN AND MILLIKEN, P.A. (AV)

Suite 63, 5915 Ponce de Leon Boulevard, 33146-2477
Telephone: 305-662-1523
Fax: 305-663-1358
Tampa, Florida Office: 615 De Leon Street 33606-2719.
Telephone: 813-251-1770.
Fax: 813-254-5436.

Reginald M. Hayden, Jr.
William Barry Milliken
William R. Boeringer
Timothy P. Shusta (Resident, Tampa, Florida Office)
Jan M. Kuylenstierna
James N. Hurley
Michael J. Cappucio
Joseph K. Birch (Resident, Tampa, Florida Office)

Representative Clients: Regency Cruise Lines; Seaboard Marine, Ltd.; Tropical Shipping and Construction Co., Ltd.; Great American Insurance Co.; Marine Office of America Corp.; St. Paul Fire and Marine Insurance Co.; Britannia P & I; New Castle P & I; Steamship Mutual; The Swedish Club; Through Transport Mutual.
Reference: Dadeland Bank.

For full biographical listings, see the Martindale-Hubbell Law Directory

NICKLAUS, VALLE, CRAIG & WICKS (AV)

15th Floor New World Tower, 100 North Biscayne Boulevard, 33132
Telephone: 305-358-2888
Facsimile: 305-358-5501
Fort Lauderdale, Florida Office: Suite 101N, Justice Building, 524 South Andrews Avenue, 33301.
Telephone: 305-523-1858.
Facsimile: 305-523-8068.

MEMBERS OF FIRM

Edward R. Nicklaus
Laurence F. Valle
Lawrance B. Craig, III
William R. Wicks, III
James W. McCready, III
Michael W. Whitaker

ASSOCIATES

Richard D. Settler
Kevin M. Fitzmaurice
Timothy Maze Hartley
Keith S. Grybowski
Patricia Blanco
Michael J. Lynott

For full biographical listings, see the Martindale-Hubbell Law Directory

PONZOLI, WASSENBERG & SPERKACZ, P.A. (AV)

302 Roland/Continental Plaza, 3250 Mary Street, 33133
Telephone: 305-442-1654

Ronald P. Ponzoli
Richard L. Wassenberg
Zorian Sperkacz
John P. Keller

Reference: City National Bank of Miami.

For full biographical listings, see the Martindale-Hubbell Law Directory

LELAND E. STANSELL, JR., P.A. (AV)

903 Biscayne Building, 19 West Flagler Street, 33130
Telephone: 305-374-5911

ASSOCIATE

Charles L. Balli

For full biographical listings, see the Martindale-Hubbell Law Directory

STUZIN AND CAMNER, PROFESSIONAL ASSOCIATION (AV)

25th Floor, 1221 Brickell Avenue, 33131-3260
Telephone: 305-577-0600

Charles B. Stuzin
Alfred R. Camner
Stanley A. Beiley
Marsha D. Bilzin
David S. Garbett
Nina S. Gordon
Barry D. Hunter
Nikki J. Nedbor
Neale J. Poller

Lisa R. Carstarphen
Maria E. Chang
Barry P. Gruher
Gustavo D. Llerena
Sherry D. McMillan
Roger A. Preziosi

OF COUNSEL

Anne Shari Camner

References: Citizens Federal Bank; City National Bank of Miami; Barnett Bank of South Florida, N.A.

For full biographical listings, see the Martindale-Hubbell Law Directory

*NAPLES,** Collier Co.

HARDT & STEWART (AV)

Suite 705 Sun Bank Building, 801 Laurel Oak Drive, 33963
Telephone: 813-598-2900
Fax: 813-598-3785

(See Next Column)

MEMBERS OF FIRM

Frederick R. Hardt
Joseph D. Stewart
John D. Kehoe

References: Northern Trust Bank of Florida/Naples, N.A.; U.S. Trust Company of Florida; Sun Bank/Naples, N.A.

For full biographical listings, see the Martindale-Hubbell Law Directory

NORTH MIAMI BEACH, Dade Co.

BUCHANAN INGERSOLL, PROFESSIONAL CORPORATION (AV)

One Turnberry Place, 19495 Biscayne Boulevard, 33180
Telephone: 305-933-5600
Telecopier: 305-933-2350
Pittsburgh, Pennsylvania Office: 5800 USX Tower, 600 Grant Street.
Telephone: 412-562-8800.
Philadelphia, Pennsylvania Office: Two Logan Square, Twelfth Floor, 18th & Arch Streets.
Telephone: 215-665-8700.
Harrisburg, Pennsylvania Office: Vartan Parc, 30 North Third Street.
Telephone: 717-237-4800.
Tampa, Florida Office: Suite 1030, 101 East Kennedy Boulevard.
Telephone: 813-222-8180.
Princeton, New Jersey Office: Buchanan Ingersoll, A Partnership, College Centre, 500 College Road East.
Telephone: 609-452-2666.
Lexington, Kentucky Office: Suite 600, PNC Bank Plaza, 200 West Vine Street.
Telephone: 606-225-5333.

Wayne M. Pathman

For Complete List of Firm Personnel, See General Section

For full biographical listings, see the Martindale-Hubbell Law Directory

*ORLANDO,** Orange Co.

McDONOUGH, O'DELL, WIELAND & WILLIAMS (AV)

19 East Central Boulevard, P.O. Drawer 1991, 32802
Telephone: 407-425-7577
Fax: 407-423-0234

John R. McDonough
Donald L. O'Dell
William J. Wieland
Donald N. Williams
Michael J. Krakar
A. Scott Toney
Nicholas a. Shannin

For full biographical listings, see the Martindale-Hubbell Law Directory

O'NEILL, CHAPIN, MARKS, LIEBMAN, COOPER & CARR (AV)

A Partnership including Professional Associations
865 Eola Park Center, 200 East Robinson Street, 32801
Telephone: 407-425-2751
Telex: 407-423-1192

Bernard C. O'Neill, Jr. (P.A.)
Bruce E. Chapin (P.A.)
Robert O. Marks (P.A.)
John B. Liebman (P.A.)
Mark O. Cooper (P.A.)
George E. Carr

ASSOCIATES

Lisa M. Cvetic
Rod C. Lundy

Reference: First Union National Bank.

For full biographical listings, see the Martindale-Hubbell Law Directory

TARASKA, GROWER, UNGER AND KETCHAM, P.A. (AV)

111 North Orange Avenue, Suite 1700, P.O. Box 538065, 32853-8065
Telephone: 407-423-9545
Telefacsimile: 407-422-1257; 425-7104

Joseph M. Taraska
Mason H. Grower, III
Martin B. Unger
Walter A. Ketcham, Jr.
Hector A. Moré
Launa K. Rutherford
Jerri L. Solomon
A. Scott Noecker
John C. Willis, IV
John M. Cacciatore
Michael C. Siboni
James M. Miller
Jeanelle G. Bronson

David B. Blessing
Eric R. Eide
Gregory D. Swartwood
Art Charles Young
S. Desiree Ellison
G. Franklin Bishop, III
George F. Indest III
David W. Henry
Patrick H. Telan
Gregory A. Fencik
Richard H. Bitner, II
Benjamin W. Newman

For full biographical listings, see the Martindale-Hubbell Law Directory

*PENSACOLA,** Escambia Co.

BELL, SCHUSTER & WHEELER, P.A. (AV)

119 West Garden Street, P.O. Box 12564, 32573-2564
Telephone: 904-438-1691
Fax: 904-438-3641

(See Next Column)

BELL, SCHUSTER & WHEELER P.A.—*Continued*

Robert D. Bell
Charles A. Schuster
Thomas E. Wheeler, Jr.
David W. Hiers

For full biographical listings, see the Martindale-Hubbell Law Directory

JANECKY, NEWELL, POTTS, HARE & WELLS, P.C. (AV)

316 South Baylen, Suite 280, 32501-5900
Telephone: 904-432-6066
Mobile, Alabama, Office: 3300 First National Bank Building, Post Office Box 2987.
Telephone: 205-432-8786.
Fax: 205-432-5900
Birmingham, Alabama Office: Suite 3120, AmSouth-Harbert Plaza, 1901 Sixth Avenue North, 35203.
Telephone: 205-252-4441.
Fax: 205-252-0320.

J. F. (Jack) Janecky
Mark A. Newell

Desmond V. Tobias
Kevin F. Masterson

Representative Clients: Alexis, Inc.; Associate Self Insurance Services, Inc.; Associated Group Services/Alabama Home Builders Self Insurers Fund; Auto-Owners Ins. Co.; Blue Cross and Blue Shield of Alabama; Canal Ins. Co.; Crum & Forster Ins. Co./U.S. Ins. Group; Electric Mutual Ins. Co.; Fireman's Fund Ins. Cos.; Nationwide Ins. Co.; Principal Mutual Life Ins. Co.

For full biographical listings, see the Martindale-Hubbell Law Directory

B. RICHARD YOUNG, P.A. (AV)

309B South Palafox Place, 32501
Telephone: 904-432-2222
Fax: 904-432-1444

B. Richard Young

For full biographical listings, see the Martindale-Hubbell Law Directory

*ST. AUGUSTINE,** St. Johns Co.

JACK A. LANGDON, P.A. (AV)

Suite 312, First Union Bank Building, 24 Cathedral Place, P.O. Box 1479, 32084
Telephone: 904-824-2667
Fax: 904-823-9742

Jack A. Langdon

For full biographical listings, see the Martindale-Hubbell Law Directory

*SARASOTA,** Sarasota Co.

DICKINSON & GIBBONS, P.A. (AV)

1750 Ringling Boulevard, P.O. Box 3979, 34230
Telephone: 813-366-4680
FAX: 813-953-3136

Francis C. Dart (1902-1972)
G. Hunter Gibbons
Ward E. Dahlgren
Lewis F. Collins, Jr.
Gary H. Larsen
Camden T. French
Ralph L. Marchbank, Jr.
A. James Rolfes
Burwell J. Jones
Richard R. Garland
Stephen G. Brannan
Deborah J. Blue
Mark A. Haskins
Jeffrey D. Peairs
Kim Carlton Bonner
Douglas R. Wight
Stephen R. Kanzer
David S. Preston
Mary Gall Jack
John A. Yanchek

OF COUNSEL

Patrick H. Dickinson

LEGAL SUPPORT PERSONNEL

Elliot J. Welch
Christine C. Menzel
Patricia L. Hunter
Nance R. Walker
Krista R. Nero
Diane Schroeder
Janet E. Gadoury (Certified Legal Assistant)

Representative Clients: Ford Motor Co.; Florida Power & Light Co.; Squibb Corp.
Insurance Clients: Liberty Mutual Insurance Co.; Allstate Insurance Co.; Nationwide Insurance Group; Ohio Casualty Insurance Co.; United States Fidelity & Guaranty Co.; State Farm Insurance Company.

For full biographical listings, see the Martindale-Hubbell Law Directory

O'RIORDEN, MANN, HOOTMAN, INGRAM & DUNKLE, P.A. (AV)

1819 Main Street, Suite 700, P.O. Box 2019, 34230
Telephone: 813-366-6885
Facsimile: 813-953-7752
Tampa, Florida Office: 1 North Dale Mabry, Suite 950, 33609.
Telephone: 813-876-3636.
Fax: 813-877-7553.

(See Next Column)

John J. O'Riorden
Keith A. Mann
Gregory W. Hootman
Paul N. Ingram
Randal C. Dunkle
Hermes Eraclides
M. Todd Merritt
Cindy Robin Galen
C. Bradley Hall, Jr.
A. Dawn Hayes
Kathi Busch Halvorsen
Elinor E. Erben
Charles Anderson Hounchell (Resident, Tampa Office)
Anne Katherine Dinan (Resident, Tampa Office)
Kristen Johannessen

For full biographical listings, see the Martindale-Hubbell Law Directory

*TALLAHASSEE,** Leon Co.

COLLINS & TRUETT, P.A. (AV)

2804 Remington Green Circle, Suite 4, Post Office Drawer 12429, 32317-2429
Telephone: 904-386-6060
Telecopier: 904-385-8220

Richard B. Collins
Gary A. Shipman

Brett Q. Lucas (Resident)
Dawn D. Caloca
Joseph E. Brooks
C. Timothy Gray
Rogelio Fontela
Charles N. Cleland, Jr.
Clifford W. Rainey

OF COUNSEL

Edgar C. Booth
James A. Dixon, Jr.

Representative Clients: Agency Rent-A-Car; Agricultural Excess and Surplus Insurance Co.; AIG Life Insurance Co.; Alliance Insurance Group; Allstate Insurance Co.; American Empire Surplus Lines Insurance Co.; American International Underwriters Inc.; Atlanta Casualty Insurance Co.; Avis Rent-A-Car; Bankers and Shippers Insurance Co.

For full biographical listings, see the Martindale-Hubbell Law Directory

HENRY, BUCHANAN, MICK, HUDSON & SUBER, P.A. (AV)

117 South Gadsden Street P.O. Drawer 1049, 32302
Telephone: 904-222-2920
Telecopier: 904-224-0034

Bryan W. Henry (1925-1986)
John D. Buchanan, Jr.
Robert A. Mick
Edwin R. Hudson
Jesse F. Suber
Harriet W. Williams
J. Steven Carter

Reference: Barnett Bank of Tallahassee, Inc.

For full biographical listings, see the Martindale-Hubbell Law Directory

MANG, RETT & MINNICK, P.A. (AV)

660 East Jefferson Street, P.O. Box 11127, 32302-3127
Telephone: 904-222-7710
1-800-342-2727
Telecopier: 904-222-6019

Douglas A. Mang
Donald A. Rett
Bruce A. Minnick
Andrew L. Granger
Steven M. Malono
Wendy Russell Wiener

LEGAL SUPPORT PERSONNEL

Teresa Z. Finley
Judy C. Rhodes
Wendy Ebbers

GOVERNMENTAL CONSULTANT

Timothy Deratany (Governmental Consultant)

For full biographical listings, see the Martindale-Hubbell Law Directory

MCFARLAIN, WILEY, CASSEDY & JONES, PROFESSIONAL ASSOCIATION (AV)

215 South Monroe Street, Suite 600, P.O. Box 2174, 32316-2174
Telephone: 904-222-2107
Telecopier: 904-222-8475

Richard C. McFarlain
William B. Wiley
Marshall R. Cassedy
Douglas P. Jones
Charles A. Stampelos
Linda McMullen
H. Darrell White, Jr.
Christopher Barkas

Harold R. Mardenborough, Jr.
Katherine Hairston LaRosa
J. Robert Griffin

OF COUNSEL

Betty J. Steffens

For full biographical listings, see the Martindale-Hubbell Law Directory

*TAMPA,** Hillsborough Co.

ALPERT, JOSEY & HUGHES, P.A. (AV)

100 South Ashley Drive, Suite 2000 (33602), P.O. Box 3270, 33601-3270
Telephone: 813-223-4131
Fax: 813-228-9612

(See Next Column)

ALPERT, JOSEY & HUGHES P.A., *Tampa—Continued*

Jonathan L. Alpert
William S. Josey
Linda Renate Hughes

Catherine A. Kyres
Patrick B. Calcutt
R. Christopher Rodems
Chris A. Barker
Kirsten K. Ullman
Gregory Joseph Blackburn
David D. Ferrentino
William J. Cook
Suzanne P. Tortorice
Matthew J. Jowanna
Daniel J. Mathis

OF COUNSEL

Stanley T. Padgett

Representative Clients: Alexander & Alexander, Inc.; American International Adjustment Co.; Colonia Insurance Co.; Hospital Underwriting Group; Maryland Casualty co.; Nationwide Insurance Co.; RLI Insurance Corp.; Scott Wetzel Services; Skandia America Group; The Seibels Bruce Insurance Companies.

For full biographical listings, see the Martindale-Hubbell Law Directory

GUNN, OGDEN & SULLIVAN, PROFESSIONAL ASSOCIATION (AV)

201 East Kennedy Boulevard, Suite 1850, P.O. Box 1006, 33601
Telephone: 813-223-5111
FAX: 813-229-2336

Timon V. Sullivan
Randy J. Ogden
Lee D. Gunn, IV

Bradley J. Goewert
Andrea L. Hairelson
Michael F. Hancock
Brian Thompson
Charles E. Mckeon
Kelly K. Griffin
Daneil M. McAuliffe

For full biographical listings, see the Martindale-Hubbell Law Directory

HAYDEN AND MILLIKEN, P.A. (AV)

615 De Leon Street, 33606-2719
Telephone: 813-251-1770
Fax: 813-254-5436
Miami, Florida Office: Suite 63, 5915 Ponce de Leon Boulevard.
Telephone: 305-662-1523.
Fax: 305-663-1358.

Reginald M. Hayden, Jr.
William Barry Milliken
Timothy P. Shusta (Resident)
Joseph K. Birch (Resident)

Representative Clients: Regency Cruise Lines; Seaboard Marine, Ltd.; Tropical Shipping and Construction Co., Ltd.; Great American Insurance Co.; Marine Office of America Corp.; St. Paul Fire and Marine Insurance Co.; Britannia P & I; New Castle P & I; Steamship Mutual; Through Transport.
Reference: Dadeland Bank.

For full biographical listings, see the Martindale-Hubbell Law Directory

LANGFORD, HILL & TRYBUS, P.A. (AV)

Suite 800, Bayshore Place, 601 Bayshore Boulevard, 33606
Telephone: 813-251-5533
Telecopier: 813-251-1900
Wats: 1-800-277-2005

E. C. Langford
Edward A. Hill
Ronald H. Trybus
Ronald G. Hock
Catherine M. Catlin
Debra M. Kubicsek
William B. Smith

Fredrique B. Boire
Muriel Desloovere
Kevin H. O'Neill
Vicki L. Page
Frederick T. Reeves
Barbara A. Sinsley
Stephens B. Woodrough (Not admitted in FL)
Anthony G. Woodward

Representative Clients: Affiliated of Florida, Inc.; American Federation Insurance Co.; Armor Insurance; Bank of Tampa; Central Bank of Tampa; Cintas Corp.; Container Corporation of America; CU Financial Services; Farm Stores, Inc.; First Union Home Equity Bank.

For full biographical listings, see the Martindale-Hubbell Law Directory

MCCLAIN & STRAUSS, P.A. (AV)

The Times Building, 1000 North Ashley Drive, Suite 105, 33602-3719
Telephone: 813-221-1331
FAX: 813-223-7881

David H. McClain
John O. Strauss
James R. Kramer
Larry K. Jackson

Representative Clients: Liberty Mutual Insurance Co.; State Farm Fire & Casualty Insurance Co.; Allstate Insurance Co.; State of Florida Risk Management; State Farm Auto Insurance Co.; Nationwide Insurance Co.; FEISCO; United States Fidelity and Guaranty Co.; Florida Physician's Insurance Co.; Tire Kingdom.

For full biographical listings, see the Martindale-Hubbell Law Directory

RYWANT, ALVAREZ, JONES & RUSSO, PROFESSIONAL ASSOCIATION (AV)

Suite 500 Perry Paint & Glass Building, 109 North Brush Street, P.O. Box 3283, 33601
Telephone: 813-229-7007
Fax: 813-223-6544
Ocala, Florida Office: 3300 S.W. 34th Avenue, Suite 124C, 32674.
Telephone: 904-237-8810.
FAX: 904-237-2022.

Manuel J. Alvarez
Jill M. Deziel
Darrell D. Dirks
Matthew D. Emerson
John A.C. Guyton, III
Gregory D. Jones
Burke G. Lopez
Kerry C. McGuinn, Jr.
Andrew F. Russo
Michael S. Rywant
Scott M. Whitley
James R. Wilson
Susan M. Zwiesler

LEGAL SUPPORT PERSONNEL

Traci D. Tew
Bradley Hugh Holt
Stephanie Dickinson Neal (Paralegal)

Representative Clients: Peerless Insurance Co.; Gulf Insurance Group; Employers Casualty Co.; Landmark Insurance Co.

For full biographical listings, see the Martindale-Hubbell Law Directory

SHOFI, SMITH, HENNEN, JENKINS, STANLEY & GRAMOVOT, P.A. (AV)

One North Dale Mabry, Suite 800, P.O. Box 10430, 33679-0430
Telephone: 813-876-7796
FAX: 813-876-0509

John D. Shofi
John S. Smith
William E. Hennen
John N. Jenkins
Donald W. Stanley, Jr.
Larry I. Gramovot
Sandra L. Peacock
Matthew R. Danahy

James E. Bogos
Augustine S. Weekley, Jr., M.D.
Bret T. Jardine
Jon A. McAuliffe
Frank Clark
Rochelle L. Lefler

Reference: City Bank of Tampa.

For full biographical listings, see the Martindale-Hubbell Law Directory

SMITH, WILLIAMS & BOWLES, P.A. (AV)

Old Hyde Park, 712 South Oregon Avenue, 33606
Telephone: 813-253-5400
Fax: 813-254-3459
Orlando, Florida Office: Smith, Williams & Humphries, P.A., Southeast Bank Building, Suite 700, 201 East Pine Street.
Telephone: 407-849-5151.
St. Cloud, Florida Office: 1700-13th Street, Suite 2, 34769.
Telephone: 407-892-5545.

David Lisle Smith
Gregory L. Williams
Margaret E. Bowles
Jana P. Andrews
Jeffrey A. Aman
J. Gregory Humphries (Resident, Orlando Office)
James A. Muench
Dale K. Bohner
Neal A. Sivyer
Robert L. Harding (Resident, Orlando Office)
Daniel William King
Rebecca H. Forest (Resident, Orlando Office)

For full biographical listings, see the Martindale-Hubbell Law Directory

STUART & STRICKLAND, P.A. (AV)

605 South Boulevard, 33606
Telephone: 813-251-8081
Fax: 813-254-2459
Brooksville, Florida Office: 217 Howell Avenue.
Telephone: 904-796-6733.
Fax: 904-799-7506.

Stephen K. Stuart
Steven A. Strickland (Resident)

Jeffrey A. Caglianone
Francis Anthony Miller

Representative Clients: Allstate Insurance Co.; Purina Mills, Inc.; Auto Owners Insurance Co.; Metropolitan Insurance Co.; Firemens Fund Insurance Co.
Reference: City Bank of Tampa.

For full biographical listings, see the Martindale-Hubbell Law Directory

WOOD, CRIST & VALENTI, P.A. (AV)

One Tampa City Center Suite 1700, 33602-5187
Telephone: 813-229-6311
Fax: 813-225-2633

J. Emory Wood
Charles J. Crist, Jr.
Lorraine A. Valenti

Marie R. Byrne
Stephen A. Barnes

Representative Clients: Casualty Indemnity Exchange; State Farm Fire & Casualty Co.; State Farm Mutual Automobile Insurance Co.; Southern Insurance Co.; Nationwide Insurance Co.; Coronet Insurance Co.; General Telephone Company of Florida; Apex Adjusting Co.; Unisource Insurance Co.

For full biographical listings, see the Martindale-Hubbell Law Directory

*WEST PALM BEACH,** Palm Beach Co.

WIEDERHOLD, MOSES, BULFIN & RUBIN, P.A. (AV)

Northbridge Centre, Suite 800, 515 North Flagler Drive, P.O. Box 3918, 33401
Telephone: 407-659-2296;
Broward: 305-763-5630
FAX: 407-659-2865

John P. Wiederhold
Robert D. Moses
John J. Bulfin
Kenneth M. Rubin

Lawrence I. Bass
Kay Seeber Hoff
Marc S. Ruderman
Bruce R. Katzell

Reference: Florida National Bank of Palm Beach Co.

For full biographical listings, see the Martindale-Hubbell Law Directory

GEORGIA

*ATLANTA,** Fulton Co.

ALEMBIK, FINE & CALLNER, P.A. (AV)

Marquis One Tower, Fourth Floor, 245 Peachtree Center Avenue, N.E., 30303
Telephone: 404-688-8800
Telecopier: 404-420-7191

Michael D. Alembik (1936-1993)
Lowell S. Fine
Bruce W. Callner
Kathy L. Portnoy
Ronald T. Gold
G. Michael Banick
Mark E. Bergeson
Russell P. Love

Z. Ileana Martinez
Kevin S. Green
Susan M. Lieppe
T. Kevin Mooney
Bruce R. Steinfeld
Janet Lichiello Franchi

For full biographical listings, see the Martindale-Hubbell Law Directory

BOVIS, KYLE & BURCH (AV)

A Partnership including Professional Corporations
Third Floor, 53 Perimeter Center East, 30346
Telephone: 404-391-9100
Telecopier: 404-668-0878
Alpharetta, Georgia Office: 41 Milton Avenue.
Telephone: 404-391-9100.
Telecopier: 404-668-0878.

MEMBERS OF FIRM

John M. Bovis (P.C.)
Steven J. Kyle (P.C.)
John V. Burch (P.C.)
C. Sam Thomas (P.C.)
James E. Singer
W. Bruce Barrickman
Gregory R. Veal

ASSOCIATES

Michaela Smith Young
Charles M. McDaniel, Jr.
Timothy J. Burson
Charles M. Medlin
Danna Farrell McBride
J.S. Scott Busby
William S. Allred
Wade H. Purcell

For full biographical listings, see the Martindale-Hubbell Law Directory

CHAMBERS, MABRY, MCCLELLAND & BROOKS (AV)

Tenth Floor, 2200 Century Parkway, N.E., 30345
Telephone: 404-325-4800
FAX: 404-325-0596
Lawrenceville, Georgia Office: Suite 377, 175 Gwinnett Drive.
Telephone: 404-339-7660.
FAX: 404-339-7060.

MEMBERS OF FIRM

Eugene P. Chambers, Jr.
E. Speer Mabry, III
Walter B. McClelland
Wilbur C. Brooks
Lawrence J. Hogan (Resident at Lawrenceville Office)
Rex D. Smith
Clyde E. Rickard, III
Genevieve L. Frazier
Virginia Jane Reed
Jan Philip Cohen
James T. Budd
Douglas F. Aholt
John C. Stivarius, Jr.
Robert M. Darroch
Cynthia J. Becker
Edwin L. Hamilton

ASSOCIATES

Benjamin T. Hughes
F. Scott Young
Beth L. Singletary
DeeAnn Boatright Waller
C. Gregory Ragsdale (Resident at Lawrenceville Office)
Vincent A. Toreno
Dale C. Ray, Jr.
Sandra G. Kirk
R. Michael Malcom
Richard H. Hill, Jr.

(See Next Column)

OF COUNSEL

H. A. Stephens, Jr.

Representative Clients: Allstate Insurance Co.; The Security Mutual Insurance Company of New York; National Automobile Insurance Co.

For full biographical listings, see the Martindale-Hubbell Law Directory

DENNIS, CORRY, PORTER & GRAY (AV)

3300 One Atlanta Plaza, 950 East Paces Ferry Road, P.O. Box 18640, 30326
Telephone: 404-240-6900
Wats: 800-735-0838
Fax: 404-240-6909
Telex: 4611041

MEMBERS OF FIRM

Robert E. Corry, Jr.
R. Clay Porter
William E. Gray, II
James S. Strawinski
Grant B. Smith

OF COUNSEL

Douglas Dennis

ASSOCIATES

Frederick D. Evans, III
Virginia M. Greer
Robert G. Ballard
Matthew J. Jewell
Pamela Jean Gray
Ronald G. Polly, Jr.
Thomas D. Trask
J. Steven Fisher
Stephanie F. Goff
Alison Roberts Solomon
Robert David Schoen
Brian DeVoe Rogers

Representative Clients: Farmers Insurance Group; Roadway Services, Inc.

For full biographical listings, see the Martindale-Hubbell Law Directory

ENGLAND & MCKNIGHT (AV)

Suite 410 River Ridge, 9040 Roswell Road, 30350
Telephone: 404-641-6010
FAX: 404-641-6003

MEMBERS OF FIRM

J. Melvin England
Robert H. McKnight, Jr.

Reference: Bank South, N.A.

For full biographical listings, see the Martindale-Hubbell Law Directory

FAIN, MAJOR & WILEY, P.C. (AV)

The Hurt Building, 50 Hurt Plaza, Suite 300, 30303
Telephone: 404-688-6633
Telecopier: 404-420-1544

Donald M. Fain
Gene A. Major
Charles A. Wiley, Jr.
Christopher E. Penna
Thomas E. Brennan
John K. Miles, Jr.
Darryl G. Haynes
David Wayne Williams
Brian Alligood
Frederic H. Pilch, III
Derek A. Mendicino

Representative Clients: Allstate Insurance Co.; Budget Rent-A-Car; Carolina Freight Carriers Corp.; Chrysler Insurance Co.; Georgia Farm Bureau Mutual Insurance Co.; Great Atlantic & Pacific Tea Co.; Hertz Corp.; Universal Underwriters Insurance Co.; Westfield Insurance co.; Winn-Dixie Stores, Inc.

For full biographical listings, see the Martindale-Hubbell Law Directory

GOLDNER, SOMMERS, SCRUDDER & BASS (AV)

2839 Paces Ferry Road, Suite 800, 30339-3774
Telephone: 404-436-4777
Facsimile: 404-436-8777

Stephen L. Goldner
Susan V. Sommers
Henry E. Scrudder, Jr.
Glenn S. Bass
C. G. Jester, Jr.
Alfred A. Quillian, Jr.

Sandra G. Chase
Linda Jacobsen Pollock
Benjamin David Ladner
Marci R. Weston
William W. Horlock, Jr.

For Complete List of Firm Personnel, See General Section

For full biographical listings, see the Martindale-Hubbell Law Directory

HARMAN, OWEN, SAUNDERS & SWEENEY, A PROFESSIONAL CORPORATION (AV)

1900 Peachtree Center Tower, 230 Peachtree Street, N.W., 30303
Telephone: 404-688-2600
Telecopier: 404-525-4347

(See Next Column)

HARMAN, OWEN, SAUNDERS & SWEENEY A PROFESSIONAL CORPORATION, *Atlanta—Continued*

H. Andrew Owen
Frederick F. Saunders, Jr.
Timothy J. Sweeney
Perry A. Phillips
Michael W. McElroy
Charles J. Cole
Rolfe M. Martin

For full biographical listings, see the Martindale-Hubbell Law Directory

MOZLEY, FINLAYSON & LOGGINS (AV)

One Premier Plaza, Suite 900, 5605 Glenridge Drive, 30342
Telephone: 404-256-0700
Telecopier: 404-250-9355

MEMBERS OF FIRM

J. Arthur Mozley
Robert M. Finlayson II
Sewell K. Loggins
William D. Harrison
Eric D. Griffin, Jr.
C. David Hailey
Deborah A. Finnerty
D. Keith Calhoun
Richard D. Hall
R. Ann Grier

ASSOCIATES

Lawrence B. Domenico
Edward C. Bresee, Jr.
Amberly A. Warner
J. Marcus Howard

For full biographical listings, see the Martindale-Hubbell Law Directory

LAW OFFICES OF J. WAYNE PIERCE, P.A. (AV)

Two Paces West, Suite 1700 4000 Cumberland Parkway, 30339
Telephone: 404-435-0500
Telecopier: 404-435-0362

J. Wayne Pierce

Dargan Scott Cole
Thomas L. Schaefer

For full biographical listings, see the Martindale-Hubbell Law Directory

SULLIVAN, HALL, BOOTH & SMITH, A PROFESSIONAL CORPORATION (AV)

One Midtown Plaza, 1360 Peachtree Street, N.E., Suite 800, 30309
Telephone: 404-870-8000
FAX: 404-870-8020

Terrance C. Sullivan
John E. Hall, Jr.
Alexander H. Booth
Rush S. Smith, Jr.
Henry D. Green, Jr.
Jack G. Slover, Jr.
Timothy H. Bendin
Michael A. Pannier
Brynda Sue Rodriguez
Roger S. Sumrall

David V. Johnson
Jeffrey T. Wise
Eleanor L. Martel
A. Spencer McManes, Jr.
David G. Goodchild, Jr.
Robert L. Shannon, Jr.
T. Andrew Graham
Earnest Redwine
Melanie P. Simon (Not admitted in GA)

Reference: Wachovia Bank of Georgia.

For full biographical listings, see the Martindale-Hubbell Law Directory

THOMAS, KENNEDY, SAMPSON & PATTERSON (AV)

1600 Bank South Building, 55 Marietta Street, N.W., 30303
Telephone: 404-688-4503
Telecopier: 404-681-2950

MEMBERS OF FIRM

John Loren Kennedy (1942-1994)
Thomas G. Sampson
P. Andrew Patterson
Myra H. Dixon
R. David Ware
Patrise M. Perkins-Hooker
Jeffrey E. Tompkins

ASSOCIATES

Rosalind T. Drakeford
Regina E. McMillan
Melynee C. Leftridge
La'Sean M. Zilton

For full biographical listings, see the Martindale-Hubbell Law Directory

WEBB, CARLOCK, COPELAND, SEMLER & STAIR (AV)

A Partnership including Professional Corporations
2600 Marquis Two Tower, 285 Peachtree Center Avenue, P.O. Box 56770, 30343-0770
Telephone: 404-522-8220
FAX: 404-523-2345

MEMBERS OF FIRM

Dennis J. Webb (P.C.)
Thomas S. Carlock (P.C.)
Robert C. Semler (P.C.)
Wade K. Copeland (P.C.)
Kent T. Stair (P.C.)
Douglas W. Smith
David F. Root
William E. Zschunke
Wayne D. McGrew, III
Douglas A. Wilde
Frederick M. Valz, III
E. Alan Miller
Johannes S. Kingma
Dennis G. Lovell, Jr.
Pat M. Anagnostakis

(See Next Column)

ASSOCIATES

Brian R. Neary
William T. Clark
Marvin D. Dikeman
Robert W. Browning
Philip P. Taylor
David D. Cookson
James T. Brieske
Todd M. Yates
Adam L. Appel
R. Michael Ethridge
Daniel J. Huff
Nora Beth Dorsey
Scott D. Huray
Gregory H. Wheeler
Christopher A. Whitlock
John W. Sandifer
Craig A. Brookes
Mary Katherine Smith
William G. Pike, Jr.
Daniel R. Ketchum, II

Counsel for: Allstate Insurance Co.

For full biographical listings, see the Martindale-Hubbell Law Directory

*AUGUSTA,** Richmond Co.

CAPERS, DUNBAR, SANDERS & BRUCKNER (AV)

Fifteenth Floor, First Union Bank Building, 30901-1454
Telephone: 706-722-7542
Telecopier: 706-724-7776

MEMBERS OF FIRM

John D. Capers
Paul H. Dunbar, III
E. Frederick Sanders
Ziva P. Bruckner

ASSOCIATE

Carl P. Dowling

For full biographical listings, see the Martindale-Hubbell Law Directory

FULCHER, HAGLER, REED, HANKS & HARPER (AV)

A Partnership including Professional Corporations
520 Greene Street, P.O. Box 1477, 30903-1477
Telephone: 706-724-0171
Telecopier: 706-724-4573

MEMBERS OF FIRM

William M. Fulcher (1902-1993)
Gould B. Hagler (Retired)
William C. Reed (Retired)
David H. Hanks (P.C.)
John I. Harper (P.C.)
Robert C. Hagler (P.C.)
Michael B. Hagler (P.C.)
James W. Purcell (P.C.)
J. Arthur Davison (P.C.)
Mark C. Wilby (P.C.)
Ronald C. Griffeth
N. Staten Bitting, Jr. (P.C.)

ASSOCIATES

David P. Dekle
Sharon R. Blair
J. Edward Enoch, Jr.
Elizabeth McLeod Kitchens
Barry A. Fleming

General Counsel for: GIW Industries, Inc.
Division Counsel for: CSX Transportation; Textron, Inc. (E-Z Go Car Division).
Counsel for: NationsBank; Georgia Natural Gas Co. (a division of Atlanta Gas Light Co.); Champion International Corp.; Aetna Life and Casualty; Liberty Mutual Insurance Company; St. Paul Fire & Marine Insurance Co.; Kimberly Clark Corporation.

For Complete List of Firm Personnel, See General Section

For full biographical listings, see the Martindale-Hubbell Law Directory

GLOVER & BLOUNT, P.C. (AV)

511 Courthouse Lane, 30901
Telephone: 706-722-3786
Fax: 706-722-5629

Gary A. Glover
Percy J. Blount

For full biographical listings, see the Martindale-Hubbell Law Directory

WILEY S. OBENSHAIN, III, P.C. (AV)

511 Courthouse Lane, 30901
Telephone: 706-722-1789
Fax: 706-722-7145

Wiley S. Obenshain, III

For full biographical listings, see the Martindale-Hubbell Law Directory

*CARROLLTON,** Carroll Co.

TISINGER, TISINGER, VANCE & GREER, A PROFESSIONAL CORPORATION (AV)

100 Wagon Yard Plaza, P.O. Box 2069, 30117
Telephone: 404-834-4467
FAX: 404-834-5426

Thomas E. Greer
Kevin B. Buice
Robert H. Sullivan
Glenn M. Jarrell
Douglas C. Vassy
J. Branson Parker
David F. Miceli

Representative Clients: Atlanta Casualty Company; Bruno's, Inc.; Cincinnati Insurance Company; Cotton States Insurance Company; Federated Electric Insurance Company; Georgia Farm Bureau Mutual Insurance Company; Merastar Insurance Company; Southern General Insurance Company; State

(See Next Column)

TISINGER, TISINGER, VANCE & GREER A PROFESSIONAL CORPORATION—*Continued*

Farm Mutual Automobile Insurance Company; State Farm Fire and Casualty Company.

For Complete List of Firm Personnel, See General Section

For full biographical listings, see the Martindale-Hubbell Law Directory

*COLUMBUS,** Muscogee Co.

HATCHER, STUBBS, LAND, HOLLIS & ROTHSCHILD (AV)

Suite 500 The Corporate Center, 233 12th Street, P.O. Box 2707, 31902-2707
Telephone: 706-324-0201
Telecopier: 706-322-7747

MEMBERS OF FIRM

William B. Hardegree — Joseph L. Waldrep
James E. Humes, II — Robert C. Martin, Jr.

ASSOCIATE

C. Morris Mullin

Division Counsel for: Georgia Power Co.
Assistant Division Counsel for: Norfolk Southern Corp.
Local Counsel for: State Farm Insurance Cos.; Liberty Mutual Insurance Co.; Home Insurance Co.; Kemper Insurance Co.; MAG Mutual Insurance Co.; Southern Guaranty Insurance Co.; Cigna Corp. (INA-Aetna); Fireman's Fund-American Insurance Cos.

For Complete List of Firm Personnel, See General Section

For full biographical listings, see the Martindale-Hubbell Law Directory

LAYFIELD, ROTHSCHILD & MORGAN (AV)

1030 First Avenue, P.O. Box 2788, 31902-2788
Telephone: 706-324-4167
FAX: 706-324-1969

MEMBERS OF FIRM

Jerome M. Rothschild — W. Donald Morgan, Jr.

ASSOCIATES

Virgil T. Theus — Neal J. Callahan

Reference: Columbus Bank and Trust Company.

For Complete List of Firm Personnel, See General Section

For full biographical listings, see the Martindale-Hubbell Law Directory

*DECATUR,** De Kalb Co.

PARKERSON & SHELFER (AV)

715 First Union Decatur Building, 250 East Ponce De Leon Avenue, 30030
Telephone: 404-377-8143
Telecopier: 404-373-6829

MEMBERS OF FIRM

William S. Shelfer (1900-1975) — I. J. Parkerson
William S. Shelfer, Jr.

Reference: Nations Bank of Georgia.

For full biographical listings, see the Martindale-Hubbell Law Directory

*GAINESVILLE,** Hall Co.

FORRESTER & BRIM (AV)

459 E.E. Butler Parkway, S.E., P.O. Box 1688, 30503-1688
Telephone: 404-531-0800
Fax: 404-536-7789

MEMBERS OF FIRM

Weymon H. Forrester — James Ernest Brim, III

ASSOCIATES

Richard Charles Bellows — Nolie J. Motes

For full biographical listings, see the Martindale-Hubbell Law Directory

SMITH, GILLIAM AND WILLIAMS (AV)

200 Old Coca-Cola Building, 301 Green Street, N.W., P.O. Box 1098, 30503
Telephone: 404-536-3381
Fax: 404-531-1491

MEMBERS OF FIRM

R. Wilson Smith, Jr. (1906-1983) — Jerry A. Williams
John H. Smith — Kelly Anne Miles
Steven P. Gilliam — Bradley J. Patten

ASSOCIATES

M. Tyler Smith — Scott Arthur Ball

General Counsel for: Gainesville Industrial Electric Co.; Georgia Mutual Insurance Co.; L & R Farms; H. Wilson Manufacturing Co.; Goforth Electrical Supply; North Georgia Petroleum Co.; Gibbs Management Group, Inc.

For full biographical listings, see the Martindale-Hubbell Law Directory

*GRIFFIN,** Spalding Co.

BECK, OWEN & MURRAY (AV)

600 First Union Tower, P.O. Box 116, 30224
Telephone: 706-227-4000
Fax: 706-229-8524

William H. Beck, Jr. (1898-1989) — John H. Goddard, Jr. (1913-1979)

MEMBERS OF FIRM

James C. Owen, Jr. — Richard L. Collier
Samuel A. Murray — Richard M. Hunter
James R. Fortune, Jr. — William M. Dallas, III

ASSOCIATE

Bradford W. Thomas

Counsel for: Griffin Federal Savings Bank; Griffin-Spalding County School System.
Local Counsel for: Atlanta Gas Light Co.; Georgia Power Co.; Southern Bell.
Representative Clients: Atlanta Casualty Co.; Cotton States Insurance Co.; Georgia Farm Bureau Mutual Ins. Co.; MAG Mutual Insurance Co.; State Farm Ins. Co.
Area Trial Counsel for: Norfolk Southern Corp.

For full biographical listings, see the Martindale-Hubbell Law Directory

*MACON,** Bibb Co.

ANDERSON, WALKER & REICHERT (AV)

Suite 404 Trust Company Bank Building, P.O. Box 6497, 31208-6497
Telephone: 912-743-8651
Telecopier: 912-743-9636

MEMBERS OF FIRM

Albert P. Reichert — Walter H. Bush, Jr.
Thomas L. Bass — Eugene S. Hatcher
Albert P. Reichert, Jr. — Robert A. B. Reichert
John D. Reeves — Elton L. Wall
John W. Collier — Susan S. Cole
Jonathan A. Alderman

ASSOCIATES

Brown W. Dennis, Jr. — Travis M. Trimble
John P. Cole — Stephen M. Welsh

Representative Clients: Riverwood International Georgia, Inc.; Hospital Corporation of America; Pepsi-Cola Bottling Company of Macon; Radiology Associates of Macon, P.C.; Thiele Kaolin Company; Trust Company Bank of Middle Georgia, N.A.
General Insurance Clients: Liberty Mutual Insurance Co.; United States Fidelity & Guaranty Co.; Continental Insurance Cos.; Alexis, Inc.

For Complete List of Firm Personnel, See General Section

For full biographical listings, see the Martindale-Hubbell Law Directory

CHAMBLESS, HIGDON & CARSON (AV)

Suite 200 Ambrose Baber Building, 577 Walnut Street, P.O. Box 246, 31298-5399
Telephone: 912-745-1181
Telecopier: 912-746-9479

MEMBERS OF FIRM

Joseph H. Davis — Thomas F. Richardson
Joseph H. Chambless — Mary Mendel Katz
David B. Higdon — Emmitte H. Griggs
James F. Carson, Jr. — Marc T. Treadwell

ASSOCIATES

Kim H. Stroup — Christopher Balch
Jon Christopher Wolfe

Local Counsel for: Atlanta Gas Light Co.; First Union National Bank of Georgia; Security National Bank.

For full biographical listings, see the Martindale-Hubbell Law Directory

HALL, BLOCH, GARLAND & MEYER (AV)

1500 Charter Medical Building, P.O. Box 5088, 31213-3199
Telephone: 912-745-1625
Telecopier: 912-741-8822

MEMBERS OF FIRM

F. Kennedy Hall — J. Steven Stewart
Benjamin M. Garland — Mark E. Toth

Representative Clients: Norfolk Southern Railway Company; Central of Georgia Railroad Company; Railway Claims Services, Inc.; United States Fidelity & Guaranty Company; Rail Tex, Inc.; Georgia Central Railway Company.

For Complete List of Firm Personnel, See General Section

For full biographical listings, see the Martindale-Hubbell Law Directory

*MARIETTA,** Cobb Co.

BARNES, BROWNING, TANKSLEY & CASURELLA (AV)

Suite 225, 166 Anderson Street, 30060
Telephone: 404-424-1500
Fax: 404-424-1740

MEMBERS OF FIRM

Roy E. Barnes
Charles B. Tanksley
Jerry A. Landers, Jr.
Jeffrey G. Casurella

For full biographical listings, see the Martindale-Hubbell Law Directory

DOWNEY & CLEVELAND (AV)

288 Washington Avenue, 30060
Telephone: 404-422-3233
Fax: 404-423-4199

OF COUNSEL

Lynn A. Downey

MEMBERS OF FIRM

Joseph C. Parker
Y. Kevin Williams
Russell B. Davis
G. Lee Welborn

ASSOCIATE

Rodney S. Shockley

Representative Clients: Allstate Insurance Co.; St. Paul Insurance Cos.; Georgia Farm Bureau Mutual Insurance Co.; State Farm Insurance Cos.; Cotton States Mutual Insurance Co.; Colonial Insurance Co. of California; Ed Voyles Oldsmobile, Honda and Chrysler-Plymouth; Chuck Clancy Ford; City of Acworth; Lockheed Aeronautical Systems Company, a Division of Lockheed Corporation.

For Complete List of Firm Personnel, See General Section

For full biographical listings, see the Martindale-Hubbell Law Directory

MOORE & ROGERS (AV)

192 Anderson Street, P.O. Box 3305, 30060
Telephone: 404-429-1499
Telecopier: 404-429-8631

MEMBERS OF FIRM

John H. Moore
William R. Johnson
Robert D. Ingram

ASSOCIATES

Jeffrey A. Watkins
Ross E. Longood

Representative Clients: Crawford & Co.; Executive Risk Consultants, Inc.; National Union Fire Insurance Co.; The PMA Group; Scottsdale Insurance Co.; Transamerica Specialty Insurance Co.; Great Central Insurance Company; Wausau Insurance Company; Georgia Oilman's Association.
Reference: C.W. Matthews Contracting Co., Inc.

For full biographical listings, see the Martindale-Hubbell Law Directory

*SAVANNAH,** Chatham Co.

BARROW, SIMS, MORROW & LEE, A PROFESSIONAL CORPORATION (AV)

111 West Congress Street, P.O. Box 8185, 31412
Telephone: 912-234-7215
Fax: 912-234-7119

Charles W. Barrow
R. Stephen Sims
Jordon D. Morrow
A. Mark Lee
Douglas P. McManamy

For full biographical listings, see the Martindale-Hubbell Law Directory

BRANNEN, SEARCY & SMITH (AV)

22 East Thirty-Fourth Street, P.O. Box 8002, 31412
Telephone: 912-234-8875
Fax: 912-232-1792

Perry Brannen (1903-1984)
Frank P. Brannen
William N. Searcy
David R. Smith
Daniel C. Cohen
Wayne L. Durden

OF COUNSEL

William T. Daniel, Jr.

ASSOCIATES

Robert L. Jenkins
Bernard F. Kistler, Jr.
Fonda L. Jackson

Counsel for: Continental Insurance Co.

For full biographical listings, see the Martindale-Hubbell Law Directory

FORBES & BOWMAN (AV)

Park South D-14, 7505 Waters Avenue, P.O. Box 13929, 31416-0929
Telephone: 912-352-1190
FAX: 912-352-1471

(See Next Column)

Morton G. Forbes
Catherine M. Bowman
John A. Foster
Isabel M. Pauley

For full biographical listings, see the Martindale-Hubbell Law Directory

KENT, WORSHAM, WILLIAMSON & BRANNON (AV)

The Callen Trust Building, 42 East Bay Street, P.O. Box 9117, 31412
Telephone: 912-238-1500
FAX: 912-238-5515

MEMBERS OF FIRM

Martin Kent
William O. Williamson III
Doris E. Brannon
Ellen S. Lyons
Hugh M. Worsham, Jr.

LEGAL SUPPORT PERSONNEL

Linda Susan Phipps

References: The Coastal Bank of Georgia; C&S National Bank.

For full biographical listings, see the Martindale-Hubbell Law Directory

MCCALLAR AND ASSOCIATES (AV)

115 Oglethorpe Avenue West, P.O. Box 9026, 31412
Telephone: 912-234-1215
Telecopier: 912-236-7549

C. James McCallar, Jr.

Mark Bulovic
Todd E. Schwartz

For full biographical listings, see the Martindale-Hubbell Law Directory

WOODALL AND MACKENZIE, P.C. (AV)

327 Tattnall Street, P.O. Box 10166, 31412
Telephone: 912-238-9999

John T. Woodall
Malcolm Mackenzie, III

Peter A. Giusti

Reference: Trust Company Bank.

For full biographical listings, see the Martindale-Hubbell Law Directory

*TOCCOA,** Stephens Co.

MCCLURE, RAMSAY & DICKERSON (AV)

400 Falls Road, P.O. Drawer 1408, 30577
Telephone: 706-886-3178
Fax: 706-886-1150

MEMBERS OF FIRM

Clyde M. McClure (1892-1976)
George B. Ramsay, Jr.
John A. Dickerson
Allan R. Ramsay
Martha B. Sikes
Marlin R. Escoe

ASSOCIATES

Alice D. Hayes
Elizabeth Felton Moore
Leon Jourolmon

OF COUNSEL

Knox Bynum

Counsel for: Coats and Clark, Inc.; Stephens Federal Savings & Loan Assn.; St. Paul Insurance Cos.; State Farm Insurance Cos.; Cotton States Insurance Cos.; City of Toccoa; Citizens Bank; Habersham Plantation Corp.; Patterson Pump Co.

For full biographical listings, see the Martindale-Hubbell Law Directory

HAWAII

*HONOLULU,** Honolulu Co.

ALCANTARA & FRAME ATTORNEYS AT LAW, A LAW CORPORATION (AV)

Suite 1100 Pioneer Plaza, 900 Fort Street Mall, 96813
Telephone: 808-536-6922
Fax: 808-521-8898
Telex: 650-225-8816
WUI: 101-650 225-8816
MCI ID: 225-8816

Leonard F. Alcantara
Robert G. Frame
Bryan Y. Y. Ho

Joy Lee Cauble
John O'Kane, Jr.
Evelyn J. Black
Mary A. Cox
Michael D. Formby
Eldon M. Ching

(See Next Column)

ALCANTARA & FRAME ATTORNEYS AT LAW, A LAW CORPORATION—*Continued*

Reference: City Bank, Honolulu.

For full biographical listings, see the Martindale-Hubbell Law Directory

ASHFORD & NAKAMURA (AV)

2910 Pacific Tower, 1001 Bishop Street, 96813
Telephone: 808-528-0444
Telex: 723-8158
Telecopier: (808) 533-0761
Cable Address: Justlaw

George W. Ashford, Jr. Lee T. Nakamura

Ann C. Kemp Francis T. O'Brien

Representative Clients: Baker Industries, Inc.; Burns International Security Services; Clark Equipment Co.; Great Lakes Chemical Corporation; California Union Insurance Co.; Fireman's Fund Insurance Companies; Great American Insurance Companies; Guaranty National Companies; Horace Mann Insurance Company; Marine Office of America Corp.

For full biographical listings, see the Martindale-Hubbell Law Directory

AYABE, CHONG, NISHIMOTO, SIA & NAKAMURA (AV)

A Partnership including a Professional Corporation
3000 Grosvenor Center, 737 Bishop Street, 96813
Telephone: 808-537-6119
Telecopier: 808-526-3491

MEMBERS OF FIRM

Sidney K. Ayabe (P.C.)
Robert A. Chong
John S. Nishimoto
Richard Nakamura
Jeffrey H. K. Sia
Kenneth T. Goya
Francis M. Nakamoto
Calvin E. Young
Diane W. Wong
Rodney S. Nishida
Patricia T. Fujii
Rhonda Nishimura
Gail M. Kang

Ann H. Aratani
Philip S. Uesato
Ronald M. Shigekane
Robin R. Horner
Nicole Jung-Shin Rhee
Stephen G. Dyer
Steven L. Goto
Daria Ann Loy
Virgil B. Prieto
Kelley G.A. Nakano

Representative Clients: Travelers Insurance Co.; St. Paul Fire and Marine Insurance Co.; The Employers Group of Insurance Companies; TIG Insurance Co.; Pacific Insurance Co.; Hartford Accident and Indemnity Co.; Continental Casualty Co.; First Insurance Company of Hawaii, Ltd.

For full biographical listings, see the Martindale-Hubbell Law Directory

GREELEY WALKER & KOWEN (AV)

A Partnership including a Law Corporation
Suite 1300 Pauahi Tower, 1001 Bishop Street, 96813
Telephone: 808-526-2211
Telecopier: 808-528-4690

MEMBERS OF FIRM

Burnham H. Greeley (A Law Corporation)
Susan P. Walker
Richard J. Kowen
Janice T. Futa

ASSOCIATES

Frank P. Richardson
Kimberly Ann Greeley (Not admitted in HI)
Andrew D. Smith
George H. Keller

Representative Clients: Abbott Laboratories; The Boeing Company; E.I. du Pont deNemours and Company, Incorporated; General Motors Corporation; Japan Tobacco International Corporation; Maytag Corporation; Phillips Petroleum Company; Sears, Roebuck and Co.; Toyota Motor Corporation; United States Aviation Underwriters, Inc.

For full biographical listings, see the Martindale-Hubbell Law Directory

MCCORRISTON MIHO MILLER MUKAI (AV)

Five Waterfront Plaza, 4th Floor, 500 Ala Moana Boulevard, 96813
Telephone: 808-529-7300
Facsimile: 808-524-8293
Cable: Attorneys, Honolulu

MEMBERS OF FIRM

William C. McCorriston
William K. Meheula
Darolyn Hatsuko Lendio
Richard B. Miller
Randall K. Schmitt
John Y. Yamano

ASSOCIATES

Lisa M. Ginoza
K. Rae McCorkle
Joel D. Kam

For Complete List of Firm Personnel, See General Section

For full biographical listings, see the Martindale-Hubbell Law Directory

LAW OFFICE OF KENNETH S. ROBBINS ATTORNEY AT LAW, A LAW CORPORATION (AV)

Suite 2220 Davies Pacific Center, 841 Bishop Street, 96813
Telephone: 808-524-2355
Fax: 808-526-0290

Kenneth S. Robbins

Vincent A. Rhodes Shinken Naitoh

For full biographical listings, see the Martindale-Hubbell Law Directory

IDAHO

*BOISE,** Ada Co.

HALL, FARLEY, OBERRECHT & BLANTON (AV)

Key Financial Center, 702 West Idaho Street, Suite 700, P.O. Box 1271, 83701-1271
Telephone: 208-336-0404
Facsimile: 208-336-5193

Richard E. Hall
Donald J. Farley
Phillip S. Oberrecht
Raymond D. Powers
Candy Wagahoff Dale
Robert B. Luce
J. Kevin West
Bart W. Harwood

J. Charles Blanton
John J. Burke
Steven J. Hippler
Thorpe P. Orton
Ronald S. Best (Not admitted in ID)

References: Boise State University; Farm Bureau Mutual Insurance Company of Idaho; Medical Insurance Exchange of California; The St. Paul Cos.

For full biographical listings, see the Martindale-Hubbell Law Directory

IMHOFF & LYNCH (AV)

1607 West Jefferson Street, P.O. Box 739, 83701
Telephone: 208-336-6900
Facsimile: 208-336-7031

MEMBERS OF FIRM

James B. Lynch
Michael W. Moore
Thomas P. Baskin, III
Paige Alan Parker

Kaaren Lynn Barr
Penny L. Dykas
Mary L. McDougal

OF COUNSEL

Joseph M. Imhoff, Jr.

Representative Clients: United State Aviation Underwriters, Aetna Casualty & Surety, Co., Yellow Freight, Underwriters at Llodys, Willis Coroon Management Co., Inc., National Union Fire Insurance Co., Capital Insurance Co., Coleman Co., Alfa Laval Agri., Inc., Admiral Insurance Co.
Reference: First Security Bank.

For full biographical listings, see the Martindale-Hubbell Law Directory

*POCATELLO,** Bannock Co.

MERRILL & MERRILL, CHARTERED (AV)

Key Bank Building, P.O. Box 991, 83204
Telephone: 208-232-2286
Fax: 208-232-2499

Wesley F. Merrill
Stephen S. Dunn
D. Russell Wight
N. Randy Smith
David C. Nye

Representative Clients: Farm Bureau Mutual Insurance Co. of Idaho; Aetna Life & Casualty; St. Paul Insurance; The Travelers Insurance Co.

For Complete List of Firm Personnel, See General Section

For full biographical listings, see the Martindale-Hubbell Law Directory

ILLINOIS

AURORA, Kane Co.

MURPHY, HUPP, FOOTE, MIELKE AND KINNALLY (AV)

North Island Center, P.O. Box 5030, 60507
Telephone: 708-844-0056
FAX: 708-844-1905

(See Next Column)

MURPHY, HUPP, FOOTE, MIELKE AND KINNALLY, *Aurora—Continued*

MEMBERS OF FIRM

William C. Murphy
Robert B. Hupp
Robert M. Foote
Craig S. Mielke
Patrick M. Kinnally
Paul G. Krentz
Joseph C. Loran
Gerald K. Hodge

Timothy D. O'Neil
Thomas U. Hipp

OF COUNSEL

Robert T. Olson

Representative Clients: American Telephone & Telegraph Co.; Fox Valley Park District; Lyon Metal Products; Kane County Forest Preserve District; Hollywood Casino; Employers Mutual Insurance Co.; Forty-Eight Insulations, Inc.; UNR Asbestos Disease Trust; Richards-Wilcox Co.; National Bank & Trust Company of Syracuse.

For full biographical listings, see the Martindale-Hubbell Law Directory

*BELLEVILLE,** St. Clair Co.

DONOVAN, ROSE, NESTER & SZEWCZYK, P.C. (AV)

8 East Washington Street, 62220
Telephone: 618-235-2020
Telecopier: 618-235-9632

Harold A. Donovan, Sr.
Michael J. Nester
Dennis E. Rose
Edward J. Szewczyk
Charles L. Joley

OF COUNSEL

Vincent J. Hatch (Retired)

Douglas R. Heise
Georgiann Oliver
Kenneth M. Nussbaumer
Bret A. Cohen

Representative Clients: State Farm Mutual Auto & Life Co.; Travelers Insurance Co.; Liberty Mutual Insurance Co.; Government Employees Insurance Co.; Great American Insurance Co.; Aetna Casualty & Surety Co.; Royal Globe Insurance Co.; Illinois Founders Insurance Co.; INA (Insurance Company of North America).

For full biographical listings, see the Martindale-Hubbell Law Directory

*CHICAGO,** Cook Co.

ARONBERG GOLDGEHN DAVIS & GARMISA (AV)

Suite 3000 One IBM Plaza, 60611-3633
Telephone: 312-828-9600
Telecopier: 312-828-9635

MEMBERS OF FIRM

Mitchell S. Goldgehn
Nathan H. Lichtenstein
James A. Smith
William W. Yotis III
Gene H. Hansen

ASSOCIATES

Christopher J. Bannon
Lisa J. Brodsky
James J. Hickey
William J. Serritella, Jr.
William C. Wilder

For Complete List of Firm Personnel, See General Section

For full biographical listings, see the Martindale-Hubbell Law Directory

BELGRADE AND O'DONNELL, A PROFESSIONAL CORPORATION (AV)

311 South Wacker Drive, Suite 2770, 60606
Telephone: 312-360-9500
Facsimile: 312-360-9550

Steven B. Belgrade
John A. O'Donnell
George M. Velcich
Kim Richard Kardas
Andrea J. McIntyre
Joseph G. Howard

For full biographical listings, see the Martindale-Hubbell Law Directory

BIXBY, LECHNER & POTRATZ, P.C. A PROFESSIONAL CORPORATION (AV)

Suite 1770, 10 South Riverside Plaza, 60606
Telephone: 312-648-4888
Telecopier: 312-648-9493

Roger A. Bixby
David C. Lechner
William G. Potratz
Robert K. Scott
Gary P. Hollander
Robert S. Pinzur

Kellie S. Halsted
Vasyl Markus, Jr.
Matthew E. Ten Eick
April A. Trob

For full biographical listings, see the Martindale-Hubbell Law Directory

BRINTON & FEDOTA (AV)

Three First National Plaza, Suite 3900, 60602
Telephone: 312-236-5015
Fax: 312-236-8559

MEMBERS OF FIRM

Howard T. Brinton
John D. Kuhn

Teresa R. Clewell
Mark J. Smith
Stephen C. Prout

For full biographical listings, see the Martindale-Hubbell Law Directory

CHAVIANO & ASSOCIATES, LTD. (AV)

10 South La Salle Street, Suite 3710, 60603-1098
Telephone: 312-759-9800
Facsimile: 312-759-1445

Hugo Chaviano

Lillian Fuentes
Edward M. Ordonez
Donna Del Principe
Jody B. Rosenbaum
Roberto Cisneros, Jr.

OF COUNSEL

Sandra Van De Kauter

For full biographical listings, see the Martindale-Hubbell Law Directory

DOWD & DOWD, LTD. (AV)

Suite 1000, 55 West Wacker Drive, 60601
Telephone: 312-704-4400
Telecopier: 312-704-4500

Joseph V. Dowd
Michael E. Dowd
Kenneth Gurber
Robert C. Yelton III
Patrick C. Dowd

S. Robert Depke
Robert J. Golden
Kevin J. Kane
Jeffrey Edward Kehl
Joseph J. Leonard
Ronald J. Lukes
Donald G. Machalinski
John M. McAndrews
Martha A. Niles
Michael G. Patrizio
Patrick J. Ruberry
Anthony R. Rutkowski
Karen W. Worsek

LEGAL SUPPORT PERSONNEL

Carrie J. Julian
Jill A. Weiseman

OF COUNSEL

Guenther Ahlf
Joel S. Ostrow

Reference: Central National Bank in Chicago.

For full biographical listings, see the Martindale-Hubbell Law Directory

EICH & FRANKLIN (AV)

Suite 1206, 22 West Monroe Street, 60603
Telephone: 312-263-0599
Fax: 312-263-6768

MEMBERS OF FIRM

Edwin W. Eich, Jr.
Charles R. Franklin

Ruth E. Farbman
Noel B. Haberek, Jr.
Harold Himelman
John J. Nash

For full biographical listings, see the Martindale-Hubbell Law Directory

GESSLER, FLYNN, FLEISCHMANN, HUGHES & SOCOL, LTD. (AV)

Three First National Plaza, Suite 2200, 60602
Telephone: 312-580-0100
Telecopy: 312-580-1994

Mark S. Dym
Michael J. Flaherty
Thomas J. Fleischmann
Terence E. Flynn
George W. Gessler
John K. Hughes
William P. Jones
Peter M. Katsaros
Mark A. LaRose
Terence J. Moran
Matthew J. Piers
David J. Pritchard
Kalman D. Resnick
Jonathan A. Rothstein
Donna Kaner Socol

Eric Berg
Benjamin P. Beringer
Anjali Dayal
Ruth M. Dunning
Jennifer Fischer
Charles J. Holley
Laura C. Liu
Kimberley Marsh
Alex W. Miller
Paul A. Reasoner
Michael P. Simkus
Marci S. Sperling
Maria L. Venturo
Vanessa J. Weathersby
Mark B. Weiner
Charles H. Winterstein

(See Next Column)

GESSLER, FLYNN, FLEISCHMANN, HUGHES & SOCOL LTD.—*Continued*

OF COUNSEL

James T. Derico, Jr.
Susan R. Gzesh
Foster Marshall, Jr.

For full biographical listings, see the Martindale-Hubbell Law Directory

GLEASON, MCGUIRE & SHREFFLER (AV)

160 North Wacker Drive, 60606
Telephone: 312-641-0580
Fax: 312-641-0380
Roseland, New Jersey Office: Three A.D.P. Boulevard.
Telephone: 201-533-1334.
Fax: 201-533-1339.

MEMBERS OF FIRM

Nancy J. Gleason
Judith A. Gleason
Philip J. McGuire
David E. Schroeder
Douglas G. Shreffler
Virginia M. Vermillion

ASSOCIATES

Bonnie F. Bagdon
Cynthia L. Bordelon
Maryterese Ceko
Henry T. French Jr.
Edward W. Gleason
Joanne Gleason
Richard E. Gottlieb
Patricia M. Kelly
Robert Nils Lane
John S. Lindemann
Anthony J. Madormo
Linda L. McCarty
Timothy M. Nolan
Michael R. Orlando
Robert C. Thurston
Hugh C. Welsh (Resident, Roseland, New Jersey Office)
J. Richard West
Vincent S. Ziccolella (Resident, Roseland, New Jersey Office)

LEGAL SUPPORT PERSONNEL

Ronald E. Feret

Stacy M. Boyle
Josephine J. Campagna
Jane W. Grimme
Monica M. Brace
Christine E. Houska
Susan E. Kelly
Kathleen A. Wrobel
Sally S. Tuxhorn

Representative Clients: Allstate Insurance Co.; Employer's Mutual Casualty Co.; Northbrook Property & Casualty; Mutual Marine Office; American Home Assurance Co.; Lexington Insurance Co.; Pacific Mutual Marine; Utica Mutual; New York Marine & General Insurance Co.

For full biographical listings, see the Martindale-Hubbell Law Directory

HASKELL & PERRIN (AV)

200 West Adams, Suite 2600, 60606
Telephone: 312-781-9393
Fax: 312-781-9178

MEMBERS OF FIRM

James Kirk Perrin
John J. Lynch
Mary Elizabeth Denefe
Jerome J. Duchowicz
Michael J. Sehr
Marsha K. Ross
Stephen Sonderby
Kevin W. Doherty
Edward J. Matushek, III
Daniel P. Caswell
Mary Jo Greene
Teresa Rooney Williams

OF COUNSEL

Donald M. Haskell

ASSOCIATES

Mark T. Banovetz
Cynthia J. Bauman
Benjamin A. Blume
Peter G. Bora
Eileen King Bower
David G. Boyer (Not admitted in IL)
Robert W. Brunner
Patrick Christopher Cremin, Jr.
Kathryn M. Frost
Myrna B. Galang
Elizabeth M. Handzel
Audrey S. Hanrahan
Elizabeth Thorne Jozefowicz
Rein F. Krammer
Daniel M. Latreille (Not admitted in IL)
Craig T. Liljestrand
Robert J. Marshall (Not admitted in IL)
David A. Nilles
Michele T. Oshman
Melissa J. Pemberton
David W. Pierdinock
Amy J. Pruess
James M. Ratzer
Nancy J. Robinson
Joseph B. Royster
Frank B. Slepicka
Michael P. Warnick
Alan S. Zelkowitz

For full biographical listings, see the Martindale-Hubbell Law Directory

JOHNSON & BELL, LTD. (AV)

Suite 2200, 222 North La Salle Street, 60601
Telephone: 312-372-0770
Facsimile: 312-372-9818
Wheaton, Illinois Office: Suite 1640, 2100 Manchester Road.
Telephone: 708-510-0880.
Facsimile: 780-510-0939.

(See Next Column)

William V. Johnson
John W. Bell
Jack T. Riley, Jr.
Brian C. Fetzer
Thomas H. Fegan
Thomas W. Murphy
Pamela L. Gellen
Thomas J. Andrews
William G. Beatty
John A. Childers
Robert L. Nora
Margaret A. Unger
Timothy J. McKay
Howard Patrick Morris
Scott W. Hoyne
James S. Stickles, Jr.
Frederick S. Mueller
Joseph R. Marconi
Frederick H. Branding
Robert M. Burke
Cornelius J. Harrington, III
Thomas W. Murphy
Michael B. Gunzburg
Charles W. Planek
Edward D. D'Arcy, Jr.
Debra A. DiMaggio
Michael P. Siavelis
William A. Geiser
Thomas J. Koch
Kurt C. Meihofer
Kevin G. Owens
Steven I. Rapaport
Dennis C. Cusack
Emilio E. Machado
Charles P. Rantis
Dean M. Athans
Robert J. Comfort
Alan Jay Goldstein
Susan Marzec Hannigan
Daniel C. Murray
Thomas F. Poelking

William J. Anaya
Frank S. Capuani
Michael A. Chabraja
Gregory D. Conforti
Larry A. Crotser
Christopher M. Daddino
Jeffrey W. Deer
Maria S. Doughty
Nancy G. Enderby
Patrick T. Garvey
Laura B. Glaser
Kevin J. Greenwood
Sean J. Hardy
Mark D. Johnson
Robert Johnson
Janet A. Kachoyeanos
Mindy L. Kallus
Andrea H. Kott
Genevie F. Labuda
Bruce M. Lichtcsien
Steven E. Lieb
Kathryn K. Loft
Mary E. Lopez
Michael J. Lynch
David M. Macksey
Robert J. Malmrose
Robert R. McNamara
Peter A. Nicholson
Eric G. Patt
Richard C. Perna
Brendan S. Power
Marilyn McCabe Reidy
Joseph D. Ryan
Ann M. Smith
Robert Spitkovsky, Jr.
Terry Takash
Paul A. Tanzillo
Kelly N. Warnick
Douglas B. Wexler
Steven F. Wittman

References available upon request.

For full biographical listings, see the Martindale-Hubbell Law Directory

KIESLER & BERMAN (AV)

Suite 1300, 188 West Randolph Street, 60601
Telephone: 312-332-2840
FAX: 312-332-4547
Wheaton Office: 2100 Manchester, Suite 504.
Telephone: 708-752-8247.
Fax: 708-665-9771.
Joliet Office: 57 West Jefferson Street.
Telephone: 815-723-2755.
Fax: 815-723-2763.
Waukegan Office: 216 Madison Street.
Telephone: 708-244-5805.
Fax: 708-244-3996.

MEMBERS OF FIRM

Marvin D. Berman
Robert L. Kiesler
Clinton J. Feil
Alan P. Miller
John R. Garofalo
Stephen B. Frew
Dale L. Schlafer
Stephen E. Ford
Edward L. Cooper
Lyle F. Koester
Mark S. Vilimek
Rory D. Cassidy
Patti Olson Deuel
David J. Kiesler

ASSOCIATES

Bradley D. Alexander
Matthew D. Creen
Jean M. French
Mary E. Haeger
Thomas J. Hendrikse
Kenneth Jones
Shari J. Kalik
Bryan W. Luce
Cynthia A. Meister
Peter R. Mennella
Jeffrey S. Pavlovich
John J. Piegore
Daniel J. Softcheck
Richard T. Valentino
Jeanne M. Zeiger

SENIOR COUNSEL

Eugene S. Goldenson
Frank N. Rago

For full biographical listings, see the Martindale-Hubbell Law Directory

KRALOVEC, MARQUARD, DOYLE & GIBBONS, CHARTERED (AV)

122 South Michigan Avenue, Suite 1720, 60603
Telephone: 312-939-4455
Fax: 312-939-8923
Wheaton, Illinois Office: 211 South Wheaton Avenue, Suite 303.
Telephone: 708-665-9750.
Fax: 708-665-9772.

(See Next Column)

KRALOVEC, MARQUARD, DOYLE & GIBBONS CHARTERED, *Chicago—Continued*

John C. Doyle
Michael J. Gibbons
Philip W. Domagalski
Michael T. Sprengnether
William E. Spizzirri
Nancy Jo Arnold
Michael J. Mullen
James F. Donovan
David T. Nani

Linda C. Abens
Michael T. Clarke
James V. Creen
Daniel J. Donnelly
Lawrence J. Drabot
Kathleen A. Johnson
Timothy E. Takash
Sara T. Wiggs

OF COUNSEL

Henry J. Marquard
Austin J. Gibbons
Sam L. Miller

Representative Clients: American Mutual Liability Insurance Co.; Mutual of Omaha Insurance Co.; Royal Insurance Cos.; Safeco Insurance Group; United States Fidelity & Guaranty Co.; American Risk Management, Inc.; American States Insurance; American Mutual Insurance Co.; Babcock Industries, Inc.; Banker's Life & Casualty.

For full biographical listings, see the Martindale-Hubbell Law Directory

---

PRETZEL & STOUFFER, CHARTERED (AV)

One South Wacker Drive Suite 2500, 60606-4673
Telephone: 312-346-1973
FAX: 312-346-8242; 346-8060

Gemma B. Allen
Richard William Austin
David M. Bennett
Richard L. Berdelle
Audrey A. Berish
Glen R. Bernfield
Paula Meyer Besler
William B. Bower
Michael G. Bruton
Barbara Condit Canning
Maryanne H. Capron
Robert Marc Chemers
Michael A. Clarke
Elizabeth Conkin
Suzanne Marie Crowley
Jeffery W. Davis
Marilyn Brock Doig
Joseph M. Dooley, III
Matthew J. Egan
Marc I. Fenton
David B. Gelman
Timothy J. Gillick (1940-1984)
Michael D. Goodman
Richard J. Gorman
Joyce M. Greene
Sally Oxley Hagerty
Brian T. Henry
Robert J. Heyne
William E. Kenny
Donald J. Kindwald
James A. Knox, Jr.
Marlene A. Kurilla
James A. LaBarge
Ronald S. Ladden
Steven M. Laduzinsky
Donald B. Lenderman
David J. Loughnane
Patrick Foran Lustig
Steven John Martin
William P. McGowen, III
Daniel B. Mills
James P. Moran
Edward H. Nielsen
Donald J. O'Meara, Jr.
Molly M. O'Reilly
Gary Arthur Peters
Paul L. Price
Neil K. Quinn
Charles F. Redden
Lynn M. Reid
Catherine Coyne Reiter
Mark D. Roth
Roger A. Rubin
Edward B. Ruff, III
Lewis M. Schneider
Betty-Jane Schrum
Alan J. Schumacher
Peter G. Skiko
John V. Smith, II
Christine Hough Speranza
Mark P. Standa
Leo M. Tarpey, Jr.
Robert D. Tuerk
Anthony J. Tunney
Stephen C. Veltman
John J. Walsh, III
Richard M. Waris
Timothy A. Weaver
Michael J. Weber
William P. White III
Richard S. Wisner

OF COUNSEL

Joseph B. Lederleitner
Paul W. Pretzel (1906-1987)
Ralph E. Stouffer, Jr.

Representative Clients: Allstate Insurance Co.; St. Paul Insurance Companies.

For Complete List of Firm Personnel, See General Section

For full biographical listings, see the Martindale-Hubbell Law Directory

---

SCARIANO, KULA, ELLCH AND HIMES, CHARTERED (AV)

Two Prudential Plaza 180 North Stetson Suite 3100, 60601-6224
Telephone: 312-565-3100
Facsimile: 312-565-0000
Chicago Heights, Illinois Office: 1450 Aberdeen.
Telephone: 708-755-1900.
Facsimile: 708-755-0000.

Anthony G. Scariano
David P. Kula
Robert H. Ellch
Alan T. Sraga
A. Lynn Himes
Justino D. Petrarca
Lawrence Jay Weiner
Kathleen Field Orr
John M. Izzo
Raymond A. Hauser

OF COUNSEL

Max A. Bailey
G. Robb Cooper
Teri E. Engler
John B. Kralovec

(See Next Column)

Daniel M. Boyle
Patrick J. Broncato
Sarah R. Carlin
Diane S. Cohen
Jon G. Crawford
Douglas D. Danielson
Anthony Ficarelli
Kelly A. Hayden
Todd K. Hayden
David A. Hemenway
Kathleen Roche Hirsman
Jonathan A. Pearl
Lisa Ann Rapacz
Shelia C. Riley
Joanne W. Schochat

For full biographical listings, see the Martindale-Hubbell Law Directory

---

SCHAFFENEGGER, WATSON & PETERSON, LTD. (AV)

Suite 3504, One East Wacker Drive, 60601-1802
Telephone: 312-527-5566
Fax: 312-527-5540

J. V. Schaffenegger (1914-1986)
Jack L. Watson
Donald G. Peterson
Jay Scott Nelson
Michael A. Strom

James L. McKnight

Reference: American National Bank & Trust Co.

For full biographical listings, see the Martindale-Hubbell Law Directory

---

SCHOEN & SMITH, LTD. (AV)

30 North La Salle Street, Suite 1500, 60602
Telephone: 312-726-5151
FAX: 312-726-0884

Lee J. Schoen
David M. Smith
Thomas W. Starck

Randall Smith
Steven Christophell
Thomas P. Mangan
Mary J. Duffy
Susan Fox Gillis

For full biographical listings, see the Martindale-Hubbell Law Directory

---

SWANSON, MARTIN & BELL (AV)

One IBM Plaza, Suite 2900, 60611
Telephone: 312-321-9100
Fax: 312-321-0990
Wheaton, Illinois Office: 605 East Roosevelt Road.
Telephone: 708-653-2266.
Fax: 708-653-2292.

MEMBERS OF FIRM

Lenard C. Swanson
David J. Cahill (Resident, Wheaton Office)
Joseph P. Switzer
Bruce S. Terlep

ASSOCIATES

Kevin V. Boyle
Matthew D. Jacboson
Joseph P. Kincaid
Sheryl A. Pethers
Barbara N. Petrungaro
Aaron T. Shepley

For full biographical listings, see the Martindale-Hubbell Law Directory

---

TAYLOR, MILLER, SPROWL, HOFFNAGLE & MERLETTI (AV)

33 North La Salle Street, Suite 2222, 60602-2691
Telephone: 312-782-6070
FAX: 312-782-6081

Orville Taylor (1885-1969)
John S. Miller (1888-1965)
James J. Hoffnagle
Roger A. Merletti
Ralph W. F. Lustgarten
Richard W. Oloffson
Frank C. Stevens
Roger LeRoy

OF COUNSEL

Charles R. Sprowl

ASSOCIATES

John R. Adams
Katherine M. Mulroy
Daniel K. Fritz
Robert W. Rohm
Hugh J. Doyle
Jack Bruce Batten
John Anthony DiSalvo
Timothy Couture

For full biographical listings, see the Martindale-Hubbell Law Directory

---

TRIBLER & ORPETT, A PROFESSIONAL CORPORATION (AV)

30 North La Salle Street, Suite 2200, 60602
Telephone: 312-201-6400
Fax: 312-201-6401

Willis R. Tribler
Mitchell A. Orpett
Douglas C. Crone
Dion J. Sartorio
Janet R. Davis
Philip R. King
Michael J. Meyer
Steven R. McMannon

H. Wesley Sunu
Jean Donath Franke
Panos T. Topalis
John W. Carver
Stanley D. Sterna
David M. Menditto

(See Next Column)

TRIBLER & ORPETT A PROFESSIONAL CORPORATION—*Continued*

OF COUNSEL

Daniel D. Drew

For full biographical listings, see the Martindale-Hubbell Law Directory

WILDMAN, HARROLD, ALLEN & DIXON (AV)

225 West Wacker Drive, 30th Floor, 60606-1229
Telephone: 312-201-2000
Cable Address: "Whad"
Fax: 312-201-2555
Aurora, Illinois Office: 1851 W. Galena Boulevard, Suite 210.
Telephone: 708-892-7021.
Fax: 708-892-7158.
Waukegan, Illinois Office: 404 West Water, P. O. Box 890.
Telephone: 708-623-0700.
Fax: 708-244-5273.
Lisle, Illinois Office: 4300 Commerce Court.
Telephone: 708-955-0555.
Libertyville, Illinois Office: 611 South Milwaukee Avenue.
Telephone: 708-680-3030.
New York, New York Office: Wildman, Harrold, Allen, Dixon & Smith. The International Building, 45 Rockefeller Plaza, Suite 353.
Telephone: 212-632-3850.
Fax: 212-632-3858.
Toronto, Ontario affiliated Office: Keel Cottrelle. 36 Toronto Street, Ninth Floor, Suite 920.
Telephone: 416-367-2900.
Telefax: 416-367-2791.
Telex: 062-18660.
Mississauga, Ontario affiliated Office: Keel Cottrelle. 100 Matatson Avenue East, Suite 104.
Telephone: 416-890-7700.
Fax: 416-890-8006.

MEMBERS OF FIRM

Thomas D. Allen
Richard C. Bartelt
Cal R. Burnton
Edward T. Butt, Jr.
James A. Christman
Steven E. Danekas
James P. Dorr
Kathy Pinkstaff Fox
Michael J. Grant
Robert E. Haley
Helaine Wachs Heydemann
Richard J. Hickey, III
Matthew A. Hurd
David A. Kanter
Leonard S. Kurfirst
Steven L. Larson (Waukegan and Libertyville Offices)
Donald R. McGarrah
Mark P. Miller
Timothy G. Nickels
Sarah L. Olson
Richard C. Palmer
Thomas E. Patterson
Douglas L. Prochnow
Robert L. Shuftan
Robert A. Strelecky (Resident Partner, DuPage County Office)
Peter A. Tomaras
Ruth E. VanDemark
James B. Vogts
Dale G. Wills

John W. Barbian
John T. Benz
James G. Bonebrake
Gary E. Dyal
Adam J. Glazer
Gerise M. Hooks
Anthony G. Hopp
Daniel Steven Kaplan
Lauren L. McFarlane
Kathryn A. Mrkonich
Richard D. Murphy Jr.
Martha D. Owens
Jeanne Walker

Representative Clients: Illinois State Medical Insurance Services, Inc.; United States Aviation Underwriters; Crawford and Co.; General Casualty Co.; CIGNA Companies; Interstate Insurance Group; CNA; Illinois Provider Trust; The Doctors Company; The Travelers Cos.

For Complete List of Firm Personnel, See General Section

For full biographical listings, see the Martindale-Hubbell Law Directory

*DANVILLE,** Vermilion Co.

HUTTON, LAURY, HESSER, LIETZ & WILCOX (AV)

16 West Madison Street, P.O. Box 1128, 61832
Telephone: 217-446-9436
FAX: 217-446-9462

MEMBERS OF FIRM

Everett L. Laury
Gary D. Hesser
Gregory G. Lietz
Roy G. Wilcox

Representative Clients: Pekin Insurance; Prudential Insurance Company; Metropolitan Life Insurance Company; Illinois State Medical Insurance Services, Inc.; Associated Physicians Insurance Company; Employers Reinsurance Corp.; Northwestern National Insurance Company; St. Paul Insurance Companies; Clarendon National Insurance Company; General Motors Corporation.

For Complete List of Firm Personnel, See General Section

For full biographical listings, see the Martindale-Hubbell Law Directory

*EDWARDSVILLE,** Madison Co.

REED, ARMSTRONG, GORMAN, COFFEY, THOMSON, GILBERT & MUDGE, PROFESSIONAL CORPORATION (AV)

One Mark Twain Plaza, Suite 300, P.O. Box 368, 62025
Telephone: 618-656-0257; 656-2244
Facsimile: 618-692-4416
Other Edwardsville Office: 125 North Buchanan.
Telephone: 618-656-2244.
Fax: 618-658-1307.
Springfield, Illinois Office: One West Old State Capital Plaza, Suite 400, Myers Building.
Telephone: 217-525-1366.
Fax: 217-525-0986.

James L. Reed (Retired)
Harry C. Armstrong
James E. Gorman
Gary R. Coffey
Stephen W. Thomson
John L. Gilbert
Stephen C. Mudge
Charles C. Compton
Martin K. Morrissey

Debra J. Meadows
Kevin J. Babb
Richard J. Behr
Michael J. Bedesky
Rodney W. Phillipe
Mitchell B. Stoddard
David Laurent
Gregory W. Coffey
Bryan L. Skelton

Representative Clients: State Farm Insurance Cos.; Country Companies; Standard Mutual Casualty Co.; General Casualty Company of Wisconsin; Western States Mutual Insurance Co.; Hawkeye-Security Insurance Co.; Shelter Insurance Co.; New Hampshire Insurance Group; Heritage Insurance Co.; Southern Illinois University of Edwardsville.

For full biographical listings, see the Martindale-Hubbell Law Directory

*HARRISBURG,** Saline Co.

JELLIFFE, FERRELL & MORRIS (AV)

108 East Walnut Street, 62946
Telephone: 618-253-7153; 253-7647
Telecopier: 618-252-1843

OF COUNSEL

Charles R. Jelliffe

MEMBERS OF FIRM

DeWitt Twente (1904-1976)
Donald V. Ferrell
Walden E. Morris

ASSOCIATES

Michal Doerge
Thomas J. Foster
Timothy L. Fornes

Representative Clients: Auto-Owners Insurance; Country Cos; Metropolitan Life Insurance; Ohio Casualty Group; Standard Mutual Insurance Co.; State Farm Cos.; Redland Insurance Co.; Aetna Casualty & Surety Co.; Kerr-McGee Coal Corp.; Sahara Coal Co.

For full biographical listings, see the Martindale-Hubbell Law Directory

*KANKAKEE,** Kankakee Co.

ACKMAN, MAREK, BOYD & SIMUTIS, LTD. (AV)

Suite 400, One Dearborn Square, 60901
Telephone: 815-933-6681
FAX: 815-933-9985
Watseka, Illinois Office: 123 South Fourth Street.
Telephone: 815-432-5215.
FAX: 815-432-3186.
Gilman, Illinois Office: 201 S. Crescent.
Telephone: 815-265-4533.

Richard L. Ackman
J. Dennis Marek
Robert W. Boyd
Frank J. Simutis (Watseka and Gilman Offices)
Deborah A. Woodruff

James A. Devine
Jack L. Haan

Representative Clients: American States Insurance Co.; Auto Owners Insurance Co.; Country Mutual Insurance Co.; Farmers Insurance Group; Hartford Accident & Indemnity Co.; Kankakee Water Co.; Medical Protective Co.; State Farm Insurance Co.; Watseka First National Bank; Economy Fire & Casualty Co.

For full biographical listings, see the Martindale-Hubbell Law Directory

LA SALLE, La Salle Co.

HERBOLSHEIMER, LANNON, HENSON, DUNCAN AND REAGAN, P.C. (AV)

State Bank Building, Suite 400, 654 First Street, P.O. Box 539, 61301
Telephone: 815-223-0111
FAX: 815-223-5829
Ottawa, Illinois Office: 200 First Federal Savings Bank Building. Ottawa, IL 61350.

(See Next Column)

HERBOLSHEIMER, LANNON, HENSON, DUNCAN AND REAGAN P.C., *La Salle—Continued*

George L. Herbolsheimer (1911-1992)
R. James Lannon, Jr.
T. Donald Henson
John S. Duncan, III
Michael T. Reagan (Resident, Ottawa Office)
Douglas A. Gift
Gary R. Eiten

Karen C. Eiten
Jonathan F. Brandt
Michael C. Jansz (Resident, Ottawa Office)
Jill W. Broderick
Murl Tod Melton

Attorneys for: Aetna Insurance Group; St. Paul Fire and Marine Insurance Co.; State Farm Insurance Co.; The La Salle National Bank; La Salle State Bank; The Daily News Tribune Company, La Salle; Eureka Savings and Loan Assn.; Illinois Valley Community Hospital; Community Hospital of Ottawa; Commonwealth Edison, Co.

For full biographical listings, see the Martindale-Hubbell Law Directory

*MARION,** Williamson Co.

MITCHELL & ARMSTRONG, LTD. (AV)

404 North Monroe, P.O. Box 488, 62959
Telephone: 618-993-2134
Telecopier: 618-993-8702

J. C. Mitchell
William A. Armstrong
Bruce W. Mitchell

Stephen R. Green

Representative Clients: St. Paul Fire & Casualty Insurance Company; Liberty Mutual Insurance Company; Shelter Insurance Company; Claims Management, Inc.; Seaboard Underwriters; Kemper Insurance; Sentry Claims; Aetna; Walmart Stores, Inc.

For full biographical listings, see the Martindale-Hubbell Law Directory

*OTTAWA,** La Salle Co.

HUPP, LANUTI, IRION & MARTIN, P.C. (AV)

227 West Madison, P.O. Box 768, 61350
Telephone: 815-433-3111
Fax: 815-433-9109

Joseph E. Lanuti
Paul V. Martin
George C. Hupp, Jr.
Richard L. Burton

Michelle Hutson

OF COUNSEL

George C. Hupp

Representative Clients: Country Mutual Insurance Co.; State Farm Mutual Automobile Insurance Co.; State Farm Fire & Casualty Co.; Economy Fire and Casualty Co.; Employee Mutual Casualty Co.; Sentry Insurance Co.; United Fire and Casualty Co.; Allstate Insurance Co.; Millers Mutual Insurance Assn.; Continental Casualty Co.

For full biographical listings, see the Martindale-Hubbell Law Directory

*PRINCETON,** Bureau Co.

JOHNSON, MARTIN, RUSSELL, ENGLISH, SCOMA & BENEKE, P.C. (AV)

Ten Park Avenue West, 61356
Telephone: 815-875-4555

Watts A. Johnson (1856-1930)
Rolla L. Russell (1864-1952)
Carey R. Johnson (1884-1951)
Joseph R. Peterson (1904-1967)
Fred G. Russell (1911-1994)
Watts C. Johnson
Donald C. Martin
Daniel K. Russell
Robert F. Russell
Michael L. English
Paul M. Scoma
William S. Beneke

For full biographical listings, see the Martindale-Hubbell Law Directory

*ROCKFORD,** Winnebago Co.

PICHA & SALISBURY (AV)

Edgebrook Court Building, 1639 North Alpine, Suite 300, 61107-1449
Telephone: 815-227-4300
FAX: 815-227-4330

MEMBERS OF FIRM

George J. Picha
Jeffrey L. Salisbury

ASSOCIATES

Lloyd R. McCumber
William A. Meister

Representative Clients: A.O. Smith Automotives Products Co.; Atwood Industries, Inc.; Chrysler Corp.; Estwing Manufacturing Co.; G.C. Thorsen, Inc.; Laidlaw Waste Systems; Ingersoll Milling Machine Co.; Sunstrand Corp.; Swedish American Hospital; Rockford Board of Education.

(See Next Column)

For full biographical listings, see the Martindale-Hubbell Law Directory

*SPRINGFIELD,** Sangamon Co.

GIFFIN, WINNING, COHEN & BODEWES, P.C. (AV)

1 West Old State Capitol Plaza, Suite 600 Myers Building, P.O. Box 2117, 62705
Telephone: 217-525-1571
Facsimile: 217-525-1710

Carol Hansen Fines
R. Mark Mifflin
Thomas P. Schanzle-Haskins, III
Gregory K. Harris

Representative Clients: Illinois Municipal League Risk Management Association; Alliance of American Insurers; Board of Regents of Regency Universities; Allstate Insurance Co.; Grinnell Mutual Reinsurance Company; Horace Mann Insurance Company; Ohio Casualty Insurance Company; Transamerica Insurance Company; Associated Beer Distributors of Illinois Risk Management Association.

For Complete List of Firm Personnel, See General Section

For full biographical listings, see the Martindale-Hubbell Law Directory

INDIANA

*BLOOMINGTON,** Monroe Co.

BUNGER & ROBERTSON (AV)

226 South College Square, P.O. Box 910, 47402-0910
Telephone: 812-332-9295
Fax: 812-331-8808

MEMBERS OF FIRM

Don M. Robertson
Joseph D. O'Connor III
James L. Whitlatch

Representative Clients: Aetna Insurance Companies; Bloomington Hospital; Commercial Union Group; Indiana Insurance Co.; Liberty Mutual Insurance; Medical Protective Co.; Monroe County Community School Corp.; Professional Golf Car, Inc.; Prudential Insurance Company of America; State Farm Automobile Insurance Co.

For Complete List of Firm Personnel, See General Section

For full biographical listings, see the Martindale-Hubbell Law Directory

KELLEY, BELCHER & BROWN, A PROFESSIONAL CORPORATION (AV)

301 West Seventh Street, P.O. Box 3250, 47402-3250
Telephone: 812-336-9963
Telecopier: 812-336-4588

William H. Kelley
Thomas J. Belcher
Barry Spencer Brown

Shannon L. Robinson
Darla Sue Brown

For full biographical listings, see the Martindale-Hubbell Law Directory

CARMEL, Hamilton Co.

COOTS, HENKE & WHEELER, PROFESSIONAL CORPORATION (AV)

255 East Carmel Drive, 46032
Telephone: 317-844-4693
Fax: 317-573-5385

E. Davis Coots
Steven H. Henke
James K. Wheeler
Jeffrey O. Meunier
James D. Crum
Jeffrey S. Zipes

Representative Clients: Chrysler Corp.; CNA Insurance Co.; Freightliner Corp.; Liberty Mutual; Allianz Insurance Co.

For Complete List of Firm Personnel, See General Section

For full biographical listings, see the Martindale-Hubbell Law Directory

*COLUMBUS,** Bartholomew Co.

SHARPNACK, BIGLEY, DAVID & RUMPLE (AV)

321 Washington Street, P.O. Box 310, 47202-0310
Telephone: 812-372-1553
Fax: 812-372-1567

MEMBERS OF FIRM

Thomas C. Bigley, Jr.
Timothy J. Vrana
John A. Stroh
Joan Tupin Crites

Representative Clients: Irwin Union Bank and Trust Co.; PSI Energy, Inc.; State Farm Mutual Insurance Cos.; American States Insurance Co.; Home News Enterprises; Cummins Federal Credit Union; Richards Elevator, Inc.

(See Next Column)

SHARPNACK, BIGLEY, DAVID & RUMPLE—*Continued*

For Complete List of Firm Personnel, See General Section

For full biographical listings, see the Martindale-Hubbell Law Directory

ELKHART, Elkhart Co.

THORNE, GRODNIK, RANSEL, DUNCAN, BYRON & HOSTETLER (AV)

228 West High Street, 46516-3176
Telephone: 219-294-7473
FAX: 219-294-5390
Mishawaka, Indiana Office: 310 Valley American Bank and Trust Building, 310 West McKinley Avenue. P.O. Box 1210.
Telephone: 219-256-5660.
FAX: 219-674-6835.

MEMBERS OF FIRM

William A. Thorne
Charles H. Grodnik
J. Richard Ransel
Glenn L. Duncan
James R. Byron
Steven L. Hostetler

ASSOCIATES

James H. Milstone
Michael A. Trippel

OF COUNSEL

F. Richard Kramer
Joseph C. Zakas

Counsel for: Witmer-McNease Music Co., Inc.; Valley American Bank and Trust Co., Mishawaka, Indiana.

For Complete List of Firm Personnel, See General Section

For full biographical listings, see the Martindale-Hubbell Law Directory

*EVANSVILLE,** Vanderburgh Co.

FINE & HATFIELD (AV)

520 N.W. Second Street, P.O. Box 779, 47705-0779
Telephone: 812-425-3592
Telecopier: 812-421-4269

MEMBERS OF FIRM

Thomas H. Bryan
Danny E. Glass
D. Timothy Born
Patricia Kay Woodring

ASSOCIATES

William H. Mullis
Debra S. McGowan

For Complete List of Firm Personnel, See General Section

For full biographical listings, see the Martindale-Hubbell Law Directory

KAHN, DEES, DONOVAN & KAHN (AV)

P.O. Box 3646, 47735-3646
Telephone: 812-423-3183
Fax: 812-423-3841

MEMBERS OF FIRM

David L. Clark
Jeffrey A. Wilhite
Jeffrey W. Ahlers
Mary Lee Franke

ASSOCIATE

Richard O. Hawley, Jr.

Representative Clients: United States Fidelity & Guaranty Insurance Co.; United Farm Bureau Mutual of Indiana; Neare, Gibbs River Marine Underwriters; I.T.T. Hartford Insurance Co.; American Family Insurance Co.; CIGNA Insurance Co.; Fireman's Fund Insurance Co.; CNA Insurance Co.; Chubb Insurance; May Lee Franke.

For Complete List of Firm Personnel, See General Section

For full biographical listings, see the Martindale-Hubbell Law Directory

STATHAM, JOHNSON & MCCRAY (AV)

215 North West Martin Luther King Jr. Boulevard, P.O. Box 3567, 47734-3567
Telephone: 812-425-5223
Facsimile: 812-421-4238

MEMBERS OF FIRM

William E. Statham
Michael McCray
Stephen Hensleigh Thomas
Gerald F. Allega
Douglas V. Jessen

ASSOCIATES

Brent Alan Raibley
Bryan S. Rudisill

Representative Clients: American Family Insurance Group; American States Insurance; Hartford Insurance Group; Indiana Insurance Cos.; Medical Protective Insurance Co.; Ohio Casualty Group; Pennsylvania Hospital Insurance Co.; Monroe Guaranty Company; St. Paul Insurance Companies; Wausau Insurance Companies.

For Complete List of Firm Personnel, See General Section

For full biographical listings, see the Martindale-Hubbell Law Directory

WRIGHT, EVANS AND DALY (AV)

425 Main Street, 47708
Telephone: 812-424-3300
Fax: 812-421-5588

MEMBERS OF FIRM

Donald R. Wright
R. Lawrence Daly

ASSOCIATE

Keith M. Wallace

Representative Clients: Allstate Insurance Company; Canal Insurance Company; Church Mutual Insurance Company; Home Insurance Companies; Liberty Mutual Insurance Company; Mutual of Omaha; Northbrook Property and Casualty Insurance Company; United Farm Bureau Mutual Insurance Company; Wausau Insurance Company; Westfield Insurance Companies of Indiana, Inc.

For Complete List of Firm Personnel, See General Section

For full biographical listings, see the Martindale-Hubbell Law Directory

GARY, Lake Co.

STULTS, STULTS, FORSZT & PAWLOWSKI, A PROFESSIONAL ASSOCIATION (AV)

3637 Grant Street, P.O. Box 15050, 46409-5050
Telephone: 219-887-7000
Fax: 219-884-1179

Fred M. Stults, Jr.
Frederick M. Stults, III
Robert P. Forszt
David R. Pawlowski

Representative Clients: American Road Insurance Co.; Employers Casualty Co.; Indiana Insurance Co.; SAFECO Insurance Co.

For full biographical listings, see the Martindale-Hubbell Law Directory

HAMMOND, Lake Co.

ABRAHAMSON, REED & ADLEY (AV)

5231 Hohman Avenue, 46320
Telephone: 219-937-1500
Fax: 219-937-3174

MEMBERS OF FIRM

Harold Abrahamson
Kenneth D. Reed
Michael C. Adley

ASSOCIATES

Scott R. Bilse
Christopher R. Karsten
Joseph L. Curosh

References: Calumet National Bank, Hammond; Mercantile National Bank, Hammond.

For full biographical listings, see the Martindale-Hubbell Law Directory

GALVIN, GALVIN & LEENEY (AV)

5231 Hohman Avenue, 46320
Telephone: 219-933-0380
Fax: 219-933-0471

MEMBERS OF FIRM

Edmond J. Leeney (1897-1978)
Timothy P. Galvin, Sr. (1894-1993)
Francis J. Galvin, Sr. (Retired)
Carl N. Carpenter
John E. Chevigny
Timothy P. Galvin, Jr.
Patrick J. Galvin
W. Patrick Downes

Brian L. Goins
William G. Crabtree II
John H. Lloyd, IV

Attorneys For: State Farm Insurance Co.; Auto Owners Insurance Co.; CIGNA; St. Margaret Mercy Healthcare Centers, Inc.; St. Anthony Hospital and Health Centers (Michigan City); Pepsi-Cola General Bottlers, Inc.; Chicago Title Insurance Company.

For full biographical listings, see the Martindale-Hubbell Law Directory

HIGHLAND, Lake Co.

BLACKMUN, BOMBERGER & MORAN (AV)

A Partnership including a Professional Corporation
Schuyler Square West, 9006 Indianapolis Boulevard, 46322
Telephone: 219-972-2200
FAX: 219-972-2404

Edwin H. Friedrich (1892-1979)
Charles G. Bomberger (1907-1980)
Stanley A. Tweedle (Retired)
Gilbert F. Blackmun
Peter C. Bomberger
William J. Moran
Leonard M. Holajter
Stephen A. Tyler
Alan R. Faulkner

Counsel for: Amtrak; Indiana Bell Telephone Co.; Metropolitan Life Insurance Co.; Prudential Insurance Co.; United States Fidelity & Guaranty Co.; CSX Transportation; Conrail; Continental National Group; The Methodist Hospitals, Inc.

For full biographical listings, see the Martindale-Hubbell Law Directory

*INDIANAPOLIS,** Marion Co.

CROMER, EAGLESFIELD & MAHER (AV)

1500 Market Tower, 10 West Market Street, 46204-2968
Telephone: 317-464-1500
Fax: 317-464-1506

John R. Cromer
R. Davy Eaglesfield, III
Kenneth W. Maher

For full biographical listings, see the Martindale-Hubbell Law Directory

GAGNON & DIEHL ATTORNEYS AT LAW A PROFESSIONAL ASSOCIATION (AV)

416 Circle Tower Building, 55 Monument Circle, 46204
Telephone: 317-632-0328
Fax: 317-236-5832

Edwin L. Gagnon
William F. Diehl

Representative Clients: Meridian Mutual Insurance Co.; MacAllister Machinery Co., Inc.
Reference: The Indiana National Bank of Indianapolis.

For full biographical listings, see the Martindale-Hubbell Law Directory

GOODIN & KRAEGE (AV)

8888 Keystone Crossing Suite 820, 46240-4616
Telephone: 317-843-2606
FAX: 317-574-3095

James A. Goodin
Richard C. Kraege
Jon C. Abernathy
Amy Loraine White
Patrick L. Miller
James W. Johnson, III

OF COUNSEL

Wilson S. Stober

Representative Clients: Allstate Insurance Companies; American National Property and Casualty Co.; Bituminous Insurance Company; Builder's Square; Commercial Union Insurance Companies; Continental Loss Adjusting Service; Construction Associates, Inc.; Continental Western Insurance Company; Economy Fire & Casualty; General Casualty Companies.

For full biographical listings, see the Martindale-Hubbell Law Directory

ICE MILLER DONADIO & RYAN (AV)

One American Square Box 82001, 46282-0002
Telephone: 317-236-2100
Fax: 317-236-2219

MEMBERS OF FIRM

James V. Donadio
Jim A. O'Neal
Evan E. Steger
Ralph A. Cohen
Arthur P. Kalleres
David M. Mattingly
James R. Fisher
Cory Brundage
David J. Mallon, Jr.
James L. Petersen
Gary J. Dankert
John F. Prescott, Jr.
Richard A. Smikle
Debra Hanley Miller
Michael D. Marine

RETIRED PARTNER

Edward J. Ohleyer

ASSOCIATES

Terri Ann Czajka
Sherry A. Fabina-Abney
Kelly Bauman Pitcher
Donald M. Snemis
Michael A. Wilkins
Kristin L. Altice
Michael R. Kerr
James Scott Fanzini
Angela K. Wade
Barbara J. Weigel
Laura B. Daghe
Jodie L. Miner
Thomas E. Mixdorf

Representative Clients: Liberty Mutual Insurance; Economy Fire & Casualty Co.; Northland Insurance Co.; National Indemnity Co.; Great West Casualty; St. Paul Fire & Marine Insurance; CNA Insurance Co.; Maryland Casualty Co.; Worldwide Insurance Co.; Employers Insurance of Wausau.

For Complete List of Firm Personnel, See General Section

For full biographical listings, see the Martindale-Hubbell Law Directory

JOHNSON, SMITH, DENSBORN, WRIGHT & HEATH (AV)

One Indiana Square Suite 1800, 46204
Telephone: 317-634-9777
Telecopier: 317-636-9061

MEMBERS OF FIRM

John F. Joyce (1948-1994)
Wayne O. Adams, III
Robert M. Baker, III
Thomas A. Barnard
David J. Carr
Peter D. Cleveland
David R. Day
Donald K. Densborn
Thomas N. Eckerle
Mark W. Ford
G. Ronald Heath
Robert B. Hebert
John David Hoover
Andrew W. Hull
Dennis A. Johnson
Richard L. Johnson
Michael J. Kaye
John R. Kirkwood

(See Next Column)

MEMBERS OF FIRM (Continued)

David Williams Russell
James T. Smith
Martha Taylor Starkey
David E. Wright

ASSOCIATES

Robert C. Wolf (1949-1993)
Carolyn H. Andretti
Maureen F. Barnard
David G. Blachly
Robert T. Buday
Sean Michael Clapp
Jeffrey S. Cohen
Charles M. Freeland
David W. Givens, Jr.
Gary P. Goodin
Patricia L. Marshall
Bradley C. Morris
Steven J. Moss
Padric K. J. O'Brien
Cathleen J. Perry
David D. Robinson
Ronald G. Sentman
David A. Tucker
Sally Franklin Zweig

OF COUNSEL

Earl Auberry (1923-1989)
Larry A. Conrad (1935-1990)
Bruce W. Claycombe
Laura S. Cohen
Paul D. Gresk
William T. Lawrence
Mark A. Palmer
Lawrence W. Schmits
Catherine A. Singleton

For full biographical listings, see the Martindale-Hubbell Law Directory

LEWIS & WAGNER (AV)

500 Place, 501 Indiana Avenue, Suite 200, 46202-3199
Telephone: 317-237-0500
Fax: 317-630-2790

Judith Trevor Kirtland (1947-1990)
Edward D. Lewis
Robert F. Wagner
David Konnersman
John C. Trimble
Thomas C. Hays
R. Robert Stommel
Kenneth P. Reese
Michael S. Huntine
Susan E. Mehringer
Daun A. Weliever
Robert K. Cowles
Richard K. Shoultz
William Owen Harrington

OF COUNSEL

Felson Bowman
Thomas P. Weliever

Representative Clients: Aetna Casualty & Surety Co.; Allstate Insurance Co.; American Southern Insurance Cos.; American States Insurance Co.; Bituminous Insurance Co.; Citizens Hanover Insurance; Erie Insurance Co.; Hoosier Insurance Co.; Key Life Insurance Co.; Associated Insurance Managers.

For full biographical listings, see the Martindale-Hubbell Law Directory

LOCKE REYNOLDS BOYD & WEISELL (AV)

1000 Capital Center South, 201 North Illinois Street, 46204
Telephone: 317-237-3800
Telecopier: 317-237-3900

Hugh E. Reynolds, Jr.
Lloyd H. Milliken, Jr.
William V. Hutchens
David S. Allen
David M. Haskett
Michael A. Bergin
David T. Kasper
Steven J. Strawbridge
Thomas L. Davis
Robert A. Fanning
Randall R. Riggs
Alan S. Brown
Mark J. Roberts
Kevin Charles Murray
Julia M. Blackwell
Richard A. Huser
Thomas J. Campbell
Diane L. Parsons
Burton M. Harris
Thomas W. Farlow
Karl M. Koons, III
Julia F. Crowe
James Dimos

Stephen L. Vaughan
Kristen K. Rollison
Thomas R. Schultz
Todd J. Kaiser
Eric A. Riegner
Kevin C. Schiferl
Ariane Schallwig Johnson
Peter H. Pogue
John H. Daerr
Robert W. Wright
Robert T. Dassow
Jeffrey J. Mortier
Kevin M. Boyle
Nicholas C. Pappas
Mary A. Schopper
Susan E. Cline
Dirk Wallsmith
Jerrilyn Powers Ramsey
Katherine Coble Dassow
Lisa A. McCallum
Kathryn Weymouth Williams
Mary Margaret Ruth Feldhake
Nelson D. Alexander

OF COUNSEL

William H. Vobach
Robert C. Riddell

Representative Clients: Associated Aviation Underwriters; Center for Claims Resolution; Citizens Insurance Co. (The Hanover Group); CNA Insurance Cos.; The Hartford Insurance Co.; The Medical Protective Co.; Nationwide Insurance Co.; PHICO Insurance Co.; Royal Insurance Cos.; U.S.F. & G. Cos.

For Complete List of Firm Personnel, See General Section

For full biographical listings, see the Martindale-Hubbell Law Directory

NORRIS, CHOPLIN & SCHROEDER (AV)

Ninth Floor, 101 West Ohio Street, 46204-1906
Telephone: 317-269-9330
FAX: 317-269-9338

(See Next Column)

NORRIS, CHOPLIN & SCHROEDER—*Continued*

MEMBERS OF FIRM

Richard L. Norris
John M. Choplin, II
Peter A. Schroeder
Bruce L. Kamplain
Raymond L. Faust
Mary Jo Hunter Wedding

ASSOCIATES

Ellen White Quigley
Kyle A. Jones
Peter Peck-Koh Ho
Nelson A. Nettles
Andrew C. Chapman

OF COUNSEL

James D. Matthews

Reference: The Indiana National Bank.

For full biographical listings, see the Martindale-Hubbell Law Directory

OSBORN HINER & LISHER P.C. (AV)

Suite 380, One Woodfield, 8330 Woodfield Crossing Boulevard, 46240
Telephone: 317-469-2100
Fax: 317-469-9011

John R. Hiner (1920-1986)
John L. Lisher

Donald G. Orzeske
Donald K. Broad

OF COUNSEL

William M. Osborn
Edward A. Straith-Miller
Janet K. Storer

For full biographical listings, see the Martindale-Hubbell Law Directory

ROCAP, WITCHGER & THRELKELD (AV)

700 Union Federal Building, 45 North Pennsylvania Street, 46204
Telephone: 317-639-6281
FAX: 317-637-9056

James E. Rocap, Sr. (1881-1969)
John T. Rocap (1909-1980)
Keith C. Reese (1920-1993)

MEMBERS OF FIRM

James E. Rocap, Jr.
James D. Witchger
W. Brent Threlkeld
Richard A. Rocap
James C. Todderud
Thomas Todd Reynolds

ASSOCIATES

Robert S. O'Dell
Nancy Grannan Curless
Michael D. Ramsey
Tara L. Becsey
Bette J. Peterson
Robert A. Durham
Jeffrey V. Crabill

OF COUNSEL

Joseph F. Quill

Representative Clients: Principal Casualty & Insurance; American Family Insurance Group; The Travelers Insurance Co.; State Farm Fire and Casualty Insurance Co.; Reliance National Insurance Co.; Statesman Insurance Co.; USAA Insurance.

For full biographical listings, see the Martindale-Hubbell Law Directory

STEPHENSON DALY MOROW AND KURNIK, P.C. (AV)

8902 North Meridian Street Suite 205, 46260-5307
Telephone: 317-844-3830
FAX: 317-573-4194

James S. Stephenson
John P. Daly, Jr.
Michael R. Morow
William W. Kurnik
Kenneth Collier-Magar
Richelle V. Cohen
Caren Lynn Pollack

Ronald J. Semler
G. Richard Potter
Kirk A. Horn

Representative Clients: Governmental Interinsurance Exchange; Interstate Insurance Group; Crum & Forster Commercial Insurance; Industrial Indemnity Insurance; Imperial Casualty Co.; National Fire and Casualty Co.; Indiana Political Subdivision Risk Management Fund; Gallagher Bassett Services; Mt. Hawley Insurance Co.; Illinois Farmers Ins. Group.; Indiana Farmers Insurance Co.; Indiana Insurance Co.; JWF Specialty; St. Paul Fire & Marine Ins. Co.; Titan Indemnity Co.; VASA North Atlantic Ins. Co.

For full biographical listings, see the Martindale-Hubbell Law Directory

STEWART DUE MILLER & PUGH (AV)

55 Monument Circle, 900 Circle Tower, 46204-5900
Telephone: 317-635-7700
Fax: 317-636-2408

MEMBERS OF FIRM

Kent O. Stewart
Danford R. Due
Larry S. Pugh
Robert J. Doyle

(See Next Column)

ASSOCIATES

Catharine Stewart
Mark A. Metzger

Representative Clients: American States Insurance; Wausau Insurance Companies; B.F. Goodrich; Carr Metal Products, Inc.; Rockwood Insurance Co.; Capital Enterprise Insurance Group; Risk Management; The Huntington National Bank of Indiana; Protective Insurance Co.; Auto Owners Insurance Company.

For full biographical listings, see the Martindale-Hubbell Law Directory

YARLING, ROBINSON, HAMMEL & LAMB (AV)

151 North Delaware, Suite 1535, P.O. Box 44128, 46204
Telephone: 317-262-8800
Fax: 317-262-3046

MEMBERS OF FIRM

Richard W. Yarling
Charles F. Robinson, Jr.
John W. Hammel
Linda Y. Hammel
Edgar H. Lamb
Douglas E. Rogers
Mark S. Gray

Representative Clients: Allstate Insurance Co.; American Family Mutual Insurance Company; Chrysler Credit Corporation; Fleet Financenter; General Motors Acceptance Corporation; Household Finance Corporation; Monroe Guaranty Insurance Company; Northbrook Property & Casualty Company; Pafco General Insurance Company; Security Pacific Finance Corporation.

For full biographical listings, see the Martindale-Hubbell Law Directory

ZEIGLER CARTER COHEN & KOCH (AV)

8500 Keystone Crossing, Suite 510, 46240
Telephone: 317-254-4400
Facsimile: 317-254-4403

Robert G. Zeigler
Michael L. Carter
Steven J. Cohen
Edna M. Koch

ASSOCIATES

David Becsey
Roger K. Kanne
Renee A. Faught (Not admitted in IN)

For full biographical listings, see the Martindale-Hubbell Law Directory

*KOKOMO,** Howard Co.

FELL, MCGARVEY, TRAURING & WILSON (AV)

515 West Sycamore Street, P.O. Box 958, 46903-0958
Telephone: 317-457-9321
Telecopier: 317-452-0882

MEMBERS OF FIRM

John E. Fell, Jr.
Eugene J. McGarvey, Jr.
Thomas J. Trauring
Alan D. Wilson

Representative Clients: Aetna Casualty & Surety Co.; American States Insurance Co.; Celina Insurance Co.; Chicago Insurance Co.; Continental Insurance Co.; Fireman's Fund Insurance Co.; Hartford Insurance Co.; Meridian Insurance Co.; Michigan Mutual Insurance Co.; State Automobile Insurance Co.

For full biographical listings, see the Martindale-Hubbell Law Directory

*LAFAYETTE,** Tippecanoe Co.

BALL, EGGLESTON, BUMBLEBURG & MCBRIDE (AV)

810 Bank One Building, P.O. Box 1535, 47902
Telephone: 317-742-9046
Fax: 317-742-1966

Cable G. Ball (1904-1981)
Owen Crook (1908-1977)
Warren N. Eggleston (1923-1991)

MEMBERS OF FIRM

Joseph T. Bumbleburg
John K. McBride
Jack L. Walkey
Michael J. Stapleton
Jeffrey J. Newell
James T. Hodson
Brian Wade Walker

ASSOCIATES

Cheryl M. Knodle
Randy J. Williams
Norman G. Printer

Representative Clients: Travelers Insurance Co.; Grain Dealers Mutual Insurance Co.; Indiana Farmers Insurance Group; Indiana Insurance Co.; American Family Insurance Co.

For full biographical listings, see the Martindale-Hubbell Law Directory

HOFFMAN, LUHMAN & BUSCH (AV)

300 Main Street, Suite 700, P.O. Box 99, 47902
Telephone: 317-423-5404
Fax: 317-742-6448

(See Next Column)

HOFFMAN, LUHMAN & BUSCH, *Lafayette—Continued*

MEMBERS OF FIRM

J. Frederick Hoffman
David W. Luhman
Thomas H. Busch

Representative Clients: Farm Bureau Mutual Insurance Co.; State Farm Insurance Company; American States Insurance Co.; Metropolitan Property & Casualty Insurance Company; Cincinnati Insurance Company; National General Insurance Company.
References: Lafayette Bank & Trust Co., Lafayette, Indiana; Farmers & Merchants Bank, Rochester, Indiana; Lafayette Savings Bank, Lafayette, Indiana.

For Complete List of Firm Personnel, See General Section

For full biographical listings, see the Martindale-Hubbell Law Directory

STUART & BRANIGIN (AV)

The Life Building, 300 Main Street, Suite 800, 47902
Telephone: 317-423-1561
Telecopier: 317-742-8175

MEMBERS OF FIRM

Allison Ellsworth Stuart (1886-1950)
Roger D. Branigin (1902-1975)
Russell H. Hart
James V. McGlone
Larry R. Fisher
Stephen R. Pennell
Anthony S. Benton
William E. Emerick
John C. Duffey
Thomas B. Parent
Laura L. Bowker
Kevin D. Nicoson

COUNSEL

George A. Rinker

ASSOCIATES

Susan K. Holtberg
John M. Stuckey
Deborah B. Trice
Brent W. Huber

General Counsel for: The Lafayette Life Insurance Co.; INB National Bank, N.W.; Lafayette Home Hospital, Inc.
State Counsel for: Norfolk & Western Railway Co.
Mr. Ryan is Counsel to: The Trustees of Purdue University.
Representative Clients: Aluminum Company of America; Liberty Mutual Insurance Group.

For Complete List of Firm Personnel, See General Section

For full biographical listings, see the Martindale-Hubbell Law Directory

*LA PORTE,** La Porte Co.

NEWBY, LEWIS, KAMINSKI & JONES (AV)

916 Lincoln Way, 46350
Telephone: 219-362-1577
Direct Line Michigan City: 219-879-6300
Fax: 219-362-2106
Mailing Address: P.O. Box 1816, La Porte, Indiana, 46352-1816

MEMBERS OF FIRM

John E. Newby (1916-1990)
Daniel E. Lewis, Jr.
Gene M. Jones
John W. Newby
Perry F. Stump, Jr.
Edward L. Volk
Mark L. Phillips
Martin W. Kus
Marsha Schatz Volk
Mark A. Lienhoop
James W. Kaminski

ASSOCIATES

John F. Lake
William S. Kaminski
Christine A. Sulewski
David P. Jones

SENIOR COUNSEL

Leon R. Kaminski

OF COUNSEL

Daniel E. Lewis

Counsel for: U. S. F. & G. Co.; State Farm Mutual Insurance Co.; Auto Owners Insurance Co.; La Porte Bank & Trust Co.; Liberty Mutual Insurance Co.; Sullair Corp.; La Porte Community School Corp.; United Farm Bureau Mutual Insurance Co.; Physicians Insurance of Indiana; Medical Protective Co.

For full biographical listings, see the Martindale-Hubbell Law Directory

*MARION,** Grant Co.

BROWNE, SPITZER, HERRIMAN, STEPHENSON, HOLDEREAD & MUSSER (AV)

One Twenty Two East Fourth Street, P.O. Box 927, 46952-0927
Telephone: 317-664-7307
Fax: 317-662-0574

MEMBERS OF FIRM

James R. Browne (1940-1993)
John R. Browne, Jr.
Herbert A. Spitzer, Jr.
Charles E. Herriman
Phillip E. Stephenson
Jerome T. Holderead
Josef D. Musser
Michael D. Conner

ASSOCIATE

Mark E. Spitzer

(See Next Column)

OF COUNSEL

Jerry W. Torrance (Semi-Retired)

Representative Clients: State Farm Mutual Insurance Company; United Farm Bureau Mutual Insurance Company; Star Financial Group; Ford Motor Company; Tulox Plastics Corp.

For full biographical listings, see the Martindale-Hubbell Law Directory

MERRILLVILLE, Lake Co.

BURKE, MURPHY, COSTANZA & CUPPY (AV)

Suite 600 8585 Broadway, 46410
Telephone: 219-769-1313
Telecopier: 219-769-6806
East Chicago, Indiana Office: First National Bank Building. 720 W. Chicago Avenue.
Telephone: 219-397-2401.
Telecopier: 219-397-0506.
Palm Harbor, Florida Office: Suite 280, 33920 U.S. Highway 19 North.
Telephone: 813-787-7799.
Telecopier: 813-787-7237.

MEMBERS OF FIRM

Lester F. Murphy (East Chicago, Indiana and Palm Harbor, Florida Offices)
Frederick M. Cuppy
David K. Ranich
Kathryn D. Schmidt
David Cerven

ASSOCIATE

Craig R. Van Schouwen

Representative Clients: Aetna Casualty & Surety Co.; Home Insurance Company.

For Complete List of Firm Personnel, See General Section

For full biographical listings, see the Martindale-Hubbell Law Directory

HOEPPNER WAGNER AND EVANS (AV)

Twin Towers, Suite 606 South, 1000 East 80th Place, 46410
Telephone: 219-769-6552; 465-0432
FAX: 219-738-2349
Valparaiso, Indiana Office: 103 East Lincolnway, P.O. Box 2357.
Telephone: 219-464-4961; 769-8995.
Fax: 219-465-0603.

RESIDENT MEMBER

F. Joseph Jaskowiak

RESIDENT ASSOCIATE

James L. Clement, Jr.

Representative Clients: State Farm Insurance; The Travelers Insurance Company; Continental Loss Adjusting Services; Auto Owners Insurance; Indiana Insurance; Allstate Insurance; General Accident Insurance.

For Complete List of Firm Personnel, See General Section

For full biographical listings, see the Martindale-Hubbell Law Directory

SPANGLER, JENNINGS & DOUGHERTY, P.C. (AV)

8396 Mississippi Street, 46410-6398
Telephone: 219-769-2323
Facsimile: 219-769-5007
Valparaiso, Indiana Office: 150 Lincolnway, Suite 3001.
Telephone: 219-462-6151.
FAX: 219-477-4935.

Ronald T. Spangler
Patrick J. Dougherty (Valparaiso Office)
Samuel J. Furlin
John P. McQuillan
Samuel J. Bernardi, Jr. (Valparaiso Office)
Jon F. Schmoll
Robert D. Hawk
David J. Hanson
Robert P. Kennedy
James T. McNiece
James D. McQuillan
David L. Abel, II
Robert P. Stoner (Valparaiso Office)
Theresa Lazar Springmann

Gregory J. Tonner
Kathleen M. Maicher
Paul B. Poracky
Robert D. Brown
Robert J. Dignam
David R. Phillips
Kristin A. Mulholland
Kisti Good Risse

Representative Clients: Allstate Insurance Cos.; American International Group; American States Insurance Co.; Associates Financial Services Co. of Indiana; Bank One, Merriville, N.A.; Bank One Leasing; Beneficial Financial Co.; Boise Cascade Corp.; CNA Insurance; Chrysler Financial Corp.

For Complete List of Firm Personnel, See General Section

For full biographical listings, see the Martindale-Hubbell Law Directory

MUNSTER, Lake Co.

LAW OFFICES OF TIMOTHY F. KELLY (AV)

Suite 2A, 9250 Columbia Avenue, 46321
Telephone: 219-836-4062
Telecopier: 219-836-0167

(See Next Column)

LAW OFFICES OF TIMOTHY F. KELLY—*Continued*

MEMBERS OF FIRM

Timothy F. Kelly
Karl K. Vanzo

ASSOCIATE

Harvey Karlovac

For Complete List of Firm Personnel, See General Section

For full biographical listings, see the Martindale-Hubbell Law Directory

*SOUTH BEND,** St. Joseph Co.

DORAN BLACKMOND READY HAMILTON & WILLIAMS (AV)

1700 Valley American Bank Building, 211 W. Washington Street, 46601
Telephone: 219-288-1800
Fax: 219-236-4265

MEMBERS OF FIRM

John E. Doran
Don G. Blackmond
David T. Ready
John C. Hamilton
A. Howard Williams

For full biographical listings, see the Martindale-Hubbell Law Directory

JONES, OBENCHAIN, FORD, PANKOW, LEWIS & WOODS (AV)

1800 Valley American Bank Building, P.O. Box 4577, 46634
Telephone: 219-233-1194
Fax: 233-8957; 233-9675

Vitus G. Jones (1879-1951)
Roland Obenchain (1890-1961)
Francis Jones (1907-1988)
Roland Obenchain (Retired)
Milton A. Johnson (Retired)

MEMBERS OF FIRM

James H. Pankow
Thomas F. Lewis, Jr.
Timothy W. Woods
John R. Obenchain
Robert W. Mysliwiec
Robert M. Edwards, Jr.
John B. Ford
Mark J. Phillipoff
John W. Van Laere

ASSOCIATES

Patrick D. Murphy
Edward P. Benchik
Wendell G. Davis, Jr.

OF COUNSEL

G. Burt Ford

Representative Clients: American Family Insurance Group; The Travelers; Ohio Casualty Group; Frankenmuth Mutual Insurance Co.; Motorists Insurance Co.; Farm Bureau of Michigan; GAB Business Services; Government Employees Insurance Co.; Transamerica Insurance; Progressive Health.

For full biographical listings, see the Martindale-Hubbell Law Directory

EDWARD N. KALAMAROS & ASSOCIATES PROFESSIONAL CORPORATION (AV)

129 North Michigan Avenue, P.O. Box 4156, 46634
Telephone: 219-232-4801
Telecopier: 219-232-9736

Edward N. Kalamaros
Timothy J. Walsh
Thomas F. Cohen
Joseph M. Forte
Robert Deane Woods
Peter J. Agostino
Patrick J. Hinkle
Bernard E. Edwards
Philip E. Kalamaros
Sally P. Norton
Kevin W. Kearney
Lynn E. Arnold

Representative Clients: Liberty Mutual Insurance Co.; Employers Mutual of Wausau; Fireman's Fund American Insurance Group; St. Paul Insurance Companies; U.S.F. & G.; Cincinnati Insurance Co.; Kemper Group; Continental Loss Adjusting Services, Inc.; Orion Group.

For full biographical listings, see the Martindale-Hubbell Law Directory

ROWE, FOLEY & GARDNER (AV)

Suite 900 Society Bank Building, 46601
Telephone: 219-233-8200

R. Kent Rowe
R. Kent Rowe, III
Edmond W. Foley
Martin J. Gardner

ASSOCIATES

Gregory J. Haines
Timothy J. Maher
Lee Korzan
Steven D. Groth
Evan S. Roberts
William James O'Mahony

For full biographical listings, see the Martindale-Hubbell Law Directory

*TERRE HAUTE,** Vigo Co.

COX, ZWERNER, GAMBILL & SULLIVAN (AV)

511 Wabash Avenue, P.O. Box 1625, 47808-1625
Telephone: 812-232-6003
Fax: 812-232-6567

(See Next Column)

MEMBERS OF FIRM

Ernest J. Zwerner (1918-1980)
Benjamin G. Cox (1915-1988)
Gilbert W. Gambill, Jr.
James E. Sullivan
Benjamin G. Cox, Jr.
David W. Sullivan
Robert L. Gowdy
Louis F. Britton
Robert D. Hepburn
Carroll D. Smeltzer
Jeffry A. Lind

ASSOCIATE

Ronald E. Jumps

Counsel for: Terre Haute First National Bank; Farmers Insurance Group; Indiana-American Water Co.; Indiana State University; Merchants National Bank of Terre Haute; Rose-Hulman Institute of Technology; Tribune-Star Publishing Co., Inc.; Weston Paper & Manufacturing Co.; Equitable Life Assurance Society of U.S.; Federated Mutual Insurance Co.; Fireman's Fund; General Accident Group; Guaranty National Insurance; Milwaukee Mutual Insurance Co.; Ohio Casualty Insurance Co.; Hartford Insurance; The Travelers Co.; United Services Auto Assn.; Vernon Insurance Co.

For full biographical listings, see the Martindale-Hubbell Law Directory

SACOPULOS, JOHNSON, CARTER & SACOPULOS (AV)

31 South Seventh Street, 47807
Telephone: 812-238-2565
FAX: 812-238-1945

MEMBERS OF FIRM

Gus Sacopulos
R. Steven Johnson
Gregory S. Carter
Peter J. Sacopulos

Representative Clients: Aetna Casualty & Surety Co.; Auto-Owners Insurance Co.; Underwriters Adjusting Co.; Indiana Insurance Co.; Cigna Insurance; American States Insurance Co.; CNA Insurance Co.; Physicians & Surgeons Insurance Co.; American Family Insurance Co.; WalMart Stores, Inc.

For full biographical listings, see the Martindale-Hubbell Law Directory

WILKINSON, GOELLER, MODESITT, WILKINSON & DRUMMY (AV)

333 Ohio Street, P.O. Box 800, 47808-0800
Telephone: 812-232-4311
Fax: 812-235-5107

MEMBERS OF FIRM

Myrl O. Wilkinson
Raymond H. Modesitt
B. Curtis Wilkinson
William W. Drummy
John C. Wall
Craig M. McKee
Scott M. Kyrouac
Jeffrey A. Boyll

ASSOCIATE

David P. Friedrich

Representative Clients: State Farm Mutual Automobile Insurance Co.; State Farm Fire & Casualty Co.; Rockwood Insurance Co. of Indiana; Medical Protective Co.; Indiana Insurance Cos.; U.S. Insurance Group; Motorists Mutual Insurance Co.; Household Bank; United Farm Bureau Mutual Insurance Company; St. Paul Insurance Companies.

For Complete List of Firm Personnel, See General Section

For full biographical listings, see the Martindale-Hubbell Law Directory

*VALPARAISO,** Porter Co.

HOEPPNER WAGNER AND EVANS (AV)

103 East Lincolnway, P.O. Box 2357, 46384-2357
Telephone: 219-464-4961; 769-8995
Fax: 219-465-0603
Merrillville, Indiana Office: Twin Towers, Suite 606 South, 1000 East 80th Place.
Telephone: 219-769-6552. Porter County: 219-465-0432.
Fax: 219-738-2349.

MEMBERS OF FIRM

Larry G. Evans
William F. Satterlee, III
John E. Hughes
James A. Cheslek
Ronald P. Kuker
F. Joseph Jaskowiak (Resident, Merrillville Office)
Richard M. Davis

ASSOCIATES

Michael P. Blaize
Mary Jill Sisson
Heidi B. Jark
James L. Clement, Jr. (Resident, Merrillville Office)
Jonathan R. Hanson
Robert L. Clark
Jeffrey W. Clymer

Representative Clients: State Farm Insurance; The Travelers Insurance Company; Continental Loss Adjusting Services; Auto Owners Insurance; Indiana Insurance; Allstate Insurance; General Accident Insurance.

For Complete List of Firm Personnel, See General Section

For full biographical listings, see the Martindale-Hubbell Law Directory

*VERSAILLES,** Ripley Co.

Eaton & Romweber (AV)

123 South Main Street, P.O. Box 275, 47042
Telephone: 812-689-5111
Fax: 812-689-5165
Batesville, Indiana Office: 13 East George Street. Telephone 812-934-5735. *Fax:* 812-934-6041.

MEMBERS OF FIRM

Larry L. Eaton
Anthony A. Romweber

ASSOCIATE

W. Gregory Coy

For full biographical listings, see the Martindale-Hubbell Law Directory

*VINCENNES,** Knox Co.

Emison, Doolittle, Kolb & Roellgen (AV)

Eighth & Busseron Streets, P.O. Box 215, 47591
Telephone: 812-882-2280
FAX: 812-885-2308

MEMBER OF FIRM

Rabb Emison

Clients Include: Security Bank & Trust Co.; Sun-Commercial Newspaper; Amoco Pipeline; Tenneco; United Farm Bureau Mutual Insurance Co.

For Complete List of Firm Personnel, See General Section

For full biographical listings, see the Martindale-Hubbell Law Directory

*WARSAW,** Kosciusko Co.

Rockhill, Pinnick, Pequignot, Helm & Landis (AV)

105 East Main Street, 46580-2742
Telephone: 219-267-6116
Telecopier: 219-269-9264

MEMBERS OF FIRM

Brooks C. Pinnick
Stanley E. Pequignot
Richard K. Helm
Vern K. Landis
Jay A. Rigdon
Jeanne A. Rondot

ASSOCIATE

Jamelyn E. Casbon

OF COUNSEL

Alvin T. Rockhill

Representative Clients: State Farm Insurance Cos.; United Farm Bureau Mutual Insurance Co.; Motorists Mutual Insurance Co.

For full biographical listings, see the Martindale-Hubbell Law Directory

IOWA

CEDAR FALLS, Black Hawk Co.

Redfern, Mason, Dieter, Larsen & Moore (AV)

315 Clay Street, P.O. Box 627, 50613
Telephone: 319-277-6830
Facsimile: 319-277-3531

MEMBERS OF FIRM

David R. Mason
Robert J. Dieter
John C. Larsen
Steven D. Moore
Donald B. Redfern
Mark W. Fransdal
Mark S. Rolinger

ASSOCIATE

Susan Bernau Staudt

Representative Clients: Norwest Bank Iowa; The National Bank of Waterloo; Don R. Havens Co.; Control-O-fax Corp.; Cedar Falls Community School District; University of Northern Iowa Foundation; United States Fidelity and Guaranty Co.; The Travelers Insurance Cos.; Fireman's Fund Insurance Companies.

For Complete List of Firm Personnel, See General Section

For full biographical listings, see the Martindale-Hubbell Law Directory

*CEDAR RAPIDS,** Linn Co.

Pickens, Barnes & Abernathy (AV)

Tenth Floor American Building, P.O. Box 74170, 52407-4170
Telephone: 319-366-7621
Fax: 319-366-3158

MEMBERS OF FIRM

Minor Barnes
Terry J. Abernathy
Mark H. Ogden
Matthew G. Novak

(See Next Column)

ASSOCIATE

JoAnne M. Lilledahl

OF COUNSEL

James F. Pickens

A list of Representative Clients furnished upon request.

For full biographical listings, see the Martindale-Hubbell Law Directory

Shuttleworth & Ingersoll, P.C. (AV)

500 Firstar Bank Building, P.O. Box 2107, 52406-2107
Telephone: 319-365-9461
Fax: 319-365-8443

John M. Bickel
Robert D. Houghton
Richard S. Fry
Richard C. Garberson
Steven J. Pace
Glenn L. Johnson
Thomas P. Peffer
Kevin H. Collins
Diane Kutzko
Mark L. Zaiger
Douglas R. Oelschlaeger
Constance M. Alt
Kurt L. Kratovil

Christine L. McLaughlin
William H. Courter

OF COUNSEL

Ralph W. Gearhart

COUNSEL

James D. Hodges, Jr.

Representative Clients: Allied Insurance Group; Auto-Owners Insurance; CIGNA Companies; CNA Insurance Companies; Crum & Forster Commercial Insurance; Farmers Insurance Group; Farmland Mutual Insurance Company; Fireman's Fund Insurance Companies; General Casualty Company of Wisconsin; IMT Insurance Company.

For Complete List of Firm Personnel, See General Section

For full biographical listings, see the Martindale-Hubbell Law Directory

Simmons, Perrine, Albright & Ellwood, L.L.P. (AV)

A Partnership including a Professional Corporation
115 Third Street S.E. Suite 1200, 52401
Telephone: 319-366-7641
Telecopier: 319-366-1917 (I,II,III)

PARTNERS

James R. Snyder
James E. Shipman
Robert M. Jilek (P.C.)
Gregory M. Lederer
James A. Gerk
Richard G. Hileman, Jr.
Roger W. Stone
Matthew J. Petrzelka
Matthew J. Brandes
James M. Peters

Representative Clients: The Home Insurance Co.; Reliance Insurance Co.; Allstate Insurance Co.; Crawford & Co.; National Union Insurance Co.; The St. Paul Insurance Co.; Grinnell Mutual Reinsurance Co.; Hawkeye-Security Insurance Co.; Milwaukee Mutual Insurance Co.

For Complete List of Firm Personnel, See General Section

For full biographical listings, see the Martindale-Hubbell Law Directory

*COUNCIL BLUFFS,** Pottawattamie Co.

Smith Peterson Law Firm (AV)

35 Main Place, Suite 300, P.O. Box 249, 51502
Telephone: 712-328-1833
Fax: 712-328-8320
Omaha, Nebraska Office: 9290 West Dodge Road, Suite 205. *Telephone:* 402-397-8500. *Fax:* 402-397-5519.

MEMBERS OF FIRM

Raymond A. Smith (1892-1977)
John LeRoy Peterson (1895-1969)
Harold T. Beckman
Robert J. Laubenthal
Richard A. Heininger
Lawrence J. Beckman
Gregory G. Barntsen
W. Curtis Hewett
Steven H. Krohn
Randy R. Ewing
Joseph D. Thornton

ASSOCIATES

Trent D. Reinert (Not admitted in IA)
T. J. Pattermann

Representative Clients: Aetna Life and Casualty Co.; Employers Mutual Co.; First National Bank of Council Bluffs; IMT Insurance Co.; Monsanto Co.; United Fire & Casualty Co.; U.S. Fidelity and Guaranty.

For full biographical listings, see the Martindale-Hubbell Law Directory

*DECORAH,** Winneshiek Co.

Miller, Pearson, Gloe, Burns, Beatty & Cowie, P.C. (AV)

301 West Broadway, 52101
Telephone: 319-382-4226
FAX: 319-382-3783

(See Next Column)

Miller, Pearson, Gloe, Burns, Beatty & Cowie P.C.—*Continued*

Frank R. Miller (1915-1977)
Donald H. Gloe
James Burns
Marion L. Beatty
Robert J. Cowie, Jr.

OF COUNSEL

Floyd S. Pearson

Counsel For: Luther College; Decorah Community School District; Winneshiek County Memorial Hospital; Decorah State Bank.
Local Counsel for: Farmers Mutual Reinsurance Co.; Ohio Casualty Insurance Co.; Iowa Farm Mutual Insurance Cos.; Employers Mutual Liability Insurance Co. of Wisconsin; Continental Casualty Co.; Employers Mutual Casualty Co.

For full biographical listings, see the Martindale-Hubbell Law Directory

*DES MOINES,** Polk Co.

Grefe & Sidney (AV)

2222 Grand Avenue, P.O. Box 10434, 50306
Telephone: 515-245-4300
Fax: 515-245-4452

MEMBERS OF FIRM

Ross H. Sidney
Henry A. Harmon
Claude H. Freeman
Stephen D. Hardy
John Werner
Patrick J. McNulty
Iris J. Post
Mark W. Thomas
Guy R. Cook

ASSOCIATES

Ken A. Winjum
David C. Duncan
Andrew D. Hall
Kevin W. Techau
Stephanie L. Glenn

Representative Clients: Easter Stores; Freeman Decorating Co.; Iowa-Nebraska Farm Equipment Association, Inc.; Pella Corp.; State Farm Mutual Insurance Companies of Bloomington, Ill.; Liberty Mutual Insurance Co.; United States Fidelity and Guaranty Co.; Koehring Co.

For Complete List of Firm Personnel, See General Section

For full biographical listings, see the Martindale-Hubbell Law Directory

Huber, Kelley, Book, Cortese & Happe (AV)

500 Liberty Building, 50309-2421
Telephone: 515-243-4148
Fax: 515-243-5481

MEMBERS OF FIRM

James C. Huber
Dorothy L. Kelley
Richard G. Book
Joseph S. Cortese II
Joseph A. Happe

ASSOCIATES

Patrick D. Smith
Cristine Kuhn

Representative Clients: Liberty Mutual Ins. Co.; Royal-Globe Group; Fireman's Fund American Insurance Companies; Continental Insurance Companies; Security Insurance Group; Home Insurance Co.; U.S. Insurance Group.
Reference: Boatmen's Bank.

For full biographical listings, see the Martindale-Hubbell Law Directory

Patterson, Lorentzen, Duffield, Timmons, Irish, Becker & Ordway (AV)

729 Insurance Exchange Building, 50309
Telephone: 515-283-2147
Fax: 515-283-1002

MEMBERS OF FIRM

G. O. Patterson (1914-1982)
James A. Lorentzen
Theodore T. Duffield
William E. Timmons
Roy M. Irish
Gary D. Ordway
Robin L. Hermann
Harry Perkins, III
Michael F. Lacey, Jr.
Jeffrey A. Boehlert
Douglas A. Haag
Charles E. Cutler
Ronald M. Rankin
Michael D. Huppert
William A. Wickett

ASSOCIATES

Jeffrey A. Baker
Janice M. Herfkens
Coreen K. Bezdicek
Scott S. Bellis

OF COUNSEL

F. H. Becker

Representative Clients: Allied Mutual Insurance Company; CNA Insurance Company; Chubb Insurance Group; Continental Western Insurance Co.; Farmers Insurance Group; Farmland Insurance Company; Grinnell Mutual Reinsurance Company; Hawkeye Security Insurance Company; Iowa Insurance Institute, St. Paul Fire & Marine Insurance Company.

For Complete List of Firm Personnel, See General Section

For full biographical listings, see the Martindale-Hubbell Law Directory

Whitfield & Eddy, P.L.C. (AV)

317 6th Avenue, Suite 1200 Locust at 6th, 50309-4110
Telephone: 515-288-6041
Fax: 515-246-1474

A. Roger Witke
Timothy J. Walker
David L. Phipps
Benjamin B. Ullem
Robert M. Kreamer
Robert L. Fanter
Bernard L. Spaeth, Jr.
Rodney P. Kubat
William L. Fairbank
Robert G. Bridges
Jaki K. Samuelson
Kevin M. Reynolds
Thomas H. Burke
Thomas Henderson
George H. Frampton
Megan Manning Antenucci
Wendy L. Carlson
Robert J. Blink
Gary A. Norton
Mark V. Hanson
Maureen Roach Tobin

Jeffrey William Courter
August B. Landis
Kent Thomas Kelsey
Richard J. Kirschman
John F. Fatino
Jason M. Casini
Nancy P. O'Brien

OF COUNSEL

Dean Dutton

General Counsel for: American Life and Casualty Co.; Hawkeye; Security Insurance Co.; The Statesman Group, Inc.; United Security Insurance Co.
Representative Clients: Crum & Forster Commercial Insurance; National Insurance Assn.; Royal Insurance; Tudor Insurance.

For Complete List of Firm Personnel, See General Section

For full biographical listings, see the Martindale-Hubbell Law Directory

*HARLAN,** Shelby Co.

Kohorst Law Firm (AV)

602 Market Street Building, P.O. Box 722, 51537-0722
Telephone: 712-755-3156
Fax: 712-755-7404

Robert Kohorst
Kathleen Schomer Kohorst

ASSOCIATES

William T. Early
Steven Elza Goodlow

Representative Clients: Employers Mutual Insurance Companies of Des Moines, Iowa; Farm Service Co-op., Harlan, Iowa; Mapco Natural Gas Liquids, Inc., Tulsa, Oklahoma; United Fire & Casualty Co.; Farmers Mutual Telephone Co., Harlan, Iowa.

For full biographical listings, see the Martindale-Hubbell Law Directory

*OSKALOOSA,** Mahaska Co.

Pothoven, Blomgren & Stravers (AV)

1201 High Avenue West, P.O. Box 1066, 52577
Telephone: 515-673-4438
Fax: 515-673-5177

MEMBERS OF FIRM

Marion H. Pothoven
James Q. Blomgren
Randall C. Stravers

For full biographical listings, see the Martindale-Hubbell Law Directory

*SIOUX CITY,** Woodbury Co.

Eidsmoe, Heidman, Redmond, Fredregill, Patterson & Schatz (AV)

A Partnership including Professional Corporations
701 Pierce Street, Suite 200, P.O. Box 3086, 51102
Telephone: 712-255-8838
Fax: 712-258-6714

MEMBERS OF FIRM

Marvin F. Heidman
James W. Redmond
Alan E. Fredregill (P.C.)
Charles T. Patterson
Kenneth C. Schatz (P.C.)
Thomas M. Plaza
Daniel D. Dykstra
Lance D. Ehmcke
Margaret M. Prahl
John Ackerman
Gregg E. Williams
Judith A. Higgs
John C. Gray
Daniel B. Shuck

ASSOCIATES

Rita C. Grimm
Ryan K. Crayne
Charles E. Trullinger
John W. Gleysteen (Retired)
Robert R. Eidsmoe (Retired)
Jacob C. Gleysteen (1883-1943)
H. Clifford Harper (1891-1959)

Representative Clients: Aetna Casualty & Surety Co.; Irving F. Jensen Co., Inc.; Marian Health Center; Medical Protective Co.; John Morrell & Co.; Pig Improvement Co.; State Farm Mutual Insurance Co.; Terra International, Inc.; The Security National Bank of Sioux City; Wal-Mart Stores, Inc.

For full biographical listings, see the Martindale-Hubbell Law Directory

Sioux City—Continued

MAYNE & MAYNE (AV)

400 Home Federal Building, P.O. Box 5049, 51102
Telephone: 712-252-3220
FAX: 712-252-1535

MEMBERS OF FIRM

Wiley Mayne
John D. Mayne

ASSOCIATE

Robert J. Pierson

Representative Clients: American Home Insurance; American Telephone & Telegraph Co.; Amoco Oil Co.; Chubb Insurance; Federated Mutual Insurance Co.; Ford Motor Credit Co.; Fremont Indemnity Co.; Ranger Insurance; Metz Baking Co.; Shell Chemical Co.

For full biographical listings, see the Martindale-Hubbell Law Directory

*WATERLOO,** Black Hawk Co.

SWISHER & COHRT (AV)

528 West Fourth Street, P.O. Box 1200, 50704
Telephone: 319-232-6555
FAX: 319-232-4835

MEMBERS OF FIRM

Benjamin F. Swisher (1878-1959)
L. J. Cohrt (1898-1974)
Charles F. Swisher (1919-1986)
Eldon R. McCann
Steven A. Weidner
Larry J. Cohrt
J. Douglas Oberman
Stephen J. Powell
Jim D. DeKoster
Jeffrey J. Greenwood
Samuel C. Anderson
Robert C. Griffin
Kevin R. Rogers

ASSOCIATES

Beth E. Hansen
Mark F. Conway
Natalie Williams Burr

Firm is Counsel for: Koehring Corp.; Clay Equipment; Chamberlain Manufacturing Co.; Waterloo Courier.
Local Counsel for: Allied Group; John Deere Insurance; Liberty Mutual Insurance Co.

For full biographical listings, see the Martindale-Hubbell Law Directory

KANSAS

*KANSAS CITY,** Wyandotte Co.

HOLBROOK, HEAVEN & FAY, P.A. (AV)

757 Armstrong, P.O. Box 171927, 66117
Telephone: 913-342-2500
Fax: 913-342-0603
Merriam, Kansas Office: 6700 Antioch Street.
Telephone: 913-677-1717.
Fax: 913-677- 0403.

Reid F. Holbrook
Lewis A. Heaven, Jr. (Resident, Merriam Office)
Ted F. Fay, Jr. (Resident, Merriam Office)
Thomas E. Osborn
Robert L. Kennedy
Janet M. Simpson
John D. Tongier (Resident, Merriam Office)
Thomas M. Sutherland
Thomas S. Busch (Resident, Merriam Office)
Vincent K. Snowbarger (Resident, Merriam Office)
Kurt S. Brack
Sally A. Howard
Brent G. Wright

For Complete List of Firm Personnel, See General Section

For full biographical listings, see the Martindale-Hubbell Law Directory

MCANANY, VAN CLEAVE & PHILLIPS, P.A. (AV)

Fourth Floor, 707 Minnesota Avenue, P.O. Box 1300, 66117
Telephone: 913-371-3838
Facsimile: 913-371-4722
Lenexa, Kansas Office: Suite 200, 11900 West 87th Street Parkway.
Telephone: 913-888-9000.
Facsimile: 913-888-7049.
Kansas City, Missouri Office: Suite 304, 819 Walnut Street.
Telephone: 816-556-9417.

John J. Jurcyk, Jr.
Robert D. Benham
Clifford T. Mueller (Resident, Lenexa Office)
Patrick D. McAnany (Resident, Lenexa Office)
Frank D. Menghini
William P. Coates, Jr. (Resident, Lenexa Office)
Douglas M. Greenwald
Terri L. Savely Bezek

Reference: UMB Commercial National Bank.

For Complete List of Firm Personnel, See General Section

For full biographical listings, see the Martindale-Hubbell Law Directory

OVERLAND PARK, Johnson Co.

FISHER, PATTERSON, SAYLER & SMITH (AV)

Suite 210, 11050 Roe Street, 66211
Telephone: 913-339-6757
FAX: 913-339-6187
Topeka, Kansas Office: 534 Kansas Avenue, Suite 400. 66603-3463.
Telephone: 913-232-7761.
Fax: 913-232-6604.

MEMBERS OF FIRM

Edwin Dudley Smith (Resident)
Michael K. Seck (Resident)
David P. Madden (Resident)

ASSOCIATE

Kurt A. Level (Resident)

For full biographical listings, see the Martindale-Hubbell Law Directory

*TOPEKA,** Shawnee Co.

DAVIS, UNREIN, HUMMER, MCCALLISTER & BUCK (AV)

100 East Ninth Street, Third Floor, P.O. Box 3575, 66601-3575
Telephone: 913-354-1100
Fax: 913-354-1113

MEMBERS OF FIRM

Byron M. Gray (1901-1986)
Maurice D. Freidberg (1902-1965)
Charles L. Davis, Jr. (1921-1992)
Michael J. Unrein
J. Franklin Hummer
Mark A. Buck
James B. Biggs
Christopher M. Rohrer
Brenda L. Head

OF COUNSEL

Gary D. McCallister

Representative Clients: American Family Group; Continental Insurance Co.; General Casualty Company; Hawkeye Security Insurance Co.; Preferred Risk Insurance Co.; Silvey Insurance Co.; Union Insurance Co.; United Fire & Casualty Co.; Utica Mutual Insurance Co.; Wausau Insurance Co.

For full biographical listings, see the Martindale-Hubbell Law Directory

FISHER, PATTERSON, SAYLER & SMITH (AV)

534 Kansas Avenue, Suite 400, 66603-3463
Telephone: 913-232-7761
Fax: 913-232-6604
Overland Park, Kansas Office: Suite 210, 11050 Roe Street. 66211.
Telephone: 913-339-6757.
Fax: 913-339-6187.

MEMBERS OF FIRM

Donald Patterson
Charles Keith Sayler
Edwin Dudley Smith (Resident, Overland Park Office)
Larry G. Pepperdine
James P. Nordstrom
Justice B. King
J. Steven Pigg
Steve R. Fabert
Ronald J. Laskowski
Michael K. Seck (Resident, Overland Park Office)
David P. Madden (Resident, Overland Park Office)
Steven K. Johnson

ASSOCIATES

Kristine A. Larscheid
Michael L. Bennett
Kurt A. Level (Resident, Overland Park Office)
Betty J. Mick

OF COUNSEL

David H. Fisher

Representative Clients: Gage Shopping Center, Inc.; Fireman's Fund-American Insurance Cos.; United States Fidelity and Guaranty Co.; Hartford Insurance Group.; The Procter & Gamble Company; American Cyanamid Company; Commercial Union Insurance Companies; Kansas Fire & Casualty Co.; National Casualty/Scottsdale Insurance Co.

For full biographical listings, see the Martindale-Hubbell Law Directory

GOODELL, STRATTON, EDMONDS & PALMER (AV)

515 South Kansas Avenue, 66603-3999
Telephone: 913-233-0593
Telecopier: 913-233-8870

MEMBERS OF FIRM

Gerald L. Goodell
Wayne T. Stratton
Arthur E. Palmer
Harold S. Youngentob
Charles R. Hay
Patrick M. Salsbury
Michael W. Merriam
John H. Stauffer, Jr.
Les E. Diehl
David E. Bruns
Daniel J. Gronniger
N. Larry Bork
John D. Ensley

ASSOCIATES

Curtis J. Waugh
Catherine Walberg
Steve A Schwarm

(See Next Column)

GOODELL, STRATTON, EDMONDS & PALMER—*Continued*

SPECIAL COUNSEL

Marta Fisher Linenberger

Local Counsel for: Farm Bureau Mutual Insurance Co.; Metropolitan Life Insurance Co.; St. Paul Fire & Marine Insurance Co.
General Counsel for: American Home Life Insurance Co.; Columbian National Title Insurance Co.; The Menninger Foundation; Stauffer Communications, Inc.; Kansas Association of Realtors; Kansas Medical Society; Kansas Hospital Association.

For Complete List of Firm Personnel, See General Section

For full biographical listings, see the Martindale-Hubbell Law Directory

WRIGHT, HENSON, SOMERS, SEBELIUS, CLARK & BAKER (AV)

Commerce Bank Building, 100 Southeast Ninth Street, 2nd Floor, P.O. Box 3555, 66601-3555
Telephone: 913-232-2200
FAX: 913-232-3344

MEMBERS OF FIRM

Thomas E. Wright
Anne Lamborn Baker

ASSOCIATES

Catherine A. Walter
Evelyn Zabel Wilson

For Complete List of Firm Personnel, See General Section

For full biographical listings, see the Martindale-Hubbell Law Directory

*WICHITA,** Sedgwick Co.

DEPEW & GILLEN (AV)

151 North Main, Suite 700, 67202-1408
Telephone: 316-265-9621
Facsimile: 316-265-3819

MEMBERS OF FIRM

Spencer L. Depew
Dennis L. Gillen
Jack Scott McInteer
David W. Nickel
Nicholas S. Daily
David E. Rogers
Charles Christian Steincamp

For full biographical listings, see the Martindale-Hubbell Law Directory

FOULSTON & SIEFKIN (AV)

(Formerly Foulston, Siefkin, Powers & Eberhardt)
700 Fourth Financial Center, Broadway at Douglas, 67202
Telephone: 316-267-6371
Facsimile: 316-267-6345
Topeka, Kansas Office: 1515 Bank IV Tower, 534 Kansas Avenue. 66603.
Telephone: 913-233-3600.
FAX: 913-233-1610.
Member: Lex Mundi, A Global Association of Independent Firms

MEMBERS OF FIRM

Frederick L. Haag
Darrell L. Warta
Jay F. Fowler
Stephen M. Kerwick
Vaughn Burkholder
Amy S. Lemley
Craig W. West

For Complete List of Firm Personnel, See General Section

For full biographical listings, see the Martindale-Hubbell Law Directory

HERSHBERGER, PATTERSON, JONES & ROTH, L.C. (AV)

600 Hardage Center, 100 South Main, 67202-3779
Telephone: 316-263-7583
Fax: 316-263-7595

William R. Smith
Greer Gsell
Jeffrey A. Roth
David J. Morgan

Tracy A. Applegate
Marc P. Clements

OF COUNSEL

H. E. Jones

Counsel for: First National Bank in Wichita; Andarko Petroleum Corporation; Mobil Oil Corp.; CNA Insurance; Royal Exchange Group; Central National Insurance Group; Transamerica Insurance Group; Northwestern National Insurance Group; St. Paul Cos.

For Complete List of Firm Personnel, See General Section

For full biographical listings, see the Martindale-Hubbell Law Directory

KAHRS, NELSON, FANNING, HITE & KELLOGG (AV)

Suite 630, 200 West Douglas Street, 67202-3089
Telephone: 316-265-7761
Telecopier: 316-267-7803

(See Next Column)

MEMBERS OF FIRM

Richard L. Honeyman
Larry A. Withers
Gary A. Winfrey
Scott J. Gunderson
Randy Troutt
Arthur S. Chalmers
Marc A. Powell
Kim R. Martens
Forrest James Robinson, Jr.
Don D. Gribble, II
Vince P. Wheeler
Alan R. Pfaff
Dennis V. Lacey

ASSOCIATE

Dana D. Preheim

Representative Clients: Attorneys Liability Protection Society; American States Ins. Co.; Chubb-Pacific Ins. Group; CNA; Cravens, Dargon & Co.; Farm Bureau Mutual Ins. Co.; Howe Associates, Inc.; Kansas Medical Mutual; Maryland Casualty Co.; The St. Paul Cos.

For Complete List of Firm Personnel, See General Section

For full biographical listings, see the Martindale-Hubbell Law Directory

KASSEBAUM & JOHNSON (AV)

River Park Place, 727 North Waco, Suite 585, 67203
Telephone: 316-263-4921
Fax: 316-263-0045

MEMBERS OF FIRM

Douglas D. Johnson
E. Craig Kennedy
David L. Dahl
Cortland Q. Clotfelter

OF COUNSEL

John Philip Kassebaum

Representative Clients: Vulcan Materials Co.; American Family Insurance Group.

For full biographical listings, see the Martindale-Hubbell Law Directory

YOUNG, BOGLE, McCAUSLAND, WELLS & CLARK, P.A. (AV)

106 West Douglas, Suite 923, 67202
Telephone: 316-265-7841
Facsimile: 316-265-3956

Jerry D. Bogle
Paul S. McCausland
Kenneth M. Clark

Representative Clients: Provident Life & Accident Insurance Co.; The Equitable Life Assurance Society of the United States; John Deere Insurance Co.; Metropolitan Life Ins. Co.; Horace Mann Ins. Co.; John Hancock Mutual Life Ins Co.; ITT Life Ins. Co.; Benefit Trust Life Ins. Co.; Home Life Insurance Co.; Minnesota Mutual Life Insurance Co.; Farmers Insurance Group.

For Complete List of Firm Personnel, See General Section

For full biographical listings, see the Martindale-Hubbell Law Directory

KENTUCKY

ASHLAND, Boyd Co.

MARTIN, PICKLESIMER, JUSTICE & VINCENT (AV)

431 Sixteenth Street, P.O. Box 2528, 41105-2528
Telephone: 606-329-8338
Fax: 606-325-8199

Richard W. Martin
Max D. Picklesimer
David Justice
John F. Vincent

ASSOCIATES

Thomas Wade Lavender, II
P. Kimberly Watson

Representative Clients: City of Ashland; FIVCO Area Development District; Boyd County Sanitation District No. 2; Mid-America Distributors, Inc.
Insurance Counsel for: State Farm Mutual Automobile Insurance Co.; State Farm Fire and Casualty Co.; Aetna Casualty Insurance Co.; Grange Mutual Insurance Co.; Great American Insurance Co.

For full biographical listings, see the Martindale-Hubbell Law Directory

*BOWLING GREEN,** Warren Co.

BRODERICK, THORNTON & PIERCE (AV)

921 College Street, Phoenix Place, P.O. Box 1137, 42102-1137
Telephone: 502-782-6700
Facsimile: 502-782-3110

David F. Broderick
Steven O. Thornton
Darell R. Pierce

ASSOCIATES

Pamela Carolyn Bratcher
B. Alan Simpson
Kenneth P. O'Brien

Representative Clients: Allstate Insurance Co.; National City Bank; American States Insurance Co.; Capital Enterprise Insurance; Fireman's Fund Insurance Co.; Imperial Casualty & Indemnity; Indiana Lumbermen's Mutual

(See Next Column)

BRODERICK, THORNTON & PIERCE, *Bowling Green—Continued*

Insurance; Kentucky Medical Insurance Co.; Scotty's Contracting & Stone, Inc.; St. Paul Insurance Co.

For full biographical listings, see the Martindale-Hubbell Law Directory

CAMPBELL, KERRICK & GRISE (AV)

1025 State Street, P.O. Box 9547, 42102-9547
Telephone: 502-782-8160
FAX: 502-782-5856

MEMBERS OF FIRM

Joe Bill Campbell
Thomas N. Kerrick
John R. Grise
Gregory N. Stivers
H. Brent Brennenstuhl
Deborah Tomes Wilkins

ASSOCIATES

H. Harris Pepper, Jr.
Lanna Martin Kilgore
Laura Hagan

Representative Clients: Aetna Life and Casualty Insurance Co.; American Resources Insurance Co.; Hartford Insurance Group; Nationwide Insurance Co.; Occidental Fire and Casualty Co.; Cincinnati Insurance Cos.; Firemans Fund Insurance Co.; Kentucky Hospital Association Trust; Kentucky Medical Insurance Company; Northland Insurance Cos.

For full biographical listings, see the Martindale-Hubbell Law Directory

CATRON, KILGORE & BEGLEY (AV)

918 State Street, P.O. Box 280, 42102-0280
Telephone: 502-842-1050
Fax: 502-842-4720

Stephen B. Catron
J. Patrick Kilgore
Ernest Edward Begley, II

Representative Clients: Kentucky Farm Bureau Mutual Insurance Company; Adriatic Insurance Company; Puritan Insurance Company; General Growth Management Corporation; Kentucky Transportation Cabinet; International Paper Company; Convention Center Authority; Camping World, Inc.; National Corvette Museum; Minit Mart Foods, Inc.

For full biographical listings, see the Martindale-Hubbell Law Directory

HARLIN & PARKER, P.S.C. (AV)

519 East Tenth Street, P.O. Box 390, 42102-0390
Telephone: 502-842-5611
Telefax: 502-842-2607
Smiths Grove, Kentucky Office: Old Farmers Bank Building.
Telephone: 502-563-4701.

William Jerry Parker
Max B. Harlin, III

Insurance Clients: Allstate Insurance Co.; American Hardware Mutual Insurance Co.; CNA; Government Employees Insurance Co.; U.S.F.&G. Co.; AIG Insurance Cos.
Railroad and Utilities Clients: District Attorneys for South Central Bell Telephone Co.
Local Counsel for: General Motors Corp.; Ford Motor Co.; Chrysler Corp.

For Complete List of Firm Personnel, See General Section

For full biographical listings, see the Martindale-Hubbell Law Directory

RUDLOFF, GOLDEN & EVANS (AV)

553 East Main Street, 42101-2256
Telephone: 502-781-7754; 781-7762

MEMBERS OF FIRM

William J. Rudloff
J. Dale Golden
R. Brian Evans

Reference: National City Bank, Bowling Green, Ky.

For full biographical listings, see the Martindale-Hubbell Law Directory

COVINGTON, Kenton Co.

ADAMS, BROOKING, STEPNER, WOLTERMANN & DUSING (AV)

421 Garrard Street, P.O. Box 861, 41012
Telephone: 606-291-7270
FAX: 606-291-7902
Florence, Kentucky Office: 8100 Burlington Pike, Suite 400, 41042.
Telephone: 606-371-6220.
FAX: 606-371-8341.

Donald L. Stepner
Gerald F. Dusing
(Resident at Florence Office)
James R. Kruer
Jeffrey C. Mando

ASSOCIATE

Stacey L. Graus

Representative Clients: CSX Transportation; Balluff, Inc., Wampler, Inc., Kisters, Inc., Krauss-Maffei, Inc., A group of German companies; State Automobile Mutual Insurance Co.; Chevron of California; Great American Insurance Co.; Grange Mutual Insurance Co.; Meridian Mutual Insurance Co.; Fifth-Third Bank of Northern Ky.; Northern Kentucky University.

(See Next Column)

For Complete List of Firm Personnel, See General Section

For full biographical listings, see the Martindale-Hubbell Law Directory

ROBERT C. CETRULO, P.S.C. (AV)

The Cetrulo Building, 620 Washington Street, 41011
Telephone: 606-491-6200
FAX: 606-491-6201

Robert C. Cetrulo

Reference: Star Bank, Covington, Kentucky.

For full biographical listings, see the Martindale-Hubbell Law Directory

GREENEBAUM DOLL & McDONALD (AV)

A Partnership including Professional Service Corporations
50 East Rivercenter Boulevard, P.O. Box 2050, 41012-2050
Telephone: 606-655-4200
Telecopier: 606-655-4239
Louisville, Kentucky Office: 3300 National City Tower.
Telephone: 502-589-4200.
Fax: 502-587-3695.
Lexington, Kentucky Office: 1400 Vine Center Tower.
Telephone: 606-231-8500.
Fax: 606-255-2742.
Cincinnati, Ohio Office: 832 Main Street.
Telephone: 513-421-8087.
Fax: 513-421-8089.

MEMBERS OF FIRM

Wm. T. Robinson, III
Roger N. Braden (Resident)

ASSOCIATES

J. Kevin King
Sheryl E. Heeter

Representative Clients: Aetna Life Insurance Co.; ANDALEX Resources, Inc.; Ashland Oil, Inc.; A T & T Communications, Inc.; Bethlehem Steel Corp.; Brown-Forman Corp.; Citizens Fidelity Bank & Trust Co.; Humana, Inc.; KFC National Cooperative Advertising Program, Inc.
*A Professional Service Corporation

For Complete List of Firm Personnel, See General Section

For full biographical listings, see the Martindale-Hubbell Law Directory

TALIAFERRO AND MEHLING (AV)

1005 Madison Avenue, P.O. Box 468, 41012-0468
Telephone: 606-291-9900
Fax: 606-291-3014

MEMBERS OF FIRM

Philip Taliaferro, III
Christopher J. Mehling

ASSOCIATES

Lucinda C. Shirooni
C. Houston Ebert
Alice G. Keys
J. David Brittingham

OF COUNSEL

Robert W. Carran
Norbert J. Bischoff

For full biographical listings, see the Martindale-Hubbell Law Directory

WARE, BRYSON, WEST & KUMMER (AV)

157 Barnwood Drive, 41017
Telephone: 606-341-0255
FAX: 606-341-1876

MEMBERS OF FIRM

Rodney S. Bryson
Larry C. West
John R. Kummer
Mark W. Howard
Greg D. Voss
Robert B. Cetrulo

ASSOCIATES

Susanne M. Cetrulo
W. L. (Skip) Hammons, Jr.
James M. West
Orie S. Ware (1882-1974)
William O. Ware (1908-1961)
James C. Ware (1913-1991)

Attorneys for: First National Bank of Northern Ky.; State Farm Insurance Co.; Reliance Insurance Group; Maryland Casualty Insurance Co.; Kemper Insurance Co.; Prudential Insurance Co.; State Farm Fire & Casualty Insurance Co.; Shelby Mutual Insurance Co.; Cincinnati Insurance Co.

For full biographical listings, see the Martindale-Hubbell Law Directory

*DANVILLE,** Boyle Co.

SHEEHAN, BARNETT & HAYS, P.S.C. (AV)

114 South Fourth Street, P.O. Box 1517, 40422
Telephone: 606-236-2641; 606-734-7552
FAX: 606-236-1483

James G. Sheehan, Jr.
James William Barnett
Edward D. Hays

Representative Clients: Bank One; Bank of Danville and Trust Co.; Great Financial Federal; Kentucky Farm Bureau Mutual Insurance Co.; Motorist Mutual Insurance Co.; R.R. Donnelley & Sons, Inc.; State Automobile Mutual Insurance Co.; City of Danville; Shelter Insurance Co.; Trim Masters, Inc.

For full biographical listings, see the Martindale-Hubbell Law Directory

*ELIZABETHTOWN,** Hardin Co.

COLLIER, ARNETT, QUICK & COLEMAN (AV)

128 West Dixie Avenue, P.O. Box 847, 42701
Telephone: 502-765-4112
Fax: 502-769-3081

MEMBERS OF FIRM

James M. Collier | Kim F. Quick
John L. Arnett | Jerry M. Coleman

ASSOCIATE

Deborah Lewis Shaw

Counsel for: City of Elizabethtown; PNC Bank; Elizabethtown Independent School District.
Representative Clients: Nationwide Insurance Co.; Shelter Insurance Co.; State Farm Insurance Co.; Government Employees Insurance Co.; Liberty Mutual Insurance Co.; Kemper Insurance Group; Motorist Mutual Insurance Co.

For full biographical listings, see the Martindale-Hubbell Law Directory

FLORENCE, Boone Co.

ADAMS, BROOKING, STEPNER, WOLTERMANN & DUSING (AV)

8100 Burlington Pike, Suite 400, 41042-0576
Telephone: 606-371-6220
FAX: 606-371-8341
Covington, Kentucky Office: 421 Garrard Street.
Telephone: 606-291-7270.
FAX: 606-291-7902.

Donald L. Stepner | Gerald F. Dusing (Resident)

Representative Clients: CSX Transportation; State Automobile Mutual Insurance Co.; Standard Oil Co. (Ky.); Great American Insurance Co.; Grange Mutual Insurance Co.; Meridian Mutual Insurance Co.; Fifth-Third Bank of Boone County; Northern Kentucky University.

For Complete List of Firm Personnel, See General Section

For full biographical listings, see the Martindale-Hubbell Law Directory

*HARLAN,** Harlan Co.

GAYLE G. HUFF (AV)

417 East Mound Street, Drawer 151, 40831-0151
Telephone: 606-573-4466
Fax: 606-573-7078

Representative Clients: Old Republic Insurance Co.; Underwriters Safety & Claims; Manalapan Mining Co.; R.B. Coal Co.; Eastover Mining Co., a division of Duke Power Co.

For full biographical listings, see the Martindale-Hubbell Law Directory

RICE & HENDRICKSON (AV)

127 Woodland Hills, P.O. Box 980, 40831
Telephone: 606-573-3955
Fax: 606-573-3956

MEMBERS OF FIRM

William A. Rice | H. Kent Hendrickson

Representative Clients: USX Corp.; Navistar International Transportation Corp.; Bituminous Casualty Corp.; Kentucky Utilities Co.; Aetna Casualty & Surety Co.; Nationwide Insurance; The Hartford Insurance Group; Arch Mineral Corp.

For full biographical listings, see the Martindale-Hubbell Law Directory

*HENDERSON,** Henderson Co.

DEEP & WOMACK (AV)

790 Bob Posey Street, P.O. Box 50, 42420
Telephone: 502-827-2522
FAX: 502-826-2870

MEMBERS OF FIRM

Charles David Deep | Zack N. Womack
James G. Womack

For full biographical listings, see the Martindale-Hubbell Law Directory

KING, DEEP AND BRANAMAN (AV)

127 North Main Street, P.O. Box 43, 42420
Telephone: 502-827-1852
FAX: 502-826-7729

MEMBERS OF FIRM

Leo King (1893-1982) | Harry L. Mathison, Jr.
William M. Deep (1920-1990) | W. Mitchell Deep, Jr.
William Branaman | H. Randall Redding
Dorin E. Luck

(See Next Column)

ASSOCIATES

Leslie M. Newman | Robert Khuon Wiederstein
Greg L. Gager

Counsel for: Allstate Insurance; MMI; Commercial Union Insurance; Farmland Insurance; Michigan Mutual Insurance Co.; Western Casualty & Surety Co.; State Auto Mutual Insurance Co.; Motorists Mutual Insurance Co.; American States Insurance Co.; Home Insurance Co.

For full biographical listings, see the Martindale-Hubbell Law Directory

*LEXINGTON,** Fayette Co.

GERALDS, MOLONEY & JONES (AV)

259 West Short Street, 40507
Telephone: 606-255-7946

R. P. Moloney (1902-1963) | John P. Schrader
Donald P. Moloney (1921-1972) | E. Douglas Stephan
Richard P. Moloney (1929-1972) | Robert L. Swisher
Oscar H. Geralds, Jr. | John G. Rice
Michael R. Moloney | Frances Geralds Rohlfing
Ernest H. Jones, II | Kathryn Ann Walton
Billy W. Sherrow | Gail Luhn Pyle

Representative Clients: Aetna Life and Casualty Co.; Allstate Insurance Co.; State Farm Mutual Automobile Insurance Co.; Nationwide Insurance Co.
Reference: Commerce National Bank.

For full biographical listings, see the Martindale-Hubbell Law Directory

LANDRUM & SHOUSE (AV)

106 West Vine Street, P.O. Box 951, 40588-0951
Telephone: 606-255-2424
Facsimile: 606-233-0308
Louisville, Kentucky Office: 400 West Market Street, Suite 1550, 40202.
Telephone: 502-589-7616.
Facsimile: 502-589-2119.

MEMBERS OF FIRM

John H. Burrus | Mark J. Hinkel
George P. Parker (Resident, Louisville Office) | Delores Hill Pregliasco (Resident, Louisville Office)
Thomas M. Cooper | Benjamin Cowgill, Jr.
William C. Shouse | John Garry McNeill
Pierce W. Hamblin | Jack E. Toliver
Mark L. Moseley | Michael J. O'Connell (Resident, Louisville Office)
Leslie Patterson Vose | R. Kent Westberry (Resident, Louisville Office)
John R. Martin, Jr. (Resident, Louisville Office) | J. Denis Ogburn (Resident, Louisville Office)
James W. Smirz | Jane Durkin Samuel
Larry C. Deener
Sandra Mendez Dawahare

ASSOCIATES

Stephen D. Milner | Douglas L. Hoots
Stephen R. Chappell | Dave Whalin (Resident, Louisville Office)
David G. Hazlett (Resident, Louisville Office) | G. Bruce Stigger (Resident, Louisville Office)
Charles E. Christian | Daniel E. Murner
Thomas E. Roma, Jr. (Resident, Louisville Office) | Courtney T. Baxter (Resident, Louisville Office)
Virginia W. Gregg | Julie A. Butcher
Timothy D. Martin (Resident, Louisville Office) | Frank M. Jenkins, III

OF COUNSEL

Weldon Shouse | Frank J. Dougherty, Jr. (Resident, Louisville Office)

District Attorneys: CSX Transportation, Inc.
Special Trial Counsel: Ford Motor Co. and Affiliates (Eastern Kentucky); Clark Equipment Co.
Representative Clients: The Continental Insurance Cos.; U.S. Insurance Group; U.S. Fidelity & Guaranty Co.; Ohio Casualty Insurance Co.; CIGNA; Royal Insurance Cos.

For Complete List of Firm Personnel, See General Section

For full biographical listings, see the Martindale-Hubbell Law Directory

PIPER, WELLMAN & BOWERS (AV)

200 North Upper Street, 40507
Telephone: 606-231-1012
FAX: 606-231-7367

MEMBERS OF FIRM

George C. Piper | Dean T. Wellman
Barbara J. Bowers

ASSOCIATE

Johann F. Herklotz

Representative Clients: Kentucky Hospital Assn. Trust; Woodford Hospital; Garrard Memorial Hospital; Century American Insurance Co.; Guaranty National Ins. Co.; Rhone Pharmaceuticals; Glaxo; Hillhaven Corp.; Sisters of Charity of Nazareth Health System, Inc.; Ky. River Medical Center; St. Josephs Hospital.

(See Next Column)

PIPER, WELLMAN & BOWERS, *Lexington—Continued*

For Complete List of Firm Personnel, See General Section

For full biographical listings, see the Martindale-Hubbell Law Directory

ROBERTS & SMITH (AV)

167 West Main Street Suite 200, 40507
Telephone: 606-233-1104

MEMBERS OF FIRM

Larry S. Roberts
Kenneth W. Smith

For full biographical listings, see the Martindale-Hubbell Law Directory

STOLL, KEENON & PARK (AV)

201 E. Main Street, Suite 1000, 40507-1380
Telephone: 606-231-3000
Telecopier: 606-253-1093; 606-253-1027
Frankfort, Kentucky Office: 326 West Main Street.
Telephone: 502-875-6000.
Telecopier: 502-875-6008.
Louisville, Kentucky Office: 400 West Market Street, Suite 2650, 40202.
Telephone: 502-568-9100.
Telecopier: 502-568-6340.

MEMBERS OF FIRM

Spencer D. Noe
J. Peter Cassidy, Jr.
Robert W. Kellerman
Eileen M. O'Brien
Perry M. Bentley

ASSOCIATE

Todd S. Page

Representative Clients: Bank One, Lexington, NA; Farmers Capital Bank Corp.; The Tokai Bank Ltd.; Link Belt Construction Equipment Co.; General Motors Corp.; International Business Machines Corp.; Ohbayashi Corp.; R. J. Reynolds Tobacco Co.; Rockwell International Corp.; Square D Co.

For Complete List of Firm Personnel, See General Section

For full biographical listings, see the Martindale-Hubbell Law Directory

STURGILL, TURNER & TRUITT (AV)

155 East Main Street, 40507
Telephone: 606-255-8581
Fax: 606-231-0851

MEMBERS OF FIRM

Stephen L. Barker
Donald P. Moloney, II
Douglas L. McSwain
Kevin G. Henry

For Complete List of Firm Personnel, See General Section

For full biographical listings, see the Martindale-Hubbell Law Directory

*LONDON,** Laurel Co.

CRABTREE & GOFORTH (AV)

120 East Fourth Street, 40741-1414
Telephone: 606-878-8888
Fax: 606-878-8899

Wm. Gary Crabtree
Michael A. Goforth

Insurance Defense Clients: National Casualty Insurance Co.; Scottsdale Insurance Co.; Crum & Forster Underwriters Group; Grange Mutual Cos.; Interstate National Insurance; Lloyds of London; Midwestern Indemnity Insurance.; Nationwide Insurance Co.; The Northbrook Co.; Preferred Risk Mutual.

For full biographical listings, see the Martindale-Hubbell Law Directory

FARMER, KELLEY & FARMER (AV)

502 West Fifth Street, Drawer 490, 40743
Telephone: 606-878-7640
Fax: 606-878-2364
Lexington Office: 121 Prosperous Place, Suite 13 B, 40509-1834.
Telephone: 606: 263-2567.
Facsimile: 606: 263-2567.

MEMBERS OF FIRM

F. Preston Farmer
John F. Kelley, Jr.
Michael P. Farmer

ASSOCIATES

Martha L. Brown
Jeffrey T. Weaver

References: The First National Bank; Cumberland Valley National Bank & Trust Company of London, Ky.; London Bank & Trust Co.

For full biographical listings, see the Martindale-Hubbell Law Directory

HAMM, MILBY & RIDINGS (AV)

120 North Main Street, 40741
Telephone: 606-864-4126
Fax: 606-878-8144

(See Next Column)

MEMBERS OF FIRM

Robert L. Milby
Marcia Milby Ridings
Kenneth H. Gilliam

James A. Ridings
Gregory A. Lay
LaDonna Lynn Koebel

Representative Clients: Acceleration National; Aetna Life & Casualty Ins. Co.; All Risk Claims Service, Inc.; Allstate Insurance Co.; Alexis; American Automobile Mutual Ins.; American Bankers; American Hardware Ins. Co.; American Home Ins.; American Inter-Fidelity Exchange.

For full biographical listings, see the Martindale-Hubbell Law Directory

TAYLOR, KELLER & DUNAWAY (AV)

802 North Main Street, P.O. Box 905, 40743-0905
Telephone: 606-878-8844
Facsimile: 606-878-5547

Boyd F. Taylor
J. Warren Keller
Bridget L. Dunaway

OF COUNSEL

Pamela Adams Chesnut

LEGAL SUPPORT PERSONNEL

Berneda Baker (Paralegal)

Representative Clients: Chubb Group; Coronet Insurance Group; ITT Hartford; Mutual of Omaha; American General Property Ins. Co.; State Farm Fire & Casualty; State Farm Mutual Automobile Insurance Co.; Lloyds of London; American Indem nity Group.

For full biographical listings, see the Martindale-Hubbell Law Directory

TOOMS & HOUSE (AV)

310 West Fifth Street, P.O. Box 520, 40743-0520
Telephone: 606-864-4145
FAX: 606-864-4279

MEMBERS OF FIRM

Murray L. Brown (1894-1980)
Roy E. Tooms (1917-1986)
R. William Tooms
Brian C. House

ASSOCIATE

Amy V. Barker

Representative Insurance Clients: State Auto Mutual Insurance Co.; Grange Mutual Casualty Co.; Kentucky Farm Bureau Mutual Insurance Co.; Canal Insurance Co.; Crawford Risk Management Services; Imperial Casualty Co.; National Union Fire Insurance Co.; Insbrok; Corporate Services, Inc.; Scottsdale Insurance Co.

For full biographical listings, see the Martindale-Hubbell Law Directory

*LOUISVILLE,** Jefferson Co.

BENNETT, BOWMAN, TRIPLETT & VITTITOW (AV)

First Trust Centre, Suite 400 South, 200 South Fifth Street, 40202
Telephone: 502-583-5581
Fax: 502-583-9622
Owensboro, Kentucky Office: 209 West Second Street, P.O. Box 765.
Telephone: 502-683-5308.
Fax: 502-685-1797.

MEMBERS OF FIRM

John L. Bennett (1918-1988)
James G. Bowman
Chester A. Vittitow, Jr.
Douglas B. Taylor
Robert R. deGolian
Robert Vic Bowers, Jr. (Resident at Owensboro Office)
D. Thomas Hansen
James P. Dilbeck, Jr.
Michael T. Lee (Resident at Owensboro Office)

OF COUNSEL

Henry A. Triplett

Representative Clients: State Farm Mutual Automobile Ins. Co.; State Farm Fire & Casualty Co.; State Farm Life Insurance Co.; Ohio Casualty Insurance Co.; West American Insurance Co.; Ohio Security Insurance Co.; American International Group; Meridian Mutual Insurance Co.; Prudential Insurance Co.; Ranger Insurance Co.

For full biographical listings, see the Martindale-Hubbell Law Directory

EWEN, HILLIARD & BUSH (AV)

The Starks Building Suite 1090, 455 S. 4th Street, 40202
Telephone: 502-584-1090
Fax: 502-584-4707

MEMBERS OF FIRM

Victor W. Ewen (1924-1989)
A. Campbell Ewen
Frank P. Hilliard
John M. Bush

(See Next Column)

EWEN, HILLIARD & BUSH—*Continued*

ASSOCIATES

Kevin P. Kinney
Scott F. Scheynost
Lawrence W. Cook
Richard G. Sloan

For full biographical listings, see the Martindale-Hubbell Law Directory

GOLDBERG & SIMPSON, P.S.C. (AV)

3000 National City Tower, 40202
Telephone: 502-589-4440
Telefax: 502-581-1344
Washington, D.C. Office: 1200 G Street, N.W. - Suite 800, 20005.
Telephone: 202-434-8968.
Telefax: 202-737-5822.

Fred M. Goldberg
David B. Ratterman
Jonathan D. Goldberg
James S. Goldberg
Mitchell A. Charney
Steven A. Goodman
A. Courtney Guild, Jr.
Edward L. Schoenbaechler
Samuel H. DeShazer
R. Thomas Carter
Cathy S. Pike
Gerald L. Stovall
Stephen E. Smith
Mary Alice Maple
Marva M. Gay
Douglas S. Haynes
Scott P. Zoppoth
Cynthia Buss Maddox
Jan M. West
Charles H. Cassis

OF COUNSEL

Ronald V. Simpson
David A. Brill
Kenneth G. Lee (Not admitted in KY; Resident, Washington, D.C. Office)

Representative Clients: First National Bank; Liberty Mutual Insurance Co.; Jewish Hospital Healthcare Services, Inc.; Louisville & Jefferson County Board of Health; Capital Holding Corp.

For full biographical listings, see the Martindale-Hubbell Law Directory

GREENEBAUM DOLL & MCDONALD (AV)

A Partnership including Professional Service Corporations
3300 National City Tower, 40202
Telephone: 502-589-4200
Fax: 502-587-3695
Lexington, Kentucky Office: 1400 Vine Center Tower.
Telephone: 606-231-8500.
Fax: 606-255-2742.
Covington, Kentucky Office: 50 East River Center Boulevard, P.O. Box 2050.
Telephone: 606-655-4200.
Fax: 606-655-4239.
Cincinnati, Ohio Office: 832 Main Street.
Telephone: 513-421-8087.
Fax: 513-421-8089.

Wm. T. Robinson, III
Barbara Reid Hartung
Roger N. Braden (Resident at Covington, Kentucky)

ASSOCIATES

J. Kevin King (Lexington and Covington, Kentucky and Cincinnati, Ohio)
Angela McCormick Bisig
Sheryl E. Heeter (Covington and Cincinnati Offices)

Representative Clients: Aetna Life Insurance Co.; ANDALEX Resources, Inc.; Ashland Oil, Inc.; A T & T Communications, Inc.; Bethlehem Steel Corp.; Brown-Forman Corp.; Humana, Inc.; Kentucky Kingdom, Inc.; KFC National Cooperative Advertising Program, Inc.
*A Professional Service Corporation

For Complete List of Firm Personnel, See General Section

For full biographical listings, see the Martindale-Hubbell Law Directory

HUMMEL & COAN (AV)

Kentucky Home Life Building, The Seventeenth Floor, 239 South Fifth Street, 40202-3268
Telephone: 502-585-3084
Fax: 502-585-3548

OF COUNSEL

Washer Kaplan Rothschild Aberson & Miller

MEMBERS OF FIRM

Dennis J. Hummel
Marvin L. Coan

ASSOCIATE

David L. Sage, II

Representative Clients: Georgia Pacific Corp.; Safeco Insurance Cos.; The Aetna Casualty & Surety Co.; Dr. Bizer's Vision World; GRE Insurance Group; Calvert Insurance Co.; Western Heritage Insurance Co.

For full biographical listings, see the Martindale-Hubbell Law Directory

LANDRUM & SHOUSE (AV)

400 West Market Street Suite 1550, 40202
Telephone: 502-589-7616
Facsimile: 502-589-2119
Lexington, Kentucky Office: 106 West Vine Street, P.O. Box 951.
Telephone: 606-255-2424.
Facsimile: 606-233-0308.

RESIDENT MEMBERS OF THE FIRM

George P. Parker
John R. Martin, Jr.
Delores Hill Pregliasco
Michael J. O'Connell
R. Kent Westberry
J. Denis Ogburn

RESIDENT ASSOCIATES

David G. Hazlett
Thomas E. Roma, Jr.
Timothy D. Martin
Dave Whalin
G. Bruce Stigger
Courtney T. Baxter
D. Sean Nilsen

OF COUNSEL

Frank J. Dougherty, Jr.

For full biographical listings, see the Martindale-Hubbell Law Directory

MIDDLETON & REUTLINGER, P.S.C. (AV)

2500 Brown and Williamson Tower, 40202-3410
Telephone: 502-584-1135
Fax: 502-561-0442
Jeffersonville, Indiana Office: 605 Watt Street, 47130.
Telephone: 812-282-4886.

O. Grant Bruton
Kenneth S. Handmaker
Charles G. Middleton, III
Charles D. Greenwell
John W. Bilby
Timothy P. O'Mara
Stewart L. Prather
D. Randall Gibson
G. Kennedy Hall, Jr.
Mark S. Fenzel
Kathiejane Oehler
William Jay Hunter, Jr.
James E. Milliman
David J. Kellerman
John M. Franck II

Julie A. Gregory
Amy B. Berge
Dennis D. Murrell
Augustus S. Herbert

Counsel for: Chevron USA; Liberty National Bank; Logan Aluminum, Inc.; Louisville Gas & Electric Co.; MCI Telecommunications Corp.; Metropolitan Life Insurance Co.; Kosmos Cement Co.; Porcelain Metal Corp.; The Home Insurance Co.; The Kroger Co.; Demars Haka Development, Inc.

For Complete List of Firm Personnel, See General Section

For full biographical listings, see the Martindale-Hubbell Law Directory

MORRIS, GARLOVE, WATERMAN & JOHNSON (AV)

Established 1925 as Morris and Garlove.
Suite 1000, One Riverfront Plaza, 40202-2959
Telephone: 502-589-3200
Fax: 502-589-3219

Louis N. Garlove
Allan Weiss
J. D. Raine, Jr.
Sheryl Kramer Smith

Representative Clients: Employers Reinsurance Corp.; Government Employees Insurance Co.; Podiatric Insurance Company of America; Mutual Security Life Insurance Co.; Scottsdale Insurance Co.; Conagra Corp. (self-insured); First Financial Insurance Co.; Ryder Services Corp.; Zurich Insurance Co.; Sedgwick James, Inc., (Risk Management).

For Complete List of Firm Personnel, See General Section

For full biographical listings, see the Martindale-Hubbell Law Directory

OGDEN NEWELL & WELCH (AV)

1200 One Riverfront Plaza, 40202-2973
Telephone: 502-582-1601
Fax: 502-581-9564

MEMBERS OF FIRM

John T. Ballantine
Stephen F. Schuster
Scott T. Wendelsdorf
David A. Harris
Gregory J. Bubalo
D. Brian Rattliff
W. Gregory King

ASSOCIATES

Susan C. Bybee
Douglas C. Ballantine
Tracy S. Prewitt
Jennifer J. Hall

Counsel for: Baptist Healthcare System; Caronia Corporation; Commercial Union Insurance Company; Kentucky Medical Insurance Company; Medical Protective Company; Ohio Casualty Insurance Company; Ophthalmic Mutual Insurance Company; Paradigm Insurance Company; Physicians Insurance Company of Indiana; Professional Risk Management Services.

For Complete List of Firm Personnel, See General Section

For full biographical listings, see the Martindale-Hubbell Law Directory

Louisville—Continued

PEDLEY, ROSS, ZIELKE & GORDINIER (AV)

1150 Starks Building, 455 South Fourth Avenue, 40202
Telephone: 502-589-4600
Fax: 502-584-0422

MEMBERS OF FIRM

Lawrence L. Pedley
Robert P. Ross
Laurence J. Zielke
John K. Gordinier
William W. Stodghill
Schuyler J. Olt
P. Stephen Gordinier
Frank G. Simpson, III
Charles F. Merz

OF COUNSEL

William C. Stone
J. Chester Porter

ASSOCIATES

William H. Mooney
William J. Shreffler
John H. Dwyer, Jr.

For full biographical listings, see the Martindale-Hubbell Law Directory

SITLINGER, McGLINCY, STEINER, THEILER & KAREM (AV)

3450 First National Tower, 101 South Fifth Street, 40202
Telephone: 502-589-2627
Fax: 502-583-3415

MEMBERS OF FIRM

Lee E. Sitlinger
Dennis R. McGlincy
Jack W. Steiner, Jr.
Charles E. Theiler, II
Edmund Pete Karem
Curt Sitlinger
Scott Edmund Karem

LEGAL SUPPORT PERSONNEL

Lynn Logsdon

Representative Clients: State Farm Mutual Automobile Insurance Co; State Farm Fire & Casualty Co.; Travelers Insurance Co.; American International Insurance Co.

For full biographical listings, see the Martindale-Hubbell Law Directory

TILFORD, DOBBINS, ALEXANDER & BUCKAWAY (AV)

Suite 1406, One Riverfront Plaza, 40202
Telephone: 502-584-6137

MEMBERS OF FIRM

Charles W. Dobbins (1916-1992)
Henry J. Tilford (1880-1968)
George S. Wetherby (1905-1954)
Lawrence W. Wetherby (1908-1994)
John T. Metcalf (1890-1974)
Stuart E. Alexander
William A. Buckaway, Jr.
Charles W. Dobbins, Jr.
Mark Wesley Dobbins
Stuart E. Alexander, III
John M. Nader
Sandra F. Keene
Thomas J.B. Hurst

OF COUNSEL

Randolph Noe
Carolyn K. Balleisen

LEGAL SUPPORT PERSONNEL

Jennifer Olvey

For full biographical listings, see the Martindale-Hubbell Law Directory

WEBER & ROSE PROFESSIONAL SERVICE CORPORATION (AV)

2700 Providian Center, 400 West Market Street, 40202
Telephone: 502-589-2200
Fax: 502-589-3400
Jeffersonville, Indiana Office: 432 East Court Avenue.
Telephone: 812-288-4372.

L. R. Curtis (1880-1968)
Shelton R. Weber
C. Alex Rose
Michael W. McGrath, Jr.
Wesley P. Adams, Jr.
Russell H. Saunders
James M. Gary
A. Andrew Draut
R. Hite Nally
Martin A. Arnett
Edward J. Smith

Bruce D. Atherton
Patrick W. Gault
Karen L. Keith

Counsel for: The Enro Shirt Co.

For full biographical listings, see the Martindale-Hubbell Law Directory

WILLIAMS & WAGONER (AV)

101 Bullitt Lane, Oxmoor Place, 40222
Telephone: 502-429-5700
FAX: 502-429-5720

MEMBERS OF FIRM

Philip Williams
James R. Wagoner
W. Kenneth Nevitt
Carole M. Pearlman
C. Thomas Hectus
L. J. (Todd) Hollenbach, IV
Dennis L. Mattingly
Carla T. Foreman

(See Next Column)

ASSOCIATES

Robert M. Beal
Mitchell L. Perry
R. Thad Keal
Maureen K. Lenihan
David Scott Dupps
James M. Burd
Robert A. Button, Jr.
Chris Joseph Mooser
M. Kathryan Manis
Mary E. Schaffner
George T. T. Kitchen III

For full biographical listings, see the Martindale-Hubbell Law Directory

WOODWARD, HOBSON & FULTON (AV)

2500 National City Tower, 101 South Fifth Street, 40202
Telephone: 502-581-8000
Fax: 502-581-8111
Lexington, Kentucky Office: National City Plaza, 301 East Main Street, Suite 650.
Telephone: 606-244-7100.
Telecopier: 606-244-7111.

MEMBERS OF FIRM

Harry K. Herren
Richard H. C. Clay
Gregory L. Smith
Elizabeth Ullmer Mendel

Representative Clients: America Home Insurance Co.; Fireman's Fund Insurance Co.; Liberty Mutual Insurance Co.; Nationwide Insurance Co., Inc.; Prudential Property and Casualty Co.; Royal Insurance Co.; Underwriters at Lloyd's London; CNA Insurance Co.; CIGNA Corp.; American International Group.

For Complete List of Firm Personnel, See General Section

For full biographical listings, see the Martindale-Hubbell Law Directory

*MOREHEAD,** Rowan Co.

DEHNER & ELLIS (AV)

206 East Main Street, 40351
Telephone: 606-783-1504
FAX: 606-784-2744

Truman L. Dehner
John J. Ellis

For full biographical listings, see the Martindale-Hubbell Law Directory

NEWPORT, Campbell Co.

JOLLY & BLAU (AV)

3699 Alexandria Pike, P.O. Box 249, 41076
Telephone: 606-441-5400
Fax: 606-441-8428

MEMBERS OF FIRM

A. J. Jolly (1924-1989)
Bernard J. Blau
Robert E. L. Blau

ASSOCIATES

Gregory B. Kriege
Carl Turner
Kenneth L. Foltz
Steven Plummer

Representative Clients: American Mutual Insurance Co.; Chubb-Pacific Indemnity Group; Firemen's Fund Insurance Co.; Beacon Insurance Co.; Kemper Insurance Co.; U.S. Insurance Group.
Approved Attorneys and Issuing Agent for: Louisville Title Division of Commonwealth Land Title Insurance Co.; Lawyers Title Insurance Corp.
References: Huntington Bank of Kenton County; Provident Bank of Campbell County.

For full biographical listings, see the Martindale-Hubbell Law Directory

*OWENSBORO,** Daviess Co.

WILSON, WILSON & PLAIN (AV)

414 Masonic Building, 42301
Telephone: 502-926-2525
Telecopier: 502-683-3812

MEMBERS OF FIRM

George S. Wilson, Jr. (1902-1966)
William L. Wilson (1912-1993)
George S. Wilson, III
R. Scott Plain
William L. Wilson, Jr.
Thomas S. Poteat
R. Scott Plain, Jr.

Representative Clients: Liberty National Bank, Owensboro, Ky.; Owensboro Board of Education; Owensboro River Sand & Gravel Co.; The Prudential Ins. Co.; Kentucky Farm Bureau Mutual Insurance Co.; Baskin Robbins; Motorist Mutual Insurance Co.; Yager Materials, Inc.
Approved Attorneys for: Louisville Title Division of Commonwealth Land Title Insurance Co.

For full biographical listings, see the Martindale-Hubbell Law Directory

*PAINTSVILLE,** Johnson Co.

WELLS, PORTER & SCHMITT (AV)

327 Main Street, 41240
Telephone: 606-789-3747; 789-3749; 789-3775
Fax: 606-789-3790

(See Next Column)

WELLS, PORTER & SCHMITT—*Continued*

MEMBERS OF FIRM

Z. Wells (1890-1946)
R. L. Wells (1894-1953)
J. K. Wells
John V. Porter, Jr.
Michael J. Schmitt
Donald L. Jones
Roger L. Massengale

ASSOCIATES

Sandra Spurgeon
Johnny L. Griffith

Representative Clients: Travelers Insurance Co.; United States Fidelity & Guaranty Co.; The Hartford Insurance Co.; Nationwide Insurance Co.; Prudential Insurance Co.; Kentucky Farm Bureau Insurance Co.; GEICO; CIGNA Insurance Co.; Allstate Insurance Co.; Fireman's Fund-American Insurance Co.

For full biographical listings, see the Martindale-Hubbell Law Directory

*PIKEVILLE,** Pike Co.

STRATTON, MAY, HAYS & HOGG, P.S.C. (AV)

232 Second Street Ward Building, P.O. Box 851, 41502
Telephone: 606-437-7300
Fax: 606-437-7569
Whitesburg, Kentucky Office: By-Pass Highway 15. 41858.
Telephone: 606-633-9922.

Henry D. Stratton (1925-1989)
Marrs Allen May
John D. Hays
Edgar N. Venters
David C. Stratton
Stephen L. Hogg
F. Byrd Hogg (Resident, Whitesburg, Kentucky Office)

LEGAL SUPPORT PERSONNEL

PARALEGALS

Carol Rowe Potter (Real Estate Paralegal)
Brenda Hays (Personnel Injury Paralegal)

Representative Clients: Commercial Union Insurance Co.; The Travelers Insurance Co.; Universal Underwriters Insurance Co.; Bituminous Casualty Co.; Kentucky Central Insurance Co.; Scottsdale Insurance Co.; Massachusetts Mutual Insurance Co.; Farmland Insurance Co., MSI Insurance; Republic Steel Corp.

For full biographical listings, see the Martindale-Hubbell Law Directory

*PRESTONSBURG,** Floyd Co.

FRANCIS, KAZEE & FRANCIS (AV)

119 East Court Street, P.O. Box 700, 41653
Telephone: 606-886-2361; 886-2362
FAX: 606-886-9603
Paintsville, Kentucky Office: 103 Main Street, P.O. Box 1275.
Telephone: 606-789-3059.

MEMBERS OF FIRM

D. B. Kazee
William G. Francis
William S. Kendrick
David H. Neeley
Mitchell D. Kinner
John T. Chafin
C. V. Reynolds
P. Franklin Heaberlin
Martin Lee Osborne
Brett D. Davis

ASSOCIATES

Robert J. Patton
William C. Mullins
Anthony Craig Davis

OF COUNSEL

Fred G. Francis (Retired)

Representative Clients: Maryland Casualty Co.; Old Republic Insurance Co.; St. Paul Insurance Cos.; Bituminous Casualty Corp.; Commercial Union Assurance Co.; Kentucky Central Insurance Cos.; Capital Enterprise Insurance Group; State Automobile Mutual Insurance Co.; Reliance Insurance Co.; Scottsdale Insurance Co.

For full biographical listings, see the Martindale-Hubbell Law Directory

*VANCEBURG,** Lewis Co.

STANLEY AND BERTRAM (AV)

P.O. Box 40, 41179-0040
Telephone: 606-796-3024; 796-3025
Fax: 606-796-2113

MEMBERS OF FIRM

Avery L. Stanley
Thomas M. Bertram, II
Anita Esham Stanley

A list of Representative Clients will be furnished upon request.

For full biographical listings, see the Martindale-Hubbell Law Directory

LOUISIANA

*ALEXANDRIA,** Rapides Parish

STAFFORD, STEWART & POTTER (AV)

3112 Jackson Street, P.O. Box 1711, 71309
Telephone: 318-487-4910
Fax: 318-487-9417

MEMBERS OF FIRM

Grove Stafford, Jr.
Larry A. Stewart
Russell L. Potter
Paul Boudreaux, Jr.
Bradley J. Gadel
James D. Kirk
Andrew P. Texada
Mark Alan Watson
Gary B. Tillman

ASSOCIATES

Mark Pearce
Randall B. Keiser

Representative Clients: Admiral Insurance Co.; Allied Insurance Co.; Asplundh Manufacturing Company; Bankers & Shippers Insurance Company of New York; Bic Corporation; John Deere Insurance Company; Government Employees Insurance Co.; Sentry Insurance Co.; Trinity Universal Insurance Company; U.S. Fidelity & Guaranty Co.

For full biographical listings, see the Martindale-Hubbell Law Directory

*BATON ROUGE,** East Baton Rouge Parish

KLEINPETER & KLEINPETER (AV)

1680 South Lobdell Avenue, Suite E, P.O. Box 66443, 70896
Telephone: 504-926-5093

MEMBERS OF FIRM

Robert L. Kleinpeter
R. Loren Kleinpeter

Representative Clients: Argonaut Insurance Co.; American Indemnity Co.; All American Assurance Co.; American Southern Insurance Co.; Louisiana Underwriters of American Indemnity Co.; American Surety Company of New York; Tri-State General Agency; State Fire & Casualty Co.; Early American Insurance Co.; Members Mutual Insurance Co.

For full biographical listings, see the Martindale-Hubbell Law Directory

LANE, FERTITTA, LANE, JANNEY & THOMAS (AV)

435 Louisiana Avenue, P.O. Box 3335, 70821
Telephone: 504-387-0241
Fax: 504-387-1238

MEMBERS OF FIRM

Horace C. Lane (1921-1989)
Frank A. Fertitta
Thomas A. Lane
William F. Janney
Richard S. Thomas

ASSOCIATE

Margaret T. Lane

Representative Clients: State Farm Mutual Automobile Insurance Co.; Credit Bureau of the South, Inc.; State Farm Fire & Casualty Co.; United States Fidelity & Guaranty Co.; Aetna Casualty & Surety Co.; Employers Liability Assurance Corp., Ltd.; Allstate Insurance Co.; Fidelity and Guaranty Underwriters, Inc.; St. Paul Fire and Marine Insurance Co.; The Medical Protective Co.

For full biographical listings, see the Martindale-Hubbell Law Directory

MATHEWS, ATKINSON, GUGLIELMO, MARKS & DAY (AV)

(Registered Limited Liability Partnership)
320 Somerulos Street, P.O. Box 3177, 70821-3177
Telephone: 504-387-6966
Fax: 504-387-8338

G. T. Owen, Jr. (1905-1972)
E. Leland Richardson (1904-1977)
Robert C. Taylor (1910-1983)
George Mathews (1914-1987)
Daniel R. Atkinson
Carey J. Guglielmo
Paul Marks, Jr.
Judith R. Atkinson
Ben L. Day
Thomas E. Balhoff
Richard G. Creed, Jr.
Charles A. Schutte, Jr.
John W. Perry, Jr.
Henry G. Terhoeve
Glen Scott Love
Leonard Cardenas, III
Daniel R. Atkinson, Jr.
Geraldine E. Fontenot
Daniel J. Balhoff
Lindsey J. Leavoy
Dawn T. Trabeau-Mire
Joseph W. Mengis

OF COUNSEL

Doug Moreau

Representative Clients: American Insurance Assn.; Liberty Mutual Insurance Co.; Commercial Union Insurance Co.; Louisiana Insurance Guarantee Association; State Farm Mutual Automobile Insurance Co.; Allstate Insurance Co.; Aetna Life & Casualty Co.; Prudential Property & Casualty Co.

For full biographical listings, see the Martindale-Hubbell Law Directory

Baton Rouge—Continued

NAVRATIL, HARDY & BOURGEOIS (AV)

445 North Boulevard, Suite 800, P.O. Box 3551, 70821-3551
Telephone: 504-343-0700
Fax: 504-343-9119

MEMBERS OF FIRM

Boris F. Navratil
David H. Hardy
André G. Bourgeois

OF COUNSEL

Robert L. Boese
Johnnie L. Matthews
George Sheram King

For full biographical listings, see the Martindale-Hubbell Law Directory

SEALE, SMITH, ZUBER & BARNETTE (AV)

Two United Plaza, Suite 200, 8550 United Plaza Boulevard, 70809
Telephone: 504-924-1600
Telecopier: 504-924-6100

Armbrust Gordon Seale (1913-1989)
Robert W. Smith (1922-1989)
Donald S. Zuber
Kenneth E. Barnette
William C. Kaufman III
John W. L. Swanner
James H. Morgan III
Ronald A. Seale
Brent E. Kinchen
Charles K. Watts
Myron A. Walker, Jr.
Daniel A. Reed
Kenner O. Miller, Jr.
William C. Rowe, Jr.
Lawrence R. Anderson, Jr.

ASSOCIATES

Richard T. Reed
Barbara G. Chatelain
Anthony J. Russo, Jr.
Catherine S. Nobile

Representative Clients: Farmers Insurance Group; St. Paul Fire and Marine Insurance Company; United Services Automobile Association; General Motors Acceptance Corporation.
Reference: City National Bank, Baton Rouge, Louisiana.

For full biographical listings, see the Martindale-Hubbell Law Directory

*DE RIDDER,** Beauregard Parish

HALL, LESTAGE & LANDRENEAU (AV)

205 Second Street, P.O. Box 880, 70634
Telephone: 318-463-8692
Fax: 318-463-2272

MEMBERS OF FIRM

William E. Hall, Jr.
H. O. Lestage, III
David R. Lestage
F. Steve Landreneau
Brian S. Lestage

Representative Clients: Boise Cascade Corp.; City Savings & Trust Co.; Crosby Land Resources; Firemen's Fund-American Cos.; Great American Insurance Co.; The Hartford Insurance Group; Pacific Marine Insurance Co.; State Farm Mutual Automobile Insurance Co.; The Travelers Insurance Co.; United States Fidelity & Guaranty Co.

For full biographical listings, see the Martindale-Hubbell Law Directory

*LAFAYETTE,** Lafayette Parish

DAVIDSON, MEAUX, SONNIER, MCELLIGOTT & SWIFT (AV)

810 South Buchanan Street, P.O. Drawer 2908, 70502
Telephone: 318-237-1660
Fax: 318-237-3676

MEMBERS OF FIRM

James J. Davidson, Jr. (1904-1990)
V. Farley Sonnier (1942-1988)
Richard C. Meaux, Sr.
James J. Davidson, III
John E. McElligott, Jr.
John G. Swift
Jeffrey A. Rhoades
Philip A. Fontenot
Kyle L. Gideon
Theodore G. Edwards, IV
Stacey L. Knight

ASSOCIATES

Jhan C. Boudreaux Beaullieu
Tracy P. Curtis

General Counsel: Southwest Louisiana Electric Membership Corp.; Power Rig Drilling Co.; Inc.; Macro Oil Co., Inc.; Dwight W. Andrus Insurance Agency; Lafayette Airport Commission.
Local Counsel: Southern Pacific Transportation Co.
Representative Clients: Highlands Insurance Co.; Wal-Mart Stores, Inc.; USAA.

For Complete List of Firm Personnel, See General Section

For full biographical listings, see the Martindale-Hubbell Law Directory

HILL & BEYER, A PROFESSIONAL LAW CORPORATION (AV)

101 LaRue France, Suite 502, P.O. Box 53006, 70505-3006
Telephone: 318-232-9733
Fax: 1-318-237-2566

(See Next Column)

John K. Hill, Jr.
Bret C. Beyer
David R. Rabalais
Lisa C. McCowen
Eugene P. Matherne
Robert B. Purser
Erin J. Sherburne
Harold Adam Lawrence

For full biographical listings, see the Martindale-Hubbell Law Directory

MANGHAM, DAVIS AND OGLESBEE (AV)

Suite 1400 First National Bank Towers, 600 Jefferson Street, P.O. Box 93110, 70509-3110
Telephone: 318-233-6200
Fax: 318-233-6521

Michael R. Mangham
Louis R. Davis
Michael G. Oglesbee
Herman E. Garner, Jr.

ASSOCIATES

Dawn Mayeux Fuqua
Lisa Hanchey Sevier

SPECIAL COUNSEL

Michael J. O'Shee

OF COUNSEL

George W. Hardy, III
Robert E. Rowe

Reference: The First National Bank of Lafayette, Lafayette, Louisiana.

For full biographical listings, see the Martindale-Hubbell Law Directory

ONEBANE, DONOHOE, BERNARD, TORIAN, DIAZ, MCNAMARA & ABELL (AV)

Suite 600, Versailles Centre, 102 Versailles Boulevard, P.O. Box 3507, 70502
Telephone: 318-237-2660
Telecopier: 318-266-1232
Cable Address: "Ondob"
Telex: 311283

Joseph Onebane (1917-1987)
John G. Torian, II (1936-1991)
Lawrence E. Donohoe, Jr.
John Allen Bernard
James E. Diaz
Timothy J. McNamara
Edward C. Abell, Jr.
Helen Onebane Mendell
Lawrence L. Lewis, III
Robert M. Mahony
Daniel G. Fournerat
Douglas W. Truxillo
Randall C. Songy
Chris G. Robbins
Michael G. Durand
Greg Guidry
Joseph L. Lemoine, Jr.
Mark L. Riley
Graham N. Smith
Gordon T. Whitman
Gary P. Kraus
Richard J. Petre, Jr.
Thomas G. Smart
James E. Diaz, Jr.
Roger E. Ishee
R. Thomas Jorden, Jr.
Kevin R. Rees
John W. Penny, Jr.
John A. Keller

Jennifer McDaniel Kleinpeter
Steven C. Lanza
Christopher H. Hebert
John W. Kolwe
Sue Nations
Joel P. Babineaux
Michael W. Landry
Ted M. Anthony
Carolyn Trahan Bertrand
Alison M. Brumley

Representative Clients: Allstate Insurance Co.; CIGNA; Continental Insurance Co.; Employers-Commercial; Fireman's Fund American Insurance Co.; Highlands Insurance Co.; Travelers Insurance Co.

For full biographical listings, see the Martindale-Hubbell Law Directory

*LAKE CHARLES,** Calcasieu Parish

BERGSTEDT & MOUNT (AV)

Second Floor, Magnolia Life Building, P.O. Drawer 3004, 70602-3004
Telephone: 318-433-3004
Facsimile: 318-433-8080

MEMBERS OF FIRM

Thomas M. Bergstedt
Benjamin W. Mount

ASSOCIATES

Van C. Seneca
Thomas J. Gayle
Gregory P. Marceaux

OF COUNSEL

Charles S. Ware

Representative Clients: Armstrong World Industries; Ashland Oil Co.; CIGNA Property & Casualty Companies; Homequity; Lake Area Medical Center; Leach Company; Olin Corporation; Terra Corporation; Town of Iowa; R. D. Werner Company.

For Complete List of Firm Personnel, See General Section

For full biographical listings, see the Martindale-Hubbell Law Directory

JONES, TÊTE, NOLEN, HANCHEY, SWIFT & SPEARS, L.L.P. (AV)

First Federal Building, P.O. Box 910, 70602
Telephone: 318-439-8315
Telefax: 436-5606; 433-5536

(See Next Column)

JONES, TÊTE, NOLEN, HANCHEY, SWIFT & SPEARS, L.L.P.—*Continued*

MEMBERS OF FIRM

Sam H. Jones (1897-1978)
William R. Tête
William M. Nolen
James C. Hanchey
Carl H. Hanchey
William B. Swift
Kenneth R. Spears
Edward J. Fonti
Charles N. Harper
Gregory W. Belfour
Robert J. Tête
Yul D. Lorio

OF COUNSEL

John A. Patin
Edward D. Myrick

ASSOCIATES

Lilynn A. Cutrer
Lydia Ann Guillory-Lee
Clint David Bischoff

Representative Clients: CIGNA Property and Casualty Companies; ITT Hartford; Life Insurance Company of the Southwest; State and County Mutual Fire Insurance Company; Federated Rural Electric Insurance Corp.

For full biographical listings, see the Martindale-Hubbell Law Directory

PLAUCHÉ SMITH & NIESET, A PROFESSIONAL LAW CORPORATION (AV)

1123 Pithon Street, P.O. Drawer 1705, 70602
Telephone: 318-436-0522
Facsimile: 318-436-9637

S. W. Plauché (1889-1952)
S. W. Plauché, Jr. (1915-1966)
A. Lane Plauché
Allen L. Smith, Jr.
James R. Nieset
Frank M. Walker, Jr.
Michael J. McNulty, III
Jeffrey M. Cole
Andrew R. Johnson, IV
Charles V. Musso, Jr.
Christopher P. Ieyoub
H. David Vaughan, II
Rebecca S. Young
Stephanie A. Landry

Representative Clients: CIGNA; CNA Insurance Cos.; Commercial Union Insurance Cos.; Crum & Forster; General Motors Corp.; Reliance Insurance Cos.; Royal Insurance Group; State Farm; U.S. Insurance Group.

For full biographical listings, see the Martindale-Hubbell Law Directory

METAIRIE, Jefferson Parish

HAILEY, MCNAMARA, HALL, LARMANN & PAPALE (AV)

A Partnership including Law Corporations
Suite 1400, One Galleria Boulevard, P.O. Box 8288, 70011
Telephone: 504-836-6500
Fax: 504-836-6565

MEMBERS OF FIRM

James W. Hailey, Jr., (P.L.C.)
Henry D. McNamara, Jr., (P.L.C.)
W. Marvin Hall (P.L.C.)
Antonio E. Papale, Jr., (P.L.C.)
Laurence E. Larmann (P.L.C.)
Richard A. Chopin (P.L.C.)
Kevin L. Cole
Michael P. Mentz
Richard T. Simmons, Jr.,(P.L.C.)
Nelson W. Wagar, III, (P.L.C.)
Michael J. Vondenstein
Brian ReBoul
David K. Persons
Thomas M. Richard
Dominic J. Ovella
Elizabeth Smyth Sirgo
C. Kelly Lightfoot
John T. Culotta (P.L.C.)
John E. Unsworth, Jr.
Julie DiFulco Robles

ASSOCIATES

William R. Seay, Jr.
Cyril B. Burck, Jr.
Claude A. Greco
Valerie T. Schexnayder
John Price McNamara
W. Evan Plauche
Brian T. Carr
Kurt D. Engelhardt
W. Glenn Burns

OF COUNSEL

John P. Volz

Representative Clients: Certain Underwriters at Lloyds of London; Diamond Offshore Drilling Inc.; First American Title Insurance Company; The Flintkote Co.; Litton Industries; Martin Marietta Manned Space Systems; Rheem Manufacturing Co.; Rowan Companies, Inc; State Farm Fire & Casualty Co.; Textron, Inc; Travelers Companies.

For full biographical listings, see the Martindale-Hubbell Law Directory

JUGE, NAPOLITANO, LEYVA & GUILBEAU (AV)

3838 North Causeway Boulevard Suite 2500, 70002-1767
Telephone: 504-831-7270
Fax: 504-831-7284

Denis Paul Juge
Jeffrey C. Napolitano
Teresa C. Leyva
Joseph B. Guilbeau
Thomas M. Ruli

Kelann Etta Larguier
Kristi L. Stroebel
Frank Whiteley
Lance E. Harwell
Lawrence B. Frieman

For full biographical listings, see the Martindale-Hubbell Law Directory

*MONROE,** Ouachita Parish

DAVENPORT, FILES & KELLY (AV)

1509 Lamy Lane, P.O. Box 4787, 71211-4787
Telephone: 318-387-6453
FAX: 318-323-6533

MEMBERS OF FIRM

Thos. W. Davenport (1909-1962)
Wm. G. Kelly, Jr.
Thomas W. Davenport, Jr.
Mike C. Sanders
Ramsey L. Ogg
Michael J. Fontenot

ASSOCIATE

M. Shane Craighead

STAFF ATTORNEY

Stacy L. Guice

Representative Clients: American International Group (AIG); Chubb Group; Commercial Aviation; GAINSCO; GEICO; Highlands Ins. Co.; Scottsdale Ins. Co.; Trinity Universal Ins. Co.; United States Aircraft Ins. Group; Zurich-American Ins. Cos.

For Complete List of Firm Personnel, See General Section

For full biographical listings, see the Martindale-Hubbell Law Directory

*NEW ORLEANS,** Orleans Parish

ADAMS AND JOHNSTON (AV)

Suite 2490, Pan American Life Center, 601 Poydras Street, 70130
Telephone: 504-581-2606
Telecopier: 504-525-1488
Boulder, Colorado Office: Vectra Bank Building, 1919 14th Street, Suite 609.
Telephone: 303-444-2993.

MEMBERS OF FIRM

Jesse R. Adams, Jr.
Robert M. Johnston
Bruce J. Oreck (Resident, Boulder, Colorado Office)
D. Russell Holwadel
Thomas S. Morse
Janet Daley Westervelt
Anne Derbes Keller
Adam W. Chase (Resident, Boulder, Colorado Office)

Representative Clients: Allianz Insurance Company; Amana Refrigeration, Inc.; Americas Insurance Company; Associated Risk Services Inc.; Aviation Underwriting Specialists, Inc.; Beech Aircraft Corporation; Dresser Industries, Inc.; Employers Casualty Company; Employers National Insurance Corporation; Fairgrounds Corporation.

For full biographical listings, see the Martindale-Hubbell Law Directory

BOGGS, LOEHN & RODRIGUE (AV)

A Partnership including Law Corporations
Suite 1800 Lykes Center, 300 Poydras Street, 70130-3597
Telephone: 504-523-7090
Fax: 504-581-6822

Charles A. Boggs (A Law Corporation)
Thomas E. Loehn (A Law Corporation)
Edward A. Rodrigue, Jr., (A Law Corporation)
Chester A. Fleming, III
Thomas W. Lewis
Terry B. Deffes
Robert I. Baudouin
Samuel M. Rosamond, III
Betty P. Westbrook
Ralph T Rabalais

Reference: First National Bank of Commerce, New Orleans, La.

For full biographical listings, see the Martindale-Hubbell Law Directory

CHRISTOVICH AND KEARNEY, L.L.P. (AV)

Suite 2300 Pan American Life Center, 601 Poydras Street, 70130-6078
Telephone: 504-561-5700
FAX: 504-561-5743
Houston, Texas Office: 700 Louisiana, Suite 4550, 77002.
Telephone: 713-225-2255.
Fax: 713-225-1112.

MEMBERS OF FIRM

Alvin R. Christovich, Jr.
William K. Christovich
J. Walter Ward, Jr.
Lawrence J. Ernst
James F. Holmes
Robert E. Peyton
C. Edgar Cloutier
Charles W. Schmidt, III
Richard K. Christovich
Terry Christovich Gay
Paul G. Preston
Michael M. Christovich
E. Phelps Gay
Thomas C. Cowan
Geoffrey P. Snodgrass
J. Warren Gardner, Jr.
Kevin R. Tully
Lance R. Rydberg
Elizabeth S. Cordes
John K. Leach
Fred T. Hinrichs
Daniel A. Rees
Charles M. Lanier, Jr.

ASSOCIATES

Lyon H. Garrison
Philip J. Borne
Anthony Reginelli, Jr.
Paige F. Rosato
J. Roslyn Lemmon
James Aristide Holmes
Richard J. Garvey, Jr.
Scott P. Yount
Patricia Broussard
Patrick W. Drouilhet (Not admitted in LA)
Cheryl A. Smith (Not admitted in LA)

(See Next Column)

CHRISTOVICH AND KEARNEY L.L.P., *New Orleans—Continued*

OF COUNSEL

Nannette Jolivette-Brown

Representative Clients: Associated Aviation Underwriters; Brown & Root, Inc.; Chubb/Pacific Indemnity Group; Continental Insurance Company; Crawford & Co.; Crum & Forster; Highlands Insurance Company; Insurance Company of North America; Liberty Mutual Insurance Company; Southern Pacific Transportation Co.

For full biographical listings, see the Martindale-Hubbell Law Directory

DEUTSCH, KERRIGAN & STILES (AV)

A Partnership including Professional Law Corporations
755 Magazine Street, 70130-3672
Telephone: 504-581-5141
Cable Address: "Dekest"
Telex: 584358
Telecopier: 504-566-1201

MEMBERS OF FIRM

Robert E. Kerrigan, Jr., (P.L.C.)
Raymon G. Jones (P.L.C.)
Philip D. Lorio, III
Marc J. Yellin (P.L.C.)
Howard L. Murphy
Darrell K. Cherry (P.L.C.)
Nancy J. Marshall
James G. Wyly, III

OF COUNSEL

Francis G. Weller (P.L.C.)

ASSOCIATES

Gary B. Roth
Barbara L. Malik
Karyn J. Vigh
Lisa C. Winter

For Complete List of Firm Personnel, See General Section

For full biographical listings, see the Martindale-Hubbell Law Directory

HABANS, BOLOGNA & CARRIERE, A PROFESSIONAL LAW CORPORATION (AV)

Suite 2323, 1515 Poydras Street, 70112
Telephone: 504-524-2323
Telex: 151514 HABA M UT
Telecopier: 504-522-7224
Cable Address: HABOL

Robert N. Habans, Jr.
William F. Bologna
James D. Carriere
John C. McNeese
Aimée Carriere
Dwight L. Acomb
Julien F. Jurgens

For full biographical listings, see the Martindale-Hubbell Law Directory

LEAKE & ANDERSSON (AV)

1700 Energy Centre, 1100 Poydras Street, 70163-1701
Telephone: 504-585-7500
Telecopier: 504-585-7775

MEMBERS OF FIRM

Robert E. Leake, Jr.
W. Paul Andersson
Lawrence A. Mann
Marta-Ann Schnabel O'Bryon
Kevin O'Bryon
George D. Fagan
Donald E. McKay, Jr.

ASSOCIATES

Stanton E. Shuler, Jr.
Rebecca Olivier Hand
Guy D. Perrier

Representative Clients: GEICO; Preferred Risk Mutual Insurance Co.; Progressive Casualty Insurance Co.; National Union Fire Insurance Co.; Nationwide Insurance Co.; U.S. Fire Insurance Co.; First Financial Insurance Co.

For full biographical listings, see the Martindale-Hubbell Law Directory

MIDDLEBERG, RIDDLE & GIANNA (AV)

31st Floor, Place St. Charles, 201 St. Charles Avenue, 70170-3100
Telephone: 504-525-7200
Telecopier: 504-581-5983
Dallas, Texas Office: 2323 Bryan Street, Suite 1600.
Telephone: 214-220-6300;
Telecopier: 214-220-2785.
Austin, Texas Office: 901 South Mopac Expressway.
Telephone: 512-329-3012.

MEMBERS OF FIRM

Ira Joel Middleberg
Michael Lee Riddle
(Resident, Dallas, Texas)
Dominic J. Gianna

Paul J. Mirabile
John D. Person
Alan Dean Weinberger
Evelyn Foley Pugh
L. Marlene Quarles
Ronald J. Vega
Edward T. Suffern, Jr.
Gary S. Brown
Tina S. Clark
E. Ralph Lupin
A.J. Herbert, III
Cynthia A. Langston

(See Next Column)

Marshall Joseph Simien, Jr.
Wade P. Webster
Brian G. Meissner
William M. Blackston
A. Elizabeth Tarver
Maria N. Rabieh

For full biographical listings, see the Martindale-Hubbell Law Directory

NESSER, KING & LEBLANC (AV)

Suite 3800 Place St. Charles, 201 St. Charles Avenue, 70170
Telephone: 504-582-3800
Telecopier: 504-582-1233

John T. Nesser, III
Henry A. King
Joseph E. LeBlanc, Jr.
David S. Bland
Patricia Ann Krebs
Robert J. Burvant
Eric Earl Jarrell
Liane K. Hinrichs

Jeffrey M. Burmaster
Jeffrey A. Mitchell
Margaret M. Sledge
Josh M. Kantrow
Elton A. Foster
Elizabeth S. Wheeler
Robert J. Bergeron
Timothy S. Madden
Elizabeth A. Meek

OF COUNSEL

Clare P. Hunter
George B. Jurgens, III
J. Grant Coleman
Len R. Brignac
George Farber, Jr.

For full biographical listings, see the Martindale-Hubbell Law Directory

O'NEIL, EICHIN, MILLER, BRECKINRIDGE & SAPORITO, A LAW CORPORATION (AV)

One Poydras Plaza, 22nd Floor, 70113
Telephone: 504-525-3200
Cable Address: ONEMILL NLN
Telex: ITT 460125
Answer Back: ONEMILL NLN
Facsimile: 504-529-7389 (Groups 1, 2 & 3)

William E. O'Neil
Earl S. Eichin, Jr.
Machale A. Miller
Alexander N. Breckinridge, IV
Jerry L. Saporito
I. Matthew Williamson
Randell E. Treadaway
Lindsay A. Larson, III
John F. Fay, Jr.
Alfred J. Rufty
Marva Jo Wyatt
Michael D. Sledge
Maria M. Bartush
Anne Flower Redd

Representative Clients: Cargill, Inc.; St. Paul Fire & Marine Insurance Company; CIGNA Companies, (P & C Group); Reliance National Insurance Company; Marine Office of America; General Motors Corp.; Toyota Motor Sales, U.S.A., Inc.; Royal Insurance Group; Hartford Insurance Company; Quaker Oats Company, Inc.

For full biographical listings, see the Martindale-Hubbell Law Directory

PREAUS, RODDY & KREBS (AV)

Suite 1650, 650 Poydras Street, 70130
Telephone: 504-523-2111
Telecopier: 504-523-2223

MEMBERS OF FIRM

Eugene R. Preaus
Virginia N. Roddy
David J. Krebs
Maura Zivalich Pelleteri

ASSOCIATES

Teresa Rose Young
Diane Lloyd Matthews
Krystil Borrouso Cook
Edward J. Parr, Jr.

Counsel for: American Society of Composers, Authors and Publishers; Fidelity and Deposit Company of Maryland; Metropolitan Life Insurance Co.; New York Life Insurance Co.; Reliance Insurance Co.; U.S. Home Corp.; Western Sizzlin, Inc.

For full biographical listings, see the Martindale-Hubbell Law Directory

PULASKI, GIEGER & LABORDE, A PROFESSIONAL LAW CORPORATION (AV)

Suite 4800, One Shell Square, 701 Poydras Street, 70139
Telephone: 504-561-0400
Telecopier: 504-561-1011

Michael T. Pulaski (P.C.)
Ernest P. Gieger, Jr., (P.C.)
Kenneth H. Laborde
Robert W. Maxwell
Keith W. McDaniel
Sharon D. Smith
Gary G. Hebert
Leo R. McAloon, III
J. Jeffrey Raborn
James E. Swinnen
Gina S. Montgomery
Diana L. Tonagel
Katherine B. Hardy
Mary Beth Meyer

For full biographical listings, see the Martindale-Hubbell Law Directory

New Orleans—Continued

RICE FOWLER (AV)

Place St. Charles, 36th Floor, 201 St. Charles Avenue, 70130
Telephone: 504-523-2600
Telecopier: 504-523-2705
Telex: 9102507910
ELN 62548910
London, England Office: Suite 692, Level 6 Lloyd's, 1 Lime Street, London EC3M 7DQ England.
Telephone: 071-327-4222.
Telecopier: 071-929-0043.
San Francisco, California Office: Embarcadero Center West, 275 Battery Street, 27th Floor, 94111.
Telephone: 415-399-9191.
Telecopier: 415-399-9192.
Telex: 451981.
San Diego, California Office: Emerald-Shapery Center, 402 W. Broadway, Suite 850, 92101.
Telephone: 619-230-0030.
Telecopier: 619-230-1350.
Beijing, China Office: Beijing International Convention Centre, Suite 7024, No. 8 Beichendong Road, Chaoyang District, 100101, P.R.C.
Telephone: (861) 493-4250.
Telecopier: (861) 493-4251.
Bogota, Colombia Office: Avenida Jimenez #4-03 Oficina 10-05.
Telephone: (571) 342-1062.
Telecopier: (571) 342-1062.

MEMBERS OF FIRM

Winston Edward Rice
George J. Fowler, III
Antonio J. Rodriguez
Thomas H. Kingsmill, III
Paul N. Vance
Delos E. Flint, Jr.
Edward F. LeBreton, III
Docia L. Dalby
Mary Campbell Hubbard
Jon W. Wise
Mat M. Gray, III

OF COUNSEL

T. C. W. Ellis

ASSOCIATES

Mary E. Kerrigan
Susan Molero Vance
Samuel A. Giberga
John F. Billera
D. Roxanne Perkins
Jeffry L. Sanford
Alanson T. Chenault, IV
Cindy T. Matherne
Barry A. Brock
Walter F. Wolf, III
Robert R. Johnston
Virginia R. Quijada
William J. Sommers, Jr.

For full biographical listings, see the Martindale-Hubbell Law Directory

WAGNER, BAGOT & GLEASON (AV)

Suite 2660, Poydras Center, 650 Poydras Street, 70130-6102
Telephone: 504-525-2141
Telecopier: 504-523-1587
TWX: 5106017673
ELN: 62928850
"INCISIVE"

Thomas J. Wagner
Michael H. Bagot, Jr.
Harvey G. Gleason
Whitney L. Cole
Eric D. Suben

For full biographical listings, see the Martindale-Hubbell Law Directory

*OPELOUSAS,** St. Landry Parish

DAUZAT, FALGOUST, CAVINESS, BIENVENU & STIPE (AV)

510 S. Court Street, P.O. Box 1450, 70571
Telephone: 318-942-5811
Fax: 318-948-9512

MEMBERS OF FIRM

Jimmy L. Dauzat
Jerry J. Falgoust
Peter F. Caviness
Steven J. Bienvenu
Jeigh L. Stipe

Representative Clients: State Farm Mutual Automobile Insurance Co.; The Travelers Insurance Co.; Farm Bureau Insurance Co's.; Audubon Insurance Co.; Kemper Insurance Group; United States Fidelity & Guaranty Co.; Louisiana Indemnity Co.; Louisiana Insurance Guaranty Assn.; Time Insurance Co.; Executive Fund Life Insurance Co.

For full biographical listings, see the Martindale-Hubbell Law Directory

*SHREVEPORT,** Caddo Parish

BARLOW AND HARDTNER L.C. (AV)

Tenth Floor, Louisiana Tower, 401 Edwards Street, 71101-3289
Telephone: 318-227-1131
Telecopier: 318-227-1141
Mailing Address: P.O. Box 8, Shreveport, Louisiana, 71161-0008

(See Next Column)

Joseph L. Shea, Jr.
Michael B. Donald
Jay A. Greenleaf

Representative Clients: Kelley Oil Corporation; NorAm Energy Corp. (formerly Arkla, Inc.); Central and South West; Panhandle Eastern Corp.; Pennzoil Producting Co.; Johnson Controls, Inc.; Ashland Oil, Inc.; Southwestern Electric Power Company; Brammer Engineering, Inc.; Goodrich Oil Company.

For Complete List of Firm Personnel, See General Section

For full biographical listings, see the Martindale-Hubbell Law Directory

BODENHEIMER, JONES, KLOTZ & SIMMONS (AV)

509 Milam Street, 71101
Telephone: 318-221-1507
Fax: 318-221-4560

MEMBERS OF FIRM

G. M. Bodenheimer, Jr.
J. W. Jones
Harry D. Simmons
F. John Reeks, Jr.
Mary Louise Coon Blackley
James P. Bodenheimer
Claude W. Bookter, Jr.

Representative Clients: American National Property & Casualty Company; Atlantic Mutual Companies; Dodson Insurance Group; Gulf Insurance Group; Kemper Insurance Group; Safeco Insurance Companies; USAA; Zurich-American Insurance Group.

For full biographical listings, see the Martindale-Hubbell Law Directory

COOK, YANCEY, KING & GALLOWAY, A PROFESSIONAL LAW CORPORATION (AV)

1700 Commercial National Tower, 333 Texas Street, P.O. Box 22260, 71120-2260
Telephone: 318-221-6277
Telecopier: 318-227-2606

Edwin L. Blewer, Jr.
Herschel E. Richard, Jr.
Samuel W. Caverlee
F. Drake Lee, Jr.
Charles G. Tutt
Albert M. Hand, Jr.
Cynthia C. Anderson
Brian A. Homza
Sidney E. Cook, Jr.
Eskridge E. Smith, Jr.
Timothy B. Burnham
Kenneth Mascagni
James R. Sterritt
Leland H. Ayres
S. Price Barker
Lisa Dunn Folsom
S. Curtis Mitchell
Gregg A. Wilkes
Tracy A. Burch

Aetna Casualty & Surety Company; Commercial Union Insurance Companies; Hartford Insurance Group; The Home Insurance Company; Kemper Group; State Farm Fire & Casualty Insurance Company; Electric Mutual Insurance Company; Louisiana Medical Mutual Insurance Company; Progressive Insurance Companies; Maryland Casualty Company.

For Complete List of Firm Personnel, See General Section

For full biographical listings, see the Martindale-Hubbell Law Directory

MAYER, SMITH & ROBERTS, L.L.P. (AV)

1550 Creswell, 71101
Telephone: 318-222-2135, 222-2268
Fax: 318-222-6420

MEMBERS OF FIRM

Caldwell Roberts
Walter O. Hunter, Jr.
Mark A. Goodwin
Ben Marshall, Jr.
Alexander S. Lyons
Kim Purdy Thomas
Richard G. Barham
David Butterfield
Vicki C. Warner
Henry N. Bellamy
John C. Turnage
Paul R. Mayer, Jr.
Steven E. Soileau

ASSOCIATES

Deborah Shea Baukman
Caldwell Roberts, Jr.
Frank K. Carroll
Dalton Roberts Ross

OF COUNSEL

Charles L. Mayer
Paul R. Mayer

Representative Clients: CNA Insurance Companies; Liberty Mutual Insurance Company; The St. Paul Companies; United States Fidelity and Guaranty Company; Schumpert Medical Center; Travelers Insurance Company; Great American Insurance Company; Insurance Corporation of America; Highlands Insurance Company; Ohio Casualty Group of Insurance Companies.

For Complete List of Firm Personnel, See General Section

For full biographical listings, see the Martindale-Hubbell Law Directory

WIENER, WEISS, MADISON & HOWELL, A PROFESSIONAL CORPORATION (AV)

333 Texas Street, Suite 2350, P.O. Box 21990, 71120-1990
Telephone: 318-226-9100
Fax: 318-424-5128

(See Next Column)

Wiener, Weiss, Madison & Howell A Professional Corporation, *Shreveport—Continued*

John M. Madison, Jr. Jeffrey W. Weiss
Larry Feldman, Jr. Mark L. Hornsby

Representative Clients: Pioneer Bank & Trust Co.; Ford Motor Credit Corp.; CNA Insurance Companies; International Paper Companies; Louisiana Homebuilders Association Self Insurers Fund; LSU-Shreveport; Sealy Realty, Inc.; Palmer Petroleum, Inc.; Brookshire Grocery Company (Louisiana); Northwest Louisiana Production Credit Association.

For Complete List of Firm Personnel, See General Section

For full biographical listings, see the Martindale-Hubbell Law Directory

Wilkinson, Carmody & Gilliam (AV)

1700 Beck Building, 400 Travis Street, P.O. Box 1707, 71166
Telephone: 318-221-4196
Telecopier: 318-221-3705

MEMBERS OF FIRM

John D. Wilkinson (1867-1929) Bobby S. Gilliam
William Scott Wilkinson (1895-1985) Mark E. Gilliam
Penny D. Sellers
Arthur R. Carmody, Jr. Brian D. Landry

Representative Clients: Farmers Insurance Group; Home Federal Savings & Loan Association of Shreveport; The Kansas City Southern Railway Co.; KTAL-TV; Lincoln National Life Insurance Co.; Mobil Oil Co.; Schumpert Medical Center; Sears, Roebuck & Co.; Southern Pacific Transportation Co.; Southwestern Electric Power Co.

For full biographical listings, see the Martindale-Hubbell Law Directory

MAINE

*AUGUSTA,** Kennebec Co.

Law Offices of Phillip E. Johnson (AV)

160 Capitol Street, P.O. Box 29, 04332-0029
Telephone: 207-623-5110
Fax: 207-622-4160

David G. Webbert

Representative Clients: Agway, Inc.; American Eagle Group; Associated Aviation Underwriters; Aviation Underwriting Specialists; AVEMCO; Central Maine Power Co.; The Doctors Company; Loss Management Services, Inc.; Progressive Casualty Insurance Co.; Shand, Morahan & Co.

For full biographical listings, see the Martindale-Hubbell Law Directory

*BANGOR,** Penobscot Co.

Eaton, Peabody, Bradford & Veague, P.A. (AV)

Fleet Center-Exchange Street, P.O. Box 1210, 04402-1210
Telephone: 207-947-0111
Telecopier: 207-942-3040
Augusta, Maine Office: 2 Central Plaza.
Telephone: 207-622-3747.
Telecopier: 207-622-9732.
Brunswick, Maine Office: 167 Park Row.
Telephone: 207-729-1144.
Telecopier: 207-729-1140.
Camden, Maine Office: 7-9 Washington Street.
Telephone: 207-236-3325.
Telecopier: 207-236-8611.
Dover-Foxcroft, Maine Office: 30 East Main Street.
Telephone: 207-564-8378.
Telecopier: 207-564-7059.

Bernard J. Kubetz Glen L. Porter
Douglas M. Smith (Resident, Dover-Foxcroft and Augusta Offices) Gordon H. S. Scott (Resident, Augusta Office)
William B. Devoe

John M. Monahan (Resident, Dover-Foxcroft Office) Judy A.S. Metcalf (Resident, Brunswick Office)
Jonathan B. Huntington (Resident, Dover-Foxcroft Office)

A List of Representative Clients available upon request.

For Complete List of Firm Personnel, See General Section

For full biographical listings, see the Martindale-Hubbell Law Directory

Richardson, Troubh & Badger, A Professional Corporation (AV)

82 Columbia Street, P.O. Box 2429, 04402-2429
Telephone: 207-945-5900
Telecopier: 207-945-0758
Portland, Maine Office: Richardson & Troubh, A Professional Corporation, 465 Congress Street. P.O. Box, 9732.
Telephone: 207-774-5821.
Telecopier: 207-761-2056.

Frederick J. Badger, Jr. (Resident) Ann M. Murray (Resident)

Frederick F. Costlow (Resident) John B. Lucy (Resident)

Representative Clients: Royal Insurance; Travelers Insurance; Peerless Insurance; CIGNA; Hanover Insurance; Liberty Mutual Insurance; Fireman's Fund American; Concord Group Insurance Company; Home Insurance.
Reference: Fleet Bank.

For full biographical listings, see the Martindale-Hubbell Law Directory

Vafiades, Brountas & Kominsky (AV)

Key Plaza, 23 Water Street, P.O. Box 919, 04402-0919
Telephone: 207-947-6915
Telecopier: 207-941-0863

MEMBERS OF FIRM

Nicholas P. Brountas Marvin H. Glazier
Susan R. Kominsky Eugene C. Coughlin, III

OF COUNSEL

Lewis V. Vafiades

Representative Clients: Allstate Insurance Company; Chubb Group; Greater New York Mutual Insurance Company; Metropolitan Property and Liability Insurance Company; National Grange Mutual Insurance Company.

For Complete List of Firm Personnel, See General Section

For full biographical listings, see the Martindale-Hubbell Law Directory

LEWISTON, Androscoggin Co.

Platz & Thompson, P.A. (AV)

95 Park Street, P.O. Box 960, 04243
Telephone: 207-783-8558
Telecopier: 207-783-9487

J. Peter Thompson Roger J. O'Donnell, III
Philip K. Hargesheimer Robert V. Hoy
Paul S. Douglass James B. Main

Representative Clients: State Farm Mutual Automobile Insurance Co.; Peerless Insurance Co.; Farm Family Mutual Insurance Co.; State Farm Fire & Casualty Co.; Patrons-Oxford Mutual Insurance Co.; Home Insurance Co.; Prudential Insurance Co.; Empire Insurance Co.; Concord General Insurance Co.; Union Mutual Insurance Co.

For Complete List of Firm Personnel, See General Section

For full biographical listings, see the Martindale-Hubbell Law Directory

*PORTLAND,** Cumberland Co.

Amerling & Burns, A Professional Association (AV)

193 Middle Street, 04101
Telephone: 207-775-3581
Facsimile: 207-775-3814
Affiliated St. Croix Office: Coon & Sanford, P.O. Box 25918, Six Chandlers's Wharf, Suite 202, 00824-0918.

W. John Amerling Arnold C. Macdonald
George F. Burns Mary DeLano
David P. Ray Joanne F. Cole
John R. Coon A. Robert Ruesch

OF COUNSEL

Bruce M. Jervis

Aetna Life & Casualty Co.; The Harford; Great American Insurance Co.; Wausau Ins. Co.

For full biographical listings, see the Martindale-Hubbell Law Directory

Friedman & Babcock (AV)

Suite 400, Six City Center, P.O. Box 4726, 04112-4726
Telephone: 207-761-0900
Telecopier: 207-761-0186

MEMBERS OF FIRM

Harold J. Friedman Thomas A. Cox
Ernest J. Babcock Karen Frink Wolf
Martha C. Gaythwaite Jennifer S. Begel
Gregory W. Powell Laurence H. Leavitt

(See Next Column)

FRIEDMAN & BABCOCK—*Continued*

ASSOCIATES

Theodore H. Irwin, Jr.
Lee H. Bals
Michelle A. Landmann
Arthur J. Lamothe
Brian L. Champion
Laurie B. Perzley
Elizabeth A. Germani
Tracey G. Burton
Jonathan Marc Dunitz
Lori A. Desjardins

For full biographical listings, see the Martindale-Hubbell Law Directory

PIERCE, ATWOOD, SCRIBNER, ALLEN, SMITH & LANCASTER (AV)

One Monument Square, 04101
Telephone: 207-773-6411
Fax: 207-773-3419
Augusta, Maine Office: 77 Winthrop Street.
Telephone: 207-622-6311.
Camden, Maine Office: 36 Chestnut Street, P.O. Box 780.
Telephone: 207-236-4333.

MEMBERS OF FIRM

Ralph I. Lancaster, Jr.
Malcolm L. Lyons (Resident, Augusta Office)
Peter W. Culley
Louise K. Thomas
Michael D. Seitzinger (Resident, Augusta Office)
John J. Aromando
David E. Barry

ASSOCIATES

Stephen G. Grygiel
Gisele M. Nadeau
Daniel J. Stevens (Resident, Augusta Office)
Michael N. Ambler, Jr.
Michael S. Wilson
Deborah L. Shaw
Jared S. des Rosiers
Debra L. Brown

For Complete List of Firm Personnel, See General Section

For full biographical listings, see the Martindale-Hubbell Law Directory

PRETI, FLAHERTY, BELIVEAU & PACHIOS (AV)

443 Congress Street, P.O. Box 11410, 04104-7410
Telephone: 207-791-3000
Telecopier: 207-791-3111
Augusta, Maine Office: 45 Memorial Circle, P.O. Box 1058, 04332-1058.
Telephone: 207-623-5300.
Telecopier: 207-623-2914.
Rumford, Maine Office: 150 Congress Street, P.O. Drawer L, 04276-2035.
Telephone: 207-364-4593.
Telecopier: 207-369-9421.

MEMBERS OF FIRM

John J. Flaherty
Albert J. Beliveau, Jr. (Rumford Office)
Severin M. Beliveau (Augusta Office)
Keith A. Powers
Christopher D. Nyhan
Jonathan S. Piper
Daniel Rapaport
Bruce C. Gerrity (Augusta Office)
Jeffrey T. Edwards
Michael G. Messerschmidt
Randall B. Weill
Evan M. Hansen
Edward R. Benjamin, Jr.
Geoffrey K. Cummings
Michael Kaplan

ASSOCIATES

Nelson J. Larkins
Stephen E. F. Langsdorf (Augusta Office)
John P. McVeigh
Elizabeth A. Olivier
Jeffrey M. Sullivan
Kevin J. Beal
Penny St. Louis
Richard L. Suter

Representative Clients: The St. Paul Companies; Maine Municipal Assn.; American International Group; MGA Insurance Services; Gallagher Bassett; Dunlap Corp.; Crawford and Co.; Maine Bonding Co.; The Travelers Insurance Co.; United States Fidelity and Guaranty Co.

For Complete List of Firm Personnel, See General Section

For full biographical listings, see the Martindale-Hubbell Law Directory

RICHARDSON & TROUBH, A PROFESSIONAL CORPORATION (AV)

465 Congress Street, P.O. Box 9732, 04104-5032
Telephone: 207-774-5821
Telecopier: 207-761-2056
Bangor, Maine Office: Richardson Troubh & Badger, A Professional Corporation, 82 Columbia Street.
Telephone: 207-945-5900.
Telecopier: 207-945-0758.

Harrison L. Richardson
Robert J. Piampiano
Richard J. Kelly
Wendell G. Large
Frederick J. Badger, Jr. (Resident, Bangor Office)
Kevin M. Gillis
Thomas E. Getchell
Michael Richards
William K. McKinley
Elizabeth G. Stouder
Barri Bloom
Daniel F. Gilligan
Ann M. Murray (Resident, Bangor Maine)

(See Next Column)

Frederick F. Costlow (Resident, Bangor Office)
John B. Lucy (Resident, Bangor Office)

Representative Clients: Commercial Union Insurance Company; Electric Mutual Insurance Company; Fireman's Fund American Insurance Companies; Great American Insurance Company; Hartford Insurance Group; Home Insurance Company.

For Complete List of Firm Personnel, See General Section

For full biographical listings, see the Martindale-Hubbell Law Directory

THOMPSON & BOWIE (AV)

Three Canal Plaza, P.O. Box 4630, 04112
Telephone: 207-774-2500
Telecopier: 207-774-3591

MEMBERS OF FIRM

Roy E. Thompson, Jr.
James M. Bowie
Daniel R. Mawhinney
Rebecca H. Farnum
Glenn H. Robinson
Frank W. DeLong, III
Michael E. Saucier
Mark V. Franco

ASSOCIATES

Elizabeth G. Knox
Cathy S. Roberts
Paul C. Catsos

Representative Clients: Aetna Casualty & Surety; CNA Insurance Co.; Chubb Group; CIGNA Property & Casualty Companies; Lexington Insurance Co.; Liberty Mutual Insurance Co.; Nationwide Mutual Insurance Co.; Prudential Insurance Co.; Travelers Insurance Co.; Continental Group.

For full biographical listings, see the Martindale-Hubbell Law Directory

PRESQUE ISLE, Aroostook Co.

STEVENS, ENGELS, BISHOP & SPRAGUE (AV)

428 Main Street, P.O. Box 311, 04769
Telephone: 207-768-5481
Telefax: 207-764-1663

MEMBERS OF FIRM

Albert M. Stevens
Richard C. Engels
Frank H. Bishop, Sr.
Jonathan W. Sprague
Michael L. Dubois

Representative Clients: Travelers Insurance Co.; Aetna Insurance Co.; Hartford Insurance Group; Liberty Mutual Insurance Co.; Peerless Insurance Co.; Union Mutual Insurance Co.; Horace Mann Insurance Co.; Patrons Mutual Insurance Co.; Mutual of Omaha Insurance; St. Paul Insurance Co.

For full biographical listings, see the Martindale-Hubbell Law Directory

MARYLAND

*BALTIMORE,** (Independent City)

ALLEN, JOHNSON, ALEXANDER & KARP, P.A. (AV)

Suite 1540, 100 East Pratt Street, 21202
Telephone: 410-727-5000
Fax: 410-727-0861
Washington, D.C. Office: 1707 L Street, N.W., Suite 1050.
Telephone: 202-828-4141.

Donald C. Allen
John D. Alexander, Jr.
Daniel Karp
D'Ana E. Johnson (Resident, Washington, D.C. Office)

Anne Marie McGinley (Resident, Washington, D.C. Office)
Denise Ramsburg Stanley
George B. Breen (Not admitted in MD; Resident, Washington, D.C. Office)
Robert G. McGinley (Resident, Washington, D.C. Office)
James X. Crogan, Jr.
Yvette M. Bryant
Kevin Bock Karpinski
Brett A. Balinsky

Representative Clients: Scottsdale Insurance Co.; Nautilus Insurance Co.; Jefferson Insurance Co.; Liberty Mutual Insurance Co.; Avis Rent-A-Car; Otis Elevator Co.; Montgomery Elevator Co.; Admiral Insurance Co.; Local Government Insurance Trust; Lancer Insurance Co.

For full biographical listings, see the Martindale-Hubbell Law Directory

JORDAN COYNE & SAVITS (AV)

400 E. Pratt Street, Suite 830, 21202
Telephone: 410-625-5080
Telecopier: 202-842-2587
Washington, D.C. Office: 1030 15th Street, N.W.
Telephone: 202-371-1800.
Telecopier: 202-842-2587.
Rockville, Maryland Office: 33 Wood Lane.
Telephone: 301-424-4161.
Automatic Telecopier: 202-842-2587.

(See Next Column)

JORDAN COYNE & SAVITS, *Baltimore—Continued*

Fairfax, Virginia Office: 10486 Armstrong Street.
Telephone: 703-246-0900.
Telecopier: 703-591-3673.
Leesburg, Virginia Office: 105 Loudoun Street, S.E.
Telephones: 703-777-6084; 202-478-1895.
Telecopier: 703-771-6383.

Joel M. Savits
D. Stephenson Schwinn
David B. Stratton

Representative Clients: Harleysville Mutual Insurance Co.; Travelers Insurance Co.

For full biographical listings, see the Martindale-Hubbell Law Directory

ROLLINS, SMALKIN, RICHARDS & MACKIE (AV)

401 North Charles Street, 21201
Telephone: 410-727-2443
Fax: 410-727-8390

MEMBERS OF FIRM

H. Beale Rollins (1898-1985)
Samuel S. Smalkin (1906-1982)
T. Benjamin Weston (1913-1980)
Thomas G. Andrew (1910-1973)
Edward C. Mackie
John F. Linsenmeyer
Thomas C. Gentner
Glenn W. Trimmer
Patrick G. Cullen
James P. O'Meara
Dennis J. Sullivan

ASSOCIATES

Francis B. Buckley
Elaine R. Wilford
Paul G. Donoghue
Ralph E. Wilson III
Kenneth G. Macleay
Donna Lynn Kolakowski-Hollen

OF COUNSEL

Raymond A. Richards (Retired)
Hartman J. Miller

For full biographical listings, see the Martindale-Hubbell Law Directory

THIEBLOT, RYAN, MARTIN & FERGUSON, P.A. (AV)

4th Floor, The World Trade Center, 21202-3091
Telephone: 410-837-1140
Washington, D.C. Line: 202-628-8223
Fax: 410-837-3282

Robert J. Thieblot
Anthony W. Ryan
J. Edward Martin, Jr.
Robert L. Ferguson, Jr.
Bruce R. Miller
Robert D. Harwick, Jr.
Thomas J. Schetelich
Christopher J. Heffernan

M. Brooke Murdock
Anne M. Hrehorovich
Donna Marie Raffaele
Michael N. Russo, Jr.
Jodi K. Ebersole
Hamilton Fisk Tyler
Peter Joseph Basile

Representative Clients: Ford Motor Credit Co.; USF & G Co.; The American Road Insurance Co.; Fidelity Engineering Corp.; The North Charles Street Design Organization; Record Collections, Inc.; Toyota Motor Credit Co.

For full biographical listings, see the Martindale-Hubbell Law Directory

VENABLE, BAETJER AND HOWARD (AV)

A Partnership including Professional Corporations
1800 Mercantile Bank & Trust Building, 2 Hopkins Plaza, 21201
Telephone: 410-244-7400
Washington, D.C. Office: Venable, Baetjer, Howard & Civiletti. Suite 1000, 1201 New York Avenue, N.W.
Telephone: 202-962-4800.
McLean, Virginia Office: Suite 400, 2010 Corporate Ridge.
Telephone: 703-760-1600.
Rockville, Maryland Office: Suite 500, One Church Street, P. O. Box 1906.
Telephone: 301-217-5600.
Towson, Maryland Office: 210 Allegheny Avenue, P. O. Box 5517.
Telephone: 410-494-6200.

MEMBERS OF FIRM

Benjamin R. Civiletti (P.C.) (Also at Washington, D.C. and Towson, Maryland Offices)
John Henry Lewin, Jr. (P.C.)
Roger W. Titus (Resident, Rockville, Maryland Office)
Ronald R. Glancz (Not admitted in MD; Resident, Washington, D.C. Office)
Douglas D. Connah, Jr. (P.C.) (Also at Washington, D.C. Office)
John H. Zink, III (Resident, Towson, Maryland Office)
Bruce E. Titus (Resident, McLean, Virginia Office)
Joel Z. Silver (Not admitted in MD; Resident, Washington, D.C. Office)
William D. Dolan, III (P.C.) (Not admitted in MD; Resident, McLean, Virginia Office)
Paul T. Glasgow (Resident, Rockville, Maryland Office)
Joseph C. Wich, Jr. (Resident, Towson, Maryland Office)
Nell B. Strachan
James K. Archibald (Also at Washington, D.C. and Towson, Maryland Offices)
Jeffrey A. Dunn (also at Washington, D.C. Office)
George F. Pappas (Also at Washington, D.C. Office)
James L. Shea (Also at Washington, D.C. Office)
Jeffrey P. Ayres (P.C.)

(See Next Column)

MEMBERS OF FIRM (Continued)

C. Carey Deeley, Jr. (Also at Towson, Maryland Office)
Kathleen Gallogly Cox (Resident, Towson, Maryland Office)
Christopher R. Mellott
Cynthia M. Hahn (Resident, Towson, Maryland Office)
M. King Hill, III (Resident, Towson, Maryland Office)
Mary E. Pivec (Also at Washington, D.C. Office)
John A. Roberts (Also at Rockville, Maryland Office)
David J. Heubeck
Herbert G. Smith, II (Not admitted in MD; Resident, McLean, Virginia Office)

ASSOCIATES

Daniel William China
Marina Lolley Dame (Resident, Towson, Maryland Office)
J. Van L. Dorsey (Resident, Towson, Maryland Office)
Mary-Dulany James (Resident, Towson, Maryland Office)
Patricia A. Malone (Resident, Towson, Maryland Office)
Christine M. McAnney (Not admitted in MD; Resident, McLean, Virginia Office)
John A. McCauley
John T. Prisbe
Nathan E. Siegel
Linda Marotta Thomas

For Complete List of Firm Personnel, See General Section

For full biographical listings, see the Martindale-Hubbell Law Directory

*ROCKVILLE,** Montgomery Co.

ANDERSON & QUINN (AV)

The Adams Law Center, 25 Wood Lane, 20850
Telephone: 301-762-3303
FAX: 301-762-3776
Washington, D.C. Office: 1220 L Street, N.W., Suite 540.
Telephone: 202-371-1245.

MEMBERS OF FIRM

Charles C. Collins (1900-1973)
Robert E. Anderson (Not admitted in MD; Retired)
Francis X. Quinn
William Ray Scanlin (Resident, Washington, D.C. Office)
Donald P. Maiberger
Robert P. Scanlon (Resident, Washington, D.C. Office)
James G. Healy

ASSOCIATES

John A. Rego
Richard L. Butler (Resident, Washington, D.C. Office)
Marie M. Gavigan (Mrs.)
Donald J. Urgo, Jr.
Laura A. Garufi

Representative Clients: C & P Telephone; Commercial Union Insurance Cos.; Allstate Insurance Co.; State Farm Mutual Automobile Insurance Co.; Liberty Mutual Insurance Co.; Northbrook Insurance Cos.; Travelers Insurance Co.; National General Insurance Co.; American International Adjustment Co.; Marriott Corp.

For Complete List of Firm Personnel, See General Section

For full biographical listings, see the Martindale-Hubbell Law Directory

ARMSTRONG, DONOHUE & CEPPOS, CHARTERED (AV)

Suite 101, 204 Monroe Street, 20850
Telephone: 301-251-0440
Telecopier: 301-279-5929

Larry A. Ceppos
H. Patrick Donohue
H. Kenneth Armstrong
Benjamin S. Vaughan
John C. Monahan

Kirk S. Burgee
Oya S. Oner
Pamela Barrow Kincheloe
Maura J. Condon
Richard S. Schrager
Sharon A. Marcial
J. Eric Rhoades

Representative Clients: Medical Mutual Liability Insurance Society of Maryland; Kaiser Permanente; Shady Grove Adventist Hospital; American Medical International, Inc.; Crum & Forster Commercial Insurance Cos.; Atlantic Mutual Insurance Co.; Nationwide Mutual Insurance Co.; Harleysville Mutual Insurance Co.; St. Paul Fire & Marine Insurance Co.; American Reliance Insurance Co.

For full biographical listings, see the Martindale-Hubbell Law Directory

JORDAN COYNE & SAVITS (AV)

33 Wood Lane, 20850-2228
Telephone: 301-424-4161
Automatic Telecopier: 202-842-2587
Washington, D.C. Office: 1030 15th Street, N.W.
Telephone: 202-371-1800.
Telecopier: 202-842-2587.
Baltimore, Maryland Office: 400 E. Pratt Street, Suite 830.
Telephone: 410-625-5080.
Telecopier: 202-842-2587.
Fairfax, Virginia Office: 10486 Armstrong Street.
Telephone: 703-246-0900.
Telecopier: 703-591-3673.

(See Next Column)

JORDAN COYNE & SAVITS—*Continued*

Leesburg, Virginia Office: 105 Loudoun Street, S.E.
Telephones: 703-777-6084; 202-478-1895.
Telecopier: 703-771-6383.

Joel M. Savits
D. Stephenson Schwinn
David B. Stratton

ASSOCIATES

William Ward Nooter
Laura Nachowitz Steel
Geoffrey T. Hervey
Deborah Murrell Whelihan
Clifton Merritt Mount
Tracy A. Cannon
Ellen Giblin Draper
Matthew L. Silverstein

Representative Clients: Harleysville Mutual Insurance Co.; Travelers Insurance Co.

For full biographical listings, see the Martindale-Hubbell Law Directory

SILVER SPRING, Montgomery Co.

LIPSHULTZ AND HONE, CHARTERED (AV)

Suite 108 Montgomery Center, 8630 Fenton Street, 20910
Telephone: 301-587-8500
Fax: 301-495-9759
Washington, D.C. Office: Suite 200, 2000 L Street, N.W.
Telephone: 202-872-0909.

Stanley L. Lipshultz
Michael T. O'Bryant (Not admitted in MD)
Stephen S. Brown
Victor I. Weiner
Joseph J. Bottiglieri
Renee R. Nebens
Andrew R. Simonson

For Complete List of Firm Personnel, See General Section

For full biographical listings, see the Martindale-Hubbell Law Directory

*TOWSON,** Baltimore Co.

HOWELL, GATELY, WHITNEY & CARTER (AV)

401 Washington Avenue, Twelfth Floor, 21204
Telephone: 410-583-8000
FAX: 410-583-8031

MEMBERS OF FIRM

H. Thomas Howell
William F. Gately
Benjamin R. Goertemiller
Daniel W. Whitney
David A. Carter
William R. Levasseur

ASSOCIATES

Una M. Perez
John S. Bainbridge, Jr.
George D. Bogris
Wendy A. Lassen
Kathleen D. Leslie

For full biographical listings, see the Martindale-Hubbell Law Directory

VENABLE, BAETJER AND HOWARD (AV)

A Partnership including Professional Corporations
210 Allegheny Avenue, P.O. Box 5517, 21204
Telephone: 410-494-6200
FAX: 410-821-0147
Baltimore, Maryland Office: 1800 Mercantile Bank & Trust Building, 2 Hopkins Plaza.
Telephone: 410-244-7400.
Washington, D.C. Office: Venable, Baetjer, Howard & Civiletti. Suite 1000, 1201 New York Avenue, N.W.
Telephone: 202-962-4800.
McLean, Virginia Office: Suite 400, 2010 Corporate Ridge.
Telephone: 703-760-1600.
Rockville, Maryland Office: Suite 500, One Church Street, P. O. Box 1906.
Telephone: 301-217-5600.

PARTNERS

Benjamin R. Civiletti (P.C.) (Also at Washington, D.C. and Baltimore, Maryland Offices)
John H. Zink, III
Joseph C. Wich, Jr.
James K. Archibald (Also at Baltimore, Maryland and Washington, D.C. Offices)
C. Carey Deeley, Jr. (Also at Baltimore, Maryland Office)
Kathleen Gallogly Cox
Cynthia M. Hahn
M. King Hill, III

ASSOCIATES

Marina Lolley Dame
J. Van L. Dorsey
Mary-Dulany James
Patricia A. Malone

For Complete List of Firm Personnel, See General Section

For full biographical listings, see the Martindale-Hubbell Law Directory

MASSACHUSETTS

*BOSTON,** Suffolk Co.

BADGER, DOLAN, PARKER & COHEN (AV)

Formerly Badger, Sullivan, Kelley & Cole
Formerly Parker & Cohen
2 Oliver Street, 02109
Telephone: 617-482-3030
Fax: 617-482-6919

MEMBERS OF FIRM

Walter I. Badger (1885-1926)
John J. Sullivan (1926-1979)
David W. Kelley (1935-1986)
George F. Parker, III
James B. Dolan, Jr.
Lawrence J. Cohen

ASSOCIATES

Audrey LaRowe Nee
Erin R. Boisvert
Lisa Cerino Cabi

OF COUNSEL

Peter D. Cole

Representative Clients: The Travelers Insurance Co.; Ford Motor Co.

For full biographical listings, see the Martindale-Hubbell Law Directory

COGAVIN AND WAYSTACK (AV)

2 Center Plaza, 02108
Telephone: 617-742-3340
Telecopier: 617-723-7563

MEMBERS OF FIRM

John J. Cogavin
Edward W. Waystack
John P. Fitzgerald
Gerard A. Butler
Kevin J. McGinty

ASSOCIATES

David T. Donnelly
John J. Jarosak
Thomas M. Franco
Mark A. Darling
Audrey Lewchik Bradley
Daniel S. McInnis
William P. Hurley
Laura E. Iannetta
Thomas G. Leonard, Jr.
John A. Dolan

Representative Clients: Fireman's Fund Insurance Co.; The Andover Companies; The Hartford Insurance Co.; The Travelers Insurance Co.; Plymouth Rock; Metropolitan Insurance Co.; Transamerica Insurance Group; Maryland Casualty Insurance Co.; Chubb Insurance Company; National Grange Mutual Insurance Co.

For full biographical listings, see the Martindale-Hubbell Law Directory

CORNELL AND GOLLUB (AV)

75 Federal Street, 02110
Telephone: 617-482-8100
Telecopier: 617-482-3917

MEMBERS OF FIRM

Robert W. Cornell (1910-1988)
Karl L. Gollub (1934-1985)
David H. Sempert
Philip J. Foley
Peter M. Durney
Paul F. Lynch

ASSOCIATES

Susan Geyer Malloy
Jane Treen Brand
Hugh M. Coxe
Janet J. Bobit
Thomas A. Pursley
David W. McGough
Susan M. Donaldson
Marie E. Chadeayne
Bruce E. Hopper
Thomas H. Dolan
Eric B. Goldberg
Kelly L. Wilkins
Martha Jane Dickey

For full biographical listings, see the Martindale-Hubbell Law Directory

GRIFFIN & GOULKA (AV)

Two Oliver Street, 02109
Telephone: 617-423-6677
Telecopier: 617-423-5755

MEMBERS OF FIRM

J. Kenneth Griffin
Joanne L. Goulka
Christopher S. Williams

ASSOCIATES

Lisa R. Pierce
Robert P. La Hait
Steven D. Weil
Lynn M. Guerriere

For full biographical listings, see the Martindale-Hubbell Law Directory

KOPELMAN AND PAIGE, P.C. (AV)

101 Arch Street, 02110
Telephone: 617-951-0007
Cable Address: "Lawkope"
Fax: 617-951-2735

(See Next Column)

KOPELMAN AND PAIGE P.C., *Boston—Continued*

Leonard Kopelman
Donald G. Paige
Elizabeth A. Lane
Joyce F. Frank
John W. Giorgio
Barbara J. Saint Andre
Joel B. Bard
Everett Joseph Marder
Patrick J. Costello

William Hewig, III

For Complete List of Firm Personnel, See General Section

For full biographical listings, see the Martindale-Hubbell Law Directory

MARTIN, MAGNUSON, MCCARTHY & KENNEY (AV)

133 Portland Street, 02114
Telephone: 617-227-3240
Telecopier: 617-227-3346

MEMBERS OF FIRM

Raymond J. Kenney, Jr. *
Charles P. Reidy, III *
Daniel J. Griffin, Jr. *
Philip E. Murray, Jr. *
Joseph L. Doherty, Jr. *
Neal M. Lerer *
Paul R. Keane *
John P. Mulvey *
Paul M. McTague *
Carol A. Kelly *
Gail L. Anderson *
Edward F. Mahoney *

COUNSEL

Harold E. Magnuson
Edward F. Hennessey

Joan L. Atlas *
Joseph B. Bertrand *
Martha A. Driscoll *
Douglas A. Robertson *
Mary T. Gibbons *
Teresa J. Farris *
Elizabeth A. Cushing *
Marie G. Leary *

Representative Clients: Allstate Insurance Company; American International Adjustment Company; Browning - Ferris Industries, Inc.; Fireman's Fund Insurance Companies; Fireman's Fund; Joint Underwriting Association of Massachusetts; Liability Limited; Multi Systems Agency LTD.; Murray Ohio Manufacturing Company; Risk Management Foundation; Shand Morhan Company.
References: Fleet Bank; Shawmut Bank, N.A.
*Employees of The Professional Corporation of McCarthy, Kenney & Reidy.

For Complete List of Firm Personnel, See General Section

For full biographical listings, see the Martindale-Hubbell Law Directory

PALMER & DODGE (AV)

(Storey Thorndike Palmer & Dodge)
One Beacon Street, 02108
Telephone: 617-573-0100
Telecopier: 617-227-4420
Telex: 951104
Cable Address: "Storeydike," Boston

MEMBERS OF FIRM

Acheson H. Callaghan, Jr.
Michael T. Gass
Michael J. Lacek
Scott P. Lewis
Steven L. Schreckinger
Craig E. Stewart
Jeffrey Swope
Tamara S. Wolfson

COUNSEL

Stephen J. Abarbanel

For Complete List of Firm Personnel, See General Section

For full biographical listings, see the Martindale-Hubbell Law Directory

SHAPIRO & ASSOCIATES (AV)

One Beacon Street, 24th Floor, 02108
Telephone: 617-227-8100

Daniel B. Shapiro

ASSOCIATE

Michael A. Mc Kinnon

Representative Clients: NLC Insurance Companies; Trust Insurance Co.; Liberty Mutual Insurance Co.

For full biographical listings, see the Martindale-Hubbell Law Directory

TAYLOR, ANDERSON & TRAVERS (AV)

75 Federal Street, 02110
Telephone: 617-654-8200
Fax: 617-482-5350
Providence, Rhode Island Office: The Wilcox Building, 42 Weybosset Street.
Telephone: 401-273-7171.
Fax: 401-273-2904.

(See Next Column)

MEMBERS OF FIRM

Allan E. Taylor
James H. Anderson
Margaret S. Travers
James J. Duane, III
Sidney W. Adler
John J. Barton
Susan H. Williams
Ellen Epstein Cohen
Pamela Slater Gilman
Alexandra B. Harvey

ASSOCIATES

Edward D. Shoulkin
Jennifer Ellis Burke
Melanie J. Gargas
A. Bernard Guekguezian
Francis A. Connor, III
Gina Witalec Verdi
Robert C. Shindell

For full biographical listings, see the Martindale-Hubbell Law Directory

WARNER & STACKPOLE (AV)

75 State Street, 02109
Telephone: 617-951-9000
Cable Address: "Warstack"
Telecopier: 617-951-9151
Telex: 940139

MEMBERS OF FIRM

Ralph T. Lepore, III
Janice Kelley Rowan
Keith C. Long
Michael DeMarco

ASSOCIATES

Charlene D. Andros
Robert A. Whitney
Daniel E. Rosenfeld

For Complete List of Firm Personnel, See General Section

For full biographical listings, see the Martindale-Hubbell Law Directory

BROCKTON, Plymouth Co.

VINCENT P. CAHALANE, P.C. (AV)

478 Torrey Street, 02401
Telephone: 508-588-1222
Fax: 508-584-4748

Vincent P. Cahalane
Robert J. Zullas
Julie A. Cahalane

LEGAL SUPPORT PERSONNEL

PARALEGALS

Joan C. Cahalane
Kristopher S. Stefani

For full biographical listings, see the Martindale-Hubbell Law Directory

MONE, D'AMBROSE & HANYEN, P.C. (AV)

529 Pearl Street, 02401
Telephone: 508-583-7010
Fax: 508-583-7062

Francis D. Mone (1930-1962)
William K. Mone (1949-1979)
James J. D'Ambrose
Clyde K. Hanyen, Jr.
Brian J. Mone
Robert E. Langway, Jr.
J. Gary Bennett
Gerard J. Good

Representative Clients: Commercial Union Insurance Cos.; Southeastern Regional Vocational School Committee; Providence-Washington Insurance Co.
Reference: Fleet Bank.

For full biographical listings, see the Martindale-Hubbell Law Directory

*CAMBRIDGE,** Middlesex Co.

GEORGE F. GORMLEY, P.C. (AV)

One Main Street, P.O. Box 965, 02142-0090
Telephone: 617-349-3750
Fax: 617-661-2576

George F. Gormley

Jackie L. Segel
John D. Colucci

For full biographical listings, see the Martindale-Hubbell Law Directory

LOWELL, Middlesex Co.

DONAHUE & DONAHUE ATTORNEYS, P.C. (AV)

21 George Street, 01852
Telephone: 508-458-6887
Fax: 508-458-3424

Daniel J. Donahue (1860-1939)
Joseph P. Donahue (1889-1973)
Charles A. Donahue (1891-1964)
Richard K. Donahue
Joseph P. Donahue, Jr.
Joseph D. Regan
Michael W. Gallagher
Peter V. Lawlor
Bradford P. Fortin
Richard K. Donahue, Jr.
Andrea S. Barisano
Matthew C. Donahue
Richard E. Cavanaugh
Kelly R. Spencer

Representative Clients: The Travelers Insurance Co.; L'Energia Cogeneration, Inc.

For full biographical listings, see the Martindale-Hubbell Law Directory

NEW BEDFORD, Bristol Co.

McLaughlin & Folan, P.C. (AV)

448 County Street, P.O. Box 2095, 02741-2095
Telephone: 508-992-9800
Fax: 508-992-9730

David A. McLaughlin
Mary Alice S. McLaughlin
John F. Folan
Michael J. McGlone
Frank H. Spillane

OF COUNSEL

John J. Kinsley, Jr.
John H. Solomito

For full biographical listings, see the Martindale-Hubbell Law Directory

*SPRINGFIELD,** Hampden Co.

Ely & King (AV)

One Financial Plaza, 1350 Main Street, 01103
Telephone: 413-781-1920
Telecopier: 413-733-3360

MEMBERS OF FIRM

Joseph Buell Ely (1905-1956)
Raymond T. King (1919-1971)
Frederick M. Kingsbury (1924-1968)
Hugh J. Corcoran (1938-1992)
Richard S. Milstein
Donald A. Beaudry
Richard F. Faille
Leland B. Seabury
Gregory A. Schmidt
Pamela Manson
Anthony T. Rice
Russell J. Mawdsley

ASSOCIATE

Donna M. Brown

Representative Clients: Hartford Accident & Indemnity Co.; Albert Steiger Cos.; Shawmut Bank N.A.; Springfield Institution for Savings; St. Paul Fire & Marine Insurance Co.; The Rouse Co.; Tighe & Bond, Inc.; Northeast Utilities.

For full biographical listings, see the Martindale-Hubbell Law Directory

*WORCESTER,** Worcester Co.

Fuller, Rosenberg, Palmer & Beliveau (AV)

14 Harvard Street, P.O. Box 764, 01613
Telephone: 508-755-5225
Telecopier: 508-757-1039

MEMBERS OF FIRM

Albert E. Fuller
Kenneth F. Rosenberg
Peter A. Palmer
Thomas W. Beliveau

ASSOCIATES

Robert W. Towle
Julie Bednarz Russell
Timothy O. Ribley
Mark W. Murphy
Lisa R. Bertonazzi
Mark C. Darling
William J. Mason
Antoinette J. Yitchinsky
Michael I. Mutter
Brian F. Welsh
John J. Finn

For full biographical listings, see the Martindale-Hubbell Law Directory

MacCarthy, Pojani & Hurley (AV)

Worcester Plaza, 446 Main Street, 01608
Telephone: 508-798-2480
Fax: 508-797-9561

Philip J. MacCarthy
Dennis Pojani
John F. Hurley, Jr.
Howard E. Stempler
John Macuga, Jr.

ASSOCIATE

William J. Ritter

Representative Clients: Shawmut Bank N.A.; Melville Corp.; Travelers Insurance Co.; Liberty Mutual Co.; United States Fidelity & Guaranty Co.; Commerce Insurance Co.; Worcester Mutual Insurance Co.; Fleet Bank of Massachusetts, N.A.; Health Plans, Inc.; Marane Oil Corp.

For full biographical listings, see the Martindale-Hubbell Law Directory

Milton, Laurence & Dixon (AV)

100 Front Street, Suite 825, 01608
Telephone: 508-791-6386
Fax: 508-799-4879

MEMBERS OF FIRM

Stanley B. Milton (1899-1992)
Robert C. Milton (1932-1977)
Gerard R. Laurence
Charles W. Dixon
Paul P. O'Connor
Stephen R. Anderson
Paul F. Benoit
Karen A. Loughlin
Beth Anne Bagley
Daniel M. Wrenn
William R. Trainor

(See Next Column)

ASSOCIATE

Karyn E. Polito

Representative Clients: Aetna Life and Casualty Co.; American Policyholders Insurance Co.; CIGNA; Chubb & Sons; Continental Insurance Co.; General Accident Group; Hanover Insurance Co.; Liberty Mutual Insurance Co.; Medical Malpractice Joint Underwriting Association of Massachusetts; St. Paul Tire and Marine Insurance Co.

For full biographical listings, see the Martindale-Hubbell Law Directory

MICHIGAN

*ANN ARBOR,** Washtenaw Co.

Hurbis, Cmejrek & Clinton (AV)

Fifth Floor, City Center Building, 48104
Telephone: 313-761-8358
Fax: 313-761-3134

Charles J. Hurbis
James R. Cmejrek
Mary F. Clinton

Robert Lipnik

Representative Clients: General Motors Corp.; ITT Hartford; Insurance Company of North America; The University of Michigan; North Oakland Medical Center; City of Pontiac; Sears Roebuck and Co.; Montgomery Ward and Co., Inc.; Sedjwick-James, Inc.; Michigan State Accident Fund.

For full biographical listings, see the Martindale-Hubbell Law Directory

Miller, Canfield, Paddock and Stone, P.L.C. (AV)

A Professional Limited Liability Company
Founded in 1852 by Sidney Davy Miller
101 North Main Street, Seventh Floor, 48104-1400
Telephone: 313-663-2445
Fax: 313-747-7147
Detroit, Michigan Office: 150 West Jefferson, Suite 2500, 48226-4415.
Telephone: 313-963-6420.
Fax: 313-496-7500.
Cable Address: "Stem Detroit."
Bloomfield Hills, Michigan Office: Suite 100, Pinehurst Office Center, 1400 North Woodward, 48303-2014.
Telephone: 313-645-5000.
Fax: 313-645-1917.
Grand Rapids, Michigan Office: 1200 Campau Square Plaza, 99 Monroe, N.W., 49503-2639.
Telephone: 616-454-8656.
Fax: 616-776-6322.
Howell, Michigan Office: 121 South Barnard Street, Suite 4, 48843-2305.
Telephone: 517-546-7600.
Telecopier: 517-546-6974.
Kalamazoo, Michigan Office: 444 West Michigan Avenue, 49007-3752.
Telephone: 616-381-7030.
Fax: 616-382-0244.
Lansing, Michigan Office: One Michigan Avenue, Suite 900, 48933-1609.
Telephone: 517-487-2070.
Fax: 517-374-6304.
Monroe, Michigan Office: The Executive Centre, 214 East Elm Avenue, 48161-2682.
Telephone: 313-243-2000.
Fax: 313-243-0901.
Washington, D.C. Office: 1225 Nineteenth Street, N.W., Suite 400. 20036.
Telephone: 202-429-5575; 785-0600.
Fax: 202-331-1118; 785-1234.
Pensacola, Florida Office: 25 West Cedar, 32501.
Telephone: 904-469-1088.
Fax: 904-432-0677.
St. Petersburg, Florida Office: 100 Second Avenue S., Suite 7045, 33701.
Telephone: 813-982-6000.
Fax: 813-892-6002.
Gdansk, Poland Office: Suite 322, Dom Technika Building, UI. Rajska 6, 80-850.
Telephone: 011-485-831-2808.
Fax: 011-485-831-4719.
Warsaw, Poland Office: UI. Marszalkowska 82, Suite 561, 00-517.
Telephone: 011-482-623-6457 and 6458.
Fax: 011-482-623-6459.

RESIDENT PARTNERS

Robert E. Gilbert
Allyn D. Kantor
David A. French

SENIOR ATTORNEY

Marta A. Manildi

Representative Firm Clients: Chrysler Corp.; Comerica, Inc.; City of Detroit, Mich.; Detroit Tigers, Inc.; First of Michigan; Fretter, Inc.; Ford Motor Co.; Ford Motor Credit Co.; Great Lakes Bancorp; Henry Ford Hospital.

(See Next Column)

MILLER, CANFIELD, PADDOCK AND STONE P.L.C., *Ann Arbor—Continued*

For Complete List of Firm Personnel, See General Section

For full biographical listings, see the Martindale-Hubbell Law Directory

BINGHAM FARMS, Oakland Co.

SMALL, TOTH, BALDRIDGE & VAN BELKUM, P.C. (AV)

30100 Telegraph Road Suite 250, 48025-4516
Telephone: 810-647-9595
Facsimile: 810-647-9599

Richard L. Small
John M. Toth
David M. Baldridge
Thomas G. Van Belkum

Michigan Physicians Mutual Liability Insurance Co.; Shelby Insurance Group; Kemper Insurance Group; Mt. Vernon Insurance Co.

For full biographical listings, see the Martindale-Hubbell Law Directory

BIRMINGHAM, Oakland Co.

KELL & LYNCH, P.C. (AV)

300 East Maple Road, Suite 200, 48009
Telephone: 810-647-2333
Fax: 810-647-2781

Michael V. Kell
Margaret A. Lynch

Lissa M. Cinat
Jose L. Patino

For full biographical listings, see the Martindale-Hubbell Law Directory

LACEY & JONES (AV)

600 South Adams Road, Suite 300, 48009-6827
Telephone: 810-433-1414
Fax: 810-433-1241
Grand Rapids, Michigan Office: Suite 330, Ledyard Building, 125 Ottawa Avenue, N.W.
Telephone: 616-776-3641.
FAX: 616-776-3516.

Ralph B. Lacey (1885-1966)
William J. Jones (1908-1991)
Robert B. Lacey (1912-1976)
Francis L. Sylvester (Retired)
Paul Van Hartesveldt (Retired)
John A. Hilgendorf (Retired)

MEMBERS OF FIRM

Theodore A. Lughezzani
Steve N. Yardley
John Hayes
Charles E. Mann
Larry P. Beidelman
Bruce C. Roberts
Lawrence G. Kozaruk
David J. Duthie (Resident, Grand Rapids)
Dennis E. Zacharski
Gerald M. Marcinkoski
Kathleen McNichol Behn

ASSOCIATES

Michael Thomas Reinholm
Johnnie B. Rambus
Sean J. Powers
Timothy M. McAree (Resident, Grand Rapids)
Timothy D. Finegan
Robert H. Orlowski, Jr.
J. Patrick O'Neill
Dawn M. Sutkiewicz

OF COUNSEL

Walter F. Reebel
Michele Kilar Kemler
Thomas J. Sullivan

Representative Clients: Alexsis, Inc.; Ameritech; Chrysler Corporation; CIGNA; Liberty Mutual Insurance Company; Meijer, Inc.; Metropolitan Prop. & Casualty; Michigan Hospital Association; Penn General Services; Travelers Insurance Company.

For full biographical listings, see the Martindale-Hubbell Law Directory

BLOOMFIELD HILLS, Oakland Co.

HOWARD & HOWARD ATTORNEYS, P.C. (AV)

The Pinehurst Office Center, Suite 101, 1400 North Woodward Avenue, 48304-2856
Telephone: 810-645-1483
Telecopier: 810-645-1568
Kalamazoo, Michigan Office: The Kalamazoo Building, Suite 400, 107 West Michigan Avenue.
Telephone: 616-382-1483.
Telecopier: 616-382-1568.
Lansing, Michigan Office: The Phoenix Building, Suite 500, 222 Washington Square, North.
Telephone: 517-485-1483.
Telecopier: 517-485-1568.
Peoria, Illinois Office: Howard & Howard, P.C., The Creve Coeur Building, Suite 200, 321 Liberty Street.
Telephone: 309-672-1483.
Telecopier: 309-672-1568.

Jon H. Kingsepp

Representative Clients: For Representative Client list, see General Practice, Bloomfield Hills, MI.

(See Next Column)

For Complete List of Firm Personnel, See General Section

For full biographical listings, see the Martindale-Hubbell Law Directory

RICHARD A. PATTERSON, P.C. (AV)

6905 Telegraph Road Suite 215, 48301
Telephone: 810-647-6950
Facsimile: 810-645-0917

Richard A. Patterson

Representative Clients: Metropolitan Life; Ohio National Life; The Credit Life Insurance Company; Travelers Insurance Co.; Imperial Casualty and Indemnity.

For full biographical listings, see the Martindale-Hubbell Law Directory

DAVID D. PATTON & ASSOCIATES, P.C. (AV)

100 Bloomfield Hills Parkway, Suite 110, 48304
Telephone: 810-258-6020
Fax: 810-258-6052

David D. Patton

Ellen Bartman Jannette
James A. Reynolds, Jr.
Patricia C. White
David H. Patton (1912-1993)

For full biographical listings, see the Martindale-Hubbell Law Directory

STROBL AND MANOOGIAN, P.C. (AV)

300 East Long Lake Road, Suite 200, 48304-2376
Telephone: 810-645-0306
Facsimile: 810-645-2690

Thomas J. Strobl
Brian C. Manoogian
John Sharp
James A. Rocchio
Kieran F. Cunningham
Michael E. Thoits
James D. Wilson

James T. Dunn
Sara S. Lisznyai
Brian M. Gottry
Thomas H. Kosik
Keith S. King
Pamela S. Ritter
Robert F. Boesiger
Douglas Young

OF COUNSEL

Glenn S. Arendsen

Representative Clients: Scibal Insurance Group; Home Insurance Company; Marsh & McLennan; Chubb Insurance Group; International Insurance Company; Republic Insurance Company; Farmers Insurance Group; K & K Insurance Group, Inc.

For full biographical listings, see the Martindale-Hubbell Law Directory

LAW OFFICES OF THOMAS J. TRENTA, P.C. (AV)

33 Bloomfield Hills Parkway Suite 145, 48304-2945
Telephone: 810-258-9610
Fax: 810-258-5132

Thomas J. Trenta

Richard A. Joslin, Jr.

OF COUNSEL

James F. Jordan

Representative Clients: National Union Fire Insurance Company; Secura Insurance Co.; Western indemnity Insurance Co.

For full biographical listings, see the Martindale-Hubbell Law Directory

*DETROIT,** Wayne Co.

BUTZEL LONG, A PROFESSIONAL CORPORATION (AV)

Suite 900, 150 West Jefferson, 48226
Telephone: 313-225-7000
Telecopier: 313-225-7080
Birmingham, Michigan Office: Suite 200, 32270 Telegraph Road.
Telephone: 810-258-1616.
Telecopier: 810-258-1439.
Lansing, Michigan Office: 118 West Ottawa Street.
Telephone: 517-372-6622.
Telecopier: 517-372-6672.
Ann Arbor, Michigan Office: Suite 400, 121 West Washington.
Telephone: 313-995-3110.
Telecopier: 313-995-1777.
Grosse Pointe Farms, Michigan Office: Suite 260, 21 Kercheval.
Telephone: 313-886-5446.
Telecopier: 313-886-2114.

Douglas G. Graham
Xhafer Orhan
John Henry Dudley, Jr.
Richard E. Rassel
Edward M. Kronk
Philip J. Kessler
Michael M. Jacob (Birmingham)
Dennis B. Schultz
Daniel P. Malone
Keefe A. Brooks

(See Next Column)

BUTZEL LONG A PROFESSIONAL CORPORATION—*Continued*

James E. Wynne
Edward M. Kalinka
Gordon J. Walker (Birmingham)
Richard P. Saslow
Dennis K. Egan
Jack J. Mazzara
Bruce L. Sendek
Susan Carino Nystrom
Leonard M. Niehoff
Lynn Abraham Sheehy
Sheldon H. Klein

William D. Vanderhoef
J. Michael Huget
Ronald E. Reynolds
Phillip C. Korovesis
Richard T. Hewlett
Eugene H. Boyle, Jr.

Representative Clients: Blue Cross/Blue Shield of Michigan; Jackson National Life Insurance Co.

For Complete List of Firm Personnel, See General Section

For full biographical listings, see the Martindale-Hubbell Law Directory

DICKINSON, WRIGHT, MOON, VAN DUSEN & FREEMAN (AV)

500 Woodward Avenue, Suite 4000, 48226-3425
Telephone: 313-223-3500
Facsimile: 313-223-3598
Bloomfield Hills, Michigan Office: 525 North Woodward Avenue, Suite 2000.
Telephone: 810-433-7200.
Facsimile: 810-433-7274.
Grand Rapids, Michigan Office: 200 Ottawa Avenue, N.W., Suite 900.
Telephone: 616-458-1300.
Facsimile: 616-458-6753.
Lansing, Michigan Office: Suite 200, 215 South Washington Square.
Telephone: 517-371-1730.
Facsimile: 517-487-4700.
Washington, D.C. Office: Suite 800, 1901 L Street, N.W.
Telephone: 202-457-0160.
Facsimile: 202-659-1559.
Chicago, Illinois Office: 225 West Washington, Suite 400.
Telephone: 312-220-0300.
Facsimile: 312-220-0021.
Warsaw, Poland Office: 46 Wilcza Street, 4th Floor, 00-679.
Telephone: (48-22) 299-241.
Facsimile: (48-2) 628-4107. Komertel Satellite Phone: (48-39) 121-510.

MEMBERS OF FIRM

Richard A. Glaser (Grand Rapids Office)
Francis R. Ortiz
Barbara Hughes Erard
Thomas G. McNeill
Jeffery V. Stuckey (Lansing Office)
Mary Elizabeth Kelly
Daniel M. Brinks (Bloomfield Hills Office)
Jerry L. Johnson
Brian K. Zahra

ASSOCIATES

Bruce R. Byrd
Stephanie Dawkins Davis
Andrew S. Doctoroff
Christine R. Essique
Michelle Thurber Freese
Nanci J. Grant (Bloomfield Hills Office)
K. Scott Hamilton
Jana L. Henkel-Benjamin
Kelli L. Kerbawy (Bloomfield Hills Office)
Douglas P. Lane
Deborah A. Lee (Lansing Office)
Sandra J. LeFevre
Edwin J. Lukas
Sarah A. McLaren
Richard W. Paige
Daniel D. Quick
Marian Keidan Seltzer
Rock A. Wood (Grand Rapids Office)

For Complete List of Firm Personnel, See General Section

For full biographical listings, see the Martindale-Hubbell Law Directory

DISE & GUREWITZ, P.C. (AV)

3600 Cadillac Tower, 48226
Telephone: 313-963-8155
Telefax: 313-963-8438

John H. Dise, Jr.
Harold Gurewitz

Gina Ursula Puzzuoli
Margaret Sind Raben
G. Gus Morris
Elizabeth M. Malone

OF COUNSEL

Timothy Downs
Gene A. Farber

For full biographical listings, see the Martindale-Hubbell Law Directory

EGGENBERGER, EGGENBERGER, MCKINNEY, WEBER & HOFMEISTER, P.C. (AV)

42nd Floor Penobscot Building, 48226
Telephone: 313-961-9722

William J. Eggenberger (1900-1984)
William D. Eggenberger
Robert E. Eggenberger
John P. McKinney
Stephen L. Weber
Paul D. Hofmeister

(See Next Column)

R. Scott Mills
Mary T. Humbert
James B. Eggenberger

Representative Clients: Central National Insurance of Omaha; Great Central Insurance Co.; Inland Mutual Insurance Co.; Midwest Mutual Insurance Co.; Motor Land Insurance Co.; Pioneer Mutual Casualty Co.; Preferred Risk Mutual Insurance Company of Des Moines Iowa; Puritan Insurance Co.; State Farm Fire and Casualty Co.; State Farm Mutual Automobile Insurance Co.

For full biographical listings, see the Martindale-Hubbell Law Directory

FOSTER, MEADOWS & BALLARD, P.C. (AV)

3200 Penobscot Building, 48226
Telephone: 313-961-3234
Cable Address: "Foster"
Telex: 23-5823
Facsimile: 313-961-6184

Sparkman D. Foster (1897-1967)
John L. Foster
Charles R. Hrdlicka
Paul D. Galea
Richard A. Dietz
Robert H. Fortunate
Robert G. Lahiff
Camille A. Raffa-Dietz

Michael J. Liddane
Paul A. Kettunen

OF COUNSEL

John F. Langs
John A. Mundell, Jr.

Representative Clients: Alexander & Alexander; Frank B. Hall & Company of New York; Great American Insurance Co.; Utica Mutual Insurance.

For full biographical listings, see the Martindale-Hubbell Law Directory

GARAN, LUCOW, MILLER, SEWARD, COOPER & BECKER, P.C. (AV)

1000 Woodbridge Place, 48207-3192
Telephone: 313-446-1530
Fax: 313-259-0450
Grand Blanc, Michigan Office: 8332 Office Park Drive.
Telephone: 810-695-3700.
Fax: 810-695-6488.
Port Huron, Michigan Office: Port Huron Office Center, 511 Fort Street, Suite 505.
Telephone: 810-985-4400.
Fax: 810-985-4107.
Ann Arbor, Michigan Office: 101 North Main Street, Suite 801.
Telephone: 313-930-5600.
Fax: 313-930-0043.
Troy, Michigan Office: 2301 West Big Beaver Road, Suite 212.
Telephone: 810-649-7600.
Fax: 810-649-5438.
Mount Clemens Office: Towne Square Development, 10 S. Main Street, Suite 307.
Telephone: 810-954-3800.
Fax: 810-954-3803.

Matthew A. Seward
David J. Cooper
James L. Borin
Thomas F. Myers
Dennis P. Partridge
John E. McSorley
Lamont E. Buffington
Thomas L. Misuraca
Rosalind Rochkind
James J. Hayes, Jr.
Thomas W. Emery
Joseph Crystal
Boyd E. Chapin, Jr.
Mark C. Smiley

Ian C. Simpson
Patricia L. Patterson
Daniel S. Saylor
Peter B. Worden, Jr.
Charlotte H. Johnson
David M. Shafer
Lloyd G. Johnson
John J. Gillooly
Robert D. Goldstein
Michael J. Paolucci
Michael J. Severyn
Michael J. DePolo
C. David Miller, II
Robert J. Squiers, Jr.
David J. Langford
Anne K. Newcomer
Robert A. Obringer
Eun (Ellen) G. Ha

OF COUNSEL

Daniel L. Garan
Albert A. Miller
Roy E. Castetter
Beth A. Andrews
Nancy J. Bourget

Counsel for: Allstate Insurance Co.; Sears, Roebuck & Co.; Liberty Mutual Insurance Co.; Continental Insurance Companies.

For Complete List of Firm Personnel, See General Section

For full biographical listings, see the Martindale-Hubbell Law Directory

HAYDUK, ANDREWS & HYPNAR, P.C. (AV)

444 Penobscot Building, 48226
Telephone: 313-962-4500
Fax: 313-964-6577

(See Next Column)

HAYDUK, ANDREWS & HYPNAR P.C., *Detroit—Continued*

Mark S. Hayduk
Robin K. Andrews
Mark A. Hypnar
Paul J. Ellison
Sean Angus McPhillips
Robert J. Heimbuch

Representative Clients: Farmers Insurance Group; Admiral Insurance Co.; Safeco Insurance Cos.; Prudential-LMI; American Modern Home Insurance; Western Heritage Insurance; Northpointe Insurance; Shelby Mutual Insurance; Scibal Ins. Co.

For full biographical listings, see the Martindale-Hubbell Law Directory

HOUGHTON, POTTER, SWEENEY & BRENNER, A PROFESSIONAL CORPORATION (AV)

The Guardian Building, 500 Griswold Street, Suite 3300, 48226-3806
Telephone: 313-964-0050
Facsimile: 313-964-4005

James E. Brenner
Mark W. McInerney

Mary C. Dirkes

LEGAL SUPPORT PERSONNEL

LEGAL ASSISTANTS

Ann E. Adams
Janet C. Driver

Representative Clients: American States Insurance Cos.; Chubb Life America; Hartford Life Cos.; Metropolitan Life Insurance Co.; Mutual of Omaha; New England Mutual Life Insurance Co.; North American Life and Casualty Co.; Phoenix Mutual Life Insurance Co.; ITT Life Insurance Co.; Fidelity and Guaranty Life Insurance Co.

For full biographical listings, see the Martindale-Hubbell Law Directory

KERR, RUSSELL AND WEBER (AV)

One Detroit Center, 500 Woodward Avenue, Suite 2500, 48226-3406
Telephone: 313-961-0200
Telecopier: 313-961-0388
Bloomfield Hills, Michigan Office: 3883 Telegraph Road.
Telephone: 810-649-5990.
East Lansing, Michigan Office: 1301 North Hagadorn Road.
Telephone: 517-336-6767.

Richard D. Weber
Roy H. Christiansen
William A. Sankbeil
Patrick McLain
Daniel G. Beyer
James R. Case
Stephen D. McGraw
Edward C. Cutlip, Jr.
Catherine Bonczak Edwards
Christopher A. Cornwall

OF COUNSEL

Robert G. Russell

For Complete List of Firm Personnel, See General Section

For full biographical listings, see the Martindale-Hubbell Law Directory

KITCH, DRUTCHAS, WAGNER & KENNEY, P.C. (AV)

One Woodward, Tenth Floor, 48226-3412
Telephone: 313-965-7900
Fax: 313-965-7403
Lansing, Michigan Office: 120 Washington Square, North, Suite 805, One Michigan Avenue, 48933-1609.
Telephone: 517-372-6430.
Fax: 517-372-0441.
Macomb County Office: Towne Square Development, 10 South Main Street, Suite 301, Mount Clemens, 48043-7903.
Telephone: 810-463-9770.
Fax: 810-463-8994.
Toledo, Ohio Office: 405 Madison Avenue, Suite 1500, 43604-1235.
Telephone: 419-243-4006.
Fax: 419-243-7333.
Troy, Michigan Office: 3001 West Big Beaver Road, Suite 200, 48084-3103.
Telephone: 810-637-3500.
Fax: 810-637-6630.
Ann Arbor, Michigan Office: 303 Detroit Street, Suite 400, P.O. Box 8610, 48107-8610.
Telephone: 313-994-7600.
Fax: 313-994-7626.

Richard A. Kitch
Ronald E. Wagner
Jeremiah J. Kenney (Managing Principal)
Ralph F. Valitutti, Jr.
Richard R. DeNardis
Mona K. Majzoub
Harry J. Sherbrook
Anthony G. Arnone
Mark D. Willmarth (Principal)
Charles W. Fisher
Clyde M. Metzger, III (Principal, Ann Arbor Office)
Thomas J. Foley
Victor J. Abela (Principal, Troy Office)
Jeffrey H. Chilton
James H. Hughesian
John P. Ryan (Principal, Lansing Office)
William D. Chaklos
Steve N. Cheolas (Principal, Macomb County Office)
Susan Healy Zitterman
William Vertes (Principal, Lansing Office)

(See Next Column)

William A. Tanoury (Principal, Ann Arbor Office)
John J. Ramar
John Stephen Wasung (Principal, Toledo, Ohio Office)
Bruce R. Shaw
Karen Bernard Berkery (Associate Principal)
Susan M. Ramage (Associate Principal, Lansing Office)
Pamela Hobbs
Daniel R. Corbet
Brian R. Garves
Daniel R. Shirey
Daniel J. Niemann (Associate Principal, Ann Arbor Office)
William P. O'Leary
David M. Kraus
Verlin R. Nafziger
Robert A. Fehniger (Macomb County Office)
Christopher P. Dinverno
Kenneth M. Essad
Steven Waclawski
Ronald S. Bowling
Sara Mae Gerbitz
Linda M. Garbarino
Antonio Mauti
Lawrence David Rosenstock
Thomas R. Shimmel
Susan Marie Beutel
Carole S. Empey (Ann Arbor Office)
Debra S. Hirsch (Lansing Office)
David R. Nauts
Richard T. Counsman
Karen Ann Smyth
Mark A. Wisniewski
Julia Kelly McNelis
J. Mark Trimble (Toledo, Ohio Office)
Sharon A. DeWaele
Arthur F. Brandt
Dean A. Etsios
Michael K. McCoy
Stephen R. Brzezinski
Kent Riesen (Toledo, Ohio Office)
Joseph P. McGill
Paula M. Burgess (Toledo, Ohio Office)
Lisa M. Iulianelli
Fred J. Fresard
Maureen Rouse-Ayoub
Matthew M. Walton (Mount Clemens Office)
Barbara A. Martin
Carol S. Allis (Ann Arbor Office)
Terese L. Farhat
Richard P. Cuneo
Kim J. Sveska
Kathleen P. Knol (Ann Arbor Office)
David A. Schoolcraft (Lansing Office)
Lauri A. Read (Troy Office)
Lisa DiPonio
John J. Koselka (Ann Arbor Office)
David J. Allen
Richard M. Mitchell
Mary Catherine Storen
Diane M. Carpentier
Robert W. Lipp, III
Cullen B. McKinney
Christine G. Strasser
Norman P. Moore, Jr.
Carla M. Calabrese
Fredericia J. Craig
Pamela A. Boland
Michael M. McNamara
Jeffrey T. Gorcyca
Laura L. Witty

Representative Clients: AETNA Casualty & Surety; Amerisure; CNA Insurance Companies; Home Insurance; Michigan Hospital Association Insurance Co.; State Farm Insurance Company; St. Paul; The Travelers.

For Complete List of Firm Personnel, See General Section

For full biographical listings, see the Martindale-Hubbell Law Directory

LUPO, KOCZKUR & PETRELLA, P.C. (AV)

1000 First National Building, 48226
Telephone: 313-964-0110
Fax: 313-964-3711

Dane A. Lupo
Paul S. Koczkur
Marisa C. Petrella
Bradley S. Mitseff
Sandra M. Vozza
Dehai Tao

Michael P. Fresard

For full biographical listings, see the Martindale-Hubbell Law Directory

MAGER, MERCER, SCOTT & ALBER, P.C. (AV)

2400 First National Building, 48226
Telephone: 313-965-1700
Facsimile: 313-965-3690
Macomb County Office: 18285 Ten Mile Road, Suite 100, Roseville, Michigan.
Telephone: 810-771-1100.

George J. Mager, Jr.
Phillip G. Alber
Lawrence M. Scott (Resident at Roseville Office)
George D. Mercer
Raymond C. McVeigh
Michael R. Alberty
Bruce H. Hoffman
Jeffrey M. Frank
Michael A. Schwartz

Representative Clients: American States Insurance Co.; CIGNA; Federal Insurance Co.; Reliance Insurance Co.; State Farm Insurance Co.; United Insurance Company of America.

For full biographical listings, see the Martindale-Hubbell Law Directory

MILLER, CANFIELD, PADDOCK AND STONE, P.L.C. (AV)

A Professional Limited Liability Company
Founded in 1852 by Sidney Davy Miller
150 West Jefferson, Suite 2500, 48226-4415
Telephone: 313-963-6420
Fax: 313-496-7500
Cable Address: "Stem Detroit"
Detroit, Michigan Office: 150 West Jefferson, Suite 2500, 48226-4415.
Telephone: 313-963-6420.
Fax: 313-496-7500.
Cable Address: "Stem Detroit."

(See Next Column)

MILLER, CANFIELD, PADDOCK AND STONE P.L.C.—*Continued*

Ann Arbor, Michigan Office: 101 North Main Street, 7th Floor, 48104-1400.
Telephone: 313-663-2445.
Fax: 313-747-7147.
Bloomfield Hills, Michigan Office: Suite 100, Pinehurst Office Center, 1400 North Woodward, 48303-2014.
Telephone: 313-645-5000.
Fax: 313-645-1917.
Grand Rapids, Michigan Office: 1200 Campau Square Plaza, 99 Monroe, N.W., 49503-2639.
Telephone: 616-454-8656.
Fax: 616-776-6322.
Howell, Michigan Office: 121 South Barnard Street, Suite 4, 48843-2305.
Telephone: 517-546-7600.
Telecopier: 517-546-6974.
Kalamazoo, Michigan Office: 444 West Michigan Avenue, 49007-3752.
Telephone: 616-381-7030.
Fax: 616-382-0244.
Lansing, Michigan Office: One Michigan Avenue, Suite 900, 48933-1609.
Telephone: 517-487-2070.
Fax: 517-374-6304.
Monroe, Michigan Office: The Executive Centre, 214 East Elm Avenue, 48161-2682.
Telephone: 313-243-2000.
Fax: 313-243-0901.
Washington, D.C. Office: 1225 Nineteenth Street, N.W., Suite 400. 20036.
Telephone: 202-429-5575; 785-0600.
Fax: 202-331-1118; 785-1234.
Pensacola, Florida Office: 25 West Cedar, 32501.
Telephone: 904-469-1088.
Fax: 904-432-0677.
St. Petersburg, Florida Office: 100 Second Avenue S., Suite 7045, 33701.
Telephone: 813-982-6000.
Fax: 813-892-6002.
Gdansk, Poland Office: Suite 322, Dom Technika Building, Ul. Rajska 6, 80-850.
Telephone: 011-485-831-2808.
Fax: 011-485-831-4719.
Warsaw, Poland Office: Ul. Marszalkowska 82, Suite 561, 00-517.
Telephone: 011-482-623-6457 and 6458.
Fax: 011-482-623-6459.

MEMBERS OF FIRM

Gilbert E. Gove
Carl H. von Ende
Allyn D. Kantor (Ann Arbor Office)
Charles E. Ritter (Kalamazoo Office)
Thomas G. Parachini
Gregory L. Curtner
W. Mack Faison
Joseph F. Galvin
Clarence L. Pozza, Jr.
Michael W. Hartmann
Larry J. Saylor
James G. Vantine, Jr. (Kalamazoo and Grand Rapids Offices)
Leland D. Barringer
Marjory G. Basile
Ryan H. Haywood
Ronald E. Baylor (Kalamazoo Office)
Stephen J. Ott
Michael P. Coakley
James E. Spurr (Kalamazoo Office)
Robert D. VanderLaan (Grand Rapids Office)
Mark T. Boonstra
David A. French (Ann Arbor Office)
Le Roy L. Asher, Jr.
Pamela Chapman Enslen (Kalamazoo Office)
Richard T. Urbis
Richard F. X. Urisko
Steven A. Roach

OF COUNSEL

George E. Bushnell, Jr.

SENIOR ATTORNEYS

Abigail Elias
Lawrence M. Dudek
Irene Bruce Hathaway
Marta A. Manildi (Ann Arbor Office)
Gary W. Faria

ASSOCIATES

Brian J. Doren
Ellen M. Tickner
Kathryn L. Ossian
Gary E. Mitchell (Grand Rapids Office)
Ballard Jay Yelton III (Kalamazoo Office)
Thomas R. Cox
Robert J. Haddad
Erich H. Hintzen
Frederick A. Acomb
Meg Hackett Carrier (Grand Rapids Office)

Representative Firm Clients: Chrysler Corp.; Comerica, Inc.; City of Detroit, Mich.; Detroit Tigers, Inc.; First of Michigan; Fretter, Inc.; Ford Motor Co.; Ford Motor Credit Co.; Great Lakes Bancorp; Henry Ford Hospital.

For Complete List of Firm Personnel, See General Section

For full biographical listings, see the Martindale-Hubbell Law Directory

RUTLEDGE, MANION, RABAUT, TERRY & THOMAS, P.C. (AV)

2300 Buhl Building, 48226
Telephone: 313-965-6100
Telefax: 313-965-6558

(*See Next Column*)

Alvin A. Rutledge
Paul J. Manion
Vincent C. Rabaut, Jr.
Christopher L. Terry
David M. Thomas
Michael A. Gunderson
Elmer L. Roller
Anthony J. Calati
Lisa Sabon Anstess
Mary L. Dresbach
Roderick W. Coons, II
David A. Brauer
Patrick D. Filbin
Karen M. Dempsey
Matthew A. Brauer

LEGAL SUPPORT PERSONNEL

PARALEGALS

Barbara J. Kennedy
Gloria A. Lambright
Laura A. Matheson
Vonya K. Gagnon
Cheryl D. Cooke
Doreen A. Honn

For full biographical listings, see the Martindale-Hubbell Law Directory

SCHUREMAN, FRAKES, GLASS & WULFMEIER (AV)

440 East Congress, Fourth Floor, 48226
Telephone: 313-961-1500
Telecopier: 313-961-1087
Harbor Springs, Michigan Office: One Spring Street Sq., 49740.
Telephone: 616-526-1145.
Telecopier: 616-526-9343.

MEMBERS OF FIRM

Jeptha W. Schureman
John C. Frakes, Jr.
Charles F. Glass
LeRoy H. Wulfmeier, III
Cheryl L. Chandler
David M. Ottenwess

ASSOCIATES

Daniel J. Dulworth
John J. Moran
Paul A. Salyers
Erane C. Washington

Reference: Comerica.

For full biographical listings, see the Martindale-Hubbell Law Directory

SIEMION, HUCKABAY, BODARY, PADILLA, MORGANTI & BOWERMAN, P.C. (AV)

1700 Penobscot Building, 48226
Telephone: 313-962-1700

Robert P. Siemion
Charles A. Huckabay
James W. Bodary
Gerald V. Padilla
Raymond W. Morganti
Cathy Rogers Bowerman
Michael J. Rinkel
Mark A. Roberts
Barbara Ann Rush
Arnold J. Matusz
Steven B. Sinkoff

Eugene Kelly Cullen
Thomas M. Caplis
Karen M. Leonetti
Donna Montano Severyn

For full biographical listings, see the Martindale-Hubbell Law Directory

TIMMIS & INMAN (AV)

300 Talon Centre, 48207
Telephone: 313-396-4200
Telecopier: 313-396-4228

MEMBERS OF FIRM

Robert E. Graziani
Mark W. Peyser

ASSOCIATE

Amy Lynn Ryntz

Representative Clients: Continental Insurance Company; Transamerica Insurance Group.

For Complete List of Firm Personnel, See General Section

For full biographical listings, see the Martindale-Hubbell Law Directory

VANDEVEER GARZIA, PROFESSIONAL CORPORATION (AV)

Suite 1600, 333 West Fort Street, 48226
Telephone: 313-961-4880
Fax: 313-961-3822
Oakland County Office: 220 Park Street, Suite 300, Birmingham, Michigan.
Telephone: 810-645-0100.
Fax: 810-645-2430.
Macomb County Office: 50 Crocker Boulevard, Mount Clemens, Michigan.
Telephone: 810-468-4880.
Fax: 810-465-7159.
Kent County Office: 510 Grand Plaza Place, 220 Lyon Square, Grand Rapids, Michigan.
Telephone: 616-366-8600.
Fax: 616-786-9095.
Holland, Michigan Office: 1121 Ottawa Beach Road, Suite 140.
Telephone: 616-399-8600.
Fax: 616-786-9095.

(*See Next Column*)

VANDEVEER GARZIA PROFESSIONAL CORPORATION, *Detroit—Continued*

Thomas P. Rockwell
James A. Sullivan
Michael M. Hathaway
John J. Lynch, III (Resident, Oakland County Office)
Thomas M. Peters
James K. Thome (Resident, Oakland County Office)
Cecil F. Boyle, Jr. (Resident, Oakland County Office)
Ronald L. Cornell (Resident, Macomb County Office)
William J. Heaphy (Kent County and Holland Offices)
Gary Alan Miller
William L. Kiriazis
Cynthia E. Merry
Dennis B. Cotter
Daniel P. Steele
Shelley K. Miller (Resident, Oakland County Office)
Terrance P. Lynch

OF COUNSEL

John M. Heaphy
Roy C. Hebert

Representative Clients: Aetna Casualty and Surety Co.; Bic Corp.; CNA Insurance Co.; Chubb Insurance; Farmers Insurance Group; Home Insurance Co.; Maryland Casualty Co.; Michigan Property & Casualty; Republic Franklin Insurance Co.; Sentry Insurance Co.; Travelers Insurance Co.; Transamerica Insurance Co.

For Complete List of Firm Personnel, See General Section

For full biographical listings, see the Martindale-Hubbell Law Directory

FARMINGTON HILLS, Oakland Co.

KAUFMAN AND PAYTON (AV)

200 Northwestern Financial Center, 30833 Northwestern Highway, 48334
Telephone: 810-626-5000
Telefacsimile: 810-626-2843
Grand Rapids, Michigan Office: 420 Trust Building.
Telephone: 616-459-4200.
Fax: 616-459-4929.
Traverse City, Michigan Office: 122 West State Street.
Telephone: 616-947-4050.
Fax: 616-947-7321.

Alan Jay Kaufman
Donald L. Payton
Kenneth C. Letherwood
Stephen R. Levine
Thomas L. Vitu
Ralph C. Chapa, Jr.
Raymond I. Foley, II
Jeffrey K. Van Hattum
Leo D. Neville

For full biographical listings, see the Martindale-Hubbell Law Directory

STILL, NEMIER, TOLARI & LANDRY, P.C. (AV)

37000 Grand River, Suite 300, 48335
Telephone: 810-476-6900
Fax: 810-476-6564

William R. Still
Craig L. Nemier
Jeffrey L. Tolari
David B. Landry
Mark R. Johnson
Rik Mazzeo
Catherine L. West
Michelle E. Mathieu
Christopher A. Todd
Thomas S. McLeod
Victoria W. Ryan

OF COUNSEL

Terry E. Pietryga
Veeder Ann Willey

Representative Clients: Amerisure/Michigan Mutual Insurance Co.; Chubb Group of Insurance Cos.; Citizens Insurance Co.; Crum & Forster (U.S. Insurance Group); Employers Insurance of Wausau; Stonewall/Dixie Insurance Co.; Travelers Insurance Co.

For full biographical listings, see the Martindale-Hubbell Law Directory

*FLINT,** Genesee Co.

GROVES, DECKER & WYATT, PROFESSIONAL CORPORATION (AV)

2357 Stone Bridge Drive, 48532
Telephone: 810-732-6920
Fax: 810-732-9015
East Lansing, Michigan Office: 2760 East Lansing Drive, Suite 4.
Telephone: 517-332-7715.
Facsimile: 517-332-4405.

Harvey R. Groves
Lee A. Decker
George H. Wyatt III
William L. Meuleman III
Thomas J. Ruth
Cameron D. Reddy

Representative Clients: Birmingham Fire Insurance Co.; Granite State Insurance Co.; Hastings Mutual Insurance Co.; Insurance Company of the State of Pennsylvania; Lake States Insurance Co.; Lexington Insurance Co.; National Union Fire Insurance Co.; New Hampshire Insurance Co.; Sumitomo Fire and Marine Insurance Co.; Zurich Insurance Co.

For full biographical listings, see the Martindale-Hubbell Law Directory

LAW OFFICES OF PATRICK M. KIRBY A PROFESSIONAL CORPORATION (AV)

G1335 South Linden Road, Suite G, 48532
Telephone: 810-230-0833
Fax: 810-230-8222

Patrick M. Kirby

Todd O. Pope

Representative Clients: Brotherhood Mutual Insurance Co.; K & K Insurance Group.

For full biographical listings, see the Martindale-Hubbell Law Directory

*GAYLORD,** Otsego Co.

BENSINGER, COTANT, MENKES & AARDEMA, P.C. (AV)

308 West Main Street, P.O. Box 1000, 49735
Telephone: 517-732-7536
Fax: 517-732-4922
Grand Rapids, Michigan Office: 983 Spaulding Avenue, S.E.
Telephone: 616-949-7963.
Fax: 616-949-5264.
Marquette, Michigan Office: 122 West Bluff.
Telephone: 906-225-1000.
Fax: 906-225-0818.

Richard G. Bensinger
James C. Cotant
Michael E. Menkes
Patrick J. Michaels
James F. Pagels
Steven C. Byram
Michael J. Harrelson
William M. Fury
Brian P. McMahon

Representative Clients: Accident Fund of Michigan; Auto-Owner Insurance Co.; Citizens/Hanover Insurance Co.; Farm Bureau Mutual Insurance Co.; Employers Reinsurance Co,; Lake State Mutual Insurance Co.; Michigan Hospital Association; Michigan Licensed Beverage Association; Physicians Insurance Co. of Michigan; State Farm Mutual Insurance Co.

For full biographical listings, see the Martindale-Hubbell Law Directory

*GRAND RAPIDS,** Kent Co.

ALLABEN, MASSIE, VANDER WEYDEN & TIMMER (AV)

Suite 850, Commerce Building, 5 Lyon Street, N.W., 49503
Telephone: 616-774-2182
Fax: 616-774-0602

MEMBERS OF FIRM

Fred Roland Allaben (1901-1985)
Sam F. Massie, Jr.
Keith A. Vander Weyden
John J. Timmer
Robert W. Bandeen

Representative Clients: American Syayes Insurance Co.; Michigan Mutual Liability Co.; National Union Insurance Cos.; Fidelity & Casualty Company of New York; U.S. Aircraft Insurance Group; Union Insurance Co.; The Continental Insurance Co.; Hanover Insurance Co.; Royal Globe Insurance Co.

For Complete List of Firm Personnel, See General Section

For full biographical listings, see the Martindale-Hubbell Law Directory

BENSINGER, COTANT, MENKES & AARDEMA, P.C. (AV)

983 Spaulding Avenue, S.E., 49546
Telephone: 616-949-7963
Fax: 616-949-5264
Gaylord, Michigan Office: 308 West Main, P.O. Box 1000.
Telephone: 517-732-7536.
Fax: 517-732-4922.
Marquette, Michigan Office: 122 West Bluff.
Telephone: 906-225-1000.
Fax: 906-225-0818.

Robert Bryan Aardema (Resident)
Kerr L. Moyer (Resident)
Brian W. Whitelaw (Resident)
Dale L. Arndt (Resident)

Representative Clients: Allstate Insurance Co.; Physicians Insurance Co. of Michigan; State Farm Mutual Insurance Co.; Foremost Insurance Co.; Northern Mutual Insurance; Auto-Owners Insurance Co.; Insurance Equities Corp.; Osteopathic Mutual Insurance Co. Northbrook Insurance Co.; Michigan Hospital Association.

For full biographical listings, see the Martindale-Hubbell Law Directory

BREMER, WADE, NELSON, LOHR & COREY (AV)

600 Three Mile Road, N.W., 49504-1601
Telephone: 616-784-4434
Fax: 616-784-7322

MEMBERS OF FIRM

William M. Bremer
Michael D. Wade
Phillip J. Nelson
James H. Lohr
Michael J. Corey

(See Next Column)

BREMER, WADE, NELSON, LOHR & COREY—*Continued*

ASSOCIATES

Michael S. Dantuma
J. Mark Cooney
Cheryl L. Bart
Barbara L. Olafsson

LEGAL SUPPORT PERSONNEL

Kathleen A. Fitzpatrick

Representative Clients: Auto Club Insurance Co.; The Continental Insurance Cos.; Continental Loss Adjustment Services; Citizens Insurance Company of America; The Doctor's Company; Insurance Equities Corp.; Medical Protective Co.; Meridian Mutual Insurance Co.; Ranger Insurance; Secura Insurance Co.

For full biographical listings, see the Martindale-Hubbell Law Directory

BUCHANAN & BOS (AV)

300 Ottawa N.W., Suite 800, 49503
Telephone: 616-458-1224
Fax: 616-458-0608

MEMBERS OF FIRM

John C. Buchanan
Carole D. Bos
Bradley K. Glazier
Lee T. Silver

ASSOCIATES

Raymond S. Kent
Jane M. Beckering
Richard A. Stevens
Susan Wilson Keener
Gwen E. Buday
Anne M. Frye
Brian K. Lawson
Nancy K. Haynes

Representative Clients: Cigna Group of Insurance Companies; Commercial Union Insurance Companies; Cranford Insurance; Kemper Group of Insurance Companies.

For full biographical listings, see the Martindale-Hubbell Law Directory

CHOLETTE, PERKINS & BUCHANAN (AV)

900 Campau Square Plaza Building, 99 Monroe Avenue, N.W., 49503
Telephone: 616-774-2131
Fax: 616-774-7016

MEMBERS OF FIRM

Calvin R. Danhof
Frederick W. Bleakley
Reynolds A. Brander, Jr.
Bruce M. Bieneman
William J. Warren
Donald C. Exelby
Thomas H. Cypher
William A. Brengle
Alfred J. Parent
Charles H. Worsfold
Michael P. McCasey
Marc A. Kidder
Michael C. Mysliwiec
Evan L. MacFarlane
John A. Quinn
Albert J. Engel, III
Stephen C. Oldstrom
William E. McDonald, Jr.
Mark E. Fatum
Richard K. Grover, Jr.
David J. DeGraw

ASSOCIATES

Kenneth L. Block
William J. Yob
Robert E. Attmore
Martin W. Buschle
Miles J. Murphy, III
Martha P. Forman
Kathrine M. West
Robert A. Kamp

Counsel for: Aetna Casualty & Surety Co.; Argonaut Insurance Co.; Auto-Owners Insurance Co.; Employers Mutual; Liberty Mutual Insurance Co.; Sentry Group; State Farm Insurance; Eastern Aviation and Marine Underwriters; Home Insurance Co.; Nationwide Insurance.

For Complete List of Firm Personnel, See General Section

For full biographical listings, see the Martindale-Hubbell Law Directory

CLARY, NANTZ, WOOD, HOFFIUS, RANKIN & COOPER (AV)

500 Calder Plaza, 250 Monroe Avenue, N.W., 49503-2244
Telephone: 616-459-9487
Telecopier: 616-459-5121

MEMBERS OF FIRM

Robert L. DeJong
Stanley J. Stek
Mark R. Smith

ASSOCIATES

Dale R. Rietberg
Douglas H. Wiegerink

Representative Clients: American Commercial Liability Insurance Co.; Celina Mutual Insurance Co.; Progressive Casualty Insurance Co.

For Complete List of Firm Personnel, See General Section

For full biographical listings, see the Martindale-Hubbell Law Directory

FARR & OOSTERHOUSE (AV)

Suite 400, Ledyard Building, 125 Ottawa Avenue, N.W., 49503
Telephone: 616-459-3355
Fax: 616-235-3350

MEMBERS OF FIRM

William S. Farr
Kenneth R. Oosterhouse
Joel E. Krissoff
John R. Oostema
Charles E. Chamberlain, Jr.

(See Next Column)

ASSOCIATE

Michelene B. Pattee

Representative Clients: Aetna Casualty & Surety Co.; Citizens Insurance Company of America; Grand Rapids Community College; Hartford Insurance Co.; J. W. Messner, Inc.; Michigan Lawyers Mutual Insurance Co.; New England Insurance Company; General Star Indemnity Co.; VASA North Atlantic Insurance Co.; Select Insured Risk Services.

For full biographical listings, see the Martindale-Hubbell Law Directory

LINSEY, STRAIN & WORSFOLD, P.C. (AV)

1200 Michigan National Bank Building, 77 Monroe Center, N.W., 49503
Telephone: 616-456-1661
Fax: 616-456-5027

Dale M. Strain
Alan R. Smith
Patrick D. Murphy
Larry D. Vander Wal
David J. Buter
Peter D. Bosch

Joseph P. Vander Veen
William D. Howard
Kurt R. Killman

Representative Clients: American States Insurance Co.; TransAmerica Insurance Co.; Auto Owners Insurance Co.; Ohio Casualty Insurance Co.; West American Insurance Co.; Fremont Mutual Insurance Co.; American Home Insurance Co.; American Intl. Adjustment Cos.; Lincoln Mutual Insurance Co.; Royal Indemnity Insurance Co.

For full biographical listings, see the Martindale-Hubbell Law Directory

RHOADES, MCKEE, BOER, GOODRICH & TITTA (AV)

161 Ottawa N.W., Suite 600, 49503-2793
Telephone: 616-235-3500
Fax: 616-459-5102
Affiliated Offices: De Francesco & De Francesco, The Shepard House, 903 Main Street, P.O. Box 769, St. Joseph, Michigan, 49085.
Telephone: 616-983-7712.
Fax: 616-983-6901.
De Francesco & De Francesco, 139 North Whittaker Street, New Buffalo, Michigan, 49117. Telephone: 616-469-0537.
Fax: 616-649-4603.

Edward B. Goodrich
Peter A. Titta
Richard G. Leonard
Arthur C. Spalding
Robert J. Dugan
Terrence L. Groesser
Thomas P. Hogan
Kurt D. Hassberger
James M. Flaggert
Mary Ann Cartwright
Joel S. Huyser
Daniel L. Elve
Laurie M. Strong
Stephen A. Hilger
Gregory G. Timmer

Mary Lynette Williams
Scott J. Steiner
Charles A. Pearce
Robert C. Shaver
Jeff A. Moyer
Kevin A. Hansen

Reference: First Michigan Bank.

For full biographical listings, see the Martindale-Hubbell Law Directory

ROBERTS, BETZ & BLOSS, P.C. (AV)

555 Riverfront Plaza Building, 55 Campau, 49503
Telephone: 616-235-9955
Telecopier: 616-235-0404

Michael J. Roberts
Michael W. Betz
David J. Bloss
Gregory A. Block
Michael T. Small
Ralph M. Reisinger
Elena C. Cardenas
Henry S. Emrich

For full biographical listings, see the Martindale-Hubbell Law Directory

SMITH, HAUGHEY, RICE & ROEGGE, P.C. (AV)

200 Calder Plaza Building, 250 Monroe Avenue, N.W., 49503-2251
Telephone: 616-774-8000
Telecopier: 616-774-2461
East Lansing, Michigan Office: 1301 North Hagadorn, 48823-2320.
Telephone: 517-332-3030.
Telecopier: 517-332-3468.
Traverse City, Michigan Office: 241 East State Street, P.O. Box 848, 49685-0804.
Telephone: 616-929-4878.
Telecopier: 616-929-4182.

Clifford A. Mitts (1902-1962)
Laurence D. Smith (1913-1980)
Robert V.V. Rice (1899-1982)
Michael S. Barnes (1944-1989)
L. Roland Roegge
Thomas F. Blackwell
P. Laurence Mulvihill
Lawrence P. Mulligan
Thomas R. Tasker
Paul H. Reinhardt
Lance R. Mather
Charles F. Behler
Gary A. Rowe
William W. Jack, Jr.
William J. Hondorp
Thomas M. Weibel
James G. Black
E. Thomas Mc Carthy, Jr.
Glenn W. House, Jr.
Thomas R. Wurst

(See Next Column)

SMITH, HAUGHEY, RICE & ROEGGE P.C., *Grand Rapids—Continued*

Craig R. Noland
Paul M. Oleniczak
Craig S. Neckers
Thomas E. Kent
Leonard M. Hickey
David N. Campos
Anthony J. Quarto
Bruce P. Rissi
John C. O'Loughlin
John M. Kruis
Paul G. Van Oostenburg
Dale Ann Iverson
William R. Jewell
Jon D. Vander Ploeg
Patrick F. Geary
Terence J. Ackert
Brian J. Kilbane
Dan C. Porter
Brian J. Plachta
Phillip K. Mowers
Carol D. Carlson

Kay L. Griffith Hammond
Ann M. Stuursma
Richard E. Holmes, Jr.
Marilyn S. Nickell
Christopher R. Genther
Beth Suzanne Kromer
Lois Marie Ens
Paul D. Fox
Robert M. Kruse
Harriet M. Hageman
John B. Combs
Aileen M. Simet
Scott W. Morgan
Matthew L. Meyer
Bret M. Hanna
Carine J. Joachim
Todd W. Millar
Elizabeth Roberts VerHey
Jennifer Jane Nasser

OF COUNSEL

A. B. Smith, Jr.
David O. Haughey
Susan Bradley Jakubowski
Thomas P. Scholler

Representative Clients: Chevron; Cincinnati Insurance Co.; General Motors Corp.; Kemper Insurance Group; Michigan Hospital Assn.; Navistar International; St. Paul Insurance Cos.; Steelcase, Inc.

For full biographical listings, see the Martindale-Hubbell Law Directory

TOLLEY, VANDENBOSCH & WALTON, P.C. (AV)

5650 Foremost Drive, S.E., 49546
Telephone: 616-942-8090
Facsimile: 616-942-4677

Peter R. Tolley
Michael C. Walton
Lawrence Korolewicz
Todd R. Dickinson
Paul L. Nelson
David A. Malson, Jr.
James B. Doezema
David L. Harrison
Richard J. Durden
Robert C. Greene
Miles J. Postema
James K. Schepers
Susan Jasper Stein
Mark J. Colon
Mark A. VandenBosch

Representative Clients: State Farm Insurance Co.; Sentry Insurance Co.; Fremont Mutual Insurance Co.; Phoenix Aviation; Admiral Insurance; Kemper Insurance; Northbrook Excess & Surplus Insurance Co.; St. Paul Companies; Aetna Insurance Co.; Wausau.

For full biographical listings, see the Martindale-Hubbell Law Directory

WHEELER UPHAM, A PROFESSIONAL CORPORATION (AV)

Second Floor, Trust Building, 40 Pearl Street, N.W., 49503
Telephone: 616-459-7100
Fax: 616-459-6366

Gordon B. Wheeler (1904-1986)
Buford A. Upham (Retired)
Robert H. Gillette
Geoffrey L. Gillis
John M. Roels
Gary A. Maximiuk
Timothy J. Orlebeke
Kenneth E. Tiews
Jack L. Hoffman
Janet C. Baxter
Peter Kladder, III
James M. Shade
Thomas A. Kuiper

Counsel for: Prudential Insurance Co.; The Travelers Insurance Co.; John Hancock Mutual Life Insurance Co.; Mutual Benefit Life Insurance Co. of Newark Penn Mutual Insurance Co.; Mutual of Omaha, Farmers Insurance Group, Massachusetts Mutual Life Insurance Co.; United Life Insurance Co.

For full biographical listings, see the Martindale-Hubbell Law Directory

GROSSE POINTE WOODS, Wayne Co.

BARBIER & BARBIER, P.C. (AV)

19251 Mack Avenue, Suite 200, 48236-2800
Telephone: 313-882-9500
Fax: 313-882-0919

Ralph W. Barbier, Jr.
Tara J. Hanley

Representative Clients: AIU Insurance Co.; All Risk Claims Services; CNA Insurance Co.; Crawford & Co.; Liberty Mutual Insurance Co.; Willis Corroon Corp. Daisy Manufacturing Co.

For full biographical listings, see the Martindale-Hubbell Law Directory

*HOUGHTON,** Houghton Co.

VAIRO, MECHLIN, TOMASI, JOHNSON & MANCHESTER (AV)

400 East Houghton Street, 49931
Telephone: 906-482-0770
Fax: 906-482-2938
Calumet, Michigan Office: 200 5th Street.
Telephone: 906-337-0312.

MEMBERS OF FIRM

Gerald G. Vairo
David R. Mechlin
Paul J. Tomasi
Frederick N. Johnson
Jeryl A. Manchester

Michael J. Mannisto

Representative Clients: U.S.F.& G., Insurance Companies; Aetna Life and Casualty Company; Auto Owners Insurance Company; Auto Club Insurance Assn.; Citizens Insurance Company of America; The Hartford Group; First of America Bank; Wausau Insurance Companies; CNA Insurance Companies; Accident Fund of Michigan.

For full biographical listings, see the Martindale-Hubbell Law Directory

*JACKSON,** Jackson Co.

BULLEN, MOILANEN, KLAASEN & SWAN, P.C. (AV)

402 South Brown Street, 49203
Telephone: 517-788-8500
Fax: 517-788-8507

Lawrence L. Bullen
Philip M. Moilanen
Terry J. Klaasen
David W. Swan

Robert M. Gordon

OF COUNSEL

T. Harrison Stanton
J. Adrian Rosenburg (1896-1983)
Frank C. Painter (1905-1976)

Representative Clients: Midland National Insurance Co.; National Grange Insurance Co.; Nationwide Insurance Group; Employers of Wausau Insurance Co.; Gulf Insurance Group; Hartford Insurance; Hastings Mutual Insurance Co.; John Hancock Insurance Co.; Michigan Millers Mutual Insurance Co.; Vesta Insurance Group.

For full biographical listings, see the Martindale-Hubbell Law Directory

*KALAMAZOO,** Kalamazoo Co.

DIETRICH, ZODY, HOWARD & VANDERROEST, P.C. (AV)

834 King Highway, Suite 110, 49001
Telephone: 616-344-9236
Fax: 616-344-0412

G. Philip Dietrich
Richard J. Howard
James W. Smith
James E. VanderRoest
Brenda Wheeler Zody

Barbara S. Weintraub

Representative Clients: John Hancock Mutual Life Insurance Co.; Prudential Property and Casualty Insurance Co.; Southern Michigan Mutual Insurance Co.; Monroe Guaranty Insurance Co.; Nationwide Insurance Co.; Brotherhood Mutual Insurance Co.; United Casualty Insurance Co.

For full biographical listings, see the Martindale-Hubbell Law Directory

EARLY, LENNON, PETERS & CROCKER, P.C. (AV)

900 Comerica Building, 49007-4752
Telephone: 616-381-8844
Fax: 616-349-8525

John T. Peters, Jr.
Harold E. Fischer, Jr.

Attorneys for: General Motors Corp.; Wal-Mart Stores; Borgess Medical Center; Aetna Insurance: Kemper Group; Medical Protective Co.; Zurich Insurance; AAA; Liberty Mutual; Home Insurance.

For Complete List of Firm Personnel, See General Section

For full biographical listings, see the Martindale-Hubbell Law Directory

HOWARD & HOWARD ATTORNEYS, P.C. (AV)

The Kalamazoo Building, Suite 400, 107 West Michigan Avenue, 49007-3956
Telephone: 616-382-1483
Telecopier: 616-382-1568
Bloomfield Hills, Michigan Office: The Pinehurst Office Center, Suite 101, 1400 North Woodward Avenue.
Telephone: 810-645-1483.
Telecopier: 810-645-1568.

(See Next Column)

HOWARD & HOWARD ATTORNEYS P.C.—*Continued*

Lansing, Michigan Office: The Phoenix Building, Suite 500, 222 Washington Square North.
Telephone: 517-485-1483.
Telecopier: 517-485-1568.
Peoria, Illinois Office: Howard & Howard, P.C., The Creve Coeur Building, Suite 200, 321 Liberty Street.
Telephone: 309-672-1483.
Telecopier: 309-672-1568.

James H. Geary — Myra L. Willis

Representative Clients: First of America Bank Corp.; Simpson Paper Company; W.R. Grace & Co.; Stryker Corp.; Kalamazoo Valley Community College.
Local Counsel for: Chrysler Motors Corp.
International Counsel for: Sony Corp.

For Complete List of Firm Personnel, See General Section

For full biographical listings, see the Martindale-Hubbell Law Directory

LILLY & LILLY, P.C. (AV)

505 South Park Street, 49007
Telephone: 616-381-7763
Fax: 616-344-6880

Charles M. Lilly (1990-1903) — Terrence J. Lilly

For full biographical listings, see the Martindale-Hubbell Law Directory

MILLER, CANFIELD, PADDOCK AND STONE, P.L.C. (AV)

A Professional Limited Liability Company
Founded in 1852 by Sidney Davy Miller
444 West Michigan Avenue, 49007-3752
Telephone: 616-381-7030
Fax: 616-382-0244
Detroit, Michigan Office: 150 West Jefferson, Suite 2500, 48226-4415.
Telephone: 313-963-6420.
Fax: 313-496-7500.
Cable Address: "Stem Detroit."
Ann Arbor, Michigan Office: 101 North Main Street, 7th Floor, 48104-1400.
Telephone: 313-663-2445.
Fax: 313-747-7147.
Bloomfield Hills, Michigan Office: Suite 100, Pinehurst Office Center, 1400 North Woodward, 48303-2014.
Telephone: 313-645-5000.
Fax: 313-645-1917.
Grand Rapids, Michigan Office: 1200 Campau Square Plaza, 99 Monroe, N.W., 49503-2639.
Telephone: 616-454-8656.
Fax: 616-776-6322.
Howell, Michigan Office: 121 South Barnard Street, Suite 4, 48843-2305.
Telephone: 517-546-7600.
Telecopier: 517-546-6974.
Lansing, Michigan Office: One Michigan Avenue, Suite 900, 48933-1609.
Telephone: 517-487-2070.
Fax: 517-374-6304.
Monroe, Michigan Office: The Executive Centre, 214 East Elm Avenue, 48161-2682.
Telephone: 313-243-2000.
Fax: 313-243-0901.
Washington, D.C. Office: 1225 Nineteenth Street, N.W., Suite 400. 20036.
Telephone: 202-429-5575; 785-0600.
Fax: 202-331-1118; 785-1234.
Pensacola, Florida Office: 25 West Cedar, 32501.
Telephone: 904-469-1088.
Fax: 904-432-0677.
St. Petersburg, Florida Office: 100 Second Avenue S., Suite 7045,33701.
Telephone: 813-982-6000.
Fax: 813-892-6002.
Gdansk, Poland Office: Suite 322, Dom Technika Building, Ul. Rajska 6, 80-850.
Telephone: 011-485-831-2808.
Fax: 011-485-831-4719.
Warsaw, Poland Office: Ul. Marszalkowska 82, Suite 561, 00-517.
Telephone: 011-482-623-6457 and 6458.
Fax: 011-482-623-6459.

MEMBERS OF FIRM

Eric V. Brown, Jr. (Resident)
James G. Vantine, Jr. (Resident)
Ronald E. Baylor (Resident)
James E. Spurr (Resident)
Pamela Chapman Enslen (Resident)

RESIDENT ASSOCIATE

Ballard Jay Yelton, III

Representative Firm Clients: Chrysler Corp.; Comerica, Inc.; City of Detroit, Mich.; Detroit Tigers, Inc.; First of Michigan; Fretter, Inc.; Ford Motor Co.; Ford Motor Credit Co.; Great Lakes Bancorp; Henry Ford Hospital.

For Complete List of Firm Personnel, See General Section

For full biographical listings, see the Martindale-Hubbell Law Directory

LANSING, Ingham Co.

* indicates certain Bar Register subscribers whose principal office is located elsewhere in the state and who have arranged for representation as a part of the state capital listings that follow

DENFIELD, TIMMER, JAMO & O'LEARY (AV)

521 Seymour Avenue, 48933
Telephone: 517-371-3500
Fax: 517-371-4514

George H. Denfield
James A. Timmer
James S. Jamo
James S. O'Leary
Kathleen A. Lopilato

Representative Clients: Auto Owners Insurance Co.; National Indemnity Insurance Co.; Pennsylvania Insurance Co.; Travelers Insurance Co.; Ohio Farmers Insurance Co.; Bankers Life & Casualty Co.; Western Casualty & Surety Co.; Indiana Insurance Co.; Western Surety Co.; United State Aviation Underwriters.

For full biographical listings, see the Martindale-Hubbell Law Directory

FOSTER, SWIFT, COLLINS & SMITH, P.C. (AV)

313 South Washington Square, 48933-2193
Telephone: 517-371-8100
Telecopier: 517-371-8200
Farmington Hills, Michigan Office: 32300 Northwestern Highway, Suite 230.
Telephone: 810-851-7500.
Fax: 810-851-7504.

John L. Collins
Webb A. Smith
William R. Schulz
David H. Aldrich
Scott A. Storey
Charles E. Barbieri
Scott L. Mandel
Michael D. Sanders
Frank A. Fleischmann
Kevin T. McGraw
Mark H. Canady
Michael W. Puerner
Matthew W. Collins

LEGAL SUPPORT PERSONNEL

LEGAL ASSISTANTS

Laurie A. Delaney — Theresa G. Solberg

Representative Clients: Citizens Insurance Company of America; Michigan Blue Cross and Blue Shield; Aetna Casualty Insurance Co.; Michigan Mutual Insurance Co.; Transamerica Insurance Co.; Royal Globe Insurance Co.; Physician Insurance Company of Michigan; Michigan Physicians Mutual Insurance Co.; Meridian Mutual Insurance Company.

For Complete List of Firm Personnel, See General Section

For full biographical listings, see the Martindale-Hubbell Law Directory

FRASER TREBILCOCK DAVIS & FOSTER, P.C. (AV)

1000 Michigan National Tower, 48933
Telephone: 517-482-5800
Fax: 517-482-0887
Okemos, Michigan Office: 2188 Commons Parkway.
Telephone: 517-349-1300.
Fax: 517-349-0922.

Peter L. Dunlap
C. Mark Hoover
Ronald R. Sutton
Brett Jon Bean
Gary C. Rogers
Mark A. Bush

Patrick K. Thornton — Brian D. Herrington

Representative Clients: Auto Owners Insurance Co.; Federated Insurance Co.; Hartford Insurance Co.; Metropolitan Life Insurance Co.; Michigan Physicians Mutual Liability Co.; Prudential Insurance Company of America; State Farm Insurance Co.

For Complete List of Firm Personnel, See General Section

For full biographical listings, see the Martindale-Hubbell Law Directory

* HONIGMAN MILLER SCHWARTZ AND COHN (AV)

A Partnership including Professional Corporations
222 North Washington Square, Suite 400, 48933
Telephone: 517-484-8282
Telecopier: 517-484-8286
Detroit, Michigan Office: 2290 First National Building.
Telephone: 313-256-7800.
West Palm Beach, Florida Office: Suite 800 Esperante Building, 222 Lakeview Avenue.
Telephone: 407-838-4500.
Tampa, Florida Office: Suite 350 One Harbour Place, 777 South Harbour Island Boulevard.
Telephone: 813-221-6600.
Orlando, Florida Office: 390 North Orange Avenue, Suite 1300.
Telephone: 407-648-0300.
Houston, Texas Office: 3100 First Interstate Bank Plaza, 1000 Louisiana.
Telephone: 713-650-2600.

(See Next Column)

HONIGMAN MILLER SCHWARTZ AND COHN, *Lansing—Continued*

Los Angeles, California Office: McNeill Plaza, Suite 820, 15260 Ventura Boulevard, 91403.
Telephone: 818-784-2900.

MEMBERS

Frederick M. Baker, Jr.
Daniel J. Demlow
Sandra L. Jasinski
Timothy Sawyer Knowlton
Mark Morton
John D. Pirich
Benjamin O. Schwendener, Jr.
Gary A. Trepod
Alan M. Valade
William C. Whitbeck
Ruth E. Zimmerman

ASSOCIATES

Ann L. Andrews
John S. Kane

Representative Clients: Aon Corporation; Continental Insurance.

For Complete List of Firm Personnel, See General Section

For full biographical listings, see the Martindale-Hubbell Law Directory

HOWARD & HOWARD ATTORNEYS, P.C. (AV)

The Phoenix Building, Suite 500, 222 Washington Square, North, 48933-1817
Telephone: 517-485-1483
Telecopier: 517-485-1568
Kalamazoo, Michigan Office: The Kalamazoo Building, Suite 400, 107 West Michigan Avenue.
Telephone: 616-382-1483.
Telecopier: 616-382-1568.
Bloomfield Hills, Michigan Office: The Pinehurst Office Center, Suite 101, 1400 North Woodward Avenue.
Telephone: 810-645-1483.
Telecopier: 810-645-1568.
Peoria, Illinois Office: Howard & Howard, P.C., The Creve Coeur Building, Suite 200, 321 Liberty Street.
Telephone: 309-672-1483.
Telecopier: 309-672-1568.

David C. Coey
James E. Lozier

Representative Clients: For Representative Client list, see General Practice, Lansing, MI.

For Complete List of Firm Personnel, See General Section

For full biographical listings, see the Martindale-Hubbell Law Directory

RAYMOND JOSEPH (AV)

1602 Michigan National Tower, 48933
Telephone: 517-372-4410
Fax: 517-372-2137

OF COUNSEL

George R. Sidwell (1899-1983)
Michael Bowman
Bruce C. Blanton

Representative Clients: Ashland Oil, Inc.; Complete Auto Transit, Inc.; Employers Insurance of Wausau; Evans Products Co.; Grain Dealers Mutl.; Harbor Insurance Co.; Interstate Motor Freight System; Lansing Symphony Assn., Inc.; RCA Service Co.; West American Insurance Co.

For full biographical listings, see the Martindale-Hubbell Law Directory

*MARQUETTE,** Marquette Co.

BENSINGER, COTANT, MENKES & AARDEMA, P.C. (AV)

122 West Bluff, 49855
Telephone: 906-225-1000
Fax: 906-225-0818
Gaylord, Michigan Office: 308 West Main, P.O. Box 1000.
Telephone: 517-732-7536.
Fax: 517-732-4922.
Grand Rapids, Michigan Office: 983 Spaulding Avenue, S.E.
Telephone: 616-949-7963.
Fax: 616-949-5264.

Gregory A. Elzinga (Resident)
William J. Maynard (Resident)
Glenn W. Smith (Resident)

Representative Clients: Allstate Insurance Co.; Auto-Owners Insurance Co.; Michigan Physicians Insurance Co.; Northern Mutual Insurance Co.; Federated Insurance Co.; Employers Reinsurance Co.; D & N Bank-FSB; Michigan Licensed Beverage Association; State Farm Insurance Co.; Farm Bureau Mutual Insurance Co.

For full biographical listings, see the Martindale-Hubbell Law Directory

WEBER, SWANSON & DETTMANN (AV)

Marquette Professional Building, 148 West Washington Street, 49855
Telephone: 906-228-7355
Fax: 906-228-7357

(See Next Column)

MEMBERS OF FIRM

John R. Weber
Keith E. Swanson
Darrell R. Dettmann

Representative Clients: Kemper Insurance Cos.; USF&G Insurance Co.; SETSEG, Inc.; Gallagher Bassett Insurance Service; North Pointe Insurance Co.; Auto Owners Insurance Co.; CoreSource, Inc.; USAA; Upper Peninsula Health Education Corp.
Reference: First of America Bank-Marquette, N.A.

For full biographical listings, see the Martindale-Hubbell Law Directory

*MONROE,** Monroe Co.

BRAUNLICH, RUSSOW & BRAUNLICH, A PROFESSIONAL CORPORATION (AV)

111 South Macomb Street, 48161
Telephone: 313-241-8300
Fax: 313-241-7715

William J. Braunlich, Jr. (1924-1992)
Thomas P. Russow
William H. Braunlich

Philip A. Costello
Patricia M. Poupard
Ann L. Nickel
Marie C. Kennedy
Susan J. Mehregan
Robert Wetzel
Michael G. Roehrig

LEGAL SUPPORT PERSONNEL

Ruth G. Flint

Representative Clients: State Farm Mutual Insurance Co.; Auto Club Insurance Assn.; Farm Bureau Insurance Co.; Home Mutual Insurance Co.; Cincinnati Insurance Co.; Board of Road Commissioners, Monroe County; Port of Monroe; Monroe County Community College; City of Luna Pier; City of Petersburg.

For full biographical listings, see the Martindale-Hubbell Law Directory

PLYMOUTH, Wayne Co.

DRAUGELIS & ASHTON (AV)

843 Penniman Avenue, 48170-1690
Telephone: 313-453-4044
Clawson, Michigan Office: 380 North Main Street.
Telephone: 313-810-7704.

MEMBERS OF FIRM

Edward F. Draugelis
John A. Ashton
Donald S. Scully
Richard T. Haynes
Lamberto DiStefano
David T. Rogers

ASSOCIATES

Debra Clancy
Dawn E. Clancy
Joseph R. Conte
Timothy M. O'Connor
Steven O. Ashton
Floyd C. Virant
Taras P. Jarema
Deborah A. Tonelli
Timothy M. McKercher
Anne K. Mayer
Sally S. Stauffer
Robert D. Wilkins
Darlene M. Germaine
Joel B. Ashton

Representative Clients: State Farm Automobile Insurance Co.; State Farm Fire and Casualty Co.

For full biographical listings, see the Martindale-Hubbell Law Directory

*PORT HURON,** St. Clair Co.

NICHOLSON, FLETCHER & DEGROW (AV)

522 Michigan Street, 48060-3893
Telephone: 810-987-8444
Facsimile: 810-987-8149

MEMBERS OF FIRM

David C. Nicholson
Gary A. Fletcher
Dan L. DeGrow

ASSOCIATES

Mark G. Clark
John D. Tomlinson
Gregory T. Stremers

Representative Clients: Fremont Mutual Insurance Co.; Westfield Insurance Co.; Michigan Municipal Risk Management Authority; City of Port Huron; City of Marysville; Port Huron Area School District; Marysville Public Schools; Wirtz Manufacturing Co.; Raymond Excavating; Relleum Real Estate Development Co.

For full biographical listings, see the Martindale-Hubbell Law Directory

ROYAL OAK, Oakland Co.

CARDELLI, SCHAEFER & MASON, P.C. (AV)

306 South Washington Avenue, Suite 500, 48067
Telephone: 810-544-1100
Telecopier: 810-544-1191

(See Next Column)

CARDELLI, SCHAEFER & MASON P.C.—*Continued*

Thomas G. Cardelli	Cheryl A. Cardelli
William C. Schaefer	Deborah A. Hebert
Laura D. Mason	Mary Ann J. O'Neil
Shelly M. Lee	

Representative Clients: Allianz Insurance Company; Allstate Insurance Company; Amerisure Insurance Company; Automobile Club Insurance Assn.; Cigna Companies; Frankenmuth Insurance Company; ITT Hartford Insurance; Indiana Insurance; Motors Insurance Company; State Auto Insurance Company.

For full biographical listings, see the Martindale-Hubbell Law Directory

*SAGINAW,** Saginaw Co.

BRAUN KENDRICK FINKBEINER (AV)

8th Floor Second National Bank Building, 48607
Telephone: 517-753-3461
Telecopier: 517-753-3951
Bay City, Michigan Office: 201 Phoenix Building, P.O. Box 2039.
Telephone: 517-895-8505.
Telecopier: 517-895-8437.

MEMBERS OF FIRM

Harold J. Blanchet, Jr.	Charles A. Gilfeather
E. Louis Ognisanti	Timothy L Curtiss
Bruce L. Dalrymple	Scott C. Strattard
Craig W. Horn	

ASSOCIATES

Brian S. Makaric	William G. Tishkoff

Representative Clients: Farm Bureau Insurance Group; Firemans Fund American Insurance; Frankenmuth Mutual Insurance Co.; Fremont Mutual Insurance Co.; Great Lakes American Life Ins. Co.; Hartford Insurance Group; Hastings Mutual Insurance Co.; Kemper Insurance Group; Michigan Mutual Liability Co.; Mutual Benefit Life Ins. Co.

For Complete List of Firm Personnel, See General Section

For full biographical listings, see the Martindale-Hubbell Law Directory

FORDNEY, DUST & PRINE (AV)

Suite 410 B Plaza North, 4800 Fashion Square Boulevard, P.O. Box 5289, 48603-0289
Telephone: 517-791-7060
Fax: 517-791-8009

J. Michael Fordney	Tobin H. Dust
Andrew W. Prine	

For full biographical listings, see the Martindale-Hubbell Law Directory

O'NEILL, WALLACE & DOYLE, P.C. (AV)

Suite 302 Four Flags Office Center, 300 St. Andrews Road, P.O. Box 1966, 48605
Telephone: 517-790-0960
Fax: 517-790-6902
Flint, Michigan Office: 611 West Court Street.
Telephone: 810-235-4031.
Fax: 810-235-5715.

Terence J. O'Neill	Thomas J. Doyle
David A. Wallace	Charles F. Filipiak

Richard L. Alger, Jr.	David Carbajal
James D. Henke	James E. O'Neill, III
John J. Danieleski, Jr.	

Representative Clients: Home Insurance Co.; Great American Insurance Co.; Farmers Insurance Co.; Cincinnati Insurance Co.; Ohio Casualty Insurance Co.; Safeco Insurance Co.; Liberty Mutual Insurance Co.; CUNA Mutual Insurance.; Pioneer State Mutual Insurance Co.; Michigan Mutual Insurance Co.

For full biographical listings, see the Martindale-Hubbell Law Directory

SOUTHFIELD, Oakland Co.

O'LEARY, O'LEARY, JACOBS, MATTSON, PERRY & MASON, P.C. (AV)

26777 Central Park Boulevard, Suite 275, 48076
Telephone: 810-799-8260

John Patrick O'Leary	C. Kenneth Perry, Jr.
Thomas M. O'Leary	Larry G. Mason
John P. Jacobs	D. Jennifer Andreou
Kenneth M. Mattson	Kevin P. Hanbury
Debra A. Reed	

For full biographical listings, see the Martindale-Hubbell Law Directory

PROVIZER, LICHTENSTEIN & PHILLIPS, P.C. (AV)

4000 Town Center, Suite 1800, 48075
Telephone: 810-352-9080
Facsimile: 810-352-1491
Los Angeles, California Office: Provizer, Lichtenstein, Phillips & Cleary, P.C. 1801 Century Park East, Suite 2400.
Telephone: 310-552-0581.
New York, N.Y. Office: Provizer, Lichtenstein, Phillips & Madon, P.C. 21 E. 40th Street, Suite 1601.
Telephone: 800-288-9080.
Fax: 212-481-6424.

Harold M. Provizer	Noel F. Beck
David S. Lichtenstein	William J. Selinsky
Randall E. Phillips	Jeffrey S. Weisswasser
Marilyn A. Madorsky	Robert I. Brown
David M. Moss	Eric J. Smith
Evan A. Zagoria	Elizabeth A. Foley
Deborah Molitz	Arnold M. Fink
Constance S. Hall	Marc Mulder
Attilio V. Colella	

For full biographical listings, see the Martindale-Hubbell Law Directory

SCHWARTZ & JALKANEN, P.C. (AV)

Suite 200, 24400 Northwestern Highway, 48075
Telephone: 810-352-2555
Facsimile: 810-352-5963

Melvin R. Schwartz	Arthur W. Jalkanen
Karl Eric Hannum	

Anne Loridas Randall	Deborah L. Laura
Lisa M. Green	

For full biographical listings, see the Martindale-Hubbell Law Directory

SOMMERS, SCHWARTZ, SILVER & SCHWARTZ, P.C. (AV)

2000 Town Center, Suite 900, 48075
Telephone: 810-355-0300
Telecopier: 810-746-4001
Plymouth, Michigan Office: 747 South Main Street.
Telephone: 313-455-4250.

Leonard B. Schwartz	Joseph E. Grinnan
John F. Vos, III	Jon J. Birnkrant
Robert G. Portnoy	Lisa K. Pernick
Allen J. Wall	Antonia Fletcher Grinnan

Representative Clients: Crum & Forster Insurance Company; Great American Insurance Company; Royal Insurance Company; Michigan Mutual/Amerisure Insurance Company; Universal Underwriters Insurance Company; ESIS, Inc.; Corporate Service, Inc.

For Complete List of Firm Personnel, See General Section

For full biographical listings, see the Martindale-Hubbell Law Directory

SULLIVAN, WARD, BONE, TYLER & ASHER, P.C. (AV)

25800 Northwestern Highway, Suite 1000, 48075
Telephone: 810-746-0700
FAX: 810-746-2760
Traverse City, Michigan Office: 3240 Racquet Club Drive.
Telephone: 616-947-1335.
Fax: 616-947-3474.
Grand Rapids, Michigan Office: 2025 East Beltline S.E., Suite 204.
Telephone: 616-940-4114.
FAX: 616-940-4142.

Richard G. Ward	Michelle A. Thomas
Richard A. Bone	Sharon S. Almonrode
David M. Tyler	Robert E. Sullivan, Jr.
Stanley G. Thayer	Colin H. John, Jr.
Lee C. Patton	Charles E. Randau
Alan S. Helmore	Michael J. Asher
Gerard J. Andree	Jeffery G. Powers
Thomas L. Auth, Jr.	Ronald S. Lederman
Kevin J. Gleeson	Sheri B. Cataldo
Scott D. Feringa	Thomas M. Slavin
Renée S. Siegan	Donald K. Warwick
John M. Simmerer	Randi P. Glanz
Eric D. Geller	Lawrence C. Bourbeau, Jr.
Dale Louis Gudenau	William J. Ewald
Steven M. Chait	Douglas H. Gaskin

Representative Clients: Allstate Insurance Co.; American International Group; American States Insurance Co.; The Great Atlantic & Pacific Tea Company; William Beaumont Hospital; Beech Aircraft; Bormans, Inc. dba/Farmer Jack Supermarkets; City of Detroit; CNA Insurance Companies; Continental Loss Adjusting Services.

For full biographical listings, see the Martindale-Hubbell Law Directory

TROY, Oakland Co.

HOLAHAN, MALLOY, MAYBAUGH & MONNICH (AV)

Suite 100, 2690 Crooks Road, 48084-4700
Telephone: 810-362-4747
Fax: 810-362-4779
East Tawas, Michigan Office: 910 East Bay Street.
Telephone: 517-362-4747.
Fax: 517-362-7331.

MEMBERS OF FIRM

J. Michael Malloy, III
James D. Maybaugh
John R. Monnich
David L. Delie, Jr.
William J. Kliffel

OF COUNSEL

Thomas H. O'Connor
Maureen Holahan (Retired; Resident, East Tawas Office)

Representative Clients: Chubb Companies; American States Insurance Co.; Travelers Insurance; Employers Reinsurance; Hartford Insurance Company.

For full biographical listings, see the Martindale-Hubbell Law Directory

POLING, MCGAW & POLING, P.C. (AV)

Suite 275, 5435 Corporate Drive, 48098
Telephone: 810-641-0500
Telecopier: 810-641-0506

Benson T. Buck (1926-1989)
Richard B. Poling
D. Douglas McGaw
Richard B. Poling, Jr.
David W. Moore
Gregory C. Hamilton
Veronica B. Winter
James R. Parker

OF COUNSEL

Ralph S. Moore

Representative Clients: County of Oakland; City of Troy; United States Fidelity & Guaranty Co.; Sentry Insurance Co.; Admiral Insurance; DeMaria Construction Co.; Leo Corporation; Aetna Casualty and Surety Co.; Concord Design; Pneumo-Abex.

For full biographical listings, see the Martindale-Hubbell Law Directory

REYNOLDS, BEEBY & MAGNUSON, P.C. (AV)

50 West Big Beaver Road Suite 400, 48084
Telephone: 810-740-9860
FAX: 810-740-9870
Detroit, Michigan Office: Ford Building.
Telephone: 810-740-9860.
Fax: 810-740-9870.

Gregory A. Reynolds
Thomas D. Beeby
Arnold N. Magnuson, Jr.
Kenneth M. Zorn
Thomas G. Grubba
Frank K. Mandlebaum

Elizabeth A. Fellows
Michael K. Sheehy
Joseph J. Wright

Representative Clients: Employers Casualty Co.; Liberty Mutual Insurance Co.; Royal Insurance Corp.; Safeco Insurance Co.

For full biographical listings, see the Martindale-Hubbell Law Directory

WEST BLOOMFIELD, Oakland Co.

CHEATHAM ACKER & SHARP, P.C. (AV)

5777 West Maple Road, Suite 130, P.O. Box 255002, 48325-5002
Telephone: 810-932-2000

Charles C. Cheatham
Lawrence J. Acker
Gary D. Sharp

William E. Osantowski
Tracy A. Leahy
Jody D. Klask
John M. Mooney
Mary E. Hollman
Adam K. Gordon

COUNSEL

Lynn L. Lower
Kyle B. Mansfield (Not admitted in MI)

For full biographical listings, see the Martindale-Hubbell Law Directory

LAW OFFICES OF LEE ESTES (AV)

5777 West Maple Road, Suite 130, P.O. Box 255002, 48325-5002
Telephone: 810-855-0770
Facsimile: 810-932-2008
(Also Of Counsel to Cheatham, Acker & Sharp, P.C.)

For full biographical listings, see the Martindale-Hubbell Law Directory

MINNESOTA

*AUSTIN,** Mower Co.

HOVERSTEN, STROM, JOHNSON & RYSAVY (AV)

807 West Oakland Avenue, 55912
Telephone: 507-433-3483
Fax: 507-433-7889

MEMBERS OF FIRM

Kermit F. Hoversten
Craig W. Johnson
Donald E. Rysavy
David V. Hoversten
John S. Beckmann
Fred W. Wellmann
Steven J Hovey

ASSOCIATE

Mary Carroll Leahy

OF COUNSEL

Kenneth M. Strom

Representative Clients: Hartford Insurance Co.; Allied Insurance Group; Travelers Insurance; American States Insurance; Royal Milbank Insurance; Prudential Insurance Co.; Independent School District 756; St. Olaf Hospital; Austin Medical Clinic; Norwest Bank, Austin.

For Complete List of Firm Personnel, See General Section

For full biographical listings, see the Martindale-Hubbell Law Directory

*BEMIDJI,** Beltrami Co.

POWELL, POWELL & AAMODT (AV)

713 Beltrami Avenue, P.O. Box 908, 56601
Telephone: 218-751-5650
FAX: 218-751-5658

MEMBERS OF FIRM

Romaine R. Powell
Charles R. Powell
Paul R. Aamodt

Representative Clients: The State Farm Insurance Companies; American Family Mutual Insurance Co..

For full biographical listings, see the Martindale-Hubbell Law Directory

*DULUTH,** St. Louis Co.

BROWN, ANDREW, HALLENBECK, SIGNORELLI & ZALLAR, P.A. (AV)

300 Alworth Building, 55802
Telephone: 218-722-1764
FAX: 218-722-6137

Gerald J. Brown
Thomas F. Andrew
Terry C. Hallenbeck
Mark T. Signorelli
Robert J. Zallar
James C. Boos

For full biographical listings, see the Martindale-Hubbell Law Directory

CRASSWELLER, MAGIE, ANDRESEN, HAAG & PACIOTTI, P.A. (AV)

1000 Alworth Building, P.O. Box 745, 55801
Telephone: 218-722-1411
Telecopier: 218-720-6817

Donald B. Crassweller
Robert H. Magie, III
Charles H. Andresen
Michael W. Haag
James P. Paciotti
Sandra E. Butterworth
Brian R. McCarthy
Bryan N. Anderson
Robert C. Barnes
Kurt D. Larson
Gerald T. Anderson

COUNSEL

John M. Donovan
Robert K. McCarthy (1915-1986)

Representative Clients: Inland Steel Co.; Allstate Insurance Co.; Liberty Mutual Insurance Co; State Farm Insurance Cos.; Great Lakes Gas Transmission Co.; Lakehead Pipe Line Co.; Trans-Canada Gas Pipeline, Ltd.

For full biographical listings, see the Martindale-Hubbell Law Directory

HALVERSON, WATTERS, BYE, DOWNS, REYELTS & BATEMAN, LTD. (AV)

700 Providence Building, 55802
Telephone: 218-727-6833
FAX: 218-727-4632

G. W. Halverson
Anthony S. Downs
Steven L. Reyelts
Charles B. Bateman
Steven W. Schneider
Eric L. D. Hylden

(See Next Column)

HALVERSON, WATTERS, BYE, DOWNS, REYELTS & BATEMAN LTD.—*Continued*

Sonia M. Sturdevant
Aaron Bransky

Representative Clients: American States Insurance Co.; CNA Group; Minnesota Lawyer's Mutual Insurance Co.; Midwest Medical Insurance Co.; Mutual Service Insurance Co.; Reinsurance Association of Minnesota; St. Paul Cos.; Wausau; Westfield Cos.

For Complete List of Firm Personnel, See General Section

For full biographical listings, see the Martindale-Hubbell Law Directory

HANFT, FRIDE, O'BRIEN, HARRIES, SWELBAR & BURNS, P.A. (AV)

1000 First Bank Place, 130 West Superior Street, 55802-2094
Telephone: 218-722-4766
Fax: 218-720-4920

Gaylord W. Swelbar
John D. Kelly
Richard J. Leighton
John R. Baumgarth
J. Kent Richards
Tim A. Strom
R. Thomas Torgerson
Cheryl M. Prince
Robin C. Merritt

Representative Clients: American International Adjustment Companies, Inc./American International Group, Inc.; Auto-Owners Insurance; Commercial Union Insurance Companies; Continental Loss Adjusting; Employers Mutual Companies; Federated Insurance Company; Great American Insurance Company; Great Central Insurance Company; Maryland Casualty Company; United States Fidelity and Guarantee Company.

For Complete List of Firm Personnel, See General Section

For full biographical listings, see the Martindale-Hubbell Law Directory

*GRAND RAPIDS,** Itasca Co.

LANO, NELSON, O'TOOLE & BENGTSON, LTD. (AV)

115 East Fifth Street, P.O. Box 20, 55744
Telephone: 218-326-9603
Fax: 218-326-1565

Neal A. Lano
Leif A. Nelson
Dennis L. O'Toole
Brian C. Bengtson

Representative Clients: State Farm Mutual Automobile Insurance Co.; Allstate Insurance Co.; Great American Insurance Co.; Firemen's Fund; Transamerica Insurance Co.; Farm Bureau Mutual Companies; American West Insurance Co.; Farmers Home Group.

For full biographical listings, see the Martindale-Hubbell Law Directory

*MANKATO,** Blue Earth Co.

FARRISH, JOHNSON & MASCHKA (AV)

200 Union Square Business Center, 201 North Broad Street, P.O. Box 550, 56002-0550
Telephone: 507-387-3002
Fax: 507-625-4002

MEMBERS OF FIRM

Robert G. Johnson
Gerald L. Maschka
William S. Partridge
Kenneth R. White
Paul J. Simonett

Representative Clients: Travelers Insurance Co.; American State Bank of Mankato, Mankato, Minn.; Hartford Insurance Group; St. Paul Insurance Cos.; Employers Mutual of Wausau; State Farm Co.; Federated Insurance Co.; Firemen's Fund American Insurance Co.; Maryland Casualty Co.; American Family Insurance Group.

For Complete List of Firm Personnel, See General Section

For full biographical listings, see the Martindale-Hubbell Law Directory

*MINNEAPOLIS,** Hennepin Co.

ARTHUR, CHAPMAN, MCDONOUGH, KETTERING & SMETAK, P.A. (AV)

500 Young Quinlan Building, 81 South Ninth Street, 55402
Telephone: 612-339-3500
Fax: 612-339-7655

Lindsay G. Arthur, Jr.
John T. Chapman
Michael P. McDonough
Robert W. Kettering, Jr.
Theodore J. Smetak
Donna D. Geck
Patrick C. Cronan
Thomas A. Pearson
Colby B. Lund
Michael R. Quinlivan
Sally J. Ferguson
James S. Pikala
Jeremiah P. Gallivan
Katherine L. MacKinnon
Blake W. Duerre
Karen Melling van Vliet
Richard C. Nelson
Eugene C. Shermoen, Jr.

(See Next Column)

Paul J. Rocheford
Lee J. Keller
Gregory J. Johnson
Paula Duggan Vraa
Joseph W. Waller

Representative Clients: American International Group; American States; Bristol Myers-Squibb, Inc.; Continental Insurance Co.; General Casualty; Home Insurance Co.; Metropolitan Property & Liability Insurance Co.; Navistar International; Safeco Insurance Co.; USAA.

For Complete List of Firm Personnel, See General Section

For full biographical listings, see the Martindale-Hubbell Law Directory

BASSFORD, LOCKHART, TRUESDELL & BRIGGS, P.A. (AV)

(Formerly Richards, Montgomery, Cobb & Bassford, P.A.)
3550 Multifoods Tower, 55402-3787
Telephone: 612-333-3000
Telecopier: 612-333-8829

Fred B. Snyder (1859-1951)
Edward C. Gale (1862-1943)
Frank A. Janes (1908-1959)
Nathan A. Cobb, Sr. (1905-1976)
Bergmann Richards (1888-1978)
Edmund T. Montgomery (1904-1987)
Charles A. Bassford (1914-1990)
Greer E. Lockhart
Lynn G. Truesdell
Jerome C. Briggs
Frederick E. Finch
John M. Degnan
Lewis A. Remele, Jr.
Kevin P. Keenan
James O. Redman
Rebecca Egge Moos
John M. Anderson
Charles E. Lundberg
Gregory P. Bulinski
Donna J. Blazevic
Mary E. Steenson
Mark P. Hodkinson
Thomas J. Niemiec
Andrew L. Marshall
Michael A. Klutho
Kathryn H. Davis
Gregory W. Deckert

Kevin P. Hickey
John P. Buckley
Bradley J. Betlach
Mark Whitmore
Christopher R. Morris
Kelly Christensen

Representative Clients: Chubb/Pacific Indemnity Group; Greyhound Lines, Inc.; John Hancock Mutual Life Insurance Co.; Medical Protective Co.; Metropolitan Life Insurance Co.; The Travelers Insurance Cos.; The St. Paul Insurance Cos.

For full biographical listings, see the Martindale-Hubbell Law Directory

COSGROVE, FLYNN & GASKINS (AV)

29th Floor, Metropolitan Centre, 333 South Seventh Street, 55402
Telephone: 612-333-9500
Fax: 612-333-9579

MEMBERS OF FIRM

Hugh J. Cosgrove
George W. Flynn
Steve Gaskins
Robert J. Terhaar
Jeannine L. Lee
Douglas R. Archibald
Barbara Jean D'Aquila
Susan D. Hall
Steven J. Pfefferle
Thomas Klosowski

ASSOCIATES

Randall J. Pattee
Bradley J. Ayers
Hal A. Shillingstad
David A. Wikoff
Gary D. Ansel
Laurie A. Willard
Sarah L. Brew
Lisa R. Griebel
Thomas F. Ascher
Lynn M. Meyer
Scott M. Rusert
Jennifer F. Rosemark
Anthony J. Kane

For full biographical listings, see the Martindale-Hubbell Law Directory

COUSINEAU, MCGUIRE & ANDERSON, CHARTERED (AV)

600 Travelers Express Tower, 1550 Utica Avenue South, 55416-5318
Telephone: 612-546-8400
Facsimile: 612-546-0628

Robert J. McGuire
Craig H. Anderson
William F. Davern
Peter G. Van Bergen
James R. Waldhauser
Thomas P. Kieselbach
Barbara A. Burke
James L. Haigh
Michael W. McNee
Jeffrey O. Knutsen
Mark A. Gwin
John T. Thul
Bruce D. Elliott
Mark A. Kleinschmidt
Michael J. Patera
Robert H. Peterson
Thomas H. McNeill

Katherine A. McBride
Michael D Barrett
Thomas J. Peterson
Richard W. Schmidt
Thomas F. Coleman
Susan M. Pasch
Scott R. West
Dale J. Evensen
Andrea E. Reisbord
Thomas V. Maguire
Robert C. Sipkins
Lisa F. Kinney
Barret W.S. Lane
Timothy K. Masterson
Jane R. McMahon
Denise D. Lemmon

(See Next Column)

COUSINEAU, MCGUIRE & ANDERSON CHARTERED, *Minneapolis—Continued*

Representative Clients: American Family Insurance; CNA; GAB Business Services; General Casualty; Great West Casualty; Minnesota Insurance Guaranty Association; Sedgwick James; St. Paul Cos.; Western National; Zurich American.

For full biographical listings, see the Martindale-Hubbell Law Directory

FETTERLY & GORDON, P.A. (AV)

808 Nicollet Mall, Suite 800, 55402
Telephone: 612-333-2003
Fax: 612-333-5950

James L. Fetterly
Gary J. Gordon
Keith A. Hanson

Stephen G. Lickteig
Diane B. Bratvold
Timothy J. Fetterly

Reference: National City Bank.

For full biographical listings, see the Martindale-Hubbell Law Directory

FOSTER, WALDECK, LIND & GRIES, LTD. (AV)

Suite 2300 Metropolitan Centre, 333 South Seventh Street, 55402
Telephone: 612-375-1550
Facsimilie: 612-375-0647
St. Michael, Minnesota Office: 100 East Central, P.O. Box 35, 55376.
Telephone: 612-497-3099. Facsimilie: 612-497-3639.

Thomas A. Foster
Timothy W. Waldeck
Peter E. Lind
John R. Gries
Rolf E. Sonnesyn
David J. Lenhardt
Byron M. Peterson
Steven E. Tomsche

Gregory J. Van Heest
Jennifer L. Kjos
Philip J. Danen

Reference: Firstar Bank of Minnesota, N.A.

For full biographical listings, see the Martindale-Hubbell Law Directory

GILMORE, AAFEDT, FORDE, ANDERSON & GRAY, P.A. (AV)

150 South Fifth Street, Suite 3100, 55402
Telephone: 612-339-8965
Fax: 612-349-6839

Curtis C. Gilmore (Retired)
John R. de Lambert (Retired)
Michael D. Aafedt
Michael Forde
Donald W. Anderson
James R. Gray
Jay T. Hartman
Roderick C. Cosgriff
Janet Monson
Steven C. Gilmore
Mary Marvin Hager

Peter M. Banovetz
Robin D. Simpson
Kirk C. Thompson
Kathy A. Endres
Miriam P. Rykken
Janet Scheel Stellpflug
Lawrence C. Miller
Adam S. Wolkoff
David J. Klaiman
David Brian Kempston
Charles S. Bierman
Sheryl A. Zaworski
Kathryn M. Hipp

Representative Clients: Aetna Casualty and Surety Company; CIGNA Companies; Crawford Risk Management Service; Kemper Insurance Group; Liberty Mutual Insurance Group; Sentry Insurance Company; St. Paul Companies; United States Fidelity and Guaranty; U.S. Insurance Group/Crum and Forster Commercial Insurance; Western National Insurance Group.

For full biographical listings, see the Martindale-Hubbell Law Directory

LOMMEN, NELSON, COLE & STAGEBERG, P.A. (AV)

1800 IDS Center, 80 South 8th Street, 55402
Telephone: 612-339-8131
Fax: 612-339-8064
Hudson, Wisconsin Office: Grandview Professional Building, 400 South Second Street, Suite 210.
Telephones: 715-386-8217 and 612-436-8085.

W. Wyman Smith (1914-1994)
John P. Lommen (1927-1988)
Michael P. Shroyer (1953-1993)
Leonard T. Juster
Alvin S. Malmon
Ronald L. Haskvitz
Phillip A. Cole
Roger V. Stageberg
Glenn R. Kessel
Thomas R. Jacobson (Resident, Hudson, Wisconsin Office)
John M. Giblin
John R. McBride
J. Christopher Cuneo
Thomas F. Dougherty
Stacey A. DeKalb
Kay N. Hunt
Richard L. Plagens
Ehrich L. Koch
Margie R. Bodas
James M. Lockhart
Stephen C. Rathke
James C. Searls
Linc S. Deter
Paul L. Dinger
Sherri D. Ulland
Reid R. Lindquist

(See Next Column)

Jill G. Doescher
James R. Johnson (Resident, Hudson, Wisconsin Office)
Terrance W. Moore
Lynn M. Starkovich
Marc A. Johannsen
Angela W. Allen
Adam Levitsky
Barry A. O'Neil
Mary I. King
Sheila A. Bjorklund

OF COUNSEL

V. Owen Nelson
Henry H. Feikema

Representative Clients: Mutual Service Insurance Co.; Employers Mutual Companies; Economy Fire and Casualty Co.

For full biographical listings, see the Martindale-Hubbell Law Directory

MAHONEY, DOUGHERTY AND MAHONEY, PROFESSIONAL ASSOCIATION (AV)

801 Park Avenue, 55404-1189
Telephone: 612-339-5863; (800)-328-4827 Ext. 1318
Fax: 612-339-1529

Richard P. Mahoney
John (Jack) M. Miller
James M. Mahoney
Kenneth P. Gleason
Dale B. Lindman
Gary C. Reiter
Randee S. Held
Mark J. Manderfeld
Gay B. Urness (Mr.)
Mary R. Watson
Patrick E. Mahoney
James M. Lehman
Thomas Scott McEachron
Gregory A. Zinn
Kelley R. Lorix
Victor E. Lund
Sandra J. Grove
Philip Sieff
Terry J. Battaglia
Lisa A. Dittmann

Representative Insurance Clients: Armour & Co.; Fireman's Fund Group; General Accident Group; Great American Insurance Company.
Reference: Norwest Bank of Minneapolis.

For full biographical listings, see the Martindale-Hubbell Law Directory

MOORE, COSTELLO & HART (AV)

Suite 1350, Craig Hallum Center, 701 Fourth Avenue South, 55415
Telephone: 612-673-0148
FAX: 612-376-1770
St. Paul, Minnesota Office: 1400 Norwest Center.
Telephone: 612-227-7683.
FAX: 612-290-1770.

MEMBERS OF FIRM

Ronald E. Martell
William M. Beadie
Leonard W. Glewwe
John G. Patterson
Timothy C. Cook
Kathryn A. Graves

Representative Clients: Associated General Contractors of Minnesota, Inc.; Macalester College; The St. Paul Cos.; United States Fidelity & Guaranty Co.; University of St. Thomas.

For full biographical listings, see the Martindale-Hubbell Law Directory

*MOORHEAD,** Clay Co.

DOSLAND, NORDHOUGEN, LILLEHAUG & JOHNSON, P.A. (AV)

Suite 203 American Bank Moorhead Building, 730 Center Avenue, P.O. Box 100, 56561-0100
Telephone: 218-233-2744
Fax: 218-233-1570

C. A. Nye (1886-1910)
C. G. Dosland (1898-1945)
G. L. Dosland (1927-1983)
W. B. Dosland (1954-1990)
John P. Dosland
Curtis A. Nordhougen
Duane A. Lillehaug
Joel D. Johnson
Bruce Romanick

General Counsel For: American Crystal Sugar Co.; American Bank Moorhead, Moorhead, Minnesota.
Representative Clients: Auto Owners Insurance Co.; Wausau Insurance Cos.; Gethsemane Episcopal Cathedral; Swift-Eckrich, Inc.; Barrett Mobile Home Transport, Inc.; Moorhead Economic Development Authority; Eventide.
Reference: American Bank Moorhead, Moorhead, Minnesota.

For full biographical listings, see the Martindale-Hubbell Law Directory

*ST. CLOUD,** Stearns, Benton & Sherburne Cos.

QUINLIVAN, SHERWOOD, SPELLACY & TARVESTAD, P.A. (AV)

Sixth Floor, Norwest Center, 400 First Street South, P.O. Box 1008, 56302
Telephone: 612-251-1414
Toll Free: 1-800-325-5650
Fax: 612-251-1415
Minneapolis, Minnesota Office: 1050 Carlson Center, 601 Lakeshore Parkway. 55303.
Telephone: 612-449-5206.
Fax: 612-449-5101.

(See Next Column)

QUINLIVAN, SHERWOOD, SPELLACY & TARVESTAD P.A.—*Continued*

John D. Quinlivan
Anthony M. Tarvestad
Kevin A. Spellacy
Michael J. Ford
Kevin S. Carpenter
Michael T. Milligan
Michael T. Feichtinger
Steven R. Schwegman
Michael D. LaFountaine
John A. Nelson
Shelly M. Davis
Brian L. Williams
Molly J. Wingate
Krister D. Johnson
Thomas A. Atkinson
Corrine L. Langerock
(Not admitted in MN)
Dyan Ebert

Representative Insurance Clients: Auto-Owners Insurance Co.; CNA Insurance Co.; Farm Bureau Mutual; Farmers Insurance Group; Grinnell Mutual Insurance Co.; Minnesota Lawyers Mutual; Prudential; State Farm Insurance; St. Paul Insurance Cos.; Travelers; Wausau Insurance; Zurich-American.

For full biographical listings, see the Martindale-Hubbell Law Directory

RAJKOWSKI HANSMEIER LTD. (AV)

Daniel Building, 11 Seventh Avenue North, P.O. Box 1433, 56302-1433
Telephone: 612-251-1055
Toll Free: 800-445-9617
Fax: 612-251-5896

Frank J. Rajkowski
Gordon H. Hansmeier
Frederick L. Grunke
Thomas G. Jovanovich
John H. Scherer
Paul A. Rajkowski
Kevin F. Gray
William J. Cashman
David T. Shay
Richard W. Sobalvarro
Michael C. Rajkowski

LEGAL SUPPORT PERSONNEL

James H. Kelly, M.D. (Forensic Medical Consultant)

Representative Clients: Independent School District No. 742 (St. Cloud, Minn.); Jim W. Miller Construction Co.; City of Waite Park; The Travelers Ins. Co.; American Family Insurance Co.; Allstate Insurance Co.; Milbank/-State Auto Insurance Companies; Safeco Insurance Co.; Employers Mutual Co.; The Agricultural Group of Monsanto Company.

For full biographical listings, see the Martindale-Hubbell Law Directory

*ST. PAUL,** Ramsey Co.

COLLINS, BUCKLEY, SAUNTRY AND HAUGH (AV)

West 1100 First National Bank Building, 332 Minnesota Street, 55101
Telephone: 612-227-0611
Telecopier: 612-227-0758

MEMBERS OF FIRM

Eugene D. Buckley
Theodore J. Collins
Michael J. Sauntry
William E. Haugh, Jr.
Mark W. Gehan, Jr.
Patrick T. Tierney
Thomas J. Germscheid
John R. Schulz
Thomas R. O'Connell
Dan C. O'Connell
Christine L. Stroemer
Sarah J. Batzli

ASSOCIATES

Bonnie J. Bennett
Thomas E. McEllistrem

Reference: First National Bank of St. Paul.

For full biographical listings, see the Martindale-Hubbell Law Directory

GERAGHTY, O'LOUGHLIN & KENNEY, PROFESSIONAL ASSOCIATION (AV)

One Capital Centre Plaza, Suite 1400, 55102-1308
Telephone: 612-291-1177
Fax: 612-297-6901

Terence J. O'Loughlin
James R. Gowling
Robert M. Mahoney
David C. Hutchinson
Timothy R. Murphy
William H. Leary, III
Richard J. Thomas
Patrick H. O'Neill, Jr
Mary H. Alcorn
Patricia Rosvold
Daniel R. Fritz
Matthew J. Hanzel
Ann D. Bray
Jean B. Rudolph
Bryon Ascheman

OF COUNSEL

James H. Geraghty
James W. Kenney (Retired)

Representative Clients: St. Paul Fire & Marine Insurance Cos.; Midwest Medical Insurance Co.; Minnesota Lawyers Mutual Insurance Co.; University of Minnesota Hospitals; American National Bank and Trust Co.; Continental National American Group; Commercial State Bank; MMI Co.; Hammel Green Abrahamson, Inc.; Lunda Construction Co.

For full biographical listings, see the Martindale-Hubbell Law Directory

JARDINE, LOGAN & O'BRIEN (AV)

2100 Piper Jaffray Plaza, 444 Cedar Street, 55101
Telephone: 612-290-6500
Fax: 612-223-5070

(See Next Column)

MEMBERS OF FIRM

Gerald M. Linnihan
Alan R. Vanasek
John M. Kennedy, Jr.
James J. Galman
Gregory G. Heacox
George W. Kuehner
Patti J. Skoglund
Sean E. Hade
Timothy S. Crom
Lawrence M. Rocheford

ASSOCIATES

Thomas M. Countryman
Karen R. Cote
Randall S. Lane
Nathan W. Hart
Ronald R. Envall

Representative Clients: American Hardware Mutual Insurance Co.; Ohio-Casualty Group; Farmers Insurance Group; Maryland-Casualty Co; CIGNA; Federated Insurance Co.; American International Group; Lumbermen's Underwriting Alliance; Dodson Insurance Group; Safeco Insurance Co.

For Complete List of Firm Personnel, See General Section

For full biographical listings, see the Martindale-Hubbell Law Directory

MOORE, COSTELLO & HART (AV)

1400 Norwest Center, 55101
Telephone: 612-227-7683
FAX: 612-290-1770
Minneapolis, Minnesota Office: Suite 1350, Craig Hallum Center, 701 Fourth Avenue, South.
Telephone: 612-673-0148.
FAX: 612-376-1770.

MEMBERS OF FIRM

James C. Otis, Sr. (1879-1949)
Roland J. Faricy (1898-1962)
Richard A. Moore (1915-1991)
Harry G. Costello (Retired)
B. Warren Hart (1923-1981)
Marvin J. Pertzik
A. Patrick Leighton
Harold R. Fotsch
Ronald E. Martell
(Resident, Minneapolis Office)
William M. Beadie
(Resident, Minneapolis Office)
Denis L. Stoddard
Larry A. Hanson
J. Patrick Plunkett
John M. Harens
Phyllis Karasov
Malcolm G. McDonald
Leonard W. Glewwe
(Resident, Minneapolis Office)
John G. Patterson
(Resident, Minneapolis Office)
Timothy C. Cook
(Resident, Minneapolis Office)
Kathryn A. Graves
(Resident, Minneapolis Office)

ASSOCIATES

Steven D. Snelling
Tara D. Mattessich
James E. Blaney
Frederick J. Putzier

OF COUNSEL

William F. Orme
Fred W. Fisher

Representative Clients: Associated General Contractors of Minnesota, Inc.; Macalester College; The St. Paul Cos., Inc.; United States Fidelity & Guaranty Co.; University of St. Thomas.

For full biographical listings, see the Martindale-Hubbell Law Directory

*WILLMAR,** Kandiyohi Co.

SCHMIDT, THOMPSON, JOHNSON & MOODY, P.A. (AV)

707 Litchfield Avenue, S.W., Suite 100, P.O. Box 913, 56201-0913
Telephone: 612-235-1980; 1-800-733-7057

Henry W. Schmidt
Joe E. Thompson
William W. Thompson
Thomas G. Johnson
David C. Moody

Bradley J. Schmidt
Kathryn N. Smith

Representative Clients: First American Bank of Willmar; First Bank Central, N.A.; Willmar School District # 347; Holiday Inn of Willmar; Hormel Foods Corp.; Roth Chevrolet, Inc.; Auto Owners Insurance Co.; American Hardware Mutual Insurance Co.; American Family Insurance Co.

For full biographical listings, see the Martindale-Hubbell Law Directory

MISSISSIPPI

*ABERDEEN,** Monroe Co.

HOLCOMB, DUNBAR, CONNELL, CHAFFIN & WILLARD, A PROFESSIONAL ASSOCIATION (AV)

109 1/2 West Commerce Street, P.O. Box 866, 39730
Telephone: 601-369-8800
Facsimile: 601-369-9404
Jackson, Mississippi Office: 111 East Capitol Street, Suite 290, P.O. Box 2990, 39207-2990.
Telephone: 601-948-0048.
Facsimile: 601-948-0050.
Clarksdale, Mississippi Office: 152 Delta Avenue, P.O. Box 368, 38614.
Telephone: 601-627-2241.
Facsimile: 601-627-9788.

(See Next Column)

HOLCOMB, DUNBAR, CONNELL, CHAFFIN & WILLARD A PROFESSIONAL ASSOCIATION, *Aberdeen—Continued*

Oxford, Mississippi Office: 1217 Jackson Avenue, P.O. Drawer 707, 38655.
Telephone: 601-234-8775.
Facsimile: 601-234-8638.
Southhaven, Mississippi Office: Suite 1, 8727 Northwest Drive, P.O. Box 190, 38671.
Telephone: 601-342-6806.
Facsimile: 601-342-6792.

Jack F. Dunbar
Guy T. Gillespie, III
John H. Dunbar
David C. Dunbar
Robert H. Faulks

OF COUNSEL

Ralph E. Pogue

Representative Clients: The Employers Group Insurance Co.; State Farm Fire & Casualty Co.; Shelter Insurance Co.; Central Mutual Insurance Co.; Commercial Union Insurance Cos.; Southern Farm Bureau Casualty Insurance Co.; Federated Mutual Insurance Co.; Shelby Mutual Insurance Co.; State Farm Mutual Automobile Insurance Co.; Horace Mann Insurance Co.

For Complete List of Firm Personnel, See General Section

For full biographical listings, see the Martindale-Hubbell Law Directory

BILOXI, Harrison Co.

PAGE, MANNINO & PERESICH (AV)

759 Vieux Marché Mall, P.O. Drawer 289, 39530
Telephone: 601-374-2100
Telecopier: 601-432-5539
Jackson, Mississippi Office: One LeFleurs Square, 4735 Old Canton Road, P.O. Box 12159.
Telephone: 601-364-1100.
Telecopier: 601-364-1118.
Gulfport, Mississippi Office: Markham Building, 2301 - 14th Street, Suite 600, Drawer 660.
Telephone: 601-863-8861.
Telecopier: 601-863-8871.

MEMBERS OF FIRM

Lyle M. Page
Frederick J. Mannino
Ronald G. Peresich
Michael B. McDermott
Stephen G. Peresich
Jess H. Dickinson
Tere Richardson Steel
David S. Raines
Michael P. Collins
Randolph Cook Wood
Mary A. Nichols
Joseph Henry Ros
Thomas William Busby
Michael E. Whitehead
Katharine Malley Samson
Douglas J. Wise

Representative Clients: United States Fidelity & Guaranty Co.; St. Paul Fire & Marine Insurance Co.; Crawford & Co.; Anheuser-Busch Corp.
General Counsel for: Peoples Bank of Biloxi, Mississippi; Biloxi Regional Medical Center; Bank of Mississippi (Gulf Coast Division).

For full biographical listings, see the Martindale-Hubbell Law Directory

*CLARKSDALE,** Coahoma Co.

HOLCOMB, DUNBAR, CONNELL, CHAFFIN & WILLARD, A PROFESSIONAL ASSOCIATION (AV)

152 Delta Avenue, P.O. Box 368, 38614
Telephone: 601-627-2241
Facsimile: 601-627-9788
Jackson, Mississippi Office: 111 East Capitol Street, Suite 290, P.O. Box 2990, 39207-2990.
Telephone: 601-948-0048.
Facsimile: 601-948-0050.
Aberdeen, Mississippi Office: 109 1/2 West Commerce Street, P.O. Box 866, 39730.
Telephone: 601-369-8800.
Facsimile: 601-369-9404.
Oxford, Mississippi Office: 1217 Jackson Avenue, P.O. Drawer 707, 38655.
Telephone: 601-234-8775.
Facsimile: 601-234-8638.
Southaven, Mississippi Office: Suite 1, 8727 Northwest Drive, 38671.
Telephone: 601-342-6806.
Facsimile: 601-342-6792.

William M. Chaffin
William G. Willard, Jr.
William A. Baskin
Jeffrey S. Dilley
David A. Burns

Representative Clients: The Employers Group Insurance Co.; State Farm Fire & Casualty Co.; Central Mutual Insurance Co.; Commercial Union Insurance Cos.; Southern Farm Bureau Casualty Insurance Co.; Federated Mutual Insurance Co.; Shelby Mutual Insurance Co.; State Farm Mutual Fire & Casualty Insurance Co.; Horace Mann Insurance Co.; Shelter Insurance Co.

For Complete List of Firm Personnel, See General Section

For full biographical listings, see the Martindale-Hubbell Law Directory

LUCKETT LAW FIRM, A PROFESSIONAL ASSOCIATION (AV)

143 Yazoo Avenue, P.O. Drawer 1000, 38614-1000
Telephone: 601-624-2591
Telecopier: 601-627-5403

William O. Luckett
William O. Luckett, Jr.

John B. Gillis
Betty W. Maynard

District and Local Counsel for: Employers Group; Firemen's Fund; Liberty Mutual Insurance Co.; CNA Group; Deere & Co.; Indiana Lumbermens Insurance Co.; Texas Gas Transmission Corp.; American Interstate Insurance Company of Georgia; Elliston, Inc.; Graward General Insurance.

For Complete List of Firm Personnel, See General Section

For full biographical listings, see the Martindale-Hubbell Law Directory

*CLEVELAND,** Bolivar Co.

JACKS, ADAMS & WESTERFIELD, P.A. (AV)

106 South Pearman Avenue, P.O. Box 1209, 38732
Telephone: 601-843-6171
FAX: 601-843-6176

Gerald H. Jacks
William S. Adams, Jr.
Andrew M. W. Westerfield
Richard L. Kimmel
S. David Norquist
Thomas B. Janoush

Representative Clients: United States Fidelity & Guaranty Co.; Audubon Insurance Co.; State Farm Mutual Automobile Ins. Co.; State Farm Fire & Casualty Co.; New Hampshire Insurance Co.; Southern Guaranty Co.; Zurich Insurance Co.; Providence Washington Ins. Co.; Aetna Life & Casualty Co.; Baxter-Travenol, Inc.; State Auto Ins. Co.

For full biographical listings, see the Martindale-Hubbell Law Directory

*COLUMBIA,** Marion Co.

AULTMAN, TYNER, MCNEESE & RUFFIN, LTD., A PROFESSIONAL LAW CORPORATION (AV)

329 Church Street, P.O. Drawer 707, 39429
Telephone: 601-736-2222
Hattiesburg, Mississippi Office: 315 Hemphill Street, P.O. Drawer 750.
Telephone: 601-583-2671.
Gulfport, Mississippi Office: 1201 25th Avenue, Suite 300, P.O. Box 607.
Telephone: 601-863-6913.

Thomas D. McNeese
Richard F. Yarborough, Jr.

Lawrence E. Hahn

OF COUNSEL

Ernest Ray Duff

Representative Clients: Hercules, Inc.; United States Steel Corp.; Ford Motor Co.; International Paper Co.; Phillips Petroleum Co.; Aetna Casualty & Surety Co.; CNA Group; Liberty Mutual Insurance Co.; St. Paul Fire & Marine Insurance Co.; Fireman's Fund.

For full biographical listings, see the Martindale-Hubbell Law Directory

*GREENWOOD,** Leflore Co.

UPSHAW, WILLIAMS, BIGGERS, PAGE & KRUGER (AV)

309 Fulton Street, P.O. Drawer 8230, 38930
Telephone: 601-455-1613
Facsimile: 601-453-9245
Jackson, Mississippi Office: One Jackson Place, 188 East Capitol Street, Suite 600. P.O. Drawer 1163, 39215.
Telephone: 601-944-0005.
Facsimile: 601-355-4269.

MEMBERS OF FIRM

James E. Upshaw
Tommie G. Williams
Marc A. Biggers
Thomas Y. Page (Resident, Jackson Office)
Stephen P. Kruger (Resident, Jackson Office)
Glenn F. Beckham
James D. Holland (Resident, Jackson Office)
F. Ewin Henson, III
Lonnie D. Bailey
Robert S. Upshaw
Clinton M. Guenther
Roger C. Riddick (Resident, Jackson Office)
Edley H. Jones, III (Resident, Jackson Office)
C. Richard Benz, Jr.
Richard C. Williams, Jr.
Wes Peters (Resident, Jackson Office)

ASSOCIATES

Brent E. Southern (Resident, Jackson Office)
R.H. Burress, III
Kathleen S. Gordon (Resident, Jackson Office)
W. Hugh Gillon, IV (Resident, Jackson Office)
William C. Helm (Resident, Jackson Office)
Bryan H. Callaway
Mark C. Carroll (Resident, Jackson Office)
Paul L. Goodman
Walter C. Morrison, IV (Resident, Jackson Office)
Patrick C. Malouf (Resident, Jackson Office)
David C. Meadors
Stuart B. Harmon (Resident, Jackson Office)

(See Next Column)

UPSHAW, WILLIAMS, BIGGERS, PAGE & KRUGER—*Continued*

OF COUNSEL

B. L. Riddick (Resident, Jackson Office)
John R. Countiss, III (Resident, Jackson Office)

Representative Clients: U.S.F. & G. Co.; State Farm Mutual Automobile Ins. Co.; ; Continental Insurance Co.; St. Paul Fire & Marine Insurance Co.; Aetna Casualty & Surety Co.; Kemper Insurance Co.; Zurich-American Ins. Group; Home Ins. Co.; Illinois Central Railroad Co.; Allstate Insurance Co.

For full biographical listings, see the Martindale-Hubbell Law Directory

*GULFPORT,** Harrison Co.

ALLEN, VAUGHN, COBB & HOOD, P.A. (AV)

One Hancock Plaza, Suite 1209, P.O. Drawer 4108, 39502-4108
Telephone: 601-864-4011
Fax: 601-864-4852

Harry R. Allen
Thomas E. Vaughn
David L. Cobb
Billy W. Hood
Robert W. Atkinson
Benjamin U. Bowden
Richard B. Tubertini
Rodney Douglas Robinson

Steven Johnson Allen (Resident)
E. Colette Towles
David W. Crane
John A. Foxworth, Jr.
H. Gray Laird, III
W. Wright Hill

OF COUNSEL

D. Knox White

For full biographical listings, see the Martindale-Hubbell Law Directory

AULTMAN, TYNER, MCNEESE & RUFFIN, LTD., A PROFESSIONAL LAW CORPORATION (AV)

1201 25th Avenue, Suite 300, P.O. Box 607, 39502
Telephone: 601-863-6913
Hattiesburg, Mississippi Office: 315 Hemphill Street, P.O. Drawer 750.
Telephone: 601-583-2671.
Columbia, Mississippi Office: 329 Church Street, P.O. Drawer 707.
Telephone: 601-736-2222.

Ben E. Sheely
Paul J. Delcambre, Jr.
Dorrance (Dee) Aultman, Jr.

For full biographical listings, see the Martindale-Hubbell Law Directory

DUKES, DUKES, KEATING AND FANECA, P.A. (AV)

2308 East Beach Boulevard, P.O. Drawer W, 39501
Telephone: 601-868-1111
FAX: 601-863-2886

William F. Dukes
Walter W. Dukes
William H. Pettey, Jr.

David Charles Goff

For full biographical listings, see the Martindale-Hubbell Law Directory

FRANKE, RAINEY & SALLOUM (AV)

2605 14th Street, P.O. Drawer 460, 39502
Telephone: 601-868-7070
Telecopier: 601-868-7090

MEMBERS OF FIRM

Paul M. Franke, Jr.
William M. Rainey
Richard P. Salloum
Paul B. Howell
Ronald T. Russell
Fredrick B. Feeney, II
Traci M. Castille

ASSOCIATES

Kaleel G. Salloum, Jr.
Ruth E. Bennett
Donald P. Moore
Roland F. Samson, III
Jeffrey S. Bruni
Stefan G. Bourn

For full biographical listings, see the Martindale-Hubbell Law Directory

HOPKINS, DODSON, CRAWLEY, BAGWELL, UPSHAW & PERSONS (AV)

2701 24th Avenue, P.O. Box 1510, 39502-1510
Telephone: 601-864-2200
Mississippi & USA Wats: 1-800-421-3629
Fax: 601-868-9358; 601-863-4227

MEMBERS OF FIRM

Alben N. Hopkins
Lisa P. Dodson
Timothy D. Crawley
Douglas Bagwell
Jessica Sibley Upshaw
James B. Persons

(See Next Column)

ASSOCIATES

Perre M. Cabell
Christopher Anthony Davis
James Robert Reeves, Jr.
Ottis B. Crocker, III
Kaye Johnson Persons (Not admitted in MS)
Matthew G. Mestayer
Regina A. Lightsey
Mary Benton-Shaw (Not admitted in MS)
K. Douglas Lee (Not admitted in MS)
Thomas A. Waller
M. Amanda Baucum (Not admitted in MS)

LEGAL SUPPORT PERSONNEL

PARALEGALS

Cherri Nickoles
Penny W. West
Jennifer Susan Regan
Justina M. Tillman
Jayme L. Evans
Tracey L. Owen
Marcia P. Henry
Anne B. Parks

Representative Clients: Avondale Shipyards; Employers Insurance of Wausau; Fireman's Fund Insurance Company; General Cable Company; Hartford Insurance Company and Its Affiliates; Insurance Company of North America; Libery Mutual Group; Reliance Insurance; USX Corporation.

For full biographical listings, see the Martindale-Hubbell Law Directory

PAGE, MANNINO & PERESICH (AV)

Markham Building, 2301 14th Street, Suite 600, Drawer 660, 39501-2095
Telephone: 601-863-8861
Telecopier: 601-863-8871
Biloxi, Mississippi Office: 759 Vieux MarchéMall, P.O. Drawer 289.
Telephone: 601-374-2100.
Telecopier: 601-432-5539.
Jackson, Mississippi Office: One Lefleurs Square, 4735 Old Canton Road, P.O. Box 12159.
Telephone: 601-364-1100.
Telecopier: 601-364-1118.

MEMBERS OF FIRM

Lyle M. Page
Frederick J. Mannino
Ronald G. Peresich
Michael B. McDermott
Stephen G. Peresich
Jess H. Dickinson
Tere Richardson Steel
David S. Raines
Michael P. Collins
Randolph Cook Wood
Mary A. Nichols
Joseph Henry Ros
Thomas William Busby
Michael E. Whitehead
Katharine Malley Samson
Douglas J. Wise

Representative Clients: United States Fidelity & Guaranty Co.; St. Paul Fire & Marine Insurance Co.; Crawford & Co.; Anheuser-Busch Corp.
General Counsel for: Peoples Bank of Biloxi, Mississippi; Biloxi Regional Medical Center; Bank of Mississippi (Gulf Coast Division).

For full biographical listings, see the Martindale-Hubbell Law Directory

*HATTIESBURG,** Forrest Co.

AULTMAN, TYNER, MCNEESE & RUFFIN, LTD., A PROFESSIONAL LAW CORPORATION (AV)

315 Hemphill Street, P.O. Drawer 750, 39403-0750
Telephone: 601-583-2671
Columbia, Mississippi Office: 329 Church Street, P.O. Drawer 707.
Telephone: 601-736-2222.
Gulfport, Mississippi Office: 1201 25th Avenue, Suite 300, P.O. Box 607.
Telephone: 601-863-6913.

Dorrance Aultman
Thomas W. Tyner
Thomas D. McNeese (Resident, Columbia Office)
Louie F. Ruffin
Richard F. Yarborough, Jr. (Resident, Columbia Office)
Ben E. Sheely (Resident, Gulfport Office)
Patrick H. Zachary
Paul J. Delcambre, Jr. (Resident, Gulfport Office)
Robert J. Dambrino, III
Vicki R. Leggett
R. Curtis Smith, II
Dorrance (Dee) Aultman, Jr. (Resident, Gulfport Office)
William Nelson Graham

James L. Quinn
Walter J. Eades
Lawrence E. Hahn (Resident, Columbia Office)
Carol Ann Estes
Victor A. DuBose

OF COUNSEL

Ernest Ray Duff (Resident, Columbia Office)

Representative Clients: Hercules, Inc.; U.S. Steel Corp.; Ford Motor Co.; Phillips Petroleum Co.; Aetna Casualty & Surety Co.; CNA Group; Liberty Mutual Insurance Co.; St. Paul Fire & Marine Insurance Co.; Fireman's Fund.

For full biographical listings, see the Martindale-Hubbell Law Directory

*JACKSON,** Hinds Co.

* indicates certain Bar Register subscribers whose principal office is located elsewhere in the state and who have arranged for representation as a part of the state capital listings that follow

ALLRED & DONALDSON (AV)

101 West Capitol Street, Suite 300, P.O. Box 3828, 39207-3828
Telephone: 601-948-2086
Telefax: 601-948-2175

MEMBERS OF FIRM

Michael S. Allred
John I. Donaldson

ASSOCIATES

Stephen M. Maloney
Kathleen H. Eiler

For full biographical listings, see the Martindale-Hubbell Law Directory

COPELAND COOK TAYLOR & BUSH (AV)

17th Floor, Capital Towers Building, 125 South Congress Street, P.O. Drawer 2132, 39225-2132
Telephone: 601-354-0123
Facsimile: 601-352-6714

MEMBERS OF FIRM

Charles G. Copeland
Thomas A. Cook
Glenn G. Taylor
C. Glen Bush, Jr.
Thomas C. Gerity
Harry E. Neblett, Jr.
James R. Moore, Jr.
Suzanna Baker
J. Tucker Mitchell
Robert P. Thompson
Thomas R. Hudson
Michael W. Baxter
Keith David Obert
James F. Noble III
Lee Howell, III
Monte L. Barton, Jr.
W. Shan Thompson
Gregory L. Kennedy
John M. Breland
C. Dale Shearer

For full biographical listings, see the Martindale-Hubbell Law Directory

HOLCOMB, DUNBAR, CONNELL, CHAFFIN & WILLARD, A PROFESSIONAL ASSOCIATION (AV)

111 East Capitol Street, Suite 290, P.O. Box 2990, 39207-2990
Telephone: 601-948-0048
Facsimile: 601-948-0050
Clarksdale, Mississippi Office: 152 Delta Avenue, P.O. Box 368, 38614.
Telephone: 601-627-2241.
Facsimile: 601-627-9788.
Aberdeen, Mississippi Office: 109 1/2 West Commerce Street, P.O. Box 866, 39730.
Telephone: 601-369-8800.
Facsimile: 601-369-9404.
Oxford, Mississippi Office: 1217 Jackson Avenue, P.O. Drawer 707, 38655.
Telephone: 601-234-8775.
Facsimile: 601-234-8638.
Southaven, Mississippi Office: Suite 1, 8727 Northwest Drive, P.O. Box 190, 38671.
Telephone: 601-342-6806.
Facsimile: 601-342-6792.

Jack F. Dunbar
William M. Chaffin
William G. Willard, Jr.
Guy T. Gillespie, III
Edward A. Moss
Thomas J. Suszek
John H. Dunbar
David C. Dunbar
Michael N. Watts
Janet G. Arnold
William A. Baskin
Thomas T. Dunbar
Robert H. Faulks
Jeffrey S. Dilley
David A. Burns
T. Swayze Alford

OF COUNSEL

Ralph E. Pogue

Representative Clients: The Employers Group Insurance Co.; State Farm Fire & Casualty Co.; Central Mutual Insurance Co.; Commercial Union Insurance Cos.; Southern Farm Bureau Casualty Insurance Co.; Federated Mutual Insurance Co.; Shelby Mutual Insurance Co.; State Farm Mutual Automobile Insurance Co.; Horace Mann Insurance Co.

For Complete List of Firm Personnel, See General Section

For full biographical listings, see the Martindale-Hubbell Law Directory

MARKOW, WALKER, REEVES & ANDERSON, P.A. (AV)

Atrium North Building, 805 South Wheatley, Suite 400, P.O. Box 13669, 39236-3669
Telephone: 601-956-8500
Telecopier: 601-956-8423

Peter J. Markow, Jr.
Christopher J. Walker
William C. Reeves
James M. Anderson
Terry B. Germany
Michael T. Estep
Richard C. Coker
Gilson Davis (Dave) Peterson
Alfonso Nuzzo

(See Next Column)

Joseph W. McDowell
Richard M. Edmonson, Jr.
Hubert Wesley Williams, III.
L. Pepper Cossar
Delia Y. Robinson
T.G. Bolen, Jr.
Alan C. Goodman

Reference: The Sunburst Bank, Jackson, Miss.

For full biographical listings, see the Martindale-Hubbell Law Directory

MCCOY, WILKINS, STEPHENS & TIPTON, P.A. (AV)

1 LeFleur Square, 4735 Old Canton Road, P.O. Box 13429, 39211
Telephone: 601-366-4343
Telecopier: 601-981-7608

Joseph L. McCoy
Joseph T. Wilkins, III
Senith C. Tipton
Robert M. Carpenter
William A. Patterson
Leland S. Smith, III
Mark C. Carlson
Betty Burton Arinder
Daniel M. Baker

Diane V. Pradat
Byron P. Hansbro
Gary K. Silberman

Representative Clients: Insurance Company of North America; Employers Insurance of Wausau.

For full biographical listings, see the Martindale-Hubbell Law Directory

PAGE, MANNINO & PERESICH (AV)

One LeFleurs Square, 4735 Old Canton Road, P.O. Box 12159, 39236-2159
Telephone: 601-364-1100
Telecopier: 601-364-1118
Biloxi, Mississippi Office: 759 Vieux MarchéMall, P.O. Drawer 289.
Telephone: 601-374-2100.
Telecopier: 601-432-5539.
Gulfport, Mississippi Office: Markham Building, 2301 - 14th Street, Suite 600, P.O. Drawer 660.
Telephone: 601-863-8861.
Telecopier: 601-863-8871.

MEMBERS OF FIRM

Lyle M. Page
Frederick J. Mannino
Ronald G. Peresich
Michael B. McDermott
Stephen G. Peresich
Jess H. Dickinson
Tere Richardson Steel
David S. Raines
Michael P. Collins
Randolph Cook Wood
Mary A. Nichols
Joseph Henry Ros
Thomas William Busby
Michael E. Whitehead
Katharine Malley Samson
Douglas J. Wise (Not admitted in MS)

Representative Clients: United States Fidelity & Guaranty Co.; St. Paul Fire & Marine Insurance Co.; Crawford & Co.; Anheuser-Busch Corp.
General Counsel for: Peoples Bank of Biloxi, Mississippi; Biloxi Regional Medical Center; Bank of Mississippi (Gulf Coast Division).

For full biographical listings, see the Martindale-Hubbell Law Directory

SHELL, BUFORD, BUFKIN, CALLICUTT & PERRY (AV)

920 Trustmark Building, P.O. Box 157, 39205
Telephone: 601-948-2291
Facsimile: 601-352-6968

MEMBERS OF FIRM

Cary E. Bufkin
K. Hayes Callicutt
Kenneth G. Perry
Douglas R. Duke
James N. Bullock
Ken R. Adcock
Eugene R. Naylor

ASSOCIATES

E. Frank Goodman
R. Scott Sellers (Not admitted in MS)

Representative Clients: Mississippi Baptist Medical Center; Mississippi Chemical Corp.; Aetna Casualty and Surety Co.; American International Group; Atlantic Mutual Insurance Co.; Commercial Union Insurance Co.; United States Fidelity and Guaranty Co.; Home Insurance Co.; The Chubb Group; Trustmark National Bank.

For full biographical listings, see the Martindale-Hubbell Law Directory

STEEN REYNOLDS DALEHITE & CURRIE (AV)

Mississippi Valley Title Building, 315 Tombigbee Street, P.O. Box 900, 39205
Telephone: 601-969-7054
Telecopier: 601-969-5120

MEMBERS OF FIRM

Jimmie B. Reynolds, Jr.
William M. Dalehite, Jr.
Edward J. Currie, Jr.
Whitman B. Johnson, III
William C. Griffin
Philip W. Gaines
Michael F. Myers

(See Next Column)

STEEN REYNOLDS DALEHITE & CURRIE—*Continued*

ASSOCIATES

Frances R. Shields
William H. Creel, Jr.
James C. Smallwood, III
F. Keith Ball
Shannon S. Clark
Lisa L. Williams
Le Robinson Brown

OF COUNSEL

Jerome B. Steen

Mississippi Counsel for: State Farm Insurance Co.
Representative Clients include: Allstate Insurance Co.; St. Paul Insurance Cos.; Indiana Lumbermens Mutual Insurance Co.; United Services Automobile Assn.; Empire Fire & Marine Ins.; Sears Roebuck & Co.
References: Trustmark National Bank, Jackson, Mississippi.

For full biographical listings, see the Martindale-Hubbell Law Directory

*** UPSHAW, WILLIAMS, BIGGERS, PAGE & KRUGER (AV)**

One Jackson Place, 188 East Capitol Street, Suite 600, P.O. Drawer 1163, 39215
Telephone: 601-944-0005
Facsimile: 601-355-4269
Greenwood, Mississippi Office: 309 Fulton Street, P.O. Drawer 8230, 38930.
Telephone: 601-455-1613.
Facsimile: 601-453-9245.

RESIDENT MEMBERS

Thomas Y. Page
Stephen P. Kruger
James D. Holland
Roger C. Riddick
Edley H. Jones, III
Wes Peters

RESIDENT ASSOCIATES

Brent E. Southern
Kathleen S. Gordon
W. Hugh Gillon, IV
William C. Helm
Mark C. Carroll
Walter C. Morrison, IV
Patrick C. Malouf
Stuart B. Harmon

OF COUNSEL

B. L. Riddick
John R. Countiss, III

Representative Clients: U.S.F. & G. Co.; State Farm Mutual Automobile Ins. Co.; Continental Insurance Co.; St. Paul Fire & Marine Insurance Co.; Aetna Casualty & Surety Co.; Kemper Insurance Co.; Zurich-America Ins. Group; Home Ins. Co.; Illinois Central Railroad Co.; Allstate Insurance Co.

For full biographical listings, see the Martindale-Hubbell Law Directory

WATKINS & EAGER (AV)

Suite 300 The Emporium Building, P.O. Box 650, 39205
Telephone: 601-948-6470
Facsimile: (601) 354-3623

OF COUNSEL

Thomas M. Murphree, Jr.

MEMBERS OF FIRM

James A. Becker, Jr.
Clifford B. Ammons
Richard T. Lawrence
Robert H. Pedersen
Robert A. Miller
Rebecca Lee Wiggs

Representative Clients: Associated Aviation Underwriters; Avemco; Cigna Property and Casualty Cos.; CNA Insurance; New York Life Insurance Co.; The Travelers.

For Complete List of Firm Personnel, See General Section

For full biographical listings, see the Martindale-Hubbell Law Directory

WELLS MARBLE & HURST (AV)

Suite 400, Lamar Life Building, 317 East Capitol Street, P.O. Box 131, 39205-0131
Telephone: 601-355-8321
Telecopier: 601-355-4217

MEMBERS OF FIRM

Erskine W. Wells
Roland D. Marble
J. Jerry Langford
John Edward Hughes, III
Wendell H. Cook, Jr.
Kenna L. Mansfield, Jr.
Steven H. Begley
Daniel H. Fairly
Roy H. Liddell
Walter D. Willson

ASSOCIATES

Kelly D. Simpkins
Lana Edwards Gillon

Counsel for: General Motors Corp.; United States Steel Corp.; International Business Machines Corp.; Illinois Central Railroad Co.; Lamar Life Insurance Co.; Metropolitan Life Insurance Co.; Prudential Insurance Company of America; Southern Natural Gas Co.; Trustmark National Bank of Jackson.

For Complete List of Firm Personnel, See General Section

For full biographical listings, see the Martindale-Hubbell Law Directory

WISE CARTER CHILD & CARAWAY, PROFESSIONAL ASSOCIATION (AV)

600 Heritage Building, 401 East Capitol Street, P.O. Box 651, 39205
Telephone: 601-968-5500
FAX: 601-968-5519

Natie P. Caraway
James L. Robertson
George Q. Evans
Charles T. Ozier
Richard D. Gamblin
David W. Clark
John D. Price
Douglas E. Levanway
F. Hall Bailey
Clifford K. Bailey, III
Andrew D. Sweat
Mark P. Caraway
George H. Ritter
R. Mark Hodges
Charles E. Ross

John W. Robinson, III.
Rachael Hetherington Lenoir

Representative Clients: Crum & Forster Managers Corp. (Ill.); Medical Assurance Company of Mississippi; National Union Life Insurance Co.; Ohio Casualty Group; St. Paul Cos.; The Home Insurance Cos.; The Travelers Insurance Cos.; United States Fidelity & Guaranty Co.; Virginia Insurance Reciprocal.

For Complete List of Firm Personnel, See General Section

For full biographical listings, see the Martindale-Hubbell Law Directory

*MERIDIAN,** Lauderdale Co.

BOURDEAUX AND JONES (AV)

505 Constitution Avenue, P.O. Box 2009, 39302-2009
Telephone: 601-693-2393
Fax: 601-693-0226

Thomas D. Bourdeaux
Thomas R. Jones
William C. Hammack
Thomas L. Webb
J. Richard Barry
E. Gregory Snowden
Michael D. Herrin
Lee Thaggard

General Counsel for: Dixie Oil Co. of Alabama; Great Southern National Bank; Meridian Housing Authority; Mississippi Loggers Group Inc.; New South Communications, Inc.; City of Meridian; Lauderdale County Board of Supervisors.
Local Counsel for: Chrysler Corporation; Louisiana-Pacific Corp.; Hartford Insurance Group; Fireman's Fund American Insurance Cos.; Mississippi Loggers Association-S.I.F.; Great River Insurance Co.; United States Fidelity and Guaranty Co.

For full biographical listings, see the Martindale-Hubbell Law Directory

EPPES, WATTS & SHANNON (AV)

4805 Poplar Springs Drive, P.O. Box 3787, 39303-3787
Telephone: 601-483-3968
Telecopier: 601-693-0416

MEMBERS OF FIRM

Walter W. Eppes, Jr.
T. Kenneth Watts
John Rex Shannon
Grace Watts Mitts
William B. Carter

Representative Clients: Allstate Insurance Co.; American International Adjusting Co.; CIGNA; Liberty Mutual Insurance Co.; Royal Globe Insurance Co.; St. Paul Insurance Cos.; State Farm Insurance Co.; General Motors Corporation; Medical Assurance Corp.; Sears, Roebuck and Co.

For full biographical listings, see the Martindale-Hubbell Law Directory

*NATCHEZ,** Adams Co.

GWIN, LEWIS & PUNCHES (AV)

319 Market Street, P.O. Box 1344, 39120
Telephone: 601-446-6621
FAX: 601-442-6175
Woodville, Mississippi Office: 457 Main Street.
Telephone: 601-446-6621.

MEMBERS OF FIRM

Lucien C. Gwin, Jr.
W. Bruce Lewis
Robert R. Punches
Lucien C. Gwin, III

Mississippi Counsel for: International Paper Company.
Representative Clients: Sammons Communications, Inc.; Britton & Koontz First National Bank; Mississippi Farm Bureau Insurance Co.

For Complete List of Firm Personnel, See General Section

For full biographical listings, see the Martindale-Hubbell Law Directory

*NEW ALBANY,** Union Co.

SUMNERS, CARTER & MCMILLIN, P.A. (AV)

104 North Central Avenue, P.O. Drawer 730, 38652
Telephone: 601-534-6326
Telecopier: 601-534-5205

(See Next Column)

SUMNERS, CARTER & MCMILLIN P.A., *New Albany—Continued*

Robert L. Smallwood, Jr. (1909-1954)
Leslie Darden (1910-1982)
Lester F. Sumners
Robert M. Carter
Roger H. McMillin, Jr.

Representative Clients: Union County Board of Supervisors; City of New Albany; USF&G Co.; Maryland Casualty Co.; First National Bank; Merchants Truck Line, Inc.; Northeast Mississippi Community College; Weyerhaeuser Co.; Baptist Memorial Hospital-Union County; Carr Oil Co.

For full biographical listings, see the Martindale-Hubbell Law Directory

*OXFORD,** Lafayette Co.

FREELAND & FREELAND (AV)

1013 Jackson Avenue, P.O. Box 269, 38655
Telephone: 601-234-3414
Telecopier: 601-234-0604

MEMBERS OF FIRM

T. H. Freeland, III
T. H. Freeland, IV
J. Hale Freeland

ASSOCIATE

Paul W. Crutcher

Representative Clients: American Republic Insurance Co.; Carolina Casualty Insurance Co.; John Deere Insurance Co.; Express Insurance Co.; Fireman's Fund Insurance; Northwestern Mutual Life Insurance Co.; Sentry Insurance; American Insurance Co.; Ohio Casualty Group; Home Insurance Co.

For full biographical listings, see the Martindale-Hubbell Law Directory

HOLCOMB, DUNBAR, CONNELL, CHAFFIN & WILLARD, A PROFESSIONAL ASSOCIATION (AV)

1217 Jackson Avenue P.O. Drawer 707, 38655
Telephone: 601-234-8775
Facsimile: 601-234-8638
Jackson, Mississippi Office: 111 East Capitol Street, Suite 290. P.O. Box 2990, 39207-2990.
Telephone: 601-948-0048.
Facsimile: 601-948-0050.
Clarksdale, Mississippi Office: 152 Delta Avenue, P.O. Box 368, 38614.
Telephone: 601-627-2241.
Facsimile: 601-627-9788.
Aberdeen, Mississippi Office: 109 1/2 West Commerce Street, P.O. Box 866, 39730.
Telephone: 601-369-8800.
Facsimile: 601-369-9404.
Southaven, Mississippi Office: Suite 1, 8727 Northwest Drive, P.O. Box 190, 38671.
Telephone: 601-342-6806.
Facsimile: 601-342-6792.

Jack F. Dunbar
Guy T. Gillespie, III
Edward A. Moss
Thomas J. Suszek
John H. Dunbar
Michael N. Watts
Janet G. Arnold
Thomas T. Dunbar
T. Swayze Alford
Nancy M. Maddox

Representative Clients: The Employers Group Insurance Co.; State Farm Fire & Casualty Co.; Central Mutual Insurance Co.; Commercial Union Insurance Cos.; Southern Farm Bureau Casualty Insurance Co.; Federated Mutual Insurance Co.; Shelby Mutual Insurance Co.; State Farm Mutual Fire & Casualty Insurance Co.; Horace Mann Insurance Co.; Shelter Insurance Co.

For Complete List of Firm Personnel, See General Section

For full biographical listings, see the Martindale-Hubbell Law Directory

*PASCAGOULA,** Jackson Co.

COLINGO, WILLIAMS, HEIDELBERG, STEINBERGER & MCELHANEY, P.A. (AV)

711 Delmas Avenue, P.O. Box 1407, 39568-0240
Telephone: 601-762-8021
FAX: 601-762-7589

Joe R. Colingo
Roy C. Williams
James H. Heidelberg
Karl R. Steinberger
Michael J. McElhaney, Jr.
James H. Colmer, Jr.
Robert W. Wilkinson
Brett K. Williams

Carol S. Noblitt
Karen N. Haarala
Stephen Walker Burrow
Scott D. Smith
Gina L. Bardwell

LEGAL SUPPORT PERSONNEL

Harry H. Carpenter

Representative Clients: International Paper Co.; R.J. Reynolds; Westinghouse Corp.; St. Paul Fire & Marine Ins. Co.; Kemper Group; Singing River Hospital System.

For full biographical listings, see the Martindale-Hubbell Law Directory

SOUTHAVEN, De Soto Co.

HOLCOMB, DUNBAR, CONNELL, CHAFFIN & WILLARD, A PROFESSIONAL ASSOCIATION (AV)

Suite 1, 8727 Northwest Drive, P.O. Box 190, 38671
Telephone: 601-342-6806
Facsimile: 601-342-6792
Jackson, Mississippi Office: 111 East Capitol Street, Suite 290, P.O. Box 2990, 39207-2990.
Telephone: 601-948-0048.
Facsimile: 601-948-0050.
Clarksdale, Mississippi Office: 152 Delta Avenue, P.O. Box 368, 38614.
Telephone: 601-627-2241.
Facsimile: 601-627-9788.
Aberdeen, Mississippi Office: 109 1/2 West Commerce Street, P.O. Box 866, 39730.
Telephone: 601-369-8800.
Facsimile: 601-369-9404.
Oxford, Mississippi Office: 1217 Jackson Avenue, P.O. Drawer 707, 38655.
Telephone: 601-234-8775.
Facsimile: 601-234-8638.

William M. Chaffin
Thomas J. Suszek
William A. Baskin
Barry C. Blackburn

Counsel For: United Southern Bank; Mississippi Power & Light Co.; Mississippi Valley Gas Co.; Aetna Casualty & Surety Co.; Southern Farm Bureau Casualty Insurance Co.; South Central Bell Telephone Co.; State Farm Mutual Fire & Casualty Insurance Co.; Deere & Co.; Navistar International Transportation Corp.; Sunburst Bank.

For Complete List of Firm Personnel, See General Section

For full biographical listings, see the Martindale-Hubbell Law Directory

*TUPELO,** Lee Co.

HOLLAND, RAY & UPCHURCH, P.A. (AV)

322 Jefferson Street, P.O. Drawer 409, 38802
Telephone: 601-842-1721
Facsimile: 601-844-6413

Sam E. Lumpkin (1908-1964)
Ralph L. Holland
James Hugh Ray
Robert K. Upchurch
W. Reed Hillen, III
Thomas A. Wicker

Michael D. Tapscott

Representative Clients: Insurance Companies - Aetna Insurance Co.; The Travelers; Continental Casualty Co.; Lloyds of London; Bankers Life & Casualty Co.; Continental National American Group; New Amsterdam Casualty Co.; Security Insurance Group; Commercial Union Insurance Cos.; Alexander Howden Insurance Services, Inc.

For full biographical listings, see the Martindale-Hubbell Law Directory

WEBB, SANDERS, DEATON, BALDUCCI & SMITH (AV)

363 North Broadway, P.O. Box 496, 38802-0496
Telephone: 601-844-2137
Facsimile: 601-842-3863
Oxford, Mississippi Office: 2154 South Lamar Boulevard, P.O. Box 148.
Telephone: 601-236-5700.
Facsimile: 601-236-5800.

MEMBERS OF FIRM

Dan W. Webb
Benjamin H. Sanders
Dana Gail Deaton
Chris H. Deaton
Timothy R. Balducci
Kent E. Smith
Danny P. Hall, Jr.
B. Wayne Williams

OF COUNSEL

Rachael Howell Webb

Representative Clients: Allstate Insurance Company; Georgia Casualty & Surety Company; GAB Business Services, Inc.; The Kroger Company; Ohio Casualty Insurance Company; Phillips and Associates; State Auto Insurance Company; State Farm Fire & Casualty Company; Transport Life Insurance Company; United States Fidelity & Guaranty Company.

For full biographical listings, see the Martindale-Hubbell Law Directory

MISSOURI

CAPE GIRARDEAU, Cape Girardeau Co.

OLIVER, OLIVER & WALTZ, P.C. (AV)

400 Broadway, P.O. Box 559, 63702-0559
Telephone: 314-335-8278
Fax: 314-334-6375

(See Next Column)

OLIVER, OLIVER & WALTZ P.C.—*Continued*

John L. Oliver, Jr.
Richard K. Kuntze
James Frederick Waltz
Jeffrey P. Hine

J. Michael Ponder
Jonah Ted Yates

Representative Clients: Mercantile Bank of Cape Girardeau; Union Electric Co.; Soutwestern Bell Corp.; Ford Motor Co.; Consolidated Drainage District No. 1; City of Charleston; MOMEDICO; CNA; The Travelers; The Hartford.

For Complete List of Firm Personnel, See General Section

For full biographical listings, see the Martindale-Hubbell Law Directory

*JEFFERSON CITY,** Cole Co.

INGLISH & MONACO, P.C. (AV)

Monroe House Law Center, 237 East High Street, P.O. Box 67, 65101
Telephone: 314-634-2522
Telecopier: 314-634-4526
California, Missouri Office: 405 North High Street.
Telephone: 314-796-4333.

John W. Inglish
Keith A. Wenzel
Nicholas M. Monaco
Ann Monaco Warren
Mark Warren

OF COUNSEL

Andrew Jackson Higgins
Charles P. Dribben (1929-1991)

LEGAL SUPPORT PERSONNEL

Lisa A. LeMaster
Wayne G Hanchey

References: Central Trust Bank; Jefferson Bank.

For full biographical listings, see the Martindale-Hubbell Law Directory

JOPLIN, Jasper Co.

BLANCHARD, VAN FLEET, MARTIN, ROBERTSON & DERMOTT (AV)

320 West Fourth Street, P.O. Box 1626, 64802
Telephone: 417-623-1515
Facsimile: 417-623-6865

MEMBERS OF FIRM

Malcolm L. Robertson
Karl W. Blanchard, Jr.
Jon Dermott
Ronald E. Mitchell
Greg B. Carter

ASSOCIATES

Ronald G. Sparlin
Theresa L. Ohler
John R. Mollenkamp

Representative Clients: Chubb Group; First National Bank of Sarcoxie; First State Bank; Liberty Mutual Insurance Co.; Missouri Southern State College; St. Paul Insurance Co.; State Farm Insurance Cos.; Southwestern Bell Telephone Co.; Tamko Asphalt Products; United States Fidelity & Guaranty Co..

For Complete List of Firm Personnel, See General Section

For full biographical listings, see the Martindale-Hubbell Law Directory

KANSAS CITY, Jackson, Clay & Platte Cos.

BAKER, STERCHI & COWDEN (AV)

Suite 2100 Commerce Tower, 911 Main Street, P.O. Box 13566, 64199-3566
Telephone: 816-471-2121
FAX: 816-472-0288
Overland Park, Kansas Office: 51 Corporate Woods, 9393 West 110th Street, Suite 508.
Telephone: 913-451-6752.

MEMBERS OF FIRM

Thomas O. Baker
Phillip C. Rouse
Thomas N. Sterchi
R. Douglas Gentile
John W. Cowden
James T. Seigfreid, Jr.
Thomas E. Rice, Jr.
Robert A. Babcock
Timothy S. Frets
Peter F. Travis
Evan A. Douthit
John P. Poland

ASSOCIATES

Quentin L. Brown
D. Gregory Stonebarger
James R. Jarrow
Kara Trouslot Stubbs
James S. Kreamer
Robert M. Carroll
Mary C. O'Connell
Stacy L. Cook
Randall L. Rhodes
Patricia A. Sexton
Brent David Thomas

Representative Clients: Aetna Casualty and Surety Co.; AIG Aviation; Allstate Insurance Co.; Associated Aviation Underwriters; Fidelity & Deposit Company of Maryland; Kemper National Insurance Companies; Lloyd's of London; MEDMARC; Safeco Insurance Co.; Yasuda Fire and Marine Insurance Co.

For full biographical listings, see the Martindale-Hubbell Law Directory

BLACKWELL SANDERS MATHENY WEARY & LOMBARDI L.C. (AV)

Suite 1100, Two Pershing Square, 2300 Main Street, 64108
Telephone: 816-274-6800
Telecopier: 816-274-6914
Overland Park, Kansas Office: 40 Corporate Woods, Suite 1200, 9401 Indian Creek Parkway.
Telephone: 913-345-8400.
Telecopier: 913-344-6375.

MEMBERS OF FIRM

Stephen T. Adams (Resident, Overland Park, Kansas Office)
James M. Ash
Jeffrey D. Ayers
Timothy M. Aylward
James Bandy
Toni Hays Blackwood
James Borthwick
John Keith Brungardt
Bruce Campbell
James D. Conkright (Resident, Overland Park, Kansas Office)
Henry R. Cox
David R. Erickson
David A. Fenley
Floyd R. Finch, Jr.
Robin V.W. Foster
Gary D. Gilson
J. Michael Grier (Resident, Overland Park, Kansas Office)
James D. Griffin (Resident, Overland Park, Kansas Office)
Allan V. Hallquist
Winn W. Halverhout
Jeffrey T. Haughey
Robert A. Horn
Charles D. Horner
Shirley Ward Keeler
William W. LaRue
Martin M. Loring
William A. Lynch
Benjamin F. Mann
Robert E. Marsh
Larry L. McMullen
Peter T. Niosi
Leslie J. Parrette, Jr.
Robert Penninger
John R. Phillips
Beverlee J. Roper (Not admitted in MO)
William H. Sanders, Jr.
William H. Sanders, Sr.
Randy P. Scheer
Douglas J. Schmidt
Roger W. Slead
Peter B. Sloan
Sally B. Surridge
Michael J. Thompson
Timothy W. Triplett (Resident, Overland Park, Kansas Office)
Thomas W. Wagstaff
James M. Warden (Resident, Overland Park, Kansas Office)
Maurice A. Watson
Daniel C. Weary
Mark D. Welker.
David L. West
Dennis P. Wilbert
John P. Williams
Ralph G. Wrobley
Karl Zobrist

SENIOR COUNSEL

Katharine S. Bunn
Neil J. Recker
Hibberd V. B. Kline, III
Gaylord G. Smith

OF COUNSEL

Menefee D. Blackwell
Cornelius E. Lombardi, Jr.
Barton P. Cohen (Resident, Overland Park, Kansas Office)
Donald F. Martin (Resident, Overland Park, Kansas Office)
Ernest M. Fleischer
Edward T. Matheny, Jr.
Stephen C. Harmon (Resident, Overland Park, Kansas Office)

STAFF ATTORNEYS

Lori H. Hill (Resident, Overland Park, Kansas Office)
Heather Nye

ASSOCIATES

Gary E. Armbrust
Jeffrey S. Austin (Resident, Overland Park, Kansas Office)
Elizabeth R. Tyndall Baucum
Richard M. Beheler (Not admitted in MO)
Kristi D. Bohling
Victoria Henges Bonavia (Resident, Overland Park, Kansas Office)
Diane Breneman (Resident, Overland Park, Kansas Office)
Kathryn B. Bussing (Not admitted in MO)
B. K. Christopher (Resident, Overland Park, Kansas Office)
J. Randall Coffey
Robert S. Conway
Marcia S. Cook
Daryl J. Douglas
Kyle W. Drefke (Not admitted in MO)
Philip Dupont
Merry Evans
Shelly L. Freeman
Michael J. Furlong
George A. Hanson
William F. High (Resident, Overland Park, Kansas Office)
Sean K. Hogan (Resident, Overland Park, Kansas Office)
Tessa K. Jacob
Phillip D. Kline (Resident, Overland Park, Kansas Office)
M. Courtney Koger
Christopher A. Koster
Michael J. Kuckelman (Resident, Overland Park, Kansas Office)
Kristopher A. Kuehn (Resident, Overland Park, Kansas Office)
James D. Langner (Resident, Overland Park, Kansas Office)
Christopher C. Lewis
John David Mandelbaum
Scott Martin
Sarah D. Mathews
John G. Mazurek
Douglas P. McLeod
Mary Elizabeth Metz
Gregory J. Minana
Diana D. Moore (Resident, Overland Park, Kansas Office)
Steven K. O'Hern (Resident, Overland Park, Kansas Office)
Peter S. Obetz (Resident, Overland Park, Kansas Office)
Michelle Y. Patterson
Cynthia L. Payseur
Michael C. Phillips
Julianne Popper
David B. Raymond
Kathryn A. Regier (Resident, Overland Park, Kansas Office)
Dora E. Reid
David L. Rein Jr.
Jana V. Richards (Resident, Overland Park, Kansas Office)
William W. Richerson, Jr.

(See Next Column)

BLACKWELL SANDERS MATHENY WEARY & LOMBARDI L.C., *Kansas City—Continued*

ASSOCIATES (Continued)

Curtis O. Roggow (Resident, Overland Park, Kansas Office)
Robert G. Rooney
Shelley Ann Runion
Brock A. Shealy
Jeffrey J. Simon
Michael A. Slaney
Price A. Sloan
Christopher S. Stachowiak
Terrance M. Summers
Michael M. Tamburini
Linda K. Tiller (Not admitted in MO)
Roger Warren
Shari L. Wright
Cori Leonard Young

Representative Clients: Black & Veatch; Carter Waters Corp.; The Coca-Cola Bottling Company of Mid-America; Commerce Bancshares, Inc.; Cook Paint and Varnish Co.; Fairbanks Morse Pump Corp.; Payless Cashways, Inc.; Puritan-Bennett Corp.; UtiliCorp United Inc.

For full biographical listings, see the Martindale-Hubbell Law Directory

SPENCER FANE BRITT & BROWNE (AV)

1400 Commerce Bank Building, 1000 Walnut Street, 64106-2140
Telephone: 816-474-8100
Overland Park, Kansas Office: Suite 500, 40 Corporate Woods, 9401 Indian Creek Parkway.
Telephone: 913-345-8100.
Washington, D.C. Office: 1133 Connecticut Avenue, N.W., Suite 1000.
Telephone: 202-775-2376.

MEMBERS OF FIRM

J. Nick Badgerow (Resident, Overland Park, Kansas Office)
Russell W. Baker, Jr.
Paul D. Cowing
Gardiner B. Davis
Donald W. Giffin
Elaine Drodge Koch
Michael F. Saunders
James A. Snyder
Richard H. Spencer
Mark A. Thornhill
Michaela M. Warden (Resident, Overland Park, Kansas Office)
Curtis E. Woods
William H. Woodson
Teresa A. Woody

ASSOCIATES

Jan P. Helder, Jr.
Nancy M. Landis (Resident, Overland Park, Kansas Office)
Samuel P. Logan
Kenneth A. Schifman
Therese M. Schuele
Brian F. Stayton (Resident, Overland Park, Kansas Office)

Representative Clients: CNA; Commercial Union Insurance Company; First American Insurance Company; Great Central Insurance Company; John Hancock Mutual Life Insurance Co.; K.C. Life Insurance Company; Medical Protective Insurance Company; Northwestern Mutual Life Insurance Co.; Scottsdale Insurance Company; USF&G.

For Complete List of Firm Personnel, See General Section

For full biographical listings, see the Martindale-Hubbell Law Directory

*KENNETT,** Dunklin Co.

CROW, REYNOLDS, PREYER AND SHETLEY (AV)

Cotton Exchange Bank Building, P.O. Box 189, 63857-0189
Telephone: 314-888-4664; 888-4665
Facsimile: 314-888-0322

MEMBERS OF FIRM

Elbert L. Ford (1899-1975)
James F. Ford (1925-1979)
Wendell W. Crow
James R. Reynolds
H. Mark Preyer
Matthew R. Shetley

Representative Clients: Merchants and Planters Bank; State Farm Mutual Auto Insurance Co.; Farm Bureau Mutual Insurance Co.; Fireman's Fund Insurance Cos.; Bank of Bootheel; Security Insurance Group; Universal Underwriters Insurance Co.; Columbia Mutual Insurance Co.; Cotton Exchange Bank; Metropolitan Life Insurance Co.; Hartford Insurance Group.

For full biographical listings, see the Martindale-Hubbell Law Directory

*POPLAR BLUFF,** Butler Co.

SPAIN, MERRELL AND MILLER (AV)

1912 Big Bend, P.O. Box 1248, 63902
Telephone: 314-686-5868
FAX: 314-686-6885

MEMBERS OF FIRM

James E. Spain
Jerry M. Merrell
Karen Jolly Miller
Samuel P. Spain
Keith D. Sorrell

For full biographical listings, see the Martindale-Hubbell Law Directory

ST. LOUIS, (Independent City)

AMELUNG, WULFF & WILLENBROCK, P.C. (AV)

17th Floor, 515 Olive Street, 63101
Telephone: 314-436-6757 Telecopier: 314-231-7305
Belleville, Illinois Office: P.O. Box 368, 62222.
Telephone: 618-233-9765.

(See Next Column)

Robert A. Wulff
Ronald C. Willenbrock
Stephen D. Hoyne
Michael C. Margherio
Robert J. Foley
Theodore G. Pashos
A. Stephen Pernoud
Robert J. Wulff

OF COUNSEL

James J. Amelung
Robert G. Brady

Timothy J. Gallagher
Joan S. Dwyer
David A. Bloch
Mark R. Dunn
Robert D. Younger
Amy L. Symons
Daniel M. Czamanske, Jr.
William J. Magrath

Representative Clients: American Family Insurance Group; Commercial Union Assurance Cos.; Continental National American Group; Farm Bureau Mutual Insurance Company of Missouri; Farmers Alliance Mutual Insurance Co.; Great Central Insurance Co.; Insurance Company of North America; Pennsylvania National Insurance Group; Ranger/Pan American Insurance Cos.; St. Paul Insurance Cos.

For full biographical listings, see the Martindale-Hubbell Law Directory

BRINKER, DOYEN & KOVACS, P.C. (AV)

Suite 500, 100 South Brentwood Boulevard (Clayton), 63105
Telephone: 314-863-6311
Telecopier: 314-863-8197

Bernard C. Brinker
John G. Doyen
Paul E. Kovacs
Gary P. Paul
Jeffrey J. Brinker
David G. Ott
Scott C. Harper
Lawrence R. Smith
James C. Thoele

Paul D. Huck
Dean R. Gallego
Anthony M. Pugliese
Patricia Bowman Howe
Aaron I. Mandel
William M. Lawson
Michael R. Cardenas
Bradley E. Wright
Timothy J. Gearin
Jon R. Sanner
Thomas B. Tobin
Paul F. Devine
John R. Kantner
Theodore D. Agniel
Michelle A. Kunin
Martin M. Clay

LEGAL SUPPORT PERSONNEL

Gayle M. Daniels (Office and Accounting Manager)
Barbara Reeves (Director, Human Resources)

Representative Clients: Aetna Casualty & Surety Co.; Farmers Insurance Group; State Farm Insurance Cos.; Transamerica Insurance Group; Avemco Insurance Co.; The Medical Protective Co.; Millers Mutual Insurance Co.; United States Fidelity & Guaranty Co.; Hensley Construction Inc.; SSM Health Care Systems.

For full biographical listings, see the Martindale-Hubbell Law Directory

EVANS & DIXON (AV)

1200 Saint Louis Place, 200 North Broadway, 63102-2749
Telephone: 314-621-7755
Kansas City, Missouri Office: City Center Square, 1100 Main Street, Suite 2000, 64105-2119.
Telephone: 816-472-4600.
Edwardsville, Illinois Office: 17 Ginger Creek Meadows, P.O. Box 405. 62025-3508.
Telephone: 618-656-8505.
Leawood, Kansas Office: 8016 State Line Road, Suite 207. 66208-3713.
Telephone: 913-649-5386.

MEMBERS OF FIRM

John F. Evans (1897-1964)
John R. Dixon (1914-1984)
James V. Gallen (1925-1985)
Ralph C. Kleinschmidt (1921-1982)
Edward W. Warner
Eugene K. Buckley
Henry D. Menghini
Robert M. Evans
Robert W. Wilson (Resident, Edwardsville, Illinois Office)
Sam P. Rynearson
Edward M. Vokoun
Harvey G. Schneider
James B. Kennedy
Jeffry S. Thomsen
James A. Thoenen
Gerre S. Langton
John A. Michener
Raymond J. Flunker
Stefan J. Glynias
James M. Gallen
Robert E. Bidstrup
Edward S. Meyer
Bradley V. Spaunhorst
Gerard T. Noce
K. Steven Jones
Robert J. Krehbiel
Robert N. Hendershot, II
Robert P. Numrich (Kansas City, Missouri and Leawood, Kansas Offices)
William F. Ringer (Resident, Kansas City, Missouri Office)
Marilyn C. Phillips
Richard F. Huck, III
David S. Ware
John F. Cooney
George T. Floros
Robert W. Haeckel
Michael F. Banahan
Carl D. Lothman
Robert D. Tucker (Resident, Edwardsville, Illinois Office)
Betsy J. Levitt
Kathi L. Chestnut
Michael Reda (Resident, Edwardsville, Illinois Office)
Brian J. Fowler (Kansas City, Missouri and Leawood, Kansas Offices)
Don A. Shaffer (Not admitted in MO; Resident, Edwardsville, Illinois Office)
Priscilla F. Gunn
Jeffrey K. Suess

(See Next Column)

EVANS & DIXON—*Continued*

MEMBERS OF FIRM (Continued)

Kevin P. Schnurbusch
Maurice D. Early
Thomas Clinkenbeard (Resident, Kansas City, Missouri Office)

OF COUNSEL

William W. Evans

ASSOCIATES

Scott C. Annunziata
Brenda G. Baum
Michael D. Bean (Resident, Edwardsville, Illinois Office)
Joan B. Bernstein
Martin J. Buckley
Thomas M. Buckley
Ann Marie Butler
Debbie S. Champion
Paul D. Chesterton
Teresa L. Cotton
Susan E. Decker (Kansas City, Missouri and Leawood, Kansas Offices)
Joseph L. Engelhard
Kim M. Fenton
Kevin L. Fritz
Philip C. Graham
Lisa A. Green
Stacey R. Hancock-Robinson
Cynthia M. Hennessey
John W. Hoffman (Resident, Edwardsville, Illinois Office)
Scott E. Huber
Amy E. Kaiser
Jill E. Kapp
Paul F. Keeven
John P. Kemppainen, Jr.
Carl Kessinger
Martin A. Klug
David C. Knieriem
Mark R. Kornblum
Paul D. Larimore
Mary Anne Lindsey
Bruce J. Magnuson
James D. Maschhoff
Cynthia A. Masterson
John S. McCollough
Jacqueline E. Moore
Susan M. Moore
James K. Muhlenbruch
Karen A. Mulroy
James M. Neimann
Patrick A. Patterson
David G. Phoenix
Carl C. Pohle
Jeffrey M. Proske
David J. Reynolds, Jr.
Betsy S. Schmidt
Steven R. Sharp
Laura E. Smith
Paul Joseph Stingley (Resident, Kansas City, Missouri Office)
Adrian P. Sulser
Timothy M. Tierney
Joy R. Urbom
Kenneth L. Voigt
Martha Madden Weast (Kansas City, Missouri and Leawood, Kansas Offices)
Alexander M. Wilson (Resident, Edwardsville, Illinois Office)
Stephen E. Winborn
Kurt E. Wolfgram

Attorneys for: Allstate Insurance Co.; Chrysler Corp.; Chubb & Son, Inc.; Kemper Insurance Group; Southwestern Bell Telephone Co.; Travelers Insurance Co.; Zurich Insurance Co.

For full biographical listings, see the Martindale-Hubbell Law Directory

LAW OFFICES OF THOMAS J. NOONAN P.C. (AV)

Gateway One on the Mall, 701 Market, Suite 650, 63101
Telephone: 314-241-4747
Fax: 314-241-2039

Thomas J. Noonan

Geri L. Dreiling
Laura Gartland Meyer
David A. Saadat

OF COUNSEL

John G. Schultz

Aetna Casualty & Surety; Auto-Owners Insurance Co.; Capitol Indemnity Corp.; Fireman's Fund Insurance Co.; Ford Motor Credit Co.; Ford Consumer Finance Co.; Grinnell Mutual Reinsurance; Miller's Mutual Insurance Assn. of Illinois; Paragon Group, Inc.; Shelter Mutual Insurance Co.

For full biographical listings, see the Martindale-Hubbell Law Directory

SIKESTON, Scott Co.

BLANTON, RICE, SIDWELL & OTTINGER (AV)

219 South Kings Highway, P.O. Box 805, 63801
Telephone: 314-471-1000
Facsimile: 314-471-1012

MEMBERS OF FIRM

Harry C. Blanton (1891-1973)
Thomas R. Gilmore (1939-1984)
David E. Blanton
Bernard C. Rice
King E. Sidwell
Terry R. Ottinger
Bruce A. Lawrence
Joseph C. Blanton, Jr.
James A. Pinkston

Representative Clients: St. Louis Southwestern Railway Lines; Employers Mutuals of Wausau; The Travelers Insurance Co.; Cigna; Commercial Union Insurance Group; Kemper Group; Continental-National Insurance Group; Shelter Insurance Cos.; First National Bank, Sikeston, Mo.; Columbia Mutual Insurance Company.

For Complete List of Firm Personnel, See General Section

For full biographical listings, see the Martindale-Hubbell Law Directory

*SPRINGFIELD,** Greene Co.

DORR, BAIRD AND LIGHTNER, A PROFESSIONAL CORPORATION (AV)

Suite 2-202 Two Corporate Centre, 1949 East Sunshine Street, 65804
Telephone: 417-887-0133
Fax: 417-887-8740

Richard E. Dorr
C. Ronald Baird
John R. Lightner

Mark J. Millsap
James Michael Bridges

Reference: First City National Bank of Springfield.

For full biographical listings, see the Martindale-Hubbell Law Directory

MONTANA

*BILLINGS,** Yellowstone Co.

CROWLEY, HAUGHEY, HANSON, TOOLE & DIETRICH (AV)

500 Transwestern II, 490 North 31st Street, P.O. Box 2529, 59103
Telephone: 406-252-3441
Fax: 406-259-4159
Helena, Montana Office: IBM Building, 100 North Park Avenue, Suite 300, 59601.
Telephone: 406-449-4165.
Fax: 406-449-5149.

OF COUNSEL

Bruce R. Toole
Neil S. Keefer

MEMBERS OF FIRM

George C. Dalthorp
Herbert I. Pierce, III
Ronald R. Lodders
Charles R. Cashmore
Lawrence B. Cozzens
Carolyn S. Ostby
Steven J. Lehman
Donald L. Harris
William J. Mattix
Peter F. Habein
Jon T. Dyre
Bruce A. Fredrickson
Janice L. Rehberg
Joe C. Maynard, Jr.

ASSOCIATES

Steven Robert Milch
Leonard H. Smith
Neil G. Westesen
Robert T. Bell

Representative Clients: Aetna; CNA Insurance; Connecticut Mutual Life; St. Paul Insurance Cos.; The Doctor's Company; The Home Insurance Cos.; Farmers Insurance Group; Fireman's Fund Insurance Co.; Kemper Insurance Group; Metropolitan Life Insurance Co.

For Complete List of Firm Personnel, See General Section

For full biographical listings, see the Martindale-Hubbell Law Directory

*GREAT FALLS,** Cascade Co.

CONKLIN, NYBO, LEVEQUE & MURPHY, P.C. (AV)

Suite 203, 9 Third Street North, P.O. Box 2049, 59403-2049
Telephone: 406-727-9270
Fax: 406-761-1406

William Conklin
L. D. Nybo
E. Lee LeVeque
Thomas J. Murphy
Allen P. Lanning

Jeffrey T. McAllister
Evan F. Danno

Representative Clients: State Farm Mutual Automobile Insurance Co.; Farmers Insurance Group; The Travelers Indemnity Co.; The American International Group; Crum & Forster Organizations; Industrial Indemnity; Metropolitan Life Ins. Co.; National Ins. Assoc.; United Pacific Reliance Ins. Co.; Coregis, Westland Farm Mutual Ins. Co.
Reference: Norwest Bank of Great Falls.

For full biographical listings, see the Martindale-Hubbell Law Directory

*HELENA,** Lewis and Clark Co.

KELLER, REYNOLDS, DRAKE, JOHNSON & GILLESPIE, P.C. (AV)

38 South Last Chance Gulch, 59601
Telephone: 406-442-0230

P. Keith Keller
Thomas Q. Johnson
Richard E. Gillespie
G. Curt Drake
Jacqueline Terrell Lenmark
Robert R. Throssell
Charles J. Seifert

(See Next Column)

KELLER, REYNOLDS, DRAKE, JOHNSON & GILLESPIE P.C., *Helena—Continued*

OF COUNSEL

Glen L. Drake

Representative Clients: Fireman's Fund American Insurance Cos.; Northwestern National Insurance Group; Government Employees Insurance Co.; Hartford Accident and Indemnity Co.; Commercial Union Assurance Cos.; Kemper Insurance Group; Crum and Forster Group; The Home Insurance Co.; CNA Insurance Cos.; Safeco Insurance.

For full biographical listings, see the Martindale-Hubbell Law Directory

*KALISPELL,** Flathead Co.

HASH, O'BRIEN & BARTLETT (AV)

Plaza West, 136 First Avenue, West, P.O. Box 1178, 59901
Telephone: 406-755-6919
Fax: 406-755-6911

MEMBERS OF FIRM

Charles L. Hash
Kenneth E. O'Brien
James C. Bartlett
C. Mark Hash

General Counsel for: Glacier Bank F.S.B.; Budget Finance; Flathead County Title Co.
Representative Clients: Western Surety Co.; Liberty Mutual Insurance Co.; Allstate Insurance Co.; Hillsteads Department Store; Montana Brokers, Inc.
Reference: Glacier Bank F.S.B.

For full biographical listings, see the Martindale-Hubbell Law Directory

MURPHY, ROBINSON, HECKATHORN & PHILLIPS, P.C. (AV)

431 1st Avenue West, 59901
Telephone: 406-752-6644
FAX: 406-752-5108

James E. Murphy (1910-1990)
C. Eugene Phillips (1932-1993)
I. James Heckathorn
John B. Dudis, Jr.
Daniel D. Johns
Donald R. Murray, Jr.
Dana L. Christensen
Steven E. Cummings
Debra D. Parker
Mikel L. Moore

OF COUNSEL

Calvin S. Robinson
James A. Robischon
M. Dean Jellison

LEGAL SUPPORT PERSONNEL

Douglas W. Wardinsky (Legal Assistant)

Representative Clients: Farmers Insurance Exchange; Kendall Insurance Co.; Farmers Alliance Insurance co.

For full biographical listings, see the Martindale-Hubbell Law Directory

NEBRASKA

*GERING,** Scotts Bluff Co.

HOLTORF, KOVARIK, ELLISON & MATHIS, P.C. (AV)

1715 11th Street, P.O. Box 340, 69341-0340
Telephone: 308-436-5297
FAX: 308-436-2297

Hans J. Holtorf, Jr. (1914-1992)
Leland K. Kovarik
James W. Ellison
James M. Mathis

Michelle M. Dreibelbis

Representative Clients: Travelers Insurance Co.; State Farm Mutual Auto Insurance Co.; Liberty Mutual Insurance Co.; Farmers Insurance Group; Hawkeye Security Insurance Co.; Aetna Life & Casualty Co.; Casualty Underwriters.
Counsel: North Platte Natural Resources District.
References: First State Bank of Gering; Gering State Bank.

For full biographical listings, see the Martindale-Hubbell Law Directory

*LINCOLN,** Lancaster Co.

BARLOW, JOHNSON, FLODMAN, SUTTER, GUENZEL & ESKE (AV)

1227 Lincoln Mall, P.O. Box 81686, 68501-1686
Telephone: 402-475-4240
Fax: 402-475-0329

MEMBERS OF FIRM

Robert A. Barlow (1921-1986)
Kile W. Johnson
Steven J. Flodman
William D. Sutter
Steven E. Guenzel
James A. Eske

ASSOCIATE

Mark T. Gokie

(See Next Column)

OF COUNSEL

Gene D. Watson

Special Counsel: Nebraska Public Power District.
Representative Clients: Allied Group; Chubb/Pacific Indemnity Group; Citizens State Bank, Polk, Nebraska; Crum & Foster; Federated Rural Electric Insurance Corp.; Runza Drive-Inns of America; United States Fidelity & Guaranty Co.; Viking Insurance Company of Wisconsin.

For Complete List of Firm Personnel, See General Section

For full biographical listings, see the Martindale-Hubbell Law Directory

DEMARS, GORDON, OLSON, RECKNOR & SHIVELY (AV)

Suite 400 Centre Terrace Building, 1225 L Street, P.O. Box 81607, 68501-1607
Telephone: 402-438-2500
Fax: 402-438-6329

MEMBERS OF FIRM

James J. DeMars
James E. Gordon
William E. Olson, Jr.
John F. Recknor
Robert W. Shively
James C. Zalewski
Danene J. Tushar

ASSOCIATE

Bruce A. Smith

For full biographical listings, see the Martindale-Hubbell Law Directory

ERICKSON & SEDERSTROM, P.C. (AV)

Suite 400, Cornhusker Plaza, 301 South 13th Street, 68508
Telephone: 402-476-1000
Fax: 402-476-6167
Omaha, Nebraska Office: Regency Westpointe, 10330 Regency Parkway Drive.
Telephone: 402-397-2200.
Fax: 402-390-7137.

Charles Thone
Charles D. Humble
Alan M. Wood
Douglas L. Curry
Mark M. Schorr
Linda W. Rohman
David C. Mussman

Representative Clients: California Public Employees Retirement Plan (CALPERS); Chase Manhattan Leasing Co.; Albertson's, Inc.; Baker's Supermarkets, Inc.; Osco Drug, Inc.; Lincoln General Hospital; Martin Luther Home; Lincoln Electric System.

For full biographical listings, see the Martindale-Hubbell Law Directory

NORFOLK, Madison Co.

DOMINA & COPPLE, P.C. (AV)

2425 Taylor Avenue, P.O. Box 78, 68702-0078
Telephone: 402-371-4300
Fax: 402-371-0790
Omaha, Nebraska Office: 1065 North 115th Street, Suite 150.
Telephone: 402-493-4100.
FAX: 402-493-9782.

David A. Domina
David E. Copple

Kathleen K. Rockey
James G. Kube
David H. Ptak
Steven D. Sunde

For full biographical listings, see the Martindale-Hubbell Law Directory

*OMAHA,** Douglas Co.

CASSEM, TIERNEY, ADAMS, GOTCH & DOUGLAS (AV)

Suite 300, 8805 Indian Hills Drive, 68114
Telephone: 402-390-0300
Telecopier: 402-390-9676

MEMBERS OF FIRM

Edwin Cassem (1902-1980)
Lawrence J. Tierney
Robert K. Adams
Charles F. Gotch
John R. Douglas
Daniel J. Duffy
Theodore J. Stouffer
Michael F. Kinney
Terry J. Grennan
Patrick B. Donahue
Ronald F. Krause
Dennis R. Riekenberg
David A. Blagg
Brien M. Welch
Michael K. Huffer

ASSOCIATES

Michael F. Scahill
Leif D. Erickson
Helarie H. Hollenbeck
Melany S. Chesterman

OF COUNSEL

Edward Shafton

Representative Clients: Aetna Casualty & Surety Co.; Chrysler Corp.; Eli Lilly & Co.; G. D. Searle & Co.; Hartford Accident & Indemnity Co.; Johnson & Johnson; Litigation Management Specialists; Merck & Co., Inc.; Safeco Insurance Co.; Travelers Insurance Co.

For full biographical listings, see the Martindale-Hubbell Law Directory

Omaha—Continued

Erickson & Sederstrom, P.C. (AV)
Regency Westpointe, 10330 Regency Parkway Drive, 68114
Telephone: 402-397-2200
Fax: 402-390-7137
Lincoln, Nebraska Office: Suite 400, Cornhusker Plaza, 301 South 13th Street.
Telephone: 402-476-1000.
Fax: 402-476-6167.

Lewis R. Leigh
Ray R. Simon
Donald H. Erickson
Daniel D. Koukol
Wm. E. Morrow, Jr.
Soren S. Jensen
Daniel B. Kinnamon
Joel Davis
Virgil K. Johnson
Charles V. Sederstrom, Jr.
Michael C. Washburn
John C. Brownrigg
Thomas J. Culhane
Richard J. Gilloon
Samuel Earle Clark
Gary L. Hoffman
J Russell Derr
Jerald L. Rauterkus
Mark Peterson
Sherry L. Hubert
Lane D. Edenburn

OF COUNSEL

Leo Eisenstatt
Roland J. Santoni
Michael A. Fortune
Anne O. Fortune

Representative Clients: Nebraska State Bank of Omaha; Berkshire Hathaway, Inc.; Bozell, Inc.; IBP, Inc.; Quaker Oats Co.; United A-G Cooperative, Inc.; Immanuel Medical Center; Cornhusker Casualty Co.; Hartford Accident & Indemnity Co.; Mortgage Guaranty Insurance Corp. (MGIC).

For Complete List of Firm Personnel, See General Section

For full biographical listings, see the Martindale-Hubbell Law Directory

Fraser, Stryker, Vaughn, Meusey, Olson, Boyer & Bloch, P.C. (AV)
500 Energy Plaza, 409 South 17th Street, 68102
Telephone: 402-341-6000
Telecopier: 402-341-8290

Joseph K. Meusey
Wayne J. Mark
Joseph E. Jones
Robert F. Rossiter, Jr.
Mary Kay Frank
Michael F. Coyle
Rex A. Rezac

John M. Ryan
Lon A. Licata
Mark C. Laughlin

Representative Clients: State Farm Insurance Cos.; Shand Morahan & Co.; Prudential Property and Casualty Insurance.

For Complete List of Firm Personnel, See General Section

For full biographical listings, see the Martindale-Hubbell Law Directory

Katskee, Henatsch & Suing (AV)
10404 Essex Court, Suite 100, 68114
Telephone: 402-391-1697
Fax: 402-391-8932

MEMBERS OF FIRM

Milton A. Katskee
Dean F. Suing
Jerry W. Katskee

ASSOCIATES

Francis T. Belsky
David A. Castello
John B. Henley
Kristine K. Kluck

OF COUNSEL

Harry R. Henatsch

References: Mid-City Bank; FirsTier Bank N.A., Omaha.

For full biographical listings, see the Martindale-Hubbell Law Directory

NEVADA

*LAS VEGAS,** Clark Co.

Albright, Stoddard, Warnick & Albright, A Professional Corporation (AV)
Quail Park I, Building D-4, 801 South Rancho Drive, 89106
Telephone: 702-384-7111
FAX: 702-384-0605

G. Vern Albright
William H. Stoddard
Whitney B. Warnick
G. Mark Albright

(See Next Column)

Albright, Stoddard, Warnick & Albright, A Professional Corporation—Continued

Michael W. Brimley
Gavin C. Jangard
D. Chris Albright

Representative Clients: Tokio Marine and Fire Ins. Co.; INAPRO, a CIGNA Co.; Nevada Ready Mix; North American Health Care, Inc. (Nursing Home); Royal Insurance; First Security Bank of Utah; Nevada Community Bank; Nationwide Insurance Co.; Liberty Mutual Insurance; CB Commercial.

For full biographical listings, see the Martindale-Hubbell Law Directory

Alverson, Taylor, Mortensen & Nelson (AV)
3821 W. Charleston Boulevard, 89102
Telephone: 702-384-7000
FAX: 702-385-7000

MEMBERS OF FIRM

J. Bruce Alverson
Eric K. Taylor
David J. Mortensen
Erven T. Nelson
LeAnn Sanders
David R. Clayson

ASSOCIATES

Milton J. Eichacker
Douglas D. Gerrard
Marie Ellerton
James H. Randall
Peter Dubowsky
Hayley B. Chambers
Michael D. Stevenson
Cookie Lea Olshein
Kenneth M. Marias
Jeffrey H. Ballin
Jeffrey W. Daly
Kenneth R. Ivory
Edward D. Boyack
Sandra Smagac
Jill M. Chase
Francis F. Lin

Representative Clients: St. Paul Fire & Marine Insurance Company; Chubb Group of Insurance Companies; Employers of Wausau Insurance Company; Farmers Home Group; General Accident Insurance; Kemper National Insurance Company; Nationwide Insurance Company; Reliance/United Pacific Insurance Company; Scottsdale Insurance Company; United States Fidelity & Guaranty.

For full biographical listings, see the Martindale-Hubbell Law Directory

Barker, Gillock, Koning & Brown, A Professional Corporation (AV)
430 South Third Street, 89101
Telephone: 702-386-1086
Fax: 702-384-5386

William S. Barker
Gerald I. Gillock
Michael A. Koning
Janice J. Brown
Jerry S. Busby
Thomas D. Sutherland
James P. Chrisman
David L. Thomas

Janet S. Markley
Antonia C. Killebrew
Terry W. Riedy
Julie A. Mersch
Lewisjohn Gazda
Robert A. Winner
Robert D. Tarte (Not admitted in NV)
Susan Arlene Winters
Stephen P. Ellis

For full biographical listings, see the Martindale-Hubbell Law Directory

Beckley, Singleton, De Lanoy, Jemison & List, Chartered, A Professional Law Corporation (AV)
530 Las Vegas Boulevard South, 89101
Telephone: 702-385-3373
Telecopier: 702-385-9447
Reno, Nevada Office: 100 West Liberty Street, Suite 700.
Telephone: 702-323-8866.
Telecopier: 702-323-5523.

J. Mitchell Cobeaga
Elizabeth Goff Gonzalez
Randal A. De Shazer
Philip M. Hymanson

Tamela L. Kahle
Paul A. Acker
James L. Edwards
Todd N. Nelson
Imanuel B. Arin
Tracey Brice Howard

OF COUNSEL

Drake De Lanoy

For Complete List of Firm Personnel, See General Section

For full biographical listings, see the Martindale-Hubbell Law Directory

Edwards & Hale, Ltd. (AV)
Suite 300, Oxford Court, 415 South Sixth Street, 89101-6937
Telephone: 702-382-1414
Fax: 702-382-1413

Keith Edwards
Floyd Hale
Gloria J. Sturman
Trevor L. Atkin
Sharon Gwin Immerman
Kym S. Cushing

(See Next Column)

EDWARDS & HALE LTD., *Las Vegas—Continued*

Erin Lee Truman
Michael L. Hermes
Thomas E. Winner
Michelle Schwarz
J. Lynn Johnson
Laura C. Rodriguez
Todd L. Moody

Representative Clients: Aetna Casualty & Surety Co.; Occidental Life Insurance Co.; State Farm Insurance Cos.; Uniguard Insurance Co.

For full biographical listings, see the Martindale-Hubbell Law Directory

KUMMER KAEMPFER BONNER & RENSHAW (AV)

Seventh Floor, 3800 Howard Hughes Parkway, 89109
Telephone: 702-792-7000
Fax: 702-796-7181

MEMBERS OF FIRM

John C. Renshaw
Thomas F. Kummer
Christopher L. Kaempfer
Martha J. Ashcraft
Michael J. Bonner
John N. Brewer
Von S. Heinz
Gerald D. Waite
Elliott R. Eisner

OF COUNSEL

H. Gregory Nasky

ASSOCIATES

Shari Cassin Patterson
Georlen K. Spangler
Sherwood N. Cook
Daurean G. Sloan
Anthony A. Zmaila
John C. Jeppsen
P. Blake Allen
L. Joe Coppedge
David A. Barksdale
George J. Claseman
Dennis M. Prince
Jeffrey W. Ray (Not admitted in NV)
Jennifer M. Settles

For full biographical listings, see the Martindale-Hubbell Law Directory

PICO & MITCHELL (AV)

2000 South Eastern Avenue, 89104
Telephone: 702-457-9099
FAX: 702-457-8451

MEMBERS OF FIRM

James F. Pico
Bert O. Mitchell
Christy Brad Escobar

ASSOCIATES

James R. Rosenberger
Gary L. Myers
E. Breen Arntz
Robert W. Cottle
Cory Hilton
Lawrence Davidson
Thomas A. Ericsson
Linda M. Graham

Representative Clients: Home Insurance Co.; State Farm Mutual Insurance Co.; Industrial Indemnity Ins. Co.; Great American Insurance Co.; Argonaut Insurance Cos.; Clark County Medical Society; Rose de Lima Hospital; Fairway Chevrolet; American States Insurance Co.; Hartford Ins.

For full biographical listings, see the Martindale-Hubbell Law Directory

RAWLINGS, OLSON & CANNON, A PROFESSIONAL CORPORATION (AV)

301 East Clark Avenue, Suite 1000, 89101
Telephone: 702-384-4012
Telecopier: 702-383-0701

Henry H. Rawlings, Jr.
James R. Olson
Walter R. Cannon
John D. Nitz
John E. Gormley
Richard E. Desruisseaux
Dana Jonathon Nitz
Janice Hodge Jensen
Brian C. Whitaker

Melissa Collins
Yvette D. Robichaud
Peter M. Angulo
Don F. Shreve, Jr.
Kenneth A. Cardone
Larry Lee Ketzenberger
Bryan W. Lewis
Michael C. Mills
Michelle D. Mullins
Michael E. Stoberski
Craig B. Friedberg
Bryan K. Scott
Joseph J. Purdy
Bradley M. Ballard

For full biographical listings, see the Martindale-Hubbell Law Directory

VANNAH COSTELLO HOWARD & CANEPA (AV)

A Partnership including a Professional Corporation
Greystone, 1850 East Flamingo, Suite 236, 89119
Telephone: 702-369-4161
Fax: 702-369-0104

MEMBERS OF FIRM

Robert D. Vannah (Chartered)
Nathan M. Costello
James W. Howard, Jr.
Scott K. Canepa

(See Next Column)

ASSOCIATE

Jerry A. Wiese

Representative Clients: Prudential Property and Casualty Insurance Co.; USF&G Co.; CNA; OUM Group Insurance Co.; American Golf Corp.; Reliance Insurance Co.

For full biographical listings, see the Martindale-Hubbell Law Directory

*RENO,** Washoe Co.

ERICKSON, THORPE & SWAINSTON, LTD. (AV)

601 S. Arlington Avenue, P.O. Box 3559, 89505
Telephone: 702-786-3930
Fax: 702-786-4160

Roger L. Erickson
Donald A. Thorpe
George W. Swainston
William G. Cobb
James L. Lundemo
Gary A. Cardinal
Thomas Peter Beko
John A. Aberasturi

Representative Clients: Allstate Insurance Co.; Coregis Insurance; Country Companies; Home Insurance; Kemper Insurance Company; International Aviation Underwriters; State Farm Fire & Casualty; TIG (Transamerica); Willis, Corroon Administrative Services.

For full biographical listings, see the Martindale-Hubbell Law Directory

GEORGESON, MCQUAID, THOMPSON & ANGARAN, CHARTERED (AV)

100 West Grove Street, Suite 500, 89509
Telephone: 702-827-6440
FAX: 702-827-9256
Mailing Address: P.O. Box 3257, Reno, Nevada, 89505

C. James Georgeson
Robert A. McQuaid, Jr.
Harold B. Thompson
Jack G. Angaran

Representative Clients: Aetna (Cravens, Dargan Co.); California State Automobile Assn.; Commercial Union Insurance Co.; Fireman's Fund Insurance Co.; Hartford Insurance Group; Industrial Indemnity Co. (Crum & Forster); Royal Insurance; St. Paul Insurance Co.

For full biographical listings, see the Martindale-Hubbell Law Directory

GUILD, RUSSELL, GALLAGHER & FULLER, LTD. (AV)

100 West Liberty, Suite 800, P.O. Box 2838, 89505
Telephone: 702-786-2366
Telecopier: 702-322-9105

Clark J. Guild (1887-1971)
Clark J. Guild, Jr.
C. David Russell
John K. Gallagher
Gary M. Fuller
Craig M. Burkett

OF COUNSEL

Reese H. Taylor, Jr.

Representative Clients: Southwest Gas Corp.; Fred H. Dressler; City of Los Angeles, Department of Water & Power; Metropolitan Water District of Southern California; Plymouth Land and Stock Co.

For full biographical listings, see the Martindale-Hubbell Law Directory

NEW HAMPSHIRE

*MANCHESTER,** Hillsborough Co.

BOUCHARD & MALLORY, P.A. (AV)

100 Middle Street, 03101
Telephone: 603-623-7222
Fax: 603-623-8953

Kenneth G. Bouchard
Mark L. Mallory

Paul B. Kleinman
Blake M. Sutton
Susan A. Vaillancourt
Christine Friedman
Robert S. Stephen

For full biographical listings, see the Martindale-Hubbell Law Directory

NEW JERSEY

BLOOMFIELD, Essex Co.

KENNEDY & KENNEDY (AV)

Bloomfield Plaza Building, 650 Bloomfield Avenue, 07003
Telephone: 201-429-7091
Fax: 201-743-5853

(See Next Column)

KENNEDY & KENNEDY—*Continued*

MEMBERS OF FIRM

William V. Kennedy
John J. Kennedy

For full biographical listings, see the Martindale-Hubbell Law Directory

*CAMDEN,** Camden Co.

BROWN & CONNERY (AV)

518 Market Street, P.O. Box 1449, 08101
Telephone: 609-365-5100
Facsimile: 609-858-4967
Westmont, New Jersey Office: 360 Haddon Avenue. P.O. Box 539.
Telephone: 609-854-8900.

MEMBERS OF FIRM

Thomas F. Connery, Jr.
William J. Cook
Warren W. Faulk
Steven G. Wolschina
Paul Mainardi
John L. Conroy, Jr.
Dennis P. Blake
Michael J. Vassalotti
John J. Mulderig
William M. Tambussi
Bruce H. Zamost
Mark P. Asselta
Stephen J. DeFeo
Jane A. Lorber

ASSOCIATES

Isabel C. Balboa
Joseph A. Zechman
Michael J. Fagan
Karen A. Peterson
Jeffrey E. Ugoretz

Representative Clients: Delaware River Port Authority; Underwood-Memorial Hospital; Garden State Water Company; Honeywell, Inc.; Philadelphia Newspapers, Inc.; Port Authority Transit Co.; Resolution Trust Corp.; General Electric; Mercedes-Benz Credit Corp.; American Red Cross.

For Complete List of Firm Personnel, See General Section

For full biographical listings, see the Martindale-Hubbell Law Directory

CHERRY HILL, Camden Co.

GARRIGLE & PALM (AV)

Suite 204, 1415 State Highway 70 East, 08034
Telephone: 609-427-9300
Fax: 609-427-9590

MEMBERS OF FIRM

William A. Garrigle
John M. Palm

ASSOCIATES

Harold H. Thomasson
Paul F Kulinski
James J. Law
Eleanore A. Rogalski

Representative Clients: Crum & Forster Group; Kemper Insurance Group; Atlantic Mutual Group; American Hardware Mutual; National General Insurance Co.; Transamerica Group; State Farm Fire Insurance Co.; Progressive Insurance Co.; United Southern Insurance Co.; New Jersey Market Transition Facility and Joint Underwriting Association.

For full biographical listings, see the Martindale-Hubbell Law Directory

MONTANO, SUMMERS, MULLEN, MANUEL, OWENS AND GREGORIO, A PROFESSIONAL CORPORATION (AV)

Two Executive Campus, Suite 400, Route 70 and Cuthbert Boulevard, 08002
Telephone: 609-665-9400
Fax: 609-665-0006
Northfield, New Jersey Office: The Executive Plaza, 2111 New Road, Suite 105.
Telephone: 609-383-8900.
Philadelphia, Pennsylvania Office: 1700 Market Street - Suite 2628.
Telephone: 215-732-3900.

Carl Kisselman (1899-1975)
James A. Mullen, Jr.
G. Wesley Manuel, Jr.
F. Herbert Owens, III
Carl J. Gregorio
Gary L. Jakob
Lawrence D. Lally
Paul F. Gilligan, Jr.
David D. Duffin
Michael G. B. David

Craig W. Summers
Mary C. Brennan
James A. Nolan, Jr.
Alfred J. Quasti, Jr.
Robert H. Ayik
Stephen D. Holtzman (Resident, Northfield Office)
Arthur E. Donnelly, III
Bruce C. Truesdale
Ronald S. Collins, Jr.
Matthew P. Lyons
William J. Rudnik (Resident, Northfield Office)

OF COUNSEL

Arthur Montano
William W. Summers

Local Counsel for: Indemnity Insurance Company of North America; Royal Group; General Motors Corp.
Reference: Midlantic National Bank, Cherry Hill, New Jersey.

For full biographical listings, see the Martindale-Hubbell Law Directory

CRANFORD, Union Co.

MCCREEDY AND COX (AV)

Second Floor, Six Commerce Drive, 07016-3509
Telephone: 908-709-0400
Fax: 908-709-0405

MEMBERS OF FIRM

Edwin J. McCreedy
Robert F. Cox

ASSOCIATE

Patrick J. Hermesmann

Reference: United Counties Trust Co.

For full biographical listings, see the Martindale-Hubbell Law Directory

FAIR LAWN, Bergen Co.

MUSCARELLA, BOCHET, LAHIFF, PECK & EDWARDS, P.C. (AV)

0-100 28th Street, P.O. Box 2770, 07410
Telephone: 201-796-3100; 201-791-9666
Telecopier: 201-791-0350

William C. Bochet
Dennis P. LaHiff
H. Shepard Peck, Jr.
Barbara Anne Edwards
James P. D'Alessandro

For full biographical listings, see the Martindale-Hubbell Law Directory

FLORHAM PARK, Morris Co.

HACK, PIRO, O'DAY, MERKLINGER, WALLACE & MCKENNA, P.A. (AV)

30 Columbia Turnpike, P.O. Box 941, 07932-0941
Telephone: 201-301-6500
Fax: 201-301-0094

David L. Hack
Peter A. Piro
William J. O'Day
M. Richard Merklinger
Joseph V. Wallace
Peter T. Melnyk
Patrick M. Sages

Bonny G. Rafel
Darlene D. Steinhart
Robert G. Alencewicz
John T. West
Scott D. Samansky
John J. Petrizzo
William F. Murphy
Thomas M. Madden

Representative Clients: Aetna Life & Casualty Co.; Avis Rent-a-Car Systems; Eastman Kodak Co.; State Farm Insurance Cos.; Trans World Airlines, Inc.; Travelers Insurance Co.; Westinghouse Electric Co.; Weyerhauser Co.

For Complete List of Firm Personnel, See General Section

For full biographical listings, see the Martindale-Hubbell Law Directory

*HACKENSACK,** Bergen Co.

BRESLIN & TROVINI (AV)

14 Washington Place, 07601
Telephone: 201-343-5678
Telefax: 201-343-0369

MEMBERS OF FIRM

Michael J. Breslin, Jr.
Vincent P. Trovini

ASSOCIATES

Daniel P. McNerney
Victoria L. Tomasella
David S. Lafferty

OF COUNSEL

J. Emmet Cassidy (1919-1989)

Reference: Bridge View Bank.

For full biographical listings, see the Martindale-Hubbell Law Directory

HARWOOD LLOYD (AV)

130 Main Street, 07601
Telephone: 201-487-1080
Facsimile: 487-4758; 487-8410
East Brunswick, New Jersey Office: Two Tower Center, 10th Floor.
Telephone: 908-214-1010.
Facsimile: 908-214-1818.
Ridgewood, New Jersey Office: 41 Oak Street.
Telephone: 201-447-1422.
Facsimile: 201-447-1926.

MEMBERS OF FIRM

Victor C. Harwood, III
Frank V. D. Lloyd
Brian J. Coyle
Michael B. Oropollo
Richard J. Ryan
Leonard P. Rosa
John D. Allen, III
Frank Holahan
Russell A. Pepe
Gregory J. Irwin
Anthony M. Carlino
Thomas B. Hanrahan
Brian R. Ade
Brian C. Gallagher
Bernadette N. Gordon
Edward Zampino
Jonathan Bubrow

(See Next Column)

HARWOOD LLOYD, *Hackensack—Continued*

OF COUNSEL

David F. McBride
Theodore W. Trautwein
August Schedler
Francis V. D. Lloyd (1896-1974)
John W. Griggs (1929-1980)
Charles C. Shenier (1905-1970)
Emil M. Wulster (1907-1978)
Daniel Gilady (1927-1975)
George A. Brown (1913-1986)

Local Counsel for: Aetna Casualty & Surety Co.; Allstate Insurance Co.; Hartford Accident & Indemnity Co.; Kemper Group; Allstate Mutual Insurance Co.; CNA Insurance Co.; U.S. Insurance Group; Selective Insurance Company of America; Royal Insurance Companies; Fireman's Fund Insurance Cos.

For Complete List of Firm Personnel, See General Section

For full biographical listings, see the Martindale-Hubbell Law Directory

HEIN, SMITH, BEREZIN, MALOOF & ROGERS (AV)

Court Plaza East, 19 Main Street, 07601-7023
Telephone: 201-487-7400
Telecopier: 201-487-4228

MEMBERS OF FIRM

Robert J. Maloof
Allan H. Rogers
Robert L. Baum
Lawrence H. Jacobs

ASSOCIATES

John L. Shanahan
Ellen W. Smith
Carla H. Madnick
Marian H. Speid

OF COUNSEL

Milton Gurny

Representative Clients: Aetna Insurance Co.; Commercial Union of New York; Employers of Wausau; Great American Insurance Cos.; Hanover Insurance Co.; Health Care Insurance Co.; Merchants Mutual Insurance Co.; St. Paul Fire & Marine Insurance Co.; U.S. Fidelity & Guaranty Co.
Reference: United Jersey Bank.

For Complete List of Firm Personnel, See General Section

For full biographical listings, see the Martindale-Hubbell Law Directory

LIVINGSTON, Essex Co.

PHILIP M. LUSTBADER & DAVID LUSTBADER A PROFESSIONAL CORPORATION (AV)

615 West Mount Pleasant Avenue, 07039
Telephone: 201-740-1000
Fax: 201-740-1520

Philip M. Lustbader
David Lustbader

John N. Holly
John L. Riordan, Jr.

OF COUNSEL

Robert J. McKenna

For full biographical listings, see the Martindale-Hubbell Law Directory

MORGAN, MELHUISH, MONAGHAN, ARVIDSON, ABRUTYN & LISOWSKI (AV)

(Formerly Schneider and Morgan)
651 West Mount Pleasant Avenue, 07039
Telephone: 201-994-2500
Fax: 201-994-3375
New York, N.Y. Office: 39 Broadway, 35th Floor.
Telephone: 212-809-1111.
Fax: 212-509-3422.

MEMBERS OF FIRM

Jacob Schneider (1910-1949)
Louis Schneider (1921-1965)
Henry G. Morgan
James L. Melhuish
Robert E. Monaghan
William F. Perry
Richard E. Arvidson
John I. Lisowski
Elliott Abrutyn
Jeffrey M. Kadish
Paul A. Tripodo
John J. Agostini
Robert J. Aste
Mary Adele Hornish
Richard E. Snyder
David M. Welt
Michael A. Sicola
Joseph DeDonato
Robert A. Assuncao

Richard Micliz
Roger C. Schechter
Richard J. Hull
Leonard C. Leicht
Nina Lynn Caroselli
Anthony M. Santoro, Jr.
Robert J. Machi
Michael H. Cohen
Timothy K. Saia
Mary Ellen Scalera
Robert G. Klinck
Linda G. O'Connell

OF COUNSEL

Vincent J. Cirlin

Represent: The Home Insurance Co.; The Insurance Company of North American Cos.; General Accident Fire & Life Assurance Corp., Ltd.; Zurich Insurance Co.; Trans America Insurance Group; Allstate Insurance Co.;

(See Next Column)

Penn Mutual Insurance Co.; State Farm Insurance; Ohio Casualty Co.; American Mutual Liability Insurance Co.

For Complete List of Firm Personnel, See General Section

For full biographical listings, see the Martindale-Hubbell Law Directory

MILLBURN, Essex Co.

KUTTNER LAW OFFICES (AV)

24 Lackawanna Plaza, P.O. Box 745, 07041-0745
Telephone: 201-467-8300
Fax: 201-467-4333

Bernard A. Kuttner
Robert D. Kuttner

Reference: Summit Bank, Millburn, New Jersey.

For full biographical listings, see the Martindale-Hubbell Law Directory

MCDERMOTT & MCGEE (AV)

64 Main Street, P.O. Box 192, 07041-0192
Telephone: 201-467-8080
FAX: 201-467-0012

MEMBERS OF FIRM

John L. McDermott
John P. McGee
Richard P. Maggi
Thomas A. Wester
Richard A. Tango
Frank P. Leanza
John L. McDermott, Jr.

ASSOCIATES

Lawrence G. Tosi
David J. Dickinson
A. Charles Lorenzo
Robert A. McDermott
Kevin John McGee

OF COUNSEL

Daniel K. Van Dorn

Representative Clients: Allstate Insurance Co.; American Hardware Mutual Insurance Co.; Argonaut Insurance Cos.; Continental Insurance Cos.; Commercial Union Insurance Cos.; General Accident Group; Maryland-American General Group; Zurich-American Insurance Co.; P.C.M. Intermediaries, Ltd.; The Hanover Insurance Cos.

For full biographical listings, see the Martindale-Hubbell Law Directory

MONTVALE, Bergen Co.

BEATTIE PADOVANO (AV)

50 Chestnut Ridge Road, P.O. Box 244, 07645-0244
Telephone: 201-573-1810
Fax: (DEX) 201-573-9736

MEMBERS OF FIRM

Ralph J. Padovano
Roger W. Breslin, Jr.
Brian R. Martinotti

ASSOCIATE

Susan Calabrese

Reference: United Jersey Bank.

For Complete List of Firm Personnel, See General Section

For full biographical listings, see the Martindale-Hubbell Law Directory

*MORRISTOWN,** Morris Co.

MCELROY, DEUTSCH AND MULVANEY (AV)

1300 Mount Kemble Avenue, P.O. Box 2075, 07962-2075
Telephone: 201-993-8100
Fax: 201-425-0161
Denver, Colorado Office: 1099 18th Street, Suite 3120.
Telephone: 303-293-8800.
Fax: 303-293-3116.

MEMBERS OF FIRM

Lorraine M. Armenti (Resident Partner, Denver Colorado Office)
Grace C. Bertone
John P. Beyel
William C. Carey
Margaret F. Catalano
Stephen H. Cohen (1938-1992)
Kevin T. Coughlin
Edward B. Deutsch
Timothy I. Duffy
Robert J. Kelly
Joseph P. La Sala
Paul A. Lisovicz
Fred A. Manley, Jr.
Michael J. Marone
William T. McElroy
Laurence M. McHeffey
Joseph P. McNulty, Jr.
James M. Mulvaney
Moira E. O'Connell
Loren L. Pierce
Warren K. Racusin
John H. Suminski
Kevin E. Wolff

OF COUNSEL

Richard G. McCarty (Not admitted in NJ)
John F. Whitteaker

(See Next Column)

McElroy, Deutsch and Mulvaney—*Continued*

ASSOCIATES

Caroline L. Beers
Christopher Robert Carroll
Edward V. Collins
Billy J. Cooper (Resident, Denver, Colorado Office)
John Thomas Coyne
Nada Leslie Wolff Culver (Resident, Denver, Colorado Office)
John J. Cummings
Anthony J. Davis
John Paul Gilfillan
Kevin M. Haas
Gary S. Kull
Matthew J. Lodge
Tracey L. Matura
Nancy McDonald
Robert McGuire
Suzanne Cocco Midlige
Robert W. Muilenburg
Gary Potters
Kathleen M. Quinn
Vincent E. Reilly
Agnes A. Reiss
Barbara C. Zimmerman Robertson
Samuel J. Samaro
Laura A. Sanom
Thomas P. Scrivo
Dennis T. Smith
Patricia Leen Sullivan
Pamela A. Tanis
Christine L. Thieman
Catharine Acker Vaughan

Representative Clients: Crum & Forster Insurance Co.; Fireman's Fund Insurance Cos.; New Jersey Manufacturers Insurance Co.; The Home Indemnity Co.; Hartford Accident & Indemnity Co.; Chubb Insurance Cos.; Aetna Casualty & Surety Co.; Admiral Insurance Company; Harleyville Insurance Co.

For full biographical listings, see the Martindale-Hubbell Law Directory

*NEWARK,** Essex Co.

Crummy, Del Deo, Dolan, Griffinger & Vecchione, A Professional Corporation (AV)

One Riverfront Plaza, 07102
Telephone: 201-596-4500
Telecopier: 201-596-0545
Cable-Telex: 138154
Brussels, Belgium Office: Crummy, Del Deo, Dolan, Griffinger & Vecchione. Avenue Louise 475, BTE. 8, B-1050.
Telephone: 011-322-646-0019.
Telecopier: 011-322-646-0152.

Ralph N. Del Deo
John T. Dolan
Michael R. Griffinger
Michael D. Loprete
John A. Ridley
David J. Sheehan (Managing Partner)
Richard S. Zackin
David M. Hyman
Arnold B. Calmann
John H. Klock
Ann G. McCormick
Brian J. McMahon
Philip W. Crawford
Ira J. Hammer
Susanne Peticolas
Kerry M. Parker
Michael F. Quinn
Anthony P. La Rocco
Gary F. Werner
Stephen R. Reynolds

Representative Clients: American Telephone & Telegraph Co.; Audit Bureau of Circulation; Hoffmann-La Roche Inc.; McGraw-Hill, Inc.; Mitsubishi Electric Corp.; Mobil Oil Corp.; The Gillette Co.; United Parcel Service, Inc.

For Complete List of Firm Personnel, See General Section

For full biographical listings, see the Martindale-Hubbell Law Directory

McCarter & English (AV)

Four Gateway Center, 100 Mulberry Street, P.O. Box 652, 07101-0652
Telephone: 201-622-4444
Telecopier: 201-624-7070
Cable Address: "McCarter" Newark
Cherry Hill, New Jersey Office: 1810 Chapel Avenue West.
Telephone: 609-662-8444.
Telecopier: 609-662-6203.
New York, New York Office: Suite 1519, One World Trade Center.
Telephone: 212-466-9018.
Telecopier: 212-432-6568.
Boca Raton, Florida Office: 2255 Glades Road, Suite 319-A.
Telephone: 407-994-6262.
Telecopier: 407-241-0798.
Wilmington, Delaware Office: Mellon Bank Center, 919 Market Street.
Telephone: 302-654-8010.
Telecopier: 302-654-0795.

MEMBERS OF FIRM

Eugene M. Haring
Thomas F. Daly
John L. McGoldrick
Richard M. Eittreim
B. John Pendleton, Jr.

COUNSEL

Joseph F. Falgiani

For Complete List of Firm Personnel, See General Section

For full biographical listings, see the Martindale-Hubbell Law Directory

Robinson, St. John & Wayne (AV)

Two Penn Plaza East, 07105-2249
Telephone: 201-491-3300
Fax: 201-491-3333
Rochester, New York Office: Robinson, St. John & Curtin. First Federal Plaza.
Telephone: 716-262-6780.
Fax: 716-262-6755.
New York, New York Office: 245 Park Avenue.
Telephone: 212-953-0700.
Fax: 212-880-6555.

MEMBERS OF FIRM

Bruce S. Edington
Mark F. Hughes, Jr.
Steven L. Lapidus

For Complete List of Firm Personnel, See General Section

For full biographical listings, see the Martindale-Hubbell Law Directory

Saiber Schlesinger Satz & Goldstein (AV)

One Gateway Center, 13th Floor, 07102-5311
Telephone: 201-622-3333
Telecopier: 201-622-3349

MEMBERS OF FIRM

David M. Satz, Jr.
Bruce I. Goldstein
William F. Maderer
David J. D'Aloia
James H. Aibel
Sean R. Kelly
John L. Conover
Lawrence B. Mink
Michael L. Allen
Michael L. Messer
Jeffrey W. Lorell
Jeffrey M. Schwartz
David J. Satz
Joan M. Schwab
Jennine DiSomma
James H. Forte
Vincent F. Papalia

OF COUNSEL

Samuel S. Saiber
Norman E. Schlesinger

COUNSEL

Andrew Alcorn
Robin B. Horn
Randi Schillinger

ASSOCIATES

Audrey M. Weinstein
Robert B. Nussbaum
Michael J. Geraghty
Jonathan S. Davis
Paul S. DeGiulio
Diana L. Sussman
Deanna M. Beacham
Robert W. Geiger
William S. Gyves
Barry P. Kramer
Susan Rozman
Michelle Viola

LEGAL SUPPORT PERSONNEL

DIRECTOR OF FINANCE AND ADMINISTRATION

Ronald Henry

For full biographical listings, see the Martindale-Hubbell Law Directory

Sills Cummis Zuckerman Radin Tischman Epstein & Gross, A Professional Corporation (AV)

One Riverfront Plaza, 07102-5400
Telephone: 201-643-7000
Fax: 201-643-6500
Telex: 820630 Sillsbeck Nwk
Atlantic City, New Jersey Office: 17 Gordon's Alley.
Telephone: 609-344-2800.
New York, N.Y. Office: 250 Park Avenue.
Telephone: 212-643-7000.

Steven S. Radin
Thomas J. Demski
Thomas S. Novak
Alan J. Cohen (Resident at Atlantic City, N.J. Office)

Stuart Rosen
Steven S. Katz
Lester Chanin
Paul F. Doda
Jeffrey M. Weinhaus
Adam Kaiser

Representative Clients: International Fidelity Insurance Co.; Integrity Insurance Co. in Liquidation; EMAR, Ltd.; American Bankers Insurance Co.; American Casualty Co.; Fidelity Mutual Life Insurance Co.; Motor Club of America.

For Complete List of Firm Personnel, See General Section

For full biographical listings, see the Martindale-Hubbell Law Directory

Tompkins, McGuire & Wachenfeld (AV)

A Partnership including a Professional Corporation
Four Gateway Center, 100 Mulberry Street, 07102-4070
Telephone: 201-622-3000
Telecopier: 201-623-7780

(See Next Column)

TOMPKINS, MCGUIRE & WACHENFELD, *Newark—Continued*

MEMBERS OF FIRM

William F. Tompkins (1913-1989)
William B. McGuire (P.A.)
Howard G. Wachenfeld
Francis X. Crahay
William J. Prout, Jr.
Rex K. Harriott
Michael F. Nestor
James F. Flanagan, III
Christopher James Carey
Marianne M. De Marco
Patrick M. Callahan
John J. Henschel
Michael S. Miller
Douglas E. Motzenbecker

ASSOCIATES

Evelyn A. Donegan
Joseph K. Cobuzio
George G. Campion
Leonore C. Lewis
Richard F. Connors, Jr.
Richard A. Ulsamer
Anthony E. Bush
Gina G. Milestone
John R. Watkins, II
Angelo Giacchi
Nadia M. Walker
Diane E. Sugrue
Brian M. English
Cynthia K. Stroud
Lisa W. Santola
David S. Blatteis
Whitney W. Bremer
Carol J. Gismondi
Albert Wesley McKee

OF COUNSEL

William T. Wachenfeld
Paul B. Thompson
Frances S. Margolis
William J. McGee

COUNSEL

Ellen Nunno Corbo
Evelyn R. Storch
William H. Trousdale

Representative Clients: Corbo Jewelers, Inc.; General Electric Co.; Hartford Insurance Group; Marriott Corp.; National Indemnity Co., Inc.; National Union Fire Insurance Co.; Underwriters at Lloyd's, London.

For Complete List of Firm Personnel, See General Section

For full biographical listings, see the Martindale-Hubbell Law Directory

*NEW BRUNSWICK,** Middlesex Co.

HOAGLAND, LONGO, MORAN, DUNST & DOUKAS (AV)

40 Paterson Street, P.O. Box 480, 08903
Telephone: 908-545-4717
Fax: 908-545-4579

MEMBERS OF FIRM

John J. Hoagland
Bartholomew A. Longo
James B. Moran
Alan I. Dunst
Kenneth J. Doukas, Jr.
Michael John Stone
Donald D. Davidson
Thaddeus J. Hubert, III
Joan Alster Weisblatt
Karen M. Buerle
Robert G. Kenny
Michael J. Baker
Robert J. Young
Andrew J. Carlowicz, Jr.
Gary J. Hoagland
Jeffrey S. Intravatola
Jamie D. Happas
Thomas J. Walsh
Robert S. Helwig
Michael F. Dolan
Douglas M. Fasciale
Carol Lonergan Perez
Marc S. Gaffrey

ASSOCIATES

John Charles Simons
Susan K. O'Connor
Stephen G. Perrella
Jacquelyn L. Poland
Gary S. Shapiro
Douglas Susan
Anne M. Weidenfeller
Edward Hoagland, Jr.
Patrick J. McDonald
Susan M. Pierce
Andrew N. Kessler
Ashley C. Paul
R. Michael Keefe
Robert B. Rogers
Carleen M. Steward
Claire N. Gallagher
Dennis P. Liloia
John P. Barnes
Daniel J. Cogan
Judith B. Moor
Kevin Nerwinski

Representative Clients: CNA/Continental Casualty; National Indemnity Co.; Providence Washington Insurance Co.; Underwriters Adjusting Co.; INA-PRO/CIGNA; Shand, Morahan & Co.; Imperial Casualty and Indemnity Co.; CSC Insurance Services; American International Group.

For Complete List of Firm Personnel, See General Section

For full biographical listings, see the Martindale-Hubbell Law Directory

NORTH BRUNSWICK, Middlesex Co.

BUSCH AND BUSCH (AV)

215 North Center Drive, Commerce Center - U.S. #1 South, P.O. Box 7448, 08902-7448
Telephone: 908-821-2300
Telecopier: 908-821-5588

OF COUNSEL

Henry Busch

MEMBERS OF FIRM

Lewis D. Busch (1901-1986)
Malcolm R. Busch
Ronald J. Busch
Bertram E. Busch
Mark N. Busch
Leonard R. Busch
Steven F. Satz

(See Next Column)

Donald J. Sears
Kenneth A. Levine

Representative Clients: Littman Jewelers; Middlesex County Mosquito Extermination Commission; Utica Mutual Insurance Co.; New Brunswick Tomorrow; Township of East Brunswick; Minnesota Mutual Life Insurance Co.; Township of Monroe, Board of Education.

For full biographical listings, see the Martindale-Hubbell Law Directory

PARSIPPANY, Morris Co.

CUYLER, BURK & MATTHEWS (AV)

Parsippany Corporate Center, Four Century Drive, 07054-4663
Telephone: 201-734-3200
Telex: 429071
Telecopier: 201-734-3201
E Mail main@cuyler.mhs.compuserve.com
New York, New York Office: 350 Fifth Avenue, Suite 3304. 10018.
Telephone: 212-312-6352.

MEMBERS OF FIRM

Stephen D. Cuyler
Jo Ann Burk
Edwin R. Matthews
Stefano Calogero
Allen E. Molnar
David L. Menzel
Peter Petrou
Richard A. Crooker
Nancy Giacumbo
Michael J. Jones
Gregg S. Sodini

COUNSEL

Anne M. Mohan

ASSOCIATES

Ellen C. Williams
Mary Fran Farley
William M. Fischer
J. Scott MacKay
Jan C. Walker
Kathleen Jane Olear
Cherie A. Hiller
Julie A. Sutton
Robert B. Flynn
Edward K. Rodgers
Ronald D. Puhala
Robert J. Pansulla
David F. Guido
Paul B. Hyman
Daniel J. Bonner
Drew D. Krause
Darin J. Winick
Kimberly A. Paw
Robert P. Lesko

LEGAL SUPPORT PERSONNEL

Frederick M. H. Currie, Jr.

For full biographical listings, see the Martindale-Hubbell Law Directory

GENNET, KALLMANN, ANTIN & ROBINSON, A PROFESSIONAL CORPORATION (AV)

6 Campus Drive, 07054-4406
Telephone: 201-285-1919
Fax: 201-285-1177

Stanley W. Kallmann
Mark L. Antin
Harry Robinson, III
Richard S. Nichols

OF COUNSEL

Samuel A. Gennet

Michael Margello
William Gary Hanft
Alan E. Burkholz
Thomas J. Olsen

Representative Clients: Aetna Insurance Co.; Hartford Fire; Lloyds of London; New England Mutuals.
Reference: United Jersey Bank.

For full biographical listings, see the Martindale-Hubbell Law Directory

PRINCETON, Mercer Co.

MEZEY & MEZEY, A PROFESSIONAL CORPORATION (AV)

Princeton Executive Campus, P.O. Box 8439, 08543
Telephone: 609-951-0200
Fax: 609-951-8677
New Brunswick, New Jersey Office: 93 Bayard Street.
Telephone: 908-545-6011.

Louis A. Mezey (1929-1982)
Frederick C. Mezey
Deborah A. Cohen (1947-1993)

OF COUNSEL

Brandon Martin
Scott M. Russ
Kevin G. Blessing

For full biographical listings, see the Martindale-Hubbell Law Directory

ROSELAND, Essex Co.

BRACH, EICHLER, ROSENBERG, SILVER, BERNSTEIN, HAMMER & GLADSTONE, A PROFESSIONAL CORPORATION (AV)

101 Eisenhower Parkway, 07068
Telephone: 201-228-5700
Telecopier: 201-228-7852

(See Next Column)

BRACH, EICHLER, ROSENBERG, SILVER, BERNSTEIN, HAMMER & GLADSTONE A PROFESSIONAL CORPORATION—*Continued*

Alan H. Bernstein
Charles X. Gormally
Alan S. Pralgever

David J. Klein
David S. Bernstein
Melissa E. Flax

OF COUNSEL

Lance A. Posner

Representative Clients: Ohio Casualty Insurance Group; New Jersey Neurological Assn.; Saint Barnabas Medical Center; Union Hospital; Radiological Society of New Jersey; Motor Club of America; Mercer Medical Center.

For Complete List of Firm Personnel, See General Section

For full biographical listings, see the Martindale-Hubbell Law Directory

CONNELL, FOLEY & GEISER (AV)

85 Livingston Avenue, 07068
Telephone: 201-535-0500
Telefax: 201-535-9217

MEMBERS OF FIRM

George W. Connell
Adrian M. Foley, Jr.
Theodore W. Geiser
John B. Lavecchia
George J. Kenny
Samuel Darrow Lord
Richard D. Catenacci
Richard J. Badolato
Peter D. Manahan
Mark L. Fleder
Jerome M. Lynes
Linda A. Palazzolo
John F. Neary
Thomas S. Cosma
Kathleen S. Murphy
Patrick J. McAuley
Peter J. Pizzi
Kevin R. Gardner
Robert E. Ryan
Michael X. McBride
Jeffrey W. Moryan
Patricia J. Pindar
Peter J. Smith
Brian G. Steller
Frank A. Lattal
Judith A. Wahrenberger
Karen Munster Cassidy
Stephen D. Kinnard
Karen Painter Randall
Liza M. Walsh

ASSOCIATES

Maureen A. Mahoney-Madarasz
Timothy E. Corriston
Ernest W. Schoellkopff
Heidi Willis Currier

OF COUNSEL

Margaret L. Moses

Representative Clients: Bethlehem Steel Corp.; Borden Inc.; Chase Manhattan Bank; CNA Insurance; Conrail; Hilton Hotels Corp.; Merrill Lynch; Microsoft; New Jersey Manufacturers Insurance.

For Complete List of Firm Personnel, See General Section

For full biographical listings, see the Martindale-Hubbell Law Directory

SELLAR, RICHARDSON, STUART & CHISHOLM, P.C. (AV)

Six Becker Farm Road, 07068
Telephone: 201-535-1400
Fax: 201-535-6522

James P. Richardson
Richard M. Chisholm
James P. Lisovicz
Wendy H. Smith
John M. Kearney

Denise M. Luckenbach
Chris William Kemprowski
Andrew M. Wolfenson
John B. D'Alessandro
Jonathan S. Fabricant
Robert P. Hoag
Shawn R. Stowell
Ian C. Doris

OF COUNSEL

Alastair J. Sellar
Anthony C. Stuart

For full biographical listings, see the Martindale-Hubbell Law Directory

WOLFF & SAMSON, P.A. (AV)

280 Corporate Center, 5 Becker Farm Road, 07068
Telephone: 201-740-0500
Fax: 201-740-1407

Ronald E. Wiss
Armen Shahinian

Darryl Weissman

Representative Clients: International Fidelity Insurance Co.; Celentano Brothers, Inc.; Chicago Title Insurance Co.; Hartz Mountain Industries; The Hillier Group; Foster Wheeler Corp.

For Complete List of Firm Personnel, See General Section

For full biographical listings, see the Martindale-Hubbell Law Directory

SADDLE RIVER, Bergen Co.

LEWIS & MCKENNA (AV)

82 East Allendale Road, 07458
Telephone: 201-934-9800
Telecopier: 201-934-8681
New York, N.Y. Office: 230 Park Avenue, Suite 2240.
Telephone: 212-772-0943.
Tallahassee, Florida Office: 820 E East Park Avenue, P.O. Box 10475.
Telephone: 904-681-3813
Telecopier: 904-222-1732.

MEMBERS OF FIRM

Paul Z. Lewis
Michael F. McKenna
Geoffrey McC. Johnson

ASSOCIATES

Sherry L. Foley
John A. Napolitano
Mariangela Chiaravalloti
Colin M. Quinn
David B. Beal
Timothy J. Foley

OF COUNSEL

Robert J. Bennett
James W. Anderson (Not admitted in NJ; Resident, Tallahassee, Florida Office)

For full biographical listings, see the Martindale-Hubbell Law Directory

*SOMERVILLE,** Somerset Co.

OZZARD WHARTON, A PROFESSIONAL PARTNERSHIP (AV)

75-77 North Bridge Street, P.O. Box 938, 08876
Telephone: 908-526-0700
Telecopier: 908-526-2246

William E. Ozzard
Victor A. Rizzolo
George A. Mauro, Jr.
Michael V. Camerino
Alan Bart Grant

Arthur D. Fialk
Frederick H. Allen, III
Wendy L. Wiebalk
Denise M. Marra

Representative Clients: New Jersey Manufacturers Insurance Co.; Travelers Insurance Co.; Porter Hayden, General Accident Insurance Company; Hanover Insurance Company.

For Complete List of Firm Personnel, See General Section

For full biographical listings, see the Martindale-Hubbell Law Directory

SPRINGFIELD, Union Co.

MCDONOUGH, KORN & EICHHORN, A PROFESSIONAL CORPORATION (AV)

Park Place Legal Center, 959 South Springfield Avenue, P.O. Box 712, 07081-0712
Telephone: 201-912-9099
Fax: 201-912-8604

Peter L. Korn
R. Scott Eichhorn
James R. Korn
William S. Mezzomo

Timothy J. Jaeger
Dona Feeney
Karen M. Lerner
Wilfred P. Coronato
Gail R. Arkin
Nancy Crosta Landale
Christopher K. Costa

OF COUNSEL

Robert P. McDonough

Representative Clients: Chubb Insurance; Medical Inter-Insurance Exchange of New Jersey; Medical Liability Mutual Insurance Co.; GRE Insurance; The Travelers; State Volunteer Insurance; Wausau Insurance; Continental Insurance; The Home.
Reference: United Counties Trust Company.

For full biographical listings, see the Martindale-Hubbell Law Directory

SUMMIT, Union Co.

HAGGERTY, DONOHUE & MONAGHAN, A PROFESSIONAL ASSOCIATION (AV)

One Springfield Avenue, 07901
Telephone: 908-277-2600
Fax: 908-273-1641

James C. Haggerty
George J. Donohue
Walter E. Monaghan

Rose Ann Haggerty
Thomas J. Haggerty
Alfred F. Carolonza, Jr.
William A. Wenzel
Mahlon H. Ortman
Michael A. Conway
James C. Haggerty, Jr.

(See Next Column)

HAGGERTY, DONOHUE & MONAGHAN A PROFESSIONAL ASSOCIATION, *Summit—Continued*

OF COUNSEL

Joseph D. Haggerty

Representative Clients: American International Group; Chubb/Pacific Indemnity Co.; Crawford & Co.; Crum & Forster; Hertz Corp.; Jefferson Insurance Group; Material Damage Adjustment Corp.; New Jersey Manufacturers; New Jersey Property Liability Guaranty Association; Royal Insurance Co.

For Complete List of Firm Personnel, See General Section

For full biographical listings, see the Martindale-Hubbell Law Directory

*TRENTON,** Mercer Co.

LENOX, SOCEY, WILGUS, FORMIDONI & CASEY (AV)

3131 Princeton Pike, 08648
Telephone: 609-896-2000
Fax: 609-895-1693

MEMBERS OF FIRM

Samuel D. Lenox (1897-1975)
Rudolph A. Socey, Jr.
George Wilgus, III
Roland R. Formidoni
Robert P. Casey
Thomas M. Brown
Gregory J. Giordano

ASSOCIATE

Elizabeth L. Tolkach
Denise M. Mariani

Representative Clients: Royal-Globe Insurance Cos.; New Jersey Bell Telephone Co.; Government Employees Insurance Co.; Pennsylvania Manufacturers Association Casualty Insurance Cos.; General Motors Corp.; Travelers Insurance Co.

For full biographical listings, see the Martindale-Hubbell Law Directory

NEEDELL & MCGLONE, A PROFESSIONAL CORPORATION (AV)

Quakerbridge Commons, 2681 Quakerbridge Road, 08619-1625
Telephone: 609-584-7700
Fax: 609-584-0123

Stanley H. Needell
Patricia Hart McGlone

Michael W. Krutman
Anthony P. Castellani
Barbara Brosnan
Douglas R. D'Antonio

For full biographical listings, see the Martindale-Hubbell Law Directory

VINELAND, Cumberland Co.

JAY H. GREENBLATT & ASSOCIATES A PROFESSIONAL CORPORATION (AV)

200 North Eighth Street, P.O. Box 883, 08360-0883
Telephone: 609-691-0424
Facsimile: 609-696-1010

M. Joseph Greenblatt (1896-1992)
Jay H. Greenblatt

Bonnie L. Laube
Nicholas Kierniesky
Charles S. Epstein
John M. Amorison

Counsel for: Newcomb Medical Center; Ware's Van & Storage Co., Inc.
Local Counsel for: CIGNA Companies (P & C Group); Coca Cola Bottlers' Association; Commercial Union Insurance Cos,; Millers Mutual Insurance Co.; Pawtucket Mutual Insurance Co.; Pennsylvania Lumbermans Mutual Insurance Co.; Vanliner Insurance Co.; Vik Brothers Insurance Group.

For full biographical listings, see the Martindale-Hubbell Law Directory

GRUCCIO, PEPPER, GIOVINAZZI, DESANTO & FARNOLY, P.A., A PROFESSIONAL CORPORATION (AV)

817 Landis Avenue, P.O. Box CN 1501, 08360
Telephone: 609-691-0100
Fax: 609-692-4095
Associated with: Stradley, Ronon, Stevens & Young, a Philadelphia Law Firm.
Woodbury, New Jersey Office: 21 Delaware Street.
Telephone: 609-848-5558.
Fax: 609-384-1181.
Avalon, New Jersey Office: 2878 Dune Drive.
Telephone: 609-967-4040.
Other New Jersey Offices:
Atlantic City Area: 609-347- 0909.
Salem Area: 609-935-3559.

James J. Gruccio
Robert A. DeSanto
Thomas P. Farnoly
Walter F. Gavigan
E. Edward Bowman

Representative Clients: State Farm Mutual Automobile Insurance Cos.; United States Fidelity & Guaranty Co.; Atlantic City Expressway Authority; County of Salem; County of Cape May; CNA Insurance Co.; Cumberland

(See Next Column)

Mutual Fire Insurance Co.; Cumberland County Guidance Center; Pizza Hut Inc.

For Complete List of Firm Personnel, See General Section

For full biographical listings, see the Martindale-Hubbell Law Directory

WAYNE, Passaic Co.

DEYOE, HEISSENBUTTEL & MATTIA (AV)

401 Hamburg Turnpike, P.O. Box 2449, 07474-2449
Telephone: 201-595-6300
Fax: 201-595-0146; 201-595-9262

MEMBERS OF FIRM

Charles P. DeYoe (1923-1973)
Wood M. DeYoe
Frederick C. Heissenbuttel
Philip F. Mattia
Gary R. Matano
Scott B. Piekarsky

ASSOCIATES

Anne Hutton
Glenn Z. Poosikian
Jo Ann G. Durr

Representative Clients: INA/Aetna Insurance Co. (Cigna); Medical Inter-Insurance Companies; Hanover-Amgro, Inc.; Maryland Casualty Co.; Ohio Casualty Insurance Co.; Motor Club of America; Selected Insurance Co.

For Complete List of Firm Personnel, See General Section

For full biographical listings, see the Martindale-Hubbell Law Directory

WILLIAMS, CALIRI, MILLER & OTLEY, A PROFESSIONAL CORPORATION (AV)

1428 Route 23, P.O. Box 995, 07474-0995
Telephone: 201-694-0800
Telecopier: 201-694-0302

Walter E. Williams (1904-1985)
David J. Caliri (Retired)
Richard S. Miller
Victor C. Otley, Jr.
Peter B. Eddy
William S. Robertson, III
David Golub
David C. Wigfield
Samuel G. Destito
John H. Hague
Stuart M. Geschwind
Steven A. Weisberger
Lawrence J. McDermott, Jr.
Darlene J. Pereksta
Hope M. Pomerantz
Cheryl H. Burstein
Joanne M. Sarubbi
Daniel Arent Colfax
David T. Miller

Representative Clients: Anchor Savings Bank, FSB; Federal Deposit Insurance Corporation (FDIC): The Hartford Accident and Indemnity Co.; The Ramapo Bank; Reliance Insurance Co.; Resolution Trust Corporation (RTC); Time-Warner Communications, Inc.; New Jersey Sports and Exposition Authority.

For full biographical listings, see the Martindale-Hubbell Law Directory

WESTMONT, Camden Co.

BROWN & CONNERY (AV)

360 Haddon Avenue, P.O. Box 539, 08108
Telephone: 609-854-8900
Facsimile: 609-858-4967
Camden, New Jersey Office: 518 Market Street, P.O. Box 1449.
Telephone: 609-365-5100.
Telecopier: 609-858-4967.

MEMBERS OF FIRM

Thomas F. Connery, Jr.
William J. Cook
Warren W. Faulk
Steven G. Wolschina
Paul Mainardi
John L. Conroy, Jr.
Dennis P. Blake
Michael J. Vassalotti
John J. Mulderig
William M. Tambussi
Bruce H. Zamost
Mark P. Asselta
Stephen J. DeFeo
Jane A. Lorber

ASSOCIATES

Isabel C. Balboa
Joseph A. Zechman
Michael J. Fagan
Karen A. Peterson
Jeffrey E. Ugoretz
Christine O'Hearn
Christine A. Campbell
Joseph T. Carney

Representative Clients: Delaware River Port Authority; Underwood-Memorial Hospital; Garden State Water Company; Honeywell, Inc.; Philadelphia Newspapers, Inc.; Port Authority Transit Co.; Resolution Trust Corp.; General Electric; Mercedez-Benz Credit Corp.; American Red Cross.

For full biographical listings, see the Martindale-Hubbell Law Directory

WEST ORANGE, Essex Co.

ZUCKER, FACHER AND ZUCKER, A PROFESSIONAL CORPORATION (AV)

100 Executive Drive, Third Floor, 07052
Telephone: 201-736-0444
Fax: 201-736-4011

(See Next Column)

ZUCKER, FACHER AND ZUCKER A PROFESSIONAL CORPORATION—*Continued*

Lionel P. Kristeller (1891-1956)
Melvin B. Cohen (1914-1966)
George R. Jackson (1895-1968)
Saul J. Zucker (1901-1984)
Morris R. Zucker
Irwin L. Facher
Roger C. Wilson
Paul J. Soderman

Judy L. Berberian
Brian Edward Tierney
James Kevin Haney

State Counsel for: Hobart; Becor Western.
Local Counsel for: United States Fidelity & Guaranty Co.; Kemper Insurance Group; Chubb & Son.

For full biographical listings, see the Martindale-Hubbell Law Directory

NEW MEXICO

*ALBUQUERQUE,** Bernalillo Co.

CIVEROLO, WOLF, GRALOW & HILL, A PROFESSIONAL ASSOCIATION (AV)

500 Marquette, N.W., Suite 1400, P.O. Drawer 887, 87103
Telephone: 505-842-8255
Telecopier: 505-764-6099

Richard C. Civerolo
Wayne C. Wolf
William P. Gralow
Lawrence H. Hill
Kathleen Davison Lebeck
Dennis E. Jontz
W. R. Logan
Roberto C. Armijo
Paul L. Civerolo
Ross L. Crown
Julia C. Roberts
Ellen M. Kelly
R. Thomas Dawe
Thomas P. Gulley
Robert James Curtis
Clinton W. Thute
Kathleen Schaechterle
Gary J. Cade
M. Clea Gutterson
Judith M. O'Neil
Lisa Entress Pullen
Leslie McCarthy Apodaca

General Counsel for: Western Bank.
Counsel for: Home Insurance Co.; Hartford Accident and Indemnity Co.; Farmers Insurance Group; Transamerica Insurance Co.; St. Joseph Hospital.
Representative Clients: AMREP Corp.; St. Vincent Hospital; Risk Management, State of New Mexico; G.D. Searle.

For Complete List of Firm Personnel, See General Section

For full biographical listings, see the Martindale-Hubbell Law Directory

THE FARLOW LAW FIRM (AV)

Suite 1020, 6501 Americas Parkway, NE, 87110
Telephone: 505-883-4975
Fax: 505-883-4992

LeRoi Farlow
Suzanne Guest
Marianne L. Bowers

Representative Clients: Allstate Insurance Co.; Commercial Insurance Co.; Sentry Insurance Co.; National Farmers Union Insurance Co.; Preferred Risk Mutual Insurance Co.; Guaranty National Insurance Co.
Reference: Bank of New Mexico.

For full biographical listings, see the Martindale-Hubbell Law Directory

GALLAGHER, CASADOS & MANN, P.C. (AV)

317 Commercial N.E., 2nd Floor, 87102
Telephone: 505-243-7848
Fax: 505-764-0153

James E. Casados
Nathan H. Mann
Michael P. Watkins
Gail S. Stewart
Doris W. Eng
Dawn T. (Penni) Adrian
Jack Carmody
Robert L. Hlady

OF COUNSEL

David R. Gallagher

Representative Clients: Great American Insurance Co.; Mutual of Omaha; Safeco Insurance Co.; Amica Insurance Co.; American International Adjustment Co.; Progressive Insurance Co.; Maryland Casualty Co.; Sentry-Dairyland; Stonewall Insurance Co.; Scottsdale Insurance Co.

For full biographical listings, see the Martindale-Hubbell Law Directory

HINKLE, COX, EATON, COFFIELD & HENSLEY (AV)

Suite 800, 500 Marquette, N.W., P.O. Box 2043, 87103
Telephone: 505-768-1500
FAX: 505-768-1529
Roswell, New Mexico Office: Suite 700, United Bank Plaza, P.O. Box 10, 88202.
Telephone: 505-622-6510.
FAX: 505-623-9332.

(See Next Column)

Midland, Texas Office: 6 Desta Drive, Suite 2800, P.O. Box 3580, 79705.
Telephone: 915-683-4691.
FAX: 915-683-6518.
Amarillo, Texas Office: 1700 Bank One Center. P.O. Box 9238, 79105-9238.
Telephone: 806-372-5569.
FAX: 806-372-9761.
Santa Fe, New Mexico Office: 218 Montezuma, P.O. Box 2068, 87504.
Telephone: 505-982-4554.
FAX: 505-982-8623.
Austin, Texas Office: 401 West 15th Street, Suite 800, 78701.
Telephone: 512-476-7137.
FAX: 512-476-5431.
Associated Office: Hoffman & Stephens, P.C., 401 West 15th Street, Suite 800, 78701.
Telephone: 512-476-5434.
Fax: 512-476-5431.

Eric D. Lanphere
Thomas J. McBride
Stanley K. Kotovsky, Jr.
Howard R. Thomas

Representative Clients: Anadarko Petroleum Corp.; Atlantic Richfield Co.; Bass Enterprises Production Co.; BHP Petroleum; Caroon & Black Management, Inc.; Chevron, USA, Inc.; CIGNA; City of Albuquerque; Coastal Oil & Gas Corp. Co.; Ethicon Inc., A Johnson & Johnson, Co.; Diagnostik; Conoco; Texaco; Presbyterian Healthcare Services.

For Complete List of Firm Personnel, See General Section

For full biographical listings, see the Martindale-Hubbell Law Directory

MILLER, STRATVERT, TORGERSON & SCHLENKER, P.A. (AV)

500 Marquette Avenue, N.W., Suite 1100, P.O. Box 25687, 87102.
Telephone: 505-842-1950
Facsimile: 505-243-4408
Farmington, New Mexico Office: Suite 300, 300 West Arrington. P.O. Box 869.
Telephone: 505-326-4521.
Facsimile: 505-325-5474.
Las Cruces, New Mexico Office: Suite 300, 277 East Amador. P.O. Drawer 1231.
Telephone: 505-523-2481.
Facsimile: 505-526-2215.
Santa Fe, New Mexico Office: 125 Lincoln Avenue, Suite 221. P.O. Box 1986.
Telephone: 505-989-9614.
Facsimile: 505-989-9857.

Ranne B. Miller
Alan C. Torgerson
Kendall O. Schlenker
Alice Tomlinson Lorenz
Gregory W. Chase
Alan Konrad
Margo J. McCormick
Lyman G. Sandy
Stephen M. Williams
Stephan M. Vidmar
Robert C. Gutierrez
Seth V. Bingham (Resident at Farmington Office)
Michael H. Hoses
James B. Collins (Resident at Farmington Office)
Timothy Ray Briggs
Walter R. Parr (Resident at Santa Fe Office)
Rudolph A. Lucero
Daniel E. Ramczyk
Dean G. Constantine
Deborah A. Solove
Gary L. Gordon
Lawrence R. White (Resident at Las Cruces Office)
Sharon P. Gross
Virginia Anderman
Marte D. Lightstone
Bradford K. Goodwin
John R. Funk (Resident at Las Cruces Office)
J. Scott Hall (Resident at Santa Fe Office)
Thomas R. Mack
Michael J. Happe (Resident at Farmington Office)
Denise Barela Shepherd
Nancy Augustus
Jill Burtram
Terri L. Sauer
Joel T. Newton (Resident at Las Cruces Office)
Judith K. Nakamura
Thomas M. Domme
David H. Thomas, III
C. Brian Charlton

COUNSEL

William K. Stratvert
Paul W. Robinson

Representative Clients: St. Paul Insurance Cos.; State Farm Mutual Automobile Insurance Co.; The Travelers; United States Fidelity & Guaranty Co.; New Mexico Physicians Mutual Liability Insurance Co.; Farmers Insurance Group; Horace Mann Insurance Co.; Worldwide Insurance Group; Gallagher Bassett Services, Inc.

For Complete List of Firm Personnel, See General Section

For full biographical listings, see the Martindale-Hubbell Law Directory

RODEY, DICKASON, SLOAN, AKIN & ROBB, P.A. (AV)

Albuquerque Plaza, Suite 2200, 201 Third Street, N.W., P.O. Box 1888, 87103-1888
Telephone: 505-765-5900
Fax: 505-768-7395
Santa Fe, New Mexico Office: Suite 101 Marcy Plaza, 123 East Marcy Street, P.O. Box 1357, 87504-1357.
Telephone: 505-984-0100.
Fax: 505-989-9542.

(See Next Column)

RODEY, DICKASON, SLOAN, AKIN & ROBB P.A., *Albuquerque—Continued*

James C. Ritchie
Joseph J. Mullins
Robert G. McCorkle
Rex D. Throckmorton
Jonathan W. Hewes
W. Robert Lasater, Jr.
Mark C. Meiering
Travis R. Collier
W. Mark Mowery (Resident, Santa Fe Office)
Patrick M. Shay
David C. Davenport, Jr. (Resident, Santa Fe Office)
Tracy E. McGee
Charles E. Stuckey
Henry M. Bohnhoff
Charles Kipps Purcell
Andrew G. Schultz
John M. Brant
Susan S. Throckmorton
Angela M. Martinez
R. Nelson Franse
Paul R. Koller

Charles J. Vigil
Sheryl S. Mahaney
Mark L. Allen
David W. Bunting

For Complete List of Firm Personnel, See General Section

For full biographical listings, see the Martindale-Hubbell Law Directory

SHEEHAN, SHEEHAN & STELZNER, P.A. (AV)

Suite 300, 707 Broadway, N.E., P.O. Box 271, 87103
Telephone: 505-247-0411
Fax: 505-842-8890

Craig T. Erickson
Juan L. Flores
Kim A. Griffith
Philip P. Larragoite
Susan C. Little
Maria O'Brien
Judith D. Schrandt
Timothy M. Sheehan
Luis G. Stelzner
Elizabeth Newlin Taylor
Robert P. Warburton

OF COUNSEL

Briggs F. Cheney
Charles T. DuMars
Thomas J. Horan
Pat Sheehan

Representative Clients: Aetna Insurance Co.; Associated Aviation Underwriters; Atlanta International Insurance Co.; Cessna Aircraft Co.; International Aviation Underwriters; KM Insurance Co.; National Aviation Underwriters; Ranger Insurance Co.; Showa Denko K.K., Inc.; Tokyo Marine & Fire Insurance Co., Ltd.

For full biographical listings, see the Martindale-Hubbell Law Directory

FARMINGTON, San Juan Co.

MILLER, STRATVERT, TORGERSON & SCHLENKER, P.A. (AV)

Suite 300, 300 West Arrington, P.O. Box 869, 87401
Telephone: 505-326-4521
Facsimile: 505-325-5474
Albuquerque, New Mexico Office: 500 Marquette Avenue, N.W., Suite 1100. P.O. Box 25687.
Telephone: 505-842-1950.
Facsimile: 505-243-4408.
Las Cruces, New Mexico Office: Suite 300, 277 East Amador. P.O. Drawer 1231.
Telephone: 505-523-2481.
Facsimile: 505-526-2215.
Santa Fe, New Mexico Office: 125 Lincoln Avenue, Suite 221. P.O. Box 1986.
Telephone: 505-989-9614.
Facsimile: 505-989-9857.

James B. Collins
Seth V. Bingham
Michael J. Happe

Representative Clients: St. Paul Insurance Cos.; State Farm Mutual Automobile Insurance Co.; The Travelers; United States Fidelity & Guaranty Co.; New Mexico Physicians Mutual Liability Insurance Co.; Farmers Insurance Group.

For full biographical listings, see the Martindale-Hubbell Law Directory

*LAS CRUCES,** Dona Ana Co.

MILLER, STRATVERT, TORGERSON & SCHLENKER, P.A. (AV)

Suite 300, 277 East Amador, P.O. Drawer 1231, 88004
Telephone: 505-523-2481
Facsimile: 505-526-2215
Albuquerque, New Mexico Office: 500 Marquette Avenue, N.W., Suite 1100. P.O. Box 25687.
Telephone: 505-842-1950.
Facsimile: 505-243-4408.
Farmington, New Mexico Office: Suite 300, 300 West Arrington. P.O. Box 869.
Telephone: 505-326-4521.
Facsimile: 505-325-5474.
Santa Fe, New Mexico Office: 125 Lincoln Avenue, Suite 221. P.O. Box 1986.
Telephone: 505-989-9614.
Facsimile: 505-989-9857.

(See Next Column)

Lawrence R. White
John R. Funk

Representative Clients: St. Paul Insurance Cos.; State Farm Mutual Automobile Insurance Co.; The Travelers; United States Fidelity & Guaranty Co.; New Mexico Physicians Mutual Liability Insurance Co.; Farmers Insurance Group; Medical Protective Co.; Qual-Med, Inc.; Penn General Southwest, Inc.; Foundation Reserve Insurance Co.

For full biographical listings, see the Martindale-Hubbell Law Directory

LAW OFFICE OF T. A. SANDENAW (AV)

545 South Melendres, Suite C, 88005
Telephone: 505-523-7500
Fax: 505-523-5600

Thomas A. Sandenaw, Jr.

Mary T. Torres
Richard L. Musick

For full biographical listings, see the Martindale-Hubbell Law Directory

WEINBRENNER, RICHARDS, PAULOWSKY & RAMIREZ, P.A. (AV)

8th Floor, First National Tower, P.O. Drawer O, 88004-1719
Telephone: 505-524-8624
Fax: 505-524-4252

Neil E. Weinbrenner
Michael T. Murphy

General Counsel for: Stahmann Farms, Inc.; First National Bank of Dona Ana County.
Representative Clients: American General Cos.; Hartford Group; CNA Insurance; Fireman's Fund; United States Fidelity & Guaranty Co.; Travelers Insurance Co.; General Accident Group.

For Complete List of Firm Personnel, See General Section

For full biographical listings, see the Martindale-Hubbell Law Directory

*ROSWELL,** Chaves Co.

HINKLE, COX, EATON, COFFIELD & HENSLEY (AV)

Suite 700, United Bank Plaza, P.O. Box 10, 88202
Telephone: 505-622-6510
FAX: 505-623-9332
Midland, Texas Office: 6 Desta Drive, Suite 2800, P.O. Box 3580, 79705.
Telephone: 915-683-4691.
FAX: 915-683-6518.
Amarillo, Texas Office: 1700 Bank One Center, P.O. Box 9238, 79105-9238.
Telephone: 806-372-5569.
FAX: 806-372-9761.
Santa Fe, New Mexico Office: 218 Montezuma, P.O. Box 2068, 87504.
Telephone: 505-982-4554.
FAX: 505-982-8623.
Albuquerque, New Mexico Office: Suite 800, 500 Marquette, N.W., P.O. Box 2043, 87103.
Telephone: 505-768-1500.
FAX: 505-768-1529.
Austin, Texas Office: 401 West 15th Street, Suite 800, 78701.
Telephone: 512-476-7137.
FAX: 512-476-5431.
Associated Office: Hoffman & Stephens, P.C., 401 West 15th Street, Suite 800, 78701.
Telephone: 512-476-5434.
Fax: 512-476-5431.

RESIDENT PARTNERS

Harold L. Hensley, Jr.
Stuart D. Shanor
Richard E. Olson
Albert L. Pitts
Thomas D. Haines, Jr.

Representative Clients: Allstate Commercial Lines; Arco Oil and Gas Co. (self-insured); Federated Insurance Co.; National Farmers Union Insurance Co.; New Mexico Subsequent Injury Fund; Phillips Petroleum Co. (self-insured); Risk Management Division of the State of New Mexico; Texaco, Inc. (self-insured); Western Farm Bureau Insurance Co.

For full biographical listings, see the Martindale-Hubbell Law Directory

*SANTA FE,** Santa Fe Co.

CARPENTER, COMEAU, MALDEGEN, BRENNAN, NIXON & TEMPLEMAN (AV)

Coronado Building, 141 East Palace Avenue, P.O. Box 669, 87504-0669
Telephone: 505-982-4611
Telecopier: 505-988-2987

MEMBERS OF FIRM

Richard N. Carpenter
Michael R. Comeau
Larry D. Maldegen
Michael W. Brennan
Sunny J. Nixon
William P. Templeman
Jon J. Indall
Stephen J. Lauer
Paula Ann Cook
Grey Handy
Joseph E. Manges

Representative Clients: Great American Insurance Co.; Agricultural Insurance Co.; Allstate; American National Fire Insurance; Primerica; UNIRISC.

For full biographical listings, see the Martindale-Hubbell Law Directory

HINKLE, COX, EATON, COFFIELD & HENSLEY (AV)

218 Montezuma, P.O. Box 2068, 87504
Telephone: 505-982-4554
FAX: 505-982-8623

Roswell, New Mexico Office: Suite 700 United Bank Plaza, P.O. Box 10, 88202.
Telephone: 505-622-6510.
FAX: 505-623-9332.

Midland, Texas Office: 6 Desta Drive, Suite 2800, P.O. Box 3580, 79705.
Telephone: 915-683-4691.
FAX: 915-683-6518.

Amarillo, Texas Office: 1700 Bank One Center, P.O. Box 9238, 79105-9238.
Telephone: 806-372-5569.
FAX: 806-372-9761.

Albuquerque, New Mexico Office: Suite 800, 500 Marquette, N.W., P.O. Box 2043, 87103.
Telephone: 505-768-1500.
FAX: 505-768-1529.

Austin, Texas Office: 401 West 15th Street, Suite 800, 78701.
Telephone: 512-476-7137.
FAX: 512-476-5431.

Associated Office: Hoffman & Stephens, P.C., 401 West 15th Street, Suite 800, 78701.
Telephone: 512-476-5434.
Fax: 512-476-5431.

RESIDENT PARTNERS

Jeffrey L. Fornaciari
Thomas M. Hnasko

Representative Clients: Federated Insurance Services: General Accident Insurance Co.; Great Plain Insurance Co., Inc.; State of New Mexico; W.R. Grace & Co.

For full biographical listings, see the Martindale-Hubbell Law Directory

---

WHITE, KOCH, KELLY & MCCARTHY, A PROFESSIONAL ASSOCIATION (AV)

433 Paseo De Peralta, P.O. Box 787, 87504-0787
Telephone: 505-982-4374
ABA/NET: 1154
Fax: 505-982-0350; 984-8631

William Booker Kelly
John F. McCarthy, Jr.
Benjamin J. Phillips
David F. Cunningham
Albert V. Gonzales
Janet Clow
Kevin V. Reilly
Charles W. N. Thompson, Jr.
M. Karen Kilgore
Sandra J. Brinck

SPECIAL COUNSEL

Paul L. Bloom

Aaron J. Wolf
Carolyn R. Glick

Representative Clients: Southern Pacific Transportation Co.; Nationwide Insurance Co.; Risk Management Division of New Mexico General Services Department; Alliance of American Insurers; Santa Fe Community College; First American Title Insurance Co.; Century Bank; Public Service Company of New Mexico; AT&SF Railway Co.; Gallager Bassett.

For full biographical listings, see the Martindale-Hubbell Law Directory

---

NEW YORK

*ALBANY,** Albany Co.

CARTER, CONBOY, CASE, BLACKMORE, NAPIERSKI AND MALONEY, P.C. (AV)

20 Corporate Woods Boulevard, 12211-2350
Telephone: 518-465-3484
Fax: 518-465-1843

J. S. Carter (1920-1954)
M. James Conboy (1920-1969)
James S. Carter
James M. Conboy
Forrest N. Case, Jr.
James C. Blackmore
Eugene E. Napierski
John T. Maloney
Gregory S. Mills
Edward D. Laird, Jr.
Susanna L. Martin
Brian P. Krzykowski
Terence S. Hannigan

(See Next Column)

John W. VanDenburgh
William J. Greagan
Anne M. Hurley
John J. Gable
Susan DiBella Harvey
Shirley Clouser Greagan
James Anthony Resila
James P. Trainor
David A. Rikard
Nancy E. May-Skinner
Christopher Lyons
Eugene Daniel Napierski
Joseph T. Perkins
Colleen H. Whalen
Paul C. Marthy

Reference: Key Bank of New York.

For Complete List of Firm Personnel, See General Section

For full biographical listings, see the Martindale-Hubbell Law Directory

---

DONOHUE, SABO, VARLEY & ARMSTRONG, P.C. (AV)

18 Computer Drive East, P.O. Box 15056, 12212-5056
Telephone: 518-458-8922
Telecopier: 518-438-4349

Paul F. Donohue, Sr. (Retired)
Alvin O. Sabo
Kenneth Varley, Jr.
Robert J. Armstrong
Fred J. Hutchison
Bruce S. Huttner
Kathleen L. Werther

Christine M. D'Addio
Walter M.B. Spiro

Representative Clients: CNA Insurance Cos.; Continental Loss Adjusting Services; Electric Insurance Co.; Electric Mutual Insurance Co.; General Accident Assurance Co.; General Electric Co.; NY Central Mutual Fire Insurance Co.; Preferred Mutual Insurance Co.; State Insurance Fund; Zurich-American Insurance Co.

For full biographical listings, see the Martindale-Hubbell Law Directory

---

ROCHE CORRIGAN MCCOY & BUSH (AV)

The Wilem Van Zandt Building, 36 South Pearl Street, 12207
Telephone: 518-436-9370

MEMBERS OF FIRM

Robert P. Roche
Peter J. Corrigan
Joseph M. McCoy
Scott W. Bush

Reference: 1st American Bank, Albany.

For full biographical listings, see the Martindale-Hubbell Law Directory

ROWLEY, FORREST, O'DONNELL & HITE, P.C. (AV)

90 State Street Suite 729, 12207-1715
Telephone: 518-434-6187
Fax: 518-434-1287

Richard R. Rowley
Thomas J. Forrest
Brian J. O'Donnell
Robert S. Hite
John H. Beaumont
Mark S. Pelersi
David C. Rowley

James J. Seaman
David P. Miranda
Kevin S. Casey
Richard W. Bader
Daniel W. Coffey
Thomas D. Spain

OF COUNSEL

Rush W. Stehlin

Reference: Norstar Bank.

For full biographical listings, see the Martindale-Hubbell Law Directory

---

THORN AND GERSHON (AV)

5 Wembley Court, New Karner Road, P.O. Box 15054, 12212
Telephone: 518-464-6770
Fax: 518-464-6778

MEMBERS OF FIRM

Richard M. Gershon
Arthur H. Thorn
Jeffrey J. Tymann
Maureen Sullivan Bonanni
Robin Bartlett Phelan

ASSOCIATES

Murry S. Brower
Noreen J. Eaton
Paul J. Catone
Nancy Nicholson Bogan
Sheila Toborg
John C. Garvey
Paul D. Jureller
Mario D. Cometti
Robert S. Bruschini

OF COUNSEL

Robert F. Doran

For full biographical listings, see the Martindale-Hubbell Law Directory

---

*BINGHAMTON,** Broome Co.

O'CONNOR, GACIOCH & POPE (AV)

One Marine Midland Plaza, East Tower-Seventh Floor, P.O. Box 1964, 13902
Telephone: 607-772-9262
Fax: 607-724-6002

(See Next Column)

O'CONNOR, GACIOCH & POPE, *Binghamton—Continued*

Thomas F. O'Connor
James C. Gacioch
Alan J. Pope
Lori Grumet Schapiro
Jeffrey A. Tait
Hugh B. Leonard
Robert N. Nielsen, Jr.
Martha Keeler Macinski
Stephen B. Atkinson
Kurt D. Schrader
Richard M. Hill
Patricia A. Cummings
Mark D. Goris
Susan E. Decker

OF COUNSEL

Walter T. Gorman

For full biographical listings, see the Martindale-Hubbell Law Directory

*BUFFALO,** Erie Co.

COHEN & LOMBARDO, P.C. (AV)

343 Elmwood Avenue, 14222
Telephone: 716-881-3010
Fax: 716-881-2755

Joseph Cohen (1909-1966)
Ernest Lombardo (1913-1993)
Richard N. Blewett
Donald A. Fisher
James I. Spandau
Robert N. Convissar
Rocco Lucente, II
Stuart Brian Shapiro

Anthony Casilio
Robert R. Goods
Neil R. Sherwood
Mark A. Doane

SPECIAL COUNSEL

Anthony M. Nosek

OF COUNSEL

Norman J. Pecora
Dean C. Stathacos

For full biographical listings, see the Martindale-Hubbell Law Directory

HURWITZ & FINE, P.C. (AV)

1300 Liberty Building, 14202-3613
Telephone: 716-849-8900
Telecopier: 716-855-0874

Sheldon Hurwitz
Theodore J. Burns
James D. Gauthier
Dan D. Kohane
Harry F. Mooney
Paul J. Suozzi
Robert M. Lippman

Amy J. Ziegler
Theresa A. Drew
Donna L. Burden
Daniel R. Archilla
Dennis J. Bischof
Paula Marie Eade Newcomb
Thomas P. Cunningham

For Complete List of Firm Personnel, See General Section

For full biographical listings, see the Martindale-Hubbell Law Directory

KOREN, BERTELL & HOEY (AV)

Suite 1820 Liberty Building, 14202
Telephone: 716-856-3631
Fax: 716-856-5457

MEMBERS OF FIRM

M. Robert Koren (1920-1992)
John T. Bertell
Benjamin J. Hoey
Bruce Kevin Koren

ASSOCIATES

Marc J. Hopkins
Richard J. Lutzel

For full biographical listings, see the Martindale-Hubbell Law Directory

RODGERS, MENARD & COPPOLA (AV)

1630 Liberty Building, 420 Main Street, 14202-3616
Telephone: 716-852-4100
Facsimile: 716-852-0002

MEMBERS OF FIRM

Douglas S. Coppola
Michael Menard
Mark C. Rodgers

ASSOCIATES

Patricia S. Stroman
Patricia S. Ciccarelli

For full biographical listings, see the Martindale-Hubbell Law Directory

LAW OFFICES OF LOUIS H. SIEGEL (AV)

602 Chemical Bank Building, 69 Delaware Avenue, 14202
Telephone: 716-854-2626
Facsimile: 716-854-2629

Reference: Fleet Bank.

For full biographical listings, see the Martindale-Hubbell Law Directory

SMITH, MURPHY & SCHOEPPERLE (AV)

786 Ellicott Square, 14203
Telephone: 716-852-1544
Telecopier: 716-852-3559

MEMBERS OF FIRM

Clayton M. Smith (1884-1967)
Esmond D. Murphy (1903-1960)
Richard K. Schoepperle
Frank G. Godson
Peter M. Collard
Lynn D. Gates
Bonnie T. Hager
Janice A. Barber
Linda J. Marsh
Robert A. Baker, Jr.
Norton T. Lowe
Edward J. Murphy, III
Dennis P. Mescall
Stephen P. Brooks

SPECIAL COUNSEL

Dennis C. Vacco

ASSOCIATES

Daniel H. Dillon
Ross J. Runfola
Susan W. Schoepperle
Michael T. Glascott

LEGAL SUPPORT PERSONNEL

LEGAL ADMINISTRATOR

Marybeth Cerrone

PARALEGALS

Michelle M. Wojciechowicz
Janice M. Beyer
Tamara Montaldi
Laurie A. Tripp

Representative Clients: Hartford Insurance Group; Dominion of Canada General Insurance Co.; Casualty Company of Canada; Royal Insurance Cos.; Chrysler Corp.; Merchants Inc., Group; Associated Aviation Underwriters; U.S. Aviation Underwriters.

For full biographical listings, see the Martindale-Hubbell Law Directory

GARDEN CITY, Nassau Co.

GALLAGHER GOSSEEN & FALLER (AV)

1010 Franklin Avenue, Suite 400, 11530-2927
Telephone: 516-742-2500
Fax: 516-742-2516
Cable: COMPROAIR
New York, New York Office: 350 Fifth Avenue.
Telephone: 212-947-5800.
FAX: 212-967-4965.

MEMBERS OF FIRM

James A. Gallagher, Jr.
Robert A. Faller
Alan D. Kaplan
Michael J. Crowley
William E. Vita

ASSOCIATES

David H. Arnsten
William A. Bales, Jr.
Jennifer Greenberg
Jeanne M. Gonsalves-Lloyd
Brian P. Morrissey
Robert A. Sparer (Resident, New York City Office)

OF COUNSEL

Edward M. O'Brien (Resident, New York City Office)
Peter F. Vetro
Daniel F. Hayes
John P. Coogan

For Complete List of Firm Personnel, See General Section

For full biographical listings, see the Martindale-Hubbell Law Directory

L'ABBATE, BALKAN, COLAVITA & CONTINI, L.L.P. (AV)

1050 Franklin Avenue, 11530
Telephone: 516-294-8844
Telecopier: 516-294-8202; 742-6563

MEMBERS OF FIRM

Donald R. L'Abbate
Kenneth J. Balkan
Anthony P. Colavita
Peter L. Contini
Monte E. Sokol
Douglas L. Pintauro
Richard P. Byrne
Ronald C. Burke
Harry Makris
Marie Ann Hoenings
Jane M. Myers
Dean L. Milber
James Plousadis

OF COUNSEL

Paula M. Gart

ASSOCIATES

Anna M. DiLonardo
David B. Kosakoff
Lewis A. Bartell
Ralph A. Catalano
Gay B. Levine
Victoria Roberts Drogin
Douglas R. Halstrom
Joseph A. Barra
Stephane Jasmin
Lawrence A. Kushnick
Diane H. Miller
Barbara Jean Romaine
Joseph V. Cambareri
Christine Andreoli

Chicago Underwriting Group, Inc.; CNA: DPIC Insurance Cos.; Evanston Insurance Co.; General Accident Insurance Co.; The Home Insurance Co.; Imperial Casualty and Indemnity Co.; Markel American Insurance Co.; Shand, Morahan & Co., Inc.; Utica Mutual Insurance Co.

For full biographical listings, see the Martindale-Hubbell Law Directory

LAKE SUCCESS, Nassau Co.

IVONE, DEVINE & JENSEN (AV)

2001 Marcus Avenue-Suite N100, 11042
Telephone: 516-326-2400
Telecopier: 516-352-4952

MEMBERS OF FIRM

Michael T. Ivone
Robert Devine
Richard C. Jensen
Brian E. Lee
Michael Ferguson

ASSOCIATES

James C. Brady
Amy S. Barash
Ann-Marie Fassl Hartline
Debora G. Nobel
Charles Costas

For full biographical listings, see the Martindale-Hubbell Law Directory

*MINEOLA,** Nassau Co.

DOMINIC J. CORNELLA ASSOCIATES, P.C. (AV)

1539 Franklin Avenue, 11501
Telephone: 516-294-1400
Fax: 516-294-1453
New York, N.Y. Office: 80 Beekman Street, 10038.
Telephone: 212-732-4042.
Fax: 212-964-3676.

Dominic J. Cornella

For full biographical listings, see the Martindale-Hubbell Law Directory

KENNEDY & COMERFORD (AV)

200 Old Country Road, 11501
Telephone: 516-741-8818
Fax: 516-741-1703
New York, N.Y. Office: 805 Third Avenue.
Telephone: 212-750-1614.
Fax: 212-750-2885.

Bernard P. Kennedy
Michael J. Comerford

ASSOCIATE

Anne Marie Caradonna

OF COUNSEL

William J. Poisson
Patrick J. Hackett

For full biographical listings, see the Martindale-Hubbell Law Directory

MCCABE & COZZENS (AV)

114 Old Country Road, P.O. Box 855, 11501
Telephone: 516-741-6266
Telecopier: 516-873-9496

MEMBERS OF FIRM

Stephen M. McCabe
R. Bruce Cozzens, Jr.
Brian J. McGeough
James J. Collins
David T. Fowler

ASSOCIATES

Patrick M. Murphy
Thomas J. Nogan
Edward B. Ehrlich
Brian J. Greenfield
William Jaffe
Michael S. Levine
Joseph P. Minasi
Thomas M. O'Connor
Michael T. Reilly
Scott L. Mathias
Philip G. Menna
Mark L. Weisenreder

OF COUNSEL

Henri P. Caubisens

For full biographical listings, see the Martindale-Hubbell Law Directory

NICOLINI & PARADISE (AV)

114 Old Country Road Suite 500, 11501
Telephone: 516-741-6355

MEMBERS OF FIRM

Anthony J. Nicolini
Vincent J. Paradise

Representative Clients: Long Island Railroad; NYS Liquidation Bureau; Avis Rent-A-Car System, Inc.; County of Nassau; Continental Excess & Select.

For full biographical listings, see the Martindale-Hubbell Law Directory

SHAYNE, DACHS, STANISCI, CORKER & SAUER (AV)

250 Old Country Road, 11501
Telephone: 516-747-1100
Telecopier: 516-747-1185

MEMBERS OF FIRM

Moe Levine (1968-1974)
Neil T. Shayne
Norman H. Dachs
Thomas W. Stanisci
W. Russell Corker
Brian J. Sauer
Kenneth J. Landau
Jonathan A. Dachs

(See Next Column)

Naomi R. Nathan

For full biographical listings, see the Martindale-Hubbell Law Directory

*NEW YORK,** New York Co.

ABRAMS & MARTIN, P.C. (AV)

120 Wall Street, 10005
Telephone: 212-422-1200
Fax: 212-968-7573

Henry H. Abrams (1910-1977)
Alan J. Martin
Mark E. Abrams
Michael E. Gorelick
Daniel J. Friedman
Glenn A. Jacobson

Melvin P. Meyer
Norman Landres
Kevin J. Spencer
Pamela R. Wolff
Martin I. Nagel
Allen A. Kolber

OF COUNSEL

Harold A. Craig, Jr.

Representative Clients: Underwriters at Lloyds; New York Property Insurance Underwriting Assn.; American International Group; Jefferson Insurance Co.; Homestead Insurance Co.

For full biographical listings, see the Martindale-Hubbell Law Directory

BEATIE, KING & ABATE (AV)

599 Lexington Avenue, Suite 1300, 10022
Telephone: 212-888-9000
Fax: 212-888-9664

Russel H. Beatie, Jr.
Kenneth J. King
Samuel J. Abate, Jr.

ASSOCIATES

Susan Kelty Law
Charna L. Gerstenhaber
Eric J. Gruber
Philip J. Miller
Peter S. Liaskos
W.H. Ramsay Lewis

For full biographical listings, see the Martindale-Hubbell Law Directory

BIGHAM ENGLAR JONES & HOUSTON (AV)

14 Wall Street, 10005-2140
Telephone: 212-732-4646
Cable: "Kedge"
RCA Telex: 235332 BEJHUR
Telefax: 2126190781 GR I II III; 2122279491 GR I II III
London, England Office: Lloyd's Suite 699, 1 Lime Street.
Telephone: 71-283-9541.
Telex: 893323 BEJH G.
Telefax: 016262382 GR I II III.
Newark, New Jersey Office: One Gateway Center.
Telephone: 201-643-1303.
Telecopier: 201-643-1124.
Washington, D.C. Office: 1919 Pennsylvania Avenue, N.W., Suite 300.
Telephone: 202-736-2150.
Telefax: 202-223-6739.
Long Beach, California Office: 301 Ocean Boulevard, Suite 800.
Telephone: 310-437-5155.
Telefax: 310-495-3273.

MEMBERS OF FIRM

Douglas A. Jacobsen
Joseph A. Kilbourn
James J. Taylor
James B. McQuillan
James S. McMahon, Jr.
John T. Kochendorfer
Louis G. Juliano
Jay Levine
George R. Daly
John E. Cone, Jr.
John MacCrate, III
Francis A. Montbach
Robert J. Phillips, Jr.
Stephen M. Marcusa
William R. Connor, III
Robert E. Hirsch
Thomas R. Pattison
Marilyn L. Lytle
Peter I. Broeman
Donald T. Rave, Jr.
Stephen V. Rible
William C. Brown, III
Adrian Mecz (Resident, London, England Office)
Helen M. Benzie
Chris Christofides
Paul Ambos
Lawrence B. Brennan
Martin J. Flannery, Jr.
John V. Coulter, Jr.
Karin A. Schlosser
Martin J. Nilsen

COUNSEL

Laurence W. Levine
William P. Sullivan, Jr.

ASSOCIATES

George S. Evans, Jr.
Aileen J. Fox
Frederick A. Lovejoy
Frank G. Sinatra
Stacey Tranchina

For Complete List of Firm Personnel, See General Section

For full biographical listings, see the Martindale-Hubbell Law Directory

New York—Continued

CALLAN, REGENSTREICH, KOSTER & BRADY (AV)

One Whitehall Street 10th Floor, 10004
Telephone: 212-248-8800
Fax: 212-248-6815
Shrewsbury, New Jersey Office: 179 Avenue of the Common, P.O. Box 7413.
Telephone: 908-389-8400.

MEMBERS OF FIRM

Paul F. Callan
Bruce N. Regenstreich
Warren S. Koster
Bruce M. Brady
Angela M. Zito
William L. Brennan
Richard D. Meadow

ASSOCIATES

Jennifer M. Woodward
Scott W. Bermack
Kenneth S. Merber
Dorothy Spinelli (Not admitted in NY)
Michael P. Kandler
Neva M. Hoffmaier
Kathleen A. Ianno
Elyse Cohen Wolfe
Walter Paterson Burrell
Raymond G. H. Waugh, Jr.
Lisa R. DeMarzo (Not admitted in NY)
Beth S. Block
Kurt E. Reinheimer (Not admitted in NY)
Vincent A. Nagler
Melissa A. Cohn
Michael I. Braverman

For full biographical listings, see the Martindale-Hubbell Law Directory

CHALOS & BROWN, P.C. (AV)

300 East 42nd Street, 10017-5982
Telephone: 212-661-5440
Telecopier: 212-697-8999
Telex: 238470 (RCA)
Clifton, New Jersey Office: 1118 Clifton Avenue.
Telephone: 201-779-1116.

Michael G. Chalos
Robert J. Brown
Harry A. Gavalas
Stephan Skoufalos
Thomas M. Russo
Martin F. Casey
Robert J. Seminara

Edward P. Flood
Timothy G. Hourican
Fred G. Wexler
Steven G. Friedberg
George J. Tsimis
Martin F. Marvet
Laurence Curran

References: Citibank, N.A.; Chase Manhattan Bank.

For full biographical listings, see the Martindale-Hubbell Law Directory

D'AMATO & LYNCH (AV)

70 Pine Street, 10270
Telephone: 212-269-0927
Cable Address: "Damcosh"
Telex: 960085 DCOS UI NYK
Telefax: 212-269-3559

MEMBERS OF FIRM

George G. D'Amato
Luke D. Lynch
Peter J. Thumser
Robert M. Makla
Kenneth A. Sagat
Howard Wildman
John J. Cullen
Luke D. Lynch, Jr.
Richard George
Richard F. Russell
Robert E. Kushner
Robert W. Lang
Neal M. Glazer
John P. Higgins
Andrew R. Simmonds
Thomas F. Breen
Alfred A. D'Agostino, Jr.
Mary Jo Barry
David A. Boyar
Barbara R. Seymour
John H. FitzSimons
Thomas Ward Hanlon, Jr.
Bill V. Kakoullis
William P. Larsen, III
Ronald H. Alenstein
Harry J. Arnold, Jr.
Philip J. Bergan

ASSOCIATES

Timothy C. Baldwin
Michael V. Baronio
Laurie P. Beatus
Frances Buckley
Nancy M. Cagan
Carla S. Caliendo
Kevin P. Carroll
Liza A. Chafiian
James D. Christo
Deborah M. Collins
Mary Lee Cunningham
Theodore Deliyannis
Michael J. Devereaux
Jeffrey J. Diecidue
John R. Edwards
Terri Green Fagan
Paul A. Ferrillo
Jeffrey R. Gaylord
John A. Goldenberg
Lloyd J. Herman
Donna Marie Hughes
Stephen Hymes
Susanne Mast Murray
Sharon A. McCloskey
Kenneth David Milbauer
Marie L. Monaco
Neil R. Morrison
Samuel F. Paniccia
Polly Schiavone
Gino D. Serpe
Lisa L. Shrewsberry
James I. Stempel
Peter A. Stroili
Maryann Taylor
Stephen F. Willig
Kevin J. Windels
Robert M. Yellen

(See Next Column)

COUNSEL

Robert E. Gilroy
Jerome Murray
Harvey Barrison
James M. Condon
Charles H. Witherwax
Richard G. McGahren

For full biographical listings, see the Martindale-Hubbell Law Directory

DOWNING & MEHRTENS, P.C. (AV)

233 Broadway, 10279
Telephone: 212-227-8090
Facsimile: 212-732-8823

John M. Downing
Thomas E. Mehrtens
Catherine Stewart Downing

Marguerite D. Peck
Brian J. Rayhill
Alison D. Metzler
Owen P. McEvoy
John M. Downing, Jr.

OF COUNSEL

Leonard M. McEvoy

For full biographical listings, see the Martindale-Hubbell Law Directory

GARBARINI & SCHER, P.C. (AV)

1114 Avenue of the Americas, 10036-7790
Telephone: 212-764-4000
Telecopier: (212) 719-5018
Telex: WUI 668964
Cable Address: "Garkrolaw NewYork"
Hackensack, New Jersey Office: 25 Main Street, Suite 300.
Telephone: 201-343-2002.
FAX: 212-719-5018.

Stanley J. Scher
Leonard Weinstock
Myrna A. Levinson
George J. Kehayas
Michael Caliguiri
Keith A. Raven
Anthony M. Fischetti
William G. Scher

Cecil E. Floyd
Jay M. Weinstein
Margery A. Budoff
Conrad Jordan
Martin K. Rowe
Gregg D. Weinstock
James W. Kachadoorian
Kurt L. Weinmann
Paul M. Paley
Timothy F. Jones
Valerie L. Drossman
Gregory D. V. Holmes
Barry Rothman
Nancy Breslow
Louise M. Cherkis

Representative Clients: Chubb & Son, Inc.; Clarendon National Insurance Co.; Farmers Insurance Group; Federation of Jewish Philanthropies; CIGNA Property and Casualty Cos.; Medical Liability Mutual Insurance Co.; St. Barnabas Hospital; The State Insurance Fund; Allstate Insurance Co.; Merchants Mutual Ins.

For full biographical listings, see the Martindale-Hubbell Law Directory

HEIDELL, PITTONI, MURPHY & BACH, P.C. (AV)

99 Park Avenue, 10016
Telephone: 212-286-8585
Telecopier: 212-490-8966
New Canaan, Connecticut Office: 49 Locust Avenue, P.O. Box 1132.
Telephone: 203-966-9983.

Luke M. Pittoni
Raymond W. Murphy
Charles L. Bach, Jr.
Rosary A. Morelli
Bruce F. Gilpatrick
Robin R. Dolsky
Elizabeth Cornacchio
Austa S. Devlin
Michael T. Walsh
Michael D. Shalhoub
Stephen R. Marshall
Louise A. Derevlany
Barbara A. Sheehan

OF COUNSEL

Robert C. Heidell

John F. Costa
Cheryl A. Harris
Michael F. McGowan
John J. Murphy, Jr.
E. Marc Hyman
Terrence P. St. John
Steven R. Goldstein
Andrea J. Fagen
Denise A. Rubin
Mitchell D. Frankel
Linda M. Ruma
Jason H. Korn
Rosemary E. Mahoney
Maria A. Onorato
William M. Wingertzahn
Janice Kirsten Lunde
John J. Peplinski
Geraldine Koeneke Russell
Diego A. Gomez
Christopher P. Foley
Marcy Blake
William D. Samers
Denise R. Melillo
Robert T. Melillo, Jr.
Katharine Demgen
Carol L. Morris-Fox
Daniel S. Ratner
George J. Tidona

For full biographical listings, see the Martindale-Hubbell Law Directory

New York—Continued

HUTTON INGRAM YUZEK GAINEN CARROLL & BERTOLOTTI (AV)

250 Park Avenue, 10177
Telephone: 212-907-9600
Facsimile: 212-907-9681

MEMBERS OF FIRM

Ernest J. Bertolotti
Daniel L. Carroll
Roger Cukras
Larry F. Gainen
G. Thompson Hutton
Samuel W. Ingram, Jr.
Paulette Kendler
Steven Mastbaum
Dean G. Yuzek
David G. Ebert
Shane O'Neill

ASSOCIATES

Warren E. Friss
Patricia Hewitt
Gail A. Buchman
Stuart A. Christie
Beth N. Green
Timish K. Hnateyko
Jeanne F. Pucci
Jane Drummey
Adam L. Sifre
Susan Ann Fennelly
Marc J. Schneider

For full biographical listings, see the Martindale-Hubbell Law Directory

JOHNSTON & MCSHANE, P.C. (AV)

Graybar Building, 420 Lexington Avenue, 10170
Telephone: 212-972-5252
Facsimilie: 212-697-2737

William R. Johnston
Bruce W. McShane
Peter F. Breheny

Dennis W. Grogan
Arthur J. Smith
Kenneth E. Moffett, Jr.
Andrew Ross
Robert D. Donahue
James M. Carman

OF COUNSEL

Charles A. Miller, II (Not admitted in NY)

For full biographical listings, see the Martindale-Hubbell Law Directory

KOPFF, NARDELLI & DOPF (AV)

440 Ninth Avenue, 10001
Telephone: 212-244-2999
Telecopier: 212-643-0862

MEMBERS OF FIRM

Peter C. Kopff
Camillo Nardelli (1936-1987)
Glenn W. Dopf
Scott F. Morgan
Charles K. Faillace
Joseph R. Cammarosano
Victoria A. Lombardi
Michael L. Manci
Martin B. Adams

ASSOCIATES

Eugene A. Ward
Mary E. Pearson
Joseph T. Belevich
Catherine R. Richter
Susan D. Noble
John A. Orbon
Denise D. Sapanara
Ronnie Michelle Grill
Richard J. Valent
Edward J. Arevalo
Edward A. Flores
Peter S. Williams
Tara K. Curcillo
Jonathan Adam Judd

Representative Clients: Aetna Casualty and Surety Co.; American International Group; Citicorp, U.S.A.; County of Nassau, State of New York; Franklin Hospital Medical Center; Guarantee National Insurance Co.; Lenox Hill Hospital; The May Department Stores Co.; Medical Inter-Insurance Exchange of New Jersey; Medical Liability Mutual Insurance Co.

For full biographical listings, see the Martindale-Hubbell Law Directory

LAVIN, COLEMAN, FINARELLI & GRAY (AV Ⓣ)

780 Third Avenue Suite 1401, 10017
Telephone: 212-319-6898
Fax: 212-319-6932
Philadelphia, Pennsylvania Office: 12th Floor, Penn Mutual Tower, 510 Walnut Street.
Telephone: 215-627-0303.
Fax: 215-627-2551.
Mount Laurel, New Jersey Office: 10000 Midlantic Drive, Suite 300 West.
Telephone: 609-778-5544.
Fax: 609-778-3383.

William J. Ricci (Not admitted in NY)
Edward A. Gray (Not admitted in NY)
Joseph A. McGinley
Michael D. Brophy

John Kieran Daly
Steven R. Kramer
Joseph F. Dunne

For full biographical listings, see the Martindale-Hubbell Law Directory

LONDON FISCHER (AV)

375 Park Avenue, 10152
Telephone: 212-888-3636
Facsimile: 212-888-3974

MEMBERS OF FIRM

Bernard London
James L. Fischer
John W. Manning
Daniel Zemann, Jr.
John E. Sparling

ASSOCIATES

Richard S. Endres
Nicholas Kalfa
Evan D. Lieberman
Amy M. Kramer
Robert S. Sunshine
Robert M. Vecchione
John P. Bruen
Christina M. Ambrosio
William C. Nanis
Michael P. Mezzacappa
Douglas W. Hammond
Michael S. Leavy
Robert L. Honig

For full biographical listings, see the Martindale-Hubbell Law Directory

MENDES & MOUNT (AV)

750 Seventh Avenue, 10019
Telephone: 212-261-8000
Telecopier: 212-261-8750
Cable Address: "Menmount"
Telex: WUI 620392; 620332
Los Angeles, California Office: Citicorp Plaza, 725 South Figueroa Street, Nineteenth Floor.
Telephone: 213-955-7700.
Telecopy: 213-955-7725.
Telex: 6831520.
Cable Address: "MNDMT."
Newark, New Jersey Office: 1 Newark Center.
Telephone: 201-639-7300.
Fax: 201-639-7350.

Joseph P. Gunset

For full biographical listings, see the Martindale-Hubbell Law Directory

MOUND, COTTON & WOLLAN (AV)

One Battery Park Plaza, 10004
Telephone: 212-804-4200
Cable Address: "Moundlaw"
Telex: 64-9063
Telecopier: 212-344-8066
San Francisco, California Office: Suite 1650, 44 Montgomery Street.
Telephone: 415-249-4919.
Telecopier: 415-391-9076.
London, England Office: Longbow House, 14-20 Chiswell Street.
Telephone: 071-638-3688.
East Hanover, New Jersey Office: 72 Eagle Rock Avenue, Building Two, P.O. Box 78.
Telephone: 201-503-9669.
Telecopier: 201-503-9494.

MEMBERS OF FIRM

Arthur N. Brook
Mitchell S. Cohen
Stuart Cotton
Leonard S. Dome
Wayne R. Glaubinger
Michael H. Goldstein
Lawrence S. Greengrass
Andrew C. Jacobson
Michael R. Koblenz
Daniel Markewich
John C. Mezzacappa
Frederic R. Mindlin
Philip C. Silverberg
Costantino P. Suriano
James D. Veach

COUNSEL

Eugene A. Leiman
Eugene Wollan

OF COUNSEL
SAN FRANCISCO, CALIFORNIA OFFICE

Alexander S. Keenan

MANAGING RESIDENT ATTORNEY
EAST HANOVER, NEW JERSEY OFFICE

Deanne Wilson

ASSOCIATES

Emilie L. Bakal
Brian F. Boardingham
Diane L. Bodenstein
Rebecca A. Buder
Mary L. Cain
Karen M. Cooke
Jeffrey C. Crawford
Guy P. Dauerty
Elisa T. Gilbert
Jeffrey B. Gold
Diana E. Goldberg
Lloyd A. Gura
Bruce R. Kaliner
Myra E. Lobel
Nancy B. London
Renee M. Plessner
Lisa S. Post
Jon Quint
Ronnie A. Rifkin
David I. Schonbrun
David A. Silva
Diane P. Simon
Sarah D. Strum
Ronald J. Theleen
Keith J. Wagner
Mark J. Weber

(See Next Column)

MOUND, COTTON & WOLLAN, *New York—Continued*

ASSOCIATES (Continued)

Jeffrey S. Weinstein
William D. Wilson
Simy C. Wolf
Rachel J. Yosevitz
Andrew L. Zalasin

For full biographical listings, see the Martindale-Hubbell Law Directory

NEWMAN SCHLAU FITCH & LANE, P.C. (AV)

305 Broadway, 10007-1198
Telephone: 212-619-4350
Fax: 212-619-3622
Glen Rock, New Jersey Office: Newman Schlau Fitch & Lane, 55 Harristown Road.
Telephone: 201-670-7040.
Fax: 201-670-4977.
Scarsdale, New York Office: 73 Greenacres Avenue.
Telephone: 914-472-0950.
Fax: 212-619-3622.

Philip Schlau
Robert A. Fitch
John C. Lane (Resident Partner, Glen Rock, New Jersey Office)
Abraham S. Altheim
Jan Kevin Myers
Jay L. Katz
Charles W. Kreines
Floyd G. Cottrell (Resident Partner, Glen Rock, New Jersey Office)
Andrew J. Cook
Olivia M. Gross

COUNSEL

William E. Bell
Howard A. Fried
Peter T. Shapiro

Ian F. Harris
Frank P. Luberti, Jr.
Kevin J. Donnelly
James K. Stern
Steven A. Carlotto
George A. Smith
Maria Sestito
Carolyn M. Green (Not admitted in NY)
Michael J. White
Ondine C. Slone
Peter C. Bobchin
Joseph P. Mooney
Ben Niderberg
Hillary P. Kahan
Ian R. Grodman (Resident, Glen Rock, New Jersey Office)
Denise Campbell
Daniel M. Schiavetta, Jr.
Debra A. Miller
Emily S. Barnett
Sim R. Shapiro
Paul A. Barkan
Andrew M. Tilem

Reference: Chase Bank, New York.

For full biographical listings, see the Martindale-Hubbell Law Directory

OHRENSTEIN & BROWN (AV)

230 Park Avenue, 10169
Telephone: 212-682-4500
Telecopier: 212-557-0910
Garden City, New York Office: 1205 Franklin Avenue.
Telephone: 516-333-1245.
Telecopier: 516-248-1947.

MEMBERS OF FIRM

Manfred Ohrenstein
Michael D. Brown
Mark J. Bunim
Terence P. Cummings
Steven D. Dreyer
John Paul Fulco, P.C.
Warren R. Graham
Abraham E. Havkins
Geoffrey W. Heineman
Christopher B. Hitchcock
Steven H. Rosenfeld

COUNSEL

Peter J. Kiernan
Stanley M. Kolber

ASSOCIATES

Peter J. Biging
Michele D. Breslow
Gerard J. Costello
Annmarie D'Amour
Joseph Francis Fields
Andrea Beth Jacobson
Bennett R. Katz
Andrew L. Margulis
Abe M. Rychik
John R. Sachs, Jr.
Robert J. Segall
Evan Shapiro
Philip Touitou

For full biographical listings, see the Martindale-Hubbell Law Directory

PARKER CHAPIN FLATTAU & KLIMPL, L.L.P. (AV)

1211 Avenue of the Americas, 10036
Telephone: 212-704-6000
Telecopier: 212-704-6288
Cable Address: "Lawpark"
Telex: 640347
Great Neck, New York Office: 175 Great Neck Road.
Telephone: 516-482-4422.
Telecopier: 516-482-4469.

MEMBERS OF FIRM

Mark Abramowitz
Robert M. Carmen
Elliot Cohen
Michael D. Friedman
Alvin M. Stein
Lee W. Stremba
Joel M. Wolosky

(See Next Column)

OF COUNSEL

Daniel S. Greenfeld

For Complete List of Firm Personnel, See General Section

For full biographical listings, see the Martindale-Hubbell Law Directory

JEFFREY SAMEL & ASSOCIATES (AV)

120 Broadway, Suite 1755, 10271
Telephone: 212-587-9690
Fax: 212-587-9673

ASSOCIATES

Robert G. Spevack
Dorothy T. Zeman
Ricardo Rengifo
James H. O'Hare
David M. Samel
David S. Gary

OF COUNSEL

Richard A. Soberman

Representative Clients: New York City Transit Authority; New York City Housing Authority; Empire Insurance Co.; National General Insurance Co.; Federal Express Corp.; Shell Oil Corp.; American Building Maintenance Corp.

For full biographical listings, see the Martindale-Hubbell Law Directory

SHEFT & SHEFT (AV)

909 Third Avenue, 10022
Telephone: 212-688-7788
Telecopier: 212-355-7373
Jersey City, New Jersey Office: Harborside Financial Center, Suite 704 Plaza Three.
Telephone: 201-332-2233.
Telecopier: 201-435-9177.

Leonard A. Sheft
Peter I. Sheft
Norman J. Golub (Resident, Jersey City, New Jersey Office)
Marjorie Heyman Mintzer
Marian S. Hertz
Leonard G. Kamlet

COUNSEL

Gerald A. Greenberger (Resident, Jersey City, New Jersey Office)

David Holmes (Resident, Jersey City, New Jersey Office)
Phillip C. Landrigan
Thomas J. Leonard
Myra Needleman
Howard K. Fishman
Mary C. Bennett
Jeffrey S. Leonard (Resident, Jersey City, New Jersey Office)
Stacy B. Parker
Edward Hayum
Daniel H. Hecht
Jerrald J. Hochman
James M. Dennis
Frank V. Kelly
Ellen G. Margolis
Guy J. Levasseur
Joseph F. Arkins
Jordan Sklar
Herbert L. Lazar
Maria E. Cannon (Resident, Jersey City, New Jersey Office)

For full biographical listings, see the Martindale-Hubbell Law Directory

SMITH MAZURE DIRECTOR WILKINS YOUNG YAGERMAN & TARALLO, P.C. (AV)

111 John Street, 10038
Telephone: 212-964-6061
Fax: 212-374-1935 (Not for Legal Service)

Gerald Director
David E. Mazure
Stanley Wilkins
Nicholas Tarallo
Jacob J. Young
Mark S. Yagerman

Lewis I. Wolf
Seymour Dicker
Marc H. Pillinger
Irwin D. Miller
Herbert Minster
Harvey Ginsberg
Michael K. Berman
John Kevin Reilly

Eugene Staub
Jeanne L. Ramasso
Irwin Bloom
Michael S. Livow
Robert P. Siegel
Mark A. Solomon
Elayna Cindy Kaplan
Jeffrey T. Miller
John Colucci
Steven P. Cahn
Beth Matus Barnett
Daniel O. Dietchweiler
Corey A. Tavel
Cary Maynard
Haydn J. Brill
Michael L. Tawil
Richard Steigman
Douglas E. Hoffer
Clara M. Villarreal-Fanizzi
Steven I. Brizel

OF COUNSEL

Robert R. MacDonnell

For full biographical listings, see the Martindale-Hubbell Law Directory

New York—Continued

WHITE, FLEISCHNER & FINO (AV)

195 Broadway, 10007
Telephone: 212-227-6292
Telex: 645255
Telecopier: 212-227-7812
Westfield, New Jersey Office: 215 North Avenue, West.
Telephone: 908-654-6266.
Telecopier: 908-654-3686.
London, England Office: Plantation House. 31/35 Fenchurch S. EC3M 3DX.
Telephone: 071-375-2037.
Telecopier: 071-375-2039.

MEMBERS OF FIRM

Allan P. White
Benjamin A. Fleischner
Paul A. Fino, Jr.
Robert G. Schenker
Marcia J. Lynn
Marisa Goetz

ASSOCIATES

Patti F. Potash
Mitchell R. Friedman
Mitchell L. Shadowitz
Debra E. Ruderman
David I. Blee
Sandra L. Bonder
Michael J. Asta
Stephanie M. Holzback
Mark R. Osherow
Virginia L. McGrane
Beth A. Goldklang
Sean Upton
Wendy K. Carrano
Nancy D. Lyness
Randy Scott Faust
Elizabeth C. Mirisola
Sheri E. Holland

LEGAL SUPPORT PERSONNEL

Darien Anderson (Paralegal)
Helen Wasey (Claims Consultant)

For full biographical listings, see the Martindale-Hubbell Law Directory

WILSON, ELSER, MOSKOWITZ, EDELMAN & DICKER (AV)

150 East 42nd Street, 10017-5639
Telephone: 212-490-3000
Telex: 177679
Facsimile: 212-490-3038; 212-557-7810
Los Angeles, California Office: Suite 2700, 1055 West Seventh Street, 90017.
Telephone: 213-624-3044.
Telex: 17-0722.
Facsimile: 213-624-8060.
San Francisco, California Office: 555 Montgomery Street, 94111.
Telephone: 415-433-0990.
Telex: 16-0768.
Facsimile: 415-434-1370.
Washington, D.C. Office: The Colorado Building, Fifth Floor, 1341 "G" Street, N.W., 20005.
Telephone: 202-626-7660.
Telex: 89453.
Facsimile: 202-628-3606.
Newark, New Jersey Office: One Gateway Center, 07102.
Telephone: 201-624-0800.
Telex: 6853589.
Facsimile: 201-624-0808.
Philadelphia, Pennsylvania Office: The Curtis Center, Independence Square West, 10604.
Telephone: 215-627-6900.
Telex: 6711203.
Facsimile: 215-627-2665.
Baltimore, Maryland Office: 250 West Pratt Street, 21201.
Telephone: 410-539-1800.
Telex: 19-8280.
Facsimile: 410-539-1820.
Miami, Florida Office: International Place, 100 Southeast Second Street, 33131.
Telephone: 305-374-1811.
Telex: 810845940.
Facsimile: 305-579-0261.
Chicago, Illinois Office: 120 N. La Salle Street, 26th Floor, 60602.
Telephone: 312-704-0550.
Telex: 1561590.
Facsimile: 312-704-1522.
White Plains, New York Office: 925 Westchester Avenue, 10604.
Telephone: 914-946-7200.
Facsimile: 914-946-7897.
Dallas, Texas Office: 5000 Renaissance Tower, 1201 Elm Street, 75270.
Telephone: 214-698-8000.
Facsimile: 214-698-1101.
Albany, New York Office: One Steuben Place, 12207.
Telephone: 518-449-8893.
Fax: 518-449-8927.
London, England Office: 141 Fenchurch Street, EC3M 6BL.
Telephone: 01-623-6723.
Telex: 885741.
Facsimile: 01-626-9774.

(See Next Column)

Tokyo, Japan Office: AIU Building, 1-3 Marunouchi 1-chome, Chiyoda-Ku, 100.
Telephone: 011-813-216-6551.
Telex: 781-2227216.
Facsimile: 011-813-216-6965.
Paris, France Office: Honig Buffat Mettetal. 21 Rue Clément Marot, 75008.
Telephone: 33 (1) 44.43.88.88.
Fax: 33 (1) 44.43.88.77.

MEMBERS OF FIRM

Thomas W. Wilson
John T. Elser
Harold J. Moskowitz
Max Edelman (1906-1989)
Herbert Dicker
Michael D. Glatt
Martin M. Ween
Marshal S. Endick
Milton Edelman
Richard S. Klein
Stephen A. Postelnek
Walter J. Smith, Jr. * (Resident Partner in Charge, Washington, D.C. Office)
Thomas W. Hyland
Vincent R. Fontana
Patrick M. Kelly * (Resident Partner in Charge, Los Angeles Office)
James P. Donovan
James Crawford Orr (Resident Partner in Charge, Newark Office)
Kenneth Scott (Resident Partner in Charge, Philadelphia Office)
Richard K. Traub
Stephen M. Marcellino
Perry I. Kreidman
Jerome N. Lerch * (Resident Partner in Charge, San Francisco Office)
Ralph W. Robinson * (Resident, San Francisco Office)
Philip J. Walsh
Edward J. Boyle
Anthony J. Mercorella
Jonathon F. Sher * (Resident, Los Angeles Office)
Robert M. Young, Jr. * (Resident, Los Angeles Office)
Jeffrey D. Robertson
Robert M. Weber
Paul J. Bottari
Michael N. Stevens
Mark K. Anesh
Daniel S. Schwartz * (Resident Partner in Charge, Miami Office)
Jerry L. McDowell * (Resident Partner in Charge, Chicago Office)
L. Victor Bilger, Jr. * (Resident, Los Angeles Office)
Steven Kent
Harry P. Brett
Glenn J. Fuerth
Phillip A. Tumbarello
Thomas M. Gambardella
Thomas W. Tobin
Eileen B. Eglin
Robert F. Roarke
Andrew S. Kaufman
Glen S. Feinberg
Jonathan C. Thau
David Florin * (Resident, Washington, D.C. Office)
Steven R. Parminter * (Resident, Los Angeles Office)
Keith G. Von Glahn (Resident, Newark Office)
Robert B. Wallace * (Resident, Washington, D.C. Office)
Louis H. Castoria * (Resident, San Francisco Office)
Martin W. Johnson * (Resident, San Francisco Office)
Jonathan Dryer * (Resident, Philadelphia Office)
Keith E. Johnston * (Resident, Philadelphia Office)
Otis D. Wright, II * (Resident, Los Angeles Office)
Arnold Kideckel
Gerald D. Freed * (Resident, Baltimore Office)
James W. Bartlett, III * (Resident, Baltimore Office)
Francis P. Manchisi
James M. Kaplan (Resident, Miami Office)
H. Michael O'Brien
Vincent P. D'Angelo * (Resident, Los Angeles, California Office)
Robert J. Kelly (Resident, Newark Office)
Bruce J. Chasan * (Resident, Philadelphia Office)
Adrian J. Gordon * (Resident, Philadelphia Office)
John Gary Luboja
Wayne I. Rabinowitz (Resident, White Plains, N.Y. Office)
Steven L. Young
Meryl R. Lieberman (Resident, White Plains, N. Y. Office)
Richard H. Rubenstein
Thomas A. Leghorn
Ricki Roer
E. Paul Dougherty, Jr. (Resident, Tokyo Office)
Wayne E. Borgeest
Thomas R. Manisero
Louis J. Isaacsohn * (Resident, Philadelphia Office)
John P. McGahey * (Resident, Chicago Office)
Thomas R. Cherry (Resident, London Office)
Jerry B. Black
Richard S. Oelsner
James A. Stankowski (Resident, Los Angeles Office)
Carl J. Pernicone
Kathleen D. Wilkinson * (Resident, Philadelphia Office)
Debra Steel Sturmer (Resident, San Francisco Office)
Carolyn Karp Schwartz
Martin K. Deniston (Resident, Los Angeles Office)
Rochelle M. Fedullo (Resident, Philadelphia Office)
Roland L. Coleman, Jr. (Resident, Los Angeles Office)
William J. Riina (Resident, Newark Office)
Robin Taylor Symons (Resident, Miami Office)
Jerold R. Ruderman (Resident, White Plains, Office)
David L. Tillem (Resident, White Plains Office)
Lee Eric Berger
Jeffrey E. Bigman
Alan Kaminsky
Robert W. Littleton
Milagros A. Matos Hunter
John Renzulli
Julianna Ryan
Edward A. Taylor
Rosario M. Vignali
David L. Wong
Bernd G. Heinze * (Resident, Philadelphia Office)
Jack A. Janov * (Resident, Los Angeles Office)
Thomas F. Quinn * (Resident, Newark Office)
Ricardo J. Cata * (Resident, Miami Office)
Edward P. Garson * (Resident, San Francisco Office)
Mark Housman
J. Marks Moore, III * (Resident, Baltimore Office)

(See Next Column)

WILSON, ELSER, MOSKOWITZ, EDELMAN & DICKER, *New York—Continued*

MEMBERS OF FIRM (Continued)

James C. Ughetta
E. Stratton Horres, Jr.
* (Resident, Dallas Office)
Jay A. Brandt
* (Resident, Dallas Office)
R. Douglas Noah, Jr.
* (Resident, Dallas Office)
Barry J. Gainey
Robert L. Joyce
Scott R. Schaffer
Timothy J. Sheehan
John D. Morio
Yongjin Park
Philip Quaranta
David S. Rutherford

OF COUNSEL

Leonard H. Minches
(Resident, Miami Office)
George H. Kolb
* (Resident, Dallas Office)

NEW YORK CITY ASSOCIATES

Don Abraham
Bonnie Greene Ackerman
Robert T. Adams
David K. Bergman
Helmut Beron
Adam Ross Bialek
Michael L. Boulhosa
Dean A. Cambourakis
Nina Cangiano
Brian T. Del Gatto
Debra A. Demarchena
Douglas Emanuel
Julie R. Evans
Joan M. Gilbride
David S. Hebbeler
Ramon D. Held
Richard M. Hunter
Maurya Crawford Keating
Colleen A. Kirchoff
Molly Klapper
Fred Knopf
Loretta A. Krez
Allison Lambert
Richard E. Lerner
Lawrence H. Lum
Edward A. Magro
Loretta T. Menkes
Richard T. Mermelstein
James Francis O'Brien
Edward J. O'Gorman
Susan M. Petrilli
Raymi Victoria Ramseur
Rolon A. Reed, III
(Not admitted in NY)
Frederick W. Reif
Angelo Rios
Michael Rosenberg
Eric J. Sauter
John J. Schwab
James K. Schwartz
Michael Schwartzberg
David S. Sheiffer
Carl L. Steccato
Stephen D. Straus
Debra Tama
Lena A. Uljanov
Steven Verveniotis
David N. Wechsler
Alexander H. Whiteaker

*(Not admitted in New York)

For full biographical listings, see the Martindale-Hubbell Law Directory

*ROCHESTER,** Monroe Co.

GOUGH, SKIPWORTH, SUMMERS, EVES & TREVETT, P.C. (AV)

700 Reynolds Arcade, 16 East Main Street, 14614
Telephone: 716-454-2181
Telecopier: 716-454-4026

Walter C. Eves (Retired)
Robert T. Skipworth (Retired)
Ronald James Summers
(Retired)
Thomas N. Trevett
Bohdan Wenglowskyj
Thomas E. Lenweaver
Thomas M. Van Strydonck
Kenneth Bersani
Richard M. Doyle
James A. Valenti
Karl F. Salzer
Peter A. Jacobson
Louis B. Cristo

Cynthia A. Constantino

Representative Clients: American Motorists Insurance Co.; Lumbermens Mutual Casualty Co.; Nationwide Mutual Insurance Co.; Interboro Mutual Indemnity Insurance Co.; Michigan Mutual Liability Insurance Co.; Virginia Surety Co.; Allstate Insurance Co.; American Hardware Insurance Co.; Pearl Assurance Co., Ltd.

For full biographical listings, see the Martindale-Hubbell Law Directory

HALLENBECK, LASCELL, NORRIS & ZORN (AV)

One Exchange Street, 14614
Telephone: 716-423-5900
Fax: 716-423-5910

MEMBERS OF FIRM

Alfred M. Hallenbeck
David M. Lascell
Michael D. Norris
Brian M. Zorn
Cheryl A. Heller

COUNSEL

Robert A. Feldman

ASSOCIATES

Audrey P. Peartree
Dandrea Lynn Ruhlmann
Rebecca A. Kirch
John R. Simon
Heidi Schenk Martinez

For full biographical listings, see the Martindale-Hubbell Law Directory

UNDERBERG & KESSLER (AV)

1800 Chase Square, 14604
Telephone: 716-258-2800
Fax: 716-258-2821

(See Next Column)

MEMBERS OF FIRM

Alan J. Underberg
Irving L. Kessler
Michael J. Beyma
Frank T. Crego
Robert W. Croessmann
John W. Crowe
Michael C. Dwyer
Bernard A. Frank
Steven R. Gersz
John L. Goldman
Lawrence P. Keller
Gordon J. Lipson
Robert F. Mechur
Paul V. Nunes
Terry M. Richman
Sharon P. Stiller
Stephen H. Waite
Russell I. Zuckerman

OF COUNSEL

Richard G. Crawford
Andrew M. Greenstein

SENIOR ATTORNEY

Thomas P. Young

ASSOCIATES

Patrick L. Cusato
Sean E. Gleason
Katherine Howk Karl
Suzanne D. Nott
Linda Prestegaard

For full biographical listings, see the Martindale-Hubbell Law Directory

ROCKVILLE CENTRE, Nassau Co.

JACOBSON & SCHWARTZ (AV)

510 Merrick Road, P.O. Box 46, 11571
Telephone: 516-536-0900
Telecopier: 516-536-2371

Jacob N. Schwartz
Ronald A. Jacobson (1935-1993)
Gary R. Schwartz
Robert M. Bridges

Paul Goodovitch
Eric P. Tosca
Thomas F. Callahan
Jeffrey D. Kadushin
Walter P. Wagner
Rhonda Hammer Barry
Deborah Sharon Ball
Susan B. Mandiberg

OF COUNSEL

Bernard Adler

For full biographical listings, see the Martindale-Hubbell Law Directory

*SYRACUSE,** Onondaga Co.

BOND, SCHOENECK & KING (AV)

18th Floor One Lincoln Center, 13202-1355
Telephone: 315-422-0121
Fax: 315-422-3598
Albany, New York Office: 111 Washington Avenue.
Telephone: 518-462-7421.
Fax: 518-462-7441.
Boca Raton, Florida Office: 5355 Town Center Road, Suite 1002.
Telephone: 407-368-1212.
Fax: 407-338-9955.
Naples, Florida Office: 1167 Third Street South.
Telephone: 813-262-6812.
Fax: 813-262-6908.
Oswego, New York Office: 130 East Second Street.
Telephone: 315-343-9116.
Fax: 315-343-1231.
Overland Park, Kansas Office: 7500 College Boulevard, Suite 910.
Telephone: 913-345-8001.
Fax: 913-345-9017.

MEMBERS OF FIRM

Francis E. Maloney, Jr.
S. Paul Battaglia
John D. Allen
Thomas E. Myers
Thomas R. Smith
David L. Dawson (Resident,
Naples, Florida Office)
David R. Sheridan
(Resident, Albany Office)
Thomas D. Keleher
John H. Callahan
John G. McGowan
Deborah H. Karalunas
Jonathan B. Fellows

General Counsel for: Syracuse University; Unity Mutual Life Insurance Co.; Manufacturers Association of Central New York.
Regional or Special Counsel for: Newhouse Broadcasting Corp. (WSYR, AM-FM); Syracuse Herald-Post Standard Newspapers.; Miller Brewing Co.; Allied Corp.; General Electric Co.; National Grange.

For Complete List of Firm Personnel, See General Section

For full biographical listings, see the Martindale-Hubbell Law Directory

*WATERTOWN,** Jefferson Co.

CONBOY, MCKAY, BACHMAN & KENDALL (AV)

407 Sherman Street, 13601
Telephone: 315-788-5100
Clayton, New York Office: 342 Riverside Drive.
Telephone: 315-686-3487.
Carthage, New York Office: 307 State Street.
Telephone: 315-493-0030.
Canton, New York Office: 24 Court Street, P.O. Box 650.
Telephone: 315-386-4539.

(See Next Column)

CONBOY, MCKAY, BACHMAN & KENDALL—*Continued*

OF COUNSEL

Joanne M. Novak (Resident, Canton Office)

MEMBERS OF FIRM

Philip A. Maphey
George K. Myrus
Floyd J. Chandler
Lawrence D. Hasseler (Resident, Carthage Office)
Stephen W. Gebo
Arthur C. Stever, III
William F. Maginn, Jr. (Resident, Canton Office)
Joseph W. Russell (Resident, Clayton Office)

ASSOCIATES

Timothy A. Farley
Edward J. Sheats, Jr.
Peter L. Walton
David B. Geurtsen

Attorneys for: Conrail; Champion International Corp.; Travelers Indemnity Co.; St. Joe Minerals Corp.; Maryland Casualty Co.; Royal Insurance Co.; Niagara Mohawk Power Corp.; Marine Midland Bank, N.A.

For full biographical listings, see the Martindale-Hubbell Law Directory

*WHITE PLAINS,** Westchester Co.

CERUSSI & SPRING, A PROFESSIONAL CORPORATION (AV)

One North Lexington Avenue, 10601-1700
Telephone: 914-948-1200
Cable Address: Cerspringlaw Whiteplainsnewyork
Facsimile: 914-948-1579
Greenwich, Connecticut Office: 66 Field Point Road.
Telephone: 203-661-4000.
Facsimile: 203-661-1197.

Michael A. Cerussi, Jr.
Ronald G. Crispi
Joseph A. D'Avanzo
Arthur J. Spring

Thomas F. Cerussi
Denise M. Cossu
Kathleen A. DePalma
Mark C. Dillon
Michael P. Fitzgerald
Matthew K. Flanagan
Thomas A. Hayes, Jr.
Anne E. Kershaw
Steven R. Lau
John J.A.M. Loveless
Curt D. Marshall
Maria J. Morreale
Owen S. Mudge, Jr.
Jeffrey C. Nagle (Not admitted in NY)
William J. Rizzo
Mary E. Toop
Gina M. Von Oehsen

For full biographical listings, see the Martindale-Hubbell Law Directory

HOFFMAN, WACHTELL, KOSTER, MAIER & MANDEL (AV)

399 Knollwood Road, 10603
Telephone: 914-682-8000
FAX: 914-682-1512
New City, New York Office: 82 Maple Avenue, 10956.
Telephone: 914-634-8169.

MEMBERS OF FIRM

Lee A. Hoffman, Jr.
Marc J. Wachtell
Eric D. Koster
Lynn J. Maier
Richard G. Mandel

Representative Clients: Mount Hope Mines, Inc.; Eastern Educational Consortium; Westchester Community College; Prime Office Systems, Inc.; Gateway Management Corp.; Purchase Environmental Protection Association, Inc.; The Jay Coalition; The Town of Greenburgh; The Town of Mamaroneck.
Reference: Citibank, N.A. (White Plains Branch).

For full biographical listings, see the Martindale-Hubbell Law Directory

O'CONNOR, MCGUINNESS, CONTE, DOYLE, OLESON & COLLINS (AV)

One Barker Avenue, 10601
Telephone: 914-948-4500
Telecopier: 914-948-0645

MEMBERS OF FIRM

Dennis L. O'Connor (1913-1989)
Rocco Conte
Dennis T. Doyle
William S. Oleson
J. Peter Collins
Richard C. Oleson
Dennis L. O'Connor, Jr.
William R. Watson
Kevin M. Loftus

ASSOCIATES

Craig P. Curcio
Louis K. Szarka
Mary Pat Burke
Patricia Lacy
Pamela R. Millian
Andrew F. Pisanelli
Montgomery Lee Effinger
Dara A. Ruderman
Philomena Basuk
Debora J. Dillon
Daniel M. Miller

OF COUNSEL

Eugene J. McGuinness
Russell J. Hauck

Attorneys for: Insurance Company of North America; Allstate Insurance Co.; Continental Insurance Group; Government Employers Insurance Co.; Merchants Mutual Insurance Co.; Prudential Insurance Co.; Consolidated Rail Corp.; Medical Liability Mutual Insurance Co.; Colonial Penn Insurance Co.

(See Next Column)

For full biographical listings, see the Martindale-Hubbell Law Directory

VOUTÉ, LOHRFINK, MAGRO & COLLINS (AV)

Formerly Mead, Dore & Vouté
170 Hamilton Avenue, 10601
Telephone: 914-946-1400
Facsimile: 914-946-8024

Arthur J. Vouté, Jr.
Richard L. Magro
Charles D. Lohrfink, Jr.
Charles A. Collins, Jr.

Elliot A. Cristantello
Stephen F. Fischer
Ralph F. Schoene
Stephen P. Falvey
Kathleen V. Gudmundsson
Dennis P. Glascott
Anthony R. Tirone
Kevin P. Fitzpatrick

Representative Clients: Allstate Insurance Co.; Crum & Forster Group; Electric Mutual Liability Insurance Co.; Commercial Union Group; General Accident Group; General Electric Co.; Liberty Mutual Insurance Co.; Medical Liability Mutual Insurance Co.

For full biographical listings, see the Martindale-Hubbell Law Directory

WILSON, BAVE, CONBOY, COZZA & COUZENS, P.C. (AV)

Two William Street, 10601
Telephone: 914-686-9010
Telecopier: 914-686-0873

William H. Bave (1919-1991)
Donald C. Wilson (1917-1994)
R. Kevin Conboy
William H. Bave, Jr.
Michael J. Cozza
John C. Couzens, Jr.
Michele A. Fournier
Joseph T. Jednak
Patricia Bave-Planell
Kevin D. Odell
Leo T. McGrath
Alexandra C. Karamitsos

LEGAL SUPPORT PERSONNEL

PARALEGAL

John R. Pearsall

Representative Clients: Royal Insurance; Kemper Insurance Co.; State Farm Mutual Automobile Insurance Co.; Continental National American Group; Utica Mutual Insurance Co.; Jefferson Insurance Co.; Nationwide Insurance Co.; Medical Liability Mutual Insurance Co.

For full biographical listings, see the Martindale-Hubbell Law Directory

NORTH CAROLINA

*CHARLOTTE,** Mecklenburg Co.

CANSLER LOCKHART & EVANS, P.A. (AV)

2030 The Carillon, 227 West Trade Street, 28202
Telephone: 704-372-1282
Fax: 704-372-1621

Edwin T. Cansler (1866-1943)
Edwin T. Cansler, Jr. (1890-1950)
John S. Cansler (1893-1978)
Thomas Ashe Lockhart
George K. Evans, Jr.
Thomas D. Garlitz
R. Michael Allen
Stacy C. Cordes

Insurance Clients: Blue Cross/Blue Shield of North Carolina, Inc.; Equitable Life Assurance Society of U.S.; Metropolitan Life Insurance Co.; New York Life Insurance Co.; Sumitomo Marine & Fire Insurance Co.; UNUM Life Insurance Co.; USAA Life Insurance Co.
General Corporate Clients: CSX Transportation, Inc.; Ford Motor Credit Co.; Wal-Mart Stores, Inc.

For full biographical listings, see the Martindale-Hubbell Law Directory

CAUDLE & SPEARS, P.A. (AV)

2600 Interstate Tower, 121 West Trade Street, 28202
Telephone: 704-377-1200
Telecopier: 704-338-5858

Lloyd C. Caudle
Harold C. Spears
Thad A. Throneburg
Patrick Jenkins
L. Cameron Caudle, Jr.
Nancy E. Walker
Timothy T. Leach
John A. Folmar
Sean M. Phelan
Jeffrey L. Helms

Counsel for: Bituminous Casualty Corp.; Baumann Springs A.G.; The A. G. Boone Co.; Consolidated Freightways; Employers Mutual Casualty Co.; Metromont Materials; Otis Elevator Co.; N.C. Farm Bureau Mutual Insurance Co.; Toyoda Textile Machinery, Inc.; U. S. Bottlers Machinery Co.

For full biographical listings, see the Martindale-Hubbell Law Directory

Charlotte—Continued

CRAIGHILL & SMITH, P.A. (AV)

(Formerly Craighill, Rendleman, Ingle & Blythe, P.A.)
1014 Cameron Brown Building, 301 South McDowell Street, 28204
Telephone: 704-374-1550
Fax: 704-374-0549

James B. Craighill   W. Lewis Smith, Jr.
Thomas E. McNeill

Representative Clients: AIG Aviation; Empire Fire & Marine Insurance Co.; Republic Claims Service; Fidelity and Deposit Company of Maryland; Zurich Insurance Co.; Transit Casualty Co. (Beneficial Insurance Group); Republic Insurance Co.; Unisun Insurance Co.; Sentry Insurance; American Hardware Mutuals; Unisun Insurance Co.; Employers Casualty Co. (TX).

For full biographical listings, see the Martindale-Hubbell Law Directory

DEAN & GIBSON (AV)

Suite 402, Cameron Brown Building, 301 South McDowell Street, 28204-2686
Telephone: 704-372-2700
Facsimile: 704-372-1804

Rodney A. Dean   Michael G. Gibson

ASSOCIATES

J. Bruce McDonald   Brien D. Stockman

OF COUNSEL

Barbara J. Dean

Representative Clients: Liberty Mutual; Nationwide Ins. Co.; St. Paul Ins. Co.; Kemper Ins. Co.; Hartford Ins. Co.; CNA Ins. Co.; Royal Ins. Co.; CIGNA, Travelers Ins. Co.; Firemans Fund Ins. Co.

For full biographical listings, see the Martindale-Hubbell Law Directory

WOMBLE CARLYLE SANDRIDGE & RICE (AV)

A Professional Limited Liability Company
3300 One First Union Center, 301 S. College Street, 28202-6025
Telephone: 704-331-4900
Telecopy: 704-331-4955
Telex: 853609
Winston-Salem, North Carolina Office: 1600 Southern National Financial Center.
Telephone: 919-721-3600.
Telecopy: 919-721-3660.
Telex: 806498.
Raleigh, North Carolina Office: 2100 First Union Capitol Center, 150 Fayetteville Street Mall, P.O. Box 831.
Telephone: 919-755-2100.
Telecopy: 919-755-2150.
Telex: 806498.
Atlanta, Georgia Office: One Ninety One Peachtree Tower, 191 Peachtree Street N.E., Suite 3250.
Telephone: 404-614-2580.
Fax: 404-614-2595.

MEMBER OF FIRM

G. Michael Barnhill

Representative Clients: Childress Klein Properties, Inc.; Food Lion, Inc.; Fieldcrest Cannon, Inc.; J.A. Jones Construction Company; Parkdale Mills, Inc.; Duke Power Company; Bowles Hollowell Conner & Company; ALLTEL Carolina, Inc.; Belk Store Services, Inc.; Philip Holzmann A.G.

For Complete List of Firm Personnel, See General Section

For full biographical listings, see the Martindale-Hubbell Law Directory

*GREENSBORO,** Guilford Co.

HENSON HENSON BAYLISS & SUE (AV)

1610 First Union Tower, P.O. Box 3525, 27402
Telephone: 910-275-0587
Facsimile: 910-273-2585

MEMBERS OF FIRM

Perry C. Henson   Jack B. Bayliss, Jr.
Perry C. Henson, Jr.   Gary K. Sue
Walter K. Burton

ASSOCIATES

Daniel L. Deuterman   Miriam S. Forbis
Brian A. Buchanan   David K. Williams, Jr.

Representative Clients: Allstate Insurance Co.; The Home Indemnity Company; Kmart Corporation; Nationwide Mutual Insurance Co.; N.C. Farm Bureau Mutual Ins. Co.; Old Dominion Freight Line; Wausau Insurance Company.

For full biographical listings, see the Martindale-Hubbell Law Directory

*RALEIGH,** Wake Co.

* indicates certain Bar Register subscribers whose principal office is located elsewhere in the state and who have arranged for representation as a part of the state capital listings that follow

BAILEY & DIXON (AV)

2500 Two Hannover Square, 434 Fayetteville Street Mall, P.O. Box 1351, 27602
Telephone: 919-828-0731
Facsimile: 919-828-6592

MEMBERS OF FIRM

Ralph McDonald   Alan J. Miles
Gary S. Parsons   Patricia P. Kerner
Carson Carmichael, III   Cathleen M. Plaut
Dorothy V. Kibler   David S. Coats

OF COUNSEL

J. Ruffin Bailey   James H. Walker (1920-1994)
Wright T. Dixon, Jr.   David M. Britt

ASSOCIATES

Marcus B. Liles, III   Kenyann G. Brown
Renee C. Riggsbee   Christopher L. Mewborn
Denise Stanford Haskell   Sylvia Stanley Wood

Representative Clients: Employers Casualty Co.; North Carolina League of Municipalities Risk Management Services; Lawyers Mutual Liability Insurance Company of North Carolina; Aetna Life and Casualty Insurance Company; Nationwide Insurance Company; Liberty Mutual Insurance Co.; Erie Insurance Company; Jefferson-Pilot Fire and Casualty Co.; ITT Hartford Insurance Group; Scottsdale Insurance Co.

For full biographical listings, see the Martindale-Hubbell Law Directory

CRANFILL, SUMNER & HARTZOG (AV)

Hillsborough Place, 225 Hillsborough Street, Suite 300, P.O. Box 27808, 27611
Telephone: 919-828-5100
Fax: 919-828-2277
Charlotte, North Carolina Office: 212 North McDowell Street, Suite 200.
Telephone: 704-332-8300.
Fax: 704-377-8880.

MEMBERS OF FIRM

Paul L. Cranfill   H. Lee Evans, Jr.
Robert W. Sumner   C. D. Taylor Pace
Dan M. Hartzog   Samuel H. Poole, Jr. (Resident, Charlotte Office)
Alene M. Mercer   Susan K. Burkhart
Richard T. Boyette   Buxton S. Copeland
David D. Ward   P. Collins Barwick, III
Patricia L. Holland   Robert H. Griffin
David H. Batten

ASSOCIATES

Kari L. Russwurm   Joseph B. Chambliss, Jr.
David A. Rhoades   Scott J. Lasso
Sheila M. Bossier   W. Scott Fuller
M. Andrew Avram (Resident, Charlotte Office)   Nicholas Peter Valaoras (Resident, Charlotte Office)
Brady W. Wells   Robin H. Terry
Anthony T. Lathrop (Resident at Charlotte Office)   William J. Garrity (Resident, Charlotte Office)
Gregory M. Kash   Edward C. LeCarpentier, III

Representative Clients: Continental Insurance Companies; Great American Insurance Group; Hartford Accident & Indemnity Co.; Liberty Mutual Insurance Co.

For full biographical listings, see the Martindale-Hubbell Law Directory

PATTERSON, DILTHEY, CLAY & BRYSON, L.L.P. (AV)

4020 WestChase Boulevard, Suite 550, 27607
Telephone: 919-821-4020
Fax: 919-829-0055
Wilmington, North Carolina Office: 116 Princess Street.
Telephone: 910-762-6544.
Fax: 910-762-4241.

MEMBERS OF FIRM

Grady S. Patterson, Jr. (Retired)   Richard Bruce Conely, Sr.
Ronald C. Dilthey   Reid Russell
Robert M. Clay   Stuart L. Egerton (Resident, Wilmington Office)
E. C. Bryson, Jr.
Mark E. Anderson

ASSOCIATES

Donna Renfrow Rutala   G. Lawrence Reeves, Jr.
Kathleen M. Millikan   Jonathan E. Hall
Phillip J. Anthony   Erle E. Peacock, Jr.
Charles George

Representative Clients: Continental Insurance Companies; Great American Insurance Group; Hartford Accident & Indemnity Co.; Liberty Mutual Insurance Co.

For full biographical listings, see the Martindale-Hubbell Law Directory

Raleigh—Continued

*** WOMBLE CARLYLE SANDRIDGE & RICE (AV)**

A Professional Limited Liability Company
2100 First Union Capitol Center, 150 Fayetteville Street Mall, P.O. Box 831, 27602
Telephone: 919-755-2100
Telecopy: 919-755-2150
Telex: 806498
Charlotte, North Carolina Office: 3300 One First Union Center, 301 South College Street.
Telephone: 704-331-4900.
Telecopy: 704-331-4955.
Telex: 853609.
Winston-Salem, North Carolina Office: 1600 Southern National Financial Center.
Telephone: 919-721-3600.
Telecopy: 919-721-3660.
Telex: 806498.
Atlanta, Georgia Office: One Ninety One Peachtree Tower, 191 Peachtree Street N.E., Suite 3250.
Telephone: 404-614-2580.
Fax: 404-614-2595.

RESIDENT PARTNER

Robert Harrison Sasser, III

RESIDENT ASSOCIATES

Elizabeth Janeway Hallyburton
Susan Sawin McFarlane

Representative Clients: Aetna Casualty and Surety Co., Inc.; ALSCO/AmeriMark Building Products, Inc.; Aoki Corporation America, Inc.; Empire of Carolina, Inc.; Hackney Brothers, Inc.; Lawyers Mutual Liability Insurance Company of North Carolina; Meredith College; Monk-Austin, Inc.; Regency Park Corporation; Wachovia Bank of North Carolina, N.A.

For Complete List of Firm Personnel, See General Section

For full biographical listings, see the Martindale-Hubbell Law Directory

YATES, MCLAMB & WEYHER, L.L.P. (AV)

Suite 350 Carolina Place, 2626 Glenwood Avenue, P.O. Box 18037, 27619
Telephone: 919-783-5300
Telecopier: 919-781-7821

MEMBERS OF FIRM

Bruce W. Berger
R. Scott Brown
Derek M. Crump
Dan J. McLamb
Andrew A. Vanore, III
Kirk G. Warner
Barbara B. Weyher
Joseph W. Yates, III

ASSOCIATES

Barry S. Cobb
Suzanne S. Lever
Cathryn M. Little
John W. Minier
Rodney E. Pettey
Shirley M. Pruitt
Beth Y. Smoot
O. Craig Tierney, Jr.
Michael W. Washburn

Representative Clients: Aetna Casualty & Surety Co.; Allstate Insurance Co.; American International Group; Chubb Group; CIGNA Cos.; Fireman's Fund Insurance Co.; Grain Dealers Mutual Insurance Co.; Harford Insurance Co.; Hartford Insurance Group; Horace Mann Insurance Co.

For full biographical listings, see the Martindale-Hubbell Law Directory

*SALISBURY,** Rowan Co.

KLUTTZ, REAMER, BLANKENSHIP & HAYES, L.L.P. (AV)

131 N. Main Street, P.O. Drawer 1617, 28145-1617
Telephone: 704-636-7100
Telecopier: 704-636-2284

Wm. Clarence Kluttz (Retired)
Lewis P. Hamlin, Jr. (1919-1988)
Richard R. Reamer
Malcolm B. Blankenship, Jr.
William C. Kluttz, Jr.
Glenn S. Hayes
James D.K.F. Randolph
Edward P. Norvell

Representative Clients: Nationwide Mutual Insurance Company; Kemper National Insurance Companies; N.C. Farm Bureau Insurance Company; Va. Mutual Insurance Company; AETNA; USAA Property & Casualty Insurance; Auto Owners; Harleysville Mutual Insurance Company.

For full biographical listings, see the Martindale-Hubbell Law Directory

*WILMINGTON,** New Hanover Co.

ANDERSON, COX & ENNIS (AV)

7225 Wrightsville Avenue, Suite 307, 28403
Telephone: 910-256-5577
FAX: 910-256-4926

MEMBERS OF FIRM

Henry L. Anderson, Jr.
J. Thomas Cox, Jr.

(See Next Column)

ASSOCIATES

Donald W. Ennis
Jacqueline A Newton
A.L. Butler Daniel

Insurance Clients: Allstate Insurance Co.; Canal Insurance Co.; Great American Insurance Cos.; Hull & Company; North Carolina Farm Bureau Mutual Insurance Co.; Pennsylvania National Insurance Group; Seibels, Bruce & Co.; Shelby Mutual Insurance Co.; State Farm Fire & Casualty Co.; Travelers Insurance Co.

For full biographical listings, see the Martindale-Hubbell Law Directory

HOGUE, HILL, JONES, NASH AND LYNCH (AV)

101 S. Third Street, P.O. Drawer 2178, 28402
Telephone: 910-763-4565
Telecopier: 910-762-6687

OF COUNSEL

Cyrus D. Hogue, Jr.

MEMBERS OF FIRM

Cyrus D. Hogue (1888-1960)
William L. Hill, II
W. Talmage Jones
David A. Nash
William O. J. Lynch
James B. Snow, III
Wayne A. Bullard
Patricia Cramer Jenkins

Representative Clients: Jefferson Standard Life Insurance Co.; St. Paul Insurance Cos.; Royal Globe Insurance Co.; Horace Mann Insurance Co.; Insurance Company of North America; New Hampshire Insurance Co.; Underwriters Adjusting Co.; CNA Insurance Co.; Canal Insurance Co.; Federated Mutual Insurance Company; Colonial Penn Insurance Co.

For full biographical listings, see the Martindale-Hubbell Law Directory

JOHNSON & LAMBETH (AV)

232 Princess Street, P.O. Box 660, 28402
Telephone: 910-763-0481
FAX: 910-251-1276

MEMBERS OF FIRM

Robert White Johnson
Carter Tate Lambeth

ASSOCIATES

Frances Youngblood Trask
Maynard M. Brown
Beth M. Bryant
John Gregory Tillery, III

References: United Carolina Bank; NCNB National Bank of North Carolina.

For full biographical listings, see the Martindale-Hubbell Law Directory

*WINSTON-SALEM,** Forsyth Co.

BENNETT & BLANCATO, L.L.P. (AV)

101 South Stratford Road, Suite 305, 27104-4227
Telephone: 910-723-1896
Fax: 910-723-8308

Richard V. Bennett
William A. Blancato

ASSOCIATES

Sherry R. Dawson
Stanley P. Dean

For full biographical listings, see the Martindale-Hubbell Law Directory

WOMBLE CARLYLE SANDRIDGE & RICE (AV)

A Professional Limited Liability Company
1600 Southern National Financial Center, P.O. Drawer 84, 27102
Telephone: 910-721-3600
Telecopy: 910-721-3660
Telex: 806498
Charlotte, North Carolina Office: 3300 One First Union Center, 301 South College Street.
Telephone: 704-331-4900.
Telecopy: 704-331-4955.
Telex: 853609.
Raleigh, North Carolina Office: 2100 First Union Capitol Center, 150 Fayetteville Street Mall, P.O. Box 831.
Telephone: 919-755-2100.
Telecopy: 919-755-2150.
Telex: 806498.
Atlanta, Georgia Office: One Ninety One Peachtree Tower, 191 Peachtree Street, N.E., Suite 3250.
Telephone: 404-614-2580.
Fax: 404-614-2595.

MEMBERS OF FIRM

Clayton M. Custer
Tyrus V. Dahl, Jr.
Allan R. Gitter
Robert S. Pierce
Richard T. Rice
Dewey W. Wells

ASSOCIATES

Ellen M. Gregg
Ursula Marie Henninger
J. Daniel McNatt
James R. Morgan, Jr.

Representative Clients: Brad Ragan, Inc.; Brenner Companies; Food Lion, Inc.; Hanes Companies, Inc.; North Carolina Baptist Hospitals, Inc.; R.J. Reynolds Tobacco Company; Summit Communications Group, Inc.; Thomasville Furniture Industries, Inc.; Wachovia Corporation; Wake Forest University.

(See Next Column)

WOMBLE CARLYLE SANDRIDGE & RICE, *Winston-Salem—Continued*

For Complete List of Firm Personnel, See General Section

For full biographical listings, see the Martindale-Hubbell Law Directory

NORTH DAKOTA

*BISMARCK,** Burleigh Co.

FLECK, MATHER & STRUTZ, LTD. (AV)

Sixth Floor, Norwest Bank Building, 400 East Broadway, P.O. Box 2798, 58502
Telephone: 701-223-6585
Telecopier: 701-222-4853

William A. Strutz
Gary R. Wolberg
Steven A. Storslee
Robert J. Udland
Curtis L. Wike
Charles S. Miller, Jr.
DeeNelle Louise Ruud

Representative Clients: ITT Hartford; American International Group; CNA Insurance Cos.; PHICO Insurance Co.; North Dakota Insurance Reserve Fund; Continental Insurance Co.; Employers Mutual Insurance Cos.; Firemen's Fund; National Farmers Union; Royal Insurance Co.

For Complete List of Firm Personnel, See General Section

For full biographical listings, see the Martindale-Hubbell Law Directory

PEARCE AND DURICK (AV)

314 East Thayer Avenue, P.O. Box 400, 58502
Telephone: 701-223-2890
Fax: 701-223-7865

MEMBERS OF FIRM

Patrick W. Durick
B. Timothy Durick
Christine A. Hogan
Joel W. Gilbertson
David E. Reich
Jerome C. Kettleson
Larry L. Boschee

ASSOCIATES

Michael F. McMahon
Stephen D. Easton

Representative Clients: American Insurance Assn.; Cigna-INA Insurance Co.; Deere & Co.; Federal Deposit Insurance Corp.; Ford Motor Co.; General Motors Corp.; MDU Resources Group, Inc.; Northwest Airlines; Royal Insurance Co.; Travelers Insurance Co.

For Complete List of Firm Personnel, See General Section

For full biographical listings, see the Martindale-Hubbell Law Directory

*FARGO,** Cass Co.

NILLES, HANSEN & DAVIES, LTD. (AV)

1800 Radisson Tower, P.O. Box 2626, 58108
Telephone: 701-237-5544

Donald R. Hansen
Timothy Q. Davies
Duane H. Ilvedson
E. Thomas Conmy, III
Stephen W. Plambeck
Leo F. J. Wilking
Richard Henderson
William P. Harrie
Mark R. Hanson
Harry M. Pippin
Thomas A. Jacobson
Douglas W. Gigler
Adele Hedley Page

Representative Clients: Fireman's Fund Insurance Group Companies; Blue Cross and Blue Shield; CNA Insurance Companies; Nodak Mutual Insurance Company; Farmers Insurance Group; U.S. Fidelity & Guaranty Company; Crum & Forster; Aetna Life & Casualty Group; U.S.A.A.; Employers Mutual Companies.

For Complete List of Firm Personnel, See General Section

For full biographical listings, see the Martindale-Hubbell Law Directory

VOGEL, BRANTNER, KELLY, KNUTSON, WEIR & BYE, LTD. (AV)

502 First Avenue North, P.O. Box 1389, 58107
Telephone: 701-237-6983
Facsimile: 701-237-0847

Carlton J. Hunke
Mart Daniel Vogel
Harlan G. Fuglesten
Pamela J. Hermes
W. Todd Haggart
Lori J. Beck
Bruce Douglas Quick
Wayne W. Carlson
Charles Alan Stock

Representative Clients: American Family Insurance Group; CIGNA Companies; CNA Insurance Comapny; Dakota Fire Insurance; Home Insurance Company; Midwest Medical Insurance Company; Milbank State Automobile Insurance Company; Phico Insurance Company; St. Paul Insurance Companies.

(See Next Column)

For Complete List of Firm Personnel, See General Section

For full biographical listings, see the Martindale-Hubbell Law Directory

*MINOT,** Ward Co.

McGEE, HANKLA, BACKES & WHEELER, P.C. (AV)

Suite 305 Norwest Center, 15 Second Avenue Southwest, P.O. Box 998, 58702-0998
Telephone: 701-852-2544
Fax: 701-838-4724

Richard H. McGee (1918-1992)
Walfrid B. Hankla
Orlin W. Backes
Robert A. Wheeler
Donald L. Peterson
Richard H. McGee, II
Collin P. Dobrovolny
Brian W. Hankla
Robert J. Hovland
Jon W. Backes

LEGAL SUPPORT PERSONNEL

Janice M. Eslinger
Jane K. Hutchison
Ardella M. Burtman
Michelle Erdmann

For full biographical listings, see the Martindale-Hubbell Law Directory

OHIO

*AKRON,** Summit Co.

NUKES, PERANTINIDES & NOLAN CO., L.P.A. (AV)

300 Courtyard Square, 80 South Summit Street, 44308-1719
Telephone: 216-253-5454
Telecopier: 216-253-6524

S. Samuel Nukes
Paul G. Perantinides
Chris T. Nolan

James J. Gutbrod
Christopher L. Parker
Peter P. Janos

References: First National Bank of Akron; National City Bank, Akron; Society Bank; Charter One Bank.

For full biographical listings, see the Martindale-Hubbell Law Directory

RODERICK, MYERS & LINTON (AV)

One Cascade Plaza, 15th Floor, 44308
Telephone: 216-434-3000
Telecopier: 216-434-9220

MEMBERS OF FIRM

George T. Roderick (1909-1994)
Robert F. Linton
Howard C. Walker, Jr.
Robert F. Orth
Frederick S. Corns
Michael A. Malyuk
Kurt R. Weitendorf
Timothy J. Truby
Lawrence R. Bach
Paul E. Weimer
James E. Davis
Matthew W. Oby

ASSOCIATES

Stephen J. Pruneski
John K. Riemenschneider

Counsel for: National City Bank, Northeast; Ohio Edison Co.; K-Mart; Westfield Cos.; The Prudential Insurance Co. of America; Maryland Casualty Co.; Summit County Medical Society.

For Complete List of Firm Personnel, See General Section

For full biographical listings, see the Martindale-Hubbell Law Directory

HARRY A. TIPPING CO. A LEGAL PROFESSIONAL ASSOCIATION (AV)

National City Center, 2200 One Cascade Plaza, 44308
Telephone: 216-434-8500
Telecopier: 216-434-5453

Harry A. Tipping
John E. Holcomb
Robert N. Woodside
John Walter Clark

OF COUNSEL

Dominic A. Olivo

For full biographical listings, see the Martindale-Hubbell Law Directory

ASHTABULA, Ashtabula Co.

WARREN AND YOUNG (AV)

134 West 46th Street, P.O. Box 2300, 44004-6951
Telephone: (216) 997-6175
Facsimile: (216) 992-9114

MEMBERS OF FIRM

William E. Riedel
Carl F. Muller

Representative Clients: Aetna Insurance; Nationwide Insurance; American States Insurance; Erie Insurance; Grange Mutual.

(See Next Column)

WARREN AND YOUNG—*Continued*

For Complete List of Firm Personnel, See General Section

For full biographical listings, see the Martindale-Hubbell Law Directory

*CANTON,** Stark Co.

DAY, KETTERER, RALEY, WRIGHT & RYBOLT (AV)

800 William R. Day Building, 121 Cleveland Avenue, South, 44702-1921
Telephone: 216-455-0173
Telecopier: 216-455-2633
Columbus, Ohio Office: Suite 1602, 50 West Broad Street.
Telephone: 614-228-3611.
Telecopier: 614-228-3663

MEMBERS OF FIRM

David B. Day (1863-1947)
John G. Ketterer (1901-1973)
Donald W. Raley (1905-1986)
Clyde H. Wright (1909-1991)
Robert M. Rybolt (Retired)
Robert P. Eshelman (Retired)
Robert E. Levitt (Retired)
Louis A. Boettler
John R. Werren
William B. Badger
James K. Brooker
E. Lang D'Atri
J. Sean Keenan
Sheila M. Markley
Fred H. Zollinger, Jr.
James R. Blake
John H. Brannen
Richard A. Princic
Tim A. Powell
Richard E. Davis, II
Douglas J. Maser (Resident, Columbus Office)
Michael S. Gruber
Alicia M. Wyler
William S. Cline
Daniel A. Minkler
Matthew Yackshaw
Raymond T. Bules
John A. Murphy, Jr.
Merle D. Evans, III
Craig G. Pelini
Darrell N. Markijohn
Robert E. Roland
Jill Freshley Otto
Sara E. Lioi

ASSOCIATES

Mark F. Fischer
J. Curtis Werren
James F. Contini, II
Thomas E. Hartnett
Andrew M. McIlvaine
Cari Fusco Evans

OF COUNSEL

John F. Buchman
Stephen A. Reilly (Resident, Columbus Office)
David M. Thomas

Representative Clients: The Timken Co.; Bank One, Akron; National City Bank; Detroit Diesel Corp.; Canton Drop Forge.

For full biographical listings, see the Martindale-Hubbell Law Directory

LESH, CASNER & MILLER A LEGAL PROFESSIONAL ASSOCIATION (AV)

606 Belden-Whipple Building, 4150 Belden Village Street, N.W., 44718
Telephone: 216-493-0040
Fax: 216-493-4108

Kenneth L. Lesh (1913-1991)
James W. Casner
Rex W. Miller
Jacob F. Hess, Jr.
Thomas J. Lombardi
Dennis J. Fox
John S. McCall, Jr.
Timothy W. Watkins
John R. Frank

OF COUNSEL

Ronald G. Figler

For full biographical listings, see the Martindale-Hubbell Law Directory

*CINCINNATI,** Hamilton Co.

BENJAMIN, YOCUM & HEATHER (AV)

1500 Central Trust Tower, 5 West 4th Street, 45202-3681
Telephone: 513-721-5672
FAX: 513-721-5910

MEMBERS OF FIRM

John A. Benjamin
Thomas R. Yocum
Timothy P. Heather
Michael J. Bergmann
Anthony J. Iaciofano

ASSOCIATES

Lisa Marie Bitter
Jeffrey Paul McSherry

For full biographical listings, see the Martindale-Hubbell Law Directory

CASH, CASH, EAGEN & KESSEL (AV)

1000 Tri State Building, 432 Walnut Street, 45202
Telephone: 513-621-4443
FAX: 513-621-5231

MEMBERS OF FIRM

Albert D. Cash
Robert B. Cash
Thomas L. Eagen, Jr.
Melvin J. Kessel
Michael J. Stegman
John R. Wykoff

(See Next Column)

ASSOCIATES

Jeffrey G. Stagnaro
Bernard C. Boggio
Christine Carey Steele
Ray C. Freudiger
Peter A. Saba

For full biographical listings, see the Martindale-Hubbell Law Directory

DINSMORE & SHOHL (AV)

1900 Chemed Center, 255 East Fifth Street, 45202-3172
Telephone: 513-977-8200
FAX: 513-977-8141
Florence, Kentucky Office: Turfway Ridge Office Park, 7300 Turfway Road, Suite 430 41042-1355.
Telephone: 606-283-0515.
FAX: 606-283-6017.
Dayton, Ohio Office: 500 Courthouse Plaza, S.W., 10 N. Ludlow Street, 45402-1834.
Telephone: 513-228-8012.
FAX: 513-461-2543.
Columbus, Ohio Office: NBD Bank Building, Suite 330, 175 South Third Street, 43215-5134.
Telephone: 614-224-7887.
FAX: 614-224-7882.

MEMBERS OF FIRM

Gordon C. Greene
Harry L. Riggs, Jr. (Resident, Florence, Kentucky Office)
Gerald V. Weigle, Jr.
Gary L. Herfel (Resident, Florence, Kentucky Office)
Michael D. Eagen
David H. Beaver
Jerry S. Sallee
Nancy J. Gill
Stephen K. Shaw
Lawrence A. Flemer
Stephen G. Schweller
Gregory A. Harrison

ASSOCIATES

Patricia B. Hogan
Brian S. Sullivan
Thomas A. Prewitt (Resident, Florence, Kentucky Office)
Nancy Korb Griffiths
Ann Collins Hindman
Michael E. Finucane
William A. Dickhaut

For Complete List of Firm Personnel, See General Section

For full biographical listings, see the Martindale-Hubbell Law Directory

FAULKNER & TEPE (AV)

2200 Central Trust Tower, 5 West Fourth Street, 45202
Telephone: 513-421-7500
FAX: 513-421-7502

MEMBERS OF FIRM

R. Edward Tepe
John C. Scott
Christopher L. Moore
Anthony W. Brock

SENIOR COUNSEL

David P. Faulkner

OF COUNSEL

A. Norman Aubin

Reference: Fifth Third Bank.

For full biographical listings, see the Martindale-Hubbell Law Directory

KEATING, MUETHING & KLEKAMP (AV)

1800 Provident Tower, One East Fourth Street, 45202
Telephone: 513-579-6400
Facsimile: 513-579-6457

ASSOCIATES

W. Keith Noel
Pamela Morgan Hodge
Daniel E. Izenson
Gail King
Mary R. True
Daniel J. Donnellon

Representative Clients: American Financial Corporation; BP America Inc.; Chiquita Brands International, Inc.; The Cincinnati Enquirer; Cintas Corporation; Comair Holdings, Inc.; Duke Associates; LSI Industries Inc.; Mosler Inc.; Provident Bankcorp, Inc.

For Complete List of Firm Personnel, See General Section

For full biographical listings, see the Martindale-Hubbell Law Directory

LINDHORST & DREIDAME CO., L.P.A. (AV)

312 Walnut Street, Suite 2300, 45202-4091
Telephone: 513-421-6630
Telecopier: 513-421-0212

Robert F. Dreidame (1914-1978)
Leo J. Breslin
James L. O'Connell
William M. Cussen
Charles J. Kelly
John A. Goldberg
William N. Kirkham
James M. Moore
James H. Smith, III
Jay R. Langenbahn
Thomas E. Martin
James F. Brockman
Michael F. Lyon
Edward S. Dorsey
Harold L. Anness
Dale A. Stalf
Gary F. Franke

Peter C. Newberry

(See Next Column)

LINDHORST & DREIDAME CO. L.P.A., *Cincinnati—Continued*

SENIOR COUNSEL

Ambrose H. Lindhorst
William J. Walsh
John A. Spain

Representative Clients: CNA; CSX Corp.; Fireman's Fund-American Group; Medical Protective Co.; Norfolk Southern Corp.; Roadway Express, Inc.; Sibcy Cline, Inc.; Jewish Hospital; T.W. Smith Aircraft, Inc.; U.S.F.&G.

For Complete List of Firm Personnel, See General Section

For full biographical listings, see the Martindale-Hubbell Law Directory

MCCASLIN, IMBUS & MCCASLIN A LEGAL PROFESSIONAL ASSOCIATION (AV)

1200 Gwynne Building, 602 Main Street, 45202
Telephone: 513-421-4646
Telecopier: 513-421-7929
Ft. Thomas, Kentucky Office: 645 Highland Ave.
Telephone: 606-781-8228.

Clement J. DeMichelis
Philip J. Marsick
John K. Hurd
Douglas E. King
R. Gary Winters
Thomas J. Gruber
Joseph K. Wehby
John J. Finnigan, Jr.

Steven C. Martin
Joseph C. Gruber
John T. Schwierling
Carter A. Beck
Laura J. Irving Murphy
Rick A. Hopkins
Valerie L. Van Valkenburg
Stephen C. Kessen
Peter J. Miller
Matthew R. Skinner
Richard G. Wendel, II
Mina Khalily
John J. Watson
Iduna D. Borger
Bernard W. Wharton

OF COUNSEL

Robert J. Imbus, Jr.

Representative Client: AETNA Casualty & Surety Co.

For full biographical listings, see the Martindale-Hubbell Law Directory

RENDIGS, FRY, KIELY & DENNIS (AV)

900 Central Trust Tower, 45202
Telephone: 513-381-9200
FAX: 513-381-9206
Courtesy Office: Kentucky National Bank Tower, Suite 1610, 50 East Rivercenter Boulevard, Covington, Kentucky.

MEMBERS OF FIRM

William H. Hutcherson, Jr.
Ralph F. Mitchell
W. Roger Fry
Thomas S. Shore, Jr.
David Winchester Peck
J. Kenneth Meagher
D. Michael Poast
Edward R. Goldman
Joseph W. Gelwicks
Leonard A. Weakley, Jr.
Carolyn A. Taggart
Donald C. Adams, Jr.
Wilson G. Weisenfelder, Jr.
Steven D. Hengehold
Thomas M. Evans
Felix J. Gora

OF COUNSEL

Robert L. McLaurin
John P. Kiely

ASSOCIATES

Jill T. O'Shea
Peter L. Ney
Terrence M. Garrigan
John M. Hands

Local Counsel for: Associated Aviation Underwriters; Commercial Union Assurance Co.; Continental National American Group; The Medical Protective Co.; St. Paul Insurance Co.; Sherwin-Williams; State Automobile Mutual Insurance Co.; U.S. Aviation Underwriters; Zurich Insurance Co.

For Complete List of Firm Personnel, See General Section

For full biographical listings, see the Martindale-Hubbell Law Directory

STRAUSS & TROY A LEGAL PROFESSIONAL ASSOCIATION (AV)

2100 PNC Center, 201 East Fifth Street, 45202-4186
Telephone: 513-621-2120
Telecopier: 513-241-8259
Northern Kentucky Office: Suite 1400, 50 East Rivercenter Boulevard, Covington, Kentucky, 41011.
Telephone: 513-621-8900; 513-621-2120.
Telecopier: 513-629-9444.

Charles G. Atkins
Mitchell B. Goldberg
R. Guy Taft
Paul B. Calico

Representative Clients: PNC Bank, N.A. (Ohio and Kentucky); Corporex Companies, Inc.; Mercantile Stores Company, Inc.; Star Bank, N.A. (Ohio and Kentucky).

For Complete List of Firm Personnel, See General Section

For full biographical listings, see the Martindale-Hubbell Law Directory

THOMPSON, HINE AND FLORY (AV)

312 Walnut Street, 14th Floor, 45202-4029
Telephone: 513-352-6700
Fax: 513-241-4771;
Telex: 938003
Akron, Ohio Office: 50 S. Main Street, Suite 502, 44308-1828.
Telephone: 216-376-8090.
Fax: 216-376-8386.
Cleveland, Ohio Office: 1100 National City Bank Building, 629 Euclid Avenue, 44114-3070.
Telephone: 216-566-5500.
Fax: 216-556-5583.
Telex: 980217.
Cable Address: "Thomflor".
Columbus, Ohio Office: One Columbus, 10 West Broad Street, 43215-3435.
Telephone: 614-469-3200.
Fax: 614-469-3361.
Dayton, Ohio Office: 2000 Courthouse Plaza, N.E., 45402-1706.
Telephone: 513-443-6600.
Fax: 513-443-6637; 443-6635.
Palm Beach, Florida Office: 125 Worth Avenue, 33480-4466.
Telephone: 407-833-5900.
Fax: 407-833-5951.
Washington, D.C. Office: 1920 N Street, N.W., 20036-1601.
Telephone: 202-331-8800.
Fax: 202-331-8330.
Telex: 904173.
Cable Address: "Caglaw".
Brussels, Belgium Office: Rue des Chevaliers / Ridderstraat 14 - B.10, B - 1050.
Telephone: 011(32-2) 511-9326.
Fax: 011(-32-2) 513-9206.

MEMBERS OF FIRM

Christopher M. Bechhold
Ethna Bennert Cooper
Jack F. Fuchs

ASSOCIATE

Robert P. Johnson

For Complete List of Firm Personnel, See General Section

For full biographical listings, see the Martindale-Hubbell Law Directory

WOOD & LAMPING (AV)

2500 Cincinnati Commerce Center, 600 Vine Street, 45202-2409
Telephone: 513-852-6000
Fax: 513-852-6087
Ft. Mitchell, Kentucky Office: Kentucky Executive Building, 2055 Dixie Highway, Suites 248-252.
Telephone: 606-344-4052; 344-4052.
Fax: 606-344-9631.

MEMBERS OF FIRM

Harold G. Korbee
David A. Caldwell
William R. Ellis
Thomas C. Korbee

ASSOCIATES

Carl J. Schmidt, III
Amy L. Tolnitch
Geraldine M. Johnson

Representative Clients: Imperial Casualty Co.; Lloyds of London; Marsh and McLennan; Neare Gibbs and Co.; Paul Revere Life Insurance Company; St. Paul Fire and Marine Insurance Company; United Southern Assurance Company; Wausau Insurance Company.

For Complete List of Firm Personnel, See General Section

For full biographical listings, see the Martindale-Hubbell Law Directory

*CLEVELAND,** Cuyahoga Co.

DAVIS AND YOUNG CO., L.P.A. (AV)

1700 Midland Building, 44115
Telephone: 216-348-1700
FAX: 216-621-0602
Cable: DANDY CLE
Akron, Ohio Office: 1015 Society Building, 159 South Main Street.
Telephone 216-376-1717.
Fax: 216-376-1797.

Rees H. Davis, Sr. (1892-1965)
Fred J. Young (1889-1946)
George W. Lutjen
Martin J. Murphy
C. Richard McDonald
Paul D. Eklund
Jan L. Roller
Thomas W. Wright
David J. Fagnilli

William Vance
Gregory H. Collins
Patrick F. Roche
Bonnie M. Gust
Dennis R. Fogarty

OF COUNSEL

R. Emmett Moran

Counsel for: Aetna Insurance Co.; Alliance Insurance Co.; Amerisure Companies; Cincinnati Insurance Co.; Central Mutual Insurance Co.; Great American Insurance Co.; John Hancock Property & Casualty Co.; Motorist

(See Next Column)

DAVIS AND YOUNG CO. L.P.A.—*Continued*

Mutual Insurance Co.; St. Paul Property & Liability; Unigard Insurance Group.

For full biographical listings, see the Martindale-Hubbell Law Directory

HERMANN, CAHN & SCHNEIDER (AV)

Suite 500, 1301 East Ninth Street, 44114
Telephone: 216-781-5515
Facsimile: 216-781-1030

MEMBERS OF FIRM

Gary D. Hermann
Kerry S. Volsky
Anthony J. Hartman
Peter J. Krembs
Timothy P. McCormick

ASSOCIATES

Thomas P. Marotta
Romney B. Cullers
Forrest A. Norman, III

Representative Clients: Allstate Insurance Co.; Farmers Insurance Companies; Great Central Insurance Co.; Foremost Insurance Co.; Transamerica Insurance Co.; Wausau Insurance Cos.; Maryland Casualty Co.; Occidental Fire & Casualty Co.; Progressive Insurance Co.

For full biographical listings, see the Martindale-Hubbell Law Directory

JANIK & DUNN (AV)

400 Park Plaza Building, 1111 Chester Avenue, 44114
Telephone: 216-781-9700
Fax: 216-781-1250
Brea, California Office: 2601 Saturn Street, Suite 300.
Telephone: 714-572-1101.
Fax: 714-572-1103.

MEMBERS OF FIRM

Steven G. Janik
Theodore M. Dunn, Jr.

ASSOCIATES

Myra Staresina
David L. Mast

For full biographical listings, see the Martindale-Hubbell Law Directory

KELLER AND CURTIN CO., L.P.A. (AV)

Suite 330 The Hanna Building, 44115-1901
Telephone: 216-566-7100
Telecopier: 216-566-5430
Akron, Ohio Office: 2304 First National Tower, 44308-1419.
Telephone: 216-376-7245.
Telecopier: 216-376-8128.

Stanley S. Keller
Walter H. Krohngold
G. Michael Curtin
James M. Johnson

Joseph G. Ritzler
Phillip A. Kuri

Reference: Bank One, Cleveland.

For full biographical listings, see the Martindale-Hubbell Law Directory

KITCHEN, DEERY & BARNHOUSE (AV)

1100 Illuminating Building, 55 Public Square, 44113
Telephone: 216-241-5614
Fax: 216-241-5255

MEMBERS OF FIRM

Charles W. Kitchen
Johanna M. Sfiscko
James W. Barnhouse
Timothy X. McGrail
Eugene B. Meador

ASSOCIATES

William F. Schmitz
Patti Jo Mooney

Representative Clients: Buckeye Union Insurance Co.; Continental Insurance Co.; Grange Mutual Casualty Co.; Erie Insurance Group; Home Insurance Cos.; Motorists Mutual Insurance Cos.; St. Paul Insurance Cos.; U.S. Aviation Underwriters; Ohio Medical Professional Liability Underwriting Assn. (J.U.A.).
Reference: National City Bank.

For full biographical listings, see the Martindale-Hubbell Law Directory

MAZANEC, RASKIN & RYDER CO., L.P.A. (AV)

100 Franklin's Row, 34305 Solon Road, 44139
Telephone: 216-248-7906
Fax: 216-248-8861
Columbus Ohio Office: Suite 980, 500 South Front Street 43215.
Telephone: 614-228-5931.
Fax: 614-228-5934.

Thomas S. Mazanec
Karen E. Lee
Todd M. Raskin
John T. McLandrich
Edward M. Ryder (Resident, Columbus Office)
James A. Climer
John T. Hanna
Richard A. Williams (Resident, Columbus, Ohio Office)
Christopher J. Russ
Michael A. Pohl
Joseph F. Nicholas, Jr.
John P. Petro (Resident, Columbus, Ohio Office)
Robert H. Stoffers (Resident, Columbus, Ohio Office)
Brenda R. Saridakis
Daniel J. Hurley (Resident, Columbus, Ohio Office)
Kimberly A. Brennan
Steven W. Ritz
Stephen F. Dobscha
Anne M. Van Devere (Not admitted in OH)

Representative Clients: Colonial Insurance Company; Crawford & Co.; Farmers Insurance Group; Leader National Insurance Company; Liberty Mutual Insurance Co.; National Casualty Insurance Co.; Progressive Casualty Insurance Co.; Scottsdale Insurance Co.; State Farm Fire & Casualty Company; Utica Mutual Insurance Co.

For full biographical listings, see the Martindale-Hubbell Law Directory

MEYERS, HENTEMANN, SCHNEIDER & REA CO., L.P.A. (AV)

21st Floor, Superior Building, 815 Superior Avenue, N.E., 44114
Telephone: 216-241-3435
Telecopier: 216-241-6568
Elyria, Ohio Office: 301 Fifth Street, 44035.
Telephone: 216-323-6920.

Kent H. Meyers (1902-1970)
Richard C. Talbert
Richard F. Stevens (1915-1981)
Thomas L. Brunn
David S. Meyers (1928-1983)
Gerald L. Jeppe
Eugene J. Gilroy (1926-1984)
Don P. Brown
John S. Rea
Lynn A. Lazzaro
Joseph G. Schneider
Joseph H. Wantz
Henry A. Hentemann
Kirk E. Roman

James C. Cochran
Sean P. Allan
Kathleen Carrabine Hopkins
Keith David Thomas
J. Michael Creagan
John Peter O'Donnell

Representative Clients: State Farm Mutual Insurance Co.; Travelers Insurance Co.; J.C. Penney Insurance, formerly Educator & Executive Insurance Co.; Lloyds Underwriters, London, England; Preferred Risk Mutual Insurance Co.; American Suzuki Motor Corp.; Detroit Automobile Inter-Insurance Exchange; Electrical Mutual; Automation Plastics, Inc.; Environmental Structures, Inc.

For full biographical listings, see the Martindale-Hubbell Law Directory

QUANDT, GIFFELS & BUCK CO., L.P.A. (AV)

800 Leader Building, 526 Superior Avenue, N.E., 44114-1460
Telephone: 216-241-2025
Telecopier: 216-241-2080

Robert G. Quandt
Beth A. Sebaugh
Walter R. Matchinga
Laurence F. Buzzelli
Joseph R. Tira
Larry C. Greathouse

OF COUNSEL

Stephen D. Richman

Hunter S. Havens
Timothy L. Kerwin
Timothy G. Sweeney
Nita Kay Smith
Jeffrey A. Schenk
Edward J. Stoll, Jr.
Ernest C. Pisanelli

Representative Clients: Physicians Insurance Company of Ohio; Royal Insurance Company; Continental Insurance Company; Heritage Insurance Company; Reliance Insurance Co.; Safeco Insurance Co.; Fireman's Fund Insurance Company.

For full biographical listings, see the Martindale-Hubbell Law Directory

SEELEY, SAVIDGE AND AUSSEM A LEGAL PROFESSIONAL ASSOCIATION (AV)

800 Bank One Center, 600 Superior Avenue, East, 44114-2655
Telephone: 216-566-8200
Cable Address: "See Sau"
Fax-Telecopier: 216-566-0213
Elyria, Ohio Office: 538 Broad Street.
Telephone: 216-236-8158.

Keith A. Savidge
Jane T. Seelie

References: Society National Bank; AmeriTrust.

For Complete List of Firm Personnel, See General Section

For full biographical listings, see the Martindale-Hubbell Law Directory

SMITH, MARSHALL AND WEAVER (AV)

500 National City East Sixth Building, 1965 East Sixth Street, 44114
Telephone: 216-781-4994
Telecopier: 216-781-9448

MEMBERS OF FIRM

Richard C. Green (1910-1967)
Wentworth J. Marshall, Jr.
Melvin M. Roberts (1911-1971)
Philip J. Weaver, Jr.
John M. Cronquist (1931-1993)
Frederick P. Vergon, Jr.
Jack F. Smith (Retired)
T. Charles Cooper

(See Next Column)

SMITH, MARSHALL AND WEAVER, *Cleveland—Continued*

ASSOCIATES

Stephen C. Merriam
David E. Ledman
Mary B. Percifull
Benjamin L. Moltman, III

Representative Clients: American States Insurance Co.; Fireman's Fund Insurance Co.; Hartford Insurance Group; State Automobile Mutual Insurance Co.

For full biographical listings, see the Martindale-Hubbell Law Directory

THOMPSON, HINE AND FLORY (AV)

1100 National City Bank Building, 629 Euclid Avenue, 44114-3070
Telephone: 216-566-5500
Fax: 216-566-5583
Telex: 980217
Cable Address: "Thomflor"
Akron, Ohio Office: 50 S. Main Street, Suite 502, 44308-1828.
Telephone: 216-376-8090.
Fax: 216-376-8386.
Cincinnati, Ohio Office: 312 Walnut Street, 14th Floor, 45202-4029.
Telephone: 513-352-6700.
Fax: 513-241-4771.
Telex: 938003.
Columbus, Ohio Office: One Columbus, 10 West Broad Street, 43215-3435.
Telephone: 614-469-3200.
Fax: 614-469-3361.
Dayton, Ohio Office: 2000 Courthouse Plaza, N.E., 45402-1706.
Telephone: 513-443-6600.
Fax: 513-443-6637; 443-6635.
Palm Beach, Florida Office: 125 Worth Avenue, Suite 117, 33480-4466.
Telephone: 407-833-5900.
Fax: 407-833-5951.
Washington, D.C. Office: 1920 N Street, N.W., 20036-1601.
Telephone: 202-331-8800.
Fax: 202-331-8330.
Telex: 904173.
Cable Address: "Caglaw".
Brussels, Belgium Office: Rue des Chevaliers, Ridderstraat 14 - B.10, B - 1050.
Telephone: 011(32-2) 511-9326.
Fax: 011(32-2) 513-9206.

MEMBERS OF FIRM

Barbara J. Arison
Brett K. Bacon
Douglas N. Barr
Stephen H. Daniels
S. Stuart Eilers
Daniel W. Hammer

For Complete List of Firm Personnel, See General Section

For full biographical listings, see the Martindale-Hubbell Law Directory

WESTON HURD FALLON PAISLEY & HOWLEY (AV)

2500 Terminal Tower, 50 Public Square, 44113-2241
Telephone: 216-241-6602;
Ohio Toll Free: 800-336-4952
FAX: 216-621-8369

MEMBERS OF FIRM

Louis Paisley
Mark O'Neill
John W. Jeffers
John M. Baker
Ronald A. Rispo
James Lincoln McCrystal, Jr.
Carolyn M. Cappel
Donald H. Switzer
Hilary Sheldon Taylor
Kenneth A. Torgerson
John S. Kluznik
Jeffrey D. Fincun
William H. Baughman, Jr.
John Winthrop Ours
Stephen D. Walters
Gary W. Johnson
Deirdre G. Henry
Harry Sigmier
Warren Rosman
Connie M. Horrigan
Jerome W. Cook
Kathryn M. Murray
Dana A. Rose
Hernan N. Visani

ASSOCIATES

John G. Farnan
Cecil Marlowe
Scott C. Smith
Raymond S. Ling
Patrick M. Dukes
Lisa G. McComas

For Complete List of Firm Personnel, See General Section

For full biographical listings, see the Martindale-Hubbell Law Directory

*COLUMBUS,** Franklin Co.

CRABBE, BROWN, JONES, POTTS & SCHMIDT (AV)

500 South Front Street, Suite 1200, 43215
Telephone: 614-228-5511
Telecopier: 614-229-4559
Cincinnati, Ohio Office: 30 Garfield Place, Suite 940, 45202.
Telephone: 513-784-1525.
Telecopier: 513-784-1250.

MEMBERS OF FIRM

J. Roth Crabbe (1906-1989)
Robert C. Potts (1913-1994)
William T. McCracken (1929-1993)
Charles E. Brown
Theodore D. Sawyer
William H. Jones
Vincent J. Lodico

(See Next Column)

MEMBERS OF FIRM (Continued)

Steven B. Ayers
Keith H. Jung
Jeffrey M. Brown
Larry H. James
Brian E. Hurley (Resident, Cincinnati Office)
Gilbert J. Gradisar
Robert J. Behal
Jeffrey M. Lewis
Richard D. Wetzel, Jr.
Jerry A. Eichenberger
James D. Gilbert
Karen A. Seawall
Luis M. Alcalde
John C. Albert
George R. McCue, III
Gregory J. Dunn

ASSOCIATES

Michael R. Henry
Robert C. Buchbinder
John A. Van Sickle
Francesca M. Tosi
Stephen L. McIntosh
Lynne K. Schoenling
Kathleen McGarvey Hidy (Resident, Cincinnati Office)
Steven A. Davis
David J. Demers
Nicholas C. York
Todd William Collis
James P. Dinsmore
Michael C. Mentel
Kristen H. Smith

OF COUNSEL

John P. Kennedy
Wilbur W. Jones
William L. Schmidt
William Page Lewis

Representative Clients: Allstate Insurance Co.; American States Insurance Co.; General Electric.

For full biographical listings, see the Martindale-Hubbell Law Directory

HAMMOND LAW OFFICE (AV)

24 East Gay Street, 43215
Telephone: 614-461-5300
FAX: 614-463-1296

MEMBER OF FIRM

Gary W. Hammond

ASSOCIATES

Frederick A. Sewards
Todd A. Cook

For full biographical listings, see the Martindale-Hubbell Law Directory

MAZANEC, RASKIN & RYDER CO., L.P.A. (AV)

Suite 980, 500 South Front Street, 43215
Telephone: 614-228-5931
Fax: 617-228-5934
Cleveland, Ohio Office: 100 Franklin's Row, 34305 Solon Road 44139.
Telephone: 216-248-7906.
Fax: 216-248-8861.

Edward M. Ryder
Richard A. Williams
Robert H. Stoffers
Daniel J. Hurley
John P. Petro

Representative Clients: Colonial Insurance Company; Crawford & Co.; Farmers Insurance Group; Leader National Insurance Company; Liberty Mutual Insurance Co.; National Casualty Insurance Co.; Progressive Casualty Insurance Co.; Scottsdale Insurance Co.; State Farm Fire & Casualty Company; Utica Mutual Insurance Co.

For full biographical listings, see the Martindale-Hubbell Law Directory

JOHN C. NEMETH & ASSOCIATES (AV)

21 East Frankfort Street, 43206-1069
Telephone: 614-443-4866
Fax: 614-443-4860

ASSOCIATES

David A. Caborn
Joseph A. Butauski
David A. Herd

Representative Clients: Anheuser-Busch, Inc.; Central Ohio Transit Authority; Crawford & Co.; Erie Insurance Group; Home Insurance Co.; Safeco Insurance Co.; Mount Carmel Hospital; The Hartford Group; Citizens Insurance Co.; State Farm Insurance Co.

For full biographical listings, see the Martindale-Hubbell Law Directory

*DAYTON,** Montgomery Co.

FREUND, FREEZE & ARNOLD A LEGAL PROFESSIONAL ASSOCIATION (AV)

Suite 1800 One Dayton Centre, One South Main Street, 45402-2017
Telephone: 513-222-2424
Telecopier: 513-222-5369
Cincinnati, Ohio Office: Suite 2110 Carew Tower, 441 Vine Street, 45202-4157.
Telephone: 513-287-8400.
FAX: 513-287-8403.

Neil F. Freund
Stephen V. Freeze
Gordon D. Arnold
Patrick J. Janis
Jane M. Lynch
Francis S. McDaniel
Stephen C. Findley
Robert N. Snyder
Christopher W. Carrigg
Scott F. McDaniel
Lisa A. Hesse
Gregory J. Berberich

(See Next Column)

FREUND, FREEZE & ARNOLD A LEGAL PROFESSIONAL ASSOCIATION—*Continued*

Mary E. Lentz	Fredric L. Young
Thomas B. Bruns	Philip D. Mervis
Shawn M. Blatt	Thomas P. Glass
Matthew K. Fox	Lori S. Kibby

August T. Janszen

Local Counsel for: Auto-Owners Insurance Co.; CNA Insurance Co.; Crum and Foster Underwriters; Employers Reinsurance Corp.; Farmers Insurance Group; Lloyds of London; Medical Protective; Midwestern Group; State Farm Mutual Automobile Insurance Co.; The Travelers Insurance Co.
Special Trial Counsel for: City of Dayton.

For full biographical listings, see the Martindale-Hubbell Law Directory

JENKS, SURDYK & COWDREY CO., L.P.A. (AV)

205 East First Street, 45402
Telephone: 513-222-2333
Fax: 513-222-1970
Cincinnati, Ohio Office: 1500 Chiquita Center, 250 East Fifth Street.
Telephone: 513-762-7622.
Fax: 513-721-4628.

Thomas E. Jenks	Edward J. Dowd
Robert J. Surdyk	Nicholas E. Subashi
Robert F. Cowdrey	Scott G. Oxley
Christopher F. Johnson	Arden Lynn Achenberg
Susan Blasik-Miller	W. Benjamin Hood, II

Representative Clients: Beta Industries, Inc.; Cessna Aircraft Co.; Miami Valley Risk Management Association, Inc.; P H Electronics, Inc.;
Local Counsel For: American States Insurance Co.; Chubb & Son, Inc.; Westfield Companies American International Group; Shelby Mutual Insurance Co.; Meridian Mutual Insurance Co.

For full biographical listings, see the Martindale-Hubbell Law Directory

PICKREL, SCHAEFFER & EBELING CO., L.P.A. (AV)

2700 Kettering Tower, 45423-2700
Telephone: 513-223-1130
Facsimile: 513-223-0339

William G. Pickrel (1931-1966)	Paul E. Zimmer
Virgil Schaeffer (1932-1958)	Richard J. Holzer
Philip C. Ebeling (1931-1963)	Alan B. Schaeffer
Bradley J. Schaeffer (1935-1992)	Janet K. Cooper
Donald G. Schweller	John W. Slagle
Harry G. Ebeling	Andrew C. Storar
Thomas J. Harrington	Jon M. Rosemeyer
Paul J. Winterhalter	David C. Korte

Beth W. Schaeffer	Diane L. Gentile
James W. Kelleher	Jeffrey S. Senney
Mary M. Biagioli	L. Michael Bly
Paul H. Spaeth	Joseph C. Hoskins

Joseph W. Meyer

OF COUNSEL

Gordon H. Savage

Representative Clients: Hearst Broadcasting Corp. (WDTN-TV); Marathon Oil Co.; Citizens Federal Bank, F.S.B., of Dayton; Allstate Insurance Co.; American Mutual Liability Co.; Miami Valley Cardiologists; American Aggregates; Sinclair Community College; Roberds Inc.; Bridgestone/Firestone; Appleton Paper Co.; SOFCO Erectors, Inc.

For full biographical listings, see the Martindale-Hubbell Law Directory

THOMPSON, HINE AND FLORY (AV)

2000 Courthouse Plaza, N.E., 45402-1706
Telephone: 513-443-6600
Fax: 513-443-6637; 443-6635
Akron, Ohio Office: 50 S. Main Street, Suite 502, 44308-1828.
Telephone: 216-376-8090.
Fax: 216-376-8386.
Cincinnati, Ohio Office: 312 Walnut Street, 14th Floor, 45202-4029.
Telephone: 513-352-6700.
Fax: 513-241-4771.
Telex: 938003.
Cleveland, Ohio Office: 1100 National City Bank Building, 629 Euclid Avenue, 44114-3070.
Telephone: 216-566-5500.
Fax: 216-556-5583.
Telex: 980217.
Cable Address: "Thomflor".
Columbus, Ohio Office: One Columbus, 10 West Broad Street, 43215-3435.
Telephone: 614-469-3200.
Fax: 614-469-3361.
Palm Beach, Florida Office: 125 Worth Avenue, 33480-4466.
Telephone: 407-833-5900.
Fax: 407-833-5951.

(See Next Column)

Washington, D.C. Office: 1920 N Street, N.W., 20036-1601.
Telephone: 202-331-8800.
Fax: 202-331-8330.
Telex: 904173.
Cable Address: "Caglaw".
Brussels, Belgium Office: Rue des Chevaliers / Ridderstraat 14 - B.10, B - 1050.
Telephone: 011(32-2) 511-9326.
Fax: 011(32-2) 513-9206.

MEMBER OF FIRM

Bruce M. Allman

For Complete List of Firm Personnel, See General Section

For full biographical listings, see the Martindale-Hubbell Law Directory

YOUNG & ALEXANDER CO., L.P.A. (AV)

Suite 100, 367 West Second Street, 45402
Telephone: 513-224-9291
Telecopier: 513-224-9679
Cincinnati, Ohio Office: 110 Boggs Lane, Suite 350.
Telephone: 513-326-5555.
FAX: 513-326-5550.

Robert F. Young (1905-1978)	Mark R. Chilson
Robert C. Alexander (1912-1982)	John A. Smalley
	A. Mark Segreti, Jr.
James M. Brennan	Margaret R. Young
Anthony R. Kidd	Steven O. Dean

James K. Hemenway

Counsel for: The Children's Medical Center, Dayton, Ohio; The Colonial Stair & Woodwork Co.; The Greater Dayton Area Hospital Assn.; Mike-Sell's Potato Chip Co.; Moorman Pontiac, Inc.
Local Counsel for: Colonial Penn Insurance Co.; John Hancock Mutual Life Insurance Co.; Hertz Corp.; State Farm Insurance Co.

For Complete List of Firm Personnel, See General Section

For full biographical listings, see the Martindale-Hubbell Law Directory

*DEFIANCE,** Defiance Co.

CLEMENS, KORHN & LIMING (AV)

Second Floor First Federal Savings Building, P.O. Box 787, 43512
Telephone: 419-782-6055
Telecopier: 419-782-3227
Hicksville, Ohio Office: Old Trustcorp Bank Building, 201 E. High Street, Box 18.
Telephone: 419-542-7705.

MEMBERS OF FIRM

Tellis T. Shaw (1868-1951)	Stephen F. Korhn
David W. Williams (1917-1987)	John M. Liming
Erwin L. Clemens	Richard L. Altman

Marc F. Warncke

Representative Clients: B & O Railroad Co. (Chessie System); First Federal Savings & Loan Association of Defiance (also Wauseon, Bryan, Montpelier and Napoleon Branches); State Automobile Mutual Insurance Co.; Defiance Hospital, Inc.; Sherwood Mutual Telephone Assn.; Allstate Insurance Co.; Auto Owners Insurance Co.; State Farm Insurance; Cincinnati Insurance.

For full biographical listings, see the Martindale-Hubbell Law Directory

*FINDLAY,** Hancock Co.

OXLEY, MALONE, FITZGERALD & HOLLISTER (AV)

301 East Main Cross Street, P.O. Box 1086, 45840
Telephone: 419-422-8713
Fax: 419-422-6495

COUNSEL

Garver Oxley

MEMBERS OF FIRM

Michael J. Malone	Dennis M. Fitzgerald

Robert B. Hollister

ASSOCIATES

Michael E. Gilb	Teresa S. Glover

OF COUNSEL

Julie A. Davenport

Representative Clients: Buckeye Union Insurance Co.; Hancock-Wood Electric Cooperative, Inc.; American States Insurance Company; Allstate Insurance Company; Auto-Owners Insurance Company; Shelby Mutual Insurance Company; Western Reserve Group; Grange Mutual Insurance Company.

For Complete List of Firm Personnel, See General Section

For full biographical listings, see the Martindale-Hubbell Law Directory

FRANKLIN, Warren Co.

RUPPERT, BRONSON, CHICARELLI & SMITH CO., L.P.A. (AV)

1063 East Second Street, P.O. Box 369, 45005
Telephone: 513-746-2832
Fax: 513-746-2855
Springboro, Ohio Office: 610 North Main, P.O. Box 186.
Telephone: 513-748-1314.

James D. Ruppert | Rupert E. Ruppert
Barbara J. Bronson | John D. Smith
David A. Chicarelli | Timothy N. Tepe

Ronald W. Ruppert | Donna K. Czechowski
Deborah Bailey | Michael J. D'Amico

For full biographical listings, see the Martindale-Hubbell Law Directory

HICKSVILLE, Defiance Co.

CLEMENS, KORHN & LIMING (AV)

Old Trustcorp Bank Building, 201 East High Street, P.O. Box Box 18, 43526
Telephone: 419-542-7705
Defiance, Ohio Office: Second Floor First Federal Savings Building, P.O. Box 787.
Telephone: 419-782-6055.
Telecopier: 419-782-3227.

MEMBERS OF FIRM

Tellis T. Shaw (1868-1951) | Stephen F. Korhn
David W. Williams (1917-1987) | John M. Liming
Erwin L. Clemens | Richard L. Altman
Marc F. Warncke

For full biographical listings, see the Martindale-Hubbell Law Directory

IRONTON,* Lawrence Co.

EDWARDS & KLEIN, CO., L.P.A. (AV)

Center and Third Streets, 45638
Telephone: 614-532-4554
Facsimile: 614-532-1554

Milton J. Andrews (1902-1958) | Charles C. Klein
James W. Byrne (1894-1958) | Thomas L. Klein
Homer M. Edwards (1921-1971) | Sara B. Klein

General Counsel for: Star Bank, N.A.
Local Counsel for: The Kroger Co.; Allied Signal Corp.; Ohio Bell; Grand Trunk Railway System; Dow Chemical Corp.; AEP Ohio Power; Ohio American Water Co.
Representative Insurance Clients: Grange Mutual Casualty Co.; State Farm Insurance Cos.

For full biographical listings, see the Martindale-Hubbell Law Directory

LIMA,* Allen Co.

GOODING, HUFFMAN, KELLEY & BECKER (AV)

127-129 North Pierce Street, P.O. Box 546, 45802
Telephone: 419-227-3423
Fax: 419-228-1937

Fred Wemmer Gooding (1914-1972) | Lawrence S. Huffman

ASSOCIATES

C. Bradford Kelley | Matthew C. Huffman
Lawrence A. Huffman | Marie A. Von der Embse
Stephen L. Becker | John C. Huffman
T. Blain Brock, II

LEGAL SUPPORT PERSONNEL

Carol L. Swem (Probate Paralegal)

Representative Clients: The Medical Protective Company; Physicians Insurance Company of Ohio; United States Fidelity and Guaranty Co.; Hamilton Mutual Insurance Company; Bank One, Lima, Ohio; Joe Ivison Chevrolet-Jeep Eagle, Inc.; Lima Contracting Company; Otis Wright & Sons Trucking, Inc.
Approved Attorneys for: Lawyers Title Insurance Corp., Richmond, Virginia.

For full biographical listings, see the Martindale-Hubbell Law Directory

MANSFIELD,* Richland Co.

BROWN, BEMILLER, MURRAY & McINTYRE (AV)

70 Park Avenue West, P.O. Box 728, 44901-0728
Telephone: 419-525-1611
FAX: 419-525-3810

MEMBERS OF FIRM

John T. Brown | William T. McIntyre
F. Loyal Bemiller | Jeffrey Molyet
D. Kim Murray | Adam Vetter, Jr.
J. Jeffrey Heck

(See Next Column)

Local Counsel for: Society Bank & Trust; Travelers Insurance Co.; United States Fidelity & Guaranty Co.; Ohio Edison Co.; Montgomery Ward & Co.; Shiloh Corp.; Westfield Ins. Co.; Commercial Union Ins. Co.; Mansfield News Journal; Peoples Federal Savings Bank.

For Complete List of Firm Personnel, See General Section

For full biographical listings, see the Martindale-Hubbell Law Directory

PAINESVILLE,* Lake Co.

BAKER, HACKENBERG & COLLINS CO., L.P.A. (AV)

77 North St. Clair Street, 44077
Telephone: 216-354-4364;
Cleveland Direct Line: 216-951-3295
Fax: 216-354-0135

I. James Hackenberg | Richard L. Collins, Jr.

OF COUNSEL

Richard A. Hennig

Representative Clients: Cleveland Electric Illuminating Co.; City of Mentor; Motorists Mutual Insurance Co.; Nationwide Insurance Co.; State Automobile Insurance Co.; Ohio Bell Telephone Co.; Hartford Insurance Group; Classic Chevrolet.

For full biographical listings, see the Martindale-Hubbell Law Directory

STEUBENVILLE,* Jefferson Co.

KINSEY, ALLEBAUGH & KING (AV)

200 Sinclair Building, P.O. Box 249, 43952
Telephone: 614-282-1900

MEMBERS OF FIRM

W. I. Kinsey (1876-1962) | Carl F. Allebaugh (1896-1970)
Robert P. King

ASSOCIATE

Robert C. Hargrave

OF COUNSEL

Adam E. Scurti | Otto A. Jack, Jr.

Solicitors for: Consolidated Rail Corporation/Penn Central Transportation Co.
Attorneys for: Ohio Power Co.; Columbia Gas Company of Ohio; Ohio Bell Telephone Co.; Ohio Edison Co.; Continental Casualty Co.; Allstate Insurance Co.; Westfield Cos.; Federal Insurance Co.; Unibank.

For full biographical listings, see the Martindale-Hubbell Law Directory

TOLEDO,* Lucas Co.

ROBERT M. ANSPACH ASSOCIATES (AV)

Suite 2100, 405 Madison Avenue, 43604-1236
Telephone: 419-246-5757
FAX: 419-321-6979

Robert M. Anspach | Mark D. Meeks
Stephen R. Serraino | J. Roy Nunn
Catherine G. Hoolahan | Paul F. Burtis

ASSOCIATES

Barry Y. Freeman | L. Nathalie Hiemstra

Representative Clients: St. Vincent Medical Center; Ohio Hospital Insurance Co.; Northland Insurance Co.; Safety-Kleen Corp.

For full biographical listings, see the Martindale-Hubbell Law Directory

DOYLE, LEWIS & WARNER (AV)

202 North Erie Street, P.O. Box 2168, 43603
Telephone: 419-248-1500
Fax: 419-248-2002

MEMBERS OF FIRM

Steven Timonere | Michael E. Hyrne
Richard F. Ellenberger | John A. Borell
Michael A. Bruno

ASSOCIATE

Kevin A. Pituch

OF COUNSEL

John R. Wanick

Representative Clients: Prudential Insurance Company of America; Equitable Life Assurance Society of U.S.; Metropolitan Life Insurance Co.; Northwestern Mutual Life Insurance Co.; John Hancock Life Insurance; Connecticut General Life Insurance Co.; National Life & Accident Insurance Co.; Fireman's Fund Insurance Cos.; Hanover Insurance; Leader National Insurance Co.

For Complete List of Firm Personnel, See General Section

For full biographical listings, see the Martindale-Hubbell Law Directory

Toledo—Continued

FULLER & HENRY (AV)

One Seagate Suite 1700, P.O. Box 2088, 43603-2088
Telephone: 419-247-2500
Telecopier: 419-247-2665
Port Clinton, Ohio Office: 125 Jefferson.
Telephone: 419-734-2153.
Telecopier: 419-732-8246.
Columbus, Ohio Office: 2210 Huntington Center, 41 South High Street.
Telephone: 614-228-6611.
Telecopier: 614-228-6623.

MEMBERS OF FIRM

Thomas L. Dalrymple
Ray A. Farris
Stephen B. Mosier
Thomas S. Zaremba
John J. Siciliano
Martin J. Witherell
Mary Ann Whipple
Sue A. Sikkema
Martin D. Carrigan
Dennis A. Lyle
Daniel T. Ellis

ASSOCIATES

Andrew K. Ranazzi
Lance Michael Keiffer
Margaret G. Beck
Mark Shaw
John Christian Everhardus

Counsel for: Chubb Group of Insurance Cos.; Great Central Insurance Co.; Kemper Insurance Company; Physicians Insurance Company of Ohio; St. Paul Fire & Marine Insurance; State Farm Mutual Auto Insurance Co.; The Hartford; Wausau Insurance Companies.

For Complete List of Firm Personnel, See General Section

For full biographical listings, see the Martindale-Hubbell Law Directory

JONES & BAHRET CO., L.P.A. (AV)

2735 N. Holland-Sylvania Road, Suite A-3, 43615-1844
Telephone: 419-536-5588
Fax: 419-536-2662

Willis P. Jones, Jr.
Robert J. Bahret

Keith J. Watkins
Peter C. Munger
Julie M. Pavelko

LEGAL SUPPORT PERSONNEL

Denise M. Conrad
Evelyn Dee Evans

Representative Clients: Auto-Owners Insurance Co.; Liberty Mutual Ins. Co.; Motorists Ins. Companies; National Casualty Ins. Co.; Podiatry Ins. Co.; Progressive Ins. Co.; State Farm Ins. Co.; Sylvania Township; Western Reserve Mutual Casualty Co.; Westfield Ins. Companies.

For full biographical listings, see the Martindale-Hubbell Law Directory

RITTER, ROBINSON, MCCREADY & JAMES (AV)

1850 National City Bank Building, 405 Madison Avenue, 43624
Telephone: 419-241-3213
Detroit, Michigan: 313-422-1610
FAX: 419-241-4925

MEMBERS OF FIRM

Ellis F. Robinson (Retired)
William S. McCready
Timothy C. James

OF COUNSEL

Milton C. Boesel, Jr.

Counsel for: Chrysler Corp.; Rubini Motors, Inc.; Ohio Casualty Insurance Co.; National Mutual Insurance Co.; Celina Mutual Insurance Co.; Westfield Insurance Co.; Northwestern National Insurance Co.; Midwestern Insurance Co.; United Ohio Insurance Co.; Toledo Auto Electric Co.

For Complete List of Firm Personnel, See General Section

For full biographical listings, see the Martindale-Hubbell Law Directory

ROBISON, CURPHEY & O'CONNELL (AV)

Ninth Floor Four Seagate, 43604
Telephone: 419-249-7900
Telecopier: 419-249-7911
Blissfield, Michigan Office: 8651 East U.S. 223, P.O. Box 59.
Telephone: 517-486-4333.
Telecopier: 517-486-4271.

MEMBERS OF FIRM

John M. Curphey
E. Thomas Maguire
Ronald S. Moening
Edwin A. Coy
David W. Stuckey
Jack Zouhary
Timothy D. Krugh
James E. Brazeau
Julia Smith Wiley
Jean Ann S. Sieler
Thomas J. Antonini

ASSOCIATES

Jean M. O'Brien
D. Casey Talbott
Charles C. Butler

Counsel for: Nationwide Insurance Cos.; St. Paul Insurance Cos.; Motorists Insurance Cos.; Physicians Insurance Company of Michigan.

(See Next Column)

For Complete List of Firm Personnel, See General Section

For full biographical listings, see the Martindale-Hubbell Law Directory

SCHNORF & SCHNORF CO., L.P.A. A PROFESSIONAL CORPORATION (AV)

1400 National City Bank Building, 405 Madison Avenue, 43604
Telephone: 419-248-2646
Facsimile: 419-248-2889

David M. Schnorf
Christopher F. Parker
Johna M. Bella

Representative Clients: Universal Underwriters Group; Cincinnati Insurance Company; Blue Cross & Blue Shield Mutual of Ohio; Bankers Multiple Line Insurance Company; GRE Insurance Group.

For Complete List of Firm Personnel, See General Section

For full biographical listings, see the Martindale-Hubbell Law Directory

SPENGLER NATHANSON (AV)

608 Madison Avenue, Suite 1000, 43604-1169
Telephone: 419-241-2201
FAX: 419-241-8599

MEMBERS OF FIRM

James R. Jeffery
James D. Jensen
Byron S. Choka
Susan B. Nelson
Joan C. Szuberla
Teresa L. Grigsby

ASSOCIATE

Renisa A. Dorner

Counsel for: CNA Insurance Companies; United States Fidelity & Guaranty Company; Great American Insurance Company; Willis Corroon Administrative Services, Inc.; Physicians Insurance Company of Ohio; Professional Mutual Insurance Co. Retention Group; Fidelity & Guaranty Insurance Underwriters, Inc.

For Complete List of Firm Personnel, See General Section

For full biographical listings, see the Martindale-Hubbell Law Directory

*TROY,** Miami Co.

SHIPMAN, UTRECHT & DIXON CO., L.P.A. (AV)

215 West Water Street, P.O. Box 310, 45373
Telephone: 513-339-1500
Fax: 513-339-1519

William M. Dixon
W. McGregor Dixon, Jr.
James D. Utrecht
Gary A. Nasal
Gary E. Zuhl

General Counsel for: Star Bank, N.A.; Milton Federal Savings and Loan Assn.; Troy Daily News Inc.; City of Troy and Troy Board of Education.
Local Counsel for: CSX Transportation, Inc.; The Dayton Power & Light Co.; Travelers Insurance Co.; Celina Group; Westfield Companies; Lawyers Title Insurance Corp.

For Complete List of Firm Personnel, See General Section

For full biographical listings, see the Martindale-Hubbell Law Directory

*WARREN,** Trumbull Co.

RICHARDS AND MEOLA (AV)

Suite 300-The First Place, 159 East Market Street, 44481-1102
Telephone: 216-373-1000
FAX: 216-394-5291

MEMBERS OF FIRM

Charles L. Richards
William Jack Meola

ASSOCIATES

Deborah E. Marik
Bruce Martin Broyles

For full biographical listings, see the Martindale-Hubbell Law Directory

*WILMINGTON,** Clinton Co.

BUCKLEY, MILLER & WRIGHT (AV)

145 North South Street, P.O. Box 311, 45177
Telephone: 513-382-0946
Fax: 513-382-1361
Sabina, Ohio Office: 34 North Howard Street.
Telephone: 513-584-4663.

MEMBERS OF FIRM

Frederick J. Buckley
James P. Miller
Jeffrey L. Wright
Karen Buckley
John P. Miller

Representative Clients: Cincinnati Insurance Co.; Grange Mutual Casualty Co.; Nationwide Mutual Insurance Co.; Ohio Casualty Insurance Co.; Ohio Mutual Insurance Co.; State Automobiel Mutual Insurance Co.; United Ohio Insurance Co.; Westfield Companies.

For full biographical listings, see the Martindale-Hubbell Law Directory

*YOUNGSTOWN,** Mahoning Co.

PFAU, PFAU & MARANDO (AV)

900 City Centre One, P.O. Box 1078, 44501-1078
Telephone: 216-747-3507
Fax: 216-747-1147

MEMBERS OF FIRM

William E. Pfau, Sr. (1889-1963)
William E. Pfau, Jr.
William E. Pfau III
John C. Pfau
Michael P. Marando

For full biographical listings, see the Martindale-Hubbell Law Directory

*ZANESVILLE,** Muskingum Co.

MICHELI, BALDWIN, BOPELEY & NORTHRUP (AV)

2806 Bell Street, P.O. Box 2687, 43702
Telephone: 614-454-2545
Fax: 614-454-6372

MEMBERS OF FIRM

Frank J. Micheli
Michael J. Micheli
James C. Micheli (1956-1992)
Steven R. Baldwin
Thomas R. Bopeley
Michael A. Northrup

Representative Clients: Bank One Cambridge, N.A.; Consolidated Rail Corp.; The Chessie System; Medical Protective Co.; Nationwide Insurance Cos.; Continental Insurance Cos.; State Farm Mutual Insurance Co.; Motorists Mutual Insurance Co.; St. Paul Insurance Co.
Reference: Mutual Federal Savings Bank

For full biographical listings, see the Martindale-Hubbell Law Directory

OKLAHOMA

*ADA,** Pontotoc Co.

DEATON & DAVISON, INC. (AV)

300 South Rennie, P.O. Box 1219, 74820
Telephone: 405-332-1752
Fax: 405-332-0827

Austin R. Deaton, Jr.
Denver N. Davison
C. Steven Kessinger

For full biographical listings, see the Martindale-Hubbell Law Directory

*DUNCAN,** Stephens Co.

ELLIS, LEONARD & BUCKHOLTS (AV)

Patterson Building, 929 West Willow, 73533-4921
Telephone: 405-252-3240
Fax: 405-252-9596

Thomas T. Ellis
Phillip H. Leonard
E. J. Buckholts, II

Reference: Security National Bank & Trust Co., Duncan, Oklahoma.

For full biographical listings, see the Martindale-Hubbell Law Directory

*OKLAHOMA CITY,** Oklahoma Co.

ABEL, MUSSER, SOKOLOSKY, MARES, HAUBRICH, BURCH & KOURI (AV)

Suite 600, One Leadership Square, 211 North Robinson, 73102
Telephone: 405-239-7046
Fax: 405-272-1090

Ed Abel
Sidney A. Musser, Jr.
Jerry D. Sokolosky
Lynn B. Mares
Greg Haubrich
Derek K. Burch
Harry J. (Trey) Kouri, III

ASSOCIATES

Kenneth G. Cole
Daniel Pines Markoff
Melvin R. Singleterry
Kelly S. Bishop
Kelly A. George
Gregory J. Ryan

OF COUNSEL

Arthur R. Angel
James A. Ikard
Warner E. Lovell, Jr.
Leo H. Whinery

For full biographical listings, see the Martindale-Hubbell Law Directory

ABOWITZ, WELCH AND RHODES (AV)

Tenth Floor 15 North Robinson, P.O. Box 1937, 73101
Telephone: 405-236-4645
Telecopier: 405-239-2843

MEMBERS OF FIRM

Murray E. Abowitz
Mort G. Welch
Sarah Jackson Rhodes

(See Next Column)

Lisa Luschen Gilbert
Denis P. Rischard
Norman Lemonik
Janice M. Dansby

Representative Clients: Jefferson Insurance Company of New York; Admiral Insurance Co.; Liberty Mutual Insurance Company; Mazda Distributors (West), Inc.; National Farmers Union Insurance Company; Oklahoma Farmers Union Mutual Insurance Company; Trinity Universal Insurance Co.

For full biographical listings, see the Martindale-Hubbell Law Directory

ANDREWS DAVIS LEGG BIXLER MILSTEN & PRICE, A PROFESSIONAL CORPORATION (AV)

500 West Main, 73102
Telephone: 405-272-9241
FAX: 405-235-8786

J. Edward Barth
John J. Breathwit
Gary S. Chilton
John F. Fischer, II
Don G. Holladay
Mona S. Lambird
Robert D. Nelon
Babette Patton
R. Brown Wallace
William D. Watts
William H. Whitehill, Jr.

Timothy D. DeGiusti
Michelle Johnson
Shelia Darling Tims

OF COUNSEL

Carolyn Gregg Hill

Representative Clients: Stewart Title & Guaranty Co.; United States Fidelity & Guaranty Co.; American Founders Life Insurance Corp.; Atlantic Casualty & Fire Insurance Co.; California Union Insurance Co.; Employers Reinsurance Corp.; Maryland Casualty Co.

For Complete List of Firm Personnel, See General Section

For full biographical listings, see the Martindale-Hubbell Law Directory

DAY, EDWARDS, FEDERMAN, PROPESTER & CHRISTENSEN, P.C. (AV)

Suite 2900 First Oklahoma Tower, 210 Park Avenue, 73102-5605
Telephone: 405-239-2121
Telecopier: 405-236-1012

Bruce W. Day
Joe E. Edwards
William B. Federman
Richard P. Propester
D. Wade Christensen
J. Clay Christensen
Kent A. Gilliland
Rodney J. Heggy
Ricki Valerie Sonders
Thomas Pitchlynn Howell, IV
John C. Platt

David R. Widdoes
Lori R. Roberts
Carolyn A. Romberg

OF COUNSEL

Herbert F. (Jack) Hewett
Jeanette Cook Timmons
Joel Warren Harmon
Jane S. Eulberg
Mark A. Cohen

Representative Clients: Aetna Life Insurance Co.; Boatmen's First National Bank of Oklahoma; Borg-Warner Chemicals, Inc.; City Bank & Trust; Federal Deposit Insurance Corp.; Bank One, Oklahoma City; Haskell Lemon Construction Co.; Merrill Lynch, Pierce, Fenner & Smith, Inc.; Prudential Securities, Inc.

For full biographical listings, see the Martindale-Hubbell Law Directory

FENTON, FENTON, SMITH, RENEAU & MOON, A PROFESSIONAL CORPORATION (AV)

Suite 800 One Leadership Square, 211 North Robinson, 73102
Telephone: 405-235-4671
Telecopier: 405-235-5247

Edgar Fenton (1890-1977)
Milton R. Moon (1921-1988)
Wm. G. Smith (1919-1993)
Dale Reneau
Donald R. Wilson
Stephen Peterson
John A. McCaleb
C. William Threlkeld
Tom E. Mullen
Brenda K. Peterson
Mary A. Kelly
Sherry L. Smith
Laurie Walker Jones
Beverly S. Pearson
Michael D. Duncan

Robin A. Wiens
Michael S. McMillin
Greg K. Ballard
R. Dale Kimsey
C. Todd Ward
John B. Vera
Kevin E. Hill
Roger Reneau

OF COUNSEL

Elliott C. Fenton
Glen D. Johnson, Jr.
Ann M. Threlkeld
James P. Kelley
Gerald E. Kelley

(See Next Column)

FENTON, FENTON, SMITH, RENEAU & MOON A PROFESSIONAL CORPORATION—*Continued*

Representative Clients: The Alliance Insurance Cos.; American Fidelity Insurance Co.; Chrysler Corp.; The Hartford Insurance Group; Insurance Company of North America; Roadway Express Inc.; The St. Paul Insurance Cos.; The Travelers Insurance Cos.; United States Fidelity & Guaranty Co.

For full biographical listings, see the Martindale-Hubbell Law Directory

FOLIART, HUFF, OTTAWAY & CALDWELL, A PROFESSIONAL CORPORATION (AV)

20th Floor, First National Center, 120 North Robinson, 73102
Telephone: 405-232-4633
FAX: 405-232-3462

James D. Foliart
Glen D. Huff
Larry D. Ottaway
M. Dan Caldwell
Monty B. Bottom
Michael C. Felty

Susan A. Short
David A. Branscum
Timothy M. Melton
Darrell W. Downs
David K. McPhail
Kevin E. McCarty
Michael T. Maloan
Jeffrey R. Atkins

For full biographical listings, see the Martindale-Hubbell Law Directory

HOLLOWAY, DOBSON, HUDSON, BACHMAN, ALDEN, JENNINGS, ROBERTSON & HOLLOWAY, A PROFESSIONAL CORPORATION (AV)

Suite 900 One Leadership Square 211 North Robinson, 73102-7102
Telephone: 405-235-8593
Fax: 405-235-1707

Page Dobson
Ronald R. Hudson
Gary C. Bachman
Charles F. Alden, III
James A. Jennings, III
Vicki Robertson
Dan L. Holloway
Don M. Vaught
John R. Denneny
Rodney L. Cook
J. William Archibald
Mark E. Duvall
James R. Baker

Lu Ann Stout
Stephen D. Bachman
Elizabeth J. Bradford
Angela D. Chancellor

OF COUNSEL

Russell B. Holloway

Representing: Associated Aviation Underwriters; Chubb Group of Insurance Cos.; Continental Insurance Cos; General Motors Corp.

For full biographical listings, see the Martindale-Hubbell Law Directory

KERR, IRVINE, RHODES & ABLES, A PROFESSIONAL CORPORATION (AV)

600 Bank of Oklahoma Plaza, 73102-4267
Telephone: 405-272-9221
Fax: 405-236-3121

Horace G. Rhodes

For Complete List of Firm Personnel, See General Section

For full biographical listings, see the Martindale-Hubbell Law Directory

KING, ROBERTS & BEELER (AV)

Suite 600, 15 N. Robinson, 73102
Telephone: 405-239-6143
Fax: 405-236-3934

MEMBERS OF FIRM

Tom L. King
K. David Roberts
Jeff R. Beeler

ASSOCIATES

Teresa Thomas Cauthorn
Tracy L. Pierce
Richard M. Glasgow
Linda Prine Brown
Phillip P. Owens II

References: Liberty Bank & Trust; City Bank & Trust.

For full biographical listings, see the Martindale-Hubbell Law Directory

MANCHESTER & PIGNATO, P.C. (AV)

Third Floor Colcord Building, 15 North Robinson, 73102
Telephone: 405-235-2222
Fax: 405-235-2204

Robert Edward Manchester
Gerard F. Pignato

Stacey L. Haws
Shannon K. Emmons
Susan Ann Knight

Representative Clients: CMI Corporation; Electric Mutual Liability Insurance Company; Otis Elevator Company; Budget Rent-A-Car Systems, Inc.; Essex Insurance Company; American Bankers Insurance Company of Florida; Motors Insurance Company; Lexington Insurance Company; City of Oklahoma City.

For full biographical listings, see the Martindale-Hubbell Law Directory

MILLS & WHITTEN, A PROFESSIONAL CORPORATION (AV)

Suite 500, One Leadership Square 211 North Robinson, 73102
Telephone: 405-239-2500
Fax: 405-235-4655

Earl D. Mills
Reggie N. Whitten
Robert B. Mills
W. Wayne Mills
Bill M. Roberts

Steve L. Lawson
Barbara K. Buratti
Kathryn D. Mansell
Glynis C. Edgar
Kent R. McGuire
Donald R. Martin, Jr.
Kay L. Hargrave
Brian E. Dittrich
Douglas A. Terry

Representative Clients: Biomet, Inc.; Crum & Forster Commercial Ins. Co.; Mid-Continent Casualty Co.; Oklahoma Farm Bureau Mutual Ins. Co.; The St. Paul Insurance Companies; OML Municipal Assurance Group; Great West Casualty; Houston General Ins. Co.; National American Ins. Co.; Progressive Casualty; Tital Indemnity.

For full biographical listings, see the Martindale-Hubbell Law Directory

OLDFIELD & COKER (AV)

4808 North Classen Boulevard, 73118
Telephone: 405-840-0555
Fax: 405-840-4808

MEMBERS OF FIRM

John S. Oldfield, Jr.
Michael G. Coker

ASSOCIATES

Rose M. J. Sloan
Matthew J. Graves

Representative Clients: CNA Insurance; Bunte Candies, Inc.; Nationwide Insurance Co.; Fine Candy Co.
Reference: Liberty Bank & Trust Co., Oklahoma City, Okla.

For full biographical listings, see the Martindale-Hubbell Law Directory

PIERCE COUCH HENDRICKSON BAYSINGER & GREEN (AV)

1109 North Francis, P.O. Box 26350, 73126
Telephone: 405-235-1611
Fax: 405-235-2904
Tulsa, Oklahoma Office: Suite 6110, 5555 East 71St. Street, 74136.
Telephone: 918-493-4944.
Fax: 918-493-6196.

MEMBERS OF FIRM

Calvin W. Hendrickson
Melvin F. Pierce
Hugh A. Baysinger
Gerald P. Green
Stephen L. Olson
James B. Durant (Resident, Tulsa Office)
D. Lynn Babb
Scott M. Rhodes
Inona Jane Harness
Russell L. Hendrickson
John Roger Hurt
Frances E. Patton
Curtis L. Smith
Charles A. Brandt
Robert S. Lafferrandre

ASSOCIATES

Jerrold Abramowitz
Kathleen J. Adler
John Christopher Condren
Steven W. Daniels
Darren B. Derryberry
Susan A. Doke
Todd Estes
Bradey T. Holler
E. Marissa Lane
Scott A. Law
G. Calvin Sharpe
Paul G. Summars
Haven Tobias
Peter L. Wheeler

OF COUNSEL

Janet Childers Pope
Larry G. Cassil, Jr.
Kevin T. Gassaway (Resident, Tulsa Office)

Representative Clients: CNA Insurance; American Fidelity Insurance Co.; Insurance Company of North America; Royal Insurance Co.; Lloyd's of London; Kemper Insurance Group; Physicians Liability Insurance Co.; Shelter Insurance Co.; Sears, Roebuck & Co.; Chubb Insurance Group.

For full biographical listings, see the Martindale-Hubbell Law Directory

*TULSA,** Tulsa Co.

ATKINSON, HASKINS, NELLIS, BOUDREAUX, HOLEMAN, PHIPPS & BRITTINGHAM (AV)

A Partnership including Professional Corporations
1500 ParkCentre, 525 South Main Street, 74103
Telephone: 918-582-8877
Fax: 918-585-8096

PARTNERS

Michael P. Atkinson, P.C.
Walter D. Haskins, P.C.
Gregory D. Nellis, P.C.
Paul T. Boudreaux, P.C.
Daniel E. Holeman, P.C.
K. Clark Phipps
Galen Lee Brittingham, P.C.
John S. Gladd

(See Next Column)

ATKINSON, HASKINS, NELLIS, BOUDREAUX, HOLEMAN, PHIPPS & BRITTINGHAM, *Tulsa—Continued*

ASSOCIATES

Martha J. Phillips
Marthanda J. Beckworth
Ann E. Allison
William A. Fiasco
Owen T. Evans
Mark W. Maguire
Jon D. Starr
Michael R. Annis
James N. Edmonds
David A. Russell
Kirsten E. Pace

OF COUNSEL

Joseph F. Glass

Representative Clients: Allstate Insurance Co.; Crum & Forester Insurance Co.; Hartford Insurance Company; National American Insurance Co.; Federated Insurance Co.; Guaranty National Insurance Co.; Liberty Mutual Insurance Co.; Physicians Liability Insurance Co.; State Farm Mutual Automobile Insurance Co.; United States Aviation Underwriters.

For full biographical listings, see the Martindale-Hubbell Law Directory

BEST, SHARP, HOLDEN, SHERIDAN, BEST & SULLIVAN, A PROFESSIONAL CORPORATION (AV)

Oneok Plaza, 100 W. 5th, Suite 808, 74103-4225
Telephone: 918-582-1234
Fax: 918-585-9447

Joseph M. Best
Joseph A. Sharp
Steven E. Holden
John H. T. Sheridan
Timothy G. Best
Daniel S. Sullivan
Steven K. Bunting
Amy Kempfert

Karen M. Grundy
Timothy E. Tipton
Philip M. Best
Malinda S. Matlock
Catherine L. Campbell
Terry S. O'Donnell
Mark Thomas Steele
Jennifer Ellen Mustain
Douglas E. Stall
Malcom D. Smith, Jr.
Bobby L. Latham, Jr.
Kenneth E. Wagner

OF COUNSEL

William E. Patten

For full biographical listings, see the Martindale-Hubbell Law Directory

GABLE & GOTWALS (AV)

2000 Bank IV Center, 15 West Sixth Street, 74119-5447
Telephone: 918-582-9201
Facsimile: 918-586-8383

Teresa B. Adwan
Pamela S. Anderson
John R. Barker
David L. Bryant
Gene C. Buzzard
Dennis Clarke Cameron
Timothy A. Carney
Renee DeMoss
Elsie C. Draper
Sidney G. Dunagan
Theodore Q. Eliot
Richard W. Gable
Jeffrey Don Hassell
Patricia Ledvina Himes
Oliver S. Howard
Richard D. Koljack, Jr.
J. Daniel Morgan
Joseph W. Morris
Elizabeth R. Muratet
Richard B. Noulles
Ronald N. Ricketts
John Henry Rule
M. Benjamin Singletary
James M. Sturdivant
Patrick O. Waddel
Michael D. Hall
David Edward Keglovits
Stephen W. Lake
Kari S. McKee
Terry D. Ragsdale
Jeffrey C. Rambach

OF COUNSEL

G. Ellis Gable
Charles P. Gotwals, Jr.

For full biographical listings, see the Martindale-Hubbell Law Directory

MCGIVERN, SCOTT, GILLIARD, CURTHOYS & ROBINSON (AV)

Legal Arts Building, 1515 S. Boulder, 74119
Telephone: 918-584-3391
Fax: 918-592-2416

Paul V. McGivern, Jr., (A Prof. Corp.)
David R. Scott
Michael Dee Gilliard
Eugene Robinson
Karen McGivern Curthoys

Riki R. Lamb
R. Jay McAtee
Ronald E. Hignight
John Brian Des Barres
Bradley A. Jackson

Reference: Bank IV of Tulsa.

For full biographical listings, see the Martindale-Hubbell Law Directory

RHODES, HIERONYMUS, JONES, TUCKER & GABLE (AV)

Bank IV Center 15 West 6th Street, Suite 2800, 74119-5430
Telephone: 918-582-1173
Fax: 918-592-3390

(See Next Column)

MEMBERS OF FIRM

Chris L. Rhodes (1902-1966)
E. D. Hieronymus (1908 -1994)
Chris L. Rhodes, III
Bert M. Jones
John H. Tucker
Robert P. Redemann
Richard M. Eldridge
Thomas E. Steichen
Jo Anne Deaton
William D. Perrine
Kevin D. Berry
Mary Quinn-Cooper
William S. Leach
Michael W. McGivern

Jim Filosa
Jill Nelson Thomas
Wilson T. White
Catherine C. Taylor
Benton T. Wheatley
David P. Reid

OF COUNSEL

Larry J. Fulton
George W. Gable
Harold C. Zuckerman

Representative Clients: Aetna Life & Casualty Group; American International Group; Chubb Group of Insurance Companies; General Motors Corporation; HCM Claims Management; Liberty Mutual Group; Nissan Motor Corporation in U.S.A.; Sheffield Steel Company; U.S. Steel Co.; Volkswagen of America, Volkswagen, A.G.

For full biographical listings, see the Martindale-Hubbell Law Directory

RICHARDS, PAUL, RICHARDS & SIEGEL (AV)

Suite 400, Reunion Center, 9 East 4th Street, 74103
Telephone: 918-584-2583
Telefax: 918-587-8521

MEMBERS OF FIRM

John R. Richards (Deceased)
John R. Paul
Phil R. Richards
Nancy Jane Siegel

ASSOCIATES

Richard E. Warzynski
Richard L. Blanchard
John G. Barnhart
Suzanne Hale Costin

OF COUNSEL

John R. Caslavka

Representative Clients: St. Paul Insurance Company; Physicians Liability Insurance Company; Hospital Casualty Company; Property & Casualty Guaranty Association; CNA Insurance Company; Oklahoma Farm Bureau; INAPRO; Employers Reinsurance Corporation; Cigna Companies.

For full biographical listings, see the Martindale-Hubbell Law Directory

SECREST, HILL & FOLLUO (AV)

7134 South Yale, Suite 900, 74136-6342
Telephone: 918-494-5905
Fax: 918-494-2847

MEMBERS OF FIRM

James K. Secrest, II
W. Michael Hill
Dan S. Folluo

Dan W. Ernst
Melvin C. Weiman
Edward John Main
Roger N. Butler, Jr.
Andrew B. Morsman
Bob D. James
Douglas M. Borochoff

Representative Clients: Aetna Casualty and Surety Co.; Allstate Insurance Co.; Automobile Club Insurance Co.; CNA Insurance Cos.; Continental Loss Adjustment Services; Hospital Casualty Co.; Kemper Group; Osteopathic Mutual Insurance Co.; Physicians Liability Insurance Co.; United Services Automobile Assn.

For full biographical listings, see the Martindale-Hubbell Law Directory

SNEED, LANG, ADAMS & BARNETT, A PROFESSIONAL CORPORATION (AV)

2300 Williams Center Tower II, Two West Second Street, 74103
Telephone: 918-583-3145
Telecopier: 918-582-0410

James C. Lang
D. Faith Orlowski
Brian S. Gaskill
G. Steven Stidham
Stephen R. McNamara
Thomas E. Black, Jr.
Robbie Emery Burke
C. Raymond Patton, Jr.
Frederick K. Slicker
Richard D. Black
John D. Russell
Jeffrey S. Swyers

OF COUNSEL

James L. Sneed
O. Edwin Adams
Howard G. Barnett, Jr.

Representative Clients: Amoco Production Company; Continental Bank; Deloitte & Touche; Enron Corporation; Halliburton Energy Services; Helmerich & Payne, Inc.; Lehman Brothers, Inc.; Shell Oil Company; Smith Barney, Inc.; State Farm Mutual Automobile Insurance Company.

For full biographical listings, see the Martindale-Hubbell Law Directory

Tulsa—Continued

WILBURN, MASTERSON & SMILING (AV)

Executive Center II, 7134 South Yale, Suite 560, 74136-6337
Telephone: 918-494-0414
Fax: 918-493-3455

Ray H. Wilburn
Michael J. Masterson
A. Mark Smiling

ASSOCIATES

Rhett Henry Wilburn
Merle L. Tyler
Jane R. Cowdery
Wendy S. Brooks

For full biographical listings, see the Martindale-Hubbell Law Directory

OREGON

*EUGENE,** Lane Co.

BROWN, ROSETA, LONG & MCCONVILLE (AV)

210 Northbank Building, 44 Club Road, 97401
Telephone: 503-686-1883
Fax: 503-686-2008

MEMBERS OF FIRM

Larry A. Brown
Philip R. McConville
Richard A. Roseta
John F. Kilcullen
Michael H. Long
Charles D. Carlson

Representative Clients: Aetna Casualty & Surety Co.; All Nation Insurance Co.; Allstate Insurance Co.; American States Insurance Co.; Crawford & Co.; Grange Mutual Insurance; Heritage Life Insurance Co.; Insurance Corp. of America; Mutual of Enumclaw; Northwest Physicians Mutual Insurance Co.

For full biographical listings, see the Martindale-Hubbell Law Directory

LUVAAS, COBB, RICHARDS & FRASER, P.C. (AV)

300 Forum Building, 777 High Street, P.O. Box 10747, 97401
Telephone: 503-484-9292
Fax: 503-343-1206

Ralph F. Cobb
Donald E. Johnson
Robert H. Fraser
Rodney B. Carter
Louis L. Kurtz
Gregory E. Skillman

Representative Clients: Farmers Insurance Group; Professional Liability Fund of the Oregon State Bar; Universal Underwriters Insurance Co.; Fireman's Fund Insurance; Northland Insurance Co.; Ohio Casualty Group; Leader National Insurance Group; Metropolitan Insurance Co.; Allstate Insurance Co.; Country Companies Group.

For Complete List of Firm Personnel, See General Section

For full biographical listings, see the Martindale-Hubbell Law Directory

*PORTLAND,** Multnomah Co.

BODYFELT, MOUNT, STROUP & CHAMBERLAIN (AV)

300 Powers Building, 65 S.W. Yamhill Street, 97204
Telephone: 503-243-1022
Fax: 503-243-2019

MEMBERS OF FIRM

Barry M. Mount
Peter R. Chamberlain
Roger K. Stroup
Richard A. Lee

Simeon D. Rapoport
Jane Paulson

OF COUNSEL

E. Richard Bodyfelt

Representative Clients: American International Group; Chrysler Corp.; CIGNA; Freightliner Corp.; Georgia Pacific; Hartford Insurance Co.; Lederle Laboratories; Safeway Stores, Inc.; Texaco, Inc.

For full biographical listings, see the Martindale-Hubbell Law Directory

COONEY & CREW, P.C. (AV)

Pioneer Tower, Suite 890, 888 S.W. Fifth Avenue, 97204
Telephone: 503-224-7600
FAX: 503-224-6740

Paul A. Cooney
Michael D. Crew
Thomas E. Cooney
Kelly T. Hagan
Thomas M. Cooney
Raymond F. Mensing, Jr.
Brent M. Crew
Robert S. Perkins

LEGAL SUPPORT PERSONNEL

Alma Weber (Paralegal)

For full biographical listings, see the Martindale-Hubbell Law Directory

HALLMARK, KEATING & ABBOTT, P.C. (AV)

800 Benj. Franklin Plaza, One Southwest Columbia, 97258-2095
Telephone: 503-222-4422
Telecopier: 503-796-0699
Seattle, Washington Office: 1600 Second and Seneca Building, 1191 Second Avenue, 98101-2910.
Telephone: 206-622-2295.
Telecopier: 206-340-0724.

Gary V. Abbott
John F. Folliard, Jr.
Jeffrey W. Bildstein
William L. Hallmark
William Alan Davis
Lindsey Harris Hughes
William G. Earle
Steven P. Jones
William E. Fitzharris, Jr. (Resident, Seattle, Washington Office)
Robert M. Keating
Daniel F. Mullin (Resident, Seattle, Washington Office)
Patrick N. Rothwell

Rickee N. Arntz
Michael B. Merchant
Lee M. Barns (Resident, Seattle, Washington Office)
Lisa L. Pan (Resident, Seattle, Washington Office)
Kathleen T. Carroll
Karin S. Phalen
Lin Harmon-Walker
Frank Joseph Steinmark (Resident, Seattle, Washington Office)
Molly K. Marcum
Barney Jay Mason (Resident, Seattle, Washington Office)
Gregory L. Ursich (Resident, Seattle, Washington Office)
Mary K. McIntyre (Resident, Seattle, Washington Office)
Karen V. Wiggins
Paul R. Xóchihua

SPECIAL COUNSEL

J. Barrett Marks
Robert C. Shoemaker, Jr.

OF COUNSEL

Lester L. Rawls
Richard E. Talbott
Douglas C. Farrell

For full biographical listings, see the Martindale-Hubbell Law Directory

MOSCATO, BYERLY & SKOPIL (AV)

A Partnership including a Professional Corporation
1100 The Bank of California Tower, 707 S.W. Washington Street, 97205
Telephone: 503-241-1442
FAX: 503-241-1458

Bruce L. Byerly
Otto R. Skopil, III
Frank A. Moscato (P.C.)
Michael T. Stone

For full biographical listings, see the Martindale-Hubbell Law Directory

WOOD TATUM SANDERS & MURPHY (AV)

1001 S.W. Fifth Avenue, Suite 1300, 97204
Telephone: 503-224-5430
Cable Address: "Linwood"
Telex: 296522
Facsimile: 503-241-7235

MEMBERS OF FIRM

Robert I. Sanders
Craig C. Murphy
John C. Mercer
Kim Jefferies
Todd A. Zilbert

ASSOCIATE

John H. Chambers

Representative Clients: Allstate Insurance Co.; Assuranceforeningen Gard; Assuranceforeningen Skuld; Britannia Steam Ship Ins. Association, Ltd.; British Marine Mutual; Carolina Casualty Ins. Co.; Colonial Ins. Co. of California; Federal Home Life Ins. Co.; The Infinity Group; Japan Ship Owners' Mutual P & I Assn.; Liverpool & London Steamship P & I; Newcastle P & I Assn.; North of England P & I Assoc.; Shipowners Claims Bureau; Shipowners Mutual P & I Assn.; Standard Steamship Owerns P & I Assoc.; Steamship Mutual Underwriting Assn.; Sveriges Angfartygs Assurans Forening; United Kingdom Mutal S.S.; West of England P & I Assn.

For Complete List of Firm Personnel, See General Section

For full biographical listings, see the Martindale-Hubbell Law Directory

PENNSYLVANIA

*BUTLER,** Butler Co.

STEPANIAN & MUSCATELLO (AV)

228 South Main Street, 16001
Telephone: 412-285-1717

MEMBERS OF FIRM

Leo M. Stepanian
Bruno A. Muscatello
William R. Shaffer

For full biographical listings, see the Martindale-Hubbell Law Directory

*CARLISLE,** Cumberland Co.

DOUGLAS, DOUGLAS & DOUGLAS (AV)

27 West High Street, 17013-0261
Telephone: 717-243-1790
Fax: 717-243-8955

MEMBERS OF FIRM

George F. Douglas, Jr.
William P. Douglas
George F. Douglas, III

Representative Client: State Farm Insurance Cos.

For full biographical listings, see the Martindale-Hubbell Law Directory

*CLARION,** Clarion Co.

LAW OFFICES OF RICHARD W. KOOMAN, II (AV)

Marianne Professional Center, P.O. Box 700, 16214
Telephone: 814-226-9100
Fax: 814-226-7361

ASSOCIATE

Terry R. Heeter

Representative Clients: Pennsylvania National Mutual Casualty Insurance Co.; Erie Insurance Exchange.

For full biographical listings, see the Martindale-Hubbell Law Directory

ELKINS PARK, Montgomery Co.

MONAGHAN & GOLD, P.C. (AV)

7837 Old York Road, 19027
Telephone: 215-782-1800
Fax: 215-782-1010

John F. X. Monaghan, Jr.
Alan Steven Gold

Brian E. Appel
Barbara Malett Weitz
Murray R. Glickman
Tanya M. Sweet

*ERIE,** Erie Co.

MARSH, SPAEDER, BAUR, SPAEDER & SCHAAF (AV)

Suite 300, 300 State Street, 16507
Telephone: 814-456-5301
Fax: 814-456-1112

MEMBERS OF FIRM

Will J. Schaaf
John C. Brydon
Ritchie T. Marsh
Thomas M. Lent
William J. Schaaf
Francis J. Klemensic
James E. Marsh, Jr.
John B. Fessler
John P. Eppinger
Eugene C. Sundberg, Jr.
James R. Fryling

Donald F. Fessler, Jr.
Kurt L. Sundberg

OF COUNSEL

Byron A. Baur

Representative Clients: Aetna Life & Casualty; Borough of Edinboro; Chase Lincoln First Bank, N.A.; Erie Parking Authority; Home Insurance Co.; Marquette Savings Assn.; Motorists Insurance Co.; Northwest Savings Bank, Pa., S.A.; Ohio Casualty Insurance Co.; Pennsylvania Medical Society Liability Insurance Co.

For Complete List of Firm Personnel, See General Section

For full biographical listings, see the Martindale-Hubbell Law Directory

FORT WASHINGTON, Montgomery Co.

DALLER GREENBERG & DIETRICH (AV)

Valley Green Corporate Center, 7111 Valley Green Road, 19034
Telephone: 215-836-1100
Facsimile: 215-836-2845
Haddon Heights, New Jersey Office: 2 White Horse Pike.
Telephone: 609-547-9068.
Telecopier: 609-547-2391.

Morton F. Daller
Nancy P. Horn
Edward A. Greenberg
A. M. Laszlo
Gerhard P. Dietrich
Tracy Canuso Nugent (Resident, Haddon Heights, New Jersey Office)
Charles E. Pugh
Eileen M. Johnson
Dennis R. Callahan
Catherine N. Walto

For full biographical listings, see the Martindale-Hubbell Law Directory

*HARRISBURG,** Dauphin Co.

BUCHANAN INGERSOLL, PROFESSIONAL CORPORATION (AV)

Vartan Parc, 30 North Third Street, 17101
Telephone: 717-237-4800
Telecopier: 717-233-0852
Pittsburgh, Pennsylvania Office: 5800 USX Tower, 600 Grant Street.
Telephone: 412-562-8800.
Philadelphia, Pennsylvania Office: Two Logan Square, Twelfth Floor, 18th & Arch Streets.
Telephone: 215-665-8700.
Tampa, Florida Office: 101 East Kennedy Boulevard, Suite 1030.
Telephone: 813-222-8180.
North Miami Beach, Florida Office: 19495 Biscayne Boulevard.
Telephone: 305-933-5600.
Lexington, Kentucky Office: 1210 Vine Center Office Tower, 333 West Vine Street.
Telephone: 606-225-5333.
Princeton, New Jersey Office: Buchanan Ingersoll, A Partnership, College Centre, 500 College Road East.
Telephone: 609-452-2666.

Andrew S. Gordon

For Complete List of Firm Personnel, See General Section

For full biographical listings, see the Martindale-Hubbell Law Directory

GOLDBERG, KATZMAN & SHIPMAN, P.C. (AV)

320 Market Street - Strawberry Square, P.O. Box 1268, 17108-1268
Telephone: 717-234-4161
Telecopier: 717-234-6808; 717-234-6810

F. Lee Shipman
James M. Sheehan
Thomas E. Brenner
John A. Statler
David C. Miller, Jr.
Guy H. Brooks
Jefferson J. Shipman

Karen S. Feuchtenberger
Michael J. Crocenzi

Representative Clients: Cincinnati Insurance Co.; Pennsylvania National Insurance Co.; Atlantic Mutual Cos.; Erie Insurance Co.; Merchant's & Businessmen's Insurance Co.; State Auto Mutual Insurance Co.; Crawford & Co.; Foremost Insurance Co.; Virginia Mutual Insurance Co.
Reference: Fulton Bank.

For Complete List of Firm Personnel, See General Section

For full biographical listings, see the Martindale-Hubbell Law Directory

HEPFORD, SWARTZ & MORGAN (AV)

111 North Front Street, P.O. Box 889, 17108-0889
Telephone: 717-234-4121
Fax: 717-232-6802
Lewistown, Pennsylvania Office: 12 South Main Street, P.O. Box 867.
Telephone: 717-248-3913.

MEMBERS OF FIRM

H. Joseph Hepford
Sandra L. Meilton
Lee C. Swartz
Stephen M. Greecher, Jr.
James G. Morgan, Jr.
Dennis R. Sheaffer

COUNSEL

Stanley H. Siegel (Resident, Lewistown Office)

ASSOCIATES

Richard A. Estacio
Michael H. Park
Andrew K. Stutzman

For full biographical listings, see the Martindale-Hubbell Law Directory

MCNEES, WALLACE & NURICK (AV)

100 Pine Street, P.O. Box 1166, 17108
Telephone: 717-232-8000
Fax: 717-237-5300

MEMBER OF FIRM

Harvey Freedenberg

ASSOCIATES

James P. DeAngelo
Michael R. Kelley
Donald B. Kaufman
Patrick J. Murphy
Carol A. Steinour

For Complete List of Firm Personnel, See General Section

For full biographical listings, see the Martindale-Hubbell Law Directory

METZGER, WICKERSHAM, KNAUSS & ERB (AV)

Mellon Bank Building, 111 Market Street, P.O. Box 93, 17108-0093
Telephone: 717-238-8187
Telefax: 717-234-9478
Other Harrisburg, Pennsylvania Office: 4813 Jonestown Road, P.O. Box 93, 17108.
Telephone: 717-652-7020.

(See Next Column)

METZGER, WICKERSHAM, KNAUSS & ERB—*Continued*

MEMBERS OF FIRM

Maurice R. Metzger (1918-1980)
F. Brewster Wickersham (1918-1974)
Edward E. Knauss, III (Retired)
Christian S. Erb, Jr.
Robert E. Yetter
James F. Carl
Robert P. Reed
Edward E. Knauss, IV
Jered L. Hock
Karl R. Hildabrand

ASSOCIATES

Richard B. Druby
Steven P. Miner
Clark DeVere

Representative Clients: Allstate Insurance Co.; Chubb Group of Insurance Companies; Fireman's Fund American Insurance Group; Liberty Mutual Insurance Co.; Continental Insurance Co.; Crum & Forster.

For full biographical listings, see the Martindale-Hubbell Law Directory

NAUMAN, SMITH, SHISSLER & HALL (AV)

Eighteenth Floor, 200 North Third Street, P.O. Box 840, 17108-0840
Telephone: 717-236-3010
Telefax: 717-234-1925

MEMBERS OF FIRM

David C. Eaton
Spencer G. Nauman, Jr.
John C. Sullivan
J. Stephen Feinour
Craig J. Staudenmaier

ASSOCIATES

Benjamin Charles Dunlap, Jr.
Stephen J. Keene

OF COUNSEL

Ralph W. Boyles, Jr.

Representative Clients: Consolidated Rail Corp.; The W.O. Hickok Mfg. Co.; Delta Dental of Pennsylvania; Mellon Bank, N.A.; PNC Bank, N.A.; General Motors Acceptance Corp.; Enders Insurance Associates; Patriot-News Co.; Chrysler Credit Corp.; Capital Area Tax Collection Bureau.

For full biographical listings, see the Martindale-Hubbell Law Directory

THOMAS, THOMAS & HAFER (AV)

305 North Front Street, 6th Floor, P.O. Box 999, 17108
Telephone: 717-237-7100
Fax: 717-237-7105
Verify: 717-255-7642

MEMBERS OF FIRM

Joseph P. Hafer
James K. Thomas, II
Jeffrey B. Rettig
Peter J. Curry
R. Burke McLemore, Jr.
Edward H. Jordan, Jr.
C. Kent Price
Randall G. Gale
David L. Schwalm
Kevin E. Osborne
Douglas B. Marcello
Peter J. Speaker
Paul J. Dellasega

OF COUNSEL

James K. Thomas

Daniel J. Gallagher
Robert A. Taylor
Sarah W. Arosell
Eugene N. McHugh
Richard C. Seneca
Stephen E. Geduldig
Paula Gayle Sanders
Karen S. Coates
Ann F. DePaulis
Margaret A. Scheaffer
Todd R. Narvol

Representative Clients: Aetna Casualty & Surety Co.; CIGNA; Commercial Union Insurance Companies; General Accident Group; Hartford Insurance Group; Liberty Mutual Insurance Co.; Maryland Casualty Co.; Ohio Casualty Co.; Pennsylvania Hospital Insurance Co.; Pennsylvania Medical Society Liability Insurance Co.

For full biographical listings, see the Martindale-Hubbell Law Directory

KING OF PRUSSIA, Montgomery Co.

POWELL, TRACHTMAN, LOGAN, CARRLE & BOWMAN, A PROFESSIONAL CORPORATION (AV)

367 South Gulph Road, 19406
Telephone: 610-354-9700
Fax: 610-354-9760
Cherry Hill, New Jersey Office: 811 Church Road, Suite 126, 08002.
Telephone: 609-663-0021.
Fax: 609-663-1590.
Harrisburg, Pennsylvania Office: 114 North Second Street, 17101.
Telephone: 717-238-9300.
Fax: 717-238-9325.

Michael G. Trachtman
Paul A. Logan
Gunther O. Carrle
C. Grainger Bowman
Richard B. Ashenfelter Jr.
Mark F. Brancato
Jonathan K. Hollin
Joel P. Perilstein

OF COUNSEL

Ralph B. Powell, Jr.
Patrick W. Liddle

(See Next Column)

Mark S. McKain
Ethan N. Halberstadt
David T. Bolger
David W. Francis
Eileen M. Coyne
Andrew P. Goode
Steven G. Bardsley

For full biographical listings, see the Martindale-Hubbell Law Directory

*MEDIA,** Delaware Co.

FRONEFIELD AND DE FURIA (AV)

107 West Third Street, P.O. Box 647, 19063
Telephone: 610-565-3100
Fax: 610-565-2349

MEMBERS OF FIRM

Frank I. Ginsburg
Rosemary C. McMunigal
F. Martin Duus
Charles F. Knapp
John R. Larkin
J. Joseph Herring, Jr.
Bruce A. Irvine
Leo A. Hackett
Francis T. Sbandi

ASSOCIATES

David C. Corujo
Jane E. Mcnerney
Donna Lynn Coyne

OF COUNSEL

Albert E. Holl, Jr.

For full biographical listings, see the Martindale-Hubbell Law Directory

GIBBONS, BUCKLEY, SMITH, PALMER & PROUD, P.C. (AV)

14 West Second Street, P.O. Box 229, 19063
Telephone: 610-565-3900
Fax: 610-565-8615
West Chester, Pennsylvania Office: 37 West Gay Street, P.O. Box 3391.
Telephone: 215-692-3924.
Fax: 215-692-2641.

D. Barry Gibbons
James C. Buckley
John Churchman Smith
Stephen H. Palmer
James F. Proud
Christopher E. Frantz
Jeffrey P. Lewis

Stuart S Smith
Denis A. Gray
Thomas X. McAndrew, Jr.
Hugh P. O'Neill, III

References: Freedom Valley Bank; Fidelity Bank.

For full biographical listings, see the Martindale-Hubbell Law Directory

*NEW CASTLE,** Lawrence Co.

LUXENBERG, GARBETT & KELLY, P.C. (AV)

303 Central Building, 16101-3763
Telephone: 412-658-8535
Fax: 412-658-8013
Ellwood City, Pennsylvania Office: 317 Seventh Street.
Telephone: 412-758-7581.
Fax: 412-758-0690.

Marvin A. Luxenberg
Charles W. Garbett
Lawrence M. Kelly
Charles P. Sapienza, Jr.

Representative Clients: Erie Insurance Exchange; Ellwood Federal Savings Bank; Ohio Casualty Insurance Co.; State Farm Insurance Co.; Beneficial Consumer Discount Co.; Church Mutual Insurance Co.; Keystone Insurance Co. Nationwide Insurance Co.; Ellwood City Hospital; Puritan Insurance Co.

For full biographical listings, see the Martindale-Hubbell Law Directory

*NORRISTOWN,** Montgomery Co.

MANNING, KINKEAD, BROOKS & BRADBURY, A PROFESSIONAL CORPORATION (AV)

412 DeKalb Street, 19404-0231
Telephone: 610-279-1800
Fax: 610-279-8682

Franklin L. Wright (1880-1965)
William Perry Manning, Jr.
William H. Kinkead, III
William H. Bradbury, III

Cheri D. Andrews

Counsel for: The Philadelphia National Bank; John Deere Co.; The Rouse Co.; Consolidated Rail Corp.; Bethlehem Steel Co.; Royal Globe Insurance Co.; Nationwide Mutual Insurance Co.

For full biographical listings, see the Martindale-Hubbell Law Directory

Norristown—Continued

Murphy & Oliver, P.C. (AV)

43 East Marshall Street, 19401-4869
Telephone: 610-272-4222; 643-5900
Fax: 610-272-2549
Mount Laurel, New Jersey Office: 1288 State Highway 73, Suite 120, 08054.
Telephone: 609-234-1495.

James J. Oliver | Frank P. Murphy

Joseph M. Hoeffel III | Barbara A. Barnes
Carla E. Connor | Paul C. Cipriano, Jr.

For full biographical listings, see the Martindale-Hubbell Law Directory

*PHILADELPHIA,** Philadelphia Co.

Anderson Greenfield & Dougherty (AV)

1525 Penn Mutual Tower 510 Walnut Street, 19106-3610
Telephone: 215-627-0789
Fax: 215-627-0813
Wayne, Pennsylvania Office: First Fidelity Bank Building, 301 West Lancaster Avenue.
Telephone: 215-341-9010.

MEMBERS OF FIRM

Susan L. Anderson | Marjorie E. Greenfield
Donna Dougherty

ASSOCIATES

John Randolph Prince, III | Linda K. Hobkirk

For full biographical listings, see the Martindale-Hubbell Law Directory

Astor Weiss Kaplan & Rosenblum (AV)

The Bellevue, 6th Floor, Broad Street at Walnut, 19102
Telephone: 215-790-0100
Fax: 215-790-0509
Bala Cynwyd, Pennsylvania Office: Suite 100, Three Bala Plaza West, P.O. Box 1665.
Telephone: 610-667-8660.
Fax: 610-667-2783.
Cherry Hill, New Jersey Office: Woodland Falls Corporate Park, 210 Lake Drive East, Suite 201.
Telephone: 609-795-1113.
Fax: 609-795-7413.

MEMBERS OF FIRM

Paul C. Astor
Alvin M. Weiss (1936-1976)
G. David Rosenblum
Arthur H. Kaplan
Barbara Oaks Silver
Richard H. Martin
Allen B. Dubroff
David S. Workman
David S. Mandel
David Gutin (Resident at Bala Cynwyd Office)
Joseph B. Finlay, Jr.
Howard K. Goldstein
Steven W. Smith
Gerald J. Schorr
Jean M. Biesecker (Resident, Bala Cynwyd Office)

ASSOCIATES

Carol L. Vassallo
Thomas J. Maiorino
John R. Poeta
Bradley J. Begelman
Andrew S. Kessler
Marc S. Zamsky
Janet G. Felgoise (Resident, Bala Cynwyd Office)
Jacqueline G. Segal (Resident, Bala Cynwyd Office)

SPECIAL COUNSEL

Neil Hurowitz (Resident, Bala Cynwyd Office)

OF COUNSEL

Erwin L. Pincus | Edward W. Silver
Lloyd Zane Remick

For full biographical listings, see the Martindale-Hubbell Law Directory

Connor & Weber, P.C. (AV)

Suite 1C-47 The Philadelphian, 2401 Pennsylvania Avenue, 19130
Telephone: 215-978-2900
Fax: 215-763-5899
Paoli, Pennsylvania Office: 171 West Lancaster Avenue.
Telephone: 610-640-2800.
Fax: 610-640-1520.
Cherry Hill, New Jersey Office: 1010 Kings Highway South, Building 2, 1st Floor.
Telephone: 609-354-9463

Joseph P. Connor, III | Thomas M. Close
William J. Weber, Jr. | Joseph M. Oberlies

Paul Nappi | Dale S. Ardizzone
James P. Curran, Jr.

For full biographical listings, see the Martindale-Hubbell Law Directory

Cozen and O'Connor, A Professional Corporation (AV)

1900 Market Street, 19103
Telephone: 215-665-2000
800-523-2900
Telecopier: 215-665-2013
Charlotte, North Carolina Office: One First Union Plaza, 28202.
Telephones: 704-376-3400; 800-762-3575.
Telecopier: 704-334-3351.
Columbia, South Carolina Office: Suite 200 The Palmetto Center, 1426 Main Street.
Telephones: 803-799-3900; 800-338-1117.
Telecopier: 803-254-7233.
Dallas, Texas Office: Suite 4100, NationsBank Plaza, 901 Main Street.
Telephones: 214-761-6700; 800-448-1207.
Telecopier: 214-761-6788.
New York, N.Y. Office: 45 Broadway Atrium.
Telephones: 212-509-9400; 800-437-9400.
Telecopier: 212-509-9492.
San Diego, California Office: Suite 1610, 501 West Broadway.
Telephones: 619-234-1700; 800-782-3366.
Telecopier: 619-234-7831.
Seattle, Washington Office: Suite 5200, Washington Mutual Tower, 1201 Third Avenue.
Telephones: 206-340-1000; 800-423-1950.
Telecopier: 206-621-8783.
Westmont, New Jersey Office: 316 Haddon Avenue.
Telephones: 609-854-4900; 800-523-2900.
Telecopier: 609-854-1782.

FIRM MEMBERS IN PHILADELPHIA

Stephen A. Cozen
Patrick J. O'Connor
Ronald B. Hamilton
Joshua Wall
John T. Thorn
Eugene J. Maginnis, Jr.
Anita B. Weinstein
Richard M. Mackowsky
William H. Howard
John T. Salvucci
Daniel C. Theveny
Denise Brinker Bense
Deborah Melamut Minkoff
Joseph H. Riches
Ann Thornton Field
James H. Heller
Jennifer Gallagher
John Dwyer
Michael R. McCarty
Cecilia M. O'Connor
Josh M. Greenbaum
Dexter R. Hamilton

FIRM ASSOCIATES IN PHILADELPHIA

Joseph J. Bellew
Barbara E. Brockman
Lori Fox
Thomas F. Gallagher
Denise H. Houghton
Stephen M. Rymal
William F. Stewart
Jeffrey R. Stoner

Representative Clients: Available upon request.

For Complete List of Firm Personnel, See General Section

For full biographical listings, see the Martindale-Hubbell Law Directory

Deasey, Mahoney, Bender & McKenna, Ltd. (AV)

Three Benjamin Franklin Parkway, Suite 1400, 19102
Telephone: 215-587-9400
Facsimile: 215-587-9456
Cherry Hill, New Jersey Office: Woodcrest Pavilion, Ten Melrose Avenue, Suite 450.
Telephone: 609-429-6331.
Facsimile: 609-429-6562.

Frank C. Bender | Harry G. Mahoney
Francis J. Deasey | James L. McKenna
James W. Daly, IV

James G. Barnes
K. Craig McChesney
Kevin B. Quinn
Lorraine B. Consorte
Gerald J. Valentini
Timothy C. Costello
James L. Barlow
Nancy C. Ryan
William R. Deasey (1917-1993)

For full biographical listings, see the Martindale-Hubbell Law Directory

John Gerard Devlin & Associates, P.C. (AV)

2100 Fidelity Building, P.O. Box 58908, 19109
Telephone: 215-545-4190
Telefax: 215-564-6732
Allentown, Pennsylvania Office: The Sovereign Building, Executive Suite 103, 609 Hamilton Mall.
Telephone: 215-820-6422.
Westmont, New Jersey Office: 216 Haddon Avenue, Suite 103, 08108.
Telephone: 609-858-1690.
FAX: 609-858-8998.
East Brunswick, New Jersey Office: 190 Route 18, Suite 3000, 08816.
Telephone: 908-214-2621.
Fax: 908-246-2917.

(See Next Column)

JOHN GERARD DEVLIN & ASSOCIATES, P.C.—*Continued*

John Gerard Devlin
James B. Corrigan, Jr.
Joseph T. Murphy, Jr.
Louis J. Mairone, Jr.
J. Brian Durkin
Thomas Paschos
Joseph A. Whip, Jr.
Michael Malarick (East Brunswick, N.J. and Westmont, N.J. Offices)
Dora R. Garcia

Representative Clients: Lloyds of London; Commercial Union; John Hancock Property and Casualty Insurance Co.; Sentry Insurance Co.; Wausau Insurance Co.; State Farms Insurance Co.; Hanseco Insurance Co.; American Family Insurance Co.; Liberty Mutual Insurance Co.; Linberg Adjustment Co.

For full biographical listings, see the Martindale-Hubbell Law Directory

FINEMAN & BACH, P.C. (AV)

19th Floor, 1608 Walnut Street, 19103
Telephone: 215-893-9300
Fax: 215-893-8719
Cherry Hill, New Jersey Office: 905 North Kings Highway.
Telephone: 609-795-1118.

Norman S. Berson
Robert J. Klein
S. David Fineman
Bonnie Brigance Leadbetter
Mitchell L. Bach
Tyler E. Wren
Richard A. Rubin
J. Randolph Lawlace
Jay Barry Harris
Richard J. Tanker (Resident, Cherry Hill, New Jersey Office)

Lee Applebaum
Diane C. Bernoff
Scott H. Brandt
June J. Essis
John C. Falls
Illene G. Greenberg
Julie Pearlman Meyers
Stefanie Newman Rabinowitz
Michael S. Saltzman
Alan J. Tauber
Alexander B. Zolfaghari

For full biographical listings, see the Martindale-Hubbell Law Directory

GALLAGHER, REILLY AND LACHAT, P.C. (AV)

Suite 1300, 2000 Market Street, 19103
Telephone: 215-299-3000
FAX: 215-299-3010
Pennsauken, New Jersey Office: Kevon Office Center, Suite 130, 2500 McClellan Boulevard, 08109.
Telephone: 609-663-8200.

Stanley S. Frazee, Jr.
Paul F. X. Gallagher
Thomas F. Reilly
Frederick T. Lachat, Jr.
Richard K. Hohn
James Emerson Egbert
Stephen A. Scheuerle
Elizabeth F. Walker

David Scott Morgan
Wilfred T. Mills, Jr.
Maureen Rowan
Charles L. McNabb
Thomas O'Neill
Laurence I. Gross
Sean F. Kennedy
Milica Novakovic
John A. Livingood, Jr.

SPECIAL COUNSEL

Dolores Rocco Kulp

For full biographical listings, see the Martindale-Hubbell Law Directory

GERMAN, GALLAGHER & MURTAGH, A PROFESSIONAL CORPORATION (AV)

Fifth Floor, The Bellevue, 200 South Broad Street, 19102
Telephone: 215-545-7700
Telecopier: 215-732-4182
Cherry Hill, New Jersey Office: Suite 643, 1040 North Kings Highway.
Telephone: 609-667-7676.
Lancaster, Pennsylvania Office: 40 East Grant Street.
Telephone: 717-293-8070.

Edward C. German
Michael D. Gallagher
Dean F. Murtagh
Philip A. Ryan
Robert P. Corbin
David P. Rovner
Kathryn A. Dux
Gary R. Gremminger
Kim Plouffe
Jeffrey N. German
John P. Shusted

Kathleen M. Carson
Kevin R. McNulty
Linda Porr Sweeney
Gary H. Hunter
Frank A. Gerolamo, III
Milan K. Mrkobrad
Thomas M. Going
Vincent J. Di Stefano, Jr.
Jack T. Ribble, Jr.
Kimberly J. Keiser
Bernard E. Jude Quinn
Gerald C. Montella
Lisa Beth Zucker
Shelby L. Mattioli
Daniel J. Divis
D. Selaine Belver
Christine L. Davis
Daniel L. Grill

(See Next Column)

Marta I. Sierra-Epperson
Paul G. Kirk
Aileen R. Thompson
Otis V. Maynard
Gregory S. Capps

For full biographical listings, see the Martindale-Hubbell Law Directory

GOLDFEIN & JOSEPH, A PROFESSIONAL CORPORATION (AV)

17th Floor, Packard Building, 111 South 15th Street, 19102-2695
Telephone: 215-977-9800
Fax: 215-988-0062
Princeton, New Jersey Office: Princeton Metro Center, Suite 115, 5 Vaughn Drive.
Telephone: 609-520-0400.
Fax: 609-520-1450.
Wilmington, Delaware Office: PNC Bank Center, Suite 1212, P.O. Box 2206, 222 Delaware Avenue.
Telephone: 302-656-3301.
Fax: 302-656-0643.

Edward B. Joseph
Fredric L. Goldfein
E. Chandler Hosmer, III
Ellen Brown Furman
Leslie Anne Miller
David C. Weinberg
James Patrick Hadden
Bernard L. Levinthal
Gary H. Kaplan (Resident, Wilmington, Delaware Office)
Roseann Lynn Brenner
Elissa J. Kahn

John A. Turlik
Susan Burton Stadtmauer
David M. Katzenstein (Resident, Princeton, New Jersey Office)
Scott I. Fegley
William J. Weiss
Michael A. Billotti (Not admitted in PA; Resident, Princeton, New Jersey Office)
Lawrence E. Currier
Robert P. Coleman
Robert T. Connor
Ann B. Cairns
Frederick A. Kiegel
Janet E. Golup
Ted Martin Berg (Resident, Wilmington, Delaware Office)

OF COUNSEL

Charles B. Burr, II

For full biographical listings, see the Martindale-Hubbell Law Directory

KELLEY, JASONS, MCGUIRE & SPINELLI (AV)

Suite 1300, 1234 Market Street, 19107-3713
Telephone: 215-854-0658
Fax: 215-854-8434
Cherry Hill, New Jersey Office: 1230 Brace Road, 08034.
Telephone: 609-429-8956.
Wilmington, Delaware Office: 1220 Market Building, P.O. Box 194, 19899.
Telephone: 302-652-8560.
Fax: 302-652-8405.

MEMBERS OF FIRM

John Patrick Kelley
Catherine N. Jasons
Joseph W. McGuire
Armand J. Della Porta, Jr.
Christopher N. Santoro
Robert N. Spinelli
Thomas P. Hanna
Thomas J. Johanson
Michael L. Turner

ASSOCIATES

Kelly J. Sasso (Resident, Wilmington, Delaware Office)
Richard L. Walker, II
Bernard E. Kueny, III
Timothy McGowan
Neal C. Glenn

OF COUNSEL

Joseph P. Green
Matthew D. Blum, M.D.
W. Matthew Reber

For full biographical listings, see the Martindale-Hubbell Law Directory

KENT & MCBRIDE, P.C. (AV)

Two Logan Square, Suite 600 18th and Arch Streets, 19103
Telephone: 215-568-1800
Fax: 215-568-1830
Audubon, New Jersey Office: 201 South Whitehorse Pike.
Telephone: 609-547-4474.
Fax: 609-547-0741.

John F. Kent
Denis P. McBride

Martin A. Durkin, Jr.
Kevin G. Dronson
Anne Manero
Jay D. Branderbit
Joseph Andrew Sellitti
John P. Shea
Laura R. Shmerler
Kimberly S. Gannon

For full biographical listings, see the Martindale-Hubbell Law Directory

KITTREDGE, DONLEY, ELSON, FULLEM & EMBICK (AV)

Fifth Floor, The Bank Building, 421 Chestnut Street, 19106
Telephone: 215-829-9900
Fax: 215-829-9888

MEMBERS OF FIRM

Patrick W. Kittredge
Joseph M. Donley
Barry R. Elson
Joseph W. Fullem, Jr.
John R. Embick

(See Next Column)

KITTREDGE, DONLEY, ELSON, FULLEM & EMBICK, *Philadelphia—Continued*

ASSOCIATES

Regina M. Harbaugh
Glenn E. Davis
Betsy F. Sternthal
Michael S. Soulé
Gary M. Marek
Patricia Powers
Daniel J. Maher
Susanne L. Longenhagen
Michael K. Smith
Richard J. Sestak

For full biographical listings, see the Martindale-Hubbell Law Directory

LAVIN, COLEMAN, FINARELLI & GRAY (AV)

12th Floor Penn Mutual Tower, 510 Walnut Street, 19106
Telephone: 215-627-0303
Fax: 215-627-2551
Mount Laurel, New Jersey Office: 10000 Midlantic Drive, Suite 300 West.
Telephone: 609-778-5544.
Fax: 609-778-3383.
New York, New York Office: 780 Third Avenue, Suite 1401.
Telephone: 212-319-6898.
Fax: 212-319-6932.

George J. Lavin, Jr.
Thomas Finarelli
William V. Coleman
Francis F. Quinn
Joseph E. O'Neil
Francis P. Burns, III
William J. Ricci
Edward A. Gray
Basil A. DiSipio
Wayne A. Graver
James Weiner
Frederick W. Rom
Gerard Cedrone
Robert Szwajkos
Mary Grace Maley
Christine O. Boyd
Michael D. Brophy
Joseph A. McGinley
Polly N. Phillippi

John J. Bateman
Stephen M. Beaudoin
Ronald W. Boak
Denise L. Carroll
Henry Michael Clinton
John J. Coughlin, IV
John Kieran Daly (Not admitted in PA)
Michael T. Droogan, Jr.
Joseph F. Dunne (Not admitted in PA)
B. Lynn Enderby
Louis Giansante
Francis J. Grey, Jr.
Mitchell Gruner
Robert J. Hafner
Eugene Hamill
Sandra Hourahan
Ernest H. Hutchinson, III
Regina A. Jones
Bridget A. Kelleher
Michael P. Kinkopf
Steven R. Kramer (Not admitted in PA)
Ellen Hatch Kueny
George J. Lavin, III
Peter W. Lee
Robert J. Martin
Karen Howard Matthews
William C. Mead, Jr.
Stephen E. Moore
Jane Elizabeth Nagle
Peter M. Newman
John J. O'Donnell
LeaNora J. Patterson
Jo E. Peifer
Michael J. Quinn
Mary D. Rafferty
Susan Ellyn Satkowski
William E. Staas, III
Fiona J. Van Dych
Thomas J. Wagner
Anne E. Walters
Maribeth Bohs Wechsler
Richard B. Wickersham, Jr.

For full biographical listings, see the Martindale-Hubbell Law Directory

MANTA AND WELGE (AV)

A Partnership of Professional Corporations
One Commerce Square, 37th Floor, 2005 Market Street, 19103
Telephone: 215-851-6600
Telecopy: 215-851-6644
Allentown, Pennsylvania Office: Suite 115 Commerce Plaza, 5050 Tilghman Street.
Telephone: 215-395-7499.
Fax: 215-398-7878.
Princeton, New Jersey Office: 101 Carnegie Center, Suite 215. P.O. Box 5306.
Telephone: 609-452-8833.
Fax: 609-452-9109.
Cherry Hill, New Jersey Office: Suite 600, 1040 North King Highway.
Telephone: 609-795-7611.
Fax: 609-795-7612.

MEMBERS OF FIRM

Joseph G. Manta
Mark A. Welge
William R. Hourican
Albert L. Piccerilli
John C. Sullivan
Joel Schneider
Joseph M. Cincotta
James V. Bielunas
Richard S. Mannella
Joanne M. Walker
Francis McGill Hadden
Walter A. Stewart

OF COUNSEL

Albert J. Bartosic

(See Next Column)

Peter F. Rosenthal
Susan Simpson-Brown
Gregory S. Thomas
Andrea L. Smith
Anton G. Marzano
Margaret E. Wenke
Wendy F. Tucker
Jacqueline Borock
David G. C. Arnold
Karen C. Buck
Laurie A. Carroll
Mark J. Manta
David S. Florig
Stephen F. Brock
Geoffrey J. Alexander
Wendy R. S. O'Connor
Kathleen K. Kerns
Fernando Santiago
Peter L. Frattarelli
Holly C. Dobrosky

For full biographical listings, see the Martindale-Hubbell Law Directory

MARGOLIS, EDELSTEIN & SCHERLIS (AV)

The Curtis Center, Fourth Floor, One Independence Square West, 19106-3304
Telephone: 215-922-1100
FAX: 215-922-1772
Telex: 62021004
Associated Law Firm: Slimm & Goldberg, 216 Haddon Avenue, Suite 750, Westmont, New Jersey, 08108-2886.
Telephone: 609-858-7200.
FAX: 609-858-1017.

MEMBERS OF FIRM

Alan Wm. Margolis
Edward L. Edelstein
Edwin L. Scherlis
Joseph S. Bekelja
Joseph Goldberg
John L. Slimm (Not admitted in PA)
Leonard S. Lipson
Michael P. McKenna
Mitchell S. Pinsly
Carl Anthony Maio
Gordon Gelfond
Donald M. Davis
Melvin R. Shuster
Christopher J. Pakuris
Marshall A. Haislup, III
Bruce E. Barrett (Resident, Westmont, New Jersey Office)
J. Vincent Roche
Gary B. Cutler
Michael D. Eiss
Mark N. Cohen
Robert M. Kaplan (Not admitted in PA)
Andrew J. Gallogly
Marc B. Zingarini
William B. Hildebrand
Richard J. Margolis
Glenn A. Ricketti
Michael J. Cawley
Anne E. Pedersen
Kenneth J. Sylvester (Resident, Westmont, New Jersey Office)
Colleen M. Ready (Resident, Westmont, New Jersey Office)
Richard T. Smith (Resident, Westmont, New Jersey Office)
H. Marc Tepper
James B. Dougherty, Jr.
Carol Ann Murphy
Janis L. Wilson

Nancy H. Resnick
Eric J. Daniel (Resident, Westmont, New Jersey Office)
R. Barry Strosnider (Resident, Westmont, New Jersey Office)
Elit R. Felix, II
James M. Prahler
Michael G. Conroy
David F. Luvara (Resident, Westmont, New Jersey Office)
James F. Wiley, III
Lawrence J. Bunis
Kevin R. Dochney (Resident, Westmont, New Jersey Office)
Peter D. Bludman
Lisa B. Flickstein
Barbara A. Thomas
Hiliary L. Remick
Mary C. Cunnane
Deborah L. Doyle
Sandra R. Craig
Debra S. Goodman
Timothy J. McCuen
Marilyn A. Della Badia
Dawn Dezii (Resident, Westmont, New Jersey Office)
John C. Farrell
Lila Wynne Williams (Resident, Westmont, New Jersey Office)
Emily H. Armstrong (Not admitted in PA; Resident, Westmont, New Jersey Office)
Donald Caruthers III (Resident, Westmont, New Jersey Office)
Jean M. Hadley
Mark A. Minicozzi
Robert D. MacMahon
Hilary Suzanne Cornell
Marie Sambor Reilly
Jill Innamorato
Michael L. Simonini (Resident, Westmont, New Jersey Office)
Peter S. Cuddihy (Resident, Westmont, New Jersey Office)
Elizabeth Horneff
Robert D. Shapiro
Sandhya M. Feltes
Kevin S. Riechelson
Jennifer A. Mullen (Resident, Westmont, New Jersey Office)
Tracy A. Tefankjian
Frank A. LaSalvia (Resident, Westmont, New Jersey Office)
James A. Tamburro (Resident, Westmont, New Jersey Office)
Laurie Harrold Rizzo (Resident, Westmont, New Jersey Office)
Stuart L. Berman
John D. Pallante
Timothy E. Games
Frank A. DiGiacomo (Resident, Westmont, New Jersey Office)
Frederic Roller
Vincent A. Vietti
Jill A. Maslynsky
Johanna E. Markind
James P. Paoli (Resident, Westmont, New Jersey Office)
Diana Brilliant
Thomas P. Donnelly
Andrea M. Jenkins
Karen E. Model
Dawn S. Osman
Scott I. Feldman
Stephen P. Yuhas (Resident, Westmont, New Jersey Office)

COUNSEL TO THE FIRM

Nathan L. Edelstein

(See Next Column)

MARGOLIS, EDELSTEIN & SCHERLIS—*Continued*

OF COUNSEL

Michael A. Orlando (Not admitted in PA; Resident, Westmont, New Jersey Office)

For full biographical listings, see the Martindale-Hubbell Law Directory

MARKS, O'NEILL, REILLY & O'BRIEN, P.C. (AV)

1880 John F. Kennedy Boulevard Suite 1200, 19103
Telephone: 215-564-6688
Fax: 215-564-2526
Norristown, Pennsylvania Office: 411 Cherry Street.
Telephone: 215-277-7601.
Westmont, New Jersey Office: 216 Haddon Avenue, Suite 403.
Telephone: 609-858-6110.
Fax: 609-858-3687.
Wilmington, Delaware Office: 1326 King Street.
Telephone: 302-652-0800.
Fax: 302-656-1993.

Jerome E. Marks
Joseph M. O'Neill
Vincent F. Reilly
Kevin J. O'Brien (Resident, Westmont, New Jersey Office)
Dawn R. Courtney
Maureen Murray-O'Toole
Lisa M. Bellino
Sean Xavier Kelly
Christine G. Boyle
William A. Fynes, III
Johanna C. Pauciulo
Arnold A. Foley
Dennis P. Herbert (Resident, Westmont, New Jersey Office)
William J. Smith
Thomas D. Smith
Gino P. Mecoli
Eva M. Candeloro (Resident, Wilmington, Delaware and Westmont, New Jersey Offices)
Jennifer Ann Lawley
Jeffrey S. Friedman
Robert E. McCann
Patrick C. Lamb
Edward F. Curtin
Richard C. Kelly
Michael J. Diamond
Steven P. Cholden
Nancy P. Brennan

For full biographical listings, see the Martindale-Hubbell Law Directory

McKISSOCK & HOFFMAN, P.C. (AV)

1700 Market Street, Suite 3000, 19103
Telephone: 215-246-2100
Fax: 215-246-2144
Mount Holly, New Jersey Office: 211 High Street.
Telephone: 609-267-1006.
Doylestown, Pennsylvania Office: 77 North Broad Street, Second Floor.
Telephone: 215-345-4501.
Harrisburg, Pennsylvania Office: 127 State Street.
Telephone: 717-234-0103.

J. Bruce McKissock
Peter J. Hoffman
Richard L. McMonigle
Jill Baratz Clarke
Marybeth Stanton Christiansen
Catherine Hill Kunda
Bryant Craig Black (Resident, Harrisburg, Office)
John M. Willis
John J. McGrath
Debra Schwaderer Dunne
Donald J. Brooks, Jr.
William J. Mundy
Elizabeth E. Davies
Christopher Thomson
Kathleen M. Kenna
K. Reed Haywood
Sara J. Thomson
Maureen P. Fitzgerald
Veronica E. Noonan
Kathleen M. Sholette
Patricia D. Shippee

For full biographical listings, see the Martindale-Hubbell Law Directory

PALMER BIEZUP & HENDERSON (AV)

Suite 956 Public Ledger Building, 620 Chestnut Street Independence Mall West, 19106-3409
Telephone: 215-625-9900
Cable Address: "Palmbee" Phila
Telex: ITT: 476-1102
FAX: 215-625-0185
New York, New York Office: 53 Wall Street, 10005.
Telephone: 212-406-1855.
Fax: 215-625-0185.
Telex: ITT 476-1102.
Wilmington, Delaware Office: 1223 Foulk Road, 19803.
Telephone: 302-594-0895.
Fax: 215-625-0185.
Telex: ITT 476-1102.
Camden, New Jersey Office: 211 North 5th Street. 08102-1203.
Telephone: 609-428-7717.
Fax: 215-625-0185.
Telex: ITT 476-1102.

MEMBERS OF FIRM

Richard W. Palmer
J. Welles Henderson
Raul Betancourt
Alfred J. Kuffler
Michael B. McCauley
Stephen M. Calder
Richard Q. Whelan
Timothy J. Abeel
Frank P. De Giulio
Kevin G. O'Donovan

(See Next Column)

David P. Thompson
Gary Francis Seitz
Richard C. Mason
Richard S. Tweedie
Peter J. Williams
Betsy A. Stone
Jon Michael Dumont
Lawrence D. Jackson
James J. Musial
Kevin Haney
Thomas P. Mundy
Paul D. Rowe, Jr.

COUNSEL

Raymond T. Letulle
H. Coleman Switkay

For full biographical listings, see the Martindale-Hubbell Law Directory

SILVERMAN COOPERSMITH HILLMAN & FRIMMER, A PROFESSIONAL CORPORATION (AV)

Two Penn Center Plaza, Suite 910, 19102
Telephone: 215-569-0000
Fax: 215-636-3999
Haddon Heights, New Jersey Office: 116 White Horse Pike.
Telephone: 609-546-4662.
Fax: 215-636-3999.

Lawrence M. Silverman
Jonathan S. Ziss

Jill Fisher
Jeffrey A. Krawitz
Dean E. Weisgold
Marna Skaletsky Friedman

Representative Clients: Boat Owners Association of the United States; Central National Insurance Company of Omaha; Delta Air Lines, Inc.; Empire Fire and Marine Insurance Co.; Protective National Insurance Co.; John Deere Transporation Services; Princeton Insurance Co.; Rider Insurance Co.; U.S. Aviation Underwriters, Inc.; Seaboard Underwriters.

For full biographical listings, see the Martindale-Hubbell Law Directory

SWARTZ, CAMPBELL & DETWEILER (AV)

1600 Land Title Building, 100 South Broad Street, 19110
Telephone: 215-564-5190
Telefax: 215-299-4301
Media, Pennsylvania Office: One Veterans Square Suite 106.
Telephone: 610-566-9222.
Fax: 610-892-0636.
Harrisburg, Pennsylvania Office: 2040 Linglestown Road, Suite 107.
Telephone: 717-540-8671.
Fax: 717-540-5481.
Allentown, Pennsylvania Office: Suite 230, 5100 Tilghman Street.
Telephone: 610-395-5903.
Fax: 610-395-7097.
Wilmington, Delaware Office: 300 Delaware Avenue, Suite 818, P.O. Box 330.
Telephone: 302-656-5935.
Fax: 302-656-1434.
Mount Laurel, New Jersey Office: Bloom Court, Suite 314. 1300 Route 73.
Telephone: 609-727-4777.
Fax: 609-727-0464.

C. Donald Swartz (1893-1976)
William T. Campbell (1896-1975)
Lynn L. Detweiler (1906-1989)

PARTNERS

Richard D. Harburg
Curtis P. Cheyney, III
Richard L. Goerwitz, Jr.
Joseph T. Bodell, Jr.
Charles S. Katz, Jr.
Joseph F. Van Horn, Jr.
Ronald F. Bové
Martin J. Fallon, Jr.
Frederick C. Fletcher, II
Stephen J. Harlen
G. Daniel Bruch, Jr.
James C. Haggerty
John A. Wetzel
John T. Carroll, III
Kevin Canavan
Walter L. McDonough
Robert B. Mulhern, Jr.
J. Eric Stedje
Charles L. Powell
Bruce W. McCullough (Resident Partner, Wilmington, Delaware Office)
David A. Pennington (Resident Partner, Allentown, Pennsylvania Office)
Joseph A. Venuti, Jr. (Resident Partner, Mount Laurel, New Jersey Office)
Sue Ellen Albert

ASSOCIATES

Gregory D. Geiss (Resident Associate, Harrisburg, Pennsylvania Office)
Michael T. Dolan
William T. Salzer
Jane Ann Lombard
William M. Bendon
Vincent J. Iozzi
Sharolyn L. Murphy
Andrew J. Reilly (Resident Associate, Media, Pennsylvania, Office)
Jeffrey B. McCarron
Louis A. Bové
Thomas More Marrone
Andrew K. Touchstone
Michael A. Cognetti (Resident, Media, Pennsylvania Office)
Daniel L. McKenty (Resident Associate, Wilmington, Delaware Office)
Paul A. Pauciulo
John J. Muldowney
Neil T. Dombrowski
Melissa Lang
Scott J. Tredwell
James D. Cella
Keith E. Donovan (Resident Associate, Wilmington, Delaware Office)

(See Next Column)

SWARTZ, CAMPBELL & DETWEILER, *Philadelphia—Continued*

ASSOCIATES (Continued)

Sheilah Anne Tone (Resident Associate, Allentown, Pennsylvania Office)
Matthew S. Wynn
Alfred J. Carlson
Nataly A. Harker
John P. Dogum
Jeffrey L. Goodman
Catherine B. Herrmann
Amy Lynne Penfil
Debra A. Matherne (Resident Associate, Harrisburg, Pennsylvania Office)
Stephen A. Seach
Susan F. Evans
Thomas E. Panzer
Sharon Simkiss Merhige
Nancy M. Harris (Resident, Allentown, Pennsylvania Office)
Robert M. Smolen (Resident, Mount Laurel, New Jersey Office)
Joseph J. Centeno

For full biographical listings, see the Martindale-Hubbell Law Directory

WILBRAHAM, LAWLER & BUBA, A PROFESSIONAL CORPORATION (AV)

The Curtis Center, Suite 450, 601 Walnut Street, 19106-3304
Telephone: 215-923-0133
Fax: 215-923-0471
Haddonfield, New Jersey Office: 24 Kings Highway West. 08033-2122.
Telephone: 609-795-4422.
Fax: 609-795-4699.

Edward J. Wilbraham
Robert B. Lawler
Barbara J. Buba
Mark A. Stevens
Michael J. Block
Kim Hollaender

Mary S. Cook
Pamela B. Hinton
Garry B. Hutchinson
James W. McCartney

For full biographical listings, see the Martindale-Hubbell Law Directory

ZARWIN, BAUM, DEVITO, KAPLAN & O'DONNELL, P.C. (AV)

Suite 700 Four Penn Center Plaza, 1616 John F. Kennedy Boulevard, 19103-2588
Telephone: 215-569-2800
Fax: 215-569-1606
Audubon, New Jersey Office: 510 White Horse Pike.
Telephone: 609-547-7555.

Norman P. Zarwin
E. Harris Baum
John R. O'Donnell
Mitchell S. Kaplan
Gary A. DeVito
Theodore M. Schaer
Lionel A. Prince

Lisa B. Wershaw
Gary Alan Zlotnick
Joseph M. Toddy
Kenneth J. Fleisher
Jane Griffin Malaspina
Edward J. McKenna
Adam M. Soll
Ronald N. Lebovits
Robert H. Prince

For full biographical listings, see the Martindale-Hubbell Law Directory

*PITTSBURGH,** Allegheny Co.

ANSTANDIG, LEVICOFF & MCDYER, A PROFESSIONAL CORPORATION (AV)

600 Gulf Tower, 15219
Telephone: 412-765-3700
Fax: 412-765-3730
Beckley, West Virgina Office: Brown, Levicoff & McDyer. 311 Prince Street. P.O. Drawer M.
Telephone: 304-253-3700.

Louis Anstandig
Avrum Levicoff
Daniel P. McDyer
Timothy J. Burdette
Edward A. Yurcon
James Michael Brown (Resident, Beckley, West Virginia Office)
Alan T. Silko

Paul G. Mayer, Jr.
Philip M.P. Buttenfield
Stephen J. Poljak
Eileen Anstandig Ziemke
William M. Adams
Elizabeth E. Deemer
Bryan J. Smith
Tracey A. Jordan
Jane E. Harkins (Resident, Beckley, West Virginia Office)
Mark A. Serge
James D. Stacy (Resident, Beckley, West Virginia Office)
R. Bruce Carlson

For full biographical listings, see the Martindale-Hubbell Law Directory

BUCHANAN INGERSOLL, PROFESSIONAL CORPORATION (AV)

5800 USX Tower, 600 Grant Street, 15219
Telephone: 412-562-8800
Telecopier: 412-562-1041
Philadelphia, Pennsylvania Office: Two Logan Square, Twelfth Floor, 18th & Arch Streets.
Telephone: 215-665-8700.
Harrisburg, Pennsylvania Office: Vartan Parc, 30 North Third Street.
Telephone: 717-237-4800.

(See Next Column)

Tampa, Florida Office: 101 East Kennedy Boulevard, Suite 1030.
Telephone: 813-222-8180.
North Miami Beach, Florida Office: 19495 Biscayne Boulevard.
Telephone: 305-933-5600.
Lexington, Kentucky Office: 1210 Vine Center Office Tower, 333 West Vine Street.
Telephone: 606-225-5333.
Princeton, New Jersey Office: Buchanan Ingersoll, A Partnership, College Centre, 500 College Road East.
Telephone: 609-452-2666.

Samuel W. Braver
Ronald W. Crouch
Deborah A. Little

John M. Cerilli

For Complete List of Firm Personnel, See General Section

For full biographical listings, see the Martindale-Hubbell Law Directory

DAVIES MCFARLAND & CARROLL, P.C. (AV)

One Gateway Center, Tenth Floor, 15222
Telephone: 412-281-0737

Ralph A. Davies
Gregg P. Otto
Edward A. McFarland
Daniel P. Carroll
William D. Geiger
Francis Garger
Lynn E. Bell
David S. Smith
James M. Poerio

C. Robert Keenan, III
David E. Lamm
Donna M. Lowman
Christopher Pierson
William S. Evans
Keith M. Hoffman
Lisa M. Montarti
Robert P. Walter

Representative Clients: CM Insurance Compnay, Inc.; Carl Watten & Company, Cincinnati Insurance Co.; Continental Insurance Co.; GAB Business Services, Inc.; John Deere Insurance Co.; Motorists Insurance Cos.; The Travelers.

For full biographical listings, see the Martindale-Hubbell Law Directory

DICKIE, MCCAMEY & CHILCOTE, A PROFESSIONAL CORPORATION (AV)

Suite 400, Two PPG Place, 15222-5402
Telephone: 412-281-7272
Fax: 412-392-5367
Wheeling, West Virginia Office: Suite 2002, 1233 Main Street, 26003-2839.
Telephone: 304-233-1022.
Facsimile: 304-233-1026.

Richard D. Klaber
Theodore O. Struk
Wilbur McCoy Otto
Richard S. Dorfzaun
M. Richard Dunlap
Charles W. Kenrick
John Edward Wall
James R. Miller
Paul W. Roman, Jr.
Joseph S. D. Christof, II
J. Lawson Johnston
Stephen R. Mlinac
David M. Neuhart
Robert J. Marino
Stephen M. Houghton
Frank M. Gianola
Leonard A. Costa, Jr.
Kenneth S. Mroz
Ingrid Medzius Lundberg
Jeffrey T. Wiley
Richard C. Polley
Thomas M. Fallert
Gloria N. Fuehrer
Robert G. Del Greco, Jr.
Edmund L. Olszewski, Jr.
Dorothy A. Davis
Richard J. Federowicz
L. John Argento
David J. Obermeier
Peter T. Stinson
Ray F. Middleman
George Monroe Schumann

Eugene G. Berry
Anthony J. Williott
George P. Kachulis
John T. Pion
Hunter A. McGeary, Jr.
Gregory A. Gross
Joseph L. Luvara
Andrew G. Kimball
W. Alan Torrance, Jr.
Howard A. Chajson
David S. Bloom
M. Suzanne McCartney
Alyson J. Kirleis
S. Jane Anderson
Paul S. Mazeski
Anthony J. Rash
Eugene A. Giotto
Vincent Scaglione, Jr.
James M. Girman
Maureen Kowalski
Michael F. Nerone
Craig M. Lee
Christopher T. Lee
Ann Michailenko Wilson
Steven W. Zoffer
Robert G. Voinchet, Jr.
Jennifer M. Kirschler
John N. Cox
Edward A. Miller
Nathan D. Bailey

OF COUNSEL

Herman C. Kimpel

For Complete List of Firm Personnel, See General Section

For full biographical listings, see the Martindale-Hubbell Law Directory

Pittsburgh—Continued

FELDSTEIN GRINBERG STEIN & MCKEE, A PROFESSIONAL CORPORATION (AV)

428 Boulevard of the Allies, 15219
Telephone: 412-471-0677
Fax: 412-263-6129
Elizabeth, Pennsylvania Office: 400 Second Street.
Telephone: 412-384-6111.
Wexford, Pennsylvania Office: 12300 Perry Highway.
Telephone: 412-935-5540.

Jay H. Feldstein
Gary M. Lang
Stanley M. Stein
James R. Hankle

Joseph L. Orszulak, II

For full biographical listings, see the Martindale-Hubbell Law Directory

GACA, MATIS & HAMILTON, A PROFESSIONAL CORPORATION (AV)

300 Four PPG Place, 15222-5404
Telephone: 412-338-4750
Fax: 412-338-4742

Giles J. Gaca
Thomas P. McGinnis
Thomas A. Matis
Bernard R. Rizza
Mark R. Hamilton
Jeffrey A. Ramaley
John W. Jordan, IV
Stephen J. Dalesio
Alan S. Baum
John Timothy Hinton, Jr.
Shawn Lynne Reed

LEGAL SUPPORT PERSONNEL

PARALEGALS

Tina M. Shanafelt
Jill M. Peterson

For full biographical listings, see the Martindale-Hubbell Law Directory

GAITENS, TUCCERI & NICHOLAS, A PROFESSIONAL CORPORATION (AV)

519 Court Place, 15219
Telephone: 412-391-6920
Fax: 412-391-1189

Larry P. Gaitens
Vincent A. Tucceri
Romel L. Nicholas

Reference: Pittsburgh National Bank.

For Complete List of Firm Personnel, See General Section

For full biographical listings, see the Martindale-Hubbell Law Directory

WILLIAM W. GUTHRIE & ASSOCIATES A PROFESSIONAL CORPORATION (AV)

416 Frick Building, 437 Grant Street, 15219
Telephone: 412-562-0556
Fax: 412-562-5920

William W. Guthrie

Reference: Pittsburgh National Bank (Potter Office).

For full biographical listings, see the Martindale-Hubbell Law Directory

HEINTZMAN, WARREN & WISE (AV)

The 35th Floor, Gulf Tower, 707 Grant Street, 15219
Telephone: 412-394-7810
Fax: 412-263-5222

MEMBERS OF FIRM

Michael D. Heintzman
Charles S. Warren
Roger L. Wise

ASSOCIATES

Jeanine L. Fonner
Kenneth F. Klanica
Joseph R. Schaper
Diane K. Wohlfarth

For full biographical listings, see the Martindale-Hubbell Law Directory

ISRAEL AND WOOD, P.C. (AV)

Suite 501, Grant Building, 15219
Telephone: 412-391-1114
Fax: 412-391-3017

James A. Wood
Ronald M. Puntil, Jr.
James F. Israel
David J. Singley

Joseph A. Ramser
Christopher S. O'Malley
Marianne C. Plant
James A. McGovern
Christopher A. Beck

For full biographical listings, see the Martindale-Hubbell Law Directory

KIGER MESSER & ALPERN (AV)

1404 Grant Building, 15219
Telephone: 412-281-7200
Fax: 412-765-0440

MEMBERS OF FIRM

Jerome W. Kiger
Howard F. Messer
Charles H. Alpern

ASSOCIATE

Alice Warner Shumlas

For Complete List of Firm Personnel, See General Section

For full biographical listings, see the Martindale-Hubbell Law Directory

MARCUS & SHAPIRA (AV)

35th Floor, One Oxford Centre, 301 Grant Street, 15219-6401
Telephone: 412-471-3490
Telecopier: 412-391-8758

MEMBERS OF FIRM

Bernard D. Marcus
Susan Gromis Flynn
Daniel H. Shapira
Darlene M. Nowak
George P. Slesinger
Glenn M. Olcerst
Robert L. Allman, II
Elly Heller-Toig
Estelle F. Comay
Sylvester A. Beozzo

OF COUNSEL

John M. Burkoff

SPECIAL COUNSEL

Jane Campbell Moriarty

ASSOCIATES

Scott D. Livingston
Lori E. McMaster
Robert M. Barnes
Melody A. Pollock
Stephen S. Zubrow
James F. Rosenberg
David B. Rodes
Amy M. Gottlieb

For full biographical listings, see the Martindale-Hubbell Law Directory

RICHARD J. MILLS & ASSOCIATES (AV)

200 Benedum Trees Building, 223 Fourth Avenue, 15222-1713
Telephone: 412-471-2442
Fax: 412-471-2456

Richard J. Mills

Austin P. Henry
Dale S. Douglas

For full biographical listings, see the Martindale-Hubbell Law Directory

MOLLICA, MURRAY & HOGUE (AV)

3400 Gulf Tower, 15219
Telephone: 412-263-5200
Fax: 412-263-5220

MEMBERS OF FIRM

James A. Mollica, Jr.
Timothy Murray
Dr. John E. Murray, Jr.
Sandra L. Lannis
Jon Geoffrey Hogue
William J. Moorhead, Jr.
Blaine A. Lucas
Jeannine A. Schuster
Cathy Ann Chromulak
Steven M. Nolan
Benjamin J. Viloski

For full biographical listings, see the Martindale-Hubbell Law Directory

PIETRAGALLO, BOSICK & GORDON (AV)

The Thirty-Eighth Floor, One Oxford Centre, 15219
Telephone: 412-263-2000
Facsimile: 412-261-5295

MEMBERS OF FIRM

William Pietragallo, II
Francis E. Pipak, Jr.
Joseph J. Bosick
LuAnn Haley
Mark Gordon
Paul K. Vey
John E. Hall
Nora Barry Fischer
Spencer D. Hirshberg
Thomas J. Sweeney, Jr.
Robert J. Behling
Daniel D. Harshman
Lawrence J. Baldasare
Robert E. Dapper, Jr.
William S. Smith
David H. Dille

ASSOCIATES

Robert H. Gustine
Vincent A Coppola
Harry J. Klucher
Clem C. Trischler, Jr.
Robert R. Leight
Anthony G. Sanchez
Christopher L. Wildfire
Kenneth T. Newman
Heather S. Heidelbaugh
C. Peter Hitson
Eric K. Falk
Raymond G. McLaughlin
James G. Orie
David Paul Franklin
Stacey F. Vernallis
Brian S. Kane
Mark F. Haak
Linda M. Gillen
Pamela G. Cochenour
Robert J. Colville
William W. Schrimpf, Sr.
Brian K. Parker
Michael P. Sosso
Sean B. Epstein
Lisa P. McQuarrie

(See Next Column)

PIETRAGALLO, BOSICK & GORDON, *Pittsburgh—Continued*

COUNSEL

Harold Gondelman
Alfred S. Pelaez

For full biographical listings, see the Martindale-Hubbell Law Directory

PLOWMAN, SPIEGEL & LEWIS, P.C. (AV)

Grant Building, Suite 925, 15219-2201
Telephone: 412-471-8521
Fax: 412-471-4481

Jack W. Plowman
John L. Spiegel
Frank J. Kernan
Clifford L. Tuttle, Jr.
Kenneth W. Lee

Marshall J. Conn
David Raves

Reference: Pittsburgh National Bank.

For Complete List of Firm Personnel, See General Section

For full biographical listings, see the Martindale-Hubbell Law Directory

ROSENBERG, KIRSHNER P.A. (AV)

1500 Grant Building, 15219-2203
Telephone: 412-281-4256
Telefax: 412-642-2380
Robinson Township, Pennsylvania Office: 5996-F Steubenville Pike, 15136.
Telephone: 412-788-0600.
Fax: 412-788-1503.
Imperial, Pennsylvania Office: 223 Main Street, 15126.
Telephone: 412-695-7888.
North Palm Beach, Florida Office: 4th Floor, 712 U.S. Highway One, 33408.
Telephone: 407-844-6206.
Telefax: 407-842-4104.

H. N. Rosenberg
Charles Kirshner
William R. Haushalter
Arthur L. Bloom
Miles A. Kirshner

Tony D. Skees

Representative Clients: Erie Insurance Co.; Keene Corporation; Liberty Mutual Insurance Co.; Kemper Insurance; Union Carbide; McDonald's Corp.; General Electric Capital Corp.; Equitable Lomas Leasing Corp.; Hyatt Legal Services; Rite Aid Corp.

For Complete List of Firm Personnel, See General Section

For full biographical listings, see the Martindale-Hubbell Law Directory

THOMPSON CALKINS & SUTTER (AV)

1412 Frick Building, 15219
Telephone: 412-261-4050
Fax: 412-261-2280

MEMBERS OF FIRM

George H. Thompson
Scott R. Calkins
Paul E. Sutter
Orlando R. Sodini
Toni J. Minner

ASSOCIATES

Hilary Sue Zakowitz
Kimberly McDaniel
Ann M. Coholan
Phyllis T. Procopio

For full biographical listings, see the Martindale-Hubbell Law Directory

THORP, REED & ARMSTRONG (AV)

One Riverfront Center, 15222
Telephone: 412-394-7711
Fax: 412-394-2555

MEMBERS OF FIRM

Michael R. Bucci, Jr.
G. Daniel Carney
Scott E. Henderson
C. James Zeszutek

ASSOCIATE

Kimberly A. Brown

For Complete List of Firm Personnel, See General Section

For full biographical listings, see the Martindale-Hubbell Law Directory

WILLMAN & ARNOLD (AV)

Suite 705-708, 700 McKnight Park Drive, 15237
Telephone: 412-366-3333
Fax: 412-366-3462

MEMBERS OF FIRM

Gene E. Arnold
R. Kenneth Willman
James W. Young, Jr.
Ruth A. Antinone
Concetta A. Silvaggio

(See Next Column)

ASSOCIATES

J. Craig Brungo
John H. Kooser, III
Glenn A. Huetter, Jr.
Jacquelyn A. Knupp
Joseph D. Silvaggio
Keith E. Whitson

For full biographical listings, see the Martindale-Hubbell Law Directory

ZIMMER KUNZ, PROFESSIONAL CORPORATION (AV)

3300 USX Tower, 600 Grant Street, 15219
Telephone: 412-281-8000
Fax: 412-281-1765

Harry J. Zimmer
Thomas A. Lazaroff
John E. Kunz
Andrew J. Banyas, III
Raymond H. Conaway
Fred C. Trenor, II
George N. Stewart
Joni M. Mangino
Joseph W. Selep
Raymond J. Conlon
Edward K. Dixon

OF COUNSEL

John W. Thomas

Nancy DeCarlo Fabi
Dara A. DeCourcy
Alexander P. Bicket
John W. Zotter
Daniel E. Krauth
George R. Farneth, II
Anthony Carone

For Complete List of Firm Personnel, See General Section

For full biographical listings, see the Martindale-Hubbell Law Directory

*SCRANTON,** Lackawanna Co.

LENAHAN & DEMPSEY, A PROFESSIONAL CORPORATION (AV)

116 North Washington Avenue, 18503-0234
Telephone: 717-346-2097
Fax: 717-346-1174
Mailing Address: P.O. Box 234, Scranton, Pennsylvania, 18501-0234

John R. Lenahan, Sr.
William J. Dempsey
John R. Lenahan, Jr.
Joseph P. Lenahan
Kathleen A. Lenahan
David E. Heisler
Timothy G. Lenahan
Matthew D. Dempsey

Marianne J. Gilmartin
Alan P. Schoen
Brian J. Lenahan
Diane Hepford Lenahan
George E. Mehalchick
Brian Yeager
Thomas R. Daniels
Myles P. McAliney
Terrence E. Dempsey
Carmina M. Rinkunas
Thomas R. Chesnick
William M. Blaum
Christine S. Mayernick
Patricia Corbett

Representative Insurance Clients: Allstate Insurance Co.; America Security Insurance Co.; Metropolitan Casualty Insurance Co.; Statesman Insurance Group; Foremost Insurance Co.; Aetna Insurance Co.; Pennsylvania National Insurance Group; Kemper Insurance Group; American Mutual Insurance Cos.; American States Insurance, Co.

For full biographical listings, see the Martindale-Hubbell Law Directory

O'MALLEY & HARRIS, P.C. (AV)

345 Wyoming Avenue, 18503
Telephone: 717-348-3711
Fax: 717-348-4092
Stroudsburg, Pennsylvania Office: 111 North Seventh Street.
Telephone: 717-421-2252.
Wilkes-Barre, Pennsylvania Office: Courthouse Square Towers, North River Street.
Telephone: 717-829-3232.
FAX: 717-829-4418.
Williamsport, Pennsylvania Office: 321 Pine Street, Suite 308.
Telephone: 717-323-4380.

Eugene Nogi (1905-1975)
Henry Nogi (1900-1976)
Russell O. O'Malley, Sr. (1904-1993)
William H. Amesbury (Resident, Wilkes-Barre Office)
Paul A. Barrett
J. Scott Brady
Bruce L. Coyer
John Q. Durkin
Gerald J. Hanchulak
Norman Harris
Richard K. Hodges
Timothy J. Holland (Resident, Wilkes-Barre Office)
Daniel Morgan
Michael Perry
Joseph R. Rydzewski
Jane M. Carlonas
James M. Tressler
Matthew P. Barrett

Representative Clients: Robert Packer Hospital; GSGS & B Architects & Engineers; Aetna Casualty & Surety Co.; Pennsylvania Hospital Insurance Co.; United States Fidelity & Guaranty Insurance Co.; Selective Insurance Co.; Maryland Casualty Insurance Co.; Robert Packer Hospital; United Gilsonite Laboratories; Electric Mutual Insurance Co.

For full biographical listings, see the Martindale-Hubbell Law Directory

SHARON, Mercer Co.

CUSICK, MADDEN, JOYCE AND McKAY (AV)

First Western Bank Building, 16146
Telephone: 412-981-2000
Fax: 412-981-2007

Martin E. Cusick (1902-1985)

MEMBERS OF FIRM

Donald R. McKay
Henry M. Ekker
P. Raymond Bartholomew
William G. McConnell
Thomas W. Kuster
Peter C. Acker

ASSOCIATE

Kevin Feeney

OF COUNSEL

William J. Joyce

Agent for: Lawyers Title Insurance Corporation.
Approved Attorneys for: Penn Attorneys Title Insurance Co.

For full biographical listings, see the Martindale-Hubbell Law Directory

*WILLIAMSPORT,** Lycoming Co.

MITCHELL, MITCHELL, GRAY & GALLAGHER, A PROFESSIONAL CORPORATION (AV)

10 West Third Street, 17701
Telephone: 717-323-8404
Fax: 717-323-8585

C. Edward S. Mitchell
Richard A. Gray
Robert A. Gallagher
Gary L. Weber

Bret J. Southard
Eric R. Linhardt

OF COUNSEL

Jacob Neafie Mitchell

For full biographical listings, see the Martindale-Hubbell Law Directory

RHODE ISLAND

*PROVIDENCE,** Providence Co.

BOYER, REYNOLDS & DEMARCO, LTD. (AV)

Suite 200, 170 Westminster Street, 02903
Telephone: 401-861-5522
Telecopier: 401-331-4861

Francis V. Reynolds (1905-1981)
Bernard W. Boyer
Paul V. Reynolds
Anthony F. DeMarco
John G. Rallis
John M. Boland
Gregory L. Boyer
Mark T. Reynolds

Representative Clients: Lumbermens Mutual Casualty Co.; American Motorists Insurance Co.; Federal Mutual Fire Insurance Co.; B. F. Goodrich Co.; Andover Group; Insurance Company of North America; Nationwide Mutual Insurance Co.; Worcester Co.; Amica Mutual Insurance Co.

For full biographical listings, see the Martindale-Hubbell Law Directory

MARTIN K. DONOVAN (AV)

Second Floor, One Park Row, 02903
Telephone: 401-831-2500
Facsimile: 401-751-7830

Reference: Fleet National Bank.

For full biographical listings, see the Martindale-Hubbell Law Directory

GIDLEY, SARLI & MARUSAK (AV)

Greater Providence Bank Building, 170 Westminster Street, 02903
Telephone: 401-274-6644
Telecopier: 401-331-9304

MEMBERS OF FIRM

Thomas D. Gidley
Michael G. Sarli
James P. Marusak
Mark C. Hadden

ASSOCIATES

Michael R. DeLuca
Linn Foster Freedman
Denise M. Lombardo
William L. Wheatley
Stuart D. Hallagan III

LEGAL SUPPORT PERSONNEL

Elaine M. Noren
Mary Repoza Caplette
Darlene E. Kotkofski

For full biographical listings, see the Martindale-Hubbell Law Directory

HANSON, CURRAN, PARKS & WHITMAN (AV)

146 Westminster Street, 02903-2218
Telephone: 401-421-2154
Telecopier: 401-521-7040

Kirk Hanson (1948-1991)

MEMBERS OF FIRM

A. Lauriston Parks
David P. Whitman
Michael T. F. Wallor
Robert D. Parrillo
Dennis J. McCarten
James T. Murphy
Seth E. Bowerman
Thomas R. Bender

ASSOCIATES

Amy Beretta
Mark W. Dana
Richard H. Burrows
Daniel P. McKiernan

OF COUNSEL

William A. Curran

General Counsel for: Medical Malpractice Joint Underwriting Association of Rhode Island.
Rhode Island Counsel for: Amica Mutual Insurance Co.; CIGNA; St. Paul Insurance Cos.; Occidental Life Insurance Co.; Exchange Mutual Insurance Co.; Aetna Casualty & Surety Co.

For full biographical listings, see the Martindale-Hubbell Law Directory

HODOSH, SPINELLA & ANGELONE (AV)

128 Dorrance Street, Shakespeare Hall, Suite 450, P.O. Box 1516, 02901-1516
Telephone: 401-274-0200
Fax: 401-274-7538

Thomas C. Angelone
Hugh L. Moore, Jr.
Kevin M. Cain

Reference: Fleet National Bank.

For Complete List of Firm Personnel, See General Section

For full biographical listings, see the Martindale-Hubbell Law Directory

KIERNAN, PLUNKETT & REDIHAN (AV)

The Remington Building, 91 Friendship Street, 02903
Telephone: 401-831-2900
Fax: 401-331-7123

MEMBERS OF FIRM

Leonard A. Kiernan, Jr.
Thomas C. Plunkett
Charles N. Redihan, Jr.
Bernard P. Healy

ASSOCIATES

Brian T. Burns
Patricia L. Sylvester
Michael R. Calise
Christopher J. O'Connor

For full biographical listings, see the Martindale-Hubbell Law Directory

WILLIAM T. MURPHY (AV)

The Calart Tower, 400 Reservoir Avenue, Suite 3L, 02907
Telephone: 401-461-7740
Telecopier: 401-461-7753

ASSOCIATE

Sean P. Lardner

Reference: Fleet National Bank.

For full biographical listings, see the Martindale-Hubbell Law Directory

RICE, DOLAN & KERSHAW (AV)

Greater Providence Bank Building, 170 Westminster Street, Suite 900, 02903
Telephone: 401-272-8800
Telecopier: 401-421-7218

OF COUNSEL

H. Eliot Rice

MEMBERS OF FIRM

John F. Dolan
John W. Kershaw
Mark P. Dolan

ASSOCIATES

Charles Garganese, Jr.
Mark A. Fay
Elizabeth Flynn Sullivan

Local Counsel for: American International Adjustment Co.; Andover Cos.; Chubb Group of Insurance Cos.; CNA/Insurance; Government Employees Insurance; Holyoke Mutual Insurance Co.; Mutual of Omaha; Providence-Washington Insurance Group; Reliance Insurance Co.; Rhode Island Hospital.

For full biographical listings, see the Martindale-Hubbell Law Directory

VOGEL, SOULS & WOODBINE (AV)

312 South Main Street, 02903
Telephone: 401-454-5350

(See Next Column)

VOGEL, SOULS & WOODBINE, *Providence—Continued*

MEMBERS OF FIRM

Netti C. Vogel
Donald A. Woodbine
James M. Souls

For full biographical listings, see the Martindale-Hubbell Law Directory

SOUTH CAROLINA

*AIKEN,** Aiken Co.

HENDERSON & SALLEY (AV)

111 Park Avenue, Southwest, P.O. Box 517, 29802-0517
Telephone: 803-648-4213
Fax: 803-648-2601

MEMBERS OF FIRM

Julian B. Salley, Jr.
William H. Tucker
Michael K. Farmer
James D. Nance

ASSOCIATE

Amy Patterson Shumpert

Attorneys for: NationsBank South Carolina (N.A.); South Carolina Electric & Gas Co.; The Graniteville Co.; Maryland Casualty Co.; Southern Bell Telephone & Telegraph Co.; Owens Corning Fiberglass Corp.; City of Aiken; United Merchants & Manufacturers, Inc.; Allstate Insurance Co.

For full biographical listings, see the Martindale-Hubbell Law Directory

*BEAUFORT,** Beaufort Co.

DAVIS, TUPPER, GRIMSLEY & SEELHOFF (AV)

611 Bay Street, P.O. Box 2055, 29901-2055
Telephone: 803-524-1116
Facsimile: 803-524-1463

MEMBERS OF FIRM

Hutson S. Davis, Jr.
James A. Grimsley, III
Ralph E. Tupper
Scott A. Seelhoff
Erin D. Dean

For full biographical listings, see the Martindale-Hubbell Law Directory

*CHARLESTON,** Charleston Co.

BARNWELL WHALEY PATTERSON & HELMS (AV)

134 Meeting Street, Suite 300, P.O. Drawer H, 29402
Telephone: 803-577-7700
Telecopier: 803-577-7708

MEMBERS OF FIRM

Robert A. Patterson
M. Dawes Cooke, Jr.
William C. Helms, III
Bruce E. Miller
Thomas J. Wills
B. C. Killough
Matthew H. Henrikson

ASSOCIATES

Aubrey R. Alvey
Lori S. Dandridge
Eleanor D. Washburn
Thomas B. Pritchard
Warren William Ariail
Heather K. Coleman
Robert P. Gritton
James E. Reeves

Representative Clients: General Accident Group; Continental Insurance Group; Hartford Insurance Cos; The Home Insurance Co.; Kemper Insurance Group; Liberty Mutual Insurance; The Travelers Insurance Co.; United States Aviation Underwriters.

For Complete List of Firm Personnel, See General Section

For full biographical listings, see the Martindale-Hubbell Law Directory

BUIST, MOORE, SMYTHE & MCGEE, P.A. (AV)

Successors to Buist, Buist, Smythe and Smythe and Moore, Mouzon and McGee.
Five Exchange Street, P.O. Box 999, 29402
Telephone: 803-722-3400
Cable Address: "Conferees"
Telex: 57-6488
Telecopier: 803-723-7398
North Charleston, South Carolina Office: Atrium Northwood Office Building, 7301 Rivers Avenue, Suite 288. Zip: 29406-2859.
Telephone: 803-797-3000.
Telecopier: 803-863-5500.

Benj. Allston Moore, Jr.
Henry B. Smythe, Jr.
Joseph H. McGee
David B. McCormack
Gordon D. Schreck
C. Allen Gibson, Jr.

David M. Collins
Elizabeth H. Warner
James D. Myrick
David S. Yandle
Douglas M. Muller
Julius H. Hines

(See Next Column)

Counsel for: CSX Transportation; NationsBank; Metropolitan Life Insurance Co.; E. I. du Pont de Nemours & Co.; AIG Aviation, Inc.; Lamorte, Burns & Co., Inc.; Allstate Insurance Co.; General Dynamics Corp.; Independent Life & Accident Insurance Co.; Georgia-Pacific Corp.

For Complete List of Firm Personnel, See General Section

For full biographical listings, see the Martindale-Hubbell Law Directory

HOOD LAW FIRM (AV)

172 Meeting Street, P.O. Box 1508, 29402
Telephone: 803-577-4435
FAX: 803-722-1630

MEMBERS OF FIRM

Robert H. Hood
G. Mark Phillips
Louis P. Herns
Carl Everette Pierce, II
John K. Blincow, Jr.

James G. Kennedy
Barbara Wynne Showers
James Dowell Gandy, III
Christine L. Companion
William R. Hearn, Jr.
Hugh Willcox Buyck
Joseph C. Wilson, IV
Jerry A. Smith
Dixon F. Pearce, III
Allan Poe Sloan, III
Margaret Allison Snead
Todd W. Smyth

For full biographical listings, see the Martindale-Hubbell Law Directory

YOUNG, CLEMENT, RIVERS & TISDALE (AV)

28 Broad Street, P.O. Box 993, 29402
Telephone: 803-577-4000
Fax: 803-724-6600
Columbia, South Carolina Office: 1901 Assembly Street, Suite 300, P.O. Box 8476.
Telephone: 803-799-4000.
Fax: 803-799-7083.
North Charleston , South Carolina Office: 2170 Ashley Phosphate Road, Suite 700, P.O. Box 61509.
Telephone: 803-720-5400.
Fax: 803-724-7796.

MEMBERS OF FIRM

Thomas S. Tisdale, Jr.
H. Michael Bowers
William J. Bates
Carol Brittain Ervin
J. Rutledge Young, Jr.
Joseph E. DaPore
Wallace G. Holland
Michael A. Molony
Bradish J. Waring
C. Michael Branham
W. Jefferson Leath, Jr.
Randell C. Stoney, Jr.
John C. Von Lehe, Jr.
Stephen P. Groves
Timothy W. Bouch
Shawn Daughtridge Wallace
William Bobo, Jr.
John Hamilton Smith

ASSOCIATES

Shawn M. Flanagan
Sally H. Rhoad
Robert W. Pearce, Jr.
E. Courtney Gruber

OF COUNSEL

Robert L. Clement, Jr.
G. L. Buist Rivers, Jr.

RETIRED

Joseph R. Young

Counsel for: Auto-Owners Insurance Co.; CIGNA Insurance Co.; Government Employees Insurance Co.; Nationwide Mutual Insurance Co.; ITT Hartford; Reliance Insurance Co.; State Farm Cos.; United Services Automobile Assn.; U.S. Fidelity & Guaranty.

For Complete List of Firm Personnel, See General Section

For full biographical listings, see the Martindale-Hubbell Law Directory

*COLUMBIA,** Richland Co.

* indicates certain Bar Register subscribers whose principal office is located elsewhere in the state and who have arranged for representation as a part of the state capital listings that follow

BARNES, ALFORD, STORK & JOHNSON, L.L.P. (AV)

1613 Main Street, P.O. Box 8448, 29202
Telephone: 803-799-1111
Telefax: 803-254-1335

James W. Alford
Richard C. Thomas
Weldon R. Johnson
Thomas C. Cofield
Robert E. Salane
Robert Thomas Strickland
Kay Gaffney Crowe
L. Elaine Mozingo

Curtis W. Dowling
Gregory G. Williams
Andrew E. Haselden

Representative Clients: First Union National Bank of South Carolina; Aetna Casualty and Surety Co.; Kline Iron & Steel Co.

For Complete List of Firm Personnel, See General Section

For full biographical listings, see the Martindale-Hubbell Law Directory

Columbia—Continued

BOWERS ORR & ROBERTSON (AV)

Suite 1100, 1401 Main Street, P.O. Box 7307, 29202
Telephone: 803-252-0494
Telefax: 803-252-1068

MEMBERS OF FIRM

Glenn Bowers
James W. Orr
William Dixon Robertson III
Thomas F. Dougall

ASSOCIATE

W. Jones Andrews, Jr.

Representative Clients: AIG Aviation, Inc.; Cardinal Casualty Co.; Houston General Insurance Co.; Insurance Company of North America; The Travelers Insurance Cos.; Phoenix Aviation Managers, Inc.; United States Fidelity & Guaranty Co.; Waite-Hill Services, Inc.; Wausau Insurance Cos.

For full biographical listings, see the Martindale-Hubbell Law Directory

FINKEL, GOLDBERG, SHEFTMAN & ALTMAN, P.A. (AV)

Suite 1800, 1201 Main Street, P.O. Box 1799, 29202
Telephone: 803-765-2935
Fax: 803-252-0786
Charleston, South Carolina Office: 12 Exchange Street, P.O. Box 225.
Telephone: 803-577-5460.
Fax: 803-577-5135.

Gerald M. Finkel
Harry L. Goldberg
Howard S. Sheftman

Representative Clients: Hewitt-Robins; 1st Union National Bank; Banc One Mortgage Co.; Motorola Communications & Electronics Corp.

For full biographical listings, see the Martindale-Hubbell Law Directory

* HAYNSWORTH, MARION, McKAY & GUÉRARD, L.L.P. (AV)

Suite 2400 A T & T Building, 1201 Main Street, P.O. Drawer 7157, 29202
Telephone: 803-765-1818
Telecopier: 803-765-2399
Greenville, South Carolina Office: Two Insignia Financial Plaza, 75 Beattie Place, P.O. Box 2048, 29602.
Telephone: 803-240-3200.
Telecopier: 803-240-3300.
Charleston, South Carolina Office: #2 Prioleau Street, P.O. Box 1119, 29402.
Telephone: 803-722-7606.
Telecopier: 803-723-5263.

MEMBERS OF FIRM

William P. Simpson
Steven Todd Moon

ASSOCIATES

Stephen F. McKinney
Boyd B. Nicholson, Jr.
Jill R. Quattlebaum
Edward Wade Mullins, III

Counsel for: St. Paul Insurance Group; Allstate Insurance Co.; Fluor-Daniel Corp.; South Carolina Jobs - Economic Development Authority; Anheuser Busch Company; CSX Transportation; Ernst & Young, LLP; Willis Corroon of South Carolina, Inc.; Westinghouse Savannah River Co.; Wachovia Bank of South Carolina, N.A.

For Complete List of Firm Personnel, See General Section

For full biographical listings, see the Martindale-Hubbell Law Directory

McCUTCHEN, BLANTON, RHODES & JOHNSON (AV)

1414 Lady Street, P.O. Drawer 11209, 29211
Telephone: 803-799-9791
Telecopier: 803-253-6084
Winnsboro, South Carolina Office: Courthouse Square, 29180.
Telephone: 803-635-6884.

MEMBERS OF FIRM

Thomas E. McCutchen
Hoover C. Blanton
Jeter E. Rhodes, Jr.
T. English McCutchen, III
Pope D. Johnson, III
William R. Taylor
Evans Taylor Barnette
G. D. Morgan, Jr.
John C. Bradley, Jr.

ASSOCIATES

Creighton B. Coleman
William E. Hopkins, Jr.

Representative Clients: Allstate Insurance Co.; Sears, Roebuck and Co.; J.B. White Co.; Anchor Continental Inc.; Western Fire Insurance Co.; Liberty Mutual Insurance Co.; Southeastern Freight Lines; American Mutual Fire Insurance Co.; Continental Life Insurance Co.; State Farm Fire & Casualty Co.

For full biographical listings, see the Martindale-Hubbell Law Directory

RICHARDSON, PLOWDEN, GRIER AND HOWSER, P.A. (AV)

1600 Marion Street, P.O. Drawer 7788, 29202
Telephone: 803-771-4400
Telecopy: 803-779-0016
Myrtle Beach, South Carolina Office: Southern National Bank Building, Suite 202, 601 21st Avenue North, P.O. Box 3646, 29578.
Telephone: 803-448-1008.
FAX: 803-448-1533.

Donald V. Richardson, III
Charles N. Plowden, Jr.
F. Barron Grier, III
R. Davis Howser
Charles E. Carpenter, Jr.
Michael A. Pulliam
George C. Beighley
William H. Hensel
Frederick A. Crawford
Francis M. Mack
Samuel F. Crews, III
Franklin Jennings Smith, Jr.
Leslie A. Cotter, Jr.
James P. Newman, Jr.

Nina Reid Mack
Deborah Harrison Sheffield
Douglas C. Baxter
William G. Besley
S. Nelson Weston Jr.
Mary L. Sowell League
Benjamin D. McCoy
Jimmy Denning, Jr.
Anne Macon Flynn
Phillip Florence, Jr.
Williams Scalise Marian

Representative Clients: Insurance: CNA Insurance Co.; The Hartford; Kemper Insurance Co.; Pennsylvania National Mutual Casualty Insurance Co.; Wausau Insurance Cos.; The Reudlinger Cos. Real Estate, Corporate and Banking: Med Corp Health Services, Inc.; First Union Bank. Construction: S.C. Department of Transportation; DPIC Insurance Companies.

For Complete List of Firm Personnel, See General Section

For full biographical listings, see the Martindale-Hubbell Law Directory

ROBINSON, McFADDEN & MOORE, P.C. (AV)

Fifteen Hundred NationsBank Plaza, 1901 Main Street, P.O. Box 944, 29202
Telephone: 803-779-8900
Telecopier: 803-252-0724

David W. Robinson, Sr. (1869-1935)
R. Hoke Robinson (1916-1977)
J. Means McFadden (1901-1990)
David W. Robinson (1899-1989)
David W. Robinson, II
D. Reece Williams, III
John S. Taylor, Jr.
James M. Brailsford, III
Daniel T. Brailsford
Frank R. Ellerbe, III
Thomas W. Bunch, II
J. Kershaw Spong
D. Clay Robinson
Jacquelyn Lee Bartley
E. Meredith Manning
R. William Metzger, Jr.
Kevin K. Bell
Annemarie B. Mathews

OF COUNSEL

Thomas T. Moore

Representative Clients: NationsBank; Chemical Financial Corp.; Transcontinental Gas Pipe Line Corp.; The Equitable Life Insurance Society of the U.S.; Metropolitan Life Insurance Co.; Firestone Tire & Rubber Co.; Mutual Life Insurance Company of New York.; South Carolina Insurance Reserve Fund; South Carolina Insurance Co.

For full biographical listings, see the Martindale-Hubbell Law Directory

TURNER, PADGET, GRAHAM & LANEY, P.A. (AV)

Seventeenth Floor, 1901 Main Street, P.O. Box 1473, 29202
Telephone: 803-254-2200
Telecopy: 803-799-3957
Florence, South Carolina Office: Fourth Floor, 1831 West Evans Street, P.O. Box 5478, 29501.
Telephone: 803-662-9008.
Telecopy: 803-667-0828.

Nathaniel A. Turner (1897-1959)
Edward W. Laney, III (1930-1980)
Harrell M. Graham (Retired)
George E. Lewis
Ronald E. Boston
Edwin P. Martin
Carl B. Epps, III
W. Duvall Spruill
Charles E. Hill
Thomas C. Salane
Danny C. Crowe
R. Wayne Byrd (Resident, Florence, SC, Office)
W. Hugh McAngus
John S. Wilkerson, III (Resident, Florence, SC, Office)
Steven W. Ouzts
Michael S. Church
Timothy D. St. Clair
Laura Callaway Hart
John E. Cuttino
Arthur E. Justice, Jr. (Resident, Florence, SC, Office)
Edward W. Laney, IV
Elbert S. Dorn
J. Russell Goudelock, II

OF COUNSEL

Henry Fletcher Padget, Jr.
Hugh M. Claytor (Resident, Florence, SC, Office)
James R. Courie

J. Kenneth Carter, Jr.

Representative Clients: Independent Life & Accident Insurance Co.; Ford Motor Co.; Insurance Company of North America; Navistar International Corp.; Winn-Dixie Stores, Inc.; Allstate Insurance Co.; Continental Insur-

(See Next Column)

TURNER, PADGET, GRAHAM & LANEY P.A., *Columbia—Continued*

ance Co.; Atlantic Soft Drink Co.; National Council on Compensation Insurance.

For Complete List of Firm Personnel, See General Section

For full biographical listings, see the Martindale-Hubbell Law Directory

*GREENVILLE,** Greenville Co.

HAYNSWORTH, MARION, MCKAY & GUÉRARD, L.L.P. (AV)

Two Insignia Financial Plaza, 75 Beattie Place, P.O. Box 2048, 29602
Telephone: 803-240-3200
Telecopier: 803-240-3300
Columbia, South Carolina Office: Suite 2400 A T & T Building, 1201 Main Street, P.O. Drawer 7157, 29202
Telephone: 803-765-1818.
Telecopier: 803-765-2399.
Charleston, South Carolina Office: #2 Prioleau Street, P.O. Box 1119, 29402.
Telephone: 803-722-7606.
Telecopier: 803-723-5263.

MEMBERS OF FIRM

Donald L. Ferguson
G. Dewey Oxner, Jr.
William E. Shaughnessy
H. Donald Sellers
Ellis M. Johnston, II
W. Francis Marion, Jr.
John B. McLeod
Richard B. Kale, Jr.
Edwin Brown Parkinson, Jr.
David Hill Keller
Floyd Matlock Elliott
Moffatt Grier McDonald

ASSOCIATES

Amy Miller Snyder
Eric Keith Englebardt
James Derrick Quattlebaum
Melissa Miller Anderson
Brent O. Clinkscale
Sarah S. (Sally) McMillan
Harry L. Phillips, Jr.
Julie Kaye Hackworth
Matthew P. Utecht
Harold J. Willson, Jr.
Jeffrey S. Jones
Cynthia Buck Brown
William David Conner

Representative Clients: Travelers Insurance Co.; United States Fidelity & Guaranty; Royal Insurance Co.; Wausau Insurance; Kemper Insurance; Liberty Mutual Ins. Co.; Fireman's Fund Insurance Co.; Companion Property & Casualty Co.; Hartford Accident & Indemnity Co.; Prudential Property & Casualty.

For Complete List of Firm Personnel, See General Section

For full biographical listings, see the Martindale-Hubbell Law Directory

LEATHERWOOD WALKER TODD & MANN, P.C. (AV)

100 East Coffee Street, P.O. Box 87, 29602
Telephone: 803-242-6440
FAX: 803-233-8461
Spartanburg, South Carolina Office: 1451 East Main Street, P.O. Box 3188.
Telephone: 803-582-4365.
Telefax: 803-583-8961.

James H. Watson
John E. Johnston
O. Doyle Martin
Joseph E. Major
Duke K. McCall, Jr.
Michael J. Giese
Bradford Neal Martin
Samuel Wright Outten

Tara H. Snyder
Sandra L. W. Miller

COUNSEL

Fletcher C. Mann

Counsel for: NationsBank; John D. Hollingsworth on Wheels, Inc.; Canal Insurance Co.; Platt Saco Lowell Corporation .
Representative Clients: Springs Industries, Inc.; American Federal Bank, F.S.B.; General Motors Acceptance Corp.; Ashland Oil, Inc.; Suitt Construction Co.

For Complete List of Firm Personnel, See General Section

For full biographical listings, see the Martindale-Hubbell Law Directory

LOVE, THORNTON, ARNOLD & THOMASON, P.A. (AV)

410 East Washington Street, P.O. Box 10045, 29603
Telephone: 803-242-6360
Telefax: 803-271-7972

William M. Hagood, III
Theron G. Cochran
Mason A. Goldsmith
Jack D. Griffeth
William A. Coates
David L. Moore, Jr.
John Robert Devlin, Jr.
Larry Lee Plumblee

James A. Blair, III

OF COUNSEL

W. Harold Arnold

Counsel for: Aetna Life & Casualty Insurance Co.; Kemper Insurance Group; Continental Insurance Companies Group; Government Employees Insurance Co.; Reliance Insurance Companies Group; American States Ins. Co.; First Citizens Bank & Trust Co.; American Federal Bank, F.S.B.; BP Oil, Inc.; Chrysler Corp.

For Complete List of Firm Personnel, See General Section

For full biographical listings, see the Martindale-Hubbell Law Directory

WYCHE, BURGESS, FREEMAN & PARHAM, PROFESSIONAL ASSOCIATION (AV)

44 East Camperdown Way, P.O. Box 728, 29602-0728
Telephone: 803-242-8200
Telecopier: 803-235-8900

William W. Kehl
Carl F. Muller
Bradford W. Wyche
Marshall Winn
Wallace K. Lightsey
William D. Herlong
Jo Watson Hackl
William P. Crawford, Jr.
J. Theodore Gentry
Gregory J. English

Counsel for: Multimedia, Inc.; Delta Woodside Industries, Inc.; Milliken & Company; Ryan's Family Steak Houses, Inc.; St. Francis Hospital; Span-America Medical Systems, Inc.; Carolina First Bank; KEMET Electronics Corp.; Builder Marts of America, Inc.; One Price Clothing, Inc.

For Complete List of Firm Personnel, See General Section

For full biographical listings, see the Martindale-Hubbell Law Directory

*SPARTANBURG,** Spartanburg Co.

LEATHERWOOD WALKER TODD & MANN, P.C. (AV)

1451 East Main Street, P.O. Box 3188, 29304-3188
Telephone: 803-582-4365
Telefax: 803-585-8961
Greenville, South Carolina Office: 100 East Coffee Street, P.O. Box 87.
Telephone: 803-242-6440.
FAX: 803-233-8461.

H. Spencer King
Russell D. Ghent

Susan A. Fretwell

For Complete List of Firm Personnel, See General Section

For full biographical listings, see the Martindale-Hubbell Law Directory

*SUMTER,** Sumter Co.

LEE, WILSON & ERTER (AV)

126 North Main Street, P.O. Drawer 580, 29150
Telephone: 803-778-2471
Telecopier: 803-778-1643

MEMBERS OF FIRM

Harry C. Wilson, Jr.
David Cornwell Holler

Representative Clients: South Carolina National Bank; Carolina Power and Light Co.; Peoples Natural Gas Company of South Carolina; First Federal Savings & Loan Assn.; Allstate Insurance Co.; American Surety Co.; Prudential Insurance Company of America; General Telephone; Korn Industries, Inc.; V-B William Furniture Company, Inc.

For Complete List of Firm Personnel, See General Section

For full biographical listings, see the Martindale-Hubbell Law Directory

SOUTH DAKOTA

*ABERDEEN,** Brown Co.

BANTZ, GOSCH, CREMER, PETERSON & SOMMERS (AV)

305 Sixth Avenue, S.E., P.O. Box 970, 57402-0970
Telephone: 605-225-2232
Fax: 605-225-2497

MEMBERS OF FIRM

Douglas W. Bantz (1909-1983)
Kennith L. Gosch
James M. Cremer
Greg L. Peterson
Richard A. Sommers
Ronald A. Wager

General Counsel for: Dacotah Bank Holding Co.
Attorneys for: Northwestern Mutual Life Insurance Co.; Transamerica Insurance Group; Employers Mutual of Wausau; Employers Mutual Casualty Cos.; Farmers & Merchants Bank, Aberdeen; United Pacific Insurance Co.; Northwestern National Insurance Co.

For full biographical listings, see the Martindale-Hubbell Law Directory

*SIOUX FALLS,** Minnehaha Co.

DAVENPORT, EVANS, HURWITZ & SMITH (AV)

513 South Main Avenue, P.O. Box 1030, 57101-1030
Telephone: 605-336-2880
Telecopier: 605-335-3639

(See Next Column)

DAVENPORT, EVANS, HURWITZ & SMITH—*Continued*

OF COUNSEL
Deming Smith
MEMBERS OF FIRM

Edwin E. Evans
Michael L. Luce
Michael J. Schaffer
Thomas M. Frankman
Rick W. Orr
Timothy M. Gebhart
Susan Jansa Brunick
Roberto A. Lange

ASSOCIATES

Michael A. Hauck
Marie Elizabeth Hovland
Cheryle M. Wiedmeier
Lori Purcell Fossen
Sandra K. Hoglund
Mark W. Haigh

Counsel for: American Society of Composers, Authors and Publishers (A.S.-C.A.P.); Burlington Northern, Inc.; Continental Insurance Cos.; The First National Bank in Sioux Falls; Ford Motor Credit Co.; General Motors Corp.; The St. Paul Cos.; The Travelers.

For Complete List of Firm Personnel, See General Section

For full biographical listings, see the Martindale-Hubbell Law Directory

NASSER LAW OFFICES, P.C. (AV)

101 South Main Avenue, Suite 613, 57102-1126
Telephone: 605-335-0001
FAX: 605-335-6269

N. Dean Nasser, Jr.

Reference: Western Bank.

For full biographical listings, see the Martindale-Hubbell Law Directory

TENNESSEE

*ATHENS,** McMinn Co.

CARTER, HARROD & CUNNINGHAM (AV)

One Madison Avenue, P.O. Box 885, 37371-0885
Telephone: 615-745-7447
FAX: 615-745-6114

MEMBERS OF FIRM

Allen H. Carter (1938-1987)
David F. Harrod
Jeffrey L. Cunningham

Counsel for: Citizens National Bank; Athens Federal Savings & Loan Assn.; Athens Utilities Board; Bowaters Incorporated.
Representative Clients: Liberty Mutual Insurance Co.; Nationwide Insurance Cos.; State Farm Mutual Automobile Insurance Co.; United States Fidelity & Guaranty Insurance Co.

For Complete List of Firm Personnel, See General Section

For full biographical listings, see the Martindale-Hubbell Law Directory

*CHATTANOOGA,** Hamilton Co.

BAKER, KINSMAN & HOLLIS, P.C. (AV)

724 First Tennessee Building, 37402
Telephone: 615-756-3333
Fax: 615-756-3337

Josiah Baker
N. Mark Kinsman
W. Joseph Hollis, Jr.

Peggie Cook Bobo

For full biographical listings, see the Martindale-Hubbell Law Directory

CAMPBELL & CAMPBELL (AV)

1200 James Building, 37402
Telephone: 615-266-1108
Fax: 615-266-8222

MEMBERS OF FIRM

Paul Campbell (1885-1974)
Paul Campbell, Jr.
Michael Ross Campbell
Paul Campbell, III
Douglas M. Campbell

ASSOCIATE
Odile M. Farrell
OF COUNSEL
James C. Lee (P.C.)

Representative Clients: Tennessee Farmers Mutual Insurance Co.; Pennsylvania National Mutual Casualty Insurance Co.; Amerisure Cos.; National Grange Mutual Insurance Co.

For full biographical listings, see the Martindale-Hubbell Law Directory

FLEISSNER, COOPER, MARCUS & QUINN (AV)

800 Vine Street, 37403
Telephone: 615-756-3595
Telecopier: 615-266-5455

Phillip A. Fleissner
Gary A. Cooper
H. Richard Marcus
J. Bartlett Quinn
Robert L. Widerkehr, Jr.

ASSOCIATE
Cynthia D. Hall

For full biographical listings, see the Martindale-Hubbell Law Directory

FOSTER, FOSTER, ALLEN & DURRENCE (AV)

Formerly Hall, Haynes & Foster
Suite 515 Pioneer Bank Building, 37402
Telephone: 615-266-1141
Telecopier: 615-266-4618

MEMBERS OF FIRM

George Lane Foster
William M. Foster
Craig R. Allen
Phillip M. Durrence, Jr.

ASSOCIATES

David J. Ward
Clayton M. Whittaker
John M. Hull

LEGAL SUPPORT PERSONNEL
Peggy Sue Bates

Division Counsel for: Alabama Great Southern Railroad Co.; C.N.O. & T.P. Railway Co.
Attorneys for: CNA/Insurance; U.S.P. & G. Co.; The Firestone Tire & Rubber Co.; Exxon, Corp.; Murphy Oil Corp.; Chicago Title Insurance Co.; City of East Ridge; Jim Walter Homes; Raymond James & Associates; Morgan Keegan & Co.

For full biographical listings, see the Martindale-Hubbell Law Directory

LUTHER, ANDERSON, CLEARY & RUTH, P.C. (AV)

99 Walnut Street, 37403-1188
Telephone: 615-756-5033
Fax: 615-266-0188

William B. Luther
Samuel R. Anderson
Jeffrey L. Cleary
R. R. Ruth, Jr.
G. Michael Luhowiak
David L. Franklin
William A. Lockett
Nora A. McCarthy
Robert W. Sauser
Gerard M. Siciliano
Grace Elaine Daniell

Steven S. Usary
John Gerard Jackson
Michael Alan Kent
Alaric Anthony Henry
Daniel J. Ripper
Lex Alan Coleman
Morgan G. Adams
David C. Nagle
Norman E. Sabin

OF COUNSEL
Robert G. Russell

For full biographical listings, see the Martindale-Hubbell Law Directory

NELSON, MCMAHAN, PARKER & NOBLETT (AV)

(An Association of Attorneys)
400 Pioneer Bank Building, 37402
Telephone: 615-756-2291
Telecopier: 615-756-0737

Randall L. Nelson
Michael A. McMahan
Wm. Shelley Parker, Jr.
Phillip A. Noblett
Douglas M. Cox
Kenneth O. Fritz
Rosalind H. Reid-Houser

OF COUNSEL
Joe E. Manuel

For full biographical listings, see the Martindale-Hubbell Law Directory

SPEARS, MOORE, REBMAN & WILLIAMS (AV)

8th Floor Blue Cross Building, 801 Pine Street, 37402
Telephone: 615-756-7000
Facsimile: 615-756-4801

MEMBERS OF FIRM

Silas Williams, Jr.
Edward Blake Moore
Joseph C. Wilson, III
W. Ferber Tracy
Lynnwood Hale Hamilton
L. Marie Williams
Joseph R. White

ASSOCIATES

Barry A. Steelman
Robert G. Norred Jr.
Rodney L. Umberger, Jr.
Howell Dean Clements
John B. Bennett
E. Brent Hill
(Not admitted in TN)
Angela A. Ripper

(See Next Column)

SPEARS, MOORE, REBMAN & WILLIAMS, *Chattanooga—Continued*

Counsel for: Pioneer Bank; Chattanooga Gas Co.; South Central Bell Telephone Co.; Tennessee-American Water Co.; Blue Cross and Blue Shield of Tennessee; State Farm Mutual Automobile Insurance Cos.; Nationwide Insurance Co.; Siskin Steel & Supply Co., Inc.; CSX Transportation, Inc.; The McCallie School; Mueller Co.

For Complete List of Firm Personnel, See General Section

For full biographical listings, see the Martindale-Hubbell Law Directory

*CLEVELAND,** Bradley Co.

BELL AND ASSOCIATES, P.C. (AV)

140 Ocoee Street, N.E., P.O. Box 1169, 37364-1169
Telephone: 615-476-8541
Facsimile: 615-339-3510

J. Hallman Bell (1896-1976)
Eddie L. Headrick (1949-1982)
L. Harlen Painter
Michael E. Callaway
John Edgar Brown, III
John F. Kimball
Marcia M. McMurray

Barrett T. Painter

OF COUNSEL

Robert L. McMurray

Local Attorneys for: Louisville & Nashville Railroad Co.; South Central Bell Telephone Co.
Representative Client: Esstee Manufacturing Co., Inc.

For full biographical listings, see the Martindale-Hubbell Law Directory

JENNE, SCOTT & BRYANT (AV)

260 Ocoee Street, P.O. Box 161, 37364-0161
Telephone: 615-476-5506
Fax: 615-476-5058

MEMBERS OF FIRM

Roger E. Jenne
D. Mitchell Bryant

For Complete List of Firm Personnel, See General Section

For full biographical listings, see the Martindale-Hubbell Law Directory

DENNY E. MOBBS (AV)

55 1/2 First Street, N.E., P.O. Box 192, 37364-0192
Telephone: 615-472-7181

Representative Clients: Liberty Mutual Ins. Co.; Shelby Mutual Insurance Co.; Carolina Casualty Co.; Maytag Corp. (Magic Chef, Inc.-Hardwick Stove Company); Industrial Development Board of Polk County; Polk County News-Citizen Advance; Ocoee Inn & Marina.

For full biographical listings, see the Martindale-Hubbell Law Directory

*COOKEVILLE,** Putnam Co.

MADEWELL & JARED (AV)

Suite One, Fourth Floor, First Tennessee Bank Building, P.O. Box 721, 38503-0721
Telephone: 615-526-6101
FAX: 615-528-1909

MEMBERS OF FIRM

James D. Madewell
William E. Halfacre, III

Representative Clients: State of Tennessee; Trial Counsel as Special Assistant to Attorney General; Bank of Putnam County; First Tennessee Bank, N.A. at Cookeville; The Maryland; Transamerica Ins. Group; Home Insurance Co.; Auto Owners Ins. Co.; Insurance Company of North America; Fireman's Fund Insurance Co.

For Complete List of Firm Personnel, See General Section

For full biographical listings, see the Martindale-Hubbell Law Directory

MOORE, RADER, CLIFT AND FITZPATRICK, P.C. (AV)

46 North Jefferson Avenue, P.O. Box 3347, 38501
Telephone: 615-526-3311
Fax: 615-526-3092

L. Dean Moore
Daniel H. Rader, III
Michael E. Clift
Walter S. Fitzpatrick, III

General Counsel for: First Tennessee Bank.
Local Counsel for: Heritage Ford-Lincoln-Mercury, Inc.
Representative Clients: Continental Insurance Co.; Kemper Group; U.S.F.&G.; Auto Owners Insurance Co.; Wausau Insurance Cos.

For full biographical listings, see the Martindale-Hubbell Law Directory

*DYERSBURG,** Dyer Co.

ASHLEY, ASHLEY & ARNOLD (AV)

322 Church Avenue, P.O. Box H, 38024
Telephone: 901-285-5074
Telecopier: 901-285-5089

MEMBERS OF FIRM

Barret Ashley
Randolph A. Ashley, Jr.
S. Leo Arnold
Stephen D. Scofield
Marianna Williams
Carol Anne Austin
Anthony Lee Winchester

OF COUNSEL

Joree G. Brownlow

Representative Clients: Illinois Central Gulf Railroad; Bekeart Steel Wire Corp.; Fidelity and Deposit Company of Maryland; St. Paul Fire and Marine Insurance Company.
Construction Company Clients: Folk Construction Co.; Ford Construction Company; Luhr Brothers, Inc.; Pine Bluff Sand & Gravel; Valley Construction Co.

For full biographical listings, see the Martindale-Hubbell Law Directory

*JACKSON,** Madison Co.

MOSS, BENTON, WALLIS & PETTIGREW (AV)

325 North Parkway, P.O. Box 2103, 38302
Telephone: 901-668-5500
Telecopier: 901-664-2840

MEMBERS OF FIRM

William P. Moss (1897-1985)
George O. Benton
John R. Moss
Edwin E. Wallis, Jr.
Charles R. Pettigrew
W. Stanworth Harris

ASSOCIATE

Jon Mark Patey

OF COUNSEL

William P. Moss, Jr.

Attorneys for: First American National Bank of Jackson; South Central Bell Telephone & Telegraph Co.; CSX Transportation, Inc.; The Equitable Life Assurance Society of the United States; Jackson Utility Division; Metropolitan Life Insurance Co.; United Services Automobile Assn.; Association of Tennessee Cola-Cola Bottlers; Central Distributors, Inc.; Combined Insurance Company of America.

For Complete List of Firm Personnel, See General Section

For full biographical listings, see the Martindale-Hubbell Law Directory

RAINEY, KIZER, BUTLER, REVIERE & BELL (AV)

105 Highland Avenue South, P.O. Box 1147, 38302-1147
Telephone: 901-423-2414
Telecopier: 901-423-1386

MEMBERS OF FIRM

Thomas H. Rainey
Jerry D. Kizer, Jr.
Clinton V. Butler, Jr.
Russell E. Reviere
John D. Burleson
Gregory D. Jordan
Robert O. Binkley, Jr.

ASSOCIATES

R. Dale Thomas
Deana C. Seymour
Mitchell Glenn Tollison
Marty R. Phillips
Stephen P. Miller
Clay M. McCormack
Milton D. Conder, Jr.

Representative Clients: CIGNA Insurance Co.; State Farm Mutual Automobile Insurance Co.; Auto-Owners Insurance Co.; USF&G; CNA Group; Allstate Insurance Co.; Nationwide Insurance Co.; Ohio Casualty Insurance Co.; Wausau Insurance Co.; General Accident Group.

For Complete List of Firm Personnel, See General Section

For full biographical listings, see the Martindale-Hubbell Law Directory

KINGSPORT, Sullivan Co.

WEST & ROSE (AV)

537 East Center Street, P.O. Box 1404, 37660
Telephone: 615-246-8176
Fax: 615-246-4028

MEMBERS OF FIRM

M. Lacy West
Steven C. Rose

ASSOCIATE

Julia C. West

For full biographical listings, see the Martindale-Hubbell Law Directory

*KNOXVILLE,** Knox Co.

BUTLER, VINES AND BABB (AV)

Suite 810, First American Center, P.O. Box 2649, 37901-2649
Telephone: 615-637-3531
Fax: 615-637-3385

MEMBERS OF FIRM

Warren Butler
William D. Vines, III
Dennis L. Babb
Martin L. Ellis
Ronald C. Koksal
James C. Wright
Bruce A. Anderson
Gregory Kevin Hardin
Steven Boyd Johnson
Edward U. Babb

ASSOCIATES

John W. Butler
Vonda M. Laughlin
Gregory F. Vines
Scarlett May

LEGAL SUPPORT PERSONNEL

PARALEGALS

Virginia H. Carver
Susie DeLozier
Dena K. Martin

Reference: First American Bank.

For full biographical listings, see the Martindale-Hubbell Law Directory

CARPENTER & O'CONNOR (AV)

1000 First American Center, P.O. Box 2485, 37901
Telephone: 615-546-1831
Fax: 615-546-0432

MEMBERS OF FIRM

Archie R. Carpenter
J. Gregory O'Connor
Robert A. Crawford
Charles F. Sterchi, III

ASSOCIATES

Louis A. McElroy, II
Christpher D. Heagerty

Representative Clients: Allstate Insurance Co.; CNA Insurance; St. Paul Fire & Marine Insurance Co.; State Farm Insurance Co.; Farmers Insurance Group; Coca Cola Co.; Food Lion; The Hyatt Corp.; The Kroger Co.; Levi Strauss & Co.

For full biographical listings, see the Martindale-Hubbell Law Directory

HODGES, DOUGHTY AND CARSON (AV)

617 Main Street, P.O. Box 869, 37901-0869
Telephone: 615-546-9611
Telecopier: 615-544-2014

MEMBERS OF FIRM

J. H. Hodges (1896-1983)
J. H. Doughty (1903-1987)
Richard L. Carson (1912-1980)
John P. Davis, Jr. (1923-1977)
Robert R. Campbell
David E. Smith
John W. Wheeler
Dalton L. Townsend
Douglas L. Dutton
William F. Alley, Jr.
Roy L. Aaron
Dean B. Farmer
David Wedekind
Julia Saunders Howard
Albert J. Harb
Edward G. White, II
Thomas H. Dickenson
J. William Coley
J. Michael Haynes
T. Kenan Smith
Wayne A. Kline

ASSOCIATES

James M. Cornelius, Jr.
W. Tyler Chastain

OF COUNSEL

Jonathan H. Burnett

Representative Clients: General Motors Corp.; Sears, Roebuck and Co.; Navistar International; Martin Marietta Energy Systems; Union Carbide Corp.; NationsBank of Tennessee; K-Mart Corporation; Aetna Life and Casualty Group; Fireman's Fund American Insurance Company; Safeco Insurance Group.

For full biographical listings, see the Martindale-Hubbell Law Directory

KENNERLY, MONTGOMERY & FINLEY, P.C. (AV)

Fourth Floor, NationsBank Center, 550 Main Avenue, P.O. Box 442, 37901-0442
Telephone: 615-546-7311
Fax: 615-524-1773

OF COUNSEL

Warren W. Kennerly

George D. Montgomery (1917-1985)
Robert A. Finley (1936-1990)
L. Anderson Galyon, III
Alexander M. Taylor
Jack M. Tallent, II
G. Wendell Thomas, Jr.
Ray J. Campbell, Jr. (1949-1986)
Steven E. Schmidt
Patti Jane Lay
Brian H. Trammell
C. Coulter Gilbert
Robert H. Green
William S. Lockett, Jr.
Rebecca Brake Murray
Robert Michael Shelor
James N. Gore, Jr.

(See Next Column)

SPECIAL COUNSEL

Jay Arthur Garrison

R. Hunter Cagle
Melody J. Bock
Rex A. Dale
Natasha K. Metcalf
Kenneth W. Ward
David Draper
James H. Price

Representative Clients: Knoxville Utilities Board; Aetna Casualty & Surety Co.; Allstate Insurance Co.; CNA Insurance Group; CIGNA Insurance; Nationwide Mutual Insurance Co.; Dow Chemical; Union Carbide; Westinghouse Electric Corp.; Mitsubishi International Corp.

For full biographical listings, see the Martindale-Hubbell Law Directory

WATSON, HOLLOW & REEVES (AV)

1700 Plaza Tower, P.O. Box 131, 37901
Telephone: 615-522-3803
Telecopier: 615-525-2514

MEMBERS OF FIRM

Robert Harmon Watson, Jr.
Richard L. Hollow
Pamela L. Reeves
Jon G. Roach
John C. Duffy
John T. Batson, Jr.
Earl Jerome Melson

ASSOCIATES

Arthur Franklin Knight, III
Robert W. Willingham

For full biographical listings, see the Martindale-Hubbell Law Directory

*MEMPHIS,** Shelby Co.

ARMSTRONG ALLEN PREWITT GENTRY JOHNSTON & HOLMES (AV)

80 Monroe Avenue Suite 700, 38103
Telephone: 901-523-8211
Telecopier: 901-524-4936
Jackson, Missippi Office: 1350 One Jackson Place, 188 East Capitol Street.
Telephone: 601-948-8020.
Telecopier: 601-948-8389.

MEMBERS OF FIRM

Gavin M. Gentry
Thomas F. Johnston
Prince C. Chambliss, Jr.
Randall D. Noel

Cannon F. Allen

For Complete List of Firm Personnel, See General Section

For full biographical listings, see the Martindale-Hubbell Law Directory

BAKER, DONELSON, BEARMAN & CALDWELL (AV)

20th Floor, First Tennessee Building, 165 Madison, 38103
Telephone: 901-526-2000
Telecopier: 901-577-2303
Nashville, Tennessee Office: 1700 Nashville City Center, 511 Union Street, 37219.
Telephone: 615-726-5600.
Telecopier: 615-726-0464.
Knoxville, Tennessee Office: 2200 Riverview Tower, 900 Gay Street, 37901.
Telephone: 615-549-7000.
Telecopier: 615-525-8569.
Chattanooga, Tennessee Office: 1800 Republic Centre, 633 Chestnut Street, 37450-1800.
Telephone: 615-752-4400.
Telecopier: 615-752-4410.
Huntsville, Tennessee Office: 3 Courthouse Square, 37756.
Telephone: 615-663-2321.
Telecopier: 615-663-2111.
Johnson City, Tennessee Office: Hamilton Bank Building, 207 Mockingbird Lane, 37604.
Telephone: 615-928-0181.
Telecopier: 615-928-5694; 615-928-3654; Kingsport: 615-246-6191.
Washington, D.C. Office: Market Square, 801 Pennsylvania Avenue, N.W., 20004.
Telephone: 202-508-3400.
Telecopier: 202-508-3402.

PARTNERS

Leo Bearman, Jr.
Larry E. Killebrew
Charles C. Harrell
Charles G. Walker
Eugene J. Podesta, Jr.
Sam B. Blair, Jr.
Jill M. Steinberg

ASSOCIATES

Monique A. Nassar
Bradley E. Trammell
Charles F. Morrow

For Complete List of Firm Personnel, See General Section

For full biographical listings, see the Martindale-Hubbell Law Directory

Memphis—Continued

BATEMAN & CHILDERS (AV)

Suite 1010 Cotton Exchange Building, 65 Union Avenue, P.O. Box 3351, 38173-0351
Telephone: 901-526-0412
Telecopier: (901) 525-8466

MEMBERS OF FIRM

William C. Bateman, Jr.
Jack Alford Childers, Jr.

ASSOCIATE

Ricky Dolan Click

For Complete List of Firm Personnel, See General Section

For full biographical listings, see the Martindale-Hubbell Law Directory

EVANS & PETREE (AV)

81 Monroe Avenue, 38103
Telephone: 901-525-6781
Telecopier: 901-521-0681; 526-0336

MEMBERS OF FIRM

Marion G. Evans (1877-1957)
Jack Petree (1921-1973)
Charles Pittman Cobb (Retired)
Elwood L. Edwards (Retired)
W. Lytle Nichol IV
John W. McQuiston II
Ernest G. Kelly, Jr.
Alan E. Glenn
Michael C. Williams
Joseph W. Barnwell, Jr.
David C. Scruggs
Leonard C. Dunavant, Jr.
E. Woods Weathersby
Henry C. Shelton III
C. Bradford Foster III
William L. Gibbons
Andrew H. Raines
Bruce M. Kahn
Frank N. Carney
P. Preston Wilson, Jr.
Paul F. T. Edwards
Patricia K. Horton
Percy H. Harvey
Katharine A. Jungkind
Michael R. Marshall
Caren Beth Fogelman

For full biographical listings, see the Martindale-Hubbell Law Directory

FARRIS, HANCOCK, GILMAN, BRANAN & HELLEN (AV)

50 North Front Street, Suite 1400, 38103
Telephone: 901-576-8200
Fax: 901-576-8250
East Memphis, Tennessee Office: Suite 400 United American Bank Building, 5384 Poplar Avenue.
Telephone: 901-763-4000.
Fax: 901-763-4095.

MEMBERS OF FIRM

Tim Wade Hellen
G. Ray Bratton
D. Edward Harvey
Rebecca P. Tuttle
Eugene Stone Forrester, Jr.

ASSOCIATE

Gregory W. O'Neal

For Complete List of Firm Personnel, See General Section

For full biographical listings, see the Martindale-Hubbell Law Directory

GLASSMAN, JETER, EDWARDS & WADE, P.C. (AV)

26 North Second Street Building, 38103
Telephone: 901-527-4673
Telecopier: 901-521-0940
Lexington, Tennessee Office: 85 East Church.
Telephone: 901-968-2561.

Richard Glassman
William M. Jeter
Tim Edwards
B. J. Wade
John Barry Burgess
Carl K. Wyatt, Jr.
Nicholas E. Bragorgos
Ben W. Keesee
Lucinda S. Murray
Robert A. Cox
Lori J. Keen
James F. Horner, Jr.

For full biographical listings, see the Martindale-Hubbell Law Directory

KRIVCHER, MAGIDS, NEAL, COTTAM & CAMPBELL, P.C. (AV)

Suite 2929 Clark Tower, 5100 Poplar Avenue, 38137
Telephone: 901-682-6431
Telecopier: 901-682-6453

Michael B. Neal
Jennie D. Latta
Shawn Alexander Tidwell

For Complete List of Firm Personnel, See General Section

For full biographical listings, see the Martindale-Hubbell Law Directory

MCDONALD KUHN (AV)

80 Monroe Avenue, Suite 550, P.O. Box 3160, 38173-0160
Telephone: 901-526-0606
Fax: 901-521-8397

(See Next Column)

MEMBERS OF FIRM

W. Percy McDonald (1890-1969)
W. Percy McDonald, Jr. (1921-1967)
Braxton C. Gandy (1915-1979)
Edward W. Kuhn (1904-1983)
Henry T. V. Miller
J. Minor Tait, Jr.
Dale H. Tuttle
William A. Lucchesi
Carol A. Mills

ASSOCIATES

Richard H. Booth
Mariann Tait

OF COUNSEL

Edward P. A. Smith
Crawford McDonald

For full biographical listings, see the Martindale-Hubbell Law Directory

THOMASON, HENDRIX, HARVEY, JOHNSON & MITCHELL (AV)

Twenty-Ninth Floor, One Commerce Square, 38103
Telephone: 901-525-8721
Telecopier: 901-525-6722

MEMBERS OF FIRM

J. Kimbrough Johnson
Jerry E. Mitchell
Stephen W. Vescovo
Robert L. Moore
Michael L. Robb

For Complete List of Firm Personnel, See General Section

For full biographical listings, see the Martindale-Hubbell Law Directory

WARING COX (AV)

Morgan Keegan Tower, 50 North Front Street, Suite 1300, 38103-1190
Telephone: 901-543-8000
Telecopy: 901-543-8030

MEMBERS OF FIRM

Louis F. Allen
William E. Frulla
Louis J. Miller
Charles W. Hill
David J. Sneed

ASSOCIATES

Robert B.C. Hale
Thomas L. Parker

Representative Clients: Federal Express Corp.; South Central Bell Telephone Co.; American States Insurance; Central Benefits National Life Insurance Co.; Delta Life and Annuity; ICAROM, PLC; Primerica Life Insurance Co.; Miles Inc.; Underwriters at Lloyds.

For Complete List of Firm Personnel, See General Section

For full biographical listings, see the Martindale-Hubbell Law Directory

WILSON, MCRAE, IVY, SEVIER, MCTYIER AND STRAIN (AV)

295 Washington Avenue, Suite Two, P.O. Box 3331, 38173
Telephone: 901-523-2364
Telecopier: 901-523-2366

MEMBERS OF FIRM

Fred P. Wilson
Albert T. McRae
Fred E. Ivy, Jr.
Charles A. Sevier
Douglas A. McTyier
Alan R. Strain

ASSOCIATES

Stuart A. Wilson
J. Whitten Gurkin
Mark L. Pittman
Charles A. Sevier, IV
Reid R. Phillips
David A. McLaughlin
Robert M. Nelson (1900-1967)

For full biographical listings, see the Martindale-Hubbell Law Directory

*NASHVILLE,** Davidson Co.

MANIER, HEROD, HOLLABAUGH & SMITH, A PROFESSIONAL CORPORATION (AV)

First Union Tower 2200 One Nashville Place, 150 Fourth Avenue North, 37219-2494
Telephone: 615-244-0030
Telecopier: 615-242-4203

Will R. Manier, Jr. (1885-1953)
Larkin E. Crouch (1882-1948)
Vincent L. Fuqua, Jr. (1930-1974)
J. Olin White (1907-1982)
Miller Manier (1897-1986)
William Edward Herod (1917-1992)
Lewis B. Hollabaugh
Don L. Smith
James M. Doran, Jr.
Stephen E. Cox
J. Michael Franks
Randall C. Ferguson
Terry L. Hill
James David Leckrone
Robert C. Evans
Tommy C. Estes
B. Gail Reese
Michael E. Evans
Laurence M. Papel
John M. Gillum
Gregory L. Cashion
Sam H. Poteet, Jr.
Samuel Arthur Butts III
David J. Deming
Mark S. LeVan
Richard McCallister Smith
Mary Paty Lynn Jetton
H. Rowan Leathers III
Jefferson C. Orr
William L. Penny

(See Next Column)

MANIER, HEROD, HOLLABAUGH & SMITH A PROFESSIONAL CORPORATION—*Continued*

Lawrence B. Hammet II
John H. Rowland
Susan C. West
John E. Quinn
John F. Floyd
Paul L. Sprader
Lela M. Hollabaugh
J. Steven Kirkham
T. Richard Travis
Stephanie M. Jennings
Jerry W. Taylor
C. Benton Patton
Kenneth A. Weber
Phillip Robert Newman
Brett A. Oeser

General Counsel for: McKinnon Bridge Co., Inc.

For full biographical listings, see the Martindale-Hubbell Law Directory

*SAVANNAH,** Hardin Co.

HOPPER & PLUNK, P.C. (AV)

404 West Main Street, P.O. Box 220, 38372
Telephone: 901-925-8076

James A. Hopper
Dennis W. Plunk

Representative Clients: United States Fidelity & Guaranty Co.; Tennessee Farmers Mutual Insurance Co.; Kemper Insurance Co.; Tennessee Municipal Insurance Pool; Savannah Electric.
References: Boatman's Bank, Savannah; The Hardin County Bank.

For Complete List of Firm Personnel, See General Section

For full biographical listings, see the Martindale-Hubbell Law Directory

*UNION CITY,** Obion Co.

ELAM, GLASGOW & ACREE (AV)

NationsBank Building, 38261
Telephone: 901-885-2011, 885-2012

MEMBERS OF FIRM

Tom Elam
James M. Glasgow
William B. Acree, Jr.
James M. Glasgow, Jr.

Attorneys for: NationsBank, Union City; Illinois Central Gulf Railroad (Obion, Lake & Weakley Counties); Louisville & Nashville Railway; United States Fidelity & Guaranty Co.; Auto Owners Insurance Co.; C.N.A. Insurance, Union City; Travelers Insurance Co.; Goodyear Tire & Rubber Co.

For full biographical listings, see the Martindale-Hubbell Law Directory

TEXAS

*ABILENE,** Taylor Co.

ROBERT D. BATJER, JR. (AV)

Suite 306, 104 Pine Street, P.O. Box 888, 79601
Telephone: 915-673-2597
Fax: 915-676-9329

Representative Clients: General Motors Corp.; International Harvester Co.; Freightliner Corp.; United States Fidelity and Guaranty Co.; Royal-Globe Insurance Cos.; Commercial Union Insurance Cos.; State Farm Mutual; USAA; Wausau Insurance Cos.; Union Standard Insurance.

For full biographical listings, see the Martindale-Hubbell Law Directory

*AMARILLO,** Potter Co.

HINKLE, COX, EATON, COFFIELD & HENSLEY (AV)

1700 Bank One Center, P.O. Box 9238, 79105-9238
Telephone: 806-372-5569
FAX: 806-372-9761
Roswell, New Mexico Office: 700 United Bank Plaza, P. O. Box 10, 88202.
Telephone: 505-622-6510.
FAX: 505-623-9332.
Midland, Texas Office: 6 Desta Drive, Suite 2800, P.O. Box 3580, 79702.
Telephone: 915-683-4691.
FAX: 915-683-6518.
Santa Fe, New Mexico Office: 218 Montezuma, P.O. Box 2068, 87504.
Telephone: 505-982-4554.
FAX: 505-982-8623.
Albuquerque, New Mexico Office: Suite 800, 500 Marquette, N.W., P.O. Box 2043, 87102.
Telephone: 505-768-1500.
FAX: 505-768-1529.
Austin, Texas Office: 401 West 15th Street, Suite 800, 78701.
Telephone: 512-476-7137.
FAX: 512-476-5431.
Associated Office: Hoffman & Stephens, P.C., 401 West 15th Street, Suite 800, 78701.
Telephone: 512-476-5434. Fax; 512-476-5431.

(See Next Column)

RESIDENT PARTNERS

Richard R. Wilfong
Russell J. Bailey
Wyatt L. Brooks
David M. Russell
Kirt E. Moelling

Representative Clients: Federated Insurance; CNA Insurance Cos.; KEmper Insurance Group; The Home Insurance Co.; Reliance Insurance Co.; The Travelers Insurance Cos.; Trinity Universal Insurance Cos.; The Prudential Insurance Co.; Royal Insurance; National Indemnity Co.; Zurich-American Insurance Co.; Farmers Insurance Group of Cos.

For full biographical listings, see the Martindale-Hubbell Law Directory

*AUSTIN,** Travis Co.

* indicates certain Bar Register subscribers whose principal office is located elsewhere in the state and who have arranged for representation as a part of the state capital listings that follow

WILL BARBER (AV)

1520 Austin Centre 701 Brazos, 78701
Telephone: 512-469-0360
Fax: 512-469-0967

Will G. Barber

For full biographical listings, see the Martindale-Hubbell Law Directory

DAVIS & DAVIS, P.C. (AV)

Arboretum Plaza One, 9th Floor, 9442 Capitol of Texas Highway, P.O. Box 1588, 78767
Telephone: 512-343-6248
Fax: 512-343-0121

C. Dean Davis
Fred E. Davis
Alexis J. Fuller, Jr.
Francis A. (Tony) Bradley
Ruth Russell-Schafer

Bill Cline, Jr.
Robert L. Hargett
Michael L. Neely
Brian Gregory Jackson
A. A. Jack Ross, IV
Kevin Wayde Morse
Mark Alan Keene
Kenda B. Dalrymple

For Complete List of Firm Personnel, See General Section

For full biographical listings, see the Martindale-Hubbell Law Directory

DAVIS & WILKERSON, P.C. (AV)

200 One American Center, Six Hundred Congress Avenue, P.O. Box 2283, 78768-2283
Telephone: 512-482-0614
Fax: 512-482-0342
Alpine, Texas Office: 1110 East Holland. P.O. Box 777. 79831-0777.
Telephone: 915-837-5547.

David M. Davis
Steven R. Welch
Jeff D. Otto
Glen Wilkerson
David A. Wright
Leonard W. Woods
Kevin A. Reed
J. Mark Holbrook
Brian E. Riewe

Fletcher H. Brown
Deborah G. Clark
Frances W. Hamermesh
Kelly Ann McDonald
Brian McElroy
Michael Wilson
Stephen G. Wohleb
Stephen A. Wood

OF COUNSEL

Pete P. Gallego
Regina C. Williams

For full biographical listings, see the Martindale-Hubbell Law Directory

FORD & FERRARO, L.L.P. (AV)

A Registered Limited Liability Partnership
98 San Jacinto Boulevard, Suite 2000, 78701-4286
Telephone: 512-476-2020
Telecopy: 512-477-5267

Joseph M. Ford (P.C.)
Peter E. Ferraro (P.C.)
Thomas D. Fritz
Daniel H. Byrne (P.C.)
William S. Rhea, IV
Lisa C. Fancher
Clint Hackney (P.C.)
John D. Head
Robert O. Renbarger

ASSOCIATES

Patricia A. Becker
Linda Cangelosi
Bruce Perkins
James A. Rodman
James V. Sylvester
Cari S. Young

SPECIAL COUNSEL

Clark Watts

OF COUNSEL

Salvatore F. Fiscina (Not admitted in TX)
Lawrence H. Brenner (Not admitted in TX)

For full biographical listings, see the Martindale-Hubbell Law Directory

Austin—Continued

HOHMANN, WERNER & TAUBE, L.L.P. (AV)

100 Congress Avenue, Suite 1600, 78701-4042
Telephone: 512-472-5997
Fax: 512-472-5248
Houston, Texas Office: 1300 Post Oak Boulevard, Suite 700.
Telephone: 713-961-3541.
Fax: 713-961-3542.

Guy M. Hohmann
Eric J. Taube
Paul Dobry Keeper

Nicholas S. Bressi
T. Wade Jefferies
Camille Johnson Mauldin
Sandra McFarland
Mitchell D. Savrick
Gary N. Schumann
Rachel J. Stroud

For full biographical listings, see the Martindale-Hubbell Law Directory

LONG, BURNER, PARKS & SEALY, A PROFESSIONAL CORPORATION (AV)

301 Congress, Suite 800, P.O. Box 2212, 78768-2212
Telephone: 512-474-1587
Fax: 512-322-0301

Tom Long (1922-1989)
Clay Cotten (1916-1991)
Burnie Burner
Larry Parks
Earl W. (Rusty) Sealy
Jane G. Noble
Wendy Kendall Schaefer
Elisabeth (Betty) DeLargy
James W. (Woody) Butler
Christopher A. McClellan
Paula A. Jones
M. Scott Holter

For full biographical listings, see the Martindale-Hubbell Law Directory

LUDLUM & LUDLUM (AV)

Second Floor The Enterprise Plaza, 13915 Burnet Road at Wells Branch Parkway, 78728
Telephone: 512-255-4000
Cable Address: "Ludlum"
Telecopier: 512-244-7000

FIRM FOUNDER

James N. Ludlum (Retired 1987)

MEMBERS OF FIRM

James Ludlum, Jr.
Catherine L. Kyle
Anthony G. Brocato, Jr
M. Winfield Atkins, IV

Representative Clients: American Hardware Insurance Group; American International Group; American International Underwriters, Inc.; Go Pro Underwriters, Inc.; National Casualty Company; New Hampshire Insurance Group; North American Specialty Insurance Group; United National Insurance Group.

For full biographical listings, see the Martindale-Hubbell Law Directory

MULLEN, MACINNES & REDDING (AV)

812 San Antonio, 6th Floor, 78701
Telephone: 512-477-6813
Fax: 512-477-7573
San Antonio, Texas Office: 434 South Main Street, Suite 208.
Telephone: 210-271-3791.
Fax: 210-271-7718.

MEMBERS OF FIRM

Pat Mullen
Robert A. MacInnes
James E. "Buck" Redding (1938-1992)
Jerri L. Ward
Gregory A. Whigham
Sam Lively

ASSOCIATES

Mark H. Siefken
Alicia A. Wilde
Karl Tiger Hanner
V. Jay Youngblood
Robert D. Wilkes
Elena N. Cablao
Connie Lynn Hawkins
Bradley P. Bengtson

For full biographical listings, see the Martindale-Hubbell Law Directory

ROAN & AUTREY, A PROFESSIONAL CORPORATION (AV)

710 First State Bank Tower, 400 West Fifteenth Street, 78701-4200
Telephone: 512-474-4200
FAX: 512-469-0470; 512-469-0474

Forrest C. Roan
Jeff W. Autrey
Stephen L. Phillips

OF COUNSEL

Robert McFarland

LEGAL SUPPORT PERSONNEL

DIRECTOR OF GOVERNMENT RELATIONS

Dana Chiodo

(See Next Column)

DIRECTOR OF WORKERS' COMPENSATION

N.J. "Nick" Huestis

For full biographical listings, see the Martindale-Hubbell Law Directory

SCOTT, DOUGLASS, LUTON & MCCONNICO, L.L.P. (AV)

A Limited Liability Partnership including a Professional Corporation
One American Center, 600 Congress Avenue, 15th Floor, 78701-3234
Telephone: 512-495-6300
Fax: 512-474-0731
Houston, Texas Office: 40th Floor, NationsBank Center, 700 Louisiana Street.
Telephone: 713-225-8400.
Dallas, Texas Office: NationsBank Plaza, 901 Main Street, Suite 2800.
Telephone: 214-651-5300.

MEMBERS OF FIRM

Wallace H. Scott, Jr.
Frank P. Youngblood
H. Philip Whitworth, Jr.
John G. Soule
Stephen E. McConnico
James N. Cowden
Richard P. Marshall, Jr.
Carroll Greer Martin
Steve Selby
Elizabeth N. Miller
John W. Camp
Daniel W. Bishop, II
Ray H. Langenberg
Thomas A. Albright
Douglas J. Dashiell
Ray N. Donley
Phyllis M. Pollard
Christopher Fuller
Casey L. Dobson
Jennifer Knauth Lipinski
Daniel C. Bitting
Sam Johnson
Robert A. Summers
Mark W. Eidman
Julie Ann Springer

OF COUNSEL

Bob Bullock
Martin L. Allday

ASSOCIATES

Jeffrey G. Henry
James P. Ray
Jane M. N. Webre
Steven J. Wingard
Elizabeth B. Pearsall
Anna M. Norris
James D. Clayton
Rebecca M. Hudson

For full biographical listings, see the Martindale-Hubbell Law Directory

*** THOMPSON & KNIGHT, A PROFESSIONAL CORPORATION** (AV)

(Attorneys and Counselors)
1200 San Jacinto Center, 98 San Jacinto Boulevard, 78701
Telephone: 512-469-6100
Telecopy: 512-469-6180
Dallas, Texas Office: 1700 Pacific Avenue, Suite 3300, 75201.
Telephone: 214-969-1700.
Telecopy: 512-969-1751.
Cable Address: "Tomtex."
Telex: 732298.
Fort Worth, Texas Office: 801 Cherry Street, Suite 1600, 76102.
Telephone: 817-347-1700.
Telecopy: 817-347-1799.
Houston, Texas Office: 1700 Texas Commerce Tower, 600 Travis, 77002.
Telephone: 713-217-2800.
Telecopy: 713-217-2828; 713-217-2882.
Monterrey, Mexico Office: Edificio Losoles PD-4, Av. Lázaro Cárdenas No. 2400 Pte., San Pedro Garza Garcia, Nuevo Léon C.P. 66220.
Telephone: (52-8) 363-0096.
Telecopy: (52-8) 363-3067.

SHAREHOLDERS

Eugene W. Brees, II
James E. Cousar IV
Frank L. Hill
Debora Beck McWilliams

ASSOCIATE

Jeffrey S. Boyd

For Complete List of Firm Personnel, See General Section

For full biographical listings, see the Martindale-Hubbell Law Directory

WALSH, ANDERSON, UNDERWOOD, SCHULZE & ALDRIDGE, P.C. (AV)

La Costa Centre, 6300 La Calma, Suite 200, P.O. Box 2156, 78768
Telephone: 512-454-6864
Fax: 512-467-9318
San Antonio, Texas Office: Renaissance Plaza, Suite 800, 70 N.E. Loop 410. P.O. Box 460606.
Telephone: 210-979-6633.
Fax: 210-979-7024.

Jim Walsh
Denise Howell Anderson
Judy Underwood
Eric W. Schulze
John S. Aldridge
Chris Garza Elizalde
Paul William Hunn
Elena M. Gallegos
Nan Porett Seidenfeld

Melissa Wiginton
Oscar G. Treviño
Dorcas A. Green
Jim Hollis
Bridget R. Robinson
Robert Russo (Resident, San Antonio Office)

For full biographical listings, see the Martindale-Hubbell Law Directory

*BEAUMONT,** Jefferson Co.

ADAMS, COFFEY & DUESLER, L.L.P. (AV)

Petroleum Tower, 550 Fannin, Suite 830, P.O. Box 7505, 77726-7505
Telephone: 409-838-6767
Fax: 409-838-6950
Houston, Texas Office: 4 Houston Center, 1221 Lamar, Suite 1175.
Telephone: 713-659-6767.
FAX: 713-739-8056.

MEMBERS OF THE FIRM

Bill Coffey
Kent M. Adams
Thomas W. Duesler
Amy Stout Bean
Kevin M. Fuller

ASSOCIATES

Arthur L. Martin
Barry C. Heslop
Mark R. Strandmo
Michael V. Ardoin
Ernest J. "Trey" Browne
Pamela N. Williams

Representative Clients: United States Fidelity and Guaranty Company (U.S.F.&G.); Chubb Group of Insurance Companies; Continental Insurance Companies; American International Group of Insurance Companies; American States Insurance Companies; G.A.B. Business Services, Inc.

For full biographical listings, see the Martindale-Hubbell Law Directory

BENCKENSTEIN, NORVELL & NATHAN, L.L.P. (AV)

2615 Calder Avenue, Suite 600, P.O. Box 551, 77704
Telephone: 409-833-4309
Telecopier: 409-833-9558
Houston, Texas Office: One Riverway, Suite 100
Telephone: 713-871-8081.
FAX: 713-871-1509.

MEMBERS OF FIRM

Lipscomb Norvell, Jr.
Jerry J. Nathan
Gerald W. Riedmueller
Michael J. Reviere
Russell W. Heald
Donald Francis Lighty
Paul A. Scheurich

ASSOCIATES

Craig H. Clendenin
Kerry B. McKnight
Floyd F. McSpadden, Jr.
Elizabeth Ellen Brown
Wayne E. Revack
Stephen R. Whalen
Dennis S. Dresden
David A. Oubre
Jacqueline M. Stroh
Douglas C. Clark (Resident, Houston, Texas Office)

Representative Clients: Chubb/Pacific Indemnity Group; Mobil Oil Corp.; Aetna Casualty Insurance Co.; Hartford Insurance Group; The Home Insurance Company; Wausau; Cigna; Fina Oil & Chemical Company; Continental Insurance Group; Kemper Group Insurance.

For full biographical listings, see the Martindale-Hubbell Law Directory

PATE & DODSON (AV)

470 Orleans Building, Suite 1201, 77701
Telephone: 409-838-6578
Fax: 409-838-6922

MEMBERS OF FIRM

Gordon R. Pate
Joe Michael Dodson
Karen L. Spivey

ASSOCIATES

Christy Amuny
Suzanne M. Wohleb

For full biographical listings, see the Martindale-Hubbell Law Directory

WELLER, GREEN, McGOWN & TOUPS, L.L.P. (AV)

5th Floor, Petroleum Tower, 550 Fannin Street, P.O. Box 350, 77704
Telephone: 409-838-0101
Telecopy: 409-838-6780

George A. Weller (1911-1986)
Edward H. Green
Michael R. McGown
Mitchell A. Toups
Raymond Lyn Stevens

John R. Dolezal
E. Hart Green, Jr.
Nicholas S. Baldo
Gene M. Zona Jones
Michael R. Walzel
B. Adam Terrell
Steven R. Thomas
Steven C. Toups
Michael K. Rose
Ellen G. Reynard
Christine M. Simoneaux (Not admitted in TX)

Representative Clients: Fireman's Fund Insurance Companies; Liberty Mutual Insurance Co.

For full biographical listings, see the Martindale-Hubbell Law Directory

KYLE WHEELUS, JR. (AV)

2358 Eastex Freeway, 77703
Telephone: 409-892-6811
Fax: 409-892-6834

For full biographical listings, see the Martindale-Hubbell Law Directory

*CONROE,** Montgomery Co.

HOPE & CAUSEY, P.C. (AV)

Commonwealth Centre, Suite 125, 2040 Loop 336 West, P.O. Box 3188, 77305-3188
Telephone: Conroe: 409-760-1599
Houston: 713-350-4352

Ruben W. Hope, Jr.
John M. Causey
Charles A. Kreger
Stephen M. Schlacks

Kenna M. Seiler
David C. Klosterboer
Ray A. Burgess

For full biographical listings, see the Martindale-Hubbell Law Directory

*CORPUS CHRISTI,** Nueces Co.

BRIN & BRIN, P.C. (AV)

1202 Third Street, 78404
Telephone: 512-881-9643
Fax: 512-883-0506
San Antonio, Texas Office: 8200 IH Ten West, Suite 610.
Telephone: 210-341-9711.
Fax: 512-341-1854.
Edinburg, Texas Office: 118 East Cano.
Telephone: 210-381-6602.
Fax: 210-381-0725.
Brownsville, Texas Office: 1205 North Expressway 83.
Telephone: 210-544-7110
Fax: 210-544-0607.

Ronald B. Brin
George G. Brin (Resident, San Antonio Office)
Richard W. Crews, Jr.
Douglas M. Kennedy
John R. Lyde (Resident, Edinburg Office)
Paul Swacina
Gerald D. McFarlen (Resident, San Antonio Office)
Bruce E. Anderson (Resident, San Antonio Office)
Tom F. Nye
Sandra C. Zamora (Resident, San Antonio Office)
Steven Mark Vidaurri (Resident, Edinburg Office)
William R. Gault (Resident, Brownsville Office)

Representative Clients: St. Paul Insurance Co.; Travelers Insurance Co.; Maryland Casualty Company; Coca Cola Bottlers Assn.; CIGNA Companies; Fireman's Fund; Texas Medical Liability Trust; Kemper Insurance Co.; National Union Insurance Co.; Medical Protective Co. (JUA).

For full biographical listings, see the Martindale-Hubbell Law Directory

DUNN & WEATHERED, P.C. (AV)

611 South Upper Broadway, 78401
Telephone: 512-883-1594
FAX: 512-883-1599

David J. Dunn
Frank E. Weathered
John A. Smith, III
Mark DeKoch

OF COUNSEL

L. Nelson Hall

Reference: Citizens Bank.

For full biographical listings, see the Martindale-Hubbell Law Directory

HUNT, HERMANSEN, McKIBBEN & ENGLISH, L.L.P. (AV)

1100 First City Tower II, 555 North Carancahua, 78478
Telephone: 512-882-6611
Telecopier: 512-883-8353

MEMBERS OF FIRM

Tom Hermansen
James F. McKibben, Jr.
Monte J. English
Ken Fields
Carlos A. Villarreal
Richard C. Woolsey

ASSOCIATES

Matthew B. Cano
Lamar G. Clemons
Jeanie D. Coltrin-Brink
Donald B. Dailey, Jr.
David W. Green
Tana S. Schlimmer
Thomas A. Silver

OF COUNSEL

Lev Hunt

Representative Clients: Reliance Insurance Co.; United States Insurance Group; Phillip Morris; St. Paul; Medical Protective.

For full biographical listings, see the Martindale-Hubbell Law Directory

*DALLAS,** Dallas Co.

BAILEY AND WILLIAMS (AV)

717 North Harwood Street Suite 1650, 75201
Telephone: 214-777-6300

OF COUNSEL

Derol Todd

MEMBERS OF FIRM

James A. Williams
Glennis E. Sims
Douglas R. Lewis
Robert C. Brown
Suzanne Caldwell Ekvall
Sidney L. Murphy

ASSOCIATES

LeAnn Wainscott Cross
Robin Janene Hill
Katherine Lee Laws

Representative Clients: American Physicians Insurance Exchange; Aetna Life & Casualty; Government Employees Insurance Co.; Vanliner Insurance Co.; Trans America Insurance Co.; Professional Risk Management; Montgomery Elevator; Akros Medico Enterprises; Childrens Medical Center of Dallas; St. Paul Medical Center of Dallas.

For Complete List of Firm Personnel, See General Section

For full biographical listings, see the Martindale-Hubbell Law Directory

E. THOMAS BISHOP, P.C. (AV)

1600 Premier Place, 5910 North Central Expressway, 75206
Telephone: 214-987-8181
Facsimile: 214-987-8180

E. Thomas Bishop

Alexander N. Beard
Richard J. Byrne
Mark Dean Johnson
Stephen C. Mahaffey
Darryl J. Silvera
J. Kevin Thompson
Kevin E. Walker
Erik E. Ekvall
Michael A. Hummert
Kathryn E. Eriksen
Robert C. Turner

For full biographical listings, see the Martindale-Hubbell Law Directory

LAW OFFICES OF ARLEN DEAN SPIDER BYNUM, P.C. (AV)

4311 Oak Lawn, Suite 444, 75219-2339
Telephone: 214-559-0500
Fax: 214-526-3805

Arlen Dean Spider Bynum

David A. Harris
Clifton M. Freeman
Michael K. Russell

For full biographical listings, see the Martindale-Hubbell Law Directory

CALHOUN & STACY (AV)

5700 NationsBank Plaza, 901 Main Street, 75202-3747
Telephone: 214-748-5000
Telecopier: 214-748-1421
Telex: 211358 CALGUMP UR

Mark Alan Calhoun
David W. Elrod
Steven D. Goldston
Parker Nelson
Roy L. Stacy

ASSOCIATES

Shannon S. Barclay
Robert A. Bragalone
Dennis D. Conder
Jane Elizabeth Diseker
Lawrence I. Fleishman
Thomas C. Jones
Katherine Johnson Knight
V. Paige Pace
Veronika Willard
Michael C. Wright

LEGAL CONSULTANT

Rees T. Bowen, III

For full biographical listings, see the Martindale-Hubbell Law Directory

GODWIN & CARLTON, A PROFESSIONAL CORPORATION (AV)

Suite 3300, 901 Main Street, 75202-3714
Telephone: 214-939-4400
Telecopier: 214-760-7332
Monterrey, Mexico Correspondent: Quintero y Quintero Abogodos. Martin De Zalva 840-3 Sur Esquinna Con Hidalgo.
Telephone: 44-07-74, 44-07-80, 44-06-56, 44-06-28.
Fax: 83-40-34-54.

George R. Carlton, Jr.
Darrell G. Adkerson
Keith A. Glover
Thomas L. Woodman
Craig A. Harris

W. Blake Hyde

(See Next Column)

Scott J. Scherr

For Complete List of Firm Personnel, See General Section

For full biographical listings, see the Martindale-Hubbell Law Directory

GOLLAHER & CHAMBERS, A PROFESSIONAL CORPORATION (AV)

Suite 1125, 2777 Stemmons Freeway, 75207
Telephone: 214-634-2582

Larry L. Gollaher
Wesley W. Chambers

James E. (Ted) Turner

For full biographical listings, see the Martindale-Hubbell Law Directory

MIDDLEBERG, RIDDLE & GIANNA (AV)

2323 Bryan Street, Suite 1600, 75201
Telephone: 214-220-6300
Telecopier: 214-220-2785
New Orleans, Louisiana Office: 31st Floor, Place St. Charles, 201 St. Charles Avenue,
Telephone: 504-525-7200.
Telecopier: 504-581-5983.
Austin, Texas Office: 901 South Mopac Expressway.
Telephone: 512-329-3012.

Ira Joel Middleberg (Not admitted in TX)
Michael Lee Riddle
Dominic J. Gianna (Not admitted in TX)

Robert M. Duval
Craig A. Eggleston
John L. Genung
Jim Jordan
Kay A. King
Kenneth J. Lambert
Marigny A. Lanier
William Andrew Messer
Carol J. Riddle
Alexandra Smith
Sheryl Weisberg
Marsha L. Williams

OF COUNSEL

Richard S. Wilensky

For full biographical listings, see the Martindale-Hubbell Law Directory

THOMPSON, COE, COUSINS & IRONS, L.L.P. (AV)

200 Crescent Court, Eleventh Floor, 75201-1840
Telephone: 214-871-8200 (Dallas)
512-480-8770 (Austin)
FAX: 214-871-8209

MEMBERS OF FIRM

Franklin H. Perry
Robert O. Lamb
Randy A. Nelson
David M. Taylor
Leo John Jordan
Robert B. Wellenberger
Rhonda Johnson Byrd
Scott Patrick Stolley
Roger D. Higgins
John L. Ross
Alison H. Moore
Belinda A. Vrielink
Richard M. Mosher
Newton J. Jones
Beth D. Bradley
Jennifer D. Aufricht

ASSOCIATES

John B. Kronenberger
Richard D. Boston
David F. Eriksen
Harrison H. Yoss
Karl A. Vogeler
Thomas A. Culpepper
James Richard Harmon
James L. Sowder
Kelley L. Heide
Kevin B. Brown
Pamela J. Touchstone

COUNSEL

R. B. Cousins

Representative Clients: Allstate Insurance Co.; American International Group; Continental Insurance Group; Crum & Forster; First State Insurance Co.; Lexington Insurance Co.; The London Agency; Transamerica Insurance Group; Zurich American.

For Complete List of Firm Personnel, See General Section

For full biographical listings, see the Martindale-Hubbell Law Directory

THOMPSON & KNIGHT, A PROFESSIONAL CORPORATION (AV)

(Attorneys and Counselors)
1700 Pacific Avenue Suite 3300, 75201
Telephone: 214-969-1700
Telecopy: 214-969-1751
Cable Address: "Tomtex"
Telex: 732298
Austin, Texas Office: 1200 San Jacinto Center, 98 San Jacinto Boulevard, 78701.
Telephone: 512-469-6100.
Telecopy: 512-469-6180.
Fort Worth, Texas Office: 801 Cherry Street, Suite 1600, 76102.
Telephone: 817-347-1700.
Telecopy: 817-347-1799.

(See Next Column)

THOMPSON & KNIGHT A PROFESSIONAL CORPORATION—*Continued*

Houston, Texas Office: 1700 Texas Commerce Tower, 600 Travis, 77002.
Telephone: 713-217-2800.
Telecopy: 713-217-2828.
Monterrey, Mexico Office: Edificio Losoles PD-4, Av. Lázaro Cárdenas No. 2400 Pte., San Pedro Garza Garcia, Nuevo Léon C.P. 66220.
Telephone: (52-8) 363-0096.
Telecopy: (52-8) 363-3067.

SHAREHOLDERS

G. Luke Ashley
P. Jefferson Ballew
William L. Banowsky
Michael R. Berry
Jane Politz Brandt
George C. Chapman
Cheryl E. Diaz
Frank Finn
Rachelle H. Glazer
Gerald H. Grissom
Deborah G. Hankinson
Craig A. Haynes
Jerry P. Jones
Stephen S. Livingston
John A. Mackintosh, Jr.
Schuyler B. Marshall, IV
John H. Martin
Maureen Murry
Joseph S. Pevsner
Stephen C. Rasch
Stephen C. Schoettmer
Molly Steele
James M. Underwood

ASSOCIATES

Steven R. Baggett
L. James Berglund, II
Beverly Ray Burlingame
Pamela Corrigan
Greg W. Curry
Lori L. Dalton
D'Lesli M. Davis
F. Barrett Davis
Katherine Romeo Gregory
Michael G. Guajardo
Craig Naveen Kakarla
Karen L. Kendrick
Jacob B. Marshall
Leasa G. McCorkle
Mindy L. McNew
Allison Roseman
Michael E. Schonberg
Lisa A. Schumacher
Pamela J. Smith
Robert V. Vitanza
David S. White
Amy K. Witherite

STAFF ATTORNEY

Dawn Marie Wright

OF COUNSEL

David S. Kidder
Malia A. Litman

For Complete List of Firm Personnel, See General Section

For full biographical listings, see the Martindale-Hubbell Law Directory

*EL PASO,** El Paso Co.

DUDLEY, DUDLEY, WINDLE & STEVENS (AV)

2501 North Mesa, Suite 200, 79902
Telephone: 915-544-3090
Fax: 915-542-2651

MEMBERS OF FIRM

William C. (Pat) Dudley
Paul W. Dudley
Wayne Windle
J. Monty Stevens
Lawrence M. Jordan
J. Malcolm Harris

ASSOCIATES

John C. Steinberger
Steven R. Hatch
Mary W. Craig
Boyd W. Naylor
Albert G. "Al" Weisenberger
Bonnie L. Jones
Jaime A. Villalobos
Regina B. Arditti

Representative Clients: Allstate Insurance Co.; A.I.G. Group; Argonaut Insurance Co.; Chubb Group of Insurance Companies; CNA Insurance Co.; Continental Loss Adjusting; Crawford & Company.

For full biographical listings, see the Martindale-Hubbell Law Directory

*FORT WORTH,** Tarrant Co.

THOMPSON & KNIGHT, A PROFESSIONAL CORPORATION (AV)

(Attorneys and Counselors)
801 Cherry Street, Suite 1600, 76102
Telephone: 817-347-1700
Telecopy: 817-347-1799
Dallas, Texas Office: 1700 Pacific Avenue, Suite 3300, 75201.
Telephone: 214-969-1700.
Telecopy: 214-969-1751.
Cable Address: "Tomtex."
Telex: 732298.
Austin, Texas Office: 1200 San Jacinto Center, 98 San Jacinto Boulevard, 78701.
Telephone: 512-469-6100.
Telecopy: 512-469-6180.
Houston, Texas Office: 1700 Texas Commerce Tower, 600 Travis, 77002.
Telephone: 713-217-2800.
Telecopy: 713-217-2828; 713-2882.
Monterrey, Mexico Office: Edificio Losoles PD-4, Av. Lázaro Cárdenas No. 2400 Pte., San Pedro Garza Garcia, Nuevo Léon C.P. 66220.
Telephone: (52-8) 363-0096.
Telecopy: (52-8) 363-3067.

SHAREHOLDERS

E. Michael Sheehan

(See Next Column)

ASSOCIATE

Jennifer Pettijohn Henry

For Complete List of Firm Personnel, See General Section

For full biographical listings, see the Martindale-Hubbell Law Directory

*HOUSTON,** Harris Co.

BOSWELL & HALLMARK, A PROFESSIONAL CORPORATION (AV)

1100 Louisiana Street, Suite 2100, 77002
Telephone: 713-650-1600
Facsimile: 713-650-1211

John H. Boswell
Jim C. Ezer
Terry M. Womac
John T. Valentine
David E. Brothers, Jr.
Gene F. Creely, II
Donald R. Hallmark (1934-1990)

Gary D. Peak
Paul C. Leggett
Lydia S. Zinkhan
Janis G. Harlan
George Andrew (Drew) Coats

LEGAL SUPPORT PERSONNEL

Dennis L. Gane (Administrator)

For full biographical listings, see the Martindale-Hubbell Law Directory

BROWN, SIMS, WISE & WHITE, A PROFESSIONAL CORPORATION (AV)

One Post Oak Central, 21st Floor, 2000 Post Oak Boulevard, 77056-4496
Telephone: 713-629-1580
Fax: 713-629-5027
Telex: 775557

G. Byron Sims
James D. Wise, Jr.
Ronald L. White
Kenneth G. Engerrand
Lyn Van Dusen
Thomas O. Deen
Innes Alexander Henderson Mackillop
James N. Isbell
Gregory M. Sullivan

OF COUNSEL

Thomas A. Brown

Polly A. Kinnibrugh
Charles M. Brackett
Deanna H. Brewer
Thomas W. Burch, III
Michael D. Williams
Richard E. Hanson
Mark C. Clemer
James R. Koecher
Randa L. Duncan
Ronnie W. Baham, Jr.
John R. Walker
William A. Galerston
Robert J. Hamm
Cynthia A. Galvan
Michael A. Varner
Stephen T. Smith
Walter Joseph Gallant
Philip Robert Brinson
Marc C. Mayfield
Gus David Oppermann, V
Douglas J. Shoemaker
Christopher A. Kesler
Monica A. Fekete
Leslie Downs Geer

For full biographical listings, see the Martindale-Hubbell Law Directory

FUNDERBURK & FUNDERBURK, L.L.P. (AV)

1080 Riviana Building, 2777 Allen Parkway, 77019
Telephone: 713-526-1801

MEMBERS OF FIRM

Weldon W. Funderburk
Larry B. Funderburk
Don Karotkin
Howard R. King
H. Dwayne Newton
John P. Cahill, Jr.
James A. Newsom
Ryan A. Beason
Cynthia L. Jones

ASSOCIATES

Thomas L. Cougill
Mark J. Courtois
J. Gregory Guy Funderburk
John L. Engvall, Jr.
David W. Funderburk
Brittian A. Featherston
Jeffrey Pierce Fultz

Representative Client: American States Insurance Co.; Citgo Petroleum Corporation; CNA Insurance; Texas Medical Liability Insurance Underwriting Association (JUA); Kemper National; Lawyers Surety Corporation; Maryland Insurance; The Medical Protective Company; The Mundy Companies; Waste Management, Inc.

For full biographical listings, see the Martindale-Hubbell Law Directory

GILPIN, PAXSON & BERSCH (AV)

A Registered Limited Liability Partnership
1900 West Loop South, Suite 2000, 77027-3259
Telephone: 713-623-8800
Telecopier: 713-993-8451

(See Next Column)

GILPIN, PAXSON & BERSCH, *Houston—Continued*

MEMBERS OF FIRM

Gary M. Alletag
Timothy R. Bersch
Deborah J. Bullion
James L. Cornell, Jr.
George R. Diaz-Arrastia
Frank W. Gerold
John D. Gilpin
William T. Little
Darryl W. Malone
Michael W. McCoy
Michael J. Pappert
Stephen Paxson
Lionel M. Schooler
Mary E. Wilson
Kevin F. Risley

ASSOCIATES

Russell T. Abney
N. Terry Adams, Jr.
John W. Burchfield
Evan N. Kramer
Dale R. Mellencamp
P. Wayne Pickering
Susan M. Schwager

OF COUNSEL

Harless R. Benthul
Thomas F. Aubry

Representative Clients: Aetna Casualty & Surety; Alexander & Alexander of Texas, Inc.; Alexis, Inc.; Arthur J. Gallagher Company; Corporate Service, Inc.; Diamond State Insurance Company; F.A. Richard & Associates, Inc.; United National Insurance Company; VASA North Atlantic Insurance Company.

For full biographical listings, see the Martindale-Hubbell Law Directory

HOHMANN, WERNER & TAUBE, L.L.P. (AV)

1300 Post Oak Boulevard, Suite 700, 77056
Telephone: 713-961-3541
Fax: 713-961-3542
Austin, Texas Office: 100 Congress, Suite 1600.
Telephone: 512-472-5997.
Fax: 512-472-5248.

Philip A. Werner
Joseph M. Heard
Mary C. Thompson

Robert W. Craft, Jr.
Leigh Whelan

For full biographical listings, see the Martindale-Hubbell Law Directory

LORANCE & THOMPSON, A PROFESSIONAL CORPORATION (AV)

303 Jackson Hill, 77007
Telephone: 713-868-5560
Fax: 713-864-4671; 868-1605
Phoenix, Arizona Office: 2525 East Camelback Road, Suite 230, 85016.
Telephone: 602-224-4000.
Fax: 602-224-4098.
San Diego, California Office: 555 West Beech Street, Suite 222, 92101.
Telephone: 800-899-1844.

Larry D. Thompson
Wayne Adams
Frank B. Stahl, Jr.
William K. Luyties
Clifford A. Lawrence, Jr.
Walter F. (Trey) Williams, III
David O. Cluck
Phillip C. Summers
David F. Webb
Richard H. Martin
Vicki F. Brann
Ronald E. Hood
Gwen W. Dobrowski
Mark D. Flanagan
F. Barham Lewis

David W. Prasifka
Gregory D. Solcher
John A. Culberson
George Eric Van Noy
James E. Simmons
John H. Thomisee, Jr.
Tracey R. Burridge
Douglas A. Haldane
Geoffrey C. Guill
Diane M. Guariglia
Kelly B. Lea
Tracey Landrum Foster
Ronnie B. Arnold
Teresa A. Carver
Terrance D. Dill, Jr.
J. Wayne Little
William T. Sebesta
Richard N. Moore
Matthew R. Pearson

OF COUNSEL

John Holman Barr
Shannon P. Davis
Alexis J. Gomez

Representative Clients: Allstate Insurance Co.; The Hartford Insurance Group.

For full biographical listings, see the Martindale-Hubbell Law Directory

MARSHALL AND GONZALEZ (AV)

3040 Post Oak Boulevard, Suite 550, 77056
Telephone: 713-622-8944
McAllen, Texas Office: The Lindberg Center, 312 Lindberg, 78501.

John C. Marshall, III
Steven M. Gonzalez

ASSOCIATES

Theodore B. Jereb
Wesley Nagorny, III
Matthew T. McCracken
Steve C. Dollinger
Matthew K. Baird
Matthew B. E. Hughes
David R. Noack
Todd J. Broussard
John Gregory Myers

(See Next Column)

LEGAL SUPPORT PERSONNEL

Barbara R. Noble

For full biographical listings, see the Martindale-Hubbell Law Directory

MCFALL, SHERWOOD & SHEEHY, A PROFESSIONAL CORPORATION (AV)

2500 Two Houston Center, 909 Fannin Street, 77010-1003
Telephone: 713-951-1000
Telecopier: 713-951-1199

Donald B. McFall
Thomas P. Sartwelle
William A. Sherwood
Richard A. Sheehy
Kent C. Sullivan
David B. Weinstein
D. Wayne Clawater
John S. Serpe
Kenneth R. Breitbeil
Shelley Rogers
Joseph A. Garnett
R. Edward Perkins
Raymond A. Neuer

Caroline E. Baker
Lauren Beck
David Brill
John M. Davidson
Robert R. Debes, Jr.
Eugene R. Egdorf
John H. Ferguson IV
Jeffrey R. Gilbert
M. Randall Jones
Christopher J. Lowman
James J. Maher
David J. McTaggart
David W. Medack
Catherine A. Mezick
Matthew G. Pletcher
Martin S. Schexnayder
David R. Tippetts
James W. K. Wilde

OF COUNSEL

Gay C. Brinson, Jr.
Edward S. Hubbard
Paul B. Radelat

Representative Clients: Dresser Industries, Inc.; The Procter & Gamble Co.; Channel Two Television; St. Paul Fire & Marine Insurance Co.; Texas Lawyers' Insurance Exchange; U.S. Aviation Underwriters; Dow Corning Corp.; Columbia Hospital Corp.; Farm & Home Savings Association.

For Complete List of Firm Personnel, See General Section

For full biographical listings, see the Martindale-Hubbell Law Directory

JAMES E. ROSS & ASSOCIATES (AV)

3209 Montrose Boulevard, 77006
Telephone: 713-523-8087
Telecopier: 713-523-8224

Edwin K. Nelson, IV

For full biographical listings, see the Martindale-Hubbell Law Directory

SCHWARTZ & CAMPBELL, L.L.P. (AV)

1221 McKinney, Suite 1000, 77010
Telephone: 713-752-0017
Telecopier: 713-752-0327

Richard A. Schwartz
Marshall S. Campbell

Monica F. Oathout
Stephen A. Mendel
Samuel E. Dunn
Harold W. Hargis
Phillip W. Bechter
Laura M. Taylor
Michael D. Hudgins

LEGAL SUPPORT PERSONNEL

PARALEGALS

Nannette Koger
Bettye Vaughan Johnson
Lenore Chomout
Maria Pinillos

For full biographical listings, see the Martindale-Hubbell Law Directory

THOMPSON & KNIGHT, A PROFESSIONAL CORPORATION (AV)

(Attorneys and Counselors)
1700 Texas Commerce Tower, 600 Travis, 77002
Telephone: 713-217-2800
Telecopy: 713-217-2828; 713-217-2882
Dallas, Texas Office: 1700 Pacific Avenue, Suite 3300, 75201.
Telephone: 214-969-1700.
Telecopy: 214-969-1751.
Cable Address: "Tomtex."
Telex: 732298.
Austin, Texas Office: 1200 San Jacinto Center, 98 San Jacinto Boulevard, 78701.
Telephone: 512-469-6100.
Telecopy: 512-469-6180.
Fort Worth, Texas Office: 801 Cherry Street, Suite 1600, 76102.
Telephone: 817-347-1700.
Telecopy: 817-347-1799.
Monterrey, Mexico Office: Edificio Losoles PD-4, Av. Lázaro Cárdenas No. 2400 PTE., San Pedro Garza Garcia, Nuevo Léon C.P. 66220.
Telephone: (52-8) 363-0096.
Telecopy: (52-8) 363-3067.

(See Next Column)

THOMPSON & KNIGHT A PROFESSIONAL CORPORATION—*Continued*

SHAREHOLDERS

David R. Noteware

ASSOCIATE

Patricia A. Nolan

For Complete List of Firm Personnel, See General Section

For full biographical listings, see the Martindale-Hubbell Law Directory

IRVING, Dallas Co.

KNOX & TOLLEFSON, P.C. (AV)

511 East Carpenter Freeway, Suite 250, 75062
Telephone: 214-869-2255
Fax: 214-869-1655
Mailing Address: P.O. Box 610863, Dallas, Texas, 75261-0863

Michael R. Knox
John C. Tollefson
Brent H. Jones

For full biographical listings, see the Martindale-Hubbell Law Directory

JACKSONVILLE, Cherokee Co.

NORMAN, THRALL, ANGLE & GUY (AV)

215 East Commerce Street, P.O. Drawer 1870, 75766
Telephone: 903-586-2595
Fax: 903-586-0524
Rusk, Texas Office: 106 East Fifth Street, P.O. Box 350.
Telephone: 903-683-2226.
FAX: 903-683-5911.

MEMBERS OF FIRM

Wyatt T. Norman (1877-1945)
Summers A. Norman (1905-1986)
Steven R. Guy (Rusk Office)
Gordon F. Thrall
Marvin J. Angle

ASSOCIATES

Forrest K. Phifer (Rusk Office)
R. Christopher Day

For full biographical listings, see the Martindale-Hubbell Law Directory

*LUBBOCK,** Lubbock Co.

CARR, FOUTS, HUNT, CRAIG, TERRILL & WOLFE, L.L.P. (AV)

1001 Texas Avenue, P.O. Box 2585, 79408
Telephone: 806-765-7491
Fax: 806-765-0553

MEMBERS OF FIRM

Robert (Bob) L. Craig, Jr.
Billy R. Wolfe
Tom H. Whiteside
Hugh N. Lyle
Leslie F. Hatch

ASSOCIATES

Lex Herrington
Leonard R. (Bud) Grossman

Representative Clients: Commercial Union Assurance Cos.; EXCEL Corp.; NCNB Texas National Bank, N.A.; The St. Paul Cos.; Utica Mutual Insurance Co.

For Complete List of Firm Personnel, See General Section

For full biographical listings, see the Martindale-Hubbell Law Directory

CRENSHAW, DUPREE & MILAM, L.L.P. (AV)

Norwest Center, P.O. Box 1499, 79408-1499
Telephone: 806-762-5281
Fax: 806-762-3510

William R. Moss
Joe H. Nagy
Brad Crawford, Jr.
William J. Wade
Philip W. Johnson
W C Bratcher
Layton Z. Woodul
Robert L. Duncan

For Complete List of Firm Personnel, See General Section

For full biographical listings, see the Martindale-Hubbell Law Directory

JONES, FLYGARE, GALEY, BROWN & WHARTON (AV)

1600 Civic Center Plaza, P.O. Box 2426, 79408
Telephone: 806-765-8851
Fax: 806-765-8829

John A. Flygare
Charles E. Galey
James L. Wharton
Jeffrey B. Jones
John P. Levick
Bradley M. Pettiet

Representative Clients: The Aetna Casualty & Surety Co.; Archers Daniels Midland Company; Farmers Insurance Group; Furr's/Bishop Cafeterias; Furr's Supermarkets, Inc.; Lee Lewis Construction, Inc.; Lummus Industries; Penn General Service Corporation; Bain Hogg Robinson; St. Joseph Health System.

For Complete List of Firm Personnel, See General Section

For full biographical listings, see the Martindale-Hubbell Law Directory

MCALLEN, Hidalgo Co.

DALE & KLEIN, L.L.P. (AV)

A Partnership including Professional Corporations
6301 North Tenth Street, 78504
Telephone: 210-687-8700
FAX: 210-687-2416
Brownsville, Texas Office: 815 Ridgewood, 78520.
Telephone: 210-546-5100.

Roy S. Dale (P.C.)
Katie Pearson Klein (P.C.)
Martin E. Morris

William D. Mount, Jr.
William L. Hubbard
Kathryn M. Flagg
Gil Peralez
Joseph A. Esparza

For full biographical listings, see the Martindale-Hubbell Law Directory

LEWIS, SKAGGS & REYNA, L.L.P. (AV)

710 Laurel, P.O. Box 2285, 78502-2285
Telephone: 210-687-8203
Fax: 210-630-6570

MEMBERS OF FIRM

John E. Lewis
John B. Skaggs
Rose Marie Guerra Reyna

Representative Clients: Farmers Insurance Group; Burlington Insurance Company; Horace Mann Insurance Company; Insurance Company of North America; The Travelers Insurance Co.; Texas Farm Bureau Insurance Cos.; Floyd West & Co.; The Home Insurance Co.; Aetna Casualty & Surety Co.; Firemen's Fund.

For full biographical listings, see the Martindale-Hubbell Law Directory

MARSHALL AND GONZALEZ (AV)

The Lindberg Center, 312 Lindberg, 78501
Telephone: 210-618-0115
Houston, Texas Office: 3040 Post Oak Boulevard, Suite 550, 77056.
Telephone: 713-622-8944.

John C. Marshall, III
Steven M. Gonzalez

ASSOCIATES

Theodore B. Jereb
Wesley Nagorny, III
Matthew T. McCracken
Steve C. Dollinger
Matthew K. Baird
Matthew B. E. Hughes
David R. Noack
Todd J. Broussard
John Gregory Myers

LEGAL SUPPORT PERSONNEL

Barbara R. Noble

For full biographical listings, see the Martindale-Hubbell Law Directory

*MIDLAND,** Midland Co.

LESLIE G. MCLAUGHLIN (AV)

1209 West Texas Avenue, 79701
Telephone: 915-687-1331
Fax: 915-687-1336

For full biographical listings, see the Martindale-Hubbell Law Directory

*PARIS,** Lamar Co.

LYLE H. JEANES, II, P.C. (AV)

805 Lamar Avenue, 75460
Telephone: 903-737-9100
Fax: 903-784-2651

Lyle H. Jeanes, II

For full biographical listings, see the Martindale-Hubbell Law Directory

*RUSK,** Cherokee Co.

NORMAN, THRALL, ANGLE & GUY (AV)

106 East Fifth Street, P.O. Box 350, 75785
Telephone: 903-683-2226
FAX: 903-683-5911
Jacksonville, Texas Office: 215 East Commerce Street, P.O. Drawer 1870.
Telephone: 903-586-2595.
FAX: 903-586-0524.

MEMBERS OF FIRM

Wyatt T. Norman (1877-1945)
Summers A. Norman (1905-1986)
Gordon F. Thrall (Jacksonville Office)
Marvin J. Angle (Jacksonville Office)
Steven R. Guy

(See Next Column)

NORMAN, THRALL, ANGLE & GUY, *Rusk—Continued*

ASSOCIATES

Forrest K. Phifer
R. Christopher Day (Jacksonville Office)

For full biographical listings, see the Martindale-Hubbell Law Directory

*SAN ANTONIO,** Bexar Co.

JONES KURTH & TREAT, P.C. (AV)

10100 Reunion Place, Suite 600, 78216
Telephone: 210-344-3900
Telecopier: 210-366-4301

David V. Jones
Laurence S. Kurth
David L. Treat
Daniel C. Andrews
Mark A. Lindow

Mark A. Giltner
Danita J. Jarreau
Carolyn D. Walker
Ray R. Ortiz
Mary M. Devine
Michael B. Angelovich

OF COUNSEL

Carol A. Jenson
John M. Sudyka

For full biographical listings, see the Martindale-Hubbell Law Directory

PLUNKETT, GIBSON & ALLEN, INC. (AV)

6243 IH - 10 West, Suite 600, P.O. Box BH002, 78201
Telephone: 210-734-7092
Fax: 210-734-0379

Lewin Plunkett
Jerry A. Gibson
Robert A. Allen
Mark R. Stein
Daniel Diaz, Jr.
Ronald Hornberger
Joseph C. Elliott
Tim T. Griesenbeck, Jr.
Keith B. O'Connell
William L. Powers
Harry S. Bates
Jennifer Gibbins Durbin
Richard N. Francis, Jr.
Ernest F. Avery
A. Dale Hicks
Richard W. Hunnicutt, III

Margaret Netemeyer
Jeffrey C. Manske
David P. Benjamin
Cathy J. Sheehan
Richard B. Copeland
John C. Howell
P. Brian Berryman
Isidro O. Castanon
Nina E. Henderson
Dan Vana
D. Ann Comerio
David L. Downs
Nancy L. Farrer
Deborah L. Klein
William J. Baine
Paul J. Janik
Tom L. Newton, Jr.
Karen H. Norris
Donald L. Crook
Peter B. Gostomski
William J. Maiberger, Jr.
Cynthia L. Beverage
Anthony A. Avey
Clayborne L. Nettleship

Representative Clients: Traveler's Insurance Co.; CIGNA; State Farm Mutual Automobile Insurance Co.; University of Texas Health Science Center at San Antonio; Commercial Union Insurance Cos.; Galen Health Care, Inc.; Ford Motor Co.; Allstate Insurance; Zurich American Insurance Group; Santa Rosa Medical Center.

For full biographical listings, see the Martindale-Hubbell Law Directory

TEXARKANA, Bowie Co.

GOODING & DODSON (AV)

A Partnership including a Professional Corporation
300 Texarkana National Bank Building, P.O. Box 1877, 75504
Telephone: 903-794-3121
FAX: 903-793-4801

William C. Gooding (P.C.)
Robert E. Dodson
Robert S. McGinnis, Jr.
Monty G. Murry
Franklin A. Poff, Jr.
Michael F. Jones
John L. Tidwell
Glen C. Hudspeth
Mark C. Burgess

Representative Clients: Aetna Life and Casualty; American General Insurance Co.; Kansas City Southern Railway Co.; Louisiana and Arkansas Railway Co.; Maryland Casualty Co.; North Texas Production Credit Assn.

For full biographical listings, see the Martindale-Hubbell Law Directory

PATTON, HALTOM, ROBERTS, MCWILLIAMS & GREER, L.L.P. (AV)

A Registered Limited Liability Partnership including Professional Corporations
700 Texarkana National Bank Building, P.O. Box 1928, 75504-1928
Telephone: 903-794-3341
Fax: 903-792-6542; 903-792-0448

James N. Haltom (P.C.)
George L. McWilliams (P.C.)
John B. Greer, III, (P.C.)
William G. Bullock

(See Next Column)

ASSOCIATES

Kristi Ingold McCasland
Caroline Malone
Ralph K. Burgess
Johanna Elizabeth Haltom Salter (1960-1993)

Representative Clients: Allstate Insurance Co.; Aetna Casualty & Surety Co.; Royal Insurance Group; Continental Insurance Group; Ranger/Pan American Insurance Cos.; The Hanover Insurance Group; American Mutual Liability Insurance Co.; American Hardware Mutual Insurance Co.; Kemper Insurance Co.; Texarkana National Bancshares, Inc.

For Complete List of Firm Personnel, See General Section

For full biographical listings, see the Martindale-Hubbell Law Directory

*VICTORIA,** Victoria Co.

CULLEN, CARSNER, SEERDEN & CULLEN, L.L.P. (AV)

119 South Main Street, P.O. Box 2938, 77902
Telephone: 512-573-6318
Fax: 512-573-2603

MEMBERS OF FIRM

Richard D. Cullen
Charles C. Carsner, Jr. (1917-1993)
William F. Seerden
Kevin D. Cullen
Jean Smetana Cullen
Juergen Koetter
Mark C. Rains
Kemper Stephen Williams, III

ASSOCIATES

Michael A. Johnson
Garland Sandhop, Jr.
Wendy Atkinson

Representative Clients: American General Insurance Co.; Aetna Casualty & Surety Co.; Hartford Accident & Indemnity Co.; U.S.F.&G. Co.; Travelers Insurance Co.; Allstate Insurance Company; Formosa Plastics Corporation and its affiliated companies; Edna Independent School District; Victoria Independent School District; Victoria County, Texas (civil only)

For full biographical listings, see the Martindale-Hubbell Law Directory

UTAH

*PROVO,** Utah Co.

JEFFS AND JEFFS, P.C. (AV)

90 North 100 East, P.O. Box 888, 84603
Telephone: 801-373-8848
Fax: 801-373-8878

M. Dayle Jeffs
A. Dean Jeffs
David D. Jeffs
Robert L. Jeffs
William M. Jeffs

Lorie D. Fowlke

Representative Clients: Farmers Insurance Group; American Service Life Insurance Co.; Central Reserve Life Insurance Co.; R.B.& G. Engineers, Inc.; Horrocks Engineers, Inc.; Duchesne County Upper Country Water Improvement District; Provo Postal Credit Union; Interwest Safety Supply, Inc.
References: Zion First National Bank; Bank of American Fork.

For full biographical listings, see the Martindale-Hubbell Law Directory

*SALT LAKE CITY,** Salt Lake Co.

HANSON, EPPERSON & SMITH, A PROFESSIONAL CORPORATION (AV)

4 Triad Center, Suite 500, P.O. Box 2970, 84110-2970
Telephone: 801-363-7611
Fax: 801-531-9747

Rex J. Hanson (1911-1980)
David H. Epperson
Lowell V. Smith
Robert R. Wallace
Scott W. Christensen
Terry M. Plant
Theodore E. Kanell
John N. Braithwaite
Richard K. Glauser
Mark J. Williams
Daniel Stoddar McConkie

Jaryl L. Rencher
Eric K. Davenport
Daniel Lee Steele
David S. Doty
Bradley R. Helsten
Bruce M. Pritchett, Jr.

Representative Clients: State Farm Ins. Co.; Continental Insurance Cos. (C.N.A.); St. Paul Fire & Marine; Kemper Insurance Group; Prudential Insurance; Transamerica Insurance Co.; Ranger Insurance; Guaranty National Ins. Co.; Utah Transit Authority; Western Surety.

For full biographical listings, see the Martindale-Hubbell Law Directory

Salt Lake City—Continued

KIMBALL, PARR, WADDOUPS, BROWN & GEE, A PROFESSIONAL CORPORATION (AV)

Suite 1300, 185 South State Street, P.O. Box 11019, 84147
Telephone: 801-532-7840
Fax: 801-532-7750

Patricia W. Christensen
Mark E. Wilkey
Heidi E. C. Leithead
Mark F. James
Gregory M. Hess

For Complete List of Firm Personnel, See General Section

For full biographical listings, see the Martindale-Hubbell Law Directory

KIPP AND CHRISTIAN, P.C. (AV)

175 East 400 South 330 City Centre I, 84111
Telephone: 801-521-3773
Fax: 801-359-9004

Carman E. Kipp
D. Gary Christian
J. Anthony Eyre
William W. Barrett
Gregory J. Sanders
Heinz J. Mahler
Michael F. Skolnick
Shawn McGarry
Kirk G. Gibbs
Sandra L. Steinvoort

Representative Clients: United States Fidelity & Guaranty Co.; E & O Professionals; Home Insurance Company; Montgomery Elevator; National Farmers Union Ins. Co.; Republic Financial Services, Inc.; Utah Medical Insurance Association (UMIA); Utah State Bar; Crum & Forster: Seaboard Underwriters.

For Complete List of Firm Personnel, See General Section

For full biographical listings, see the Martindale-Hubbell Law Directory

KIRTON & MCCONKIE, A PROFESSIONAL CORPORATION (AV)

1800 Eagle Gate Tower, 60 East South Temple, 84111
Telephone: 801-328-3600
Telecopier: 801-321-4893

Wilford W. Kirton, Jr.
Oscar W. McConkie, Jr.
Raymond W. Gee
Anthony I. Bentley, Jr.
J. Douglas Mitchell
Richard R. Neslen
Myron L. Sorensen
Robert W. Edwards
B. Lloyd Poelman
Raeburn G. Kennard
Jerry W. Dearinger
R. Bruce Findlay
Charles W. Dahlquist, II
M. Karlynn Hinman
Robert P. Lunt
Brinton R. Burbidge
Gregory S. Bell
Lee Ford Hunter
Larry R. White
William H. Wingo
David M. McConkie
Read R. Hellewell
Rolf H. Berger
Oscar W. McConkie, III
Marc Nick Mascaro
Lorin C. Barker
David M. Wahlquist
Robert S. Prince
Wallace O. Felsted
Merrill F. Nelson
Paul H. Matthews
Fred D. Essig
Clark B. Fetzer
Samuel D. McVey
Blake T. Ostler
Daniel Bay Gibbons
Gregory M. Simonsen
Von G. Keetch
Patrick Hendrickson
Stuart F. Weed
Thomas D. Walk
James E. Ellsworth
Daniel V. Goodsell
David J. Hardy
Randy T. Austin

For Complete List of Firm Personnel, See General Section

For full biographical listings, see the Martindale-Hubbell Law Directory

MORGAN & HANSEN (AV)

Kearns Building, Eighth Floor, 136 South Main Street, 84101
Telephone: 801-531-7888
Telefax: 801-531-9732

MEMBERS OF FIRM

Stephen G. Morgan
Darwin C. Hansen
John C. Hansen
Cynthia K.C. Meyer
Mitchel T. Rice
Joseph E. Minnock
Eric C. Singleton

OF COUNSEL

Dennis R. James

Representative Clients: Albertson's Inc.; Smith Food and Drug Centers, Inc.; Colorado Casualty; Farmers Insurance Group; SLC Airport Authority; St. Paul Fire and Marine Insurance Co.; State Farm Fire and Casualty; State Farm Mutual Automobile Insurance Co.; Utah Farm Bureau Insurance Co.; Utah Local Government's Insurance Trust.

For full biographical listings, see the Martindale-Hubbell Law Directory

RAY, QUINNEY & NEBEKER, A PROFESSIONAL CORPORATION (AV)

Suite 400 Deseret Building, 79 South Main Street, P.O. Box 45385, 84145-0385
Telephone: 801-532-1500
Telecopier: 801-532-7543
Provo, Utah Office: 210 First Security Bank Building, 92 North University Avenue.
Telephone: 801-226-7210.
Telecopier: 801-375-8379.

Stephen B. Nebeker
James L. Wilde (Resident at Provo)
Paul S. Felt
John A. Adams
Craig Carlile (Resident at Provo)
Steven J. Aeschbacher
Rick L. Rose
Rick B. Hoggard
Lisa A. Yerkovich

Representative Clients: Aetna Casualty & Surety Co.; Cigna Cos.; Great American Insurance Co.; Home Insurance Co.; New York Life Insurance Co.; Teachers Insurance and Annuity; Travelers Insurance Co.

For Complete List of Firm Personnel, See General Section

For full biographical listings, see the Martindale-Hubbell Law Directory

RICHARDS, BRANDT, MILLER & NELSON, A PROFESSIONAL CORPORATION (AV)

Suite 700 50 South Main Street, P.O. Box 2465, 84110
Telephone: 801-531-2000
Fax: 801-532-5506

Robert W. Brandt
Robert W. Miller (1940-1983)
P. Keith Nelson
Gary D. Stott
Robert L. Stevens
David L. Barclay
John L. Young
Brett F. Paulsen
David K. Lauritzen
Lynn S. Davies
Robert G. Gilchrist
Russell C. Fericks
Michael K. Mohrman
Michael N. Emery
Michael P. Zaccheo
Gary L. Johnson
Curtis J. Drake
George T. Naegle
Craig C. Coburn
Lloyd A. Hardcastle

JoAnn E. Carnahan
Brad C. Betebenner
Robert G. Wright
Barbara K. Berrett
Nathan R. Hyde
Christian W. Nelson
Craig Aramaki
Elizabeth A. Hruby-Mills
Bret M. Hanna (Not admitted in UT)

OF COUNSEL

William S. Richards
Wallace R. Lauchnor

Reference: Key Bank of Utah.

For full biographical listings, see the Martindale-Hubbell Law Directory

SCALLEY & READING, A PROFESSIONAL CORPORATION (AV)

261 East 300 South, Suite 200, 84111
Telephone: 801-531-7870
Fax: 801-531-7968

Ford G. Scalley
J. Bruce Reading
Steven K. Walkenhorst
Michael W. Spence
Marlon L. Bates
John Edward Hansen
Scott N. Rasmussen

John E. Swallow
Steven B. Smith
Wesley Hutchins
James W. Claflin, Jr.

For full biographical listings, see the Martindale-Hubbell Law Directory

STRONG & HANNI, A PROFESSIONAL CORPORATION (AV)

Sixth Floor Boston Building, 9 Exchange Place, 84111
Telephone: 801-532-7080
Fax: 801-596-1508

Gordon R. Strong (1909-1969)
Glenn C. Hanni
Henry E. Heath
Philip R. Fishler
Roger H. Bullock
Robert A. Burton
R. Scott Williams
Dennis M. Astill (Managing Partner)
S. Baird Morgan
Stuart H. Schultz
Paul M. Belnap
Stephen J. Trayner
Joseph J. Joyce
Bradley Wm. Bowen

Robert L. Janicki
Elizabeth L. Willey
Peter H. Christensen
H. Burt Ringwood
David R. Nielson
Adam Trupp
Catherine M. Larson

Representative Clients: State Farm Mutual Automobile Insurance Co.; Standard Accident Insurance Co.; United Services Automobile Assn.; Western Casualty & Surety Co.; Government Employees Insurance Co.; Guaranty Mutual Life Co.

For full biographical listings, see the Martindale-Hubbell Law Directory

Salt Lake City—Continued

Van Cott, Bagley, Cornwall & McCarthy, A Professional Corporation (AV)

Suite 1600, 50 South Main Street, P.O. Box 45340, 84145
Telephone: 801-532-3333
Telex: 453149
Telecopier: 801-534-0058
Ogden, Utah Office: Suite 900, 2404 Washington Boulevard.
Telephone: 801-394-5783.
Park City, Utah Office: 314 Main Street, Suite 205.
Telephone: 801-649-3889.
Reno, Nevada Office: Jeppson & Lee, 100 West Liberty, Suite 990.
Telephone: 702-333-6800.

Kenneth W. Yeates
Scott M. Hadley (Resident, Ogden, Utah Office)
Timothy W. Blackburn (Resident, Ogden, Utah Office)

For Complete List of Firm Personnel, See General Section

For full biographical listings, see the Martindale-Hubbell Law Directory

VERMONT

*MIDDLEBURY,** Addison Co.

Conley & Foote (AV)

11 South Pleasant Street, P.O. Drawer 391, 05753
Telephone: 802-388-4061
Fax: 802-388-0210

MEMBERS OF FIRM

John T. Conley (1900-1971)
Ralph A. Foote
Charity A. Downs
D. Michael Mathes
Richard P. Foote
Janet P. Shaw

For full biographical listings, see the Martindale-Hubbell Law Directory

*MONTPELIER,** Washington Co.

Theriault & Joslin, P.C. (AV)

141 Main Street, P.O. Box 249, 05601-0249
Telephone: 802-223-2381
Fax: 802-223-1461

William N. Theriault (1877-1961)
Peter B. Joslin
Fletcher Brian (Ted) Joslin

Peter S. Cullen
John Davis Buckley
Robert S. Behrens

OF COUNSEL

Fletcher B. Joslin
Jeffry W. White

LEGAL SUPPORT PERSONNEL

Betsy A. LaFlame

Representative Clients: Allstate Insurance Co.; American International Cos.; Hartford Insurance Group; St. Paul Insurance Cos.; Nationwide Insurance Cos.; Metropolitan Insurance Co.; American Home Group; Commercial Union Insurance Cos.; Prudential Insurance Cos.; PHICO Insurance Co.

For full biographical listings, see the Martindale-Hubbell Law Directory

*RUTLAND,** Rutland Co.

David L. Cleary Associates A Professional Corporation (AV)

110 Merchants Row, P.O. Box 6740, 05702-6740
Telephone: 802-775-8800
Telefax: 802-775-8809

David L. Cleary

Kaveh S. Shahi
George A. Holoch, Jr.
Ellen J. Abbott
Thomas P. Aicher
Karen S. Heald

For full biographical listings, see the Martindale-Hubbell Law Directory

Hull, Webber & Reis (AV)

(Formerly Dick, Hackel & Hull)
60 North Main Street, P.O. Box 890, 05702-0890
Telephone: 802-775-2361
Fax: 802-775-0739

Donald H. Hackel (1925-1985)
John B. Webber
Robert K. Reis
John C. Holler
Lisa L. Chalidze

(See Next Column)

ASSOCIATES

Phyllis R. McCoy
Karen Abatiell Kalter

OF COUNSEL

Richard A. Hull (P.C.)
Steven D. Vogl

Representative Clients: Aetna Insurance Co.; Great American Insurance Cos.; Crum & Forster.

For full biographical listings, see the Martindale-Hubbell Law Directory

Miller & Faignant, A Professional Corporation (AV)

36 Merchants Row, P.O. Box 6688, 05702-6688
Telephone: 802-775-2521
Fax: 802-775-8274

Lawrence Miller
John Paul Faignant

Barbara R. Blackman
Christopher J. Whelton

LEGAL SUPPORT PERSONNEL

Cynthia L. Bonvouloir
Marie T. Fabian

Representative Clients: Travelers Insurance Co.; Government Employees Insurance Co.; Utica Mutual Insurance Co.; Universal Underwriters Insurance Co.
Reference: Travelers Insurance Co.

For full biographical listings, see the Martindale-Hubbell Law Directory

VIRGINIA

*ARLINGTON,** Arlington Co.

Law Offices of George W. Campbell, Jr. & Associates A Professional Corporation (AV)

Suite 507, Arlington Plaza, 2000 15th Street, North, 22201
Telephone: 703-525-8500
Fax: 703-525-8214

George W. Campbell, Jr.

Philip G. Evans

For full biographical listings, see the Martindale-Hubbell Law Directory

BRISTOL, (Independent City)

Woodward, Miles & Flannagan, P.C. (AV)

Suite 200, Executive Plaza, 510 Cumberland Street, P.O. Box 789, 24203-0789
Telephone: 703-669-0161
Telecopier: 703-669-7376

S. Bruce Jones (1892-1966)
Jno. W. Flannagan, Jr. (1885-1955)
Waldo G. Miles (1911-1973)
Wm. H. Woodward (1907-1992)
Francis W. Flannagan
John E. Kieffer
Larry B. Kirksey
Elizabeth Smith Jones
Christen W. Burkholder
Beth Osborne Skinner

Representative Clients: CNA Companies; Cooper Tire and Rubber; Hanover Insurance Companies; Lawyers Title Insurance Company; Nationwide Mutual Co.; United Telephone-Southeast, Inc.; Universal Underwriters Group; USAA; Worldwide Insurance Group.

For full biographical listings, see the Martindale-Hubbell Law Directory

*CHARLOTTESVILLE,** (Ind. City; Seat of Albemarle Co.)

Richmond and Fishburne (AV)

Queen Charlotte Square, 214 East High Street, P.O. Box 559, 22902
Telephone: 804-977-8590
Telefax: 804-296-9861

MEMBER OF FIRM

Matthew B. Murray

Representative Clients: Albemarle Home Mutual Fire Insurance Co.; Fireman's Fund; Horace Mann Insurance Co.; Nationwide Insurance Co.; Norfolk-Southern Corp.; State Farm Insurance Co.; USAA; Virginia Farm Bureau Insurance Service; The Windsor Group.

For Complete List of Firm Personnel, See General Section

For full biographical listings, see the Martindale-Hubbell Law Directory

Taylor, Zunka, Milnor & Carter, Ltd. (AV)

414 Park Street, P.O. Box 1567, 22902
Telephone: 804-977-0191
FAX: 804-977-0198

(See Next Column)

TAYLOR, ZUNKA, MILNOR & CARTER LTD.—*Continued*

Robert Edward Taylor (Retired) Richard H. Milnor
John W. Zunka Richard E. Carter

Representative Clients: State Farm Insurance Companies; Allstate Insurance Company; The Travelers Insurance Companies; The Harleysville Insurance Companies; Kemper National Insurance Company; Commercial Union Insurance Co.; Selective Insurance Co.; Blue Cross and Blue Shield of Virginia; Crestar Bank.

For Complete List of Firm Personnel, See General Section

For full biographical listings, see the Martindale-Hubbell Law Directory

*FAIRFAX,** (Ind. City; Seat of Fairfax Co.)

DOHERTY, SHERIDAN & GRIMALDI, L.L.P. (AV)

8408 Arlington Boulevard, Suite 200, 22031
Telephone: 703-698-7700
Facsimile: 703-641-9645
Washington, D.C. Office: Suite 901, 1825 K Street, N.W.
Telephone: 202-293-1059.

MEMBERS OF FIRM

Cornelius H. Doherty, Jr. Anthony E. Grimaldi
Edwin A. Sheridan William J. Virgulak, Jr.
Dana L. Scott, Jr.

ASSOCIATE

Eric M. Persian

For full biographical listings, see the Martindale-Hubbell Law Directory

GODARD, WEST & ADELMAN, P.C. (AV)

Suite 220, 3975 University Drive, P.O. Box 1287, 22030
Telephone: 703-273-4800
Facsimile: 703-691-0804
Rockville, Maryland Office: Suite 310, 200-A Monroe Street.
Telephone: 301-340-1140.

Gary A. Godard
Norman A. West
S. Allan Adelman (Not admitted in VA; Resident, Rockville, Maryland Office)
Vicki Layman Jasper
Kenneth J. Barton, Jr.
Nomi Irene Lowy (Not admitted in VA; Resident, Rockville, Maryland Office)
Edward A. Gonsalves
William J. Minor, Jr.
Michael I. Joseph (Resident, Rockville, Maryland Office)
John S. Twinam (Resident, Rockville, Maryland Office)

LEGAL SUPPORT PERSONNEL

Arleta G. Cosby
Sharon I. Spinks
Leslie C. Jelacic
Judith H. Caldwell
Susan Kabatchnick-Klein (Resident, Rockville, Maryland Office)

For full biographical listings, see the Martindale-Hubbell Law Directory

JORDAN COYNE & SAVITS (AV)

10486 Armstrong Street, 22030
Telephone: 703-246-0900
Telecopier: 703-591-3673
Washington, D.C. Office: 1030 15th Street, N.W.
Telephone: 202-371-1800.
Telecopier: 202-842-2587.
Baltimore, Maryland Office: 400 E. Pratt Street, Suite 830.
Telephone: 410-625-5080.
Telecopier: 202-842-2587.
Rockville, Maryland Office: 33 Wood Lane.
Telephone: 301-424-4161.
Leesburg, Virginia Office: 105 Loudoun Street, S.E.
Telephones: 703-777-6084; 202-478-1895.
Telecopier: 703-771-6383.

MEMBERS OF FIRM

John O. Easton Carol Thomas Stone
John H. Carstens

ASSOCIATES

William F. Pugh James P. Fisher
Terry L. Lazaron Deborah A. Farson
Michael E. Reheuser

OF COUNSEL

Daniel D. Smith (P.C.)

Representative Clients: Aetna Casualty & Surety Co.; American International Group; Budget Car Rental; Design Professionals Insurance Co.; Giant Food; The Home Insurance Co.; Marriott Corp.; Minnesota Mining & Manufacturing; Scottsdale Insurance Co.; Washington Adventist Hospital.

For full biographical listings, see the Martindale-Hubbell Law Directory

LEWIS, TRICHILO, BANCROFT, MCGAVIN & HORVATH, P.C. (AV)

Fairfax Bank & Trust Building, Suite 400, 4117 Chain Bridge Road, P.O. Box 22, 22030-0022
Telephone: 703-385-1000
Telecopier: 703-385-1555

Benjamin J. Trichilo John D. McGavin
Steven W. Bancroft Stephen A. Horvath
Julia Bougie Judkins

Elaina Holmes Melissa S. Hogue
Alicia M. Lehnes Dawn E. Boyce
William M. Dupray

OF COUNSEL

Richard H. Lewis

References: Continental Insurance Co; Virginia Farm Bureau Insurance Cos.; Amoco Oil Co.; Cigna Insurance Cos.; Erie Insurance Exchange; Hartford Insurance Co.; State Farm Insurance Cos.; Harford Mutual Insurance Co.; Ohio Casualty Group; Chubb Group of Insurance Cos.; Atlantic Mutual Insurance Co.; USAA; Allstate Insurance Co.

For full biographical listings, see the Martindale-Hubbell Law Directory

*HARRISONBURG,** (Ind. City; Seat of Rockingham Co.)

WHARTON, ALDHIZER & WEAVER, P.L.C. (AV)

100 South Mason Street, 22801
Telephone: 703-434-0316
Fax: 703-434-5502

M. Bruce Wallinger Mark D. Obenshain
Ronald D. Hodges Thomas E. Ullrich
Douglas L. Guynn Marshall H. Ross
Gregory T. St. Ours Jeffrey S. Zurbuch
Charles F. Hilton Jennifer E. Kirkland
Daniel L. Fitch Cathleen P. Welsh
G. Rodney Young, II

Representative Clients: Fireman's Fund; Home Insurance; PMA Group; Royal Insurance Group; St. Paul Insurance Co.; State Farm Mutual Ins. Co.; The Travelers; Virginia Insurance Reciprocal; Wausau Insurance Company.

For Complete List of Firm Personnel, See General Section

For full biographical listings, see the Martindale-Hubbell Law Directory

*LEESBURG,** Loudoun Co.

JORDAN COYNE & SAVITS (AV)

105 Loudoun Street, S.E., 22075
Telephone: 703-777-6084; 202-478-1895
Telecopier: 703-771-6383
Washington, D.C. Office: 1030 15th Street, N.W.
Telephone: 202-371-1800.
Telecopier: 202-842-2587.
Rockville, Maryland Office: 33 Wood Lane.
Telephone: 301-424-4161.
Baltimore, Maryland Office: 400 E. Pratt Street, Suite 830.
Telephone: 410-625-5080.
Telecopier: 202-842-2587.
Fairfax, Virginia Office: 10486 Armstrong Street.
Telephone: 703-246-0900.
Telecopier: 703-591-3673.

John O. Easton

ASSOCIATE

William F. Pugh

OF COUNSEL

Daniel D. Smith (P.C.)

Representative Clients: Aetna Casualty & Surety Co.; American International Group; Budget Car Rental; Design Professionals Insurance Co.; Giant Food; The Home Insurance Co.; Marriott Corp.; Minnesota Mining & Manufacturing; Scottsdale Insurance Co.; Washington Adventist Hospital.

For full biographical listings, see the Martindale-Hubbell Law Directory

MCLEAN, Fairfax Co.

PLEDGER & SANTONI (AV)

Suite 204, 1489 Chain Bridge Road, 22101
Telephone: 703-821-1250
Fax: 703-790-7250

R. Harrison Pledger, Jr. Cynthia Vancil Santoni

Bernard G. Feord, Jr. Cherie Kay Dibbell Durand

For full biographical listings, see the Martindale-Hubbell Law Directory

NEWPORT NEWS, (Independent City)

PHILLIPS M. DOWDING (AV)

12335 Warwick Boulevard, 23606
Telephone: 804-595-0338
FAX: 804-595-3979

Representative Clients: The Aetna Casualty & Surety Co.; The Hartford Insurance Group; Security Group; Utica Mutual Insurance Co.; Riverside Hospital; PENTRAN; CIGNA Insurance Group; Selective Insurance Group; Commercial Union; Moore Group, Inc.

For full biographical listings, see the Martindale-Hubbell Law Directory

NORFOLK, (Independent City)

STACKHOUSE, SMITH & NEXSEN (AV)

1600 First Virginia Tower, 555 Main Street, P.O. Box 3640, 23514
Telephone: 804-623-3555
FAX: 804-624-9245

MEMBERS OF FIRM

Robert C. Stackhouse
William W. Nexsen
Peter W. Smith, IV
R. Clinton Stackhouse, Jr.
Janice McPherson Doxey

ASSOCIATES

Mary Painter Opitz
Timothy P. Murphy
Carl J. Khalil

Representative Clients: Heritage Bank & Trust; The Atlantic Group, Inc.; Roughton Pontiac Corp; Federal National Mortgage Association; Kemper National Insurance Cos.; Shearson/American Express Mortgage Corp.; Harleysville Mutual Insurance Co.; Heritage Bankshares, Inc.; Presbyterian League of the Presbytery of Eastern Virginia, Inc.; Oakwood Acceptance Corp.

For full biographical listings, see the Martindale-Hubbell Law Directory

*PULASKI,** Pulaski Co.

GILMER, SADLER, INGRAM, SUTHERLAND & HUTTON (AV)

Midtown Professional Building, 65 East Main Street, P.O. Box 878, 24301
Telephone: 703-980-1360; 703-639-0027
Telecopier: 703-980-5264
Blacksburg (Montgomery County), Virginia Office: 201 West Roanoke Street, P.O. Box 908.
Telephone: 703-552-1061.
Telecopier: 703-552-8227.

MEMBERS OF FIRM

Howard C. Gilmer, Jr. (1906-1975)
Roby K. Sutherland (1909-1975)
Philip M. Sadler (1915-1994)
Robert J. Ingram
James L. Hutton (Resident, Blacksburg Office)
Thomas J. McCarthy, Jr.
John J. Gill
Gary C. Hancock
Jackson M. Bruce
Michael J. Barbour
Deborah Wood Dobbins
Todd G. Patrick (Resident, Blacksburg Office)
Debra Fitzgerald-O'Connell
Scott A. Rose
Timothy Edmond Kirtner

OF COUNSEL

James R. Montgomery

Representative Clients: Appalachian Power Co.; Chevron; Liberty Mutual Insurance Co.; Norfolk Southern Railway Co.; Pulaski Furniture Corp.; NationsBank; Travelers Insurance Group; Renfro, Inc.; Magnox, Inc.; Corning Glass Works.

For full biographical listings, see the Martindale-Hubbell Law Directory

*RICHMOND,** (Ind. City; Seat of Henrico Co.)

COWAN & OWEN, P.C. (AV)

1930 Huguenot Road, P.O. Box 35655, 23235-0655
Telephone: 804-320-8918
Fax: 804-330-3140

Frank N. Cowan
John H. O'Brion, Jr.
W. Joseph Owen, III
Deborah S. O'Toole
David H. Gates
Frank F. Rennie, IV
Michael C. Hall
F. Neil Cowan, Jr.

Derrick Thomas
Mary Burkey Owens

References: Crestar Bank; Central Fidelity Bank.

For full biographical listings, see the Martindale-Hubbell Law Directory

DUANE AND SHANNON, P.C. (AV)

10 East Franklin Street, 23219
Telephone: 804-644-7400
Fax: 804-649-8329

(See Next Column)

Harley W. Duane, III
James C. Shannon
B. Craig Dunkum
David L. Hauck
Arnold B. Snukals
William V. Riggenbach
Carl R. Schwertz

Martha P. Smith

For full biographical listings, see the Martindale-Hubbell Law Directory

THOMPSON, SMITHERS, NEWMAN & WADE (AV)

5911 West Broad Street, P.O. Box 6357, 23230
Telephone: 804-288-4007
Telecopier: 804-282-5379

MEMBERS OF FIRM

Harry L. Thompson
William S. Smithers, Jr.
Nathaniel S. Newman
Winfrey T. Wade
R. Paul Childress, Jr.
Kimberly Smithers Wright
R. Ferrell Newman
Anton J. Stelly
Robert S. Carter

ASSOCIATES

James C. Bodie
Paul D. Georgiadis
Suzanne Elizabeth Wade
Glenn S. Phelps

Approved Attorneys for: Lawyers Title Insurance Corp.

For full biographical listings, see the Martindale-Hubbell Law Directory

WILLIAMS, MULLEN, CHRISTIAN & DOBBINS, A PROFESSIONAL CORPORATION (AV)

Two James Center, 1021 East Cary Street, P.O. Box 1320, 23210-1320
Telephone: 804-643-1991
Fax: 804-783-6456
Glen Allen, Virginia Office: 4401 Waterfront Drive, Suite 140.
Telephone: 804-965-9168.
Fax: 804-965-0955.
Washington, D.C. Office: 1575 Eye Street, N.W.
Telephone: 202-289-6200.
Fax: 202-289-4126.

David George Ball (Resident, Washington, D.C. Office)
Stephen E. Baril
William D. Bayliss
W. F. Drewry Gallalee
Andrea Rowse Stiles

Theodore J. Edlich, IV
Calvin W. Fowler, Jr.
Glen Andrew Lea
George W. Marget, III
John L. Walker, III

For Complete List of Firm Personnel, See General Section

For full biographical listings, see the Martindale-Hubbell Law Directory

ROANOKE, (Independent City)

JOHNSON, AYERS & MATTHEWS (AV)

Southwest Virginia Savings Bank Building Second Floor, 302 Second Street, S.W., P.O. Box 2200, 24009
Telephone: 703-982-3666
Fax: 703-982-1552

MEMBERS OF FIRM

James F. Johnson
Ronald M. Ayers
Joseph A. Matthews, Jr.
John D. Eure
William P. Wallace, Jr.
Kenneth J. Ries
Jonnie L. Speight
David B. Carson

ASSOCIATES

Robert S. Ballou
Philip O. Garland
L. Johnson Sarber, III

Representative Clients: Bell Atlantic-Virginia, Inc.; Blue Cross and Blue Shield of Virginia (Trigon); Federated Mutual Insurance Co.; General Motors Corp.; Nationwide Mutual Insurance Company; Norfolk and Western Railway Co.; Progressive Insurance Cos.; Royal Insurance Co.; State Farm Insurance Cos.; The Travelers Cos.

For full biographical listings, see the Martindale-Hubbell Law Directory

WOOTEN & HART, A PROFESSIONAL CORPORATION (AV)

Suite 310, 707 Building, P.O. Box 12247, 24024
Telephone: 703-343-2451
Telecopier: 703-345-6417

George W. Wooten
David B. Hart
Gary E. Tegenkamp
M. Lanier Woodrum
L. Thompson Hanes
Susan Waddell Spangler
Bradley D. McGraw
John L. Cooley
Robert M. McAdam

Michael Scott Fell
Robert A. Mullen
Thomas W. Farrell
Jeffrey J. Hatch
Peter D. Vieth
S. Jan Hueber
Katherine Cabell Londos

(See Next Column)

WOOTEN & HART A PROFESSIONAL CORPORATION—*Continued*

Representative Clients: St. Paul Insurance Cos.; United States Fidelity and Guaranty Co.
Approved Attorneys for: Lawyers Title Insurance Corp.
Reference: First Union National Bank.

For full biographical listings, see the Martindale-Hubbell Law Directory

SUFFOLK, (Independent City)

GLASSCOCK, GARDY AND SAVAGE (AV)

4th Floor National Bank Building, P.O. Box 1876, 23434
Telephone: 804-539-3474
FAX: 804-925-1419

MEMBERS OF FIRM

J. Samuel Glasscock
Jeffrey L. Gardy
William R. Savage, III

Representative Clients: Seaboard Railway System; Planters Peanuts (Division of Nabisco); Norfolk Southern Railway Co.; Nationwide Mutual Insurance Co.; State Farm Mutual Automobile Insurance Co.; Virginia Power Co.; Virginia Farm Bureau Mutual Insurance Co.; Suffolk Redevelopment and Housing Authority.
Approved Attorneys for: Lawyers Title Insurance Corp.

WASHINGTON

*OLYMPIA,** Thurston Co.

BEAN & GENTRY (AV)

Columbia Square, 320 North Columbia, P.O. Box 2317, 98507
Telephone: 206-943-8040
Fax: 206-786-6943

MEMBERS OF FIRM

Stephen J. Bean
Fred D. Gentry

ASSOCIATES

Mary G. Gentry
Cecilia Marie Clynch

Reference: Key Bank of Puget Sound.

For full biographical listings, see the Martindale-Hubbell Law Directory

*SEATTLE,** King Co.

BETTS, PATTERSON & MINES, P.S. (AV)

800 Financial Center, 1215 Fourth Avenue, 98161-1090
Telephone: 206-292-9988
Fax: 206-343-7053

Frederick V. Betts
Michael Mines
William P. Fite
Christopher W. Tompkins
Kenneth S. McEwan
Steven Goldstein
David L. Hennings
S. Karen Bamberger

OF COUNSEL

Mark M. Miller
Martin T. Collier

Samual S. Chapin
Glenn S. Draper

Representative Clients: Chicago Title Insurance Company; Chrysler Insurance Company; Crum & Forster Insurance Company; Fireman's Fund Insurance Company; GEICO; Highlands Insurance Company; John Deere Insurance Co.; Nationwide Mutual Insurance Company; Provident Life Insurance Company; State Farm Insurance Companies.

For full biographical listings, see the Martindale-Hubbell Law Directory

GAITÁN & CUSACK (AV)

30th Floor Two Union Square, 601 Union Street, 98101-2324
Telephone: 206-521-3000
Facsimile: 206-386-5259
Anchorage, Alaska Office: 425 G Street, Suite 760.
Telephone: 907-278-3001.
Facsimile: 907-278-6068.
San Francisco, California Office: 275 Battery Street, 20th Floor.
Telephone: 415-398-5562.
Fax: 415-398-4033.
Washington, D.C. Office: 2000 L Street, Suite 200.
Telephone: 202-296-4637.
Fax: 202-296-4650.

MEMBERS OF FIRM

José E. Gaitán
Kenneth J. Cusack (Resident, Anchorage, Alaska Office)
William F. Knowles
Ronald L. Bozarth

OF COUNSEL

Howard K. Todd
Gary D. Gayton
Michel P. Stern (Also practicing alone, Bellevue, Washington)
Christopher A. Byrne
Patricia D. Ryan

(See Next Column)

ASSOCIATES

Mary F. O'Boyle
Bruce H. Williams
David J. Onsager
Diana T. Jimenez
Robert T. Mimbu
Cristina C. Kapela
Camilla M. Hedberg
John E. Lenker
Kathleen C. Healy

Representative Clients: The Chubb Group of Insurance Companies; CNA Insurance Companies; CIGNA Insurance Companies; Central National Insurance Company of Omaha; Switzerland Insurance Company; Hartford Insurance Company; Allstate Insurance Companies; Northbrook Property and Casualty; Commercial Union Insurance Company.

For full biographical listings, see the Martindale-Hubbell Law Directory

KELLER ROHRBACK (AV)

1201 Third Avenue, Suite 3200, 98101-3052
Telephone: 206-623-1900
FAX: 206-623-3384
Bremerton, Washington Office: 400 Warren Avenue.
Telephone: 360-479-5151.
Fax: 360-479-7403.

MEMBERS OF FIRM

Pinckney M. Rohrback (1923-1994)
Fred R. Butterworth
Harold Fardal
Glen P. Garrison
Laurence Ross Weatherly
Lynn Lincoln Sarko (Mr.)
John H. Bright
William C. Smart
Lawrence B. Linville
Irene M. Hecht
Kirk S. Portmann
Kathleen Kim Coghlan
David R. Major
Benson D. Wong
Nikki L. Anderson (Ms.)
John T. Mellen
Karen E. Boxx
Thomas A. Heller
Stephen J. Henderson
Michael Woerner

ASSOCIATES

T. David Copley
Rob J. Crichton
Juli E. Farris
Mark A. Griffin
William A. Linton
Paulette Peterson
Stella L. Pitts
Roberta N. Riley
Britt L. Tinglum
John H. Wiegenstein

OF COUNSEL

Burton C. Waldo
Melvin F. Buol

Attorneys For: Allstate Insurance Company; American Honda Motor Co., Inc.; American States Insurance Co.; American Suzuki Motor Corp.; Bell Helmets, Inc.; Kemper Insurance Group; Ohio Casualty Group; Pacific Northwest Bank; Ticor Title; United Services Automobile Association.

For Complete List of Firm Personnel, See General Section

For full biographical listings, see the Martindale-Hubbell Law Directory

OLES, MORRISON & RINKER (AV)

3300 Columbia Center, 701 Fifth Avenue, 98104-7082
Telephone: 206-623-3427
Telecopier: 206-682-6234

MEMBERS OF FIRM

Seth W. Morrison
David C. Stewart
Sam E. Baker, Jr.
Arthur D. McGarry
B. Michael Schestopol
Theodore L. Preg
Robert J. Burke
David H. Karlen
Bradley L. Powell
Douglas S. Oles
Peter N. Ralston
Mark F. O'Donnell
John Lukjanowicz
James F. Nagle
Glenn R. Nelson
J. Craig Rusk
T. Daniel Heffernan
Harlan M. Hatfield
Robert W. Sargeant

ASSOCIATES

Todd M. Nelson
Traeger Machetanz
Richard T. Black
Evalyn K. Hodges
William D Garcia (Not admitted in WA)
George T. Schroth

OF COUNSEL

Stuart G. Oles

For full biographical listings, see the Martindale-Hubbell Law Directory

WEST VIRGINIA

*BECKLEY,** Raleigh Co.

FILE, PAYNE, SCHERER & FILE (AV)

Law Building, 130 Main Street, P.O. Drawer L, 25801
Telephone: 304-253-3358
Fax: 304-255-5136

(See Next Column)

FILE, PAYNE, SCHERER & FILE, *Beckley—Continued*

MEMBERS OF FIRM

Edward M. Payne, III
Robert N. File
John Payne Scherer
William H. File, III

ASSOCIATE

C. Michael Griffith

OF COUNSEL

William Henry File, Jr.

Representative Clients: Federal Insurance Co.; Globe Indemnity Co.; Insurance Company of America; Horace Mann Insurance Co.; Metropolitan Property and Liability Insurance Co.; Prudential Insurance; Federated Insurance; Kemper Insurance; Professional Medical Insurance Company; Lloyd's of London.

For full biographical listings, see the Martindale-Hubbell Law Directory

LYNCH, MANN, SMITH & MANN (AV)

108 1/2 South Heber Street, P.O. Box 1600, 25802-1600
Telephone: 304-253-3349

MEMBERS OF FIRM

Jack A. Mann
Clyde A. Smith, Jr.
Kimberly G. Mann

Representative Clients: State Farm Insurance Companies; Horace Mann Insurance Co.; Erie Insurance Company; Sears, Roebuck and Co.; Dairyland Insurance Company; Allstate Insurance Co.; U.S.F.&G. Insurance Company; American States Insurance Company; Atlantic Mutual Insurance Company; Transamerica Corporation.

For full biographical listings, see the Martindale-Hubbell Law Directory

*CHARLESTON,** Kanawha Co.

GOODWIN & GOODWIN (AV)

1500 One Valley Square, 25301
Telephone: 304-346-7000
Fax: 304-344-9692
Ripley, West Virginia Office: 500 Church Street, P.O. Box 349.
Telephone: 304-372-2651.
Parkersburg, West Virginia Office: 201 Third Street, Town Square.
Telephone: 304-485-2345.
Fax: 304-485-3459.

MEMBERS OF FIRM

Joseph R. Goodwin
Richard E. Rowe
Stephen P. Goodwin
Robert Q. Sayre, Jr.
Richard D. Owen

ASSOCIATE

Jeffry H. Hall

Representative Clients: Bucyrus-Erie Co.; CSX Corp.; Eastern American Energy Corp.; The Eureka Pipe Line Company.

For Complete List of Firm Personnel, See General Section

For full biographical listings, see the Martindale-Hubbell Law Directory

JACKSON & KELLY (AV)

1600 Laidley Tower, P.O. Box 553, 25322
Telephone: 304-340-1000
Fax: 304-340-1130
Martinsburg, West Virginia Office: 300 Foxcroft Avenue, P.O. Box 1068.
Telephone: 304-263-8800.
Morgantown, West Virginia Office: 6000 Hampton Center, P.O. Box 619.
Telephone: 304-599-3000.
New Martinsville, West Virginia Office: 256 Russell Avenue, P.O. Box 68.
Telephone: 304-455-1751.
Charles Town, West Virginia Office: 700 East Washington Street, P.O. Box 983.
Telephone: 304-728-6088.
Clarksburg, West Virginia Office: 203 Main Street, P.O. Box 1587.
Telephone: 304-623-3002.
Lexington, Kentucky Office: 175 East Main Street, Suite 500, P.O. Box 2150.
Telephone: 606-255-9500.
Washington, D. C. Office: 2401 Pennsylvania Avenue, N.W., Suite 400.
Telephone: 202-973-0200.
Denver, Colorado Office: Suite 2710, 1660 Lincoln Street.
Telephone: 303-837-0003.

MEMBERS OF FIRM

Winfield T. Shaffer
Lynn Oliver Frye
Wm. Richard McCune, Jr.
Gale Reddie Lea
(Martinsburg and Charles Town, West Virginia Offices)

Representative Clients: Home; Hartford; Reliance: Crum & Forster; Farm Family; Government Employees; Metropolitan Life; Prudential; Transamerican; Anthem Personal Insurance.

For Complete List of Firm Personnel, See General Section

For full biographical listings, see the Martindale-Hubbell Law Directory

SHUMAN, ANNAND & POE (AV)

Suite 1007, 405 Capitol Street, P.O. Box 3953, 25339
Telephone: 304-345-1400
Telecopier: 304-343-1826
Wheeling, West Virginia Office: Suite 3002, 1233 Main Street, 26003.
Telephone: 304-233-3100.
Telecopier: 304-233-0201.

MEMBERS OF FIRM

David L. Shuman
R. Ford Francis
Stephen Darley Annand
David E. Schumacher
Edgar A. Poe, Jr.
David Venable Moore
Charles R. Bailey
H. Gerard Kelley
Richard L. Earles
Mark William Browning
David L. Wyant (Resident, Wheeling Office)
William R. Slicer

ASSOCIATES

Jon L. Brown (Resident, Wheeling Office)
Belinda Bartley Neal
G. Kenneth Robertson
Jay W. Craig
Elizabeth Summers Lawton
Desireé Halkias Haden
W. Christopher Wickham
Paul L. Weber
George J. Joseph
David F. Nelson
Roberta F. Green
Shaun L. Peck

COUNSEL

Harry P. Henshaw, III

Representative Clients: CNA Insurance Companies; Insurance Corporation of America; Metropolitan Property & Liability Ins. Co.; MMI Companies, Inc.; Motorists Insurance Cos.; Travelers Insurance Cos.; Westfield Companies.
Reference: One Valley Bank.

For full biographical listings, see the Martindale-Hubbell Law Directory

STEPTOE & JOHNSON (AV)

Seventh Floor, Bank One Center, P.O. Box 1588, 25326-1588
Telephone: 304-353-8000
Fax: 304-353-8180
Clarksburg, West Virginia Office: Bank One Center, P.O. Box 2190, 26302-2190.
Telephone: 304-624-8000.
Fax: 304-624-8183.
Morgantown, West Virginia Office: 1000 Hampton Center, P.O. Box 1616, 26507-1616.
Telephone: 304-598-8000.
Fax: 304-598-8116.
Martinsburg, West Virginia Office: 126 East Burke Street, P.O. Box 2629, 25401-5429.
Telephone: 304-263-6991.
Fax: 304-263-4785.
Charles Town, West Virginia Office: 104 West Congress Street, P.O. Box 100, 25414-0100.
Telephone: 304-725-1414.
Fax: 304-725-1913.
Hagerstown, Maryland Office: The Bryan Centre, 82 West Washington Street, Fourth Floor, P.O. Box 570, 21740-0570.
Telephone: 301-739-8600.
Fax: 301-739-8742.
Wheeling, West Virginia Office: The Riley Building, Suite 400, 14th & Chapline Streets, P.O. Box 150, 26008-0020.
Telephone: 304-233-0000.
Fax: 304-233-0014.

MEMBERS OF FIRM

James R. Watson
Daniel R. Schuda
Patrick D. Kelly

ASSOCIATES

Cynthia R. Cokeley
Janet N. Kawash
Robert D. Pollitt
Jeffrey K. Phillips
Luci R. Wellborn
Richard J. Wolf
Susan L. Basile
Michael J. Funk
Joanna I. Tabit
Marc B. Lazenby

Representative Clients: Ameribank; ARCO Chemical Co.; City National Bank of Charleston; Federal Kemper Insurance Co.; Goodyear Tire & Rubber Co.; The Hartford Group; Hope Gas, Inc.; Olin Corp.; South Charleston Stamping & Manufacturing Co.; State Farm Insurance Cos.

For Complete List of Firm Personnel, See General Section

For full biographical listings, see the Martindale-Hubbell Law Directory

*CLARKSBURG,** Harrison Co.

MCNEER, HIGHLAND & MCMUNN (AV)

Empire Building, P.O. Drawer 2040, 26301
Telephone: 304-623-6636
Facsimile: 304-623-3035
Morgantown Office: McNeer, Highland & McMunn, Baker & Armistead, 168 Chancery Row, P.O. Box 1615.
Telephone: 304-292-8473.
Fax: 304-292-1528.
Martinsburg, Office: 1446-1 Edwin Miller Boulevard. P.O. Box 2509.
Telephone: 304-264-4621.
Fax: 304-264-8623.

(See Next Column)

MCNEER, HIGHLAND & MCMUNN—*Continued*

MEMBERS OF FIRM

C. David McMunn
J. Cecil Jarvis
James A. Varner
George B. Armistead (Resident, Morgantown Office)
Catherine D. Munster
Robert W. Trumble (Resident, Martinsburg Office)
Dennis M. Shreve
Geraldine S. Roberts
Harold M. Sklar
Jeffrey S. Bolyard
Steven R. Bratke
Michael J. Novotny (Resident, Martinsburg Office)

OF COUNSEL

James E. McNeer
Cecil B. Highland, Jr.
William L. Fury

Representative Clients: One Valley Bank of Clarksburg, National Association; Bruceton Bank; Harrison County Bank; Nationwide Mutual Insurance Cos.; Clarksburg Publishing Co.; C.I.T. Financial Services; State Automobile Mutual Insurance Co.; United Hospital Center, Inc.; West Virginia Coals, Inc.; Swanson Plating Company.

For Complete List of Firm Personnel, See General Section

For full biographical listings, see the Martindale-Hubbell Law Directory

STEPTOE & JOHNSON (AV)

Bank One Center, P.O. Box 2190, 26302-2190
Telephone: 304-624-8000
Fax: 304-624-8183
Mailing Address: P.O. Box 2190, 26302-2190
Charleston, West Virginia Office: Seventh Floor, Bank One Center, P.O. Box 1588, 25326-1588.
Telephone: 304-353-8000
Fax: 304-353-8180.
Morgantown, West Virginia Office: 1000 Hampton Center, P.O. Box 1616, 26507-1616.
Telephone: 304-598-8000.
Fax: 304-598-8116.
Martinsburg, West Virginia Office: 126 East Burke Street, P.O. Box 2629, 25401-5429.
Telephone: 304-263-6991.
Fax: 304-263-4785.
Charles Town, West Virginia Office: 104 West Congress Street, P.O. Box 100, 25414-0100.
Telephone: 304-725-1414.
Fax: 304-725-1913.
Hagerstown, Maryland Office: The Bryan Centre, 82 West Washington Street, Fourth Floor, P.O. Box 570, 21740-0570.
Telephone: 301-739-8600.
Fax: 301-739-8742.
Wheeling, West Virginia Office: The Riley Building, Suite 400, 14th & Chapline Streets, P.O. Box 150, 26003-0020.
Telephone: 304-233-0000.
Fax: 304-233-0014.

MEMBERS OF FIRM

Herbert G. Underwood
Robert G. Steele
James M. Wilson
James D. Gray
J. Greg Goodykoontz
Walter L. Williams
W. Henry Lawrence IV
Gordon H. Copland
Richard M. Yurko, Jr.

ASSOCIATES

Matthew J. Mullaney
Michael Kozakewich, Jr.
Daniel C. Cooper
Timothy R. Miley
Jacqueline A. Wilson

Representative Clients: Consolidated Gas Transmission Corp.; Consolidated Coal Co.; CNA; E.I. DuPont de Nemours & Co.; Equitable Resources, Inc.; The Hartford Group; Peabody Coal Co.; PPG Industries; Union National Bank of West Virginia; Ogden Newspapers, Inc.

For Complete List of Firm Personnel, See General Section

For full biographical listings, see the Martindale-Hubbell Law Directory

WATERS, WARNER & HARRIS (AV)

Formerly Stathers & Cantrall
701 Goff Building, P.O. Box 1716, 26301
Telephone: 304-624-5571
Fax: 304-624-7228

Birk S. Stathers (1884-1945)
W. G. Stathers (1889-1970)
Arch M. Cantrall (1896-1967)
Stuart R. Waters
Boyd L. Warner
James A. Harris
Scott E. Wilson
James C. Turner
Francis L. Warder, Jr.
G. Thomas Smith
Thomas G. Dyer

ASSOCIATES

Michael J. Folio
Katherine M. Carpenter
Ernest Glen Hentschel, II
Katrina L. Gallagher

Representative Clients: Bethlehem Steel Corp.; United States Fidelity and Guaranty Co.; State Farm Insurance Companies; Dowell Schlumberger, Inc.; Westfield Insurance Company; Grafton Coal Company; Harry Green Chevrolet, Inc.; Emax Oil Co.; Southern Steel Products Co.

(See Next Column)

For full biographical listings, see the Martindale-Hubbell Law Directory

*FAIRMONT,** Marion Co.

ROSE PADDEN & PETTY, L.C. (AV)

612 WesBanco Building, 26555
Telephone: 304-363-4260
Fax: 304-363-4284
Morgantown, West Virginia Office: 201 Walnut Street, P.O. Box 1618.
Telephone: 304-292-5036.
Fax: 304-296-0846.

Herschel Rose (1912-1992)
Timothy J. Padden
Philip C. Petty
Elisabeth H. Rose
Bruce A. Kayuha
Charles J. Crooks

Jeffery D. Taylor

Representative Clients: Chessie System; Consolidated Gas Supply Corp.; General Motors Corp.; Aetna Life & Casualty; Hartford Insurance Group; Insurance Company, North America; First National Bank in Fairmont; Travelers Insurance Co.; United States Fidelity & Guaranty Insurance Co.
Reference: WesBanco Bank, Fairmont.

For full biographical listings, see the Martindale-Hubbell Law Directory

*HUNTINGTON,** Cabell & Wayne Cos.

JENKINS, FENSTERMAKER, KRIEGER, KAYES, FARRELL & AGEE (AV)

Eleventh Floor Coal Exchange Building, P.O. Drawer 2688, 25726
Telephone: 304-523-2100
Charleston, WV 304-345-3100
Facsimile: 304-523-2347; 304-523-9279

MEMBERS OF FIRM

John E. Jenkins (1897-1961)
P. Thomas Krieger
Henry M. Kayes
Michael J. Farrell
Wesley F. Agee
Barry M. Taylor

ASSOCIATES

Suzanne McGinnis Oxley
Charlotte A. Hoffman
Robert H. Sweeney, Jr.
Patricia A. Jennings
Stephen J. Golder
William J. McGee, Jr.
Anne Maxwell McGee
Tamela J. White
Lee Murray Hall
Thomas J. Obrokta

OF COUNSEL

John E. Jenkins, Jr.
Susan B. Saxe

For full biographical listings, see the Martindale-Hubbell Law Directory

*MADISON,** Boone Co.

SHAFFER AND SHAFFER (AV)

330 State Street, P.O. Box 38, 25130
Telephone: 304-369-0511
Fax: 304-369-5431
Charleston, West Virginia Office: 1710 Bank One Center, P.O. Box 3973.
Telephone: 304-344-8716.
Fax: 304-342-1105.

MEMBERS OF FIRM

James J. MacCallum
Charles S. Piccirillo
Harry G. Shaffer, III (Resident, Charleston Office)

Representative Clients: Bank One, West Virginia, N.A., Boone; Armco Inc.; Westmoreland Coal Co.; State Farm Mutual Insurance Cos.; Nationwide Insurance Co.

For Complete List of Firm Personnel, See General Section

For full biographical listings, see the Martindale-Hubbell Law Directory

*MARTINSBURG,** Berkeley Co.

MCNEER, HIGHLAND & MCMUNN (AV)

1446-1 Edwin Miller Boulevard, P.O. Box 2509, 25401-2509
Telephone: 304-264-4621
Facsimile: 304-264-8623
Morgantown Office: McNeer, Highland & McMunn, Baker & Armistead, 168 Chancery Row. P.O. Box 1615.
Telephone: 304-292-8473.
Fax: 304-292-1528.
Clarksburg Office: Empire Building. P.O. Drawer 2040.
Telephone: 304-623-6636.
Facsimile: 304-623-3035.

Robert W. Trumble

Representative Clients: Westfield Companies; West Virginia Fire & Casualty; Home Insurance Co.; Bruceton Bank; Celina Insurance Company.

For Complete List of Firm Personnel, See General Section

For full biographical listings, see the Martindale-Hubbell Law Directory

*MORGANTOWN,** Monongalia Co.

McNeer, Highland & McMunn, Baker & Armistead (AV)

168 Chancery Row, P.O. Box 1615, 26507-1615
Telephone: 304-292-8473
Fax: 304-292-1528
Clarksburg Office: McNeer, Highland & McMunn, Empire Building, P.O. Drawer 2040.
Telephone: 304-623-6636.
Facsimile: 304-623-3035.
Martinsburg Office: McNeer, Highland & McMunn, 1446-1 Edwin Miller Boulevard, P.O. Box 2509.
Telephone: 304-264-4621.
Facsimile: 304-264-8623.

OF COUNSEL

Charles S. Armistead

Representative Clients: The Chesapeake and Potomac Telephone Company of West Virginia; Federal Kemper Insurance Co.; Home Insurance Co.

For Complete List of Firm Personnel, See General Section

For full biographical listings, see the Martindale-Hubbell Law Directory

Rose Padden & Petty, L.C. (AV)

201 Walnut Street, P.O. Box 1618, 26507
Telephone: 304-292-5036
Fax: 304-296-0846
Fairmont, West Virginia Office: 612 WesBanco Building.
Telephone: 304-363-4260.
Fax: 304-363-4284.

Timothy J. Padden
Bruce A. Kayuha
Charles J. Crooks

For full biographical listings, see the Martindale-Hubbell Law Directory

*PARKERSBURG,** Wood Co.

Ruley & Everett (AV)

The PMC Building, Suite 101, 417 Grand Park Drive, P.O. Box 628, 26102
Telephone: 304-422-6463
FAX: 304-422-6462

MEMBERS OF FIRM

Daniel Avery Ruley, Jr.
Diana Everett

Representative Clients: Camden-Clark Memorial Hospital; Cabot Corp.; United National Bank; Gatewood Products, Inc.; Aetna Casualty Co.; Commercial Union.

For Complete List of Firm Personnel, See General Section

For full biographical listings, see the Martindale-Hubbell Law Directory

*PRINCETON,** Mercer Co.

Whites Law Offices (AV)

1426 Main Street, 24740
Telephone: 304-425-8781

MEMBERS OF FIRM

Ben B. White, Jr.
Ben B. White, III

ASSOCIATES

Edward K. Rotenberry
Dwayne E. Cyrus

References: Mercer County Bank; Princeton Bank & Trust Co.

For full biographical listings, see the Martindale-Hubbell Law Directory

*WHEELING,** Ohio Co.

Bachmann, Hess, Bachmann & Garden (AV)

1226 Chapline Street, P.O. Box 351, 26003
Telephone: 304-233-3511
Fax: 304-233-3199

MEMBERS OF FIRM

Carl G. Bachmann (1890-1980)
Lester C. Hess (1903-1971)
John B. Garden (1925-1994)
Gilbert S. Bachmann
Lester C. Hess, Jr.
John L. Allen
R. Noel Foreman
Paul T. Tucker
George E. McLaughlin
Jeffrey R. Miller
Suzanne Quinn
Anthony Ira Werner

ASSOCIATES

Rhonda L. Wade
Jeffrey A. Grove
Elizabeth A. Abraham
Samuel H. Foreman

Representative Clients: Allstate Insurance Co.; Erie Insurance Group; Shelby Mutual Insurance Co.; The Cincinnati Insurance Co.; Worldwide Insurance Co.; Horace Mann Insurance Co.; Canal Insurance Co.; Metropolitan Life Insurance Co.; Nationwide Insurance Co.; The Travelers Insurance Co.; Continental Insurance Cos.; Oak Casualty Insurance Co.

For full biographical listings, see the Martindale-Hubbell Law Directory

Schrader, Recht, Byrd, Companion & Gurley (AV)

1000 Hawley Building, 1025 Main Street, P.O. Box 6336, 26003
Telephone: 304-233-3390
Fax: 304-233-2769
Martins Ferry, Ohio Office: 205 North Fifth Street, P.O. Box 309.
Telephone: 614-633-8976.
Fax: 614-633-0400.

PARTNERS

Henry S. Schrader (Retired)
Arthur M. Recht
Ray A. Byrd
James F. Companion
Terence M. Gurley
Frank X. Duff
Teresa Rieman-Camilletti
Yolonda G. Lambert
Patrick S. Casey
Sandra M. Chapman
Daniel P. Fry (Resident, Martins Ferry, Ohio Office)
James P. Mazzone

ASSOCIATES

Sandra K. Law
D. Kevin Coleman
Denise A. Jebbia
Edythe A. Nash
Robert G. McCoid
Denise D. Klug
Thomas E. Johnston

OF COUNSEL

James A. Byrum, Jr.

General Counsel: WesBanco Bank-Elm Grove.
Representative Clients: CIGNA Property and Casualty Cos.; Columbia Gas Transmission Corp.; Commercial Union Assurance Co.; Hazlett, Burt & Watson, Inc.; Stone & Thomas Department Stores; Transamerica Commercial Finance Corp.; Wheeling-Pittsburgh Steel Corp.

For full biographical listings, see the Martindale-Hubbell Law Directory

Seibert, Kasserman, Farnsworth, Gillenwater, Glauser, Richardson & Curtis, L.C. (AV)

1217 Chapline Street, P.O. Box 311, 26003
Telephone: 304-233-1220
Fax: 304-233-4813

Carl B. Galbraith (1903-1972)
George H. Seibert, Jr. (1913-1986)
Ronald W. Kasserman
Sue Seibert Farnsworth
James E. Seibert
Elba Gillenwater, Jr.
M. Jane Glauser
Randolf E. Richardson
Ronald William Kasserman
Linda Weatherholt Curtis
Donald A. Nickerson, Jr.

Representative Clients: Ohio Valley Medical Center, Inc.; Ohio Valley Window Co.; The Travelers Cos.
Reference: United National Bank - Wheeling, W. Va.

For full biographical listings, see the Martindale-Hubbell Law Directory

WISCONSIN

*APPLETON,** Outagamie Co.

McCanna, Konz, Dudas & Associates, S.C. (AV)

47 Park Place, P.O. Box 1857, 54913-1857
Telephone: 414-734-2825
Fax: 414-734-9770

Michael R. McCanna
Michael P. Konz
David G. Dudas

Representative Clients: Allstate Insurance Co.; American States Insurance Co.; Auto Owners Insurance Co.; Custom Marine Engineering, Inc.; Economy Fire & Casualty Co.; General Casualty Companies; C. R. Meyer & Sons Company; Northbrook Property & Casualty Co.; State Farm Cos.; West Bend Mutual Insurance Co.

For full biographical listings, see the Martindale-Hubbell Law Directory

Menn, Nelson, Sharratt, Teetaert & Beisenstein, Ltd. (AV)

(Formerly, Fulton, Menn & Nehs, Ltd.)
222 North Oneida Street, P.O. Box 785, 54912-0785
Telephone: 414-731-6631
FAX: 414-734-0981

Homer H. Benton (1886-1957)
Alfred C. Bosser (1890-1965)
Franklin L. Nehs (1922-1979)
David L. Fulton (1911-1985)
Glenn L. Sharratt (Retired)
John B. Menn
Peter S. Nelson
John R. Teetaert
Joseph J. Beisenstein
Mark R. Feldmann
Joseph A. Bielinski
Jonathan M. Menn
Douglas D. Hahn
Keith W. Kostecke
Robert N. Duimstra

(See Next Column)

MENN, NELSON, SHARRATT, TEETAERT & BEISENSTEIN LTD.—*Continued*

LEGAL SUPPORT PERSONNEL

Kathy J. Krause

Representative Clients: Allstate Insurance Co.; American Family Insurance Co.; General Casualty Company of Wisconsin; Hartford Insurance Group; Heritage Mutual Insurance Co.; Liberty Mutual Insurance Co.; St. Paul Insurance Cos.; Travelers Insurance Co.; Sentry Insurance Co.; Wausau Insurance Cos.

For full biographical listings, see the Martindale-Hubbell Law Directory

BROOKFIELD, Waukesha Co.

NELSON, DRIES & ZIMMERMAN, S.C. (AV)

150 North Sunnyslope Road, Suite 305, 53005
Telephone: 414-789-5880
Facsimile: 414-789-5888

Craig W. Nelson
Christine K. Nelson
James J. Dries
Jerry D. Zimmerman
Robert W. Connell
Mark S. Nelson
Mark R. Kramer
Christopher J. Conrad
Kurt R. Anderson
Sherri A. Wolske

For full biographical listings, see the Martindale-Hubbell Law Directory

*EAU CLAIRE,** Eau Claire Co.

CARROLL, POSTLEWAITE, GRAHAM & PENDERGAST, S.C. (AV)

419 South Barstow Street, P.O. Box 1207, 54702
Telephone: 715-834-7774
Fax: 715-834-1298

Bailey E. Ramsdell (1890-1963)
George Y. King (1892-1966)
George M. Carroll
Jack A. Postlewaite
Thomas J. Graham, Jr.
Raymond K. Hughes

Attorneys for: Metropolitan Life Insurance Co.; The Continental Insurance Cos.; Indemnity Insurance Company of N.A.; Travelers Insurance Co.; Sentry Insurance Company; CNA Insurance Companies; State Farm Insurance Companies.

For Complete List of Firm Personnel, See General Section

For full biographical listings, see the Martindale-Hubbell Law Directory

GARVEY, ANDERSON, JOHNSON, GABLER & GERACI, S.C. (AV)

402 Graham Avenue, P.O. Box 187, 54702-0187
Telephone: 715-834-3425
FAX: 715-834-9240

James E. Garvey
Douglas M. Johnson
William M. Gabler
Carol S. Dittmar

Representative Clients: Aetna Life & Casualty Co.; Eau Claire-Chippewa Board of Realtors; Employer's Insurance of Wausau; Great American Insurance Co.; Lyman Lumber, Inc.; Northern States Power Co.; Pope & Talbot.

For Complete List of Firm Personnel, See General Section

For full biographical listings, see the Martindale-Hubbell Law Directory

KELLY & RYBERG, S.C. (AV)

1620 Ohm Avenue, P.O. Box 479, 54702-0479
Telephone: 715-833-9640
Facsimile: 715-833-9711

Richard J. Kelly
J. Drew Ryberg

Michael F. O'Brien
Kristina Marie Bourget

Reference: Firstar Bank.

For full biographical listings, see the Martindale-Hubbell Law Directory

WILCOX, WILCOX, DUPLESSIE, WESTERLUND & ENRIGHT (AV)

1030 Regis Court, P.O. Box 128, 54701
Telephone: 715-832-6645
Fax: 715-832-8438

MEMBERS OF FIRM

Roy P. Wilcox (1873-1946)
Francis J. Wilcox
Roy S. Wilcox
Richard D. Duplessie
William J. Westerlund
Daniel A. Enright
John F. Wilcox

Attorneys for: Aetna Insurance Group; Medical Protective Assn.; American Surety Co.; Viking Insurance Co.; American Mutual Liability Ins. Co.; Continental Cas. Co.; Farmers Insurance Group.

For full biographical listings, see the Martindale-Hubbell Law Directory

*GREEN BAY,** Brown Co.

DENISSEN, KRANZUSH, MAHONEY & EWALD, S.C. (AV)

3000 Riverside Drive, P.O. Box 10597, 54307-0597
Telephone: 414-435-4391
Fax: 414-435-0730

Cletus G. Chadek (1900-1957)
Frank P. Cornelisen (1902-1967)
Charles M. Denissen (1906-1991)
Shannon D. Mahoney (1935-1993)
William J. Ewald
Mark A. Pennow
Mary Beth Callan
F. Scott Wochos
John K. Gorton
James R. Gorton
Erik J. Pless
Beth Rahmig Pless

OF COUNSEL

Eugene D. Kranzush

Representative Clients: Aetna Casualty & Surety Co.; Wausau Insurance Cos.; The Home Insurance Cos.; CIGNA/Insurance Company of North America; Maryland Casualty Co.; Firemans' Fund American Insurance Cos.; Sentry-Dairyland Claims Service; Underwriters Adjusting Co.; The Hartford.

For full biographical listings, see the Martindale-Hubbell Law Directory

SCHOBER & ULATOWSKI, S.C. (AV)

414 East Walnut Street, Suite 150, 54305-1780
Telephone: 414-432-5355
Facsimile: 414-432-5967

Thomas L. Schober

Michael J. Kirschling

For full biographical listings, see the Martindale-Hubbell Law Directory

*LA CROSSE,** La Crosse Co.

WILLIAM SKEMP LAW FIRM, S.C. (AV)

505 King Street, Suite 209, 54601
Telephone: 608-791-2500
Facsimile: 608-791-2510

William P. Skemp
William G. Skemp

For full biographical listings, see the Martindale-Hubbell Law Directory

*MADISON,** Dane Co.

BELL, METZNER, GIERHART & MOORE, S.C. (AV)

44 East Mifflin Street, P.O. Box 1807, 53701
Telephone: 608-257-3764
FAX: 608-257-3757

Carroll E. Metzner
Roger L. Gierhart
John M. Moore
Steven J. Caulum
Ward I. Richter
Mary L. McDaniel

W. Scott McAndrew
David J. Pliner
Teresa Ann Mueller

Counsel for: American Family Mutual Insurance Group; Superior Water, Light & Power Co.; North-West Telecommunications, Inc.; Wisconsin Southern Gas Co., Inc.; St. Paul Fire and Marine Insurance Cos.; Allstate Insurance Co.; Fireman's Fund Insurance Co.

For Complete List of Firm Personnel, See General Section

For full biographical listings, see the Martindale-Hubbell Law Directory

*MILWAUKEE,** Milwaukee Co.

GIBBS, ROPER, LOOTS & WILLIAMS, S.C. (AV)

735 North Water Street, 53202
Telephone: 414-273-7000
Fax: 414-273-7897

Clay R. Williams
Terry E. Nilles

For Complete List of Firm Personnel, See General Section

For full biographical listings, see the Martindale-Hubbell Law Directory

GUTGLASS ERICKSON & BONVILLE, S.C. (AV)

Suite 1400, 735 North Water Street, 53202-4267
Telephone: 414-273-1144
Fax: 414-273-3821

James R. Gutglass
Paul R. Erickson
Kathleen E. Bonville

Mark E. Larson
Judith P. Sullivan
Colleen M. Fleming
Bradley I. Dallet

For full biographical listings, see the Martindale-Hubbell Law Directory

Milwaukee—Continued

KASDORF, LEWIS & SWIETLIK, S.C. (AV)

(Formerly Kivett and Kasdorf)
1551 South 108th Street, 53214
Telephone: 414-257-1055
Facsimile: 414-257-3759
Green Bay Office: 414 East Walnut Street, Suite 260, 54301.
Telephone: 414-436-0304.

Austin W. Kivett (1898-1993)
Clifford C. Kasdorf
John M. Swietlik
James P. Reardon
Werner E. Scherr
Terrance E. Davczyk
Jeff Schmeckpeper
Gregory J. Cook
Michael J. Cieslewicz
Michael A. Mesirow
William J. Katt
Joseph J. Ferris
James J. Kriva
David L. Styer
Robert J. Lauer
Emile H. Banks, Jr.
James M. Ryan
Robert P. Ochowicz

Michael C. Frohman
Charles G. Maris
John E. Cain
Vicki L. Arrowood
Christine M. Benson
Denise M. Harron
Kevin A. Christensen
Michael S. Murray
Cecilia M. McCormack
Denise Y. Bowen
Timothy S. Trecek
Christopher D. Stombaugh
Kristin M. Cafferty

OF COUNSEL

Kenton E. Kilmer
Hugh E. Russell
Robert B. Corris
Patti J. Kurth

Representative Clients: State Farm Insurance Cos.; Crum & Forster; Kemper Insurance Cos.; Allstate Insurance Cos.; Employers Mutual Insurance Cos.; Fireman's Fund Insurance Cos.; American International Group; Liberty Mutual Insurance; Progressive Insurance Cos.

For full biographical listings, see the Martindale-Hubbell Law Directory

PIETTE & JACOBSON, S.C. (AV)

1233 North Mayfair Road, Suite 204, 53226-3255
Telephone: 414-257-3700
Fax: 414-257-3729

Ronald L. Piette
Amory O. Moore
James J. Jacobson
Michael T. Steber
Brian J. Frank
Therese M. Lyons
William J. Richards
Thomas A. Piette
Mark T. McNabb
L. John Ratzel, Jr.
Robert M. Piette

For full biographical listings, see the Martindale-Hubbell Law Directory

REINHART, BOERNER, VAN DEUREN, NORRIS & RIESELBACH, S.C. (AV)

1000 North Water Street, P.O. Box 92900, 53202-0900
Telephone: 414-298-1000
Facsimile: 414-298-8097
Denver, Colorado Office: One Norwest Center, 1700 Lincoln Street, Suite 3725.
Telephone: 303-831-0909.
Fax: 303-831-4805.
Madison, Wisconsin Office: 7617 Mineral Point Road, 53701-2020.
Telephone: 608-283-7900.
Fax: 608-283-7919.
Washington, D.C. Office: 601 Pennsylvania Avenue, N.W., North Building, Suite 750.
Telephone: 202-393-3636.
Fax: 202-393-0796.

Paul V. Lucke
William R. Steinmetz
Stephen T. Jacobs
Scott W. Hansen
Richard P. Carr
Anne Willis Reed
Francis W. Deisinger
Steven P. Bogart

R. Timothy Muth
Anne Morgan Hlavacka
Kathleen S. Donius
Christine L. Thierfelder
David J. Sisson
Patrick J. Hodan
Katherine McConahay Nealon
Colleen D. Ball
Dean E. Mabie
Geri Krupp-Gordon
Daniel J. La Fave
David G. Hanson

For Complete List of Firm Personnel, See General Section

For full biographical listings, see the Martindale-Hubbell Law Directory

SCHELLINGER & DOYLE, S.C. (AV)

Suite 110 Deer Creek Office Building, 445 South Mooreland Road (Brookfield), 53005
Telephone: 414-785-0200
Fax: 414-785-1446

(See Next Column)

Stanley F. Schellinger (1923-1983)
James G. Doyle
Timothy J. Strattner
James M. Fergal
Paul J. Kelly

Donald P. Schneider
Linda Vogt Meagher
Amy J. Doyle
Clare T. Ryan
Mark K. Lougua

Representative Clients: Wisconsin Health Care Liability Insurance Plan; Wausau Insurance Cos.; The Medical Protective Co.; The Professional Insurance Co.; Admiral Insurance Co.; Fireman's Fund Insurance Cos.; Unigard Insurance Co.; Commercial Union; Physicians Insurance Co. of Wisconsin; Carolina Casualty Insurance Co.

For full biographical listings, see the Martindale-Hubbell Law Directory

SLATTERY, HAUSMAN & HOEFLE, LTD. (AV)

The Milwaukee Center, Suite 1800, 111 East Kilbourn Avenue, 53202
Telephone: 414-271-4555
Facsimile: 414-271-9045

Robert A. Slattery
C. Michael Hausman
Paul R. Hoefle

Alan E. Gesler
Steven J. Snedeker

For full biographical listings, see the Martindale-Hubbell Law Directory

NEENAH, Winnebago Co.

DI RENZO AND BOMIER (AV)

231 East Wisconsin Avenue, P.O. Box 788, 54957-0788
Telephone: 414-725-8464
Fax: 414-725-8568

MEMBERS OF FIRM

Jerome T. Bomier
Philip A. Munroe
Samuel J. Bomier

Representative Clients: Aetna Casualty and Surety Company; Employers Mutual Companies; American Family Mutual Insurance Co.; Insurance Company of North America; General Casualty Insurance Co. of Wisconsin; West Bend Mutual Insurance Co.; Employers Insurance of Wausau; Harco National Insurance Company; United Heartland Insurance Company.

For Complete List of Firm Personnel, See General Section

For full biographical listings, see the Martindale-Hubbell Law Directory

*RACINE,** Racine Co.

PAULSON, HANKEL, BRUNER & NICHOLS, S.C. (AV)

6921 Mariner Drive, 53406
Telephone: 414-886-0206
Fax: 414-886-6748
Union Grove, Wisconsin Office: 1222 Main Street.
Telephone: 414-878-3749.

David W. Paulson
Edward J. Bruner, Jr.

For Complete List of Firm Personnel, See General Section

For full biographical listings, see the Martindale-Hubbell Law Directory

*RHINELANDER,** Oneida Co.

ECKERT & STINGL (AV)

158 South Anderson Street, P.O. Box 1247, 54501-1247
Telephone: 715-369-1624
FAX: 715-369-1273

MEMBERS OF FIRM

Michael L. Eckert
Michael J. Stingl
James O. Moermond, III
Timothy B. Melms

OF COUNSEL

John R. Lund

Reference: M & I Merchants Bank.

For full biographical listings, see the Martindale-Hubbell Law Directory

RICE LAKE, Barron Co.

THRASHER, DOYLE, PELISH & FRANTI, LTD. (AV)

13 East Eau Claire Street, P.O. Box 31, 54868
Telephone: 715-234-8105
Fax: 715-234-2985

Timothy M. Doyle
James A. Pelish
Theodore A. Franti

William E. Morgan
Larry S. Schifano

Representative Clients: General Casualty Co. of Wisconsin; Sentry Insurance Co.; Allstate Insurance Co.; The Medical Protective Co.; American Family Insurance Co.; M S I; Fireman's Fund Insurance Co.; Employers Insurance of Wausau; Integrity Mutual Insurance Co.; Threshermen's Insurance Co.

For full biographical listings, see the Martindale-Hubbell Law Directory

WYOMING

*CASPER,** Natrona Co.

BROWN & DREW (AV)

Casper Business Center, Suite 800, 123 West First Street, 82601-2486
Telephone: 307-234-1000
800-877-6755
Telefax: 307-265-8025

MEMBERS OF FIRM

W. Thomas Sullins, II
Donn J. McCall
J. Kenneth Barbe
Jeffrey C. Brinkerhoff

ASSOCIATES

Jon B. Huss
Courtney Robert Kepler
Drew A. Perkins

Attorneys for: Aetna Casualty & Surety Co.; CIGNA; Commercial Union Insurance Co.; Crum & Forster Managers Corp.; The Doctor's Co.; MED-MARC; The Home Insurance Company; United Pacific Insurance; Willis Coroon Administrative Services Corp.

For Complete List of Firm Personnel, See General Section

For full biographical listings, see the Martindale-Hubbell Law Directory

WILLIAMS, PORTER, DAY & NEVILLE, P.C. (AV)

Suite 300 Durbin Center, 145 South Durbin Street, 82601
Telephone: 307-265-0700
Fax: 307-266-2306

Richard E. Day
Frank D. Neville
Patrick J. Murphy
Stuart R. Day
Ann M. Rochelle
Mark L. Carman
Stephenson D. Emery
Scott E. Ortiz

Representative Clients: ITT Hartford Insurance Group; Fireman's Fund Insurance Co.; Continental Insurance Co.; National Farmers Union Insurance Co.; Wausau Insurance Co.; Home Insurance Co.; The Doctors Company; The Prudential Insurance Co.; Ohio Casualty Insurance Co.; Guaranty National Insurance Co.; Bituminous Insurance Companies; Attorneys Liability Protection Society.

For Complete List of Firm Personnel, See General Section

For full biographical listings, see the Martindale-Hubbell Law Directory

*CHEYENNE,** Laramie Co.

LATHROP & RUTLEDGE, A PROFESSIONAL CORPORATION (AV)

Suite 500 City Center Building, 1920 Thomes Avenue, P.O. Box 4068, 82003-4068
Telephone: 307-632-0554
Telecopier: 307-635-4502

Carl L. Lathrop
J. Kent Rutledge
Corinne E. Rutledge
Loyd E. Smith

Roger E. Cockerille
James T. Dinneen

OF COUNSEL

Arthur Kline
Byron Hirst

General Counsel for: Cheyenne Internal Medicine and Neurology, P.C.; Laramie County School District No. 2; Cheyenne Newspapers, Inc.; Wyoming Hospital Assn.
Insurance Clients: Omaha Property Casualty Insurance Co.; National Chiropractic Insurance Co.; Underwriters at Lloyds; Omaha Property Casualty; Underwriters at Lloyds; CIGNA Insurance Group.

For full biographical listings, see the Martindale-Hubbell Law Directory

SUNDAHL, POWERS, KAPP & MARTIN (AV)

American National Bank Building, 1912 Capitol Avenue, Suite 300, P.O. Box 328, 82001
Telephone: 307-632-6421
FAX: 307-632-7216

MEMBERS OF FIRM

John Alan Sundahl
George E. Powers, Jr.
Paul Kapp
Raymond W. Martin

ASSOCIATES

John A. Coppede
Kay Lynn Bestol

A list of Representative Clients will be furnished upon request.

For full biographical listings, see the Martindale-Hubbell Law Directory

*SHERIDAN,** Sheridan Co.

DAVIS AND CANNON (AV)

Formerly Burgess, Davis & Cannon
40 South Main Street, P.O. Box 728, 82801
Telephone: 307-672-7491
Fax: 307-672-8955
Cheyenne, Wyoming Office: 2710 Thomes Avenue, P.O. Box 43, 82003.
Telephone: 307-634-3210.
Fax: 307-778-7118.

MEMBERS OF FIRM

Richard M. Davis, Jr.
Kim D. Cannon
Anthony T. Wendtland
Kate M. Fox

Representative Clients: Consol, Inc.; Hesston Corporation; Mutual of New York; Peter Kiewit Sons, Inc.; Wichita River Oil Corporation; Phillips Petroleum; First Interstate Bank of Commerce; Merrell Dow Pharmaceuticals, Inc.; Philip Morris, Inc.; Range Telephone Cooperative.

For Complete List of Firm Personnel, See General Section

For full biographical listings, see the Martindale-Hubbell Law Directory

LONABAUGH AND RIGGS (AV)

50 East Loucks Street, P.O. Drawer 5059, 82801
Telephone: 307-672-7444
Telecopier: 307-672-2230

MEMBERS OF FIRM

E. E. Lonabaugh (1861-1938)
A. W. Lonabaugh (1896-1971)
Ellsworth E. Lonabaugh
Dan B. Riggs
Jeffrey J. Gonda
Robert G. Berger
E. Michael Weber
Robert W. Brown
Haultain E. Corbett
Thomas J. Klepperich
Harold E. Meier

ASSOCIATE

Jonathan A. Botten

Representative Clients: American States Insurance Co.; Allstate Insurance Co.; CNA Group; Liberty Mutual Insurance Co.; Safeco Insurance Co.; St. Paul Insurance Cos.; U.S.F. & G. Insurance Co.

For full biographical listings, see the Martindale-Hubbell Law Directory

PUERTO RICO

SAN JUAN, San Juan Dist.

FIDDLER, GONZÁLEZ & RODRÍGUEZ

Chase Manhattan Bank Building (Hato Rey), P.O. Box 363507, 00936-3507
Telephone: 809-753-3113
Telecopier: 809-759-3123

MEMBERS OF FIRM

Pedro J. Polanco
Clara E. Lopez-Baralt

SENIOR ASSOCIATES

Pedro I. Vidal-Cordero
Cesar T. Alcover-Acosta

Representative Clients: Metropolitan Life Insurance Co.; John Hancock.

For Complete List of Firm Personnel, See General Section

For full biographical listings, see the Martindale-Hubbell Law Directory

GONZALEZ & BENNAZAR

Capital Center Building South Tower - 9th Floor, Arterial Hostos Avenue (Hato Rey), 00918
Telephone: 809-754-9191
Fax: 809-754-9325

MEMBERS OF FIRM

Raul E. González Díaz
A. J. Bennazar-Zequeira

Representative Clients: American Express Life Insurance; Federal Deposit Insurance Corp.; Resolution Trust Co.; GIGNA Insurance Group; Zurich-American Insurance Group; Pacific Employers Insurance Co.; Transamerica Insurance.

For Complete List of Firm Personnel, See General Section

For full biographical listings, see the Martindale-Hubbell Law Directory

JIMÉNEZ, GRAFFAM & LAUSELL

Formerly Jiménez & Fusté
Suite 505, Midtown Building, 421 Muñoz Rivera Avenue, Hato Rey, P.O. Box 366104, 00936-6104
Telephone: 809-767-1030; 767-1000; 767-1061; 767-1064
Telefax: 809-751-4068;
Cable: "Nezte"; RCA
Telex: 325-2730

(See Next Column)

JIMÉNEZ, GRAFFAM & LAUSELL, *San Juan—Continued*

MEMBERS OF FIRM

Nicolás Jiménez
William A. Graffam
Steven C. Lausell
J. Ramón Rivera-Morales
José Juan Torres-Escalera
Raquel M. Dulzaides
Manuel San Juan

ASSOCIATES

Manolo T. Rodríguez-Bird
Patricia Garrity
Carlos E. Bayrón
Isabel J. Vélez-Serrano
Edgardo A. Vega-López
Alexandra M. Serracante-Cadilla
Luis Saldaña-Roman

Representative Clients: Underwriters at Lloyds; Ropner Insurance Co.; Evanston Insurance Co.; Continental Insurance/Commercial Life Insurance Co.; The United Kingdom Steamship P & I Association.

For full biographical listings, see the Martindale-Hubbell Law Directory

VIRGIN ISLANDS

*CHRISTIANSTED, ST. CROIX,** St. Croix

JEAN-ROBERT ALFRED

46B-47 King Street, 00820
Telephone: 809-773-2156
Telecopier: 809-773-4301

COUNSEL

Jane Wells Kleeger

For full biographical listings, see the Martindale-Hubbell Law Directory

CANADA
ALBERTA

*EDMONTON,** Edmonton Jud. Dist.

PARLEE McLAWS (AV)

15th Floor Manulife Place, 10180 101st Street, T5J 4K1
Telephone: 403-423-8500
Telecopier: 403-423-2870
Calgary, Alberta Office: 3400, Western Canadian Place, 707 - 8th Avenue, S.W.
Telephone: 403-294-7000.
Telecopier: 403-265-8263.

MEMBERS OF FIRM

C. H. Kerr, Q.C.
M. D. MacDonald
K. F. Bailey, Q.C.
R. B. Davison, Q.C.
F. R. Haldane
P. E. J. Curran
D. G. Finlay
J. K. McFadyen
R. C. Secord
D. L. Kennedy
D. C. Rolf
D. F. Pawlowski
A. A. Garber
R. P. James
D. C. Wintermute
J. L. Cairns
R. A. Newton, Q.C.
T. A. Cockrall, Q.C.
H. D. Montemurro
F. J. Niziol
R. W. Wilson
I. L. MacLachlan
R. O. Langley
R. G. McBean
J. T. Neilson
E. G. Rice
J. F. McGinnis
J. H. H. Hockin
G. W. Jaycock
M. J. K. Nikel
B. J. Curial
S. L. May
M. S. Poretti

ASSOCIATES

C. R. Head
A.W. Slemko
L. H. Hamdon
K.A. Smith
K. D. Fallis-Howell
D. S. Tam
J.W. McClure
F.H. Belzil
R.A. Renz
J.G. Paulson
K. E. Buss
B. L. Andriachuk
P. E. S. J. Kennedy
R. Feraco
R.J. Billingsley
N.B.R. Thompson
P. A. Shenher
I. C. Johnson
K.G. Koshman
D.D. Dubrule
G. T. Lund
W.D. Johnston
G. E. Flemming
K. P. Nayyer

For full biographical listings, see the Martindale-Hubbell Law Directory

CANADA
BRITISH COLUMBIA

*VANCOUVER,** Vancouver Co.

ALEXANDER, HOLBURN, BEAUDIN & LANG (AV)

P.O. Box 10057 2700 Toronto Dominion Bank Tower, 700 West Georgia Street, V7Y 1B8
Telephone: 604-688-1351
Fax: 604-669-7642
Hong Kong, In Association with Lawrence Ong & Chung: 8th Floor, Chekiang First Bank Centre, 1 Duddell Street. Central.
Telephone: (852-2) 526-1171.
Fax: (852-2) 845-0686.
Taipei, Taiwan Office, In Association with Perennial Law Office: c/o 7F-2, No. 9, Roosevelt Road, Section 2.
Telephone: (886-2) 395-6989.
Fax: (886-2) 391-4235.

PARTNERS

William M. Holburn, Q.C.
Michael P. Ragona, Q.C.
David A. Gooderham
James A. Dowler
Robert G. Payne
Robert B. Kennedy
R. Patrick Saul
Gregory J. Nash
J.J. McIntyre
Jo Ann Carmichael
Bruno De Vita
David B. Wende
Terry C. Vos
Gary M. Nijman
Judith P. Kennedy
Ross Shamenski
J. Dale Stewart
Kenneth H. Crook

ASSOCIATES

Darcie A. Laurient
Glen A. McEachran
Sharleen L. Dumont
Barbara L. Devlin
Peggy M. Tugwood
Eileen E. Vanderburgh
Janet L. Winteringham
Renee T. E. Goult
Susan Grattan-Doyle
Dana G. Graves
D. Christopher Fong
David T. McKnight
Todd R. Davies
Jean-Marc F. Hébert

A list of Representative Clients will be furnished on request.

For Complete List of Firm Personnel, See General Section

For full biographical listings, see the Martindale-Hubbell Law Directory

HARPER GREY EASTON (AV)

3100 Vancouver Centre, 650 West Georgia Street, P.O. Box 11504, V6B 4P7
Telephone: 604-687-0411
Telex: 04-55448
Telecopier: 604-669-9385

MEMBERS OF FIRM

Harvey J. Grey, Q.C.
M. Donald Easton
L. N. Matheson
Terrence C. O'Brien
Isidor M. Wolfe
Terrence L. Robertson, Q.C.
W. J. McJannet
James M. Lepp
Bryan G. Baynham
John B. Brown
C. E. Hinkson, Q.C.
Howard A. Barends
Gordon G. Hilliker
M. M. Skorah
Kathryn E. Neilson, Q.C.
G. Bruce Butler
Paul T. McGivern
Scott W. Fleming
Larry H. Koo
Stephen P. Grey
Peter M. Willcock
James A. Doyle
Maureen L. A. Lundell
Victor P. Harwardt
Laura B. Gerow
Barbara J. Norell
David A. Gagnon
Guy Patrick Brown
Bernard S. Buettner
Loreen M. Williams

ASSOCIATES

Robert J. Rose
Kieron G. Grady
Juliet A. Donnici
Geoffrey L. K. Yeung
Cheryl L. Talbot
William S. Clark
M. Lynn McBride
Douglas L. Long
David W. Pilley
Anu K. Khanna
Bena Wendy Stock
Katherine E. Armstrong

Anne F. Cameron
Janet E. Currie
Andrea Finch
Marion (Mara) E. Stickland

RETIRED PARTNERS

Arthur M. Harper, Q.C. (Retired)
David Sigler, Q.C. (Retired)

Solicitors for: Commercial Union Assurance Company of Canada; Lumbermens Mutual Casualty Co.; State Farm Fire and Casualty Co.

For full biographical listings, see the Martindale-Hubbell Law Directory

Vancouver—Continued

PAINE EDMONDS (AV)

Suite 1100 Montreal Trust Centre, 510 Burrard Street, V6C 3A8
Telephone: 604-683-1211
Facsimile: 604-681-5084
Abbotsford, British Columbia Office: 31205 Old Yale Road. V2T 5E5.
Telephone: (604) 864-2880.
Fax: (604) 864-8445.

W. H. Kemp Edmonds, Q.C. (1916-1986)

MEMBERS OF FIRM

Leonard C. Dudley
J. Lyle Woodley, Q.C.
James C. Taylor
Elmer A. Yusep
Owen G. Jones
Henry D.M. Edmonds
Steven H. Heringa
John J. Hyde

ASSOCIATES

Eric B. Heringa
John Bancroft-Jones
Bradford D.S. Garside
Anthony E. Thomas
P. L. (Lee) Quinton
Robert D. Kirkham
Kirsten J. Madsen
Clay Bruce Williams

Reference: Toronto Dominion Bank.

For full biographical listings, see the Martindale-Hubbell Law Directory

RUSSELL & DUMOULIN (AV)

2100-1075 West Georgia Street, V6E 3G2
Telephone: 604-631-3131
Fax: 604-631-3232
A Member of the national association of Borden DuMoulin Howard Gervais, comprising Russell & DuMoulin, Vancouver, British Columbia; Howard Mackie, Calgary, Alberta; Borden & Elliot, Toronto, Ontario; Mackenzie Gervais, Montreal, Quebec and Borden DuMoulin Howard Gervais, London, England.
Strategic Alliance with Perkins Coie with offices in Seattle, Spokane and Bellevue, Washington; Portland, Oregon; Anchorage, Alaska; Los Angeles, California; Washington, D.C.; Hong Kong and Taipei, Taiwan.
Represented in Hong Kong by Vincent T.K. Cheung, Yap & Co.

MEMBERS OF FIRM

James H. MacMaster
Avon M. Mersey

Representative Clients: Alcan Smelters & Chemicals Ltd.; The Bank of Nova Scotia; Canada Trust Co.; The Canada Life Assurance Co.; Forest Industrial Relations Ltd.; Honda Canada Inc.; IBM Canada Ltd.; Macmillan Bloedel Ltd.; Nissho Iwai Canada Ltd.; The Toronto-Dominion Bank.

For Complete List of Firm Personnel, See General Section

For full biographical listings, see the Martindale-Hubbell Law Directory

SINGLETON URQUHART MACDONALD (AV)

1200 - 1125 Howe Street, V6Z 2K8
Telephone: 604-682-7474
Fax: 604-682-1283
Calgary, Alberta Office: 203 - 200 Barclay Parade, S.W., T2P 0J1.
Telephone: 403-261-9043.
Fax: 403-265-4632.

Glenn A. Urquhart
A. Webster Macdonald, Jr., Q.C. (Resident, Calgary
John R. Singleton
Derek A. Brindle
Nathan H. Smith

Representative Clients: Encon Insurance Managers, Inc.; Insurance Bureau of Canada; Municipal Insurance Association; Prudential Assurance Co.; GAN Canada; St. Paul Fire & Marine Insurance Co.

For Complete List of Firm Personnel, See General Section

For full biographical listings, see the Martindale-Hubbell Law Directory

CANADA MANITOBA

*WINNIPEG,** Eastern Jud. Dist.

AIKINS, MACAULAY & THORVALDSON (AV)

Thirtieth Floor, Commodity Exchange Tower, 360 Main Street, R3C 4G1
Telephone: 204-957-0050
Fax: 204-957-0840

MEMBERS OF FIRM

Knox B. Foster, Q.C.
Daryl J. Rosin
L. William Bowles
D. Salín Guttormsson
Rod E. Stephenson, Q.C.
G. Todd Campbell
Thor J. Hansell
Helga D. Van Iderstine
Barbara S. MacDonald

Representative Clients: Canadian Medical Protective Assn.; Cigna Insurance Co.; Zurich Insurance Co.; Gerat-West Life Assurance Co.; Sovereign General Insurance Co.; Wasanes Mutual Insurance Co.; Royal Insurance Co.;

(See Next Column)

American Home Insurance Co.; Paul Revere Insurance Co.; Dominion of Canada Group.

For Complete List of Firm Personnel, See General Section

For full biographical listings, see the Martindale-Hubbell Law Directory

CANADA NEW BRUNSWICK

*SAINT JOHN,** Saint John Co.

CLARK, DRUMMIE & COMPANY (AV)

40 Wellington Row, P.O. Box 6850 Station "A", E2L 4S3
Telephone: 506-633-3800
Telecopier (Automatic): 506-633-3811

MEMBERS OF FIRM

Barry R. Morrison, Q.C.
Norman J. Bossé
Timothy M. Hopkins

Reference: Royal Bank of Canada.

For Complete List of Firm Personnel, See General Section

For full biographical listings, see the Martindale-Hubbell Law Directory

GILBERT, MCGLOAN, GILLIS (AV)

Suite 710, Mercantile Centre, 55 Union Street P.O. Box 7174, Station "A", E2L 4S6
Telephone: 506-634-3600
Telecopier: 506-634-3612

T. Louis McGloan, Q.C. (1896-1986)
Adrian B. Gilbert, Q.C. (1895-1986)

MEMBERS OF FIRM

Donald M. Gillis, Q.C.
Thomas L. McGloan, Q.C.
A. G. Warwick Gilbert, Q.C.
Rodney J. Gillis, Q.C.
Douglas A. M. Evans, Q.C.
Brenda J. Lutz
David N. Rogers

ASSOCIATES

Paulette C. Garnett, Q.C.
Edward Veitch
Hugh J. Flemming, Q.C.
Anne F. MacNeill
Nancy E. Forbes
Marie T. Bérubé
Guy C. Spavold
Claire B.N. Porter
Michael J. Murphy
Mark A. Canty

Representative Clients: Bank of Montreal; Canada Packers Ltd.; McCain Foods Ltd.; The Sunderland Steamship Protecting & Indemnity Association; Steamship Mutual Underwriting Association (Bermuda) Limited; Royal Insurance Co.; Wawanesa Mutual Insurance Co.; Dominion of Canada General Insurance Co.; Canadian General Insurance Co.

For full biographical listings, see the Martindale-Hubbell Law Directory

CANADA NOVA SCOTIA

*HALIFAX,** Halifax Co.

MCINNES COOPER & ROBERTSON (AV)

1601 Lower Water Street, P.O. Box 730, B3J 2V1
Telephone: 902-425-6500
Fax: 902-425-6350
St. John's, Newfoundland Office: Suite 602, Scotia Centre, 235 Water Street, P.O. Box 547. A1C, 5K8.
Telephone: 709-726-9500.
Fax: 709-726-9550.

Harry E. Wrathall, Q.C.
George W. MacDonald, Q.C.
Christopher C. Robinson
David A. Graves
David B. Ritcey, Q.C.
Robert G. Belliveau, Q.C.
Thomas E. Hart
Scott C. Norton
Eric LeDrew

ASSOCIATE

John Kulik

Attorneys for: Bank of Nova Scotia; Imperial Oil, Limited; Frank B. Hall & Co., Inc. (New York); American Steamship Owners Protection & Indemnity Association, Inc.; Coca-Cola, Ltd.; Scott Worldwide Inc.; Hong Kong Bank of Canada.

For Complete List of Firm Personnel, See General Section

For full biographical listings, see the Martindale-Hubbell Law Directory

CANADA ONTARIO

KITCHENER, Regional Munic. of Waterloo

GIFFEN, LEE, WAGNER, MORLEY & GARBUTT (AV)

50 Queen Street North, P.O. Box 2396, N2H 6M3
Telephone: 519-578-4150
Fax: 519-578-8740

MEMBERS OF FIRM

Jeffrey J. Mansfield (1955-1991)
J. Peter Giffen, Q.C.
Bruce L. Lee
J. Scott Morley
Brian R. Wagner
Philip A. Garbutt

ASSOCIATES

Edward J. Vanderkloet
Keith C. Masterman
Daniel J. Fife
Jeffrey W. Boich

For full biographical listings, see the Martindale-Hubbell Law Directory

*TORONTO,** Regional Munic. of York

BORDEN & ELLIOT (AV)

Barristers & Solicitors
Scotia Plaza, 40 King Street West, M5H 3Y4
Telephone: 416-367-6000
Telecopier: 416-367-6749
Internet: @ borden.com
A Member of the national association of Borden DuMoulin Howard Gervais, comprising Borden & Elliot in Toronto, Ontario, Russell & DuMoulin in Vancouver, British Columbia, Howard, Mackie in Calgary, Alberta and Mackenzie Gervais in Montréal, Québec. Borden DuMoulin Howard Gervais also operates an office in London, England.

MEMBER AND ASSOCIATES

Edward A. Ayers, Q.C.

For Complete List of Firm Personnel, See General Section

For full biographical listings, see the Martindale-Hubbell Law Directory

HUGHES, AMYS (AV)

Royal Bank Plaza North Tower, 200 Bay Street 24th Floor Box 45, M5J 2P6
Telephone: 416-367-1608
Fax: 416-367-8821
Hamilton, Ontario Office: One King Street, West, Suite 1401.
Telephone: 905-577-4050.
Fax: 905-577-6301.

MEMBERS OF FIRM

Wendell S. Wigle, Q.C.
Darcy G. Duke, Q.C.
Lloyd G. Harlock, Q.C.
Michael T. J. McGoey, Q.C.
Paul J. French
James J. Keaney
Richard F. Horak
Pamela M. Stevens
D. Bruce Garrow
Jack F. Fitch
Donald J. Ross
Michael S. Teitelbaum
Weir H. Milne
William J. McCorriston
Mario R. Pietrangeli
Michael E. Girard
Albert M. Conforzi
A. Jarvis Scott
William S. Chalmers
Alan N. West

ASSOCIATES

Bruce L. Desmond
Jamie K. Trimble
Martha S. Binks
Mary Ann Teal
Christopher John Wheeler
Barbara McAfee
Peter W. Gutelius
Petra de Lima

For full biographical listings, see the Martindale-Hubbell Law Directory

PATERSON, MACDOUGALL (AV)

Suite 2100, 1 Queen Street, East, P.O. Box 100, M5C 2W5
Telephone: 416-366-9607
Fax: 416-366-3743

MEMBERS OF FIRM

Alastair R. Paterson, O.B.E., Q.C. (1908-1990)
D. Bruce MacDougall, Q.C.
Vasaris R. P. Bersenas
Peter F. M. Jones
Carol E. McCall
Peter M. Jacobsen
Gerard A. Chouest
James P. Thomson
W. Brian Dawe
Janice E. Blackburn

ASSOCIATES

Brenda Spaulding
Vivian Bercovici
Adrienne R. Rutherford
K. Bruce B. Chambers
Timothy Bruce Trembley

For full biographical listings, see the Martindale-Hubbell Law Directory

CANADA PRINCE EDWARD ISLAND

*CHARLOTTETOWN,** Queen's Co.

CAMPBELL, LEA, MICHAEL, MCCONNELL & PIGOT (AV)

15 Queen Street, P.O. Box 429, C1A 7K7
Telephone: 902-566-3400
Telecopier: 902-566-9266

MEMBERS OF FIRM

William G. Lea, Q.C.
Robert A. McConnell
Paul D. Michael, Q.C.
Kenneth L. Godfrey

General Counsel in Prince Edward Island for: Canadian Imperial Bank of Commerce; Maritime Electric Co., Ltd.; Michelin Tires (Canada) Ltd.; Newsco Investments Ltd. (Dundas Farms); Queen Elizabeth Hospital Inc.; Imperial Oil Limited; General Motors of Canada; Co-op Atlantic; Liberty Mutual; Employers Reinsurance Group.

For Complete List of Firm Personnel, See General Section

For full biographical listings, see the Martindale-Hubbell Law Directory

CANADA QUEBEC

*MONTREAL,** Montreal Dist.

MCMASTER MEIGHEN (AV)

A General Partnership
7th Floor, 630 René-Lévesque Boulevard West, H3B 4H7
Telephone: 514-879-1212
Telecopier: 514-878-0605
Cable Address: "Cammerall"
Telex: "Cammerall MTL" 05-268637
Affiliated with Fraser & Beatty in Toronto, North York, Ottawa and Vancouver.

MEMBERS OF FIRM

Alex K. Paterson, O.C., O.Q., Q.C.
Alexis P. Bergeron
Daniel Ayotte
Michel A. Pinsonnault
P. Jeremy Bolger
Nicholas J. Spillane
Robert J. Torralbo
Peter G. Pamel
Douglas C. Mitchell
Luc Bĕliveau
Kurt A. Johnson
Jacques Brien
Colin K. Irving
Sean J. Harrington
Jon H. Scott
Diane Quenneville
Marc Duchesne
Richard R. Provost
Jacques Gauthier
Yvan Houle
John G. Murphy
Valérie Beaudin
Bruce W. Johnston

COUNSEL

A. Stuart Hyndman, Q.C.

For Complete List of Firm Personnel, See General Section

For full biographical listings, see the Martindale-Hubbell Law Directory

CANADA SASKATCHEWAN

*SASKATOON,** Saskatoon Jud. Centre

MCKERCHER, MCKERCHER & WHITMORE (AV)

374 Third Avenue, South, S7K 1M5
Telephone: 306-653-2000
Fax: 306-244-7335
Regina, Saskatchewan Office: 1000 - 1783 Hamilton Street.
Telephone: 306-352-7661.
Fax: 306-781-7113.

MEMBERS OF FIRM

Robert H. McKercher, Q.C.
J. D. Denis Pelletier
Gregory A. Thompson

ASSOCIATES

Shaunt Parthev
David E. Thera
Catherine A. Sloan
J. Denis Bonthoux

For Complete List of Firm Personnel, See General Section

For full biographical listings, see the Martindale-Hubbell Law Directory

INTERNATIONAL BUSINESS LAW

ALABAMA

*BIRMINGHAM,** Jefferson Co.

BRADLEY, ARANT, ROSE & WHITE (AV)

1400 Park Place Tower, 2001 Park Place, 35203
Telephone: 205-521-8000
Telex: 494-1324
Facsimile: 205-251-8611, 251-8665, 252-0264
Facsimile (Southtrust Office): 205-251-9915
Huntsville, Alabama Office: 200 Clinton Avenue West, Suite 900.
Telephone: 205-517-5100.
Facsimile: 205-533-5069.

MEMBERS OF FIRM

Thomas Neely Carruthers, Jr. Laurence Duncan Vinson, Jr.

For Complete List of Firm Personnel, See General Section

For full biographical listings, see the Martindale-Hubbell Law Directory

SIROTE & PERMUTT, P.C. (AV)

2222 Arlington Avenue, South, P.O. Box 55727, 35255
Telephone: 205-933-7111
Facsimile: 205-930-5301
Huntsville, Alabama Office: 200 Clinton Avenue, N.W., Suite 1000.
Telephone: 205-536-1711.
Facsimile: 205-534-9650.
Mobile, Alabama Office: One St. Louis Centre, Suite 1000.
Telephone: 205-432-1671.
Facsimile: 205-434-0196.
Montgomery, Alabama Office: Colonial Commerce Center, Suite 305 One Commerce Street.
Telephone: 205-261-3400.
Facsimile: 205-261-3434.
Tuscaloosa, Alabama Office: 2216 14th Street.
Telephone: 205-752-2089.

James C. Wilson, Jr. Kim E. Rosenfield

OF COUNSEL

Joseph W. Blackburn

Representative Clients: International Business Machines (IBM); General Motors Corp.; Colonial Bank; Bruno's, Inc.; University of Alabama Hospitals; Westinghouse Electric Corp.; First Alabama Bank; Monsanto Chemical Company; South Central Bell; Prudential Insurance Company; American Home Products, Inc.; Minnesota Mining and Manufacturing, Inc. (3M).

For Complete List of Firm Personnel, See General Section

For full biographical listings, see the Martindale-Hubbell Law Directory

*HUNTSVILLE,** Madison Co.

SIROTE & PERMUTT, P.C. (AV)

Suite 1000, 200 Clinton Avenue, N.W., 35801
Telephone: 205-536-1711
Facsimile: 205-534-9650
Birmingham, Alabama Office: 2222 Arlington Avenue, South, P.O. Box 55727.
Telephone: 205-933-7111.
Facsimile: 205-930-5301.
Mobile, Alabama Office: One St. Louis Centre, Suite 1000.
Telephone: 205-432-1671.
Facsimile: 205-434-0196.
Montgomery, Alabama Office: Colonial Commerce Center, Suite 305, One Commerce Street.
Telephone: 205-261-3400.
Facsimile: 205-261-3434.
Tuscaloosa, Alabama Office: 2216 14th Street.
Telephone: 205-752-2089.

George W. Royer, Jr. June Wang

For Complete List of Firm Personnel, See General Section

For full biographical listings, see the Martindale-Hubbell Law Directory

ARIZONA

*NOGALES,** Santa Cruz Co.

O'CONNOR, CAVANAGH, ANDERSON, WESTOVER, KILLINGSWORTH & BESHEARS, A PROFESSIONAL ASSOCIATION (AV)

1827 North Mastick Way, 85621
Telephone: 602-761-4215
FAX: 602-761-3505
Phoenix, Arizona Office: One East Camelback Road, Suite 1100, 85012.
Telephone: 602-263-2400.
FAX: 602-263-2900.
Tucson, Arizona Office: Suite 2200, One South Church Avenue, 85701.
Telephone: 602-882-8912.
FAX: 602-624-9564.
Sun City, Arizona Office: 13250 North Del Webb Boulevard, Suite B, 85351.
Telephone: 602-263-2808.
FAX: 602-933-3100.

Hector G. Arana Kimberly A. Howard Arana

Representative Clients: Omega Produce Co.; Frank's Distributing, Inc.; City of Nogales; Collectron of Ariz., Inc.; James K. Wilson Produce Co.; Agricola Bon, S. de R.L. de C.V.; Angel Demerutis E.; Rene Carrillo C.; Arturo Lomeli; Theojary Crisantes E.

For Complete List of Firm Personnel, See General Section

For full biographical listings, see the Martindale-Hubbell Law Directory

*PHOENIX,** Maricopa Co.

O'CONNOR, CAVANAGH, ANDERSON, WESTOVER, KILLINGSWORTH & BESHEARS, A PROFESSIONAL ASSOCIATION (AV)

One East Camelback Road, Suite 1100, 85012-1656
Telephone: 602-263-2400
FAX: 602-263-2900
Sun City, Arizona Office: 13250 North Del Webb Boulevard, Suite B, 85351.
Telephone: 602-263-2808.
FAX: 602-933-3100.
Tucson, Arizona Office: Suite 2200, One South Church Avenue, 85701.
Telephone: 602-882-8912.
FAX: 602-624-9564.
Nogales, Arizona Office: 1827 North Mastick Way, 85621.
Telephone: 602-761-4215.
FAX: 602-761-3505.

Gerald L. Jacobs Raymond S. Heyman
John B. Furman David L. Lansky

Steven M. Rudner

OF COUNSEL

Shoshana B. Tancer

Representative Clients: Rural/Metro Corp.; ITT Cannon; Cerprobe Corp.; Viasoft, Inc.

For Complete List of Firm Personnel, See General Section

For full biographical listings, see the Martindale-Hubbell Law Directory

CALIFORNIA

BEVERLY HILLS, Los Angeles Co.

DANA B. TASCHNER, P.C. (AV🅃)

9454 Wilshire Boulevard, Suite 550, 90212-2915
Telephone: 310-592-2600
Fax: 310-592-2640
Dallas, Texas Office: 350 St. Paul Street. 75201.
Liechtenstein Associated Office: DDr. Proksch & Partner. ITA P&A Bürotel Building. Landstrasse 161-163. FL 9494 Schaan.
Telephone: 41 75 2332303, 2322614, 2324121.
Facsimile: 41 75 2323562, 2324133, 2329181.
Telex: 899520 ita fl E-Mail:100415,1733 @ compuserve.com

Dana B. Taschner

OF COUNSEL

Reinhard J. Proksch (Not admitted in CA)

For full biographical listings, see the Martindale-Hubbell Law Directory

DIAMOND BAR, Los Angeles Co.

JOHN W. TULAC (AV)

1575 South Valley Vista Drive, Suite 140, 91765
Telephone: 909-860-5852
FAX: 909-860-3741

Reference: Marine National Bank, Irvine.

For full biographical listings, see the Martindale-Hubbell Law Directory

IRVINE, Orange Co.

BROWN, PISTONE, HURLEY, VAN VLEAR & SELTZER, A PROFESSIONAL CORPORATION (AV)

Suite 900 AT&T Building, 8001 Irvine Center Drive, 92718
Telephone: 714-727-0559
Fax: 714-727-0656
Tempe, Arizona Office: 1501 West Fountainhead Parkway, Suite 540.
Telephone: 602-968-2427.
Fax: 602-968-2401.
San Francisco, California Office: Suite 1300, Steuart Street Tower, One Market Plaza.
Telephone: 415-281-2154.
Fax: 415-281-2194.

Ernest C. Brown
Thomas A. Pistone
Gregory F. Hurley
John E. Van Vlear
Margaret A. Seltzer (Resident, San Francisco Office)

Michael K. Wolder
Francis T. Donohue, III
Kedric L. Francis
Michael W. Foster (Resident, Tempe, Arizona Office)
Robert C. Schneider (Resident, Tempe, Arizona Office)
Sarah Namnama Saria
Sheila Patterson
Michael Ray Gandee

OF COUNSEL

Robert G. Mahan
Stephen M. Wontrobski
Brian A. Runkel (Not admitted in CA)

For full biographical listings, see the Martindale-Hubbell Law Directory

WATT, TIEDER & HOFFAR (AV⊤)

3 Park Plaza, Suite 1530, 92714
Telephone: 714-852-6700
Telecopier: 714-261-0771
McLean Virginia Office: 7929 Westpark Drive, Suite 400,
Telephone: 703-749-1000.
Telex: 248797 WATTR.
Telecopier: 703-893-8029.
Washington, D.C. Office: 601 Pennsylvania Avenue, N.W. Suite 900,
Telephone: 202-462-4697.

MEMBERS OF FIRM

John B. Tieder, Jr. (Not admitted in CA)
Robert M. Fitzgerald (Not admitted in CA)
Michael G. Long

ASSOCIATE

Christopher P. Pappas

For full biographical listings, see the Martindale-Hubbell Law Directory

LONG BEACH, Los Angeles Co.

FLYNN, DELICH & WISE (AV)

One World Trade Center, Suite 1800, 90831-1800
Telephone: 310-435-2626
Fax: 310-437-7555
San Francisco, California Office: Suite 1750, 580 California Street.
Telephone: 415-693-5566.
Fax: 415-693-0410.

Erich P. Wise
Nicholas S. Politis

Representative Clients: American Hawaii Cruises; Holland America Line; Through Transport Mutual Insurance Association, Ltd.; The Britannia Steam Ship Insurance Association Limited; The Steamship Mutual Underwriting Association (Bermuda) Ltd.; General Steamship Corp., Ltd.; Commodore Cruise Line, Ltd.; Interocean Steamship Corporation; Sea-Land Service, Inc.; Hatteras Yachts.

For full biographical listings, see the Martindale-Hubbell Law Directory

RUSSELL & MIRKOVICH (AV)

One World Trade Center, Suite 1450, 90831-1450
Telephone: 310-436-9911
FAX: 310-436-1897

Carlton E. Russell
Joseph N. Mirkovich

ASSOCIATE

Maria Cecilia Inawati Tjandrasuwita

For full biographical listings, see the Martindale-Hubbell Law Directory

WILLIAMS WOOLLEY COGSWELL NAKAZAWA & RUSSELL (AV)

111 West Ocean Boulevard, Suite 2000, 90802-4614
Telephone: 310-495-6000
Telecopier: 310-435-1359
Telex: ITT: 4933872; WU: 984929

MEMBERS OF FIRM

Reed M. Williams
David E. R. Woolley
Forrest R. Cogswell
Alan Nakazawa
Blake W. Larkin
Thomas A. Russell

ASSOCIATES

B. Alexander Moghaddam
Dennis R. Acker

For full biographical listings, see the Martindale-Hubbell Law Directory

*LOS ANGELES,** Los Angeles Co.

LAW OFFICES OF RICHARD I. FINE & ASSOCIATES A PROFESSIONAL CORPORATION (AV)

Suite 1000, 10100 Santa Monica Boulevard (Century City), 90067-4090
Telephone: 310-277-5833
Rapifax: 310-277-1543

Richard I. Fine

OF COUNSEL

Brian D. Krantz

LEGAL SUPPORT PERSONNEL

Mary Benson (Senior Paralegal)

For full biographical listings, see the Martindale-Hubbell Law Directory

GOLBERT KIMBALL & WEINER (AV)

555 South Flower Street Suite 2800, 90071
Telephone: 213-891-9641
Telecopier: 213-623-6130

Albert S. Golbert
George Kimball
Jeffrey M. Weiner

ASSOCIATES

Andrew H. Kopkin
Matthew F. Maccoby

For full biographical listings, see the Martindale-Hubbell Law Directory

LYN H. MARCUS (AV)

30 Driftwood Street, No. 7, 90292
Telephone: 310-822-6454
Fax: 310-822-9368

Reference: Bank of America, Marina del Rey Branch.

MATTHIAS & BERG (AV)

Seventh Floor, 515 South Flower Street, 90071
Telephone: 213-895-4200
Telecopier: 213-895-4058

Michael R. Matthias
Jeffrey P. Berg
Stuart R. Singer
Kenneth M. H. Hoff

Representative Clients: N-Viro Recovery, Inc.; Supercart International, Inc.; Mexalit, S.A.; Allstar Inns; Chatsworth Products, Inc.; International Meta Systems, Inc.; MedGroup, Inc.; Palm Springs Golf Company, Inc.; Residential Resources, Inc.
Reference: First Professional Bank.

For full biographical listings, see the Martindale-Hubbell Law Directory

ROBERT P. PALAZZO (AV)

3002 Midvale Avenue, Suite 209, 90034
Telephone: 310-474-5483
Inyo County Law Office: 230 South Main Street, Darwin, California 93522.
Telephone: 619-876-5941.

For full biographical listings, see the Martindale-Hubbell Law Directory

*MODESTO,** Stanislaus Co.

RICHARD DOUGLAS BREW A PROFESSIONAL LAW CORPORATION (AV)

Suite 350 / Judge Frank C. Damrell Building, 1601 I Street, 95354-1110
Telephone: 209-572-3157
Telefax: 209-572-4641

Richard Douglas Brew

For full biographical listings, see the Martindale-Hubbell Law Directory

NEWPORT BEACH, Orange Co.

CAPRETZ & RADCLIFFE (AV)

5000 Birch Street, West Tower Suite 2500, 92660-2139
Telephone: 714-724-3000
Fax: 714-757-2635

(See Next Column)

CAPRETZ & RADCLIFFE—*Continued*

James T. Capretz
Richard J. Radcliffe

LEGAL SUPPORT PERSONNEL

Rosanna S. Bertheola

For full biographical listings, see the Martindale-Hubbell Law Directory

FRANK B. MYERS (AV)

Suite 720, 4400 MacArthur Boulevard, 92660
Telephone: 714-752-2001
Facsimile: 714-955-3670

For full biographical listings, see the Martindale-Hubbell Law Directory

*SAN DIEGO,** San Diego Co.

LAW OFFICES OF J. ERNESTO GRIJALVA (AV)

550 West B Street, Suite 340, 92101
Telephone: 619-234-1776
Facsimile: 619-235-6749

ASSOCIATE

Margarita Haugaard

For full biographical listings, see the Martindale-Hubbell Law Directory

PAGE, POLIN, BUSCH & BOATWRIGHT, A PROFESSIONAL CORPORATION (AV)

350 West Ash Street, Suite 900, 92101-3404
Telephone: 619-231-1822
Fax: 619-231-1877
FAX: 619-231-1875

David C. Boatwright
Michael E. Busch
Robert K. Edmunds
Kathleen A. Cashman-Kramer
Richard L. Moskitis
Richard W. Page
Kenneth D. Polin
Steven G. Rowles

OF COUNSEL

Richard Edward Ball, Jr.

Rod S. Fiori
Christina B. Gamache
Dorothy A. Johnson
Theresa McCarthy
Jolene L. Parker
Deidre L. Schneider
Sandra L. Shippey

For full biographical listings, see the Martindale-Hubbell Law Directory

RICE FOWLER BOOTH & BANNING (AV)

Emerald - Shapery Center, 402 W. Broadway, Suite 850, 92101
Telephone: 619-230-0030
Telecopier: 619-230-1350
New Orleans, Louisiana Office: 36th Floor, Place St. Charles, 201 St. Charles Avenue, 70130
Telephone: 504-523-2600.
Telecopier: 504-523-2705.
Telex: 9102507910. ELN: 62548910.
London, England Office: Suite 692, Level 6 Lloyd's, 1 Lime Street, London EC3M 7DQ England.
Telephone: 071-327-4222.
Telecopier: 071-929-0043.
San Francisco, California Office: Embarcadero Center West, 275 Battery Street, 27th Floor, 94111.
Telephone: 415-399-9191.
Telecopier: 415-399-9192.
Telex: 451981.
Beijing, China Office: Beijing International Convention Centre, Suite 7024, No. 8 Beichendong Road, Chaoyang District, 100101, P.R.C.
Telephone: (861) 493-4250.
Telecopier: (861) 493-4251.
Bogota, Colombia Office: Avenida Jimenez #4-03 Officina 10-05.
Telephone: (571) 342-1062.
Telecopier: (571) 342-1062.

PARTNERS

William L. Banning
Keith Zakarin
Robert B. Krueger, Jr.

ASSOCIATE

Juan Carlos Dominguez

For full biographical listings, see the Martindale-Hubbell Law Directory

*SAN FRANCISCO,** San Francisco Co.

LAW OFFICE OF KEVIN W. FINCK (AV)

601 Montgomery Street, Suite 1900, 94111
Telephone: 415-296-9100
Facsimile: 415-394-6446

(See Next Column)

Marla Raucher Osborn

For full biographical listings, see the Martindale-Hubbell Law Directory

FLEISCHMANN & FLEISCHMANN (AV)

650 California Street, Suite 2550, 94108-2606
Telephone: 415-981-0140
FAX: 415-788-6234

MEMBERS OF FIRM

Hartly Fleischmann
Roger Justice Fleischmann

Stella J. Kim
Mark S. Molina

OF COUNSEL

Grace C. Shohet

LEGAL SUPPORT PERSONNEL

Lissa Dirrim

For full biographical listings, see the Martindale-Hubbell Law Directory

FLYNN, DELICH & WISE (AV)

Suite 1750, 580 California Street, 94104
Telephone: 415-693-5566
Fax: 415-693-0410
Long Beach, California Office: 1 World Trade Center, Suite 1800.
Telephone: 310-435-2626.
Fax: 310-437-7555.

John Allen Flynn
Sam D. Delich
James B. Nebel

Representative Clients: American Hawaii Cruises; Holland America Line; Through Transport Mutual Insurance Association, Ltd.; The Britannia Steam Ship Insurance Association Limited; The Steamship Mutual Underwriting Association (Bermuda) Ltd.; General Steamship Corp., Ltd.; Commodore Cruise Line, Ltd.; Interocean Steamship Corporation; Sea-Land Service, Inc.; Hatteras Yachts.

For full biographical listings, see the Martindale-Hubbell Law Directory

RICE FOWLER BOOTH & BANNING (AV)

Embarcadero Center West, 275 Battery Street, 27th Floor, 94111
Telephone: 415-399-9191
Telecopier: 415-399-9192
Telex: 451981
New Orleans, Louisiana Office: Place St. Charles, 36th Floor, 201 St. Charles Avenue, 70130.
Telephone: 504-523-2600.
Telecopier: 504-523-2705.
Telex: 9102507910. ELN 62548910.
San Diego, California Office: Emerald-Shapery Center, 402 W. Broadway, Suite 850, 92101.
Telephone: 619-230-0030.
Telecopier: 619-230-1350.
London, England Office: Suite 692, Level 6 Lloyd's, 1 Lime Street, London EC3M 7DQ England.
Telephone: 071-327-4222.
Telecopier: 071-929-0043.
Beijing, China Office: Beijing International Convention Centre, Suite 7024, No. 8 Beichendong Road, Chaoyang District, 100101, P.R.C.
Telephone: (861) 493-4250.
Telecopier: (861) 493-4251.
Bogota, Colombia Office: Avenida Jimenez #4-03 Oficina 10-05, Bogota, Colombia.
Telephone: (571) 342-1062.
Telecopier: (571) 342-1062.

MEMBERS OF FIRM

Forrest Booth
Kurt L. Micklow
Norman J. Ronneberg, Jr.

ASSOCIATES

Cynthia L. Mitchell
Lynn Haggerty King
Edward M. Bull, III
Kim O. Dincel
Amy Jo Poor
Janice Amenta-Jones
Heidi Loken Benas

For full biographical listings, see the Martindale-Hubbell Law Directory

COLORADO

*DENVER,** Denver Co.

HARRY L. ARKIN & ASSOCIATES (AV)

Suite 2750 Lincoln Center, 1660 Lincoln Street, 80264
Telephone: 303-863-8400
Telefax: 303-832-4703
London, England Office: Verulam Chambers, Peer House, 8-14 Verulam Street, WCIX 8LZ.
Telephone: 071 813-2400.
Fax: 071 405-3870.

ASSOCIATE

Simon L. Krauss

For full biographical listings, see the Martindale-Hubbell Law Directory

ENGEL & RUDMAN, P.C. (AV)

The Quadrant, 5445 DTC Parkway, Suite 1025 (Englewood), 80111
Telephone: 303-741-1111
Fax: 303-694-4028

Barry S. Engel
Ronald L. Rudman

For full biographical listings, see the Martindale-Hubbell Law Directory

HOLME ROBERTS & OWEN LLC (AV)

Suite 4100, 1700 Lincoln, 80203
Telephone: 303-861-7000
Telex: 45-4460
Telecopier: 303-866-0200
Boulder, Colorado Office: Suite 400, 1401 Pearl Street.
Telephone: 303-444-5955.
Telecopier: 303-444-1063.
Colorado Springs, Colorado Office: Suite 1300, 90 South Cascade Avenue.
Telephone: 719-473-3800.
Telecopier: 719-633-1518.
Salt Lake City, Utah Office: Suite 1100, 111 East Broadway.
Telephone: 801-521-5800.
Telecopier: 801-521-9639.
London, England Office: 4th Floor, Mellier House, 26a Albemarle Street.
Telephone: 44-171-499-8776.
Telecopier: 44-171-499-7769.
Moscow, Russia Office: 14 Krivokolenny Pr., Suite 30, 101000.
Telephone: 095-925-7816.
Telecopier: 095-923-2726.

MEMBERS OF FIRM

Bruce R. Kohler (Resident Managing Member, London, England Office; Co-Director, Moscow, Russia Office)
Judith L. L. Roberts (Co-Director, Moscow Office; London Office)
Garth B. Jensen

ASSOCIATES

John Adams Barrett, Jr. (On Leave of Absence)
Margaret B. McLean (Resident Managing Lawyer, Moscow, Russia Office)
Paul G. Thompson

For Complete List of Firm Personnel, See General Section

For full biographical listings, see the Martindale-Hubbell Law Directory

DISTRICT OF COLUMBIA

WASHINGTON, D.C. Co.

ADDUCI, MASTRIANI, SCHAUMBERG & SCHILL (AV)

In Affiliation with Russin & Vecchi
1140 Connecticut Avenue, N.W., Suite 250, 20036
Telephone: 202-467-6300
Telecopier: 202-466-2006; 467-4732
New York, N.Y. Office: 330 Madison Avenue.
Telephone: 212-949-7120.
Telecopier: 212-949-7271.

MEMBERS OF FIRM

V. James Adduci, II
Louis S. Mastriani
Charles F. Schill
Barbara A. Murphy
Tom M. Schaumberg
Ralph H. Sheppard (Not admitted in DC; Resident, New York Office)
Ronald J. Kubovcik
James C. Lydon (Not admitted in DC)

(See Next Column)

Larry L. Shatzer, II
Anri Suzuki
Lisa Levaggi Borter (Resident, New York Office)
Gregory C. Anthes
Peter B. Martine
Robert J. Leo (Not admitted in DC; Resident, New York Office)
David A. Guth

A list of Representative Clients and References will be furnished upon request.

For full biographical listings, see the Martindale-Hubbell Law Directory

BERLINER, CORCORAN & ROWE (AV)

A Partnership including a Professional Corporation
1101 Seventeenth Street, N.W., 20036-4798
Telephone: 202-293-5555
FAX: 202-293-9035

MEMBERS OF FIRM

Thomas G. Corcoran, Jr.
Neal E. Krucoff
Henry M. Lloyd (P.C.)
Wayne H. Rusch
Michael W. Beasley
Clemens J. M. Kochinke
John L. Simson

COUNSEL

Henry A. Berliner, Jr.
Rufus King
Peter Heidenberger

ASSOCIATES

Kathleen S. Rice
Jay A. Rosenthal

For full biographical listings, see the Martindale-Hubbell Law Directory

CAMERON & HORNBOSTEL (AV)

Suite 700, 818 Connecticut Avenue, N.W., 20006
Telephone: 202-293-4690
Cable Address: "Continent"
Telecopier: 202-293-1877
New York, N.Y. Office: 230 Park Avenue.
Telephone: 212-682-4902.
Cable Address: "Continents, New York".
Telecopier: 212-697-0946.

MEMBERS OF FIRM

Duncan H. Cameron
Bertrand J. Delanney (Resident, New York, N.Y. Office)
Peter A. Hornbostel
William K. Ince
Dennis James, Jr.
Alexander W. Sierck
Frederick Simpich
Larry W. Thomas
Howard L. Vickery (Resident, New York, N.Y. Office)
Bruce Zagaris

ASSOCIATES

Gregory J. Bendlin
Rachel F. Herold (Resident at the New York Office)
Michele C. Sherman

OF COUNSEL

Carolyn W. Davenport (Resident at New York, N.Y. Office)
Richard Pu (Resident, New York, N.Y. Office)

For full biographical listings, see the Martindale-Hubbell Law Directory

MURPHY & ASSOCIATES (AV)

818 Connecticut Avenue, N.W., 20006
Telephone: 202-833-9211
Fax: 202-293-1877
Associated Office: Kiskalt, Dielmann & Schoenberger, Frankfurt, Germany.

MEMBERS OF FIRM

Terence Roche Murphy
Charles A. Weber

OF COUNSEL

Heinz J. Dielmann

For full biographical listings, see the Martindale-Hubbell Law Directory

REICHLER, MILTON & MEDEL (AV)

Suite 1200, 1747 Pennsylvania Avenue, N.W., 20006-4604
Telephone: 202-223-1200
Telex: 494-3588
Fax: 202-785-6687

Paul S. Reichler
Kathleen M. Milton
Arthur V. Medel

ASSOCIATES

Janis H. Brennan
Padideh Ala'i
Traci Duvall Humes
Alima Joned (Not admitted in DC)

For full biographical listings, see the Martindale-Hubbell Law Directory

SHAWN, MANN & NIEDERMAYER, L.L.P. (AV)

1850 M Street, N.W., Suite 280, 20036-5803
Telephone: 202-331-7900
Fax: 202-331-0726

(See Next Column)

SHAWN, MANN & NIEDERMAYER L.L.P.—*Continued*

MEMBERS OF FIRM

William H. Shawn
Eshel Bar-Adon

For full biographical listings, see the Martindale-Hubbell Law Directory

WATT, TIEDER & HOFFAR (AV)

601 Pennsylvania Avenue, N.W., Suite 900, 20004
Telephone: 202-462-4697
Telecopier: 703-893-8029
McLean Virginia Office: 7929 Westpark Drive, Suite 400,
Telephone: 703-749-1000.
Telecopier: 703-893-8029.
Irvine California Office: 3 Park Plaza, Suite 1530.
Telephone: 714-852-6700.

MEMBERS OF FIRM

John B. Tieder, Jr.
Robert K. Cox
David C. Romm

For full biographical listings, see the Martindale-Hubbell Law Directory

WILMER, CUTLER & PICKERING (AV)

2445 M Street, N.W., 20037-1420
Telephone: 202-663-6000
Facsimile: 202-663-6363
Internet: Law@Wilmer.Com
European Offices:
4 Carlton Gardens, London, SW1Y 5AA, England. Telephone: 011 (4471) 839-4466.
Facsimile: 011 (4471) 839-3537.
Rue de la Loi 15 Wetstraat, B-1040 Brussels, Belgium. Telephone: 011 (322) 231-0903.
Facsimile: 011 (322) 230-4322.
Friedrichstrasse 95, D-10117 Berlin, Germany. Telephone: 011 (4930) 2643-3601.
Facsimile: 011 (4930) 2643-3630.

MEMBERS OF FIRM

Daniel K. Mayers
James S. Campbell
Louis R. Cohen
F. David Lake, Jr.
Paul J. Mode, Jr.
C. Loring Jetton, Jr.
William T. Lake
Dieter G. F. Lange (Not admitted in DC; Resident, European Office, London, England)
Charles S. Levy
A. Douglas Melamed
Dr. Manfred Balz (Not admitted in the United States); (Resident, European Office, Berlin, Germany)
Richard W. Cass
Kenneth W. Gideon
Arthur L. Marriott (Resident, European Office, London, England)
Robert C. Cassidy, Jr.
John D. Greenwald (Not admitted in DC)
John H. Harwood II
Stephen P. Doyle
Russell J. Bruemmer
William J. Wilkins
Andrew N. Vollmer
James S. Venit (Not admitted in DC; Resident, European Office, Brussels, Belgium)
W. Scott Blackmer (Resident, European Office, Brussels, Belgium)
Gary B. Born (Resident, European Office, London, England)
Paul A. von Hehn (Not admitted in DC; Resident, European Office, Brussels, Belgium)
Bryan Slone (Not admitted in DC; Resident, European Office, Berlin, Germany)
Andrew K. Parnell (Resident, European Office, London, England)

SENIOR COUNSEL

Lloyd N. Cutler
John H. Pickering

COUNSEL

Lester Nurick
Leonard M. Shambon
Dr. Andreas Weitbrecht (Not admitted in DC; Resident, European Office, Brussels, Belgium)
Jeffrey N. Shane
Marc C. Hansen (Resident, European Office, Brussels, Belgium)

SPECIAL COUNSEL

John J. Kallaugher (Not admitted in DC; Resident, European Office, London, England)

For Complete List of Firm Personnel, See General Section

For full biographical listings, see the Martindale-Hubbell Law Directory

FLORIDA

*KISSIMMEE,** Osceola Co.

POHL & BROWN, P.A.

(See Winter Park)

*MIAMI,** Dade Co.

BIERMAN, SHOHAT, LOEWY & PERRY, PROFESSIONAL ASSOCIATION (AV)

Penthouse Two, 800 Brickell Avenue, 33131-2944
Telephone: 305-358-7000
Facsimile: 305-358-4010

Donald I. Bierman
Edward R. Shohat
Ira N. Loewy
Pamela I. Perry
Maria C. Beguiristain

Reference: United National Bank of Miami.

For full biographical listings, see the Martindale-Hubbell Law Directory

LIVINGSTON & KALETA (AV)

Third Floor, 150 S.E. Second Avenue, 33131
Telephone: 305-373-5766
FAX: 305-374-4194

MEMBERS OF FIRM

Robert E. Livingston
Charles J. Kaleta, Jr.

Representative Clients: Banque Paribas; City of Coral Gables; The Kern Company; L.D. Pankey Dental Foundation; Metropolitan Life Insurance Company; Nichols Partnership, Inc.

For full biographical listings, see the Martindale-Hubbell Law Directory

MURAI, WALD, BIONDO & MORENO, P.A. (AV)

9th Floor Ingraham Building, 25 Southeast 2nd Avenue, 33131
Telephone: 305-358-5900
Fax: 305-358-9490

Rene V. Murai
Gerald B. Wald
Gerald J. Biondo
M. Cristina Moreno
William E. Davis

Cristina Echarte Brochin
Ana Maria Escagedo
Manuel Kadre
Lynette Ebeoglu McGuinness
Mary Leslie Smith

Reference: Republic National Bank of Miami.

For full biographical listings, see the Martindale-Hubbell Law Directory

PATTERSON, CLAUSSEN, SANTOS & HUME (AV)

A Partnership of Professional Associations
18th Floor, Courthouse Tower, 44 West Flagler Street, 33130-1808
Telephone: 305-350-9000
Fax: 305-372-3940

John H. Patterson (P.A.)
Kenneth F. Claussen (P.A.)
Jose A. Santos, Jr. (P.A.)
John H. Patterson, Jr. (P.A.)
Charles Lea Hume (P.A.)

OF COUNSEL

James H. Sweeny, III (P.A.)

For Complete List of Firm Personnel, See General Section

For full biographical listings, see the Martindale-Hubbell Law Directory

SHEEHE & VENDITTELLI, P.A. (AV)

Miami Center, Suite 1800, 201 South Biscayne Boulevard, 33131
Telephone: 305-379-3515
Telecopier: 305-379-5404

Phillip J. Sheehe
Louis V. Vendittelli
Henry E. Mendia

Reference: First Union Bank of Florida; Northern Trust Bank of Florida, N.A.

For full biographical listings, see the Martindale-Hubbell Law Directory

SPENCER AND KLEIN, PROFESSIONAL ASSOCIATION (AV)

Suite 1901, 801 Brickell Avenue, 33131
Telephone: 305-374-7700
Telecopier: 305-374-4890

Thomas R. Spencer, Jr.

Representative Clients: America Publishing Group; Amerivend Corp.; Buen Hogar Magazine; Editorial America; Gold Star Medical Management, Inc.; Grupo Anaya, S.A.; Independent Living Care, Inc.; Lourdes Health Services, Inc.; Managed Care of America, Inc.

For Complete List of Firm Personnel, See General Section

For full biographical listings, see the Martindale-Hubbell Law Directory

*ORLANDO,** Orange Co.

BOROUGHS, GRIMM, BENNETT & MORLAN, P.A. (AV)

201 East Pine Street, Suite 500, P.O. Box 3309, 32802-3309
Telephone: 407-841-3353
Telecopier: 407-843-9587

R. Lee Bennett
Thomas Boroughs
William A. Grimm
Harold E. Morlan, II
John R. Simpson, Jr.
Douglas E. Starcher
Robert J. Stovash

Edward R. Alexander, Jr.
Kenneth P. Hazouri

OF COUNSEL

Robert W. Boyd

General Counsel for: Autonomous Technologies Corporation; Bubble Room, Inc.; The Civil Design Group, Inc.; Datamax Corporation; The Investment Counsel Company; Sawtek Inc.

For full biographical listings, see the Martindale-Hubbell Law Directory

POHL & BROWN, P.A.

(See Winter Park)

*SARASOTA,** Sarasota Co.

WILLIAMS, PARKER, HARRISON, DIETZ & GETZEN, PROFESSIONAL ASSOCIATION (AV)

1550 Ringling Boulevard, 34230-3258
Telephone: 813-366-4800
Telecopier: 813-366-5109
Mailing Address: P.O. Box 3258, Sarasota, Florida, 34230-3258

J. J. Williams, Jr. (1886-1968)
W. Davis Parker (1920-1982)
William T. Harrison, Jr.
George A. Dietz
Monte K. Marshall
James L. Ritchey
Hugh McPheeters, Jr.
William G. Lambrecht
John T. Berteau
John V. Cannon, III
Charles D. Bailey, Jr.
J. Michael Hartenstine
Michele Boardman Grimes
James L. Turner
William M. Seider
Elizabeth C. Marshall
Robert W. Benjamin
Frank Strelec
David A. Wallace
Terri Jayne Salt
Jeffrey A. Grebe
John Leslie Moore
Mark A. Schwartz
Stephanie Edwards
Ric Gregoria
Morgan R. Bentley
Susan Barrett Jewell
Linda R. Getzen
Kimberly J. Page
Phillip D. Eck

OF COUNSEL

Frazer F. Hilder
William E. Getzen
Elvin W. Phillips

Counsel for: Sarasota-Manatee Airport Authority; Sarasota County Public Hospital Board; William G. & Marie Selby Foundation; Taylor Woodrow Homes Ltd.; The School Board of Sarasota County.
Local Counsel for: NationsBank of Florida; Arvida/JMB Partners.

For full biographical listings, see the Martindale-Hubbell Law Directory

WINTER PARK, Orange Co.

POHL & BROWN, P.A. (AV)

280 West Canton Avenue, Suite 410, P.O. Box 3208, 32789
Telephone: 407-647-7645; 407-647-POHL
Telefax: 407-647-2314

Frank L. Pohl
Usher L. Brown
Houston E. Short
Dwight I. Cool
William W. Pouzar
Mary B. Van Leuven

OF COUNSEL

Frederick W. Peirsol

Representative Clients: Orange County Comptroller; Osceola County; School Board of Osceola County, Florida; Osceola Tourist Development Council; NationsBank of Florida, N.A.; SunBank, N.A.; The Bank of Winter Park; Bekins Moving and Storage Co., Inc.; Champion Boats, Inc.; KeyCom Telephone Systems, Inc.

For full biographical listings, see the Martindale-Hubbell Law Directory

GEORGIA

*ATLANTA,** Fulton Co.

BOOTH, WADE & CAMPBELL (AV)

Cumberland Center II, 3100 Cumberland Circle, Suite 1500, 30339
Telephone: 404-850-5000
FAX: 404-850-5079

MEMBERS OF FIRM

Allison Wade
Gordon Dean Booth, Jr.
Douglas N. Campbell
L. Dale Owens
Walter E. Jospin
Larry D. Ledbetter
Harry V. Lamon, Jr., (P.C.)
Carl I. Gable, Jr., (P.C.)

ASSOCIATES

Allen Buckley
Steven W. Hardy (Not admitted in GA)
Randolph H. Houchins
Randall W. Johnson
Edward C. Konieczny (Not admitted in GA)
Courtney G. Lytle
Edward H. Nicholson, Jr.
Nancy P. Parson
Scott A. Wharton

Representative Clients: American Airlines, Inc.; Apple South, Inc.; British Airports; Columbia/HCA Healthcare Corporation; Delta Air Lines, Inc.; Life Insurance Company of Georgia; Merrill Lynch & Co.; Prudential Securities Incorporated; Southwire Company.

For full biographical listings, see the Martindale-Hubbell Law Directory

GLASS, MCCULLOUGH, SHERRILL & HARROLD (AV)

1409 Peachtree Street, N.E., 30309
Telephone: 404-885-1500
Telecopier: 404-892-1801
Buckhead Office: Monarch Plaza, 3414 Peachtree Road, N.E., Suite 450, Atlanta, Georgia, 30326-1162.
Telephone: 404-885-1500.
Telecopier: 404-231-1978.
Washington, D.C. Office: 1155 15th Street, N.W., Suite 400, Washington, D.C., 20005.
Telephone: 202-785-8118.
Telecopier: 202-785-0128.

MEMBER OF FIRM

Thomas J. Harrold, Jr.
W. Clayton Sparrow, Jr.

For Complete List of Firm Personnel, See General Section

For full biographical listings, see the Martindale-Hubbell Law Directory

HARKLEROAD & HERMANCE, A PROFESSIONAL CORPORATION (AV)

2500 Cain Tower-Peachtree Center, 229 Peachtree Street, N.E., 30303
Telephone: 404-588-9211
Telex II: 810-751-3228
Telecopier: 404-659-0860

Donald R. Harkleroad

For full biographical listings, see the Martindale-Hubbell Law Directory

HAWAII

*HONOLULU,** Honolulu Co.

DAVID F. DAY (AV)

Amfac Center, Hawaii Building, Suite 1840, 745 Fort Street, 96813
Telephone: 808-531-8020
Fax: 808-521-0962

For full biographical listings, see the Martindale-Hubbell Law Directory

FOLEY MAEHARA NIP & CHANG (AV)

2700 Grosvenor Center, 737 Bishop Street, 96813
Telephone: 808-526-3011
Telecopier: 808-523-1171, 808-526-0121, 808-533-4814

MEMBERS OF FIRM

Thomas M. Foley
Eric T. Maehara
Renton L. K. Nip
Wesley Y. S. Chang
Carl Tom
Edward R. Brooks
Arlene S. Kishi
Susan M. Ichinose
Robert F. Miller
Christian P. Porter

ASSOCIATES

Paula W. Chong
Lenore H. Lee
Leanne A. N. Nikaido
Jordan D. Wagner
Donna H. Yamamoto
Mark J. Bernardin
Jenny K. T. Wakayama

(See Next Column)

FOLEY MAEHARA NIP & CHANG—*Continued*

OF COUNSEL

Elizabeth A. Ivey

References: First Hawaiian Bank; Bank of Honolulu; Bank of Hawaii.

For full biographical listings, see the Martindale-Hubbell Law Directory

MCCORRISTON MIHO MILLER MUKAI (AV)

Five Waterfront Plaza, 4th Floor, 500 Ala Moana Boulevard, 96813
Telephone: 808-529-7300
Facsimile: 808-524-8293
Cable: Attorneys, Honolulu

MEMBERS OF FIRM

William C. McCorriston
Jon T. Miho
Clifford J. Miller
Franklin K. Mukai
Calvert G. Chipchase, III
David N. Kuriyama
Eric T. Kawatani
Keith K. Suzuka

ASSOCIATES

Andrew W. Char
Randall F. Sakumoto
Alexander R. Jampel

OF COUNSEL

Stanley Y. Mukai

For Complete List of Firm Personnel, See General Section

For full biographical listings, see the Martindale-Hubbell Law Directory

ILLINOIS

*CHICAGO,** Cook Co.

BOWLES, KEATING, HERING & LOWE, CHARTERED (AV)

135 South La Salle Street, Suite 1040, 60603-4295
Telephone: 312-263-6300
Fax: 312-263-0415
Italy Office: 10, Via Pietro Verri, 20121 Milan, Italy.
Telephone: 2-798609.
Fax: 276001473.
European Associated Offices:
Italy Office: Studio Legale Ippolito, viale Astichello, 6, 36100 Vicenza, Italy.
Telephone: 444-300957.
Fax: 444-300827..
Sweden Office: Advokatgruppen i Stockholm AB, Kommendorsgatan 26,114 48 Stockholm, Sweden.
Telephone: 8-667-0765.
Fax: 8-660-9827.
France Office: Allain - Kaltenbach - Plaisant - Raimon, 14 Rue Lejemptel, 94302 Vincennes (Paris), France.
Telephone: 1-4374 7494.
Fax: 1-4374 3222.
Asian Cooperative Offices:
China Offices: Liaoning Law Office For Foreign Affairs, 11 Liaohe Street, Shenyang Liaoning 110032, China.
Telephone: 652125.
Telex: 808305 LCPIT CN.
FAX: (24) 664791. Dalian Foreign Economic Law Office: No. 2 S. Square, Dalian, Liaoning, China.
Telephone: 332532.
FAX: 332532. Shenyang Foreign Economic Law Office, 230-3, Quingnian Street, Shenhe District, Shenyang Liaoning 110014, China.
Telephone: 290123.

Clyde O. Bowles, Jr. (Chicago Office)
Mario Bruno
Roberto N. Bruno
Nicola Fiordalisi (Chicago Office)
Glenn Z. Hering (Chicago Office)
Kathryn R. Ingrim (Chicago Office)
Christopher L. Ingrim (Chicago Office)
Thomas M. Keating (Chicago Office)
Jung Y. Lowe (Chicago Office)
Lynne R. Ostfeld (Chicago Office)
Arnold A. Silvestri (Chicago Office)

COUNSEL

Malcolm A. Chandler (Chicago Office)

For full biographical listings, see the Martindale-Hubbell Law Directory

PATTISHALL, MCAULIFFE, NEWBURY, HILLIARD & GERALDSON (AV)

Suite 5000, 311 South Wacker Drive, 60606
Telephone: 312-554-8000
Facsimile: 312-554-8015
Telex: 27-0500
Washington, D.C. Office: 320 Watergate, Six Hundred 20037.
Telephone: 202-338-1300.
Facsimile: 202-388-9349.
Telex: 89-7453.

MEMBERS OF FIRM

Beverly W. Pattishall
Jeremiah D. McAuliffe
Robert M. Newbury
Benjamin S. Warren III (Resident Partner, Washington, D.C. Office)
Raymond I. Geraldson, Jr.
David Craig Hilliard
Edward G. Wierzbicki
Robert W. Sacoff
Mark V. B. Partridge
Joseph N. Welch II
Mark H. Hellmann
Jean Marie R. Pechette

Daniel D. Frohling
John Thompson Brown
Mary E. Innis
Douglas N. Masters
Brett A. August
Jonathan S. Jennings
John Michael Murphy
Paul R. Garcia
Kimberly White Alcantara
Maxine S. Lans
Nancy L. Clarke

For full biographical listings, see the Martindale-Hubbell Law Directory

LOMBARD, Du Page Co.

ARTHUR FAKES, P.C. (AV)

929 South Main Street, Suite 109, 60148
Telephone: 708-268-0600
Telecopier: 708-268-0642

Arthur Fakes

For full biographical listings, see the Martindale-Hubbell Law Directory

INDIANA

*INDIANAPOLIS,** Marion Co.

ICE MILLER DONADIO & RYAN (AV)

One American Square Box 82001, 46282-0002
Telephone: 317-236-2100
Fax: 317-236-2219

MEMBERS OF FIRM

Donald G. Sutherland
Richard E. Parker
Harry L. Gonso

ASSOCIATES

Dale E. Stackhouse
Timothy A. Brooks

Representative Clients: Avesta Sheffield Plate, Inc.; Biomet, Inc.; DeMars-Haka Development, Inc.; Reilly Industries, Inc.; Thomson Consumer Electronics, Inc.; INTAT Precision, Inc. (Aisin Takaoka Co., Ltd.); Onkyo America, Inc. (Onkyo Corporation); Toyota Equipment Mfg. Inc. (Toyoda Automatic Loom Works, Ltd.); Sony Corporation of America (Sony Corporation); Stewart Warner South Wind Corporation.

For Complete List of Firm Personnel, See General Section

For full biographical listings, see the Martindale-Hubbell Law Directory

KANSAS

*WICHITA,** Sedgwick Co.

FOULSTON & SIEFKIN (AV)

(Formerly Foulston, Siefkin, Powers & Eberhardt)
700 Fourth Financial Center, Broadway at Douglas, 67202
Telephone: 316-267-6371
Facsimile: 316-267-6345
Topeka, Kansas Office: 1515 Bank IV Tower, 534 Kansas Avenue. 66603.
Telephone: 913-233-3600.
FAX: 913-233-1610.
Member: Lex Mundi, A Global Association of Independent Firms

MEMBERS OF FIRM

Benjamin C. Langel
Harvey R. Sorensen
Larry G. Rapp

For Complete List of Firm Personnel, See General Section

For full biographical listings, see the Martindale-Hubbell Law Directory

LOUISIANA

*NEW ORLEANS,** Orleans Parish

GAINSBURGH, BENJAMIN, FALLON, DAVID & ATES (AV)

A Partnership including Professional Law Corporations
2800 Energy Centre, 1100 Poydras, 70163-2800
Telephone: 504-522-2304
Telecopier: 504-528-9973

OF COUNSEL

Samuel C. Gainsburgh (P.L.C.)

MEMBERS OF FIRM

Jack C. Benjamin (P.L.C.)
Eldon E. Fallon (P.L.C.)
Robert J. David
George S. Meyer (1939-1977)
J. Robert Ates (P.L.C.)
Gerald E. Meunier
Nick F. Noriea, Jr.
Irving J. Warshauer
Stevan C. Dittman
Madeleine M. Landrieu

ASSOCIATES

Darryl M. Phillips
Andrew A. Lemmon
Michael G. Calogero

For full biographical listings, see the Martindale-Hubbell Law Directory

RICE FOWLER (AV)

Place St. Charles, 36th Floor, 201 St. Charles Avenue, 70130
Telephone: 504-523-2600
Telecopier: 504-523-2705
Telex: 9102507910
ELN 62548910
London, England Office: Suite 692, Level 6 Lloyd's, 1 Lime Street, London EC3M 7DQ England.
Telephone: 071-327-4222.
Telecopier: 071-929-0043.
San Francisco, California Office: Embarcadero Center West, 275 Battery Street, 27th Floor, 94111.
Telephone: 415-399-9191.
Telecopier: 415-399-9192.
Telex: 451981.
San Diego, California Office: Emerald-Shapery Center, 402 W. Broadway, Suite 850, 92101.
Telephone: 619-230-0030.
Telecopier: 619-230-1350.
Beijing, China Office: Beijing International Convention Centre, Suite 7024, No. 8 Beichendong Road, Chaoyang District, 100101, P.R.C.
Telephone: (861) 493-4250.
Telecopier: (861) 493-4251.
Bogota, Colombia Office: Avenida Jimenez #4-03 Oficina 10-05.
Telephone: (571) 342-1062.
Telecopier: (571) 342-1062.

MEMBERS OF FIRM

Winston Edward Rice
George J. Fowler, III
Antonio J. Rodriguez
Thomas H. Kingsmill, III
Paul N. Vance
Delos E. Flint, Jr.
Edward F. LeBreton, III
Docia L. Dalby
Mary Campbell Hubbard
Jon W. Wise
Mat M. Gray, III

OF COUNSEL

T. C. W. Ellis

ASSOCIATES

Mary E. Kerrigan
Susan Molero Vance
Samuel A. Giberga
John F. Billera
D. Roxanne Perkins
Jeffry L. Sanford
Alanson T. Chenault, IV
Cindy T. Matherne
Barry A. Brock
Walter F. Wolf, III
Robert R. Johnston
Virginia R. Quijada
William J. Sommers, Jr.

For full biographical listings, see the Martindale-Hubbell Law Directory

WAGNER, BAGOT & GLEASON (AV)

Suite 2660, Poydras Center, 650 Poydras Street, 70130-6102
Telephone: 504-525-2141
Telecopier: 504-523-1587
TWX: 5106017673
ELN: 62928850
"INCISIVE"

Thomas J. Wagner
Michael H. Bagot, Jr.
Harvey G. Gleason
Whitney L. Cole
Eric D. Suben

For full biographical listings, see the Martindale-Hubbell Law Directory

MAINE

BAR HARBOR, Hancock Co.

FENTON, CHAPMAN, FENTON, SMITH & KANE, P.A. (AV)

109 Main Street, P.O. Box B, 04609
Telephone: 207-288-3331
FAX: 207-288-9326

William Fenton
Hancock Griffin, Jr. (1912-1980)
Douglas B. Chapman
Nathaniel R. Fenton
Chadbourn H. Smith
Daniel H. Kane

Margaret A. Timothy
Eric Lindquist

OF COUNSEL

David Einhorn
Edwin R. Smith

Reference: Bar Harbor Banking and Trust Co.

For full biographical listings, see the Martindale-Hubbell Law Directory

MASSACHUSETTS

*BOSTON,** Suffolk Co.

ARESTY INTERNATIONAL LAW OFFICES (AV)

Bay 107, Union Wharf, 02109
Telephone: 617-367-8393
FAX: 617-742-6452
Kaohsiung, Taiwan Office: Suite 2, Fourth Floor, 143 Ta-Tung 2nd Road.
Telephone: 07-291-3051.
Fax: 08-732-7500.

Jeffrey M. Aresty

ASSOCIATE

Andrew S. Breines

INTERNATIONAL LAW CONSULTANT

Yi-Fu (Eve) Sun

LEGAL SUPPORT PERSONNEL

INTERNATIONAL BUSINESS CONSULTANTS

Victor J. Aresty
Yeichun Wang

For full biographical listings, see the Martindale-Hubbell Law Directory

PALMER & DODGE (AV)

(Storey Thorndike Palmer & Dodge)
One Beacon Street, 02108
Telephone: 617-573-0100
Telecopier: 617-227-4420
Telex: 951104
Cable Address: "Storeydike," Boston

MEMBERS OF FIRM

F. Andrew Anderson
Neil P. Arkuss
F. Kingston Berlew
Robert Duggan
Robert E. Sullivan
John Taylor Williams

COUNSEL

Kevin R. McNamara
Alan S. Musgrave

For Complete List of Firm Personnel, See General Section

For full biographical listings, see the Martindale-Hubbell Law Directory

MICHIGAN

*ANN ARBOR,** Washtenaw Co.

MILLER, CANFIELD, PADDOCK AND STONE, P.L.C. (AV)

A Professional Limited Liability Company
Founded in 1852 by Sidney Davy Miller
101 North Main Street, Seventh Floor, 48104-1400
Telephone: 313-663-2445
Fax: 313-747-7147
Detroit, Michigan Office: 150 West Jefferson, Suite 2500, 48226-4415.
Telephone: 313-963-6420.
Fax: 313-496-7500.
Cable Address: "Stem Detroit."
Bloomfield Hills, Michigan Office: Suite 100, Pinehurst Office Center, 1400 North Woodward, 48303-2014.
Telephone: 313-645-5000.
Fax: 313-645-1917.

(See Next Column)

MILLER, CANFIELD, PADDOCK AND STONE P.L.C.—*Continued*

Grand Rapids, Michigan Office: 1200 Campau Square Plaza, 99 Monroe, N.W., 49503-2639.
Telephone: 616-454-8656.
Fax: 616-776-6322.
Howell, Michigan Office: 121 South Barnard Street, Suite 4, 48843-2305.
Telephone: 517-546-7600.
Telecopier: 517-546-6974.
Kalamazoo, Michigan Office: 444 West Michigan Avenue, 49007-3752.
Telephone: 616-381-7030.
Fax: 616-382-0244.
Lansing, Michigan Office: One Michigan Avenue, Suite 900, 48933-1609.
Telephone: 517-487-2070.
Fax: 517-374-6304.
Monroe, Michigan Office: The Executive Centre, 214 East Elm Avenue, 48161-2682.
Telephone: 313-243-2000.
Fax: 313-243-0901.
Washington, D.C. Office: 1225 Nineteenth Street, N.W., Suite 400. 20036.
Telephone: 202-429-5575; 785-0600.
Fax: 202-331-1118; 785-1234.
Pensacola, Florida Office: 25 West Cedar, 32501.
Telephone: 904-469-1088.
Fax: 904-432-0677.
St. Petersburg, Florida Office: 100 Second Avenue S., Suite 7045, 33701.
Telephone: 813-982-6000.
Fax: 813-892-6002.
Gdansk, Poland Office: Suite 322, Dom Technika Building, Ul. Rajska 6, 80-850.
Telephone: 011-485-831-2808.
Fax: 011-485-831-4719.
Warsaw, Poland Office: Ul. Marszalkowska 82, Suite 561, 00-517.
Telephone: 011-482-623-6457 and 6458.
Fax: 011-482-623-6459.

RESIDENT PARTNERS

Erik H. Serr — J. David Reck

RESIDENT ASSOCIATES

A. Paul Thowsen — Linda M. Ledbetter

Representative Firm Clients: Chrysler Corp.; Comerica, Inc.; City of Detroit, Mich.; Detroit Tigers, Inc.; First of Michigan; Fretter, Inc.; Ford Motor Co.; Ford Motor Credit Co.; Great Lakes Bancorp; Henry Ford Hospital.

For Complete List of Firm Personnel, See General Section

For full biographical listings, see the Martindale-Hubbell Law Directory

BLOOMFIELD HILLS, Oakland Co.

MILLER, CANFIELD, PADDOCK AND STONE, P.L.C. (AV)

A Professional Limited Liability Company
Founded in 1852 by Sidney Davy Miller
Suite 100 Pinehurst Office Center, 1400 North Woodward, P.O. Box 2014, 48303-2014
Telephone: 810-645-5000
Fax: 810-645-1917
Fax: 810-258-3036
Detroit, Michigan Office: 150 West Jefferson, Suite 2500, 48226-4415.
Telephone: 313-963-6420.
Fax: 313-496-7500.
Cable Address: "Stem Detroit."
Ann Arbor, Michigan Office: 101 North Main Street, 7th Floor, 48104-1400.
Telephone: 313-663-2445.
Fax: 313-747-7147.
Grand Rapids, Michigan Office: 1200 Campau Square Plaza, 99 Monroe, N.W., 49503-2639.
Telephone: 616-454-8656.
Fax: 616-776-6322.
Howell, Michigan Office: 121 South Barnard Street, Suite 4, 48843-2305.
Telephone: 517-546-7600.
Telecopier: 517-546-6974.
Kalamazoo, Michigan Office: 444 West Michigan Avenue, 49007-3752.
Telephone: 616-381-7030.
Fax: 616-382-0244.
Lansing, Michigan Office: One Michigan Avenue, Suite 900, 48933-1609.
Telephone: 517-487-2070.
Fax: 517-374-6304.
Monroe, Michigan Office: The Executive Centre, 214 East Elm Avenue, 48161-2682.
Telephone: 313-243-2000.
Fax: 313-243-0901.
Washington, D.C. Office: 1225 Nineteenth Street, N.W., Suite 400. 20036.
Telephone: 202-429-5575; 785-0600.
Fax: 202-331-1118; 785-1234.
Pensacola, Florida Office: 25 West Cedar, 32501.
Telephone: 904-469-1088.
Fax: 904-432-0677.
St. Petersburg, Florida Office: 100 Second Avenue S., Suite 7045, 33701.
Telephone: 813-982-6000.
Fax: 813-892-6002.

(See Next Column)

Gdansk, Poland Office: Suite 322, Dom Technika Building, Ul. Rajska 6, 80-850.
Telephone: 011-485-831-2808.
Fax: 011-485-831-4719.
Warsaw, Poland Office: Ul. Marszalkowska 82, Suite 561, 00-517.
Telephone: 011-482-623-6457 and 6458.
Fax: 011-482-623-6459.

RESIDENT MEMBERS

John A. Thurber (P.C.) — John A. Marxer (P.C.)

RESIDENT OF COUNSEL

Henry R. Nolte, Jr.

RESIDENT ASSOCIATE

Jereen G. Trudell

Representative Firm Clients: Chrysler Corp.; Comerica, Inc.; City of Detroit, Mich.; Detroit Tigers, Inc.; First of Michigan; Fretter, Inc.; Ford Motor Co.; Ford Motor Credit Co.; Great Lakes Bancorp; Henry Ford Hospital.

For Complete List of Firm Personnel, See General Section

For full biographical listings, see the Martindale-Hubbell Law Directory

*DETROIT,** Wayne Co.

BUTZEL LONG, A PROFESSIONAL CORPORATION (AV)

Suite 900, 150 West Jefferson, 48226
Telephone: 313-225-7000
Telecopier: 313-225-7080
Birmingham, Michigan Office: Suite 200, 32270 Telegraph Road.
Telephone: 810-258-1616.
Telecopier: 810-258-1439.
Lansing, Michigan Office: 118 West Ottawa Street.
Telephone: 517-372-6622.
Telecopier: 517-372-6672.
Ann Arbor, Michigan Office: Suite 400, 121 West Washington.
Telephone: 313-995-3110.
Telecopier: 313-995-1777.
Grosse Pointe Farms, Michigan Office: Suite 260, 21 Kercheval.
Telephone: 313-886-5446.
Telecopier: 313-886-2114.

Morris Milmet
Robert J. Battista
Xhafer Orhan
C. Peter Theut
Robert M. Vercruysse
Richard E. Rassel
Jack D. Shumate
John P. Hancock, Jr.
James C. Bruno
Gregory V. Murray
Mark R. Lezotte
James L. Hughes
Gordon W. Didier
Alan S. Levine
Brian P. Henry (Birmingham and Lansing)

Brian J. Miles
Clara DeMatteis Mager
Nicholas J. Stasevich
Guglielmo A. Pezza
Debra Auerbach Clephane
Caridad Pastor-Klucens

Representative Clients: Bridgestone/Firestone, Inc.; The Detroit News, Inc.; Detroit Diesel Corp.; Kelly Services; Kelsey Hayes Co.; Merrill Lynch & Co., Inc.; Stroh Brewery Co.; Takata Corp.; United Parcel Services of America, Inc.; The University of Michigan.

For Complete List of Firm Personnel, See General Section

For full biographical listings, see the Martindale-Hubbell Law Directory

DICKINSON, WRIGHT, MOON, VAN DUSEN & FREEMAN (AV)

500 Woodward Avenue, Suite 4000, 48226-3425
Telephone: 313-223-3500
Facsimile: 313-223-3598
Bloomfield Hills, Michigan Office: 525 North Woodward Avenue, Suite 2000.
Telephone: 810-433-7200.
Facsimile: 810-433-7274.
Grand Rapids, Michigan Office: 200 Ottawa Avenue, N.W., Suite 900.
Telephone: 616-458-1300.
Facsimile: 616-458-6753.
Lansing, Michigan Office: Suite 200, 215 South Washington Square.
Telephone: 517-371-1730.
Facsimile: 517-487-4700.
Washington, D.C. Office: Suite 800, 1901 L Street, N.W.
Telephone: 202-457-0160.
Facsimile: 202-659-1559.
Chicago, Illinois Office: 225 West Washington, Suite 400.
Telephone: 312-220-0300.
Facsimile: 312-220-0021.
Warsaw, Poland Office: 46 Wilcza Street, 4th Floor, 00-679.
Telephone: (48-22) 299-241.
Facsimile: (48-2) 628-4107. Komertel Satellite Phone: (48-39) 121-510.

MEMBERS OF FIRM

Douglas D. Roche
Thomas G. Kienbaum
Julia Donovan Darlow
John K. Lawrence
Roger H. Cummings
Bruce C. Thelen
Larry J. Stringer
Peter Swiecicki (Warsaw, Poland Office)
Tomoaki Ikenaga

(See Next Column)

DICKINSON, WRIGHT, MOON, VAN DUSEN & FREEMAN, *Detroit—Continued*

ASSOCIATES

Julie T. Emerick
Matthew V. Piwowar
(Warsaw, Poland Office)
Linda J. Truitt

For Complete List of Firm Personnel, See General Section

For full biographical listings, see the Martindale-Hubbell Law Directory

DYKEMA GOSSETT (AV)

400 Renaissance Center, 48243-1668
Telephone: 313-568-6800
Cable Address: "Dyke-Detroit"
Telex: 23-0121
Fax: 313-568-6594
Ann Arbor, Michigan Office: 315 East Eisenhower Parkway, Suite 100, 48108-3306.
Telephone: 313-747-7660.
Fax: 313-747-7696.
Bloomfield Hills, Michigan Office: 1577 North Woodward Avenue, Suite 300, 48304-2820.
Telephone: 810-540-0700.
Fax: 810-540-0763.
Grand Rapids, Michigan Office: 200 Oldtown Riverfront Building, 248 Louis Campau Promenade, N.W., 49503-2668.
Telephone: 616-776-7500.
Fax: 616-776-7573.
Lansing, Michigan Office: 800 Michigan National Tower, 48933-1707.
Telephone: 517-374-9100.
Fax: 517-374-9191.
Washington, D.C. Office: Franklin Square, Suite 300 West Tower, 1300 I Street, N.W., 20005-3306.
Telephone: 202-522-8600.
Fax: 202-522-8669.
Chicago, Illinois Office: Three First National Plaza, Suite 1400, 70 W. Madison, 60602-4270.
Telephone: 312-214-3380.
Fax: 312-214-3441.

MEMBERS OF FIRM

Teresa A. Brooks (Resident at Washington, D.C. Office)
B. Kingsley Buhl (Resident at Bloomfield Hills Office)
Joseph F. Dillon
Michael D. Fishman (Resident at Bloomfield Hills Office)
Steven E. Grob
J. Timothy Hobbs (Not admitted in MI; Resident at Washington, D.C. Office)
Gregory M. Kopacz
Bruce A. McDonald (Not admitted in MI; Resident at Washington, D.C. Office)
Richard D. McLellan (Resident at Lansing Office)
Janet L. Neary (Resident at Ann Arbor Office)
Rex E. Schlaybaugh, Jr. (Resident at Bloomfield Hills Office)
Daniel J. Scully, Jr.
Lloyd A. Semple
Daniel G. Wyllie

ASSOCIATE

Dennis M. Pousak

For Complete List of Firm Personnel, See General Section

For full biographical listings, see the Martindale-Hubbell Law Directory

MILLER, CANFIELD, PADDOCK AND STONE, P.L.C. (AV)

A Professional Limited Liability Company
Founded in 1852 by Sidney Davy Miller
150 West Jefferson, Suite 2500, 48226-4415
Telephone: 313-963-6420
Fax: 313-496-7500
Cable Address: "Stem Detroit"
Detroit, Michigan Office: 150 West Jefferson, Suite 2500, 48226-4415.
Telephone: 313-963-6420.
Fax: 313-496-7500.
Cable Address: "Stem Detroit."
Ann Arbor, Michigan Office: 101 North Main Street, 7th Floor, 48104-1400.
Telephone: 313-663-2445.
Fax: 313-747-7147.
Bloomfield Hills, Michigan Office: Suite 100, Pinehurst Office Center, 1400 North Woodward, 48303-2014.
Telephone: 313-645-5000.
Fax: 313-645-1917.
Grand Rapids, Michigan Office: 1200 Campau Square Plaza, 99 Monroe, N.W., 49503-2639.
Telephone: 616-454-8656.
Fax: 616-776-6322.
Howell, Michigan Office: 121 South Barnard Street, Suite 4, 48843-2305.
Telephone: 517-546-7600.
Telecopier: 517-546-6974.
Kalamazoo, Michigan Office: 444 West Michigan Avenue, 49007-3752.
Telephone: 616-381-7030.
Fax: 616-382-0244.

(See Next Column)

Lansing, Michigan Office: One Michigan Avenue, Suite 900, 48933-1609.
Telephone: 517-487-2070.
Fax: 517-374-6304.
Monroe, Michigan Office: The Executive Centre, 214 East Elm Avenue, 48161-2682.
Telephone: 313-243-2000.
Fax: 313-243-0901.
Washington, D.C. Office: 1225 Nineteenth Street, N.W., Suite 400. 20036.
Telephone: 202-429-5575; 785-0600.
Fax: 202-331-1118; 785-1234.
Pensacola, Florida Office: 25 West Cedar, 32501.
Telephone: 904-469-1088.
Fax: 904-432-0677.
St. Petersburg, Florida Office: 100 Second Avenue S., Suite 7045, 33701.
Telephone: 813-982-6000.
Fax: 813-892-6002.
Gdansk, Poland Office: Suite 322, Dom Technika Building, Ul. Rajska 6, 80-850.
Telephone: 011-485-831-2808.
Fax: 011-485-831-4719.
Warsaw, Poland Office: Ul. Marszalkowska 82, Suite 561, 00-517.
Telephone: 011-482-623-6457 and 6458.
Fax: 011-482-623-6459.

MEMBERS OF FIRM

John W. Gelder
Robert S. Ketchum
Rocque E. Lipford (P.C.) (Monroe Office)
Eric V. Brown, Jr. (Kalamazoo Office)
Bruce D. Birgbauer
John A. Thurber (P.C.) (Bloomfield Hills Office)
Erik H. Serr (Ann Arbor Office)
John A. Marxer (P.C.) (Bloomfield Hills Office)
John J. Collins, Jr.
Thomas G. Appleman
J. David Reck (Ann Arbor and Howell Offices)
Richard A. Walawender

OF COUNSEL

George J. Slykhouse (Grand Rapids Office)
Gerard Thomas (Kalamazoo Office)
Henry R. Nolte, Jr. (Bloomfield Hills Office)

SENIOR ATTORNEYS

Elise Levasseur Rohn
David F. Dixon

ASSOCIATES

Jereen G. Trudell (Bloomfield Hills Office)
A. Paul Thowsen (Ann Arbor Office)
Terry Xiaotian Gao (Washington, D.C. Office)
Linda M. Ledbetter (Ann Arbor Office)

Representative Firm Clients: Chrysler Corp.; Comerica, Inc.; City of Detroit, Mich.; Detroit Tigers, Inc.; First of Michigan; Fretter, Inc.; Ford Motor Co.; Ford Motor Credit Co.; Great Lakes Bancorp; Henry Ford Hospital.

For Complete List of Firm Personnel, See General Section

For full biographical listings, see the Martindale-Hubbell Law Directory

FARMINGTON HILLS, Oakland Co.

KAUFMAN AND PAYTON (AV)

200 Northwestern Financial Center, 30833 Northwestern Highway, 48334
Telephone: 810-626-5000
Telefacsimile: 810-626-2843
Grand Rapids, Michigan Office: 420 Trust Building.
Telephone: 616-459-4200.
Fax: 616-459-4929.
Traverse City, Michigan Office: 122 West State Street.
Telephone: 616-947-4050.
Fax: 616-947-7321.

Alan Jay Kaufman
Donald L. Payton
Kenneth C. Letherwood
Stephen R. Levine
Thomas L. Vitu
Ralph C. Chapa, Jr.
Raymond I. Foley, II
Jeffrey K. Van Hattum
Leo D. Neville

For full biographical listings, see the Martindale-Hubbell Law Directory

*GRAND RAPIDS,** Kent Co.

MILLER, CANFIELD, PADDOCK AND STONE, P.L.C. (AV)

A Professional Limited Liability Company
Founded in 1852 by Sidney Davy Miller
1200 Campau Square Plaza, 99 Monroe, N.W., P.O. Box 329, 49503-2639
Telephone: 616-454-8656
Fax: 616-776-6322
Detroit, Michigan Office: 150 West Jefferson, Suite 2500, 48226-4415.
Telephone: 313-963-6420.
Fax: 313-496-7500.
Cable Address: "Stem Detroit."
Ann Arbor, Michigan Office: 101 North Main Street, 7th Floor, 48104-1400.
Telephone: 313-663-2445.
Fax: 313-747-7147.

(See Next Column)

MILLER, CANFIELD, PADDOCK AND STONE P.L.C.—*Continued*

Bloomfield Hills, Michigan Office: Suite 100, Pinehurst Office Center, 1400 North Woodward, 48303-2014.
Telephone: 313-645-5000.
Fax: 313-645-1917.
Howell, Michigan Office: 121 South Barnard Street, Suite 4, 48843-2305.
Telephone: 517-546-7600.
Telecopier: 517-546-6974.
Kalamazoo, Michigan Office: 444 West Michigan Avenue, 49007-3752.
Telephone: 616-381-7030.
Fax: 616-382-0244.
Lansing, Michigan Office: One Michigan Avenue, Suite 900, 48933-1609.
Telephone: 517-487-2070.
Fax: 517-374-6304.
Monroe, Michigan Office: The Executive Centre, 214 East Elm Avenue, 48161-2682.
Telephone: 313-243-2000.
Fax: 313-243-0901.
Washington, D.C. Office: 1225 Nineteenth Street, N.W., Suite 400. 20036.
Telephone: 202-429-5575; 785-0600;
Fax: 202-331-1118; 785-1234.
Pensacola, Florida Office: 25 West Cedar 32501.
Telephone: 904-469-1088.
Fax: 904-432-0677.
St. Petersburg Florida Office: 100 Second Avenue S., Suite 7045, 33701.
Telephone: 813-982-6000.
Fax: 813-892-6002.
Gdansk, Poland Office: Suite 322, Dom Technika Building, UI. Rajska 6, 80-850.
Telephone: 011-485-831-2808.
Fax: 011-485-831-4719.
Warsaw, Poland Office: UI. Marszalkowska 82, Suite 561, 00-517.
Telephone: 011-482-623-6457 and 6458.
Fax: 011-482-623-6459.

OF COUNSEL

George J. Slykhouse (Resident)

Representative Firm Clients: Chrysler Corp.; Comerica, Inc.; City of Detroit, Mich.; Detroit Tigers, Inc.; First of Michigan; Fretter, Inc.; Ford Motor Co.; Ford Motor Credit Co.; Great Lakes Bancorp; Henry Ford Hospital.

For Complete List of Firm Personnel, See General Section

For full biographical listings, see the Martindale-Hubbell Law Directory

PRICE, HENEVELD, COOPER, DEWITT & LITTON (AV)

695 Kenmoor, S.E., P.O. Box 2567, 49501
Telephone: 616-949-9610
Cable Address: "Preld"
Telex: 226-402
Telecopier: 616-957-8196

MEMBERS OF FIRM

Lloyd A. Heneveld
Richard C. Cooper
William W. DeWitt
Randall G. Litton
James A. Mitchell
Daniel Van Dyke
Harold W. Reick
Donald S. Gardner
Thomas M. McKinley
Carl S. Clark
Terence J. Linn
Frederick S. Burkhart

ASSOCIATES

James E. Bartek
Daniel L. Girdwood
Mark E. Bandy
Barry C. Kane

Representative Clients: Amway Corp.; Donnelly Corp.; Dow Chemical Co.; Gerber Products Co.; Kysor Industrial Corp.; L. Perrigo Co.; Prince Corp.; Ralston Purina Co.; Steelcase, Inc.; Wolverine World Wide, Inc.

For full biographical listings, see the Martindale-Hubbell Law Directory

*KALAMAZOO,** Kalamazoo Co.

MILLER, CANFIELD, PADDOCK AND STONE, P.L.C. (AV)

A Professional Limited Liability Company
Founded in 1852 by Sidney Davy Miller
444 West Michigan Avenue, 49007-3752
Telephone: 616-381-7030
Fax: 616-382-0244
Detroit, Michigan Office: 150 West Jefferson, Suite 2500, 48226-4415.
Telephone: 313-963-6420.
Fax: 313-496-7500.
Cable Address: "Stem Detroit."
Ann Arbor, Michigan Office: 101 North Main Street, 7th Floor, 48104-1400.
Telephone: 313-663-2445.
Fax: 313-747-7147.
Bloomfield Hills, Michigan Office: Suite 100, Pinehurst Office Center, 1400 North Woodward, 48303-2014.
Telephone: 313-645-5000.
Fax: 313-645-1917.
Grand Rapids, Michigan Office: 1200 Campau Square Plaza, 99 Monroe, N.W., 49503-2639.
Telephone: 616-454-8656.
Fax: 616-776-6322.

(See Next Column)

Howell, Michigan Office: 121 South Barnard Street, Suite 4, 48843-2305.
Telephone: 517-546-7600.
Telecopier: 517-546-6974.
Lansing, Michigan Office: One Michigan Avenue, Suite 900, 48933-1609.
Telephone: 517-487-2070.
Fax: 517-374-6304.
Monroe, Michigan Office: The Executive Centre, 214 East Elm Avenue, 48161-2682.
Telephone: 313-243-2000.
Fax: 313-243-0901.
Washington, D.C. Office: 1225 Nineteenth Street, N.W., Suite 400. 20036.
Telephone: 202-429-5575; 785-0600.
Fax: 202-331-1118; 785-1234.
Pensacola, Florida Office: 25 West Cedar, 32501.
Telephone: 904-469-1088.
Fax: 904-432-0677.
St. Petersburg, Florida Office: 100 Second Avenue S., Suite 7045,33701.
Telephone: 813-982-6000.
Fax: 813-892-6002.
Gdansk, Poland Office: Suite 322, Dom Technika Building, UI. Rajska 6, 80-850.
Telephone: 011-485-831-2808.
Fax: 011-485-831-4719.
Warsaw, Poland Office: UI. Marszalkowska 82, Suite 561, 00-517.
Telephone: 011-482-623-6457 and 6458.
Fax: 011-482-623-6459.

MEMBER OF FIRM

Eric V. Brown, Jr. (Resident)

RESIDENT OF COUNSEL

Gerard Thomas

Representative Firm Clients: Chrysler Corp.; Comerica, Inc.; City of Detroit, Mich.; Detroit Tigers, Inc.; First of Michigan; Fretter, Inc.; Ford Motor Co.; Ford Motor Credit Co.; Great Lakes Bancorp; Henry Ford Hospital.

For Complete List of Firm Personnel, See General Section

For full biographical listings, see the Martindale-Hubbell Law Directory

LANSING, Ingham Co.

FOSTER, SWIFT, COLLINS & SMITH, P.C. (AV)

313 South Washington Square, 48933-2193
Telephone: 517-371-8100
Telecopier: 517-371-8200
Farmington Hills, Michigan Office: 32300 Northwestern Highway, Suite 230.
Telephone: 810-851-7500.
Fax: 810-851-7504.

Gary J. McRay
Robert L. Knechtel

General Counsel for: First American Bank-Central; Story, Inc.; Michigan Milk Producers Assn.; Edward W. Sparrow Hospital; St. Lawrence Hospital; Demmer Corp.; Michigan Financial Corp.
Local Counsel for: Shell Oil Co.; Michigan-Mutual Insurance Co.; Century Cellunet.

For Complete List of Firm Personnel, See General Section

For full biographical listings, see the Martindale-Hubbell Law Directory

*MONROE,** Monroe Co.

MILLER, CANFIELD, PADDOCK AND STONE, P.L.C. (AV)

A Professional Limited Liability Company
Founded in 1852 by Sidney Davy Miller
The Executive Centre, 214 East Elm Avenue, 48161-2682
Telephone: 313-243-2000
Fax: 313-243-0901
Detroit, Michigan Office: 150 West Jefferson, Suite 2500, 48226-4415.
Telephone: 313-963-6420.
Fax: 313-496-7500.
Cable Address: "Stem Detroit."
Ann Arbor, Michigan Office: 101 North Main Street, 7th Floor, 48104-1400.
Telephone: 313-663-2445.
Fax: 313-747-7147.
Bloomfield Hills, Michigan Office: Suite 100, Pinehurst Office Center, 1400 North Woodward, 48303-2014.
Telephone: 313-645-5000.
Fax: 313-645-1917.
Grand Rapids, Michigan Office: 1200 Campau Square Plaza, 99 Monroe, N.W., 49503-2639.
Telephone: 616-454-8656.
Fax: 616-776-6322.
Howell, Michigan Office: 121 South Barnard Street, Suite 4, 48843-2305.
Telephone: 517-546-7600.
Telecopier: 517-546-6974.
Kalamazoo, Michigan Office: 444 West Michigan Avenue, 49007-3752.
Telephone: 616-381-7030.
Fax: 616-382-0244.
Lansing, Michigan Office: One Michigan Avenue, Suite 900, 48933-1609.
Telephone: 517-487-2070.
Fax: 517-374-6304.

(See Next Column)

MILLER, CANFIELD, PADDOCK AND STONE P.L.C., *Monroe—Continued*

Washington, D.C. Office: 1225 Nineteenth Street, N.W., Suite 400. 20036.
Telephone: 202-429-5575; 785-0600.
Fax: 202-331-1118; 785-1234.
Pensacola, Florida Office: 25 West Cedar, 32501.
Telephone: 904-469-1088.
Fax: 904-432-0677.
St. Petersburg, Florida Office: 100 Second Avenue S., Suite 7045, 33701.
Telephone: 813-982-6000.
Fax: 813-892-6002.
Gdansk, Poland Office: Suite 322, Dom Technika Building, Ul. Rajska 6, 80-850.
Telephone: 011-485-831-2808.
Fax: 011-485-831-4719.
Warsaw, Poland Office: Ul. Marszalkowska 82, Suite 561, 00-517.
Telephone: 011-482-623-6457 and 6458.
Fax: 011-482-623-6459.

RESIDENT MEMBER

Rocque E. Lipford (P.C.)

Representative Firm Clients: Chrysler Corp.; Comerica, Inc.; City of Detroit, Mich.; Detroit Tigers, Inc.; First of Michigan; Fretter, Inc.; Ford Motor Co.; Ford Motor Credit Co.; Great Lakes Bancorp; Henry Ford Hospital.

For full biographical listings, see the Martindale-Hubbell Law Directory

MINNESOTA

*MINNEAPOLIS,** Hennepin Co.

HAUGEN AND NIKOLAI, P.A. (AV)

820 International Centre, 900 Second Avenue South, 55402
Telephone: 612-339-7461
Telecopier: 612-349-6556

Orrin M. Haugen — James T. Nikolai
Thomas J. Nikolai — Charles G. Mersereau

Frederick W. Niebuhr — Catherine C. Maresh
Eric O. Haugen — Paul T. Dietz

Reference: Norwest Bank.

For full biographical listings, see the Martindale-Hubbell Law Directory

MISSISSIPPI

*JACKSON,** Hinds Co.

LILLY & WISE (AV)

Suite 2180 Deposit Guaranty Plaza, 210 East Capitol Street, 39201-2305
Telephone: 601-354-4040; 601-354-0078
Fax: DATA 601-354-2244

Thomas G. Lilly — Joseph P. Wise

For full biographical listings, see the Martindale-Hubbell Law Directory

MISSOURI

KANSAS CITY, Jackson, Clay & Platte Cos.

DETLEF G. LEHNARDT (AV Ⓣ)

911 Main Street, Suite 1322, 64105
Telephone: 816-221-2440
Facsimile: 816-221-5665
New York, New York Office: 90 Park Avenue, 17th Floor.
Telephone: 212-972-4263.
Facsimile: 212-972-4264.

LEGAL SUPPORT PERSONNEL

Stephen K. Lehnardt

For full biographical listings, see the Martindale-Hubbell Law Directory

MILLER & COMPANY P.C. (AV)

2320 Commerce Tower, 911 Main Street, 64105
Telephone: 816-221-1777
Fax: 816-221-1782
Washington, D.C. Office: International Square, 1825 "I" Street, N.W., Suite 400, 20006.
Telephone: 202-429-2017.
Fax: 202-659-6848.

(See Next Column)

Marshall V. Miller

D. Brooks Pavilack — Melissa Farley Sebree

For full biographical listings, see the Martindale-Hubbell Law Directory

ST. LOUIS, (Independent City)

SCHRAMM & PINES, L.L.C. (AV)

Suite 1404 Chromalloy Plaza, 120 South Central Avenue, 63105
Telephone: 314-721-5321
Telecopier: 314-721-0790

MEMBERS OF FIRM

Paul H. Schramm — M. Harvey Pines
Daniel R. Schramm

Norman S. Newmark — Dean A. Schramm
Peter L. Hoffman

Reference: The Boatmen's National Bank of St. Louis.

For full biographical listings, see the Martindale-Hubbell Law Directory

NEBRASKA

*OMAHA,** Douglas Co.

MCGILL, GOTSDINER, WORKMAN & LEPP, P.C. (AV)

Suite 500 - First National Plaza, 11404 West Dodge Road, 68154
Telephone: 402-492-9200
Telecopier: 402-492-9222

R. Thomas Workman — George O. Rebensdorf

Representative Clients: Telenational Deutschland; Informat, Gmbh; Behlen Mfg., Co.

For Complete List of Firm Personnel, See General Section

For full biographical listings, see the Martindale-Hubbell Law Directory

NEVADA

*LAS VEGAS,** Clark Co.

GOOLD, PATTERSON, DEVORE & RONDEAU (AV)

905 Bank of America Plaza, 300 South Fourth Street, 89101
Telephone: 702-386-0038
Telecopier: 702-385-2484

Barry Stephen Goold — Thomas J. DeVore
Jeffrey D. Patterson — Thomas Rondeau

ASSOCIATES

Wilbur M. Roadhouse — Bryan K. Day
Kathryn S. Wonders

Representative Clients: Gateway Development Group; Hanshaw Partnership; Jack Tarr Development; Meridian Point Properties, Inc.; NationsBank; Pacific Cellular; Plaster Development Co.; RS Development; U.S.A. Capital Land Fund.
Reference: Bank of America.

For full biographical listings, see the Martindale-Hubbell Law Directory

NEW JERSEY

MAPLEWOOD, Essex Co.

FOYEN & PARTNERS (AV Ⓣ)

108 Baker Street, 07040
Telephone: 201-762-5800
Telefax: 212-762-5801
New York, N.Y. Office: 800 Third Avenue, 23rd Floor, NTC.
Telephone: 212-265-2555.
Telefax: 212-838-0374.
Affiliated Offices: Oslo, Norway Office: Advokatfirmaet Foyen & Co. ANS, Oscargate 52, N-0258 Olso 2.
Telephone: 02-44 46 40.
Telefax: 02-44 89 27.
Stockholm, Sweden Office: Advokatfirman Foyen & Partners, Nybrogatan 15, S-10246 Stockholm.
Telephone: 8-663-02-90.
Telefax: 8-662-15-90.

(See Next Column)

FOYEN & PARTNERS—*Continued*

MEMBERS OF FIRM

Steven B. Peri
Michael T. Stewart

OF COUNSEL

Stein A. Føyen (Resident, Oslo, Norway Office)
Michael P. DiRaimondo (Resident, New York Office)

For full biographical listings, see the Martindale-Hubbell Law Directory

PRINCETON, Mercer Co.

JOHN KUHN BLEIMAIER (AV)

15 Witherspoon Street, 08542
Telephone: 609-924-7273
Fax: 609-924-7030

For full biographical listings, see the Martindale-Hubbell Law Directory

ROSELAND, Essex Co.

MARGARET L. MOSES (AV)

85 Livingston Avenue, 07068
Telephone: 201-533-0233
Telecopier: 201-535-9217

References: National Westminster Bank; Midlantic Bank.

For full biographical listings, see the Martindale-Hubbell Law Directory

WESTWOOD, Bergen Co.

BARRY G. LEVEEN (AV)

99 Kinderkamack Road, P.O. Box 977, 07675
Telephone: 201-666-3232
Telefax: 201-666-6993

Reference: Citizens First National Bank of New Jersey.

For full biographical listings, see the Martindale-Hubbell Law Directory

NEW MEXICO

*ALBUQUERQUE,** Bernalillo Co.

RODEY, DICKASON, SLOAN, AKIN & ROBB, P.A. (AV)

Albuquerque Plaza, Suite 2200, 201 Third Street, N.W., P.O. Box 1888, 87103-1888
Telephone: 505-765-5900
Fax: 505-768-7395
Santa Fe, New Mexico Office: Suite 101 Marcy Plaza, 123 East Marcy Street, P.O. Box 1357, 87504-1357.
Telephone: 505-984-0100.
Fax: 505-989-9542.

John D. Robb
DeWitt Michael Morgan

For Complete List of Firm Personnel, See General Section

For full biographical listings, see the Martindale-Hubbell Law Directory

NEW YORK

*NEW YORK,** New York Co.

BELLER & KELLER (AV)

415 Madison Avenue, 10017
Telephone: 212-754-2700
Facsimile: 212-754-2708

Barry Beller
Arthur Keller
Gary D. Roth
Jill D. Block
Roy H. Carlin (P.C.)
William E. Hammond
Robert S. Herbst
Jean Kim
Leonard D. Levin
Stephen A. Linde
Anna E. Panayotou
Elisabeth N. Radow
Harriet Rubin Roberts
Dan L. Rosenbaum
Bianca M. Scaramellino
Marc S. Shapiro
Paul S. Shapses
Richard S. Weisman

For full biographical listings, see the Martindale-Hubbell Law Directory

BRAUNSCHWEIG RACHLIS FISHMAN & RAYMOND, P.C. (AV)

1114 Avenue of the Americas, 10036
Telephone: 212-944-5200
Telecopier: 212-944-5210

(See Next Column)

Robert Braunschweig
Stephen P. H. Rachlis
Bernard H. Fishman
Richard C. Raymond

OF COUNSEL

Jeffrey M. Herrmann
Jeffrey H. Teitel (Not admitted in NY)
William G. Halby
Gerard C. Smetana (P.C.)
Martin W. McCormack
Jacob Dolinger (Not admitted in NY)

Bruce D. Osborne

LEGAL SUPPORT PERSONNEL

William Hershkowitz

For full biographical listings, see the Martindale-Hubbell Law Directory

DAVIS HOXIE FAITHFULL & HAPGOOD (AV)

45 Rockefeller Plaza, 10111
Telephone: 212-757-2200
Cable Address: "Explicit"
International Telex: 421236
Telecopiers: (212) 586-1461; 969-9805

MEMBERS OF FIRM

Caspar Carl Schneider, Jr.
Charles W. Bradley
Stanley L. Amberg
John B. Pegram
William J. Hone
Thomas E. Spath
Richard P. Ferrara
Peter Bucci
Lawrence B. Goodwin
Peter H. Priest
Bradford S. Breen
Robert M. Isackson

COUNSEL

Richard Whiting
Cyrus S. Hapgood
Brandon N. Sklar

ASSOCIATES

Andrew T. D'Amico, Jr.
Stephan J. Filipek
Robert A. Cote
James J. Murtha
Wayne S. Breyer
Robert E. Rudnick
Robert T. Canavan
Harold C. Moore
Davy E. Zoneraich
Joseph B. Ryan
Kevin M. Mason
Samuel Borodach
William A. Munck

For full biographical listings, see the Martindale-Hubbell Law Directory

HUTTON INGRAM YUZEK GAINEN CARROLL & BERTOLOTTI (AV)

250 Park Avenue, 10177
Telephone: 212-907-9600
Facsimile: 212-907-9681

MEMBERS OF FIRM

Ernest J. Bertolotti
Daniel L. Carroll
Roger Cukras
Larry F. Gainen
G. Thompson Hutton
Samuel W. Ingram, Jr.
Paulette Kendler
Steven Mastbaum
Dean G. Yuzek
David G. Ebert
Shane O'Neill

ASSOCIATES

Warren E. Friss
Patricia Hewitt
Gail A. Buchman
Stuart A. Christie
Beth N. Green
Timish K. Hnateyko
Jeanne F. Pucci
Jane Drummey
Adam L. Sifre
Susan Ann Fennelly
Marc J. Schneider

For full biographical listings, see the Martindale-Hubbell Law Directory

MOUND, COTTON & WOLLAN (AV)

One Battery Park Plaza, 10004
Telephone: 212-804-4200
Cable Address: "Moundlaw"
Telex: 64-9063
Telecopier: 212-344-8066
San Francisco, California Office: Suite 1650, 44 Montgomery Street.
Telephone: 415-249-4919.
Telecopier: 415-391-9076.
London, England Office: Longbow House, 14-20 Chiswell Street.
Telephone: 071-638-3688.
East Hanover, New Jersey Office: 72 Eagle Rock Avenue, Building Two, P.O. Box 78.
Telephone: 201-503-9669.
Telecopier: 201-503-9494.

MEMBERS OF FIRM

Arthur N. Brook
Mitchell S. Cohen
Stuart Cotton
Leonard S. Dome
Wayne R. Glaubinger
Michael H. Goldstein
Lawrence S. Greengrass
Andrew C. Jacobson
Michael R. Koblenz
Daniel Markewich
John C. Mezzacappa
Frederic R. Mindlin
Philip C. Silverberg
Costantino P. Suriano
James D. Veach

(See Next Column)

MOUND, COTTON & WOLLAN, *New York—Continued*

COUNSEL

Eugene A. Leiman
Eugene Wollan

OF COUNSEL
SAN FRANCISCO, CALIFORNIA OFFICE

Alexander S. Keenan

MANAGING RESIDENT ATTORNEY
EAST HANOVER, NEW JERSEY OFFICE

Deanne Wilson

ASSOCIATES

Emilie L. Bakal
Brian F. Boardingham
Diane L. Bodenstein
Rebecca A. Buder
Mary L. Cain
Karen M. Cooke
Jeffrey C. Crawford
Guy P. Dauerty
Elisa T. Gilbert
Jeffrey B. Gold
Diana E. Goldberg
Lloyd A. Gura
Bruce R. Kaliner
Myra E. Lobel
Nancy B. London
Renee M. Plessner
Lisa S. Post
Jon Quint
Ronnie A. Rifkin
David I. Schonbrun
David A. Silva
Diane P. Simon
Sarah D. Strum
Ronald J. Theleen
Keith J. Wagner
Mark J. Weber
Jeffrey S. Weinstein
William D. Wilson
Simy C. Wolf
Rachel J. Yosevitz
Andrew L. Zalasin

For full biographical listings, see the Martindale-Hubbell Law Directory

ORANS, ELSEN & LUPERT (AV)

33rd Floor, One Rockefeller Plaza, 10020
Telephone: 212-586-2211
Cable Address: "ORELSLU"
Telecopier: 212-765-3662

MEMBERS OF FIRM

Sheldon H. Elsen
Leslie A. Lupert
Gary H. Greenberg
Lawrence Solan
Robert L. Plotz

ASSOCIATES

Melissa A. Cohen
Amelia Anne Nickles
Jonathan J. Englander

For full biographical listings, see the Martindale-Hubbell Law Directory

OTTERBOURG, STEINDLER, HOUSTON & ROSEN, P.C. (AV)

230 Park Avenue, 10169
Telephone: 212-661-9100
Cable Address: "Otlerton";
Telecopier: 212-682-6104
Telex: 960916

Donald N. Gellert
William M. Silverman
Alan R. Weiskopf
Daniel Wallen
Albert F. Reisman
David W. Morse

For Complete List of Firm Personnel, See General Section

For full biographical listings, see the Martindale-Hubbell Law Directory

SERKO & SIMON (AV)

Suite 3371, 1 World Trade Center, 10048
Telephone: 212-775-0055
Telex: 426816 TRADE
Cable Address: "Trade Attys"
Facsimile: 212-839-9103.
Washington, D.C. Office: Metropolitan Square, Suite 300, 655 15th Street, N.W.
Telephone: 202-639-4017.
Facsimile: 202-347-1945.
Atlanta, Georgia Office: Suite 1400 Bank South Building.
Telephone: 404-659-4488.
San Juan, Puerto Rico Office: Banco de San Juan Building, Suite 302, P.O. Box 3222.
Telephone: 809-723-3672.
Facsimile: 809-725-4133.
Taipei, Taiwan, R.O.C. Office: 3rd Fl. Rose Mansion, No. 162 Shin-Yi Rd., Sec. 3, 10632.
Telephone: 866-2-707-2847.

MEMBERS OF FIRM

David Serko
Joel K. Simon
Daniel J. Gluck

ASSOCIATES

Christopher M. Kane
Arlen Tobias Epstein
Barbara Y. Wierbicki

(See Next Column)

OF COUNSEL-NEW YORK

Leibert L. Greenberg
David S. Chang
Beryl B. Farris (Not admitted in NY; Resident, Atlanta, Georgia Office)
Rafael F. Castro-Lang (Not admitted in NY)
Dr. Jhy-Mou Shih (Not admitted in NY; Resident, Taipei, Taiwan Office)

LEGAL SUPPORT PERSONNEL

Kenneth Pukel

For full biographical listings, see the Martindale-Hubbell Law Directory

SULLIVAN, DONOVAN, BOND & BONNER (AV)

A Partnership including a Professional Corporation
415 Madison Avenue, 10017
Telephone: 212-935-5100
Cable Address: "Navillus"
Telecopier: 935-5106
Albany, New York Office: 109 State Street, 12207.
Telephone: 518-434-1121.
Telecopier: 518-463-0815.
East Meadow, New York Office: 90 Merrick Avenue, 11554.
Telephone: 516-794-5454.
Telecopier: 516-296-7111.
Greenwich, Connecticut Office: 21 Benedict Place, 06830.
Telephone: 203-869-3553.
Telecopier: 203-625-0226.

MEMBERS OF FIRM

Cornelius J. Sullivan (1870-1932)
Gerald Donovan (1891-1987)
Edmond M. Hanrahan (1905-1979)
Richard P. Donovan
Kenneth W. Bond
Robert H. Carey
Thomas J. Bonner (P.C.)
James A. Moyer (Resident, East Meadow Office)
Thomas H. Bach
Lloyd N. Hull (Resident, Greenwich, Connecticut Office)

ASSOCIATES

John J. Mattras, Jr.
Gary E. Ireland

OF COUNSEL

Joseph G. Krassy
Robert A. Klipstein
John P. Dowling
Michael C. Magguilli (Resident, Albany Office)

For full biographical listings, see the Martindale-Hubbell Law Directory

NORTH CAROLINA

*CHARLOTTE,** Mecklenburg Co.

WOMBLE CARLYLE SANDRIDGE & RICE (AV)

A Professional Limited Liability Company
3300 One First Union Center, 301 S. College Street, 28202-6025
Telephone: 704-331-4900
Telecopy: 704-331-4955
Telex: 853609
Winston-Salem, North Carolina Office: 1600 Southern National Financial Center.
Telephone: 919-721-3600.
Telecopy: 919-721-3660.
Telex: 806498.
Raleigh, North Carolina Office: 2100 First Union Capitol Center, 150 Fayetteville Street Mall, P.O. Box 831.
Telephone: 919-755-2100.
Telecopy: 919-755-2150.
Telex: 806498.
Atlanta, Georgia Office: One Ninety One Peachtree Tower, 191 Peachtree Street N.E., Suite 3250.
Telephone: 404-614-2580.
Fax: 404-614-2595.

MEMBERS OF FIRM

J. Carlton Fleming
William C. Raper

Representative Clients: Childress Klein Properties, Inc.; Food Lion, Inc.; Fieldcrest Cannon, Inc.; J.A. Jones Construction Company; Parkdale Mills, Inc.; Duke Power Company; Bowles Hollowell Conner & Company; ALLTEL Carolina, Inc.; Belk Store Services, Inc.; Philip Holzmann A.G.

For Complete List of Firm Personnel, See General Section

For full biographical listings, see the Martindale-Hubbell Law Directory

*RALEIGH,** Wake Co.

* indicates certain Bar Register subscribers whose principal office is located elsewhere in the state and who have arranged for representation as a part of the state capital listings that follow

ALLEN AND PINNIX (AV)

20 Market Plaza, Suite 200, P.O. Drawer 1270, 27602
Telephone: 919-755-0505
Telecopier: 919-829-8098
Woodlawn Green, Charlotte, North Carolina Telephone: 704-522-8069

MEMBERS OF FIRM

Noel L. Allen
John L. Pinnix
C. Lynn Calder
Paul Christian Ridgeway

General Counsel for: North Carolina State Board of CPA Examiners; North Carolina Board of Architecture.

For full biographical listings, see the Martindale-Hubbell Law Directory

*** WOMBLE CARLYLE SANDRIDGE & RICE (AV)**

A Professional Limited Liability Company
2100 First Union Capitol Center, 150 Fayetteville Street Mall, P.O. Box 831, 27602
Telephone: 919-755-2100
Telecopy: 919-755-2150
Telex: 806498
Charlotte, North Carolina Office: 3300 One First Union Center, 301 South College Street.
Telephone: 704-331-4900.
Telecopy: 704-331-4955.
Telex: 853609.
Winston-Salem, North Carolina Office: 1600 Southern National Financial Center.
Telephone: 919-721-3600.
Telecopy: 919-721-3660.
Telex: 806498.
Atlanta, Georgia Office: One Ninety One Peachtree Tower, 191 Peachtree Street N.E., Suite 3250.
Telephone: 404-614-2580.
Fax: 404-614-2595.

RESIDENT ASSOCIATE

Simmons I. Patrick, Jr.

Representative Clients: Aetna Casualty and Surety Co., Inc.; ALSCO/AmeriMark Building Products, Inc.; Aoki Corporation America, Inc.; Empire of Carolina, Inc.; Hackney Brothers, Inc.; Lawyers Mutual Liability Insurance Company of North Carolina; Meredith College; Monk-Austin, Inc.; Regency Park Corporation; Wachovia Bank of North Carolina, N.A.

For Complete List of Firm Personnel, See General Section

For full biographical listings, see the Martindale-Hubbell Law Directory

*WINSTON-SALEM,** Forsyth Co.

WOMBLE CARLYLE SANDRIDGE & RICE (AV)

A Professional Limited Liability Company
1600 Southern National Financial Center, P.O. Drawer 84, 27102
Telephone: 910-721-3600
Telecopy: 910-721-3660
Telex: 806498
Charlotte, North Carolina Office: 3300 One First Union Center, 301 South College Street.
Telephone: 704-331-4900.
Telecopy: 704-331-4955.
Telex: 853609.
Raleigh, North Carolina Office: 2100 First Union Capitol Center, 150 Fayetteville Street Mall, P.O. Box 831.
Telephone: 919-755-2100.
Telecopy: 919-755-2150.
Telex: 806498.
Atlanta, Georgia Office: One Ninety One Peachtree Tower, 191 Peachtree Street, N.E., Suite 3250.
Telephone: 404-614-2580.
Fax: 404-614-2595.

MEMBER OF FIRM

James K. Phillips

Representative Clients: Brad Ragan, Inc.; Brenner Companies; Food Lion, Inc.; Hanes Companies, Inc.; North Carolina Baptist Hospitals, Inc.; R.J. Reynolds Tobacco Company; Summit Communications Group, Inc.; Thomasville Furniture Industries, Inc.; Wachovia Corporation; Wake Forest University.

For Complete List of Firm Personnel, See General Section

For full biographical listings, see the Martindale-Hubbell Law Directory

OHIO

*CINCINNATI,** Hamilton Co.

KATZ, GREENBERGER & NORTON (AV)

105 East Fourth Street, 9th Floor, 45202-4011
Telephone: 513-721-5151
FAX: 513-621-9285

Leonard H. Freiberg (1885-1954)
Alfred B. Katz
Mark Alan Greenberger
Louis H. Katz
Richard L. Norton
Steven M. Rothstein
Robert Gray Edmiston
Ellen Essig

ASSOCIATES

Scott P. Kadish
Stephen E. Imm
Stephen L. Robison
Jeffrey J. Greenberger

OF COUNSEL

Charles Weiner

For full biographical listings, see the Martindale-Hubbell Law Directory

WAITE, SCHNEIDER, BAYLESS & CHESLEY CO., L.P.A. (AV)

1513 Central Trust Tower, Fourth and Vine Streets, 45202
Telephone: 513-621-0267
Fax: 513-381-2375; 621-0262

Stanley M. Chesley

Thomas F. Rehme
Fay E. Stilz
Louise M. Roselle
Dwight Tillery
D. Arthur Rabourn
Jerome L. Skinner
Janet G. Abaray
Paul M. De Marco
Terrence L. Goodman
Sherrill P. Hondorf
Colleen M. Hegge
Dianna Pendleton
Randy F. Fox
Glenn D. Feagan
Theresa L. Groh
Theodore N. Berry
Jane H. Walker
Renée Infante
Allen P. Grunes

OF COUNSEL

Jos. E. Rosen
James F. Keller

For full biographical listings, see the Martindale-Hubbell Law Directory

*COLUMBUS,** Franklin Co.

HARRIS, CARTER & MAHOTA (AV)

500 South Front Street, Suite 1010, 43215
Telephone: 614-221-2112
Fax: 614-221-2217
Washington, D.C. Office: 1747 Pennsylvania Avenue, N.W., Suite 704.
Telephone: 202-223-4723.

MEMBERS OF FIRM

Kenneth E. Harris
James M. Carter (Not admitted in OH; Resident, Washington D.C. Office)
John M. Mahota

ASSOCIATES

Robin L. Canowitz
Thomas G. St. Pierre

For full biographical listings, see the Martindale-Hubbell Law Directory

OKLAHOMA

*OKLAHOMA CITY,** Oklahoma Co.

DAY, EDWARDS, FEDERMAN, PROPESTER & CHRISTENSEN, P.C. (AV)

Suite 2900 First Oklahoma Tower, 210 Park Avenue, 73102-5605
Telephone: 405-239-2121
Telecopier: 405-236-1012

Bruce W. Day
Joe E. Edwards
William B. Federman
Richard P. Propester
D. Wade Christensen
J. Clay Christensen
Kent A. Gilliland
Rodney J. Heggy
Ricki Valerie Sonders
Thomas Pitchlynn Howell, IV
John C. Platt

David R. Widdoes
Lori R. Roberts
Carolyn A. Romberg

OF COUNSEL

Herbert F. (Jack) Hewett
Jeanette Cook Timmons
Joel Warren Harmon
Jane S. Eulberg
Mark A. Cohen

(See Next Column)

DAY, EDWARDS, FEDERMAN, PROPESTER & CHRISTENSEN P.C., *Oklahoma City—Continued*

Representative Clients: Aetna Life Insurance Co.; Boatmen's First National Bank of Oklahoma; Borg-Warner Chemicals, Inc.; City Bank & Trust; Federal Deposit Insurance Corp.; Bank One, Oklahoma City; Haskell Lemon Construction Co.; Merrill Lynch, Pierce, Fenner & Smith, Inc.; Prudential Securities, Inc.

For full biographical listings, see the Martindale-Hubbell Law Directory

*TULSA,** Tulsa Co.

BOESCHE, MCDERMOTT & ESKRIDGE (AV)

Suite 800 Oneok Plaza, 100 West Fifth Street, 74103
Telephone: 918-583-1777
Fax: 918-592-5809
Muskogee, Oklahoma Office: 420 Broadway, 74101.
Telephone: 918-683-6100.

MEMBER OF FIRM

David A. Johnson

Representative Clients: Apache Corp.; Atlantic Richfield; Oxy USA, Inc.; Dillon, Reed Co., Inc.; Elf Atochem North America, Inc.; The Chase Manhattan Bank (N.A.); Transwestern Pipeline Co.

For Complete List of Firm Personnel, See General Section

For full biographical listings, see the Martindale-Hubbell Law Directory

OREGON

*PORTLAND,** Multnomah Co.

CAROL A. EMORY (AV)

1990 Benj. Franklin Plaza, 1 S.W. Columbia, 97258
Telephone: 503-226-6499
Facsimile: 503-226-2201

Representative Clients: Bear Creek Corporation; Viking International, Inc.; For Counsel, Inc.; Jackson & Perkins Co.; Harry & David; Cost Technology, Inc.; Ventura Institute of Psychiatry; Linaeum Corporation.
Reference: US Bank, Portland, Oregon.

For full biographical listings, see the Martindale-Hubbell Law Directory

PENNSYLVANIA

NARBERTH, Montgomery Co.

EDWARD M. MEZVINSKY (AV)

815 Woodbine Avenue, 19072
Telephone: 610-664-7115
Fax: 610-664-7225

For full biographical listings, see the Martindale-Hubbell Law Directory

*PHILADELPHIA,** Philadelphia Co.

BRUCE G. CASSIDY & ASSOCIATES, P.A. (AV)

Suite 1040, 21 South 12th Street, 19107
Telephone: 215-568-6700
Fax: 215-568-4077
Collingswood, New Jersey Office: 915 Haddon Avenue, 08108.
Telephone: 609-869-3535.

Bruce G. Cassidy

OF COUNSEL

Dr. Peter H. Feuerstein (Not admitted United States)
James A. Dunleavy

For full biographical listings, see the Martindale-Hubbell Law Directory

CORSON, GETSON & SCHATZ (AV)

Suite 300 The Carlton Business Center, 1819 John F. Kennedy Boulevard, 19103
Telephone: 215-564-3030; 568-2525
Fax: 215-564-5477

MEMBERS OF FIRM

Lawrence Corson
Allan Getson
Robert B. B. Schatz

For full biographical listings, see the Martindale-Hubbell Law Directory

BERNARD G. HEINZEN, LTD. (AV)

Suite 2500, One Liberty Place, 1650 Market Street, 19103
Telephone: 215-988-0290
Telex: 834615 HQPHA
Telecopier: 215-851-1420

Bernard G. Heinzen

For full biographical listings, see the Martindale-Hubbell Law Directory

ROGER A. JOHNSEN (AV)

50th Floor, 1650 Market Street, 19103
Telephone: 215-561-3400
Fax: 215-851-9759

Reference: Constitution Bank.

For full biographical listings, see the Martindale-Hubbell Law Directory

*PITTSBURGH,** Allegheny Co.

DICKIE, MCCAMEY & CHILCOTE, A PROFESSIONAL CORPORATION (AV)

Suite 400, Two PPG Place, 15222-5402
Telephone: 412-281-7272
Fax: 412-392-5367
Wheeling, West Virginia Office: Suite 2002, 1233 Main Street, 26003-2839.
Telephone: 304-233-1022.
Facsimile: 304-233-1026.

Clayton A. Sweeney
John W. Lewis, II
George Randal Fox, III

Donald E. Evans

For Complete List of Firm Personnel, See General Section

For full biographical listings, see the Martindale-Hubbell Law Directory

SOUTH CAROLINA

*COLUMBIA,** Richland Co.

BERRY, DUNBAR, DANIEL, O'CONNOR & JORDAN (AV)

A Partnership including Professional Associations
1200 Main Street, Eighth Floor, P.O. Box 11645, Capitol Station, 29211-1645
Telephone: 803-765-1030
Facsimile: 803-799-5536
Spartanburg, South Carolina Office: 112 West Daniel Morgan Avenue.
Telephone: 803-583-3975.
Atlanta, Georgia Office: 2400 Cain Tower, Peachtree Center.
Telephone: 404-588-0500.
Facsimile: 404-523-6714.

MEMBER OF FIRM

James V. Dunbar, Jr.

ASSOCIATE

John A. Hill

Approved Attorneys for: Lawyers Title Insurance Corporation of Richmond.

For Complete List of Firm Personnel, See General Section

For full biographical listings, see the Martindale-Hubbell Law Directory

TENNESSEE

*MEMPHIS,** Shelby Co.

THE BOGATIN LAW FIRM (AV)

A Partnership including Professional Corporations
(Formerly Bogatin Lawson & Chiapella)
860 Ridge Lake Boulevard, Suite 360, 38120
Telephone: 901-767-1234
Telecopier: 901-767-2803 & 901-767-4010

MEMBERS OF FIRM

G. Patrick Arnoult
Irvin Bogatin (P.C.)
H. Stephen Brown
Susan Callison (P.C.)
Tillman C. Carroll
Matthew P. Cavitch
John André Chiapella (P.C.)
David J. Cocke
Russell J. Hensley
Arlie C. Hooper
Charles M. Key
William H. Lawson, Jr., (P.C.)
David C. Porteous
Arthur E. Quinn
Thaddeus S. Rodda, Jr., (P.C.)

(See Next Column)

THE BOGATIN LAW FIRM—*Continued*

ASSOCIATES

Robert F. Beckmann
James Q. Carr, II
C. William Denton, Jr.
Thomas M. Federico (Not admitted in TN)
James S. King
John F. Murrah

For full biographical listings, see the Martindale-Hubbell Law Directory

TEXAS

*AUSTIN,** Travis Co.

* indicates certain Bar Register subscribers whose principal office is located elsewhere in the state and who have arranged for representation as a part of the state capital listings that follow

*** THOMPSON & KNIGHT, A PROFESSIONAL CORPORATION** (AV)

(Attorneys and Counselors)
1200 San Jacinto Center, 98 San Jacinto Boulevard, 78701
Telephone: 512-469-6100
Telecopy: 512-469-6180
Dallas, Texas Office: 1700 Pacific Avenue, Suite 3300, 75201.
Telephone: 214-969-1700.
Telecopy: 512-969-1751.
Cable Address: "Tomtex."
Telex: 732298.
Fort Worth, Texas Office: 801 Cherry Street, Suite 1600, 76102.
Telephone: 817-347-1700.
Telecopy: 817-347-1799.
Houston, Texas Office: 1700 Texas Commerce Tower, 600 Travis, 77002.
Telephone: 713-217-2800.
Telecopy: 713-217-2828; 713-217-2882.
Monterrey, Mexico Office: Edificio Losoles PD-4, Av. Lázaro Cárdenas No. 2400 Pte., San Pedro Garza Garcia, Nuevo Léon C.P. 66220.
Telephone: (52-8) 363-0096.
Telecopy: (52-8) 363-3067.

SHAREHOLDERS

Carrie Parker Tiemann

For Complete List of Firm Personnel, See General Section

For full biographical listings, see the Martindale-Hubbell Law Directory

WOODWARD AND ASSOCIATES (AV)

2630 Exposition Boulevard, Suite 10, 78703
Telephone: 512-474-1820
Telecopier: 512-474-1847
Miami, Florida Affiliated Office: Law Office of J. Bruce Irving, Suite 300 Courvoisier Centre, 501 Brickell Key Drive.
Telephone: 305-374-5505.
Telecopier: 305-374-6715.
Caracas, Venezuela Affiliated Office: Anzola Boveda Rafalli Rodriguez y Redondo, Torre Británica, 10th Floor, Av. José Felix Sosa, Altamira Sur.
Telephone: (58 2) 261-8580; 261-9604; 263-2003; 263-4329; 263-4782; 322836.
FAX: (58 2) 263-4286.
Mexico Affiliated Office: Law Office of Fernando Cabrera, Campo Eliseos 345, 11560 Mexico, D.F.
Telephone: 202-1666.
Telefax: 596-13-89.
Dominican Republic Affiliated Office: Law Office of Cristóbal J. Gómez Saviñon, Alvarez de Tejeda, Condominio Naco 5, Suite 6 A, Norte Sto. Domingo, The Dominican Republic.
Telephone: (809) 686-6747; The Peoples Republic of China, Beijing Affiliated Office: Office of Dr. Fred C. Chandler, Jr. (Non-legal, international consulting only)

M. Kenneth Woodward, Jr.

OF COUNSEL

M. Kenneth Woodward, Sr.
Frank E. Nattier
Fred C. Chandler, Jr.

VENEZUELA COUNSEL

J. Eloy Anzola E.

MIAMI, FLORIDA COUNSEL

J. Bruce Irving

MEXICO COUNSEL

Fernando Cabrera (Not admitted in TX)

DOMINICAN REPUBLIC COUNSEL

Cristóbal J. Gómez Saviñon

Representative Clients: Channel Trust Limited; St. Peter Port C.I., Legal Resources Development Inc.; Baba Kingdom, Inc.; O'Brien Operating Co.; Michael Halface Fashion Designs, Inc.; Fabricas Unidas de Hielo, S.A., Mexico D.F.; Dura Investments Inc.; Corporacion Internacional Tecnica S.A. Mexico D.F.; Bays of Huatalco Resort Land Management Group; Dominican Resort Villa Assoc.

(See Next Column)

For full biographical listings, see the Martindale-Hubbell Law Directory

*DALLAS,** Dallas Co.

LAW OFFICES OF DANA B. TASCHNER (AV⊤)

350 St. Paul Street, 75201
Telephone: 1-800-448-5800
Fax: 818-583-8825
Pasadena, California Office: 1115 East Cordova, Suite 404. 91106.
Telephone: 818-583-8500.
Fax: 818-583-8825.
Beverly Hills, California Office: 9454 Wilshire Boulevard, Suite 550. 90212-2915.
Telephone: 310-275-5077; 800-448-5800.

For full biographical listings, see the Martindale-Hubbell Law Directory

THOMPSON & KNIGHT, A PROFESSIONAL CORPORATION (AV)

(Attorneys and Counselors)
1700 Pacific Avenue Suite 3300, 75201
Telephone: 214-969-1700
Telecopy: 214-969-1751
Cable Address: "Tomtex"
Telex: 732298
Austin, Texas Office: 1200 San Jacinto Center, 98 San Jacinto Boulevard, 78701.
Telephone: 512-469-6100.
Telecopy: 512-469-6180.
Fort Worth, Texas Office: 801 Cherry Street, Suite 1600, 76102.
Telephone: 817-347-1700.
Telecopy: 817-347-1799.
Houston, Texas Office: 1700 Texas Commerce Tower, 600 Travis, 77002.
Telephone: 713-217-2800.
Telecopy: 713-217-2828.
Monterrey, Mexico Office: Edificio Losoles PD-4, Av. Lázaro Cárdenas No. 2400 Pte., San Pedro Garza Garcia, Nuevo Léon C.P. 66220.
Telephone: (52-8) 363-0096.
Telecopy: (52-8) 363-3067.

SHAREHOLDERS

Dorothy H. Bjorck
Sam P. Burford, Jr.
Frederick W. Burnett, Jr.
Robert D. Campbell
James B. Harris
Gregory S. C. Huffman
David E. Morrison
Peter J. Riley
Joe A. Rudberg

ASSOCIATES

Ann Marie Bixby
John R. Cohn
David L. Emmons

For Complete List of Firm Personnel, See General Section

For full biographical listings, see the Martindale-Hubbell Law Directory

*FORT WORTH,** Tarrant Co.

THOMPSON & KNIGHT, A PROFESSIONAL CORPORATION (AV)

(Attorneys and Counselors)
801 Cherry Street, Suite 1600, 76102
Telephone: 817-347-1700
Telecopy: 817-347-1799
Dallas, Texas Office: 1700 Pacific Avenue, Suite 3300, 75201.
Telephone: 214-969-1700.
Telecopy: 214-969-1751.
Cable Address: "Tomtex."
Telex: 732298.
Austin, Texas Office: 1200 San Jacinto Center, 98 San Jacinto Boulevard, 78701.
Telephone: 512-469-6100.
Telecopy: 512-469-6180.
Houston, Texas Office: 1700 Texas Commerce Tower, 600 Travis, 77002.
Telephone: 713-217-2800.
Telecopy: 713-217-2828; 713-217-2882.
Monterrey, Mexico Office: Edificio Losoles PD-4, Av. Lázaro Cárdenas No. 2400 Pte., San Pedro Garza Garcia, Nuevo Léon C.P. 66220.
Telephone: (52-8) 363-0096.
Telecopy: (52-8) 363-3067.

SHAREHOLDERS

Stephen B. Norris

For Complete List of Firm Personnel, See General Section

For full biographical listings, see the Martindale-Hubbell Law Directory

*HOUSTON,** Harris Co.

PAUL P. BAZELIDES (AV)

Suite 550, 9821 Katy Freeway, 77024-1210
Telephone: 713-722-0008
Telecopier: 713-722-0009

For full biographical listings, see the Martindale-Hubbell Law Directory

UTAH

*SALT LAKE CITY,** Salt Lake Co.

PARSONS BEHLE & LATIMER, A PROFESSIONAL CORPORATION (AV)

One Utah Center, 201 South Main Street, Suite 1800, P.O. Box 45898, 84145-0898
Telephone: 801-532-1234
Telecopy: 801-536-6111

J. Gordon Hansen
Daniel M. Allred
W. Jeffery Fillmore
David W. Tundermann
Neil Orloff
James M. Elegante
Val R. Antczak
Lee Kapaloski
Stephen J. Hull
Lawrence R. Barusch
R. Craig Johnson (Not admitted in UT)
Lorna Rogers Burgess
Jim B. Butler
Craig D. Galli

Representative Clients: Albion Laboratories; American Barrick Resources Corporation; Kennecott Corporation; Gentner Communications Corporation.

For full biographical listings, see the Martindale-Hubbell Law Directory

VIRGINIA

MCLEAN, Fairfax Co.

WATT, TIEDER & HOFFAR (AV)

7929 Westpark Drive, Suite 400, 22102
Telephone: 703-749-1000
Telecopier: 703-893-8029
Washington, D.C. Office: 601 Pennsylvania Ave, N.W., Suite 900.
Telephone: 202-462-4697.
Irvine California Office: 3 Park Plaza, Suite 1530.
Telephone: 714-852-6700.

MEMBERS OF FIRM

John B. Tieder, Jr.
Robert G. Watt
Julian F. Hoffar
Robert M. Fitzgerald
Robert K. Cox
William R. Chambers
David C. Romm
Charles E. Raley (Not admitted in VA)
Francis X. McCullough
Barbara G. Werther (Not admitted in VA)
Garry R. Boehlert
Thomas B. Newell
Lewis J. Baker
Benjamin T. Riddles, II
Timothy F. Brown
Richard G. Mann, Jr.
David C. Mancini
David C. Haas
Henry D. Danforth
Carter B. Reid
Donna S. McCaffrey
Mark J. Groff (Not admitted in VA)
Mark A. Sgarlata
Daniel E. Cohen
Michael G. Long (Resident, Irvine, California Office)

OF COUNSEL

Avv. Roberto Tassi
Clyde Harold Slease (Not admitted in VA)

ASSOCIATES

Thomas J. Powell
Douglas C. Proxmire
Tara L. Vautin
Edward Parrott
Steven G. Schassler
Joseph H. Bucci
Steven J. Weber
Paul A. Varela
Vivian Katsantonis
Charlie Lee
Kathleen A. Olden
Christopher P. Pappas (Resident, Irvine, California Office)
Shelly L. Ewald
Christopher J. Brasco
Jean V. Misterek
Charles W. Durant
Susan Latham Timoner
Fred A. Mendicino
Susan G. Sisskind
Robert G. Barbour
Keith C. Phillips
Marybeth Zientek Gaul
Timothy E. Heffernan (Not admitted in VA)
William Drew Mallender
James Moore Donahue
Heidi Brown Hering
Kerrin Maureen McCormick (Not admitted in VA)
Gretal J. Toker

For full biographical listings, see the Martindale-Hubbell Law Directory

*RICHMOND,** (Ind. City; Seat of Henrico Co.)

WILLIAMS, MULLEN, CHRISTIAN & DOBBINS, A PROFESSIONAL CORPORATION (AV)

Two James Center, 1021 East Cary Street, P.O. Box 1320, 23210-1320
Telephone: 804-643-1991
Fax: 804-783-6456
Glen Allen, Virginia Office: 4401 Waterfront Drive, Suite 140.
Telephone: 804-965-9168.
Fax: 804-965-0955.
Washington, D.C. Office: 1575 Eye Street, N.W.
Telephone: 202-289-6200.
Fax: 202-289-4126.

Theodore L. Chandler, Jr.
Louis Armand Dejoie (Resident, Washington, D.C. Office)
Alexander C. Graham, Jr.
David R. Johnson
Thomas B. McVey (Not admitted in VA; Resident, Washington, D.C. Office)
Julious P. Smith, Jr.
Robin Robertson Starr
William J. Benos

For Complete List of Firm Personnel, See General Section

For full biographical listings, see the Martindale-Hubbell Law Directory

WASHINGTON

*SEATTLE,** King Co.

THE BELES GROUP (AV)

Counselors At Law-A Sole Proprietorship in Association with Attorneys "Of Counsel" and Correspondent Offices Worldwide
Grand Central on The Park, 216 First Avenue South, Suite 300, 98104
Telephone: 206-623-9119
Facsimile: 206-622-3812

MEMBER OF FIRM

Craig C. Beles

For full biographical listings, see the Martindale-Hubbell Law Directory

GAITÁN & CUSACK (AV)

30th Floor Two Union Square, 601 Union Street, 98101-2324
Telephone: 206-521-3000
Facsimile: 206-386-5259
Anchorage, Alaska Office: 425 G Street, Suite 760.
Telephone: 907-278-3001.
Facsimile: 907-278-6068.
San Francisco, California Office: 275 Battery Street, 20th Floor.
Telephone: 415-398-5562.
Fax: 415-398-4033.
Washington, D.C. Office: 2000 L Street, Suite 200.
Telephone: 202-296-4637.
Fax: 202-296-4650.

MEMBERS OF FIRM

José E. Gaitán
Kenneth J. Cusack (Resident, Anchorage, Alaska Office)
William F. Knowles
Ronald L. Bozarth

OF COUNSEL

Howard K. Todd
Gary D. Gayton
Michel P. Stern (Also practicing alone, Bellevue, Washington)
Christopher A. Byrne
Patricia D. Ryan

ASSOCIATES

Mary F. O'Boyle
Bruce H. Williams
David J. Onsager
Diana T. Jimenez
Robert T. Mimbu
Cristina C. Kapela
Camilla M. Hedberg
John E. Lenker
Kathleen C. Healy

Representative Clients: Hosho America, Inc.; Toshi Products; HFI Foods; Elscint, Inc.; Switzerland Insurance Company; Zurich-America Insurance Company; K & S Engineering, Inc.

For full biographical listings, see the Martindale-Hubbell Law Directory

JUNKER & THOMPSON, A PROFESSIONAL CORPORATION (AV)

The Financial Center, 1215 4th Avenue, Suite 1501, 98161-1001
Telephone: 206-625-9211
Facsimile: 206-625-9115

Joel R. Junker
Lindsay T. Thompson

Representative Clients: Ace Novelty Co., Inc.; Augat Communications, Inc.; Basic American Foods, Inc.; Basic Vegetable Products, Ltd.; Cominco Fertilizers; Columbia Transport, Inc.; Cowlitz County Washington; Hampton Power Products, Inc.; "K" Line America, Inc.

(See Next Column)

JUNKER & THOMPSON A PROFESSIONAL CORPORATION—*Continued*

Reference: The Commerce Bank of Washington.

For full biographical listings, see the Martindale-Hubbell Law Directory

WISCONSIN

*MILWAUKEE,** Milwaukee Co.

QUARLES & BRADY (AV)

411 East Wisconsin Avenue, 53202-4497
Telephone: 414-277-5000
Cable Address: "Lawdock"
Fax: 414-271-3552.
TWX: 910-262-3426
Madison, Wisconsin Office: Firstar Plaza, One South Pinckney Street, P.O. Box 2113.
Telephone: 608-251-5000.
Fax: 608-251-9166.
West Palm Beach, Florida Office: 222 Lakeview Avenue, 4th Floor.
Telephone: 407-653-5000.
Fax: 407-653-5333.
Naples, Florida Office: Barnett Center, 4501 Tamiami Trail North.
Telephone: 813-262-5959.
Fax: 813-434-4999.
Phoenix, Arizona Office: One Camelback Building, One East Camelback Road, Suite 400.
Telephone: 602-230-5500.
Fax: 602-230-5598.

MEMBERS OF FIRM
(ALPHABETICALLY BY YEAR OF ADMISSION TO BAR)

Thad F. Kryshak
Thomas O. Kloehn
Anthony W. Asmuth, III
P. Robert Moya (Resident, Phoenix, Arizona Office)
James D. Friedman
Thomas J. Phillips
Darryl S. Bell
Carl R. Schwartz
David G. Beauchamp (Resident, Phoenix, Arizona Office)
Thomas A. Simonis

ASSOCIATES

Kurt A. Johnson (Resident, Phoenix, Arizona Office)
Harold O.M. Rocha

For Complete List of Firm Personnel, See General Section

For full biographical listings, see the Martindale-Hubbell Law Directory

VIRGIN ISLANDS

*CHARLOTTE AMALIE, ST. THOMAS,** St. Thomas

GRUNERT STOUT BRUCH & MOORE

24-25 Kongensgade, P.O. Box 1030, 00804
Telephone: 809-774-1320
Fax: 809-774-7839

MEMBERS OF FIRM

John E. Stout
Susan Bruch Moorehead
Treston E. Moore

ASSOCIATES

Maryleen Thomas
Richard F. Taylor
H. Kevin Mart (Not admitted in VI)

OF COUNSEL

William L. Blum

For full biographical listings, see the Martindale-Hubbell Law Directory

CANADA ALBERTA

*CALGARY,** Calgary Jud. Dist.

BENNETT JONES VERCHERE (AV)

4500 Bankers Hall East, 855-2nd Street S.W., T2P 4K7
Telephone: (403) 298-3100
Facsimile: (403) 265-7219
Edmonton, Alberta Office: 1000, 10035-105 Street.
Telephone: (403) 421-8133.
Facsimile: (403) 421-7951.
Toronto, Ontario Office: 3400 1 First Canadian Place. P.O. Box 130.
Telephone: (416) 863-1200.
Facsimile: (416) 863-1716.

(See Next Column)

Ottawa, Ontario Office: Suite 1800. 350 Alberta Street, Box 25, K1R 1A4.
Telephone: (613) 230-4935.
Facsimile: (613) 230-3836.
Montreal, Quebec Office: Suite 1600, 1 Place Ville Marie.
Telephone: (514) 871-1200.
Facsimile: (514) 871-8115.

MEMBER OF FIRM

John F. Curran, Q.C.

For Complete List of Firm Personnel, See General Section

For full biographical listings, see the Martindale-Hubbell Law Directory

*EDMONTON,** Edmonton Jud. Dist.

PARLEE MCLAWS (AV)

15th Floor Manulife Place, 10180 101st Street, T5J 4K1
Telephone: 403-423-8500
Telecopier: 403-423-2870
Calgary, Alberta Office: 3400, Western Canadian Place, 707 - 8th Avenue, S.W.
Telephone: 403-294-7000.
Telecopier: 403-265-8263.

MEMBERS OF FIRM

C. H. Kerr, Q.C.
M. D. MacDonald
K. F. Bailey, Q.C.
R. B. Davison, Q.C.
F. R. Haldane
P. E. J. Curran
D. G. Finlay
J. K. McFadyen
R. C. Secord
D. L. Kennedy
D. C. Rolf
D. F. Pawlowski
A. A. Garber
R. P. James
D. C. Wintermute
J. L. Cairns
R. A. Newton, Q.C.
T. A. Cockrall, Q.C.
H. D. Montemurro
F. J. Niziol
R. W. Wilson
I. L. MacLachlan
R. O. Langley
R. G. McBean
J. T. Neilson
E. G. Rice
J. F. McGinnis
J. H. H. Hockin
G. W. Jaycock
M. J. K. Nikel
B. J. Curial
S. L. May
M. S. Poretti

ASSOCIATES

C. R. Head
A.W. Slemko
L. H. Hamdon
K.A. Smith
K. D. Fallis-Howell
D. S. Tam
J.W. McClure
F.H. Belzil
R.A. Renz
J.G. Paulson
K. E. Buss
B. L. Andriachuk
P. E. S. J. Kennedy
R. Feraco
R.J. Billingsley
N.B.R. Thompson
P. A. Shenher
I. C. Johnson
K.G. Koshman
D.D. Dubrule
G. T. Lund
W.D. Johnston
G. E. Flemming
K. P. Nayyer

For full biographical listings, see the Martindale-Hubbell Law Directory

CANADA ONTARIO

*TORONTO,** Regional Munic. of York

BORDEN & ELLIOT (AV)

Barristers & Solicitors
Scotia Plaza, 40 King Street West, M5H 3Y4
Telephone: 416-367-6000
Telecopier: 416-367-6749
Internet: @ borden.com

A Member of the national association of Borden DuMoulin Howard Gervais, comprising Borden & Elliot in Toronto, Ontario, Russell & DuMoulin in Vancouver, British Columbia, Howard, Mackie in Calgary, Alberta and Mackenzie Gervais in Montréal, Québec. Borden DuMoulin Howard Gervais also operates an office in London, England.

MEMBER AND ASSOCIATES

J. Fraser Mann

For Complete List of Firm Personnel, See General Section

For full biographical listings, see the Martindale-Hubbell Law Directory

LIECHTENSTEIN

*VADUZ,**

DDr. Proksch & Partner

ITA P&A Bürotel Building, Landstrasse 161-163 FL-9494 Schaan, Vaduz
Telephone: 41 75 2332303, 2322614, 2324121
Fax: 41 75 2323562, 2324133, 2329181
Telex: 899520 ita fl E-Mail: 100415,1733@compuserve.com
Vienna, Austria Office: resident counsel: ERICH PROKSCH, Auhofgasse 1, A-1130
London, England/UK Office: resident counsel: JOSEPH KANAAN, 33 Jermyne Street, SW1
Beverley Hills, CA/USA Office: resident counsel: DANA B TASCHNER, 9545 Wilshire Boulevard, Suite 550, 90212 (offices also in Pasadena, California and Dallas, Texas)

MEMBERS OF FIRM

Reinhard J. Proksch
Werner Walser

OF COUNSEL

Christian Hopp
Erich Proksch
Dana B. Taschner (Not admitted in Liechtenstein)

INTERNATIONAL TAX COUNSEL

Joseph N. Kanaan

MEXICO

MONTERREY, NUEVO LEÓN,

Monterrey, Nuevo León

Thompson & Knight, A Professional Corporation

(Attorneys and Counselors)
Edificio Losoles PD-4, Av. Lázaro Cárdenas No. 2400 PTE San Pedro Garza Garcia, Monterrey, Nuevo León 66220
Telephone: (52-8) 363-0096
Telecopy: (52-8) 363-3067
Dallas, Texas Office: 1700 Pacific Avenue, Suite 3300, 75201.
Telephone: 214-969-1700.
Telecopy: 214-969-1751.
Cable Address: "Tomtex."
Telex: 732298.
Austin, Texas Office: 1200 San Jacinto Center, 98 San Jacinto Boulevard, 78701.
Telephone: 512-469-6100.
Telecopy: 512-469-6180.
Fort Worth, Texas Office: 801 Cherry Street, Suite 1600, 76102.
Telephone: 817-347-1700.
Telecopy: 817-347-1799.
Houston, Texas Office: 1700 Texas Commerce Tower, 600 Travis, 77002.
Telephone: 713-217-2800.
Telecopy: 713-217-2828; 713-217-2882.

SHAREHOLDERS

Joe A. Rudberg
Michael C. Titens

For full biographical listings, see the Martindale-Hubbell Law Directory

LABOR AND EMPLOYMENT LAW

ALABAMA

*BIRMINGHAM,** Jefferson Co.

BALCH & BINGHAM (AV)

1710 Sixth Avenue North, P.O. Box 306, 35201
Telephone: 205-251-8100
Facsimile: 205-226-8798
Other Birmingham, Alabama Office: 1901 Sixth Avenue North, 35203.
Telephone: 205-251-8100.
Facsimile: 205-226-8799.
Montgomery, Alabama Office: The Winter Building, 2 Dexter Avenue, 36101.
Telephone: 205-834-6500.
Facsimile: 205-269-3115.
Huntsville, Alabama Office: Suite 810, 200 West Court Square, 35801.
Telephone: 205-551-0171.
Facsimile: 205-551-0174.
Washington, D.C. Office: Suite 800, 1101 Connecticut Avenue, N.W., 20036.
Telephone: 202-296-0387.
Facsimile: 202-452-8180.

MEMBERS OF FIRM

Harold A. Bowron, Jr.
John Richard Carrigan
Edward S. Allen
John J. Coleman, III
M. Stanford Blanton

SENIOR ATTORNEY

T. Dwight Sloan

ASSOCIATE

Debra Carter White

Counsel for: Alabama Power Co.; Blue Cross and Blue Shield of Alabama; The Boeing Company; Brasfield & Gorrie, Inc.; Compass Bancshares, Inc.; Harbert Corp.; Kimberly-Clark Corp.; Southern Company Services, Inc.; Southern Research Institute; Vesta Insurance Group, Inc.

For Complete List of Firm Personnel, See General Section

For full biographical listings, see the Martindale-Hubbell Law Directory

BERKOWITZ, LEFKOVITS, ISOM & KUSHNER, A PROFESSIONAL CORPORATION (AV)

1600 SouthTrust Tower, 420 North Twentieth Street, 35203
Telephone: 205-328-0480
Telecopier: 205-322-8007

Lee H. Zell
Frank S. James III
Wesley C. Redmond

Lisa B. Singer

Representative Clients: AlaTenn Resources, Inc.; B.A.S.S., Inc.; CLP Corporation (McDonald's Franchise); Daniel Corp.; Hanna Steel Co., Inc.; Jefferson Home Furniture, Inc.; Liberty Trouser Co., Inc.; Parisian, Inc.; Southern Pipe & Supply Co., Inc.; The Personnel Board of Jefferson County, Alabama.

For Complete List of Firm Personnel, See General Section

For full biographical listings, see the Martindale-Hubbell Law Directory

BRADLEY, ARANT, ROSE & WHITE (AV)

1400 Park Place Tower, 2001 Park Place, 35203
Telephone: 205-521-8000
Telex: 494-1324
Facsimile: 205-251-8611, 251-8665, 252-0264
Facsimile (Southtrust Office): 205-251-9915
Huntsville, Alabama Office: 200 Clinton Avenue West, Suite 900.
Telephone: 205-517-5100.
Facsimile: 205-533-5069.

MEMBERS OF FIRM

John James Coleman, Jr.
W. Braxton Schell, Jr.
James Patrick Alexander
James Walker May
Robert K. Spotswood
Jay D. St. Clair
John William Hargrove

ASSOCIATES

Forrest K. Covington
Anne R. Yuengert
Warne S. Heath (Resident, Huntsville Office)
Amy K. Myers
Arnold W. Umbach, III
James W. Davis

(See Next Column)

For Complete List of Firm Personnel, See General Section

For full biographical listings, see the Martindale-Hubbell Law Directory

BURR & FORMAN (AV)

3000 SouthTrust Tower, 420 North 20th Street, 35203
Telephone: 205-251-3000
Telecopier: 205-458-5100
Huntsville, Alabama Office: Suite 204, Regency Center, 400 Meridian Street.
Telephone: 205-551-0010.

MEMBERS OF FIRM

C. V. Stelzenmuller
J. Patrick Logan
J. Fredric Ingram
F. A. Flowers, III
Mark Taliaferro, Jr.
Michael L. Lucas
D. Frank Davis
Dent M. Morton
T. Thomas Cottingham, III
Sue Ann Willis

OF COUNSEL

Samuel H. Burr

For Complete List of Firm Personnel, See General Section

For full biographical listings, see the Martindale-Hubbell Law Directory

CONSTANGY, BROOKS & SMITH (AV)

Suite 1410 AmSouth/Harbert Plaza, 1901 Sixth Avenue North, 35203-2602
Telephone: 205-252-9321
Atlanta, Georgia Office: Suite 2400 Peachtree Center Building, 230 Peachtree Street, N.W.
Telephone: 404-525-8622.
Nashville, Tennessee Office: Suite 1080 Vanderbilt Plaza, 2100 West End Avenue.
Telephone: 615-321-5891.
Columbia, South Carolina Office: Suite 810 NationsBank Tower. 1301 Gervais Street,
Telephone: 803-256-3200.
Washington, D.C. Office: Suite 1200, 1015 Fifteenth Street, N.W.
Telephone: 202-789-8676.
Winston-Salem, North Carolina Office: Suite 300, 101 South Stratford Road.
Telephone: 910-721-1001, 704-344-1040 (Charlotte).

RESIDENT MEMBERS

J. Richard Walton
Richard O. Brown
Chris Mitchell
Carol Sue Nelson

RESIDENT ASSOCIATES

Thomas A. Davis
Michael D. Giles
Lisa Narrell-Mead

Representative Clients: Blockbuster Entertainment Corp.; Blue Cross/Blue Shield of Alabama; Consolidated Freightways, Inc.; Delta Woodside Industries; McDonald's; Merck & Co., Inc.; Philip-Morris Cos., Inc.; Phillips Van Heusen Corp.; Sara Lee Corp.; Trust Company Bank.

For full biographical listings, see the Martindale-Hubbell Law Directory

COOPER, MITCH, CRAWFORD, KUYKENDALL & WHATLEY (AV)

1100 Financial Center, 505 20th Street North, 35203-2605
Telephone: 205-328-9576
Telecopier: 205-328-9669

MEMBERS OF FIRM

Jerome A. Cooper
John D. Saxon
William E. Mitch
Glen M. Connor
Thomas N. Crawford, Jr.
Patricia Guthrie Fraley
Frederick T. Kuykendall, III
Jay Smith (On Leave of Absence)
Joe R. Whatley, Jr.

ASSOCIATES

Candis A. McGowan
G. Patterson Keahey
Andrew C. Allen
Maureen Kane Berg
William Z. Cullen
Gerald B. Taylor, Jr.
Samuel H. Heldman
Rebecca Higgins Hunt
Hilary E. Ball-Walker
Marcel L. Debruge
Patrick F. Clark
Peter H. Burke

Counsel for: United Steelworkers of America, AFL-CIO; United Mine Workers of America, District 20; Birmingham Plumbers & Steamfitters Local Union No. 91 Pension Fund.
Reference: AMSouth Bank of Birmingham.

For full biographical listings, see the Martindale-Hubbell Law Directory

GORDON, SILBERMAN, WIGGINS & CHILDS, A PROFESSIONAL CORPORATION (AV)

1400 SouthTrust Tower, 420 North 20th Street, 35203
Telephone: 205-328-0640
Telecopier: 205-254-1500

Robert L. Wiggins, Jr.
Robert F. Childs, Jr.
C. Michael Quinn

(See Next Column)

GORDON, SILBERMAN, WIGGINS & CHILDS A PROFESSIONAL CORPORATION, *Birmingham—Continued*

James Mendelsohn
Richard J. Ebbinghouse
Ann K. Norton
Samuel Fisher
Ann C. Robertson
Elizabeth Evans Courtney
Byron R. Perkins
Jon C. Goldfarb
Gregory O. Wiggins
Lee Winston
Deborah A. Mattison
Amelia H. Griffith
Rocco Calamusa, Jr.

For Complete List of Firm Personnel, See General Section

For full biographical listings, see the Martindale-Hubbell Law Directory

HASKELL SLAUGHTER YOUNG & JOHNSTON, PROFESSIONAL ASSOCIATION (AV)

1200 AmSouth/Harbert Plaza, 1901 Sixth Avenue North, 35203
Telephone: 205-251-1000
Facsimile: 205-324-1133
Montgomery, Alabama Office: Haskell Slaughter Young Johnston & Gallion. Bailey Building, Suite 375, 400 South Union Street, P.O. Box 4660. 36104
Telephone: 205-265-8573.
Facsimile: 205-264-7945.

Frank M. Young, III
Beverly P. Baker
Ross N. Cohen
Richard H. Walston

Michael K. K. Choy
Paula J. Baker

Representative Clients: Baxter Healthcare Corporation; The Bradford Group, Inc.; The Coalition for Employee Healthcare, Inc.; Jefferson County Racing Association; Jones Plumbing Systems, Inc.; Manpower Temporary Services (Alabama); Marshall Durbin Companies; Montgomery County, Alabama; Ridout's-Brown-Service Inc.; Webster Industries, Inc.

For Complete List of Firm Personnel, See General Section

For full biographical listings, see the Martindale-Hubbell Law Directory

JOHNSTON, BARTON, PROCTOR, SWEDLAW & NAFF (AV)

2900 AmSouth/Harbert Plaza, 1901 Sixth Avenue North, 35203-2618
Telephone: 205-458-9400
Telecopier: 205-458-9500

MEMBERS OF FIRM

Harvey Deramus (1904-1970)
Alfred M. Naff (1923-1993)
James C. Barton
G. Burns Proctor, Jr.
Sydney L. Lavender
Jerome K. Lanning
Don B. Long, Jr.
Charles L. Robinson
J. William Rose, Jr.
Gilbert E. Johnston, Jr.
David P. Whiteside, Jr.
Ralph H. Smith II
James C. Barton, Jr.
Thomas E. Walker
Anne P. Wheeler
Raymond P. Fitzpatrick, Jr.
Hollinger F. Barnard
William D. Jones III
David W. Proctor
Oscar M. Price III
W. Hill Sewell
Robert S. Vance, Jr.
Richard J. Brockman
Anthony A. Joseph

OF COUNSEL

Gilbert E. Johnston
Alfred Swedlaw
Alan W. Heldman

ASSOCIATES

William K. Hancock
James P. Pewitt
Scott Wells Ford
David M. Hunt
Lee M. Pope
Haskins W. Jones
James M. Parker, Jr.
Michael H. Johnson
Russell L. Irby, III
R. Scott Clark
Helen Kathryn Downs

General Counsel for: Anderson News Co.; The Baptist Medical Centers; The Birmingham News Co.; Process Equipment, Inc.
Counsel for: BellSouth Services, Inc.; Continental Grain Co.; Times-Mirror Broadcasting (WVTM-TV, Channel 13).

For full biographical listings, see the Martindale-Hubbell Law Directory

LEHR, MIDDLEBROOKS & PROCTOR, P.C. (AV)

Suite 300, 2021 Third Avenue North, 35203
Telephone: 205-326-3002
Telecopier: 205-326-3008

Richard I. Lehr
David J. Middlebrooks
R. David Proctor
Albert L. Vreeland, II
Brent L. Crumpton
Steven M. Stastny

For full biographical listings, see the Martindale-Hubbell Law Directory

POWELL & FREDERICK (AV)

Suite 700 2100 First Avenue North, 35203
Telephone: 205-324-4996
Telecopier: 205-324-4120

(See Next Column)

MEMBERS OF FIRM

Charles A. Powell, III
Barry V. Frederick
William G. Somerville, III

ASSOCIATE

John W. Sheffield

OF COUNSEL

Paul E. Toppins

For full biographical listings, see the Martindale-Hubbell Law Directory

SIROTE & PERMUTT, P.C. (AV)

2222 Arlington Avenue, South, P.O. Box 55727, 35255
Telephone: 205-933-7111
Facsimile: 205-930-5301
Huntsville, Alabama Office: 200 Clinton Avenue, N.W., Suite 1000.
Telephone: 205-536-1711.
Facsimile: 205-534-9650.
Mobile, Alabama Office: One St. Louis Centre, Suite 1000.
Telephone: 205-432-1671.
Facsimile: 205-434-0196.
Montgomery, Alabama Office: Colonial Commerce Center, Suite 305 One Commerce Street.
Telephone: 205-261-3400.
Facsimile: 205-261-3434.
Tuscaloosa, Alabama Office: 2216 14th Street.
Telephone: 205-752-2089.

John C. Falkenberry
Frances Heidt
David W. Long
Matthew A. Vega

Representative Clients: International Business Machines (IBM); General Motors Corp.; Colonial Bank; Bruno's, Inc.; University of Alabama Hospitals; Westinghouse Electric Corp.; First Alabama Bank; Monsanto Chemical Company; South Central Bell; Prudential Insurance Company; American Home Products, Inc.; Minnesota Mining and Manufacturing, Inc. (3M).

For Complete List of Firm Personnel, See General Section

For full biographical listings, see the Martindale-Hubbell Law Directory

SPAIN, GILLON, GROOMS, BLAN & NETTLES (AV)

The Zinszer Building, 2117 2nd Avenue North, 35203
Telephone: 205-328-4100
Telecopier: 205-324-8866

MEMBERS OF FIRM

Samuel H. Frazier
Alton B. Parker, Jr.
Thomas M. Eden, III

General Counsel for: Liberty National Life Insurance Co.; United States Fidelity & Guaranty Co.; Piggly Wiggly Alabama Distributing Co.; AmSouth Mortgage Co., Inc.; Alabama Insurance Guaranty Association; Alabama Life and Disability Insurance Guaranty Association; Alabama Insurance Underwriters Association.
Counsel for: The Prudential Insurance Company of America; Government Employees Insurance Co.; Massachusetts Mutual Life Insurance Co.

For Complete List of Firm Personnel, See General Section

For full biographical listings, see the Martindale-Hubbell Law Directory

*HUNTSVILLE,** Madison Co.

BERRY, ABLES, TATUM, LITTLE & BAXTER, P.C. (AV)

Legal Building, 315 Franklin Street, S.E., P.O. Box 165, 35804-0165
Telephone: 205-533-3740
Facsimile: 205-533-3751

William H. Blanton (1889-1973)
Joe M. Berry
L. Bruce Ables
James T. Tatum, Jr.
Loyd H. Little, Jr.
James T. Baxter, III
Thomas E. Parker, Jr.
Bill G. Hall

Representative Clients: AmSouth Bank, N.A.; First Alabama Bank; General Shale Products Co.; The Hartz Corp.; Litton Industries, Inc.; Farmers Tractor Co.; Colonial Bank; Farm Credit Bank of Texas; Resolution Trust Corp.
Reference: First Alabama Bank.

For full biographical listings, see the Martindale-Hubbell Law Directory

BRADLEY, ARANT, ROSE & WHITE (AV)

200 Clinton Avenue West, Suite 900, 35801
Telephone: 205-517-5100
Facsimile: 205-533-5069
Birmingham, Alabama Office: 1400 Park Place Tower, 2001 Park Place.
Telephone: 205-521-8000.
Telex: 494-1324.
Facsimile: 205-251-8611, 251-8665, 252-0264. Facsimile (Southtrust Office): 205-251-9915.

RESIDENT PARTNER

E. Cutter Hughes, Jr.

(See Next Column)

BRADLEY, ARANT, ROSE & WHITE—*Continued*

RESIDENT ASSOCIATE

Warne S. Heath

For Complete List of Firm Personnel, See General Section

For full biographical listings, see the Martindale-Hubbell Law Directory

SIROTE & PERMUTT, P.C. (AV)

Suite 1000, 200 Clinton Avenue, N.W., 35801
Telephone: 205-536-1711
Facsimile: 205-534-9650
Birmingham, Alabama Office: 2222 Arlington Avenue, South, P.O. Box 55727.
Telephone: 205-933-7111.
Facsimile: 205-930-5301.
Mobile, Alabama Office: One St. Louis Centre, Suite 1000.
Telephone: 205-432-1671.
Facsimile: 205-434-0196.
Montgomery, Alabama Office: Colonial Commerce Center, Suite 305, One Commerce Street.
Telephone: 205-261-3400.
Facsimile: 205-261-3434.
Tuscaloosa, Alabama Office: 2216 14th Street.
Telephone: 205-752-2089.

Julian D. Butler
George W. Royer, Jr.
Roderic G. Steakley

For Complete List of Firm Personnel, See General Section

For full biographical listings, see the Martindale-Hubbell Law Directory

*MOBILE,** Mobile Co.

ARMBRECHT, JACKSON, DEMOUY, CROWE, HOLMES & REEVES (AV)

1300 AmSouth Center, P.O. Box 290, 36601
Telephone: 334-432-6751
Facsimile: 334-432-6843; 433-3821

MEMBERS OF FIRM

Marshall J. DeMouy
Kirk C. Shaw
William B. Harvey
James Donald Hughes
Broox G. Holmes, Jr.

Representative Clients: Ryan-Walsh, Inc.; Gulf City Fisheries, Inc.; Automation Technology, Inc.; Microtie, Inc.; Loyal American Life Insurance Co.; WKRG-TV, Inc.; The Great Atlantic and Pacific Tea Co.; Circle K Corp.; Coca-Cola Bottling Co.; Consolidated Office Automation Systems, Inc.

For Complete List of Firm Personnel, See General Section

For full biographical listings, see the Martindale-Hubbell Law Directory

GARDNER, MIDDLEBROOKS & FLEMING, P.C. (AV)

64 North Royal Street, P.O. Drawer 3103, 36652
Telephone: 334-433-8100
Telecopier: 334-433-8181

J. Cecil Gardner
Charles J. Fleming
Sherwood C. Middlebrooks, III
W. Michael Hamilton (Not admitted in AL)

John D. Gibbons
Christopher E. Krafchak
William H. Reece

Representative Clients: Alabama AFL-CIO; Southwest Alabama Labor Council, AFL-CIO; Greater Mobile Port Council, AFL-CIO; Mobile/Pensacola; Building Trades Council, AFL-C10; United Paperworkers International Union, AFL CIO, CLC; Oil, Chemical & Atomic Workers International Union, AFL-CIO; International Organization of Masters, Mates & Pilots, AFL-CIO; International Brotherhood of Boilermakers, AFL-CIO; International Alliance of Theatrical Stage Employees & Moving Picture Machine Operators, AFL-CIO.

For full biographical listings, see the Martindale-Hubbell Law Directory

HAND, ARENDALL, BEDSOLE, GREAVES & JOHNSTON (AV)

3000 First National Bank Building, P.O. Box 123, Drawer C, 36601
Telephone: 334-432-5511
Fax: 334-694-6375
Washington, D.C. Office: 410 First Street, S.E., Suite 300. 20003.
Telephone: 202-863-0053.
Fax: 202-863-0096.

MEMBERS OF FIRM

William C. Tidwell, III
M. Mallory Mantiply
George M. Walker
Walter T. Gilmer, Jr.

For Complete List of Firm Personnel, See General Section

For full biographical listings, see the Martindale-Hubbell Law Directory

JOHNSTONE, ADAMS, BAILEY, GORDON AND HARRIS (AV)

Royal St. Francis Building, 104 St. Francis Street, P.O. Box 1988, 36633
Telephone: 334-432-7682
Facsimile: 334-432-2800
Telex: 782040

MEMBERS OF FIRM

Brock B. Gordon
Gregory C. Buffalow
Wade B. Perry, Jr.
Celia J. Collins

Representative Clients: The Lerio Corp.; First Alabama Bank, Mobile; Infirmary Health System/Mobile Infirmary Medical Center/Rotary Rehabilitation Hospital (Multi-hospital system); Aluminum Company of America; Transportation Leasing Co.; Clark County Board of Education; Mobile Mental Health Center, Inc.

For Complete List of Firm Personnel, See General Section

For full biographical listings, see the Martindale-Hubbell Law Directory

LYONS, PIPES & COOK, P.C. (AV)

2 North Royal Street, P.O. Box 2727, 36652-2727
Telephone: 334-432-4481
Cable Address: "Lysea"
Telecopier: 334-433-1820

G. Sage Lyons
Charles L. Miller, Jr.
W. David Johnson, Jr.

Representative Clients: Carriers Container Council, Inc.; Crawford & Company; Inchcape Shipping Services, Inc.; INSBROK; International Systems, Inc.; Jordan Industries, Inc.; Marriott Corporation; Massachusetts Mutual Life Insurance Co.; Spectacor Management Group; United States Fidelity & Guaranty.

For Complete List of Firm Personnel, See General Section

For full biographical listings, see the Martindale-Hubbell Law Directory

SIROTE & PERMUTT, P.C. (AV)

One St. Louis Centre, Suite 1000, P.O. Drawer 2025, 36652-2025
Telephone: 334-432-1671
Facsimile: 334-434-0196
Birmingham, Alabama Office: 2222 Arlington Avenue, South, P.O. Box 55727.
Telephone: 205-933-7111.
Facsimile: 205-930-5301.
Huntsville, Alabama Office: 200 Clinton Avenue, N.W., Suite 1000.
Telephone: 205-536-1711.
Facsimile: 205-534-9650.
Montgomery, Alabama Office: Colonial Commerce Center, Suite 305, One Commerce Street.
Telephone: 205-261-3400.
Facsimile: 205-261-3434.
Tuscaloosa, Alabama Office: 2216 14th Street.
Telephone: 205-752-2089.

T. Julian Motes

For Complete List of Firm Personnel, See General Section

For full biographical listings, see the Martindale-Hubbell Law Directory

*MONTGOMERY,** Montgomery Co.

* indicates certain Bar Register subscribers whose principal office is located elsewhere in the state and who have arranged for representation as a part of the state capital listings that follow

* **BALCH & BINGHAM** (AV)

The Winter Building, 2 Dexter Avenue, P.O. Box 78, 36101
Telephone: 334-834-6500
Facsimile: 334-269-3115
Birmingham, Alabama Offices: 1710 Sixth Avenue North, 35203.
Telephone: 205-251-8100.
Facsimile: 205-226-8798. 1901 Sixth Avenue North, 35203.
Telephone: 205-251-8100.
Facsimile: 205-226-8799.
Huntsville, Alabama Office: Suite 810, 200 West Court Square, 35801.
Telephone: 205-551-0171.
Facsimile: 205-551-0174.
Washington, D.C. Office: Suite 800, 1101 Connecticut Avenue, N.W., 20036.
Telephone: 202-296-0387.
Facsimile: 202-452-8180.

RESIDENT MEMBERS OF FIRM

Thomas W. Thagard, Jr.
David R. Boyd
William P. Cobb, II

RESIDENT ASSOCIATE

Leslie M. Allen

Counsel for: Alabama Power Co.; Blue Cross and Blue Shield of Alabama; The Boeing Company; Brasfield & Gorrie, Inc.; Compass Bancshares, Inc.; Harbert Corp.; Kimberly-Clark Corp.; Southern Company Services, Inc.; Southern Research Institute; Vesta Insurance Group, Inc.

(See Next Column)

BALCH & BINGHAM, *Montgomery—Continued*

For Complete List of Firm Personnel, See General Section

For full biographical listings, see the Martindale-Hubbell Law Directory

CAPELL, HOWARD, KNABE & COBBS, P.A. (AV)

57 Adams Avenue, P.O. Box 2069, 36102-2069
Telephone: 334-241-8000

Jack L. Capell	Henry C. Barnett, Jr.
Fontaine M. Howard (1908-1985)	Palmer Smith Lehman
	Richard F. Allen
Walter J. Knabe (1898-1979)	Neal H. Acker
Edward E. Cobbs (1909-1982)	Henry H. Hutchinson
L. Lister Hill (1936-1993)	Shapard D. Ashley
Herman H. Hamilton, Jr.	D. Kyle Johnson
Rufus M. King	J. Lister Hubbard
Robert S. Richard	James N. Walter, Jr.
John B. Scott, Jr.	James H. McLemore
John F. Andrews	H. Dean Mooty, Jr.
James M. Scott	Jim B. Grant, Jr.
Thomas S. Lawson, Jr.	Wyeth Holt Speir, III
John L. Capell, III	Chad S. Wachter
William D. Coleman	Ellen M. Hastings
William K. Martin	Debra Deames Spain
Bruce J. Downey III	William Rufus King

C. Clay Torbert, III

OF COUNSEL

Timothy Sullivan

For full biographical listings, see the Martindale-Hubbell Law Directory

CAPOUANO, WAMPOLD, PRESTWOOD & SANSONE, P.A. (AV)

350 Adams Avenue, P.O. Box 1910, 36102-1910
Telephone: 334-264-6401
Fax: 334-834-4954

Leon M. Capouano	Ellis D. Hanan
Alvin T. Prestwood	Joseph P. Borg
Jerome D. Smith	Joseph W. Warren

OF COUNSEL

Charles H. Wampold, Jr.

Thomas B. Klinner	Linda Smith Webb

James M. Sizemore, Jr.

Counsel for: First Alabama Bank of Montgomery, N.A.; Union Bank and Trust Co.; Real Estate Financing, Inc.; SouthTrust Bank; AmSouth Bank; Central Bank; City Federal Savings & Loan Assoc.; Colonial Mortgage Co.; Lomas & Nettleton; First Bank of Linden.

For full biographical listings, see the Martindale-Hubbell Law Directory

HASKELL SLAUGHTER YOUNG JOHNSTON & GALLION, PROFESSIONAL ASSOCIATION (AV)

Suite 375 Bailey Building, 400 South Union Street, P.O. Box 4660, 36104
Telephone: 334-265-8573
Facsimile: 334-264-7945
Birmingham, Alabama Office: Haskell Slaughter Young & Johnston. 1200 AmSouth/Harbert Plaza, 1901 Sixth Avenue North. 35203
Telephone: 205-251-1000.
Facsimile: 205-324-1133.

Thomas T. Gallion, III	Constance A. Caldwell

Representative Clients: Baxter Healthcare Corporation; The Bradford Group, Inc.; The Coalition for Employee Healthcare, Inc.; Jefferson County Racing Association; Jones Plumbing Systems, Inc.; Manpower Temporary Services (Alabama); Marshall Durbin Companies; Montgomery County, Alabama; Ridout's-Brown-Service Inc.; Webster Industries, Inc.

For Complete List of Firm Personnel, See General Section

For full biographical listings, see the Martindale-Hubbell Law Directory

ARIZONA

*PHOENIX,** Maricopa Co.

BROWN & BAIN, A PROFESSIONAL ASSOCIATION (AV)

2901 North Central Avenue, P.O. Box 400, 85001-0400
Telephone: 602-351-8000
Cable: TWX 910-951-0646
Telecopier: 602-351-8516
Palo Alto, California Affiliated Office: Brown & Bain, 600 Hansen Way.
Telephone: 415-856-9411.
Telecopier: 415-856-6061.

(See Next Column)

Tucson, Arizona Affiliated Office: Brown & Bain, A Professional Association. One South Church Avenue, Nineteenth Floor, P.O. Box 2265.
Telephone: 602-798-7900
Telecopier: 602-798-7945.

Daniel C. Barr	Sarah R. Simmons (Resident at Tucson Office)
Amy J. Gittler	Charles Van Cott
Philip R. Higdon (Resident at Tucson Office)	

Diane Madenci (Resident at Tucson Office)	Lee Stein

For Complete List of Firm Personnel, See General Section

For full biographical listings, see the Martindale-Hubbell Law Directory

DAUGHTON, HAWKINS, BROCKELMAN, GUINAN & PATTERSON (AV)

40 North Central Avenue, Suite 2500, 85004
Telephone: 602-271-4400
Fax: 602-271-4300

Donald Daughton	Michael D. Guinan
Michael D. Hawkins	Bart J. Patterson
Kent Brockelman	Leslie Kyman Cooper

For Complete List of Firm Personnel, See General Section

For full biographical listings, see the Martindale-Hubbell Law Directory

FENNEMORE CRAIG, A PROFESSIONAL CORPORATION (AV)

Two North Central, Suite 2200, 85004
Telephone: 602-257-8700
Fax: 602-257-8527
Scottsdale, Arizona Office: 6263 North Scottsdale Road, Suite 290, 85250.
Telephone: 602-257-5400.
Fax: 602-945-4932.
Tucson, Arizona Office: One South Church Avenue, Suite 1030, 85701.
Telephone: 602-624-9312.
Fax: 602-882-7383.

C. Webb Crockett	Loral Deatherage
Donald R. Gilbert	Christopher P. Staring
Ronald J. Stolkin	John J. Balitis, Jr.

Janice Procter-Murphy	Keith L. Hendricks

Polly S. Rapp

Representative Clients: ASARCO Incorporated; AT&T Communications; Bridgestone/Firestone, Inc.; Catellus Development Corp.; Citibank (Arizona); First Interstate Bank of Arizona; GIANT Industries; Phelps Dodge Corporation; The Atchison, Topeka & Santa Fe Railway, Co.; US WEST Communications.

For Complete List of Firm Personnel, See General Section

For full biographical listings, see the Martindale-Hubbell Law Directory

JEROME L. FROIMSON (AV)

340 East Palm Lane #275, 85004
Telephone: 602-252-4990
Fax: 602-271-9308

For full biographical listings, see the Martindale-Hubbell Law Directory

DAVID F. GOMEZ A PROFESSIONAL CORPORATION (AV)

2525 East Camelback Road Suite 860, 85016
Telephone: 602-957-8686
Telecopier: 602-956-9854

David F. Gomez

Michael J. Petitti, Jr.

For full biographical listings, see the Martindale-Hubbell Law Directory

JENNINGS, STROUSS AND SALMON, P.L.C. (AV)

A Professional Limited Liability Company
One Renaissance Square, Two North Central, 85004-2393
Telephone: 602-262-5911
Fax: 602-253-3255

Gerald W. Alston	Glenn J. Carter
Rita A. Meiser	Ernest Calderon
Gary L. Lassen	John J. Egbert

Robert D. Haws	Gordon Lewis

For Complete List of Firm Personnel, See General Section

For full biographical listings, see the Martindale-Hubbell Law Directory

Phoenix—Continued

LEWIS AND ROCA (AV)

A Partnership including Professional Corporations
40 North Central Avenue, 85004-4429
Telephone: 602-262-5311
Fax: 602-262-5747
Tucson, Arizona Office: One South Church Avenue, Suite 700.
Telephone: 602-622-2090.
Fax: 602-622-3088.

MEMBERS OF FIRM

Marty Harper
Barbara J. Muller
Steven J. Hulsman
Richard S. Cohen
Allen R. Clarke
Jane E. Reddin

ASSOCIATES

Barbara A. Anstey
David A. Kelly
Julia A. Kossak-Fuller

Representative Clients: Arizona Public Service Co.; City of Phoenix; General Electric Co.; Gosnell Builders Corp.; Maricopa Community College District; McKesson Corp.; Phoenix Memorial Hospital; Skymall, Inc.; Southwest Risk Services; United Parcel Service, Inc.

For Complete List of Firm Personnel, See General Section

For full biographical listings, see the Martindale-Hubbell Law Directory

LAW OFFICE OF STANLEY LUBIN (AV)

Suite 875, 2700 North Central Avenue, 85004
Telephone: 602-234-1082
Fax: 602-234-0008

Scott J. Cooley

Representative Clients: American Federation of Government Employees, Arizona State Council and its Locals 1662, 2924 and 3954; Arizona Education Assn.; American Federation of State, County and Municipal Employees Council 97; Bakery Confectionary & Tobacco Workers, Local Union 232; IATSE Stage Employees Local No. 294 and 336; International Brotherhood of Electrical Workers, Locals #266, #640 and G.C.C. #1; Mailhandlers Local Union #320; Phoenix Federation of Musicians, AFM #586; Roofers Union, Local #135; United Fire Fighters Association, Phoenix Local 493, I.A.F.F.

For full biographical listings, see the Martindale-Hubbell Law Directory

MEYER, HENDRICKS, VICTOR, OSBORN & MALEDON, A PROFESSIONAL ASSOCIATION (AV)

2929 North Central Avenue Suite 2100, 85012-2794
Telephone: 602-640-9000
Facsimile: (24 Hrs.) 602-640-9050
Mailing Address: P.O. Box 33449, 85067-3449,

Don Bivens
David B. Rosenbaum
Bruce E. Meyerson
Mary E. Berkheiser
Brent Ghelfi
Mark Andrew Fuller

Ronald R. Gallegos

Reference: Bank One Arizona, NA.

For Complete List of Firm Personnel, See General Section

For full biographical listings, see the Martindale-Hubbell Law Directory

O'CONNOR, CAVANAGH, ANDERSON, WESTOVER, KILLINGSWORTH & BESHEARS, A PROFESSIONAL ASSOCIATION (AV)

One East Camelback Road, Suite 1100, 85012-1656
Telephone: 602-263-2400
FAX: 602-263-2900
Sun City, Arizona Office: 13250 North Del Webb Boulevard, Suite B, 85351.
Telephone: 602-263-2808.
FAX: 602-933-3100.
Tucson, Arizona Office: Suite 2200, One South Church Avenue, 85701.
Telephone: 602-882-8912.
FAX: 602-624-9564.
Nogales, Arizona Office: 1827 North Mastick Way, 85621.
Telephone: 602-761-4215.
FAX: 602-761-3505.

Charles L. Fine
Janice H. Moore

Arthur T. Carter

Steven G. Biddle

Representative Clients: American Fence Corp.; Arden Corporation; Arizona Independent Electrical Contractors Association; Carnation Dairy Co.; Computer Power Group; Glendale Union High School District; Resort Management of America; Smith's Food & Drug Centers, Inc.; Stanton Industries; Trico Electric Cooperative, Inc.

(See Next Column)

For Complete List of Firm Personnel, See General Section

For full biographical listings, see the Martindale-Hubbell Law Directory

SHIMMEL, HILL, BISHOP & GRUENDER, P.C. (AV)

3700 North 24th Street, 85016
Telephone: 602-224-9500
Telecopier: 602-955-6176

Daniel F. Gruender
Michael V. Perry

Representative Clients: Bashas' Stores; Phoenix Newspapers, Inc.; Revlon, Inc.; Silo, Inc.; Black Mesa Pipeline Co.; Associated General Contractors of America; The Ashton Companies.

For Complete List of Firm Personnel, See General Section

For full biographical listings, see the Martindale-Hubbell Law Directory

SNELL & WILMER (AV)

One Arizona Center, 85004-0001
Telephone: 602-382-6000
Fax: 602-382-6070
Tucson, Arizona Office: 1500 Norwest Tower, One South Church Avenue 85701-1612.
Telephone: 602-882-1200.
Fax: 602-884-1294.
Orange County Office: 1920 Main Street, Suite 1200, P.O. Box 19601, Irvine, California, 92714.
Telephone: 714-253-2700.
Fax: 714-955-2507.
Salt Lake City, Utah Office: Broadway Centre, 111 East Broadway, Suite 900, 84111.
Telephone: 801-237-1900.
Fax: 801-237-1950.

MEMBERS OF FIRM

Frederick K. Steiner, Jr.
William R. Hayden
Robert J. Deeny
Gerard Morales
Rebecca A. Winterscheidt

SENIOR ATTORNEY

William P. Allen

ASSOCIATE

Charles P. Keller

Representative Clients: Arizona Public Service Company; Brown & Root, Inc.; Chase Bank of Arizona; Coca Cola Enterprises, Inc.; Intel Corporation; Mrs. Field's Cookies; Samaritan Health Service; Safeway, Inc.; Bank One, Arizona, N.A.; Ford Motor Co.

For Complete List of Firm Personnel, See General Section

For full biographical listings, see the Martindale-Hubbell Law Directory

SCOTTSDALE, Maricopa Co.

JEFFREY A. MATZ A PROFESSIONAL CORPORATION (AV Ⓣ)

6711 East Camelback Road, Suite 8, 85251
Telephone: 602-955-0900
Fax: 602-955-1885

Jeffrey A. Matz (Not admitted in AZ)

*TUCSON,** Pima Co.

ERNEST ALLEN COHEN (AV)

6426 Calle de Los Seris, P.O. Box 37273, 85740
Telephone: 602-297-4100
Fax: 602-297-4105
(Also Of Counsel, Billet & Connor, Philadelphia, PA; Billet & Connor, Turnersville, N.J.; Langer & Charles, New York, N.Y.)

Representative Clients: International Organization of Masters, Mates & Pilots, ILA, AFL-CIO; Lawyers Mediation Service Corp.; Childtime Children's Centers; Co-Counsel; MRR International Corp.; 1701 Realty Corp.; Therapeutic Sleep Products of New Jersey; IOMMP Health and Benefits Plan.

For full biographical listings, see the Martindale-Hubbell Law Directory

COREY & FARRELL, P.C. (AV)

Suite 830, Norwest Tower, One South Church Avenue, 85701-1620
Telephone: 602-882-4994
Telefax: 602-884-7757

Barry M. Corey
Kristen B. Klotz

Representative Clients: Amphitheater Public School District; Civil Service Commission of the City of Tucson; La Quinta Homes, Inc.; Pima County Merit System Commission; DANKA-Uni-Copy Corp.; Introspect Health Care Corp.

For full biographical listings, see the Martindale-Hubbell Law Directory

Tucson—Continued

FENNEMORE CRAIG, A PROFESSIONAL CORPORATION (AV)

Suite 1030, One South Church Avenue, 85701-1620
Telephone: 602-624-9312
Fax: 602-882-7383
Phoenix, Arizona Office: Two North Central Avenue, Suite 2200, 85004.
Telephone: 602-257-8700.
Fax: 602-257-8527.
Scottsdale, Arizona Office: 6263 North Scottsdale Road, Suite 290, 85250.
Telephone: 602-257-5400.
Fax: 602-945-4932.

Ronald J. Stolkin   Christopher P. Staring

Representative Clients: ASARCO Incorporated; AT&T Communications; Bridgestone/Firestone, Inc.; Catellus Development Corp.; Cyprus Amax Minerals Co.; First Interstate Bank of Arizona; GFC Financial Corp.; GIANT Industries; PETsMART, Inc.; Phelps Dodge Corporation.

For Complete List of Firm Personnel, See General Section

For full biographical listings, see the Martindale-Hubbell Law Directory

O'CONNOR, CAVANAGH, ANDERSON, WESTOVER, KILLINGSWORTH & BESHEARS, A PROFESSIONAL ASSOCIATION (AV)

Suite 2200 One South Church Avenue, 85701-1621
Telephone: 602-882-8912
FAX: 602-624-9564
Phoenix, Arizona Office: One East Camelback Road, Suite 1100, 85012.
Telephone: 602-263-2400.
FAX: 602-263-2900.
Sun City, Arizona Office: 13250 North Del Webb Boulevard, Suite B, 85351.
Telephone: 602-263-2808.
FAX: 602-933-3100.
Nogales, Arizona Office: 1827 North Mastick Way, 85621.
Telephone: 602-761-4215.
FAX: 602-761-3505.

Jenne S. Forbes

Representative Client: Jeffco, Inc.
Reference: Citibank.

For Complete List of Firm Personnel, See General Section

For full biographical listings, see the Martindale-Hubbell Law Directory

RAVEN, KIRSCHNER & NORELL, P.C. (AV)

Suite 1600, One South Church Avenue, 85701-1612
Telephone: 602-628-8700
Telefax: 602-798-5200

Donald T. Awerkamp   Barry Kirschner

Representative Clients: Pace American Bonding Company; Citibank (Arizona); Continental Medical Systems, Inc.; El Paso Natural Gas Co.; Norwest Bank Arizona; El Rio-Santa Cruz Neighborhood Health Center, Inc.; Resolution Trust Corp.; Sierra Vista Community Hospital; Southern Arizona Rehabilitation Hospital; Ford Motor Credit.

For Complete List of Firm Personnel, See General Section

For full biographical listings, see the Martindale-Hubbell Law Directory

ARKANSAS

*LITTLE ROCK,** Pulaski Co.

FRIDAY, ELDREDGE & CLARK (AV)

A Partnership including Professional Associations
Formerly, Smith, Williams, Friday, Eldredge & Clark
2000 First Commercial Building, 400 West Capitol, 72201-3493
Telephone: 501-376-2011
Telecopier: 501-376-2147; 376-6369

MEMBERS OF FIRM

James W. Moore   Walter A. Paulson, II, (P.A.)
Oscar E. Davis, Jr., (P.A.)   Christopher J. Heller (P.A.)
Michael Scott Moore (P.A.)

ASSOCIATE

Andrew T. Turner

COUNSEL

B. S. Clark

Counsel for: Union Pacific System; St. Paul Insurance Co.; Liberty Mutual Insurance Co.; Cigna Property & Casualty Co.; Arkansas Power & Light Co.; Dillard Department Stores, Inc.; First Commercial Corp.; Browning Arms Co.; Phillips Petroleum Co.; Aetna Casualty & Surety Co.

(See Next Column)

For Complete List of Firm Personnel, See General Section

For full biographical listings, see the Martindale-Hubbell Law Directory

HILBURN, CALHOON, HARPER, PRUNISKI & CALHOUN, LTD. (AV)

P.O. Box 1256, 72203-1256
Telephone: 501-372-0110
FAX: 501-372-2029
North Little Rock, Arkansas Office: Eighth Floor, The Twin City Bank Building, One Riverfront Place, P.O. Box 5551, 72119.
Telephone: 501-372-0110.
FAX: 501-372-2029.

David M. Fuqua   James M. McHaney, Jr.
Phillip W. Campbell

Representative Clients: The Twin City Bank; Merril Lynch Pierce Fenner & Smith, Inc.; Central Arkansas Risk Management Association; Smith Barney Shearson, Inc.; The Kroger Co.

For Complete List of Firm Personnel, See General Section

For full biographical listings, see the Martindale-Hubbell Law Directory

ROSE LAW FIRM, A PROFESSIONAL ASSOCIATION (AV)

120 East Fourth Street, 72201
Telephone: 501-375-9131
Telecopy: 501-375-1309

Tim Boe   James Hunter Birch
James M. Gary

Mark Alan Peoples

Representative Clients: Acxiom Corporation, ALCOA; Aromatique, Inc.; Harvest Foods; Georgia-Pacific Corporation; Merico, Inc., d/b/a Colonial Bakery; Pat Salmon & Sons, Inc.; Schering-Plough Corporation; Wal-Mart Stores, Inc.; Weyerhaeuser Company.

For Complete List of Firm Personnel, See General Section

For full biographical listings, see the Martindale-Hubbell Law Directory

WRIGHT, LINDSEY & JENNINGS (AV)

2200 Worthen Bank Building, 200 West Capitol Avenue, 72201
Telephone: 501-371-0808
Fax: 501-376-9442
Fayetteville, Arkansas Office: 101 West Mountain Street, Suite 206, 72701.
Telephone: 501-575-0808.
Fax: 501-575-0999.
Russellville, Arkansas Office: Suite E, 1110 West B Street.
Telephone: 501-968-7995.

Kathlyn Graves   John D. Davis

Representative Clients: First Electric Cooperative Corp. Reynolds Metals Co.; Timex Corp.; United Parcel Service; Worthen National Bank of Arkansas; Meyer's Bakery; Hudson Foods, Inc.; Amtran Corp.; Northern Arkansas Telephone Corp.; St. Joseph's Regional Health Center.

For Complete List of Firm Personnel, See General Section

For full biographical listings, see the Martindale-Hubbell Law Directory

CALIFORNIA

*BAKERSFIELD,** Kern Co.

KLEIN, WEGIS, DENATALE, GOLDNER & MUIR (AV)

A Partnership including Professional Corporations
(Formerly Di Giorgio, Davis, Klein, Wegis, Duggan & Friedman)
ARCO Tower, 4550 California Avenue, Second Floor, P.O. Box 11172, 93389-1172
Telephone: 805-395-1000
Telecopier: 805-326-0418
Santa Ana, California Office: Park Tower Building #610, 200 W. Santa Ana Boulevard, 92701.
Telephone: 714-285-0711.
Fax: 714-285-9003.

MEMBERS OF FIRM

Anthony J. Klein (Inc.)   Jay L. Rosenlieb

ASSOCIATES

Barry E. Rosenberg   Jeffrey W. Noe

Representative Clients: Smith International, Inc.; Sandrini Brothers Company; Nahama & Weagany Energy Co.; EIU of California, Inc.; Kern County Hay Growers Association, Inc.

For Complete List of Firm Personnel, See General Section

For full biographical listings, see the Martindale-Hubbell Law Directory

BEVERLY HILLS, Los Angeles Co.

SWERDLOW, FLORENCE & SANCHEZ, A LAW CORPORATION (AV)

Suite 828, 9401 Wilshire Boulevard, 90212
Telephone: 310-201-4700
Fax: 310-273-8680

Seymour Swerdlow
Kenneth J. Florence
Millicent N. Sanchez
Sandy K. Rathbun
Cynthia A. Woodruff
Paul C. Dempsey

For full biographical listings, see the Martindale-Hubbell Law Directory

CLAREMONT, Los Angeles Co.

JOHN C. McCARTHY (AV)

401 Harvard Avenue, 91711
Telephone: 909-621-4984
Telecopier: 909-621-5757

Reference: Bank of America, Claremont Branch.

For full biographical listings, see the Martindale-Hubbell Law Directory

COSTA MESA, Orange Co.

RUTAN & TUCKER (AV)

A Partnership including Professional Corporations
611 Anton Boulevard, Suite 1400, P.O. Box 1950, 92626
Telephone: 714-641-5100; 213-625-7586
Telecopier: 714-546-9035

MEMBERS OF FIRM

David C. Larsen (P.C.)
James L. Morris
Ernest W. Klatte, III

For Complete List of Firm Personnel, See General Section

For full biographical listings, see the Martindale-Hubbell Law Directory

*FRESNO,** Fresno Co.

DOWLING, MAGARIAN, AARON & HEYMAN, INCORPORATED (AV)

Suite 200, 6051 North Fresno Street, 93710
Telephone: 209-432-4500
Fax: 209-432-4590

Kent F. Heyman

James C. Sherwood
Mark D. Magarian

Reference: Wells Fargo Bank (Main).

For Complete List of Firm Personnel, See General Section

For full biographical listings, see the Martindale-Hubbell Law Directory

JORY, PETERSON, WATKINS & SMITH (AV)

555 West Shaw, Suite C-1, P.O. Box 5394, 93755
Telephone: 209-225-6700
Telecopier: 209-225-3416

MEMBERS OF FIRM

Jay V. Jory
John E. Peterson
Cal B. Watkins, Jr.
Michael Jens F. Smith

ASSOCIATES

William M. Woolman
Marcia A. Ross
Mark A. Pasculli

Reference: Valliwide Bank.

For full biographical listings, see the Martindale-Hubbell Law Directory

LANG, RICHERT & PATCH, A PROFESSIONAL CORPORATION (AV)

Fig Garden Financial Center, 5200 North Palm Avenue, 4th Floor, P.O. Box 40012, 93755
Telephone: 209-228-6700
Fax: 209-228-6727

Frank H. Lang
William T. Richert (1937-1993)
Robert L. Patch, II
Val W. Saldaña
Douglas E. Noll
Michael T. Hertz
Victoria J. Salisch
Bradley A. Silva
David R. Jenkins
Charles Trudrung Taylor
Mark L. Creede
Peter N. Zeitler
Charles L. Doerksen

Randall C. Nelson
Barbara A. McAuliffe
Laurie Quigley Cardot
Douglas E. Griffin
Nabil E. Zumout

(See Next Column)

References: Wells Fargo Bank (Fresno Main Office); First Interstate Bank (Fresno Main Office).

For full biographical listings, see the Martindale-Hubbell Law Directory

IRVINE, Orange Co.

ANDRADE & ASSOCIATES (AV)

Marine National Bank Building, 18401 Von Karman, Suite 350, 92715
Telephone: 714-553-1951
Telecopier: 714-553-0655

Richard B. Andrade

ASSOCIATES

Jack W. Fleming
Andrew C. Muzi
Steven S. Hanagami

OF COUNSEL

Kurt Kupferman

Representative Clients: American International Cos.; American Home Assurance; Insurance Company of North America (INA); National Union Fire Insurance of Pittsburgh, PA; Aetna Insurance Co.; Fremont Insurance Co.; Maryland Casualty; Commercial Union Insurance Co.; Superior National Insurance Co.

For full biographical listings, see the Martindale-Hubbell Law Directory

A. PATRICK NAGEL (AV)

18881 Von Karman Avenue, Suite 1450, 92715
Telephone: 714-644-1001
FAX: 714-644-1005

For full biographical listings, see the Martindale-Hubbell Law Directory

LAGUNA HILLS, Orange Co.

MICHELLE A. REINGLASS (AV)

Suite 170 23161 Millcreek Road, 92653
Telephone: 714-587-0460
FAX: 714-587-1004

For full biographical listings, see the Martindale-Hubbell Law Directory

*LOS ANGELES,** Los Angeles Co.

ADAMS, DUQUE & HAZELTINE (AV)

A Partnership including Professional Corporations
777 South Figueroa Street, Tenth Floor, 90017
Telephone: 213-620-1240
FAX: 213-896-5500
San Francisco, California Office: 500 Washington Street.
Telephone: 415-982-1240.
FAX: 415-982-0130.

MEMBERS OF FIRM

Richard R. Terzian
Lonnie E. Woolverton (P.C.)
James R. Willcox (San Francisco Office)
David L. Bacon
Ronald F. Frank
Margaret Lynn Oldendorf
Remy Kessler

For Complete List of Firm Personnel, See General Section

For full biographical listings, see the Martindale-Hubbell Law Directory

BAKER & HOSTETLER (AV)

600 Wilshire Boulevard, 90017-3212
Telephone: 213-624-2400
FAX: 213-975-1740
In Cleveland, Ohio, 3200 National City Center, 1900 East Ninth Street. Telephone: 216-621-0200.
In Columbus, Ohio, Capitol Square, Suite 2100, 65 East State Street. Telephone: 614-228-1541.
In Denver, Colorado, 303 East 17th Avenue, Suite 1100. Telephone: 303-861-0600.
In Houston, Texas, 1000 Louisiana, Suite 2000. Telephone: 713-236-0020.
In Long Beach, California: 300 Oceangate, Suite 620. *Telephone:* 310-432-2827.
In Orlando, Florida, SunBank Center, Suite 2300, 200 South Orange Avenue. Telephone: 407-649-4000.
In Washington, D. C., Washington Square, Suite 1100, 1050 Connecticut Avenue, N. W. Telephone: 202-861-1500.
In College Park, Maryland, 9658 Baltimore Boulevard, Suite 206. Telephone: 301-441-2781.
In Alexandria, Virginia, 437 North Lee Street. Telephone: 703-549-1294.
In San Francisco, California: One Sansome Street, Suite 2000. *Telephone:* 415-951-4705.

PARTNERS

Michael M. Johnson
Teresa R. Tracy

ASSOCIATE

Keith A. Fink

For Complete List of Firm Personnel, See General Section

For full biographical listings, see the Martindale-Hubbell Law Directory

Los Angeles—Continued

BUCHALTER, NEMER, FIELDS & YOUNGER, A PROFESSIONAL CORPORATION (AV)

24th Floor, 601 South Figueroa Street, 90017
Telephone: 213-891-0700
Fax: 213-896-0400
Cable Address: "Buchnem"
Telex: 68-7485
New York, New York Office: 19th Floor, 237 Park Avenue.
Telephone: 212-490-8600.
Fax: 212-490-6022.
San Francisco, California Office: 29th Floor, 333 Market Street.
Telephone: 415-227-0900.
Fax: 415-227-0770.
San Jose, California Office: 12th Floor, 50 West San Fernando Street.
Telephone: 408-298-0350.
Fax: 408-298-7683.
Newport Beach, California Office: Suite 300, 620 Newport Center Drive.
Telephone: 714-760-1121.
Fax: 714-720-0182.
Century City, California Office: Suite 2400, 1801 Century Park East.
Telephone: 213-891-0700.
Fax: 310-551-0233.

Arthur Chinski

Jamie Rudman

References: City National Bank; Wells Fargo Bank; Metrobank.

For Complete List of Firm Personnel, See General Section

For full biographical listings, see the Martindale-Hubbell Law Directory

CLARK & TREVITHICK, A PROFESSIONAL CORPORATION (AV)

800 Wilshire Boulevard, 12th Floor, 90017
Telephone: 213-629-5700
Telecopier: 213-624-9441

Philip W. Bartenetti
Dolores Cordell

References: Wells Fargo Bank (Los Angeles Main Office); National Bank of California.

For Complete List of Firm Personnel, See General Section

For full biographical listings, see the Martindale-Hubbell Law Directory

FORD & HARRISON (AV)

333 South Grand Avenue Suite 3680, 90071
Telephone: 213-680-3410
FAX: 213-680-4161
Atlanta, Georgia Office: 600 Peachtree at the Circle Building, 1275 Peachtree Street, N.E., 30309.
Telephone: 404-888-3800.
Fax: 404-888-3863.
Washington, D.C. Office: 1920 N Street, N.W., Suite 200, 20036.
Telephone: 202-463-6633.
Fax: 202-466-5705.

Michael L. Lowry
Glen H. Mertens (Resident)

ASSOCIATES

Maral Donoyan (Resident)
Kari Haugen (Resident)

Representative Clients: Coca-Cola Enterprises; Delta Air Lines, Inc.; Federal Express Corporation; Knight Publishing Company; Landmark Communications, Inc.; LIN Television Corp.; Regional Airline Assn.; Rheem Manufacturing Co.; The Standard Register Co.

For full biographical listings, see the Martindale-Hubbell Law Directory

GARTNER & YOUNG, A PROFESSIONAL CORPORATION (AV)

1925 Century Park East, Suite 2050, 90067-2709
Telephone: 310-556-3576
Fax: 310-556-8459

Naomi Young
Lawrence J. Gartner

Christopher Adams Thorn
Kimberly M. Talley
Mark E. Goldsmith
Tracy A. Chriss
Ruth de V. Bolden
Jennifer L. Futch
Philip G. Paccione

For full biographical listings, see the Martindale-Hubbell Law Directory

HAWKINS, SCHNABEL, LINDAHL & BECK (AV)

660 South Figueroa Street, Suite 1500, 90017
Telephone: 213-488-3900
Telecopier: 213-486-9883
Cable Address: "Haslin"

(See Next Column)

MEMBERS OF FIRM

Laurence H. Schnabel
George M. Lindahl
Timothy A. Gonzales

For full biographical listings, see the Martindale-Hubbell Law Directory

HILL, FARRER & BURRILL (AV)

A Partnership including Professional Corporations
35th Floor, Union Bank Square, 445 South Figueroa Street, 90071
Telephone: 213-620-0460
Fax: 213-624-4840; 488-1593

MEMBERS OF FIRM

Stanley E. Tobin (P.C.)
Jonathan M. Brandler (P.C.)
Kyle D. Brown (P.C.)
James A. Bowles (P.C.)
Stuart H. Young, Jr., (P.C.)
Ronald W. Novotny (P.C.)
James G. Johnson (P.C.)
Suzanne J. Holland
G. Cresswell Templeton III

OF COUNSEL

Edwin H. Franzen (P.C.)

ASSOCIATE

Ondrea D. Hidley

For Complete List of Firm Personnel, See General Section

For full biographical listings, see the Martindale-Hubbell Law Directory

KINDEL & ANDERSON (AV)

A Partnership including Professional Corporations
Twenty-Ninth Floor, 555 South Flower Street, 90071
Telephone: 213-680-2222
Cable Address: "Kayanda"
Telex: 67-7497
FAX: 213-688-7564
Irvine, California Office: 5 Park Plaza, Suite 1000.
Telephone: 714-752-0777.
Woodland Hills, California Office: Suite 244, 5959 Topanga Canyon Boulevard.
Telephone: 818-712-0036.
San Francisco, California Office: 580 California Street, 15th Floor.
Telephone: 415-398-0110.

MEMBERS OF FIRM

Paul J. Coady
Victor F. Yacullo (P.C.)

ASSOCIATES

Mark G. Kisicki
Mark A. McLean
Mary E. Wright

For Complete List of Firm Personnel, See General Section

For full biographical listings, see the Martindale-Hubbell Law Directory

KNEE & MASON (AV)

A Partnership
Suite 2050, 2049 Century Park East, 90067
Telephone: 310-551-0909
Fax: 310-552-9818

Howard M. Knee
Melanie C. Ross
Belle C. Mason
Lora Silverman
Gregory N. Karasik
Stephen M. Benardo

For full biographical listings, see the Martindale-Hubbell Law Directory

LANGBERG, LESLIE & GABRIEL (AV)

An Association including a Professional Corporation
2049 Century Park East Suite 3030, 90067
Telephone: 310-286-7700
Telecopier: 310-284-8355

Barry B. Langberg (A Professional Corporation)
Jody R. Leslie
Joseph M. Gabriel

Eileen M. Cohn
Michael M. Baranov
Deborah Drooz
Beth F. Dumas
Richard J. Wynne
Dwayne A. Watts
Beatrice L. Hoffman
Mitchell J. Langberg

LEGAL SUPPORT PERSONNEL

PARALEGALS

Patricia Urban
Patricia Ann Essig
Jeanne A. Logé

For full biographical listings, see the Martindale-Hubbell Law Directory

Los Angeles—Continued

LOEB AND LOEB (AV)

A Partnership including Professional Corporations
Suite 1800, 1000 Wilshire Boulevard, 90017-2475
Telephone: 213-688-3400
Telecopier: 213-688-3460; 688-3461; 688-3462
Century City, California Office: Suite 2200, 10100 Santa Monica Boulevard, Los Angeles, 90067-4164.
Telephone: 310-282-2000.
Telecopier: 310-282-2191; 282-2192.
New York, N.Y. Office: 345 Park Avenue, 10154-0037.
Telephone: 212-407-4000.
Facsimile: 212-407-4990.
Nashville, Tennessee Office: 45 Music Square West, 37203-3205.
Telephone: 615-749-8300;
Facsimile: 615-749-8308.
Rome, Italy Office: Piazza Digione 1, 00197.
Telephone: 011-396-808-8456.
Telecopier: 011-396-674-8223.

MEMBERS OF FIRM

Fred B. Griffin (Century City Office)
Richard W. Kopenhefer (Century City Office)
Raymond W. Thomas (Century City Office)

ASSOCIATES

Marita T. Covarrubias (Century City Office)
Richard Frey (Century City Office)
Joanne B. O'Donnell
Richard S. Zuniga (Century City Office)

For Complete List of Firm Personnel, See General Section

For full biographical listings, see the Martindale-Hubbell Law Directory

MITCHELL, SILBERBERG & KNUPP (AV)

A Partnership of Professional Corporations
11377 West Olympic Boulevard, 90064
Telephone: 310-312-2000
Cable Address: "Silmitch"
Telex: 69-1347
Telecopier: 310-312-3200

MEMBERS OF FIRM

Steven M. Schneider (A Professional Corporation)
Deborah P. Koeffler (A Professional Corporation)
William L. Cole (A Professional Corporation)
Lawrence A. Ginsberg (A Professional Corporation)
Mark A. Wasserman (A Professional Corporation)
Allen J. Gross (A Professional Corporation)
Lawrence A. Michaels (A Professional Corporation)
Larry C. Drapkin (A Professional Corporation)

ASSOCIATES

Anthony J. Amendola
Mary M. Courtney
Brian S. Arbetter
Michelle L. Abend
Adam Levin

Reference: First Interstate Bank of California (Headquarters, Los Angeles, California).

For Complete List of Firm Personnel, See General Section

For full biographical listings, see the Martindale-Hubbell Law Directory

MUSICK, PEELER & GARRETT (AV)

Suite 2000, One Wilshire Boulevard, 90017-3321
Telephone: 213-629-7600
Cable Address: "Peelgar"
Facsimile: 213-624-1376
San Diego, California Office: 1900 Home Savings Tower, 225 Broadway.
Telephone: 619-231-2500.
Facsimile: 619-231-1234.
San Francisco, California Office: Suite 1300, Steuart Street Tower, One Market Plaza.
Telephone: 415-281-2000.
Facsimile: 415-281-2010.
Sacramento, California Office: Suite 100, 1121 L Street.
Telephone: 916-442-1200.
Facsimile: 916-442-8644.
Fresno, California Office: 6041 North First Street.
Telephone: 209-228-1000.
Facsimile: 209-447-4670.

MEMBERS OF FIRM

Stuart W. Rudnick
Gary F. Overstreet
Robert M. Stone
Steven D. Weinstein
Richard J. Simmons
Michael W. Monk
Mark H. Van Brussel (Resident at Sacramento Office)
Linda S. Husar
Thomas E. Hill
Douglas R. Hart
Cheryl L. Schreck
David M. Lester
Philip Ewen

(See Next Column)

ASSOCIATES

Caroline G. Smith (Resident at San Francisco Office)
Kelly L. Hensley
Araceli K. Cole
Greg S. Labate
Michael R. Goldstein
S. Ellen D'Arcangelo
Son Young Kahng
Carole M. Wertheim (Resident at San Diego Office)
James T. Cahalan (Resident at Sacramento Office)
Jennifer A. Woo
Michael G. Morgan

For Complete List of Firm Personnel, See General Section

For full biographical listings, see the Martindale-Hubbell Law Directory

O'MELVENY & MYERS (AV)

400 South Hope Street, 90071-2899
Telephone: 213-669-6000
Cable Address: "Moms"
Facsimile: 213-669-6407
Century City, California Office: 1999 Avenue of the Stars, 7th Floor, 90067-6035.
Telephone: 310-553-6700.
Facsimile: 310-246-6779.
Newport Beach, California Office: 610 Newport Center Drive, Suite 1700, 92660.
Telephone: 714-760-9600.
Cable Address: "Moms".
Facsimile: 714-669-6994.
San Francisco, California Office: Embarcadero Center West Tower, 275 Battery Street, Suite 2600, 94111.
Telephone: 415-984-8700.
Facsimile: 415-984-8701.
New York, N.Y. Office: Citicorp Center, 153 East 53rd Street, 54th Floor, 10022-4611.
Telephone: 212-326-2000.
Facsimile: 212-326-2061.
Washington, D.C. Office: 555 13th Street, N.W., Suite 500 West, 20004-1109.
Telephone: 202-383-5300.
Cable Address: "Moms".
Facsimile: 202-383-5414.
Newark, New Jersey Office: One Gateway Center, 7th Floor, 07102.
Telephone: 201-639-8600.
Facsimile: 201-639-8630.
London, England Office: 10 Finsbury Square, London, EC2A 1LA.
Telephone: 011-44-171-256 8451.
Facsimile: 011-44-171-638-8205.
Tokyo, Japan Office: Sanbancho KB-6 Building, 6 Sanbancho, Chiyoda-ku, Tokyo 102, Japan.
Telephone: 011-81-3-3239-2800.
Facsimile: 011-81-3-3239-2432.
Hong Kong Office: 1104 Lippo Tower, Lippo Centre, 89 Queensway, Central Hong Kong.
Telephone: 011-852-523-8266.
Facsimile: 011-852-522-1760.

MEMBERS OF FIRM

Michael A. Curley (New York, N.Y. Office)
Scott H. Dunham
Richard N. Fisher
Cliff H. Fonstein (New York, N.Y. Office)
Catherine Burcham Hagen (Newport Beach Office)
Tom A. Jerman
F. Curt Kirschner, Jr. (San Francisco Office)
Jeffrey I. Kohn (Not admitted in CA; New York, N.Y. Office)
Gordon E. Krischer
Stephen P. Pepe
Robert A. Siegel
Victoria Dagy Stratman
Framroze M. Virjee

OF COUNSEL

Charles G. Bakaly, Jr.

SPECIAL COUNSEL

Douglas E. Dexter (San Francisco Office)
Kenneth E. Johnson
Michael G. McGuinness
Mia E. Montpas
Thomas H. Reilly (Newport Beach Office)

ASSOCIATES

Diane Wasil Biagianti (Newport Beach Office)
Debra L. Boyd
Renée Turkell Brook
William R. Burford (San Francisco Office)
K. Leigh Chapman
Apalla U. Chopra
Ira A. Daves, III
Elena Bocca Dietrich (San Francisco Office)
Kate W. Duchene
Kenneth A. Goldberg (Not admitted in CA; New York, N.Y. Office)
Edward Gregory
Peter R. Herman (Not admitted in CA; New York, N.Y. Office)
David L. Herron
Chris Hollinger
Jennifer L. Isenberg (San Francisco Office)
Patricia H. Kim (Not admitted in CA; New York, N.Y. Office)
Kathleen E. Kinney (Newport Beach Office)
Michael Cary Levine
Michele Logan Lynch
Marion K. McDonald (Washington, D.C. Office)

(See Next Column)

O'MELVENY & MYERS, *Los Angeles—Continued*

ASSOCIATES (Continued)

Linda M. Mealey-Lohmann
David J. Reis (San Francisco Office)
Pamela D. Samuels
Sam S. Shaulson (New York, N.Y. Office)
Albert J. Solecki, Jr. (Not admitted in CA; New York, N.Y. Office)
Michael I. Stockman
Janet I. Swerdlow
Kenneth J. Turnbull (Not admitted in CA; New York, N.Y. Office)
Larry A. Walraven (Newport Beach Office)
David A. Wimmer
Todd R. Wulffson (Newport Beach Office)

For Complete List of Firm Personnel, See General Section

For full biographical listings, see the Martindale-Hubbell Law Directory

SCHWARTZ, STEINSAPIR, DOHRMANN & SOMMERS (AV)

Suite 1820, 3580 Wilshire Boulevard, 90010
Telephone: 213-487-5700
Fax: 213-487-5548

MEMBERS OF FIRM

Laurence D. Steinsapir
Robert M. Dohrmann
Richard D. Sommers
Stuart Libicki
Michael R. Feinberg
Michael D. Four
Margo A. Feinberg
Henry M. Willis
Dennis J. Murphy
D. William Heine, Jr.
Claude Cazzulino
Dolly M. Gee
William T. Payne

ASSOCIATES

Kathy A. Finn
Brenda E. Sutton

For full biographical listings, see the Martindale-Hubbell Law Directory

SHEPPARD, MULLIN, RICHTER & HAMPTON (AV)

A Partnership including Professional Corporations
Forty-Eighth Floor, 333 South Hope Street, 90071-1406
Telephone: 213-620-1780
Telecopier: 213-620-1398
Cable Address: "Sheplaw"
Telex: 19-4424
Orange County, California Office: Seventh Floor, 4695 MacArthur Court, Newport Beach.
Telephone: 714-752-6400.
Telecopier: 714-851-0739.
Telex: 19-4424.
San Francisco, California Office: Seventeenth Floor, Four Embarcadero Center.
Telephone: 415-434-9100.
Telecopier: 415-434-3947.
Telex: 19-4424.
San Diego, California Office: Nineteenth Floor, 501 West Broadway.
Telephone: 619-338-6500.
Telecopier: 619-234-3815.
Telex: 19-4424.

MEMBERS OF FIRM

Charles F. Barker
Dennis Childs (San Diego Office)
John D. Collins * (San Diego Office)
John C. Cook (San Francisco Office)
Richard M. Freeman * (San Diego Office)
Guy N. Halgren (San Diego Office)
Richard L. Lotts *
David A. Maddux *
Susan Herbst Roos (San Francisco Office)
Ann Kane Smith
Dianne Baquet Smith
Daniel P. Westman (San Francisco Office)

SPECIAL COUNSEL

William V. Whelan (San Diego Office)

ASSOCIATES

Scott Brutocao
David B. Chidlaw (San Diego Office)
Katherine H. Cowan (San Francisco Office)
Angela A. Dahl (San Diego Office)
Dana DuFrane (San Francisco Office)
Stephen J. Duggan (San Francisco Office)
Laura C. Fentonmiller
Teresa M. Fitzgerald
Anna E. Goodwin (San Francisco Office)
Tracey A. Kennedy
Bridget Lanouette (San Francisco Office)
Ryan D. McCortney
Lisa Goodwin Michael
Felicia R. Reid (San Francisco Office)
Kay S. Solomon
Michael E. Wilbur (San Francisco Office)
Tara L. Wilcox (San Diego Office)

*Professional Corporation

For Complete List of Firm Personnel, See General Section

For full biographical listings, see the Martindale-Hubbell Law Directory

STOCKWELL, HARRIS, ANDERSON & WIDOM, A PROFESSIONAL CORPORATION (AV)

6222 Wilshire Boulevard, Sixth Floor, P.O. Box 48917, 90048-0917
Telephone: 213-935-6669; 818-784-6222; 310-277-6669
Fax: 213-935-0198
Santa Ana, California Office: Suite 500, 1551 N. Tustin Avenue, P.O. Box 11979.
Telephone: 714-479-1180.
Fax: 714-479-1190.
Pomona, California Office: Suite 200, 363 South Park Avenue.
Telephone: 909-623-1459; 213-622-7427.
Fax: 909-623-5554.
Ventura, California Office: Suite 270, 2151 Alessandro Drive.
Telephone: 805-653-2710; 213-617-7290.
Fax: 805-653-2731.
San Bernardino, California Office: Suite 303, 215 North "D" Street.
Telephone: 909-381-5553.
Fax: 909-384-9981.
San Diego, California Office: Suite 400, 402 West Broadway.
Telephone: 619-235-6054.
Fax: 619-231-0129.
Grover Beach, California Office: Suite 307, 200 South 13th Street.
Telephone: 805-473-0720.
Fax: 805-473-0635.

Steven I. Harris (Managing Attorney)
Patricia A. Olive
David L. Slucter (Resident, San Bernardino Office)
Richard M. Widom (Managing Attorney)
Jeffrey T. Landres (Resident, Ventura Office)
Linda S. Freeman (Santa Ana and San Diego Offices)
Michael L. Terry (Resident, Grover Beach Office)
William M. Carero
Brian R. Horan
David F. Grant (Resident, Pomona Office)
Ian D. Paige
Edward S. Muehl (Resident, Pomona Office)
Lawrence S. Mendelsohn
Edwin H. McKnight, Jr. (Resident, Santa Ana Office)
Steven A. Meline (Resident, Santa Ana Office)
Michael K. McKibbin (Resident, San Bernardino Office)
Ted L. Hirschberger
Lawrence B. Madans
Jeffrey M. Williams (Resident, Ventura Office)
Lester D. Marshall
Jeffery M. Klein (Resident, Santa Ana Office)
John R. Payne

For full biographical listings, see the Martindale-Hubbell Law Directory

LOS GATOS, Santa Clara Co.

SWEENEY, MASON & WILSON, A PROFESSIONAL LAW CORPORATION (AV)

983 University Avenue, Suite 104C, 95030
Telephone: 408-356-3000
Fax: 408-354-8839

Joseph M. Sweeney
Roger M. Mason
Kurt E. Wilson
Bradley D. Bosomworth
Allan James Manzagol

For full biographical listings, see the Martindale-Hubbell Law Directory

MENLO PARK, San Mateo Co.

LAW OFFICES OF JOHN C. SHAFFER, JR. A PROFESSIONAL LAW CORPORATION (AV)

750 Menlo Avenue, Suite 250, 94025
Telephone: 415-324-0622
Fax: 415-321-0198

John C. Shaffer, Jr.
Douglas N. Thomason

For full biographical listings, see the Martindale-Hubbell Law Directory

NEWPORT BEACH, Orange Co.

FISHER & PHILLIPS (AV)

A Partnership including Professional Corporations and Associations
4675 MacArthur Court, Suite 550, 92660
Telephone: 714-851-2424
Telecopier: 714-851-0152
Atlanta, Georgia Office: 1500 Resurgens Plaza, 945 East Paces Ferry Road, N.E., 30326.
Telephone: 404-231-1400.
Telecopier: 404-240-4249.
Telex: 54-2331.
Fort Lauderdale, Florida Office: Suite 2310 NationsBank Tower, One Financial Plaza, 33394.
Telephone: 305-525-4800.
Telecopier: 305-525-8739.
Redwood City, California Office: Suite 345, Three Lagoon Drive, 94065.
Telephone: 415-592-6160.
Telecopier: 415-592-6385.

(See Next Column)

FISHER & PHILLIPS—*Continued*

New Orleans, Louisiana Office: 3710 Place St. Charles, 201 St. Charles Avenue, 70170.
Telephone: 504-522-3303.
Telecopier: 504-529-3850.

RESIDENT MEMBERS

Robert J. Bekken
James J. McDonald, Jr.
Karl R. Lindegren

RESIDENT ASSOCIATES

Robert V. Schnitz
Georgia V. Ingram
John M. Polson
David A. Pierce
Karen Ardon
Jeffrey B. Freid
Anne M. Terra

Representative Clients: Behr Process Corp.; California Motor Car Dealers Assn.; Marie Callendar Pie Shops, Inc.; Motor Car Dealers Association of Orange County; New Car Dealers Association of San Diego; Textron, Inc.

For full biographical listings, see the Martindale-Hubbell Law Directory

McDERMOTT, WILL & EMERY (AV)

A Partnership including Professional Corporations
1301 Dove Street, Suite 500, 92660-2444
Telephone: 714-851-0633
Facsimile: 714-851-9348
Chicago, Illinois Office: 227 West Monroe Street.
Telephone: 312-372-2000.
Telex: 253565 MILAM CGO.
Facsimile: 312-984-7700.
Boston, Massachusetts Office: 75 State Street, Suite 1700.
Telephone: 617-345-5000.
Telex: 951324 MILAM BSN.
Facsimile: 617-345-5077.
Miami, Florida Office: 201 South Biscayne Boulevard.
Telephone: 305-358-3500.
Telex: 441777 LEYES.
Facsimile: 305-347-6500.
Washington, D.C. Office: 1850 K Street, N.W.
Telephone: 202-887-8000.
Telex: 253565 MILAM CGO.
Facsimile: 202-778-8087.
Los Angeles, California Office: 2049 Century Park East.
Telephone: 310-277-4110.
Facsimile: 310-277-4730.
New York, N.Y. Office: 1211 Avenue of the Americas.
Telephone: 212-768-5400.
Facsimile: 212-768-5444.
St. Petersburg, Russia Office: 2/2 Tchaikovsky Street, #517, 191187 St. Petersburg, Russia.
Telephone: (7) (812) 273-9831.
Facsimile: (7) (812) 9831.
Vilnius, Lithuania Office: Smetonos 6, 2600 Vilnius, Lithuania.
Telephone: 370 2 61-43-08.
Facsimile: 370 2 22-79-55.
Associated (Independent) Offices:
Brussels, Blegium: Uettwiller Grelon Lippens Dekeyser, 73 avenue Vandendriessche, 1150 Brussels, Belgium.
Telephone: (32) (2) 772-87-50.
Facsimile: (32) (2) 772-87-52.
London, England: Paisner & Co, Bouverie House, 154 Fleet Street, London EC4A 2DQ, England.
Telephone: (44) (71) 353-0299.
Facsimile: (44) (71) 583-8621.
Paris, France: Uettwiller Grelon Gout Canat & Associes, 68, boulevard de Courcelles, 75017 Paris, France.
Telephone: (33) (1) 48 88 89 00.
Facsimile: (33) (1) 48 88 05 50.

MEMBER OF FIRM

Peter D. Holbrook

For Complete List of Firm Personnel, See General Section

For full biographical listings, see the Martindale-Hubbell Law Directory

*OAKLAND,** Alameda Co.

CORBETT & KANE, A PROFESSIONAL CORPORATION (AV)

2000 Powell Street, Suite 1450 (Emeryville), 94608
Telephone: 510-547-2434
Fax: 510-658-5014
San Francisco Office: Suite 1800, Spear Street Tower, One Market Plaza.
Telephone: 415-956-4100.
Fax: 415-956-1552.

Gerald R. Lucey
Judith Droz Keyes
W. Daniel Clinton
Joseph E. Wiley
Mary Maloney Roberts
Sharon J. Grodin
Tim J. Emert
Suzanne I. Price
Monna R. Radulovich

(See Next Column)

Patricia M. Kelly
Douglas J. Farmer
Douglas N. Freifeld
Aron Cramer
Philip Obbard
Ian P. Fellerman
Darren E. Temkin-Nadel
Denise M. DeRose
Peter M. Chester
Joan Pugh Newman

SPECIAL COUNSEL

Glenn J. Borromeo

OF COUNSEL

Laurence P. Corbett

For full biographical listings, see the Martindale-Hubbell Law Directory

SAPERSTEIN, GOLDSTEIN, DEMCHAK & BALLER, A PROFESSIONAL CORPORATION (AV)

1300 Clay Street, 11th Floor, 94612
Telephone: 510-763-9800

Barry Goldstein
Teresa Demchak
Morris J. Baller

OF COUNSEL

Guy T. Saperstein

David Borgen
Linda M. Dardarian
Jollee C. Faber
Jeremy Friedman
Susan Guberman-Garcia
Antonio M. Lawson
Jack W. Lee
David E. Pesonen
Kristine A. Poplawski
Sheila Y. Thomas

For full biographical listings, see the Martindale-Hubbell Law Directory

*REDWOOD CITY,** San Mateo Co.

FISHER & PHILLIPS (AV)

A Partnership including Professional Corporations and Associations
Suite 345, Three Lagoon Drive, 94065
Telephone: 415-592-6160
Telecopier: 415-592-6385
Atlanta, Georgia Office: 1500 Resurgens Plaza, 945 East Paces Ferry Road, N.E., 30326.
Telephone: 404-231-1400.
Telecopier: 404-240-4249.
Telex: 54-2331.
Fort Lauderdale, Florida Office: Suite 2310 NationsBank Tower, One Financial Plaza, 33394.
Telephone: 305-525-4800.
Telecopier: 305-525-8739.
Newport Beach, California Office: 4675 MacArthur Court, Suite 550, 92660.
Telephone: 714-851-2424.
Telecopier: 714-851-0152.
New Orleans, Louisiana Office: 3710 Place St. Charles, 201 St. Charles Avenue, 70170.
Telephone: 504-522-3303.
Telecopier: 504-529-3850.

RESIDENT MEMBERS

Ned A. Fine
John D. McLachlan

RESIDENT ASSOCIATES

Lynn D. Lieber
Annette Marie Houck
Donald E. Cope
John Phillip Boggs

Representative Clients: California Motor Car Dealers Assn.; Centex Cement; Consolidated Freightways, Inc.; The Limited; Nestle Beverage Co.; Waste Management of North America; Willamette Industries, Inc.; Zurn Nepco.

For full biographical listings, see the Martindale-Hubbell Law Directory

*SACRAMENTO,** Sacramento Co.

WILKE, FLEURY, HOFFELT, GOULD & BIRNEY (AV)

A Partnership including Professional Corporations
400 Capitol Mall, Suite 2200, 95814-4408
Telephone: 916-441-2430
Telefax: 916-442-6664
Mailing Address: P.O. Box 15559, 95852-0559

MEMBERS OF FIRM

Richard H. Hoffelt (Inc.)
William A. Gould, Jr., (Inc.)
Philip R. Birney (Inc.)
Thomas G. Redmon (Inc.)
Scott L. Gassaway
Donald Rex Heckman II (Inc.)
Alan G. Perkins
Bradley N. Webb
Ernest James Krtil
Robert R. Mirkin
Matthew W. Powell
Mark L. Andrews
Stephen K. Marmaduke
David A. Frenznick
John R. Valencia
Angus M. MacLeod

(See Next Column)

WILKE, FLEURY, HOFFELT, GOULD & BIRNEY, *Sacramento—Continued*

ASSOCIATES

Paul A. Dorris
Kelli M. Kennaday
Tracy S. Hendrickson
Joseph G. De Angelis
Jennifer L. Kennedy
Anthony J. DeCristoforo
Rachel N. Kook
Alicia F. From
Michael Polis
Matthew J. Smith
Wayne L. Ordos

OF COUNSEL

Sherman C. Wilke
Anita Seipp Marmaduke
Benjamin G. Davidian

Representative Clients: NOR-CAL Mutual Insurance Co.; California Optometric Assn.; KPMG Peat Marwick; Glaxo, Inc.

For full biographical listings, see the Martindale-Hubbell Law Directory

*SAN BERNARDINO,** San Bernardino Co.

GRESHAM, VARNER, SAVAGE, NOLAN & TILDEN (AV)

Suite 300, 600 North Arrowhead Avenue, 92401
Telephone: 909-884-2171
Fax: 909-888-2120
Victorville, California Office: 14011 Park Avenue, Suite 140.
Telephone: 619-243-2889.
Fax: 619-243-3057.
Riverside, California Office: 3737 Main Street, Suite 420.
Telephone: 714-274-7777.
Fax: 714-274-7770.

MEMBERS OF FIRM

Allen B. Gresham
Stephan G. Saleson
Richard D. Marca

Representative Clients: Kaiser Resources, Inc.; Southern California Edison Co.; General Telephone Company of California; Southern California Gas Co.; General Motors Corp.; North American Chemical Co.; TTX Company; Sunwest Materials; California Portland Cement Co.; Amax Gold, Inc.; Stater Bros. Markets.

For Complete List of Firm Personnel, See General Section

For full biographical listings, see the Martindale-Hubbell Law Directory

*SAN DIEGO,** San Diego Co.

FERRIS & BRITTON, A PROFESSIONAL CORPORATION (AV)

1600 First National Bank Center, 401 West A Street, 92101
Telephone: 619-233-3131
Fax: 619-232-9316

Alfred G. Ferris
Christopher Q. Britton
Steven J. Pynes
Michael R. Weinstein

Representative Clients: Allstate Insurance Co.; Cox Communications, Inc.; Enterprise Rent-a-Car; Exxon; Immuno Pharmaceutics, Inc.; Invitrogen Corporation; Teleport Communications Group; Southwest Airlines; Times-Mirror Cable Television.

For Complete List of Firm Personnel, See General Section

For full biographical listings, see the Martindale-Hubbell Law Directory

GRAY CARY WARE & FREIDENRICH, A PROFESSIONAL CORPORATION (AV)

Gray Cary Established in 1927
Ware & Freidenrich Established in 1969
401 "B" Street, Suite 1700, 92101
Telephone: 619-699-2700
Telecopier: 619-236-1048
Palo Alto, California Office: 400 Hamilton Avenue.
Telephone: 415-328-6561.
La Jolla, California Office: Suite 575, 1200 Prospect Street.
Telephone: 619-454-9101.
El Centro, California Office: 1224 State Street, P.O. Box 2890.
Telephone: 619-353-6140.

Robert W. Bell, Jr.
J. Rod Betts
David B. Geerdes
Peter N. Larrabee
Josiah L. Neeper
Richard A. Paul
Fred M. Plevin
William B. Sailer
James K. Smith
Merrill F. Storms, Jr.

Therese H. Hymer
Nancy Kawano
Michael C. Sullivan

Representative Clients: San Diego Transit Corp.; General Dynamics Corp.; Imperial Savings Assn.; Zoological Society of San Diego; Mercy Hospital and Medical Center; Sony Manufacturing Company of America.

For Complete List of Firm Personnel, See General Section

For full biographical listings, see the Martindale-Hubbell Law Directory

LUCE, FORWARD, HAMILTON & SCRIPPS (AV)

A Partnership including Professional Corporations
600 West Broadway, Suite 2600, 92101
Telephone: 619-236-1414
Fax: 619-232-8311
La Jolla, California Office: 4275 Executive Square, Suite 800, 92037.
Telephone: 619-535-2639.
Fax: 619-453-2812.
Los Angeles, California Office: 777 South Figueroa, 36th Floor, 90017.
Telephone: 213-892-4992.
Fax: 213-892-7731.
San Francisco, California Office: 100 Bush Street, 20th Floor, 94104.
Telephone: 415-395-7900.
Fax: 415-395-7949.
New York, N.Y. Office: Citicorp Center, 153 East 53rd Street, 26th Floor, 10022.
Telephone: 212-754-1414.
Fax: 212-644-9727.

MEMBERS OF FIRM

George S. Howard, Jr.
Michael L. Jensen
Albert T. Harutunian III
Craig A. Schloss
Robert A. Levy
Daniel N. Riesenberg
Kathryn A. Bernert
Mary L. Russell

ASSOCIATES

William T. Earley
Maria C. Rodriguez
Jeffrey K. Brown
Tami L. Johnson Penner
Kelly Capen Douglas

For Complete List of Firm Personnel, See General Section

For full biographical listings, see the Martindale-Hubbell Law Directory

OLINS, FOERSTER & HAYES (AV)

A Partnership including Professional Corporations
2214 Second Avenue, 92101
Telephone: 619-238-1601
Fax: 619-238-1613

MEMBERS OF FIRM

Douglas F. Olins (A P.C.)
Barrett J. Foerster (A P.C.)
Dennis J. Hayes

ASSOCIATE

Julia Houchin Guroff

Representative Clients: United Food and Commercial Workers International Union, AFL-CIO; United Food and Commercial Workers, Locals 1036 and 1428; American Federation of State, County and Municipal Employees, Local 127; American Postal Workers Union, California Area Local; American Postal Workers Union, San Diego Chapter; Association of Orange County Deputy Sheriffs; Sacramento County Deputy Sheriffs Assn.; Santa Ana Firemen's Benevolent Association; San Bernardino Public Employees Association.

For full biographical listings, see the Martindale-Hubbell Law Directory

*SAN FRANCISCO,** San Francisco Co.

ALTSHULER, BERZON, NUSSBAUM, BERZON & RUBIN (AV)

Suite 300, 177 Post Street, 94108
Telephone: 415-421-7151
Telecopier: 415-362-8064

Fred H. Altshuler
Marsha S. Berzon
Stephen P. Berzon
Peter D. Nussbaum
Michael Rubin
Lowell Finley
Jeffrey B. Demain
Indira Talwani
Daniel T. Purtell
Scott A. Kronland

For full biographical listings, see the Martindale-Hubbell Law Directory

BREON, O'DONNELL, MILLER, BROWN & DANNIS (AV)

19th Floor, Stevenson Place, 71 Stevenson Street, 94105
Telephone: 415-543-4111
Fax: 415-543-4384
Palos Verdes Estates, California Office: Suite 3A, 2550 Via Tejon, 90274.
Telephone: 310-373-6857.
FAX: 310-373-6808.
Salinas, California Office: Suite H120, 17842 Moro Road, Suite F120, 93907.
Telephone: 408-663-0470.

MEMBERS OF FIRM

Keith V. Breon
Margaret E. O'Donnell
David G. Miller (Resident, Palos Verdes Estates Office)
Priscilla Brown
Gregory J. Dannis
Emi R. Uyehara
Bridget A. Flanagan
Nancy B. Bourne

(See Next Column)

BREON, O'DONNELL, MILLER, BROWN & DANNIS—*Continued*

Kathryn Luhe
Laurie S. Juengert
Marilyn J. Cleveland
Joan Birdt (Resident, Palos Verdes Estates Office)
David A. Wolf
Brant T. Lee
Claudia L. Madrigal
Randall O. Parent
Peter W. Sturges
Laurie E. Reynolds
Guy A. Bryant
Jane E. Mitchell

SPECIAL COUNSEL

Martha Buell Scott

Representative Clients: Monterey Peninsula Unified School Dist.; Mt. Diablo Unified School Dist.; Palo Alto Unified School Dist.; Santa Cruz City Schools.

For full biographical listings, see the Martindale-Hubbell Law Directory

BRONSON, BRONSON & MCKINNON (AV)

A Partnership including Professional Corporations
505 Montgomery Street, 94111-2514
Telephone: 415-986-4200
Fax: 415-982-1394
Telex: 255921 KINBR UR
Los Angeles, California Office: 444 South Flower Street, 24th Floor.
Telephone: 213-627-2000.
Santa Rosa, California Office: 100 B Street, Suite 400.
Telephone: 707-527-8110.
San Jose, California Office: 10 Almaden Boulevard, Suite 600.
Telephone: 408-293-0599.

MEMBERS OF FIRM

Edwin L. Currey, Jr.
Gilmore F. Diekmann, Jr.
Robert W. Tollen
Patricia H. Cullison

OF COUNSEL

David L. Hall

ASSOCIATES

Lynn A. Bersch
Evelyn G. Heilbrunn
Sarah Robertson McCuaig
Mary Bossart Halfpenny

For Complete List of Firm Personnel, See General Section

For full biographical listings, see the Martindale-Hubbell Law Directory

BUELL & BERNER (AV)

A Partnership of Professional Corporations
101 California Street, 22nd Floor, 94111
Telephone: 415-391-5011
Fax: 415-391-7383

MEMBERS OF FIRM

E. Rick Buell, II, (P.C.)
Curtis William Berner (P.C.)

For full biographical listings, see the Martindale-Hubbell Law Directory

CORBETT & KANE, A PROFESSIONAL CORPORATION (AV)

Suite 1800, Spear Street Tower, One Market Plaza, 94105
Telephone: 415-956-4100
Fax: 415-956-1552
Oakland, California Office: 2000 Powell Street, Suite 1450 (Emeryville).
Telephone: 510-547-2434.
Fax: 510-658-5014.

Gerald R. Lucey
Judith Droz Keyes
W. Daniel Clinton
Joseph E. Wiley
Mary Maloney Roberts
Sharon J. Grodin
Tim J. Emert
Suzanne I. Price
Monna R. Radulovich

Patricia M. Kelly
Douglas J. Farmer
Douglas N. Freifeld
Aron Cramer
Philip Obbard
Ian P. Fellerman
Darren E. Temkin-Nadel
Denise M. DeRose
Peter M. Chester
Joan Pugh Newman
Matthew H. Burrows

SPECIAL COUNSEL

Glenn J. Borromeo

OF COUNSEL

Laurence P. Corbett

For full biographical listings, see the Martindale-Hubbell Law Directory

LIEFF, CABRASER & HEIMANN (AV)

Embarcadero Center West, 30th Floor, 275 Battery Street, 94111
Telephone: 415-956-1000
Telecopier: 415-956-1008

(See Next Column)

Robert L. Lieff
Elizabeth J. Cabraser
Richard M. Heimann
William Bernstein
William B. Hirsch
James M. Finberg
Karen E. Karpen
Michael F. Ram
William M. Audet
Joseph R. Saveri
Steven E. Fineman
Donald C. Arbitblit
Robert J. Nelson

Kristine E. Bailey
Suzanne A. Barr
Kelly M. Dermody
Deborah A. Kemp
Anthony K. Lee
Jacqueline E. Mottek
Kimberly W. Pate
Melanie M. Piech
Morris A. Ratner
Rhonda L. Woo

For full biographical listings, see the Martindale-Hubbell Law Directory

KATHLEEN M. LUCAS (AV)

Suite 500, 530 Bush Street, 94108
Telephone: 415-433-6166
FAX: 415-433-6517

ASSOCIATES

David S. Schwartz
Erika A. Zucker

For full biographical listings, see the Martindale-Hubbell Law Directory

ROSEN, BIEN & ASARO (AV)

Eighth Floor, 155 Montgomery Street, 94104
Telephone: 415-433-6830
Fax: 415-433-7104

Sanford Jay Rosen
Michael W. Bien
Andrea G. Asaro

Stephen M. Liacouras
Hilary A. Fox
Thomas Nolan
Mary Ann Cryan (Not admitted in CA)
Donna Petrine

For full biographical listings, see the Martindale-Hubbell Law Directory

SCHACHTER, KRISTOFF, ORENSTEIN & BERKOWITZ (AV)

505 Montgomery Street, 14th Floor, 94111
Telephone: 415-391-3333
Telecopier: 415-392-6589

MEMBERS OF FIRM

Victor Schachter
Robert P. Kristoff
Morton H. Orenstein
Alan R. Berkowitz
Thomas E. Geidt
Ronald J. Souza (APLC, Chief Counsel)
Steven R. Blackburn

ASSOCIATES

Allen M. Kato
Kathleen Dillon Hunt
Daniel A. Briskin
Lisa Bradley
Joseph D. Miller
Gil B. Fried
Chandler A. Rand
Lo Mei Seh
Sharon Zezima

OF COUNSEL

Gale Heuman Borden
John F. Penrose

For full biographical listings, see the Martindale-Hubbell Law Directory

M. GERALD SCHWARTZBACH (AV)

901 Market Street, Suite 230, 94103
Telephone: 415-777-3828
Fax: 415-777-3584

For full biographical listings, see the Martindale-Hubbell Law Directory

*SAN JOSE,** Santa Clara Co.

FERRARI, ALVAREZ, OLSEN & OTTOBONI, A PROFESSIONAL CORPORATION (AV)

333 West Santa Clara Street, Suite 700, 95113
Telephone: 408-280-0535
Fax: 408-280-0151
Palo Alto, California Office: 550 Hamilton Avenue.
Telephone: 415-327-3233.

Clarence J. Ferrari, Jr.
Kent E. Olsen
John M. Ottoboni
Richard S. Bebb
James J. Eller
Robert C. Danneskiold
Terence M. Kane
Emma Peña Madrid
John P. Thurau
Roger D. Wintle
Christopher E. Cobey

Michael D. Brayton
Lisa Intrieri Caputo
Jil Dalesandro
Gregory R. Dietrich
J. Timothy Maximoff
Joseph W. Mell, Jr.
George P. Mulcaire
Eleanor C. Schuermann
Melva M. Vollersen

(See Next Column)

FERRARI, ALVAREZ, OLSEN & OTTOBONI A PROFESSIONAL CORPORATION, *San Jose—Continued*

OF COUNSEL

Edward M. Alvarez

For full biographical listings, see the Martindale-Hubbell Law Directory

MCPHARLIN & SPRINKLES (AV)

Fairmont Plaza, 50 West San Fernando, Suite 810, 95113
Telephone: 408-293-1900
Fax: 408-293-1999

MEMBERS OF FIRM

Linda Hendrix McPharlin | Catherine C. Sprinkles

ASSOCIATES

Timothy B. McCormick | Mary Lee Malysz

For full biographical listings, see the Martindale-Hubbell Law Directory

*SANTA ANA,** Orange Co.

RICKS & ANDERSON, A LAW CORPORATION (AV)

Suite 970, Griffin Towers, 5 Hutton Centre Drive, 92707-5754
Telephone: 714-966-9190

Cecil E. Ricks, Jr. | Annette L. Anderson

For full biographical listings, see the Martindale-Hubbell Law Directory

SANTA MONICA, Los Angeles Co.

FOGEL, FELDMAN, OSTROV, RINGLER & KLEVENS, A LAW CORPORATION (AV)

1620 26th Street, Suite 100 South, 90404-4040
Telephone: 310-453-6711
Fax: 310-828-2191

Daniel Fogel (1923-1991) | Robert M. Turner
Lester G. Ostrov | Jerome L. Ringler
Larry R. Feldman | Richard L. Rosett
Joel N. Klevens | Jon H. Levenstein

Gerald J. Miller | Leighanne Lake
Stephen D. Rothschild | Thomas H. Peters

OF COUNSEL

Carol S. May

Reference: Republic Bank of California, Beverly Hills, California.

For full biographical listings, see the Martindale-Hubbell Law Directory

HAIGHT, BROWN & BONESTEEL (AV)

A Partnership including Professional Corporations
1620 26th Street, Suite 4000 North, P.O. Box 680, 90404
Telephone: 310-449-6000
Telecopier: 310-829-5117
Telex: 705837
Santa Ana, California Office: Suite 900, 5 Hutton Centre Drive.
Telephone: 714-754-1100.
Telecopier: 714-754-0826.
Riverside, California Office: 3750 University Avenue, Suite 650.
Telephone: 909-341-8300.
Fax: 909-341-8309.
San Francisco, California Office: Suite 300, 201 Sansome Street.
Telephone: 415-986-7700.
Fax: 415-986-6945.

MEMBERS OF FIRM

Harold Hansen Brown (A Professional Corporation) | George Christensen
Neil G. McNiece

For Complete List of Firm Personnel, See General Section

For full biographical listings, see the Martindale-Hubbell Law Directory

STOKES & MURPHY (AV)

520 Broadway, Suite 300, 90401
Telephone: 310-451-3337
Atlanta, Georgia Office: Waterstone Suite 350, 4751 Best Road.
Telephone: 404-766-0076,
Fax: 404-766-8823.

Robert L. Murphy

RESIDENT ASSOCIATES

Tricia D. Mading | Coleen P. Hennig

For full biographical listings, see the Martindale-Hubbell Law Directory

*SANTA ROSA,** Sonoma Co.

BELDEN, ABBEY, WEITZENBERG & KELLY, A PROFESSIONAL CORPORATION (AV)

1105 North Dutton Avenue, P.O. Box 1566, 95402
Telephone: 707-542-5050
Telecopier: 707-542-2589

Thomas P. Kelly, Jr. | Richard W. Abbey

Representative Clients: Exchange Bank of Santa Rosa; Westamerica Bank; North Bay Title Co.; Northwestern Title Security Co.; Geyser Peak Winery; Arrowood Vineyards & Winery; Hansel Ford; Santa Rosa City School District.

For Complete List of Firm Personnel, See General Section

For full biographical listings, see the Martindale-Hubbell Law Directory

COLORADO

*DENVER,** Denver Co.

DUFFORD & BROWN, P.C. (AV)

1700 Broadway, Suite 1700, 80290-1701
Telephone: 303-861-8013
Facsimile: 303-832-3804

Thomas G. Brown | Douglas P. Ruegsegger
David W. Furgason | Scott J. Mikulecky

Thomas E. J. Hazard

Representative Clients: CF&I Steel, L.P.; Reorganized CF&I Steel Corporation; Reorganized Colorado & Wyoming Railway Company; Colorado Permanente Medical Group, P.C.; Colorado Company Insurance Authority.

For Complete List of Firm Personnel, See General Section

For full biographical listings, see the Martindale-Hubbell Law Directory

EIBERGER, STACY, SMITH & MARTIN (AV)

A Partnership including Professional Corporations
3500 Republic Plaza, 370 Seventeenth Street, 80202-5635
Telephone: 303-534-3500
Telecopier: 303-595-9554

MEMBERS OF FIRM

Carl F. Eiberger | Rodney L. Smith (P.C.)
David H. Stacy (P.C.) | Raymond W. Martin (P.C.)
Lawrence D. Stone (P.C.)

ASSOCIATES

Paul F. Hodapp | David M. Bost
Susan M. Schaecher | Kim L. Ritter

Representative Clients: U.S. West, Inc.; Super Valu, Inc.; The Denver Post Corp.; Cub Foods; Rocky Mountain Motorist d/b/a/ AAA; Enterprise Rent-A-Car Co.; Times Mirror Corp.; Service Merchandise, Inc.; Wright-McGill/Eagle Claw; EG&G - Rocky Flats.

For full biographical listings, see the Martindale-Hubbell Law Directory

GREGSON LAW OFFICES, P.C. (AV)

1775 Mellon Financial Center, 1775 Sherman Street, 80203
Telephone: 303-861-2702
Fax: 303-861-2706

Ronald E. Gregson

Hugh S. Pixler | Bradley M. Knepper

For full biographical listings, see the Martindale-Hubbell Law Directory

LARRY F. HOBBS, P.C. (AV)

Colorado State Bank Building, 1600 Broadway, Suite 1900, 80202
Telephone: 303-861-7070
Telecopier: 303-861-7511

Larry F. Hobbs

For full biographical listings, see the Martindale-Hubbell Law Directory

HOLLAND & HART (AV)

Suite 2900, 555 Seventeenth Street, P.O. Box 8749, 80201
Telephone: 303-295-8000
Cable Address: "Holhart Denver"
Telecopier: 303-295-8261
TWX: 910-931-0568
Denver Tech Center, Colorado Office: Suite 1050, 4601 DTC Boulevard.
Telephone: 303-290-1600.
Telecopier: 303-290-1606.

(See Next Column)

HOLLAND & HART—*Continued*

Aspen, Colorado Office: 600 East Main Street.
Telephone: 303-925-3476.
Telecopier: 303-925-9367.
Boulder, Colorado Office: Suite 500, 1050 Walnut.
Telephone: 303-473-2700.
Telecopier: 303-473-2720.
Colorado Springs, Colorado Office: Suite 1000, 90 S. Cascade Avenue.
Telephone: 719-475-7730.
Telex: 82077 SHHTLX.
Telecopier: 719-634-2461.
Washington, D.C. Office: Suite 310, 1001 Pennsylvania Avenue, N.W.
Telephone: 202-638-5500.
Telecopier: 202-737-8998.
Boise, Idaho Office: Suite 1400, West One Plaza, 101 South Capitol Boulevard, P.O. Box 2527.
Telephone: 208-342-5000.
Telecopier: 208-343-8869.
Billings, Montana Office: Suite 1500, First Interstate Center, 401 North 31st Street, P.O. Box 639.
Telephone: 406-252-2166.
Telecopier: 406-252-1669.
Salt Lake City, Utah Office: Suite 880, 111 East Broadway.
Telephone: 801-578-6000.
FAX: 801-578-6010.
Cheyenne, Wyoming Office: Holland & Hart, A Partnership including Professional Corporations, Suite 500, 2020 Carey Avenue, P.O. Box 1347.
Telephone: 307-778-4200.
Telecopier: 307-778-8175.
Jackson, Wyoming Office: Holland & Hart, A Partnership including Professional Corporations, Suite 2, 175 South King Street, P.O. Box 68.
Telephone: 307-739-9741.
Telecopier: 307-739-9744.

MEMBERS OF FIRM

Warren L. Tomlinson (Retired)
Gregory A. Eurich
John M. Husband
Brian Muldoon
Jeffrey T. Johnson
Sandra R. Goldman
Renée W. O'Rourke

SPECIAL COUNSEL

James J. Gonzales
Brian M. Mumaugh

ASSOCIATES

Judith A. (Jude) Biggs
Sunhee Juhon
David D. Powell, Jr.
Carlos A. Samour, Jr.

DENVER TECH CENTER, COLORADO RESIDENT PARTNER

Michael S. Beaver

BOULDER, COLORADO ASSOCIATE

Judith A. (Jude) Biggs

COLORADO SPRINGS, COLORADO RESIDENT SPECIAL COUNSEL

Elaine Holland Turner

WASHINGTON, D.C. RESIDENT ASSOCIATE

C. William Groscup

BOISE, IDAHO RESIDENT OF COUNSEL

Debra K. Ellers
Brian J. King

BILLINGS, MONTANA PARTNER

Paul D. Miller

CHEYENNE, WYOMING PARTNER

Edward W. Harris

CHEYENNE, WYOMING RESIDENT ASSOCIATE

Bradley T. Cave

For Complete List of Firm Personnel, See General Section

For full biographical listings, see the Martindale-Hubbell Law Directory

HOLME ROBERTS & OWEN LLC (AV)

Suite 4100, 1700 Lincoln, 80203
Telephone: 303-861-7000
Telex: 45-4460
Telecopier: 303-866-0200
Boulder, Colorado Office: Suite 400, 1401 Pearl Street.
Telephone: 303-444-5955.
Telecopier: 303-444-1063.
Colorado Springs, Colorado Office: Suite 1300, 90 South Cascade Avenue.
Telephone: 719-473-3800.
Telecopier: 719-633-1518.
Salt Lake City, Utah Office: Suite 1100, 111 East Broadway.
Telephone: 801-521-5800.
Telecopier: 801-521-9639.
London, England Office: 4th Floor, Mellier House, 26a Albemarle Street.
Telephone: 44-171-499-8776.
Telecopier: 44-171-499-7769.
Moscow, Russia Office: 14 Krivokolenny Pr., Suite 30, 101000.
Telephone: 095-925-7816.
Telecopier: 095-923-2726.

(See Next Column)

MEMBERS OF FIRM

David T. Mitzner
John R. Webb
Richard L. Nagl (Colorado Springs Office)
Carolyn E. Daniels
Brent E. Rychener (Colorado Springs Office)
Susan E. Duffey Campbell (Colorado Springs Office)

For Complete List of Firm Personnel, See General Section

For full biographical listings, see the Martindale-Hubbell Law Directory

LONG & JAUDON, P.C. (AV)

The Bailey Mansion, 1600 Ogden Street, 80218-1414
Telephone: 303-832-1122
FAX: 303-832-1348

James A. Dierker
Gary B. Blum
Margaret J. Walton

Representative Clients: St. Joseph Hospital; King Soopers, Inc. (Dillon Companies, Inc.).

For Complete List of Firm Personnel, See General Section

For full biographical listings, see the Martindale-Hubbell Law Directory

LAW OFFICES OF JOHN W. MCKENDREE (AV)

Creswell Mansion, 1244 Grant Street, 80203
Telephone: 303-861-8906
Fax: 303-861-7773

John W. McKendree

ASSOCIATES

Deana L. Vogel Goodman
Shelley Wittevrongel
Elizabeth G. McKendree

Counsel For: Colorado-Wyoming Teamsters Construction Workers Local Union No. 13; United Brotherhood of Carpenters and Joiners of America Local 1583; International Federation of Petroleum and Chemical Workers; International Labor Relations Services, Inc.; Teamsters Local 13 Health and Welfare Trust Fund; Teamsters Local 13 Vacation Trust Fund; Colorado Centennial District Counsel of Carpenters; Boilermakers Lodge 101; Brakemans' Association of America; Boilermakers National Pension Trust.

For full biographical listings, see the Martindale-Hubbell Law Directory

ROBERT L. MORRIS & ASSOCIATES, P.C. (AV)

Suite 630, 7800 East Union Avenue, Denver Technological Center, 80237
Telephone: 303-779-4664
Telecopier: 303-779-4854

Robert L. Morris
Robert T. Clark

SEMPLE & JACKSON, P.C. (AV)

The Chancery Building, Suite 1603, 1120 Lincoln Street, 80203
Telephone: 303-595-0941
Fax: 303-861-9608

Martin Semple
Michael H. Jackson
Franklin A. Nachman
Patrick B. Mooney

Representative Clients: Denver Public Schools; Adams County School District No. 50; City of Aurora; Denver Center for the Performing Arts; Intermountain Rural Electric Association; City of Thornton; Aspen Imaging International, Inc.; National Printing & Packaging Corp.; City of Englewood.

For full biographical listings, see the Martindale-Hubbell Law Directory

SHERMAN & HOWARD L.L.C. (AV)

Attorneys at Law
633 Seventeenth Street, Suite 3000, 80202
Telephone: 303-297-2900
Telecopier: 303-298-0940
Colorado Springs, Colorado Office: Suite 1500, 90 South Cascade Avenue, 80903.
Telephone: 719-475-2440.
Las Vegas, Nevada Office: Swendseid & Stern a member in Sherman & Howard L.L.C., 317 Sixth Street, 89101.
Telephone: 702-387-6073.
Reno, Nevada Office: Swendseid & Stern, a member in Sherman & Howard L.L.C., 50 West Liberty Street, Suite 660, 89501.
Telephone: 702-323-1980.

James E. Hautzinger
E. Lee Dale
Charles W. Newcom
Raymond M. Deeny (Colorado Springs Office)
W.V. Bernie Siebert
J. Mark Baird
Andrew W. Volin
Theodore A. Olsen
N. Dawn Webber (Colorado Springs Office)
Glenn H. Schlabs (Colorado Springs Office)
Elizabeth I. Kiovsky
Wayne W. Williams (Colorado Springs Office)

Representative Clients: AT&T Corp.; Eastman Kodak Co.; Newmont Gold Corp.; Rockwell International Corp.; Public Service Company of Colorado.

(See Next Column)

SHERMAN & HOWARD L.L.C., *Denver—Continued*

For Complete List of Firm Personnel, See General Section

For full biographical listings, see the Martindale-Hubbell Law Directory

STETTNER, MILLER AND COHN, P.C. (AV)

Lawrence Street Center, Suite 1000, 1380 Lawrence Street, 80204-2058
Telephone: 303-534-0273
Fax: 303-534-5036

Kenneth R. Stettner
Robert R. Miller
Robert I. Cohn
Katherine Ann Raabe
John S. Finn
Bruce C. Anderson
William C. Berger
Daniel Grossman

Representative Clients: Associated General Contractors of Colorado, Building Chapter, Inc.; Swedish Medical Center; The Aetna Casualty and Surety Co.; McDonald's Corp; Hensel Phelps Construction Co.; Adams County School District No. 14; Weitz-Cohen Construction Co.; Federal Express Corporation; McLane Co., Inc.; Health One.

For full biographical listings, see the Martindale-Hubbell Law Directory

*GOLDEN,** Jefferson Co.

BRADLEY, CAMPBELL, CARNEY & MADSEN, PROFESSIONAL CORPORATION (AV)

1717 Washington Avenue, 80401-1994
Telephone: 303-278-3300
Fax: 303-278-3379

Earl K. Madsen
Russell Carparelli
John N. Galbavy

Counsel for: Adolph Coors Co.; Coors Brewing Co.; Evergreen National Bank, Evergreen, Colorado; Coors Ceramics Co.; Clear Creek National Bank, Georgetown, Colorado; ASARCO, Inc.; Morrison-Knudsen; Westinghouse Electric Corp.
Local Counsel for: Public Service Company of Colorado.
Reference: Colorado National Bank, Denver, Colorado.

For Complete List of Firm Personnel, See General Section

For full biographical listings, see the Martindale-Hubbell Law Directory

LAKEWOOD, Jefferson Co.

PLAUT LIPSTEIN MORTIMER PC (AV)

Suite C-400, 12600 West Colfax Avenue, 80215
Telephone: 303-232-5151
Fax: 303-232-5161
Denver, Colorado Office: 2750 Lincoln Center. 1660 Lincoln Street, 80264.
Telephone: 303-232-5154.

Frank Plaut
Evan S. Lipstein
Charles E. Mortimer, Jr.

For full biographical listings, see the Martindale-Hubbell Law Directory

CONNECTICUT

*HARTFORD,** Hartford Co.

SHIPMAN & GOODWIN (AV)

One American Row, 06103
Telephone: 203-251-5000
Telecopier: 203-251-5099
Lakeville, Connecticut Office: Porter Street.
Telephone: 203-435-2539.
Stamford, Connecticut Office: Three Landmark Square.
Telephone: 203-359-4544.

MEMBERS OF FIRM

Paul W. Orth
Brian Clemow
Brenda A. Eckert
Thomas B. Mooney
Saranne P. Murray
Linda L. Yoder
Richard A. Mills, Jr.

ASSOCIATES

Patrick J. McHale
Christine L. Chinni
Kimberly A. Mango
Carolyn A. Ikari
Stephen J. Courtney
Raymond M. Bernstein

Representative Labor Clients: American Red Cross; Blue Cross & Blue Shield of Connecticut; City of Bristol; Institute of Living; Keeney Manufacturing Co.; Stamford Board of Education; City of Danbury; Trinity College; West Hartford Board of Education.

For Complete List of Firm Personnel, See General Section

For full biographical listings, see the Martindale-Hubbell Law Directory

SIEGEL, O'CONNOR, SCHIFF & ZANGARI, P.C. (AV)

370 Asylum Street, 06103
Telephone: 203-727-8900
New Haven, Connecticut Office: 171 Orange Street, P.O. Box 906.
Telephone: 203-789-0001.

Peter A. Janus
Richard D. O'Connor
Edward F. O'Donnell, Jr.
Robert J. Percy
Donald W. Strickland

OF COUNSEL

Jay S. Siegel
Robert E. Jackson

Carole Williams Briggs
Nicholas J. Grello, Jr.
Dana Shaw MacKinnon

Representative Clients: Federal Paper Board Co., Inc.; Stanadyne, Inc.; Associated General Contractors; Yale University; Mystic Seaport, Inc.; General Motors Corp.; UNISYS Corp.

For full biographical listings, see the Martindale-Hubbell Law Directory

MILFORD, New Haven Co.

BERCHEM, MOSES & DEVLIN, A PROFESSIONAL CORPORATION (AV)

75 Broad Street, 06460
Telephone: 203-783-1200
Telecopiers: 203-878-2235; 877-8422

Robert L. Berchem
Marsha Belman Moses
Michael P. Devlin
Stephen W. Studer
Robert W. Blythe
Richard J. Buturla
Floyd J. Dugas

Winthrop S. Smith, Jr.
David F. Weber
Brian A. Lema
Lawrence B. Pellegrino
Warren L. Holcomb
Gregory B. Ladewski

OF COUNSEL

John J. Kelly
Brian M. Stone

For full biographical listings, see the Martindale-Hubbell Law Directory

NEW BRITAIN, Hartford Co.

EISENBERG, ANDERSON, MICHALIK & LYNCH (AV)

136 West Main Street, P.O. Box 2950, 06050-2950
Telephone: 203-229-4855; 225-8403
Fax: 203-223-4026

MEMBERS OF FIRM

Stephen J. Anderson
Robert A. Michalik
Edward T. Lynch, Jr.
Charles W. Bauer
Dennis G. Ciccarillo
Paul T. Czepiga

COUNSEL

Harold J. Eisenberg (Retired)
Denise Magnoli McNair

ASSOCIATES

David K. Jaffe
Carl R. Ficks, Jr.
Bruce A. Zawodniak
Joann Centrilla-Silvia
Thomas A. Pavano
Kenneth R. Slater, Jr.
Jeffrey F. Gostyla

Representative Clients: Burritt InterFinancial Bancorporation; Magson Uniform Corp.; TILCON Connecticut Inc.

For full biographical listings, see the Martindale-Hubbell Law Directory

*NEW HAVEN,** New Haven Co.

HOGAN & RINI, P.C. (AV)

Gold Building, 8th Floor 234 Church Street, 06510
Telephone: 203-787-4191
Telecopier: 203-777-4032

John W. Hogan, Jr.
Joseph L. Rini
Sue A. Cousineau

OF COUNSEL

Mark S. Cousineau

For full biographical listings, see the Martindale-Hubbell Law Directory

LYNCH, TRAUB, KEEFE AND ERRANTE, A PROFESSIONAL CORPORATION (AV)

52 Trumbull Street, P.O. Box 1612, 06506
Telephone: 203-787-0275
Fax: 203-782-0278

Stephen I. Traub
Hugh F. Keefe
Steven J. Errante
John J. Keefe, Jr.
Donn A. Swift
Charles E. Tiernan, III
Robert W. Lynch
Richard W. Lynch

(See Next Column)

LYNCH, TRAUB, KEEFE AND ERRANTE A PROFESSIONAL CORPORATION—*Continued*

Mary Beattie Schairer
John M. Walsh, Jr.
Suzanne L. McAlpine
David J. Vegliante
Christopher M. Licari
David S. Monastersky

OF COUNSEL

William C. Lynch

Local Counsel for: Transport Insurance Co., Dallas, Texas; American Trucking Associations; Roadway Express, Inc., Akron, Ohio; A.R.A. Philadelphia, Penn.; Consolidated Freightways, Menlo Park, California; Ogden Corp. *Labor Counsel:* Coca-Cola, U.S.A., Atlanta, Georgia (Private Truck Operation); The Dow Chemical Co.; Cincinnati Milacron.

For full biographical listings, see the Martindale-Hubbell Law Directory

SIEGEL, O'CONNOR, SCHIFF & ZANGARI, P.C. (AV)

171 Orange Street, P.O. Box 906, 06504
Telephone: 203-789-0001
Hartford, Connecticut Office: 370 Asylum Street.
Telephone: 203-727-8900.

Hugh W. Cuthbertson
Frederick L. Dorsey
Mario J. Zangari

Glenn A. Duhl
William A. Ryan
Lauren H. Soloff

Representative Clients: State of Connecticut Judicial Dept.; Blue Cross/Blue Shield of Connecticut; Kimberly-Clark Corp.; General Dynamics Electric Boa Div.; Sheraton Hotel Waterbury; City of New London.

For full biographical listings, see the Martindale-Hubbell Law Directory

WIGGIN & DANA (AV)

One Century Tower, 06508-1832
Telephone: 203-498-4400
Telefax: 203-782-2889
Hartford, Connecticut Office: One CityPlace.
Telephone: 203-297-3700.
FAX: 203-525-9380.
Stamford, Connecticut Office: Three Stamford Plaza, 301 Tresser Boulevard.
Telephone: 203-363-7600.
Telefax: 203-363-7676.

MEMBERS OF FIRM

Peter J. Lefeber
John G. Zandy
Penny Quinn Seaman

ASSOCIATES

Joan M. Allen
Stephen B. Harris (Not admitted in CT; Resident at Hartford)
Claudia Damsky Heyman
Bernard E. Jacques (Not admitted in CT; Resident at Hartford)
Marcia Kenny Keegan (Resident at Hartford)
Sigismund L. Sapinski

For Complete List of Firm Personnel, See General Section

For full biographical listings, see the Martindale-Hubbell Law Directory

STAMFORD, Fairfield Co.

CASPER & DE TOLEDO (AV)

600 Summer Street, 06901-1418
Telephone: 203-325-8600
Fax: 203-323-5970

Stewart M. Casper
Victoria de Toledo

ASSOCIATES

Renée Mayerson Cannella
Daniel S. Fabricant

For full biographical listings, see the Martindale-Hubbell Law Directory

SILVER, GOLUB & TEITELL (AV)

184 Atlantic Street, P.O. Box 389, 06904
Telephone: 203-325-4491
FAX: 203-325-3769

MEMBERS OF FIRM

Richard A. Silver
David S. Golub
Ernest F. Teitell
Patricia M. Haugh (1942-1988)
Elaine T. Silver

John D. Josel
Mario DiNatale
Jonathan M. Levine
Marilyn J. Ramos
Jack Zaremski (Not admitted in CT)

For full biographical listings, see the Martindale-Hubbell Law Directory

WEST HARTFORD, Hartford Co.

WILLIAM S. ZEMAN (AV)

18 North Main Street, P.O. Box 270067, 06127-0067
Telephone: 203-521-4430
Fax: 203-561-0723

COUNSEL

Joel M. Ellis

For full biographical listings, see the Martindale-Hubbell Law Directory

DELAWARE

*WILMINGTON,** New Castle Co.

SMITH, KATZENSTEIN & FURLOW (AV)

1220 Market Building, P.O. Box 410, 19899
Telephone: 302-652-8400
FAX: 302-652-8405

MEMBERS OF FIRM

Craig B. Smith
David A. Jenkins
Vicki A. Hagel
Laurence V. Cronin

For Complete List of Firm Personnel, See General Section

For full biographical listings, see the Martindale-Hubbell Law Directory

THE LAW OFFICES OF RICHARD R. WIER, JR. A PROFESSIONAL ASSOCIATION (AV)

1220 Market Street, Suite 600, 19801
Telephone: 302-888-3222
Fax: 302-888-3225

Richard R. Wier, Jr.

For full biographical listings, see the Martindale-Hubbell Law Directory

DISTRICT OF COLUMBIA

WASHINGTON, D.C. Co.

* indicates certain Bar Register subscribers, in cities of comparable size and importance, who maintain an additional office in Washington, D.C. and who have arranged for representation as a part of the Washington, D.C. listings that follow

BAKER & HOSTETLER (AV)

Washington Square, Suite 1100, 1050 Connecticut Avenue, N.W., 20036-5304
Telephone: 202-861-1500
In Cleveland, Ohio: 3200 National City Center, 1900 East Ninth Street.
Telephone: 216-621-0200.
In Columbus, Ohio: Capitol Square, Suite 2100, 65 East State Street.
Telephone: 614-228-1541.
In Denver, Colorado: 303 East 17th Avenue, Suite 1100.
Telephone: 303-861-0600.
In Houston, Texas: 1000 Louisiana, Suite 2000.
Telephone: 713-751-1600.
In Long Beach, California: 300 Oceangate, Suite 620.
Telephone: 310-432-2827.
In Los Angeles, California: 600 Wilshire Boulevard.
Telephone: 213-624-2400.
In Orlando, Florida: SunBank Center, Suite 2300, 200 South Orange Avenue.
Telephone: 305-841-1111.
In College Park, Maryland: 9658 Baltimore Boulevard, Suite 206.
Telephone: 301-441-2781.
In Alexandria, Virginia: 437 North Lee Street.
Telephone: 703-549-1294.
In San Francisco, California: One Sansome Street, Suite 2000.
Telephone: 415-951-4705.

PARTNERS

David Alistair Grant
Brian S. Harvey
Sargent Karch
Betty Southard Murphy

ASSOCIATES

John S. Farrington (Not admitted in DC)
Elizabeth M. Yeonas

For Complete List of Firm Personnel, See General Section

For full biographical listings, see the Martindale-Hubbell Law Directory

Washington—Continued

BUTSAVAGE & ASSOCIATES, P.C. (AV)

1150 Connecticut Avenue, N.W., Ninth Floor, 20036
Telephone: 202-862-4355
Fax: 202-828-4130

Carey R. Butsavage
George Wiszynski
Dianna Marie Louis (Not admitted in DC)
Marc A. Stefan

For full biographical listings, see the Martindale-Hubbell Law Directory

CONSTANGY, BROOKS & SMITH (AV)

1015 Fifteenth Street, N.W., Suite 1200, 20005-2685
Telephone: 202-789-8676
Atlanta, Georgia Office: 2400 Peachtree Center Building, 230 Peachtree Street, N.W.
Telephone: 404-525-8622.
Birmingham, Alabama Office: Suite 1410 AmSouth/Harbert Plaza, 1901 Sixth Avenue North.
Telephone: 205-252-9321.
Nashville, Tennessee Office: Suite 1080 Vanderbilt Plaza, 2100 West End Avenue.
Telephone: 615-320-5200.
Columbia, South Carolina Office: Suite 810 NationsBank Tower, 1301 Gervais Street.
Telephone: 803-256-3200.
Winston-Salem, North Carolina Office: Suite 300, 101 South Stratford Road.
Telephone: 910-721-1001, 704-344-1040 (Charlotte).

MEMBERS OF FIRM

Frank A. Constangy (1911-1971)
Lovic A. Brooks, Jr. (Not admitted in DC)
Edward Katze
Patrick R. Tyson (Not admitted in DC)

Representative Clients: Blockbuster Entertainment Corp.; Blue Cross/Blue Shield of Alabama; Consolidated Freightways, Inc.; Delta Woodside Industries; McDonald's Merck & Co., Inc.; Philip-Morris Cos., Inc.; Phillips Van Heusen Corp.; Sara Lee Corp.; Trust Company Bank.

For full biographical listings, see the Martindale-Hubbell Law Directory

THE FALK LAW FIRM A PROFESSIONAL LIMITED COMPANY (AV)

Suite 260 One Westin Center, 2445 M Street, N.W., 20037
Telephone: 202-833-8700
Telecopier: 202-872-1725

James H. Falk, Sr.
James H. Falk, Jr.
John M. Falk
Rose Burks Emery (Not admitted in DC)
Robert K. Tompkins (Not admitted in DC)

OF COUNSEL

Pierre E. Murphy

For full biographical listings, see the Martindale-Hubbell Law Directory

KENNETH R. FEINBERG & ASSOCIATES (AV)

1120 20th Street, N.W. Suite 740 South, 20036
Telephone: 202-371-1110
Fax: 202-962-9290
New York, N.Y. Office: 780 3rd Avenue, Suite 2202.
Telephone: 212-527-9600.
Fax: 212-527-9611.

ASSOCIATES

Deborah E. Greenspan
Michael K. Rozen (Not admitted in DC)
Peter H. Woodin (Not admitted in DC)

For full biographical listings, see the Martindale-Hubbell Law Directory

HIGHSAW, MAHONEY & CLARKE, P.C. (AV)

Suite 210, 1050 Seventeenth Street, N.W., 20036
Telephone: 202-296-8500
Fax: 202-296-7143

James L. Highsaw (1970-1992)
William G. Mahoney
John O'B. Clarke, Jr.
Richard S. Edelman
L. Pat Wynns
Donald F. Griffin
Elizabeth A. Nadeau (Not admitted in DC)

For full biographical listings, see the Martindale-Hubbell Law Directory

O'DONOGHUE & O'DONOGHUE (AV)

4748 Wisconsin Avenue, N.W., 20016
Telephone: 202-362-0041
Telecopier: 202-362-2640
Philadelphia, Pennsylvania Office: 1056 Public Ledger Building, Independence Square.
Telephone: 215-574-3250.
Telecopier: 215-629-4996.

(See Next Column)

MEMBERS OF FIRM

Martin F. O'Donoghue (1903-1973)
Patrick C. O'Donoghue (1930-1979)
Donald J. Capuano
James R. O'Connell
Robert Matisoff
Joyce A. Mader
Sally M. Tedrow
Brian A. Powers
John L. Bohman
Joseph P. Boyle (Resident, Philadelphia, Pennsylvania Office)
Francis J. Martorana
Nicholas R. Femia
Ellen O. Boardman
Charles W. Gilligan
Louis P. Malone III

ASSOCIATES

Mary Capuano Feller
John Leary (Not admitted in DC)
John R. Harney
Gerard M. Waites (Not admitted in DC)
Scott A. Cronin (Resident, Philadelphia, Pennsylvania Office)
R. Richard Hopp
W. Iris Carter
Marc D. Keffer (Not admitted in DC)
Linda J. Tarlow (Not admitted in DC)
David D. Capuano (Not admitted in DC)
John M. McIntire (Not admitted in DC)
Mark William Kunst

For full biographical listings, see the Martindale-Hubbell Law Directory

*** OGLETREE, DEAKINS, NASH, SMOAK & STEWART (AV)**

Fifth Floor, 2400 N Street, N.W., 20037
Telephone: 202-887-0855
Facsimile: 202-887-0866
Atlanta, Georgia Office: 3800 One Atlantic Center, 1201 West Peachtree Street, N.W.
Telephone: 404-881-1300.
Greenville, South Carolina Office: The Ogletree Building, 300 North Main Street, P.O. Box 2757.
Telephone: 803-271-1300.
Charleston, South Carolina Office: First Union Building, Suite 310, 177 Meeting Street, P.O. Box 1808.
Telephone: 803-853-1300.
Columbia, South Carolina Office: Palmetto Center, Suite 1820, 1426 Main Street, P.O. Box 11206.
Telephone: 803-252-1300.
Nashville, Tennessee Office: St. Cloud Corner, 500 Church Street.
Telephone: 615-254-1900.
Raleigh, North Carolina Office: Suite 511, 4101 Lake Boone Trail, P.O. Box 31608.
Telephone: 919-787-9700.
Albany, New York Office: 4th Floor, One Steuben Place.
Telephone: 518-434-1300.

MEMBERS OF FIRM

Homer L. Deakins, Jr.
Lewis Tyson Smoak
J. Hamilton Stewart, III
Michael A. Taylor
Peter H. Kiefer
Marshall B. Babson
Bernard P. Jeweler
Jonathan R. Mook
Joel A. Daniel
Robert T. Lee
David Edward Jones (Not admitted in DC)
Celeste M. Wasielewski
Michael J. Murphy
Elizabeth I. Torphy-Donzella

OF COUNSEL

Stanley R. Strauss

For full biographical listings, see the Martindale-Hubbell Law Directory

THOMPSON AND HUTSON (AV)

Suite 900, 1317 F Street, N.W., 20004
Telephone: 202-783-1900
Fax: 202-783-5995
Greenville, South Carolina Office: NationsBank Plaza, Suite 100.
Telephone: 803-242-3200.
Fax: 803-233-7867.

MEMBERS OF FIRM

Robert T. Thompson
David L. Thompson (Resident, Washington, D.C. Office)

For full biographical listings, see the Martindale-Hubbell Law Directory

*** VEDDER, PRICE, KAUFMAN, KAMMHOLZ & DAY (AV)**

A Partnership including Vedder, Price, Kaufman & Kammholz, P.C.
1600 M. Street, N.W., 20036
Telephone: 202-296-0500
Fax: 202-296-2339
Chicago, Illinois Office: Vedder, Price, Kaufman & Kammholz, 222 North La Salle Street.
Telephone: 312-609-7500.
Rockford, Illinois Office: Vedder, Price, Kaufman & Kammholz, 4615 East State Street, Suite 201.
Telephone: 815-226-7700.
New York, N.Y. Office: Vedder, Price, Kaufman, Kammholz & Day, 805 Third Avenue.
Telephone: 212-407-7700.

(See Next Column)

VEDDER, PRICE, KAUFMAN, KAMMHOLZ & DAY—*Continued*

MEMBERS OF FIRM

Virgil B. Day (P.C.)
George J. Pantos

For Complete List of Firm Personnel, See General Section

For full biographical listings, see the Martindale-Hubbell Law Directory

*** VENABLE, BAETJER, HOWARD & CIVILETTI** (AV)

A Partnership including Professional Corporations
Suite 1000, 1201 New York Avenue, N.W., 20005
Telephone: 202-962-4800
Fax: 202-962-8300
Baltimore, Maryland Office: Venable, Baetjer and Howard, 1800 Mercantile Bank & Trust Building, 2 Hopkins Plaza.
Telephone: 410-244-7400.
McLean, Virginia Office: Venable, Baetjer and Howard, Suite 400, 2010 Corporate Ridge.
Telephone: 703-760-1600.
Rockville, Maryland Office: Venable, Baetjer and Howard, Suite 500, One Church Street, P. O. Box 1906.
Telephone: 301-217-5600.
Towson, Maryland Office: Venable, Baetjer and Howard, 210 Allegheny Avenue, P. O. Box 5517.
Telephone: 410-494-6200.

MEMBERS OF FIRM

Douglas D. Connah, Jr. (P.C.) (Also at Baltimore, Maryland Office)
Kenneth C. Bass, III (Also at McLean, Virginia Office)
Joseph G. Block
Robert G. Ames (Also at Baltimore, Maryland Office)
Jeffrey A. Dunn (Also at Baltimore, Maryland Office)
George F. Pappas (Also at Baltimore, Maryland Office)
James L. Shea (Not admitted in DC; also at Baltimore, Maryland Office)
Maurice Baskin
James A. Dunbar (Also at Baltimore, Maryland Office)
Mary E. Pivec (Not admitted in DC; Also at Baltimore, Maryland Office)
Patrick J. Stewart (Also at Baltimore, Maryland Office)
Gary M. Hnath

ASSOCIATES

David W. Goewey
Samuel T. Morison
Traci H. Mundy (Not admitted in DC)
Karen D. Woodard

For Complete List of Firm Personnel, See General Section

For full biographical listings, see the Martindale-Hubbell Law Directory

VERNER, LIIPFERT, BERNHARD, MCPHERSON AND HAND, CHARTERED (AV)

901 15th Street, N.W., 20005-2301
Telephone: 202-371-6000
Cable Address: "Verlip"
Telex: 1561792 VERLIP UT
Fax: 202-371-6279
McLean, Virginia Office: Sixth Floor, 8280 Greensboro Drive, 22102.
Telephone: 703-749-6000.
Fax: 703-749-6027.
Houston, Texas Office: 2600 Texas Commerce Tower, 600 Travis, 77002.
Telephone: 713-237-9034.
Fax: 713-237-1216.

John P. Campbell
J. Richard Hammett (Resident, Houston, Texas Office)
Lawrence Z. Lorber
Joseph L. Manson, III
Ronald B. Natalie

OF COUNSEL

J. Robert Kirk

For Complete List of Firm Personnel, See General Section

For full biographical listings, see the Martindale-Hubbell Law Directory

FLORIDA

*FORT LAUDERDALE,** Broward Co.

FISHER & PHILLIPS (AV)

A Partnership including Professional Corporations and Associations
Suite 2310 NationsBank Tower, One Financial Plaza, 33394
Telephone: 305-525-4800
Telecopier: 305-525-8739
Atlanta, Georgia Office: 1500 Resurgens Plaza, 945 East Paces Ferry Road, N.E., 30326.
Telephone: 404-231-1400.
Telecopier: 404-240-4249.
Telex: 54-2331.

(See Next Column)

Redwood City, California Office: Suite 345, Three Lagoon Drive, 94065.
Telephone: 415-592-6160.
Telecopier: 415-592-6385.
Newport Beach, California Office: 4675 MacArthur Court, Suite 550, 92660.
Telephone: 714-851-2424.
Telecopier: 714-851-0152.
New Orleans, Louisiana Office: 3710 Place St. Charles, 201 St. Charles Avenue, 70170.
Telephone: 504-522-3303.
Telecopier: 504-529-3850.

RESIDENT MEMBERS

Charles S. Caulkins (P.A.)
Christopher D. Robinson

RESIDENT OF COUNSEL

James C. Polkinghorn

RESIDENT ASSOCIATES

Kenneth A. Knox
David H. Spalter
Suzanne K. Sleep
Michael A. Puchades

Representative Clients: Boca Raton Resort & Club; Dean Foods/T.G. Lee Foods, Inc.; Hyatt Corp.; Independent Life & Accident Insurance Co.; Miller Brewing Co.; Textron, Inc.; The Prudential Insurance Company of America; United States Sugar Corp./South Bay Growers.

For full biographical listings, see the Martindale-Hubbell Law Directory

*FORT MYERS,** Lee Co.

KUNKEL MILLER & HAMENT (AV)

Sun Bank Financial Center, Suite 416, 12730 New Brittany Boulevard, 33907
Telephone: 813-278-1600
Telecopier: 813-278-9056
Sarasota, Florida Office: Southtrust Bank Plaza, Suite 785, 1800 Second Street, 34236.
Telephone: 813-365-6006.
Fax: 813-365-6209.
Tampa, Florida Office: 15438 North Florida Avenue, Suite 106.
Telephone: 813-963-7736.
Telefax: 813-969-3639.

Daniel H. Kunkel
Michael R. Miller
John M. Hament

Jody A. O'Konski
Michele M. DiGello (Not admitted in FL)

LEGAL SUPPORT PERSONNEL

Chris C. Garringer (Wage and Hour Consultant)

Representative Clients: Florida Health Care Assn.; Florida Employee Leasing Assn.; Godl & Diamond Source; New London, Connecticut Convalescent Center; Mid-Hudson, NY Cablevision; The Hillhaven Corp.; Bon Secours Hospital; Polyplastex International; Central Park Lodges.

For full biographical listings, see the Martindale-Hubbell Law Directory

*FORT PIERCE,** St. Lucie Co.

RICHESON AND BROWN, P.A. (AV)

317 South 2nd Street, P.O. Box 4048, 34948
Telephone: 407-465-5111
FAX: 407-466-0378
Orlando, Florida Office: 135 North Magnolia Avenue, P.O Box 3006, 32802.
Telephone: 407-425-7755.
West Palm Beach, Florida Office: Suite 900 Forum III Building, 1655 Palm Beach Lakes Boulevard, 33401.
Telephone: 407-689-6660.

J. David Richeson
James G. Brown
Joseph J. Mancini
Dorothy F. Green
Helen E. Scott

For full biographical listings, see the Martindale-Hubbell Law Directory

*JACKSONVILLE,** Duval Co.

COFFMAN, COLEMAN, ANDREWS & GROGAN, PROFESSIONAL ASSOCIATION (AV)

2065 Herschel Street, P.O. Box 40089, 32203
Telephone: 904-389-5161
Telecopier: 904-387-9340

Daniel R. Coffman, Jr.
Patrick D. Coleman
William H. Andrews
Michael K. Grogan
Eric J. Holshouser
Mary W. Jarrett
Robert G. Riegel, Jr.
Marc M. Mayo
Joann M. Bricker
Michael G. Prendergast
Timothy B. Strong

(See Next Column)

COFFMAN, COLEMAN, ANDREWS & GROGAN PROFESSIONAL ASSOCIATION, *Jacksonville—Continued*

Gregory D. Holland | Margaret W. Means
Heather A. Owen | Kelly B. Pritchard

Representative Clients: American Home Products Corp.; Anheuser-Busch Companies, Inc.; Atlantic Marine and Drydock, Inc.; Baptist Medical Center; Blue Cross and Blue Shield of Florida, Inc.; Container Corporation of America, Fernandina Beach, Florida; Winn-Dixie Stores, Inc.; Xerox Corp.

For full biographical listings, see the Martindale-Hubbell Law Directory

CORBIN, DICKINSON, DUVALL & MARGULIES (AV)

121 West Forsyth Street, Suite 1000, P.O. Box 41566, 32203
Telephone: 904-356-8073
Telecopier: 904-358-2319

MEMBERS OF FIRM

Peter Reed Corbin | John E. Duvall
John F. Dickinson | Richard N. Margulies

ASSOCIATE

Frank Damon Kitchen

Representative Clients: Allied Signal Corp.; Carolina Freight Carriers Corp.; Consolidated Freightways Corp.; The Haskell Co.; International Speedway Corp.; Mobil Oil Corp.; Sears, Roebuck and Co.; State of Florida; University of North Florida; Lanier Worldwide, Inc.

For full biographical listings, see the Martindale-Hubbell Law Directory

HAYNSWORTH, BALDWIN, JOHNSON AND HARPER (AV)

Formerly Hamilton & Bowden
1506 Prudential Drive, P.O. Box 40593, 32203
Telephone: 904-396-3000
Facsimile: 904-396-9999
Tampa, Florida Office: 600 North Westshore Boulevard, Suite 200.
Telephone: 813-289-1247.
Macon, Georgia Office: 577 Mulberry Street, Suite 710, P.O. Box 1975.
Telephone: 912-746-0262.
Greenville, South Carolina Office: Haynsworth, Baldwin, Johnson & Greaves, P.A., 918 South Pleasantburg Drive, P.O. Box 10888.
Telephone: 803-271-7410.
Columbia, South Carolina Office: Haynsworth, Baldwin, Johnson & Greaves, P.A., 1201 Main Street, Suite 1230.
Telephone: 803-799-5858.
Raleigh, North Carolina Office: Haynsworth, Baldwin, Johnson & Greaves, P.A., 3605 Glenwood Avenue, Suite 210, P.O. Box 10035.
Telephone: 919-782-3340.
Greensboro, North Carolina Office: Haynsworth, Baldwin, Johnson & Greaves, P.A., 2709 Henry Street, P.O. Box 13310.
Telephone: 910-375-9737.
Charlotte, North Carolina Office: Haynsworth, Baldwin, Johnson & Greaves, P.A., 400 West Trade Street.
Telephone: 704-342-2588.

MEMBERS OF FIRM

Knox L. Haynsworth, Jr. (Not admitted in FL) | G. Thomas Harper (Resident)
| Charles F. Henley, Jr. (Resident)

Kimberly T. Acuna (Resident) | Elizabeth A. Maas (Resident)

Representative Clients: Belk Department Stores; The Coca-Cola Company Foods Division; Continental Cablevision of Jacksonville; Florida Mining & Materials, Inc.; Florida Steel Corp.; Great Dane Trailers, Inc.; Kmart Corp.; Lockheed Missiles and Space Company, Inc.; Stone Container Corp.; Winn-Dixie Stores, Inc.

For full biographical listings, see the Martindale-Hubbell Law Directory

*KISSIMMEE,** Osceola Co.

POHL & BROWN, P.A.

(See Winter Park)

*MIAMI,** Dade Co.

ALLEY AND ALLEY, CHARTERED (AV)

612 Ingraham Building, 25 S.E. 2nd Avenue, 33131
Telephone: 305-371-6753
Tampa, Florida Office: 205 Brush Street, P.O. Box 1427.
Telephone: 813-229-6481.

Granville M. Alley, Jr. (1929-1976) | John-Edward Alley

Representative Clients: The Wackenhut Corporation and subsidiaries; Publix Super Markets, Inc.; The Miami Herald Publishing Company/Knight-Ridder, Inc.; Southern Air Transport; Sysco Corp.; Skyline Mobile Homes, Inc.; Associated Grocers of Florida; Baxter Healthcare Corp. (Dade Div.); Edron Fixture Corp.

For full biographical listings, see the Martindale-Hubbell Law Directory

CLARKE & SILVERGLATE, PROFESSIONAL ASSOCIATION (AV)

100 North Biscayne Boulevard, Suite 2401, 33132
Telephone: 305-377-0700
Fax: 305-377-3001

Mercer K. Clarke | Spencer H. Silverglate
Kelly Anne Luther

For full biographical listings, see the Martindale-Hubbell Law Directory

JOSEPH Z. FLEMING, P.A. (AV)

620 Ingraham Building, 25 Southeast Second Avenue, 33131
Telephone: 305-373-0791
Telecopier: 305-358-5933

Joseph Z. Fleming

For full biographical listings, see the Martindale-Hubbell Law Directory

GREENE & BELL, P.A. (AV)

Suite 1406, One Datran Center, 9100 South Dadeland Boulevard, 33156
Telephone: 305-670-5999
Facsimile: 305-670-8373

Alan Douglas Greene | Felicia Greene Bell

Representative Clients: Birdsall, Inc.; CBM Industries, Inc.; Club Corporation of America; Florida Blacktop, Inc.; General Electric Co.; Lillie Rubin Affiliates, Inc.; Martin Marietta Services, Inc.; RCA Corp.; SeaSpecialties, Inc.; Tursair Fueling, Inc.

For full biographical listings, see the Martindale-Hubbell Law Directory

McDERMOTT, WILL & EMERY (AV)

A Partnership including Professional Corporations
201 South Biscayne Boulevard, 33131-4336
Telephone: 305-358-3500
Telex: 441777 LEYES
Facsimile: 305-347-6500
Chicago, Illinois Office: 227 West Monroe Street.
Telephone: 312-372-2000.
Telex: 253565 MILAM CGO.
Facsimile: 312-984-7700.
Boston, Massachusetts Office: 75 State Street, Suite 1700.
Telephone: 617-345-5000.
Telex: 951324 MILAM BSN.
Facsimile: 617-345-5077.
Washington, D.C. Office: 1850 K Street, N.W.
Telephone: 202-887-8000.
Telex: 904261 MILAM CGO.
Facsimile: 202-778-8087.
Los Angeles, California Office: 2049 Century Park East.
Telephone: 310-277-4110.
Facsimile: 310-277-4730.
Newport Beach, California Office: 1301 Dove Street, Suite 500.
Telephone: 714-851-0633.
Facsimile: 714-851-9348.
New York, N.Y. Office: 1211 Avenue of the Americas.
Telephone: 212-768-5400.
Facsimile: 212-768-5444.
St. Petersburg, Russia Office: 2/2 Tchaikovsky Street, #517, 191187 St. Petersburg, Russia.
Telephone: (7) (812) 273-9831.
Facsimile: (7) (812) 273-9831.
Tallinn, Estonia Office: Tallinn Business Center, 6 Harju Street, EE0001 Tallinn, Estonia.
Telephone: 372 6 31-05-53.
Facsimile: 372 6 31-05-54.
Vilnius, Lithuania Office: Smetonos 6, 2600 Vilnius, Lithuania.
Telephone: 370 2 61-43-08.
Facsimile: 370 2 22-79-55.
Associated (Independent) Offices:
Brussels, Belgium: Uettwiller Grelon Lippens Dekeyser, 73 avenue Vandendriessche, 1150 Brussels, Belgium.
Telephone: (32) (2) 772-87-50.
Facsimile: (32) (2) 772-87-52.
London, England: Paisner & Co, Bouverie House, 154 Fleet Street, London EC4A 2DQ, England.
Telephone: (44) (71) 353-0299.
Facsimile: (44) (71) 583-8621.
Paris, France: Uettwiller Grelon Gout Canat & Associes, 68, boulevard de Courcelles, 75017 Paris, France.
Telephone: (33) (1) 48 88 89 00.
Facsimile: (33) (1) 48 88 05 50.

MEMBER OF FIRM

Steven E. Siff

For Complete List of Firm Personnel, See General Section

For full biographical listings, see the Martindale-Hubbell Law Directory

Miami—Continued

MERSHON, SAWYER, JOHNSTON, DUNWODY & COLE (AV)

A Partnership including Professional Associations
Suite 4500 First Union Financial Center, 200 South Biscayne Boulevard, 33131-2387
Telephone: 305-358-5100
Cable Address: "Mercole"
Telex: 515705
Fax: 305-376-8654
Naples, Florida Office: Pelican Bay Corporate Centre, Suite 501, 5551 Ridgewood Drive.
Telephone: 813-598-1055.
Fax: 813-598-1868.
West Palm Beach, Florida Office: 777 South Flagler Drive, Suite 900.
Telephone: 407-659-5990.
Fax: 407-659-6313.
Key West, Florida Office: 3132 North Side Drive, Suite 102.
Telephone: 305-296-1774.
Fax: 305-296-1715
London, England Office: Blake Lodge, Bridge Lane, London SW11 3AD, England.
Telephone: 44-71-978-7748.
Fax: 44-71-350-0156.

MEMBERS OF FIRM

W. I. Evans (1893-1938)
O. B. Simmons, Jr. (1900-1962)
M. L. Mershon (1891-1968)
Herbert S. Sawyer (1889-1978)
Aubrey V. Kendall (P.A.)
Osmond C. Howe, Jr., (P.A.)
William J. Dunaj (P.A.)
Henry H. Raattama, Jr., (P.A.)
Brian P. Tague
Richard C. Grant (P.A.) (Resident, Naples Office)
Robert D. W. Landon, II, (P.A.)
James M. McCann, Jr. (Resident, West Palm Beach Office)
Barry G. Craig (P.A.)
Robert T. Wright, Jr.
Russell T. Kamradt (Resident, West Palm Beach Office)
Dennis M. Campbell (P.A.)
Douglas F. Darbut
Timothy J. Norris (P.A.)
Harvey W. Gurland, Jr.
Jeffrey D. Fridkin (Resident, Naples Office)
Jose E. Castro (P.A.)
Carlos M. Sires
David F. Parish
Richard M. Bezold
David B. McCrea (P.A.)
Philip M. Sprinkle, II (Resident, West Palm Beach Office)
Thomas E. Streit (Resident, West Palm Beach Office)
John C. Shawde
Jorge R. Gutierrez (P.A.)
Ronald L. Fick (P.A.) (Resident, West Palm Beach Office)
Marjie C. Nealon (P.A.)
Michael T. Lynott (P.A.)
William M. Pearson (P.A.)
Jack A. Falk, Jr
John F. Halula
John J. Grundhauser
Neil R. Chrystal
Mary Ellen Valletta

OF COUNSEL

Atwood Dunwody
Robert B. Cole
Robert A. White (P.A.)
Alexander Penelas
Jeri A. Poller
Ron Saunders
John S. Schwartz
Jose R. Cuervo
William T. Muir
Charles L. Brackbill, Jr. (Not admitted in FL)
Griffith F. Pitcher
A. Patrick Giles (Resident, London, England Office)
James P. Reeder (1896-1985)
W. E. Dunwody, Jr. (1910-1988)
Claude Pepper (1900-1989)
Thos. McE. Johnston (1897-1989)
John D. Armstrong (1918-1992)

ASSOCIATES

Lawrence P. Rochefort
Mitchell E. Silverstein
G. Helen Athan (Resident, Naples Office)
Jonna Stukel Brown
Doreen S. Moloney
Rona F. Morrow
Nancy A. Romfh (Resident, West Palm Beach Office)
John D. Eaton
Mario David Carballo
Elizabeth Cassidy Barber
Natalie Scharf
Gregg Metzger
Martha de Zayas
Phillip T. Ridolfo, Jr. (Resident, West Palm Beach Office)
Floyd Brantley Chapman (Resident, West Palm Beach Office)
Kurt E. Lee (Resident, Naples Office)
Michael A. Feldman (Resident, Naples Office)
Robin C. Thomes (Resident, Naples Office)
Brenda Ozaki (Resident, West Palm Beach Office)
G. Michael Deacon

Representative Clients: Arvida/JMB Partners; Bankers Trust Co.; Biscayne Kennel Club, Inc.; The Chase Manhattan Bank, N.A.; Lennar Corp.; Reynolds Metals Co.; United States Sugar Corp.; University of Miami.

For full biographical listings, see the Martindale-Hubbell Law Directory

MULLER, MINTZ, KORNREICH, CALDWELL, CASEY, CROSLAND & BRAMNICK, P.A. (AV)

Suite 3600 First Union Financial Center, 200 South Biscayne Boulevard, 33131
Telephone: 305-358-5500
Broward: 305-522-0393
Orlando, Florida Office: Suite 1525 Firstate Tower, 255 South Orange Avenue.
Telephone: 407-843-1400.

(See Next Column)

David V. Kornreich
Michael W. Casey, III
James C. Crosland
James S. Bramnick
Paul C. Heidmann
Gordon D. Rogers
John D. Gronda
Elizabeth S. Syger
Carmen S. Johnson
Debra A. Abbott
Jeffrey E. Mandel
Denise M. Heekin
Richard D. Tuschman
Andrew K. Williams
Donna M. DiChiara
Paul T. Ryder
William P. Burns
Frank H. Henry
Teresa A. Adamson Herrmann
Sara B. Riley
Betsy M. Santini

OF COUNSEL

Joseph A. Caldwell

Representative Clients: Florida Power & Light Co.; Universal Studios; American Telephone & Telegraph Co.; J.C. Penney Co.; Columbia Broadcasting Systems, Inc. (CBS Inc.); National Car Rental Systems, Inc.; Motorola, Inc.; Palm Beach County; Volusia County; South Miami Hospital.

For full biographical listings, see the Martindale-Hubbell Law Directory

*ORLANDO,** Orange Co.

DEMPSEY & ASSOCIATES, P.A. (AV)

605 East Robinson Street, P.O. Box 1980, 32802-1980
Telephone: 407-422-5166
Mailing Address: 1031 West Morse Boulevard, Suite 200, Winter Park, Florida, 32789
Winter Park, Florida Office: 1031 West Morse Boulevard, Suite 200, 32789.
Telephone: 407-740-7778.
Telecopier: 407-740-0911.

Bernard H. Dempsey, Jr.
Michael C. Sasso

M. Susan Sacco
William P. Weatherford, Jr.
Daniel N. Brodersen
Lori R. Benton
Barbara B. Smithers

OF COUNSEL

Gary S. Salzman

Reference: First Union National Bank of Florida.

For full biographical listings, see the Martindale-Hubbell Law Directory

FOLEY & LARDNER (AV)

Suite 1800, 111 North Orange Avenue, P.O. Box 2193, 32802-2193
Telephone: 407-423-7656
Telex: 441781 (HQ ORL)
Facsimile: 407-648-1743
Milwaukee, Wisconsin Office: Firstar Center, 777 East Wisconsin Avenue.
Telephone: 414-271-2400.
Telex: 26-819 (Foley Lard Mil).
Facsimile: 414-297-4900.
Madison, Wisconsin Office: Firstar Plaza, One South Pinckney Street, P.O. Box 1497.
Telephone: 608-257-5035.
Telex: 262051 (F L Madison).
Facsimile: 608-258-4258.
Chicago, Illinois Office: Suite 3300, One IBM Plaza, 330 N. Wabash Avenue.
Telephone: 312-755-1900.
Facsimile: 312-755-1925.
Washington, D.C. Office: Washington Harbour, Suite 500, 3000 K Street, N.W.
Telephone: 202-672-5300.
Telex: 904136 (Foley Lard Wsh).
Facsimile: 202-672-5399.
Annapolis, Maryland Office: Suite 102, 175 Admiral Cochrane Drive.
Telephone: 301-266-8077.
Telex: 899149 (Oldtownpat).
Facsimile: 301-266-8664.
Jacksonville, Florida Office: The Greenleaf Building, 200 Laura Street, P.O. Box 240.
Telephone: 904-359-2000.
Facsimile: 904-359-8700.
Tallahassee, Florida Office: Suite 450, 215 South Monroe Street, P.O. Box 508.
Telephone: 904-222-6100.
Facsimile: 904-224-0496.
Tampa, Florida Office: Suite 2700, One Hundred N. Tampa Street, P.O. Box 3391.
Telephones: 813-229-2300; Pinellas County: 813-442-3296.
Facsimile: 813-221-4210
West Palm Beach, Florida Office: Suite 200, Phillips Point East Tower, 777 South Flagler Drive.
Telephone: 407-655-5050.
Facsimile: 407-655-6925.

RESIDENT PARTNER

Christopher C. Skambis, Jr.

(See Next Column)

FOLEY & LARDNER, *Orlando—Continued*

RETIRED PARTNER

Norman F. Burke

General Counsel for: The Greater Orlando Aviation Authority.
Attorneys for: United Parcel Service of America, Inc.; Citrus Central, Inc.

For Complete List of Firm Personnel, See General Section

For full biographical listings, see the Martindale-Hubbell Law Directory

MULLER, MINTZ, KORNREICH, CALDWELL, CASEY, CROSLAND & BRAMNICK, P.A. (AV)

Suite 1525 Firstate Tower, 255 South Orange Avenue, 32801
Telephone: 407-843-1400
Miami, Florida Office: Suite 3600 First Union Financial Center, 200 South Biscayne Boulevard.
Telephone: 305-358-5500, Broward: 305-522-0393.

David V. Kornreich
Michael W. Casey, III
James C. Crosland
James S. Bramnick
Debra A. Abbott
Jeffrey E. Mandel
Teresa A. Adamson Herrmann

Representative Clients: Florida Power & Light Co.; Universal Studios; American Telephone & Telegraph Co.; J.C. Penney Co.; Columbia Broadcasting Systems, Inc. (CBS Inc.); National Car Rental Systems, Inc.; Motorola, Inc.; Palm Beach County; Volusia County; South Miami Hospital.

For full biographical listings, see the Martindale-Hubbell Law Directory

POHL & BROWN, P.A.

(See Winter Park)

RICHESON AND BROWN, P.A. (AV)

135 North Magnolia Avenue, P.O. Box 3006, 32802
Telephone: 407-425-7755
Fort Pierce, Florida Office: 317 South 2nd Street, P.O. Box 4048, 34948.
Telephone: 407-465-5111.
West Palm Beach, Florida Office: Suite 900 Forum III Building, 1655 Palm Beach Lakes Boulevard, 33401.
Telephone: 407-689-6660.

J. David Richeson
James G. Brown
Joseph J. Mancini
Dorothy F. Green
Helen E. Scott

For full biographical listings, see the Martindale-Hubbell Law Directory

*SARASOTA,** Sarasota Co.

KUNKEL MILLER & HAMENT (AV)

Southtrust Bank Plaza, Suite 785, 1800 Second Street, 34236
Telephone: 813-365-6006
Telecopier: 813-365-6209
Fort Myers, Florida Office: Sunbank Financial Center, Suite 400, 12730 New Brittany Boulevard.
Telephone: 813-278-1600.
Telecopier: 813-278-9056.
Tampa, Florida Office: 15438 North Florida Avenue, Suite 106.
Telephone: 813-963-7736.
Telefax: 813-969-3639.

MEMBERS OF FIRM

Daniel H. Kunkel
Michael R. Miller
John M. Hament

Jody A. O'Konski
Michele M. DiGello (Not admitted in FL)

LEGAL SUPPORT PERSONNEL

Chris C. Garringer (Wage and Hour Consultant)

Representative Clients: S & E Contractors, Inc.; Asolo Center For The Performing Arts; Sun Coast Closures, Inc.; Sun Coast Media Group, Inc.; Manatee Memorial Hospital; Florida Aluminum and Steel Fabricators; Safetronics, Inc.; Sarasota University Club; Mote Marine Laboratory; First of Englewood.

For full biographical listings, see the Martindale-Hubbell Law Directory

*TALLAHASSEE,** Leon Co.

MANG, RETT & MINNICK, P.A. (AV)

660 East Jefferson Street, P.O. Box 11127, 32302-3127
Telephone: 904-222-7710
1-800-342-2727
Telecopier: 904-222-6019

Douglas A. Mang
Donald A. Rett
Bruce A. Minnick
Andrew L. Granger
Steven M. Malono
Wendy Russell Wiener

LEGAL SUPPORT PERSONNEL

Teresa Z. Finley
Judy C. Rhodes
Wendy Ebbers

(See Next Column)

GOVERNMENTAL CONSULTANT

Timothy Deratany (Governmental Consultant)

For full biographical listings, see the Martindale-Hubbell Law Directory

*TAMPA,** Hillsborough Co.

ALLEY AND ALLEY, CHARTERED (AV)

205 Brush Street, P.O. Box 1427, 33601
Telephone: 813-229-6481
Fax: 813-223-7029
Miami, Florida Office: 612 Ingraham Building, 25 S.E. 2nd Avenue.
Telephone: 305-371-6753.

Granville M. Alley, Jr. (1929-1976)
John-Edward Alley
Robert D. Hall, Jr.
Tony B. Griffin
James M. Craig
David S. Shankman
Mark P. Graves

Representative Clients: Better Business Forms; Florida Southern College; Opus South Corp.; City of Panama City, Florida; Publix Super Markets, Inc.; Santa Fe Healthcare Systems; Skyline Mobile Homes, Inc.; Southwest Florida Water Management District; Payroll Transfers, Inc.; Val-Pak Direct Marketing System.

For full biographical listings, see the Martindale-Hubbell Law Directory

GOLD, RESNICK & SEGALL, P.A. (AV)

704 West Bay Street, 33606
Telephone: 813-254-2071
FAX: (813) 251-0616

Aaron J. Gold
Eddy R. Resnick
Larry M. Segall

Nancy J. Cass

Reference: Barnett Bank of Tampa.

For full biographical listings, see the Martindale-Hubbell Law Directory

HAYNSWORTH, BALDWIN, JOHNSON AND HARPER (AV)

600 North Westshore Boulevard, Suite 200, 33609
Telephone: 813-289-1247
Facsimile: 813-289-6530
Jacksonville, Florida Office: 1506 Prudential Drive, P.O. Box 40593.
Telephone: 904-396-3000.
Macon, Georgia Office: 577 Mulberry Street, Suite 710, P.O. Box 1975.
Telephone: 912-746-0262.
Greenville, South Carolina Office: Haynsworth, Baldwin, Johnson & Greaves, P.A., 918 South Pleasantburg Drive, P.O. Box 10888.
Telephone: 803-271-7410.
Columbia, South Carolina Office: Haynsworth, Baldwin, Johnson & Greaves, P.A., 1201 Main Street, Suite 1230.
Telephone: 803-799-5858.
Raleigh, North Carolina Office: Haynsworth, Baldwin, Johnson & Greaves, P.A., 3605 Glenwood Avenue, Suite 210, P.O. Box 10035.
Telephone: 919-782-3340.
Greensboro, North Carolina Office: Haynsworth, Baldwin, Johnson & Greaves, P.A., 2709 Henry Street, P.O. Box 13310.
Telephone: 910-375-9737.
Charlotte, North Carolina Office: Haynsworth, Baldwin, Johnson & Greaves, P.A., 400 West Trade Street.
Telephone: 704-342-2588.

MEMBERS OF FIRM

Knox L. Haynsworth, Jr. (Not admitted in FL)
Bradley R. Johnson (Resident)
Grant D. Petersen (Resident)

M. Kristen Allman (Resident)
Donna M. Griffin (Resident)
Eduardo Alberto Suarez-Solar (Resident)

Representative Clients: Florida Steel Corp.; Kmart Corp.; Manatee Memorial Hospital; Tropical Garment Manufacturing Co.

For full biographical listings, see the Martindale-Hubbell Law Directory

KUNKEL MILLER & HAMENT (AV)

Magdalene Center, Suite 106, 15438 North Florida Avenue, 33631
Telephone: 813-963-7736
Fax: 813-969-3639
Sarasota, Florida Office: Suite 785, 1800 Second Street.
Telephone: 813-365-6006.
Telecopier: 813-365-6209.
Fort Myers, Florida Office: Sunbank Financial Center, Suite 400, 12730 New Brittany Boulevard.
Telephone: 813-278-1600.
Telecopier: 813-278-9056.

Daniel H. Kunkel
Michael R. Miller
John M. Hament

Jody A. O'Konski
Michele M. DiGello (Not admitted in FL)

(See Next Column)

KUNKEL MILLER & HAMENT—*Continued*

LEGAL SUPPORT PERSONNEL

Chris C. Garringer (Wage and Hour Consultant)

Representative Clients: Florida Health Care Assn.; Florida Employee Leasing Assn.; Godl & Diamond Source; New London, Connecticut Convalescent Center; Mid-Hudson, NY Cablevision; The Hillhaven Corp.; Bon Secours Hospital; Polyplastex International; Central Park Lodges.

For full biographical listings, see the Martindale-Hubbell Law Directory

ZINOBER & MCCREA, P.A. (AV)

Enterprise Plaza, 201 East Kennedy Boulevard Suite 1750, P.O. Box 1378, 33602
Telephone: 813-224-9004
Telecopier: 813-223-4881
Also Available for Consultation at: Summit Building, 13575 58th Street, N., Suite 265, Clearwater, 34620.
Telephone: 813-224-9004.

Peter W. Zinober | Richard C. McCrea, Jr.

Edwin J. Turanchik | Jacqueline Ley Brown
Frank E. Brown | Nancy A. Roslow
D. Michael Pointer, II | Cynthia L. May
Charles A. Powell, IV | Scott T. Silverman

LEGAL SUPPORT PERSONNEL

Debra A. Douglas (Administrator)

For full biographical listings, see the Martindale-Hubbell Law Directory

*WEST PALM BEACH,** Palm Beach Co.

RICHESON AND BROWN, P.A. (AV)

Suite 900 Forum III Building, 1655 Palm Beach Lakes Boulevard, 33401
Telephone: 407-689-6660
Orlando, Florida Office: 135 North Magnolia Avenue, P.O Box 3006, 32802.
Telephone: 407-425-7755.
Fort Pierce, Florida Office: 317 South 2nd Street, P.O. Box 4048, 34948.
Telephone: 407-465-5111.

J. David Richeson | Joseph J. Mancini
James G. Brown | Dorothy F. Green
Helen E. Scott

For full biographical listings, see the Martindale-Hubbell Law Directory

WINTER PARK, Orange Co.

POHL & BROWN, P.A. (AV)

280 West Canton Avenue, Suite 410, P.O. Box 3208, 32789
Telephone: 407-647-7645; 407-647-POHL
Telefax: 407-647-2314

Frank L. Pohl | Dwight I. Cool
Usher L. Brown | William W. Pouzar
Houston E. Short | Mary B. Van Leuven

OF COUNSEL

Frederick W. Peirsol

Representative Clients: Orange County Comptroller; Osceola County; School Board of Osceola County, Florida; Osceola Tourist Development Council; NationsBank of Florida, N.A.; SunBank, N.A.; The Bank of Winter Park; Bekins Moving and Storage Co., Inc.; Champion Boats, Inc.; KeyCom Telephone Systems, Inc.

For full biographical listings, see the Martindale-Hubbell Law Directory

GEORGIA

*ATLANTA,** Fulton Co.

ALSTON & BIRD (AV)

A Partnership including Professional Corporations
One Atlantic Center, 1201 West Peachtree Street, 30309-3424
Telephone: 404-881-7000
Telecopier: 404-881-7777
Cable Address: AMGRAM GA
Telex: 54-2996
Easylink: 62985848
Washington, D.C. Office: 700 Thirteenth Street, Suite 350 20005-3960.
Telephone: 202-508-3300.
Telecopier: 202-508-3333.

MEMBERS OF FIRM

Alexander E. Wilson III | Anne S. Rampacek
Robert H. Buckler | Robert P. Riordan
Forrest W. Hunter | Clare H. Draper IV
R. Steve Ensor

(See Next Column)

COUNSEL

E. Bruce Mather

ASSOCIATES

Lisa H. Cassilly | Charles H. Morgan
Frederick C. Dawkins | Eileen M. G. Scofield
Brian D. Edwards | Debra K. Scott
Michael D. Kaufman | (Not admitted in GA)

Representative Clients: Atlantic Steel Industries, Inc.; Georgia-Pacific Corporation; National Data Corporation; Printpack, Inc.

For Complete List of Firm Personnel, See General Section

For full biographical listings, see the Martindale-Hubbell Law Directory

ARNOLD & ANDERSON (AV)

1200 Peachtree Center Cain Tower, 229 Peachtree Street, N.E., 30303
Telephone: 404-584-0200
Fax: 404-584-0845

MEMBERS OF FIRM

John M. Arnold | David H. Grigereit
John K. Anderson | Kevin P. Hishta
R. Bryan Struble, Jr.

ASSOCIATE

Steven C. Ellingson

OF COUNSEL

James P. Swann, Jr.

Representative Clients: EBCO Manufacturing Co.; Flowers Industries, Inc.; Golf Host Resorts, Inc. d/b/a "Innisbrook Hilton Resort, Inc." and "Tamarron"; Life Care Centers of America; MagneTek National Electric Coil; M.O.D.E., Inc.; Mother's Cake & Cookie Co.; Petrie Stores Corp.; President Baking Co., Inc.

For full biographical listings, see the Martindale-Hubbell Law Directory

CLARK, PAUL, HOOVER & MALLARD (AV)

One Midtown Plaza, Suite 900, 1360 Peachtree Street, N.E., 30309-3214
Telephone: 404-874-7500
FAX: 404-874-0001

MEMBERS OF FIRM

William B. Paul | Bennet D. Alsher
James C. Hoover | Peter F. Munger
David C. Hagaman | Jon M. Gumbel
Norman A. Quandt | Robert E. Rigrish

ASSOCIATES

Paul T. Ryan | Steven J. Lewengrub
Patricia Greene Butler | J. Stephen O'Donnell (Not admitted in GA)

OF COUNSEL

Wade V. Mallard, Jr. | Frederick J. Lewis (Not admitted in GA)
Fletcher L. Hudson (Not admitted in GA)

Representative Clients: BTR; Georgia-Pacific Corp.; Johnson Controls; Melville Corp.; Miami Children's Hospital; Mississippi Power Co.; Motorola, Inc.; Nestle USA, Inc.; Pratt & Whitney, Division of United Technologies Corp.; Reliance Electric Co.

For full biographical listings, see the Martindale-Hubbell Law Directory

CONSTANGY, BROOKS & SMITH (AV)

2400 Peachtree Center Building, 230 Peachtree Street, N.W., 30303-1557
Telephone: 404-525-8622
Birmingham, Alabama Office: Suite 1410 AmSouth/Harbert Plaza, 1901 Sixth Avenue North.
Telephone: 205-252-9321.
Nashville, Tennessee Office: Suite 1080 Vanderbilt Plaza, 2100 West End Avenue.
Telephone: 615-320-5200.
Columbia, South Carolina Office: Suite 810 NationsBank Tower, 1301 Gervais Street.
Telephone: 803-256-3200.
Washington, D.C. Office: 1015 Fifteenth Street, N.W., Suite 1200.
Telephone: 202-789-8676.
Winston-Salem, North Carolina Office: Suite 300, 101 South Stratford Road.
Telephone: 910-721-1001. Charlotte: 704-344-1040.

MEMBERS OF FIRM

Frank A. Constangy (1911-1971) | Lee E. Boeke
Lovic A. Brooks, Jr. | Chris Mitchell (Resident, Birmingham, Alabama Office)
James F. Smith | Townsell G. Marshall, Jr.
George B. Smith | Lovic A. Brooks, III (Resident, Columbia, South Carolina Office)
Kathryn S. James (1922-1980) | Daniel P. Murphy
Michael J. Shershin, Jr. | Richard O. Brown (Resident, Birmingham, Alabama Office)
Herman L. Allison | Larry W. Bridgesmith (Resident, Nashville, Tennessee Office)
J. Richard Walton (Resident, Birmingham, Alabama Office)
Alan L. Rolnick
Edward Katze
Fred M. Richardson

(See Next Column)

CONSTANGY, BROOKS & SMITH, *Atlanta—Continued*

MEMBERS OF FIRM (Continued)

Patrick R. Tyson
William Keith Principe
Carol Sue Nelson (Resident, Birmingham, Alabama Office)
Neil H. Wasser
Terry Price
R. Carl Cannon
W. Randolph Loftis, Jr. (Resident, Winston-Salem, North Carolina Office)
William A. Blue, Jr. (Resident, Nashville, Tennessee Office)
John J. Doyle, Jr. (Resident, Winston-Salem, North Carolina Office)
Steven S. Greene
Mitchell S. Allen
Gregory W. Blount
Donald W. Benson
Frank B. Shuster

ASSOCIATES

Michael L. Blumenthal
Thomas A. Davis (Resident, Birmingham, Alabama Office)
Timothy A. Davis
Ruth L. Flemister
Michael D. Giles (Resident, Birmingham, Alabama Office)
J. Michael Kettle
Neil D. Kodsi
Robert C. Lemert, Jr.
Rosemary C. Lumpkins
Michael P. Mac Harg
Stephen Craig Moore (Resident, Nashville, Tennessee Office)
Lisa Narrell-Mead (Resident, Birmingham, Alabama Office)
Timothy R. Newton
John Charles Ormond, Jr. (Resident, Columbia, South Carolina Office)
Robin E. Shea (Resident, Winston-Salem, North Carolina Office)
David L. Smith
Kristine L. Thompson (Resident, Columbia, South Carolina Office)
Kimberly A. Weber
Nedra L. Wick
Wayne W. Wisong

OF COUNSEL

Edgar L. McGowan (Resident, Columbia, South Carolina Office)

Representative Clients: Blockbuster Entertainment Corp.; Blue Cross/Blue Shield of Alabama; Consolidated Freightways, Inc.; Delta Woodside Industries; McDonald's; Merck & Co., Inc.; Philip-Morris Cos., Inc.; Phillips Van Heusen Corp.; Sara Lee Corp.; Trust Company Bank.

For full biographical listings, see the Martindale-Hubbell Law Directory

ELARBEE, THOMPSON & TRAPNELL (AV)

800 Peachtree-Cain Tower, 229 Peachtree Street, N.E., 30303
Telephone: 404-659-6700
Fax: 404-222-9718

MEMBERS OF FIRM

Fred W. Elarbee, Jr. (1925-1986)
Robert L. Thompson
John R. Trapnell
David M. Vaughan
John Lewis Sapp
William M. Earnest
Charles K. Howard, Jr.
Walter O. Lambeth, Jr.
Robert J. Martin, Jr.
Joseph M. Freeman
Stanford G. Wilson
Brent L. Wilson
Victor A. Cavanaugh
Nancy F. Reynolds

ASSOCIATES

Sharon Parker Morgan
Mark D. Halverson
R. Read Gignilliat
Douglas H. Duerr
Victor J. Maya
Jan M. Harrison
William Drummond Deveney
Patrick L. Lail
Bernard L. McNamee, II
Kelly Michael Hundley
Kenneth N. Winkler
Frederick L. Douglas (Not admitted in GA)

Representative Clients: Cox Communications, Inc.; Dunlop Tire Corp.; National Service Industries; Atlanta Gas Light Co.; Brown & Williamson Tobacco Corp.; Engelhard Corp.; Louisiana-Pacific Corp.; MCI Communications Corp.; Florida Power and Light Co.; Southwire Co.

For full biographical listings, see the Martindale-Hubbell Law Directory

FAIN, MAJOR & WILEY, P.C. (AV)

The Hurt Building, 50 Hurt Plaza, Suite 300, 30303
Telephone: 404-688-6633
Telecopier: 404-420-1544

Donald M. Fain
Gene A. Major
Charles A. Wiley, Jr.
Thomas E. Brennan
Darryl G. Haynes
David Wayne Williams
Brian Alligood
Frederic H. Pilch, III
Derek A. Mendicino

Representative Clients: Allstate Insurance Co.; Budget Rent-A-Car; Carolina Freight Carriers Corp.; Chrysler Insurance Co.; Georgia Farm Bureau Mutual Insurance Co.; Great Atlantic & Pacific Tea Co.; Hertz Corp.; Universal Underwriters Insurance Co.; Westfield Insurance co.; Winn-Dixie Stores, Inc.

For Complete List of Firm Personnel, See General Section
For full biographical listings, see the Martindale-Hubbell Law Directory

FISHER & PHILLIPS (AV)

A Partnership including Professional Corporations and Associations
1500 Resurgens Plaza, 945 East Paces Ferry Road, N.E., 30326
Telephone: 404-231-1400
Telecopier: 404-240-4249;
Telex: 54-2331
Fort Lauderdale, Florida Office: Suite 2310 NationsBank Tower, One Financial Plaza, 33394.
Telephone: 305-525-4800.
Telecopier: 305-525-8739.
Redwood City, California Office: Suite 345, Three Lagoon Drive, 94065.
Telephone: 415-592-6160.
Telecopier: 415-592-6385.
Newport Beach, California Office: 4675 MacArthur Court, Suite 550, 92660.
Telephone: 714-851-2424.
Telecopier: 714-851-0152.
New Orleans, Louisiana Office: 3710 Place St. Charles, 201 St. Charles Avenue, 70170.
Telephone: 504-522-3303.
Telecopier: 504-522-3850.

MEMBERS OF FIRM

I. Walter Fisher (P.C.)
Erle Phillips (P.C.)
Robert J. Berghel (P.C.)
Donald E. Wright (P.C.)
Charles Kelso
Donald B. Harden (P.C.)
H. Victor Hansen (P.C.)
Robert W. Ashmore
John M. Capron
James M. Walters (P.C.)
Claud L. McIver, III, (P.C.)
Henry A. Huettner
Ned A. Fine (Resident, Redwood City, California Office)
Griffin B. Bell, Jr.
William F. Kaspers (P.C.)
Dean E. Rice (P.C.)
Reginald J. Bell
Michael C. Towers
Robert C. Christenson
Ralph J. Zatzkis (Resident, New Orleans, Louisiana Office)
Charles S. Caulkins (P.A.) (Resident, Fort Lauderdale, Florida Office)
Robert J. Bekken (Resident, Newport Beach, California Office)
Ann Margaret Pointer
Michael S. Mitchell (Resident, New Orleans, Louisiana Office)
F. Kytle Frye, III
John E. Donovan
John E. Thompson
Thomas P. Rebel
Benjamin B. Culp, Jr.
Ruth W. Woodling
Douglas R. Sullenberger
Mairen C. Kelly
James D. Morgan (Resident, New Orleans, Louisiana Office)
Sandra Mills Feingerts (Resident, New Orleans, Louisiana Office)
Roger K. Quillen
John B. Gamble, Jr.
Walter J. Kruger, III
John D. McLachlan (Resident, Redwood City, California Office)
Burton F. Dodd
Christopher D. Robinson (Resident, Fort Lauderdale, Florida Office)
Lawrence S. McGoldrick
D. Albert Brannen
James J. McDonald, Jr. (Resident, Newport Beach, California Office)
Howard A. Mavity
Robert P. Foster
David R. Kresser
David C. Whitlock
Keith B. Romich
Charles A. Hawkins

OF COUNSEL

James C. Polkinghorn (Resident, Fort Lauderdale, Florida Office)

ASSOCIATES

Daniel R. Kopti
Andria Lure Ryan
Cynthia L. Gleason
Kurt N. Peterson
Karl R. Lindegren (Resident, Newport Beach, California Office)
Kenneth A. Knox (Resident, Fort Lauderdale, Florida Office)
David E. Duclos
Robert V. Schnitz (Resident, Newport Beach, California Office)
Lynn D. Lieber (Resident, Redwood City, California Office)
Jeffrey A. Schwartz (Resident, New Orleans, Louisiana Office)
Cameron S. Pierce
Steven M. Bernstein
Annette Marie Houck (Resident, Redwood City, California Office)
Joseph M. English
Georgia V. Ingram (Resident, Newport Beach, California Office)
Stephen J. Roppolo (Resident, New Orleans, Louisiana Office)
Lynne M. Murphy (Resident, New Orleans, Louisiana Office)
Christine E. Howard
Kenneth J. Barr
Michael D. Kabat
Hilary M. Lancaster
John M. Polson (Resident, Newport Beach, California Office)
Gary E. Thomas
Ilene Weisbard Berman
Bardeen H. Dunphy
Tillman Y. Coffey
Timothy R. Maguire
David H. Spalter (Resident, Fort Lauderdale, Florida Office)
Robert A. Lippitt
David A. Pierce (Resident, Newport Beach, California Office)
Myra K. Creighton
Richard H. Kimberly, Jr.
Audrey N. Browne (Resident, New Orleans, Louisiana Office)
Suzanne K. Sleep (Resident, Fort Lauderdale, Florida Office)
C. R. Wright

(See Next Column)

FISHER & PHILLIPS—*Continued*

ASSOCIATES (Continued)

Donald E. Cope (Resident, Redwood City, California Office)	Anderson B. Scott
Tracy L. Moon, Jr.	Gordon J. Rose
Stephanie M. Baldauff	Michelle C. Hamilton (Resident, New Orleans, Louisiana Office)
Jeffrey B. Freid (Resident, Newport Beach, California Office)	Susan Rinehart Ashcom
	Howard B. Jackson

Representative Clients: Airborne Express Corp.; Alaska International Industries, Inc.; Emory University; The Henley Group, Inc.; Miller Brewing Co.; The Prudential Insurance Company of America; United States Sugar Corp.; Yellow Freight System, Inc.

For full biographical listings, see the Martindale-Hubbell Law Directory

FORD & HARRISON (AV)

600 Peachtree at the Circle Building, 1275 Peachtree Street, N.E., 30309
Telephone: 404-888-3800
FAX: 404-888-3863
Los Angeles, California Office: 333 South Grand Avenue, Suite 3680, 90071.
Telephone: 213-680-3410.
Fax: 213-680-4161.
Washington, D.C. Office: 1920 N Street, N.W., Suite 200, 20036.
Telephone: 202-463-6633.
Fax: 202-466-5705.

MEMBERS OF FIRM

William F. Ford (1936-1990)	Thomas J. Kassin
C. Lash Harrison	E. Scott Smith
Michael L. Lowry	Glen H. Mertens (Not admitted in GA; Resident, Los Angeles, California Office)
Ronald R. Kimzey	Jack B. Albanese
Ronald C. Henson (Resident, Washington, D.C. Office)	Patricia G. Griffith
Michael H. Campbell	Karin A. Verdon
D. Gerald Coker	F. Carter Tate
Paul David Jones	William N. Hiers, Jr.
Jeffrey W. Bell	Mallory E. Phillips, III
Paula A. Hilburn	

SENIOR COUNSEL

Claude T. Sullivan	Joshua M. Javits (Resident, Washington, D.C. Office)
Frederick L. Warren, III	

ASSOCIATES

Rebecca D. Cottingham	Steven K. Kirson
Maral Donoyan (Resident, Los Angeles, California Office)	Andrew D. McClintock
Terry P. Finnerty	John L. Monroe, Jr.
David N. Goldman	M. Elizabeth Ortega
Kari Haugen (Resident, Los Angeles, California Office)	Sarah B. Pierce
Ruth H. Heinzman	Chad A. Shultz
John P. Kelly	John S. Snelling
	John R. Sumner, Jr (Resident, Washington, D.C. Office)

OF COUNSEL

F. Carlton King, Jr.	Glenn R. Bunting
Steven J. Ross	

Representative Clients: Coca-Cola Enterprises; Delta Air Lines, Inc.; Publix Super Markets, Inc.; Federal Express Corporation; Knight Publishing Company; LIN Television Corp.; Regional Airline Assn.; Rheem Manufacturing Co.; The Standard Register Co.

For full biographical listings, see the Martindale-Hubbell Law Directory

JONES, DAY, REAVIS & POGUE (AV)

3500 One Peachtree Center, 303 Peachtree Street, N.E., 30308-3242
Telephone: 404-521-3939
Cable Address: "Attorneys Atlanta"
Telex: 54-2711
Telecopier: 404-581-8330
In Brussels, Belgium: Avenue Louise 480, 7th Floor, B-1050 Brussels.
Telephone: 011-32-2-645-14-11.
Telecopier: 011-32-2-645-14-45.
In Chicago, Illinois: 77 West Wacker.
Telephone: 312-782-3939.
Telecopier: 312-782-8585.
In Cleveland, Ohio: North Point. 901 Lakeside Avenue.
Telephone: 216-586-3939.
Cable Address: "Attorneys Cleveland".
Telex: 980389.
Telecopier: 216-579-0212.
In Columbus, Ohio: 1900 Huntington Center.
Telephone: 614-469-3939.
Cable Address: "Attorneys Columbus".
Telecopier: 614-461-4198.
In Dallas, Texas: 2300 Trammell Crow Center, 2001 Ross Avenue.
Telephone: 214-220-3939.
Cable Address: "Attorneys Dallas."
Telex: 730852.
Telecopier: 214-969-5100.

(See Next Column)

In Frankfurt, Germany: Westendstrasse 41, 60325 Frankfurt am Main.
Telephone: 011-49-69-7438-3939.
Telecopier: 011-49-69-741-1686.
In Geneva, Switzerland: 20, rue de Candolle.
Telephone: 011-41-22-320-2339.
Telecopier: 011-41-22-320-1232.
In Hong Kong: 1501 One Exchange Square, 8 Connaught Place.
Telephone: 011-852-526-6895.
Telecopier: 011-852-810-5787.
In Irvine, California: 2603 Main Street, Suite 900.
Telephone: 714-851-3939.
Telex: 194911 Lawyers LSA.
Telecopier: 714-553-7539.
In London, England: One Mount Street.
Telephone: 011-44-71-493-9361.
Cable Address: "Surgoe London WI."
Telecopier: 011-44-71-493-9666.
In Los Angeles, California: 555 West Fifth Street, Suite 4600.
Telephone: 213-489-3939.
Telex: 181439 UD.
Telecopier: 213-243-2539.
In New York, New York: 599 Lexington Avenue.
Telephone: 212-326-3939.
Cable Address: "JONESDAY NEWYORK."
Telex: 237013 JDRP UR.
Telecopier: 212-755-7306.
In Paris, France: 62, rue du Faubourg Saint-Honore.
Telephone: 011-33-1-44-71-3939.
Cable Address: "Surgoe Paris."
Telex: 290156 Surgoe.
Telecopier: 011-33-1-49-24-0471.
In Pittsburgh, Pennsylvania: 500 Grant Street, 31st Floor.
Telephone: 412-391-3939.
Cable Address: "Attorneys Pittsburgh".
Telecopier: 412-394-7959.
In Riyadh, Saudi Arabia: Law Offices of Saud M.A. Shawwaf, P.O. Box 2700.
Telephones: 011 (966-1) 465-6543, 011 (966-1) 464-8534 or 011 (966-1) 464-8540.
Telex: 401831 SAUCON SJ.
Telecopier: (966-1) 464-8480.
In Taipei, Taiwan: 7th Floor, 2 Tun Hwa South Road, Section 2.
Telephone: 011 (886-2) 704-6808 and 704-6809.
Telecopier: 011 (886-2) 704-6791.
In Tokyo, Japan: Shiroyama JT Mori Bldg., 15th Floor, 3-1, Toranomon 4-chome Minato-ku.
Telephone: 011-81-3-3433-3939.
Telecopier: 011-81-3-5401-2725.
In Washington, D.C.: Metropolitan Square, 1450 G Street, N.W.
Telephone: 202-879-3939.
Cable Address: "Attorneys Washington."
Telex: 89-2410 ATTORNEYS WASH.
Telecopier: 202-737-2832. 2-737-2832.

MEMBER OF FIRM IN ATLANTA

Deborah A. Sudbury

For Complete List of Firm Personnel, See General Section

For full biographical listings, see the Martindale-Hubbell Law Directory

KILPATRICK & CODY (AV)

Suite 2800, 1100 Peachtree Street, 30309-4530
Telephone: 404-815-6500
Telephone Copier: 404-815-6555
Telex: 54-2307
Washington, D.C. Office: Suite 800, 700 13th Street, N.W., 20005.
Telephone: 202-508-5800. Telephone Copier: 202-508-5858.
Brussels, Belgium Office: Avenue Louise 65, BTE 3, 1050 Brussels.
Telephone: (32) (2) 533-03-00.
Telecopier: (32) (2) 534-86-38.
London, England Office: 68 Pall Mall, London, SW1Y 5ES, England.
Telephone: (44) (71) 321 0477.
Telecopier: (44) (71) 930 9733.
Augusta, Georgia Office: Suite 1400 First Union Bank Building, P.O. Box 2043, 30903. Telephone (706) 724-2622. Telecopier (706) 722-0219.

MEMBERS OF FIRM

Duane C. Aldrich	William H. Boice
Susan A. Cahoon	Edmund M. Kneisel
Richard R. Boisseau	Thomas H. Christopher
James H. Coil III	R. Slaton Tuggle, III
Diane L. Prucino	

COUNSEL

G. Paris Sykes, Jr.

ASSOCIATES

Kevin E. Hooks	Jane W. Robbins
Walter E. Johnson	Lori J. Shapiro
Charles M. Rice	Jeffrey A. Van Detta
Amy Weinstein	

Representative Clients: Frito-Lay, Inc.; The Pepsi-Cola Company; Pizza Hut, Inc.; Scientific-Atlanta, Inc.; Bank South Corporation; Intermet Corp.; Lockheed Aeronautical Systems Co.; The Grand Union Co.; Pullman Power Products Corporation.

(See Next Column)

KILPATRICK & CODY, *Atlanta—Continued*

For Complete List of Firm Personnel, See General Section

For full biographical listings, see the Martindale-Hubbell Law Directory

LONG ALDRIDGE & NORMAN (AV)

A Partnership including Professional Corporations
One Peachtree Center, Suite 5300, 303 Peachtree Street, 30308
Telephone: 404-527-4000
Telecopier: 404-527-4198
Washington, D.C. Office: Suite 950, 1615 L Street, 20036.
Telephone: 202-223-7033.
Telecopier: 202-223-7013.

MEMBERS OF FIRM

Phillip A. Bradley — Deborah S. Ebel

ASSOCIATES

J. Michell Philpott — Sheryl L. Thomson

For Complete List of Firm Personnel, See General Section

For full biographical listings, see the Martindale-Hubbell Law Directory

McKEE & BARGE (AV)

Suite 400, The Candler Building, 127 Peachtree Street, N.E., 30303
Telephone: 404-577-8300
Fax: 404-577-4902

MEMBERS OF FIRM

Patrick W. McKee — Richmond Mason Barge
Christopher J. Ramig

ASSOCIATE

Richard H. Barbe

OF COUNSEL

J. Robert Thompson

For full biographical listings, see the Martindale-Hubbell Law Directory

OGLETREE, DEAKINS, NASH, SMOAK & STEWART (AV)

3800 One Atlantic Center, 1201 West Peachtree Street, N.W., 30309
Telephone: 404-881-1300
Facsimile: 404-870-1732
Washington, D.C. Office: Fifth Floor, 2400 N Street, N.W.
Telephone: 202-887-0855.
Greenville, South Carolina Office: The Ogletree Building, 300 North Main Street, P.O. Box 2757.
Telephone: 803-271-1300.
Charleston, South Carolina Office: First Union Building, Suite 310, 177 Meeting Street, P.O. Box 1808.
Telephone: 803-853-1300.
Columbia, South Carolina Office: Palmetto Center, Suite 1820, 1426 Main Street, P.O. Box 11206.
Telephone: 803-252-1300.
Nashville, Tennessee Office: St. Cloud Corner, 500 Church Street.
Telephone: 615-254-1900.
Raleigh, North Carolina Office: 4101 Lake Boone Trail, Suite 511, P.O. Box 31608.
Telephone: 919-787-9700.
Albany, New York Office: 4th Floor, One Steuben Place.
Telephone: 518-434-1300.

MEMBERS OF FIRM

Homer L. Deakins, Jr.
J. Roy Weathersby
M. Baker Wyche, III
Martha C. Perrin
Robert O. Sands
William A. Gray
Michael L. Chapman
Margaret Hutchins Campbell
Dara L. DeHaven
Michael S. Thwaites
Dion Y. Kohler
William S. Myers
Charles E. Feuss
David Edward Jones
Jay Michael Barber
Phillip Lee Conner
C. Thomas Davis
Kristofer K. Strasser
Janet Quick Lewis
Devin M. Ehrlich
Lewis F. Gossett
Gregory J. Hare
Mark L. Keenan
Rosemary Globetti
Dionysia L. Johnson
Gail E. Farr

For full biographical listings, see the Martindale-Hubbell Law Directory

SCHULTEN & WARD (AV)

Suite 930 The Hurt Building, 50 Hurt Plaza, 30303
Telephone: 404-688-6800
Fax: 404-688-6840

MEMBERS OF FIRM

Wm. Scott Schulten — Kevin L. Ward

ASSOCIATES

David L. Turner — Susan Kastan Murphey
Erik V. Huey

Reference: NationsBank of Georgia, N.A.

For full biographical listings, see the Martindale-Hubbell Law Directory

SHAPIRO, FUSSELL, WEDGE, SMOTHERMAN & MARTIN (AV)

One Midtown Plaza, Suite 1200, 1360 Peachtree Street, 30309
Telephone: 404-870-2200
Facsimile: 404-870-2222

MEMBERS OF FIRM

J. Ben Shapiro, Jr.
Ira J. Smotherman, Jr.
Herman L. Fussell
Robert B. Wedge
Ronald J. Garber
Charles F. Williams
Nicholas S. Papleacos
Seth Price
Michael P. Davis
Cyrell E. Lynch
David L. Tank

ASSOCIATES

Connie H. Buffington — Daniel M. Jennings
Scott I. Zucker

Representative Clients: McKenney's Inc.; PPG Industries, Inc.; The Pinkerton and Laws Co.; Cleveland Electric Co.; Acousti Engineering Co.; Georgia Marble Co.; Owen Steel Co., Inc.; The Glidden Co.; Intrepid Enterprises.

For full biographical listings, see the Martindale-Hubbell Law Directory

SMITH, CURRIE & HANCOCK (AV)

2600 Harris Tower-Peachtree Center, 233 Peachtree Street, N.E., 30303-1530
Telephone: 404-521-3800
Telecopier: 404-688-0671

MEMBERS OF FIRM

G. Maynard Smith (1907-1992).
Overton A. Currie
E. Reginald Hancock (Retired)
Luther P. House, Jr.
Glower W. Jones
Robert B. Ansley, Jr.
George K. McPherson, Jr.
Bert R. Oastler
James Allan Smith
John G. Skinner
J. Thomas Kilpatrick
Aubrey L. Coleman, Jr.
Larry E. Forrester
Thomas E. Abernathy, IV
Philip L. Fortune
John C. Stout, Jr.
Daniel M. Shea
Thomas J. Kelleher, Jr.
Frank E. Riggs, Jr.
Ronald G. Robey
Dan T. Carter
William E. Dorris
Brian G. Corgan
Charles W. Surasky
Robert N. Godfrey
John T. Flynn
James F. Butler, III
Joseph C. Staak
Hubert J. Bell, Jr.
Philip E. Beck
Neal J. Sweeney
Frederick L. Wright
James K. Bidgood, Jr.
Randall F. Hafer
S. Gregory Joy
Fredric W. Stearns
Robert C. Chambers
Karl Dix, Jr.
George Q. Sewell

OF COUNSEL

James E. Stephenson — Frank O. Hendrick III

ASSOCIATES

D. Lee Roberts, Jr.
William R. Poplin, Jr.
Ivor J. Longo
Joseph Paul Henner
John E. Menechino, Jr.
Marty N. Martenson
Edward A. Arnold
Charles A. Bledsoe, Jr.
Daniel F. DuPré
Catherine M. Hobart
George Papaioanou
M. Craig Hall
Christine M. MacIver
Craig P. Siegenthaler
Suzanne Jones
R. Randy Edwards

Labor Relations Clients: Atlanta Symphony Orchestra; Babcock & Wilcox Co.; Diversified Products Corp.; Echlin, Inc.; Genuine Parts Co. (NAPA); Proctor & Gamble Co.; Oxford Industries; Sears Roebuck and Co.
Construction Clients: Seaboard Surety Co.; Travelers Indemnity Co.

For full biographical listings, see the Martindale-Hubbell Law Directory

STOKES LAZARUS & CARMICHAEL (AV)

80 Peachtree Park Drive, N.E., 30309-1320
Telephone: 404-352-1465
Fax: 404-352-8463

MEMBERS OF FIRM

Marion B. Stokes — William K. Carmichael
Wayne H. Lazarus — Michael J. Ernst

ASSOCIATES

C. W. Tab Billingsley, Jr. — Douglas L. Brooks
Derek W. Johanson

For full biographical listings, see the Martindale-Hubbell Law Directory

STOKES & MURPHY (AV)

Waterstone, Suite 350, 4751 Best Road, 30337
Telephone: 404-766-0076
Fax: 404-766-8823
Santa Monica, California Office: 520 Broadway, Suite 300.
Telephone: 310-451-3337.

(See Next Column)

STOKES & MURPHY—*Continued*

Arch Y. Stokes
McNeill Stokes
Robert L. Murphy (Resident, Santa Monica Office)
John R. Hunt
Margaret Mead Stokes
Karl M. Terrell

ASSOCIATES

Cassandra Kirk
Debra Gordon
Michael Pepperman (Not admitted in GA)
Anne-Marie Mizel (Not admitted in GA)
Annette Sanford Werner (Not admitted in GA)

For full biographical listings, see the Martindale-Hubbell Law Directory

*GAINESVILLE,** Hall Co.

HARBEN & HARTLEY (AV)

539 Green Street, P.O. Box 2975, 30503
Telephone: 404-534-7341
FAX: 404-532-0399

MEMBERS OF FIRM

Sam S. Harben, Jr.
Phillip L. Hartley
Martha McMasters Pearson

ASSOCIATE

Emily Bagwell Harben

LEGAL SUPPORT PERSONNEL

Barbara J. Smith
Lisa A. Rosetti

For full biographical listings, see the Martindale-Hubbell Law Directory

*MACON,** Bibb Co.

ANDERSON, WALKER & REICHERT (AV)

Suite 404 Trust Company Bank Building, P.O. Box 6497, 31208-6497
Telephone: 912-743-8651
Telecopier: 912-743-9636

MEMBERS OF FIRM

John W. Collier
Susan S. Cole

ASSOCIATE

John P. Cole

Representative Clients: Riverwood International Georgia, Inc.; Hospital Corporation of America; Pepsi-Cola Bottling Company of Macon; Radiology Associates of Macon, P.C.; Thiele Kaolin Company; Trust Company Bank of Middle Georgia, N.A.
General Insurance Clients: Liberty Mutual Insurance Co.; United States Fidelity & Guaranty Co.; Continental Insurance Cos.; Alexis, Inc.

For Complete List of Firm Personnel, See General Section

For full biographical listings, see the Martindale-Hubbell Law Directory

HAYNSWORTH, BALDWIN, JOHNSON AND HARPER (AV)

577 Mulberry Street, Suite 710, P.O. Box 1975, 31202-1975
Telephone: 912-746-0262
Facsimile: 912-746-0797
Tampa, Florida Office: 600 North Westshore Boulevard, Suite 200.
Telephone: 813-289-1247.
Jacksonville, Florida Office: 1506 Prudential Drive, P.O. Box 40593.
Telephone: 904-396-3000.
Greenville, South Carolina Office: Haynsworth, Baldwin, Johnson & Greaves, P.A., 918 South Pleasantburg Drive, P.O. Box 10888.
Telephone: 803-271-7410.
Columbia, South Carolina Office: Haynsworth, Baldwin, Johnson & Greaves, P.A., 1201 Main Street, Suite 1230.
Telephone: 803-799-5858.
Raleigh, North Carolina Office: Haynsworth, Baldwin, Johnson & Greaves, P.A., 3605 Glenwood Avenue, Suite 210. P.O. Box 10035.
Telephone: 919-782-3340.
Greensboro, North Carolina Office: Haynsworth, Baldwin, Johnson & Greaves, P.A., 230 North Elm Street, Suite 1650.
Telephone: 910-373-0325.
Charlotte, North Carolina Office: Haynsworth, Baldwin, Johnson & Greaves, P.A., 400 West Trade Street.
Telephone: 704-342-2588.

MEMBERS OF FIRM

Knox L. Haynsworth, Jr. (Not admitted in GA)
John G. Creech
W. Melvin Haas, III (Resident)

Jeffery L. Thompson (Resident)

OF COUNSEL

Edgar W. Ennis, Jr. (Resident)

Representative Clients: Boeing Georgia, Inc.; Fieldcrest Cannon, Inc.; General Mills; Georgia Employers Assn.; Gold Kist, Inc.; The Kroger Co.; McDonnell Douglas Corp.; Northrop Corp.; St. Joseph Hospital; Wm. Wrigley Jr. Co.

For full biographical listings, see the Martindale-Hubbell Law Directory

HAWAII

*HONOLULU,** Honolulu Co.

DWYER IMANAKA SCHRAFF KUDO MEYER & FUJIMOTO ATTORNEYS AT LAW, A LAW CORPORATION (AV)

1800 Pioneer Plaza, 900 Fort Street Mall, 96813
Telephone: 808-524-8000
Telecopier: 808-526-1419
Mailing Address: P.O. Box 2727, 96803

John R. Dwyer, Jr.
Mitchell A. Imanaka
Paul A. Schraff
Benjamin A. Kudo (Atty. at Law, A Law Corp.)
William G. Meyer, III
Wesley M. Fujimoto
Ronald Van Grant
Jon M. H. Pang
Blake W. Bushnell
Kenn N. Kojima

Adelbert Green
Richard T. Asato, Jr.
Scott W. Settle
Darcie S. Yoshinaga
Tracy Timothy Woo
Lawrence I. Kawasaki
Douglas H. Inouye
Christine A. Low

OF COUNSEL

Randall Y. Iwase

For full biographical listings, see the Martindale-Hubbell Law Directory

TORKILDSON, KATZ, JOSSEM, FONSECA, JAFFE, MOORE & HETHERINGTON ATTORNEYS AT LAW, A LAW CORPORATION (AV)

Amfac Building, 15th Floor, 700 Bishop Street, 96813-4187
Telephone: 808-521-1051
Cable Address: "Counsel"
Telex: RCA 723-8185
Telecopier: 808-521-8239
Kailua-Kona, Hawaii Office: 75-5706 Kuakini Highway, Suite 105.
Telephone: 808-329-8581.
Telecopier: 808-329-3837.
Hilo, Hawaii Office: 100 Pauahi Street, Suite 206.
Telephone: 808-961-0406.
Telecopier: 808-935-1225.

Raymond M. Torkildson
Robert S. Katz
Jared H. Jossem
Ernest C. Moore, III
Richard M. Rand
Jeffrey S. Harris
Gregory M. Sato
John L. Knorek
Sabrina R. Toma
Perry W. Confalone
Wayne S. Yoshigai

Kitty K. Kamaka
Clayton A. Kamida (Not admitted in HI)

Representative Clients: Alexander & Baldwin, Inc.; Aloha Airlines, Inc.; Amfac, Inc.; Castle and Cooke, Inc.; Castle Medical Center; Theo H. Davies and Co., Ltd.; First Hawaiian Bank; General Motors Corp.; Council of Hawaii Hotels.

For Complete List of Firm Personnel, See General Section

For full biographical listings, see the Martindale-Hubbell Law Directory

IDAHO

*BOISE,** Ada Co.

ELAM & BURKE, A PROFESSIONAL ASSOCIATION (AV)

Key Financial Center, 702 West Idaho Street, P.O. Box 1539, 83701
Telephone: 208-343-5454
Telecopier: 208-384-5844

James D. LaRue
Ryan P. Armbruster
Bobbi Killian Dominick

Representative Clients: Morrison-Knudsen, Inc.; Texas Instruments, Inc.; Prudential Securities, Inc.; Pechiney Corp.; Dow Corning Corporation; U.S. West Communications; State Farm Insurance Cos.; Sinclair Oil Company d/b/a Sun Valley Company; Farmers Insurance Group; Hecla Mining Company.

For Complete List of Firm Personnel, See General Section

For full biographical listings, see the Martindale-Hubbell Law Directory

IMHOFF & LYNCH (AV)

1607 West Jefferson Street, P.O. Box 739, 83701
Telephone: 208-336-6900
Facsimile: 208-336-7031

(See Next Column)

IMHOFF & LYNCH, *Boise—Continued*

MEMBERS OF FIRM

James B. Lynch
Thomas P. Baskin, III
Michael W. Moore
Paige Alan Parker

Kaaren Lynn Barr
Penny L. Dykas
Mary L. McDougal

OF COUNSEL

Joseph M. Imhoff, Jr.

Representative Clients: United State Aviation Underwriters, Aetna Casualty & Surety, Co., Yellow Freight, Underwriters at Llodys, Willis Coroon Management Co., Inc., National Union Fire Insurance Co., Capital Insurance Co., Coleman Co., Alfa Laval Agri., Inc., Admiral Insurance Co.
Reference: First Security Bank.

For full biographical listings, see the Martindale-Hubbell Law Directory

MOFFATT, THOMAS, BARRETT, ROCK & FIELDS, CHARTERED (AV)

First Security Building, 911 West Idaho Street, Suite 300, P.O. Box 829, 83701
Telephone: 208-345-2000
FAX: 208-385-5384
Idaho Falls Office: 525 Park Avenue, Suite 2D, P.O. Box 1367, 83403.
Telephone: 208-522-6700.
FAX: 208-522-5111.
Pocatello, Idaho Office: 1110 Call Creek Drive, P.O. Box 4941, 83201.
Telephone: 208-233-2001.

Richard C. Fields

Representative Clients: BMC West Corporation; Chevron, U.S.A.; First Security Bank of Idaho, N.A.; General Motors Corp.; Idaho Potato Commission; Intermountain Gas Co.; John Alden Life Insurance Co.; Micron, Inc.; Royal Insurance Cos.; St. Luke's Regional Medical Center & Mountain States Tumor Institute.

For Complete List of Firm Personnel, See General Section
For full biographical listings, see the Martindale-Hubbell Law Directory

ILLINOIS

*BELLEVILLE,** St. Clair Co.

THOMPSON & MITCHELL (AV)

525 West Main Street, 62220
Telephone: 618-277-4700; 314-271-1800
Telecopier: 618-236-3434
St. Louis, Missouri Office: One Mercantile Center, Suite 3300.
Telephone: 314-231-7676.
Telecopier: 314-342-1717.
St. Charles, Missouri Office: 200 North Third Street.
Telephone: 314-946-7717.
Telecopier: 314-946-4938.
Washington, D.C. Office: 700 14th Street, N.W., Suite 900.
Telephone: 202-508-1000.
Telecopier: 202-508-1010.

MEMBERS OF FIRM

David F. Yates
Charles M. Poplstein
Allan McD. Goodloe, Jr.
Harry W. Wellford, Jr.

OF COUNSEL

Robert L. Broderick

ASSOCIATES

Kelly M. Brown
Karen A. Carr

Representative Clients: First Illinois Bank; Harcros Pigments, Inc.; Magna Group, Inc.; Memorial Hospital of Belleville; Monterey Coal Company, a division of Exxon Corporation; Norfolk Southern Corp. & affiliates; Peabody Coal Company; Zeigler Coal Company; City of Belleville.

For Complete List of Firm Personnel, See General Section
For full biographical listings, see the Martindale-Hubbell Law Directory

*CHICAGO,** Cook Co.

BATES MECKLER BULGER & TILSON (AV)

8300 Sears Tower, 233 South Wacker, 60606
Telephone: 312-474-7900
Facsimile: 312-474-7898

MEMBERS OF FIRM

Robert J. Bates, Jr.
Brian W. Bulger
Scott L. Carey
Patrick J. Foley
J. Stuart Garbutt
Paul R. Garry
Maryann C. Hayes
Mari Henry Leigh
Michael M. Marick
Bruce R. Meckler
Steven D. Pearson
Joseph E. Tilson

(See Next Column)

ASSOCIATES

Dina L. Brantman
Catherine M. Crisham
Robin Edelstein
Maria G. Enriquez
Stanley V. Figura
Judith Y. Gaston
Mary E. Gootjes
Michael J. Gray
Robert C. Heist
Julie Marie Hextell
Darlene M. Jarzyna
Kathleen H. Jensen
Michael I. Leonard
Mary F. Licari
James A. Lupo, Jr.
Susan M. Narimatsu
Brett G. Rawitz
John E. Rodewald
Scott M. Seaman
Mark G. Sheridan
Frederick W. Stein
Monica T. Sullivan
Timothy A. Wolfe

For full biographical listings, see the Martindale-Hubbell Law Directory

BELL, BOYD & LLOYD (AV)

Three First National Plaza Suite 3300, 70 West Madison Street, 60602
Telephone: 312-372-1121
FAX: 312-372-2098
Washington, D.C. Office: 1615 L Street, N.W.
Telephone: 202-466-6300.
FAX: 202-463-0678.

MEMBERS OF FIRM

Nancy E. Bertoglio
Jeffrey A. Blevins
James P. Daley
Stanley J. Garber
John P. (Pete) Morrison
David M. Novak
Gregory J. Schroedter
Alan M. Serwer
Edwin C. Thomas, III

OF COUNSEL

William B. Hanley

ASSOCIATE

Joanne L. Hyman

For Complete List of Firm Personnel, See General Section
For full biographical listings, see the Martindale-Hubbell Law Directory

SUSAN BOGART (AV)

Twenty North Clark Street, Suite 808, 60602
Telephone: 312-726-9060
Fax: 312-726-9248

For full biographical listings, see the Martindale-Hubbell Law Directory

THE LAW OFFICES OF EDNA SELAN EPSTEIN (AV)

321 South Plymouth Court Suite 800, 60603
Telephone: 312-408-2750
FAX: 312-408-2760

Edna Selan Epstein

For full biographical listings, see the Martindale-Hubbell Law Directory

FOX & GROVE, CHARTERED (AV)

311 South Wacker Drive Suite 6200, 60606
Telephone: 312-876-0500
Telecopier: 312-362-0700
St. Petersburg, Florida Office: Fox, Grove, Abbey, Adams, Reynolds, Byclick & Kiernan, Eleventh Floor, 360 Central Avenue.
Telephone: 813-821-2080.
Tampa, Florida Office: Fox, Grove, Abbey, Adams, Reynolds, Byclick & Kiernan, 500 East Kennedy Boulevard, Suite 200.
Telephone: 813-253-0745.
San Francisco, California Office: 240 Stockton Street, Suite 900.
Telephone: 415-956-1360.

Shayle P. Fox
Lawrence M. Cohen
S. Richard Pincus
Russell M. Kofoed
Jeffrey S. Goldman
Marty Denis
Steven L. Gillman
William Henry Barrett
Allison C. Blakley
Jeffrey E. Beeson

OF COUNSEL

Kalvin M. Grove
Joseph M. Kehoe, Jr.

Tamra S. Domeyer
Jill J. Gladney
Mari Rose Hatzenbuehler
Davi L. Hirsch
Joshua D. Holleb
Diane Kristen
Steven H. Kuh
Steven I. Locke
Daniel R. Madock
Robert M. Mintz
Paul A. Olsen
Michael Paull
Joel W. Rice
Peter S. Rukin
Kerry Evan Saltzman
Michael L. Sullivan
Douglas M. Werman

Labor Counsel for: Sears Roebuck and Co.; National Association of Independent Insurers; Alliance of American Insurers.
Representative Labor Client: Liberty Mutual Insurance Co.

For full biographical listings, see the Martindale-Hubbell Law Directory

Chicago—Continued

GESSLER, FLYNN, FLEISCHMANN, HUGHES & SOCOL, LTD. (AV)

Three First National Plaza, Suite 2200, 60602
Telephone: 312-580-0100
Telecopy: 312-580-1994

Mark S. Dym
Michael J. Flaherty
Thomas J. Fleischmann
Terence E. Flynn
George W. Gessler
John K. Hughes
William P. Jones
Peter M. Katsaros
Mark A. LaRose
Terence J. Moran
Matthew J. Piers
David J. Pritchard
Kalman D. Resnick
Jonathan A. Rothstein
Donna Kaner Socol

Eric Berg
Benjamin P. Beringer
Anjali Dayal
Ruth M. Dunning
Jennifer Fischer
Charles J. Holley
Laura C. Liu
Kimberley Marsh
Alex W. Miller
Paul A. Reasoner
Michael P. Simkus
Marci S. Sperling
Maria L. Venturo
Vanessa J. Weathersby
Mark B. Weiner
Charles H. Winterstein

OF COUNSEL

James T. Derico, Jr.
Susan R. Gzesh
Foster Marshall, Jr.

For full biographical listings, see the Martindale-Hubbell Law Directory

LANER, MUCHIN, DOMBROW, BECKER, LEVIN AND TOMINBERG, LTD. (AV)

515 North State Street, Suite 2800, 60610
Telephone: 312-467-9800
Fax: 312-467-9479

Richard W. Laner
Lawrence F. Doppelt (1935-1979)
Arthur B. Muchin
Anthony E. Dombrow
William L. Becker
Alan M. Levin
Carl S. Tominberg
Mark L. Juster
Gary Alan Wincek
Robert M. Klein
Michael Klupchak
Joseph H. Yastrow
Joseph M. Gagliardo
Robert H. Brown
James J. Convery
Robert S. Letchinger
Violet M. Clark
James F. Vanek

Thomas Bradley
Beth A. Clukey
Maureen A. Gorman
Jill P. O'Brien
Clifford R. Perry, III
Dawn E. Sellstrom
Jane E. Shaffer
Thomas Vasiljevich

OF COUNSEL

Isaiah S. Dorfman
Herman J. De Koven
Seymour Cohen

References: NBD Bank Chicago; Illinois; La Salle National Bank & Trust Co.

For full biographical listings, see the Martindale-Hubbell Law Directory

MCBRIDE BAKER & COLES (AV)

500 West Madison Street 40th Floor, 60661
Telephone: 312-715-5700
Cable Address: "Chilaw"
Telex: 270258
Telecopier: 312-993-9350

MEMBERS OF FIRM

William J. Cooney
Kenneth A. Jenero
Steven B. Varick

ASSOCIATES

Patrick W. Kocian
Richard F. Nelson

For Complete List of Firm Personnel, See General Section

For full biographical listings, see the Martindale-Hubbell Law Directory

MCDERMOTT, WILL & EMERY (AV)

A Partnership including Professional Corporations
227 West Monroe Street, 60606-5096
Telephone: 312-372-2000
Telex: 253565 Milam CGO
Facsimile: 312-984-7700
Boston, Massachusetts Office: 75 State Street, Suite 1700.
Telephone: 617-345-5000.
Telex: 951324 MILAM BSN.
Facsimile: 617-345-5077.
Miami, Florida Office: 201 South Biscayne Boulevard.
Telephone: 305-358-3500.
Telex: 441777 LEYES.
Facsimile: 305-347-6500.

(See Next Column)

Washington, D.C. Office: 1850 K Street, N.W.
Telephone: 202-887-8000.
Telex: 253565 MILAM CGO.
Facsimile: 202-778-8087.
Los Angeles, California Office: 2049 Century Park East.
Telephone: 310-277-4110.
Facsimile: 310-277-4730.
Newport Beach, California Office: 1301 Dove Street, Suite 500.
Telephone: 714-851-0633.
Facsimile: 714-851-9348.
New York, N.Y. Office: 1211 Avenue of the Americas.
Telephone: 212-768-5400.
Facsimile: 212-768-5444.
St. Petersburg, Russia Office: 2/2 Tchaikovsky Street, #517, 191187 St. Petersburg, Russia.
Telephone: (7) (812) 273-9831.
Facsimile: (7) (812) 273-9831.
Tallinn, Estonia Office: Tallinn Business Center, 6 Harju Street, EE0001 Tallinn, Estonia.
Telephone: 372 6 31-05-53.
Facsimile: 372 6 31-05-54.
Vilnius, Lithuania Office: Smetonos 6, 2600 Vilnius, Lithuania.
Telephone: 370 2 61-43-08.
Facsimile: 370 2 22-79-55.
Associated (Independent) Offices:
Brussels, Belgium: Uettwiller Grelon Lippens Dekeyser, 73 avenue Vandendriessche, 1150 Brussels, Belgium.
Telephone: (32) (2) 772-87-50.
Facsimile: (32) (2) 772-87-52.
London, England: Paisner & Co, Bouverie House, 154 Fleet Street, London EC4A 2DQ, England.
Telephone: (44) (71) 353-0299.
Facsimile: (44) (71) 583-8621.
Paris, France: Uettwiller Grelon Gout Canat & Associes, 68, boulevard de Courcelles, 75017 Paris, France.
Telephone: (33) (1) 48 88 89 00.
Facsimile: (33) (1) 48 88 05 50.

MEMBERS OF FIRM

Julie Badel
Stephen D. Erf
Howard L. Kastel *
Nancy G. Ross
Alan S. Rutkoff
Harry M. Sangerman *

ASSOCIATES

Kathryn T. Ditmars
Christine M. Drylie
David B. Montgomery
Susan Rifken

*Denotes a lawyer employed by a Professional Corporation which is a member of the Firm.

For Complete List of Firm Personnel, See General Section

For full biographical listings, see the Martindale-Hubbell Law Directory

MURPHY, SMITH & POLK, A PROFESSIONAL CORPORATION (AV)

Twenty-Fifth Floor, Two First National Plaza 20 South Clark Street, 60603-1891
Telephone: 312-558-1220
Telecopier: 807-3619

Charles E. Murphy
Arthur B. Smith, Jr.
Lee T. Polk
Robert P. Casey
Michael T. Roumell
Peter M. Kelly, II
Richard L. Samson
Carol A. Poplawski
Daniel J. Ashley
James M. O'Brien

Dwight D. Pancottine
Tracey L. Truesdale
Julia A. Donnelly
Caran L. Joseph
Richard P. McArdle
Peter A. Steinmeyer
Charles R. Marcordes

OF COUNSEL

Karl W. Grabemann

For full biographical listings, see the Martindale-Hubbell Law Directory

SCARIANO, KULA, ELLCH AND HIMES, CHARTERED (AV)

Two Prudential Plaza 180 North Stetson Suite 3100, 60601-6224
Telephone: 312-565-3100
Facsimile: 312-565-0000
Chicago Heights, Illinois Office: 1450 Aberdeen.
Telephone: 708-755-1900.
Facsimile: 708-755-0000.

Anthony G. Scariano
David P. Kula
Robert H. Ellch
Alan T. Sraga
A. Lynn Himes
Justino D. Petrarca
Lawrence Jay Weiner
Kathleen Field Orr
John M. Izzo
Raymond A. Hauser

OF COUNSEL

Max A. Bailey
G. Robb Cooper
Teri E. Engler
John B. Kralovec

(See Next Column)

SCARIANO, KULA, ELLCH AND HIMES CHARTERED, *Chicago—Continued*

Daniel M. Boyle
Patrick J. Broncato
Sarah R. Carlin
Diane S. Cohen
Jon G. Crawford
Douglas D. Danielson
Anthony Ficarelli
Kelly A. Hayden
Todd K. Hayden
David A. Hemenway
Kathleen Roche Hirsman
Jonathan A. Pearl
Lisa Ann Rapacz
Shelia C. Riley
Joanne W. Schochat

For full biographical listings, see the Martindale-Hubbell Law Directory

VEDDER, PRICE, KAUFMAN & KAMMHOLZ (AV)

A Partnership including Vedder, Price, Kaufman & Kammholz, P.C.
222 North La Salle Street, 60601-1003
Telephone: 312-609-7500
Fax: 312-609-5005
Rockford, Illinois Office: Vedder, Price, Kaufman & Kammholz, 4615 East State Street, Suite 201.
Telephone: 815-226-7700.
Washington, D.C. Office: Vedder, Price, Kaufman, Kammholz & Day, 1600 M. Street, N.W.
Telephone: 202-296-0500.
New York, New York Office: Vedder, Price, Kaufman, Kammholz & Day, 805 Third Avenue.
Telephone: 212-407-7700.

MEMBERS OF FIRM

William W. McKittrick
Robert C. Claus
James S. Petrie
George P. Blake
Richard H. Schnadig
John Jacoby
Paul F. Gleeson
Theodore J. Tierney
Allan E. Lapidus
Richard C. Robin
Nina Gidden Stillman
Lawrence L. Summers
Thomas G. Abram
Michael G. Cleveland
Lawrence J. Casazza
Charles B. Wolf
Michael W. Sculnick
James A. Spizzo
Edward C. Jepson, Jr.
Bruce R. Alper
Carol L. Van Hal Browne
Janet M. Hedrick

ASSOCIATES

William C. Glynn
Randall Marc Lending
Philip L. Mowery
C. Elizabeth Belmont
Steven G. Rudolf
Malory N. Harriman
Karen L. Taylor
Carla Rendina Owen
Edward N. Druck
Michael P. Nicolai
Nancy M. Gerrity

PARTNER AT ROCKFORD, ILLINOIS

Greg A. Cheney

ASSOCIATE AT ROCKFORD, ILLINOIS

Mary K. Osborn

PARTNERS AT NEW YORK CITY

Virgil B. Day
John C. Grosz
Alan M. Koral
John H. Eickemeyer
Neal I. Korval

ASSOCIATES AT NEW YORK CITY

Marc S. Wenger
Jonathan A. Wexler
Neil A. Capobianco

PARTNER AT DISTRICT OF COLUMBIA

George J. Pantos

For Complete List of Firm Personnel, See General Section

For full biographical listings, see the Martindale-Hubbell Law Directory

INDIANA

*EVANSVILLE,** Vanderburgh Co.

BERGER AND BERGER (AV)

313 Main Street, 47708-1485
Telephone: 812-425-8101;
Indiana Only: 800-622-3604;
Outside Indiana: 800-327-0182
Fax: 812-421-5909

MEMBERS OF FIRM

Sydney L. Berger (1917-1988)
Charles L. Berger
Sheila M. Corcoran
Mark W. Rietman
Robert J. Pigman
Andrew S. Ward

References: Citizens National Bank of Evansville; Old National Bank in Evansville.

For full biographical listings, see the Martindale-Hubbell Law Directory

BOWERS, HARRISON, KENT & MILLER (AV)

25 N.W. Riverside Drive, P.O. Box 1287, 47706-1287
Telephone: 812-426-1231
Fax: 812-464-3676

MEMBERS OF FIRM

Arthur D. Rutkowski
James P. Casey

Division Counsel in Indiana for: Southern Railway Co.
District Attorneys for the Southern District of Indiana: CSX Transportation, Inc.
Representative Clients: Permanent Federal Savings Bank; Citizens Realty & Insurance, Inc.

For Complete List of Firm Personnel, See General Section

For full biographical listings, see the Martindale-Hubbell Law Directory

FINE & HATFIELD (AV)

520 N.W. Second Street, P.O. Box 779, 47705-0779
Telephone: 812-425-3592
Telecopier: 812-421-4269

MEMBERS OF FIRM

Ronald R. Allen
Danny E. Glass

ASSOCIATE

Shannon Scholz Frank

For Complete List of Firm Personnel, See General Section

For full biographical listings, see the Martindale-Hubbell Law Directory

KAHN, DEES, DONOVAN & KAHN (AV)

P.O. Box 3646, 47735-3646
Telephone: 812-423-3183
Fax: 812-423-3841

MEMBERS OF FIRM

Thomas O. Magan
Larry R. Downs
Wm. Michael Schiff
Robert H. Brown
Jon D. Goldman
David L. Clark
Mary Lee Franke

OF COUNSEL

Arthur R. Donovan

Representative Clients: University of Evansville; University of Southern Indiana; St. Mary's Medical Center of Evansville, Inc.; Welborn Hospital; Big Rivers Electric Corp.; Hoosier Energy Rural Electric; Lewis Bakeries, Inc.; Deaconess Hospital, Inc.; St. Anthony's Medical Center; Orion Electric (American), Inc.

For Complete List of Firm Personnel, See General Section

For full biographical listings, see the Martindale-Hubbell Law Directory

STATHAM, JOHNSON & McCRAY (AV)

215 North West Martin Luther King Jr. Boulevard, P.O. Box 3567, 47734-3567
Telephone: 812-425-5223
Facsimile: 812-421-4238

MEMBER OF FIRM

William E. Statham

ASSOCIATE

Keith E. Rounder

Representative Clients: Bootz Manufacturing Company, Inc.; Bootz Plumbingware Company; Evansville Association for Retarded Citizens; Lamasco Transfer Crane & Rigging Corp.; McDonald's Corporation; The Medical Center of Southern Indiana; Peerless Pottery, Inc.; Research Systems Corp.

For Complete List of Firm Personnel, See General Section

For full biographical listings, see the Martindale-Hubbell Law Directory

*FORT WAYNE,** Allen Co.

GALLUCCI, HOPKINS & THEISEN, P.C. (AV)

229 West Berry Street, Suite 400, P.O. Box 12663, 46864-2663
Telephone: 219-424-3800
Telecopier: 219-420-1260

William T. Hopkins, Jr.
John C. Theisen
John T. Menzie
M. Scott Hall
Loren K. Allison

Michael A. Scheer
Thomas N. O'Malley
Mark S. Kittaka
Tonya S. Shea
Kristen L. Maly
Eric H. J. Stahlhut
Jeffrey S. Schafer
Anthony G. Genakos (Not admitted in IN)
Frank L. Gallucci

For full biographical listings, see the Martindale-Hubbell Law Directory

GREENWOOD, Johnson Co.

VAN VALER WILLIAMS & HEWITT (AV)

Suite 400 National City Bank Building, 300 South Madison Avenue, P.O. Box 405, 46142
Telephone: 317-888-1121
Fax: 317-887-4069

MEMBERS OF FIRM

Joe N. Van Valer
Jon E. Williams
Brian C. Hewitt

ASSOCIATES

J. Lee Robbins
John M. White
William M. Waltz
Kim Van Valer Shilts
Mark E. Need

For full biographical listings, see the Martindale-Hubbell Law Directory

*INDIANAPOLIS,** Marion Co.

BAKER & DANIELS (AV)

300 North Meridian Street, 46204
Telephone: 317-237-0300
FAX: 317-237-1000
Fort Wayne, Indiana Office: 2400 Fort Wayne National Bank Building.
Telephone: 219-424-8000.
South Bend, Indiana Office: First Bank Building, 205 West Jefferson Boulevard.
Telephone: 219-234-4149.
Elkhart, Indiana Office: 301 South Main Street, Suite 307.
Telephone: 219-296-6000.
Washington, D.C. Office: 1701 K Street, N.W., Suite 400.
Telephone: 202-785-1565.

MEMBERS OF FIRM

Michael R. Maine
Wendell R. Tucker
David N. Shane
John W. Purcell
John T. Neighbours
Roberta Sabin Recker
David W. Miller
Irene T. Adamczyk
Gayle L. Skolnik
Hudnall A. Pfeiffer
Mitzi Harris Martin
Todd Murray Nierman

ASSOCIATES

Debra L. Hinshaw
Nancy J. Futterknecht
Gregory N. Dale
Cynthia Pearson Purvis
Michael J. MacLean
Kenneth B. Siepman
Ji-Qing Liu
Mark J. Sifferlen

LEGAL SUPPORT PERSONNEL

Vicki L. Beckenbaugh
Susan L. Davis

Representative Clients: Associated Insurance Companies, Inc.; Bank One, Indianapolis, N.A.; Borg-Warner Corp.; City of Indianapolis; Cummins Engine Co.; Eli Lilly and Company; General Motors Corp.; Indiana Bell; Indianapolis Public Schools; United Airlines.

For Complete List of Firm Personnel, See General Section

For full biographical listings, see the Martindale-Hubbell Law Directory

BOSE MCKINNEY & EVANS (AV)

2700 First Indiana Plaza, 135 North Pennsylvania Street, 46204
Telephone: 317-684-5000
Facsimile: 317-684-5173
Indianapolis North Office: Suite 1201, 8888 Keystone Crossing, 46240.
Telephone: 317-574-3700.
Facsimile: 317-574-3716.

MEMBERS OF FIRM

Charles R. Rubright
Daniel C. Emerson
Margaret Bannon Miller
Keith E. White
David L. Swider
Jon M. Bailey

ASSOCIATES

Jeffrey S. Koehlinger
Karen Glasser Sharp
Gregory W. Guevara

Representative Clients: Anacomp, Inc.; First Indiana Bank; United Parcel Service, Inc.; Metropolitan School District of Wayne Township Marion County, Indiana; Conseco, Inc.; Indianapolis Colts, Inc.; The Somerset Group, Inc.; The Quaker Oats Co.; National Football League; Cellular One Indianapolis.

For Complete List of Firm Personnel, See General Section
For full biographical listings, see the Martindale-Hubbell Law Directory

ICE MILLER DONADIO & RYAN (AV)

One American Square Box 82001, 46282-0002
Telephone: 317-236-2100
Fax: 317-236-2219

(See Next Column)

MEMBERS OF FIRM

Leland B. Cross, Jr.
William R. Riggs
S. R. Born
Martin J. Klaper
Richard E. Parker
Michael H. Boldt
Susan B. Tabler
Byron L. Myers
Michael A. Blickman
Robert B. Bush
Todd W. Ponder
Melissa Proffitt Reese

RETIRED PARTNER

Alan T. Nolan

ASSOCIATES

Kevin C. Woodhouse
Michael L. Tooley
Brian L. McDermott

Counsel for: AMAX Coal Co.; Associated General Contractors of Indiana, Inc.; Citizens Gas and Coke Utility; Community Hospital, Indianapolis; Cummins Engine Company, Columbus; General Housewares Corp.; Terre Haute; Grote Industries, Inc., Madison; Indiana University; Indiana Vocational Technical College; Reilly Industries, Inc.; Target Stores.

For Complete List of Firm Personnel, See General Section

For full biographical listings, see the Martindale-Hubbell Law Directory

LOCKE REYNOLDS BOYD & WEISELL (AV)

1000 Capital Center South, 201 North Illinois Street, 46204
Telephone: 317-237-3800
Telecopier: 317-237-3900

James S. Haramy
Paul S. Mannweiler
Michael T. Bindner
Kim F. Ebert
Charles B. Baldwin
Julia F. Crowe

Ariane Schallwig Johnson
Lisa Drees Tobin
Charles S. Eberhardt, II

OF COUNSEL

Sarah R. Galvarro

Representative Clients: Ameritech Indiana; IDS Financial Corp.; Indiana State University; Kraft General Foods; The Kroger Co.; Methodist Hospital of Indiana, Inc.; Miller Pipeline Corporation; Navistar International Transportation Corp.; Phelps Dodge Magnet Wire Co. Subaru-Isuzu Automotive, Inc.

For Complete List of Firm Personnel, See General Section

For full biographical listings, see the Martindale-Hubbell Law Directory

OWEN SHOUP & KINZIE (AV)

Suite 3680 Bank One Tower, 111 Monument Circle, 46204-5136
Telephone: 317-267-3595
Fax: 317-267-3597
Fremont, Michigan Office: 3918 Skyline Drive.
Telephone: 616-924-7045.
Seattle, Washington Office: 4118 Greenwood Avenue.
Telephone: 206-633-4363.
Cedar Mountain, North Carolina Office: 54 Robin Hood Road.
Telephone: 704-862-3548.

MEMBERS OF FIRM

Michael W. Owen
Steven V. Shoup
Jan J. Kinzie

OF COUNSEL

F. Pen Cosby
Charles V. Traylor
Warren D. Krebs
Amanda A. Owen (Not admitted in IN; Resident, Seattle, Washington Office)

Reference: Bank One Indianapolis.

For full biographical listings, see the Martindale-Hubbell Law Directory

RUCKELSHAUS, ROLAND, HASBROOK & O'CONNOR (AV)

Suite 1100, 129 East Market Street, 46204
Telephone: 317-634-4356
Fax: 317-634-8635

MEMBERS OF FIRM

John C. Ruckelshaus
Paul G. Roland
William A. Hasbrook
John F. Kautzman
David T. Hasbrook

ASSOCIATES

Leo T. Blackwell
M. Elizabeth Bemis

OF COUNSEL

John C. O'Connor

Representative Clients: State Lodge Fraternal Order of Police; Professional Firefighters Union of Indiana AFL-CIO; Indianapolis Yellow Cab, Inc.; Roselyn Bakeries, Inc.; United Consulting Engineers, Inc. St. Vincent Hospital.

Indianapolis—Continued

SOMMER & BARNARD, ATTORNEYS AT LAW, PC (AV)

4000 Bank One Tower, 111 Monument Circle, P.O. Box 44363, 46244-0363
Telephone: 317-630-4000
FAX: 317-236-9802
North Office: 8900 Keystone Crossing, Suite 1046, Indianapolis, Indiana, 46240-2134.
Telephone: 317-630-4000.
FAX: 317-844-4780.

Frederick M. King
Lynn Brundage Jongleux

Representative Clients: Dow Chemical Co.; Farm Bureau Insurance Co.; Wabash National Corp.; Indiana Veneers Corp.; MCL Cafeterias; MPD, Inc.; Regency Electronics, Inc.; Syndicate Sales, Inc.; Woods Wire Products, Inc.; Yellow Freight System, Inc.

For Complete List of Firm Personnel, See General Section

For full biographical listings, see the Martindale-Hubbell Law Directory

*LA PORTE,** La Porte Co.

NEWBY, LEWIS, KAMINSKI & JONES (AV)

916 Lincoln Way, 46350
Telephone: 219-362-1577
Direct Line Michigan City: 219-879-6300
Fax: 219-362-2106
Mailing Address: P.O. Box 1816, La Porte, Indiana, 46352-1816

MEMBERS OF FIRM

John E. Newby (1916-1990)
Daniel E. Lewis, Jr.
Gene M. Jones
John W. Newby
Perry F. Stump, Jr.
Edward L. Volk
Mark L. Phillips
Martin W. Kus
Marsha Schatz Volk
Mark A. Lienhoop
James W. Kaminski

ASSOCIATES

John F. Lake
William S. Kaminski
Christine A. Sulewski
David P. Jones

SENIOR COUNSEL

Leon R. Kaminski

OF COUNSEL

Daniel E. Lewis

Counsel for: U. S. F. & G. Co.; State Farm Mutual Insurance Co.; Auto Owners Insurance Co.; La Porte Bank & Trust Co.; Liberty Mutual Insurance Co.; Sullair Corp.; La Porte Community School Corp.; United Farm Bureau Mutual Insurance Co.; Physicians Insurance of Indiana.

For full biographical listings, see the Martindale-Hubbell Law Directory

MERRILLVILLE, Lake Co.

HOEPPNER WAGNER AND EVANS (AV)

Twin Towers, Suite 606 South, 1000 East 80th Place, 46410
Telephone: 219-769-6552; 465-0432
FAX: 219-738-2349
Valparaiso, Indiana Office: 103 East Lincolnway, P.O. Box 2357.
Telephone: 219-464-4961; 769-8995.
Fax: 219-465-0603.

RESIDENT MEMBER

F. Joseph Jaskowiak

Representative Clients: Bethlehem Steel Corporation; National Steel Corporation; Valparaiso University; Town of Lowell, Indiana; Powdertech Industries.

For Complete List of Firm Personnel, See General Section

For full biographical listings, see the Martindale-Hubbell Law Directory

MUNSTER, Lake Co.

LAW OFFICES OF TIMOTHY F. KELLY (AV)

Suite 2A, 9250 Columbia Avenue, 46321
Telephone: 219-836-4062
Telecopier: 219-836-0167

MEMBERS OF FIRM

Timothy F. Kelly
Karl K. Vanzo

ASSOCIATE

Harvey Karlovac

For Complete List of Firm Personnel, See General Section

For full biographical listings, see the Martindale-Hubbell Law Directory

*SOUTH BEND,** St. Joseph Co.

JONES, OBENCHAIN, FORD, PANKOW, LEWIS & WOODS (AV)

1800 Valley American Bank Building, P.O. Box 4577, 46634
Telephone: 219-233-1194
Fax: 233-8957; 233-9675

(See Next Column)

Vitus G. Jones (1879-1951)
Roland Obenchain (1890-1961)
Francis Jones (1907-1988)
Roland Obenchain (Retired)
Milton A. Johnson (Retired)

MEMBERS OF FIRM

James H. Pankow
Thomas F. Lewis, Jr.
Timothy W. Woods
John R. Obenchain
Robert W. Mysliwiec
Robert M. Edwards, Jr.
John B. Ford
Mark J. Phillipoff
John W. Van Laere

ASSOCIATES

Patrick D. Murphy
Edward P. Benchik
Wendell G. Davis, Jr.

OF COUNSEL

G. Burt Ford

Attorneys For: Koontz-Wagner Electric Co.; South Bend Controls; McDaniel Fire Systems; Network Field Services; Miles Inc.; Kuert Concrete, Inc.

For full biographical listings, see the Martindale-Hubbell Law Directory

*VALPARAISO,** Porter Co.

HOEPPNER WAGNER AND EVANS (AV)

103 East Lincolnway, P.O. Box 2357, 46384-2357
Telephone: 219-464-4961; 769-8995
Fax: 219-465-0603
Merrillville, Indiana Office: Twin Towers, Suite 606 South, 1000 East 80th Place.
Telephone: 219-769-6552. Porter County: 219-465-0432.
Fax: 219-738-2349.

MEMBERS OF FIRM

Larry G. Evans
William F. Satterlee, III
James L. Jorgensen
Ronald P. Kuker
F. Joseph Jaskowiak (Resident, Merrillville Office)
Mark E. Schmidtke

ASSOCIATES

Michael P. Blaize
Jonathan R. Hanson
Lauren K. Kroeger

Representative Clients: Bethlehem Steel Corporation; National Steel Corporation; Valparaiso University; Town of Lowell, Indiana; Powdertech Industries.

For Complete List of Firm Personnel, See General Section

For full biographical listings, see the Martindale-Hubbell Law Directory

IOWA

*CEDAR RAPIDS,** Linn Co.

SHUTTLEWORTH & INGERSOLL, P.C. (AV)

500 Firstar Bank Building, P.O. Box 2107, 52406-2107
Telephone: 319-365-9461
Fax: 319-365-8443

Glenn L. Johnson
Mark L. Zaiger
Constance M. Alt

Representative Clients: Amana Society; Archer-Daniels-Midland Co.; Cargill, Inc.; Cryovac, Inc., a Division of W. R. Grace & Co.; Firstar Bank Cedar Rapids, N.A.; General Mills, Inc.; MCI; PMX Industries, Inc.; Rockwell International - Graphic Systems Division.

For Complete List of Firm Personnel, See General Section

For full biographical listings, see the Martindale-Hubbell Law Directory

SIMMONS, PERRINE, ALBRIGHT & ELLWOOD, L.L.P. (AV)

A Partnership including a Professional Corporation
115 Third Street S.E. Suite 1200, 52401
Telephone: 319-366-7641
Telecopier: 319-366-1917 (I,II,III)

PARTNERS

Iris E. Muchmore
James M. Peters

Representative Clients: Amana Refrigeration, Inc.; Norwest Bank Iowa, N.A.; Sheaffer Pen; Weyerhaeuser Co.; Grand Wood Area Education Agency; Howard R. Green Co.; Varied Investments, Inc.; Norand Corp.; Universal Gym Equipment Co.; Hall Foundation.

For Complete List of Firm Personnel, See General Section

For full biographical listings, see the Martindale-Hubbell Law Directory

*COUNCIL BLUFFS,** Pottawattamie Co.

SMITH PETERSON LAW FIRM (AV)

35 Main Place, Suite 300, P.O. Box 249, 51502
Telephone: 712-328-1833
Fax: 712-328-8320
Omaha, Nebraska Office: 9290 West Dodge Road, Suite 205.
Telephone: 402-397-8500.
Fax: 402-397-5519.

MEMBERS OF FIRM

Raymond A. Smith (1892-1977)
John LeRoy Peterson (1895-1969)
Harold T. Beckman
Robert J. Laubenthal
Richard A. Heininger
Lawrence J. Beckman
Gregory G. Barntsen
W. Curtis Hewett
Steven H. Krohn
Randy R. Ewing
Joseph D. Thornton

ASSOCIATES

Trent D. Reinert (Not admitted in IA)
T. J. Pattermann

Representative Clients: Aetna Life and Casualty Co.; Employers Mutual Co.; First National Bank of Council Bluffs; IMT Insurance Co.; Monsanto Co.; United Fire & Casualty Co.; U.S. Fidelity and Guaranty.

For full biographical listings, see the Martindale-Hubbell Law Directory

*DES MOINES,** Polk Co.

AHLERS, COONEY, DORWEILER, HAYNIE, SMITH & ALLBEE, P.C. (AV)

100 Court Avenue, Suite 600, 50309-2231
Telephone: 515-243-7611
Fax: 515-243-2149

Edgar H. Bittle
Elizabeth Gregg Kennedy
Peter L. J. Pashler
Ronald L. Peeler

Representative Clients: Des Moines Independent Community School District; Drake University; Insurance Company of North America; Iowa Association of School Boards; Koss Construction Co.; Pittsburg-Des Moines Steel Co.; Sears, Roebuck & Co.; Travelers Insurance Co.

For Complete List of Firm Personnel, See General Section

For full biographical listings, see the Martindale-Hubbell Law Directory

DICKINSON, MACKAMAN, TYLER & HAGEN, P.C. (AV)

Suite 1600 Hub Tower, 699 Walnut Street, 50309-3986
Telephone: 515-244-2600
Telecopier: 515-246-4550

L. J. Dickinson (1873-1968)
L. Call Dickinson (1905-1974)
Addison M. Parker (Retired)
John H. Raife (Retired)
Robert B. Throckmorton (Retired)
Helen C. Adams
Brent R. Appel
Barbara G. Barrett
John W. Blyth
L. Call Dickinson, Jr.
Jeanine M. Freeman
David J. Grace
Craig F. Graziano
Howard O. Hagen
J. Russell Hixson
Paul E. Horvath
F. Richard Lyford
John R. Mackaman
Richard A. Malm
James W. O'Brien
Arthur F. Owens
Rebecca Boyd Parrott
David M. Repp
Robert C. Rouwenhorst
Russell L. Samson
David S. Steward
Philip E. Stoffregen
Francis (Frank) J. Stork
Jon P. Sullivan
Celeste L. Tito (Not admitted in IA)
Paul R. Tyler
John K. Vernon
J. Marc Ward
Linda S. Weindruch

OF COUNSEL

Robert E. Mannheimer

Representative Clients: Archer-Daniels-Midland Co.; Board of Water Works Trustees, Des Moines, Iowa; Merchants Bonding Co. (Mutual); Norwest Bank, N.A.

For full biographical listings, see the Martindale-Hubbell Law Directory

SHEARER, TEMPLER, PINGEL & KAPLAN, A PROFESSIONAL CORPORATION (AV)

Suite 437 3737 Woodland Avenue (West Des Moines, 50266), P.O. Box 1991, 50309
Telephone: 515-225-3737
Fax: 515-225-9510

Thomas M. Cunningham
Leon R. Shearer
Brenton D. Soderstrum
Ann M. Ver Heul

For Complete List of Firm Personnel, See General Section

For full biographical listings, see the Martindale-Hubbell Law Directory

*SIOUX CITY,** Woodbury Co.

SMITH, McELWAIN & WENGERT (AV)

632-636 Badgerow Building, P.O. Box 1194, 51101
Telephone: 712-255-8094

MEMBERS OF FIRM

Harry H. Smith
MacDonald Smith
Dennis M. McElwain
Patricia K. Wengert

Representative Clients: Iowa Federation of Labor; Iowa State Building & Construction Trades Council; Bakers' Pension Fund; Iowa State Educational Assn.
Reference: Norwest Bank, N.A.

For full biographical listings, see the Martindale-Hubbell Law Directory

*WATERLOO,** Black Hawk Co.

SWISHER & COHRT (AV)

528 West Fourth Street, P.O. Box 1200, 50704
Telephone: 319-232-6555
FAX: 319-232-4835

MEMBERS OF FIRM

Benjamin F. Swisher (1878-1959)
L. J. Cohrt (1898-1974)
Charles F. Swisher (1919-1986)
Eldon R. McCann
Steven A. Weidner
Larry J. Cohrt
J. Douglas Oberman
Stephen J. Powell
Jim D. DeKoster
Jeffrey J. Greenwood
Samuel C. Anderson
Robert C. Griffin
Kevin R. Rogers

ASSOCIATES

Beth E. Hansen
Mark F. Conway
Natalie Williams Burr

Firm is Counsel for: Koehring Corp.; Clay Equipment; Chamberlain Manufacturing Co.; Waterloo Courier.
Local Counsel for: Allied Group; John Deere Insurance; Liberty Mutual Insurance Co.

For full biographical listings, see the Martindale-Hubbell Law Directory

KANSAS

PRAIRIE VILLAGE, Johnson Co.

HOLMAN, McCOLLUM & HANSEN, P.C. (AV Ⓣ)

9400 Mission Road Suite 205, 66206
Telephone: 913-648-7272
Fax: 913-383-9596
Kansas City, Missouri Office: 644 West 57th Terrace.
Telephone: 816-333-8522.
Fax: 913-383-9596.

Joseph Y. Holman
Frank B. W. McCollum
Eric L. Hansen
Dana L. Parks
Nancy Merrill Wilson
Amy L. Brown
E. John Edwards III (Not admitted in KS)
Katherine E. Rich

For full biographical listings, see the Martindale-Hubbell Law Directory

*TOPEKA,** Shawnee Co.

GOODELL, STRATTON, EDMONDS & PALMER (AV)

515 South Kansas Avenue, 66603-3999
Telephone: 913-233-0593
Telecopier: 913-233-8870

MEMBERS OF FIRM

Arthur E. Palmer
Harold S. Youngentob
Michael W. Merriam
John H. Stauffer, Jr.
Les E. Diehl
John D. Ensley

Local Counsel for: Farm Bureau Mutual Insurance Co.; Metropolitan Life Insurance Co.; St. Paul Fire & Marine Insurance Co.
General Counsel for: American Home Life Insurance Co.; Columbian National Title Insurance Co.; The Menninger Foundation; Stauffer Communications, Inc.; Kansas Association of Realtors; Kansas Medical Society; Kansas Hospital Association.

For Complete List of Firm Personnel, See General Section

For full biographical listings, see the Martindale-Hubbell Law Directory

WRIGHT, HENSON, SOMERS, SEBELIUS, CLARK & BAKER (AV)

Commerce Bank Building, 100 Southeast Ninth Street, 2nd Floor, P.O. Box 3555, 66601-3555
Telephone: 913-232-2200
FAX: 913-232-3344

(See Next Column)

WRIGHT, HENSON, SOMERS, SEBELIUS, CLARK & BAKER, *Topeka—Continued*

MEMBER OF FIRM

K. Gary Sebelius

ASSOCIATE

Catherine A. Walter

Representative Client: Western Resources, Inc.; KPL/Gas Service Company; St. Francis Hospital and Medical Center; Adams Business Forms; The May Department Stores, Inc.; Payless ShoeSource, Inc.; IBP, Inc.

For Complete List of Firm Personnel, See General Section

For full biographical listings, see the Martindale-Hubbell Law Directory

*WICHITA,** Sedgwick Co.

FLEESON, GOOING, COULSON & KITCH, L.L.C. (AV)

125 North Market Street, Suite 1600, P.O. Box 997, 67201-0997
Telephone: 316-267-7361
Telecopier: 316-267-1754

Gerrit H. Wormhoudt — Susan P. Selvidge
William P. Tretbar — Lyndon W. Vix

Attorneys for: Bank IV, Wichita, N.A; Intrust Bank, N.A.; Wichita Eagle and Beacon Publishing Co., Inc.; Southwest Kansas Royalty Owners Assn.; Liberty Mutual Insurance Co.; Grant Thornton; The Law Company; Vulcan Materials Co.; The Wichita State University Board of Trustees.

For Complete List of Firm Personnel, See General Section

For full biographical listings, see the Martindale-Hubbell Law Directory

FOULSTON & SIEFKIN (AV)

(Formerly Foulston, Siefkin, Powers & Eberhardt)
700 Fourth Financial Center, Broadway at Douglas, 67202
Telephone: 316-267-6371
Facsimile: 316-267-6345
Topeka, Kansas Office: 1515 Bank IV Tower, 534 Kansas Avenue. 66603.
Telephone: 913-233-3600.
FAX: 913-233-1610.
Member: Lex Mundi, A Global Association of Independent Firms

MEMBERS OF FIRM

William H. Dye — Gloria G. Farha Flentje
Mary Kathleen Babcock — Douglas L. Stanley
J. Steven Massoni

For Complete List of Firm Personnel, See General Section

For full biographical listings, see the Martindale-Hubbell Law Directory

MARTIN, CHURCHILL, OVERMAN, HILL & COLE, CHARTERED (AV)

500 North Market Street, 67214
Telephone: 316-263-3200
Telecopier: 316-263-6298

W. Stanley Churchill — Charles E. Cole, Jr.
Robert D. Overman — Ross A. Hollander
Donald E. Hill — Jeffrey B. Hurt
Paul C. Herr

RETIRED

Marvin J. Martin

Anthony J. Powell — Kasey Alan Rogg

Representative Clients: Labor Relations: Koch Industries, Inc.; Southwest Petro-Chem., (Division of Witco Corp.); Wescon Products Co. (Division of Latshaw Enterprises).

For full biographical listings, see the Martindale-Hubbell Law Directory

RUPE & GIRARD LAW OFFICES, P.A. (AV)

Market Centre Suite 305, 155 North Market, 67202-1816
Telephone: 316-263-0505; 800-Rupe-Law
Fax: 316-263-0658

Alan L. Rupe — Barbara Scott Girard

Edward L. Keeley — Thomas L. Steele
Steven J. Rupp — Todd Nicholas Tedesco
Sean M. Dwyer — Jeff A. VanZandt
Lisa J. Lewis

For full biographical listings, see the Martindale-Hubbell Law Directory

KENTUCKY

ASHLAND, Boyd Co.

VANANTWERP, MONGE, JONES & EDWARDS (AV)

1544 Winchester Avenue Fifth Floor, P.O. Box 1111, 41105-1111
Telephone: 606-329-2929
Fax: 606-329-0490
Ironton, Ohio Office: Cooper & VanAntwerp, A Legal Professional Association, 407 Center Street.
Telephone: 614-532-4366.

MEMBERS OF FIRM

Howard VanAntwerp, III — William H. Jones, Jr.
Gregory Lee Monge — Carl D. Edwards, Jr.
Kimberly Scott McCann

ASSOCIATES

Matthew J. Wixsom — James D. Keffer
William Mitchell Hall — Stephen S. Burchett

Representative Clients: Armco; Bank of Ashland; Calgon Carbon Corp.; King's Daughters' Hospital; Allstate Insurance Co.; Kemper Insurance Group; Commercial Union Cos.; The Mayo Coal Cos.; Maryland Casualty Co.; Merck & Co.

For full biographical listings, see the Martindale-Hubbell Law Directory

*BOWLING GREEN,** Warren Co.

CAMPBELL, KERRICK & GRISE (AV)

1025 State Street, P.O. Box 9547, 42102-9547
Telephone: 502-782-8160
FAX: 502-782-5856

MEMBERS OF FIRM

Joe Bill Campbell — Gregory N. Stivers
Thomas N. Kerrick — H. Brent Brennenstuhl
John R. Grise — Deborah Tomes Wilkins

ASSOCIATES

H. Harris Pepper, Jr. — Lanna Martin Kilgore
Laura Hagan

Representative Clients: Dollar General Corp.; Greenview Hospital; Hospital Corporation of America; Hardin Memorial Hospital; Monarch Environmental, Inc.; Mid-South Management Group, Inc.; Western Kentucky University; Service One Credit Union; Trans Financial Bank; TKR Cable.

For full biographical listings, see the Martindale-Hubbell Law Directory

CATRON, KILGORE & BEGLEY (AV)

918 State Street, P.O. Box 280, 42102-0280
Telephone: 502-842-1050
Fax: 502-842-4720

Stephen B. Catron — J. Patrick Kilgore
Ernest Edward Begley, II

Representative Clients: Bowling Green Bank & Trust Company, N.A.; General Growth Management Corporation; Kentucky Transportation Cabinet; Resolution Trust Corporation; International Paper Company; Convention Center Authority; Bowling Green-Warren County Industrial Park Authority, Inc.; Camping World, Inc.; National Corvette Museum; Minit Mart Foods, Inc.

For full biographical listings, see the Martindale-Hubbell Law Directory

ENGLISH, LUCAS, PRIEST & OWSLEY (AV)

1101 College Street, P.O. Box 770, 42102-0770
Telephone: 502-781-6500
Telecopier: 502-782-7782

MEMBERS OF FIRM

James H. Lucas — Michael A. Owsley

For Complete List of Firm Personnel, See General Section

For full biographical listings, see the Martindale-Hubbell Law Directory

*HARLAN,** Harlan Co.

GAYLE G. HUFF (AV)

417 East Mound Street, Drawer 151, 40831-0151
Telephone: 606-573-4466
Fax: 606-573-7078

Representative Clients: Old Republic Insurance Co.; Underwriters Safety & Claims; Manalapan Mining Co.; R.B. Coal Co.; Eastover Mining Co., a division of Duke Power Co.

For full biographical listings, see the Martindale-Hubbell Law Directory

RICE & HENDRICKSON (AV)

127 Woodland Hills, P.O. Box 980, 40831
Telephone: 606-573-3955
Fax: 606-573-3956

(See Next Column)

RICE & HENDRICKSON—*Continued*

MEMBERS OF FIRM

William A. Rice
H. Kent Hendrickson

Representative Clients: USX Corp.; Navistar International Transportation Corp.; Bituminous Casualty Corp.; Kentucky Utilities Co.; Aetna Casualty & Surety Co.; Nationwide Insurance; The Hartford Insurance Group; Arch Mineral Corp.

For full biographical listings, see the Martindale-Hubbell Law Directory

*LEXINGTON,** Fayette Co.

LANDRUM & SHOUSE (AV)

106 West Vine Street, P.O. Box 951, 40588-0951
Telephone: 606-255-2424
Facsimile: 606-233-0308
Louisville, Kentucky Office: 400 West Market Street, Suite 1550, 40202.
Telephone: 502-589-7616.
Facsimile: 502-589-2119.

MEMBERS OF FIRM

Mark L. Moseley
Leslie Patterson Vose
Sandra Mendez Dawahare

ASSOCIATES

David G. Hazlett (Resident, Louisville Office)
Timothy D. Martin (Resident, Louisville Office)
Thomas E. Roma, Jr. (Resident, Louisville Office)

District Attorneys: CSX Transportation, Inc.
Special Trial Counsel: Ford Motor Co. and Affiliates (Eastern Kentucky); Clark Equipment Co.
Representative Clients: The Continental Insurance Cos.; U.S. Insurance Group; U.S. Fidelity & Guaranty Co.; Ohio Casualty Insurance Co.; CIGNA; Royal Insurance Cos.

For Complete List of Firm Personnel, See General Section

For full biographical listings, see the Martindale-Hubbell Law Directory

STOLL, KEENON & PARK (AV)

201 E. Main Street, Suite 1000, 40507-1380
Telephone: 606-231-3000
Telecopier: 606-253-1093; 606-253-1027
Frankfort, Kentucky Office: 326 West Main Street.
Telephone: 502-875-6000.
Telecopier: 502-875-6008.
Louisville, Kentucky Office: 400 West Market Street, Suite 2650, 40202.
Telephone: 502-568-9100.
Telecopier: 502-568-6340.

MEMBERS OF FIRM

Robert F. Houlihan
Gary W. Barr
Bennett Clark
Donald P. Wagner
Richard C. Stephenson
Larry A. Sykes
Robert F. Houlihan, Jr.
Denise Kirk Ash
Bonnie Hoskins

ASSOCIATES

Mary Beth Griffith
James D. Allen
James L. Thomerson
Susan Beverly Jones

Representative Clients: Consolidated Freightways, Inc.; IBM Corp.; Johnson Controls, Inc.; Kentucky Utilities Co.; Peabody Coal Co.; Rockwell International Corp.; Square D Co.; The Trane Co.; Transylvania University.

For Complete List of Firm Personnel, See General Section

For full biographical listings, see the Martindale-Hubbell Law Directory

VIMONT & WILLS (AV)

Suite 300, 155 East Main Street, 40507-1317
Telephone: 606-252-2202
Telecopier: 606-259-2927

MEMBER OF FIRM

Timothy C. Wills

ASSOCIATE

Barbara Booker Wills

For Complete List of Firm Personnel, See General Section

For full biographical listings, see the Martindale-Hubbell Law Directory

*LOUISVILLE,** Jefferson Co.

JOHN S. GREENBAUM, P.S.C. (AV)

2700 First National Tower, 40202
Telephone: 502-585-1750
Fax: 502-581-1066

John S. Greenebaum

For full biographical listings, see the Martindale-Hubbell Law Directory

OGDEN NEWELL & WELCH (AV)

1200 One Riverfront Plaza, 40202-2973
Telephone: 502-582-1601
Fax: 502-581-9564

MEMBERS OF FIRM

Joseph C. Oldham
Scott T. Wendelsdorf
Stephen F. Schuster
Walter Lapp Sales

ASSOCIATES

Susan C. Bybee
Jennifer J. Hall

Counsel for: KU Energy Corp.; Kentucky Utilities Co.; Brown-Forman Corp.; B.F. Goodrich Co.; Interlock Industries, Inc.; Akzo Coatings, Inc.; United Distillers Manufacturing, Inc.; SYSCO/Louisville Food Service, Inc.; Rhone-Poulenc, Ins.; Kentucky Metals, Inc.

For Complete List of Firm Personnel, See General Section

For full biographical listings, see the Martindale-Hubbell Law Directory

RICH & D'AMBROSIO, P.S.C. (AV)

Sterling Place Business Park, 3044 Breckenridge Lane Suite 103, 40220
Telephone: 502-493-0503
Fax: 502-493-0504
Louisville, Kentucky, Downtown Office: 513 South Fifth Street, Suites 11 & 12B, 40202.
Telephone: 502-585-6328.
Fax: 502-585-6333.

Ivan H. Rich, Jr. (Resident, Downtown Office)
Joseph G. D'Ambrosio
Kathleen Archer

For full biographical listings, see the Martindale-Hubbell Law Directory

SMITH AND SMITH (AV)

400 North, First Trust Centre, 200 South Fifth Street, 40202-3204
Telephone: 502-587-0761
Fax: 502-589-5345

James U. Smith, Jr. (1914-1977)
Andrew J. Russell
S. Russell Smith (1921-1973)
S. Russell Smith, Jr.
Joseph A. Worthington
W. Kevin Smith
James U. Smith, III
Kay W. Brown
John O. Sheller

Representative Clients: Associated Builders and Contractors, Inc.; Blount, Inc.; Container Corporation of America; Hall Contracting Corp.; Henry Vogt Machine Co.; Highlands Regional Medical Center; Pepsi-Cola General Bottlers, Inc.; The Rogers Group; Whayne Supply Co.; W.R. Grace & Co.

For full biographical listings, see the Martindale-Hubbell Law Directory

WOODWARD, HOBSON & FULTON (AV)

2500 National City Tower, 101 South Fifth Street, 40202
Telephone: 502-581-8000
Fax: 502-581-8111
Lexington, Kentucky Office: National City Plaza, 301 East Main Street, Suite 650.
Telephone: 606-244-7100.
Telecopier: 606-244-7111.

MEMBER OF FIRM

William A. Blodgett, Jr.

ASSOCIATE

Kathryn A. Quesenberry

Representative Clients: Brown-Forman Corp.; Brownsville Garment Co.; Our Lady of Peace Hospital; CSX Transportation; Fischer Packing; Ralston Purina; Purina Mills; Nu-kote International.

For Complete List of Firm Personnel, See General Section

For full biographical listings, see the Martindale-Hubbell Law Directory

*MADISONVILLE,** Hopkins Co.

MITCHELL, JOINER, HARDESTY & LOWTHER (AV)

113 East Center Street, Drawer 659, 42431-0659
Telephone: 502-825-4455
Telefax: 502-825-9600

Thomas A. Mitchell
Richard M. Joiner
Charles E. Lowther

Representative Clients: Aetna Life & Casualty; American Resources Insurance Co.; Commercial Union Insurance Co.; Willis Corroon Administrative Services Corp.; Fireman's Fund Insurance Co.; MAPCO, Inc.; Costain Coal, Inc.

For Complete List of Firm Personnel, See General Section
For full biographical listings, see the Martindale-Hubbell Law Directory

*OWENSBORO,** Daviess Co.

LOVETT & LAMAR (AV)

208 West Third Street, 42303-4121
Telephone: 502-926-3000
FAX: 502-685-2625

MEMBERS OF FIRM

Wells T. Lovett
John T. Lovett
Charles L. Lamar
Marty G. Jacobs

Representative Clients: Bel Cheese; Ensign-Bickford Co.; Fern Terrace Rest Homes, Inc.; Hausner Hard-Chrome, Inc.; Owensboro-Daviess County Labor-Management Committee; Trace Die Cast, Inc.; United L-N (Libbey-Nippon) Glass, Inc.; Willamette Industries, Inc.

For full biographical listings, see the Martindale-Hubbell Law Directory

*PADUCAH,** McCracken Co.

WHITLOW, ROBERTS, HOUSTON & RUSSELL (AV)

Old National Bank Building, 300 Broadway, P.O. Box 995, 42001
Telephone: 502-443-4516
FAX: 502-443-4571

MEMBER OF FIRM

Mark C. Whitlow

ASSOCIATE

Ronald F. Kupper

Representative Clients: Westvaco Corporation; Elf Atochem North America, Inc.; WPSD-TV; Paxton Media Group, Inc.; Crounse Corporation; Martin Marietta Energy Systems, Inc.; Austin Management Group; Fisher-Price, Inc.

For Complete List of Firm Personnel, See General Section

For full biographical listings, see the Martindale-Hubbell Law Directory

LOUISIANA

*BATON ROUGE,** East Baton Rouge Parish

BREAZEALE, SACHSE & WILSON, L.L.P. (AV)

Twenty-Third Floor, One American Place, P.O. Box 3197, 70821-3197
Telephone: 504-387-4000
Fax: 504-387-5397
New Orleans, Louisiana Office: Place St. Charles, Suite 4214, 201 St. Charles Avenue.
Telephone: 504-582-1170.
Fax: 504-582-1164.

MEMBERS OF FIRM

Gordon A. Pugh
Murphy J. Foster, III

ASSOCIATE

Leo C. Hamilton

Counsel for: Hibernia National Bank; South Central Bell Telephone Co.; Allied-Signal Corp.; Reynolds Metal Co.; Illinois Central Railroad Co.; The Continental Insurance Cos.; Fireman's Fund American Group; Chicago Bridge & Iron Co.; Montgomery Ward & Co.

For Complete List of Firm Personnel, See General Section

For full biographical listings, see the Martindale-Hubbell Law Directory

KEAN, MILLER, HAWTHORNE, D'ARMOND, MCCOWAN & JARMAN, L.L.P. (AV)

22nd Floor, One American Place, P.O. Box 3513, 70821
Telephone: 504-387-0999
Fax: 504-388-9133
New Orleans, Louisiana Office: Energy Centre, Suite 1470, 1100 Poydras Street.
Telephone: 504-585-3050.
Fax: 504-585-3051.

MEMBERS OF FIRM

William R. D'Armond
Melanie M. Hartmann
Michael C. Garrard
Cynthia M. Chemay

Gregg R. Kronenberger
D. Scott Landry
Theresa R. Hagen

Representative Clients: Anco Industries, Inc., Baton Rouge, La.; BASF Corporation, Parsippany, N.J.; Cajun Electric Power Co-op., Baton Rouge, La.; City of Baton Rouge/Parish of East Baton Rouge; DSM Copolymer, Inc., Baton Rouge, La.; Georgia Gulf Corporation, Atlanta, Ga.; The Lamar Corporation, Baton Rouge, La.; Piccadilly Cafeterias, Inc., Baton Rouge, La.; Turner Industries, Ltd., Baton Rouge, La.; Vulcan Materials Company, Geismar, La.

(See Next Column)

For Complete List of Firm Personnel, See General Section

For full biographical listings, see the Martindale-Hubbell Law Directory

*LAFAYETTE,** Lafayette Parish

HILL & BEYER, A PROFESSIONAL LAW CORPORATION (AV)

101 LaRue France, Suite 502, P.O. Box 53006, 70505-3006
Telephone: 318-232-9733
Fax: 1-318-237-2566

John K. Hill, Jr.
Eugene P. Matherne
Bret C. Beyer
Robert B. Purser
David R. Rabalais
Erin J. Sherburne
Lisa C. McCowen
Harold Adam Lawrence

For full biographical listings, see the Martindale-Hubbell Law Directory

*LAKE CHARLES,** Calcasieu Parish

JONES, TÊTE, NOLEN, HANCHEY, SWIFT & SPEARS, L.L.P. (AV)

First Federal Building, P.O. Box 910, 70602
Telephone: 318-439-8315
Telefax: 436-5606; 433-5536

MEMBERS OF FIRM

Sam H. Jones (1897-1978)
Kenneth R. Spears
William R. Tête
Edward J. Fonti
William M. Nolen
Charles N. Harper
James C. Hanchey
Gregory W. Belfour
Carl H. Hanchey
Robert J. Tête
William B. Swift
Yul D. Lorio

OF COUNSEL

John A. Patin
Edward D. Myrick

ASSOCIATES

Lilynn A. Cutrer
Lydia Ann Guillory-Lee
Clint David Bischoff

General Counsel for: First Federal Savings & Loan Association of Lake Charles; Beauregard Electric Cooperative, Inc.
Representative Clients: Atlantic Richfield Company; CITGO Petroleum Corp.; Conoco Inc.; HIMONT U.S.A., Inc.; ITT Hartford; Olin Corporation; OXY USA Inc.; Premier Bank, National Association; W.R. Grace & Co.

For full biographical listings, see the Martindale-Hubbell Law Directory

METAIRIE, Jefferson Parish

JUGE, NAPOLITANO, LEYVA & GUILBEAU (AV)

3838 North Causeway Boulevard Suite 2500, 70002-1767
Telephone: 504-831-7270
Fax: 504-831-7284

Denis Paul Juge
Teresa C. Leyva
Jeffrey C. Napolitano
Joseph B. Guilbeau
Thomas M. Ruli

Kelann Etta Larguier
Frank Whiteley
Kristi L. Stroebel
Lance E. Harwell
Lawrence B. Frieman

For full biographical listings, see the Martindale-Hubbell Law Directory

*NEW ORLEANS,** Orleans Parish

CHAFFE, MCCALL, PHILLIPS, TOLER & SARPY (AV)

A Partnership including a Professional Law Corporation
2300 Energy Centre, 1100 Poydras Street, 70163-2300
Telephone: 504-585-7000
Telecopier: 504-585-7075
Cable Address: "Denegre"
Telex: (AT&T) 460122 CMPTS
Baton Rouge, Louisiana Office: 202 Two United Plaza, 8550 United Plaza Boulevard.
Telephone: 504-922-4300.
Fax: 504-922-4304.

MEMBERS OF FIRM

G. Phillip Shuler, III
Dona J. Dew
Julie D. Livaudais
Robert B. Landry, III
Andrew C. Partee, Jr.

ASSOCIATE

Skye C. Henry

Representative Clients: Associated Builders and Contractors, Inc.; Dillard Department Stores, Inc.; Hills Bros. Coffee Co.; Marriott Corporation; Roadway Express, Inc.; Seventh Ward General Hospital; Schwrgmann Giant Super Markets, Inc.; Tulane University; Tulane University Hospital and Clinic.

For Complete List of Firm Personnel, See General Section

For full biographical listings, see the Martindale-Hubbell Law Directory

New Orleans—Continued

DEUTSCH, KERRIGAN & STILES (AV)

A Partnership including Professional Law Corporations
755 Magazine Street, 70130-3672
Telephone: 504-581-5141
Cable Address: "Dekest"
Telex: 584358
Telecopier: 504-566-1201

MEMBERS OF FIRM

Bernard Marcus (P.L.C.)
Charles K. Reasonover (P.L.C.)
Ellis B. Murov (P.L.C.)

For Complete List of Firm Personnel, See General Section

For full biographical listings, see the Martindale-Hubbell Law Directory

MILLING, BENSON, WOODWARD, HILLYER, PIERSON & MILLER (AV)

A Partnership including Professional Law Corporations
Suite Twenty-Three Hundred, 909 Poydras Street, 70112-1017
Telephone: 504-569-7000
Cable Address: "Milling"
Telex: 58-4211
Telecopier: 504-569-7001
ABA net: 15656
MCI Mail: "Milling"
Lafayette, Louisiana Office: 101 LaRue France, Suite 200.
Telephone: 318-232-3929.
Telecopier: 318-233-4957.
Baton Rouge, Louisiana Office: Suite 402, 8555 United Plaza Blvd.
Telephone: 504-928-688.
Fax: 504-928-6881.

PARTNER EMERITUS

M. Truman Woodward, Jr., (P.C.)

MEMBERS OF FIRM

Haywood H. Hillyer, Jr., (P.C.)
G. Henry Pierson, Jr., (P.C.)
Joseph B. Miller
David J. Conroy (P.C.)
Wilson S. Shirley, Jr., (P.C.)
Guy C. Lyman, Jr., (P.C.)
Neal D. Hobson (P.C.)
F. Frank Fontenot (P.C.)
William C. Gambel (P.C.)
Charles A. Snyder (P.C.)
Richard A. Whann (P.C.)
Emile A. Wagner, III, (P.C.)
Charles D. Marshall, Jr. (P.C.)
James K. Irvin (P.C.)
Hilton S. Bell (P.C.)
Katherine Goldman (P.C.)
John W. Colbert (P.C.)
Bruce R. Hoefer, Jr. (P.C.)
David N. Schell, Jr. (P.C.)
Patrick A. Talley (P.C.)
Mary L. Grier Holmes (P.C.)
Jean M. Sweeney (P.C.)

SPECIAL COUNSEL

J. Clifford Rogillio (P.C.)
Patrick J. Butler, Jr.
Timothy T. Roniger
Peter M. Meisner

ASSOCIATES

Mark P. Dauer
Julia M. Pearce
Jay Corenswet
Ann C. Dowling
Alanna S. Arnold
Benjamin O. Schupp
J. Timothy Betbeze
F. Paul Simoneaux, III
Robert T. Lorio
Mary Sprague Langston

LAFAYETTE OFFICE
RESIDENT MEMBERS OF FIRM

Jack C. Caldwell
Robert L. Cabes (P.C.)

SPECIAL COUNSEL

John E. Castle, Jr.

RESIDENT ASSOCIATES

Karen T. Bordelon
Thomas C. Stewart

BATON ROUGE OFFICE
RESIDENT OF COUNSEL

Stephen C. Carleton

See General Section for list of Representative Clients.

For full biographical listings, see the Martindale-Hubbell Law Directory

PHELPS DUNBAR, L.L.P. (AV)

Texaco Center, 400 Poydras Street, 70130-3245
Telephone: 504-566-1311
Telecopier: 504-568-9130, 504-568-9007
Cable Address: "Howspencer"
Telex: 584125 WU
Telex: 6821155 WUI
Baton Rouge, Louisiana Office: Suite 701, City National Bank Building, P.O. Box 4412.
Telephone: 504-346-0285.
Telecopier: 504-381-9197.
Jackson, Mississippi Office: Suite 500, Security Centré North, 200 South Lamar Street, P.O. Box 23066.
Telephone: 601-352-2300.
Telecopier: 601-360-9777.

(See Next Column)

Tupelo, Mississippi Office: Seventh Floor, One Mississippi Plaza, P.O. Box 1220.
Telephone: 601-842-7907.
Telecopier: 601-842-3873.
Houston, Texas Office: Suite 501, 4 Houston Center, 1331 Lamar Street.
Telephone: 713-659-1386.
Telecopier: 713-659-1388.
London, England Office: Suite 976, Level 9, Lloyd's, 1 Lime Street, London EC3M 7DQ England.
Telephone: 011-44-71-929-4765.
Telecopier: 011-44-71-929-0046.
Telex: 987321.

MEMBERS OF FIRM

Harry Rosenberg
Paul O. Miller, III (Not admitted in LA; Resident, Jackson, Mississippi Office)
Armin J. Moeller, Jr. (Resident, Jackson, Mississippi Office)
Gary E. Friedman (Not admitted in LA; Resident, Jackson, Mississippi Office)
William D. Aaron, Jr.
W. Thomas Siler, Jr. (Not admitted in LA; Jackson and Tupelo, Mississippi Offices)
R. Pepper Crutcher, Jr. (Jackson and Tupelo, Mississippi Offices)
M. Nan Alessandra
William I. Gault, Jr. (Not admitted in LA; Resident, Jackson, Mississippi Office)
Susan Fahey Desmond (Not admitted in LA; Resident, Jackson, Mississippi Office)
Thomas H. Kiggans (Resident, Baton Rouge, Louisiana Office)

COUNSEL

Jane E. Armstrong

ASSOCIATES

John Wilson Eaton III (Not admitted in LA; Jackson and Tupelo, Mississippi Offices)
Robert S. Eitel
Ken Fairly (Not admitted in LA; Resident, Jackson, Mississippi Office)
Susan W. Furr (Resident, Baton Rouge, Louisiana Office)
James M. Jacobs
David M. Korn
Wendy L. Moore (Not admitted in LA; Resident, Jackson, Mississippi Office)
Chelye E. Prichard (Not admitted in LA; Resident, Jackson, Mississippi Office)
David M. Thomas, II (Not admitted in LA; Resident, Jackson, Mississippi Office)

Representative Clients: Beech Aerospace Services; Dow Chemical USA; General Motors; ITT; Louisiana Lottery Corporation; Mississippi Municipal Liability Plan; Philip Morris, Inc.; Pulitzer Broadcasting Corp.; Southern Farm Bureau Life Insurance Company; Union Pacific Railroad Company.

For Complete List of Firm Personnel, See General Section

For full biographical listings, see the Martindale-Hubbell Law Directory

WAGNER, BAGOT & GLEASON (AV)

Suite 2660, Poydras Center, 650 Poydras Street, 70130-6102
Telephone: 504-525-2141
Telecopier: 504-523-1587
TWX: 5106017673
ELN: 62928850
"INCISIVE"

Thomas J. Wagner
Michael H. Bagot, Jr.
Harvey G. Gleason
Whitney L. Cole
Eric D. Suben

For full biographical listings, see the Martindale-Hubbell Law Directory

*SHREVEPORT,** Caddo Parish

BARLOW AND HARDTNER L.C. (AV)

Tenth Floor, Louisiana Tower, 401 Edwards Street, 71101-3289
Telephone: 318-227-1131
Telecopier: 318-227-1141
Mailing Address: P.O. Box 8, Shreveport, Louisiana, 71161-0008

Joseph L. Shea, Jr.
Clair F. White
Philip E. Downer, III
Michael B. Donald
Jay A. Greenleaf

Representative Clients: AmCom General Corporation; Johnson Controls, Inc.; NorAm Energy Corp. (formerly Arkla, Inc.); Panhandle Eastern Corp.; Kelley Oil Corporation; Central and South West; Pennzoil Producing Co.; Johnson Controls, Inc.; General Electric Co.

For Complete List of Firm Personnel, See General Section

For full biographical listings, see the Martindale-Hubbell Law Directory

COOK, YANCEY, KING & GALLOWAY, A PROFESSIONAL LAW CORPORATION (AV)

1700 Commercial National Tower, 333 Texas Street, P.O. Box 22260, 71120-2260
Telephone: 318-221-6277
Telecopier: 318-227-2606

(See Next Column)

COOK, YANCEY, KING & GALLOWAY A PROFESSIONAL LAW CORPORATION, *Shreveport—Continued*

Bryce J. Denny | S. Price Barker

Representative Clients: Schumpert Medical Center; Specialty Oil Company; Caddo Parish Sheriff's Office; Crystal Oil Company; Commercial National Bank in Shreveport; Fibrebond Corporation; Ironclad, Inc.; General Motors Corporation; Library Glass Division, Owens-Illinois Corp.; Beall-Ladymon Corporation.

For Complete List of Firm Personnel, See General Section

For full biographical listings, see the Martindale-Hubbell Law Directory

WILKINSON, CARMODY & GILLIAM (AV)

1700 Beck Building, 400 Travis Street, P.O. Box 1707, 71166
Telephone: 318-221-4196
Telecopier: 318-221-3705

MEMBERS OF FIRM

John D. Wilkinson (1867-1929)
William Scott Wilkinson (1895-1985)
Arthur R. Carmody, Jr.
Bobby S. Gilliam
Mark E. Gilliam
Penny D. Sellers
Brian D. Landry

Representative Clients: Farmers Insurance Group; Home Federal Savings & Loan Association of Shreveport; The Kansas City Southern Railway Co.; KTAL-TV; Lincoln National Life Insurance Co.; Mobil Oil Co.; Schumpert Medical Center; Sears, Roebuck & Co.; Southern Pacific Transportation Co.; Southwestern Electric Power Co.

For full biographical listings, see the Martindale-Hubbell Law Directory

MAINE

*AUGUSTA,** Kennebec Co.

LAW OFFICES OF PHILLIP E. JOHNSON (AV)

160 Capitol Street, P.O. Box 29, 04332-0029
Telephone: 207-623-5110
Fax: 207-622-4160

David G. Webbert

Representative Clients: Agway, Inc.; American Eagle Group; Associated Aviation Underwriters; Aviation Underwriting Specialists; AVEMCO; Central Maine Power Co.; The Doctors Company; Loss Management Services, Inc.; Progressive Casualty Insurance Co.; Shand, Morahan & Co.

For full biographical listings, see the Martindale-Hubbell Law Directory

*BANGOR,** Penobscot Co.

EATON, PEABODY, BRADFORD & VEAGUE, P.A. (AV)

Fleet Center-Exchange Street, P.O. Box 1210, 04402-1210
Telephone: 207-947-0111
Telecopier: 207-942-3040
Augusta, Maine Office: 2 Central Plaza.
Telephone: 207-622-3747.
Telecopier: 207-622-9732.
Brunswick, Maine Office: 167 Park Row.
Telephone: 207-729-1144.
Telecopier: 207-729-1140.
Camden, Maine Office: 7-9 Washington Street.
Telephone: 207-236-3325.
Telecopier: 207-236-8611.
Dover-Foxcroft, Maine Office: 30 East Main Street.
Telephone: 207-564-8378.
Telecopier: 207-564-7059.

Malcolm E. Morrell, Jr.
Thomas C. Johnston
Clare Hudson Payne

Michael A. Duddy

A List of Representative Clients available upon request.

For Complete List of Firm Personnel, See General Section

For full biographical listings, see the Martindale-Hubbell Law Directory

*BATH,** Sagadahoc Co.

CONLEY, HALEY & O'NEIL (AV)

Thirty Front Street, 04530
Telephone: 207-443-5576
Telefax: 207-443-6665

Mark L. Haley
Constance P. O'Neil
Arlyn H. Weeks
Laura M. O'Hanlon

Representative Clients: Bath Iron Works Corporation; Central Maine Power Company; Saco Defense, Inc.; Sugarloaf Mountain Corporation.

(See Next Column)

References: Casco Northern Bank, N.A.; First Federal Savings & Loan Association of Bath; Shawmut Bank.

For Complete List of Firm Personnel, See General Section

For full biographical listings, see the Martindale-Hubbell Law Directory

*PORTLAND,** Cumberland Co.

HERBERT H. BENNETT AND ASSOCIATES, P.A. (AV)

Suite 300, 121 Middle Street, P.O. Box 7799, 04112-7799
Telephone: 207-773-4775
Telecopier: 207-774-2366

Herbert H. Bennett (1928-1992)
Peter Bennett
Jeffrey Bennett
Frederick B. Finberg
Melinda J. Caterine
Hilary A. Rapkin

Counsel for: Associated Grocers of New England; Casco Northern Bank, N.A.; Coca Cola Bottling Company of Northern New England, Inc.; Northern Utilities/Bay State Gas; Pratt & Whitney (Division of United Technologies); Primerica Financial Services; Sprague Energy (C.H. Sprague & Son); Perrier Group of America, Inc.; Lepage Bakeries, Inc. (Country Kitchen); Table Talk Pies, Inc.; Texaco, Inc.

For full biographical listings, see the Martindale-Hubbell Law Directory

PIERCE, ATWOOD, SCRIBNER, ALLEN, SMITH & LANCASTER (AV)

One Monument Square, 04101
Telephone: 207-773-6411
Fax: 207-773-3419
Augusta, Maine Office: 77 Winthrop Street.
Telephone: 207-622-6311.
Camden, Maine Office: 36 Chestnut Street, P.O. Box 780.
Telephone: 207-236-4333.

MEMBERS OF FIRM

S. Mason Pratt, Jr.
Charles S. Einsiedler, Jr.
Peter H. Jacobs
Robert A. Moore
James R. Erwin, II
Margaret Coughlin LePage
William H. Nichols

ASSOCIATES

Anthony R. Derosby
Eric D. Altholz
Barney Simeon Goldstein
Allan M. Muir

For Complete List of Firm Personnel, See General Section

For full biographical listings, see the Martindale-Hubbell Law Directory

PRETI, FLAHERTY, BELIVEAU & PACHIOS (AV)

443 Congress Street, P.O. Box 11410, 04104-7410
Telephone: 207-791-3000
Telecopier: 207-791-3111
Augusta, Maine Office: 45 Memorial Circle, P.O. Box 1058, 04332-1058.
Telephone: 207-623-5300.
Telecopier: 207-623-2914.
Rumford, Maine Office: 150 Congress Street, P.O. Drawer L, 04276-2035.
Telephone: 207-364-4593.
Telecopier: 207-369-9421.

MEMBERS OF FIRM

Albert J. Beliveau, Jr. (Rumford Office)
Keith A. Powers
Daniel Rapaport
Michael G. Messerschmidt
Randall B. Weill
Evan M. Hansen
Geoffrey K. Cummings

ASSOCIATES

Nelson J. Larkins
Stephen E. F. Langsdorf (Augusta Office)
Elizabeth A. Olivier
Jeffrey M. Sullivan

Representative Clients: Bronze Craft Corp.; Northern New England Benefit Trust; Maine Turnpike Authority; Maine Maritime Academy; Guy Gannett Publishing Co.

For Complete List of Firm Personnel, See General Section

For full biographical listings, see the Martindale-Hubbell Law Directory

PRESQUE ISLE, Aroostook Co.

STEVENS, ENGELS, BISHOP & SPRAGUE (AV)

428 Main Street, P.O. Box 311, 04769
Telephone: 207-768-5481
Telefax: 207-764-1663

MEMBERS OF FIRM

Albert M. Stevens
Richard C. Engels
Frank H. Bishop, Sr.
Jonathan W. Sprague
Michael L. Dubois

Representative Clients: Commercial Union Cos.; Travelers Insurance Co.; Aetna Insurance Co.; Firemans Fund Group; Hartford Insurance Group; Home Indemnity Co.; Maine Bonding and Casualty Co.; New Hampshire Group; Liberty Mutual Insurance Co.; Peoples Heritage Bank.

For full biographical listings, see the Martindale-Hubbell Law Directory

MARYLAND

*BALTIMORE,** (Independent City)

GORDON, FEINBLATT, ROTHMAN, HOFFBERGER & HOLLANDER (AV)

The Garrett Building, 233 East Redwood Street, 21202
Telephone: 410-576-4000
Telex: 908041 BAL

MEMBERS OF FIRM

Sander L. Wise
Robert C. Kellner (Chairman)
Matthew P. Mellin
Bradford W. Warbasse

ASSOCIATE

Cheryl F. Kitt

For Complete List of Firm Personnel, See General Section

For full biographical listings, see the Martindale-Hubbell Law Directory

LAW OFFICES OF MARCY M. HALLOCK, P.A. (AV)

Suite 1820, 36 South Charles Street, 21201
Telephone: 410-234-0300
FAX: 410-234-0332

Marcy M. Hallock

Elizabeth G. Jacobs

Representative Clients: Big Yank Corp.; Farberware; Metroplex Communications, Inc.; Broadway Services, Inc.; W.R. Berkley & Co.
Reference: Signet Bank.

For full biographical listings, see the Martindale-Hubbell Law Directory

KAHN, SMITH & COLLINS, P.A. (AV)

110 Saint Paul Street, 6th Floor, 21202
Telephone: 410-244-1010
Telecopier: 410-244-8001

Andrew H. Kahn
Joel A. Smith
Francis J. Collins

David Vernon Diggs
Christyne L. Neff

For full biographical listings, see the Martindale-Hubbell Law Directory

KOLLMAN & SHEEHAN, P.A. (AV)

Sun Life Building, 20 South Charles Street, 21201
Telephone: 410-727-4300
Telecopier: 410-727-4391

Frank L. Kollman
David M. Sheehan
Peter S. Saucier

Charles J. Morton, Jr.
Jessica V. Carter
Clifford B. Geiger

For full biographical listings, see the Martindale-Hubbell Law Directory

E. FREMONT MAGEE, P.A. (AV)

The Legg Mason Tower, 111 South Calvert Street, Suite 2700, 21202
Telephone: 410-385-5295; 410-625-7540
FAX: 410-385-5201

E. Fremont Magee

Lynn K. Edwards

For full biographical listings, see the Martindale-Hubbell Law Directory

PIPER & MARBURY (AV)

Charles Center South, 36 South Charles Street, 21201-3010
Telephone: 410-539-2530
FAX: 410-539-0489
Washington, D.C. Office: 1200 Nineteenth Street, N.W., 20036-2430.
Telephone: 202-861-3900.
FAX: 202-223-2085.
Easton, Maryland Office: 117 Bay Street, 21601-2703.
Telephone: 410-820-4460.
FAX: 410-820-4463.
Garrison, New York Office: Garrison Landing.
Telephone: 914-424-3711.
Fax: 914-424-3045.
New York, N.Y. Office: 31 West 52nd Street, 10019-6118.
Telephone: 212-261-2000.
FAX: 212-261-2001.

(See Next Column)

Philadelphia, Pennsylvania Office: Suite 1500, 2 Penn Center Plaza, 19102-1715.
Telephone: 215-656-3300.
FAX: 215-656-3301.
London, England Office: 14 Austin Friars, EC2N 2HE.
Telephone: 071-638-3833.
FAX: 071-638-1208.

MEMBERS OF FIRM

Leonard E. Cohen
Robert B. Barnhouse
Russell H. Gardner
Richard J. Hafets
Emmett F. McGee, Jr.

ASSOCIATES

Lynette M. Phillips
Stephen B. Lebau
Eric Paltell
Ann L. Lamdin

For Complete List of Firm Personnel, See General Section

For full biographical listings, see the Martindale-Hubbell Law Directory

SHAWE & ROSENTHAL (AV)

Sun Life Building, 20 South Charles Street, 21201
Telephone: 410-752-1040
Telecopier: 410-752-8861

MEMBERS OF FIRM

Earle K. Shawe
William J. Rosenthal
Carrol Hament (Retired)
Stephen D. Shawe
Arthur M. Brewer
Bruce S. Harrison
Patrick M. Pilachowski
Eric Hemmendinger
J. Michael McGuire
Mark J. Swerdlin
Gary L. Simpler
Frances O. Taylor
R. Michael Smith
Alisa H. Reff
Robert H. Ingle, III
Alice Paige Estill

Representative Clients: Amdahl Corp.; Baltimore Gas & Electric Co.; Bethlehem Steel Corp.; Black & Decker (U.S.) Inc.; Federal Reserve Bank of Richmond; Food Lion; The May Department Stores Co. (Hecht's, Washington, D.C.; Filene's); McDonald's Corp.; Thiokol Corp.; United States Fidelity & Guaranty Co.

For full biographical listings, see the Martindale-Hubbell Law Directory

VENABLE, BAETJER AND HOWARD (AV)

A Partnership including Professional Corporations
1800 Mercantile Bank & Trust Building, 2 Hopkins Plaza, 21201
Telephone: 410-244-7400
Washington, D.C. Office: Venable, Baetjer, Howard & Civiletti. Suite 1000, 1201 New York Avenue, N.W.
Telephone: 202-962-4800.
McLean, Virginia Office: Suite 400, 2010 Corporate Ridge.
Telephone: 703-760-1600.
Rockville, Maryland Office: Suite 500, One Church Street, P. O. Box 1906.
Telephone: 301-217-5600.
Towson, Maryland Office: 210 Allegheny Avenue, P. O. Box 5517.
Telephone: 410-494-6200.

MEMBERS OF FIRM

John Henry Lewin, Jr. (P.C.)
Stanley Mazaroff (P.C.)
Roger W. Titus (Resident, Rockville, Maryland Office)
N. Peter Lareau (P.C.)
Douglas D. Connah, Jr. (P.C.) (Also at Washington, D.C. Office)
David T. Stitt (Not admitted in MD; Resident, McLean, Virginia Office)
Kenneth C. Bass, III (Not admitted in MD; Also at Washington, D.C. and McLean, Virginia Offices)
John H. Zink, III (Resident, Towson, Maryland Office)
Paul T. Glasgow (Resident, Rockville, Maryland Office)
Joseph C. Wich, Jr. (Resident, Towson, Maryland Office)
Joseph G. Block (Not admitted in MD; Resident, Washington, D.C. Office)
Sondra Harans Block (Resident, Rockville, Maryland Office)
Craig E. Smith
Robert G. Ames (Also at Washington, D.C. Office)
Nell B. Strachan
Barbara E. Schlaff
L. Paige Marvel
Susan K. Gauvey (Also at Towson, Maryland Office)
G. Stewart Webb, Jr.
George W. Johnston (P.C.)
H. Russell Frisby, Jr.
Jana Howard Carey (P.C.)
Jeffrey A. Dunn (also at Washington, D.C. Office)
George F. Pappas (Also at Washington, D.C. Office)
James L. Shea (Also at Washington, D.C. Office)
Jeffrey P. Ayres (P.C.)
Maurice Baskin (Resident, Washington, D.C. Office)
C. Carey Deeley, Jr. (Also at Towson, Maryland Office)
Christopher R. Mellott
James A. Dunbar (Also at Washington, D.C. Office)
Ronald W. Taylor
Robert L. Waldman
Mary E. Pivec (Also at Washington, D.C. Office)
John A. Roberts (Also at Rockville, Maryland Office)
Patrick J. Stewart (Also at Washington, D.C. Office)
Gary M. Hnath (Resident, Washington, D.C. Office)
Darrell R. VanDeusen

OF COUNSEL

A. Samuel Cook (P.C.) (Resident, Towson, Maryland Office)

(See Next Column)

VENABLE, BAETJER AND HOWARD, *Baltimore—Continued*

ASSOCIATES

Scharon L. Ball
Paul D. Barker, Jr.
Elizabeth Marzo Borinsky
Patrick L. Clancy (Resident, Rockville, Maryland Office)
Patricia Gillis Cousins (Resident, Rockville, Maryland Office)
David W. Goewey (Not admitted in MD; Resident, Washington, D.C. Office)
E. Anne Hamel
Todd J. Horn
Gregory L. Laubach (Resident, Rockville, Maryland Office)
Vicki Margolis
Christine M. McAnney (Not admitted in MD; Resident, McLean, Virginia Office)
John A. McCauley
Timothy J. McEvoy
Mitchell Y. Mirviss
Samuel T. Morison (Not admitted in MD; Resident, Washington, D.C. Office)
Traci H. Mundy (Not admitted in MD; Resident, Washington, D.C. Office)
Valerie Floyd Portner
John T. Prisbe
Michael W. Robinson (Not admitted in MD; Resident, McLean, Virginia Office)
Nathan E. Siegel
Linda Marotta Thomas
J. Preston Turner
Karen D. Woodard (Resident, Washington, D.C. Office)

For Complete List of Firm Personnel, See General Section

For full biographical listings, see the Martindale-Hubbell Law Directory

WHITEFORD, TAYLOR & PRESTON (AV)

7 Saint Paul Street, 21202-1626
Telephone: 410-347-8700
Telex: 5101012334
Fax: 410-752-7092
Towson, Maryland Office: 210 West Pennsylvania Avenue.
Telephone: 410-832-2000.
Washington, D.C. Office: 888 17th Street, N.W.
Telephone: 202-659-6800.

MEMBERS OF FIRM

Larry M. Wolf
Arthur P. Rogers (Resident Washington, D.C. Office)
Joseph K. Pokempner
Robert S. Hillman
Steven E. Bers
Jeanne M. Phelan
Kevin C. McCormick

ASSOCIATES

Peter D. Guattery
John L. Senft

For Complete List of Firm Personnel, See General Section

For full biographical listings, see the Martindale-Hubbell Law Directory

*ROCKVILLE,** Montgomery Co.

STEIN, SPERLING, BENNETT, DE JONG, DRISCOLL, GREENFEIG & METRO, P.A. (AV)

25 West Middle Lane, 20850
Telephone: 301-340-2020; 800-435-5230
Telecopier: 301-340-8217

David C. Driscoll, Jr.
Jack A. Garson
A. Howard Metro
Jeffrey M. Schwaber
Donald N. Sperling

For Complete List of Firm Personnel, See General Section

For full biographical listings, see the Martindale-Hubbell Law Directory

VENABLE, BAETJER AND HOWARD (AV)

A Partnership including Professional Corporations
Suite 500, One Church Street, P.O. Box 1906, 20850-4129
Telephone: 301-217-5600
FAX: 301-217-5617
Baltimore, Maryland Office: 1800 Mercantile Bank & Trust Building, 2 Hopkins Plaza.
Telephone: 410-244-7400.
Washington, D.C. Office: Venable, Baetjer, Howard & Civiletti. Suite 1000, 1201 New York Avenue, N.W.
Telephone: 202-962-4800.
McLean, Virginia Office: Suite 400, 2010 Corporate Ridge.
Telephone: 703-760-1600.
Towson, Maryland, Office: 210 Allegheny Avenue, P. O. Box 5517.
Telephone: 410-494-6200.

MEMBERS OF FIRM

Roger W. Titus
Paul T. Glasgow
Sondra Harans Block
John A. Roberts (Also at Baltimore, Maryland Office)

ASSOCIATES

Patrick L. Clancy
Patricia Gillis Cousins
Gregory L. Laubach

For Complete List of Firm Personnel, See General Section

For full biographical listings, see the Martindale-Hubbell Law Directory

SILVER SPRING, Montgomery Co.

ALEXANDER, GEBHARDT, APONTE & MARKS, L.L.C. (AV)

Lee Plaza-Suite 805, 8601 Georgia Avenue, 20910
Telephone: 301-589-2222
Facsimile: 301-589-2523
Washington, D.C. Office: 1314 Nineteenth Street, N.W., 20036.
Telephone: 202-835-1555.
New York, New York Office: 330 Madison Avenue, 36th Floor.
Telephone: 212-808-0008.
Fax: 212-599-1028.

Joseph D. Gebhardt
Abbey G. Hairston

Gregory E. Gaskins
Adrian Van Nelson II

Reference: Riggs National Bank of Washington, D.C.

For full biographical listings, see the Martindale-Hubbell Law Directory

*TOWSON,** Baltimore Co.

VENABLE, BAETJER AND HOWARD (AV)

A Partnership including Professional Corporations
210 Allegheny Avenue, P.O. Box 5517, 21204
Telephone: 410-494-6200
FAX: 410-821-0147
Baltimore, Maryland Office: 1800 Mercantile Bank & Trust Building, 2 Hopkins Plaza.
Telephone: 410-244-7400.
Washington, D.C. Office: Venable, Baetjer, Howard & Civiletti. Suite 1000, 1201 New York Avenue, N.W.
Telephone: 202-962-4800.
McLean, Virginia Office: Suite 400, 2010 Corporate Ridge.
Telephone: 703-760-1600.
Rockville, Maryland Office: Suite 500, One Church Street, P. O. Box 1906.
Telephone: 301-217-5600.

PARTNERS

John H. Zink, III
Joseph C. Wich, Jr.
Susan K. Gauvey (Also at Baltimore, Maryland Office)
C. Carey Deeley, Jr. (Also at Baltimore, Maryland Office)

OF COUNSEL

A. Samuel Cook (P.C.)

For Complete List of Firm Personnel, See General Section

For full biographical listings, see the Martindale-Hubbell Law Directory

MASSACHUSETTS

*BOSTON,** Suffolk Co.

CUDDY BIXBY (AV)

One Financial Center, 02111
Telephone: 617-348-3600
Telecopier: 617-348-3643
Wellesley, Massachusetts Office: 60 Walnut Street.
Telephone: 617-235-1034.

Francis X. Cuddy (Retired)
Wayne E. Hartwell
Brian D. Bixby
Anthony M. Ambriano
William E. Kelly
Paul G. Boylan
Robert A. Vigoda
Paul J. Murphy
Alexander L. Cataldo
Duncan S. Payne
Stephen T. Kunian
Arthur P. Menard
Joseph H. Walsh
Michael J. Owens
Robert J. O'Regan
Andrew R. Menard
David F. Hendren
Glenn B. Asch
Timothy E. McAllister
William R. Moriarty
Kevin P. Sweeney
Denise I. Murphy

For full biographical listings, see the Martindale-Hubbell Law Directory

FOLEY, HOAG & ELIOT (AV)

One Post Office Square, 02109
Telephone: 617-482-1390
Cable Address: "Foleyhoag"
Telex: 94-0693
Telecopier: 617-482-7347
Washington, D.C. Office: 1615 L Street, N.W.
Telephone: 202-775-0600.
Telecopier: 202-857-0140.

(See Next Column)

FOLEY, HOAG & ELIOT—*Continued*

MEMBERS OF FIRM

David B. Ellis
Peter B. Ellis
Philip Burling
Paul V. Lyons
Arthur G. Telegen
Stephen B. Deutsch
William B. Koffel
Kevin J. Fitzgerald
James T. Montgomery, Jr. (Resident at Washington, D.C. Office)

ASSOCIATES

James W. Bucking
Lynda B. Furash
Jeffrey M. Hahn
Amy B. G. Katz
Jonathan A. Keselenko
Michael L. Rosen
Michele A. Whitham

For Complete List of Firm Personnel, See General Section

For full biographical listings, see the Martindale-Hubbell Law Directory

GLOVSKY & ASSOCIATES (AV)

Suite 810, 31 Milk Street, 02109
Telephone: 617-423-7100
Telecopier: 617-482-8034
Washington, D.C. Office: 1101 17th Street, N.W.
Telephone: 202-659-9119.

Richard D. Glovsky

ASSOCIATES

Melinda Milberg
Daniel S. Tarlow
Loretta A. Healy
Peter M. Kelley
John F. Tocci
Debra L. Feldstein

OF COUNSEL

Lynne K. Zusman (Not admitted in MA; Resident, Washington, D.C. Office)
Paul S. Davis

For full biographical listings, see the Martindale-Hubbell Law Directory

GOODWIN, PROCTER & HOAR (AV)

A Partnership including Professional Corporations
Exchange Place, 02109-2881
Telephone: 617-570-1000
Cable Address: "Goodproct, Boston"
Telex: 94-0640
Telecopier: 617-523-1231
Washington, D.C. Office: 901 Fifteenth Street, N.W., Suite 410.
Telephone: 202-414-6160.
Telecopier: 202-789-1720.
Albany, New York Office: One Steuben Place.
Telephone: 518-472-9460.
Telecopier: 518-472-9472.

MEMBERS OF FIRM

Jerome H. Somers (P.C.)
James W. Nagle
Wilfred J. Benoit, Jr.
Robert M. Hale

For Complete List of Firm Personnel, See General Section

For full biographical listings, see the Martindale-Hubbell Law Directory

HANIFY & KING, PROFESSIONAL CORPORATION (AV)

One Federal Street, 02110-2007
Telephone: 617-423-0400
Telefax: 617-423-0498

James Coyne King
John D. Hanify
Harold B. Murphy
David Lee Evans
Daniel J. Lyne
Donald F. Farrell, Jr.
Barbara Wegener Pfirrman
Gerard P. Richer
Timothy P. O'Neill

Gordon M. Jones, III
Kara L. Thornton
Jean A. Musiker
Ann M. Chiacchieri
Melissa J. Cassedy
Kara M. Lucciola
Philip C. Silverman
Michael R. Perry
Jeffrey S. Cedrone
Charles A. Dale, III
Joseph F. Cortellini
Hiram N. Pan
Amy Conroy
Michael S. Bloom
Andrew G. Lizotte
Peter D. Lee
Martin F. Gaynor, III

For full biographical listings, see the Martindale-Hubbell Law Directory

McDERMOTT, WILL & EMERY (AV)

A Partnership including Professional Corporations
75 State Street, Suite 1700, 02109-1807
Telephone: 617-345-5000
Telex: 951324 MILAM BSN
Facsimile: 617-345-5077
Chicago, Illinois Office: 227 West Monroe Street.
Telephone: 312-372-2000.
Telex: 253565 MILAM CGO.
Facsimile: 312-984-7700.
Miami, Florida Office: 201 South Biscayne Boulevard.
Telephone: 305-358-3500.
Telex: 441777 LEYES.
Facsimile: 305-347-6500.
Washington, D.C. Office: 1850 K Street, N.W.
Telephone: 202-887-8000.
Telex: 253565 MILAM CGO.
Facsimile: 202-778-8087.
Los Angeles, California Office: 2049 Century Park East.
Telephone: 310-277-4110.
Facsimile: 310-277-4730.
Newport Beach, California Office: 1301 Dove Street, Suite 500.
Telephone: 714-851-0633.
Facsimile: 714-851-9348.
New York, N.Y. Office: 1211 Avenue of the Americas.
Telephone: 212-768-5400.
Facsimile: 212-768-5444.
St. Petersburg, Russia Office: 2/2 Tchaikovsky Street, #517, 191187 St. Petersburg, Russia.
Telephone: (7) (812) 273-9831.
Facsimile: (7) (812) 273-9831.
Tallinn, Estonia Office: Tallinn Business Center, 6 Harju Street, EE0001 Tallinn, Estonia.
Telephone: 372 6 31-05-53.
Facsimile: 372 6 31-05-54.
Vilnius, Lithuania Office: Smetonos 6, 2600 Vilnius, Lithuania.
Telephone: 370 2 61-43-08.
Facsimile: 370 2 22-79-55.
Associated (Independent) Offices:
Brussels, Belgium: Uettwiller Grelon Lippens Dekeyser, 73 avenue Vandendriessche, 1150 Brussels, Belgium.
Telephone: (32) (2) 772-87-50.
Facsimile: (32) (2) 772-87-52.
London, England: Paisner & Co, Bouverie House, 154 Fleet Street, London EC4A 2DQ, England.
Telephone: (44) (71) 353-0299.
Facsimile: (44) (71) 583-8621.
Paris, France: Uettwiller Grelon Gout Canat & Associes, 68, Boulevard de Courcelles, 75017 Paris, France.
Telephone: (33) (1) 48 88 89 00.
Facsimile: (33) (1) 48 88 05 50.

MEMBER OF FIRM

Dustin F. Hecker

For Complete List of Firm Personnel, See General Section

For full biographical listings, see the Martindale-Hubbell Law Directory

MORGAN, BROWN & JOY (AV)

One Boston Place, 02108
Telephone: 617-523-6666
Facsimile: 617-367-3125

MEMBERS OF FIRM

John W. Morgan (1898-1974)
William F. Joy
Harold N. Mack
Alan I. Kaplan
James M. Paulson
Nicholas DiGiovanni, Jr.
William F. Joy, Jr.
Robert P. Joy
Nathan L. Kaitz
Keith H. McCown
Keith B. Muntyan
Laurence J. Donoghue

ASSOCIATES

Robert P. Morris
Carol A. Merchasin
Dorothy L. Gruenberg
Susan L. Lipsitz
Jaclyn L. Kugell
Richard J. Joy
Joseph P. McConnell

OF COUNSEL

Murray Brown

Representative Clients: Acushnet Company; American Telephone & Telegraph; Boston Edison Co.; Combustion Engineering; Data General Corp.; Federated Department Stores; General Electric; Hasbro, Inc.; John Hancock Mutual Life Insurance Co.; Kraft General Foods.

For full biographical listings, see the Martindale-Hubbell Law Directory

Boston—Continued

PALMER & DODGE (AV)

(Storey Thorndike Palmer & Dodge)
One Beacon Street, 02108
Telephone: 617-573-0100
Telecopier: 617-227-4420
Telex: 951104
Cable Address: "Storeydike," Boston

MEMBERS OF FIRM

Michael R. Brown
Andrew L. Eisenberg
Judith A. Malone
Henry G. Stewart
Jerome N. Weinstein

For Complete List of Firm Personnel, See General Section

For full biographical listings, see the Martindale-Hubbell Law Directory

---

RICH, MAY, BILODEAU & FLAHERTY, P.C. (AV)

The Old South Building, 294 Washington Street, 02108-4675
Telephone: 617-482-1360
FAX: 617-556-3889

John F. Rich (1908-1987)
Thomas H. Bilodeau (1915-1987)
Gerald May
Harold B. Dondis
Walter L. Landergan, Jr.
Edwin J. Carr
Arthur F. Flaherty
Franklin M. Hundley
Michael F. Donlan
Joseph F. Sullivan, Jr.
Owen P. Maher
Nicolas A. Kensington
Daniel T. Clark
Gerald V. May, Jr.
Eric J. Krathwohl
Michael J. McHugh
James M. Behnke
James M. Avery
Stephen M. Kane
Mark C. O'Connor
Walter A. Wright, III
Emmett E. Lyne

Nicholas F. Kourtis
James T. Finnigan
Carol E. Kazmer
Robert P. Snell

For full biographical listings, see the Martindale-Hubbell Law Directory

---

SHERBURNE, POWERS & NEEDHAM, P.C. (AV)

One Beacon Street, 02108
Telephone: 617-523-2700
Fax: 617-523-6850

William D. Weeks
John T. Collins
Allan J. Landau
John L. Daly
Stephen A. Hopkins
Alan I. Falk
C. Thomas Swaim
James Pollock
William V. Tripp III
Stephen S. Young
William F. Machen
W. Robert Allison
Jacob C. Diemert
Philip J. Notopoulos
Richard J. Hindlian
Paul E. Troy
Harold W. Potter, Jr.
Dale R. Johnson
Philip S. Lapatin
Pamela A. Duckworth
Mark Schonfeld
James D. Smeallie
Paul Killeen
Gordon P. Katz
Joseph B. Darby, III
Richard M Yanofsky
James E. McDermott
Robert V. Lizza
Miriam Goldstein Altman
John J. Monaghan
Margaret J. Palladino
Mark C. Michalowski
David Scott Sloan
M. Chrysa Long
Lawrence D. Bradley
Miriam J. McKendall

Cynthia A. Brown
Cynthia M. Hern
Dianne R. Phillips
Paul M. James
Theodore F. Hanselman
Joshua C. Krumholz
Ieuan G. Mahony
Kenneth L. Harvey
Christopher J. Trombetta
Edwin F. Landers, Jr.
Amy J. Mastrobattista
William Howard McCarthy, Jr.
Douglas W. Clapp
Tamara E. Goulston
Nicholas J. Psyhogeos

COUNSEL

Haig Der Manuelian
Mason M. Taber, Jr.
Karl J. Hirshman
Benjamin Volinski
Kenneth P. Brier

OF COUNSEL

John Barr Dolan

For full biographical listings, see the Martindale-Hubbell Law Directory

---

WARNER & STACKPOLE (AV)

75 State Street, 02109
Telephone: 617-951-9000
Cable Address: "Warstack"
Telecopier: 617-951-9151
Telex: 940139

MEMBERS OF FIRM

William B. Hetzel, Jr.
Stephen E. Moore
Henry T. Goldman
Ronald F. Kehoe
Douglas F. Seaver

(See Next Column)

ASSOCIATE

Laurie C. Buck

For Complete List of Firm Personnel, See General Section

For full biographical listings, see the Martindale-Hubbell Law Directory

---

*SPRINGFIELD,** Hampden Co.

COOLEY, SHRAIR P.C. (AV)

5th Floor, 1380 Main Street, 01103
Telephone: 413-781-0750
Telecopier: 413-733-3042

David A. Shrair
Irving D. Labovitz
Robert L. Dambrov
Alan S. Dambrov
Alice E. Zaft
Rona S. Fingold
Peter W. Shrair
Norman C. Michaels
Mark A. NeJame
Mary E. Hurley
Mark D. Mason

OF COUNSEL

Edward B. Cooley
Sidney M. Cooley

Representative Clients: Peter Pan Bus Lines, Inc.; Buxton Co.; State Line Potato Chip Co.; Park West Bank and Trust Company; Westfield Savings Bank; Merrill, Lynch, Pierce, Fenner and Smith; City of Springfield, Mass.; Dairy Mart; Western Region; Town of Longmeadow, Mass.; Springfield College.

For full biographical listings, see the Martindale-Hubbell Law Directory

---

ELY & KING (AV)

One Financial Plaza, 1350 Main Street, 01103
Telephone: 413-781-1920
Telecopier: 413-733-3360

MEMBERS OF FIRM

Joseph Buell Ely (1905-1956)
Raymond T. King (1919-1971)
Frederick M. Kingsbury (1924-1968)
Hugh J. Corcoran (1938-1992)
Richard S. Milstein
Donald A. Beaudry
Richard F. Faille
Leland B. Seabury
Gregory A. Schmidt
Pamela Manson
Anthony T. Rice
Russell J. Mawdsley

ASSOCIATE

Donna M. Brown

Representative Clients: Hartford Accident & Indemnity Co.; Albert Steiger Cos.; Shawmut Bank N.A.; Springfield Institution for Savings; St. Paul Fire & Marine Insurance Co.; The Rouse Co.; Tighe & Bond, Inc.; Northeast Utilities.

For full biographical listings, see the Martindale-Hubbell Law Directory

---

SKOLER, ABBOTT & PRESSER, P.C. (AV)

Suite 2000, One Monarch Place, 01144
Telephone: 413-737-4753
Fax: 413-787-1941
Worcester, Massachusetts Office: 30 Park Avenue.
Telephone: 508-757-5335.

Martin E. Skoler (1932-1991)
Ralph F. Abbott, Jr.
Jay M. Presser
John H. Glenn
Rosemary J. Nevins

Toby G. Hartt
Richard U. Stubbs, Jr.
Jeffrey C. Hummel

OF COUNSEL

Martin Fleisher

LEGAL SUPPORT PERSONNEL

Chelsey Ugolik

Representative Clients: Baystate Medical Center; Erving Paper Mills; Hanover Insurance Company; Monarch Life Insurance Company; Monsanto Co.; Smith & Wesson; Spalding & Evenflo; The Waltham-Weston Hospital & Medical Center.

For full biographical listings, see the Martindale-Hubbell Law Directory

---

*WORCESTER,** Worcester Co.

SKOLER, ABBOTT & PRESSER, P.C. (AV)

30 Park Avenue, 01605
Telephone: 508-757-5335
Springfield, Massachusetts Office: Suite 2000, One Monarch Place.
Telephone: 413-737-4753.
Fax: 413-787-1941.

Martin E. Skoler (1932-1991)
Ralph F. Abbott, Jr.
Jay M. Presser
John H. Glenn
Rosemary J. Nevins

Toby G. Hartt
Richard U. Stubbs, Jr.
Jeffrey C. Hummel

(See Next Column)

SKOLER, ABBOTT & PRESSER P.C.—*Continued*

OF COUNSEL
Martin Fleisher

Representative Clients: Baystate Medical Center; Erving Paper Mills; Hanover Insurance Company; Monsanto Company; National Envelope Co,; Smith & Wesson; Spalding & Evenflo; The Waltham-Weston Hospital & Medical Center.

For full biographical listings, see the Martindale-Hubbell Law Directory

MICHIGAN

*ANN ARBOR,** Washtenaw Co.

HOOPER, HATHAWAY, PRICE, BEUCHE & WALLACE (AV)

126 South Main Street, 48104
Telephone: 313-662-4426
Fax: 313-662-9559

Joseph C. Hooper (1899-1980)
Alan E. Price
James R. Beuche
Bruce T. Wallace
Charles W. Borgsdorf
Mark R. Daane
Gregory A. Spaly
Robert W. Southard
William J. Stapleton
Bruce C. Conybeare, Jr.
Anthony P. Patti
Marcia J. Major

OF COUNSEL

James A. Evashevski
Roderick K. Daane

Representative Clients: Michigan Livestock Exchange; Michigan Livestock Credit Corporation; City of Ann Arbor; Glacier Hill; Cimage Corporation; Domtar Gypsum, Inc.

For Complete List of Firm Personnel, See General Section

For full biographical listings, see the Martindale-Hubbell Law Directory

MILLER, CANFIELD, PADDOCK AND STONE, P.L.C. (AV)

A Professional Limited Liability Company
Founded in 1852 by Sidney Davy Miller
101 North Main Street, Seventh Floor, 48104-1400
Telephone: 313-663-2445
Fax: 313-747-7147
Detroit, Michigan Office: 150 West Jefferson, Suite 2500, 48226-4415.
Telephone: 313-963-6420.
Fax: 313-496-7500.
Cable Address: "Stem Detroit."
Bloomfield Hills, Michigan Office: Suite 100, Pinehurst Office Center, 1400 North Woodward, 48303-2014.
Telephone: 313-645-5000.
Fax: 313-645-1917.
Grand Rapids, Michigan Office: 1200 Campau Square Plaza, 99 Monroe, N.W., 49503-2639.
Telephone: 616-454-8656.
Fax: 616-776-6322.
Howell, Michigan Office: 121 South Barnard Street, Suite 4, 48843-2305.
Telephone: 517-546-7600.
Telecopier: 517-546-6974.
Kalamazoo, Michigan Office: 444 West Michigan Avenue, 49007-3752.
Telephone: 616-381-7030.
Fax: 616-382-0244.
Lansing, Michigan Office: One Michigan Avenue, Suite 900, 48933-1609.
Telephone: 517-487-2070.
Fax: 517-374-6304.
Monroe, Michigan Office: The Executive Centre, 214 East Elm Avenue, 48161-2682.
Telephone: 313-243-2000.
Fax: 313-243-0901.
Washington, D.C. Office: 1225 Nineteenth Street, N.W., Suite 400. 20036.
Telephone: 202-429-5575; 785-0600.
Fax: 202-331-1118; 785-1234.
Pensacola, Florida Office: 25 West Cedar, 32501.
Telephone: 904-469-1088.
Fax: 904-432-0677.
St. Petersburg, Florida Office: 100 Second Avenue S., Suite 7045, 33701.
Telephone: 813-982-6000.
Fax: 813-892-6002.
Gdansk, Poland Office: Suite 322, Dom Technika Building, Ul. Rajska 6, 80-850.
Telephone: 011-485-831-2808.
Fax: 011-485-831-4719.
Warsaw, Poland Office: Ul. Marszalkowska 82, Suite 561, 00-517.
Telephone: 011-482-623-6457 and 6458.
Fax: 011-482-623-6459.

RESIDENT PARTNER
Robert E. Gilbert

(See Next Column)

SENIOR ATTORNEY
Charles A. Duerr, Jr.

Representative Firm Clients: Chrysler Corp.; Comerica, Inc.; City of Detroit, Mich.; Detroit Tigers, Inc.; First of Michigan; Fretter, Inc.; Ford Motor Co.; Ford Motor Credit Co.; Great Lakes Bancorp; Henry Ford Hospital.

For Complete List of Firm Personnel, See General Section

For full biographical listings, see the Martindale-Hubbell Law Directory

PEAR SPERLING EGGAN & MUSKOVITZ, P.C. (AV)

Domino's Farms, 24 Frank Lloyd Wright Drive, 48105
Telephone: 313-665-4441
Fax: 313-665-8788
Ypsilanti, Michigan Offices: 5 South Washington Street.
Telephone: 313-483-3626 and 2164 Bellevue at Washtenaw.
Telephone: 313-483-7177.

Melvin J. Muskovitz
Thomas E. Daniels
Paul R. Fransway
Francyne Stacey
Helen Conklin Vick
David E. Kempner

Counsel for: Domino's Pizza, Inc.; Townsend and Bottum, Inc.; Gelman Sciences, Inc.; Bank One, Ypsilanti, N.A.; Thomas Design and Engineering Services, Inc.; Mechanical Dynamics, Inc.; Meadowbrook Insurance Group; City of Brighton; City of Ypsilanti; Ann Arbor Transportation Authority.

For Complete List of Firm Personnel, See General Section

For full biographical listings, see the Martindale-Hubbell Law Directory

BATTLE CREEK, Calhoun Co.

VARNUM, RIDDERING, SCHMIDT & HOWLETT (AV)

4950 West Dickman Road, Suite B-1, 49015
Telephone: 616-962-7144
Grand Rapids, Michigan Office: Bridgewater Place, P.O. Box 352, 49501-0352.
Telephone: 616-336-6000; 800-262-0011.
Facsimile: 616-336-7000.
Telex: 1561593 VARN.
Lansing, Michigan Office: The Victor Center, Suite 810, 201 North Washington Square, 48933.
Telephone: 517-482-6237.
Facsimile: 517-482-6937.
Kalamazoo, Michigan Office: 350 East Michigan Avenue, 49007.
Telephone: 616-382-2300.
Facsimile: 616-382-2382.
Grand Haven, Michigan Office: 321 Washington Street, P.O. Box 288, 49417.
Telephone: 616-846-7100.
Facsimile: 616-846-7101.
Detroit, Michigan Office: 440 East Congress, Fourth Floor, 48226.
Telephone: 313-961-1600.
Facsimile: 313-961-1636.

MEMBER OF FIRM
Carl E. Ver Beek

For full biographical listings, see the Martindale-Hubbell Law Directory

*BAY CITY,** Bay Co.

BRAUN KENDRICK FINKBEINER (AV)

201 Phoenix Building, P.O. Box 2039, 48708
Telephone: 517-895-8505
Telecopier: 517-895-8437
Saginaw, Michigan Office: 8th Floor Second National Bank Building.
Telephone: 517-753-3461.
Telecopier: 517-753-3951.

MEMBERS OF FIRM

Ralph J. Isackson
Patrick D. Neering
George F. Gronewold, Jr.
Frank M. Quinn
Gregory E. Meter
Daniel S. Opperman
Gregory T. Demers

Representative Clients: APV Chemical Machinery, Inc.; Bay Health Systems; Berger and Co.; Catholic Federal Credit Union; Charter Township of Bridgeport; City of Saginaw; City of Vassar; City of Zilwaukee; Corporate Service; Cox Cable.

For Complete List of Firm Personnel, See General Section

For full biographical listings, see the Martindale-Hubbell Law Directory

BINGHAM FARMS, Oakland Co.

SOTIROFF ABRAMCZYK & RAUSS, P.C. (AV)

30400 Telegraph Road, Suite 444, 48025-4541
Telephone: 810-642-6000
Facsimile: 810-642-9001

(See Next Column)

SOTIROFF ABRAMCZYK & RAUSS P.C., *Bingham Farms—Continued*

Philip Sotiroff
Lawrence R. Abramczyk
Dennis M. Rauss
Lawrence A. Tower
Robert B. Goldi
Keith A. Sotiroff
Edward S. Toth

OF COUNSEL

John N. Kaspers

For full biographical listings, see the Martindale-Hubbell Law Directory

BIRMINGHAM, Oakland Co.

KORNEY & HELDT (AV)

30700 Telegraph Road, Suite 1551, 48025
Telephone: 810-646-1050
Fax: 810-646-1054

J. Douglas Korney
Jeffrey A. Heldt

For full biographical listings, see the Martindale-Hubbell Law Directory

BLOOMFIELD HILLS, Oakland Co.

HOWARD & HOWARD ATTORNEYS, P.C. (AV)

The Pinehurst Office Center, Suite 101, 1400 North Woodward Avenue, 48304-2856
Telephone: 810-645-1483
Telecopier: 810-645-1568
Kalamazoo, Michigan Office: The Kalamazoo Building, Suite 400, 107 West Michigan Avenue.
Telephone: 616-382-1483.
Telecopier: 616-382-1568.
Lansing, Michigan Office: The Phoenix Building, Suite 500, 222 Washington Square, North.
Telephone: 517-485-1483.
Telecopier: 517-485-1568.
Peoria, Illinois Office: Howard & Howard, P.C., The Creve Coeur Building, Suite 200, 321 Liberty Street.
Telephone: 309-672-1483.
Telecopier: 309-672-1568.

Martha A. Proctor
Brad A. Rayle

Representative Clients: For Representative Client list, see General Practice, Bloomfield Hills, MI.

For Complete List of Firm Personnel, See General Section

For full biographical listings, see the Martindale-Hubbell Law Directory

DAVID D. PATTON & ASSOCIATES, P.C. (AV)

100 Bloomfield Hills Parkway, Suite 110, 48304
Telephone: 810-258-6020
Fax: 810-258-6052

David D. Patton

Ellen Bartman Jannette
James A. Reynolds, Jr.
Patricia C. White
David H. Patton (1912-1993)

For full biographical listings, see the Martindale-Hubbell Law Directory

*DETROIT,** Wayne Co.

ABBOTT, NICHOLSON, QUILTER, ESSHAKI & YOUNGBLOOD, P.C. (AV)

19th Floor, One Woodward Avenue, 48226
Telephone: 313-963-2500
Telecopier: 313-963-7882

C. Richard Abbott
John R. Nicholson
Thomas R. Quilter III
Gene J. Esshaki
John F. Youngblood
Donald E. Conley
James B. Perry
Carl F. Jarboe
Jay A. Kennedy
Timothy A. Stoepker
Timothy J. Kramer
Norbert T. Madison, Jr.
William D. Gilbride, Jr.

Mary P. Nelson
Michael R. Blum
Thomas Ferguson Hatch
Anne D. Warren Bagno
Mark E. Mueller
Eric J. Girdler

OF COUNSEL

Thomas C. Shumaker
Roy R. Hunsinger

For full biographical listings, see the Martindale-Hubbell Law Directory

BODMAN, LONGLEY & DAHLING (AV)

34th Floor 100 Renaissance Center, 48243
Telephone: 313-259-7777
Fax: 313-393-7579
Troy, Michigan Office: Suite 2020, 755 West Big Beaver Road.
Telephone: 810-362-2110.

(See Next Column)

Ann Arbor, Michigan Office: 110 Miller, Suite 300.
Telephone: 313-761-3780.
Northern Michigan Office: 229 Court Street, P.O. Box 405, Cheboygan.
Telephone: 616-627-4351.

MEMBERS OF FIRM

Richard D. Rohr
James T. Heimbuch
James J. Walsh
John C. Cashen (Troy Office)
Lloyd C. Fell (Northern Michigan Office)
Kathleen A. Lieder (Northern Michigan Office)
Karen L. Piper
R. Craig Hupp
Henry N. Carnaby (Troy Office)

Representative Clients: Abitibi Price Group; Archdiocese of Detroit; Comerica Bank; The Detroit Lions, Inc.; Ford Estates; General Motors Corporation; Charles Stewart Mott Foundation; Norfolk Southern Corporation; Panhandle Eastern Corporation; State Farm Mutual Automobile Insurance Company.

For Complete List of Firm Personnel, See General Section

For full biographical listings, see the Martindale-Hubbell Law Directory

BRADY HATHAWAY, PROFESSIONAL CORPORATION (AV)

1330 Buhl Building, 48226-3602
Telephone: 313-965-3700
Telecopier: 313-965-2830

Thomas M. J. Hathaway

Representative Clients: Beam Stream, Inc.; Bundy Tubing Company; Century 21 Real Estate Corp.; Datamedia Corporation; Energy Conversion Devices, Inc.; Michigan Gas Utilities; Pony Express Courier Corp,; Schering Corporation; Warner-Lambert; Wolverine Technologies.

For Complete List of Firm Personnel, See General Section

For full biographical listings, see the Martindale-Hubbell Law Directory

BUTZEL LONG, A PROFESSIONAL CORPORATION (AV)

Suite 900, 150 West Jefferson, 48226
Telephone: 313-225-7000
Telecopier: 313-225-7080
Birmingham, Michigan Office: Suite 200, 32270 Telegraph Road.
Telephone: 810-258-1616.
Telecopier: 810-258-1439.
Lansing, Michigan Office: 118 West Ottawa Street.
Telephone: 517-372-6622.
Telecopier: 517-372-6672.
Ann Arbor, Michigan Office: Suite 400, 121 West Washington.
Telephone: 313-995-3110.
Telecopier: 313-995-1777.
Grosse Pointe Farms, Michigan Office: Suite 260, 21 Kercheval.
Telephone: 313-886-5446.
Telecopier: 313-886-2114.

William M. Saxton
Robert J. Battista
John Henry Dudley, Jr.
Robert M. Vercruysse
Donald B. Miller
John P. Hancock, Jr.
Virginia F. Metz
Gregory V. Murray
Mark T. Nelson
Barbara S. Kendzierski
Raymond J. Carey
David B. Calzone
Lynne E. Deitch
Diane M. Soubly
Daniel B. Tukel
Carey A. DeWitt
Robert A. Boonin
Andrea Roumell Dickson

Barbara T. Pichan
James S. Rosenfeld
Jordan S. Schreier
Nicholas J. Stasevich
Bernice M. Tatarelli
Jeffrey S. Wilke
Maria T. Harshe
Sherri A. Krause
Ann M. Kelly

Representative Clients: Associated General Contractors of America, Detroit Chapter, Inc.; William Beaumont Hospital; General Dynamics Corp.; Michigan Road Builders Assoc.; The Stroh Brewery Co.; Teledyne, Inc.; Tishken Products, Inc.; United Parcel Service, Inc.; The University of Michigan.

For Complete List of Firm Personnel, See General Section

For full biographical listings, see the Martindale-Hubbell Law Directory

CHARFOOS, REITER, PETERSON, HOLMQUIST & PILCHAK, P.C. (AV)

476 State of Michigan Plaza Building, 1200 Sixth Street, 48226
Telephone: 313-961-7011
Farmington Hills, Michigan Office: 30500 Northwestern Highway, Suite 400.
Telephone: 810-626-7300.
Fax: 810-626-7305.

(See Next Column)

CHARFOOS, REITER, PETERSON, HOLMQUIST & PILCHAK P.C.—*Continued*

Myron B. Charfoos	Michael P. Krut
James A. Reiter	Kenneth E. Jones
Daniel Peterson	Marianne G. Talon
C. John Holmquist, Jr.	Deborah S. Dorland
William E. Pilchak	Daniel G. Cohen

Danial J. Hébert

Representative Clients: Little Caesars Enterprises; Modern Engineering/CDI Corporation of Michigan; Detroit Board of Education; Michigan Plastic Processors Association; Alexis Risk Management Services; Michigan Auto Dealers Workers Compensation; Michigan National Bank; Faygo Beverages; Michigan Tooling Assoc.; Michigan Hospital Assoc.; Forty-Sixth District Court.

For full biographical listings, see the Martindale-Hubbell Law Directory

CLARK, KLEIN & BEAUMONT (AV)

1600 First Federal Building, 1001 Woodward Avenue, 48226
Telephone: 313-965-8300
Facsimile: 313-962-4348
Bloomfield Hills Office: 1533 North Woodward Avenue, Suite 220, 48304.
Telephone: 810-258-2900.
Facsimile: 810-258-2949.

MEMBERS OF FIRM

David P. Wood	David H. Paruch
Dwight H. Vincent	Suanne Tiberio Trimmer
Henry Earle, III	Rachelle G. Silberberg
Fred W. Batten	Dorothy Hanigan Basmaji

ASSOCIATES

Jennifer M. Sweeney Buckley	Patricia Bordman
Keith James	Donica Tolee Thomas

Representative Clients: American Red Cross; Bally's Health & Tennis Corp. of America; BASF Corporation; Bechtel Eastern Power Corp.; The Budd Company; The Canteen Corporation; First Federal of Michigan; Dow Corning Corporation; La-Z-Boy Chair Company; Michigan Consolidated Gas Company.

For Complete List of Firm Personnel, See General Section

For full biographical listings, see the Martindale-Hubbell Law Directory

CONKLIN, BENHAM, DUCEY, LISTMAN & CHUHRAN, P.C. (AV)

1740 First National Building, 48226
Telephone: 313-961-8690
Traverse City, Michigan Office: 415 East Front Street.
Telephone: 616-947-4300.

S. Gerard Conklin (1903-1975)	David J. Watts
Donald G. Ducey	Martin L. Critchell
William R. Listman	Thomas A. Plagens
Thomas P. Chuhran	John S. Chapman
Thomas J. McNally	David J. Berge
Dwight D. Labadie	Martin M. Summer

Reference: National Bank of Detroit.

For full biographical listings, see the Martindale-Hubbell Law Directory

DICKINSON, WRIGHT, MOON, VAN DUSEN & FREEMAN (AV)

500 Woodward Avenue, Suite 4000, 48226-3425
Telephone: 313-223-3500
Facsimile: 313-223-3598
Bloomfield Hills, Michigan Office: 525 North Woodward Avenue, Suite 2000.
Telephone: 810-433-7200.
Facsimile: 810-433-7274.
Grand Rapids, Michigan Office: 200 Ottawa Avenue, N.W., Suite 900.
Telephone: 616-458-1300.
Facsimile: 616-458-6753.
Lansing, Michigan Office: Suite 200, 215 South Washington Square.
Telephone: 517-371-1730.
Facsimile: 517-487-4700.
Washington, D.C. Office: Suite 800, 1901 L Street, N.W.
Telephone: 202-457-0160.
Facsimile: 202-659-1559.
Chicago, Illinois Office: 225 West Washington, Suite 400.
Telephone: 312-220-0300.
Facsimile: 312-220-0021.
Warsaw, Poland Office: 46 Wilcza Street, 4th Floor, 00-679.
Telephone: (48-22) 299-241.
Facsimile: (48-2) 628-4107. Komertel Satellite Phone: (48-39) 121-510.

MEMBERS OF FIRM

John Corbett O'Meara	Gregory L. McClelland (Lansing Office)
Thomas G. Kienbaum	Noel D. Massie
Henry W. Saad (Bloomfield Hills Office)	Theodore R. Opperwall
Timothy H. Howlett	John M. Lichtenberg (Grand Rapids Office)
Joseph C. Marshall, III	Jon Robert Steiger (Bloomfield Hills Office)
George R. Ashford (Bloomfield Hills Office)	

(See Next Column)

MEMBERS OF FIRM (Continued)

Elizabeth Phelps Hardy	Elizabeth M. Pezzetti (Bloomfield Hills Office)
Andrea Andrews Larkin (Lansing Office)	Johanna H. Armstrong

Eric J. Pelton

OF COUNSEL

Thomas D. McLennan (Bloomfield Hills Office)

ASSOCIATES

William C. Bertrand, Jr. (Lansing Office)	Mary Keizer Kalmink
Robert E. Carr (Bloomfield Hills Office)	Richard D. McNulty (Lansing Office)
David R. Deromedi	Louis Theros (Chicago, Illinois Office)
Sherisse Eddy Fiorvento	Jennifer A. Zinn

For Complete List of Firm Personnel, See General Section

For full biographical listings, see the Martindale-Hubbell Law Directory

DYKEMA GOSSETT (AV)

400 Renaissance Center, 48243-1668
Telephone: 313-568-6800
Cable Address: "Dyke-Detroit"
Telex: 23-0121
Fax: 313-568-6594
Ann Arbor, Michigan Office: 315 East Eisenhower Parkway, Suite 100, 48108-3306.
Telephone: 313-747-7660.
Fax: 313-747-7696.
Bloomfield Hills, Michigan Office: 1577 North Woodward Avenue, Suite 300, 48304-2820.
Telephone: 810-540-0700.
Fax: 810-540-0763.
Grand Rapids, Michigan Office: 200 Oldtown Riverfront Building, 248 Louis Campau Promenade, N.W., 49503-2668.
Telephone: 616-776-7500.
Fax: 616-776-7573.
Lansing, Michigan Office: 800 Michigan National Tower, 48933-1707.
Telephone: 517-374-9100.
Fax: 517-374-9191.
Washington, D.C. Office: Franklin Square, Suite 300 West Tower, 1300 I Street, N.W., 20005-3306.
Telephone: 202-522-8600.
Fax: 202-522-8669.
Chicago, Illinois Office: Three First National Plaza, Suite 1400, 70 W. Madison, 60602-4270.
Telephone: 312-214-3380.
Fax: 312-214-3441.

MEMBERS OF FIRM

Timothy K. Carroll	James P. Greene (Resident at Ann Arbor Office)
Bruce G. Davis (Resident at Ann Arbor Office)	Patrick F. Hickey
Robert L. Duty (Resident at Bloomfield Hills Office)	Debra M. McCulloch
	Joseph A. Ritok, Jr.
John A. Entenman	Ronald J. Santo
Martin Jay Galvin	Paul H. Townsend, Jr.

RETIRED PARTNERS

Earl R. Boonstra	James D. Tracy

ASSOCIATES

John F. Birmingham, Jr.	Anne E. MacIntyre (Resident at Ann Arbor Office)
Elizabeth M. Donovan	
Jennifer J. Howe	Steven H. Schwartz
Cathleen C. Jansen	Todd J. Shoudy
Sheri B. Katzman	Jeffrey N. Silveri

For Complete List of Firm Personnel, See General Section

For full biographical listings, see the Martindale-Hubbell Law Directory

HAISCH & BOYDA (AV)

100 Renaissance Center, Suite 1750, 48243
Telephone: 313-259-4370
Facsimile: 313-259-6487

Anthony A. Haisch	John M. Boyda

ASSOCIATE

Donald C. Wheaton, Jr.

Representative Clients: AT&T Corp.; AT&T Universal Card Services Corp.; Amoco Corp.; North American Philips Corp.; Empire Blue Cross & Blue Shield; Lyon Financial Services, Inc.; Schwans' Sales Enterprises; Marshalls, Inc.; Access America Inc.; Grant Industries, Inc.

For full biographical listings, see the Martindale-Hubbell Law Directory

Detroit—Continued

HONIGMAN MILLER SCHWARTZ AND COHN (AV)

A Partnership including Professional Corporations
2290 First National Building, 48226
Telephone: 313-256-7800
Telecopier: 313-962-0176
Telex: 235705
Lansing, Michigan Office: Phoenix Building, 222 North Washington Square, Suite 400.
Telephone: 517-484-8282.
West Palm Beach, Florida Office: Suite 800 Esperante Building, 222 Lakeview Avenue.
Telephone: 407-838-4500.
Tampa, Florida Office: 2700 Landmark Centre, 401 E. Jackson Street.
Telephone: 813-221-6600.
Orlando, Florida Office: 390 North Orange Avenue, Suite 1300.
Telephone: 407-648-0300.
Houston, Texas Office: 3100 First Interstate Bank Plaza, 1000 Louisiana.
Telephone: 713-650-2600.
Los Angeles, California Office: McNeill Plaza, Suite 820, 15260 Ventura Boulevard, 91403.
Telephone: 818-784-2900.

MEMBERS OF FIRM

Ingrid K. Brey
Norman D. Hawkins
Linn A. Hynds
Frank T. Mamat
A. David Mikesell
William D. Sargent

ASSOCIATES

Ann L. Andrews (Lansing, Michigan Office)
Cameron J. Evans
Claudia D. Orr
Barbara A. Van Zanten

Representative Clients: White Castle System, Inc.; Koepplinger's Bakery, Inc.; Handleman Co.; Gantos, Inc.; Guardian Industries, Inc.; Detroit Edison Company; General Motors Corporation; Associated Builders and Contractors (Southeast Michigan Chapters); Frank's Nursery and Crafts; Children's Hospital of Michigan.

For Complete List of Firm Personnel, See General Section

For full biographical listings, see the Martindale-Hubbell Law Directory

HOUGHTON, POTTER, SWEENEY & BRENNER, A PROFESSIONAL CORPORATION (AV)

The Guardian Building, 500 Griswold Street, Suite 3300, 48226-3806
Telephone: 313-964-0050
Facsimile: 313-964-4005

Ralph H. Houghton, Jr.
James E. Brenner

LEGAL SUPPORT PERSONNEL

LEGAL ASSISTANTS

Ann E. Adams
Janet C. Driver

Representative Clients: Wayne Center; Sevakis Industries, Inc.; Macauley's, Inc.; Molded Materials, Inc.; Village of Grosse Pointe Shores; Hartford Life Companies; APAC Paper and Packaging Corporation; Marathon Linen Service, Inc.; Douglas Cleaners, Inc.

For full biographical listings, see the Martindale-Hubbell Law Directory

KELLER, THOMA, SCHWARZE, SCHWARZE, DUBAY & KATZ, P.C. (AV)

440 E. Congress, 5th Floor, 48226
Telephone: 313-965-7610
Bloomfield Hills, Michigan Office: Suite 122, 100 West Long Lake Road.
Telephone: 313-647-3114.

Leonard A. Keller (1906-1970)
Charles E. Keller
Frederick B. Schwarze
Thomas H. Schwarze
Dennis B. DuBay
James R. Miller
Stewart J. Katz
Anthony J. Heckemeyer
Thomas L. Fleury
Terrence J. Miglio
Gary P. King
Donna R. Nuyen
Robert A. Lusk
Linda M. Foster
Bruce M. Bagdady
Carl F. Schwarze
George P. Butler, III
Christopher M. Murray
Brian A. Kreucher
Kenneth C. Howell

OF COUNSEL

Richard J. Thoma

Counsel for: Livonia Public Schools; Ludington News Co., Inc.
Representative Clients: Borg-Warner Corp.; E & L Transport Co.; The Kroger Co.; Holnam, Inc.
Public Employer Clients: City of Farmington Hills; City of Flint; City of Grosse Pointe Woods; Saginaw Public Schools.

For Complete List of Firm Personnel, See General Section

For full biographical listings, see the Martindale-Hubbell Law Directory

KERR, RUSSELL AND WEBER (AV)

One Detroit Center, 500 Woodward Avenue, Suite 2500, 48226-3406
Telephone: 313-961-0200
Telecopier: 313-961-0388
Bloomfield Hills, Michigan Office: 3883 Telegraph Road.
Telephone: 810-649-5990.
East Lansing, Michigan Office: 1301 North Hagadorn Road.
Telephone: 517-336-6767.

Richard D. Weber
William A. Sankbeil
Monte D. Jahnke
Michael B. Lewis
Curtis J. DeRoo
Daniel G. Beyer
George J. Christopoulos
Paul M. Shirilla
Stephen D. McGraw
Thomas R. Williams
Edward C. Cutlip, Jr.
Robert J. Pineau
Jeffrey A. Brantley
Catherine Bonczak Edwards
Patrick J. Haddad
Eric I. Lark
James E. DeLine
Daniel J. Schulte

For Complete List of Firm Personnel, See General Section

For full biographical listings, see the Martindale-Hubbell Law Directory

KITCH, DRUTCHAS, WAGNER & KENNEY, P.C. (AV)

One Woodward, Tenth Floor, 48226-3412
Telephone: 313-965-7900
Fax: 313-965-7403
Lansing, Michigan Office: 120 Washington Square, North, Suite 805, One Michigan Avenue, 48933-1609.
Telephone: 517-372-6430.
Fax: 517-372-0441.
Macomb County Office: Towne Square Development, 10 South Main Street, Suite 301, Mount Clemens, 48043-7903.
Telephone: 810-463-9770.
Fax: 810-463-8994.
Toledo, Ohio Office: 405 Madison Avenue, Suite 1500, 43604-1235.
Telephone: 419-243-4006.
Fax: 419-243-7333.
Troy, Michigan Office: 3001 West Big Beaver Road, Suite 200, 48084-3103.
Telephone: 810-637-3500.
Fax: 810-637-6630.
Ann Arbor, Michigan Office: 303 Detroit Street, Suite 400, P.O. Box 8610, 48107-8610.
Telephone: 313-994-7600.
Fax: 313-994-7626.

Jeremiah J. Kenney (Managing Principal)
Ralph F. Valitutti, Jr.
Mark D. Willmarth (Principal)
Victor J. Abela (Principal, Troy Office)
Susan Healy Zitterman
Karen Bernard Berkery (Associate Principal)
Gregory P. Sweda (Troy Office)
Maureen Rouse-Ayoub

Representative Clients: Browning-Ferris Industries, Inc.; Clarkston-Potomac Group, Inc.; CPI Corporation; St. John-Bon Secour Senior Community; St. John Hospital; Venture Service Corp.; W.A. Forte Memorial Hospital, Inc.; Wayne State University; Wickes Lumber Company.

For Complete List of Firm Personnel, See General Section

For full biographical listings, see the Martindale-Hubbell Law Directory

LAW OFFICES OF THOMAS E. MARSHALL (AV)

Ford Building, Suite 1805, 615 Griswold, 48226-3583
Telephone: 313-963-4483
Telecopier: 313-963-4736

ASSOCIATES

Rachel K. Eickemeyer
Phyllis Leah Hurks-Hill

OF COUNSEL

Andrew J. Bean

For full biographical listings, see the Martindale-Hubbell Law Directory

MILLER, CANFIELD, PADDOCK AND STONE, P.L.C. (AV)

A Professional Limited Liability Company
Founded in 1852 by Sidney Davy Miller
150 West Jefferson, Suite 2500, 48226-4415
Telephone: 313-963-6420
Fax: 313-496-7500
Cable Address: "Stem Detroit"
Detroit, Michigan Office: 150 West Jefferson, Suite 2500, 48226-4415.
Telephone: 313-963-6420.
Fax: 313-496-7500.
Cable Address: "Stem Detroit."
Ann Arbor, Michigan Office: 101 North Main Street, 7th Floor, 48104-1400.
Telephone: 313-663-2445.
Fax: 313-747-7147.
Bloomfield Hills, Michigan Office: Suite 100, Pinehurst Office Center, 1400 North Woodward, 48303-2014.
Telephone: 313-645-5000.
Fax: 313-645-1917.

(See Next Column)

MILLER, CANFIELD, PADDOCK AND STONE P.L.C.—*Continued*

Grand Rapids, Michigan Office: 1200 Campau Square Plaza, 99 Monroe, N.W., 49503-2639.
Telephone: 616-454-8656.
Fax: 616-776-6322.
Howell, Michigan Office: 121 South Barnard Street, Suite 4, 48843-2305.
Telephone: 517-546-7600.
Telecopier: 517-546-6974.
Kalamazoo, Michigan Office: 444 West Michigan Avenue, 49007-3752.
Telephone: 616-381-7030.
Fax: 616-382-0244.
Lansing, Michigan Office: One Michigan Avenue, Suite 900, 48933-1609.
Telephone: 517-487-2070.
Fax: 517-374-6304.
Monroe, Michigan Office: The Executive Centre, 214 East Elm Avenue, 48161-2682.
Telephone: 313-243-2000.
Fax: 313-243-0901.
Washington, D.C. Office: 1225 Nineteenth Street, N.W., Suite 400. 20036.
Telephone: 202-429-5575; 785-0600.
Fax: 202-331-1118; 785-1234.
Pensacola, Florida Office: 25 West Cedar, 32501.
Telephone: 904-469-1088.
Fax: 904-432-0677.
St. Petersburg, Florida Office: 100 Second Avenue S., Suite 7045, 33701.
Telephone: 813-982-6000.
Fax: 813-892-6002.
Gdansk, Poland Office: Suite 322, Dom Technika Building, Ul. Rajska 6, 80-850.
Telephone: 011-485-831-2808.
Fax: 011-485-831-4719.
Warsaw, Poland Office: Ul. Marszalkowska 82, Suite 561, 00-517.
Telephone: 011-482-623-6457 and 6458.
Fax: 011-482-623-6459.

MEMBERS OF FIRM

Leonard D. Givens
Thomas P. Hustoles (Kalamazoo Office)
Jerome R. Watson
Donna J. Donati
Richard J. Seryak
Kevin M. McCarthy (Kalamazoo Office)
Beverly Hall Burns
Charles S. Mishkind (Grand Rapids, Lansing and Kalamazoo Offices)
Walter Briggs Connolly, Jr.
Alison B. Marshall (Washington, D.C. Office)

OF COUNSEL

James E. Tobin

SENIOR ATTORNEY

Charles A. Duerr, Jr. (Ann Arbor Office)

ASSOCIATES

George D. Mesritz
Megan P. Norris
Kurt N. Sherwood (Kalamazoo Office)
John H. Willems
Joseph G. Sullivan
Mark A. Randon

Representative Firm Clients: Chrysler Corp.; Comerica, Inc.; City of Detroit, Mich.; Detroit Tigers, Inc.; First of Michigan; Fretter, Inc.; Ford Motor Co.; Ford Motor Credit Co.; Great Lakes Bancorp; Henry Ford Hospital.

For Complete List of Firm Personnel, See General Section

For full biographical listings, see the Martindale-Hubbell Law Directory

PRATHER & ASSOCIATES, P.C. (AV)

3800 Penobscot Building, 48226-4220
Telephone: 313-962-7722
Facsimile: 313-962-2653

Kenneth E. Prather

Jan Rewers McMillan

For full biographical listings, see the Martindale-Hubbell Law Directory

RILEY AND ROUMELL, P.C. (AV)

7th Floor, Ford Building, 48226-3986
Telephone: 313-962-8255
Telefax: 313-962-2937

Wallace D. Riley
George T. Roumell, Jr.
William F. Dennis
Steven M. Zarowny
Amy E. Newberg
Alfred John Eppens
Wilber M. Brucker III
Allen J. Lippitt
Gregory T. Schultz

OF COUNSEL

Wilber M. Brucker, Jr.
William D. Cohan
Emmet E. Tracy, Jr.

Representative Clients: Detroit Board of Education; Wayne County; City of Livonia; Lapeer County Road Commission; Manistee County Road Commission; Lake Superior State University; Village of Lake Orion; White Chapel Memorial Assn.

For full biographical listings, see the Martindale-Hubbell Law Directory

STRINGARI, FRITZ, KREGER, AHEARN & CRANDALL, P.C. (AV)

650 First National Building, 48226-3538
Telephone: 313-961-6474
Fax: 313-961-5688

Richard J. Fritz
Conrad W. Kreger
Brian S. Ahearn
Martin E. Crandall
Kenneth S. Wilson

Dallas G. Moon
John C. Dickinson

OF COUNSEL

Karl R. Bennett, Jr.

Representative Clients: Automotive Moulding Co.; American Sunroof Corp.; Erb Lumber Co.; City of Detroit; Children's Hospital of Michigan; City Management Corp.; Variety Foodservices, Inc.

For full biographical listings, see the Martindale-Hubbell Law Directory

TIMMIS & INMAN (AV)

300 Talon Centre, 48207
Telephone: 313-396-4200
Telecopier: 313-396-4228

MEMBERS OF FIRM

Michael T. Timmis
Wayne C. Inman
George A. Peck
Richard L. Levin
Henry J. Brennan, III
Mark W. Peyser
Richard M. Miettinen
Lisa R. Gorman

ASSOCIATES

Bradley J. Knickerbocker
George M. Malis
Amy Lynn Ryntz
Mark Robert Adams
Daniel G. Kielczewski
Michael F. Wais
Kevin S. Kendall
David J. Galbenski

Representative Clients: Talon, Inc.; F & M Distributors.

For Complete List of Firm Personnel, See General Section

For full biographical listings, see the Martindale-Hubbell Law Directory

*ESCANABA,** Delta Co.

BUTCH, QUINN, ROSEMURGY, JARDIS, BUSH, BURKHART & STROM, P.C. (AV)

816 Ludington Street, 49829
Telephone: 906-786-4422
Fax: 906-786-5128
Gladstone, Michigan Office: 201 First National Bank Building.
Telephone: 906-428-3123.
Marquette, Michigan Office: 300 South Front Street.
Telephone: 906-228-4440.
Iron Mountain, Michigan Office: 500 South Stephenson Avenue.
Telephone: 906-774-4460.
Marinette, Wisconsin Office: 2008 Ella Court.
Telephone: 715-732-4154.

Thomas L. Butch
Terry F. Burkhart
Peter W. Strom
Steven C. Parks
John A. Lewandowski
Bonnie Lee Hoff
James E. Soderberg

Representative Clients: Escanaba Area Public Schools; Gwinn Area Community Schools; County of Delta; Delta County Community Mental Health Board; Alger-Delta Cooperative Electric Association; Rapid Electric Sales & Service; MFC First National Bank of Escanaba; City of Gladstone; St. Francis Hospital; Delta-Schoolcraft Intermediate School District.

For Complete List of Firm Personnel, See General Section

For full biographical listings, see the Martindale-Hubbell Law Directory

FARMINGTON HILLS, Oakland Co.

CHARFOOS, REITER, PETERSON, HOLMQUIST & PILCHAK, P.C. (AV)

Suite 400, 30500 Northwestern Highway, 48334-3179
Telephone: 810-626-7300
Facsimile: 810-626-7305
Detroit, Michigan Office: 1200 Sixth Street.
Telephone: 313-961-7011.

Myron B. Charfoos
James A. Reiter
Daniel Peterson
C. John Holmquist, Jr.
William E. Pilchak
Michael P. Krut
Kenneth E. Jones
Marianne G. Talon
Deborah S. Dorland
Daniel G. Cohen
Danial J. Hébert

Representative Clients: Little Caesars Enterprises; Modern Engineering/CDI Corporation of Michigan; Detroit Board of Education; Michigan Plastic Processors Association; Alexis Risk Management Services; Michigan Auto Dealers Workers Compensation; Faygo Beverages; Michigan Tooling Assoc.; Michigan Hospital Assoc.; Forty-Sixth District Court.

For full biographical listings, see the Martindale-Hubbell Law Directory

Farmington Hills—Continued

JOHNSON, ROSATI, GALICA, SHIFMAN, LABARGE, ASELTYNE, SUGAMELI & FIELD, P.C. (AV)

34405 W. Twelve Mile Road, Suite 200, 48331
Telephone: 810-489-4100
Fax: 810-489-1726
Bay City, Michigan Office: 420 Shearer Building, 311 Center Avenue, 48708.
Telephone: 517-894-2600; 517-894-7191.
Fax: 517-894-7177.
Lansing, Michigan Office: 303 S. Waverly Road, 48917.
Telephone: 517-886-3800.
Fax: 517-886-9154.
St. Clair Shores, Michigan Office: 19900 E. 10 Mile Road, 48080.
Telephone: 313-777-3377.

Christopher J. Johnson
Carol A. Rosati
Kenneth G. Galica
Howard L. Shifman
J. Russell LaBarge, Jr.
S. Randall Field
Patrick A. Aseltyne
Michael E. Rosati
Michael J. Sugameli
Kenneth A. Slusser
Laura Amtsbuechler
Edward M. Olson
Daniel P. Dalton
Margaret T. Debler
David R. Brinks
Marcelyn A. Stepanski

Representative Clients: Michigan Municipal Risk Management Authority; Metropolitan Association for Improved School Legislation Risk Management Trust; Indiana Insurance Company; County of Lapeer; County of Van Buren; County of Otsego, City of Romulus; City of Harper Woods; City of Hazel Park; Chirco Realty.

For full biographical listings, see the Martindale-Hubbell Law Directory

*FLINT,** Genesee Co.

DEAN, DEAN, SEGAR, HART & SHULMAN, P.C. (AV)

1616 Genesee Towers, One East First Street, 48502
Telephone: 810-235-5631
Fax: 810-235-8983

Max Dean
Robert L. Segar
Clifford H. Hart

Representative Clients: Flint Industrial Sales & Equipment Co.; P&H Plumbing & Heating, Inc.; Genesee County Dental Society; City of Montrose; Royalite Electric Co.; King of All Manufacturing, Inc.; Executive Travel Service.
Local Counsel for: Detroit Automobile Inter-Insurance Exchange.
References: NBD Bank, N.A.; Citizens Bank.

For Complete List of Firm Personnel, See General Section

For full biographical listings, see the Martindale-Hubbell Law Directory

GROVES, DECKER & WYATT, PROFESSIONAL CORPORATION (AV)

2357 Stone Bridge Drive, 48532
Telephone: 810-732-6920
Fax: 810-732-9015
East Lansing, Michigan Office: 2760 East Lansing Drive, Suite 4.
Telephone: 517-332-7715.
Facsimile: 517-332-4405.

Harvey R. Groves
Lee A. Decker
George H. Wyatt III
William L. Meuleman III
Thomas J. Ruth
Cameron D. Reddy

Representative Clients: American International Adjustment Co.; Crawford & Co.; General Motors Corp.; Johnson Controls, Inc.; Kmart Corp.; Masco Corp.; National Union Fire Insurance Co.; New Hampshire Insurance Co.; Scibal, Inc.

For full biographical listings, see the Martindale-Hubbell Law Directory

LAW OFFICES OF PATRICK M. KIRBY A PROFESSIONAL CORPORATION (AV)

G1335 South Linden Road, Suite G, 48532
Telephone: 810-230-0833
Fax: 810-230-8222

Patrick M. Kirby

Todd O. Pope

Representative Clients: Brotherhood Mutual Insurance Co.; City of Flint; K&K Insurance Group; Merchants and Medical Credit Corp.; Nero Plastics; Rent-A-Center.

For full biographical listings, see the Martindale-Hubbell Law Directory

WINEGARDEN, SHEDD, HALEY, LINDHOLM & ROBERTSON (AV)

501 Citizens Bank Building, 48502-1983
Telephone: 810-767-3600
Telecopier: 810-767-8776

(See Next Column)

MEMBERS OF FIRM

William C. Shedd
Dennis M. Haley
John T. Lindholm
Donald H. Robertson
L. David Lawson
John R. Tucker

ASSOCIATES

Alan F. Himelhoch
Suellen J. Parker
Damion Frasier
Peter T. Mooney

Representative Clients: Citizens Commercial and Savings Bank; R.L. White Development Corporation; Interstate Traffic Consultants (Intracon) Inc.; Downtown Development Authority of Flint; Young Olds-Cadillac, Inc.; First American Title Insurance Co.; Sorensen Gross Construction Co.; Genesee County; Insight, Inc..; Flint Counsel, National Bank of Detroit.

For Complete List of Firm Personnel, See General Section

For full biographical listings, see the Martindale-Hubbell Law Directory

*GRAND RAPIDS,** Kent Co.

CLARY, NANTZ, WOOD, HOFFIUS, RANKIN & COOPER (AV)

500 Calder Plaza, 250 Monroe Avenue, N.W., 49503-2244
Telephone: 616-459-9487
Telecopier: 616-459-5121

MEMBERS OF FIRM

Jack R. Clary
Philip W. Nantz
Philip F. Wood
Leo H. Litowich
John H. Gretzinger
Marshall W. Grate
Steven K. Girard

ASSOCIATES

Mark D. Pakkala
Peter H. Peterson

Representative Clients: Extruded Metals, Inc.; Coca Cola Foods; F&M Distributors, Inc.; City of Cadillac; D & W Food Centers, Inc.; Hesperia Public Schools; Kent County; City of South Haven; USG Interiors, Inc.; Weather Shield Mfg., Inc.

For Complete List of Firm Personnel, See General Section

For full biographical listings, see the Martindale-Hubbell Law Directory

DICKINSON, WRIGHT, MOON, VAN DUSEN & FREEMAN (AV)

200 Ottawa Avenue, N.W., Suite 900, 49503-2423
Telephone: 616-458-1300
Facsimile: 616-458-6753
Detroit, Michigan Office: 500 Woodward Avenue, Suite 4000.
Telephone: 313-223-3500.
Facsimile: 313-223-3598.
Bloomfield Hills, Michigan Office: 525 North Woodward Avenue, Suite 2000.
Telephone: 810-433-7200.
Facsimile: 810-433-7274.
Lansing, Michigan Office: Suite 200, 215 South Washington Square.
Telephone: 517-371-1730.
Facsimile: 517-487-4700.
Washington, D.C. Office: Suite 800, 1901 L Street, N.W.
Telephone: 202-457-0160.
Facsimile: 202-659-1559.
Chicago, Illinois Office: 225 West Washington, Suite 400.
Telephone: 312-220-0300.
Facsimile: 312-220-0021.
Warsaw, Poland Office: 46 Wilcza Street, 4th Floor, 00-679.
Telephone: (48-22) 299-241.
Facsimile: (48-2) 628-4107. Komertel Satellite Phone: (48-39) 121-510.

RESIDENT PARTNER

John M. Lichtenberg

Representative Clients: Federal-Mogul Corp.; Florists' Transworld Delivery Assn.; GMF Robotics Corp.; Kmart Corp.; Kuhlman Corp.; Michigan Consolidated Gas Co.; NBD Bank, N.A.

For Complete List of Firm Personnel, See General Section

For full biographical listings, see the Martindale-Hubbell Law Directory

VARNUM, RIDDERING, SCHMIDT & HOWLETT (AV)

Bridgewater Place, P.O. Box 352, 49501-0352
Telephone: 616-336-6000
800-262-0011
Facsimile: 616-336-7000
Telex: 1561593 VARN
Lansing, Michigan Office: The Victor Center, Suite 810, 210 North Washington Square, 48933.
Telephone: 517-482-6237.
Facsimile: 517-482-6937.
Kalamazoo, Michigan Office: 350 East Michigan Avenue, 49007.
Telephone: 616-382-2300.
Facsimile: 616-382-2382.
Grand Haven, Michigan Office: 321 Washington Street, P.O. Box 288, 49417.
Telephone: 616-846-7100.
Facsimile: 616-846-7101.

(See Next Column)

VARNUM, RIDDERING, SCHMIDT & HOWLETT—*Continued*

Battle Creek, Michigan Office: 4950 West Dickman Road, Suite B-1, 49015.
Telephone: 616-962-7144.
Detroit, Michigan Office: 440 East Congress, Fourth Floor, 48226.
Telephone: 313-961-1600.
Facsimile: 313-961-1636.

COUNSEL

Eugene Alkema
Karen S. Kienbaum (Resident at Detroit Office)
James R. Viventi (Resident at Lansing Office)

MEMBERS OF FIRM

Kent J. Vana
Carl E. Ver Beek
Gary P. Skinner
H. Edward Paul
Thomas J. Barnes
Larry J. Titley
Richard A. Hooker (Resident at Kalamazoo Office)
Joseph J. Vogan
John Patrick White
Paul M. Kara
Gregory M. Palmer
David E. Khorey
Timothy J. Tornga
David A. Rhem
Donald P. Lawless

ASSOCIATES

Jeffrey J. Fraser
James R. Stadler
Richard R. Symons
Eric J. Guerin (Kalamazoo Office)
Mary C. Bonnema
Linda L. Oldford

Counsel for: Babcock Industries, Inc.; Battle Creek Unlimited; CMI International, Inc.; Canteen Service Co.; Donnelly Corporation; Excel Industries, Inc.; Georgia Pacific Corp.; Grand Valley State University; Hanson Industries; Teledyne, RJR Nabisco.

For Complete List of Firm Personnel, See General Section

For full biographical listings, see the Martindale-Hubbell Law Directory

WARNER, NORCROSS & JUDD (AV)

900 Old Kent Building, 111 Lyon Street, N.W., 49503-2489
Telephone: 616-752-2000
Fax: 616-752-2500
Muskegon, Michigan Office: 400 Terrace Plaza, P.O. Box 900.
Telephone: 616-727-2600.
Fax: 616-727-2699.
Holland, Michigan Office: Curtis Center, Suite 300, 170 College Avenue.
Telephone: 616-396-9800.
Fax: 616-396-3656.

OF COUNSEL

Lawson E. Becker

MEMBERS OF FIRM

Donald J. Veldman (Resident at Muskegon Office)
Jack B. Combs
Joseph F. Martin
Robert J. Chovanec
Robert W. Sikkel (Muskegon and Holland Offices)
Louis C. Rabaut
Stephen B. Grow

Representative Clients: Blodgett Memorial Center; Guardsman Products, Inc.; Kysor Industrial Corp.; Michigan Bankers Assn.; Old Kent Financial Corp.; Muskegon Community College; Michigan Civil Service Commission; Hart & Cooley Manufacturing.

For Complete List of Firm Personnel, See General Section

For full biographical listings, see the Martindale-Hubbell Law Directory

*KALAMAZOO,** Kalamazoo Co.

HOWARD & HOWARD ATTORNEYS, P.C. (AV)

The Kalamazoo Building, Suite 400, 107 West Michigan Avenue, 49007-3956
Telephone: 616-382-1483
Telecopier: 616-382-1568
Bloomfield Hills, Michigan Office: The Pinehurst Office Center, Suite 101, 1400 North Woodward Avenue.
Telephone: 810-645-1483.
Telecopier: 810-645-1568.
Lansing, Michigan Office: The Phoenix Building, Suite 500, 222 Washington Square North.
Telephone: 517-485-1483.
Telecopier: 517-485-1568.
Peoria, Illinois Office: Howard & Howard, P.C., The Creve Coeur Building, Suite 200, 321 Liberty Street.
Telephone: 309-672-1483.
Telecopier: 309-672-1568.

Richard D. Fries
Lawrence J. Murphy

Representative Clients: First of America Bank Corp.; Simpson Paper Company; W.R. Grace & Co.; Stryker Corp.; Kalamazoo Valley Community College.
Local Counsel for: Chrysler Motors Corp.
International Counsel for: Sony Corp.

For Complete List of Firm Personnel, See General Section

For full biographical listings, see the Martindale-Hubbell Law Directory

KREIS, ENDERLE, CALLANDER & HUDGINS, A PROFESSIONAL CORPORATION (AV)

One Moorsbridge, 49002
Telephone: 616-324-3000
Telecopier: 616-324-3010

Douglas L. Callander
John F. Koryto

For Complete List of Firm Personnel, See General Section

For full biographical listings, see the Martindale-Hubbell Law Directory

LILLY & LILLY, P.C. (AV)

505 South Park Street, 49007
Telephone: 616-381-7763
Fax: 616-344-6880

Charles M. Lilly (1990-1903)
Terrence J. Lilly

For full biographical listings, see the Martindale-Hubbell Law Directory

MILLER, CANFIELD, PADDOCK AND STONE, P.L.C. (AV)

A Professional Limited Liability Company
Founded in 1852 by Sidney Davy Miller
444 West Michigan Avenue, 49007-3752
Telephone: 616-381-7030
Fax: 616-382-0244
Detroit, Michigan Office: 150 West Jefferson, Suite 2500, 48226-4415.
Telephone: 313-963-6420.
Fax: 313-496-7500.
Cable Address: "Stem Detroit."
Ann Arbor, Michigan Office: 101 North Main Street, 7th Floor, 48104-1400.
Telephone: 313-663-2445.
Fax: 313-747-7147.
Bloomfield Hills, Michigan Office: Suite 100, Pinehurst Office Center, 1400 North Woodward, 48303-2014.
Telephone: 313-645-5000.
Fax: 313-645-1917.
Grand Rapids, Michigan Office: 1200 Campau Square Plaza, 99 Monroe, N.W., 49503-2639.
Telephone: 616-454-8656.
Fax: 616-776-6322.
Howell, Michigan Office: 121 South Barnard Street, Suite 4, 48843-2305.
Telephone: 517-546-7600.
Telecopier: 517-546-6974.
Lansing, Michigan Office: One Michigan Avenue, Suite 900, 48933-1609.
Telephone: 517-487-2070.
Fax: 517-374-6304.
Monroe, Michigan Office: The Executive Centre, 214 East Elm Avenue, 48161-2682.
Telephone: 313-243-2000.
Fax: 313-243-0901.
Washington, D.C. Office: 1225 Nineteenth Street, N.W., Suite 400. 20036.
Telephone: 202-429-5575; 785-0600.
Fax: 202-331-1118; 785-1234.
Pensacola, Florida Office: 25 West Cedar, 32501.
Telephone: 904-469-1088.
Fax: 904-432-0677.
St. Petersburg, Florida Office: 100 Second Avenue S., Suite 7045,33701.
Telephone: 813-982-6000.
Fax: 813-892-6002.
Gdansk, Poland Office: Suite 322, Dom Technika Building, Ul. Rajska 6, 80-850.
Telephone: 011-485-831-2808.
Fax: 011-485-831-4719.
Warsaw, Poland Office: Ul. Marszalkowska 82, Suite 561, 00-517.
Telephone: 011-482-623-6457 and 6458.
Fax: 011-482-623-6459.

MEMBERS OF FIRM

Eric V. Brown, Jr. (Resident)
Thomas P. Hustoles (Resident)
Kevin M. McCarthy (Resident)

RESIDENT ASSOCIATE

Kurt N. Sherwood

Representative Firm Clients: Chrysler Corp.; Comerica, Inc.; City of Detroit, Mich.; Detroit Tigers, Inc.; First of Michigan; Fretter, Inc.; Ford Motor Co.; Ford Motor Credit Co.; Great Lakes Bancorp; Henry Ford Hospital.

For Complete List of Firm Personnel, See General Section

For full biographical listings, see the Martindale-Hubbell Law Directory

LANSING, Ingham Co.

DUNNINGS & FRAWLEY, P.C. (AV)

Duncan Building, 530 South Pine Street, 48933-2299
Telephone: 517-487-8222
Fax: 517-487-2026

Stuart J. Dunnings, Jr.
John J. Frawley

(See Next Column)

DUNNINGS & FRAWLEY P.C., *Lansing—Continued*

Stuart J. Dunnings, III
Steven D. Dunnings

Representative Clients: Lansing Board of Education; Lansing Housing Commission; Ford Motor Co.
References: First of America; Michigan National Bank.

For full biographical listings, see the Martindale-Hubbell Law Directory

FOSTER, SWIFT, COLLINS & SMITH, P.C. (AV)

313 South Washington Square, 48933-2193
Telephone: 517-371-8100
Telecopier: 517-371-8200
Farmington Hills, Michigan Office: 32300 Northwestern Highway, Suite 230.
Telephone: 810-851-7500.
Fax: 810-851-7504.

Theodore W. Swift
Stephen O. Schultz
William R. Schulz
Scott L. Mandel
Kathryn M. Niemer (Resident, Farmington Hills Office)
David J. Houston
Michael J. Bommarito
Melissa J. Jackson
Peter R. Albertins

General Counsel for: First American Bank-Central; Story, Inc.; Michigan Milk Producers Assn.; Edward W. Sparrow Hospital; St. Lawrence Hospital; Demmer Corp.; Michigan Financial Corp.
Local Counsel for: Shell Oil Co.; Michigan-Mutual Insurance Co.; Century Cellunet.

For Complete List of Firm Personnel, See General Section

For full biographical listings, see the Martindale-Hubbell Law Directory

FRASER TREBILCOCK DAVIS & FOSTER, P.C. (AV)

1000 Michigan National Tower, 48933
Telephone: 517-482-5800
Fax: 517-482-0887
Okemos, Michigan Office: 2188 Commons Parkway.
Telephone: 517-349-1300.
Fax: 517-349-0922.

Michael E. Cavanaugh
John J. Loose
Brandon W. Zuk

Sharon A. Bruner

Counsel for: Auto Owners Insurance Company; Dowleg Manufacturing; Michigan Education Association; Michigan Non-Profit Homes; Tri-State Hospital Supply Corporation.

For Complete List of Firm Personnel, See General Section

For full biographical listings, see the Martindale-Hubbell Law Directory

HOWARD & HOWARD ATTORNEYS, P.C. (AV)

The Phoenix Building, Suite 500, 222 Washington Square, North, 48933-1817
Telephone: 517-485-1483
Telecopier: 517-485-1568
Kalamazoo, Michigan Office: The Kalamazoo Building, Suite 400, 107 West Michigan Avenue.
Telephone: 616-382-1483.
Telecopier: 616-382-1568.
Bloomfield Hills, Michigan Office: The Pinehurst Office Center, Suite 101, 1400 North Woodward Avenue.
Telephone: 810-645-1483.
Telecopier: 810-645-1568.
Peoria, Illinois Office: Howard & Howard, P.C., The Creve Coeur Building, Suite 200, 321 Liberty Street.
Telephone: 309-672-1483.
Telecopier: 309-672-1568.

Todd D. Chamberlain

Representative Clients: For Representative Client list, see General Practice, Lansing, MI.

For Complete List of Firm Personnel, See General Section

For full biographical listings, see the Martindale-Hubbell Law Directory

MILLER, CANFIELD, PADDOCK AND STONE, P.L.C. (AV)

A Professional Limited Liability Company
Founded in 1852 by Sidney Davy Miller
Suite 900, One Michigan Avenue, 48933-1609
Telephone: 517-487-2070
Fax: 517-374-6304
Detroit, Michigan Office: 150 West Jefferson, Suite 2500, 48226-4415.
Telephone: 313-963-6420.
Fax: 313-496-7500.
Cable Address: "Stem Detroit."

(See Next Column)

Ann Arbor, Michigan Office: 101 North Main Street, 7th Floor, 48104-1400.
Telephone: 313-663-2445.
Fax: 313-747-7147.
Bloomfield Hills, Michigan Office: Suite 100, Pinehurst Office Center, 1400 North Woodward, 48303-2014.
Telephone: 313-645-5000.
Fax: 313-645-1917.
Grand Rapids, Michigan Office: 1200 Campau Square Plaza, 99 Monroe, N.W., 49503-2639.
Telephone: 616-454-8656.
Fax: 616-776-6322.
Howell, Michigan Office: 121 South Barnard Street, Suite 4, 48843-2305.
Telephone: 517-546-7600.
Telecopier: 517-546-6974.
Kalamazoo, Michigan Office: 444 West Michigan Avenue, 49007-3752.
Telephone: 616-381-7030.
Fax: 616-382-0244.
Monroe, Michigan Office: The Executive Centre, 214 East Elm Avenue, 48161-2682.
Telephone: 313-243-2000.
Fax: 313-243-0901.
Washington, D.C. Office: 1225 Nineteenth Street, N.W., Suite 400. 20036.
Telephone: 202-429-5575; 785-0600.
Fax: 202-331-1118; 785-1234.
Pensacola, Florida Office: 25 West Cedar, 32501.
Telephone: 904-469-1088.
Fax: 904-432-0677.
St. Petersburg Office: 100 Second Avenue S., Suite 7045, 33701.
Telephone: 813-982-6000.
Fax: 813-892-6002.
Gdansk, Poland Office: Suite 322, Dom Technika Building, UI. Rajska 6, 80-850.
Telephone: 011-485-831-2808.
Fax: 011-485-831-4719.
Warsaw, Poland Office: UI. Marszalkowska 82, Suite 561, 00-517.
Telephone: 011-482-623-6457 and 6458.
Fax: 011-482-623-6459.

MEMBER OF FIRM

William J. Danhof (Resident)

Representative Firm Clients: Chrysler Corp.; Comerica, Inc.; City of Detroit, Mich.; Detroit Tigers, Inc.; First of Michigan; Fretter, Inc.; Ford Motor Co.; Ford Motor Credit Co.; Great Lakes Bancorp; Henry Ford Hospital.

For Complete List of Firm Personnel, See General Section

For full biographical listings, see the Martindale-Hubbell Law Directory

*PORT HURON,** St. Clair Co.

NICHOLSON, FLETCHER & DEGROW (AV)

522 Michigan Street, 48060-3893
Telephone: 810-987-8444
Facsimile: 810-987-8149

MEMBERS OF FIRM

David C. Nicholson
Gary A. Fletcher

ASSOCIATE

Mark G. Clark

Representative Clients: Wirtz MFG.; Raymond Excavating; City of Port Huron; City of Marsville; St. Clair County; Port Huron Area School District; Intermediate School District of St. Clair County; East China School District; Marysville School District; Algonac School District.

For Complete List of Firm Personnel, See General Section

For full biographical listings, see the Martindale-Hubbell Law Directory

*SAGINAW,** Saginaw Co.

BRAUN KENDRICK FINKBEINER (AV)

8th Floor Second National Bank Building, 48607
Telephone: 517-753-3461
Telecopier: 517-753-3951
Bay City, Michigan Office: 201 Phoenix Building, P.O. Box 2039.
Telephone: 517-895-8505.
Telecopier: 517-895-8437.

MEMBERS OF FIRM

J. Richard Kendrick
James V. Finkbeiner
E. Louis Ognisanti
Robert A. Kendrick
John A. Decker

ASSOCIATES

Irenna M. Garapetian
Carolyn Pollock Cary

Representative Clients: The Dow Chemical Co.; General Motors Corp.; Lobdell Emery Manufacturing Co.; Merrill, Lynch, Inc.; Saginaw General Hospital; Saginaw News; The Wickes Foundation.

For Complete List of Firm Personnel, See General Section

For full biographical listings, see the Martindale-Hubbell Law Directory

Saginaw—Continued

MASUD, GILBERT & PATTERSON, P.C. (AV)

4449 Fashion Square Boulevard, 48603-1242
Telephone: 517-792-4499
Fax: 517-792-7725

David John Masud | Donald A. Gilbert
Gary D. Patterson

Curtis R. Willner | Kraig M. Schutter

Representative Clients: Dow Corning Corporation; Boritz Health Care Facilities; Associated Builders & Contractors; Michigan Sugar Co.; Saginaw Charter Township; Saginaw Township Community School; Aetna Insurance Co.; Central Michigan Railway; St. Mary's Medical Center; Forward Corp.

For full biographical listings, see the Martindale-Hubbell Law Directory

SMITH & BROOKER, P.C. (AV)

3057 Davenport Avenue, 48602
Telephone: 517-799-1891
Bay City, Michigan Office: 703 Washington Avenue.
Telephone: 517-892-2595.
Flint, Michigan Office: 3506 Lennon Road.
Telephone: 810-733-0140.

RESIDENT ATTORNEYS

Francis B. Drinan | Michael J. Huffman

BAY CITY, MICHIGAN OFFICE

Carl H. Smith, Jr. | Richard C. Sheppard
Albert C. Hicks | George B. Mullison
Glenn F. Doyle | Charles T. Hewitt

FLINT, MICHIGAN OFFICE

Thomas A. Connolly | Peter L. Diesel

Representative Clients: CIGNA; Citizens Insurance Co.; City of Saginaw; General Motors Corp.; Saginaw Township Community Schools; Saginaw Intermediate School District; State Farm Mutual Automobile Insurance Co.; Tri-City Airport Commission; CSX Transportation; Tittabawasee Township.

For full biographical listings, see the Martindale-Hubbell Law Directory

*ST. JOSEPH,** Berrien Co.

TROFF, PETZKE & AMMESON (AV)

Law and Title Building, 811 Ship Street, P.O. Box 67, 49085
Telephone: 616-983-0161
Facsimile: 616-983-0166

MEMBERS OF FIRM

Theodore E. Troff | Roger A. Petzke
Charles F. Ammeson

ASSOCIATES

Bennett S. Schwartz | Daniel G. Lambrecht
Deborah L. Berecz

Representative Clients: Auto Owners Insurance Co.; CSX Transportation, Inc.; NBD Bank, N.A.

For full biographical listings, see the Martindale-Hubbell Law Directory

SOUTHFIELD, Oakland Co.

SOMMERS, SCHWARTZ, SILVER & SCHWARTZ, P.C. (AV)

2000 Town Center, Suite 900, 48075
Telephone: 810-355-0300
Telecopier: 810-746-4001
Plymouth, Michigan Office: 747 South Main Street.
Telephone: 313-455-4250.

Donald J. Gasiorek | David A. Kotzian
Justin C. Ravitz | Patricia A. Stamler
Joseph A. Golden | Sam G. Morgan
Daniel D. Swanson | Gary E. Abeska

Representative Clients: Automatic Data Processing; Vlasic & Co.; C. A. Muer Corp.; O/E Automation, Inc.; Woodland Physicians; City of Taylor; Township of Van Buren; Vesco Oil Corp.; Royal Insurance Co.; Michigan Mutual-/Amerisure Insurance Co.

For Complete List of Firm Personnel, See General Section

For full biographical listings, see the Martindale-Hubbell Law Directory

*TRAVERSE CITY,** Grand Traverse Co.

MURCHIE, CALCUTT & BOYNTON (AV)

109 East Front Street, Suite 300, 49684
Telephone: 616-947-7190
Fax: 616-947-4341

Robert B. Murchie (1894-1975) | William B. Calcutt
Harry Calcutt | Mark A. Burnheimer
Jack E. Boynton | Dawn M. Rogers

(See Next Column)

ASSOCIATES

George W. Hyde, III | Ralph J. Dilley (Not admitted in MI)

General Counsel for: Old Kent Bank-Grand Traverse; Northwestern Savings Bank & Trust; Central-State Bancorp; Traverse City Record Eagle; WPNB-7 & WTOM-4; Emergency Consultants, Inc.; National Guardian Risk Retention Group, Inc.; Farmers Mutual Insurance Co.; Environmental Solutions, Inc.
Local Counsel For: Consumers Power Co.

For full biographical listings, see the Martindale-Hubbell Law Directory

TROY, Oakland Co.

BARLOW & LANGE, P.C. (AV)

3290 West Big Beaver Road Suite 310, 48084
Telephone: 810-649-3150
Facsimile: 810-649-3175

Thomas W. H. Barlow | Donna A. Lavoie
Craig W. Lange | Matthew S. Derby
Paul W. Coughenour | Julie Benson Valice
Craig S. Schwartz | John K. Ausdemore

For full biographical listings, see the Martindale-Hubbell Law Directory

CHANDLER, BUJOLD & CHANDLER (AV)

755 West Big Beaver Road Suite 1114, 48084
Telephone: 810-362-2277
Telecopier: 810-362-3760

Dan W. Chandler | W. Robert Chandler
Frank J. Bujold | R. Joseph Chandler
Francis X. Bujold, II

For full biographical listings, see the Martindale-Hubbell Law Directory

KEYWELL AND ROSENFELD (AV)

Suite 600, 2301 West Big Beaver Road, 48084
Telephone: 810-649-3200
Fax: 810-649-0454

MEMBERS OF FIRM

Gary W. Klotz | Norman E. Greenfield

ASSOCIATE

Miriam R. Rosen

OF COUNSEL

Robert S. Rosenfeld

Reference: National Bank of Detroit.

For full biographical listings, see the Martindale-Hubbell Law Directory

MATHESON, PARR, SCHULER, EWALD, ESTER & JOLLY (AV)

2555 Crooks Road, Suite 200, 48084
Telephone: 810-643-7900
Telecopier: 810-643-0417

MEMBERS OF FIRM

Robert Alan Parr | Terence K. Jolly
James D. Osmer

Representative Clients: National Automobile Transporters Labor Division; Brink's Inc.; Expertec, Inc.; Advance Technology, Inc.; Digital Electronic Automation, Inc.; Frito-Lay, Inc.
Reference: Comerica Bank.

For Complete List of Firm Personnel, See General Section

For full biographical listings, see the Martindale-Hubbell Law Directory

STEPHEN K. VALENTINE, JR., P.C. (AV)

600 Columbia Center, 201 West Big Beaver Road, 48084
Telephone: 810-851-3010
West Bloomfield, Michigan Office: Suite 400, 5767 West Maple Road.
Telephone: 810-851-3010.

Stephen K. Valentine, Jr.

For full biographical listings, see the Martindale-Hubbell Law Directory

WEST BLOOMFIELD, Oakland Co.

STEPHEN K. VALENTINE, JR., P.C. (AV)

5767 West Maple Road, Suite 400, 48322
Telephone: 810-851-3010
Troy, Michigan Office: 600 Columbia Center. 201 West Big Beaver Road.
Telephone: 810-851-3010.

Stephen K. Valentine, Jr.

OF COUNSEL

Philip G. Meyer

For full biographical listings, see the Martindale-Hubbell Law Directory

MINNESOTA

MINNEAPOLIS, * Hennepin Co.

ARTHUR, CHAPMAN, MCDONOUGH, KETTERING & SMETAK, P.A. (AV)

500 Young Quinlan Building, 81 South Ninth Street, 55402
Telephone: 612-339-3500
Fax: 612-339-7655

Michael R. Quinlivan
Sally J. Ferguson
Jeremiah P. Gallivan
Katherine L. MacKinnon
Lee J. Keller
Joseph W. Waller
Christine L. Tuft

Representative Clients: American International Group; American States; Bristol Myers-Squibb, Inc.; Continental Insurance Co.; General Casualty; Home Insurance Co.; Metropolitan Property & Liability Insurance Co.; Navistar International; Safeco Insurance Co.; USAA.

For Complete List of Firm Personnel, See General Section

For full biographical listings, see the Martindale-Hubbell Law Directory

GREGG M. CORWIN & ASSOCIATES (AV)

Parkdale Plaza Building, 1660 South Highway 100, 55416
Telephone: 612-544-7774
FAX: 612-544-7151

ASSOCIATES

Karin E. Peterson
Mary L. Setter
Ann E. Walther

For full biographical listings, see the Martindale-Hubbell Law Directory

FELHABER, LARSON, FENLON AND VOGT, PROFESSIONAL ASSOCIATION (AV)

Suite 4200, First Bank Place 601 2nd Avenue South, 55402-4302
Telephone: 612-339-6321
Facsimile: 612-338-0535
St. Paul, Minnesota Office: Suite 2100, Minnesota World Trade Center.
Telephone: 612-222-6321. Facsimilie: 612-222-8905.

Robert L. Bach
Edward J. Bohrer
Stephen J. Burton
Paul H. Cady
James J. Cronin
James M. Dawson
Robert J. Fenlon
Robert S. Halagan
Jan Douglas Halverson
David R. Hols
Lee A. Lastovich
William F. Mohrman
Karen G. Schanfield
Thomas M. Vogt
Paul J. Zech

For Complete List of Firm Personnel, See General Section

For full biographical listings, see the Martindale-Hubbell Law Directory

FREDRIKSON & BYRON, P.A. (AV)

1100 International Centre, 900 Second Avenue South, 55402-3397
Telephone: 612-347-7000
Telex: 290569 FREDRIKSON MPS
Telecopier: 612-347-7077
European Office: 79 Knightsbridge, London SW1X 7RB England.
Telephone: 44-71-823-2338.
Telecopier: 44-71-235-2683.

Kathleen A. Hughes
Paul L. Landry
Richard A. Ross
Robert C. Boisvert, Jr.
Anne M. Radolinski
Mary Anne Colovic
Mary M. Krakow
Mary E. Hanton

For Complete List of Firm Personnel, See General Section

For full biographical listings, see the Martindale-Hubbell Law Directory

HVASS, WEISMAN & KING, CHARTERED (AV)

Suite 450, 100 South Fifth Street, 55402
Telephone: 612-333-0201
FAX: 612-342-2606

Charles T. Hvass (Retired)
Si Weisman (1912-1992)
Robert J. King
Frank J. Brixius
Richard A. Williams, Jr.
Charles T. Hvass, Jr.
Robert J. King, Jr.
Michael W. Unger

John E. Daly
John M. Dornik
Mark T. Porter

For full biographical listings, see the Martindale-Hubbell Law Directory

LEONARD, STREET AND DEINARD, PROFESSIONAL ASSOCIATION (AV)

Suite 2300, 150 South Fifth Street, 55402
Telephone: 612-335-1500
Telecopier: 612-335-1657

James V. Roth
Angela M. Bohmann
Ellen G. Sampson
Robert Zeglovitch
Gregg J. Cavanagh
Susan M. Robiner

Thomas J. Conley
Daniel L. Palmquist
Daniel Oberdorfer

OF COUNSEL

Michelle A. Miller

Representative Clients: Pillsbury Co.; Nabisco Brands, Inc.; F.M.C. Corporation; Minnesota Historical Society; The Stroh Brewery Co.

For Complete List of Firm Personnel, See General Section

For full biographical listings, see the Martindale-Hubbell Law Directory

MANSFIELD & TANICK, P.A. (AV)

International Centre, 900 Second Avenue South, 15th Floor, 55402
Telephone: 612-339-4295
Fax: 612-339-3161

Seymour J. Mansfield
Marshall H. Tanick
Earl H. Cohen
Robert A. Johnson
Teresa J. Ayling
Sholly A. Blustin
Catherine M. Klimek
Phillip J. Trobaugh
Richard J. Fuller

OF COUNSEL

Daniel S. Kleinberger

For full biographical listings, see the Martindale-Hubbell Law Directory

ST. PAUL, * Ramsey Co.

BRIGGS AND MORGAN, PROFESSIONAL ASSOCIATION (AV)

2200 First National Bank Building, 55101
Telephone: 612-223-6600
Telecopier: 612-223-6450
Minneapolis, Minnesota Office: 2400 IDS Center, 80 South Eighth Street.
Telephone: 612-334-8400.
Telecopier: 612-334-8650.

RESIDENT PERSONNEL

Neal T. Buethe
Michael J. Galvin, Jr.
R. Ann Huntrods
Elena L. Ostby
Sally A. Scoggin
Daniel R. Wachtler

MINNEAPOLIS OFFICE

R. Scott Davies
Michael Thomas Miller
Gregory J. Stenmoe
Karin L. Wille

For Complete List of Firm Personnel, See General Section

For full biographical listings, see the Martindale-Hubbell Law Directory

GERAGHTY, O'LOUGHLIN & KENNEY, PROFESSIONAL ASSOCIATION (AV)

One Capital Centre Plaza, Suite 1400, 55102-1308
Telephone: 612-291-1177
Fax: 612-297-6901

Terence J. O'Loughlin
James R. Gowling
Robert M. Mahoney
David C. Hutchinson
Timothy R. Murphy
William H. Leary, III
Richard J. Thomas
Patrick H. O'Neill, Jr
Mary H. Alcorn
Patricia Rosvold
Daniel R. Fritz
Matthew J. Hanzel
Ann D. Bray
Jean B. Rudolph
Bryon Ascheman

OF COUNSEL

James H. Geraghty
James W. Kenney (Retired)

Representative Clients: St. Paul Fire & Marine Insurance Cos.; Midwest Medical Insurance Co.; Minnesota Lawyers Mutual Insurance Co.; University of Minnesota Hospitals; American National Bank and Trust Co.; Continental National American Group; Commercial State Bank; MMI Co.; Hammel Green Abrahamson, Inc.; Lunda Construction Co.

For full biographical listings, see the Martindale-Hubbell Law Directory

MISSISSIPPI

*ABERDEEN,** Monroe Co.

HOLCOMB, DUNBAR, CONNELL, CHAFFIN & WILLARD, A PROFESSIONAL ASSOCIATION (AV)

109 1/2 West Commerce Street, P.O. Box 866, 39730
Telephone: 601-369-8800
Facsimile: 601-369-9404
Jackson, Mississippi Office: 111 East Capitol Street, Suite 290, P.O. Box 2990, 39207-2990.
Telephone: 601-948-0048.
Facsimile: 601-948-0050.
Clarksdale, Mississippi Office: 152 Delta Avenue, P.O. Box 368, 38614.
Telephone: 601-627-2241.
Facsimile: 601-627-9788.
Oxford, Mississippi Office: 1217 Jackson Avenue, P.O. Drawer 707, 38655.
Telephone: 601-234-8775.
Facsimile: 601-234-8638.
Southhaven, Mississippi Office: Suite 1, 8727 Northwest Drive, P.O. Box 190, 38671.
Telephone: 601-342-6806.
Facsimile: 601-342-6792.

Jack F. Dunbar

Counsel for: United Southern Bank; Mississippi Power & Light Co.; Mississippi Valley Gas Co.; Aetna Casualty & Surety Co.; Southern Farm Bureau Casualty Insurance Co.; South Central Bell Telephone Co.; State Farm Mutual Automobile Insurance Co.; Fireman's Fund Insurance Cos.; Deere & Co.; Navistar International Transportation Corp.

For Complete List of Firm Personnel, See General Section

For full biographical listings, see the Martindale-Hubbell Law Directory

PATTERSON & PATTERSON (AV)

304 East Jefferson Street, P.O. Box 663, 39730
Telephone: 601-369-2476
1-800-523-9975
FAX: 601-369-9806

MEMBERS OF FIRM

Robert D. Patterson
Jan P. Patterson

Local Counsel for: National Bank of Commerce of Mississippi; American Colloid Company; Vista Chemical Co.; Pruet Production Co.; Arco Oil & Gas Co.; Chemical Corporation; Unimin Corporation.

For Complete List of Firm Personnel, See General Section

For full biographical listings, see the Martindale-Hubbell Law Directory

*GULFPORT,** Harrison Co.

DUKES, DUKES, KEATING AND FANECA, P.A. (AV)

2308 East Beach Boulevard, P.O. Drawer W, 39501
Telephone: 601-868-1111
FAX: 601-863-2886

Hugh D. Keating
Cy Faneca

For full biographical listings, see the Martindale-Hubbell Law Directory

*JACKSON,** Hinds Co.

HOLCOMB, DUNBAR, CONNELL, CHAFFIN & WILLARD, A PROFESSIONAL ASSOCIATION (AV)

111 East Capitol Street, Suite 290, P.O. Box 2990, 39207-2990
Telephone: 601-948-0048
Facsimile: 601-948-0050
Clarksdale, Mississippi Office: 152 Delta Avenue, P.O. Box 368, 38614.
Telephone: 601-627-2241.
Facsimile: 601-627-9788.
Aberdeen, Mississippi Office: 109 1/2 West Commerce Street, P.O. Box 866, 39730.
Telephone: 601-369-8800.
Facsimile: 601-369-9404.
Oxford, Mississippi Office: 1217 Jackson Avenue, P.O. Drawer 707, 38655.
Telephone: 601-234-8775.
Facsimile: 601-234-8638.
Southaven, Mississippi Office: Suite 1, 8727 Northwest Drive, P.O. Box 190, 38671.
Telephone: 601-342-6806.
Facsimile: 601-342-6792.

Jack F. Dunbar
Edward A. Moss
Thomas J. Suszek
John H. Dunbar
David C. Dunbar
Louis H. Watson, Jr.

Counsel for: United Southern Bank; Mississippi Power & Light Co.; Mississippi Valley Gas Co.; Aetna Casualty & Surety Co.; Southern Farm Bureau Casualty Insurance Co.; South Central Bell Telephone Co.; State Farm Fire & Casualty Insurance Co.; Fireman's Fund Insurance Cos.; Deere & Co.; Navistar International Transportation Corp.

(See Next Column)

For Complete List of Firm Personnel, See General Section

For full biographical listings, see the Martindale-Hubbell Law Directory

PHELPS DUNBAR, L.L.P. (AV)

Suite 500, Security Centre North, 200 South Lamar Street, P.O. Box 23066, 39225-3066
Telephone: 601-352-2300
Telecopier: 601-360-9777
New Orleans, Louisiana Office: Texaco Center, 400 Poydras Street.
Telephone: 504-566-1311.
Telecopier: 504-568-9130; 504-568-9007.
Cable Address: "Howspencer."
Telex: 584125 WU.
Telex: 6821155 WUI.
Baton Rouge, Louisiana Office: Suite 701, City National Bank Building, P.O. Box 4412.
Telephone: 504-346-0285.
Telecopier: 504-381-9197.
Tupelo, Mississippi Office: Seventh Floor, One Mississippi Plaza, P.O. Box 1220.
Telephone: 601-842-7907.
Telecopier: 601-842-3873.
Houston, Texas Office: Suite 501, 4 Houston Center, 1331 Lamar Street.
Telephone: 713-659-1386.
Telecopier: 713-659-1388.
London, England Office: Suite 976, Level 9, Lloyd's, 1 Lime Street, London EC3M 7DQ England.
Telephone: 011-44-171-929-4765.
Telecopier: 011-44-171-929-0046.
Telex: 987321.

MEMBERS OF FIRM

Paul O. Miller, III
Armin J. Moeller, Jr.
Gary E. Friedman
W. Thomas Siler, Jr. (Also at Tupelo, Mississippi Office)
R. Pepper Crutcher, Jr. (Also at Tupelo, Mississippi Office)
William I. Gault, Jr.
Susan Fahey Desmond

ASSOCIATES

John Wilson Eaton III (Also at Tupelo, Mississippi Office)
Ken Fairly
Wendy L. Moore
A. Matt Pesnell
Chelye E. Prichard
David M. Thomas, II

Representative Clients: Associated Builders and Contractors; Beech Aerospace Services; BellSouth Telecommunications, Inc.; General Motors Corporation; ITT; The Kroger Co.; Mississippi Hospital Association; Mississippi Municipal Liability Plan; Philip Morris, Incorporated; Southern Farm Bureau Life Insurance Company.

For Complete List of Firm Personnel, See General Section

For full biographical listings, see the Martindale-Hubbell Law Directory

WATKINS & EAGER (AV)

Suite 300 The Emporium Building, P.O. Box 650, 39205
Telephone: 601-948-6470
Facsimile: (601) 354-3623

MEMBER OF FIRM

Kenneth E. Milam

ASSOCIATE

Walter J. Brand

Representative Clients: UPS; MTEL; Hughes Aircraft; La-Z-Boy; Mississippi Baptist Medical Center; South Mississippi Electrical Power Association; Kerr-McGee Chemical Corp.

For Complete List of Firm Personnel, See General Section

For full biographical listings, see the Martindale-Hubbell Law Directory

*OXFORD,** Lafayette Co.

HOLCOMB, DUNBAR, CONNELL, CHAFFIN & WILLARD, A PROFESSIONAL ASSOCIATION (AV)

1217 Jackson Avenue P.O. Drawer 707, 38655
Telephone: 601-234-8775
Facsimile: 601-234-8638
Jackson, Mississippi Office: 111 East Capitol Street, Suite 290, P.O. Box 2990, 39207-2990.
Telephone: 601-948-0048.
Facsimile: 601-948-0050.
Clarksdale, Mississippi Office: 152 Delta Avenue, P.O. Box 368, 38614.
Telephone: 601-627-2241.
Facsimile: 601-627-9788.
Aberdeen, Mississippi Office: 109 1/2 West Commerce Street, P.O. Box 866, 39730.
Telephone: 601-369-8800.
Facsimile: 601-369-9404.
Southaven, Mississippi Office: Suite 1, 8727 Northwest Drive, P.O. Box 190, 38671.
Telephone: 601-342-6806.
Facsimile: 601-342-6792.

(See Next Column)

HOLCOMB, DUNBAR, CONNELL, CHAFFIN & WILLARD A PROFESSIONAL ASSOCIATION, *Oxford—Continued*

Jack F. Dunbar
Edward A. Moss
Thomas J. Suszek
John H. Dunbar
Louis H. Watson, Jr.

Counsel for: United Southern Bank; Mississippi Power & Light Co.; Mississippi Valley Gas Co.; Aetna Casualty & Surety Co.; Southern Farm Bureau Casualty Insurance Co.; South Central Bell Telephone Co.; State Farm Mutual Fire & Casualty Insurance Co.; Fireman's Fund Insurance Cos.; Deere & Co.; Navistar International Transportation Corp.

For Complete List of Firm Personnel, See General Section

For full biographical listings, see the Martindale-Hubbell Law Directory

SOUTHAVEN, De Soto Co.

HOLCOMB, DUNBAR, CONNELL, CHAFFIN & WILLARD, A PROFESSIONAL ASSOCIATION (AV)

Suite 1, 8727 Northwest Drive, P.O. Box 190, 38671
Telephone: 601-342-6806
Facsimile: 601-342-6792
Jackson, Mississippi Office: 111 East Capitol Street, Suite 290, P.O. Box 2990, 39207-2990.
Telephone: 601-948-0048.
Facsimile: 601-948-0050.
Clarksdale, Mississippi Office: 152 Delta Avenue, P.O. Box 368, 38614.
Telephone: 601-627-2241.
Facsimile: 601-627-9788.
Aberdeen, Mississippi Office: 109 1/2 West Commerce Street, P.O. Box 866, 39730.
Telephone: 601-369-8800.
Facsimile: 601-369-9404.
Oxford, Mississippi Office: 1217 Jackson Avenue, P.O. Drawer 707, 38655.
Telephone: 601-234-8775.
Facsimile: 601-234-8638.

Jack F. Dunbar
Thomas J. Suszek

Counsel For: United Southern Bank; Mississippi Power & Light Co.; Mississippi Valley Gas Co.; Aetna Casualty & Surety Co.; Southern Farm Bureau Casualty Insurance Co.; South Central Bell Telephone Co.; State Farm Mutual Fire & Casualty Insurance Co.; Deere & Co.; Navistar International Transportation Corp.; Sunburst Bank.

For Complete List of Firm Personnel, See General Section

For full biographical listings, see the Martindale-Hubbell Law Directory

*TUPELO,** Lee Co.

HOLLAND, RAY & UPCHURCH, P.A. (AV)

322 Jefferson Street, P.O. Drawer 409, 38802
Telephone: 601-842-1721
Facsimile: 601-844-6413

Sam E. Lumpkin (1908-1964)
Ralph L. Holland
James Hugh Ray
Robert K. Upchurch
W. Reed Hillen, III
Thomas A. Wicker

Michael D. Tapscott

Representative Clients: The Travelers; Continental Casualty Co.; South Central Bell Telephone Co.; The Greyhound Corp.; Mississippi Valley Gas Co.; Bryan-Rogers, Inc.; The Housing Authority of the City of Tupelo; Action Industries, Inc.; American Cable Systems, Inc.; American Funeral Assurance Co.

For full biographical listings, see the Martindale-Hubbell Law Directory

MISSOURI

KANSAS CITY, Jackson, Clay & Platte Cos.

BAKER, STERCHI & COWDEN (AV)

Suite 2100 Commerce Tower, 911 Main Street, P.O. Box 13566, 64199-3566
Telephone: 816-471-2121
FAX: 816-472-0288
Overland Park, Kansas Office: 51 Corporate Woods, 9393 West 110th Street, Suite 508.
Telephone: 913-451-6752.

MEMBERS OF FIRM

Thomas O. Baker
Thomas N. Sterchi
John W. Cowden
Thomas E. Rice, Jr.
Timothy S. Frets
Evan A. Douthit
Phillip C. Rouse
R. Douglas Gentile
James T. Seigfreid, Jr.
Robert A. Babcock
Peter F. Travis
John P. Poland

(See Next Column)

ASSOCIATES

Quentin L. Brown
James R. Jarrow
James S. Kreamer
Mary C. O'Connell
Randall L. Rhodes
D. Gregory Stonebarger
Kara Trouslot Stubbs
Robert M. Carroll
Stacy L. Cook
Patricia A. Sexton
Brent David Thomas

For full biographical listings, see the Martindale-Hubbell Law Directory

BLACKWELL SANDERS MATHENY WEARY & LOMBARDI L.C. (AV)

Suite 1100, Two Pershing Square, 2300 Main Street, 64108
Telephone: 816-274-6800
Telecopier: 816-274-6914
Overland Park, Kansas Office: 40 Corporate Woods, Suite 1200, 9401 Indian Creek Parkway.
Telephone: 913-345-8400.
Telecopier: 913-344-6375.

MEMBERS OF FIRM

Toni Hays Blackwood
John R. Phillips
Maurice A. Watson

ASSOCIATES

Gary E. Armbrust
Shelly L. Freeman
Brock A. Shealy

Representative Clients: Capitol Federal Savings & Loan Association; Commerce Bancshares; Hallmark Cards; Kimberly Quality Care; Percy Kent Bag Company; Puritan-Bennett; Saint Luke's Hospital; Utilicorp United Inc.

For Complete List of Firm Personnel, See General Section

For full biographical listings, see the Martindale-Hubbell Law Directory

SHUGHART THOMSON & KILROY, A PROFESSIONAL CORPORATION (AV)

Twelve Wyandotte Plaza, 120 West 12th Street, 64105
Telephone: 816-421-3355
Overland Park, Kansas Office: Suite 1100, 32 Corporate Woods, 9225 Indian Creek Parkway 66210.
Telephone: 913-451-3355.

Jack L. Campbell
W. Terrence Kilroy
Gregory M. Bentz
Thomas A. Sheehan
Adam P. Sachs

OF COUNSEL

William C. Nulton

For Complete List of Firm Personnel, See General Section

For full biographical listings, see the Martindale-Hubbell Law Directory

SPENCER FANE BRITT & BROWNE (AV)

1400 Commerce Bank Building, 1000 Walnut Street, 64106-2140
Telephone: 816-474-8100
Overland Park, Kansas Office: Suite 500, 40 Corporate Woods, 9401 Indian Creek Parkway.
Telephone: 913-345-8100.
Washington, D.C. Office: 1133 Connecticut Avenue, N.W., Suite 1000.
Telephone: 202-775-2376.

MEMBERS OF FIRM

J. Nick Badgerow (Resident, Overland Park, Kansas Office)
James G. Baker
Stanley E. Craven
Michael F. Delaney
Mark P. Johnson
William C. Martucci
James R. Willard
David L. Wing
Jack L. Whitacre

OF COUNSEL

Georgann H. Eglinski

ASSOCIATES

Daniel B. Boatright
Aaron C. Johnson
Nancy M. Landis (Resident, Overland Park, Kansas Office)

Representative Clients: Allsop Venture Partners; AT&T Technologies, Inc.; Baird Kurtz & Dobson; Bedford Properties; Builders Association of Missouri; City of Kansas City, Missouri; Daniels-McCray Lumber Co.; Heavy Constructors Assn.; Kansas City Power & Light Co.; Missouri Hospital Assn.

For Complete List of Firm Personnel, See General Section

For full biographical listings, see the Martindale-Hubbell Law Directory

SWANSON, MIDGLEY, GANGWERE, KITCHIN & MCLARNEY, L.L.C. (AV)

1500 Commerce Trust Building, 922 Walnut, 64106-1848
Telephone: 816-842-6100
Overland Park, Kansas Office: The NCAA Building, Suite 350, 6201 College Boulevard.
Telephone: 816-842-6100.

(See Next Column)

SWANSON, MIDGLEY, GANGWERE, KITCHIN & MCLARNEY L.L.C.—*Continued*

John J. Kitchin
Robert W. McKinley
Lawrence M. Maher

Linda J. Salfrank
Tedrick A. Housh, III

Counsel for: General Electric Co.; Chrysler Corp.; Yellow Freight System, Inc.; The Prudential Insurance Co. of America; Metropolitan Life Insurance Co.; National Collegiate Athletic Assn.; Safeway Stores, Inc.; The Lee Apparel Co.; Mutual of Omaha Insurance Co.; Maryland Casualty.

For Complete List of Firm Personnel, See General Section

For full biographical listings, see the Martindale-Hubbell Law Directory

ST. LOUIS, (Independent City)

ARMSTRONG, TEASDALE, SCHLAFLY & DAVIS (AV)

A Partnership including Professional Corporations
One Metropolitan Square, 63102-2740
Telephone: 314-621-5070
Facsimile: 314-621-5065
Twx: 910 761-2246
Cable: ATKV LAW
Kansas City, Missouri Office: 1700 City Center Square. 1100 Main Street, 64105.
Telephone: 816-221-3420.
Facsimile: 816-221-0786.
Belleville, Illinois Office: 23 South First Street, 62220.
Telephone: 618-397-4411.
Olathe, Kansas Office: 100 East Park, 66061.
Telephone: 913-345-0706.

MEMBERS OF FIRM

Fred Leicht, Jr., (P.C.)
Timothy K. Kellett (P.C.)
Wilbur L. Tomlinson (P.C.)
Joan Z. Cohen

ASSOCIATE

James G. Nowogrocki

OF COUNSEL

John P. Emde (P.C.)

Representative Clients: Western Lithotech; National Super Markets, Inc.; Ralston Purina Co; Cupples Company Manufacturers; Gusdorf Corporation; St. Louis Community College; Willert Home Products, Inc.; Absorbent Cotton Company; Midland Container Corp.; The Western Group, Inc.

For Complete List of Firm Personnel, See General Section

For full biographical listings, see the Martindale-Hubbell Law Directory

KOHN, SHANDS, ELBERT, GIANOULAKIS & GILJUM (AV)

24th Floor, One Mercantile Center, 63101
Telephone: 314-241-3963
Telecopier: 314-241-2509

Alan C. Kohn
Courtney Shands, Jr.
Harold I. Elbert
John Gianoulakis
Joseph P. Giljum
John A. Klobasa
Mark J. Bremer
Charles S. Elbert
Robert T. Haar
Robert A. Useted
Peter C. Woods
Lisa A. Pake

ASSOCIATES

Rebecca S. Stith
Lori Jeanette Baskins
Susan E. Bindler
Robert F. Murray

For full biographical listings, see the Martindale-Hubbell Law Directory

LEWIS, RICE & FINGERSH (AV)

A Partnership including Partnerships and Individuals
500 North Broadway, Suite 2000, 63102-2147
Telephone: 314-444-7600
Telecopier: 314-241-6056
Clayton, Missouri Office: Suite 400, 8182 Maryland Avenue.
Telephone: 314-444-7600.
Belleville, Illinois Office: 325 South High Street.
Telephone: 618-234-8636.
Hays, Kansas Office: 201 W. 11th St.
Telephone: 913-625-3997.
Leawood, Kansas Office: Suite 375, 8900 State Line.
Telephone: 913-381-8898.
Kansas City, Missouri Office: 1010 Walnut, Suite 500.
Telephone: 816-421-2500.

RESIDENT PARTNERS

Walter J. Taylor
John J. Moellering

For Complete List of Firm Personnel, See General Section

For full biographical listings, see the Martindale-Hubbell Law Directory

PEPER, MARTIN, JENSEN, MAICHEL AND HETLAGE (AV)

720 Olive Street, Twenty-Fourth Floor, 63101
Telephone: 314-421-3850
Fax: 314-621-4834
Fort Myers, Florida Office: 2080 McGregor Boulevard, Third Floor.
Telephone: 813-337-3850.
Fax: 813-337-0970.
Punta Gorda, Florida Office: 1625 West Marion Avenue, Suite 2.
Telephone: 813-637-1955.
Fax: 813-637-8485.
Naples, Florida Office: 850 Park Shore Drive, Suite 202.
Telephone: 813-261-6525.
Fax: 813-649-1805.
Belleville, Illinois Office: 720 West Main Street, Suite 140.
Telephone: 618-234-9574.
Fax: 618-234-9846.

MEMBERS OF FIRM

Richard E. Jaudes
Thomas A. Mickes
Thomas E. Tueth
Bradley S. Hiles
Clifford A. Godiner
Peter H. Ruger

ASSOCIATES

Celynda L. Brasher
Cathleen S. Bumb
Teri B. Goldman
Peter C. Johnson
Melanie Gurley Keeney
James G. Thomeczek
Robert J. Tomaso
Peter G. Yelkovac

For Complete List of Firm Personnel, See General Section

For full biographical listings, see the Martindale-Hubbell Law Directory

THOMPSON & MITCHELL (AV)

One Mercantile Center, Suite 3300, 63101
Telephone: 314-231-7676
Telecopier: 314-342-1717
Belleville, Illinois Office: 525 West Main Street.
Telephone: 618-277-4700; 314-271-1800.
Telecopier: 618-236-3434.
St. Charles, Missouri Office: 200 North Third Street.
Telephone: 314-946-7717.
Telecopier: 314-946-4938.
Washington, D.C. Office: 700 14th Street, N.W., Suite 900.
Telephone: 202-508-1000.
Telecopier: 202-508-1010.

MEMBERS OF FIRM

Charles B. Baron
David F. Yates
Charles A. Newman
Allen D. Allred
Charles M. Poplstein
Harry W. Wellford, Jr.
Patricia L. Cohen

ASSOCIATES

Kelly M. Brown
Ellen F. Cruickshank
Gerard K. Rodriguez
Stephen D. Smith

Representative Clients: Angelica Corporation; The Dial Corporation; Chrysler Corp.; City of St. Peters, Missouri; Home Builders Association of St. Louis; Magna Group, Inc.; Mercantile Bancorporation Inc.; Monterey Coal Co., a division of Exxon Corporation; St. Anthony's Medical Center; Fred Weber, Inc.

For Complete List of Firm Personnel, See General Section

For full biographical listings, see the Martindale-Hubbell Law Directory

WEINHAUS AND DOBSON (AV)

Suite 900, 906 Olive Street, 63101
Telephone: 314-621-8363
Telecopier: 314-621-8366

MEMBERS OF FIRM

S. Sheldon Weinhaus
Jerome J. Dobson

ASSOCIATES

Michael Craig Goldberg
Jonathan Charles Berns

OF COUNSEL

Mark E. Moreland

Reference: The Boatmen's National Bank of St. Louis.

For full biographical listings, see the Martindale-Hubbell Law Directory

MONTANA

*BILLINGS,** Yellowstone Co.

CROWLEY, HAUGHEY, HANSON, TOOLE & DIETRICH (AV)

500 Transwestern II, 490 North 31st Street, P.O. Box 2529, 59103
Telephone: 406-252-3441
Fax: 406-259-4159
Helena, Montana Office: IBM Building, 100 North Park Avenue, Suite 300, 59601.
Telephone: 406-449-4165.
Fax: 406-449-5149.

MEMBERS OF FIRM

Gareld F. Krieg
Terry B. Cosgrove
Steven J. Lehman
Laura A. Mitchell
William J. Mattix
Joe C. Maynard, Jr.

ASSOCIATES

Michael S. Lahr
Lori A. Harper

Representative Clients: Xerox Corporation; Valley Motor Supply; Montana Power Company; Armstrong World Industries; Peabody Coal Co.; United Parcel Service; Billings Clinic; Yellowstone County; MDU Resources Group, Inc.; General Electric Co.

For Complete List of Firm Personnel, See General Section

For full biographical listings, see the Martindale-Hubbell Law Directory

*BOZEMAN,** Gallatin Co.

KIRWAN & BARRETT, P.C. (AV)

215 West Mendenhall, P.O. Box 1348, 59771-1348
Telephone: 406-586-1553
Fax: 406-586-8971

Peter M. Kirwan
Stephen M. Barrett

Tom W. Stonecipher

For full biographical listings, see the Martindale-Hubbell Law Directory

NEBRASKA

*LINCOLN,** Lancaster Co.

BARLOW, JOHNSON, FLODMAN, SUTTER, GUENZEL & ESKE (AV)

1227 Lincoln Mall, P.O. Box 81686, 68501-1686
Telephone: 402-475-4240
Fax: 402-475-0329

MEMBER OF FIRM

Steven E. Guenzel

Special Counsel: Nebraska Public Power District.
Representative Clients: Allied Group; Chubb/Pacific Indemnity Group; Citizens State Bank, Polk, Nebraska; Crum & Foster; Federated Rural Electric Insurance Corp.; Runza Drive-Inns of America; United States Fidelity & Guaranty Co.; Viking Insurance Company of Wisconsin.

For Complete List of Firm Personnel, See General Section

For full biographical listings, see the Martindale-Hubbell Law Directory

ERICKSON & SEDERSTROM, P.C. (AV)

Suite 400, Cornhusker Plaza, 301 South 13th Street, 68508
Telephone: 402-476-1000
Fax: 402-476-6167
Omaha, Nebraska Office: Regency Westpointe, 10330 Regency Parkway Drive.
Telephone: 402-397-2200.
Fax: 402-390-7137.

Douglas L. Curry
Mark M. Schorr

Representative Clients: A T & T; Dubuque Packing Co.; General Motors Corp.; Hershey Foods, Inc.; IBP, Inc.; Mutual of Omaha; Nash Finch Co.; Omaha World Herald; Sun-Husker Foods, Inc.

For Complete List of Firm Personnel, See General Section

For full biographical listings, see the Martindale-Hubbell Law Directory

SCUDDER LAW FIRM, P.C. (AV)

Second Floor, 411 South 13th Street, P.O. Box 81277, 68508
Telephone: 402-435-3223
Fax: 402-435-4239

(See Next Column)

Beverly Evans Grenier
Christine C. Schwartzkopf Schroff
Earl H. Scudder, Jr.
Mark A. Scudder

For full biographical listings, see the Martindale-Hubbell Law Directory

*OMAHA,** Douglas Co.

ANDERSEN, BERKSHIRE, LAURITSEN & BROWER (AV)

A Partnership including a Professional Corporation
Suite 200, 8805 Indian Hills Drive, 68114-4070
Telephone: 402-397-0666
Facsimile: 397-4633

Thomas C. Lauritsen
John C. Hewitt

Representative Clients: Wilson Trailer Co.; U.S. Cold Storage; Affiliated Foods Cooperative, Inc.; KMTV; United Affiliated Grocers; Lisle Corp.; CMI-Load King; Owen Industries, Inc.; Goodkind & Goodkind, Inc.; Interstate Printing, Inc.

For Complete List of Firm Personnel, See General Section

For full biographical listings, see the Martindale-Hubbell Law Directory

BERENS & TATE, P.C. (AV)

Suite 400, 10050 Regency Circle, 68114
Telephone: 402-391-1991
Fax: 402-391-7363

Kelvin C. Berens
Joseph Dreesen
Timothy D. Loudon
Christopher E. Hoyme
Mark E. McQueen
Jerylyn R. Bridgeford
Christopher R. Hedican
Scott S. Moore
Mark A. Fahleson
Michelle Pribil

OF COUNSEL

John E. Tate
Donald E. Leonard (1933-1994)

For full biographical listings, see the Martindale-Hubbell Law Directory

ERICKSON & SEDERSTROM, P.C. (AV)

Regency Westpointe, 10330 Regency Parkway Drive, 68114
Telephone: 402-397-2200
Fax: 402-390-7137
Lincoln, Nebraska Office: Suite 400, Cornhusker Plaza, 301 South 13th Street.
Telephone: 402-476-1000.
Fax: 402-476-6167.

Soren S. Jensen
J Russell Derr

Representative Clients: A T & T; Boise Cascade Corp.; Dubuque Packing Co.; Eaton Corp.; General Motors Corp.; Hershey Foods, Inc.; IBP, Inc.; Mutual of Omaha; Omaha World Herald.

For Complete List of Firm Personnel, See General Section

For full biographical listings, see the Martindale-Hubbell Law Directory

FRASER, STRYKER, VAUGHN, MEUSEY, OLSON, BOYER & BLOCH, P.C. (AV)

500 Energy Plaza, 409 South 17th Street, 68102
Telephone: 402-341-6000
Telecopier: 402-341-8290

George C. Rozmarin
Robert F. Rossiter, Jr.
Mary Kay Frank

For Complete List of Firm Personnel, See General Section

For full biographical listings, see the Martindale-Hubbell Law Directory

MCGRATH, NORTH, MULLIN & KRATZ, P.C. (AV)

Suite 1400, One Central Park Plaza, 68102
Telephone: 402-341-3070
Telecopy: 402-341-0216
Telex: 797122 MNMKOM

Dean G. Kratz
Roger J. Miller
A. Stevenson Bogue
Patrick J. Barrett

Representative Clients: AT&T; Blue Cross/Blue Shield of Western Iowa, South Dakota and Nebraska; ConAgra, Inc.; Memorial Hospital of Dodge County; Physicians Mutual Insurance Co.; Richman-Gordman Stores, Inc.; Roberts Dairy Co.; Sioux Tools, Inc.; Weyerhauser Company; 1/2 Price Stores.

For Complete List of Firm Personnel, See General Section

For full biographical listings, see the Martindale-Hubbell Law Directory

NEVADA

*LAS VEGAS,** Clark Co.

JOLLEY, URGA, WIRTH & WOODBURY (AV)

Suite 800 Bank of America Plaza, 300 South Fourth Street, 89101
Telephone: 702-385-5161
Telecopier: 702-382-6814
Boulder City, Nevada Office: Suite 105, 1000 Nevada Highway.
Telephone: 702-293-3674.

MEMBERS OF FIRM

William R. Urga
Jay Earl Smith
Stephanie M. Smith

ASSOCIATE

Elissa F. Cadish

Representative Client: First Interstate Bank of Nevada; Nevada State Bank; Chicago Title Insurance Co.; Melvin Simon & Associates, Inc.; General Motors Acceptance Corp.; Toyota Motor Credit Corporation; Owens-Corning Fiberglas Corp.; Champion Home Builders Co.; Circus Circus Casinos, Inc.; Southwest Gas Corp.

For Complete List of Firm Personnel, See General Section

For full biographical listings, see the Martindale-Hubbell Law Directory

KAMER & RICCIARDI (AV)

3000 West Charleston Suite 3, 89102
Telephone: 702-259-8640
Fax: 702-259-8646
Cable Address: "Kamerlaw"

MEMBERS OF FIRM

Gregory J. Kamer
Mark J. Ricciardi

ASSOCIATES

S. Scott Greenberg
Scott M. Abbott
Lisa G. Salevitz

For full biographical listings, see the Martindale-Hubbell Law Directory

KIRSHMAN, HARRIS & COOPER, A PROFESSIONAL CORPORATION (AV)

411 East Bonneville Avenue Suite 300, 89101
Telephone: 702-384-3877
Fax: 702-384-7057; 702-384-4250
Los Angeles, California Office: Kirshman & Harris, A Professional Corporation. 11500 West Olympic Boulevard, Suite 605.
Telephone: 310-312-4544.

Norman H. Kirshman
Michael S. Harris
William E. Cooper
Sheldon M. Markel
Robert Zentz
Gary G. Branton

Representative Clients: Associated General Contractors of America Southern Nevada Chapter; Caesars World, Inc.; City of Henderson, Nevada; Employers Association of Southern Nevada; L.A. Yuma Freight Lines; Prime Cable; Sahara Hotel & Casino; San Gabriel Valley Tribune; Western Cab Co.

For full biographical listings, see the Martindale-Hubbell Law Directory

LIONEL SAWYER & COLLINS (AV)

1700 Bank of America Plaza, 300 South Fourth Street, 89101
Telephone: 702-383-8888
Fax: 702-383-8845
Reno, Nevada Office: Suite 1100, Bank of America Plaza, 50 West Liberty Street.
Telephone: 702-788-8666.
Fax: 702-788-8682.

MEMBER OF FIRM

Dan C. Bowen (Resident, Reno Office)

ASSOCIATE

Howard E. Cole

Representative Clients: Caesars Palace; Humana, Inc.; General Motors Corporation; Kerr McGee Corporation; Lewis Homes of Nevada; Citicorp; Hilton Hotels Corporation; Sprint/Central Telephone-Nevada; Tropicana Hotel and Country Club.

For Complete List of Firm Personnel, See General Section

For full biographical listings, see the Martindale-Hubbell Law Directory

MORRIS BRIGNONE & PICKERING (AV)

1203 Bank of America Plaza, 300 South Fourth Street, 89101
Telephone: 702-474-9400
Facsimile: 702-474-9422
Reno, Nevada Office: Wiegand Center, 165 West Liberty, #100, 89501.
Telephone: 702-322-7777.
Facsimile: 702-322-7791.

MEMBERS OF FIRM

Andrew S. Brignone
Mary Kristina Pickering

(See Next Column)

ASSOCIATES

José León
Ann Lyter Thomas

For full biographical listings, see the Martindale-Hubbell Law Directory

THE LAW FIRM OF SABBATH & MEHESAN CHARTERED (AV)

850 E. Bonneville Avenue, 89101
Telephone: 702-385-2004
Fax: 702-384-7268

Dennis M. Sabbath
Thomas C. Mehesan

Patricia McAllister Brame
Martha D. Macomber

Representative Clients: International Brotherhood of Electrical Workers Local Union #357, AFL-CIO; American Federation of Musicians; Musicians Union of Las Vegas Local #369, AFM, AFL-CIO; Floor Covers Local 2001; Clark County Fire Fighters; U.S. Steelworkers; Ventura Enterprises; Maricopa Turf, Inc.; P Hendley & Associates; Vista Investments, Inc.

For full biographical listings, see the Martindale-Hubbell Law Directory

SCHRECK, JONES, BERNHARD, WOLOSON & GODFREY, CHARTERED (AV)

600 East Charleston Boulevard, 89104
Telephone: 702-382-2101
Fax: 702-382-8135

Frank A. Schreck
Leslie Terry Jones
Peter C. Bernhard
Kenneth A. Woloson
John A. Godfrey
David D. Johnson
James R. Chamberlain
Michelle L. Morgando
Lance C. Earl
Thomas R. Canham
Sean T. McGowan
Dawn M. Cica
F. Edward Mulholland, II
Todd L. Bice
James J. Pisanelli
Ellen L. Schulhofer
John M. McManus

OF COUNSEL

Howard W. Cannon

For full biographical listings, see the Martindale-Hubbell Law Directory

SMITH & KOTCHKA, LTD. (AV)

317 South Sixth Street, 89101
Telephone: 702-382-1707
Telecopier: 702-382-9370

Gregory E. Smith
Malani L. Kotchka

Keith E. Kizer
L. Steven Demaree
Rose Marie Reynolds

Representative Clients: California Hotel and Casino; Housing Authority of the City of Las Vegas; Lincoln Management; Greyhound Exposition Services, Inc.; Las Vegas Valley Water District; Lucky Stores, Inc.; MGM-Desert Inn Hotel & Casino; Showboat Hotel and Casino; Tropicana; United Air Lines.

For full biographical listings, see the Martindale-Hubbell Law Directory

*RENO,** Washoe Co.

McDONALD, CARANO, WILSON, McCUNE, BERGIN, FRANKOVICH & HICKS (AV)

241 Ridge Street, 89505
Telephone: 702-322-0635
Telecopier: 702-786-9532
Las Vegas, Nevada Office: Suite 1000, 2300 West Sahara Avenue.
Telephone: 702-873-4100.
Telecopier: 702-873-9966.

MEMBERS OF FIRM

John J. McCune
Timothy E. Rowe
James W. Bradshaw
Lenard T. Ormsby

ASSOCIATES

Pat Lundvall
James P. Stefflre

Representative Clients: Associated General Contractors of America; Clark & Sullivan Constructors, Inc.; Eldorado Hotel & Casino; Hamilton Group of Companies; Jackpot Enterprises, Inc.; Regional Emergency Medical Services Authority; Sierra Nevada Production Credit Association.

For Complete List of Firm Personnel, See General Section

For full biographical listings, see the Martindale-Hubbell Law Directory

NEW HAMPSHIRE

*CONCORD,** Merrimack Co.

ORR & RENO, PROFESSIONAL ASSOCIATION (AV)

One Eagle Square, P.O. Box 3550, 03302-3550
Telephone: 603-224-2381
Fax: 603-224-2318

William L. Chapman

Representative Clients: Beach Aircraft Corporation; Chubb Life America; Fleet Bank; Dartmouth-Hitchcock Medical Center; EnergyNorth, Inc.; National Grange Mutual Co.; New England College; New England Electric System Co.; Newspapers of New England, Inc.; St. Paul's School.

For Complete List of Firm Personnel, See General Section

For full biographical listings, see the Martindale-Hubbell Law Directory

NEW JERSEY

HADDONFIELD, Camden Co.

TOMAR, SIMONOFF, ADOURIAN & O'BRIEN, A PROFESSIONAL CORPORATION (AV)

41 South Haddon Avenue, 08033
Telephone: 609-429-1100
Telecopier: 609-429-8164
Camden, New Jersey Office: 501 Cooper Street.
Telephone: 609-338-0553.
Telecopier: 609-338-0321.
Atlantic City, New Jersey Office: Commerce Building, Suite 220, 1200 Atlantic Avenue.
Telephone: 609-348-5900.
Northfield, New Jersey Office: The Executive Plaza, Suite 202, 2111 New Road.
Telephone: 609-485-0800.
Telecopier: 609-484-9388.
Wilmington, Delaware Office: Tomar, Simonoff, Adourian & O'Brien, The Mellon Bank Center, Suite 1701, 919 Market Street.
Telephone: 302-655-0500.
Telecopier: 302-428-0963.
Media, Pennsylvania Office: 115 North Jackson Street.
Telephone: 215-574-0635.

Howard S. Simonoff
Robert F. O'Brien
Ronald A. Graziano
Mary L. Crangle
James Katz
Mark E. Belland

For full biographical listings, see the Martindale-Hubbell Law Directory

LIBERTY CORNER, Somerset Co.

APRUZZESE, MCDERMOTT, MASTRO & MURPHY, A PROFESSIONAL CORPORATION (AV)

25 Independence Boulevard, P.O. Box 112, 07938
Telephone: 908-580-1776
Fax: 908-647-1492

Vincent J. Apruzzese
Frank X. McDermott
Francis A. Mastro
James F. Murphy (1938-1990)
Frederick T. Danser, III
Maurice J. Nelligan, Jr.
Richard C. Mariani
Barry Marell
Robert T. Clarke
Melvin L. Gelade
Jerrold J. Wohlgemuth

Sharon P. Margello
Tarquin Jay Bromley
Daniel F. Crowe
James M. Cooney
James L. Plosia, Jr.

Representative Clients: General Public Utilities Corp.; Public Service Electric & Gas Co.; Jersey Central Power & Light Co.; Smithkline; Beecham, Inc.; U. S. Metals & Refining Co.; Kelly-Springfield Tire Co.; ASEA Brown-Boveri; Foster Wheeler Corp.; Prudential Insurance Co.; General Electric; Schering Plough Corp.

For full biographical listings, see the Martindale-Hubbell Law Directory

LIVINGSTON, Essex Co.

GENOVA, BURNS, TRIMBOLI & VERNOIA (AV)

Eisenhower Plaza II, 354 Eisenhower Parkway, 07039
Telephone: 201-533-0777
Facsimile: 201-533-1112
Trenton, New Jersey Office: Suite One, 160 West State Street.
Telephone: 609-393-1131.

MEMBERS OF FIRM

Angelo J. Genova
James M. Burns
Stephen E. Trimboli
Francis J. Vernoia

(See Next Column)

ASSOCIATES

Meryl G. Nadler
John C. Petrella
James J. McGovern, III
Kathleen M. Connelly
Joseph Licata
Elaine M. Reyes
Lynn S. Degen
James J. Gillespie
T. Sean Jackson

For full biographical listings, see the Martindale-Hubbell Law Directory

SCHWARTZ, SIMON, EDELSTEIN, CELSO & KESSLER (AV)

(A Partnership including a Professional Corporation)
Presidential Center Suite 300, 293 Eisenhower Parkway, 07039
Telephone: 201-740-1600
Telecopier: 201-740-0891

Lawrence S. Schwartz (P.C.)
Stephen J. Edelstein
Nathanya Guritzky Simon
Nicholas Celso, III
Donald A. Kessler

Michael S. Rubin
David L. Rosenberg
Denise Pamela Coleman
Alan R. Niedz
Joel G. Scharff
Andrew B. Brown
John B. Mariano, Jr.
Joyce A. Brauer-Weston
Wendi F. Weill
Jeffrey A. Bennett
Alison C. Leonard
Joseph P. Kreoll
Pamela T. Hanback
Thomas Russo

OF COUNSEL

Miguel A. Maza

For full biographical listings, see the Martindale-Hubbell Law Directory

*MORRISTOWN,** Morris Co.

BRODERICK, NEWMARK & GRATHER, A PROFESSIONAL CORPORATION (AV)

20 South Street, 07960
Telephone: 201-538-0084
Fax: 201-538-2509

Edward F. Broderick, Jr.
Martin A. Newmark
Francis G. Grather
Alan J. Baldwin

OF COUNSEL

Edward F. Broderick (1905-1987)
I. Ezra Newmark (1901-1979)
George F. Sweeny (P.C.)

Stephen I. Weichert

For full biographical listings, see the Martindale-Hubbell Law Directory

PITNEY, HARDIN, KIPP & SZUCH (AV)

Park Avenue at Morris County, P.O. Box 1945, 07962-1945
Telephone: 201-966-6300
New York City: 212-926-0331
Telex: 642014
Telecopier: 201-966-1550

MEMBERS OF FIRM

S. Joseph Fortunato
Edward P. Lynch
Gregory C. Parliman
Patrick J. McCarthy
Kathy A. Lawler
Theresa Donahue Egler

COUNSEL

David P. Doyle

ASSOCIATES

Sean T. Quinn
Jonathan E. Hill
Theresa A. Kelly
Donna M. Murphy
Rosalie J. Shoeman
Susan R. Kohn

Representative Clients: AlliedSignal Inc.; AT&T; Base Ten Systems, Inc.; Exxon Corp.; Ford Motor Co.; Midlantic National Bank; Sony Electronics, Inc.; Union Carbide Corp.; United Parcel Services, Inc.; Warner-Lambert Co.

For Complete List of Firm Personnel, See General Section

For full biographical listings, see the Martindale-Hubbell Law Directory

SHANLEY & FISHER, A PROFESSIONAL CORPORATION (AV)

131 Madison Avenue, 07962-1979
Telephone: 201-285-1000
Telecopier: 1-201-285-1098
Telex: 475-4255 (I.T.T.)
Cable Address: "Shanley"
New York, N.Y. Office: 89th Floor, One World Trade Center.
Telephone: 212-321-1812.
Telecopier: 1-212-466-0569.

Paul G. Nittoly
Patrick M. Stanton

(See Next Column)

SHANLEY & FISHER A PROFESSIONAL CORPORATION—*Continued*

Peter O. Hughes
Mark Diana
Douglas S. Zucker
Lisa M. Plinio
Nicholas J. Taldone
Suzanne Cerra

For Complete List of Firm Personnel, See General Section

For full biographical listings, see the Martindale-Hubbell Law Directory

*NEWARK,** Essex Co.

APRUZZESE, MCDERMOTT, MASTRO & MURPHY, A PROFESSIONAL CORPORATION

(See Liberty Corner)

BARRY & MCMORAN, A PROFESSIONAL CORPORATION (AV)

One Newark Center, 07102
Telephone: 201-624-6500
Telecopier: 201-624-4052

John J. Barry
Bruce P. McMoran
Salvatore T. Alfano
Mark Falk
John A. Avery
John P. Flanagan

Mark F. Kluger
Madeline E. Cox
Joann K. Dobransky
Adam N. Saravay
Thomas F. Doherty
Judson L. Hand
Carmen J. Di Maria

For full biographical listings, see the Martindale-Hubbell Law Directory

CARPENTER, BENNETT & MORRISSEY (AV)

(Formerly Carpenter, Gilmour & Dwyer)
Three Gateway Center, 17th Floor, 100 Mulberry Street, 07102-4079
Telephone: 201-622-7711
New York City: 212-943-6530
Telex: 139405
Telecopier: 201-622-5314
EasyLink: 62827845
ABA/net: CARPENTERB

MEMBERS OF FIRM

Edward F. Ryan
James J. Crowley, Jr.
Donald A. Romano
Francis X. Dee
Irving L. Hurwitz
John J. Peirano
Linda B. Celauro
John K. Bennett
Patrick G. Brady
James E. Patterson

ASSOCIATES

Kevin C. Donovan
James Peter Lidon
David J. Reilly
John J. Shea
Joseph Gerard Lee
Michele L. Fliegel
L. Julius M. Turman
Karen L. Mayer
David A. Cohen
Vimal K. Shah (Not admitted in NJ)

Representative Clients: General Motors Corp.; AT&T; Bell Atlantic; Anheuser-Busch, Inc.; Litton Industries; GAF Corporation; Merck & Company; Johnson & Johnson; Prudential Insurance Company of America; Rutgers, The State University.

For Complete List of Firm Personnel, See General Section

For full biographical listings, see the Martindale-Hubbell Law Directory

CRUMMY, DEL DEO, DOLAN, GRIFFINGER & VECCHIONE, A PROFESSIONAL CORPORATION (AV)

One Riverfront Plaza, 07102
Telephone: 201-596-4500
Telecopier: 201-596-0545
Cable-Telex: 138154
Brussels, Belgium Office: Crummy, Del Deo, Dolan, Griffinger & Vecchione. Avenue Louise 475, BTE. 8, B-1050.
Telephone: 011-322-646-0019.
Telecopier: 011-322-646-0152.

John A. Ridley
Richard S. Zackin
Ira J. Hammer
Kerry M. Parker

Anthony J. Cincotta
David G. Uffelman
Patricia A. Barbieri

Representative Clients: Claremont Companies; Hoffmann-La Roche Inc.; McGraw Hill, Inc.; Toshiba America Consumer Products; Interbank Card Assn. (Mastercard).

For Complete List of Firm Personnel, See General Section

For full biographical listings, see the Martindale-Hubbell Law Directory

DEMARIA, ELLIS, HUNT, SALSBERG & FRIEDMAN (AV)

Suite 1400, 744 Broad Street, 07102
Telephone: 201-623-1699
Telecopier: 201-623-0954

MEMBERS OF FIRM

H. Reed Ellis
Ronald H. DeMaria
William J. Hunt
Richard M. Salsberg
Paul A. Friedman
Brian N. Flynn
Richard H. Bauch
Lee H. Udelsman

ASSOCIATES

Mitchell A. Schley
Joseph D. Olivieri
Joanne M. Maxwell
Robyn L. Aversa
George W. Rettig
David S. Catuogno
Debra S. Friedman
Kathryn A. Calista

For full biographical listings, see the Martindale-Hubbell Law Directory

JASINSKI AND PARANAC, A PROFESSIONAL CORPORATION (AV)

Ten Park Place, 8th Floor, 07102
Telephone: 201-824-9700
Telecopier: 201-824-6061
Philadelphia, Pennsylvania Office: Architects Building, 117 South 17th Street, Suite 2100, 19103.
Telephone: 215-568-1200.
Telecopier: 215-563-1534.

David F. Jasinski
Joseph P. Paranac, Jr.

Karen McGlashan Williams

Representative Clients: American Bureau of Shipping; Bradco Supply Corp.; Building Contractors Association, Atlantic County; Core States Bank; Freehold Rehabilitation and Nursing Center; GAB Business Services, Inc.; Graphnet, Inc.; City of Harrisburg, Pennsylvania; Hunterdon Convalescent Center.

For full biographical listings, see the Martindale-Hubbell Law Directory

MCCARTER & ENGLISH (AV)

Four Gateway Center, 100 Mulberry Street, P.O. Box 652, 07101-0652
Telephone: 201-622-4444
Telecopier: 201-624-7070
Cable Address: "McCarter" Newark
Cherry Hill, New Jersey Office: 1810 Chapel Avenue West.
Telephone: 609-662-8444.
Telecopier: 609-662-6203.
New York, New York Office: Suite 1519, One World Trade Center.
Telephone: 212-466-9018.
Telecopier: 212-432-6568.
Boca Raton, Florida Office: 2255 Glades Road, Suite 319-A.
Telephone: 407-994-6262.
Telecopier: 407-241-0798.
Wilmington, Delaware Office: Mellon Bank Center, 919 Market Street.
Telephone: 302-654-8010.
Telecopier: 302-654-0795.

MEMBERS OF FIRM

Thomas F. Daly
Richard C. Cooper
John E. Flaherty
John B. Brescher, Jr.
Rosemary Alito
Theodore D. Moskowitz
Mark A. Daniele

For Complete List of Firm Personnel, See General Section

For full biographical listings, see the Martindale-Hubbell Law Directory

SILLS CUMMIS ZUCKERMAN RADIN TISCHMAN EPSTEIN & GROSS, A PROFESSIONAL CORPORATION (AV)

One Riverfront Plaza, 07102-5400
Telephone: 201-643-7000
Fax: 201-643-6500
Telex: 820630 Sillsbeck Nwk
Atlantic City, New Jersey Office: 17 Gordon's Alley.
Telephone: 609-344-2800.
New York, N.Y. Office: 250 Park Avenue.
Telephone: 212-643-7000.

Lester Aron
Mark J. Blunda

Cherie L. Maxwell
Derlys Maria Gutierrez

Representative Clients: Becton Dickinson & Company; Stevens Institute of Technology; Bally Manufacturing Corporation; Walgreen Company; Fairleigh Dickinson University; BMW of North America, Inc.; Ridgewood Board of Education; Highland Park Board of Education.

For Complete List of Firm Personnel, See General Section

For full biographical listings, see the Martindale-Hubbell Law Directory

Newark—Continued

ZAZZALI, ZAZZALI, FAGELLA & NOWAK, A PROFESSIONAL CORPORATION (AV)

One Riverfront Plaza, 07102-5410
Telephone: 201-623-1822
Telecopier: 201-623-2209
Trenton, New Jersey Office: 150 West State Street.
Telephone: 609-392-8172.
Telecopier: 609-392-8933.

Andrew F. Zazzali (1925-1969)
Andrew F. Zazzali, Jr.
James R. Zazzali
Robert A. Fagella
Kenneth I. Nowak

Paul L. Kleinbaum
Richard A. Friedman
Kathleen Anne Naprstek
Michael J. Buonoaguro
Aileen M. O'Driscoll
Charles J. Farley, Jr.
Edward H. O'Hare

For full biographical listings, see the Martindale-Hubbell Law Directory

---

NORTHFIELD, Atlantic Co.

TOMAR, SIMONOFF, ADOURIAN & O'BRIEN, A PROFESSIONAL CORPORATION (AV)

The Executive Plaza, Suite 202, 2111 New Road, 08225
Telephone: 609-485-0800
Telecopier: 609-484-9388
Camden, New Jersey Office: 501 Cooper Street.
Telephone: 609-338-0553.
Telecopier: 609-338-0321.
Haddonfield, New Jersey Office: 41 South Haddon Avenue.
Telephone: 609-429-1100.
Telecopier: 609-429-8164.
Atlantic City, New Jersey Office: Commerce Building, Suite 220, 1200 Atlantic Avenue.
Telephone: 609-348-5900.
Wilmington, Delaware Office: Tomar, Simonoff, Adourian & O'Brien, The Mellon Bank Center, Suite 1701, 919 Market Street.
Telephone: 302-655-0500.
Telecopier: 302-428-0963.
Media, Pennsylvania Office: 115 North Jackson Street.
Telephone: 215-574-0635.

Howard S. Simonoff
Robert F. O'Brien
Ronald A. Graziano
James Katz

For full biographical listings, see the Martindale-Hubbell Law Directory

---

RAHWAY, Union Co.

DORF & DORF, A PROFESSIONAL CORPORATION (AV)

2376 St. Georges Avenue, 07065
Telephone: 908-574-9700
Fax: 908-574-0340
Boca Raton, Florida Office: 7764 Wind Key Drive.
Telephone: 407-488-3123.

Gerald L. Dorf
Mitchell L. Dorf

Richard B. Robins

For full biographical listings, see the Martindale-Hubbell Law Directory

---

ROSELAND, Essex Co.

HANNOCH WEISMAN, A PROFESSIONAL CORPORATION (AV)

4 Becker Farm Road, 07068-3788
Telephone: 201-535-5300
New York: 212-732-3262
Telecopier: 201-994-7198
Mailing Address: P.O. Box 1040, Newark, New Jersey, 07101-9819
Washington, D.C. Office: Suite 600, 1150 Seventeenth Street, N.W.
Telephone: 202-296-3432.

Carmine A. Iannaccone

James P. Flynn
Terri L. Freeman
Marie A. Latoff

For Complete List of Firm Personnel, See General Section

For full biographical listings, see the Martindale-Hubbell Law Directory

POST, POLAK, GOODSELL & MACNEILL, P.A. (AV)

65 Livingston Avenue, 07068
Telephone: 201-994-1100
Telecopier: 201-994-1705
New York, New York Office: Suite 1006, 575 Madison Avenue.
Telephone: 212-486-1455.

(See Next Column)

John N. Post
Charles R. Church
David L. Epstein

Allison D. B. Liebowitz

For full biographical listings, see the Martindale-Hubbell Law Directory

---

SPRINGFIELD, Union Co.

APRUZZESE, MCDERMOTT, MASTRO & MURPHY, A PROFESSIONAL CORPORATION

(See Liberty Corner)

JARDINE & PAGANO, A PROFESSIONAL CORPORATION (AV)

11 Cleveland Place, 07081
Telephone: 201-467-1620
Fax: 201-467-5562

Thomas V. Jardine
Joseph R. Pagano

For full biographical listings, see the Martindale-Hubbell Law Directory

---

*TRENTON,** Mercer Co.

SCHRAGGER, LAVINE & NAGY, A PROFESSIONAL CORPORATION (AV)

The Atrium at Lawrence, 133 Franklin Corner Road (Lawrenceville), 08648
Telephone: 609-896-9777
Fax: 609-895-1373

Alan S. Lavine
Bruce M. Schragger
Raymond L. Nagy
James A. Schragger

OF COUNSEL

Henry C. Schragger
A. Jerome Moore

Representative Clients: Sears, Roebuck & Co.; New Jersey Manufacturers Insurance Co.; Mercer County Community College; Mercer Mutual Insurance Co..

For Complete List of Firm Personnel, See General Section

For full biographical listings, see the Martindale-Hubbell Law Directory

---

VINELAND, Cumberland Co.

GRUCCIO, PEPPER, GIOVINAZZI, DESANTO & FARNOLY, P.A., A PROFESSIONAL CORPORATION (AV)

817 Landis Avenue, P.O. Box CN 1501, 08360
Telephone: 609-691-0100
Fax: 609-692-4095
Associated with: Stradley, Ronon, Stevens & Young, a Philadelphia Law Firm.
Woodbury, New Jersey Office: 21 Delaware Street.
Telephone: 609-848-5558.
Fax: 609-384-1181.
Avalon, New Jersey Office: 2878 Dune Drive.
Telephone: 609-967-4040.
Other New Jersey Offices:
Atlantic City Area: 609-347- 0909.
Salem Area: 609-935-3559.

Lawrence Pepper, Jr.
Cosmo A. Giovinazzi, III
Stephen D. Barse

Representative Clients: State Farm Mutual Automobile Insurance Cos.; United States Fidelity & Guaranty Co.; Atlantic City Expressway Authority; County of Salem; County of Cape May; CNA Insurance Co.; Cumberland Mutual Fire Insurance Co.; Cumberland County Guidance Center; Pizza Hut Inc.; Cities of Millville, Cape May, Wildwood, North Wildwood, Stone Harbor, Avalon, Sea Isle City, Margate, Farmers and Merchants National Bank.

For Complete List of Firm Personnel, See General Section

For full biographical listings, see the Martindale-Hubbell Law Directory

---

WESTFIELD, Union Co.

LINDABURY, MCCORMICK & ESTABROOK, A PROFESSIONAL CORPORATION (AV)

53 Cardinal Drive, P.O. Box 2369, 07091
Telephone: 908-233-6800
Fax: 908-233-5078

Peter A. Somers
John H. Schmidt, Jr.
Donald F. Nicolai
James K. Estabrook

Richard J. Cino

OF COUNSEL

Kenneth L. Estabrook

Representative Clients: Elizabeth General Medical Center; Kessler Institute for Rehabilitation; Mechanical Contractors Association of New Jersey; St. Joseph's Hospital and Medical Center; DeDietrich (USA), Inc.; Plunkett-

(See Next Column)

LINDABURY, MCCORMICK & ESTABROOK A PROFESSIONAL CORPORATION—*Continued*

Webster, Inc.; Union Trucking Co.; Visiting Nurse Association of Trenton, Inc.

For Complete List of Firm Personnel, See General Section

For full biographical listings, see the Martindale-Hubbell Law Directory

WOODBRIDGE, Middlesex Co.

WILENTZ, GOLDMAN & SPITZER, A PROFESSIONAL CORPORATION (AV)

90 Woodbridge Center Drive Suite 900, Box 10, 07095
Telephone: 908-636-8000
Telecopier: 908-855-6117
Eatontown, New Jersey Office: Meridian Center I, Two Industrial Way West, 07724.
Telephone: 908-493-1000.
Telecopier: 908-493-8387.
New York, New York Office: Wall Street Plaza, 88 Pine Street, 9th Floor, 10005.
Telephone: 212-267-3091.
Telecopier: 212-267-3828.

Alfred J. Hill
Alan M. Darnell
Stephen A. Spitzer

Glen D. Savits
Fred Hopke
George L. Kimmel
Laura J. Bogaards

Representative Clients: Suburban Transit Corp.; Co-Steel Raritan; Local 358 International Brotherhood of Electrical Workers.

For Complete List of Firm Personnel, See General Section

For full biographical listings, see the Martindale-Hubbell Law Directory

NEW MEXICO

*ALBUQUERQUE,** Bernalillo Co.

PETER J. ADANG, P.C. (AV)

500 Marquette N.W., Suite 630, 87102
Telephone: 505-242-3999
Fax: 505-242-3939

Peter J. Adang

For full biographical listings, see the Martindale-Hubbell Law Directory

CHERPELIS & ASSOCIATES, P.A. (AV)

1208 Hideaway Lane SE, 87123
Telephone: 505-294-0200
Fax: 505-294-5771

George Cherpelis

Representative Clients: General Motors Corp.; Gas Company of New Mexico; Public Service Company of New Mexico; Siemens Transmission Systems, Inc.; Sandia National Laboratories; Martin Marietta Corporation; Avonite; Hoffman Corporation; Kelly Services.

For full biographical listings, see the Martindale-Hubbell Law Directory

HINKLE, COX, EATON, COFFIELD & HENSLEY (AV)

Suite 800, 500 Marquette, N.W., P.O. Box 2043, 87103
Telephone: 505-768-1500
FAX: 505-768-1529
Roswell, New Mexico Office: Suite 700, United Bank Plaza, P.O. Box 10, 88202.
Telephone: 505-622-6510.
FAX: 505-623-9332.
Midland, Texas Office: 6 Desta Drive, Suite 2800, P.O. Box 3580, 79705.
Telephone: 915-683-4691.
FAX: 915-683-6518.
Amarillo, Texas Office: 1700 Bank One Center. P.O. Box 9238, 79105-9238.
Telephone: 806-372-5569.
FAX: 806-372-9761.
Santa Fe, New Mexico Office: 218 Montezuma, P.O. Box 2068, 87504.
Telephone: 505-982-4554.
FAX: 505-982-8623.
Austin, Texas Office: 401 West 15th Street, Suite 800, 78701.
Telephone: 512-476-7137.
FAX: 512-476-5431.
Associated Office: Hoffman & Stephens, P.C., 401 West 15th Street, Suite 800, 78701.
Telephone: 512-476-5434.
Fax: 512-476-5431.

(See Next Column)

Robert P. Tinnin, Jr.
Ellen S. Casey (Santa Fe Office)
Nicholas J. Noeding
Margaret Carter Ludewig
Stanley K. Kotovsky, Jr.
William P. Slattery (Santa Fe Office)

Representative Clients: Diagnostek, Inc.; Ethicon, Inc., a Johnson & Johnson Co.; First National Bank of Albuquerque; Gulton Data Systems, a division of Mark IV; Maloof Cos.; Martin Marietta Information Systems; Nobel/-Sysco, Inc.; Plains Electric Transmission & Generation Cooperative, Inc.; Presbyterian Healthcare Services; St. Vincent Hospital.

For Complete List of Firm Personnel, See General Section

For full biographical listings, see the Martindale-Hubbell Law Directory

KELLY, RAMMELKAMP, MUEHLENWEG, LUCERO & LEÓN, A PROFESSIONAL ASSOCIATION (AV)

Simms Tower, 400 Gold Avenue S.W., Suite 500, P.O. Box 25127, 87125-5127
Telephone: 505-247-8860
Fax: 505-247-8881

David A. Rammelkamp

Todd M. Stafford

Representative Clients: Galles Motor Company; John L. Rust Co. (Caterpillar); Envirco Corp.; Rehoboth-McKinley Christian Health Care Services; Pace Membership Warehouse, Inc.; City of Albuquerque; Barnard Construction Company, Inc.; Albuquerque-Bernalillo County Economic Opportunity Board; Eberline Instrument Corporation; House of Fabrics, Inc.

For Complete List of Firm Personnel, See General Section

For full biographical listings, see the Martindale-Hubbell Law Directory

RODEY, DICKASON, SLOAN, AKIN & ROBB, P.A. (AV)

Albuquerque Plaza, Suite 2200, 201 Third Street, N.W., P.O. Box 1888, 87103-1888
Telephone: 505-765-5900
Fax: 505-768-7395
Santa Fe, New Mexico Office: Suite 101 Marcy Plaza, 123 East Marcy Street, P.O. Box 1357, 87504-1357.
Telephone: 505-984-0100.
Fax: 505-989-9542.

Duane C. Gilkey
Angela M. Martinez
Jo Saxton Brayer
Theresa W. Parrish
Scott D. Gordon
Barbara G. Stephenson

Charles J. Vigil
Thomas L. Stahl
Charles W. Weese, III

For Complete List of Firm Personnel, See General Section

For full biographical listings, see the Martindale-Hubbell Law Directory

FARMINGTON, San Juan Co.

TANSEY, ROSEBROUGH, GERDING & STROTHER, P.C. (AV)

621 West Arrington Street, P.O. Box 1020, 87499
Telephone: 505-325-1801
Telecopier: 505-325-4675

Haskell D. Rosebrough
Douglas A. Echols
Austin E. Roberts (1921-1983)
James B. Payne
Richard L. Gerding
Michael T. O'Loughlin
Robin D. Strother
Tommy Roberts
Karen L. Townsend

OF COUNSEL

Charles M. Tansey, Jr.

Representative Clients: American International Adjustment Co.; New Mexico Newspapers, Inc.; CIGNA Insurance Co.; Commercial Union Insurance Cos.; United Indian Traders Association, Inc.; Farmington Municipal Schools; Risk Management Division, State of New Mexico; San Juan Regional Medical Center; Merrion Oil & Gas Co; Giant Exploration and Production Co.

For full biographical listings, see the Martindale-Hubbell Law Directory

*SANTA FE,** Santa Fe Co.

CAMPBELL, CARR, BERGE & SHERIDAN, P.A. (AV)

110 North Guadalupe, P.O. Box 2208, 87504-2208
Telephone: 505-988-4421
Telecopier: 505-983-6043

Michael B. Campbell
Bradford C. Berge
William F. Carr
Mark F. Sheridan

Michael H. Feldewert
Tanya M. Trujillo
Nancy A. Rath

(See Next Column)

CAMPBELL, CARR, BERGE & SHERIDAN P.A., *Santa Fe—Continued*

OF COUNSEL

Jack M. Campbell

For full biographical listings, see the Martindale-Hubbell Law Directory

MONTGOMERY & ANDREWS, PROFESSIONAL ASSOCIATION (AV)

325 Paseo de Peralta, P.O. Box 2307, 87504-2307
Telephone: 505-982-3873
Albuquerque, New Mexico Office: Suite 1300 Albuquerque Plaza, 201 Third Street, N.W., P.O. Box 26927.
Telephone: 505-242-9677.
FAX: 505-243-2542.

Bruce Herr
Paula G. Maynes
R. Michael Shickich

Representative Clients: El Paso Natural Gas Co.; St. Vincent Hospital; State of New Mexico, Risk Management Division; Las Campanas Limited Partnership; Los Alamos National Laboratory; Giant Industries Arizona, Inc.; Los Alamos Technical Associates, Inc.; St. John's College; Southwest Airlines Co.; Johnson Controls World Services, Inc.

For Complete List of Firm Personnel, See General Section

For full biographical listings, see the Martindale-Hubbell Law Directory

SCHEUER, YOST & PATTERSON, A PROFESSIONAL CORPORATION (AV)

125 Lincoln Avenue, Suite 223, P.O. Drawer 9570, 87504
Telephone: 505-982-9911
Fax: 505-982-1621

Ralph H. Scheuer
Mel E. Yost
John N. Patterson
Holly A. Hart
Roger L. Prucino
Elizabeth A. Jaffe
Tracy Erin Conner
Ruth M. Fuess

OF COUNSEL

Melvin T. Yost

Representative Clients: Cyprus-AMAX, Inc.; Century Bank, FSB; Chicago Insurance Co.; GEICO; Pepsico, Inc.; Rocky Mountain Bankcard System; St. John's College; Sun Loan Companies; Territorial Abstract & Title Co.; Tosco Corporation.

For full biographical listings, see the Martindale-Hubbell Law Directory

WHITE, KOCH, KELLY & MCCARTHY, A PROFESSIONAL ASSOCIATION (AV)

433 Paseo De Peralta, P.O. Box 787, 87504-0787
Telephone: 505-982-4374
ABA/NET: 1154
Fax: 505-982-0350; 984-8631

William Booker Kelly
John F. McCarthy, Jr.
Benjamin J. Phillips
David F. Cunningham
Albert V. Gonzales
Janet Clow
Kevin V. Reilly
Charles W. N. Thompson, Jr.
M. Karen Kilgore
Sandra J. Brinck

SPECIAL COUNSEL

Paul L. Bloom

Aaron J. Wolf
Carolyn R. Glick

Representative Clients: Southern Pacific Transportation Co.; Nationwide Insurance Co.; Risk Management Division of New Mexico General Services Department; Alliance of American Insurers; Santa Fe Community College; First American Title Insurance Co.; Century Bank; Public Service Company of New Mexico; AT&SF Railway Co.; Gallager Bassett.

For full biographical listings, see the Martindale-Hubbell Law Directory

NEW YORK

*ALBANY,** Albany Co.

DREYER, BOYAJIAN & TUTTLE (AV)

75 Columbia Street, 12210
Telephone: 518-463-7784
Telecopier: 518-463-4039

William J. Dreyer
Donald W. Boyajian
James B. Tuttle
Daniel J. Stewart
Brian W. Devane
Christopher M. Scaringe
Damon J. Stewart
Jill A. Dunn

For full biographical listings, see the Martindale-Hubbell Law Directory

KOHN, BOOKSTEIN & KARP, P.C. (AV)

Ninety State Street Suite 929, 12207-1888
Telephone: 518-449-8810
Fax: 518-449-1029

Edward L. Bookstein
Richard A. Kohn

Representative Clients: Adirondack Transit Lines, Inc.; Amfast Corp.; Simmons Fastener Corp.; Tagsons Papers, Inc.; Thermo Products, Inc.

For Complete List of Firm Personnel, See General Section

For full biographical listings, see the Martindale-Hubbell Law Directory

ROWLEY, FORREST, O'DONNELL & HITE, P.C. (AV)

90 State Street Suite 729, 12207-1715
Telephone: 518-434-6187
Fax: 518-434-1287

Richard R. Rowley
Thomas J. Forrest
Brian J. O'Donnell
Robert S. Hite
John H. Beaumont
Mark S. Pelersi
David C. Rowley

James J. Seaman
David P. Miranda
Kevin S. Casey
Richard W. Bader
Daniel W. Coffey
Thomas D. Spain

OF COUNSEL

Rush W. Stehlin

Reference: Norstar Bank.

For full biographical listings, see the Martindale-Hubbell Law Directory

TOBIN AND DEMPF (AV)

33 Elk Street, 12207
Telephone: 518-463-1177
Telecopier: 518-463-7489

MEMBERS OF FIRM

Charles J. Tobin (1882-1954)
Charles J. Tobin, Jr. (1915-1987)
James W. Sanderson (1937-1992)
Louis Dempf, Jr.
Michael L. Costello
John W. Clark
John T. Mitchell
David A. Ruffo
Kevin A. Luibrand
R. Christopher Dempf

ASSOCIATES

Mark A. Mainello
Gayle E. Hartz
William H. Reynolds
Raul A. Tabora, Jr.

General Counsel for: Adirondack Beverages, Inc.; MLB Industries, Inc.; College of St. Rose; Siena College; Orange Motor Co., Inc.; The Roman Catholic Diocese of Albany, New York; Teresian House Nursing Home Co.

For full biographical listings, see the Martindale-Hubbell Law Directory

*BINGHAMTON,** Broome Co.

HINMAN, HOWARD & KATTELL (AV)

700 Security Mutual Building, 80 Exchange Street, 13901
Telephone: 607-723-5341
Fax: 607-723-6605
Norwich, New York Office: 600 South Broad Street, Suite 200.
Telephone: 607-334-5896.
Fax: 607-336-6240.

MEMBERS OF FIRM

John C. Fish
Peter J. Vivona
James S. Gleason
James R. Franz
Kenneth F. Tomko

Representative Clients: First-City Division, Chase Lincoln First Bank, N.A.; Binghamton Savings Bank; International Business Machines Corp.; Universal Instruments Corp.; Security Mutual Life Insurance Company of New York; New York Telephone Co.; Travelers Insurance Co.; New York State Electric & Gas Corp.; Exxon Corp.; Columbia Gas System, Inc.

For Complete List of Firm Personnel, See General Section

For full biographical listings, see the Martindale-Hubbell Law Directory

O'CONNOR, GACIOCH & POPE (AV)

One Marine Midland Plaza, East Tower-Seventh Floor, P.O. Box 1964, 13902
Telephone: 607-772-9262
Fax: 607-724-6002

Thomas F. O'Connor
James C. Gacioch
Alan J. Pope
Lori Grumet Schapiro
Jeffrey A. Tait
Hugh B. Leonard
Robert N. Nielsen, Jr.
Martha Keeler Macinski
Stephen B. Atkinson
Kurt D. Schrader
Richard M. Hill
Patricia A. Cummings
Mark D. Goris
Susan E. Decker

OF COUNSEL

Walter T. Gorman

For full biographical listings, see the Martindale-Hubbell Law Directory

*BUFFALO,** Erie Co.

FLAHERTY, COHEN, GRANDE, RANDAZZO & DOREN, P.C. (AV)

Suite 210 Firstmark Building, 135 Delaware Avenue, 14202
Telephone: 716-853-7262
Fax: 716-854-6430

Edward D. Flaherty (1903-1971)
Jeremy V. Cohen
Genuino J. Grande
Joseph L. Randazzo
Robert A. Doren
Daniel P. Forsyth
Dennis J. Campagna

Colleen M. O'Connell Jancevski
Susan Moslander McClaren
Laura Scirri Dudley

For full biographical listings, see the Martindale-Hubbell Law Directory

HODGSON, RUSS, ANDREWS, WOODS & GOODYEAR (AV)

A Partnership including Professional Associations
Suite 1800, One M & T Plaza, 14203
Telephone: 716-856-4000
Cable Address: "Magna Carta" Buffalo, N.Y.
Telecopier: 716-849-0349
Albany, New York Office: Three City Square.
Telephone: 518-465-2333.
Telecopier: 518-465-1567.
Rochester, New York Office: 400 East Avenue.
Telephone: 716-454-6950.
Telecopier: 716-454-4698.
Boca Raton, Florida Office: Suite 400, Nations Bank Building, 2000 Glades Road.
Telephone: 407-394-0500.
Telecopier: 305-427-4303.
Mississauga, Ontario, Canada Office: Suite 880, 3 Robert Speck Parkway.
Telephone: 905-566-5061.
Telecopier: 905-566-2049.
New York, New York Office: 330 Madison Avenue, 11th Floor. Telephone 212-297-3370.
Telecopier: 212-972-6521.

MEMBERS OF FIRM
(ALPHABETICALLY BY YEAR OF ADMISSION TO BAR)

Robert M. Walker
David E. Hall
Karl W. Kristoff
Anne Smith Simet
David A. Farmelo
Joseph L. Braccio
Karen S. Martell (Albany Office)
John J. Christopher

COUNSEL

Arnold T. Olena

ASSOCIATES
(ALPHABETICALLY BY YEAR OF ADMISSION TO BAR)

Mary Thomas Scott
Jeffrey F. Swiatek

Counsel for: Manufacturers and Traders Trust Company; Rich Products Corp.; Children's Hospital of Buffalo; Domtar Industries, Inc.; General Mills, Inc.; City of Olean; Buffalo Public School System; American Red Cross; Gibraltar Steel; Steuben Foods.

For Complete List of Firm Personnel, See General Section

For full biographical listings, see the Martindale-Hubbell Law Directory

LIPSITZ, GREEN, FAHRINGER, ROLL, SALISBURY & CAMBRIA (AV)

42 Delaware Avenue, Suite 300, 14202
Telephone: 716-849-1333
Fax: 716-855-1580
New York, N.Y. Office: 110 East 59th Street.
Telephone: 212-909-9670.
East Aurora, New York Office: 164 Quaker Road.
Telephone: 716-652-4290.
Alden, New York Office: 1472 Exchange Street.
Telephone: 716-937-9494.

MEMBER OF FIRM

Eugene W. Salisbury

OF COUNSEL

Richard Lipsitz

Representative Clients: Buffalo Bills; Marine Midland Bank, N.A.
Reference: Marine Midland Bank.

For Complete List of Firm Personnel, See General Section

For full biographical listings, see the Martindale-Hubbell Law Directory

PHILLIPS, LYTLE, HITCHCOCK, BLAINE & HUBER (AV)

(Formerly Kenefick, Letchworth, Baldy, Phillips & Emblidge)
3400 Marine Midland Center, 14203
Telephone: 716-847-8400
Telecopier: 716-852-6100
Jamestown, New York Office: 307 Chase Bank Building, 8 E. Third Street.
Telephone: 716-664-3906.
Telecopier: 716-664-4230.
Rochester, New York Office: 1400 First Federal Plaza.
Telephone: 716-238-2000.
Telecopier: 716-232-3141.
New York, New York Office: 437 Madison Avenue.
Telephone: 212-759-4888.
Telecopier: 212-308-9079.
Fredonia, New York Office: 11 East Main Street.
Telephone: 716-672-2164.
FAX: 716-672-7979.

OF COUNSEL

John F. Donovan

PARTNERS

James D. Donathen
Michael R. Moravec
Gerald L. Paley (Resident, Rochester Office)

ASSOCIATES

Robert A. Colón (Resident, Rochester Office)
Mark L. Suher (Resident, Rochester Office)

General Counsel for: Astronics Corporation; Bryant & Stratton Business Institute; Canisius College; Chase Manhattan Bank, N.A.; Columbus McKinnon Corp.
Local Counsel for: A.O. Smith Corp.; Allied Signal; Bethleham Steel Corp.; Chrysler Motor Corp.; E.I. DuPont deNemours Co., Inc.

For Complete List of Firm Personnel, See General Section

For full biographical listings, see the Martindale-Hubbell Law Directory

EAST SYRACUSE, Onondaga Co.

FERRARA, FIORENZA, LARRISON, BARRETT & REITZ, P.C. (AV)

5010 CampusWood Drive, 13057
Telephone: 315-437-7600
Fax: 315-437-7744

Benjamin J. Ferrara
Nicholas J. Fiorenza
David W. Larrison
Dennis T. Barrett
Marc H. Reitz
Henry F. Sobota
Susan T. Johns
Norman H. Gross
Craig M. Atlas
Michael L. Dodd

For full biographical listings, see the Martindale-Hubbell Law Directory

GARDEN CITY, Nassau Co.

COLLERAN, O'HARA & MILLS (AV)

1225 Franklin Avenue, 11530
Telephone: 516-248-5757
Telecopier: 516-742-1765

Walter M. Colleran (Retired)
Richard L. O'Hara
John F. Mills
Edward J. Groarke
Christopher P. O'Hara

ASSOCIATES

Scott P. Shelkin
Carol L. O'Rourke
James A. Brown
Jennifer Berlingieri
John W. Dunne

COUNSEL

Glenn A. Krebs
Elizabeth Pollina Donlon

LEGAL SUPPORT PERSONNEL

Stephanie Suarez
Robin Young
Madeleine Olaciregui
Ann Carolan
Laura Harrington

Representative Clients: New York State AFL-CIO; New York City Building and Construction Trades Council; Local 40 Iron Workers; Local 100 Transport Workers Union; Garden City Professional Firefighters; Local 252 Transport Workers Union; Local 1087; Merble Industry Funds of NY, Inc.; Local 154 United Roofers; Local 580 Iron Workers.

For full biographical listings, see the Martindale-Hubbell Law Directory

EHRLICH, FRAZER & FELDMAN (AV)

1415 Kellum Place, 11530-1690
Telephone: 516-742-7777
Facsimile: 516-742-7868

Jerome H. Ehrlich
Florence T. Frazer
Jacob S. Feldman
James H. Pyun

For full biographical listings, see the Martindale-Hubbell Law Directory

Garden City—Continued

GALLAGHER GOSSEEN & FALLER (AV)

1010 Franklin Avenue, Suite 400, 11530-2927
Telephone: 516-742-2500
Fax: 516-742-2516
Cable: COMPROAIR
New York, New York Office: 350 Fifth Avenue.
Telephone: 212-947-5800.
FAX: 212-967-4965.

MEMBERS OF FIRM

Robert I. Gosseen (Resident, New York City Office)

ASSOCIATES

Robert A. Sparer (Resident, New York City Office)

For Complete List of Firm Personnel, See General Section

For full biographical listings, see the Martindale-Hubbell Law Directory

JASPAN, GINSBERG, SCHLESINGER, SILVERMAN & HOFFMAN (AV)

300 Garden City Plaza, 11530
Telephone: 516-746-8000
Telecopier: 516-746-0552

MEMBERS OF FIRM

Arthur W. Jaspan
Eugene S. Ginsberg
Steven R. Schlesinger
Kenneth P. Silverman
Carol M. Hoffman
Stanley A. Camhi
Eugene P. Cimini, Jr.
Holly Juster
Stephen P. Epstein
Gary F. Herbst
Allen Perlstein

For Complete List of Firm Personnel, See General Section

For full biographical listings, see the Martindale-Hubbell Law Directory

MELVILLE, Suffolk Co.

KAUFMAN, NANESS, SCHNEIDER & ROSENSWEIG, P.C. (AV)

425 Broad Hollow Road, Suite 315, 11747-4730
Telephone: 516-756-9110
Fax: 516-756-9098

Arthur R. Kaufman
Richard M. Naness
Peter A. Schneider
Dorothy Rosensweig
Elliot J. Mandel

Thomas J. Bianco
Carmelo Grimaldi
Alesia J. Kantor
Michael A. Kaufman
Jeffrey N. Naness

OF COUNSEL

Clifford P. Chaiet

For full biographical listings, see the Martindale-Hubbell Law Directory

*MINEOLA,** Nassau Co.

RAINS & POGREBIN, P.C. (AV)

210 Old Country Road, 11501
Telephone: 516-742-1470
Cable Address: "Rainslaw"
Telecopier: 516-742-1473
New York City Office: 375 Park Avenue.
Telephone: 212-980-3560; 914-668-6166.
Telecopier: 516-742-1473.

Bertrand B. Pogrebin
Mona N. Glanzer
Terence M. O'Neil
Frederick D. Braid
Bruce R. Millman
David M. Wirtz
Ernest R. Stolzer
Alan C. Becker
Richard K. Zuckerman
Richard G. Kass
Mark N. Reinharz
Craig R. Benson
John T. Bauer

Sharon N. Berlin
Susan H. Joffe
Jessica S. Weinstein

OF COUNSEL

Harry H. Rains

Representative Clients: New York City Board of Education; I.B.M.; Federated Department Stores; Parsons, Brickerhoff, Quade & Douglas, Inc.; South Oaks Hospital; Trans-Lux Corp.; Fulton Fish Market Employers Assn.; Building Contractors, Assn., Inc.; Polygram Records, Inc.; Northern Telecom.

For full biographical listings, see the Martindale-Hubbell Law Directory

MOUNT KISCO, Westchester Co.

ANDERSON, BANKS, CURRAN & DONOGHUE (AV)

61 Smith Avenue, 10549
Telephone: 914-666-2161
Telecopier: 914-666-3292

(See Next Column)

MEMBERS OF FIRM

Stanley E. Anderson (1928-1965)
William F. Banks
Stanley E. Anderson, Jr.
Maurice F. Curran
Lawrence W. Thomas
John M. Donoghue
Gregory Keefe
James P. Drohan
Rochelle J. Auslander

ASSOCIATES

Barbara Banks Schwam
Suzanne Johnston
Daniel Petigrow
Stuart Waxman

OF COUNSEL

Margaret A. Clark

Representative Clients: The Centennial Life Insurance Company of America.

For full biographical listings, see the Martindale-Hubbell Law Directory

*NEW YORK,** New York Co.

BENETAR BERNSTEIN SCHAIR & STEIN (AV)

A Partnership of Professional Corporations
330 Madison Avenue, 10017-5001
Telephone: 212-697-4433
FAX: 212-697-3510

MEMBERS OF FIRM

David L. Benetar (1906-1986)
Michael I. Bernstein (P.C.)
Stanley Schair (P.C.)
Kenneth D. Stein (P.C.)

ASSOCIATE

David Michael Safon

COUNSEL

Eric D. Witkin

For full biographical listings, see the Martindale-Hubbell Law Directory

BURKE HORAN & MACRI (AV)

555 Fifth Avenue, 10017-2416
Telephone: 212-557-4600
Telecopier: 212-557-0526

MEMBERS OF FIRM

Edward J. Burke
David F. Horan
Michele Costanza Horan
Stephen J. Macri

ASSOCIATES

Mercedes Marie Maldonado
Eileen D. Brennan
John L. Harrisingh

COUNSEL

Thomas A. Brennan, Sr.

For full biographical listings, see the Martindale-Hubbell Law Directory

GANZ, HOLLINGER & TOWE (AV)

1394 Third Avenue, 10021
Telephone: 212-517-5500; 838-9600
Cable Address: "Ganzlaw New York"
Telex: 852970 GANZLAW NYK
FAX: 212-772-2720; 772-2216

David L. Ganz
Jerrietta R. Hollinger
Teri Noel Towe

ASSOCIATE

Nancy A. Torres (Not admitted in NY)

For full biographical listings, see the Martindale-Hubbell Law Directory

KREITZMAN, MORTENSEN & SIMON (AV)

521 Fifth Avenue, 10175
Telephone: 212-986-4177
Facsimile: 212-986-1884

MEMBERS OF FIRM

David Kreitzman
Philip S. Mortensen
Eric P. Simon

Scott L. Irgang
Brian K. Saltz
Carissa A. Barletta

For full biographical listings, see the Martindale-Hubbell Law Directory

LIDDLE, ROBINSON & SHOEMAKER (AV)

685 Third Avenue, 10017
Telephone: 212-687-8500
Telecopier: 212-687-1505

MEMBERS OF FIRM

Samuel Finkelstein (Retired)
Jeffrey L. Liddle
Miriam M. Robinson
Paul T. Shoemaker
Laurence S. Moy
W. Dan Boone

(See Next Column)

LIDDLE, ROBINSON & SHOEMAKER—*Continued*

ASSOCIATES

James A. Batson
Blaine H. Bortnick
Ethan A. Brecher
Linda A. Danovitch
Jeffrey A. Koslowsky
Douglas A. Lopp

For full biographical listings, see the Martindale-Hubbell Law Directory

McDERMOTT, WILL & EMERY (AV)

A Partnership including Professional Corporations
1211 Avenue of the Americas, 10036-8701
Telephone: 212-768-5400
Facsimile: 212-768-5444
Chicago, Illinois Office: 227 West Monroe Street.
Telephone: 312-372-2000.
Telex: 253565 MILAM CGO.
Facsimile: 312-984-7700.
Boston, Massachusetts Office: 75 State Street, Suite 1700.
Telephone: 617-345-5000.
Telex: 951324 MILAM BSN.
Facsimile: 617-345-5077.
Miami, Florida Office: 201 South Biscayne Boulevard.
Telephone: 305-358-3500.
Telex: 441777 LEYES.
Facsimile: 305-347-6500.
Washington, D.C. Office: 1850 K Street, N.W.
Telephone: 202-887-8000.
Telex: 253565 MILAM CGO.
Facsimile: 202-778-8087.
Los Angeles, California Office: 2049 Century Park East.
Telephone: 310-277-4110.
Facsimile: 310-277-4730.
Newport Beach, California Office: 1301 Dove Street, Suite 500.
Telephone: 714-851-0633.
Facsimile: 714-851-9348.
St. Petersburg, Russia Office: 2/2 Tchaikovsky Street, #517, 191187 St. Petersburg, Russia.
Telephone: (7) (812) 273-9831.
Facsimile: (7) (812) 273-9831.
Vilnius, Lithuania Office: Smetonos 6, 2600 Vilnius, Lithuania.
Telephone: 370 2 61-43-08.
Facsimile: 370 2 22-79-55.
Associated (Independent) Offices:
Brussels, Belgium: Uettwiller Grelon Lippens Dekeyser, 73 avenue Vandendriessche, 1150 Brussels, Belgium.
Telephone: (32) (2) 772-87-50.
Facsimile: (32) (2) 772-87-52.
London, England: Paisner & Co, Bouverie House, 154 Fleet Street, London EC4A 2DQ, England.
Telephone: (44) (71) 353-0299.
Facsimile: (44) (71) 583-8621.
Paris, France: Uettwiller Grelon Gout Canat & Associes, 68, boulevard de Courcelles, 75017 Paris, France.
Telephone: (33) (1) 48 88 89 00.
Facsimile: (33) (1) 48 88 05 50.

MEMBERS OF FIRM

William L. Kandel
Richard J. Reibstein

For Complete List of Firm Personnel, See General Section

For full biographical listings, see the Martindale-Hubbell Law Directory

McGUIRE, KEHL & NEALON (AV)

230 Park Avenue, Suite 2830, 10169
Telephone: 212-557-0040
Telecopier: 212-953-0768

MEMBERS OF FIRM

Harold F. McGuire, Jr.
Jeffrey A. Kehl
Arthur V. Nealon
Terri E. Simon

COUNSEL

Marion C. Katzive
Shelley Sanders Kehl

For full biographical listings, see the Martindale-Hubbell Law Directory

MUDGE ROSE GUTHRIE ALEXANDER & FERDON (AV)

(Mudge, Stern, Baldwin & Todd)
(Caldwell, Trimble & Mitchell)
180 Maiden Lane, 10038
Telephone: 212-510-7000
Cable Address: "Baltuchins, New York"
Telex: 127889 & 703729
Telecopier: 212-248-2655/57
Los Angeles, California Office: 21st Floor, 333 South Grand Avenue, 90071.
Telephone: 213-613-1112.
Telecopier: 213-680-1358.

(See Next Column)

Washington, D.C. Office: 2121 K Street, N.W., 20037.
Telephone: 202-429-9355.
Telecopier: 202-429-9367.
Telex: MRGA 440264.
Cable Address: "Baltuchins, Washington, DC"
West Palm Beach, Florida Office: Suite 900, 515 North Flagler Drive, 33401.
Telephone: 407-650-8100.
Telecopier: 407-833-1722.
Telex: 514847 MRWPB.
Parsippany, New Jersey Office: Morris Corporate Center Two, Building D, One Upper Pond Road, 07054-1075.
Telephone: 201-335-0004.
Telecopier: 201-402-1593.
European Office: 12, Rue de la Paix, 75002 Paris, France.
Telephone: 42.61.57.71.
Telecopier: 42.61.79.21.
Cable Address: "Baltuchins, Paris".
Tokyo, Japan Office: Infini Akasaka, 8-7-15 Akasaka, Minato-Ku, Tokyo 107, Japan.
Telephone: (03) 3423-3970.
Fax: (03) 3423-3971.

MEMBERS OF FIRM

Ned H. Bassen
Joel E. Cohen
Rita A. Hernandez

ASSOCIATE

Patrick J. Della Valle

For Complete List of Firm Personnel, See General Section

For full biographical listings, see the Martindale-Hubbell Law Directory

PARKER CHAPIN FLATTAU & KLIMPL, L.L.P. (AV)

1211 Avenue of the Americas, 10036
Telephone: 212-704-6000
Telecopier: 212-704-6288
Cable Address: "Lawpark"
Telex: 640347
Great Neck, New York Office: 175 Great Neck Road.
Telephone: 516-482-4422.
Telecopier: 516-482-4469.

MEMBERS OF FIRM

Peter M. Panken
B. Michael Thrope

OF COUNSEL

Michael Starr

ASSOCIATES

Stacey B. Babson-Smith
Christine L. Wilson

For Complete List of Firm Personnel, See General Section

For full biographical listings, see the Martindale-Hubbell Law Directory

PROSKAUER ROSE GOETZ & MENDELSOHN LLP (AV)

1585 Broadway, 10036
Telephone: 212-969-3000
Cable Address: "Roput"
Telex: TRT 175719 ROPUT NY
FAX: 212-969-2900
Washington, D.C. Office: 1233 Twentieth Street, N.W., Suite 800.
Telephone: 202-416-6800.
Los Angeles, California Office: 2121 Avenue of the Stars, Suite 2700.
Telephone: 310-557-2900.
San Francisco, California Office: 555 California Street, Suite 4604.
Telephone: 415-956-2218.
Boca Raton, Florida Office: One Boca Place, Suite 340 West, 2255 Glades Road.
Telephone: 407-241-7400.
Clifton, New Jersey Office: 1373 Broad Street. P.O. Box 4444.
Telephone: 201-779-6300.
Paris, France Office: 9 rue Le Tasse.
Telephone: (33-1) 45 27 43 01

MEMBERS OF FIRM

Rory Judd Albert
L. Robert Batterman
Joseph Baumgarten
Edward A. Brill
Peter D. Conrad
David H. Diamond
Allen I. Fagin
Howard L. Ganz
Murray Gartner
Bernard Gold
Ira M. Golub
Jerold D. Jacobson
Alan S. Jaffe
Saul G. Kramer
Carole O'Blenes
Martin J. Oppenheimer
Bettina B. Plevan
Bernard M. Plum
Sara S. Portnoy
Myron D. Rumeld
Paul Salvatore
Donald W. Savelson
Neal S. Schelberg
Aaron J. Schindel
Ronald F. Storette
M. David Zurndorfer

SPECIAL COUNSEL

Toby R. Hyman
Fredric C. Leffler
Richard A. Levin

(See Next Column)

PROSKAUER ROSE GOETZ & MENDELSOHN LLP, *New York—Continued*

ASSOCIATES

Neil H. Abramson
Cigdem A. Acar
Jeffrey S. Agnew
Jennifer A. Borg
Roberta K. Chevlowe
Christopher J. Collins
Michael D. Davis
Maria F. Gandarez
Daniel R. Halem
Gwen J. Lourie
Seth M. Popper
Rafael A. Vargas (Not admitted in NY)
Bernard Weinreb
William G. Wright (Not admitted in NY)
Miriam Wugmeister

LOS ANGELES, CALIFORNIA PARTNERS

Jeffrey A. Berman
Harold M. Brody
Steven G. Drapkin
Howard D. Fabrick
Bernard D. Gold

SPECIAL COUNSEL

Walter Cochran-Bond

LOS ANGELES, CALIFORNIA ASSOCIATES

Nicholas P. Connon
Antonia Ozeroff
Scott J. Witlin

SAN FRANCISCO, CALIFORNIA PARTNERS

Dennis T. Daniels
Thomas J. Dowdalls
John H. Feldmann, III
J. Mark Montobbio

SAN FRANCISCO, CALIFORNIA ASSOCIATE

Philip L. Ross

BOCA RATON, FLORIDA PARTNER

Allan H. Weitzman

CLIFTON, NEW JERSEY PARTNER

Kathleen M. McKenna

CLIFTON, NEW JERSEY ASSOCIATE

David W. MacGregor

For Complete List of Firm Personnel, See General Section

For full biographical listings, see the Martindale-Hubbell Law Directory

---

SEHAM SEHAM MELTZ & PETERSEN (AV)

380 Madison Avenue, Suite 17, 10017-2513
Telephone: 212-557-9577

Martin C. Seham
Lee Seham
Louis S. Meltz
Scott C. Petersen

For full biographical listings, see the Martindale-Hubbell Law Directory

---

SHACK & SIEGEL, P.C. (AV)

530 Fifth Avenue, 10036
Telephone: 212-782-0700
Fax: 212-730-1964

Charles F. Crames
Pamela E. Flaherty
Paul S. Goodman
Ronald S. Katz
Donald D. Shack
Jeffrey N. Siegel
Jeffrey B. Stone

Paul A. Lucido
Steven M. Lutt
Ruby S. Teich
Keith D. Wellner
Adam F. Wergeles (Not admitted in NY)

For full biographical listings, see the Martindale-Hubbell Law Directory

---

SKADDEN, ARPS, SLATE, MEAGHER & FLOM (AV)

919 Third Avenue, 10022
Telephone: 212-735-3000
Telex: 645899 SKARSLAW
Fax: 212-735-2000; 212-735-2001
Boston, Massachusetts Office: One Beacon Street, 02108.
Telephone: 617-573-4800.
Fax: 617-573-4822.
Washington, D.C. Office: 1440 New York Avenue, N.W., 20005.
Telephone: 202-371-7000.
Fax: 202-393-5760.
Wilmington, Delaware Office: One Rodney Square, 19899.
Telephone: 302-651-3000.
Fax: 302-651-3001.
Los Angeles, California Office: 300 South Grand Avenue, 90071.
Telephone: 213-687-5000.
Fax: 213-687-5600.
Chicago, Illinois Office: 333 West Wacker Drive, 60606.
Telephone: 312-407-0700.
Fax: 312-407-0411.
San Francisco, California Office: Four Embarcadero Center, 94111.
Telephone: 415-984-6400.
Fax: 415-984-2698.
Houston, Texas Office: 1600 Smith Street, Suite 4460, 77002.
Telephone: 713-655-5100.
Fax: 713-655-5181.

(See Next Column)

Newark, New Jersey Office: One Riverfront Plaza, 07102.
Telephone: 201-596-4440.
Fax: 201-596-4444.
Tokyo, Japan Office: 12th Floor, The Fukoku Seimei Building, 2-2-2, Uchisaiwaicho, Chiyoda-ku, 100.
Telephone: 011-81-3-3595-3850.
Fax: 011-81-3-3504-2780.
London, England Office: 25 Bucklersbury EC4N 8DA.
Telephone: 011-44-71-248-9929.
Fax: 011-44-71-489-8533.
Hong Kong Office: 30/F Peregrine Tower, Lippo Centre, 89 Queensway, Central.
Telephone: 011-852-820-0700.
Fax: 011-852-820-0727.
Sydney, New South Wales, Australia Office: Level 26-State Bank Centre, 52 Martin Place, 2000.
Telephone: 011-61-2-224-6000.
Fax: 011-61-2-224-6044.
Toronto, Ontario Office: Suite 1820, North Tower, P.O. Box 189, Royal Bank Plaza, M5J 2J4.
Telephone: 416-777-4700.
Fax: 416-777-4747.
Paris, France Office: 105 rue du Faubourg Saint-Honoré, 75008.
Telephone: 011-33-1-40-75-44-44.
Fax: 011-33-1-49-53-09-99.
Brussels, Belgium Office: 523 avenue Louise, Box 30, 1050.
Telephone: 011-32-2-648-7666.
Fax: 011-32-2-640-3032.
Frankfurt, Germany Office: MesseTurm, 27th Floor, 60308.
Telephone: 011-49-69-9757-3000.
Fax: 011-49-69-9757-3050.
Beijing, China Office: 1605 Capital Mansion Tower, No. 6 Xin Yuan Nan Road, Chao Yang District, 100004.
Telephone: 011-86-1-466-8800.
Fax: 011-86-1-466-8822.
Budapest, Hungary Office: Mahart Building, H-1052 Apáczai Csere János u.11, Vl.em.
Telephone: 011-36-1-266-2145.
Fax: 011-36-1-266-4033.
Prague, Czech Republic Office: Revolucni 16, 110 00.
Telephone: 011-42-2-231-75-18.
Fax: 011-42-2-231-47-33.
Moscow, Russia Office: Pleteshkovsky Pereulok 1, 107005.
Telephone: 011-7-501-940-2304.
Fax: 011-7-501-940-2511.

MEMBERS OF FIRM

Michael M. Connery
John P. Furfaro

OF COUNSEL

Henry P. Baer

SPECIAL COUNSEL

Jay S. Berke

LOS ANGELES, CALIFORNIA OFFICE PARTNER

Martha W. Hammer

NEW YORK, N.Y. OFFICE ASSOCIATES

Julie B. Carlin-Sasaki
Carolyn M. Duffy
Lisa K. Howlett
Maury B. Josephson
Lawrence A. Marcus

LOS ANGELES, CALIFORNIA ASSOCIATE

Karen Leili Corman

For Complete List of Firm Personnel, See General Section

For full biographical listings, see the Martindale-Hubbell Law Directory

---

VLADECK, WALDMAN, ELIAS & ENGELHARD, P.C. (AV)

1501 Broadway, Suite 800, 10036
Telephone: 212-403-7300
FAX: 212-221-3172

Stephen C. Vladeck (1920-1979)
Judith P. Vladeck
Seymour M. Waldman
Sylvan H. Elias
Sheldon Engelhard
Irwin Bluestein
Daniel Engelstein
Patricia McConnell
Anne C. Vladeck
Karen Honeycutt
Laura S. Schnell
Linda E. Rodd
Debra L. Raskin
Julian R. Birnbaum
Larry Cary
James I. Wasserman
Owen M. Rumelt
Hanan B. Kolko (Not admitted in NY)
Jay P. Levy-Warren
Ivan D. Smith

John A. Beranbaum
Anne L. Clark
Maureen Maria Stampp
Mary Josephine E. Provenzano
James D. Esseks (Not admitted in NY)
Suja A. Thomas

OF COUNSEL

Burton M. Epstein

(See Next Column)

VLADECK, WALDMAN, ELIAS & ENGELHARD P.C.—*Continued*

LEGAL SUPPORT PERSONNEL

Patricia Francisco
Karen Sais-Metzger
John Stauder
Robert G. Ridenour
Edward Heldman
Christopher Antilla

For full biographical listings, see the Martindale-Hubbell Law Directory

WISEHART & KOCH (AV)

Suite 412, 19 West 44th Street, 10036
Telephone: 212-730-0044

Arthur M. Wisehart
Francis E. Koch (1922-1978)

ASSOCIATE

Michael H. Prince

For full biographical listings, see the Martindale-Hubbell Law Directory

*ROCHESTER,** Monroe Co.

HARTER, SECREST & EMERY (AV)

700 Midtown Tower, 14604-2070
Telephone: 716-232-6500
Telecopier: 716-232-2152
Naples, Florida Office: Suite 400, 800 Laurel Oak Drive.
Telephone: 813-598-4444.
Telecopier: 813-598-2781.
Albany, New York Office: One Steuben Place.
Telephone: 518-434-4377.
Telecopier: 518-449-4025.
Syracuse, New York Office: 431 East Fayette Street.
Telephone: 315-474-4000.
Telecopier: 315-474-7789.

MEMBERS OF FIRM

Barry R. Whitman
Peter G. Smith
Jack D. Eisenberg
Eric A. Evans
Ronald J. Mendrick
Maureen T. Alston

ASSOCIATES

Judith E. Christiansen
Kathleen M. Beckman

For Complete List of Firm Personnel, See General Section

For full biographical listings, see the Martindale-Hubbell Law Directory

*SYRACUSE,** Onondaga Co.

BLITMAN AND KING (AV)

Suite 1100 The 500 Building, 500 South Salina Street, 13202
Telephone: 315-422-7111
FAX: 315-471-2623
Rochester, New York Office: The Powers Building, Suite 207, 16 West Main Street.
Telephone: 716-232-5600.
FAX: 716-232-7738.

MEMBERS OF FIRM

J. Norman Crannage (1908-1950)
Nathan H. Blitman (1909-1990)
Bernard T. King
Charles E. Blitman
Jules L. Smith (Resident at Rochester Office)
James R. LaVaute
Donald D. Oliver
Jennifer A. Clark
Melvin H. Pizer
Frederick W. Trump
Monica Robinson Heath

ASSOCIATES

Kenneth L. Wagner
Susan B. Marris
John E. Hebert IV (Not admitted in NY)
Harry Bernard Bronson (Resident at Rochester Office)
Amy M. Bittner
William D. Perun, Jr.
Timothy R. Bauman

OF COUNSEL

William A. Pizio
Harold J. Cohen (Resident at Rochester)

For full biographical listings, see the Martindale-Hubbell Law Directory

BOND, SCHOENECK & KING (AV)

18th Floor One Lincoln Center, 13202-1355
Telephone: 315-422-0121
Fax: 315-422-3598
Albany, New York Office: 111 Washington Avenue.
Telephone: 518-462-7421.
Fax: 518-462-7441.
Boca Raton, Florida Office: 5355 Town Center Road, Suite 1002.
Telephone: 407-368-1212.
Fax: 407-338-9955.
Naples, Florida Office: 1167 Third Street South.
Telephone: 813-262-6812.
Fax: 813-262-6908.
Oswego, New York Office: 130 East Second Street.
Telephone: 315-343-9116.
Fax: 315-343-1231.

(See Next Column)

Overland Park, Kansas Office: 7500 College Boulevard, Suite 910.
Telephone: 913-345-8001.
Fax: 913-345-9017.

MEMBERS OF FIRM

Tracy H. Ferguson
Francis D. Price
Raymond W. Murray, Jr.
Robert W. Kopp
William L. Bergan
Thomas J. Grooms
Stephen J. Vollmer
L. Lawrence Tully
Paul M. Sansoucy
David M. Pellow
Louis P. DiLorenzo
John Gaal
R. Daniel Bordoni
Larry P. Malfitano
Robert A. LaBerge

ASSOCIATES

Raymond J. Pascucci
Thomas G. Eron
David M. Ferrara
John E. Higgins (Resident, Albany Office)
Joseph C. Dole
Kevin G. Martin
Peter A. Jones
John G. Mc Donald

General Counsel for: Syracuse University; Unity Mutual Life Insurance Co.; Manufacturers Association of Central New York.
Regional or Special Counsel for: Newhouse Broadcasting Corp. (WSYR, AM-FM); Syracuse Herald-Post Standard Newspapers.; Miller Brewing Co.; Allied Corp.; General Electric Co.; National Grange.

For Complete List of Firm Personnel, See General Section

For full biographical listings, see the Martindale-Hubbell Law Directory

GROSSMAN KINNEY DWYER & HARRIGAN, P.C. (AV)

5720 Commons Park, 13057
Telephone: 315-449-2131
Telecopier: 315-449-2905

Richard D. Grossman
John P. Kinney
James F. Dwyer
C. Frank Harrigan
Robert E. Hornik, Jr.
Harris N. Lindenfeld

Ruth Moors D'Eredita
Edward P. Dunn
Joseph G. Shields

Representative Clients: County of Onondaga; County of Tompkins; Therm, Incorporated, Ithaca, New York; Village of Marcellus; Smith Barney Shearson; The Mitsubishi Bank, Limited (New York Branch); C&S Engineers, Inc.; Town of Harrietstown, New York.

For full biographical listings, see the Martindale-Hubbell Law Directory

*WHITE PLAINS,** Westchester Co.

KEANE & BEANE, P.C. (AV)

One North Broadway, 10601
Telephone: 914-946-4777
Telecopier: 914-946-6868
Rye, New York Office: 49 Purchase Street.
Telephone: 914-967-3936.

Thomas F. Keane, Jr. (1932-1991)

Edward F. Beane
David Glasser
Ronald A. Longo
Richard L. O'Rourke
Lawrence Praga
Joel H. Sachs
Steven A. Schurkman
Judson K. Siebert

Debbie G. Jacobs
Lance H. Klein
Donna E. Frosco
Nicholas M. Ward-Willis

LEGAL SUPPORT PERSONNEL

Barbara S. Durkin
Toni Ann Huff

OF COUNSEL

Eric F. Jensen
Peter A. Borrok

For full biographical listings, see the Martindale-Hubbell Law Directory

NORTH CAROLINA

*CHARLOTTE,** Mecklenburg Co.

BLAKENEY & ALEXANDER (AV)

3700 NationsBank Plaza, 101 South Tryon Street, 28280
Telephone: 704-372-3680
Facsimile: 704-332-2611

MEMBERS OF FIRM

Whiteford S. Blakeney (1906-1991)
J. W. Alexander, Jr. (1919-1990)
John O. Pollard
W. T. Cranfill, Jr.
Richard F. Kane
David L. Terry
Michael V. Matthews

(See Next Column)

BLAKENEY & ALEXANDER, *Charlotte—Continued*

ASSOCIATES

Jay L. Grytdahl
Robert B. Meyer
Kevin V. Parsons

Counsel for: Overnite Transportation Company; Old Dominion Freight Line, Inc.; Freightliner Corporation; U.S. Air; Trinity Industries; NationsBank Corporation; Vaughan Furniture Cos.; The Lane Company, Inc.; Ingles Markets, Inc.; Lance, Inc.

For full biographical listings, see the Martindale-Hubbell Law Directory

HAYNSWORTH, BALDWIN, JOHNSON AND GREAVES, P.A. (AV)

Federal Plaza Building, 400 West Trade Street, 28202
Telephone: 704-342-2588
Facsimile: 704-342-4379
Greenville, South Carolina Office: 918 South Pleasantburg Drive, P.O. Box 10888.
Telephone: 803-271-7410.
Columbia, South Carolina Office: 1201 Main Street, Suite 1230.
Telephone: 803-799-5858.
Raleigh, North Carolina Office: 3605 Glenwood Avenue, Suite 210, P.O. Box 10035.
Telephone: 919-782-3340.
Greensboro, North Carolina Office: 2709 Henry Street, P.O. Box 13310.
Telephone: 910-375-9737.
Jacksonville, Florida Office: Haynsworth, Baldwin, Johnson and Harper, 1506 Prudential Drive, P.O. Box 40593.
Telephone: 904-396-3000.
Tampa, Florida Office: Haynsworth, Baldwin, Johnson and Harper, 600 North Westshore Boulevard, Suite 200.
Telephone: 813-289-1247.
Macon, Georgia Office: Haynsworth, Baldwin, Johnson and Harper, 577 Mulberry Street, Suite 710, P.O. Box 1975.
Telephone: 912-746-0262.

Knox L. Haynsworth, Jr. (Not admitted in NC)
James B. Spears, Jr. (Resident)
Robert S. Phifer (Resident)

Lilli K. Lindbeck (Resident)
Stephen D. Dellinger (Resident)
Jacob J. Modla (Resident)
John D. Cole (Not admitted in NC; Resident)

OF COUNSEL

James J. Baldwin (Not admitted in NC)

Representative Clients: Belk Stores Services, Inc.; Carolina Freight Corp.; Charlotte Pipe and Foundry Co.; Drexel Heritage Furnishings, Inc.; Interstate Johnson Lane; Nucor Steel Corp.; Rexham Corp.; Sears Merchandise Group; Sunhealth Corp.

For full biographical listings, see the Martindale-Hubbell Law Directory

LESESNE & CONNETTE (AV)

1001 Elizabeth Avenue, Suite 1-D, 28204-2209
Telephone: 704-372-5700
Fax: 704-377-2008

MEMBERS OF FIRM

Louis L. Lesesne, Jr.
Edward G. Connette, III
Martha L. Clark

For full biographical listings, see the Martindale-Hubbell Law Directory

SMITH HELMS MULLISS & MOORE, L.L.P. (AV)

227 North Tryon Street, P.O. Box 31247, 28231
Telephone: 704-343-2000
Telecopier: 704-334-8467
Telex: 572460
Greensboro, North Carolina Office: Smith Helms Mulliss & Moore, Suite 1400 First Union Tower, 300 North Greene Street, P.O. Box 21927.
Telephone: 910-378-5200.
Telecopier: 910-379-9558.
Raleigh, North Carolina Office: 316 West Edenton Street, P.O. Box 27525.
Telephone: 919-755-8700.
Telecopier: 919-828-7938.

MEMBERS OF FIRM

Catherine E. Thompson
H. Landis Wade, Jr.
L. D. Simmons, II

ASSOCIATE

Brian D. Barger

For Complete List of Firm Personnel, See General Section

For full biographical listings, see the Martindale-Hubbell Law Directory

VAN HOY, REUTLINGER & TAYLOR (AV)

737 East Boulevard, 28203
Telephone: 704-375-6022
Fax: 704-375-6024

(See Next Column)

MEMBERS OF FIRM

Philip M. Van Hoy
Craig A. Reutlinger
Paul B. Taylor

Representative Clients: Duke Power Company; Sunstrand Corporation; CIGNA Corporation; Pic 'N Pay Stores, Inc.; Parsons Main, Inc.; City of Fayetteville, North Carolina; McDowell Hospital; Medical Review of North Carolina; National Health Labs, Inc.; Dawson Consumer Products.

For full biographical listings, see the Martindale-Hubbell Law Directory

*GREENSBORO,** Guilford Co.

ADAMS KLEEMEIER HAGAN HANNAH & FOUTS (AV)

North Carolina Trust Center, 301 N. Elm Street, P.O. Box 3463, 27402
Telephone: 910-373-1600
Fax: 910-273-5357

MEMBERS OF FIRM

John A. Kleemeier, Jr. (1911-1973)
William J. Adams, Jr. (1908-1993)
Walter L. Hannah
Daniel W. Fouts
Robert G. Baynes
Joseph W. Moss
Clinton Eudy, Jr.
M. Jay DeVaney
Michael H. Godwin
W. Winburne King III
F. Cooper Brantley
Bruce H. Connors
Charles T. Hagan III
Larry I. Moore III
Elizabeth Dunn White
W. B. Rodman Davis
Thomas W. Brawner
Margaret Shea Burnham
Peter G. Pappas
William M. Wilcox IV
Katherine Bonan McDiarmid
David A. Senter
J. Alexander S. Barrett
Christine L. Myatt

OF COUNSEL

Charles T. Hagan, Jr.
Horace R. Kornegay

ASSOCIATES

Trudy A. Ennis
A. Scott Jackson
Amiel J. Rossabi
James W. Bryan
Betty Pincus Balcomb
Edward L. Bleynat, Jr.
Stephen A. Mayo
Louise Anderson Maultsby
R. Harper Heckman
Dena Beth Langley
David S. Pokela

Representative Clients: NationsBank of North Carolina, N.A.; Hafele America Co.; Duke Power Co.; U.S. Fidelity & Guaranty Co.; Dillard Paper Co.; Carolina Steel Corp.; Electrical South Inc.

For full biographical listings, see the Martindale-Hubbell Law Directory

HAYNSWORTH, BALDWIN, JOHNSON AND GREAVES, P.A. (AV)

2709 Henry Street, P.O. Box 13310, 27415
Telephone: 910-375-9737
Facsimile: 910-375-4430
Greenville, South Carolina Office: 918 South Pleasantburg Drive, P.O. Box 10888.
Telephone: 803-271-7410.
Columbia, South Carolina Office: 1201 Main Street, Suite 1230.
Telephone: 803-799-5858.
Raleigh, North Carolina Office: 3605 Glenwood Avenue, Suite 210, P.O. Box 10035.
Telephone: 919-782-3340.
Charlotte, North Carolina Office: 400 West Trade Street.
Telephone: 704-342-2588.
Jacksonville, Florida Office: Haynsworth, Baldwin, Johnson and Harper, 1506 Prudential Drive, P.O. Box 40593.
Telephone: 904-396-3000.
Tampa, Florida Office: Haynsworth, Baldwin, Johnson and Harper, 600 North Westshore Boulevard, Suite 200.
Telephone: 813-289-1247.
Macon, Georgia Office: Haynsworth, Baldwin, Johnson and Harper, 577 Mulberry Street, Suite 710, P.O. Box 1975.
Telephone: 912-746-0262.

Knox L. Haynsworth, Jr. (Not admitted in NC)
James M. Powell (Resident)
Charles P. Roberts III (Resident)

Gregory P. McGuire (Resident)
Brian M. Freedman (Resident)
Lucretia D. Smith (Resident)
Martha B. Perkowski (Resident)
D. Ross Hamilton, Jr. (Resident)

OF COUNSEL

James J. Baldwin (Not admitted in NC)

Representative Clients: Carter Machinery Corp.; Coca-Cola Bottling Co., Consolidated; Cone Mills Corp.; GKN Automotive Components, Inc.; Honda Power Equipment Co.; Integon Corp.; The Moses H. Cone Memorial Hospital; Piedmont Triad Airport Authority; VF Corp.; Volvo GM Heavy Truck Corp.;

For full biographical listings, see the Martindale-Hubbell Law Directory

Greensboro—Continued

SMITH HELMS MULLISS & MOORE, L.L.P. (AV)

Suite 1400 First Union Tower, 300 North Greene Street, P.O. Box 21927, 27420
Telephone: 910-378-5200
Telecopier: 910-379-9558
Charlotte, North Carolina Office: Smith Helms Mulliss & Moore, L.L.P., 227 North Tryon Street, P.O. Box 31247.
Telephone: 704-343-2000.
Telecopier: 704-334-8467.
Telex: 572460.
Raleigh, North Carolina Office: Smith Helms Mulliss & Moore, L.L.P., 316 West Edenton Street, P.O. Box 27525.
Telephone: 919-755-8700.
Telecopier: 919-828-7938.

MEMBERS OF FIRM

Martin N. Erwin
Michael E. Kelly
Allan L. Shackelford
Julianna C. Theall

ASSOCIATES

Dayna J. Kelly
Todd W. Cline

For Complete List of Firm Personnel, See General Section

For full biographical listings, see the Martindale-Hubbell Law Directory

HIGH POINT, Guilford Co.

ROBERT E. SHEAHAN & ASSOCIATES (AV)

603-B Eastchester Drive, P.O. Box 29, 27261
Telephone: 910-889-2711
Fax: 910-885-7940

ASSOCIATES

Ronda Leigh Lowe
Randle L. Jones
Lawrence H. Schultz, Jr.

For full biographical listings, see the Martindale-Hubbell Law Directory

*RALEIGH,** Wake Co.

* indicates certain Bar Register subscribers whose principal office is located elsewhere in the state and who have arranged for representation as a part of the state capital listings that follow

HAYNSWORTH, BALDWIN, JOHNSON AND GREAVES, P.A. (AV)

3605 Glenwood Avenue, Suite 210, P.O. Box 10035, 27605
Telephone: 919-782-3340
Facsimile: 919-782-3346
Greenville, South Carolina Office: 918 South Pleasantburg Drive, P.O. Box 10888.
Telephone: 803-271-7410.
Columbia, South Carolina Office: 1201 Main Street, Suite 1230.
Telephone: 803-799-5858.
Greensboro, North Carolina Office: 2709 Henry Street, P.O. Box 13310.
Telephone: 910-375-9737.
Charlotte, North Carolina Office: 400 West Trade Street.
Telephone: 704-342-2588.
Jacksonville, Florida Office: Haynsworth, Baldwin, Johnson and Harper, 1506 Prudential Drive, P.O. Box 40593.
Telephone: 904-396-3000.
Tampa, Florida Office: Haynsworth, Baldwin, Johnson and Harper, 600 North Westshore Boulevard, Suite 200.
Telephone: 813-289-1247.
Macon, Georgia Office: Haynsworth, Baldwin, Johnson and Harper, 577 Mulberry Street, Suite 710, P.O. Box 1975.
Telephone: 912-746-0262.

Knox L. Haynsworth, Jr. (Not admitted in NC)
Bruce A. Petesch (Resident)

Rodolfo R. Agraz (Resident)

OF COUNSEL

James J. Baldwin (Not admitted in NC)

Representative Clients: Cone Mills Corp.; Fieldcrest Cannon, Inc.; Flagstar Companies, Inc.; Frigidaire Company Dishwasher Products; Golden Corral Corp.; Mitsubishi Semiconductor America, Inc.; Perdue Farms, Inc.; Public Service Company of North Carolina; S.T. Wooten Construction Co.

For full biographical listings, see the Martindale-Hubbell Law Directory

MAUPIN TAYLOR ELLIS & ADAMS, P.A. (AV)

Suite 500, 3200 Beechleaf Court, P.O. Drawer 19764, 27619
Telephone: 919-981-4000
Telecopier: 919-981-4300
Rock Hill, South Carolina Office: 448 Lakeshore Parkway, Suite 200.
Telephone: 803-324-8118.
Telecopier: 803-324-2093.
Durham, North Carolina Office: 411 Andrews Road, Suite 150.
Telephone: 919-382-0188.
Telecopier: 919-383-9771.

(See Next Column)

Robert A. Valois
Frank P. Ward, Jr.
Richard M. Lewis
Margie Toy Case
Thomas A. Farr
James A. Roberts, III
Steven M. Rudisill (Resident, Rock Hill, SC Office)
Timothy S. Riordan
Winston L. Page, Jr.
Jack Spain Holmes
Gretchen W. Ewalt
Michael C. Lord
Robert J. Reeves (Not admitted in NC; Resident, Rock Hill, SC Office)
William P. Barrett
James C. Dever, III
Julie Ann Alagna
John D. Elvers
M. Reid Acree, Jr.

Representative Clients: American Airlines; Lenox, Inc.; Capital Cities/ABC Inc.; Fluor Daniel; McDonald's Corp.; Glaxo, Inc.; Northern Telecom, Inc.; United Parcel Service; CSX Transportation.

For Complete List of Firm Personnel, See General Section

For full biographical listings, see the Martindale-Hubbell Law Directory

OGLETREE, DEAKINS, NASH, SMOAK & STEWART (AV)

Suite 511, 4101 Lake Boone Trail, P.O. Box 31608, 27622
Telephone: 919-787-9700
Facsimile: 919-783-9412
Atlanta, Georgia Office: 3800 One Atlantic Center, 1201 West Peachtree Street, N.W.
Telephone: 404-881-1300.
Washington, D.C. Office: Fifth Floor, 2400 N Street, N.W.
Telephone: 202-887-0855.
Nashville, Tennessee Office: 500 Church Street.
Telephone: 615-254-1900.
Greenville, South Carolina Office: The Ogletree Building, 300 North Main Street, P.O. Box 2757.
Telephone: 803-271-1300.
Charleston, South Carolina Office: First Union Building, Suite 310, 177 Meeting Street, P.O. Box 1808.
Telephone: 803-853-1300.
Columbia, South Carolina Office: Palmetto Center, Suite 1820, 1426 Main Street, P.O. Box 11206.
Telephone: 803-252-1300.
Albany, New York Office: 4th Floor, One Steuben Place.
Telephone: 518-434-1300.

MEMBERS OF FIRM

Homer L. Deakins, Jr. (Not admitted in NC)
Lewis Tyson Smoak (Not admitted in NC)
J. Hamilton Stewart, III (Not admitted in NC)
L. Gray Geddie, Jr. (Not admitted in NC)
Stuart M. Vaughan, Jr.
M. Baker Wyche III (Not admitted in NC)
L. Franklin Elmore (Not admitted in NC)
John S. Burgin
James M. Kuszaj
A. Bruce Clarke
Joel A. Daniel (Not admitted in NC)
C. Matthew Keen
Clyde H. Jarrett, III
Robin Adams Anderson

OF COUNSEL

Thomas C. Bradley, Jr. (Not admitted in NC)

Representative Clients: Burlington Industries, Inc.; Duke Power Co.; Eastman Chemical Co.; General Electric Co.; W. R. Grace & Co.; Hercules, Inc.; Union Carbide Corp.

For full biographical listings, see the Martindale-Hubbell Law Directory

* **WOMBLE CARLYLE SANDRIDGE & RICE** (AV)

A Professional Limited Liability Company
2100 First Union Capitol Center, 150 Fayetteville Street Mall, P.O. Box 831, 27602
Telephone: 919-755-2100
Telecopy: 919-755-2150
Telex: 806498
Charlotte, North Carolina Office: 3300 One First Union Center, 301 South College Street.
Telephone: 704-331-4900.
Telecopy: 704-331-4955.
Telex: 853609.
Winston-Salem, North Carolina Office: 1600 Southern National Financial Center.
Telephone: 919-721-3600.
Telecopy: 919-721-3660.
Telex: 806498.
Atlanta, Georgia Office: One Ninety One Peachtree Tower, 191 Peachtree Street N.E., Suite 3250.
Telephone: 404-614-2580.
Fax: 404-614-2595.

RESIDENT PARTNER

Charles A. Edwards

Representative Clients: Aetna Casualty and Surety Co., Inc.; ALSCO/AmeriMark Building Products, Inc.; Aoki Corporation America, Inc.; Empire of Carolina, Inc.; Hackney Brothers, Inc.; Lawyers Mutual Liability Insurance Company of North Carolina; Meredith College; Monk-Austin, Inc.; Regency Park Corporation; Wachovia Bank of North Carolina, N.A.

(See Next Column)

WOMBLE CARLYLE SANDRIDGE & RICE, *Raleigh—Continued*

For Complete List of Firm Personnel, See General Section

For full biographical listings, see the Martindale-Hubbell Law Directory

*WINSTON-SALEM,** Forsyth Co.

CONSTANGY, BROOKS & SMITH (AV)

Suite 300, 101 South Stratford Road, 27104-4213
Telephone: 910-721-1001
Charlotte Telephone: 704-344-1040
Fax: 910-748-9112
Atlanta, Georgia Office: 2400 Peachtree Center Building, 200 Peachtree Street, N.W.
Telephone: 404-525-8622.
Birmingham, Alabama Office: 1410 AmSouth/Harbert Plaza, 1901 Sixth Avenue North.
Telephone: 205-252-9321.
Columbia, South Carolina Office: Suite 810 NationsBank Tower, 1301 Gervais Street.
Telephone: 803-256-3200.
Nashville, Tennessee Office: Suite 1080, Vanderbilt Plaza, 2100 West End Avenue.
Telephone: 615-320-5200.
Washington, D.C. Office: Suite 1200, 1015 Fifteenth Street, N.W.
Telephone: 202-789-8676.

RESIDENT MEMBERS

John J. Doyle, Jr. — W. Randolph Loftis, Jr.

RESIDENT ASSOCIATE

Robin E. Shea

Representative Clients: Blockbuster Entertainment Corp.; Blue Cross/Blue Shield of Alabama; Consolidated Freightways, Inc.; Delta Woodside Industries; McDonald's; Merck & Co., Inc.; Philip-Morris Cos., Inc.; Phillips Van Heusen Corp.; Sara Lee Corp.; Trust Company Bank.

For full biographical listings, see the Martindale-Hubbell Law Directory

WOMBLE CARLYLE SANDRIDGE & RICE (AV)

A Professional Limited Liability Company
1600 Southern National Financial Center, P.O. Drawer 84, 27102
Telephone: 910-721-3600
Telecopy: 910-721-3660
Telex: 806498
Charlotte, North Carolina Office: 3300 One First Union Center, 301 South College Street.
Telephone: 704-331-4900.
Telecopy: 704-331-4955.
Telex: 853609.
Raleigh, North Carolina Office: 2100 First Union Capitol Center, 150 Fayetteville Street Mall, P.O. Box 831.
Telephone: 919-755-2100.
Telecopy: 919-755-2150.
Telex: 806498.
Atlanta, Georgia Office: One Ninety One Peachtree Tower, 191 Peachtree Street, N.E., Suite 3250.
Telephone: 404-614-2580.
Fax: 404-614-2595.

MEMBERS OF FIRM

Guy F. Driver, Jr. — David A. Irvin
Gusti W. Frankel — Charles F. Vance, Jr.

Representative Clients: Brad Ragan, Inc.; Brenner Companies, Inc.; Food Lion, Inc.; Hanes Companies, Inc.; North Carolina Baptist Hospitals, Inc.; R.J. Reynolds Tobacco Company; Summit Communications Group, Inc.; Thomasville Furniture Industries, Inc.; Wachovia Bank of North Carolina, National Association; Wake Forest University.

For Complete List of Firm Personnel, See General Section

For full biographical listings, see the Martindale-Hubbell Law Directory

NORTH DAKOTA

*BISMARCK,** Burleigh Co.

FLECK, MATHER & STRUTZ, LTD. (AV)

Sixth Floor, Norwest Bank Building, 400 East Broadway, P.O. Box 2798, 58502
Telephone: 701-223-6585
Telecopier: 701-222-4853

Ernest R. Fleck — Robert J. Udland
Gary R. Wolberg — DeeNelle Louise Ruud

Representative Clients: The North American Coal Corp.; North Dakota Insurance Reserve Fund; American Home Products Co.; Employers Mutual Cos.; Basin Electric Power Coop.; Mid-Dakota Medical Clinic; Chubb Group; OMF Office Products; United Bank; Midwest Motor Express, Inc.

(See Next Column)

For Complete List of Firm Personnel, See General Section

For full biographical listings, see the Martindale-Hubbell Law Directory

PEARCE AND DURICK (AV)

314 East Thayer Avenue, P.O. Box 400, 58502
Telephone: 701-223-2890
Fax: 701-223-7865

MEMBERS OF FIRM

William P. Pearce — Gary R. Thune
Patrick W. Durick — David E. Reich

Representative Clients: American Insurance Assn.; Cigna-INA Insurance Co.; Deere & Co.; Federal Deposit Insurance Corp.; Ford Motor Co.; General Motors Corp.; MDU Resources Group, Inc.; Northwest Airlines; Royal Insurance Co.; North Dakota School Boards Assn.

For Complete List of Firm Personnel, See General Section

For full biographical listings, see the Martindale-Hubbell Law Directory

*FARGO,** Cass Co.

NILLES, HANSEN & DAVIES, LTD. (AV)

1800 Radisson Tower, P.O. Box 2626, 58108
Telephone: 701-237-5544

Thomas A. Jacobson

Representative Clients: Metropolitan Federal Bank (fsb); First Bank of North Dakota (N.A.); Red River Valley and Western Railroad; Cass Clay Creamery, Inc.; Maintenance Engineering; The Village Family Service Center; Northwest Professional Color; Cossette Trucking; Northern School Supply.

For Complete List of Firm Personnel, See General Section

For full biographical listings, see the Martindale-Hubbell Law Directory

VOGEL, BRANTNER, KELLY, KNUTSON, WEIR & BYE, LTD. (AV)

502 First Avenue North, P.O. Box 1389, 58107
Telephone: 701-237-6983
Facsimile: 701-237-0847

John D. Kelly — Douglas R. Herman
Pamela J. Hermes

Representative Clients: Associated General Contractors of North Dakota; Clark Equipment Co.; Dakota Hospital; Forum Communications Company; Merit Care Medical Group; Northern Improvement Co.; Dakota Clinic; Gateway Chevrolet, Inc.; West Acres Development Company; Fargo Glass & Paint Company.

For Complete List of Firm Personnel, See General Section

For full biographical listings, see the Martindale-Hubbell Law Directory

OHIO

*AKRON,** Summit Co.

THOMPSON, HINE AND FLORY (AV)

50 S. Main Street, Suite 502, 44308-1828
Telephone: 216-376-8090
Fax: 216-376-8386
Cincinnati, Ohio Office: 312 Walnut Street, 14th Floor, 45202-4029.
Telephone: 513-352-6700.
Fax: 513-241-4771.
Telex: 938003.
Cleveland, Ohio Office: 1100 National City Bank Building, 629 Euclid Avenue, 44114-3070.
Telephone: 216-566-5500.
Fax: 216-556-5583.
Telex: 980217.
Cable Address: "Thomflor".
Columbus, Ohio Office: One Columbus, 10 West Broad Street, 43215-3435.
Telephone: 614-469-3200.
Fax: 614-469-3361.
Dayton, Ohio Office: 2000 Courthouse Plaza, 45402-1706.
Telephone: 513-443-6600.
Fax: 513-443-6637; 443-6635.
Palm Beach, Florida Office: 125 Worth Avenue, 33480-4466.
Telephone: 407-833-5900.
Fax: 407-833-5951.
Washington, D.C. Office: 1920 N Street, N.W., 20036-1601.
Telephone: 202-331-8800.
Fax: 202-331-8330.
Telex: 904173.
Cable Address: "Caglaw".
Brussels, Belgium Office: Rue des Chevaliers / Ridderstraat 14 - B.10, B - 1050.
Telephone: 011(32-2) 511-9326.
Fax: 011(32-2) 513-9206.

(See Next Column)

THOMPSON, HINE AND FLORY—*Continued*

MEMBER OF FIRM

Joseph S. Ruggie, Jr.

For Complete List of Firm Personnel, See General Section

For full biographical listings, see the Martindale-Hubbell Law Directory

HARRY A. TIPPING CO. A LEGAL PROFESSIONAL ASSOCIATION (AV)

National City Center, 2200 One Cascade Plaza, 44308
Telephone: 216-434-8500
Telecopier: 216-434-5453

Harry A. Tipping
John E. Holcomb
Robert N. Woodside
John Walter Clark

OF COUNSEL

Dominic A. Olivo

For full biographical listings, see the Martindale-Hubbell Law Directory

ASHTABULA, Ashtabula Co.

WARREN AND YOUNG (AV)

134 West 46th Street, P.O. Box 2300, 44004-6951
Telephone: (216) 997-6175
Facsimile: (216) 992-9114

MEMBER OF FIRM

Carl F. Muller

Representative Clients: Ashtabula County Medical Center; Iten Industries; Molded Fiber Glass Cos.; Premix; Plasticolors.

For Complete List of Firm Personnel, See General Section

For full biographical listings, see the Martindale-Hubbell Law Directory

*CINCINNATI,** Hamilton Co.

BROWN, CUMMINS & BROWN CO., L.P.A. (AV)

3500 Carew Tower, 441 Vine Street, 45202
Telephone: 513-381-2121
Fax: 513-381-2125

J. W. Brown (Retired)
Robert S Brown
Lynne Skilken
Melanie S. Corwin

Counsel for: Paramount's Kings Island; Squeri Food Products; Public Library of Cincinnati and Hamilton County; Maisonette-LaNormandie; United Air Specialists, Inc.; Drake Center, Inc.; Cincinnati Gardens, Inc.; WYZZ-TV; WSMH-TV.
Reference: Star Bank of Cincinnati.

For full biographical listings, see the Martindale-Hubbell Law Directory

CORS & BASSETT (AV)

1200 Carew Tower, 45202-2990
Telephone: 513-852-8200
FAX: 513-852-8222
Covington, Kentucky Office: 250 Grandview Drive, Suite 200, Ft. Mitchell, 41017.
Telephone: 606-341-4666.

MEMBERS OF FIRM

Paul R. Moran
Joseph H. Vahlsing
Robert J. Hollingsworth
David L. Barth
Stephen S. Holmes

ASSOCIATES

Katharine C. Weber
Curtis L. Cornett

OF COUNSEL

Hal F. Franke

Representative Clients: Belcan Corporation; Consolidated Freightways; Dorman Products; Dugan & Meyers Construction Co., Inc.; Keco Industries, Inc.; State of Kentucky; Zonic Corporation.

For Complete List of Firm Personnel, See General Section

For full biographical listings, see the Martindale-Hubbell Law Directory

DENLINGER, ROSENTHAL & GREENBERG (AV)

2310 Star Bank Center, 425 Walnut Street, 45202
Telephone: 513-621-3440
Fax: 513-621-4449

MEMBERS OF FIRM

Dean E. Denlinger
Daniel G. Rosenthal
Gary L. Greenberg
John W. Fischer, II
Mark E. Lutz
James A. Mills

(See Next Column)

ASSOCIATE

Robert M. Lamb

Representative Clients: Columbia Sussex Corp.; Duro Bag Manufacturing Co.; Eagle-Picher Co.; Georgia-Pacific Corp.; The City of Kettering; The Kroger Co.; Moraine Materials Co.; The Ohio Masonic Home; Riverwood International Corp.; Spectra Physics Corp.

For full biographical listings, see the Martindale-Hubbell Law Directory

DINSMORE & SHOHL (AV)

1900 Chemed Center, 255 East Fifth Street, 45202-3172
Telephone: 513-977-8200
FAX: 513-977-8141
Florence, Kentucky Office: Turfway Ridge Office Park, 7300 Turfway Road, Suite 430 41042-1355.
Telephone: 606-283-0515.
FAX: 606-283-6017.
Dayton, Ohio Office: 500 Courthouse Plaza, S.W., 10 N. Ludlow Street, 45402-1834.
Telephone: 513-228-8012.
FAX: 513-461-2543.
Columbus, Ohio Office: NBD Bank Building, Suite 330, 175 South Third Street, 43215-5134.
Telephone: 614-224-7887.
FAX: 614-224-7882.

MEMBERS OF FIRM

Harold S. Freeman
Michael W. Hawkins
Michael S. Glassman
Lawrence A. Flemer
Charles M. Roesch

ASSOCIATES

Jeffrey S. Shoskin
Colleen P. Lewis
Ann L. Munson
Christopher Ragonesi
Robert J. Reid
Corey M. MacGillivray

For Complete List of Firm Personnel, See General Section

For full biographical listings, see the Martindale-Hubbell Law Directory

FROST & JACOBS (AV)

2500 PNC Center, 201 East Fifth Street, P.O. Box 5715, 45201-5715
Telephone: 513-651-6800
Cable Address: "Frostjac"
Telex: 21-4396 F & J CIN
Telecopier: 513-651-6981
Columbus, Ohio Office: One Columbus, 10 West Broad Street.
Telephone: 614-464-1211.
Telecopier: 614-464-1737.
Lexington, Kentucky Office: 1100 Vine Center Tower, 333 West Vine Street.
Telephone: 606-254-1100.
Telecopier: 606-253-2990.
Middletown, Ohio Office: 400 First National Bank Building, 2 North Main Street.
Telephone: 513-422-2001.
Telecopier: 513-422-3010.
Naples, Florida Office: 4001 Tamiami Trail North, Suite 220.
Telephone: 813-261-0582.
Telecopier: 813-261-2083.

MEMBERS OF FIRM

James K. L. Lawrence
Robert A. Dimling
George E. Yund
David T. Croall
Deborah S. Adams
Gregory P. Adams

SENIOR ATTORNEYS

William W. Ford, III
Raymond D. Neusch

ASSOCIATES

Nancy Dirkse DeWitt
Hilla M. Zerbst
Douglas Halpert (Not admitted in OH)
Patrice Baughman Borders

SENIOR PARTNER

Daniel P. Dooley

COLUMBUS, OHIO OFFICE
MEMBER OF FIRM

Thomas V. Williams

MIDDLETOWN OFFICE
MEMBERS OF FIRM

Thomas A. Swope
Donald L. Crain

Representative Clients: Armco Inc.; Arthur Andersen & Co.; Champion International; Cincinnati Bell Inc.; Cincinnati Milacron Inc.; Federated Department Stores Inc.; Mercy Health Systems; PNC Bank, Ohio, National Association; U.S. Shoe Corp.; Sencorp.; Champion International.

For Complete List of Firm Personnel, See General Section

For full biographical listings, see the Martindale-Hubbell Law Directory

Cincinnati—Continued

KLAINE, WILEY, HOFFMANN & MEURER A LEGAL PROFESSIONAL ASSOCIATION (AV)

Suite 1850, 105 East Fourth Street, 45202-4080
Telephone: 513-241-0202
Fax: 513-241-9322

Franklin A. Klaine, Jr. — Gregory J. Meurer

For Complete List of Firm Personnel, See General Section

For full biographical listings, see the Martindale-Hubbell Law Directory

SIRKIN PINALES MEZIBOV & SCHWARTZ (AV)

920 Fourth & Race Tower, 105 West Fourth Street, 45202-2776
Telephone: 513-721-4876
Telecopier: 513-721-0876

MEMBER OF FIRM

Marc D. Mezibov

References: The Central Trust Co.; The Huntington National Bank.

For full biographical listings, see the Martindale-Hubbell Law Directory

THOMPSON, HINE AND FLORY (AV)

312 Walnut Street, 14th Floor, 45202-4029
Telephone: 513-352-6700
Fax: 513-241-4771;
Telex: 938003
Akron, Ohio Office: 50 S. Main Street, Suite 502, 44308-1828.
Telephone: 216-376-8090.
Fax: 216-376-8386.
Cleveland, Ohio Office: 1100 National City Bank Building, 629 Euclid Avenue, 44114-3070.
Telephone: 216-566-5500.
Fax: 216-556-5583.
Telex: 980217.
Cable Address: "Thomflor".
Columbus, Ohio Office: One Columbus, 10 West Broad Street, 43215-3435.
Telephone: 614-469-3200.
Fax: 614-469-3361.
Dayton, Ohio Office: 2000 Courthouse Plaza, N.E., 45402-1706.
Telephone: 513-443-6600.
Fax: 513-443-6637; 443-6635.
Palm Beach, Florida Office: 125 Worth Avenue, 33480-4466.
Telephone: 407-833-5900.
Fax: 407-833-5951.
Washington, D.C. Office: 1920 N Street, N.W., 20036-1601.
Telephone: 202-331-8800.
Fax: 202-331-8330.
Telex: 904173.
Cable Address: "Caglaw".
Brussels, Belgium Office: Rue des Chevaliers / Ridderstraat 14 - B.10, B - 1050.
Telephone: 011(32-2) 511-9326.
Fax: 011(-32-2) 513-9206.

MEMBERS OF FIRM

Edward B. Mitchell — Edna V. Scheuer
Peter E. Tamborski

ASSOCIATES

Sarah A. Barlage — Stacie A. Seiler
Michael Soto

For Complete List of Firm Personnel, See General Section

For full biographical listings, see the Martindale-Hubbell Law Directory

WAITE, SCHNEIDER, BAYLESS & CHESLEY CO., L.P.A. (AV)

1513 Central Trust Tower, Fourth and Vine Streets, 45202
Telephone: 513-621-0267
Fax: 513-381-2375; 621-0262

Stanley M. Chesley

Thomas F. Rehme — Sherrill P. Hondorf
Fay E. Stilz — Colleen M. Hegge
Louise M. Roselle — Dianna Pendleton
Dwight Tillery — Randy F. Fox
D. Arthur Rabourn — Glenn D. Feagan
Jerome L. Skinner — Theresa L. Groh
Janet G. Abaray — Theodore N. Berry
Paul M. De Marco — Jane H. Walker
Terrence L. Goodman — Renée Infante
Allen P. Grunes

OF COUNSEL

Jos. E. Rosen — James F. Keller

For full biographical listings, see the Martindale-Hubbell Law Directory

*CLEVELAND,** Cuyahoga Co.

ARTER & HADDEN (AV)

1100 Huntington Building, 925 Euclid Avenue, 44115-1475
Telephone: 216-696-1100
Telex: 98-5384
In Columbus, Ohio: 21st Floor, One Columbus, 10 West Broad Street. 43215-3422.
Telephone: 614-221-3155.
In Washington, D.C.: 1801 K Street, N.W., Suite 400K. 20006-3480.
Telephone: 202-775-7100.
In Dallas, Texas: 1717 Main Street, Suite 4100. 75201-4605.
Telephone: 214-761-2100.
In Los Angeles, California: 700 South Flower Street. 90017-4101.
Telephone: 213-629-9300.
In Irvine, California: Two Park Plaza, Suite 700, Jamboree Center.
Telephone: 714-252-7500.
In Austin, Texas: 100 Congress Avenue, Suite 1800.
Telephone: 512-479-6403.
In San Antonio, Texas: Suite 540, Harte-Hanks Tower, 7710 Jones Maltsberger Road.
Telephone: 210-805-8497.

MEMBERS OF FIRM

Richard D. DeLuce — James S. Bryan
Joseph A. Rotolo — John B. Lewis
Dennis D. Grant — Michael V. Abcarian
Edwin W. Duncan — Tom McDonald
Gregory V. Mersol

For Complete List of Firm Personnel, See General Section

For full biographical listings, see the Martindale-Hubbell Law Directory

BAKER & HOSTETLER (AV)

3200 National City Center, 1900 East Ninth Street, 44114-3485
Telephone: 216-621-0200
Telecopier: 216-696-0740
TWX: 810 421 8375
RCA Telex: 215032
In Columbus, Ohio: Capitol Square, Suite 2100, 65 East State Street.
Telephone: 614-228-1541.
In Denver, Colorado: 303 East 17th Avenue, Suite 1100.
Telephone: 303-861-0600.
In Houston, Texas: 1000 Louisiana, Suite 2000.
Telephone: 713-751-1600.
In Long Beach, California: 300 Oceangate, Suite 620.
Telephone: 310-432-2827.
In Los Angeles, California: 600 Wilshire Boulevard.
Telephone: 213-624-2400.
In Orlando, Florida: SunBank Center, Suite 2300, 200 South Orange Avenue.
Telephone: 407-649-4000.
In Washington, D. C.: Washington Square, Suite 1100, 1050 Connecticut Avenue, N.W.
Telephone: 202-861-1500.
In College Park, Maryland: 9658 Baltimore Boulevard, Suite 206.
Telephone: 301-441-2781.
In Alexandria, Virginia: 437 North Lee Street.
Telephone: 703-549-1294.
In San Francisco, California: One Sansome Street, Suite 2000.
Telephone: 415-951-4705.

PARTNERS

Elliot Stephen Azoff — W. James Ollinger
John H. M. Fenix — Charles T. Price
Paula L. Friedman — Thomas M. Seger
David G. Holcombe — Robert G. Stinchcomb
Earl M. Leiken — Victor Strimbu, Jr.
Richard H. Leukart, II — Paul D. White
John F. Novatney, Jr. — John H. Wilharm, Jr.
John A. Zangerle

ASSOCIATES

Thomas F. Cooke, II — Tom A. King
Robert C. Petrulis

RETIRED PARTNERS

William L. Calfee — James P. Garner

For Complete List of Firm Personnel, See General Section

For full biographical listings, see the Martindale-Hubbell Law Directory

BELKIN & HARROLD CO., L.P.A. (AV)

Signature Square II, 25101 Chagrin Boulevard, Suite 210, 44122
Telephone: 216-831-3377
Telecopier: 216-831-1326

Jeffrey A. Belkin — Thomas J. Wiencek
Linda Hauserman Harrold — Lester W. Armstrong

For full biographical listings, see the Martindale-Hubbell Law Directory

Cleveland—Continued

BENESCH, FRIEDLANDER, COPLAN & ARONOFF (AV)

2300 BP America Building, 200 Public Square, 44114-2378
Telephone: 216-363-4500
Telecopier: 216-363-4588
Columbus, Ohio Office: 88 East Broad Street, 43215-3506.
Telephone: 614-223-9300.
Telecopier: 614-223-9330.
Cincinnati, Ohio Office: 2800 Cincinnati Commerce Center, 600 Vine Street, 45202-2409.
Telephone: 713-762-6200.
Telecopier: 513-762-6245.

MEMBERS OF FIRM

Maynard A. Buck, III
Margaret A. Kennedy
Howard A. Levy

ASSOCIATES

Joseph N. Gross
Mary E. Reid

COLUMBUS, OHIO
RESIDENT MEMBER

N. Victor Goodman

CINCINNATI, OHIO
RESIDENT MEMBER

Robin E. Harvey

CINCINNATI, OHIO
RESIDENT ASSOCIATE

Shelley B. Jones

For Complete List of Firm Personnel, See General Section

For full biographical listings, see the Martindale-Hubbell Law Directory

CHATTMAN, SUTULA, FRIEDLANDER & PAUL A LEGAL PROFESSIONAL ASSOCIATION (AV)

6200 Rockside Road, 44131
Telephone: 216-328-8000
Telecopier: 216-328-8018
Red Bank, New Jersey Office: 241 Maple Street. 07701.
Telephone: 908-219-9000.
Facsimile: 908-219-9020.

Gerald B. Chattman
Richard G. Ross
Fred N. Carmen

For full biographical listings, see the Martindale-Hubbell Law Directory

DUVIN, CAHN & BARNARD A LEGAL PROFESSIONAL ASSOCIATION (AV)

Erieview Tower, 20th Floor, 1301 East Ninth Street, 44114
Telephone: 216-696-7600
Telecopier: 216-696-2038

Robert P. Duvin
Stephen J. Cahn
Thomas H. Barnard
Gerald A. Messerman
Marc J. Bloch
Andrew C. Meyer
Lee J. Hutton
Martin S. List
Craig M. Brown
Frank W. Buck
Gale S. Messerman
Neal B. Wainblat
Kenneth B. Stark
Martin T. Wymer
Barton A. Bixenstine
Robert M. Wolff
Jane P. Wilson

Richard C. Hubbard, III
Lisa Froimson Mann
Philip S. Kushner
Stephen J. Sferra
Linda E. Tawil
Steven K. Aronoff
Kenneth Michael Haneline
Kevin M. Norchi
Paul A. Monahan
Jon M. Dileno
David A. Posner
Scott A. Moorman
Vincent T. Norwillo
Marc A. Duvin
Suellen Oswald
Stephen C. Sutton
Michele H. Schmidt
William Joseph Evans
Carole O. Heyward

Representative Clients: Cleveland-Akron-Canton Supermarket Industry; The Scott-Fetzer Co.; Greater Cleveland Regional Transit Authority; Forest City Enterprises, Inc.; Cleveland Board of Education; Electronic Data Systems-General Motors Corp.; B.P. America; The Cleveland Clinic; Lamson & Sessions Co.; Progressive Insurance Companies.

For full biographical listings, see the Martindale-Hubbell Law Directory

GOLDFARB & REZNICK (AV)

Suite 1800, 55 Public Square, 44113
Telephone: 216-781-0383
Telecopier: 216-781-0393

MEMBERS OF FIRM

Bernard S. Goldfarb
Morris M. Reznick
Mark V. Webber

(See Next Column)

ASSOCIATES

Carl E. Cormany
Sergio A. Carano

For full biographical listings, see the Martindale-Hubbell Law Directory

JANIK & DUNN (AV)

400 Park Plaza Building, 1111 Chester Avenue, 44114
Telephone: 216-781-9700
Fax: 216-781-1250
Brea, California Office: 2601 Saturn Street, Suite 300.
Telephone: 714-572-1101.
Fax: 714-572-1103.

MEMBERS OF FIRM

Steven G. Janik
Theodore M. Dunn, Jr.

ASSOCIATES

Myra Staresina
David L. Mast

For full biographical listings, see the Martindale-Hubbell Law Directory

JONES, DAY, REAVIS & POGUE (AV)

North Point, 901 Lakeside Avenue, 44114
Telephone: 216-586-3939
Cable Address: "Attorneys Cleveland"
Telex: 980389
Telecopier: 216-579-0212
In Columbus, Ohio: 1900 Huntington Center.
Telephone: 614-469-3939.
Cable Address: "Attorneys Columbus."
Telecopier: 614-461-4198.
In Atlanta, Georgia: 3500 One Peachtree Center, 303 Peachtree Street, N.E.
Telephone: 404-521-3939.
Cable Address: "Attorneys Atlanta".
Telex: 54-2711.
Telecopier: 404-581-8330.
In Brussels, Belgium: Avenue Louise 480, 7th Floor. B-1050 Brussels.
Telephone: 011-32-2-645-14-11.
Telecopier: 011-32-2-645-14-45.
In Chicago, Illinois: 77 West Wacker.
Telephone: 312-782-3939.
Telecopier: 312-782-8585.
In Dallas, Texas: 2300 Trammell Crow Center, 2001 Ross Avenue.
Telephone: 214-220-3939.
Cable Address: "Attorneys Dallas."
Telex: 730852.
Telecopier: 214-969-5100.
In Frankfurt, Germany: Triton Haus, Bockenheimer Landstrasse 42, 60323 Frankfurt am Main.
Telephone: 49-69-9726-3939.
Telecopier: 49-69-9726-3993.
In Geneva, Switzerland: 20, rue de Candolle.
Telephone: 011-41-22-320-2339.
Telecopier: 011-41-22-320-1232.
In Hong Kong: 1501 One Exchange Square, 8 Connaught Place.
Telephone: 011-852-2526-6895.
Telecopier: 011-852-2810-5787.
In Irvine, California: 2603 Main Street, Suite 900.
Telephone: 714-851-3939.
Telex: 194911 Lawyers LSA.
Telecopier: 714-553-7539.
In London, England: One Mount Street.
Telephone: 011-44-71-493-9361.
Cable Address: "Surgoe London WI."
Telecopier: 011-44-71-493-9666.
In Los Angeles, California: 555 West Fifth Street, Suite 4600.
Telephone: 213-489-3939.
Telex: 181439 UD.
Telecopier: 213-243-2539.
In New York, New York: 599 Lexington Avenue.
Telephone: 212-326-3939.
Cable Address: "JONESDAY NEWYORK."
Telex: 237013 JDRP UR.
Telecopier: 212-755-7306.
In Paris, France: 62, rue du Faubourg Saint-Honore.
Telephone: 011-33-1-44-71-3939.
Cable Address: "Surgoe Paris."
Telex: 290156 Surgoe.
Telecopier: 011-33-1-49-24-0471.
In Pittsburgh, Pennsylvania: 500 Grant Street, 31st Floor.
Telephone: 412-391-3939.
Cable Address: "Attorneys Pittsburgh".
Telecopier: 412-394-7959.
In Riyadh, Saudi Arabia: Law Offices of Saud M.A. Shawwaf, P.O. Box 2700.
Telephones: 011 (966-1) 465-6543, 011 (966-1) 464-8534 or 011 (966-1) 464-8540.
Telex: 401831 SAUCON SJ.
Telecopier: (966-1) 464-8480.
In Taipei, Taiwan: 8th Floor, Tun Hwa South Road, Section 2.
Telephone: 011 (886-2) 704-6808.
Telecopier: 011 (886-2) 704-6791.

(See Next Column)

JONES, DAY, REAVIS & POGUE, *Cleveland—Continued*

In Tokyo, Japan: Toranomon MT Building, 4th Floor, 10-3, Toranomon 3-Chome, Minato-Ku, Tokyo 105, Japan.
Telephone: 011-81-3-3433-3939.
Telecopier: 011-81-3-5401-2725.
In Washington, D.C.: Metropolitan Square, 1450 G Street, N.W.
Telephone: 202-879-3939.
Cable Address: "Attorneys Washington."
Telex: 89-2410 ATTORNEYS WASH.
Telecopier: 202-737-2832.

MEMBERS OF FIRM

Andrew M. Kramer | Kathleen B. Burke
James A. Rydzel | Barbara J. Leukart

For Complete List of Firm Personnel, See General Section

For full biographical listings, see the Martindale-Hubbell Law Directory

MILLISOR & NOBIL A LEGAL PROFESSIONAL ASSOCIATION (AV)

9150 South Hills Boulevard, 44147-3599
Telephone: 216-838-8800 Cleveland
216-253-5500 Akron
Telefax: 216-838-8805
Columbus, Ohio Office: 41 South High Street, 3737 Huntington Center, 43215-6101.
Telephone: 614-224-1010.
Telefax: 614-365-9411.

Kenneth R. Millisor | Michael J. Hickey
Steven M. Nobil | Maribeth Gavin
Thomas D. Rooney | Douglas B. Brown
Harley M. Kastner | Linda S. Wilkins
David E. Schreiner | Jodi L. Wood
David P. Hiller | Kelly E. Drushel
Preston J. Garvin | Mark M. McCarthy
James P. Wilkins | Christine C. Covey
Michael J. Ranallo | Richard A. Millisor
Paul H. Malesick | Lisa A. Kainec
Keith L. Pryatel | Jeffrey B. Keiper (Not admitted in OH)
John J. Krimm, Jr.
Bruce H. Fahey

LEGAL SUPPORT PERSONNEL
DIRECTORS

James M. Kitchin | Bruce W. Baylor
Christine Belz | Bryan D. Richert

PARALEGALS

Vicki Barnette | Irene G. Frye
Angela M. Bertka | Barbara L. Micale
Robert C. Dowd | Yvonne M. Shaw
Rita M. Filer | Laurie L. Tolbert
Shelia Wenger

Labor Counsel for: Bridgestone/Firestone, Inc.; BFGoodrich Co.; Uniroyal-Goodrich Tire Co.; Cooper Industries; May Department Stores, Co. (Kaufmann's and Payless Shoe Source); Federated Department Stores (Lazarus); Union Metal Corp.; Ohio Automobile Dealers Assn.; Children's Hospital; Kent State University.

For full biographical listings, see the Martindale-Hubbell Law Directory

LAWRENCE M. OBERDANK CO., L.P.A. (AV)

Suite 1717, Superior Building, 815 Superior Avenue, N.E., 44114
Telephone: 216-771-8008
FAX: 216-771-8234

Lawrence M. Oberdank

For full biographical listings, see the Martindale-Hubbell Law Directory

ROSS, BRITTAIN & SCHONBERG CO., L.P.A. (AV)

6000 Freedom Square Drive, Suite 540, 44131
Telephone: 216-447-1551
Telecopier: 216-447-1554

Alan G. Ross | Brian K. Brittain
Evelyn P. Schonberg

Richard E. Walters | Patrick J. Harrington
Debra G. Simms | Susan C. Margulies (Not admitted in OH)

LEGAL SUPPORT PERSONNEL
PARALEGALS

Justine Schlund | Deena Dinapoli
Renee Mezera | Tonya Gentry Camarda
Lauri Cochran

For full biographical listings, see the Martindale-Hubbell Law Directory

SEELEY, SAVIDGE AND AUSSEM A LEGAL PROFESSIONAL ASSOCIATION (AV)

800 Bank One Center, 600 Superior Avenue, East, 44114-2655
Telephone: 216-566-8200
Cable Address: "See Sau"
Fax-Telecopier: 216-566-0213
Elyria, Ohio Office: 538 Broad Street.
Telephone: 216-236-8158.

Keith A. Savidge | Jane T. Seelie

Patrick J. McIntyre | Carter R. Dodge
Robert C. White

References: Society National Bank; AmeriTrust.

For Complete List of Firm Personnel, See General Section

For full biographical listings, see the Martindale-Hubbell Law Directory

TIMOTHY A. SHIMKO & ASSOCIATES A LEGAL PROFESSIONAL ASSOCIATION (AV)

2010 Huntington Building, 925 Euclid Avenue, 44115
Telephone: 216-241-8300
Fax: 216-241-2702

Timothy A. Shimko

Janet I. Stich | Ronald K. Starkey
Theresa A. Tarchinski | Frank E. Piscitelli, Jr.

OF COUNSEL

Frank B. Mazzone

Reference: National City Bank, Cleveland.

For full biographical listings, see the Martindale-Hubbell Law Directory

SPIETH, BELL, MCCURDY & NEWELL CO., L.P.A. (AV)

2000 Huntington Building, 925 Euclid Avenue, 44115-1496
Telephone: 216-696-4700
Telecopier: 216-696-6569; 216-696-2706; 216-696-1052

Glen O. Smith, Jr. | Bruce G. Hearey
Stanley Dan Pace | Dianne Foley Hearey
Wade M. Fricke

Representative Clients: Cleveland Cavaliers; Nationwide Advertising Services, Inc.; Independent Steel Co.; Baldwin Wallace College; The Tool-Die Engineering Company.
Representative Labor Relations Clients (Management Only): Parker Hannifin Corp.; Reliance Electric Co.; Brush Wellman Co.

For Complete List of Firm Personnel, See General Section

For full biographical listings, see the Martindale-Hubbell Law Directory

THOMPSON, HINE AND FLORY (AV)

1100 National City Bank Building, 629 Euclid Avenue, 44114-3070
Telephone: 216-566-5500
Fax: 216-566-5583
Telex: 980217
Cable Address: "Thomflor"
Akron, Ohio Office: 50 S. Main Street, Suite 502, 44308-1828.
Telephone: 216-376-8090.
Fax: 216-376-8386.
Cincinnati, Ohio Office: 312 Walnut Street, 14th Floor, 45202-4029.
Telephone: 513-352-6700.
Fax: 513-241-4771.
Telex: 938003.
Columbus, Ohio Office: One Columbus, 10 West Broad Street, 43215-3435.
Telephone: 614-469-3200.
Fax: 614-469-3361.
Dayton, Ohio Office: 2000 Courthouse Plaza, N.E., 45402-1706.
Telephone: 513-443-6600.
Fax: 513-443-6637; 443-6635.
Palm Beach, Florida Office: 125 Worth Avenue, Suite 117, 33480-4466.
Telephone: 407-833-5900.
Fax: 407-833-5951.
Washington, D.C. Office: 1920 N Street, N.W., 20036-1601.
Telephone: 202-331-8800.
Fax: 202-331-8330.
Telex: 904173.
Cable Address: "Caglaw".
Brussels, Belgium Office: Rue des Chevaliers, Ridderstraat 14 - B.10, B - 1050.
Telephone: 011(32-2) 511-9326.
Fax: 011(32-2) 513-9206.

MEMBERS OF FIRM

Keith A. Ashmus | Robert L. Larson
T. Merritt Bumpass, Jr. | Joseph S. Ruggie, Jr.
Michael J. Frantz | Daniel A. Ward
Joel R. Hlavaty | Richard V. Whelan, Jr.

(See Next Column)

THOMPSON, HINE AND FLORY—*Continued*

ASSOCIATES

Colleen P. Battle
Carl H. Gluek
Mauritia G. Kamer
Thomas J. Piatak
Keith P. Spiller
(In Cincinnati, Ohio)

OF COUNSEL

Gregory A. Jacobs

SENIOR ATTORNEY

Judith M. Woo

For Complete List of Firm Personnel, See General Section

For full biographical listings, see the Martindale-Hubbell Law Directory

VORYS, SATER, SEYMOUR AND PEASE (AV)

2100 One Cleveland Center, 1375 East Ninth Street, 44114
Telephone: 216-479-6100
Telecopier: 216-479-6060
Columbus, Ohio Office: 52 East Gay Street, P.O. Box 1008, 43216-1008.
Telephone: 614-464-6400.
Telex: 241348.
Telecopier: 614-464-6350.
Cable Address: "Vorysater".
Cincinnati, Ohio Office: Suite 2100, 221 East Fourth Street, P.O. Box 0236, 45201-0236.
Telephone: 513-723-4000.
Telecopier: 513-723-4056.
Washington, D.C. Office: Suite 1111, 1828 L Street, N.W., 20036-5104.
Telephone: 202-467-8800.
Telex: 440693.
Telecopier: 202-467-8900.

MEMBER OF FIRM

Charles J. French, III

For Complete List of Firm Personnel, See General Section

For full biographical listings, see the Martindale-Hubbell Law Directory

WALTER & HAVERFIELD (AV)

1300 Terminal Tower, 44113-2253
Telephone: 216-781-1212
Telecopier: 216-575-0911
Columbus, Ohio Office: 88 East Broad Street.
Telephone: 614-221-7371.

MEMBERS OF FIRM

Robert T. Rosenfeld
Michael T. McMenamin
Marcia E. Hurt
Nancy A. Noall
Kenneth A. Zirm

ASSOCIATES

Patricia F. Weisberg
Jonathan D. Greenberg
Michael P. Harvey
R. Todd Hunt

Representative Clients: AGA Gas, Inc.; Air Products and Chemicals, Inc.; American Crane Corp.; Andrews Moving & Storage, Inc.; Applied Medical Technology, Inc.; Aribica Cafes, Inc.; Associated Aviation Underwriters; The Associated Press; Beverly Enterprises, Inc.; Brookfield Wire Company.

For Complete List of Firm Personnel, See General Section

For full biographical listings, see the Martindale-Hubbell Law Directory

*COLUMBUS,** Franklin Co.

* indicates certain Bar Register subscribers whose principal office is located elsewhere in the state and who have arranged for representation as a part of the state capital listings that follow

*** BAKER & HOSTETLER (AV)**

Capitol Square, Suite 2100, 65 East State Street, 43215-4260
Telephone: 614-228-1541
Telecopier: 614-462-2616
In Cleveland, Ohio: 3200 National City Center, 1900 East Ninth Street.
Telephone: 216-621-0200.
In Denver, Colorado: 303 East 17th Avenue, Suite 1100.
Telephone: 202-861-1500.
In Houston, Texas: 1000 Louisiana, Suite 2000.
Telephone: 713-751-1600.
In Long Beach, California: 300 Oceangate, Suite 620.
Telephone: 310-432-2827.
In Los Angeles, California: 600 Wilshire.
Telephone: 213-624-2400.
In Orlando, Florida: SunBank Center, Suite 2300, 200 South Orange Avenue.
Telephone: 407-649-4000.
In Washington, D. C.: Washington Square, Suite 1100, 1050 Connecticut Avenue, N.W.
Telephone: 202-861-1500.
In College Park, Maryland: 9658 Baltimore Boulevard, Suite 301.
Telephone: 301-441-2781.
In Alexandria, Virginia: 437 North Lee Street.
Telephone: 703-549-1294.

(See Next Column)

In San Francisco, California: One Sansome Street, Suite 2000.
Telephone: 415-951-4705.

PARTNERS

M.J. Asensio, III
Stephen J. Habash
Ronald G. Linville
W. Irl Reasoner, III
David M. Selcer

ASSOCIATES

R. Christopher Doyle
Ellen J. Garling

For Complete List of Firm Personnel, See General Section

For full biographical listings, see the Martindale-Hubbell Law Directory

*** BENESCH, FRIEDLANDER, COPLAN & ARONOFF (AV)**

88 East Broad Street, 43215-3506
Telephone: 614-223-9300
Telecopier: 614-223-9330
Cleveland, Ohio Office: 2300 BP American Building, 200 Public Square, 44114-2378.
Telephone: 216-363-4500.
Telecopier: 216-363-4588.
Cincinnati, Ohio Office: 2800 Cincinnati Commerce Center, 600 Vine Street, 45202-2409.
Telephone: 513-762-6200.
Telecopier: 513-762-6245.

MEMBER OF FIRM

N. Victor Goodman

For Complete List of Firm Personnel, See General Section

For full biographical listings, see the Martindale-Hubbell Law Directory

BRICKER & ECKLER (AV)

100 South Third Street, 43215-4291
Telephone: 614-227-2300
Telecopy: 614-227-2390
Cleveland, Ohio Office: 600 Superior Avenue East, Suite 800.
Telephone: 216-771-0720. Fax 216-771-7702.

Jerry E. Nathan
Donald R. Keller
Timothy J. Owens

Betsy A. Swift

Representative Clients: Nationwide Insurance Companies; CompuServe, Inc.; American Chemical Society; Robertshaw Controls Company; Columbus Board of Education; Ohio Hospital Association; City of Columbus; Health Care & Retirement Corporation of America; Cardinal Foods Inc.

For Complete List of Firm Personnel, See General Section

For full biographical listings, see the Martindale-Hubbell Law Directory

CLOPPERT, PORTMAN, SAUTER, LATANICK & FOLEY (AV)

225 East Broad Street, 43215-3709
Telephone: 614-461-4455
Fax: 614-461-0072
Portsmouth, Ohio Office: 812 6th Street.
Telephone: 614-354-2553.
Fax: 614-353-5293.

MEMBERS OF FIRM

Mark A. Foley
Frederick G. Cloppert, Jr.
Frederic A. Portman
David G. Latanick
Robert W. Sauter
Robert L. Washburn, Jr.
Walter J. Gerhardstein
Michael J. Hunter
Russell E. Carnahan
Grant D. Shoub
Susan Hayest Kozlowski
Charles J. Smith

William J. Steele
Nancy E. Leech
Debra D. Paxson

LEGAL SUPPORT PERSONNEL

Victoria L. Wythe

Reference: Bank One of Columbus, N.A.

For full biographical listings, see the Martindale-Hubbell Law Directory

EMENS, KEGLER, BROWN, HILL & RITTER (AV)

Capitol Square Suite 1800, 65 East State Street, 43215-4294
Telephone: 614-462-5400
Telecopier: 614-464-2634
Cable Address: "Law EKBHR"
Telex: 246671

Lawrence F. Feheley
Ronald L. Mason
Frank A. Titus

COUNSEL

Joseph M. Millious

(See Next Column)

EMENS, KEGLER, BROWN, HILL & RITTER, *Columbus—Continued*

Todd F. Palmer Timothy T. Tullis

Representative Clients: Associated Builders & Contractors, Inc.; Borden, Inc.; Columbus Metropolitan Housing Authority; Continental Airlines, Inc.; Diocese of Columbus; Farmers Insurance Group; The Fishel Co.; National Ground Water Association; Nationwise Automotive, Inc.; Patrick Petroleum Co.

For Complete List of Firm Personnel, See General Section

For full biographical listings, see the Martindale-Hubbell Law Directory

MILLISOR & NOBIL A LEGAL PROFESSIONAL ASSOCIATION (AV)

41 South High Street, 3737 Huntington Center, 43215-6101
Telephone: 614-224-1010
Telefax: 614-365-9411
Cleveland, Ohio Office: 9150 South Hills Boulevard, 44147-3599.
Telephone: 216-838-8800.
Telefax: 216-838-8805.

David P. Hiller John J. Krimm, Jr.
Preston J. Garvin Michael J. Hickey
Mark M. McCarthy

Labor Counsel for: Bridgestone/Firestone, Inc.; BF Goodrich Co.; Uniroyal-Goodrich Tire Co.; Cooper Industries; May Department Stores, Co. (Kaufmann's and Payless Shoe Source); Federated Department Stores (Lazarus); Union Metal Corp.; Ohio Automobile Dealers Assn.; Children's Hospital; Kent State University.

For full biographical listings, see the Martindale-Hubbell Law Directory

MOOTS, COPE & STANTON A LEGAL PROFESSIONAL ASSOCIATION (AV)

3600 Olentangy River Road, 43214-3913
Telephone: 614-459-4140
FAX: 614-459-4503

Philip R. Moots Jon M. Cope
Elizabeth M. Stanton

Wanda L. Carter Catherine A. Cunningham

OF COUNSEL

Benson A. Wolman

For full biographical listings, see the Martindale-Hubbell Law Directory

PORTER, WRIGHT, MORRIS & ARTHUR (AV)

41 South High Street, 43215-6194
Telephone: 614-227-2000; (800-533-2794)
Telex: 6503213584 MCI
Fax: 614-227-2100
Dayton, Ohio Office: One Dayton Centre, One South Main Street, 45402.
Telephones: 513-228-2411; (800-533-4434).
Fax: 513-449-6820.
Cincinnati, Ohio Office: 250 E. Fifth Street, 45202-4166.
Telephones: 513-381-4700; (800-582-5813).
Fax: 513-421-0991.
Cleveland, Ohio Office: 925 Euclid Avenue, 44115-1483.
Telephones: 216-443-9000; (800-824-1980).
Fax: 216-443-9011.
Washington, D.C. Office: 1233 20th Street, N.W., 20036-2395.
Telephones: 202-778-3000; (800-456-7962).
Fax: 202-778-3063.
Naples, Florida Office: 4501 Tamiami Trail North, 33940-3060.
Telephones: 813-263-8898;(800-876-7962).
Fax: 813-436-2990.

MEMBERS OF FIRM
COLUMBUS, OHIO OFFICE

Daniel A. Brown Fred G. Pressley, Jr.
Stuart M. Gordon Diane C. Reichwein
Brian D. Hall Bradd N. Siegel
David A. Laing Mark S. Stemm
Alvin J. McKenna John M. Stephen
D. Michael Miller Michael J. Underwood
Adele Ellen O'Conner Charles C. Warner
Franck G. Wobst

ASSOCIATES
COLUMBUS, OHIO OFFICE

Charles H. Cooper, Jr. Kevin E. Griffith
Christopher C. Russell

OF COUNSEL
COLUMBUS, OHIO OFFICE

Warren H. Morse

DAYTON, OHIO OFFICE
RESIDENT MEMBERS

John J. Heron Robert E. Portune
R. Bruce Snyder

(See Next Column)

CINCINNATI, OHIO OFFICE
RESIDENT ASSOCIATE

Duane A. Boggs

CLEVELAND, OHIO OFFICE
RESIDENT MEMBER

Terrance L. Ryan

CLEVELAND, OHIO OFFICE
RESIDENT ASSOCIATE

Robert G. Cohn

Representative Clients: American Electric Power, Inc; American Mobile Communications, Inc.; AT&T; Battelle Memorial Institute; The Huntington National Bank; Kroger Co.; The Longaberger Co.; Metropolitan Life Insurance Co.; Rockwell International; United Parcel Service.

For Complete List of Firm Personnel, See General Section

For full biographical listings, see the Martindale-Hubbell Law Directory

SCHOTTENSTEIN, ZOX & DUNN A LEGAL PROFESSIONAL ASSOCIATION (AV)

The Huntington Center, 41 South High Street, 43215
Telephone: 614-221-3211
Telecopier: 614-464-1135
Telex: 650 24 444 365

James M. L. Ferber James E. Davidson
Robert D. Weisman David A. Kadela
Felix C. Wade Susan Porter

Corey V. Crognale Robert M. Robenalt
William J. Barath Michael A. Womack
Marie-Joëlle C. Khouzam

Reference: Bank One of Columbus, N.A.

For Complete List of Firm Personnel, See General Section

For full biographical listings, see the Martindale-Hubbell Law Directory

*** THOMPSON, HINE AND FLORY (AV)**

One Columbus, 10 West Broad Street, 43215-3435
Telephone: 614-469-3200
Fax: 614-469-3361
Akron, Ohio Office: 50 S. Main Street, Suite 502, 44308-1828.
Telephone: 216-376-8090.
Fax: 216-376-8386.
Cincinnati, Ohio Office: 312 Walnut Street, 14th Floor, 45202-4029.
Telephone: 513-352-6700.
Fax: 513-241-4771.
Telex: 938003.
Cleveland, Ohio Office: 1100 National City Bank Building, 629 Euclid Avenue, 44114-3070.
Telephone: 216-566-5500.
Fax: 216-556-5583.
Telex: 980217.
Cable Address: "Thomflor".
Dayton, Ohio Office: 2000 Courthouse Plaza, N.E., 45402-1706.
Telephone: 513-443-6600.
Fax: 513-443-6637; 443-6635.
Palm Beach, Florida Office: 125 Worth Avenue, 33480-4466.
Telephone: 407-833-5900.
Fax: 407-833-5951.
Washington, D.C. Office: 1920 N Street, N.W., 20036-1601.
Telephone: 202-331-8800.
Fax: 202-331-8330.
Telex: 904173.
Cable Address: "Caglaw".
Brussels, Belgium Office: Rue des Chevaliers / Ridderstraat 14 - B.10, B - 1050.
Telephone: 011(32-2) 511-9326.
Fax: 011(32-2) 513-9206.

MEMBERS OF FIRM

William C. Moul Janis B. Rosenthal

ASSOCIATE

Helen Mac Murray

SENIOR ATTORNEY

Philip B. Cochran

For Complete List of Firm Personnel, See General Section

For full biographical listings, see the Martindale-Hubbell Law Directory

Columbus—Continued

VORYS, SATER, SEYMOUR AND PEASE (AV)

52 East Gay Street, P.O. Box 1008, 43216-1008
Telephone: 614-464-6400
Telex: 241348
Telecopier: 614-464-6350
Cable Address: "Vorysater"
Washington, D.C. Office: Suite 1111, 1828 L Street, N.W., 20036-5104.
Telephone: 202-467-8800.
Telex: 440693.
Telecopier: 202-467-8900.
Cleveland, Ohio Office: 2100 One Cleveland Center, 1375 East Ninth Street, 44114-1724.
Telephone: 216-479-6100.
Telecopier: 216-479-6060.
Cincinnati, Ohio Office: Suite 2100, 221 East Fourth Street, P.O. Box 0236, 45201-0236.
Telephone: 513-723-4000.
Telecopier: 513-723-4056.

MEMBERS OF FIRM

Lester S. Lash
James P. Friedt
Thomas M. Tarpy
G. Ross Bridgman
Robert A. Minor
Jonathan M. Norman
Nanci L. Danison
John W. Wilmer, Jr. (Resident, Washington, D.C. Office)
Chris J. North
Jonathan R. Vaughn
Andrew C. Smith

Bradley K. Sinnott
Allen S. Kinzer
Bradley A. Smith
Richard T. Miller

OF COUNSEL

Charles D. Minor
Anne C. Griffin

Local Counsel: Anheuser-Busch, Inc.; General Motors Corp.; The Kroger Co.; Ohio Manufacturers Assn.; Ranco Inc.; Liebert Corp.; Big Bear Stores Co.; Asahi Glass; Worthington Industries, Inc.; Honda of America Mfg., Inc.

For Complete List of Firm Personnel, See General Section

For full biographical listings, see the Martindale-Hubbell Law Directory

*DAYTON,** Montgomery Co.

LOGOTHETIS & PENCE (AV)

Suite 1100, 111 West First Street, 45402-1156
Telephone: 513-461-5310
Fax: 513-461-7219
Cincinnati, Ohio Office: 1300 Gwynne Building, 602 Main Street.
Telephone: 513-651-0559.

MEMBERS OF FIRM

Sorrell Logothetis
Bruce E. Pence
John R. Doll

ASSOCIATES

Susan D. Jansen
Julie C. Ford

OF COUNSEL

Thomas F. Phalen, Jr. (Manager, Cincinnati, Ohio Office)

Reference: National City Bank.

For full biographical listings, see the Martindale-Hubbell Law Directory

PICKREL, SCHAEFFER & EBELING CO., L.P.A. (AV)

2700 Kettering Tower, 45423-2700
Telephone: 513-223-1130
Facsimile: 513-223-0339

Thomas J. Harrington
Richard J. Holzer
Janet K. Cooper
David C. Korte

Mary M. Biagioli

Representative Clients: Appleton Paper; E.G. and G.; Archdiocese of Cincinnati; Dayton Board of Education; Kettering Board of Education; City of Englewood; Sinclair Community College; Marathon Oil; American Aggregates; Miami Valley Cardiologists.

For Complete List of Firm Personnel, See General Section

For full biographical listings, see the Martindale-Hubbell Law Directory

SEBALY, SHILLITO & DYER (AV)

1300 Courthouse Plaza, NE, P.O. Box 220, 45402-0220
Telephone: 513-222-2500
Telefax: 513-222-6554; 222-8279
Springfield, Ohio Office: National City Bank Building, 4 West Main Street, Suite 530, P.O. Box 1346, 45501-1346.
Telephone: 513-325-7878.
Telefax: 513-325-6151.

(See Next Column)

MEMBERS OF FIRM

James A. Dyer
Gale S. Finley
William W. Lambert
Michael P. Moloney
Mary Lynn Readey
Jon M. Sebaly
Beverly F. Shillito
Jeffrey B. Shulman
Karl R. Ulrich
Robert A. Vaughn (Resident, Springfield Office)

Martin A. Beyer
Daniel A. Brown
Anne L. Rhoades
Orly R. Rumberg
Juliana M. Spaeth
Kendra F. Thompson

For full biographical listings, see the Martindale-Hubbell Law Directory

THOMPSON, HINE AND FLORY (AV)

2000 Courthouse Plaza, N.E., 45402-1706
Telephone: 513-443-6600
Fax: 513-443-6637; 443-6635
Akron, Ohio Office: 50 S. Main Street, Suite 502, 44308-1828.
Telephone: 216-376-8090.
Fax: 216-376-8386.
Cincinnati, Ohio Office: 312 Walnut Street, 14th Floor, 45202-4029.
Telephone: 513-352-6700.
Fax: 513-241-4771.
Telex: 938003.
Cleveland, Ohio Office: 1100 National City Bank Building, 629 Euclid Avenue, 44114-3070.
Telephone: 216-566-5500.
Fax: 216-556-5583.
Telex: 980217.
Cable Address: "Thomflor".
Columbus, Ohio Office: One Columbus, 10 West Broad Street, 43215-3435.
Telephone: 614-469-3200.
Fax: 614-469-3361.
Palm Beach, Florida Office: 125 Worth Avenue, 33480-4466.
Telephone: 407-833-5900.
Fax: 407-833-5951.
Washington, D.C. Office: 1920 N Street, N.W., 20036-1601.
Telephone: 202-331-8800.
Fax: 202-331-8330.
Telex: 904173.
Cable Address: "Caglaw".
Brussels, Belgium Office: Rue des Chevaliers / Ridderstraat 14 - B.10, B - 1050.
Telephone: 011(32-2) 511-9326.
Fax: 011(32-2) 513-9206.

MEMBER OF FIRM

Robert J. Brown

ASSOCIATE

Teresa D. Jones

For Complete List of Firm Personnel, See General Section

For full biographical listings, see the Martindale-Hubbell Law Directory

*TOLEDO,** Lucas Co.

ROBERT M. ANSPACH ASSOCIATES (AV)

Suite 2100, 405 Madison Avenue, 43604-1236
Telephone: 419-246-5757
FAX: 419-321-6979

Robert M. Anspach
Stephen R. Serraino
Catherine G. Hoolahan
Mark D. Meeks
J. Roy Nunn
Paul F. Burtis

ASSOCIATES

Barry Y. Freeman
L. Nathalie Hiemstra

For full biographical listings, see the Martindale-Hubbell Law Directory

EASTMAN & SMITH (AV)

One Seagate, Twenty-Fourth Floor, 43604
Telephone: 419-241-6000
Telecopier: 419-247-1777
Columbus, Ohio Office: 65 East State Street, Suite 1000, 43215.
Telephone: 614-460-3556.
Telecopier: 614-228-5371.

MEMBERS OF FIRM

Patrick J. Johnson
John T. Landwehr
Robert J. Gilmer, Jr.
Thomas A. Dixon
Thomas J. Gibney

ASSOCIATES

Kimberly S. Stepleton
Michael J. Niedzielski

Counsel for: Chrysler Corp.; Roadway Express, Inc.; Dana Corp.; A P Parts Co.; City of Wauseon; Fayette Tubular Products, Inc.; Fulton Industries; Ludlow Composites Corp.; Coulton Chemical Co., L.P.

For Complete List of Firm Personnel, See General Section

For full biographical listings, see the Martindale-Hubbell Law Directory

Toledo—Continued

FULLER & HENRY (AV)

One Seagate Suite 1700, P.O. Box 2088, 43603-2088
Telephone: 419-247-2500
Telecopier: 419-247-2665
Port Clinton, Ohio Office: 125 Jefferson.
Telephone: 419-734-2153.
Telecopier: 419-732-8246.
Columbus, Ohio Office: 2210 Huntington Center, 41 South High Street.
Telephone: 614-228-6611.
Telecopier: 614-228-6623.

MEMBERS OF FIRM

Charles R. Leech, Jr. — Stephen J. Stanford
Raymond G. Esch — John J. Siciliano
Mary Ann Whipple

COUNSEL

Warren D. Wolfe

ASSOCIATES

Scott G. Deller — James B. Yates

Representative Clients: Owens-Illinois, Inc.; Campbell Soup Company; The Toledo Blade Company; Glass Container Industrial Relations Council; Savannah Foods & Industries, Inc.; Harris Corporation; Hunt-Wesson, Inc.; Dentsply International, Inc.; BP Oil Company; G.M.P.-Employers Retiree Trust.

For Complete List of Firm Personnel, See General Section

For full biographical listings, see the Martindale-Hubbell Law Directory

LACKEY, NUSBAUM, HARRIS, RENY & TORZEWSKI A LEGAL PROFESSIONAL ASSOCIATION (AV)

Two Maritime Plaza Third Floor, 43604
Telephone: 419-243-1105
Fax: 419-243-8953

Joan Torzewski — John D. Franklin

References: Fifth Third Bank; Society Bank.

For full biographical listings, see the Martindale-Hubbell Law Directory

SCHNORF & SCHNORF CO., L.P.A. A PROFESSIONAL CORPORATION (AV)

1400 National City Bank Building, 405 Madison Avenue, 43604
Telephone: 419-248-2646
Facsimile: 419-248-2889

David M. Schnorf — Barry F. Hudgin

Representative Clients: American Federation of Teachers, AFL-CIO; Ohio Federation of Teachers, AFL-CIO; Toledo Federation of Teachers, AFL-CIO.

For Complete List of Firm Personnel, See General Section

For full biographical listings, see the Martindale-Hubbell Law Directory

SPENGLER NATHANSON (AV)

608 Madison Avenue, Suite 1000, 43604-1169
Telephone: 419-241-2201
FAX: 419-241-8599

MEMBERS OF FIRM

Frank T. Pizza — Cheryl F. Wolff
B. Gary McBride — James M. Sciarini
Theodore M. Rowen — Susan B. Nelson
Ward Summerville — Lisa E. Pizza

Counsel for: Seaway Food Town, Inc.; The University of Toledo; Toledo Board of Education; Washington Local Board of Education; Toledo-Lucas County Port Authority; Fifth-Third Bank of Northwestern Ohio, N.A.; Sun Refining and Marketing; Ottawa County; City of Perrysburg; Toledo Metropolitan Park District.

For Complete List of Firm Personnel, See General Section

For full biographical listings, see the Martindale-Hubbell Law Directory

OKLAHOMA

*OKLAHOMA CITY,** Oklahoma Co.

ANDREWS DAVIS LEGG BIXLER MILSTEN & PRICE, A PROFESSIONAL CORPORATION (AV)

500 West Main, 73102
Telephone: 405-272-9241
FAX: 405-235-8786

(See Next Column)

Mona S. Lambird — R. Brown Wallace
William D. Watts

OF COUNSEL

Carolyn Gregg Hill

Representative Clients: Marathon Oil Co.; USF&G; Kerr McGee Corp.; Local Federal Bank, N.A.; Globe Life & Accident Insurance Co.; Panhandle Telephone Cooperative, Inc.; Martinaire of Oklahoma, Inc.; Southwestern Bell Telephone Co.

For Complete List of Firm Personnel, See General Section

For full biographical listings, see the Martindale-Hubbell Law Directory

CROWE & DUNLEVY, A PROFESSIONAL CORPORATION (AV)

1800 Mid-America Tower, 20 North Broadway, 73102-8273
Telephone: 405-235-7700
Fax: 405-239-6651
Tulsa, Oklahoma Office: Crowe & Dunlevy, 500 Kennedy Building, 321 South Boston.
Telephone: 918-592-9800.
Fax: 918-592-9801.
Norman, Oklahoma Office: Crowe & Dunlevy, Luttrell, Pendarvis & Rawlinson, 104 East Eufaula Street.
Telephone: 405-321-7317.
Fax: 405-360-4002.

L. E. Stringer — Leonard Court
James L. Hall, Jr. — Marie Weston Evans
Arlen E. Fielden — Gayle L. Barrett

Peggy L. Clay — Dana M. Tacker
Joel S. Allen

For Complete List of Firm Personnel, See General Section

For full biographical listings, see the Martindale-Hubbell Law Directory

DAY, EDWARDS, FEDERMAN, PROPESTER & CHRISTENSEN, P.C. (AV)

Suite 2900 First Oklahoma Tower, 210 Park Avenue, 73102-5605
Telephone: 405-239-2121
Telecopier: 405-236-1012

Bruce W. Day — J. Clay Christensen
Joe E. Edwards — Kent A. Gilliland
William B. Federman — Rodney J. Heggy
Richard P. Propester — Ricki Valerie Sonders
D. Wade Christensen — Thomas Pitchlynn Howell, IV
John C. Platt

David R. Widdoes — Lori R. Roberts
Carolyn A. Romberg

OF COUNSEL

Herbert F. (Jack) Hewett — Joel Warren Harmon
Jeanette Cook Timmons — Jane S. Eulberg
Mark A. Cohen

Representative Clients: Aetna Life Insurance Co.; Boatmen's First National Bank of Oklahoma; Borg-Warner Chemicals, Inc.; City Bank & Trust; Federal Deposit Insurance Corp.; Bank One, Oklahoma City; Haskell Lemon Construction Co.; Merrill Lynch, Pierce, Fenner & Smith, Inc.; Prudential Securities, Inc.

For full biographical listings, see the Martindale-Hubbell Law Directory

HARTZOG CONGER & CASON, A PROFESSIONAL CORPORATION (AV)

1600 Bank of Oklahoma Plaza, 73102
Telephone: 405-235-7000
Facsimile: 405-235-7329

Larry D. Hartzog — Valerie K. Couch
J. William Conger — Mark D. Dickey
Len Cason — Joseph P. Hogsett
James C. Prince — John D. Robertson
Alan Newman — Kurt M. Rupert
Steven C. Davis — Laura Haag McConnell

Susan B. Shields — Armand Paliotta
Ryan S. Wilson — Julia Watson
Melanie J. Jester — J. Leslie LaReau

OF COUNSEL

Kent F. Frates

For full biographical listings, see the Martindale-Hubbell Law Directory

Oklahoma City—Continued

McCaffrey & Tawwater (AV)

Bank of Oklahoma Plaza, Suite 1100 201 Robert S. Kerr Avenue, 73102
Telephone: 405-235-2900
Fax: 405-235-4932
Other Oklahoma City, Oklahoma Offices: Suite 1950, One Leadership Square, 211 North Robinson.

MEMBERS OF FIRM

George J. McCaffrey
Larry A. Tawwater

ASSOCIATES

Robert M. Behlen
Charles L. Cashion
Jo Lynn Slama
Gloria E. Trout
Loren F. Gibson
David Little
Steven R. Davis
Piper E. Mills

For full biographical listings, see the Martindale-Hubbell Law Directory

Oldfield & Coker (AV)

4808 North Classen Boulevard, 73118
Telephone: 405-840-0555
Fax: 405-840-4808

MEMBERS OF FIRM

John S. Oldfield, Jr.
Michael G. Coker

ASSOCIATES

Rose M. J. Sloan
Matthew J. Graves

Representative Clients: CNA Insurance; Bunte Candies, Inc.; Nationwide Insurance Co.; Fine Candy Co.
Reference: Liberty Bank & Trust Co., Oklahoma City, Okla.

For full biographical listings, see the Martindale-Hubbell Law Directory

*TULSA,** Tulsa Co.

Doerner, Stuart, Saunders, Daniel & Anderson (AV)

Suite 500, 320 South Boston Avenue, 74103-3725
Telephone: 918-582-1211
FAX: 918-591-5360

MEMBERS OF FIRM

C. B. Stuart (1857-1936)
Erwin J. Doerner (1897-1980)
Samuel P. Daniel
William C. Anderson
Varley H. Taylor, Jr.
G. Michael Lewis
William B. Morgan
Lawrence T. Chambers, Jr.
Dallas E. Ferguson
Sam G. Bratton, II
Gary M. McDonald
H. Wayne Cooper
Kevin C. Coutant
Richard P. Hix
Lynn Paul Mattson
William F. Riggs
Lewis N. Carter
Linda Crook Martin
James Patrick McCann
Richard H. Foster
Charles S. Plumb
Leonard I. Pataki
S. Douglas Dodd
Elise Dunitz Brennan
Kathy R. Neal
John J. Carwile
Jon E. Brightmire
L. Dru McQueen
Tom Q. Ferguson

ASSOCIATES

Richard J. Eagleton
Rebecca McCarthy Fowler
Kristen L. Brightmire
Michael C. Redman
Steven K. Metcalf
Benjamin J. Chapman
R. Michael Cole
David B. Auer
Shelly L. Dalrymple
Russell W. Kroll
John R. Pinkerton
Robert A. Burk

OF COUNSEL

Dickson M. Saunders
R. Robert Huff

Representative Clients: Public Service Company of Oklahoma; Burlington Northern Railroad Co.; Atlas Life Insurance Co.; Minnehoma Insurance Co.; Oklahoma Ordnance Works Authority & KYRI Corp.; Sand Springs Railway Co.; St. John Medical Center, Inc.

For full biographical listings, see the Martindale-Hubbell Law Directory

Gable & Gotwals (AV)

2000 Bank IV Center, 15 West Sixth Street, 74119-5447
Telephone: 918-582-9201
Facsimile: 918-586-8383

Teresa B. Adwan
Pamela S. Anderson
John R. Barker
David L. Bryant
Gene C. Buzzard
Dennis Clarke Cameron
Timothy A. Carney
Renee DeMoss
Elsie C. Draper
Sidney G. Dunagan
Theodore Q. Eliot
Richard W. Gable
Jeffrey Don Hassell
Patricia Ledvina Himes
Oliver S. Howard
Richard D. Koljack, Jr.
J. Daniel Morgan
Joseph W. Morris
Elizabeth R. Muratet
Richard B. Noulles
Ronald N. Ricketts
John Henry Rule
M. Benjamin Singletary
James M. Sturdivant
Patrick O. Waddel
Michael D. Hall

(See Next Column)

David Edward Keglovits
Stephen W. Lake
Kari S. McKee
Terry D. Ragsdale
Jeffrey C. Rambach

OF COUNSEL

G. Ellis Gable
Charles P. Gotwals, Jr.

For full biographical listings, see the Martindale-Hubbell Law Directory

McGivern, Scott, Gilliard, Curthoys & Robinson (AV)

Legal Arts Building, 1515 S. Boulder, 74119
Telephone: 918-584-3391
Fax: 918-592-2416

Paul V. McGivern, Jr., (A Prof. Corp.)
David R. Scott
Michael Dee Gilliard
Eugene Robinson
Karen McGivern Curthoys

Riki R. Lamb
R. Jay McAtee
Ronald E. Hignight
John Brian Des Barres
Bradley A. Jackson

Reference: Bank IV of Tulsa.

For full biographical listings, see the Martindale-Hubbell Law Directory

Shipley, Inhofe & Strecker (AV)

Suite 3600 First National Tower, 15 East Fifth Street, 74103-4307
Telephone: 918-582-1720
FAX: 918-584-7681

MEMBERS OF FIRM

Charles W. Shipley
Douglas L. Inhofe
David E. Strecker
Mark B. Jennings
Blake K. Champlin

ASSOCIATES

Leslie C. Rinn
Jamie Taylor Boyd
Connie L. Kirkland
Mark Alston Waller

Reference: Western National Bank, Tulsa.

For full biographical listings, see the Martindale-Hubbell Law Directory

Ungerman & Iola (AV)

Riverbridge Office Park, 1323 East 71st Street, Suite 300, P.O. Box 701917, 74170-1917
Telephone: 918-495-0550
Fax: 918-495-0561

MEMBERS OF FIRM

Irvine E. Ungerman (1908-1980)
Maynard I. Ungerman
Mark H. Iola

ASSOCIATE

Randall L. Iola

Representative Client: Northeastern Oklahoma Building and Construction Trades Council.

For full biographical listings, see the Martindale-Hubbell Law Directory

OREGON

*PORTLAND,** Multnomah Co.

Cooney & Crew, P.C. (AV)

Pioneer Tower, Suite 890, 888 S.W. Fifth Avenue, 97204
Telephone: 503-224-7600
FAX: 503-224-6740

Paul A. Cooney
Thomas E. Cooney
Thomas M. Cooney
Brent M. Crew
Michael D. Crew
Kelly T. Hagan
Raymond F. Mensing, Jr.
Robert S. Perkins

LEGAL SUPPORT PERSONNEL

Alma Weber (Paralegal)

For full biographical listings, see the Martindale-Hubbell Law Directory

Lane Powell Spears Lubersky (AV)

520 S.W. Yamhill Street, Suite 800, 97204-1383
Telephone: 503-226-6151
Telecopier: 224-0388
Other Offices at: Seattle, Mount Vernon and Olympia, Washington; Los Angeles and San Francisco, California; Anchorage, Alaska; London, England.

(See Next Column)

LANE POWELL SPEARS LUBERSKY, *Portland—Continued*

MEMBERS OF FIRM

Nelson D. Atkin II
Richard F. Liebman
Paula A. Barran
Mark M. Loomis
C. Akin Blitz
William F. Lubersky
Edwin A. Harnden
Lewis K. Scott
Michael G. Holmes
Leigh D. Stephenson
Richard C. Hunt
John C. Stevason
Richard N. Van Cleave

ASSOCIATES

Nancy J. Brown
Monique S. Matheson
Scott Joseph Fortmann
John C. Walsh

For Complete List of Firm Personnel, See General Section

For full biographical listings, see the Martindale-Hubbell Law Directory

MILLER, NASH, WIENER, HAGER & CARLSEN (AV)

111 S.W. Fifth Avenue, 97204-3699
Telephone: 503-224-5858
Telex: 364462, Kingmar PTL
Facsimile: 503-224-0155, 503-224-2450
Seattle, Washington Office: 4400 Two Union Square, 601 Union Street, 98101-2322.
Telephone: 206-622-8484.
Facsimile: 206-622-7485.

PORTLAND, OREGON PARTNERS

Donald A. Burns
Louis B. Livingston
Donna M. Cameron
Linda L. Marshall
Brian B. Doherty
James B. Ruyle
Maureen R. Sloane

SEATTLE, WASHINGTON PARTNERS

James R. Dickens
Francis L. Van Dusen, Jr.

PORTLAND, OREGON ASSOCIATES

Victoria Lee Rudometkin
Sharon L. Toncray

SEATTLE, WASHINGTON ASSOCIATE

James W. Allen

Representative Clients: U. S. Bancorp; United States National Bank of Oregon; Louisiana-Pacific Corp.; Willamette Industries, Inc.; Portland Public Schools; St. Vincent Hospital and Medical Center; Merrill Lynch, Pierce, Fenner & Smith, Inc.

For Complete List of Firm Personnel, See General Section

For full biographical listings, see the Martindale-Hubbell Law Directory

O'DONNELL, RAMIS, CREW, CORRIGAN & BACHRACH (AV)

Ballow & Wright Building, 1727 N.W. Hoyt Street, 97209
Telephone: 503-222-4402
FAX: 503-243-2944
Clackamas County Office: Suite 202, 181 N. Grant, Canby.
Telephone: 503-266-1149.

MEMBERS OF FIRM

Mark P. O'Donnell
Stephen F. Crew
Timothy V. Ramis
Charles E. Corrigan
Jeff H. Bachrach

SPECIAL COUNSEL

James M. Coleman

ASSOCIATES

Pamela J. Beery
G. Frank Hammond
Mark L. Busch
William A. Monahan
Gary Firestone
William J. Stalnaker
Ty K. Wyman

LEGAL SUPPORT PERSONNEL

Margaret M. Daly
G. William Selzer
Mary C. Meyers
Dawna S. Shattuck
Laurel L. Ramsey
(Legal Assistant)

For full biographical listings, see the Martindale-Hubbell Law Directory

PENNSYLVANIA

ELKINS PARK, Montgomery Co.

MONAGHAN & GOLD, P.C. (AV)

7837 Old York Road, 19027
Telephone: 215-782-1800
Fax: 215-782-1010

John F. X. Monaghan, Jr.
Alan Steven Gold

(See Next Column)

Brian E. Appel
Barbara Malett Weitz
Murray R. Glickman
Tanya M. Sweet

*ERIE,** Erie Co.

ELDERKIN, MARTIN, KELLY & MESSINA, P.C. (AV)

Jones School Square, 150 East Eighth Street, P.O. Box 1819, 16507-0819
Telephone: 814-456-4000
FAX: 814-454-7411

Harry D. Martin
Thomas J. Minarcik
William J. Kelly
Gery T. Nietupski
Joseph T. Messina
Elizabeth K. Kelly
Kenneth G. Vasil
Evan C. Rudert
James H. Richardson, Jr.
Edward J. Betza
Ronald L. Slater
James F. Geronimo
John B. Enders
Craig A. Zonna
Robert C. LeSuer
Michael T. Reynolds
Craig A. Markham
William J. Kelly, Jr.

OF COUNSEL

Vernon H. Elderkin, Jr.

Representative Clients: Commonwealth Land Title Insurance Co.; Times Publishing Co.; Integra Bank/North; Gannon University; Sears, Roebuck & Co.; Waste Management, Inc.; Allstate Insurance Co.; State Farm Fire and Casualty Co.; Autoclave Engineers, Inc.

For Complete List of Firm Personnel, See General Section

For full biographical listings, see the Martindale-Hubbell Law Directory

*HARRISBURG,** Dauphin Co.

BECKLEY & MADDEN (AV)

Cranberry Court, 212 North Third Street, P.O. Box 11998, 17108
Telephone: 717-233-7691
FAX: 717-233-3740

MEMBERS OF FIRM

Thomas A. Beckley
John G. Milakovic

ASSOCIATE

Charles O. Beckley, II

For full biographical listings, see the Martindale-Hubbell Law Directory

BOSWELL, SNYDER, TINTNER & PICCOLA (AV)

315 North Front Street, P.O. Box 741, 17108-0741
Telephone: 717-236-9377
Telecopier: 717-236-9316

MEMBERS OF FIRM

William D. Boswell
Jeffrey R. Boswell
Donn L. Snyder
Brigid Q. Alford
Leonard Tintner
Mark R. Parthemer
Jeffrey E. Piccola
Charles J. Hartwell

OF COUNSEL

Richard B. Wickersham

Representative Clients: Conley Frog & Switch Co.; Borough of Camp Hill; Capitol Area Transit; Dauphin County; Perry County; Susquehanna Township; United Restaurant Equipment; West Shore Country Club.

For full biographical listings, see the Martindale-Hubbell Law Directory

BUCHANAN INGERSOLL, PROFESSIONAL CORPORATION (AV)

Vartan Parc, 30 North Third Street, 17101
Telephone: 717-237-4800
Telecopier: 717-233-0852
Pittsburgh, Pennsylvania Office: 5800 USX Tower, 600 Grant Street.
Telephone: 412-562-8800.
Philadelphia, Pennsylvania Office: Two Logan Square, Twelfth Floor, 18th & Arch Streets.
Telephone: 215-665-8700.
Tampa, Florida Office: 101 East Kennedy Boulevard, Suite 1030.
Telephone: 813-222-8180.
North Miami Beach, Florida Office: 19495 Biscayne Boulevard.
Telephone: 305-933-5600.
Lexington, Kentucky Office: 1210 Vine Center Office Tower, 333 West Vine Street.
Telephone: 606-225-5333.
Princeton, New Jersey Office: Buchanan Ingersoll, A Partnership, College Centre, 500 College Road East.
Telephone: 609-452-2666.

John R. Johnson

SENIOR ATTORNEY

Kathryn Speaker MacNett

Samuel M. First

For Complete List of Firm Personnel, See General Section

For full biographical listings, see the Martindale-Hubbell Law Directory

Harrisburg—Continued

KILLIAN & GEPHART (AV)

218 Pine Street, P.O. Box 886, 17108
Telephone: 717-232-1851
Telecopier: 717-238-0592

MEMBERS OF FIRM

John D. Killian
Thomas W. Scott
Jane Penny Malatesta
Ronda K. Kiser

ASSOCIATE

J. Paul Helvy

Reference: Dauphin Deposit Bank & Trust Co.

For full biographical listings, see the Martindale-Hubbell Law Directory

MCNEES, WALLACE & NURICK (AV)

100 Pine Street, P.O. Box 1166, 17108
Telephone: 717-232-8000
Fax: 717-237-5300

MEMBERS OF FIRM

Bruce D. Bagley
Norman I. White

ASSOCIATES

Eric N. Athey
Robert J. Goduto
Robert G. Haas
Brian F. Jackson
Catherine E. Walters

For Complete List of Firm Personnel, See General Section

For full biographical listings, see the Martindale-Hubbell Law Directory

THOMAS, THOMAS & HAFER (AV)

305 North Front Street, 6th Floor, P.O. Box 999, 17108
Telephone: 717-237-7100
Fax: 717-237-7105
Verify: 717-255-7642

MEMBERS OF FIRM

Joseph P. Hafer
James K. Thomas, II
Jeffrey B. Rettig
Peter J. Curry
R. Burke McLemore, Jr.
Edward H. Jordan, Jr.
C. Kent Price
Randall G. Gale
David L. Schwalm
Kevin E. Osborne
Douglas B. Marcello
Peter J. Speaker
Paul J. Dellasega

OF COUNSEL

James K. Thomas

Daniel J. Gallagher
Robert A. Taylor
Sarah W. Arosell
Eugene N. McHugh
Richard C. Seneca
Stephen E. Geduldig
Paula Gayle Sanders
Karen S. Coates
Ann F. DePaulis
Margaret A. Scheaffer
Todd R. Narvol

Representative Clients: Aetna Casualty & Surety Co.; Bethlehem Steel Corp.; Commercial Union Insurance Companies; Geisinger Medical Center; Hartford Insurance Group; Liberty Mutual Insurance Co.; Pennsylvania Hospital Insurance Co.; Roadway Services, Inc.; UGI Corp.; Weis Markets, Inc.;

For full biographical listings, see the Martindale-Hubbell Law Directory

LANSDALE, Montgomery Co.

PEARLSTINE/SALKIN ASSOCIATES (AV)

1250 South Broad Street Suite 1000, P.O. Box 431, 19446
Telephone: 215-699-6000
Fax: 215-699-0231

MEMBERS OF FIRM

Philip Salkin
Ronald E. Robinson
Barry Cooperberg
Frederick C. Horn
Marc B. Davis
William R. Wanger
F. Craig La Rocca
Jeffrey T. Sultanik
Neal R. Pearlstine
Wendy G. Rothstein
Alan L. Eisen
Glenn D. Fox

Wilhelm L. Gruszecki
Brian E. Subers
Mark S. Cappuccio
James R. Hall
Michael S. Paul
David J. Draganosky
Lawrence P. Kempner

For full biographical listings, see the Martindale-Hubbell Law Directory

*MEDIA,** Delaware Co.

FRONEFIELD AND DE FURIA (AV)

107 West Third Street, P.O. Box 647, 19063
Telephone: 610-565-3100
Fax: 610-565-2349

(See Next Column)

MEMBERS OF FIRM

Frank I. Ginsburg
Rosemary C. McMunigal
F. Martin Duus
Charles F. Knapp
John R. Larkin
J. Joseph Herring, Jr.
Bruce A. Irvine
Leo A. Hackett
Francis T. Sbandi

ASSOCIATES

David C. Corujo
Jane E. Mcnerney
Donna Lynn Coyne

OF COUNSEL

Albert E. Holl, Jr.

For full biographical listings, see the Martindale-Hubbell Law Directory

KASSAB ARCHBOLD JACKSON & O'BRIEN (AV)

Lawyers-Title Building, 214 North Jackson Street, P.O. Box 626, 19063
Telephone: 610-565-3800
Telecopier: 610-892-6888
Wilmington, Delaware Office: 1326 King Street.
Telephone: 302-656-3393.
Fax: 302-656-1993.
Wildwood, New Jersey Office: 5201 New Jersey Avenue.
Telephone: 609-522-6559.

MEMBERS OF FIRM

Edward Kassab
William C. Archbold, Jr.
Robert James Jackson
Joseph Patrick O'Brien
Richard A. Stanko
Roy T. J. Stegena

OF COUNSEL

Matthew J. Ryan
John W. Nilon, Jr.

ASSOCIATES

Kevin William Gibson
Cynthia Kassab Larosa
Marc S. Stein
Terrance A. Kline
George C. McFarland, Jr.
Jill E. Aversa
Pamela A. La Torre
Kenneth D. Kynett

Representative Clients furnished upon request.

For full biographical listings, see the Martindale-Hubbell Law Directory

*PHILADELPHIA,** Philadelphia Co.

ANDERSON GREENFIELD & DOUGHERTY (AV)

1525 Penn Mutual Tower 510 Walnut Street, 19106-3610
Telephone: 215-627-0789
Fax: 215-627-0813
Wayne, Pennsylvania Office: First Fidelity Bank Building, 301 West Lancaster Avenue.
Telephone: 215-341-9010.

MEMBERS OF FIRM

Susan L. Anderson
Marjorie E. Greenfield
Donna Dougherty

ASSOCIATES

John Randolph Prince, III
Linda K. Hobkirk

For full biographical listings, see the Martindale-Hubbell Law Directory

BALLARD SPAHR ANDREWS & INGERSOLL (AV)

1735 Market Street, 51st Floor, 19103-7599
Telephone: 215-665-8500
Fax: 215-864-8999
Denver, Colorado Office: Seventeenth Street Plaza Building, Suite 2300, 1225 17th Street.
Telephone: 303-292-2400.
Fax: 303-296-3956.
Kaunas, Lithuania Office: Donelaicio g., 71-2, Kaunas 3000.
Telephone: (370-7) 20 56 66.
Fax: (370-7) 20 56 91.
Salt Lake City, Utah Office: One Utah Center, Suite 1200, 201 South Main Street.
Telephone: 801-531-3000.
Fax: 801-531-3001.
Washington, D.C. Office: Suite 900 East, 555 13th Street, N.W.
Telephone: 202-383-8800.
Fax: 202-383-8877; 383-8893.
Baltimore, Maryland Office: 300 East Lombard Street. 19th Floor.
Telephone: 410-528-5600.
Fax: 410-528-5650.
Camden, New Jersey Office: 800 Hudson Square, 5th Floor.
Telephone: 609-541-5577.
Fax: 609-541-8272.

John B. Langel
Maureen M. Rayborn
Charisse R. Lillie
Richard L. Strouse
Suzanne E. Turner

James H. Bocchinfuso
David S. Fryman
James Bucci
Brian D. Pedrow

For Complete List of Firm Personnel, See General Section

For full biographical listings, see the Martindale-Hubbell Law Directory

Philadelphia—Continued

BUCHANAN INGERSOLL, PROFESSIONAL CORPORATION (AV)

Two Logan Square Twelfth Floor, 18th & Arch Streets, 19103
Telephone: 215-665-8700
Telecopier: 215-569-2066
Pittsburgh, Pennsylvania Office: 5800 USX Tower, 600 Grant Street.
Telephone: 412-562-8800.
Harrisburg, Pennsylvania Office: Vartan Parc, 30 North Third Street.
Telephone: 717-237-4800.
Tampa, Florida Office: 101 East Kennedy Boulevard, Suite 1030.
Telephone: 813-222-8180.
North Miami Beach, Florida Office: 19495 Biscayne Boulevard.
Telephone: 305-933-5600.
Lexington, Kentucky Office: 1210 Vine Center Office Tower, 333 West Vine Street.
Telephone: 606-225-5333.
Princeton, New Jersey Office: Buchanan Ingersoll, A Partnership, College Centre, 500 College Road East.
Telephone: 609-452-2666.

SENIOR ATTORNEY

Mary Ellen Krober

For Complete List of Firm Personnel, See General Section

For full biographical listings, see the Martindale-Hubbell Law Directory

DUANE, MORRIS & HECKSCHER (AV)

Suite 4200 One Liberty Place, 19103-7396
Telephone: 215-979-1000
FAX: 215-979-1020
Harrisburg, Pennsylvania Office: 305 North Front Street, 5th Floor, P.O. Box 1003.
Telephone: 717-237-5500.
Fax: 717-232-4015.
Wilmington, Delaware Office: Suite 1500, 1201 Market Street.
Telephone: 302-571-5550.
Fax: 302-571-5560.
New York, N.Y. Office: 112 E. 42nd Street, Suite 2125.
Telephone: 212-499-0410.
Fax: 212-499-0420.
Wayne, Pennsylvania Office 735 Chesterbrook Boulevard, Suite 300.
Telephone: 610-647-3555.
Allentown, Pennsylvania Office: 968 Postal Road, Suite 200.
Telephone: 610-266-3650.
Fax: 610-640-2619.
Cherry Hill, New Jersey Office: 51 Haddonfield Road, Suite 340.
Telephone: 609-488-7300.
Fax: 609-488-7021.

MEMBERS OF FIRM

Frank L. White, Jr. (Resident, Wayne Office)
Jane Leslie Dalton
Edward M. Feege (Resident, Allentown, Office)
John S. Hayes (Resident, Allentown Office)
Bruce J. Kasten
Paul J. Schneider
Amy E. Wilkinson

ASSOCIATES

Thomas G. Servodidio
David L. Frank
Jeffrey M. Zimskind (Resident, Allentown Office)
John K. Baker (Resident, Allentown, Pennsylvania Office)
Nancy Conrad
Robert J. Bohner, Jr.
Deborah Tate Pecci
Linda Marie Doyle

For Complete List of Firm Personnel, See General Section

For full biographical listings, see the Martindale-Hubbell Law Directory

KITTREDGE, DONLEY, ELSON, FULLEM & EMBICK (AV)

Fifth Floor, The Bank Building, 421 Chestnut Street, 19106
Telephone: 215-829-9900
Fax: 215-829-9888

MEMBERS OF FIRM

Patrick W. Kittredge
Barry R. Elson
Joseph M. Donley
Joseph W. Fullem, Jr.
John R. Embick

ASSOCIATES

Regina M. Harbaugh
Patricia Powers
Glenn E. Davis
Daniel J. Maher
Betsy F. Sternthal
Susanne L. Longenhagen
Michael S. Soulé
Michael K. Smith
Gary M. Marek
Richard J. Sestak

For full biographical listings, see the Martindale-Hubbell Law Directory

KLEINBARD, BELL & BRECKER (AV)

Suite 700, 1900 Market Street, 19103
Telephone: 215-568-2000
Telecopier: 215-568-0140
TWX: 710-670-1345 KLEINBELBR
Cherry Hill, New Jersey Office: Building B, 102 Browning Lane, 08003.
Telephone: 609-783-4448.

MEMBERS OF FIRM

Arthur S. Keyser
Fred D. Furman
Paul E. Bomze
Howard J. Davis
Murray I. Blackman
Imogene E. Hughes
Howard N. Greenberg
John P. Hickey
Kevin M. McKenna

ASSOCIATES

Jay R. Goldstein
Ralph J. Mauro

COUNSEL

Joseph Bell
Robert John Brecker

For Complete List of Firm Personnel, See General Section

For full biographical listings, see the Martindale-Hubbell Law Directory

MAGER LIEBENBERG & WHITE (AV)

Two Penn Center, Suite 415, 19102
Telephone: 215-569-6921
Telecopier: 215-569-6931

MEMBERS OF FIRM

Carol A. Mager
Roberta D. Liebenberg
Ann D. White

ASSOCIATES

Matthew D. Baxter
Michael J. Salmanson
Brett M. L. Blyshak
W. Scott Magargee
Nancy F. DuBoise

OF COUNSEL

Anna M. Durbin

For full biographical listings, see the Martindale-Hubbell Law Directory

MERANZE AND KATZ (AV)

Twelfth Floor, Lewis Tower Building, N.E. Corner 15th & Locust Street, 19102-3977
Telephone: 215-546-4183
Fax: 215-790-1382

MEMBERS OF FIRM

Bernard N. Katz
Michael N. Katz

ASSOCIATES

Lynne Pava Fox
Elissa B. Katz
David A. Gaudioso

OF COUNSEL

Joseph B. Meranze
Marc E. Levitt
Michelle L. Janick
Ronald A. Kovler

For full biographical listings, see the Martindale-Hubbell Law Directory

NEIL A. MORRIS ASSOCIATES, P.C. (AV)

The Curtis Center, Suite 1100, Independence Square West 601 Walnut Street, 19106
Telephone: 215-923-0970
Telefax: 215-925-0218
Telex: 83-4201
Westmont, New Jersey Office: Sentry Office Plaza, 216 Haddon Avenue, Suite 500.
Telephone: 609-645-3993.
Telefax: 609-858-6707.

Neil A. Morris

Laurence L. Smith
Lloyd T. Hoppe, Jr.

LEGAL SUPPORT PERSONNEL

Jacqueline J. Simon

For full biographical listings, see the Martindale-Hubbell Law Directory

SAMUEL AND BALLARD, A PROFESSIONAL CORPORATION (AV)

225 South 15th Street, Suite 1700, 19102
Telephone: 215-893-9990

Ralph David Samuel
Alice W. Ballard

OF COUNSEL

Babette Josephs

Shari Reed
Lynn Malmgren

For full biographical listings, see the Martindale-Hubbell Law Directory

SCANLAN AND SCANLAN, A PROFESSIONAL CORPORATION (AV)

Suite 701, One Penn Square West, 30 South 15th Street, 19102
Telephone: 215-564-6399
Cable Address: "Scanlan"
Telecopier: 215-564-2242

Francis A. Scanlan
Francis X. Scanlan
Ricardo A. Byron

For full biographical listings, see the Martindale-Hubbell Law Directory

Philadelphia—Continued

SCHNADER, HARRISON, SEGAL & LEWIS (AV)

Suite 3600, 1600 Market Street, 19103
Telephone: 215-751-2000
Cable Address: "Walew"
Fax: 215-751-2205; 215-751-2313
Washington, D.C. Office: Suite 600, 1913 Eye Street, N.W.
Telephone: 202-463-2900.
Cable Address: "Dejuribus, Washington."
Fax: 202-296-8930; 202-775-8741.
New York, N.Y. Office: 330 Madison Avenue.
Telephone: 212-973-8000.
Cable Address: "Dejuribus, New York."
Fax: 212-972-8798.
Harrisburg, Pennsylvania: Suite 700, 30 North Third Street.
Telephone: 717-231-4000.
Fax: 717-231-4012.
Norristown, Pennsylvania Office: Suite 901, One Montgomery Plaza.
Telephone: 215-277-7700.
Fax: 215-277-3211.
Pittsburgh, Pennsylvania Office: Suite 2700, Fifth Avenue Place, 120 Fifth Avenue.
Telephone: 412-577-5200.
Fax: 412-765-3858.
Scranton, Pennsylvania Office: Suite 700, 108 North Washington Avenue.
Telephone: 717-342-6100.
Fax: 717-342-6147.
Washington, Pennsylvania Office: 8 East Pine Street.
Telephone: 412-222-7378.
Fax: 412-222-0771.
Cherry Hill, New Jersey Office: Suite 200, Woodland Falls Corporate Park, 220 Lake Drive East.
Telephone: 609-482-5222.
Fax: 609-482-6980.
Atlanta, Georgia Office: Suite 2550 Marquis Two Tower, 285 Peachtree Center Avenue, N.E.
Telephone: 404-215-8100.
Fax: 404-223-5164.

MEMBERS OF THE FIRM

William H. Brown III
Jake Hart
Nicholas N. Price
Frank C. Sabatino
Barry Simon
Martin Wald

COUNSEL TO THE FIRM

Brenda C. Kinney

RETIRED MEMBERS OF THE FIRM

Frank H. Abbott
John H. Leddy

ASSOCIATES

Michael G. Tierce
Gary M. Tocci

For Complete List of Firm Personnel, See General Section

For full biographical listings, see the Martindale-Hubbell Law Directory

WOLF, BLOCK, SCHORR AND SOLIS-COHEN (AV)

Twelfth Floor, Packard Building, S.E. Corner 15th and Chestnut Streets, 19102-2678
Telephone: 215-977-2000
Cable Address: "WOLBLORR PHA"
TWX: 710-670-1927
Telecopiers: 977-2334; 977-2346
Malvern, Pennsylvania Office: 20 Valley Stream Parkway.
Telephone: 215-889-4900.
Fax: 215-889-4916.
Harrisburg, Pennsylvania Office: 305 North Front Street, Suite 401.
Telephone: 717-237-7160.
Fax: 717-237-7161.

MEMBERS OF FIRM

James R. Redeker
Philip E. Garber
Robert M. Goldich
Laurance E. Baccini
Barry M. Klayman
Roma Skeen Young
Jay A. Dorsch

OF COUNSEL

Daniel C. Cohen
Robert E. Wachs

For Complete List of Firm Personnel, See General Section

For full biographical listings, see the Martindale-Hubbell Law Directory

*PITTSBURGH,** Allegheny Co.

BUCHANAN INGERSOLL, PROFESSIONAL CORPORATION (AV)

5800 USX Tower, 600 Grant Street, 15219
Telephone: 412-562-8800
Telecopier: 412-562-1041
Philadelphia, Pennsylvania Office: Two Logan Square, Twelfth Floor, 18th & Arch Streets.
Telephone: 215-665-8700.
Harrisburg, Pennsylvania Office: Vartan Parc, 30 North Third Street.
Telephone: 717-237-4800.

(See Next Column)

Tampa, Florida Office: 101 East Kennedy Boulevard, Suite 1030.
Telephone: 813-222-8180.
North Miami Beach, Florida Office: 19495 Biscayne Boulevard.
Telephone: 305-933-5600.
Lexington, Kentucky Office: 1210 Vine Center Office Tower, 333 West Vine Street.
Telephone: 606-225-5333.
Princeton, New Jersey Office: Buchanan Ingersoll, A Partnership, College Centre, 500 College Road East.
Telephone: 609-452-2666.

Richard J. Antonelli
John S. Brendel
Mark Raymond Hornak
Donald T. O'Connor
P. Jerome Richey
Jacques M. Wood
Sidney Zonn

John M. Cerilli
Paul J. Corrado
John P. O'Connor
Mark T. Phillis
Lisa G. Silverman
Patricia L. Wozniak

For Complete List of Firm Personnel, See General Section

For full biographical listings, see the Martindale-Hubbell Law Directory

DEFOREST & KOSCELNIK (AV)

3000 Koppers Building, 436 Seventh Avenue, 15219
Telephone: 412-227-3100
Fax: 412-227-3130

Walter P. DeForest, III
Jacqueline A. Koscelnik

Representative Clients: Carnegie Mellon University; Blue Cross of Western Pennsylvania; Ohio Valley Medical Center; Cox Enterprises, Inc.; Shamrock Broadcasting, Inc.; General Electric Co.

For full biographical listings, see the Martindale-Hubbell Law Directory

GACA, MATIS & HAMILTON, A PROFESSIONAL CORPORATION (AV)

300 Four PPG Place, 15222-5404
Telephone: 412-338-4750
Fax: 412-338-4742

Giles J. Gaca
Thomas A. Matis
Mark R. Hamilton
John W. Jordan, IV
Alan S. Baum
Thomas P. McGinnis
Bernard R. Rizza
Jeffrey A. Ramaley
Stephen J. Dalesio
John Timothy Hinton, Jr.
Shawn Lynne Reed

LEGAL SUPPORT PERSONNEL

PARALEGALS

Tina M. Shanafelt
Jill M. Peterson

For full biographical listings, see the Martindale-Hubbell Law Directory

KLETT LIEBER ROONEY & SCHORLING, A PROFESSIONAL CORPORATION (AV)

40th Floor, One Oxford Centre, 15219-6498
Telephone: 412-392-2000
FAX: 412-392-2128; 412-392-2129
Harrisburg, Pennsylvania Office: 240 North Third Street, Suite 600.
Telephone: 717-231-7700.
Philadelphia, Pennsylvania Office: 28th Floor, One Logan Square.
Telephone: 215-567-7500

SHAREHOLDERS

Thomas S. Giotto
Richard T. Kennedy
Elizabeth A. Malloy
Terrence H. Murphy

ASSOCIATES

John C. Pekar
Donald S. Prophete
Joseph F. Quinn
Leonard C. Sherer

For Complete List of Firm Personnel, See General Section

For full biographical listings, see the Martindale-Hubbell Law Directory

MARCUS & SHAPIRA (AV)

35th Floor, One Oxford Centre, 301 Grant Street, 15219-6401
Telephone: 412-471-3490
Telecopier: 412-391-8758

MEMBERS OF FIRM

Bernard D. Marcus
Daniel H. Shapira
George P. Slesinger
Robert L. Allman, II
Estelle F. Comay
Susan Gromis Flynn
Darlene M. Nowak
Glenn M. Olcerst
Elly Heller-Toig
Sylvester A. Beozzo

OF COUNSEL

John M. Burkoff

SPECIAL COUNSEL

Jane Campbell Moriarty

(See Next Column)

MARCUS & SHAPIRA, *Pittsburgh—Continued*

ASSOCIATES

Scott D. Livingston
Robert M. Barnes
Stephen S. Zubrow
David B. Rodes
Lori E. McMaster
Melody A. Pollock
James F. Rosenberg
Amy M. Gottlieb

For full biographical listings, see the Martindale-Hubbell Law Directory

POLITO & SMOCK, P.C. (AV)

Suite 400, Four Gateway Center, 15222
Telephone: 412-394-3333
Fax: 412-232-1799

Anthony J. Polito
Thomas A. Smock
Leonard Fornella
David J. Laurent
Michael D. Glass
John C. Artz
J. Michael Klutch
Sally Griffith Cimini

Robert J. Henderson
Thomas B. Bacon

For full biographical listings, see the Martindale-Hubbell Law Directory

REED SMITH SHAW & MCCLAY (AV)

James H. Reed Building, Mellon Square, 435 Sixth Avenue, 15219-1886
Telephone: 412-288-3131
Cable Address: "Reedsmith Pgh"
TWX: 710-664-2083
FAX: 412-288-3063
Mailing Address: P.O. Box 2009, 15230
Washington, D.C. Office: Ring Building, 1200 18th Street, N.W., 20036-2506.
Telephone: 202-457-6100.
FAX: 202-457-6113.
Philadelphia, Pennsylvania Office: 2500 One Liberty Place, 19103-7301.
Telephone: 215-851-8100.
FAX: 215-851-1420.
Harrisburg, Pennsylvania Office: 213 Market Street, 17101-2132.
Telephone: 717-234-5988.
McLean, Virginia Office: Suite 1100, 8251 Greensboro Drive, 22102-3844.
Telephone: 703-734-4600.
Princeton, New Jersey Office: 136 Main Street, 08540-5799.
Telephone: 609-987-0050.
FAX: 609-951-0824.

MEMBERS OF FIRM

William Bevan, III
Walter G. Bleil
Eugene K. Connors
Steven P. Fulton
James R. Haggerty
Robert W. Hartland
Carole S. Katz
David J. McAllister
Martha Hartle Munsch
Peter D. Post
Robert F. Prorok
Patrick W. Ritchey
Leonard L. Scheinholtz
Edward N. Stoner, II
Harley N. Trice, II
John C. Unkovic
Scott F. Zimmerman

COUNSEL

Henry J. Wallace, Jr.

For Complete List of Firm Personnel, See General Section

For full biographical listings, see the Martindale-Hubbell Law Directory

ROSE, SCHMIDT, HASLEY & DISALLE, P.C. (AV)

900 Oliver Building, 15222-2310
Telephone: 412-434-8600
Fax: 412-263-2829
Washington, Pennsylvania Office: 7th Floor, Millcraft Center.
Telephone: 412-228-8883.

Edmund M. Carney
R. Stanley Mitchel

For Complete List of Firm Personnel, See General Section

For full biographical listings, see the Martindale-Hubbell Law Directory

ROTHMAN GORDON FOREMAN & GROUDINE, P.C. (AV)

Third Floor-Grant Building, 15219
Telephone: 412-338-1100
Telefax: 412-281-7304
Washington, D.C. Office: 1120 Connecticut Avenue, N.W. Suite 440.
Telephone: 202-338-3248.

Louis B. Kushner
Stephen H. Jordan
Ronald G. Backer
Shelley W. Elovitz

Sandra Reiter Kushner
Alan Carlos Blanco

For Complete List of Firm Personnel, See General Section

For full biographical listings, see the Martindale-Hubbell Law Directory

SPRINGER, BUSH & PERRY, A PROFESSIONAL CORPORATION (AV)

Two Gateway Center, Fifteenth Floor, 15222
Telephone: 412-281-4900
Fax: 412-261-1645
Moon Township, Pennsylvania Office: 500 Cherrington Parkway, Suite 420, Coraopolis, Pennsylvania, 15108.
Telephone: 412-269-4200.
Fax: 412-269-9638.

Donald C. Bush
Thomas P. Peterson
Gerri L. Sperling

For Complete List of Firm Personnel, See General Section

For full biographical listings, see the Martindale-Hubbell Law Directory

THORP, REED & ARMSTRONG (AV)

One Riverfront Center, 15222
Telephone: 412-394-7711
Fax: 412-394-2555

MEMBERS OF FIRM

Thomas E. Lippard
Joseph Mack, III
Kurt A. Miller
Barbara K. Ross
Martin J. Saunders
Robert H. Shoop, Jr.
Richard V. Sica
Richard I. Thomas

ASSOCIATES

Craig A. Barr
Philip J. Murray III

For Complete List of Firm Personnel, See General Section

For full biographical listings, see the Martindale-Hubbell Law Directory

TUCKER ARENSBERG, P.C. (AV)

1500 One PPG Place, 15222
Telephone: 412-566-1212
Telex: 902914
Fax: 412-594-5619
Harrisburg, Pennsylvania Office: 116 Pine Street.
Telephone: 717-238-2007.
Fax: 717-238-2242.
Pittsburgh Airport Area Office: Airport Professional Office Center, 1150 Thorn Run Road Ext., Moon Township, Pennsylvania, 15108.
Telephone: 412-262-3730.
Fax: 412-262-2576.

Charles F. C. Arensberg (1879-1974)
Frank R. S. Kaplan (1886-1957)
Donald L. Very (1933-1979)
Linda A. Acheson
W. Theodore Brooks
Matthew J. Carl
Richard W. Cramer
J. Kent Culley
Donald P. Eriksen
Paul F. Fagan
Gary J. Gushard
William T. Harvey
Joel M. Helmrich
Gary P. Hunt
Raymond M. Komichak
Jeffrey J. Leech
Beverly Weiss Manne
Garland H. McAdoo, Jr.
John M. McElroy
Robert L. McTiernan
John B. Montgomery
Stanley V. Ostrow
William A. Penrod
Daniel J. Perry
Henry S. Pool
Richard B. Tucker, III
Bradley S. Tupi
Charles J. Vater
Gary E. Wieczorek
G. Ashley Woolridge

Donald E. Ambrose
Robin K. Capozzi
Diane Hernon Chavis
Toni L. DiGiacobbe
Donna M. Donaher
John E. Graf
Mark L. Heleen
David P. Hvizdos
Timothy S. Johnson
Joni L. Landy
Jonathan S. McAnney
G. Ross Rhodes
Christopher J. Richardson
Eric M. Schumann
Steven H. Seel
Steven B. Silverman
Michael J. Tobak, III
Homer L. Walton

HARRISBURG OFFICE

J. Kent Culley

John G. Di Leonardo

SPECIAL COUNSEL

Richard S. Crone
Elliott W. Finkel
Michael J. Laffey
John P. Papuga
William J. Staley
Richard B. Tucker, Jr.

For full biographical listings, see the Martindale-Hubbell Law Directory

VOLK, ROBERTSON & HELLERSTEDT (AV)

Three Gateway Center 15th Floor East, 15222
Telephone: 412-392-2300
Facsimile: 412-263-2230
Weirton, West Virginia Office: 384 Penco Road.
Telephone: 304-723-4442.
Fax: 304-723-3826.

(See Next Column)

VOLK, ROBERTSON & HELLERSTEDT—*Continued*

MEMBERS OF FIRM

Charles R. Volk
David L. Robertson
Carl H. Hellerstedt, Jr.
James G. Connolly
John A. McCreary, Jr.

ASSOCIATES

Jane Lewis Volk
Timothy M. Volk
Thomas E. Buck
Henry L. Clement III

For full biographical listings, see the Martindale-Hubbell Law Directory

*WILKES-BARRE,** Luzerne Co.

HOURIGAN, KLUGER, SPOHRER & QUINN, A PROFESSIONAL CORPORATION (AV)

700 Mellon Bank Center, 8 West Market Street, 18701-1867
Telephone: 717-825-9401
FAX: 717-829-3460
Scranton, Pennsylvania Office: Suite 200, 434 Lackawanna Avenue.
Telephone: 717-346-8414.
Allentown, Pennsylvania Office: Sovereign Building, 609 Hamilton Mall.
Telephone: 610-437-1584.
Hazelton, Pennsylvania Office: CAN DO Building, One South Church Street.
Telephone: 717-455-5141.

Allan M. Kluger
Richard M. Goldberg
Alexia Kita Blake

Representative Client: Teamsters, Pope & Talbot, Topp, Inc.

For Complete List of Firm Personnel, See General Section

For full biographical listings, see the Martindale-Hubbell Law Directory

ROSENN, JENKINS & GREENWALD (AV)

15 South Franklin Street, 18711-0075
Telephone: 717-826-5600
Fax: 717-826-5640

MEMBERS OF FIRM

Donald H. Brobst
James P. Valentine
Mark A. Van Loon

ASSOCIATES

James C. Oschal
Joseph G. Ferguson
Jennifer Glor Dressler

Representative Clients: Allstate Insurance Co.; C-TEC Corporation; Chicago Title Insurance Co.; Franklin First Savings Bank; The Geisinger Medical Center; Guard Insurance Group; The Mays Department Stores Company; Student LoanMarketing Association (Sallie Mae); Subaru of America, Inc.

For Complete List of Firm Personnel, See General Section

For full biographical listings, see the Martindale-Hubbell Law Directory

*WILLIAMSPORT,** Lycoming Co.

MCNERNEY, PAGE, VANDERLIN & HALL (AV)

433 Market Street, 17701
Telephone: 717-326-6555
Fax: 717-326-3170
Muncy, Pennsylvania Office: R.D. #6, Box 260-1.
Telephone: 717-546-5111.

MEMBERS OF FIRM

Joseph M. McNerney (1909-1967)
Allen P. Page, Jr. (1923-1975)
O. William Vanderlin
T. Max Hall
George V. Cohen
Charles J. McKelvey
E. Eugene Yaw
Michael H. Collins
Ann Pepperman
Brett O. Feese
Thomas A. Marino

ASSOCIATES

Robin A. Read
Thomas C. Marshall
Peter G. Facey
Joy Reynolds McCoy

Approved Agent for: American Title Insurance.
Representative Clients: Williamsport National Bank; Textron Lycoming; Underwriters Adjustment Co.; Continental Insurance Co.; Little League Baseball, Inc.; The West Co.; Shop Vac Corp.; Divine Providence Hospital; Pennsylvania College of Technology.

For full biographical listings, see the Martindale-Hubbell Law Directory

*YORK,** York Co.

STOCK AND LEADER (AV)

35 South Duke Street, P.O. Box 5167, 17401-5167
Telephone: 717-846-9800
Fax: 717-843-6134
Hallam, Pennsylvania Office: 450 West Market Street.
Telephone: 717-840-4491.
Stewartstown, Pennsylvania Office: 5 South Main Street.
Telephone: 717-993-2845.

(See Next Column)

Shrewsbury, Pennsylvania Office: 28 Northbrook Drive, Suite 2F.
Telephone: 717-235-3608.

MEMBERS OF FIRM

Raymond L. Hovis
Michael W. King
Emily J. Leader

General Counsel: The Drovers & Mechanics Bank; Paradise Mutual Insurance Co.; Yorktowne Paper Mills, Inc.; York Electrical Supply Co.; Eisenhart Wallcoverings Co.; York Suburban School District; York Township; Central York School District.

For Complete List of Firm Personnel, See General Section

For full biographical listings, see the Martindale-Hubbell Law Directory

RHODE ISLAND

*PROVIDENCE,** Providence Co.

BLISH & CAVANAGH (AV)

Commerce Center, 30 Exchange Terrace, 02903
Telephone: 401-831-8900
Telecopier: 401-751-7542

MEMBERS OF FIRM

John H. Blish
Joseph V. Cavanagh, Jr.
William R. Landry
Michael DiBiase
Stephen J. Reid, Jr.

Karen A. Pelczarski
Raymond A. Marcaccio
Scott P. Tierney

Representative Clients: Providence Journal Co.; Fleet Financial Group; Rhode Island Hospital Trust National Bank; Allstate Insurance Co.; U-Haul International, Inc.; Delta Dental of Rhode Island; Gilbane Building Co.; Colony Communications; Providence Housing Authority.

For full biographical listings, see the Martindale-Hubbell Law Directory

EDWARDS & ANGELL (AV)

2700 Hospital Trust Tower, 02903
Telephone: 401-274-9200
Telecopier: 401-276-6611
Cable Address: "Edwangle Providence"
Telex: 952001 "E A PVD"
Boston, Massachusetts Office: 101 Federal Street, 02110.
Telephone: 617-439-444.
Telecopier: 617-439-4170.
New York, New York Office: 750 Lexington Avenue, 10022.
Telephone: 212-308-4411.
Telecopier: 212-308-4844.
Palm Beach, Florida Office: 250 Royal Palm Way, 33480.
Telephone: 407-833-7700.
Telecopier: 407-655-8719.
Newark, New Jersey Office: Gateway three, 07120.
Telephone: 201-623-7717.
Telecopier: 201-623-7717.
Hartford, Connecticut Office: 750 Main Street, 14th Floor, 06103.
Telephone: 203-525-5065.
Telecopier: 203-527-4198.
Newport, Rhode Island Office: 130 Bellevue Avenue, 02840.
Telephone: 401-849-7800.
Telecopier: 401-849-7887.

MEMBERS OF FIRM

Alvin M. Glazerman (Not admitted in RI; Resident Boston, Massachusetts Office)
Richard A. Perras (Not admitted in RI; Resident Boston, Massachusetts Office)
Walter C. Hunter
William E. Smith

COUNSEL

John B. Rosenquest III
Carla J. L. Spacone

For Complete List of Firm Personnel, See General Section

For full biographical listings, see the Martindale-Hubbell Law Directory

FLANDERS + MEDEIROS INC. (AV)

One Turks Head Place, Suite 700, 02903
Telephone: 401-831-0700
Telecopier: 401-274-2752

Matthew F. Medeiros
Robert G. Flanders, Jr.
Robert Karmen

Neal J. McNamara
Fausto C. Anguilla
Amelia E. Edwards
Stacey P. Nakasian

For full biographical listings, see the Martindale-Hubbell Law Directory

Providence—Continued

GIDLEY, SARLI & MARUSAK (AV)

Greater Providence Bank Building, 170 Westminster Street, 02903
Telephone: 401-274-6644
Telecopier: 401-331-9304

MEMBERS OF FIRM

Thomas D. Gidley
Michael G. Sarli
James P. Marusak
Mark C. Hadden

ASSOCIATES

Michael R. DeLuca
Linn Foster Freedman
Denise M. Lombardo
William L. Wheatley
Stuart D. Hallagan III

LEGAL SUPPORT PERSONNEL

Elaine M. Noren
Mary Repoza Caplette
Darlene E. Kotkofski

For full biographical listings, see the Martindale-Hubbell Law Directory

HANSON, CURRAN, PARKS & WHITMAN (AV)

146 Westminster Street, 02903-2218
Telephone: 401-421-2154
Telecopier: 401-521-7040

Kirk Hanson (1948-1991)

MEMBERS OF FIRM

A. Lauriston Parks
David P. Whitman
Michael T. F. Wallor
Robert D. Parrillo
Dennis J. McCarten
James T. Murphy
Seth E. Bowerman
Thomas R. Bender

ASSOCIATES

Amy Beretta
Mark W. Dana
Richard H. Burrows
Daniel P. McKiernan

OF COUNSEL

William A. Curran

General Counsel for: Medical Malpractice Joint Underwriting Association of Rhode Island.
Rhode Island Counsel for: Amica Mutual Insurance Co.; CIGNA; St. Paul Insurance Cos.; Occidental Life Insurance Co.; Exchange Mutual Insurance Co.; Aetna Casualty & Surety Co.

For full biographical listings, see the Martindale-Hubbell Law Directory

WILLIAM T. MURPHY (AV)

The Calart Tower, 400 Reservoir Avenue, Suite 3L, 02907
Telephone: 401-461-7740
Telecopier: 401-461-7753

ASSOCIATE

Sean P. Lardner

Reference: Fleet National Bank.

For full biographical listings, see the Martindale-Hubbell Law Directory

FRANK J. WILLIAMS, LTD. (AV)

2 Williams Street, (At South Main Street), 02903
Telephone: 401-331-2222
Cable Address: "LINCOLN"
Telecopier: 401-751-5257

Frank J. Williams

Michael A. Ursillo

References: Shawmut Bank of R.I.; Citizens Trust Co.

For full biographical listings, see the Martindale-Hubbell Law Directory

WESTERLY, Washington Co.

URSO, LIGUORI AND URSO (AV)

85 Beach Street, P.O. Box 1277, 02891
Telephone: 401-596-7751
Telecopier: 401-596-7963

MEMBERS OF FIRM

Natale Louis Urso
Thomas J. Liguori, Jr.
M. Linda Urso

General Counsel for: National Education Association Rhode Island; Westerly Broadcasting Co.
Approved Attorneys for: Lawyers Title Insurance Corporation of Richmond, Virginia.
Reference: Fleet National Bank.

For full biographical listings, see the Martindale-Hubbell Law Directory

SOUTH CAROLINA

*CHARLESTON,** Charleston Co.

GIBBS & HOLMES (AV)

171 Church Street, P.O. Box 938, 29402
Telephone: 803-722-0033
Fax: 803-722-0114

MEMBERS OF FIRM

Coming B. Gibbs, Jr.
Allan R. Holmes

ASSOCIATES

Anne M. Payne
Michele E. Bateman
P. Steven Barkowitz

For full biographical listings, see the Martindale-Hubbell Law Directory

OGLETREE, DEAKINS, NASH, SMOAK & STEWART (AV)

First Union Building, Suite 310, 177 Meeting Street, P.O. Box 1808, 29402
Telephone: 803-853-1300
Facsimile: 803-853-9992
Atlanta, Georgia Office: 3800 One Atlantic Center, 1201 West Peachtree Street, N.W.
Telephone: 404-881-1300.
Washington, D.C. Office: Fifth Floor, 2400 N Street, N.W.
Telephone: 202-887-0855.
Greenville, South Carolina Office: The Ogletree Building, 300 North Main Street, P.O. Box 2757.
Telephone: 803-271-1300.
Columbia, South Carolina Office: Palmetto Center, Suite 1820, 1426 Main Street, P.O. Box 11206.
Telephone: 803-252-1300.
Raleigh, North Carolina Office: Suite 511, 4101 Lake Boone Trail, P.O. Box 31608.
Telephone: 919-787-9700.
Nashville, Tennessee Office: St. Cloud Corner, 500 Church Street.
Telephone: 615-254-1900.
Albany, New York Office: 4th Floor, One Steuben Place.
Telephone: 518-434-1300.

MEMBERS OF FIRM

J. Frank Ogletree, Jr. (1930-1985)
Peter G. Nash (1937-1993)
Dixie L. Atwater (1948-1992)
J. Hamilton Stewart, III
Mark H. Wall
Cheryl D. Shoun
Richard Allison Phinney
G. Waring Parker
C. C. Harness, III
Robert T. Lyles, Jr.
Neil S. Haldrup
Robert L. Wylie, IV
Charles F. Castner

OF COUNSEL

Thomas E. Pedersen

Representative Clients: Alumax of South Carolina, Inc.; Baxter Healthcare Corporation; Bi-Lo, Inc.; Laidlaw Environmental Services, Inc.; Metropolitan Life Insurance; Nissan Motor Manufacturing Corporation U.S.A.; S.C. Insurance Reserve Fund; St. Paul Insurance Company; Union Camp Corporation; Wachovia Corporation.

For full biographical listings, see the Martindale-Hubbell Law Directory

ROSEN, ROSEN & HAGOOD, P.A. (AV)

134 Meeting Street, Suite 200, P.O. Box 893, 29402
Telephone: 803-577-6726

Morris D. Rosen
Robert N. Rosen
Alice F. Paylor
Susan Corner Rosen

Alexander B. Cash
Daniel F. Blanchard, III

Reference: NationsBank of South Carolina, N.A.

For Complete List of Firm Personnel, See General Section

For full biographical listings, see the Martindale-Hubbell Law Directory

YOUNG, CLEMENT, RIVERS & TISDALE (AV)

28 Broad Street, P.O. Box 993, 29402
Telephone: 803-577-4000
Fax: 803-724-6600
Columbia, South Carolina Office: 1901 Assembly Street, Suite 300, P.O. Box 8476.
Telephone: 803-799-4000.
Fax: 803-799-7083.
North Charleston , South Carolina Office: 2170 Ashley Phosphate Road, Suite 700, P.O. Box 61509.
Telephone: 803-720-5400.
Fax: 803-724-7796.

MEMBERS OF FIRM

Carol Brittain Ervin
Shawn Daughtridge Wallace

(See Next Column)

YOUNG, CLEMENT, RIVERS & TISDALE—*Continued*

ASSOCIATES

Elizabeth B. Luzuriaga | Wilbur E. Johnson

Counsel for: Charleston Memorial Hospital; Charleston Southern University; Provost, Inc.; Roper Hospital; Santee Cooper; Unisun.

For Complete List of Firm Personnel, See General Section

For full biographical listings, see the Martindale-Hubbell Law Directory

*COLUMBIA,** Richland Co.

CONSTANGY, BROOKS & SMITH (AV)

Suite 810 NationsBank Tower, 1301 Gervais Street, 29201-3326
Telephone: 803-256-3200
Atlanta, Georgia Office: Suite 2400 Peachtree Center Building, 230 Peachtree Street, N.W.
Telephone: 404-525-8622.
Birmingham, Alabama Office: Suite 1410 AmSouth/Harbert Plaza, 1901 Sixth Avenue, North.
Telephone: 205-252-9321.
Nashville, Tennessee Office: Suite 1080 Vanderbilt Plaza, 2100 West End Avenue.
Telephone: 615-320-5200.
Washington, D.C. Office: Suite 1200, 1015 Fifteenth Street, N.W.
Telephone: 202-789-8676.
Winston-Salem, North Carolina Office: Suite 300, 101 South Stratford Road.
Telephone: 910-721-1001. Charlotte: 704-344-1040.

MEMBERS OF FIRM

Lovic A. Brooks, Jr. | Lovic A. Brooks, III (Resident)

OF COUNSEL

Edgar L. McGowan (Resident)

ASSOCIATES

Kristine L. Thompson (Resident) | John Charles Ormond, Jr. (Resident)

Representative Clients: Blockbuster Entertainment Corp.; Blue Cross/Blue Shield of Alabama; Consolidated Freightways, Inc.; Delta Woodside Industries; McDonald's; Merck & Co., Inc.; Philip-Morris Cos., Inc.; Phillips Van Heusen Corp.; Sara Lee Corp.; Trust Company Bank.

For full biographical listings, see the Martindale-Hubbell Law Directory

HAYNSWORTH, BALDWIN, JOHNSON AND GREAVES, P.A. (AV)

1201 Main Street, Suite 1230, 29201
Telephone: 803-799-5858
Facsimile: 803-799-7168
Greenville, South Carolina Office: 918 South Pleasantburg Drive, P.O. Box 10888.
Telephone: 803-271-7410.
Raleigh, North Carolina Office: 3605 Glenwood Avenue, Suite 210, P.O. Box 10035.
Telephone: 919-782-3340.
Greensboro, North Carolina Office: 2709 Henry Street, P.O. Box 13310.
Telephone: 910-375-9737.
Charlotte, North Carolina Office: 400 West Trade Street.
Telephone: 704-342-2588.
Jacksonville, Florida Office: Haynsworth, Baldwin, Johnson and Harper, 1506 Prudential Drive, P.O. Box 40593.
Telephone: 904-396-3000.
Tampa, Florida Office: Haynsworth, Baldwin, Johnson and Harper, 600 North Westshore Boulevard, Suite 200.
Telephone: 813-289-1247.
Macon, Georgia Office: Haynsworth, Baldwin, Johnson and Harper, 577 Mulberry Street, Suite 710, P.O. Box 1975.
Telephone: 912-746-0262.

Knox L. Haynsworth, Jr. | Charles T. Speth II (Resident)

Katherine Dudley Helms (Resident)
Leigh Mullikin Nason (Resident)
Levan J. Wingate (Resident)
Scott T. Justice (Resident)
Georgia Anna M. Rashley (Resident)
T. Lowndes Pope (Resident)
M. Brian Magargle (Resident)
Janis M. Wilson (Resident)

OF COUNSEL

James J. Baldwin

Representative Clients: AT&T; Colonial Life & Accident Insurance Co.; FMC Corp.; McLeod Regional Medical Center; Owen Steel Co.; Piggly Wiggly Carolina Company, Inc.; Sonoco Products Co.; South Carolina Bankers Assn.; State of South Carolina (Insurance Reserve Fund).

For full biographical listings, see the Martindale-Hubbell Law Directory

OGLETREE, DEAKINS, NASH, SMOAK & STEWART (AV)

Palmetto Center, Suite 1820, 1426 Main Street, P.O. Box 11206, 29211
Telephone: 803-252-1300
Facsimile: 803-254-6517
Greenville, South Carolina Office: The Ogletree Building, 300 North Main Street, P.O. Box 2757.
Telephone: 803-271-1300.

(See Next Column)

Charleston, South Carolina Office: First Union Building, Suite 310, 177 Meeting Street, P.O. Box 1808.
Telephone: 803-853-1300.
Atlanta, Georgia Office: 3800 One Atlantic Center, 1201 West Peachtree Street, N.W.
Telephone: 404-881-1300.
Washington, D.C. Office: Fifth Floor, 2400 N Street, N.W.
Telephone: 202-887-0855.
Raleigh, North Carolina Office: Suite 511, 4101 Lake Boone Trail, P.O. Box 31608.
Telephone: 919-787-9700.
Nashville, Tennessee Office: St. Cloud Corner, 500 Church Street.
Telephone: 615-254-1900.
Albany, New York Office: 4th Floor, One Steuben Place.
Telephone: 518-434-1300.

MEMBERS OF FIRM

G. Daniel Ellzey
M. Baker Wyche III
Jonathan P. Pearson
James L. Werner
Ethan R. Ware
Mason G. Alexander, Jr.
Michael D. Carrouth
Lawrence J. Needle
George W. Lampl, III
Charles F. Thompson, Jr.
Weston Adams, III
Stephen Carrington Mitchell

OF COUNSEL

Thomas Ross Haggard

Representative Clients: Allied Signal, Inc.; Alumax of South Carolina, Inc.; BE&K, Inc.; Carolina Eastman Co.; Georgetown Steel Corp.; Gerber Products Company, Inc.; Nissan Motor Manufacturing Corporation U.S.A.; Union Camp Corp.; Wachovia Corporation; Wellman, Inc.

For full biographical listings, see the Martindale-Hubbell Law Directory

*GREENVILLE,** Greenville Co.

HAYNSWORTH, BALDWIN, JOHNSON AND GREAVES, P.A. (AV)

918 South Pleasantburg Drive, P.O. Box 10888, 29603
Telephone: 803-271-7410
Facsimile: 803-233-1481
Columbia, South Carolina Office: 1201 Main Street, Suite 1230.
Telephone: 803-799-5858.
Raleigh, North Carolina Office: 3605 Glenwood Avenue, Suite 210, P.O. Box 10035.
Telephone: 919-782-3340.
Greensboro, North Carolina Office: 2709 Henry Street, P.O. Box 13310.
Telephone: 910-375-9737.
Charlotte, North Carolina Office: 400 West Trade Street.
Telephone: 704-342-2588.
Jacksonville, Florida Office: Haynsworth, Baldwin, Johnson and Harper, 1506 Prudential Drive, P.O. Box 40593.
Telephone: 904-396-3000.
Tampa, Florida Office: Haynsworth, Baldwin, Johnson and Harper, 600 North Westshore Boulevard, Suite 200.
Telephone: 813-289-1247.
Macon, Georgia Office: Haynsworth, Baldwin, Johnson and Harper, 577 Mulberry Street, Suite 710, P.O. Box 1975.
Telephone: 912-746-0262.

Knox L. Haynsworth, Jr.
Bradley R. Johnson (Resident, Tampa, Florida Office)
Thomas G. Greaves III
John G. Creech
Bruce A. Petesch (Resident, Raleigh, North Carolina Office)
Wm. Ross McKibbon, Jr.
G. Thomas Harper (Resident, Jacksonville, Florida Office)
James B. Spears, Jr. (Resident, Charlotte, North Carolina Office)
J. Howard Daniel
Robert S. Phifer (Resident, Charlotte, North Carolina Office)
Joseph A. Rhodes, Jr.
David R. Wylie
James M. Powell (Resident, Greensboro, North Carolina Office)
Charles T. Speth II (Resident, Columbia, South Carolina Office)
Charles P. Roberts III (Resident, Greensboro, North Carolina Office)
Thomas A. Bright
W. Melvin Haas, III (Resident, Macon, Georgia Office)
Grant D. Petersen (Resident, Tampa, Florida Office)
Charles F. Henley, Jr. (Resident, Jacksonville, Florida Office)

Lilli K. Lindbeck (Resident, Charlotte, North Carolina Office)
Katherine Dudley Helms (Resident, Columbia, South Carolina Office)
M. Kristen Allman (Resident, Tampa, Florida Office)
M. Susan Eglin
Thomas T. Hodges
Gregory P. McGuire (Resident, Greensboro, North Carolina Office)
Leigh Mullikin Nason (Resident, Columbia, South Carolina Office)
Rodolfo R. Agraz (Resident, Raleigh, North Carolina Office)
Andreas N. Satterfield, Jr.
Jeffery L. Thompson (Resident, Macon, Georgia Office)
Brian M. Freedman (Resident, Greensboro, North Carolina Office)
Stephen D. Dellinger (Resident, Charlotte, North Carolina Office)
Jacob J. Modla (Resident, Charlotte, North Carolina Office)
Anna Maria Conner

(See Next Column)

HAYNSWORTH, BALDWIN, JOHNSON AND GREAVES P.A., *Greenville—Continued*

Lucretia D. Smith (Resident, Greensboro, North Carolina Office)
Donna M. Griffin (Resident, Tampa, Florida Office)
Levan J. Wingate (Resident, Columbia, South Carolina Office)
Gretchen Bonds Gleason
D. Christopher Lauderdale
John D. Cole (Resident, Charlotte, North Carolina Office)
Scott T. Justice (Resident, Columbia, South Carolina Office)
Kimberly T. Acuna (Resident, Jacksonville, Florida Office)
Elizabeth A. Maas (Resident, Jacksonville, Florida Office)
Vance E. Drawdy
Georgia Anna M. Rashley (Resident, Columbia, South Carolina Office)
Eduardo Alberto Suarez-Solar (Resident, Tampa, Florida Office)
T. Lowndes Pope (Resident, Columbia, South Carolina Office)
Thomas Bailey Smith
Aaron M. Christensen
M. Brian Magargle (Resident, Columbia, South Carolina Office)
Martha B. Perkowski (Resident, Greensboro, North Carolina Office)
Glenn L. Spencer
Ellison F. McCoy
Janis M. Wilson (Resident, Columbia, South Carolina Office)
D. Ross Hamilton, Jr. (Resident, Greensboro, North Carolina Office)

OF COUNSEL

Edgar W. Ennis, Jr. (Resident, Macon, Georgia Office)
James J. Baldwin
Thomas M. Christina (Not admitted in SC)

Representative Clients: Ball-InCon Glass Packaging Corp.; Coca-Cola Bottling Co. Consolidated; Greenville Hospital System; The Liberty Corp.; McDonnell Douglas Corp.; Multimedia, Inc. (Greenville News); Nucor Steel Corp.; The Stouffer Corporation.; VF Corp.; Wal-Mart Stores, Inc.

For full biographical listings, see the Martindale-Hubbell Law Directory

OGLETREE, DEAKINS, NASH, SMOAK & STEWART (AV)

The Ogletree Building, 300 North Main Street, P.O. Box 2757, 29602
Telephone: 803-271-1300
Facsimile: 803-235-8806
Atlanta, Georgia Office: 3800 One Atlantic Center, 1201 West Peachtree Street, N.W.
Telephone: 404-881-1300.
Washington, D.C. Office: Fifth Floor, 2400 N Street, N.W.
Telephone: 202-887-0855.
Charleston, South Carolina Office: First Union Building, Suite 310, 177 Meeting Street, P.O. Box 1808.
Telephone: 803-853-1300.
Columbia, South Carolina Office: Palmetto Center, Suite 1820, 1426 Main Street, P.O. Box 11206.
Telephone: 803-252-1300.
Raleigh, North Carolina Office: 4101 Lake Boone Trail, Suite 511, P.O. Box 31608.
Telephone: 919-787-9700.
Nashville, Tennessee Office: St. Cloud Corner, 500 Church Street.
Telephone: 615-254-1900.
Albany, New York Office: 4th Floor, One Steuben Place.
Telephone: 518-434-1300.

MEMBERS OF FIRM

Homer L. Deakins, Jr.
Lewis Tyson Smoak
J. Hamilton Stewart, III
L. Gray Geddie, Jr.
Ralph M. Mellom
Robert Oliver King
Stuart M. Vaughan, Jr.
G. Daniel Ellzey
Fred W. Suggs, Jr.
Eric C. Schweitzer
M. Baker Wyche III
Richard R. Parker
Donald A. Cockrill
L. Franklin Elmore
Mark H. Wall
John S. Burgin
John W. Hoag, III
Jonathan P. Pearson
Michael S. Thwaites
Joel A. Daniel
Cheryl D. Shoun
Phillip A. Kilgore
Richard Allison Phinney
James L. Werner
Charles E. Feuss
Ronald E. Cardwell
Ethan R. Ware
Mary Lou Hill
Ingrid J. Blackwelder
Steven M. Wynkoop
G. Waring Parker
C. C. Harness, III
Phillip Lee Conner
William H. Floyd, III
Mason G. Alexander, Jr.
Kristofer K. Strasser
Janet Quick Lewis
Nancy Walker Monts
Devin M. Ehrlich
Michael D. Carrouth
Mark M. Stubley
William S. Rutchow
Glenn R. Goodwin
Robert T. Lyles, Jr.
G. Scott Humphrey
Neil S. Haldrup
Kimila Lynn Wooten
Lawrence J. Needle
Lewis F. Gossett
Stephen F. Fisher
Michael T. Brittingham
Robert L. Wylie, IV
John St. C. White
E. Grantland Burns
Charles F. Thompson, Jr.
George W. Lampl, III
Weston Adams, III
Keven K. Kenison
Oscar Eugene Prioleau, Jr.
Stephen Carrington Mitchell
Ellisa Huguley Culp

(See Next Column)

OF COUNSEL

Thomas C. Bradley, Jr.
Thomas Ross Haggard
Thomas E. Pedersen

Representative Clients: Chevron USA Products Co.; Duke Power Co.; Eastman Kodak Company; Fluor Corporation; General Electric Co.; W.R. Grace & Co.; Hitachi Electronics Devices (USA), Inc.; Laidlaw Environmental Services, Inc.; Nissan Motor Manufacturing Corporation U.S.A.; WestPoint Stevens, Inc.

For full biographical listings, see the Martindale-Hubbell Law Directory

THOMPSON AND HUTSON (AV)

NationsBank Plaza, Suite 100, 29601
Telephone: 803-242-3200
FAX: 803-233-7867
Mailing Address: P.O. Box 88, Greenville, South Carolina, 29602-0088
Washington, D.C. Office: 1317 F Street, N.W., Suite 900.
Telephone: 202-783-1900.
Fax: 202-783-5995.

MEMBERS OF FIRM

Robert T. Thompson
Melvin Hutson
David L. Thompson (Resident, Washington, D.C. Office)

ASSOCIATE

Dallas G. Kingsbury (Not admitted in SC)

For full biographical listings, see the Martindale-Hubbell Law Directory

WYCHE, BURGESS, FREEMAN & PARHAM, PROFESSIONAL ASSOCIATION (AV)

44 East Camperdown Way, P.O. Box 728, 29602-0728
Telephone: 803-242-8200
Telecopier: 803-235-8900

Jo Watson Hackl
J. Theodore Gentry

Counsel for: Multimedia, Inc.; Delta Woodside Industries, Inc.; Milliken & Company; Ryan's Family Steak Houses, Inc.; St. Francis Hospital; Span-America Medical Systems, Inc.; Carolina First Bank; KEMET Electronics Corp.; Builder Marts of America, Inc.; One Price Clothing, Inc.

For Complete List of Firm Personnel, See General Section

For full biographical listings, see the Martindale-Hubbell Law Directory

MYRTLE BEACH, Horry Co.

STEVENS, STEVENS & THOMAS, P.C. (AV)

1215 48th Avenue North, 29577-2468
Telephone: 803-449-9675
Fax: 803-497-2262
Loris, South Carolina Office: 3341 Broad Street.
Telephone: 803-756-7652.
Fax: 803-756-3785.

James P. Stevens, Jr. (Resident, Loris Office)
J. Jackson Thomas

Angela T. Jordan (Resident Loris Office)

OF COUNSEL

James P. Stevens

For full biographical listings, see the Martindale-Hubbell Law Directory

SOUTH DAKOTA

*ABERDEEN,** Brown Co.

MALONEY & MALONEY (AV)

Twelve Second Avenue, Southwest, P.O. Box 755, 57402-0755
Telephone: 605-229-2752
Fax: 605-226-0276

MEMBERS OF FIRM

Dennis Maloney
Marilyn Marshall Maloney

For full biographical listings, see the Martindale-Hubbell Law Directory

*RAPID CITY,** Pennington Co.

BANGS, McCULLEN, BUTLER, FOYE & SIMMONS (AV)

818 St. Joseph Street, P.O. Box 2670, 57709
Telephone: 605-343-1040
Telecopier: 605-343-1503

MEMBERS OF FIRM

Thomas E. Simmons
Michael M. Hickey

Representative Clients: Norwest Bank South Dakota, N.A., Rapid City, S.D.; Pete Lien & Sons; The Travelers Insurance Co.; Rapid City Regional Hospital; Dakota Steel & Supply Co.; Great American Insurance Co.; Fireman's

(See Next Column)

BANGS, MCCULLEN, BUTLER, FOYE & SIMMONS—*Continued*

Fund Insurance; United States Automobile Association; Moyle Petroleum; Rapid City Area School District 51-4.

For Complete List of Firm Personnel, See General Section

For full biographical listings, see the Martindale-Hubbell Law Directory

TENNESSEE

*CHATTANOOGA,** Hamilton Co.

BROWN, DOBSON, BURNETTE & KESLER (AV)

713 Cherry Street, 37402
Telephone: 615-266-2121
Fax: 615-266-3324

MEMBERS OF FIRM

Harry F. Burnette
Anita B Hardeman
Michael S. Pineda

Reference: First Tennessee Bank.

For full biographical listings, see the Martindale-Hubbell Law Directory

CHAMBLISS & BAHNER (AV)

1000 Tallan Building, Two Union Square, 37402-2500
Telephone: 615-756-3000
Fax: 615-265-9574

MEMBER OF FIRM

William H. Pickering

ASSOCIATES

K. Scott Graham
Collette R. Jones

General Counsel for: McKee Foods Corporation; Porter Warner Inds., Inc.; SCT Yarns, Inc.; Stein Construction Co., Inc.
Representative Clients: United States Pipe & Foundry Company; Hamilton County Department of Education; First American National Bank; Health Stream Corp.; Fortwood Center, Inc.; HealthCorp, Inc.

For Complete List of Firm Personnel, See General Section

For full biographical listings, see the Martindale-Hubbell Law Directory

FLEISSNER, COOPER, MARCUS & QUINN (AV)

800 Vine Street, 37403
Telephone: 615-756-3595
Telecopier: 615-266-5455

Phillip A. Fleissner
H. Richard Marcus
Gary A. Cooper
J. Bartlett Quinn
Robert L. Widerkehr, Jr.

ASSOCIATE

Cynthia D. Hall

For full biographical listings, see the Martindale-Hubbell Law Directory

SPEARS, MOORE, REBMAN & WILLIAMS (AV)

8th Floor Blue Cross Building, 801 Pine Street, 37402
Telephone: 615-756-7000
Facsimile: 615-756-4801

MEMBERS OF FIRM

Joseph C. Wilson, III
L. Marie Williams
W. Ferber Tracy
Harry L. Dadds, II

ASSOCIATES

Howell Dean Clements
John B. Bennett
Angela A. Ripper

Counsel for: Pioneer Bank; Chattanooga Gas Co.; South Central Bell Telephone Co.; Tennessee-American Water Co.; Blue Cross and Blue Shield of Tennessee; State Farm Mutual Automobile Insurance Cos.; Nationwide Insurance Co.; Siskin Steel & Supply Co., Inc.; CSX Transportation, Inc.; The McCallie School; Mueller Co.

For Complete List of Firm Personnel, See General Section

For full biographical listings, see the Martindale-Hubbell Law Directory

SUMMERS, MCCREA & WYATT, P.C. (AV)

500 Lindsay Street, 37402
Telephone: 615-265-2385
Fax: 615-266-5211

Jerry H. Summers
Thomas L. Wyatt
Sandra K. McCrea
Jeffrey W. Rufolo

For full biographical listings, see the Martindale-Hubbell Law Directory

WITT, GAITHER & WHITAKER, P.C. (AV)

1100 American National Bank Building, 37402-2608
Telephone: 615-265-8881
Telefax: 615-266-4138; 615-756-5612

William P. Hutcheson (1923-1991)
Frank P. Pinchak
Philip B. Whitaker
K. Stephen Powers
Hugh J. Moore, Jr.
Rosemarie Luise Bryan
Douglas E. Peck

Representative Clients: American National Bank & Trust Company; Chattanooga Cetropolitan Airport Authority; Chrysler Insurance Co.; Coca-Cola Bottling Co. Consolidated; Dean Witter Reynolds, Inc.; Dixie Yarns, Inc.; E.I. du Pont de Nemours & Company; Signal Apparel Company, Inc.; Southwest Motor Freight, Inc.; University of Chattanooga Foundation, Inc.

For Complete List of Firm Personnel, See General Section

For full biographical listings, see the Martindale-Hubbell Law Directory

KINGSPORT, Sullivan Co.

HUNTER, SMITH & DAVIS (AV)

1212 North Eastman Road, P.O. Box 3740, 37664
Telephone: 615-378-8800;
Johnson City: 615-282-4186;
Bristol: 615-968-7604
Telecopier: 615-378-8801
Johnson City, Tennessee Office: Suite 500 First American Center, 208 Sunset Drive, 37604.
Telephone: 615-283-6300.
Telecopier: 615-283-6301.

MEMBERS OF FIRM

William C. Bovender
Michael L. Forrester
Douglas S. Tweed
Stephen M. Darden

ASSOCIATE

Julie Poe Bennett

COUNSEL

Shelburne Ferguson, Jr.

Representative Clients: Arcata Graphics; The Mead Corp.; AFG Industries, Inc.; United Telephone System-Southeast Group; Eastman Chemical Co.; Bristol Regional Medical Center; Ball Corp.; Land-O-Sun Dairies; Plus Mark, Inc. (Subsidiary of American Greetings Corp.); General Shale Products Corp.

For Complete List of Firm Personnel, See General Section

For full biographical listings, see the Martindale-Hubbell Law Directory

MOORE, STOUT, WADDELL & LEDFORD (AV)

238 Broad Street, P.O. Box 1345, 37662
Telephone: 615-246-2344
Fax: 615-246-2210

MEMBER OF FIRM

Robert Lane Arrington

ASSOCIATE

Angela R. Kelley

Representative Clients: Kinsport Housing Authority; Donihe Graphics, Inc.; Form Rite LTD; Impact Plastics, Inc.; Intermountain Pathology Associates, P.C.; Kingsport Radiology Group, P.C.; Bice Chapman & Smith, M.D., P.C.

For Complete List of Firm Personnel, See General Section

For full biographical listings, see the Martindale-Hubbell Law Directory

SHINE & MASON LAW OFFICE (AV)

Suite 201, 433 East Center Street, 37660
Telephone: 615-246-8433
FAX: 615 247 2241
Washington, D.C. Office: Suite 200, 4427-A Wisconsin Avenue, N.W., 20016.
Telephone: 202-895-2699.

MEMBERS OF FIRM

D. Bruce Shine
Donald F. Mason, Jr.

Reference: Citizens Bank, Kingsport, TN.

For full biographical listings, see the Martindale-Hubbell Law Directory

*KNOXVILLE,** Knox Co.

ARNETT, DRAPER & HAGOOD (AV)

Suite 2300 Plaza Tower, 37929-2300
Telephone: 615-546-7000
Telecopier: 615-546-0423

MEMBERS OF FIRM

Lewis R. Hagood
Robert N. Townsend

Representative Clients: United Parcel Service, Inc.; Philips Consumer Electronics Co.; Consolidation Coal Co.; Indian Head Industries, Inc.; Fort Sanders Regional Medical Center; Blue Diamond Coal Co.; Shoney's of

(See Next Column)

ARNETT, DRAPER & HAGOOD, *Knoxville—Continued*

Knoxville, Inc.; American Airlines, Inc.; Liberty Healthcare, Inc.; Rexnord Corp.

For Complete List of Firm Personnel, See General Section

For full biographical listings, see the Martindale-Hubbell Law Directory

WATSON, HOLLOW & REEVES (AV)

1700 Plaza Tower, P.O. Box 131, 37901
Telephone: 615-522-3803
Telecopier: 615-525-2514

MEMBERS OF FIRM

Robert Harmon Watson, Jr.
Richard L. Hollow
Pamela L. Reeves
Jon G. Roach
John C. Duffy
John T. Batson, Jr.
Earl Jerome Melson

ASSOCIATES

Arthur Franklin Knight, III
Robert W. Willingham

For full biographical listings, see the Martindale-Hubbell Law Directory

*MEMPHIS,** Shelby Co.

ARMSTRONG ALLEN PREWITT GENTRY JOHNSTON & HOLMES (AV)

80 Monroe Avenue Suite 700, 38103
Telephone: 901-523-8211
Telecopier: 901-524-4936
Jackson, Missippi Office: 1350 One Jackson Place, 188 East Capitol Street.
Telephone: 601-948-8020.
Telecopier: 601-948-8389.

MEMBERS OF FIRM

J. Edward Wise
Paul E. Prather
John W. Simmons

Steven W. Likens

For Complete List of Firm Personnel, See General Section

For full biographical listings, see the Martindale-Hubbell Law Directory

BAKER, DONELSON, BEARMAN & CALDWELL (AV)

20th Floor, First Tennessee Building, 165 Madison, 38103
Telephone: 901-526-2000
Telecopier: 901-577-2303
Nashville, Tennessee Office: 1700 Nashville City Center, 511 Union Street, 37219.
Telephone: 615-726-5600.
Telecopier: 615-726-0464.
Knoxville, Tennessee Office: 2200 Riverview Tower, 900 Gay Street, 37901.
Telephone: 615-549-7000.
Telecopier: 615-525-8569.
Chattanooga, Tennessee Office: 1800 Republic Centre, 633 Chestnut Street, 37450-1800.
Telephone: 615-752-4400.
Telecopier: 615-752-4410.
Huntsville, Tennessee Office: 3 Courthouse Square, 37756.
Telephone: 615-663-2321.
Telecopier: 615-663-2111.
Johnson City, Tennessee Office: Hamilton Bank Building, 207 Mockingbird Lane, 37604.
Telephone: 615-928-0181.
Telecopier: 615-928-5694; 615-928-3654; Kingsport: 615-246-6191.
Washington, D.C. Office: Market Square, 801 Pennsylvania Avenue, N.W., 20004.
Telephone: 202-508-3400.
Telecopier: 202-508-3402.

PARTNERS

Maurice Wexler
Stephen H. Biller
Stephen D. Wakefield

ASSOCIATE

Robbin T. Sarrazin

For Complete List of Firm Personnel, See General Section

For full biographical listings, see the Martindale-Hubbell Law Directory

BOWLING, BOWLING & ASSOCIATES (AV)

766 South White Station Road, Suite 4, 38117
Telephone: 901-761-3440
FAX: 901-761-3484
Cookeville, Tennessee Office: Suite One, Fourth Floor, First Tennessee Bank, 345 S. Jefferson Avenue, 38501.
Telephone: 615-526-6101; 615-484-7237.

PRINCIPALS OF FIRM

W. Kerby Bowling
W. Kerby Bowling, II

For full biographical listings, see the Martindale-Hubbell Law Directory

HARKAVY, SHAINBERG, KOSTEN & PINSTEIN (AV)

Oak Court Office Building, 530 Oak Court Drive, Suite 350, P.O. Box 241450, 38124-1450
Telephone: 901-761-1263
Telecopier: 901-763-3340

MEMBERS AND ASSOCIATES

Ronald M. Harkavy
Raymond M. Shainberg
Alan L. Kosten
Robert J. Pinstein
Michael D. Kaplan
Allen C. Dunstan
Neil Harkavy
Laurie A. Cooper
Jerome A. Broadhurst
Dixie White Ishee
Alan M. Harkavy

OF COUNSEL

Ira D. Pruitt, Jr.

For full biographical listings, see the Martindale-Hubbell Law Directory

MCKNIGHT, HUDSON, LEWIS & HENDERSON (AV)

6750 Poplar Avenue, Suite 301, P.O. Box 171375, 38187-1375
Telephone: 901-756-1550
Telecopier: 901-756-1016

MEMBERS OF FIRM

Robert L. McKnight (1906-1976)
Fletcher L. Hudson
Frederick J. Lewis
Kenneth D. Henderson
Donna K. Fisher
Keith A. Warren
Louis P. Britt, III
Thomas L. Henderson

ASSOCIATES

Charles V. Holmes
Mary K. Kallaher
Kelly S. Gooch
Delaine R. Smith
Theofilos G. Galoozis
J. Gregory Addison
Conielyn Lowry Abernathy
Rhonda M. Taylor
Mark K. Braswell
Morrison Carl Knox
Thomas H. Lawrence (Not admitted in TN)

OF COUNSEL

William B. Paul (Not admitted in TN)
James C. Hoover (Not admitted in TN)

For full biographical listings, see the Martindale-Hubbell Law Directory

WARING COX (AV)

Morgan Keegan Tower, 50 North Front Street, Suite 1300, 38103-1190
Telephone: 901-543-8000
Telecopy: 901-543-8030

MEMBERS OF FIRM

Louis F. Allen
Charles W. Hill

ASSOCIATE

Robert B.C. Hale

Representative Clients: Federal Express Corp.; South Central Bell Telephone Co.; Flavorite Laboratories, Inc.; Fred's Inc.; Seabrook Wallcovering, Inc.; Health First Medical Group, P.C.

For Complete List of Firm Personnel, See General Section

For full biographical listings, see the Martindale-Hubbell Law Directory

WEINTRAUB, ROBINSON, WEINTRAUB, STOCK & BENNETT, P.C. (AV)

Suite 2560 One Commerce Square, 38103
Telephone: 901-526-0431
1-800-467-0435
Facsimile: 901-526-8183

Samuel J. Weintraub (1917-1993)
Earl W. DeHart (1933-1977)
Jay R. Robinson
Jeff Weintraub
James H. Stock, Jr.
Richard D. Bennett

Cindy Cole Ettingoff
J. Gregory Grisham
George H. Rieger, II
Elizabeth A. Holloway

For full biographical listings, see the Martindale-Hubbell Law Directory

YOUNG & PERL, P.C. (AV)

Suite 2380, One Commerce Square, 38103
Telephone: 901-525-2761
FAX: 901-526-2702

Edward R. Young
Arnold E. Perl
Jay W. Kiesewetter
Jonathan E. Kaplan
Cary Schwimmer
W. Stephen Gardner

Karen W. Grochau (Resident)
James C. Holland
Leigh A. Hollingsworth
John Marshall Jones
Shawn R. Lillie
Todd L. Sarver (Not admitted in TN)
James M. Simpson
Mark Theodore (Not admitted in TN)

(See Next Column)

YOUNG & PERL P.C.—*Continued*

For Complete List of Firm Personnel, See General Section

For full biographical listings, see the Martindale-Hubbell Law Directory

*NASHVILLE,** Davidson Co.

BASS, BERRY & SIMS (AV)

2700 First American Center, 37238-2700
Telephone: 615-742-6200
Telecopy: 615-742-6293
Knoxville, Tennessee Office: 1700 Riverview Tower, 900 S. Gay Street, P.O. Box 1509, 37901-1509.
Telephone: 615-521-6200.
Telecopy: 615-521-6234.

MEMBERS OF FIRM

Russell F. Morris, Jr. | Karen L.C. Ellis
William N. Ozier | Tim K. Garrett
Stafford F. McNamee, Jr. | Bennett L. Ross

Representative Clients: Vanderbilt University; Quebecor Printing, Inc.; ; General Electric Co.; Toshiba America Consumer Products, Inc.; Oshkosh B'Gosh, Inc.; Goodyear Tire & Rubber Co.; Peterbilt Motors Company; Cracker Barrel Old Country Stores, Inc.; Springs Industries, Inc.; Service Merchandise Co., Inc.

For full biographical listings, see the Martindale-Hubbell Law Directory

CONSTANGY, BROOKS & SMITH (AV)

Suite 1080 Vanderbilt Plaza, 2100 West End Avenue, 37203-5231
Telephone: 615-320-5200
Atlanta, Georgia Office: 2400 Peachtree Center Building, 230 Peachtree Street, N.W.
Telephone: 404-525-8622.
Birmingham, Alabama Office: Suite 1410 AmSouth/Harbert Plaza, 1901 Sixth Avenue North.
Telephone: 205-252-9321.
Columbia, South Carolina Office: Suite 810 NationsBank Tower, 1301 Gervais Street.
Telephone: 803-256-3200.
Washington, D.C. Office: Suite 1200, 1015 Fifteenth Street., N.W.
Telephone: 202-789-8676.
Winston-Salem, North Carolina Office: Suite 300, 101 South Stratford Road.
Telephone: 910-721-1001, 704-344-1040 (Charlotte).

Frank A. Constangy (1911-1971)

RESIDENT MEMBERS

Larry W. Bridgesmith | William A. Blue, Jr.

RESIDENT ASSOCIATE

Stephen Craig Moore

Representative Clients: Blockbuster Entertainment Corp.; Blue Cross/Blue Shield of Tennessee; Consolidated Freightways, Inc.; Delta Woodside Industries;McDonald's; Merck & Co., Inc.; Philip-Morris Cos., Inc.; Phillips Van Heusen Corp.; Sara Lee Corp.; Trust Company Bank.

For full biographical listings, see the Martindale-Hubbell Law Directory

KING & BALLOW (AV)

1200 Noel Place, 200 Fourth Avenue, North, 37219
Telephone: 615-259-3456
Fax: 615-254-7907
San Diego, California Office: 2700 Symphony Towers, 750 B Street, 92101.
Telephone: 619-236-9401.
Fax: 619-236-9437.
San Francisco, California Office: 100 First Street, Suite 2700, 94105.
Telephone: 415-541-7803.
Fax: 415-541-7805.

MEMBERS OF FIRM

Frank S. King, Jr. | Steven C. Douse
Robert L. Ballow | Douglas R. Pierce
Richard C. Lowe | James P. Thompson
R. Eddie Wayland | Howard M. Kastrinsky
Larry D. Crabtree | Kenneth E. Douthat
Alan L. Marx | Mark E. Hunt
Paul H. Duvall (Resident, San Diego, California Office) | John J. Matchulat
| M. Kim Vance

ASSOCIATES

R. Brent Ballow | Paul H. Derrick
Michael D. Oesterle | Richard S. Busch

Representative Clients: American Airlines, Nashville, Tennessee; Capital Cities/ABC, Inc., New York, New York; Denver Post, Denver, Colorado; Houston Post, Houston, Texas; Knight-Rider, Inc, Miami, Florida; Northern Telecom, Inc., Nashville, Tennessee; Opryland USA, Inc., Nashville, Tennessee; Parade Magazine, Inc., New York, New York; Pulitzer Publishing Company, St. Louis, Missouri; Tribune Company, Chicago, Illinois; Union Tribune Publishing Co., San Diego, California.

For Complete List of Firm Personnel, See General Section

For full biographical listings, see the Martindale-Hubbell Law Directory

ZINSER AND DOMINA (AV)

150 Second Avenue North, 37201
Telephone: 615-244-9700
Fax: 615-244-9734

MEMBERS OF FIRM

L. Michael Zinser | Rebecca E. Domina
Bruce H. Henderson

ASSOCIATES

Michael E. Heston | James McMahan Patterson, Jr.
Mark Posten Reineke

Representative Clients: Houston Chronicle; The Hearst Corporation; The Tennessean; Guy Gannett Publishing Co.; Vista Metropolitan Media Co.; Donrey Media Group; Stauffer Communications, Inc.; Patrick Media Group, Inc.; American Publishing Co.; Southern Newspapers, Inc.

For full biographical listings, see the Martindale-Hubbell Law Directory

TEXAS

*AUSTIN,** Travis Co.

DAVIS & DAVIS, P.C. (AV)

Arboretum Plaza One, 9th Floor, 9442 Capitol of Texas Highway, P.O. Box 1588, 78767
Telephone: 512-343-6248
Fax: 512-343-0121

C. Dean Davis | Alexis J. Fuller, Jr.
Fred E. Davis | Francis A. (Tony) Bradley
Ruth Russell-Schafer

Kevin Wayde Morse

For Complete List of Firm Personnel, See General Section

For full biographical listings, see the Martindale-Hubbell Law Directory

DAVIS & WILKERSON, P.C. (AV)

200 One American Center, Six Hundred Congress Avenue, P.O. Box 2283, 78768-2283
Telephone: 512-482-0614
Fax: 512-482-0342
Alpine, Texas Office: 1110 East Holland. P.O. Box 777. 79831-0777.
Telephone: 915-837-5547.

David M. Davis | David A. Wright
Steven R. Welch | Leonard W. Woods
Jeff D. Otto | Kevin A. Reed
Glen Wilkerson | J. Mark Holbrook
Brian E. Riewe

Fletcher H. Brown | Brian McElroy
Deborah G. Clark | Michael Wilson
Frances W. Hamermesh | Stephen G. Wohleb
Kelly Ann McDonald | Stephen A. Wood

OF COUNSEL

Pete P. Gallego | Regina C. Williams

For full biographical listings, see the Martindale-Hubbell Law Directory

MATTHEWS & BRANSCOMB, A PROFESSIONAL CORPORATION (AV)

301 Congress Avenue, Suite 2050, 78701
Telephone: 512-305-4400
Facsimile: 512-305-4413
San Antonio, Texas Office: One Alamo Center. 106 S. St. Mary's Street, Suite 800.
Telephone: 210-226-4211.
Facsimile: 210-226-0521.
Telex: 5106009283. Cable Code: MBLAW.
Corpus Christi, Texas Office: 802 N. Caranachua, Suite 1900.
Telephone: 512-888-9261.
Facsimile: 512-888-8504.
Eagle Pass, Texas Office: 675 Main Street.
Telephone: 210-773-6700.
Facsimile: 210-757-4045.
Uvalde, Texas Office: 200 E. Nopal # 208.
Telephone: 210-278-4597.
Facsimile: 210-278-4806.
(Associated with Hall, Quintanilla & Alarcon, L.C., Laredo, Texas, under the name of Hall, Quintanilla, Alarcon, Matthews & Branscomb, P.L.L.C.).

Lacey L. Gourley | Holly Claghorn

For Complete List of Firm Personnel, See General Section

For full biographical listings, see the Martindale-Hubbell Law Directory

*CORPUS CHRISTI,** Nueces Co.

MATTHEWS & BRANSCOMB, A PROFESSIONAL CORPORATION (AV)

802 North Carancahua, Suite 1900, 78470-0700
Telephone: 512-888-9261
Facsimile: 512-888-8504
Austin, Texas Office: 301 Congress Avenue, Suite 2050.
Telephone: 512-305-4400.
Facsimile: 512-305-4413.
San Antonio, Texas Office: One Alamo Center, 106 S. St. Mary's Street, Suite 800.
Telephone: 210-226-4211.
Facsimile: 210-226-0521.
Telex: 51060009283. Cable Code: MBLAW.
Eagle Pass, Texas Office: 675 Main Street.
Telephone: 210-773-6700.
Facsimile: 210-757-4045.
Uvalde, Texas Office: 200 E. Nopal #208.
Telephone: 210-278-4597.
Facsimile: 210-278-4806.
(Associated with Hall, Quintanilla & Alarcon, L.C., Laredo, Texas, under the name of Hall, Quintanilla, Alarcon, Matthews & Branscomb, P.L.L.C.).

M. Colleen McHugh
Robert S. Nichols
Keith B. Sieczkowski

For Complete List of Firm Personnel, See General Section

For full biographical listings, see the Martindale-Hubbell Law Directory

*DALLAS,** Dallas Co.

BAKER & BOTTS, L.L.P. (AV)

2001 Ross Avenue, 75201
Telephone: 214-953-6500
Fax: 214-953-6503
Houston, Texas Office: One Shell Plaza, 910 Louisiana.
Telephone: 713-229-1234.
Washington, D.C. Office: The Warner, 1299 Pennsylvania Avenue, N.W.
Telephone: 202-639-7700.
Austin, Texas Office: 1600 San Jacinto Center, 98 San Jacinto Boulevard.
Telephone: 512-322-2500.
New York, New York Office: 885 Third Avenue, Suite 2000.
Telephone: 212-705-5000.
Moscow, Russian Federation Office: 10 ul. Pushkinskaya, 103031.
Telephone: 7095/921-5300 (Local); 7095/929-7070.

MEMBERS OF FIRM

Larry D. Carlson
George C. Lamb III
Sarah R. Saldana

ASSOCIATES

Mary L. Scott
Lynn S. Switzer

For Complete List of Firm Personnel, See General Section

For full biographical listings, see the Martindale-Hubbell Law Directory

CALHOUN & STACY (AV)

5700 NationsBank Plaza, 901 Main Street, 75202-3747
Telephone: 214-748-5000
Telecopier: 214-748-1421
Telex: 211358 CALGUMP UR

Mark Alan Calhoun
Steven D. Goldston
David W. Elrod
Parker Nelson
Roy L. Stacy

ASSOCIATES

Shannon S. Barclay
Thomas C. Jones
Robert A. Bragalone
Katherine Johnson Knight
Dennis D. Conder
V. Paige Pace
Jane Elizabeth Diseker
Veronika Willard
Lawrence I. Fleishman
Michael C. Wright

LEGAL CONSULTANT

Rees T. Bowen, III

For full biographical listings, see the Martindale-Hubbell Law Directory

CANTERBURY, STUBER, PRATT, ELDER & GOOCH, A PROFESSIONAL CORPORATION (AV)

One Lincoln Centre, 5400 LBJ Freeway, Suite 1300, 75240
Telephone: 214-239-7493
Telefax: 214-490-7739
San Antonio, Texas Office: Centre Plaza, 45 N.E. Loop 410, Suite 600.
Telephone: 210-366-3850.

Joseph F. Canterbury, Jr.
Charles W. Stuber
Donald O. Pratt
Robert C. Elder, Jr.
W. Kyle Gooch
Stanley W. Curry, Jr. (Resident, San Antonio Office)
Frederic Gover
David G. Surratt
Steve Kennedy

(See Next Column)

Paul H. Sanderford
Jeffrey A. Brannen

For full biographical listings, see the Martindale-Hubbell Law Directory

GARDERE & WYNNE, L.L.P. (AV)

Thanksgiving Tower, 1601 Elm Street, Suite 3000, 75201
Telephone: 214-999-3000
Fax: 214-999-4667
Cable Address: "Garwyn Dallas"
Telex: 73-0197
Tulsa, Oklahoma Office: 401 South Boston, Mid-Continent Tower, Suite 2000.
Telephone: 918-560-2900.
Fax: 918-560-2929.
Houston, Texas Office: 600 Travis Street, Suite 5000.
Telephone: 713-547-3500.
Fax: 713-547-3535.
Mexico City, Mexico Office: Sèneca 245, Col. Chapultepec Polanco, 11560 Mèxico, D.F. Telèfonos: 011 (525) 282-0031; 011 (525) 282-0156; 011 (525) 282-0414; 011 (525) 282-0507; 011 (525) 282-1696.
FAX: 011 (525) 282-1821.

MEMBERS OF FIRM

Ronald M. Gaswirth
Dan Hartsfield
Steven M. Ladik

ASSOCIATES

Michele T. Baird
Brian A. King

Representative Clients: Atlantic Richfield Co.; Campbell Taggart, Inc.; Cronus Industries, Inc.; E-Systems, Inc.; National Gysum Co.; First RepublicBank; Tandy Corp.; Trammell Crow Co.; Tyler Corp.; Zale Corp.

For Complete List of Firm Personnel, See General Section

For full biographical listings, see the Martindale-Hubbell Law Directory

GODWIN & CARLTON, A PROFESSIONAL CORPORATION (AV)

Suite 3300, 901 Main Street, 75202-3714
Telephone: 214-939-4400
Telecopier: 214-760-7332
Monterrey, Mexico Correspondent: Quintero y Quintero Abogodos. Martin De Zalva 840-3 Sur Esquinna Con Hidalgo.
Telephone: 44-07-74, 44-07-80, 44-06-56, 44-06-28.
Fax: 83-40-34-54.

Donald E. Godwin
Harvey M. Shapan
Steven T. Polino

For Complete List of Firm Personnel, See General Section

For full biographical listings, see the Martindale-Hubbell Law Directory

THOMPSON, COE, COUSINS & IRONS, L.L.P. (AV)

200 Crescent Court, Eleventh Floor, 75201-1840
Telephone: 214-871-8200 (Dallas)
512-480-8770 (Austin)
FAX: 214-871-8209

MEMBERS OF FIRM

John L. Ross
Jennifer D. Aufricht

ASSOCIATE

Karl A. Vogeler

Representative Clients: Bridgestone, Inc.; Republic Parking Corp.; Tyler Independent School District; United Stationers Supply Co.; H.S. Fox Corp.; Gates, McDonald & Co.; Fort Worth Country Day School, Inc.; Garland Independent School District; LD Brinkman; Wal-Mart; Hawkins Independent School District.

For Complete List of Firm Personnel, See General Section

For full biographical listings, see the Martindale-Hubbell Law Directory

THOMPSON & KNIGHT, A PROFESSIONAL CORPORATION (AV)

(Attorneys and Counselors)
1700 Pacific Avenue Suite 3300, 75201
Telephone: 214-969-1700
Telecopy: 214-969-1751
Cable Address: "Tomtex"
Telex: 732298
Austin, Texas Office: 1200 San Jacinto Center, 98 San Jacinto Boulevard, 78701.
Telephone: 512-469-6100.
Telecopy: 512-469-6180.
Fort Worth, Texas Office: 801 Cherry Street, Suite 1600, 76102.
Telephone: 817-347-1700.
Telecopy: 817-347-1799.
Houston, Texas Office: 1700 Texas Commerce Tower, 600 Travis, 77002.
Telephone: 713-217-2800.
Telecopy: 713-217-2828.

(See Next Column)

THOMPSON & KNIGHT A PROFESSIONAL CORPORATION—*Continued*

Monterrey, Mexico Office: Edificio Losoles PD-4, Av. Lázaro Cárdenas No. 2400 Pte., San Pedro Garza Garcia, Nuevo Léon C.P. 66220.
Telephone: (52-8) 363-0096.
Telecopy: (52-8) 363-3067.

SHAREHOLDERS

Bennett W. Cervin
Stephen F. Fink
Steven W. Sloan
Arlene Switzer Steinfield

ASSOCIATES

Marc H. Klein
Mia M. Martin
Bryan P. Neal
Elizabeth A. Schartz

For Complete List of Firm Personnel, See General Section

For full biographical listings, see the Martindale-Hubbell Law Directory

*EL PASO,** El Paso Co.

KEMP, SMITH, DUNCAN & HAMMOND, A PROFESSIONAL CORPORATION (AV)

2000 State National Bank Plaza, 79901, P.O. Drawer 2800, 79999
Telephone: 915-533-4424
Fax: 915-546-5360
Albuquerque, New Mexico Office: 500 Marquette, N.W., Suite 1200, P.O. Box 1276.
Telephone: 505-247-2315.
Fax: 505-764-5480.

Charles C. High, Jr.
Michael D. McQueen
Kenneth R. Carr
Mark R. Flora

Clara B. Burns
Robert L. Blumenfeld

Attorneys for: State National Bank; Southern Pacific Transportation Co.; Pet Inc.; Asarco; Tony Lama Co.; Tri-State Wholesale Associated Grocers.

For Complete List of Firm Personnel, See General Section

For full biographical listings, see the Martindale-Hubbell Law Directory

MOUNCE & GALATZAN, A PROFESSIONAL CORPORATION (AV)

7th Floor, Texas Commerce Bank Building, 79901-1334
Telephone: 915-532-3911
Fax: 915-541-1597

Carl H. Green
Steven L. Hughes
Mark D. Dore

Clyde A. Pine, Jr.
Bruce A. Koehler
Carrie D. Helmcamp
Lisa Anne Elizondo

Attorneys for: El Paso Natural Gas Co.; Texas Commerce Bank National Association; El Paso Independent School District; Commercial Union Assurance Cos.; State Farm Mutual Automobile Insurance Co.; Employers Insurance of Texas; Greater El Paso Association of Realtors; Farah Incorporated; El Paso Apparel Co., Inc.; Mack Massey Motors, Inc.; Roadrunner Trucking, Inc.; Danny Herman Trucking Co., Inc.; Greenwood Mills, Inc.; Vulcraft, A Division of Nucor Corporation.

For Complete List of Firm Personnel, See General Section

For full biographical listings, see the Martindale-Hubbell Law Directory

*FORT WORTH,** Tarrant Co.

CANTEY & HANGER (AV)

A Registered Limited Liability Partnership
2100 Burnett Plaza, 801 Cherry Street, 76102-6899
Telephone: 817-877-2800, Metro Line: 429-3815
Telex: 758631 FAX: 877-2807
Dallas
Dallas, Texas Office: Suite 500, 300 Crescent Court.
Telephone: 214-978-4100.
FAX: 214-978-4150.

MEMBERS OF FIRM

Edward L. Kemble
Donald K. Buckman
Clay Dean Humphries

ASSOCIATE

Farolito Parco (Not admitted in TX)

Represent: General Motors Corp.; Texas-New Mexico Power Co.; Miller Brewing Co.; The Medical Protective Co.; Union Oil Co.; Texas Utilities Electric Co.; NationsBank of Texas, N.A.; Union Pacific Resources; Kimbell Art Foundation; Texas Commerce Bank.

For Complete List of Firm Personnel, See General Section

For full biographical listings, see the Martindale-Hubbell Law Directory

*HOUSTON,** Harris Co.

BAKER & BOTTS, L.L.P. (AV)

One Shell Plaza, 910 Louisiana, 77002
Telephone: 713-229-1234
Cable Address: "Boterlove"
Fax: 713-229-1522
Washington, D.C. Office: The Warner, 1299 Pennsylvania Avenue, N.W.
Telephone: 202-639-7700.
New York, New York Office: 885 Third Avenue, Suite 2000.
Telephone: 212-705-5000.
Austin, Texas Office: 1600 San Jacinto Center, 98 San Jacinto Boulevard.
Telephone: 512-322-2500.
Dallas, Texas Office: 2001 Ross Avenue.
Telephone: 214-953-6500.
Moscow, Russian Federation Office: 10 ul. Pushkinskaya, 103031.
Telephone: 7095/921-5300 (Local); 7095/929-7070 (International).

MEMBERS OF FIRM

Richard R. Brann
L. Chapman Smith
Tony P. Rosenstein
Paul L. Mitchell

ASSOCIATES

Maria Wyckoff Boyce
Ross E. Cockburn
Robin Elizabeth Curtis
Phillip L. Douglass
Matthew P. Eastus
John K. Rentz
Suzanne H. Stenson
Rebecca S. Stierna
M. Virginia Stockbridge
Teresa Slowen Valderrama
Kathryn S. Vaughn
Shira R. Yoshor

For Complete List of Firm Personnel, See General Section

For full biographical listings, see the Martindale-Hubbell Law Directory

BRUCKNER & SYKES, L.L.P. (AV)

2700 Post Oak Boulevard, Suite 2100, 77056
Telephone: 713-877-8788
FAX: 713-877-8065

William H. Bruckner
Charles E. Sykes
Judith Batson Sadler
Sylvia Davidow

ASSOCIATE

Douglas H. Maddux, Jr.

For full biographical listings, see the Martindale-Hubbell Law Directory

FARNSWORTH & VONBERG (AV)

A Partnership of Professional Corporations
333 North Sam Houston Parkway, Suite 300, 77060
Telephone: 713-931-8902
Telecopy: 713-931-6032

T Brooke Farnsworth (P.C.)
Mary Frances vonBerg (P.C.)

ASSOCIATES

Diane B. Gould
Bennett S. Bartlett

LEGAL SUPPORT PERSONNEL

Lucille P. Poole

For full biographical listings, see the Martindale-Hubbell Law Directory

DAVID T. LOPEZ & ASSOCIATES (AV)

3900 Montrose Boulevard, 77006-4908
Telephone: 713-523-3900
Telecopier: 713-523-3908

ASSOCIATES

Thomas H. Padgett, Jr.
David V. de Cordova, Jr.
David J. Guillory

For full biographical listings, see the Martindale-Hubbell Law Directory

NEEL, HOOPER & KALMANS, P.C. (AV)

1700 West Loop South, Suite 1400, 77027-3008
Telephone: 713-629-1800
Fax: 713-629-1812

James M. Neel
Samuel E. Hooper
Raymond L. Kalmans
Joseph G. Galagaza

Cherry K. Bounds
Donna Smith Cude
Eric R. Miller

For full biographical listings, see the Martindale-Hubbell Law Directory

SCHWARTZ & CAMPBELL, L.L.P. (AV)

1221 McKinney, Suite 1000, 77010
Telephone: 713-752-0017
Telecopier: 713-752-0327

Richard A. Schwartz
Marshall S. Campbell

(See Next Column)

SCHWARTZ & CAMPBELL L.L.P., *Houston—Continued*

Monica F. Oathout
Stephen A. Mendel
Samuel E. Dunn
Harold W. Hargis
Phillip W. Bechter
Laura M. Taylor
Michael D. Hudgins

LEGAL SUPPORT PERSONNEL

PARALEGALS

Nannette Koger
Bettye Vaughan Johnson
Lenore Chomout
Maria Pinillos

For full biographical listings, see the Martindale-Hubbell Law Directory

VINSON & ELKINS L.L.P. (AV)

2300 First City Tower, 1001 Fannin, 77002-6760
Telephone: 713-758-2222
Fax: 713-758-2346
International Telex: 6868314
Cable Address: Vinelkins
Austin, Texas Office: One American Center, 600 Congress Avenue.
Telephone: 512-495-8400.
Fax: 512-495-8612.
Dallas, Texas Office: 3700 Trammell Crow Center, 2001 Ross Avenue.
Telephone: 214-220-7700.
Fax: 214-220-7716.
Washington, D.C. Office: The Willard Office Building, 1455 Pennsylvania Avenue, N.W.
Telephone: 202-639-6500.
Fax: 202-639-6604.
Cable Address: Vinelkins.
London, England Office: 47 Charles Street, Berkeley Square, London, W1X 7PB, England.
Telephone: 011 (44-171) 491-7236.
Fax: 011 (44-71) 499-5320.
Cable Address: Vinelkins London W.1.
Moscow, Russian Federation Office: 16 Alexey Tolstoy Street, Second Floor, Moscow, 103001 Russian Federation.
Telephone: 011 (70-95) 956-1995.
Telecopy: 011 (70-95) 956-1996.
Mexico City, Mexico Office: Aristóteles 77, 5°Piso, Colonia Chapultepec Polanco, 11560 Mexico, D.F.
Telephone: (52-5) 280-7828.
Fax: (52-5) 280-9223.
Singapore Office: 50 Raffles Place, #19-05 Shell Tower, 0104. U.S. Voice Mailbox: 713-758-3500.
Telephone: (65) 536-8300.
Fax: (65) 536-8311.

Douglas E. Hamel
W. Carl Jordan
John H. Smither
Thomas H. Wilson

ASSOCIATES

Dorene Aber
Anissa M. Albro
Sherrard L. Hayes, Jr.
Robert W. Horton
Robert L. Ivey
Suzanne M. Lehman
Anne M. Pike
Bryant Siddoway
Shadow Sloan
Sara A. Welch
Steven J Wright

For Complete List of Firm Personnel, See General Section

For full biographical listings, see the Martindale-Hubbell Law Directory

*SAN ANTONIO,** Bexar Co.

COX & SMITH INCORPORATED (AV)

112 East Pecan Street, Suite 1800, 78205
Telephone: 210-554-5500
Telecopier: 210-226-8395

William H. Lemons, III
Donna K. McElroy
Britannia Hobbs Hardee

Representative Clients: Bartlett Cocke Jr. Construction Co.; The Dee Howard Co.; Fairchild Aircraft Incorporated; Karena Hotels, Inc.; QVC Network, Inc.; Schindler Elevator Corporation; South Texas Radiology Group; Trinity University; Camla Care Centers, Inc.

For Complete List of Firm Personnel, See General Section

For full biographical listings, see the Martindale-Hubbell Law Directory

FOSTER, HELLER & KILGORE, P.C. (AV)

Suite 401, 4040 Broadway, 78209-6392
Telephone: 210-828-4040
FAX: 210-828-5964

Ramon D. Bissmeyer
Ben F. Foster, Jr.
Richard G. Garza
Jeffrey A. Goldberg
John A. Heller
Michael L. Holland
E. Burke Huber, Jr.
Robert D. Kilgore
Daniel R. Stern
Susan Stone

(See Next Column)

LEGAL SUPPORT PERSONNEL

PARALEGALS

Rose Magallanes
Mary Radicke
Valerie Thomas

Reference: Frost National Bank.

For full biographical listings, see the Martindale-Hubbell Law Directory

MATTHEWS & BRANSCOMB, A PROFESSIONAL CORPORATION (AV)

One Alamo Center, 106 S. St. Mary's Street, Suite 800, 78205
Telephone: 210-226-4211
Facsimile: 210-226-0521
Telex: 5106009283
Cable Code: MBLAW
Austin, Texas Office: 301 Congress Avenue, Suite 2050.
Telephone: 512-305-4400.
Facsimile: 512-305-4413.
Corpus Christi, Texas Office: 802 N. Carancahua, Suite 1900.
Telephone: 512-888-9261.
Facsimile: 512-888-8504.
Eagle Pass, Texas Office: 675 Main Street.
Telephone: 210-773-6700.
Facsimile: 210-757-4045.
Uvalde, Texas Office: 200 E. Nopal #208.
Telephone: 210-278-4597.
Facsimile: 210-278-4806.
(Associated with Hall, Quintanilla & Alarcon, L.C., Laredo, Texas, under the name of Hall, Quintanilla, Alarcon, Matthews & Branscomb, P.L.L.C.)

J. Joe Harris
George P. Parker, Jr.
J. Tullos Wells
James H. Kizziar, Jr.
Leslie Selig Byrd
Dawn Bruner Finlayson
John A. Ferguson, Jr.
Judy K. Jetelina
Robert Shaw-Meadow
Mary Helen Medina

Representative Clients: Coca Cola Bottling Company of the Southwest; Concord Oil Co.; Ellison Enterprises, Inc.; H. E. Butt Grocery Co.; Frank B. Hall & Co., Inc.; The Hearst Corp., San Antonio Light Division; San Antonio Gas & Electric Utilities (City Board); Southern Pacific Transportation Co.; Southwest Texas Methodist Hospital.

For Complete List of Firm Personnel, See General Section

For full biographical listings, see the Martindale-Hubbell Law Directory

UTAH

*SALT LAKE CITY,** Salt Lake Co.

JONES, WALDO, HOLBROOK & MCDONOUGH, A PROFESSIONAL CORPORATION (AV)

1500 First Interstate Plaza, 170 South Main Street, 84101
Telephone: 801-521-3200
Telecopier: 801-328-0537
Mailing Address: P.O. Box 45444, 84145-0444
St. George, Utah Office: The Tabernacle Tower Building, 249 East Tabernacle.
Telephone: 801-628-1627.
Telecopier: 801-628-5225.
Washington, D.C. Office: Suite 900, 2300 M Street, N.W.
Telephone: 202-296-5950.
Telecopier: 202-293-2509.

James S. Lowrie
James W. Stewart
Keven M. Rowe
Michael Patrick O'Brien

Deno G. Himonas

Representative Clients: American Stores Cos.; First Interstate Bank of Utah; Blue Cross and Blue Shield of Utah; Utah Power & Light; Lucas Western, Inc.; Mrs. Fields, Inc.; Unisys Corp.; Newspaper Agency Corp.; Thiokol Corp.

For Complete List of Firm Personnel, See General Section

For full biographical listings, see the Martindale-Hubbell Law Directory

PARSONS BEHLE & LATIMER, A PROFESSIONAL CORPORATION (AV)

One Utah Center, 201 South Main Street, Suite 1800, P.O. Box 45898, 84145-0898
Telephone: 801-532-1234
Telecopy: 801-536-6111

Keith E. Taylor
Gordon L. Roberts
Kent W. Winterholler
Barbara K. Polich
Charles H. Thronson
Francis M. Wikstrom
Chris Wangsgard
James M. Elegante

(See Next Column)

PARSONS BEHLE & LATIMER A PROFESSIONAL CORPORATION—*Continued*

Spencer E. Austin
David A. Anderson
Lois A. Baar
Derek Langton
Lorna Rogers Burgess
W. Mark Gavre
Douglas R. Davis
Elisabeth R. Blattner
David W. Zimmerman
Michael A. Zody

Representative Clients: AT&T Information Systems; American Express Company; Hercules, Inc.; Kennecott Corporation; McDonnell Douglas Corporation; Pepperidge Farm, Inc.; USX Corporation; United Parcel Service of America.

For full biographical listings, see the Martindale-Hubbell Law Directory

PRINCE, YEATES & GELDZAHLER (AV)

City Centre I, Suite 900, 175 East 400 South, 84111
Telephone: 801-524-1000
Fax: 801-524-1099
Park City, Utah Office: 614 Main Street, P.O. Box 38.
Telephones: 801-524-1000; 649-7440.

MEMBERS OF FIRM

Robert M. Yeates
John S. Chindlund

ASSOCIATE

Roger J. McConkie

Representative Clients: Albertson's Inc.; Associated General Contractors of Utah; Gilbert Western Corp. (a division of Peter Kiewit); Intermountain Retail, Health & Welfare Pension; Smith's Food and Drug Centers, Inc.; Utah Power & Light Company; Magnesium Corp. of America.

For Complete List of Firm Personnel, See General Section

For full biographical listings, see the Martindale-Hubbell Law Directory

RAY, QUINNEY & NEBEKER, A PROFESSIONAL CORPORATION (AV)

Suite 400 Deseret Building, 79 South Main Street, P.O. Box 45385, 84145-0385
Telephone: 801-532-1500
Telecopier: 801-532-7543
Provo, Utah Office: 210 First Security Bank Building, 92 North University Avenue.
Telephone: 801-226-7210.
Telecopier: 801-375-8379.

D. Jay Curtis
Janet Hugie Smith
Michael E. Blue

Representative Clients: First Security Bank of Utah, N.A.; Borden, Inc.; Southern Pacific Transportation; Utah Power & Light Co.; Travelers Insurance Co.; Greyhound Leasing & Financial; Holy Cross Hospital and Health System; Amoco Production Co.

For Complete List of Firm Personnel, See General Section

For full biographical listings, see the Martindale-Hubbell Law Directory

STRONG & HANNI, A PROFESSIONAL CORPORATION (AV)

Sixth Floor Boston Building, 9 Exchange Place, 84111
Telephone: 801-532-7080
Fax: 801-596-1508

Gordon R. Strong (1909-1969)
Glenn C. Hanni
Henry E. Heath
Philip R. Fishler
Roger H. Bullock
Robert A. Burton
R. Scott Williams
Dennis M. Astill (Managing Partner)
S. Baird Morgan
Stuart H. Schultz
Paul M. Belnap
Stephen J. Trayner
Joseph J. Joyce
Bradley Wm. Bowen

Robert L. Janicki
Elizabeth L. Willey
Peter H. Christensen
H. Burt Ringwood
David R. Nielson
Adam Trupp
Catherine M. Larson

Representative Clients: State Farm Mutual Automobile Insurance Co.; Standard Accident Insurance Co.; United Services Automobile Assn.; Western Casualty & Surety Co.; Government Employees Insurance Co.; Guaranty Mutual Life Co.

For full biographical listings, see the Martindale-Hubbell Law Directory

VAN COTT, BAGLEY, CORNWALL & MCCARTHY, A PROFESSIONAL CORPORATION (AV)

Suite 1600, 50 South Main Street, P.O. Box 45340, 84145
Telephone: 801-532-3333
Telex: 453149
Telecopier: 801-534-0058
Ogden, Utah Office: Suite 900, 2404 Washington Boulevard.
Telephone: 801-394-5783.
Park City, Utah Office: 314 Main Street, Suite 205.
Telephone: 801-649-3889.

(See Next Column)

Reno, Nevada Office: Jeppson & Lee, 100 West Liberty, Suite 990.
Telephone: 702-333-6800.

Brent J. Giauque
E. Scott Savage
Danny C. Kelly
Steven D. Woodland
Patricia M. Leith
Ronald G. Moffitt
John A. Anderson
Wayne D. Swan
Donald L. Dalton
David L. Arrington
Casey K. McGarvey
Phyllis J. Vetter
Bryon J. Benevento

Elizabeth D. Winter
Jon E. Waddoups
Melyssa D. Davidson
Michele Ballantyne
Matthew M. Durham

For Complete List of Firm Personnel, See General Section

For full biographical listings, see the Martindale-Hubbell Law Directory

VIRGINIA

ALEXANDRIA, (Independent City)

GRAD, LOGAN & KLEWANS, P.C. (AV)

112 North Columbus Street, P.O. Box 1417-A44, 22313
Telephone: 703-548-8400
Facsimile: 703-836-6289

John D. Grad
Michael P. Logan
Samuel N. Klewans

Sean C. E. McDonough
Claire R. Pettrone
David A. Damiani

OF COUNSEL

Jeanne F. Franklin

For full biographical listings, see the Martindale-Hubbell Law Directory

THOMAS, BALLENGER, VOGELMAN AND TURNER, P.C. (AV)

124 South Royal Street, 22314
Telephone: 703-836-3400
Fax: 703-836-3549

Jeffrey A. Vogelman

References: First Union National Bank of Virginia; Burke & Herbert Bank & Trust Co.

For Complete List of Firm Personnel, See General Section

For full biographical listings, see the Martindale-Hubbell Law Directory

BRISTOL, (Independent City)

ELLIOTT LAWSON & POMRENKE (AV)

Sixth Floor, First Union Bank Building, P.O. Box 8400, 24203-8400
Telephone: 703-466-8400
Fax: 703-466-8161

James Wm. Elliott, Jr.
Mark M. Lawson
Kurt J. Pomrenke
Steven R. Minor
Kyle P. Macione
Lisa King Crockett

For full biographical listings, see the Martindale-Hubbell Law Directory

*FAIRFAX,** (Ind. City; Seat of Fairfax Co.)

ODIN, FELDMAN & PITTLEMAN, P.C. (AV)

9302 Lee Highway, Suite 1100, 22031
Telephone: 703-218-2100
Facsimile: 703-218-2160

Dexter S. Odin
John S. Wisiackas
Robert K. Richardson
F. Douglas Ross
Bruce M. Blanchard
Leslye S. Fenton
Frances P. Dwornik

For Complete List of Firm Personnel, See General Section

For full biographical listings, see the Martindale-Hubbell Law Directory

MCLEAN, Fairfax Co.

MANDELL, LEWIS & GOLDBERG, A PROFESSIONAL CORPORATION (AV)

Tysons Executive Plaza, Suite 1075, 2000 Corporate Ridge (Tysons Corner), 22102
Telephone: 703-734-9622
Facsimile: 703-356-0005
Washington, D.C. Office: Suite 200, 4427A Wisconsin Avenue, N.W.
Telephone: 202-296-1666.

(See Next Column)

MANDELL, LEWIS & GOLDBERG A PROFESSIONAL CORPORATION, *McLean—Continued*

Sterling, Virginia Office: Suite 340, Pidgeon Hill Drive.
Telephone: 703-430-0828.

Steve A. Mandell
David M. Lewis
Michael L. Goldberg

Adam P. Feinberg

OF COUNSEL

Seidman & Associates, P.C., , Washington, D.C.

For full biographical listings, see the Martindale-Hubbell Law Directory

NORFOLK, (Independent City)

HEILIG, MCKENRY, FRAIM & LOLLAR, A PROFESSIONAL CORPORATION (AV)

700 Newtown Road, 23502
Telephone: 804-461-2500
Fax: 804-461-2341

George H. Heilig, Jr.
James R. McKenry
John A. Heilig
Paul D. Fraim
George J. Dancigers
Charles M. Lollar
Carolyn P. Oast
Teresa R. Warner
Peter S. Lake
Thomas C. Dawson, Jr.
Stewart Penney Oast
Debra L. Mosley
Todd M. Fiorella
Robert E. Moreland
Philip R. Trapani
A. William Charters
Tena Touzos Canavos

Jason Evans Dodd
Lisa L. Howlett
Colleen Treacy Dickerson
Lynn E. Watson

Representative Clients: American International Insurance Group; Blue Cross of Virginia; Blue Shield of Virginia; The Home Insurance Company; Horace Mann Mutual Insurance Co.; Nationwide Mutual Insurance Co.; TranSouth Financial Corp.

For full biographical listings, see the Martindale-Hubbell Law Directory

VANDEVENTER, BLACK, MEREDITH & MARTIN (AV)

500 World Trade Center, 23510
Telephone: 804-446-8600
Cable Address: "Hughsvan"
Telex: 823-671
Telecopier: 446-8670
North Carolina, Kitty Hawk Office: 6 Juniper Trail.
Telephone: 919-261-5055.
Fax: 919-261-8444.
London, England Office: Suite 692, Level 6, Lloyd's, 1 Lime Street.
Telephone: (071) 623-2081.
Facsimile: (071) 929-0043.
Telex: 987321.

MEMBERS OF FIRM

John M. Ryan
F. Nash Bilisoly
R. John Barrett
Thomas M. Lucas

For Complete List of Firm Personnel, See General Section

For full biographical listings, see the Martindale-Hubbell Law Directory

*RICHMOND,** (Ind. City; Seat of Henrico Co.)

LEVIT & MANN (AV)

419 North Boulevard, 23220
Telephone: 804-355-7766
Fax: 804-358-4018

MEMBERS OF FIRM

Jay J. Levit
John B. Mann

For full biographical listings, see the Martindale-Hubbell Law Directory

MCGUIRE, WOODS, BATTLE & BOOTHE (AV)

One James Center, 901 East Cary Street, 23219-4030
Telephone: 804-775-1000
Fax: 804-775-1061
Alexandria, Virginia Office: Transpotomac Plaza, Suite 1000, 1199 North Fairfax Street, 22314-1437.
Telephone: 703-739-6200.
Fax: 703-739-6270.
Baltimore, Maryland Office: The Blaustein Building, One North Charles Street, 21201-3793.
Telephone: 410-659-4400.
Fax: 410-659-4599.
Charlottesville, Virginia Office: Court Square Building, P.O. Box 1288, 22902-1288.
Telephone: 804-977-2500.
Fax: 804-980-2222.

(See Next Column)

Jacksonville, Florida Office: Barnett Center, Suite 2750, 50 North Laura Street, 32202-3635.
Telephone: 904-798-3200.
Fax: 904-798-3207.
McLean, (Tysons Corner) Virginia Office: 8280 Greensboro Drive, Suite 900, Tysons Corner, 22102-3892.
Telephone: 703-712-5000.
Fax: 703-712-5050.
Norfolk, Virginia Office: World Trade Center, Suite 9000, 101 West Main Street, 23510-1655.
Telephone: 804-640-3700.
Fax: 804-640-3701.
Washington, D.C. Office: The Army and Navy Club Building, 1627 Eye Street, N.W., 20006-4007.
Telephone: 202-857-1700.
Fax: 202-857-1737.
Brussels, Belgium Office: 250 Avenue Louise, Ste. 64, 1050.
Telephone: (32 2) 629 42 11.
Fax: (32 2) 629 42 22.
Zürich, Switzerland Office: P.O. Box 4930, Bahnhofstrasse 3, 8022.
Telephone: (41 1) 225 20 00.
Fax: (41 1) 225 20 20.

MEMBERS OF FIRM

J. Robert Brame III
Donald F. Burke (Resident, Baltimore, Maryland Office)
Scott S. Cairns
Alan C. Cason (Resident, Baltimore, Maryland Office)
Ann-Mac Cox (Resident, McLean (Tysons Corner) Office)
Gary S. Marshall
James P. McElligott, Jr.
Stephen W. Robinson (Resident, Washington, D.C. Office)
Dana L. Rust
Eva S. Tashjian-Brown
William E. Twomey, Jr.
R. Craig Wood (Resident, Charlottesville Office)
W. Carter Younger

OF COUNSEL

Jean Bilger Arnold (Resident, Charlottesville Office)
Elizabeth Land Lewis (Resident, McLean (Tysons Corner) Office)
Clifford R. Oviatt, Jr. (Resident, Washington, D.C. Office)

ASSOCIATES

Lisa Ann Bertini (Resident, Norfolk Office)
David F. Dabbs
Mark S. Davis (Resident, Norfolk Office)
Valerie A. Fant (Resident, Washington, D.C. Office)
Cynthia E. Hudson
Kimberly S. Hugo
John J. Michels, Jr.
Arlene Paul (Resident, McLean (Tysons Corner) Office)
Deanna L. Ruddock
Rodney A. Satterwhite
Bruce M. Steen (Resident, Charlottesville Office)

For Complete List of Firm Personnel, See General Section

For full biographical listings, see the Martindale-Hubbell Law Directory

WILLIAMS, MULLEN, CHRISTIAN & DOBBINS, A PROFESSIONAL CORPORATION (AV)

Two James Center, 1021 East Cary Street, P.O. Box 1320, 23210-1320
Telephone: 804-643-1991
Fax: 804-783-6456
Glen Allen, Virginia Office: 4401 Waterfront Drive, Suite 140.
Telephone: 804-965-9168.
Fax: 804-965-0955.
Washington, D.C. Office: 1575 Eye Street, N.W.
Telephone: 202-289-6200.
Fax: 202-289-4126.

Lynn F. Jacob
James V. Meath
Douglas M. Nabhan

M. Peebles Harrison
Charles B. Scher

For Complete List of Firm Personnel, See General Section

For full biographical listings, see the Martindale-Hubbell Law Directory

ROANOKE, (Independent City)

THE CENTER FOR EMPLOYMENT LAW, P.C. (AV)

Suite 333, 2965 Colonnade Drive, S.W., P.O. Box 21669, 24018-0580
Telephone: 703-989-1021
FAX: 703-989-1485

Bayard E. Harris
P. Douglas Henson, II
Agnis C. Chakravorty

For full biographical listings, see the Martindale-Hubbell Law Directory

VIENNA, Fairfax Co.

BORING, PARROTT & PILGER, P.C. (AV)

307 Maple Avenue West, Suite D, 22180-4368
Telephone: 703-281-2161
FAX: 703-281-9464

(See Next Column)

BORING, PARROTT & PILGER P.C.—*Continued*

W. Thomas Parrott, III — Thomas J. Sawyer

Representative Clients: Balmar, Inc.; Hewlett-Packard Co.; Toshiba America Information Systems, Inc.; King Wholesale, Inc.; FSM Leasing, Inc.; KDI Sylvan Pools, Inc.; Brobst International, Inc.; Telematics, Inc.; Northern Virginia Surgical Associates, P.C.; Rainbow Industries, Inc.

For full biographical listings, see the Martindale-Hubbell Law Directory

WASHINGTON

*SEATTLE,** King Co.

GAITÁN & CUSACK (AV)

30th Floor Two Union Square, 601 Union Street, 98101-2324
Telephone: 206-521-3000
Facsimile: 206-386-5259
Anchorage, Alaska Office: 425 G Street, Suite 760.
Telephone: 907-278-3001.
Facsimile: 907-278-6068.
San Francisco, California Office: 275 Battery Street, 20th Floor.
Telephone: 415-398-5562.
Fax: 415-398-4033.
Washington, D.C. Office: 2000 L Street, Suite 200.
Telephone: 202-296-4637.
Fax: 202-296-4650.

MEMBERS OF FIRM

José E. Gaitán
Kenneth J. Cusack (Resident, Anchorage, Alaska Office)
William F. Knowles
Ronald L. Bozarth

OF COUNSEL

Howard K. Todd
Gary D. Gayton
Michel P. Stern (Also practicing alone, Bellevue, Washington)
Christopher A. Byrne
Patricia D. Ryan

ASSOCIATES

Mary F. O'Boyle
Bruce H. Williams
David J. Onsager
Diana T. Jimenez
Robert T. Mimbu
Cristina C. Kapela
Camilla M. Hedberg
John E. Lenker
Kathleen C. Healy

Representative Clients: National Insurance Professional Corporation; King County Police Union.

For full biographical listings, see the Martindale-Hubbell Law Directory

LANE POWELL SPEARS LUBERSKY (AV)

A Partnership including Professional Corporations
1420 Fifth Avenue, Suite 4100, 98101-2338
Telephone: 206-223-7000
Cable Address: "Embe"
Telex: 32-8808
Telecopier: 206-223-7107
Other Offices at: Mount Vernon and Olympia, Washington; Los Angeles and San Francisco, California; Anchorage, Alaska; Portland, Oregon; London, England.

MEMBERS OF FIRM

Wayne W. Hansen — Ralph C. Pond

Representative Clients: A. B. Dick Co.; AT&T; Fred Hutchinson Cancer Research Center; Heath Tecna Aerospace Co.; J. C. Penney Co., Inc.; K-Mart Corp.; Nordstrom, Ltd.; Pacific Medical Center, Inc.; Target Stores, Inc.; Union Pacific Railroad Co.

For Complete List of Firm Personnel, See General Section

For full biographical listings, see the Martindale-Hubbell Law Directory

PERKINS COIE (AV)

A Law Partnership including Professional Corporations
Strategic Alliance with Russell & DuMoulin
1201 Third Avenue, 40th Floor, 98101-3099
Telephone: 206-583-8888
Facsimile: 206-583-8500
Cable Address: "Perki ns Seattle."
Telex: 32-0319 PERKINS SEA
Anchorage, Alaska Office: 1029 West Third Avenue, Suite 300.
Telephone: 907-279-8561.
Facsimile: 907-276-3108.
Telex: 32-0319 PERKINS SEA.
Los Angeles, California Office: 1999 Avenue of the Stars, Ninth Floor.
Telephone: 310-788-9900.
Telex: 32-0319 PERKINS SEA.
Facsimile: 310-788-3399.

(See Next Column)

Washington, D.C. Office: 607 Fourteenth Street, N.W.
Telephone: 202-628-6600.
Facsimile: 202-434-1690.
Telex: 44-0277 PCSO.
Portland, Oregon Office: U.S. Bancorp Tower, Suite 2500, 111 S.W. Fifth Avenue.
Telephone: 503-295-4400.
Facsimile: 503-295-6793.
Telex: 32-0319 PERKINS SEA.
Bellevue, Washington Office: Suite 1800, One Bellevue Center, 411 - 108th Avenue N.E.
Telephone: 206-453-6980.
Facsimile: 206-453-7350.
Telex: 32-0319 PERKINS SEA.
Spokane, Washington Office: North 221 Wall Street, Suite 600.
Telephone: 509-624-2212.
Facsimile: 509-458-3399.
Telex: 32-0319 PERKINS SEA.
Olympia, Washington Office: 1110 Capitol Way South, Suite 405.
Telephone: 206-956-3300.
Strategic Alliance with Russell & DuMoulin, 1700-1075 West Georgia Street, Vancouver, B.C. V6E 3G2. Telephone: 604-631-3131.
Hong Kong Office: 23rd Floor Asia Pacific Finance Tower, Citibank Plaza, 3 Garden Road.
Telephone: 852-2878-1177.
Facsimile: 852-2524-9988. DX-9230-IC.
London, England Office: 36/38 Cornhill, ECV3 3ND.
Telephone: 071-369-9966.
Facsimile: 071-369-9968.
Taipei, Taiwan Office: 8/F TFIT Tower, 85 Jen AiRoad, Sec. 4,Taipei 106, Taiwan, R.O.C.
Telephone: 886-2-778-1177.
Facsimile: 086-2-777-9898.

PARTNERS/SHAREHOLDERS

J. David Andrews, P.S.
John F. Aslin
Bruce M. Brooks
Bruce D. Corker
Bruce Michael Cross
Kevin J. Hamilton
Jeffrey A. Hollingsworth
Philip S. Morse
Russell L. Perisho
Thomas E. Platt
Richard Ottesen Prentke
Michael T. Reynvaan
Bart Waldman
Nancy Williams

RESIDENT ASSOCIATES

Karen P. Clark — Karin L. Foster

Counsel for: The Boeing Company; Puget Sound Power & Light Company; Seattle School District; Swedish Hospital and Medical Center.

For Complete List of Firm Personnel, See General Section

For full biographical listings, see the Martindale-Hubbell Law Directory

STOKES, EITELBACH & LAWRENCE, P.S. (AV)

800 Fifth Avenue, Suite 4000, 98104-3199
Telephone: 206-626-6000
Fax: 206-464-1496

Steven D. Brown
Carolyn Cairns
Suzanne J. Thomas

Alexander J. Higgins — Kelly Twiss Noonan

For full biographical listings, see the Martindale-Hubbell Law Directory

WILLIAMS, KASTNER & GIBBS (AV)

4100 Two Union Square, 601 Union Street, P.O. Box 21926, 98111-3926
Telephone: 206-628-6600
Fax: 206-628-6611
Bellevue, Washington Office: 2000 Skyline Tower, 10900 N.E. Fourth Street, P.O. Box 1800, 98004-5841.
Telephone: 206-462-4700.
Fax: 206-451-0714.
Tacoma, Washington Office: 1000 Financial Center, 1145 Broadway, 98402-3502.
Telephone: 206-593-5620; Seattle: 628-2420.
Fax: 206-593-5625.
Vancouver, Washington Office: First Independent Place, 1220 Main Street, Suite 510.
Telephone: 206-696-0248.
Fax: 206-696-2051.

MEMBERS OF FIRM

Franklin L. Dennis
Josephine B. Vestal (Resident Partner, Bellevue Office)
Sheryl J. Willert
Judd H. Lees (Resident Partner, Bellevue Office)
Ronald J. Knox
Daniel W. Ferm

ASSOCIATES

Carmen L. Cook (Resident Associate, Bellevue Office)
Elizabeth K. Maurer
Rebekah R. Ross

Representative Clients: Aetna Casulaty & Surety Co.; Atlantic-Richfield Co.; CIGNA; CNA Insurance; Continental Can Company, Inc.; Cushman & Wakefield of Washington, Inc.; General Motors Acceptance Corp.; Loomis Armored, Inc.; Mayne Nickless Incorporated; UNICO Properties, Inc.

(See Next Column)

WILLIAMS, KASTNER & GIBBS, *Seattle—Continued*

For Complete List of Firm Personnel, See General Section

For full biographical listings, see the Martindale-Hubbell Law Directory

WEST VIRGINIA

*CHARLESTON,** Kanawha Co.

JACKSON & KELLY (AV)

1600 Laidley Tower, P.O. Box 553, 25322
Telephone: 304-340-1000
Fax: 304-340-1130
Martinsburg, West Virginia Office: 300 Foxcroft Avenue, P.O. Box 1068.
Telephone: 304-263-8800.
Morgantown, West Virginia Office: 6000 Hampton Center, P.O. Box 619.
Telephone: 304-599-3000.
New Martinsville, West Virginia Office: 256 Russell Avenue, P.O. Box 68.
Telephone: 304-455-1751.
Charles Town, West Virginia Office: 700 East Washington Street, P.O. Box 983.
Telephone: 304-728-6088.
Clarksburg, West Virginia Office: 203 Main Street, P.O. Box 1587.
Telephone: 304-623-3002.
Lexington, Kentucky Office: 175 East Main Street, Suite 500, P.O. Box 2150.
Telephone: 606-255-9500.
Washington, D. C. Office: 2401 Pennsylvania Avenue, N.W., Suite 400.
Telephone: 202-973-0200.
Denver, Colorado Office: Suite 2710, 1660 Lincoln Street.
Telephone: 303-837-0003.

MEMBERS OF FIRM

Charles Q. Gage
Roger A. Wolfe
Michael D. Foster
Charles M. Surber, Jr.
Cheryl Harris Wolfe
Larry W. Blalock (Administrative Manager, New Martinsville, West Virginia Office)
Daniel L. Stickler
L. Anthony George
Albert F. Sebok

ASSOCIATES

Gene W. Bailey, II
Jacqueline Syers Duncan (Resident, Lexington, Kentucky Office)
Timothy Ray Coleman (Not admitted in WV; Resident, Lexington, Kentucky Office)
Tammy A. Mitchell-Bittorf (Martinsburg and Charles Town, West Virginia Offices)
Erin E. Magee
Katherine Shand Larkin (Resident, Denver, Colorado Office)

OF COUNSEL

David D. Johnson (Retired)

Representative Clients: A.T. Massey Coal Company, Inc.; CONSOL Inc.; Ashland Coal, Inc.; One Valley Bankcorp of West Virginia, Inc.; West Virginia-American Water Co.; Ramsay Health Care, Inc.; Charleston Newspapers; Union Carbide Corp.; Kmart Corp.; Old Republic Insurance Co.

For Complete List of Firm Personnel, See General Section

For full biographical listings, see the Martindale-Hubbell Law Directory

STEPTOE & JOHNSON (AV)

Seventh Floor, Bank One Center, P.O. Box 1588, 25326-1588
Telephone: 304-353-8000
Fax: 304-353-8180
Clarksburg, West Virginia Office: Bank One Center, P.O. Box 2190, 26302-2190.
Telephone: 304-624-8000.
Fax: 304-624-8183.
Morgantown, West Virginia Office: 1000 Hampton Center, P.O. Box 1616, 26507-1616.
Telephone: 304-598-8000.
Fax: 304-598-8116.
Martinsburg, West Virginia Office: 126 East Burke Street, P.O. Box 2629, 25401-5429.
Telephone: 304-263-6991.
Fax: 304-263-4785.
Charles Town, West Virginia Office: 104 West Congress Street, P.O. Box 100, 25414-0100.
Telephone: 304-725-1414.
Fax: 304-725-1913.
Hagerstown, Maryland Office: The Bryan Centre, 82 West Washington Street, Fourth Floor, P.O. Box 570, 21740-0570.
Telephone: 301-739-8600.
Fax: 301-739-8742.
Wheeling, West Virginia Office: The Riley Building, Suite 400, 14th & Chapline Streets, P.O. Box 150, 26008-0020.
Telephone: 304-233-0000.
Fax: 304-233-0014.

(See Next Column)

MEMBERS OF FIRM

Bryan R. Cokeley
W. Randolph Fife

ASSOCIATES

Cynthia R. Cokeley
Wendy D. Young

Representative Clients: PPG Industries, Inc.; Consolidation Coal Co.; Peabody Coal Co.; Union Carbide Corp.; Ogden Newspapers, Inc.; Tree Preservation Co., Inc.; United Hospital Center; Glenmark Associates, Inc.; CNG Transmission Corp.; Salem-Teikyo University.

For Complete List of Firm Personnel, See General Section

For full biographical listings, see the Martindale-Hubbell Law Directory

*CLARKSBURG,** Harrison Co.

STEPTOE & JOHNSON (AV)

Bank One Center, P.O. Box 2190, 26302-2190
Telephone: 304-624-8000
Fax: 304-624-8183
Mailing Address: P.O. Box 2190, 26302-2190
Charleston, West Virginia Office: Seventh Floor, Bank One Center, P.O. Box 1588, 25326-1588.
Telephone: 304-353-8000
Fax: 304-353-8180.
Morgantown, West Virginia Office: 1000 Hampton Center, P.O. Box 1616, 26507-1616.
Telephone: 304-598-8000.
Fax: 304-598-8116.
Martinsburg, West Virginia Office: 126 East Burke Street, P.O. Box 2629, 25401-5429.
Telephone: 304-263-6991.
Fax: 304-263-4785.
Charles Town, West Virginia Office: 104 West Congress Street, P.O. Box 100, 25414-0100.
Telephone: 304-725-1414.
Fax: 304-725-1913.
Hagerstown, Maryland Office: The Bryan Centre, 82 West Washington Street, Fourth Floor, P.O. Box 570, 21740-0570.
Telephone: 301-739-8600.
Fax: 301-739-8742.
Wheeling, West Virginia Office: The Riley Building, Suite 400, 14th & Chapline Streets, P.O. Box 150, 26003-0020.
Telephone: 304-233-0000.
Fax: 304-233-0014.

MEMBERS OF FIRM

Robert M. Steptoe, Jr.
C. David Morrison
Clement D. Carter, III
Richard M. Yurko, Jr.
Gary W. Nickerson

ASSOCIATES

Carolyn A. Wade
Douglas G. Lee
John R. Merinar, Jr.
Stephen D. Williams

Representative Clients: PPG Industries, Inc.; Consolidation Coal Co.; Peabody Coal Co.; Union Carbide Corp.; Ogden Newspapers, Inc.; Tree Preservation Co., Inc.; United Hospital Center; Glenmark Associates, Inc.; CNG Transmission Corp.; Salem-Teikyo University.

For Complete List of Firm Personnel, See General Section

For full biographical listings, see the Martindale-Hubbell Law Directory

*WHEELING,** Ohio Co.

SCHRADER, RECHT, BYRD, COMPANION & GURLEY (AV)

1000 Hawley Building, 1025 Main Street, P.O. Box 6336, 26003
Telephone: 304-233-3390
Fax: 304-233-2769
Martins Ferry, Ohio Office: 205 North Fifth Street, P.O. Box 309.
Telephone: 614-633-8976.
Fax: 614-633-0400.

PARTNERS

Henry S. Schrader (Retired)
Arthur M. Recht
Ray A. Byrd
James F. Companion
Terence M. Gurley
Frank X. Duff
Teresa Rieman-Camilletti
Yolonda G. Lambert
Patrick S. Casey
Sandra M. Chapman
Daniel P. Fry (Resident, Martins Ferry, Ohio Office)
James P. Mazzone

ASSOCIATES

Sandra K. Law
D. Kevin Coleman
Denise A. Jebbia
Edythe A. Nash
Robert G. McCoid
Denise D. Klug
Thomas E. Johnston

OF COUNSEL

James A. Byrum, Jr.

General Counsel: WesBanco Bank-Elm Grove.
Representative Clients: CIGNA Property and Casualty Cos.; Columbia Gas Transmission Corp.; Commercial Union Assurance Co.; Hazlett, Burt & Watson, Inc.; Stone & Thomas Department Stores; Transamerica Commercial Finance Corp.; Wheeling-Pittsburgh Steel Corp.

For full biographical listings, see the Martindale-Hubbell Law Directory

WISCONSIN

*MADISON,** Dane Co.

LAWTON & CATES, S.C. (AV)

214 West Mifflin Street, 53703-2594
Telephone: 608-256-9031
Fax: 608-256-4670

Bruce F. Ehlke
Richard Graylow
Victor M. Arellano
Aaron N. Halstead
John C. Talis

OF COUNSEL

John H. Bowers

Reference: Bank One, Madison.

For full biographical listings, see the Martindale-Hubbell Law Directory

MELLI, WALKER, PEASE & RUHLY, S.C. (AV)

Suite 600, 119 Martin Luther King, Jr. Boulevard, P.O. Box 1664, 53701
Telephone: 608-257-4812
Telefax: 608-258-7470

Joseph A. Melli
Jack D. Walker
James K. Pease, Jr.
James K. Ruhly
Thomas R. Crone
John R. Sweeney
Philip J. Bradbury
JoAnn M. Hart
Susan C. Sheeran
Douglas E. Witte
Dana J. Erlandsen
Lora H. Woods
Christopher B. Hughes
Lisa A. Polinske
Devon R. Baumbach

OF COUNSEL

John H. Shiels

Representative Clients: Oshkosh Truck Corp.; Coca-Cola Bottling Company of Madison; Wisconsin Road Builders Assn.; Associated Builders & Contractors of Wisconsin, Inc.; Marshall Erdman & Associates, Inc.; Research Products Corp.; Wells Manufacturing Corp.; JJ Security, Inc.; Perry Printing Co.; Racine Unified School District.

For full biographical listings, see the Martindale-Hubbell Law Directory

*MILWAUKEE,** Milwaukee Co.

BRIGDEN & PETAJAN, S.C. (AV)

600 East Mason Street, 53202-3831
Telephone: 414-291-0666
Facsimile: 414-291-9204

Patrick H. Brigden (1931-1984)
Douglas A. Cairns (1944-1987)
Albert H. Petajan
John C. Patzke

Marna M. Tess-Mattner

LEGAL SUPPORT PERSONNEL

Mary T. Silver

For full biographical listings, see the Martindale-Hubbell Law Directory

DAVIS & KUELTHAU, S.C. (AV)

111 East Kilbourn Avenue, Suite 1400, 53202-6613
Telephone: 414-276-0200
Facsimile: 414-276-9369
Cable Address: "Shiplaw"

James E. Braza
Clifford B. Buelow
Robert H. Buikema
Walter S. Davis
Mark L. Olson
Gary M. Ruesch
Mark F. Vetter
Daniel G. Vliet
Roger E. Walsh

Michael Aldana
Mary L. Hubacher
Jane M. Knasinski
Nancy L. Pirkey

Special Labor Relations Counsel For: Chromalloy American Corp.; Grunau Co.; Grede Foundries; Hamilton Industries, Inc.; The Manitowoc Cos.; Mayline, Inc.; Leach Co.; SNC Manufacturing Co.; Beloit, Elmbrook, Glendale-River Hills, Kenosha, Sturgeon Bay, Watertown, Wauwatosa and Whitefish Bay School Districts; Municipalities of Hales Corners, Oak Creek and Thiensville.

For full biographical listings, see the Martindale-Hubbell Law Directory

KRUKOWSKI & COSTELLO, S.C. (AV)

7111 West Edgerton Avenue, 53220
Telephone: 414-423-1330
Telefax: 414-423-1694
Washington, D.C. Office: 2011 Pennsylvania Avenue, N.W., Suite 500, 20006-1832.
Telephone: 202-659-4799.
Fax: 202-457-9121.

Thomas P. Krukowski
Timothy G. Costello
Robert J. Bartel
Kevin J. Kinney
Marty R. Howard

David Loeffler
Robert A. Hirsch (Not admitted in WI; Resident, Washington, D.C. Office)
Jill Pedigo Hall
Sarah V. Lewis
Charles B. Palmer
Shelly A. Ranus
Elizabeth A. McDuffie
Janice M. Pogorelec
Debra L. Haselow Rolfs
Robert C. Johnson
John D. Finerty, Jr.
Gregory L. Peters
Thomas Revnew
Heather L. MacDougall
C. H. Stuart Charlson

Representative Clients: Briggs & Stratton; Firstar Corporation; Bemis Corporation; Roundy's, Inc.; Yellow Freight Systems,Inc.; Schreiber Foods, Inc.; Ryder Truck Rental, Inc.; Kerry Ingredients; Lutheran Hospital, La Crosse; Roadmaster Corporation.

For full biographical listings, see the Martindale-Hubbell Law Directory

LINDNER & MARSACK, S.C. (AV)

411 East Wisconsin Avenue, 53202
Telephone: 414-273-3910
FAX: 414-273-0522

Leon B. Lamfrom (1884-1970)
Egon W. Peck (1903-1979)
Dennis G. Lindner
Gary A. Marsack
Robert E. Schreiber, Jr.
Jonathan T. Swain
James S. Clay
James R. Scott
Thomas W. Mackenzie
Donald J. Cairns
Charles P. Stevens
Douglas M. Feldman
Lisa M. Leemon
Alan M. Levy
Laurie A. Petersen
Gail M. Olsen
Gerald A. Einsohn
John E. Drana

OF COUNSEL

Eugene J. Hayman

Representative Corporate Labor Clients: Ansul Co.; Beloit Corp.; Caterpillar Tractor Co.; Roundy's Inc.; Lennox International.

For full biographical listings, see the Martindale-Hubbell Law Directory

MICHAEL, BEST & FRIEDRICH (AV)

100 East Wisconsin Avenue, 53202-4108
Telephone: 414-271-6560
Telecopier: 414-277-0656
Cable Address: "Mibef"
Madison, Wisconsin Office: One South Pinckney Street, Firstar Plaza, P.O. Box 1806, 53701-1806.
Telephone: 608-257-3501.
Telecopier: 283-2275.
Chicago, Illinois Office: 135 South LaSalle Street, Suite 1610, 60603-4391.
Telephone: 312-845-5800.
Telecopier: 312-845-5828.
Affiliated Law Firm: Edward D. Heffernan, Penthouse One, 1019 19th Street, N.W., Washington, D.C. 20036.
Telephone: 202-331-7444.

PARTNERS

Marshall R. Berkoff
Jacob L. Bernheim
David W. Croysdale
Scott H. Engroff
Thomas E. Obenberger
John R. Sapp
Paul E. Prentiss
John C. Lapinski
Thomas W. Scrivner
Thomas P. Godar (Resident Partner, Madison, Wisconsin Office)
José A. Olivieri
Robert W. Mulcahy
Robert D. Rothacker, Jr.
Paul Jordan Cherner (Resident Partner, Chicago, Illinois Office)
Eric E. Hobbs

OF COUNSEL

James C. Mallatt

ASSOCIATES

Jonathan O. Levine
Scott C. Beightol
Eric H. Rumbaugh
Paul D. Windsor
Mitchell W. Quick
Daniel A. Kaufman (Resident Associate, Chicago, Illinois Office)
Robin M. Sheridan

For Complete List of Firm Personnel, See General Section

For full biographical listings, see the Martindale-Hubbell Law Directory

Milwaukee—Continued

PREVIANT, GOLDBERG, UELMEN, GRATZ, MILLER & BRUEGGEMAN, S.C. (AV)

1555 North River Center Drive, 53212
Telephone: 414-271-4500
Fax: 414-271-6308

David Previant
David L. Uelmen
Richard M. Goldberg
Gerald A. Goldberg
Gerry M. Miller
Larry B. Brueggeman
Matthew R. Robbins
Marianne Goldstein Robbins
Scott D. Soldon
Thomas J. Flanagan
Dean M. Horwitz
Frederick Perillo
Daniel E. Goldberg
Hope K. Olson
Kenneth R. Loebel
Philip R. O'Brien
Bernard O. Westler
John J. Brennan
Michael D. Riegert
Shawn R. Crain
Frank G. Locante
Steven G. Kluender
Naomi E. Eisman
Renata Krawczyk
Ronald G. Tays
Ruth Elaine Canan
John T. Schomisch, Jr.
Lisa A. Bangert

Representative Clients: Wisconsin State AFL-CIO; Milwaukee Building and Construction Trades Council; Central Conference of Teamsters; Wisconsin Teamsters Joint Council 39; Machinists Dist. 10; United Paperworks International Union.

For full biographical listings, see the Martindale-Hubbell Law Directory

QUARLES & BRADY (AV)

411 East Wisconsin Avenue, 53202-4497
Telephone: 414-277-5000
Cable Address: "Lawdock"
Fax: 414-271-3552.
TWX: 910-262-3426
Madison, Wisconsin Office: Firstar Plaza, One South Pinckney Street, P.O. Box 2113.
Telephone: 608-251-5000.
Fax: 608-251-9166.
West Palm Beach, Florida Office: 222 Lakeview Avenue, 4th Floor.
Telephone: 407-653-5000.
Fax: 407-653-5333.
Naples, Florida Office: Barnett Center, 4501 Tamiami Trail North.
Telephone: 813-262-5959.
Fax: 813-434-4999.
Phoenix, Arizona Office: One Camelback Building, One East Camelback Road, Suite 400.
Telephone: 602-230-5500.
Fax: 602-230-5598.

MEMBERS OF FIRM
(ALPHABETICALLY BY YEAR OF ADMISSION TO BAR)

Fred G. Groiss
George K. Whyte, Jr.
Charles W. Herf (Resident, Phoenix, Arizona Office)
David E. Jarvis
Patrick W. Schmidt
Fred Gants (Resident, Madison Office)
Mary Pat Ninneman
Jon E. Pettibone (Resident, Phoenix, Arizona Office)
Patricia K. McDowell
Carolyn A. Gnaedinger
David B. Kern
Ely A. Leichtling
Robert H. Duffy

OF COUNSEL

Laurence E. Gooding, Jr.

ASSOCIATES

Cynthia L. Jewett (Resident, Phoenix, Arizona Office)
Anthony A. Tomaselli (Resident, Madison Office)
Gregg M. Formella
Carmella A. Huser
Jose L. Martinez (Resident, Phoenix, Arizona Office)
Wendy L. Gerlach (Resident, Phoenix, Arizona Office)
Kevin P. Crooks

For Complete List of Firm Personnel, See General Section

For full biographical listings, see the Martindale-Hubbell Law Directory

REINHART, BOERNER, VAN DEUREN, NORRIS & RIESELBACH, S.C. (AV)

1000 North Water Street, P.O. Box 92900, 53202-0900
Telephone: 414-298-1000
Facsimile: 414-298-8097
Denver, Colorado Office: One Norwest Center, 1700 Lincoln Street, Suite 3725.
Telephone: 303-831-0909.
Fax: 303-831-4805.
Madison, Wisconsin Office: 7617 Mineral Point Road, 53701-2020.
Telephone: 608-283-7900.
Fax: 608-283-7919.
Washington, D.C. Office: 601 Pennsylvania Avenue, N.W., North Building, Suite 750.
Telephone: 202-393-3636.
Fax: 202-393-0796.

(See Next Column)

Paul V. Lucke
Robert K. Sholl
Steven P. Bogart

David J. Sisson
Geri Krupp-Gordon

For Complete List of Firm Personnel, See General Section

For full biographical listings, see the Martindale-Hubbell Law Directory

*OSHKOSH,** Winnebago Co.

CURTIS WILDE & NEAL LAW OFFICES (AV)

1010 West 20th Avenue, P.O. Box 2845, 54903-2845
Telephone: 414-233-1010
Markesan, Wisconsin Office: 10 East Water Street.
Telephone: 414-398-2314.

George W. Curtis
William R. Wilde
John A. Neal

Scott C. Woldt

Reference: Valley Bank.

For full biographical listings, see the Martindale-Hubbell Law Directory

WYOMING

*CASPER,** Natrona Co.

BROWN & DREW (AV)

Casper Business Center, Suite 800, 123 West First Street, 82601-2486
Telephone: 307-234-1000
800-877-6755
Telefax: 307-265-8025

MEMBERS OF FIRM

Morris R. Massey
W. Thomas Sullins, II
Donn J. McCall
Thomas F. Reese
J. Kenneth Barbe
Jeffrey C. Brinkerhoff

ASSOCIATES

Carol Warnick
P. Jaye Rippley
Courtney Robert Kepler
Drew A. Perkins

Attorneys for: First Interstate Bank of Wyoming, N.A.; Norwest Bank Wyoming, N.A.; The CIT Group/Industrial Financing; Aetna Casualty & Surety Co.; The Doctor's Co.; MEDMARC; WOTCO, Inc.; Chevron USA; Kerr-McGee Corp.; Chicago and NorthWestern Transportation Company.

For Complete List of Firm Personnel, See General Section

For full biographical listings, see the Martindale-Hubbell Law Directory

PUERTO RICO

SAN JUAN, San Juan Dist.

FIDDLER, GONZÁLEZ & RODRÍGUEZ

Chase Manhattan Bank Building (Hato Rey), P.O. Box 363507, 00936-3507
Telephone: 809-753-3113
Telecopier: 809-759-3123

MEMBERS OF FIRM

Pedro Pumarada
Juan Carlos Pérez-Otero
Tristán Reyes-Gilestra
José A. Silva-Cofresí
Arturo Bauermeister-Baldrich
José Luis Verdiales Morales
José J. Santiago
Carlos V. J. Dávila

Representative Clients: The Chase Manhattan Bank, N.A.; Citibank, N.A.; Pfizer, Inc.; Merck & Co., Inc.; American Cyanamid Co.; Baxter Healthcare Corp.; Citibank, N.A.; The San Juan Star and Telemundo Group, Inc.

For Complete List of Firm Personnel, See General Section

For full biographical listings, see the Martindale-Hubbell Law Directory

GOLDMAN ANTONETTI & CÓRDOVA

American International Plaza Fourteenth & Fifteenth Floors, 250 Muñoz Rivera Avenue (Hato Rey), P.O. Box 70364, 00936-0364
Telephone: 809-759-8000
Telecopiers: 809-767-9333 (Main)
809-767-9177 (Litigation Department)
809-767-8660 (Labor & Corporate Law Departments)
809-767-9325 (Tax & Environmental Law Departments)

(See Next Column)

GOLDMAN ANTONETTI & CÓRDOVA—*Continued*

MEMBERS OF FIRM

Vicente J. Antonetti
Luis F. Antonetti
Luis D. Ortiz-Abreu
Gregory T. Usera
Raymond E. Morales
Howard Pravda

ASSOCIATES

Jorge R. Rodriguez-Micheo
José M. Lorié Velasco
Edwin J. Seda-Fernández
Migdalia Davila-Garcia
Manuel E. Lopez-Fernandez
Roberto Ariel Fernández
Josefina Cruz-Melendez
Ruben Colon-Morales
Lora J. Espada-Medina
Aileen M. Navas-Auger
Artemio Rivera Rivera

Representative Clients: American Airlines; Upjohn Manufacturing Corp.; Federal Express Corp.; Bumble Bee Puerto Rico, Inc.; Mayagüez Hilton International; Seven-Up Bottling Co.; Star Kist Caribe, Inc.; Westinghouse Electric Corp.; Abbott Laboratories.

For Complete List of Firm Personnel, See General Section

For full biographical listings, see the Martindale-Hubbell Law Directory

JIMÉNEZ, GRAFFAM & LAUSELL

Formerly Jiménez & Fusté
Suite 505, Midtown Building, 421 Muñoz Rivera Avenue, Hato Rey, P.O. Box 366104, 00936-6104
Telephone: 809-767-1030; 767-1000; 767-1061; 767-1064
Telefax: 809-751-4068;
Cable: "Nezte"; RCA
Telex: 325-2730

MEMBERS OF FIRM

Nicolás Jiménez
William A. Graffam
Steven C. Lausell
J. Ramón Rivera-Morales
José Juan Torres-Escalera
Raquel M. Dulzaides
Manuel San Juan

ASSOCIATES

Manolo T. Rodríguez-Bird
Patricia Garrity
Carlos E. Bayrón
Isabel J. Vélez-Serrano
Edgardo A. Vega-López

Representative Clients: Sea-Land Service, Inc.; McAllister Brothers; Crowley Maritime Corp.; Crowley Marine Services.

For Complete List of Firm Personnel, See General Section

For full biographical listings, see the Martindale-Hubbell Law Directory

MÁRTINEZ ODELL & CALABRIA

Banco Popular Center, 16th Floor, (Hato Rey), P.O. Box 190998, 00919-0998
Telephone: 809-753-8914
Facsimile: 809-753-8402; 809-759-9075; 809-764-5664

MEMBERS OF FIRM

Francisco M. Ramirez-Rivera
Graciela J. Belaval
Roberto E. Vega Pacheco
Francisco L. Acevedo-Nogueras

ASSOCIATES

Amelia Fortuño-Ruiz
Luis R. Perez-Giusti
Jose G. Fagot-Diaz

Representative Clients: A.T. & T. Corp.; Pepsi-Cola P.R. Bottling Co.; Banco Popular de Puerto Rico; I.T.T. Financial Corp.; John H. Harland Company of Puerto Rico, Inc.; Lutron Electronics Co., Inc.; Paine Webber, Inc.; Lotus Development Corp.; Western Digital.

For Complete List of Firm Personnel, See General Section

For full biographical listings, see the Martindale-Hubbell Law Directory

O'NEILL & BORGES

10th Floor, Chase Manhattan Bank Building (Hato Rey), 254 Muñoz Rivera Avenue, 00918-1995
Telephone: 809-764-8181
Telecopier: 809-753-8944

MEMBER OF FIRM

Jorge L. Capó-Matos

ASSOCIATES

María de Lourdes Medina
Ramón L. Velasco
María del Carmen Betancourt

Representative Clients: Abbott Laboratories, Inc.; American Airlines, Inc.; Ashland Chemical Co.; Caribbean Restaurants, Inc.; Edison Brothers Stores, Inc.; Hanes Menswear, Inc.,; Marshalls, Inc.; McCann-Erickson Corp.; Mitsubishi Motor Sales of Caribbean, Inc.; Pall Corp.; The Procter & Gamble Commercial Co.; Puerto Rico Harbor Pilots Pension & Welfare Benefits Plan; Stewart Enterprises, Inc.

For Complete List of Firm Personnel, See General Section

For full biographical listings, see the Martindale-Hubbell Law Directory

VIRGIN ISLANDS

*CHARLOTTE AMALIE, ST. THOMAS,** St. Thomas

BORNN BORNN HANDY

No. 8 Norre Gade, P.O. Box 1500, 00804
Telephone: 809-774-1400
Fax: 809-774-9607

PARTNERS

David A. Bornn
Veronica J. Handy

References: Bank of Nova Scotia; Banco Popular de P.R., St. Thomas, U.S. Virgin Islands.

For Complete List of Firm Personnel, See General Section

For full biographical listings, see the Martindale-Hubbell Law Directory

CANADA
ALBERTA

*EDMONTON,** Edmonton Jud. Dist.

LUCAS BOWKER & WHITE (AV)

Esso Tower - Scotia Place, 1201-10060 Jasper Avenue, T5J 4E5
Telephone: 403-426-5330
Telecopier: 403-428-1066

MEMBERS OF FIRM

Gerald A. I. Lucas, Q.C.
George E. Bowker, Q.C.
Robert B. White, Q.C.
David J. Stratton, Q.C.
E. James Kindrake
Elizabeth A. Johnson
Norman J. Pollock
Kent H. Davidson
Alan R. Gray
Robert A. Seidel
David J. Stam
Donald J. Wilson

ASSOCIATES

Deborah L. Hughes
Douglas A. Bodner
Michael Alexander Kirk
Mark E. Lesniak
Eric C. Lund

Reference: Canadian Imperial Bank of Commerce.

For Complete List of Firm Personnel, See General Section

For full biographical listings, see the Martindale-Hubbell Law Directory

MCLENNAN ROSS (AV)

600 West Chambers, 12220 Stony Plain Road, P.O. Box 12040, T5J 3L2
Telephone: 403-482-9200
Telecopier: 403-482-9100; 403-482-9101; 403-482-9102
INTERNET: mross@supernet.ab.ca

Roderick A. McLennan, Q.C. *
John Sterk, Q.C. *
Philip G. Ponting, Q.C.
Havelock B. Madill, Q.C.
Brian R. Burrows, Q.C.
Johanne L. Amonson, Q.C. *
Kevin J. Anderson *
Douglas G. Gorman
Glenn D. Tait
Yolanda S. Van Wachem
Michelle G. Crighton
Walter J. Pavlic
Donald J. McGarvey
Donald W. Dear
Scott A. Watson
Stephen J. Livingstone
Doreen C. Mueller
Douglas J. Boyer
John K. Gormley
Timothy C. Mavko
David J. Ross, Q.C.
Peter P. Taschuk, Q.C.
D. Mark Gunderson *
Darren Becker *
Frederick A. Day, Q.C. *
Hugh J. D. McPhail
Jonathan P. Rossall *
R. Graham McLennan *
William S. Rosser *
Ronald M. Kruhlak
Gerhard J. Seifner
Rodney R. Neys
Damon S. Bailey
Christopher J. Lane
Clay K. Hamdon
Sandra J. Weber
Steven J. Ferner
Karen J.A. Metcalfe
Katharine L. Hurlburt
Lucien R. Lamoureux
Timothy F. Garvin

*Denotes Lawyer Whose Professional Corporation is a Member of the Partnership.

For Complete List of Firm Personnel, See General Section

For full biographical listings, see the Martindale-Hubbell Law Directory

CANADA BRITISH COLUMBIA

*VANCOUVER,** Vancouver Co.

ALEXANDER, HOLBURN, BEAUDIN & LANG (AV)

P.O. Box 10057 2700 Toronto Dominion Bank Tower, 700 West Georgia Street, V7Y 1B8
Telephone: 604-688-1351
Fax: 604-669-7642
Hong Kong, In Association with Lawrence Ong & Chung: 8th Floor, Chekiang First Bank Centre, 1 Duddell Street. Central.
Telephone: (852-2) 526-1171.
Fax: (852-2) 845-0686.
Taipei, Taiwan Office, In Association with Perennial Law Office: c/o 7F-2, No. 9, Roosevelt Road, Section 2.
Telephone: (886-2) 395-6989.
Fax: (886-2) 391-4235.

PARTNERS

Thomas A. Roper
R. Patrick Saul
Frances R. Watters
Patrick M. Gilligan-Hackett

ASSOCIATES

Matthew Cooperwilliams
Delayne M. Sartison
Andrea A. Rayment
Cheryl E. Shizgal

A list of Representative Clients will be furnished on request.

For Complete List of Firm Personnel, See General Section

For full biographical listings, see the Martindale-Hubbell Law Directory

HARRIS & COMPANY (AV)

Twenty-Second Floor, 1111 West Georgia Street, V6E 4M3
Telephone: 604-684-6633
Telecopier: 604-684-6632

PARTNERS

Judith C. Anderson
James P. Carwana
J. Stuart Clyne, Q.C.
Peter A. Csiszar
Wendy Devine Harris
R. Alan Francis
Eric J. Harris
John L. McConchie
D. Murray Tevlin
Adriana F. Wills

ASSOCIATES

Adam S. Albright
Shafik Bhalloo
Janice R. Dillon
Frances C. Doyle
Michael Hancock
Geoffrey J. Litherland
Enid J. Marion

RESEARCH LAWYERS

Barbara L. Armstrong

For full biographical listings, see the Martindale-Hubbell Law Directory

RUSSELL & DuMOULIN (AV)

2100-1075 West Georgia Street, V6E 3G2
Telephone: 604-631-3131
Fax: 604-631-3232
A Member of the national association of Borden DuMoulin Howard Gervais, comprising Russell & DuMoulin, Vancouver, British Columbia; Howard Mackie, Calgary, Alberta; Borden & Elliot, Toronto, Ontario; Mackenzie Gervais, Montreal, Quebec and Borden DuMoulin Howard Gervais, London, England.
Strategic Alliance with Perkins Coie with offices in Seattle, Spokane and Bellevue, Washington; Portland, Oregon; Anchorage, Alaska; Los Angeles, California; Washington, D.C.; Hong Kong and Taipei, Taiwan.
Represented in Hong Kong by Vincent T.K. Cheung, Yap & Co.

MEMBERS OF FIRM

Bruce R. Grist
Gavin H. G. Hume, Q.C.

Representative Clients: Alcan Smelters & Chemicals Ltd.; The Bank of Nova Scotia; Canada Trust Co.; The Canada Life Assurance Co.; Forest Industrial Relations Ltd.; Honda Canada Inc.; IBM Canada Ltd.; Macmillan Bloedel Ltd.; Nissho Iwai Canada Ltd.; The Toronto-Dominion Bank.

For Complete List of Firm Personnel, See General Section

For full biographical listings, see the Martindale-Hubbell Law Directory

CANADA NEW BRUNSWICK

*SAINT JOHN,** Saint John Co.

CLARK, DRUMMIE & COMPANY (AV)

40 Wellington Row, P.O. Box 6850 Station "A", E2L 4S3
Telephone: 506-633-3800
Telecopier (Automatic): 506-633-3811

(See Next Column)

MEMBERS OF FIRM

John M. McNair
William B. Richards
Patrick J. P. Ervin
Frederick A. Welsford

Reference: Royal Bank of Canada.

For Complete List of Firm Personnel, See General Section

For full biographical listings, see the Martindale-Hubbell Law Directory

CANADA NOVA SCOTIA

*HALIFAX,** Halifax Co.

McINNES COOPER & ROBERTSON (AV)

1601 Lower Water Street, P.O. Box 730, B3J 2V1
Telephone: 902-425-6500
Fax: 902-425-6350
St. John's, Newfoundland Office: Suite 602, Scotia Centre, 235 Water Street, P.O. Box 547. A1C, 5K8.
Telephone: 709-726-9500.
Fax: 709-726-9550.

Eric Durnford, Q.C.
Brian G. Johnston
Peter McLellan, Q.C.
Maureen E. Reid
Malcolm D. Boyle

ASSOCIATE

Noella Martin

Attorneys for: Bank of Nova Scotia; Imperial Oil, Limited; Frank B. Hall & Co., Inc. (New York); American Steamship Owners Protection & Indemnity Association, Inc.; Coca-Cola, Ltd.; Scott Worldwide Inc.; Hong Kong Bank of Canada.

For Complete List of Firm Personnel, See General Section

For full biographical listings, see the Martindale-Hubbell Law Directory

CANADA ONTARIO

*TORONTO,** Regional Munic. of York

BORDEN & ELLIOT (AV)

Barristers & Solicitors
Scotia Plaza, 40 King Street West, M5H 3Y4
Telephone: 416-367-6000
Telecopier: 416-367-6749
Internet: @ borden.com
A Member of the national association of Borden DuMoulin Howard Gervais, comprising Borden & Elliot in Toronto, Ontario, Russell & DuMoulin in Vancouver, British Columbia, Howard, Mackie in Calgary, Alberta and Mackenzie Gervais in Montréal, Québec. Borden DuMoulin Howard Gervais also operates an office in London, England.

MEMBER AND ASSOCIATES

Barry W. Earle, Q.C.

For Complete List of Firm Personnel, See General Section

For full biographical listings, see the Martindale-Hubbell Law Directory

MATHEWS, DINSDALE & CLARK (AV)

1 Queen Street East, Suite 2500, M5C 2Z1
Telephone: 416-862-8280
FAX: 416-862-8247

Stanley E. Dinsdale, Q.C.
Bruce W. Binning
William S. Cook
William G. Phelps, Q.C.
Raymond A. Werry
Brian R. Baldwin
Stephen C. Bernardo
Robert M. Parry
Paula M. Rusak
Mark D. Contini
Steven F. Wilson
Norman A. Keith
Joseph Liberman
Walter R. Thornton
Mark D. Mills
Neil A. Ornstein
S. David Gorelle
David C. Daniels
M. Elizabeth Keenan
David M. Chondon
David Cowling
Joni E. Smith
Jeffrey E. Canto-Thaler
Karen L. Fields
John Barrack
Susan Lynn Crawford

For full biographical listings, see the Martindale-Hubbell Law Directory

Toronto—Continued

Stringer, Brisbin, Humphrey (AV)

110 Yonge Street, Suite 1100, M5C 1T4
Telephone: 416-862-1616
Fax: 416-363-7358

MEMBERS OF FIRM

Edwin L. Stringer, Q.C.
David L. Brisbin
Charles E. Humphrey
Barbara G. Humphrey

ASSOCIATES

Marilyn Silverman
Cheryl A. Edwards
Jeffrey E. Goodman
Michael G. Sherrard
Maryann Crnekovic
Keith Murray

OF COUNSEL

Lynn Bevan

For full biographical listings, see the Martindale-Hubbell Law Directory

*WINDSOR,** Essex Co.

McTague Law Firm (AV)

455 Pelissier Street, N9A 6Z9
Telephone: 519-255-4300
Detroit, Michigan Telephone: 313-965-1332
Fax: 519-255-4360(Corporate/Labor)
Fax: 519-255-4384 (Litigation/Real Estate)

MEMBERS OF FIRM

H. M. McTague, Miss, Q.C. (1900-1986)
Alexander R. Szalkai, Q.C.
Michael K. Coughlin
Jerry B. Udell
Josephine Stark
J. Douglas Lawson, Q.C.
Roger A. Skinner
George W. King
Peter J. Kuker
Theodore Crljenica
Gerri L. Wong
R. Paul Layfield

ASSOCIATES

John D. Leslie
Tom Serafimovski
Marilee Marcotte

For full biographical listings, see the Martindale-Hubbell Law Directory

CANADA
QUEBEC

*MONTREAL,** Montreal Dist.

Byers Casgrain (AV)

A Member of McMillan Bull Casgrain
Suite 3900, 1 Place Ville-Marie, H3B 4M7
Telephone: 514-878-8800
Telecopier: 514-866-2241
Cable Address: "Magee"
Telex: 05-24195

Hon. Jean Bazin, Q.C.
Michel Towner
Denis Manzo
Guy Lavoie
Francine Mercure
Yves Turgeon
Christian Létourneau

For Complete List of Firm Personnel, See General Section

For full biographical listings, see the Martindale-Hubbell Law Directory

McMaster Meighen (AV)

A General Partnership
7th Floor, 630 René-Lévesque Boulevard West, H3B 4H7
Telephone: 514-879-1212
Telecopier: 514-878-0605
Cable Address: "Cammerall"
Telex: "Cammerall MTL" 05-268637
Affiliated with Fraser & Beatty in Toronto, North York, Ottawa and Vancouver.

MEMBERS OF FIRM

Pierre Flageole
Thomas M. Davis
Philippe C. Vachon
André Royer

For Complete List of Firm Personnel, See General Section

For full biographical listings, see the Martindale-Hubbell Law Directory

MEDICAL MALPRACTICE LAW

ALABAMA

*BIRMINGHAM,** Jefferson Co.

HARRIS, EVANS, BERG & ROGERS, P.C. (AV)

Historic 2007 Building, 2007 Third Avenue North, 35203-2366
Telephone: 205-328-2366
Telecopier: 205-328-0013

Lyman H. Harris
Judy Whalen Evans
Lonette Lamb Berg
Susan Rogers

Matthew J. Dougherty
David L. Selby, II
Jeffrey K. Hollis
Stephen J. Bumgarner

For full biographical listings, see the Martindale-Hubbell Law Directory

HOGAN, SMITH, ALSPAUGH, SAMPLES & PRATT, P.C. (AV)

2323 Second Avenue, North, 35203
Telephone: 205-324-5635
Telecopier: 205-324-5637

S. Shay Samples
Ronald R. Crook

Reference: First Alabama Bank.

For Complete List of Firm Personnel, See General Section

For full biographical listings, see the Martindale-Hubbell Law Directory

HUIE, FERNAMBUCQ AND STEWART (AV)

Suite 800 First Alabama Bank Building, 35203
Telephone: 205-251-1193
Telecopy: 205-251-1256

MEMBERS OF FIRM

Stanley A. Cash
Robert M. Girardeau
M. Keith Gann
J. Allen Sydnor, Jr.

Representative Clients: Allstate Insurance Co.; Royal Insurance Company; Safeco Insurance Company; Employers-Commercial Union Group; Zurich-American Insurance Company; Home Insurance Company; CIGNA Insurance; Kemper Insurance; AETNA Casualty & Surety; American States Insurance.

For full biographical listings, see the Martindale-Hubbell Law Directory

PITTMAN, HOOKS, MARSH, DUTTON & HOLLIS, P.C. (AV)

1100 Park Place Tower, 35203
Telephone: 205-322-8880
Telecopier: 205-328-2711

W. Lee Pittman
Kenneth W. Hooks
David H. Marsh
Tom Dutton
L. Andrew Hollis, Jr.
Jeffrey C. Kirby
Ralph Bohanan, Jr.
Nat Bryan

Jeffrey C. Rickard
Susan J. Silvernail
Nici F. Williams
Chris T. Hellums
Adam P. Morel

OF COUNSEL

James H. Davis (Not admitted in AL)
Myra B. Staggs

For full biographical listings, see the Martindale-Hubbell Law Directory

PORTERFIELD, HARPER & MILLS, P.A. (AV)

22 Inverness Center Parkway, Suite 600, P.O. Box 530790, 35253-0790
Telephone: 205-980-5000
Fax: 205-980-5001

Larry W. Harper
William T. Mills, II
William Dudley Motlow, Jr.
Stanley K. Smith
Philip F. Hutcheson
H. C. "Trey" Ireland, III

Representative Clients: CIGNA; Equitable Life Assurance Society of the U.S.; Figge International; The Hanover Insurance Co.; Ingersoll-Rand Co.; New York Life Insurance Co.; The St. Paul Insurance Co.; Terex Corp.; The Travelers.

For Complete List of Firm Personnel, See General Section

For full biographical listings, see the Martindale-Hubbell Law Directory

PRITCHARD, MCCALL & JONES (AV)

800 Financial Center, 35203
Telephone: 205-328-9190

(See Next Column)

MEMBERS OF FIRM

William S. Pritchard (1890-1967)
Alexander W. Jones (1914-1988)
William S. Pritchard, Jr.
Madison W. O'Kelley, Jr.
Julian P. Hardy, Jr.
Alexander W. Jones, Jr.
F. Hilton-Green Tomlinson
James G. Henderson
William S. Pritchard, III

ASSOCIATES

Michael L. McKerley
Robert Bond Higgins
Nina Michele LaFleur
Mary W. Burge

Representative Clients: First National Bank of Columbiana; Central State Bank of Calera; Buffalo Rock-Pepsi-Cola Bottling Co.; Gillis Advertising, Inc.; Liberty Mutual Insurance Co.; Reliance Insurance Company; SouthTrust Bank, N.A.; Bromberg & Company, Inc.; Farmers Furniture Company; First Commercial Bank.

For full biographical listings, see the Martindale-Hubbell Law Directory

STARNES & ATCHISON (AV)

100 Brookwood Place, P.O. Box 598512, 35259-8512
Telephone: 205-868-6000
Telecopier: 205-868-6099

MEMBERS OF FIRM

W. Stancil Starnes
W. Michael Atchison
Michael A. Florie
Randal H. Sellers
Walter William Bates
Michael K. Wright
Robert P. Mackenzie, III
Laura Howard Peck

ASSOCIATES

Mark Christopher Eagan
Ann Sybil Vogtle
Joseph S. Miller
Scott M. Salter
Ashley E. Watkins

Representative Clients: Mutual Assurance, Inc.; AMI Brookwood Medical Center; American Medical International; Medical Care International; Mobile Infirmary Medical Center; CNA Insurance Co.

For full biographical listings, see the Martindale-Hubbell Law Directory

ARIZONA

*FLAGSTAFF,** Coconino Co.

ASPEY, WATKINS & DIESEL (AV)

123 North San Francisco, 86001
Telephone: 602-774-1478
Facsimile: 602-774-1043
Sedona, Arizona Office: 120 Soldier Pass Road.
Telephone: 602-282-5955.
Facsimile: 602-282-5962.
Page, Arizona Office: 904 North Navajo.
Telephone: 602-645-9694.
Winslow, Arizona Office: 205 North Williamson.
Telephone: 602-289-5963.
Cottonwood, Arizona Office: 905 Cove Parkway, Unite 201.
Telephone: 602-639-1881.

MEMBERS OF FIRM

Frederick M. Fritz Aspey
Harold L. Watkins
Louis M. Diesel
Bruce S. Griffen
Donald H. Bayles, Jr.
Kaign N. Christy
John J. Dempsey

Zachary Markham
James E. Ledbetter
Whitney Cunningham
Holly S. Karris

LEGAL SUPPORT PERSONNEL

Deborah D. Roberts (Legal Assistant)
C. Denece Pruett (Legal Assistant)
Dominic M. Marino, Jr, (Paralegal Assistant)

Representative Clients: Farmer's Insurance Company of Arizona; Kelley-Moore Paint Co.; Pepsi-Cola Bottling Company of Northern Arizona; Bill Luke's Chrysler-Plymouth, Inc.; First American Title Insurance Company ; Transamerica Title Insurance Co.; Page Electric Utility; Comprehensive Access Health Plan, Inc.

Reference: First Interstate Bank-Arizona, N.A., Flagstaff, Arizona.

For full biographical listings, see the Martindale-Hubbell Law Directory

*PHOENIX,** Maricopa Co.

BEGAM, LEWIS, MARKS, WOLFE & DASSE A PROFESSIONAL ASSOCIATION OF LAWYERS (AV)

111 West Monroe Street, Suite 1400, 85003-1787
Telephone: 602-254-6071
Fax: 602-252-0042

(See Next Column)

Begam, Lewis, Marks, Wolfe & Dasse A Professional Association of Lawyers, *Phoenix—Continued*

Robert G. Begam
Frank Lewis
Stanley J. Marks
Elliot G. Wolfe
Thomas F. Dasse
Cora Perez
Kelly J. McDonald
Daniel J. Adelman
Lisa Kurtz
Dena Rosen Epstein

Reference: National Bank of Arizona.

For full biographical listings, see the Martindale-Hubbell Law Directory

Michael E. Bradford (AV)

4131 North 24th Street Building C Suite 201, 85016
Telephone: 602-955-0088
FAX: 602-955-6445

LEGAL SUPPORT PERSONNEL

Sandra M. Bryant

OF COUNSEL

Jerry Steele

For full biographical listings, see the Martindale-Hubbell Law Directory

Burch & Cracchiolo, P.A. (AV)

702 East Osborn Road, Suite 200, 85014
Telephone: 602-274-7611
Fax: 602-234-0341
Mailing Address: P.O. Box 16882, Phoenix, AZ, 85011

Daniel Cracchiolo
David G. Derickson
Linda A. Finnegan
Jess A. Lorona

Representative Clients: Bashas' Inc.; Farmers Insurance Group; U-Haul International, Inc.

For Complete List of Firm Personnel, See General Section

For full biographical listings, see the Martindale-Hubbell Law Directory

Fennemore Craig, A Professional Corporation (AV)

Two North Central, Suite 2200, 85004
Telephone: 602-257-8700
Fax: 602-257-8527
Scottsdale, Arizona Office: 6263 North Scottsdale Road, Suite 290, 85250.
Telephone: 602-257-5400.
Fax: 602-945-4932.
Tucson, Arizona Office: One South Church Avenue, Suite 1030, 85701.
Telephone: 602-624-9312.
Fax: 602-882-7383.

John D. Everroad
Phillip F. Fargotstein
Andrew M. Federhar

Debra L. Runbeck
Jean Marie Sullivan
Marc H. Lamber

Representative Clients: ASARCO Incorporated; AT&T Communications; Bridgestone/Firestone, Inc.; Catellus Development Corp.; Citibank (Arizona); First Interstate Bank of Arizona; GIANT Industries; Phelps Dodge Corporation; The Atchison, Topeka & Santa Fe Railway, Co.; US WEST Communications.

For Complete List of Firm Personnel, See General Section

For full biographical listings, see the Martindale-Hubbell Law Directory

Friedl, Richter & Buri (AV)

Suite 200, 1440 East Washington Street, 85034
Telephone: 602-495-1000
Fax: 602-271-4733

MEMBERS OF FIRM

William J. Friedl
Charles E. Buri

For full biographical listings, see the Martindale-Hubbell Law Directory

Harris & Palumbo, A Professional Corporation (AV)

361 East Coronado, Suite 101, P.O. Box 13568, 85002-3568
Telephone: 602-271-9344
Fax: 602-252-2099

Anthony J. Palumbo
John David Harris
Kevin W. Keenan
Gene M. Cullan
Frank I. Powers
Shawn M. Cunningham

For full biographical listings, see the Martindale-Hubbell Law Directory

Jennings, Strouss and Salmon, P.L.C. (AV)

A Professional Limited Liability Company
One Renaissance Square, Two North Central, 85004-2393
Telephone: 602-262-5911
Fax: 602-253-3255

(See Next Column)

William T. Birmingham
W. Michael Flood
Gary L. Stuart
Douglas L. Christian
John A. Micheaels
Barry E. Lewin
Jay A. Fradkin
Jon D. Schneider
Frederick M. Cummings
Michael J. O'Connor

For Complete List of Firm Personnel, See General Section

For full biographical listings, see the Martindale-Hubbell Law Directory

Jones, Skelton & Hochuli (AV)

2901 North Central, Suite 800, 85012
Telephone: 602-263-1700
Telefax: 602-263-1784

MEMBERS OF FIRM

William R. Jones, Jr.
Peter G. Kline
Bruce D. Crawford

ASSOCIATE

Lori A. Shipley

For full biographical listings, see the Martindale-Hubbell Law Directory

Mark & Pearlstein, P.A. (AV)

Suite 150 The Brookstone, 2025 North Third Street, 85004
Telephone: 602-257-0200

Leonard J. Mark
Lynn M. Pearlstein, Mr.

OF COUNSEL

Stephen G. Campbell

For full biographical listings, see the Martindale-Hubbell Law Directory

Miller & Miller, Ltd. (AV)

Suite 2250, 3200 North Central Avenue, 85012
Telephone: 602-266-8440
Fax: 602-266-8453

Murray Miller
Richard K. Miller
Robert M. Miller
Marcus Westervelt

For full biographical listings, see the Martindale-Hubbell Law Directory

Law Offices of Raymond J. Slomski, P.C. (AV)

2901 North Central Avenue, Suite 1150, 85012
Telephone: 602-230-8777
Fax: 602-230-8707

Raymond J. Slomski

Kevin L. Beckwith
James M. Abernethy

LEGAL SUPPORT PERSONNEL

PARALEGAL

Patti A. Hibbeler

For full biographical listings, see the Martindale-Hubbell Law Directory

SCOTTSDALE, Maricopa Co.

Jeffrey A. Matz A Professional Corporation (AV Ⓣ)

6711 East Camelback Road, Suite 8, 85251
Telephone: 602-955-0900
Fax: 602-955-1885

Jeffrey A. Matz (Not admitted in AZ)

*TUCSON,** Pima Co.

Healy and Beal, P.C. (AV)

5255 E. Williams Circle Suite 6000-West Tower, 85711
Telephone: 602-790-6200
Fax: 602-790-1619

William T. Healy
Robert L. Beal
William D. Nelson

Dora Fitzpatrick

References: Bank of America; Merrill Lynch.

For full biographical listings, see the Martindale-Hubbell Law Directory

Stompoly, Stroud, Giddings & Glicksman, P.C. (AV)

1820 Citibank Tower, One South Church Avenue, 85702
Telephone: 602-628-8300
Telefax: 602-628-9948
Mailing Address: P.O. Box 190, Tucson, AZ, 85702-0190

John G. Stompoly

For Complete List of Firm Personnel, See General Section

For full biographical listings, see the Martindale-Hubbell Law Directory

Tucson—Continued

STRICKLAND & O'HAIR, P.C. (AV)

4400 E. Broadway, Suite 700, 85711-3517
Telephone: 602-795-8727
Fax: 602-795-5649

William E. Strickland | William E. Strickland, Jr.
Jennele Morris O'Hair

Representative Clients: AkChin Indian Community; City of Sierra Vista; City of Benson; Golf 36 Corp.; Town of Mammoth; Town of Patagonia; Fertilizer Company of Arizona, Inc.; Gila Valley Irrigation District; Franklin Irrigation District; City of Globe.
Reference: Bank One (formerly Valley National Bank).

ARKANSAS

*JONESBORO,** Craighead Co.

SNELLGROVE, LASER, LANGLEY, LOVETT & CULPEPPER (AV)

Second Floor, 111 East Huntington, P.O. Box 1346, 72403-1346
Telephone: 501-932-8357
Fax: 501-932-5488

MEMBERS OF FIRM

G. D. Walker (1910-1989)
Frank Snellgrove, Jr.
David N. Laser
Stanley R. Langley
Glenn Lovett, Jr.
Malcolm Culpepper
D. Todd Williams
Michael E. Mullally

ASSOCIATE

P. Sanders Huckabee

Representative Clients: Mercantile Bank; First Bank of Arkansas; Travelers Insurance Co.; Aetna Insurance Co.; ITT Hartford Insurance Co.; Commercial Union Insurance Co.; CNA Insurance Group; State Farm Insurance Cos.; Columbia Mutual Insurance Co.; Bituminous Insurance Co.

For full biographical listings, see the Martindale-Hubbell Law Directory

*LITTLE ROCK,** Pulaski Co.

HUCKABAY, MUNSON, ROWLETT & TILLEY, P.A. (AV)

First Commercial Building, Suite 1900, 400 West Capitol, 72201
Telephone: 501-374-6535
FAX: 501-374-5906

Mike Huckabay
Bruce E. Munson
Beverly A. Rowlett
James W. Tilley
John E. Moore
Tim Boone
Rick Runnells
Sarah Ann Presson

Lizabeth Lookadoo
Valerie Denton
Edward T. Oglesby
D. Michael Huckabay, Jr.
Carol Lockard Worley
Mark S. Breeding
Elizabeth Fletcher Rogers
Jeffrey A. Weber

Representative Clients: American Medical International; Columbia/HCA Healthcare Corporation; Sisters of Charity of Nazareth Health System d/b/a St. Vincent Infirmary Medical Center.

For full biographical listings, see the Martindale-Hubbell Law Directory

LASER, SHARP, WILSON, BUFFORD & WATTS, P.A. (AV)

101 S. Spring Street, Suite 300, 72201-2488
Telephone: 501-376-2981
Telecopier: 501-376-2417

Sam Laser | J. Kendal "Ken" Cook

Representative Clients: Allstate Insurance Co.; American International Insurance Group; Continental Insurance Cos.; Farm Bureau Insurance Cos. (Casualty & Fire); Farmers Insurance Group; GAB Business Services, Inc.; St. Paul Insurance Cos.; Scottsdale Insurance Co.; State Farm Auto (Fire) Insurance Cos.

For Complete List of Firm Personnel, See General Section

For full biographical listings, see the Martindale-Hubbell Law Directory

MCHENRY AND MITCHELL (AV)

124 West Capitol Avenue Suite 1500, 72201
Telephone: 501-372-3425
Fax: 501-372-3428

MEMBERS OF FIRM

Robert M. McHenry, Jr. | David S. Mitchell
Donna J. Wolfe

References: First Commercial Bank, N.A., Little Rock, Arkansas; Worthen Bank & Trust, Little Rock, Ark.

For full biographical listings, see the Martindale-Hubbell Law Directory

THE MCMATH LAW FIRM, P.A. (AV)

711 West Third Street, P.O. Box 1401, 72203
Telephone: 501-376-3021
FAX: 501-374-5118

Sidney S. McMath
Leland F. Leatherman
Sandy S. McMath
Phillip H. McMath
James Bruce McMath
Mart Vehik
Winslow Drummond
Paul E. Harrison
Sandra L. Sanders

For full biographical listings, see the Martindale-Hubbell Law Directory

*TEXARKANA,** Miller Co.

SMITH, STROUD, MCCLERKIN, DUNN & NUTTER (AV)

State Line Plaza, Box 8030, 75502-5945
Telephone: 501-773-5651
Telecopier: 501-772-2037

MEMBERS OF FIRM

Winford L. Dunn, Jr. | R. Gary Nutter
William David Carter

LEGAL SUPPORT PERSONNEL

LEGAL ASSISTANTS

Myra J. Conaway

Representative Clients: CNA Insurance Cos.; Cigna Insurance Cos.; St. Michael Hospital.

For Complete List of Firm Personnel, See General Section

For full biographical listings, see the Martindale-Hubbell Law Directory

CALIFORNIA

COSTA MESA, Orange Co.

LAW OFFICES OF W. DOUGLAS EASTON (AV)

3200 Park Center Drive, Suite 1000, 92626
Telephone: 714-850-4590
Fax: 714-850-4500

Anderson L. Washburn

For full biographical listings, see the Martindale-Hubbell Law Directory

*FRESNO,** Fresno Co.

LANG, RICHERT & PATCH, A PROFESSIONAL CORPORATION (AV)

Fig Garden Financial Center, 5200 North Palm Avenue, 4th Floor, P.O. Box 40012, 93755
Telephone: 209-228-6700
Fax: 209-228-6727

Frank H. Lang
William T. Richert (1937-1993)
Robert L. Patch, II
Val W. Saldaña
Douglas E. Noll
Michael T. Hertz
Victoria J. Salisch
Bradley A. Silva
David R. Jenkins
Charles Trudrung Taylor
Mark L. Creede
Peter N. Zeitler
Charles L. Doerksen

Randall C. Nelson
Barbara A. McAuliffe
Laurie Quigley Cardot
Douglas E. Griffin
Nabil E. Zumout

References: Wells Fargo Bank (Fresno Main Office); First Interstate Bank (Fresno Main Office).

For full biographical listings, see the Martindale-Hubbell Law Directory

MILES, SEARS & EANNI, A PROFESSIONAL CORPORATION (AV)

2844 Fresno Street, P.O. Box 1432, 93716
Telephone: 209-486-5200
Fax: 209-486-5240

Wm. M. Miles (1909-1991)
Robert E. Sears (1918-1992)
Carmen A. Eanni
Richard C. Watters
Gerald J. Maglio
William J. Seiler
Douglas L. Gordon

For full biographical listings, see the Martindale-Hubbell Law Directory

GLENDALE, Los Angeles Co.

JAMES J. PAGLIUSO (AV)

801 North Brand Boulevard Suite 320, 91203
Telephone: 818-244-2253; 213-744-1330
Fax: 818-547-0283

Reference: Bank of America, West Glenoaks Branch.

For full biographical listings, see the Martindale-Hubbell Law Directory

LARKSPUR, Marin Co.

WEINBERG, HOFFMAN & CASEY (AV)

A Partnership including a Professional Corporation
700 Larkspur Landing Circle, Suite 280, 94939
Telephone: 415-461-9666
Fax: 415-461-9681

Ivan Weinberg
Joseph Hoffman
A. Michael Casey

For full biographical listings, see the Martindale-Hubbell Law Directory

LONG BEACH, Los Angeles Co.

BENNETT & KISTNER (AV)

301 East Ocean Boulevard, Suite 800, 90802
Telephone: 310-435-6675
Fax: 310-437-8375
Riverside, California Office: 3403 Tenth Street, Suite 605. 92501-3676.
Telephone: 909-341-9360.
Fax: 909-341-9362.

Charles J. Bennett
Wayne T. Kistner

ASSOCIATES

Richard R. Bradbury
Mary A. Estante (Resident, Riverside Office)
Todd R. Becker
Karen H. Beckman (Resident, Riverside Office)

Representative Clients: The Hertz Corporation; Thrifty Oil Co.; Golden West Refining Co.; Standard Brands Paint Co.; Mattel, Inc.; Di Salvo Trucking Co.; County of Riverside; Southern California Rapid Transit District.
Reference: First Interstate Bank of California, The Market Place Office, Long Beach, California.

For full biographical listings, see the Martindale-Hubbell Law Directory

BURNS, AMMIRATO, PALUMBO, MILAM & BARONIAN, A PROFESSIONAL LAW CORPORATION (AV)

One World Trade Center, Suite 1200, 90831-1200
Telephone: 310-436-8338; 714-952-1047
Fax: 310-432-6049
Pasadena, California Office: 65 North Raymond Avenue, 2nd Floor.
Telephone: 818-796-5053; 213-258-8282.
Fax: 818-792-3078.

Vincent A. Ammirato

Thomas L. Halliwell
Robert Gary Mendoza
Joseph F. O'Hara
Michael P. Vicencia
Michael E. Wenzel

For full biographical listings, see the Martindale-Hubbell Law Directory

*LOS ANGELES,** Los Angeles Co.

BONNE, BRIDGES, MUELLER, O'KEEFE & NICHOLS, PROFESSIONAL CORPORATION (AV)

3699 Wilshire Boulevard, 10th Floor, 90010-2719
Telephone: 213-480-1900
Fax: 213-738-5888
Santa Ana, California Office: 801 Civic Center Drive West, Suite 400, P.O. Box 22018, 92702-2018.
Telephone: 714-835-1157.
Fax: 714-835-5913.
Santa Barbara, California Office: 801 Garden Street, Suite 300, 93101-5502.
Telephone: 805-965-2992.
Fax: 805-962-6509.
Riverside, California Office: 3801 University Avenue, Suite 710, 92501-3229.
Telephone: 909-788-1944.
Fax: 909-683-7827.
San Luis Obispo, California Office: 1060 Palm Street, 93401-3221.
Telephone: 805-541-8350.
Fax: 805-541-6817.

Ried Bridges
Kenneth N. Mueller
David J. O'Keefe
James D. Nichols
George E. Peterson
Joel Bruce Douglas
Alexander B. T. Cobb
Peter R. Osinoff
Margaret Manton Holm (Resident in Santa Ana Office)

(See Next Column)

Mark V. Franzen (Resident in Santa Ana Office)
Jeffrey C. Moffat
N. Denise Taylor
Patricia K. Ramsey (Resident in Santa Barbara Office)
Theodore H. O'Leary
Michael D. Lubrani (Resident at Riverside Office)
Peter A. Schneider
Christopher B. Marshall (Resident in Riverside Office)
Thomas M. O'Neil

Louis W. Pappas
Thomas R. Bradford (Resident in Santa Barbara Office)
Carol Kurke Lucas
JoAnna Jesperson
Yuk Kwong Law
Mary A. Seliger
Thomas G. Scully (Resident in Santa Ana Office)
Janice B. Lee
Martha A. H. Berman
John Aitelli
Steven C. Porath
Carmen Vigil
Kathryn S. Cook
Mark B. Connely (Resident in San Luis Obispo Office)
Robert W. Bates
Douglas C. Smith (Resident at Riverside Office)
Peter G. Bertling (Resident in Santa Barbara Office)
Donna Bruce Koch
Jerry S. Akita (Resident in Santa Ana Office)
Julianne M. DeMarco
John H. Dodd
Keith M. Staub
Kippy L. Wood (Resident in Santa Ana Office)
Jeffrey L. Tobin (Resident in Santa Ana Office)
Michael A. Shekey
Sara E. Hersh
Heather J. Higson (Resident, Santa Ana Office)
Barbara D. Springe (Resident in Santa Barbara Office)
Mary Lawrence Test
Gregory Reyna Bunch
George E. Nowotny, III (Resident in Santa Ana Office)
Marie E. Colmey
Gregory D. Werre
Brian L. Hoffman
Alison J. Vitacolonna (Resident in Santa Ana Office)
David D. Ernst
Ralph Godoy
Kathleen M. Walker
Mark E. Elliott
Jennifer L. Sturges
David Bricker
David J. Murray (Resident in Santa Ana Office)
Linda T. Pierce
Andrew S. Levey
Brian H. Clausen (Resident in Santa Barbara Office)
Michael B. Horrow
Mary-Lynn L. Pirner
Patricia M. Egan
Lisa L. Werries (Resident in Santa Ana Office)
Donna M. San Agustin
Melanie L. Goodman (Resident in Riverside Office)
Paul F. Arentz
Daniel E. Kenney
Jeannette Lynne Van Horst
Marc J. Gamberdella
Robert A. Madison
Barbara Kamenir Frankel
Raymond J. Mc Mahon
Lawrence Ronald Smith
Daniel J. Alexander
Mitzie L. Dobson

OF COUNSEL

Bruce J. Bonne

Representative Clients: Southern California Physicians Insurance Exchange, Doctor's Co.; Cooperative of American Physicians; Norcal Mutual Insurance Co.; Physician's Interindemnity Cooperative Corp.

For full biographical listings, see the Martindale-Hubbell Law Directory

WILLIAM J. GARGARO, JR. A PROFESSIONAL CORPORATION (AV)

Suite 1800, 2049 Century Park East, 90067
Telephone: 310-552-0633
FAX: 310-552-9760

William J. Gargaro, Jr.

Reference: First Interstate Bank of California.

For full biographical listings, see the Martindale-Hubbell Law Directory

HAMRICK, GARROTTO, BRISKIN & PENE, A PROFESSIONAL CORPORATION (AV)

3580 Wilshire Boulevard, 10th Floor, 90010
Telephone: 213-252-0041
Fax: 213-386-5414
Long Beach, California Office: 300 Oceangate, Suite 600.
Telephone: 310-435-4553.
Fax: 310-435-6442.

Robert S. Hamrick (A P.C.)
Greg W. Garrotto
Jeffrey F. Briskin (Resident, Long Branch Office)
Katherine B. Pene
John J. Latzanich, II

Craig A. McDougall (Resident, Long Beach Office)
Marla (Beth) Shah
Terry Porvin
Jana L. Gordon
Peter E. Garrell (Resident, Long Beach Office)
Roman Y. Nykolyshyn
Lori M. Levine
Nancy J. Lemkin (Resident, Long Beach Office)
Norman Goldman
Maureen A. McKinley
Linda L. Hamlin (Resident, Long Beach Office)

For full biographical listings, see the Martindale-Hubbell Law Directory

Los Angeles—Continued

LAW OFFICES OF DAVID M. HARNEY (AV)

Suite 1300 Figueroa Plaza, 201 North Figueroa Street, 90012-2636
Telephone: 213-482-0881
Fax: 213-250-4042

SPECIAL COUNSEL

Thomas Kallay

ASSOCIATES

Carl A. McMahan
Julie A. Harney
David T. Harney
Andrew J. Nocas
Vincent McGowan
Peter J. Polos
Thomas A. Schultz
Christopher P. Leyel
Jeffrey B. Smith
Robert H. Pourvali
C. Michael Alder
Daniel S. Glaser

OF COUNSEL

Gert K. Hirschberg

Reference: Bank of America.

For full biographical listings, see the Martindale-Hubbell Law Directory

KUSSMAN & WHITEHILL (AV)

A Partnership including a Professional Corporation
Suite 1470, 10866 Wilshire Boulevard, 90024
Telephone: 310-474-4411
Fax: 310-474-6530

Russell S. Kussman (A Professional Corporation)
Michael H. Whitehill

Steven G. Mehta

For full biographical listings, see the Martindale-Hubbell Law Directory

LA FOLLETTE, JOHNSON, DE HAAS, FESLER & AMES, A PROFESSIONAL CORPORATION (AV)

865 South Figueroa Street, Suite 3100, 90017-5443
Telephone: 213-426-3600
Fax: 213-426-3650
San Francisco, California Office: 50 California Street, Suite 3350.
Telephone: 415-433-7610.
Telecopier: 415-392-7541.
Santa Ana, California Office: 2677 North Main Street, Suite 901.
Telephone: 714-558-7008.
Telecopier: 714-972-0379.
Riverside, California Office: 3403 Tenth Street, Suite 820.
Telephone: 714-275-9192.
Fax: 714-275-9249.

John T. La Follette (1922-1990)
Daren T. Johnson
Louis H. De Haas
Donald C. Fesler
Dennis K. Ames (Resident, Santa Ana Office)
Alfred W. Gerisch, Jr.
Brian W. Birnie
Peter J. Zomber
Robert E. Kelly, Jr.
Leon A. Zallen
G. Kelley Reid, Jr. (Resident, San Francisco Office)
Dennis J. Sinclitico
Christopher C. Cannon (Resident, Santa Ana Office)
Dorothy B. Reyes
Steven R. Odell (Santa Ana and Riverside Offices)
Christopher L. Thomas (Santa Ana and Riverside Offices)
Robert K. Warford (Resident, Riverside Office)
John L. Supple (Resident, San Francisco Office)
Vincent D. Lapointe
Steven J. Joffe
Mark M. Stewart
Bradley J. McGirr (Resident, Santa Ana Office)
Sydney La Branche Merritt

Peter R. Bing
Larry P. Nathenson
Donald R. Beck (Resident, Santa Ana Office)
Donna R. Evans
David J. Ozeran
Mark B. Guterman
Terry A. Woodward (Resident, Santa Ana Office)
Stephen C. Dreher (Resident, Santa Ana Office)
Tatiana M. Schultz (Resident, San Francisco Office)
Peter E. Theophilos (Resident, San Francisco Office)
Deborah A. Cowley
Thomas S. Alch
Kenton E. Moore
Kent T. Brandmeyer
Garry O. Moses
Jeffery R. Erickson (Resident, Riverside Office)
Michael J. O'Connor
Elizabeth Anne Scherer (Resident, Santa Ana Office)
Hugh R. Burns
Stephen K. Hiura
James G. Wold
Eileen S. Lemmon (Resident, Riverside, Office)
David M. Wright
Larry E. White (Resident, Riverside Office)
Laurie Miyamoto Johnson
David James Reinard
Michelle Louise McCoy
Duane A. Newton (Resident, Riverside Office)
Adriaan F. van der Capellen (Resident, Santa Ana Office)
William T. Gray (Resident, Santa Ana Office)
Thomas J. Lo (Resident, Santa Ana Office)
Daniel D. Sorenson (Resident, Riverside Office)
Joanne Rosendin (Resident, San Francisco Office)
Henry P. Canvel (Resident, San Francisco Office)

(See Next Column)

Peter D. Busciglio (Resident, Santa Ana Office)
Mark S. Rader (Resident, Riverside Office)
Jay B. Lake
Erin L. Muellenberg (Resident, Riverside Office)
Phyllis M. Winston (Resident, Riverside Office)
John Calfee Mulvana (Resident, Santa Ana Office)
David L. Bell
Brian T. Chu (Resident, Santa Ana Office)
John Hammond
Laurent C. Vonderweidt
David Peim
Daniel V. Kohls (Resident, San Francisco Office)
Joel E. D. Odou
Robert T. Bergsten
Marcelo A. D'Asero
Natasha M. Riggs
Henry M. Su
Richard K. Kay
Annette A. Apperson

A list of References will be furnished upon request.

For full biographical listings, see the Martindale-Hubbell Law Directory

VEATCH, CARLSON, GROGAN & NELSON (AV)

A Partnership including a Professional Corporation
3926 Wilshire Boulevard, 90010
Telephone: 213-381-2861
Telefax: 213-383-6370

MEMBERS OF FIRM

Wayne Veatch
Henry R. Thomas (1905-1963)
James R. Nelson (1925-1987)
James C. Galloway, Jr. (A Professional Corporation)
C. Snyder Patin
Anthony D. Seine
Mark A. Weinstein
John A. Peterson

ASSOCIATES

Michael Eric Wasserman
Richard A. Wood
Michael A. Kramer
Mark M. Rudy
André S. Goodchild
Lyn A. Woodward
Kevin L. Henderson
Betty Rubin-Elbaz
John B. Loomis
Judith Randel Cooper
Karen J. Travis
Amy W. Lyons
Wayne Rozenberg
Gilbert A. Garcia
Judy Lew
James A. Jinks

OF COUNSEL

Robert C. Carlson (A Professional Corporation)
Stephen J. Grogan
David J. Aisenson

For full biographical listings, see the Martindale-Hubbell Law Directory

ROBERT D. WALKER A PROFESSIONAL CORPORATION (AV)

Suite 1208, One Park Plaza, 3250 Wilshire Boulevard, 90010-1606
Telephone: 213-382-8010
Fax: 213-388-1033

Robert D. Walker

Delia Flores
René M. Faucher

Reference: Bank of America (Los Angeles Main Office)

For full biographical listings, see the Martindale-Hubbell Law Directory

NEWPORT BEACH, Orange Co.

DONALD PETERS A LAW CORPORATION (AV)

1300 Dove Street, Suite 200, 92660
Telephone: 714-955-3818
Fax: 714-955-1341

Donald Peters

For full biographical listings, see the Martindale-Hubbell Law Directory

*OAKLAND,** Alameda Co.

RANKIN, SPROAT & POLLACK (AV)

An Association including Professional Corporations
Suite 1616, 1800 Harrison Street, 94612
Telephone: 510-465-3922
Fax: 510-452-3006
San Francisco, California Office: 369 Pine Street, Suite 400.
Telephone: 415-392-4346.

Joseph F. Rankin (-1977)
Patrick T. Rankin (1943-1990)
Ronald G. Sproat (Member of Rankin & Sproat, Professional Corporation)
Edward Vail Pollack (A Professional Corporation) (Resident, San Francisco Office)
Geoffrey A. Mires
Thomas A. Trapani
Michael J. Reiser

Gregory P. Menzel (Resident, San Francisco)
Lynne P. McGhee
David T. Shuey
G. Trent Morrow
Eugene Ashley

(See Next Column)

RANKIN, SPROAT & POLLACK, *Oakland—Continued*

LEGAL SUPPORT PERSONNEL

Jennifer L. Rankin
Betty E. Evans (Nurse Paralegal)
Sue Perata (Medical Paralegal)
Erika K. Ambacher (Paralegal)

Reference: Security Pacific Bank.

For full biographical listings, see the Martindale-Hubbell Law Directory

VAN BLOIS & KNOWLES (AV)

Suite 2245 Ordway Building, One Kaiser Plaza, 94612
Telephone: 510-444-1906
Contra Costa County 510-947-1055
Fax: 510-444-1294
Livermore, California Office: 2109 Fourth Street.
Telephone: 510-455-0193.

MEMBERS OF FIRM

R. Lewis Van Blois
Thomas C. Knowles
Ellen R. Schwartz
Richard J. Baskin

For full biographical listings, see the Martindale-Hubbell Law Directory

PALM SPRINGS, Riverside Co.

REGAR & PARKINSON (AV)

255 North El Cielo, Suite 200, 92262-6974
Telephone: 619-327-1516
Fax: 619-327-3291

MEMBERS OF FIRM

Barry Regar
James W. Parkinson

ASSOCIATE

Sigrid R. Hilkey

For full biographical listings, see the Martindale-Hubbell Law Directory

PASADENA, Los Angeles Co.

BURNS, AMMIRATO, PALUMBO, MILAM & BARONIAN, A PROFESSIONAL LAW CORPORATION (AV)

65 North Raymond Avenue, 2nd Floor, 91103-3919
Telephone: 818-796-5053; 213-258-8282
Fax: 818-792-3078
Long Beach, California Office: One World Trade Center, Suite 1200.
Telephone: 310-436-8338; 714-952-1047.
Fax: 310-432-6049.

Michael A. Burns
Bruce Palumbo
Jeffrey L. Milam
Robert H. Baronian
Steven J. Banner

Normand A. Ayotte
Colleen Clark
Vincent F. De Marzo
William D. Dodson
Valerie Julien-Peto
Susan E. Luhring
Grace C. Mori

Reference: First Los Angeles Bank.

For full biographical listings, see the Martindale-Hubbell Law Directory

FREEBURG, JUDY, MACCHIAGODENA & NETTELS (AV)

600 South Lake Avenue, 91106
Telephone: 818-585-4150
FAX: 818-585-0718
Santa Ana, California Office: Xerox Centre. 1851 East First Street, Suite 120. 92705-4017.
Telephone: 714-569-0950.
Facsimile: 714-569-0955.

Steven J. Freeburg
J. Lawrence Judy
Marina A. Macchiagodena
Charles F. Nettels

ASSOCIATES

Ingall W. Bull, Jr.
Richard B. Castle
Cynthia B. Schaldenbrand (Resident, Santa Ana Office)
Robert S. Brody
Sheral A. Hyde
Holly A. McNulty
Karen S. Freeburg
Jennifer D. Helsel
James P. Habel
Marianne L. Offermans

For full biographical listings, see the Martindale-Hubbell Law Directory

GEORGE E. MOORE A PROFESSIONAL LAW CORPORATION (AV)

Wells Fargo Building, 350 West Colorado Boulevard Suite 400, 91105-1894
Telephone: 818-440-1111
Fax: 818-440-9456

George E. Moore

For full biographical listings, see the Martindale-Hubbell Law Directory

*SACRAMENTO,** Sacramento Co.

PORTER, SCOTT, WEIBERG & DELEHANT, A PROFESSIONAL CORPORATION (AV)

350 University Avenue, Suite 200, 95825
Telephone: 916-929-1481
Fax: 916-927-3706

Russell G. Porter
A. Irving Scott, Jr.
Edwin T. Weiberg
John W. Delehant
Anthony S. Warburg
Ned P. Telford
James K. Mirabell
Craig A. Caldwell
Terence J. Cassidy
Tom H. Bailey
Carl J. Calnero
Russ J. Wunderli
Nancy J. Sheehan
Norman V. Prior
Timothy M. Blaine
Stephen E. Horan

Amanda R. Lowe
Mark L. Hardy
John R. Thacker
David R. Lane
Clay A. Jackson
Elisa Ungerman
Jesse Cardenas
Fred G. Wiesner
John Carl Padrick
Dennis M. Beaty
Molly Geremia Wiese
David E. Faliszek
Michael J. LeVangie
Carissa A. Shubb
Erik Z. Revai
Karen Beth Ebel
Carl L. Fessenden
Shannon I. Sutherland
Grant Collins Woodruff
Dana K. Astrachan
Paul William Naso

For full biographical listings, see the Martindale-Hubbell Law Directory

SCHUERING ZIMMERMAN SCULLY & NOLEN (AV)

400 University Avenue, 95825
Telephone: 916-567-0400
Fax: 916-568-0400

MEMBERS OF FIRM

Leo H. Schuering, Jr.
Robert H. Zimmerman
Steven T. Scully
Rhudolph Nolen, Jr.
Thomas J. Doyle
Lawrence S. Giardina
Anthony D. Lauria

Keith D. Chidlaw
Regina A. Favors
Raymond R. Gates
Scott A. Linn
Donna W. Low
Dominique A. Pollara
Theodore D. Poppinga
Janet Marie Richmond
John J. Sillis

For full biographical listings, see the Martindale-Hubbell Law Directory

WILKE, FLEURY, HOFFELT, GOULD & BIRNEY (AV)

A Partnership including Professional Corporations
400 Capitol Mall, Suite 2200, 95814-4408
Telephone: 916-441-2430
Telefax: 916-442-6664
Mailing Address: P.O. Box 15559, 95852-0559

MEMBERS OF FIRM

Richard H. Hoffelt (Inc.)
William A. Gould, Jr., (Inc.)
Philip R. Birney (Inc.)
Thomas G. Redmon (Inc.)
Scott L. Gassaway
Donald Rex Heckman II (Inc.)
Alan G. Perkins
Bradley N. Webb
Ernest James Krtil
Robert R. Mirkin
Matthew W. Powell
Mark L. Andrews
Stephen K. Marmaduke
David A. Frenznick
John R. Valencia
Angus M. MacLeod

ASSOCIATES

Paul A. Dorris
Kelli M. Kennaday
Tracy S. Hendrickson
Joseph G. De Angelis
Jennifer L. Kennedy
Anthony J. DeCristoforo
Rachel N. Kook
Alicia F. From
Michael Polis
Matthew J. Smith
Wayne L. Ordos

OF COUNSEL

Sherman C. Wilke
Anita Seipp Marmaduke
Benjamin G. Davidian

Representative Clients: NOR-CAL Mutual Insurance Co.; California Optometric Assn.; KPMG Peat Marwick; Glaxo, Inc.

For full biographical listings, see the Martindale-Hubbell Law Directory

*SAN DIEGO,** San Diego Co.

BELSKY & ASSOCIATES (AV)

610 West Ash Street, Suite 700, 92101
Telephone: 619-232-8300
Fax: 619-338-0066

Daniel S. Belsky

(See Next Column)

BELSKY & ASSOCIATES—*Continued*

Gabriel M. Benrubi
Cynthia Brack McGrew
Vincent J. Iuliano
Laura L. Waterman

References: First National Bank; Kaiser Foundation Health Plan, Inc.; Norcal Mutual Insurance Company; Sharp Rees-Stealy Medical Group; Sharp Mission Park Medical Group; Southern California Physician Insurance Exchange.

For full biographical listings, see the Martindale-Hubbell Law Directory

NEIL, DYMOTT, PERKINS, BROWN & FRANK, A PROFESSIONAL CORPORATION (AV)

1010 Second Avenue, Suite 2500, 92101-4959
Telephone: 619-238-1712
Fax: 619-238-1562

Michael I. Neil
David G. Brown
Robert W. Frank
Robert W. Harrison
Sheila S. Trexler

Reference: 1st Interstate Bank - San Diego.

For full biographical listings, see the Martindale-Hubbell Law Directory

*SAN FRANCISCO,** San Francisco Co.

BOSTWICK & TEHIN (AV)

A Partnership including Professional Corporations
Bank of America Center, 555 California Street, 33rd Floor, 94104-1609
Telephone: 415-421-5500
Fax: 415-421-8144
Honolulu, Hawaii Office: Suite 900, 333 Queen Street.
Telephone: 808-536-7771.

MEMBERS OF FIRM

James S. Bostwick (Professional Corporation)
Nikolai Tehin (Professional Corporation)
Pamela J. Stevens

ASSOCIATES

James J. O'Donnell
Sara A. Smith
Baron J. Drexel

For full biographical listings, see the Martindale-Hubbell Law Directory

JOHN GARDENAL A PROFESSIONAL CORPORATION (AV)

Suite 800 Cathedral Hill Office Building, 1255 Post Street, 94109
Telephone: 415-771-2700
FAX: 415-771-2072

John Gardenal

For full biographical listings, see the Martindale-Hubbell Law Directory

ROBERT A. HARLEM, INC. & ASSOCIATES A PROFESSIONAL CORPORATION (AV)

120 Montgomery Street, Suite 2410, 94104
Telephone: 415-981-1801
Fax: 415-981-5815

Robert A. Harlem

B. Mark Fong

OF COUNSEL

Patricia Knight
Jack Miller

For full biographical listings, see the Martindale-Hubbell Law Directory

MOLLIGAN, COX & MOYER, A PROFESSIONAL CORPORATION (AV)

703 Market Street, Suite 1800, 94103
Telephone: 415-543-9464
Fax: 415-777-1828

Ingemar E. Hoberg (1903-1971)
John H. Finger (1913-1991)
Phillip E. Brown (Retired)
Peter N. Molligan
Stephen T. Cox
David W. Moyer

John C. Hentschel
Guy D. Loranger
Nicholas J. Piediscazzi

OF COUNSEL

Kenneth W. Rosenthal
Barbara A. Zuras

For full biographical listings, see the Martindale-Hubbell Law Directory

MURPHY, PEARSON, BRADLEY & FEENEY, A PROFESSIONAL CORPORATION (AV)

88 Kearny Street, 11th Floor, 94108
Telephone: 415-788-1900
Telecopier: 415-393-8087
Sacramento, California Office: Suite 200, 3600 American River Drive, 95864.
Telephone: 916-483-6074.
Telecopier: 916-483-6088.

James A. Murphy
Arthur V. Pearson
Michael P. Bradley
John H. Feeney
Gregory A. Bastian (Resident, Sacramento Office)
Timothy J. Halloran
Karen M. Goodman (Resident, Sacramento Office)
Mark S. Perelman
Mark Ellis (Resident, Sacramento Office)
William S. Kronenberg

Peter L. Isola
Gregg Anthony Thornton
Anne F. Marchant
Antoinette Waters Farrell
Tomislav (Tom) Peraic
Douglas L. Johnson (Resident, Sacramento Office)
Michael K. Pazdernik (Resident, Sacramento Office)
Reed R. Johnson (Resident, Sacramento Office)
Alexander J. Berline
Alec Hunter Boyd
Amy Bisson Holloway (Resident, Sacramento Office)
Peter W. Thompson (Resident, Sacramento Office)
Gregory S. Maple
Rita K. Johnson
Jane L. O'Hara Gamp
Joseph E. Addiego, III
Kevin T. Burton (Resident at Sacramento, California Office)
Stacy Marie Howard (Resident, Sacramento Office)

LEGAL SUPPORT PERSONNEL

Wilfred A. Fregeau

For full biographical listings, see the Martindale-Hubbell Law Directory

O'CONNOR, COHN, DILLON & BARR, A LAW CORPORATION (AV)

The Folger Coffee Building, 101 Howard Street, Fifth Floor, 94105-1619
Telephone: 415-281-8888
Fax: 415-281-8890

Joseph T. O'Connor (Deceased, 1959)
Harold H. Cohn (1910-1992)
James L. Dillon
Duncan Barr
Janet L. Grove
Mark Oium
Jerald W. F. Jamison
Lisa T. Ungerer
Joel C. Lamp
Michael J. FitzSimons

Thomas G. Manning
Susan Reifel Goins
Dexter B. Louie
Deborah L. Panter
Marirose Piciucco
Keith Reyen
Deems A. Fishman
Jeanine M. Donohue
Karen K. Smith
Daniel J. Herp
James A. Beltzer (Not admitted in CA)

For full biographical listings, see the Martindale-Hubbell Law Directory

WALKUP, MELODIA, KELLY & ECHEVERRIA, A PROFESSIONAL CORPORATION (AV)

30th Floor, 650 California Street, 94108
Telephone: 415-981-7210
Fax: 415-391-6965

Bruce Walkup
Paul V. Melodia
Daniel J. Kelly
John Echeverria
Richard B. Goethals, Jr.
Ronald H. Wecht
Michael A. Kelly
Kevin L. Domecus
Jeffrey P. Holl
Daniel Dell'Osso

Mary E. Elliot
Richard H. Schoenberger
Cynthia F. Newton
Ann M. Richardson
Erik Brunkal
Michael J. Recupero

OF COUNSEL

John D. Link
Wesley Sokolosky

Reference: Bank of California, San Francisco Main Office, 400 California Street, San Francisco, Calif. 94104.

For full biographical listings, see the Martindale-Hubbell Law Directory

*SAN JOSE,** Santa Clara Co.

THE BOCCARDO LAW FIRM (AV)

Eleventh Floor, 111 West St. John Street, 95115
Telephone: 408-298-5678
Fax: 408-298-7503

MEMBERS OF FIRM

James F. Boccardo
John W. McDonald
Brian N. Lawther
John C. Stein
Richard L. Bowers
Russell L. Moore, Jr.

(See Next Column)

THE BOCCARDO LAW FIRM, *San Jose—Continued*

ASSOCIATES

Stephen Foster
David P. Moyles
Byron C. Foster
Victor F. Stefan
Robert W. Thayer
G. Matthew Fick
Charles A. Browning
Diego F. MacWilliam
Stephen A. Roberts

For full biographical listings, see the Martindale-Hubbell Law Directory

CAMPBELL, WARBURTON, BRITTON, FITZSIMMONS & SMITH, A PROFESSIONAL CORPORATION (AV)

Suite 1200, 101 Park Center Plaza, P.O. Box 1867, 95113
Telephone: 408-295-7701
Fax: 408-295-1423

Frank Valpey Campbell (1892-1971)
Frank L. Custer (1902-1962)
Alfred B. Britton, Jr. (1919-1991)
Austen D. Warburton
Willard R. Campbell
John R. Fitzsimmons, Jr.
C. Michael Smith
Ralph E. Mendell
Nicholas Pastore
J. Michael Fitzsimmons

William R. Colucci
Carolyn M. Rose

LEGAL SUPPORT PERSONNEL

Susan Frederick

Representative Corporate Clients: Marriott Corp.; Swenson Builders; Helene Curtis, Inc.; Viking Freight Systems.
Representative Insurance Clients: California State Automobile Assn.; Farmers Insurance Group; Travelers Insurance Co.; Westfield Insurance Cos.; Michelin Tire Corp. (Self Insured).

For full biographical listings, see the Martindale-Hubbell Law Directory

COLLINS & SCHLOTHAUER (AV)

An Association of Attorneys including a Professional Corporation
60 South Market Street, Suite 1100, 95113-2369
Telephone: 408-298-5161
Fax: 408-297-5766

Mark Scott Collins (Inc.)
Steven J. Plas
David N. Poll
Linda L. Duiven
Michael P. Dunn
Jovita Prestoza

OF COUNSEL

Thomas L. Schlothauer
Todd E. Macaluso

Representative Clients: Unigard Insurance; Farmers Insurance Co.; Fire Insurance Exchange; National American Insurance Co.; American Hardware Mutual Insurance; ABAG (Association of Bay Area Governmental Entities).

For full biographical listings, see the Martindale-Hubbell Law Directory

RUOCCO, SAUCEDO & CORSIGLIA, A LAW CORPORATION (AV)

RiverPark Towers, Suite 600, 333 West San Carlos Street, 95110
Telephone: 408-289-1417
Fax: 408-289-8127

Norman W. Saucedo
Bradley M. Corsiglia

For full biographical listings, see the Martindale-Hubbell Law Directory

TYNDALL & CAHNERS (AV)

An Association of Attorneys including a Professional Corporation
96 North Third Street, Suite 580, 95112
Telephone: 408-297-3700
Fax: 408-297-3721

John G. Tyndall, III (P.C.)
John D. Cahners

Michael Francis Brown

For full biographical listings, see the Martindale-Hubbell Law Directory

*SANTA ANA,** Orange Co.

RINOS & PACKER (AV)

A Partnership including Professional Corporations
550 North Parkcenter Drive, Suite 100, 92705
Telephone: 714-834-1500
Fax: 714-834-0480
Riverside, California Office: 1770 Iowa Avenue, Suite 170.
Telephone: 909-686-3380.
Fax: 909-686-2732.

MEMBERS OF FIRM

Dimitrios C. Rinos (A Professional Corporation)
Michael R. Packer (A Professional Corporation)
Linda B. Martin
Douglas G. Dickson
Robert C. Shephard

(See Next Column)

Michael E. Huff
Caleb W. Sullivan
Sandra G. Foraker
Deborah L. Tallon
Keith A. Weaver
Robert C. Risbrough
Matthew D. Barton
John A. Dragonette
Jennifer Lynn Zager
Jill E. Siegel

For full biographical listings, see the Martindale-Hubbell Law Directory

*SANTA CRUZ,** Santa Cruz Co.

DUNLAP, BURDICK AND MCCORMACK, A PROFESSIONAL LAW CORPORATION (AV)

121 Jewell Street, 95060
Telephone: 408-426-7040
FAX: 408-426-1095

Michael E. Dunlap
Paul P. Burdick

OF COUNSEL

Sandra C. McCormack

For full biographical listings, see the Martindale-Hubbell Law Directory

SANTA MONICA, Los Angeles Co.

DICKSON, CARLSON & CAMPILLO (AV)

120 Broadway, Suite 300, P.O. Box 2122, 90407-2122
Telephone: 310-451-2273
Telecopier: 310-451-9071

Robert L. Dickson
Jeffery J. Carlson
Ralph A. Campillo
Debra E. Pole
Roxanne M. Wilson
David J. Fleming
George E. Berry
William A. Hanssen
Mario Horwitz
Frederick J. Ufkes

Karen S. Bril
Pamela J. Yates

For Complete List of Firm Personnel, See General Section

For full biographical listings, see the Martindale-Hubbell Law Directory

*SANTA ROSA,** Sonoma Co.

BELDEN, ABBEY, WEITZENBERG & KELLY, A PROFESSIONAL CORPORATION (AV)

1105 North Dutton Avenue, P.O. Box 1566, 95402
Telephone: 707-542-5050
Telecopier: 707-542-2589

W. Barton Weitzenberg

Wayne R. Wolski

Representative Clients: Exchange Bank of Santa Rosa; Westamerica Bank; North Bay Title Co.; Northwestern Title Security Co.; Geyser Peak Winery; Arrowood Vineyards & Winery; Hansel Ford; Santa Rosa City School District.

For Complete List of Firm Personnel, See General Section

For full biographical listings, see the Martindale-Hubbell Law Directory

*VENTURA,** Ventura Co.

LAW OFFICES OF FREDERICK H. BYSSHE, JR. (AV)

10 South California Street, 93001
Telephone: 805-648-3224
Fax: 805-653-0267

Terence Geoghegan

For full biographical listings, see the Martindale-Hubbell Law Directory

ENGLE & BRIDE (AV)

353 San Jon Road, 93001
Telephone: 805-643-2200
Fax: 805-643-3062

MEMBERS OF FIRM

Benjamin J. Engle
Robert F. Bride

ASSOCIATES

Walter M. Leighton
Daniel J. Carobine

For Complete List of Firm Personnel, See General Section

For full biographical listings, see the Martindale-Hubbell Law Directory

WALNUT CREEK, Contra Costa Co.

ANDERSON, GALLOWAY & LUCCHESE, A PROFESSIONAL CORPORATION (AV)

1676 North California Boulevard, Suite 500, 94596-4183
Telephone: 510-943-6383
Facsimile: 510-943-7542

(See Next Column)

ANDERSON, GALLOWAY & LUCCHESE A PROFESSIONAL CORPORATION—*Continued*

Robert L. Anderson
George Patrick Galloway
David R. Lucchese
Martin J. Everson
Thomas J. Donnelly
Ralph J. Smith
James M. Nelson
Scott E. Murray
Henry E. Needham
Stephen F. Lucey
David A. Depolo
Karen A. Sparks
Stephen J. Brooks
James J. Zenere
Joseph S. Picchi
Coleen L. Welch
Deborah C. Moritz-Farr
Marc G. Cowden
Lauren E. Tate
Erin C. Ruddy
Lea K. McMahan

For full biographical listings, see the Martindale-Hubbell Law Directory

COLORADO

*ASPEN,** Pitkin Co.

FREEMAN & JENNER, P.C. (AV Ⓣ)

215 South Monarch Street, Suite 202, 81611
Telephone: 303-925-3400
FAX: 303-925-4043
Bethesda, Maryland Office: 3 Bethesda Metro Center, Suite 1410.
Telephone: 301-907-7747.
FAX: 301-907-9877.
Washington, D.C. Office: 1000 16th Street, N.W., Suite 300.
Telephone: 301-907-7747.

Martin H. Freeman

*DENVER,** Denver Co.

FEDER, MORRIS, TAMBLYN & GOLDSTEIN, P.C. (AV)

150 Blake Street Building, 1441 Eighteenth Street, 80202
Telephone: 303-292-1441
FAX: 303-292-1126

Harold A. Feder
Leonard M. Goldstein

Reference: Guaranty Bank & Trust Co., Denver, Colorado.

For full biographical listings, see the Martindale-Hubbell Law Directory

JOHNSON, RUDDY, NORMAN & McCONATY, A PROFESSIONAL CORPORATION (AV)

Ptarmigan Place - Suite 801, 3773 Cherry Creek Drive North, 80209-3866
Telephone: 303-388-7711
Telecopier: 303-388-1749

Roger F. Johnson
Robert Ruddy
Brian G. McConaty
Collie E. Norman

Thomas H. Anderson
Phil C. Pearson
Marci L. Laddusaw
Craig A. Sargent

OF COUNSEL

Gary H. Hemminger
Christine Ann Mullen

For full biographical listings, see the Martindale-Hubbell Law Directory

KENNEDY & CHRISTOPHER, P.C. (AV)

1616 Wynkoop Street, Suite 900, 80202
Telephone: 303-825-2700
Fax: 303-825-0434

Frank R. Kennedy
Daniel R. Christopher
Kim B. Childs
Elizabeth A. Starrs
Richard B. Caschette
Mark A. Fogg
Michael T. Mihm
Charles R. Ledbetter
Lisa B. Heintz
Ronald H. Nemirow
Barbara H. Glogiewicz
Dawn E. Mitzner
John R. Mann
Daniel R. McCune

OF COUNSEL

Paul E. Scott

Douglas J. Cox
Dean A. McConnell
Matthew S. Feigenbaum
Catherine O'Brien-Crum
Steven J. Picardi
Cheryl K. Hara
Nancy Hart-Edwards

Representative Clients: AETNA Casualty and Surety Co.; American Medical International; Blue Cross/Blue Shield of Colorado; COPIC; The Doctors Co.; Hartford Insurance Co.; Home Insurance Co.; St. Paul Fire and Marine Insurance Co.; PRMS, Colorado Insurance Guaranty Association.

For full biographical listings, see the Martindale-Hubbell Law Directory

LONG & JAUDON, P.C. (AV)

The Bailey Mansion, 1600 Ogden Street, 80218-1414
Telephone: 303-832-1122
FAX: 303-832-1348

Joseph C. Jaudon, Jr.
Gary B. Blum
Michael T. McConnell
Alan D. Avery
Walter N. Houghtaling
Carla M. LaRosa
Thomas C. Kearns, Jr.
Michael Shaefer Drew
David H. Yun

Representative Clients: St. Joseph Hospital; Aetna Life & Casualty Company; The Doctors Company; Home Insurance Company; Baxter Healthcare.

For Complete List of Firm Personnel, See General Section

For full biographical listings, see the Martindale-Hubbell Law Directory

MYERS, HOPPIN, BRADLEY AND DEVITT, P.C. (AV)

Suite 420, 4704 Harlan Street, 80212
Telephone: 303-433-8527
Fax: 303-433-8219

Frederick J. Myers
Charles T. Hoppin
Jon T. Bradley
Jerald J. Devitt

Gregg W. Fraser

OF COUNSEL

Kent E. Hanson

Reference: Bank One Lakeside Banking Center.

For full biographical listings, see the Martindale-Hubbell Law Directory

PRYOR, CARNEY AND JOHNSON, A PROFESSIONAL CORPORATION (AV)

Carrara Place, Suite 400, 6200 South Syracuse Way (Englewood), P.O. Box 22003, 80222-0003
Telephone: 303-771-6200
Facsimile: 303-779-0740

Peter W. Pryor
Irving G. Johnson
David D. Karr
Edward D. Bronfin
Scott S. Nixon
Bruce A. Montoya
JoAnne M. Zboyan
Michael J. McNally
Elizabeth C. Moran
C. Gregory Tiemeier
Daniel M. Hubbard
Nick S. Kaluk, Jr.

Representative Clients: The Doctors' Company; Kaiser Foundation Health Plan of Colorado; COPIC (Colorado Physicians Insurance Company); Ophthalmic Mutual Insurance Company; Professional Medical Insurance Company; Physicians & Surgeons Insurance Company; AMS of Oral Surgeons; The Colorado Dental Trust; PHICO and MMI Companies, Inc.

For Complete List of Firm Personnel, See General Section

For full biographical listings, see the Martindale-Hubbell Law Directory

SCHADEN, LAMPERT & LAMPERT (AV)

1610 Emerson Street, 80218-1412
Telephone: 303-832-2771
Broomfield, Colorado Office: 11870 Airport Way, 80021.
Telephone: 303-465-3663.
Birmingham, Michigan Office: Schaden, Wilson and Katzman. 800 N. Woodward Avenue, Suite 102.
Telephone: 313-258-4800.

MEMBERS OF FIRM

Richard F. Schaden (Resident, Broomfield Office)
Bruce A. Lampert
Brian J. Lampert

ASSOCIATES

Kathleen M. Schaden (Resident, Boulder Office)
Susanna L. Meissner-Cutler
Patricia M. Jarzobski

For full biographical listings, see the Martindale-Hubbell Law Directory

TREECE, ALFREY & MUSAT, P.C. (AV)

Denver Place, 999 18th Street, Suite 1600, 80202
Telephone: 303-292-2700
Facsimile: 303-295-0414

Thomas N. Alfrey

OF COUNSEL

Duncan W. Cameron

For full biographical listings, see the Martindale-Hubbell Law Directory

ENGLEWOOD, Arapahoe Co.

THOMAS J. TOMAZIN, P.C. (AV)

Suite 200, 5655 South Yosemite, 80111
Telephone: 303-771-1900
FAX: 303-793-0923

(See Next Column)

THOMAS J. TOMAZIN, P.C., *Englewood—Continued*

Thomas J. Tomazin

Reference: Key Bank.

For full biographical listings, see the Martindale-Hubbell Law Directory

LAKEWOOD, Jefferson Co.

BUSCH AND COHEN, P.C. (AV)

Suite A-130, 12600 West Colfax Avenue, 80215
Telephone: 303-232-0362
Fax: 303-232-1125

Robert G. Busch
Michael A. Cohen

For full biographical listings, see the Martindale-Hubbell Law Directory

CONNECTICUT

*BRIDGEPORT,** Fairfield Co.

WILLIAMS, COONEY & SHEEHY (AV)

One Lafayette Circle, 06604
Telephone: 203-331-0888
Telecopier: 203-331-0896

MEMBERS OF FIRM

Ronald D. Williams
Robert J. Cooney
Edward Maum Sheehy
Peter D. Clark
Peter J. Dauk
Dion W. Moore
Ronald D. Williams, Jr.
Francis A. Smith, Jr. (1951-1989)

Lawrence F. Reilly
Michael P. Bowler
Michael Cuff Deakin

Representative Clients: Aetna Life & Casualty Co.; Nationwide Insurance Co.; Connecticut Medical Insurance Co.; Zimmer Manufacturing Co.; The Travelers; Preferred Physicians Mutual; Podiatary Insurance Company of America; Medical Liability Mutual Insurance Company.

For full biographical listings, see the Martindale-Hubbell Law Directory

CHESHIRE, New Haven Co.

HITT, SACHNER & COLEMAN (AV)

673 South Main Street, P.O. Box 724, 06410
Telephone: 203-272-0371
FAX: 203-272-9854

MEMBERS OF FIRM

Fred A. Hitt
Stephen P. Sachner
Andrew D. Coleman

ASSOCIATE

James M. Miele

Representative Clients: The Aetna Casualty & Surety Division; Lafayette American Bank & Trust; Liberty Mutual Insurance Co.; National Paint Distributors, Inc.; Ravenswood Properties, Inc.; Harte Nissan, Inc.; Dowling Ford, Inc.; Shawmut Bank Connecticut, N.A.; Frank R. DiNatali Inc.; Doug Calcagni Associates, Inc.

For Complete List of Firm Personnel, See General Section

For full biographical listings, see the Martindale-Hubbell Law Directory

*HARTFORD,** Hartford Co.

GORDON, MUIR AND FOLEY (AV)

Hartford Square North, Ten Columbus Boulevard, 06106-1944
Telephone: 203-525-5361
Telecopier: 203-525-4849

MEMBERS OF FIRM

William S. Gordon, Jr. (1946-1956)
George Muir (1939-1976)
Edward J. Foley (1955-1983)
Peter C. Schwartz
John J. Reid
John H. Goodrich, Jr.
R. Bradley Wolfe
Jon Stephen Berk
William J. Gallitto
Gerald R. Swirsky
Robert J. O'Brien
Philip J. O'Connor
Kenneth G. Williams
Chester J. Bukowski
Mary Ann Santacroce

ASSOCIATES

J. Lawrence Price
Mary Anne Alicia Charron
James G. Kelly
Kevin F. Morin
Claudia A. Baio
Patrick T. Treacy
Andrew J. Hern
Eileen Geel
Christopher L. Slack
Renee W. Dwyer
David B. Heintz

(See Next Column)

OF COUNSEL

Stephen M. Riley

Reference: Fleet Bank.

For full biographical listings, see the Martindale-Hubbell Law Directory

JACKSON, O'KEEFE AND PHELAN (AV)

36 Russ Street, 06106-1571
Telephone: 203-278-4040
Fax: 203-527-2500
West Hartford, Connecticut Office: 62 LaSalle Road.
Telephone: 203-521-7500.
Fax: 203-561-5399.
Bethlehem, Connecticut Office: 423 Munger Lane.
Telephone: 203-266-5255.

MEMBERS OF FIRM

Jay W. Jackson
Andrew J. O'Keefe
Denise Martino Phelan
Matthew J. O'Keefe
Peter K. O'Keefe
Philip R. Dunn, Jr.
Michael J. Walsh
Anna M. Carbonaro
Denise Rodosevich

OF COUNSEL

Maureen Sullivan Dinnan

Representative Clients: Aetna Casualty & Surety Co.; ITT Hartford; Liberty Mutual Insurance Co.; Connecticut Medical Insurance Co.

For full biographical listings, see the Martindale-Hubbell Law Directory

KENNY, BRIMMER, MELLEY & MAHONEY (AV)

5 Grand Street, 06106
Telephone: 203-527-4226
FAX: 203-527-0214

Joseph P. Kenny (1920-1993)

MEMBERS OF FIRM

Leslie R. Brimmer
William J. Melley, III
Richard C. Mahoney

ASSOCIATES

Anita M. Varunes
Dennis F. McCarthy
Maurice M. O'Shea
Beverly Johns

For full biographical listings, see the Martindale-Hubbell Law Directory

*NEW HAVEN,** New Haven Co.

JACOBS & JACOBS (AV)

555 Long Wharf Drive, Suite 13A, 06511
Telephone: 203-777-2300
Fax: 203-787-5628

MEMBERS OF FIRM

Israel J. Jacobs (1918-1963)
Stanley A. Jacobs
Bruce D. Jacobs
Irene Prosky Jacobs
Carol Wolven

Reference: Connecticut National Bank.

For full biographical listings, see the Martindale-Hubbell Law Directory

LYNCH, TRAUB, KEEFE AND ERRANTE, A PROFESSIONAL CORPORATION (AV)

52 Trumbull Street, P.O. Box 1612, 06506
Telephone: 203-787-0275
Fax: 203-782-0278

Stephen I. Traub
Hugh F. Keefe
Steven J. Errante
John J. Keefe, Jr.
Donn A. Swift
Charles E. Tiernan, III
Robert W. Lynch
Richard W. Lynch

Mary Beattie Schairer
John M. Walsh, Jr.
Suzanne L. McAlpine
David J. Vegliante
Christopher M. Licari
David S. Monastersky

OF COUNSEL

William C. Lynch

Local Counsel for: Transport Insurance Co., Dallas, Texas; American Trucking Associations; Roadway Express, Inc., Akron, Ohio; A.R.A. Philadelphia, Penn.; Consolidated Freightways, Menlo Park, California; Ogden Corp. *Labor Counsel:* Coca-Cola, U.S.A., Atlanta, Georgia (Private Truck Operation); The Dow Chemical Co.; Cincinnati Milacron.

For full biographical listings, see the Martindale-Hubbell Law Directory

NEW LONDON, New London Co.

REARDON & NAZZARO, P.C. (AV)

160 Hempstead Street, Drawer 1430, 06320
Telephone: 203-442-0444
Telecopier: 203-444-6445

(See Next Column)

REARDON & NAZZARO P.C.—*Continued*

Robert I. Reardon, Jr. John J. Nazzaro
Maryann Diaz

Angelo A. Ziotas Stephen J. MacKinnon

LEGAL SUPPORT PERSONNEL

Bette B. Beam (Legal Administrator) Carolyn B. Dickey (Paralegal)
Kelly G. MacDonald (Paralegal)
Jillene B. Mattern (Paralegal)

For full biographical listings, see the Martindale-Hubbell Law Directory

STAMFORD, Fairfield Co.

ROSENBLUM & FILAN (AV Ⓣ)

One Landmark Square, 06901
Telephone: 203-358-9200
Fax: 203-969-6140
White Plains, New York Office: 50 Main Street. 10606.
Telephone: 914-686-6100.
Fax: 914-686-6140.
New York, New York Office: 400 Madison Avenue. 10017.
Telephone: 212-888-8001.
Fax: 212-888-3331.

MEMBERS OF FIRM

Patrick J. Filan James B. Rosenblum

Jeannine M. Foran Kate E. Maguire
James F. Walsh M. Karen Noble
James Newfield

OF COUNSEL

Lee Judy Johnson (Not admitted in CT) Theodore J. Greene
Katherine Benesch (Not admitted in CT) Jack L. Most
Richard M. Schwartz (Not admitted in CT)

For full biographical listings, see the Martindale-Hubbell Law Directory

SILVER, GOLUB & TEITELL (AV)

184 Atlantic Street, P.O. Box 389, 06904
Telephone: 203-325-4491
FAX: 203-325-3769

MEMBERS OF FIRM

Richard A. Silver Ernest F. Teitell
David S. Golub Patricia M. Haugh (1942-1988)
Elaine T. Silver

John D. Josel Marilyn J. Ramos
Mario DiNatale Jack Zaremski
Jonathan M. Levine (Not admitted in CT)

For full biographical listings, see the Martindale-Hubbell Law Directory

WATERBURY, New Haven Co.

THOMAS L. BRAYTON, P.C. (AV)

Suite 301, 37 Leavenworth Street, P.O. Box 2757, 06723-2757
Telephone: 203-574-3233
Facsimile: 203-597-0855

Thomas L. Brayton Thomas L. Brayton, III

For full biographical listings, see the Martindale-Hubbell Law Directory

WESTPORT, Fairfield Co.

LAWRENCE W. KANAGA (AV)

830 Post Road East, 06880-5291
Telephone: 203-221-0696
Fax: 203-226-6866

For full biographical listings, see the Martindale-Hubbell Law Directory

DELAWARE

*WILMINGTON,** New Castle Co.

BURT & BURT (AV)

Suite 1700 Mellon Bank Center, 919 Market Street, 19801
Telephone: 302-429-9430
Fax: 302-429-9427

Warren B. Burt David H. Burt

(See Next Column)

Richard D. Abrams Michael F. Duggan

For full biographical listings, see the Martindale-Hubbell Law Directory

DALEY, ERISMAN & VAN OGTROP (AV)

1224 King Street, 19801
Telephone: 302-658-4000
FAX: 302-652-8975
Newark, Delaware Office: 206 East Delaware Avenue.
Telephone: 302-368-0133.
FAX: 302-368-4587.

MEMBERS OF FIRM

Robert E. Daley James A. Erisman
Piet H. van Ogtrop

References: Wilmington Trust Company; Beneficial National Bank.

For full biographical listings, see the Martindale-Hubbell Law Directory

SMITH, KATZENSTEIN & FURLOW (AV)

1220 Market Building, P.O. Box 410, 19899
Telephone: 302-652-8400
FAX: 302-652-8405

MEMBERS OF FIRM

Robert J. Katzenstein Susan L. Parker
Vicki A. Hagel

Stephen M. Miller

For Complete List of Firm Personnel, See General Section

For full biographical listings, see the Martindale-Hubbell Law Directory

TYBOUT, REDFEARN & PELL (AV)

Suite 1100, PNC Bank Building, 300 Delaware Avenue, P.O. Box 2092, 19899
Telephone: 302-658-6901
FAX: 658-4018

F. Alton Tybout Anne L. Naczi
B. Wilson Redfearn Nancy E. Chrissinger
Richard W. Pell David G. Culley

ASSOCIATES

Sherry Ruggiero Fallon Michael I. Silverman
Sean A. Dolan Bernadette M. Plaza
Elizabeth Daniello Maron Joel R. Brown
Francis X. Nardo John J. Klusman, Jr.
Todd M. Finchler

Representative Clients: CIGNA Ins., Co.; Liberty Mutual Ins., Co.; Hartford Ins., Co.; Universal Underwriters; PHICO; State of Delaware; GAB Business Services Inc.; State Farm Ins., Co.; Alliance of American Insurers; Insurance Guarantee Assn.

For full biographical listings, see the Martindale-Hubbell Law Directory

DISTRICT OF COLUMBIA

WASHINGTON, D.C. Co.

THE ABELSON LAW FIRM (AV)

Suite 300, 1000 Sixteenth Street, N.W., 20036
Telephone: 202-331-0600
Fax: 202-429-9088

Michael A. Abelson

For full biographical listings, see the Martindale-Hubbell Law Directory

BRAULT, GRAHAM, SCOTT & BRAULT (AV)

1906 Sunderland Place, N.W., 20036
Telephone: 202-785-1200
Fax: 202-785-4301
Rockville, Maryland Office: 101 South Washington Street.
Telephone: 301-424-1060.
FAX: 301-424-7991.
Arlington, Virginia Office: Suite 1201, 2300 North Clarendon Boulevard, Courthouse Plaza.
Telephone: 703-522-1781.

OF COUNSEL

Laurence T. Scott

MEMBERS OF FIRM

Denver H. Graham (1922-1987) James S. Wilson (Resident, Rockville, Maryland Office)
Albert E. Brault (Retired) Ronald G. Guziak (Resident, Rockville, Maryland Office)
Albert D. Brault (Resident, Rockville, Maryland Office)
Leo A. Roth, Jr.

(See Next Column)

BRAULT, GRAHAM, SCOTT & BRAULT, *Washington—Continued*

MEMBERS OF FIRM (Continued)

Daniel L. Shea (Resident, Rockville, Maryland Office)
Keith M. Bonner
M. Kathleen Parker (Resident, Rockville, Maryland Office)
Regina Ann Casey (Resident, Rockville, Maryland Office)
James M. Brault (Resident, Rockville, Maryland Office)

ASSOCIATES

David G. Mulquin (Not admitted in DC; Resident, Rockville, Maryland Office)
Sanford A. Friedman
Holly D. Shupert (Not admitted in DC; Resident, Rockville, Maryland Office)
Eric A. Spacek
Joan F. Brault (Resident, Rockville, Maryland Office)

Representative Clients: American Oil Co.; Crum & Forster Group; Fireman's Fund American Insurance Cos.; Kemper Group; Reliance Insurance Cos.; Safeco Group; Government Employees Insurance Co.; Medical Mutual Society of Maryland; Legal Mutual Liability Insurance Society of Maryland.

For Complete List of Firm Personnel, See General Section

For full biographical listings, see the Martindale-Hubbell Law Directory

THE FALK LAW FIRM A PROFESSIONAL LIMITED COMPANY (AV)

Suite 260 One Westin Center, 2445 M Street, N.W., 20037
Telephone: 202-833-8700
Telecopier: 202-872-1725

James H. Falk, Sr.
James H. Falk, Jr.
John M. Falk
Rose Burks Emery (Not admitted in DC)
Robert K. Tompkins (Not admitted in DC)

OF COUNSEL

Pierre E. Murphy

For full biographical listings, see the Martindale-Hubbell Law Directory

KENNETH R. FEINBERG & ASSOCIATES (AV)

1120 20th Street, N.W. Suite 740 South, 20036
Telephone: 202-371-1110
Fax: 202-962-9290
New York, N.Y. Office: 780 3rd Avenue, Suite 2202.
Telephone: 212-527-9600.
Fax: 212-527-9611.

ASSOCIATES

Deborah E. Greenspan
Michael K. Rozen (Not admitted in DC)
Peter H. Woodin (Not admitted in DC)

For full biographical listings, see the Martindale-Hubbell Law Directory

JACK H. OLENDER AND ASSOCIATES, P.C. (AV)

One Farragut Square South 11th Floor, 1634 Eye Street, N.W., 20006
Telephone: 202-879-7777

Jack H. Olender

Harlow R. Case
Gary S. Freeman
Sandra H. Robinson
Kim M. Keenan
Dan L. Gray, Jr.
Marian K. Riedy

For full biographical listings, see the Martindale-Hubbell Law Directory

PAULSON, NACE & NORWIND (AV)

1814 N Street, N.W., 20036
Telephone: 202-463-1999
Fax: 202-223-6824

MEMBERS OF FIRM

Richard S. Paulson (1928-1986)
Barry J. Nace
Edward L. Norwind

ASSOCIATES

John S. Lopatto, III
Mark R. Lightfoot

OF COUNSEL

Irving R. M. Panzer

For full biographical listings, see the Martindale-Hubbell Law Directory

FLORIDA

*BARTOW,** Polk Co.

FROST, O'TOOLE & SAUNDERS, P.A. (AV)

395 South Central Avenue, P.O. Box 2188, 33830
Telephone: 813-533-0314; 800-533-0967
Telecopier: 813-533-8985

(See Next Column)

John W. Frost, II
Neal L. O'Toole
Thomas C. Saunders
Richard E. "Rick" Dantzler
Robert A. Carr
Robert H. Van Hart
James R. Franklin
John Marc Tamayo

Reference: Community National Bank, Bartow.

For full biographical listings, see the Martindale-Hubbell Law Directory

*BRADENTON,** Manatee Co.

MULOCK, COLEMAN & THOMPSON, P.A. (AV)

519 13th Street West, 34205
Telephone: 813-748-2104
Fax: 813-748-6588

Edwin T. Mulock
Larry K. Coleman
W. Wade Thompson

LEGAL SUPPORT PERSONNEL

Nancy A. Martin (Certified Legal Assistant)

Representative Clients: Clerk of Circuit Court of Manatee County; The Bradenton Herald; Belk-Lindsey Department Stores; Bill Graham Ford Co.; Walgreen Co.
Approved Attorneys for: Attorneys' Title Insurance Fund.

For full biographical listings, see the Martindale-Hubbell Law Directory

CRYSTAL RIVER, Citrus Co.

BEST & ANDERSON, P.A. (AV)

7655 West Gulf to Lake Highway, Suite 6, 34429
Telephone: 904-795-1107
Orlando, Florida Office: 20 North Orange Avenue, Suite 505.
Telephone: 407-425-2985.

David R. Best
George H. "Dutch" Anderson, III

Mark S. Walker
Perry M. Nardi
G. Clay Morris
Lawrence I. Hauser

For full biographical listings, see the Martindale-Hubbell Law Directory

DAYTONA BEACH, Volusia Co.

EUBANK, HASSELL & LEWIS (AV)

Suite 301, 149 South Ridgewood Avenue, P.O. Box 2229, 32015-2229
Telephone: 904-238-1357
Telecopier: 904-258-7406

MEMBERS OF FIRM

James O. Eubank, II
F. Bradley Hassell
Lester A. Lewis

ASSOCIATES

Jennifer M. Dehn
Alfred Truesdell
Timothy A. Traster
Joseph D. Tessitore

For full biographical listings, see the Martindale-Hubbell Law Directory

SMITH, SCHODER, ROUSE & BOUCK, P.A. (AV)

605 South Ridgewood Avenue, 32014
Telephone: 904-255-0505
FAX: 904-252-4794
Other Daytona Beach Office: 214 Loomis Avenue.
Telephone: 904-255-6711.

James W. Smith
Robert K. Rouse, Jr.

For full biographical listings, see the Martindale-Hubbell Law Directory

*FORT LAUDERDALE,** Broward Co.

COONEY, HALICZER, MATTSON, LANCE, BLACKBURN, PETTIS & RICHARDS, P.A. (AV)

301 East Las Olas Boulevard, P.O. Box 14546, 33302
Telephone: Telephone: 305-779-1900
WATS: 1-800-745-3864
Telecopier: 305-779-1910

David F. Cooney
James S. Haliczer
Michael C. Mattson
Victor Lance
Ace J. Blackburn, Jr.
Eugene K. Pettis
John H. Richards
Kenneth E. White
Kieran O'Connor
Lorna E. Brown-Burton
Bruce Michael Trybus
Pamela R. Kittrell
Lawrence E. Brownstein
Christopher D. Malin
Amy B. Talisman

For full biographical listings, see the Martindale-Hubbell Law Directory

*JACKSONVILLE,** Duval Co.

Liles, Gavin & Costantino (AV)

One Enterprise Center, Suite 1500, 225 Water Street, 32202
Telephone: 904-634-1100
Fax: 904-634-1234

Rutledge R. Liles
R. Kyle Gavin
R. Scott Costantino
F. Bay Neal III

For full biographical listings, see the Martindale-Hubbell Law Directory

*MIAMI,** Dade Co.

Angones, Hunter, McClure, Lynch & Williams, P.A. (AV)

Ninth Floor-Concord Building, 66 West Flagler Street, 33130
Telephone: 305-371-5000
Fort Lauderdale: 305-728-9112
FAX: 305-371-3948

Frank R. Angones
Steven Kent Hunter
John McClure
Christopher J. Lynch
Stewart D. Williams
B. Scott Hunter

Leopoldo Garcia, Jr.
Thomas W. Paradise
Donna Joy Hunter
Lourdes Alfonsin Ruiz
Matthew K. Mitchell
Kara D. Phinney

Insurance Clients: Allstate Insurance Co.; Prudential Property & Casualty Insurance Company; State Farm Fire & Casualty Insurance Company; Rollins Hudig Hall Healthcare Risk, Inc.

For Complete List of Firm Personnel, See General Section

For full biographical listings, see the Martindale-Hubbell Law Directory

Deutsch & Blumberg, P.A. (AV)

Suite 2802 New World Tower, 100 North Biscayne Boulevard, 33132
Telephone: 305-358-6329
Fax: 305-358-9304

Steven K. Deutsch
Edward R. Blumberg
Louis Thaler

For full biographical listings, see the Martindale-Hubbell Law Directory

George, Hartz, Lundeen, Flagg & Fulmer (AV)

4800 LeJeune Road (Coral Gables), 33146
Telephone: 305-662-4800
FAX: 305-667-8015
Fort Lauderdale, Florida Office: Suite 333 Justice Building East, 524 South Andrews Avenue.
Telephone: 305-462-1620. Palm Beach County
Telephone: 407-736-3620.
Fort Myers, Florida Office: Sun Bank Financial Center, Suite 403, 12730 New Brittany Boulevard.
Telephone: 813-939-3006.

Charles K. George
Charles Michael Hartz
Mitchell L. Lundeen
Clinton D. Flagg
Liana C. Silsby (Resident, Fort Lauderdale Office)
C. Richard Fulmer, Jr. (Resident, Fort Lauderdale Office)
A. Scott Lundeen
David V. King (Resident, Fort Lauderdale Office)
Stanley V. Buky (Resident, Fort Lauderdale Office)
Crane A. Johnstone (Resident, Fort Lauderdale Office)
Tracy E. Tomlin
Douglas W. Barnes

ASSOCIATES

John R. Buchholz
Maria A. Santoro
Esther E. Galicia
Matthew F. Minno
Craig R. Stevens (Resident at Ft. Myers Office)
Michael A. Petruccelli (Resident, Fort Lauderdale Office)
Keith J. Lambdin (Resident, Fort Lauderdale Office)
Mitchell H. Katler (Resident, Fort Lauderdale Office)
Michael H. Imber (Resident, Fort Lauderdale Office)
Peter K. Spillis
Loren Sonesen
Frederick W. Hoethke (Resident, Ft. Myers Office)
Michael T. Tomlin
Susan D. Bernhardt (Resident at Ft. Lauderdale Office)
Timonty Bunbrack (Resident at Ft. Lauderdale Office)

For full biographical listings, see the Martindale-Hubbell Law Directory

Haddad, Josephs, Jack, Gaebe & Markarian (AV)

1493 Sunset Drive (Coral Gables), P.O. Box 345118, 33114
Telephone: Dade County: 305-666-6006
Broward County: 305-463-6699
Telecopier: 305-662-9931

MEMBERS OF FIRM

Gil Haddad
Michael R. Josephs
Lewis N. Jack, Jr.
John S. Gaebe
David K. Markarian

(See Next Column)

ASSOCIATES

Amarillys E. Garcia-Perez
Elisabeth M. McClosky

For full biographical listings, see the Martindale-Hubbell Law Directory

*ORLANDO,** Orange Co.

Best & Anderson, P.A. (AV)

20 North Orange Avenue, Suite 505, 32801
Telephone: 407-425-2985
Crystal River, Florida Office: 7655 West Gulf to Lake Highway, Suite 6.
Telephone: 904-795-1107.

David R. Best
George H. "Dutch" Anderson, III

Mark S. Walker
Perry M. Nardi
Jeffrey B. Sexton
G. Clay Morris
Lawrence I. Hauser

For full biographical listings, see the Martindale-Hubbell Law Directory

Law Offices of Jack F. (Jay) Durie, Jr. (AV)

1000 East Robinson Street, 32801
Telephone: 407-841-6000; 1-800-940-0442
Fax: 407-841-2425

Jack F. (Jay) Durie, Jr.

ASSOCIATE

Jean Marie Steedley

For full biographical listings, see the Martindale-Hubbell Law Directory

Maher, Gibson and Guiley A Professional Association of Lawyers (AV)

Suite 200, 90 East Livingston Street, 32801
Telephone: 407-839-0866
Fax: 407-425-7958

Michael Maher
Patricia M. Gibson
David D. Guiley

Steven R. Maher
Robin M. Orosz
Monique M. Edwards

OF COUNSEL

John Edward Jones (P.A.)

LEGAL SUPPORT PERSONNEL

INSURANCE CLAIM COORDINATOR

Charles R. Simpson

For full biographical listings, see the Martindale-Hubbell Law Directory

Martinez & Dalton, Professional Association (AV)

719 Vassar Street, 32804
Telephone: 407-425-0712
Fax: 407-425-1856

Mel R. Martinez
Roy B. Dalton, Jr.
Robert H. Dellecker
Brian T. Wilson

Yvonne M. Yegge
Leticia Marques

For full biographical listings, see the Martindale-Hubbell Law Directory

Parrish, Bailey & Morsch, P.A. (AV)

116 America Street, 32801
Telephone: 407-849-1776

Sidney H. Parrish
Michael K. Bailey
Mark V. Morsch

Jay M. Fisher
Donald A. Myers, Jr.

For full biographical listings, see the Martindale-Hubbell Law Directory

*PENSACOLA,** Escambia Co.

Bell, Schuster & Wheeler, P.A. (AV)

119 West Garden Street, P.O. Box 12564, 32573-2564
Telephone: 904-438-1691
Fax: 904-438-3641

Robert D. Bell
Charles A. Schuster
Thomas E. Wheeler, Jr.
David W. Hiers

For full biographical listings, see the Martindale-Hubbell Law Directory

ST. PETERSBURG, Pinellas Co.

WILLIAMS, BRASFIELD, WERTZ, FULLER, GOLDMAN, FREEMAN & LOVELL, P.A. (AV)

2553 First Avenue, North, P.O. Box 12349, 33733-2349
Telephone: 813-327-2258, Tampa: 813-224-0430
Fax: 813-328-1340

John W. Williams
J. Scott Brasfield
Larry W. Wertz
Jeffrey R. Fuller
Carl A. Goldman
Stuart J. Freeman
Maron E. "Ron" Lovell
Billie Ann O'Hern
Karen A. Dean
D. Keith Thomas
Robert A. Santa Lucia

For full biographical listings, see the Martindale-Hubbell Law Directory

*SARASOTA,** Sarasota Co.

DICKINSON & GIBBONS, P.A. (AV)

1750 Ringling Boulevard, P.O. Box 3979, 34230
Telephone: 813-366-4680
FAX: 813-953-3136

G. Hunter Gibbons
Ralph L. Marchbank, Jr.
Burwell J. Jones
Stephen G. Brannan

Representative Clients: Venice Hospital; Physicians Protective Trust Fund; Florida Physicians Insurance Co.; Lee Memorial Hospital; Manatee Memorial Hospital; Sarasota Memorial Hospital; Columbia Hospital Corp.; Florida Physicians Trust; Alexis; Squibb Corp.

For Complete List of Firm Personnel, See General Section

For full biographical listings, see the Martindale-Hubbell Law Directory

*TALLAHASSEE,** Leon Co.

COLLINS & TRUETT, P.A. (AV)

2804 Remington Green Circle, Suite 4, Post Office Drawer 12429, 32317-2429
Telephone: 904-386-6060
Telecopier: 904-385-8220

Richard B. Collins
Gary A. Shipman

Brett Q. Lucas (Resident)
Dawn D. Caloca
Joseph E. Brooks
C. Timothy Gray
Rogelio Fontela
Charles N. Cleland, Jr.
Clifford W. Rainey

OF COUNSEL

Edgar C. Booth
James A. Dixon, Jr.

Representative Clients: Agency Rent-A-Car; Agricultural Excess and Surplus Insurance Co.; AIG Life Insurance Co.; Alliance Insurance Group; Allstate Insurance Co.; American Empire Surplus Lines Insurance Co.; American International Underwriters Inc.; Atlanta Casualty Insurance Co.; Avis Rent-A-Car; Bankers and Shippers Insurance Co.

For full biographical listings, see the Martindale-Hubbell Law Directory

FONVIELLE & HINKLE (AV)

3375-A Capital Circle Northeast, 32308
Telephone: 904-422-7773
Fax: 904-422-3449

MEMBERS OF FIRM

C. David Fonvielle
Donald M. Hinkle
Halley B. Lewis, III

For full biographical listings, see the Martindale-Hubbell Law Directory

*TAMPA,** Hillsborough Co.

BARBAS, WEED, GLENN, MORGAN & WHEELEY (AV)

A Partnership including a Professional Association
1802 West Cleveland Street, 33605
Telephone: 813-254-6575
FAX: 813-254-4690
New Port Richey Office: 6014 U.S. 19, Suite 101-4.
Telephone: 813-849-0592.
Palm Harbor Office: 2708 Alternate U.S. 19 North, Suite 701.
Telephone: 813-786-5866.

Rex Martin Barbas

References: First Florida Bank, N.A.; Sun Bank.

For full biographical listings, see the Martindale-Hubbell Law Directory

GUNN, OGDEN & SULLIVAN, PROFESSIONAL ASSOCIATION (AV)

201 East Kennedy Boulevard, Suite 1850, P.O. Box 1006, 33601
Telephone: 813-223-5111
FAX: 813-229-2336

(See Next Column)

Timon V. Sullivan
Randy J. Ogden
Lee D. Gunn, IV

Bradley J. Goewert
Andrea L. Hairelson
Michael F. Hancock
Brian Thompson
Charles E. Mckeon
Kelly K. Griffin
Daneil M. McAuliffe

For full biographical listings, see the Martindale-Hubbell Law Directory

*VERO BEACH,** Indian River Co.

MOSS, HENDERSON, VAN GAASBECK, BLANTON & KOVAL, P.A. (AV)

817 Beachland Boulevard, P.O. Box 3406, 32964-3406
Telephone: 407-231-1900
Fax: 407-231-4387

George H. Moss, II
Steve L. Henderson
Everett J. Van Gaasbeck
Robin A. Blanton
Thomas A. Koval
Clinton W. Lanier
Kevin S. Doty

Donald E. Feuerbach
Fred L. Kretschmer, Jr.
Margaret Sue Lyon
Lisa D. Harpring
Kathleen W. Stratton
Lewis W. Murphy, Jr.
E. Clayton Yates
Judith Goodman Hill

OF COUNSEL

Charles E. Garris
Ford J. Fegert

Representative Clients: Aetna Life & Casualty; Alcoa Florida, Inc.; Florida Power & Light Co.; Insurance Company of North America; Liberty Mutual Insurance Co.; Sears, Roebuck & Co.; Sugar Cane Growers Cooperative of Florida; Norfolk Southern Corporation/North American Van Lines, Inc.

For full biographical listings, see the Martindale-Hubbell Law Directory

*WEST PALM BEACH,** Palm Beach Co.

BABBITT, HAZOURI AND JOHNSON, P.A. (AV)

1801 Australian Avenue South, Suite 200, P.O. Drawer 024426, 33402
Telephone: 407-684-2500
Fax: 407-684-6308

Theodore Babbitt
Fred A. Hazouri
Joseph R. Johnson

For full biographical listings, see the Martindale-Hubbell Law Directory

FREEMAN & ROSS, P.A. (AV)

811 North Olive Avenue, 33401-3709
Telephone: 407-655-6025
Fax: 407-655-5759
Palatka Office: 415 St. Johns Avenue.
Telephone: 904-325-6239.
Fax: 904-329-9626.

Terry N. Freeman
Robert C. Ross

OF COUNSEL

Henry P. Ruffolo

LEGAL SUPPORT PERSONNEL

Debra J. McPherson
E.I. "Chuck" Engelking

For full biographical listings, see the Martindale-Hubbell Law Directory

STUART E. KOCHA, P.A. (AV)

118 Clematis Street, P.O. Box 1427, 33402
Telephone: 407-659-5611
Fax: 407-659-5636

Stuart E. Kocha

LEGAL SUPPORT PERSONNEL

David L. Halderman (Chief Investigator)
Steve L. Sheehy (Investigator)

References: NationsBank; Admiralty Bank.

For full biographical listings, see the Martindale-Hubbell Law Directory

LYTAL & REITER (AV)

A Partnership including Professional Associations
Tenth Floor, 515 North Flagler Drive, 33401
Telephone: 407-655-1990
Fax: 407-832-2932
Mailing Address: P.O. Box 4056, 33402

Lake Lytal, Jr. (P.A.)
Joseph J. Reiter (P.A.)
Mark W. Clark
Tracy R. Sharpe

(See Next Column)

LYTAL & REITER—*Continued*

Donald R. Fountain, Jr.
Rafael J. Roca
William S. Williams
Michael J. Overbeck
Yvette Trelles Murray
Kevin C. Smith
Gerald T. McCarthy

Reference: United National Bank.

For full biographical listings, see the Martindale-Hubbell Law Directory

PRUITT & PRUITT, P.A. (AV)

Suite 400 Flagler Tower, 505 South Flagler Drive, 33401
Telephone: 407-655-8080
Fax: 407-655-4134

William H. Pruitt
William E. Pruitt

Reference: Flagler National Bank.

For full biographical listings, see the Martindale-Hubbell Law Directory

GARY ROBERTS & ASSOCIATES, P.A. (AV)

1675 Palm Beach Lakes Boulevard Seventh Floor, 33401
Telephone: 407-686-1800
FAX: 407-686-1533
Mailing Address: P.O. Drawer 4178, 33402,
New Port Richey, Florida Office: Roberts, Sojka & Doran, P.A., 5841 Main Street, 34652.
Telephone: 813-847-1103.

Gary W. Roberts

For full biographical listings, see the Martindale-Hubbell Law Directory

SEARCY DENNEY SCAROLA BARNHART & SHIPLEY, PROFESSIONAL ASSOCIATION (AV)

2139 Palm Beach Lakes Boulevard, P.O. Drawer 3626, 33402-3626
Telephone: 407-686-6300
800-780-8607
Fax: 407-478-0754

Christian D. Searcy, Sr.
Earl L. Denney, Jr.
John Scarola
F. Gregory Barnhart
John A. Shipley
Lois J. Frankel
David K. Kelley, Jr.
Lawrence J. Block, Jr.
C. Calvin Warriner, III
William A. Norton
David J. Sales

James N. Nance
Katherine Ann Martinez
T. Michael Kennedy
Todd S. Stewart
Christopher K. Speed

LEGAL SUPPORT PERSONNEL

Deane L. Cady (Paralegal/Investigator)
James E. Cook (Paralegal/Investigator)
Emilio Diamantis (Paralegal/Investigator)
David W. Gilmore (Paralegal/Investigator)
John C. Hopkins (Paralegal/Investigator)
Thaddeus E. Kulesa (Paralegal/Investigator)
J. Peter Love (Paralegal/Investigator)
Marjorie A. Morgan (Paralegal)
Joel C. Padgett (Paralegal/Investigator)
William H. Seabold (Paralegal/Investigator)
Kathleen Simon (Paralegal)
Steve M. Smith (Paralegal/Investigator)
Judson Whitehorn (Paralegal/Investigator)
Marcia Yarnell Dodson (Not admitted in FL; Law Clerk)
Kelly Lynn Hopkins (Paralegal/Investigator)
Frank Cotton (Paralegal/Investigator)

For full biographical listings, see the Martindale-Hubbell Law Directory

GEORGIA

*ATLANTA,** Fulton Co.

BEDFORD, KIRSCHNER AND VENKER, P.C. (AV)

Suite 450, 600 West Peachtree Street, N.W., 30308
Telephone: 404-872-6646

T. Jackson Bedford, Jr.
Andrew R. Kirschner
Thomas J. Venker

For full biographical listings, see the Martindale-Hubbell Law Directory

BIRD, BALLARD & STILL (AV)

14 Seventeenth Street, Suite 5, P.O. Box 7009, 30357
Telephone: 404-873-4696
Fax: 404-872-3745

(See Next Column)

William Q. Bird

For full biographical listings, see the Martindale-Hubbell Law Directory

DAVID WM. BOONE, P.C. (AV)

3155 Roswell Road Suite 100, The Cotton Exchange, 30305
Telephone: 404-239-0305
FAX: 404-239-0520

David William Boone

Leigh McCranie Smith

For full biographical listings, see the Martindale-Hubbell Law Directory

BUTLER, WOOTEN, OVERBY & CHEELEY (AV)

2719 Buford Highway, 30324
Telephone: 404-321-1700
WATS 1-800-242-2962
FAX: 404-321-1713
Columbus, Georgia Office: 1500 Second Avenue, P.O. Box 2766.
Telephone: 706-322-1990; National Wats: 1-800-233-4086.
FAX: 706-323-2962.

MEMBERS OF FIRM

James E. Butler, Jr.
Joel O. Wooten, Jr.
C. Frederick Overby
Robert D. Cheeley
Albert M. Pearson, III
George W. Fryhofer, III

ASSOCIATES

Peter J. Daughtery
J. Frank Myers, III
Patrick A. Dawson
Lee Tarte
Jason L. Crawford
Keith A. Pittman

Reference: Columbus Bank and Trust, Columbus, Ga.

For full biographical listings, see the Martindale-Hubbell Law Directory

CARR & KESSLER (AV)

An Association of Attorneys, Not a Partnership
3379 Peachtree Road, N.E., Suite 980, 30326
Telephone: 404-233-5008
FAX: 404-233-4713

James C. Carr, Jr.
Kathleen Kessler

For full biographical listings, see the Martindale-Hubbell Law Directory

CHAMBERS, MABRY, MCCLELLAND & BROOKS (AV)

Tenth Floor, 2200 Century Parkway, N.E., 30345
Telephone: 404-325-4800
FAX: 404-325-0596
Lawrenceville, Georgia Office: Suite 377, 175 Gwinnett Drive.
Telephone: 404-339-7660.
FAX: 404-339-7060.

MEMBER OF FIRM

Eugene P. Chambers, Jr.

ASSOCIATE

Dale C. Ray, Jr.

Representative Clients: Allstate Insurance Co.; The Security Mutual Insurance Company of New York; National Automobile Insurance Co.

For full biographical listings, see the Martindale-Hubbell Law Directory

DREW ECKL & FARNHAM (AV)

880 West Peachtree Street, P.O. Box 7600, 30357
Telephone: 404-885-1400
Facsimile: 404-876-0992

MEMBERS OF FIRM

W. Wray Eckl
Hall F. McKinley III

ASSOCIATE

Jeffrey B. Grimm

Representative Clients: American International Adjustment Co.; Chicago Title Insurance Co.; CIGNA; Crum & Forster Commercial Insurance; Ford Motor Co.; Frito-Lay, Inc.; General Motors; Georgia Pacific Corp.; Liberty Mutual Insurance Co.; Parthenon/Hospital Corporation of America.

For Complete List of Firm Personnel, See General Section

For full biographical listings, see the Martindale-Hubbell Law Directory

DWYER & WHITE (AV)

A Partnership including a Professional Corporation
Suite 700, 2100 Riveredge Parkway, 30328-4654
Telephone: 404-956-1984
FAX: 404-956-1381

MEMBER

J. Matthew Dwyer, Jr. (P.C.)

(See Next Column)

DWYER & WHITE, *Atlanta—Continued*

ASSOCIATES

Anne Woolf Sapp Carmen D. Smith

For full biographical listings, see the Martindale-Hubbell Law Directory

EICHELBERGER & PERROTTA (AV)

The Hurt Building, 50 Hurt Plaza, Suite 902, 30303
Telephone: 404-524-1957
Telecopier: 404-577-9490

MEMBERS OF FIRM

James A. Eichelberger Theodore B. Eichelberger
Joseph D. Perrotta

For full biographical listings, see the Martindale-Hubbell Law Directory

ENGLAND & MCKNIGHT (AV)

Suite 410 River Ridge, 9040 Roswell Road, 30350
Telephone: 404-641-6010
FAX: 404-641-6003

MEMBERS OF FIRM

J. Melvin England Robert H. McKnight, Jr.

Reference: Bank South, N.A.

For full biographical listings, see the Martindale-Hubbell Law Directory

GARLAND, SAMUEL & LOEB, P.C. (AV)

3151 Maple Drive, N.E., 30305
Telephone: 404-262-2225
FAX: 404-365-5041

Donald F. Samuel Robin N. Loeb

For full biographical listings, see the Martindale-Hubbell Law Directory

GOLDNER, SOMMERS, SCRUDDER & BASS (AV)

2839 Paces Ferry Road, Suite 800, 30339-3774
Telephone: 404-436-4777
Facsimile: 404-436-8777

Stephen L. Goldner Susan V. Sommers

Benjamin David Ladner Tammy Spivack Skinner

For Complete List of Firm Personnel, See General Section

For full biographical listings, see the Martindale-Hubbell Law Directory

HART & MCINTYRE (AV)

Promenade Two Suite 3775, 1230 Peachtree Street, N.E., 30309
Telephone: 800-521-3775 (Nationwide); 404-876-3775
Fax: 404-873-3799

MEMBERS OF FIRM

George W. Hart John C. McIntyre, Jr.
Bonnie M. Wharton

Reference: BankSouth.

For full biographical listings, see the Martindale-Hubbell Law Directory

HILL AND BLEIBERG (AV)

Suite 200, 47 Perimeter Center East, 30346
Telephone: 404-394-7800
Fax: 404-394-7802

MEMBERS OF FIRM

Robert P. Bleiberg Gary Hill

For full biographical listings, see the Martindale-Hubbell Law Directory

LAW OFFICES OF J. WAYNE PIERCE, P.A. (AV)

Two Paces West, Suite 1700 4000 Cumberland Parkway, 30339
Telephone: 404-435-0500
Telecopier: 404-435-0362

J. Wayne Pierce

Dargan Scott Cole Thomas L. Schaefer

For full biographical listings, see the Martindale-Hubbell Law Directory

SAMUEL P. PIERCE, JR., P.C. (AV)

One Buckhead Plaza, Suite 850, 3060 Peachtree Road, N.W., 30305
Telephone: 404-364-2890
FAX: 404-240-0232

Samuel P. Pierce, Jr.

For full biographical listings, see the Martindale-Hubbell Law Directory

POPE, MCGLAMRY, KILPATRICK & MORRISON (AV)

A Partnership including Professional Corporations
83 Walton Street, N.W., P.O. Box 1733, 30303
Telephone: 404-523-7706;
Phenix City, Alabama: 205-298-7354
Columbus, Georgia Office: 318 11th Street, 2nd Floor, P.O. Box 2128, 31902-2128.
Telephone: 706-324-0050.

MEMBERS OF FIRM

C. Neal Pope (P.C.)
Max R. McGlamry (P.C.) (Resident, Columbus, Georgia Office)
Paul V. Kilpatrick, Jr. (Resident, Columbus, Georgia Office)
R. Timothy Morrison
Michael L. McGlamry
Earle F. Lasseter
William J. Cornwell
Jay F. Hirsch
Daniel W. Sigelman
Wade H. Tomlinson, III
William Usher Norwood, III

RESIDENT ASSOCIATE

C. Elizabeth Pope

Reference: Columbus Bank & Trust Co.

For full biographical listings, see the Martindale-Hubbell Law Directory

REYNOLDS & MCARTHUR (AV)

A Partnership including a Professional Corporation
Suite 1010, One Buckhead Plaza, 3060 Peachtree Road, N.W., 30305
Telephone: 404-240-0265
Fax: 404-262-3557
Macon, Georgia Office: 850 Walnut Street.
Telephone: 912-741-6000.
Fax: 912-742-0750.
Asheville, North Carolina Office: The Jackson Building, 22 South Pack Square, Suite 1200.
Telephone: 704-254-8523.
Fax: 704-254-3038.

MEMBERS OF FIRM

W. Carl Reynolds (P.C.)
Katherine L. McArthur
Steve Ray Warren (Not admitted in GA)
Charles M. Cork, III
Bradley J. Survant
Laura D. Hogue

For full biographical listings, see the Martindale-Hubbell Law Directory

ANDREW M. SCHERFFIUS, P.C. (AV)

3166 Mathieson Drive, P.O. Box 53299, 30355
Telephone: 404-261-3562; 1-800-521-2867
Fax: 404-841-0861

Andrew M. Scherffius

Tamara McDowell Ayres

For full biographical listings, see the Martindale-Hubbell Law Directory

SULLIVAN, HALL, BOOTH & SMITH, A PROFESSIONAL CORPORATION (AV)

One Midtown Plaza, 1360 Peachtree Street, N.E., Suite 800, 30309
Telephone: 404-870-8000
FAX: 404-870-8020

Terrance C. Sullivan
John E. Hall, Jr.
Alexander H. Booth
Rush S. Smith, Jr.
Henry D. Green, Jr.
Jack G. Slover, Jr.
Timothy H. Bendin
Michael A. Pannier
Brynda Sue Rodriguez
Roger S. Sumrall

David V. Johnson
Jeffrey T. Wise
Eleanor L. Martel
A. Spencer McManes, Jr.
David G. Goodchild, Jr.
Robert L. Shannon, Jr.
T. Andrew Graham
Earnest Redwine
Melanie P. Simon (Not admitted in GA)

Reference: Wachovia Bank of Georgia.

For full biographical listings, see the Martindale-Hubbell Law Directory

THOMAS, KENNEDY, SAMPSON & PATTERSON (AV)

1600 Bank South Building, 55 Marietta Street, N.W., 30303
Telephone: 404-688-4503
Telecopier: 404-681-2950

MEMBERS OF FIRM

John Loren Kennedy (1942-1994)
Thomas G. Sampson
P. Andrew Patterson
Myra H. Dixon
R. David Ware
Patrise M. Perkins-Hooker
Jeffrey E. Tompkins

ASSOCIATES

Rosalind T. Drakeford
Regina E. McMillan
Melynee C. Leftridge
La'Sean M. Zilton

For full biographical listings, see the Martindale-Hubbell Law Directory

*CARROLLTON,** Carroll Co.

TISINGER, TISINGER, VANCE & GREER, A PROFESSIONAL CORPORATION (AV)

100 Wagon Yard Plaza, P.O. Box 2069, 30117
Telephone: 404-834-4467
FAX: 404-834-5426

David H. Tisinger
Kevin B. Buice
John A. Harris

Representative Clients: CNA; MMI Companies, Inc.; St. Paul Fire and Marine Insurance Company.

For Complete List of Firm Personnel, See General Section

For full biographical listings, see the Martindale-Hubbell Law Directory

*COLUMBUS,** Muscogee Co.

BUTLER, WOOTEN, OVERBY & CHEELEY (AV)

1500 Second Avenue, P.O. Box 2766, 31902
Telephone: 706-322-1990;
National Wats: 1-800-233-4086
FAX: 706-323-2962
Atlanta, Georgia Office: 2719 Buford Highway, 30324.
Telephone: 404-321-1700.
FAX: 404-321-1713. Wats Line: 1-800-242-2962.

MEMBERS OF FIRM

James E. Butler, Jr.
Joel O. Wooten, Jr.
C. Frederick Overby
Robert D. Cheeley
Albert M. Pearson, III
George W. Fryhofer, III

ASSOCIATES

Peter J. Daughtery
J. Frank Myers, III
Patrick A. Dawson
Lee Tarte
Jason L. Crawford
Keith A. Pittman

For full biographical listings, see the Martindale-Hubbell Law Directory

POPE, MCGLAMRY, KILPATRICK & MORRISON (AV)

A Partnership including Professional Corporations
318 11th Street, 2nd Floor, P.O. Box 2128, 31902-2128
Telephone: 706-324-0050;
Phenix City, Alabama: 205-298-7354
Atlanta, Georgia Office: 83 Walton Street, N.W., P.O. Box 1733, 30303.
Telephone: 404-523-7706.

MEMBERS OF FIRM

C. Neal Pope (P.C.)
Max R. McGlamry (P.C.) (Resident)
Paul V. Kilpatrick, Jr. (Resident)
R. Timothy Morrison (Resident, Atlanta, Georgia Office)
Michael L. McGlamry
Earle F. Lasseter
William J. Cornwell
Jay F. Hirsch
Daniel W. Sigelman
Wade H. Tomlinson, III (Resident, Atlanta Office)
William Usher Norwood, III (Resident, Atlanta Office)

RESIDENT ASSOCIATES

Joan S. Redmond
Teresa Pike Majors

Reference: Columbus Bank & Trust Co.

For full biographical listings, see the Martindale-Hubbell Law Directory

*GAINESVILLE,** Hall Co.

FORRESTER & BRIM (AV)

459 E.E. Butler Parkway, S.E., P.O. Box 1688, 30503-1688
Telephone: 404-531-0800
Fax: 404-536-7789

MEMBERS OF FIRM

Weymon H. Forrester
James Ernest Brim, III

ASSOCIATES

Richard Charles Bellows
Nolie J. Motes

For full biographical listings, see the Martindale-Hubbell Law Directory

*MACON,** Bibb Co.

CHAMBLESS, HIGDON & CARSON (AV)

Suite 200 Ambrose Baber Building, 577 Walnut Street, P.O. Box 246, 31298-5399
Telephone: 912-745-1181
Telecopier: 912-746-9479

MEMBERS OF FIRM

Joseph H. Davis
Joseph H. Chambless
David B. Higdon
James F. Carson, Jr.
Thomas F. Richardson
Mary Mendel Katz
Emmitte H. Griggs
Marc T. Treadwell

(See Next Column)

ASSOCIATES

Kim H. Stroup
Christopher Balch
Jon Christopher Wolfe

Local Counsel for: Atlanta Gas Light Co.; First Union National Bank of Georgia; Security National Bank.

For full biographical listings, see the Martindale-Hubbell Law Directory

REYNOLDS & MCARTHUR (AV)

A Partnership including a Professional Corporation
850 Walnut Street, 31201
Telephone: 912-741-6000
Fax: 912-742-0750
Atlanta, Georgia Office: Suite 1010, One Buckhead Plaza, 3060 Peachtree Road, N.W.
Telephone: 404-240-0265.
Fax: 404-262-3557.
Asheville, North Carolina Office: The Jackson Building, 22 South Pack Square, Suite 1200.
Telephone: 704-254-8523.
Fax: 704-254-3038.

MEMBERS OF FIRM

W. Carl Reynolds (P.C.)
Katherine L. McArthur
Steve Ray Warren (Not admitted in GA)
Charles M. Cork, III
O. Wendell Horne, III
Bradley J. Survant
Laura D. Hogue

For full biographical listings, see the Martindale-Hubbell Law Directory

*MARIETTA,** Cobb Co.

BARNES, BROWNING, TANKSLEY & CASURELLA (AV)

Suite 225, 166 Anderson Street, 30060
Telephone: 404-424-1500
Fax: 404-424-1740

MEMBERS OF FIRM

Roy E. Barnes
Charles B. Tanksley
Jerry A. Landers, Jr.
Jeffrey G. Casurella

For full biographical listings, see the Martindale-Hubbell Law Directory

DOWNEY & CLEVELAND (AV)

288 Washington Avenue, 30060
Telephone: 404-422-3233
Fax: 404-423-4199

OF COUNSEL

Lynn A. Downey

MEMBERS OF FIRM

Robert H. Cleveland (1940-1989)
Joseph C. Parker
Y. Kevin Williams
Russell B. Davis
G. Lee Welborn

ASSOCIATES

Rodney S. Shockley
W. Curtis Anderson
Scott D. Clay
Todd E. Hatcher

Representative Clients: Allstate Insurance Co.; St. Paul Insurance Cos.; Georgia Farm Bureau Mutual Insurance Co.; State Farm Insurance Cos.; Cotton States Mutual Insurance Co.; Colonial Insurance Co. of California; Ed Voyles Oldsmobile, Honda and Chrysler-Plymouth; Chuck Clancy Ford; City of Acworth; Lockheed Aeronautical Systems Company, a Division of Lockheed Corporation.

For full biographical listings, see the Martindale-Hubbell Law Directory

HAWAII

*HONOLULU,** Honolulu Co.

AYABE, CHONG, NISHIMOTO, SIA & NAKAMURA (AV)

A Partnership including a Professional Corporation
3000 Grosvenor Center, 737 Bishop Street, 96813
Telephone: 808-537-6119
Telecopier: 808-526-3491

MEMBERS OF FIRM

Sidney K. Ayabe (P.C.)
John S. Nishimoto
Jeffrey H. K. Sia

Representative Clients: Travelers Insurance Co.; St. Paul Fire and Marine Insurance Co.; The Employers Group of Insurance Companies; TIG Insurance Co.; Pacific Insurance Co.; Hartford Accident and Indemnity Co.; Continental Casualty Co.; First Insurance Company of Hawaii, Ltd.

For Complete List of Firm Personnel, See General Section

For full biographical listings, see the Martindale-Hubbell Law Directory

Honolulu—Continued

CRONIN, FRIED, SEKIYA, KEKINA & FAIRBANKS ATTORNEYS AT LAW, A LAW CORPORATION (AV)

1900 Davies Pacific Center, 841 Bishop Street, 96813
Telephone: 808-524-1433
FAX: 808-536-2073

Paul F. Cronin
L. Richard Fried, Jr.
Gerald Y. Sekiya
Wayne K. Kekina
David L. Fairbanks
John D. Thomas, Jr.
Stuart A. Kaneko
Bert S. Sakuda
Allen K. Williams
Keith K. H. Young

Patrick W. Border
Gregory L. Lui-Kwan
Patrick F. McTernan
Irene M. Nakano

For full biographical listings, see the Martindale-Hubbell Law Directory

LEE, KIM, WONG, YEE & LAU ATTORNEYS AT LAW, A LAW CORPORATION (AV)

Suite 700 The Queen Street Building, 345 Queen Street, 96813
Telephone: 808-536-4421
Telecopier: 808-521-3566

Douglas T. Y. Lee
Wayson W. S. Wong
Edmund K. U. Yee
Eric T. W. Kim
Gene K. Lau

Arthur H. Kuwahara
Walter E. Hebelethwaite

For full biographical listings, see the Martindale-Hubbell Law Directory

PRICE OKAMOTO HIMENO & LUM ATTORNEYS AT LAW, A LAW CORPORATION (AV)

Suite 728, Ocean View Center, 707 Richards Street, 96813
Telephone: 808-538-1113
FAX: 808-533-0549

Warren Price, III
Kenneth T. Okamoto
Sharon R. Himeno
Bettina W. J. Lum
Terence S. Yamamoto

John H. Yuen

OF COUNSEL

Stuart M. Cowan

For full biographical listings, see the Martindale-Hubbell Law Directory

LAW OFFICE OF KENNETH S. ROBBINS ATTORNEY AT LAW, A LAW CORPORATION (AV)

Suite 2220 Davies Pacific Center, 841 Bishop Street, 96813
Telephone: 808-524-2355
Fax: 808-526-0290

Kenneth S. Robbins

Vincent A. Rhodes
Shinken Naitoh

For full biographical listings, see the Martindale-Hubbell Law Directory

WEINBERG & BELL ATTORNEYS AT LAW, A LAW CORPORATION (AV)

Suite 1200, 1164 Bishop Street, 96813
Telephone: 808-523-9477
FAX: 808-521-4681

Jan M. Weinberg
Roy J. Bell, III

For full biographical listings, see the Martindale-Hubbell Law Directory

IDAHO

*BOISE,** Ada Co.

HALL, FARLEY, OBERRECHT & BLANTON (AV)

Key Financial Center, 702 West Idaho Street, Suite 700, P.O. Box 1271, 83701-1271
Telephone: 208-336-0404
Facsimile: 208-336-5193

Richard E. Hall
Donald J. Farley
Phillip S. Oberrecht
Raymond D. Powers
Candy Wagahoff Dale
Robert B. Luce
J. Kevin West
Bart W. Harwood

(See Next Column)

J. Charles Blanton
John J. Burke
Steven J. Hippler
Thorpe P. Orton
Ronald S. Best
(Not admitted in ID)

References: Boise State University; Farm Bureau Mutual Insurance Company of Idaho; Medical Insurance Exchange of California; The St. Paul Cos.

For full biographical listings, see the Martindale-Hubbell Law Directory

ILLINOIS

*CHICAGO,** Cook Co.

BRINTON & FEDOTA (AV)

Three First National Plaza, Suite 3900, 60602
Telephone: 312-236-5015
Fax: 312-236-8559

MEMBERS OF FIRM

Mark C. Fedota
Edward J. Melia
Brian C. Rocca

David H. Brinton
Timothy J. Mahoney
Mark J. Smith

For full biographical listings, see the Martindale-Hubbell Law Directory

CORBOY • DEMETRIO • CLIFFORD, P.C. (AV)

33 North Dearborn Street 21st Floor, 60602
Telephone: 312-346-3191
FAX: 312-346-5562
TDD: 312-236-3191

Philip H. Corboy
Thomas A. Demetrio
Robert A. Clifford

Kevin G. Burke
Keith A. Hebeisen
Susan J. Schwartz

Susan A. Capra
Mary E. Doherty
Margaret M. Power

OF COUNSEL

Phillip Taxman

Reference: The American National Bank & Trust Company, Chicago, Illinois.

For full biographical listings, see the Martindale-Hubbell Law Directory

EPSTEIN, ZAIDEMAN & ESRIG, P.C. (AV)

120 South Riverside Plaza, Suite 1150, 60606
Telephone: 312-207-0005
Fax: 312-207-1332

James R. Epstein
Robert J. Zaideman
Jerry A. Esrig

Jeffrey L. Whitcomb
Elizabeth A. Kaveny
David R. Nordwall

OF COUNSEL

Donald W. Aaronson

For full biographical listings, see the Martindale-Hubbell Law Directory

JOHNSON & BELL, LTD. (AV)

Suite 2200, 222 North La Salle Street, 60601
Telephone: 312-372-0770
Facsimile: 312-372-9818
Wheaton, Illinois Office: Suite 1640, 2100 Manchester Road.
Telephone: 708-510-0880.
Facsimile: 780-510-0939.

Brian C. Fetzer
Pamela L. Gellen
Timothy J. McKay
Charles W. Planek

Kathryn K. Loft
Marilyn McCabe Reidy
Terry Takash

References available upon request.

For full biographical listings, see the Martindale-Hubbell Law Directory

PETER D. KASDIN, LTD. (AV)

Suite 1960, 135 South La Salle Street, 60603
Telephone: 312-630-1990
Facsimile: 312-630-1103

Peter D. Kasdin

(See Next Column)

PETER D. KASDIN, LTD.—*Continued*

David W. Hepplewhite
Regina Picone Etherton
Meredith H. Emerson

OF COUNSEL

David W. Horan

For full biographical listings, see the Martindale-Hubbell Law Directory

KENNETH C. MILLER, LTD. (AV)

33 North Dearborn Street, Suite 1930, 60602
Telephone: 312-236-8634
Telecopier: 312-236-1882

Kenneth C. Miller
James W. O'Connor
Joy L. Sparling

For full biographical listings, see the Martindale-Hubbell Law Directory

STEPHEN M. PASSEN, LTD. (AV)

Suite 2900, 120 North La Salle Street, 60602
Telephone: 312-236-5878
Facsimile: 312-236-1162

Stephen M. Passen

David G. Susler

For full biographical listings, see the Martindale-Hubbell Law Directory

PAVALON & GIFFORD (AV)

Two North La Salle Street, Suite 1600, 60602
Telephone: 312-419-7400
FAX: 312-419-7408
Rockford, Illinois Office: 501 Seventh Street, Suite 501, 61104.
Telephone: 815-968-5100.

MEMBERS OF FIRM

Eugene I. Pavalon
Geoffrey L. Gifford
Gary K. Laatsch
Frank C. Marino

Kathleen A. Russell
Jodi L. Habush
Richard S. Goode

OF COUNSEL

Henry Phillip Gruss

For full biographical listings, see the Martindale-Hubbell Law Directory

POWER ROGERS & SMITH, P.C. (AV)

35 West Wacker Drive, Suite 3700, 60601
Telephone: 312-236-9381
Fax: 312-236-0920

Joseph A. Power, Jr.
Larry R. Rogers
Todd A. Smith
Thomas G. Siracusa
Paul L. Salzetta
Thomas M. Power

Larry R. Rogers, Jr.
Ruth M. Degnan

For full biographical listings, see the Martindale-Hubbell Law Directory

JOHN B. SCHWARTZ & ASSOCIATES (AV)

Suite 408, Thirty-Nine South La Salle Street, 60603
Telephone: 312-332-1586
Fax: 312-332-7009

ASSOCIATES

Stephen J. Caron
David J. Spira

OF COUNSEL

Thomas W. Duda

For full biographical listings, see the Martindale-Hubbell Law Directory

SWANSON, MARTIN & BELL (AV)

One IBM Plaza, Suite 2900, 60611
Telephone: 312-321-9100
Fax: 312-321-0990
Wheaton, Illinois Office: 605 East Roosevelt Road.
Telephone: 708-653-2266.
Fax: 708-653-2292.

MEMBERS OF FIRM

Lenard C. Swanson
Kevin T. Martin
Brian W. Bell
Stanley V. Boychuck
Kay L. Schichtel
Lawrence Helms
Joseph P. Switzer
David E. Kawala
Bruce S. Terlep

(See Next Column)

ASSOCIATES

Kevin V. Boyle
Matthew D. Jacboson
Joseph P. Kincaid
Patricia S. Kocour
Robert J. Meyer
Sheryl A. Pethers
Barbara N. Petrungaro
Aaron T. Shepley
William Blake Weiler

For full biographical listings, see the Martindale-Hubbell Law Directory

EAST ST. LOUIS, St. Clair Co.

CARR, KOREIN, TILLERY, KUNIN, MONTROY & GLASS (AV)

412 Missouri Avenue, 62201
Telephone: 618-274-0434
Telecopier: 618-274-8369
St. Louis, Missouri Office: 701 Market Street, Suite 300.
Telephone: 314-241-4844.
Telecopier: 314-241-3525.
Belleville, Illinois Office: 5520 West Main.
Telephone: 618-277-1180.

MEMBERS OF FIRM

Rex Carr
Stephen M. Tillery
Gerald L. Montroy

ASSOCIATES

Martin L. Perron
Robert L. King

References: Union Bank; First National Bank.

For Complete List of Firm Personnel, See General Section

For full biographical listings, see the Martindale-Hubbell Law Directory

PERU, La Salle Co.

ANTHONY C. RACCUGLIA & ASSOCIATES (AV)

1200 Maple Drive, 61354
Telephone: 815-223-0230
Ottawa, Illinois Office: 633 La Salle Street.
Telephone: 815-434-2003.

ASSOCIATES

James A. McPhedran
Louis L. Bertrand

References: La Salle National Bank; Citizens First National Bank of Peru, Illinois.

For full biographical listings, see the Martindale-Hubbell Law Directory

*WAUKEGAN,** Lake Co.

LAW OFFICES OF PATRICK A. SALVI, P.C. (AV)

218 North Utica Street, 60085
Telephone: 708-249-1227
Telefax: 708-249-0138

Patrick A. Salvi

Michael P. Schostok
Megan E. Chadwick
Terrence S. Carden, III
Dorothy Lupton Moran
John Andrew Kornak

OF COUNSEL

Bernard E. Grysen

References: First Midwest Bank, Waukegan, Illinois; Northern Trust Bank, Lake Forest, Illinois.

For full biographical listings, see the Martindale-Hubbell Law Directory

INDIANA

*EVANSVILLE,** Vanderburgh Co.

STATHAM, JOHNSON & McCRAY (AV)

215 North West Martin Luther King Jr. Boulevard, P.O. Box 3567, 47734-3567
Telephone: 812-425-5223
Facsimile: 812-421-4238

MEMBERS OF FIRM

William E. Statham
Michael McCray
Stephen Hensleigh Thomas
Douglas V. Jessen

Representative Clients: American Family Insurance Group; American States Insurance; Hartford Insurance Group; Indiana Insurance Company; the Medical Protective Company; Meridian Mutual Insurance; Pennsylvania Hospital Insurance Company; Royal Insurance; St. Paul Insurance Cos.; Shelter Insurance Companies.

For Complete List of Firm Personnel, See General Section

For full biographical listings, see the Martindale-Hubbell Law Directory

*INDIANAPOLIS,** Marion Co.

CONOUR • DOEHRMAN (AV)
Suite 1725, One Indiana Square, 46204
Telephone: 317-269-3550
Fax: 317-269-3564

MEMBERS OF FIRM

William F. Conour — Thomas C. Doehrman

ASSOCIATES

Rex E. Baker — Daniel S. Chamberlain
Daniel J. Mages

LEGAL SUPPORT PERSONNEL

Linda S. Carmichael (Legal Administrator) — Kimberly N. Beasley (Legal Assistant)
Stacey M. Merchant — Sarah E. Stites
Paula M. Roseman (Legal Assistant)

For full biographical listings, see the Martindale-Hubbell Law Directory

HALL, RENDER, KILLIAN, HEATH & LYMAN, PROFESSIONAL CORPORATION (AV)
Suite 2000, One American Square Box 82064, 46282
Telephone: 317-633-4884
Telecopier: 317-633-4878
North Office: Suite 820, 8402 Harcourt Road, 46260.
Telephone: 317-871-6222.

William S. Hall — Kevin P. Speer
Timothy W. Kennedy — Richard W. McMinn
N. Kent Smith — Rebekah N. Murphy

For Complete List of Firm Personnel, See General Section
For full biographical listings, see the Martindale-Hubbell Law Directory

ICE MILLER DONADIO & RYAN (AV)
One American Square Box 82001, 46282-0002
Telephone: 317-236-2100
Fax: 317-236-2219

MEMBERS OF FIRM

James V. Donadio — Mary Nold Larimore
David J. Mallon, Jr. — L. Alan Whaley
Bonnie L. Gallivan

OF COUNSEL

Nancy Menard Riddle — Gloria A. Aplin

ASSOCIATES

Sherry A. Fabina-Abney — Laure V. Flaniken
Kelly Bauman Pitcher — Kevin R. Knight
Gerald B. Coleman

Representative Clients: Indiana University; PHICO Insurance Co.; St. Paul Insurance Co.; MultiMutual Insurance; Physicians Insurance Company of Indiana; St. Francis Hospital; St. Vincent's Hospital.

For Complete List of Firm Personnel, See General Section
For full biographical listings, see the Martindale-Hubbell Law Directory

LOCKE REYNOLDS BOYD & WEISELL (AV)
1000 Capital Center South, 201 North Illinois Street, 46204
Telephone: 317-237-3800
Telecopier: 317-237-3900

David S. Allen — Kevin Charles Murray
Karl M. Koons, III

Todd J. Kaiser — Dirk Wallsmith
Susan E. Cline — Jerrilyn Powers Ramsey
Mary Margaret Ruth Feldhake

OF COUNSEL

Robert C. Riddell

Representative Clients: Charter Medical Corporation; MMI Companies; The Medical Protective Company; Methodist Hospital of Indiana, Inc.; PHICO Insurance Company; Physicians Insurance Company of Indiana, Inc.; Riverview Hospital; St. Francis Hospital Center; Wishard Memorial Hospital; The Women's Hospital-Indianapolis.

For Complete List of Firm Personnel, See General Section
For full biographical listings, see the Martindale-Hubbell Law Directory

MILLER MULLER MENDELSON & KENNEDY (AV)
8900 Keystone Crossing Suite 1250, 46240
Telephone: 317-574-4500
1-800-394-3094
Fax: 317-574-4501

MEMBERS OF FIRM

Michael S. Miller — Tilden Mendelson
John Muller — Timothy J. Kennedy
Faith L. Pottschmidt

For full biographical listings, see the Martindale-Hubbell Law Directory

MITCHELL HURST JACOBS & DICK (AV)
152 East Washington Street, 46204
Telephone: 317-636-0808
1-800-636-0808
Fax: 317-633-7680

(See Next Column)

MEMBERS OF FIRM

Marvin H. Mitchell — Richard J. Dick
William W. Hurst — Marshall S. Hanley
Samuel L. Jacobs — Steven K. Huffer
Robert W. Strohmeyer, Jr.

ASSOCIATES

Danielle A. Takla — Michael T. McNelis
John M. Reames — Michael P. Kilkenny

LEGAL SUPPORT PERSONNEL

L. Kathleen Hughes Brown, R.N.

General Counsel for: Premium Optical Co.; Calderon Bros. Vending Machines, Inc.; Grocers Supply Co., Inc.; Power Train Services, Inc.; Frank E. Irish, Inc.; Bedding Liquidators; Galyan's Trading Co.; Harcourt Management Co., Inc.; Kosene & Kosene Mgt. & Dev. Co., Inc.; Hasten Bancorp.

For full biographical listings, see the Martindale-Hubbell Law Directory

PARDIECK, GILL & VARGO, A PROFESSIONAL CORPORATION (AV)
The Old Bailey Building, 244 North College Avenue, 46202
Telephone: 317-639-3321
FAX: 317-639-3318
Seymour, Indiana Office: 100 North Chestnut Street. P.O. Box 608.
Telephone: 812-523-8686.

Roger L. Pardieck — W. Brent Gill
John F. Vargo

Thomas L. Landwerlen — Janet O. Vargo
Robert C. Rothkopf

For full biographical listings, see the Martindale-Hubbell Law Directory

PRICE & BARKER (AV)
The Hammond Block Building, 301 Massachusetts Avenue, 46204
Telephone: 317-633-8787
Telecopier: 317-633-8797

PARTNERS

Henry J. Price — Mary Arlien Findling

ASSOCIATES

Stephanie L. Franco — Barbara J. Germano
Deborah K. Pennington

For full biographical listings, see the Martindale-Hubbell Law Directory

TOWNSEND, HOVDE & MONTROSS (AV)
230 East Ohio Street, 46204
Telephone: 317-264-4444
FAX: 317-264-2080

F. Boyd Hovde — W. Scott Montross
Frederick R. Hovde

Reference: The Indiana National Bank of Indianapolis.

For full biographical listings, see the Martindale-Hubbell Law Directory

TOWNSEND & TOWNSEND (AV)
151 East Market Street, 46204
Telephone: 317-631-7777; 800-272-5720
FAX: 317-686-4449
Roscommon, Michigan Office: 603 Lake Street.
Telephone: 517-821-9114.

Earl C. Townsend, Jr. — Earl C. Townsend, III

For full biographical listings, see the Martindale-Hubbell Law Directory

YOSHA, LADENDORF & TODD (AV)
2220 North Meridian Street, 46208
Telephone: 317-925-9200
FAX: 317-923-5759

MEMBERS OF FIRM

Louis Buddy Yosha — Mark C. Ladendorf
William Levy — Teresa L. Todd

ASSOCIATE

David C. Krahulik

OF COUNSEL

Irwin J. Prince — Irving L. Fink
Theodore F. Smith, Jr.

References: NBD Indiana; Bank One, Indianapolis.

For full biographical listings, see the Martindale-Hubbell Law Directory

MUNSTER, Lake Co.

Law Offices of Timothy F. Kelly (AV)

Suite 2A, 9250 Columbia Avenue, 46321
Telephone: 219-836-4062
Telecopier: 219-836-0167

MEMBERS OF FIRM

Timothy F. Kelly — Karl K. Vanzo

ASSOCIATE

Harvey Karlovac

For Complete List of Firm Personnel, See General Section

For full biographical listings, see the Martindale-Hubbell Law Directory

SEYMOUR, Jackson Co.

Pardieck, Gill & Vargo, A Professional Corporation (AV)

100 North Chestnut Street, P.O. Box 608, 47274
Telephone: 812-523-8686
FAX: 812-522-4199
Indianapolis, Indiana Office: The Old Bailey Building, 244 North College Avenue.
Telephone: 317-639-3321.

Roger L. Pardieck — W. Brent Gill

Bruce A. MacTavish

OF COUNSEL

Barbara Stevens

References: Home Federal Savings Bank, Seymour, Indiana.

For full biographical listings, see the Martindale-Hubbell Law Directory

*SOUTH BEND,** St. Joseph Co.

Hardig, Lee and Groves, Professional Association (AV)

Suite 502, First Bank Building, 205 West Jefferson Boulevard, 46601
Telephone: 219-232-5923
Fax: 219-232-5942

Edward W. Hardig — Robert D. Lee
James F. Groves

William T. Webb

Representative Client: South Bend-Mishawaka New Car Dealers Assn.
Reference: First Interstate Bank of South Bend.

For full biographical listings, see the Martindale-Hubbell Law Directory

IOWA

*DES MOINES,** Polk Co.

Roxanne B. Conlin and Associates, P.C. (AV)

The Plaza, 300 Walnut Street - Suite 5, 50309-2239
Telephone: 515-282-3333
Fax: 515-282-0318

Roxanne B. Conlin

For full biographical listings, see the Martindale-Hubbell Law Directory

Finley, Alt, Smith, Scharnberg, May & Craig, P.C. (AV)

Fourth Floor Equitable Building, 50309
Telephone: 515-288-0145
Telecopier: 515-288-2724

Thomas A. Finley

Representative Clients: Aetna Casualty & Surety Co.; Aetna Life Insurance Co.; ALAS; American Society of Composers, Authors and Publishers; Equitable Life Assurance Society of the U.S.; Federated Insurance Co.; Meredith Corp.; Catholic Health Corp.; Iowa Methodist Medical Center.
Iowa Attorneys for: Midwest Medical Insurance Co.

For Complete List of Firm Personnel, See General Section

For full biographical listings, see the Martindale-Hubbell Law Directory

The James Law Firm, P.C. (AV)

630 Equitable Building, 50309
Telephone: 515-246-8484
Fax: 515-246-8767

(See Next Column)

Dwight W. James — Michael J. Carroll
Frederick W. James — Scott L. Bandstra

Reference: Norwest Bank.

For full biographical listings, see the Martindale-Hubbell Law Directory

*OSKALOOSA,** Mahaska Co.

Pothoven, Blomgren & Stravers (AV)

1201 High Avenue West, P.O. Box 1066, 52577
Telephone: 515-673-4438
Fax: 515-673-5177

MEMBERS OF FIRM

Marion H. Pothoven — James Q. Blomgren
Randall C. Stravers

For full biographical listings, see the Martindale-Hubbell Law Directory

KANSAS

OVERLAND PARK, Johnson Co.

Fisher, Patterson, Sayler & Smith (AV)

Suite 210, 11050 Roe Street, 66211
Telephone: 913-339-6757
FAX: 913-339-6187
Topeka, Kansas Office: 534 Kansas Avenue, Suite 400. 66603-3463.
Telephone: 913-232-7761.
Fax: 913-232-6604.

MEMBERS OF FIRM

Edwin Dudley Smith (Resident) — Michael K. Seck (Resident)
David P. Madden (Resident)

ASSOCIATE

Kurt A. Level (Resident)

For full biographical listings, see the Martindale-Hubbell Law Directory

Shamberg, Johnson, Bergman & Morris, Chartered (AV)

Suite 355, 4551 West 107th Street, 66207
Telephone: 913-642-0600
Fax: 913-642-9629
Kansas City, Kansas Office: Suite 860, New Brotherhood Building, 8th and State Streets.
Telephone: 913-281-1900.
Kansas City, Missouri Office: Suite 205, Scarritt Arcade Building, 819 Walnut.
Telephone: 816-556-9431.

Lynn R. Johnson — David R. Morris
Victor A. Bergman — John M. Parisi

Steven G. Brown — Anthony L. DeWitt (Not admitted in KS)
John E. Rogers — Patrick A. Hamilton
Steve N. Six

OF COUNSEL

John E. Shamberg

For full biographical listings, see the Martindale-Hubbell Law Directory

*TOPEKA,** Shawnee Co.

Palmer & Lowry (AV)

Suite 102 Columbian Building, 112 West Sixth, 66603-3862
Telephone: 913-233-1836
Fax: 913-233-3703

MEMBERS OF FIRM

Jerry R. Palmer — Kirk W. Lowry

ASSOCIATE

L J Leatherman

References: Commerce State Bank; Merchants National Bank.

For full biographical listings, see the Martindale-Hubbell Law Directory

Wright, Henson, Somers, Sebelius, Clark & Baker (AV)

Commerce Bank Building, 100 Southeast Ninth Street, 2nd Floor, P.O. Box 3555, 66601-3555
Telephone: 913-232-2200
FAX: 913-232-3344

MEMBERS OF FIRM

Thomas E. Wright — K. Gary Sebelius
Charles N. Henson — Bruce J. Clark
Dale L. Somers — Anne Lamborn Baker

(See Next Column)

WRIGHT, HENSON, SOMERS, SEBELIUS, CLARK & BAKER, *Topeka—Continued*

ASSOCIATES

Catherine A. Walter
Theron L. Sims, Jr.
Evelyn Zabel Wilson
J. Lyn Entrikin Goering

For full biographical listings, see the Martindale-Hubbell Law Directory

*WICHITA,** Sedgwick Co.

FOULSTON & SIEFKIN (AV)

(Formerly Foulston, Siefkin, Powers & Eberhardt)
700 Fourth Financial Center, Broadway at Douglas, 67202
Telephone: 316-267-6371
Facsimile: 316-267-6345
Topeka, Kansas Office: 1515 Bank IV Tower, 534 Kansas Avenue. 66603.
Telephone: 913-233-3600.
FAX: 913-233-1610.
Member: Lex Mundi, A Global Association of Independent Firms

MEMBERS OF FIRM

Jay F. Fowler
Amy S. Lemley
Craig W. West

For Complete List of Firm Personnel, See General Section

For full biographical listings, see the Martindale-Hubbell Law Directory

KENTUCKY

*BOWLING GREEN,** Warren Co.

CAMPBELL, KERRICK & GRISE (AV)

1025 State Street, P.O. Box 9547, 42102-9547
Telephone: 502-782-8160
FAX: 502-782-5856

MEMBERS OF FIRM

Joe Bill Campbell
Gregory N. Stivers
Thomas N. Kerrick
H. Brent Brennenstuhl
John R. Grise
Deborah Tomes Wilkins

ASSOCIATES

H. Harris Pepper, Jr.
Lanna Martin Kilgore
Laura Hagan

Representative Clients: Greenview Hospital; Riverdell Hospital; Hospital Corporation of America; Russell County Hospital; Wayne County Hospital; Hardin Memorial Hospital; Kentucky Hospital Association Trust.

For full biographical listings, see the Martindale-Hubbell Law Directory

ENGLISH, LUCAS, PRIEST & OWSLEY (AV)

1101 College Street, P.O. Box 770, 42102-0770
Telephone: 502-781-6500
Telecopier: 502-782-7782

MEMBERS OF FIRM

James H. Lucas
Murry A. Raines
Keith M. Carwell
Charles E. English, Jr.

ASSOCIATE

D. Gaines Penn

For Complete List of Firm Personnel, See General Section

For full biographical listings, see the Martindale-Hubbell Law Directory

HARLIN & PARKER, P.S.C. (AV)

519 East Tenth Street, P.O. Box 390, 42102-0390
Telephone: 502-842-5611
Telefax: 502-842-2607
Smiths Grove, Kentucky Office: Old Farmers Bank Building.
Telephone: 502-563-4701.

William Jerry Parker
Max B. Harlin, III

Insurance Clients: Allstate Insurance Co.; CNA Insurance Companies; Maryland Casualty Co.
Railroad and Utilities Clients: District Attorneys for South Central Bell Telephone Co.; CSX Transportation, Inc.
Local Counsel for: General Motors Corp.
Representative Clients: Graves Gilbert Clinic.

For Complete List of Firm Personnel, See General Section

For full biographical listings, see the Martindale-Hubbell Law Directory

MILLIKEN LAW FIRM (AV)

426 East Main Street, P.O. Box 1640, 42102-1640
Telephone: 502-843-0800
Fax: 502-842-1237

(See Next Column)

W. Currie Milliken
Morris Lowe

Reference: Trans Financial Bank, Bowling Green, Kentucky.

For full biographical listings, see the Martindale-Hubbell Law Directory

COVINGTON, Kenton Co.

ROBERT E. SANDERS AND ASSOCIATES, P.S.C. (AV)

The Charles H. Fisk House, 1017 Russell Street, 41011
Telephone: 606-491-3000
FAX: 606-655-4642

Robert E. Sanders

Julie Lippert Duncan

LEGAL SUPPORT PERSONNEL

Shirley L. Sanders
Harry E. Holtkamp
Sandra A. Head
Joseph E. Schmiade, Sr.

For full biographical listings, see the Martindale-Hubbell Law Directory

*LEXINGTON,** Fayette Co.

SAVAGE, GARMER & ELLIOTT, P.S.C. (AV)

Opera House Office Building, 141 North Broadway, 40507
Telephone: 606-254-9351
Fax: 606-233-9769

Joe C. Savage
William R. Garmer
Robert L. Elliott

For full biographical listings, see the Martindale-Hubbell Law Directory

*LONDON,** Laurel Co.

FARMER, KELLEY & FARMER (AV)

502 West Fifth Street, Drawer 490, 40743
Telephone: 606-878-7640
Fax: 606-878-2364
Lexington Office: 121 Prosperous Place, Suite 13 B, 40509-1834.
Telephone: 606: 263-2567.
Facsimile: 606: 263-2567.

MEMBERS OF FIRM

F. Preston Farmer
John F. Kelley, Jr.
Michael P. Farmer

ASSOCIATES

Martha L. Brown
Jeffrey T. Weaver

References: The First National Bank; Cumberland Valley National Bank & Trust Company of London, Ky.; London Bank & Trust Co.

For full biographical listings, see the Martindale-Hubbell Law Directory

*LOUISVILLE,** Jefferson Co.

FRANKLIN AND HANCE, P.S.C. (AV)

The Speed House, 505 West Ormsby Avenue, 40203
Telephone: 502-637-6000
Fax: 502-637-1413

Larry B. Franklin
Michael R. Hance

David B. Gray

Reference: First National Bank.

For full biographical listings, see the Martindale-Hubbell Law Directory

GARDNER, EWING & SOUZA (AV)

1600 Meidinger Tower, 462 South 4th Street, 40202-3467
Telephone: 502-585-5800
Fax: 502-585-5858

MEMBERS OF FIRM

Gary L. Gardner
C. David Ewing
Joseph C. Souza

ASSOCIATE

Anne Milton McMillin

Reference: PNC National City Bank & Trust Co.

For full biographical listings, see the Martindale-Hubbell Law Directory

HARGADON, LENIHAN, HARBOLT, & HERRINGTON (AV)

713 West Main Street, 40202
Telephone: 502-583-9701
FAX: 502-589-1144

MEMBERS OF FIRM

James B. Lenihan
Harry L. Hargadon, Jr.
A. Neal Herrington

ASSOCIATES

Michael T. Cooper
Mark A. Weis

(See Next Column)

HARGADON, LENIHAN, HARBOLT, & HERRINGTON—*Continued*

OF COUNSEL

John L. Harbolt

References: Liberty National Bank and Trust Co.; Citizens Fidelity Bank & Trust Co.

For full biographical listings, see the Martindale-Hubbell Law Directory

OGDEN NEWELL & WELCH (AV)

1200 One Riverfront Plaza, 40202-2973
Telephone: 502-582-1601
Fax: 502-581-9564

MEMBERS OF FIRM

John T. Ballantine
Stephen F. Schuster
Scott T. Wendelsdorf
David A. Harris
Gregory J. Bubalo
W. Gregory King

ASSOCIATES

Susan C. Bybee
Douglas C. Ballantine
Tracy S. Prewitt
Jennifer J. Hall

Counsel for: Baptist Healthcare System; Caronia Corporation; Kentucky Medical Insurance Company; Medical Protective Company; Ophtharmic Mutual Insurance Company; Paradigm Insurance Company; Physicians Insurance Company of Indiana; Professional Risk Management Services.

For Complete List of Firm Personnel, See General Section

For full biographical listings, see the Martindale-Hubbell Law Directory

OLDFATHER & MORRIS (AV)

One Mezzanine The Morrissey Building, 304 West Liberty Street, 40202
Telephone: 502-589-5500
Fax: 502-589-5338

Ann B. Oldfather
Douglas H. Morris, II
William F. McMurry
James Barrett
Teresa A. Talbott

For full biographical listings, see the Martindale-Hubbell Law Directory

TAUSTINE, POST, SOTSKY, BERMAN, FINEMAN & KOHN (AV)

8th Floor Marion E. Taylor Building, 40202
Telephone: 502-589-5760
Telecopier: 502-584-5927

MEMBERS OF FIRM

Hugo Taustine (1899-1987)
Edward M. Post (1929-1986)
Marvin M. Sotsky
Jerome D. Berman
Joseph E. Fineman
Robert A. Kohn
Alex Berman
H. Philip Grossman
Stanley W. Whetzel, Jr.
Maria A. Fernandez

ASSOCIATE

Sandra Sotsky Harrison

OF COUNSEL

W. David Shearer, Jr.
David A. Friedman
Martin R. Snyder
Jerald R. Steinberg (Also Practicing individually as Steinberg & Steinberg)
Craig I. Lustig

For full biographical listings, see the Martindale-Hubbell Law Directory

WEBER & ROSE PROFESSIONAL SERVICE CORPORATION (AV)

2700 Providian Center, 400 West Market Street, 40202
Telephone: 502-589-2200
Fax: 502-589-3400
Jeffersonville, Indiana Office: 432 East Court Avenue.
Telephone: 812-288-4372.

L. R. Curtis (1880-1968)
Shelton R. Weber
C. Alex Rose
Michael W. McGrath, Jr.
Wesley P. Adams, Jr.
Russell H. Saunders
James M. Gary
A. Andrew Draut
R. Hite Nally
Martin A. Arnett
Edward J. Smith

Bruce D. Atherton
Patrick W. Gault
Karen L. Keith

Counsel for: The Enro Shirt Co.

For full biographical listings, see the Martindale-Hubbell Law Directory

LOUISIANA

*BATON ROUGE,** East Baton Rouge Parish

WATSON, BLANCHE, WILSON & POSNER (AV)

505 North Boulevard, P.O. Drawer 2995, 70821-2995
Telephone: 504-387-5511
Fax: 504-387-5972
Other Baton Rouge, Louisiana Office: 4000 South Sherwood Forest Boulevard, Suite 504.
Telephone: 504-291-5280.
Fax: 504-293-8075.

Peter T. Dazzio
Felix R. Weill
William E. Scott, III
Mary H. Thompson
Michael M. Remson
P. Chauvin Wilkinson, Jr.
Randall L. Champagne
René J. Pfefferle

ASSOCIATES

P. Scott Jolly
Raymond A. Daigle, Jr.

Representative Clients: Baton Rouge General Medical Center; Louisiana Hospital Association; Woman's Hospital.

For Complete List of Firm Personnel, See General Section

For full biographical listings, see the Martindale-Hubbell Law Directory

*LAFAYETTE,** Lafayette Parish

ROY, BIVINS, JUDICE & HENKE, A PROFESSIONAL LAW CORPORATION (AV)

600 Jefferson Street, Suite 800, P.O. Drawer Z, 70502
Telephone: 318-233-7430
Telecopier: 318-233-8403
Telex: 9102505130

Harmon F. Roy
John A. Bivins
Ronald J. Judice
Kenneth M. Henke
W. Alan Lilley
Philip E. Roberts
Patrick M. Wartelle

Representative Clients: Employers Insurance of Wausau; Louisiana Medical Mutual Ins. Co.; St. Paul Fire & Marine Ins. Co.; Our Lady of Lourdes Regional Medical Center, Inc.; Midwest Medical Ins. Co.

For full biographical listings, see the Martindale-Hubbell Law Directory

*NEW ORLEANS,** Orleans Parish

BOGGS, LOEHN & RODRIGUE (AV)

A Partnership including Law Corporations
Suite 1800 Lykes Center, 300 Poydras Street, 70130-3597
Telephone: 504-523-7090
Fax: 504-581-6822

Charles A. Boggs (A Law Corporation)
Thomas E. Loehn (A Law Corporation)
Edward A. Rodrigue, Jr., (A Law Corporation)
Chester A. Fleming, III
Thomas W. Lewis
Terry B. Deffes
Robert I. Baudouin
Samuel M. Rosamond, III
Betty P. Westbrook
Ralph T Rabalais

Reference: First National Bank of Commerce, New Orleans, La.

For full biographical listings, see the Martindale-Hubbell Law Directory

GAINSBURGH, BENJAMIN, FALLON, DAVID & ATES (AV)

A Partnership including Professional Law Corporations
2800 Energy Centre, 1100 Poydras, 70163-2800
Telephone: 504-522-2304
Telecopier: 504-528-9973

OF COUNSEL

Samuel C. Gainsburgh (P.L.C.)

MEMBERS OF FIRM

Jack C. Benjamin (P.L.C.)
Eldon E. Fallon (P.L.C.)
Robert J. David
George S. Meyer (1939-1977)
J. Robert Ates (P.L.C.)
Gerald E. Meunier
Nick F. Noriea, Jr.
Irving J. Warshauer
Stevan C. Dittman
Madeleine M. Landrieu

ASSOCIATES

Darryl M. Phillips
Andrew A. Lemmon
Michael G. Calogero

For full biographical listings, see the Martindale-Hubbell Law Directory

*PLAQUEMINE,** Iberville Parish

BORRON, DELAHAYE, EDWARDS & DORÉ (AV)

58065 Meriam Street, P.O. Box 679, 70765-0679
Telephone: 504-687-3571; 343-3148
Fax: 504-687-9695

MEMBERS OF FIRM

Paul G. Borron (1874-1960)
Charles Ory Dupont (1919-1976)
Paul G. Borron, III
Allen M. Edwards
James P. Doré
John L. Delahaye

(See Next Column)

BORRON, DELAHAYE, EDWARDS & DORÉ, *Plaquemine—Continued*

OF COUNSEL

Paul G. Borron, Jr. J. Evan Delahaye

Representative Clients: Iberville Building & Loan Assn.; American Sugar Cane League; Iberville Trust & Savings Bank; South Central Bell Telephone Co.; Citizens Bank & Trust Co.; Iberville Motors, Inc.; A. Wilbert's Sons Limited Partnership; Surgical Associates of Baton Rouge, Inc.; Vascular Surgery Associates; Vascular Associates Laboratory, Inc.

For full biographical listings, see the Martindale-Hubbell Law Directory

MAINE

*AUGUSTA,** Kennebec Co.

* indicates certain Bar Register subscribers whose principal office is located elsewhere in the state and who have arranged for representation as a part of the state capital listings that follow

*** PIERCE, ATWOOD, SCRIBNER, ALLEN, SMITH & LANCASTER** (AV)

77 Winthrop Street, 04330
Telephone: 207-622-6311
Fax: 207-623-9367
Portland, Maine Office: One Monument Square.
Telephone: 207-773-6411.
Camden, Maine Office: 36 Chestnut Street, P.O. Box 780.
Telephone: 207-236-4333.

MEMBERS OF FIRM

Malcolm L. Lyons John C. Nivison

For Complete List of Firm Personnel, See General Section

For full biographical listings, see the Martindale-Hubbell Law Directory

*PORTLAND,** Cumberland Co.

PRETI, FLAHERTY, BELIVEAU & PACHIOS (AV)

443 Congress Street, P.O. Box 11410, 04104-7410
Telephone: 207-791-3000
Telecopier: 207-791-3111
Augusta, Maine Office: 45 Memorial Circle, P.O. Box 1058, 04332-1058.
Telephone: 207-623-5300.
Telecopier: 207-623-2914.
Rumford, Maine Office: 150 Congress Street, P.O. Drawer L, 04276-2035.
Telephone: 207-364-4593.
Telecopier: 207-369-9421.

MEMBERS OF FIRM

John J. Flaherty Christopher D. Nyhan
Daniel Rapaport

ASSOCIATES

Elizabeth A. Olivier Kevin J. Beal
Penny St. Louis

Representative Clients: St. Paul Fire and Marine Insurance Co.; PHICO Insurance Co.

For Complete List of Firm Personnel, See General Section

For full biographical listings, see the Martindale-Hubbell Law Directory

SMITH ELLIOTT SMITH & GARMEY, P.A. (AV)

100 Commercial Street, Suite 304, 04101
Telephone: 207-774-3199
Telefax: 207-774-2235
Kennebunk, Maine Office: Route One South, P.O. Box 980.
Telephone: 207-985-4464.
Telefax: 207-985-3946.
Saco, Maine Office: 199 Main Street, P.O. Box 1179.
Telephone: 207-282-1527.
Telefax: 207-283-4412. Sanford
Telephone: 207-324-1560. Wells
Telephone: 207-464-0970.

Randall E. Smith Terrence D. Garmey

Representative Clients: Towns of Waterboro and Kennebunk, Maine; City of Biddeford; Saco and Biddeford Savings Institution; Ocean Communities Federal Credit Union.
Local Counsel for: Mutual Fire Insurance Company.
Reference: Casco Northern Bank, N. A. (Saco Branch); Saco & Biddeford Savings Institution.

For Complete List of Firm Personnel, See General Section

For full biographical listings, see the Martindale-Hubbell Law Directory

SACO, York Co.

SMITH ELLIOTT SMITH & GARMEY, P.A. (AV)

199 Main Street, P.O. Box 1179, 04072
Telephone: 207-282-1527
Telefax: 207-283-4412
Sanford Telephone: 207-324-1560
Portland Telephone: 207-774-3199
Wells Telephone: 207-646-0970
Kennebunk, Maine Office: Route One South, P.O. Box 980.
Telephone: 207-985-4464.
Telefax: 207-985-3946.
Portland, Maine Office: 100 Commercial Street, Suite 304.
Telephone: 207-774-3199.
Telefax: 207-774-2235.

Randall E. Smith Terrence D. Garmey
John H. O'Neil, Jr.

Representative Clients: City of Biddeford; Towns of Waterboro and Kennebunk, Maine; Saco and Biddeford Savings Institution; Ocean Communities Federal Credit Union;
Local Counsel for: Mutual Fire Insurance Company.
References: Casco Northern Bank, N.A. (Saco Branch); Saco & Biddeford Savings Institution.

For Complete List of Firm Personnel, See General Section

For full biographical listings, see the Martindale-Hubbell Law Directory

MARYLAND

*BALTIMORE,** (Independent City)

ELLIN AND BAKER (AV)

Second Floor, 1101 St. Paul Street, 21202
Telephone: 410-727-1787
FAX: 410-752-4838

MEMBER OF FIRM

Marvin Ellin LaVonna Lee Vice

Jack David Lebowitz Michael P. Smith

For full biographical listings, see the Martindale-Hubbell Law Directory

ISRAELSON, SALSBURY, CLEMENTS & BEKMAN (AV)

300 West Pratt Street, Suite 450, 21201
Telephone: 410-539-6633
FAX: 410-625-9554

MEMBERS OF FIRM

Stuart Marshall Salsbury Daniel M. Clements
Paul D. Bekman Matthew Zimmerman
Laurence A. Marder

Suzanne K. Farace Scott R. Scherr
Carol J. Glover

COUNSEL TO THE FIRM

Max R. Israelson

OF COUNSEL

Samuel Omar Jackson, Jr. (Semi-Retired)

For full biographical listings, see the Martindale-Hubbell Law Directory

JANET & STRAUSBERG (AV)

A Partnership of Professional Associations
Executive Centre at Hooks Lane, 8 Reservoir Circle, Suite 200, 21208
Telephone: 410-653-3200
Fax: 410-653-9030

MEMBERS OF FIRM

Howard A. Janet (P.A.) Gary I. Strausberg (P.A.)

ASSOCIATES

Wayne M. Willoughby Randal D. Getz
Zev T. Gershon Sammie Lee Mouton

For full biographical listings, see the Martindale-Hubbell Law Directory

KAHN, SMITH & COLLINS, P.A. (AV)

110 Saint Paul Street, 6th Floor, 21202
Telephone: 410-244-1010
Telecopier: 410-244-8001

Andrew H. Kahn Joel A. Smith
Francis J. Collins

(See Next Column)

KAHN, SMITH & COLLINS P.A.—*Continued*

David Vernon Diggs
Christyne L. Neff

For full biographical listings, see the Martindale-Hubbell Law Directory

ROBINETTE, DUGAN & JAKUBOWSKI, P.A. (AV)
The Robinette-Dugan Building, 801 St. Paul Street, 21202
Telephone: 410-659-6700
FAX: 410-752-0456

Gilbert H. Robinette
Ruth A. Jakubowski
Henry E. Dugan, Jr.
Bruce J. Babij

Pamela S. Foresman
George S. Tolley, III

OF COUNSEL
Marian V. Fleming

For full biographical listings, see the Martindale-Hubbell Law Directory

SCHOCHOR, FEDERICO AND STATON, P.A. (AV)
The Paulton, 1211 St. Paul Street, 21202
Telephone: 410-234-1000
FAX: 410-234-1010
Washington D.C. Office: 777 North Capitol Street, N.E., Suite 910.
Telephone: 202-408-3300.
Fax: 202-408-3304.

Jonathan Schochor
Philip C. Federico
Kerry D. Staton

Louis G. Close, III
Diane M. Littlepage
Christopher P. Kennedy

For full biographical listings, see the Martindale-Hubbell Law Directory

BETHESDA, Montgomery Co.

FREEMAN & JENNER, P.C. (AV)
3 Bethesda Metro Center, Suite 1410, 20814
Telephone: 301-907-7747
FAX: 301-907-9877
Washington, D.C. Office: 1000 16th Street, N.W., Suite 300.
Telephone: 301-907-7747.
Aspen, Colorado Office: 215 South Monarch Street, Suite 202.
Telephone: 303-925-3400.
FAX: 303-925-4043.

Martin H. Freeman
Robert K. Jenner

Barbara E. Hirsch
Mark Allan Freeman

Reference: Crestar Bank of Maryland.

For full biographical listings, see the Martindale-Hubbell Law Directory

*LA PLATA,** Charles Co.

DAVID NEWMAN & ASSOCIATES, P.C. (AV)
Centennial Square, P.O. Box 2728, 20646-2728
Telephone: 301-934-6100; 202-842-8400
Facsimile: 301-934-5782

David B. Newman, Jr.

Suzin C. Bailey

LEGAL SUPPORT PERSONNEL
TECHNICAL ADVISORS
Dr. Christopher J. Newman
Dr. Amy Hauck Newman

For full biographical listings, see the Martindale-Hubbell Law Directory

*ROCKVILLE,** Montgomery Co.

ARMSTRONG, DONOHUE & CEPPOS, CHARTERED (AV)
Suite 101, 204 Monroe Street, 20850
Telephone: 301-251-0440
Telecopier: 301-279-5929

Larry A. Ceppos
H. Kenneth Armstrong
Benjamin S. Vaughan

Oya S. Oner
Sharon A. Marcial
Pamela Barrow Kincheloe
J. Eric Rhoades

For full biographical listings, see the Martindale-Hubbell Law Directory

BRAULT, GRAHAM, SCOTT & BRAULT (AV)
101 South Washington Street, 20850
Telephone: 301-424-1060
Fax: 301-424-7991
Washington, D.C. Office: 1906 Sunderland Place, N.W.
Telephone: 202-785-1200.
FAX: 202-785-4301.
Arlington, Virginia Office: Suite 1201, 2300 North Clarendon Boulevard, Courthouse Plaza.
Telephone: 703-522-1781.

OF COUNSEL
Laurence T. Scott

MEMBERS OF FIRM
Denver H. Graham (1922-1987)
Ronald G. Guziak (Resident)
Albert E. Brault (Retired)
Daniel L. Shea (Resident)
Albert D. Brault (Resident)
Keith M. Bonner
Leo A. Roth, Jr.
M. Kathleen Parker (Resident)
James S. Wilson (Resident)
Regina Ann Casey (Resident)
James M. Brault (Resident)

ASSOCIATES
David G. Mulquin (Resident)
Eric A. Spacek (Not admitted in MD)
Sanford A. Friedman
Holly D. Shupert (Resident)
Joan F. Brault (Resident)

Representative Clients: American Oil Co.; Crum & Forster Group; Fireman's Fund American Insurance Cos.; Kemper Group; Reliance Insurance Cos.; Safeco Group; Government Employees Insurance Co.; Medical Mutual Insurance Society of Maryland; Legal Mutual Liability Insurance Society of Maryland.

For Complete List of Firm Personnel, See General Section

For full biographical listings, see the Martindale-Hubbell Law Directory

PAULSON, NACE, NORWIND & SELLINGER (AV)
31 Wood Lane, 20850
Telephone: 301-294-8060
Washington, D.C. Office: 1814 N Street, N.W.
Telephone: 202-463-1999.
Fax: 202-223-6824.

John J. Sellinger

For full biographical listings, see the Martindale-Hubbell Law Directory

SHADOAN AND MICHAEL (AV)
108 Park Avenue, 20850
Telephone: 301-762-5150

MEMBERS OF FIRM
George W. Shadoan
Robert R. Michael

ASSOCIATE
David J. Kaminow

Reference: Crestar Bank, N.A.

For full biographical listings, see the Martindale-Hubbell Law Directory

MASSACHUSETTS

*BOSTON,** Suffolk Co.

CORNELL AND GOLLUB (AV)
75 Federal Street, 02110
Telephone: 617-482-8100
Telecopier: 617-482-3917

MEMBERS OF FIRM
Robert W. Cornell (1910-1988)
Philip J. Foley
Karl L. Gollub (1934-1985)
Peter M. Durney
David H. Sempert
Paul F. Lynch

ASSOCIATES
Susan Geyer Malloy
Susan M. Donaldson
Jane Treen Brand
Marie E. Chadeayne
Hugh M. Coxe
Bruce E. Hopper
Janet J. Bobit
Thomas H. Dolan
Thomas A. Pursley
Eric B. Goldberg
David W. McGough
Kelly L. Wilkins
Martha Jane Dickey

For full biographical listings, see the Martindale-Hubbell Law Directory

LAW OFFICES OF LEONARD GLAZER, P.C. & ASSOCIATES (AV)
One Longfellow Place Suite 3408, 02114
Telephone: 617-523-4411
Fax: 617-523-7433

Leonard Glazer

(See Next Column)

LAW OFFICES OF LEONARD GLAZER, P.C. & ASSOCIATES, *Boston—Continued*

Frank E. Glazer
Georgia A. Saylor

For full biographical listings, see the Martindale-Hubbell Law Directory

SUGARMAN AND SUGARMAN, P.C. (AV)

One Beacon Street, 02108
Telephone: 617-542-1000
Telecopier: 617-542-1359

Nathan Fink (1920-1974)
Paul R. Sugarman
Neil Sugarman
W. Thomas Smith
Steven L. Hoffman
Robert W. Casby
Kerry Paul Choi
Valerie A. Yarashus
Charlotte E. Glinka

Jodi M. Petrucelli
Darin Michael Colucci
Kimberly Ellen Nelson Winter
Marianne Camille LeBlanc

For full biographical listings, see the Martindale-Hubbell Law Directory

SWARTZ & SWARTZ (AV)

10 Marshall Street, 02108
Telephone: 617-742-1900
Fax: 617-367-7193

Edward M. Swartz
Alan L. Cantor
Joseph A. Swartz
Victor A. Denaro
Joan E. Swartz
James A. Swartz
Robert S. Berger
Harold David Levine

OF COUNSEL

Fredric A. Swartz

For full biographical listings, see the Martindale-Hubbell Law Directory

*CAMBRIDGE,** Middlesex Co.

McCARTHY, BOULEY, FOSTER & ELDRIDGE, P.C. (AV)

One Main Street, 02142
Telephone: 617-225-4800
Fax: 617-225-4849

Edward D. McCarthy
Robert L. Bouley
Martin C. Foster
Joan Eldridge
James J. Barry

Steven M. O'Brien
John DiPietrantonio
Elaine M. Angelone

For full biographical listings, see the Martindale-Hubbell Law Directory

*SPRINGFIELD,** Hampden Co.

ELY & KING (AV)

One Financial Plaza, 1350 Main Street, 01103
Telephone: 413-781-1920
Telecopier: 413-733-3360

MEMBERS OF FIRM

Joseph Buell Ely (1905-1956)
Raymond T. King (1919-1971)
Frederick M. Kingsbury (1924-1968)
Hugh J. Corcoran (1938-1992)
Richard S. Milstein
Donald A. Beaudry
Richard F. Faille
Leland B. Seabury
Gregory A. Schmidt
Pamela Manson
Anthony T. Rice
Russell J. Mawdsley

ASSOCIATE

Donna M. Brown

Representative Clients: Hartford Accident & Indemnity Co.; Albert Steiger Cos.; Shawmut Bank N.A.; Springfield Institution for Savings; St. Paul Fire & Marine Insurance Co.; The Rouse Co.; Tighe & Bond, Inc.; Northeast Utilities.

For full biographical listings, see the Martindale-Hubbell Law Directory

THOMAS A. KENEFICK, III (AV)

73 Chestnut Street, 01103
Telephone: 413-734-7000
Fax: 413-731-1302

For full biographical listings, see the Martindale-Hubbell Law Directory

MICHIGAN

*ANN ARBOR,** Washtenaw Co.

BOOTHMAN, HEBERT & ELLER, P.C. (AV)

300 N. Fifth Avenue, Suite 140, 48108
Telephone: 313-995-9050
Fax: 313-995-8966
Detroit, Michigan Office: One Kennedy Square, Suite 2006.
Telephone: 313-964-0150.
Fax: 313-964-2226.

Richard C. Boothman (Resident)

For full biographical listings, see the Martindale-Hubbell Law Directory

DAVIS AND FAJEN, P.C. (AV)

Suite 400, 320 North Main Street, 48104
Telephone: 313-995-0066
Facsimile: 313-995-0184
Grand Haven, Michigan Office: Davis, Fajen & Miller. Harbourfront Place, 41 Washington Street, Suite 260.
Telephone: 616-846-9875.
Facsimile: 616-846-4920.

Peter A. Davis
James A. Fajen
Nelson P. Miller
Richard B. Bailey
Catherine G. Tennant

Reference: First of America Bank-Ann Arbor.

For full biographical listings, see the Martindale-Hubbell Law Directory

BINGHAM FARMS, Oakland Co.

SMALL, TOTH, BALDRIDGE & VAN BELKUM, P.C. (AV)

30100 Telegraph Road Suite 250, 48025-4516
Telephone: 810-647-9595
Facsimile: 810-647-9599

Richard L. Small
John M. Toth
David M. Baldridge
Thomas G. Van Belkum

Representative Clients: The Medical Protective Co.; Michigan Physicians Mutual Liability Insurance Co.; Physicians Insurance Company of Michigan; Shelby Insurance Group; Kemper Insurance Group; Michigan Society of Oral and Maxillofacial Surgeons; Michigan Association of Orthodontists; Michigan Association of Endodontists; AAMOS Mutual; Mt Vernon Insurance Company.

For full biographical listings, see the Martindale-Hubbell Law Directory

BIRMINGHAM, Oakland Co.

CARSON FISCHER, P.L.C. (AV)

Third Floor, 300 East Maple Road, 48009-6317
Telephone: 810-644-4840
Facsimile: 810-644-1832

Robert M. Carson
Kathleen A. Stibich

For full biographical listings, see the Martindale-Hubbell Law Directory

GOREN & GOREN, P.C. (AV)

Suite 470, 30400 Telegraph Road, 48025
Telephone: 810-540-3100

Robert Goren
Steven E. Goren

Reference: Michigan National Bank-Oakland.

BLOOMFIELD HILLS, Oakland Co.

DAVID D. PATTON & ASSOCIATES, P.C. (AV)

100 Bloomfield Hills Parkway, Suite 110, 48304
Telephone: 810-258-6020
Fax: 810-258-6052

David D. Patton

Ellen Bartman Jannette
James A. Reynolds, Jr.
Patricia C. White
David H. Patton (1912-1993)

For full biographical listings, see the Martindale-Hubbell Law Directory

PORTNOY, PIDGEON & ROTH, P.C. (AV)

3883 Telegraph, Suite 103, 48302
Telephone: 810-647-4242
Fax: 810-647-8251

Bernard N. Portnoy
James M. Pidgeon
Robert P. Roth
Marc S. Berlin
Berton K. May

(See Next Column)

PORTNOY, PIDGEON & ROTH P.C.—*Continued*

Representative Clients: North Oakland Medical Center, Pontiac General Hospital Division; Hurly Medical Center, Flint, Michigan; McLaren Regional Medical Center, Flint, Michigan; William Beaumont Hospital, Royal Oak, Michigan; Detroit Osteopathic Hospital; Horizon Health Systems; Bi-County Community Hospital; Riverside Osteopathic; Crittenton Hospital, Rochester, Michigan.

For full biographical listings, see the Martindale-Hubbell Law Directory

LAW OFFICES OF THOMAS J. TRENTA, P.C. (AV)

33 Bloomfield Hills Parkway Suite 145, 48304-2945
Telephone: 810-258-9610
Fax: 810-258-5132

Thomas J. Trenta

Richard A. Joslin, Jr.
OF COUNSEL
James F. Jordan

For full biographical listings, see the Martindale-Hubbell Law Directory

*DETROIT,** Wayne Co.

BOOTHMAN, HEBERT & ELLER, P.C. (AV)

One Kennedy Square, Suite 2006 719 Griswold, 48226
Telephone: 313-964-0150; 1-800-572-8022
Fax: 313-964-2226
Ann Arbor, Michigan Office: 300 N. Fifth Avenue, Suite 140.
Telephone: 313-995-9050.
Fax: 313-995-8966.

Dale L. Hebert
Richard C. Boothman (Resident, Ann Arbor Office)
Gary S. Eller

George D. Moustakas
Roy A. Luttmann
Marta J. Hoffman
Sharon E. Hollins
Joyce E. Taylor
OF COUNSEL
L. Stewart Hastings, Jr.
Kathryn A. Kerka

Representative Clients: University of Michigan; CNA Insurance Companies; Michigan Physicians Mutual Liability Co.; Emergency Physicians Medical Group; Kaiser Permanente; Physicians Insurance Co. of Michigan.
Reference: Comerica Bank-Detroit.

For full biographical listings, see the Martindale-Hubbell Law Directory

COTICCHIO, ZOTTER, SULLIVAN, MOLTER, SKUPIN & TURNER, PROFESSIONAL CORPORATION (AV)

155 West Congress, Suite 300, 48226
Telephone: 313-961-0425

George W. Coticchio
Walter J. Zotter
Timothy J. Sullivan
Ronald A. Molter
Charles G. Skupin
James Howard Turner
Stephen A. Coticchio
Joseph F. Lucas
Donald N. Payne, II

For full biographical listings, see the Martindale-Hubbell Law Directory

DENARDIS, MCCANDLESS & MULLER, P.C. (AV)

800 Buhl Building, 48226-3602
Telephone: 313-963-9050
Fax: 313-963-4553

Ronald F. DeNardis
William McCandless
Gregory J. Muller
Mark F. Miller
Lawrence M. Hintz
Michael D. Dolenga

For full biographical listings, see the Martindale-Hubbell Law Directory

FEIKENS, VANDER MALE, STEVENS, BELLAMY & GILCHRIST, P.C. (AV)

One Detroit Center Suite 3400, 500 Woodward Avenue, 48226-3406
Telephone: 313-962-5909
Fax: 313-962-3125

Jack E. Vander Male
L. Neal Kennedy
Bruce A. VandeVusse
William C. Hurley
Linda M. Galbraith

Richard G. Koefod
Joseph E. Kozely, Jr.
Jeffrey Feikens
Michael B. Barey
Gary T. Tandberg
Susan Tillotson Mills

For Complete List of Firm Personnel, See General Section

For full biographical listings, see the Martindale-Hubbell Law Directory

KERR, RUSSELL AND WEBER (AV)

One Detroit Center, 500 Woodward Avenue, Suite 2500, 48226-3406
Telephone: 313-961-0200
Telecopier: 313-961-0388
Bloomfield Hills, Michigan Office: 3883 Telegraph Road.
Telephone: 810-649-5990.
East Lansing, Michigan Office: 1301 North Hagadorn Road.
Telephone: 517-336-6767.

Richard D. Weber
Roy H. Christiansen
Monte D. Jahnke
Patrick McLain
Daniel G. Beyer
Stephen D. McGraw
Joanne Geha Swanson
Robert J. Pineau
Catherine Bonczak Edwards
Christopher A. Cornwall
Patrick J. Haddad
Eric I. Lark
James E. DeLine

For Complete List of Firm Personnel, See General Section

For full biographical listings, see the Martindale-Hubbell Law Directory

KITCH, DRUTCHAS, WAGNER & KENNEY, P.C. (AV)

One Woodward, Tenth Floor, 48226-3412
Telephone: 313-965-7900
Fax: 313-965-7403
Lansing, Michigan Office: 120 Washington Square, North, Suite 805, One Michigan Avenue, 48933-1609.
Telephone: 517-372-6430.
Fax: 517-372-0441.
Macomb County Office: Towne Square Development, 10 South Main Street, Suite 301, Mount Clemens, 48043-7903.
Telephone: 810-463-9770.
Fax: 810-463-8994.
Toledo, Ohio Office: 405 Madison Avenue, Suite 1500, 43604-1235.
Telephone: 419-243-4006.
Fax: 419-243-7333.
Troy, Michigan Office: 3001 West Big Beaver Road, Suite 200, 48084-3103.
Telephone: 810-637-3500.
Fax: 810-637-6630.
Ann Arbor, Michigan Office: 303 Detroit Street, Suite 400, P.O. Box 8610, 48107-8610.
Telephone: 313-994-7600.
Fax: 313-994-7626.

Richard A. Kitch
Ronald E. Wagner
Jeremiah J. Kenney (Managing Principal)
Ralph F. Valitutti, Jr.
Richard R. DeNardis
Mona K. Majzoub
Harry J. Sherbrook
Anthony G. Arnone
Mark D. Willmarth (Principal)
Charles W. Fisher
Clyde M. Metzger, III (Principal, Ann Arbor Office)
Thomas J. Foley
Victor J. Abela (Principal, Troy Office)
Jeffrey H. Chilton
James H. Hughesian
John P. Ryan (Principal, Lansing Office)
William D. Chaklos
Steve N. Cheolas (Principal, Macomb County Office)
Susan Healy Zitterman
William Vertes (Principal, Lansing Office)
William A. Tanoury (Principal, Ann Arbor Office)
John J. Ramar
John Stephen Wasung (Principal, Toledo, Ohio Office)
Bruce R. Shaw
Karen Bernard Berkery (Associate Principal)
Susan M. Ramage (Associate Principal, Lansing Office)
Pamela Hobbs
Daniel R. Corbet
Brian R. Garves
Daniel R. Shirey
Daniel J. Niemann (Associate Principal, Ann Arbor Office)
John Paul Hessburg
William P. O'Leary
David M. Kraus
Verlin R. Nafziger
Robert A. Fehniger (Macomb County Office)
Christopher P. Dinverno
Kenneth M. Essad
Steven Waclawski
Ronald S. Bowling
Sara Mae Gerbitz
Linda M. Garbarino
Antonio Mauti
Lawrence David Rosenstock
Thomas R. Shimmel
Susan Marie Beutel
Carole S. Empey (Ann Arbor Office)
Debra S. Hirsch (Lansing Office)
David R. Nauts
Richard T. Counsman
Karen Ann Smyth
Mark A. Wisniewski
Julia Kelly McNelis
J. Mark Trimble (Toledo, Ohio Office)
Sharon A. DeWaele
Arthur F. Brandt
Dean A. Etsios
Michael K. McCoy
Stephen R. Brzezinski
Joseph P. McGill
Paula M. Burgess (Toledo, Ohio Office)
Lisa M. Iulianelli
Fred J. Fresard
Maureen Rouse-Ayoub
Matthew M. Walton (Mount Clemens Office)
Barbara A. Martin
Carol S. Allis (Ann Arbor Office)
Terese L. Farhat
Richard P. Cuneo
Kim J. Sveska
Kathleen P. Knol (Ann Arbor Office)
David A. Schoolcraft (Lansing Office)
Lauri A. Read (Troy Office)

(See Next Column)

KITCH, DRUTCHAS, WAGNER & KENNEY P.C., *Detroit—Continued*

Lisa DiPonio
John J. Koselka (Ann Arbor Office)
David J. Allen
Richard M. Mitchell
Mary Catherine Storen
Diane M. Carpentier
Robert W. Lipp, III
Cullen B. McKinney
Christine G. Strasser
Norman P. Moore, Jr.
Carla M. Calabrese
Fredericia J. Craig
Pamela A. Boland
Michael M. McNamara
Jeffrey T. Gorcyca
Laura L. Witty

For Complete List of Firm Personnel, See General Section

For full biographical listings, see the Martindale-Hubbell Law Directory

LOPATIN, MILLER, FREEDMAN, BLUESTONE, HERSKOVIC & HEILMANN, A PROFESSIONAL CORPORATION (AV)

1301 East Jefferson, 48207
Telephone: 313-259-7800

Albert Lopatin
Sheldon L. Miller
Stuart G. Freedman
Saul Bluestone
Maurice Herskovic
Michael G. Heilmann

Michael A. Gantz (1939-1990)
David F. Dickinson
Richard E. Shaw
Ronald Robinson
Jeffrey A. Danzig
B. J. Belcoure
David R. Berndt
Stephen I. Kaufman
Jeffrey S. Cook
Robert J. Boyd, III
Patrick M. Horan
Richard R. Mannausa
Alan Wittenberg

OF COUNSEL

Harry Okrent (1912-1990)
Lee R. Franklin (Ms.)
Bernard L. Humphrey

For full biographical listings, see the Martindale-Hubbell Law Directory

MILLER, CANFIELD, PADDOCK AND STONE, P.L.C. (AV)

A Professional Limited Liability Company
Founded in 1852 by Sidney Davy Miller
150 West Jefferson, Suite 2500, 48226-4415
Telephone: 313-963-6420
Fax: 313-496-7500
Cable Address: "Stem Detroit"
Detroit, Michigan Office: 150 West Jefferson, Suite 2500, 48226-4415.
Telephone: 313-963-6420.
Fax: 313-496-7500.
Cable Address: "Stem Detroit."
Ann Arbor, Michigan Office: 101 North Main Street, 7th Floor, 48104-1400.
Telephone: 313-663-2445.
Fax: 313-747-7147.
Bloomfield Hills, Michigan Office: Suite 100, Pinehurst Office Center, 1400 North Woodward, 48303-2014.
Telephone: 313-645-5000.
Fax: 313-645-1917.
Grand Rapids, Michigan Office: 1200 Campau Square Plaza, 99 Monroe, N.W., 49503-2639.
Telephone: 616-454-8656.
Fax: 616-776-6322.
Howell, Michigan Office: 121 South Barnard Street, Suite 4, 48843-2305.
Telephone: 517-546-7600.
Telecopier: 517-546-6974.
Kalamazoo, Michigan Office: 444 West Michigan Avenue, 49007-3752.
Telephone: 616-381-7030.
Fax: 616-382-0244.
Lansing, Michigan Office: One Michigan Avenue, Suite 900, 48933-1609.
Telephone: 517-487-2070.
Fax: 517-374-6304.
Monroe, Michigan Office: The Executive Centre, 214 East Elm Avenue, 48161-2682.
Telephone: 313-243-2000.
Fax: 313-243-0901.
Washington, D.C. Office: 1225 Nineteenth Street, N.W., Suite 400. 20036.
Telephone: 202-429-5575; 785-0600.
Fax: 202-331-1118; 785-1234.
Pensacola, Florida Office: 25 West Cedar, 32501.
Telephone: 904-469-1088.
Fax: 904-432-0677.
St. Petersburg, Florida Office: 100 Second Avenue S., Suite 7045, 33701.
Telephone: 813-982-6000.
Fax: 813-892-6002.
Gdansk, Poland Office: Suite 322, Dom Technika Building, Ul. Rajska 6, 80-850.
Telephone: 011-485-831-2808.
Fax: 011-485-831-4719.
Warsaw, Poland Office: Ul. Marszalkowska 82, Suite 561, 00-517.
Telephone: 011-482-623-6457 and 6458.
Fax: 011-482-623-6459.

(See Next Column)

MEMBERS OF FIRM

Charles E. Ritter (Kalamazoo Office)
Thomas G. Parachini
James C. Foresman
Leland D. Barringer

SENIOR ATTORNEY

Irene Bruce Hathaway

ASSOCIATE

Brian J. Doren

Representative Firm Clients: Chrysler Corp.; Comerica, Inc.; City of Detroit, Mich.; Detroit Tigers, Inc.; First of Michigan; Fretter, Inc.; Ford Motor Co.; Ford Motor Credit Co.; Great Lakes Bancorp; Henry Ford Hospital.

For Complete List of Firm Personnel, See General Section

For full biographical listings, see the Martindale-Hubbell Law Directory

MARIETTA S. ROBINSON (AV)

The Globe Building, 407 East Fort Street, Suite 101, 48226
Telephone: 313-964-4460

ASSOCIATE

Ramona C. Howard

For full biographical listings, see the Martindale-Hubbell Law Directory

JOSEPH C. SMITH, P.C. (AV)

600 Renaissance Center Suite 1500, 48243
Telephone: 313-567-8300
Fax: 313-567-0892

Joseph C. Smith

For full biographical listings, see the Martindale-Hubbell Law Directory

EAST LANSING, Ingham Co.

FARHAT, STORY & KRAUS, P.C. (AV)

Beacon Place, 4572 South Hagadorn Road, Suite 3, 48823
Telephone: 517-351-3700
Fax: 517-332-4122

Leo A. Farhat
James E. Burns (1925-1979)
Monte R. Story
Richard C. Kraus
Max R. Hoffman Jr.
Chris A. Bergstrom
Kitty L. Groh
Charles R. Toy
David M. Platt

Lawrence P. Schweitzer
Jeffrey J. Short
Kathy A. Breedlove
Thomas L. Sparks

Reference: Capitol National Bank.

For full biographical listings, see the Martindale-Hubbell Law Directory

SMITH, HAUGHEY, RICE & ROEGGE, P.C. (AV)

1301 North Hagadorn, 48823-2320
Telephone: 517-332-3030
Telecopier: 517-332-3468
Grand Rapids, Michigan Office: 200 Calder Plaza Building, 250 Monroe Avenue, N.W., 49503-2251.
Telephone: 616-774-8000.
Telecopier: 616-774-2461.
Traverse City, Michigan Office: 241 East State Street, P.O. Box 848, 49685-0848.
Telephone: 616-929-4878.
Telecopier: 616-929-4182.

Douglas G. Powe

Loretta B. Passanante
Daniel N. Stephens
James R. Duby, Jr.
Veronica A. Marsich

For full biographical listings, see the Martindale-Hubbell Law Directory

FARMINGTON HILLS, Oakland Co.

KAUFMAN AND PAYTON (AV)

200 Northwestern Financial Center, 30833 Northwestern Highway, 48334
Telephone: 810-626-5000
Telefacsimile: 810-626-2843
Grand Rapids, Michigan Office: 420 Trust Building.
Telephone: 616-459-4200.
Fax: 616-459-4929.
Traverse City, Michigan Office: 122 West State Street.
Telephone: 616-947-4050.
Fax: 616-947-7321.

(See Next Column)

KAUFMAN AND PAYTON—*Continued*

Alan Jay Kaufman
Donald L. Payton
Kenneth C. Letherwood
Stephen R. Levine
Thomas L. Vitu
Ralph C. Chapa, Jr.
Raymond I. Foley, II
Jeffrey K. Van Hattum
Leo D. Neville

For full biographical listings, see the Martindale-Hubbell Law Directory

STILL, NEMIER, TOLARI & LANDRY, P.C. (AV)

37000 Grand River, Suite 300, 48335
Telephone: 810-476-6900
Fax: 810-476-6564

William R. Still
Craig L. Nemier
Jeffrey L. Tolari
David B. Landry
Mark R. Johnson
Rik Mazzeo
Catherine L. West
Michelle E. Mathieu
Christopher A. Todd
Thomas S. McLeod
Victoria W. Ryan

OF COUNSEL

Terry E. Pietryga
Veeder Ann Willey

For full biographical listings, see the Martindale-Hubbell Law Directory

*GRAND RAPIDS,** Kent Co.

BREMER, WADE, NELSON, LOHR & COREY (AV)

600 Three Mile Road, N.W., 49504-1601
Telephone: 616-784-4434
Fax: 616-784-7322

MEMBERS OF FIRM

William M. Bremer
Michael D. Wade
Phillip J. Nelson
James H. Lohr
Michael J. Corey

ASSOCIATES

Michael S. Dantuma
J. Mark Cooney
Cheryl L. Bart
Barbara L. Olafsson

LEGAL SUPPORT PERSONNEL

Kathleen A. Fitzpatrick

For full biographical listings, see the Martindale-Hubbell Law Directory

BUCHANAN & BOS (AV)

300 Ottawa N.W., Suite 800, 49503
Telephone: 616-458-1224
Fax: 616-458-0608

MEMBERS OF FIRM

John C. Buchanan
Carole D. Bos
Bradley K. Glazier
Lee T. Silver

ASSOCIATES

Raymond S. Kent
Jane M. Beckering
Richard A. Stevens
Susan Wilson Keener
Gwen E. Buday
Anne M. Frye
Brian K. Lawson
Nancy K. Haynes

For full biographical listings, see the Martindale-Hubbell Law Directory

GRUEL, MILLS, NIMS AND PYLMAN (AV)

50 Monroe Place, Suite 700 West, 49503
Telephone: 616-235-5500
Fax: 616-235-5550

MEMBERS OF FIRM

Grant J. Gruel
William F. Mills
J. Clarke Nims
Norman H. Pylman, II
Scott R. Melton
Brion J. Brooks
Thomas R. Behm
J. Paul Janes

Representative Clients: Aquinas College; Bell Helmet Co.; Blodgett Memorial Medical Center; Butterworth Hospital; Chem Central, Inc.; Cook Pump Co.; Grove, Inc.; NBDC; Heim Corp.

For full biographical listings, see the Martindale-Hubbell Law Directory

SMITH, HAUGHEY, RICE & ROEGGE, P.C. (AV)

200 Calder Plaza Building, 250 Monroe Avenue, N.W., 49503-2251
Telephone: 616-774-8000
Telecopier: 616-774-2461
East Lansing, Michigan Office: 1301 North Hagadorn, 48823-2320.
Telephone: 517-332-3030.
Telecopier: 517-332-3468.
Traverse City, Michigan Office: 241 East State Street, P.O. Box 848, 49685-0804.
Telephone: 616-929-4878.
Telecopier: 616-929-4182.

(See Next Column)

Clifford A. Mitts (1902-1962)
Laurence D. Smith (1913-1980)
Robert V.V. Rice (1899-1982)
Michael S. Barnes (1944-1989)
L. Roland Roegge
Thomas F. Blackwell
P. Laurence Mulvihill
Lawrence P. Mulligan
Thomas R. Tasker
Paul H. Reinhardt
Lance R. Mather
Charles F. Behler
Gary A. Rowe
William W. Jack, Jr.
William J. Hondorp
Thomas M. Weibel
James G. Black
E. Thomas Mc Carthy, Jr.
Glenn W. House, Jr.
Thomas R. Wurst
Craig R. Noland
Paul M. Oleniczak
Craig S. Neckers
Thomas E. Kent
Leonard M. Hickey
David N. Campos
Anthony J. Quarto
Bruce P. Rissi
John C. O'Loughlin
John M. Kruis
Paul G. Van Oostenburg
Dale Ann Iverson
William R. Jewell
Jon D. Vander Ploeg
Patrick F. Geary
Terence J. Ackert
Brian J. Kilbane
Dan C. Porter
Brian J. Plachta
Phillip K. Mowers
Carol D. Carlson

Kay L. Griffith Hammond
Ann M. Stuursma
Richard E. Holmes, Jr.
Marilyn S. Nickell
Christopher R. Genther
Beth Suzanne Kromer
Lois Marie Ens
Paul D. Fox
Robert M. Kruse
Harriet M. Hageman
John B. Combs
Aileen M. Simet
Scott W. Morgan
Matthew L. Meyer
Bret M. Hanna
Carine J. Joachim
Todd W. Millar
Elizabeth Roberts VerHey
Jennifer Jane Nasser

OF COUNSEL

A. B. Smith, Jr.
David O. Haughey
Susan Bradley Jakubowski
Thomas P. Scholler

For full biographical listings, see the Martindale-Hubbell Law Directory

*KALAMAZOO,** Kalamazoo Co.

MILLER, CANFIELD, PADDOCK AND STONE, P.L.C. (AV)

A Professional Limited Liability Company
Founded in 1852 by Sidney Davy Miller
444 West Michigan Avenue, 49007-3752
Telephone: 616-381-7030
Fax: 616-382-0244
Detroit, Michigan Office: 150 West Jefferson, Suite 2500, 48226-4415.
Telephone: 313-963-6420.
Fax: 313-496-7500.
Cable Address: "Stem Detroit."
Ann Arbor, Michigan Office: 101 North Main Street, 7th Floor, 48104-1400.
Telephone: 313-663-2445.
Fax: 313-747-7147.
Bloomfield Hills, Michigan Office: Suite 100, Pinehurst Office Center, 1400 North Woodward, 48303-2014.
Telephone: 313-645-5000.
Fax: 313-645-1917.
Grand Rapids, Michigan Office: 1200 Campau Square Plaza, 99 Monroe, N.W., 49503-2639.
Telephone: 616-454-8656.
Fax: 616-776-6322.
Howell, Michigan Office: 121 South Barnard Street, Suite 4, 48843-2305.
Telephone: 517-546-7600.
Telecopier: 517-546-6974.
Lansing, Michigan Office: One Michigan Avenue, Suite 900, 48933-1609.
Telephone: 517-487-2070.
Fax: 517-374-6304.
Monroe, Michigan Office: The Executive Centre, 214 East Elm Avenue, 48161-2682.
Telephone: 313-243-2000.
Fax: 313-243-0901.
Washington, D.C. Office: 1225 Nineteenth Street, N.W., Suite 400. 20036.
Telephone: 202-429-5575; 785-0600.
Fax: 202-331-1118; 785-1234.
Pensacola, Florida Office: 25 West Cedar, 32501.
Telephone: 904-469-1088.
Fax: 904-432-0677.
St. Petersburg, Florida Office: 100 Second Avenue S., Suite 7045,33701.
Telephone: 813-982-6000.
Fax: 813-892-6002.
Gdansk, Poland Office: Suite 322, Dom Technika Building, Ul. Rajska 6, 80-850.
Telephone: 011-485-831-2808.
Fax: 011-485-831-4719.
Warsaw, Poland Office: Ul. Marszalkowska 82, Suite 561, 00-517.
Telephone: 011-482-623-6457 and 6458.
Fax: 011-482-623-6459.

(See Next Column)

MILLER, CANFIELD, PADDOCK AND STONE P.L.C., *Kalamazoo—Continued*

MEMBER OF FIRM

Charles E. Ritter (Resident)

Representative Firm Clients: Chrysler Corp.; Comerica, Inc.; City of Detroit, Mich.; Detroit Tigers, Inc.; First of Michigan; Fretter, Inc.; Ford Motor Co.; Ford Motor Credit Co.; Great Lakes Bancorp; Henry Ford Hospital.

For Complete List of Firm Personnel, See General Section

For full biographical listings, see the Martindale-Hubbell Law Directory

---

LANSING, Ingham Co.

CHURCH, KRITSELIS, WYBLE & ROBINSON, P.C. (AV)

3939 Capital City Boulevard, 48906-9962
Telephone: 517-323-4770

William N. Kritselis
J. Richard Robinson
James T. Heos
David S. Mittleman

D. Michael Dudley
Catherine Groll
James M. Hofer

For full biographical listings, see the Martindale-Hubbell Law Directory

DENFIELD, TIMMER, JAMO & O'LEARY (AV)

521 Seymour Avenue, 48933
Telephone: 517-371-3500
Fax: 517-371-4514

George H. Denfield
James A. Timmer
James S. Jamo
James S. O'Leary
Kathleen A. Lopilato

Representative Clients: Auto-Owners Insurance Co.; National Indemnity Insurance Co.; Travelers Insurance Co.; Ohio Farmers Insurance Co.; Bankers Life & Casualty Co.; Western Casualty & Surety Co.; Indiana Insurance Group; Western Surety Co.; Michigan Municipal League; Preston Trucking.

For full biographical listings, see the Martindale-Hubbell Law Directory

FRASER TREBILCOCK DAVIS & FOSTER, P.C. (AV)

1000 Michigan National Tower, 48933
Telephone: 517-482-5800
Fax: 517-482-0887
Okemos, Michigan Office: 2188 Commons Parkway.
Telephone: 517-349-1300.
Fax: 517-349-0922.

Joe C. Foster, Jr.
Eugene Townsend (1926-1982)
Ronald R. Pentecost
Donald A. Hines
Peter L. Dunlap
Everett R. Zack
Douglas J. Austin
Robert W. Stocker, II
Michael E. Cavanaugh
John J. Loose
David E. S. Marvin
Stephen L. Burlingame
C. Mark Hoover
Darrell A. Lindman
Ronald R. Sutton
Iris K. Socolofsky-Linder
Brett Jon Bean
Richard C. Lowe
Gary C. Rogers
Mark A. Bush
Michael H. Perry
Brandon W. Zuk
David D. Waddell
Thomas J. Waters

John E. Bos
Michael C. Levine
Mark R. Fox
Nancy L. Little
Sharon A. Bruner
Michael S. Ashton
Michael James Reilly
Michelyn E. Pastuer
Patrick K. Thornton
Charyn K. Hain
Brian D. Herrington
Michael J. Laramie
Marcy R. Meyer

OF COUNSEL

Archie C. Fraser
Everett R. Trebilcock
James R. Davis

Counsel for: Auto Club Insurance Assn. (ACIA); Auto Owners Insurance Co.; City of Mackinac Island; Federal Insurance Co.; General Motors Corp.; Grand Trunk Ry. Co.; Prudential Insurance Company of America; State Farm Automobile Insurance Co.

For full biographical listings, see the Martindale-Hubbell Law Directory

---

*MOUNT CLEMENS,** Macomb Co.

MARTIN, BACON & MARTIN, P.C. (AV)

44 First Street, 48043
Telephone: 810-979-6500
Fax: 810-468-7016

James N. Martin
John G. Bacon
Jonathan E. Martin
Paul R. VanTol
Michael R. Janes
Kevin L. Moffatt
John W. Crimando
Victor T. Van Camp

(See Next Column)

Deborah S. Forster

Reference: First National Bank of Mt. Clemens.

For full biographical listings, see the Martindale-Hubbell Law Directory

---

*MOUNT PLEASANT,** Isabella Co.

GRAY, SOWLE & IACCO, A PROFESSIONAL CORPORATION (AV)

600 East Broadway, 48858
Telephone: 517-772-5932
Fax: 517-773-0538

Loren E. Gray
Donald N. Sowle
Daniel A. Iacco

References: Isabella Bank & Trust; First of American of Mount Pleasant.

For full biographical listings, see the Martindale-Hubbell Law Directory

---

*SAGINAW,** Saginaw Co.

FORDNEY, DUST & PRINE (AV)

Suite 410 B Plaza North, 4800 Fashion Square Boulevard, P.O. Box 5289, 48603-0289
Telephone: 517-791-7060
Fax: 517-791-8009

J. Michael Fordney
Tobin H. Dust
Andrew W. Prine

For full biographical listings, see the Martindale-Hubbell Law Directory

---

*ST. JOSEPH,** Berrien Co.

GLOBENSKY, GLEISS, BITTNER & HYRNS, P.C. (AV)

610 Ship Street, P.O. Box 290, 49085
Telephone: 616-983-0551
FAX: 616-983-5858

H. S. Gray (1867-1961)
Luman H. Gray (1902-1952)
John L. Globensky
Henry W. Gleiss
Rodger V. Bittner
Randy S. Hyrns

J. Joseph Daly
Charles T. LaSata

LEGAL SUPPORT PERSONNEL

Robin J. Jollay

General Counsel for: Inter-City Bank; Southern Michigan Cold Storage Co.; Pearson Construction Co., Inc.
Approved Attorneys for: Lawyers Title Insurance Corp.
Reference: Inter-City Bank of Benton Harbor.

For full biographical listings, see the Martindale-Hubbell Law Directory

---

SOUTHFIELD, Oakland Co.

FIEGER, FIEGER & SCHWARTZ, A PROFESSIONAL CORPORATION (AV)

19390 West Ten Mile Road, 48075-2463
Telephone: 810-355-5555
FAX: 810-355-5148

Bernard J. Fieger (1922-1988)
Geoffrey N. Fieger
Michael Alan Schwartz
Dennis Fuller
Pamela A. Hamway
Dean W. Amburn
Ronald S. Glaser
Gary S. Fields
Todd J. Weglarz

OF COUNSEL

Barry Fayne
Stephen L. Witenoff
Beverly Hires Brode

For full biographical listings, see the Martindale-Hubbell Law Directory

HIGHLAND & ZANETTI (AV)

Suite 205, 24445 Northwestern Highway, 48075
Telephone: 810-352-9580

John N. Highland
J. R. Zanetti, Jr.
R. Michael John

Duncan Hall Brown
Joseph M. LaBella
James S. Meyerand

For full biographical listings, see the Martindale-Hubbell Law Directory

O'LEARY, O'LEARY, JACOBS, MATTSON, PERRY & MASON, P.C. (AV)

26777 Central Park Boulevard, Suite 275, 48076
Telephone: 810-799-8260

(See Next Column)

O'LEARY, O'LEARY, JACOBS, MATTSON, PERRY & MASON P.C.—*Continued*

John Patrick O'Leary
Thomas M. O'Leary
John P. Jacobs
Kenneth M. Mattson
C. Kenneth Perry, Jr.
Larry G. Mason
D. Jennifer Andreou
Kevin P. Hanbury
Debra A. Reed

For full biographical listings, see the Martindale-Hubbell Law Directory

SCHWARTZ & JALKANEN, P.C. (AV)

Suite 200, 24400 Northwestern Highway, 48075
Telephone: 810-352-2555
Facsimile: 810-352-5963

Melvin R. Schwartz
Arthur W. Jalkanen
Karl Eric Hannum

Anne Loridas Randall
Deborah L. Laura
Lisa M. Green

For full biographical listings, see the Martindale-Hubbell Law Directory

SOMMERS, SCHWARTZ, SILVER & SCHWARTZ, P.C. (AV)

2000 Town Center, Suite 900, 48075
Telephone: 810-355-0300
Telecopier: 810-746-4001
Plymouth, Michigan Office: 747 South Main Street.
Telephone: 313-455-4250.

Stanley S. Schwartz
Jeffrey N. Shillman
Jeremy L. Winer
David R. Getto
Norman D. Tucker
Paul W. Hines
Stephen N. Leuchtman
Richard D. Fox
Frank Mafrice
Richard L. Groffsky
David J. Winter
B. A. Tyler
Michael J. Cunningham
Matthew G. Curtis
Helen K. Joyner
John L. Runco
Susanne Pryce
David J. Shea
Anne M. Schoepfle
Gary D. Dodds
Kenneth T. Watkins
James A. Carlin

OF COUNSEL

Howard Silver

General Counsel for: City of Taylor; Foodland Distributors; C.A. Muer Corporation; Vlasic & Company; Nederlander Corporation; Woodland Physicians; Midwest Health Centers, P.C.
Representative Clients: Crum & Forster Insurance Company; City of Pontiac; Michigan National Bank; Perry Drugs.

For Complete List of Firm Personnel, See General Section

For full biographical listings, see the Martindale-Hubbell Law Directory

*TRAVERSE CITY,** Grand Traverse Co.

SMITH, HAUGHEY, RICE & ROEGGE, P.C. (AV)

241 East State Street, P.O. Box 848, 49685-0848
Telephone: 616-929-4878
Telecopier: 616-929-4182
Grand Rapids, Michigan Office: 200 Calder Plaza Building, 250 Monroe Avenue, N.W., 49503-2251.
Telephone: 616-774-8000.
Telecopier: 616-774-2461.
East Lansing, Michigan Office: 1301 North Hagadorn, 48823-2320.
Telephone: 517-332-3030.
Telecopier: 517-332-3468.

George Frederick Bearup
Mark P. Bickel
P. David Vinocur
R. Jay Hardin
Robert W. Tubbs
Robert M. Faulkner

Thomas C. Kates
John R. Vander Veen
Mark D. Williams
Jeffrey R. Wonacott
Ann M. Kling

For full biographical listings, see the Martindale-Hubbell Law Directory

THOMPSON, PARSONS & O'NEIL (AV)

309 East Front Street, P.O. Box 429, 49685
Telephone: 616-929-9700; 1-800-678-1307
Fax: 616-929-7262

MEMBERS OF FIRM

George R. Thompson
Grant W. Parsons
Daniel P. O'Neil

William J. Brooks

For full biographical listings, see the Martindale-Hubbell Law Directory

TROY, Oakland Co.

HOLAHAN, MALLOY, MAYBAUGH & MONNICH (AV)

Suite 100, 2690 Crooks Road, 48084-4700
Telephone: 810-362-4747
Fax: 810-362-4779
East Tawas, Michigan Office: 910 East Bay Street.
Telephone: 517-362-4747.
Fax: 517-362-7331.

MEMBERS OF FIRM

J. Michael Malloy, III
James D. Maybaugh
John R. Monnich
David L. Delie, Jr.
William J. Kliffel

OF COUNSEL

Thomas H. O'Connor
Maureen Holahan (Retired; Resident, East Tawas Office)

For full biographical listings, see the Martindale-Hubbell Law Directory

WEST BLOOMFIELD, Oakland Co.

CHEATHAM ACKER & SHARP, P.C. (AV)

5777 West Maple Road, Suite 130, P.O. Box 255002, 48325-5002
Telephone: 810-932-2000

Charles C. Cheatham
Lawrence J. Acker
Gary D. Sharp

William E. Osantowski
Tracy A. Leahy
Jody D. Klask
John M. Mooney
Mary E. Hollman
Adam K. Gordon

COUNSEL

Lynn L. Lower
Kyle B. Mansfield (Not admitted in MI)

For full biographical listings, see the Martindale-Hubbell Law Directory

MINNESOTA

*MINNEAPOLIS,** Hennepin Co.

HVASS, WEISMAN & KING, CHARTERED (AV)

Suite 450, 100 South Fifth Street, 55402
Telephone: 612-333-0201
FAX: 612-342-2606

Charles T. Hvass (Retired)
Si Weisman (1912-1992)
Robert J. King
Frank J. Brixius
Richard A. Williams, Jr.
Charles T. Hvass, Jr.
Robert J. King, Jr.
Michael W. Unger

John E. Daly
John M. Dornik
Mark T. Porter

For full biographical listings, see the Martindale-Hubbell Law Directory

MESHBESHER & SPENCE, LTD. (AV)

1616 Park Avenue, 55404
Telephone: 612-339-9121
Fax: 612-339-9188
St. Paul, Minnesota Office: World Trade Center.
Telephone: 612-227-0799.
St. Cloud, Minnesota Office: 400 Zapp Bank Plaza.
Telephone: 612-656-0484.

Kenneth Meshbesher
Ronald I. Meshbesher
Russell M. Spence (Resident, St. Paul Office)
James H. Gilbert
John P. Clifford
Dennis R. Johnson
Jack Nordby
Paul W. Bergstrom (Resident, St. Paul Office)
Patrick K. Horan (Resident, St. Paul Office)
Daniel J. Boivin
Michael C. Snyder
James A. Wellner
John P. Sheehy
Mark D. Streed
Randall Spence
Howard I. Bass
Daniel C. Guerrero
Katherine S. Flom
Pamela R. Finney
Jeffrey P. Oistad (Resident, St. Cloud Office)
Jeffrey A. Olson
Daniel E. Meshbesher
Anthony J. Nemo
Colleen M. Christianson
Russell Spence, Jr.

For full biographical listings, see the Martindale-Hubbell Law Directory

SIEBEN, GROSE, VON HOLTUM, MCCOY & CAREY, LTD. (AV)

900 Midwest Plaza East, 800 Marquette Avenue, 55402
Telephone: 612-333-4500
Fairfax, Minnesota Office: 117 South Park Street.
Telephone: 507-426-8211.

(See Next Column)

SIEBEN, GROSE, VON HOLTUM, MCCOY & CAREY LTD., *Minneapolis—Continued*

Duluth, Minnesota Office: 220 Missabe Building.
Telephone: 218-722-6848. Toll Free (Minnesota): 800-422-0612.

Harry A. Sieben, Jr. | John W. Carey

For full biographical listings, see the Martindale-Hubbell Law Directory

*ST. PAUL,** Ramsey Co.

GERAGHTY, O'LOUGHLIN & KENNEY, PROFESSIONAL ASSOCIATION (AV)

One Capital Centre Plaza, Suite 1400, 55102-1308
Telephone: 612-291-1177
Fax: 612-297-6901

Terence J. O'Loughlin
James R. Gowling
Robert M. Mahoney
David C. Hutchinson
Timothy R. Murphy
William H. Leary, III
Richard J. Thomas

OF COUNSEL

James H. Geraghty
James W. Kenney (Retired)

Representative Clients: St. Paul Fire & Marine Insurance Cos.; Midwest Medical Insurance Co.; Minnesota Lawyers Mutual Insurance Co.; University of Minnesota Hospitals; American National Bank and Trust Co.; Continental National American Group; Commercial State Bank; MMI Co.; Hammel Green Abrahamson, Inc.; Lunda Construction Co.

For full biographical listings, see the Martindale-Hubbell Law Directory

MISSISSIPPI

BILOXI, Harrison Co.

PAGE, MANNINO & PERESICH (AV)

759 Vieux Marché Mall, P.O. Drawer 289, 39530
Telephone: 601-374-2100
Telecopier: 601-432-5539
Jackson, Mississippi Office: One LeFleurs Square, 4735 Old Canton Road, P.O. Box 12159.
Telephone: 601-364-1100.
Telecopier: 601-364-1118.
Gulfport, Mississippi Office: Markham Building, 2301 - 14th Street, Suite 600, Drawer 660.
Telephone: 601-863-8861.
Telecopier: 601-863-8871.

MEMBERS OF FIRM

Lyle M. Page
Frederick J. Mannino
Ronald G. Peresich
Michael B. McDermott
Stephen G. Peresich
Jess H. Dickinson
Tere Richardson Steel
David S. Raines
Michael P. Collins
Randolph Cook Wood
Mary A. Nichols
Joseph Henry Ros
Thomas William Busby
Michael E. Whitehead
Katharine Malley Samson
Douglas J. Wise

Representative Clients: United States Fidelity & Guaranty Co.; St. Paul Fire & Marine Insurance Co.; Crawford & Co.; Anheuser-Busch Corp.
General Counsel for: Peoples Bank of Biloxi, Mississippi; Biloxi Regional Medical Center; Bank of Mississippi (Gulf Coast Division).

For full biographical listings, see the Martindale-Hubbell Law Directory

*CLARKSDALE,** Coahoma Co.

MERKEL & COCKE, A PROFESSIONAL ASSOCIATION (AV)

30 Delta Avenue, P.O. Box 1388, 38614
Telephone: 601-627-9641
Fax: 601-627-3592

Charles M. Merkel
John H. Cocke
Walter Stephens Cox
Cynthia I. Mitchell
William B. Raiford, III
Jack R. Dodson, Jr.

Reference: United Southern Bank, Clarksdale, Miss.

For full biographical listings, see the Martindale-Hubbell Law Directory

*GULFPORT,** Harrison Co.

PAGE, MANNINO & PERESICH (AV)

Markham Building, 2301 14th Street, Suite 600, Drawer 660, 39501-2095
Telephone: 601-863-8861
Telecopier: 601-863-8871
Biloxi, Mississippi Office: 759 Vieux MarchéMall, P.O. Drawer 289.
Telephone: 601-374-2100.
Telecopier: 601-432-5539.

(See Next Column)

Jackson, Mississippi Office: One Lefleurs Square, 4735 Old Canton Road, P.O. Box 12159.
Telephone: 601-364-1100.
Telecopier: 601-364-1118.

MEMBERS OF FIRM

Lyle M. Page
Frederick J. Mannino
Ronald G. Peresich
Michael B. McDermott
Stephen G. Peresich
Jess H. Dickinson
Tere Richardson Steel
David S. Raines
Michael P. Collins
Randolph Cook Wood
Mary A. Nichols
Joseph Henry Ros
Thomas William Busby
Michael E. Whitehead
Katharine Malley Samson
Douglas J. Wise

Representative Clients: United States Fidelity & Guaranty Co.; St. Paul Fire & Marine Insurance Co.; Crawford & Co.; Anheuser-Busch Corp.
General Counsel for: Peoples Bank of Biloxi, Mississippi; Biloxi Regional Medical Center; Bank of Mississippi (Gulf Coast Division).

For full biographical listings, see the Martindale-Hubbell Law Directory

*HERNANDO,** De Soto Co.

GERALD W. CHATHAM, SR. (AV)

291 Losher Street, 38632
Telephone: 601-429-9871
Telecopier: 601-429-0242

ASSOCIATE

Claude M. Purvis

Representative Clients: Allstate Insurance Co.; Ranger Insurance Co.; Paracelsus Senatobia Community Hospital; National Bank of Commerce, Memphis, TN; Balboa Insurance Co.; Wausau Insurance Co.; Premier Alliance Insurance Co.; Nationwide Insurance Co.; Alumax Extrusions, Inc.; National Home Insurance Co.

For full biographical listings, see the Martindale-Hubbell Law Directory

*JACKSON,** Hinds Co.

MARKOW, WALKER, REEVES & ANDERSON, P.A. (AV)

Atrium North Building, 805 South Wheatley, Suite 400, P.O. Box 13669, 39236-3669
Telephone: 601-956-8500
Telecopier: 601-956-8423

Peter J. Markow, Jr.
Christopher J. Walker
William C. Reeves
James M. Anderson
Terry B. Germany
Michael T. Estep
Richard C. Coker
Gilson Davis (Dave) Peterson
Alfonso Nuzzo

Joseph W. McDowell
Richard M. Edmonson, Jr.
Hubert Wesley Williams, III.
L. Pepper Cossar
Delia Y. Robinson
T.G. Bolen, Jr.
Alan C. Goodman

Reference: The Sunburst Bank, Jackson, Miss.

For full biographical listings, see the Martindale-Hubbell Law Directory

PAGE, MANNINO & PERESICH (AV)

One LeFleurs Square, 4735 Old Canton Road, P.O. Box 12159, 39236-2159
Telephone: 601-364-1100
Telecopier: 601-364-1118
Biloxi, Mississippi Office: 759 Vieux MarchéMall, P.O. Drawer 289.
Telephone: 601-374-2100.
Telecopier: 601-432-5539.
Gulfport, Mississippi Office: Markham Building, 2301 - 14th Street, Suite 600, P.O. Drawer 660.
Telephone: 601-863-8861.
Telecopier: 601-863-8871.

MEMBERS OF FIRM

Lyle M. Page
Frederick J. Mannino
Ronald G. Peresich
Michael B. McDermott
Stephen G. Peresich
Jess H. Dickinson
Tere Richardson Steel
David S. Raines
Michael P. Collins
Randolph Cook Wood
Mary A. Nichols
Joseph Henry Ros
Thomas William Busby
Michael E. Whitehead
Katharine Malley Samson
Douglas J. Wise (Not admitted in MS)

Representative Clients: United States Fidelity & Guaranty Co.; St. Paul Fire & Marine Insurance Co.; Crawford & Co.; Anheuser-Busch Corp.
General Counsel for: Peoples Bank of Biloxi, Mississippi; Biloxi Regional Medical Center; Bank of Mississippi (Gulf Coast Division).

For full biographical listings, see the Martindale-Hubbell Law Directory

Jackson—Continued

STEEN REYNOLDS DALEHITE & CURRIE (AV)

Mississippi Valley Title Building, 315 Tombigbee Street, P.O. Box 900, 39205
Telephone: 601-969-7054
Telecopier: 601-969-5120

MEMBERS OF FIRM

Jimmie B. Reynolds, Jr.
William M. Dalehite, Jr.
Edward J. Currie, Jr.
Whitman B. Johnson, III
William C. Griffin
Philip W. Gaines
Michael F. Myers

ASSOCIATES

Frances R. Shields
William H. Creel, Jr.
James C. Smallwood, III
F. Keith Ball
Shannon S. Clark
Lisa L. Williams
Le Robinson Brown

OF COUNSEL

Jerome B. Steen

Mississippi Counsel for: State Farm Insurance Co.
Representative Clients include: Allstate Insurance Co.; St. Paul Insurance Cos.; Indiana Lumbermens Mutual Insurance Co.; United Services Automobile Assn.; Empire Fire & Marine Ins.; Sears Roebuck & Co.
References: Trustmark National Bank, Jackson, Mississippi.

For full biographical listings, see the Martindale-Hubbell Law Directory

WISE CARTER CHILD & CARAWAY, PROFESSIONAL ASSOCIATION (AV)

600 Heritage Building, 401 East Capitol Street, P.O. Box 651, 39205
Telephone: 601-968-5500
FAX: 601-968-5519

George Q. Evans
Douglas E. Levanway
Mark P. Caraway
George H. Ritter
R. Mark Hodges

Representative Clients: St. Paul Fire and Marine Insurance Co.; Virginia Insurance Reciprocal; Professional Risk Management Services; Medical Assurance Company of Mississippi.

For Complete List of Firm Personnel, See General Section

For full biographical listings, see the Martindale-Hubbell Law Directory

*PASCAGOULA,** Jackson Co.

COLINGO, WILLIAMS, HEIDELBERG, STEINBERGER & McELHANEY, P.A. (AV)

711 Delmas Avenue, P.O. Box 1407, 39568-0240
Telephone: 601-762-8021
FAX: 601-762-7589

Joe R. Colingo
Roy C. Williams
James H. Heidelberg
Karl R. Steinberger
Michael J. McElhaney, Jr.
James H. Colmer, Jr.
Robert W. Wilkinson
Brett K. Williams

Carol S. Noblitt
Karen N. Haarala
Stephen Walker Burrow
Scott D. Smith
Gina L. Bardwell

LEGAL SUPPORT PERSONNEL

Harry H. Carpenter

Representative Clients: International Paper Co.; R.J. Reynolds; Westinghouse Corp.; St. Paul Fire & Marine Ins. Co.; Kemper Group; Singing River Hospital System.

For full biographical listings, see the Martindale-Hubbell Law Directory

*TUPELO,** Lee Co.

HOLLAND, RAY & UPCHURCH, P.A. (AV)

322 Jefferson Street, P.O. Drawer 409, 38802
Telephone: 601-842-1721
Facsimile: 601-844-6413

Sam E. Lumpkin (1908-1964)
Ralph L. Holland
James Hugh Ray
Robert K. Upchurch
W. Reed Hillen, III
Thomas A. Wicker

Michael D. Tapscott

Representative Clients: The Travelers; Continental Casualty Co.; South Central Bell Telephone Co.; The Greyhound Corp.; Mississippi Valley Gas Co.; Bryan-Rogers, Inc.; The Housing Authority of the City of Tupelo; Action Industries, Inc.; American Cable Systems, Inc.; American Funeral Assurance Co.

For full biographical listings, see the Martindale-Hubbell Law Directory

MISSOURI

KANSAS CITY, Jackson, Clay & Platte Cos.

BARTIMUS, KAVANAUGH & FRICKLETON, A PROFESSIONAL CORPORATION (AV)

23rd Floor City Center Square, 1100 Main Street, 64105
Telephone: 816-842-2300
FAX: 816-421-2111

James R. Bartimus
Paul F. Kavanaugh
James P. Frickleton
Kirk R. Presley

OF COUNSEL

Max W. Foust

LEGAL SUPPORT PERSONNEL

LEGAL ASSISTANTS

Janet L. Smith-Lierman
Tammy J. Gilliams
Stephanie Lang
Laura M. Burbach
Arnella R. McNichols

For full biographical listings, see the Martindale-Hubbell Law Directory

HANOVER & TURNER (AV)

700 Commerce Trust Building, 922 Walnut Street, 64106
Telephone: 816-221-2888
Fax: 816-221-4453

MEMBERS OF FIRM

Hollis H. Hanover
John E. Turner

For full biographical listings, see the Martindale-Hubbell Law Directory

REDFEARN & BROWN, A PROFESSIONAL CORPORATION (AV)

Suite 814, 1125 Grand Avenue, 64106
Telephone: 816-421-5301
FAX: 816-421-3785

Paul L. Redfearn
Daniel R. Brown

For full biographical listings, see the Martindale-Hubbell Law Directory

ST. LOUIS, (Independent City)

GREENBERG & PLEBAN (AV)

100 South Fourth Street, Suite 600, 63102
Telephone: 314-241-4141
Telecopier: 314-241-1038

Burton M. Greenberg
C. John Pleban

ASSOCIATES

Karen A. Greenberg
George A. Kiser
Michael J. Schaller

OF COUNSEL

Sarah Shelledy Pleban

Reference: Boatmen's National Bank.

For full biographical listings, see the Martindale-Hubbell Law Directory

PADBERG, McSWEENEY, SLATER & MERZ, A PROFESSIONAL CORPORATION (AV)

Suite 800, 1015 Locust Street, 63101
Telephone: 314-621-3787
Telecopier: 314-621-7396

Godfrey P. Padberg
Edward P. McSweeney
R. J. Slater
Charles L. Merz

Richard J. Burke, Jr.
Matthew J. Padberg
James P. Leonard
Anthony J. Soukenik
Thomas C. Simon
Mary K. Munroe
Marty Daesch

For full biographical listings, see the Martindale-Hubbell Law Directory

MONTANA

*BILLINGS,** Yellowstone Co.

CROWLEY, HAUGHEY, HANSON, TOOLE & DIETRICH (AV)

500 Transwestern II, 490 North 31st Street, P.O. Box 2529, 59103
Telephone: 406-252-3441
Fax: 406-259-4159
Helena, Montana Office: IBM Building, 100 North Park Avenue, Suite 300, 59601.
Telephone: 406-449-4165.
Fax: 406-449-5149.

(See Next Column)

CROWLEY, HAUGHEY, HANSON, TOOLE & DIETRICH, *Billings—Continued*

MEMBERS OF FIRM

Herbert I. Pierce, III
Ronald R. Lodders
Joe C. Maynard, Jr.

ASSOCIATE

Steven Robert Milch

Representative Clients: Montana Power Co.; First Interstate Bank of Commerce; MDU Resources Group, Inc.; Chevron U.S.A., Inc.; Noranda Minerals Corp.; United Parcel Service.
Insurance Clients: Farmers Insurance Group; New York Life Insurance Co.

For Complete List of Firm Personnel, See General Section

For full biographical listings, see the Martindale-Hubbell Law Directory

NEVADA

*LAS VEGAS,** Clark Co.

ALVERSON, TAYLOR, MORTENSEN & NELSON (AV)

3821 W. Charleston Boulevard, 89102
Telephone: 702-384-7000
FAX: 702-385-7000

MEMBERS OF FIRM

J. Bruce Alverson
Eric K. Taylor
David J. Mortensen
Erven T. Nelson
LeAnn Sanders
David R. Clayson

ASSOCIATES

Milton J. Eichacker
Douglas D. Gerrard
Marie Ellerton
James H. Randall
Peter Dubowsky
Hayley B. Chambers
Michael D. Stevenson
Cookie Lea Olshein
Kenneth M. Marias
Jeffrey H. Ballin
Jeffrey W. Daly
Kenneth R. Ivory
Edward D. Boyack
Sandra Smagac
Jill M. Chase
Francis F. Lin

Representative Clients: St. Paul Fire & Marine Insurance Company; The Doctors' Company; Medical Insurance Exchange of California (MIEC); MEDMARC; National Chiropractic Mutual Insurance Company; Lake Mead Hospital Medical Center; University Medical Center of Southern Nevada; American Healthcare Management; Ophthalmic Mutual Insurance Company; Osteopathic Mutual Insurance Company.

For full biographical listings, see the Martindale-Hubbell Law Directory

GALATZ, EARL & BULLA (AV)

710 South Fourth Street, 89101
Telephone: 702-386-0000
Fax: 702-384-0394

Neil G. Galatz
Allan R. Earl
Bonnie A. Bulla

For full biographical listings, see the Martindale-Hubbell Law Directory

GARY LOGAN (AV)

Third Floor, First Interstate Bank Building, 302 East Carson Avenue, 89101
Telephone: 702-385-9900
Telecopier: 702-382-4800

OF COUNSEL

Richard I. Feinberg

References: Bank of America-Nevada; The Chase Manhattan Bank, N.A.

For full biographical listings, see the Martindale-Hubbell Law Directory

VANNAH COSTELLO HOWARD & CANEPA (AV)

A Partnership including a Professional Corporation
Greystone, 1850 East Flamingo, Suite 236, 89119
Telephone: 702-369-4161
Fax: 702-369-0104

MEMBERS OF FIRM

Robert D. Vannah (Chartered)
Nathan M. Costello
James W. Howard, Jr.
Scott K. Canepa

ASSOCIATE

Jerry A. Wiese

Representative Clients: Prudential Property and Casualty Insurance Co.; USF&G Co.; CNA; OUM Group Insurance Co.; American Golf Corp.; Reliance Insurance Co.

For full biographical listings, see the Martindale-Hubbell Law Directory

NEW HAMPSHIRE

*CONCORD,** Merrimack Co.

RATH, YOUNG, PIGNATELLI AND OYER, P.A. (AV)

Two Capital Plaza, P.O. Box 854, 03302-0854
Telephone: 603-226-2600
Telecopier: 603-226-2700; 228-2294
Nashua, New Hampshire Office: The Glass Tower, 20 Trafalgar Square.
Telephone: 603-889-9952.
Telecopier: 603-595-7489.

Thomas D. Rath
Sherilyn Burnett Young
Michael A. Pignatelli
Eve H. Oyer
Ann McLane Kuster
David M. Howe
William F. J. Ardinger
M. Curtis Whittaker
Andrew W. Serell
Brian T. Tucker
Constance P. Powers
Andrew J. Harmon
Charles George Willing, Jr.
Diane Murphy Quinlan
Elise S. Feldman
Ian D. Hecker

LEGAL SUPPORT PERSONNEL

Eugene A. Savage
Lindsey Dalton

For full biographical listings, see the Martindale-Hubbell Law Directory

*MANCHESTER,** Hillsborough Co.

ABRAMSON, REIS AND BROWN (AV)

1819 Elm Street, 03104
Telephone: 603-647-0300
Fax: 603-666-4227
Nashua, New Hampshire Office: 11 Concord Street.
Telephone: 603-886-0308.

MEMBERS OF FIRM

Stanley M. Brown
Kenneth C. Brown
Randolph J. Reis
Mark A. Abramson
Kevin F. Dugan

For full biographical listings, see the Martindale-Hubbell Law Directory

NEW JERSEY

CHATHAM, Morris Co.

O'CONNOR & RHATICAN, A PROFESSIONAL CORPORATION (AV)

383 Main Street, 07928
Telephone: 201-635-2210
FAX: 201-635-2622

Gerald B. O'Connor
Peter E. Rhatican
Vivian Demas

Paul A. O'Connor, III

OF COUNSEL

Patricia J. Cooney

For full biographical listings, see the Martindale-Hubbell Law Directory

CRANFORD, Union Co.

MCCREEDY AND COX (AV)

Second Floor, Six Commerce Drive, 07016-3509
Telephone: 908-709-0400
Fax: 908-709-0405

MEMBERS OF FIRM

Edwin J. McCreedy
Robert F. Cox

ASSOCIATE

Patrick J. Hermesmann

Reference: United Counties Trust Co.

For full biographical listings, see the Martindale-Hubbell Law Directory

*HACKENSACK,** Bergen Co.

BRESLIN AND BRESLIN, P.A. (AV)

41 Main Street, 07601
Telephone: 201-342-4014; 342-4015
Fax: 201-342-0068; 201-342-3077

John J. Breslin, Jr. (1899-1987)
James A. Breslin, Sr. (1900-1980)
Charles Rodgers
E. Carter Corriston
Donald A. Caminiti

(See Next Column)

BRESLIN AND BRESLIN P.A.—*Continued*

Michael T. Fitzpatrick
Angelo A. Bello
Terrence J. Corriston
Kevin C. Corriston
Karen Boe Gatlin
Lawrence Farber
E. Carter Corriston, Jr.

Representative Clients: Bergen County Housing Authority; Phillips Fuel Co.; Prudential Insurance Co.; Rent Leveling Board of Township of North Bergen; Housing Authority of Passaic.
Reference: United Jersey Bank.

For Complete List of Firm Personnel, See General Section

For full biographical listings, see the Martindale-Hubbell Law Directory

HEIN, SMITH, BEREZIN, MALOOF & ROGERS (AV)

Court Plaza East, 19 Main Street, 07601-7023
Telephone: 201-487-7400
Telecopier: 201-487-4228

MEMBERS OF FIRM

Allan H. Rogers
Robert L. Baum
Lawrence H. Jacobs

ASSOCIATES

John L. Shanahan
Marian H. Speid

Representative Clients: Aetna Insurance Co.; Commercial Union of New York; Employers of Wausau; Great American Insurance Cos.; Hanover Insurance Co.; Health Care Insurance Co.; Merchants Mutual Insurance Co.; St. Paul Fire & Marine Insurance Co.; U.S. Fidelity & Guaranty Co.
Reference: United Jersey Bank.

For Complete List of Firm Personnel, See General Section

For full biographical listings, see the Martindale-Hubbell Law Directory

LIVINGSTON, Essex Co.

PHILIP M. LUSTBADER & DAVID LUSTBADER A PROFESSIONAL CORPORATION (AV)

615 West Mount Pleasant Avenue, 07039
Telephone: 201-740-1000
Fax: 201-740-1520

Philip M. Lustbader
David Lustbader

John N. Holly
John L. Riordan, Jr.

OF COUNSEL

Robert J. McKenna

For full biographical listings, see the Martindale-Hubbell Law Directory

MILLBURN, Essex Co.

MCDERMOTT & MCGEE (AV)

64 Main Street, P.O. Box 192, 07041-0192
Telephone: 201-467-8080
FAX: 201-467-0012

MEMBERS OF FIRM

John L. McDermott
John P. McGee
Richard P. Maggi
Thomas A. Wester
Richard A. Tango
Frank P. Leanza
John L. McDermott, Jr.

ASSOCIATES

Lawrence G. Tosi
David J. Dickinson
A. Charles Lorenzo
Robert A. McDermott
Kevin John McGee

OF COUNSEL

Daniel K. Van Dorn

Representative Clients: Allstate Insurance Co.; American Hardware Mutual Insurance Co.; Argonaut Insurance Cos.; Continental Insurance Cos.; Commercial Union Insurance Cos.; General Accident Group; Maryland-American General Group; Zurich-American Insurance Co.; P.C.M. Intermediaries, Ltd.; The Hanover Insurance Cos.

For full biographical listings, see the Martindale-Hubbell Law Directory

MOORESTOWN, Burlington Co.

CHIERICI & WRIGHT, A PROFESSIONAL CORPORATION (AV)

Blason Campus - III, 509 South Lenola Road Building Six, 08057-1561
Telephone: 609-234-6300
Fax: 609-234-9490

(See Next Column)

Donald R. Chierici, Jr.
David B. Wright
Elizabeth Coleman Chierici
Julie C. Smith
Sheri Nelson Oliano
Jaunice M. Canning
Rhonda J. Eiger
Michael A. Foresta
Linda M. Novosel

For full biographical listings, see the Martindale-Hubbell Law Directory

*MORRISTOWN,** Morris Co.

MASKALERIS & ASSOCIATES (AV)

30 Court Street, 07960
Telephone: 201-267-0222
Newark, New Jersey Office: Federal Square Station, P.O. Box 20207.
Telephone: 201-622-4300.
Far Hills, New Jersey Office: Route 202 Station Plaza.
Telephone: 201-234-0600.
New York, New York Office: 123 Bank Street.
Telephone: 212-724-8669.
Athens, Greece Office: Stadio 28, Fourth Floor.
Telephone: 322-6790.

Stephen N. Maskaleris

ASSOCIATES

Peter C. Ioannou
Christopher P. Luongo

For full biographical listings, see the Martindale-Hubbell Law Directory

STEPHEN S. WEINSTEIN A PROFESSIONAL CORPORATION (AV)

20 Park Place, Suite 301, 07960
Telephone: 201-267-5200
FAX: 201-538-1779

Stephen S. Weinstein

Gail S. Boertzel
Peter N. Gilbreth
William A. Johnson
Melissa H. Luce

For full biographical listings, see the Martindale-Hubbell Law Directory

*NEWARK,** Essex Co.

BROWN & BROWN, P.C. (AV)

One Gateway Center, Fifth Floor, 07102
Telephone: 201-622-1846
Fax: 201-622-2223
Jersey City, New Jersey Office:
Telephone: 201-656-2381.

Raymond A. Brown
Raymond M. Brown

Reference: National Westminster Bank, NJ.

For full biographical listings, see the Martindale-Hubbell Law Directory

LAW OFFICES OF IRA J. ZARIN (AV)

One Gateway Center, Suite 1612, 07102
Telephone: 201-622-3533
Telecopier: 201-622-1338

ASSOCIATE

Jeffrey E. Strauss

For full biographical listings, see the Martindale-Hubbell Law Directory

RED BANK, Monmouth Co.

PHILIP G. AUERBACH A PROFESSIONAL CORPORATION (AV)

231 Maple Avenue, P.O. Box Y, 07701
Telephone: 908-842-6660

Philip G. Auerbach

Edward A. Genz
John J. Ryan

For full biographical listings, see the Martindale-Hubbell Law Directory

ROSELAND, Essex Co.

POST, POLAK, GOODSELL & MACNEILL, P.A. (AV)

65 Livingston Avenue, 07068
Telephone: 201-994-1100
Telecopier: 201-994-1705
New York, New York Office: Suite 1006, 575 Madison Avenue.
Telephone: 212-486-1455.

Jay Scott MacNeill

Peter A. Bogaard
Lauren F. Koffler

For full biographical listings, see the Martindale-Hubbell Law Directory

SPRINGFIELD, Union Co.

McDONOUGH, KORN & EICHHORN, A PROFESSIONAL CORPORATION (AV)

Park Place Legal Center, 959 South Springfield Avenue, P.O. Box 712, 07081-0712
Telephone: 201-912-9099
Fax: 201-912-8604

Peter L. Korn
James R. Korn
R. Scott Eichhorn
William S. Mezzomo

Timothy J. Jaeger
Wilfred P. Coronato
Dona Feeney
Gail R. Arkin
Karen M. Lerner
Nancy Crosta Landale
Christopher K. Costa

OF COUNSEL

Robert P. McDonough

Representative Clients: Chubb; Medical Inter-Insurance Exchange of New Jersey; Medical Liability Mutual Insurance Co.; Columbia Presbyterian Medical Center; Greater New York Blood Center; University of Medicine and Dentistry of New Jersey; Wausau Insurance Co.; New Jersey Property-Liability Ins. Guaranty Assoc.; Cigna Insurance; National Chiropractic Mutual Ins. Co.
Reference: United Counties Trust Company.

For full biographical listings, see the Martindale-Hubbell Law Directory

*TRENTON,** Mercer Co.

DESTRIBATS, CAMPBELL, DESANTIS & MAGEE (AV)

247 White Horse Avenue, 08610
Telephone: 609-585-2443
Telefax: 609-585-9508

MEMBERS OF FIRM

Jay G. Destribats
Dennis M. DeSantis
Bernard A. Campbell, Jr.
Michael H. Magee

ASSOCIATE

Daniel J. O'Donnell

OF COUNSEL

Henry F. Gill

For full biographical listings, see the Martindale-Hubbell Law Directory

DEVLIN, CITTADINO & SHAW, P.C. (AV)

3131 Princeton Pike, Building 1-A, 08648
Telephone: 609-896-2222
Fax: 609-896-2279

Robert A. Shaw (1964-1992)
John W. Devlin
Benjamin N. Cittadino

John G. Devlin

Reference: United Jersey Bank.

For full biographical listings, see the Martindale-Hubbell Law Directory

LENOX, SOCEY, WILGUS, FORMIDONI & CASEY (AV)

3131 Princeton Pike, 08648
Telephone: 609-896-2000
Fax: 609-895-1693

MEMBERS OF FIRM

Samuel D. Lenox (1897-1975)
Roland R. Formidoni
Rudolph A. Socey, Jr.
Robert P. Casey
George Wilgus, III
Thomas M. Brown
Gregory J. Giordano

ASSOCIATE

Elizabeth L. Tolkach
Denise M. Mariani

Representative Clients: Royal-Globe Insurance Cos.; New Jersey Bell Telephone Co.; Government Employees Insurance Co.; Pennsylvania Manufacturers Association Casualty Insurance Cos.; General Motors Corp.; Travelers Insurance Co.

For full biographical listings, see the Martindale-Hubbell Law Directory

WAYNE, Passaic Co.

DEYOE, HEISSENBUTTEL & MATTIA (AV)

401 Hamburg Turnpike, P.O. Box 2449, 07474-2449
Telephone: 201-595-6300
Fax: 201-595-0146; 201-595-9262

MEMBERS OF FIRM

Charles P. DeYoe (1923-1973)
Philip F. Mattia
Wood M. DeYoe
Gary R. Matano
Frederick C. Heissenbuttel
Scott B. Piekarsky

(See Next Column)

ASSOCIATES

Anne Hutton
Frank A. Campana
Glenn Z. Poosikian
John E. Clarke
Jo Ann G. Durr
Jason T. Shafron
Frank D. Samperi
Maura Waters Brady

LEGAL SUPPORT PERSONNEL

Marilyn Moore (Office Manager)

Representative Clients: INA/Aetna Insurance Co. (Cigna); Medical Inter-Insurance Companies; Hanover-Amgro, Inc.; Maryland Casualty Co.; Ohio Casualty Insurance Co.; Motor Club of America; Selected Insurance Co.

For full biographical listings, see the Martindale-Hubbell Law Directory

NEW MEXICO

*ALBUQUERQUE,** Bernalillo Co.

HINKLE, COX, EATON, COFFIELD & HENSLEY (AV)

Suite 800, 500 Marquette, N.W., P.O. Box 2043, 87103
Telephone: 505-768-1500
FAX: 505-768-1529
Roswell, New Mexico Office: Suite 700, United Bank Plaza, P.O. Box 10, 88202.
Telephone: 505-622-6510.
FAX: 505-623-9332.
Midland, Texas Office: 6 Desta Drive, Suite 2800, P.O. Box 3580, 79705.
Telephone: 915-683-4691.
FAX: 915-683-6518.
Amarillo, Texas Office: 1700 Bank One Center. P.O. Box 9238, 79105-9238.
Telephone: 806-372-5569.
FAX: 806-372-9761.
Santa Fe, New Mexico Office: 218 Montezuma, P.O. Box 2068, 87504.
Telephone: 505-982-4554.
FAX: 505-982-8623.
Austin, Texas Office: 401 West 15th Street, Suite 800, 78701.
Telephone: 512-476-7137.
FAX: 512-476-5431.
Associated Office: Hoffman & Stephens, P.C., 401 West 15th Street, Suite 800, 78701.
Telephone: 512-476-5434.
Fax: 512-476-5431.

Thomas J. McBride
William P. Slattery (Santa Fe Office)

Representative Clients: The Medical Protective Company Media; Professional Insurance Co.

For Complete List of Firm Personnel, See General Section

For full biographical listings, see the Martindale-Hubbell Law Directory

RODEY, DICKASON, SLOAN, AKIN & ROBB, P.A. (AV)

Albuquerque Plaza, Suite 2200, 201 Third Street, N.W., P.O. Box 1888, 87103-1888
Telephone: 505-765-5900
Fax: 505-768-7395
Santa Fe, New Mexico Office: Suite 101 Marcy Plaza, 123 East Marcy Street, P.O. Box 1357, 87504-1357.
Telephone: 505-984-0100.
Fax: 505-989-9542.

W. Robert Lasater, Jr.
Ellen G. Thorne
Angela M. Martinez

Sheryl S. Mahaney
Paul C. Collins

For Complete List of Firm Personnel, See General Section

For full biographical listings, see the Martindale-Hubbell Law Directory

*LAS CRUCES,** Dona Ana Co.

LAW OFFICE OF T. A. SANDENAW (AV)

545 South Melendres, Suite C, 88005
Telephone: 505-523-7500
Fax: 505-523-5600

Thomas A. Sandenaw, Jr.

Richard L. Musick

For full biographical listings, see the Martindale-Hubbell Law Directory

NEW YORK

*BROOKLYN,** Kings Co.

BONINA & BONINA, P.C. (AV)
Suite 1608, 16 Court Street, 11241
Telephone: 718-522-1786
Fax: 718-243-0414

John Anthony Bonina
John Bonina, III
Elizabeth Bonina
Andrea E. Bonina

Deborah A. Trerotola
Michael Campanile
Louise Gleason

OF COUNSEL
Sandra Krevitsky Janin

LEGAL SUPPORT PERSONNEL
Pedro Cintron
Inez M. Diaz
Shari Resnick

Reference: Republic Bank of New York.

For full biographical listings, see the Martindale-Hubbell Law Directory

GARDEN CITY, Nassau Co.

SAWYER, DAVIS & HALPERN (AV)
600 Old Country Road, 11530
Telephone: 516-222-4567
Telecopier: 516-222-4585

MEMBER OF FIRM
James Sawyer

ASSOCIATE
Adam C. Demetri

For Complete List of Firm Personnel, See General Section
For full biographical listings, see the Martindale-Hubbell Law Directory

GREAT NECK, Nassau Co.

PEGALIS & WACHSMAN, P.C. (AV)
175 East Shore Road, 11023
Telephone: 718-895-7492; 212-936-2662; 516-487-1990
Outside New York: 1-800-522-0170
Telecopier: 516-487-4304
Philadelphia, Pennsylvania Office: 1601 Market Street, Suite 1040.
Telephone: 215-564-6838.
FAX: 215-564-6840.

Steven E. Pegalis
Harvey F. Wachsman

Kathryn M. Wachsman
Alice F. Collopy
Annamarie Bondi-Stoddard
Michael A. Carlucci
Gilbert G. Spencer, Jr.
James B. Baydar
Sanford Nagrotsky
Rhonda L. Meyer
Glenn C. McCarthy (Not admitted in NY)
Michael Aronoff
Daniel Albert Thomas

For full biographical listings, see the Martindale-Hubbell Law Directory

LAKE SUCCESS, Nassau Co.

IVONE, DEVINE & JENSEN (AV)
2001 Marcus Avenue-Suite N100, 11042
Telephone: 516-326-2400
Telecopier: 516-352-4952

MEMBERS OF FIRM
Michael T. Ivone
Robert Devine
Richard C. Jensen
Brian E. Lee
Michael Ferguson

ASSOCIATES
James C. Brady
Amy S. Barash
Ann-Marie Fassl Hartline
Debora G. Nobel
Charles Costas

For full biographical listings, see the Martindale-Hubbell Law Directory

*MINEOLA,** Nassau Co.

SHAYNE, DACHS, STANISCI, CORKER & SAUER (AV)
250 Old Country Road, 11501
Telephone: 516-747-1100
Telecopier: 516-747-1185

MEMBERS OF FIRM
Moe Levine (1968-1974)
Neil T. Shayne
Norman H. Dachs
Thomas W. Stanisci
W. Russell Corker
Brian J. Sauer
Kenneth J. Landau
Jonathan A. Dachs

(See Next Column)

Naomi R. Nathan

For full biographical listings, see the Martindale-Hubbell Law Directory

*NEW YORK,** New York Co.

COSTELLO, SHEA & GAFFNEY (AV)
One Battery Park Plaza, 10004
Telephone: 212-483-9600
Fax: 212-344-7680

MEMBERS OF FIRM
Joseph M. Costello
Mortimer C. Shea
Frederick N. Gaffney
Steven E. Garry
William A. Goldstein
Donald J. Scialabba
Paul E. Blutman
Alan T. Blutman

ASSOCIATES
Robert R. Arena
Edward S. Benson
J Mcgarry Costello
Mario J. DiRe
Leo V. Duval, III
Cathy Ann Gallagher
Jozef K. Goscilo
Adam Charles Kandell
Timothy M. McCann
Kevin B. McHugh
Samuel Mark Mizrahi
Margaret Sullivan O'Connell
Manuel Ortega
John F. Parker
Neil B. Ptashnik
David Schrager
Lydia P. Shure
David N. Zane
Craig F. Wilson
Brian G. Winter

OF COUNSEL
James F. Corcoran

For full biographical listings, see the Martindale-Hubbell Law Directory

DEBLASIO & ALTON, P.C. (AV)
Woolworth Building, 233 Broadway, 10279
Telephone: 212-732-2620
Fax: 212-571-2045

Peter E. DeBlasio
Walter G. Alton, Jr.
Steven A. Epstein
Rhoda Grossberg Faller
Stephen S. La Rocca

For full biographical listings, see the Martindale-Hubbell Law Directory

EVANS, ORR, LAFFAN, TORRES & DEMAGGIO, P.C. (AV)
225 Broadway, Suite 1405, 10007-3001
Telephone: 212-267-1800
FAX: 212-964-0958
Long Island Office: 25 Jackson Avenue, Syosset, 11791.
Telephone: 516-364-0300.

Walter G. Evans (1886-1981)
William F. Laffan, Jr.
Frank Torres
David DeMaggio

Seymour I. Yanofsky
Eugene Guarneri
Angelantonio Bianchi
Cari E. Pepkin
Maura V. Laffan
Christian A. Rofrano
Paula T. Amsterdam
Donald G. Derrico
Patricia Ann Cavagnaro
Thomas P. Ryan, Jr.
Lambert C Sheng
Richard Fama

OF COUNSEL
Steven DeMaggio

OF COUNSEL EMERITUS
Alexander Orr, Jr.
Alfred V. Norton, Jr.
Edward J. Pacelli

LEGAL SUPPORT PERSONNEL
PARALEGALS
Alicia Carrano
Susan Dunphy
Damian L. Calemmo
Diana L. Cohen

For full biographical listings, see the Martindale-Hubbell Law Directory

FINKELSTEIN BRUCKMAN WOHL MOST & ROTHMAN (AV)
575 Lexington Avenue, 10022-6102
Telephone: 212-754-3100
Telecopier: 212-371-2980
Stamford, Connecticut Office: 1 Landmark Square.
Telephone: 203-358-9200.
Telecopier: 203-969-6140.
Hackensack, New Jersey Office: 20 Court Street.
Telephone: 201-525-1800.
Telecopier: 201-489-4509.

MEMBERS OF FIRM
Ronald Gene Wohl
Joan Levin
T. Lawrence Tabak

ASSOCIATE
David B. Bruckman

(See Next Column)

FINKELSTEIN BRUCKMAN WOHL MOST & ROTHMAN, *New York—Continued*

OF COUNSEL

James B. Rosenblum
Patrick J. Filan

For Complete List of Firm Personnel, See General Section

For full biographical listings, see the Martindale-Hubbell Law Directory

---

GAIR, GAIR, CONASON, STEIGMAN & MACKAUF (AV)

80 Pine Street, 10005
Telephone: 212-943-1090

MEMBERS OF FIRM

Robert L. Conason
Herbert H. Hirschhorn
Seymour Boyers
Herman Schmertz
Ernest R. Steigman
Stephen H. Mackauf
Warren J. Willinger
Ronald Berson
Jerome I. Katz
David G. Miller
Candice Singer Ram
Jeffrey B. Bloom
Anthony H. Gair
Mary Nicholls
Gayle F. Bertoldo
Vincent F. Maher
Robert E. Godosky
Rick S. Conason
Ben B. Rubinowitz
Rhonda E. Kay

COUNSEL

Harriet E. Gair

For full biographical listings, see the Martindale-Hubbell Law Directory

---

GARBARINI & SCHER, P.C. (AV)

1114 Avenue of the Americas, 10036-7790
Telephone: 212-764-4000
Telecopier: (212) 719-5018
Telex: WUI 668964
Cable Address: "Garkrolaw NewYork"
Hackensack, New Jersey Office: 25 Main Street, Suite 300.
Telephone: 201-343-2002.
FAX: 212-719-5018.

Stanley J. Scher
Leonard Weinstock
Myrna A. Levinson
George J. Kehayas
Michael Caliguiri
Keith A. Raven
Anthony M. Fischetti
William G. Scher

Cecil E. Floyd
Jay M. Weinstein
Margery A. Budoff
Conrad Jordan
Martin K. Rowe
Gregg D. Weinstock
James W. Kachadoorian
Kurt L. Weinmann
Paul M. Paley
Timothy F. Jones
Valerie L. Drossman
Gregory D. V. Holmes
Barry Rothman
Nancy Breslow
Louise M. Cherkis

Representative Clients: Chubb & Son, Inc.; Clarendon National Insurance Co.; Farmers Insurance Group; Federation of Jewish Philanthropies; CIGNA Property and Casualty Cos.; Medical Liability Mutual Insurance Co.; St. Barnabas Hospital; The State Insurance Fund; Allstate Insurance Co.; Merchants Mutual Ins.

For full biographical listings, see the Martindale-Hubbell Law Directory

---

GINSBERG & BROOME (AV)

225 Broadway, Suite 3105, 10007
Telephone: 212-227-4225

Robert M. Ginsberg
Alvin H. Broome

ASSOCIATE

Michael Finkelstein

For full biographical listings, see the Martindale-Hubbell Law Directory

---

HARLEY & BROWNE (AV)

18 East 41st Street, 10017
Telephone: 212-545-7900

MEMBERS OF FIRM

J. Austin Browne
Robert G. Harley
Bridget Asaro

Robert E. Fein

OF COUNSEL

Richard H. Dreyfuss

Reference: Chemical Bank.

For full biographical listings, see the Martindale-Hubbell Law Directory

---

HEIDELL, PITTONI, MURPHY & BACH, P.C. (AV)

99 Park Avenue, 10016
Telephone: 212-286-8585
Telecopier: 212-490-8966
New Canaan, Connecticut Office: 49 Locust Avenue, P.O. Box 1132.
Telephone: 203-966-9983.

(See Next Column)

Luke M. Pittoni
Raymond W. Murphy
Charles L. Bach, Jr.
Rosary A. Morelli
Bruce F. Gilpatrick
Robin R. Dolsky
Elizabeth Cornacchio
Austa S. Devlin
Michael T. Walsh
Michael D. Shalhoub
Stephen R. Marshall
Louise A. Derevlany
Barbara A. Sheehan

OF COUNSEL

Robert C. Heidell

John F. Costa
Cheryl A. Harris
Michael F. McGowan
John J. Murphy, Jr.
E. Marc Hyman
Terrence P. St. John
Steven R. Goldstein
Andrea J. Fagen
Denise A. Rubin
Mitchell D. Frankel
Linda M. Ruma
Jason H. Korn
Rosemary E. Mahoney
Maria A. Onorato
William M. Wingertzahn
Janice Kirsten Lunde
John J. Peplinski
Geraldine Koeneke Russell
Diego A. Gomez
Christopher P. Foley
Marcy Blake
William D. Samers
Denise R. Melillo
Robert T. Melillo, Jr.
Katharine Demgen
Carol L. Morris-Fox
Daniel S. Ratner
George J. Tidona

For full biographical listings, see the Martindale-Hubbell Law Directory

---

JULIEN & SCHLESINGER, P.C. (AV)

150 William Street, 19th Floor, 10038
Telephone: 212-962-8020

Alfred S. Julien (1910-1989)
Stuart A. Schlesinger
Denise Mortner Kranz
Ira M. Newman
David B. Turret

OF COUNSEL

Louis Fusco, Jr.

Mary Elizabeth Burns
Richard A. Robbins
Michael J. Taub
Marla L. Schiff
Alvin Craig Gordon
Adam Schlesinger
Robert J. Epstein

For full biographical listings, see the Martindale-Hubbell Law Directory

---

KOPFF, NARDELLI & DOPF (AV)

440 Ninth Avenue, 10001
Telephone: 212-244-2999
Telecopier: 212-643-0862

MEMBERS OF FIRM

Peter C. Kopff
Camillo Nardelli (1936-1987)
Glenn W. Dopf
Scott F. Morgan
Charles K. Faillace
Joseph R. Cammarosano
Victoria A. Lombardi
Michael L. Manci
Martin B. Adams

ASSOCIATES

Eugene A. Ward
Mary E. Pearson
Joseph T. Belevich
Catherine R. Richter
Susan D. Noble
John A. Orbon
Denise D. Sapanara
Ronnie Michelle Grill
Richard J. Valent
Edward J. Arevalo
Edward A. Flores
Peter S. Williams
Tara K. Curcillo
Jonathan Adam Judd

Representative Clients: Aetna Casualty and Surety Co.; American International Group; Citicorp, U.S.A.; County of Nassau, State of New York; Franklin Hospital Medical Center; Guarantee National Insurance Co.; Lenox Hill Hospital; The May Department Stores Co.; Medical Inter-Insurance Exchange of New Jersey; Medical Liability Mutual Insurance Co.

For full biographical listings, see the Martindale-Hubbell Law Directory

---

LITMAN, ASCHE, LUPKIN, GIOIELLA & BASSIN (AV)

45 Broadway Atrium, 10006
Telephone: 212-809-4500
Telecopier: GP II, III (212) 509-8403

MEMBERS OF FIRM

Richard M. Asche
Jack T. Litman
Stanley N. Lupkin
Russell M. Gioiella
Steven Jay Bassin

ASSOCIATES

Mary Lou Chatterton
Frederick L. Sosinsky

OF COUNSEL

Alan C. Rothfeld
Ronald S. Pohl

For full biographical listings, see the Martindale-Hubbell Law Directory

---

MCALOON & FRIEDMAN, P.C. (AV)

116 John Street, 10038
Telephone: 212-732-8700

(See Next Column)

McALOON & FRIEDMAN P.C.—*Continued*

Edward H. McAloon (1908-1986)
Stanley D. Friedman
Gunther H. Kilsch
Theodore B. Rosenzweig
Gary A. Greenfield
Brendan J. Lantier
Lawrence W. Mumm
Laura R. Shapiro

Rose Candeloro
Regina E. Schneller
Lisa B. Goldstein
John Langell
Barbara A. Dalton
Michelle E. Just
Eleanor M. Kanzler
Paul Nasta
Kim R. Kleppel
Kenneth Gordon Ellison
Evette E. Harrison
Thomas Medardo Oliva
Adam R. Goldsmith
Christopher B. O'Malley
Arlene Bergman

For full biographical listings, see the Martindale-Hubbell Law Directory

STEVEN E. NORTH, P.C. (AV)

148 East 74th Street, 10021
Telephone: 212-861-5000
Telecopier: 212-861-4055

Steven E. North

For full biographical listings, see the Martindale-Hubbell Law Directory

PARKER CHAPIN FLATTAU & KLIMPL, L.L.P. (AV)

1211 Avenue of the Americas, 10036
Telephone: 212-704-6000
Telecopier: 212-704-6288
Cable Address: "Lawpark"
Telex: 640347
Great Neck, New York Office: 175 Great Neck Road.
Telephone: 516-482-4422.
Telecopier: 516-482-4469.

MEMBER OF FIRM

Jesse J. Graham, II

For Complete List of Firm Personnel, See General Section

For full biographical listings, see the Martindale-Hubbell Law Directory

QUELLER & FISHER (AV)

A Law Partnership including Professional Corporations
110 Wall Street, 10005-3851
Telephone: 212-422-3600
Cable Address: "Quelfish, New York"
Facsimile: 212-422-2828

MEMBERS OF FIRM

Fred Queller (P.C.)
Bertram D. Fisher (P.C.)
Walter F. Benson

ASSOCIATES

Ira Bartfield
Marshall Schmeizer
Kevin S. McDonald
Phillip P. Nikolis
Edmund L. Rothschild
Dorothy S. Morrill
David P. Horowitz
Glenn Verchick
Ira Fogelgaren
Frances I. Beaupierre (Not admitted in NY)

For full biographical listings, see the Martindale-Hubbell Law Directory

ROSENBLUM & FILAN (AV)

400 Madison Avenue, 10017
Telephone: 212-888-8001
Fax: 212-888-3331
Stamford, Connecticut Office: One Landmark Square. 06901.
Telephone: 203-358-9200.
Fax: 203-969-6140.
White Plains, New York Office: 50 Main Street. 10606.
Telephone: 914-686-6100.
Fax: 914-686-6140.

MEMBERS OF FIRM

Patrick J. Filan
James B. Rosenblum

Jeannine M. Foran
James F. Walsh
Kate E. Maguire
M. Karen Noble (Not admitted in NY)
James S. Newfield

OF COUNSEL

Lee Judy Johnson
Katherine Benesch (Not admitted in NY)
Theodore J. Greene
Jack L. Most
Richard M. Schwartz

For full biographical listings, see the Martindale-Hubbell Law Directory

SCHNEIDER, KLEINICK, WEITZ, DAMASHEK, GODOSKY & GENTILE (AV)

233 Broadway, Fifth Floor, 10279-0003
Telephone: 212-553-9000
Fax: 212-804-0820

Ivan S. Schneider
Arnold L. Kleinick
Harvey Weitz
Philip M. Damashek
Richard Godosky
Anthony P. Gentile
Gregory J. Cannata
Robert B. Jackson
Brian J. Shoot

Richard B. Ancowitz
Jeffrey R. Brecker
Scott A. Buxbaum
Dawn S. DeWeil
Steven M. Fink
Steven Gold
Keith H. Gross
Wilma Guzman
Leslie Debra Kelmachter
Keith A. Kleinick
Matthew R. Kreinces
Ruth Frances Leve
Gerard Anthony Lucciola
Grace Carreras McCallen
Charles J. Nolet, Jr.
Harlan Platz
Lloyd M. Roberts
Paul Bryan Schneider
Perry D. Silver
Clifford J. Stern
Paul B. Weitz

For full biographical listings, see the Martindale-Hubbell Law Directory

SHEFT & SHEFT (AV)

909 Third Avenue, 10022
Telephone: 212-688-7788
Telecopier: 212-355-7373
Jersey City, New Jersey Office: Harborside Financial Center, Suite 704 Plaza Three.
Telephone: 201-332-2233.
Telecopier: 201-435-9177.

Leonard A. Sheft
Peter I. Sheft
Norman J. Golub (Resident, Jersey City, New Jersey Office)
Marjorie Heyman Mintzer
Marian S. Hertz
Leonard G. Kamlet

COUNSEL

Gerald A. Greenberger (Resident, Jersey City, New Jersey Office)

David Holmes (Resident, Jersey City, New Jersey Office)
Phillip C. Landrigan
Thomas J. Leonard
Myra Needleman
Howard K. Fishman
Mary C. Bennett
Jeffrey S. Leonard (Resident, Jersey City, New Jersey Office)
Stacy B. Parker
Edward Hayum
Daniel H. Hecht
Jerrald J. Hochman
James M. Dennis
Frank V. Kelly
Ellen G. Margolis
Guy J. Levasseur
Joseph F. Arkins
Jordan Sklar
Herbert L. Lazar
Maria E. Cannon (Resident, Jersey City, New Jersey Office)

For full biographical listings, see the Martindale-Hubbell Law Directory

SIMONSON HESS & LEIBOWITZ, P.C. (AV)

15 Maiden Lane, 10038
Telephone: 212-233-5000

Paul Simonson
Alan B. Leibowitz
Steven L. Hess

Nancy S. Stuzin
Kathleen Marie O'Neill
Jennifer Levine

For full biographical listings, see the Martindale-Hubbell Law Directory

WHITE, FLEISCHNER & FINO (AV)

195 Broadway, 10007
Telephone: 212-227-6292
Telex: 645255
Telecopier: 212-227-7812
Westfield, New Jersey Office: 215 North Avenue, West.
Telephone: 908-654-6266.
Telecopier: 908-654-3686.
London, England Office: Plantation House. 31/35 Fenchurch S. EC3M 3DX.
Telephone: 071-375-2037.
Telecopier: 071-375-2039.

MEMBERS OF FIRM

Allan P. White
Benjamin A. Fleischner
Paul A. Fino, Jr.
Robert G. Schenker
Marcia J. Lynn
Marisa Goetz

ASSOCIATES

Patti F. Potash
Mitchell R. Friedman
Mitchell L. Shadowitz
Debra E. Ruderman
David I. Blee
Sandra L. Bonder
Michael J. Asta
Stephanie M. Holzback

(See Next Column)

WHITE, FLEISCHNER & FINO, *New York—Continued*

ASSOCIATES (Continued)

Mark R. Osherow
Virginia L. McGrane
Beth A. Goldklang
Sean Upton
Wendy K. Carrano
Nancy D. Lyness
Randy Scott Faust
Elizabeth C. Mirisola
Sheri E. Holland

LEGAL SUPPORT PERSONNEL

Darien Anderson (Paralegal)
Helen Wasey (Claims Consultant)

For full biographical listings, see the Martindale-Hubbell Law Directory

*ROCHESTER,** Monroe Co.

ROBERT J. MICHAEL (AV)

39 State Street, Suite 420, 14614
Telephone: 716-232-3460
Fax: 716-232-4583

OF COUNSEL

Mark H. Tiernan

Reference: Chemical Bank.

For full biographical listings, see the Martindale-Hubbell Law Directory

STANFORDVILLE, Dutchess Co.

WILLIAM E. STANTON (AV)

Village Centre, Route 82, P.O. Box 370, 12581
Telephone: 914-868-7514
FAX: 914-868-7761

Representative Clients: Dupont de Nemours & Co.; Millbrook School; Hanover Insurance Co.; New York Telephone Co.
Reference: Fishkill National Bank.

For full biographical listings, see the Martindale-Hubbell Law Directory

*WHITE PLAINS,** Westchester Co.

ROSENBLUM & FILAN (AV)

50 Main Street, 10606
Telephone: 914-686-6100
Fax: 914-686-6140
Stamford, Connecticut Office: One Landmark Square. 06901.
Telephone: 203-358-9200.
Fax: 203-969-6140.
New York, New York Office: 400 Madison Avenue. 10017.
Telephone: 212-888-8001.
Fax: 212-888-3331.

MEMBERS OF FIRM

Patrick J. Filan
James B. Rosenblum

Jeannine M. Foran
James F. Walsh
Kate E. Maguire
M. Karen Noble (Not admitted in NY)
James S. Newfield

OF COUNSEL

Lee Judy Johnson
Katherine Benesch (Not admitted in NY)
Theodore J. Greene
Jack L. Most
Richard M. Schwartz

For full biographical listings, see the Martindale-Hubbell Law Directory

NORTH CAROLINA

*ASHEVILLE,** Buncombe Co.

REYNOLDS & McARTHUR (AV Ⓣ)

A Partnership including a Professional Corporation
The Jackson Building, 22 South Pack Square Suite 1200, 28801
Telephone: 704-254-8523
Fax: 704-254-3038
Macon, Georgia Office: 850 Walnut Street.
Telephone: 912-741-6000.
Fax: 912-742-0750.
Atlanta, Georgia Office: Suite 1080, One Buckhead Plaza, 3060 Peachtree Road, N.W.
Telephone: 404-240-0265.
Fax: 404-262-3557.

MEMBERS OF FIRM

W. Carl Reynolds (P.C.) (Not admitted in NC)
Katherine L. McArthur
Charles M. Cork, III (Not admitted in NC)
O. Wendell Horne, III (Not admitted in NC)
Bradley J. Survant (Not admitted in NC)
Steve Ray Warren

For full biographical listings, see the Martindale-Hubbell Law Directory

*CHARLOTTE,** Mecklenburg Co.

TIM L. HARRIS AND ASSOCIATES (AV)

4000 Tuckaseegee Road, 28208
Telephone: 704-392-4111
Fax: 704-391-1905
Gastonia, North Carolina Office: 223 West Main Avenue, P.O. Box 249.
Telephone: 704-864-3409.
Fax: 704-853-1040.

MEMBER OF FIRM

Tim L. Harris
Jerry Neil Ragan

For full biographical listings, see the Martindale-Hubbell Law Directory

*GASTONIA,** Gaston Co.

TIM L. HARRIS AND ASSOCIATES (AV)

223 West Main Avenue, P.O. Box 249, 28053-0249
Telephone: 704-864-3409
Fax: 704-853-1040
Charlotte, North Carolina Office: 4000 Tuckaseegee Road.
Telephone: 704-392-4111.

MEMBERS OF FIRM

Tim L. Harris
Jerry Neil Ragan

For Complete List of Firm Personnel, See General Section

For full biographical listings, see the Martindale-Hubbell Law Directory

*GREENSBORO,** Guilford Co.

VANCE BARRON, JR. (AV)

301 South Greene Street, Suite 310, 27401
Telephone: 910-274-4782
FAX: 910-379-8592
Mailing Address: P.O. Box 2370, Greensboro, NC, 27402-2370

For full biographical listings, see the Martindale-Hubbell Law Directory

*GREENVILLE,** Pitt Co.

MARVIN K. BLOUNT, JR. (AV)

400 West First Street, P.O. Drawer 58, 27835-0058
Telephone: 919-752-6000
FAX: 919-752-2174

ASSOCIATES

Joseph T. Edwards
James F. Hopf
Sharron R. Edwards

Reference: Branch Banking & Trust Co., Greenville, N.C.

For full biographical listings, see the Martindale-Hubbell Law Directory

*RALEIGH,** Wake Co.

FULLER, BECTON, BILLINGS, SLIFKIN & BELL, P.A. (AV)

4020 Westchase Boulevard Suite 575, 27607
Telephone: 919-755-1068
FAX: 919-828-7543

James C. Fuller, Jr.
Charles L. Becton
James G. Billings
Anne R. Slifkin

Asa L. Bell, Jr.
Michele L. Flowers
Maria J. Mangano

For full biographical listings, see the Martindale-Hubbell Law Directory

ELIZABETH F. KUNIHOLM (AV)

4101 Lake Boone Trail, Suite 200, P.O. Box 30303, 27622
Telephone: 919-782-4494
Telecopier: 919-782-4517

For full biographical listings, see the Martindale-Hubbell Law Directory

*SMITHFIELD,** Johnston Co.

ARMSTRONG & ARMSTRONG, P.A. (AV)

P.O. Box 27, 27577-4352
Telephone: 919-934-1575
FAX: 919-934-1846

L. Lamar Armstrong, Jr.
Angela D. Matney

For full biographical listings, see the Martindale-Hubbell Law Directory

*WINSTON-SALEM,** Forsyth Co.

BENNETT & BLANCATO, L.L.P. (AV)

101 South Stratford Road, Suite 305, 27104-4227
Telephone: 910-723-1896
Fax: 910-723-8308

(See Next Column)

BENNETT & BLANCATO L.L.P.—*Continued*

Richard V. Bennett   William A. Blancato

ASSOCIATES

Sherry R. Dawson   Stanley P. Dean

For full biographical listings, see the Martindale-Hubbell Law Directory

NORTH DAKOTA

*BISMARCK,** Burleigh Co.

PETERSON, SCHMITZ, MOENCH & SCHMIDT, A PROFESSIONAL CORPORATION (AV)

Second Floor, Suite 200, 116 North Fourth Street, P.O. Box 2076, 58502-2076
Telephone: 701-224-0400
Fax: 701-224-0399

David L. Peterson   Dale W. Moench
Orell D. Schmitz   William D. Schmidt

OF COUNSEL

Gerald Glaser

LEGAL SUPPORT PERSONNEL

Vicki J. Kunz   Traci L. Albers

For full biographical listings, see the Martindale-Hubbell Law Directory

OHIO

*AKRON,** Summit Co.

A. RUSSELL SMITH (AV)

503 Society Building, 159 South Main Street, 44308
Telephone: 216-434-7167
FAX: 216-434-7195

A. Russell Smith

R. Bryan Nace

For full biographical listings, see the Martindale-Hubbell Law Directory

A. WILLIAM ZAVARELLO CO., L.P.A. (AV)

313 South High Street, Corner South High and Buchtel, 44308-1532
Telephone: 216-762-9700
Fax: 216-762-1680

A. William Zavarello   Rhonda G. Davis

References: First National Bank of Ohio; National City Bank, Akron.

For full biographical listings, see the Martindale-Hubbell Law Directory

*CINCINNATI,** Hamilton Co.

DINSMORE & SHOHL (AV)

1900 Chemed Center, 255 East Fifth Street, 45202-3172
Telephone: 513-977-8200
FAX: 513-977-8141
Florence, Kentucky Office: Turfway Ridge Office Park, 7300 Turfway Road, Suite 430 41042-1355.
Telephone: 606-283-0515.
FAX: 606-283-6017.
Dayton, Ohio Office: 500 Courthouse Plaza, S.W., 10 N. Ludlow Street, 45402-1834.
Telephone: 513-228-8012.
FAX: 513-461-2543.
Columbus, Ohio Office: NBD Bank Building, Suite 330, 175 South Third Street, 43215-5134.
Telephone: 614-224-7887.
FAX: 614-224-7882.

MEMBERS OF FIRM

Frank C. Woodside, III   Nancy J. Gill
Gordon C. Greene   Stephen K. Shaw
Deborah R. Lydon   Lawrence A. Flemer
John E. Jevicky   K. C. Green
June Smith Tyler

(See Next Column)

ASSOCIATES

James A. Comodeca   Laurie H. Schwab
John J. Hoffmann (Resident, Dayton, Ohio Office)   Mary-Jo Middelhoff
Sara Simrall Rorer   Ann Collins Hindman
Melissa A. Fetters   Christopher L. Riegler (Resident, Dayton, Ohio Office)

For Complete List of Firm Personnel, See General Section

For full biographical listings, see the Martindale-Hubbell Law Directory

HERMANIES, MAJOR, CASTELLI & GOODMAN (AV)

Suite 740-Cincinnati Club Building, 30 Garfield Place, 45202-4396
Telephone: 513-621-2345
Fax: 513-621-2519

MEMBERS OF FIRM

Ronald D. Major   Richard Lanahan Goodman
Anthony D. Castelli   Mark Allen Ferestad

References: Southern Ohio Bank; First National Bank of Cincinnati; The PNC Bank.

For full biographical listings, see the Martindale-Hubbell Law Directory

KEATING, MUETHING & KLEKAMP (AV)

1800 Provident Tower, One East Fourth Street, 45202
Telephone: 513-579-6400
Facsimile: 513-579-6457

MEMBERS OF FIRM

Louis F. Gilligan   William A. Posey
Gregory M. Utter

Representative Clients: American Financial Corporation; BP America Inc.; Chiquita Brands International, Inc.; The Cincinnati Enquirer; Cintas Corporation; Comair Holdings, Inc.; Duke Associates; LSI Industries Inc.; Mosler Inc.; Provident Bankcorp, Inc.

For Complete List of Firm Personnel, See General Section

For full biographical listings, see the Martindale-Hubbell Law Directory

RICHARD D. LAWRENCE AND ASSOCIATES CO., L.P.A. (AV)

Suite 2020, CBLD Building, 36 East Seventh Street, 45202
Telephone: 513-651-4130
FAX: Available upon request

Richard D. Lawrence   James B. McGrath, Jr.

Jill Gustafson

For full biographical listings, see the Martindale-Hubbell Law Directory

LINDHORST & DREIDAME CO., L.P.A. (AV)

312 Walnut Street, Suite 2300, 45202-4091
Telephone: 513-421-6630
Telecopier: 513-421-0212

Leo J. Breslin   John A. Goldberg
Michael F. Lyon

Representative Clients: Medical Protective Co.; Fireman's Fund-American Group; CNA; U.S.F.&G.; Ohio Hospital Insurance Co.; Middletown Hospital; Scottsdale Insurance Co.

For Complete List of Firm Personnel, See General Section

For full biographical listings, see the Martindale-Hubbell Law Directory

GATES T. RICHARDS (AV)

3807 Carew Tower, 441 Vine Street, 45202
Telephone: 513-621-1991

Reference: First National Bank, Cincinnati, Ohio.

For full biographical listings, see the Martindale-Hubbell Law Directory

SANTEN & HUGHES A LEGAL PROFESSIONAL ASSOCIATION (AV)

Suite 3100, 312 Walnut Street, 45202
Telephone: 513-721-4450
FAX: 513-721-7644; 721-0109

William E. Santen   John D. Holschuh, Jr.
William E. Santen, Jr.

LEGAL SUPPORT PERSONNEL

Karen W. Crane (Corporate Paralegal)   Karen L. Jansen (Litigation Paralegal)
Deborah M. McKinney (Trust/Estate Paralegal)   Bobbie S. Ebbers (Paralegal)

For Complete List of Firm Personnel, See General Section

For full biographical listings, see the Martindale-Hubbell Law Directory

Cincinnati—Continued

LAW OFFICES OF JOSEPH W. SHEA III (AV)

36 East 7th Street, Suite 2650, 45202-4459
Telephone: 513-621-8333
Telecopier: 513-651-3272

ASSOCIATE

Shirley A. Coffey

LEGAL SUPPORT PERSONNEL

NURSE - LEGAL ASSISTANT

Marianne E. Alf

For full biographical listings, see the Martindale-Hubbell Law Directory

STRAUSS & TROY A LEGAL PROFESSIONAL ASSOCIATION (AV)

2100 PNC Center, 201 East Fifth Street, 45202-4186
Telephone: 513-621-2120
Telecopier: 513-241-8259
Northern Kentucky Office: Suite 1400, 50 East Rivercenter Boulevard, Covington, Kentucky, 41011.
Telephone: 513-621-8900; 513-621-2120.
Telecopier: 513-629-9444.

Charles G. Atkins

Thomas L. Stachler

Representative Clients: PNC Bank, N.A. (Ohio and Kentucky); Corporex Companies, Inc.; Mercantile Stores Company, Inc.; Star Bank, N.A. (Ohio and Kentucky).

For Complete List of Firm Personnel, See General Section

For full biographical listings, see the Martindale-Hubbell Law Directory

WAITE, SCHNEIDER, BAYLESS & CHESLEY CO., L.P.A. (AV)

1513 Central Trust Tower, Fourth and Vine Streets, 45202
Telephone: 513-621-0267
Fax: 513-381-2375; 621-0262

Stanley M. Chesley

Thomas F. Rehme
Fay E. Stilz
Louise M. Roselle
Dwight Tillery
D. Arthur Rabourn
Jerome L. Skinner
Janet G. Abaray
Paul M. De Marco
Terrence L. Goodman
Sherrill P. Hondorf
Colleen M. Hegge
Dianna Pendleton
Randy F. Fox
Glenn D. Feagan
Theresa L. Groh
Theodore N. Berry
Jane H. Walker
Renée Infante
Allen P. Grunes

OF COUNSEL

Jos. E. Rosen
James F. Keller

For full biographical listings, see the Martindale-Hubbell Law Directory

*CLEVELAND,** Cuyahoga Co.

NURENBERG, PLEVIN, HELLER & MCCARTHY CO., L.P.A. (AV)

1370 Ontario Street First Floor, 44113-1792
Telephone: 216-621-2300
FAX: 216-771-2242

A. H. Dudnik (1905-1963)
S. F. Komito (1902-1984)
Marshall I. Nurenberg
Leon M. Plevin
Maurice L. Heller
John J. McCarthy
Thomas Mester
Harlan M. Gordon
Andrew P. Krembs
Anne L. Kilbane
David M. Paris
Richard C. Alkire
Richard L. Demsey
Joel Levin
Jamie R. Lebovitz
William S. Jacobson

Dean C. Nieding
Jeffrey A. Leikin
Robin J. Peterson
Robert S. Zeller
James T. Schumacher
Ellen M. McCarthy
J. Charles Ruiz-Bueno
Sandra J. Rosenthal
Kathleen St. John
Jessica F. Kahn

Reference: Society Key Corp.

For full biographical listings, see the Martindale-Hubbell Law Directory

RUBENSTEIN, NOVAK, EINBUND, PAVLIK & CELEBREZZE (AV)

Suite 270, Skylight Office Tower Tower City Center, 44113-1498
Telephone: 216-781-8700
Telecopier: 216-781-9227

MEMBER OF FIRM

William J. Novak

For full biographical listings, see the Martindale-Hubbell Law Directory

TIMOTHY A. SHIMKO & ASSOCIATES A LEGAL PROFESSIONAL ASSOCIATION (AV)

2010 Huntington Building, 925 Euclid Avenue, 44115
Telephone: 216-241-8300
Fax: 216-241-2702

Timothy A. Shimko

Janet I. Stich
Theresa A. Tarchinski
Ronald K. Starkey
Frank E. Piscitelli, Jr.

OF COUNSEL

Frank B. Mazzone

Reference: National City Bank, Cleveland.

For full biographical listings, see the Martindale-Hubbell Law Directory

*COLUMBUS,** Franklin Co.

BUTLER, CINCIONE, DICUCCIO & DRITZ (AV)

Suite 700 LeVeque Lincoln Tower, 50 West Broad Street, 43215
Telephone: 614-221-3151
Fax: 614-221-8196

MEMBERS OF FIRM

Robert A. Butler
Alphonse P. Cincione
N. Gerald DiCuccio
Stanley B. Dritz
David B. Barnhart

Matthew P. Cincione
Gail M. Zalimeni

References: National City Bank, Columbus, Ohio; Bank One, Columbus, Ohio.

For full biographical listings, see the Martindale-Hubbell Law Directory

CLARK, PERDUE, ROBERTS & SCOTT CO., L.P.A. (AV)

471 East Broad Street Suite 1400, 43215
Telephone: 614-469-1400
Fax: 614-469-0900

Dale K. Perdue
Paul O. Scott
Douglas S. Roberts
Edward L. Clark
Glen R. Pritchard
Robert W. Kerpsack, Jr.
D. Andrew List
Brian W. Palmer

For full biographical listings, see the Martindale-Hubbell Law Directory

MICHAEL F. COLLEY CO., L.P.A. (AV)

Hoster & High Building, 536 South High Street, 43215-5674
Telephone: 614-228-6453
Fax: 614-228-7122

Michael F. Colley

David I. Shroyer
Daniel N. Abraham
Elizabeth Schorpp Burkett
Jennifer K. Thivener
Thomas F. Martello, Jr.

OF COUNSEL

Marvin Sloin
David K. Frank

Reference: Bank One of Columbus, NA.

For full biographical listings, see the Martindale-Hubbell Law Directory

LAMKIN, VAN EMAN, TRIMBLE, BEALS & ROURKE (AV)

Suite 200, 500 South Front Street, 43215-5671
Telephone: 614-224-8187
Fax: 614-224-4943

MEMBERS OF FIRM

William W. Lamkin
Timothy L. Van Eman
Thomas W. Trimble
David A. Beals
Michael J. Rourke

ASSOCIATE

Kathy A. Dougherty

Reference: Huntington National Bank.

For full biographical listings, see the Martindale-Hubbell Law Directory

MALOON, MALOON & BARCLAY CO., L.P.A. (AV)

475 East Town Street, 43215-4706
Telephone: 614-469-7833
Fax: 614-469-1733

Jerry L. Maloon
Jeffrey Lee Maloon
Craig D. Barclay
Melissa Ann Pollock

For full biographical listings, see the Martindale-Hubbell Law Directory

Columbus—Continued

McCarthy, Palmer, Volkema, Boyd & Thomas A Legal Professional Association (AV)

140 East Town Street, Suite 1100, 43215
Telephone: Telephone: 614-221-4400
Telecopier: 614-221-6010

Dennis M. McCarthy
Robert Gray Palmer
Daniel R. Volkema
Jeffrey D. Boyd
Warner M. Thomas, Jr.

Craig P. Scott

COUNSEL

Russell H. Volkema
Stanton G. Darling, II

Reference: Huntington National Bank.

For full biographical listings, see the Martindale-Hubbell Law Directory

Ray, Todaro & Alton Co., L.P.A. (AV)

175 South Third Street, Suite 350, 43215-5100
Telephone: 614-221-7791
Fax: 614-221-8957

Frank A. Ray
John M. Alton
Frank E. Todaro

Gregory W. Kirstein

For full biographical listings, see the Martindale-Hubbell Law Directory

Scherner & Hanson (AV)

130 Northwoods Boulevard, 43235-4725
Telephone: 614-431-7200
Fax: 614-431-7262
Delaware, Ohio Office: 5300 David Road.
Telephone: 614-595-3366.

Hans Scherner
Robert E. Hanson

For full biographical listings, see the Martindale-Hubbell Law Directory

Wolske & Blue A Legal Professional Association (AV)

580 South High Street, 43215-5672
Telephone: 614-228-6969
Cincinnati, Ohio Office: The Society Bank Center, 36 East Seventh Street, Suite 2120.
Telephone: 513-579-1181.

Walter J. Wolske, Jr.
Jason A. Blue
Gerald S. Leeseberg
Michael S. Miller

Anne M. Valentine
William Mann
David B. Shaver
Douglas J. Blue
Maryellen C. Spirito
Sarah Meirson

Reference: Bank One of Columbus, N.A.

For full biographical listings, see the Martindale-Hubbell Law Directory

*DAYTON,** Montgomery Co.

Freund, Freeze & Arnold A Legal Professional Association (AV)

Suite 1800 One Dayton Centre, One South Main Street, 45402-2017
Telephone: 513-222-2424
Telecopier: 513-222-5369
Cincinnati, Ohio Office: Suite 2110 Carew Tower, 441 Vine Street, 45202-4157.
Telephone: 513-287-8400.
FAX: 513-287-8403.

Neil F. Freund
Robert N. Snyder
Mary E. Lentz

Local Counsel for: Auto-Owners Insurance Co.; CNA Insurance Co.; Crum and Foster Underwriters; Employers Reinsurance Corp.; Farmers Insurance Group; Lloyds of London; Medical Protective; Midwestern Group; State Farm Mutual Automobile Insurance Co.; The Travelers Insurance Co.
Special Trial Counsel for: City of Dayton.

For full biographical listings, see the Martindale-Hubbell Law Directory

Young & Alexander Co., L.P.A. (AV)

Suite 100, 367 West Second Street, 45402
Telephone: 513-224-9291
Telecopier: 513-224-9679
Cincinnati, Ohio Office: 110 Boggs Lane, Suite 350.
Telephone: 513-326-5555.
FAX: 513-326-5550.

(See Next Column)

James M. Brennan
Anthony R. Kidd
Mark R. Chilson
Margaret R. Young
Barbara A. Lahmann

James K. Hemenway
Kenneth J. Ignozzi

Counsel for: The Children's Medical Center, Dayton, Ohio; The Colonial Stair & Woodwork Co.; The Greater Dayton Area Hospital Assn.; Mike-Sell's Potato Chip Co.; Moorman Pontiac, Inc.
Local Counsel for: Colonial Penn Insurance Co.; John Hancock Mutual Life Insurance Co.; Hertz Corp.; State Farm Insurance Co.

For Complete List of Firm Personnel, See General Section

For full biographical listings, see the Martindale-Hubbell Law Directory

*ELYRIA,** Lorain Co.

Spike & Meckler (AV)

1551 West River Street North, 44035
Telephone: 216-324-5353
Fax: 216-324-6529

MEMBERS OF FIRM

Allen S. Spike
Stephen G. Meckler
Douglas M. Brill

For full biographical listings, see the Martindale-Hubbell Law Directory

FRANKLIN, Warren Co.

Ruppert, Bronson, Chicarelli & Smith Co., L.P.A. (AV)

1063 East Second Street, P.O. Box 369, 45005
Telephone: 513-746-2832
Fax: 513-746-2855
Springboro, Ohio Office: 610 North Main, P.O. Box 186.
Telephone: 513-748-1314.

James D. Ruppert
Barbara J. Bronson
David A. Chicarelli
Rupert E. Ruppert
John D. Smith
Timothy N. Tepe

Ronald W. Ruppert
Deborah Bailey
Donna K. Czechowski
Michael J. D'Amico

For full biographical listings, see the Martindale-Hubbell Law Directory

*TOLEDO,** Lucas Co.

Robert M. Anspach Associates (AV)

Suite 2100, 405 Madison Avenue, 43604-1236
Telephone: 419-246-5757
FAX: 419-321-6979

Robert M. Anspach
Stephen R. Serraino
Catherine G. Hoolahan
Mark D. Meeks
J. Roy Nunn
Paul F. Burtis

ASSOCIATES

Barry Y. Freeman
L. Nathalie Hiemstra

For full biographical listings, see the Martindale-Hubbell Law Directory

Connelly, Soutar & Jackson (AV)

405 Madison Avenue Suite 1600, 43604
Telephone: 419-243-2100
Fax: 419-243-7119

MEMBERS OF FIRM

David M. Soutar (1937-1981)
William M. Connelly
Reginald S. Jackson, Jr.
Steven R. Smith
Steven P. Collier
Kevin E. Joyce
Anthony P. Georgetti
Michael A. Bonfiglio

ASSOCIATES

Thomas G. Mackin
Beverly J. Cox
Janine T. Avila
Sarah Steele Riordan (Not admitted in OH)

OF COUNSEL

Gerald P. Openlander

For full biographical listings, see the Martindale-Hubbell Law Directory

Robison, Curphey & O'Connell (AV)

Ninth Floor Four Seagate, 43604
Telephone: 419-249-7900
Telecopier: 419-249-7911
Blissfield, Michigan Office: 8651 East U.S. 223, P.O. Box 59.
Telephone: 517-486-4333.
Telecopier: 517-486-4271.

(See Next Column)

ROBISON, CURPHEY & O'CONNELL, *Toledo—Continued*

MEMBERS OF FIRM

John M. Curphey
E. Thomas Maguire
Ronald S. Moening
Edwin A. Coy
David W. Stuckey
Jack Zouhary
Timothy D. Krugh
James E. Brazeau
Julia Smith Wiley
Jean Ann S. Sieler
Thomas J. Antonini

ASSOCIATES

Jean M. O'Brien
D. Casey Talbott
Charles C. Butler

Counsel for: Nationwide Insurance Cos.; St. Paul Insurance Cos.; Motorists Insurance Cos.; Physicians Insurance Company of Michigan.

For Complete List of Firm Personnel, See General Section

For full biographical listings, see the Martindale-Hubbell Law Directory

OKLAHOMA

*OKLAHOMA CITY,** Oklahoma Co.

GARY L. BROOKS (AV)

6303 Waterford Boulevard, Suite 220, 73118-1122
Telephone: 405-840-1066
Fax: 405-843-8446
Dayton, Ohio Office: First National Plaza, Suite 1700, 45402.
Telephone: 513-224-3400.
Fax: 513-228-0331.

ASSOCIATE

Ann Jarrard

For full biographical listings, see the Martindale-Hubbell Law Directory

DURLAND & DURLAND (AV)

300 Bank IV Tower, 1601 Northwest Expressway, 73118
Telephone: 405-840-0060
FAX: 405-842-8547

Jack R. Durland, Jr.
Harvey L. Harmon, Jr.
Kathleen Garewal

OF COUNSEL

Jack R. Durland
Robert D. Allen

For full biographical listings, see the Martindale-Hubbell Law Directory

FENTON, FENTON, SMITH, RENEAU & MOON, A PROFESSIONAL CORPORATION (AV)

Suite 800 One Leadership Square, 211 North Robinson, 73102
Telephone: 405-235-4671
Telecopier: 405-235-5247

Edgar Fenton (1890-1977)
Milton R. Moon (1921-1988)
Wm. G. Smith (1919-1993)
Dale Reneau
Donald R. Wilson
Stephen Peterson
John A. McCaleb
C. William Threlkeld
Tom E. Mullen
Brenda K. Peterson
Mary A. Kelly
Sherry L. Smith
Laurie Walker Jones
Beverly S. Pearson
Michael D. Duncan

Robin A. Wiens
Michael S. McMillin
Greg K. Ballard
R. Dale Kimsey
C. Todd Ward
John B. Vera
Kevin E. Hill
Roger Reneau

OF COUNSEL

Elliott C. Fenton
Glen D. Johnson, Jr.
Ann M. Threlkeld
James P. Kelley
Gerald E. Kelley

Representative Clients: The Alliance Insurance Cos.; American Fidelity Insurance Co.; Chrysler Corp.; The Hartford Insurance Group; Insurance Company of North America; Roadway Express Inc.; The St. Paul Insurance Cos.; The Travelers Insurance Cos.; United States Fidelity & Guaranty Co.

For full biographical listings, see the Martindale-Hubbell Law Directory

FOLIART, HUFF, OTTAWAY & CALDWELL, A PROFESSIONAL CORPORATION (AV)

20th Floor, First National Center, 120 North Robinson, 73102
Telephone: 405-232-4633
FAX: 405-232-3462

James D. Foliart
Glen D. Huff
Larry D. Ottaway
M. Dan Caldwell
Monty B. Bottom
Michael C. Felty

(See Next Column)

Susan A. Short
David A. Branscum
Timothy M. Melton
Darrell W. Downs
David K. McPhail
Kevin E. McCarty
Michael T. Maloan
Jeffrey R. Atkins

For full biographical listings, see the Martindale-Hubbell Law Directory

MCCAFFREY & TAWWATER (AV)

Bank of Oklahoma Plaza, Suite 1100 201 Robert S. Kerr Avenue, 73102
Telephone: 405-235-2900
Fax: 405-235-4932
Other Oklahoma City, Oklahoma Offices: Suite 1950, One Leadership Square, 211 North Robinson.

MEMBERS OF FIRM

George J. McCaffrey
Larry A. Tawwater

ASSOCIATES

Robert M. Behlen
Charles L. Cashion
Jo Lynn Slama
Gloria E. Trout
Loren F. Gibson
David Little
Steven R. Davis
Piper E. Mills

For full biographical listings, see the Martindale-Hubbell Law Directory

MILLS & WHITTEN, A PROFESSIONAL CORPORATION (AV)

Suite 500, One Leadership Square 211 North Robinson, 73102
Telephone: 405-239-2500
Fax: 405-235-4655

Earl D. Mills
Reggie N. Whitten
Robert B. Mills
W. Wayne Mills
Bill M. Roberts

Steve L. Lawson
Barbara K. Buratti
Kathryn D. Mansell
Glynis C. Edgar
Kent R. McGuire
Donald R. Martin, Jr.
Kay L. Hargrave
Brian E. Dittrich
Douglas A. Terry

Representative Clients: Biomet, Inc.; Crum & Forster Commercial Ins. Co.; Mid-Continent Casualty Co.; Oklahoma Farm Bureau Mutual Ins. Co.; The St. Paul Insurance Companies; OML Municipal Assurance Group; Great West Casualty; Houston General Ins. Co.; National American Ins. Co.; Progressive Casualty; Titan Indemnity.

For full biographical listings, see the Martindale-Hubbell Law Directory

PIERCE COUCH HENDRICKSON BAYSINGER & GREEN (AV)

1109 North Francis, P.O. Box 26350, 73126
Telephone: 405-235-1611
Fax: 405-235-2904
Tulsa, Oklahoma Office: Suite 6110, 5555 East 71St. Street, 74136.
Telephone: 918-493-4944.
Fax: 918-493-6196.

MEMBERS OF FIRM

Calvin W. Hendrickson
Inona Jane Harness
Russell L. Hendrickson
John Roger Hurt
Frances E. Patton

ASSOCIATES

John Christopher Condren
E. Marissa Lane
Scott A. Law
G. Calvin Sharpe

OF COUNSEL

Janet Childers Pope

Representative Clients: Physicians Liability Insurance Co.; Physicians Casualty Insurance Co.; Continental Insurance Healthcare; Texas Medical Liability Trust; Sterling Medical Associates; Physicians Mutual Insurance Co.; Pennsylvania Healthcare Insurance Corp.

For Complete List of Firm Personnel, See General Section

For full biographical listings, see the Martindale-Hubbell Law Directory

*TULSA,** Tulsa Co.

ATKINSON, HASKINS, NELLIS, BOUDREAUX, HOLEMAN, PHIPPS & BRITTINGHAM (AV)

A Partnership including Professional Corporations
1500 ParkCentre, 525 South Main Street, 74103
Telephone: 918-582-8877
Fax: 918-585-8096

PARTNERS

Michael P. Atkinson, P.C.
Walter D. Haskins, P.C.
Gregory D. Nellis, P.C.
Paul T. Boudreaux, P.C.
Daniel E. Holeman, P.C.
K. Clark Phipps
Galen Lee Brittingham, P.C.
John S. Gladd

(See Next Column)

ATKINSON, HASKINS, NELLIS, BOUDREAUX, HOLEMAN, PHIPPS & BRITTINGHAM—*Continued*

ASSOCIATES

Martha J. Phillips
Marthanda J. Beckworth
Ann E. Allison
William A. Fiasco
Owen T. Evans
Mark W. Maguire
Jon D. Starr
Michael R. Annis
James N. Edmonds
David A. Russell
Kirsten E. Pace

OF COUNSEL

Joseph F. Glass

Representative Clients: Allstate Insurance Co.; Crum & Forester Insurance Co.; Hartford Insurance Company; National American Insurance Co.; Federated Insurance Co.; Guaranty National Insurance Co.; Liberty Mutual Insurance Co.; Physicians Liability Insurance Co.; State Farm Mutual Automobile Insurance Co.; United States Aviation Underwriters.

For full biographical listings, see the Martindale-Hubbell Law Directory

BEST, SHARP, HOLDEN, SHERIDAN, BEST & SULLIVAN, A PROFESSIONAL CORPORATION (AV)

Oneok Plaza, 100 W. 5th, Suite 808, 74103-4225
Telephone: 918-582-1234
Fax: 918-585-9447

Joseph M. Best
Joseph A. Sharp
Steven E. Holden
Timothy G. Best
Daniel S. Sullivan
Amy Kempfert

Karen M. Grundy
Malinda S. Matlock
Terry S. O'Donnell
Douglas E. Stall
Bobby L. Latham, Jr.
Kenneth E. Wagner

For full biographical listings, see the Martindale-Hubbell Law Directory

FELDMAN, HALL, FRANDEN, WOODARD & FARRIS (AV)

1400 Park Centre, 525 South Main, 74103-4409
Telephone: 918-583-7129
Telecopier: 918-584-3814

MEMBERS OF FIRM

W. E. Green (1889-1977)
William S. Hall (1930-1991)
Raymond G. Feldman
Robert A. Franden
John R. Woodard, III
Joseph R. Farris
Larry G. Taylor
Victor R. Seagle
Tony M. Graham

ASSOCIATES

Jacqueline O'Neil Haglund
Jody Nathan
R. Jack Freeman
J. David Mustain
Margaret E. Dunn
Ellen Caslavka Edwards
Douglass R. Elliott
Cathy G. Stricker
R. Daniel Scroggins

Representative Clients: CIGNA; The Equitable Life Assurance Society of the United States; Browning-Ferris Industries, Inc.; American Cyanamid Co.; American Home Assurance Co.; Oklahoma Bar Professional Liability Insurance Co.; American Motors Corp.; Sunbeam Corp.; Aviation Underwriters Inc.; Progressive Casualty Insurance Co.

For full biographical listings, see the Martindale-Hubbell Law Directory

RICHARDS, PAUL, RICHARDS & SIEGEL (AV)

Suite 400, Reunion Center, 9 East 4th Street, 74103
Telephone: 918-584-2583
Telefax: 918-587-8521

MEMBERS OF FIRM

John R. Richards (Deceased)
John R. Paul
Phil R. Richards
Nancy Jane Siegel

ASSOCIATES

Richard E. Warzynski
Richard L. Blanchard
John G. Barnhart
Suzanne Hale Costin

OF COUNSEL

John R. Caslavka

Reference: Bank of Oklahoma, Tulsa, Oklahoma.

For full biographical listings, see the Martindale-Hubbell Law Directory

SECREST, HILL & FOLLUO (AV)

7134 South Yale, Suite 900, 74136-6342
Telephone: 918-494-5905
Fax: 918-494-2847

MEMBERS OF FIRM

James K. Secrest, II
W. Michael Hill
Dan S. Folluo

(See Next Column)

Dan W. Ernst
Melvin C. Weiman
Edward John Main
Roger N. Butler, Jr.
Andrew B. Morsman
Bob D. James
Douglas M. Borochoff

For full biographical listings, see the Martindale-Hubbell Law Directory

WILBURN, MASTERSON & SMILING (AV)

Executive Center II, 7134 South Yale, Suite 560, 74136-6337
Telephone: 918-494-0414
Fax: 918-493-3455

Ray H. Wilburn
Michael J. Masterson
A. Mark Smiling

ASSOCIATES

Rhett Henry Wilburn
Jane R. Cowdery
Merle L. Tyler
Wendy S. Brooks

For full biographical listings, see the Martindale-Hubbell Law Directory

OREGON

*PORTLAND,** Multnomah Co.

COONEY & CREW, P.C. (AV)

Pioneer Tower, Suite 890, 888 S.W. Fifth Avenue, 97204
Telephone: 503-224-7600
FAX: 503-224-6740

Paul A. Cooney
Thomas E. Cooney
Thomas M. Cooney
Brent M. Crew
Michael D. Crew
Kelly T. Hagan
Raymond F. Mensing, Jr.
Robert S. Perkins

LEGAL SUPPORT PERSONNEL

Alma Weber (Paralegal)

For full biographical listings, see the Martindale-Hubbell Law Directory

PENNSYLVANIA

*EASTON,** Northampton Co.

GUS MILIDES (AV)

654 Wolf Avenue, 18042
Telephone: 610-258-0433

ASSOCIATE

Beth Ann Milides

For full biographical listings, see the Martindale-Hubbell Law Directory

ELKINS PARK, Montgomery Co.

MONAGHAN & GOLD, P.C. (AV)

7837 Old York Road, 19027
Telephone: 215-782-1800
Fax: 215-782-1010

John F. X. Monaghan, Jr.
Alan Steven Gold

Brian E. Appel
Murray R. Glickman
Barbara Malett Weitz
Tanya M. Sweet

*HARRISBURG,** Dauphin Co.

ANGINO & ROVNER, P.C. (AV)

4503 North Front Street, 17110-1799
Telephone: 717-238-6791
Fax: 717-238-5610

Richard C. Angino
Neil J. Rovner

Joseph M. Melillo
Terry S. Hyman
David L. Lutz
Michael E. Kosik
Pamela G. Shuman
Catherine M. Mahady-Smith
Richard A. Sadlock
David S. Wisneski
Nijole C. Olson
Michael J. Navitsky
Robin J. Marzella
Lawrence F. Barone
Dawn L. Jennings
Stephen R. Pedersen

References: Harrisburg Credit Exchange; Hamilton Bank.

For full biographical listings, see the Martindale-Hubbell Law Directory

Harrisburg—Continued

CALDWELL & KEARNS, A PROFESSIONAL CORPORATION (AV)

3631 North Front Street, 17110-1533
Telephone: 717-232-7661
Fax: 717-232-2766

Richard L. Kearns
James L. Goldsmith
James G. Nealon, III

Representative Clients: Allstate Insurance Co.; Erie Insurance Exchange; Government Employees Insurance Co.; Royal Globe Insurance Cos.; United States Fidelity & Guaranty Insurance; The Home Insurance Co.; Pennsylvania Institute of Certified Public Accountants; Pennsylvania Association of Realtors; Motor Truck Equipment Co.; Mack Sales and Service, Inc.
Reference: Fulton Bank.

For full biographical listings, see the Martindale-Hubbell Law Directory

GOLDBERG, KATZMAN & SHIPMAN, P.C. (AV)

320 Market Street - Strawberry Square, P.O. Box 1268, 17108-1268
Telephone: 717-234-4161
Telecopier: 717-234-6808; 717-234-6810

F. Lee Shipman
James M. Sheehan
April L. Strang-Kutay
Guy H. Brooks

Representative Client: Fulton Bank.

For Complete List of Firm Personnel, See General Section

For full biographical listings, see the Martindale-Hubbell Law Directory

HEPFORD, SWARTZ & MORGAN (AV)

111 North Front Street, P.O. Box 889, 17108-0889
Telephone: 717-234-4121
Fax: 717-232-6802
Lewistown, Pennsylvania Office: 12 South Main Street, P.O. Box 867.
Telephone: 717-248-3913.

MEMBERS OF FIRM

H. Joseph Hepford
Lee C. Swartz
James G. Morgan, Jr.
Sandra L. Meilton
Stephen M. Greecher, Jr.
Dennis R. Sheaffer

COUNSEL

Stanley H. Siegel (Resident, Lewistown Office)

ASSOCIATES

Richard A. Estacio
Michael H. Park
Andrew K. Stutzman

For full biographical listings, see the Martindale-Hubbell Law Directory

JOSEPH A. KLEIN A PROFESSIONAL CORPORATION (AV)

100 Chestnut Street, Suite 210, P.O. Box 1152, 17108
Telephone: 717-233-0132
Fax: 717-233-2516

Joseph A. Klein
Mark S. Silver

For full biographical listings, see the Martindale-Hubbell Law Directory

METZGER, WICKERSHAM, KNAUSS & ERB (AV)

Mellon Bank Building, 111 Market Street, P.O. Box 93, 17108-0093
Telephone: 717-238-8187
Telefax: 717-234-9478
Other Harrisburg, Pennsylvania Office: 4813 Jonestown Road, P.O. Box 93, 17108.
Telephone: 717-652-7020.

MEMBERS OF FIRM

Maurice R. Metzger (1918-1980)
F. Brewster Wickersham (1918-1974)
Edward E. Knauss, III (Retired)
Christian S. Erb, Jr.
Robert E. Yetter
James F. Carl
Robert P. Reed
Edward E. Knauss, IV
Jered L. Hock
Karl R. Hildabrand

ASSOCIATES

Richard B. Druby
Steven P. Miner
Clark DeVere

Representative Clients: Allstate Insurance Co.; Chubb Group of Insurance Companies; Fireman's Fund American Insurance Group; Liberty Mutual Insurance Co.; Continental Insurance Co.; Crum & Forster.

For full biographical listings, see the Martindale-Hubbell Law Directory

THOMAS, THOMAS & HAFER (AV)

305 North Front Street, 6th Floor, P.O. Box 999, 17108
Telephone: 717-237-7100
Fax: 717-237-7105
Verify: 717-255-7642

(See Next Column)

MEMBERS OF FIRM

Joseph P. Hafer
James K. Thomas, II
Jeffrey B. Rettig
Peter J. Curry
R. Burke McLemore, Jr.
Edward H. Jordan, Jr.
C. Kent Price
Randall G. Gale
David L. Schwalm
Kevin E. Osborne
Douglas B. Marcello
Peter J. Speaker
Paul J. Dellasega

OF COUNSEL

James K. Thomas

Daniel J. Gallagher
Robert A. Taylor
Sarah W. Arosell
Eugene N. McHugh
Richard C. Seneca
Stephen E. Geduldig
Paula Gayle Sanders
Karen S. Coates
Ann F. DePaulis
Margaret A. Scheaffer
Todd R. Narvol

Representative Clients: Aetna Casualty & Surety Co.; Commercial Union Insurance Companies; Geisinger Medical Center; Hartford Insurance Group; Liberty Mutual Insurance Co.; Medical Inter-Insurance Exchange; Medical Protective Co.; Pennsylvania Hospital Insurance Co.; Pennsylvania Medical Society Liability Insurance Co.

For full biographical listings, see the Martindale-Hubbell Law Directory

*LANCASTER,** Lancaster Co.

ATLEE & HALL (AV)

8 North Queen Street, P.O. Box 449, 17603
Telephone: 717-393-9596
FAX: 717-393-2138

MEMBERS OF FIRM

William A. Atlee, Jr.
Thomas W. Hall

ASSOCIATES

Steven D. Costello
Dan M. Brookhart
Jan S. Barnett
Terri L. Ackerman

For full biographical listings, see the Martindale-Hubbell Law Directory

*MEDIA,** Delaware Co.

BEATTY, YOUNG, OTIS & LINCKE (AV)

300 West State Street, Suite 200, P.O. Box 901, 19063-0901
Telephone: 610-565-8800
Fax: 610-565-8127

MEMBERS OF FIRM

Lewis B. Beatty, Jr.
David J. Otis
William P. Lincke

ASSOCIATES

Natalie M. Habert
Peter W. Dicce
Carol E. Tucci
Katherine J. Dickinson (Not admitted in PA)

OF COUNSEL

Robert C. Grasberger
Joseph R. Young (1921-1993)

Representative Clients: Suburban Federal Savings Bank; Elwyn Inc.; Delaware County School Employees Health and Welfare Trust.

For full biographical listings, see the Martindale-Hubbell Law Directory

KASSAB ARCHBOLD JACKSON & O'BRIEN (AV)

Lawyers-Title Building, 214 North Jackson Street, P.O. Box 626, 19063
Telephone: 610-565-3800
Telecopier: 610-892-6888
Wilmington, Delaware Office: 1326 King Street.
Telephone: 302-656-3393.
Fax: 302-656-1993.
Wildwood, New Jersey Office: 5201 New Jersey Avenue.
Telephone: 609-522-6559.

MEMBERS OF FIRM

Edward Kassab
William C. Archbold, Jr.
Robert James Jackson
Joseph Patrick O'Brien
Richard A. Stanko
Roy T. J. Stegena

OF COUNSEL

Matthew J. Ryan
John W. Nilon, Jr.

ASSOCIATES

Kevin William Gibson
Cynthia Kassab Larosa
Marc S. Stein
Terrance A. Kline
George C. McFarland, Jr.
Jill E. Aversa
Pamela A. La Torre
Kenneth D. Kynett

Representative Clients furnished upon request.

For full biographical listings, see the Martindale-Hubbell Law Directory

JOHN A. LUCHSINGER (AV)

25 East Second Street, P.O. Box 955, 19063
Telephone: 610-565-2930
Fax: 610-565-9242

(See Next Column)

JOHN A. LUCHSINGER—*Continued*

Thomas J. O'Malley, Jr.

Representative Clients: State Farm Mutual Insurance Co.; The St. Paul Co.; Crum & Foster Group; Metropolitan Tile Abstract Co.; Chester County Radiologic Associates; The Central Cos.; State Farm Fire and Casualty Co.; Penn Mutual Fire Insurance Co.; University of Pennsylvania Hospital; United States Fire Insurance Co.; Scott Paper; Employer's of Wausau Insurance Co.; CHUBB Group of Insurance Co.;The Medical Protection Co.; Children's Hospital of Philadelphia; Weaver Corp.; J.C. Penney Life Insurance Co.
Reference: Fidelity Bank.

For full biographical listings, see the Martindale-Hubbell Law Directory

*NORRISTOWN,** Montgomery Co.

LINDLEY M. COWPERTHWAIT, JR., P.C. (AV)

17 East Airy Street, 19401
Telephone: 610-277-6622
Fax: 610-277-6601
Cherry Hill, New Jersey Office: 1040 North Kings Highway, Suite 600, 08034.
Telephone: 609-482-8600.

Lindley M. Cowperthwait, Jr.
Adam D. Zucker

For full biographical listings, see the Martindale-Hubbell Law Directory

RAYMOND M. VICTOR, P.C. (AV)

616 DeKalb Street, 19401
Telephone: 610-272-5253
Fax: 610-272-7422

Raymond M. Victor
Dolores Victor

For full biographical listings, see the Martindale-Hubbell Law Directory

*PHILADELPHIA,** Philadelphia Co.

FARAGE AND MCBRIDE (AV)

836 Suburban Station Building, 1617 John F. Kennedy Boulevard, 19103
Telephone: 215-563-3973
Fax: 215-563-3094
CHerry Hill, New Jersey Office: 1040 N. Kings Highway, 08034.
Telephone: 609-321-0442.

MEMBERS OF FIRM

Donald J. Farage
James F. McBride

Dennis L. Scanlon
Thomas C. Sullivan

Reference: Girard Trust Co.

For full biographical listings, see the Martindale-Hubbell Law Directory

GALLAGHER, REILLY AND LACHAT, P.C. (AV)

Suite 1300, 2000 Market Street, 19103
Telephone: 215-299-3000
FAX: 215-299-3010
Pennsauken, New Jersey Office: Kevon Office Center, Suite 130, 2500 McClellan Boulevard, 08109.
Telephone: 609-663-8200.

Stanley S. Frazee, Jr.
Paul F. X. Gallagher
Thomas F. Reilly
Frederick T. Lachat, Jr.
Richard K. Hohn
James Emerson Egbert
Stephen A. Scheuerle
Elizabeth F. Walker

David Scott Morgan
Wilfred T. Mills, Jr.
Maureen Rowan
Charles L. McNabb
Thomas O'Neill
Laurence I. Gross
Sean F. Kennedy
Milica Novakovic
John A. Livingood, Jr.

SPECIAL COUNSEL

Dolores Rocco Kulp

For full biographical listings, see the Martindale-Hubbell Law Directory

GERMAN, GALLAGHER & MURTAGH, A PROFESSIONAL CORPORATION (AV)

Fifth Floor, The Bellevue, 200 South Broad Street, 19102
Telephone: 215-545-7700
Telecopier: 215-732-4182
Cherry Hill, New Jersey Office: Suite 643, 1040 North Kings Highway.
Telephone: 609-667-7676.
Lancaster, Pennsylvania Office: 40 East Grant Street.
Telephone: 717-293-8070.

(See Next Column)

Edward C. German
Michael D. Gallagher
Dean F. Murtagh
Philip A. Ryan
Robert P. Corbin
David P. Rovner
Kathryn A. Dux
Gary R. Gremminger
Kim Plouffe
Jeffrey N. German
John P. Shusted

Kathleen M. Carson
Kevin R. McNulty
Linda Porr Sweeney
Gary H. Hunter
Frank A. Gerolamo, III
Milan K. Mrkobrad
Thomas M. Going
Vincent J. Di Stefano, Jr.
Jack T. Ribble, Jr.
Kimberly J. Keiser
Bernard E. Jude Quinn
Gerald C. Montella
Lisa Beth Zucker
Shelby L. Mattioli
Daniel J. Divis
D. Selaine Belver
Christine L. Davis
Daniel L. Grill
Marta I. Sierra-Epperson
Paul G. Kirk
Aileen R. Thompson
Otis V. Maynard
Gregory S. Capps

For full biographical listings, see the Martindale-Hubbell Law Directory

GOLDFEIN & JOSEPH, A PROFESSIONAL CORPORATION (AV)

17th Floor, Packard Building, 111 South 15th Street, 19102-2695
Telephone: 215-977-9800
Fax: 215-988-0062
Princeton, New Jersey Office: Princeton Metro Center, Suite 115, 5 Vaughn Drive.
Telephone: 609-520-0400.
Fax: 609-520-1450.
Wilmington, Delaware Office: PNC Bank Center, Suite 1212, P.O. Box 2206, 222 Delaware Avenue.
Telephone: 302-656-3301.
Fax: 302-656-0643.

Edward B. Joseph
Fredric L. Goldfein
E. Chandler Hosmer, III
Ellen Brown Furman
Leslie Anne Miller
David C. Weinberg
James Patrick Hadden
Bernard L. Levinthal
Gary H. Kaplan (Resident, Wilmington, Delaware Office)
Roseann Lynn Brenner
Elissa J. Kahn

John A. Turlik
Susan Burton Stadtmauer
David M. Katzenstein (Resident, Princeton, New Jersey Office)
Scott I. Fegley
William J. Weiss
Michael A. Billotti (Not admitted in PA; Resident, Princeton, New Jersey Office)
Lawrence E. Currier
Robert P. Coleman
Robert T. Connor
Ann B. Cairns
Frederick A. Kiegel
Janet E. Golup
Ted Martin Berg (Resident, Wilmington, Delaware Office)

OF COUNSEL

Charles B. Burr, II

For full biographical listings, see the Martindale-Hubbell Law Directory

KELLEY, JASONS, MCGUIRE & SPINELLI (AV)

Suite 1300, 1234 Market Street, 19107-3713
Telephone: 215-854-0658
Fax: 215-854-8434
Cherry Hill, New Jersey Office: 1230 Brace Road, 08034.
Telephone: 609-429-8956.
Wilmington, Delaware Office: 1220 Market Building, P.O. Box 194, 19899.
Telephone: 302-652-8560.
Fax: 302-652-8405.

MEMBERS OF FIRM

John Patrick Kelley
Catherine N. Jasons
Joseph W. McGuire
Armand J. Della Porta, Jr.
Christopher N. Santoro
Robert N. Spinelli
Thomas P. Hanna
Thomas J. Johanson
Michael L. Turner

ASSOCIATES

Kelly J. Sasso (Resident, Wilmington, Delaware Office)
Richard L. Walker, II
Bernard E. Kueny, III
Timothy McGowan
Neal C. Glenn

OF COUNSEL

Joseph P. Green
Matthew D. Blum, M.D.
W. Matthew Reber

For full biographical listings, see the Martindale-Hubbell Law Directory

KOLSBY, GORDON, ROBIN, SHORE & ROTHWEILER, A PROFESSIONAL CORPORATION (AV)

One Liberty Place, 22nd Floor, 1650 Market Street, 19103
Telephone: 215-851-9700
Fax: 215-851-9701

(See Next Column)

KOLSBY, GORDON, ROBIN, SHORE & ROTHWEILER A PROFESSIONAL CORPORATION, *Philadelphia—Continued*

Herbert F. Kolsby
Allan H. Gordon
F. Philip Robin
Mitchell J. Shore
Kenneth Michael Rothweiler
Nadeem A. Bezar
Daniel Jeck

For full biographical listings, see the Martindale-Hubbell Law Directory

LEVIN, FISHBEIN, SEDRAN & BERMAN (AV)

Suite 600, 320 Walnut Street, 19106
Telephone: 215-592-1500
Fax: 215-592-4663

MEMBERS OF FIRM

Arnold Levin
Michael D. Fishbein
Howard J. Sedran
Laurence S. Berman
Frederick S. Longer

Robert M. Unterberger
Craig D. Ginsburg
Jonathan Shub
Cheryl R. Brown Hill
Roberta Shaner

For full biographical listings, see the Martindale-Hubbell Law Directory

MCKISSOCK & HOFFMAN, P.C. (AV)

1700 Market Street, Suite 3000, 19103
Telephone: 215-246-2100
Fax: 215-246-2144
Mount Holly, New Jersey Office: 211 High Street.
Telephone: 609-267-1006.
Doylestown, Pennsylvania Office: 77 North Broad Street, Second Floor.
Telephone: 215-345-4501.
Harrisburg, Pennsylvania Office: 127 State Street.
Telephone: 717-234-0103.

J. Bruce McKissock
Peter J. Hoffman
Richard L. McMonigle
Jill Baratz Clarke
Marybeth Stanton Christiansen
Catherine Hill Kunda
Bryant Craig Black (Resident, Harrisburg, Office)
John M. Willis
John J. McGrath
Debra Schwaderer Dunne
Donald J. Brooks, Jr.
William J. Mundy
Elizabeth E. Davies
Christopher Thomson
Kathleen M. Kenna
K. Reed Haywood
Sara J. Thomson
Maureen P. Fitzgerald
Veronica E. Noonan
Kathleen M. Sholette
Patricia D. Shippee

For full biographical listings, see the Martindale-Hubbell Law Directory

MCWILLIAMS AND MINTZER, P.C. (AV)

Eight Penn Center, 20th Floor, 1628 John F. Kennedy Boulevard, 19103-2708
Telephone: 215-981-1060
Fax: 215-981-0133

Edward C. Mintzer, Jr.
Anthony F. Zabicki, Jr.
Kenneth D. Powell, Jr.

OF COUNSEL

Daniel T. McWilliams

Patrick S. Mintzer
John Michael Skrocki
Patricia A. Powell
Regina Spause McGraw

LEGAL SUPPORT PERSONNEL

Frances Kelly McCaffery

Representative Clients: Pennsylvania Hospital Insurance Co.; Frankford Hospital & Health Care Systems; Thomas Jefferson University Hospital; Princeton Insurance Co.; Pawtucket Insurance Co.; Medical Inter-Insurance Exchange; Medical Protective Co.; ITT Hartford; Common of Pennsylvania Medical Professional Liability Catastrophe Loss Fund.

For full biographical listings, see the Martindale-Hubbell Law Directory

PERRY, FIALKOWSKI & PERRY (AV)

Suite 1802 One Penn Square West, 19102
Telephone: 215-561-4110
Fax: 215-981-1472
Clementon, New Jersey Office: 180 White Horse Pike.
Telephone: 609-627-1005.

MEMBERS OF FIRM

David Perry
Anne E. Fialkowski
Sherryl R. Perry
Marcia F. Rosenbaum

For full biographical listings, see the Martindale-Hubbell Law Directory

SARAH M. THOMPSON (AV)

1710 Spruce Street, 19103
Telephone: 215-790-4568
Fax: 215-735-2211

For full biographical listings, see the Martindale-Hubbell Law Directory

*PITTSBURGH,** Allegheny Co.

BERGER KAPETAN MEYERS ROSEN LOUIK & RAIZMAN, P.C. (AV)

Suite 200 The Frick Building, 15219-6003
Telephone: 412-281-4200
Fax: 412-281-3262

Daniel M. Berger
Alex N. Kapetan
Jerry I. Meyers
Neil R. Rosen
Dorothy L. Raizman

For full biographical listings, see the Martindale-Hubbell Law Directory

JOHN A. CAPUTO & ASSOCIATES (AV)

Fifth Floor, Three Gateway Center, 15222
Telephone: 412-391-4990

Allan Meyers Cox
Bernard C. Caputo

For full biographical listings, see the Martindale-Hubbell Law Directory

DAVIES MCFARLAND & CARROLL, P.C. (AV)

One Gateway Center, Tenth Floor, 15222
Telephone: 412-281-0737

Ralph A. Davies
Gregg P. Otto
Edward A. McFarland
Daniel P. Carroll
William D. Geiger
Francis Garger
Lynn E. Bell
David S. Smith
James M. Poerio

C. Robert Keenan, III
David E. Lamm
Donna M. Lowman
Christopher Pierson
William S. Evans
Keith M. Hoffman
Lisa M. Montarti
Robert P. Walter

Representative Clients: Cincinnati Insurance Co.; Pennsylvania Medical Society Liability Insurance Co.; Physicians Insurance Company; Medical Protective Co.

For full biographical listings, see the Martindale-Hubbell Law Directory

DICKIE, MCCAMEY & CHILCOTE, A PROFESSIONAL CORPORATION (AV)

Suite 400, Two PPG Place, 15222-5402
Telephone: 412-281-7272
Fax: 412-392-5367
Wheeling, West Virginia Office: Suite 2002, 1233 Main Street, 26003-2839.
Telephone: 304-233-1022.
Facsimile: 304-233-1026.

David B. Fawcett
Theodore O. Struk
Wilbur McCoy Otto
Richard S. Dorfzaun
Daniel P. Stefko
James F. Malone, III
Eugene F. Scanlon, Jr.
Charles W. Kenrick
James R. Miller
Paul W. Roman, Jr.
Joseph S. D. Christof, II
Stewart M. Flam
J. Lawson Johnston
David M. Neuhart
Robert J. Marino
Stephen M. Houghton
Larry A. Silverman
Arthur L. Schwarzwaelder
Kenneth S. Mroz
Ingrid Medzius Lundberg
Frederick W. Bode, III
Jeffrey T. Wiley
Thomas M. Fallert
Edmund L. Olszewski, Jr.
Richard J. Federowicz
John C. Conti
Ray F. Middleman
Terry C. Cavanaugh

Anthony J. Williott
George P. Kachulis
John T. Pion
Hunter A. McGeary, Jr.
Bonnie Pearce Webster
Joseph L. Luvara
Howard A. Chajson
Marcelle M. Theis
Brian T. Must
Alyson J. Kirleis
Paul S. Mazeski
Steven W. Zoffer
Robert G. Voinchet, Jr.
Jennifer M. Kirschler
Edward A. Miller
Laurel A. Peters

For Complete List of Firm Personnel, See General Section

For full biographical listings, see the Martindale-Hubbell Law Directory

EVANS, IVORY P.C. (AV)

1311 Frick Building, 15219
Telephone: 412-471-3740
Fax: 412-471-3457

(See Next Column)

EVANS, IVORY P.C.—*Continued*

Paul E. Moses
Robin S. Wertkin
Thomas Hollander
Dennis M. Morgenstern
J. Bradley Kearns

For full biographical listings, see the Martindale-Hubbell Law Directory

EVANS, PORTNOY & QUINN (AV)

36th Floor, One Oxford Centre, 301 Grant Street, 15219-6401
Telephone: 412-765-3800
Fax: 412-765-3747

Charles E. Evans
Irving M. Portnoy
John E. Quinn

ASSOCIATES

Anita Amato Scaglione
Herbert B. Cohen
Mark E. Milsop

For full biographical listings, see the Martindale-Hubbell Law Directory

GAITENS, TUCCERI & NICHOLAS, A PROFESSIONAL CORPORATION (AV)

519 Court Place, 15219
Telephone: 412-391-6920
Fax: 412-391-1189

Larry P. Gaitens
Vincent A. Tucceri
Romel L. Nicholas

Suzanne Bernard Merrick
Gregory G. Schwab
Anthony T. Colangelo
Michele A. McPeak
Patricia A. Monahan
Donald J. Garwood
Gregory Gleason

Reference: Pittsburgh National Bank.

For full biographical listings, see the Martindale-Hubbell Law Directory

HEINTZMAN, WARREN & WISE (AV)

The 35th Floor, Gulf Tower, 707 Grant Street, 15219
Telephone: 412-394-7810
Fax: 412-263-5222

MEMBERS OF FIRM

Michael D. Heintzman
Charles S. Warren

For full biographical listings, see the Martindale-Hubbell Law Directory

TARASI & JOHNSON, P.C. (AV)

510 Third Avenue, 15219
Telephone: 412-391-7135
Fax: 412-471-2673

Louis M. Tarasi, Jr.

For Complete List of Firm Personnel, See General Section

For full biographical listings, see the Martindale-Hubbell Law Directory

*SCRANTON,** Lackawanna Co.

FOLEY, MCLANE, NEALON, FOLEY & MCDONALD (AV)

Linden Plaza, 600 Linden Street, P.O. Box 1108, 18501-1108
Telephone: 717-342-8194
Fax: 717-342-4658
Stroudsburg, Pennsylvania Office: 26 North Sixth Street.
Telephone: 717-424-1757.
Fax: 717-424-2764.

Thomas J. Foley, Jr.
John T. McLane
Terrence R. Nealon
Michael J. Foley
Michael J. McDonald
Thomas J. Foley, III (Resident, Stroudsburg Office)
Kevin P. Foley
Malcolm L. MacGregor
M. Colleen Foley Canovas

For full biographical listings, see the Martindale-Hubbell Law Directory

O'MALLEY & HARRIS, P.C. (AV)

345 Wyoming Avenue, 18503
Telephone: 717-348-3711
Fax: 717-348-4092
Stroudsburg, Pennsylvania Office: 111 North Seventh Street.
Telephone: 717-421-2252.
Wilkes-Barre, Pennsylvania Office: Courthouse Square Towers, North River Street.
Telephone: 717-829-3232.
FAX: 717-829-4418.
Williamsport, Pennsylvania Office: 321 Pine Street, Suite 308.
Telephone: 717-323-4380.

(See Next Column)

Eugene Nogi (1905-1975)
Henry Nogi (1900-1976)
Russell O. O'Malley, Sr. (1904-1993)
William H. Amesbury (Resident, Wilkes-Barre Office)
Paul A. Barrett
J. Scott Brady
Bruce L. Coyer
John Q. Durkin
Gerald J. Hanchulak
Norman Harris
Richard K. Hodges
Timothy J. Holland (Resident, Wilkes-Barre Office)
Daniel Morgan
Michael Perry
Joseph R. Rydzewski
Jane M. Carlonas
James M. Tressler
Matthew P. Barrett

Representative Clients: Robert Packer Hospital; GSGS & B Architects & Engineers; Aetna Casualty & Surety Co.; Pennsylvania Hospital Insurance Co.; United States Fidelity & Guaranty Insurance Co.; Selective Insurance Co.; Maryland Casualty Insurance Co.; Robert Packer Hospital; United Gilsonite Laboratories; Electric Mutual Insurance Co.

For full biographical listings, see the Martindale-Hubbell Law Directory

SCANLON, HOWLEY, SCANLON & DOHERTY (AV)

321 Spruce Street, 10th Floor, 18503
Telephone: 717-346-7651

MEMBERS OF FIRM

James M. Howley
James M. Scanlon
James A. Doherty, Jr.
Thomas R. Nealon
Thomas B. Helbig
Patrick R. Casey

OF COUNSEL

James W. Scanlon

Counsel for: CNA Insurance Company; Selective Insurance Company of America; The Medical Protective Co.; Harleysville Insurance Co.; Mutual Benefit Insurance Co.; The Procter & Gamble Co.; Prudential-Bach Securities, Inc.; Zurich-American Insurance Co.; The Coca-Cola Bottling Co.; The Home Insurance Co.

For full biographical listings, see the Martindale-Hubbell Law Directory

*WELLSBORO,** Tioga Co.

SPENCER, GLEASON, HEBE & RAGUE (AV)

17 Central Avenue, P.O. Box 507, 16901
Telephone: 717-724-1832
FAX: 717-724-7610

MEMBERS OF FIRM

Warren H. Spencer (1921-1991)
Gary M. Gleason
William A. Hebe
James T. Rague

ASSOCIATE

Jeffrey S. Loomis

References: Citizens & Northern Bank; Commonwealth Bank & Trust Co.

For full biographical listings, see the Martindale-Hubbell Law Directory

*WILKES-BARRE,** Luzerne Co.

HOURIGAN, KLUGER, SPOHRER & QUINN, A PROFESSIONAL CORPORATION (AV)

700 Mellon Bank Center, 8 West Market Street, 18701-1867
Telephone: 717-825-9401
FAX: 717-829-3460
Scranton, Pennsylvania Office: Suite 200, 434 Lackawanna Avenue.
Telephone: 717-346-8414.
Allentown, Pennsylvania Office: Sovereign Building, 609 Hamilton Mall.
Telephone: 610-437-1584.
Hazelton, Pennsylvania Office: CAN DO Building, One South Church Street.
Telephone: 717-455-5141.

Joseph A. Quinn, Jr.
Joseph P. Mellody, Jr.
David W. Saba
Neil L. Conway (Resident, Allentown Office)
Joseph A. Lach (Managing Partner)
Neil E. Wenner (Resident, Allentown Office)
Shawn P. Phillips (Resident, Allentown Office)
Mark T. Perry
David J. Selingo
Lara J. Endler
John R. Hill (Resident, Allentown Office)
Malachy E. Mannion (Resident, Scranton Office)
Kathleen Quinn DePillis (Resident, Allentown Office)

Representative Clients: Physicians Insurance Co.; Pennsylvania Medical Society Libility Insurance Co.; The Medical Protective Co.

For Complete List of Firm Personnel, See General Section

For full biographical listings, see the Martindale-Hubbell Law Directory

*WILLIAMSPORT,** Lycoming Co.

McCormick, Reeder, Nichols, Bahl, Knecht & Person (AV)

(Formerly McCormick, Herdic & Furst).
835 West Fourth Street, 17701
Telephone: 717-326-5131
Fax: 717-326-5529

OF COUNSEL

Henry Clay McCormick

MEMBERS OF FIRM

S. Dale Furst, Jr. (1904-1969)
Robert J. Sarno (1941-1982)
Paul W. Reeder
William E. Nichols
David R. Bahl
William L. Knecht
John E. Person, III
J. David Smith
Robert A. Eckenrode
Cynthia Ranck Person

ASSOCIATES

Joanne C. Ludwikowski
R. Matthew Patch
Sean P. Roman
Kenneth B. Young

General Counsel for: Northern Central Bank; Jersey Shore Steel Co.
Representative Clients: Pennsylvania Power & Light Co.; Consolidated Rail Corp.; Royal Insurance Co.; State Automobile Insurance Association.

For full biographical listings, see the Martindale-Hubbell Law Directory

Mitchell, Mitchell, Gray & Gallagher, A Professional Corporation (AV)

10 West Third Street, 17701
Telephone: 717-323-8404
Fax: 717-323-8585

C. Edward S. Mitchell
Richard A. Gray
Robert A. Gallagher
Gary L. Weber

Bret J. Southard
Eric R. Linhardt

OF COUNSEL

Jacob Neafie Mitchell

For full biographical listings, see the Martindale-Hubbell Law Directory

Rieders, Travis, Mussina, Humphrey & Harris (AV)

161 West Third Street, P.O. Box 215, 17703-0215
Telephone: 717-323-8711
1-800-326-9259
Fax: 717-323-4192

MEMBERS OF FIRM

Gary T. Harris
John M. Humphrey
Malcolm S. Mussina
Clifford A. Rieders
Ronald C. Travis
Thomas Waffenschmidt
C. Scott Waters

ASSOCIATES

Robert H. Vesely
Jeffrey C. Dohrmann
James Michael Wiley

LEGAL SUPPORT PERSONNEL

Kimberly A. Paulhamus

Representative Clients: Jersey Shore State Bank; Gamble Twp.; Crown American Corp.; Fowler Motors, Inc.; Twin Hills oldsmobile, Inc.; Brady Twp.; Cascade Twp.; Cogan House Twp.; Susquehana Twp.; Upper Fairfield Twp.; Borough of Picture Rocks.

For full biographical listings, see the Martindale-Hubbell Law Directory

RHODE ISLAND

*PROVIDENCE,** Providence Co.

Decof & Grimm, A Professional Corporation (AV)

One Smith Hill, 02903
Telephone: 401-272-1110
Facsimile: 401-351-6641
Newport, Rhode Island Office: 130 Bellevue Avenue, 02840.
Telephone: 401-848-5700.
Facsimile: 401-847-3391.

Leonard Decof
E. Paul Grimm
Mark B. Decof
John S. Foley
Vincent T. Cannon
Donna M. Di Donato
David Morowitz
Daniel J. Schatz
Howard B. Klein
Suzanne M. McGrath
Peri Ann Aptaker (Not admitted in RI)
Christine M. Renda (Not admitted in RI)

(See Next Column)

OF COUNSEL

Arthur I. Fixler

For full biographical listings, see the Martindale-Hubbell Law Directory

Gidley, Sarli & Marusak (AV)

Greater Providence Bank Building, 170 Westminster Street, 02903
Telephone: 401-274-6644
Telecopier: 401-331-9304

MEMBERS OF FIRM

Thomas D. Gidley
Michael G. Sarli
James P. Marusak
Mark C. Hadden

ASSOCIATES

Michael R. DeLuca
Linn Foster Freedman
Denise M. Lombardo
William L. Wheatley
Stuart D. Hallagan III

LEGAL SUPPORT PERSONNEL

Elaine M. Noren
Mary Repoza Caplette
Darlene E. Kotkofski

For full biographical listings, see the Martindale-Hubbell Law Directory

Vincent D. Morgera (AV)

One Old Stone Square, 02903-7104
Telephone: 401-456-0300
Telecopier: 401-456-0303

For full biographical listings, see the Martindale-Hubbell Law Directory

Rice, Dolan & Kershaw (AV)

Greater Providence Bank Building, 170 Westminster Street, Suite 900, 02903
Telephone: 401-272-8800
Telecopier: 401-421-7218

OF COUNSEL

H. Eliot Rice

MEMBERS OF FIRM

John F. Dolan
John W. Kershaw
Mark P. Dolan

ASSOCIATES

Charles Garganese, Jr.
Mark A. Fay
Elizabeth Flynn Sullivan

Local Counsel for: American International Adjustment Co.; Andover Cos.; Chubb Group of Insurance Cos.; CNA/Insurance; Government Employees Insurance; Holyoke Mutual Insurance Co.; Mutual of Omaha; Providence-Washington Insurance Group; Reliance Insurance Co.; Rhode Island Hospital.

For full biographical listings, see the Martindale-Hubbell Law Directory

SOUTH CAROLINA

*BEAUFORT,** Beaufort Co.

Davis, Tupper, Grimsley & Seelhoff (AV)

611 Bay Street, P.O. Box 2055, 29901-2055
Telephone: 803-524-1116
Facsimile: 803-524-1463

MEMBERS OF FIRM

Hutson S. Davis, Jr.
Ralph E. Tupper
James A. Grimsley, III
Scott A. Seelhoff
Erin D. Dean

For full biographical listings, see the Martindale-Hubbell Law Directory

*CHARLESTON,** Charleston Co.

Grimball & Cabaniss (AV)

The Franke Building, 171 Church Street, Suite 120, P.O. Box 816, 29402-0816
Telephone: 803-722-0311
Fax: 803-722-1374

MEMBERS OF FIRM

William H. Grimball
Joseph W. Cabaniss
Henry E. Grimball
Frank E. Grimball
Max G. Mahaffee
Eugene Patrick Corrigan, III
E. Warren Moise
Michael J. Ferri

ASSOCIATES

Kathryn S. Craven
Julie L. Weinheimer
E. Charles Grose, Jr.
Henry H. Cabaniss

Representative Clients: Chubb Group; CIGNA; CNA Insurance Cos.; Nationwide Mutual Insurance Co.; Prudential Insurance Co.; State Farm Insurance Cos.

(See Next Column)

GRIMBALL & CABANISS—*Continued*

Local Counsel for: Exxon Corp.; The Greyhound Corp.; Norfolk-Southern Corp.; Baker Hospital.

For full biographical listings, see the Martindale-Hubbell Law Directory

HAYNSWORTH, MARION, MCKAY & GUÉRARD, L.L.P (AV)

#2 Prioleau Street, P.O. Box 1119, 29402
Telephone: 803-722-7606
Telecopier: 803-723-5263
Columbia, South Carolina Office: Suite 2400 AT&T Building, 1201 Main Street, P.O. Drawer 7157, 29202.
Telephone: 803-765-1818.
Telecopier: 803-765-2399.
Greenville, South Carolina Office: Two Insignia Financial Plaza, 75 Beattie Place, P.O. Box 2048, 29602.
Telephone: 803-240-3200.
Telecopier: 803-240-3300.

MEMBERS OF FIRM

W. E. Applegate, III
James J. Hinchey, Jr. (Resident)

ASSOCIATES

Coleman Miller Legerton
Meredith Grier Buyck

Counsel for: Bank of South Carolina; Baker Hospital; Healthsources of South Carolina; Allstate Insurance Co.; CSX Corporation; Lloyd's Underwriters; Coward-Hund Construction Co.; South Carolina Public Service Authority; South Carolina Jobs - Economic Development Authority; City of Hanahan.

For Complete List of Firm Personnel, See General Section

For full biographical listings, see the Martindale-Hubbell Law Directory

HOOD LAW FIRM (AV)

172 Meeting Street, P.O. Box 1508, 29402
Telephone: 803-577-4435
FAX: 803-722-1630

MEMBERS OF FIRM

Robert H. Hood
Louis P. Herns
G. Mark Phillips
Carl Everette Pierce, II
John K. Blincow, Jr.

James G. Kennedy
James Dowell Gandy, III
William R. Hearn, Jr.
Joseph C. Wilson, IV
Dixon F. Pearce, III
Margaret Allison Snead
Barbara Wynne Showers
Christine L. Companion
Hugh Willcox Buyck
Jerry A. Smith
Allan Poe Sloan, III
Todd W. Smyth

For full biographical listings, see the Martindale-Hubbell Law Directory

ROSEN, ROSEN & HAGOOD, P.A. (AV)

134 Meeting Street, Suite 200, P.O. Box 893, 29402
Telephone: 803-577-6726

Morris D. Rosen
Richard S. Rosen
Susan Corner Rosen

Reference: NationsBank of South Carolina, N.A.

For Complete List of Firm Personnel, See General Section

For full biographical listings, see the Martindale-Hubbell Law Directory

YOUNG, CLEMENT, RIVERS & TISDALE (AV)

28 Broad Street, P.O. Box 993, 29402
Telephone: 803-577-4000
Fax: 803-724-6600
Columbia, South Carolina Office: 1901 Assembly Street, Suite 300, P.O. Box 8476.
Telephone: 803-799-4000.
Fax: 803-799-7083.
North Charleston , South Carolina Office: 2170 Ashley Phosphate Road, Suite 700, P.O. Box 61509.
Telephone: 803-720-5400.
Fax: 803-724-7796.

MEMBERS OF FIRM

J. Rutledge Young, Jr.
Carol Brittain Ervin
John Hamilton Smith

ASSOCIATES

Elizabeth B. Luzuriaga
F. Drake Rogers

Counsel for: American International Group; Continental Insurance health Ca re; Medical Society Health Systems Inc.; Roper Hospital Inc.; Ropers Self Insurers Trust; S.C. Medical Malpractice Joint Underwriters Assn.; The Virginia Insurance Reciprocal.

For Complete List of Firm Personnel, See General Section

For full biographical listings, see the Martindale-Hubbell Law Directory

*COLUMBIA,** Richland Co.

* indicates certain Bar Register subscribers whose principal office is located elsewhere in the state and who have arranged for representation as a part of the state capital listings that follow

BARNES, ALFORD, STORK & JOHNSON, L.L.P. (AV)

1613 Main Street, P.O. Box 8448, 29202
Telephone: 803-799-1111
Telefax: 803-254-1335

James W. Alford
Weldon R. Johnson
Robert E. Salane
Kay Gaffney Crowe

Representative Clients: First Union National Bank of South Carolina; Aetna Casualty and Surety Co.; Kline Iron & Steel Co.

For Complete List of Firm Personnel, See General Section

For full biographical listings, see the Martindale-Hubbell Law Directory

FURR AND HENSHAW (AV)

A Partnership of Professional Corporations
1534 Blanding Street, 29201
Telephone: 803-252-4050
Fax: 803-254-7513
Myrtle Beach, South Carolina Office: 1900 Oak Street, P.O. Box 2909.
Telephone: 803-626-7621.
FAX: 803-448-6445.

O. Fayrell Furr, Jr. (P.C.)
Charles L. Henshaw, Jr. (P.C.)

Karolan Furr Ohanesian (Resident, Myrtle Beach Office)

Reference: Anchor Bank, Myrtle Beach, S.C.

For full biographical listings, see the Martindale-Hubbell Law Directory

*** HAYNSWORTH, MARION, MCKAY & GUÉRARD, L.L.P. (AV)**

Suite 2400 A T & T Building, 1201 Main Street, P.O. Drawer 7157, 29202
Telephone: 803-765-1818
Telecopier: 803-765-2399
Greenville, South Carolina Office: Two Insignia Financial Plaza, 75 Beattie Place, P.O. Box 2048, 29602.
Telephone: 803-240-3200.
Telecopier: 803-240-3300.
Charleston, South Carolina Office: #2 Prioleau Street, P.O. Box 1119, 29402.
Telephone: 803-722-7606.
Telecopier: 803-723-5263.

MEMBERS OF FIRM

William P. Simpson
Steven Todd Moon

Counsel for: St. Paul Insurance Group; Allstate Insurance Co.; Fluor-Daniel Corp.; South Carolina Jobs - Economic Development Authority; Anheuser Busch Company; CSX Transportation; Ernst & Young, LLP; Willis Corroon of South Carolina, Inc.; Westinghouse Savannah River Co.; Wachovia Bank of South Carolina, N.A.

For Complete List of Firm Personnel, See General Section

For full biographical listings, see the Martindale-Hubbell Law Directory

MCKAY, MCKAY, HENRY & FOSTER, P.A. (AV)

1325 Laurel Street, P.O. Box 7217, 29202
Telephone: 803-256-4645
FAX: 803-765-1839

Douglas McKay, Jr.
Julius W. McKay, II
Angela L. Henry
Ruskin C. Foster

Representative Clients: Americlaim Adjustment Corp.; Britanco Underwriters, Inc.; Homestead Insurance Co.; Lincoln National Life Ins. Co.; Pennsylvania Manufactuers Association Co. (PMA); Schneider National Carriers; South Carolina Division of General Services-Insurance Reserve Fund (IRF); South Carolina Medical Malpractice Joint Underwriting Assn. (JUA); Underwriters Laboratories, Inc.; Union Bankers Ins. Co.

For Complete List of Firm Personnel, See General Section

For full biographical listings, see the Martindale-Hubbell Law Directory

ERNEST J. NAUFUL, JR., P.C. (AV)

1330 Lady Street Suite 615, P.O. Box 5907, 29250
Telephone: 803-256-4045
Facsimile: 803-254-0776

Ernest J. Nauful, Jr.

For full biographical listings, see the Martindale-Hubbell Law Directory

Columbia—Continued

RICHARDSON, PLOWDEN, GRIER AND HOWSER, P.A. (AV)

1600 Marion Street, P.O. Drawer 7788, 29202
Telephone: 803-771-4400
Telecopy: 803-779-0016
Myrtle Beach, South Carolina Office: Southern National Bank Building, Suite 202, 601 21st Avenue North, P.O. Box 3646, 29578.
Telephone: 803-448-1008.
FAX: 803-448-1533.

Donald V. Richardson, III
George C. Beighley
William H. Hensel

Phillip Florence, Jr.
Williams Scalise Marian

Representative Clients: St. Paul Insurance Co.; S.C. Medical Malpractice Joint Underwriting Assn.; S.C. Division of General Services Insurance Reserve; Continental Insurance Co.

For Complete List of Firm Personnel, See General Section

For full biographical listings, see the Martindale-Hubbell Law Directory

*GREENVILLE,** Greenville Co.

HAYNSWORTH, MARION, MCKAY & GUÉRARD, L.L.P. (AV)

Two Insignia Financial Plaza, 75 Beattie Place, P.O. Box 2048, 29602
Telephone: 803-240-3200
Telecopier: 803-240-3300
Columbia, South Carolina Office: Suite 2400 A T & T Building, 1201 Main Street, P.O. Drawer 7157, 29202
Telephone: 803-765-1818.
Telecopier: 803-765-2399.
Charleston, South Carolina Office: #2 Prioleau Street, P.O. Box 1119, 29402.
Telephone: 803-722-7606.
Telecopier: 803-723-5263.

MEMBERS OF FIRM

G. Dewey Oxner, Jr.
W. Francis Marion, Jr.
Edwin Brown Parkinson, Jr.

ASSOCIATES

Sarah S. (Sally) McMillan
Matthew P. Utecht

Counsel for: Duke Power Co.; Liberty Mutual Insurance Co.; Equitable Life Assurance Society of the United States; St. Paul Insurance Group; Allstate Insurance Co.; Fluor-Daniel Corp.; Snyalloy Corporation; Greenville Hospital System.

For Complete List of Firm Personnel, See General Section

For full biographical listings, see the Martindale-Hubbell Law Directory

LOVE, THORNTON, ARNOLD & THOMASON, P.A. (AV)

410 East Washington Street, P.O. Box 10045, 29603
Telephone: 803-242-6360
Telefax: 803-271-7972

William M. Hagood, III
Theron G. Cochran
V. Clark Price

Counsel for: Aetna Life & Casualty Insurance Co.; Kemper Insurance Group; Continental Insurance Companies Group; Government Employees Insurance Co.; Reliance Insurance Companies Group; American States Ins. Co.; First Citizens Bank & Trust Co.; American Federal Bank, F.S.B.; BP Oil, Inc.; Chrysler Corp.

For Complete List of Firm Personnel, See General Section

For full biographical listings, see the Martindale-Hubbell Law Directory

PARHAM & SMITH (AV)

Suite 200 Falls Place, 531 South Main, 29601
Telephone: 803-235-5692; 242-9008

MEMBERS OF FIRM

Michael Parham
Barney O. Smith, Jr.

For full biographical listings, see the Martindale-Hubbell Law Directory

*WALHALLA,** Oconee Co.

LARRY C. BRANDT, P.A. (AV)

205 West Main Street, P.O. Drawer 738, 29691
Telephone: 803-638-5406
803-638-7873

Larry C. Brandt

D. Bradley Jordan
J. Bruce Schumpert

LEGAL SUPPORT PERSONNEL

Debra C. Miller

For full biographical listings, see the Martindale-Hubbell Law Directory

SOUTH DAKOTA

*RAPID CITY,** Pennington Co.

JOHNSON HUFFMAN A PROFESSIONAL CORPORATION OF LAWYERS (AV)

3202 West Main Street, P.O. Box 6100, 57709-6100
Telephone: 605-348-7300
FAX: 605-348-4757

Glen H. Johnson
Richard E. Huffman
Scott Sumner
Wayne F. Gilbert
Timothy J. Becker
John J. Delaney
Courtney R. Clayborne
Jay A. Alderman

LEGAL SUPPORT PERSONNEL
PARALEGALS

Cynthia J. Johnson
Renee Lehr
Dory M. Maks
Timothy Crawford

For full biographical listings, see the Martindale-Hubbell Law Directory

TENNESSEE

*CHATTANOOGA,** Hamilton Co.

FOSTER, FOSTER, ALLEN & DURRENCE (AV)

Formerly Hall, Haynes & Foster
Suite 515 Pioneer Bank Building, 37402
Telephone: 615-266-1141
Telecopier: 615-266-4618

MEMBERS OF FIRM

George Lane Foster
William M. Foster
Craig R. Allen
Phillip M. Durrence, Jr.

ASSOCIATES

David J. Ward
Clayton M. Whittaker
John M. Hull

LEGAL SUPPORT PERSONNEL

Peggy Sue Bates

Division Counsel for: Alabama Great Southern Railroad Co.; C.N.O. & T.P. Railway Co.
Attorneys for: CNA/Insurance; U.S.P. & G. Co.; The Firestone Tire & Rubber Co.; Exxon, Corp.; Murphy Oil Corp.; Chicago Title Insurance Co.; City of East Ridge; Jim Walter Homes; Raymond James & Associates; Morgan Keegan & Co.

For full biographical listings, see the Martindale-Hubbell Law Directory

SUMMERS, MCCREA & WYATT, P.C. (AV)

500 Lindsay Street, 37402
Telephone: 615-265-2385
Fax: 615-266-5211

Jerry H. Summers

For Complete List of Firm Personnel, See General Section

For full biographical listings, see the Martindale-Hubbell Law Directory

*KNOXVILLE,** Knox Co.

BUTLER, VINES AND BABB (AV)

Suite 810, First American Center, P.O. Box 2649, 37901-2649
Telephone: 615-637-3531
Fax: 615-637-3385

MEMBERS OF FIRM

Warren Butler
William D. Vines, III
Dennis L. Babb
Martin L. Ellis
Ronald C. Koksal
James C. Wright
Bruce A. Anderson
Gregory Kevin Hardin
Steven Boyd Johnson
Edward U. Babb

ASSOCIATES

John W. Butler
Vonda M. Laughlin
Gregory F. Vines
Scarlett May

LEGAL SUPPORT PERSONNEL
PARALEGALS

Virginia H. Carver
Susie DeLozier
Dena K. Martin

Reference: First American Bank.

For full biographical listings, see the Martindale-Hubbell Law Directory

Knoxville—Continued

GILREATH & ASSOCIATES (AV)

550 Main Avenue, Suite 600, P.O. Box 1270, 37901
Telephone: 615-637-2442
FAX: 615-971-4116
Nashville, Tennessee Office: Sidney W. Gilreath, 2828 Stouffer Tower, 611 Commerce Street.
Telephone: 615-256-3388.

Sidney W. Gilreath

ASSOCIATES

Meridith C. Bond
Donna Keene Holt
Richard Baker, Jr.
Mark W. Strange
Paul Kaufman
Richard L. Duncan

LEGAL SUPPORT PERSONNEL

Janie Turpin (Paralegal)
Janet L. Tucker (Paralegal)
Pamela Smith Wise (Legal Assistant to Senior Partner)
Susan Stogner (Legal Assistant to Senior Partner)
Bryan L. Capps (Legal Administrator)

Reference: Third National Bank.
Representative Client: Transportation Communications International Union.

For full biographical listings, see the Martindale-Hubbell Law Directory

HODGES, DOUGHTY AND CARSON (AV)

617 Main Street, P.O. Box 869, 37901-0869
Telephone: 615-546-9611
Telecopier: 615-544-2014

MEMBERS OF FIRM

J. H. Hodges (1896-1983)
J. H. Doughty (1903-1987)
Richard L. Carson (1912-1980)
John P. Davis, Jr. (1923-1977)
Robert R. Campbell
David E. Smith
John W. Wheeler
Dalton L. Townsend
Douglas L. Dutton
William F. Alley, Jr.
Roy L. Aaron
Dean B. Farmer
David Wedekind
Julia Saunders Howard
Albert J. Harb
Edward G. White, II
Thomas H. Dickenson
J. William Coley
J. Michael Haynes
T. Kenan Smith
Wayne A. Kline

ASSOCIATES

James M. Cornelius, Jr.
W. Tyler Chastain

OF COUNSEL

Jonathan H. Burnett

Representative Clients: General Motors Corp.; Sears, Roebuck and Co.; Navistar International; Martin Marietta Energy Systems; Union Carbide Corp.; NationsBank of Tennessee; K-Mart Corporation; Aetna Life and Casualty Group; Fireman's Fund American Insurance Company; Safeco Insurance Group.

For full biographical listings, see the Martindale-Hubbell Law Directory

PRYOR, FLYNN, PRIEST & HARBER (AV)

Suite 600 Two Centre Square, 625 Gay Street, P.O. Box 870, 37901
Telephone: 615-522-4191
Telecopier: 615-522-0910

Robert E. Pryor
Frank L. Flynn, Jr.
Timothy A. Priest
John K. Harber

ASSOCIATES

Mark E. Floyd
Donald R. Coffey
M. Christopher Coffey

References: Third National Bank; First National Bank.

For full biographical listings, see the Martindale-Hubbell Law Directory

RAINWATER, HUMBLE & VOWELL (AV)

2037 Plaza Tower, P.O. Box 2775, 37901
Telephone: 615-525-0321
Fax: 615-525-2431

MEMBERS OF FIRM

J. Earl Rainwater
J. Randolph Humble
Donald K. Vowell

Representative Clients: Acme Construction, Inc.; Curtis Construction Co., Inc.; Knoxville Pediatric Associates, P.C.; National Gas Distributors, Inc.; Neel's Wholesale Produce Co., Inc.; Oldham Insurance Inc.; Sherrod Electric Co., Inc.; Towe Iron Works, Inc.; Wm. S. Trimble Co., Inc.

For full biographical listings, see the Martindale-Hubbell Law Directory

WATSON, HOLLOW & REEVES (AV)

1700 Plaza Tower, P.O. Box 131, 37901
Telephone: 615-522-3803
Telecopier: 615-525-2514

(See Next Column)

MEMBERS OF FIRM

Robert Harmon Watson, Jr.
Richard L. Hollow
Pamela L. Reeves
Jon G. Roach
John C. Duffy
John T. Batson, Jr.
Earl Jerome Melson

ASSOCIATES

Arthur Franklin Knight, III
Robert W. Willingham

For full biographical listings, see the Martindale-Hubbell Law Directory

*NASHVILLE,** Davidson Co.

MANIER, HEROD, HOLLABAUGH & SMITH, A PROFESSIONAL CORPORATION (AV)

First Union Tower 2200 One Nashville Place, 150 Fourth Avenue North, 37219-2494
Telephone: 615-244-0030
Telecopier: 615-242-4203

Will R. Manier, Jr. (1885-1953)
Larkin E. Crouch (1882-1948)
Vincent L. Fuqua, Jr. (1930-1974)
J. Olin White (1907-1982)
Miller Manier (1897-1986)
William Edward Herod (1917-1992)
Lewis B. Hollabaugh
Don L. Smith
James M. Doran, Jr.
Stephen E. Cox
J. Michael Franks
Randall C. Ferguson
Terry L. Hill
James David Leckrone
Robert C. Evans
Tommy C. Estes
B. Gail Reese
Michael E. Evans
Laurence M. Papel
John M. Gillum
Gregory L. Cashion
Sam H. Poteet, Jr.
Samuel Arthur Butts III
David J. Deming
Mark S. LeVan
Richard McCallister Smith
Mary Paty Lynn Jetton
H. Rowan Leathers III
Jefferson C. Orr
William L. Penny

Lawrence B. Hammet II
John H. Rowland
Susan C. West
John E. Quinn
John F. Floyd
Paul L. Sprader
Lela M. Hollabaugh
J. Steven Kirkham
T. Richard Travis
Stephanie M. Jennings
Jerry W. Taylor
C. Benton Patton
Kenneth A. Weber
Phillip Robert Newman
Brett A. Oeser

General Counsel for: McKinnon Bridge Co., Inc.

For full biographical listings, see the Martindale-Hubbell Law Directory

TEXAS

*AUSTIN,** Travis Co.

* indicates certain Bar Register subscribers whose principal office is located elsewhere in the state and who have arranged for representation as a part of the state capital listings that follow

DAVIS & DAVIS, P.C. (AV)

Arboretum Plaza One, 9th Floor, 9442 Capitol of Texas Highway, P.O. Box 1588, 78767
Telephone: 512-343-6248
Fax: 512-343-0121

C. Dean Davis
Fred E. Davis
Alexis J. Fuller, Jr.
Francis A. (Tony) Bradley
Ruth Russell-Schafer

Bill Cline, Jr.
Robert L. Hargett
Michael L. Neely
Brian Gregory Jackson
A. A. Jack Ross, IV
Kevin Wayde Morse
Mark Alan Keene
Kenda B. Dalrymple

For Complete List of Firm Personnel, See General Section

For full biographical listings, see the Martindale-Hubbell Law Directory

DAVIS & WILKERSON, P.C. (AV)

200 One American Center, Six Hundred Congress Avenue, P.O. Box 2283, 78768-2283
Telephone: 512-482-0614
Fax: 512-482-0342
Alpine, Texas Office: 1110 East Holland. P.O. Box 777. 79831-0777.
Telephone: 915-837-5547.

David M. Davis
Steven R. Welch
Jeff D. Otto
Glen Wilkerson
David A. Wright
Leonard W. Woods
Kevin A. Reed
J. Mark Holbrook
Brian E. Riewe

(See Next Column)

DAVIS & WILKERSON P.C., *Austin—Continued*

Fletcher H. Brown
Brian McElroy
Deborah G. Clark
Michael Wilson
Frances W. Hamermesh
Stephen G. Wohleb
Kelly Ann McDonald
Stephen A. Wood

OF COUNSEL

Pete P. Gallego
Regina C. Williams

For full biographical listings, see the Martindale-Hubbell Law Directory

GIBBINS, WINCKLER & HARVEY, L.L.P. (AV)

500 West 13th Street, P.O. Box 1452, 78767
Telephone: 512-474-2441

Bob Gibbins
Jay L. Winckler
Jay Harvey

ASSOCIATES

Steven Gibbins
Wayne Prosperi
Susan P. Russell
Neil M. Bonavita

Reference: Nationsbank, Austin.

For full biographical listings, see the Martindale-Hubbell Law Directory

LUDLUM & LUDLUM (AV)

Second Floor The Enterprise Plaza, 13915 Burnet Road at Wells Branch Parkway, 78728
Telephone: 512-255-4000
Cable Address: "Ludlum"
Telecopier: 512-244-7000

FIRM FOUNDER

James N. Ludlum (Retired 1987)

MEMBERS OF FIRM

James Ludlum, Jr.
Anthony G. Brocato, Jr
Catherine L. Kyle
M. Winfield Atkins, IV

Representative Clients: American Hardware Insurance Group; American International Group; American International Underwriters, Inc.; Go Pro Underwriters, Inc.; National Casualty Company; New Hampshire Insurance Group; North American Specialty Insurance Group; United National Insurance Group.

For full biographical listings, see the Martindale-Hubbell Law Directory

*** THOMPSON & KNIGHT, A PROFESSIONAL CORPORATION** (AV)

(Attorneys and Counselors)
1200 San Jacinto Center, 98 San Jacinto Boulevard, 78701
Telephone: 512-469-6100
Telecopy: 512-469-6180
Dallas, Texas Office: 1700 Pacific Avenue, Suite 3300, 75201.
Telephone: 214-969-1700.
Telecopy: 512-969-1751.
Cable Address: "Tomtex."
Telex: 732298.
Fort Worth, Texas Office: 801 Cherry Street, Suite 1600, 76102.
Telephone: 817-347-1700.
Telecopy: 817-347-1799.
Houston, Texas Office: 1700 Texas Commerce Tower, 600 Travis, 77002.
Telephone: 713-217-2800.
Telecopy: 713-217-2828; 713-217-2882.
Monterrey, Mexico Office: Edificio Losoles PD-4, Av. Lázaro Cárdenas No. 2400 Pte., San Pedro Garza Garcia, Nuevo Léon C.P. 66220.
Telephone: (52-8) 363-0096.
Telecopy: (52-8) 363-3067.

SHAREHOLDERS

Eugene W. Brees, II
Frank L. Hill

For Complete List of Firm Personnel, See General Section

For full biographical listings, see the Martindale-Hubbell Law Directory

*DALLAS,** Dallas Co.

BARBER, HART & O'DELL, L.L.P. (AV)

4310 Gaston Avenue, 75246-1398
Telephone: 214-821-8840
Fax: 214-821-3834

James C. Barber
David G. Hart
David M. O'Dell

For full biographical listings, see the Martindale-Hubbell Law Directory

LAW OFFICES OF FRANK L. BRANSON, P.C. (AV)

18th Floor, Highland Park Place, 4514 Cole Avenue, 75205
Telephone: 214-522-0200;
Metro: 817-263-7452
Fax: 214-521-5485

(See Next Column)

Frank L. Branson
J. Stephen King
Debbie D. Branson
Christopher A. Payne
George A. Quesada, Jr.
Michael L. Parham
Jerry M. White
Joel M. Fineberg

OF COUNSEL

Ted Z. Robertson
J. Hadley Edgar, Jr.

For full biographical listings, see the Martindale-Hubbell Law Directory

CALHOUN & STACY (AV)

5700 NationsBank Plaza, 901 Main Street, 75202-3747
Telephone: 214-748-5000
Telecopier: 214-748-1421
Telex: 211358 CALGUMP UR

Mark Alan Calhoun
Steven D. Goldston
David W. Elrod
Parker Nelson
Roy L. Stacy

ASSOCIATES

Shannon S. Barclay
Thomas C. Jones
Robert A. Bragalone
Katherine Johnson Knight
Dennis D. Conder
V. Paige Pace
Jane Elizabeth Diseker
Veronika Willard
Lawrence I. Fleishman
Michael C. Wright

LEGAL CONSULTANT

Rees T. Bowen, III

For full biographical listings, see the Martindale-Hubbell Law Directory

LAW OFFICES OF ALAN K. LAUFMAN, J.D., M.D. A PROFESSIONAL CORPORATION (AV)

Suite 1000 Turtle Creek Centre, 3811 Turtle Creek Boulevard, 75219
Telephone: 214-559-3300
Fax: 214-526-1150

Alan K. Laufman

For full biographical listings, see the Martindale-Hubbell Law Directory

MISKO, HOWIE & SWEENEY (AV)

Turtle Creek Centre, Suite 1900, 3811 Turtle Creek Boulevard, 75219
Telephone: 214-443-8000
Fax: 214-443-8000

Fred Misko, Jr.
John R. Howie
Paula Sweeney

ASSOCIATES

Charles S. Siegel
Raymond A. Williams, III
James L. Mitchell, Jr.
Christopher D. Jones
Bryan D. Pope

For full biographical listings, see the Martindale-Hubbell Law Directory

GEORGE A. OTSTOTT & ASSOCIATES A PROFESSIONAL CORPORATION (AV)

3611 Fairmount, 75219
Telephone: 214-522-9999
Terrell, Texas Office: 304 East Wheeler.
Telephone: 214-563-2222.
Jefferson, Texas Office: 117 West Lafayette Street.
Telephone: 903-665-3300.
Denton, Texas Office: 1010 Dallas Drive.
Telephone: 817-383-8080.
Greenville, Texas Office: 2718 Wesley.
Telephone: 903-454-4444.
Waxahachie, Texas Office: 303 South Elm Street.
Telephone: 214-937-3000.

George A. Otstott

Jerry D. Andrews
Jean A. Robb
David Townsend

For full biographical listings, see the Martindale-Hubbell Law Directory

THE LAW FIRM OF C.L. MIKE SCHMIDT, P.C. (AV)

3102 Oak Lawn, Suite 730, LB 158, 75219
Telephone: 214-521-4898
Toll Free No. 1-800-677-4898
Fax: 214-521-9995

C. L. Mike Schmidt

Ronald D. Wren
Michael E. Schmidt

For full biographical listings, see the Martindale-Hubbell Law Directory

Dallas—Continued

THOMPSON & KNIGHT, A PROFESSIONAL CORPORATION (AV)

(Attorneys and Counselors)
1700 Pacific Avenue Suite 3300, 75201
Telephone: 214-969-1700
Telecopy: 214-969-1751
Cable Address: "Tomtex"
Telex: 732298
Austin, Texas Office: 1200 San Jacinto Center, 98 San Jacinto Boulevard, 78701.
Telephone: 512-469-6100.
Telecopy: 512-469-6180.
Fort Worth, Texas Office: 801 Cherry Street, Suite 1600, 76102.
Telephone: 817-347-1700.
Telecopy: 817-347-1799.
Houston, Texas Office: 1700 Texas Commerce Tower, 600 Travis, 77002.
Telephone: 713-217-2800.
Telecopy: 713-217-2828.
Monterrey, Mexico Office: Edificio Losoles PD-4, Av. Lázaro Cárdenas No. 2400 Pte., San Pedro Garza Garcia, Nuevo Léon C.P. 66220.
Telephone: (52-8) 363-0096.
Telecopy: (52-8) 363-3067.

SHAREHOLDERS

P. Jefferson Ballew
Michael R. Berry
Jane Politz Brandt
Cheryl E. Diaz
Gerald H. Grissom
Deborah G. Hankinson
John A. Mackintosh, Jr.
John H. Martin
Maureen Murry
Stephen C. Rasch
James M. Underwood

ASSOCIATES

L. James Berglund, II
Beverly Ray Burlingame
Greg W. Curry
Lori L. Dalton
D'Lesli M. Davis
Michael G. Guajardo
Craig Naveen Kakarla
Michael E. Schonberg
Lisa A. Schumacher
Robert V. Vitanza
David S. White
Amy K. Witherite

OF COUNSEL

Malia A. Litman

For Complete List of Firm Personnel, See General Section

For full biographical listings, see the Martindale-Hubbell Law Directory

*EL PASO,** El Paso Co.

CHARLES A. DEASON, JR. (AV)

1141 East Rio Grande, 79902-1371
Telephone: 915-544-1371
Fax: 915-544-2013

For full biographical listings, see the Martindale-Hubbell Law Directory

VOLK & MONTES, P.C. (AV)

609 Montana, 79902
Telephone: 915-533-3773
Fax: 915-533-9920

Michael D. Volk
Jose Montes, Jr.

Reference: State National Bank El Paso.

For full biographical listings, see the Martindale-Hubbell Law Directory

*FORT WORTH,** Tarrant Co.

LAW FIRM OF DARRELL KEITH, P.C. (AV)

201 Main Street, Suite 1400, 76102
Telephone: 817-338-1400
Telefax: 817-870-2448

Darrell L. Keith
Sue S. Walker

Jane A. Freese

LEGAL SUPPORT PERSONNEL

E. Earl Hauss (Senior Nurse Legal Assistant, Litigation Section)
Judy Renfrow (Senior Legal Assistant, Litigation Section; Legal Administrator, Legal Administration Section)
Kena W. Lewis
Patricia N. Ford (Legal Assistant, Evaluation Section)
Christi Lester (Associate Legal Assistant, Litigation Section)
Leslie A. Edwards (Administrative Assistant, Legal Administration Section)

For full biographical listings, see the Martindale-Hubbell Law Directory

RUSSELL, TURNER, LAIRD & JONES, L.L.P. (AV)

One Colonial Place, 2400 Scott Avenue, 76103-2200
Telephone: 817-531-3000; 1-800-448-2889
Fax: 817-535-3046
Dallas, Texas Office: Williams Square, Central Tower, Suite 700, 5215 North O'Connor Boulevard, Las Colinas Urban Center.
Telephone: 214-444-0444; 1-800-448-2889.

Wm. Greg Russell
Randall E. Turner
Steven C. Laird
Gregory G. Jones

For full biographical listings, see the Martindale-Hubbell Law Directory

THOMPSON & KNIGHT, A PROFESSIONAL CORPORATION (AV)

(Attorneys and Counselors)
801 Cherry Street, Suite 1600, 76102
Telephone: 817-347-1700
Telecopy: 817-347-1799
Dallas, Texas Office: 1700 Pacific Avenue, Suite 3300, 75201.
Telephone: 214-969-1700.
Telecopy: 214-969-1751.
Cable Address: "Tomtex."
Telex: 732298.
Austin, Texas Office: 1200 San Jacinto Center, 98 San Jacinto Boulevard, 78701.
Telephone: 512-469-6100.
Telecopy: 512-469-6180.
Houston, Texas Office: 1700 Texas Commerce Tower, 600 Travis, 77002.
Telephone: 713-217-2800.
Telecopy: 713-217-2828; 713-2882.
Monterrey, Mexico Office: Edificio Losoles PD-4, Av. Lázaro Cárdenas No. 2400 Pte., San Pedro Garza Garcia, Nuevo Léon C.P. 66220.
Telephone: (52-8) 363-0096.
Telecopy: (52-8) 363-3067.

SHAREHOLDERS

R Gordon Appleman
Stephen B. Norris
E. Michael Sheehan

ASSOCIATES

Susan E. Coleman
Jennifer Pettijohn Henry
Mary M. Penrose

For full biographical listings, see the Martindale-Hubbell Law Directory

*HOUSTON,** Harris Co.

JAMES R. BOSTON & ASSOCIATES, P.C. (AV)

1330 Post Oak Boulevard Suite 1600, 77056
Telephone: 713-963-2955
Fax: 713-965-0883

James R. Boston, Jr.

Lee D. Thibodeaux

For full biographical listings, see the Martindale-Hubbell Law Directory

CRUSE, SCOTT, HENDERSON & ALLEN, L.L.P. (AV)

Two Houston Center, Suite 1850, 909 Fannin Street, 77010-1007
Telephone: 713-650-6600
Fax: 713-650-1720

Sam W. Cruse, Jr.
John P. Scott
Jay H. Henderson
T. Scott Allen, Jr.
Samuel A. Houston
George W. (Billy) Shepherd, III
John R. Strawn, Jr.

ASSOCIATES

Stephen R. Bailey
Michael F. Hord, Jr.
Jana F. Lohse
Debra Lynn Sales
Louis B. Sullivan, III
John D. Vogel

For full biographical listings, see the Martindale-Hubbell Law Directory

LORANCE & THOMPSON, A PROFESSIONAL CORPORATION (AV)

303 Jackson Hill, 77007
Telephone: 713-868-5560
Fax: 713-864-4671; 868-1605
Phoenix, Arizona Office: 2525 East Camelback Road, Suite 230, 85016.
Telephone: 602-224-4000.
Fax: 602-224-4098.
San Diego, California Office: 555 West Beech Street, Suite 222, 92101.
Telephone: 800-899-1844.

Larry D. Thompson
Wayne Adams
Frank B. Stahl, Jr.
William K. Luyties
Clifford A. Lawrence, Jr.
Walter F. (Trey) Williams, III
David O. Cluck
Phillip C. Summers
David F. Webb
Richard H. Martin
Vicki F. Brann
Ronald E. Hood
Gwen W. Dobrowski
Mark D. Flanagan
F. Barham Lewis

(See Next Column)

LORANCE & THOMPSON A PROFESSIONAL CORPORATION, *Houston—Continued*

David W. Prasifka
Gregory D. Solcher
John A. Culberson
George Eric Van Noy
James E. Simmons
John H. Thomisee, Jr.
Tracey R. Burridge
Douglas A. Haldane
Geoffrey C. Guill
Diane M. Guariglia
Kelly B. Lea
Tracey Landrum Foster
Ronnie B. Arnold
Teresa A. Carver
Terrance D. Dill, Jr.
J. Wayne Little
William T. Sebesta
Richard N. Moore
Matthew R. Pearson

OF COUNSEL

John Holman Barr
Shannon P. Davis
Alexis J. Gomez

Representative Clients: Allstate Insurance Co.; The Hartford Insurance Group.

For full biographical listings, see the Martindale-Hubbell Law Directory

---

MCFALL, SHERWOOD & SHEEHY, A PROFESSIONAL CORPORATION (AV)

2500 Two Houston Center, 909 Fannin Street, 77010-1003
Telephone: 713-951-1000
Telecopier: 713-951-1199

Donald B. McFall
Thomas P. Sartwelle
William A. Sherwood
John S. Serpe

Representative Clients: Dresser Industries, Inc.; The Procter & Gamble Co.; Channel Two Television; St. Paul Fire & Marine Insurance Co.; Texas Lawyers' Insurance Exchange; U.S. Aviation Underwriters; Dow Corning Corp.; Columbia Hospital Corp.; Farm & Home Savings Association.

For Complete List of Firm Personnel, See General Section

For full biographical listings, see the Martindale-Hubbell Law Directory

---

PERDUE & CLORE, L.L.P. (AV)

2727 Allen Parkway, Suite 800, 77019
Telephone: 713-520-2500

Jim M. Perdue
Mark D. Clore

ASSOCIATES

Joann V. Bennett
Jo Emma Arechiga
John Walter Lewis

For full biographical listings, see the Martindale-Hubbell Law Directory

---

THOMPSON & KNIGHT, A PROFESSIONAL CORPORATION (AV)

(Attorneys and Counselors)
1700 Texas Commerce Tower, 600 Travis, 77002
Telephone: 713-217-2800
Telecopy: 713-217-2828; 713-217-2882
Dallas, Texas Office: 1700 Pacific Avenue, Suite 3300, 75201.
Telephone: 214-969-1700.
Telecopy: 214-969-1751.
Cable Address: "Tomtex."
Telex: 732298.
Austin, Texas Office: 1200 San Jacinto Center, 98 San Jacinto Boulevard, 78701.
Telephone: 512-469-6100.
Telecopy: 512-469-6180.
Fort Worth, Texas Office: 801 Cherry Street, Suite 1600, 76102.
Telephone: 817-347-1700.
Telecopy: 817-347-1799.
Monterrey, Mexico Office: Edificio Losoles PD-4, Av. Lázaro Cárdenas No. 2400 PTE., San Pedro Garza Garcia, Nuevo Léon C.P. 66220.
Telephone: (52-8) 363-0096.
Telecopy: (52-8) 363-3067.

SHAREHOLDERS

David R. Noteware

For Complete List of Firm Personnel, See General Section

For full biographical listings, see the Martindale-Hubbell Law Directory

---

*SAN ANTONIO,** Bexar Co.

TINSMAN & HOUSER, INC. (AV)

One Riverwalk Place, 14th Floor, 700 North St. Mary's Street, 78205
Telephone: 210-225-3121
Texas Wats: 1-800-292-9999
Fax: 210-225-6235

(See Next Column)

Richard Tinsman
Franklin D. Houser
Margaret M. Maisel
David G. Jayne
Robert C. Scott
Daniel J. T. Sciano
Rey Perez
Bernard Wm. Fischman
Sharon L. Cook
Christopher Pettit
Ronald J. Salazar
Sue Dodson

For full biographical listings, see the Martindale-Hubbell Law Directory

---

*VICTORIA,** Victoria Co.

CULLEN, CARSNER, SEERDEN & CULLEN, L.L.P. (AV)

119 South Main Street, P.O. Box 2938, 77902
Telephone: 512-573-6318
Fax: 512-573-2603

MEMBERS OF FIRM

Richard D. Cullen
Charles C. Carsner, Jr. (1917-1993)
William F. Seerden
Kevin D. Cullen
Jean Smetana Cullen
Juergen Koetter
Mark C. Rains
Kemper Stephen Williams, III

ASSOCIATES

Michael A. Johnson
Garland Sandhop, Jr.
Wendy Atkinson

Representative Clients: Citizens Medical Center; Medical Protective Company; Texas Medical Liability Trust; Insurance Corporation of America; Texas Medical Liability Insurance Underwriting Association (JUA); The Home Insurance Company.

For full biographical listings, see the Martindale-Hubbell Law Directory

---

UTAH

---

*SALT LAKE CITY,** Salt Lake Co.

HANSON, EPPERSON & SMITH, A PROFESSIONAL CORPORATION (AV)

4 Triad Center, Suite 500, P.O. Box 2970, 84110-2970
Telephone: 801-363-7611
Fax: 801-531-9747

Rex J. Hanson (1911-1980)
David H. Epperson
Lowell V. Smith
Robert R. Wallace
Scott W. Christensen
Terry M. Plant
Theodore E. Kanell
John N. Braithwaite
Richard K. Glauser
Mark J. Williams
Daniel Stoddar McConkie

Jaryl L. Rencher
Eric K. Davenport
Daniel Lee Steele
David S. Doty
Bradley R. Helsten
Bruce M. Pritchett, Jr.

Representative Clients: HealthTrust, Inc. (10 Utah Hospitals); St. Paul Fire and Marine; Continental Insurance Cos. (C.N.A.); The Doctor's Company; American Continental Ins. Co. (M.M.I.); The Salt Lake Clinic; Insurance Corporation of America; Mentor Corporation; Duchesne County Hospital; Intermountain Surgical Center.

For full biographical listings, see the Martindale-Hubbell Law Directory

---

PARSONS BEHLE & LATIMER, A PROFESSIONAL CORPORATION (AV)

One Utah Center, 201 South Main Street, Suite 1800, P.O. Box 45898, 84145-0898
Telephone: 801-532-1234
Telecopy: 801-536-6111

Gordon L. Roberts
Charles H. Thronson
Daniel W. Hindert
Mark S. Webber
Elizabeth S. Conley
William J. Evans

For full biographical listings, see the Martindale-Hubbell Law Directory

---

STRONG & HANNI, A PROFESSIONAL CORPORATION (AV)

Sixth Floor Boston Building, 9 Exchange Place, 84111
Telephone: 801-532-7080
Fax: 801-596-1508

Gordon R. Strong (1909-1969)
Glenn C. Hanni
Henry E. Heath
Philip R. Fishler
Roger H. Bullock
Robert A. Burton
R. Scott Williams
Dennis M. Astill (Managing Partner)
S. Baird Morgan
Stuart H. Schultz
Paul M. Belnap
Stephen J. Trayner
Joseph J. Joyce
Bradley Wm. Bowen

(See Next Column)

STRONG & HANNI A PROFESSIONAL CORPORATION—*Continued*

Robert L. Janicki
Elizabeth L. Willey
Peter H. Christensen
H. Burt Ringwood
David R. Nielson
Adam Trupp
Catherine M. Larson

Representative Clients: State Farm Mutual Automobile Insurance Co.; Standard Accident Insurance Co.; United Services Automobile Assn.; Western Casualty & Surety Co.; Government Employees Insurance Co.; Guaranty Mutual Life Co.

For full biographical listings, see the Martindale-Hubbell Law Directory

VAN COTT, BAGLEY, CORNWALL & MCCARTHY, A PROFESSIONAL CORPORATION (AV)

Suite 1600, 50 South Main Street, P.O. Box 45340, 84145
Telephone: 801-532-3333
Telex: 453149
Telecopier: 801-534-0058
Ogden, Utah Office: Suite 900, 2404 Washington Boulevard.
Telephone: 801-394-5783.
Park City, Utah Office: 314 Main Street, Suite 205.
Telephone: 801-649-3889.
Reno, Nevada Office: Jeppson & Lee, 100 West Liberty, Suite 990.
Telephone: 702-333-6800.

Kenneth W. Yeates
Michael F. Richman
Jeffrey E. Nelson

Elizabeth D. Winter
Jon E. Waddoups

For Complete List of Firm Personnel, See General Section

For full biographical listings, see the Martindale-Hubbell Law Directory

VERMONT

*BURLINGTON,** Chittenden Co.

LISMAN & LISMAN, A PROFESSIONAL CORPORATION (AV)

84 Pine Street, P.O. Box 728, 05402-0728
Telephone: 802-864-5756
Fax: 802-864-3629

Carl H. Lisman
Allen D. Webster
Mary G. Kirkpatrick
E. William Leckerling, III
Douglas K. Riley

Judith Lillian Dillon
Richard W. Kozlowski

OF COUNSEL

Bernard Lisman
Louis Lisman

For full biographical listings, see the Martindale-Hubbell Law Directory

MANCHESTER LAW OFFICES, PROFESSIONAL CORPORATION (AV)

One Lawson Lane, P.O. Box 1459, 05402-1459
Telephone: 802-658-7444
Fax: 802-658-2078

Robert E. Manchester
Patricia S. Orr

LEGAL SUPPORT PERSONNEL

LEGAL NURSE CONSULTANTS

Tina L Mulvey
Rosemeryl S. Harple
Maureen P. Tremblay

For full biographical listings, see the Martindale-Hubbell Law Directory

SYLVESTER & MALEY, INC. (AV)

78 Pine Street, P.O. Box 1053, 05402-1053
Telephone: 802-864-5722
Fax: 802-658-6124

Alan F. Sylvester
John P. Maley
Michael S. Brow

Geoffrey M. Fitzgerald
Amy E. Sylvester

For full biographical listings, see the Martindale-Hubbell Law Directory

*MONTPELIER,** Washington Co.

THERIAULT & JOSLIN, P.C. (AV)

141 Main Street, P.O. Box 249, 05601-0249
Telephone: 802-223-2381
Fax: 802-223-1461

(See Next Column)

Peter B. Joslin
Fletcher Brian (Ted) Joslin

Representative Clients: Allstate Insurance Co.; American International Cos.; Hartford Insurance Group; St. Paul Insurance Cos.; Nationwide Insurance Cos.; Metropolitan Insurance Co.; American Home Group; Commercial Union Insurance Cos.; Prudential Insurance Cos.; PHICO Insurance Co.

For Complete List of Firm Personnel, See General Section

For full biographical listings, see the Martindale-Hubbell Law Directory

*RUTLAND,** Rutland Co.

DAVID L. CLEARY ASSOCIATES A PROFESSIONAL CORPORATION (AV)

110 Merchants Row, P.O. Box 6740, 05702-6740
Telephone: 802-775-8800
Telefax: 802-775-8809

David L. Cleary

Kaveh S. Shahi
George A. Holoch, Jr.
Karen S. Heald

For Complete List of Firm Personnel, See General Section

For full biographical listings, see the Martindale-Hubbell Law Directory

HULL, WEBBER & REIS (AV)

(Formerly Dick, Hackel & Hull)
60 North Main Street, P.O. Box 890, 05702-0890
Telephone: 802-775-2361
Fax: 802-775-0739

Donald H. Hackel (1925-1985)
John B. Webber
Robert K. Reis
John C. Holler
Lisa L. Chalidze

ASSOCIATES

Phyllis R. McCoy
Karen Abatiell Kalter

OF COUNSEL

Richard A. Hull (P.C.)
Steven D. Vogl

Representative Clients: Phico Insurance Co.; National Chiropractic Mutual Insurance Co.; The Doctor's Company.

For full biographical listings, see the Martindale-Hubbell Law Directory

MILLER & FAIGNANT, A PROFESSIONAL CORPORATION (AV)

36 Merchants Row, P.O. Box 6688, 05702-6688
Telephone: 802-775-2521
Fax: 802-775-8274

Lawrence Miller
John Paul Faignant

Barbara R. Blackman
Christopher J. Whelton

LEGAL SUPPORT PERSONNEL

Cynthia L. Bonvouloir
Marie T. Fabian

Representative Clients: Travelers Insurance Co.; Government Employees Insurance Co.; Utica Mutual Insurance Co.; Universal Underwriters Insurance Co.
Reference: Travelers Insurance Co.

For full biographical listings, see the Martindale-Hubbell Law Directory

VIRGINIA

*ARLINGTON,** Arlington Co.

WILLIAM E. ARTZ A PROFESSIONAL CORPORATION (AV)

1010 Rosslyn Metro Center, 1700 North Moore Street, 22209
Telephone: 703-243-3500
Facsimile: 703-524-8770

William E. Artz

Dominique D. Michel

For full biographical listings, see the Martindale-Hubbell Law Directory

SCHWARTZ AND ELLIS, LTD. (AV)

6950 North Fairfax Drive, 22213
Telephone: 703-532-9300
Telex: 892320
Facsimile: 703-534-0329

John P. Ellis

John S. Petrillo

References: First Virginia Bank; Signet Bank; First Union National Bank.

For full biographical listings, see the Martindale-Hubbell Law Directory

*FAIRFAX,** (Ind. City; Seat of Fairfax Co.)

GODARD, WEST & ADELMAN, P.C. (AV)

Suite 220, 3975 University Drive, P.O. Box 1287, 22030
Telephone: 703-273-4800
Facsimile: 703-691-0804
Rockville, Maryland Office: Suite 310, 200-A Monroe Street.
Telephone: 301-340-1140.

Gary A. Godard
Norman A. West
S. Allan Adelman (Not admitted in VA; Resident, Rockville, Maryland Office)
Vicki Layman Jasper
Kenneth J. Barton, Jr.
Nomi Irene Lowy (Not admitted in VA; Resident, Rockville, Maryland Office)
Edward A. Gonsalves
William J. Minor, Jr.
Michael I. Joseph (Resident, Rockville, Maryland Office)
John S. Twinam (Resident, Rockville, Maryland Office)

LEGAL SUPPORT PERSONNEL

Arleta G. Cosby
Sharon I. Spinks
Leslie C. Jelacic
Judith H. Caldwell
Susan Kabatchnick-Klein (Resident, Rockville, Maryland Office)

For full biographical listings, see the Martindale-Hubbell Law Directory

MCLEAN, Fairfax Co.

PLEDGER & SANTONI (AV)

Suite 204, 1489 Chain Bridge Road, 22101
Telephone: 703-821-1250
Fax: 703-790-7250

R. Harrison Pledger, Jr.
Cynthia Vancil Santoni

Bernard G. Feord, Jr.
Cherie Kay Dibbell Durand

Representative Clients: St. Paul Insurance Companies; National Capital Reciprocal Ins. Co.; Phico Insurance Company; Insurance Corporation of America; Kaiser Foundation Health Plan of the Mid-Atlantic States, Inc.; The Medical Protective Company; The Virginia Insurance Reciprocal.

For full biographical listings, see the Martindale-Hubbell Law Directory

MIDLOTHIAN, Chesterfield Co.

ROGER L. TUTTLE (AV)

3801 Commodore Point Place, 23112
Telephone: 804-744-0040
FAX: 804-744-0608

NORFOLK, (Independent City)

THOMAS J. HARLAN, JR., P.C. (AV)

1200 Dominion Tower, 999 Waterside Drive, 23510
Telephone: 804-625-8300
FAX: 804-625-3714

Thomas J. Harlan, Jr.

John M. Flora
Kevin M. Thompson (Not admitted in VA)

LEGAL SUPPORT PERSONNEL

Mary Hayse Grant Wareing (Paralegal)
Barry Wade Vanderhoof (Paralegal)

Reference: Commerce Bank.

For full biographical listings, see the Martindale-Hubbell Law Directory

HEILIG, MCKENRY, FRAIM & LOLLAR, A PROFESSIONAL CORPORATION (AV)

700 Newtown Road, 23502
Telephone: 804-461-2500
Fax: 804-461-2341

George H. Heilig, Jr.
James R. McKenry
John A. Heilig
Paul D. Fraim
George J. Dancigers
Charles M. Lollar
Carolyn P. Oast
Teresa R. Warner
Peter S. Lake
Thomas C. Dawson, Jr.
Stewart Penney Oast
Debra L. Mosley
Todd M. Fiorella
Robert E. Moreland
Philip R. Trapani
A. William Charters
Tena Touzos Canavos

(See Next Column)

Jason Evans Dodd
Lisa L. Howlett
Colleen Treacy Dickerson
Lynn E. Watson

Representative Clients: American International Insurance Group; Blue Cross of Virginia; Blue Shield of Virginia; The Home Insurance Company; Horace Mann Mutual Insurance Co.; Nationwide Mutual Insurance Co.; TranSouth Financial Corp.

For full biographical listings, see the Martindale-Hubbell Law Directory

ROANOKE, (Independent City)

MUNDY, ROGERS & FRITH (AV)

Third Street and Woods Avenue, S.W., P.O. Box 2240, 24009
Telephone: 703-982-2900
FAX: 703-982-1362

MEMBERS OF FIRM

G. Marshall Mundy
Frank W. Rogers, III
T. Daniel Frith, III
Cheryl Watson Smith

Reference: First Union.

For full biographical listings, see the Martindale-Hubbell Law Directory

WASHINGTON

*SEATTLE,** King Co.

GAITÁN & CUSACK (AV)

30th Floor Two Union Square, 601 Union Street, 98101-2324
Telephone: 206-521-3000
Facsimile: 206-386-5259
Anchorage, Alaska Office: 425 G Street, Suite 760.
Telephone: 907-278-3001.
Facsimile: 907-278-6068.
San Francisco, California Office: 275 Battery Street, 20th Floor.
Telephone: 415-398-5562.
Fax: 415-398-4033.
Washington, D.C. Office: 2000 L Street, Suite 200.
Telephone: 202-296-4637.
Fax: 202-296-4650.

MEMBERS OF FIRM

José E. Gaitán
Kenneth J. Cusack (Resident, Anchorage, Alaska Office)
William F. Knowles
Ronald L. Bozarth

OF COUNSEL

Howard K. Todd
Gary D. Gayton
Michel P. Stern (Also practicing alone, Bellevue, Washington)
Christopher A. Byrne
Patricia D. Ryan

ASSOCIATES

Mary F. O'Boyle
Bruce H. Williams
David J. Onsager
Diana T. Jimenez
Robert T. Mimbu
Cristina C. Kapela
Camilla M. Hedberg
John E. Lenker
Kathleen C. Healy

Representative Clients: The Chubb Group of Insurance Companies; CNA Insurance Companies; Transamerica Insurance Companies; CIGNA Insurance Companies; Central National Insurance Company of Omaha; Zurich-American Insurance Companies; Switzerland Insurance Company; Hartford Insurance Company; Allstate Insurance Companies.

For full biographical listings, see the Martindale-Hubbell Law Directory

*TACOMA,** Pierce Co.

ROSENOW, JOHNSON, GRAFFE, KEAY, POMEROY & MONIZ (AV)

Suite 101, 2115 North 30th Street, 98403
Telephone: 206-572-5323; Seattle: 838-1767
Fax: 206-572-5413
Seattle
Seattle, Washington Office: 1111 Third Avenue, Suite 3000.
Telephone: 206-223-4770.
Fax: 206-386-7344.

MEMBERS OF FIRM

Jack G. Rosenow
A. Clarke Johnson
Christopher W. Keay
Clifford L. Peterson
Marilyn W. Schultheis
Cheryl A. Asche

OF COUNSEL

Jeffrey F. Hale
W. Ben Blackett

Representative Clients: American States Insurance Company; Continental Casualty Company; Group Health Cooperative of Puget Sound; Johnson & Johnson; National General Insurance Company; Physicians Insurance Exchange; The Doctors' Company; Transamerica Insurance Group; Washington Casualty Company.

For full biographical listings, see the Martindale-Hubbell Law Directory

WEST VIRGINIA

*CHARLESTON,** Kanawha Co.

CICCARELLO, DEL GIUDICE & LAFON (AV)

Suite 100, 1219 Virginia Street, East, 25301
Telephone: 304-343-4440
Telecopier: 304-343-4464

MEMBERS OF FIRM

Arthur T. Ciccarello
Michael J. Del Giudice
Timothy J. LaFon

For full biographical listings, see the Martindale-Hubbell Law Directory

HUNT, LEES, FARRELL & KESSLER (AV)

7 Players Club Drive, P.O. Box 2506, 25329-2506
Telephone: 304-344-9651
Telecopier: 304-343-1916
Huntington, West Virginia Office: Prichard Building, 601 Ninth Street, P.O. Box 2191, 25722.
Telephone: 304-529-1999.
Martinsburg, West Virginia Office: 1012 B Winchester Avenue. P.O. Box 579. 25401.
Telephone: 304-267-3100.

MEMBERS OF FIRM

James B. Lees, Jr.
Joseph M. Farrell, Jr. (Resident, Huntington Office)
John A. Kessler

ASSOCIATES

James A. McKowen
Jeffrey T. Jones
Marion Eugene Ray
Mark Jenkinson (Resident, Martinsburg Office)
Meikka A. Cutlip (Resident, Huntington Office)
Sharon M. Fedorochko

OF COUNSEL

L. Alvin Hunt

For full biographical listings, see the Martindale-Hubbell Law Directory

MASINTER & LACY (AV)

Suite 1401 Bank One Center, 707 Virginia Street East, 25301
Telephone: 304-344-3532
Fax: 304-346-2306

Allan H. Masinter
Gerald R. Lacy

For full biographical listings, see the Martindale-Hubbell Law Directory

*CLARKSBURG,** Harrison Co.

JOHNSON, SIMMERMAN & BROUGHTON, L.C. (AV)

Suite 210, Goff Building, P.O. Box 150, 26301
Telephone: 304-624-6555
Telecopier: 304-623-4933

Charles G. Johnson
Frank E. Simmerman, Jr.
Marcia Allen Broughton

For full biographical listings, see the Martindale-Hubbell Law Directory

WEST & JONES (AV)

360 Washington Avenue, P.O. Box 2348, 26302
Telephone: 304-624-5501
FAX: 304-624-4454

MEMBERS OF FIRM

James C. West, Jr.
Jerald E. Jones
John S. Kaull

ASSOCIATES

Kathryn K. Allen
Norman T. Farley

Reference: The Union National Bank of West Virginia.

For Complete List of Firm Personnel, See General Section

For full biographical listings, see the Martindale-Hubbell Law Directory

*HUNTINGTON,** Cabell & Wayne Cos.

JENKINS, FENSTERMAKER, KRIEGER, KAYES, FARRELL & AGEE (AV)

Eleventh Floor Coal Exchange Building, P.O. Drawer 2688, 25726
Telephone: 304-523-2100
Charleston, WV 304-345-3100
Facsimile: 304-523-2347; 304-523-9279

(See Next Column)

MEMBERS OF FIRM

John E. Jenkins (1897-1961)
P. Thomas Krieger
Henry M. Kayes
Michael J. Farrell
Wesley F. Agee
Barry M. Taylor

ASSOCIATES

Suzanne McGinnis Oxley
Charlotte A. Hoffman
Robert H. Sweeney, Jr.
Patricia A. Jennings
Stephen J. Golder
William J. McGee, Jr.
Anne Maxwell McGee
Tamela J. White
Lee Murray Hall
Thomas J. Obrokta

OF COUNSEL

John E. Jenkins, Jr.
Susan B. Saxe

For full biographical listings, see the Martindale-Hubbell Law Directory

*PRINCETON,** Mercer Co.

GIBSON & ASSOCIATES (AV)

1345 Mercer Street, 24740
Telephone: 304-425-8276
800-742-3545

MEMBER OF FIRM

Michael F. Gibson

ASSOCIATES

Derrick Ward Lefler
Bill Huffman
Kelly R. Charnock

LEGAL SUPPORT PERSONNEL

SOCIAL SECURITY PARALEGALS

Nancy Belcher

PERSONAL INJURY PARALEGALS

Kathy Richards

WORKERS COMPENSATION PARALEGAL

Carol Hylton

MEDICAL NEGLIGENCE PARALEGAL

Deborah Fye

For full biographical listings, see the Martindale-Hubbell Law Directory

*WHEELING,** Ohio Co.

SCHRADER, RECHT, BYRD, COMPANION & GURLEY (AV)

1000 Hawley Building, 1025 Main Street, P.O. Box 6336, 26003
Telephone: 304-233-3390
Fax: 304-233-2769
Martins Ferry, Ohio Office: 205 North Fifth Street, P.O. Box 309.
Telephone: 614-633-8976.
Fax: 614-633-0400.

PARTNERS

Henry S. Schrader (Retired)
Arthur M. Recht
Ray A. Byrd
James F. Companion
Terence M. Gurley
Frank X. Duff
Teresa Rieman-Camilletti
Yolonda G. Lambert
Patrick S. Casey
Sandra M. Chapman
Daniel P. Fry (Resident, Martins Ferry, Ohio Office)
James P. Mazzone

ASSOCIATES

Sandra K. Law
D. Kevin Coleman
Denise A. Jebbia
Edythe A. Nash
Robert G. McCoid
Denise D. Klug
Thomas E. Johnston

OF COUNSEL

James A. Byrum, Jr.

General Counsel: WesBanco Bank-Elm Grove.
Representative Clients: CIGNA Property and Casualty Cos.; Columbia Gas Transmission Corp.; Commercial Union Assurance Co.; Hazlett, Burt & Watson, Inc.; Stone & Thomas Department Stores; Transamerica Commercial Finance Corp.; Wheeling-Pittsburgh Steel Corp.

For full biographical listings, see the Martindale-Hubbell Law Directory

WISCONSIN

*MILWAUKEE,** Milwaukee Co.

KERSTEN & MCKINNON, S.C. (AV)

231 West Wisconsin Avenue, Suite 1200, 53203
Telephone: 414-271-0054
Fax: 414-271-7131

(See Next Column)

KERSTEN & MCKINNON S.C., *Milwaukee—Continued*

Charles J. Kersten (1925-1972)
J. P. McKinnon (1943-1973)
Arlo McKinnon
E. Campion Kersten
George P. Kersten
Kenan J. Kersten
Dyan Evans Barbeau
Leslie Van Buskirk
Sheila M. Hanrahan

For full biographical listings, see the Martindale-Hubbell Law Directory

*WAUSAU,** Marathon Co.

JEROME A. MAEDER LAW OFFICES, S.C. (AV)

602 Jackson Street, P.O. Box 1626, 54401
Telephone: 715-842-2281
FAX: 715-842-1046

Jerome A. Maeder

Vincent A. Maeder
William D. Mansell
Robert J. Gray

For full biographical listings, see the Martindale-Hubbell Law Directory

WYOMING

*CASPER,** Natrona Co.

DUNCAN & KOFAKIS (AV)

Suite 325, Key Bank Building, 300 South Wolcott Street, 82601
Telephone: 307-265-0934
Fax: 307-237-0718

Hugh M. Duncan

For full biographical listings, see the Martindale-Hubbell Law Directory

CANADA
ALBERTA

*CALGARY,** Calgary Jud. Dist.

BENNETT JONES VERCHERE (AV)

4500 Bankers Hall East, 855-2nd Street S.W., T2P 4K7
Telephone: (403) 298-3100
Facsimile: (403) 265-7219
Edmonton, Alberta Office: 1000, 10035-105 Street.
Telephone: (403) 421-8133.
Facsimile: (403) 421-7951.
Toronto, Ontario Office: 3400 1 First Canadian Place. P.O. Box 130.
Telephone: (416) 863-1200.
Facsimile: (416) 863-1716.
Ottawa, Ontario Office: Suite 1800. 350 Alberta Street, Box 25, K1R 1A4.
Telephone: (613) 230-4935.
Facsimile: (613) 230-3836.
Montreal, Quebec Office: Suite 1600, 1 Place Ville Marie.
Telephone: (514) 871-1200.
Facsimile: (514) 871-8115.

MEMBER OF FIRM

John G. Martland, Q.C.

For Complete List of Firm Personnel, See General Section

For full biographical listings, see the Martindale-Hubbell Law Directory

*EDMONTON,** Edmonton Jud. Dist.

LUCAS BOWKER & WHITE (AV)

Esso Tower - Scotia Place, 1201-10060 Jasper Avenue, T5J 4E5
Telephone: 403-426-5330
Telecopier: 403-428-1066

MEMBERS OF FIRM

George E. Bowker, Q.C.
Robert B. White, Q.C.
E. James Kindrake
Norman J. Pollock
Kent H. Davidson
Alan R. Gray
David J. Stam
Donald J. Wilson

ASSOCIATES

Kevin J. Smith
Gordon V. Garside
Deborah L. Hughes
Annette E. Koski
Douglas A. Bodner
Michael Alexander Kirk
Mark E. Lesniak
Eric C. Lund

COUNSEL

Joan C. Copp

Reference: Canadian Imperial Bank of Commerce.

For Complete List of Firm Personnel, See General Section

For full biographical listings, see the Martindale-Hubbell Law Directory

CANADA
ONTARIO

*TORONTO,** Regional Munic. of York

BORDEN & ELLIOT (AV)

Barristers & Solicitors
Scotia Plaza, 40 King Street West, M5H 3Y4
Telephone: 416-367-6000
Telecopier: 416-367-6749
Internet: @ borden.com
A Member of the national association of Borden DuMoulin Howard Gervais, comprising Borden & Elliot in Toronto, Ontario, Russell & DuMoulin in Vancouver, British Columbia, Howard, Mackie in Calgary, Alberta and Mackenzie Gervais in Montréal, Québec. Borden DuMoulin Howard Gervais also operates an office in London, England.

MEMBER AND ASSOCIATES

William A. McClelland

For Complete List of Firm Personnel, See General Section

For full biographical listings, see the Martindale-Hubbell Law Directory

MUNICIPAL AND ZONING LAW

ALABAMA

*BIRMINGHAM,** Jefferson Co.

BRADLEY, ARANT, ROSE & WHITE (AV)

1400 Park Place Tower, 2001 Park Place, 35203
Telephone: 205-521-8000
Telex: 494-1324
Facsimile: 205-251-8611, 251-8665, 252-0264
Facsimile (Southtrust Office): 205-251-9915
Huntsville, Alabama Office: 200 Clinton Avenue West, Suite 900.
Telephone: 205-517-5100.
Facsimile: 205-533-5069.

MEMBER OF FIRM

Charles A. J. Beavers, Jr.

ASSOCIATE

Frank C. Galloway, III

For Complete List of Firm Personnel, See General Section

For full biographical listings, see the Martindale-Hubbell Law Directory

*MOBILE,** Mobile Co.

FINKBOHNER AND LAWLER (AV)

169 Dauphin Street Suite 300, P.O. Box 3085, 36652
Telephone: 334-438-5871
Fax: 334-432-8052

MEMBERS OF FIRM

George W. Finkbohner, Jr.
John L. Lawler
George W. Finkbohner, III
Royce A. Ray, III

For full biographical listings, see the Martindale-Hubbell Law Directory

ARIZONA

*PHOENIX,** Maricopa Co.

DUSHOFF MCCALL, A PROFESSIONAL CORPORATION (AV)

Two Renaissance Square, 40 North Central, 14th Floor, 85004
Telephone: 602-254-3800
Fax: 602-258-2551

Jay Dushoff
Jack E. McCall
Michael J. McGivern
Denise J. Henslee
Jean Weaver Rice
Janice Sloan Feinberg Massey

OF COUNSEL

Dawn Stoll Zeitlin (P.C.)

LEGAL SUPPORT PERSONNEL

Thomas M. Flynn

For full biographical listings, see the Martindale-Hubbell Law Directory

FENNEMORE CRAIG, A PROFESSIONAL CORPORATION (AV)

Two North Central, Suite 2200, 85004
Telephone: 602-257-8700
Fax: 602-257-8527
Scottsdale, Arizona Office: 6263 North Scottsdale Road, Suite 290, 85250.
Telephone: 602-257-5400.
Fax: 602-945-4932.
Tucson, Arizona Office: One South Church Avenue, Suite 1030, 85701.
Telephone: 602-624-9312.
Fax: 602-882-7383.

Michael Preston Green
Graeme E. M. Hancock
Andrew M. Federhar

Representative Clients: ASARCO Incorporated; AT&T Communications; Bridgestone/Firestone, Inc.; Catellus Development Corp.; Citibank (Arizona); First Interstate Bank of Arizona; GIANT Industries; Phelps Dodge Corporation; The Atchison, Topeka & Santa Fe Railway, Co.; US WEST Communications.

For Complete List of Firm Personnel, See General Section

For full biographical listings, see the Martindale-Hubbell Law Directory

GAMMAGE & BURNHAM (AV)

One Renaissance Square, Two North Central Avenue, Suite 1800, 85004
Telephone: 602-256-0566
Fax: 602-256-4475

MEMBERS OF FIRM

Grady Gammage, Jr.
Michael B. Withey

Representative Clients: Kaufman & Broad of Arizona, Inc.; Viehmann Martin & Associates; Homes by Dave Brown; Evans Withycombe, Inc.; Waste Management, Inc.; Opus Southwest; Samaritan Health System; W.M. Grace Development Co.

For Complete List of Firm Personnel, See General Section

For full biographical listings, see the Martindale-Hubbell Law Directory

MEYER, HENDRICKS, VICTOR, OSBORN & MALEDON, A PROFESSIONAL ASSOCIATION (AV)

2929 North Central Avenue Suite 2100, 85012-2794
Telephone: 602-640-9000
Facsimile: (24 Hrs.) 602-640-9050
Mailing Address: P.O. Box 33449, 85067-3449,

Jones Osborn II
Jeffrey L. Sellers
Gary A. Gotto
Jeffrey C. Zimmerman
Lucia Fakonas Howard
Robert V. Kerrick

Reference: Bank One Arizona, NA.

For Complete List of Firm Personnel, See General Section

For full biographical listings, see the Martindale-Hubbell Law Directory

CALIFORNIA

COSTA MESA, Orange Co.

RUTAN & TUCKER (AV)

A Partnership including Professional Corporations
611 Anton Boulevard, Suite 1400, P.O. Box 1950, 92626
Telephone: 714-641-5100; 213-625-7586
Telecopier: 714-546-9035

MEMBERS OF FIRM

Leonard A. Hampel, Jr.
David C. Larsen (P.C.)
Michael D. Rubin
Jeffrey M. Oderman (P.C.)
Stan Wolcott (P.C.)
Robert S. Bower
David J. Aleshire
William M. Marticorena
Philip D. Kohn
Joel D. Kuperberg
William W. Wynder
M. Katherine Jenson
Richard Montevideo
Elizabeth L. (Hanna) Dixon

For Complete List of Firm Personnel, See General Section

For full biographical listings, see the Martindale-Hubbell Law Directory

EL MONTE, Los Angeles Co.

MICHAEL B. MONTGOMERY A LAW CORPORATION (AV)

10501 Valley Boulevard, Suite 121, 91731
Telephone: 818-452-1222
Fax: 818-452-8323

Michael B. Montgomery

Reference: Bank of America (San Marino Branch).

For full biographical listings, see the Martindale-Hubbell Law Directory

GLENDALE, Los Angeles Co.

LASKIN & GRAHAM (AV)

Suite 840, 800 North Brand Boulevard, 91203
Telephone: 213-665-6955; 818-547-4800; 714-957-3031
Telecopier: 818-547-3100

MEMBERS OF FIRM

Arnold K. Graham
Susan L. Vaage
John S. Peterson
Michael Anthony Cisneros
Gregson M. Perry
Lynn I. Ibara
Jason L. Glovinsky

OF COUNSEL

Richard Laskin

For full biographical listings, see the Martindale-Hubbell Law Directory

*MARTINEZ,** Contra Costa Co.

CHARLES J. WILLIAMS A PROFESSIONAL CORPORATION (AV)

1320 Arnold Drive Suite 160, 94553
Telephone: 510-228-3840
Fax: 510-228-1703

(See Next Column)

CHARLES J. WILLIAMS A PROFESSIONAL CORPORATION, *Martinez—Continued*

Charles J. Williams
Elizabeth B. Hearey
Teresa L. Highsmith

PALM DESERT, Riverside Co.

CRANDALL & TRAVER (AV)

43-645 Monterey Avenue, Suite D, 92260
Telephone: 619-346-7557
Telecopier: 619-773-3589

Lynn D. Crandall
Walter J.R. Traver

Lisa A. Garvin
Elizabeth Olivier
Toni Eggebraaten
Kimberly G. Oleson

Reference: Eldorado Bank, Palm Desert Office.

For full biographical listings, see the Martindale-Hubbell Law Directory

PASADENA, Los Angeles Co.

LAGERLOF, SENECAL, BRADLEY & SWIFT (AV)

301 North Lake Avenue, 10th Floor, 91101-4107
Telephone: 818-793-9400
FAX: 818-793-5900

MEMBERS OF FIRM

Joseph J. Burris (1913-1980)
Stanley C. Lagerlof
H. Melvin Swift, Jr.
H. Jess Senecal
Jack T. Swafford
John F. Bradley
Timothy J. Gosney
William F. Kruse
Thomas S. Bunn, III
Andrew D. Turner
Rebecca J. Thyne

ASSOCIATES

Paul M. Norman
John F. Machtinger
James D. Ciampa
Ellen M. Burkhart

LEGAL SUPPORT PERSONNEL

Ronald E. Hagler

Representative Clients: Anchor Glass Container Corporation; Bethlehem Steel Corp.; Orthopaedic Hospital; Palmdale Water District; Public Water Agencies Group; Walnut Valley Water District.
Special Counsel: City of Redondo Beach, Calif.; Ventura Port Dist., Calif.

For full biographical listings, see the Martindale-Hubbell Law Directory

*SAN DIEGO,** San Diego Co.

HOVEY, KIRBY, THORNTON & HAHN, A PROFESSIONAL CORPORATION (AV)

101 West Broadway, Suite 1100, 92101-8297
Telephone: 619-685-4000
Fax: 619-685-4004

Gregg B. Hovey

For full biographical listings, see the Martindale-Hubbell Law Directory

*SANTA CRUZ,** Santa Cruz Co.

ATCHISON, ANDERSON, HURLEY & BARISONE, A PROFESSIONAL CORPORATION (AV)

333 Church Street, 95060
Telephone: 408-423-8383
Fax: 408-423-9401
Salinas, California Office: 137 Central Avenue, Suite 6. 93901.
Telephone: 408-755-7833.
Fax: 408-753-0293.

Rodney R. Atchison
Neal R. Anderson (1947-1986)
Vincent P. Hurley
John G. Barisone

Justin B. Lighty
Mitchell A. Jackman
David Y. Imai
Anthony P. Condotti
Mary C. Logan

Counsel for: City of Santa Cruz.

For full biographical listings, see the Martindale-Hubbell Law Directory

COLORADO

*ASPEN,** Pitkin Co.

AUSTIN, PEIRCE & SMITH, P.C. (AV)

Suite 205, 600 East Hopkins Avenue, 81611
Telephone: 303-925-2600
FAX: 303-925-4720

(See Next Column)

Ronald D. Austin
Frederick F. Peirce
Thomas Fenton Smith

Rhonda J. Bazil

Counsel for: Clark's Market; Coates, Reid & Waldron Realtors; Crystal Palace Corp.; Snowmass Shopping Center; Coldwell Banker; William Poss & Assoc., Architects; Snowmass Resort Association; Real Estate Affiliates, Inc.; Raleigh Enterprises.

For full biographical listings, see the Martindale-Hubbell Law Directory

*CASTLE ROCK,** Douglas Co.

FOLKESTAD, KOKISH & FAZEKAS, P.C. (AV)

316 Wilcox Street, 80104-2495
Telephone: 303-688-3045
FAX: 303-688-3189

James B. Folkestad
John Kokish
Ernest F. Fazekas, II

Susan B. Shoemaker
Douglas E. Saunders

Representative Clients: Bank of Douglas County; Johnson & Sons Construction, Inc.; B & W Construction Co.; Proto Construction & Paving, Inc.; Grimm Construction Co.; Ashcroft Homes of Denver LLC.
References: Bank of Douglas County; First National Bank of Castle Rock; First Bank of Castle Rock; Colorado National Bank.

For full biographical listings, see the Martindale-Hubbell Law Directory

*DENVER,** Denver Co.

HAYES, PHILLIPS & MALONEY, P.C. (AV)

Suite 450, The Market Center, 1350 Seventeenth Street, 80202-1517
Telephone: 303-825-6444
Fax: 303-825-1269

John E. Hayes
Herbert C. Phillips
James S. Maloney
Kathleen E. Haddock
M. Susan Lombardi
Bradley N. Shefrin

Representative Clients: City of Northglenn; City of Sheridan; Metropolitan Denver Water Authority; Parker Water and Sanitation District; Town of Winter Park; City of Black Hawk; Town of Hudson; Town of Parker; Town of Superior; Town of Alma.

For full biographical listings, see the Martindale-Hubbell Law Directory

MYERS, HOPPIN, BRADLEY AND DEVITT, P.C. (AV)

Suite 420, 4704 Harlan Street, 80212
Telephone: 303-433-8527
Fax: 303-433-8219

Frederick J. Myers
Charles T. Hoppin
Jon T. Bradley
Jerald J. Devitt

Gregg W. Fraser

OF COUNSEL

Kent E. Hanson

Reference: Bank One Lakeside Banking Center.

For full biographical listings, see the Martindale-Hubbell Law Directory

CONNECTICUT

CHESHIRE, New Haven Co.

JOHN K. KNOTT, JR. (AV)

325 South Main Street, 06410
Telephone: 203-271-3031

ASSOCIATE

Priscilla C. Mulvaney

For full biographical listings, see the Martindale-Hubbell Law Directory

GREENWICH, Fairfield Co.

ALBERT, WARD & JOHNSON, P.C. (AV)

125 Mason Street, P.O. Box 1668, 06836
Telephone: 203-661-8600
Telecopier: 203-661-8051

OF COUNSEL

David Albert

Tom S. Ward, Jr.
Scott R. Johnson
Jane D. Hogeman
Howard R. Wolfe

(See Next Column)

ALBERT, WARD & JOHNSON P.C.—*Continued*

Christopher A. Kristoff

For full biographical listings, see the Martindale-Hubbell Law Directory

*NEW HAVEN,** New Haven Co.

HOGAN & RINI, P.C. (AV)

Gold Building, 8th Floor 234 Church Street, 06510
Telephone: 203-787-4191
Telecopier: 203-777-4032

John W. Hogan, Jr.
Joseph L. Rini
Sue A. Cousineau

OF COUNSEL

Mark S. Cousineau

For full biographical listings, see the Martindale-Hubbell Law Directory

NEW LONDON, New London Co.

WALLER, SMITH & PALMER, P.C. (AV)

52 Eugene O'Neill Drive, P.O. Box 88, 06320
Telephone: 203-442-0367
Telecopier: 203-447-9915
Old Lyme, Connecticut Office: 103-A Halls Road.
Telephone: 203-434-8063.

Birdsey G. Palmer (Retired)
William W. Miner
Robert P. Anderson, Jr.
Robert W. Marrion
Hughes Griffis
Edward B. O'Connell
Frederick B. Gahagan
Linda D. Loucony
Mary E. Driscoll
William E. Wellette

Tracy M. Collins
Donna Richer Skaats
David P. Condon
Valerie Ann Votto
Charles C. Anderson

OF COUNSEL

Suzanne Donnelly Kitchings

General Counsel for: Colotone Group.
Counsel for: Union Trust Co.; Coastal Savings Bank; Cash Home Center, Inc.
Local Counsel for: Metropolitan Insurance Co.; Connecticut General Life Insurance Co.

For Complete List of Firm Personnel, See General Section
For full biographical listings, see the Martindale-Hubbell Law Directory

WESTPORT, Fairfield Co.

WILLIAM L. SCHEFFLER (AV(T))

315 Post Road West, 06880
Telephone: 203-226-6600; 212-795-7800
Telecopier: 203-227-1873

For full biographical listings, see the Martindale-Hubbell Law Directory

WEISMAN & LUBELL (AV)

5 Sylvan Road South, P.O. Box 3184, 06880
Telephone: 203-226-8307
Telecopier: 203-221-7279

MEMBERS OF FIRM

Lawrence P. Weisman
Ellen B. Lubell

Andrew R. Tarshis

For full biographical listings, see the Martindale-Hubbell Law Directory

DISTRICT OF COLUMBIA

WASHINGTON, D.C. Co.

FRANK W. FRISK, JR., P.C. (AV)

Suite 125, Canal Square, 1054 Thirty-First Street, N.W., 20007
Telephone: 202-333-8433
Fax: 202-333-8431

Frank W. Frisk, Jr.

For full biographical listings, see the Martindale-Hubbell Law Directory

FLORIDA

*BRADENTON,** Manatee Co.

MCGUIRE, PRATT, MASIO & FARRANCE, P.A. (AV)

Suite 600, 1001 3rd Avenue West, P.O. Box 1866, 34206
Telephone: 813-748-7076
FAX: 813-747-9774

Hugh E. McGuire, Jr.
Charles J. Pratt, Jr.
Carol A. Masio
Robert A. Farrance
Richard G. Groff

OF COUNSEL

Carter H. Parry

Reference: Barnett Bank of Manatee County.

For full biographical listings, see the Martindale-Hubbell Law Directory

DESTIN, Okaloosa Co.

J. JEROME MILLER (AV)

Suite 3, 415 Mountain Drive, 32541
Telephone: 904-837-3860
Fax: 904-837-6158

Lamar A. Conerly, Jr.

For full biographical listings, see the Martindale-Hubbell Law Directory

*KISSIMMEE,** Osceola Co.

POHL & BROWN, P.A.

(See Winter Park)

*MIAMI,** Dade Co.

FERRELL & FERTEL, P.A. (AV)

Suite 1920 Miami Center, 201 South Biscayne Boulevard, 33131-2305
Telephone: 305-371-8585
Telecopier: 305-371-5732

Milton M. Ferrell, Jr.

Reference: City National Bank of Florida.

For full biographical listings, see the Martindale-Hubbell Law Directory

STEARNS WEAVER MILLER WEISSLER ALHADEFF & SITTERSON, P.A. (AV)

Suite 2200 Museum Tower, 150 West Flagler Street, 33130
Telephone: 305-789-3200
FAX: 305-789-3395
Tampa, Florida Office: Suite 2200 Landmark Centre, 401 East Jackson Street.
Telephone: 813-223-4800.
Fort Lauderdale, Florida Office: 200 East Broward Boulevard, Suite 1900.
Telephone: 305-462-9500.

E. Richard Alhadeff
Louise Jacowitz Allen
Stuart D. Ames
Thomas P. Angelo (Resident, Fort Lauderdale Office)
Lawrence J. Bailin (Resident, Tampa Office)
Patrick A. Barry (Resident, Fort Lauderdale Office)
Lisa K. Bennett (Resident, Fort Lauderdale Office)
Susan Fleming Bennett (Resident, Tampa Office)
Mark J. Bernet (Resident, Tampa Office)
Claire Bailey Carraway (Resident, Tampa Office)
Seth T. Craine (Resident, Tampa Office)
Piero Luciano Desiderio (Resident, Fort Lauderdale Office)
Mark P. Dikeman
Sharon Quinn Dixon
Alan H. Fein
Owen S. Freed
Dean M. Freitag
Robert E. Gallagher, Jr.
Alice R. Huneycutt (Resident, Tampa Office)
Theodore A. Jewell
Elizabeth J. Keeler
Teddy D. Klinghoffer
Robert T. Kofman
Thomas A. Lash (Resident, Tampa Office)
Joy Spillis Lundeen
Brian J. McDonough
Francisco J. Menendez
Antonio R. Menendez
Alison W. Miller
Vicki Lynn Monroe
Harold D. Moorefield, Jr.
John N. Muratides (Resident, Tampa Office)
John K. Olson (Resident, Tampa Office)
Robert C. Owens
Patricia A. Redmond
Carl D. Roston
Steven D. Rubin
Mark A. Schneider
Curtis H. Sitterson
Mark D. Solov
Eugene E. Stearns
Bradford Swing
Dennis R. Turner
Ronald L. Weaver (Resident, Tampa Office)
Robert I. Weissler
Patricia G. Welles
Martin B. Woods (Resident, Fort Lauderdale Office)

(See Next Column)

STEARNS WEAVER MILLER WEISSLER ALHADEFF & SITTERSON P.A., *Miami—Continued*

Shawn M. Bayne (Resident, Fort Lauderdale Office)
Lisa Berg
Hans C. Beyer (Resident, Tampa Office)
Dawn A. Carapella (Resident, Tampa Office)
Christina Maria Diaz
Robert I. Finvarb
Patricia K. Green
Marilyn D. Greenblatt
Richard B. Jackson
Aimee C. Jimenez
Cheryl A. Kaplan
Michael I. Keyes
Vernon L. Lewis
Kevin Bruce Love
Adam Coatsworth Mishcon
Elizabeth G. Rice (Resident, Tampa Office)
Glenn M. Rissman
Claudia J. Saenz
Richard E. Schatz
Robert P. Shantz (Resident, Tampa Office)
Martin S. Simkovic
Ronni D. Solomon
Jo Claire Spear (Resident, Tampa Office)
Gail Marie Stage (Resident, Fort Lauderdale Office)
Annette Torres
Barbara L. Wilhite

OF COUNSEL

Stephen A. Bennett

For full biographical listings, see the Martindale-Hubbell Law Directory

*NAPLES,** Collier Co.

VEGA, BROWN, STANLEY, MARTIN & ZELMAN, P.A. (AV)

2660 Airport Road, South, 33962
Telephone: 813-774-3333
Fax: 813-774-6420

George Vega, Jr.
John F. Stanley

Thomas J. Wood
John G. Vega

OF COUNSEL

Thomas R. Brown

General Counsel for: Lely Estates; Naples Community Hospital.
Local Counsel: Fleischmann Trust; Quail Creek Developments.

For Complete List of Firm Personnel, See General Section

For full biographical listings, see the Martindale-Hubbell Law Directory

*ORLANDO,** Orange Co.

POHL & BROWN, P.A.

(See Winter Park)

*TALLAHASSEE,** Leon Co.

HOPPING BOYD GREEN & SAMS (AV)

123 South Calhoun Street, P.O. Box 6526, 32314
Telephone: 904-222-7500
Fax: 904-224-8551

MEMBERS OF FIRM

Carlos Alvarez
James S. Alves
Brian H. Bibeau
Kathleen L. Blizzard
Elizabeth C. Bowman
William L. Boyd, IV
Richard S. Brightman
Peter C. Cunningham
Ralph A. DeMeo
Thomas M. DeRose
William H. Green
Wade L. Hopping
Frank E. Matthews
Richard D. Melson
David L. Powell
William D. Preston
Carolyn S. Raepple
Gary P. Sams
Robert P. Smith
Cheryl G. Stuart

ASSOCIATES

Kristin M. Conroy
Charles A. Culp, Jr.
Connie C. Durrence
Jonathan S. Fox
James Calvin Goodlett
Gary K. Hunter, Jr.
Dalana W. Johnson
Jonathan T. Johnson
Angela R. Morrison
Gary V. Perko
Karen Peterson
Michael P. Petrovich
Douglas S. Roberts
R. Scott Ruth
Julie Rome Steinmeyer

OF COUNSEL

W. Robert Fokes

Representative Clients: ITT Community Development Corp.; Florida Power & Light Co.; Florida Electric Power Coordinating Group; Hollywood, Inc.; CF Industries, Inc.; Association of Physical Fitness Centers; Sunniland Pipe Line Company, Inc.; Florida Chemical Industries Council; Mobil Oil Co.; Waste Management, Inc.

For full biographical listings, see the Martindale-Hubbell Law Directory

*TAMPA,** Hillsborough Co.

MORRISON, MORRISON & MILLS, P.A. (AV)

1200 West Platt Street Suite 100, 33606
Telephone: 813-258-3311
Telecopier: 813-258-3209

Thomas K. Morrison
Susan B. Morrison
Frederick J. Mills
Tracey Karen Jaensch
James E. Holmes, Jr.

Representative Clients: SouthTrust Bank of West Florida; SouthTrust Bank of Alabama, National Association; NationsBank of Florida, N.A.; Mercantile Bank; Barnett Banks, Inc.; Southern Commerce Bank; Sun Bank of Pasco County; Hillsborough County Industrial Development Authority; Automation Packaging, Inc.; Medical Data Management, Inc.

For full biographical listings, see the Martindale-Hubbell Law Directory

RYDBERG, GOLDSTEIN & BOLVES, P.A. (AV)

Suite 200, 500 East Kennedy Boulevard, 33602
Telephone: 813-229-3900
Telecopier: 813-229-6101

Marsha Griffin Rydberg
Bruce S. Goldstein
Brian A. Bolves
Robert E. V. Kelley, Jr.
Homer Duvall, III
Richard Thomas Petitt
Donald Alan Workman
David M. Corry
Leenetta Blanton
Peter Baker
Jeffery R. Ward
Roy J. Ford, Jr.
John J. Dingfelder

For full biographical listings, see the Martindale-Hubbell Law Directory

WINTER PARK, Orange Co.

POHL & BROWN, P.A. (AV)

280 West Canton Avenue, Suite 410, P.O. Box 3208, 32789
Telephone: 407-647-7645; 407-647-POHL
Telefax: 407-647-2314

Frank L. Pohl
Usher L. Brown
Houston E. Short
Dwight I. Cool
William W. Pouzar
Mary B. Van Leuven

OF COUNSEL

Frederick W. Peirsol

Representative Clients: Orange County Comptroller; Osceola County; School Board of Osceola County, Florida; Osceola Tourist Development Council; NationsBank of Florida, N.A.; SunBank, N.A.; The Bank of Winter Park; Bekins Moving and Storage Co., Inc.; Champion Boats, Inc.; KeyCom Telephone Systems, Inc.

For full biographical listings, see the Martindale-Hubbell Law Directory

GEORGIA

*ATLANTA,** Fulton Co.

FREEMAN & HAWKINS (AV)

4000 One Peachtree Center, 303 Peachtree Street, N.E., 30308-3243
Telephone: 404-614-7400
Fax: 404-614-750
CompuServe address: 73541,1626
Internet address: 73451.1626@compuserve.com

MEMBERS OF FIRM

H. Lane Young, II
Robert U. Wright

ASSOCIATES

Kimberly Houston Ridley
Cullen Christie Wilkerson, Jr.

Representative Clients: ACCG-IRMA; G-IRMA; Willis Corroon Administrative Services; Titan Insurance Co.; American International Group.

For Complete List of Firm Personnel, See General Section

For full biographical listings, see the Martindale-Hubbell Law Directory

HOLT, NEY, ZATCOFF & WASSERMAN (AV)

A Partnership including Professional Corporations
100 Galleria Parkway, Suite 600, 30339
Telephone: 404-956-9600
Facsimile Number: 404-956-1490

MEMBER OF FIRM

James M. Ney (P.C.)

Representative Clients: Equitable Real Estate Investment Management, Inc.; NationsBank of Georgia, N.A.; Roberts Properties, Inc.; Trammell Crow Residential; John Weiland Homes, Inc.; Childress Klein Properties; Home Depot, Inc.; Genuine Parts Co.; Brookwood Hills Homeowner Assn.; Mt. Paran/Northside Citizens Assn.

(See Next Column)

HOLT, NEY, ZATCOFF & WASSERMAN—*Continued*

For Complete List of Firm Personnel, See General Section

For full biographical listings, see the Martindale-Hubbell Law Directory

*MCDONOUGH,** Henry Co.

SMITH, WELCH & STUDDARD (AV)

41 Keys Ferry Street, P.O. Box 31, 30253
Telephone: 404-957-3937
Fax: 404-957-9165
Stockbridge, Georgia Office: 1231-A Eagle's Landing Parkway.
Telephone: 404-389-4864.
FAX: 404-389-5157.

MEMBERS OF FIRM

Ernest M. Smith (1911-1992)
A. J. Welch, Jr.
Ben W. Studdard, III
J. Mark Brittain (Resident, Stockbridge Office)

ASSOCIATES

Patrick D. Jaugstetter
E. Gilmore Maxwell
J.V. Dell, Jr. (Resident, Stockbridge Office)

Representative Clients: Alliance Corp.; Atlanta Motor Speedway, Inc.; Bellamy-Strickland Chevrolet, Inc.; Ceramic and Metal Coatings Corp.; City of Hampton; City of Locust Grove; City of Stockbridge.

For full biographical listings, see the Martindale-Hubbell Law Directory

*NEWNAN,** Coweta Co.

GLOVER & DAVIS, P.A. (AV)

10 Brown Street, P.O. Box 1038, 30264
Telephone: 404-253-4330;
Atlanta: 404-463-1100
Fax: 404-251-7152
Peachtree City, Georgia Office: Suite 130, 200 Westpark Drive.
Telephone: 404-487-5834.
Fax: 404-487-3492.

J. Littleton Glover, Jr.
Asa M. Powell, Jr.
Jerry Ann Conner

Representative Clients: Newnan Savings Bank; Pike Transfer Co.; Batson-Cook Company, General Corporate and Construction Divisions; Coweta County, Georgia; Heard County, Georgia.
Local Counsel for: International Latex Corp.; First Union National Bank of Georgia; West Georgia Farm Credit, ACA.

For Complete List of Firm Personnel, See General Section

For full biographical listings, see the Martindale-Hubbell Law Directory

HAWAII

*HONOLULU,** Honolulu Co.

DWYER IMANAKA SCHRAFF KUDO MEYER & FUJIMOTO ATTORNEYS AT LAW, A LAW CORPORATION (AV)

1800 Pioneer Plaza, 900 Fort Street Mall, 96813
Telephone: 808-524-8000
Telecopier: 808-526-1419
Mailing Address: P.O. Box 2727, 96803

John R. Dwyer, Jr.
Mitchell A. Imanaka
Paul A. Schraff
Benjamin A. Kudo (Atty. at Law, A Law Corp.)
William G. Meyer, III
Wesley M. Fujimoto
Ronald Van Grant
Jon M. H. Pang
Blake W. Bushnell
Kenn N. Kojima

Adelbert Green
Richard T. Asato, Jr.
Scott W. Settle
Darcie S. Yoshinaga
Tracy Timothy Woo
Lawrence I. Kawasaki
Douglas H. Inouye
Christine A. Low

OF COUNSEL

Randall Y. Iwase

For full biographical listings, see the Martindale-Hubbell Law Directory

FOLEY MAEHARA NIP & CHANG (AV)

2700 Grosvenor Center, 737 Bishop Street, 96813
Telephone: 808-526-3011
Telecopier: 808-523-1171, 808-526-0121, 808-533-4814

MEMBERS OF FIRM

Thomas M. Foley
Eric T. Maehara
Renton L. K. Nip
Wesley Y. S. Chang
Carl Tom
Edward R. Brooks
Arlene S. Kishi
Susan M. Ichinose
Robert F. Miller
Christian P. Porter

(See Next Column)

ASSOCIATES

Paula W. Chong
Lenore H. Lee
Leanne A. N. Nikaido
Jordan D. Wagner
Donna H. Yamamoto
Mark J. Bernardin
Jenny K. T. Wakayama

OF COUNSEL

Elizabeth A. Ivey

References: First Hawaiian Bank; Bank of Honolulu; Bank of Hawaii.

For full biographical listings, see the Martindale-Hubbell Law Directory

IDAHO

*TWIN FALLS,** Twin Falls Co.

ROSHOLT, ROBERTSON & TUCKER, CHARTERED (AV)

142 Third Avenue North, P.O. Box 1906, 83303-1906
Telephone: 208-734-0700
Fax: 208-736-0041
Boise, Idaho Office: Suite 600, 1221 W. Idaho, P.O. Box 2139.
Telephone: 208-336-0700.
Fax: 208-344-6034.

J. Evan Robertson
Gary D. Slette

Thomas J. Ryan
Timothy J. Stover

For full biographical listings, see the Martindale-Hubbell Law Directory

ILLINOIS

*CHICAGO,** Cook Co.

EARL L. NEAL & ASSOCIATES (AV)

Suite 1700, 111 West Washington Street, 60602
Telephone: 312-641-7144
Fax: 312-641-5137

Earl Langdon Neal

ASSOCIATES

Michael D. Leroy
Anne L. Fredd
Richard F. Friedman
Terrance Lee Diamond
Langdon D. Neal
Roxanne M. Ward
D. Rainell Rains
Francine D. Lynch
Grady B. Murdock, Jr.
Valda D. Staton
Jeanette Sublett

OF COUNSEL

George N. Leighton
Earl J. Barnes

For full biographical listings, see the Martindale-Hubbell Law Directory

SCARIANO, KULA, ELLCH AND HIMES, CHARTERED (AV)

Two Prudential Plaza 180 North Stetson Suite 3100, 60601-6224
Telephone: 312-565-3100
Facsimile: 312-565-0000
Chicago Heights, Illinois Office: 1450 Aberdeen.
Telephone: 708-755-1900.
Facsimile: 708-755-0000.

Anthony G. Scariano
David P. Kula
Robert H. Ellch
Alan T. Sraga
A. Lynn Himes
Justino D. Petrarca
Lawrence Jay Weiner
Kathleen Field Orr
John M. Izzo
Raymond A. Hauser

OF COUNSEL

Max A. Bailey
G. Robb Cooper
Teri E. Engler
John B. Kralovec

Daniel M. Boyle
Patrick J. Broncato
Sarah R. Carlin
Diane S. Cohen
Jon G. Crawford
Douglas D. Danielson
Anthony Ficarelli
Kelly A. Hayden
Todd K. Hayden
David A. Hemenway
Kathleen Roche Hirsman
Jonathan A. Pearl
Lisa Ann Rapacz
Shelia C. Riley
Joanne W. Schochat

For full biographical listings, see the Martindale-Hubbell Law Directory

CRYSTAL LAKE, McHenry Co.

ZUKOWSKI, ROGERS, FLOOD & McARDLE (AV)

50 Virginia Street, 60014
Telephone: 815-459-2050
Facsimile: 815-459-9057
Chicago, Illinois Office: 100 South Wacker Drive, Suite 1502.
Telephone: 312-407-7700.
Facsimile: 312-332-1901.

MEMBERS OF FIRM

Richard R. Zukowski
H. David Rogers
Richard G. Flood
David W. McArdle
Andrew T. Freund
Jeannine A. Thoms
Stuart D. Gordon

ASSOCIATES

William P. Stanton
Valeree D. Marek
Melissa J. Cooney
Rita W. Garry
Kelly A. Cahill
Michael J. Smoron
Michael J. Chmiel

OF COUNSEL

Timothy J. Curran
Francis S. Lorenz

Representative Clients: Scottsdale Insurance Co.; Illinois Municipal League Risk Management Association-Martin Boyer Companies; Village of Algonquin; Village of Lake in the Hills; Village of Johnsburg; Village of Lakewood; Village of Bull Valley; Village of Hebron; City of Harvard; City of McHenry.

For full biographical listings, see the Martindale-Hubbell Law Directory

*GENEVA,** Kane Co.

SMITH, LANDMEIER & SKAAR, P.C. (AV)

15 North Second Street, 60134
Telephone: 708-232-2880
Fax: 708-232-2889

Howard E. Smith, Jr.
Allen L. Landmeier

Representative Clients: City of St. Charles; Cog Hill Golf & Country Club; Wasco Sanitary District; Testing Service Corp.

For Complete List of Firm Personnel, See General Section

For full biographical listings, see the Martindale-Hubbell Law Directory

*JOLIET,** Will Co.

HERSCHBACH, TRACY, JOHNSON, BERTANI & WILSON (AV)

Two Rialto Square, 116 North Chicago Street, Sixth Floor, 60431
Telephone: 815-723-8500
Fax: 815-727-4846

Thomas R. Wilson
George F. Mahoney, III
Raymond E. Meader
David J. Silverman

General Counsel For: First National Bank of Joliet.
Representative Clients: Villages of Channahon, Frankfort and Shorewood; City of Wilmington; Gallaher & Henry; Tope Corporation; Vulcan Materials; Waste Management, Inc.; Crosfield Chemicals, Inc.

For Complete List of Firm Personnel, See General Section

For full biographical listings, see the Martindale-Hubbell Law Directory

INDIANA

*FORT WAYNE,** Allen Co.

HELMKE, BEAMS, BOYER & WAGNER (AV)

300 Metro Building, Berry & Harrison Streets, 46802-2242
Telephone: 219-422-7422
Telecopier: 219-422-6764

MEMBERS OF FIRM

Walter E. Helmke (1901-1976)
Walter P. Helmke
R. David Boyer
Robert A. Wagner
J. Timothy McCaulay
Daniel J. Borgmann

ASSOCIATE

Trina Glusenkamp Gould

OF COUNSEL

Glen J. Beams
John G. Reiber

Representative Clients: Aalco Distributing Co., Inc.; Brotherhood Mutual Insurance Co.; Fremont Community Schools; Teco, Inc.; Air-O-Mat, Inc.; Leo Distributors, Inc.

For full biographical listings, see the Martindale-Hubbell Law Directory

*INDIANAPOLIS,** Marion Co.

CLARK, QUINN, MOSES & CLARK (AV)

One Indiana Square, Suite 2200, 46204-2011
Telephone: 317-637-1321
Fax: 317-687-2344

MEMBERS OF FIRM

Thomas Michael Quinn
J. Murray Clark
Matthew R. Clark

ASSOCIATES

Michael D. Keele
Cameron F. Clark

Representative Clients: Justus; The Shorewood Corporation; Marina Limited Partnership; Lafarge Corporation; Meijer Realty, Inc.; Lowe's; Kite Development; U-Stor Self Storage Warehouses; Mechanic's Laundry; Davis Homes.

For full biographical listings, see the Martindale-Hubbell Law Directory

*LAFAYETTE,** Tippecanoe Co.

BALL, EGGLESTON, BUMBLEBURG & McBRIDE (AV)

810 Bank One Building, P.O. Box 1535, 47902
Telephone: 317-742-9046
Fax: 317-742-1966

Cable G. Ball (1904-1981)
Owen Crook (1908-1977)
Warren N. Eggleston (1923-1991)

MEMBERS OF FIRM

Joseph T. Bumbleburg
John K. McBride
Jack L. Walkey
Michael J. Stapleton
Jeffrey J. Newell
James T. Hodson
Brian Wade Walker

ASSOCIATES

Cheryl M. Knodle
Randy J. Williams
Norman G. Printer

General Counsel for: The Lafayette Union Railway Co.; Bank One, Lafayette, N.A.
Representative Clients: Farmers Insurance Group; General Accident Fire & Life Assurance Corp.; City of Lafayette Board of Parks and Recreation; West Lafayette Community School Corp.; Travelers Insurance Co.; Trustees, West Lafayette Public Library.

For full biographical listings, see the Martindale-Hubbell Law Directory

MUNSTER, Lake Co.

LAW OFFICES OF EUGENE M. FEINGOLD (AV)

707 Ridge Road, Suite 204, 46321
Telephone: 219-836-8800
Fax: 219-836-8944

ASSOCIATES

Steven P. Kennedy
Barbara Richards Campbell

For full biographical listings, see the Martindale-Hubbell Law Directory

IOWA

*IOWA CITY,** Johnson Co.

MEARDON, SUEPPEL, DOWNER & HAYES P.L.C. (AV)

122 South Linn Street, 52240
Telephone: 319-338-9222
Fax: 319-338-7250

William L. Meardon
William F. Sueppel

William J. Sueppel

Representative Clients: United Technologies-Automotive; Perpetual Savings Bank; Farmers Savings Bank of Kalona; Metro Pavers, Inc.; League of Iowa Municipalities; Hills Bank and Trust Co.; J.M. Swank Co.; City of Muscatine; McComas-Lacina Construction Co., Inc.; Diamond Dave's Taco Company, Inc.

For Complete List of Firm Personnel, See General Section

For full biographical listings, see the Martindale-Hubbell Law Directory

KENTUCKY

*BOWLING GREEN,** Warren Co.

CATRON, KILGORE & BEGLEY (AV)

918 State Street, P.O. Box 280, 42102-0280
Telephone: 502-842-1050
Fax: 502-842-4720

Stephen B. Catron
J. Patrick Kilgore
Ernest Edward Begley, II

Representative Clients: City-County Planning Commission of Warren County; Chicago Title Insurance Company; Commonwealth Land Title Insurance Company; Bowling Green Bank & Trust Company, N.A.; Trans Financial Bank, N.A.; Convention Ce nter Authority; Bowling Green-Warren County Industrial Park Authority, Inc.; Camping World, Inc.; International Paper Company; National Corvette Museum.

For full biographical listings, see the Martindale-Hubbell Law Directory

COVINGTON, Kenton Co.

GREENEBAUM DOLL & McDONALD (AV)

A Partnership including Professional Service Corporations
50 East Rivercenter Boulevard, P.O. Box 2050, 41012-2050
Telephone: 606-655-4200
Telecopier: 606-655-4239
Louisville, Kentucky Office: 3300 National City Tower.
Telephone: 502-589-4200.
Fax: 502-587-3695.
Lexington, Kentucky Office: 1400 Vine Center Tower.
Telephone: 606-231-8500.
Fax: 606-255-2742.
Cincinnati, Ohio Office: 832 Main Street.
Telephone: 513-421-8087.
Fax: 513-421-8089.

MEMBERS OF FIRM

Wm. T. Robinson, III
Jeffrey A. McKenzie

Representative Clients: Aetna Life Insurance Co.; ANDALEX Resources, Inc.; Ashland Oil, Inc.; A T & T Communications, Inc.; Bethlehem Steel Corp.; Brown-Forman Corp.; Citizens Fidelity Bank & Trust Co.; Humana, Inc.; KFC National Cooperative Advertising Program, Inc.
*A Professional Service Corporation

For Complete List of Firm Personnel, See General Section

For full biographical listings, see the Martindale-Hubbell Law Directory

*LEXINGTON,** Fayette Co.

GREENEBAUM DOLL & McDONALD (AV)

A Partnership including Professional Service Corporations
1400 Vine Center Tower, 40508
Telephone: 606-231-8500
Telecopier: 606-255-2742
Telex: 213029
Louisville, Kentucky Office: 3300 National City Tower.
Telephone: 502-589-4200.
Fax: 502-587-3695.
Covington, Kentucky Office: 50 East River Center Boulevard, P.O. Box 2050.
Telephone: 606-655-4200.
Fax: 606-655-4239.
Cincinnati, Ohio Office: 832 Main Street.
Telephone: 513-421-8087.
Fax: 513-421-8089.

MEMBERS OF FIRM

Wm. T. Robinson, III
Job D. Turner, III (Resident)

Representative Clients: Aetna Life Insurance Co.; ANDALEX Resources, Inc.; Ashland Oil, Inc.; AT&T Communications, Inc.; Bethlehem Steel Corp.; Brown-Forman Corp.; Columbia Gas & Transmission Co.; Commonwealth Aluminum Corp.; Consolidation Coal Co.; Costain Coal, Inc.

For Complete List of Firm Personnel, See General Section

For full biographical listings, see the Martindale-Hubbell Law Directory

STOLL, KEENON & PARK (AV)

201 E. Main Street, Suite 1000, 40507-1380
Telephone: 606-231-3000
Telecopier: 606-253-1093; 606-253-1027
Frankfort, Kentucky Office: 326 West Main Street.
Telephone: 502-875-6000.
Telecopier: 502-875-6008.
Louisville, Kentucky Office: 400 West Market Street, Suite 2650, 40202.
Telephone: 502-568-9100.
Telecopier: 502-568-6340.

MEMBERS OF FIRM

Samuel D. Hinkle, IV
Rena Gardner Wiseman

(See Next Column)

ASSOCIATE

Lea Pauley Goff

Representative Clients: Bank One, Lexington, NA; Farmers Capital Bank Corp.; The Tokai Bank Ltd.; Link Belt Construction Equipment Co.; General Motors Corp.; International Business Machines Corp.; Ohbayashi Corp.; R. J. Reynolds Tobacco Co.; Rockwell International Corp.; Square D Co.

For Complete List of Firm Personnel, See General Section

For full biographical listings, see the Martindale-Hubbell Law Directory

*LOUISVILLE,** Jefferson Co.

GREENEBAUM DOLL & McDONALD (AV)

A Partnership including Professional Service Corporations
3300 National City Tower, 40202
Telephone: 502-589-4200
Fax: 502-587-3695
Lexington, Kentucky Office: 1400 Vine Center Tower.
Telephone: 606-231-8500.
Fax: 606-255-2742.
Covington, Kentucky Office: 50 East River Center Boulevard, P.O. Box 2050.
Telephone: 606-655-4200.
Fax: 606-655-4239.
Cincinnati, Ohio Office: 832 Main Street.
Telephone: 513-421-8087.
Fax: 513-421-8089.

Wm. T. Robinson, III
Job D. Turner, III (Resident at Lexington, Kentucky)
Jeffrey A. McKenzie

Representative Clients: Aetna Life Insurance Co.; ANDALEX Resources, Inc.; Ashland Oil, Inc.; A T & T Communications, Inc.; Bethlehem Steel Corp.; Brown-Forman Corp.; Humana, Inc.; Kentucky Kingdom, Inc.; KFC National Cooperative Advertising Program, Inc.
*A Professional Service Corporation

For Complete List of Firm Personnel, See General Section

For full biographical listings, see the Martindale-Hubbell Law Directory

MAINE

*PORTLAND,** Cumberland Co.

PIERCE, ATWOOD, SCRIBNER, ALLEN, SMITH & LANCASTER (AV)

One Monument Square, 04101
Telephone: 207-773-6411
Fax: 207-773-3419
Augusta, Maine Office: 77 Winthrop Street.
Telephone: 207-622-6311.
Camden, Maine Office: 36 Chestnut Street, P.O. Box 780.
Telephone: 207-236-4333.

MEMBERS OF FIRM

Richard A. McKittrick (Resident, Camden Office)
Peter G. Warren (Resident, Camden Office)
Dennis C. Keeler
Elaine S. Falender

ASSOCIATES

Jennie L. Clegg
Nancy V. Savage
Pamela C. Morris

STAFF ATTORNEY

Judith A. Fletcher Woodbury

For Complete List of Firm Personnel, See General Section

For full biographical listings, see the Martindale-Hubbell Law Directory

MARYLAND

*BALTIMORE,** (Independent City)

VENABLE, BAETJER AND HOWARD (AV)

A Partnership including Professional Corporations
1800 Mercantile Bank & Trust Building, 2 Hopkins Plaza, 21201
Telephone: 410-244-7400
Washington, D.C. Office: Venable, Baetjer, Howard & Civiletti. Suite 1000, 1201 New York Avenue, N.W.
Telephone: 202-962-4800.
McLean, Virginia Office: Suite 400, 2010 Corporate Ridge.
Telephone: 703-760-1600.

(See Next Column)

VENABLE, BAETJER AND HOWARD, *Baltimore—Continued*

Rockville, Maryland Office: Suite 500, One Church Street, P. O. Box 1906.
Telephone: 301-217-5600.
Towson, Maryland Office: 210 Allegheny Avenue, P. O. Box 5517.
Telephone: 410-494-6200.

MEMBERS OF FIRM

Thomas P. Perkins, III (P.C.)
John B. Howard (Resident, Towson, Maryland Office)
John G. Milliken (Not admitted in MD; Also at Washington, D.C. and McLean, Virginia Offices)
Cynthia M. Hahn (Resident, Towson, Maryland Office)
Robert A. Hoffman (Resident, Towson, Maryland Office)
Michael H. Davis (Resident, Towson, Maryland Office)

OF COUNSEL

Judith A. Armold

ASSOCIATE

G. Page Wingert (Resident, Towson, Maryland Office)

For Complete List of Firm Personnel, See General Section

For full biographical listings, see the Martindale-Hubbell Law Directory

*BEL AIR,** Harford Co.

STARK & KEENAN, A PROFESSIONAL ASSOCIATION (AV)

30 Office Street, 21014
Telephone: 410-838-5522
Baltimore: 410-879-2222
Fax: 410-879-0688

Elwood V. Stark, Jr.
Charles B. Keenan, Jr.
Thomas E. Marshall
Edwin G. Carson
Judith C. H. Cline
Gregory A. Szoka
Robert S. Lynch

Claire Prin Blomquist
Kimberly Kahoe Muenter
Paul W. Ishak

For full biographical listings, see the Martindale-Hubbell Law Directory

SILVER SPRING, Montgomery Co.

ALEXANDER, GEBHARDT, APONTE & MARKS, L.L.C. (AV)

Lee Plaza-Suite 805, 8601 Georgia Avenue, 20910
Telephone: 301-589-2222
Facsimile: 301-589-2523
Washington, D.C. Office: 1314 Nineteenth Street, N.W., 20036.
Telephone: 202-835-1555.
New York, New York Office: 330 Madison Avenue, 36th Floor.
Telephone: 212-808-0008.
Fax: 212-599-1028.

Koteles Alexander (Not admitted in MD)
Joseph D. Gebhardt
Mari Carmen Aponte (Not admitted in MD; Resident Washington, D.C. Office)
Kenneth H. Marks, Jr. (Not admitted in MD)
S. Ricardo Narvaiz (Not admitted in MD)
James L. Bearden (Not admitted in MD)
Abbey G. Hairston
Glenn K. Garnes

OF COUNSEL

Eduardo Peña, Jr. (Not admitted in MD)
Jack M. Platt (Not admitted in MD; Resident, New York Office)
Michelle C. Clay (Not admitted in MD)

Susan C. Lee (Not admitted in MD)
Gregory E. Gaskins
J. Darrell Peterson
Suelyn Smith
Eleanor Pelta (Not admitted in MD)
Donna Rucker Williams (Not admitted in MD)
David B. Johnson
Michelle J. Hamilton (Not admitted in MD)
Y. Kris Oh (Ms.) (Not admitted in MD)
Mimi (Mildred) Steward (Not admitted in MD)
Adrienne P. Byrd
Andrea R. Littlejohn (Not admitted in MD)
Norma J.S. Mendelson
Ellen C. Ha (Not admitted in MD)
Adrian Van Nelson II
Suzette Wynn Blackwell
Nihar R. Mohanty
John L. Machado (Not admitted in MD)
Lynn R. Estes
Todd A. Harrison
Afshin Pishevar
John S. Rah
Dawana D. Merritt
Darius B. Withers

Reference: Riggs National Bank of Washington, D.C.

For full biographical listings, see the Martindale-Hubbell Law Directory

MASSACHUSETTS

ANDOVER, Essex Co.

ROBERT S. ZOLLNER (AV)

15 Central Street, 01810-3708
Telephone: 508-470-3768
Fax: 508-475-7836

For full biographical listings, see the Martindale-Hubbell Law Directory

*BOSTON,** Suffolk Co.

KOPELMAN AND PAIGE, P.C. (AV)

101 Arch Street, 02110
Telephone: 617-951-0007
Cable Address: "Lawkope"
Fax: 617-951-2735

Leonard Kopelman
Donald G. Paige
Elizabeth A. Lane
Joyce F. Frank
John W. Giorgio
Barbara J. Saint Andre
Joel B. Bard
Everett Joseph Marder
Patrick J. Costello

For Complete List of Firm Personnel, See General Section

For full biographical listings, see the Martindale-Hubbell Law Directory

SHERBURNE, POWERS & NEEDHAM, P.C. (AV)

One Beacon Street, 02108
Telephone: 617-523-2700
Fax: 617-523-6850

William D. Weeks
John T. Collins
Allan J. Landau
John L. Daly
Stephen A. Hopkins
Alan I. Falk
C. Thomas Swaim
James Pollock
William V. Tripp III
Stephen S. Young
William F. Machen
W. Robert Allison
Jacob C. Diemert
Philip J. Notopoulos
Richard J. Hindlian
Paul E. Troy
Harold W. Potter, Jr.
Dale R. Johnson
Philip S. Lapatin
Pamela A. Duckworth
Mark Schonfeld
James D. Smeallie
Paul Killeen
Gordon P. Katz
Joseph B. Darby, III
Richard M Yanofsky
James E. McDermott
Robert V. Lizza
Miriam Goldstein Altman
John J. Monaghan
Margaret J. Palladino
Mark C. Michalowski
David Scott Sloan
M. Chrysa Long
Lawrence D. Bradley
Miriam J. McKendall

Cynthia A. Brown
Cynthia M. Hern
Dianne R. Phillips
Paul M. James
Theodore F. Hanselman
Joshua C. Krumholz
Ieuan G. Mahony
Kenneth L. Harvey
Christopher J. Trombetta
Edwin F. Landers, Jr.
Amy J. Mastrobattista
William Howard McCarthy, Jr.
Douglas W. Clapp
Tamara E. Goulston
Nicholas J. Psyhogeos

COUNSEL

Haig Der Manuelian
Mason M. Taber, Jr.
Karl J. Hirshman
Benjamin Volinski
Kenneth P. Brier

OF COUNSEL

John Barr Dolan

For full biographical listings, see the Martindale-Hubbell Law Directory

FRANKLIN, Norfolk Co.

ROCHE AND MURPHY (AV)

Franklin Office Park West, 38 Pond Street, Suite 308, P.O. Box 267, 02038
Telephone: 508-528-8300
FAX: 508-528-8889

MEMBERS OF FIRM

Neil J. Roche
Paul G. Murphy

ASSOCIATE

John J. Roche

For full biographical listings, see the Martindale-Hubbell Law Directory

MICHIGAN

BIRMINGHAM, Oakland Co.

CARSON FISCHER, P.L.C. (AV)

Third Floor, 300 East Maple Road, 48009-6317
Telephone: 810-644-4840
Facsimile: 810-644-1832

Robert M. Carson
Peter L. Wanger

For full biographical listings, see the Martindale-Hubbell Law Directory

WILLIAMS, SCHAEFER, RUBY & WILLIAMS, PROFESSIONAL CORPORATION (AV)

Suite 300, 380 North Woodward Avenue, 48009
Telephone: 810-642-0333
Telecopy: 810-642-0856

James A. Williams
Thomas G. Plunkett
Richard D. Rattner
William E. Hosler, III

Representative Clients: Beachum & Roeser Development Corporation; Groveland Township; Marriott Corporation; McDonald's Corporation; KinderCare Learning Centers; Michigan National Bank; Morgan-Mitsubishi Development Corporation; Sanilac County; Walmart; Western Development Company.

For full biographical listings, see the Martindale-Hubbell Law Directory

*DETROIT,** Wayne Co.

BODMAN, LONGLEY & DAHLING (AV)

34th Floor 100 Renaissance Center, 48243
Telephone: 313-259-7777
Fax: 313-393-7579
Troy, Michigan Office: Suite 2020, 755 West Big Beaver Road.
Telephone: 810-362-2110.
Ann Arbor, Michigan Office: 110 Miller, Suite 300.
Telephone: 313-761-3780.
Northern Michigan Office: 229 Court Street, P.O. Box 405, Cheboygan.
Telephone: 616-627-4351.

MEMBERS OF FIRM

Herold McC. Deason
James A. Smith
Joseph N. Brown
Randolph S. Perry (Ann Arbor Office)
James J. Walsh
F. Thomas Lewand
Michael A. Stack (Northern Michigan Office)
Harvey W. Berman (Ann Arbor Office)
Jerold Lax (Ann Arbor Office)

COUNSEL

John S. Dobson (Ann Arbor Office)

Representative Clients: Abitibi Price Group; Archdiocese of Detroit; Comerica Bank; The Detroit Lions, Inc.; Ford Estates; General Motors Corporation; Charles Stewart Mott Foundation; Norfolk Southern Corporation; Panhandle Eastern Corporation; State Farm Mutual Automobile Insurance Company.

For Complete List of Firm Personnel, See General Section

For full biographical listings, see the Martindale-Hubbell Law Directory

HOUGHTON, POTTER, SWEENEY & BRENNER, A PROFESSIONAL CORPORATION (AV)

The Guardian Building, 500 Griswold Street, Suite 3300, 48226-3806
Telephone: 313-964-0050
Facsimile: 313-964-4005

Ralph H. Houghton, Jr.
Mark W. McInerney

For full biographical listings, see the Martindale-Hubbell Law Directory

JAFFE, RAITT, HEUER & WEISS, PROFESSIONAL CORPORATION (AV)

One Woodward Avenue, Suite 2400, 48226
Telephone: 313-961-8380
Telecopier: 313-961-8358
Cable Address: "Jafsni"
Southfield,Michigan Office: Travelers Tower, Suite 1520.
Telephone: 313-961-8380.
Monroe, Michigan Office: 212 East Front Street, Suite 3.
Telephone: 313-241-6470.
Telefacsimile: 313-241-3849.

Julia Blakeslee
Robert S. Bolton

Kerry Gross-Bondy (Resident, Monroe, Michigan Office)

See General Practice Section for List of Representative Clients.

For Complete List of Firm Personnel, See General Section

For full biographical listings, see the Martindale-Hubbell Law Directory

VANDEVEER GARZIA, PROFESSIONAL CORPORATION (AV)

Suite 1600, 333 West Fort Street, 48226
Telephone: 313-961-4880
Fax: 313-961-3822
Oakland County Office: 220 Park Street, Suite 300, Birmingham, Michigan.
Telephone: 810-645-0100.
Fax: 810-645-2430.
Macomb County Office: 50 Crocker Boulevard, Mount Clemens, Michigan.
Telephone: 810-468-4880.
Fax: 810-465-7159.
Kent County Office: 510 Grand Plaza Place, 220 Lyon Square, Grand Rapids, Michigan.
Telephone: 616-366-8600.
Fax: 616-786-9095.
Holland, Michigan Office: 1121 Ottawa Beach Road, Suite 140.
Telephone: 616-399-8600.
Fax: 616-786-9095.

Thomas M. Peters
Cecil F. Boyle, Jr. (Resident, Oakland County Office)
Leonard A. Krzyzaniak, Jr.

Dawn Twydell Gladhill

Representative Clients: Aetna Casualty and Surety Co.; Bic Corp.; CNA Insurance Group; Travelers Insurance Co.; United States Aviation Underwriters; Goodyear Tire & Rubber Co.

For Complete List of Firm Personnel, See General Section

For full biographical listings, see the Martindale-Hubbell Law Directory

WACHLER & KOPSON, PROFESSIONAL CORPORATION (AV)

1028 Buhl Building, 48226
Telephone: 313-963-1700
Fax: 313-963-8598

Andrew B. Wachler
Mark S. Kopson

Vicki Sherman Myckowiak
Phyllis A. Avery

Representative Clients: United Dental Associates, Inc.

For full biographical listings, see the Martindale-Hubbell Law Directory

FARMINGTON HILLS, Oakland Co.

COOPER, FINK & ZAUSMER, P.C. (AV)

31700 Middlebelt Road, Suite 150, 48334
Telephone: 810-851-4111
Telefax: 810-851-0100
Detroit, Michigan Office: 1917 Penobscot Building.
Telephone: 313-963-3873.
Telefax: 313-961-6879.
Lansing, Michigan Office: One Michigan Avenue, Suite 1050.
Telephone: 517-372-2020.
Telefax: 517-371-3207.

Daniel S. Cooper
David H. Fink
Mark J. Zausmer
Avery K. Williams
Sarah D. Lile

Ruben Acosta
Michael L. Caldwell
Barbara B. Vacketta
Alan D. Wasserman
Amy M. Sitner
Karen S. Libertiny

OF COUNSEL

John T. Peters, Jr.

For full biographical listings, see the Martindale-Hubbell Law Directory

JOHNSON, ROSATI, GALICA, SHIFMAN, LABARGE, ASELTYNE, SUGAMELI & FIELD, P.C. (AV)

34405 W. Twelve Mile Road, Suite 200, 48331
Telephone: 810-489-4100
Fax: 810-489-1726
Bay City, Michigan Office: 420 Shearer Building, 311 Center Avenue, 48708.
Telephone: 517-894-2600; 517-894-7191.
Fax: 517-894-7177.
Lansing, Michigan Office: 303 S. Waverly Road, 48917.
Telephone: 517-886-3800.
Fax: 517-886-9154.
St. Clair Shores, Michigan Office: 19900 E. 10 Mile Road, 48080.
Telephone: 313-777-3377.

Christopher J. Johnson
Carol A. Rosati
Kenneth G. Galica
Howard L. Shifman
J. Russell LaBarge, Jr.
S. Randall Field
Patrick A. Aseltyne
Michael E. Rosati
Michael J. Sugameli
Kenneth A. Slusser
Laura Amtsbuechler
Edward M. Olson

(See Next Column)

JOHNSON, ROSATI, GALICA, SHIFMAN, LABARGE, ASELTYNE, SUGAMELI & FIELD P.C., *Farmington Hills—Continued*

Daniel P. Dalton
Margaret T. Debler
David R. Brinks
Marcelyn A. Stepanski

Representative Clients: Michigan Municipal Risk Management Authority; Metropolitan Association for Improved School Legislation Risk Management Trust; Indiana Insurance Company; County of Lapeer; County of Van Buren; County of Otsego, City of Romulus; City of Harper Woods; City of Hazel Park; Chirco Realty.

For full biographical listings, see the Martindale-Hubbell Law Directory

*KALAMAZOO,** Kalamazoo Co.

KREIS, ENDERLE, CALLANDER & HUDGINS, A PROFESSIONAL CORPORATION (AV)

One Moorsbridge, 49002
Telephone: 616-324-3000
Telecopier: 616-324-3010

Alan G. Enderle
Douglas L. Callander
Thomas G. King

For Complete List of Firm Personnel, See General Section

For full biographical listings, see the Martindale-Hubbell Law Directory

LANSING, Ingham Co.

CHURCH, KRITSELIS, WYBLE & ROBINSON, P.C. (AV)

3939 Capital City Boulevard, 48906-9962
Telephone: 517-323-4770

William N. Kritselis
J. Richard Robinson
James T. Heos
David S. Mittleman

D. Michael Dudley
Catherine Groll
James M. Hofer

For full biographical listings, see the Martindale-Hubbell Law Directory

*MONROE,** Monroe Co.

BRAUNLICH, RUSSOW & BRAUNLICH, A PROFESSIONAL CORPORATION (AV)

111 South Macomb Street, 48161
Telephone: 313-241-8300
Fax: 313-241-7715

William J. Braunlich, Jr. (1924-1992)
Thomas P. Russow
William H. Braunlich

Philip A. Costello
Patricia M. Poupard
Ann L. Nickel
Marie C. Kennedy
Susan J. Mehregan
Robert Wetzel
Michael G. Roehrig

LEGAL SUPPORT PERSONNEL

Ruth G. Flint

Representative Clients: State Farm Mutual Insurance Co.; Auto Club Insurance Assn.; Farm Bureau Insurance Co.; Home Mutual Insurance Co.; Cincinnati Insurance Co.; Board of Road Commissioners, Monroe County; Port of Monroe; Monroe County Community College; City of Luna Pier; City of Petersburg.

For full biographical listings, see the Martindale-Hubbell Law Directory

JAFFE, RAITT, HEUER & WEISS, PROFESSIONAL CORPORATION (AV)

212 East Front Street, Suite 3, 48161
Telephone: 313-241-6470
Telefacsimile: 313-241-3849
Detroit, Michigan Office: One Woodward Avenue, Suite 2400.
Telephone: 313-961-8380.
Telecopier: 313-961-8358.
Southfield, Michigan Office: Suite 1520, Travelers Tower.
Telephone: 313-961-8380.

John A. Hohman, Jr. (Resident)

Kerry Gross-Bondy (Resident)

Representative Clients: Berlin Township; Frenchtown Charter Township.

For Complete List of Firm Personnel, See General Section

For full biographical listings, see the Martindale-Hubbell Law Directory

*PONTIAC,** Oakland Co.

BOOTH, PATTERSON, LEE, NEED & ADKISON, P.C. (AV)

1090 West Huron Street, 48328
Telephone: 810-681-1200
FAX: 810-681-1754

(See Next Column)

Douglas W. Booth (1918-1992)
Calvin E. Patterson (1913-1987)
Parvin Lee, Jr.
J. Timothy Patterson
David J. Lee
Gregory K. Need
Phillip G. Adkison
Martin L. Kimmel
Allan T. Motzny
Ann DeCaminada Christ
Kathryn Niazy Nichols

Representative Clients: City of South Lyon; Village of Leonard; Charter Township of Commerce; Holly Township; Charter Township of Orion; Township of Rose; Charter Township of Springfield; Charter Township of White Lake.

For full biographical listings, see the Martindale-Hubbell Law Directory

*PORT HURON,** St. Clair Co.

NICHOLSON, FLETCHER & DEGROW (AV)

522 Michigan Street, 48060-3893
Telephone: 810-987-8444
Facsimile: 810-987-8149

MEMBERS OF FIRM

David C. Nicholson
Gary A. Fletcher

ASSOCIATE

Mark G. Clark

Representative Clients: Clay Township; City of Memphis; City of Port Huron; City of Marysville; Port Huron Area School District; Marysville Public Schools; Relleum Real Estate Development Co.

For Complete List of Firm Personnel, See General Section

For full biographical listings, see the Martindale-Hubbell Law Directory

*ST. JOSEPH,** Berrien Co.

GLOBENSKY, GLEISS, BITTNER & HYRNS, P.C. (AV)

610 Ship Street, P.O. Box 290, 49085
Telephone: 616-983-0551
FAX: 616-983-5858

H. S. Gray (1867-1961)
Luman H. Gray (1902-1952)
John L. Globensky
Henry W. Gleiss
Rodger V. Bittner
Randy S. Hyrns

J. Joseph Daly
Charles T. LaSata

LEGAL SUPPORT PERSONNEL

Robin J. Jollay

General Counsel for: Inter-City Bank; Southern Michigan Cold Storage Co.; Pearson Construction Co., Inc.
Approved Attorneys for: Lawyers Title Insurance Corp.
Reference: Inter-City Bank of Benton Harbor.

For full biographical listings, see the Martindale-Hubbell Law Directory

MINNESOTA

*ST. PAUL,** Ramsey Co.

BANNIGAN & KELLY, P.A. (AV)

Suite 1750, North Central Life Tower, 445 Minnesota Street, 55101
Telephone: 612-224-3781
FAX: 612-223-8019

John F. Bannigan, Jr.
Patrick J. Kelly
James J. Hanton
Janet M. Wilebski
John W. Quarnstrom

For full biographical listings, see the Martindale-Hubbell Law Directory

MISSISSIPPI

*GULFPORT,** Harrison Co.

DUKES, DUKES, KEATING AND FANECA, P.A. (AV)

2308 East Beach Boulevard, P.O. Drawer W, 39501
Telephone: 601-868-1111
FAX: 601-863-2886

Hugh D. Keating

For full biographical listings, see the Martindale-Hubbell Law Directory

MISSOURI

KANSAS CITY, Jackson, Clay & Platte Cos.

Sherwin L. Epstein & Associates (AV)

Suite 1700, 1006 Grand Avenue, 64106
Telephone: 816-421-6200
FAX: 816-421-6201

John W. Roe

ASSOCIATE

Mark H. Epstein

LEGAL SUPPORT PERSONNEL

Amy L. Edwards
Christine Marie Leete

For full biographical listings, see the Martindale-Hubbell Law Directory

MONTANA

*BOZEMAN,** Gallatin Co.

Kirwan & Barrett, P.C. (AV)

215 West Mendenhall, P.O. Box 1348, 59771-1348
Telephone: 406-586-1553
Fax: 406-586-8971

Janice K. Whetstone
Stephen M. Barrett

Tom W. Stonecipher

For full biographical listings, see the Martindale-Hubbell Law Directory

NEVADA

*LAS VEGAS,** Clark Co.

Leavitt, Sully & Rivers (AV)

An Association of Professional Corporations
601 East Bridger Avenue, 89101
Telephone: 702-382-5111
Telecopier: 702-382-2892

K. Michael Leavitt (Chartered)
W. Leslie Sully, Jr. (Chartered)
David J. Rivers, II (Chartered)

For full biographical listings, see the Martindale-Hubbell Law Directory

*RENO,** Washoe Co.

McDonald, Carano, Wilson, McCune, Bergin, Frankovich & Hicks (AV)

241 Ridge Street, 89505
Telephone: 702-322-0635
Telecopier: 702-786-9532
Las Vegas, Nevada Office: Suite 1000, 2300 West Sahara Avenue.
Telephone: 702-873-4100.
Telecopier: 702-873-9966.

MEMBERS OF FIRM

Leo P. Bergin, III
John J. Frankovich

ASSOCIATES

Matthew C. Addison
David F. Grove

Representative Clients: Associated General Contractors of America; AT & T; Eldorado Hotel & Casino; Scolari's Warehouse Markets, Inc.

For Complete List of Firm Personnel, See General Section

For full biographical listings, see the Martindale-Hubbell Law Directory

NEW HAMPSHIRE

*EXETER,** Rockingham Co.

Holland, Donovan, Beckett & Hermans, Professional Association (AV)

151 Water Street, P.O. Box 1090, 03833
Telephone: 603-772-5956
Fax: 603-778-1434

(See Next Column)

John W. Perkins (1902-1973)
Everett P. Holland (1915-1993)
Robert B. Donovan
William H. M. Beckett
Stephen G. Hermans

Ronald G. Sutherland

For full biographical listings, see the Martindale-Hubbell Law Directory

*KEENE,** Cheshire Co.

Bell, Falk & Norton, P.A. (AV)

8 Middle Street, P.O. Box F, 03431
Telephone: 603-352-5950
FAX: 603-352-5930

Ernest L. Bell, Jr. (1925-1961)
Ernest L. Bell
Arnold R. Falk
John C. Norton

William James Robinson

For full biographical listings, see the Martindale-Hubbell Law Directory

NEW JERSEY

ELMWOOD PARK, Bergen Co.

Andora, Palmisano & Geaney, A Professional Corporation (AV)

303 Molnar Drive, P.O. Box 431, 07407-0431
Telephone: 201-791-0100
Fax: 201-791-8922

Anthony D. Andora
John P. Palmisano
John F. Geaney, Jr.
Vincent A. Siano
Joseph M. Andresini
Patrick J. Spina
Melissa A. Muilenburg
Joseph A. Venti

Representative Client: City of Jersey City.

For full biographical listings, see the Martindale-Hubbell Law Directory

MONTVILLE, Morris Co.

Edward J. Buzak (AV)

Montville Office Park, 150 River Road, Suite N-4, 07045
Telephone: 201-335-0600
Fax: 201-335-1145

ASSOCIATES

Jacquelin P. Gioioso
Robert B. Campbell
Jeanne Ann McManus
Laura C. Tharney

For full biographical listings, see the Martindale-Hubbell Law Directory

MOORESTOWN, Burlington Co.

Frederick W. Hardt (AV)

Suite 101, 300 Chester Avenue, P.O. Box 840, 08057
Telephone: 609-234-4141
FAX: 609-273-8617

ASSOCIATE

Pamela O. Adriano

PARAMUS, Bergen Co.

Stern Steiger Croland, A Professional Corporation (AV)

One Mack Centre Drive, Mack Centre II, 07652
Telephone: 201-262-9400
Telecopier: 201-262-6055

Howard Stern
Joel J. Steiger
Barry I. Croland
Gerald Goldman
Donald R. Sorkow (1930-1985)
Norman Tanenbaum
Barry L. Baime
Jay Rubenstein
Frank L. Brunetti
Kenneth S. Goldrich
Bruce J. Ackerman
Thomas Loikith
John J. Stern
Stuart Reiser
William J. Heimbuch
Edward P. D'Alessio
E. Drew Britcher
Meridith J. Bronson
Valerie D. Solimano

William R. Kugelman
Mindy Michaels Roth
Neil E. Kozek
Lizabeth Sarakin
Joanne T. Nowicki
Armand Leone, Jr.
Craig P. Caggiano
Jeffrey P. Gardner
David Torchin

(See Next Column)

STERN STEIGER CROLAND A PROFESSIONAL CORPORATION, *Paramus—Continued*

OF COUNSEL

Harvey R. Sorkow

Representative Clients: K Mart Corp.; Meyer Brothers Department Stores.

For full biographical listings, see the Martindale-Hubbell Law Directory

---

*SOMERVILLE,** Somerset Co.

OZZARD WHARTON, A PROFESSIONAL PARTNERSHIP (AV)

75-77 North Bridge Street, P.O. Box 938, 08876
Telephone: 908-526-0700
Telecopier: 908-526-2246

William E. Ozzard
William B. Savo
Edward M. Hogan
Michael V. Camerino

Michael G. Friedman
Suzette Nanovic Berrios
Frederick H. Allen, III

Representative Clients: Mack Development Co.; New Jersey Savings Bank; Somerset Raritan Valley Sewerage Authority, Borough of Raritan, East Amwell Township, Frenchtown, Delaware Township.

For Complete List of Firm Personnel, See General Section

For full biographical listings, see the Martindale-Hubbell Law Directory

---

VERONA, Essex Co.

SALERNO, COZZARELLI, MAUTONE, DE SALVO & NUSSBAUM, A PROFESSIONAL CORPORATION (AV)

155 Pompton Avenue, 07044
Telephone: 201-239-2222
Fax: 201-239-0463

Ralph J. Salerno
Frank J. Cozzarelli
Dennis M. Mautone
Peter De Salvo, Jr.
Gary Nussbaum

Robert Ricci
John Motta

OF COUNSEL

Frank Cozzarelli, Jr.

References: Peoples Bank, N.A.; The Howard Savings Bank.

For full biographical listings, see the Martindale-Hubbell Law Directory

---

NEW YORK

---

*ALBANY,** Albany Co.

WHITEMAN OSTERMAN & HANNA (AV)

One Commerce Plaza, 12260
Telephone: 518-487-7600
Telecopier: 518-487-7777
Cable Address: "Advocate Albany"
Buffalo, New York Office: 1700 Liberty Building.
Telephone: 716-854-4420.
Telecopier: 716-854-4428.

MEMBERS OF FIRM

Michael Whiteman
Melvin H. Osterman
John Hanna, Jr.
Joel L. Hodes
Philip H. Gitlen
Scott N. Fein
Alice J. Kryzan (Resident, Buffalo Office)
Daniel A. Ruzow
Philip H. Dixon
Günter Dully
James W. Lytle
Richard E. Leckerling
Margaret J. Gillis
Jonathan P. Nye
Heather D. Diddel
Neil L. Levine
Mary Jane Bendon Couch
John T. Kolaga (Resident, Buffalo Office)

SENIOR COUNSEL

Howard T. Sprow

COUNSEL

John R. Dunne
Thomas H. Lynch

OF COUNSEL

Leslie K. Thiele

ASSOCIATES

Kenneth S. Ritzenberg
Jean F. Gerbini
Jeffrey S. Baker
Terresa M. Bakner
Elizabeth M. Morss
Carla E. Hogan
Paul C. Rapp
D. Scott Bassinson
Alan J. Goldberg (Not admitted in NY)
James H. Hoeksema, Jr.
Mary Walsh Snyder

(See Next Column)

ASSOCIATES (Continued)

Maria E. Villa
Beth A. Bourassa
Boty McDonald
Martin J. Ricciardi
Alicia C. Rood (Resident, Buffalo Office)
Sonya Kumari Del Peral
Carolyn Dick
David R. Everett
Michael G. Sterthous
John J. Henry
Lisa S. Kwong
Ellen M. Bach
Molly M.A. Brown
Judith Gaies Kahn
Ana-Maria Galeano
Alexandra J. Streznewski
Wayne Barr, Jr.

For full biographical listings, see the Martindale-Hubbell Law Directory

---

EAST MEADOW, Nassau Co.

CERTILMAN BALIN ADLER & HYMAN, LLP (AV)

90 Merrick Avenue, 11554
Telephone: 516-296-7000
Telecopier: 516-296-7111

MEMBERS OF FIRM

Ira J. Adler
Dale Allinson
Herbert M. Balin
Bruce J. Bergman
Michael D. Brofman
Morton L. Certilman
Murray Greenberg
David Z. Herman
Richard Herzbach
M. Allan Hyman
Bernard Hyman
Donna-Marie Korth
Steven J. Kuperschmid
Thomas J. McNamara
Fred S. Skolnik
Louis Soloway
Harold Somer
Howard M. Stein
Brian K. Ziegler

OF COUNSEL

Daniel S. Cohan
Norman J. Levy
Marilyn Price

ASSOCIATES

Howard B. Busch
Scott M. Gerber
Jodi S. Hoffman
Glenn Kleinbaum
Michael C. Manniello
Jaspreet S. Mayall
Stacey R. Miller
Lawrence S. Novak
Kim J. Radbell

For full biographical listings, see the Martindale-Hubbell Law Directory

---

HUNTINGTON, Suffolk Co.

GOLDSTEIN & RUBINTON, P.C. (AV)

18 West Carver Street, 11743
Telephone: 516-421-9051
Telefax: 516-421-9122

Arthur Goldstein
Peter D. Rubinton
Ronald L. Goldstein
S. Russ Di Fazio

References: Chemical Bank; New York Trust Co.; Town of Huntingdon.

For full biographical listings, see the Martindale-Hubbell Law Directory

---

*NEW CITY,** Rockland Co.

GRANIK SILVERMAN SANDBERG CAMPBELL NOWICKI RESNIK HEKKER (AV)

254 South Main Street, 10956
Telephone: 914-634-8822; 800-822-1238

MEMBERS OF FIRM

Joseph F. X. Nowicki (1922-1976)
Robert R. Granik (1922-1994)
David W. Silverman
Martin L. Sandberg
Patrick M. Campbell
Kenneth H. Resnik
John M. Hekker
Ricki Hollis Berger

ASSOCIATE

Catherine T. O'Toole Lauritano

OF COUNSEL

Morrie Slifkin

For full biographical listings, see the Martindale-Hubbell Law Directory

---

*POUGHKEEPSIE,** Dutchess Co.

CORBALLY, GARTLAND AND RAPPLEYEA (AV)

35 Market Street, 12601
Telephone: 914-454-1110
FAX: 914-454-4857
Millbrook, New York Office: Bank of Millbrook Building, Franklin Avenue.
Telephone: 914-677-5539.
Clearwater, Florida Office: Citizens Bank Building, Suite 250, 1130 Cleveland Street.
Telephone: 813-461-3144.

(See Next Column)

CORBALLY, GARTLAND AND RAPPLEYEA—*Continued*

MEMBERS OF FIRM

John Hackett (Died 1916)
James L. Williams (Died 1908)
Charles J. Corbally (1888-1966)
John J. Gartland, Jr.
Allan E. Rappleyea
Daniel F. Curtin
Fred W. Schaeffer
Michael G. Gartland
Jon H. Adams
Vincent L. DeBiase
Paul O. Sullivan
William F. Bogle, Jr.

ASSOCIATES

Rena Muckenhoupt O'Connor
Allan B. Rappleyea, Jr.

OF COUNSEL

Joseph F. Hawkins (1916-1986)
Milton M. Haven
Edward J. Murtaugh

Representative Clients: Hudson Valley Farm Credit, A.C.A.; St. Francis Hospital; Marist College; Merritt-Meridian Construction Corp.
Counsel for: Poughkeepsie Savings Bank, F.S.B.; Bank of New York; Farm Credit Bank of Springfield; Equitable Life Assurance Society of the United States; McCann Foundation, Inc.
Reference: Bank of New York.

For full biographical listings, see the Martindale-Hubbell Law Directory

*WHITE PLAINS,** Westchester Co.

HOFFMAN, WACHTELL, KOSTER, MAIER & MANDEL (AV)

399 Knollwood Road, 10603
Telephone: 914-682-8000
FAX: 914-682-1512
New City, New York Office: 82 Maple Avenue, 10956.
Telephone: 914-634-8169.

MEMBERS OF FIRM

Lee A. Hoffman, Jr.
Marc J. Wachtell
Eric D. Koster
Lynn J. Maier
Richard G. Mandel

Representative Clients: Mount Hope Mines, Inc.; Eastern Educational Consortium; Westchester Community College; Prime Office Systems, Inc.; Gateway Management Corp.; Purchase Environmental Protection Association, Inc.; The Jay Coalition; The Town of Greenburgh; The Town of Mamaroneck.
Reference: Citibank, N.A. (White Plains Branch).

For full biographical listings, see the Martindale-Hubbell Law Directory

KEANE & BEANE, P.C. (AV)

One North Broadway, 10601
Telephone: 914-946-4777
Telecopier: 914-946-6868
Rye, New York Office: 49 Purchase Street.
Telephone: 914-967-3936.

Thomas F. Keane, Jr. (1932-1991)

Edward F. Beane
David Glasser
Ronald A. Longo
Richard L. O'Rourke
Lawrence Praga
Joel H. Sachs
Steven A. Schurkman
Judson K. Siebert

Debbie G. Jacobs
Lance H. Klein
Donna E. Frosco
Nicholas M. Ward-Willis

LEGAL SUPPORT PERSONNEL

Barbara S. Durkin
Toni Ann Huff

OF COUNSEL

Eric F. Jensen
Peter A. Borrok

For full biographical listings, see the Martindale-Hubbell Law Directory

STEPHENS, BARONI, REILLY & LEWIS (AV)

Northcourt Building, 175 Main Street, 10601
Telephone: 914-761-0300; 683-5185
Telecopier: 914-761-0995; 683-1323
Cross River, New York Office: Northern Westchester Office, Old Post Road Professional Building, 10518.
Telephone: 914-763-3232.

MEMBERS OF FIRM

Gerald D. Reilly
Roland A. Baroni, Jr.
Stephen R. Lewis

ASSOCIATE

Claudia Guerrino

OF COUNSEL

Thomas J. Stephens
Michael Fuller Sirignano
James R. Caruso (1906-1994)

For full biographical listings, see the Martindale-Hubbell Law Directory

JOHN E. WATKINS, JR. (AV)

175 Main Street, 10601
Telephone: 914-428-1292
Telecopier: 914-428-4104
Local 800 Service: 1-800-33WATKINS
New York, New York Office: 29 Broadway.
Telephone: 212-968-1500.

Reference: Bankers Trust Co.

For full biographical listings, see the Martindale-Hubbell Law Directory

NORTH CAROLINA

*GREENSBORO,** Guilford Co.

ISAACSON ISAACSON & GRIMES (AV)

Suite 400 NationsBank Building, 101 West Friendly Avenue, P.O. Box 1888, 27402
Telephone: 910-275-7626
FAX: 910-273-7293

MEMBERS OF FIRM

Henry H. Isaacson
Marc L. Isaacson
L. Charles Grimes

ASSOCIATE

Thomas B. Kobrin

For full biographical listings, see the Martindale-Hubbell Law Directory

*WINSTON-SALEM,** Forsyth Co.

WOMBLE CARLYLE SANDRIDGE & RICE (AV)

A Professional Limited Liability Company
1600 Southern National Financial Center, P.O. Drawer 84, 27102
Telephone: 910-721-3600
Telecopy: 910-721-3660
Telex: 806498
Charlotte, North Carolina Office: 3300 One First Union Center, 301 South College Street.
Telephone: 704-331-4900.
Telecopy: 704-331-4955.
Telex: 853609.
Raleigh, North Carolina Office: 2100 First Union Capitol Center, 150 Fayetteville Street Mall, P.O. Box 831.
Telephone: 919-755-2100.
Telecopy: 919-755-2150.
Telex: 806498.
Atlanta, Georgia Office: One Ninety One Peachtree Tower, 191 Peachtree Street, N.E., Suite 3250.
Telephone: 404-614-2580.
Fax: 404-614-2595.

MEMBERS OF FIRM

Anthony H. Brett
Roddey M. Ligon, Jr.

ASSOCIATES

Joel M. Leander
Celeste Elizabeth O'Keeffe

Representative Clients: Brad Ragan, Inc.; Brenner Companies; Food Lion, Inc.; Hanes Companies, Inc.; North Carolina Baptist Hospitals, Inc.; R.J. Reynolds Tobacco Company; Summit Communications Group, Inc.; Thomasville Furniture Industries, Inc.; Wachovia Corporation; Wake Forest University.

For Complete List of Firm Personnel, See General Section

For full biographical listings, see the Martindale-Hubbell Law Directory

OHIO

*CINCINNATI,** Hamilton Co.

BARRETT & WEBER A LEGAL PROFESSIONAL ASSOCIATION (AV)

400 Atlas Building, 524 Walnut Street, 45202-3114
Telephone: 513-721-2120
Facsimile: 513-721-2139

C. Francis Barrett

For full biographical listings, see the Martindale-Hubbell Law Directory

Cincinnati—Continued

DINSMORE & SHOHL (AV)

1900 Chemed Center, 255 East Fifth Street, 45202-3172
Telephone: 513-977-8200
FAX: 513-977-8141
Florence, Kentucky Office: Turfway Ridge Office Park, 7300 Turfway Road, Suite 430 41042-1355.
Telephone: 606-283-0515.
FAX: 606-283-6017.
Dayton, Ohio Office: 500 Courthouse Plaza, S.W., 10 N. Ludlow Street, 45402-1834.
Telephone: 513-228-8012.
FAX: 513-461-2543.
Columbus, Ohio Office: NBD Bank Building, Suite 330, 175 South Third Street, 43215-5134.
Telephone: 614-224-7887.
FAX: 614-224-7882.

MEMBERS OF FIRM

Mark A. Vander Laan
Patrick D. Lane

ASSOCIATES

Lynn Marmer
Robert A. Williams

For Complete List of Firm Personnel, See General Section

For full biographical listings, see the Martindale-Hubbell Law Directory

*CLEVELAND,** Cuyahoga Co.

KELLEY, MCCANN & LIVINGSTONE (AV)

35th Floor, BP America Building, 200 Public Square, 44114-2302
Telephone: 216-241-3141
FAX: 216-241-3707

MEMBERS OF FIRM

Fred J. Livingstone
Stephen M. O'Bryan
John D. Brown
Margaret Anne Cannon
Mark J. Valponi
Thomas J. Lee

ASSOCIATES

Kurt D. Weaver
Robert A. Brindza, II
Sylvester Summers, Jr.

For Complete List of Firm Personnel, See General Section

For full biographical listings, see the Martindale-Hubbell Law Directory

SEELEY, SAVIDGE AND AUSSEM A LEGAL PROFESSIONAL ASSOCIATION (AV)

800 Bank One Center, 600 Superior Avenue, East, 44114-2655
Telephone: 216-566-8200
Cable Address: "See Sau"
Fax-Telecopier: 216-566-0213
Elyria, Ohio Office: 538 Broad Street.
Telephone: 216-236-8158.

Gregory D. Seeley
Gary A. Ebert

William E. Blackie, III

OF COUNSEL

William E. Blackie

References: Society National Bank; AmeriTrust.

For Complete List of Firm Personnel, See General Section

For full biographical listings, see the Martindale-Hubbell Law Directory

THOMPSON, HINE AND FLORY (AV)

1100 National City Bank Building, 629 Euclid Avenue, 44114-3070
Telephone: 216-566-5500
Fax: 216-566-5583
Telex: 980217
Cable Address: "Thomflor"
Akron, Ohio Office: 50 S. Main Street, Suite 502, 44308-1828.
Telephone: 216-376-8090.
Fax: 216-376-8386.
Cincinnati, Ohio Office: 312 Walnut Street, 14th Floor, 45202-4029.
Telephone: 513-352-6700.
Fax: 513-241-4771.
Telex: 938003.
Columbus, Ohio Office: One Columbus, 10 West Broad Street, 43215-3435.
Telephone: 614-469-3200.
Fax: 614-469-3361.
Dayton, Ohio Office: 2000 Courthouse Plaza, N.E., 45402-1706.
Telephone: 513-443-6600.
Fax: 513-443-6637; 443-6635.
Palm Beach, Florida Office: 125 Worth Avenue, Suite 117, 33480-4466.
Telephone: 407-833-5900.
Fax: 407-833-5951.

(See Next Column)

Washington, D.C. Office: 1920 N Street, N.W., 20036-1601.
Telephone: 202-331-8800.
Fax: 202-331-8330.
Telex: 904173.
Cable Address: "Caglaw".
Brussels, Belgium Office: Rue des Chevaliers, Ridderstraat 14 - B.10, B - 1050.
Telephone: 011(32-2) 511-9326.
Fax: 011(32-2) 513-9206.

MEMBER OF FIRM

David L. Parham

For Complete List of Firm Personnel, See General Section

For full biographical listings, see the Martindale-Hubbell Law Directory

WALTER & HAVERFIELD (AV)

1300 Terminal Tower, 44113-2253
Telephone: 216-781-1212
Telecopier: 216-575-0911
Columbus, Ohio Office: 88 East Broad Street.
Telephone: 614-221-7371.

MEMBERS OF FIRM

Charles T. Riehl, III
John H. Gibbon
James E. Betts
Christopher L. Gibbon
Frederick W. Whatley
Carl E. Anderson

ASSOCIATES

Jonathan D. Greenberg
R. Todd Hunt

Representative Clients: AGA Gas, Inc.; Air Products and Chemicals, Inc.; American Crane Corp.; Andrews Moving & Storage, Inc.; Applied Medical Technology, Inc.; Aribica Cafes, Inc.; Associated Aviation Underwriters; The Associated Press; Beverly Enterprises, Inc.; Brookfield Wire Company.

For Complete List of Firm Personnel, See General Section

For full biographical listings, see the Martindale-Hubbell Law Directory

*COLUMBUS,** Franklin Co.

* indicates certain Bar Register subscribers whose principal office is located elsewhere in the state and who have arranged for representation as a part of the state capital listings that follow

EMENS, KEGLER, BROWN, HILL & RITTER (AV)

Capitol Square Suite 1800, 65 East State Street, 43215-4294
Telephone: 614-462-5400
Telecopier: 614-464-2634
Cable Address: "Law EKBHR"
Telex: 246671

William J. Brown
R. Kevin Kerns
Roger P. Sugarman
Michael E. Zatezalo

Michael J. Galeano
Robert G. Schuler

Representative Clients: Chambers Development Company, Inc.; Diocese of Columbus; Integrity Supply, Inc.; Medco Containment Services, Inc.; Mid-American Waste Systems, Inc.; Ohio Manufactured Housing Association.

For Complete List of Firm Personnel, See General Section

For full biographical listings, see the Martindale-Hubbell Law Directory

* **THOMPSON, HINE AND FLORY** (AV)

One Columbus, 10 West Broad Street, 43215-3435
Telephone: 614-469-3200
Fax: 614-469-3361
Akron, Ohio Office: 50 S. Main Street, Suite 502, 44308-1828.
Telephone: 216-376-8090.
Fax: 216-376-8386.
Cincinnati, Ohio Office: 312 Walnut Street, 14th Floor, 45202-4029.
Telephone: 513-352-6700.
Fax: 513-241-4771.
Telex: 938003.
Cleveland, Ohio Office: 1100 National City Bank Building, 629 Euclid Avenue, 44114-3070.
Telephone: 216-566-5500.
Fax: 216-556-5583.
Telex: 980217.
Cable Address: "Thomflor".
Dayton, Ohio Office: 2000 Courthouse Plaza, N.E., 45402-1706.
Telephone: 513-443-6600.
Fax: 513-443-6637; 443-6635.
Palm Beach, Florida Office: 125 Worth Avenue, 33480-4466.
Telephone: 407-833-5900.
Fax: 407-833-5951.
Washington, D.C. Office: 1920 N Street, N.W., 20036-1601.
Telephone: 202-331-8800.
Fax: 202-331-8330.
Telex: 904173.
Cable Address: "Caglaw".

(See Next Column)

THOMPSON, HINE AND FLORY—*Continued*

Brussels, Belgium Office: Rue des Chevaliers / Ridderstraat 14 - B.10, B - 1050.
Telephone: 011(32-2) 511-9326.
Fax: 011(32-2) 513-9206.

MEMBER OF FIRM

Michael T. Shannon

For Complete List of Firm Personnel, See General Section

For full biographical listings, see the Martindale-Hubbell Law Directory

*TOLEDO,** Lucas Co.

EASTMAN & SMITH (AV)

One Seagate, Twenty-Fourth Floor, 43604
Telephone: 419-241-6000
Telecopier: 419-247-1777
Columbus, Ohio Office: 65 East State Street, Suite 1000, 43215.
Telephone: 614-460-3556.
Telecopier: 614-228-5371.

MEMBERS OF FIRM

Bruce L. Smith
Richard T. Sargeant
Dirk P. Plessner

ASSOCIATES

Oksana M. Ludd
Beth J. Olson
Albin Bauer, II

For Complete List of Firm Personnel, See General Section

For full biographical listings, see the Martindale-Hubbell Law Directory

RITTER, ROBINSON, MCCREADY & JAMES (AV)

1850 National City Bank Building, 405 Madison Avenue, 43624
Telephone: 419-241-3213
Detroit, Michigan: 313-422-1610
FAX: 419-241-4925

MEMBER OF FIRM

William S. McCready

Counsel for: Chrysler Corp.; Rubini Motors, Inc.; Ohio Casualty Insurance Co.; National Mutual Insurance Co.; Celina Mutual Insurance Co.; Westfield Insurance Co.; Northwestern National Insurance Co.; Midwestern Insurance Co.; United Ohio Insurance Co.; Toledo Auto Electric Co.

For Complete List of Firm Personnel, See General Section

For full biographical listings, see the Martindale-Hubbell Law Directory

OREGON

*PORTLAND,** Multnomah Co.

JOSSELSON, POTTER & ROBERTS (AV)

53 S.W. Yamhill Street, 97204
Telephone: 503-228-1455
Facsimile: 503-228-0171

MEMBERS OF FIRM

Frank Josselson
Irving W. Potter
Leslie M. Roberts

OF COUNSEL

Lawrence R. Derr

For full biographical listings, see the Martindale-Hubbell Law Directory

O'DONNELL, RAMIS, CREW, CORRIGAN & BACHRACH (AV)

Ballow & Wright Building, 1727 N.W. Hoyt Street, 97209
Telephone: 503-222-4402
FAX: 503-243-2944
Clackamas County Office: Suite 202, 181 N. Grant, Canby.
Telephone: 503-266-1149.

MEMBERS OF FIRM

Timothy V. Ramis
Jeff H. Bachrach

ASSOCIATE

William A. Monahan

LEGAL SUPPORT PERSONNEL

Margaret M. Daly
G. William Selzer

For full biographical listings, see the Martindale-Hubbell Law Directory

PENNSYLVANIA

*ALLENTOWN,** Lehigh Co.

WEAVER, MOSEBACH, PIOSA, HIXSON & MARLES (AV)

One Windsor Plaza, Suite 200, 7535 Windsor Drive, 18195-1014
Telephone: 610-366-8000
FAX: 610-366-8001

MEMBERS OF FIRM

Thomas E. Weaver, Jr.
Barry N. Mosebach
Michael J. Piosa
Boyd G. Hixson
Blake C. Marles
John F. Hacker
Donald E. Wieand, Jr.
Donald H. Lipson
William H. Dayton, Jr.
David G. Knerr
Thomas E. Reilly, Jr.

ASSOCIATES

Thomas F. Smida
Paul D. North, Jr.
Robert J. Hobaugh, Jr.
Thomas A. Capehart
Irene Chiavaroli Johns

OF COUNSEL

Thomas E. Weaver
William H. Eckensberger, Jr.
Murray Mackson

LEGAL SUPPORT PERSONNEL

Jacqui Petch
Francine H. Glazier

For full biographical listings, see the Martindale-Hubbell Law Directory

*EASTON,** Northampton Co.

HERSTER, NEWTON & MURPHY (AV)

127 North Fourth Street, P.O. Box 1087, 18042
Telephone: 610-258-6219

MEMBERS OF FIRM

Andrew L. Herster, Jr.
Henry R. Newton
William K. Murphy

General Counsel For: Valley Federal Savings & Loan Assn.; Lafayette Bank; Easton Printing Co.; Northampton Community College; Eisenhardt Mills, Inc.; Delaware Wood Products, Inc.; Panuccio Construction, Inc.
References: Merchants Bank, N.A.; Lafayette Bank; Valley Federal Savings and Loan.

*HARRISBURG,** Dauphin Co.

GOLDBERG, KATZMAN & SHIPMAN, P.C. (AV)

320 Market Street - Strawberry Square, P.O. Box 1268, 17108-1268
Telephone: 717-234-4161
Telecopier: 717-234-6808; 717-234-6810

Ronald M. Katzman
Neil Hendershot
Jesse Jay Cooper

Arnold B. Kogan

Representative Clients: Dauphin County General Authority; Hampden Township Sewer Authority.
Reference: Fulton Bank.

For Complete List of Firm Personnel, See General Section

For full biographical listings, see the Martindale-Hubbell Law Directory

JOSEPH A. KLEIN A PROFESSIONAL CORPORATION (AV)

100 Chestnut Street, Suite 210, P.O. Box 1152, 17108
Telephone: 717-233-0132
Fax: 717-233-2516

Joseph A. Klein
Mark S. Silver

For full biographical listings, see the Martindale-Hubbell Law Directory

*MEDIA,** Delaware Co.

BEATTY, YOUNG, OTIS & LINCKE (AV)

300 West State Street, Suite 200, P.O. Box 901, 19063-0901
Telephone: 610-565-8800
Fax: 610-565-8127

MEMBERS OF FIRM

Lewis B. Beatty, Jr.
David J. Otis
William P. Lincke

ASSOCIATES

Natalie M. Habert
Peter W. Dicce
Carol E. Tucci
Katherine J. Dickinson (Not admitted in PA)

OF COUNSEL

Robert C. Grasberger
Joseph R. Young (1921-1993)

Representative Clients: Suburban Federal Savings Bank; Elwyn Inc.; Delaware County School Employees Health and Welfare Trust.

For full biographical listings, see the Martindale-Hubbell Law Directory

*PITTSBURGH,** Allegheny Co.

BUCHANAN INGERSOLL, PROFESSIONAL CORPORATION (AV)

5800 USX Tower, 600 Grant Street, 15219
Telephone: 412-562-8800
Telecopier: 412-562-1041
Philadelphia, Pennsylvania Office: Two Logan Square, Twelfth Floor, 18th & Arch Streets.
Telephone: 215-665-8700.
Harrisburg, Pennsylvania Office: Vartan Parc, 30 North Third Street.
Telephone: 717-237-4800.
Tampa, Florida Office: 101 East Kennedy Boulevard, Suite 1030.
Telephone: 813-222-8180.
North Miami Beach, Florida Office: 19495 Biscayne Boulevard.
Telephone: 305-933-5600.
Lexington, Kentucky Office: 1210 Vine Center Office Tower, 333 West Vine Street.
Telephone: 606-225-5333.
Princeton, New Jersey Office: Buchanan Ingersoll, A Partnership, College Centre, 500 College Road East.
Telephone: 609-452-2666.

A. Bruce Bowden
Mark Raymond Hornak
Robert Y. Kopf, Jr.
Stanley Yorsz

SENIOR ATTORNEY

Philip J. Weis

For Complete List of Firm Personnel, See General Section

For full biographical listings, see the Martindale-Hubbell Law Directory

MOLLICA, MURRAY & HOGUE (AV)

3400 Gulf Tower, 15219
Telephone: 412-263-5200
Fax: 412-263-5220

MEMBERS OF FIRM

James A. Mollica, Jr.
Dr. John E. Murray, Jr.
Jon Geoffrey Hogue
Blaine A. Lucas
Cathy Ann Chromulak
Timothy Murray
Sandra L. Lannis
William J. Moorhead, Jr.
Jeannine A. Schuster
Steven M. Nolan
Benjamin J. Viloski

For full biographical listings, see the Martindale-Hubbell Law Directory

THORP, REED & ARMSTRONG (AV)

One Riverfront Center, 15222
Telephone: 412-394-7711
Fax: 412-394-2555

MEMBERS OF FIRM

John H. Bingler, Jr.
Clifford B. Levine
Mark F. Nowak
Robert H. Shoop, Jr.
Timothy M. Slavish

ASSOCIATE

Kimberly L. Wakim

For Complete List of Firm Personnel, See General Section

For full biographical listings, see the Martindale-Hubbell Law Directory

*WEST CHESTER,** Chester Co.

CRAWFORD, WILSON, RYAN & AGULNICK, P.C. (AV)

220 West Gay Street, 19380
Telephone: 610-431-4500
Fax: 610-430-8718
Radnor, Pennsylvania Office: 252 Radnor-Chester Road, P. O. Box 8333, 19087.
Telephone: 215-688-1205.
Fax: 215-688-7802.

Ronald M. Agulnick
Fronefield Crawford, Jr.
Thomas R. Wilson
Kevin J. Ryan

John J. Mahoney
Kim Denise Morton
Steven L. Mutart
Rita Kathryn Borzillo
Patricia T. Brennan
Richard H. Morton
Patricia J. Kelly
Charles W. Tucker

Reference: First National Bank of West Chester.

For full biographical listings, see the Martindale-Hubbell Law Directory

JOHN E. GOOD (AV)

331 West Miner Street, 19382
Telephone: 610-436-6565
Reference: First National Bank of West Chester.

For full biographical listings, see the Martindale-Hubbell Law Directory

LAMB, WINDLE & MCERLANE, P.C. (AV)

24 East Market Street, P.O. Box 565, 19381-0565
Telephone: 610-430-8000
Telecopier: 610-692-0877

COUNSEL

Theodore O. Rogers

William H. Lamb
Susan Windle Rogers
James E. McErlane
E. Craig Kalemjian
James C. Sargent, Jr.
John D. Snyder
William P. Mahon
Guy A. Donatelli
Vincent M. Pompo
James J. McEntee III

Tracy Blake DeVlieger
P. Andrew Schaum
Lawrence J. Persick
Thomas K. Schindler
Daniel A. Loewenstern
Thomas F. Oeste
John W. Pauciulo
Andrea B. Pettine
John J. Cunningham

Representative Clients: Chester County; First Financial Savings Bank, PaSA; Bank of Chester County; Jefferson Bank; Downingtown Area and Great Valley School Districts; Philadelphia Electric Company; Central and Western Chester County Industrial Development Authority; Valley Forge Sewer Authority; Manito Title Insurance Company.

For full biographical listings, see the Martindale-Hubbell Law Directory

RHODE ISLAND

*PROVIDENCE,** Providence Co.

GIDLEY, SARLI & MARUSAK (AV)

Greater Providence Bank Building, 170 Westminster Street, 02903
Telephone: 401-274-6644
Telecopier: 401-331-9304

MEMBERS OF FIRM

Thomas D. Gidley
Michael G. Sarli
James P. Marusak
Mark C. Hadden

ASSOCIATES

Michael R. DeLuca
Linn Foster Freedman
Denise M. Lombardo
William L. Wheatley
Stuart D. Hallagan III

LEGAL SUPPORT PERSONNEL

Elaine M. Noren
Mary Repoza Caplette
Darlene E. Kotkofski

For full biographical listings, see the Martindale-Hubbell Law Directory

SOUTH CAROLINA

*CHARLESTON,** Charleston Co.

REGAN & CANTWELL (AV)

18 Broad Street, Suite 610, P.O. Box 1001, 29402
Telephone: 803-722-4064
Fax: 803-722-3320

William B. Regan
Frances I. Cantwell

References: The Citizens & Southern National Bank of South Carolina; South Carolina National Bank.

For full biographical listings, see the Martindale-Hubbell Law Directory

TENNESSEE

*CHATTANOOGA,** Hamilton Co.

NELSON, MCMAHAN, PARKER & NOBLETT (AV)

(An Association of Attorneys)
400 Pioneer Bank Building, 37402
Telephone: 615-756-2291
Telecopier: 615-756-0737

Randall L. Nelson
Michael A. McMahan
Wm. Shelley Parker, Jr.
Phillip A. Noblett
Douglas M. Cox
Kenneth O. Fritz
Rosalind H. Reid-Houser

(See Next Column)

NELSON, MCMAHAN, PARKER & NOBLETT—*Continued*

OF COUNSEL

Joe E. Manuel

For full biographical listings, see the Martindale-Hubbell Law Directory

*MEMPHIS,** Shelby Co.

FARRIS, HANCOCK, GILMAN, BRANAN & HELLEN (AV)

50 North Front Street, Suite 1400, 38103
Telephone: 901-576-8200
Fax: 901-576-8250
East Memphis, Tennessee Office: Suite 400 United American Bank Building, 5384 Poplar Avenue.
Telephone: 901-763-4000.
Fax: 901-763-4095.

MEMBERS OF FIRM

Homer B. Branan, III
John M. Farris

ASSOCIATE

Dedrick Brittenum, Jr.

For Complete List of Firm Personnel, See General Section

For full biographical listings, see the Martindale-Hubbell Law Directory

TEXAS

*AUSTIN,** Travis Co.

* indicates certain Bar Register subscribers whose principal office is located elsewhere in the state and who have arranged for representation as a part of the state capital listings that follow

KAUFMAN, REIBACH & RICHIE, INC. (AV)

2150 One American Center, 600 Congress Avenue, 78701
Telephone: 512-320-7220
Fax: 512-320-7230
San Antonio, Texas Office: 300 Convent Street, Suite 900.
Telephone: 210-227-2000.
Telecopier: 210-229-1307.

Sheldon E. Richie

Katherine J. Walters

For full biographical listings, see the Martindale-Hubbell Law Directory

SANFORD, SPELLINGS, KUHL & PERKINS, L.L.P. (AV)

400 West 15th Street, Suite 1630, 78701
Telephone: 512-472-9090
FAX: 512-472-9182
Houston, Texas Office: 1180 Galleria Financial Center, 5075 Westheime.
Telephone: 713-850-9000.
Fax: 713-850-1330.

RESIDENT MEMBERS

Marion Sanford, Jr.
Robert D. Spellings

For full biographical listings, see the Martindale-Hubbell Law Directory

* **THOMPSON & KNIGHT, A PROFESSIONAL CORPORATION** (AV)

(Attorneys and Counselors)
1200 San Jacinto Center, 98 San Jacinto Boulevard, 78701
Telephone: 512-469-6100
Telecopy: 512-469-6180
Dallas, Texas Office: 1700 Pacific Avenue, Suite 3300, 75201.
Telephone: 214-969-1700.
Telecopy: 512-969-1751.
Cable Address: "Tomtex."
Telex: 732298.
Fort Worth, Texas Office: 801 Cherry Street, Suite 1600, 76102.
Telephone: 817-347-1700.
Telecopy: 817-347-1799.
Houston, Texas Office: 1700 Texas Commerce Tower, 600 Travis, 77002.
Telephone: 713-217-2800.
Telecopy: 713-217-2828; 713-217-2882.
Monterrey, Mexico Office: Edificio Losoles PD-4, Av. Lázaro Cárdenas No. 2400 Pte., San Pedro Garza Garcia, Nuevo Léon C.P. 66220.
Telephone: (52-8) 363-0096.
Telecopy: (52-8) 363-3067.

SHAREHOLDERS

James E. Cousar IV

For Complete List of Firm Personnel, See General Section

For full biographical listings, see the Martindale-Hubbell Law Directory

*DALLAS,** Dallas Co.

CALHOUN & STACY (AV)

5700 NationsBank Plaza, 901 Main Street, 75202-3747
Telephone: 214-748-5000
Telecopier: 214-748-1421
Telex: 211358 CALGUMP UR

Mark Alan Calhoun
David W. Elrod
Steven D. Goldston
Parker Nelson
Roy L. Stacy

ASSOCIATES

Shannon S. Barclay
Robert A. Bragalone
Dennis D. Conder
Jane Elizabeth Diseker
Lawrence I. Fleishman
Thomas C. Jones
Katherine Johnson Knight
V. Paige Pace
Veronika Willard
Michael C. Wright

LEGAL CONSULTANT

Rees T. Bowen, III

For full biographical listings, see the Martindale-Hubbell Law Directory

THOMPSON & KNIGHT, A PROFESSIONAL CORPORATION (AV)

(Attorneys and Counselors)
1700 Pacific Avenue Suite 3300, 75201
Telephone: 214-969-1700
Telecopy: 214-969-1751
Cable Address: "Tomtex"
Telex: 732298
Austin, Texas Office: 1200 San Jacinto Center, 98 San Jacinto Boulevard, 78701.
Telephone: 512-469-6100.
Telecopy: 512-469-6180.
Fort Worth, Texas Office: 801 Cherry Street, Suite 1600, 76102.
Telephone: 817-347-1700.
Telecopy: 817-347-1799.
Houston, Texas Office: 1700 Texas Commerce Tower, 600 Travis, 77002.
Telephone: 713-217-2800.
Telecopy: 713-217-2828.
Monterrey, Mexico Office: Edificio Losoles PD-4, Av. Lázaro Cárdenas No. 2400 Pte., San Pedro Garza Garcia, Nuevo Léon C.P. 66220.
Telephone: (52-8) 363-0096.
Telecopy: (52-8) 363-3067.

SHAREHOLDERS

James B. Harris
Geoffrey D. Osborn
Clint Shouse

For Complete List of Firm Personnel, See General Section

For full biographical listings, see the Martindale-Hubbell Law Directory

*HOUSTON,** Harris Co.

GREGG & MIESZKUC, P.C. (AV)

17044 El Camino Real (Clear Lake City), 77058-2686
Telephone: 713-488-8680
Facsimile: 713-488-8531

Dick H. Gregg, Jr.
Marilyn Mieszkuc
Polly P. Lewis
Charles A. Daughtry

Elizabeth E. Scott
Dick H. Gregg, III

For full biographical listings, see the Martindale-Hubbell Law Directory

*SAN ANTONIO,** Bexar Co.

KAUFMAN, REIBACH & RICHIE, INC. (AV)

300 Convent Street, Suite 900, 78205-3791
Telephone: 210-227-2000
Fax: 210-229-1307
Austin, Texas Office: 2150 One American Center, 600 Congress Avenue.
Telephone: 512-320-7220.
Fax: 512-320-7320.

William T. Kaufman
Robert E. Reibach
Jack H. Kaufman
James H. Barrow
Robert S. Glass

Gay Gueringer
Holly H. Fuller
Nancy H. Reyes

For full biographical listings, see the Martindale-Hubbell Law Directory

VERMONT

*BURLINGTON,** Chittenden Co.

Burak & Anderson (AV)

Executive Square, 346 Shelburne Street, P.O. Box 64700, 05406-4700
Telephone: 802-862-0500
Telecopier: 802-862-8176

MEMBERS OF FIRM

Michael L. Burak
Jon Anderson

ASSOCIATES

Brian J. Sullivan
Josephine L. Peyser

For Complete List of Firm Personnel, See General Section

For full biographical listings, see the Martindale-Hubbell Law Directory

Gravel and Shea, A Professional Corporation (AV)

Corporate Plaza, 76 St. Paul Street, P.O. Box 369, 05402-0369
Telephone: 802-658-0220
Fax: 802-658-1456

Stephen R. Crampton
John R. Ponsetto
Dennis R. Pearson

OF COUNSEL

Clarke A. Gravel

SPECIAL COUNSEL

Norman Williams

For Complete List of Firm Personnel, See General Section

For full biographical listings, see the Martindale-Hubbell Law Directory

VIRGINIA

*FAIRFAX,** (Ind. City; Seat of Fairfax Co.)

Rust, Rust & Silver, A Professional Corporation (AV)

4103 Chain Bridge Road Fourth Floor, P.O. Box 460, 22030
Telephone: 703-591-7000
Telecopier: 703-591-7336

John H. Rust, Jr.
Glenn H. Silver
C. Thomas Brown

James E. Kane
Paulo E. Franco, Jr.
Andrew W. White

RETIRED, EMERITUS

John H. Rust, Sr. (Retired)

Representative Clients: Crestar Bank; Commonwealth Land Title Insurance Co.; Patriot National Bank; Century Graphics Corp.

For full biographical listings, see the Martindale-Hubbell Law Directory

*RICHMOND,** (Ind. City; Seat of Henrico Co.)

Williams, Mullen, Christian & Dobbins, A Professional Corporation (AV)

Two James Center, 1021 East Cary Street, P.O. Box 1320, 23210-1320
Telephone: 804-643-1991
Fax: 804-783-6456
Glen Allen, Virginia Office: 4401 Waterfront Drive, Suite 140.
Telephone: 804-965-9168.
Fax: 804-965-0955.
Washington, D.C. Office: 1575 Eye Street, N.W.
Telephone: 202-289-6200.
Fax: 202-289-4126.

Ralph L. Axselle, Jr.
Charles L. Cabell
Howard W. Dobbins
Sarah Hopkins Finley
A. Brooks Hock
Philip deB. Rome

Heidi Wilson Abbott

For Complete List of Firm Personnel, See General Section

For full biographical listings, see the Martindale-Hubbell Law Directory

WASHINGTON

*SEATTLE,** King Co.

Buck & Gordon (AV)

902 Waterfront Place, 1011 Western Avenue, 98104-1097
Telephone: 206-382-9540
Telecopier: 206-626-0675

MEMBERS OF FIRM

William H. Block
Peter L. Buck
Brent Carson
Jay P. Derr
Joel M. Gordon
Amy L. Kosterlitz
Keith E. Moxon

ASSOCIATES

Alison D. Birmingham
Shelley E. Kneip

OF COUNSEL

Madeleine A. F. Brenner

Reference: Seafirst Bank, Seattle, Washington (Metropolitan Branch).

For full biographical listings, see the Martindale-Hubbell Law Directory

Preston Gates & Ellis (AV)

5000 Columbia Seafirst Center, 701 Fifth Avenue, 98104-7011
Telephone: 206-623-7580
Telex: 4740035
Telecopy: 206-623-7022
Anchorage, Alaska Office: 4th Floor, 420 L Street, 99501-1937.
Telephone: 907-276-1969.
Telecopier: 907-276-1365.
Los Angeles, California Office: 3450 Sanwa Bank Plaza, 601 South Figueroa Street.
Telephone: 213-892-4700.
Telecopier: 213-892-4701.
Coeur d'Alene, Idaho Office: 1200 Ironwood Drive, Suite 315. 83814.
Telephone: 208-667-1839.
Telecopier: 208-667-3567.
Washington, D.C. Office: Preston Gates Ellis & Rouvelas Meeds, Suite 500, 1735 New York Avenue, N.W., 20006-4759.
Telephone: 202-628-1700.
Telecopier: 202-331-1024.
Portland, Oregon Office: 3200 US Bancorp Tower 111 S.W. Fifth Avenue, 97204-3688.
Telephone: 503-228-3200.
Telecopier: 503-248-9085.
Spokane, Washington Office: 1400 Seafirst Financial Center, W. 601 Riverside Avenue, 99201-0636.
Telephone: 509-624-2100.
Telecopier: 509-456-0146.
Tacoma, Washington Office: 1500 First Interstate Plaza, 1201 Pacific Avenue, 98402-4301.
Telephone: 206-272-1500.
Telecopier: 206-272-2913.

MEMBERS OF FIRM

Frank M. Preston (1895-1985)
George W. McBroom (1923-1986)
Richard Thorgrimson (1909-1975)
Roger L. Shidler (1900-1988)
Donald L. Holman (1927-1986)
Deborah A. Allard
Thomas G. Allison
Carol Slayden Arnold
Lawrence B. Bailey
Hugh F. Bangasser
Marc L. Barreca
Mark R. Beatty
Judith A. Bigelow
David H. Binney
John C. Bjorkman
Paula E. Boggs
William H. Burkhart
Charles R. Bush
Christopher M. Carletti
C. Kent Carlson
Larry M. Carter
William H. Chapman
Connie R. Collingsworth
Gordon G. Conger
Stephan H. Coonrod
Ronald E. Cox
Lance Christopher Dahl
Scott L. David
Martha J. Dawson
Mabry C. De Buys
James K. Doane
Richard B. Dodd
Kirk A. Dublin
James R. Ellis (Retired)
David E. Fennell
Richard D. Ford
Bart J. Freedman
Michele A. Gammer
William H. Gates
Carl P. Gilmore
Peter J. Glase
Karen E. Glover
John A. Gose
G. Scott Greenburg
Robert L. Gunter
James R. Irwin
Robert S. Jaffe
B. Gerald Johnson
Susan Delanty Jones
Alan H. Kane
Thomas E. Kelly, Jr.
Paul J. Lawrence
Ross A. Macfarlane
William E. Mantle
James Markham Marshall
Pamela A. Martin
Scott A. Milburn
Yoram Milo
Robert B. Mitchell
Donald H. Mullins
Nancy M. Neraas
Robert D. Neugebauer
James L. Phillips
Charles H. Purcell
Jay A. Reich
Douglas H. Rosenberg
John A. Seethoff
James D. Sherman
Beryl N. Simpson
Shannon J. Skinner

(See Next Column)

PRESTON GATES & ELLIS—*Continued*

MEMBERS OF FIRM (Continued)

Martin F. Smith
Stephen A. Smith
Peter C. Spratt
Diane R. Stokke
Clyde W. Summerville
David K.Y. Tang
Fredric C. Tausend
Elizabeth Thomas
Holly K. Towle
Scott R. Vokey
Forrest W. Walls
Cynthia M. Weed
Kenneth S. Weiner
Alan Wicks
Thomas H. Wolfendale

OF COUNSEL

John N. Rupp

ASSOCIATES

Sherri M. Anderson
Thomas Eli Backer
Carol Eads Bailey
Jennifer Belk
Shawn M. Carter
J. Alan Clark
Cheri Y. Cornell
Christopher H. Cunningham
Kenneth Ray Davis, II
Elizabeth J. Deckman
Keith R. Dolliver
Ramona M. Emerson
Jesse Owen Franklin IV
John D. Fugate
Michel Gahard
Michael J. Gearin
Dean George-Falvy
Adam W. Gravley
Frederick W. Green
Thomas F. Haensly
Margaret Chieko Inouye
Lisa L. Johnsen
Madeline June Kass
Aaron Keyt
Brian K. Knox
Gary J. Kocher
(Not admitted in WA)
Eric S. Laschever
Liam Burgess Lavery
Jessica Stone Levy
Marc C. Levy
Konrad J. Liegel
Kirk A. Lilley
Douglas M. Love
Knoll D. Lowney
Douglas A. Luetjen
Cestjon L. McFarland
Kathleen M. McGinnis
Mary Megan McLemore
Teresa C. McNally
Jonathan T. McPhee
Richard Archibald Montfort, Jr.
Robin L. Nielsen
Margaret A. Niles
Sarah E. Oyer
Faith L. Pettis
J. Michael Philips
Anne Diehl Rees
Floyd G. Short
John D. Sullivan
Susan Naomi Takemoto
William V. Taylor
Lori A. Terry
David O. Thompson
Ruth A. Tressel
Perry S. Weinberg
Eileen Weresch-Doornink
Herbert E. Wilgis III
Mary L. Williamson
Chapin E. Wilson, III
Roger D. Wynne
Grace Tsuang Yuan

For full biographical listings, see the Martindale-Hubbell Law Directory

---

JON G. SCHNEIDLER (AV)

4100 First Interstate Center, 999 Third Avenue, 98104
Telephone: 206-624-9400
Telecopier: 206-464-9559

Reference: Key Bank of Washington.

For full biographical listings, see the Martindale-Hubbell Law Directory

---

WISCONSIN

*MILWAUKEE,** Milwaukee Co.

QUARLES & BRADY (AV)

411 East Wisconsin Avenue, 53202-4497
Telephone: 414-277-5000
Cable Address: "Lawdock"
Fax: 414-271-3552.
TWX: 910-262-3426
Madison, Wisconsin Office: Firstar Plaza, One South Pinckney Street, P.O. Box 2113.
Telephone: 608-251-5000.
Fax: 608-251-9166.
West Palm Beach, Florida Office: 222 Lakeview Avenue, 4th Floor.
Telephone: 407-653-5000.
Fax: 407-653-5333.
Naples, Florida Office: Barnett Center, 4501 Tamiami Trail North.
Telephone: 813-262-5959.
Fax: 813-434-4999.
Phoenix, Arizona Office: One Camelback Building, One East Camelback Road, Suite 400.
Telephone: 602-230-5500.
Fax: 602-230-5598.

MEMBERS OF FIRM
(ALPHABETICALLY BY YEAR OF ADMISSION TO BAR)

Theodore F. Zimmer
James H. Baxter III
Michael L. Roshar
Paul R. Schilling
Julianna Ebert
Brian G. Lanser

OF COUNSEL

Richard W. Cutler

(See Next Column)

ASSOCIATES

Kevin A. Delorey
(Resident, Madison Office)
Rebecca A. Speckhard

For Complete List of Firm Personnel, See General Section

For full biographical listings, see the Martindale-Hubbell Law Directory

---

CANADA ALBERTA

*EDMONTON,** Edmonton Jud. Dist.

PARLEE MCLAWS (AV)

15th Floor Manulife Place, 10180 101st Street, T5J 4K1
Telephone: 403-423-8500
Telecopier: 403-423-2870.
Calgary, Alberta Office: 3400, Western Canadian Place, 707 - 8th Avenue, S.W.
Telephone: 403-294-7000.
Telecopier: 403-265-8263.

MEMBERS OF FIRM

C. H. Kerr, Q.C.
M. D. MacDonald
K. F. Bailey, Q.C.
R. B. Davison, Q.C.
F. R. Haldane
P. E. J. Curran
D. G. Finlay
J. K. McFadyen
R. C. Secord
D. L. Kennedy
D. C. Rolf
D. F. Pawlowski
A. A. Garber
R. P. James
D. C. Wintermute
J. L. Cairns
R. A. Newton, Q.C.
T. A. Cockrall, Q.C.
H. D. Montemurro
F. J. Niziol
R. W. Wilson
I. L. MacLachlan
R. O. Langley
R. G. McBean
J. T. Neilson
E. G. Rice
J. F. McGinnis
J. H. H. Hockin
G. W. Jaycock
M. J. K. Nikel
B. J. Curial
S. L. May
M. S. Poretti

ASSOCIATES

C. R. Head
A.W. Slemko
L. H. Hamdon
K.A. Smith
K. D. Fallis-Howell
D. S. Tam
J.W. McClure
F.H. Belzil
R.A. Renz
J.G. Paulson
K. E. Buss
B. L. Andriachuk
P. E. S. J. Kennedy
R. Feraco
R.J. Billingsley
N.B.R. Thompson
P. A. Shenher
I. C. Johnson
K.G. Koshman
D.D. Dubrule
G. T. Lund
W.D. Johnston
G. E. Flemming
K. P. Nayyer

For full biographical listings, see the Martindale-Hubbell Law Directory

---

CANADA NEW BRUNSWICK

*SAINT JOHN,** Saint John Co.

CLARK, DRUMMIE & COMPANY (AV)

40 Wellington Row, P.O. Box 6850 Station "A", E2L 4S3
Telephone: 506-633-3800
Telecopier (Automatic): 506-633-3811

MEMBER OF FIRM

Deno P. Pappas, Q.C.

OF COUNSEL

L. Paul Zed, M.P.

Reference: Royal Bank of Canada.

For Complete List of Firm Personnel, See General Section

For full biographical listings, see the Martindale-Hubbell Law Directory

CANADA
NOVA SCOTIA

*HALIFAX,** Halifax Co.

McInnes Cooper & Robertson (AV)

1601 Lower Water Street, P.O. Box 730, B3J 2V1
Telephone: 902-425-6500
Fax: 902-425-6350
St. John's, Newfoundland Office: Suite 602, Scotia Centre, 235 Water Street, P.O. Box 547. A1C, 5K8.
Telephone: 709-726-9500.
Fax: 709-726-9550.

Peter J. E. McDonough, Q.C.

ASSOCIATE

J. David Connolly

Attorneys for: Bank of Nova Scotia; Imperial Oil, Limited; Frank B. Hall & Co., Inc. (New York); American Steamship Owners Protection & Indemnity Association, Inc.; Coca-Cola, Ltd.; Scott Worldwide Inc.; Hong Kong Bank of Canada.

For Complete List of Firm Personnel, See General Section

For full biographical listings, see the Martindale-Hubbell Law Directory

CANADA
ONTARIO

*TORONTO,** Regional Munic. of York

Borden & Elliot (AV)

Barristers & Solicitors
Scotia Plaza, 40 King Street West, M5H 3Y4
Telephone: 416-367-6000
Telecopier: 416-367-6749
Internet: @ borden.com
A Member of the national association of Borden DuMoulin Howard Gervais, comprising Borden & Elliot in Toronto, Ontario, Russell & DuMoulin in Vancouver, British Columbia, Howard, Mackie in Calgary, Alberta and Mackenzie Gervais in Montréal, Québec. Borden DuMoulin Howard Gervais also operates an office in London, England.

MEMBER AND ASSOCIATES

Stanley M. Makuch

For Complete List of Firm Personnel, See General Section

For full biographical listings, see the Martindale-Hubbell Law Directory

MUNICIPAL BOND/PUBLIC AUTHORITY FINANCING LAW

ALABAMA

ALBERTVILLE, Marshall Co.

GULLAHORN & HARE, P.C. (AV)

310 West Main Street, P.O. Box 1669, 35950
Telephone: 205-878-1891
FAX: 205-878-1965

Charles R. Hare, Jr. John C. Gullahorn

Representative Clients: First Bank of Boaz; The Home Bank; Bank of Albertville; Peoples Independent Bank of Boaz; AmSouth Bank; Compass Bank of the South; Albertville Industrial Development Board; Boaz Industrial Development Board; Marshall-Dekalb Electric Cooperative; Olympia Construction, Inc.

For full biographical listings, see the Martindale-Hubbell Law Directory

*BIRMINGHAM,** Jefferson Co.

BALCH & BINGHAM (AV)

1710 Sixth Avenue North, P.O. Box 306, 35201
Telephone: 205-251-8100
Facsimile: 205-226-8798
Other Birmingham, Alabama Office: 1901 Sixth Avenue North, 35203.
Telephone: 205-251-8100.
Facsimile: 205-226-8799.
Montgomery, Alabama Office: The Winter Building, 2 Dexter Avenue, 36101.
Telephone: 205-834-6500.
Facsimile: 205-269-3115.
Huntsville, Alabama Office: Suite 810, 200 West Court Square, 35801.
Telephone: 205-551-0171.
Facsimile: 205-551-0174.
Washington, D.C. Office: Suite 800, 1101 Connecticut Avenue, N.W., 20036.
Telephone: 202-296-0387.
Facsimile: 202-452-8180.

MEMBERS OF FIRM

William J. Ward
A. Key Foster, Jr.
Walter M. Beale, Jr.
J. Foster Clark
Richard L. Pearson
J. Thomas Francis, Jr.

Counsel for: Alabama Power Co.; Blue Cross and Blue Shield of Alabama; The Boeing Company; Brasfield & Gorrie, Inc.; Compass Bancshares, Inc.; Harbert Corp.; Kimberly-Clark Corp.; Southern Company Services, Inc.; Southern Research Institute; Vesta Insurance Group, Inc.

For Complete List of Firm Personnel, See General Section

For full biographical listings, see the Martindale-Hubbell Law Directory

BRADLEY, ARANT, ROSE & WHITE (AV)

1400 Park Place Tower, 2001 Park Place, 35203
Telephone: 205-521-8000
Telex: 494-1324
Facsimile: 205-251-8611, 251-8665, 252-0264
Facsimile (Southtrust Office): 205-251-9915
Huntsville, Alabama Office: 200 Clinton Avenue West, Suite 900.
Telephone: 205-517-5100.
Facsimile: 205-533-5069.

MEMBERS OF FIRM

John P. Adams
John G. Harrell
Robert C. Walthall
P. Nicholas Greenwood
Alan K. Zeigler
John K. Molen
J. David Dresher

ASSOCIATE

Stephen K. Greene

Counsel for: University of Alabama; Auburn University; University of Alabama at Birmingham; University of South Alabama; City of Huntsville; City of Mobile; Huntsville-Madison County Airport Authority; Mobile Airport Authority; Decatur General Hospital; Southeast Alabama Medical Center.

For Complete List of Firm Personnel, See General Section

For full biographical listings, see the Martindale-Hubbell Law Directory

BURR & FORMAN (AV)

3000 SouthTrust Tower, 420 North 20th Street, 35203
Telephone: 205-251-3000
Telecopier: 205-458-5100
Huntsville, Alabama Office: Suite 204, Regency Center, 400 Meridian Street.
Telephone: 205-551-0010.

MEMBERS OF FIRM

Joseph G. Stewart
Eric L. Carlton
George M. Taylor, III
Dwight L. Mixson, Jr.

For Complete List of Firm Personnel, See General Section

For full biographical listings, see the Martindale-Hubbell Law Directory

HASKELL SLAUGHTER YOUNG & JOHNSTON, PROFESSIONAL ASSOCIATION (AV)

1200 AmSouth/Harbert Plaza, 1901 Sixth Avenue North, 35203
Telephone: 205-251-1000
Facsimile: 205-324-1133
Montgomery, Alabama Office: Haskell Slaughter Young Johnston & Gallion. Bailey Building, Suite 375, 400 South Union Street, P.O. Box 4660. 36104
Telephone: 205-265-8573.
Facsimile: 205-264-7945.

Wyatt Rushton Haskell
William M. Slaughter
Benjamin B. Spratling III
E. Alston Ray
Mark Edward Ezell
Beverly P. Baker

Robert D. Shattuck, Jr. Paula J. Baker

For Complete List of Firm Personnel, See General Section

For full biographical listings, see the Martindale-Hubbell Law Directory

SIROTE & PERMUTT, P.C. (AV)

2222 Arlington Avenue, South, P.O. Box 55727, 35255
Telephone: 205-933-7111
Facsimile: 205-930-5301
Huntsville, Alabama Office: 200 Clinton Avenue, N.W., Suite 1000.
Telephone: 205-536-1711.
Facsimile: 205-534-9650.
Mobile, Alabama Office: One St. Louis Centre, Suite 1000.
Telephone: 205-432-1671.
Facsimile: 205-434-0196.
Montgomery, Alabama Office: Colonial Commerce Center, Suite 305 One Commerce Street.
Telephone: 205-261-3400.
Facsimile: 205-261-3434.
Tuscaloosa, Alabama Office: 2216 14th Street.
Telephone: 205-752-2089.

J. Mason Davis
David M. Wooldridge
John H. Cooper
Joseph T. Ritchey

Representative Clients: International Business Machines (IBM); General Motors Corp.; Colonial Bank; Bruno's, Inc.; University of Alabama Hospitals; Westinghouse Electric Corp.; First Alabama Bank; Monsanto Chemical Company; South Central Bell; Prudential Insurance Company; American Home Products, Inc.; Minnesota Mining and Manufacturing, Inc. (3M).

For Complete List of Firm Personnel, See General Section

For full biographical listings, see the Martindale-Hubbell Law Directory

SPAIN, GILLON, GROOMS, BLAN & NETTLES (AV)

The Zinszer Building, 2117 2nd Avenue North, 35203
Telephone: 205-328-4100
Telecopier: 205-324-8866

MEMBERS OF FIRM

John P. McKleroy, Jr.
Samuel H. Frazier
Glenn E. Estess, Jr.

General Counsel for: Liberty National Life Insurance Co.; United States Fidelity & Guaranty Co.; Piggly Wiggly Alabama Distributing Co.; AmSouth Mortgage Co., Inc.; Alabama Insurance Guaranty Association; Alabama Life and Disability Insurance Guaranty Association; Alabama Insurance Underwriters Association.
Counsel for: The Prudential Insurance Company of America; Government Employees Insurance Co.; Massachusetts Mutual Life Insurance Co.

For Complete List of Firm Personnel, See General Section

For full biographical listings, see the Martindale-Hubbell Law Directory

*HUNTSVILLE,** Madison Co.

SIROTE & PERMUTT, P.C. (AV)

Suite 1000, 200 Clinton Avenue, N.W., 35801
Telephone: 205-536-1711
Facsimile: 205-534-9650
Birmingham, Alabama Office: 2222 Arlington Avenue, South, P.O. Box 55727.
Telephone: 205-933-7111.
Facsimile: 205-930-5301.
Mobile, Alabama Office: One St. Louis Centre, Suite 1000.
Telephone: 205-432-1671.
Facsimile: 205-434-0196.
Montgomery, Alabama Office: Colonial Commerce Center, Suite 305, One Commerce Street.
Telephone: 205-261-3400.
Facsimile: 205-261-3434.
Tuscaloosa, Alabama Office: 2216 14th Street.
Telephone: 205-752-2089.

Joe H. Ritch
Johnnie Frank Vann

For Complete List of Firm Personnel, See General Section

For full biographical listings, see the Martindale-Hubbell Law Directory

*MOBILE,** Mobile Co.

LYONS, PIPES & COOK, P.C. (AV)

2 North Royal Street, P.O. Box 2727, 36652-2727
Telephone: 334-432-4481
Cable Address: "Lysea"
Telecopier: 334-433-1820

G. Sage Lyons
W. David Johnson, Jr.

Representative Clients: Industrial Development Board of the City of Mobile; Mobile Airport Authority.

For Complete List of Firm Personnel, See General Section

For full biographical listings, see the Martindale-Hubbell Law Directory

SIROTE & PERMUTT, P.C. (AV)

One St. Louis Centre, Suite 1000, P.O. Drawer 2025, 36652-2025
Telephone: 334-432-1671
Facsimile: 334-434-0196
Birmingham, Alabama Office: 2222 Arlington Avenue, South, P.O. Box 55727.
Telephone: 205-933-7111.
Facsimile: 205-930-5301.
Huntsville, Alabama Office: 200 Clinton Avenue, N.W., Suite 1000.
Telephone: 205-536-1711.
Facsimile: 205-534-9650.
Montgomery, Alabama Office: Colonial Commerce Center, Suite 305, One Commerce Street.
Telephone: 205-261-3400.
Facsimile: 205-261-3434.
Tuscaloosa, Alabama Office: 2216 14th Street.
Telephone: 205-752-2089.

Gordon O. Tanner
Steven L. Nicholas

For Complete List of Firm Personnel, See General Section

For full biographical listings, see the Martindale-Hubbell Law Directory

*MONTGOMERY,** Montgomery Co.

CAPELL, HOWARD, KNABE & COBBS, P.A. (AV)

57 Adams Avenue, P.O. Box 2069, 36102-2069
Telephone: 334-241-8000

Jack L. Capell
Fontaine M. Howard (1908-1985)
Walter J. Knabe (1898-1979)
Edward E. Cobbs (1909-1982)
L. Lister Hill (1936-1993)
Herman H. Hamilton, Jr.
Rufus M. King
Robert S. Richard
John B. Scott, Jr.
John F. Andrews
James M. Scott
Thomas S. Lawson, Jr.
John L. Capell, III
William D. Coleman
William K. Martin
Bruce J. Downey III
Henry C. Barnett, Jr.
Palmer Smith Lehman
Richard F. Allen
Neal H. Acker
Henry H. Hutchinson
Shapard D. Ashley
D. Kyle Johnson
J. Lister Hubbard
James N. Walter, Jr.
James H. McLemore
H. Dean Mooty, Jr.
Jim B. Grant, Jr.
Wyeth Holt Speir, III
Chad S. Wachter
Ellen M. Hastings
Debra Deames Spain
William Rufus King
C. Clay Torbert, III

OF COUNSEL

Timothy Sullivan

For full biographical listings, see the Martindale-Hubbell Law Directory

SIROTE & PERMUTT, P.C. (AV)

Colonial Commerce Center, Suite 305, One Commerce Street, 36104
Telephone: 334-261-3400
Facsimile: 334-261-3434
Birmingham, Alabama Office: 2222 Arlington Avenue, South, P.O. Box 55727.
Telephone: 205-933-7111.
Facsimile: 205-930-5301.
Huntsville, Alabama Office: 200 Clinton Avenue, N.W., Suite 1000.
Telephone: 205-536-1711.
Facsimile: 205-534-9650.
Mobile, Alabama Office: One St. Louis Centre, Suite 1000.
Telephone: 205-432-1671.
Facsimile: 205-434-0196.
Tuscaloosa, Alabama Office: 2216 14th Street.
Telephone: 205-752-2089.

M. Fredrick Simpler, Jr.

For Complete List of Firm Personnel, See General Section

For full biographical listings, see the Martindale-Hubbell Law Directory

ARIZONA

*PHOENIX,** Maricopa Co.

JENNINGS, STROUSS AND SALMON, P.L.C. (AV)

A Professional Limited Liability Company
One Renaissance Square, Two North Central, 85004-2393
Telephone: 602-262-5911
Fax: 602-253-3255

Anne L. Kleindienst
Robert E. Coltin

For Complete List of Firm Personnel, See General Section

For full biographical listings, see the Martindale-Hubbell Law Directory

SNELL & WILMER (AV)

One Arizona Center, 85004-0001
Telephone: 602-382-6000
Fax: 602-382-6070
Tucson, Arizona Office: 1500 Norwest Tower, One South Church Avenue 85701-1612.
Telephone: 602-882-1200.
Fax: 602-884-1294.
Orange County Office: 1920 Main Street, Suite 1200, P.O. Box 19601, Irvine, California, 92714.
Telephone: 714-253-2700.
Fax: 714-955-2507.
Salt Lake City, Utah Office: Broadway Centre, 111 East Broadway, Suite 900, 84111.
Telephone: 801-237-1900.
Fax: 801-237-1950.

MEMBERS OF FIRM

William A. Hicks, III
Richard W. Sheffield

ASSOCIATE

Sandra L. Seamans

Representative Clients: Arizona Board of Regents/Arizona State University; Arizona Health Facilities Authority; City of Tucson; Madison Elementary School District; Roosevelt Elementary School District; Scottsdale Unified School District; State of Arizona Department of Transportation; Sunnyside Unified School District; Tucson Airport Authority.

For Complete List of Firm Personnel, See General Section

For full biographical listings, see the Martindale-Hubbell Law Directory

*TUCSON,** Pima Co.

RAVEN, KIRSCHNER & NORELL, P.C. (AV)

Suite 1600, One South Church Avenue, 85701-1612
Telephone: 602-628-8700
Telefax: 602-798-5200

Mark B. Raven

Representative Clients: Pace American Bonding Company; Citibank (Arizona); Continental Medical Systems, Inc.; El Paso Natural Gas Co.; Norwest Bank Arizona; El Rio-Santa Cruz Neighborhood Health Center, Inc.; Resolution Trust Corp.; Sierra Vista Community Hospital; Southern Arizona Rehabilitation Hospital; Ford Motor Credit.

For Complete List of Firm Personnel, See General Section

For full biographical listings, see the Martindale-Hubbell Law Directory

ARKANSAS

*LITTLE ROCK,** Pulaski Co.

FRIDAY, ELDREDGE & CLARK (AV)

A Partnership including Professional Associations
Formerly, Smith, Williams, Friday, Eldredge & Clark
2000 First Commercial Building, 400 West Capitol, 72201-3493
Telephone: 501-376-2011
Telecopier: 501-376-2147; 376-6369

MEMBERS OF FIRM

John C. Echols (P.A.)
James A. Buttry (P.A.)
Thomas P. Leggett, (P.A.)
J. Shepherd Russell, III, (P.A.)
Robert B. Beach, Jr., (P.A.)

ASSOCIATE

R. Christopher Lawson

COUNSEL

William L. Patton, Jr.

Counsel for: Union Pacific System; St. Paul Insurance Co.; Liberty Mutual Insurance Co.; Cigna Property & Casualty Co.; Arkansas Power & Light Co.; Dillard Department Stores, Inc.; First Commercial Corp.; Browning Arms Co.; Phillips Petroleum Co.; Aetna Casualty & Surety Co.

For Complete List of Firm Personnel, See General Section

For full biographical listings, see the Martindale-Hubbell Law Directory

GILL LAW FIRM (AV)

3801 TCBY Tower, Capitol and Broadway, 72201
Telephone: 501-376-3800
Fax: 501-372-3359

John P. Gill
Charles C. Owen
W. W. Elrod, II
Victor A. Fleming
Heartsill Ragon, III
Joseph D. Calhoun, III

ASSOCIATES

Glenn E. Kelley
C. Tad Bohannon

OF COUNSEL

John A. Fogleman

For full biographical listings, see the Martindale-Hubbell Law Directory

ROSE LAW FIRM, A PROFESSIONAL ASSOCIATION (AV)

120 East Fourth Street, 72201
Telephone: 501-375-9131
Telecopy: 501-375-1309

George E. Campbell
M. Jane Dickey
Les R. Baledge
Gordon M. Wilbourn

Franklin M. Faust
Marti S. Toennies

Representative Clients: Arkansas Development Finance Authority; Arkansas Soil and Water Conservation Commission; Beverly Enterprises; Crews & Associates, Inc.; City of Little Rock, Arkansas Airport Commission, Waste-water Commission and Residential Housing and Public Facilities Board; Llama Co.; PainWebber Incorporated; Stephens Inc.

For Complete List of Firm Personnel, See General Section

For full biographical listings, see the Martindale-Hubbell Law Directory

WILLIAMS & ANDERSON (AV)

Twenty-Second Floor, 111 Center Street, 72201
Telephone: 501-372-0800
FAX: 501-372-6453

MEMBERS OF FIRM

W. Jackson Williams
David F. Menz
James E. Hathaway III
Rush B. Deacon

Thomas G. Williams
J. Madison Barker
Jeanne L. Seewald

Representative Clients: Arkansas Development Finance Authority; Coregis; Dean Witter Reynolds Inc.; Entergy Power, Inc.; Little Rock Newspapers, Inc. d/b/a/ Arkansas Democrat-Gazette; Texaco, Inc.; Transport Indemnity Insurance Co.; Wal-Mart Stores, Inc.

For Complete List of Firm Personnel, See General Section

For full biographical listings, see the Martindale-Hubbell Law Directory

WRIGHT, LINDSEY & JENNINGS (AV)

2200 Worthen Bank Building, 200 West Capitol Avenue, 72201
Telephone: 501-371-0808
Fax: 501-376-9442
Fayetteville, Arkansas Office: 101 West Mountain Street, Suite 206, 72701.
Telephone: 501-575-0808.
Fax: 501-575-0999.

(See Next Column)

Russellville, Arkansas Office: Suite E, 1110 West B Street.
Telephone: 501-968-7995.

John R. Tisdale
John William Spivey, III
Charles C. Price
Walter E. May
Walter McSpadden
Kevin W. Kennedy
R. Gregory Aclin
Fred M. Perkins, III

Representative Clients: Arkansas Development Finance Authority; Pulaski County, Arkansas; City of Little Rock, Arkansas; Board of Trustees, University of Arkansas; Arkansas Industrial Development Commission; Arkansas Soil and Water Conservation Commission.

For Complete List of Firm Personnel, See General Section

For full biographical listings, see the Martindale-Hubbell Law Directory

CALIFORNIA

*BAKERSFIELD,** Kern Co.

KUHS, PARKER & STANTON (AV)

Suite 200, 1200 Truxtun Avenue, P.O. Box 2205, 93303
Telephone: 805-322-4004
FAX: 805-322-2906

William C. Kuhs
James R. Parker, Jr.
David B. Stanton

Lorraine G. Adams
John P. Doering, III
Robert G. Kuhs

Reference: First Interstate Bank (Bakersfield Main Branch).

For full biographical listings, see the Martindale-Hubbell Law Directory

COSTA MESA, Orange Co.

RUTAN & TUCKER (AV)

A Partnership including Professional Corporations
611 Anton Boulevard, Suite 1400, P.O. Box 1950, 92626
Telephone: 714-641-5100; 213-625-7586
Telecopier: 714-546-9035

MEMBERS OF FIRM

Stan Wolcott (P.C.)
William M. Marticorena

For Complete List of Firm Personnel, See General Section

For full biographical listings, see the Martindale-Hubbell Law Directory

EL MONTE, Los Angeles Co.

MICHAEL B. MONTGOMERY A LAW CORPORATION (AV)

10501 Valley Boulevard, Suite 121, 91731
Telephone: 818-452-1222
Fax: 818-452-8323

Michael B. Montgomery

Reference: Bank of America (San Marino Branch).

For full biographical listings, see the Martindale-Hubbell Law Directory

*FRESNO,** Fresno Co.

JACKSON EMERICH PEDREIRA & NAHIGIAN, A PROFESSIONAL CORPORATION (AV)

7108 North Fresno Street, Suite 400, 93720-2938
Telephone: 209-261-0200
Facsimile: 209-261-0910

Donald A. Jackson
David R. Emerich
Thomas A. Pedreira
Eliot S. Nahigian
David A. Fike

John W. Phillips
John M. Cardot
Nicholas A. Tarjoman
Jeffrey B. Pape
David G. Hansen

Reference: Bank of California.

For full biographical listings, see the Martindale-Hubbell Law Directory

IRVINE, Orange Co.

JONES, DAY, REAVIS & POGUE (AV)

2603 Main Street, Suite 900, 92714-6232
Telephone: 714-851-3939
Telex: 194911 Lawyers LSA
Telecopier: 714-553-7539
In Los Angeles, California: 555 West Fifth Street, Suite 4600.
Telephone: 213-489-3939.
Telex: 181439 UD.
Telecopier: 213-243-2539.

(See Next Column)

JONES, DAY, REAVIS & POGUE, *Irvine—Continued*

In Atlanta, Georgia: 3500 One Peachtree Center, 303 Peachtree Street, N.E.
Telephone: 404-521-3939.
Cable Address: "Attorneys Atlanta".
Telex: 54-2711.
Telecopier: 404-581-8330.
In Brussels, Belgium: Avenue Louise 480, 7th Floor, B-1050 Brussels.
Telephone: 011-32-2-645-14-11.
Telecopier: 011-32-2-645-14-45.
In Chicago, Illinois: 77 West Wacker.
Telephone: 312-782-3939.
Telecopier: 312-782-8585.
In Cleveland, Ohio: North Point, 901 Lakeside Avenue.
Telephone: 216-586-3939.
Cable Address: "Attorneys Cleveland."
Telex: 980389.
Telecopier: 216-579-0212.
In Columbus, Ohio: 1900 Huntington Center.
Telephone: 614-469-3939.
Cable Address: "Attorneys Columbus."
Telecopier: 614-461-4198.
In Dallas, Texas: 2300 Trammell Crow Center, 2001 Ross Avenue.
Telephone: 214-220-3939.
Cable Address: "Attorneys Dallas."
Telex: 730852.
Telecopier: 214-969-5100.
In Frankfurt, Germany: Triton Haus, Bockenheimer Landstrasse 42, 60323, Franfurt am Main.
Telephone: 49-69-9726-3939.
Telecopier: 49-69-9726-3993.
In Geneva, Switzerland: 20, rue de Candolle.
Telephone: 011-41-22-320-2339.
Telecopier: 011-41-22-320-1232.
In Hong Kong: 1501 One Exchange Square, 8 Connaught Place.
Telephone: 011-852-2526-6895.
Telecopier: 011-852-2810-5787.
In London, England: One Mount Street.
Telephone: 011-44-71-493-9361.
Cable Address: "Surgoe London WI."
Telecopier: 011-44-71-493-9666.
In New York, New York: 599 Lexington Avenue.
Telephone: 212-326-3939.
Cable Address: "JONESDAY NEWYORK."
Telex: 237013 JDRP UR.
Telecopier: 212-755-7306.
In Paris, France: 62, rue du Faubourg Saint-Honore.
Telephone: 011-33-1-44-71-3939.
Cable Address: "Surgoe Paris."
Telex: 290156 Surgoe.
Telecopier: 011-33-1-49-24-0471.
In Pittsburgh, Pennsylvania: 500 Grant Street, 31st Floor.
Telephone: 412-391-3939.
Cable Address: "Attorneys Pittsburgh."
Telecopier: 412-394-7959.
In Riyadh, Saudi Arabia: Law Offices of Saud M.A. Shawwaf, P.O. Box 2700.
Telephones: 011 (966-1) 465-6543, 011 (966-1) 464-8534 or 011 (966-1) 464-8540.
Telex: 401831 SAUCON SJ.
Telecopier: (966-1) 464-8480.
In Taipei, Taiwan: 8th Floor, 2 Tun Hwa South Road, Section 2.
Telephone: 011 (886-2) 704-6808.
Telecopier: 011 (886-2) 704-6791.
In Tokyo, Japan: Toranomon MT Building, 4th Floor, 10-3, Toranomon 3-Chome, Minato-Ku, Tokyo 105, Japan.
Telephone: 011-81-3-3433-3939.
Telecopier: 011-81-3-5401-2725.
In Washington, D.C.: Metropolitan Square, 1450 G Street, N.W.
Telephone: 202-879-3939.
Cable Address: "Attorneys Washington."
Telex: 89-2410 ATTORNEYS WASH.
Telecopier: 202-737-2832.

MEMBERS OF FIRM IN IRVINE

Thomas R. Malcolm	John F. Della Grotta
Peter J. Tennyson	Dulcie D. Brand (Not admitted in CA)

For Complete List of Firm Personnel, See General Section

For full biographical listings, see the Martindale-Hubbell Law Directory

*LOS ANGELES,** Los Angeles Co.

JONES, DAY, REAVIS & POGUE (AV)

555 West Fifth Street Suite 4600, 90013-1025
Telephone: 213-489-3939
Telex: 181439 UD
Telecopier: 213-243-2539
In Irvine, California: 2603 Main Street, Suite 900.
Telephone: 714-851-3939.
Telex: 194911 Lawyers LSA.
Telecopier: 714-553-7539.

(See Next Column)

In Atlanta, Georgia: 3500 One Peachtree Center, 303 Peachtree Street, N.E.
Telephone: 404-521-3939.
Cable Address: "Attorneys Atlanta".
Telex: 54-2711.
Telecopier: 404-581-8330.
In Brussels, Belgium: Avenue Louise 480, 7th Floor, B-1050 Brussels.
Telephone: 011-32-2-645-14-11.
Telecopier: 011-32-2-645-14-45.
In Chicago, Illinois: 77 West Wacker.
Telephone: 312-782-3939.
Telecopier: 312-782-8585.
In Cleveland, Ohio: North Point, 901 Lakeside Avenue.
Telephone: 216-586-3939.
Cable Address: "Attorneys Cleveland."
Telex: 980389.
Telecopier: 216-579-0212.
In Columbus, Ohio: 1900 Huntington Center.
Telephone: 614-469-3939.
Cable Address: "Attorneys Columbus."
Telecopier: 614-461-4198.
In Dallas, Texas: 2300 Trammell Crow Center, 2001 Ross Avenue.
Telephone: 214-220-3939.
Cable Address: "Attorneys Dallas."
Telex: 730852.
Telecopier: 214-969-5100.
In Frankfurt, Germany: Triton Haus, Bockenheimer Landstrasse 42, 60323 Frankfurt am Main.
Telephone: 49-69-9726-3939.
Telecopier: 49-69-9726-3993.
In Geneva, Switzerland: 20, rue de Candolle.
Telephone: 011-41-22-320-2339.
Telecopier: 011-41-22-320-1232.
In Hong Kong: 1501 One Exchange Square, 8 Connaught Place.
Telephone: 011-852-2526-6895.
Telecopier: 011-852-2810-5787.
In London England: One Mount Street.
Telephone: 011-44-71-493-9361.
Cable Address: "Surgoe London WI."
Telecopier: 011-44-71-493-9666.
In New York, New York: 599 Lexington Avenue.
Telephone: 212-326-3939.
Cable Address: "JONESDAY NEWYORK."
Telex: 237013 JDRP UR.
Telecopier: 212-755-7306.
In Paris, France: 62, rue du Faubourg Saint-Honore.
Telephone: 011-33-1-44-71-3939.
Cable Address: "Surgoe Paris."
Telex: 290156 Surgoe.
Telecopier: 011-33-1-49-24-0471.
In Pittsburgh, Pennsylvania: 500 Grant Street, 31st Floor.
Telephone: 412-391-3939.
Cable Address: "Attorneys Pittsburgh".
Telecopier: 412-394-7959.
In Riyadh, Saudi Arabia: Law Offices of Saud M.A. Shawwaf, P.O. Box 2700.
Telephones: 011 (966-1) 465-6543, 011 (966-1) 464-8534 or 011 (966-1) 464-8540.
Telex: 401831 SAUCON SJ.
Telecopier: (966-1) 464-8480.
In Taipei, Taiwan: 8th Floor, 2 Tun Hwa South Road, Section 2.
Telephone: 011 (886-2) 704-6808.
Telecopier: 011 (886-2) 704-6791.
In Tokyo, Japan: Toranomon MT Building, 4th Floor, 10-3, Toranomon 3-Chome, Minato-Ku, Tokyo 105, Japan.
Telephone: 011-81-3-3433-3939.
Telecopier: 011-81-3-5401-2725.
In Washington, D.C.: Metropolitan Square, 1450 G Street, N.W.
Telephone: 202-879-3939.
Cable Address: "Attorneys Washington."
Telex: 89-2410 ATTORNEYS WASH.
Telecopier: 202-737-2832.

MEMBERS OF FIRM IN LOS ANGELES

Robert Dean Avery	Thomas R. Mueller
Richard A. Shortz	Scott D. Harvel (Not admitted in CA)
James L. Baumoel (Not admitted in CA)	Erich Lawson Spangenberg (Not admitted in CA)

ASSOCIATES

Catherine A. Ehrgott	Ann K. Bowman
Valerie A. Brown	Christopher B. Donahoe

For Complete List of Firm Personnel, See General Section

For full biographical listings, see the Martindale-Hubbell Law Directory

Los Angeles—Continued

O'MELVENY & MYERS (AV)

400 South Hope Street, 90071-2899
Telephone: 213-669-6000
Cable Address: "Moms"
Facsimile: 213-669-6407
Century City, California Office: 1999 Avenue of the Stars, 7th Floor, 90067-6035.
Telephone: 310-553-6700.
Facsimile: 310-246-6779.
Newport Beach, California Office: 610 Newport Center Drive, Suite 1700, 92660.
Telephone: 714-760-9600.
Cable Address: "Moms".
Facsimile: 714-669-6994.
San Francisco, California Office: Embarcadero Center West Tower, 275 Battery Street, Suite 2600, 94111.
Telephone: 415-984-8700.
Facsimile: 415-984-8701.
New York, N.Y. Office: Citicorp Center, 153 East 53rd Street, 54th Floor, 10022-4611.
Telephone: 212-326-2000.
Facsimile: 212-326-2061.
Washington, D.C. Office: 555 13th Street, N.W., Suite 500 West, 20004-1109.
Telephone: 202-383-5300.
Cable Address: "Moms".
Facsimile: 202-383-5414.
Newark, New Jersey Office: One Gateway Center, 7th Floor, 07102.
Telephone: 201-639-8600.
Facsimile: 201-639-8630.
London, England Office: 10 Finsbury Square, London, EC2A 1LA.
Telephone: 011-44-171-256 8451.
Facsimile: 011-44-171-638-8205.
Tokyo, Japan Office: Sanbancho KB-6 Building, 6 Sanbancho, Chiyoda-ku, Tokyo 102, Japan.
Telephone: 011-81-3-3239-2800.
Facsimile: 011-81-3-3239-2432.
Hong Kong Office: 1104 Lippo Tower, Lippo Centre, 89 Queensway, Central Hong Kong.
Telephone: 011-852-523-8266.
Facsimile: 011-852-522-1760.

MEMBERS OF FIRM

Travis C. Gibbs
Richard M. Jones
Marie L. Martineau
Michael Newman
Gilbert T. Ray
Kathryn A. Sanders
Masood Sohaili
Stephen J. Stern
Dean M. Weiner
Charles C. Wolf

SPECIAL COUNSEL

Daniel A. Deshon, IV (San Francisco Office)

For Complete List of Firm Personnel, See General Section

For full biographical listings, see the Martindale-Hubbell Law Directory

*SAN FRANCISCO,** San Francisco Co.

JONES HALL HILL & WHITE,, A PROFESSIONAL LAW CORPORATION (AV)

Four Embarcadero Center, Nineteenth Floor, 94111
Telephone: 415-391-5780
Telecopier: 415-391-5784

Andrew C. Hall, Jr.
Sharon Stanton White
Charles F. Adams
Stephen R. Casaleggio
William H. Madison
Paul J. Thimmig
Brian D. Quint
Thomas A. Downey
David J. Oster
Michael D. Castelli
Greg Harrington
David A. Walton
Christopher K. Lynch

OF COUNSEL

Kenneth I. Jones

For full biographical listings, see the Martindale-Hubbell Law Directory

SAN MATEO, San Mateo Co.

G. A. LASTER (AV)

The Wilson Building, 630 North San Mateo Drive, P.O. Box 152, 94401-2328
Telephone: 415-342-3523
Telecopier: 415-342-6392

Gerald A. Laster

Representative Clients: Cities of Colma; King City; Mt. Shasta; Plymouth; San Carlos; Castroville Water District; Franklin County Water District; Quartz Hill Water District; Granada Sanitary District; Montara Sanitary District.

For full biographical listings, see the Martindale-Hubbell Law Directory

COLORADO

*DENVER,** Denver Co.

BALLARD SPAHR ANDREWS & INGERSOLL (AV)

Seventeenth Street Plaza Building, Suite 2300, 1225 17th Street, 80202-5596
Telephone: 303-292-2400
Fax: 303-296-3956
Philadelphia, Pennsylvania Office: 1735 Market Street, 51st Floor.
Telephone: 215-665-8500.
Fax: 215-864-8999.
Kaunas, Lithuania Office: Donelaičio 71-2, Kaunas 3000.
Telephone: (370-7) 20 56 66.
Fax: (370-7) 20 56 91.
Salt Lake City, Utah Office: One Utah Center, 201 South Main Street, Suite 1200.
Telephone: 801-531-3000.
Fax: 801-531-3001.
Washington, D.C. Office: Suite 900 East, 555 13th Street, N.W.
Telephone: 202-383-8800.
Fax: 202-383-8877; 383-8893.
Baltimore, Maryland Office: 300 East Lombard Street, 19th Floor.
Telephone: 410-528-5600.
Fax: 410-528-5650.
Camden, New Jersey Office: 800 Hudson Square, 5th Floor.
Telephone: 609-541-5577.
Fax: 609-541-8272.

John M. Gardner
Loring E. Harkness III

Matthew J. Hogan

For Complete List of Firm Personnel, See General Section

For full biographical listings, see the Martindale-Hubbell Law Directory

BROWNSTEIN HYATT FARBER & STRICKLAND, P.C. (AV)

Twenty-Second Floor, 410 Seventeenth Street, 80202-4437
Telephone: 303-534-6335
Telecopier: 303-623-1956

Steven M. Sommers
Michael R. McGinnis
Thomas J. Mancuso

Gregory W. Berger

Representative Clients: A.G. Edwards & Sons, Inc.; George K. Baum & Co.; City and County of Denver; City of Glenwood Springs, CO; Coughlin & Company, Inc.; Dougherty, Dawkins, Strand & Bigelow, Inc.; Hanifen, Imhoff, Inc.; Lakewood Fire Protection District; Norwest Investment Services, Inc.; Rose Medical Center/Rose Health Care Systems.

For Complete List of Firm Personnel, See General Section

For full biographical listings, see the Martindale-Hubbell Law Directory

HOLLAND & HART (AV)

Suite 2900, 555 Seventeenth Street, P.O. Box 8749, 80201
Telephone: 303-295-8000
Cable Address: "Holhart Denver"
Telecopier: 303-295-8261
TWX: 910-931-0568
Denver Tech Center, Colorado Office: Suite 1050, 4601 DTC Boulevard.
Telephone: 303-290-1600.
Telecopier: 303-290-1606.
Aspen, Colorado Office: 600 East Main Street.
Telephone: 303-925-3476.
Telecopier: 303-925-9367.
Boulder, Colorado Office: Suite 500, 1050 Walnut.
Telephone: 303-473-2700.
Telecopier: 303-473-2720.
Colorado Springs, Colorado Office: Suite 1000, 90 S. Cascade Avenue.
Telephone: 719-475-7730.
Telex: 82077 SHHTLX.
Telecopier: 719-634-2461.
Washington, D.C. Office: Suite 310, 1001 Pennsylvania Avenue, N.W.
Telephone: 202-638-5500.
Telecopier: 202-737-8998.
Boise, Idaho Office: Suite 1400, West One Plaza, 101 South Capitol Boulevard, P.O. Box 2527.
Telephone: 208-342-5000.
Telecopier: 208-343-8869.
Billings, Montana Office: Suite 1500, First Interstate Center, 401 North 31st Street, P.O. Box 639.
Telephone: 406-252-2166.
Telecopier: 406-252-1669.
Salt Lake City, Utah Office: Suite 880, 111 East Broadway.
Telephone: 801-578-6000.
FAX: 801-578-6010.

(See Next Column)

HOLLAND & HART, *Denver—Continued*

Cheyenne, Wyoming Office: Holland & Hart, A Partnership including Professional Corporations, Suite 500, 2020 Carey Avenue, P.O. Box 1347.
Telephone: 307-778-4200.
Telecopier: 307-778-8175.
Jackson, Wyoming Office: Holland & Hart, A Partnership including Professional Corporations, Suite 2, 175 South King Street, P.O. Box 68.
Telephone: 307-739-9741.
Telecopier: 307-739-9744.

MEMBERS OF FIRM

Dennis M. Jackson — Mark D. Safty

COLORADO SPRINGS, COLORADO PARTNER

Ronald A. Lehmann (Resident)

BILLINGS, MONTANA PARTNER

David R. Chisholm

CHEYENNE, WYOMING RESIDENT ASSOCIATE

James R. Belcher

For Complete List of Firm Personnel, See General Section

For full biographical listings, see the Martindale-Hubbell Law Directory

HOLME ROBERTS & OWEN LLC (AV)

Suite 4100, 1700 Lincoln, 80203
Telephone: 303-861-7000
Telex: 45-4460
Telecopier: 303-866-0200
Boulder, Colorado Office: Suite 400, 1401 Pearl Street.
Telephone: 303-444-5955.
Telecopier: 303-444-1063.
Colorado Springs, Colorado Office: Suite 1300, 90 South Cascade Avenue.
Telephone: 719-473-3800.
Telecopier: 719-633-1518.
Salt Lake City, Utah Office: Suite 1100, 111 East Broadway.
Telephone: 801-521-5800.
Telecopier: 801-521-9639.
London, England Office: 4th Floor, Mellier House, 26a Albemarle Street.
Telephone: 44-171-499-8776.
Telecopier: 44-171-499-7769.
Moscow, Russia Office: 14 Krivokolenny Pr., Suite 30, 101000.
Telephone: 095-925-7816.
Telecopier: 095-923-2726.

MEMBERS OF FIRM

Nick Nimmo
Steve L. Gaines (Colorado Springs Office)
R. Bruce Johnson (Salt Lake City Office)
David Harold Little (Salt Lake City Office)
Patricia C. Tisdale
Mary L. Groves

SPECIAL COUNSEL

Diane S. Barrett

SENIOR COUNSEL

Kathryn B. Stoker

ASSOCIATE

Robert J. Kaukol (Colorado Springs Office)

For Complete List of Firm Personnel, See General Section

For full biographical listings, see the Martindale-Hubbell Law Directory

SHERMAN & HOWARD L.L.C. (AV)

Attorneys at Law
633 Seventeenth Street, Suite 3000, 80202
Telephone: 303-297-2900
Telecopier: 303-298-0940
Colorado Springs, Colorado Office: Suite 1500, 90 South Cascade Avenue, 80903.
Telephone: 719-475-2440.
Las Vegas, Nevada Office: Swendseid & Stern a member in Sherman & Howard L.L.C., 317 Sixth Street, 89101.
Telephone: 702-387-6073.
Reno, Nevada Office: Swendseid & Stern, a member in Sherman & Howard L.L.C., 50 West Liberty Street, Suite 660, 89501.
Telephone: 702-323-1980.

Kurt A. Kaufmann
Robert P. Mitchell
John O. Swendseid (Las Vegas and Reno, Nevada Offices)
Dee P. Wisor
Stanley M. Raine
Calvin T. Hanson
Jennifer Stern (Las Vegas and Reno, Nevada Offices)
Ann Marie (Amy) Kennedy

COUNSEL

Michael D. Groshek — Carolyn Lubchenco

Amy L. Hirter — Maria L. Prevedel
Sarah J. Kilgore

Representative Clients: Colorado Health Facilities Authority; Colorado Student Obligation Bond Authority; Jefferson County, Colorado; Platte River Power Authority; Clark County, Nevada; Farmington, New Mexico.; City of Thornton, Colorado; Colorado Housing and Finance Authority.

(See Next Column)

For Complete List of Firm Personnel, See General Section

For full biographical listings, see the Martindale-Hubbell Law Directory

CONNECTICUT

WESTPORT, Fairfield Co.

WEISMAN & LUBELL (AV)

5 Sylvan Road South, P.O. Box 3184, 06880
Telephone: 203-226-8307
Telecopier: 203-221-7279

MEMBERS OF FIRM

Lawrence P. Weisman — Ellen B. Lubell

Andrew R. Tarshis

For full biographical listings, see the Martindale-Hubbell Law Directory

DELAWARE

*WILMINGTON,** New Castle Co.

POTTER ANDERSON & CORROON (AV)

350 Delaware Trust Building, P.O. Box 951, 19899-0951
Telephone: 302-658-6771
FAX: 658-1192; 655-1190; 655-1199

MEMBERS OF FIRM

Richard L. McMahon — David A. Anderson
Charles S. McDowell

ASSOCIATES

Harold I. Salmons, III — Scott E. Waxman

Counsel for: The State of Delaware; Delaware Transportation Authority; DE Health Facilities Authority; New Castle County; Kent County; Sussex County; City of Dover; Delaware Trust Co.; Delmarva Power & Light Co.; Hercules Inc.; General Motors Corp.

For Complete List of Firm Personnel, See General Section

For full biographical listings, see the Martindale-Hubbell Law Directory

DISTRICT OF COLUMBIA

WASHINGTON, D.C. Co.

* indicates certain Bar Register subscribers, in cities of comparable size and importance, who maintain an additional office in Washington, D.C. and who have arranged for representation as a part of the Washington, D.C. listings that follow

*** BALLARD SPAHR ANDREWS & INGERSOLL** (AV)

Suite 900 East, 555 13th Street, N.W., 20004-1112
Telephone: 202-383-8800
Fax: 202-383-8877
Philadelphia, Pennsylvania Office: 1735 Market Street, 51st Floor.
Telephone: 215-665-8500.
Fax: 215-864-8999.
Denver, Colorado Office: Seventeenth Street Plaza Building, Suite 2300, 1225 17th Street.
Telephone: 303-292-2400.
Fax: 303-296-3956.
Kaunas, Lithuania Office: Donelaičio 71-2 Kaunas 3000.
Telephone: (370-7) 20 56 66.
Fax: (370-7) 20 56 91.
Salt Lake City, Utah Office: One Utah Center, 201 South Main Street, Suite 1200.
Telephone: 801-531-3000.
Fax: 801-531-3001.
Baltimore, Maryland Office: 300 East Lombard Street, 19th Floor.
Telephone: 410-528-5600.
Fax: 410-528-5650.
Camden, New Jersey Office: 800 Hudson Square, 5th Floor.
Telephone: 609-541-5577.
Fax: 609-541-8272.

Frederic L. Ballard, Jr. — Charles S. Henck

For Complete List of Firm Personnel, See General Section

For full biographical listings, see the Martindale-Hubbell Law Directory

Washington—Continued

*** Jones, Day, Reavis & Pogue (AV)**

Metropolitan Square, 1450 G Street, N.W., 20005-2088
Telephone: 202-879-3939
Cable Address: "Attorneys Washington"
Telex: W.U. (Domestic) 89-2410 ATTORNEYS WASH (International) 64363 ATTORNEYS WASH
Telecopier: 202-737-2832
In Atlanta, Georgia: 3500 One Peachtree Center, 303 Peachtree Street, N.E.
Telephone: 404-521-3939.
Cable Address: "Attorneys Atlanta".
Telex: 54-2711.
Telecopier: 404-581-8330.
In Brussels, Belgium: Avenue Louise 480, 7th Floor, B-1050 Brussels.
Telephone: 011-32-2-645-14-11.
Telecopier: 011-32-2-645-14-45.
In Chicago, Illinois: 77 West Wacker.
Telephone: 312-782-3939.
Telecopier: 312-782-8585.
In Cleveland, Ohio: North Point, 901 Lakeside Avenue.
Telephone: 216-586-3939.
Cable Address: "Attorneys Cleveland."
Telex: 980389.
Telecopier: 216-579-0212.
In Columbus, Ohio: 1900 Huntington Center.
Telephone: 614-469-3939.
Cable Address: "Attorneys Columbus."
Telecopier: 614-461-4198.
In Dallas, Texas: 2300 Trammell Crow Center, 2001 Ross Avenue.
Telephone: 214-220-3939.
Cable Address: "Attorneys Dallas."
Telex: 730852.
Telecopier: 214-969-5100.
In Frankfurt, Germany: Triton Haus, Bockenheimer Landstrasse 42, 60323 Frankfurt am Main.
Telephone: 49-69-9726-3939.
Telecopier: 49-69-9726-3993.
In Geneva, Switzerland: 20, rue de Candolle.
Telephone: 011-41-22-320-2339.
Telecopier: 011-41-22-320-1232.
In Hong Kong: 1501 One Exchange Square, 8 Connaught Place.
Telephone: 011-852-2526-6895.
Telecopier: 011-852-2810-5787.
In Irvine, California: 2603 Main Street, Suite 900 .
Telephone: 714-851-3939.
Telex: 194911 Lawyers LSA.
Telecopier: 714-553-7539.
In London, England: One Mount Street.
Telephone: 011-44-71-493-9361.
Cable Address: "Surgoe London WI."
Telecopier: 011-44-71-493-9666.
In Los Angeles, California: 555 West Fifth Street, Suite 4600.
Telephone: 213-489-3939.
Telex: 181439 UD.
Telecopier: 213-243-2539.
In New York, New York: 599 Lexington Avenue.
Telephone: 212-326-3939.
Cable Address: "JONESDAY NEWYORK."
Telex: 237013 JDRP UR.
Telecopier: 212-755-7306.
In Paris, France: 62, rue du Faubourg Saint-Honore.
Telephone: 011-33-1-44-71-3939.
Cable Address: "Surgoe Paris."
Telex: 290156 Surgoe.
Telecopier: 011-33-1-49-24-0471.
In Pittsburgh, Pennsylvania: 500 Grant Street, 31st Floor.
Telephone: 412-391-3939.
Cable Address: "Attorneys Pittsburgh".
Telecopier: 412-394-7959.
In Riyadh, Saudi Arabia: Law Offices of Saud M.A. Shawwaf, P.O. Box 2700.
Telephones: 011 (966-1) 465-6543, 011 (966-1) 464-8534 or 011 (966-1) 464-8540.
Telex: 401831 SAUCON SJ.
Telecopier: (966-1) 464-8480.
In Taipai, Taiwan: 8th Floor, 2 Tun Hwa South Road, Section 2.
Telephone: 011 (886-2) 704-6808.
Telecopier: 011 (886-2) 704-6791.
In Tokyo, Japan: Toranomon MT Building, 4th Floor, 10-3, Toranomon 3-Chome, Minato-Ku, Tokyo 105, Japan.
Telephone: 011-81-3-3433-3939.
Telecopier: 011-81-3-5401-2725.

MEMBERS OF FIRM IN WASHINGTON, D.C.

Frieda K. Wallison
Mark K. Sisitsky

ASSOCIATES

Dennis D. Dillon (Not admitted in DC)
Richard J. Caplan (Not admitted in DC)
Debra A. Ulven (Not admitted in DC)

(See Next Column)

For Complete List of Firm Personnel, See General Section

For full biographical listings, see the Martindale-Hubbell Law Directory

*** Lewis, White & Clay, A Professional Corporation (AV)**

1250 K Street, N.W., Suite 630, 20005
Telephone: 202-408-5419
Fax: 202-408-5456
Detroit, Michigan Office: 1300 First National Building, 660 Woodward Avenue.
Telephone: 313-961-2550.

Kathleen Miles (Resident)
Karen Kendrick Brown (Resident)
Werten F. W. Bellamy, Jr. (Not admitted in DC; Resident)

OF COUNSEL

Inez Smith Reid (Resident)

For full biographical listings, see the Martindale-Hubbell Law Directory

FLORIDA

*FORT LAUDERDALE,** Broward Co.

Doumar, Curtis, Cross, Laystrom & Perloff (AV)

A Partnership of Professional Corporations
1177 Southeast Third Avenue, 33316
Telephone: 305-525-3441
Fax: 305-525-3423
Direct Miami Line: 305-945-3172

MEMBERS OF FIRM

Raymond A. Doumar (P.C.)
Charles L. Curtis (P.C.)
William S. Cross (P.C.)
C. William Laystrom, Jr. (P.C.)
John W. Perloff (P.C.)
E. Scott Allsworth (P.C.)
John D. Voigt (P.C.)
Jeffrey S. Wachs (P.C.)

ASSOCIATE

Mark E. Allsworth

Representative Clients: Albertson's, Inc.; Robinson-Humphrey/American Express; Deutsch-Ireland Properties; Massey-Yardley Chrysler Plymouth, Inc.; Waste Management, Inc.; Planned Development Corp.; Toys-R-Us Inc.; Lumbermans Mutual Casualty Co.; Melvin Simon And Associates.

For full biographical listings, see the Martindale-Hubbell Law Directory

*ORLANDO,** Orange Co.

Baker & Hostetler (AV)

SunBank Center, Suite 2300, 200 South Orange Avenue, 32802-3432
Telephone: 407-649-4000
In Cleveland, Ohio: 3200 National City Center, 1900 East Ninth Street.
Telephone: 216-621-0200.
In Columbus, Ohio: Capitol Square, Suite 2100, 65 East State Street.
Telephone: 614-228-1541.
In Denver, Colorado: 303 East 17th Avenue, Suite 1100.
Telephone: 303-861-0600.
In Houston, Texas: 1000 Louisiana, Suite 2000.
Telephone: 713-751-1600.
In Long Beach, California: 300 Oceangate, Suite 620.
Telephone: 310-432-2827.
In Los Angeles, California: 600 Wilshire Boulevard.
Telephone: 213-624-2400.
In Washington, D.C.: Washington Square, Suite 1100, 1050 Connecticut Avenue, N.W., Suite 1100.
Telephone: 202-861-1500.
In College Park, Maryland: 9658 Baltimore Boulevard, Suite 206.
Telephone: 301-441-2781.
In Alexandria, Virginia: 437 North Lee Street.
Telephone: 703-549-1294.
In San Francisco, California: One Sansome Street, Suite 2000.
Telephone: 415-951-4705.

PARTNER

Jerry R. Linscott

For Complete List of Firm Personnel, See General Section

For full biographical listings, see the Martindale-Hubbell Law Directory

Honigman Miller Schwartz and Cohn (AV)

A Partnership including Professional Corporations
390 North Orange Avenue, Suite 1300, 32801-1632
Telephone: 407-648-0300
Telecopier: 407-648-1155
West Palm Beach, Florida Office: Suite 800 Esperante Building, 222 Lakeview Avenue.
Telephone: 407-838-4500.
Tampa, Florida Office: 2700 Landmark Centre, 401 E. Jackson Street.
Telephone: 813-221-6600.

(See Next Column)

HONIGMAN MILLER SCHWARTZ AND COHN, *Orlando—Continued*

Detroit, Michigan Office: 2290 First National Building.
Telephone: 313-256-7800.
Lansing, Michigan Office: 222 North Washington Square, Suite 400.
Telephone: 517-484-8282.
Houston, Texas Office: 3100 First Interstate Bank Plaza, 1000 Louisiana.
Telephone: 713-650-2600.
Los Angeles, California Office: Watt Plaza, Suite 2200, 1875 Century Park East.
Telephone: 310-789-3800.
Fax: 310-789-3814.

MEMBER

Brad M. Tomtishen

General Counsel For: Osceola County Health Facilities Authority; Osceola County Industrial Development Authority; Osceola County Housing Finance Authority.
Local or Special Counsel for: Florida Housing Finance Agency (Co-Counsel); City of Winter Springs, City Attorney; Palm Beach County (Co-Bond Counsel); City of Ft. Pierce (Bond Counsel); City of Sebring (Bond Counsel).

For Complete List of Firm Personnel, See General Section

For full biographical listings, see the Martindale-Hubbell Law Directory

PALM BEACH, Palm Beach Co.

CALDWELL & PACETTI (AV)

324 Royal Palm Way, P.O. Box 2775, 33480-2775
Telephone: 407-655-0620
Fax: 407-655-3775

MEMBERS OF FIRM

Manley P. Caldwell (1901-1971)
Madison F. Pacetti (1914-1994)
Manley P. Caldwell, Jr.
Kenneth W. Edwards
Mary M. Viator
Charles F. Schoech
Elizabeth S. (Betsy) Burden
John A. Weig

OF COUNSEL

Arthur E. Barrow (Retired)

Representative Clients: Shawano Drainage District; Acme Improvement District; Northern Palm Beach County Water Control District; Indian Trail Water Control District; Siemens Information Systems; Town Of Hypoluxo; Everglades Agricultural Area Environmental Protection District; East County Water Control District; Town of Lake Clarke Shores.

For full biographical listings, see the Martindale-Hubbell Law Directory

*SARASOTA,** Sarasota Co.

WILLIAMS, PARKER, HARRISON, DIETZ & GETZEN, PROFESSIONAL ASSOCIATION (AV)

1550 Ringling Boulevard, 34230-3258
Telephone: 813-366-4800
Telecopier: 813-366-5109
Mailing Address: P.O. Box 3258, Sarasota, Florida, 34230-3258

William T. Harrison, Jr.
George A. Dietz
Monte K. Marshall
James L. Ritchey
Hugh McPheeters, Jr.
William G. Lambrecht
John T. Berteau
John V. Cannon, III
Charles D. Bailey, Jr.
J. Michael Hartenstine
Michele Boardman Grimes
James L. Turner
William M. Seider
Elizabeth C. Marshall
Robert W. Benjamin
Frank Strelec
David A. Wallace
Terri Jayne Salt
Jeffrey A. Grebe
John Leslie Moore
Mark A. Schwartz
Stephanie Edwards

OF COUNSEL

Frazer F. Hilder
William E. Getzen
Elvin W. Phillips

Counsel for: Sarasota-Manatee Airport Authority; Sarasota County Public Hospital Board; William G. & Marie Selby Foundation; Taylor Woodrow Homes Ltd.; The School Board of Sarasota County.
Local Counsel for: NationsBank of Florida; Arvida/JMB Partners.

For Complete List of Firm Personnel, See General Section

For full biographical listings, see the Martindale-Hubbell Law Directory

*TAMPA,** Hillsborough Co.

MORRISON, MORRISON & MILLS, P.A. (AV)

1200 West Platt Street Suite 100, 33606
Telephone: 813-258-3311
Telecopier: 813-258-3209

Thomas K. Morrison
Susan B. Morrison
Frederick J. Mills
Tracey Karen Jaensch
James E. Holmes, Jr.

Representative Clients: SouthTrust Bank of West Florida; SouthTrust Bank of Alabama, National Association; NationsBank of Florida, N.A.; Mercantile Bank; Barnett Banks, Inc.; Southern Commerce Bank; Sun Bank of Pasco County; Hillsborough County Industrial Development Authority; Automation Packaging, Inc.; Medical Data Management, Inc.

For full biographical listings, see the Martindale-Hubbell Law Directory

GEORGIA

*ATLANTA,** Fulton Co.

ALSTON & BIRD (AV)

A Partnership including Professional Corporations
One Atlantic Center, 1201 West Peachtree Street, 30309-3424
Telephone: 404-881-7000
Telecopier: 404-881-7777
Cable Address: AMGRAM GA
Telex: 54-2996
Easylink: 62985848
Washington, D.C. Office: 700 Thirteenth Street, Suite 350 20005-3960.
Telephone: 202-508-3300.
Telecopier: 202-508-3333.

MEMBERS OF FIRM

L. Clifford Adams, Jr.
H. Sadler Poe
Peter M. Wright
Gerald W. Bowling
Glenn R. Thomson
Terence J. Greene
Robert J. Middleton, Jr.
Karol V. Mason

Representative Client: The Fulton-DeKalb Hospital Authority.

For Complete List of Firm Personnel, See General Section

For full biographical listings, see the Martindale-Hubbell Law Directory

JONES, DAY, REAVIS & POGUE (AV)

3500 One Peachtree Center, 303 Peachtree Street, N.E., 30308-3242
Telephone: 404-521-3939
Cable Address: "Attorneys Atlanta"
Telex: 54-2711
Telecopier: 404-581-8330
In Brussels, Belgium: Avenue Louise 480, 7th Floor, B-1050 Brussels.
Telephone: 011-32-2-645-14-11.
Telecopier: 011-32-2-645-14-45.
In Chicago, Illinois: 77 West Wacker.
Telephone: 312-782-3939.
Telecopier: 312-782-8585.
In Cleveland, Ohio: North Point. 901 Lakeside Avenue.
Telephone: 216-586-3939.
Cable Address: "Attorneys Cleveland".
Telex: 980389.
Telecopier: 216-579-0212.
In Columbus, Ohio: 1900 Huntington Center.
Telephone: 614-469-3939.
Cable Address: "Attorneys Columbus".
Telecopier: 614-461-4198.
In Dallas, Texas: 2300 Trammell Crow Center, 2001 Ross Avenue.
Telephone: 214-220-3939.
Cable Address: "Attorneys Dallas."
Telex: 730852.
Telecopier: 214-969-5100.
In Frankfurt, Germany: Westendstrasse 41, 60325 Frankfurt am Main.
Telephone: 011-49-69-7438-3939.
Telecopier: 011-49-69-741-1686.
In Geneva, Switzerland: 20, rue de Candolle.
Telephone: 011-41-22-320-2339.
Telecopier: 011-41-22-320-1232.
In Hong Kong: 1501 One Exchange Square, 8 Connaught Place.
Telephone: 011-852-526-6895.
Telecopier: 011-852-810-5787.
In Irvine, California: 2603 Main Street, Suite 900.
Telephone: 714-851-3939.
Telex: 194911 Lawyers LSA.
Telecopier: 714-553-7539.
In London, England: One Mount Street.
Telephone: 011-44-71-493-9361.
Cable Address: "Surgoe London WI."
Telecopier: 011-44-71-493-9666.
In Los Angeles, California: 555 West Fifth Street, Suite 4600.
Telephone: 213-489-3939.
Telex: 181439 UD.
Telecopier: 213-243-2539.
In New York, New York: 599 Lexington Avenue.
Telephone: 212-326-3939.
Cable Address: "JONESDAY NEWYORK."
Telex: 237013 JDRP UR.
Telecopier: 212-755-7306.
In Paris, France: 62, rue du Faubourg Saint-Honore.
Telephone: 011-33-1-44-71-3939.
Cable Address: "Surgoe Paris."
Telex: 290156 Surgoe.
Telecopier: 011-33-1-49-24-0471.

(See Next Column)

JONES, DAY, REAVIS & POGUE—*Continued*

In Pittsburgh, Pennsylvania: 500 Grant Street, 31st Floor.
Telephone: 412-391-3939.
Cable Address: "Attorneys Pittsburgh".
Telecopier: 412-394-7959.
In Riyadh, Saudi Arabia: Law Offices of Saud M.A. Shawwaf, P.O. Box 2700.
Telephones: 011 (966-1) 465-6543, 011 (966-1) 464-8534 or 011 (966-1) 464-8540.
Telex: 401831 SAUCON SJ.
Telecopier: (966-1) 464-8480.
In Taipei, Taiwan: 7th Floor, 2 Tun Hwa South Road, Section 2.
Telephone: 011 (886-2) 704-6808 and 704-6809.
Telecopier: 011 (886-2) 704-6791.
In Tokyo, Japan: Shiroyama JT Mori Bldg., 15th Floor, 3-1, Toranomon 4-chome Minato-ku.
Telephone: 011-81-3-3433-3939.
Telecopier: 011-81-3-5401-2725.
In Washington, D.C.: Metropolitan Square, 1450 G Street, N.W.
Telephone: 202-879-3939.
Cable Address: "Attorneys Washington."
Telex: 89-2410 ATTORNEYS WASH.
Telecopier: 202-737-2832. 2-737-2832.

MEMBERS OF FIRM IN ATLANTA

Dom H. Wyant — John E. Zamer
Lizanne Thomas

ASSOCIATE

Joel C. Ross

For Complete List of Firm Personnel, See General Section

For full biographical listings, see the Martindale-Hubbell Law Directory

KILPATRICK & CODY (AV)

Suite 2800, 1100 Peachtree Street, 30309-4530
Telephone: 404-815-6500
Telephone Copier: 404-815-6555
Telex: 54-2307
Washington, D.C. Office: Suite 800, 700 13th Street, N.W., 20005.
Telephone: 202-508-5800. Telephone Copier: 202-508-5858.
Brussels, Belgium Office: Avenue Louise 65, BTE 3, 1050 Brussels.
Telephone: (32) (2) 533-03-00.
Telecopier: (32) (2) 534-86-38.
London, England Office: 68 Pall Mall, London, SW1Y 5ES, England.
Telephone: (44) (71) 321 0477.
Telecopier: (44) (71) 930 9733.
Augusta, Georgia Office: Suite 1400 First Union Bank Building, P.O. Box 2043, 30903. Telephone (706) 724-2622. Telecopier (706) 722-0219.

MEMBERS OF FIRM

Barry Phillips — Frederick K. Heller, Jr. (Resident, Brussels, Belgium Office)

Representative Clients: Southern Bell Telephone and Telegraph Co.; Lockheed Aeronautical Systems Co.; Frito-Lay, Inc.; Scientific-Atlanta, Inc.; Scripto-Tokai, Inc.; Interface, Inc.; Bank South Corporation; PepsiCo; Prudential Capital Corporation; Aaron Rents, Inc.

For Complete List of Firm Personnel, See General Section

For full biographical listings, see the Martindale-Hubbell Law Directory

LONG ALDRIDGE & NORMAN (AV)

A Partnership including Professional Corporations
One Peachtree Center, Suite 5300, 303 Peachtree Street, 30308
Telephone: 404-527-4000
Telecopier: 404-527-4198
Washington, D.C. Office: Suite 950, 1615 L Street, 20036.
Telephone: 202-223-7033.
Telecopier: 202-223-7013.

MEMBERS OF FIRM

Barbara L. Blackford — Margaret M. Joslin
R. William Ide III — John E. Ramsey
Edgar H. Sims, Jr. (P.C.)

ASSOCIATES

Thomas P. Lauth, III — Kenneth B. Pollock

For Complete List of Firm Personnel, See General Section

For full biographical listings, see the Martindale-Hubbell Law Directory

POWELL, GOLDSTEIN, FRAZER & MURPHY (AV)

191 Peachtree Street, N.E., Sixteenth Floor, 30303
Telephone: 404-572-6600
Telex: 542864
Telecopier: 404-572-6999
Cable Address: "Pgfm"
Washington, D.C. Office: Sixth Floor, 1001 Pennsylvania Avenue, N.W., 20004.
Telephone: 202-347-0066.

(See Next Column)

MEMBERS OF FIRM

Lewis C. Horne, Jr. — Robert C. Lewinson
Ronald D. Stallings

ASSOCIATES

Michael I. Diamond — Debra L. Skal

For Complete List of Firm Personnel, See General Section

For full biographical listings, see the Martindale-Hubbell Law Directory

SUTHERLAND, ASBILL & BRENNAN (AV)

999 Peachtree Street, N.E., 30309-3996
Telephone: 404-853-8000
Facsimile: 404-853-8806
Washington, D.C. Office: 1275 Pennsylvania Avenue, N.W., 20004-2404.
Telephone: 202-383-0100.
New York, N.Y. Office: 1270 Avenue of the Americas, 10020-1700.
Telephone: 212-332-3000.
Austin, Texas Office: 111 Congress Avenue, 23rd Floor, 78701-4079.
Telephone: 512-469-3350.

James L. Henderson, III — John H. Mobley, II

For Complete List of Firm Personnel, See General Section

For full biographical listings, see the Martindale-Hubbell Law Directory

THOMAS, KENNEDY, SAMPSON & PATTERSON (AV)

1600 Bank South Building, 55 Marietta Street, N.W., 30303
Telephone: 404-688-4503
Telecopier: 404-681-2950

MEMBERS OF FIRM

John Loren Kennedy (1942-1994) — Myra H. Dixon
Thomas G. Sampson — R. David Ware
P. Andrew Patterson — Patrise M. Perkins-Hooker
Jeffrey E. Tompkins

ASSOCIATES

Rosalind T. Drakeford — Melynee C. Leftridge
Regina E. McMillan — La'Sean M. Zilton

For full biographical listings, see the Martindale-Hubbell Law Directory

*COLUMBUS,** Muscogee Co.

HATCHER, STUBBS, LAND, HOLLIS & ROTHSCHILD (AV)

Suite 500 The Corporate Center, 233 12th Street, P.O. Box 2707, 31902-2707
Telephone: 706-324-0201
Telecopier: 706-322-7747

MEMBERS OF FIRM

J. Barrington Vaught — James E. Humes, II
John M. Tanzine, III

General Counsel for: Trust Company Bank of Columbus, N.A.; TOM'S Foods Inc.; Muscogee County Board of Education; Columbus Georgia Water Board; St. Francis Hospital, Inc.
Local Counsel for: First Union National Bank of Georgia.

For Complete List of Firm Personnel, See General Section

For full biographical listings, see the Martindale-Hubbell Law Directory

*MARIETTA,** Cobb Co.

AWTREY AND PARKER, P.C. (AV)

211 Roswell Street, P.O. Box 997, 30061
Telephone: 404-424-8000
Fax: 404-424-1594

L. M. Awtrey, Jr. (1915-1986) — Michael L. Marsh
George L. Dozier, Jr. — Barbara H. Martin
Harvey D. Harkness — A. Sidney Parker
Mike Harrison — Toby B. Prodgers
Dana L. Jackel — J. Lynn Rainey
Donald A. Mangerie (1924-1988) — Annette M. Risse (Mrs.)
Robert B. Silliman

Gregg A. Landau — Lisa G. Gunn
Alan H. Sheldon

OF COUNSEL

Allan J. Hall — J. Ben Moore
S. Alan Schlact

General Counsel for: Kennesaw Finance Co.; Cobb Electric Membership Corporation; Development Authority of Cobb County.
Local Counsel for: Coats & Clark; Bell South Mobility; Lockheed-Georgia Corp.; Post Properties, Inc.; CSX Transportation, Inc.

For full biographical listings, see the Martindale-Hubbell Law Directory

IDAHO

*BOISE,** Ada Co.

ELAM & BURKE, A PROFESSIONAL ASSOCIATION (AV)

Key Financial Center, 702 West Idaho Street, P.O. Box 1539, 83701
Telephone: 208-343-5454
Telecopier: 208-384-5844

Ryan P. Armbruster

Representative Clients: Morrison-Knudsen, Inc.; Texas Instruments, Inc.; Prudential Securities, Inc.; Pechiney Corp.; Dow Corning Corporation; U.S. West Communications; State Farm Insurance Cos.; Sinclair Oil Company d/b/a Sun Valley Company; Farmers Insurance Group; Hecla Mining Company.

For Complete List of Firm Personnel, See General Section

For full biographical listings, see the Martindale-Hubbell Law Directory

ILLINOIS

*CHICAGO,** Cook Co.

BELL, BOYD & LLOYD (AV)

Three First National Plaza Suite 3300, 70 West Madison Street, 60602
Telephone: 312-372-1121
FAX: 312-372-2098
Washington, D.C. Office: 1615 L Street, N.W.
Telephone: 202-466-6300.
FAX: 202-463-0678.

MEMBERS OF FIRM

Lawrence C. Eppley
Jeffrey R. Ladd
Paul T. Metzger
Thomas J. Murphy
William S. Price

For Complete List of Firm Personnel, See General Section

For full biographical listings, see the Martindale-Hubbell Law Directory

CHAPMAN AND CUTLER (AV)

111 West Monroe Street, 60603
Telephone: 312-845-3000
TWX: 910-221-2103
Fax: 312-701-2361
Salt Lake City, Utah Office: Suite 800, Key Bank Tower, 50 South Main Street.
Telephone: 801-533-0066.
Fax: 801-533-9595.
Phoenix, Arizona Office: Suite 1100, One Renaissance Square, 2 North Central Avenue.
Telephone: 602-256-4060.
Fax: 602-256-4099.

Daniel J. Bacastow
Andrea G. Bacon
Daniel C. Bird, Jr.
Deborah Thomas Boye
Lee A. Boye
James C. Burr (Not admitted in IL; Resident, Salt Lake City Office)
George D. Buzard, III
Steven L. Clark
Lynn Leland Coe
William E. Corbin, Jr.
Richard A. Cosgrove
Patricia M. Curtner
C. Robert Foltz
Lynda K. Given
Richard H. Goss
Howard H. Hush, Jr.
Charles L. Jarik
Daniel L. Johnson
Darrell R. Larsen, Jr. (Not admitted in IL; Resident, Salt Lake City Office)
Matthew R. Lewin
William M. Libit
James E. Luebchow
Timothy V. McGree
Michael J. Mitchell
Robert W. Ollis, Jr.
John S. Overdorff (Resident, Phoenix Office)
S. Louise Rankin
James R. Richardson
Richard J. Scott (Resident, Salt Lake City Office)
Stephen F. Stroh
Harold C. Sutter
William M. Taylor
M. John Trofa
John L. Tuohy
John A. Ward
David G. Williams
Steven N. Wohl

John F. Bibby, Jr.
James M. Broeking
Nancy A. Burke
William A. Callison
William R. DeHaan (Resident, Phoenix Office)
Peter R. Freund
Marie I. Jordan
Scott A. Kolar
Kelly K. Kost
Kenneth A. Peterson, Jr.
Donald B. Rohbock (Not admitted in IL; Resident, Salt Lake City Office)
Susan E. Rollins
Cynthia A. Rybak

(See Next Column)

Robert D. Stephan
Elizabeth D. Swanson
Richard K. Tomei
Deanne M. Tomse
Christopher F. Walrath

For Complete List of Firm Personnel, See General Section

For full biographical listings, see the Martindale-Hubbell Law Directory

JONES, DAY, REAVIS & POGUE (AV)

77 West Wacker, 60601-1692
Telephone: 312-782-3939
Telecopier: 312-782-8585
In Atlanta, Georgia: 3500 One Peachtree Center, 303 Peachtree Street, N.E.
Telephone: 404-521-3939.
Cable Address: "Attorneys Atlanta".
Telex: 54-2711.
Telecopier: 404-581-8330.
In Brussels, Belgium: Avenue Louise 480, 7th Floor, B-1050 Brussels.
Telephone: 011-32-2-645-14-11.
Telecopier: 011-32-2-645-14-45.
In Cleveland, Ohio: North Point, 901 Lakeside Avenue.
Telephone: 216-586-3939.
Cable Address: "Attorneys Cleveland."
Telex: 980389.
Telecopier: 216-579-0212.
In Columbus, Ohio: 1900 Huntington Center.
Telephone: 614-469-3939.
Cable Address: "Attorneys Columbus."
Telecopier: 614-461-4198.
In Dallas, Texas: 2300 Trammell Crow Center, 2001 Ross Avenue.
Telephone: 214-220-3939.
Cable Address: "Attorneys Dallas."
Telex: 730852.
Telecopier: 214-969-5100.
In Frankfurt, Germany: Westendstrasse 41, 60325 Frankfurt am Main.
Telephone: 011-49-69-7438-3939.
Telecopier: 011-49-69-741-1686.
In Geneva, Switzerland: 20, rue de Candolle.
Telephone: 011-41-22-320-2339.
Telecopier: 011-41-22-320-1232.
In Hong Kong: 1501 One Exchange Square, 8 Connaught Place.
Telephone: 011-852-526-6895.
Telecopier: 011-852-810-5787.
In Irvine, California: 2603 Main Street, Suite 900.
Telephone: 714-851-3939.
Telex: 194911 Lawyers LSA.
Telecopier: 714-553-7539.
In London, England: One Mount Street.
Telephone: 011-44-71-493-9361.
Cable Address: "Surgoe London WI."
Telecopier: 011-44-71-493-9666.
In Los Angeles, California: 555 West Fifth Street, Suite 4600.
Telephone: 213-489-3939.
Telex: 181439 UD.
Telecopier: 213-243-2539.
In New York, New York: 599 Lexington Avenue.
Telephone: 212-326-3939.
Cable Address: "JONESDAY NEWYORK."
Telex: 237013 JDRP UR.
Telecopier: 212-755-7306.
In Paris, France: 62, rue du Faubourg Saint-Honore.
Telephone: 011-33-1-44-71-3939.
Cable Address: "Surgoe Paris."
Telex: 290156 Surgoe.
Telecopier: 011-33-1-49-24-0471.
In Pittsburgh, Pennsylvania: 500 Grant Street, 31st Floor.
Telephone: 412-391-3939.
Cable Address: "Attorneys Pittsburgh."
Telecopier: 412-394-7959.
In Riyadh, Saudi Arabia: Law Offices of Saud M.A. Shawwaf, P.O. Box 2700.
Telephones: 011 (966-1) 465-6543, 011 (966-1) 464-8534 or 011 (966-1) 464-8540.
Telex: 401831 SAUCON SJ.
Telecopier: (966-1) 464-8480.
In Taipei, Taiwan: 7th Floor, 2 Tun Hwa South Road, Section 2.
Telephone: 011 (886-2) 704-6808 and 704-6809.
Telecopier: 011 (886-2) 704-6791.
In Tokyo, Japan: Shiroyama JT Mori Bldg., 15th Floor, 3-1, Toranomon 4-chome, Minato-Ku.
Telephone: 011-81-3-3433-3939.
Telecopier: 011-81-3-5401-2725.
In Washington, D.C.: Metropolitan Square, 1450 G Street, N.W.
Telephone: 202-879-3939.
Cable Address: "Attorneys Washington."
Telex: 89-2410 ATTORNEYS WASH.
Telecopier: 202-737-2832.

MEMBERS OF FIRM IN CHICAGO

Robert A. Yolles
Robert H. Baker
Robert J. Graves

OF COUNSEL

William J. Harmon

(See Next Column)

Jones, Day, Reavis & Pogue—*Continued*

ASSOCIATES

Timothy J. Melton
Mary Jo Quinn
(Not admitted in IL)
Elizabeth Haber Lacy

For Complete List of Firm Personnel, See General Section

For full biographical listings, see the Martindale-Hubbell Law Directory

Scariano, Kula, Ellch and Himes, Chartered (AV)

Two Prudential Plaza 180 North Stetson Suite 3100, 60601-6224
Telephone: 312-565-3100
Facsimile: 312-565-0000
Chicago Heights, Illinois Office: 1450 Aberdeen.
Telephone: 708-755-1900.
Facsimile: 708-755-0000.

Anthony G. Scariano
David P. Kula
Robert H. Ellch
Alan T. Sraga
A. Lynn Himes
Justino D. Petrarca
Lawrence Jay Weiner
Kathleen Field Orr
John M. Izzo
Raymond A. Hauser

OF COUNSEL

Max A. Bailey
G. Robb Cooper
Teri E. Engler
John B. Kralovec

Daniel M. Boyle
Patrick J. Broncato
Sarah R. Carlin
Diane S. Cohen
Jon G. Crawford
Douglas D. Danielson
Anthony Ficarelli
Kelly A. Hayden
Todd K. Hayden
David A. Hemenway
Kathleen Roche Hirsman
Jonathan A. Pearl
Lisa Ann Rapacz
Shelia C. Riley
Joanne W. Schochat

For full biographical listings, see the Martindale-Hubbell Law Directory

Vedder, Price, Kaufman & Kammholz (AV)

A Partnership including Vedder, Price, Kaufman & Kammholz, P.C.
222 North La Salle Street, 60601-1003
Telephone: 312-609-7500
Fax: 312-609-5005
Rockford, Illinois Office: Vedder, Price, Kaufman & Kammholz, 4615 East State Street, Suite 201.
Telephone: 815-226-7700.
Washington, D.C. Office: Vedder, Price, Kaufman, Kammholz & Day, 1600 M. Street, N.W.
Telephone: 202-296-0500.
New York, New York Office: Vedder, Price, Kaufman, Kammholz & Day, 805 Third Avenue.
Telephone: 212-407-7700.

MEMBERS OF FIRM

William W. McKittrick
Michael L. Igoe, Jr.
Robert J. Stucker
Robert J. Moran
Daniel O'Rourke
Lawrence J. Casazza
E. Wayne Robinson
John R. Obiala
James A. Spizzo
Benjamin J. Baker
Dalius F. Vasys
Daniel T. Sherlock
Jennifer R. Evans

ASSOCIATES

Michael A. Nemeroff
Mark J. Handfelt

For Complete List of Firm Personnel, See General Section

For full biographical listings, see the Martindale-Hubbell Law Directory

Watt & Sawyier (AV)

Amalgamated Bank Annex Building, 55 West Van Buren Street, Suite 500, 60605
Telephone: 312-663-1440
Telecopier: 312-663-1410

MEMBER OF FIRM

Garland W. Watt

Representative Clients: First National Bank of Chicago; Chicago Title & Trust Company; North Carolina Mutual Life Insurance Company (Durham, North Carolina); Supreme Life Insurance Company of America; Illinois/Service Federal Savings and Loan Association of Chicago; Sonicraft, Inc.; Universal Casket Company (Cassopolis, Michigan).

For full biographical listings, see the Martindale-Hubbell Law Directory

INDIANA

*INDIANAPOLIS,** Marion Co.

Baker & Daniels (AV)

300 North Meridian Street, 46204
Telephone: 317-237-0300
FAX: 317-237-1000
Fort Wayne, Indiana Office: 2400 Fort Wayne National Bank Building.
Telephone: 219-424-8000.
South Bend, Indiana Office: First Bank Building, 205 West Jefferson Boulevard.
Telephone: 219-234-4149.
Elkhart, Indiana Office: 301 South Main Street, Suite 307,
Telephone: 219-296-6000.
Washington, D.C. Office: 1701 K Street, N.W., Suite 400.
Telephone: 202-785-1565.

MEMBERS OF FIRM

Theodore J. Esping
David Lawther Johnson
Thomas A. Pitman
Jill Harris Tanner
Richard C. Starkey

ASSOCIATES

Robert M. Bond
Thomas C. Froehle Jr.
Amy E. Kosnoff

Representative Clients: Associated Insurance Companies, Inc.; Bank One, Indianapolis, N.A.; Borg-Warner Corp.; City of Indianapolis; Cummins Engine Co.; Eli Lilly and Company; General Motors Corp.; Indiana Bell; Indianapolis Public Schools; United Airlines.

For Complete List of Firm Personnel, See General Section

For full biographical listings, see the Martindale-Hubbell Law Directory

Bose McKinney & Evans (AV)

2700 First Indiana Plaza, 135 North Pennsylvania Street, 46204
Telephone: 317-684-5000
Facsimile: 317-684-5173
Indianapolis North Office: Suite 1201, 8888 Keystone Crossing, 46240.
Telephone: 317-574-3700.
Facsimile: 317-574-3716.

MEMBERS OF FIRM

Lewis C. Bose
Thomas M. Johnston
David A. Travelstead
Ronald M. Soskin
L. Parvin Price
Jon M. Bailey
Karl R. Sturbaum
Roderick H. Morgan

Representative Clients: Indiana Health Facilities; Financing Authority; Metropolitan School District of Wayne Township, Marion County, Indiana; Metropolitan School District of Lawrence Township; Kemper Securities, Inc.; Gibson County Water District; DeKalb County Jail Building Corp.; The Indianapolis Bond Bank, Local Public Improvement; Hendricks County; Avon Community Schools; The Indiana Bond Bank.

For Complete List of Firm Personnel, See General Section

For full biographical listings, see the Martindale-Hubbell Law Directory

Ice Miller Donadio & Ryan (AV)

One American Square Box 82001, 46282-0002
Telephone: 317-236-2100
Fax: 317-236-2219

MEMBERS OF FIRM

Bruce A. Polizotto
Terry A. M. Mumford
Philip C. Genetos
James A. Shanahan
Jeffrey O. Lewis
Thomas K. Downs
Brenda S. Horn
Todd W. Ponder
Lucy A. Emison
Thomas W. Peterson
Patricia A. Zelmer

OF COUNSEL

William P. Diener
James B. Burroughs
Karen Little Arland

ASSOCIATES

Bette J. Dodd
Jane Neuhauser Herndon
Elizabeth P. Rippy
Robert A. Anderson
Christopher J. Franzmann
Michael J. Melliere
Charles A. Compton

Counsel for: Indiana University; Purdue University; Indiana Bond Bank; Indiana Municipal Power Agency; Indiana Housing Finance Authority; Indiana Health Facility Financing Authority; Indiana Development Finance Authority; Citizens Gas & Coke Utility; Indianapolis International Airport Authority.

For Complete List of Firm Personnel, See General Section

For full biographical listings, see the Martindale-Hubbell Law Directory

*NOBLESVILLE,** Hamilton Co.

CHURCH, CHURCH, HITTLE & ANTRIM (AV)

938 Conner Street, P.O. Box 10, 46060-0010
Telephone: 317-773-2190
Telecopier: 317-773-5320

MEMBERS OF FIRM

Manson E. Church
Douglas D. Church
Jack G. Hittle
J. Michael Antrim
Martin E. Risacher
Bruce M. Bittner

ASSOCIATES

Brian J. Zaiger
David Joseph Barker
Leslie Craig Henderzahs

OF COUNSEL

Gary D. Beerbower

Representative Clients: Noblesville Schools; Westfield-Washington Schools; Indiana School Finance Corp.; Community Bank; Metrobank; Towns of Westfield, Fishers and Noblesville; Reynolds Farm Equipment Co.; Weihe Engineering.

For full biographical listings, see the Martindale-Hubbell Law Directory

IOWA

*DES MOINES,** Polk Co.

AHLERS, COONEY, DORWEILER, HAYNIE, SMITH & ALLBEE, P.C. (AV)

100 Court Avenue, Suite 600, 50309-2231
Telephone: 515-243-7611
Fax: 515-243-2149

Philip J. Dorweiler
Kenneth H. Haynie
John F. McKinney, Jr.
Edgar H. Bittle
Lance A. Coppock
William J. Noth
Linda L. Kniep
Ivan T. Webber

Carole A. Tillotson

Representative Clients: Cities of Cedar Rapids, Council Bluffs, Des Moines, Dubuque, Iowa City, Mason City and Sioux City, Iowa; Dain Bosworth, Inc.; Drake University; Iowa Department of National Resources; Iowa Finance Authority; Iowa School Cash Program; Iowa State Board of Regents; Iowa Western Community College; John Nuveen & Co. Inc.; Kirkwood Community College.

For Complete List of Firm Personnel, See General Section

For full biographical listings, see the Martindale-Hubbell Law Directory

KANSAS

*WICHITA,** Sedgwick Co.

HINKLE, EBERHART & ELKOURI, L.L.C. (AV)

Suite 2000 Epic Center, 301 North Main Street, 67202
Telephone: 316-267-2000
Fax: 316-264-1518

Winton M. Hinkle
John E. Caton
Thomas R. Powell

J. T. Klaus
L. Dale Ward
Kim A. Bell

Representative Clients: City of Wichita, Kansas; Wichita Public Schools; Wichita Public Building Commission; Sedgwick County, Kansas; Kansas Development Finance Authority.

For Complete List of Firm Personnel, See General Section

For full biographical listings, see the Martindale-Hubbell Law Directory

KENTUCKY

*BOWLING GREEN,** Warren Co.

ENGLISH, LUCAS, PRIEST & OWSLEY (AV)

1101 College Street, P.O. Box 770, 42102-0770
Telephone: 502-781-6500
Telecopier: 502-782-7782

(See Next Column)

MEMBERS OF FIRM

Whayne C. Priest, Jr.
Keith M. Carwell

For Complete List of Firm Personnel, See General Section

For full biographical listings, see the Martindale-Hubbell Law Directory

*LEXINGTON,** Fayette Co.

STOLL, KEENON & PARK (AV)

201 E. Main Street, Suite 1000, 40507-1380
Telephone: 606-231-3000
Telecopier: 606-253-1093; 606-253-1027
Frankfort, Kentucky Office: 326 West Main Street.
Telephone: 502-875-6000.
Telecopier: 502-875-6008.
Louisville, Kentucky Office: 400 West Market Street, Suite 2650, 40202.
Telephone: 502-568-9100.
Telecopier: 502-568-6340.

MEMBERS OF FIRM

Gary L. Stage
Douglas P. Romaine
J. David Smith, Jr.

Representative Clients: Bank One, Lexington, NA; Kentucky Association of Counties; Smith Barney, Harris Upham & Co. Inc.

For Complete List of Firm Personnel, See General Section

For full biographical listings, see the Martindale-Hubbell Law Directory

*LOUISVILLE,** Jefferson Co.

HARPER, FERGUSON & DAVIS (AV)

1730 Meidinger Tower, 40202
Telephone: 502-582-3871
Telecopier: 502-582-3905

MEMBERS OF FIRM

Spencer E. Harper, Jr.
William W. Davis

OF COUNSEL

Jo M. Ferguson (Retired)

Representative Clients: Kentucky Housing Corp.; Kentucky Higher Education Student Loan Corp.; Cities of Louisville and Covington; Kenton County Airport Board (Cincinnati/No. Kentucky International Airport); Regional Airport Authority of Louisville and Jefferson County; Toyota Motor Mfg., U.S.A., Inc.; Scott Paper Company; Delta Air Lines, Inc.; Kentucky Utilities Co.; Louisville Gas & Electric Co.; Baptist Healthcare System, Inc.

For full biographical listings, see the Martindale-Hubbell Law Directory

OGDEN NEWELL & WELCH (AV)

1200 One Riverfront Plaza, 40202-2973
Telephone: 502-582-1601
Fax: 502-581-9564

MEMBERS OF FIRM

Richard F. Newell
James S. Welch
Ernest W. Williams
Robert E. Thieman
James B. Martin, Jr.
Lisa Ann Vogt

ASSOCIATES

John Wade Hendricks
Thomas E. Rutledge

Counsel for: KU Energy Corp.; Kentucky Utilities Co.; Brown-Forman Corp.; B.F. Goodrich Co.; Brown & Williamson Tobacco Corp.; J.J.B. Hilliard, W.L. Lyons, Inc.; Interlock Industries, Inc.; Akzo Coatings, Inc.; United Medical Corp.; Bank of Louisville.

For Complete List of Firm Personnel, See General Section

For full biographical listings, see the Martindale-Hubbell Law Directory

RUBIN HAYS & FOLEY (AV)

First Trust Centre 200 South Fifth Street, 40202
Telephone: 502-569-7550
Telecopier: 502-569-7555

MEMBERS OF FIRM

Wm. Carl Fust
Harry Lee Meyer
David W. Gray
Irvin D. Foley
Joseph R. Gathright, Jr.
Lisa Koch Bryant
Sharon C. Hardy
Charles S. Musson
W. Randall Jones
K. Gail Russell

ASSOCIATE

Christian L. Juckett

OF COUNSEL

James E. Fahey
Newman T. Guthrie

Representative Clients: J.C. Bradford & Co., Inc.; J.J.B. Hilliard, W.L. Lyons, Inc.; Huntington National Bank; Liberty National Bank and Trust Company; National City Bank; PNC Bank; Prudential Bache & Co., Inc.; Prudential Securities, Inc.; Society Bank; Stock Yards Bank and Trust Co.

For full biographical listings, see the Martindale-Hubbell Law Directory

Louisville—Continued

STITES & HARBISON (AV)

Formerly Stites, McElwain & Fowler and Harbison, Kessinger, Lisle & Bush
400 West Market Street, Suite 1800, 40202
Telephone: 502-587-3400
Frankfort, Kentucky Office: 421 West Main Street.
Telephone: 502-223-3477.
Lexington, Kentucky Office: 2300 Lexington Financial Center.
Telephone: 606-226-2300.
Jeffersonville, Indiana Office: 323 East Court Avenue.
Telephone: 812-282-7566.

MEMBERS OF FIRM

Robert W. Lanum (Jeffersonville, Indiana Office)
William H. Haden, Jr.
William E. Hellmann

Representative Clients: South Central Bell Telephone Co.; Glenmore Distilleries Co.; New York Life Insurance Co.; Chrysler Financial Corp.; ARCO Metals Co.; Aetna Life & Casualty Insurance Cos.; Illinois Central Railroad Co.

For Complete List of Firm Personnel, See General Section

For full biographical listings, see the Martindale-Hubbell Law Directory

LOUISIANA

*BATON ROUGE,** East Baton Rouge Parish

BREAZEALE, SACHSE & WILSON, L.L.P. (AV)

Twenty-Third Floor, One American Place, P.O. Box 3197, 70821-3197
Telephone: 504-387-4000
Fax: 504-387-5397
New Orleans, Louisiana Office: Place St. Charles, Suite 4214, 201 St. Charles Avenue.
Telephone: 504-582-1170.
Fax: 504-582-1164.

MEMBERS OF FIRM

Leonard R. Nachman, II
Richard D. Leibowitz

Counsel for: Hibernia National Bank; South Central Bell Telephone Co.; Allied-Signal Corp.; Reynolds Metal Co.; Illinois Central Railroad Co.; The Continental Insurance Cos.; Fireman's Fund American Group; Chicago Bridge & Iron Co.; Montgomery Ward & Co.

For Complete List of Firm Personnel, See General Section

For full biographical listings, see the Martindale-Hubbell Law Directory

*NEW ORLEANS,** Orleans Parish

THE GODFREY FIRM A PROFESSIONAL LAW CORPORATION (AV)

2500 Energy Centre, 1100 Poydras Street, 70163-2500
Telephone: 504-585-7538
Fax: 504-585-7535

Jarrell E. Godfrey, Jr.
Jacob S. Capraro
Glenn J. Reames
Paul F. Guarisco

For full biographical listings, see the Martindale-Hubbell Law Directory

MAINE

*BANGOR,** Penobscot Co.

EATON, PEABODY, BRADFORD & VEAGUE, P.A. (AV)

Fleet Center-Exchange Street, P.O. Box 1210, 04402-1210
Telephone: 207-947-0111
Telecopier: 207-942-3040
Augusta, Maine Office: 2 Central Plaza.
Telephone: 207-622-3747.
Telecopier: 207-622-9732.
Brunswick, Maine Office: 167 Park Row.
Telephone: 207-729-1144.
Telecopier: 207-729-1140.
Camden, Maine Office: 7-9 Washington Street.
Telephone: 207-236-3325.
Telecopier: 207-236-8611.
Dover-Foxcroft, Maine Office: 30 East Main Street.
Telephone: 207-564-8378.
Telecopier: 207-564-7059.

John W. Conti
Michael B. Trainor

A List of Representative Clients available upon request.

(See Next Column)

For Complete List of Firm Personnel, See General Section

For full biographical listings, see the Martindale-Hubbell Law Directory

*PORTLAND,** Cumberland Co.

PIERCE, ATWOOD, SCRIBNER, ALLEN, SMITH & LANCASTER (AV)

One Monument Square, 04101
Telephone: 207-773-6411
Fax: 207-773-3419
Augusta, Maine Office: 77 Winthrop Street.
Telephone: 207-622-6311.
Camden, Maine Office: 36 Chestnut Street, P.O. Box 780.
Telephone: 207-236-4333.

MEMBERS OF FIRM

Bruce A. Coggeshall
James B. Zimpritch
Christopher E. Howard

OF COUNSEL

Charles W. Allen

For Complete List of Firm Personnel, See General Section

For full biographical listings, see the Martindale-Hubbell Law Directory

PRETI, FLAHERTY, BELIVEAU & PACHIOS (AV)

443 Congress Street, P.O. Box 11410, 04104-7410
Telephone: 207-791-3000
Telecopier: 207-791-3111
Augusta, Maine Office: 45 Memorial Circle, P.O. Box 1058, 04332-1058.
Telephone: 207-623-5300.
Telecopier: 207-623-2914.
Rumford, Maine Office: 150 Congress Street, P.O. Drawer L, 04276-2035.
Telephone: 207-364-4593.
Telecopier: 207-369-9421.

MEMBERS OF FIRM

John J. Flaherty
Severin M. Beliveau (Augusta Office)
Michael J. Gentile (Augusta Office)
Richard H. Spencer, Jr.
Eric P. Stauffer
James C. Pitney, Jr. (Augusta Office)

ASSOCIATE

James E. Phipps

Representative Clients: Prudential Securities Incorporated; Kidder, Peabody & Co., Inc.; Paine Webber Incorporated; State of Maine; Town of Jay, Maine; A. G. Edwards, Inc.; Merrill Lynch & Co.; Chemical Securities Inc.; Goldman, Sachs & Co.

For Complete List of Firm Personnel, See General Section

For full biographical listings, see the Martindale-Hubbell Law Directory

MARYLAND

*BALTIMORE,** (Independent City)

MILES & STOCKBRIDGE, A PROFESSIONAL CORPORATION (AV)

10 Light Street, 21202-1487
Telephone: 410-727-6464
Telecopier: 385-3700
Towson, Maryland Office: 600 Washington Avenue, Suite 300.
Telephone: 410-821-6565.
Telecopier: 823-8123.
Easton, Maryland Office: 101 Bay Street.
Telephone: 410-822-5280.
Telecopier: 822-5450.
Cambridge, Maryland Office: 300 Academy Street.
Telephone: 410-228-4545.
Telecopier: 228-5652.
Rockville, Maryland Office: 22 West Jefferson Street.
Telephone: 301-762-1600.
Telecopier: 762-0363.
Frederick, Maryland Office: 30 West Patrick Street.
Telephone: 301-662-5155.
Telecopier: 662-3647.
Washington, D.C. Office: 1450 G. Street, N.W., Suite 445.
Telephone: 202-737-9600.
Telecopier: 737-0097.
Fairfax, Virginia Office: Fair Oaks Plaza, 11350 Random Hills Road.
Telephone: 703-273-2440.
Telecopier: 273-4446.

James C. Doub
Robert L. Doory, Jr.
Harold Altscher
John A. Stalfort
Katherine L. Bishop
Patrick K. Arey

(See Next Column)

MILES & STOCKBRIDGE A PROFESSIONAL CORPORATION, *Baltimore—Continued*

Theodore A. Shields John R. Devine

Representative Clients: Maryland National Bank; Lloyd's of London; The Black & Decker Corp.; Aetna Life & Casualty Co.; Martin Marietta Corp.; Employers Mutual Casualty Co.; Transcontinental Gas Pipeline Corp.; Westinghouse Electric Corp.; Crum & Forster Group; NationsBank Corporation.

For Complete List of Firm Personnel, See General Section

For full biographical listings, see the Martindale-Hubbell Law Directory

PIPER & MARBURY (AV)

Charles Center South, 36 South Charles Street, 21201-3010
Telephone: 410-539-2530
FAX: 410-539-0489
Washington, D.C. Office: 1200 Nineteenth Street, N.W., 20036-2430.
Telephone: 202-861-3900.
FAX: 202-223-2085.
Easton, Maryland Office: 117 Bay Street, 21601-2703.
Telephone: 410-820-4460.
FAX: 410-820-4463.
Garrison, New York Office: Garrison Landing.
Telephone: 914-424-3711.
Fax: 914-424-3045.
New York, N.Y. Office: 31 West 52nd Street, 10019-6118.
Telephone: 212-261-2000.
FAX: 212-261-2001.
Philadelphia, Pennsylvania Office: Suite 1500, 2 Penn Center Plaza, 19102-1715.
Telephone: 215-656-3300.
FAX: 215-656-3301.
London, England Office: 14 Austin Friars, EC2N 2HE.
Telephone: 071-638-3833.
FAX: 071-638-1208.

MEMBERS OF FIRM

Donald P. McPherson, III
Francis X. Wright
Mark Pollak
Edward C. Sledge
Ronald B. Sheff
John P. Machen
Stewart K. Diana
Elizabeth A. McKennon
William L. Henn, Jr.
Paul A. Tiburzi
Paul D. Shelton
Kurt J. Fischer
James A. Gede, Jr.
Kristin H. R. Franceschi

OF COUNSEL

Edward Owen Clarke, Jr.

For Complete List of Firm Personnel, See General Section

For full biographical listings, see the Martindale-Hubbell Law Directory

VENABLE, BAETJER AND HOWARD (AV)

A Partnership including Professional Corporations
1800 Mercantile Bank & Trust Building, 2 Hopkins Plaza, 21201
Telephone: 410-244-7400
Washington, D.C. Office: Venable, Baetjer, Howard & Civiletti. Suite 1000, 1201 New York Avenue, N.W.
Telephone: 202-962-4800.
McLean, Virginia Office: Suite 400, 2010 Corporate Ridge.
Telephone: 703-760-1600.
Rockville, Maryland Office: Suite 500, One Church Street, P. O. Box 1906.
Telephone: 301-217-5600.
Towson, Maryland Office: 210 Allegheny Avenue, P. O. Box 5517.
Telephone: 410-494-6200.

MEMBERS OF FIRM

William J. McCarthy (P.C.)
Thomas P. Perkins, III (P.C.)
Lee M. Miller (P.C.)
Robert A. Shelton
Thomas J. Kenney, Jr. (P.C.) (Also at Washington, D.C. Office)
David J. Levenson (Not admitted in MD; Resident, Washington, D.C. Office)
Lars E. Anderson (Not admitted in MD; Resident, McLean, Virginia Office)
Joel Z. Silver (Not admitted in MD; Resident, Washington, D.C. Office)
Paul T. Glasgow (Resident, Rockville, Maryland Office)
Sondra Harans Block (Resident, Rockville, Maryland Office)
H. Russell Frisby, Jr.
Edward L. Wender (P.C.)
Mitchell Kolkin
Peter P. Parvis
Bruce H. Jurist (Also at Washington, D.C. Office)
Paul A. Serini (Also at Washington, D.C. Office)
James E. Cumbie

ASSOCIATE

Davis V. R. Sherman

For Complete List of Firm Personnel, See General Section

For full biographical listings, see the Martindale-Hubbell Law Directory

WHITEFORD, TAYLOR & PRESTON (AV)

7 Saint Paul Street, 21202-1626
Telephone: 410-347-8700
Telex: 5101012334
Fax: 410-752-7092
Towson, Maryland Office: 210 West Pennsylvania Avenue.
Telephone: 410-832-2000.
Washington, D.C. Office: 888 17th Street, N.W.
Telephone: 202-659-6800.

MEMBERS OF FIRM

Priscilla C. Caskey James C. Holman

For Complete List of Firm Personnel, See General Section

For full biographical listings, see the Martindale-Hubbell Law Directory

RIVERDALE, Prince Georges Co.

MEYERS, BILLINGSLEY, SHIPLEY, RODBELL & ROSENBAUM, P.A. (AV)

Suite 400 Berkshire Building, 6801 Kenilworth Avenue, 20737-1385
Telephone: 301-699-5800
Fax: 301-779-5746

Lance W. Billingsley Frederick Stichnoth

Reference: First National Bank of Maryland.

For Complete List of Firm Personnel, See General Section

For full biographical listings, see the Martindale-Hubbell Law Directory

SILVER SPRING, Montgomery Co.

ALEXANDER, GEBHARDT, APONTE & MARKS, L.L.C. (AV)

Lee Plaza-Suite 805, 8601 Georgia Avenue, 20910
Telephone: 301-589-2222
Facsimile: 301-589-2523
Washington, D.C. Office: 1314 Nineteenth Street, N.W., 20036.
Telephone: 202-835-1555.
New York, New York Office: 330 Madison Avenue, 36th Floor.
Telephone: 212-808-0008.
Fax: 212-599-1028.

Kenneth H. Marks, Jr. (Not admitted in MD)

Y. Kris Oh (Ms.) (Not admitted in MD)
Adrienne P. Byrd
Suzette Wynn Blackwell

Reference: Riggs National Bank of Washington, D.C.

For full biographical listings, see the Martindale-Hubbell Law Directory

*TOWSON,** Baltimore Co.

VENABLE, BAETJER AND HOWARD (AV)

A Partnership including Professional Corporations
210 Allegheny Avenue, P.O. Box 5517, 21204
Telephone: 410-494-6200
FAX: 410-821-0147
Baltimore, Maryland Office: 1800 Mercantile Bank & Trust Building, 2 Hopkins Plaza.
Telephone: 410-244-7400.
Washington, D.C. Office: Venable, Baetjer, Howard & Civiletti. Suite 1000, 1201 New York Avenue, N.W.
Telephone: 202-962-4800.
McLean, Virginia Office: Suite 400, 2010 Corporate Ridge.
Telephone: 703-760-1600.
Rockville, Maryland Office: Suite 500, One Church Street, P. O. Box 1906.
Telephone: 301-217-5600.

PARTNERS

John B. Howard
Cynthia M. Hahn
Robert A. Hoffman
Michael H. Davis

ASSOCIATE

G. Page Wingert

For Complete List of Firm Personnel, See General Section

For full biographical listings, see the Martindale-Hubbell Law Directory

MASSACHUSETTS

*BOSTON,** Suffolk Co.

BINGHAM, DANA & GOULD (AV)

150 Federal Street, 02110
Telephone: 617-951-8000
Cable Address: "Blodgham Bsn"
Telex: 275147 BDGBSN UR
Telecopy: 617-951-8736
Hartford, Connecticut Office: 100 Pearl Street.
Telephone: 203-244-3770.
Telecopy: 203-527-5188.
London, England Office: 39 Victoria Street, SWIH 0EE.
Telephone: 011-44-71-799-2646.
Telecopy: 011-44-71-799-2654.
Telex: 888179 BDGLDN G.
Cable Address: "Blodgham Ldn".
Washington, D.C. Office: 1550 M Street, N.W.
Telephone: 202-822-9320.
Telecopy: 202-833-1506.

MEMBERS OF FIRM

James N. Rice
James C. Stokes

OF COUNSEL

J. Patrick Dowdall

For Complete List of Firm Personnel, See General Section

For full biographical listings, see the Martindale-Hubbell Law Directory

GOODWIN, PROCTER & HOAR (AV)

A Partnership including Professional Corporations
Exchange Place, 02109-2881
Telephone: 617-570-1000
Cable Address: "Goodproct, Boston"
Telex: 94-0640
Telecopier: 617-523-1231
Washington, D.C. Office: 901 Fifteenth Street, N.W., Suite 410.
Telephone: 202-414-6160.
Telecopier: 202-789-1720.
Albany, New York Office: One Steuben Place.
Telephone: 518-472-9460.
Telecopier: 518-472-9472.

MEMBERS OF FIRM

Robert B. Fraser (P.C.)
Richard E. Floor (P.C.)
F. Beirne Lovely, Jr.
Edward Matson Sibble, Jr., (P.C.)

For Complete List of Firm Personnel, See General Section

For full biographical listings, see the Martindale-Hubbell Law Directory

MINTZ, LEVIN, COHN, FERRIS, GLOVSKY AND POPEO, P.C. (AV)

One Financial Center, 02111
Telephone: 617-542-6000
FAX: 617-542-2241
Washington, D.C. Office: 701 Pennsylvania Avenue, N.W. Suite 900.
Telephone: 202-434-7300.
Fax: 202-434-7400.

Francis X. Meaney
Gregory A. Sandomirsky
Maxwell D. Solet

Linda B. Port
Meghan B. Burke

For Complete List of Firm Personnel, See General Section

For full biographical listings, see the Martindale-Hubbell Law Directory

PALMER & DODGE (AV)

(Storey Thorndike Palmer & Dodge)
One Beacon Street, 02108
Telephone: 617-573-0100
Telecopier: 617-227-4420
Telex: 951104
Cable Address: "Storeydike," Boston

MEMBERS OF FIRM

Norman P. Cohen
Jean M. DeLuca
John G. Faria
Ruth E. Fitch
Robert H. Hale
Thomas W. Merrill
Walter J. St. Onge, III
John M. Thomas
Roger P. Vacco
Donald F. Winter

(See Next Column)

OF COUNSEL

James W. Perkins

For Complete List of Firm Personnel, See General Section

For full biographical listings, see the Martindale-Hubbell Law Directory

WARNER & STACKPOLE (AV)

75 State Street, 02109
Telephone: 617-951-9000
Cable Address: "Warstack"
Telecopier: 617-951-9151
Telex: 940139

MEMBERS OF FIRM

William B. Hetzel, Jr.
John C. Hutchins
Timothy B. Bancroft

COUNSEL

George E. Curtis

For Complete List of Firm Personnel, See General Section

For full biographical listings, see the Martindale-Hubbell Law Directory

MICHIGAN

BLOOMFIELD HILLS, Oakland Co.

HOWARD & HOWARD ATTORNEYS, P.C. (AV)

The Pinehurst Office Center, Suite 101, 1400 North Woodward Avenue, 48304-2856
Telephone: 810-645-1483
Telecopier: 810-645-1568
Kalamazoo, Michigan Office: The Kalamazoo Building, Suite 400, 107 West Michigan Avenue.
Telephone: 616-382-1483.
Telecopier: 616-382-1568.
Lansing, Michigan Office: The Phoenix Building, Suite 500, 222 Washington Square, North.
Telephone: 517-485-1483.
Telecopier: 517-485-1568.
Peoria, Illinois Office: Howard & Howard, P.C., The Creve Coeur Building, Suite 200, 321 Liberty Street.
Telephone: 309-672-1483.
Telecopier: 309-672-1568.

Gustaf R. Andreasen

Representative Clients: For Representative Client list, see General Practice, Bloomfield Hills, MI.

For Complete List of Firm Personnel, See General Section

For full biographical listings, see the Martindale-Hubbell Law Directory

*DETROIT,** Wayne Co.

BODMAN, LONGLEY & DAHLING (AV)

34th Floor 100 Renaissance Center, 48243
Telephone: 313-259-7777
Fax: 313-393-7579
Troy, Michigan Office: Suite 2020, 755 West Big Beaver Road.
Telephone: 810-362-2110.
Ann Arbor, Michigan Office: 110 Miller, Suite 300.
Telephone: 313-761-3780.
Northern Michigan Office: 229 Court Street, P.O. Box 405, Cheboygan.
Telephone: 616-627-4351.

MEMBERS OF FIRM

Herold McC. Deason
Joseph N. Brown
F. Thomas Lewand
Barbara Bowman Bluford
Christopher J. Dine (Troy Office)
Jerold Lax (Ann Arbor Office)
Patrick C. Cauley

Representative Clients: Abitibi Price Group; Archdiocese of Detroit; Comerica Bank; The Detroit Lions, Inc.; Ford Estates; General Motors Corporation; Charles Stewart Mott Foundation; Norfolk Southern Corporation; Panhandle Eastern Corporation; State Farm Mutual Automobile Insurance Company.

For Complete List of Firm Personnel, See General Section

For full biographical listings, see the Martindale-Hubbell Law Directory

BUTZEL LONG, A PROFESSIONAL CORPORATION (AV)

Suite 900, 150 West Jefferson, 48226
Telephone: 313-225-7000
Telecopier: 313-225-7080
Birmingham, Michigan Office: Suite 200, 32270 Telegraph Road.
Telephone: 810-258-1616.
Telecopier: 810-258-1439.

(See Next Column)

BUTZEL LONG A PROFESSIONAL CORPORATION, *Detroit—Continued*

Lansing, Michigan Office: 118 West Ottawa Street.
Telephone: 517-372-6622.
Telecopier: 517-372-6672.
Ann Arbor, Michigan Office: Suite 400, 121 West Washington.
Telephone: 313-995-3110.
Telecopier: 313-995-1777.
Grosse Pointe Farms, Michigan Office: Suite 260, 21 Kercheval.
Telephone: 313-886-5446.
Telecopier: 313-886-2114.

David W. Berry (Birmingham)
Carl Rashid, Jr.
Gordon J. Walker (Birmingham)
Brian P. Henry (Birmingham and Lansing)

Ronald E. Reynolds
Susan Klein Friedlaender (Birmingham)

Representative Clients: Bridgestone/Firestone, Inc.; The Detroit News, Inc.; Detroit Diesel Corp.; Kelly Services; Kelsey Hayes Co.; Merrill Lynch & Co., Inc.; Stroh Brewery Co.; Takata Corp.; United Parcel Services of America, Inc.; The University of Michigan.

For Complete List of Firm Personnel, See General Section

For full biographical listings, see the Martindale-Hubbell Law Directory

---

DICKINSON, WRIGHT, MOON, VAN DUSEN & FREEMAN (AV)

500 Woodward Avenue, Suite 4000, 48226-3425
Telephone: 313-223-3500
Facsimile: 313-223-3598
Bloomfield Hills, Michigan Office: 525 North Woodward Avenue, Suite 2000.
Telephone: 810-433-7200.
Facsimile: 810-433-7274.
Grand Rapids, Michigan Office: 200 Ottawa Avenue, N.W., Suite 900.
Telephone: 616-458-1300.
Facsimile: 616-458-6753.
Lansing, Michigan Office: Suite 200, 215 South Washington Square.
Telephone: 517-371-1730.
Facsimile: 517-487-4700.
Washington, D.C. Office: Suite 800, 1901 L Street, N.W.
Telephone: 202-457-0160.
Facsimile: 202-659-1559.
Chicago, Illinois Office: 225 West Washington, Suite 400.
Telephone: 312-220-0300.
Facsimile: 312-220-0021.
Warsaw, Poland Office: 46 Wilcza Street, 4th Floor, 00-679.
Telephone: (48-22) 299-241.
Facsimile: (48-2) 628-4107. Komertel Satellite Phone: (48-39) 121-510.

MEMBERS OF FIRM

Judson Werbelow (Lansing Office)
John A. Everhardus
Frank G. Pollock (Bloomfield Hills Office)
Terence M. Donnelly
James W. Bliss (Lansing Office)
David R. Bruegel (Bloomfield Hills Office)
Kester K. So (Lansing Office)
Thomas V. Yates
Paul M. Wyzgoski

CONSULTING PARTNER

Charles R. Moon

ASSOCIATES

Kirk E. Grable (Lansing Office)
Craig W. Hammond
Mark A. McDowell (Lansing Office)

Counsel for: State of Michigan and Authorities; Michigan Public Power Agency; City of Flint; City of Auburn Hills; City of Holland; City of Farmington Hills; County of Oakland; County of Genesee; County of Ottawa; Township of West Bloomfield.

For Complete List of Firm Personnel, See General Section

For full biographical listings, see the Martindale-Hubbell Law Directory

---

DYKEMA GOSSETT (AV)

400 Renaissance Center, 48243-1668
Telephone: 313-568-6800
Cable Address: "Dyke-Detroit"
Telex: 23-0121
Fax: 313-568-6594
Ann Arbor, Michigan Office: 315 East Eisenhower Parkway, Suite 100, 48108-3306.
Telephone: 313-747-7660.
Fax: 313-747-7696.
Bloomfield Hills, Michigan Office: 1577 North Woodward Avenue, Suite 300, 48304-2820.
Telephone: 810-540-0700.
Fax: 810-540-0763.
Grand Rapids, Michigan Office: 200 Oldtown Riverfront Building, 248 Louis Campau Promenade, N.W., 49503-2668.
Telephone: 616-776-7500.
Fax: 616-776-7573.
Lansing, Michigan Office: 800 Michigan National Tower, 48933-1707.
Telephone: 517-374-9100.
Fax: 517-374-9191.

(See Next Column)

Washington, D.C. Office: Franklin Square, Suite 300 West Tower, 1300 I Street, N.W., 20005-3306.
Telephone: 202-522-8600.
Fax: 202-522-8669.
Chicago, Illinois Office: Three First National Plaza, Suite 1400, 70 W. Madison, 60602-4270.
Telephone: 312-214-3380.
Fax: 312-214-3441.

MEMBERS OF FIRM

Bowden V. Brown (Resident at Bloomfield Hills Office)
John K. Cannon (Resident at Bloomfield Hills Office)
J. Theodore Everingham
Jane Forbes
James P. Kiefer (Resident at Lansing Office)
Robert L. Nelson (Resident at Grand Rapids Office)
Brian J. Page (Resident at Grand Rapids Office)
Brad S. Rutledge (Resident at Lansing Office)
Raynold A. Schmick (Resident at Ann Arbor Office)
Robert L. Schwartz (Resident at Bloomfield Hills Office)
Leamon R. Sowell, Jr.

ASSOCIATES

Ann D. Fillingham (Resident at Lansing Office)
Julia A. Goatley Moreno (Resident at Lansing Office)
Gina M. Torielli (Resident at Lansing Office)

For Complete List of Firm Personnel, See General Section

For full biographical listings, see the Martindale-Hubbell Law Directory

---

HONIGMAN MILLER SCHWARTZ AND COHN (AV)

A Partnership including Professional Corporations
2290 First National Building, 48226
Telephone: 313-256-7800
Telecopier: 313-962-0176
Telex: 235705
Lansing, Michigan Office: Phoenix Building, 222 North Washington Square, Suite 400.
Telephone: 517-484-8282.
West Palm Beach, Florida Office: Suite 800 Esperante Building, 222 Lakeview Avenue.
Telephone: 407-838-4500.
Tampa, Florida Office: 2700 Landmark Centre, 401 E. Jackson Street.
Telephone: 813-221-6600.
Orlando, Florida Office: 390 North Orange Avenue, Suite 1300.
Telephone: 407-648-0300.
Houston, Texas Office: 3100 First Interstate Bank Plaza, 1000 Louisiana.
Telephone: 713-650-2600.
Los Angeles, California Office: McNeill Plaza, Suite 820, 15260 Ventura Boulevard, 91403.
Telephone: 818-784-2900.

MEMBERS OF FIRM

Maurice S. Binkow
William M. Cassetta
Carl W. Herstein
John M. Kamins
Stuart M. Lockman
David K. Page
G. Scott Romney
Samuel T. Stahl

RESIDENT IN TAMPA, FLORIDA OFFICE

MEMBER

Brad M. Tomtishen (P.A.)

RESIDENT IN ORLANDO, FLORIDA OFFICE

MEMBERS

Thomas F. Lang (P.A.)
Brad M. Tomtishen (P.A.)

Representative Clients: Michigan State Hospital Finance Authority; City of Plymouth, Michigan; Lapeer County, Michigan; School Board of Orange County, Florida; Orange County Housing Finance Authority; PaineWebber Incorporated; Morgan Stanley & Company, Inc.; William R. Hough & Co.; Dillon, Read & Co., Inc.; Roney & Co.

For Complete List of Firm Personnel, See General Section

For full biographical listings, see the Martindale-Hubbell Law Directory

---

JAFFE, RAITT, HEUER & WEISS, PROFESSIONAL CORPORATION (AV)

One Woodward Avenue, Suite 2400, 48226
Telephone: 313-961-8380
Telecopier: 313-961-8358
Cable Address: "Jafsni"
Southfield,Michigan Office: Travelers Tower, Suite 1520.
Telephone: 313-961-8380.
Monroe, Michigan Office: 212 East Front Street, Suite 3.
Telephone: 313-241-6470.
Telefacsimile: 313-241-3849.

Gail A. Anderson
Robert S. Bolton
Gary R. Glenn
Robert J. Gordon
Larry K. Griffis
Ralph R. Margulis
Lawrence C. Patrick, Jr.
David H. Raitt
Stephen G. Schafer
Susan M. Sutton

See General Practice Section for List of Representative Clients.

(See Next Column)

JAFFE, RAITT, HEUER & WEISS PROFESSIONAL CORPORATION—*Continued*

For Complete List of Firm Personnel, See General Section

For full biographical listings, see the Martindale-Hubbell Law Directory

LEWIS, WHITE & CLAY, A PROFESSIONAL CORPORATION (AV)

1300 First National Building, 660 Woodward Avenue, 48226-3531
Telephone: 313-961-2550
Washington, D.C. Office: 1250 Connecticut Avenue, N.W., Suite 630, 20036.
Telephone: 202-835-0616.
Fax: 202-833-3316.

David Baker Lewis
Richard Thomas White
Eric Lee Clay
Reuben A. Munday
Ulysses Whittaker Boykin
S. Allen Early, III
Carl F. Stafford
Helen Francine Strong
Derrick P. Mayes
Frank E. Barbee
Camille Stearns Miller
Melvin J. Hollowell, Jr.
Michael T. Raymond
Jacqueline H. Sellers
Thomas R. Paxton
Kathleen Miles (Resident, Washington, D.C. Office)
David N. Zacks

Karen Kendrick Brown (Resident, Washington, D.C. Office)
J. Taylor Teasdale
Wade Harper McCree
Tyrone A. Powell
Blair A. Person
Susan D. Hoffman
Stephon E. Johnson
John J. Walsh
Andrea L. Powell
Teresa N. Gueyser
Hans J. Massaquoi, Jr.
Werten F. W. Bellamy, Jr. (Resident, Washington, D.C. Office)
Akin O. Akindele
Regina P. Freelon-Solomon
Calita L. Elston
Nancy C. Borland
Terrence Randall Haugabook
Lynn R. Westfall
Lance W. Mason

OF COUNSEL

Otis M. Smith (1922-1994)
Inez Smith Reid (Resident, Washington, D.C. Office)

Representative Clients: Omnicare Health Plan; Aetna Life & Casualty Co.; Chrysler Motors Corp.; Chrysler Financial Corp.; MCI Communications Corp.; City of Detroit; City of Detroit Building Authority; City of Detroit Downtown Development Authority; Consolidated Rail Corp. (Conrail); Equitable Life Assurance Society of the United States.

For full biographical listings, see the Martindale-Hubbell Law Directory

MILLER, CANFIELD, PADDOCK AND STONE, P.L.C. (AV)

A Professional Limited Liability Company
Founded in 1852 by Sidney Davy Miller
150 West Jefferson, Suite 2500, 48226-4415
Telephone: 313-963-6420
Fax: 313-496-7500
Cable Address: "Stem Detroit"
Detroit, Michigan Office: 150 West Jefferson, Suite 2500, 48226-4415.
Telephone: 313-963-6420.
Fax: 313-496-7500.
Cable Address: "Stem Detroit."
Ann Arbor, Michigan Office: 101 North Main Street, 7th Floor, 48104-1400.
Telephone: 313-663-2445.
Fax: 313-747-7147.
Bloomfield Hills, Michigan Office: Suite 100, Pinehurst Office Center, 1400 North Woodward, 48303-2014.
Telephone: 313-645-5000.
Fax: 313-645-1917.
Grand Rapids, Michigan Office: 1200 Campau Square Plaza, 99 Monroe, N.W., 49503-2639.
Telephone: 616-454-8656.
Fax: 616-776-6322.
Howell, Michigan Office: 121 South Barnard Street, Suite 4, 48843-2305.
Telephone: 517-546-7600.
Telecopier: 517-546-6974.
Kalamazoo, Michigan Office: 444 West Michigan Avenue, 49007-3752.
Telephone: 616-381-7030.
Fax: 616-382-0244.
Lansing, Michigan Office: One Michigan Avenue, Suite 900, 48933-1609.
Telephone: 517-487-2070.
Fax: 517-374-6304.
Monroe, Michigan Office: The Executive Centre, 214 East Elm Avenue, 48161-2682.
Telephone: 313-243-2000.
Fax: 313-243-0901.
Washington, D.C. Office: 1225 Nineteenth Street, N.W., Suite 400. 20036.
Telephone: 202-429-5575; 785-0600.
Fax: 202-331-1118; 785-1234.
Pensacola, Florida Office: 25 West Cedar, 32501.
Telephone: 904-469-1088.
Fax: 904-432-0677.
St. Petersburg, Florida Office: 100 Second Avenue S., Suite 7045, 33701.
Telephone: 813-982-6000.
Fax: 813-892-6002.

(See Next Column)

Gdansk, Poland Office: Suite 322, Dom Technika Building, Ul. Rajska 6, 80-850.
Telephone: 011-485-831-2808.
Fax: 011-485-831-4719.
Warsaw, Poland Office: Ul. Marszalkowska 82, Suite 561, 00-517.
Telephone: 011-482-623-6457 and 6458.
Fax: 011-482-623-6459.

MEMBERS OF FIRM

Robert E. Hammell
Joel L. Piell
Robert E. Gilbert (Ann Arbor Office)
George T. Stevenson
Charles L. Burleigh, Jr.
Dennis R. Neiman
William J. Danhof (Lansing Office)
Jerry T. Rupley
Thomas W. Linn
Donald W. Keim
Christopher J. Dembowski (Lansing Office)
Gary A. Bruder (Ann Arbor Office)
Amanda Van Dusen
Cynthia B. Faulhaber
Michael L. Lencione
Harold W. Bulger, Jr.
Michael P. McGee
Richard A. Walawender

OF COUNSEL

Stratton S. Brown
Richard B. Gushée
Richard I. Lott (Pensacola, Florida Office)

ASSOCIATES

Janet R. Chrzanowski
Amy S. Davis
Patrick F. McGow

Representative Firm Clients: Chrysler Corp.; Comerica, Inc.; City of Detroit, Mich.; Detroit Tigers, Inc.; First of Michigan; Fretter, Inc.; Ford Motor Co.; Ford Motor Credit Co.; Great Lakes Bancorp; Henry Ford Hospital.

For Complete List of Firm Personnel, See General Section

For full biographical listings, see the Martindale-Hubbell Law Directory

*GRAND RAPIDS,** Kent Co.

CLARY, NANTZ, WOOD, HOFFIUS, RANKIN & COOPER (AV)

500 Calder Plaza, 250 Monroe Avenue, N.W., 49503-2244
Telephone: 616-459-9487
Telecopier: 616-459-5121

MEMBERS OF FIRM

Robert P. Cooper
Richard A. Wendt
Scott G. Smith

Representative Clients: City of Cadillac; Hesperia Community Schools; Economic Development Corporation of Grand Rapids; City of Grand Rapids; City of Greenville; City of Coopersville; City of Lowell; Michigan Job Development Authority; City of Kentwood; Michigan Municipal Bond Authority.

For Complete List of Firm Personnel, See General Section

For full biographical listings, see the Martindale-Hubbell Law Directory

VARNUM, RIDDERING, SCHMIDT & HOWLETT (AV)

Bridgewater Place, P.O. Box 352, 49501-0352
Telephone: 616-336-6000
800-262-0011
Facsimile: 616-336-7000
Telex: 1561593 VARN
Lansing, Michigan Office: The Victor Center, Suite 810, 210 North Washington Square, 48933.
Telephone: 517-482-6237.
Facsimile: 517-482-6937.
Kalamazoo, Michigan Office: 350 East Michigan Avenue, 49007.
Telephone: 616-382-2300.
Facsimile: 616-382-2382.
Grand Haven, Michigan Office: 321 Washington Street, P.O. Box 288, 49417.
Telephone: 616-846-7100.
Facsimile: 616-846-7101.
Battle Creek, Michigan Office: 4950 West Dickman Road, Suite B-1, 49015.
Telephone: 616-962-7144.
Detroit, Michigan Office: 440 East Congress, Fourth Floor, 48226.
Telephone: 313-961-1600.
Facsimile: 313-961-1636.

MEMBERS OF FIRM

Jon F. DeWitt
Jeffrey L. Schad
John W. Pestle
Randall W. Kraker
Susan M. Wyngaarden

Counsel for: City of Evart Local Development Finance Authority; City of Grandville; City of Plainwell Tax Increment Finance Authority; City of Walker; City of Walker Downtown Development Authority; Charter Township of Grand Rapids Economic Development Corp.; County of Kent; Kent County Building Authority; Newaygo Public Schools; Township of Ada.

For Complete List of Firm Personnel, See General Section

For full biographical listings, see the Martindale-Hubbell Law Directory

GROSSE POINTE FARMS, Wayne Co.

JOHN R. AXE AND ASSOCIATES (AV)

Suite 360, 21 Kercheval Avenue, 48236
Telephone: 313-884-1550; 1-800-383-MFCI
Fax: 313-884-0626

ASSOCIATE

Peter S. Ecklund

OF COUNSEL

Robert P. Allen

References: First of America Bank.

For full biographical listings, see the Martindale-Hubbell Law Directory

MINNESOTA

*MINNEAPOLIS,** Hennepin Co.

LEONARD, STREET AND DEINARD, PROFESSIONAL ASSOCIATION (AV)

Suite 2300, 150 South Fifth Street, 55402
Telephone: 612-335-1500
Telecopier: 612-335-1657

Richard H. Martin
Robyn Hansen

Debra G. Strehlow
Tammie S. Ptacek
Steven J. Rindsig
John E. King

Representative Clients: Piper Jaffray, Inc.; Dougherty Dawkins; Miller & Schroeder Financial, Inc.

For Complete List of Firm Personnel, See General Section

For full biographical listings, see the Martindale-Hubbell Law Directory

O'CONNOR & HANNAN (AV)

3800 IDS Center, 80 South Eighth Street, 55402-2254
Telephone: 612-343-1200
Telecopy: 612-343-1256
Washington, D.C. Office: 1919 Pennsylvania Avenue, N.W., Suite 800.
Telephone: 202-887-1400.
Telecopy: 202-466-2198.

MEMBERS OF FIRM

Frederick W. Thomas (1911-1986)
William C. Kelly (1918-1970)
Patrick J. O'Connor
Joe A. Walters
Robert J. Tennessen
John S. Jagiela

OF COUNSEL

Michael E. McGuire

WASHINGTON, D.C. OFFICE

William T. Hannan (1911-1985)
John J. Flynn (1925-1990)
H. Robert Halper (1931-1988)
Patrick J. O'Connor
Edward W. Brooke *
Thomas H. Quinn *
David R. Melincoff *
Hope S. Foster *
Patrick E. O'Donnell *
Joseph H. Blatchford *
F. Gordon Lee *
George J. Mannina, Jr. *
John J. McDermott *
James W. Symington *
Donald R. Dinan *
Michael Colopy **
Thomas J. Schneider *
David L. Hill *
Thomas J. Corcoran **
Peter M. Kazon *
Christina W. Fleps *
Timothy W. Jenkins *
Gary C. Adler *
Wayne M. Zell *
J. Timothy O'Neill *
Mark R. Paoletta *
David L. Anderson *
Audrey P. Rasmussen *

Stephen C. Fogleman *
Elissa Garber Kon *
Craig A. Koenigs *

OF COUNSEL

David C. Treen *
E. William Crotty *
Charles R. McCarthy, Jr. *
William W. Nickerson *
H. George Schweitzer *

A List of Representative Clients will be furnished upon request.
*Not admitted in Minn.
**Non-Lawyer Partner

For full biographical listings, see the Martindale-Hubbell Law Directory

*ST. PAUL,** Ramsey Co.

BRIGGS AND MORGAN, PROFESSIONAL ASSOCIATION (AV)

2200 First National Bank Building, 55101
Telephone: 612-223-6600
Telecopier: 612-223-6450
Minneapolis, Minnesota Office: 2400 IDS Center, 80 South Eighth Street.
Telephone: 612-334-8400.
Telecopier: 612-334-8650.

RESIDENT PERSONNEL

Mary M. Dyrseth
Bernard P. Friel
Mary L. Ippel
James P. O'Meara
Peter S. Popovich
Peter H. Seed
Tony R. Stemberger

MINNEAPOLIS OFFICE

Brian G. Belisle
William T. Dolan
Trudy J. Halla
Andrew R. Kintzinger
David M. Lebedoff

For Complete List of Firm Personnel, See General Section

For full biographical listings, see the Martindale-Hubbell Law Directory

MISSISSIPPI

*JACKSON,** Hinds Co.

STENNETT, WILKINSON & PEDEN, A PROFESSIONAL ASSOCIATION (AV)

100 Congress Street South, P.O. Box 22627, 39225-2627
Telephone: 601-948-3000
Telefax: 601-948-3019

Gene A. Wilkinson
Derryl W. Peden

Representative Clients: State of Mississippi; Mississippi Hospital Equipment and Facilities Authority; The Mississippi Home Corporation; Gulfport Community Development Commission; Vicksburg Housing Authority; City of Clarksdale; Thorn, Alvis, Welch Investment Securities, Inc.; The Mitchell Company; Farm Credit Bank of Texas; Mississippi Bankers Association.

For Complete List of Firm Personnel, See General Section

For full biographical listings, see the Martindale-Hubbell Law Directory

MISSOURI

ST. LOUIS, (Independent City)

LEWIS, RICE & FINGERSH (AV)

A Partnership including Partnerships and Individuals
500 North Broadway, Suite 2000, 63102-2147
Telephone: 314-444-7600
Telecopier: 314-241-6056
Clayton, Missouri Office: Suite 400, 8182 Maryland Avenue.
Telephone: 314-444-7600.
Belleville, Illinois Office: 325 South High Street.
Telephone: 618-234-8636.
Hays, Kansas Office: 201 W. 11th St.
Telephone: 913-625-3997.
Leawood, Kansas Office: Suite 375, 8900 State Line.
Telephone: 913-381-8898.
Kansas City, Missouri Office: 1010 Walnut, Suite 500.
Telephone: 816-421-2500.

RESIDENT PARTNERS

Henry F. Luepke, Jr.
Joseph H. Weyhrich

For Complete List of Firm Personnel, See General Section

For full biographical listings, see the Martindale-Hubbell Law Directory

THOMPSON & MITCHELL (AV)

One Mercantile Center, Suite 3300, 63101
Telephone: 314-231-7676
Telecopier: 314-342-1717
Belleville, Illinois Office: 525 West Main Street.
Telephone: 618-277-4700; 314-271-1800.
Telecopier: 618-236-3434.
St. Charles, Missouri Office: 200 North Third Street.
Telephone: 314-946-7717.
Telecopier: 314-946-4938.
Washington, D.C. Office: 700 14th Street, N.W., Suite 900.
Telephone: 202-508-1000.
Telecopier: 202-508-1010.

(See Next Column)

THOMPSON & MITCHELL—*Continued*

MEMBERS OF FIRM

Michael F. Lause
Claire Halpern
Rhonda C. Thomas
Henry A. Bettendorf
Charles R. Saulsberry

ASSOCIATES

Sara E. Kotthoff
Steven B. Mitchell
Denette C. Kuhlman
Deborah K. Rush

ST. CHARLES, MISSOURI OFFICE

MEMBERS OF FIRM

Rollin J. Moerschel
Wm. Randolph Weber

Representative Clients: A. G. Edwards & Sons, Inc.; Bi-State Development Authority; Health and Educational Facilities Authority of the State of Missouri; Magna Banks; Mercantile Bancorporation Inc.; The Metropolitan St. Louis Sewer District; Regional Convention and Sports Complex Authority; St. Charles County, Missouri; Stifel Nicolaus & Co.; University of Missouri.

For Complete List of Firm Personnel, See General Section

For full biographical listings, see the Martindale-Hubbell Law Directory

MONTANA

*BILLINGS,** Yellowstone Co.

CROWLEY, HAUGHEY, HANSON, TOOLE & DIETRICH (AV)

500 Transwestern II, 490 North 31st Street, P.O. Box 2529, 59103
Telephone: 406-252-3441
Fax: 406-259-4159
Helena, Montana Office: IBM Building, 100 North Park Avenue, Suite 300, 59601.
Telephone: 406-449-4165.
Fax: 406-449-5149.

MEMBERS OF FIRM

Gareld F. Krieg
Terry B. Cosgrove
Michael S. Dockery

Representative Clients: Montana Power Co.; First Interstate Bank of Commerce; MDU Resources Group, Inc.; Chevron U.S.A., Inc.; Noranda Minerals Corp.; United Parcel Service.
Insurance Clients: Farmers Insurance Group; New York Life Insurance Co.

For Complete List of Firm Personnel, See General Section

For full biographical listings, see the Martindale-Hubbell Law Directory

NEVADA

*LAS VEGAS,** Clark Co.

ALVERSON, TAYLOR, MORTENSEN & NELSON (AV)

3821 W. Charleston Boulevard, 89102
Telephone: 702-384-7000
FAX: 702-385-7000

MEMBERS OF FIRM

J. Bruce Alverson
Erven T. Nelson
Eric K. Taylor
LeAnn Sanders
David J. Mortensen
David R. Clayson

ASSOCIATES

Milton J. Eichacker
Kenneth M. Marias
Douglas D. Gerrard
Jeffrey H. Ballin
Marie Ellerton
Jeffrey W. Daly
James H. Randall
Kenneth R. Ivory
Peter Dubowsky
Edward D. Boyack
Hayley B. Chambers
Sandra Smagac
Michael D. Stevenson
Jill M. Chase
Cookie Lea Olshein
Francis F. Lin

Representative Clients: The City of Las Vegas, Nevada; The County of Clark, Nevada; Clark County McCarran International Airport.

For full biographical listings, see the Martindale-Hubbell Law Directory

SWENDSEID & STERN (AV)

a member in Sherman & Howard L.L.C.
317 Sixth Street, 89101
Telephone: 702-387-6073
Telecopier: 702-382-9370
Reno, Nevada Office: 50 West Liberty Street, Suite 660, 89501.
Telephone: 702-323-1980.
Denver, Colorado Office: Sherman & Howard L.L.C., 633 Seventeenth Street, Suite 3000, 80202.
Telephone: 303-297-2900.

(See Next Column)

Colorado Springs, Colorado Office: Sherman & Howard L.L.C., Suite 1500, 90 South Cascade Avenue, 80903.
Telephone: 719-475-2440.

John O. Swendseid
Dee P. Wisor
Jennifer Stern
(Not admitted in NV)

Daniel J. Tangeman

Representative Clients: State of Nevada; Clark County; Clark County School District; Washoe County School District; University of Nevada System; Las Vegas Valley Water District; Clark County Sanitation District; Washoe County; Carson City; Douglas County; City of Las Vegas; City of Reno.
Reference: Bank of America Nevada.

For full biographical listings, see the Martindale-Hubbell Law Directory

*RENO,** Washoe Co.

SWENDSEID & STERN (AV)

a member in Sherman & Howard L.L.C.
50 West Liberty Street Suite 660, 89501
Telephone: 702-323-1980
Telecopier: 702-323-2339
Las Vegas, Nevada Office: 317 Sixth Street, 89101.
Telephone: 702-387-6073.
Denver, Colorado Office: Sherman & Howard L.L.C., 633 17th Street, Suite 3000, 80202.
Telephone: 303-297-2900.
Colorado Springs, Colorado Office: Sherman & Howard L.L.C., Suite 1500, 90 South Cascade Avenue, 80903.
Telephone: 719-475-2440.

John O. Swendseid
Jennifer Stern

Daniel J. Tangeman

Representative Clients: State of Nevada; Clark County; Clark County School District; Washoe County School District, University of Nevada System; Las Vegas Valley Water District; Clark County Sanitation District; Washoe County; Carson City; Douglas County; City of Las Vegas; City of Reno.
Reference: Bank of America Nevada.

For full biographical listings, see the Martindale-Hubbell Law Directory

NEW JERSEY

BAYONNE, Hudson Co.

FITZPATRICK & WATERMAN (AV)

90 West 40th Street, P.O. Box 1227, 07002
Telephone: 201-339-4000
1-800 BOND LAW
Secaucus, New Jersey Office: 400 Plaza Drive, 07096-3159.
Telephone: 201-865-9100.
Facsimile: 201-865-4805.

Harold F. Fitzpatrick

For full biographical listings, see the Martindale-Hubbell Law Directory

HAWTHORNE, Passaic Co.

JEFFER, HOPKINSON, VOGEL, COOMBER & PEIFFER (AV)

(Formerly Jeffer, Walter, Tierney, DeKorte, Hopkinson & Vogel)
Law Building, 1600 Route 208N, P.O. Box 507, 07507
Telephone: 201-423-0100
Fax: 201-423-5614
Tequesta, Florida Office: 250 Tequesta Drive.
Telephone: 407-747-6000.
Fax: 407-575-9167.
New York, N.Y. Office: Suite 2206, 150 Broadway.
Telephone: 212-406-7260.

MEMBERS OF FIRM

Herman M. Jeffer
Reginald F. Hopkinson
Jerome A. Vogel

Counsel for: Brioschi, Inc.; Opici Wine Co.; Gas Pumpers of America Corp.; Jupiter Tequesta National Bank; John Royle & Sons; Christian Health Care Center; Valley Hospital.

For Complete List of Firm Personnel, See General Section

For full biographical listings, see the Martindale-Hubbell Law Directory

*NEWARK,** Essex Co.

BATHGATE, WEGENER, DUGAN & WOLF, P.C. (AV)

Three Gateway Center, Fifteenth Floor, 07102
Telephone: 201-623-6663
Telecopier: 201-623-5464
Lakewood, New Jersey Office: One Airport Road, Lakewood, New Jersey 08701.
Telephone: 908-363-0666.
Telecopier: 908-363-9864.

Lawrence E. Bathgate, II

For Complete List of Firm Personnel, See General Section

For full biographical listings, see the Martindale-Hubbell Law Directory

MCCARTER & ENGLISH (AV)

Four Gateway Center, 100 Mulberry Street, P.O. Box 652, 07101-0652
Telephone: 201-622-4444
Telecopier: 201-624-7070
Cable Address: "McCarter" Newark
Cherry Hill, New Jersey Office: 1810 Chapel Avenue West.
Telephone: 609-662-8444.
Telecopier: 609-662-6203.
New York, New York Office: Suite 1519, One World Trade Center.
Telephone: 212-466-9018.
Telecopier: 212-432-6568.
Boca Raton, Florida Office: 2255 Glades Road, Suite 319-A.
Telephone: 407-994-6262.
Telecopier: 407-241-0798.
Wilmington, Delaware Office: Mellon Bank Center, 919 Market Street.
Telephone: 302-654-8010.
Telecopier: 302-654-0795.

MEMBERS OF FIRM

John J. Scally, Jr.
Jeffrey H. Aminoff (Resident Partner, New York, New York Office)
Scott A. Kobler
Stephen B. Pearlman
Jacqueline P. Shanes

COUNSEL

Gary Duescher

ASSOCIATES

Steven N. J. Wlodychak
Claudia J. Keefe
Deborah S. Verderame
Richard T. Nolan, Jr.
Francis A. Henry

For Complete List of Firm Personnel, See General Section

For full biographical listings, see the Martindale-Hubbell Law Directory

MCMANIMON & SCOTLAND (AV)

One Gateway Center, 18th Floor, 07102-5311
Telephone: 201-622-1800
Fax: 201-622-7333; 201-622-3744
Atlantic City, New Jersey Office: 26 South Pennsylvania Avenue.
Telephone: 609-347-0040.
Fax: 609-347-0866.
Trenton, New Jersey Office: 172 West State Street.
Telephone: 609-278-1800.
Fax: 609-278-9222.
Washington, D.C. Office: 1275 Pennsylvania Avenue, N.W.
Telephone: 202-638-3100.
Fax: 202-638-4222.

MEMBERS OF FIRM

Joseph P. Baumann, Jr.
Carla J. Brundage
John V. Cavaliere
Edward F. Clark
Christopher H. Falcon
Felicia L. Garland
James R. Gregory
John B. Hall
Thomas A. Hart, Jr. (Resident, Washington, D.C. Office)
Leah C. Healey
Ronald J. Ianoale
Andrea L. Kahn
Jeffrey G. Kramer
Michael A. Lampert
Joseph J. Maraziti, Jr.
Edward J. McManimon, III
Steven P. Natko
Martin C. Rothfelder
Steven Schaars (Resident, Washington, D.C. Office)
Glenn F. Scotland
Michael A. Walker

ASSOCIATES

Carl E. Ailara, Jr.
Diane Alexander-McCabe
Leslie G. London
Cheryl A. Maier
Daniel E. McManus
Sheryl L. Newman
Steven J. Reed
Erik F. Remmler
David J. Ruitenberg
Bradford M. Stern

OF COUNSEL

John R. Armstrong
Carl H. Fogler (Not admitted in NJ)

LEGAL SUPPORT PERSONNEL

Helen Lysaght

(See Next Column)

PARALEGALS

Jane Folmer
Zulmira Donahue

References: First Fidelity Bank, N.A., New Jersey; Midlantic National Bank.

For full biographical listings, see the Martindale-Hubbell Law Directory

ROBINSON, ST. JOHN & WAYNE (AV)

Two Penn Plaza East, 07105-2249
Telephone: 201-491-3300
Fax: 201-491-3333
Rochester, New York Office: Robinson, St. John & Curtin. First Federal Plaza.
Telephone: 716-262-6780.
Fax: 716-262-6755.
New York, New York Office: 245 Park Avenue.
Telephone: 212-953-0700.
Fax: 212-880-6555.

MEMBERS OF FIRM

Lee A. Albanese
Timothy R. Curtin (Resident at Rochester, New York Office)
Bernard S. Davis
Timothy R. McGill (Resident at Rochester, New York Office)
Bryan G. Petkanics (Resident at New York, New York Office)

For Complete List of Firm Personnel, See General Section

For full biographical listings, see the Martindale-Hubbell Law Directory

SILLS CUMMIS ZUCKERMAN RADIN TISCHMAN EPSTEIN & GROSS, A PROFESSIONAL CORPORATION (AV)

One Riverfront Plaza, 07102-5400
Telephone: 201-643-7000
Fax: 201-643-6500
Telex: 820630 Sillsbeck Nwk
Atlantic City, New Jersey Office: 17 Gordon's Alley.
Telephone: 609-344-2800.
New York, N.Y. Office: 250 Park Avenue.
Telephone: 212-643-7000.

Clive S. Cummis
Stephen J. Moses
Gerald Span
Cecil J. Banks
Alan E. Sherman
Jerry Genberg
William M. Russell

Glenn E. Davis

Representative Clients: County of Essex; Hudson County Improvement Authority; GAF Corp.; Jersey City Medical Center; U.S. Generating Co.; Six Flags Great Adventure; The Lefrak Organization; New Jersey Economic Development Authority; City of Newark; J.P. Morgan Securities, Inc.

For Complete List of Firm Personnel, See General Section

For full biographical listings, see the Martindale-Hubbell Law Directory

ROSELAND, Essex Co.

CARELLA, BYRNE, BAIN, GILFILLAN, CECCHI, STEWART & OLSTEIN, A PROFESSIONAL CORPORATION (AV)

Six Becker Farm Road, 07068-1739
Telephone: 201-994-1700
Telecopier: 201-994-1744
Lyndhurst, New Jersey Office: Carella, Byrne, Bain, Gilfillan, Cecchi, Stewart & Olstein. 37 Park Avenue.
Telephone: 201-935-6900;
Telecopier: 201-804-9414.

Herbert M. Rinaldi
Peter G. Stewart
Elliot M. Olstein
Arthur T. Vanderbilt, II
James T. Byers

Representative Clients: Passaic Valley Sewerage Commissioners, Newark, N.J.; NJ Educational Facilities Authority, Lawrenceville, N.J.; NJ Economic Development Authority, Trenton, N.J.; NJ Health Care Facilities Financing Authority, Trenton, N.J.; NJ Highway Authority, Woodbridge, N.J.

For Complete List of Firm Personnel, See General Section

For full biographical listings, see the Martindale-Hubbell Law Directory

WOLFF & SAMSON, P.A. (AV)

280 Corporate Center, 5 Becker Farm Road, 07068
Telephone: 201-740-0500
Fax: 201-740-1407

Arthur S. Goldstein
Daniel A. Schwartz
Morris Bienenfeld

Representative Clients: International Fidelity Insurance Co.; Celentano Brothers, Inc.; Chicago Title Insurance Co.; Hartz Mountain Industries; The Hillier Group; Foster Wheeler Corp.

For Complete List of Firm Personnel, See General Section

For full biographical listings, see the Martindale-Hubbell Law Directory

SECAUCUS, Hudson Co.

FITZPATRICK & WATERMAN (AV)

400 Plaza Drive, P.O. Box 3159, 07096-3159
Telephone: 201-865-9100
1-800 BOND LAW
Facsimile: 201-865-4805
Bayonne, New Jersey Office: 90 West 40th Street. 07002,
Telephone: 201339-4000; 1-800 BOND LAW.

Harold F. Fitzpatrick | Stephen P. Waterman

ASSOCIATES

James F. McDonough | Glenn C. Merritt
Jeanette M. Samra

OF COUNSEL

Andre Shramenko

For full biographical listings, see the Martindale-Hubbell Law Directory

*SOMERVILLE,** Somerset Co.

OZZARD WHARTON, A PROFESSIONAL PARTNERSHIP (AV)

75-77 North Bridge Street, P.O. Box 938, 08876
Telephone: 908-526-0700
Telecopier: 908-526-2246

William E. Ozzard

Ellen M. Gillespie | Suzette Nanovic Berrios

OF COUNSEL

Mark F. Strauss

Representative Clients: Somerset Raritan Valley Sewerage Authority; Somerset Pollution Control Financing Authority, Middlesex County, Township of Hillsborough, Borough of Raritan.

For Complete List of Firm Personnel, See General Section

For full biographical listings, see the Martindale-Hubbell Law Directory

WESTFIELD, Union Co.

LINDABURY, McCORMICK & ESTABROOK, A PROFESSIONAL CORPORATION (AV)

53 Cardinal Drive, P.O. Box 2369, 07091
Telephone: 908-233-6800
Fax: 908-233-5078

Richard R. Width | J. Ferd Convery III
Robert S. Burney

Representative Clients: A list of representative clients will be furnished upon request.

For Complete List of Firm Personnel, See General Section

For full biographical listings, see the Martindale-Hubbell Law Directory

WOODBRIDGE, Middlesex Co.

WILENTZ, GOLDMAN & SPITZER, A PROFESSIONAL CORPORATION (AV)

90 Woodbridge Center Drive Suite 900, Box 10, 07095
Telephone: 908-636-8000
Telecopier: 908-855-6117
Eatontown, New Jersey Office: Meridian Center I, Two Industrial Way West, 07724.
Telephone: 908-493-1000.
Telecopier: 908-493-8387.
New York, New York Office: Wall Street Plaza, 88 Pine Street, 9th Floor, 10005.
Telephone: 212-267-3091.
Telecopier: 212-267-3828.

Charles S. Zucker | Anthony J. Pannella, Jr.

Robert C. Kautz | Cheryl J. Oberdorf
Lisa A. Gorab

Representative Clients: Middlesex County Utilities Authority; City of New Brunswick; Middlesex County Improvement Authority; Borough of Lodi; Perth Amboy Board of Education; Southeast Morris County Municipal Utilities Authority; New Brunswick Housing Authority; City of South Amboy; New Brunswick Parking Authority.

For Complete List of Firm Personnel, See General Section

For full biographical listings, see the Martindale-Hubbell Law Directory

NEW YORK

*BINGHAMTON,** Broome Co.

HINMAN, HOWARD & KATTELL (AV)

700 Security Mutual Building, 80 Exchange Street, 13901
Telephone: 607-723-5341
Fax: 607-723-6605
Norwich, New York Office: 600 South Broad Street, Suite 200.
Telephone: 607-334-5896.
Fax: 607-336-6240.

COUNSEL

A. Edward Hill

MEMBER OF FIRM

M. Elizabeth Bradley

Representative Clients: First-City Division, Chase Lincoln First Bank, N.A.; Binghamton Savings Bank; International Business Machines Corp.; Universal Instruments Corp.; Security Mutual Life Insurance Company of New York; New York Telephone Co.; Travelers Insurance Co.; New York State Electric & Gas Corp.; Exxon Corp.; Columbia Gas System, Inc.

For Complete List of Firm Personnel, See General Section

For full biographical listings, see the Martindale-Hubbell Law Directory

*NEW YORK,** New York Co.

CAHILL GORDON & REINDEL (AV)

A Partnership including a Professional Corporation
(Cotton & Franklin)
80 Pine Street, 10005
Telephone: 212-701-3000
Cable Address: "Cottofrank New York"
Telex: (ATT) 127068 Cottofrank NYK; (MCI) 232184 CAGO UR
Facsimile: 212-269-5420
Confirmation: 212-701-3557
European Office: 19 rue Francois 1er, 75008, Paris, France.
Telephone: 33.1-47.20.10.50.
Facsimile: 33.1-47.23.06.38.
Telex: 842-642331; CGR 642331F.
Cable Address: "Cottofrank Paris."
District of Columbia Office: 1990 K Street, N.W., Washington, D.C., 20006.
Telephone: 202-862-8900.
Facsimile: 202-862-8958.
Cable Address: "Cottofrank Washington."

MEMBERS OF FIRM

Roger Andrus
Michael A. Becker
James J. Clark
Walter C. Cliff (P.C.)
Benjamin J. Cohen
W. Leslie Duffy
Bart Friedman
Ciro A. Gamboni
William B. Gannett
Stephen A. Greene
Robert M. Hallman
William M. Hartnett
Lawrence A. Kobrin
Immanuel Kohn
Jonathan I. Mark
Gerard M. Meistrell
Roger Meltzer
Clifford L. Michel
John P. Mitchell
Kenneth W. Orce
Richard J. Sabella
Jonathan A. Schaffzin
John J. Schuster
Gerald S. Tanenbaum
Robert Usadi
Gary W. Wolf
Daniel J. Zubkoff

SENIOR COUNSEL

Joseph P. Conway

For Complete List of Firm Personnel, See General Section

For full biographical listings, see the Martindale-Hubbell Law Directory

DEWEY BALLANTINE (AV)

1301 Avenue of the Americas, 10019-6092
Telephone: 212-259-8000
Cable Address: "Dewbalaw"
Telex: 12-6825
Facsimile: 212-259-6333
Washington, D.C. Office: 1775 Pennsylvania Avenue, N.W., 20006-4605.
Telephone: 202-862-1000.
Fax: 202-862-1093.
Los Angeles, California Office: 333 South Hope Street, 90071-1406.
Telephone: 213-626-3399.
Fax: 213-625-0562.
London, England Office: 150 Aldersgate Street, London EC1A 4EJ, England.
Telephone: 011-44-71-606-6121.
Fax: 011-44-71-600-3754.
Hong Kong Office: Asia Pacific Finance Tower, Suite 3907, Citibank Plaza, 3 Garden Road, Central, Hong Kong.
Telephone: 011-852-2509-7000.
Fax: 011-852-2509-7088.

(See Next Column)

DEWEY BALLANTINE, *New York—Continued*

Budapest, Hungary Office: Dewey Ballantine Theodore Goddard, Vadasz utca 31, H-1054 Budapest Hungary.
Telephone: (36-1) 111-9620.
Fax: (36-1) 112-2272.
Prague, Czech Republic Office: Dewey Ballantine Theodore Goddard, Revolucni 13, 110 00 Prague 1, Czech Republic.
Telephone: (42-2) 2481-0283.
Fax: (42-2) 231-0983.
Warsaw, Poland Office: Dewey Ballantine Theodore Goddard, ul. Klonowa 8, 00-591 Warsaw, Poland.
Telephone: 48-22-49-32-88.
Fax: 48-22-49-80-23.
Kraków, Poland Office: Dewey Ballantine Theodore Goddard, Pl. Axentowicza 6. 30-034 Kraków Poland.
Telephone: 48-12-340-339.
Fax: 48-12-333-624.

MEMBERS OF FIRM

Michael J. Close
C. Brooke Dormire
John G. Fritzinger, Jr.
E. Ann Gill
David M. Irwin
Frederick W. Kanner
Bernard E. Kury
Richard A. Stenberg

OF COUNSEL

Horace B. B. Robinson

For Complete List of Firm Personnel, See General Section

For full biographical listings, see the Martindale-Hubbell Law Directory

JONES, DAY, REAVIS & POGUE (AV)

599 Lexington Avenue, 10022
Telephone: 212-326-3939
Cable Address: "JONESDAY NEWYORK"
Telex: 237013 JDRP UR
Telecopier: 212-755-7306
In Atlanta, Georgia: 3500 One Peachtree Center, 303 Peachtree Street, N.E.
Telephone: 404-521-3939.
Cable Address: "Attorneys Atlanta".
Telex: 54-2711.
Telecopier: 404-581-8330.
In Brussels, Belgium: Avenue Louise 480, 7th Floor, B-1050 Brussels.
Telephone: 011-32-2-645-14-11.
Telecopier: 011-32-2-645-14-45.
In Chicago, Illinois: 77 West Wacker.
Telephone: 312-782-3939.
Telecopier: 312-782-8585.
In Cleveland, Ohio: North Point, 901 Lakeside Avenue.
Telephone: 216-586-3939.
Cable Address: "Attorneys Cleveland."
Telex: 980389.
Telecopier: 216-579-0212.
In Columbus, Ohio: 1900 Huntington Center.
Telephone: 614-469-3939.
Cable Address: "Attorneys Columbus."
Telecopier: 614-461-4198.
In Dallas, Texas: 2300 Trammell Crow Center, 2001 Ross Avenue.
Telephone: 214-220-3939.
Cable Address: "Attorneys Dallas."
Telex: 730852.
Telecopier: 214-969-5100.
In Frankfurt, Germany: Triton Haus, Bockenheimer Landstrasse 42, 60323 Frankfurt am Main.
Telephone: 49-69-9726-3939.
Telecopier: 49-69-9726-3993.
In Geneva, Switzerland: 20, rue de Candolle.
Telephone: 011-41-22-320-2339.
Telecopier: 011-41-22-320-1232.
In Hong Kong: 1501 One Exchange Square, 8 Connaught Place.
Telephone: 011-852-2526-6895.
Telecopier: 011-852-2810-5787.
In Irvine, California: 2603 Main Street, Suite 900.
Telephone: 714-851-3939.
Telex: 194911 Lawyers LSA.
Telecopier: 714-553-7539.
In London, England: One Mount Street.
Telephone: 011-44-71-493-9361.
Cable Address: "Surgoe London WI."
Telecopier: 011-44-71-493-9666.
In Los Angeles, California: 555 West Fifth Street, Suite 4600.
Telephone: 213-489-3939.
Telex: 181439 UD.
Telecopier: 213-243-2539.
In Paris, France: 62, rue du Faubourg Saint-Honore.
Telephone: 011-33-1-44-71-3939.
Cable Address: "Surgoe Paris."
Telex: 290156 Surgoe.
Telecopier: 011-33-1-49-24-0471.
In Pittsburgh, Pennsylvania: 500 Grant Street, 31st Floor.
Telephone: 412-391-3939.
Cable Address: "Attorneys Pittsburgh".
Telecopier: 412-394-7959.

(See Next Column)

In Riyadh, Saudi Arabia: Law Offices of Saud M.A. Shawwaf, P.O. Box 2700.
Telephones: 011 (966-1) 465-6543, 011 (966-1) 464-8534 or 011 (966-1) 464-8540.
Telex: 401831 SAUCON SJ.
Telecopier: (966-1) 464-8480.
In Taipei, Taiwan: 8th Floor, 2 Tun Hwa South Road, Section 2.
Telephone: 011 (886-2) 704-6808.
Telecopier: 011 (886-2) 704-6791.
In Tokyo, Japan: Toranomon MT Building, 4th Floor, 10-3, Toranomon 3-Chome, Minato-Ku, Tokyo 105, Japan.
Telephone: 011-81-3-3433-3939.
Telecopier: 011-81-3-5401-2725.
In Washington, D.C.: Metropolitan Square, 1450 G Street, N.W.
Telephone: 202-879-3939.
Cable Address: "Attorneys Washington."
Telex: 89-2410 ATTORNEYS WASH.
Telecopier: 202-737-2832.

MEMBERS OF FIRM IN NEW YORK

David M. Mahle
Donald F. Devine
William F. Henze, II
Dean M. Erger
Richard H. Sauer

OF COUNSEL

Linda L. D'Onofrio

ASSOCIATES

Andrew G. Kent
Torsten M. Marshall

For Complete List of Firm Personnel, See General Section

For full biographical listings, see the Martindale-Hubbell Law Directory

MUDGE ROSE GUTHRIE ALEXANDER & FERDON (AV)

(Mudge, Stern, Baldwin & Todd)
(Caldwell, Trimble & Mitchell)
180 Maiden Lane, 10038
Telephone: 212-510-7000
Cable Address: "Baltuchins, New York"
Telex: 127889 & 703729
Telecopier: 212-248-2655/57
Los Angeles, California Office: 21st Floor, 333 South Grand Avenue, 90071.
Telephone: 213-613-1112.
Telecopier: 213-680-1358.
Washington, D.C. Office: 2121 K Street, N.W., 20037.
Telephone: 202-429-9355.
Telecopier: 202-429-9367.
Telex: MRGA 440264.
Cable Address: "Baltuchins, Washington, DC"
West Palm Beach, Florida Office: Suite 900, 515 North Flagler Drive, 33401.
Telephone: 407-650-8100.
Telecopier: 407-833-1722.
Telex: 514847 MRWPB.
Parsippany, New Jersey Office: Morris Corporate Center Two, Building D, One Upper Pond Road, 07054-1075.
Telephone: 201-335-0004.
Telecopier: 201-402-1593.
European Office: 12, Rue de la Paix, 75002 Paris, France.
Telephone: 42.61.57.71.
Telecopier: 42.61.79.21.
Cable Address: "Baltuchins, Paris".
Tokyo, Japan Office: Infini Akasaka, 8-7-15 Akasaka, Minato-Ku, Tokyo 107, Japan.
Telephone: (03) 3423-3970.
Fax: (03) 3423-3971.

MEMBERS OF FIRM

Nathan Abramowitz
John G. Bove
Joseph J. Carroll
Martin J. Dockery
Robert E. Ferdon
F. Susan Gottlieb
Judah Gribetz
Michael J. Hannigan
Eugene W. Harper, Jr.
H. Sidney Holmes III
Stanford G. Ladner
Carl F. Lyon, Jr.
James P. Marlin
Arthur F. McMahon, Jr.
Craig M. Scully
Christopher M. Waterman
Neil T. Wolk

COUNSEL

Walter E. Breen
Edward W. Long (Resident Counsel, Los Angeles, California Office)

ASSOCIATES

Robert P. Coyne
David L. Dubrow
Stephanie L. Jones
James R. Levine
Pamela J. McNair
Virginia O'Connell
Stuart S. Poloner
Mark R. Pronk
Richard J. Reilly, Jr.
Timothy K. Saunders, Jr.
Brendan R. Sheehan
Robert R. Viducich
Lore E. Wall
Richard C. Wong

(See Next Column)

MUDGE ROSE GUTHRIE ALEXANDER & FERDON—*Continued*

PARSIPPANY, NEW JERSEY
RESIDENT COUNSEL

John T. Kelly

For Complete List of Firm Personnel, See General Section

For full biographical listings, see the Martindale-Hubbell Law Directory

---

SATTERLEE STEPHENS BURKE & BURKE (AV)

230 Park Avenue, 10169-0079
Telephone: 212-818-9200
Cable Address: "Saterfield," New York
Telex: 233437
Telecopy or Facsimile: (212) 818-9606 or 818-9607
Summit, New Jersey Office: 47 Maple Street.
Telephone: 908-277-2221.
Westfield, New Jersey Office: 105 Elm Street.
Telephone: 908-654-4200.

MEMBERS OF FIRM

Bernard M. Althoff
Dwight A. Kinsey

For Complete List of Firm Personnel, See General Section

For full biographical listings, see the Martindale-Hubbell Law Directory

---

SKADDEN, ARPS, SLATE, MEAGHER & FLOM (AV)

919 Third Avenue, 10022
Telephone: 212-735-3000
Telex: 645899 SKARSLAW
Fax: 212-735-2000; 212-735-2001
Boston, Massachusetts Office: One Beacon Street, 02108.
Telephone: 617-573-4800.
Fax: 617-573-4822.
Washington, D.C. Office: 1440 New York Avenue, N.W., 20005.
Telephone: 202-371-7000.
Fax: 202-393-5760.
Wilmington, Delaware Office: One Rodney Square, 19899.
Telephone: 302-651-3000.
Fax: 302-651-3001.
Los Angeles, California Office: 300 South Grand Avenue, 90071.
Telephone: 213-687-5000.
Fax: 213-687-5600.
Chicago, Illinois Office: 333 West Wacker Drive, 60606.
Telephone: 312-407-0700.
Fax: 312-407-0411.
San Francisco, California Office: Four Embarcadero Center, 94111.
Telephone: 415-984-6400.
Fax: 415-984-2698.
Houston, Texas Office: 1600 Smith Street, Suite 4460, 77002.
Telephone: 713-655-5100.
Fax: 713-655-5181.
Newark, New Jersey Office: One Riverfront Plaza, 07102.
Telephone: 201-596-4440.
Fax: 201-596-4444.
Tokyo, Japan Office: 12th Floor, The Fukoku Seimei Building, 2-2-2, Uchisaiwaicho, Chiyoda-ku, 100.
Telephone: 011-81-3-3595-3850.
Fax: 011-81-3-3504-2780.
London, England Office: 25 Bucklersbury EC4N 8DA.
Telephone: 011-44-71-248-9929.
Fax: 011-44-71-489-8533.
Hong Kong Office: 30/F Peregrine Tower, Lippo Centre, 89 Queensway, Central.
Telephone: 011-852-820-0700.
Fax: 011-852-820-0727.
Sydney, New South Wales, Australia Office: Level 26-State Bank Centre, 52 Martin Place, 2000.
Telephone: 011-61-2-224-6000.
Fax: 011-61-2-224-6044.
Toronto, Ontario Office: Suite 1820, North Tower, P.O. Box 189, Royal Bank Plaza, M5J 2J4.
Telephone: 416-777-4700.
Fax: 416-777-4747.
Paris, France Office: 105 rue du Faubourg Saint-Honoré, 75008.
Telephone: 011-33-1-40-75-44-44.
Fax: 011-33-1-49-53-09-99.
Brussels, Belgium Office: 523 avenue Louise, Box 30, 1050.
Telephone: 011-32-2-648-7666.
Fax: 011-32-2-640-3032.
Frankfurt, Germany Office: MesseTurm, 27th Floor, 60308.
Telephone: 011-49-69-9757-3000.
Fax: 011-49-69-9757-3050.
Beijing, China Office: 1605 Capital Mansion Tower, No. 6 Xin Yuan Nan Road, Chao Yang District, 100004.
Telephone: 011-86-1-466-8800.
Fax: 011-86-1-466-8822.
Budapest, Hungary Office: Mahart Building, H-1052 Apáczai Csere János u.11, Vl.em.
Telephone: 011-36-1-266-2145.
Fax: 011-36-1-266-4033.

(See Next Column)

Prague, Czech Republic Office: Revolucni 16, 110 00.
Telephone: 011-42-2-231-75-18.
Fax: 011-42-2-231-47-33.
Moscow, Russia Office: Pleteshkovsky Pereulok 1, 107005.
Telephone: 011-7-501-940-2304.
Fax: 011-7-501-940-2511.

MEMBER OF FIRM

Christopher J. Kell

SPECIAL COUNSEL

Barbara Mendel Mayden

CHICAGO, ILLINOIS OFFICE

PARTNER

Ronald J. Clapham

NEW YORK, N.Y. OFFICE
CHICAGO, ILLINOIS OFFICE
ASSOCIATES

Ronald J. Clapham
Marguerite M. Elias
Eric David Hargan

For Complete List of Firm Personnel, See General Section

For full biographical listings, see the Martindale-Hubbell Law Directory

---

SULLIVAN, DONOVAN, BOND & BONNER (AV)

A Partnership including a Professional Corporation
415 Madison Avenue, 10017
Telephone: 212-935-5100
Cable Address: "Navillus"
Telecopier: 935-5106
Albany, New York Office: 109 State Street, 12207.
Telephone: 518-434-1121.
Telecopier: 518-463-0815.
East Meadow, New York Office: 90 Merrick Avenue, 11554.
Telephone: 516-794-5454.
Telecopier: 516-296-7111.
Greenwich, Connecticut Office: 21 Benedict Place, 06830.
Telephone: 203-869-3553.
Telecopier: 203-625-0226.

MEMBERS OF FIRM

Cornelius J. Sullivan (1870-1932)
Gerald Donovan (1891-1987)
Edmond M. Hanrahan (1905-1979)
Richard P. Donovan
Kenneth W. Bond
Robert H. Carey
Thomas J. Bonner (P.C.)
James A. Moyer (Resident, East Meadow Office)
Thomas H. Bach
Lloyd N. Hull (Resident, Greenwich, Connecticut Office)

ASSOCIATES

John J. Mattras, Jr.
Gary E. Ireland

OF COUNSEL

Joseph G. Krassy
Robert A. Klipstein
John P. Dowling
Michael C. Magguilli (Resident, Albany Office)

For full biographical listings, see the Martindale-Hubbell Law Directory

---

WILLKIE FARR & GALLAGHER (AV)

One Citicorp Center, 153 East 53rd Street, 10022-4669
Telephone: 212-821-8000
Fax: 212-821-8111
Telex: RCA 233780-WFGUR; RCA 238805-WFGUR
Washington, D.C. Office: Three Lafayette Centre, 1155 21st Street, N.W., 6th Floor, 20036-3384.
Telephone: 202-328-8000.
Fax: 202-887-8979; 202-331-8187.
Telex: RCA 229800-WFGIG; WU 89-2762.
Paris, France Office: 6, Avenue Velasquez 75008.
Telephone: 011-33-1-44-35-44-35.
Fax: 011-331-42-89-87-01.
Telex: 652740-WFG Paris.
London, England Office: 3rd Floor, 35 Wilson Street, EC2M 2SJ.
Telephone: 011-44-71-696-9060.
Fax: 011-44-71-417-9191.

MEMBERS OF FIRM

Dennis R. Deveney
Robert M. Drillings
Alexander T. Galloway II
William E. Hiller
Peter J. Kenny
Leslie M. Mazza
Thomas M. Rothman
Richard C. Sammis
Brent W. White

For Complete List of Firm Personnel, See General Section

For full biographical listings, see the Martindale-Hubbell Law Directory

*SYRACUSE,** Onondaga Co.

BOND, SCHOENECK & KING (AV)

18th Floor One Lincoln Center, 13202-1355
Telephone: 315-422-0121
Fax: 315-422-3598
Albany, New York Office: 111 Washington Avenue.
Telephone: 518-462-7421.
Fax: 518-462-7441.
Boca Raton, Florida Office: 5355 Town Center Road, Suite 1002.
Telephone: 407-368-1212.
Fax: 407-338-9955.
Naples, Florida Office: 1167 Third Street South.
Telephone: 813-262-6812.
Fax: 813-262-6908.
Oswego, New York Office: 130 East Second Street.
Telephone: 315-343-9116.
Fax: 315-343-1231.
Overland Park, Kansas Office: 7500 College Boulevard, Suite 910.
Telephone: 913-345-8001.
Fax: 913-345-9017.

MEMBERS OF FIRM

John A. Beach (Resident, Albany Office)
Robert E. Moses
Anthony R. Pittarelli
Stephen L. Johnson
Richard D. Hole
Joseph Zagraniczny
Edwin J. Kelley, Jr.

ASSOCIATE

Steven J. Ford

General Counsel for: Syracuse University; Unity Mutual Life Insurance Co.; Manufacturers Association of Central New York.
Regional or Special Counsel for: Newhouse Broadcasting Corp. (WSYR, AM-FM); Syracuse Herald-Post Standard Newspapers.; Miller Brewing Co.; Allied Corp.; General Electric Co.; National Grange.

For Complete List of Firm Personnel, See General Section

For full biographical listings, see the Martindale-Hubbell Law Directory

HANCOCK & ESTABROOK (AV)

Mony Tower 1, P.O. Box 4976, 13221-4976
Telephone: 315-471-3151
Telecopier: 315-471-3167
Albany, New York Office: Suite 505, 125 Wolf Road.
Telephone: 518-458-7660.
Telecopier: 518-458-7731.

MEMBERS OF FIRM

Richard W. Cook
Gerald F. Stack
Jeffrey B. Andrus

General Counsel for: Marine Midland Bank, (Mid-State Region); Deanco.
Representative Clients: Anheuser-Busch, Inc.; Bristol Laboratories, Division of Bristol-Meyers Squibb; Mutual Benefit Life Insurance Co.; Hartford Insurance Group; Metropolitan Life Insurance Co.; Foremost Insurance Co.

For Complete List of Firm Personnel, See General Section

For full biographical listings, see the Martindale-Hubbell Law Directory

*WHITE PLAINS,** Westchester Co.

SMITH, RANSCHT, CONNORS, MUTINO, NORDELL & SIRIGNANO, P.C. (AV)

235 Main Street, 10601
Telephone: 914-946-8800
Telecopier: 914-946-8861
Cable Address: "Smiran" White Plains, New York
Greenwich, Connecticut Office: P.O. Box 4847, 06830-0605.
Telephone: 203-622-6660.

Peter T. Manos (1923-1991)
James P. Connors, Jr.
William F. Ranscht, Jr.
Peter J. Mutino
Michael Nordell
George A. Sirignano, Jr.

OF COUNSEL

Gary E. Bashian
James M. Pollock
Anthony J. Enea

Counsel for: The Corham Artificial Flower Co.; Universal Builders Supply, Inc.; Kalman Floor Co., Inc.; The Walter Karl Companies.

For full biographical listings, see the Martindale-Hubbell Law Directory

NORTH CAROLINA

*CHARLOTTE,** Mecklenburg Co.

SMITH HELMS MULLISS & MOORE, L.L.P. (AV)

227 North Tryon Street, P.O. Box 31247, 28231
Telephone: 704-343-2000
Telecopier: 704-334-8467
Telex: 572460
Greensboro, North Carolina Office: Smith Helms Mulliss & Moore, Suite 1400 First Union Tower, 300 North Greene Street, P.O. Box 21927.
Telephone: 910-378-5200.
Telecopier: 910-379-9558.
Raleigh, North Carolina Office: 316 West Edenton Street, P.O. Box 27525.
Telephone: 919-755-8700.
Telecopier: 919-828-7938.

COUNSEL

James H. Guterman

MEMBERS OF FIRM

R. Malloy McKeithen
Kenneth C. Day
Boyd C. Campbell, Jr.
J. Richard Hazlett
Charles F. Bowman
Stephen L. Cordell

ASSOCIATE

Melissa Garrett Burns

For Complete List of Firm Personnel, See General Section

For full biographical listings, see the Martindale-Hubbell Law Directory

WOMBLE CARLYLE SANDRIDGE & RICE (AV)

A Professional Limited Liability Company
3300 One First Union Center, 301 S. College Street, 28202-6025
Telephone: 704-331-4900
Telecopy: 704-331-4955
Telex: 853609
Winston-Salem, North Carolina Office: 1600 Southern National Financial Center.
Telephone: 919-721-3600.
Telecopy: 919-721-3660.
Telex: 806498.
Raleigh, North Carolina Office: 2100 First Union Capitol Center, 150 Fayetteville Street Mall, P.O. Box 831.
Telephone: 919-755-2100.
Telecopy: 919-755-2150.
Telex: 806498.
Atlanta, Georgia Office: One Ninety One Peachtree Tower, 191 Peachtree Street N.E., Suite 3250.
Telephone: 404-614-2580.
Fax: 404-614-2595.

MEMBERS OF FIRM

James R. Bryant, III
Joe B. Cogdell, Jr.

Representative Clients: Childress Klein Properties, Inc.; Food Lion, Inc.; Fieldcrest Cannon, Inc.; J.A. Jones Construction Company; Parkdale Mills, Inc.; Duke Power Company; Bowles Hollowell Conner & Company; ALLTEL Carolina, Inc.; Belk Store Services, Inc.; Philip Holzmann A.G.

For Complete List of Firm Personnel, See General Section

For full biographical listings, see the Martindale-Hubbell Law Directory

*RALEIGH,** Wake Co.

* indicates certain Bar Register subscribers whose principal office is located elsewhere in the state and who have arranged for representation as a part of the state capital listings that follow

*** WOMBLE CARLYLE SANDRIDGE & RICE** (AV)

A Professional Limited Liability Company
2100 First Union Capitol Center, 150 Fayetteville Street Mall, P.O. Box 831, 27602
Telephone: 919-755-2100
Telecopy: 919-755-2150
Telex: 806498
Charlotte, North Carolina Office: 3300 One First Union Center, 301 South College Street.
Telephone: 704-331-4900.
Telecopy: 704-331-4955.
Telex: 853609.
Winston-Salem, North Carolina Office: 1600 Southern National Financial Center.
Telephone: 919-721-3600.
Telecopy: 919-721-3660.
Telex: 806498.
Atlanta, Georgia Office: One Ninety One Peachtree Tower, 191 Peachtree Street N.E., Suite 3250.
Telephone: 404-614-2580.
Fax: 404-614-2595.

RESIDENT PARTNER

Donald A. Donadio

(See Next Column)

WOMBLE CARLYLE SANDRIDGE & RICE—*Continued*

RESIDENT ASSOCIATE

Andrea Harris Fox

Representative Clients: Aetna Casualty and Surety Co., Inc.; ALSCO/AmeriMark Building Products, Inc.; Aoki Corporation America, Inc.; Empire of Carolina, Inc.; Hackney Brothers, Inc.; Lawyers Mutual Liability Insurance Company of North Carolina; Meredith College; Monk-Austin, Inc.; Regency Park Corporation; Wachovia Bank of North Carolina, N.A.

For Complete List of Firm Personnel, See General Section

For full biographical listings, see the Martindale-Hubbell Law Directory

*WINSTON-SALEM,** Forsyth Co.

WOMBLE CARLYLE SANDRIDGE & RICE (AV)

A Professional Limited Liability Company
1600 Southern National Financial Center, P.O. Drawer 84, 27102
Telephone: 910-721-3600
Telecopy: 910-721-3660
Telex: 806498
Charlotte, North Carolina Office: 3300 One First Union Center, 301 South College Street.
Telephone: 704-331-4900.
Telecopy: 704-331-4955.
Telex: 853609.
Raleigh, North Carolina Office: 2100 First Union Capitol Center, 150 Fayetteville Street Mall, P.O. Box 831.
Telephone: 919-755-2100.
Telecopy: 919-755-2150.
Telex: 806498.
Atlanta, Georgia Office: One Ninety One Peachtree Tower, 191 Peachtree Street, N.E., Suite 3250.
Telephone: 404-614-2580.
Fax: 404-614-2595.

MEMBERS OF FIRM

Roddey M. Ligon, Jr. Robert Louis Quick

Representative Clients: Brad Ragan, Inc.; Brenner Companies; Food Lion, Inc.; Hanes Companies, Inc.; North Carolina Baptist Hospitals, Inc.; R.J. Reynolds Tobacco Company; Summit Communications Group, Inc.; Thomasville Furniture Industries, Inc.; Wachovia Corporation; Wake Forest University.

For Complete List of Firm Personnel, See General Section

For full biographical listings, see the Martindale-Hubbell Law Directory

NORTH DAKOTA

WEST FARGO, Cass Co.

OHNSTAD TWICHELL, P.C. (AV)

901 13th Avenue East, P.O. Box 458, 58078-0458
Telephone: 701-282-3249
FAX: 701-282-0825
Hillsboro, North Dakota Office: West Caledonia Avenue, P.O. Box 220.
Telephone: 701-436-5700.
FAX: 701-436-4025.
Mayville, North Dakota Office: 12 Third Street, S.E., P.O. Box 547.
Telephone: 701-786-3251.
FAX: 701-786-4243.
Fargo, North Dakota Office: 15 Broadway, Suite 202.
Telephone: 701-280-5801.
Fax: 701-280-5803.

Daniel R. Twichell Brian D. Neugebauer

Representative Clients: First National Bank North Dakota; Quality Boneless Beef; City of West Fargo; Bond Counsel for Cities of Fargo, Jamestown, West Fargo and Valley City; Insurance Company of North America; Reliance Insurance Co.; The Continental Insurance Cos.; Underwriters Adjusting Co.; Industrial Indemnity Co.; Integrity Insurance Co.

For Complete List of Firm Personnel, See General Section

For full biographical listings, see the Martindale-Hubbell Law Directory

OHIO

*CINCINNATI,** Hamilton Co.

THOMPSON, HINE AND FLORY (AV)

312 Walnut Street, 14th Floor, 45202-4029
Telephone: 513-352-6700
Fax: 513-241-4771;
Telex: 938003
Akron, Ohio Office: 50 S. Main Street, Suite 502, 44308-1828.
Telephone: 216-376-8090.
Fax: 216-376-8386.
Cleveland, Ohio Office: 1100 National City Bank Building, 629 Euclid Avenue, 44114-3070.
Telephone: 216-566-5500.
Fax: 216-556-5583.
Telex: 980217.
Cable Address: "Thomflor".
Columbus, Ohio Office: One Columbus, 10 West Broad Street, 43215-3435.
Telephone: 614-469-3200.
Fax: 614-469-3361.
Dayton, Ohio Office: 2000 Courthouse Plaza, N.E., 45402-1706.
Telephone: 513-443-6600.
Fax: 513-443-6637; 443-6635.
Palm Beach, Florida Office: 125 Worth Avenue, 33480-4466.
Telephone: 407-833-5900.
Fax: 407-833-5951.
Washington, D.C. Office: 1920 N Street, N.W., 20036-1601.
Telephone: 202-331-8800.
Fax: 202-331-8330.
Telex: 904173.
Cable Address: "Caglaw".
Brussels, Belgium Office: Rue des Chevaliers / Ridderstraat 14 - B.10, B - 1050.
Telephone: 011(32-2) 511-9326.
Fax: 011(-32-2) 513-9206.

MEMBER OF FIRM

Robert A. Selak

For Complete List of Firm Personnel, See General Section

For full biographical listings, see the Martindale-Hubbell Law Directory

*CLEVELAND,** Cuyahoga Co.

BAKER & HOSTETLER (AV)

3200 National City Center, 1900 East Ninth Street, 44114-3485
Telephone: 216-621-0200
Telecopier: 216-696-0740
TWX: 810 421 8375
RCA Telex: 215032
In Columbus, Ohio: Capitol Square, Suite 2100, 65 East State Street.
Telephone: 614-228-1541.
In Denver, Colorado: 303 East 17th Avenue, Suite 1100.
Telephone: 303-861-0600.
In Houston, Texas: 1000 Louisiana, Suite 2000.
Telephone: 713-751-1600.
In Long Beach, California: 300 Oceangate, Suite 620.
Telephone: 310-432-2827.
In Los Angeles, California: 600 Wilshire Boulevard.
Telephone: 213-624-2400.
In Orlando, Florida: SunBank Center, Suite 2300, 200 South Orange Avenue.
Telephone: 407-649-4000.
In Washington, D. C.: Washington Square, Suite 1100, 1050 Connecticut Avenue, N.W.
Telephone: 202-861-1500.
In College Park, Maryland: 9658 Baltimore Boulevard, Suite 206.
Telephone: 301-441-2781.
In Alexandria, Virginia: 437 North Lee Street.
Telephone: 703-549-1294.
In San Francisco, California: One Sansome Street, Suite 2000.
Telephone: 415-951-4705.

PARTNERS

Albert T. Adams Edward S. Ginsburg
Richard R. Hollington, Jr.

For Complete List of Firm Personnel, See General Section

For full biographical listings, see the Martindale-Hubbell Law Directory

JONES, DAY, REAVIS & POGUE (AV)

North Point, 901 Lakeside Avenue, 44114
Telephone: 216-586-3939
Cable Address: "Attorneys Cleveland"
Telex: 980389
Telecopier: 216-579-0212
In Columbus, Ohio: 1900 Huntington Center.
Telephone: 614-469-3939.
Cable Address: "Attorneys Columbus."
Telecopier: 614-461-4198.

(See Next Column)

JONES, DAY, REAVIS & POGUE, *Cleveland—Continued*

In Atlanta, Georgia: 3500 One Peachtree Center, 303 Peachtree Street, N.E.
Telephone: 404-521-3939.
Cable Address: "Attorneys Atlanta".
Telex: 54-2711.
Telecopier: 404-581-8330.
In Brussels, Belgium: Avenue Louise 480, 7th Floor. B-1050 Brussels.
Telephone: 011-32-2-645-14-11.
Telecopier: 011-32-2-645-14-45.
In Chicago, Illinois: 77 West Wacker.
Telephone: 312-782-3939.
Telecopier: 312-782-8585.
In Dallas, Texas: 2300 Trammell Crow Center, 2001 Ross Avenue.
Telephone: 214-220-3939.
Cable Address: "Attorneys Dallas."
Telex: 730852.
Telecopier: 214-969-5100.
In Frankfurt, Germany: Triton Haus, Bockenheimer Landstrasse 42, 60323 Frankfurt am Main.
Telephone: 49-69-9726-3939.
Telecopier: 49-69-9726-3993.
In Geneva, Switzerland: 20, rue de Candolle.
Telephone: 011-41-22-320-2339.
Telecopier: 011-41-22-320-1232.
In Hong Kong: 1501 One Exchange Square, 8 Connaught Place.
Telephone: 011-852-2526-6895.
Telecopier: 011-852-2810-5787.
In Irvine, California: 2603 Main Street, Suite 900.
Telephone: 714-851-3939.
Telex: 194911 Lawyers LSA.
Telecopier: 714-553-7539.
In London, England: One Mount Street.
Telephone: 011-44-71-493-9361.
Cable Address: "Surgoe London WI."
Telecopier: 011-44-71-493-9666.
In Los Angeles, California: 555 West Fifth Street, Suite 4600.
Telephone: 213-489-3939.
Telex: 181439 UD.
Telecopier: 213-243-2539.
In New York, New York: 599 Lexington Avenue.
Telephone: 212-326-3939.
Cable Address: "JONESDAY NEWYORK."
Telex: 237013 JDRP UR.
Telecopier: 212-755-7306.
In Paris, France: 62, rue du Faubourg Saint-Honore.
Telephone: 011-33-1-44-71-3939.
Cable Address: "Surgoe Paris."
Telex: 290156 Surgoe.
Telecopier: 011-33-1-49-24-0471.
In Pittsburgh, Pennsylvania: 500 Grant Street, 31st Floor.
Telephone: 412-391-3939.
Cable Address: "Attorneys Pittsburgh".
Telecopier: 412-394-7959.
In Riyadh, Saudi Arabia: Law Offices of Saud M.A. Shawwaf, P.O. Box 2700.
Telephones: 011 (966-1) 465-6543, 011 (966-1) 464-8534 or 011 (966-1) 464-8540.
Telex: 401831 SAUCON SJ.
Telecopier: (966-1) 464-8480.
In Taipei, Taiwan: 8th Floor, Tun Hwa South Road, Section 2.
Telephone: 011 (886-2) 704-6808.
Telecopier: 011 (886-2) 704-6791.
In Tokyo, Japan: Toranomon MT Building, 4th Floor, 10-3, Toranomon 3-Chome, Minato-Ku, Tokyo 105, Japan.
Telephone: 011-81-3-3433-3939.
Telecopier: 011-81-3-5401-2725.
In Washington, D.C.: Metropolitan Square, 1450 G Street, N.W.
Telephone: 202-879-3939.
Cable Address: "Attorneys Washington."
Telex: 89-2410 ATTORNEYS WASH.
Telecopier: 202-737-2832.

MEMBERS OF FIRM

John W. Sager
Zachary T. Paris
Anthony R. Moore
Louis Rorimer
John D. Currivan
David P. Porter

SENIOR ATTORNEY

Martha L. Sjogreen (Not admitted in OH)

ASSOCIATE

Stephen Gold

For Complete List of Firm Personnel, See General Section

For full biographical listings, see the Martindale-Hubbell Law Directory

THOMPSON, HINE AND FLORY (AV)

1100 National City Bank Building, 629 Euclid Avenue, 44114-3070
Telephone: 216-566-5500
Fax: 216-566-5583
Telex: 980217
Cable Address: "Thomflor"
Akron, Ohio Office: 50 S. Main Street, Suite 502, 44308-1828.
Telephone: 216-376-8090.
Fax: 216-376-8386.
Cincinnati, Ohio Office: 312 Walnut Street, 14th Floor, 45202-4029.
Telephone: 513-352-6700.
Fax: 513-241-4771.
Telex: 938003.
Columbus, Ohio Office: One Columbus, 10 West Broad Street, 43215-3435.
Telephone: 614-469-3200.
Fax: 614-469-3361.
Dayton, Ohio Office: 2000 Courthouse Plaza, N.E., 45402-1706.
Telephone: 513-443-6600.
Fax: 513-443-6637; 443-6635.
Palm Beach, Florida Office: 125 Worth Avenue, Suite 117, 33480-4466.
Telephone: 407-833-5900.
Fax: 407-833-5951.
Washington, D.C. Office: 1920 N Street, N.W., 20036-1601.
Telephone: 202-331-8800.
Fax: 202-331-8330.
Telex: 904173.
Cable Address: "Caglaw".
Brussels, Belgium Office: Rue des Chevaliers, Ridderstraat 14 - B.10, B - 1050.
Telephone: 011(32-2) 511-9326.
Fax: 011(32-2) 513-9206.

MEMBER OF FIRM

Raymond T. Sawyer

For Complete List of Firm Personnel, See General Section

For full biographical listings, see the Martindale-Hubbell Law Directory

*COLUMBUS,** Franklin Co.

* indicates certain Bar Register subscribers whose principal office is located elsewhere in the state and who have arranged for representation as a part of the state capital listings that follow

BRICKER & ECKLER (AV)

100 South Third Street, 43215-4291
Telephone: 614-227-2300
Telecopy: 614-227-2390
Cleveland, Ohio Office: 600 Superior Avenue East, Suite 800.
Telephone: 216-771-0720. Fax 216-771-7702.

Richard F. Kane
Richard C. Simpson
David A. Rogers
Randall Edwin Moore
David K. Conrad
Rebecca Coleman Princehorn

Price D. Finley
Luther L. Liggett, Jr.

Representative Clients: City of Columbus; County of Franklin; County of Union; Ehrlich Bober & Co., Inc.; The Ohio Company; A.G. Edwards & Co.; Dublin City School District; Columbus City School District; City of Findlay; City of Huber Heights.

For Complete List of Firm Personnel, See General Section

For full biographical listings, see the Martindale-Hubbell Law Directory

*** JONES, DAY, REAVIS & POGUE (AV)**

1900 Huntington Center, 43215
Telephone: 614-469-3939
Cable Address: "Attorneys Columbus"
Telecopier: 614-461-4198
In Cleveland, Ohio: North Point, 901 Lakeside Avenue.
Telephone: 216-586-3939.
Cable Address: "Attorneys Cleveland."
Telex: 980389.
Telecopier: 216-579-0212.
In Atlanta, Georgia: 3500 One Peachtree Center, 303 Peachtree Street, N.E.
Telephone: 404-521-3939.
Cable Address: "Attorneys Atlanta".
Telex: 54-2711.
Telecopier: 404-581-8330.
In Brussels, Belgium: Avenue Louise 480, 7th Floor, B-1050 Brussels.
Telephone: 011-32-2-645-14-11.
Telecopier: 011-32-2-645-14-45.
In Chicago, Illinois: 77 West Wacker.
Telephone: 312-782-3939.
Telecopier: 312-782-8585.
In Dallas, Texas: 2300 Trammell Crow Center, 2001 Ross Avenue.
Telephone: 214-220-3939.
Cable Address: "Attorneys Dallas."
Telex: 730852.
Telecopier: 214-969-5100.

(See Next Column)

JONES, DAY, REAVIS & POGUE—*Continued*

In Frankfurt, Germany: Triton Haus, Bockenheimer Landstrasse 42, 60323 Frankfurt am Main.
Telephone: 49-69-9726-3939.
Telecopier: 49-69-9726-3993.
In Geneva, Switzerland: 20, rue de Candolle.
Telephone: 011-41-22-320-2339.
Telecopier: 011-41-22-320-1232.
In Hong Kong: 1501 One Exchange Square, 8 Connaught Place.
Telephone: 011-852-2526-6895.
Telecopier: 011-852-2810-5787. Irvine, California: 2603 Main Street, Suite 900.
Telephone: 714-851-3939.
Telex: 194911 Lawyers LSA.
Telecopier: 714-553-7539.
In London, England: One Mount Street.
Telephone: 011-44-71-493-9361.
Cable Address: "Surgoe London WI."
Telecopier: 011-44-71-493-9666.
In Los Angeles, California: 555 West Fifth Street, Suite 4600.
Telephone: 213-489-3939.
Telex: 181439 UD.
Telecopier: 213-243-2539.
In New York, New York: 599 Lexington Avenue.
Telephone: 212-326-3939.
Cable Address: "JONESDAY NEWYORK."
Telex: 237013 JDRP UR.
Telecopier: 212-755-7306.
In Paris, France: 62, rue du Faubourg Saint-Honore.
Telephone: 011-33-1-44-71-3939.
Cable Address: "Surgoe Paris."
Telex: 290156 Surgoe.
Telecopier: 011-33-1-49-24-0471.
In Pittsburgh, Pennsylvania: 500 Grant Street, 31st Floor.
Telephone: 412-391-3939.
Cable Address: "Attorneys Pittsburgh".
Telecopier: 412-394-7959.
In Riyadh, Saudi Arabia: Law Offices of Saud M.A. Shawwaf, P.O. Box 2700.
Telephones: 011 (966-1) 465-6543, 011 (966-1) 464-8534 or 011 (966-1) 464-8540.
Telex: 401831 SAUCON SJ.
Telecopier: (966-1) 464-8480.
In Taipei, Taiwan: 8th Floor, 2 Tun Hwa South Road, Section 2.
Telephone: 011 (886-2) 704-6808.
Telecopier: 011 (886-2) 704-6791.
In Tokyo, Japan: Toranomon MT Building, 4th Floor, 10-3, Toranomon 3-Chome, Minato-Ku, Tokyo 105, Japan.
Telephone: 011-81-3-3433-3939.
Telecopier: 011-81-3-5401-2725.
In Washington, D.C.: Metropolitan Square, 1450 G Street, N.W.
Telephone: 202-879-3939.
Cable Address: "Attorneys Washington."
Telex: 89-2410 ATTORNEYS WASH.
Telecopier: 202-737-2832.

MEMBERS OF FIRM IN COLUMBUS

Harry J. Lehman
Roger R. Stinehart
Robert J. Gilker
Gary D. Begeman

For Complete List of Firm Personnel, See General Section

For full biographical listings, see the Martindale-Hubbell Law Directory

PORTER, WRIGHT, MORRIS & ARTHUR (AV)

41 South High Street, 43215-6194
Telephone: 614-227-2000; (800-533-2794)
Telex: 6503213584 MCI
Fax: 614-227-2100
Dayton, Ohio Office: One Dayton Centre, One South Main Street, 45402.
Telephones: 513-228-2411; (800-533-4434).
Fax: 513-449-6820.
Cincinnati, Ohio Office: 250 E. Fifth Street, 45202-4166.
Telephones: 513-381-4700; (800-582-5813).
Fax: 513-421-0991.
Cleveland, Ohio Office: 925 Euclid Avenue, 44115-1483.
Telephones: 216-443-9000; (800-824-1980).
Fax: 216-443-9011.
Washington, D.C. Office: 1233 20th Street, N.W., 20036-2395.
Telephones: 202-778-3000; (800-456-7962).
Fax: 202-778-3063.
Naples, Florida Office: 4501 Tamiami Trail North, 33940-3060.
Telephones: 813-263-8898;(800-876-7962).
Fax: 813-436-2990.

MEMBERS OF FIRM
COLUMBUS, OHIO OFFICE

Anthony J. Celebrezze, Jr.
Thomas C. Coady
Ronald W. Gabriel
William G. Martin
Nancy Belville Young

ASSOCIATE
COLUMBUS, OHIO OFFICE

Steven M. McCarty

(See Next Column)

DAYTON, OHIO OFFICE
RESIDENT MEMBER

Thomas A. Holton

CLEVELAND, OHIO OFFICE
RESIDENT MEMBERS

Craig S. Miller
John W. Waldeck, Jr.

CLEVELAND, OHIO OFFICE
RESIDENT ASSOCIATE

David C. Tryon

Representative Clients: Ohio Building Authority; The Huntington National Bank; Red Roof Inns, Inc.; City of Grandview Heights, Ohio.

For Complete List of Firm Personnel, See General Section

For full biographical listings, see the Martindale-Hubbell Law Directory

* THOMPSON, HINE AND FLORY (AV)

One Columbus, 10 West Broad Street, 43215-3435
Telephone: 614-469-3200
Fax: 614-469-3361
Akron, Ohio Office: 50 S. Main Street, Suite 502, 44308-1828.
Telephone: 216-376-8090.
Fax: 216-376-8386.
Cincinnati, Ohio Office: 312 Walnut Street, 14th Floor, 45202-4029.
Telephone: 513-352-6700.
Fax: 513-241-4771.
Telex: 938003.
Cleveland, Ohio Office: 1100 National City Bank Building, 629 Euclid Avenue, 44114-3070.
Telephone: 216-566-5500.
Fax: 216-556-5583.
Telex: 980217.
Cable Address: "Thomflor".
Dayton, Ohio Office: 2000 Courthouse Plaza, N.E., 45402-1706.
Telephone: 513-443-6600.
Fax: 513-443-6637; 443-6635.
Palm Beach, Florida Office: 125 Worth Avenue, 33480-4466.
Telephone: 407-833-5900.
Fax: 407-833-5951.
Washington, D.C. Office: 1920 N Street, N.W., 20036-1601.
Telephone: 202-331-8800.
Fax: 202-331-8330.
Telex: 904173.
Cable Address: "Caglaw".
Brussels, Belgium Office: Rue des Chevaliers / Ridderstraat 14 - B.10, B - 1050.
Telephone: 011(32-2) 511-9326.
Fax: 011(32-2) 513-9206.

MEMBER OF FIRM

Raymond T. Sawyer (In Columbus and Cleveland, Ohio)

For Complete List of Firm Personnel, See General Section

For full biographical listings, see the Martindale-Hubbell Law Directory

VORYS, SATER, SEYMOUR AND PEASE (AV)

52 East Gay Street, P.O. Box 1008, 43216-1008
Telephone: 614-464-6400
Telex: 241348
Telecopier: 614-464-6350
Cable Address: "Vorysater"
Washington, D.C. Office: Suite 1111, 1828 L Street, N.W., 20036-5104.
Telephone: 202-467-8800.
Telex: 440693.
Telecopier: 202-467-8900.
Cleveland, Ohio Office: 2100 One Cleveland Center, 1375 East Ninth Street, 44114-1724.
Telephone: 216-479-6100.
Telecopier: 216-479-6060.
Cincinnati, Ohio Office: Suite 2100, 221 East Fourth Street, P.O. Box 0236, 45201-0236.
Telephone: 513-723-4000.
Telecopier: 513-723-4056.

MEMBERS OF FIRM

Roger A. Yurchuck (Resident, Cincinnati, Ohio Office)
George L. Jenkins
Philip C. Johnston
Daniel H. Schoedinger
Phillip L. Nunnally
George N. Corey
Bruce R. Henke
Douglas L. Rogers
Carole A. Mitchell

David A. Gurwin
Russell R. Rosler
Amy Haynes Geis

Local Counsel: Abbott Laboratories; Connecticut General Life Insurance Co.; Exxon Company U.S.A.; General Motors Corp.; The Kroger Co.; Navistar International Corporation; Wendy's International, Inc.; Honda of America Mfg., Inc.; Worthington Industries, Inc.; Bank One.

For Complete List of Firm Personnel, See General Section

For full biographical listings, see the Martindale-Hubbell Law Directory

*DAYTON,** Montgomery Co.

THOMPSON, HINE AND FLORY (AV)

2000 Courthouse Plaza, N.E., 45402-1706
Telephone: 513-443-6600
Fax: 513-443-6637; 443-6635
Akron, Ohio Office: 50 S. Main Street, Suite 502, 44308-1828.
Telephone: 216-376-8090.
Fax: 216-376-8386.
Cincinnati, Ohio Office: 312 Walnut Street, 14th Floor, 45202-4029.
Telephone: 513-352-6700.
Fax: 513-241-4771.
Telex: 938003.
Cleveland, Ohio Office: 1100 National City Bank Building, 629 Euclid Avenue, 44114-3070.
Telephone: 216-566-5500.
Fax: 216-556-5583.
Telex: 980217.
Cable Address: "Thomflor".
Columbus, Ohio Office: One Columbus, 10 West Broad Street, 43215-3435.
Telephone: 614-469-3200.
Fax: 614-469-3361.
Palm Beach, Florida Office: 125 Worth Avenue, 33480-4466.
Telephone: 407-833-5900.
Fax: 407-833-5951.
Washington, D.C. Office: 1920 N Street, N.W., 20036-1601.
Telephone: 202-331-8800.
Fax: 202-331-8330.
Telex: 904173.
Cable Address: "Caglaw".
Brussels, Belgium Office: Rue des Chevaliers / Ridderstraat 14 - B.10, B - 1050.
Telephone: 011(32-2) 511-9326.
Fax: 011(32-2) 513-9206.

MEMBERS OF FIRM

David A. Neuhardt
Arik A. Sherk

For Complete List of Firm Personnel, See General Section

For full biographical listings, see the Martindale-Hubbell Law Directory

*TOLEDO,** Lucas Co.

SPENGLER NATHANSON (AV)

608 Madison Avenue, Suite 1000, 43604-1169
Telephone: 419-241-2201
FAX: 419-241-8599

MEMBERS OF FIRM

David A. Katz
Frank T. Pizza
B. Gary McBride
Gary D. Sikkema

Counsel for: Fifth-Third Bank of Northwestern Ohio, N.A.; Huntington Bank of Toledo; Society Bank & Trust; Toledo Lucas County Port Authority; The University of Toledo; Toledo Board of Education; Metropolitan Park District; Seaway Food Town, Inc.; AP Parts.

For Complete List of Firm Personnel, See General Section

For full biographical listings, see the Martindale-Hubbell Law Directory

OKLAHOMA

*OKLAHOMA CITY,** Oklahoma Co.

CROWE & DUNLEVY, A PROFESSIONAL CORPORATION (AV)

1800 Mid-America Tower, 20 North Broadway, 73102-8273
Telephone: 405-235-7700
Fax: 405-239-6651
Tulsa, Oklahoma Office: Crowe & Dunlevy, 500 Kennedy Building, 321 South Boston.
Telephone: 918-592-9800.
Fax: 918-592-9801.
Norman, Oklahoma Office: Crowe & Dunlevy, Luttrell, Pendarvis & Rawlinson, 104 East Eufaula Street.
Telephone: 405-321-7317.
Fax: 405-360-4002.

Earl A. Skarky
Kenni B. Merritt

Randy D. Gordon

OF COUNSEL

James C. Gibbens

For Complete List of Firm Personnel, See General Section

For full biographical listings, see the Martindale-Hubbell Law Directory

SHIRK, WORK, ROBINSON & WORK, A PROFESSIONAL CORPORATION (AV)

800 Colcord Building, 73102
Telephone: 405-236-3571
FAX: 405- 236-8028

James E. Work
William J. Robinson

Representative Clients: AMF Inc.; Oklahoma County Finance Authority; Pizza Hut, Inc.; Oklahoma City Industrial Cultural Facilities Trust; Weyerhaeuser Co.; Federal Corp.; Little Giant Corp.; Bank IV Oklahoma; Fred Jones Manufacturing Co.; Southeastern Oklahoma Industries Authority.

For Complete List of Firm Personnel, See General Section

For full biographical listings, see the Martindale-Hubbell Law Directory

*TULSA,** Tulsa Co.

STONE JESSUP, P.C. (AV)

21st Floor, 320 South Boston, 74103
Telephone: 918-583-1178
FAX: 918-583-0277

Samuel C. Stone
James R. Jessup (1936-1991)

For full biographical listings, see the Martindale-Hubbell Law Directory

PENNSYLVANIA

*HARRISBURG,** Dauphin Co.

GOLDBERG, KATZMAN & SHIPMAN, P.C. (AV)

320 Market Street - Strawberry Square, P.O. Box 1268, 17108-1268
Telephone: 717-234-4161
Telecopier: 717-234-6808; 717-234-6810

Ronald M. Katzman
Neil Hendershot
Jesse Jay Cooper
Michael A. Finio

Arnold B. Kogan

Representative Client: Dauphin County General Authority.
Reference: Fulton Bank.

For Complete List of Firm Personnel, See General Section

For full biographical listings, see the Martindale-Hubbell Law Directory

METTE, EVANS & WOODSIDE, A PROFESSIONAL CORPORATION (AV)

3401 North Front Street, P.O. Box 5950, 17110-0950
Telephone: 717-232-5000
Telecopier: 717-236-1816

Howell C. Mette
Robert Moore
Charles B. Zwally
James A. Ulsh

Counsel for: City of Lebanon Authority; Dauphin County General Authority; Mifflin County Hospital Authority; Central Dauphin School District; Northern York School District; Bloomsburg Area School District; Mercersburg Borough Authority.

For Complete List of Firm Personnel, See General Section

For full biographical listings, see the Martindale-Hubbell Law Directory

RHOADS & SINON (AV)

One South Market Square, 12th Floor, P.O. Box 1146, 17108-1146
Telephone: 717-233-5731
Fax: 717-232-1459
Boca Raton, Florida Affiliated Office: Suite 301, 299 West Camino Gardens Boulevard.
Telephone: 407-395-5595.
Fax: 407-395-9497.
Lancaster, Pennsylvania Office: 15 North Lime Street.
Telephone: 717-397-5127.
Fax: 717-397-5267.

MEMBERS OF FIRM

Robert H. Long, Jr.
Richard B. Wood
Frank J. Leber
Paul A. Lundeen
Nathan H. Waters, Jr.
David O. Twaddell
Jens H. Damgaard
Dean H. Dusinberre

ASSOCIATE

Kimberly A. Noel

For Complete List of Firm Personnel, See General Section

For full biographical listings, see the Martindale-Hubbell Law Directory

*MEDIA,** Delaware Co.

KASSAB ARCHBOLD JACKSON & O'BRIEN (AV)

Lawyers-Title Building, 214 North Jackson Street, P.O. Box 626, 19063
Telephone: 610-565-3800
Telecopier: 610-892-6888
Wilmington, Delaware Office: 1326 King Street.
Telephone: 302-656-3393.
Fax: 302-656-1993.
Wildwood, New Jersey Office: 5201 New Jersey Avenue.
Telephone: 609-522-6559.

MEMBERS OF FIRM

Edward Kassab
William C. Archbold, Jr.
Robert James Jackson
Joseph Patrick O'Brien
Richard A. Stanko
Roy T. J. Stegena

OF COUNSEL

Matthew J. Ryan
John W. Nilon, Jr.

ASSOCIATES

Kevin William Gibson
Cynthia Kassab Larosa
Marc S. Stein
Terrance A. Kline
George C. McFarland, Jr.
Jill E. Aversa
Pamela A. La Torre
Kenneth D. Kynett

Representative Clients furnished upon request.

For full biographical listings, see the Martindale-Hubbell Law Directory

*PHILADELPHIA,** Philadelphia Co.

BALLARD SPAHR ANDREWS & INGERSOLL (AV)

1735 Market Street, 51st Floor, 19103-7599
Telephone: 215-665-8500
Fax: 215-864-8999
Denver, Colorado Office: Seventeenth Street Plaza Building, Suite 2300, 1225 17th Street.
Telephone: 303-292-2400.
Fax: 303-296-3956.
Kaunas, Lithuania Office: Donelaicio g., 71-2, Kaunas 3000.
Telephone: (370-7) 20 56 66.
Fax: (370-7) 20 56 91.
Salt Lake City, Utah Office: One Utah Center, Suite 1200, 201 South Main Street.
Telephone: 801-531-3000.
Fax: 801-531-3001.
Washington, D.C. Office: Suite 900 East, 555 13th Street, N.W.
Telephone: 202-383-8800.
Fax: 202-383-8877; 383-8893.
Baltimore, Maryland Office: 300 East Lombard Street. 19th Floor.
Telephone: 410-528-5600.
Fax: 410-528-5650.
Camden, New Jersey Office: 800 Hudson Square, 5th Floor.
Telephone: 609-541-5577.
Fax: 609-541-8272.

Jeffrey T. Chappelle
Thomas Jay Ellis
Brian T. Hirai
William P. Scott
Kevin R. Cunningham
Dianne Coady Fisher
H. David Prior
Jere G. Thompson
J. Brian Walsh

OF COUNSEL

Joseph P. Flanagan, Jr.
Frank L. Newburger, III

Kendra S. Follett
Marie Keeley

For Complete List of Firm Personnel, See General Section

For full biographical listings, see the Martindale-Hubbell Law Directory

DILWORTH, PAXSON, KALISH & KAUFFMAN (AV)

3200 Mellon Bank Center, 1735 Market Street, 19103
Telephone: 215-575-7000
Fax: 215-575-7200
Harrisburg, Pennsylvania Office: 305 N. Front Street, Suite 403.
Telephone: 717-236-4812.
Fax: 717-236-7811.
Plymouth Meeting, Pennsylvania Office: 630 West Germantown Pike, Suite 160.
Telephone: 610-941-4444.
Fax: 610-941-9880.
Westmont, New Jersey Office: 222 Haddon Avenue.
Telephone: 609-854-5150.
Fax: 609-854-2316.
Media, Pennsylvania Office: 606 E. Baltimore Pike.
Telephone: 610-565-4322.
Fax: 610-565-4131.

MEMBERS OF FIRM

Ross J. Reese
Marc A. Feller

For Complete List of Firm Personnel, See General Section

For full biographical listings, see the Martindale-Hubbell Law Directory

SAUL, EWING, REMICK & SAUL (AV)

3800 Centre Square West, 19102
Telephone: 215-972-7777
Cable Address: "Bidsal"
TWX: 83-4798
Telecopier: XEROX 7020 215-972-7725
Wilmington, Delaware Office: 222 Delaware Avenue, P.O. Box 1266, 19899-1266. For Courier Delivery: 222 Delaware Avenue, Suite 1200, 19801.
Telephone: 302-421-6800.
Cable Address: "Bidsal."
TWX: 83-4798.
Telecopier: XEROX 7020 302-421-6813.
New York, N.Y. Office: Twenty-first Floor, 237 Park Avenue.
Telephone: 212-551-3502.
TWX: 425170.
Telecopier: 212-697-8486.
Malvern, Pennsylvania Office: Suite 200, Great Valley Corporate Center, 300 Chester Field Parkway.
Telephone: 215-251-5050.
Cable Address: "BIDSAL".
TWX: 83-4798.
Telecopier: 215-651-5930.
Voorhees, New Jersey Office: Plaza 1000, Main Street, Suite 206 Evesham & Kresson Roads.
Telephone: 609-424-0098.
Telecopier: XEROX 7020 609-424-2204.
Harrisburg, Pennsylvania Office: 240 North 3rd Street, P.O. Box 1291, 17108-1291. For Courier Delivery: 240 N. 3rd Street, Suite 700, 17101.
Telephone: 717-238-8300.
Telecopier: 717-238-4622.
Trenton, New Jersey Office: Capital Center, 50 East State Street, 08608.
Telephone: 609-393-0057.
Fax: 609-393-5962.

MEMBERS OF FIRM

Russell C. Bellavance
Thomas J. Capano (Not admitted in PA; Resident, Wilmington, Delaware Office)
Timothy J. Carson
Timothy A. Frey (Resident, Wilmington, Delaware Office)
Robert J. Jones
George T. Magnatta
David Unkovic
William W. Warren, Jr. (Resident, Harrisburg, Pennsylvania Office)
Mark R. Zehner

OF COUNSEL

Arthur R. G. Solmssen

SPECIAL COUNSEL

Robert W. O'Donnell
Robert S. Price

ASSOCIATES

Mark S. Arena
Steven A. Goldfield
Suzanne Serianni Mayes
Bonnie S. Milavec

For Complete List of Firm Personnel, See General Section

For full biographical listings, see the Martindale-Hubbell Law Directory

WOLF, BLOCK, SCHORR AND SOLIS-COHEN (AV)

Twelfth Floor, Packard Building, S.E. Corner 15th and Chestnut Streets, 19102-2678
Telephone: 215-977-2000
Cable Address: "WOLBLORR PHA"
TWX: 710-670-1927
Telecopiers: 977-2334; 977-2346
Malvern, Pennsylvania Office: 20 Valley Stream Parkway.
Telephone: 215-889-4900.
Fax: 215-889-4916.
Harrisburg, Pennsylvania Office: 305 North Front Street, Suite 401.
Telephone: 717-237-7160.
Fax: 717-237-7161.

MEMBERS OF FIRM

E. Gerald Riesenbach
William J. Morehouse
John S. Roberts, Jr.
Dennis L. Cohen
Ronald M. Wiener
Ivan I. Light
Arthur A. Zatz
Michael Allan Budin

OF COUNSEL

Albert J. Feldman

For Complete List of Firm Personnel, See General Section

For full biographical listings, see the Martindale-Hubbell Law Directory

*PITTSBURGH,** Allegheny Co.

BUCHANAN INGERSOLL, PROFESSIONAL CORPORATION (AV)

5800 USX Tower, 600 Grant Street, 15219
Telephone: 412-562-8800
Telecopier: 412-562-1041
Philadelphia, Pennsylvania Office: Two Logan Square, Twelfth Floor, 18th & Arch Streets.
Telephone: 215-665-8700.
Harrisburg, Pennsylvania Office: Vartan Parc, 30 North Third Street.
Telephone: 717-237-4800.

(See Next Column)

BUCHANAN INGERSOLL PROFESSIONAL CORPORATION, *Pittsburgh—Continued*

Tampa, Florida Office: 101 East Kennedy Boulevard, Suite 1030.
Telephone: 813-222-8180.
North Miami Beach, Florida Office: 19495 Biscayne Boulevard.
Telephone: 305-933-5600.
Lexington, Kentucky Office: 1210 Vine Center Office Tower, 333 West Vine Street.
Telephone: 606-225-5333.
Princeton, New Jersey Office: Buchanan Ingersoll, A Partnership, College Centre, 500 College Road East.
Telephone: 609-452-2666.

Patricia J. Marley | John M. Rumin

COUNSEL

Margaret B. Angel

Frances Magovern O'Connor

For Complete List of Firm Personnel, See General Section

For full biographical listings, see the Martindale-Hubbell Law Directory

JONES, DAY, REAVIS & POGUE (AV)

500 Grant Street 31st Floor, 15219
Telephone: 412-391-3939
Cable Address: "Attorneys Pittsburgh".
Telecopier: 412-394-7959
In Atlanta, Georgia: 3500 One Peachtree Center, 303 Peachtree Street, N.E.
Telephone: 404-521-3939.
Cable Address: "Attorneys Atlanta".
Telex: 54-2711.
Telecopier: 404-581-8330.
In Brussels, Belgium: Avenue Louise 480, 7th Floor, B-1050 Brussels.
Telephone: 011-32-2-645-14-11.
Telecopier: 011-32-2-645-14-45.
In Chicago, Illinois: 77 West Wacker.
Telephone: 312-782-3939.
Telecopier: 312-782-8585.
In Cleveland, Ohio: North Point, 901 Lakeside Avenue.
Telephone: 216-586-3939.
Cable Address: "Attorneys Cleveland."
Telex: 980389.
Telecopier: 216-579-0212.
In Columbus, Ohio: 1900 Huntington Center.
Telephone: 614-469-3939.
Cable Address: "Attorneys Columbus."
Telecopier: 614-461-4198.
In Dallas, Texas: 2300 Trammell Crow Center, 2001 Ross Avenue.
Telephone: 214-220-3939.
Cable Address: "Attorneys Dallas."
Telex: 730852.
Telecopier: 214-969-5100.
In Frankfurt, Germany: Triton Haus, Bockenheimer Landstrasse 42, 60323 Frankfurt am Main.
Telephone: 49-69-9726-3939.
Telecopier: 49-69-9726-3993.
In Geneva, Switzerland: 20, rue de Candolle.
Telephone: 011-41-22-320-2339.
Telecopier: 011-41-22-320-1232.
In Hong Kong: 1501 One Exchange Square, 8 Connaught Place.
Telephone: 011-852-2526-6895.
Telecopier: 011-852-2810-5787.
In Irvine, California: 2603 Main Street, Suite 900.
Telephone: 714-851-3939.
Telex: 194911 Lawyers LSA.
Telecopier: 714-553-7539.
In London, England: One Mount Street.
Telephone: 011-44-71-493-9361.
Cable Address: "Surgoe London WI."
Telecopier: 011-44-71-493-9666.
In Los Angeles, California: 555 West Fifth Street, Suite 4600.
Telephone: 213-489-3939.
Telex: 181439 UD.
Telecopier: 213-243-2539.
In New York, New York: 599 Lexington Avenue.
Telephone: 212-326-3939.
Cable Address: "JONESDAY NEWYORK."
Telex: 237013 JDRP UR.
Telecopier: 212-755-7306.
In Paris, France: 62, rue du Faubourg Saint-Honore.
Telephone: 011-33-1-44-71-3939.
Cable Address: "Surgoe Paris."
Telex: 290156 Surgoe.
Telecopier: 011-33-1-49-24-0471.
In Riyadh, Saudi Arabia: Law Offices of Saud M.A. Shawwaf, P.O. Box 2700.
Telephones: 011 (966-1) 465-6543, 011 (966-1) 464-8534 or 011 (966-1) 464-8540.
Telex: 401831 SAUCON SJ.
Telecopier: (966-1) 464-8480.

(See Next Column)

In Taipei, Taiwan: 8th Floor, 2 Tun Hwa South Road, Section 2.
Telephone: 011 (886-2) 704-6808.
Telecopier: 011 (886-2) 704-6791.
In Tokyo, Japan: Toranomon MT Building, 4th Floor, 10-3, Toranomon 3-Chome, Minato-Ku, Tokyo 105, Japan.
Telephone: 011-81-3-3433-3939.
Telecopier: 011-81-3-5401-2725.
In Washington, D.C.: Metropolitan Square, 1450 G Street, N.W.
Telephone: 202-879-3939.
Cable Address: "Attorneys Washington."
Telex: 89-2410 ATTORNEYS WASH.
Telecopier: 202-737-2832.

MEMBER OF FIRM IN PITTSBURGH

Charles A. Schliebs

For Complete List of Firm Personnel, See General Section

For full biographical listings, see the Martindale-Hubbell Law Directory

KLETT LIEBER ROONEY & SCHORLING, A PROFESSIONAL CORPORATION (AV)

40th Floor, One Oxford Centre, 15219-6498
Telephone: 412-392-2000
FAX: 412-392-2128; 412-392-2129
Harrisburg, Pennsylvania Office: 240 North Third Street, Suite 600.
Telephone: 717-231-7700.
Philadelphia, Pennsylvania Office: 28th Floor, One Logan Square.
Telephone: 215-567-7500

SHAREHOLDERS

Mary Jo Howard Dively | Michael M. Lyons
Kenneth R. Luttinger | William A. K. Titelman

ASSOCIATE

Barbara A. Fure Hollinshead

For Complete List of Firm Personnel, See General Section

For full biographical listings, see the Martindale-Hubbell Law Directory

REED SMITH SHAW & MCCLAY (AV)

James H. Reed Building, Mellon Square, 435 Sixth Avenue, 15219-1886
Telephone: 412-288-3131
Cable Address: "Reedsmith Pgh"
TWX: 710-664-2083
FAX: 412-288-3063
Mailing Address: P.O. Box 2009, 15230
Washington, D.C. Office: Ring Building, 1200 18th Street, N.W., 20036-2506.
Telephone: 202-457-6100.
FAX: 202-457-6113.
Philadelphia, Pennsylvania Office: 2500 One Liberty Place, 19103-7301.
Telephone: 215-851-8100.
FAX: 215-851-1420.
Harrisburg, Pennsylvania Office: 213 Market Street, 17101-2132.
Telephone: 717-234-5988.
McLean, Virginia Office: Suite 1100, 8251 Greensboro Drive, 22102-3844.
Telephone: 703-734-4600.
Princeton, New Jersey Office: 136 Main Street, 08540-5799.
Telephone: 609-987-0050.
FAX: 609-951-0824.

MEMBERS OF FIRM

Edward Hoopes | William J. Smith
John F. LeBlond | Leonard L. Stewart
Glenn R. Mahone | Thomas Todd

Harry H. Weil

COUNSEL

John H. Demmler

For Complete List of Firm Personnel, See General Section

For full biographical listings, see the Martindale-Hubbell Law Directory

SPRINGER, BUSH & PERRY, A PROFESSIONAL CORPORATION (AV)

Two Gateway Center, Fifteenth Floor, 15222
Telephone: 412-281-4900
Fax: 412-261-1645
Moon Township, Pennsylvania Office: 500 Cherrington Parkway, Suite 420, Coraopolis, Pennsylvania, 15108.
Telephone: 412-269-4200.
Fax: 412-269-9638.

Joseph Friedman | James H. Webster
W. Ronald Stout | Edward R. Lawrence, Jr. (Resident, Moon Township, Coraopolis, Pennsylvania Office)
Robert E. Harper (Resident, Moon Township, Coraopolis, Pennsylvania Office)

COUNSEL

Paul G. Perry | John E. Perry

For Complete List of Firm Personnel, See General Section

For full biographical listings, see the Martindale-Hubbell Law Directory

Pittsburgh—Continued

Thorp, Reed & Armstrong (AV)

One Riverfront Center, 15222
Telephone: 412-394-7711
Fax: 412-394-2555

MEMBERS OF FIRM

James D. Chiafullo
Melissa A. Jad
Ralph F. Scalera
Timothy M. Slavish

For Complete List of Firm Personnel, See General Section

For full biographical listings, see the Martindale-Hubbell Law Directory

*READING,** Berks Co.

Stevens & Lee, A Professional Corporation (AV)

111 North Sixth Street, P.O. Box 679, 19603
Telephone: 610-478-2000
Fax: 610-376-5610
Wayne, Pennsylvania Office: One Glenhardie Corporate Center, 1275 Drummers Lane, P. O. Box 236.
Telephone: 610-964-1480.
Fax: 610-687-1384.
Lancaster, Pennsylvania Office: One Penn Square, P.O. Box 1594.
Telephone: 717-291-1031.
Fax: 717-394-7726.
Allentown, Pennsylvania Office: 740 North Hamilton Mall, P. O. Box 8838.
Telephone: 610-439-4195.
Fax: 610-439-8415.
Harrisburg, Pennsylvania Office: 208 North Third Street. Suite 310. P.O. Box 12090. 17101.
Telephone: 717-234-1250.
Fax: 717-234-1939.
Philadelphia, Pennsylvania Office: Two Penn Center Plaza, Suite 200.
Telephone: 215-854-6370.
Fax: 215-569-0216.
Wilkes-Barre, Pennsylvania Office: 289 North Main Street.
Telephone: 717-823-6116.
Fax: 717-823-1149.

Edward A. Fedok (Resident, Allentown Office)
Joseph M. Harenza
John W. Espenshade (Resident, Lancaster Office)
David A. Vind
Michael A. Setley

Peter T. Edelman
Douglas P. Rauch

For Complete List of Firm Personnel, See General Section

For full biographical listings, see the Martindale-Hubbell Law Directory

*WEST CHESTER,** Chester Co.

Lamb, Windle & McErlane, P.C. (AV)

24 East Market Street, P.O. Box 565, 19381-0565
Telephone: 610-430-8000
Telecopier: 610-692-0877

COUNSEL

Theodore O. Rogers

William H. Lamb
Susan Windle Rogers
James E. McErlane
E. Craig Kalemjian
James C. Sargent, Jr.
John D. Snyder
William P. Mahon
Guy A. Donatelli
Vincent M. Pompo
James J. McEntee III

Tracy Blake DeVlieger
P. Andrew Schaum
Lawrence J. Persick
Thomas K. Schindler
Daniel A. Loewenstern
Thomas F. Oeste
John W. Pauciulo
Andrea B. Pettine
John J. Cunningham

Representative Clients: Chester County; First Financial Savings Bank, PaSA; Bank of Chester County; Jefferson Bank; Downingtown Area and Great Valley School Districts; Philadelphia Electric Company; Central and Western Chester County Industrial Development Authority; Valley Forge Sewer Authority; Manito Title Insurance Company.

For full biographical listings, see the Martindale-Hubbell Law Directory

*YORK,** York Co.

Stock and Leader (AV)

35 South Duke Street, P.O. Box 5167, 17401-5167
Telephone: 717-846-9800
Fax: 717-843-6134
Hallam, Pennsylvania Office: 450 West Market Street.
Telephone: 717-840-4491.
Stewartstown, Pennsylvania Office: 5 South Main Street.
Telephone: 717-993-2845.

(See Next Column)

Shrewsbury, Pennsylvania Office: 28 Northbrook Drive, Suite 2F.
Telephone: 717-235-3608.

MEMBERS OF FIRM

Raymond L. Hovis
Marietta Harte Barbour

General Counsel: The Drovers & Mechanics Bank; Paradise Mutual Insurance Co.; Yorktowne Paper Mills, Inc.; York Electrical Supply Co.; Eisenhart Wallcoverings Co.; York Suburban School District; York Township; Central York School District.

For Complete List of Firm Personnel, See General Section

For full biographical listings, see the Martindale-Hubbell Law Directory

RHODE ISLAND

*PROVIDENCE,** Providence Co.

Edwards & Angell (AV)

2700 Hospital Trust Tower, 02903
Telephone: 401-274-9200
Telecopier: 401-276-6611
Cable Address: "Edwangle Providence"
Telex: 952001 "E A PVD"
Boston, Massachusetts Office: 101 Federal Street, 02110.
Telephone: 617-439-444.
Telecopier: 617-439-4170.
New York, New York Office: 750 Lexington Avenue, 10022.
Telephone: 212-308-4411.
Telecopier: 212-308-4844.
Palm Beach, Florida Office: 250 Royal Palm Way, 33480.
Telephone: 407-833-7700.
Telecopier: 407-655-8719.
Newark, New Jersey Office: Gateway three, 07120.
Telephone: 201-623-7717.
Telecopier: 201-623-7717.
Hartford, Connecticut Office: 750 Main Street, 14th Floor, 06103.
Telephone: 203-525-5065.
Telecopier: 203-527-4198.
Newport, Rhode Island Office: 130 Bellevue Avenue, 02840.
Telephone: 401-849-7800.
Telecopier: 401-849-7887.

MEMBERS OF FIRM

Alvin M. Glazerman (Not admitted in RI; Resident Boston, Massachusetts Office)
James J. Skeffington
James R. McGuirk
Kurt J. von Boeselager
Pamela S. Robertson

ASSOCIATE

Adele Geffen Eil

For Complete List of Firm Personnel, See General Section

For full biographical listings, see the Martindale-Hubbell Law Directory

SOUTH CAROLINA

*CHARLESTON,** Charleston Co.

Haynsworth, Marion, McKay & Guérard, L.L.P (AV)

#2 Prioleau Street, P.O. Box 1119, 29402
Telephone: 803-722-7606
Telecopier: 803-723-5263
Columbia, South Carolina Office: Suite 2400 AT&T Building, 1201 Main Street, P.O. Drawer 7157, 29202.
Telephone: 803-765-1818.
Telecopier: 803-765-2399.
Greenville, South Carolina Office: Two Insignia Financial Plaza, 75 Beattie Place, P.O. Box 2048, 29602.
Telephone: 803-240-3200.
Telecopier: 803-240-3300.

OF COUNSEL

Theodore B. Guérard

MEMBERS OF FIRM

W. E. Applegate, III
J. Paul Trouche
Samuel W. Howell, IV
Carol L. Clark

Counsel for: South Carolina Public Service Authority; University of South Carolina; South Carolina Jobs - Economic Development Authority; School District Richland County; College of Charleston; Dorchester County; City of North Charleston; City of Beaufort; Town of Mt. Pleasant; Mt. Pleasant Water and Sewer Commission.

For Complete List of Firm Personnel, See General Section

For full biographical listings, see the Martindale-Hubbell Law Directory

Charleston—Continued

SINKLER & BOYD, P.A. (AV)

160 East Bay Street, P.O. Box 340, 29402-0340
Telephone: 803-722-3366
FAX: 803-722-2266
Columbia, South Carolina Office: Suite 1200 The Palmetto Center, 1426 Main Street, P.O. Box 11889.
Telephone: 803-779-3080.
FAX: 803-765-1243.
Greenville, South Carolina Office: 15 South Main Street, Suite 500, Wachovia Building, P.O. Box 275.
Telephone: 803-467-1100.
FAX: 803-467-1521.

George S. King, Jr. (Resident, Columbia Office)
Margaret Christian Pope (Resident, Columbia Office)
Charlton deSaussure, Jr.
F. Mitchell Johnson, Jr.
Robert S. Galloway, III (Resident, Greenville Office)
Steve A. Matthews (Resident, Columbia Office)
Theodore B. DuBose (Resident, Columbia Office)
John K. Van Duys (Resident, Columbia Office)

OF COUNSEL

Albert Simons, Jr.
Martin C. McWilliams, Jr. (Resident, Columbia Office)

Attorneys for: The South Carolina National Bank; Westvaco Corporation; Palmetto Shipping & Stevedoring Co.; The City of Charleston, S.C.; The South Carolina State Housing Finance and Development Authority; Bowater, Incorporated; Carolina Shipping Co.

For Complete List of Firm Personnel, See General Section

For full biographical listings, see the Martindale-Hubbell Law Directory

*COLUMBIA,** Richland Co.

* indicates certain Bar Register subscribers whose principal office is located elsewhere in the state and who have arranged for representation as a part of the state capital listings that follow

*** HAYNSWORTH, MARION, MCKAY & GUÉRARD, L.L.P.** (AV)

Suite 2400 A T & T Building, 1201 Main Street, P.O. Drawer 7157, 29202
Telephone: 803-765-1818
Telecopier: 803-765-2399
Greenville, South Carolina Office: Two Insignia Financial Plaza, 75 Beattie Place, P.O. Box 2048, 29602.
Telephone: 803-240-3200.
Telecopier: 803-240-3300.
Charleston, South Carolina Office: #2 Prioleau Street, P.O. Box 1119, 29402.
Telephone: 803-722-7606.
Telecopier: 803-723-5263.

OF COUNSEL

Theodore B. Guérard

MEMBER OF FIRM

Samuel W. Howell, IV

ASSOCIATE

Edward G. Kluiters

Counsel for: South Carolina Jobs-Economic Development Authority; South Carolina Public Service Authority; Richland County; Town of Lexington; Town of Winnsboro; The State of South Carolina; Business Development Corp. of South Carolina; Santee Cooper Electric Cooperative; Cooper River Park and Playground Commission; John Deere Industrial Development, Inc.; School District of Richland County.

For Complete List of Firm Personnel, See General Section

For full biographical listings, see the Martindale-Hubbell Law Directory

SINKLER & BOYD, P.A. (AV)

Suite 1200 The Palmetto Center, 1426 Main Street, P.O. Box 11889, 29211-1889
Telephone: 803-779-3080
FAX: 803-765-1243
Charleston, South Carolina Office: 160 East Bay Street, P.O. Box 340.
Telephone: 803-722-3366.
FAX: 803-722-2266.
Greenville, South Carolina Office: 15 South Main Street, Suite 500, Wachovia Building, P.O. Box 275.
Telephone: 803-467-1100.
FAX: 803-467-1521.

George S. King, Jr.
Margaret Christian Pope
Charlton deSaussure, Jr. (Resident, Charleston Office)
F. Mitchell Johnson, Jr. (Resident, Charleston Office)
Robert S. Galloway, III (Resident, Greenville Office)
Steve A. Matthews
Theodore B. DuBose
John K. Van Duys

(See Next Column)

OF COUNSEL

Albert Simons, Jr. (Resident, Charleston Office)
Martin C. McWilliams, Jr.

Counsel For: South Carolina State Housing Finance and Development Authority; City of Charleston, S.C.; Clemson University; Western Carolina Regional Sewer Authority; York County, S.C.

For Complete List of Firm Personnel, See General Section

For full biographical listings, see the Martindale-Hubbell Law Directory

*GREENVILLE,** Greenville Co.

SINKLER & BOYD, P.A. (AV)

Suite 500, Wachovia Building, 15 South Main Street, P.O. Box 275, 29602-0275
Telephone: 803-467-1100
FAX: 803-467-1521
Columbia, South Carolina Office: Suite 1200 The Palmetto Center, 1426 Main Street, P.O. Box 11889.
Telephone: 803-779-3080.
FAX: 803-765-1243.
Charleston, South Carolina Office: 160 East Bay Street, P.O. Box 340.
Telephone: 803-722-3366.
FAX: 803-722-2266.

Robert S. Galloway, III
George S. King, Jr. (Resident, Columbia Office)
Margaret Christian Pope (Resident, Columbia Office)
Charlton deSaussure, Jr. (Resident, Charleston Office)
F. Mitchell Johnson, Jr. (Resident, Charleston Office)
Steve A. Matthews (Resident, Columbia Office)
Theodore B. DuBose (Resident, Columbia Office)
John K. Van Duys (Resident, Columbia Office)

OF COUNSEL

Albert Simons, Jr. (Resident, Charleston Office)
Martin C. McWilliams, Jr. (Resident, Columbia Office)

Attorneys for: The South Carolina National Bank; Westvaco Corporation; Palmetto Shipping & Stevedoring Co.; The City of Charleston, S.C.; The South Carolina State Housing Finance and Development Authority; Bowater, Incorporated; Carolina Shipping Co.

For full biographical listings, see the Martindale-Hubbell Law Directory

WYCHE, BURGESS, FREEMAN & PARHAM, PROFESSIONAL ASSOCIATION (AV)

44 East Camperdown Way, P.O. Box 728, 29602-0728
Telephone: 803-242-8200
Telecopier: 803-235-8900

C. Thomas Wyche
Carl F. Muller
Eric B. Amstutz

Counsel for: Multimedia, Inc.; Delta Woodside Industries, Inc.; Milliken & Company; Ryan's Family Steak Houses, Inc.; St. Francis Hospital; Span-America Medical Systems, Inc.; Carolina First Bank; KEMET Electronics Corp.; Builder Marts of America, Inc.; One Price Clothing, Inc.

For Complete List of Firm Personnel, See General Section

For full biographical listings, see the Martindale-Hubbell Law Directory

TENNESSEE

*CHATTANOOGA,** Hamilton Co.

CHAMBLISS & BAHNER (AV)

1000 Tallan Building, Two Union Square, 37402-2500
Telephone: 615-756-3000
Fax: 615-265-9574

MEMBERS OF FIRM

Kirk Snouffer
William P. Aiken, Jr.
Gary D. Lander
David R. Evans
Jay A. Young
Penelope W. Register

General Counsel for: McKee Foods Corporation; SCT Yarns, Inc.; Stein Construction Co., Inc.
Representative Clients: Tri-County Hospital Authority (N.GA); First American National Bank; Retirement Services of America, Inc.; First Tennessee Bank.

For Complete List of Firm Personnel, See General Section

For full biographical listings, see the Martindale-Hubbell Law Directory

KINGSPORT, Sullivan Co.

HUNTER, SMITH & DAVIS (AV)

1212 North Eastman Road, P.O. Box 3740, 37664
Telephone: 615-378-8800;
Johnson City: 615-282-4186;
Bristol: 615-968-7604
Telecopier: 615-378-8801
Johnson City, Tennessee Office: Suite 500 First American Center, 208 Sunset Drive, 37604.
Telephone: 615-283-6300.
Telecopier: 615-283-6301.

MEMBERS OF FIRM

T. Arthur Scott, Jr. William C. Argabrite

ASSOCIATES

Cynthia S. Kessler Gary Dean Miller

Representative Clients: The Industrial Development Board of the City of Kingsport, Tennessee; The Industrial Development Board of the City of Bristol, Tennessee; The Industrial Development Board of the County of Sullivan, Tennessee; The Industrial Development Board of Washington County, Tennessee; The Health and Educational Facilities Board of Sullivan County, Tennessee; The Health and Educational Facilities Board of the City of Bristol, Tennessee; The Industrial Development Board of Johnson City, Tennessee; The Industrial Development Authority of the City of Bristol, Virginia.

For Complete List of Firm Personnel, See General Section

For full biographical listings, see the Martindale-Hubbell Law Directory

*MEMPHIS,** Shelby Co.

ARMSTRONG ALLEN PREWITT GENTRY JOHNSTON & HOLMES (AV)

80 Monroe Avenue Suite 700, 38103
Telephone: 901-523-8211
Telecopier: 901-524-4936
Jackson, Missippi Office: 1350 One Jackson Place, 188 East Capitol Street.
Telephone: 601-948-8020.
Telecopier: 601-948-8389.

MEMBERS OF FIRM

Elmore Holmes, III James B. McLaren, Jr.

For Complete List of Firm Personnel, See General Section

For full biographical listings, see the Martindale-Hubbell Law Directory

BAKER, DONELSON, BEARMAN & CALDWELL (AV)

20th Floor, First Tennessee Building, 165 Madison, 38103
Telephone: 901-526-2000
Telecopier: 901-577-2303
Nashville, Tennessee Office: 1700 Nashville City Center, 511 Union Street, 37219.
Telephone: 615-726-5600.
Telecopier: 615-726-0464.
Knoxville, Tennessee Office: 2200 Riverview Tower, 900 Gay Street, 37901.
Telephone: 615-549-7000.
Telecopier: 615-525-8569.
Chattanooga, Tennessee Office: 1800 Republic Centre, 633 Chestnut Street, 37450-1800.
Telephone: 615-752-4400.
Telecopier: 615-752-4410.
Huntsville, Tennessee Office: 3 Courthouse Square, 37756.
Telephone: 615-663-2321.
Telecopier: 615-663-2111.
Johnson City, Tennessee Office: Hamilton Bank Building, 207 Mockingbird Lane, 37604.
Telephone: 615-928-0181.
Telecopier: 615-928-5694; 615-928-3654; Kingsport: 615-246-6191.
Washington, D.C. Office: Market Square, 801 Pennsylvania Avenue, N.W., 20004.
Telephone: 202-508-3400.
Telecopier: 202-508-3402.

PARTNERS

Charles T. Tuggle, Jr. Allan J. Wade

OF COUNSEL

Frierson M. Graves, Jr.

For Complete List of Firm Personnel, See General Section

For full biographical listings, see the Martindale-Hubbell Law Directory

WARING COX (AV)

Morgan Keegan Tower, 50 North Front Street, Suite 1300, 38103-1190
Telephone: 901-543-8000
Telecopy: 901-543-8030

MEMBERS OF FIRM

Robert L. Cox Frank L. Watson, Jr.
Jerald H. Sklar B. Douglas Earthman

(See Next Column)

ASSOCIATE

Michael B. Chance

Representative Clients: Federal Express Corp.; South Central Bell Telephone Co.; Delta Life and Annuity; Miles, Inc.; Underwriters at Lloyd's; United States Fidelity and Guaranty Co.; Vining-Sparks IBG; Flavorite Laboratories, Inc.; Perkins Family Restaurants.

For Complete List of Firm Personnel, See General Section

For full biographical listings, see the Martindale-Hubbell Law Directory

*NASHVILLE,** Davidson Co.

BASS, BERRY & SIMS (AV)

2700 First American Center, 37238-2700
Telephone: 615-742-6200
Telecopy: 615-742-6293
Knoxville, Tennessee Office: 1700 Riverview Tower, 900 S. Gay Street, P.O. Box 1509, 37901-1509.
Telephone: 615-521-6200.
Telecopy: 615-521-6234.

MEMBERS OF FIRM

Charles K. Wray G. Mark Mamantov (Resident, Knoxville, Tennessee Office)
Keith B. Simmons N. B. Forrest Shoaf
George H. Masterson
Karen Scott Neal

Representative Clients: Our lawyers have been involved in bond issues in every County in Tennessee.

For full biographical listings, see the Martindale-Hubbell Law Directory

TEXAS

*AUSTIN,** Travis Co.

SANFORD, SPELLINGS, KUHL & PERKINS, L.L.P. (AV)

400 West 15th Street, Suite 1630, 78701
Telephone: 512-472-9090
FAX: 512-472-9182
Houston, Texas Office: 1180 Galleria Financial Center, 5075 Westheime.
Telephone: 713-850-9000.
Fax: 713-850-1330.

RESIDENT MEMBERS

Marion Sanford, Jr. Robert D. Spellings

For full biographical listings, see the Martindale-Hubbell Law Directory

*DALLAS,** Dallas Co.

HUTCHISON BOYLE BROOKS & FISHER, A PROFESSIONAL CORPORATION (AV)

1700 Pacific Avenue Suite 3900, 75201-4622
Telephone: 214-754-8600
Fax: 214-754-0840
Austin, Texas Office: 98 San Jacinto Boulevard, Suite 1000.
Telephone: 512-477-4121.
Fax: 512-477-4136.

Ray Hutchison Bob C. Griffo (Not admitted in TX)
John F. Boyle, Jr. Sara Tangen
Ben A. Brooks, III Leroy Grawunder, Jr.
David C. Petruska L. Stanton Lowry
Roger E. Beecham

For full biographical listings, see the Martindale-Hubbell Law Directory

JONES, DAY, REAVIS & POGUE (AV)

2300 Trammell Crow Center, 2001 Ross Avenue, 75201
Telephone: 214-220-3939
Cable Address: "Attorneys Dallas"
Telex: 730852
Telecopier: 214-969-5100
In Atlanta, Georgia: 3500 One Peachtree Center, 303 Peachtree Street, N.E.
Telephone: 404-521-3939.
Cable Address: "Attorneys Atlanta".
Telex: 54-2711.
Telecopier: 404-581-8330.
In Brussels, Belgium: Avenue Louise 480, 7th Floor, B-1050 Brussels.
Telephone: 011-32-2-645-14-11.
Telecopier: 011-32-2-645-14-45.
In Chicago, Illinois: 77 West Wacker.
Telephone: 312-782-3939.
Telecopier: 312-782-8585.
In Cleveland, Ohio: North Point, 901 Lakeside Avenue.
Telephone: 216-586-3939.
Cable Address: "Attorneys Cleveland."
Telex: 980389.
Telecopier: 216-579-0212.

(See Next Column)

JONES, DAY, REAVIS & POGUE, *Dallas—Continued*

In Columbus, Ohio: 1900 Huntington Center.
Telephone: 614-469-3939.
Cable Address: "Attorneys Columbus."
Telecopier: 614-461-4198.
In Frankfurt, Germany: Triton Haus, Bockenheimer Landstrasse 42, 60323 Frankfurt am Main.
Telephone: 49-69-9726-3939.
Telecopier: 49-69-9726-3993.
In Geneva, Switzerland: 20, rue de Candolle.
Telephone: 011-41-22-320-2339.
Telecopier: 011-41-22-320-1232.
In Hong Kong: 1501 One Exchange Square, 8 Connaught Place.
Telephone: 011-852-2526-6895.
Telecopier: 011-852-2810-5787.
In Irvine, California: 2603 Main Street, Suite 900.
Telephone: 714-851-3939.
Telex: 194911 Lawyers LSA.
Telecopier: 714-553-7539.
In London, England: One Mount Street.
Telephone: 011-44-71-493-9361.
Cable Address: "Surgoe London WI."
Telecopier: 011-44-71-493-9666.
In Los Angeles, California: 555 West Fifth Street, Suite 4600.
Telephone: 213-489-3939.
Telex: 181439 UD.
Telecopier: 213-243-2539.
In New York, New York: 599 Lexington Avenue.
Telephone: 212-326-3939.
Cable Address: "JONESDAY NEWYORK."
Telex: 237013 JDRP UR.
Telecopier: 212-755-7306.
In Paris, France: 62, rue du Faubourg Saint-Honore.
Telephone: 011-33-1-44-71-3939.
Cable Address: "Surgoe Paris."
Telex: 290156 Surgoe.
Telecopier: 011-33-1-49-24-0471.
In Pittsburgh, Pennsylvania: 500 Grant Street, 31st Floor.
Telephone: 412-391-3939.
Cable Address: "Attorneys Pittsburgh".
Telecopier: 412-394-7959.
In Riyadh, Saudi Arabia: Law Offices of Saud M.A. Shawwaf, P.O. Box 2700.
Telephones: 011 (966-1) 465-6543, 011 (966-1) 464-8534 or 011 (966-1) 464-8540.
Telex: 401831 SAUCON SJ.
Telecopier: (966-1) 464-8480.
In Taipei, Taiwan: 8th Floor, 2 Tun Hwa South Road, Section 2.
Telephone: 011 (886-2) 704-6808.
Telecopier: 011 (886-2) 704-6791.
In Tokyo, Japan: Toranomon MT Building, 4th Floor, 10-3, Toranomon, 3-Chome, Minato-Ku, Tokyo 105, Japan.
Telephone: 011-81-3-3433-3939.
Telecopier: 011-81-3-5401-2725.
In Washington, D.C.: Metropolitan Square, 1450 G Street, N.W.
Telephone: 202-879-3939.
Cable Address: "Attorneys Washington."
Telex: 89-2410 ATTORNEYS WASH.
Telecopier: 202-737-2832.

MEMBERS OF FIRM IN DALLAS

Francis P. Hubach, Jr.
John T. McCafferty
Michael K. Ording

For Complete List of Firm Personnel, See General Section

For full biographical listings, see the Martindale-Hubbell Law Directory

*EL PASO,** El Paso Co.

DIAMOND RASH GORDON & JACKSON, P.C. (AV)

300 East Main Drive, 7th Floor, 79901
Telephone: 915-533-2277
Fax: 915-545-4623

Tom Diamond
Alan V. Rash
Norman J. Gordon
Ronald L. Jackson
John R. Batoon
Robert J. Truhill

Russell D. Leachman

Representative Clients: City of El Paso; El Paso Housing Finance Corp.; City of El Paso Industrial Development Authority; Ysleta del sur Pueblo Indian Tribe; Alabama and Coushatta Indian Tribe of Texas; Metropolitan Life Insurance Company; De Bruyn, Cooper, Maldonada Advertising, Inc.

For full biographical listings, see the Martindale-Hubbell Law Directory

*FORT WORTH,** Tarrant Co.

HAYNES AND BOONE, L.L.P. (AV)

1300 Burnett Plaza, 801 Cherry Street, 76102-4706
Telephone: 817-347-6600
Metro: 817-654-3308
Telecopy: 817-347-6650
Austin, Texas Office: 1600 One American Center, 600 Congress Avenue.
Telephone: 512-867-8400.
Telecopy: 512-867-8470.
Dallas, Texas Office: 3100 NationsBank Plaza, 901 Main Street.
Telephone: 214-651-5000. Metro: 214-263-2310.
Telecopy: 214-651-5940.
Telex: 73-0187.
Houston, Texas Office: 4300 First Interstate Bank Plaza, 1000 Louisiana Street.
Telephone: 713-547-2000.
Telecopy: 713-547-2600.
San Antonio, Texas Office: 112 East Pecan Street, Suite 1600.
Telephone: 210-978-7000.
Telecopy: 210-978-7450.
Washington, D.C. Office: 919 Eighteenth Street, N.W., Suite 800.
Telephone: 202-393-3502.
Telecopy: 202-296-8680.
Mexico City Office: Monte Pelvoux 111, 1er Piso, Col. Lomas de Chapultepec.
Telephone: 011-525-596-7390.
Telecopy: 011-525-596-7798.

MEMBERS OF FIRM

Brian D. Barnard
Keith D. Calcote
Lawrence Andrew Gaydos
William D. Greenhill
Mark C. Hill
David E. Keltner
Wade H. McMullen
John D. Penn
William D. Ratliff, III
G. Dennis Sheehan
Bettye S. Springer

OF COUNSEL

Robert M. Burnett
Michael L. Williams

ASSOCIATES

Terry S. Boone
Richard K. Casner
Matthew D. Goetz
David S. Goldberg
Kight L. Higgins
Amy Nickell Jacobs
Kathleen R. Parker (Not admitted in TX)
Lu Pham
Karen S. Precella
Craig M. Price

For full biographical listings, see the Martindale-Hubbell Law Directory

*HOUSTON,** Harris Co.

VINSON & ELKINS L.L.P. (AV)

2300 First City Tower, 1001 Fannin, 77002-6760
Telephone: 713-758-2222
Fax: 713-758-2346
International Telex: 6868314
Cable Address: Vinelkins
Austin, Texas Office: One American Center, 600 Congress Avenue.
Telephone: 512-495-8400.
Fax: 512-495-8612.
Dallas, Texas Office: 3700 Trammell Crow Center, 2001 Ross Avenue.
Telephone: 214-220-7700.
Fax: 214-220-7716.
Washington, D.C. Office: The Willard Office Building, 1455 Pennsylvania Avenue, N.W.
Telephone: 202-639-6500.
Fax: 202-639-6604.
Cable Address: Vinelkins.
London, England Office: 47 Charles Street, Berkeley Square, London, W1X 7PB, England.
Telephone: 011 (44-171) 491-7236.
Fax: 011 (44-71) 499-5320.
Cable Address: Vinelkins London W.1.
Moscow, Russian Federation Office: 16 Alexey Tolstoy Street, Second Floor, Moscow, 103001 Russian Federation.
Telephone: 011 (70-95) 956-1995.
Telecopy: 011 (70-95) 956-1996.
Mexico City, Mexico Office: Aristóteles 77, 5°Piso, Colonia Chapultepec Polanco, 11560 Mexico, D.F.
Telephone: (52-5) 280-7828.
Fax: (52-5) 280-9223.
Singapore Office: 50 Raffles Place, #19-05 Shell Tower, 0104. U.S. Voice Mailbox: 713-758-3500.
Telephone: (65) 536-8300.
Fax: (65) 536-8311.

Joe B. Allen
Kenneth M. Anderson
Larry G. Barbour
James R. Bertrand
James A. Boone
Francis J. Coleman, Jr.
John C. Dawson, Jr.
Ted A. Hodges
Patricia Hunt Holmes
Donald L. Howell
Lynne B. Humphries
David R. Keyes
Frank E. McCreary, III
Craig W. Murray

(See Next Column)

VINSON & ELKINS L.L.P.—*Continued*

Robert R. Randolph
Stephen C. Tarry
Carolyn Truesdell
Terry A. Yates
Clifford W. Youngblood

ASSOCIATES

Ann Ainsworth
Lori Auray
Trina Hill Chandler
Cristen Cline
Susan M. Edwards
Joel N. Ephross
Paul Steven Hacker
Sheila R. Jones
Jeffrey Scott Lynn
Jeanne H. McDonald
Vincent S. Moreland
Richard H. Mourglia
Robert René Rabalais
Patricia F. Reilly
Terrie L. Sechrist
Annette Faubion Stephens

For Complete List of Firm Personnel, See General Section

For full biographical listings, see the Martindale-Hubbell Law Directory

*SAN ANTONIO,** Bexar Co.

HARDY JACOBSON GAZDA & JACOBSON, P.C. (AV)

400 GPM Building - South Tower, 800 N.W. Loop 410, 78216-5610
Telephone: 210-341-1333
Fax: 210-341-8016

Harvey L. Hardy
Adolph D. Jacobson
Peter F. Gazda
Dana D. Jacobson

For full biographical listings, see the Martindale-Hubbell Law Directory

MATTHEWS & BRANSCOMB, A PROFESSIONAL CORPORATION (AV)

One Alamo Center, 106 S. St. Mary's Street, Suite 800, 78205
Telephone: 210-226-4211
Facsimile: 210-226-0521
Telex: 5106009283
Cable Code: MBLAW
Austin, Texas Office: 301 Congress Avenue, Suite 2050.
Telephone: 512-305-4400.
Facsimile: 512-305-4413.
Corpus Christi, Texas Office: 802 N. Carancahua, Suite 1900.
Telephone: 512-888-9261.
Facsimile: 512-888-8504.
Eagle Pass, Texas Office: 675 Main Street.
Telephone: 210-773-6700.
Facsimile: 210-757-4045.
Uvalde, Texas Office: 200 E. Nopal #208.
Telephone: 210-278-4597.
Facsimile: 210-278-4806.
(Associated with Hall, Quintanilla & Alarcon, L.C., Laredo, Texas, under the name of Hall, Quintanilla, Alarcon, Matthews & Branscomb, P.L.L.C.)

Wilbur L. Matthews
Jon C. Wood
W. Roger Wilson
Howard D. Bye
Kay L. Reamey

Representative Clients: Coca Cola Bottling Company of the Southwest; Concord Oil Co.; Ellison Enterprises, Inc.; H. E. Butt Grocery Co.; Frank B. Hall & Co., Inc.; The Hearst Corp., San Antonio Light Division; San Antonio Gas & Electric Utilities (City Board); Southern Pacific Transportation Co.; Southwest Texas Methodist Hospital.

For Complete List of Firm Personnel, See General Section

For full biographical listings, see the Martindale-Hubbell Law Directory

UTAH

*SALT LAKE CITY,** Salt Lake Co.

BALLARD SPAHR ANDREWS & INGERSOLL (AV)

201 South Main Street, Suite 1200, 84111-2215
Telephone: 801-531-3000
Fax: 801-531-3001
Philadelphia, Pennsylvania Office: 1735 Market Street, 51st Floor.
Telephone: 215-665-8500.
Fax: 215-864-8999.
Denver, Colorado Office: Seventeenth Street Plaza Building, Suite 2300, 1225 17th Street.
Telephone: 303-292-2400.
Fax: 303-296-3956.
Kaunas, Lithuania Office: Donelaičio Kaunas 3000.
Telephone: (370-7) 20 56 66.
Fax: (370-7) 20 56 91.
Washington, D.C. Office: Suite 900 East, 555 13th Street, N.W.
Telephone: 202-383-8800.
Fax: 202-383-8877; 383-8893.
Baltimore, Maryland Office: 300 East Lombard Street, 19th Floor.
Telephone: 410-528-5600.
Fax: 410-528-5650.

(See Next Column)

Camden, New Jersey Office: 800 Hudson Square, 5th Floor.
Telephone: 609-541-5577.
Fax: 609-541-8272.

Blaine L. Carlton
Richard S. Fox
Fredrick H. Olsen
Blake K. Wade

For full biographical listings, see the Martindale-Hubbell Law Directory

CALLISTER, NEBEKER & MCCULLOUGH, A PROFESSIONAL CORPORATION (AV)

800 Kennecott Building, 84133
Telephone: 801-530-7300
Telecopier: 801-364-9127

Louis H. Callister
Fred W. Finlinson
Dorothy C. Pleshe
George E. Harris, Jr.

Representative Clients: Zions First National Bank; Discount Corporation of New York (formerly Smith Capital Markets); State of Utah; Sandy City; Logan City School District; American Fork City; Salt Lake City Suburban Sanitary District No. 1; North Davis County Sewer District; Utah State University; Bank One Arizona, N.A.

For Complete List of Firm Personnel, See General Section

For full biographical listings, see the Martindale-Hubbell Law Directory

RAY, QUINNEY & NEBEKER, A PROFESSIONAL CORPORATION (AV)

Suite 400 Deseret Building, 79 South Main Street, P.O. Box 45385, 84145-0385
Telephone: 801-532-1500
Telecopier: 801-532-7543
Provo, Utah Office: 210 First Security Bank Building, 92 North University Avenue.
Telephone: 801-226-7210.
Telecopier: 801-375-8379.

Brent W. Todd
Dale M. Okerlund
Boyd A. Ferguson

Representative Clients: First Security Bank of Utah, N.A.; Borden, Inc.; Southern Pacific Transportation; Utah Power & Light Co.; Travelers Insurance Co.; Greyhound Leasing & Financial; Holy Cross Hospital and Health System; Amoco Production Co.

For Complete List of Firm Personnel, See General Section

For full biographical listings, see the Martindale-Hubbell Law Directory

VERMONT

*BURLINGTON,** Chittenden Co.

BURAK & ANDERSON (AV)

Executive Square, 346 Shelburne Street, P.O. Box 64700, 05406-4700
Telephone: 802-862-0500
Telecopier: 802-862-8176

MEMBERS OF FIRM

Michael L. Burak
Thomas R. Melloni

For Complete List of Firm Personnel, See General Section

For full biographical listings, see the Martindale-Hubbell Law Directory

VIRGINIA

*RICHMOND,** (Ind. City; Seat of Henrico Co.)

MCGUIRE, WOODS, BATTLE & BOOTHE (AV)

One James Center, 901 East Cary Street, 23219-4030
Telephone: 804-775-1000
Fax: 804-775-1061
Alexandria, Virginia Office: Transpotomac Plaza, Suite 1000, 1199 North Fairfax Street, 22314-1437.
Telephone: 703-739-6200.
Fax: 703-739-6270.
Baltimore, Maryland Office: The Blaustein Building, One North Charles Street, 21201-3793.
Telephone: 410-659-4400.
Fax: 410-659-4599.
Charlottesville, Virginia Office: Court Square Building, P.O. Box 1288, 22902-1288.
Telephone: 804-977-2500.
Fax: 804-980-2222.

(See Next Column)

McGuire, Woods, Battle & Boothe, *Richmond—Continued*

Jacksonville, Florida Office: Barnett Center, Suite 2750, 50 North Laura Street, 32202-3635.
Telephone: 904-798-3200.
Fax: 904-798-3207.
McLean, (Tysons Corner) Virginia Office: 8280 Greensboro Drive, Suite 900, Tysons Corner, 22102-3892.
Telephone: 703-712-5000.
Fax: 703-712-5050.
Norfolk, Virginia Office: World Trade Center, Suite 9000, 101 West Main Street, 23510-1655.
Telephone: 804-640-3700.
Fax: 804-640-3701.
Washington, D.C. Office: The Army and Navy Club Building, 1627 Eye Street, N.W., 20006-4007.
Telephone: 202-857-1700.
Fax: 202-857-1737.
Brussels, Belgium Office: 250 Avenue Louise, Ste. 64, 1050.
Telephone: (32 2) 629 42 11.
Fax: (32 2) 629 42 22.
Zürich, Switzerland Office: P.O. Box 4930, Bahnhofstrasse 3, 8022.
Telephone: (41 1) 225 20 00.
Fax: (41 1) 225 20 20.

MEMBERS OF FIRM

Arthur E. Anderson II
Ann Ramsey Bergan (Resident, Baltimore, Maryland Office)
Steven W. Blaine (Resident, Charlottesville Office)
Alan C. Cason (Resident, Baltimore, Maryland Office)
Curtis M. Coward (Resident, McLean, (Tysons Corner) Office)
Bonnie M. France
Stanley M. Franklin (Resident, McLean (Tysons Corner) Office)
Nancy Ruth Little
Laura R. Lucas (Resident, Norfolk Office)
George Keith Martin
R. Dennis McArver (McLean (Tysons Corner) and Baltimore, Maryland Offices)
Charles L. Menges
David L. Richardson II
George L. Scruggs, Jr.
William J. Strickland
Robert E. Stroud (Resident, Charlottesville Office)
John S. Stump (Resident, McLean (Tysons Corner) Office)
Ernest G. Wilson (Resident, Baltimore, Maryland Office)

OF COUNSEL

John V. Murray
Joseph C. Reid (Resident, Baltimore, Maryland Office)
John H. Toole (Resident, McLean (Tysons Corner) Office)

ASSOCIATES

Stephanie L. Hamlett
Michael L. Jennings (Resident, Baltimore, Maryland Office)
Emery B. McRill (Resident, Baltimore, Maryland Office)
Lloyd M. Richardson

For Complete List of Firm Personnel, See General Section

For full biographical listings, see the Martindale-Hubbell Law Directory

Williams, Mullen, Christian & Dobbins, A Professional Corporation (AV)

Two James Center, 1021 East Cary Street, P.O. Box 1320, 23210-1320
Telephone: 804-643-1991
Fax: 804-783-6456
Glen Allen, Virginia Office: 4401 Waterfront Drive, Suite 140.
Telephone: 804-965-9168.
Fax: 804-965-0955.
Washington, D.C. Office: 1575 Eye Street, N.W.
Telephone: 202-289-6200.
Fax: 202-289-4126.

R. Hart Lee

For Complete List of Firm Personnel, See General Section

For full biographical listings, see the Martindale-Hubbell Law Directory

WASHINGTON

*SEATTLE,** King Co.

Perkins Coie (AV)

A Law Partnership including Professional Corporations
Strategic Alliance with Russell & DuMoulin
1201 Third Avenue, 40th Floor, 98101-3099
Telephone: 206-583-8888
Facsimile: 206-583-8500
Cable Address: "Perki ns Seattle."
Telex: 32-0319 PERKINS SEA
Anchorage, Alaska Office: 1029 West Third Avenue, Suite 300.
Telephone: 907-279-8561.
Facsimile: 907-276-3108.
Telex: 32-0319 PERKINS SEA.

(See Next Column)

Los Angeles, California Office: 1999 Avenue of the Stars, Ninth Floor.
Telephone: 310-788-9900.
Telex: 32-0319 PERKINS SEA.
Facsimile: 310-788-3399.
Washington, D.C. Office: 607 Fourteenth Street, N.W.
Telephone: 202-628-6600.
Facsimile: 202-434-1690.
Telex: 44-0277 PCSO.
Portland, Oregon Office: U.S. Bancorp Tower, Suite 2500, 111 S.W. Fifth Avenue.
Telephone: 503-295-4400.
Facsimile: 503-295-6793.
Telex: 32-0319 PERKINS SEA.
Bellevue, Washington Office: Suite 1800, One Bellevue Center, 411 - 108th Avenue N.E.
Telephone: 206-453-6980.
Facsimile: 206-453-7350.
Telex: 32-0319 PERKINS SEA.
Spokane, Washington Office: North 221 Wall Street, Suite 600.
Telephone: 509-624-2212.
Facsimile: 509-458-3399.
Telex: 32-0319 PERKINS SEA.
Olympia, Washington Office: 1110 Capitol Way South, Suite 405.
Telephone: 206-956-3300.
Strategic Alliance with Russell & DuMoulin, 1700-1075 West Georgia Street, Vancouver, B.C. V6E 3G2. Telephone: 604-631-3131.
Hong Kong Office: 23rd Floor Asia Pacific Finance Tower, Citibank Plaza, 3 Garden Road.
Telephone: 852-2878-1177.
Facsimile: 852-2524-9988. DX-9230-IC.
London, England Office: 36/38 Cornhill, ECV3 3ND.
Telephone: 071-369-9966.
Facsimile: 071-369-9968.
Taipei, Taiwan Office: 8/F TFIT Tower, 85 Jen AiRoad, Sec. 4,Taipei 106, Taiwan, R.O.C.
Telephone: 886-2-778-1177.
Facsimile: 086-2-777-9898.

PARTNERS/SHAREHOLDERS

Richard E. McCann

OF COUNSEL

Wayne C. Booth, Jr.

Counsel for: Seattle School District; Burlington Northern Inc.; Children's Hospital and Medical Center; Economic Development Corporation of Pierce County, State of Washington; King County Hospital District No. 1.

For Complete List of Firm Personnel, See General Section

For full biographical listings, see the Martindale-Hubbell Law Directory

WEST VIRGINIA

*CHARLESTON,** Kanawha Co.

Goodwin & Goodwin (AV)

1500 One Valley Square, 25301
Telephone: 304-346-7000
Fax: 304-344-9692
Ripley, West Virginia Office: 500 Church Street, P.O. Box 349.
Telephone: 304-372-2651.
Parkersburg, West Virginia Office: 201 Third Street, Town Square.
Telephone: 304-485-2345.
Fax: 304-485-3459.

MEMBERS OF FIRM

Joseph R. Goodwin
Michael I. Spiker
Steven F. White
Leonard S. Coleman
Susan C. Wittemeier

Representative Clients: Pennzoil Co.; CSX Corp.; The Eureka Pipe Line Company.

For Complete List of Firm Personnel, See General Section

For full biographical listings, see the Martindale-Hubbell Law Directory

Hamb & Poffenbarger (AV)

Bank One Center, Suite 515, P.O. Box 1671, 25301-1671
Telephone: 304-343-4128
Telecopier: 304-344-1974

MEMBERS OF FIRM

William E. Hamb
John T. Poffenbarger

ASSOCIATE

Robert W. Kiefer, Jr.

Representative Clients: Old Colony Co.; Simonton Building Products, Inc.; Storck Baking Company; Fisher-Brison Properties, Incorporated; First Empire Federal Savings & Loan Assn.; Eagle Bancorp.; SBR, Inc.; Travelers Insurance Companies; Yorel Development Co.; Bays, Inc.

For full biographical listings, see the Martindale-Hubbell Law Directory

Charleston—Continued

JACKSON & KELLY (AV)

1600 Laidley Tower, P.O. Box 553, 25322
Telephone: 304-340-1000
Fax: 304-340-1130
Martinsburg, West Virginia Office: 300 Foxcroft Avenue, P.O. Box 1068.
Telephone: 304-263-8800.
Morgantown, West Virginia Office: 6000 Hampton Center, P.O. Box 619.
Telephone: 304-599-3000.
New Martinsville, West Virginia Office: 256 Russell Avenue, P.O. Box 68.
Telephone: 304-455-1751.
Charles Town, West Virginia Office: 700 East Washington Street, P.O. Box 983.
Telephone: 304-728-6088.
Clarksburg, West Virginia Office: 203 Main Street, P.O. Box 1587.
Telephone: 304-623-3002.
Lexington, Kentucky Office: 175 East Main Street, Suite 500, P.O. Box 2150.
Telephone: 606-255-9500.
Washington, D. C. Office: 2401 Pennsylvania Avenue, N.W., Suite 400.
Telephone: 202-973-0200.
Denver, Colorado Office: Suite 2710, 1660 Lincoln Street.
Telephone: 303-837-0003.

MEMBERS OF FIRM

James Knight Brown
Lee O. Hill
Taunja Willis Miller
Samme L. Gee

Representative Clients: West Virginia Water Development Authority; City of Charleston; West Virginia Regional Jail & Correctional Facility Authority; West Virginia Public Energy Authority; West Virginia University (University of West Virginia Board of Trustees); CAMC; Davis Memorial Hospital; Southern West Virginia Regional Airport Authority; One Valley Bank; National Association; Morgantown Energy Associates.

For Complete List of Firm Personnel, See General Section

For full biographical listings, see the Martindale-Hubbell Law Directory

*CLARKSBURG,** Harrison Co.

STEPTOE & JOHNSON (AV)

Bank One Center, P.O. Box 2190, 26302-2190
Telephone: 304-624-8000
Fax: 304-624-8183
Mailing Address: P.O. Box 2190, 26302-2190
Charleston, West Virginia Office: Seventh Floor, Bank One Center, P.O. Box 1588, 25326-1588.
Telephone: 304-353-8000
Fax: 304-353-8180.
Morgantown, West Virginia Office: 1000 Hampton Center, P.O. Box 1616, 26507-1616.
Telephone: 304-598-8000.
Fax: 304-598-8116.
Martinsburg, West Virginia Office: 126 East Burke Street, P.O. Box 2629, 25401-5429.
Telephone: 304-263-6991.
Fax: 304-263-4785.
Charles Town, West Virginia Office: 104 West Congress Street, P.O. Box 100, 25414-0100.
Telephone: 304-725-1414.
Fax: 304-725-1913.
Hagerstown, Maryland Office: The Bryan Centre, 82 West Washington Street, Fourth Floor, P.O. Box 570, 21740-0570.
Telephone: 301-739-8600.
Fax: 301-739-8742.
Wheeling, West Virginia Office: The Riley Building, Suite 400, 14th & Chapline Streets, P.O. Box 150, 26003-0020.
Telephone: 304-233-0000.
Fax: 304-233-0014.

MEMBERS OF FIRM

Vincent A. Collins
Walter L. Williams
Louis E. Enderle, Jr.

ASSOCIATE

Francesca Tan

Representative Clients: Consolidated Gas Transmission Corp.; Consolidated Coal Co.; CNA; E.I. DuPont de Nemours & Co.; Equitable Resources, Inc.; The Hartford Group; Peabody Coal Co.; PPG Industries; Union National Bank of West Virginia; Ogden Newspapers, Inc.

For Complete List of Firm Personnel, See General Section

For full biographical listings, see the Martindale-Hubbell Law Directory

WISCONSIN

*MILWAUKEE,** Milwaukee Co.

DAVIS & KUELTHAU, S.C. (AV)

111 East Kilbourn Avenue, Suite 1400, 53202-6613
Telephone: 414-276-0200
Facsimile: 414-276-9369
Cable Address: "Shiplaw"

James A. Brindley
Robert H. Buikema
James H. Gormley, Jr.
Thomas E. Mountin
Mark L. Olson
Gary M. Ruesch
Roger E. Walsh

For full biographical listings, see the Martindale-Hubbell Law Directory

MICHAEL, BEST & FRIEDRICH (AV)

100 East Wisconsin Avenue, 53202-4108
Telephone: 414-271-6560
Telecopier: 414-277-0656
Cable Address: "Mibef"
Madison, Wisconsin Office: One South Pinckney Street, Firstar Plaza, P.O. Box 1806, 53701-1806.
Telephone: 608-257-3501.
Telecopier: 283-2275.
Chicago, Illinois Office: 135 South LaSalle Street, Suite 1610, 60603-4391.
Telephone: 312-845-5800.
Telecopier: 312-845-5828.
Affiliated Law Firm: Edward D. Heffernan, Penthouse One, 1019 19th Street, N.W., Washington, D.C. 20036.
Telephone: 202-331-7444.

PARTNERS

Frank J. Pelisek
James S. Levin
John J. McHugh (Resident Partner, Chicago, Illinois Office)
Robert A. Schnur
David J. Hanson (Resident Partner, Madison, Wisconsin Office)
Nelson D. Flynn (Resident Partner, Madison, Wisconsin Office)
Peggy E. Brever
Thomas E. Klancnik (Resident Partner, Madison, Wisconsin Office)
Charles A. Brizzolara (Resident Partner, Chicago, Illinois Office)
Jesse S. Ishikawa (Resident Partner, Madison, Wisconsin Office)
Peter L. Coffey
Thomas C. Judge (Resident Partner, Chicago, Illinois Office)

ASSOCIATES

Raymond P. Taffora (Resident Associate, Madison, Wisconsin Office)
Lynda R. Templen (Resident Associate, Madison, Wisconsin Office)

For Complete List of Firm Personnel, See General Section

For full biographical listings, see the Martindale-Hubbell Law Directory

QUARLES & BRADY (AV)

411 East Wisconsin Avenue, 53202-4497
Telephone: 414-277-5000
Cable Address: "Lawdock"
Fax: 414-271-3552.
TWX: 910-262-3426
Madison, Wisconsin Office: Firstar Plaza, One South Pinckney Street, P.O. Box 2113.
Telephone: 608-251-5000.
Fax: 608-251-9166.
West Palm Beach, Florida Office: 222 Lakeview Avenue, 4th Floor.
Telephone: 407-653-5000.
Fax: 407-653-5333.
Naples, Florida Office: Barnett Center, 4501 Tamiami Trail North.
Telephone: 813-262-5959.
Fax: 813-434-4999.
Phoenix, Arizona Office: One Camelback Building, One East Camelback Road, Suite 400.
Telephone: 602-230-5500.
Fax: 602-230-5598.

MEMBERS OF FIRM
(ALPHABETICALLY BY YEAR OF ADMISSION TO BAR)

John S. Holbrook, Jr. (Resident, Madison Office)
Stephen E. Richman
Michael L. Roshar
Paul R. Schilling
Judith M. Bailey (Resident, Phoenix, Arizona Office)
John T. Whiting (Resident, Madison Office)
Ann M. Murphy
Julianna Ebert
Brian G. Lanser

ASSOCIATE

Rebecca A. Speckhard

For Complete List of Firm Personnel, See General Section

For full biographical listings, see the Martindale-Hubbell Law Directory

Milwaukee—Continued

REINHART, BOERNER, VAN DEUREN, NORRIS & RIESELBACH, S.C. (AV)

1000 North Water Street, P.O. Box 92900, 53202-0900
Telephone: 414-298-1000
Facsimile: 414-298-8097
Denver, Colorado Office: One Norwest Center, 1700 Lincoln Street, Suite 3725.
Telephone: 303-831-0909.
Fax: 303-831-4805.
Madison, Wisconsin Office: 7617 Mineral Point Road, 53701-2020.
Telephone: 608-283-7900.
Fax: 608-283-7919.
Washington, D.C. Office: 601 Pennsylvania Avenue, N.W., North Building, Suite 750.
Telephone: 202-393-3636.
Fax: 202-393-0796.

William R. Steinmetz
William F. Flynn

For Complete List of Firm Personnel, See General Section

For full biographical listings, see the Martindale-Hubbell Law Directory

PUERTO RICO

SAN JUAN, San Juan Dist.

FIDDLER, GONZÁLEZ & RODRÍGUEZ

Chase Manhattan Bank Building (Hato Rey), P.O. Box 363507, 00936-3507
Telephone: 809-753-3113
Telecopier: 809-759-3123

MEMBERS OF FIRM

Julio L. Aguirre
José Julián Alvarez-Maldonado

Representative Clients: Chase Securities; Shearson, Lehman, Hutton; Banco Santander; Government Development Bank for Puerto Rico.

For Complete List of Firm Personnel, See General Section

For full biographical listings, see the Martindale-Hubbell Law Directory

GOLDMAN ANTONETTI & CÓRDOVA

American International Plaza Fourteenth & Fifteenth Floors, 250 Muñoz Rivera Avenue (Hato Rey), P.O. Box 70364, 00936-0364
Telephone: 809-759-8000
Telecopiers: 809-767-9333 (Main)
809-767-9177 (Litigation Department)
809-767-8660 (Labor & Corporate Law Departments)
809-767-9325 (Tax & Environmental Law Departments)

MEMBERS OF FIRM

Jorge Souss
Pedro Morell Losada
Thelma Rivera-Miranda
Francisco J. García-García

ASSOCIATE

Mercedes M. Barreras Soler

Representative Clients: Banque Paribas; Scotiabank de Puerto Rico.

For Complete List of Firm Personnel, See General Section

For full biographical listings, see the Martindale-Hubbell Law Directory

CANADA
QUEBEC

*MONTREAL,** Montreal Dist.

McMASTER MEIGHEN (AV)

A General Partnership
7th Floor, 630 René-Lévesque Boulevard West, H3B 4H7
Telephone: 514-879-1212
Telecopier: 514-878-0605
Cable Address: "Cammerall"
Telex: "Cammerall MTL" 05-268637
Affiliated with Fraser & Beatty in Toronto, North York, Ottawa and Vancouver.

MEMBERS OF FIRM

Thomas C. Camp, Q.C.
Richard W. Shannon
R. Jamie Plant
Jean Daigle
H. John Godber

For Complete List of Firm Personnel, See General Section

For full biographical listings, see the Martindale-Hubbell Law Directory

NATURAL RESOURCES LAW

ALABAMA

*BIRMINGHAM,** Jefferson Co.

BALCH & BINGHAM (AV)

1710 Sixth Avenue North, P.O. Box 306, 35201
Telephone: 205-251-8100
Facsimile: 205-226-8798
Other Birmingham, Alabama Office: 1901 Sixth Avenue North, 35203.
Telephone: 205-251-8100.
Facsimile: 205-226-8799.
Montgomery, Alabama Office: The Winter Building, 2 Dexter Avenue, 36101.
Telephone: 205-834-6500.
Facsimile: 205-269-3115.
Huntsville, Alabama Office: Suite 810, 200 West Court Square, 35801.
Telephone: 205-551-0171.
Facsimile: 205-551-0174.
Washington, D.C. Office: Suite 800, 1101 Connecticut Avenue, N.W., 20036.
Telephone: 202-296-0387.
Facsimile: 202-452-8180.

MEMBERS OF FIRM

Marshall Timberlake
William H. Satterfield
Steven G. McKinney

ASSOCIATES

David B. Champlin
Glenn G. Waddell

Counsel for: Alabama Power Co.; Alabama River Pulp Co., Inc.; Blue Cross and Blue Shield of Alabama; Brasfield & Gorrie, Inc.; Compass Bancshares, Inc.; Harbert Corp.; Kimberly-Clark Corp.; National Energy Partners; Southern Company Services, Inc.; Southern Research Institute.

For Complete List of Firm Personnel, See General Section

For full biographical listings, see the Martindale-Hubbell Law Directory

BRADLEY, ARANT, ROSE & WHITE (AV)

1400 Park Place Tower, 2001 Park Place, 35203
Telephone: 205-521-8000
Telex: 494-1324
Facsimile: 205-251-8611, 251-8665, 252-0264
Facsimile (Southtrust Office): 205-251-9915
Huntsville, Alabama Office: 200 Clinton Avenue West, Suite 900.
Telephone: 205-517-5100.
Facsimile: 205-533-5069.

MEMBERS OF FIRM

Macbeth Wagnon, Jr.
Gary C. Huckaby (Resident, Huntsville Office)
John G. Harrell
Andrew Robert Greene
Walter H. Monroe, III
G. Edward Cassady, III
John E. Hagefstration, Jr.

ASSOCIATES

Frank C. Galloway, III
Anne R. Yuengert

Counsel for: SouthTrust Bank of Alabama, National Association; Energen, Corporation (formerly Alagasco, Inc.); Blount, Inc.; Coca-Cola Bottling Company; United, Inc.; The New York Times Co.; Russell Corp.; Ford Motor Co.; Volkswagen of America, Inc.; Rust International Corp.; Dexter Corporation; Goodyear Tire & Rubber Co.

For Complete List of Firm Personnel, See General Section

For full biographical listings, see the Martindale-Hubbell Law Directory

*MOBILE,** Mobile Co.

ARMBRECHT, JACKSON, DEMOUY, CROWE, HOLMES & REEVES (AV)

1300 AmSouth Center, P.O. Box 290, 36601
Telephone: 334-432-6751
Facsimile: 334-432-6843; 433-3821

MEMBERS OF FIRM

Wm. H. Armbrecht, III
Broox G. Holmes
Conrad P. Armbrecht
Edward G. Hawkins
Grover E. Asmus II
Dabney Bragg Foshee
David E. Hudgens
Duane A. Graham

Representative Clients: Scott Paper Co.; UNOCAL; Exxon Co. (USA); Texaco, Inc.; Mobil Oil Corp.; Pacific Enterprises Oil Co. (USA); Callon Petroleum Co.; BP Exploration, Inc.; Jim Walter Resources, Inc.; Champion International Corp.

For Complete List of Firm Personnel, See General Section

For full biographical listings, see the Martindale-Hubbell Law Directory

(See Next Column)

JOHNSTONE, ADAMS, BAILEY, GORDON AND HARRIS (AV)

Royal St. Francis Building, 104 St. Francis Street, P.O. Box 1988, 36633
Telephone: 334-432-7682
Facsimile: 334-432-2800
Telex: 782040

MEMBERS OF FIRM

Charles B. Bailey, Jr.
Brock B. Gordon
Ben H. Harris, Jr.
William H. Hardie, Jr.
I. David Cherniak
Alan C. Christian

Representative Clients: Exxon Corp.; Conoco Inc.; Amerada Hess.

For Complete List of Firm Personnel, See General Section

For full biographical listings, see the Martindale-Hubbell Law Directory

LYONS, PIPES & COOK, P.C. (AV)

2 North Royal Street, P.O. Box 2727, 36652-2727
Telephone: 334-432-4481
Cable Address: "Lysea"
Telecopier: 334-433-1820

G. Sage Lyons
Wesley Pipes
Norton W. Brooker, Jr.
John Patrick Courtney, III
Caroline C. McCarthy

Representative Clients: Champion International Corp.; Chevron U.S.A., Inc.; Coastal Corp.; Conoco, Inc.; Shell Oil Co.; Sonat, Inc.; Phillips Petroleum Co.; Kerr McGee Corp.; The Nature Conservancy; Atlantic Richfield Co.

For Complete List of Firm Personnel, See General Section

For full biographical listings, see the Martindale-Hubbell Law Directory

*MONTGOMERY,** Montgomery Co.

* indicates certain Bar Register subscribers whose principal office is located elsewhere in the state and who have arranged for representation as a part of the state capital listings that follow

*** BALCH & BINGHAM (AV)**

The Winter Building, 2 Dexter Avenue, P.O. Box 78, 36101
Telephone: 334-834-6500
Facsimile: 334-269-3115
Birmingham, Alabama Offices: 1710 Sixth Avenue North, 35203.
Telephone: 205-251-8100.
Facsimile: 205-226-8798. 1901 Sixth Avenue North, 35203.
Telephone: 205-251-8100.
Facsimile: 205-226-8799.
Huntsville, Alabama Office: Suite 810, 200 West Court Square, 35801.
Telephone: 205-551-0171.
Facsimile: 205-551-0174.
Washington, D.C. Office: Suite 800, 1101 Connecticut Avenue, N.W., 20036.
Telephone: 202-296-0387.
Facsimile: 202-452-8180.

RESIDENT MEMBER OF FIRM

Dorman Walker

Counsel for: Alabama Power Co.; Alabama River Pulp Co., Inc.; Blue Cross and Blue Shield of Alabama; Brasfield & Gorrie, Inc.; Compass Bancshares, Inc.; Harbert Corp.; Kimberly-Clark Corp.; National Energy Partners; Southern Company Services, Inc.; Southern Research Institute.

For Complete List of Firm Personnel, See General Section

For full biographical listings, see the Martindale-Hubbell Law Directory

ARIZONA

*PHOENIX,** Maricopa Co.

APKER, APKER, HAGGARD & KURTZ, P.C. (AV)

2111 East Highland Avenue, Suite 230, 85016
Telephone: 602-381-0085
Telecopier: 602-956-3457

Burton M. Apker
Jerry L. Haggard
David B. Apker
Gerrie Apker Kurtz

Cynthia M. Chandley
Kevin M. Moran

Representative Clients: ASARCO Incorporated; Douglas Land Corp.; Frito-Lay, Inc.; Lawyers Title Insurance Corp.; Nevada Power Company; The North West Life Assurance Co.; Phelps Dodge Corporation; Santa Fe Pacific Gold Corporation; Santa Fe Pacific Industrials; Western Federal Savings & Loan Assn.

For full biographical listings, see the Martindale-Hubbell Law Directory

FENNEMORE CRAIG, A PROFESSIONAL CORPORATION (AV)

Two North Central, Suite 2200, 85004
Telephone: 602-257-8700
Fax: 602-257-8527
Scottsdale, Arizona Office: 6263 North Scottsdale Road, Suite 290, 85250.
Telephone: 602-257-5400.
Fax: 602-945-4932.
Tucson, Arizona Office: One South Church Avenue, Suite 1030, 85701.
Telephone: 602-624-9312.
Fax: 602-882-7383.

Calvin H. Udall
James M. Bush
James W. Johnson
Lauren J. Caster
Timothy Berg
Margaret R. Gallogly
Robert D. Anderson

Douglas C. Northup

Representative Clients: ASARCO Incorporated; AT&T Communications; Bridgestone/Firestone, Inc.; Catellus Development Corp.; Citibank (Arizona); First Interstate Bank of Arizona; GIANT Industries; Phelps Dodge Corporation; The Atchison, Topeka & Santa Fe Railway, Co.; US WEST Communications.

For Complete List of Firm Personnel, See General Section

For full biographical listings, see the Martindale-Hubbell Law Directory

JENNINGS, STROUSS AND SALMON, P.L.C. (AV)

A Professional Limited Liability Company
One Renaissance Square, Two North Central, 85004-2393
Telephone: 602-262-5911
Fax: 602-253-3255

M. Byron Lewis
John B. Weldon, Jr.
James D. Vieregg
Richard N. Morrison
Joseph A. Drazek
Stephen E. Crofton
James M. Ackerman
George Esahak-Gage
Lisa M. McKnight

Mark A. McGinnis

For Complete List of Firm Personnel, See General Section

For full biographical listings, see the Martindale-Hubbell Law Directory

KIMBALL & CURRY, P.C. (AV)

2600 North Central Avenue Suite 1600, 85004
Telephone: 602-222-5920
Fax: 602-222-5929

David P. Kimball, III
J. Stanton Curry
Dalva L. Moellenberg
Laura W. Janzik
David L. Wallis
Todd W. Rallison
John C. Giles
D. Lee Decker
Cameron T. Chandler
Walter E. Rusinek
Lisa A. Schuh (Not admitted in AZ)
Karilee S. Ramaley
Mara G. Linder

Representative Clients: Phelps Dodge Corp.; Talley Industries, Inc.; Arizona Public Service Co.; Motorola, Inc.; Reynolds Metals Co.; Kaibab Industries; U-Haul International, Inc.; Cyprus Amax Minerals Co.; United Industrial Corp.; Southern Pacific Transportation Co.

For full biographical listings, see the Martindale-Hubbell Law Directory

MEYER, HENDRICKS, VICTOR, OSBORN & MALEDON, A PROFESSIONAL ASSOCIATION (AV)

2929 North Central Avenue Suite 2100, 85012-2794
Telephone: 602-640-9000
Facsimile: (24 Hrs.) 602-640-9050
Mailing Address: P.O. Box 33449, 85067-3449,

Jay I. Moyes
James G. Derouin
Jeffrey C. Zimmerman
Lee Herold Storey

Reference: Bank One Arizona, NA.

For Complete List of Firm Personnel, See General Section

For full biographical listings, see the Martindale-Hubbell Law Directory

SNELL & WILMER (AV)

One Arizona Center, 85004-0001
Telephone: 602-382-6000
Fax: 602-382-6070
Tucson, Arizona Office: 1500 Norwest Tower, One South Church Avenue 85701-1612.
Telephone: 602-882-1200.
Fax: 602-884-1294.

(See Next Column)

Orange County Office: 1920 Main Street, Suite 1200, P.O. Box 19601, Irvine, California, 92714.
Telephone: 714-253-2700.
Fax: 714-955-2507.
Salt Lake City, Utah Office: Broadway Centre, 111 East Broadway, Suite 900, 84111.
Telephone: 801-237-1900.
Fax: 801-237-1950.

MEMBERS OF FIRM

George H. Lyons
Robert B. Hoffman
E. Jeffrey Walsh
Steven M. Wheeler
Martha E. Gibbs
G. Van Velsor Wolf, Jr.

ASSOCIATES

Jeffrey Webb Crockett
Thomas L. Mumaw
Clinton J Elliott
Carlos D. Ronstadt
Steve C. Thornton

Representative Clients: Arizona Public Service Company; Coca Cola Enterprises; El Paso Natural Gas Company; Hughes Aircraft; Magma Copper Company; Metro Mobile CTS, Inc.; Mitsubishi Motor Sales of America; Toyota Technical Center; Tucson Airport Authority; Bank One, Arizona, NA.

For Complete List of Firm Personnel, See General Section

For full biographical listings, see the Martindale-Hubbell Law Directory

STREICH LANG, A PROFESSIONAL ASSOCIATION (AV)

Renaissance One, Two N. Central Avenue, 85004-2391
Telephone: 602-229-5200
Fax: 602-229-5690
Tucson, Arizona Office: One S. Church Avenue, Suite 1700.
Telephone: 602-770-8700.
Fax: 602-623-2518.
Las Vegas, Nevada Affiliated Office: Dawson & Associates, 3800 Howard Hughes Parkway, Suite 1500.
Telephone: 702-792-2727.
Fax: 702-792-2676.
Los Angeles, California Office: 444 S. Flower Street, Suite 1530.
Telephone: 213-896-0484.

Steven A. Betts
Roger K. Ferland

Lance L. Shea
Dana Stagg Belknap

Representative Clients: Arizona Portland Cement; Allied-Signal Aerospace Company; Burr-Brown Corporation; Browning-Ferris Industries, Inc.; First Interstate Bank of Arizona, N.A.; Magma Copper Company; Univar Corporation; Valley National Bank of Arizona, N.A.; W.L. Gore and Associates, Inc.

For Complete List of Firm Personnel, See General Section

For full biographical listings, see the Martindale-Hubbell Law Directory

*TUCSON,** Pima Co.

CHANDLER, TULLAR, UDALL & REDHAIR (AV)

1700 Bank of America Plaza, 33 North Stone Avenue, 85701
Telephone: 602-623-4353
Telefax: 602-792-3426

MEMBERS OF FIRM

Thomas Chandler
D. B. Udall
Jack Redhair
Joe F. Tarver, Jr.
Steven Weatherspoon
S. Jon Trachta
Edwin M. Gaines, Jr.
Dwight M. Whitley, Jr.
E. Hardy Smith
John J. Brady
Christopher J. Smith
Charles V. Harrington
Bruce G. MacDonald

ASSOCIATES

Margaret A. Barton
Joel T. Ireland
Mark Fredenberg
Mariann T. Shinoskie
Kurt Kroese

Representative Clients: Arizona Electric Power Cooperative, Inc.; Atlantic Richfield Co.; CNA Insurance; Farmers Insurance Exchange; MICA; Chubb Insurance Group; Aetna Casualty; State Farm Mutual Insurance Companies; Santa Cruz Valley Water Authority.
Reference: Arizona Bank.

For full biographical listings, see the Martindale-Hubbell Law Directory

STRICKLAND & O'HAIR, P.C. (AV)

4400 E. Broadway, Suite 700, 85711-3517
Telephone: 602-795-8727
Fax: 602-795-5649

William E. Strickland
William E. Strickland, Jr.
Jennele Morris O'Hair

Representative Clients: AkChin Indian Community; City of Sierra Vista; City of Benson; Golf 36 Corp.; Town of Mammoth; Town of Patagonia; Fertilizer Company of Arizona, Inc.; Gila Valley Irrigation District; Franklin Irrigation District; City of Globe.
Reference: Bank One (formerly Valley National Bank).

ARKANSAS

*TEXARKANA,** Miller Co.

SMITH, STROUD, MCCLERKIN, DUNN & NUTTER (AV)

State Line Plaza, Box 8030, 75502-5945
Telephone: 501-773-5651
Telecopier: 501-772-2037

MEMBERS OF FIRM

John F. Stroud, Jr.
Hayes C. McClerkin
Charles A. Morgan
Demaris A. Hart

LEGAL SUPPORT PERSONNEL

LEGAL ASSISTANTS

Myra J. Conaway
Sonja L. Oliver

Representative Clients: North American Energy Corporation (NorAm); Southwest Arkansas Water District; Southwest Arkansas Electric Cooperative Corp.; Red River Commission of Arkansas; Mobil Oil Co.; Oryx Energy Co.; Ethyl Corp.; Miller County Levee District No. 2; Miller County Improvement and Drainage District; Oxy, USA, Inc.

For Complete List of Firm Personnel, See General Section

For full biographical listings, see the Martindale-Hubbell Law Directory

CALIFORNIA

COSTA MESA, Orange Co.

MCCORMICK, KIDMAN & BEHRENS (AV)

A Partnership of Professional Corporations
Imperial Bank Building, 695 Town Center Drive Suite 1400, 92626-1924
Telephone: 714-755-3100
Fax: 714-755-3110

MEMBERS OF FIRM

Homer L. (Mike) McCormick, Jr., (P.C.)
Arthur G. Kidman (P.C.)
Russell G. Behrens (P.C.)
Suzanne M. Tague (P.C.)
Michael D. Michaels (P.C.)
Janet R. Morningstar (P.C.)
Douglas J. Evertz (P.C.)

ASSOCIATES

Keith E. McCullough
Allison C. Hargrave
Frank W. Battaile

For full biographical listings, see the Martindale-Hubbell Law Directory

IRVINE, Orange Co.

BROWN, PISTONE, HURLEY, VAN VLEAR & SELTZER, A PROFESSIONAL CORPORATION (AV)

Suite 900 AT&T Building, 8001 Irvine Center Drive, 92718
Telephone: 714-727-0559
Fax: 714-727-0656
Tempe, Arizona Office: 1501 West Fountainhead Parkway, Suite 540.
Telephone: 602-968-2427.
Fax: 602-968-2401.
San Francisco, California Office: Suite 1300, Steuart Street Tower, One Market Plaza.
Telephone: 415-281-2154.
Fax: 415-281-2194.

Ernest C. Brown
Thomas A. Pistone
Gregory F. Hurley
John E. Van Vlear
Margaret A. Seltzer (Resident, San Francisco Office)

Michael K. Wolder
Francis T. Donohue, III
Kedric L. Francis
Michael W. Foster (Resident, Tempe, Arizona Office)
Robert C. Schneider (Resident, Tempe, Arizona Office)
Sarah Namnama Saria
Sheila Patterson
Michael Ray Gandee

OF COUNSEL

Robert G. Mahan
Stephen M. Wontrobski
Brian A. Runkel (Not admitted in CA)

For full biographical listings, see the Martindale-Hubbell Law Directory

LAW OFFICES OF SUSAN M. TRAGER A PROFESSIONAL CORPORATION (AV)

The Landmark Building, Suite 104, 2100 S. E. Main Street, 92714
Telephone: 714-752-8971
Telefax: 714-863-9804

Susan M. Trager

(See Next Column)

Robert C. Hawkins
Michele A. Staples
Larry B. McKenney

Representative Client: San Luis Rey Municipal Water District.
Reference: Sanwa Bank California.

For full biographical listings, see the Martindale-Hubbell Law Directory

*LOS ANGELES,** Los Angeles Co.

DEMETRIOU, DEL GUERCIO, SPRINGER & MOYER (AV)

801 South Grand Avenue, 10th Floor, 90017
Telephone: 213-624-8407
Telecopy: 213-624-0174

MEMBERS OF FIRM

Ronald J. Del Guercio
Craig A. Moyer
Michael A. Francis
Kermit D. Marsh
Priscilla Fritz Adler
Kelly A. Sakir

Reference: Bank of America, L.A. Main Office, Los Angeles, Calif.

For full biographical listings, see the Martindale-Hubbell Law Directory

HANNA AND MORTON (AV)

A Partnership including Professional Corporations
Seventeenth Floor, Wilshire-Grand Building, 600 Wilshire Boulevard, 90017
Telephone: 213-628-7131

MEMBERS OF FIRM

Edward S. Renwick (A Professional Corporation)
James P. Lower
David A. Ossentjuk

OF COUNSEL

Bela G. Lugosi (A Professional Corporation)

ASSOCIATES

Stephen G. Mason
Robert J. Roche
Allison L. Malin

Representative Clients: Atlantic Richfield Co.; Air Liquide America Corp.; Carrier Corp.; Conservation Committee of California Oil & Gas Producers; Mobil Oil Corp.; Occidental Petroleum Corp.; Shell Oil Corp.; Texaco, Inc.; Union Pacific Resources Co.; Unocal.

For Complete List of Firm Personnel, See General Section

For full biographical listings, see the Martindale-Hubbell Law Directory

SHEPPARD, MULLIN, RICHTER & HAMPTON (AV)

A Partnership including Professional Corporations
Forty-Eighth Floor, 333 South Hope Street, 90071-1406
Telephone: 213-620-1780
Telecopier: 213-620-1398
Cable Address: "Sheplaw"
Telex: 19-4424
Orange County, California Office: Seventh Floor, 4695 MacArthur Court, Newport Beach.
Telephone: 714-752-6400.
Telecopier: 714-851-0739.
Telex: 19-4424.
San Francisco, California Office: Seventeenth Floor, Four Embarcadero Center.
Telephone: 415-434-9100.
Telecopier: 415-434-3947.
Telex: 19-4424.
San Diego, California Office: Nineteenth Floor, 501 West Broadway.
Telephone: 619-338-6500.
Telecopier: 619-234-3815.
Telex: 19-4424.

MEMBERS OF FIRM

Lawrence M. Braun
Domenic C. Drago (San Diego Office)
Guy N. Halgren (San Diego Office)
Brent R. Liljestrom (Orange County Office)
Gary J. Nevolo (San Francisco Office)
Jon W. Newby
Prentice L. O'Leary *
Stephen J. O'Neil
Mark T. Okuma
Jack H. Rubens
Stephen C. Taylor *
Timothy B. Taylor (San Diego Office)
Robert E. Williams
Roy G. Wuchitech (Director, The Sheppard, Mullin Environmental Practice Group)

ASSOCIATES

Justine Mary Casey (Orange County Office)
Angela A. Dahl (San Diego Office)
Karin A. Dougan (San Diego Office)

*Professional Corporation

For Complete List of Firm Personnel, See General Section

For full biographical listings, see the Martindale-Hubbell Law Directory

ORANGE, Orange Co.

WALSWORTH, FRANKLIN & BEVINS (AV)

1 City Boulevard West, Suite 308, 92668
Telephone: 714-634-2522
LAW-FAX: 714-634-0686
San Francisco, California Office: 580 California Street, Suite 1335.
Telephone: 415-781-7072.
Fax: 415-391-6258.

Jeffrey P. Walsworth
Ferdie F. Franklin
Ronald H. Bevins, Jr.
Michael T. McCall
Noel Edlin (Resident, San Francisco Office)
Lawrence E. Duffy, Jr.
Sheldon J. Fleming
J. Wayne Allen
James A. Anton
Ingrid K. Campagne (Resident, San Francisco Office)
Robert M. Channel (Resident, San Francisco Office)
Nicholas A. Cipiti
Sharon L. Clisham (Resident, San Francisco Office)
David W. Epps (Resident, San Francisco Office)
Richard M. Hills (Resident, San Francisco Office)
Sandra G. Kennedy
Randall J. Lee (Resident, San Francisco Office)
Kimberly K. Mays
Bruce A. Nelson (Resident, San Francisco Office)
Kevin Pegan
Allan W. Ruggles
Jonathan M. Slipp
Cyrian B. Tabuena (Resident, San Francisco Office)
John L. Trunko
Houston M. Watson, II
Mary A. Watson

For full biographical listings, see the Martindale-Hubbell Law Directory

PASADENA, Los Angeles Co.

LAGERLOF, SENECAL, BRADLEY & SWIFT (AV)

301 North Lake Avenue, 10th Floor, 91101-4107
Telephone: 818-793-9400
FAX: 818-793-5900

MEMBERS OF FIRM

Joseph J. Burris (1913-1980)
Stanley C. Lagerlof
H. Melvin Swift, Jr.
H. Jess Senecal
Jack T. Swafford
John F. Bradley
Timothy J. Gosney
William F. Kruse
Thomas S. Bunn, III
Andrew D. Turner
Rebecca J. Thyne

ASSOCIATES

Paul M. Norman
John F. Machtinger
James D. Ciampa
Ellen M. Burkhart

LEGAL SUPPORT PERSONNEL

Ronald E. Hagler

Representative Clients: Anchor Glass Container Corporation; Bethlehem Steel Corp.; Orthopaedic Hospital; Palmdale Water District; Public Water Agencies Group; Walnut Valley Water District.
Special Counsel: City of Redondo Beach, Calif.; Ventura Port Dist., Calif.

For full biographical listings, see the Martindale-Hubbell Law Directory

*SACRAMENTO,** Sacramento Co.

DOWNEY, BRAND, SEYMOUR & ROHWER (AV)

Suite 1050, 555 Capitol Mall, 95814
Telephone: 916-441-0131
FAX: 916-441-4021

MEMBERS OF FIRM

George D. Basye
Philip A. Stohr
James M. Day, Jr.
Keith E. Pershall
Kevin M. O'Brien
David E. Lindgren
Julie A. Carter
Steven H. Goldberg

ASSOCIATES

David R.E. Aladjem
Wendy M. Fisher
Ronald Liebert
JudyAnne McGinley
Scott L. Shapiro

Counsel for: Las Vegas Valley Water District; East Contra Costa Irrigation District; Enron Oil and Gas Co.; Benton Oil and Gas Co.; Sacramento Municipal Utility District; Reclamation District No. 1000; Amerada Hess; General Motors Corp.; Anheuser-Busch Cos.; Mobil Oil Corp.

For Complete List of Firm Personnel, See General Section

For full biographical listings, see the Martindale-Hubbell Law Directory

COLORADO

*ASPEN,** Pitkin Co.

AUSTIN, PEIRCE & SMITH, P.C. (AV)

Suite 205, 600 East Hopkins Avenue, 81611
Telephone: 303-925-2600
FAX: 303-925-4720

Ronald D. Austin
Frederick F. Peirce
Thomas Fenton Smith

Rhonda J. Bazil

Counsel for: Clark's Market; Coates, Reid & Waldron Realtors; Crystal Palace Corp.; Snowmass Shopping Center; Coldwell Banker; William Poss & Assoc., Architects; Snowmass Resort Association; Real Estate Affiliates, Inc.; Raleigh Enterprises.

For full biographical listings, see the Martindale-Hubbell Law Directory

KEVIN L. PATRICK, P.C. (AV)

Suite 300, 205 South Mill Street, 81611
Telephone: 303-920-1028
FAX: 303-925-6847

Kevin L. Patrick

Brian L. Stowell
Kelly Elizabeth Archer

Representative Clients: Aspcol Corporation, N.V.; McCloskey Enterprises, Inc.; Snowmass Land Company, a joint venture of Heitman Financial, Ltd. and Golub & Co.; Aspen Highlands Ski Area/Hines Highlands Limited Partnership; Dallas Creek Water Company; Fairway Pines Estates Golf Club/Loghill Village Inv.; Telluride Regional Airport Authority; Town of Gypsum; B.C. Ziegler & Company; Velocity Peak, Inc.

For full biographical listings, see the Martindale-Hubbell Law Directory

*BOULDER,** Boulder Co.

VRANESH AND RAISCH, L.L.C. (AV)

1720 14th Street, P.O. Box 871, 80306
Telephone: 303-443-6151
Telecopier: 303-443-9586

MEMBERS OF FIRM

Jerry W. Raisch
John R. Henderson
Michael D. Shimmin
Eugene J. Riordan
Paul J. Zilis
Douglas A. Goulding
George Vranesh (Retired)

Thomas Morris

Representative Clients: Cyprus Climax Metals Co.; City of Fort Collins; Colorado Association of Commerce and Industry; County of Arapahoe; Eastman Kodak Company; Hendricks Mining Company; Horizon Gold Corporation, Inc.; Metro Wastewater Reclamation District; Phillips Petroleum Company; Waste Management of North America.

For full biographical listings, see the Martindale-Hubbell Law Directory

*DENVER,** Denver Co.

ROBERT L. BARTHOLIC (AV)

Suite 600, 1600 Broadway, 80202
Telephone: 303-830-0500
Fax: 303-860-7855

OF COUNSEL

Clarence L. Bartholic

Approved Attorney for: Mid-South Title Insurance Corp; Lawyers Title Insurance Co.
Representative Clients: Anschutz Corp.; Denver and Rio Grande Western Railroad Co.; Johnson Anderson Mortgage Co.; Arco Environmental Affairs; Burlington Northern Railroad Co. and Subsidiaries; American Association of Private Railroad Car Owners, Inc.
References: Colorado National Bank; Colorado State Bank.

For full biographical listings, see the Martindale-Hubbell Law Directory

BURNS WALL SMITH AND MUELLER, A PROFESSIONAL CORPORATION (AV)

Suite 800, 303 East Seventeenth Avenue, 80203-1260
Telephone: 303-830-7000
Telecopier: 303-830-6708
Telex: 650-278-8717 (MCI UW)

Peter J. Wall
Gregory J. Smith
George W. Mueller
James E. Bosik
Steven F. Mueller
Robert T. Cosgrove

(See Next Column)

BURNS WALL SMITH AND MUELLER A PROFESSIONAL CORPORATION—*Continued*

James P. Rouse, Donald D. Farlow, Gretchen L. Aultman, Mark D. Masters

OF COUNSEL

Thomas M. Burns, Darrell C. Miller, Frank H. Houck, Anthony van Westrum

SPECIAL COUNSEL

John D. Amen, Robert Neece, Jack M. Merritts

Representative Clients: Snyder Oil Corporation; Amoco Production Company; Cabot Oil & Gas Production Corp.; Mull Drilling Company, Inc.; Presidio Exploration, Inc.; Advance Geophysical Corporation; Northern Geophysical of America Inc.; Bannon Energy Incorporated; Harvard Gold Mining Co.; Pacific Industrial Systems, Inc.

For full biographical listings, see the Martindale-Hubbell Law Directory

CLANAHAN, TANNER, DOWNING AND KNOWLTON, P.C. (AV)

Suite 2400, 1600 Broadway, 80202
Telephone: 303-830-9111
Telecopier: 303-830-0299

David C. Knowlton, Jack D. Henderson, Thomas C. McKee, Peter T. Moore, Denis B. Clanahan, Judith M. Matlock, Michael J. Wozniak, C. Kevin Cahill, James M. Colosky, Gary P. LaPlante, J. David Arkell, Richard L. Shearer, James T. Ayers, Jr., David M. Rich, Janet N. Harris, Langdon J. Jorgensen, Sheryl L. Howe, Brian D. Fitzgerald

Robert J. Bricmont, Jr., Robert M. O'Hayre, Dino A. Ross, Richard J. Gognat

SPECIAL COUNSEL

Joseph K. Reynolds, Leslie Abrams Pizzi

OF COUNSEL

Barkley L. Clanahan, Ira E. Tanner, Jr., Richard Downing, Jr.

Representative Clients: Amoco Production Company; Ampol Exploration (U.S.A.), Inc.; Apache Corporation; Barrett Resources Corp.; Enron Oil and Gas Co.; KN Production Company; Maxus Exploration Company; Oryx Energy Company; Snyder Oil Corporation; Western Natural Gas and Transmission Co.

For Complete List of Firm Personnel, See General Section

For full biographical listings, see the Martindale-Hubbell Law Directory

DUFFORD & BROWN, P.C. (AV)

1700 Broadway, Suite 1700, 80290-1701
Telephone: 303-861-8013
Facsimile: 303-832-3804

Philip G. Dufford, Phillip D. Barber, William C. Robb, Jack F. Ross, Richard L. Fanyo, Eugene F. Megyesy, Jr.

SPECIAL COUNSEL

Morris B. Hecox, Jr., Deborah L. Freeman

Representative Clients: BHP-Minerals, Inc.; CF&I Steel Corp.; Chevron Shale Oil Company; Coors Brewing Company; Echo Bay-Sunnyside Gold; Powderhorn Coal Co.; Energy Fuels Coal, Inc.; Equitable Resources Energy Company (Balcron Oil Division); Gold Express Corporation; Howell Petroleum Company.

For Complete List of Firm Personnel, See General Section

For full biographical listings, see the Martindale-Hubbell Law Directory

HOLLAND & HART (AV)

Suite 2900, 555 Seventeenth Street, P.O. Box 8749, 80201
Telephone: 303-295-8000
Cable Address: "Holhart Denver"
Telecopier: 303-295-8261
TWX: 910-931-0568
Denver Tech Center, Colorado Office: Suite 1050, 4601 DTC Boulevard.
Telephone: 303-290-1600.
Telecopier: 303-290-1606.
Aspen, Colorado Office: 600 East Main Street.
Telephone: 303-925-3476.
Telecopier: 303-925-9367.
Boulder, Colorado Office: Suite 500, 1050 Walnut.
Telephone: 303-473-2700.
Telecopier: 303-473-2720.

(See Next Column)

Colorado Springs, Colorado Office: Suite 1000, 90 S. Cascade Avenue.
Telephone: 719-475-7730.
Telex: 82077 SHHTLX.
Telecopier: 719-634-2461.
Washington, D.C. Office: Suite 310, 1001 Pennsylvania Avenue, N.W.
Telephone: 202-638-5500.
Telecopier: 202-737-8998.
Boise, Idaho Office: Suite 1400, West One Plaza, 101 South Capitol Boulevard, P.O. Box 2527.
Telephone: 208-342-5000.
Telecopier: 208-343-8869.
Billings, Montana Office: Suite 1500, First Interstate Center, 401 North 31st Street, P.O. Box 639.
Telephone: 406-252-2166.
Telecopier: 406-252-1669.
Salt Lake City, Utah Office: Suite 880, 111 East Broadway.
Telephone: 801-578-6000.
FAX: 801-578-6010.
Cheyenne, Wyoming Office: Holland & Hart, A Partnership including Professional Corporations, Suite 500, 2020 Carey Avenue, P.O. Box 1347.
Telephone: 307-778-4200.
Telecopier: 307-778-8175.
Jackson, Wyoming Office: Holland & Hart, A Partnership including Professional Corporations, Suite 2, 175 South King Street, P.O. Box 68.
Telephone: 307-739-9741.
Telecopier: 307-739-9744.

MEMBERS OF FIRM

Frank H. Morison (Retired), John Arthur Ramsey, William E. Murane, Paul D. Phillips, H. Gregory Austin, John F. Shepherd, Dennis M. Jackson, Davis O. O'Connor, Stephen H. Foster (Not admitted in CO), Jeanine Feriancek, Anne J. Castle, Robert T. Connery, Brian R. Hanson, Denise W. Kennedy

OF COUNSEL

Lawrence E. Volmert

ASSOCIATES

Douglas L. Abbott, Steven W. Black, Margaret Althoff, Jane Lowell Montgomery

DENVER TECH CENTER, COLORADO RESIDENT PARTNER

Robert M. Pomeroy, Jr.

ASPEN, COLORADO RESIDENT PARTNERS

James T. Moran, Arthur C. Daily, Arthur B. Ferguson, Jr.

ASPEN, COLORADO OF COUNSEL

James B. Boyd

COLORADO SPRINGS, COLORADO PARTNERS

Jack W. Foutch (Retired), Edward H. Flitton (Resident)

WASHINGTON, D.C. RESIDENT PARTNERS

J. Peter Luedtke, Michael J. Brennan, William F. Demarest, Jr., Steven G. Barringer

OF COUNSEL

Thomas L. Sansonetti

WASHINGTON, D.C. SPECIAL COUNSEL

Adelia Smith Borrasca

WASHINGTON, D.C. RESIDENT ASSOCIATE

Kelly Anne Johnson

BOISE, IDAHO RESIDENT OF COUNSEL

Brian J. King

BOISE, IDAHO RESIDENT ASSOCIATES

Murray D. Feldman, Linda B. Jones

BILLINGS, MONTANA PARTNER

Donald W. Quander

BILLINGS, MONTANA SPECIAL COUNSEL

Robert A. Lorenz

CHEYENNE, WYOMING PARTNERS

Jack D. Palma, II (P.C.), Edward W. Harris, Donald I. Schultz (P.C.), Lawrence J. Wolfe (P.C.)

CHEYENNE, WYOMING RESIDENT ASSOCIATES

James R. Belcher, Lynnette J. Boomgaarden, Catherine W. Hansen

JACKSON, WYOMING RESIDENT PARTNERS

John L. Gallinger (P.C.), Marilyn S. Kite (P.C.)

SALT LAKE CITY UTAH RESIDENT PARTNER

Lawrence J. Jensen

For Complete List of Firm Personnel, See General Section

For full biographical listings, see the Martindale-Hubbell Law Directory

Denver—Continued

HOLME ROBERTS & OWEN LLC (AV)

Suite 4100, 1700 Lincoln, 80203
Telephone: 303-861-7000
Telex: 45-4460
Telecopier: 303-866-0200
Boulder, Colorado Office: Suite 400, 1401 Pearl Street.
Telephone: 303-444-5955.
Telecopier: 303-444-1063.
Colorado Springs, Colorado Office: Suite 1300, 90 South Cascade Avenue.
Telephone: 719-473-3800.
Telecopier: 719-633-1518.
Salt Lake City, Utah Office: Suite 1100, 111 East Broadway.
Telephone: 801-521-5800.
Telecopier: 801-521-9639.
London, England Office: 4th Floor, Mellier House, 26a Albemarle Street.
Telephone: 44-171-499-8776.
Telecopier: 44-171-499-7769.
Moscow, Russia Office: 14 Krivokolenny Pr., Suite 30, 101000.
Telephone: 095-925-7816.
Telecopier: 095-923-2726.

MEMBERS OF FIRM

Paul D. Holleman
Frank Erisman
William R. Roberts (Boulder Office)
David K. Detton (Salt Lake City Office)
Thomas F. Cope
Lynn Parker Hendrix
Jan N. Steiert
Marla J. Williams
Steven B. Richardson

OF COUNSEL

A. Edgar Benton

ASSOCIATES

John Adams Barrett, Jr. (On Leave of Absence)
James F. Cress
Staunton L. T. Golding

For Complete List of Firm Personnel, See General Section

For full biographical listings, see the Martindale-Hubbell Law Directory

LOHF, SHAIMAN & JACOBS, P.C. (AV)

900 Cherry Tower, 950 South Cherry Street, 80222
Telephone: 303-753-9000
Telecopier: 303-753-9997

David G. Ebner
J. Michael Morgan

Reference: Professional Bank.

For full biographical listings, see the Martindale-Hubbell Law Directory

NETZORG & MCKEEVER, PROFESSIONAL CORPORATION (AV)

5251 DTC Parkway (Englewood) Penthouse One, 80111
Telephone: 303-770-8200
Fax: 303-770-8342

Gordon W. Netzorg
J. Nicholas McKeever, Jr.
Susan Bernhardt
Cecil E. Morris, Jr.

For full biographical listings, see the Martindale-Hubbell Law Directory

POULSON, ODELL & PETERSON (AV)

Suite 1400, 1775 Sherman Street, 80203
Telephone: 303-861-4400
Telecopier: 303-861-1225

MEMBERS OF FIRM

William G. Odell
C. M. Peterson (Retired)
Randall M. Case
Stephen M. Thompson
Carleton L. Ekberg
Alan B. Cameron

SPECIAL COUNSEL

MaryBeth Sobel

OF COUNSEL

Robert D. Poulson
Arthur Thad Smith
Gary H. Hoff
James W. Campbell (Retired)

ASSOCIATES

Daniel E. Evans
William F. Leonard
Scott M. Campbell

Representative Clients: Amoco Production Co.; Anadarko Petroleum Corp.; Conoco, Inc.; Enron Oil and Gas Co.; Exxon Co., USA; Fort Collins Consolidated Royalties, Inc.; Meridian Oil Inc.; Mobil Oil Corp.; Pennzoil Exploration and Production Co.

For full biographical listings, see the Martindale-Hubbell Law Directory

SHERMAN & HOWARD L.L.C. (AV)

Attorneys at Law
633 Seventeenth Street, Suite 3000, 80202
Telephone: 303-297-2900
Telecopier: 303-298-0940
Colorado Springs, Colorado Office: Suite 1500, 90 South Cascade Avenue, 80903.
Telephone: 719-475-2440.

(See Next Column)

Las Vegas, Nevada Office: Swendseid & Stern a member in Sherman & Howard L.L.C., 317 Sixth Street, 89101.
Telephone: 702-387-6073.
Reno, Nevada Office: Swendseid & Stern, a member in Sherman & Howard L.L.C., 50 West Liberty Street, Suite 660, 89501.
Telephone: 702-323-1980.

Alan J. Gilbert
Ronald M. Eddy
Leanne B. DeVos

COUNSEL

Gary L. Greer

Richard T. Galanits

Representative Clients: Newmont Gold Corp.; Benson Mineral Co.; Bow Valley Exploration (U.S.), Inc.; Union Oil Company of America (UNOCAL).

For Complete List of Firm Personnel, See General Section

For full biographical listings, see the Martindale-Hubbell Law Directory

WELBORN SULLIVAN MECK & TOOLEY, P.C. (AV)

Mellon Financial Center, 1775 Sherman Street, Suite 1800, 80203
Telephone: 303-830-2500
Facsimile: 303-832-2366

John F. Welborn
Stephen J. Sullivan
John F. Meck
Molly Sommerville
Marla E. Valdez
Karen Ostrander-Krug

Scott L. Sells

For Complete List of Firm Personnel, See General Section

For full biographical listings, see the Martindale-Hubbell Law Directory

LOUISVILLE, Boulder Co.

STEPHEN T. WILLIAMSON (AV)

813 Main, P.O. Box 850, 80027
Telephone: 303-666-4060
Fax: 303-666-4426

ASSOCIATE

Alan G. Hill

For full biographical listings, see the Martindale-Hubbell Law Directory

DISTRICT OF COLUMBIA

WASHINGTON, D.C. Co.

* indicates certain Bar Register subscribers, in cities of comparable size and importance, who maintain an additional office in Washington, D.C. and who have arranged for representation as a part of the Washington, D.C. listings that follow

* **BAKER & BOTTS, L.L.P.** (AV)

A Registered Limited Liability Partnership
The Warner, 1299 Pennsylvania Avenue, N.W., 20004-2400
Telephone: 202-639-7700
Fax: 202-639-7832
Houston, Texas Office: One Shell Plaza, 910 Louisiana.
Telephone: 713-229-1234.
Austin, Texas Office: 1600 San Jacinto Center, 98 San Jacinto Boulevard.
Telephone: 512-322-2500.
Dallas, Texas Office: 2001 Ross Avenue.
Telephone: 214-953-6500.
New York, New York Office: 805 Third Avenue, Suite 2000.
Telephone: 212-705-5000.
Moscow, Russian Federation Office: 10 ul. Pushkinskaya, 103031.
Telephone: 7095/921-5300 (Local); 7501/929-7070 (International).

MEMBERS OF FIRM

Bruce F. Kiely
Charles M. Darling, IV
Randolph Quaile McManus
J. Patrick Berry
Thomas J. Eastment
Steven R. Hunsicker
Hugh Tucker
John B. Veach, III

ASSOCIATES

Debra Raggio Bolton
Drew J. Fossum
Jennifer S. Leete (Not admitted in DC)
Mark K. Lewis

For Complete List of Firm Personnel, See General Section

For full biographical listings, see the Martindale-Hubbell Law Directory

Washington—Continued

Balch & Bingham (AV)

1101 Connecticut Avenue, N.W., Suite 800, 20036
Telephone: 202-296-0387
Facsimile: 202-452-8180
Birmingham, Alabama Offices: 1710 Sixth Avenue North, 35203.
Telephone: 205-251-8100.
Facsimile: 205-226-8798. 1901 Sixth Avenue North, 35203.
Telephone: 205-251-8100.
Facsimile: 205-226-8799.
Montgomery, Alabama Office: The Winter Building, 2 Dexter Avenue, 36101.
Telephone: 205-834-6500.
Facsimile: 205-269-3115.
Huntsville, Alabama Office: Suite 810, 200 West Court Square, 35801.
Telephone: 205-551-0171.
Facsimile: 205-551-0174.

RESIDENT MEMBER OF FIRM

Karl R. Moor (Not admitted in DC)

Counsel for: Alabama Power Co.; Alabama River Pulp Co., Inc.; Blue Cross and Blue Shield of Alabama; Brasfield & Gorrie, Inc.; Compass Bancshares, Inc.; Harbert Corp.; Kimberly-Clark Corp.; National Energy Partners; Southern Company Services, Inc.; Southern Research Institute.

For Complete List of Firm Personnel, See General Section

For full biographical listings, see the Martindale-Hubbell Law Directory

Brickfield, Burchette & Ritts, P.C. (AV)

8th Floor, West Tower, 1025 Thomas Jefferson Street, N.W., 20007-0805
Telephone: 202-342-0800
Fax: 202-342-0807
Austin, Texas Office: Suite 1050, 1005 Congress Avenue.
Telephone: 512-472-1081.

Peter J. P. Brickfield
William H. Burchette
Mark C. Davis (Not admitted in DC; Resident, Austin, Texas Office)
Daniel C. Kaufman
Michael E. Kaufmann
Peter J. Mattheis
Michael N. McCarty
Frederick H. Ritts
Fernando Rodriguez (Not admitted in DC; Resident, Austin, Texas Office)
Christine C. Ryan
Garrett A. Stone

COUNSEL

Philip L. Chabot, Jr.
Foster De Reitzes
Robert L. McCarty
A. Hewitt Rose

Lisa A. Cottle (Not admitted in DC)
Vincent P. Duane
Julie B. Greenisen (Not admitted in DC)
Stephen J. Karina (Not admitted in DC)
Sandra E. Rizzo
Sonnet C. Schmidt (Not admitted in DC)

LEGAL SUPPORT PERSONNEL

Jean Levicki

For full biographical listings, see the Martindale-Hubbell Law Directory

Freedman, Levy, Kroll & Simonds (AV)

Suite 825, 1050 Connecticut Avenue, N.W., 20036-5366
Telephone: 202-457-5100
Cable Address: "Attorneys"
Telecopier: 202-457-5151

MEMBER OF FIRM

Lawrence G. McBride

OF COUNSEL

Arnold Levy
Jerome H. Simonds

For Complete List of Firm Personnel, See General Section

For full biographical listings, see the Martindale-Hubbell Law Directory

Frank W. Frisk, Jr., P.C. (AV)

Suite 125, Canal Square, 1054 Thirty-First Street, N.W., 20007
Telephone: 202-333-8433
Fax: 202-333-8431

Frank W. Frisk, Jr.

For full biographical listings, see the Martindale-Hubbell Law Directory

John, Hengerer & Esposito (AV)

Suite 600, 1200 17th Street, N.W., 20036
Telephone: 202-429-8800
Telecopier: 202 429-8805

MEMBERS OF FIRM

Douglas F. John
Edward W. Hengerer
Peter G. Esposito
Kevin M. Sweeney
Kim M. Clark

(See Next Column)

ASSOCIATES

Gordon J. Smith (Not admitted in DC)
Kathryn L. Patton (Not admitted in DC)

For full biographical listings, see the Martindale-Hubbell Law Directory

Morley Caskin (AV)

1225 Eye Street, N.W., Suite 402, 20005
Telephone: 202-789-1100
Facsimile: 202-289-3928

OF COUNSEL

Stanley M. Morley (1912-1991)

MEMBERS OF FIRM

Joel F. Zipp
William A. Mogel
George H. Williams, Jr.
Paul W. Diehl

For full biographical listings, see the Martindale-Hubbell Law Directory

Sutherland, Asbill & Brennan (AV)

1275 Pennsylvania Avenue, N.W., 20004-2404
Telephone: 202-383-0100
Cable Address: "Sutab Wash"
Telex: 89-501
Facsimile: 202-637-3593
Atlanta, Georgia Office: 999 Peachtree Street, N. E., 30309-3996.
Telephone: 404-853-8000.
New York, N.Y. Office: 1270 Avenue of the Americas, 10020-1700.
Telephone: 212-332-3000.
Austin, Texas Office: 111 Congress Avenue, 23rd Floor, 78701-4079.
Telephone: 512-469-3350.

Robert W. Clark
Philip R. Ehrenkranz
Edward J. Grenier, Jr.
Glen S. Howard
Keith R. McCrea
Michael T. Mishkin
William H. Penniman

COUNSEL

Sterling H. Smith

For Complete List of Firm Personnel, See General Section

For full biographical listings, see the Martindale-Hubbell Law Directory

*** Venable, Baetjer, Howard & Civiletti (AV)**

A Partnership including Professional Corporations
Suite 1000, 1201 New York Avenue, N.W., 20005
Telephone: 202-962-4800
Fax: 202-962-8300
Baltimore, Maryland Office: Venable, Baetjer and Howard, 1800 Mercantile Bank & Trust Building, 2 Hopkins Plaza.
Telephone: 410-244-7400.
McLean, Virginia Office: Venable, Baetjer and Howard, Suite 400, 2010 Corporate Ridge.
Telephone: 703-760-1600.
Rockville, Maryland Office: Venable, Baetjer and Howard, Suite 500, One Church Street, P. O. Box 1906.
Telephone: 301-217-5600.
Towson, Maryland Office: Venable, Baetjer and Howard, 210 Allegheny Avenue, P. O. Box 5517.
Telephone: 410-494-6200.

MEMBERS OF FIRM

Benjamin R. Civiletti (P.C.) (Also at Baltimore and Towson, Maryland Offices)
Anthony M. Carey (Not admitted in DC; Also at Baltimore, Maryland Office)
John G. Milliken (Also at McLean, Virginia Office)
Max Stul Oppenheimer (P.C.) (Also at Baltimore and Towson, Maryland Offices)
Joseph G. Block
Michael Schatzow (Also at Baltimore and Towson, Maryland Offices)
John F. Cooney
James K. Archibald (Also at Baltimore and Towson, Maryland Offices)
Judson W. Starr (Also at Baltimore and Towson, Maryland Offices)
Jeffrey A. Dunn (Also at Baltimore, Maryland Office)
James L. Shea (Not admitted in DC; also at Baltimore, Maryland Office)
John J. Pavlick, Jr.
James A. Dunbar (Also at Baltimore, Maryland Office)
Thomas J. Kelly, Jr.

ASSOCIATES

Gregory S. Braker (Not admitted in DC)
Andrew R. Herrup
Valerie K. Mann

For Complete List of Firm Personnel, See General Section

For full biographical listings, see the Martindale-Hubbell Law Directory

Washington—Continued

VERNER, LIIPFERT, BERNHARD, MCPHERSON AND HAND, CHARTERED (AV)

901 15th Street, N.W., 20005-2301
Telephone: 202-371-6000
Cable Address: "Verlip"
Telex: 1561792 VERLIP UT
Fax: 202-371-6279
McLean, Virginia Office: Sixth Floor, 8280 Greensboro Drive, 22102.
Telephone: 703-749-6000.
Fax: 703-749-6027.
Houston, Texas Office: 2600 Texas Commerce Tower, 600 Travis, 77002.
Telephone: 713-237-9034.
Fax: 713-237-1216.

Douglas Ochs Adler
J. Cathy Fogel
Andrea Jill Grant
Gary J. Klein
Glen L. Ortman
Clinton A. Vince
Bernhardt K. Wruble
John H. Zentay

For Complete List of Firm Personnel, See General Section

For full biographical listings, see the Martindale-Hubbell Law Directory

FLORIDA

*MIAMI,** Dade Co.

EARL, BLANK, KAVANAUGH & STOTTS, PROFESSIONAL ASSOCIATION (AV)

Suite 3636, One Biscayne Tower, Two South Biscayne Boulevard, 33131
Telephone: 305-358-3000
FAX: 305-358-5079
Sarasota, Florida Office: 1800 Second Street.
Telephone: 813-366-1180.
FAX: 813-366-1183.
Tallahassee, Florida Office: 116 E. Jefferson Street.
Telephone: 904-681-1900.
Fax: 904-681-0989.

William L. Earl
Robert H. Blank
Judith Smith Kavanaugh
Dennis M. Stotts
Mark T. Kobelinski
Stephen R. Verbit

Reference: NationsBank, N.A.

For full biographical listings, see the Martindale-Hubbell Law Directory

JOSEPH Z. FLEMING, P.A. (AV)

620 Ingraham Building, 25 Southeast Second Avenue, 33131
Telephone: 305-373-0791
Telecopier: 305-358-5933

Joseph Z. Fleming

For full biographical listings, see the Martindale-Hubbell Law Directory

STEARNS WEAVER MILLER WEISSLER ALHADEFF & SITTERSON, P.A. (AV)

Suite 2200 Museum Tower, 150 West Flagler Street, 33130
Telephone: 305-789-3200
FAX: 305-789-3395
Tampa, Florida Office: Suite 2200 Landmark Centre, 401 East Jackson Street.
Telephone: 813-223-4800.
Fort Lauderdale, Florida Office: 200 East Broward Boulevard, Suite 1900.
Telephone: 305-462-9500.

E. Richard Alhadeff
Louise Jacowitz Allen
Stuart D. Ames
Thomas P. Angelo (Resident, Fort Lauderdale Office)
Lawrence J. Bailin (Resident, Tampa Office)
Patrick A. Barry (Resident, Fort Lauderdale Office)
Lisa K. Bennett (Resident, Fort Lauderdale Office)
Susan Fleming Bennett (Resident, Tampa Office)
Mark J. Bernet (Resident, Tampa Office)
Claire Bailey Carraway (Resident, Tampa Office)
Seth T. Craine (Resident, Tampa Office)
Piero Luciano Desiderio (Resident, Fort Lauderdale Office)
Mark P. Dikeman
Sharon Quinn Dixon
Alan H. Fein
Owen S. Freed
Dean M. Freitag
Robert E. Gallagher, Jr.
Alice R. Huneycutt (Resident, Tampa Office)
Theodore A. Jewell
Elizabeth J. Keeler
Teddy D. Klinghoffer
Robert T. Kofman
Thomas A. Lash (Resident, Tampa Office)
Joy Spillis Lundeen
Brian J. McDonough

(See Next Column)

Francisco J. Menendez
Antonio R. Menendez
Alison W. Miller
Vicki Lynn Monroe
Harold D. Moorefield, Jr.
John N. Muratides (Resident, Tampa Office)
John K. Olson (Resident, Tampa Office)
Robert C. Owens
Patricia A. Redmond
Carl D. Roston
Steven D. Rubin
Mark A. Schneider
Curtis H. Sitterson
Mark D. Solov
Eugene E. Stearns
Bradford Swing
Dennis R. Turner
Ronald L. Weaver (Resident, Tampa Office)
Robert I. Weissler
Patricia G. Welles
Martin B. Woods (Resident, Fort Lauderdale Office)

Shawn M. Bayne (Resident, Fort Lauderdale Office)
Lisa Berg
Hans C. Beyer (Resident, Tampa Office)
Dawn A. Carapella (Resident, Tampa Office)
Christina Maria Diaz
Robert I. Finvarb
Patricia K. Green
Marilyn D. Greenblatt
Richard B. Jackson
Aimee C. Jimenez
Cheryl A. Kaplan
Michael I. Keyes
Vernon L. Lewis
Kevin Bruce Love
Adam Coatsworth Mishcon
Elizabeth G. Rice (Resident, Tampa Office)
Glenn M. Rissman
Claudia J. Saenz
Richard E. Schatz
Robert P. Shantz (Resident, Tampa Office)
Martin S. Simkovic
Ronni D. Solomon
Jo Claire Spear (Resident, Tampa Office)
Gail Marie Stage (Resident, Fort Lauderdale Office)
Annette Torres

Barbara L. Wilhite

OF COUNSEL

Stephen A. Bennett

For full biographical listings, see the Martindale-Hubbell Law Directory

THOMSON MURARO RAZOOK & HART, P.A. (AV)

17th Floor, One Southeast Third Avenue, 33131
Telephone: 305-350-7200
Telecopier: 305-374-1005

Parker Davidson Thomson
Robert E. Muraro
Carol A. Licko
Sarah L. Schweitzer

Representative Clients: State of Florida; United States Sugar Corporation.

For Complete List of Firm Personnel, See General Section

For full biographical listings, see the Martindale-Hubbell Law Directory

PALM BEACH GARDENS, Palm Beach Co.

SCOTT, ROYCE, HARRIS, BRYAN, BARRA & JORGENSEN, PROFESSIONAL ASSOCIATION (AV)

4400 PGA Boulevard, Suite 900, 33410
Telephone: 407-624-3900
Fax: 407-524-3533

Raymond W. Royce
J. Richard Harris
John L. Bryan, Jr.
John M. Jorgensen
Richard K. Barra
Robert A. Schaeffer
Mark P. Gagnon
Barry B. Byrd

Representative Clients: John D. and Catherine T. MacArthur Foundation; First Union National Bank of Florida, N.A.; North Palm Beach County Association of Realtors, Inc.; Lost Tree Village; Jupiter Hills, Pappalardo Contractors, Inc.; Art Moran Pontiac, Inc.; Wal-Mart Stores, Inc.; Whitworth Farms; Hendrix Farms; DuBois Growers.

For Complete List of Firm Personnel, See General Section

For full biographical listings, see the Martindale-Hubbell Law Directory

*SARASOTA,** Sarasota Co.

EARL, BLANK, KAVANAUGH & STOTTS, PROFESSIONAL ASSOCIATION (AV)

1800 Second Street, Suite 888, 34236
Telephone: 813-366-1180
FAX: 813-366-1183
Miami, Florida Office: Suite 3636, One Biscayne Tower, Two South Biscayne Boulevard.
Telephone: 305-358-3000.
FAX: 305-358-5079.
Tallahassee, Florida Office: 116 E. Jefferson Street.
Telephone: 904-681-1900.
FAX: 904-681-0989.

William L. Earl
Robert H. Blank
Judith Smith Kavanaugh
Dennis M. Stotts
Mark T. Kobelinski
Stephen R. Verbit

Reference: NationsBank, N.A.

For full biographical listings, see the Martindale-Hubbell Law Directory

*TALLAHASSEE,** Leon Co.

EARL, BLANK, KAVANAUGH & STOTTS, PROFESSIONAL ASSOCIATION (AV)

116 East Jefferson Street, 32301
Telephone: 904-681-1900
FAX: 904-681-0989
Miami, Florida Office: Suite 3636, One Biscayne Tower, Two South Biscayne Boulevard.
Telephone: 305-358-3000.
FAX: 305-358-5079.
Sarasota, Florida Office: 1800 Second Street.
Telephone: 813-366-1180.
FAX: 813-366-1183.

William L. Earl
Robert H. Blank
Judith Smith Kavanaugh
Dennis M. Stotts
Mark T. Kobelinski
Stephen R. Verbit

Reference: NationsBank, N.A.

For full biographical listings, see the Martindale-Hubbell Law Directory

HOPPING BOYD GREEN & SAMS (AV)

123 South Calhoun Street, P.O. Box 6526, 32314
Telephone: 904-222-7500
Fax: 904-224-8551

MEMBERS OF FIRM

Carlos Alvarez
James S. Alves
Brian H. Bibeau
Kathleen L. Blizzard
Elizabeth C. Bowman
William L. Boyd, IV
Richard S. Brightman
Peter C. Cunningham
Ralph A. DeMeo
Thomas M. DeRose
William H. Green
Wade L. Hopping
Frank E. Matthews
Richard D. Melson
David L. Powell
William D. Preston
Carolyn S. Raepple
Gary P. Sams
Robert P. Smith
Cheryl G. Stuart

ASSOCIATES

Kristin M. Conroy
Charles A. Culp, Jr.
Connie C. Durrence
Jonathan S. Fox
James Calvin Goodlett
Gary K. Hunter, Jr.
Dalana W. Johnson
Jonathan T. Johnson
Angela R. Morrison
Gary V. Perko
Karen Peterson
Michael P. Petrovich
Douglas S. Roberts
R. Scott Ruth
Julie Rome Steinmeyer

OF COUNSEL

W. Robert Fokes

Representative Clients: ITT Community Development Corp.; Florida Power & Light Co.; Florida Electric Power Coordinating Group; Hollywood, Inc.; CF Industries, Inc.; Association of Physical Fitness Centers; Sunniland Pipe Line Company, Inc.; Florida Chemical Industries Council; Mobil Oil Co.; Waste Management, Inc.

For full biographical listings, see the Martindale-Hubbell Law Directory

*TAMPA,** Hillsborough Co.

HONIGMAN MILLER SCHWARTZ AND COHN (AV)

A Partnership including Professional Corporations
2700 Landmark Centre, 401 E. Jackson Street, 33602
Telephone: 813-221-6600
Telecopier: 813-223-4410
West Palm Beach, Florida Office: Suite 800 Esperante Building, 222 Lakeview Avenue.
Telephone: 407-838-4500.
Orlando, Florida Office: 390 North Orange Avenue, Suite 1300.
Telephone: 407-648-0300.
Detroit, Michigan Office: 2290 First National Building.
Telephone: 313-256-7800.
Lansing, Michigan Office: 222 North Washington Square, Suite 400.
Telephone: 517-484-8282.
Houston, Texas Office: 3100 First Interstate Bank Plaza, 1000 Louisiana.
Telephone: 713-650-2600.
Los Angeles, California Office: Watt Plaza, Suite 2200, 1875 Century Park East.
Telephone: 310-789-3800.
Fax: 310-789-3814.

MEMBER

Michael G. Cooke (P.A.)

ASSOCIATE

Susan M. Salvatore

For Complete List of Firm Personnel, See General Section

For full biographical listings, see the Martindale-Hubbell Law Directory

*WEST PALM BEACH,** Palm Beach Co.

HONIGMAN MILLER SCHWARTZ AND COHN (AV)

A Partnership including Professional Corporations
Suite 800 Esperante Building, 222 Lakeview Avenue, 33401-6112
Telephone: 407-838-4500
Telecopier: 407-832-3036; 832-2645
Tampa, Florida Office: 2700 Landmark Centre, 401 E. Jackson Street.
Telephone: 813-221-6600.
Orlando, Florida Office: 390 North Orange Avenue, Suite 1300.
Telephone: 407-648-0300.
Detroit, Michigan Office: 2290 First National Building.
Telephone: 313-256-7800.
Lansing, Michigan Office: 222 North Washington Square, Suite 400.
Telephone: 517-484-8282.
Houston, Texas: 3100 First Interstate Bank Plaza, 1000 Louisiana.
Telephone: 713-650-2600.
Los Angeles, California Office: Watt Plaza, Suite 2200, 1875 Century Park East.
Telephone: 310-789-3800.
Fax: 310-789-3814.

MEMBERS

Carla L. Brown
Donald H. Reed, Jr.
E. Lee Worsham (P.A.)

Representative Clients: Adler Group, Inc.; Chiquita Brands, Inc.; E. Llwyd Ecclestone, Jr.; Forbes/Cohen Properties; ITT-Rayonier, Inc.; National Advertising Company; PHM Corporation (Pulte Home Corp.); Thos. J. White Development Corp.; Linpro, Inc.; Rubin Periodical Group-FEC News.

For Complete List of Firm Personnel, See General Section

For full biographical listings, see the Martindale-Hubbell Law Directory

JONES, FOSTER, JOHNSTON & STUBBS, P.A. (AV)

Flagler Center Tower, 505 South Flagler Drive, P.O. Box 3475, 33402-3475
Telephone: 407-659-3000
Fax: 407-832-1454

Sidney A. Stubbs, Jr.
John Blair McCracken
John C. Randolph
Herbert Adams Weaver, Jr.
Larry B. Alexander
Thornton M. Henry
Margaret L. Cooper
D. Culver Smith III (P.A.)
Allen R. Tomlinson
Peter S. Holton
Michael P. Walsh
Peter A. Sachs
Michael T. Kranz
John S. Trimper
Mark B. Kleinfeld
Andrew R. Ross
Scott Gardner Hawkins
Steven J. Rothman
Rebecca G. Doane

Joyce A. Conway
Stephen J. Aucamp
Christopher S. Duke
Scott L. McMullen
John C. Rau
Tracey Biagiotti
Edward Diaz

Counsel For: U.S. Trust Co.; NationsBank of Florida, N.A.; Island National Bank; Bankers Trust Company of Florida; Sun Bank/South Florida, N.A.; General Motors Acceptance Corp.

For full biographical listings, see the Martindale-Hubbell Law Directory

HAWAII

*HONOLULU,** Honolulu Co.

DWYER IMANAKA SCHRAFF KUDO MEYER & FUJIMOTO ATTORNEYS AT LAW, A LAW CORPORATION (AV)

1800 Pioneer Plaza, 900 Fort Street Mall, 96813
Telephone: 808-524-8000
Telecopier: 808-526-1419
Mailing Address: P.O. Box 2727, 96803

John R. Dwyer, Jr.
Mitchell A. Imanaka
Paul A. Schraff
Benjamin A. Kudo (Atty. at Law, A Law Corp.)
William G. Meyer, III
Wesley M. Fujimoto
Ronald Van Grant
Jon M. H. Pang
Blake W. Bushnell
Kenn N. Kojima

Adelbert Green
Richard T. Asato, Jr.
Scott W. Settle
Darcie S. Yoshinaga
Tracy Timothy Woo
Lawrence I. Kawasaki
Douglas H. Inouye
Christine A. Low

OF COUNSEL

Randall Y. Iwase

For full biographical listings, see the Martindale-Hubbell Law Directory

IDAHO

*BOISE,** Ada Co.

Eberle, Berlin, Kading, Turnbow & McKlveen, Chartered (AV)

Capitol Park Plaza, 300 North Sixth Street, P.O. Box 1368, 83701
Telephone: 208-344-8535
Facsimile: 208-344-8542

William J. McKlveen | Bradley G. Andrews
Scott D. Hess | Stephen A. Bradbury

Ronald L. Williams

Representative Clients: Idaho Timber Corporation; Canfor U.S.A. Corporation.

For Complete List of Firm Personnel, See General Section

For full biographical listings, see the Martindale-Hubbell Law Directory

Elam & Burke, A Professional Association (AV)

Key Financial Center, 702 West Idaho Street, P.O. Box 1539, 83701
Telephone: 208-343-5454
Telecopier: 208-384-5844

Carl P. Burke | John Magel
Scott L. Campbell

Kristen R. Thompson

Representative Clients: Morrison-Knudsen, Inc.; Texas Instruments, Inc.; Prudential Securities, Inc.; Pechiney Corp.; Dow Corning Corporation; U.S. West Communications; State Farm Insurance Cos.; Sinclair Oil Company d/b/a Sun Valley Company; Farmers Insurance Group; Hecla Mining Company.

For Complete List of Firm Personnel, See General Section

For full biographical listings, see the Martindale-Hubbell Law Directory

Moffatt, Thomas, Barrett, Rock & Fields, Chartered (AV)

First Security Building, 911 West Idaho Street, Suite 300, P.O. Box 829, 83701
Telephone: 208-345-2000
FAX: 208-385-5384
Idaho Falls Office: 525 Park Avenue, Suite 2D, P.O. Box 1367, 83403.
Telephone: 208-522-6700.
FAX: 208-522-5111.
Pocatello, Idaho Office: 1110 Call Creek Drive, P.O. Box 4941, 83201.
Telephone: 208-233-2001.

Eugene C. Thomas | Morgan W. Richards, Jr.

Representative Clients: BMC West Corporation; Chevron, U.S.A.; First Security Bank of Idaho, N.A.; General Motors Corp.; Idaho Potato Commission; Intermountain Gas Co.; John Alden Life Insurance Co.; Micron, Inc.; Royal Insurance Cos.; St. Luke's Regional Medical Center & Mountain States Tumor Institute.

For Complete List of Firm Personnel, See General Section

For full biographical listings, see the Martindale-Hubbell Law Directory

Rosholt, Robertson & Tucker, Chartered (AV)

Suite 600, 1221 W. Idaho, P.O. Box 2139, 83701-2139
Telephone: 208-336-0700
Fax: 208-344-6034
Twin Falls, Idaho Office: 142 Third Avenue North, P.O. Box 1906.
Telephone: 208-734-0700.
Fax: 208-736-0041.

James C. Tucker

Bruce Smith | Gary L. Quigley
John K. Simpson

For full biographical listings, see the Martindale-Hubbell Law Directory

KETCHUM, Blaine Co.

James L. Kennedy, Jr. (AV)

340 Second Street East, P.O. Box 2165, 83340
Telephone: 208-726-8255

Reference: First Interstate Bank of Idaho, N.A. (Ketchum-Sun Valley Branch); First Security Bank of Idaho, N.A. (Ketchum Branch)

For full biographical listings, see the Martindale-Hubbell Law Directory

*TWIN FALLS,** Twin Falls Co.

Rosholt, Robertson & Tucker, Chartered (AV)

142 Third Avenue North, P.O. Box 1906, 83303-1906
Telephone: 208-734-0700
Fax: 208-736-0041
Boise, Idaho Office: Suite 600, 1221 W. Idaho, P.O. Box 2139.
Telephone: 208-336-0700.
Fax: 208-344-6034.

John A. Rosholt | Gary D. Slette

Norman M. Semanko

For full biographical listings, see the Martindale-Hubbell Law Directory

ILLINOIS

*PINCKNEYVILLE,** Perry Co.

Hohlt, House, DeMoss & Johnson (AV)

1 North Main Street, 62274
Telephone: 618-357-2178
Telecopier: 618-357-3314
Nashville, Illinois Office: Holston Building.
Telephone: 618-327-8241.
Telecopier: 618-327-4079.
Du Quoin, Illinois Office: 13 North Division.
Telephone: 618-542-4703.

MEMBERS

Don E. Johnson | Roger H. Seibert
Donald Bigham

Counsel for: Nashville Savings & Loan Assn.; Murphy-Wall State Bank & Trust Company of Pinckneyville; First National Bank of Pinckneyville; Farmers & Merchants National Bank of Nashville; Oakdale State Bank.
Local Counsel for: Consolidation Coal Co.; Natural Gas Pipeline Company of America; Amax Coal Co.; Zeigler Coal Co.

For full biographical listings, see the Martindale-Hubbell Law Directory

INDIANA

*INDIANAPOLIS,** Marion Co.

Ice Miller Donadio & Ryan (AV)

One American Square Box 82001, 46282-0002
Telephone: 317-236-2100
Fax: 317-236-2219

MEMBERS OF FIRM

G. Daniel Kelley, Jr. | W. C. Blanton
Phillip L. Bayt

For Complete List of Firm Personnel, See General Section

For full biographical listings, see the Martindale-Hubbell Law Directory

Plews Shadley Racher & Braun (AV)

1346 North Delaware Street, 46202-2415
Telephone: 317-637-0700
Telecopier: 317-637-0710

MEMBERS OF FIRM

George M. Plews | Peter M. Racher
Sue A. Shadley | Christopher J. Braun

ASSOCIATES

Harinder Kaur | Jeffrey D. Claflin
Leonardo D. Robinson | John E. Klarquist
Frederick D. Emhardt | Jeffrey D. Featherstun
S. Curtis DeVoe | Amy K. Luigs
Donna C. Marron

OF COUNSEL

Craig A. Wood | Christine C. H. Plews
M. Scott Barrett

For full biographical listings, see the Martindale-Hubbell Law Directory

*MT. VERNON,** Posey Co.

Hawley, Hudson & Almon (AV)

309 Main Street, P.O. Box 716, 47620
Telephone: 812-838-4495

(See Next Column)

HAWLEY, HUDSON & ALMON—*Continued*

MEMBERS OF FIRM

K. Richard Hawley
Henry C. Hudson
S. Brent Almon
Marc E. Hawley

Representative Clients: Sohio Supply Co.; Farm Bureau Oil Co.; Wade Oil Corp.; Conyers Oil Service, Inc.; Coy Oil, Inc.; Trey Exploration, Inc.; Jarvis Drilling, Inc.; K.C. Oil Corp.; Ecus Corp.; Quinn Energy Corp.

For Complete List of Firm Personnel, See General Section

For full biographical listings, see the Martindale-Hubbell Law Directory

*PRINCETON,** Gibson Co.

HALL, PARTENHEIMER & KINKLE (AV)

219 North Hart Street, P.O. Box 313, 47670
Telephone: 812-386-0050
FAX: 812-385-2575

MEMBERS OF FIRM

Verner P. Partenheimer
J. Robert Kinkle
R. Scott Partenheimer

Representative Clients: Interlake Inc.; Gibson County Bank; Old Ben Coal Co.
Approved Attorneys for: Lawyers Title Insurance; Ticor Title Insurance.

For full biographical listings, see the Martindale-Hubbell Law Directory

KANSAS

*WICHITA,** Sedgwick Co.

ADAMS, JONES, ROBINSON AND MALONE, CHARTERED (AV)

600 Market Centre, 155 Nortn Market, P.O. Box 1034, 67201-1034
Telephone: 316-265-8591
Telecopier: 316-265-9719

Clifford L. Malone
Donald W. Bostwick
Teresa J. James

Representative Clients: Williams Natural Gas Co.; Oxy U.S.A., Inc.; BHP Petroleum (Americas) Inc.; Mesa Operating Limited Partnership.

For Complete List of Firm Personnel, See General Section

For full biographical listings, see the Martindale-Hubbell Law Directory

FLEESON, GOOING, COULSON & KITCH, L.L.C. (AV)

125 North Market Street, Suite 1600, P.O. Box 997, 67201-0997
Telephone: 316-267-7361
Telecopier: 316-267-1754

Thomas D. Kitch
Gregory J. Stucky
Charles E. Millsap
Stephen M. Stark

Scott Jensen

OF COUNSEL

Dale M. Stucky

Attorneys for: Bank IV, Wichita, N.A; Intrust Bank, N.A.; Wichita Eagle and Beacon Publishing Co., Inc.; Southwest Kansas Royalty Owners Assn.; Liberty Mutual Insurance Co.; Grant Thornton; The Law Company; Vulcan Materials Co.; The Wichita State University Board of Trustees.

For Complete List of Firm Personnel, See General Section

For full biographical listings, see the Martindale-Hubbell Law Directory

FOULSTON & SIEFKIN (AV)

(Formerly Foulston, Siefkin, Powers & Eberhardt)
700 Fourth Financial Center, Broadway at Douglas, 67202
Telephone: 316-267-6371
Facsimile: 316-267-6345
Topeka, Kansas Office: 1515 Bank IV Tower, 534 Kansas Avenue. 66603.
Telephone: 913-233-3600.
FAX: 913-233-1610.
Member: Lex Mundi, A Global Association of Independent Firms

MEMBERS OF FIRM

Charles J. Woodin
Jim H. Goering

For Complete List of Firm Personnel, See General Section

For full biographical listings, see the Martindale-Hubbell Law Directory

HERSHBERGER, PATTERSON, JONES & ROTH, L.C. (AV)

600 Hardage Center, 100 South Main, 67202-3779
Telephone: 316-263-7583
Fax: 316-263-7595

(See Next Column)

Jerome E. Jones
Robert J. Roth
Evan J. Olson

Representative Clients: Anadarko Petroleum Corporation; Mobil Oil Co.; Murfin Drilling; J.M. Huber Corporation; Oxy Oil & Gas USA, Inc.; Panhandle Eastern Pipeline Co.; Rine Drilling & Exploration Company; Tesoro Petroleum Corp.; Triad Drilling Co.

For Complete List of Firm Personnel, See General Section

For full biographical listings, see the Martindale-Hubbell Law Directory

MORRIS, LAING, EVANS, BROCK & KENNEDY, CHARTERED (AV)

Fourth Floor, 200 West Douglas, 67202-3084
Telephone: 316-262-2671
FAX: 316-262-6226; 262-5991
Topeka Office: 800 S.W. Jackson, Suite 914. 66612-2214.
Telephone: 913-232-2662.
Fax: 913-232-9983.

Ralph R. Brock
Joseph W. Kennedy
Donald E. Schrag
Robert K. Anderson
Susan R. Schrag
Robert E. Nugent
Michael Lennen
Karl R. Swartz
Gerald N. Capps
Bruce A. Ney

References: The Emprise Banks of Kansas; Mellon Bank; N.A.; The Merchants National Bank of Topeka; Southwest National Bank; Twin Lakes Bank & Trust.

For Complete List of Firm Personnel, See General Section

For full biographical listings, see the Martindale-Hubbell Law Directory

YOUNG, BOGLE, MCCAUSLAND, WELLS & CLARK, P.A. (AV)

106 West Douglas, Suite 923, 67202
Telephone: 316-265-7841
Facsimile: 316-265-3956

Glenn D. Young, Jr.
Paul S. McCausland

Mark R. Maloney

Representative Clients: Bridgestone/Firestone Inc.; Deere & Co.; Citibank; Metropolitan Life Insurance Co.; Equitable Life Assurance Society of the United States; New York Life Insurance Co.

For Complete List of Firm Personnel, See General Section

For full biographical listings, see the Martindale-Hubbell Law Directory

KENTUCKY

*BOWLING GREEN,** Warren Co.

ENGLISH, LUCAS, PRIEST & OWSLEY (AV)

1101 College Street, P.O. Box 770, 42102-0770
Telephone: 502-781-6500
Telecopier: 502-782-7782

MEMBERS OF FIRM

Charles E. English
James H. Lucas
Whayne C. Priest, Jr.
Michael A. Owsley
Keith M. Carwell
Murry A. Raines
Kurt W. Maier
Charles E. English, Jr.
Wade T. Markham, II

ASSOCIATES

D. Gaines Penn
Robert A. Young

General Counsel for: Medical Center at Bowling Green; Warren Rural Electric Cooperative Corporation; Trans Financial Bank, N.A.; Southern Sanitation, Inc.
Representative Clients: Commercial Union Insurance Cos.; Kemper Insurance Group; St. Paul Insurance Co.; Eaton Corp.; Desa International; Sumitomo Electric Wiring Systems, Inc.

For Complete List of Firm Personnel, See General Section

For full biographical listings, see the Martindale-Hubbell Law Directory

*HAZARD,** Perry Co.

GULLETT & COMBS (AV)

109 Broadway, Second Floor, P.O. Box 1039, 41702-5039
Telephone: 606-439-1373
Fax: 606-439-4450

MEMBERS OF FIRM

Asa P. Gullett, III
Ronald G. Combs

(See Next Column)

GULLETT & COMBS, *Hazard—Continued*

ASSOCIATES

Teresa C. Reed | Matthew Lawton Bowling

Reference: Peoples Bank and Trust Co.

For full biographical listings, see the Martindale-Hubbell Law Directory

*HENDERSON,** Henderson Co.

BENJAMIN C. CUBBAGE (AV)

600 Barret Boulevard, P.O. Drawer 17, 42420
Telephone: 502-827-5635
Fax: 502-826-3763

For full biographical listings, see the Martindale-Hubbell Law Directory

KING, DEEP AND BRANAMAN (AV)

127 North Main Street, P.O. Box 43, 42420
Telephone: 502-827-1852
FAX: 502-826-7729

MEMBERS OF FIRM

Leo King (1893-1982)
William M. Deep (1920-1990)
William Branaman
Harry L. Mathison, Jr.
W. Mitchell Deep, Jr.
H. Randall Redding
Dorin E. Luck

ASSOCIATES

Leslie M. Newman
Robert Khuon Wiederstein
Greg L. Gager

Counsel for: Reynolds Metals Co.; P B & S Chemical Co.; Jim R. Smith Coal Co.; Har-Ken Oil Co.; MAPCO, Inc.; Webster County Coal Co.; American Electric Power; Texas Gas Exploration; Ashland Oil, Inc.; Hercules Petroleum.

For full biographical listings, see the Martindale-Hubbell Law Directory

*HINDMAN,** Knott Co.

WEINBERG, CAMPBELL, SLONE & SLONE, P.S.C. (AV)

Main Street, P.O. Box 727, 41822
Telephone: 606-785-5048; 785-5049
FAX: 606-785-3021

William R. Weinberg
Randy A. Campbell
Jerry Wayne Slone
Randy G. Slone

References: Bank of Hindman; Thacker & Grigsby Telephone Co.

For full biographical listings, see the Martindale-Hubbell Law Directory

*LEXINGTON,** Fayette Co.

BUCHANAN INGERSOLL, PROFESSIONAL CORPORATION (AV)

Suite 1210, Vine Center Office Tower, 333 West Vine Street, 40507
Telephone: 606-225-5333
Telecopier: 606-225-5334
Pittsburgh, Pennsylvania Office: 5800 USX Tower, 600 Grant Street.
Telephone: 412-562-8800.
Philadelphia, Pennsylvania Office: Two Logan Square, Twelfth Floor, 18th & Arch Streets.
Telephone: 215-665-8700.
Harrisburg, Pennsylvania Office: Vartan Parc, 30 North Third Street.
Telephone: 717-237-4800.
Tampa, Florida Office: 101 East Kennedy Boulevard, Suite 1030.
Telephone: 813-222-8180.
North Miami Beach, Florida Office: 19495 Biscayne Boulevard.
Telephone: 305-933-5600.
Princeton, New Jersey Office: Buchanan Ingersoll, A Partnership, College Centre, 500 College Road East.
Telephone: 609-452-2666.

John R. Leathers

Stephen G. Allen | Sam P. Burchett

For full biographical listings, see the Martindale-Hubbell Law Directory

GREENEBAUM DOLL & MCDONALD (AV)

A Partnership including Professional Service Corporations
1400 Vine Center Tower, 40508
Telephone: 606-231-8500
Telecopier: 606-255-2742
Telex: 213029
Louisville, Kentucky Office: 3300 National City Tower.
Telephone: 502-589-4200.
Fax: 502-587-3695.
Covington, Kentucky Office: 50 East River Center Boulevard, P.O. Box 2050.
Telephone: 606-655-4200.
Fax: 606-655-4239.
Cincinnati, Ohio Office: 832 Main Street.
Telephone: 513-421-8087.
Fax: 513-421-8089.

(See Next Column)

MEMBERS OF FIRM

Marcus P. McGraw (Resident)
John V. Wharton (Resident)
Bruce E. Cryder
John C. Bender (Resident)
David A. Owen (Resident)

ASSOCIATE

Bryan R. Reynolds (Resident)

Representative Clients: American Synthetic Rubber Corp.; Andalex Resources, Inc.; Ashland Oil, Inc.; BHP-Utah International Inc.; Columbia Gas Transmission Corp.; Consolidation Coal Co.; National Southwire Aluminum; Rohm and Haas Co.; Toyota Motor Manufacturing, U.S.A., Inc.
*A Professional Service Corporation

For Complete List of Firm Personnel, See General Section

For full biographical listings, see the Martindale-Hubbell Law Directory

STITES & HARBISON (AV)

Formerly Stites, McElwain & Fowler and Harbison, Kessinger, Lisle & Bush
2300 Lexington Financial Center, 40507
Telephone: 606-226-2300
Louisville, Kentucky Office: 400 West Market Street, Suite 1800.
Telephone: 502-587-3400.
Frankfort, Kentucky Office: 421 West Main Street.
Telephone: 502-223-3477.
Jeffersonville, Indiana Office: 323 East Court Avenue.
Telephone: 812-282-7566.

MEMBERS OF FIRM

Calvert T. Roszell
Thomas E. Meng
Laura D. Keller

For Complete List of Firm Personnel, See General Section

For full biographical listings, see the Martindale-Hubbell Law Directory

STOLL, KEENON & PARK (AV)

201 E. Main Street, Suite 1000, 40507-1380
Telephone: 606-231-3000
Telecopier: 606-253-1093; 606-253-1027
Frankfort, Kentucky Office: 326 West Main Street.
Telephone: 502-875-6000.
Telecopier: 502-875-6008.
Louisville, Kentucky Office: 400 West Market Street, Suite 2650, 40202.
Telephone: 502-568-9100.
Telecopier: 502-568-6340.

MEMBERS OF FIRM

Lindsey W. Ingram, Jr.
Spencer D. Noe
Charles E. Shivel, Jr.
Maxwell P. Barret, Jr.
Diane M. Carlton
Kendall S. Barret
Dan M. Rose
J. Mel Camenisch, Jr.

Representative Clients: A. T. Massey Coal Co., Inc.; Chevron, U.S.A.; Cyprus Minerals Co.; Delta Natural Gas Co., Inc.; Drummand Coal Co.; Mapco; Noranda Mines, Ltd.; Peabody Coal Co.; United Coal Co.; Western Pocahontas Corp.

For Complete List of Firm Personnel, See General Section

For full biographical listings, see the Martindale-Hubbell Law Directory

STURGILL, TURNER & TRUITT (AV)

155 East Main Street, 40507
Telephone: 606-255-8581
Fax: 606-231-0851

MEMBERS OF FIRM

Don S. Sturgill
Gardner L. Turner
Jerry D. Truitt
Stephen L. Barker
Donald P. Moloney, II
Ann D. Sturgill
Phillip M. Moloney
Douglas L. McSwain
Kevin G. Henry
Gene Lynn Humphreys

For Complete List of Firm Personnel, See General Section

For full biographical listings, see the Martindale-Hubbell Law Directory

*PRESTONSBURG,** Floyd Co.

COMBS AND STEVENS (AV)

99 North Lake Drive, P.O. Box 189, 41653
Telephone: 606-886-2391; 886-1000
Fax: 606-886-2776

MEMBERS OF FIRM

James A. Combs | Ralph H. Stevens

ASSOCIATE

Gregory A. Isaac

For full biographical listings, see the Martindale-Hubbell Law Directory

Prestonsburg—Continued

Francis, Kazee & Francis (AV)

119 East Court Street, P.O. Box 700, 41653
Telephone: 606-886-2361; 886-2362
FAX: 606-886-9603
Paintsville, Kentucky Office: 103 Main Street, P.O. Box 1275.
Telephone: 606-789-3059.

MEMBERS OF FIRM

D. B. Kazee
William G. Francis
William S. Kendrick
David H. Neeley
Mitchell D. Kinner
John T. Chafin
C. V. Reynolds
P. Franklin Heaberlin
Martin Lee Osborne
Brett D. Davis

ASSOCIATES

Robert J. Patton
William C. Mullins
Anthony Craig Davis

OF COUNSEL

Fred G. Francis (Retired)

Representative Clients: Island Creek Coal Co.; The Elk Horn Coal Corp.; First Commonwealth Bank; Old Republic Insurance Co.; Zurich American Insurance Co.; Maryland Casualty Co.; Bituminous Casualty Corp.; Mack Financial Corp.; Nationwide Insurance; Kentucky May Coal Co., Inc.

For full biographical listings, see the Martindale-Hubbell Law Directory

LOUISIANA

*BATON ROUGE,** East Baton Rouge Parish

Breazeale, Sachse & Wilson, L.L.P. (AV)

Twenty-Third Floor, One American Place, P.O. Box 3197, 70821-3197
Telephone: 504-387-4000
Fax: 504-387-5397
New Orleans, Louisiana Office: Place St. Charles, Suite 4214, 201 St. Charles Avenue.
Telephone: 504-582-1170.
Fax: 504-582-1164.

MEMBERS OF FIRM

Victor A. Sachse, III
Emile C. Rolfs, III
John W. Barton, Jr.
Jude C. Bursavich

ASSOCIATES

William F. Ridlon, II
Luis A. Leitzelar

Counsel for: Hibernia National Bank; South Central Bell Telephone Co.; Allied-Signal Corp.; Reynolds Metal Co.; Illinois Central Railroad Co.; The Continental Insurance Cos.; Fireman's Fund American Group; Chicago Bridge & Iron Co.; Montgomery Ward & Co.

For Complete List of Firm Personnel, See General Section

For full biographical listings, see the Martindale-Hubbell Law Directory

Gordon, Arata, McCollam & Duplantis, L.L.P. (AV)

A Partnership including Professional Law Corporations
1710 One American Place, 70825-0012
Telephone: 504-381-9643
Fax: 504-336-9763
New Orleans, Louisiana Office: Place St. Charles, Suite 4000, 201 St. Charles Avenue.
Telephone: 504-582-1111.
Fax: 504-582-1121.
Lafayette, Louisiana Office: 625 East Kaliste Saloom Road.
Telephone: 318-237-0132.
Fax: 318-237-3451.

RESIDENT MEMBER OF FIRM

Richard E. Matheny

RESIDENT ASSOCIATE

Teanna West Neskora

Representative Clients: Amoco Production Co.; Bass Enterprises; BHP Petroleum (Americas); Chevron U.S.A. Inc.; CNG Producing Co.; Enron Corp.; Freeport-McMoran Oil & Gas Co.; Union Oil Company of California.

For full biographical listings, see the Martindale-Hubbell Law Directory

Kean, Miller, Hawthorne, D'Armond, McCowan & Jarman, L.L.P. (AV)

22nd Floor, One American Place, P.O. Box 3513, 70821
Telephone: 504-387-0999
Fax: 504-388-9133
New Orleans, Louisiana Office: Energy Centre, Suite 1470, 1100 Poydras Street.
Telephone: 504-585-3050.
Fax: 504-585-3051.

(See Next Column)

MEMBERS OF FIRM

G. William Jarman
Leonard L. Kilgore III
Gary A. Bezet
M. Dwayne Johnson
J. Carter Wilkinson
Sandra Louise Edwards
Linda Sarradet Akchin
Katherine W. King

Kelly Wilkinson
Charles S. McCowan III
Esteban Herrera, Jr.
Susan Knight Carter (Resident, New Orleans Office)
William Ellis Latham II
Robert Neill Aguiluz
Robert M. Hoyland

Representative Clients: Amoco Production Company, Houston, Tx.; BASF Corporation, Parsippany, N.J.; Exxon Company, U.S.A., Baton Rouge, La.; Freeport McMoRan, Inc., New Orleans, La.; Georgia-Pacific Corporation, Atlanta, Ga.; Mobil Oil Corporation, Fairfax, Va.; Rhone-Poulenc Basic Chemicals Company, Shelton, Ct.; Tenneco, Inc., Houston, Tx.; Texaco Inc., New Orleans, La.; Transcontinental Gas Pipe Line Company, Houston, Tx.

For Complete List of Firm Personnel, See General Section

For full biographical listings, see the Martindale-Hubbell Law Directory

*HOMER,** Claiborne Parish

Shaw and Shaw, A Professional Law Corporation (AV)

522 East Main Street, P.O. Box 420, 71040
Telephone: 318-927-6149

William M. Shaw

Reference: Homer National Bank.

*LAFAYETTE,** Lafayette Parish

Gordon, Arata, McCollam & Duplantis, L.L.P. (AV)

A Partnership including Professional Law Corporations
625 East Kaliste Saloom Road, 70508-2508
Telephone: 318-237-0132
Fax: 318-237-3451
New Orleans, Louisiana Office: Place St. Charles, Suite 4000, 201 St. Charles Avenue.
Telephone: 504-582-1111.
Fax: 504-582-1121.
Baton Rouge, Louisiana Office: 1710 One American Place.
Telephone: 504-381-9643.
Fax: 504-336-9763.

RESIDENT MEMBERS OF FIRM

B. J. Duplantis (A P.L.C.)
Benjamin B. Blanchet
Margaret D. Swords
William F. Bailey
James E. Slatten, III
Samuel E. Masur

RESIDENT ASSOCIATES

Rebecca Wormser Comeaux
Denis C. Swords

Representative Clients: Amoco Production Co.; Bass Enterprises ; BHP Petroleum (Americas); Chevron U.S.A. Inc.; CNG Producing Co.; Enron Corp.; Freeport-McMoran Oil & Gas Co.; Union Oil Company of California.

For full biographical listings, see the Martindale-Hubbell Law Directory

Mangham, Davis and Oglesbee (AV)

Suite 1400 First National Bank Towers, 600 Jefferson Street, P.O. Box 93110, 70509-3110
Telephone: 318-233-6200
Fax: 318-233-6521

Michael R. Mangham
Louis R. Davis
Michael G. Oglesbee
Herman E. Garner, Jr.

ASSOCIATES

Dawn Mayeux Fuqua
Lisa Hanchey Sevier

SPECIAL COUNSEL

Michael J. O'Shee

OF COUNSEL

George W. Hardy, III
Robert E. Rowe

Reference: The First National Bank of Lafayette, Lafayette, Louisiana.

For full biographical listings, see the Martindale-Hubbell Law Directory

*NEW ORLEANS,** Orleans Parish

Chaffe, McCall, Phillips, Toler & Sarpy (AV)

A Partnership including a Professional Law Corporation
2300 Energy Centre, 1100 Poydras Street, 70163-2300
Telephone: 504-585-7000
Telecopier: 504-585-7075
Cable Address: "Denegre"
Telex: (AT&T) 460122 CMPTS
Baton Rouge, Louisiana Office: 202 Two United Plaza, 8550 United Plaza Boulevard.
Telephone: 504-922-4300.
Fax: 504-922-4304.

(See Next Column)

CHAFFE, MCCALL, PHILLIPS, TOLER & SARPY, *New Orleans—Continued*

MEMBERS OF FIRM

B. Lloyd Magruder
James A. Barton, III
Harry R. Holladay
Raymond G. Hoffman, Jr.
David R. Richardson

OF COUNSEL

E. Harold Saer, Jr.
Gordon O. Ewin

Representative Clients: Amoco Production Co.; Texaco, Inc.; Samedan Oil Co.; Phillips Petroleum Co.; Placid Oil Co.

For Complete List of Firm Personnel, See General Section

For full biographical listings, see the Martindale-Hubbell Law Directory

GORDON, ARATA, MCCOLLAM & DUPLANTIS, L.L.P. (AV)

A Partnership including Professional Law Corporations
Place St. Charles, Suite 4000, 201 St. Charles Avenue, 70170-4000
Telephone: 504-582-1111
Fax: 504-582-1121
Lafayette, Louisiana Office: 625 East Kaliste Saloom Road.
Telephone: 318-237-0132.
Fax: 318-237-3451.
Baton Rouge, Louisiana Office: 1710 One American Place.
Telephone: 504-381-9643.
Fax: 504-336-9763.

MEMBERS OF FIRM

John A. Gordon (A P.L.C.)
Blake G. Arata (A P.L.C.)
John M. McCollam (A P.L.C.)
Marcel Garsaud, Jr.
Philip N. Asprodites
Guy E. Wall
Cynthia A. Nicholson
Alan C. Wolf
Paul E. Bullington
James L. Weiss
Loulan J. Pitre, Jr.
Jason A. T. Jumonville

ASSOCIATES

Anthony C. Marino
Martin E. Landrieu
Scott A. O'Connor
C. Peck Hayne, Jr.
Douglas H. McCollam
Elizabeth L. Gordon
Marcy V. Massengale

LAFAYETTE OFFICE
RESIDENT MEMBERS OF FIRM

B. J. Duplantis (A P.L.C.)
Benjamin B. Blanchet
Margaret D. Swords
William F. Bailey
James E. Slatten, III
Samuel E. Masur

RESIDENT ASSOCIATES

Rebecca Wormser Comeaux
Denis C. Swords

BATON ROUGE OFFICE
RESIDENT MEMBER OF FIRM

Richard E. Matheny

Representative Clients: Amoco Production Co.; Bass Enterprises; CNG Producing Co.; Enron Corp; BHP Petroleum (Americas); Chevron U.S.A. Inc.; Freeport-McMoran Oil & Gas Co.; Union Oil Company of California.

For Complete List of Firm Personnel, See General Section

For full biographical listings, see the Martindale-Hubbell Law Directory

LEMLE & KELLEHER, L.L.P. (AV)

A Partnership including Professional Law Corporations
21st Floor, Pan-American Life Center, 601 Poydras Street, 70130-6097
Telephone: 504-586-1241
FAX: 504-584-9142
Cable Address: "Lemmor"
Telex: WU 584272
Baton Rouge, Louisiana Office: One American Place, 301 Main Street, Suite 1800, 70825.
Telephone: 504-387-5068.
FAX: 504-387-4995.
London, England Office: 1 Seething Lane, EC3N 4AX.
Telephone: 071-702-1446.
FAX: 071-702-1447.

MEMBERS OF FIRM

Ernest L. Edwards, Jr. (A Professional Law Corp.)
James M. Petersen
George Frazier
W. L. West
B. Richard Moore, Jr.
Stephen G. Lindsey
Randall A. Fish
Amy L. Baird

ASSOCIATES

Wayne K. McNeil
Robert P. Hutchinson

Representative Clients: American Cyanamid Co.; Kaiser Energy, Inc.; Monsanto Co.; Shell Oil Co.; Southern Natural Gas Co.; United Energy Resources, Inc.

For Complete List of Firm Personnel, See General Section

For full biographical listings, see the Martindale-Hubbell Law Directory

MILLING, BENSON, WOODWARD, HILLYER, PIERSON & MILLER (AV)

A Partnership including Professional Law Corporations
Suite Twenty-Three Hundred, 909 Poydras Street, 70112-1017
Telephone: 504-569-7000
Cable Address: "Milling"
Telex: 58-4211
Telecopier: 504-569-7001
ABA net: 15656
MCI Mail: "Milling"
Lafayette, Louisiana Office: 101 LaRue France, Suite 200.
Telephone: 318-232-3929.
Telecopier: 318-233-4957.
Baton Rouge, Louisiana Office: Suite 402, 8555 United Plaza Blvd.
Telephone: 504-928-688.
Fax: 504-928-6881.

MEMBERS OF FIRM

Haywood H. Hillyer, Jr., (P.C.)
Joseph B. Miller
Wilson S. Shirley, Jr., (P.C.)
Charles D. Marshall, Jr. (P.C.)
David N. Schell, Jr. (P.C.)
Mary L. Grier Holmes (P.C.)

SPECIAL COUNSEL

J. Clifford Rogillio (P.C.)

ASSOCIATES

Jay Corenswet
Alanna S. Arnold
Robert T. Lorio

LAFAYETTE OFFICE
RESIDENT MEMBERS OF FIRM

Jack C. Caldwell
Robert L. Cabes (P.C.)

RESIDENT ASSOCIATE

Thomas C. Stewart

Counsel for: Arthur Andersen & Co.; Chevron U.S.A., Inc.; Chrysler Corp.; The Dow Chemical Co.; E.I. duPont de Nemours & Co., Inc.; Exxon Corp.; Louisiana & Arkansas Railway Co.; The Louisiana Land & Exploration Co.; McDermott Incorporated; Whitney National Bank of New Orleans.

For Complete List of Firm Personnel, See General Section

For full biographical listings, see the Martindale-Hubbell Law Directory

PHELPS DUNBAR, L.L.P. (AV)

Texaco Center, 400 Poydras Street, 70130-3245
Telephone: 504-566-1311
Telecopier: 504-568-9130, 504-568-9007
Cable Address: "Howspencer"
Telex: 584125 WU
Telex: 6821155 WUI
Baton Rouge, Louisiana Office: Suite 701, City National Bank Building, P.O. Box 4412.
Telephone: 504-346-0285.
Telecopier: 504-381-9197.
Jackson, Mississippi Office: Suite 500, Security Centré North, 200 South Lamar Street, P.O. Box 23066.
Telephone: 601-352-2300.
Telecopier: 601-360-9777.
Tupelo, Mississippi Office: Seventh Floor, One Mississippi Plaza, P.O. Box 1220.
Telephone: 601-842-7907.
Telecopier: 601-842-3873.
Houston, Texas Office: Suite 501, 4 Houston Center, 1331 Lamar Street.
Telephone: 713-659-1386.
Telecopier: 713-659-1388.
London, England Office: Suite 976, Level 9, Lloyd's, 1 Lime Street, London EC3M 7DQ England.
Telephone: 011-44-71-929-4765.
Telecopier: 011-44-71-929-0046.
Telex: 987321.

MEMBERS OF FIRM

Robert U. Soniat
Harvey D. Wagar, III
Edward B. Poitevent, II
Bruce V. Schewe
James A. Stuckey
David M. Hunter

ASSOCIATE

Charles G. Duffy, III

Representative Clients: Acadian Gas Pipeline System; CNG Transmission Corp.; Columbia Gas Development Corp.; Energy Development Corp.; Laurel Operating Company, Inc.; Phibro Energy USA, Inc.; Sabine Royalty Trust; Texas Gas Transmission Corp.; Transco Energy Co.; Unocal Exploration Corp.

For Complete List of Firm Personnel, See General Section

For full biographical listings, see the Martindale-Hubbell Law Directory

*SHREVEPORT,** Caddo Parish

BARLOW AND HARDTNER L.C. (AV)

Tenth Floor, Louisiana Tower, 401 Edwards Street, 71101-3289
Telephone: 318-227-1131
Telecopier: 318-227-1141
Mailing Address: P.O. Box 8, Shreveport, Louisiana, 71161-0008

(See Next Column)

BARLOW AND HARDTNER L.C.—*Continued*

Ray A. Barlow
Malcolm S. Murchison
Kay Cowden Medlin
Joseph L. Shea, Jr.
David R. Taggart
Clair F. White
Stephen E. Ramey
Philip E. Downer, III
Michael B. Donald
Jay A. Greenleaf

Representative Clients: Anderson Oil & Gas, Inc.; Bass Enterprises Production Co.; Brammer Engineering, Inc.; Goodrich Oil Company; Grigsby Petroleum, Inc.; Hilliard Petroleum; Kelley Oil Corporation; NorAm Energy Corp. (formerly Arkla, Inc.); Texas Eastern Corp.

For Complete List of Firm Personnel, See General Section

For full biographical listings, see the Martindale-Hubbell Law Directory

BODENHEIMER, JONES, KLOTZ & SIMMONS (AV)

509 Milam Street, 71101
Telephone: 318-221-1507
Fax: 318-221-4560

MEMBERS OF FIRM

David B. Klotz
C. Gary Mitchell
F. John Reeks, Jr.

Representative Clients: Scurlock Oil & Gas Co.; SONAT Exploration Co.; TXO Production Corp.; Texaco Exploration & Production Inc.; Texaco Inc.

For full biographical listings, see the Martindale-Hubbell Law Directory

COOK, YANCEY, KING & GALLOWAY, A PROFESSIONAL LAW CORPORATION (AV)

1700 Commercial National Tower, 333 Texas Street, P.O. Box 22260, 71120-2260
Telephone: 318-221-6277
Telecopier: 318-227-2606

Stephen R. Yancey II
J. William Fleming
James H. Campbell
Frank M. Dodson
Albert M. Hand, Jr.

A list of representative clients will be furnished upon request.

For Complete List of Firm Personnel, See General Section

For full biographical listings, see the Martindale-Hubbell Law Directory

WIENER, WEISS, MADISON & HOWELL, A PROFESSIONAL CORPORATION (AV)

333 Texas Street, Suite 2350, P.O. Box 21990, 71120-1990
Telephone: 318-226-9100
Fax: 318-424-5128

Donald P. Weiss
James Fleet Howell
Neil T. Erwin
Lawrence Russo, III
Susie Morgan
Katherine Clark Hennessey
Jeffrey W. Weiss
Donald B. Wiener

Representative Clients: Pioneer Bank & Trust Co.; Ford Motor Credit Corp.; CNA Insurance Companies; International Paper Companies; Louisiana Homebuilders Association Self Insurers Fund; LSU-Shreveport; Sealy Realty, Inc.; Palmer Petroleum, Inc.; Brookshire Grocery Company (Louisiana); Northwest Louisiana Production Credit Association.

For Complete List of Firm Personnel, See General Section

For full biographical listings, see the Martindale-Hubbell Law Directory

MAINE

*PORTLAND,** Cumberland Co.

PIERCE, ATWOOD, SCRIBNER, ALLEN, SMITH & LANCASTER (AV)

One Monument Square, 04101
Telephone: 207-773-6411
Fax: 207-773-3419
Augusta, Maine Office: 77 Winthrop Street.
Telephone: 207-622-6311.
Camden, Maine Office: 36 Chestnut Street, P.O. Box 780.
Telephone: 207-236-4333.

MEMBERS OF FIRM

Daniel E. Boxer
John O'Leary
John D. Delahanty
Thomas R. Doyle
Philip F. W. Ahrens, III
Kenneth Fairbanks Gray
Elizabeth R. Butler
William E. Taylor

ASSOCIATES

Dixon P. Pike
Kate L. Geoffroy
Matthew D. Manahan
Adam H. Steinman
David P. Littell

(See Next Column)

For Complete List of Firm Personnel, See General Section

For full biographical listings, see the Martindale-Hubbell Law Directory

MARYLAND

*BALTIMORE,** (Independent City)

VENABLE, BAETJER AND HOWARD (AV)

A Partnership including Professional Corporations
1800 Mercantile Bank & Trust Building, 2 Hopkins Plaza, 21201
Telephone: 410-244-7400
Washington, D.C. Office: Venable, Baetjer, Howard & Civiletti. Suite 1000, 1201 New York Avenue, N.W.
Telephone: 202-962-4800.
McLean, Virginia Office: Suite 400, 2010 Corporate Ridge.
Telephone: 703-760-1600.
Rockville, Maryland Office: Suite 500, One Church Street, P. O. Box 1906.
Telephone: 301-217-5600.
Towson, Maryland Office: 210 Allegheny Avenue, P. O. Box 5517.
Telephone: 410-494-6200.

MEMBERS OF FIRM

Benjamin R. Civiletti (P.C.) (Also at Washington, D.C. and Towson, Maryland Offices)
Anthony M. Carey (Also at Washington, D.C. Office)
John Henry Lewin, Jr. (P.C.)
Robert G. Smith (P.C.)
David T. Stitt (Not admitted in MD; Resident, McLean, Virginia Office)
John G. Milliken (Not admitted in MD; Also at Washington, D.C. and McLean, Virginia Offices)
Max Stul Oppenheimer (P.C.) (Also at Washington, D.C. and Towson, Maryland Offices)
Joseph C. Wich, Jr. (Resident, Towson, Maryland Office)
Joseph G. Block (Not admitted in MD; Resident, Washington, D.C. Office)
Michael Schatzow (Also at Washington, D.C. and Towson, Maryland Offices)
John F. Cooney (Not admitted in MD; Resident, Washington, D.C. Office)
Susan K. Gauvey (Also at Towson, Maryland Office)
James K. Archibald (Also at Washington, D.C. and Towson, Maryland Offices)
Judson W. Starr (Not admitted in MD; Also at Washington, D.C. and Towson, Maryland Offices)
Jeffrey A. Dunn (also at Washington, D.C. Office)
James L. Shea (Also at Washington, D.C. Office)
Brigid E. Kenney
John J. Pavlick, Jr. (Not admitted in MD; Resident, Washington, D. C. Office)
Kathleen Gallogly Cox (Resident, Towson, Maryland Office)
Christopher R. Mellott
M. King Hill, III (Resident, Towson, Maryland Office)
James A. Dunbar (Also at Washington, D.C. Office)
Thomas J. Kelly, Jr. (Not admitted in MD; Resident, Washington, D. C. Office)
Kevin L. Shepherd

OF COUNSEL

Judith A. Armold

ASSOCIATES

Gregory S. Braker (Resident, Washington, D.C. Office)
J. Van L. Dorsey (Resident, Towson, Maryland Office)
Andrew R. Herrup (Resident, Washington, D.C. Office)
Matthew L. Iwicki
Mary-Dulany James (Resident, Towson, Maryland Office)
Paula Titus Laboy (Resident, Rockville, Maryland Office)
Thomas M. Lingan
Valerie K. Mann (Not admitted in MD; Resident, Washington, D.C. Office)
Laura K. McAfee
Mitchell Y. Mirviss

For Complete List of Firm Personnel, See General Section

For full biographical listings, see the Martindale-Hubbell Law Directory

MICHIGAN

*ANN ARBOR,** Washtenaw Co.

MILLER, CANFIELD, PADDOCK AND STONE, P.L.C. (AV)

A Professional Limited Liability Company
Founded in 1852 by Sidney Davy Miller
101 North Main Street, Seventh Floor, 48104-1400
Telephone: 313-663-2445
Fax: 313-747-7147
Detroit, Michigan Office: 150 West Jefferson, Suite 2500, 48226-4415.
Telephone: 313-963-6420.
Fax: 313-496-7500.
Cable Address: "Stem Detroit."

(See Next Column)

MILLER, CANFIELD, PADDOCK AND STONE P.L.C., *Ann Arbor—Continued*

Bloomfield Hills, Michigan Office: Suite 100, Pinehurst Office Center, 1400 North Woodward, 48303-2014.
Telephone: 313-645-5000.
Fax: 313-645-1917.
Grand Rapids, Michigan Office: 1200 Campau Square Plaza, 99 Monroe, N.W., 49503-2639.
Telephone: 616-454-8656.
Fax: 616-776-6322.
Howell, Michigan Office: 121 South Barnard Street, Suite 4, 48843-2305.
Telephone: 517-546-7600.
Telecopier: 517-546-6974.
Kalamazoo, Michigan Office: 444 West Michigan Avenue, 49007-3752.
Telephone: 616-381-7030.
Fax: 616-382-0244.
Lansing, Michigan Office: One Michigan Avenue, Suite 900, 48933-1609.
Telephone: 517-487-2070.
Fax: 517-374-6304.
Monroe, Michigan Office: The Executive Centre, 214 East Elm Avenue, 48161-2682.
Telephone: 313-243-2000.
Fax: 313-243-0901.
Washington, D.C. Office: 1225 Nineteenth Street, N.W., Suite 400. 20036.
Telephone: 202-429-5575; 785-0600.
Fax: 202-331-1118; 785-1234.
Pensacola, Florida Office: 25 West Cedar, 32501.
Telephone: 904-469-1088.
Fax: 904-432-0677.
St. Petersburg, Florida Office: 100 Second Avenue S., Suite 7045, 33701.
Telephone: 813-982-6000.
Fax: 813-892-6002.
Gdansk, Poland Office: Suite 322, Dom Technika Building, Ul. Rajska 6, 80-850.
Telephone: 011-485-831-2808.
Fax: 011-485-831-4719.
Warsaw, Poland Office: Ul. Marszalkowska 82, Suite 561, 00-517.
Telephone: 011-482-623-6457 and 6458.
Fax: 011-482-623-6459.

RESIDENT PARTNER

Robert E. Gilbert

Representative Firm Clients: Chrysler Corp.; Comerica, Inc.; City of Detroit, Mich.; Detroit Tigers, Inc.; First of Michigan; Fretter, Inc.; Ford Motor Co.; Ford Motor Credit Co.; Great Lakes Bancorp; Henry Ford Hospital.

For Complete List of Firm Personnel, See General Section

For full biographical listings, see the Martindale-Hubbell Law Directory

*BAY CITY,** Bay Co.

BRAUN KENDRICK FINKBEINER (AV)

201 Phoenix Building, P.O. Box 2039, 48708
Telephone: 517-895-8505
Telecopier: 517-895-8437
Saginaw, Michigan Office: 8th Floor Second National Bank Building.
Telephone: 517-753-3461.
Telecopier: 517-753-3951.

MEMBERS OF FIRM

Ralph J. Isackson
Patrick D. Neering
George F. Gronewold, Jr.
Frank M. Quinn
Gregory E. Meter
Daniel S. Opperman
Gregory T. Demers

Representative Clients: APV Chemical Machinery, Inc.; Bay Health Systems; Berger and Co.; Catholic Federal Credit Union; Charter Township of Bridgeport; City of Saginaw; City of Vassar; City of Zilwaukee; Corporate Service; Cox Cable.

For Complete List of Firm Personnel, See General Section

For full biographical listings, see the Martindale-Hubbell Law Directory

*DETROIT,** Wayne Co.

BODMAN, LONGLEY & DAHLING (AV)

34th Floor 100 Renaissance Center, 48243
Telephone: 313-259-7777
Fax: 313-393-7579
Troy, Michigan Office: Suite 2020, 755 West Big Beaver Road.
Telephone: 810-362-2110.
Ann Arbor, Michigan Office: 110 Miller, Suite 300.
Telephone: 313-761-3780.
Northern Michigan Office: 229 Court Street, P.O. Box 405, Cheboygan.
Telephone: 616-627-4351.

MEMBERS OF FIRM

Carson C. Grunewald
James A. Smith
Robert G. Brower

Representative Clients: Abitibi Price Group; Archdiocese of Detroit; Comerica Bank; The Detroit Lions, Inc.; Ford Estates; General Motors Corporation; Charles Stewart Mott Foundation; Norfolk Southern Corporation; Panhandle Eastern Corporation; State Farm Mutual Automobile Insurance Company.

(See Next Column)

For Complete List of Firm Personnel, See General Section

For full biographical listings, see the Martindale-Hubbell Law Directory

HONIGMAN MILLER SCHWARTZ AND COHN (AV)

A Partnership including Professional Corporations
2290 First National Building, 48226
Telephone: 313-256-7800
Telecopier: 313-962-0176
Telex: 235705
Lansing, Michigan Office: Phoenix Building, 222 North Washington Square, Suite 400.
Telephone: 517-484-8282.
West Palm Beach, Florida Office: Suite 800 Esperante Building, 222 Lakeview Avenue.
Telephone: 407-838-4500.
Tampa, Florida Office: 2700 Landmark Centre, 401 E. Jackson Street.
Telephone: 813-221-6600.
Orlando, Florida Office: 390 North Orange Avenue, Suite 1300.
Telephone: 407-648-0300.
Houston, Texas Office: 3100 First Interstate Bank Plaza, 1000 Louisiana.
Telephone: 713-650-2600.
Los Angeles, California Office: McNeill Plaza, Suite 820, 15260 Ventura Boulevard, 91403.
Telephone: 818-784-2900.

MEMBERS OF FIRM

Christopher J. Dunsky
Kenneth C. Gold
Philip A. Grashoff, Jr.
Robert A. Hykan
Brian Negele
John D. Pirich (Lansing, Michigan Office)
Joseph M. Polito
Paul Revere, III
Gary A. Trepod (Lansing, Michigan Office)
Grant R. Trigger
John W. Voelpel
William A. Wichers II

ASSOCIATES

Sally J. Churchill
S. Lee Johnson
Walter J. Kramarz
Jeffrey L. Woolstrum

RESIDENT IN WEST PALM BEACH, FLORIDA OFFICE

MEMBER

E. Lee Worsham (P.A.)

RESIDENT IN TAMPA, FLORIDA OFFICE

MEMBER

Michael G. Cooke (P.A.)

RESIDENT IN ORLANDO, FLORIDA OFFICE

MEMBER

J.A. Jurgens (P.A.)

ASSOCIATES

Jan A. Albanese
Roseanna J. Lee

Representative Clients: Auto Alliance International (formerly Mazda Motor Mfg. (USA) Corp.); Consumers Power Co.; The Detroit Edison Co.; Ford Motor Co.; General Motors Corp.; Edw. C. Levy Co.; Hughes Aircraft Company; Masco Corporation/MascoTech, Inc.; McLouth Steel Products Corp.; Morton International, Inc.; Weyerhaeuser Company.

For Complete List of Firm Personnel, See General Section

For full biographical listings, see the Martindale-Hubbell Law Directory

MILLER, CANFIELD, PADDOCK AND STONE, P.L.C. (AV)

A Professional Limited Liability Company
Founded in 1852 by Sidney Davy Miller
150 West Jefferson, Suite 2500, 48226-4415
Telephone: 313-963-6420
Fax: 313-496-7500
Cable Address: "Stem Detroit"
Detroit, Michigan Office: 150 West Jefferson, Suite 2500, 48226-4415.
Telephone: 313-963-6420.
Fax: 313-496-7500.
Cable Address: "Stem Detroit."
Ann Arbor, Michigan Office: 101 North Main Street, 7th Floor, 48104-1400.
Telephone: 313-663-2445.
Fax: 313-747-7147.
Bloomfield Hills, Michigan Office: Suite 100, Pinehurst Office Center, 1400 North Woodward, 48303-2014.
Telephone: 313-645-5000.
Fax: 313-645-1917.
Grand Rapids, Michigan Office: 1200 Campau Square Plaza, 99 Monroe, N.W., 49503-2639.
Telephone: 616-454-8656.
Fax: 616-776-6322.
Howell, Michigan Office: 121 South Barnard Street, Suite 4, 48843-2305.
Telephone: 517-546-7600.
Telecopier: 517-546-6974.
Kalamazoo, Michigan Office: 444 West Michigan Avenue, 49007-3752.
Telephone: 616-381-7030.
Fax: 616-382-0244.

(See Next Column)

MILLER, CANFIELD, PADDOCK AND STONE P.L.C.—*Continued*

Lansing, Michigan Office: One Michigan Avenue, Suite 900, 48933-1609.
Telephone: 517-487-2070.
Fax: 517-374-6304.
Monroe, Michigan Office: The Executive Centre, 214 East Elm Avenue, 48161-2682.
Telephone: 313-243-2000.
Fax: 313-243-0901.
Washington, D.C. Office: 1225 Nineteenth Street, N.W., Suite 400. 20036.
Telephone: 202-429-5575; 785-0600.
Fax: 202-331-1118; 785-1234.
Pensacola, Florida Office: 25 West Cedar, 32501.
Telephone: 904-469-1088.
Fax: 904-432-0677.
St. Petersburg, Florida Office: 100 Second Avenue S., Suite 7045, 33701.
Telephone: 813-982-6000.
Fax: 813-892-6002.
Gdansk, Poland Office: Suite 322, Dom Technika Building, UI. Rajska 6, 80-850.
Telephone: 011-485-831-2808.
Fax: 011-485-831-4719.
Warsaw, Poland Office: UI. Marszalkowska 82, Suite 561, 00-517.
Telephone: 011-482-623-6457 and 6458.
Fax: 011-482-623-6459.

MEMBERS OF FIRM

Frank L. Andrews (Detroit and Bloomfield Hills Offices)
Thomas C. Phillips (Grand Rapids and Lansing Offices)
Steven D. Weyhing (Lansing Office)

Representative Firm Clients: Chrysler Corp.; Comerica, Inc.; City of Detroit, Mich.; Detroit Tigers, Inc.; First of Michigan; Fretter, Inc.; Ford Motor Co.; Ford Motor Credit Co.; Great Lakes Bancorp; Henry Ford Hospital.

For Complete List of Firm Personnel, See General Section

For full biographical listings, see the Martindale-Hubbell Law Directory

*GRAND RAPIDS,** Kent Co.

CLARY, NANTZ, WOOD, HOFFIUS, RANKIN & COOPER (AV)

500 Calder Plaza, 250 Monroe Avenue, N.W., 49503-2244
Telephone: 616-459-9487
Telecopier: 616-459-5121

MEMBERS OF FIRM

Leonard M. Hoffius
Scott G. Smith

OF COUNSEL

Richard J. Rankin, Jr.

Representative Clients: United Bank of Michigan; FMB First Michigan Bank-Grand Rapids; Goodrich Theatres, Inc.; S. Abraham & Sons, Inc.; Garb-Ko, Inc., d/b/a 7-Eleven; Weather Shield Manufacturing Co.; JET Electronics & Technology, Inc.; Inc.; Westinghouse Credit Corp.

For Complete List of Firm Personnel, See General Section

For full biographical listings, see the Martindale-Hubbell Law Directory

WARNER, NORCROSS & JUDD (AV)

900 Old Kent Building, 111 Lyon Street, N.W., 49503-2489
Telephone: 616-752-2000
Fax: 616-752-2500
Muskegon, Michigan Office: 400 Terrace Plaza, P.O. Box 900.
Telephone: 616-727-2600.
Fax: 616-727-2699.
Holland, Michigan Office: Curtis Center, Suite 300, 170 College Avenue.
Telephone: 616-396-9800.
Fax: 616-396-3656.

MEMBERS OF FIRM

John D. Tully
Peter L. Gustafson
Michael L. Robinson
Eugene E. Smary
Paul T. Sorensen
John D. Dunn
John V. Byl
Tracy T. Larsen

General Counsel for: Bissell Inc.; Blodgett Memorial Medical Center; Guardsman Products, Inc.; Haworth, Inc.; Kysor Industrial Corp.; Michigan Bankers Assn.; Old Kent Financial Corp.; Steelcase, Inc.; Wolverine World Wide, Inc.

For Complete List of Firm Personnel, See General Section

For full biographical listings, see the Martindale-Hubbell Law Directory

LANSING, Ingham Co.

* indicates certain Bar Register subscribers whose principal office is located elsewhere in the state and who have arranged for representation as a part of the state capital listings that follow

* HONIGMAN MILLER SCHWARTZ AND COHN (AV)

A Partnership including Professional Corporations
222 North Washington Square, Suite 400, 48933
Telephone: 517-484-8282
Telecopier: 517-484-8286
Detroit, Michigan Office: 2290 First National Building.
Telephone: 313-256-7800.
West Palm Beach, Florida Office: Suite 800 Esperante Building, 222 Lakeview Avenue.
Telephone: 407-838-4500.
Tampa, Florida Office: Suite 350 One Harbour Place, 777 South Harbour Island Boulevard.
Telephone: 813-221-6600.
Orlando, Florida Office: 390 North Orange Avenue, Suite 1300.
Telephone: 407-648-0300.
Houston, Texas Office: 3100 First Interstate Bank Plaza, 1000 Louisiana.
Telephone: 713-650-2600.
Los Angeles, California Office: McNeill Plaza, Suite 820, 15260 Ventura Boulevard, 91403.
Telephone: 818-784-2900.

MEMBERS

Mark Morton
John D. Pirich
Gary A. Trepod

Representative Clients: Central Wayne County Sanitation Authority; Granger Land Development Company; Greater Detroit Resource Recovery Authority; Landfill Management Company; Michigan Disposal Service Corporation; Republic Waste Industries; Wayne Disposal, Inc.

For Complete List of Firm Personnel, See General Section

For full biographical listings, see the Martindale-Hubbell Law Directory

*MOUNT PLEASANT,** Isabella Co.

LYNCH, GALLAGHER, LYNCH & MARTINEAU (AV)

555 North Main Street, P.O. Box 446, 48858
Telephone: 517-773-9961
Fax: 517-773-2107
Lansing, Michigan Office: 2400 Lake Lansing Road, Suite B.
Telephone: 517-485-0400.
Fax: 517-485-0402.

MEMBERS OF FIRM

Byron P. Gallagher
John J. Lynch
Steven W. Martineau
Sue A. Jeffers
Paula K. Manis (Resident at Lansing Office)
William M. McClintic
Michael J. Hackett
Byron P. Gallagher, Jr. (Resident at Lansing Office)
Denise A. Koehler

Representative Clients: Amoco Production Co.; Mosbacher Production Co.; Muskegon Development Co.; Lease Management, Inc.; Dow Chemical Co.; Dresser Industries, Inc.; North Michigan Oil & Gas Corp; Scanda Energy Co., Inc.

For Complete List of Firm Personnel, See General Section

For full biographical listings, see the Martindale-Hubbell Law Directory

*SAGINAW,** Saginaw Co.

BRAUN KENDRICK FINKBEINER (AV)

8th Floor Second National Bank Building, 48607
Telephone: 517-753-3461
Telecopier: 517-753-3951
Bay City, Michigan Office: 201 Phoenix Building, P.O. Box 2039.
Telephone: 517-895-8505.
Telecopier: 517-895-8437.

MEMBERS OF FIRM

J. Richard Kendrick
James V. Finkbeiner
Thomas R. Luplow
John A. Decker
Barry M. Levine

ASSOCIATES

Brian S. Makaric
Glenn L. Fitkin

Representative Clients: The Dow Chemical Co.; General Motors Corp.; Lobdell Emery Manufacturing Co.; Merrill, Lynch, Inc.; Saginaw General Hospital; Saginaw News; The Wickes Foundation.

For Complete List of Firm Personnel, See General Section

For full biographical listings, see the Martindale-Hubbell Law Directory

MINNESOTA

*MINNEAPOLIS,** Hennepin Co.

LEONARD, STREET AND DEINARD, PROFESSIONAL ASSOCIATION (AV)

Suite 2300, 150 South Fifth Street, 55402
Telephone: 612-335-1500
Telecopier: 612-335-1657

Charles K. Dayton
Byron E. Starns, Jr.
John H. Herman (P.A.)
Edward M. Moersfelder
Martha C. Brand
Joseph M. Finley, Jr.
Ellen G. Sampson
Joan Ericksen Lancaster
Susan M. Robiner
Shaun C. McElhatton
James J. Bertrand

Carolyn V. Wolski
William H. Koch
Edward A. Murphy
Gregory L. Poe
Joshua J. Kanassatega
Jann M. Eichlersmith
I. Daniel Colton

OF COUNSEL

Peter H. Bachman

Representative Clients: Blount Energy Resources Corp.; Lundgren Bros. Construction Co.; Minneapolis Community Development Agency; PCL Construction-PCL Enterprises, Inc.; Terra International, Inc.; Waste Management of Minnesota, Inc.

For Complete List of Firm Personnel, See General Section

For full biographical listings, see the Martindale-Hubbell Law Directory

MISSISSIPPI

*ABERDEEN,** Monroe Co.

PATTERSON & PATTERSON (AV)

304 East Jefferson Street, P.O. Box 663, 39730
Telephone: 601-369-2476
1-800-523-9975
FAX: 601-369-9806

MEMBERS OF FIRM

Robert D. Patterson
Jan P. Patterson

Local Counsel for: National Bank of Commerce of Mississippi; American Colloid Company; Vista Chemical Co.; Pruet Production Co.; Arco Oil & Gas Co.; Chemical Corporation; Unimin Corporation.

For Complete List of Firm Personnel, See General Section

For full biographical listings, see the Martindale-Hubbell Law Directory

*CLARKSDALE,** Coahoma Co.

ROSS, HUNT, SPELL & ROSS, A PROFESSIONAL ASSOCIATION (AV)

123 Court Street, P.O. Box 1196, 38614
Telephone: 601-627-5251
Telecopier No.: 601-627-5254
Clinton, Mississippi Office: 203 Monroe Street.
Telephone: 601-924-2655.

Tom T. Ross (1903-1993)
David R. Hunt
Tom T. Ross, Jr.

Representative Client: Beech Aircraft Corp., Wichita, Kansas.

For Complete List of Firm Personnel, See General Section

For full biographical listings, see the Martindale-Hubbell Law Directory

*JACKSON,** Hinds Co.

ALSTON, RUTHERFORD, TARDY & VAN SLYKE (AV)

121 North State Street, P.O. Drawer 1532, 39215-1532
Telephone: 601-948-6882
Fax: 601-948-6902

MEMBERS OF FIRM

Alex A. Alston, Jr.
Kenneth A. Rutherford
Thomas W. Tardy, III
Julie E. Chaffin

Counsel for: Southland Oil Co.; Georgia-Pacific Corp.; Forest Oil Corp.; Conoco, Inc.; Transcontinental Gas Pipeline, Inc.; Chemrich, Inc.; E. I. Du Pont de Nemours & Co.; The Dow Chemical Co.; Hunt Energy Corp.; The Travelers Ins. Cos.; The Trans Co.

For Complete List of Firm Personnel, See General Section

For full biographical listings, see the Martindale-Hubbell Law Directory

MCDAVID, NOBLIN & WEST (AV)

Suite 1000, Security Centre North, 200 South Lamar Street, 39201
Telephone: 601-948-3305
Telecopier: 601-354-4789

MEMBERS OF FIRM

John Land McDavid
William C. Noblin, Jr.
W. Eric West
John Sanford McDavid
John C. Robertson

OF COUNSEL

Lowell F. Stephens

For full biographical listings, see the Martindale-Hubbell Law Directory

LAW OFFICES OF MCKIBBEN, GRANT & ASSOCIATES A PROFESSIONAL ASSOCIATION (AV)

501 Riverhill Tower, 1675 Lakeland Drive, 39216
Telephone: 601-982-7200
Telecopier: 601-982-7203

Dale H. McKibben
Russell P. Grant, Jr.

For full biographical listings, see the Martindale-Hubbell Law Directory

WATKINS & EAGER (AV)

Suite 300 The Emporium Building, P.O. Box 650, 39205
Telephone: 601-948-6470
Facsimile: (601) 354-3623

MEMBERS OF FIRM

William F. Goodman, Jr.
P. Nicholas Harkins, III
John G. Corlew
Paul H. Stephenson, III

Representative Clients: Ashland Oil, Inc.; Chevron U.S.A. Inc.; First Energy Corp.; International Paper Co.; Blossman Gas, Inc.; Pruet Production Co.; Shell Oil Co.; Texaco Inc.; Trustmark National Bank; Union Pacific Resources Co.

For Complete List of Firm Personnel, See General Section

For full biographical listings, see the Martindale-Hubbell Law Directory

MISSOURI

KANSAS CITY, Jackson, Clay & Platte Cos.

SWANSON, MIDGLEY, GANGWERE, KITCHIN & MCLARNEY, L.L.C. (AV)

1500 Commerce Trust Building, 922 Walnut, 64106-1848
Telephone: 816-842-6100
Overland Park, Kansas Office: The NCAA Building, Suite 350, 6201 College Boulevard.
Telephone: 816-842-6100.

Robert W. McKinley

Craig T. Kenworthy

Counsel for: General Electric Co.; Chrysler Corp.; Conoco, Inc.; Yellow Freight System, Inc.; The Prudential Insurance Co. of America; Metropolitan Life Insurance Co.; National Collegiate Athletic Assn.; Land Title Insurance Co.; Safeway Stores, Inc.; The Lee Apparel Co.

For Complete List of Firm Personnel, See General Section

For full biographical listings, see the Martindale-Hubbell Law Directory

MONTANA

*BILLINGS,** Yellowstone Co.

CROWLEY, HAUGHEY, HANSON, TOOLE & DIETRICH (AV)

500 Transwestern II, 490 North 31st Street, P.O. Box 2529, 59103
Telephone: 406-252-3441
Fax: 406-259-4159
Helena, Montana Office: IBM Building, 100 North Park Avenue, Suite 300, 59601.
Telephone: 406-449-4165.
Fax: 406-449-5149.

OF COUNSEL

Bruce R. Toole

MEMBERS OF FIRM

Louis R. Moore
Arthur F. Lamey, Jr.
Kemp J. Wilson
Steven P. Ruffatto
Carolyn S. Ostby
Christopher Mangen, Jr.
Michael E. Webster
Janice L. Rehberg

(See Next Column)

CROWLEY, HAUGHEY, HANSON, TOOLE & DIETRICH—*Continued*

ASSOCIATES

John R. Lee Michael S. Lahr

Representative Clients: Noranda Minerals Corp.; Chevron U.S.A., Inc.; Kennecott Corporation; Conoco, Inc.; Pegasus Gold Corp.; Norfolk Energy, Inc.; Sinclair Oil Corp.; Peabody Coal Co.; Decker Coal Co.; Montana Power Company.

For Complete List of Firm Personnel, See General Section

For full biographical listings, see the Martindale-Hubbell Law Directory

NEVADA

*LAS VEGAS,** Clark Co.

JOLLEY, URGA, WIRTH & WOODBURY (AV)

Suite 800 Bank of America Plaza, 300 South Fourth Street, 89101
Telephone: 702-385-5161
Telecopier: 702-382-6814
Boulder City, Nevada Office: Suite 105, 1000 Nevada Highway.
Telephone: 702-293-3674.

MEMBERS OF FIRM

R. Gardner Jolley
Mark A. James
Donald E. Brookhyser

ASSOCIATES

Allen D. Emmel
Gregory J. Walch

Representative Clients: First Interstate Bank of Nevada; Nevada State Bank; Melvin Simon & Associates, Inc.; Nevada Mobilehome Park Owners Association; Continental National Bank; First Nationwide Bank; PriMerit Bank; Wells Cargo, Inc.; Dean Roofing Co.; Lincoln Property Co.

For Complete List of Firm Personnel, See General Section

For full biographical listings, see the Martindale-Hubbell Law Directory

WOODBURN AND WEDGE (AV)

Suite 620 Bank of America Plaza, 300 South Fourth Street, 89101
Telephone: 702-387-1000
Reno, Nevada Office: 16th Floor, First Interstate Bank Building. P.O. Box 2311.
Telephone: 702-688-3000.
Telecopier: 702-688-3088.

MEMBERS OF FIRM

Casey Woodburn Vlautin
W. Chris Wicker
Charles A. Jeannes

ASSOCIATE

Andrew J. Driggs

Representative Clients: Atlantic Richfield Co.; Sierra Pacific Power Co.; The Union Pacific Railroad Co.; Western Union Telegraph Co.; Cyprus Minerals Corp.; The Roman Catholic Bishop of Reno, A Corporation Sole.

For full biographical listings, see the Martindale-Hubbell Law Directory

*RENO,** Washoe Co.

HALE, LANE, PEEK, DENNISON AND HOWARD (AV)

Porsche Building, 100 West Liberty Street, Tenth Floor, P.O. Box 3237, 89501
Telephone: 702-786-7900
Telefax: 702-786-6179
Las Vegas, Nevada Office: Suite 800, Nevada Financial Center, 2300 West Sahara Avenue, Box 8.
Telephone: 702-362-5118.
Fax: 702-365-6940.

MEMBERS OF FIRM

R. Craig Howard
Alex J. Flangas

Representative Clients: Western Water Development Co.; Washoe County; Caughlin Ranch; Northern Nevada Water Resources, Limited Partnership.

For Complete List of Firm Personnel, See General Section

For full biographical listings, see the Martindale-Hubbell Law Directory

WOODBURN AND WEDGE (AV)

16th Floor, First Interstate Bank Building, One East First Street, P.O. Box 2311, 89505
Telephone: 702-688-3000
Telecopier: 702-688-3088
Las Vegas, Nevada Office: Suite 620 Bank of American Plaza, 300 South Court Street.
Telephone: 702-387-1000.

MEMBERS OF FIRM

Casey Woodburn Vlautin
W. Chris Wicker
Charles A. Jeannes

(See Next Column)

ASSOCIATE

Andrew J. Driggs

Representative Clients: Atlantic Richfield Co.; Sierra Pacific Power Co.; The Union Pacific Railroad Co.; Western Union Telegraph Co.; Bank of America; Cyprus Minerals Corp.; The Roman Catholic Bishop of Reno, A Corporation Sole; Placer Dome, Inc.; Amax Gold, Inc.; Glamis Gold, Inc.

For full biographical listings, see the Martindale-Hubbell Law Directory

NEW JERSEY

HADDONFIELD, Camden Co.

TOMAR, SIMONOFF, ADOURIAN & O'BRIEN, A PROFESSIONAL CORPORATION (AV)

41 South Haddon Avenue, 08033
Telephone: 609-429-1100
Telecopier: 609-429-8164
Camden, New Jersey Office: 501 Cooper Street.
Telephone: 609-338-0553.
Telecopier: 609-338-0321.
Atlantic City, New Jersey Office: Commerce Building, Suite 220, 1200 Atlantic Avenue.
Telephone: 609-348-5900.
Northfield, New Jersey Office: The Executive Plaza, Suite 202, 2111 New Road.
Telephone: 609-485-0800.
Telecopier: 609-484-9388.
Wilmington, Delaware Office: Tomar, Simonoff, Adourian & O'Brien, The Mellon Bank Center, Suite 1701, 919 Market Street.
Telephone: 302-655-0500.
Telecopier: 302-428-0963.
Media, Pennsylvania Office: 115 North Jackson Street.
Telephone: 215-574-0635.

William Tomar
David Jacoby
Alan H. Sklarsky
Joshua M. Spielberg

For full biographical listings, see the Martindale-Hubbell Law Directory

*NEWARK,** Essex Co.

CARPENTER, BENNETT & MORRISSEY (AV)

(Formerly Carpenter, Gilmour & Dwyer)
Three Gateway Center, 17th Floor, 100 Mulberry Street, 07102-4079
Telephone: 201-622-7711
New York City: 212-943-6530
Telex: 139405
Telecopier: 201-622-5314
EasyLink: 62827845
ABA/net: CARPENTERB

MEMBERS OF FIRM

John F. Lynch, Jr.
Francis X. O'Brien
Edward F. Day, Jr.
John D. Goldsmith
Louis M. DeStefano
Jane Andrews

ASSOCIATES

Jennifer L. Kapell
Lois H. Goodman
Dennis M. Helewa
Patrick J. McNamara
Bonnie E. Bershad
Lisa A. Breen
Judith A. Eisenberg

Representative Clients: General Motors Corp.; Texaco Inc.; International Flavors & Fragrances Inc.; Allied Signal; Hoechst-Celanese; Miller Brewing Co.; FMC Corp.; General Electric Corp.; Hercules Inc.

For Complete List of Firm Personnel, See General Section

For full biographical listings, see the Martindale-Hubbell Law Directory

HELLRING LINDEMAN GOLDSTEIN & SIEGAL (AV)

One Gateway Center, 07102-5386
Telephone: 201-621-9020
Telecopier: 201-621-7406

Philip Lindeman, II
Joel D. Siegal
Jonathan L. Goldstein
Margaret Dee Hellring
Richard D. Shapiro
Charles Oransky
Richard B. Honig
Richard K. Coplon
Robert S. Raymar
Ronny Jo Greenwald Siegal
Stephen L. Dreyfuss
John A. Adler
Judah I. Elstein
Ronnie F. Liebowitz
Bruce S. Etterman
Matthew E. Moloshok
Rachel N. Davidson
Sarah Jane Jelin
Eric A. Savage
David N. Narciso
Sheryl E. Koomer

For Complete List of Firm Personnel, See General Section

For full biographical listings, see the Martindale-Hubbell Law Directory

Newark—Continued

McCarter & English (AV)

Four Gateway Center, 100 Mulberry Street, P.O. Box 652, 07101-0652
Telephone: 201-622-4444
Telecopier: 201-624-7070
Cable Address: "McCarter" Newark
Cherry Hill, New Jersey Office: 1810 Chapel Avenue West.
Telephone: 609-662-8444.
Telecopier: 609-662-6203.
New York, New York Office: Suite 1519, One World Trade Center.
Telephone: 212-466-9018.
Telecopier: 212-432-6568.
Boca Raton, Florida Office: 2255 Glades Road, Suite 319-A.
Telephone: 407-994-6262.
Telecopier: 407-241-0798.
Wilmington, Delaware Office: Mellon Bank Center, 919 Market Street.
Telephone: 302-654-8010.
Telecopier: 302-654-0795.

MEMBERS OF FIRM

Alfred L. Ferguson
John A. McKinney, Jr.
Lanny S. Kurzweil
Frank E. Ferruggia
Keith E. Lynott
James J. Maron (Resident, Wilmington, Delaware Office)

COUNSEL

Gary T. Hall
J. Forrest Jones

ASSOCIATES

Brenda C. Liss
David C. Apy
Paul C. Dritsas
Joseph M. Aronds
Lisa W.S. Bonsall
D. Mark Leonard
Gerard G. Brew
Sherilyn Pastor
Vito A. Pinto
William P. Higgins, Jr.
Kathleen A. Pierce
Karen L. Blinder
Anthony J. Del Piano

For Complete List of Firm Personnel, See General Section

For full biographical listings, see the Martindale-Hubbell Law Directory

ROSELAND, Essex Co.

Post, Polak, Goodsell & MacNeill, P.A. (AV)

65 Livingston Avenue, 07068
Telephone: 201-994-1100
Telecopier: 201-994-1705
New York, New York Office: Suite 1006, 575 Madison Avenue.
Telephone: 212-486-1455.

Frederick B. Polak
Robert A. Goodsell
Paul D. Strauchler

Robert P. Merenich

For full biographical listings, see the Martindale-Hubbell Law Directory

NEW MEXICO

*ALBUQUERQUE,** Bernalillo Co.

Hinkle, Cox, Eaton, Coffield & Hensley (AV)

Suite 800, 500 Marquette, N.W., P.O. Box 2043, 87103
Telephone: 505-768-1500
FAX: 505-768-1529
Roswell, New Mexico Office: Suite 700, United Bank Plaza, P.O. Box 10, 88202.
Telephone: 505-622-6510.
FAX: 505-623-9332.
Midland, Texas Office: 6 Desta Drive, Suite 2800, P.O. Box 3580, 79705.
Telephone: 915-683-4691.
FAX: 915-683-6518.
Amarillo, Texas Office: 1700 Bank One Center. P.O. Box 9238, 79105-9238.
Telephone: 806-372-5569.
FAX: 806-372-9761.
Santa Fe, New Mexico Office: 218 Montezuma, P.O. Box 2068, 87504.
Telephone: 505-982-4554.
FAX: 505-982-8623.
Austin, Texas Office: 401 West 15th Street, Suite 800, 78701.
Telephone: 512-476-7137.
FAX: 512-476-5431.
Associated Office: Hoffman & Stephens, P.C., 401 West 15th Street, Suite 800, 78701.
Telephone: 512-476-5434.
Fax: 512-476-5431.

Marshall G. Martin
Mark C. Dow

Representative Clients: Anadarko Petroleum Corp.; Atlantic Richfield Co.; Bass Enterprises Production Co.; BHP Petroleum; Caroon & Black Management, Inc.; Chevron, USA, Inc.; CIGNA; City of Albuquerque; Coastal Oil & Gas Corp. Co.; Ethicon Inc., A Johnson & Johnson, Co.; Diagnostik; Conoco; Texaco; Presbyterian Healthcare Services.

(See Next Column)

For Complete List of Firm Personnel, See General Section

For full biographical listings, see the Martindale-Hubbell Law Directory

Miller, Stratvert, Torgerson & Schlenker, P.A. (AV)

500 Marquette Avenue, N.W., Suite 1100, P.O. Box 25687, 87102
Telephone: 505-842-1950
Facsimile: 505-243-4408
Farmington, New Mexico Office: Suite 300, 300 West Arrington. P.O. Box 869.
Telephone: 505-326-4521.
Facsimile: 505-325-5474.
Las Cruces, New Mexico Office: Suite 300, 277 East Amador. P.O. Drawer 1231.
Telephone: 505-523-2481.
Facsimile: 505-526-2215.
Santa Fe, New Mexico Office: 125 Lincoln Avenue, Suite 221. P.O. Box 1986.
Telephone: 505-989-9614.
Facsimile: 505-989-9857.

Ranne B. Miller
Alan C. Torgerson
Kendall O. Schlenker
Alice Tomlinson Lorenz
Gregory W. Chase
Alan Konrad
Margo J. McCormick
Lyman G. Sandy
Stephen M. Williams
Stephan M. Vidmar
Robert C. Gutierrez
Seth V. Bingham (Resident at Farmington Office)
Michael H. Hoses
James B. Collins (Resident at Farmington Office)
Timothy Ray Briggs
Walter R. Parr (Resident at Santa Fe Office)
Rudolph A. Lucero
Daniel E. Ramczyk
Dean G. Constantine
Deborah A. Solove
Gary L. Gordon
Lawrence R. White (Resident at Las Cruces Office)
Sharon P. Gross
Virginia Anderman
Marte D. Lightstone
Bradford K. Goodwin
John R. Funk (Resident at Las Cruces Office)
J. Scott Hall (Resident at Santa Fe Office)
Thomas R. Mack
Michael J. Happe (Resident at Farmington Office)
Denise Barela Shepherd
Nancy Augustus
Jill Burtram
Terri L. Sauer
Joel T. Newton (Resident at Las Cruces Office)
Judith K. Nakamura
Thomas M. Domme
David H. Thomas, III
C. Brian Charlton

COUNSEL

William K. Stratvert
Paul W. Robinson

Representative Clients: St. Paul Insurance Cos.; State Farm Mutual Automobile Insurance Co.; The Travelers; United States Fidelity & Guaranty Co.; New Mexico Physicians Mutual Liability Insurance Co.; Farmers Insurance Group; Amoco Production Co.; Aztec Well Servicing Co.; Mesa Limited Partnership.

For Complete List of Firm Personnel, See General Section

For full biographical listings, see the Martindale-Hubbell Law Directory

Rodey, Dickason, Sloan, Akin & Robb, P.A. (AV)

Albuquerque Plaza, Suite 2200, 201 Third Street, N.W., P.O. Box 1888, 87103-1888
Telephone: 505-765-5900
Fax: 505-768-7395
Santa Fe, New Mexico Office: Suite 101 Marcy Plaza, 123 East Marcy Street, P.O. Box 1357, 87504-1357.
Telephone: 505-984-0100.
Fax: 505-989-9542.

John D. Robb
Mark K. Adams
John P. Salazar
James P. Fitzgerald
Joseph B. Rochelle
Brian H. Lematta

Mary P. Keleher

For Complete List of Firm Personnel, See General Section

For full biographical listings, see the Martindale-Hubbell Law Directory

FARMINGTON, San Juan Co.

Miller, Stratvert, Torgerson & Schlenker, P.A. (AV)

Suite 300, 300 West Arrington, P.O. Box 869, 87401
Telephone: 505-326-4521
Facsimile: 505-325-5474
Albuquerque, New Mexico Office: 500 Marquette Avenue, N.W., Suite 1100. P.O. Box 25687.
Telephone: 505-842-1950.
Facsimile: 505-243-4408.
Las Cruces, New Mexico Office: Suite 300, 277 East Amador. P.O. Drawer 1231.
Telephone: 505-523-2481.
Facsimile: 505-526-2215.

(See Next Column)

MILLER, STRATVERT, TORGERSON & SCHLENKER P.A.—*Continued*

Santa Fe, New Mexico Office: 125 Lincoln Avenue, Suite 221. P.O. Box 1986.
Telephone: 505-989-9614.
Facsimile: 505-989-9857.

James B. Collins
Seth V. Bingham
Michael J. Happe

Representative Clients: St. Paul Insurance Cos.; State Farm Mutual Automobile Insurance Co.; The Travelers; United States Fidelity & Guaranty Co.; New Mexico Physicians Mutual Liability Insurance Co.; Farmers Insurance Group.

For full biographical listings, see the Martindale-Hubbell Law Directory

*LAS CRUCES,** Dona Ana Co.

MILLER, STRATVERT, TORGERSON & SCHLENKER, P.A. (AV)

Suite 300, 277 East Amador, P.O. Drawer 1231, 88004
Telephone: 505-523-2481
Facsimile: 505-526-2215
Albuquerque, New Mexico Office: 500 Marquette Avenue, N.W., Suite 1100. P.O. Box 25687.
Telephone: 505-842-1950.
Facsimile: 505-243-4408.
Farmington, New Mexico Office: Suite 300, 300 West Arrington. P.O. Box 869.
Telephone: 505-326-4521.
Facsimile: 505-325-5474.
Santa Fe, New Mexico Office: 125 Lincoln Avenue, Suite 221. P.O. Box 1986.
Telephone: 505-989-9614.
Facsimile: 505-989-9857.

Lawrence R. White
John R. Funk

Representative Clients: St. Paul Insurance Cos.; State Farm Mutual Automobile Insurance Co.; The Travelers; United States Fidelity & Guaranty Co.; New Mexico Physicians Mutual Liability Insurance Co.; Farmers Insurance Group; Amoco Production Co.; Mesa Limited Partnership.

For full biographical listings, see the Martindale-Hubbell Law Directory

*ROSWELL,** Chaves Co.

HINKLE, COX, EATON, COFFIELD & HENSLEY (AV)

Suite 700, United Bank Plaza, P.O. Box 10, 88202
Telephone: 505-622-6510
FAX: 505-623-9332
Midland, Texas Office: 6 Desta Drive, Suite 2800, P.O. Box 3580, 79705.
Telephone: 915-683-4691.
FAX: 915-683-6518.
Amarillo, Texas Office: 1700 Bank One Center, P.O. Box 9238, 79105-9238.
Telephone: 806-372-5569.
FAX: 806-372-9761.
Santa Fe, New Mexico Office: 218 Montezuma, P.O. Box 2068, 87504.
Telephone: 505-982-4554.
FAX: 505-982-8623.
Albuquerque, New Mexico Office: Suite 800, 500 Marquette, N.W., P.O. Box 2043, 87103.
Telephone: 505-768-1500.
FAX: 505-768-1529.
Austin, Texas Office: 401 West 15th Street, Suite 800, 78701.
Telephone: 512-476-7137.
FAX: 512-476-5431.
Associated Office: Hoffman & Stephens, P.C., 401 West 15th Street, Suite 800, 78701.
Telephone: 512-476-5434.
Fax: 512-476-5431.

RESIDENT PARTNERS

Harold L. Hensley, Jr.
Stuart D. Shanor
Douglas L. Lunsford
T. Calder Ezzell, Jr.
Richard E. Olson
Gregory J. Nibert

Counsel for: Southwestern Public Service Co.; United New Mexico Bank of Roswell.
Representative Clients: Atlantic Richfield Co.; Equitable Life Assurance Society; Exxon Corp.; Insurance Company of North America; Phillips Petroleum Co.; Sun Oil Co.; Texaco; Western Farm Bureau Mutual Insurance Co.

For full biographical listings, see the Martindale-Hubbell Law Directory

*SANTA FE,** Santa Fe Co.

CAMPBELL, CARR, BERGE & SHERIDAN, P.A. (AV)

110 North Guadalupe, P.O. Box 2208, 87504-2208
Telephone: 505-988-4421
Telecopier: 505-983-6043

Michael B. Campbell
William F. Carr
Bradford C. Berge
Mark F. Sheridan

(See Next Column)

Michael H. Feldewert
Tanya M. Trujillo
Nancy A. Rath

For Complete List of Firm Personnel, See General Section

For full biographical listings, see the Martindale-Hubbell Law Directory

CARPENTER, COMEAU, MALDEGEN, BRENNAN, NIXON & TEMPLEMAN (AV)

Coronado Building, 141 East Palace Avenue, P.O. Box 669, 87504-0669
Telephone: 505-982-4611
Telecopier: 505-988-2987

MEMBERS OF FIRM

Richard N. Carpenter
Michael R. Comeau
Larry D. Maldegen
Michael W. Brennan
Sunny J. Nixon
William P. Templeman
Jon J. Indall
Stephen J. Lauer
Paula Ann Cook
Grey Handy
Joseph E. Manges

Representative Clients: Homestake Mining Co.; N. M. Electric Cooperatives; Plains Electric G & T Cooperative; Southern California Edison Co.; United Nuclear Corp.; Uranium Producers of America; BHP Minerals.

For full biographical listings, see the Martindale-Hubbell Law Directory

GALLEGOS LAW FIRM, P.C. (AV)

141 East Palace Avenue, 87501
Telephone: 505-983-6686
Telefax: 505-986-0741

J. E. Gallegos
Mary E. Walta
Michael J. Condon
David Sandoval
Glenn Theriot

Representative Clients: Doyle Hartman Oil Operator; Cuesta Production Co.; Graham Royalty Ltd.; Windward Energy and Marketing Co.; The Northern Trust Co.; San Rio Oil & Gas Co.

For full biographical listings, see the Martindale-Hubbell Law Directory

HINKLE, COX, EATON, COFFIELD & HENSLEY (AV)

218 Montezuma, P.O. Box 2068, 87504
Telephone: 505-982-4554
FAX: 505-982-8623
Roswell, New Mexico Office: Suite 700 United Bank Plaza, P.O. Box 10, 88202.
Telephone: 505-622-6510.
FAX: 505-623-9332.
Midland, Texas Office: 6 Desta Drive, Suite 2800, P.O. Box 3580, 79705.
Telephone: 915-683-4691.
FAX: 915-683-6518.
Amarillo, Texas Office: 1700 Bank One Center, P.O. Box 9238, 79105-9238.
Telephone: 806-372-5569.
FAX: 806-372-9761.
Albuquerque, New Mexico Office: Suite 800, 500 Marquette, N.W., P.O. Box 2043, 87103.
Telephone: 505-768-1500.
FAX: 505-768-1529.
Austin, Texas Office: 401 West 15th Street, Suite 800, 78701.
Telephone: 512-476-7137.
FAX: 512-476-5431.
Associated Office: Hoffman & Stephens, P.C., 401 West 15th Street, Suite 800, 78701.
Telephone: 512-476-5434.
Fax: 512-476-5431.

RESIDENT PARTNERS

Conrad E. Coffield
Jeffrey L. Fornaciari
James Bruce
Thomas M. Hnasko

Representative Clients: Atlantic Richfield Co.; Exxon Corp.; Fernandez Co., Ltd.; Pennzoil Exploration and Production; Western Ag/Minerals Co.

For full biographical listings, see the Martindale-Hubbell Law Directory

HUFFAKER & BARNES, A PROFESSIONAL CORPORATION (AV)

155 Grant Avenue, P.O. Box 1868, 87504-1868
Telephone: 505-988-8921
Fax: 505-983-3927

Gregory D. Huffaker, Jr.
Julia Hosford Barnes
Bradley C. Barron
Sharon A. Higgins
(Not admitted in NM)

Representative Clients: Chevron U.S.A. Products Inc.; Federal Deposit Insurance Corp.; Resolution Trust Corporation; Alphagraphics of Santa Fe and Los Alamos; Basis International, Ltd.; San Juan Concrete Co.

For full biographical listings, see the Martindale-Hubbell Law Directory

Santa Fe—Continued

KELLAHIN AND KELLAHIN (AV)

El Patio Building, 117 North Guadalupe, P.O. Box 2265, 87504-2265
Telephone: 505-982-4285
Fax: 505-982-2047

MEMBERS OF FIRM

W. Thomas Kellahin
Jason Kellahin (Retired, 1991)

Representative Clients: Conoco, Inc.; OXY USA; Phillips Petroleum Co.; Oryx Energy; Meridian Oil Inc.; Marathon Oil Co.; Bass Enterprises Production Co.; Chevron USA, Inc.

For full biographical listings, see the Martindale-Hubbell Law Directory

MONTGOMERY & ANDREWS, PROFESSIONAL ASSOCIATION (AV)

325 Paseo de Peralta, P.O. Box 2307, 87504-2307
Telephone: 505-982-3873
Albuquerque, New Mexico Office: Suite 1300 Albuquerque Plaza, 201 Third Street, N.W., P.O. Box 26927.
Telephone: 505-242-9677.
FAX: 505-243-2542.

Gary Kilpatric
John B. Draper
Nancy M. Anderson King
Sarah Michael Singleton
Galen M. Buller
Edmund H. Kendrick
Louis W. Rose

Representative Clients: Meridian Oil, Inc.; El Paso Natural Gas Co.; Mobil Exploration and Producing U.S., Inc.; US WEST Communications; Phillips Petroleum Co.; LAC Minerals (USA) Inc.; Giant Industries, Inc.; Duke City Lumber Co.; State of Kansas.

For Complete List of Firm Personnel, See General Section

For full biographical listings, see the Martindale-Hubbell Law Directory

NEW YORK

*BINGHAMTON,** Broome Co.

HINMAN, HOWARD & KATTELL (AV)

700 Security Mutual Building, 80 Exchange Street, 13901
Telephone: 607-723-5341
Fax: 607-723-6605
Norwich, New York Office: 600 South Broad Street, Suite 200.
Telephone: 607-334-5896.
Fax: 607-336-6240.

MEMBERS OF FIRM

N. Theodore Sommer
James F. Lee
Lee R. Cirba
Katherine A. Fitzgerald
Albert J. Millus, Jr.

Representative Clients: First-City Division, Chase Lincoln First Bank, N.A.; Binghamton Savings Bank; International Business Machines Corp.; Universal Instruments Corp.; Security Mutual Life Insurance Company of New York; New York Telephone Co.; Travelers Insurance Co.; New York State Electric & Gas Corp.; Exxon Corp.; Columbia Gas System, Inc.

For Complete List of Firm Personnel, See General Section

For full biographical listings, see the Martindale-Hubbell Law Directory

*NEW YORK,** New York Co.

SATTERLEE STEPHENS BURKE & BURKE (AV)

230 Park Avenue, 10169-0079
Telephone: 212-818-9200
Cable Address: "Saterfield," New York
Telex: 233437
Telecopy or Facsimile: (212) 818-9606 or 818-9607
Summit, New Jersey Office: 47 Maple Street.
Telephone: 908-277-2221.
Westfield, New Jersey Office: 105 Elm Street.
Telephone: 908-654-4200.

MEMBERS OF FIRM

Randolph G. Abood
Bernard M. Althoff
Peter A. Basilevsky
Gilman S. Burke
Robert M. Callagy
Robert W. Cockren
Seth H. Dubin
Mark A. Fowler
Robert H. Goldie
Daniel G. Gurfein
William M. Jackson
Dwight A. Kinsey
Stanley Mailman
Howard A. Neuman
Denis R. Pinkernell
Paul J. Powers, Jr.
James F. Rittinger
John Gregory Saver
Kenneth A. Schultz

COUNSEL

Maurice Hahn
Robert C. Hubbard
Karen C. Hunter
Wallace B. Liverance, Jr.
William A. Moore
Bryan Webb
Barbara L. Zinsser

(See Next Column)

ASSOCIATES

Barbara B. Cadigan (Not admitted in NY; Resident, Summit, New Jersey Office)
Geraldine Donovan (Not admitted in NY)
William T. McCue
Kirk H. O'Ferrall
Carla N. Barone
Jan R. Uhrbach

For Complete List of Firm Personnel, See General Section

For full biographical listings, see the Martindale-Hubbell Law Directory

*SYRACUSE,** Onondaga Co.

GROSSMAN KINNEY DWYER & HARRIGAN, P.C. (AV)

5720 Commons Park, 13057
Telephone: 315-449-2131
Telecopier: 315-449-2905

Richard D. Grossman
John P. Kinney
James F. Dwyer
C. Frank Harrigan
Robert E. Hornik, Jr.
Harris N. Lindenfeld

Ruth Moors D'Eredita
Edward P. Dunn
Joseph G. Shields

Representative Clients: County of Onondaga; County of Tompkins; Therm, Incorporated, Ithaca, New York; Village of Marcellus; Smith Barney Shearson; The Mitsubishi Bank, Limited (New York Branch); C&S Engineers, Inc.; Town of Harrietstown, New York.

For full biographical listings, see the Martindale-Hubbell Law Directory

NORTH CAROLINA

*CHARLOTTE,** Mecklenburg Co.

WOMBLE CARLYLE SANDRIDGE & RICE (AV)

A Professional Limited Liability Company
3300 One First Union Center, 301 S. College Street, 28202-6025
Telephone: 704-331-4900
Telecopy: 704-331-4955
Telex: 853609
Winston-Salem, North Carolina Office: 1600 Southern National Financial Center.
Telephone: 919-721-3600.
Telecopy: 919-721-3660.
Telex: 806498.
Raleigh, North Carolina Office: 2100 First Union Capitol Center, 150 Fayetteville Street Mall, P.O. Box 831.
Telephone: 919-755-2100.
Telecopy: 919-755-2150.
Telex: 806498.
Atlanta, Georgia Office: One Ninety One Peachtree Tower, 191 Peachtree Street N.E., Suite 3250.
Telephone: 404-614-2580.
Fax: 404-614-2595.

OF COUNSEL

Bradford A. DeVore

Representative Clients: Childress Klein Properties, Inc.; Food Lion, Inc.; Fieldcrest Cannon, Inc.; J.A. Jones Construction Company; Parkdale Mills, Inc.; Duke Power Company; Bowles Hollowell Conner & Company; ALLTEL Carolina, Inc.; Belk Store Services, Inc.; Philip Holzmann A.G.

For Complete List of Firm Personnel, See General Section

For full biographical listings, see the Martindale-Hubbell Law Directory

*RALEIGH,** Wake Co.

*** indicates certain Bar Register subscribers whose principal office is located elsewhere in the state and who have arranged for representation as a part of the state capital listings that follow**

*** WOMBLE CARLYLE SANDRIDGE & RICE** (AV)

A Professional Limited Liability Company
2100 First Union Capitol Center, 150 Fayetteville Street Mall, P.O. Box 831, 27602
Telephone: 919-755-2100
Telecopy: 919-755-2150
Telex: 806498
Charlotte, North Carolina Office: 3300 One First Union Center, 301 South College Street.
Telephone: 704-331-4900.
Telecopy: 704-331-4955.
Telex: 853609.

(See Next Column)

WOMBLE CARLYLE SANDRIDGE & RICE—*Continued*

Winston-Salem, North Carolina Office: 1600 Southern National Financial Center.
Telephone: 919-721-3600.
Telecopy: 919-721-3660.
Telex: 806498.
Atlanta, Georgia Office: One Ninety One Peachtree Tower, 191 Peachtree Street N.E., Suite 3250.
Telephone: 404-614-2580.
Fax: 404-614-2595.

RESIDENT ASSOCIATE

Yvonne C. Bailey

Representative Clients: Aetna Casualty and Surety Co., Inc.; ALSCO/AmeriMark Building Products, Inc.; Aoki Corporation America, Inc.; Empire of Carolina, Inc.; Hackney Brothers, Inc.; Lawyers Mutual Liability Insurance Company of North Carolina; Meredith College; Monk-Austin, Inc.; Regency Park Corporation; Wachovia Bank of North Carolina, N.A.

For Complete List of Firm Personnel, See General Section

For full biographical listings, see the Martindale-Hubbell Law Directory

*WINSTON-SALEM,** Forsyth Co.

WOMBLE CARLYLE SANDRIDGE & RICE (AV)

A Professional Limited Liability Company
1600 Southern National Financial Center, P.O. Drawer 84, 27102
Telephone: 910-721-3600
Telecopy: 910-721-3660
Telex: 806498
Charlotte, North Carolina Office: 3300 One First Union Center, 301 South College Street.
Telephone: 704-331-4900.
Telecopy: 704-331-4955.
Telex: 853609.
Raleigh, North Carolina Office: 2100 First Union Capitol Center, 150 Fayetteville Street Mall, P.O. Box 831.
Telephone: 919-755-2100.
Telecopy: 919-755-2150.
Telex: 806498.
Atlanta, Georgia Office: One Ninety One Peachtree Tower, 191 Peachtree Street, N.E., Suite 3250.
Telephone: 404-614-2580.
Fax: 404-614-2595.

MEMBERS OF FIRM

Karen Estelle Carey
R. Howard Grubbs
Keith W. Vaughan
G. Criston Windham

ASSOCIATES

Jeffrey L. Furr
Lori Privette Hinnant
Celeste Elizabeth O'Keeffe

Representative Clients: Brad Ragan, Inc.; Brenner Companies; Food Lion, Inc.; Hanes Companies, Inc.; North Carolina Baptist Hospitals, Inc.; R.J. Reynolds Tobacco Company; Summit Communications Group, Inc.; Thomasville Furniture Industries, Inc.; Wachovia Corporation; Wake Forest University.

For Complete List of Firm Personnel, See General Section

For full biographical listings, see the Martindale-Hubbell Law Directory

NORTH DAKOTA

*BISMARCK,** Burleigh Co.

FLECK, MATHER & STRUTZ, LTD. (AV)

Sixth Floor, Norwest Bank Building, 400 East Broadway, P.O. Box 2798, 58502
Telephone: 701-223-6585
Telecopier: 701-222-4853

Ernest R. Fleck
Russell R. Mather
Gary R. Wolberg
Paul W. Summers
Brian R. Bjella
John W. Morrison, Jr.
Craig Cordell Smith

Representative Clients: Amerada Hess Corporation; Amoco Production Co.; Apache Corporation; Columbia Gas Development Corp.; Conoco Inc.; Duncan Energy Co.; Meridian Oil, Inc.; The North American Coal Corp.; Petro-Hunt Corporation; True Oil Co.

For Complete List of Firm Personnel, See General Section

For full biographical listings, see the Martindale-Hubbell Law Directory

PEARCE AND DURICK (AV)

314 East Thayer Avenue, P.O. Box 400, 58502
Telephone: 701-223-2890
Fax: 701-223-7865

(See Next Column)

MEMBERS OF FIRM

William P. Pearce
Lawrence Bender

Representative Clients: Amoco Oil Co.; MDU Resources Group, Inc.; Amerada Hess Corp.; Chevron U.S.A., Inc.; Conoco, Inc.; Phillips Petroleum Co.; Shell Oil Co.; Texaco, Inc.; American Hunter Exploration, Ltd.

For Complete List of Firm Personnel, See General Section

For full biographical listings, see the Martindale-Hubbell Law Directory

OHIO

ALLIANCE, Stark Co.

GEIGER, TEEPLE, SMITH & HAHN (AV)

260 East Main Street, P.O. Box 2446, 44601
Telephone: 216-821-1430
Canton Office Phone: 216-478-4915
Fax: 216-821-2217

MEMBERS OF FIRM

Milton S. Geiger (1900-1991)
John N. Teeple
Bruce E. Smith
B. Scott Hahn
J. Michael Gatien

ASSOCIATE

Richard C. Ogline

Representative Clients: Jerry Moore, Inc.; Damon Chemical Co.; M B Operating Co., Inc.; The American Simmental Assn.; Electronic Circuits & Design Co.; Atlas Energy Group, Inc.

For full biographical listings, see the Martindale-Hubbell Law Directory

*CLEVELAND,** Cuyahoga Co.

NOBLE & SULLIVAN (AV)

1025 Huron Road, 44115
Telephone: 216-771-1212
FAX: 216-771-1272

MEMBERS OF FIRM

David D. Noble
John E. Sullivan, III

Reference: Lanier Resources, Inc., Lewisville, Texas; Stocker & Sitler Oil Co., Inc., Newark, Ohio.

For full biographical listings, see the Martindale-Hubbell Law Directory

*COLUMBUS,** Franklin Co.

EMENS, KEGLER, BROWN, HILL & RITTER (AV)

Capitol Square Suite 1800, 65 East State Street, 43215-4294
Telephone: 614-462-5400
Telecopier: 614-464-2634
Cable Address: "Law EKBHR"
Telex: 246671

Jack A. Bjerke
J. Richard Emens
Allen L. Handlan
Samuel C. Randazzo
Paul D. Ritter, Jr.
Richard P. Rosenberry
O. Judson Scheaf, III
Kevin L. Sykes
Beatrice E. Wolper

Representative Clients: Aluminum Company of America; The Benatty Corp.; Nalco Chemical Co.; National Ground Water Association; Ohio Gas Co.; Ohio Oil and Gas Assn.; Owens-Corning Fiberglass Corp.; Patrick Petroleum Co.

For Complete List of Firm Personnel, See General Section

For full biographical listings, see the Martindale-Hubbell Law Directory

VORYS, SATER, SEYMOUR AND PEASE (AV)

52 East Gay Street, P.O. Box 1008, 43216-1008
Telephone: 614-464-6400
Telex: 241348
Telecopier: 614-464-6350
Cable Address: "Vorysater"
Washington, D.C. Office: Suite 1111, 1828 L Street, N.W., 20036-5104.
Telephone: 202-467-8800.
Telex: 440693.
Telecopier: 202-467-8900.
Cleveland, Ohio Office: 2100 One Cleveland Center, 1375 East Ninth Street, 44114-1724.
Telephone: 216-479-6100.
Telecopier: 216-479-6060.
Cincinnati, Ohio Office: Suite 2100, 221 East Fourth Street, P.O. Box 0236, 45201-0236.
Telephone: 513-723-4000.
Telecopier: 513-723-4056.

(See Next Column)

VORYS, SATER, SEYMOUR AND PEASE, *Columbus—Continued*

MEMBERS OF FIRM

Sheldon A. Taft
John W. Hoberg
Joseph D. Lonardo
W. Jonathan Airey
John K. Keller
William S. Newcomb, Jr.
John W. Wilmer, Jr. (Resident, Washington, D.C. Office)
M. Howard Petricoff
Benita A. Kahn
Robert H. Maynard
Robert J. Styduhar
Mark A. Norman (Resident, Cincinnati, Ohio Office)
Elizabeth E. Tulman
Scott M. Doran

Stephen M. Howard
Elizabeth M. Campbell
Anthony J. Giuliani
Paul J. Coval
Joseph M. Brooker
Kristin L. Watt
Theodore A. Boggs
William D. Hayes (Resident, Cincinnati, Ohio Office)
Victor A. Walton, Jr. (Resident, Cincinnati, Ohio Office)

OF COUNSEL

Martyn T. Brodnik

Local Counsel: National Gas & Oil Corp.; General Motors Corp.; Viking Resources Corp.; Clinton Gas Systems, Inc.; Access Energy Corporation; The Ohio Manufacturers Association; Honda of America Mfg., Inc.; Stone Container Corporation; Chemical Waste Management.

For Complete List of Firm Personnel, See General Section

For full biographical listings, see the Martindale-Hubbell Law Directory

---

*TOLEDO,** Lucas Co.

FULLER & HENRY (AV)

One Seagate Suite 1700, P.O. Box 2088, 43603-2088
Telephone: 419-247-2500
Telecopier: 419-247-2665
Port Clinton, Ohio Office: 125 Jefferson.
Telephone: 419-734-2153.
Telecopier: 419-732-8246.
Columbus, Ohio Office: 2210 Huntington Center, 41 South High Street.
Telephone: 614-228-6611.
Telecopier: 614-228-6623.

MEMBERS OF FIRM

Louis E. Tosi
William L. Patberg
Douglas G. Haynam
Michael E. Born

COUNSEL

Nirav D. Parikh

ASSOCIATES

Michael J. O'Callaghan
Joseph S. Simpson
Craig A. Sturtz
John Christian Everhardus
Linda S. Woggon

Representative Clients: General Motors Corp.; Ohio Electric Utility Institute Environmental Committee, The Toledo Edison Co.; Centerior Energy Corp.; The Goodyear Tire & Rubber Co.; The BF Goodrich Co.; Owens-Illinois, Inc.; GSX Chemical Services of Ohio; BP America.

For Complete List of Firm Personnel, See General Section

For full biographical listings, see the Martindale-Hubbell Law Directory

---

OKLAHOMA

---

*OKLAHOMA CITY,** Oklahoma Co.

ANDREWS DAVIS LEGG BIXLER MILSTEN & PRICE, A PROFESSIONAL CORPORATION (AV)

500 West Main, 73102
Telephone: 405-272-9241
FAX: 405-235-8786

J. Edward Barth
C. Temple Bixler
John J. Breathwit
Charles C. Callaway, Jr.
James F. Davis
Richard B. Kells, Jr.
William J. Legg
Babette Patton
R. Brown Wallace
William D. Watts

Lynn O. Holloman
Shelia Darling Tims

Representative Clients: ANR Pipeline Company; El Paso Natural Gas Co.; Marathon Oil Co.; Tennessee Gas Pipeline Company; Enron Corp.; Exxon Corp.; Conoco, Inc.; Union Oil Company of California; Smith Cogeneration, Inc.; New Jersey Natural Resources Co.

For Complete List of Firm Personnel, See General Section

For full biographical listings, see the Martindale-Hubbell Law Directory

CROWE & DUNLEVY, A PROFESSIONAL CORPORATION (AV)

1800 Mid-America Tower, 20 North Broadway, 73102-8273
Telephone: 405-235-7700
Fax: 405-239-6651
Tulsa, Oklahoma Office: Crowe & Dunlevy, 500 Kennedy Building, 321 South Boston.
Telephone: 918-592-9800.
Fax: 918-592-9801.
Norman, Oklahoma Office: Crowe & Dunlevy, Luttrell, Pendarvis & Rawlinson, 104 East Eufaula Street.
Telephone: 405-321-7317.
Fax: 405-360-4002.

Gary W. Davis
John J. Griffin, Jr.
Mark D. Christiansen
Arthur F. Hoge III
L. Mark Walker
Stephen L. DeGiusti
Kevin D. Gordon

Paul D. Trimble

OF COUNSEL

Val R. Miller
James A. Peabody
James W. George

For Complete List of Firm Personnel, See General Section

For full biographical listings, see the Martindale-Hubbell Law Directory

---

DAY, EDWARDS, FEDERMAN, PROPESTER & CHRISTENSEN, P.C. (AV)

Suite 2900 First Oklahoma Tower, 210 Park Avenue, 73102-5605
Telephone: 405-239-2121
Telecopier: 405-236-1012

Bruce W. Day
Joe E. Edwards
William B. Federman
Richard P. Propester
D. Wade Christensen
J. Clay Christensen
Kent A. Gilliland
Rodney J. Heggy
Ricki Valerie Sonders
Thomas Pitchlynn Howell, IV
John C. Platt

David R. Widdoes
Lori R. Roberts
Carolyn A. Romberg

OF COUNSEL

Herbert F. (Jack) Hewett
Jeanette Cook Timmons
Joel Warren Harmon
Jane S. Eulberg
Mark A. Cohen

Representative Clients: Aetna Life Insurance Co.; Boatmen's First National Bank of Oklahoma; Borg-Warner Chemicals, Inc.; City Bank & Trust; Federal Deposit Insurance Corp.; Bank One, Oklahoma City; Haskell Lemon Construction Co.; Merrill Lynch, Pierce, Fenner & Smith, Inc.; Prudential Securities, Inc.

For full biographical listings, see the Martindale-Hubbell Law Directory

---

HARTZOG CONGER & CASON, A PROFESSIONAL CORPORATION (AV)

1600 Bank of Oklahoma Plaza, 73102
Telephone: 405-235-7000
Facsimile: 405-235-7329

Larry D. Hartzog
J. William Conger
Len Cason
James C. Prince
Alan Newman
Steven C. Davis
Valerie K. Couch
Mark D. Dickey
Joseph P. Hogsett
John D. Robertson
Kurt M. Rupert
Laura Haag McConnell

Susan B. Shields
Ryan S. Wilson
Melanie J. Jester
Armand Paliotta
Julia Watson
J. Leslie LaReau

OF COUNSEL

Kent F. Frates

For full biographical listings, see the Martindale-Hubbell Law Directory

---

MCAFEE & TAFT, A PROFESSIONAL CORPORATION (AV)

Tenth Floor, Two Leadership Square, 73102
Telephone: 405-235-9621
Cable Address: "Oklaw"
TWX: 910-831-3294
Facsimile: (405) 235-0439 (405) 232-2404

Stewart W. Mark (1915-1993)
Judson S. Woodruff (Retired)
Terry R. Barrett
Gary W. Catron
Stanley L. Cunningham
Philip D. Hart
Laurence M. Huffman
C. David Stinson
Steven R. Welch

(See Next Column)

McAfee & Taft A Professional Corporation—*Continued*

OF COUNSEL

Eugene Kuntz

Representative Clients: Boatman's First National Bank of Oklahoma; Amoco Production Company; Beard Oil Company; Devon Resource Investors, LP; Exxon Corporation; Forest Oil Corporation; Mustang Fuel Corporation; Mobil Oil Corporation.

For Complete List of Firm Personnel, See General Section

For full biographical listings, see the Martindale-Hubbell Law Directory

Mock, Schwabe, Waldo, Elder, Reeves & Bryant, A Professional Corporation (AV)

Fifteenth Floor, One Leadership Square, 211 North Robinson Avenue, 73102
Telephone: 405-235-5500
Telecopy: 405-235-2875

James R. Waldo
John R. Reeves
Steven L. Barghols
Jay C. Jimerson

OF COUNSEL

Michael J. Hunter

Representative Clients: Amoco Production Co.; Anadarko Petroleum Corporation; Apache Corporation; Abuckle Enterprises, Inc.; Atlantic Richfield Co.; Cabot Oil & Gas Corporation; Conoco Inc.; Enogex, Inc.; Farm Credit Bank of Wichita; Federal Deposit Insurance Corporation.

For Complete List of Firm Personnel, See General Section

For full biographical listings, see the Martindale-Hubbell Law Directory

Monnet, Hayes, Bullis, Thompson & Edwards (AV)

Suite 1719 First National Center, West, 73102
Telephone: 405-232-5481
Fax: 405-235-9159

MEMBERS OF FIRM

John T. Edwards
James M. Peters
James S. Drennan
Sarah H. Stuhr
Gayle Freeman Cook
Robert C. Smith, Jr.
Steven K. McKinney

Representative Clients: Natural Gas Pipeline Company of America; Grace Petroleum Corp.; Chevron, U.S.A.; Mid-Con Corp.; Deminex USA Oil, Inc.; Enron Oil & Gas co.; Mobil Oil; Oryx Energy Co.; OXY USA, Inc.; Apache Corp.

For Complete List of Firm Personnel, See General Section

For full biographical listings, see the Martindale-Hubbell Law Directory

Self, Giddens & Lees, Inc. (AV)

2725 Oklahoma Tower, 210 Park Avenue, 73102-5604
Telephone: 405-232-3001
Telecopier: 405-232-5553

Jared D. Giddens
C. Ray Lees
Shannon T. Self

Thomas J. Blalock
Christopher R. Graves
W. Shane Smithton
Bryan J. Wells

For full biographical listings, see the Martindale-Hubbell Law Directory

*TULSA,** Tulsa Co.

Boesche, McDermott & Eskridge (AV)

Suite 800 Oneok Plaza, 100 West Fifth Street, 74103
Telephone: 918-583-1777
Fax: 918-592-5809
Muskogee, Oklahoma Office: 420 Broadway, 74101.
Telephone: 918-683-6100.

MEMBERS OF FIRM

Bradley K. Beasley
Frank D. Spiegelberg
David A. Johnson

OF COUNSEL

Nik Jones
Clifford K. Cate, Jr. (Resident at Muskogee)

Representative Clients: Amax Oil & Gas, Inc.; Amoco Production Corp.; Apache Corp.; Atlantic Richfield; Atochem North America, Inc.; Enogex Corp.; Enron Corp.; Oxy USA, Inc.; Helmerich & Payne, Inc.; Unit Corp.

For Complete List of Firm Personnel, See General Section

For full biographical listings, see the Martindale-Hubbell Law Directory

Conner & Winters, A Professional Corporation (AV)

15 East 5th Street, Suite 2400, 74103-4391
Telephone: 918-586-5711
Fax: 918-586-8982
Oklahoma City, Oklahoma Office: 204 North Robinson, Suite 950, 73102.
Telephone: 405-232-7711.
Facsimile: 405-232-2695.

Lynnwood R. Moore, Jr.
Randolph L. Jones, Jr. (Not admitted in OK)
R. Kevin Redwine

For Complete List of Firm Personnel, See General Section

For full biographical listings, see the Martindale-Hubbell Law Directory

Doerner, Stuart, Saunders, Daniel & Anderson (AV)

Suite 500, 320 South Boston Avenue, 74103-3725
Telephone: 918-582-1211
FAX: 918-591-5360

MEMBERS OF FIRM

C. B. Stuart (1857-1936)
Erwin J. Doerner (1897-1980)
Samuel P. Daniel
William C. Anderson
Varley H. Taylor, Jr.
G. Michael Lewis
William B. Morgan
Lawrence T. Chambers, Jr.
Dallas E. Ferguson
Sam G. Bratton, II
Gary M. McDonald
H. Wayne Cooper
Kevin C. Coutant
Richard P. Hix
Lynn Paul Mattson
William F. Riggs
Lewis N. Carter
Linda Crook Martin
James Patrick McCann
Richard H. Foster
Charles S. Plumb
Leonard I. Pataki
S. Douglas Dodd
Elise Dunitz Brennan
Kathy R. Neal
John J. Carwile
Jon E. Brightmire
L. Dru McQueen
Tom Q. Ferguson

ASSOCIATES

Richard J. Eagleton
Rebecca McCarthy Fowler
Kristen L. Brightmire
Michael C. Redman
Steven K. Metcalf
Benjamin J. Chapman
R. Michael Cole
David B. Auer
Shelly L. Dalrymple
Russell W. Kroll
John R. Pinkerton
Robert A. Burk

OF COUNSEL

Dickson M. Saunders
R. Robert Huff

Representative Clients: Public Service Company of Oklahoma; Atlas Life Insurance Co.; Minnehoma Insurance Co.; Valley National Bank; Health Concepts IV, Inc.; Local Americ Bank; Bank of the Lakes.

For full biographical listings, see the Martindale-Hubbell Law Directory

Gable & Gotwals (AV)

2000 Bank IV Center, 15 West Sixth Street, 74119-5447
Telephone: 918-582-9201
Facsimile: 918-586-8383

Teresa B. Adwan
Pamela S. Anderson
John R. Barker
David L. Bryant
Gene C. Buzzard
Dennis Clarke Cameron
Timothy A. Carney
Renee DeMoss
Elsie C. Draper
Sidney G. Dunagan
Theodore Q. Eliot
Richard W. Gable
Jeffrey Don Hassell
Patricia Ledvina Himes
Oliver S. Howard
Richard D. Koljack, Jr.
J. Daniel Morgan
Joseph W. Morris
Elizabeth R. Muratet
Richard B. Noulles
Ronald N. Ricketts
John Henry Rule
M. Benjamin Singletary
James M. Sturdivant
Patrick O. Waddel
Michael D. Hall
David Edward Keglovits
Stephen W. Lake
Kari S. McKee
Terry D. Ragsdale
Jeffrey C. Rambach

OF COUNSEL

G. Ellis Gable
Charles P. Gotwals, Jr.

For full biographical listings, see the Martindale-Hubbell Law Directory

Holliman, Langholz, Runnels, Holden, Forsman & Sellers, A Professional Corporation (AV)

Suite 500 Holarud Building, Ten East Third Street, 74103-3695
Telephone: 918-584-1471
FAX: 918-587-9652,
Telex: 251773 GRC UR
Oklahoma City, Oklahoma Office: Suite 160, Two Broadway Executive Park, 205 N.W. 63rd Street.
Telephone: 405-848-6999.
Fax: 405-840-3312.

(See Next Column)

HOLLIMAN, LANGHOLZ, RUNNELS, HOLDEN, FORSMAN & SELLERS A PROFESSIONAL CORPORATION, *Tulsa—Continued*

Robert W. Langholz
Michael S. Forsman
Gail R. Runnels
Keith F. Sellers
David W. Holden
James D. Bryant

Matthew James Browne, III
Ann Nicholson Smith
Laurence Langholz

AFFILIATES

David L. Sobel
Roderick Oxford

OF COUNSEL

Joe M. Holliman
Ted P. Holshouser (Resident, Oklahoma City Office)

Representative Clients: The F & M Bank and Trust Company, Tulsa, Ok.; Transportation Leasing Co., Inc.; The Sterling Group, Inc.; Albert Investments; Bryan Industries, Inc.; Enserch Corp.; Kaiser-Francis Oil Co.; Family & Children's Service, Inc.; Junior League of Tulsa; Anadarko Bank and Trust Co.

For full biographical listings, see the Martindale-Hubbell Law Directory

SNEED, LANG, ADAMS & BARNETT, A PROFESSIONAL CORPORATION (AV)

2300 Williams Center Tower II, Two West Second Street, 74103
Telephone: 918-583-3145
Telecopier: 918-582-0410

James C. Lang
Robbie Emery Burke
D. Faith Orlowski
C. Raymond Patton, Jr.
Brian S. Gaskill
Frederick K. Slicker
G. Steven Stidham
Richard D. Black
Stephen R. McNamara
John D. Russell
Thomas E. Black, Jr.
Jeffrey S. Swyers

OF COUNSEL

James L. Sneed
O. Edwin Adams
Howard G. Barnett, Jr.

Representative Clients: Amoco Production Company; Continental Bank; Deloitte & Touche; Enron Corporation; Halliburton Energy Services; Helmerich & Payne, Inc.; Lehman Brothers, Inc.; Shell Oil Company; Smith Barney, Inc.; State Farm Mutual Automobile Insurance Company.

For full biographical listings, see the Martindale-Hubbell Law Directory

OREGON

*PORTLAND,** Multnomah Co.

BLACK HELTERLINE (AV)

1200 The Bank of California Tower, 707 S.W. Washington Street, 97205
Telephone: 503-224-5560
Telecopier: 503-224-6148

MEMBERS OF FIRM

Paul R. Hribernick
Gerald H. Robinson
Steven R. Schell

ASSOCIATE

Stark Ackerman

Representative Clients: Ataka Lumber America, Inc.; Bayview Transit Mix, Inc.; Cavenham Forest Industries, Inc.; Duke City Lumber Company, Inc.; Eagle-Picher Minerals, Inc.; Morse Bros., Inc.; Oregon Concrete and Aggregate Producers Association, Inc.; Quartz Hill Mining Co.; R-DMAC, Inc.; Sato America, Inc.;

For Complete List of Firm Personnel, See General Section

For full biographical listings, see the Martindale-Hubbell Law Directory

PENNSYLVANIA

*GREENSBURG,** Westmoreland Co.

SEAN CASSIDY (AV)

118 North Main Street, 15601
Telephone: 412-836-4900
Fax: 412-836-2090

Representative Clients: CNG Producing Co.; CNG Transmission Corp.; Consolidation Coal Co.; Mitchell Energy Corp.; Cabot Oil and Gas Corp.; Mark Resources Corp.; Angerman Associates, Inc.; Quaker State Corp.; Pennzoil Co.; Equitrans, Inc.

For full biographical listings, see the Martindale-Hubbell Law Directory

*HARRISBURG,** Dauphin Co.

BUCHANAN INGERSOLL, PROFESSIONAL CORPORATION (AV)

Vartan Parc, 30 North Third Street, 17101
Telephone: 717-237-4800
Telecopier: 717-233-0852
Pittsburgh, Pennsylvania Office: 5800 USX Tower, 600 Grant Street.
Telephone: 412-562-8800.
Philadelphia, Pennsylvania Office: Two Logan Square, Twelfth Floor, 18th & Arch Streets.
Telephone: 215-665-8700.
Tampa, Florida Office: 101 East Kennedy Boulevard, Suite 1030.
Telephone: 813-222-8180.
North Miami Beach, Florida Office: 19495 Biscayne Boulevard.
Telephone: 305-933-5600.
Lexington, Kentucky Office: 1210 Vine Center Office Tower, 333 West Vine Street.
Telephone: 606-225-5333.
Princeton, New Jersey Office: Buchanan Ingersoll, A Partnership, College Centre, 500 College Road East.
Telephone: 609-452-2666.

SENIOR ATTORNEY

Richard H. Friedman

For Complete List of Firm Personnel, See General Section

For full biographical listings, see the Martindale-Hubbell Law Directory

*PHILADELPHIA,** Philadelphia Co.

BUCHANAN INGERSOLL, PROFESSIONAL CORPORATION (AV)

Two Logan Square Twelfth Floor, 18th & Arch Streets, 19103
Telephone: 215-665-8700
Telecopier: 215-569-2066
Pittsburgh, Pennsylvania Office: 5800 USX Tower, 600 Grant Street.
Telephone: 412-562-8800.
Harrisburg, Pennsylvania Office: Vartan Parc, 30 North Third Street.
Telephone: 717-237-4800.
Tampa, Florida Office: 101 East Kennedy Boulevard, Suite 1030.
Telephone: 813-222-8180.
North Miami Beach, Florida Office: 19495 Biscayne Boulevard.
Telephone: 305-933-5600.
Lexington, Kentucky Office: 1210 Vine Center Office Tower, 333 West Vine Street.
Telephone: 606-225-5333.
Princeton, New Jersey Office: Buchanan Ingersoll, A Partnership, College Centre, 500 College Road East.
Telephone: 609-452-2666.

Stephen C. Braverman
Antoinette R. Stone

Fern L. McGovern

For Complete List of Firm Personnel, See General Section

For full biographical listings, see the Martindale-Hubbell Law Directory

*PITTSBURGH,** Allegheny Co.

BUCHANAN INGERSOLL, PROFESSIONAL CORPORATION (AV)

5800 USX Tower, 600 Grant Street, 15219
Telephone: 412-562-8800
Telecopier: 412-562-1041
Philadelphia, Pennsylvania Office: Two Logan Square, Twelfth Floor, 18th & Arch Streets.
Telephone: 215-665-8700.
Harrisburg, Pennsylvania Office: Vartan Parc, 30 North Third Street.
Telephone: 717-237-4800.
Tampa, Florida Office: 101 East Kennedy Boulevard, Suite 1030.
Telephone: 813-222-8180.
North Miami Beach, Florida Office: 19495 Biscayne Boulevard.
Telephone: 305-933-5600.
Lexington, Kentucky Office: 1210 Vine Center Office Tower, 333 West Vine Street.
Telephone: 606-225-5333.
Princeton, New Jersey Office: Buchanan Ingersoll, A Partnership, College Centre, 500 College Road East.
Telephone: 609-452-2666.

Samuel W. Braver
Henry McC. Ingram
David B. Fawcett III
R. Henry Moore
Stanley R. Geary
Thomas C. Reed

SENIOR ATTORNEY

Gary R. Walker

Stephen C. Smith
Heather A. Wyman

For Complete List of Firm Personnel, See General Section

For full biographical listings, see the Martindale-Hubbell Law Directory

Pittsburgh—Continued

KLETT LIEBER ROONEY & SCHORLING, A PROFESSIONAL CORPORATION (AV)

40th Floor, One Oxford Centre, 15219-6498
Telephone: 412-392-2000
FAX: 412-392-2128; 412-392-2129
Harrisburg, Pennsylvania Office: 240 North Third Street, Suite 600.
Telephone: 717-231-7700.
Philadelphia, Pennsylvania Office: 28th Floor, One Logan Square.
Telephone: 215-567-7500

SHAREHOLDERS

Howard J. Wein

ASSOCIATE

Paul A. Supowitz

For Complete List of Firm Personnel, See General Section

For full biographical listings, see the Martindale-Hubbell Law Directory

WELLER, WICKS & WALLACE, PROFESSIONAL CORPORATION (AV)

1800 Benedum-Trees Building, 15222
Telephone: 412-471-1751
Fax: 412-471-8117

John S. Weller (1866-1944)
John O. Wicks (1880-1947)
C. L. Wallace (1885-1953)
Henry A. Bergstrom (1911-1993)
J. Murray Egan
Donald W. Shaffer
Henry A. Bergstrom, Jr.
Thomas A. Woodward

Reference: Pittsburgh National Bank.

For full biographical listings, see the Martindale-Hubbell Law Directory

RHODE ISLAND

*PROVIDENCE,** Providence Co.

EDWARDS & ANGELL (AV)

2700 Hospital Trust Tower, 02903
Telephone: 401-274-9200
Telecopier: 401-276-6611
Cable Address: "Edwangle Providence"
Telex: 952001 "E A PVD"
Boston, Massachusetts Office: 101 Federal Street, 02110.
Telephone: 617-439-444.
Telecopier: 617-439-4170.
New York, New York Office: 750 Lexington Avenue, 10022.
Telephone: 212-308-4411.
Telecopier: 212-308-4844.
Palm Beach, Florida Office: 250 Royal Palm Way, 33480.
Telephone: 407-833-7700.
Telecopier: 407-655-8719.
Newark, New Jersey Office: Gateway three, 07120.
Telephone: 201-623-7717.
Telecopier: 201-623-7717.
Hartford, Connecticut Office: 750 Main Street, 14th Floor, 06103.
Telephone: 203-525-5065.
Telecopier: 203-527-4198.
Newport, Rhode Island Office: 130 Bellevue Avenue, 02840.
Telephone: 401-849-7800.
Telecopier: 401-849-7887.

MEMBERS OF FIRM

Deming E. Sherman
Gail E. McCann
Lynn Wright (Not admitted in RI; New York, New York and Newark, New Jersey Office)
Lorne W. McDougall
Mark A. Pogue

COUNSEL

Rosemary Healey

For Complete List of Firm Personnel, See General Section

For full biographical listings, see the Martindale-Hubbell Law Directory

SOUTH DAKOTA

*BELLE FOURCHE,** Butte Co.

BENNETT, MAIN & FREDERICKSON, A PROFESSIONAL CORPORATION (AV)

618 State Street, 57717-1489
Telephone: 605-892-2011
Fax: 605-892-4084

(See Next Column)

Max Main
John R. Frederickson

OF COUNSEL

Donn Bennett

Representative Clients: Atlantic Richfield Co.; Chevron, USA, Inc.; Exxon U.S.A., Co.; Inland Oil & Gas Co.; Royal Bank of Canada; Bank of Montreal; Security Pacific National Bank; Timberline Oil & Gas Co.; Wyoming Resources Corp; Bald Mountain Mining Co.; Homestake Mining Co.

For Complete List of Firm Personnel, See General Section

For full biographical listings, see the Martindale-Hubbell Law Directory

*RAPID CITY,** Pennington Co.

JOHNSON HUFFMAN A PROFESSIONAL CORPORATION OF LAWYERS (AV)

3202 West Main Street, P.O. Box 6100, 57709-6100
Telephone: 605-348-7300
FAX: 605-348-4757

Glen H. Johnson
Richard E. Huffman
Scott Sumner
Wayne F. Gilbert
Timothy J. Becker
John J. Delaney
Courtney R. Clayborne
Jay A. Alderman

LEGAL SUPPORT PERSONNEL
PARALEGALS

Cynthia J. Johnson
Renee Lehr
Dory M. Maks
Timothy Crawford

For full biographical listings, see the Martindale-Hubbell Law Directory

TENNESSEE

JOHNSON CITY, Washington Co.

BAKER, DONELSON, BEARMAN & CALDWELL (AV)

Hamilton Bank Building, 207 Mockingbird Lane, 37604
Telephone: 615-928-0181
Telecopier: 615-928-5694; 928-3654; Kingsport: 615-246-6191
Memphis, Tennessee Office: 20th Floor, First Tennessee Building, 165 Madison, 38103.
Telephone: 901-526-2000.
Telecopier: 901-577-2303.
Nashville, Tennessee Office: 1700 Nashville City Center, 511 Union Street, 37219.
Telephone: 615-726-5600.
Telecopier: 615-726-0464.
Knoxville, Tennessee Office: 2200 Riverview Tower, 900 Gay Street, 37901.
Telephone: 615-549-7000.
Telecopier: 615-525-8569.
Chattanooga, Tennessee Office: 1800 Republic Centre, 633 Chestnut Street, 37450-1800.
Telephone: 615-752-4400.
Telecopier: 615-752-4410.
Huntsville, Tennessee Office: 3 Courthouse Square, 37756.
Telephone: 615-663-2321.
Telecopier: 615-663-2111.
Washington, D.C. Office: Market Square, 801 Pennsylvania Avenue, N.W., 20004.
Telephone: 202-508-3400.
Telecopier: 202-508-3402.

PARTNERS

Ed E. Williams, III
Gary C. Shockley
Melissa M. McGuire

For Complete List of Firm Personnel, See General Section

For full biographical listings, see the Martindale-Hubbell Law Directory

KINGSPORT, Sullivan Co.

HUNTER, SMITH & DAVIS (AV)

1212 North Eastman Road, P.O. Box 3740, 37664
Telephone: 615-378-8800;
Johnson City: 615-282-4186;
Bristol: 615-968-7604
Telecopier: 615-378-8801
Johnson City, Tennessee Office: Suite 500 First American Center, 208 Sunset Drive, 37604.
Telephone: 615-283-6300.
Telecopier: 615-283-6301.

MEMBERS OF FIRM

T. Arthur Scott, Jr.
Douglas S. Tweed
William C. Argabrite

ASSOCIATE

James E. Kaiser

(See Next Column)

HUNTER, SMITH & DAVIS, *Kingsport—Continued*

PARALEGALS

Pam Talbott (Mineral Title Examiner-Paralegal)
Janet L. Snyder (Mineral Title Examiner-Paralegal)

Representative Clients: Equitable Resources Exploration, Inc.; Alamco, Inc.; Commonwealth of Virginia Department of Mines, Minerals and Energy; ArakisEnergy Corp.; Champ Oil Corp.; Hi-Tech Exploration, Inc.; Valley and Ridge Exploration, LLC.

For Complete List of Firm Personnel, See General Section

For full biographical listings, see the Martindale-Hubbell Law Directory

*KNOXVILLE,** Knox Co.

McCAMPBELL & YOUNG, A PROFESSIONAL CORPORATION (AV)

2021 Plaza Tower, P.O. Box 550, 37901-0550
Telephone: 615-637-1440
Telecopier: 615-546-9731

Herbert H. McCampbell, Jr. (1905-1974)
F. Graham Bartlett (1920-1982)
Robert S. Young
Lindsay Young
Robert S. Marquis
Robert S. Stone
J. Christopher Kirk
Mark K. Williams

Janie C. Porter
Gregory E. Erickson
R. Scott Elmore
Tammy Kaousias
Benét S. Theiss
Allen W. Blevins

Representative Clients: Union Zinc, Inc.; Mountain, Inc.; Premium Coal Company; Lindsay Land Company; Garland Coal Co.; Sun Coal Company (Sun Company); Kentucky River Coal Corp.

For full biographical listings, see the Martindale-Hubbell Law Directory

WAGNER, MYERS & SANGER, A PROFESSIONAL CORPORATION (AV)

1801 Plaza Tower, P.O. Box 1308, 37929
Telephone: 615-525-4600
Fax: 615-524-5731

Herbert S. Sanger, Jr.
Charles A. Wagner III

Joseph N. Clarke, Jr.

Representative Clients: Beazer East, Inc.; Costain Coal Co.; Colquest Energy, Inc.; Cullman Electric Membership Corp.; Facts About Coal in Tennessee; Gatliff Coal Co., Inc.; Kopper-Glo Fuels, Inc.; A. B. Long Cos.; Nerco Coal Co.; Skyline Coal Company.

For Complete List of Firm Personnel, See General Section

For full biographical listings, see the Martindale-Hubbell Law Directory

TEXAS

*AMARILLO,** Potter Co.

HINKLE, COX, EATON, COFFIELD & HENSLEY (AV)

1700 Bank One Center, P.O. Box 9238, 79105-9238
Telephone: 806-372-5569
FAX: 806-372-9761
Roswell, New Mexico Office: 700 United Bank Plaza, P. O. Box 10, 88202.
Telephone: 505-622-6510.
FAX: 505-623-9332.
Midland, Texas Office: 6 Desta Drive, Suite 2800, P.O. Box 3580, 79702.
Telephone: 915-683-4691.
FAX: 915-683-6518.
Santa Fe, New Mexico Office: 218 Montezuma, P.O. Box 2068, 87504.
Telephone: 505-982-4554.
FAX: 505-982-8623.
Albuquerque, New Mexico Office: Suite 800, 500 Marquette, N.W., P.O. Box 2043, 87102.
Telephone: 505-768-1500.
FAX: 505-768-1529.
Austin, Texas Office: 401 West 15th Street, Suite 800, 78701.
Telephone: 512-476-7137.
FAX: 512-476-5431.
Associated Office: Hoffman & Stephens, P.C., 401 West 15th Street, Suite 800, 78701.
Telephone: 512-476-5434. Fax; 512-476-5431.

RESIDENT PARTNERS

Paul W. Eaton
Maston C. Courtney
William F. Countiss
Gary D. Compton

Representative Clients: Amoco Production Company; Conoco, Inc.; Mesa Limited Partnership; Mitchell Energy Corp.; Natural Gas Pipeline Company; OXY U.S.A., CNG Producing Company; POGO Producing Com-

(See Next Column)

pany; Pennzoil Exploration and Production Company; R.B. Operating Company.

For full biographical listings, see the Martindale-Hubbell Law Directory

*AUSTIN,** Travis Co.

McGINNIS, LOCHRIDGE & KILGORE, L.L.P. (AV)

1300 Capitol Center, 919 Congress Avenue, 78701
Telephone: 512-495-6000
Houston, Texas Office: 3200 One Houston Center, 1221 McKinney Street.
Telephone: 713-615-8500.

RETIRED PARTNER

Robert C. McGinnis (Retired)

MEMBERS OF FIRM

Barry L. Wertz
Robert Wilson
S. Jack Balagia, Jr.
W. Timothy George
David E. Jackson
Edmond R. McCarthy, Jr.

For Complete List of Firm Personnel, See General Section

For full biographical listings, see the Martindale-Hubbell Law Directory

SCOTT, DOUGLASS, LUTON & McCONNICO, L.L.P. (AV)

A Limited Liability Partnership including a Professional Corporation
One American Center, 600 Congress Avenue, 15th Floor, 78701-3234
Telephone: 512-495-6300
Fax: 512-474-0731
Houston, Texas Office: 40th Floor, NationsBank Center, 700 Louisiana Street.
Telephone: 713-225-8400.
Dallas, Texas Office: NationsBank Plaza, 901 Main Street, Suite 2800.
Telephone: 214-651-5300.

MEMBERS OF FIRM

Wallace H. Scott, Jr.
Frank P. Youngblood
H. Philip Whitworth, Jr.
John G. Soule
Stephen E. McConnico
James N. Cowden
Richard P. Marshall, Jr.
Carroll Greer Martin
Steve Selby
Elizabeth N. Miller
John W. Camp
Daniel W. Bishop, II
Ray H. Langenberg
Thomas A. Albright
Douglas J. Dashiell
Ray N. Donley
Phyllis M. Pollard
Christopher Fuller
Casey L. Dobson
Jennifer Knauth Lipinski
Daniel C. Bitting
Sam Johnson
Robert A. Summers
Mark W. Eidman
Julie Ann Springer

OF COUNSEL

Bob Bullock
Martin L. Allday

ASSOCIATES

Jeffrey G. Henry
James P. Ray
Jane M. N. Webre
Steven J. Wingard
Elizabeth B. Pearsall
Anna M. Norris
James D. Clayton
Rebecca M. Hudson

For full biographical listings, see the Martindale-Hubbell Law Directory

*BEAUMONT,** Jefferson Co.

BENCKENSTEIN & OXFORD, L.L.P. (AV)

First Interstate Bank Building, P.O. Box 150, 77704
Telephone: 409-833-9182
Cable Address: "Bmor"
Telex: 779485
Telefax: 409-833-8819
Austin, Texas Office: Suite 810, 400 West 15th Street, 78701.
Telephone: 512-474-8586.
Telefax: 512-478-3064.

MEMBERS OF FIRM

L. J. Benckenstein (1894-1966)
F. L. Benckenstein (1918-1987)
Hubert Oxford, III
Alan G. Sampson
Frank D. Calvert
Dana Timaeus
Mary Ellen Blade
William H. Yoes
William M. Tolin, III
Kip Kevin Lamb
Frances Blair Bethea
Robert J. Rose, Sr.

ASSOCIATES

Susan J. Oliver
F. Blair Clarke
Keith A. Pardue (Resident, Austin, Texas Office)
Josiah Wheat, Jr.
Steve Johnson
Michael Keith Eaves
Nikki L. Redden

Representative Clients: Marine Office of American Corporation (MOAC); Moran Towing and Transportation Co., Inc.

For Complete List of Firm Personnel, See General Section

For full biographical listings, see the Martindale-Hubbell Law Directory

*CORPUS CHRISTI,** Nueces Co.

MATTHEWS & BRANSCOMB, A PROFESSIONAL CORPORATION (AV)

802 North Carancahua, Suite 1900, 78470-0700
Telephone: 512-888-9261
Facsimile: 512-888-8504
Austin, Texas Office: 301 Congress Avenue, Suite 2050.
Telephone: 512-305-4400.
Facsimile: 512-305-4413.
San Antonio, Texas Office: One Alamo Center, 106 S. St. Mary's Street, Suite 800.
Telephone: 210-226-4211.
Facsimile: 210-226-0521.
Telex: 51060009283. Cable Code: MBLAW.
Eagle Pass, Texas Office: 675 Main Street.
Telephone: 210-773-6700.
Facsimile: 210-757-4045.
Uvalde, Texas Office: 200 E. Nopal #208.
Telephone: 210-278-4597.
Facsimile: 210-278-4806.
(Associated with Hall, Quintanilla & Alarcon, L.C., Laredo, Texas, under the name of Hall, Quintanilla, Alarcon, Matthews & Branscomb, P.L.L.C.).

Gerald E. Thornton, Jr. J. A. (Andy) Carson

For Complete List of Firm Personnel, See General Section

For full biographical listings, see the Martindale-Hubbell Law Directory

*DALLAS,** Dallas Co.

JOE B. ABBEY (AV)

1717 Main Street, Suite 2220, 75201
Telephone: 214-748-0423
Fax: 214-748-0426

For full biographical listings, see the Martindale-Hubbell Law Directory

COCKRELL & WEED (AV)

3811 Turtle Creek, Suite 200, 75219-4421
Telephone: 214-522-5300
Fax: 214-526-1120

M. W. (Mel) Cockrell, Jr. Allen Ray Weed

For full biographical listings, see the Martindale-Hubbell Law Directory

KILGORE & KILGORE, A PROFESSIONAL CORPORATION (AV)

700 McKinney Place, 3131 McKinney Avenue - LB 103, 75204-2471
Telephone: 214-969-9099
Fax: 214-953-0133; 214-953-0242

Wilmer D. Masterson, III
W. Stephen Swayze
Robert M. Thornton
Roger F. Claxton
Theodore C. Anderson, III

For Complete List of Firm Personnel, See General Section

For full biographical listings, see the Martindale-Hubbell Law Directory

THOMPSON & KNIGHT, A PROFESSIONAL CORPORATION (AV)

(Attorneys and Counselors)
1700 Pacific Avenue Suite 3300, 75201
Telephone: 214-969-1700
Telecopy: 214-969-1751
Cable Address: "Tomtex"
Telex: 732298
Austin, Texas Office: 1200 San Jacinto Center, 98 San Jacinto Boulevard, 78701.
Telephone: 512-469-6100.
Telecopy: 512-469-6180.
Fort Worth, Texas Office: 801 Cherry Street, Suite 1600, 76102.
Telephone: 817-347-1700.
Telecopy: 817-347-1799.
Houston, Texas Office: 1700 Texas Commerce Tower, 600 Travis, 77002.
Telephone: 713-217-2800.
Telecopy: 713-217-2828.
Monterrey, Mexico Office: Edificio Losoles PD-4, Av. Lázaro Cárdenas No. 2400 Pte., San Pedro Garza Garcia, Nuevo Léon C.P. 66220.
Telephone: (52-8) 363-0096.
Telecopy: (52-8) 363-3067.

SHAREHOLDERS

Robert B. Allen
Dennis J. Grindinger
Samuel D. Haas
Thornton Hardie III
James L. Irish
Karen E. Lynch
Jeffrey A. Zlotky

ASSOCIATES

Linda S. Crawley
Mary A. McNulty
Kirkmichael T. Moore

(See Next Column)

OF COUNSEL

Fred L. Hamric John W. Rutland, Jr.

For Complete List of Firm Personnel, See General Section

For full biographical listings, see the Martindale-Hubbell Law Directory

*HOUSTON,** Harris Co.

ALSUP BEVIS & PETTY (AV)

333 Clay Suite 4930, 77098
Telephone: 713-739-1313
Fax: 713-739-7095

Richard C. Alsup
Randall F. Bevis
Andrew H. Petty

ASSOCIATE

Michael J. Short

For full biographical listings, see the Martindale-Hubbell Law Directory

JOHN R. BONICA, P.C. (AV)

1000 Louisiana, Suite 6600, 77002
Telephone: 713-754-9212
Telecopier: 713-659-1231

John R. Bonica

For full biographical listings, see the Martindale-Hubbell Law Directory

FARNSWORTH & VONBERG (AV)

A Partnership of Professional Corporations
333 North Sam Houston Parkway, Suite 300, 77060
Telephone: 713-931-8902
Telecopy: 713-931-6032

T Brooke Farnsworth (P.C.) Mary Frances vonBerg (P.C.)

ASSOCIATES

Diane B. Gould Bennett S. Bartlett

LEGAL SUPPORT PERSONNEL

Lucille P. Poole

For full biographical listings, see the Martindale-Hubbell Law Directory

CHARLES H. PUCKETT, III (AV)

2390 Five Post Oak Park, 77027
Telephone: 713-871-8881
Fax: 713-871-8898

For full biographical listings, see the Martindale-Hubbell Law Directory

THOMPSON & KNIGHT, A PROFESSIONAL CORPORATION (AV)

(Attorneys and Counselors)
1700 Texas Commerce Tower, 600 Travis, 77002
Telephone: 713-217-2800
Telecopy: 713-217-2828; 713-217-2882
Dallas, Texas Office: 1700 Pacific Avenue, Suite 3300, 75201.
Telephone: 214-969-1700.
Telecopy: 214-969-1751.
Cable Address: "Tomtex."
Telex: 732298.
Austin, Texas Office: 1200 San Jacinto Center, 98 San Jacinto Boulevard, 78701.
Telephone: 512-469-6100.
Telecopy: 512-469-6180.
Fort Worth, Texas Office: 801 Cherry Street, Suite 1600, 76102.
Telephone: 817-347-1700.
Telecopy: 817-347-1799.
Monterrey, Mexico Office: Edificio Losoles PD-4, Av. Lázaro Cárdenas No. 2400 PTE., San Pedro Garza Garcia, Nuevo Léon C.P. 66220.
Telephone: (52-8) 363-0096.
Telecopy: (52-8) 363-3067.

SHAREHOLDERS

Michael K. Pierce

For Complete List of Firm Personnel, See General Section

For full biographical listings, see the Martindale-Hubbell Law Directory

VINSON & ELKINS L.L.P. (AV)

2300 First City Tower, 1001 Fannin, 77002-6760
Telephone: 713-758-2222
Fax: 713-758-2346
International Telex: 6868314
Cable Address: Vinelkins
Austin, Texas Office: One American Center, 600 Congress Avenue.
Telephone: 512-495-8400.
Fax: 512-495-8612.
Dallas, Texas Office: 3700 Trammell Crow Center, 2001 Ross Avenue.
Telephone: 214-220-7700.
Fax: 214-220-7716.

(See Next Column)

VINSON & ELKINS L.L.P., *Houston—Continued*

Washington, D.C. Office: The Willard Office Building, 1455 Pennsylvania Avenue, N.W.
Telephone: 202-639-6500.
Fax: 202-639-6604.
Cable Address: Vinelkins.
London, England Office: 47 Charles Street, Berkeley Square, London, W1X 7PB, England.
Telephone: 011 (44-171) 491-7236.
Fax: 011 (44-71) 499-5320.
Cable Address: Vinelkins London W.1.
Moscow, Russian Federation Office: 16 Alexey Tolstoy Street, Second Floor, Moscow, 103001 Russian Federation.
Telephone: 011 (70-95) 956-1995.
Telecopy: 011 (70-95) 956-1996.
Mexico City, Mexico Office: Aristóteles 77, 5°Piso, Colonia Chapultepec Polanco, 11560 Mexico, D.F.
Telephone: (52-5) 280-7828.
Fax: (52-5) 280-9223.
Singapore Office: 50 Raffles Place, #19-05 Shell Tower, 0104. U.S. Voice Mailbox: 713-758-3500.
Telephone: (65) 536-8300.
Fax: (65) 536-8311.

John C. Ale
Christopher B. Amandes
Marcia E. Backus
Robert F. Barrett
Charles L. Berry
Bruce R. Bilger
Douglas S. Bland
Fielding B. Cochran, III
Joseph C. Dilg
Carol E. Dinkins
Kenneth B. Fenelon
Douglas B. Glass
Alberto R. Gonzales
Barry Hunsaker, Jr.
Sharon M. Mattox
Sidney S. McClendon, III
Richard Kelly McGee
William S. Moss, Jr.
Arthur E. Murphy, III
Larry W. Nettles
Benjamin H. Powell, III
James "Rell" Tipton, Jr.

HOUSTON OF COUNSEL

Philip M. Kinkaid

ASSOCIATES

James Mark Brazzil
David T. Cindric
Timothy J. Dorsey
Robin S. Fredrickson
Valerie K. Friedrich
Catherine Legro Gentry
Bruce C. Herzog
L. DeWayne Layfield
Kimberly Z. Lesniak
Jeffrey Scott Mũnoz
Larry J. Pechacek
Frederick Paul Phillips, IV
Pamela L. Roger
John Walter Van Schwartzenburg
Charles A. Spears, Jr.
Lewis C. Sutherland
Fernando Tovar
David J. Tuckfield
Dirk P. Walker
Wayne Wiesen
George O. Wilkinson, Jr.

For Complete List of Firm Personnel, See General Section

For full biographical listings, see the Martindale-Hubbell Law Directory

*MIDLAND,** Midland Co.

HINKLE, COX, EATON, COFFIELD & HENSLEY (AV)

6 Desta Drive, Suite 2800, P.O. Box 3580, 79702
Telephone: 915-683-4691
FAX: 915-683-6518
Roswell, New Mexico Office: 700 United Bank Plaza, P.O. Box 10.
Telephone: 505-622-6510.
FAX: 505-623-9332.
Amarillo, Texas Office: 1700 Bank One Center, P.O. Box 9238.
Telephone: 806-372-5569.
FAX: 806-372-9761.
Santa Fe, New Mexico Office: 218 Montezuma, P.O. Box 2068.
Telephone: 505-982-4554.
FAX: 505-982-8623.
Albuquerque, New Mexico Office: Suite 800, 500 Marquette, N.W., P.O. Box 2043.
Telephone: 505-768-1500.
FAX: 505-768-1529.
Austin, Texas Office: 401 West 15th Street, Suite 800, 78701.
Telephone: 512-476-7137.
FAX: 512-476-5431.
Associated Office: Hoffman & Stephens, P.C., 401 West 15th Street, Suite 800, 78701.
Telephone: 512-476-5434.
FAX: 512-476-5431.

RESIDENT PARTNERS

C. D. Martin
William B. Burford
Jeffrey D. Hewett
James M. Hudson

Representative Clients: Atlantic Richfield Co.; BHP Petroleum (Americas) Inc.; Bass Enterprises Production Co.; Coastal Oil and Gas Corp.; Exxon Corp.; Hondo Oil & Gas Co.; Midland National Bank; Mobil Producing Texas & New Mexico Inc.; NationsBank of Texas; Pennzoil Co.; Pogo Producing Co.; Texaco; Texas National Bank of Midland.

For full biographical listings, see the Martindale-Hubbell Law Directory

LYNCH, CHAPPELL & ALSUP, A PROFESSIONAL CORPORATION (AV)

The Summit, Suite 700, 300 North Marienfeld, 79701
Telephone: 915-683-3351
Fax: 915-683-2587

Robert A. Spears
David W. Childress
James C. Brown

OF COUNSEL

Clovis G. Chappell

Representative Clients: Tom Brown, Inc.; NationsBank of Texas, N.A.; Parker & Parsley Development Company; Chevron U.S.A. Inc.; Texas National Bank of Midland; Wagner & Brown, Ltd.

For Complete List of Firm Personnel, See General Section

For full biographical listings, see the Martindale-Hubbell Law Directory

*PERRYTON,** Ochiltree Co.

LEMON, SHEARER, EHRLICH, PHILLIPS & GOOD, A PROFESSIONAL CORPORATION (AV)

311 South Main Street, P.O. Box 1066, 79070
Telephone: 806-435-6544
FAX: 806-435-4377
Booker, Texas Office: 122 South Main Street, P.O. Box 348.
Telephone: 806-658-4545.
FAX: 806-658-4524.

Robert D. Lemon
Otis C. Shearer
Mitchell Ehrlich
Randall M. Phillips
F. Keith Good

Representative Clients: The Perryton National Bank; The Perryton Equity Exchange; The North Plains Ground Water Conservation District; Natural Gas Anadarko Company; Courson Oil & Gas, Inc.; The City of Perryton; The Booker Equity Exchange; The Follett National Bank; Lyco Energy Corporation; Unit Petroleum Company.

For full biographical listings, see the Martindale-Hubbell Law Directory

*SAN ANTONIO,** Bexar Co.

COX & SMITH INCORPORATED (AV)

112 East Pecan Street, Suite 1800, 78205
Telephone: 210-554-5500
Telecopier: 210-226-8395

Paul H. Smith
Richard T. Brady
Jon R. Ray
Barron W. Dowling
Kevin M. Beiter
Raymond E. Gallaway, Jr.
Margaret Pedrick Sullivan

Representative Clients: Abraxas Petroleum Corporation; Clayton Williams Energy, Inc.; Coates Energy Trust; Conoco Inc.; International Bank of Commerce; George A. Musselman Estate; Tri-C Resources, Inc.; Venus Oil Company; Victoria Operating, Inc.; Oxy USA, Inc.

For Complete List of Firm Personnel, See General Section

For full biographical listings, see the Martindale-Hubbell Law Directory

MATTHEWS & BRANSCOMB, A PROFESSIONAL CORPORATION (AV)

One Alamo Center, 106 S. St. Mary's Street, Suite 800, 78205
Telephone: 210-226-4211
Facsimile: 210-226-0521
Telex: 5106009283
Cable Code: MBLAW
Austin, Texas Office: 301 Congress Avenue, Suite 2050.
Telephone: 512-305-4400.
Facsimile: 512-305-4413.
Corpus Christi, Texas Office: 802 N. Carancahua, Suite 1900.
Telephone: 512-888-9261.
Facsimile: 512-888-8504.
Eagle Pass, Texas Office: 675 Main Street.
Telephone: 210-773-6700.
Facsimile: 210-757-4045.
Uvalde, Texas Office: 200 E. Nopal #208.
Telephone: 210-278-4597.
Facsimile: 210-278-4806.
(Associated with Hall, Quintanilla & Alarcon, L.C., Laredo, Texas, under the name of Hall, Quintanilla, Alarcon, Matthews & Branscomb, P.L.L.C.)

William H. Robison
C. Michael Montgomery
W. Roger Wilson
Howard D. Bye
Craig A. Arnold

Representative Clients: Coca Cola Bottling Company of the Southwest; Concord Oil Co.; Ellison Enterprises, Inc.; H. E. Butt Grocery Co.; Frank B. Hall & Co., Inc.; The Hearst Corp., San Antonio Light Division; San Antonio Gas & Electric Utilities (City Board); Southern Pacific Transportation Co.; Southwest Texas Methodist Hospital.

For Complete List of Firm Personnel, See General Section

For full biographical listings, see the Martindale-Hubbell Law Directory

*TYLER,** Smith Co.

SAM B. COBB, JR. (AV)

415 South Bois D'Arc, P.O. Box 6996, 75711
Telephone: 903-595-6711
Fax: 903-592-7319

For full biographical listings, see the Martindale-Hubbell Law Directory

UTAH

*SALT LAKE CITY,** Salt Lake Co.

CALLISTER, NEBEKER & MCCULLOUGH, A PROFESSIONAL CORPORATION (AV)

800 Kennecott Building, 84133
Telephone: 801-530-7300
Telecopier: 801-364-9127

Fred W. Finlinson
James R. Holbrook
R. Willis Orton
Brian W. Burnett
Jan M. Bergeson

Representative Clients: Central Valley Water Reclamation Facility Board; Washington County Conservancy District; Sinclair Oil (Little America).

For Complete List of Firm Personnel, See General Section

For full biographical listings, see the Martindale-Hubbell Law Directory

JONES, WALDO, HOLBROOK & MCDONOUGH, A PROFESSIONAL CORPORATION (AV)

1500 First Interstate Plaza, 170 South Main Street, 84101
Telephone: 801-521-3200
Telecopier: 801-328-0537
Mailing Address: P.O. Box 45444, 84145-0444
St. George, Utah Office: The Tabernacle Tower Building, 249 East Tabernacle.
Telephone: 801-628-1627.
Telecopier: 801-628-5225.
Washington, D.C. Office: Suite 900, 2300 M Street, N.W.
Telephone: 202-296-5950.
Telecopier: 202-293-2509.

Elizabeth M. Haslam
Robert G. Pruitt, III
Gregory Cropper

OF COUNSEL

Sidney G. Baucom

Representative Clients: Arch Mineral Corp.; Colorado Interstate Gas Co.; GW Petroleum, Inc.; Gold Standard, Inc.

For Complete List of Firm Personnel, See General Section

For full biographical listings, see the Martindale-Hubbell Law Directory

KIMBALL, PARR, WADDOUPS, BROWN & GEE, A PROFESSIONAL CORPORATION (AV)

Suite 1300, 185 South State Street, P.O. Box 11019, 84147
Telephone: 801-532-7840
Fax: 801-532-7750

Clayton J. Parr
Scott W. Loveless
Daniel A. Jensen
Clay W. Stucki

For Complete List of Firm Personnel, See General Section

For full biographical listings, see the Martindale-Hubbell Law Directory

PARSONS BEHLE & LATIMER, A PROFESSIONAL CORPORATION (AV)

One Utah Center, 201 South Main Street, Suite 1800, P.O. Box 45898, 84145-0898
Telephone: 801-532-1234
Telecopy: 801-536-6111

Keith E. Taylor
James B. Lee
Gordon L. Roberts
Lawrence E. Stevens
Daniel M. Allred
Dallin W. Jensen
Kent W. Winterholler
David R. Bird
David W. Tundermann
Neil Orloff
Lee Kapaloski
Stephen J. Hull
Patricia J. Winmill
Maxwell A. Miller
R. Craig Johnson (Not admitted in UT)
David G. Mangum
Lucy B. Jenkins
David L. Deisley
Hal J. Pos
J. Michael Bailey
M. Lindsay Ford
Jim B. Butler
Craig D. Galli

(See Next Column)

James E. Karkut
Michael J. Malmquist
Lisa A. Kirschner
Elizabeth Kitchens Jones
Clare Russell Davis
Michael J. Tomko

Representative Clients: American Barrick Resources Corporation; Battle Mountain Gold Company; Coastal States Energy Company; Energy Fuels Nuclear, Inc.; Hercules, Inc.; Kennecott Corporation; Pegasus Gold Corporation; Questar Corporation; Rio Algom Mining Corporation.

For full biographical listings, see the Martindale-Hubbell Law Directory

PRUITT, GUSHEE & BACHTELL (AV)

Suite 1850 Beneficial Life Tower, 36 South State Street, 84111
Telephone: 801-531-8446
Fax: 801-531-8468; 533-9223

MEMBERS OF FIRM

Robert G. Pruitt, Jr.
Oliver W. Gushee, Jr.
Thomas W. Bachtell
A. John Davis, III
John W. Anderson
Frederick M. MacDonald
Angela L. Franklin

OF COUNSEL

John F. Waldo
Brent A. Bohman

Representative Clients: Pennzoil Co.; Enron Oil & Gas Co.; Marathon Oil Co.; Flying J Inc.; Pegasus Gold Corp.; Brush Wellman, Inc.; Texasgulf, Inc.; LAC Minerals Ltd.; Shoshone Irrigation District.

For full biographical listings, see the Martindale-Hubbell Law Directory

RAY, QUINNEY & NEBEKER, A PROFESSIONAL CORPORATION (AV)

Suite 400 Deseret Building, 79 South Main Street, P.O. Box 45385, 84145-0385
Telephone: 801-532-1500
Telecopier: 801-532-7543
Provo, Utah Office: 210 First Security Bank Building, 92 North University Avenue.
Telephone: 801-226-7210.
Telecopier: 801-375-8379.

Mitchell Melich
Alan A. Enke
Robert P. Hill
Richard G. Allen
John P. Harrington
John A. Adams

Representative Clients: First Security Bank of Utah, N.A.; Borden, Inc.; Southern Pacific Transportation; Utah Power & Light Co.; Travelers Insurance Co.; Greyhound Leasing & Financial; Holy Cross Hospital and Health System; Amoco Production Co.

For Complete List of Firm Personnel, See General Section

For full biographical listings, see the Martindale-Hubbell Law Directory

VAN COTT, BAGLEY, CORNWALL & MCCARTHY, A PROFESSIONAL CORPORATION (AV)

Suite 1600, 50 South Main Street, P.O. Box 45340, 84145
Telephone: 801-532-3333
Telex: 453149
Telecopier: 801-534-0058
Ogden, Utah Office: Suite 900, 2404 Washington Boulevard.
Telephone: 801-394-5783.
Park City, Utah Office: 314 Main Street, Suite 205.
Telephone: 801-649-3889.
Reno, Nevada Office: Jeppson & Lee, 100 West Liberty, Suite 990.
Telephone: 702-333-6800.

Gregory P. Williams
Richard C. Skeen
John T. Nielsen
H. Michael Keller
Matthew F. McNulty, III
Roger W. Jeppson (Resident, Reno, Nevada)

OF COUNSEL

Leonard J. Lewis
Richard K. Sager
John Crawford, Jr.

Bradley R. Cahoon
Thomas W. Clawson
R. Blain Andrus (Resident, Reno, Nevada Office)

Representative Clients: Atlantic Richfield Co.; Atlas Corp.; Chevron USA, Inc; FMC Corp.; Kerr McGee Corp.; Monsanto Co.; Phillips Petroleum Co.; RTZ Corp.; Shell Oil Co.; Union Pacific Resources, Inc.

For Complete List of Firm Personnel, See General Section

For full biographical listings, see the Martindale-Hubbell Law Directory

VERMONT

*BURLINGTON,** Chittenden Co.

MANCHESTER LAW OFFICES, PROFESSIONAL CORPORATION (AV)

One Lawson Lane, P.O. Box 1459, 05402-1459
Telephone: 802-658-7444
Fax: 802-658-2078

Robert E. Manchester
Patricia S. Orr

LEGAL SUPPORT PERSONNEL
LEGAL NURSE CONSULTANTS

Tina L Mulvey
Rosemeryl S. Harple
Maureen P. Tremblay

For full biographical listings, see the Martindale-Hubbell Law Directory

WEST VIRGINIA

*CHARLESTON,** Kanawha Co.

JACKSON & KELLY (AV)

1600 Laidley Tower, P.O. Box 553, 25322
Telephone: 304-340-1000
Fax: 304-340-1130
Martinsburg, West Virginia Office: 300 Foxcroft Avenue, P.O. Box 1068.
Telephone: 304-263-8800.
Morgantown, West Virginia Office: 6000 Hampton Center, P.O. Box 619.
Telephone: 304-599-3000.
New Martinsville, West Virginia Office: 256 Russell Avenue, P.O. Box 68.
Telephone: 304-455-1751.
Charles Town, West Virginia Office: 700 East Washington Street, P.O. Box 983.
Telephone: 304-728-6088.
Clarksburg, West Virginia Office: 203 Main Street, P.O. Box 1587.
Telephone: 304-623-3002.
Lexington, Kentucky Office: 175 East Main Street, Suite 500, P.O. Box 2150.
Telephone: 606-255-9500.
Washington, D. C. Office: 2401 Pennsylvania Avenue, N.W., Suite 400.
Telephone: 202-973-0200.
Denver, Colorado Office: Suite 2710, 1660 Lincoln Street.
Telephone: 303-837-0003.

MEMBERS OF FIRM

James Knight Brown
John L. McClaugherty
Thomas E. Potter
Charles Q. Gage
William K. Bodell, II (Resident, Lexington, Kentucky Office)
Henry Chajet (Resident, Washington, D.C. Office)
Mark N. Savit (Resident, Washington, D.C. Office)
James R. Snyder
Thomas N. McJunkin
Laura E. Beverage (Resident, Denver, Colorado Office)
Robert G. McLusky
Thad S. Huffman (Resident, Washington, D.C. Office)
Kevin M. McGuire (Resident, Lexington, Kentucky Office)
L. Poe Leggette (Resident, Washington, D.C. Office)
Wendel B. Turner
Dean K. Hunt (Resident, Lexington, Kentucky Office)

ASSOCIATES

Brooks K. Barkwill (New Martinsville, West Virginia Office)
Robert K. Parsons
James Zissler (Resident, Washington, D.C. Office)
Linden R. Evans
Katherine Shand Larkin (Resident, Denver, Colorado Office)
William C. Miller, II

Representative Clients: A.T. Massey Coal Company, Inc.; ANR Coal Co.; Ashland Coal, Inc.; Cabot Corp.; Carbon Industries, Inc.; Consol Inc.; Cyprus Amax Minerals Co.; Pittston Coal Co.; West Virginia Coal Assn.; Westvaco Corp.

For Complete List of Firm Personnel, See General Section

For full biographical listings, see the Martindale-Hubbell Law Directory

*CLARKSBURG,** Harrison Co.

WATERS, WARNER & HARRIS (AV)

Formerly Stathers & Cantrall
701 Goff Building, P.O. Box 1716, 26301
Telephone: 304-624-5571
Fax: 304-624-7228

Birk S. Stathers (1884-1945)
W. G. Stathers (1889-1970)
Arch M. Cantrall (1896-1967)
Stuart R. Waters
Boyd L. Warner
James A. Harris
Scott E. Wilson
James C. Turner
Francis L. Warder, Jr.
G. Thomas Smith
Thomas G. Dyer

(See Next Column)

ASSOCIATES

Michael J. Folio
Katherine M. Carpenter
Ernest Glen Hentschel, II
Katrina L. Gallagher

Representative Clients: Bethlehem Steel Corp.; Alamco, Inc.; Equitable Resources, Inc.; Equitrans, Inc.; Brooklyn Union Gas Co.; Dowell Schlumberger, Inc.; FIVE-J Energy, Inc.; Fuel Resources Production and Development Company, Inc.; Grafton Coal Co.; Emax Oil Company; Tygart Coal Co.; B & R Construction, Inc.

For full biographical listings, see the Martindale-Hubbell Law Directory

WISCONSIN

*MILWAUKEE,** Milwaukee Co.

MICHAEL, BEST & FRIEDRICH (AV)

100 East Wisconsin Avenue, 53202-4108
Telephone: 414-271-6560
Telecopier: 414-277-0656
Cable Address: "Mibef"
Madison, Wisconsin Office: One South Pinckney Street, Firstar Plaza, P.O. Box 1806, 53701-1806.
Telephone: 608-257-3501.
Telecopier: 283-2275.
Chicago, Illinois Office: 135 South LaSalle Street, Suite 1610, 60603-4391.
Telephone: 312-845-5800.
Telecopier: 312-845-5828.
Affiliated Law Firm: Edward D. Heffernan, Penthouse One, 1019 19th Street, N.W., Washington, D.C. 20036.
Telephone: 202-331-7444.

PARTNERS

Arvid A. Sather (Resident Partner, Madison, Wisconsin Office)
David J. Hanson (Resident Partner, Madison, Wisconsin Office)
Paul E. Prentiss
Gary A. Ahrens
David V. Meany
Linda H. Bochert (Resident Partner, Madison, Wisconsin Office)
Raymond R. Krueger
Charles V. Sweeney (Resident Partner, Madison, Wisconsin Office)
Donald P. Gallo
Donald F. Kiesling

ASSOCIATES

Peter R. Reckmeyer
Grant C. Killoran
David A. Crass (Resident Associate, Madison, Wisconsin Office)
Thomas J. Basting, Jr.
Lisa S. Keyes (Resident Associate, Madison, Wisconsin Office)
Cynthia E. Smith
Lisa M. Toussaint

For Complete List of Firm Personnel, See General Section

For full biographical listings, see the Martindale-Hubbell Law Directory

REINHART, BOERNER, VAN DEUREN, NORRIS & RIESELBACH, S.C. (AV)

1000 North Water Street, P.O. Box 92900, 53202-0900
Telephone: 414-298-1000
Facsimile: 414-298-8097
Denver, Colorado Office: One Norwest Center, 1700 Lincoln Street, Suite 3725.
Telephone: 303-831-0909.
Fax: 303-831-4805.
Madison, Wisconsin Office: 7617 Mineral Point Road, 53701-2020.
Telephone: 608-283-7900.
Fax: 608-283-7919.
Washington, D.C. Office: 601 Pennsylvania Avenue, N.W., North Building, Suite 750.
Telephone: 202-393-3636.
Fax: 202-393-0796.

Michael H. Simpson
Jeffrey P. Clark
Steven P. Bogart
John M. Van Lieshout

William P. Scott
Carolyn A. Sullivan
Patricia S. Novacheck

For Complete List of Firm Personnel, See General Section

For full biographical listings, see the Martindale-Hubbell Law Directory

WYOMING

*BUFFALO,** Johnson Co.

OMOHUNDRO, PALMERLEE AND DURRANT (AV)

An Association of Attorneys
130 South Main Street, 82834
Telephone: 307-684-2207
Telecopier: 307-684-9364
Gillette, Wyoming Office: East Entrance, Suite 700, 201 West Lakeway Road.
Telephone: 307-682-7826.

William D. Omohundro (P.C.) David F. Palmerlee
Sean P. Durrant

Representative Clients: Crook County Irrigation District; North Fork Irrigation District; Crazy Woman Watershed Improvement District (Water Quality Development); Little Horn Energy Wyoming, Inc. (Hydro Electric); Cannon Land & Livestock Co. (Water Rights Transfer); Platte County, Wyoming (Ad Valorem Valuation of Power Plant - Litigation).

For full biographical listings, see the Martindale-Hubbell Law Directory

*CASPER,** Natrona Co.

BROWN & DREW (AV)

Casper Business Center, Suite 800, 123 West First Street, 82601-2486
Telephone: 307-234-1000
800-877-6755
Telefax: 307-265-8025

MEMBERS OF FIRM

Morris R. Massey Donn J. McCall
Harry B. Durham, III Thomas F. Reese

ASSOCIATES

Jon B. Huss P. Jaye Rippley

Attorneys for: Chevron USA Inc.; Santa Fe Industries; Unocal and subsidiaries; Enron Group of Energy Cos.; North American Resources Co.; Kerr-McGee Corp.; Marathon Oil Co.; OXY USA Inc.; Allied Signal; Wold Trona Co., Inc.

For Complete List of Firm Personnel, See General Section

For full biographical listings, see the Martindale-Hubbell Law Directory

CRAIG NEWMAN (AV)

242 South Park Street, P.O. Box 530, 82601
Telephone: 307-235-0480
FAX: 307-235-0482

For full biographical listings, see the Martindale-Hubbell Law Directory

*SHERIDAN,** Sheridan Co.

DAVIS AND CANNON (AV)

Formerly Burgess, Davis & Cannon
40 South Main Street, P.O. Box 728, 82801
Telephone: 307-672-7491
Fax: 307-672-8955
Cheyenne, Wyoming Office: 2710 Thomes Avenue, P.O. Box 43, 82003.
Telephone: 307-634-3210.
Fax: 307-778-7118.

MEMBERS OF FIRM

Richard M. Davis, Jr. Kim D. Cannon
Kate M. Fox

Representative Clients: Consol, Inc.; Hesston Corporation; Mutual of New York; Peter Kiewit Sons, Inc.; Wichita River Oil Corporation; Phillips Petroleum; First Interstate Bank of Commerce; Merrell Dow Pharmaceuticals, Inc.; Philip Morris, Inc.; Range Telephone Cooperative.

For Complete List of Firm Personnel, See General Section

For full biographical listings, see the Martindale-Hubbell Law Directory

LONABAUGH AND RIGGS (AV)

50 East Loucks Street, P.O. Drawer 5059, 82801
Telephone: 307-672-7444
Telecopier: 307-672-2230

MEMBERS OF FIRM

E. E. Lonabaugh (1861-1938) Robert G. Berger
A. W. Lonabaugh (1896-1971) E. Michael Weber
Ellsworth E. Lonabaugh Robert W. Brown
Dan B. Riggs Haultain E. Corbett
Jeffrey J. Gonda Thomas J. Klepperich
Harold E. Meier

(See Next Column)

ASSOCIATE

Jonathan A. Botten

Representative Clients: Kaneb Services, Inc.; Scurlock-Permian Corp.; First Interstate Bank of Commerce; Oxy, U.S.A.; TOTAL Minatome Corp.; Decker Coal Co.

For full biographical listings, see the Martindale-Hubbell Law Directory

PUERTO RICO

SAN JUAN, San Juan Dist.

GOLDMAN ANTONETTI & CÓRDOVA

American International Plaza Fourteenth & Fifteenth Floors, 250 Muñoz Rivera Avenue (Hato Rey), P.O. Box 70364, 00936-0364
Telephone: 809-759-8000
Telecopiers: 809-767-9333 (Main)
809-767-9177 (Litigation Department)
809-767-8660 (Labor & Corporate Law Departments)
809-767-9325 (Tax & Environmental Law Departments)

MEMBERS OF FIRM

José A. Cepeda-Rodriguez Braulio García Jiménez
Francis Torres-Fernández Karín G. Díaz-Toro

ASSOCIATES

Eli Matos-Alicea Carlos E. Colón-Franceschi
John A. Uphoff-Figueroa Gretchen M. Mendez-Vilella
Orlando Cabrera-Rodriguez

Representative Clients: Baxter Health Care Corp.; Chevron U.S.A.; Conagra, Inc.; Esso Standard Oil; Owen-Illinois; Puerto Rico Manufacturers Association; Britol Myers Squibb.

For Complete List of Firm Personnel, See General Section

For full biographical listings, see the Martindale-Hubbell Law Directory

CANADA ALBERTA

*CALGARY,** Calgary Jud. Dist.

BENNETT JONES VERCHERE (AV)

4500 Bankers Hall East, 855-2nd Street S.W., T2P 4K7
Telephone: (403) 298-3100
Facsimile: (403) 265-7219
Edmonton, Alberta Office: 1000, 10035-105 Street.
Telephone: (403) 421-8133.
Facsimile: (403) 421-7951.
Toronto, Ontario Office: 3400 1 First Canadian Place. P.O. Box 130.
Telephone: (416) 863-1200.
Facsimile: (416) 863-1716.
Ottawa, Ontario Office: Suite 1800. 350 Alberta Street, Box 25, K1R 1A4.
Telephone: (613) 230-4935.
Facsimile: (613) 230-3836.
Montreal, Quebec Office: Suite 1600, 1 Place Ville Marie.
Telephone: (514) 871-1200.
Facsimile: (514) 871-8115.

MEMBER OF FIRM

W. Gordon Brown, Q.C.

For Complete List of Firm Personnel, See General Section

For full biographical listings, see the Martindale-Hubbell Law Directory

*EDMONTON,** Edmonton Jud. Dist.

PARLEE McLAWS (AV)

15th Floor Manulife Place, 10180 101st Street, T5J 4K1
Telephone: 403-423-8500
Telecopier: 403-423-2870
Calgary, Alberta Office: 3400, Western Canadian Place, 707 - 8th Avenue, S.W.
Telephone: 403-294-7000.
Telecopier: 403-265-8263.

MEMBERS OF FIRM

C. H. Kerr, Q.C. R. A. Newton, Q.C.
M. D. MacDonald T. A. Cockrall, Q.C.
K. F. Bailey, Q.C. H. D. Montemurro
R. B. Davison, Q.C. F. J. Niziol
F. R. Haldane R. W. Wilson
P. E. J. Curran I. L. MacLachlan
D. G. Finlay R. O. Langley
J. K. McFadyen R. G. McBean
R. C. Secord J. T. Neilson
D. L. Kennedy E. G. Rice

(See Next Column)

PARLEE MCLAWS, *Edmonton—Continued*

D. C. Rolf
D. F. Pawlowski
A. A. Garber
R. P. James
D. C. Wintermute
J. L. Cairns
J. F. McGinnis
J. H. H. Hockin
G. W. Jaycock
M. J. K. Nikel
B. J. Curial
S. L. May
M. S. Poretti

ASSOCIATES

C. R. Head
A.W. Slemko
L. H. Hamdon
K.A. Smith
K. D. Fallis-Howell
D. S. Tam
J.W. McClure
F.H. Belzil
R.A. Renz
J.G. Paulson
K. E. Buss
B. L. Andriachuk
P. E. S. J. Kennedy
R. Feraco
R.J. Billingsley
N.B.R. Thompson
P. A. Shenher
I. C. Johnson
K.G. Koshman
D.D. Dubrule
G. T. Lund
W.D. Johnston
G. E. Flemming
K. P. Nayyer

For full biographical listings, see the Martindale-Hubbell Law Directory

CANADA BRITISH COLUMBIA

*VANCOUVER,** Vancouver Co.

RUSSELL & DUMOULIN (AV)

2100-1075 West Georgia Street, V6E 3G2
Telephone: 604-631-3131
Fax: 604-631-3232
A Member of the national association of Borden DuMoulin Howard Gervais, comprising Russell & DuMoulin, Vancouver, British Columbia; Howard Mackie, Calgary, Alberta; Borden & Elliot, Toronto, Ontario; Mackenzie Gervais, Montreal, Quebec and Borden DuMoulin Howard Gervais, London, England.
Strategic Alliance with Perkins Coie with offices in Seattle, Spokane and Bellevue, Washington; Portland, Oregon; Anchorage, Alaska; Los Angeles, California; Washington, D.C.; Hong Kong and Taipei, Taiwan.
Represented in Hong Kong by Vincent T.K. Cheung, Yap & Co.

MEMBERS OF FIRM

J. M. McCormick
Gary W. Ott

Representative Clients: Alcan Smelters & Chemicals Ltd.; The Bank of Nova Scotia; Canada Trust Co.; The Canada Life Assurance Co.; Forest Industrial Relations Ltd.; Honda Canada Inc.; IBM Canada Ltd.; Macmillan Bloedel Ltd.; Nissho Iwai Canada Ltd.; The Toronto-Dominion Bank.

For Complete List of Firm Personnel, See General Section

For full biographical listings, see the Martindale-Hubbell Law Directory

CANADA NOVA SCOTIA

*HALIFAX,** Halifax Co.

MCINNES COOPER & ROBERTSON (AV)

1601 Lower Water Street, P.O. Box 730, B3J 2V1
Telephone: 902-425-6500
Fax: 902-425-6350
St. John's, Newfoundland Office: Suite 602, Scotia Centre, 235 Water Street, P.O. Box 547. A1C, 5K8.
Telephone: 709-726-9500.
Fax: 709-726-9550.

Wylie Spicer
F. V. W. Penick
Brian G. Johnston

ASSOCIATES

David S. Mac Dougall
Aidan J. Meade

Attorneys for: Bank of Nova Scotia; Imperial Oil, Limited; Frank B. Hall & Co., Inc. (New York); American Steamship Owners Protection & Indemnity Association, Inc.; Coca-Cola, Ltd.; Scott Worldwide Inc.; Hong Kong Bank of Canada.

For Complete List of Firm Personnel, See General Section

For full biographical listings, see the Martindale-Hubbell Law Directory

CANADA ONTARIO

*TORONTO,** Regional Munic. of York

BORDEN & ELLIOT (AV)

Barristers & Solicitors
Scotia Plaza, 40 King Street West, M5H 3Y4
Telephone: 416-367-6000
Telecopier: 416-367-6749
Internet: @ borden.com
A Member of the national association of Borden DuMoulin Howard Gervais, comprising Borden & Elliot in Toronto, Ontario, Russell & DuMoulin in Vancouver, British Columbia, Howard, Mackie in Calgary, Alberta and Mackenzie Gervais in Montréal, Québec. Borden DuMoulin Howard Gervais also operates an office in London, England.

MEMBER AND ASSOCIATES

Edmund F. Merringer

For Complete List of Firm Personnel, See General Section

For full biographical listings, see the Martindale-Hubbell Law Directory

CANADA QUEBEC

*MONTREAL,** Montreal Dist.

BYERS CASGRAIN (AV)

A Member of McMillan Bull Casgrain
Suite 3900, 1 Place Ville-Marie, H3B 4M7
Telephone: 514-878-8800
Telecopier: 514-866-2241
Cable Address: "Magee"
Telex: 05-24195

Philippe Casgrain, Q.C.
Hon. Jean Bazin, Q.C.
Pierre Langlois
William S. Grodinsky
John Hurley
Martin Bernard
Serge Tousignant
Sébastien Grammond

For Complete List of Firm Personnel, See General Section

For full biographical listings, see the Martindale-Hubbell Law Directory

CANADA SASKATCHEWAN

*REGINA,** Regina Jud. Centre

MACPHERSON LESLIE & TYERMAN (AV)

1500-1874 Scarth Street, S4P 4E9
Telephone: 306-347-8000
Telecopier: 306-352-5250
Saskatoon, Saskatchewan Office: 1500-410 22nd Street East, S7K 5T6.
Telephone: 306-975-7100.
Telecopier: 306-975-7145.

MEMBERS OF FIRM

Harold H. MacKay, Q.C.
A. Robson Garden, Q.C. (Resident, Saskatoon Office)
Stephen A. Arsenych
Danny R. Anderson (Resident, Saskatoon Office)

For Complete List of Firm Personnel, See General Section

For full biographical listings, see the Martindale-Hubbell Law Directory

PATENT, TRADEMARK, COPYRIGHT AND UNFAIR COMPETITION LAW

(See also listings under Trademark, Copyright and Unfair Competition Law)

ALABAMA

*BIRMINGHAM,** Jefferson Co.

BALCH & BINGHAM (AV)

1710 Sixth Avenue North, P.O. Box 306, 35201
Telephone: 205-251-8100
Facsimile: 205-226-8798
Other Birmingham, Alabama Office: 1901 Sixth Avenue North, 35203.
Telephone: 205-251-8100.
Facsimile: 205-226-8799.
Montgomery, Alabama Office: The Winter Building, 2 Dexter Avenue, 36101.
Telephone: 205-834-6500.
Facsimile: 205-269-3115.
Huntsville, Alabama Office: Suite 810, 200 West Court Square, 35801.
Telephone: 205-551-0171.
Facsimile: 205-551-0174.
Washington, D.C. Office: Suite 800, 1101 Connecticut Avenue, N.W., 20036.
Telephone: 202-296-0387.
Facsimile: 202-452-8180.

MEMBERS OF FIRM

Walter M. Beale, Jr.
Susan B. Bevill
Will Hill Tankersley, Jr.

Counsel for: Alabama Power Co.; Blue Cross and Blue Shield of Alabama; The Boeing Company; Brasfield & Gorrie, Inc.; Compass Bancshares, Inc.; Harbert Corp.; Kimberly-Clark Corp.; Southern Company Services, Inc.; Southern Research Institute; Vesta Insurance Group, Inc.

For Complete List of Firm Personnel, See General Section

For full biographical listings, see the Martindale-Hubbell Law Directory

BRADLEY, ARANT, ROSE & WHITE (AV)

1400 Park Place Tower, 2001 Park Place, 35203
Telephone: 205-521-8000
Telex: 494-1324
Facsimile: 205-251-8611, 251-8665, 252-0264
Facsimile (Southtrust Office): 205-251-9915
Huntsville, Alabama Office: 200 Clinton Avenue West, Suite 900.
Telephone: 205-517-5100.
Facsimile: 205-533-5069.

MEMBERS OF FIRM

Thad Gladden Long
James W. Gewin
Linda A. Friedman

ASSOCIATES

J. David Pugh
Frank M. Caprio (Resident, Huntsville Office)

Counsel for: SouthTrust Bank of Alabama, National Association; Energen, Corporation (formerly Alagasco, Inc.); Blount, Inc; Coca-Cola Bottling Company United, Inc.; The New York Times Co.; Russell Corp.; Walter Industries, Inc.; ASCAP, Auburn University.

For Complete List of Firm Personnel, See General Section

For full biographical listings, see the Martindale-Hubbell Law Directory

SIROTE & PERMUTT, P.C. (AV)

2222 Arlington Avenue, South, P.O. Box 55727, 35255
Telephone: 205-933-7111
Facsimile: 205-930-5301
Huntsville, Alabama Office: 200 Clinton Avenue, N.W., Suite 1000.
Telephone: 205-536-1711.
Facsimile: 205-534-9650.
Mobile, Alabama Office: One St. Louis Centre, Suite 1000.
Telephone: 205-432-1671.
Facsimile: 205-434-0196.
Montgomery, Alabama Office: Colonial Commerce Center, Suite 305 One Commerce Street.
Telephone: 205-261-3400.
Facsimile: 205-261-3434.

(See Next Column)

Tuscaloosa, Alabama Office: 2216 14th Street.
Telephone: 205-752-2089.

Jerry E. Held
Timothy A. Bush
Kim E. Rosenfield
Robert R. Baugh
Gail Crummie Washington
J. Scott Sims

Representative Clients: International Business Machines (IBM); General Motors Corp.; Colonial Bank; Bruno's, Inc.; University of Alabama Hospitals; Westinghouse Electric Corp.; First Alabama Bank; Monsanto Chemical Company; South Central Bell; Prudential Insurance Company; American Home Products, Inc.; Minnesota Mining and Manufacturing, Inc. (3M).

For Complete List of Firm Personnel, See General Section

For full biographical listings, see the Martindale-Hubbell Law Directory

*HUNTSVILLE,** Madison Co.

BALCH & BINGHAM (AV)

Suite 810, 200 West Court Square, P.O. Box 18668, 35804-8668
Telephone: 205-551-0171
Facsimile: 205-551-0174
Birmingham, Alabama Offices: 1710 Sixth Avenue North, 35203.
Telephone: 205-251-8100.
Facsimile: 205-226-8798. 1901 Sixth Avenue North, 35203.
Telephone: 205-251-8100.
Facsimile: 205-226-8799.
Montgomery, Alabama Office: The Winter Building, 2 Dexter Avenue, 36101.
Telephone: 205-834-6500.
Facsimile: 205-269-3115.
Washington, D.C. Office: Suite 800, 1101 Connecticut Avenue, N.W., 20036.
Telephone: 202-296-0387.
Facsimile: 202-452-8180.

RESIDENT MEMBER OF FIRM

S. Revelle Gwyn

Counsel for: Alabama Power Co.; Blue Cross and Blue Shield of Alabama; The Boeing Company; Brasfield & Gorrie, Inc.; Compass Bancshares, Inc.; Harbert Corp.; Kimberly-Clark Corp.; Southern Company Services, Inc.; Southern Research Institute; Vesta Insurance Group, Inc.

For Complete List of Firm Personnel, See General Section

For full biographical listings, see the Martindale-Hubbell Law Directory

SIROTE & PERMUTT, P.C. (AV)

Suite 1000, 200 Clinton Avenue, N.W., 35801
Telephone: 205-536-1711
Facsimile: 205-534-9650
Birmingham, Alabama Office: 2222 Arlington Avenue, South, P.O. Box 55727.
Telephone: 205-933-7111.
Facsimile: 205-930-5301.
Mobile, Alabama Office: One St. Louis Centre, Suite 1000.
Telephone: 205-432-1671.
Facsimile: 205-434-0196.
Montgomery, Alabama Office: Colonial Commerce Center, Suite 305, One Commerce Street.
Telephone: 205-261-3400.
Facsimile: 205-261-3434.
Tuscaloosa, Alabama Office: 2216 14th Street.
Telephone: 205-752-2089.

Joe H. Ritch
George W. Royer, Jr.
Roderic G. Steakley
June Wang

For Complete List of Firm Personnel, See General Section

For full biographical listings, see the Martindale-Hubbell Law Directory

*MOBILE,** Mobile Co.

SIROTE & PERMUTT, P.C. (AV)

One St. Louis Centre, Suite 1000, P.O. Drawer 2025, 36652-2025
Telephone: 334-432-1671
Facsimile: 334-434-0196
Birmingham, Alabama Office: 2222 Arlington Avenue, South, P.O. Box 55727.
Telephone: 205-933-7111.
Facsimile: 205-930-5301.
Huntsville, Alabama Office: 200 Clinton Avenue, N.W., Suite 1000.
Telephone: 205-536-1711.
Facsimile: 205-534-9650.
Montgomery, Alabama Office: Colonial Commerce Center, Suite 305, One Commerce Street.
Telephone: 205-261-3400.
Facsimile: 205-261-3434.
Tuscaloosa, Alabama Office: 2216 14th Street.
Telephone: 205-752-2089.

(See Next Column)

SIROTE & PERMUTT P.C., *Mobile—Continued*

Gordon O. Tanner Steven L. Nicholas

For Complete List of Firm Personnel, See General Section

For full biographical listings, see the Martindale-Hubbell Law Directory

ARIZONA

*PHOENIX,** Maricopa Co.

BROWN & BAIN, A PROFESSIONAL ASSOCIATION (AV)

2901 North Central Avenue, P.O. Box 400, 85001-0400
Telephone: 602-351-8000
Cable: TWX 910-951-0646
Telecopier: 602-351-8516
Palo Alto, California Affiliated Office: Brown & Bain, 600 Hansen Way.
Telephone: 415-856-9411.
Telecopier: 415-856-6061.
Tucson, Arizona Affiliated Office: Brown & Bain, A Professional Association. One South Church Avenue, Nineteenth Floor, P.O. Box 2265.
Telephone: 602-798-7900
Telecopier: 602-798-7945.

Robert E. B. Allen
Michael F. Bailey
C. Randall Bain
Alan H. Blankenheimer
Jack E. Brown
H. Michael Clyde
Paul F. Eckstein
Terry E. Fenzl
Michael F. McNulty (Resident at Tucson Office)
Joseph W. Mott
Charles S. Price
Daniel P. Quigley
Lawrence G. D. Scarborough
Craig W. Soland
Antonio T. Viera
Kim E. Williamson

Charles A. Blanchard
Patricia A. Hubbard
Jonathan M. James
C. Mark Kittredge
Deborah Henscheid Lyon
Anthony L. Marks
Christopher J. Raboin

For Complete List of Firm Personnel, See General Section

For full biographical listings, see the Martindale-Hubbell Law Directory

FENNEMORE CRAIG, A PROFESSIONAL CORPORATION (AV)

Two North Central, Suite 2200, 85004
Telephone: 602-257-8700
Fax: 602-257-8527
Scottsdale, Arizona Office: 6263 North Scottsdale Road, Suite 290, 85250.
Telephone: 602-257-5400.
Fax: 602-945-4932.
Tucson, Arizona Office: One South Church Avenue, Suite 1030, 85701.
Telephone: 602-624-9312.
Fax: 602-882-7383.

C. Owen Paepke
Ray K. Harris
Lesa J. Storey

Stacie K. Smith

Representative Clients: ASARCO Incorporated; AT&T Communications; Bridgestone/Firestone, Inc.; Catellus Development Corp.; Citibank (Arizona); First Interstate Bank of Arizona; GIANT Industries; Phelps Dodge Corporation; The Atchison, Topeka & Santa Fe Railway, Co.; US WEST Communications.

For Complete List of Firm Personnel, See General Section

For full biographical listings, see the Martindale-Hubbell Law Directory

O'CONNOR, CAVANAGH, ANDERSON, WESTOVER, KILLINGSWORTH & BESHEARS, A PROFESSIONAL ASSOCIATION (AV)

One East Camelback Road, Suite 1100, 85012-1656
Telephone: 602-263-2400
FAX: 602-263-2900
Sun City, Arizona Office: 13250 North Del Webb Boulevard, Suite B, 85351.
Telephone: 602-263-2808.
FAX: 602-933-3100.
Tucson, Arizona Office: Suite 2200, One South Church Avenue, 85701.
Telephone: 602-882-8912.
FAX: 602-624-9564.
Nogales, Arizona Office: 1827 North Mastick Way, 85621.
Telephone: 602-761-4215.
FAX: 602-761-3505.

Donald R. Greene (Not admitted in AZ)

John D. Titus

For Complete List of Firm Personnel, See General Section

For full biographical listings, see the Martindale-Hubbell Law Directory

STREICH LANG, A PROFESSIONAL ASSOCIATION (AV)

Renaissance One, Two N. Central Avenue, 85004-2391
Telephone: 602-229-5200
Fax: 602-229-5690
Tucson, Arizona Office: One S. Church Avenue, Suite 1700.
Telephone: 602-770-8700.
Fax: 602-623-2518.
Las Vegas, Nevada Affiliated Office: Dawson & Associates, 3800 Howard Hughes Parkway, Suite 1500.
Telephone: 702-792-2727.
Fax: 702-792-2676.
Los Angeles, California Office: 444 S. Flower Street, Suite 1530.
Telephone: 213-896-0484.

Charles W. Jirauch

Representative Clients: Allied-Signal Aerospace Company; America West Airlines, Inc.; Atlantic Richfield Co.; Chicago Title; First Interstate Bank of Arizona, N.A.; Magma Copper Co.; Motorola, Inc.; Phelps Dodge Development Corp.; TRW Inc.; The Travelers Companies.

For Complete List of Firm Personnel, See General Section

For full biographical listings, see the Martindale-Hubbell Law Directory

SCOTTSDALE, Maricopa Co.

CATES & HOLLOWAY (AV)

Suite D-218, 6991 East Camelback Road, 85251
Telephone: 602-248-0982
Fax: 602-234-3330

MEMBER OF FIRM

Charles E. Cates

ASSOCIATES

Karl M. Gauby
Richard G. Harrer (Not admitted in AZ)
Edward C. Jason (Not admitted in AZ)

OF COUNSEL

A. Donald Messenheimer (Not admitted in AZ)
William W. Holloway

Representative Clients: Albers Technologies, Inc.; Applied Computer Research; ARA Leisure Services, Inc.; Bank One of Arizona; Claridge Casino Hotel; Courtaulds Performance Films; The Dial Corp.; Discount Tire Co., Inc.; Performance Industries, Inc.; Pilkington Visioncare, Inc.

For full biographical listings, see the Martindale-Hubbell Law Directory

ARKANSAS

*LITTLE ROCK,** Pulaski Co.

IVESTER, SKINNER & CAMP, P.A. (AV)

Suite 1200, 111 Center Street, 72201
Telephone: 501-376-7788
FAX: 501-376-8536

Hermann Ivester
Todd A. Lewellen

For Complete List of Firm Personnel, See General Section

For full biographical listings, see the Martindale-Hubbell Law Directory

CALIFORNIA

BEVERLY HILLS, Los Angeles Co.

DRUCKER & SOMMERS (AV)

A Partnership including a Professional Corporation
Suite 328 Wilshire-Beverly Center, 9465 Wilshire Boulevard, 90212
Telephone: 310-278-6852
Fax: 310-274-3482

MEMBERS OF FIRM

I. Morley Drucker (A Professional Corporation)
Howard N. Sommers

(See Next Column)

DRUCKER & SOMMERS—*Continued*

ASSOCIATES

Avis Frazier-Thomas
Daniel R. Kimbell
Muriel C. Haritchabalet

For full biographical listings, see the Martindale-Hubbell Law Directory

*FRESNO,** Fresno Co.

KIMBLE, MACMICHAEL & UPTON, A PROFESSIONAL CORPORATION (AV)

Fig Garden Financial Center, 5260 North Palm Avenue, Suite 221, P.O. Box 9489, 93792-9489
Telephone: 209-435-5500
Telecopier: 209-435-1500

Joseph C. Kimble (1910-1972)
Thomas A. MacMichael (1920-1990)
Jon Wallace Upton
Robert E. Bergin
Jeffrey G. Boswell
Steven D. McGee
Robert E. Ward
John P. Eleazarian
Robert H. Scribner
Michael E. Moss
David D. Doyle
Mark D. Miller
Michael F. Tatham
W. Richard Lee
D. Tyler Tharpe
Sylvia Halkousis Coyle

Michael J. Jurkovich
S. Brett Sutton
Douglas V. Thornton
Robert William Branch
Brian N. Folland
Christopher L. Wanger
Elise M. Krause
Donald J. Pool
Susan King Hatmaker

For full biographical listings, see the Martindale-Hubbell Law Directory

WORREL & WORREL (AV)

Suite 130, Civic Center Square, 2444 Main Street, 93721-1984
Telephone: 209-486-4526
Fax: 209-486-6948

Richard M. Worrel (Retired)
Rodney K. Worrel

Representative Clients: Bank of America; California State University, Fresno; California State University, Bakersfield; Duncan Enterprises; Fresno Pacific College; J. G. Boswell Co.; The Vendo Company; City of Visalia.

For full biographical listings, see the Martindale-Hubbell Law Directory

IRVINE, Orange Co.

POMS, SMITH, LANDE & ROSE, PROFESSIONAL CORPORATION (AV)

1920 Main Street, Suite 1050, 92714
Telephone: 714-263-8250
FAX: 714-263-8260
Los Angeles, California Office: 2029 Century Park East, 38th Floor, 90067.
Telephone: 310-788-5000.
FAX: 310-277-1297.
San Jose, California Office: 95 South Market Street, Suite 550, 95113.
Telephone: 408-275-8790.
FAX: 408-275-8793.

Richard L. Gausewitz
Kurt A. MacLean
Edward F. O'Connor
Michael A. Kondzella
Terry L. Miller

OF COUNSEL

Richard F. Carr
Allan Rothenberg

Reference: First Los Angeles Bank (Century Plaza Office, Century City).

For full biographical listings, see the Martindale-Hubbell Law Directory

LAGUNA HILLS, Orange Co.

STETINA, BRUNDA AND BUYAN, A PROFESSIONAL CORPORATION (AV)

Suite 401, 24221 Calle De La Louisa, 92653
Telephone: 714-855-1246
Telex: 704355
Facsimile: 714-855-6371

Kit M. Stetina (Mr.)
Bruce B. Brunda
Robert Dean Buyan

Mark B. Garred
William J. Brucker
Matt A. Newboles
Robert J. Lauson

LEGAL SUPPORT PERSONNEL

Norman E. Carte
Kristy Kay Moore

Representative Clients: Smith-Kline Diagnostics; Northrop-Grumman Aerospace Corp.; No Fear, Inc.; Dunn Edwards, Inc.; Ankly Systems; Baxter Corp.; Pick Systems; Bird Products Corp.; Tyco Industries, Inc.; Kalnan Floor Co.

For full biographical listings, see the Martindale-Hubbell Law Directory

*LOS ANGELES,** Los Angeles Co.

BRIGHT & LORIG, A PROFESSIONAL CORPORATION (AV)

633 West Fifth Street, Suite 3330, 90071
Telephone: 213-627-7774
Telecopier: 213-627-8508

Frederick A. Lorig
Patrick F. Bright

Lois A. Stone
Sidford Lewis Brown
Edward C. Schewe

Reference: Manufacturers Bank (Headquarters Office).

For full biographical listings, see the Martindale-Hubbell Law Directory

FULWIDER, PATTON, LEE & UTECHT (AV)

10877 Wilshire Boulevard, 10th Floor, 90024
Telephone: 310-824-5555
Cable Address: "Fulpat"
FAX: 310-824-9696
Long Beach, California Office: Fifth Floor, 200 Oceangate, Suite 1550.
Telephone: 310-432-0453.
Fax: 310-435-6014.

MEMBERS OF FIRM

Robert W. Fulwider (1903-1979)
John M. Lee (1921-1978)
Warren L. Patton (1912-1985)
Francis A. Utecht (Long Beach Resident Partner)
Richard A. Bardin
Gilbert G. Kovelman
Vern Schooley (Long Beach Resident Partner)
James W. Paul
Craig B. Bailey
John S. Nagy
Stephen J. Strauss

OF COUNSEL

Joseph F. McLellan

ASSOCIATES

David G. Parkhurst
Paul M. Stull
Thomas H. Majcher
Gunther Hanke (Long Beach Resident Associate)
Gary M. Anderson (Long Beach Resident Associate)
Thomas A. Runk
Ronald E. Perez
Clifton W. Thompson
Robert L. Kovelman
Pamela G. Maher
John V. Hanley
Rex A. Wilcox (Long Beach Resident Associate)
John K. Fitzgerald
David G. Duckworth (Long Beach Resident Associate)

For full biographical listings, see the Martindale-Hubbell Law Directory

JOSEPH H. GOLANT (AV)

1901 Avenue of the Stars, Suite 1100, 90067
Telephone: 310-556-0055
Facsimile: 310-556-1880

For full biographical listings, see the Martindale-Hubbell Law Directory

HARRIS, WALLEN, MACDERMOTT & TINSLEY (AV)

Top Floor Quinby Building, 650 South Grand Avenue, 90017-3878
Telephone: 213-626-5251
Fax: 213-626-0123

MEMBERS OF FIRM

Ford W. Harris, Jr. (1907-1977)
Warren L. Kern (1915-1984)
Walton Eugene Tinsley
Richard A. Wallen
Michael J. MacDermott

Reference: First Interstate Bank.

For full biographical listings, see the Martindale-Hubbell Law Directory

JONES, DAY, REAVIS & POGUE (AV)

555 West Fifth Street Suite 4600, 90013-1025
Telephone: 213-489-3939
Telex: 181439 UD
Telecopier: 213-243-2539
In Irvine, California: 2603 Main Street, Suite 900.
Telephone: 714-851-3939.
Telex: 194911 Lawyers LSA.
Telecopier: 714-553-7539.
In Atlanta, Georgia: 3500 One Peachtree Center, 303 Peachtree Street, N.E.
Telephone: 404-521-3939.
Cable Address: "Attorneys Atlanta".
Telex: 54-2711.
Telecopier: 404-581-8330.
In Brussels, Belgium: Avenue Louise 480, 7th Floor, B-1050 Brussels.
Telephone: 011-32-2-645-14-11.
Telecopier: 011-32-2-645-14-45.
In Chicago, Illinois: 77 West Wacker.
Telephone: 312-782-3939.
Telecopier: 312-782-8585.

(See Next Column)

JONES, DAY, REAVIS & POGUE, *Los Angeles—Continued*

In Cleveland, Ohio: North Point, 901 Lakeside Avenue.
Telephone: 216-586-3939.
Cable Address: "Attorneys Cleveland."
Telex: 980389.
Telecopier: 216-579-0212.
In Columbus, Ohio: 1900 Huntington Center.
Telephone: 614-469-3939.
Cable Address: "Attorneys Columbus."
Telecopier: 614-461-4198.
In Dallas, Texas: 2300 Trammell Crow Center, 2001 Ross Avenue.
Telephone: 214-220-3939.
Cable Address: "Attorneys Dallas."
Telex: 730852.
Telecopier: 214-969-5100.
In Frankfurt, Germany: Triton Haus, Bockenheimer Landstrasse 42, 60323 Frankfurt am Main.
Telephone: 49-69-9726-3939.
Telecopier: 49-69-9726-3993.
In Geneva, Switzerland: 20, rue de Candolle.
Telephone: 011-41-22-320-2339.
Telecopier: 011-41-22-320-1232.
In Hong Kong: 1501 One Exchange Square, 8 Connaught Place.
Telephone: 011-852-2526-6895.
Telecopier: 011-852-2810-5787.
In London England: One Mount Street.
Telephone: 011-44-71-493-9361.
Cable Address: "Surgoe London WI."
Telecopier: 011-44-71-493-9666.
In New York, New York: 599 Lexington Avenue.
Telephone: 212-326-3939.
Cable Address: "JONESDAY NEWYORK."
Telex: 237013 JDRP UR.
Telecopier: 212-755-7306.
In Paris, France: 62, rue du Faubourg Saint-Honore.
Telephone: 011-33-1-44-71-3939.
Cable Address: "Surgoe Paris."
Telex: 290156 Surgoe.
Telecopier: 011-33-1-49-24-0471.
In Pittsburgh, Pennsylvania: 500 Grant Street, 31st Floor.
Telephone: 412-391-3939.
Cable Address: "Attorneys Pittsburgh".
Telecopier: 412-394-7959.
In Riyadh, Saudi Arabia: Law Offices of Saud M.A. Shawwaf, P.O. Box 2700.
Telephones: 011 (966-1) 465-6543, 011 (966-1) 464-8534 or 011 (966-1) 464-8540.
Telex: 401831 SAUCON SJ.
Telecopier: (966-1) 464-8480.
In Taipei, Taiwan: 8th Floor, 2 Tun Hwa South Road, Section 2.
Telephone: 011 (886-2) 704-6808.
Telecopier: 011 (886-2) 704-6791.
In Tokyo, Japan: Toranomon MT Building, 4th Floor, 10-3, Toranomon 3-Chome, Minato-Ku, Tokyo 105, Japan.
Telephone: 011-81-3-3433-3939.
Telecopier: 011-81-3-5401-2725.
In Washington, D.C.: Metropolitan Square, 1450 G Street, N.W.
Telephone: 202-879-3939.
Cable Address: "Attorneys Washington."
Telex: 89-2410 ATTORNEYS WASH.
Telecopier: 202-737-2832.

MEMBER OF FIRM IN LOS ANGELES

Louis L. Touton

For Complete List of Firm Personnel, See General Section

For full biographical listings, see the Martindale-Hubbell Law Directory

---

LEOPOLD, PETRICH & SMITH, A PROFESSIONAL CORPORATION (AV)

(Formerly Youngman, Hungate & Leopold)
Suite 3110, 2049 Century Park East (Century City), 90067
Telephone: 310-277-3333
Telecopier: 310-277-7444

Gordon E. Youngman (1903-1983)
A. Fredric Leopold
Louis P. Petrich
Joel McCabe Smith
Edward A. Ruttenberg
Vincent Cox
Donald R. Gordon
Walter R. Sadler
Daniel M. Mayeda

OF COUNSEL

Richard Hungate

Paul M. Krekorian
David Aronoff
Gary M. Grossenbacher
Robert S. Gutierrez

For full biographical listings, see the Martindale-Hubbell Law Directory

---

NILSSON, WURST & GREEN (AV)

707 Wilshire Boulevard Thirty Second Floor, 90017
Telephone: 213-243-8000
Telecopier: 213-243-8050

(See Next Column)

MEMBERS OF FIRM

Byard G. Nilsson
Harold E. Wurst
Robert A. Green
Jai ho Rho

ASSOCIATES

Anne Wang
Clarke A. Wixon
Stephen D. Burbach

OF COUNSEL

William P. Green (Law Corporation)

LEGAL SUPPORT PERSONNEL

Reena Kuyper

For full biographical listings, see the Martindale-Hubbell Law Directory

---

POMS, SMITH, LANDE & ROSE, PROFESSIONAL CORPORATION (AV)

2029 Century Park East, 38th Floor, 90067
Telephone: 310-788-5000
FAX: 310-277-1297
Orange County Office: 1920 Main Street, Suite 1050, Irvine, California, 92714.
Telephone: 714-263-8250.
FAX: 714-263-8260.
San Jose, California Office: 95 South Market Street, Suite 550, 95113.
Telephone: 408-275-8790.
FAX: 408-275-8793.

William Poms
Guy Porter Smith
Gary E. Lande
Alan C. Rose
Louis J. Bovasso
Bernard R. Gans
David J. Oldenkamp
Christopher Darrow
Kurt A. MacLean (Resident, Irvine Office)
Michael D. Harris
Charles Rosenberg
Marc E. Brown
Breton August Bocchieri
Michael B. Lachuk (Resident, San Jose Office)
James A. Henricks
Edward F. O'Connor (Resident, Irvine Office)
J. Patrick Weir
Richard L. Gausewitz (Resident, Irvine Office)
Alan P. Block
Paul Y. Feng
Michael A. Kondzella (Resident, Irvine Office)
Terry L. Miller (Resident, Irvine Office)
Steven E. Shapiro
Kevin D. DeBré
Steven W. Smyrski
Scott R. Hansen
Miriam C. Beezy
Thomas E. Malone
Douglas N. Larson
U. P. Peter Eng
James W. Inskeep
Craig A. Slavin
Peter L. Holmes

OF COUNSEL

Richard F. Carr (Resident, Irvine Office)
Allan Rothenberg (Resident, Irvine Office)

LEGAL SUPPORT PERSONNEL

David G. Alexander (Patent Agent)
Paula M. Theismann (Legal Assistant)
Sheiron Y. Allen (Legal Assistant)
Larry L. Peters (Legal Assistant)
Antonia D. Espinoza (Legal Assistant)

Reference: Bank of America (Century Plaza Office, Century City).

For full biographical listings, see the Martindale-Hubbell Law Directory

---

PRETTY, SCHROEDER, BRUEGGEMANN & CLARK, A PROFESSIONAL CORPORATION (AV)

Suite 2000, 444 South Flower Street, 90071
Telephone: 213-622-7700
Telecopier: 213-489-4210
San Diego, California Office: Suite 600, 4370 La Jolla Village Drive.
Telephone: 619-546-4737.
Telecopier: 619-546-9392.

Laurence H. Pretty
Robert A. Schroeder
James R. Brueggemann
Gary A. Clark
Craig S. Summers
Edward G. Poplawski
Stephen E. Reiter (Resident, San Diego Office)

Marc Philip Schuyler
Wendy A. Whiteford
Steven J. Kirschner
Mark Garscia
Jeffrey F. Craft
Suzanne R. Jones
Robroy R. Fawcett
Paul D. Tripodi, II
Marc H. Cohen
Keith A. Newburry
Michael L. Crapenhoft
Deborah A. Dugan (Resident, San Diego Office)
Robert Troy Ramos (Resident, San Diego Office)
Sharon M. Fujita
J. Chris James
John A. Griecci

For full biographical listings, see the Martindale-Hubbell Law Directory

---

ROBBINS, BERLINER & CARSON (AV)

Fifth Floor, Figueroa Plaza, 201 North Figueroa Street, 90012-2628
Telephone: 213-977-1001
Telecopier: 213-977-1003

(See Next Column)

ROBBINS, BERLINER & CARSON—*Continued*

MEMBERS OF FIRM

Billy A. Robbins
Robert Berliner
John Carson
Michael S. Elkind
Leonard D. Messinger
John M. May
Norman E. Brunell
Clark D. Gross

ASSOCIATES

Ying-Kit Lau
Horacio A. Farach (Not admitted in CA)
Sharon Wong
Deborah M. Nesset
Pete A. Smits
Wean Khing Wong

OF COUNSEL

John P. Spitals

For full biographical listings, see the Martindale-Hubbell Law Directory

SMALL LARKIN & KIDDÉ (AV)

10940 Wilshire Boulevard, Eighteenth Floor, 90024
Telephone: 310-209-4400
Fax: 310-209-4450
Cable Address: SLK MARK
Telex: 49616151

MEMBERS OF FIRM

Thomas M. Small
Joan Kupersmith Larkin
Thomas S. Kiddé
Jon E. Hokanson
Janet A. Kobrin

Kenneth L. Wilton
Mary B. Scott
Donald J. Cox, Jr.
Barry Seaton
Kamran Fattahi
Karen E. Samuels

LEGAL SUPPORT PERSONNEL

Susan Brady Blasco

For full biographical listings, see the Martindale-Hubbell Law Directory

MENLO PARK, San Mateo Co.

FISH & RICHARDSON P.C. (AV)

2200 Sand Hill Road Suite 100, 94025
Telephone: 415-854-5277
Telecopier: 415-854-0875
Washington, D.C. Office: 601 13th Street, N.W.
Telephone: 202-783-5070.
Telecopier: 202-783-2331.
Houston, Texas Office: One Riverway, Suite 1200.
Telephone: 713-629-5070.
Telecopier: 713-629-7811.
Boston, Massachusetts Office: 225 Franklin Street.
Telephone: 617-542-5070.
Fax: 617-542-8906.
Telex: 200154.
Minneapolis, Minnesota Office: Fish & Richardson P.C., P.A., 2500 One Financial Plaza, 120 South Sixth Street.
Telephone: 612-335-5070.
Facsimile: 612-288-9696.

Frederick P. Fish (1855-1930)
W.K. Richardson (1859-1951)
James H. A. Pooley
Hans R. Troesch
David A. Henderson
John E. Gartman
John R. Schiffhauer (Not admitted in CA)
Karl Bozicevic

Christopher J. Palermo
Frank E. Scherkenbach
Jodi L. Sutton
Shelley K. Wessels
John W. Thornburgh
Wayne P. Sobon
Valeta A. Gregg-Emery (Not admitted in CA)

For full biographical listings, see the Martindale-Hubbell Law Directory

NEWPORT BEACH, Orange Co.

HARNESS, DICKEY & PIERCE (AV)

4041 MacArthur Boulevard, Suite 400, 92660
Telephone: 714-760-6233
Telefacsimile: 714-760-6123
Troy, Michigan Office: 5445 Corporate Drive, Suite 400.
Telephone: 810-641-1600. Telefacsimile (All Groups): 810-641-0270.
Ann Arbor, Michigan Office: Suite 555, 301 East Liberty Street.
Telephone: 313-662-5653.
Telefacsimile: 313-662-7813.
San Diego, California Office: 900 First Interstate Plaza, 401 B Street.
Telephone: 619-238-4122.
Telefacsimile: 619-238-0970.
Washington, D.C. Office: 888 Sixteenth Street, N.W.
Telephone: 202-835-7480.
Telefacsimile: 202-835-7487.

(See Next Column)

MEMBER OF FIRM

William G. Lane (Resident)

Representative Clients: Chrysler Corp.; The Black and Decker Manufacturing Co.; Thermos Co.; Monroe Auto Equipment Co.; La-Z-Boy Chair Co.; Hughes Aircraft; Budd Co.; Dow Chemical Co.; Procter & Gamble; Kmart Properties.

For full biographical listings, see the Martindale-Hubbell Law Directory

KNOBBE, MARTENS, OLSON & BEAR (AV)

A Partnership including Professional Corporations
620 Newport Center Drive, 16th Floor, 92660
Telephone: 714-760-0404
Telex: 183513 Knobbe NPBH
Fax: 714-760-9502
San Diego, California Office: 501 West Broadway, Suite 1400.
Telephone: 619-235-8550.
Telex: 183513 Knobbe NPBH.
Fax: 619-235-0176.
Riverside, California Office: 3801 University Avenue, Suite 260.
Telephone: 909-781-9231.
Fax: 909-781-4507.

Louis J. Knobbe (P.C.)
Don W. Martens (P.C.)
Gordon H. Olson (P.C.)
James B. Bear
Darrell L. Olson (P.C.)
William B. Bunker
William H. Nieman
Lowell Anderson
Arthur S. Rose
James F. Lesniak
Jerry T. Sewell
John B. Sganga, Jr.
Edward A. Schlatter
W. Gerard von Hoffmann, III
Gregory M. Edalatpour
Joseph R. Re
Catherine J. Tobin
Karen J. Vogel
Andrew H. Simpson
Jeffrey L. Van Hoosear
Daniel E. Altman
Ernest A. Beutler, Jr.
Marguerite L. Gunn
Stephen C. Jensen
Vito A. Canuso, III
Lynda J. Zadra-Symes
William H. Shreve
Steven J. Nataupsky
Michael F. Fedrick
Paul A. Stewart
Joseph F. Jennings
Brenton R. Babcock
Edward J. Treska
Diane M. Reed
Glenn R. Smith
Johnathan A. Barney
William S. Reimus
John R. King
Ronald J. Schoenbaum
Michael G. Del Monte
Richard C. Gilmore
Deborah S. Shepherd
Stephen S. Korniczky
Christine A. Gritzmacher
Raymond T. Chen
John Phillip Giezentanner
Adeel S. Akhtar
Kent M. Chen
Frederick S. Berretta

Representative Clients: AST Research Inc., Irvine; ASM America-Phoenix; NIH Washington, D.C.

For full biographical listings, see the Martindale-Hubbell Law Directory

*OAKLAND,** Alameda Co.

PEZZOLA & REINKE, A PROFESSIONAL CORPORATION (AV)

Suite 1300, Lake Merritt Plaza, 1999 Harrison Street, 94612
Telephone: 510-839-1350
Telecopier: 510-834-7440
San Francisco, California Office: 50 California Street, Suite 470. 94111.
Telephone: 415-989-9710.

Stephen P. Pezzola
Donald C. Reinke
Thomas A. Maier
Thomas C. Armstrong
Bruce D. Whitley

OF COUNSEL

Robert E. Krebs

LEGAL SUPPORT PERSONNEL

Loretta H. Hintz
Mary A. Fitzpatrick

For full biographical listings, see the Martindale-Hubbell Law Directory

PALO ALTO, Santa Clara Co.

ARNOLD, WHITE & DURKEE, A PROFESSIONAL CORPORATION

Five Palo Alto Square Suite 700, 94306-2122
Telephone: 415-812-2929
Facsimile: 415-812-2949
Houston, Texas Office: 750 Bering Drive, 77057-2198; P.O. Box 4433, 77210-4433.
Telephone: 713-787-1400.
Facsimile: 713-789-2679.
Telex: 79-0924.
Austin, Texas Office: 1900 One American Center, 600 Congress Avenue, 78701-3248.
Telephone: 512-418-3000.
Facsimile: 512-474-7577.
Arlington, Virginia Office: 2001 Jefferson Davis Highway, Suite 401, 22202-3604.
Telephone: 703-415-1720.
Facsimile: 703-415-1728.

(See Next Column)

ARNOLD, WHITE & DURKEE A PROFESSIONAL CORPORATION, *Palo Alto—Continued*

Chicago, Illinois Office: 800 Quaker Tower, 321 North Clark Street, 60610-4714.
Telephone: 312-744-0090.
Facsimile: 312-755-4489.
Minneapolis, Minnesota Office: 4850 First Bank Place, 601 Second Avenue South, 55402-4320.
Telephone: 612-321-2800.
Facsimile: 612-321-9600.

Patricia N. Brantley
Michelle D. Kahn
David L. Bilsker
James F. Valentine
Mark K. Dickson

For full biographical listings, see the Martindale-Hubbell Law Directory

BROWN & BAIN (AV)

600 Hansen Way, 94306
Telephone: 415-856-9411
Telecopier: 415-856-6061
Phoenix, Arizona Affiliated Office: Brown & Bain, A Professional Association, 2901 North Central Avenue, P.O. Box 400.
Telephone: 602-351-8000.
Telecopier: 602-351-8516.
Tucson, Arizona Affiliated Office: Brown & Bain, A Professional Association. One South Church Avenue, Nineteenth Floor, P.O. Box 2265.
Telephone: 602-798-7900
Telecopier: 602-798-7945.

RESIDENT PERSONNEL

Lois W. Abraham
Philip P. Berelson
Karl J. Kramer
Don F. Kumamoto
Martin L. Lagod
Christopher R. Ottenweller
Jeffrey G. Randall
D. Bruce Sewell

Susan D. Berney-Key
Chuck P. Ebertin
Robin M. Lightner

COUNSEL

Roger S. Borovoy

For Complete List of Firm Personnel, See General Section

For full biographical listings, see the Martindale-Hubbell Law Directory

FLEHR, HOHBACH, TEST, ALBRITTON & HERBERT (AV)

Suite 200, 850 Hansen Way, 94304-1017
Telephone: 415-494-8700
Telefax: 415-494-8771
San Francisco, California Office: Suite 3400, Four Embarcadero Center.
Telephone: 415-781-1989.

RESIDENT ATTORNEYS

Harold C. Hohbach
Aldo J. Test
Thomas O. Herbert
Edward S. Wright
James A. Sheridan
Gary S. Williams
C. Michael Zimmerman
Steven F. Caserza

ASSOCIATES

William S. Galliani
Janet Elizabeth Muller
Edward N. Bachand
Kevin James Zimmer
Richard Aron Osman
R. Michael Ananian
David C. Ashby
Dennis Y. Lee
Bret Field

OF COUNSEL

Edward B. Gregg
Julian Caplan

For full biographical listings, see the Martindale-Hubbell Law Directory

TOWNSEND AND TOWNSEND KHOURIE AND CREW (AV)

A Partnership including a Professional Corporation
379 Lytton Avenue, 94301-1431
Telephone: 415-326-2400
Telecopier: 415-326-2422
San Francisco, California Office: Twentieth Floor, Steuart Street Tower, One Market Plaza.
Telephone: 415-543-9600.
Telecopier: 415-543-5043.
Seattle, Washington Office: 601 Union Street, Suite 5400.
Telephone: 206-467-9600.
Telecopier: 206-623-6793.

MEMBERS OF FIRM

Kenneth R. Allen (Resident)
Robert C. Colwell (Resident)
Daniel J. Furniss (Resident)
David N. Slone (Resident)
James M. Heslin
Gary T. Aka (Resident)
William M. Smith
Paul C. Haughey (Resident)
Theodore G. Brown, III
Vernon A. Norviel (Resident)
William J. Bohler (Resident)
Karen B. Dow (Resident)

OF COUNSEL

John L. McGannon (Resident)
Henry K. Woodward (Resident)

(See Next Column)

ASSOCIATES

Tracy J. Dunn (Not admitted in CA; Resident)
Joe Liebeschuetz (Resident)
Joseph M. Villeneuve (Resident)
William L. Shaffer
James F. Kurkowski
Richard Takashi Ogawa (Resident)
Theodore T. Herhold (Resident)
Stephen J. Le Blanc
Dexter K. Chin (Not admitted in CA)
Darin J. Gibby
Stephen Y.F. Pang
Heather Slotnick Vance
Michael J. Ritter
Matthew B. Murphy
Mark D. Barrish
Melvin D. Chan
Rosa S. Kim
Margaret A. Powers
John R. Storella (Not admitted in CA)

For full biographical listings, see the Martindale-Hubbell Law Directory

PASADENA, Los Angeles Co.

FREDERICK GOTHA (AV)

Suite 823, 80 South Lake Avenue, 91101
Telephone: 818-796-1849
Telecopier: 818-405-0952

For full biographical listings, see the Martindale-Hubbell Law Directory

*SACRAMENTO,** Sacramento Co.

GERBER, RITCHEY & O'BANION (AV)

5441 Fair Oaks Boulevard, Suite B-1, 95608
Telephone: 916-971-1010
Facsimile: 916-487-0706

MEMBERS OF FIRM

Joseph E. Gerber
James M. Ritchey
John P. O'Banion

For full biographical listings, see the Martindale-Hubbell Law Directory

*SAN DIEGO,** San Diego Co.

BAKER, MAXHAM, JESTER & MEADOR, A PROFESSIONAL CORPORATION (AV)

Symphony Towers, 750 B Street, Suite 2770, 92101
Telephone: 619-233-9004
Facsimile: 619-544-1246 (Groups I, II, III)

Freling E. Baker
Lawrence A. Maxham
Michael H. Jester
Terrance A. Meador
Walter W. Duft

James A. Ward
David A. Hall
R. Kevin Perkins
Dan L. Hubert

OF COUNSEL

Ervin F. Johnston
John C. Lambertsen

Reference: Bank of Southern California.

For full biographical listings, see the Martindale-Hubbell Law Directory

FITCH, EVEN, TABIN & FLANNERY (AV)

4250 Executive Square, Suite 510, 92037
Telephone: 619-552-1311
Telecopier: 619-552-0095
Chicago, Illinois Office: 135 South La Salle Street.
Telephone: 312-372-7842.
Cable Address: "Patlaw".
Telex: 20 6566 Patlaw Cgo.
Telecopier: 312-372-7848.
Washington, D.C. Office: 2305 Wilson Boulevard (Arlington, Virginia, 22201).
Telephone: 703-243-9236.
Telecopier: 703-243-9207.

MEMBERS OF FIRM

Julius Tabin
James J. Schumann (Not admitted in CA)
Bryant R. Gold

OF COUNSEL

Robert R. Meads

Thomas F. Lebens
Robert J. Hampsch (Not admitted in CA)

For full biographical listings, see the Martindale-Hubbell Law Directory

San Diego—Continued

GRAY CARY WARE & FREIDENRICH, A PROFESSIONAL CORPORATION (AV)

Gray Cary Established in 1927
Ware & Freidenrich Established in 1969
401 "B" Street, Suite 1700, 92101
Telephone: 619-699-2700
Telecopier: 619-236-1048
Palo Alto, California Office: 400 Hamilton Avenue.
Telephone: 415-328-6561.
La Jolla, California Office: Suite 575, 1200 Prospect Street.
Telephone: 619-454-9101.
El Centro, California Office: 1224 State Street, P.O. Box 2890.
Telephone: 619-353-6140.

John Allcock
David E. Monahan
Anthony M. Stiegler
James C. Weseman

Cathy A. Bencivengo
Rodney S. Edmonds
Alexander H. Rogers

Representative Clients: Automobile Club of South California; Bank of America; Brooktree Corp.; C. A. Parr (Agencies), Ltd.; IMED; Pacific Bell; McMillin Development Co.; Scripps Clinic and Research Fdtn.; SeaWorld, Inc.; Underwriters at Lloyds; Wells Fargo Bank.

For Complete List of Firm Personnel, See General Section

For full biographical listings, see the Martindale-Hubbell Law Directory

HARNESS, DICKEY & PIERCE (AV)

900 First Interstate Plaza, 401 B Street, 92101
Telephone: 619-238-4122
Telefacsimile: 619-238-0970
Troy, Michigan Office: 5445 Corporate Drive, Suite 400.
Telephone: 810-641-1600. Telefacsimile (All Groups): 810-641-0270.
Ann Arbor, Michigan Office: Suite 555, 301 East Liberty Street.
Telephone: 313-662-5653.
Telefacsimile: 313-662-7813.
Newport Beach, California Office: 4041 MacArthur Boulevard, Suite 400.
Telephone: 714-760-6233.
Telefacsimile: 714-760-6123.
Washington, D.C. Office: 888 Sixteenth Street, N.W.
Telephone: 202-835-7480.
Telefacsimile: 202-835-7487.

Welton B. Whann (Resident)

RESIDENT ASSOCIATE

Donald L. Wenskay (Not admitted in CA)

Representative Clients: Chrysler Corp.; The Black and Decker Manufacturing Co.; Thermos Co.; Monroe Auto Equipment Co.; La-Z-Boy Chair Co.; Hughes Aircraft; Budd Co.; Dow Chemical Co.; Procter & Gamble; Kmart Properties.

For full biographical listings, see the Martindale-Hubbell Law Directory

ROYCE, GRIMM, VRANJES, MCCORMICK & GRAHAM (AV)

A Partnership including Professional Corporations
185 West "F" Street, Suite 200, 92101-6098
Telephone: 619-231-8802
Fax: 619-233-6039
Temecula, California Office: 41877 Enterprise Circle North, Suite 100. 92590.
Telephone: 909-695-3220.

MEMBERS OF FIRM

Gene E. Royce (Professional Corporation)
W. Patrick Grimm (Professional Corporation)
Mark Vranjes (Professional Corporation)
Kathleen McCormick
Kevin R. Graham
A. Carl Yaeckel
Jeffrey Y. Greer

Charles A. Phillips
Stephen M. Hogan
Lisa F. Butler
Gregory D. Stephan
Brian L. Frary
Leslie H. Roe
Michael B. Martin
Larry D. Letofsky
Laurel L. Barry
Michael B Schaefer

For full biographical listings, see the Martindale-Hubbell Law Directory

*SAN FRANCISCO,** San Francisco Co.

FLEHR, HOHBACH, TEST, ALBRITTON & HERBERT (AV)

Suite 3400, Four Embarcadero Center, 94111-4187
Telephone: 415-781-1989
Telefax: 415-398-3249
TWX: 910-372-6669 "FLEHR SFO"
Palo Alto, California Office: Suite 200, 850 Hansen Way.
Telephone: 415-494-8700.
Telefax: 415-494-8771.

(See Next Column)

MEMBERS OF FIRM

Paul D. Flehr (1898-1992)
Elmer S. Albritton (1922-1988)
Harold C. Hohbach (Resident, Palo Alto Office)
Aldo J. Test (Resident, Palo Alto Office)
Thomas O. Herbert (Resident, Palo Alto Office)
Donald N. MacIntosh
Jerry G. Wright
Edward S. Wright (Resident, Palo Alto Office)
David J. Brezner
Richard E. Backus
James A. Sheridan (Resident, Palo Alto Office)
Robert B. Chickering
Gary S. Williams (Resident, Palo Alto Office)
Richard F. Trecartin
C. Michael Zimmerman
Walter H. Dreger
Steven F. Caserza (Resident, Palo Alto Office)

ASSOCIATES

Karen S. Smith
William S. Galliani
Laura L. Kulhanjian
Michael A. Kaufman
Michael L. Louie
Janet Elizabeth Muller (Resident, Palo Alto)
Kevin James Zimmer (Resident, Palo Alto)
Edward N. Bachand (Resident, Palo Alto Office)
Richard Aron Osman (Resident, Palo Alto)
R. Michael Ananian (Resident, Palo Alto Office)
Stephen M. Knauer
Jan P. Brunelle
Bret Field (Resident, Palo Alto Office)
Robin M. Silva
David C. Ashby (Resident, Palo Alto Office)
Dennis Y. Lee (Resident, Palo Alto Office)
Lisa E. Alexander

OF COUNSEL

Edward B. Gregg (Resident, Palo Alto Office)
Julian Caplan (Resident, Palo Alto Office)

LEGAL SUPPORT PERSONNEL

Robert L. McCarthy
Wendy Dea
Laura Forslund
Steven D. Dennison
Cheryl Ann Hernandez
Holly A. Metz

Representative Clients: Genentec; McKesson, Inc.; Safeway Stores, Inc.; Systron Donner Corp.; Watkins-Johnson Co.

For full biographical listings, see the Martindale-Hubbell Law Directory

FLYNN, DELICH & WISE (AV)

Suite 1750, 580 California Street, 94104
Telephone: 415-693-5566
Fax: 415-693-0410
Long Beach, California Office: 1 World Trade Center, Suite 1800.
Telephone: 310-435-2626.
Fax: 310-437-7555.

Sam D. Delich

Representative Clients: American Hawaii Cruises; Holland America Line; Through Transport Mutual Insurance Association, Ltd.; The Britannia Steam Ship Insurance Association Limited; The Steamship Mutual Underwriting Association (Bermuda) Ltd.; General Steamship Corp., Ltd.; Commodore Cruise Line, Ltd.; Interocean Steamship Corporation; Sea-Land Service, Inc.; Hatteras Yachts.

For full biographical listings, see the Martindale-Hubbell Law Directory

THOMAS A. GALLAGHER A PROFESSIONAL CORPORATION (AV)

100 Green Street-3rd Floor, 94111-1302
Telephone: 415-989-8080
Facsimile: 415-989-0910

Thomas A. Gallagher

David N. Lathrop

HAVERSTOCK, MEDLEN & CARROLL (AV)

220 Montgomery Street, Suite 2200, 94104
Telephone: 415-705-8410
Facsimile: 415-397-8338
Norwood, Massachusetts Office: 477 Washington Street, Suite 19.
Telephone: 617-769-0960.
Facsimile: 617-769-0798.
Toledo, Ohio Office: One Seagate, Suite 960.
Telephone: 419-247-1010.
Facsimile: 419-247-1011.

MEMBERS OF FIRM

Thomas B. Haverstock
Virginia Shaw Medlen
Peter G. Carroll

ASSOCIATES

Jonathan O. Owens
Cynthia Soumoff
Diane E. Ingolia
Kamrin T. MacKnight
Lisa K. Levine
Chadd T. Kawai
Todd A. Lorenz
Christopher John Smith

LEGAL SUPPORT PERSONNEL

TECHNICAL CONSULTANTS

Michael Y. Han
Elsebeth M. Baumgartner

(See Next Column)

HAVERSTOCK, MEDLEN & CARROLL, *San Francisco—Continued*

INTERNATIONAL TRADEMARK DEPARTMENT

Daw Aye Cho (Manager)

For full biographical listings, see the Martindale-Hubbell Law Directory

LIMBACH & LIMBACH (AV)

A Partnership including Professional Corporations
2001 Ferry Building, 94111
Telephone: 415-433-4150
Fax: 415-433-8716
San Jose, California Office: 10 Almaden, Suite 1210.
Telephone: 408-291-5225.

MEMBERS OF FIRM

Karl A. Limbach (P.C.)
George C. Limbach (P.C.)
John K. Uilkema (P.C.)
J. William Wigert, Jr., (P.C.)
Philip M. Shaw, Jr., (P.C.)
Neil A. Smith (P.C.)
Carrie L. Walthour
Veronica Colby Devitt
Ronald L. Yin
Gerald T. Sekimura
Michael A. Stallman
Philip A. Girard
Michael J. Pollock
Stephen M. Everett
Deborah A. Bailey-Wells
Maria S. Cefalu
Alfred A. Equitz
W. Patrick Bengtsson
Mark A. Dalla Valle
Charles P. Sammut

ASSOCIATES

Richard A. Nebb
Ian Hardcastle
Richard E. Wawrzyniak
Alan D. Minsk
Mark C. Pickering
Kathleen A. Frost
Harvey J. Anderson, II
David B. Woycechowsky
Alan S. Hodes
Jens E. Hoekendijk
Patricia Coleman James
Alan A. Limbach
Slade E. Smith

OF COUNSEL

J. Thomas McCarthy
Ted Naccarella (Not admitted in CA)

LEGAL SUPPORT PERSONNEL

PATENT AGENTS

Douglas C. Limbach
Michael R. Ward

For full biographical listings, see the Martindale-Hubbell Law Directory

PHILLIPS, MOORE, LEMPIO & FINLEY (AV)

455 Market Street, Suite 1940, 94105-2440
Telephone: 415-882-7024
Facsimile: 415-882-7034
Palo Alto, California Office: 385 Sherman Avenue, Suite 6, 94306-1827.
Telephone: 415-324-1677.
Telefax: 415-324-1678.

MEMBERS OF FIRM

Leonard Phillips (1924-1985)
Hugh D. Finley
Howard M. Peters (Resident at Palo Alto, California Office)
Hana Dolezalova (Resident at Palo Alto, California Office)
Allston L. Jones (Resident at Palo Alto, California Office)
Michael N. Berg

OF COUNSEL

Carlisle M. Moore
Paul S. Lempio

Representative Clients: COM 21, Inc.; Ampro Corp.; Applied Biosystems, Inc.; Barrier Systems, inc.; Bay Packaging & Converting, Inc.; BINDCO Corp.; Blentech Corp.; Brayer Lighting, Inc.; Cable Data; Cable Car Sunglasses.

For full biographical listings, see the Martindale-Hubbell Law Directory

SKJERVEN, MORRILL, MACPHERSON, FRANKLIN & FRIEL (AV)

Suite 800, 601 California Street, 94104
Telephone: 415-986-8383
Telecopier: 415-982-7372
San Jose, California Office: Suite 700, 25 Metro Drive.
Telephone: 408-283-1222.
Telecopier: 408-283-1233.
Austin, Texas Office: Suite 1050, 100 Congress Street.
Telephone: 512-404-3600.
Telecopier: 512-404-3601.

MEMBERS OF FIRM

Richard H. Skjerven (At San Jose, California and Austin, Texas Offices)
Robert B. Morrill
Alan H. MacPherson (Resident, San Jose Office)
Richard K. Franklin (Resident, San Jose Office)
Thomas J. Friel, Jr.
Marc David Freed (Resident, San Jose Office)
Anthony de Alcuaz (Resident, San Jose Office)
Paul J. Winters (Resident, San Jose Office)
Justin T. Beck (Resident, San Jose Office)
Joseph A. Greco (Resident, San Jose Office)
David W. Heid (Resident, San Jose Office)
David H. Carroll (Resident, Austin, Texas Office)
Forrest Gunnison (Resident, San Jose Office)

(See Next Column)

MEMBERS OF FIRM (Continued)

Norman R. Klivans, Jr. (Resident, San Jose Office)
Charles D. Chalmers (Resident, San Jose Office)
Kenneth E. Leeds (Resident, San Jose Office)
Brian Ogonowsky (Resident, San Jose Office)
David E. Steuber (Resident, San Jose Office)
Laura Terlizzi (Resident, San Jose Office)
Edward V. Anderson (Resident, San Jose Office)
Edward C. Kwok (Resident, San Jose Office)
Michelle G. Breit (Resident, San Jose Office)

ASSOCIATES

Michael Shenker (Resident, San Jose Office)
Kimberly Paul Zapata (Resident, San Jose Office)
Scott R. Brown (Resident, San Jose Office)
Patrick T. Bever (Resident, San Jose Office)
James E. Parsons (Resident, San Jose Office)
T. Lester Wallace (Resident, San Jose Office)
Peter H. Kang (Resident, San Jose Office)
Alexandra J. Horne (Resident, San Jose Office)
David T. Millers (Resident, San Jose Office)
E. Eric Hoffman (Resident, San Jose Office)
Omkarmurthy K. Suryadevara (Resident, San Jose Office)
Emily M. Haliday (Resident, San Jose Office)
Elizabeth Ann Hemphill (Resident, San Jose Office)
Philip J. McKay (Resident, San Jose Office)
Lawrence E. Lycke (Resident, San Jose Office)
L. Scott Primak (Resident, San Jose Office)
H. Fredrick Zimmermann (Resident, San Jose Office)
Thomas E. Rossmeissl (Resident, San Jose Office)
Steven M. Levitan (Resident, San Jose Office)
Michael A. Gelblum (Resident, San Jose Office)
Arthur J. Behiel (Resident, San Jose Office)
Michael J. Halbert (Resident, San Jose Office)
Jennifer A. Ochs (Resident, San Jose Office)

SPECIAL COUNSEL

Guy W. Shoup (Resident, San Jose Office)

OF COUNSEL

Thomas S. MacDonald (Resident, San Jose Office)
Ronald J. Meetin (Resident, San Jose Office)

PATENT AGENT

Anthony G. Dervan (Resident, San Jose Office)

Reference: Bank of America.

For full biographical listings, see the Martindale-Hubbell Law Directory

TOWNSEND AND TOWNSEND KHOURIE AND CREW (AV)

A Partnership including a Professional Corporation
Twentieth Floor, Steuart Street Tower, One Market Plaza, 94105-1492
Telephone: 415-543-9600
Cable Address: "Dewey"
TWX: 910-372-6566 Townsend SFO
Telecopier: 415-543-5043
Palo Alto, California Office: 379 Lytton Avenue.
Telephone: 415-326-2400.
Telecopier: 415-326-2422.
Seattle, Washington Office: 601 Union Street, Suite 5400.
Telephone: 206-467-9600.
Telecopier: 206-623-6793.

MEMBERS OF FIRM

Charles E. Townsend (1868-1944)
Anthony B. Diepenbrock
Eugene Crew
William M. Hynes (A Professional Corporation)
Bruce W. Schwab
George M. Schwab
Kenneth R. Allen (Resident, Palo Alto Office)
Daniel J. Furniss (Resident, Palo Alto Office)
James F. Hann
M. Henry Heines
Gary T. Aka (Resident, Palo Alto Office)
James G. Gilliland, Jr.
Mark A. Steiner
E. Lynn Perry
Theodore G. Brown, III (Resident, Palo Alto Office)
Mark T. Jansen
Vernon A. Norviel (Resident, Palo Alto Office)
William J. Bohler (Resident, Palo Alto Office)
Duane H. Mathiowetz
K. T. (Sunny) Cherian
Stephen S. Townsend (1917-1986)
Albert J. Hillman
Paul W. Vapnek
J. Georg Seka
Roger L. Cook
William L. Jaeger
Robert J. Bennett
Robert C. Colwell (Resident, Palo Alto Office)
David N. Slone (Resident, Palo Alto Office)
James M. Heslin (Resident, Palo Alto Office)
William M. Smith (Palo Alto and Seattle)
Charles E. Krueger
Richard L. Grossman
Paul C. Haughey (Resident, Palo Alto Office)
Guy W. Chambers
Kenneth A. Weber
Steven W. Parmelee (Resident in Seattle)
Ellen Lauver Weber
Karen B. Dow (Resident, Palo Alto Office)
A. James Isbester

(See Next Column)

TOWNSEND AND TOWNSEND KHOURIE AND CREW—*Continued*

OF COUNSEL

Charles E. Townsend, Jr.
Dirks B. Foster
Henry K. Woodward (Resident, Palo Alto Office)
Michael N. Khourie
John L. McGannon (Resident, Palo Alto Office)
Edward J. Keeling
John A. Hughes

ASSOCIATES

Michael E. Woods
Margaret C. McHugh
Kevin L. Bastian
Susan M. Spaeth
Philip H. Albert
Tracy J. Dunn (Resident, Palo Alto Office)
R. Gwen Lipsey
Joe Liebeschuetz (Resident, Palo Alto Office)
William L. Shaffer (Resident, Palo Alto Office)
Richard Takashi Ogawa (Resident, Palo Alto Office)
Stephen J. Le Blanc (Resident, Palo Alto Office)
Tom Hunter
William B. Kezer
Darin J. Gibby (Resident, Palo Alto Office)
Larry Mendenhall
Stephen Y.F. Pang (Resident, Palo Alto Office)
Michael J. Ritter (Resident, Palo Alto Office)
David G. Beck
Roger Kennedy
Jonathan Alan Quine
Melvin D. Chan (Resident, Palo Alto Office)
Margaret A. Powers (Resident, Palo Alto Office)
William T. Gallagher
Mark Lee Pettinari
Victoria M. Kalmanson
Paul F. Kirsch
Jennifer C. Pizer
Charles J. Kulas
Paula Chertok
Eugenia Garrett-Wackowski
Babak Sadegh Sani
Joseph M. Villeneuve (Resident, Palo Alto Office)
James F. Kurkowski (Resident, Palo Alto Office)
Norman J. Kruse
Theodore T. Herhold (Resident, Palo Alto Office)
Kurt M. Maschoff (Resident in Seattle)
Dexter K. Chin (Resident, Palo Alto Office)
Shailendra C. Bhumralkar
Marc M. Gorelnik
Dan H. Lang
Heather Lynn Slotnick (Resident, Palo Alto Office)
John Thomas Raffle
Matthew B. Murphy (Resident, Palo Alto Office)
Mark D. Barrish (Resident, Palo Alto Office)
Rosa S. Kim (Resident, Palo Alto Office)
John R. Storella (Resident, Palo Alto Office)

For full biographical listings, see the Martindale-Hubbell Law Directory

*SAN JOSE,** Santa Clara Co.

SKJERVEN, MORRILL, MACPHERSON, FRANKLIN & FRIEL (AV)

Suite 700, 25 Metro Drive, 95110
Telephone: 408-283-1222
Telecopier: 408-283-1233
San Francisco, California Office: Suite 800, 601 California Street.
Telephone: 415-986-8383.
Telecopier: 415-982-7372.
Austin, Texas Office: Suite 1050, 100 Congress Street.
Telephone: 512-404-3600.
Telecopier: 512-404-3601.

MEMBERS OF FIRM

Richard H. Skjerven
Robert B. Morrill (Resident, San Francisco Office)
Alan H. MacPherson
Richard K. Franklin
Thomas J. Friel, Jr. (Resident, San Francisco Office)
Marc David Freed
Anthony de Alcuaz
Paul J. Winters
Justin T. Beck
Joseph A. Greco
David W. Heid
David H. Carroll (Resident, Austin, Texas Office)
Forrest Gunnison
Norman R. Klivans, Jr.
Charles D. Chalmers (Resident, San Francisco Office)
Kenneth E. Leeds
Brian Ogonowsky
David E. Steuber
Laura Terlizzi
Edward V. Anderson
Edward C. Kwok
Michelle G. Breit

ASSOCIATES

Michael Shenker
Kimberly Paul Zapata
Scott R. Brown
Patrick T. Bever
James E. Parsons
T. Lester Wallace
Peter H. Kang
Alexandra J. Horne
David T. Millers
E. Eric Hoffman
Omkarmurthy K. Suryadevara
Emily M. Haliday
Elizabeth Ann Hemphill
Philip J. McKay
Lawrence E. Lycke
William L. Paradice III
L. Scott Primak
H. Fredrick Zimmermann
Thomas E. Rossmeissl
Steven M. Levitan
Michael A. Gelblum
Arthur J. Behiel
Michael J. Halbert
Jennifer A. Ochs

SPECIAL COUNSEL

Guy W. Shoup

OF COUNSEL

Thomas S. MacDonald
Ronald J. Meetin

(See Next Column)

PATENT AGENT

Anthony G. Dervan

Reference: Bank of America.

For full biographical listings, see the Martindale-Hubbell Law Directory

WOODLAND HILLS, Los Angeles Co.

KELLY, BAUERSFELD & LOWRY (AV)

6320 Canoga Avenue Suite 1650, 91367
Telephone: 818-347-7900
Telex: 510 601 8309 KELPAT CA UQ
FAX: 818-340-2859

Ralph B. Pastoriza (1923-1985)
John E. Kelly
Stuart O. Lowry
John D. Bauersfeld
Scott W. Kelley
Janine Rickman Novatt

Representative Clients: J.R. Simplot Co.; Rainbird Sprinkler Manufacturing Corp.; Pudenz-Schulte Medical Research Corp.; Softub, Inc.; Hydrotechnology, Inc.; Center for Homewares Design; Medical Packaging Corp.; Mrs. Gooch's Natural Foods, Inc.

For full biographical listings, see the Martindale-Hubbell Law Directory

COLORADO

*ASPEN,** Pitkin Co.

FREEMAN & JENNER, P.C. (AV Ⓣ)

215 South Monarch Street, Suite 202, 81611
Telephone: 303-925-3400
FAX: 303-925-4043
Bethesda, Maryland Office: 3 Bethesda Metro Center, Suite 1410.
Telephone: 301-907-7747.
FAX: 301-907-9877.
Washington, D.C. Office: 1000 16th Street, N.W., Suite 300.
Telephone: 301-907-7747.

Martin H. Freeman

*BOULDER,** Boulder Co.

GREENLEE AND WINNER, P.C. (AV)

5370 Manhattan Circle, Suite 201, 80303
Telephone: 303-499-8080
Facsimile: 303-499-8089
E-mail: Winner @ Greenwin . Com

Lorance L. Greenlee
Ellen P. Winner

Barbara A. Gyure
Charles E. Rohrer

LEGAL SUPPORT PERSONNEL
PATENT AGENTS

Sally A. Sullivan
Jennie M. Caruthers
Donna M. Ferber
Alison A. Langford

Reference: Bank One.

For full biographical listings, see the Martindale-Hubbell Law Directory

*COLORADO SPRINGS,** El Paso Co.

HANES & SCHUTZ, P.C. (AV)

7222 Commerce Center Drive Suite 243, 80916
Telephone: 719-260-7900
Denver Line: 303-740-9694
Fax: 719-260-7904

Richard W. Hanes
Tim Schutz

For full biographical listings, see the Martindale-Hubbell Law Directory

*DENVER,** Denver Co.

DORR, CARSON, SLOAN & PETERSON, P.C. (AV)

3010 East Sixth Avenue, 80206
Telephone: 303-333-3010
FAX: 303-333-1470

Robert C. Dorr
W. Scott Carson
Jack C. Sloan
Gary H. Peterson
Thomas S. Birney
Stuart Langley

OF COUNSEL

Christopher H. Munch
Steve A. Mains

Representative Clients: Winegard Co.; Ball Corp.; Hewlett Packard; Colorado State University Research Foundation; Colorado Memory Systems, Inc.; Steam Way International; Big Sur Waterbeds; Taco John's International; Micron Technology; University of Denver; The Denver Post Co.

For full biographical listings, see the Martindale-Hubbell Law Directory

Denver—Continued

HOLLAND & HART (AV)

Suite 2900, 555 Seventeenth Street, P.O. Box 8749, 80201
Telephone: 303-295-8000
Cable Address: "Holhart Denver"
Telecopier: 303-295-8261
TWX: 910-931-0568
Denver Tech Center, Colorado Office: Suite 1050, 4601 DTC Boulevard.
Telephone: 303-290-1600.
Telecopier: 303-290-1606.
Aspen, Colorado Office: 600 East Main Street.
Telephone: 303-925-3476.
Telecopier: 303-925-9367.
Boulder, Colorado Office: Suite 500, 1050 Walnut.
Telephone: 303-473-2700.
Telecopier: 303-473-2720.
Colorado Springs, Colorado Office: Suite 1000, 90 S. Cascade Avenue.
Telephone: 719-475-7730.
Telex: 82077 SHHTLX.
Telecopier: 719-634-2461.
Washington, D.C. Office: Suite 310, 1001 Pennsylvania Avenue, N.W.
Telephone: 202-638-5500.
Telecopier: 202-737-8998.
Boise, Idaho Office: Suite 1400, West One Plaza, 101 South Capitol Boulevard, P.O. Box 2527.
Telephone: 208-342-5000.
Telecopier: 208-343-8869.
Billings, Montana Office: Suite 1500, First Interstate Center, 401 North 31st Street, P.O. Box 639.
Telephone: 406-252-2166.
Telecopier: 406-252-1669.
Salt Lake City, Utah Office: Suite 880, 111 East Broadway.
Telephone: 801-578-6000.
FAX: 801-578-6010.
Cheyenne, Wyoming Office: Holland & Hart, A Partnership including Professional Corporations, Suite 500, 2020 Carey Avenue, P.O. Box 1347.
Telephone: 307-778-4200.
Telecopier: 307-778-8175.
Jackson, Wyoming Office: Holland & Hart, A Partnership including Professional Corporations, Suite 2, 175 South King Street, P.O. Box 68.
Telephone: 307-739-9741.
Telecopier: 307-739-9744.

MEMBERS OF FIRM

Ralph F. Crandell
Gary M. Polumbus
Jane Michaels
James E. Hartley
John R. Ley
Gregg I. Anderson
Kevin S. Crandell
William J. Kubida

ASSOCIATES

Carol W. Burton
Charles C. Cary (Not admitted in CO)
Donald A. Degnan
Robert H. Kelly (Not admitted in CO)
Lee R. Osman
John B. Phillips

BOULDER, COLORADO PARTNER

Scott Havlick

OF COUNSEL

Homer L. Knearl
Earl C. Hancock
Francis A. Sirr

BOULDER, COLORADO ASSOCIATE

Jennifer L. Bales

COLORADO SPRINGS, COLORADO PARTNER

Gary R. Burghart (Resident)

BOISE, IDAHO RESIDENT ASSOCIATES

Kim J. Dockstader
Dana Lieberman Hofstetter

BILLINGS, MONTANA PARTNER

James M. Ragain

CHEYENNE, WYOMING RESIDENT ASSOCIATE

Susan E. Laser-Bair

For Complete List of Firm Personnel, See General Section

For full biographical listings, see the Martindale-Hubbell Law Directory

HOLME ROBERTS & OWEN LLC (AV)

Suite 4100, 1700 Lincoln, 80203
Telephone: 303-861-7000
Telex: 45-4460
Telecopier: 303-866-0200
Boulder, Colorado Office: Suite 400, 1401 Pearl Street.
Telephone: 303-444-5955.
Telecopier: 303-444-1063.
Colorado Springs, Colorado Office: Suite 1300, 90 South Cascade Avenue.
Telephone: 719-473-3800.
Telecopier: 719-633-1518.
Salt Lake City, Utah Office: Suite 1100, 111 East Broadway.
Telephone: 801-521-5800.
Telecopier: 801-521-9639.

(See Next Column)

London, England Office: 4th Floor, Mellier House, 26a Albemarle Street.
Telephone: 44-171-499-8776.
Telecopier: 44-171-499-7769.
Moscow, Russia Office: 14 Krivokolenny Pr., Suite 30, 101000.
Telephone: 095-925-7816.
Telecopier: 095-923-2726.

MEMBERS OF FIRM

Randy G. Bobier (Colorado Springs Office)
Paul E. Smith (Boulder Office)

SPECIAL COUNSEL

David Akers Weinstein

ASSOCIATE

Robert J. Kaukol (Colorado Springs Office)

For Complete List of Firm Personnel, See General Section

For full biographical listings, see the Martindale-Hubbell Law Directory

SHERIDAN ROSS & MCINTOSH, A PROFESSIONAL CORPORATION (AV)

1700 Lincoln Street Suite 3500, 80203
Telephone: 303-863-9700
Facsimile: 303-863-0223

Michael D. McIntosh
David F. Zinger
Lesley Witt Craig
George G. Matava
Thomas R. Marsh
Craig C. Groseth
Michael L. Tompkins
Todd P. Blakely
Gary J. Connell
Susan Pryor Willson
Christopher J. Kulish
Sabrina Crowley Stavish
James L. Johnson
Lewis D. Hansen
Joseph E. Kovarik
Robert R. Brunelli
Kent A. Fischmann
Douglas W. Swartz
John R. Posthumus
Ross E. Breyfogle
Mark H. Snyder
Kevin P. Moran
Bruce A. Kugler
Jeffrey A. Divney
Jed W. Caven
David F. Dockery

OF COUNSEL

Philip H. Sheridan (P.C.)

LEGAL SUPPORT PERSONNEL

TECHNICAL SPECIALISTS

Carol Talkington Verser
Dennis J. Dupray
Nadine C. Chien

PARALEGALS

Cynthia Rapp
Janet E. Balent
Peggy West
Michele McCoy

Representative Clients: Band-It-Houdaille, Inc.; Celestial Seasonings, Inc.; Norgren Co.
Reference: Norwest Bank.

For full biographical listings, see the Martindale-Hubbell Law Directory

CONNECTICUT

FAIRFIELD, Fairfield Co.

PERMAN & GREEN (AV)

425 Post Road, 06430-6232
Telephone: 203-259-1800
Facsimile: 203-255-5170

MEMBER OF FIRM

Clarence A. Green

ASSOCIATES

David M. Warren (Not admitted in CT)
Albert W. Hilburger
Harry F. Smith
Mark F. Harrington
Thomas L. Tully
David N. Koffsky
Michael J. Tully (Not admitted in CT)
John J. Goodwin (Not admitted in CT)

OF COUNSEL

Donald C. Caulfield

For full biographical listings, see the Martindale-Hubbell Law Directory

*HARTFORD,** Hartford Co.

HAYES & REINSMITH (AV)

Thirty-Fourth Floor, CityPlace, 185 Asylum Street, 06103-3406
Telephone: 203-727-9956
Telecopier: 203-727-9765

MEMBERS OF FIRM

Donald J. Hayes
R. William Reinsmith

For full biographical listings, see the Martindale-Hubbell Law Directory

MILFORD, New Haven Co.

MELVIN I. STOLTZ (AV)

51 Cherry Street, 06460
Telephone: 203-874-8183
Facsimile: 203-878-9607

For full biographical listings, see the Martindale-Hubbell Law Directory

*NEW HAVEN,** New Haven Co.

BACHMAN & LAPOINTE, P.C. (AV)

900 Chapel Street, Suite 1201, 06510
Telephone: 203-777-6628
Cable Address: "Balapat" New Haven
Telex: 710-465-4066
FAX: 203-865-0297

Robert H. Bachman (Not admitted in CT)
Gregory P. LaPointe
Barry L. Kelmachter

Richard S. Strickler (Not admitted in CT)
George A. Coury
Bryan D. Rockwell

For full biographical listings, see the Martindale-Hubbell Law Directory

WIGGIN & DANA (AV)

One Century Tower, 06508-1832
Telephone: 203-498-4400
Telefax: 203-782-2889
Hartford, Connecticut Office: One CityPlace.
Telephone: 203-297-3700.
FAX: 203-525-9380.
Stamford, Connecticut Office: Three Stamford Plaza, 301 Tresser Boulevard.
Telephone: 203-363-7600.
Telefax: 203-363-7676.

MEMBERS OF FIRM

J. Drake Turrentine (Resident at Stamford)
Mary R. Norris

COUNSEL

Dale L. Carlson
William A. Simons (Not admitted in CT)

ASSOCIATES

Gregory S. Rosenblatt (Not admitted in CT)
Laura Wright Wooton (Resident at Stamford)

For Complete List of Firm Personnel, See General Section

For full biographical listings, see the Martindale-Hubbell Law Directory

SIMSBURY, Hartford Co.

LAW OFFICE OF VICTOR E. LIBERT (AV)

965 Hopmeadow Street, P.O. Box 538, 06070-0538
Telephone: 203-651-9321
Fax: 203-651-5735

ASSOCIATE

Frederick A. Spaeth

For full biographical listings, see the Martindale-Hubbell Law Directory

STAMFORD, Fairfield Co.

CHAPMAN & FENNELL (AV)

Three Landmark Square, 06901
Telephone: 203-353-8000
Telecopier: 203-353-8799
New York, New York Office: 330 Madison Avenue.
Telephone: 212-687-3600.
Washington, D.C. Office: 2000 L Street, N.W., Suite 200.
Telephone: 202-822-9351.

MEMBERS OF FIRM

John Haven Chapman
Philip M. Chiappone (Resident, New York, N.Y. Office)
Darrell K. Fennell (Resident, New York, N.Y. Office)
Peter S. Gummo
D. Seeley Hubbard
Eric S. Kamisher (Resident, New York, N.Y. Office)
Brian E. Moran
Victor L. Zimmermann, Jr.

ASSOCIATE

Barton Meyerhoff (Not admitted in CT)

OF COUNSEL

Kevin T. Hoffman
Carol E. Meltzer (Resident, New York, N.Y. Office)
Brainard S. Patton
E. Gabriel Perle (Not admitted in CT)
Victor J. Toth (Resident, Washington, D.C. Office)
Michael Winger (Resident, New York, N.Y. Office)

For full biographical listings, see the Martindale-Hubbell Law Directory

ST. ONGE STEWARD JOHNSTON & REENS (AV)

986 Bedford Street, 06905
Telephone: 203-324-6155
Telecopier: 203-327-1096
New Haven, Connecticut Office: 88 Prospect Street.
Telephone: 203-562-4043.

Ronald J. St. Onge
Louis H. Reens
Thaddius J. Carvis
Gene S. Winter
William J. Speranza
James R. Cartiglia
Stephen P. McNamara
Mary M. Krinsky
Wesley W. Whitmyer, Jr.
Martha B. Allard

COUNSEL

Albert C. Johnston

For full biographical listings, see the Martindale-Hubbell Law Directory

DELAWARE

*WILMINGTON,** New Castle Co.

CONNOLLY, BOVE, LODGE & HUTZ (AV)

1220 Market Street, P.O. Box 2207, 19899-2207
Telephone: 302-658-9141
Telecopier: 302-658-5614
Cable Address: "Artcon"
Telex: 83-5477

Arthur G. Connolly (Emeritus)
James M. Mulligan, Jr.
Arthur G. Connolly, Jr.
Rudolf E. Hutz
Harold Pezzner
John D. Fairchild (Not admitted in DE)
Richard M. Beck (Not admitted in DE)
Paul E. Crawford
Stanley C. Macel, III
Thomas M. Meshbesher
George Pazuniak
N. Richard Powers
Jeffrey B. Bove
Collins J. Seitz, Jr.
Patricia Smink Rogowski
Mary W. Bourke
R. Eric Hutz
Robert G. McMorrow, Jr. (Not admitted in DE)
Ashley I. Pezzner (Not admitted in DE)
William E. McShane (Not admitted in DE)
James T. Moore (Not admitted in DE)
Gerard M. O'Rourke

For Complete List of Firm Personnel, See General Section

For full biographical listings, see the Martindale-Hubbell Law Directory

DISTRICT OF COLUMBIA

WASHINGTON, D.C. Co.

* indicates certain Bar Register subscribers, in cities of comparable size and importance, who maintain an additional office in Washington, D.C. and who have arranged for representation as a part of the Washington, D.C. listings that follow

*** BAKER & BOTTS, L.L.P.** (AV)

A Registered Limited Liability Partnership
The Warner, 1299 Pennsylvania Avenue, N.W., 20004-2400
Telephone: 202-639-7700
Fax: 202-639-7832
Houston, Texas Office: One Shell Plaza, 910 Louisiana.
Telephone: 713-229-1234.
Austin, Texas Office: 1600 San Jacinto Center, 98 San Jacinto Boulevard.
Telephone: 512-322-2500.
Dallas, Texas Office: 2001 Ross Avenue.
Telephone: 214-953-6500.
New York, New York Office: 805 Third Avenue, Suite 2000.
Telephone: 212-705-5000.
Moscow, Russian Federation Office: 10 ul. Pushkinskaya, 103031.
Telephone: 7095/921-5300 (Local); 7501/929-7070 (International).

MEMBERS OF FIRM

Scott F. Partridge
Rodger L. Tate

ASSOCIATES

James B. Arpin
Christopher C. Campbell
James G. Gatto
Jay B. Johnson
Charles B. Lobsenz
James Remenick

For Complete List of Firm Personnel, See General Section

For full biographical listings, see the Martindale-Hubbell Law Directory

Washington—Continued

BANNER, BIRCH, MCKIE & BECKETT (AV)

Eleventh Floor, 1001 G Street, N.W., 20001-4597
Telephone: 202-508-9100
Cable Address: "Bankett"
Telex: 197430 BBMB UT
Facsimile: 202-508-9299; 508-9298; 508-9297

MEMBERS OF FIRM

Donald W. Banner
Edward F. McKie, Jr.
William W. Beckett
Dale H. Hoscheit
Alan S. Cooper
Joseph M. Potenza
Alan I. Cantor
James A. Niegowski
Barry L. Grossman
Joseph M. Skerpon
Kathy J. McKnight
Thomas L. Peterson
Nina L. Medlock
William J. Fisher
Thomas H. Jackson

ASSOCIATES

Lance G. Johnson
Sarah A. Kagan
Bruce S. Shapiro
Mary Gronlund
Steven P. Schad
Victor W. Marton (Not admitted in DC)
Eric T. Fingerhut
Wendi L. Weinstein
Michael J. Shea (Not admitted in DC)
Christopher L. McKee
Scott M. Alter
Richild A. Stewart
Laurence H. Posorske (Not admitted in DC)
Robert S. Katz
Robert F. Altherr, Jr.
Daniel E. Fisher
Lucille Pratt Nichols
Gary D. Fedorochko (Not admitted in DC)
Nathan W. McCutcheon (Not admitted in DC)
John D. Zele (Not admitted in DC)
Patricia E. Hong
Adriana C.L. Suringa
Susan A. Wolffe

COUNSEL

Harold J. Birch
Edward P. Grattan (Not admitted in DC)
Franklin D. Wolffe

For full biographical listings, see the Martindale-Hubbell Law Directory

BEVERIDGE, DEGRANDI, WEILACHER & YOUNG (AV)

Suite 800, 1850 M Street, N.W., 20036
Telephone: 202-659-2811
Cable Address: "Jemead"
Telex: WUI 64470; WU 89-2393;
Telecopier: 202-659-1462

MEMBERS OF FIRM

Andrew B. Beveridge (1915-1972)
Joseph A. DeGrandi
Robert G. Weilacher
Richard G. Young
Michael A. Makuch
Bernard A. Meany (Not admitted in DC)
Dennis C. Rodgers
Maurice U. Cahn
William J. Bundren

CONSULTANT ON THE LAWS OF JAPAN

Yoichiro Yamaguchi (Not admitted in DC)

ASSOCIATES

Helen M. McCarthy
Helen Hill Minsker
G. Byron Stover
William Frank Rauchholz
Robert Jones Worrall
Thomas L. Evans (Not admitted in DC)

OF COUNSEL

Leroy G. Sinn

PATENT AGENT

Qixia Zhang

LEGAL SUPPORT PERSONNEL

Joseph E. Washington

Reference: First American Bank, Washington, D.C.

For full biographical listings, see the Martindale-Hubbell Law Directory

CUSHMAN DARBY & CUSHMAN, L.L.P. (AV)

1100 New York Avenue, N.W. Ninth Floor, East Tower, 20005
Telephone: 202-861-3000
Telex: 6714627 CUSH;
Telefax G 3/2: 202-822-0944; 202-822-0678; 202-822-0679

Arlon V. Cushman (1892-1950)
John J. Darby (1920-1950)
William Michael Cushman (1925-1964)

MEMBERS OF FIRM

Paul N. Kokulis
Raymond F. Lippitt
Gearry Lloyd Knight, Jr.
Carl G. Love
Edgar H. Martin
William K. West, Jr.
Kevin E. Joyce
Edward M. Prince
Donald B. Deaver
David W. Brinkman
George M. Sirilla
Donald J. Bird
W. Warren Taltavull, III
Susan Tucker Brown
Peter W. Gowdey
Dale S. Lazar
Glenn J. Perry
Kendrew H. Colton
Chris Comuntzis
Richard L. Kirkpatrick

(See Next Column)

MEMBERS OF FIRM (Continued)

Lawrence Harbin
Wallace G. Walter
Paul E. White, Jr.
Stephen L. Sulzer
Sheldon H. Klein
Michelle N. Lester
Jeffrey A. Simenauer
Robert A. Molan
G. Paul Edgell

ASSOCIATES

William P. Atkins
Jack S. Barufka (Not admitted in DC)
Brian J. Beatus (Not admitted in DC)
James D. Berquist
Thomas M. Blasey
William H. Bollman
Gregory P. Brummett (Not admitted in DC)
Marlana Kathryn Chapin
Barry P. Golob
Michael W. Haas (Not admitted in DC)
Adam R. Hess (Not admitted in DC)
Stuart T. F. Huang
David A. Jakopin
Timothy J. Klima
Kevin T. Kramer
Jeffrey Scott Melcher
Mark G. Paulson (Not admitted in DC)
Dante J. Picciano (Not admitted in DC)
Edward J. Stemberger
Joerg-Uwe Szipl

COUNSEL

Howard D. Doescher
Frederick S. Frei
Lawrence A. Hymo
Allen Kirkpatrick
John P. Moran
Gary J. Rinkerman
Thomas G. Wiseman (Not admitted in DC)

Reference: Sovran Bank/D.C. National, Washington D.C.

For full biographical listings, see the Martindale-Hubbell Law Directory

*** DICKINSON, WRIGHT, MOON, VAN DUSEN & FREEMAN (AV)**

Suite 800, 1901 L Street, N.W., 20036-3506
Telephone: 202-457-0160
Facsimile: 202-659-1559
Detroit, Michigan Office: 500 Woodward Avenue, Suite 4000.
Telephone: 313-223-3500.
Facsimile: 313-223-3598.
Bloomfield Hills, Michigan Office: 525 North Woodward Avenue, Suite 2000.
Telephone: 810-433-7200.
Facsimile: 810-433-7274.
Grand Rapids, Michigan Office: 200 Ottawa Avenue, N.W., Suite 900.
Telephone: 616-458-1300.
Facsimile: 616-458-6753.
Lansing, Michigan Office: Suite 200, 215 South Washington Square.
Telephone: 517-371-1730.
Facsimile: 517-487-4700.
Chicago, Illinois Office: 225 West Washington, Suite 400.
Telephone: 312-220-0300.
Facsimile: 312-220-0021.
Warsaw, Poland Office: 46 Wilcza Street, 4th Floor, 00-679.
Telephone: (48-22) 299-241.
Facsimile: (48-2) 628-4107. Komertel Satellite Phone: (48-39) 121-510.

RESIDENT PARTNERS

Michael T. Platt
Jeffrey M. Petrash
Kirk Howard Betts
William E. Elwood
Samuel D. Littlepage
Conrad J. Clark

RESIDENT OF COUNSEL

Lucien N. Nedzi
Bruce A. Tassan
Marc A. Bergsman
Jill M. Barker

For full biographical listings, see the Martindale-Hubbell Law Directory

KENNETH R. FEINBERG & ASSOCIATES (AV)

1120 20th Street, N.W. Suite 740 South, 20036
Telephone: 202-371-1110
Fax: 202-962-9290
New York, N.Y. Office: 780 3rd Avenue, Suite 2202.
Telephone: 212-527-9600.
Fax: 212-527-9611.

ASSOCIATES

Deborah E. Greenspan
Michael K. Rozen (Not admitted in DC)
Peter H. Woodin (Not admitted in DC)

For full biographical listings, see the Martindale-Hubbell Law Directory

FINNEGAN, HENDERSON, FARABOW, GARRETT & DUNNER (AV)

Suite 700, 1300 I Street, N.W., 20005-3315
Telephone: 202-408-4000
Cable Address: "Finderbow"
Telex: 440275 ITT; 248740 RCA;
Facsimile: 202-408-4400
Tokyo, Japan Office: Richard V. Burgujian, Gaikokuho Jimu Bengoshi Jimusho, Toranomon No. 45 Mori Building, Third Floor, 1-5, Toranomon 5-chome Minato-Ku.
Telephone: 0081-3-3431-6943.
Facsimile: 0081-3-3431-6945.

(See Next Column)

FINNEGAN, HENDERSON, FARABOW, GARRETT & DUNNER—*Continued*

Brussels, Belgium Office: Avenue Louise 326, Box 37, 1050.
Telephone: 011-322-646-0353.
Facsimile: 011-322-646-2135.

MEMBERS OF FIRM

Marcus B. Finnegan (1927-1979)
Douglas B. Henderson
Ford F. Farabow, Jr.
Arthur S. Garrett
Donald R. Dunner
Brian G. Brunsvold
Tipton D. Jennings IV
Jerry D. Voight
Laurence R. Hefter
Kenneth E. Payne
Herbert H. Mintz
C. Larry O'Rourke
Albert J. Santorelli
Michael C. Elmer
Richard H. Smith
Stephen L. Peterson
John M. Romary
Bruce C. Zotter
Dennis P. O'Reilley
Allen M. Sokal
Robert D. Bajefsky
Richard Lee Stroup
David W. Hill
Thomas L. Irving (Resident Partner, Brussels, Belgium Office)
Charles E. Lipsey
Thomas W. Winland
Basil J. Lewris
Robert J. Gaybrick
Martin I. Fuchs
E. Robert Yoches
Barry W. Graham
Susan Haberman Griffen
Richard B. Racine
Thomas H. Jenkins III
Robert E. Converse, Jr.
Clair X. Mullen, Jr.
Christopher P. Foley
John C. Paul
Roger D. Taylor
Griffith B. Price, Jr.
John F. Hornick
Robert D. Litowitz
David M. Kelly
Kenneth John Meyers
Carol P. Einaudi
Walter Y. Boyd, Jr.
Steven M. Anzalone
Darrel C. Karl (Not admitted in DC)
Jean Burke Fordis
Barbara Clarke McCurdy
James K. Hammond (Not admitted in DC)
Richard V. Burgujian (Resident, Tokyo, Japan Office)
John Michael Jakes
John C. Lowe

COUNSEL

Arthur J. Levine
George E. Hutchinson
Herbert W. Patterson (Not admitted in DC)
William T. McClain
Wilford L. Wisner (Not admitted in DC)
Robert F. Ziems
Edward F. Possessky
Robert J. Eichelburg
Ernest F. Chapman (Not admitted in DC)
Charles S. Hall
Wayne W. Herrington
Don O. Burley
Robert A. Cahill (Not admitted in DC)
Liam O'Grady (Not admitted in DC)
Gerard P. Rooney

ASSOCIATES

Dirk D. Thomas
Thomas W. Banks
Christopher P. Isaac
Bryan C. Diner
William H. Pratt
M. Paul Barker
Gerson S. Panitch
David S. Forman
Vincent P. Kovalick (Not admitted in DC)
James W. Edmondson
Michael R. McGurk
Mark S. Sommers
Jeffrey A. Berkowitz (Not admitted in DC)
Mark R. Shanks
Cheri M. Taylor
Joann M. Neth
Michael D. Kaminski
Kenneth M. Frankel
Bruce K. Lagerman
Mark W. Lauroesch
Michael R. Kelly
Judy Garcia Barrett
Michael J. Bell
Luke Andrew Kilyk (Not admitted in DC)
Jane E. R. Potter
Kenneth J. Nunnenkamp
Michael K. Kirschner
Toni-Junell Herbert (Not admitted in DC)
David C. Gardiner, Jr.
Linda S. Evans
Jeffrey M. Karmilovich
Jeffrey David Karceski
Glenn E. J. Murphy (Not admitted in DC)
Michael L. Leetzow
Carla C. Calcagno
John G. Smith
David Avrum Manspeizer
Linda A. Wadler
Lori-Ann Johnson (Not admitted in DC)
Michael J. Blake
Andrew E. Rawlins (Not admitted in DC)
Brian C. Altmiller (Not admitted in DC)
Jeffrey A. Lindeman (Not admitted in DC)
James P. Longfellow
Donald C. Kordich
R. Bruce Bower
Mary S. Jones (Not admitted in DC)
Colleen Superko (Not admitted in DC)
Thomas H. Martin (Not admitted in DC)
Lavanya S. Ratnam (Not admitted in DC)
David L. Soltz (Not admitted in DC)
Lisa F. Peller
Stuart H. Kupinsky
Randi S. Kremer (Not admitted in DC)
Susan L. Christenberry (Not admitted in DC)
Ronald S. Hermenau
Thalia V. Warnement
Michele C. Bosch (Not admitted in DC)
Howard Warren Levine (Not admitted in DC)
Michele M. Schafer
Leslie I. Bookoff (Not admitted in DC)
Stacey A. Barlow
Alan W. Hammond (Not admitted in DC)
Linda S. Paine-Powell
John R. Alison
Stasia L. Ogden (Not admitted in DC)
Anthony M. Gutowski (Not admitted in DC)
Donald R. McPhail

(See Next Column)

ASSOCIATES (Continued)

Robert C. Millonig
Barbara R. Rudolph (Not admitted in DC)
Jeff E. Schwartz
James B. Monroe (Not admitted in DC)

Reference: Crestar Bank, N.A., Washington, D.C.

For full biographical listings, see the Martindale-Hubbell Law Directory

FISH & RICHARDSON (AV)

601 13th Street N.W., 20005
Telephone: 202-783-5070
Telecopier: 202-783-2331
Boston, Massachusetts Office: 225 Franklin Street.
Telephone: 617-542-5070.
Telecopier: 617-542-8906.
Houston, Texas Office: One Riverway, Suite 1200.
Telephone: 713-629-5070.
Telecopier: 713-629-7811.
Menlo Park, California Office: 2200 Sand Hill Road, Suite 100.
Telephone: 415-854-5277.
Telecopier: 415-854-0875.
Minneapolis, Minnesota Office: 2500 One Financial Plaza, 120 South Sixth Street.
Telephone: 612-335-5070.
Facsimile: 612-288-9696.

Frederick P. Fish (1855-1930)
W. K. Richardson (1859-1951)
Rene D. Tegtmeyer
Steven E. Lipman
Ralph A. Mittelberger
Barry E. Bretschneider
Terry G. Mahn
Walter E. Steimel, Jr. (Not admitted in DC)
Arnold P. Lutzker
Scott C. Harris

Randolph A. Smith (Not admitted in DC)
Lynn E. Eccleston
Michael R. Dzwonczyk
Gary S. Levenson
Monique L. Cordray
Keith A. Barritt
John F. Hayden (Not admitted in DC)

For full biographical listings, see the Martindale-Hubbell Law Directory

* FITZPATRICK, CELLA, HARPER & SCINTO (AV)

1001 Pennsylvania Avenue, N.W., 20004-2505
Telephone: 202-347-8100
Facsimile: 202-347-8136
New York, N.Y. Office: 277 Park Avenue.
Telephone: 212-758-2400. International-
Telex: FCHS 236262.
Cable Address: "Fitzcel New York".
Facsimile: 212-758-2982.
Orange County, California Office: 650 Town Center Drive, Suite 740, Costa Mesa.
Telephone: 714-540-8700.
Facsimile: 714-540-9823.

RESIDENT PARTNERS

Robert C. Kline
John W. Behringer
Lawrence A. Stahl
William M. Wannisky
Warren E. Olsen
Richard P. Bauer

RESIDENT ASSOCIATES

Christopher Philip Wrist
Gary M. Jacobs
Scott D. Malpede (Not admitted in DC)
Steven E. Warner
Thomas J. O'Connell
Mark A. Williamson
John T. Whelan
Jean K. Dudek
Anne M. Maher (Not admitted in DC)
William J. Zak, Jr. (Not admitted in DC)
Daniel S. Glueck (Not admitted in DC)
Brian Lee Klock (Not admitted in DC)

For full biographical listings, see the Martindale-Hubbell Law Directory

HENDERSON & STURM (AV)

Suite 701, 1747 Pennsylvania Avenue, N.W., 20006-4604
Telephone: 202-296-3854
Fax: 202-223-9606
Des Moines, Iowa Office: 1213 Midland Building, 206 Sixth Avenue.
Telephone: 515-288-9589.
Fax: 515-288-4860.
Davenport, Iowa Office: 204 Northwest Bank Building-Downtown, 101 West Second Street.
Telephone: 319-323-9731.
Fax: 319-323-9709.
Omaha, Nebraska Office: Suite 330, 1125 South 103rd Street.
Telephone: 402-398-9000.
Fax: 402-398-9005.

MEMBERS OF FIRM

William H. Wright (Resident)
Martin G. Mullen (Not admitted in DC; Resident)

For full biographical listings, see the Martindale-Hubbell Law Directory

Washington—Continued

JACOBSON, PRICE, HOLMAN & STERN (AV)

The Jenifer Building, 400 Seventh Street, N.W., 20004
Telephone: 202-638-6666
Cable Address: "Lawpat"
Telex: RCA 248593 IDEA UR
Telefax: 202-393-5350; 202-393-5351; 202-393-5352 E-Mail: MC I MAILBOX 502-8614

MEMBERS OF FIRM

Harvey B. Jacobson, Jr.
D. Douglas Price
John Clarke Holman
Marvin R. Stern
Simor L. Moskowitz
Michael R. Slobasky
Marsha G. Gentner
Jonathan L. Scherer
Stanford W. Berman
Irwin M. Aisenberg

ASSOCIATES

Leesa N. Weiss
John E. McKie
Carmen B. Pili-Curtis

LEGAL SUPPORT PERSONNEL
PATENT AGENTS

Homer A. Smith
Gordon C. Fell
David W. Selesnick
Guillermo Enrique Baeza
Tania J. Keeble

OF COUNSEL

Thomas A. Mauro
Randall G. Erdley
(Not admitted in DC)
William E. Player

For full biographical listings, see the Martindale-Hubbell Law Directory

*** KENYON & KENYON** (AV)

1025 Connecticut Avenue, N.W., 20036
Telephone: 202-429-1776
Telecopier: (202) 429-0796, Groups II & III
New York, N.Y. Office: One Broadway.
Telephone: 212-425-7200.
Frankfurt, Germany Office: Bockenheimer Landstrasse 97-99, 60325 Frankfurt am Main.
Telephone: (69) 97-58-050.
Telecopier: (69) 97-58-05-99.

RESIDENT PARTNERS

Richard G. Kline
John C. Altmiller
Philip J. McCabe
Edward T. Colbert
William K. Wells, Jr.

RESIDENT COUNSEL

Donald Knox Duvall

RESIDENT OF COUNSEL

John M. Rommel

RESIDENT ASSOCIATES

Frank Pietrantonio
James Prizant
Patrick J. Fay
(Not admitted in DC)
Suzanne M. Parker
Robert D. Anderson
P. McCoy Smith
(Not admitted in DC)
Joseph A. Micallef
(Not admitted in DC)
Mark M. Supko
(Not admitted in DC)
Shawn W. O'Down
William T. Enos

For full biographical listings, see the Martindale-Hubbell Law Directory

LANE, AITKEN & MCCANN (AV)

Watergate Office Building, 2600 Virginia Avenue, N.W., 20037
Telephone: 202-337-5556
Telecopier: 202-337-8073

MEMBERS OF FIRM

Richard L. Aitken
Clifton E. McCann
John P. Shannon, Jr.
Laurence J. Marhoefer
(Not admitted in DC)
Andrew C. Aitken
(Not admitted in DC)

ASSOCIATE

David D'Zurilla

OF COUNSEL

Joseph M. Lane

For full biographical listings, see the Martindale-Hubbell Law Directory

MORGAN & FINNEGAN, L.L.P. (AV)

A Registered Liability Partnership
1299 Pennsylvania Avenue, N.W., Suite 960, 20004
Telephone: 202-857-7887
Facsimile: 202-857-7929
New York, N.Y. Office: 345 Park Avenue.
Telephone: 212-758-4800.
Cable Address: "Findurpine".
Telecopier: (212) 751-6849.
Telex: ITT 421792.

(See Next Column)

RESIDENT PARTNERS

Harry F. Manbeck, Jr.
Frederick F. Calvetti

ASSOCIATES

Edward A. Pennington
Mark L. Hogge
Michael S. Marcus
Howard N. Flaxman

For full biographical listings, see the Martindale-Hubbell Law Directory

*** PENNIE & EDMONDS** (AV)

1701 Pennsylvania Avenue, N.W., 20006
Telephone: 202-393-0177
Facsimile: GI/GII (202) 737-7950
GIII (202) 393-0462
New York, New York Office: 1155 Avenue of the Americas.
Telephone: 212-790-9090.
Telex: (WUI) 66141-Pennie.
Cable Address: "Penangold."
Facsimile: GI/GII/GIII (212) 869-9741, GIII (212) 869-8864.
Menlo Park, California Office: 2730 Sand Hill Road.
Telephone: 415-854-3660.
Facsimile: 415-854-3694.

John C. Pennie (1858-1921)
Dean S. Edmonds (1879-1972)

RESIDENT PARTNERS

Joseph V. Colaianni
Arthur Wineburg

RESIDENT ASSOCIATES

Wilma F. Triebwasser
(Not admitted in DC)
Lyle Kimms
George C. Summerfield, Jr.
(Not admitted in DC)
Melissa Lanni Robertson
Theresa M. Smith
Christine E. Lehman
(Not admitted in DC)

COUNSEL

Marcia H. Sundeen

For full biographical listings, see the Martindale-Hubbell Law Directory

ROYLANCE, ABRAMS, BERDO & GOODMAN (AV)

1225 Connecticut Avenue, N.W., 20036-2680
Telephone: 202-659-9076
Cable Address: "Roypat"
Telex: 64416
Facsimile: 202-659-9344

D. C. Roylance (Retired)
David S. Abrams
Robert H. Berdo
Alfred N. Goodman
Mark S. Bicks
Richard A. Flynt
Darle M. Short
David L. Tarnoff
Michael T. Murphy
Garrett V. Davis
Stacey J. Longanecker
(Not admitted in DC)

SENIOR OF COUNSEL

Frank E. Robbins

OF COUNSEL

John E. Holmes
Susan Neuberger Weller

For full biographical listings, see the Martindale-Hubbell Law Directory

SPENCER, FRANK & SCHNEIDER (AV)

1100 New York Avenue, N.W., Suite 300 East, 20005-3955
Telephone: 202-414-4000
Telefax: 202-414-4040
Telex: Spencer 64267

George H. Spencer
Norman N. Kunitz
Robert J. Frank
Gabor J. Kelemen
(Not admitted in DC)
Mark B. Harrison
Robert Kinberg
Jerold I. Schneider
John W. Schneller
Jeffrey M. Samuels

ASSOCIATES

Ashley J. Wells
Christopher H. Lynt
Barbara Schmidt Twardzik
(Not admitted in DC)
Joseph Paul Curtin
Robert H. Berdo, Jr.
(Not admitted in DC)

COUNSEL

Jay M. Cantor (P.C.)
Julie A. Petruzzelli
Douglas B. Comer

LEGAL SUPPORT PERSONNEL

Mark G. Toohey
Houri Khalilian
Lauren L. Fuller

TRANSLATORS

Holly A. Neuuenschwander
Barbara Rosenbaum

For full biographical listings, see the Martindale-Hubbell Law Directory

Washington—Continued

* VENABLE, BAETJER, HOWARD & CIVILETTI (AV)

A Partnership including Professional Corporations
Suite 1000, 1201 New York Avenue, N.W., 20005
Telephone: 202-962-4800
Fax: 202-962-8300
Baltimore, Maryland Office: Venable, Baetjer and Howard, 1800 Mercantile Bank & Trust Building, 2 Hopkins Plaza.
Telephone: 410-244-7400.
McLean, Virginia Office: Venable, Baetjer and Howard, Suite 400, 2010 Corporate Ridge.
Telephone: 703-760-1600.
Rockville, Maryland Office: Venable, Baetjer and Howard, Suite 500, One Church Street, P. O. Box 1906.
Telephone: 301-217-5600.
Towson, Maryland Office: Venable, Baetjer and Howard, 210 Allegheny Avenue, P. O. Box 5517.
Telephone: 410-494-6200.

MEMBERS OF FIRM

Thomas J. Kenney, Jr. (P.C.) (Not admitted in DC)
Douglas D. Connah, Jr. (P.C.) (Also at Baltimore, Maryland Office)
Kenneth C. Bass, III (Also at McLean, Virginia Office)
Max Stul Oppenheimer (P.C.) (Also at Baltimore and Towson, Maryland Offices)
Edward F. Glynn, Jr.
James R. Myers
Jeffrey D. Knowles
Jeffrey A. Dunn (Also at Baltimore, Maryland Office)
George F. Pappas (Also at Baltimore, Maryland Office)
William D. Coston
William D. Quarles (Also at Towson, Maryland Office)
Jeffrey L. Ihnen
James A. Dunbar (Also at Baltimore, Maryland Office)
Mary E. Pivec (Not admitted in DC; Also at Baltimore, Maryland Office)
Robert J. Bolger, Jr. (Not admitted in DC; Also at Baltimore, Maryland Office)
Paul A. Serini (Not admitted in DC; Also at Baltimore, Maryland Office)
Gary M. Hnath

OF COUNSEL

Fred W. Hathaway

ASSOCIATES

Royal W. Craig (Not admitted in DC)
David W. Goewey
Edward Brendan Magrab (Not admitted in DC)
Barbara L. Waite

For Complete List of Firm Personnel, See General Section

For full biographical listings, see the Martindale-Hubbell Law Directory

WENDEROTH, LIND & PONACK (AV)

Suite 700 Southern Building, 805 Fifteenth Street, N.W., 20005
Telephone: 202-371-8850
Fascimile: 202-371-8856 (G-III)
202-371-5681 (G-III)
202-371-8310 (G-III)
202-646-1179 (G-IV)
(24 Hours)

MEMBERS OF FIRM

E. F. Wenderoth (1886-1974)
John E. Lind (1892-1983)
A. Ponack (1900-1969)
John T. Miller
John T. Fedigan
Michael R. Davis
Matthew M. Jacob
Jeffrey Nolton
Henry M. Zykorie
Michael Stone
Warren M. Cheek, Jr.
Adam C. Volentine

OF COUNSEL

Vincent M. Creedon

ASSOCIATES

Nils E. Pedersen
Charles R. Watts
Bennett M. Celsa
Mary Frances Love

For full biographical listings, see the Martindale-Hubbell Law Directory

JOHN F. WITHERSPOON (AV)

The Army and Navy Club Building, 1627 I Street, N.W., 20006
Telephone: 202-835-3700
Facsimile: 202-775-1168

For full biographical listings, see the Martindale-Hubbell Law Directory

FLORIDA

*FORT LAUDERDALE,** Broward Co.

MALIN, HALEY, DIMAGGIO AND CROSBY, P.A. (AV)

Suite 1609, 1 East Broward Boulevard, 33301
Telephone: 305-763-3303
Fax: 305-522-6507
Miami, Florida Office: 2000 South Dixie Highway, Suite 203, 33133.
Telephone: 305-374-4082.
West Palm Beach, Florida Office: Suite 600, 500 South Australian Avenue, 33401.
Telephone: 407-832-6341.

Eugene F. Malin (1936-1990)
Barry L. Haley
Dale Paul DiMaggio
Kevin P. Crosby

Daniel S. Polley
Mario J. Donato, Jr.
David P. Lhota
Mark David Bowen
John M. Miller

OF COUNSEL

John C. Black (Not admitted in FL)

Representative Clients: Sea Ray Boats, Inc., Merritt Island; IBM; American Hydro-Surgical Instruments, Inc.; News and Sun-Sentinel; Flagler National Bank, West Palm Beach; Delta Industrial Systems Corp., Hialeah; Nova University, Fort Lauderdale; Mission Bay, Boca Raton; Computer Products, Inc., Fort Lauderdale; Huron Machine Products, Inc., Fort Lauderdale; CAE-Link Corporation, Binghamton, NY.
Reference: Barnett Bank.

For full biographical listings, see the Martindale-Hubbell Law Directory

OLTMAN AND FLYNN (AV)

415 Galleria Professional Building, 915 Middle River Drive, 33304-3585
Telephone: 305-563-4814
Facsimile: 305-947-3888
Miami, Florida Office: Suite 2750 International Place, 100 S.E. 2nd Street.
Telephone: 305-947-3888.
Boca Raton, Florida Office: Suite 801 Crocker Plaza, 5355 Town Center Road.
Telephone: 407-391-4900.

John H. Oltman

Representative Clients: Clairson International Corp.; New York Institute of Technology; Jensen Corp.; M & W Pump Corp.; Hollywood Federal Savings and Loan Assn.; Adaptive Systems, Inc.; Oki Telecom, Division of Oki America, Inc.; Security Plastics, Inc.; Eaton Oil Co.
Reference: Nations Bank, Fort Lauderdale.

For full biographical listings, see the Martindale-Hubbell Law Directory

*MIAMI,** Dade Co.

DOMINIK, STEIN, SACCOCIO, REESE, COLITZ & VAN DER WALL (AV)

Suite 225, 6175 N.W. 153rd Street (Miami Lakes), 33014
Telephone: 305-556-7000
Fax: 305-556-6577
Tampa, Florida Office: Suite 400, 3030 North Rocky Point Drive West.
Telephone: 813-289-2966.
Telex: 155238469 PAT LAW.
Fax: 813-289-2967.

Jack E. Dominik
Stefan V. Stein
Richard M. Saccocio
Benjamin P. Reese, II
Michael J. Colitz, Jr.
Robert J. Van Der Wall
Stephan A. Pendorf

OF COUNSEL

Leon Chasan (Not admitted in FL)

For full biographical listings, see the Martindale-Hubbell Law Directory

MALIN, HALEY, DIMAGGIO AND CROSBY, P.A. (AV)

2000 South Dixie Highway, Suite 203, 33133
Telephone: 305-374-4082
Fort Lauderdale, Florida Office: Suite 1609, 1 East Broward Boulevard.
Telephone: 305-763-3303.
Fax: 305-522-6507.
West Palm Beach, Florida Office: Suite 600, 500 South Australian Avenue.
Telephone: 407-832-6341.

Eugene F. Malin (1936-1990)
Barry L. Haley
Dale Paul DiMaggio
Kevin P. Crosby

Daniel S. Polley
Mario J. Donato, Jr.
David P. Lhota
Mark David Bowen
John M. Miller

(See Next Column)

MALIN, HALEY, DIMAGGIO AND CROSBY P.A., *Miami—Continued*

OF COUNSEL

John C. Black (Not admitted in FL)

For full biographical listings, see the Martindale-Hubbell Law Directory

JOHN CYRIL MALLOY (AV)

Suite 1480 701 Buckell Avenue, 33131
Telephone: 305-374-1003

For full biographical listings, see the Martindale-Hubbell Law Directory

*ORLANDO,** Orange Co.

ALLEN, DYER, DOPPELT, FRANJOLA & MILBRATH (AV)

255 South Orange Avenue, Suite 1401, P.O. Box 3791, 32802-3791
Telephone: 407-841-2330
Fax: 407-841-2343

Herbert L. Allen
Robert Dyer
Ava K. Doppelt
George Franjola
Stephen D. Milbrath
Brian R. Gilchrist
Lisa N. Kaufman
Virginia M. Zock
Stephen Murphy (Not admitted in FL)

For full biographical listings, see the Martindale-Hubbell Law Directory

MAGUIRE, VOORHIS & WELLS, P.A. (AV)

Two South Orange Plaza, P.O. Box 633, 32802
Telephone: 407-244-1100
Telecopier: 407-423-8796
Melbourne, Florida Office: 1499 South Harbor City Boulevard.
Telephone: 407-951-1776.
Fax: 407-951-1849.
Tavares, Florida Office: 131 West Main Street, Post Office Box 39.
Telephone: 904-343-5900.
Fax: 904-343-3524.

Robert W. Duckworth

Robert L. Wolter

For full biographical listings, see the Martindale-Hubbell Law Directory

*TAMPA,** Hillsborough Co.

ADKINS & KISE, P.A. (AV)

2175 Barnett Plaza, 101 East Kennedy Boulevard, 33602
Telephone: 813-221-2200
Fax: 813-221-8850

Edward C. Adkins
Christopher M. Kise

For full biographical listings, see the Martindale-Hubbell Law Directory

DOMINIK, STEIN, SACCOCIO, REESE, COLITZ & VAN DER WALL (AV)

Suite 400, 3030 Rocky Point Drive West, 33607-5904
Telephone: 813-289-2966
Telex: 155238469 PAT LAW
Fax: 813-289-2967
Miami, Florida Office: Suite 225, 6175 N.W. 153rd Street (Miami Lakes).
Telephone: 305-556-7000.
Fax: 305-556-6577.

Jack E. Dominik
Stefan V. Stein
Richard M. Saccocio
Benjamin P. Reese, II
Michael J. Colitz, Jr.
Robert J. Van Der Wall
Stephan A. Pendorf

OF COUNSEL

Leon Chasan (Not admitted in FL)

For full biographical listings, see the Martindale-Hubbell Law Directory

FRIJOUF, RUST & PYLE, P.A. (AV)

201 East Davis Boulevard (Davis Islands), 33606-3787
Telephone: 813-254-5100
Toll Free: 1-800-226-4332
Cable Address: "Patents"
Telecopier: 813-254-5400

Robert F. Frijouf
Charles R. Rust
Ray S. Pyle

Reference: Sun Bank of Tampa Bay.

For full biographical listings, see the Martindale-Hubbell Law Directory

PETTIS & MCDONALD, P.A. (AV)

Suite 700, 501 East Kennedy Boulevard, P.O. Box 1528, 33601-1528
Telephone: 813-229-8176
Telex: 522613 ITS INC TPA; 441898 ITS INC TPA UI (Via ITT)
Facsimile: 813-229-8073

(See Next Column)

David W. Pettis, Jr.
C. Douglas McDonald, Jr.

William S. Van Royen
Max N. Langen

For full biographical listings, see the Martindale-Hubbell Law Directory

*WEST PALM BEACH,** Palm Beach Co.

MALIN, HALEY, DIMAGGIO AND CROSBY, P.A. (AV)

Suite 600, 500 South Australian Avenue, 33401
Telephone: 407-832-6341
Fort Lauderdale, Florida Office: Suite 1609, 1 East Broward Boulevard.
Telephone: 305-763-3303.
Miami, Florida Office: 2000 South Dixie Highway, Suite 203.
Telephone: 305-374-4082.

Eugene F. Malin (1936-1990)
Barry L. Haley
Dale Paul DiMaggio
Kevin P. Crosby

Daniel S. Polley
Mario J. Donato, Jr.
David P. Lhota
Mark David Bowen
John M. Miller

OF COUNSEL

John C. Black (Not admitted in FL)

For full biographical listings, see the Martindale-Hubbell Law Directory

GEORGIA

*ATLANTA,** Fulton Co.

DEVEAU, COLTON & MARQUIS (AV)

Two Midtown Plaza Suite 1400, 1360 Peachtree Street, N.E., 30309-3209
Telephone: 404-875-3555
Facsimile: 404-875-8505

MEMBERS OF FIRM

Todd Deveau
Laurence P. Colton
Harold L. Marquis

ASSOCIATES

Arthur A. Gardner
Kenneth Southall
Jennifer Williams Colton

For full biographical listings, see the Martindale-Hubbell Law Directory

HOPKINS & THOMAS (AV)

Suite 1500, 100 Galleria Parkway N.W., 30339
Telephone: 404-951-0931
Facsimile: 404-951-0933

MEMBERS OF FIRM

George M. M. Hopkins
George M. Thomas
James F. Vaughan
James W. Kayden (Managing Partner)
Steven D. Kerr
David S. Sudderth
Scott A. Horstemeyer

ASSOCIATES

Stephen R. Risley
M.U. Griffin, III
Collen A. Beard
Jon M. Jurgovan (Not admitted in GA)

OF COUNSEL

David P. Kelley (Not admitted in GA)
Charles H. Fails

LEGAL SUPPORT PERSONNEL

Geoff L. Sutcliffe (Registered Patent Agent)
Pelham H. Anderson, III
Denise Humphrey

Representative Clients: American Family Life Assurance Co.; Alexander Seewald Co.; Allwaste Manufacturing Co.; American Telephone & Telegraph Co.; Atlanta Attachment Co.; B.G. 300, Inc.; Bankhead Enterprises, Inc.; Bio-Plus, Inc.; Board of Regents - UGA; Char-Broil.

For full biographical listings, see the Martindale-Hubbell Law Directory

KILPATRICK & CODY (AV)

Suite 2800, 1100 Peachtree Street, 30309-4530
Telephone: 404-815-6500
Telephone Copier: 404-815-6555
Telex: 54-2307
Washington, D.C. Office: Suite 800, 700 13th Street, N.W., 20005.
Telephone: 202-508-5800. Telephone Copier: 202-508-5858.
Brussels, Belgium Office: Avenue Louise 65, BTE 3, 1050 Brussels.
Telephone: (32) (2) 533-03-00.
Telecopier: (32) (2) 534-86-38.
London, England Office: 68 Pall Mall, London, SW1Y 5ES, England.
Telephone: (44) (71) 321 0477.
Telecopier: (44) (71) 930 9733.
Augusta, Georgia Office: Suite 1400 First Union Bank Building, P.O. Box 2043, 30903. Telephone (706) 724-2622. Telecopier (706) 722-0219.

OF COUNSEL

Thomas C. Shelton

MEMBERS OF FIRM

Miles J. Alexander
Matthew H. Patton
Jerre B. Swann
Virginia S. Taylor
John S. Pratt
James L. Ewing, IV
Christopher P. Bussert
Patrea L. Pabst
William H. Brewster
Dean W. Russell

ASSOCIATE

Cheryl Knowles Zalesky

Representative Clients: Southern Bell Telephone and Telegraph Co.; Lockheed Aeronautical Systems Co.; Frito-Lay, Inc.; Scientific-Atlanta, Inc.; Scripto-Tokai, Inc.; Bank South Corporation; PepsiCo.; University of Georgia Research Foundation.

(See Next Column)

KILPATRICK & CODY—*Continued*

For Complete List of Firm Personnel, See General Section

For full biographical listings, see the Martindale-Hubbell Law Directory

HAWAII

*HONOLULU,** Honolulu Co.

CADES SCHUTTE FLEMING & WRIGHT (AV)

Formerly Smith, Wild, Beebe & Cades
1000 Bishop Street, P.O. Box 939, 96808
Telephone: 808-521-9200
Telex: 7238589
Telecopier: 808-531-8738
Affiliated Law Firm: Udom-Prok Associates Law Offices, 105/36 Tharinee Mansion, Borom Raj Chananee Road Bangkoknoi, Bangkok, Thailand, 10700.
Telephone: 011 660 435-4146.
Kailua-Kona, Hawaii Office: Hualalai Center, Suite B-303, 75-170 Hualalai Road.
Telephone: 808-329-5811.
Telecopier: 808-326-1175.

MEMBER OF FIRM

Martin E. Hsia

Counsel for: Amfac, Inc.; First Hawaiian Bank; Alexander & Baldwin, Inc.; Theo. H. Davies & Co., Ltd.; C. Brewer & Company, Ltd.; Bank of America, FSB; Fun Factory, Inc.

For Complete List of Firm Personnel, See General Section

For full biographical listings, see the Martindale-Hubbell Law Directory

IDAHO

*BOISE,** Ada Co.

MOFFATT, THOMAS, BARRETT, ROCK & FIELDS, CHARTERED (AV)

First Security Building, 911 West Idaho Street, Suite 300, P.O. Box 829, 83701
Telephone: 208-345-2000
FAX: 208-385-5384
Idaho Falls Office: 525 Park Avenue, Suite 2D, P.O. Box 1367, 83403.
Telephone: 208-522-6700.
FAX: 208-522-5111.
Pocatello, Idaho Office: 1110 Call Creek Drive, P.O. Box 4941, 83201.
Telephone: 208-233-2001.

Paul S. Street
Thomas C. Morris

Representative Clients: BMC West Corporation; Chevron, U.S.A.; First Security Bank of Idaho, N.A.; General Motors Corp.; Idaho Potato Commission; Intermountain Gas Co.; John Alden Life Insurance Co.; Micron, Inc.; Royal Insurance Cos.; St. Luke's Regional Medical Center & Mountain States Tumor Institute.

For Complete List of Firm Personnel, See General Section

For full biographical listings, see the Martindale-Hubbell Law Directory

ILLINOIS

BARRINGTON, Cook & Lake Cos.

VIGIL & HANRATH (AV)

Successor to Thomas R. Vigil & Associates 1975-1991
836 South Northwest Highway, 60010-4683
Telephone: 708-382-6500
Facsimile: 708-382-6895
Cable: USPATLAW

Thomas R. Vigil
James P. Hanrath
John G. Bisbikis

For full biographical listings, see the Martindale-Hubbell Law Directory

*CHICAGO,** Cook Co.

ALLEGRETTI & WITCOFF, LTD. (AV)

Established In 1920 - Predecessor Parent
Ten South Wacker Drive, 60606
Telephone: 312-715-1000
Telecopier: 312-715-1234
Boston, Massachusetts Office: 75 State Street.
Telephone: 617-345-9100.
Telecopier: 617-345-9111.

D. Dennis Allegretti (Resident, Boston, Massachusetts Office)
Sheldon W. Witcoff
Seymour Rothstein
James V. Callahan
Jon O. Nelson
Charles F. Pigott
Charles G. Call (Resident, Boston, Massachusetts Office)
Ronald E. Larson
Edward W. Remus
Denis A. Berntsen
John J. McDonnell
Robert M. Ward
Charles W. Shifley
Daniel A. Boehnen
Jamie S. Smith
Mark T. Banner
Bradley J. Hulbert
Paul H. Berghoff
Jerry A. Riedinger
Peter D. McDermott (Resident, Boston, Massachusetts Office)
Charles C. Kinne
Michael H. Shanahan (Resident, Boston, Massachusetts Office)
Dale A. Malone (Resident, Boston, Massachusetts Office)
Robert H. Resis
Grantland G. Drutchas
James C. Gumina
Christopher J. Renk
David M. Frischkorn
Marc S. Cooperman
Kyle K. Kappes
Barbara A. Heaphy
Richard A. Clegg
John P. Iwanicki (Resident, Boston, Massachusetts Office)
A. Blair Hughes
Lawrence H. Aaronson
Thomas A. Fairhall
Kenneth J. Rudofski
Steven J. Sarussi
Michael S. Greenfield
J. Pieter Van Es
Thomas K. Pratt
Sanjay Prasad (Resident, Boston, Massachusetts Office)
Kevin E. Noonan
Leon R. Yankwich (Resident, Boston, Massachusetts Office)

OF COUNSEL

George B. Newitt

For full biographical listings, see the Martindale-Hubbell Law Directory

ARNOLD, WHITE & DURKEE, A PROFESSIONAL CORPORATION (AV)

800 Quaker Tower, 321 North Clark Street, 60610
Telephone: 312-744-0090
Facsimile: 312-755-4489
Houston, Texas Office: 750 Bering Drive, P.O. Box 4433.
Telephone: 713-787-1400.
Facsimile: 713-789-2679.
Telex: 79-0924.
Cable Address: "ARNWHITEHOU".
Austin, Texas Office: 1900 One American Center, 600 Congress Avenue.
Telephone: 512-418-3000.
Facsimile: 512-474-7577.
Arlington, Virginia Office: 2001 Jefferson Davis Highway, Suite 401.
Telephone: 703-415-1720.
Facsimile: 703-415-1728.
Palo Alto, California Office: Five Palo Alto Square, Suite 700.
Telephone: 415-812-2929.
Facsimile: 415-812-2949.

Stephen G. Rudisill
Ronald B. Coolley
J. Bradford Leaheey
Barry D. Blount
Michael J. Blankstein
Julio A. Garceran
Paul R. Kitch

For full biographical listings, see the Martindale-Hubbell Law Directory

BAILEY, BORLACK, NADELHOFFER & CARROLL (AV)

Suite 2000, 135 South La Salle Street, 60603
Telephone: 312-629-2700
Telecopier: 312-629-0174

Robert C. Bailey
Alan R. Borlack
Clement J. Carroll, Jr.
Sarah K. Nadelhoffer
Eric G. Grossman

For full biographical listings, see the Martindale-Hubbell Law Directory

COOK, EGAN, MCFARRON & MANZO, LTD., A PROFESSIONAL CORPORATION (AV)

Suite 4100, 135 South La Salle Street, 60603
Telephone: 312-236-8500
Cable Address: "Cowegan"
Fax: 312-236-8176

Granger Cook, Jr.
Donald E. Egan
Gary W. McFarron
Edward D. Manzo
Dean A. Monco
Stephen B. Heller

(See Next Column)

COOK, EGAN, MCFARRON & MANZO, LTD. A PROFESSIONAL CORPORATION, *Chicago—Continued*

Andrew G. Kolomayets
Mark J. Murphy
Ted K. Ringsred
David M. Thimmig
James P. Riek
Paul C. Craane

For full biographical listings, see the Martindale-Hubbell Law Directory

DICK AND HARRIS (AV)

Suite 3800, 181 West Madison Street, 60602
Telephone: 312-726-4000
Telecopier: 312-726-5834

MEMBERS OF FIRM

Richard Eugene Dick
Richard D. Harris
Max Shaftal
Howard E. Silverman

ASSOCIATES

John S. Pacocha
Douglas B. Teaney
Jody L. Factor
Herbert H. Finn
Jordan A. Sigale
Jordan Herzog

For full biographical listings, see the Martindale-Hubbell Law Directory

DORN, MCEACHRAN, JAMBOR & KEATING (AV)

55 East Monroe Street, Suite 2940, 60603
Telephone: 312-726-4421; 236-1112
Facsimile: 312-726-9756

MEMBERS OF FIRM

Alfred H. Plyer, Jr. (1925-1991)
Thomas E. Dorn
Daniel C. McEachran
Robert V. Jambor
Edward M. Keating
James L. Kurtz
Joel H. Bock

ASSOCIATES

Vangelis Economou
Troy M. Schmelzer

OF COUNSEL

James B. Kinzer

For full biographical listings, see the Martindale-Hubbell Law Directory

DRESSLER, GOLDSMITH, SHORE & MILNAMOW, LTD. (AV)

Two Prudential Plaza, Suite 4700, 60601
Telephone: 312-616-5400
Facsimile: 312-616-5460
Arlington, Virginia Office: 2001 Jefferson Davis Highway.
Telephone: 703-415-0880.
Facsimile: 703-415-0883.

Albert J. Brunett
Ernest Cheslow
Todd M. Crissey
Max Dressler
Karl R. Fink
Stephen D. Geimer
Allen J. Hoover
Martin L. Katz
Annette M. McGarry
Gerson E. Meyers
John P. Milnamow
Paul M. Odell
Jack Shore
Joel E. Siegel
Paul M. Vargo
Mitchell J. Weinstein

OF COUNSEL

David D. Kaufman

LEGAL SUPPORT PERSONNEL

Lois P. Besanko

For full biographical listings, see the Martindale-Hubbell Law Directory

FITCH, EVEN, TABIN & FLANNERY (AV)

135 South La Salle Street, 60603-4277
Telephone: 312-372-7842
Cable Address: "Patlaw"
Telex: 20 6566 Patlaw Cgo
Telecopier: 312-372-7848
San Diego, California Office: 4250 Executive Square, Suite 510.
Telephone: 619-552-1311.
Telecopier: 619-552-0095.

MEMBERS OF FIRM

Morgan L. Fitch, Jr.
Francis A. Even
Julius Tabin
John F. Flannery
Robert B. Jones
James J. Schumann (Resident, San Diego, California Office)
R. Steven Pinkstaff
James J. Hamill
Phillip H. Watt
Timothy E. Levstik
Joseph E. Shipley
Bryant R. Gold (Resident, San Diego, California, Office)
Robert J. Fox
Kenneth H. Samples
Philip T. Petti
John S. Paniaguas
Donald A. Peterson
John J. Cavanaugh
James R. McBride
James A. Sprowl
Bruce R. Mansfield
Stanley J. Tomsa (1941-1993)
Joseph T. Nabor
Richard P. Beem
James E. Turner, Jr. (Not admitted in IL)

(See Next Column)

OF COUNSEL

Louis Bernat
Robert R. Meads (Resident, San Diego, California Office)

Jack D. Nimz
Mark A. Hamill
Perry Jay Hoffman
Richard A. Kaba (Not admitted in IL)
James P. Krueger
Mark W. Hetzler
Timothy P. Maloney
Jay A. Saltzman
Thomas F. Lebens (Resident, San Diego, California Office)
Robert J. Hampsch (Resident, San Diego, California Office)

For full biographical listings, see the Martindale-Hubbell Law Directory

KEGAN & KEGAN, LTD. (AV)

79 West Monroe Street, Suite 1320, 60603-4969
Telephone: 312-782-6495
Telex: 650-286-7010 MCI UW
Telecopier: (fax) 312-782-6494

Albert I. Kegan (1908-1963)
Esther O. Kegan
Daniel L. Kegan

Cynthia L. Scott
Diane Lidman Prendiville
Patrick A. Flynn

OF COUNSEL

Marvin N. Benn

For full biographical listings, see the Martindale-Hubbell Law Directory

LAFF, WHITESEL, CONTE & SARET, LTD., A PROFESSIONAL CORPORATION (AV)

Suite 1700, 401 North Michigan Avenue, 60611-4212
Telephone: 312-661-2100
Cable Address: "Lawyer"
Telex: 20-6024
Telecopiers: 312-661-0029 312-527-3001

Charles A. Laff
J. Warren Whitesel
Robert F. I. Conte
Larry L. Saret
Martin L. Stern
Louis Altman
Joseph F. Schmidt
Barry W. Sufrin
Marshall W. Sutker
Jennifer A. Dunner
Judith L. Grubner
John T. Gabrielides
Neil R. Ormos
Kevin C. Trock
Diana Flynn
Richard P. Gilly

OF COUNSEL

Jack R. Halvorsen

For full biographical listings, see the Martindale-Hubbell Law Directory

LEYDIG, VOIT & MAYER, LTD. (AV)

Two Prudential Plaza, 180 North Stetson Avenue, Suite 4900, 60601-6780
Telephone: 312-616-5600
Telecopier: 312-616-5700
Telex: 25-3533
Rockford, Illinois Office: 815 North Church Street.
Telephone: 815-963-7661.
Telecopier: 815-963-7664.
Telex: 25-3533.
Washington, D.C. Office: 700 Thirteenth Street, N.W., Suite 300.
Telephone: 202-737-6770.
Telecopier: 202-737-6776.
Telex: 25-3533.
St. Louis, Missouri Office: 8182 Maryland, Suite 400.
Telephone: 314-721-5868.
Telecopier: 314-854-8530.

C. Frederick Leydig
John P. Bundock, Jr. (Washington, D.C. Office)
Paul L. Ahern
Berton Scott Sheppard
James B. Muskal
Dennis R. Schlemmer
Gordon R. Coons
Michael C. Payden (Rockford, Illinois Office)
John E. Rosenquist
John W. Kozak
Charles S. Oslakovic
Mark E. Phelps
H. Michael Hartmann
Lawrence S. Wick
Bruce M. Gagala
Charles H. Mottier
Donald W. Peterson (Not admitted in IL; St. Louis, Missouri Office)
John Kilyk, Jr.
Robert F. Green
John B. Conklin
James D. Zalewa
Mark J. Liss
John M. Belz (Washington, D.C. Office)
Herbert C. Rose (Not admitted in IL; Washington, D.C. Office)
Brett A. Hesterberg
Keith B. Willhelm
Jeffrey S. Ward
Jeffrey A. Wyand (Not admitted in IL; Washington, D.C. Office)
Richard M. Johnson
Theodore W. Anderson
Noel I. Smith

(See Next Column)

LEYDIG, VOIT & MAYER LTD.—*Continued*

Paul J. Korniczky
Pamela J. Ruschau
Christopher T. Griffith
Amy N. Cohen
Lynn A. Tannehill
D. Bartley Eppenauer
Frederick N. Samuels (Not admitted in IL; Washington, D.C. Office)
Steven P. Petersen
John M. Augustyn
Wesley O. Mueller
Jeremy M. Jay (Not admitted in IL; Washington, D.C. Office)
Jeffrey B. Burgan
Eley O. Thompson
Neil P. Calvin
Mark Joy
Regina M. Anderson
Matthew C. McNeill
Donald J. Silvert
James A. Flight
Frederic M. Meeker (Not admitted in IL; Washington, D.C. Office)
Albert S. Michalik
Daniel R. McClure
Allen E. Hoover
David M. Airan
Maureen R. Smith
Michael H. Tobias (Not admitted in IL; Washington, D.C. Office)
Keith Frantz (Rockford, Illinois Office)
Carl J. Evens (Not admitted in IL; Washington, D.C. Office)
Kenneth J. Rose (Not admitted in IL; Washington, D.C. Office)

OF COUNSEL

Richard L. Voit
Phillip H. Mayer
Homer J. Schneider
Arthur G. Gilkes
John D. Foster (Washington, D.C. Office)
Arthur A. Olson, Jr.
William J. Birmingham
Ralph C. Medhurst

For full biographical listings, see the Martindale-Hubbell Law Directory

MASON, KOLEHMAINEN, RATHBURN & WYSS (AV)

Suite 2400, 300 South Wacker Drive, 60606-6701
Telephone: 312-697-2400
Telecopier: 312-697-2415
Cable Address: "Makraw"

MEMBERS OF FIRM

Richard D. Mason (1906-1982)
Waino M. Kolehmainen (1906-1985)
M. Hudson Rathburn (1908-1973)
Walther E. Wyss (1909-1990)
Philip M. Kolehmainen
Joseph Krieger
Joan Pennington

OF COUNSEL

Philip C. Peterson

For full biographical listings, see the Martindale-Hubbell Law Directory

MCANDREWS, HELD & MALLOY, LTD. (AV)

Northwestern Atrium Center Suite 3400, 500 West Madison Street, 60661
Telephone: 312-707-8889
Telecopier: 312-707-9155
Telex: 650-388-1248

George P. McAndrews
John J. Held
Timothy J. Malloy
William M. Wesley
Lawrence M. Jarvis
Robert C. Ryan
Gregory J. Vogler
Jean Dudek Kuelper
Herbert D. Hart III
Robert W. Fieseler
D. David Hill
Thomas J. Wimbiscus
Steven J. Hampton
Alejandro Menchaca
Priscilla F. Gallagher
Stephen F. Sherry
Patrick J. Arnold, Jr.
Robert B. Polit
George Wheeler
Christopher C. Winslade
Edward A. Mas, II
Gregory C. Schodde
John S. Artz
David D. Headrick
Sharon A. Hwang
Phyllis T. Turner Brim
Jeff D. Wheeler

OF COUNSEL

S. Jack Sauer
Donald P. Reynolds

For full biographical listings, see the Martindale-Hubbell Law Directory

NIRO, SCAVONE, HALLER & NIRO (AV)

181 West Madison, Suite 4600, 60602-4515
Telephone: 312-236-0733
Facsimile: 312-236-3137
Telex: 18-1162 US

Raymond P. Niro
Thomas G. Scavone
Timothy J. Haller
William L. Niro
Joseph N. Hosteny, III
Robert A. Vitale, Jr.
John C. Janka

Samuel L. Alberstadt
Michael P. Mazza
Larry D. Taylor (1959-1993)
Dean D. Niro
Raymond P. Niro, Jr.
Keith A. Vogt
Arthur A. Gasey
Christopher J. Lee

For full biographical listings, see the Martindale-Hubbell Law Directory

PATULA & ASSOCIATES (AV)

A Professional Partnership
116 South Michigan Avenue 14th Floor, 60603
Telephone: 312-201-8220
FAX: 312-372-8681

Timothy T. Patula

OF COUNSEL

Joanne Daley

LEGAL SUPPORT PERSONNEL

Charles T. Riggs Jr. (Patent Agent)
John F. Rollins (Patent Agent)

For full biographical listings, see the Martindale-Hubbell Law Directory

ROCKEY, RIFKIN AND RYTHER (AV)

Two First National Plaza 20 South Clark Street Suite 2900, 60603
Telephone: 312-704-5600
Facsimile: 312-704-5616

MEMBERS OF FIRM

Keith V. Rockey
James P. Ryther
William T. Rifkin
Thomas C. Elliott, Jr.
Kathleen A. Lyons
Henry S. Kaplan
Mary Spalding Burns
Stanley M. Parmerter

ASSOCIATES

Dennis J. Williamson
Jeffrey W. Salmon

OF COUNSEL

H. Vincent Harsha

For full biographical listings, see the Martindale-Hubbell Law Directory

TREXLER, BUSHNELL, GIANGIORGI & BLACKSTONE, LTD. (AV)

105 West Adams Street 36th Floor, 60603-6299
Telephone: 312-704-1890
FAX: 312-704-8023
Washington, D.C. Office: 3231 Reservoir Road, N.W.
Telephone: 202-337-5723.

Richard Bushnell
Richard A. Giangiorgi
Raiford A. Blackstone, Jr.
Roger J. French
Cynthia Bushnell Stevens
David J. Marr
Geoffrey M. Novelli
Grant H. Peters

OF COUNSEL

Richard R. Trexler

WASHINGTON, D.C. RESIDENT

Charles L. Sturtevant

For full biographical listings, see the Martindale-Hubbell Law Directory

WOOD, PHILLIPS, VAN SANTEN, HOFFMAN & ERTEL (AV)

Northwestern Atrium Center, Suite 3800, 500 West Madison Street, 60661-2511
Telephone: 312-876-1800
Cable Address: "Chipat"
TWX: 910-221-5147
Telecopier: 312-876-2020

MEMBERS OF FIRM

Jeffrey L. Clark
Patrick D. Ertel
Lee F. Grossman
John R. Hoffman
Stephen J. Manich
F. William McLaughlin
John S. Mortimer
Richard S. Phillips
William A. Van Santen
Gomer W. Walters

ASSOCIATES

Stephen S. Favakeh
Michael L. Korniczky
Steven J. Soucar

RETIRED PARTNERS

Stanley C. Dalton
Lloyd W. Mason
Charles L. Rowe
James C. Wood

OF COUNSEL

William E. Recktenwald
John W. Hofeldt
William G. Lawler, Jr.
G. Michael Perry

For full biographical listings, see the Martindale-Hubbell Law Directory

LLOYD L. ZICKERT (AV)

79 West Monroe Street, Suite 1100, 60603
Telephone: 312-236-1888
Fax: 312-236-1885

ASSOCIATE

Adam H. Masia

For full biographical listings, see the Martindale-Hubbell Law Directory

*ROCKFORD,** Winnebago Co.

LEYDIG, VOIT & MAYER, LTD. (AV)

815 North Church Street, 61103
Telephone: 815-963-7661
Telecopier: 815-963-7664.
Telex: 25-3533
Chicago, Illinois Office: Two Prudential Plaza, 180 North Stetson Avenue, Suite 4900.
Telephone: 312-616-5600.
Telecopier: 312-616-5700.
Telex: 25-3533.
Washington, D.C. Office: 700 Thirteenth Street, N.W., Suite 300.
Telephone: 202-737-6770.
Telecopier: 202-737-6776.
Telex: 25-3533.
St. Louis, Missouri Office: 8182 Maryland, Suite 400.
Telephone: 314-721-5868.
Telecopier: 314-854-8530.

Michael C. Payden
Keith Frantz

INDIANA

*FORT WAYNE,** Allen Co.

BAKER & DANIELS (AV)

2400 Fort Wayne National Bank Building, 46802
Telephone: 219-424-8000
FAX: (219) 460-1700
Indianapolis, Indiana Office: 300 North Meridian Street.
Telephone: 317-237-0300.
South Bend, Indiana Office: First Bank Building, 205 West Jefferson Boulevard.
Telephone: 219-234-4149.
Elkhart, Indiana Office: 301 South Main Street, Suite 307.
Telephone: 219-296-6000.
Washington, D.C. Office: 1701 K Street, N.W. Suite 400.
Telephone: 202-785-1565.

MEMBERS OF FIRM

John F. Hoffman
Anthony Niewyk

ASSOCIATES

Kevin R. Erdman
Randall J. Knuth
Michael T. Bates
Todd T. Taylor

Representative Clients: Central Soya Co., Inc.; Essex Group, Inc.; ITT Corp.; Lincoln National Corp.; Lutheran Hospital of Indiana; Norwest Bank, Fort Wayne; Tokheim Corp.; Shambaugh & Son, Inc.; General Motors Corp.; Eli Lilly and Company.

For Complete List of Firm Personnel, See General Section

For full biographical listings, see the Martindale-Hubbell Law Directory

DAVID A. LUNDY (AV)

1020 Anthony Wayne Building, 203 East Berry Street, 46802
Telephone: 219-422-1534
Telecopier: 219-423-1590
Indianapolis, Indiana Office: 233 Circle Tower Building. 55 Monument Circle.
Telephone: 317-634-5552.

Reference: Fort Wayne National Bank.

For full biographical listings, see the Martindale-Hubbell Law Directory

*INDIANAPOLIS,** Marion Co.

BAKER & DANIELS (AV)

300 North Meridian Street, 46204
Telephone: 317-237-0300
FAX: 317-237-1000
Fort Wayne, Indiana Office: 2400 Fort Wayne National Bank Building.
Telephone: 219-424-8000.
South Bend, Indiana Office: First Bank Building, 205 West Jefferson Boulevard.
Telephone: 219-234-4149.
Elkhart, Indiana Office: 301 South Main Street, Suite 307,
Telephone: 219-296-6000.
Washington, D.C. Office: 1701 K Street, N.W., Suite 400.
Telephone: 202-785-1565.

MEMBERS OF FIRM

Lawrence A. Steward
John B. Swarbrick, Jr.

COUNSEL

Arthur R. Whale

(See Next Column)

ASSOCIATE

Edward J. Prein

Representative Clients: Associated Insurance Companies, Inc.; Bank One, Indianapolis, N.A.; Borg-Warner Corp.; City of Indianapolis; Cummins Engine Co.; Eli Lilly and Company; General Motors Corp.; Indiana Bell; Indianapolis Public Schools; United Airlines.

For Complete List of Firm Personnel, See General Section

For full biographical listings, see the Martindale-Hubbell Law Directory

LOCKE REYNOLDS BOYD & WEISELL (AV)

1000 Capital Center South, 201 North Illinois Street, 46204
Telephone: 317-237-3800
Telecopier: 317-237-3900

Stephen J. Dutton
Richard A. Huser
David E. Jose
Charles B. Baldwin
Andrew James Richardson

Stephen L. Vaughan
Robert A. Burtzlaff
James O. Waanders
Charles S. Eberhardt, II

OF COUNSEL

David S. Klinestiver
Jeffrey S. Dible

Representative Clients: Boehringer Mannheim Corp.; Constar Plastics, Inc.; Electra Form, Inc.; France Telecom; Indiana University; Monon Corporation; National Wine & Spirits, Inc.; Noble Romans, Inc.; The Spaghetti Shop, Inc.; VonDuprin, Inc.

For Complete List of Firm Personnel, See General Section

For full biographical listings, see the Martindale-Hubbell Law Directory

DAVID A. LUNDY (AV)

233 Circle Tower Building, 55 Monument Circle, 46204
Telephone: 317-634-5552
Telecopier: 219-422-1535
Fort Wayne, Indiana Office: 1020 Anthony Wayne Building. 203 East Berry Street.
Telephone: 219-422-1534.

References: Fort Wayne National Bank; Anthony Wayne Bank.

For full biographical listings, see the Martindale-Hubbell Law Directory

WOODARD, EMHARDT, NAUGHTON, MORIARTY & MCNETT (AV)

Bank One Center/Tower, 111 Monument Circle, Suite 3700, 46204-5137
Telephone: 317-634-3456
Telecopier: 317-637-7561
Telex: 810-341-3283
Cable Address: "Patents Ind"

MEMBERS OF FIRM

Harold R. Woodard
Vincent O. Wagner
C. David Emhardt
Stephen E. Zlatos
Joseph A. Naughton, Jr.
Spiro Bereveskos
John V. Moriarty
William F. Bahret
John C. McNett
Clifford W. Browning
Thomas Q. Henry
R. Randall Frisk
James M. Durlacher
Daniel J. Lueders
Charles R. Reeves
Michael D. Beck
Kenneth A. Gandy

ASSOCIATES

Timothy N. Thomas
Kurt N. Jones
Kerry Pauline Sisselman
Jeffrey A. Michael
Deborah Rae Knoll

STAFF ATTORNEY

Linda C. Shelby

OF COUNSEL

James L. Rowe

For full biographical listings, see the Martindale-Hubbell Law Directory

*SOUTH BEND,** St. Joseph Co.

BAKER & DANIELS (AV)

First Bank Building, 205 West Jefferson Boulevard, 46601
Telephone: 219-234-4149
Fax: 219-239-1900
Indianapolis, Indiana Office: 300 North Meridian Street.
Telephone: 317-237-0300.
Fort Wayne, Indiana Office: 2400 Fort Wayne National Bank Building.
Telephone: 219-424-8000.
Elkhart, Indiana Office: 301 South Main Street, Suite 307.
Telephone: 219-296-6000.
Washington, D.C. Office: 1701 K Street, N.W., Suite 400.
Telephone: 202-785-1565.

(See Next Column)

BAKER & DANIELS—*Continued*

MEMBER OF FIRM

James D. Hall (Resident)

Representative Clients: City of South Bend; 1st Source Bank; Jack-Post Corp.; Society Corp.; South Bend Drug Co.; WSBT, Inc.; General Motors Corp.; Indiana Bell; Eli Lilly and Company; Borg-Warner Corporation.

For Complete List of Firm Personnel, See General Section

For full biographical listings, see the Martindale-Hubbell Law Directory

IOWA

*CEDAR RAPIDS,** Linn Co.

SHUTTLEWORTH & INGERSOLL, P.C. (AV)

500 Firstar Bank Building, P.O. Box 2107, 52406-2107
Telephone: 319-365-9461
Fax: 319-365-8443

James C. Nemmers
Glenn L. Johnson

Representative Clients: Aegon USA, Inc.; Iowa Electric Light and Power Co.; Met-Coil Systems Corporation; Parsons Technology, Inc.

For Complete List of Firm Personnel, See General Section

For full biographical listings, see the Martindale-Hubbell Law Directory

*DAVENPORT,** Scott Co.

HENDERSON & STURM (AV)

204 Northwest Bank Building-Downtown, 101 West Second Street, 52801-1813
Telephone: 319-323-9731
Fax: 319-323-9709
Washington, D.C. Office: Suite 701, 1747 Pennsylvania Avenue, N.W.
Telephone: 202-296-3854.
Fax: 202-223-9606.
Des Moines, Iowa Office: 1213 Midland Building, 206 Sixth Avenue.
Telephone: 515-288-9589.
Fax: 515-288-4860.
Omaha, Nebraska Office: Suite 330, 1125 South 103rd Street.
Telephone: 402-398-9000.
Fax: 402-398-9005.

MEMBERS OF FIRM

H. Robert Henderson
John E. Cepican (Resident)

For full biographical listings, see the Martindale-Hubbell Law Directory

*DES MOINES,** Polk Co.

DAVIS, HOCKENBERG, WINE, BROWN, KOEHN & SHORS, P.C. (AV)

The Financial Center, 666 Walnut Street, Suite 2500, 50309-3993
Telephone: 515-288-2500
Cable: Davis Law
Facsimile: 515-243-0654
Affiliated London, England Office: Vizards, Solicitors, 42 Bedford Row. London WC1R 4JL England.
Telephone: 071-405-6302.
Facsimile: 071-405-6248.

Kent A. Herink
Brian J. Laurenzo

Brett J. Trout

For Complete List of Firm Personnel, See General Section

For full biographical listings, see the Martindale-Hubbell Law Directory

HENDERSON & STURM (AV)

1213 Midland Building, 206 Sixth Avenue, 50309-4076
Telephone: 515-288-9589
Fax: 515-288-4860
Washington, D.C. Office: Suite 701, 1747 Pennsylvania Avenue, N.W.
Telephone: 202-296-3854.
Fax: 202-223-9606.
Davenport, Iowa Office: 204 Northwest Bank Building-Downtown, 101 West Second Street.
Telephone: 319-323-9731.
Fax: 319-323-9709.
Omaha, Nebraska Office: Suite 330, 1125 South 103rd Street.
Telephone: 402-398-9000.
Fax: 402-398-9005.

MEMBERS OF FIRM

H. Robert Henderson
Michael O. Sturm
John E. Cepican (Resident at Davenport, Iowa Office)
Richard L. Fix
William H. Wright (Resident at Washington, D.C. Office)

(See Next Column)

Martin G. Mullen (Resident at Washington, D.C. Office)
Robert J. Jondle (Resident at Omaha, Nebraska Office)
Curtis A. Bell (Resident)
Daniel B. Greenwood (Resident at Omaha, Nebraska Office)

Reference: Norwest Bank Iowa, N.A.

For full biographical listings, see the Martindale-Hubbell Law Directory

ZARLEY, MCKEE, THOMTE, VOORHEES & SEASE (AV)

801 Grand, Suite 3200, 50309-2721
Telephone: 515-288-3667
Telex: 706625
Telecopier: 515-288-1338
Omaha, Nebraska Office: 1111 Commercial Federal Tower, 2120 South 72nd Street.
Telephone: 402-392-2280.
Telecopier: 402-392-0734.
Toronto, Ontario, Canada Office: 40 King Street West, Suite 4300.
Telephone: 416-367-1576.
Telecopier: 416-367-6749.

MEMBERS OF FIRM

Donald H. Zarley
Bruce W. McKee
Dennis L. Thomte
Michael G. Voorhees
Edmund J. Sease
Mark D. Hansing
Kirk M. Hartung
Mark D. Frederiksen

ASSOCIATES

Denise C. Mazour (Not admitted in IA)
Daniel J. Cosgrove
Heidi Sease Nebel
Michael R. Crabb
Bruce A. Johnson
Wendy K. Hartung

OF COUNSEL

Dale L. Porter

Reference: Boatmen's National Bank of Des Moines (Des Moines, Iowa).

For full biographical listings, see the Martindale-Hubbell Law Directory

KANSAS

*TOPEKA,** Shawnee Co.

WRIGHT, HENSON, SOMERS, SEBELIUS, CLARK & BAKER (AV)

Commerce Bank Building, 100 Southeast Ninth Street, 2nd Floor, P.O. Box 3555, 66601-3555
Telephone: 913-232-2200
FAX: 913-232-3344

MEMBERS OF FIRM

Thomas E. Wright
Bruce J. Clark

Representative Client: Newtek, Inc.

For Complete List of Firm Personnel, See General Section

For full biographical listings, see the Martindale-Hubbell Law Directory

KENTUCKY

*LEXINGTON,** Fayette Co.

KING AND SCHICKLI (AV)

Corporate Gateway, Suite 210, 3070 Harrodsburg Road, 40503
Telephone: 606-223-4050
Telecopier: 606-224-9445

J. Ralph King
Warren D. Schickli

ASSOCIATE

Larry M. Bauman (Not admitted in KY)

For full biographical listings, see the Martindale-Hubbell Law Directory

*LOUISVILLE,** Jefferson Co.

MIDDLETON & REUTLINGER, P.S.C. (AV)

2500 Brown and Williamson Tower, 40202-3410
Telephone: 502-584-1135
Fax: 502-561-0442
Jeffersonville, Indiana Office: 605 Watt Street, 47130.
Telephone: 812-282-4886.

James R. Higgins, Jr.
Charles G. Lamb

(See Next Column)

MIDDLETON & REUTLINGER P.S.C., *Louisville—Continued*

Beach A. Craigmyle
Amy B. Berge
David W. Carrithers
James C. Eaves, Jr.

Representative Clients: Brown & Williamson Tobacco Co., Inc.; Campbell Tobacco Rehandling Co., Inc.; Corhart Refractories Corp.; DeTer Co., Inc.; Porcelain Metals Corp.; Rosalco, Inc.; Tube Turns, Inc.; Universal Denim Services; Vermont American Corp.; Whip Mix, Inc.

For Complete List of Firm Personnel, See General Section

For full biographical listings, see the Martindale-Hubbell Law Directory

ROBERT & MILLER (AV)

10000 Shelbyville Road, Suite 112, 40223
Telephone: 502-245-7717
Fax: 502-245-7932

MEMBERS OF FIRM

Arthur F. Robert (1901-1985)
M. Larry Miller

For full biographical listings, see the Martindale-Hubbell Law Directory

MAINE

BAR HARBOR, Hancock Co.

FENTON, CHAPMAN, FENTON, SMITH & KANE, P.A. (AV)

109 Main Street, P.O. Box B, 04609
Telephone: 207-288-3331
FAX: 207-288-9326

William Fenton
Hancock Griffin, Jr. (1912-1980)
Douglas B. Chapman
Nathaniel R. Fenton
Chadbourn H. Smith
Daniel H. Kane

Margaret A. Timothy
Eric Lindquist

OF COUNSEL

David Einhorn
Edwin R. Smith

Reference: Bar Harbor Banking and Trust Co.

For full biographical listings, see the Martindale-Hubbell Law Directory

MARYLAND

*BALTIMORE,** (Independent City)

VENABLE, BAETJER AND HOWARD (AV)

A Partnership including Professional Corporations
1800 Mercantile Bank & Trust Building, 2 Hopkins Plaza, 21201
Telephone: 410-244-7400
Washington, D.C. Office: Venable, Baetjer, Howard & Civiletti. Suite 1000, 1201 New York Avenue, N.W.
Telephone: 202-962-4800.
McLean, Virginia Office: Suite 400, 2010 Corporate Ridge.
Telephone: 703-760-1600.
Rockville, Maryland Office: Suite 500, One Church Street, P. O. Box 1906.
Telephone: 301-217-5600.
Towson, Maryland Office: 210 Allegheny Avenue, P. O. Box 5517.
Telephone: 410-494-6200.

MEMBERS OF FIRM

George Cochran Doub (P.C.)
Thomas J. Kenney, Jr. (P.C.) (Also at Washington, D.C. Office)
Douglas D. Connah, Jr. (P.C.) (Also at Washington, D.C. Office)
Kenneth C. Bass, III (Not admitted in MD; Also at Washington, D.C. and McLean, Virginia Offices)
Max Stul Oppenheimer (P.C.) (Also at Washington, D.C. and Towson, Maryland Offices)
Edward F. Glynn, Jr. (Not admitted in MD; Resident, Washington, D.C. Office)
G. Stewart Webb, Jr.
James R. Myers (Not admitted in MD; Resident, Washington, D.C. Office)
Jeffrey D. Knowles (Not admitted in MD; Resident, Washington, D.C. Office)
F. Dudley Staples, Jr. (Also at Towson, Maryland Office)
Jeffrey A. Dunn (also at Washington, D.C. Office)
George F. Pappas (Also at Washington, D.C. Office)
William D. Coston (Not admitted in MD; Resident, Washington, D.C. Office)
William D. Quarles (Also at Washington, D.C. and Towson, Maryland Offices)
Jeffrey L. Ihnen (Not admitted in MD; Resident, Washington, D. C. Office)
James A. Dunbar (Also at Washington, D.C. Office)
Mary E. Pivec (Also at Washington, D.C. Office)

(See Next Column)

MEMBERS OF FIRM (Continued)

Robert J. Bolger, Jr. (Also at Washington, D.C. Office)
David J. Heubeck
Paul A. Serini (Also at Washington, D.C. Office)
Gary M. Hnath (Resident, Washington, D.C. Office)

OF COUNSEL

Fred W. Hathaway (Not admitted in MD; Resident, Washington, D.C. Office)

ASSOCIATES

Paul D. Barker, Jr.
Royal W. Craig (Resident, Washington, D.C. Office)
Newton B. Fowler, III
David W. Goewey (Not admitted in MD; Resident, Washington, D.C. Office)
Mary-Dulany James (Resident, Towson, Maryland Office)
Edward Brendan Magrab (Resident, Washington, D.C. Office)
Vicki Margolis
John T. Prisbe
J. Preston Turner
Barbara L. Waite (Not admitted in MD; Resident, Washington, D.C. Office)

For Complete List of Firm Personnel, See General Section

For full biographical listings, see the Martindale-Hubbell Law Directory

BETHESDA, Montgomery Co.

FREEMAN & JENNER, P.C. (AV)

3 Bethesda Metro Center, Suite 1410, 20814
Telephone: 301-907-7747
FAX: 301-907-9877
Washington, D.C. Office: 1000 16th Street, N.W., Suite 300.
Telephone: 301-907-7747.
Aspen, Colorado Office: 215 South Monarch Street, Suite 202.
Telephone: 303-925-3400.
FAX: 303-925-4043.

Martin H. Freeman
Robert K. Jenner

Barbara E. Hirsch
Mark Allan Freeman

Reference: Crestar Bank of Maryland.

For full biographical listings, see the Martindale-Hubbell Law Directory

*LA PLATA,** Charles Co.

DAVID NEWMAN & ASSOCIATES, P.C. (AV)

Centennial Square, P.O. Box 2728, 20646-2728
Telephone: 301-934-6100; 202-842-8400
Facsimile: 301-934-5782

David B. Newman, Jr.

Suzin C. Bailey

LEGAL SUPPORT PERSONNEL
TECHNICAL ADVISORS

Dr. Christopher J. Newman
Dr. Amy Hauck Newman

For full biographical listings, see the Martindale-Hubbell Law Directory

MASSACHUSETTS

*BOSTON,** Suffolk Co.

CESARI AND MCKENNA (AV)

30 Rowes Wharf, 02110
Telephone: 617-261-6800
Telecopier: 617-261-6801

Robert A. Cesari
John F. McKenna
Martin J. O'Donnell
Thomas C. O'Konski
Joseph H. Born
Patricia A. Sheehan
Michael E. Attaya
Steven J. Frank
David J. Thibodeau, Jr.

Charles J. Barbas
Philip L. Conrad
Patrick J. O'Shea

OF COUNSEL

Paul E. Kudirka

LEGAL SUPPORT PERSONNEL

George J. Jakobsche (Law Clerk)
Dora V. Dodin (Patent Engineer)

For full biographical listings, see the Martindale-Hubbell Law Directory

Boston—Continued

DIKE, BRONSTEIN, ROBERTS & CUSHMAN (AV)

A Partnership including Professional Corporations
130 Water Street, 02109
Telephone: 617-523-3400
Telex: 200291 STRE UR
Telefax: 617-523-6440; 523-7318
Marlborough, Massachusetts Office: 62 Cotting Avenue. P.O. Box 556.
Telephone: 508-485-7772.
Fax: 508-485-0363.

Sewall P. Bronstein (P.C.)
Donald Brown (P.C.)
Robert L. Goldberg
Robert F. O'Connell
David G. Conlin (P.C.)
George W. Neuner (P.C.)
Ernest V. Linek
Linda M. Buckley
Ronald I. Eisenstein
Henry D. Pahl, Jr.

David S. Resnick
Peter F. Corless
Kevin J. Fournier
Cara Zucker Lowen

OF COUNSEL

Peter J. Manus
John L. Welch
Milton M. Oliver

For full biographical listings, see the Martindale-Hubbell Law Directory

FISH & RICHARDSON (AV)

225 Franklin Street, 02110-2804
Telephone: 617-542-5070
Telecopier: 617-542-8906
Cable Address: "Fishrich, Boston".
Telex: RCA 200154 Fishr Ur
Washington, D.C. Office: 601 13th Street, N.W.
Telephone: 202-783-5070.
Telecopier: 202-783-2331.
Houston, Texas Office: One Riverway, Suite 1200.
Telephone: 713-629-5070.
Telecopier: 713-629-7811.
Menlo Park, California Office: 2200 Sand Hill Road, Suite 100.
Telephone: 415-854-5277.
Telecopier: 415-854-0875.
Minneapolis, Minneapolis Office: 2500 One Financial Plaza, 120 South Sixth Street.
Telephone: 612-335-5070.
Facsimile: 612-288-9696.

Frederick P. Fish (1855-1930)
W. K. Richardson (1859-1951)

MEMBERS OF FIRM

John N. Williams
Charles C. Winchester
Robert E. Hillman
Frank P. Porcelli
Gregory A. Madera
David L. Feigenbaum
John M. Skenyon
G. Roger Lee
Paul T. Clark
Charles Hieken
Gilbert H. Hennessey, III
John W. Freeman
William E. Booth
Timothy A. French
Eric L. Prahl
Robert C. Nabinger
Mark J. Hebert
Peter J. Devlin
Ronald E. Myrick
Gary A. Walpert
Janis K. Fraser
Richard M. Sharkansky

OF COUNSEL

Willis M. Ertman
Blair L. Perry

ASSOCIATES

Eileen M. Herlihy
Heidi E. Harvey
J. Peter Fasse
Mary (Molly) Mosley-Goren
James E. Mrose
Y. Rocky Tsao
Jennifer T. Miller
Donna M. Weinstein
Kenneth M. Fagin
John J. Gagel
Kurt L. Glitzenstein
Jolynn M. Lussier
Alan Dean Smith (Not admitted in MA)
Laurie J. Whitaker (Not admitted in MA)
Robert E. Rigby, Jr.

For full biographical listings, see the Martindale-Hubbell Law Directory

SHERBURNE, POWERS & NEEDHAM, P.C. (AV)

One Beacon Street, 02108
Telephone: 617-523-2700
Fax: 617-523-6850

William D. Weeks
John T. Collins
Allan J. Landau
John L. Daly
Stephen A. Hopkins
Alan I. Falk
C. Thomas Swaim
James Pollock
William V. Tripp III
Stephen S. Young
William F. Machen
W. Robert Allison
Jacob C. Diemert
Philip J. Notopoulos
Richard J. Hindlian
Paul E. Troy
Harold W. Potter, Jr.
Dale R. Johnson
Philip S. Lapatin
Pamela A. Duckworth
Mark Schonfeld
James D. Smeallie
Paul Killeen
Gordon P. Katz

(See Next Column)

Joseph B. Darby, III
Richard M Yanofsky
James E. McDermott
Robert V. Lizza
Miriam Goldstein Altman
John J. Monaghan
Margaret J. Palladino
Mark C. Michalowski
David Scott Sloan
M. Chrysa Long
Lawrence D. Bradley
Miriam J. McKendall

Cynthia A. Brown
Cynthia M. Hern
Dianne R. Phillips
Paul M. James
Theodore F. Hanselman
Joshua C. Krumholz
Ieuan G. Mahony
Kenneth L. Harvey
Christopher J. Trombetta
Edwin F. Landers, Jr.
Amy J. Mastrobattista
William Howard McCarthy, Jr.
Douglas W. Clapp
Tamara E. Goulston
Nicholas J. Psyhogeos

COUNSEL

Haig Der Manuelian
Mason M. Taber, Jr.
Karl J. Hirshman
Benjamin Volinski
Kenneth P. Brier

OF COUNSEL

John Barr Dolan

For full biographical listings, see the Martindale-Hubbell Law Directory

WILLCOX, PIROZZOLO AND MCCARTHY, PROFESSIONAL CORPORATION (AV)

50 Federal Street, 02110
Telephone: 617-482-5470
Telecopier: 617-423-1572
Worcester, Massachusetts Office: 421 Main Street.
Telephone: 508-799-7446.

Harold M. Willcox (1925-1975)
Jack R. Pirozzolo
Richard F. McCarthy

Richard L. Binder
Richard E. Bennett
Judith Seplowitz Ziss
Kelly M. Bird

OF COUNSEL

Richard P. Crowley
Thomas A. Kahrl

For full biographical listings, see the Martindale-Hubbell Law Directory

LONGMEADOW, Hampden Co.

HOLLAND & ASSOCIATES (AV)

Longmeadow Professional Park, 171 Dwight Road, 01106
Telephone: 413-567-2076
Fax: 413-567-2079
Springfield, Massachusetts Office: 1441 Main Street, 01103.
Telephone: 413-737-5524

Donald S. Holland

ASSOCIATES

Mary R. Bonzagni
Richard H. Kosakowski

For full biographical listings, see the Martindale-Hubbell Law Directory

*SPRINGFIELD,** Hampden Co.

HOLLAND & ASSOCIATES (AV)

1441 Main Street, 01103
Telephone: 413-737-5524
FAX: 413-567-2079
Longmeadow, Massachusetts Office: Longmeadow Professional Park, 171 Dwight Road, 01106.
Telephone: 413-567-2076.
Fax: 413-567-2079.

Donald S. Holland

For full biographical listings, see the Martindale-Hubbell Law Directory

MICHIGAN

*ANN ARBOR,** Washtenaw Co.

BODMAN, LONGLEY & DAHLING (AV)

110 Miller, Suite 300, 48104
Telephone: 313-761-3780
Fax: 313-930-2494
Detroit, Michigan Office: 34th Floor, 100 Renaissance Center.
Telephone: 313-259-7777.
Troy, Michigan Office: Suite 2020, 755 West Big Beaver Road.
Telephone: 810-362-2110.
Northern Michigan Office: 229 Court Street, P.O. Box 405, Cheboygan.
Telephone: 616-627-4351.

(See Next Column)

BODMAN, LONGLEY & DAHLING, *Ann Arbor—Continued*

RESIDENT PARTNERS

Mark W. Griffin | Harvey W. Berman
Thomas A. Roach | Jerold Lax
Randolph S. Perry | Susan M. Kornfield

RESIDENT COUNSEL

John S. Dobson | Patricia D. White

RESIDENT ASSOCIATES

Sandra L. Sorini | Stephen K. Postema
Lydia Pallas Loren

For full biographical listings, see the Martindale-Hubbell Law Directory

HARNESS, DICKEY & PIERCE (AV)

Suite 555, 301 East Liberty Street, 48104
Telephone: 313-662-5653
Telex: 287637 HARNES UR
Telefacsimile (All Groups): 313-662-7813
Troy, Michigan Office: 5445 Corporate Drive, Suite 400.
Telephone: 810-641-1600. Telefacsimile (All Groups): 810-641-0270.
Newport Beach California Office: 4041 MacArthur Boulevard, Suite 400.
Telephone: 714-760-6233.
Telefacsimile: 714-760-6123.
San Diego, California Office: 900 First Interstate Plaza, 401 B Street.
Telephone: 619-238-4122.
Telefacsimile: 619-238-0970.

MEMBERS OF FIRM

James E. Stephenson (Resident) | Steven L. Oberholtzer (Resident)

RESIDENT ASSOCIATES

Charles T. Graham | Eric J. Sosenko
Keith D. Grzelak

Representative Clients: Chrysler Corp.; The Black and Decker Manufacturing Co.; Thermos Co.; Monroe Auto Equipment Co.; La-Z-Boy Chair Co.; Hughes Aircraft; Budd Co.; Dow Chemical Co.; Procter & Gamble; Kmart Properties.

For full biographical listings, see the Martindale-Hubbell Law Directory

BLOOMFIELD HILLS, Oakland Co.

DYKEMA GOSSETT (AV)

1577 North Woodward Avenue Suite 300, 48304-2820
Telephone: 810-540-0700
Telex: 23-0121
Fax: 810-540-0763
Detroit, Michigan Office: 400 Renaissance Center, 48243-1668.
Telephone: 313-568-6800.
Fax: 313-568-6594.
Ann Arbor, Michigan Office: 315 East Eisenhower Parkway, Suite 100, 48108-3306.
Telephone: 313-747-7660.
Fax: 313-747-7696.
Grand Rapids, Michigan Office: 200 Oldtown Riverfront Building, 248 Louis Campau Promenade, N.W., 49503-2668.
Telephone: 616-776-7500.
Fax: 616-776-7573.
Lansing, Michigan Office: 800 Michigan National Tower, 48933.
Telephone: 517-374-9100.
Fax: 517-374-9191.
Washington, D.C. Office: Franklin Square, Suite 300 West Tower, 1300 I Street, N.W., 20005-3306.
Telephone: 202-522-8600.
Fax: 202-522-86697
Chicago, Illinois Office: Three First National Plaza, Suite 1400, 70 W. Madison, 60602-4270.
Telephone: 312-214-3380.
Fax: 312-214-3441.

RESIDENT MEMBERS

Michael D. Fishman | Ralph T. Rader
Richard D. Grauer | Charles R. Rutherford
Robert L. Kelly | Randy W. Tung

RETIRED MEMBER

Robert A. Sloman

RESIDENT ASSOCIATES

Joseph V. Coppola, Sr. | John W. Rees
David John Gaskey | Stephen L. Scharf
Kevin M. Hinman | Michael B. Stewart

For Complete List of Firm Personnel, See General Section

For full biographical listings, see the Martindale-Hubbell Law Directory

HOWARD & HOWARD ATTORNEYS, P.C. (AV)

The Pinehurst Office Center, Suite 101, 1400 North Woodward Avenue, 48304-2856
Telephone: 810-645-1483
Telecopier: 810-645-1568
Kalamazoo, Michigan Office: The Kalamazoo Building, Suite 400, 107 West Michigan Avenue.
Telephone: 616-382-1483.
Telecopier: 616-382-1568.
Lansing, Michigan Office: The Phoenix Building, Suite 500, 222 Washington Square, North.
Telephone: 517-485-1483.
Telecopier: 517-485-1568.
Peoria, Illinois Office: Howard & Howard, P.C., The Creve Coeur Building, Suite 200, 321 Liberty Street.
Telephone: 309-672-1483.
Telecopier: 309-672-1568.

Fernando A. Borrego | Theodore W. Olds III
William J. Clemens | Jeffrey G. Raphelson
William H. Honaker | Deborah M. Schneider
Raymond E. Scott

Representative Clients: For Representative Client list, see General Practice, Bloomfield Hills, MI.

For Complete List of Firm Personnel, See General Section

For full biographical listings, see the Martindale-Hubbell Law Directory

*DETROIT,** Wayne Co.

BARNES, KISSELLE, RAISCH, CHOATE, WHITTEMORE & HULBERT, P.C. (AV)

3500 Penobscot Building, 48226
Telephone: 313-962-4790
Telecopier: 313-962-0158
Cable Address: "Barkl"

Stuart C. Barnes (1885-1968) | L. Gaylord Hulbert (1895-1980)
John M. Kisselle (1894-1980) | Basil C. Foussianes
Arthur Raisch (1902-1991) | William H. Griffith
Lacey Laughlin (1896-1956) | William J. Waugaman
Prescott M. Hulbert (1865-1961) | Chester L. Davis, Jr.
Laurence J. Whittemore (1871-1946) | William H. Francis
| Robert C. Collins
William J. Belknap (1883-1941) | Linda M. Deschere

David D. Stein | James L. Wolfe
Bryan J. Lempia

OF COUNSEL

Robert A. Choate | Alfonse John D'Amico

Representative Clients: General Motors Corporation; Goodyear Tire & Rubber Co.; Henry Ford Hospital; Motor Wheel Corp.; Owens-Illinois, Inc.; SPX Corp.; Vickers, Inc.; Walbro Corp.

For full biographical listings, see the Martindale-Hubbell Law Directory

BODMAN, LONGLEY & DAHLING (AV)

34th Floor 100 Renaissance Center, 48243
Telephone: 313-259-7777
Fax: 313-393-7579
Troy, Michigan Office: Suite 2020, 755 West Big Beaver Road.
Telephone: 810-362-2110.
Ann Arbor, Michigan Office: 110 Miller, Suite 300.
Telephone: 313-761-3780.
Northern Michigan Office: 229 Court Street, P.O. Box 405, Cheboygan.
Telephone: 616-627-4351.

MEMBERS OF FIRM

Henry E. Bodman (1874-1963) | Joseph J. Kochanek
Clifford B. Longley (1888-1954) | Randolph S. Perry (Ann Arbor Office)
Louis F. Dahling (1892-1992) | James J. Walsh
Pierre V. Heftler | David G. Chardavoyne
Richard D. Rohr | David W. Hipp
Theodore Souris | Robert G. Brower
Joseph A. Sullivan | Larry R. Shulman
Carson C. Grunewald | Charles N. Raimi
Walter O. Koch (Troy Office) | Terrence B. Larkin (Troy Office)
Alfred C. Wortley, Jr. | Thomas Van Dusen (Troy Office)
Michael B. Lewiston | Fredrick J. Dindoffer
George D. Miller, Jr. | Robert J. Diehl, Jr.
Mark W. Griffin (Ann Arbor Office) | John C. Cashen (Troy Office)
Thomas A. Roach (Ann Arbor Office) | James C. Conboy, Jr. (Northern Michigan Office)
Kenneth R. Lango (Troy Office) | Lloyd C. Fell (Northern Michigan Office)
James T. Heimbuch | F. Thomas Lewand
Herold McC. Deason | Michael A. Stack (Northern Michigan Office)
James A. Smith | Kathleen A. Lieder (Northern Michigan Office)
James R. Buschmann |
George G. Kemsley |
Joseph N. Brown |
David M. Hempstead |

(See Next Column)

BODMAN, LONGLEY & DAHLING—*Continued*

MEMBERS OF FIRM (Continued)

Karen L. Piper	Linda J. Throne (Northern Michigan Office)
Martha Bedsole Goodloe (Troy Office)	Diane L. Akers
Harvey W. Berman (Ann Arbor Office)	Ralph E. McDowell
Barbara Bowman Bluford	Susan M. Kornfield (Ann Arbor Office)
R. Craig Hupp	Stephen I. Greenhalgh
Lawrence P. Hanson (Northern Michigan Office)	Kathleen O'Callaghan Hickey
Christopher J. Dine (Troy Office)	Patrick C. Cauley
Henry N. Carnaby (Troy Office)	Dennis J. Levasseur
Jerold Lax (Ann Arbor Office)	David P. Larsen
	Gail Pabarue Bennett (Troy Office)

Kay E. Malaney (Troy Office)

COUNSEL

Robert A. Nitschke	Lewis A. Rockwell
John S. Dobson (Ann Arbor Office)	Patricia D. White (Ann Arbor Office)

ASSOCIATES

Gary D. Reeves (Troy Office)	Louise-Annette Marcotty
Joseph W. Girardot	William L. Hoey
Barnett Jay Colvin	Laurie A. Allen (Troy Office)
David W. Barton (Northern Michigan Office)	Marc M. Bakst
Susan E. Conboy (Northern Michigan Office)	A. Craig Klomparens (Northern Michigan Office)
Sandra L. Sorini (Ann Arbor Office)	Kim M. Williams
Stephen K. Postema (Ann Arbor Office)	David P. Rea
Bonnie S. Sherr	Jodee Fishman Raines
Lisa M. Panourgias	Nicholas P. Scavone, Jr.
R. Carl Lanfear	Lydia Pallas Loren (Ann Arbor Office)
	Robert C. Skramstad
	Deanna L. Dixon

Arthur F. deVaux (Troy Office)

Representative Clients: Abitibi Price Group; Archdiocese of Detroit; Comerica Bank; The Detroit Lions, Inc.; Ford Estates; General Motors Corporation; Charles Stewart Mott Foundation; Norfolk Southern Corporation; Panhandle Eastern Corporation; State Farm Mutual Automobile Insurance Company.

For full biographical listings, see the Martindale-Hubbell Law Directory

DICKINSON, WRIGHT, MOON, VAN DUSEN & FREEMAN (AV)

500 Woodward Avenue, Suite 4000, 48226-3425
Telephone: 313-223-3500
Facsimile: 313-223-3598
Bloomfield Hills, Michigan Office: 525 North Woodward Avenue, Suite 2000.
Telephone: 810-433-7200.
Facsimile: 810-433-7274.
Grand Rapids, Michigan Office: 200 Ottawa Avenue, N.W., Suite 900.
Telephone: 616-458-1300.
Facsimile: 616-458-6753.
Lansing, Michigan Office: Suite 200, 215 South Washington Square.
Telephone: 517-371-1730.
Facsimile: 517-487-4700.
Washington, D.C. Office: Suite 800, 1901 L Street, N.W.
Telephone: 202-457-0160.
Facsimile: 202-659-1559.
Chicago, Illinois Office: 225 West Washington, Suite 400.
Telephone: 312-220-0300.
Facsimile: 312-220-0021.
Warsaw, Poland Office: 46 Wilcza Street, 4th Floor, 00-679.
Telephone: (48-22) 299-241.
Facsimile: (48-2) 628-4107. Komertel Satellite Phone: (48-39) 121-510.

MEMBERS OF FIRM

Michael T. Platt (Washington, D.C. Office)	Conrad J. Clark (Washington, D.C. Office)
Samuel D. Littlepage (Washington, D.C. Office)	

OF COUNSEL

Bruce A. Tassan (Washington, D.C. Office)

For Complete List of Firm Personnel, See General Section

For full biographical listings, see the Martindale-Hubbell Law Directory

MILLER, CANFIELD, PADDOCK AND STONE, P.L.C. (AV)

A Professional Limited Liability Company
Founded in 1852 by Sidney Davy Miller
150 West Jefferson, Suite 2500, 48226-4415
Telephone: 313-963-6420
Fax: 313-496-7500
Cable Address: "Stem Detroit"
Detroit, Michigan Office: 150 West Jefferson, Suite 2500, 48226-4415.
Telephone: 313-963-6420.
Fax: 313-496-7500.
Cable Address: "Stem Detroit."

(See Next Column)

Ann Arbor, Michigan Office: 101 North Main Street, 7th Floor, 48104-1400.
Telephone: 313-663-2445.
Fax: 313-747-7147.
Bloomfield Hills, Michigan Office: Suite 100, Pinehurst Office Center, 1400 North Woodward, 48303-2014.
Telephone: 313-645-5000.
Fax: 313-645-1917.
Grand Rapids, Michigan Office: 1200 Campau Square Plaza, 99 Monroe, N.W., 49503-2639.
Telephone: 616-454-8656.
Fax: 616-776-6322.
Howell, Michigan Office: 121 South Barnard Street, Suite 4, 48843-2305.
Telephone: 517-546-7600.
Telecopier: 517-546-6974.
Kalamazoo, Michigan Office: 444 West Michigan Avenue, 49007-3752.
Telephone: 616-381-7030.
Fax: 616-382-0244.
Lansing, Michigan Office: One Michigan Avenue, Suite 900, 48933-1609.
Telephone: 517-487-2070.
Fax: 517-374-6304.
Monroe, Michigan Office: The Executive Centre, 214 East Elm Avenue, 48161-2682.
Telephone: 313-243-2000.
Fax: 313-243-0901.
Washington, D.C. Office: 1225 Nineteenth Street, N.W., Suite 400. 20036.
Telephone: 202-429-5575; 785-0600.
Fax: 202-331-1118; 785-1234.
Pensacola, Florida Office: 25 West Cedar, 32501.
Telephone: 904-469-1088.
Fax: 904-432-0677.
St. Petersburg, Florida Office: 100 Second Avenue S., Suite 7045, 33701.
Telephone: 813-982-6000.
Fax: 813-892-6002.
Gdansk, Poland Office: Suite 322, Dom Technika Building, Ul. Rajska 6, 80-850.
Telephone: 011-485-831-2808.
Fax: 011-485-831-4719.
Warsaw, Poland Office: Ul. Marszalkowska 82, Suite 561, 00-517.
Telephone: 011-482-623-6457 and 6458.
Fax: 011-482-623-6459.

MEMBER OF FIRM

Marjory G. Basile

Representative Firm Clients: Chrysler Corp.; Comerica, Inc.; City of Detroit, Mich.; Detroit Tigers, Inc.; First of Michigan; Fretter, Inc.; Ford Motor Co.; Ford Motor Credit Co.; Great Lakes Bancorp; Henry Ford Hospital.

For Complete List of Firm Personnel, See General Section

For full biographical listings, see the Martindale-Hubbell Law Directory

*GRAND RAPIDS,** Kent Co.

PRICE, HENEVELD, COOPER, DEWITT & LITTON (AV)

695 Kenmoor, S.E., P.O. Box 2567, 49501
Telephone: 616-949-9610
Cable Address: "Preld"
Telex: 226-402
Telecopier: 616-957-8196

MEMBERS OF FIRM

Lloyd A. Heneveld	Harold W. Reick
Richard C. Cooper	Donald S. Gardner
William W. DeWitt	Thomas M. McKinley
Randall G. Litton	Carl S. Clark
James A. Mitchell	Terence J. Linn
Daniel Van Dyke	Frederick S. Burkhart

ASSOCIATES

James E. Bartek	Mark E. Bandy
Daniel L. Girdwood	Barry C. Kane

Representative Clients: Amway Corp.; Donnelly Corp.; Dow Chemical Co.; Gerber Products Co.; Kysor Industrial Corp.; L. Perrigo Co.; Prince Corp.; Ralston Purina Co.; Steelcase, Inc.; Wolverine World Wide, Inc.

For full biographical listings, see the Martindale-Hubbell Law Directory

VARNUM, RIDDERING, SCHMIDT & HOWLETT (AV)

Bridgewater Place, P.O. Box 352, 49501-0352
Telephone: 616-336-6000
800-262-0011
Facsimile: 616-336-7000
Telex: 1561593 VARN
Lansing, Michigan Office: The Victor Center, Suite 810, 210 North Washington Square, 48933.
Telephone: 517-482-6237.
Facsimile: 517-482-6937.
Kalamazoo, Michigan Office: 350 East Michigan Avenue, 49007.
Telephone: 616-382-2300.
Facsimile: 616-382-2382.
Grand Haven, Michigan Office: 321 Washington Street, P.O. Box 288, 49417.
Telephone: 616-846-7100.
Facsimile: 616-846-7101.

(See Next Column)

VARNUM, RIDDERING, SCHMIDT & HOWLETT, *Grand Rapids—Continued*

Battle Creek, Michigan Office: 4950 West Dickman Road, Suite B-1, 49015.
Telephone: 616-962-7144.
Detroit, Michigan Office: 440 East Congress, Fourth Floor, 48226.
Telephone: 313-961-1600.
Facsimile: 313-961-1636.

COUNSEL

Peter Visserman

MEMBERS OF FIRM

John E. McGarry | H. Lawrence Smith
Thomas L. Lockhart | Timothy E. Eagle
Joel E. Bair

ASSOCIATES

Richard J. McKenna | Mark A. Davis

Counsel for: Cadillac Rubber & Plastics, Inc.; Cascade Engineering; Herman Miller, Inc.; Neway Anchorlok, Inc.; Smith's Industries; X-Rite, Inc.

For Complete List of Firm Personnel, See General Section

For full biographical listings, see the Martindale-Hubbell Law Directory

WARNER, NORCROSS & JUDD (AV)

900 Old Kent Building, 111 Lyon Street, N.W., 49503-2489
Telephone: 616-752-2000
Fax: 616-752-2500
Muskegon, Michigan Office: 400 Terrace Plaza, P.O. Box 900.
Telephone: 616-727-2600.
Fax: 616-727-2699.
Holland, Michigan Office: Curtis Center, Suite 300, 170 College Avenue.
Telephone: 616-396-9800.
Fax: 616-396-3656.

MEMBERS OF FIRM

James H. Breay | John G. Cameron, Jr.
Peter L. Gustafson | Stephen C. Waterbury
Charles E. Burpee

Representative Clients: Amstore Corp; Guardsman Products; H.H. Cutler Co.; High Q Manufacturing Co.; Morbark Industries, Inc.; ODL Incorporated; Pandrol Jackson, Inc.; Plascore, Inc.; Rockford Corp.; The Zondervan Corp.

For Complete List of Firm Personnel, See General Section

For full biographical listings, see the Martindale-Hubbell Law Directory

HOLLAND, Ottawa Co.

MCKINNON AND MCKINNON (AV)

A Partnership including a Professional Corporation
305 Hoover Boulevard, 49423
Telephone: 616-393-6400
Fax: 616-393-4931
Williamston, Michigan Office: One Energy Center, 148 East Grand River, P.O. Box 102.
Telephone: 517-349-0780.
Fax: 517-349-0781.

Malcolm R. McKinnon (P.C.) | Malcolm L. McKinnon

For full biographical listings, see the Martindale-Hubbell Law Directory

*KALAMAZOO,** Kalamazoo Co.

MILLER, CANFIELD, PADDOCK AND STONE, P.L.C. (AV)

A Professional Limited Liability Company
Founded in 1852 by Sidney Davy Miller
444 West Michigan Avenue, 49007-3752
Telephone: 616-381-7030
Fax: 616-382-0244
Detroit, Michigan Office: 150 West Jefferson, Suite 2500, 48226-4415.
Telephone: 313-963-6420.
Fax: 313-496-7500.
Cable Address: "Stem Detroit."
Ann Arbor, Michigan Office: 101 North Main Street, 7th Floor, 48104-1400.
Telephone: 313-663-2445.
Fax: 313-747-7147.
Bloomfield Hills, Michigan Office: Suite 100, Pinehurst Office Center, 1400 North Woodward, 48303-2014.
Telephone: 313-645-5000.
Fax: 313-645-1917.
Grand Rapids, Michigan Office: 1200 Campau Square Plaza, 99 Monroe, N.W., 49503-2639.
Telephone: 616-454-8656.
Fax: 616-776-6322.
Howell, Michigan Office: 121 South Barnard Street, Suite 4, 48843-2305.
Telephone: 517-546-7600.
Telecopier: 517-546-6974.
Lansing, Michigan Office: One Michigan Avenue, Suite 900, 48933-1609.
Telephone: 517-487-2070.
Fax: 517-374-6304.

(See Next Column)

Monroe, Michigan Office: The Executive Centre, 214 East Elm Avenue, 48161-2682.
Telephone: 313-243-2000.
Fax: 313-243-0901.
Washington, D.C. Office: 1225 Nineteenth Street, N.W., Suite 400. 20036.
Telephone: 202-429-5575; 785-0600.
Fax: 202-331-1118; 785-1234.
Pensacola, Florida Office: 25 West Cedar, 32501.
Telephone: 904-469-1088.
Fax: 904-432-0677.
St. Petersburg, Florida Office: 100 Second Avenue S., Suite 7045,33701.
Telephone: 813-982-6000.
Fax: 813-892-6002.
Gdansk, Poland Office: Suite 322, Dom Technika Building, UI. Rajska 6, 80-850.
Telephone: 011-485-831-2808.
Fax: 011-485-831-4719.
Warsaw, Poland Office: UI. Marszalkowska 82, Suite 561, 00-517.
Telephone: 011-482-623-6457 and 6458.
Fax: 011-482-623-6459.

MEMBER OF FIRM

Eric V. Brown, Jr. (Resident)

Representative Firm Clients: Chrysler Corp.; Comerica, Inc.; City of Detroit, Mich.; Detroit Tigers, Inc.; First of Michigan; Fretter, Inc.; Ford Motor Co.; Ford Motor Credit Co.; Great Lakes Bancorp; Henry Ford Hospital.

For Complete List of Firm Personnel, See General Section

For full biographical listings, see the Martindale-Hubbell Law Directory

LANSING, Ingham Co.

FOSTER, SWIFT, COLLINS & SMITH, P.C. (AV)

313 South Washington Square, 48933-2193
Telephone: 517-371-8100
Telecopier: 517-371-8200
Farmington Hills, Michigan Office: 32300 Northwestern Highway, Suite 230.
Telephone: 810-851-7500.
Fax: 810-851-7504.

Gary J. McRay | Robert L. Knechtel

General Counsel for: First American Bank-Central; Story, Inc.; Michigan Milk Producers Assn.; Edward W. Sparrow Hospital; St. Lawrence Hospital; Demmer Corp.; Michigan Financial Corp.
Local Counsel for: Shell Oil Co.; Michigan-Mutual Insurance Co.; Century Cellunet.

For Complete List of Firm Personnel, See General Section

For full biographical listings, see the Martindale-Hubbell Law Directory

OKEMOS, Ingham Co.

IAN C. MCLEOD, P.C. (AV)

2190 Commons Parkway, 48864
Telephone: 517-347-4100
Telecopier: 517-347-4103

Ian C. McLeod | Mary M. Moyne

Representative Clients: Ash Stevens, Inc., Detroit, Michigan; Quest International, Inc., Sarasota, Florida; Michigan State University, East Lansing, Michigan; Wayne State University, Detroit, Michigan; Technical Advisors, Inc., Wayne, Michigan; Unilever, Netherlands, Prototypes, England; Lumigen Inc., Detroit, Michigan.
References: Michigan National Bank; First of America; Bank of Lansing, Lansing, Michigan.

For full biographical listings, see the Martindale-Hubbell Law Directory

*SAGINAW,** Saginaw Co.

LEARMAN & MCCULLOCH AND REISING, ETHINGTON, BARNARD, PERRY & MILTON (AV)

5291 Colony Drive, North, 48603
Telephone: 517-799-5300
Telecopier: 792-8585
Troy, Michigan Office: Reising, Ethington, Barnard, Perry & Milton and Learman & McCulloch. Suite 400, 201 West Big Beaver Road. P.O. Box 4390.
Telephone: 810-689-3500.

RESIDENT PARTNERS

John F. Learman | John K. McCulloch

RESIDENT ASSOCIATES

Robert L. Farris | Robert L. Stearns

For full biographical listings, see the Martindale-Hubbell Law Directory

TROY, Oakland Co.

HARNESS, DICKEY & PIERCE (AV)

5445 Corporate Drive, Suite 400, 48098
Telephone: 810-641-1600
Cable Address: "PATENTS TROYMICHIGAN"
Telex: 287637 HARNES UR
Telefacsimile (All Groups): 810-641-0270
Ann Arbor, Michigan Office: Suite 555, 301 East Liberty Street.
Telephone: 313-662-5653.
Telefacsimile: 313-662-7813.
Newport Beach, California Office: 4041 MacArthur Boulevard, Suite 400.
Telephone: 714-760-6233.
Telefacsimile: 714-760-6123.
San Diego, California Office: 900 First Interstate Plaza, 401 B Street.
Telephone: 619-238-4122.
Telefacsimile: 619-238-0970.

MEMBERS OF FIRM

J. King Harness (1897-1977)
Arthur W. Dickey (1897-1964)
Hodgson S. Pierce (1896-1947)
Charles H. Blair
Joseph R. Papp
H. Keith Miller
James E. Stephenson (Resident at Ann Arbor Office)
Bernard J. Cantor
Welton B. Whann (Resident at San Diego, California Office)
William G. Lane (Resident at Newport Beach, California Office)
Christopher M. Brock
Richard L. Carlson
Ronald L. Hofer
Jeffrey A. Sadowski
Paul A. Keller
William Jude Coughlin
G. Gregory Schivley
Ronald W. Wangerow
Gregory A. Stobbs
Steven L. Oberholtzer (Resident at Ann Arbor Office)
Michael P. Brennan
Gordon K. Harris, Jr.
Stephen J. Foss
Gary L. Newtson
W. R. Duke Taylor
Richard P. Vitek
Robert S. Nolan
Philip R. Warn
Thomas A. Hallin
Philip E. Rettig
Eric M. Dobrusin

ASSOCIATES

Garrett C. Donley
Mark D. Elchuk
Stanley M. Erjavac
Monte Lee Falcoff
Charles T. Graham (Resident at Ann Arbor Office)
Keith D. Grzelak (Resident at Ann Arbor Office)
Kevin T. Grzelak
Joseph M. Lafata
Douglas P. LaLone
David A. McClaughry
John A. Miller
Thomas Traian Moga
Stephen T. Olson
Michael J. Schmidt
George T. Schooff
Robert M. Siminski
DeAnn Foran Smith
Eric J. Sosenko (Resident at Ann Arbor Office)
David P. Utykanski
Richard W. Warner
Donald L. Wenskay (Resident, San Diego, California Office)
Michael D. Wiggins

COUNSEL

Sally Lee Foley
Robert J. Wallace, Sr.
Lisabeth H. Coakley
Rebecca Birchmore Campen (Not admitted in MI)

Representative Clients: Chrysler Corp.; Diamond Crystal Salt Co.; The Black and Decker Manufacturing Co.; King-Seeley Thermos Co.; Monroe Auto Equipment Co.; La-Z-Boy Chair Co.; Hughes Aircraft; Budd Co.; Dow Chemical Co.; Procter & Gamble; Kmart Properties.

For full biographical listings, see the Martindale-Hubbell Law Directory

LYMAN R. LYON (AV)

755 West Big Beaver Road, Suite 2224, 48084
Telephone: 810-362-2600
Facsimile: 810-362-1094

For full biographical listings, see the Martindale-Hubbell Law Directory

REISING, ETHINGTON, BARNARD, PERRY & MILTON AND LEARMAN & McCULLOCH (AV)

Suite 400, 201 West Big Beaver, P.O. Box 4390, 48099
Telephone: 810-689-3500
Fax: 810-689-4071
Saginaw, Michigan Office: Learman & McCulloch and Reising, Ethington, Barnard, Perry & Milton. 5291 Colony Drive North, Saginaw, Michigan, 48603.
Telephone: 517-799-5300.
FAX: 517-792-8585.

MEMBERS OF FIRM

Richard P. Barnard (1924-1993)
Paul J. Reising (1923-1993)
Laurie A. Ebling
Paul J. Ethington
John C. Evans
Francis J. Fodale
Richard W. Hoffmann
Kenneth I. Kohn
John F. Learman (Resident, Saginaw, Michigan Office)
Jeanne-Marie Marshall
John K. McCulloch (Resident Saginaw, Michigan Office)
Harold W. Milton, Jr.
Steven L. Permut
Owen E. Perry

(See Next Column)

ASSOCIATES

Robin W. Asher
Craig A. Baldwin
Edward J. Biskup
Robert L. Farris (Resident, Saginaw, Michigan Office)
David R. Kurlandsky
Ilene Nowicki Montgomery
John P. Moran
Ronald L. Phillips
Jon E. Shackelford
David J. Simonelli
Robert L. Stearns (Resident, Saginaw, Michigan Office)
James D. Stevens
Charles R. White

OF COUNSEL

David A. Greenlee
Stanley C. Thorpe

Reference: Michigan National Bank of Detroit.

For full biographical listings, see the Martindale-Hubbell Law Directory

MINNESOTA

*MINNEAPOLIS,** Hennepin Co.

HAUGEN AND NIKOLAI, P.A. (AV)

820 International Centre, 900 Second Avenue South, 55402
Telephone: 612-339-7461
Telecopier: 612-349-6556

Orrin M. Haugen
Thomas J. Nikolai
James T. Nikolai
Charles G. Mersereau

Frederick W. Niebuhr
Eric O. Haugen
Catherine C. Maresh
Paul T. Dietz

Reference: Norwest Bank.

For full biographical listings, see the Martindale-Hubbell Law Directory

KINNEY & LANGE, P.A. (AV)

Suite 1500 625 Fourth Avenue South, 55415-1659
Telephone: 612-339-1863
Telex: 9103805042
Cable Address: Protek
Facsimile Transmission: 612-339-6580

Harold J. Kinney (1907-1986)
Frederick E. Lange (Retired-1987)
William A. Braddock (Retired-1991)
David R. Fairbairn
Jo M. Fairbairn
Zbigniew Peter Sawicki
James L. Young
Theodore F. Neils
Robert M. Angus
Vytas M. Rimas
Thomas J. Stueber
Julie Esther Witte
Deirdre A. Megley
Kevin B. Sullivan
Paul S. Grunzweig
Jeffrey D. Shewchuk
Michael L. Traino
John M. Weyrauch
Michael R. Binzak
Lawrence C. Chasin
Philip F. Fox
Mony R. Ghose
Todd A. Rathe
John D. Veldhuis-Kroeze
David D. Brush
David Plettner
John M. Vasuta
Patrick G. Billig
Michael A. Bondi
Gena M. Chapman
Timothy A. Czaja
Paul P. Kempf
Matthew B. McNutt
Paul W. Stanga

For full biographical listings, see the Martindale-Hubbell Law Directory

MERCHANT, GOULD, SMITH, EDELL, WELTER & SCHMIDT, PROFESSIONAL ASSOCIATION (AV)

3100 Norwest Center, 90 South 7th Street, 55402
Telephone: 612-332-5300
Telex: 290593
Facsimile: 612-332-9081 (GI, GII, GIII)
St. Paul, Minnesota Office: Suite One Thousand, Norwest Center, 55 E. 5th Street.
Telephone: 612-298-1055.
Facsimile: 612-298-1160.
Los Angeles, California Office: Merchant & Gould, Suite 400, 11150 Santa Monica Boulevard.
Telephone: 310-445-1140.
Facsimile: 310-445-9031.

Frank D. Merchant (1867-1943)
Ralph F. Merchant (1907-1980)
John D. Gould
Phillip H. Smith (Retired)
Robert T. Edell
Paul A. Welter
Cecil C. Schmidt (Resident at St. Paul Office)
John S. Sumners
Alan G. Carlson
Earl D. Reiland
Charles E. Golla (Resident at St. Paul Office)
Douglas J. Williams
Douglas A. Strawbridge
Albert L. Underhill
D. Randall King
Michael B. Lasky
Curtis B. Hamre
Michael D. Schumann
Michael L. Mau (Resident at St. Paul Office)

(See Next Column)

MERCHANT, GOULD, SMITH, EDELL, WELTER & SCHMIDT PROFESSIONAL ASSOCIATION, *Minneapolis—Continued*

John A. Clifford
Mark J. DiPietro (Resident at St. Paul Office)
Raymond A. Bogucki (Resident at Los Angeles Office)
Timothy R. Conrad
Alan W. Kowalchyk
Daniel W. McDonald
Randall A. Hillson
John P. Sumner
Wendy M. McDonald
Linda M. Byrne (Resident at St. Paul Office)
Mark D. Schuman
Albin James Nelson
Gregory B. Wood (Resident, Los Angeles, California Office)
George Henry Gates, III (Resident Los Angeles Office)
Brian H. Batzli (Resident at St. Paul Office)
David K. Tellekson
Charles Berman (Resident at Los Angeles Office)
John J. Gresens (Resident at St. Paul Office)
John L. Beard

Paul E. Lacy
Philip P. Caspers
Gregory A. Sebald
Robert C. Beck
Kristine M. Strodthoff
Steven C. Bruess
Andrew D. Sorensen (Resident at St. Paul Office)
Katherine M. Kowalchyk
J. Derek Vandenburgh
Mark A. Krull (Resident at St. Paul Office)
Alan G. Gorman
Philip S. Yip
Joseph M. Kastelic
Theodore R. Plunkett
John C. Reich
Caroline G. Kadievitch
Thomas E. Bejin
David W. Lynch (Resident, Los Angeles, California Office)
Dennis R. Daley
Ronald A. Daignault (Resident at St. Paul Office)
Scott A. Stinebruner (Resident at St. Paul Office)
Charles G. Carter
Edmond Arthur DeFrank (Resident at Los Angeles Office)
Jerome R. Smith, Jr.
Dawn M. Larsen (Not admitted in MN)
Karen D. McDaniel
Lance L. Vietzke
Michael B. Farber (Resident at Los Angeles Office)
Sarah B. Adriano (Resident at Los Angeles Office)
Michael R. Cohen
Mark A. Hollingsworth (Not admitted in MN)
Robert J. Crawford (Not admitted in MN)
Leslie E. B. Dalglish (Not admitted in MN)

Representative Clients: Cray Research, Inc.; Donaldson Co., Inc.; Honeywell, Inc.; Medtronic, Inc.; Minnetonka, Inc.; Norwest Corp.; Northwestern National Life Insurance Co.; The Toro Co.; Tonka Corp.; University of Minnesota.

For full biographical listings, see the Martindale-Hubbell Law Directory

---

MOORE & HANSEN (AV)

3000 Norwest Center, 90 South Seventh Street, 55402-4101
Telephone: 612-332-8200
Toll-free WATS: 1-800-362-1493
Fax: 612-332-1780

MEMBERS OF FIRM

Malcolm L. Moore
Conrad A. Hansen

ASSOCIATES

Chad A. Klingbeil
Daniel J. Polglaze (Not admitted in MN)

LEGAL SUPPORT PERSONNEL

Allen H. Erickson (Patent Agent)

Representative Clients: Liberty Diversified Industries; MedAmicus, Inc.; Stratesys, Inc.; Regis Corp.; Services Ideas, Inc.; Domain, Inc., New Richmond, Wis.; Dodger Industries, Inc., Eldora, Iowa; Slidell, Inc., Owatonna, Mn.

For full biographical listings, see the Martindale-Hubbell Law Directory

---

PALMATIER, SJOQUIST & HELGET, P.A. (AV)

2000 Norwest Financial Center, 7900 Xerxes Avenue, South, 55431
Telephone: 612-831-5454
Telex: 4310015
Fax: 612-831-8561

H. Dale Palmatier
Paul L. Sjoquist
Gerald E. Helget
Edwin E. Voigt II

Douglas J. Christensen
Nelson R. Capes

Representative Clients: Graco, Inc.; Magnepan, Inc.; Fluoroware, Inc.; FSI Corp.; IBM; Modern Controls, Inc.; Skyline Displays, Inc.; Michael Foods, Inc.

For full biographical listings, see the Martindale-Hubbell Law Directory

*ST. PAUL,** Ramsey Co.

* indicates certain Bar Register subscribers whose principal office is located elsewhere in the state and who have arranged for representation as a part of the state capital listings that follow

*** MERCHANT, GOULD, SMITH, EDELL, WELTER & SCHMIDT, PROFESSIONAL ASSOCIATION (AV)**

Suite One Thousand Norwest Center, 55 E. 5th Street, 55101
Telephone: 612-298-1055
Facsimile: 612-298-1160 (GI, GII, GIII)
Minneapolis Office: 3100 Norwest Center, 90 South 7th Street.
Telephone: 612-332-5300.
Los Angeles, California Office: Merchant & Gould, Suite 400, 11150 Santa Monica Boulevard.
Telephone: 310-445-1140.
Facsimile: 310-445-9031.

Frank D. Merchant (1868-1943)
Ralph F. Merchant (1907-1980)
Cecil C. Schmidt (Resident)
Charles E. Golla (Resident)
D. Randall King (Resident)
Michael L. Mau (Resident)
Mark J. DiPietro (Resident)
Linda M. Byrne (Resident)
Brian H. Batzli (Resident)
John J. Gresens (Resident)

Andrew D. Sorensen (Resident)
Mark A. Krull
Ronald A. Daignault (Not admitted in MN)
Scott A. Stinbruner

Representative Clients: Andersen Corp.; Animal Fair, Inc.; CPT Corp.; Donaldson Co.; Economics Laboratory, Inc.; H. B. Fuller; Ideal Security Hardware Corp.; McQuay, Inc.

For full biographical listings, see the Martindale-Hubbell Law Directory

MISSISSIPPI

*JACKSON,** Hinds Co.

ALSTON, RUTHERFORD, TARDY & VAN SLYKE (AV)

121 North State Street, P.O. Drawer 1532, 39215-1532
Telephone: 601-948-6882
Fax: 601-948-6902

MEMBERS OF FIRM

Terryl K. Rushing
C. Jackson Williams

Counsel for : Anheuser-Busch Companies, Inc.; Motion Picture Association of America, Inc.; E. I. Du Pont de Nemours & Co.; The Dow Chemical Co.; Dean Witter Reynolds Inc.; Ford Motor Co.; Yellow Freight Systems, Inc.; Xerox Corp.; Gannett Co. Inc.; Mississippi Baptist Foundation.

For Complete List of Firm Personnel, See General Section

For full biographical listings, see the Martindale-Hubbell Law Directory

MISSOURI

KANSAS CITY, Jackson, Clay & Platte Cos.

HOVEY, WILLIAMS, TIMMONS & COLLINS (AV)

A Partnership of Professional Corporations
1400 Mercantile Bank Tower, 1101 Walnut Street, 64106-2165
Telephone: 816-474-9050
Watts: 800-445-3460
Cable Address: "Patlawkc"
Telex: 434363
Telefacsimile: 816-474-9057
Overland Park, Kansas Office: 9401 Indian Creek Parkway, Suite 870, Building 40 Corporate Woods.
Telephone: 913-338-1047.

MEMBERS OF FIRM

C. Earl Hovey (1897-1959)
Gordon D. Schmidt (1915-1985)
Donald E. Johnson (1921-1992)
Robert D. Hovey (P.C.)
Warren N. Williams (P.C.)
Stephen D. Timmons (P.C.)
John M. Collins (P.C.)
Steven R. Dickey (P.C.)
Thomas H. Van Hoozer (P.C.)
John A. Weresh

ASSOCIATE

Jill D. Singer

OF COUNSEL

William A. Rudy

For full biographical listings, see the Martindale-Hubbell Law Directory

Kansas City—Continued

KOKJER, KIRCHER, BOWMAN & JOHNSON, A PROFESSIONAL CORPORATION (AV)

2414 Commerce Tower, 911 Main Street, 64105-2088
Telephone: 816-474-5300
Telex: 42-4210 PATMARK KSC
Telecopier: 816-474-5304

Carter H. Kokjer
William B. Kircher
Joseph B. Bowman
Richard R. Johnson
K. Penny R. Slicer

Taylor J. Ross
Devon A. Rolf
Dean D. Small

For full biographical listings, see the Martindale-Hubbell Law Directory

LITMAN, MCMAHON AND BROWN (AV)

Formerly Fishburn, Gold and Litman
Suite 1600 One Kansas City Place, 1200 Main Street, 64105
Telephone: 816-842-1590
Facsimile: 816-472-5974

MEMBERS OF FIRM

Orville O. Gold (1908-1980)
Claude A. Fishburn (1896-1982)
Malcolm A. Litman
Gerald M. Kraai
John C. McMahon
Mark E. Brown
Michael Elbein
Kent R. Erickson

ASSOCIATES

Gerald L. Brigance
Marcia J. Rodgers

OF COUNSEL

David W. Clark

LEGAL SUPPORT PERSONNEL

PATENT AGENT

Dennis A. Crawford

For full biographical listings, see the Martindale-Hubbell Law Directory

ST. LOUIS, (Independent City)

POLSTER, LIEDER, WOODRUFF & LUCCHESI, L.C. (AV)

763 South New Ballas Road, 63141-8750
Telephone: 314-872-8118
Fax: 314-991-2178
Louisville, Kentucky Office: 2303 Tuckaho Road.
Telephone: 505-895-4672.

Roy Lieder (1924-1991)
Philip B. Polster
Frederick M. Woodruff
J. Philip Polster
Lionel L. Lucchesi
William B. Cunningham, Jr.
William G. Bruns
Edward A. Boeschenstein
Gregory E. Upchurch
Michael Kovac
J. Joseph Muller
Ralph B. Brick (Resident, Louisville, Kentucky Office)

Jonathan P. Soifer
Ned W. Randle
M. Lee Watson Gerdelman

OF COUNSEL

Martha A. Michaels
Richard J. Sher

For full biographical listings, see the Martindale-Hubbell Law Directory

ROGERS, HOWELL & HAFERKAMP (AV)

Suite 1400, Pierre Laclede Building, 7733 Forsyth Boulevard, 63105-1783
Telephone: 314-727-5188
Telex: 510-600-4342
Telecopier: 314-727-6092

OF COUNSEL

Edmund C. Rogers

MEMBERS OF FIRM

John M. Howell
Richard E. Haferkamp
Stanley M. Tarter
Kenneth Solomon
Joseph M. Rolnicki

ASSOCIATES

Daniel G. Feder
David E. Crawford, Jr.
Joseph E. Walsh, Jr.
Donald R. Holland (Not admitted in MO)

For full biographical listings, see the Martindale-Hubbell Law Directory

MONTANA

*BOZEMAN,** Gallatin Co.

PAUL R. WYLIE A PROFESSIONAL CORPORATION (AV(T))

1805 West Dickerson #2, Suite 3, 59715
Telephone: 406-585-7344
Telecopier: 406-585-7358

Paul R. Wylie

Reference: First Security Bank, Bozeman, Montana.

For full biographical listings, see the Martindale-Hubbell Law Directory

*MISSOULA,** Missoula Co.

HARRY M. CROSS, JR. (AV(T))

436 South 3rd West, P.O. Box 280, 59806-0280
Telephone: 406-728-5300
Fax: 406-549-9252
Bothell, Washington Office: 19119 Northcreek Parkway, Suite 207.
Telephone: 206-485-0899.
Fax: 206-488-5812.

Harry M. Cross, Jr. (Not admitted in MT)

Representative Clients: York International Corp.; Thompson Dental Manufacturing Co.; Creative Sales & Manufacturing Co.; Rawlings Manufacturing, Inc.

NEBRASKA

*OMAHA,** Douglas Co.

HENDERSON & STURM (AV)

Suite 330, 1125 South 103rd Street, 68124-1076
Telephone: 402-398-9000
Fax: 402-398-9005
Washington, D.C. Office: Suite 701, 1747 Pennsylvania Avenue, N.W.
Telephone: 202-296-3854.
Fax: 202-223-9606.
Des Moines, Iowa Office: 1213 Midland Building, 206 Sixth Avenue.
Telephone: 515-288-9589.
Fax: 515-288-4860.
Davenport, Iowa Office: 204 Northwest Bank Building-Downtown, 101 West Second Street.
Telephone: 319-323-9731.
Fax: 319-323-9709.

MEMBERS OF FIRM

H. Robert Henderson
Michael O. Sturm
Richard L. Fix

Robert J. Jondle (Resident)
Daniel B. Greenwood (Resident)

For full biographical listings, see the Martindale-Hubbell Law Directory

ZARLEY, MCKEE, THOMTE, VOORHEES & SEASE (AV)

1111 Commercial Federal Tower, 2120 South 72nd Street, 68124
Telephone: 402-392-2280
Telecopier: 402-392-0734
Des Moines, Iowa Office: 801 Grand, Suite 3200.
Telephone: 515-288-3667. Telex 706625.
Telecopier: 515-288-1338.
Toronto, Ontario, Canada Office: 40 King Street West, Suite 4300.
Telephone: 416-367-1576.
Telecopier: 416-367-6749.

MEMBERS OF FIRM

Donald H. Zarley (Not admitted in NE)
Bruce W. McKee (Not admitted in NE)
Dennis L. Thomte
Michael G. Voorhees (Not admitted in NE)
Edmund J. Sease (Not admitted in NE)
Mark D. Hansing (Not admitted in NE)
Kirk M. Hartung (Not admitted in NE)
Mark D. Frederiksen

ASSOCIATES

Denise C. Mazour
Daniel J. Cosgrove (Not admitted in NE)
Heidi Sease Nebel (Not admitted in NE)
Michael R. Crabb (Not admitted in NE)
Bruce A. Johnson (Not admitted in NE)
Wendy K. Hartung (Not admitted in NE)

OF COUNSEL

Dale L. Porter (Not admitted in NE)

Reference: Boatmen's National Bank of Des Moines (Des Moines, Iowa).

For full biographical listings, see the Martindale-Hubbell Law Directory

NEW HAMPSHIRE

*MANCHESTER,** Hillsborough Co.

DAVIS, BUJOLD & STRECK, PROFESSIONAL ASSOCIATION (AV)

175 Canal Street, 03101
Telephone: 603-624-9220
Telecopier: 603-624-9229

Anthony G. M. Davis (Not admitted in NH)
Michael J. Bujold
Donald A. Streck (Not admitted in NH)

For full biographical listings, see the Martindale-Hubbell Law Directory

PORTSMOUTH, Rockingham Co.

LORUSSO & LOUD (AV)

93 State Street, 02109
Telephone: 603-427-0070
Fax: 603-427-5530
Boston, Massachusetts Office: 440 Commercial Street.
Telephone: 617-227-0700.
Telefax: 617-723-4609.
Arlington, Virginia Office: 745 South 23rd Street, Suite 301.

Anthony M. Lorusso (Not admitted in NH)

For full biographical listings, see the Martindale-Hubbell Law Directory

NEW JERSEY

*HACKENSACK,** Bergen Co.

KLAUBER & JACKSON (AV)

Continental Plaza, 411 Hackensack Avenue, 07601
Telephone: 201-487-5800
Telex: 133521
Fax: 201-343-1684; 343-7544

MEMBERS OF FIRM

Stefan J. Klauber
David A. Jackson

ASSOCIATES

Barbara L. Renda
Lawrence D. Mandel

OF COUNSEL

Jeffrey L. Miller
Herbert H. Waddell

LEGAL SUPPORT PERSONNEL

Thomas E. Anderson

For full biographical listings, see the Martindale-Hubbell Law Directory

SAMUELSON & JACOB (AV)

25 East Salem Street, P.O. Box 686, 07602
Telephone: 201-488-8700
Telecopier: 201-488-3884

MEMBERS OF FIRM

Cyrus D. Samuelson
Arthur Jacob

For full biographical listings, see the Martindale-Hubbell Law Directory

*NEWARK,** Essex Co.

SILLS CUMMIS ZUCKERMAN RADIN TISCHMAN EPSTEIN & GROSS, A PROFESSIONAL CORPORATION (AV)

One Riverfront Plaza, 07102-5400
Telephone: 201-643-7000
Fax: 201-643-6500
Telex: 820630 Sillsbeck Nwk
Atlantic City, New Jersey Office: 17 Gordon's Alley.
Telephone: 609-344-2800.
New York, N.Y. Office: 250 Park Avenue.
Telephone: 212-643-7000.

Charles J. Walsh
Jeffrey J. Greenbaum
Jeffrey Barton Cahn
Ira A. Rosenberg
Marc S. Klein
Robert M. Axelrod

Representative Clients: Dominos Pizza, Inc.; Alpine Lace Brands.

For Complete List of Firm Personnel, See General Section

For full biographical listings, see the Martindale-Hubbell Law Directory

PRINCETON, Mercer Co.

BUCHANAN INGERSOLL (AV)

A Partnership
College Centre, 500 College Road East, 08540-6615
Telephone: 609-452-2666
Telecopier: 609-520-0360
Pittsburgh, Pennsylvania Office: Buchanan Ingersoll, Professional Corporation, 5800 USX Tower, 600 Grant Street.
Telephone: 412-562-8800.
Philadelphia, Pennsylvania Office: Buchanan Ingersoll, Professional Corporation, Two Logan Square, Twelfth Floor, 18th & Arch Streets.
Telephone: 215-665-8700.
Harrisburg, Pennsylvania Office: Buchanan Ingersoll, Professional Corporation, Vartan Parc, 30 North Third Street.
Telephone: 717-237-4800.
Tampa, Florida Office: Buchanan Ingersoll, Professional Corporation, 101 East Kennedy Boulevard, Suite 1030.
Telephone: 813-222-8180.
North Miami Beach, Florida Office: Buchanan Ingersoll, Professional Corporation, 19495 Biscayne Boulevard.
Telephone: 305-933-5600.
Lexington, Kentucky Office: Buchanan Ingersoll, Professional Corporation, 1210 Vine Center Office Tower, 333 West Vine Street.
Telephone: 606-225-5333.

Frank S. Chow

For Complete List of Firm Personnel, See General Section

For full biographical listings, see the Martindale-Hubbell Law Directory

ROSELAND, Essex Co.

CARELLA, BYRNE, BAIN, GILFILLAN, CECCHI, STEWART & OLSTEIN, A PROFESSIONAL CORPORATION (AV)

Six Becker Farm Road, 07068-1739
Telephone: 201-994-1700
Telecopier: 201-994-1744
Lyndhurst, New Jersey Office: Carella, Byrne, Bain, Gilfillan, Cecchi, Stewart & Olstein. 37 Park Avenue.
Telephone: 201-935-6900;
Telecopier: 201-804-9414.

John N. Bain
John G. Gilfillan, III
Elliot M. Olstein

Raymond J. Lillie
Charles J. Herron (Not admitted in NJ)
William Squire
Gregory D. Ferraro

OF COUNSEL

Donald S. Brooks

Representative Clients: Carter Wallace, Inc., New York, N.Y.; UA-Columbia Cablevision of New Jersey, Oakland, N.J.; FL Industries, Inc., Livingston, N.J.; Becton-Dickinson, Franklin Lakes, N.J.; Werner and Pfeiderer Corp., Ramsey, N.J.; Ausimont, USA.; E.J. Brooks Co.; Russ Berrie and Co., Inc.; The Pullman Co.; Fortex Industries.

For Complete List of Firm Personnel, See General Section

For full biographical listings, see the Martindale-Hubbell Law Directory

WESTFIELD, Union Co.

LERNER, DAVID, LITTENBERG, KRUMHOLZ & MENTLIK (AV)

600 South Avenue West, 07090-1497
Telephone: 908-654-5000
Cable Address: "Littpat", Westfield, N.J.
Telex: 139-125
Facsimile: 908-654-7866

MEMBERS OF FIRM

Lawrence I. Lerner
Sidney David
Joseph S. Littenberg
Arnold H. Krumholz
William L. Mentlik
John R. Nelson
Roy H. Wepner
Stephen B. Goldman
Charles P. Kennedy
Paul H. Kochanski
Marcus J. Millet
Bruce H. Sales
Arnold B. Dompieri

Peter J. Butch III
Keith E. Gilman
Robert B. Cohen
Michael H. Teschner
Jeffrey S. Dickey
Gregory S. Gewirtz
Jonathan A. David
Shawn P. Foley (Not admitted in NJ)
Lawrence G. Fridman (Not admitted in NJ)

OF COUNSEL

Daniel H. Bobis
W. Drew Kastner

For full biographical listings, see the Martindale-Hubbell Law Directory

NEW MEXICO

*ALBUQUERQUE,** Bernalillo Co.

MONTGOMERY & ANDREWS, PROFESSIONAL ASSOCIATION (AV)

Suite 1300 Albuquerque Plaza, 201 Third Street, N.W., P.O. Box 26927, 87125-6927
Telephone: 505-242-9677
FAX: 505-243-2542
Santa Fe, New Mexico Office: 325 Paseo De Peralta, P.O. Box 2307.
Telephone: 505-982-3873.

Deborah A. Peacock
Rod D. Baker
Jeffrey D. Myers
Donovan F. Duggan
(Not admitted in NM)

OF COUNSEL

Roberta Marie Price

Representative Clients: Sandia National Laboratories; New Mexico State University; New Mexico Tech Research Foundation; University of New Mexico; R.C. Gorman; The Georgia O'Keeffe Foundation.

For full biographical listings, see the Martindale-Hubbell Law Directory

*SANTA FE,** Santa Fe Co.

JONES, SNEAD, WERTHEIM, RODRIGUEZ & WENTWORTH, P.A. (AV)

215 Lincoln Avenue, P.O. Box 2228, 87504-2228
Telephone: 505-982-0011
Fax: 505-989-6288

O. Russell Jones (1912-1978)
James E. Snead
Jerry Wertheim
Manuel J. Rodriguez
John Wentworth
Arturo L. Jaramillo
Peter V. Culbert
James G. Whitley
Francis J. Mathew

Jerry Todd Wertheim
Carol A. Clifford

LEGAL SUPPORT PERSONNEL

PARALEGALS

Linda A. Zieba

General Counsel for: Charter Bank for Savings, F.S.B.; National Education Association of New Mexico.
Representative Clients: Century Bank, F.S.B.; 3M; Scurlock Permian Corp.; Merchants' Fast Motor Lines; Billy Walker Trucking, Inc.; Centel Cellular, Inc.; Santa Fe Properties, Inc.
Reference: Bank of Santa Fe.

For full biographical listings, see the Martindale-Hubbell Law Directory

NEW YORK

*ALBANY,** Albany Co.

HESLIN & ROTHENBERG, P.C. (AV)

5 Columbia Circle, 12203
Telephone: 518-452-5600
Facsimile: 518-452-5579
Telex: 710-110-1708 (PMS CAP BUS SVC)

Robert E. Heslin
Jeff Rothenberg
Kevin P. Radigan
Susan E. Farley
Nicholas Mesiti

Blanche E. Schiller
Wayne F. Reinke
Douglas H. Tulley, Jr.
John T. Johnson
Jeffrey R. Klembczyk
David Barron
Martha Linton Boden
Francis T. Coppa
(Not admitted in NY)
Walter D. Fields
(Not admitted in NY)

PATENT AGENT

Philip E. Hansen

For full biographical listings, see the Martindale-Hubbell Law Directory

*BUFFALO,** Erie Co.

HODGSON, RUSS, ANDREWS, WOODS & GOODYEAR (AV)

A Partnership including Professional Associations
Suite 1800, One M & T Plaza, 14203
Telephone: 716-856-4000
Cable Address: "Magna Carta" Buffalo, N.Y.
Telecopier: 716-849-0349
Albany, New York Office: Three City Square.
Telephone: 518-465-2333.
Telecopier: 518-465-1567.
Rochester, New York Office: 400 East Avenue.
Telephone: 716-454-6950.
Telecopier: 716-454-4698.
Boca Raton, Florida Office: Suite 400, Nations Bank Building, 2000 Glades Road.
Telephone: 407-394-0500.
Telecopier: 305-427-4303.
Mississauga, Ontario, Canada Office: Suite 880, 3 Robert Speck Parkway.
Telephone: 905-566-5061.
Telecopier: 905-566-2049.
New York, New York Office: 330 Madison Avenue, 11th Floor. Telephone 212-297-3370.
Telecopier: 212-972-6521.

MEMBERS OF FIRM

(ALPHABETICALLY BY YEAR OF ADMISSION TO BAR)

Edwin T. Bean, Jr.
Martin G. Linihan
Tricia Thomas Semmelhack
Paul I. Perlman
James C. Simmons

ASSOCIATES

(ALPHABETICALLY BY YEAR OF ADMISSION TO BAR)

Michael F. Scalise
M. Bud Nelson

Counsel For: Tops Markets, Inc.; SKW Alloys, Inc.; Wilson Greatbatch Ltd.; Zippo Manufacturing Co.; Eastman Machine Co.

For Complete List of Firm Personnel, See General Section

For full biographical listings, see the Martindale-Hubbell Law Directory

McGEE & GELMAN (AV)

200 Summer Street, 14222
Telephone: 716-883-7272
Fax: 716-883-7084

MEMBERS OF FIRM

Michael R. McGee
Warren B. Gelman
F. Brendan Burke, Jr.
James P. Giambrone, Jr.
Laura A. Colca

For full biographical listings, see the Martindale-Hubbell Law Directory

JERICHO, Nassau Co.

HOFFMANN & BARON (AV)

350 Jericho Turnpike, 11753
Telephone: 516-822-3550
Telex: 6972994 INTELLAW
Telecopier: 516-822-3582
Parsippany, New Jersey Office: 1055 Parsippany Boulevard. 07054
Telephone: 201-331-1700.
Telecopier: 201-331-1717.

MEMBERS OF FIRM

Charles R. Hoffmann
Ronald J. Baron
Gerald T. Bodner

ASSOCIATES

Alan M. Sack
A. Thomas Kammer
Arlene D. Morris
Daniel A. Scola, Jr. (Resident, Parsippany, New Jersey Office)
Robert P. Michal
R. Glenn Schroeder
Glenn T. Henneberger
Louise A. Foutch
Livia Boyadjian
Sean W. O'Dea
(Not admitted in NY)
Salvatore J. Abbruzzese
Lindsay S. Adams
Kirk M. Miles (Resident, Parsippany, New Jersey Office)
Jessica H. Tran
(Not admitted in NY)

For full biographical listings, see the Martindale-Hubbell Law Directory

*NEW YORK,** New York Co.

BRUMBAUGH, GRAVES, DONOHUE & RAYMOND (AV)

30 Rockefeller Plaza, 10112
Telephone: 212-408-2500
Facsimile: 212-765-2519
MCI Mail: 611-1063
Telex: 650 6111063

(See Next Column)

BRUMBAUGH, GRAVES, DONOHUE & RAYMOND, *New York—Continued*

MEMBERS OF FIRM

Francis J. Hone
Joseph D. Garon
Arthur S. Tenser
Ronald B. Hildreth
Thomas R. Nesbitt, Jr.
Robert Neuner
Richard G. Berkley
Richard S. Clark
Thomas D. MacBlain
Bradley B. Geist
Russell H. Falconer
James J. Maune
John D. Murnane
Henry Y. S. Tang
Doreen Leavens Costa
Robert C. Scheinfeld
Parker H. Bagley
John A. Fogarty, Jr.

OF COUNSEL

Dana M. Raymond
Frank W. Ford, Jr.
Frederick C. Carver

SPECIAL COUNSEL

Peter A. Businger (Not admitted in NY)

ASSOCIATES

Louis S. Sorell
Gary M. Butter
Marta E. Delsignore
Dr. Kay-Ellen Smith
Alex L. Yip
Jong H. Lee
Thomas J. Parker
Stephen J. Quigley
Neil P. Sirota
Steven C. Gray
David S. Benyacar
Rochelle K. Seide
Steven R. Gustavson (Not admitted in NY)
Andrew T. Block
Michael J. Doherty
Paul A. Ragusa
Adan Ayala
David T. Cunningham

For full biographical listings, see the Martindale-Hubbell Law Directory

---

CHAPMAN & FENNELL (AV)

330 Madison Avenue, 10017
Telephone: 212-687-3600
Telex: WUI 880411 (ETOSHA NY)
Telefax: 212-972-5368
Stamford, Connecticut Office: Three Landmark Square.
Telephone: 203-353-8000.
Telefax: 203-353-8799.
Washington D.C. Office: 2000 L. Street, N.W., Suite 200.
Telephone: 202-822-9351.

MEMBERS OF FIRM

Darrell K. Fennell
Philip M. Chiappone

OF COUNSEL

Michael Winger
Carol E. Meltzer
Eric S. Kamisher

For full biographical listings, see the Martindale-Hubbell Law Directory

---

COBRIN GITTES & SAMUEL (AV)

750 Lexington Avenue, 10022
Telephone: 212-486-4000
Telecopier: 212-486-4007

Peter T. Cobrin
Marvin S. Gittes
Richard I. Samuel (Not admitted in NY)

David Jacobs
Kerry P.L. Miller
Eileen M. Ebel
Richard M. Lehrer
David J. Garrod
Jill C. Greenwald

For full biographical listings, see the Martindale-Hubbell Law Directory

---

COOPER & DUNHAM (AV)

1185 Avenue of the Americas, 10036
Telephone: 212-278-0400
Facsimile: 212-391-0525

MEMBERS OF FIRM

Gerald W. Griffin
Christopher C. Dunham
Ivan S. Kavrukov
Norman H. Zivin
Peter D. Murray
John P. White
Thomas G. Carulli
Lewis H. Eslinger
Jay H. Maioli
Robert B. G. Horowitz
Donald S. Dowden
Robert D. Katz
William E. Pelton
Peter J. Phillips
Donna A. Tobin

ASSOCIATES

Wendy E. Miller
Richard S. Milner
Robert M. Bauer
Albert Wai-Kit Chan
Matthew J. Golden
Matthew B. Tropper
Lewis J. Kreisler
Jeffrey L. Snow
Jeffrey A. Hovden
Kristina L. Konstas
Robert T. Maldonado
Mark S. Cohen

OF COUNSEL

John N. Cooper
Thomas F. Moran

(See Next Column)

LEGAL SUPPORT PERSONNEL

SCIENTIFIC ADVISORS

Nathan P. Letts
Elizabeth Ann Bogosian
A. David Joran
Thomas E. Phalen
Adrian Gerard Looney
Keum A. Yoon
Victor DeVito (Patent Agent)

For full biographical listings, see the Martindale-Hubbell Law Directory

---

CURTIS, MORRIS & SAFFORD, P.C. (AV)

530 Fifth Avenue, 10036
Telephone: 212-840-3333
Cable Address: "Cumosa"
Telex: 425066 CURTMS
Telecopier: 212-840-0712; 764-5574

Edward G. Curtis (1886-1970)
Truman S. Safford (1903-1993)
Gregor N. Neff
A. Thomas S. Safford
Fred A. Keire
Barry Evans
Leonard J. Santisi
William S. Frommer
George B. Snyder
William F. Lawrence
Edgar H. Haug
Robert F. Kirchner
Marilyn Matthes Brogan
Matthew K. Ryan
William J. Spatz
Theodore F. Shiells
Eugene L. Flanagan, III
Adam L. Brookman
Barry S. White
Thomas J. Kowalski
John R. Lane

OF COUNSEL

Alvin Sinderbrand

Dennis M. Smid (Not admitted in NY)
Brenda Pomerance
Howard J. Susser
Lawrence E. Russ
Mark Montague
Robert G. Winkle
Daniel G. Brown
John E. Boyd
Pamela G. Salkeld

For full biographical listings, see the Martindale-Hubbell Law Directory

---

DARBY & DARBY, PROFESSIONAL CORPORATION (AV)

805 Third Avenue, 10022-7513
Telephone: 212-527-7700
Telecopier: 212-753-6237
Telex: 236687

Samuel E. Darby (1867-1936)
Samuel E. Darby, Jr. (1891-1947)
Morris Relson
William F. Dudine, Jr.
Michael J. Sweedler
S. Peter Ludwig
Paul Fields
Joseph B. Lerch
Melvin C. Garner
Ethan Horwitz
Beverly B. Goodwin
Adda C. Gogoris
Martin E. Goldstein
Bert J. Lewen
Henry Sternberg
Andrew Baum
Peter C. Schechter
Robert Schaffer
David R. Francescani

OF COUNSEL

Gordon D. Coplein
Peter K. Kontler
Amanda Laura Nye
James W. Falk
Walt T. Zielinski

Robert C. Sullivan, Jr.
Robert J. Hess
Ira Jay Levy
Francis J. Duffin
Alexandra D. Malatestinic
Robert S. Weisbein
Joseph R. Robinson
Amy J. Benjamin
David Leason
Eugene L. Szczecina, Jr. (Not admitted in NY)
Bonnie Kramer Carney
Pierre R. Yanney
Michelle M. Carniaux
Eric A. Prager
Elizabeth M. Koch
Seth H. Jacobs

LEGAL SUPPORT PERSONNEL

PATENT AGENTS

Howard M. Frankfort
Scott L. Sullivan
William F. Prout
Tobias Lewenstein
Reza Green
Karen G. Horowitz

TECHNICAL ADVISERS

Samuel P. Wertheimer
Philip M. Sass

For full biographical listings, see the Martindale-Hubbell Law Directory

---

DAVIS HOXIE FAITHFULL & HAPGOOD (AV)

45 Rockefeller Plaza, 10111
Telephone: 212-757-2200
Cable Address: "Explicit"
International Telex: 421236
Telecopiers: (212) 586-1461; 969-9805

(See Next Column)

DAVIS HOXIE FAITHFULL & HAPGOOD—*Continued*

MEMBERS OF FIRM

Caspar Carl Schneider, Jr.
Charles W. Bradley
Stanley L. Amberg
John B. Pegram
William J. Hone
Thomas E. Spath
Richard P. Ferrara
Peter Bucci
Lawrence B. Goodwin
Peter H. Priest
Bradford S. Breen
Robert M. Isackson

COUNSEL

Richard Whiting
Cyrus S. Hapgood
Brandon N. Sklar

ASSOCIATES

Andrew T. D'Amico, Jr.
Stephan J. Filipek
Robert A. Cote
James J. Murtha
Wayne S. Breyer
Robert E. Rudnick
Robert T. Canavan
Harold C. Moore
Davy E. Zoneraich
Joseph B. Ryan
Kevin M. Mason
Samuel Borodach
William A. Munck

For full biographical listings, see the Martindale-Hubbell Law Directory

FISH & NEAVE (AV)

Fish, Richardson & Neave, New York (1916-1969)
1251 Avenue of the Americas, 10020
Telephone: 212-596-9000
Telex: 14-8367
Cable Address: Fishneave
Telecopier: 212-596-9090
Palo Alto, California Office: 525 University Avenue, Suite 300, 94301.
Telephone: 415-617-4000.
Telecopier: 415-617-4090.

Frederick P. Fish (1855-1930)
Charles Neave (1867-1937)

PARTNERS

David W. Plant
Albert E. Fey
John O. Tramontine
Herbert F. Schwartz
Lars I. Kulleseid
William J. Gilbreth (Resident, Palo Alto, California Office)
Eric C. Woglom
John E. Nathan
Robert C. Morgan
Kenneth B. Herman
Edward F. Mullowney (Resident, Palo Alto, California Office)
Robert R. Jackson
Jesse J. Jenner
W. Edward Bailey
David J. Lee
Patricia A. Martone
James F. Haley, Jr.
Richard M. Barnes
Laurence S. Rogers
Thomas L. Giannetti
Vincent N. Palladino
Robert J. Goldman
Thomas L. Secrest
Daniel M. Gantt
Norman H. Beamer (Resident, Palo Alto, California Office)
Kevin J. Culligan
Glenn A. Ousterhout
Susan Progoff
Margaret A. Pierri
Douglas J. Gilbert
Denise L. Loring
Jeffrey H. Ingerman
Mark H. Bloomberg
Jane A. Massaro
Duane-David Hough
Mark D. Rowland (Resident, Palo Alto, California Office)

RETIRED PARTNERS

W. Philip Churchill
Harry R. Pugh, Jr.
William K. Kerr
Rynn Berry
Henry J. Zafian
Donald E. Degling
Charles B. Smith

SENIOR ATTORNEYS

A. Peter Adler
Richard A. Inz
Thomas J. Vetter

ASSOCIATES

Lisa E. Cristal
Edward J. DeFranco (Resident, Palo Alto, California Office)
Mark D. Engelmann
Eric R. Hubbard
David A. Loewenstein
John J. Cassingham
Kelsey I. Nix
Joseph H. Guth
Marta E. Gross
John Michael Hintz
William J. McCabe
Vicki S. Veenker (Resident, Palo Alto, California Office)
Leslie A. McDonell
Christopher P. Godziela
Kristin H. Neuman
Karen T. Judlowe
Andrew Steven Marks
Nicola A. Pisano (Resident, Palo Alto, California Office)
Donald K. Reedy
Gabrielle E. Higgins (Resident, Palo Alto, California Office)
Brenda J. Panichi
Jeremy Lack
James P. Bergin
Ivor R. Elrifi
Frances M. Lynch
Ronald A. Krasnow
Lianna C. Kalmar
Bradford L. Friedman (Resident, Palo Alto, California Office)
Christopher J. Harnett
Marie Hagarty MacNichol
Richard G. Gervase, Jr.
Alison Joy Arnold
K. Iain Mc Ausland (Resident, Palo Alto, California Office)
Lydia T. McNally
William H. Steinmetz
Keith T. Takeda
Kathryn Frances Reyburn
Elizabeth C. Schuler

(See Next Column)

ASSOCIATES (Continued)

Elizabeth Shieldkret
Karen J. Choi
Steven C. Cherny
Carlos Dennis
Lewis V. Popovski
Joseph M. Guiliano
Gerald J. Flattmann, Jr.
Jaime A. Siegel
Esther H. Steinhauer
Michael Phillipps
Gene W. Lee
Audrey F. Sher
Kevin P.B. Johnson (Resident, Palo Alto, California Office)
Elaine Anne Drager
Sara B. Goldstein
Kevin E. Flynn
William L. Leschensky
Chun-Yeong Yang
Gregory S. Arovas
Susan L. Loring
John C. Carey
Ashley J. Chadowitz
Caroline S. Chua-Rocco
Cynthia H. Ho
George A. Xixis
Ronald E. Cahill
Avinash S. Lele
John Clifton Vetter
Jane Tower Gunnison
Kevin R. Hansbro
Bradley A. Greenwald (Resident, Palo Alto, California Office)
Leo L. Lam
Petrina S. Hsi

For full biographical listings, see the Martindale-Hubbell Law Directory

FITZPATRICK, CELLA, HARPER & SCINTO (AV)

277 Park Avenue, 10172
Telephone: 212-758-2400
Cable Address: "Fitzcel New York"
International-Telex: FCHS 236262
Facsimile: 212-758-2982
Washington, D.C. Office: 1001 Pennsylvania Avenue, N.W.
Telephone: 202-347-8100.
Facsimile: 202-347-8136.
Orange County, California Office: 650 Town Center Drive, Suite 740, Costa Mesa.
Telephone: 714-540-8700.
Facsimile: 714-540-9823.

MEMBERS OF FIRM

Joseph M. Fitzpatrick
Lawrence F. Scinto
William J. Brunet
Robert L. Baechtold
John A. O'Brien
Robert C. Kline (Washington, D.C. Office)
John A. Krause
Henry J. Renk
David F. Ryan
Peter Saxon
Anthony M. Zupcic
Charles P. Baker
Stevan J. Bosses
Edward E. Vassallo
Ronald A. Clayton
Nicholas M. Cannella
Hugh C. Barrett
David M. Quinlan
Pasquale A. Razzano
John W. Behringer (Washington, D.C. Office)
Lawrence A. Stahl (Washington, D.C. Office)
Leonard P. Diana
William M. Wannisky (Washington, D.C. Office)
Nina Shreve
Robert H. Fischer
Donald J. Curry
Warren E. Olsen (Washington, D.C. Office)
Nicholas N. Kallas
Bruce C. Haas
Abigail F. Cousins
Thomas H. Beck
Lawrence S. Perry
Michael K. O'Neill (Orange County, California Office)
Richard P. Bauer (Washington, D.C. Office)
Errol B. Taylor
Nicholas Groombridge
Leslie K. Mitchell
Scott K. Reed
Fredrick M. Zullow

ASSOCIATES

Laura A. Bauer
Christopher Philip Wrist (Washington, D.C. Office)
Gary M. Jacobs (Washington, D.C. Office)
Scott D. Malpede (Washington, D.C. Office)
Steven E. Warner (Washington, D.C. Office)
Thomas J. O'Connell (Washington, D.C. Office)
Victor J. Geraci
MaryAnne Dickey
Aaron C. Deditch
Penina Wollman
Steven C. Kline
David L. Schaeffer
Jack S. Cubert (Not admitted in NY)
Mark A. Williamson (Washington, D.C. Office)
John T. Whelan (Washington, D.C. Office)
Jean K. Dudek (Washington, D.C. Office)
Raymond R. Mandra
Lisa A. Pieroni
Dominick A. Conde
Lori B. Riker
Pamela A. Mayer
Steven C. Bauman
Anne M. Maher (Washington, D.C. Office)
Mark J. Itri (Orange County, California Office)
Brian V. Slater
Diego Scambia
Daniel Chung
Timothy J. Kelly
Karin L. Williams
Benjamin C. Hsing
Michael P. Sandonato
William C. Hwang
Joseph M. O'Malley, Jr.
Ronald J. McGaw
John D. Carlin
Jack M. Arnold (Not admitted in NY)
Donna Marie Werner
Joseph W. Ragusa
William J. Zak, Jr. (Washington, D.C. Office)
Daniel S. Glueck (Washington, D.C. Office)
Paul A. Pysher (Orange County, California Office)
Bruce M. Wexler
Brian Lee Klock (Washington, D.C. Office)

(See Next Column)

FITZPATRICK, CELLA, HARPER & SCINTO, *New York—Continued*

TECHNICAL ADVISORS

Dr. Peter J. Knudsen
Jay H. Anderson

For full biographical listings, see the Martindale-Hubbell Law Directory

LAW OFFICES OF PHILIP FURGANG (AV)

205 Lexington Avenue, 10016
Telephone: 212-725-1818
Telecopier: Group III 212-941-9711; 914-353-1996
West Nyack, New York Office: Suite 210 Centerock East, 2 Crosfield Avenue.
Telephone: 914-353-1818.

ASSOCIATE

Stephanie Furgang-Adwar

For full biographical listings, see the Martindale-Hubbell Law Directory

JORDAN AND HAMBURG (AV)

122 East 42nd Street, 10168
Telephone: 212-986-2340
Cable Address: "Patentmark"
Telex: 237057 JAH UR
Telecopier: 212-953-7733
e mail 6446099@mcimail.com
Washington, D.C. Area Office: Suite 520, 2361 Jefferson Davis Highway, Arlington, Virginia.

C. Bruce Hamburg
Frank J. Jordan

ASSOCIATES

Lainie Elyse Dolinger
Herbert F. Ruschmann
Marvin Turken
Alfred A. D'Andrea, Jr. (Not admitted in NY)

OF COUNSEL

Martin P. Hoffman (Not admitted in NY; Resident, Arlington, Virginia)

For full biographical listings, see the Martindale-Hubbell Law Directory

KANE, DALSIMER, SULLIVAN, KURUCZ, LEVY, EISELE AND RICHARD (AV)

711 Third Avenue, 10017-4059
Telephone: 212-687-6000
Fax: 212-682-3485
Cable Address: "Duelson"
ITT Telex: 426767

MEMBERS OF FIRM

Joseph C. Sullivan
John Kurucz
David H. T. Kane
Siegrun D. Kane
Gerald Levy
Joseph T. Eisele
Virginia R. Richard
Ronald R. Santucci

ASSOCIATES

William E. Marames
Ronald E. Brown
John F. Gulbin
Richard J. Danyko, Jr.
Maribel Figueredo
Karl M. Zielaznicki
Kathleen E. McCarthy
Keri A. Christ
Neal D. Marcus
Lara A. Holzman
Chrystal A. LeRoy

OF COUNSEL

Daniel H. Kane

For full biographical listings, see the Martindale-Hubbell Law Directory

KENYON & KENYON (AV)

One Broadway, 10004
Telephone: 212-425-7200
Telecopier: Dex (212) 425-5288
Washington, D.C. Office: 1025 Connecticut Avenue, N.W.
Telephone: 202-429-1776.
Telecopier: (202) 429-0796.
Frankfurt, Germany Office: Bockenheimer Landstrassee 97-99, 60325 Frankfurt am Main.
Telephone: (69) 97-58-05-0.
Telecopier: (69) 97-58-05-99.

MEMBERS OF FIRM

Francis T. Carr
Hugh A. Chapin
Richard A. Huettner
Edward W. Greason
William T. Boland, Jr.
Robert D. Fier
Charles R. Brainard
Kenneth E. Madsen
Richard L. Mayer
Richard G. Kline (Resident, Washington, D.C. Office)
Douglas G. Brace
Edward J. Handler, III
Robert T. Tobin
Paul Lempel
Alan T. Bowes
Paul H. Heller
Arthur D. Gray
Albert J. Breneisen
Stuart J. Sinder
George E. Badenoch
John C. Altmiller (Resident, Washington, D.C. Office)
Michael J. Lennon
Philip J. McCabe (Resident, Washington, D.C. Office)
James Galbraith
Walter E. Hanley, Jr.

(See Next Column)

MEMBERS OF FIRM (Continued)

Richard L. DeLucia
James E. Rosini
Edward T. Colbert (Resident, Washington, D.C. Office)
William K. Wells, Jr. (Resident, Washington, D.C. Office)
Jonathan D. Reichman
Patrick J. Birde (Resident, Frankfurt, Germany Office)
Howard J. Shire
Richard S. Gresalfi
Michael D. Loughnane
William A. Tanenbaum
Steven J. Lee
John Flock

RESIDENT COUNSEL
WASHINGTON, D.C. OFFICE

Donald Knox Duvall

OF COUNSEL

Charles B. Spencer
Charles E. Hepner
John M. Rommel (Resident, Washington, D.C. Office)

SENIOR ATTORNEYS

John J. Kelly, Jr.
Lynne Darcy
Thomas F. Meagher

ASSOCIATES

Richard M. Rosati
Frank Pietrantonio (Resident, Washington, D.C. Office)
Allen J. Baden
John E. Tsavaris, II
Andrea Harris Scheidt
James Prizant (Resident, Washington, D.C. Office)
Robert F. Perry
Donna M. Praiss
Thomas J. Meloro
Frederick H. Rein
Joseph F. Nicholson
Gerard A. Messina
Patrick J. Fay (Resident, Washington, D.C. Office)
Maria L. Palmese
Suzanne M. Parker (Resident, Washington, D.C. Office)
Rajesh Vallabh
Jeffrey M. Butler (Resident, Frankfurt, Germany Office)
Michael P. Straub
Robert A. Whitman
Joseph P. Kirk, Jr.
John V. Swinson
John R. Kenny
Robert D. Anderson (Resident, Washington, D.C. Office)
Elizabeth Gardner
P. McCoy Smith (Resident, Washington, D.C. Office)
Leslye B. Davidson
Joseph A. Micallef (Resident, Washington, D.C. Office)
Michael R. Graif
Ronald J. Campbell (Not admitted in NY)
Howard O. Bell
Joshua Bressler
William C. Gehris (Resident, Frankfurt, Germany Office)
Cary S. Kappel
Cheryl A. Milone
John R. Moore
Paul J. Richter, Jr.
Douglas E. Ringel (Not admitted in NY)
Hector A. Alicea
Mark M. Supko (Resident, Washington, D.C. Office)
John R. Witcher, III
Benjamin Hershkowitz
Robert S. MacWright
Jonathan S. Caplan
Joel Bock
Maria Anita Pamintuan
Shawn W. O'Down (Resident, Washington, D.C. Office)
William T. Enos (Not admitted in NY)
Henry S. Hadad
John C. Pokotyho
Chris Kolefas

For full biographical listings, see the Martindale-Hubbell Law Directory

LIDDY SULLIVAN GALWAY & BEGLER, P.C. (AV)

41 Madison Avenue, 10010
Telephone: 212-481-3000
Cable Address: "LISHADS"
Telex: 422743
Telecopier: 212-481-8043

Sylvester J. Liddy (1927-1975)
Francis J. Sullivan (1932-1978)
Andrew V. Galway, Sr. (1905-1980)
Andrew V. Galway
Jay H. Begler
Arlana S. Cohen
Marcella A. Stapor

Mark J. Speciner
Nancy J. Deckinger
Janet M. Russo

For full biographical listings, see the Martindale-Hubbell Law Directory

MORGAN & FINNEGAN, L.L.P. (AV)

A Registered Liability Partnership
345 Park Avenue, 10154
Telephone: 212-758-4800
Cable Address: "Findurpine"
Telecopier: (212) 751-6849
Telex: ITT 421792
Washington, D.C. Office: 1299 Pennsylvania Avenue, N.W., Suite 960.
Telephone: 202-857-7887.
Facsimile: 202-857-7929.

MEMBERS OF FIRM

John D. Morgan (1893-1939)
Hobart N. Durham (1930-1969)
John D. Foley
John A. Diaz
Thomas P. Dowling
John C. Vassil
Warren H. Rotert
Alfred P. Ewert
David H. Pfeffer
Harry C. Marcus
Robert E. Paulson
Stephen R. Smith
Kurt E. Richter
J. Robert Dailey
Eugene Moroz
John F. Sweeney
Arnold I. Rady
Christopher A. Hughes

(See Next Column)

MORGAN & FINNEGAN L.L.P.—*Continued*

MEMBERS OF FIRM (Continued)

William S. Feiler
Janet Dore
Joseph A. Calvaruso
James W. Gould
Richard C. Komson
Israel Blum
Christopher K. Hu
Bartholomew Verdirame
Dickerson M. Downing
Maria C. H. Lin
Joseph A. DeGirolamo
Christopher E. Chalsen
Michael A. Nicodema
Michael P. Dougherty

SENIOR COUNSEL

George B. Finnegan, Jr.
Jerome G. Lee

COUNSEL

Thomas I. O'Brien
Richard C. Witte (Not admitted in NY)
John P. Sinnott
Ned W. Branthover
Roger S. Smith

ASSOCIATES

Thomas M. Hammond (Not admitted in NY)
Eugene C. Rzucidlo (Not admitted in NY)
Andrew M. Riddles
Seth J. Atlas
Scott D. Greenberg
Bruce D. DeRenzi
Midge M. Hyman
Mark J. Abate
Barry J. Schindler
John T. Gallagher
Steven F. Meyer
Gabriel P. Kralik
Tony V. Pezzano
Bruce D. Radin
Andrea L. Wayda
Elaine J. Kaman
Desireé M. Stahl
Mary J. Morry
Robert K. Goethals
Kenneth H. Sonnenfeld
John W. Osborne
Richard K. Warther
Michael M. Murray (Not admitted in NY)
Laurence J. Bromberg
Jean E. Shimotake
M. Caragh Noone
Walter G. Hanchuk
Jeffrey J. Oelke
Charles M. Fish
Oliver A. Zitzmann
Scott B. Howard
Richard B. LeBlanc
Peter N. Fill
Kenneth S. Weitzman
Richard Straussman
Heather L. Creps
James M. Gibson
Leif R. Sigmond, Jr. (Not admitted in NY)

For full biographical listings, see the Martindale-Hubbell Law Directory

NOTARO & MICHALOS P.C. (AV)

Suite 6902 Empire State Building, 350 Fifth Avenue, 10118-6985
Telephone: 212-564-0200
Fax: 212-564-0217
Rockland County Office: 100 Dutch Hill Road, Suite 110, Orangeburg, New York, 10962-2100.
Telephone: 914-359-7700.
Fax: 914-359-7798.

Angelo Notaro
Peter C. Michalos

For full biographical listings, see the Martindale-Hubbell Law Directory

PENNIE & EDMONDS (AV)

1155 Avenue of the Americas, 10036
Telephone: 212-790-9090
Telex: (WUI) 66141 PENNIE
Cable Address: "Penangold"
Facsimile: GI/GII/GIII (212) 869-9741
GIII (212) 869-8864
Washington, D.C. Office: 1701 Pennsylvania Avenue, N.W.
Telephone: 202-393-0177.
Facsimile: GI/GII (202) 737-7950; GIII (202) 393-0462.
Menlo Park, California Office: 2730 Sand Hill Road.
Telephone: 415-854-3660.
Facsimile: 415-854-3694.

John C. Pennie (1858-1921)
Dean S. Edmonds (1879-1972)

MEMBERS OF FIRM

S. Leslie Misrock
Harry C. Jones, III
Berj A. Terzian
Gerald J. Flintoft
David Weild, III
Jonathan A. Marshall
Barry D. Rein
Stanton T. Lawrence, III
Charles E. Miller
Francis E. Morris
Gidon D. Stern
John J. Lauter
Brian M. Poissant
Brian D. Coggio
Mercer L. Stockell
Isaac Jarkovsky
Joseph V. Colaianni (Managing Partner, Washington, D.C. Office)
Charles E. McKenney
Philip T. Shannon
John M. Richardson
Rory J. Radding
Robert M. Kunstadt
Stephen J. Harbulak
Donald J. Goodell
James N. Palik
William G. Pecau
Joseph Diamante
Thomas E. Friebel
Laura A. Coruzzi
Jennifer Gordon
Jon R. Stark (Resident, Menlo Park, California Office)
James W. Dabney
Arthur Wineburg (Resident, Washington, D.C. Office)
Paul R. De Stefano (Not admitted in NY; Resident, Menlo Park, California Office)
Allan A. Fanucci
Geraldine F. Baldwin

(See Next Column)

MEMBERS OF FIRM (Continued)

Victor N. Balancia
Peter D. Vogl
Catherine H. Stockell
John J. Normile, Jr.
Albert P. Halluin

COUNSEL

Constance Golden
Samuel B. Abrams
Marcia H. Sundeen (Resident, Washington, D.C. Office)

ASSOCIATES

Mark A. Farley
Thomas A. Canova
Steven I. Wallach
James G. Markey
Walter E. Stalzer
Paul J. Zegger
Edmond R. Bannon
Bruce J. Barker
Jonathan E. Moskin
Ilene B. Tannen
Adriane M. Antler
Margaret M. Coyne
Darren W. Saunders
Thomas G. Rowan
Wilma F. Triebwasser (Resident, Washington, D.C. Office)
Thomas D. Kohler
Kenneth K. Sharples (Resident, Menlo Park, California Office)
Hope H. Liebke
Scott D. Stimpson
Nancy A. Zoubek
Kent H. Cheng
Ann L. Gisolfi
Lyle Kimms (Not admitted in NY; Resident, Washington, D.C. Office)
Hailing Zhang
Mikhail Lotvin
Scott B. Familant
Brian M. Rothery
Brian D. Siff
Todd A. Wagner
George C. Summerfield, Jr. (Resident, Washington, D.C. Office)
Deborah J. Barnett
John G. de la Rosa
Robert S. Broder
F. Dominic Cerrito
Ronald M. Daignault
Lori S. Gentile
Stephen Michael Patton
William J. Sipio
Laurence Manber
Charles F. Hoyng (Not admitted in NY)
Warren S. Heit (Resident, Menlo Park, California Office)
Barry W. Elledge (Resident, Menlo Park, California Office)
Jacqueline M. Lesser
Michael J. Lyons
Maria E. Pasquale
Melissa Lanni Robertson (Resident, Washington, D.C. Office)
Stephen R. Schaefer
Susan C. Shin
Carol M. Wilhelm
Sandra A. Bresnick
Alan C. Wong (Resident, Menlo Park, California Office)
Bernard H. Chao (Resident, Menlo Park, California Office)
Laurence Stein (Resident, Washington, D.C. Office)
Louis A. Piccone (Not admitted in NY)
Theresa Stevens Smith (Resident, Washington, D.C. Office)
Linda A. Sasaki (Not admitted in NY)
Daniel Hansburg
Troy R. Lester
H.T. Than
Michael Joel Blum
Bryan W. Butler
Alan Leonard Koller
Lawrence Burton Ebert
Kenneth L. Stein
Christine E. Lehman (Resident, Washington, D.C. Office)
Gianni P. Servodidio
Richard J. Gallagher (Not admitted in NY)
Joyce M. Ferraro
Leslie A. Tilly (Not admitted in NY)
David M. O'Neill
Scott R. Bortner (Resident, Menlo Park, California Office)
Alan Tenenbaum
Rashida A. Karmali
Frederick F. Hadidi (Resident, Menlo Park, California Office)
Kelly D. Talcott
Alan P. Force (Not admitted in NY)
John D. Garretson
Lance K. Ishimoto (Resident, Menlo Park, California Office)
Dwight H. Renfrew, Jr.
Katharine E. Smith
William L. Wang (Resident, Menlo Park, California Office)
Mark R. Scadina (Resident, Menlo Park, California Office)

For full biographical listings, see the Martindale-Hubbell Law Directory

ROLAND PLOTTEL (AV)

30 Rockefeller Plaza, 10112-0025
Telephone: 212-489-7073
Telex: 225708R&H
FAX: 212 974-3059

For full biographical listings, see the Martindale-Hubbell Law Directory

ROSEN, DAINOW & JACOBS (AV)

Limited Liability Partnership
489 Fifth Avenue, 10017
Telephone: 212-692-7000; 800-332-4994
Fax: 212-370-5998
E Mail: postmastar@rdjlaw.com

MEMBERS OF FIRM

Daniel M. Rosen (1940-1994)
J. David Dainow
James David Jacobs
Frank J. De Rosa
Eugene D. Berman
Frederick H. Rabin

ASSOCIATES

Dinah H. Lewitan
Tzvi Hirshaut
Donna L. Angotti
Seth H. Ostrow

COUNSEL

Jack Oisher

For full biographical listings, see the Martindale-Hubbell Law Directory

New York—Continued

SUTTON, BASSECHES, MAGIDOFF & AMARAL (AV)

Graybar Building Suite 2310, 420 Lexington Avenue, 10170
Telephone: 212-490-7900
Telefacsimile: 212-370-5559

MEMBERS OF FIRM

Paul J. Sutton
Mark T. Basseches
Barry G. Magidoff
Anthony Amaral, Jr.

SENIOR COUNSEL

Arthur B. Colvin (P.C.)

COUNSEL

David Teschner (Not admitted in NY)
John G. Costa
Steven H. Bazerman
Harold A. Gell (Not admitted in NY)

For full biographical listings, see the Martindale-Hubbell Law Directory

ROSLYN, Nassau Co.

COLLARD & ROE, P.C. (AV)

1077 Northern Boulevard, 11576
Telephone: 516-365-9802
Telex: 261176 CRG(UR)
Facsimile: 516-365-9805

Edward G. Roe (1902-1977)
Allison C. Collard

Edward R. Freedman
Stewart J. Bellus
Edwin H. Keusey
John G. Tutunjian

OF COUNSEL

Joseph R. McPhee, Jr.
James M. Heilman (Not admitted in NY)

For full biographical listings, see the Martindale-Hubbell Law Directory

WINDHAM, Greene Co.

BROWN, KELLEHER, ZWICKEL & WILHELM (AV)

Main Street, 12496
Telephone: 518-734-3800
Fax: 518-734-4226
Catskill, New York Office: 370 Main Street 12414.
Telephone: 518-943-1111.
Fax: 518-943-4549.

MEMBERS OF FIRM

Charles J. Brown
Kevin M. Kelleher
Charles Zwickel
Terry J. Wilhelm

ASSOCIATE

Carol D. Stevens

For full biographical listings, see the Martindale-Hubbell Law Directory

NORTH CAROLINA

*CHARLOTTE,** Mecklenburg Co.

BELL, SELTZER, PARK & GIBSON, PROFESSIONAL ASSOCIATION (AV)

1211 East Morehead Street, P.O. Drawer 34009, 28234
Telephone: 704-331-6000
Fax: 704-334-2014
Raleigh, North Carolina Office (Research Triangle Area): 310 UCB Plaza, P.O. Drawer 31107, 27622.
Telephone: 919-420-2200.
Fax: 919-881-3175.

Charles B. Park, III
Floyd A. Gibson
Samuel G. Layton, Jr.
Joell T. Turner
Charles B. Elderkin
John L. Sullivan, Jr.
John J. Barnhardt, III
Raymond O. Linker, Jr.
James D. Myers (Resident, Research Triangle Area Office)
Michael D. McCoy
Blas P. Arroyo
Philip Summa
Mitchell S. Bigel (Resident, Research Triangle Area Office)
Kenneth D. Sibley (Resident, Research Triangle Area Office)
Dickson M. Lupo
Stephen M. Bodenheimer, Jr.
F. Michael Sajovec (Resident, Research Triangle Area Office)
John H. Thomas
Martha G. Barber
Larry C. Jones
Paul F. Pedigo
Michael S. Connor
Christopher F. Regan (Resident, Research Triangle Area Office)
William M. Atkinson
Frank Burkhead Wyatt, II
George M. Taulbee
Melissa B. Pendleton
Timothy J. O'Sullivan (Resident, Research Triangle Area Office)

(See Next Column)

Robert W. Glatz (Resident, Research Triangle Area Office)
James R. Cannon (Resident, Research Triangle Area Office)
Grant J. Scott (Resident, Research Triangle Area Office)
Jeffrey S. Whittle
Guy R. Gosnell
Virginia C. Bennett (Resident, Research Triangle Area Office)
Jason P. Cooper
Ernest B. Lipscomb, III
Christopher C. Dremann
Bruce J. Rose
Lorie Ann Herington (Resident, Research Triangle Area Office)
Thomas C. McThenia, Jr. (Resident, Research Triangle Area Office)
Scott C. Hatfield (Resident, Research Triangle Area Office)
John P. Higgins
J. Rick Taché
Robert J. Smith
Sara M. Current
Needham J. Boddie, II (Resident, Research Triangle Area Office)
Albert P. Allan
Rachel M. Healey
D. Randall Ayers (Resident, Research Triangle Area Office)
Sorojini J. Biswas (Resident, Research Triangle Area Office)
Richard M. McDermott

OF COUNSEL

Paul B. Bell
Donald M. Seltzer
Paul B. Eaton (1895-1960)
Julian E. Carnes, Jr. (1924-1992)

Representative Clients: Burroughs Wellcome Company; General Electric Company; Kobe Development Corporation; MCNC (Microelectronics Center of North Carolina); NationsBank Corporation; North Carolina State University; Semiconductor Research Corporation; Sonoco Products Company; Springs Industries, Inc.; The Coca-Cola Company.

For full biographical listings, see the Martindale-Hubbell Law Directory

SHEFTE, PINCKNEY & SAWYER (AV)

3740 One First Union Center, 301 South College Street, 28202-6020
Telephone: 704-375-9181
Telex: 221213
ANSWBK: TTC UR
Fax: 704-333-3675

MEMBERS OF FIRM

Channing L. Richards (1912-1979)
Dalbert U. Shefte
Francis M. Pinckney
Karl S. Sawyer, Jr.

Robert J. Walters
Mark A. Taylor
Chad Dustin Tillman

Representative Clients: Conbraco Industries, Inc.; Duff-Norton Co., Inc.; First Union Corporation; Gaston County Dyeing Machine Co.; Guilford Mills, Inc.; Owen Steel Company, Inc.; Pneumafil Corp.; Star Paper Tube, Inc.; Stockhauser, Inc.; United Dominion Industries; W. Schlafhorst A.G. & Co.

For full biographical listings, see the Martindale-Hubbell Law Directory

*DURHAM,** Durham Co.

RICHARD E. JENKINS (AV)

Suite 1600 University Tower, 3100 Tower Boulevard, 27707
Telephone: 919-493-8000
Telecopier: 919-419-0383;
Cable Address: "Durhampat"

Jennifer L. Skord

Representative Clients: Adams Products Co.; Duke University; Freudenberg Spunweb Co. (The Lutravil Co.); Glaxo Inc. (Glaxo Holdings p.l.c.); Isotechnologies, Inc.; Liggett Group, Inc. (Liggett & Myers Tobacco Co.); Newton Instrument Co.; North Carolina State University; Sumitomo Electric Fiber Optics Corp.; The University of North Carolina at Chapel Hill.

For full biographical listings, see the Martindale-Hubbell Law Directory

OLIVE AND OLIVE, P.A. (AV)

500 Memorial Street, P.O. Box 2049, 27702-2049
Telephone: 919-683-5514
FAX: 919-688-3781

B. B. Olive
Susan Freya Olive
Lynn Eileen Barber

Michael R. Philips
Tara J. Gray
Bruce Vrana

Reference: North Carolina Bar Assn.

For full biographical listings, see the Martindale-Hubbell Law Directory

*GREENSBORO,** Guilford Co.

RHODES COATS AND BENNETT, L.L.P. (AV)

1600 First Union Tower, 300 North Greene Street, P.O. Box 2974, 27402
Telephone: 910-273-4422
FAX: 910-271-2830
Raleigh, North Carolina Office: 909 Glenwood Avenue, P.O. Box 5.
Telephone: 919-832-3946.
Fax: 919-831-9056.
Wilmington, North Carolina Office: 201 N. Front Street.
Telephone: 910-763-2382.
Fax: 910-763-2386.

MEMBERS OF FIRM

Charles Robert Rhodes
Larry L. Coats (Resident, Raleigh Office)
David E. Bennett (Resident, Raleigh Office)
Edward W. Rilee
Howard A. MacCord, Jr.

ASSOCIATES

Jack B. Hicks
David G. Matthews (Resident, Raleigh Office)
David D. Beatty

Reference: Wachovia Bank and Trust Co.

For full biographical listings, see the Martindale-Hubbell Law Directory

*RALEIGH,** Wake Co.

* indicates certain Bar Register subscribers whose principal office is located elsewhere in the state and who have arranged for representation as a part of the state capital listings that follow

BELL, SELTZER, PARK & GIBSON, PROFESSIONAL ASSOCIATION (AV)

310 UCB Plaza, P.O. Drawer 31107, 27622
Telephone: 919-420-2200
Fax: 919-881-3175
Charlotte, North Carolina Office: 1211 East Morehead Street, P.O. Drawer 34009, 28234.
Telephone: 704-331-6000.
Fax: 704-334-2014.

RESIDENT ATTORNEYS

James D. Myers
Mitchell S. Bigel
Kenneth D. Sibley
F. Michael Sajovec
Christopher F. Regan
Timothy J. O'Sullivan
Robert W. Glatz
James R. Cannon
Grant J. Scott
Virginia C. Bennett
Lorie Ann Herington
Thomas C. McThenia, Jr.
Scott C. Hatfield
Needham J. Boddie, II
D. Randall Ayers
Sorojini J. Biswas

Representative Clients: Burroughs Wellcome Company; General Electric Company; Kobe Development Corporation; MCNC (Microelectronics Center of North Carolina); NationsBank Corporation; North Carolina State University; Semiconductor Research Corporation; Sonoco Products Company; Springs Industries, Inc.; The Coca-Cola Company.

For full biographical listings, see the Martindale-Hubbell Law Directory

RHODES COATS AND BENNETT, L.L.P. (AV)

909 Glenwood Avenue, P.O. Box 5, 27602
Telephone: 919-832-3946
FAX: 919-831-9056
Greensboro, North Carolina Office: 1600 First Union Tower, 300 North Greene Street, P.O. Box 2974.
Telephone: 910-273-4422.
FAX: 910-271-2830.
Wilmington, North Carolina Office: 201 N. Front Street.
Telephone: 910-763-2382.
FAX: 910-763-2386.

MEMBERS OF FIRM

Charles Robert Rhodes
Larry L. Coats (Resident)
David E. Bennett (Resident)
Edward W. Rilee
Howard A. MacCord, Jr.

ASSOCIATES

Jack B. Hicks
David G. Matthews (Resident)

For full biographical listings, see the Martindale-Hubbell Law Directory

*** WOMBLE CARLYLE SANDRIDGE & RICE (AV)**

A Professional Limited Liability Company
2100 First Union Capitol Center, 150 Fayetteville Street Mall, P.O. Box 831, 27602
Telephone: 919-755-2100
Telecopy: 919-755-2150
Telex: 806498
Charlotte, North Carolina Office: 3300 One First Union Center, 301 South College Street.
Telephone: 704-331-4900.
Telecopy: 704-331-4955.
Telex: 853609.
Winston-Salem, North Carolina Office: 1600 Southern National Financial Center.
Telephone: 919-721-3600.
Telecopy: 919-721-3660.
Telex: 806498.
Atlanta, Georgia Office: One Ninety One Peachtree Tower, 191 Peachtree Street N.E., Suite 3250.
Telephone: 404-614-2580.
Fax: 404-614-2595.

RESIDENT PARTNER

M. Christopher Bolen

RESIDENT ASSOCIATE

Maury M. Tepper, III

Representative Clients: Aetna Casualty and Surety Co., Inc.; ALSCO/AmeriMark Building Products, Inc.; Aoki Corporation America, Inc.; Empire of Carolina, Inc.; Hackney Brothers, Inc.; Lawyers Mutual Liability Insurance Company of North Carolina; Meredith College; Monk-Austin, Inc.; Regency Park Corporation; Wachovia Bank of North Carolina, N.A.

For Complete List of Firm Personnel, See General Section

For full biographical listings, see the Martindale-Hubbell Law Directory

*WINSTON-SALEM,** Forsyth Co.

WOMBLE CARLYLE SANDRIDGE & RICE (AV)

A Professional Limited Liability Company
1600 Southern National Financial Center, P.O. Drawer 84, 27102
Telephone: 910-721-3600
Telecopy: 910-721-3660
Telex: 806498
Charlotte, North Carolina Office: 3300 One First Union Center, 301 South College Street.
Telephone: 704-331-4900.
Telecopy: 704-331-4955.
Telex: 853609.
Raleigh, North Carolina Office: 2100 First Union Capitol Center, 150 Fayetteville Street Mall, P.O. Box 831.
Telephone: 919-755-2100.
Telecopy: 919-755-2150.
Telex: 806498.
Atlanta, Georgia Office: One Ninety One Peachtree Tower, 191 Peachtree Street, N.E., Suite 3250.
Telephone: 404-614-2580.
Fax: 404-614-2595.

ASSOCIATE

Jeffrey R. McFadden

Representative Clients: Brad Ragan, Inc.; Brenner Companies; Food Lion, Inc.; Hanes Companies, Inc.; North Carolina Baptist Hospitals, Inc.; R.J. Reynolds Tobacco Company; Summit Communications Group, Inc.; Thomasville Furniture Industries, Inc.; Wachovia Corporation; Wake Forest University.

For Complete List of Firm Personnel, See General Section

For full biographical listings, see the Martindale-Hubbell Law Directory

OHIO

*AKRON,** Summit Co.

RENNER, KENNER, GREIVE, BOBAK, TAYLOR & WEBER A LEGAL PROFESSIONAL ASSOCIATION (AV)

Sixteenth Floor, First National Tower, 44308-1456
Telephone: 216-376-1242; 216-376-1034
Cable Address: "Patlaw"
Telex: PATLAW AKR 98 6317
Facsimile: 216-376-9646

Jack L. Renner
Reese Taylor
Phillip L. Kenner
Edward G. Greive
Donald J. Bobak
Ray L. Weber
Sylvia A. Petrosky
Joseph G. Curatolo
Douglas J. Hura

(See Next Column)

RENNER, KENNER, GREIVE, BOBAK, TAYLOR & WEBER A LEGAL PROFESSIONAL ASSOCIATION, *Akron—Continued*

Rodney Lee Skoglund
Andrew B. Morton
W. Michael Dixon
Fred H. Zollinger, III

Reference: Society National Bank.

For full biographical listings, see the Martindale-Hubbell Law Directory

*CINCINNATI,** Hamilton Co.

DINSMORE & SHOHL (AV)

1900 Chemed Center, 255 East Fifth Street, 45202-3172
Telephone: 513-977-8200
FAX: 513-977-8141
Florence, Kentucky Office: Turfway Ridge Office Park, 7300 Turfway Road, Suite 430 41042-1355.
Telephone: 606-283-0515.
FAX: 606-283-6017.
Dayton, Ohio Office: 500 Courthouse Plaza, S.W., 10 N. Ludlow Street, 45402-1834.
Telephone: 513-228-8012.
FAX: 513-461-2543.
Columbus, Ohio Office: NBD Bank Building, Suite 330, 175 South Third Street, 43215-5134.
Telephone: 614-224-7887.
FAX: 614-224-7882.

MEMBERS OF FIRM

Thomas S. Calder
Lynda E. Roesch
Ronald J. Snyder
James D. Liles

ASSOCIATES

Patricia B. Hogan
Randel S. Springer
Ernamarie Messenger
Patrick E. Beck
Gregory S. Lampert

For Complete List of Firm Personnel, See General Section

For full biographical listings, see the Martindale-Hubbell Law Directory

FROST & JACOBS (AV)

2500 PNC Center, 201 East Fifth Street, P.O. Box 5715, 45201-5715
Telephone: 513-651-6800
Cable Address: "Frostjac"
Telex: 21-4396 F & J CIN
Telecopier: 513-651-6981
Columbus, Ohio Office: One Columbus, 10 West Broad Street.
Telephone: 614-464-1211.
Telecopier: 614-464-1737.
Lexington, Kentucky Office: 1100 Vine Center Tower, 333 West Vine Street.
Telephone: 606-254-1100.
Telecopier: 606-253-2990.
Middletown, Ohio Office: 400 First National Bank Building, 2 North Main Street.
Telephone: 513-422-2001.
Telecopier: 513-422-3010.
Naples, Florida Office: 4001 Tamiami Trail North, Suite 220.
Telephone: 813-261-0582.
Telecopier: 813-261-2083.

PATENT, TRADEMARK AND COPYRIGHT ATTORNEYS
MEMBERS OF FIRM

Gibson R. Yungblut
James H. Hayes
David E. Schmit
Kenneth B. Germain
Steven J. Goldstein
Edwin R. Acheson, Jr.

ASSOCIATES

Frederick H. Gribbell
Martin J. Miller
Scott T. Piering (Not admitted in OH)
Jay R. Deshmukh

Representative Clients: Chiquita, Kirschner Medical Corporation; Cincinnati Bell Inc.; Cincinnati Milacron Inc.; Hilton Davis Chemical Co.; Mercantile Stores Company, Inc.; Senco Products, Inc.; Standard Textile Company, Inc.; U.S. Shoe Corp.; University of Cincinnati;

For Complete List of Firm Personnel, See General Section

For full biographical listings, see the Martindale-Hubbell Law Directory

WOOD, HERRON & EVANS (AV)

2700 Carew Tower, 45202
Telephone: 513-241-2324

MEMBERS OF FIRM

Edmund E. Wood (1868-1916)
William R. Wood (1893-1935)
Edmund P. Wood (1923-1968)
Truman A. Herron (1935-1976)
Edward B. Evans (1937-1971)
Richard H. Evans
John D. Poffenberger
Bruce Tittel
Donald F. Frei
David J. Josephic
A. Ralph Navaro, Jr.
David S. Stallard
J. Robert Chambers
Gregory J. Lunn
Kurt L. Grossman
Clement H. Luken, Jr.
Thomas J. Burger

(See Next Column)

ASSOCIATES

Gregory F. Ahrens
Joseph R. Jordan
David M. Lockman
Wayne L. Jacobs
Kurt Andrew Summe
Keith R. Haupt
Kevin G. Rooney
C. Richard Eby
Theodore R. Remaklus
David E. Pritchard
Thomas W. Humphrey

OF COUNSEL

Herbert C. Brinkman

For full biographical listings, see the Martindale-Hubbell Law Directory

*CLEVELAND,** Cuyahoga Co.

FAY, SHARPE, BEALL, FAGAN, MINNICH & MCKEE (AV)

1100 Superior Avenue, Suite 700, 44114
Telephone: 216-861-5582
Telex: 980162
FAX: 216-241-1666; 216-241-5147
Alexandria, Virginia Office: 104 East Hume Avenue.
Telephone: 703-684-1120.
Fax: 703-684-1157.

MEMBERS OF FIRM

Albert P. Sharpe, III
Thomas E. Beall, Jr. (Not admitted in OH; Resident, Alexandria, Virginia Office)
Christopher B. Fagan
Richard J. Minnich
James W. McKee
Patrick R. Roche
Thomas E. Kocovsky, Jr.
Jay F. Moldovanyi
John X. Garred
Timothy E. Nauman
Richard M. Klein
Alan J. Ross
John R. Mattingly (Not admitted in OH; Resident, Alexandria, Virginia Office)
Philip J. Moy, Jr.

ASSOCIATES

Sandra M. Koenig
Mark S. Svat
Michael E. Hudzinski
Daniel J. Stanger (Resident, Alexandria, Virginia Office)
Jude A. Fry
Joseph D. Dreher
Sue Ellen Phillips
Eric A. Stephenson
Scott Andrew McCollister

OF COUNSEL

John C. Tiernan
Daniel G. Blackhurst

For full biographical listings, see the Martindale-Hubbell Law Directory

JONES, DAY, REAVIS & POGUE (AV)

North Point, 901 Lakeside Avenue, 44114
Telephone: 216-586-3939
Cable Address: "Attorneys Cleveland"
Telex: 980389
Telecopier: 216-579-0212
In Columbus, Ohio: 1900 Huntington Center.
Telephone: 614-469-3939.
Cable Address: "Attorneys Columbus."
Telecopier: 614-461-4198.
In Atlanta, Georgia: 3500 One Peachtree Center, 303 Peachtree Street, N.E.
Telephone: 404-521-3939.
Cable Address: "Attorneys Atlanta".
Telex: 54-2711.
Telecopier: 404-581-8330.
In Brussels, Belgium: Avenue Louise 480, 7th Floor. B-1050 Brussels.
Telephone: 011-32-2-645-14-11.
Telecopier: 011-32-2-645-14-45.
In Chicago, Illinois: 77 West Wacker.
Telephone: 312-782-3939.
Telecopier: 312-782-8585.
In Dallas, Texas: 2300 Trammell Crow Center, 2001 Ross Avenue.
Telephone: 214-220-3939.
Cable Address: "Attorneys Dallas."
Telex: 730852.
Telecopier: 214-969-5100.
In Frankfurt, Germany: Triton Haus, Bockenheimer Landstrasse 42, 60323 Frankfurt am Main.
Telephone: 49-69-9726-3939.
Telecopier: 49-69-9726-3993.
In Geneva, Switzerland: 20, rue de Candolle.
Telephone: 011-41-22-320-2339.
Telecopier: 011-41-22-320-1232.
In Hong Kong: 1501 One Exchange Square, 8 Connaught Place.
Telephone: 011-852-2526-6895.
Telecopier: 011-852-2810-5787.
In Irvine, California: 2603 Main Street, Suite 900.
Telephone: 714-851-3939.
Telex: 194911 Lawyers LSA.
Telecopier: 714-553-7539.
In London, England: One Mount Street.
Telephone: 011-44-71-493-9361.
Cable Address: "Surgoe London WI."
Telecopier: 011-44-71-493-9666.

(See Next Column)

JONES, DAY, REAVIS & POGUE—*Continued*

In Los Angeles, California: 555 West Fifth Street, Suite 4600.
Telephone: 213-489-3939.
Telex: 181439 UD.
Telecopier: 213-243-2539.
In New York, New York: 599 Lexington Avenue.
Telephone: 212-326-3939.
Cable Address: "JONESDAY NEWYORK."
Telex: 237013 JDRP UR.
Telecopier: 212-755-7306.
In Paris, France: 62, rue du Faubourg Saint-Honore.
Telephone: 011-33-1-44-71-3939.
Cable Address: "Surgoe Paris."
Telex: 290156 Surgoe.
Telecopier: 011-33-1-49-24-0471.
In Pittsburgh, Pennsylvania: 500 Grant Street, 31st Floor.
Telephone: 412-391-3939.
Cable Address: "Attorneys Pittsburgh".
Telecopier: 412-394-7959.
In Riyadh, Saudi Arabia: Law Offices of Saud M.A. Shawwaf, P.O. Box 2700.
Telephones: 011 (966-1) 465-6543, 011 (966-1) 464-8534 or 011 (966-1) 464-8540.
Telex: 401831 SAUCON SJ.
Telecopier: (966-1) 464-8480.
In Taipei, Taiwan: 8th Floor, Tun Hwa South Road, Section 2.
Telephone: 011 (886-2) 704-6808.
Telecopier: 011 (886-2) 704-6791.
In Tokyo, Japan: Toranomon MT Building, 4th Floor, 10-3, Toranomon 3-Chome, Minato-Ku, Tokyo 105, Japan.
Telephone: 011-81-3-3433-3939.
Telecopier: 011-81-3-5401-2725.
In Washington, D.C.: Metropolitan Square, 1450 G Street, N.W.
Telephone: 202-879-3939.
Cable Address: "Attorneys Washington."
Telex: 89-2410 ATTORNEYS WASH.
Telecopier: 202-737-2832.

MEMBERS OF FIRM

Hal D. Cooper
Barry L. Springel
Richard H. Sayler
Regan J. Fay
Kenneth R. Adamo
Robert Conley Kahrl
James L. Wamsley, III
Robert P. Ducatman
Michael W. Vary
Timothy J. O'Hearn

SENIOR ATTORNEYS

H. Duane Switzer
Leozino Agozzino

For Complete List of Firm Personnel, See General Section

For full biographical listings, see the Martindale-Hubbell Law Directory

PEARNE, GORDON, McCOY & GRANGER (AV)

1200 Leader Building, 44114-1401
Telephone: 216-579-1700
Facsimile: 216-579-6073

MEMBERS OF FIRM

John F. Pearne (1912-1981)
Charles B. Gordon
William C. McCoy, Jr.
Louis V. Granger
Richard H. Dickinson, Jr.
Thomas P. Schiller
David B. Deioma
Joseph J. Corso
Howard G. Shimola
Jeffrey J. Sopko
John P. Murtaugh
James M. Moore

David E. Spaw
Michael W. Garvey
Richard M. Mescher

For full biographical listings, see the Martindale-Hubbell Law Directory

RENNER, OTTO, BOISSELLE & SKLAR (AV)

Nineteenth Floor, 1621 Euclid Avenue, 44115-2183
Telephone: 216-621-1113
Cable: "Oldpat"
Telex: 8104212034 Oldpat Clv
FAX: 216-621-6165

John F. Oberlin (1880-1971)
Edwin E. Donnelly, Jr. (1925-1976)

MEMBERS OF FIRM

John W. Renner
Donald L. Otto
Armand P. Boisselle
Warren A. Sklar
Neil A. DuChez
Don W. Bulson
Gordon D. Kinder

ASSOCIATES

William C. Tritt
Jay R. Campbell
Mark D. Saralino
Gregory Turocy
Andrew J. Rudd

OF COUNSEL

Walter Maky

For full biographical listings, see the Martindale-Hubbell Law Directory

WESTON HURD FALLON PAISLEY & HOWLEY (AV)

2500 Terminal Tower, 50 Public Square, 44113-2241
Telephone: 216-241-6602;
Ohio Toll Free: 800-336-4952
FAX: 216-621-8369

MEMBERS OF FIRM

John S. Kluznik
David R. Posteraro

For Complete List of Firm Personnel, See General Section

For full biographical listings, see the Martindale-Hubbell Law Directory

*COLUMBUS,** Franklin Co.

BIEBEL & FRENCH A LEGAL PROFESSIONAL ASSOCIATION (AV)

620 Leveque Tower, 50 West Broad Street, 43215
Telephone: 614-464-2902
Fax: 513-443-0861
Dayton, Ohio Office: 2500 Kettering Tower.
Telephone: 513-461-4543.
Cable Address: "Daypat".
Telex: 288272.
Telecopier: (Grp. III) 513-443-0861.

Edward Paul Forgrave (Resident)
Patrick P. Phillips (Resident)

For full biographical listings, see the Martindale-Hubbell Law Directory

EMENS, KEGLER, BROWN, HILL & RITTER (AV)

Capitol Square Suite 1800, 65 East State Street, 43215-4294
Telephone: 614-462-5400
Telecopier: 614-464-2634
Cable Address: "Law EKBHR"
Telex: 246671

COUNSEL

John L. Gray

Holly Robinson Fischer
Robert G. Schuler
Shawnell Williams

Representative Clients: Borden, Inc.; Drug Emporium, Inc.; The Ohio State University; Owens-Corning Fiberglas Corp.

For Complete List of Firm Personnel, See General Section

For full biographical listings, see the Martindale-Hubbell Law Directory

MUELLER AND SMITH A LEGAL PROFESSIONAL ASSOCIATION (AV)

Mueller-Smith Building, 7700 Rivers Edge Drive, 43235
Telephone: 614-436-0600
Telecopier: 614-436-0057

Jerry K. Mueller, Jr.
Gerald L. Smith

James R. Eley
John A. Molnar, Jr.
Philip S. Lyren

Representative Clients: Ashland Chemical Co.; Battelle Columbus Laboratories; General Electric Co.; IRD Mechanalysis, Inc.; Liebert Corp.; OCLC Online Computer Library Center, Inc.
Reference: Bank One of Columbus.

For full biographical listings, see the Martindale-Hubbell Law Directory

PORTER, WRIGHT, MORRIS & ARTHUR (AV)

41 South High Street, 43215-6194
Telephone: 614-227-2000; (800-533-2794)
Telex: 6503213584 MCI
Fax: 614-227-2100
Dayton, Ohio Office: One Dayton Centre, One South Main Street, 45402.
Telephones: 513-228-2411; (800-533-4434).
Fax: 513-449-6820.
Cincinnati, Ohio Office: 250 E. Fifth Street, 45202-4166.
Telephones: 513-381-4700; (800-582-5813).
Fax: 513-421-0991.
Cleveland, Ohio Office: 925 Euclid Avenue, 44115-1483.
Telephones: 216-443-9000; (800-824-1980).
Fax: 216-443-9011.
Washington, D.C. Office: 1233 20th Street, N.W., 20036-2395.
Telephones: 202-778-3000; (800-456-7962).
Fax: 202-778-3063.
Naples, Florida Office: 4501 Tamiami Trail North, 33940-3060.
Telephones: 813-263-8898;(800-876-7962).
Fax: 813-436-2990.

MEMBERS OF FIRM
COLUMBUS, OHIO OFFICE

Edwin M. Baranowski
Marjorie Crowder Briggs
Deborah S. Clifton

ASSOCIATES
COLUMBUS, OHIO OFFICE

Laurie N. Jacques
Michael D. Steffensmeier

(See Next Column)

PORTER, WRIGHT, MORRIS & ARTHUR, *Columbus—Continued*

CINCINNATI, OHIO OFFICE
RESIDENT MEMBER

Wm. Cates Rambo

CINCINNATI, OHIO OFFICE
RESIDENT ASSOCIATE

Stephen P. Kenkel

Representative Clients: Battelle Memorial Institute; Bank One; The Huntington Bancshares Inc.; The Longaberger Co.; Nestle Ice Cream Company; Tech International; The Peerless Saw Co.; Red Roof Inns; Warner Books, Inc.; White Castle System, Inc.

For Complete List of Firm Personnel, See General Section

For full biographical listings, see the Martindale-Hubbell Law Directory

*DAYTON,** Montgomery Co.

BIEBEL & FRENCH A LEGAL PROFESSIONAL ASSOCIATION (AV)

2500 Kettering Tower, 45423
Telephone: 513-461-4543
Fax: 513-443-0861
Columbus, Ohio Office: 620 Leveque Tower, 50 W. Broad Street.
Telephone: 614-464-2902.
Fax: 614-464-1058.

Lawrence B. Biebel (1906-1989)
Gilbert N. Henderson
Edward Paul Forgrave (Resident, Columbus Office)
Thomas W. Flynn
Bruce E. Peacock
Patrick P. Phillips (Resident, Columbus Office)
Matthew R. Jenkins
Michael D. Folkerts

James P. Davidson
Steven D. A. McCarthy
R. Scott Speroff

COUNSEL

Nathaniel R. French
John W. Donahue

For full biographical listings, see the Martindale-Hubbell Law Directory

KILLWORTH, GOTTMAN, HAGAN & SCHAEFF (AV)

One Dayton Centre, One South Main Street, Suite 500, 45402-2023
Telephone: 513-223-2050
FAX: 513-223-0724

MEMBERS OF FIRM

Richard A. Killworth
James F. Gottman
Timothy W. Hagan
B. Joseph Schaeff
Richard C. Stevens
Robert L. Showalter
Kimberly Gambrel

ASSOCIATES

Brian M. Bolam
Brent M. Peebles (Not admitted in OH)
Harold C. Knecht, III

OF COUNSEL

John R. Flanagan
Charles R. Wilson

For full biographical listings, see the Martindale-Hubbell Law Directory

THOMPSON, HINE AND FLORY (AV)

2000 Courthouse Plaza, N.E., 45402-1706
Telephone: 513-443-6600
Fax: 513-443-6637; 443-6635
Akron, Ohio Office: 50 S. Main Street, Suite 502, 44308-1828.
Telephone: 216-376-8090.
Fax: 216-376-8386.
Cincinnati, Ohio Office: 312 Walnut Street, 14th Floor, 45202-4029.
Telephone: 513-352-6700.
Fax: 513-241-4771.
Telex: 938003.
Cleveland, Ohio Office: 1100 National City Bank Building, 629 Euclid Avenue, 44114-3070.
Telephone: 216-566-5500.
Fax: 216-556-5583.
Telex: 980217.
Cable Address: "Thomflor".
Columbus, Ohio Office: One Columbus, 10 West Broad Street, 43215-3435.
Telephone: 614-469-3200.
Fax: 614-469-3361.
Palm Beach, Florida Office: 125 Worth Avenue, 33480-4466.
Telephone: 407-833-5900.
Fax: 407-833-5951.
Washington, D.C. Office: 1920 N Street, N.W., 20036-1601.
Telephone: 202-331-8800.
Fax: 202-331-8330.
Telex: 904173.
Cable Address: "Caglaw".
Brussels, Belgium Office: Rue des Chevaliers / Ridderstraat 14 - B.10, B - 1050.
Telephone: 011(32-2) 511-9326.
Fax: 011(32-2) 513-9206.

(See Next Column)

MEMBERS OF FIRM

Mark P. Levy
Theodore D. Lienesch

For Complete List of Firm Personnel, See General Section

For full biographical listings, see the Martindale-Hubbell Law Directory

OKLAHOMA

*OKLAHOMA CITY,** Oklahoma Co.

DOUGHERTY, HESSIN, BEAVERS & GILBERT, A PROFESSIONAL CORPORATION (AV)

Two Leadership Square, Suite 1400, 211 North Robinson, 73102
Telephone: 405-232-5586
Fax: 405-232-5597
Tulsa, Oklahoma Office: Suite 1110, Williams Center Tower 1, One West Third Street.
Telephone: 918-592-6970.
Fax: 918-583-6122.

William R. Laney (1930-1992)
C. Clark Dougherty, Jr.
Lucian Wayne Beavers
E. Harry Gilbert, III
Neal R. Kennedy
Clifford Clark Dougherty, III
Lawrence R. Watson (Resident at Tulsa, Oklahoma Office)
Dennis D. Brown (Resident, Tulsa Office)

Anthony L. Rahhal
Michael J. LaBrie

OF COUNSEL

Robert M. Hessin

Representative Clients: Conoco Inc.; Halliburton Co.; Phillips Petroleum Co.; Kerr McGee Refining Corp.; B. S. & B. Safety Systems; John Zink Co.; Koch Engineering Co., Inc.; Continental Carlisle.

For full biographical listings, see the Martindale-Hubbell Law Directory

DUNLAP, CODDING & LEE, P.C. (AV)

Suite 420, 9400 North Broadway, 73114
Telephone: 405-478-5344
Fax: 405-478-5349

Jerry J. Dunlap
Charles A. Codding
Mary M. Lee

John F. McPhail
Sue Corbett
Joseph P. Titterington
Quentin R. Rakestraw (Not admitted in OK)
Jerry J. Dunlap, II
Nicholas D. Rouse
Glen M. Burdick

PATENT AGENT

Christopher W. Corbett, Ph.D.

Reference: The Oklahoma Bank, Oklahoma City.

For full biographical listings, see the Martindale-Hubbell Law Directory

OREGON

*PORTLAND,** Multnomah Co.

WILLIAM A. BIRDWELL & ASSOCIATES (AV)

Suite 1260 900 S.W. Fifth Avenue, 97204-1221
Telephone: 503-228-1841
Facsimile: 503-228-2635

Michael E. Schmitt
Bradley M. Ganz
Garth Janke

Representative Clients: Audio Precision, Inc.; Ideas For Medicine, Inc.; In Focus Systems, Inc.; Metheus Corporation; Tektronix, Inc.; II Morrow, Inc.

For full biographical listings, see the Martindale-Hubbell Law Directory

CHERNOFF, VILHAUER, MCCLUNG & STENZEL (AV)

600 Benj. Franklin Plaza, One S.W. Columbia, 97258
Telephone: 503-227-5631
Cable Address: "Patents"
FAX: 503-228-4373

MEMBERS OF FIRM

Daniel P. Chernoff
Jacob E. Vilhauer, Jr.
Dennis E. Stenzel
Charles D. McClung
Donald B. Haslett
J. Peter Staples
William O. Geny

(See Next Column)

CHERNOFF, VILHAUER, MCCLUNG & STENZEL—*Continued*

Nancy J. Moriarty
Julianne R. Davis
Douglas B. Ferguson
Judy A. Peterson
Kevin L. Russell
Karen Dana Fienberg (Not admitted in OR)

LEGAL SUPPORT PERSONNEL

David Sylvan Fine

Representative Clients: Bend Research, Inc.; Cascade Corp.; Columbia Sportswear Co.; Gunderson, Inc.; Jeld-Wen, Inc.; Longview Fibre Co.; Planar Systems, Inc.; Soloflex, Inc.; Videx, Inc.; White's Electronics, Inc.
Reference: U.S. National Bank of Oregon.

For full biographical listings, see the Martindale-Hubbell Law Directory

KLARQUIST, SPARKMAN, CAMPBELL, LEIGH & WHINSTON (AV)

One World Trade Center, Suite 1600, 121 S.W. Salmon Street, 97204
Telephone: 503-226-7391
FAX: 503-228-9446
Telex: 910-464-5089 PATLAW PTL

MEMBERS OF FIRM

Mark L. Becker
James Campbell
William Y. Conwell
Patrick W. Hughey
Kenneth S. Klarquist
Ramon A. Klitzke, II
James S. Leigh
David P. Petersen
Richard J. Polley
Joseph B. Sparkman (Retired)
John W. Stuart
John D. Vandenberg
Arthur L. Whinston

ASSOCIATES

Timothy M. Carlson
Alan E. Dow
Scott D. Eads
James E. Geringer (Not admitted in OR)
Douglas D. Hancock
Joseph T. Jakubek (Not admitted in OR)
Joel R. Meyer
Mark A. Porter
Robert Scotti
Stacey C. Slater
Donald L. Stephens, Jr.
Stephen A. Wight
Garth A. Winn

OF COUNSEL

William D. Noonan, M.D.

LEGAL SUPPORT PERSONNEL

David J. Earp

Representative Clients: Battelle Pacific Northwest; Boise Cascade Corp.; Freightliner Corp.; Hewlett-Packard Co.; Lamb-Weston, Inc.; Mentor Graphics Corp.; Omark Division of Blount Industries; Precision Castparts, Inc.; Advanced Silicon Materials Inc.; Microsoft, Inc.

For full biographical listings, see the Martindale-Hubbell Law Directory

KOLISCH HARTWELL DICKINSON MCCORMACK & HEUSER, A PROFESSIONAL CORPORATION (AV)

200 Pacific Building, 520 S.W. Yamhill Street, 97204
Telephone: 503-224-6655
FAX: 503-295-6679
Palo Alto, California Office: 420 Florence Street.
Telephone: 415-325-8673.
FAX: 415-325-9041.

J. Pierre Kolisch
Jon M. Dickinson
John M. McCormack (Not admitted in OR)
Peter E. Heuser
James G. Stewart
David A. Fanning
David P. Cooper

Walter W. Karnstein
Pierre C. Van Rysselberghe
Charles DeVoe
Kasey C. Christie (Not admitted in OR)
Stephen F. Gass
Lance Richard Sadler

OF COUNSEL

Mortimer H. Hartwell, Jr.

For full biographical listings, see the Martindale-Hubbell Law Directory

MARGER, JOHNSON, MCCOLLOM & STOLOWITZ, P.C. (AV)

650 American Bank Building, 621 S.W. Morrison Street, 97205
Telephone: 503-222-3613
FAX: 503-274-4622
Internet: inquiry@techlaw.com

Jerome S. Marger
Alexander C. Johnson, Jr.
Micah D. Stolowitz
Alan T. McCollom

Glenn C. Brown
Stephen S. Ford
Gerald D. Haynes

LEGAL SUPPORT PERSONNEL

PATENT AGENT

Peter J. Ayers

(See Next Column)

PARALEGAL

Kimberly A. Hubbell

For full biographical listings, see the Martindale-Hubbell Law Directory

MILLER, NASH, WIENER, HAGER & CARLSEN (AV)

111 S.W. Fifth Avenue, 97204-3699
Telephone: 503-224-5858
Telex: 364462, Kingmar PTL
Facsimile: 503-224-0155, 503-224-2450
Seattle, Washington Office: 4400 Two Union Square, 601 Union Street, 98101-2322.
Telephone: 206-622-8484.
Facsimile: 206-622-7485.

PORTLAND, OREGON PARTNERS

Erich W. Merrill, Jr.
Dennis P. Rawlinson

SEATTLE, WASHINGTON PARTNER

James P. Donohue

Representative Clients: U. S. Bancorp; United States National Bank of Oregon; Louisiana-Pacific Corp.; Willamette Industries, Inc.; Portland Public Schools; St. Vincent Hospital and Medical Center; Merrill Lynch, Pierce, Fenner & Smith, Inc.

For Complete List of Firm Personnel, See General Section

For full biographical listings, see the Martindale-Hubbell Law Directory

PENNSYLVANIA

*ALLENTOWN,** Lehigh Co.

ECKERT SEAMANS CHERIN & MELLOTT (AV)

Sovereign Building, 609 Hamilton Mall, 3rd Floor, 18101
Telephone: 610-432-3000
Facsimile: 610-432-8827
Pittsburgh, Pennsylvania Office: 600 Grant Street, 42nd Floor.
Telephone: 412-566-6000.
Telex: 866172.
Facsimile: 412-566-6099.
Harrisburg, Pennsylvania Office: One South Market Square Building, 213 Market Street.
Telephone: 717-237-6000.
Facsimile: 717-237-6019.
Philadelphia, Pennsylvania Office: 1700 Market Street, Suite 3232.
Telephone: 215-575-6000.
Telex: 845226.
Facsimile: 215-575-6015.
Boston, Massachusetts Office: One International Place, 18th Floor.
Telephone: 617-342-6800.
Facsimile: 617-342-6899.
Buffalo, New York Office: 606 Liberty Building.
Telephone: 716-854-4100.
Facsimile: 716-854-4227.
Fort Lauderdale, Florida Office: First Fort Lauderdale Place, Suite 900, 100 Northeast Third Avenue.
Telephone: 305-523-0400.
Facsimile: 305-523-7002.
Boca Raton, Florida Office: Suite 902, The Plaza, 5355 Town Center Road.
Telephone: 407-394-7775.
Facsimile: 407-394-9998.
Miami, Florida Office: Barnett Tower, 18th Floor, 701 Brickell Avenue.
Telephone: 305-373-9100.
Facsimile: 305-372-9400.
Tallahassee, Florida Office: 206 South Adams Street.
Telephone: 904-222-2515.
Facsimile: 904-222-3452.
Washington, D.C. Office: 2100 Pennsylvania Avenue, N.W., Suite 600.
Telephone: 202-659-6600.
Telex: 62030761.
Facsimile: 202-659-6699.

PATENT AND TRADEMARK PARTNERS

Lewis F. Gould, Jr.
Stephan P. Gribok

For full biographical listings, see the Martindale-Hubbell Law Directory

*HARRISBURG,** Dauphin Co.

MCNEES, WALLACE & NURICK (AV)

100 Pine Street, P.O. Box 1166, 17108
Telephone: 717-232-8000
Fax: 717-237-5300

MEMBERS OF FIRM

Michael A. Doctrow
W. Jeffry Jamouneau
Franklin A. Miles, Jr.
Gary F. Yenkowski

(See Next Column)

McNEES, WALLACE & NURICK, *Harrisburg—Continued*

ASSOCIATES

Kathleen A. Dunst | P. Nicholas Guarneschelli

For Complete List of Firm Personnel, See General Section

For full biographical listings, see the Martindale-Hubbell Law Directory

*MEDIA,** Delaware Co.

ELMAN WILF & FRIED, A PROFESSIONAL CORPORATION (AV)

20 West Third Street, P.O. Box 1969, 19063
Telephone: 610-892-9580
Fax: 610-892-9577
CompuServe 72245,556
Internet info@elman.com

Gerry J. Elman
Frederic M. Wilf
Allan H. Fried

OF COUNSEL

Allan J. Jacobson
Ash Tankha (Not admitted in PA)
Jeffrey Keith Rucker

SCIENCE ADVISORS

Michael D. Davis (Science Advisor)
Kenneth F. Mitchell (Science Advisor)

LEGAL SUPPORT PERSONNEL

PARALEGAL

Dana L. Kushwara

For full biographical listings, see the Martindale-Hubbell Law Directory

*PHILADELPHIA,** Philadelphia Co.

CAESAR, RIVISE, BERNSTEIN, COHEN & POKOTILOW, LTD. (AV)

12th Floor, 1635 Market Street, 19103-2212
Telephone: 215-567-2010
Telecopier: 215-751-1142

Alan H. Bernstein
Stanley H. Cohen
Manny D. Pokotilow
Barry A. Stein
Martin L. Faigus
Eric S. Marzluf
Robert S. Silver
Michael J. Berkowitz
Scott M. Slomowitz

OF COUNSEL

Abraham D. Caesar
Max Goldman

For full biographical listings, see the Martindale-Hubbell Law Directory

DANN, DORFMAN, HERRELL AND SKILLMAN, A PROFESSIONAL CORPORATION (AV)

Suite 720, 1601 Market Street, 19103-2307
Telephone: 215-563-4100
Cable Address: "Skilpatent" Philadelphia
Fax: 215-563-4044

John Charles Dorfman
Henry Howson Skillman
Roger Wayne Herrell
Patrick J. Hagan
Donald R. Piper, Jr.
Vincent T. Pace

Janet E. Reed

OF COUNSEL

Curtis Marshall Dann
John S. Child, Jr.
Charles N. Quinn

LEGAL SUPPORT PERSONNEL

PATENT AGENTS

John B. Berryhill
Mitchell R. Brustein

For full biographical listings, see the Martindale-Hubbell Law Directory

DUANE, MORRIS & HECKSCHER (AV)

Suite 4200 One Liberty Place, 19103-7396
Telephone: 215-979-1000
FAX: 215-979-1020
Harrisburg, Pennsylvania Office: 305 North Front Street, 5th Floor, P.O. Box 1003.
Telephone: 717-237-5500.
Fax: 717-232-4015.
Wilmington, Delaware Office: Suite 1500, 1201 Market Street.
Telephone: 302-571-5550.
Fax: 302-571-5560.
New York, N.Y. Office: 112 E. 42nd Street, Suite 2125.
Telephone: 212-499-0410.
Fax: 212-499-0420.
Wayne, Pennsylvania Office 735 Chesterbrook Boulevard, Suite 300.
Telephone: 610-647-3555.
Allentown, Pennsylvania Office: 968 Postal Road, Suite 200.
Telephone: 610-266-3650.
Fax: 610-640-2619.

(See Next Column)

Cherry Hill, New Jersey Office: 51 Haddonfield Road, Suite 340.
Telephone: 609-488-7300.
Fax: 609-488-7021.

MEMBERS OF FIRM

Peter J. Cronk
Scott J. Fields

ASSOCIATE

John F. "Jack" Daniels

SPECIAL COUNSEL

Jeffrey M. Navon

*Hasday & Margulis, A Professional Corporation

For Complete List of Firm Personnel, See General Section

For full biographical listings, see the Martindale-Hubbell Law Directory

ECKERT SEAMANS CHERIN & MELLOTT (AV)

1700 Market Street, Suite 3232, 19103
Telephone: 215-575-6000
Telex: 845226
Facsimile: 215-575-6015
Pittsburgh, Pennsylvania Office: 600 Grant Street, 42nd Floor.
Telephone: 412-566-6000.
Telex: 866172.
Facsimile: 412-566-6099.
Harrisburg, Pennsylvania Office: One South Market Square Building, 213 Market Street.
Telephone: 717-237-6000.
Facsimile: 717-237-6019.
Allentown, Pennsylvania Office: Sovereign Building, 609 Hamilton Mall, 3rd Floor.
Telephone: 610-432-3000.
Facsimile: 610-432-8827.
Boston, Massachusetts Office: One International Place, 18th Floor.
Telephone: 617-342-6800.
Facsimile: 617-342-6899.
Buffalo, New York Office: 606 Liberty Building.
Telephone: 716-854-4100.
Facsimile: 716-854-4227.
Fort Lauderdale, Florida Office: First Fort Lauderdale Place, Suite 900, 100 Northeast Third Avenue.
Telephone: 305-523-0400.
Facsimile: 305-523-7002.
Boca Raton, Florida Office: Suite 902, The Plaza, 5355 Town Center Road.
Telephone: 407-394-7775.
Facsimile: 407-394-9998.
Miami, Florida Office: Barnett Tower, 18th Floor, 701 Brickell Avenue.
Telephone: 305-373-9100.
Facsimile: 305-372-9400.
Tallahassee, Florida Office: 206 South Adams Street.
Telephone: 904-222-2515.
Facsimile: 904-222-3452.
Washington, D.C. Office: 2100 Pennsylvania Avenue, N.W., Suite 600.
Telephone: 202-659-6600.
Telex: 62030761.
Facsimile: 202-659-6699.

PATENT AND TRADEMARK PARTNERS

Lewis F. Gould, Jr.
Stephan P. Gribok

RESIDENT PATENT AND TRADEMARK OF COUNSEL

Karl L. Spivak

RESIDENT ASSOCIATES

Jonathan A. Bay
Steven C. Benjamin
Daniel S. Goldberg
J. Mark Hand
John V. Silverio

For full biographical listings, see the Martindale-Hubbell Law Directory

MILLER & CHRISTENBURY, P.C. (AV)

44th Floor One Liberty Place, 1650 Market Street, 19103
Telephone: 215-563-1810
FAXES: 215-568-6946; 215-564-2535

Austin R. Miller
T. Daniel Christenbury

Joshua L. Cohen

OF COUNSEL

A. Newton Huff

LEGAL SUPPORT PERSONNEL

PATENT AGENT

Frank A. Cona

References: Core States First Pennsylvania Bank; Knoblauch State Bank.

For full biographical listings, see the Martindale-Hubbell Law Directory

Philadelphia—Continued

PANITCH SCHWARZE JACOBS & NADEL, P.C. (AV)

36th Floor, 1601 Market Street, 19103-2398
Telephone: 215-567-2020
Cable Address: Patents
Telex: 831-494
Fax: 215-567-2991

Ronald L. Panitch
William W. Schwarze
Roberta Jacobs-Meadway
Alan S. Nadel
Leslie L. Kasten, Jr.
Joel S. Goldhammer
John Jamieson, Jr.

James R. Meyer
Wallace D. Newcomb
Jay K. Meadway
Martin Belisario
Karol A. Kepchar
Lynda L. Calderone (Not admitted in PA)
Steven H. Meyer
Frank M. Linguiti
David W. Parker
Charles E. Bergere
Michael L. Lovitz
Ned E. Barlas
John A. Parrish

For full biographical listings, see the Martindale-Hubbell Law Directory

PAUL & PAUL (AV)

2900 Two Thousand Market Street, 19103
Telephone: 215-568-4900
Cable Address: "Caveat"
Telex: 710-670-1352 Dex
Telecopier: 215-567-5057

MEMBERS OF FIRM

James C. McConnon
John F. McNulty
Alex R. Sluzas

ASSOCIATES

Joseph E. Chovanes
Frank J. Bonini, Jr.
Paul A. Taufer
Craig M. Bell
Alan G. Towner
Gary A. Greene
Joseph A. Tessari

For full biographical listings, see the Martindale-Hubbell Law Directory

SEIDEL, GONDA, LAVORGNA & MONACO, P.C. (AV)

Suite 1800 Two Penn Center Plaza, 19102
Telephone: 215-568-8383
Telecopiers: 215-568-9214; 568-5549

Edward C. Gonda (1960-1985)
Arthur H. Seidel
Gregory J. Lavorgna
Daniel A. Monaco
Thomas J. Durling
John J. Marshall

Stephen J. Meyers
Nancy A. Rubner-Frandsen
Harriet M Sinton
David Crichton
Raymond I. Bruttomesso, Jr.
Joseph R. DelMaster, Jr.
Peter B. Ritz
Joan E. Switzer
Robert E. Cannuscio

PATENT AGENTS

Clark A. Jablon

For full biographical listings, see the Martindale-Hubbell Law Directory

WOODCOCK WASHBURN KURTZ MACKIEWICZ & NORRIS (AV)

One Liberty Place - 46th Floor, 17th & Market Streets, 19103
Telephone: 215-568-3100
Fax: 215-568-3439
Cable Address: "Woodcock"
TWX: 1334

Virgil E. Woodcock (1905-1974)
Lawrence T. Phelan (1900-1969)
Robert B. Washburn
Richard E. Kurtz
John J. Mackiewicz
Norman L. Norris
Albert W. Preston, Jr.
Dale M. Heist
Philip S. Johnson
John W. Caldwell
Gary H. Levin
Steven J. Rocci
Dianne B. Elderkin
Francis A. Paintin
John P. Donohue, Jr.
Henrik D. Parker
Suzanne E. Miller

ASSOCIATES

Albert T. Keyack
Lynn Bavaro Morreale
Laura Genovese Miller
Joseph Lucci
Michael P. Dunnam
Michael D. Stein
Albert J. Marcellino
David R. Bailey
Rebecca Lynne Ralph
John L. Knoble
Michele K. Herman
Barbara Lynn Mullin
Ken Ichiro Yoshida
Mark DeLuca
Steven B. Samuels
Lynn A. Malinoski
Lori Yanisko Beardell
Frederick A. Tecce
Doreen Y. Trujillo
Michael P. Straher (Not admitted in PA)
Merle W. Richman III

OF COUNSEL

Raymond M. Speer (Not admitted in PA)

(See Next Column)

SCIENTIFIC ADVISORS

Paul K. Legaard
Kathryn Leary

For full biographical listings, see the Martindale-Hubbell Law Directory

*PITTSBURGH,** Allegheny Co.

BUCHANAN INGERSOLL, PROFESSIONAL CORPORATION (AV)

5800 USX Tower, 600 Grant Street, 15219
Telephone: 412-562-8800
Telecopier: 412-562-1041
Philadelphia, Pennsylvania Office: Two Logan Square, Twelfth Floor, 18th & Arch Streets.
Telephone: 215-665-8700.
Harrisburg, Pennsylvania Office: Vartan Parc, 30 North Third Street.
Telephone: 717-237-4800.
Tampa, Florida Office: 101 East Kennedy Boulevard, Suite 1030.
Telephone: 813-222-8180.
North Miami Beach, Florida Office: 19495 Biscayne Boulevard.
Telephone: 305-933-5600.
Lexington, Kentucky Office: 1210 Vine Center Office Tower, 333 West Vine Street.
Telephone: 606-225-5333.
Princeton, New Jersey Office: Buchanan Ingersoll, A Partnership, College Centre, 500 College Road East.
Telephone: 609-452-2666.

Lynn J. Alstadt
George P. Baier
Paul A. Beck
Michael L. Dever

SENIOR ATTORNEY

George Raynovich, Jr.

John F. O'Rourke
Robert J. Pugh

For Complete List of Firm Personnel, See General Section

For full biographical listings, see the Martindale-Hubbell Law Directory

DICKIE, MCCAMEY & CHILCOTE, A PROFESSIONAL CORPORATION (AV)

Suite 400, Two PPG Place, 15222-5402
Telephone: 412-281-7272
Fax: 412-392-5367
Wheeling, West Virginia Office: Suite 2002, 1233 Main Street, 26003-2839.
Telephone: 304-233-1022.
Facsimile: 304-233-1026.

M. Richard Dunlap
Robert F. Wagner
Leland P. Schermer

Barry I. Friedman
John N. Cox

For Complete List of Firm Personnel, See General Section

For full biographical listings, see the Martindale-Hubbell Law Directory

ECKERT SEAMANS CHERIN & MELLOTT (AV)

600 Grant Street, 42nd Floor, 15219-2787
Telephone: 412-566-6000
Telex: 866172
Facsimile: 412-566-6099
Harrisburg, Pennsylvania Office: One South Market Square Building, 213 Market Street.
Telephone: 717-237-6000.
Facsimile: 717-237-6019.
Allentown, Pennsylvania Office: Sovereign Building, 609 Hamilton Mall, 3rd Floor.
Telephone: 610-432-3000.
Facsimile: 610-432-8827.
Philadelphia, Pennsylvania Office: 1700 Market Street, Suite 3232.
Telephone: 215-575-6000.
Telex: 845226.
Facsimile: 215-575-6015.
Boston, Massachusetts Office: One International Place, 18th Floor.
Telephone: 617-342-6800.
Facsimile: 617-342-6899.
Buffalo, New York Office: 606 Liberty Building.
Telephone: 716-854-4100.
Facsimile: 716-854-4227.
Fort Lauderdale, Florida Office: First Fort Lauderdale Place, Suite 900, 100 Northeast Third Avenue.
Telephone: 305-523-0400.
Facsimile: 305-523-7002.
Boca Raton, Florida Office: Suite 902, The Plaza, 5355 Town Center Road.
Telephone: 407-394-7775.
Facsimile: 407-394-9998.
Miami, Florida Office: Barnett Tower, 18th Floor, 701 Brickell Avenue.
Telephone: 305-373-9100.
Facsimile: 305-372-9400.
Tallahassee, Florida Office: 206 South Adams Street.
Telephone: 904-222-2515.
Facsimile: 904-222-3452.

(See Next Column)

ECKERT SEAMANS CHERIN & MELLOTT, *Pittsburgh—Continued*

Washington, D.C. Office: 2100 Pennsylvania Avenue, N.W., Suite 600.
Telephone: 202-659-6600.
Telex: 62030761.
Facsimile: 202-659-6699.

PATENT AND TRADEMARK COUNSEL

David V. Radack — Arnold B. Silverman
Richard V. Westerhoff

COUNSEL

Walter J. Blenko, Jr.

ASSOCIATES

Jolene W. Appleman — George K. Stacey

For Complete List of Firm Personnel, See General Section

For full biographical listings, see the Martindale-Hubbell Law Directory

GACA, MATIS & HAMILTON, A PROFESSIONAL CORPORATION (AV)

300 Four PPG Place, 15222-5404
Telephone: 412-338-4750
Fax: 412-338-4742

Giles J. Gaca
Thomas A. Matis
Mark R. Hamilton
John W. Jordan, IV
Alan S. Baum
Thomas P. McGinnis
Bernard R. Rizza
Jeffrey A. Ramaley
Stephen J. Dalesio
John Timothy Hinton, Jr.
Shawn Lynne Reed

LEGAL SUPPORT PERSONNEL

PARALEGALS

Tina M. Shanafelt — Jill M. Peterson

For full biographical listings, see the Martindale-Hubbell Law Directory

WEBB ZIESENHEIM BRUENING LOGSDON ORKIN & HANSON, P.C. (AV)

700 Koppers Building, 436 Seventh Avenue, 15219-1818
Telephone: 412-471-8815
Cable Address: "Webblaw"
Fax: 412-471-4094
Harrisburg, Pennsylvania Office: 100 Pine Street. 17106-1166.
Telephone: 717-238-1555.
Fax: 717-238-1755.

William Hess Webb
David C. Bruening
William H. Logsdon
Russell D. Orkin
David C. Hanson
Richard L. Byrne
Frederick B. Ziesenheim
Kent E. Baldauf
Barbara E. Johnson

Paul M. Reznick
Raymond J. Harmuth
John W. McIlvaine, III
Michael I. Shamos
Blynn L. Shideler
Julie W. Meder
Lester N. Fortney

For full biographical listings, see the Martindale-Hubbell Law Directory

VALLEY FORGE, Chester Co.

MICHAEL F. PETOCK (AV)

46 The Commons at Valley Forge, 1220 Valley Forge Road, P.O. Box 856, 19482-0856
Telephone: 610-935-8600; 215-922-5550
Fax: 610-933-9300

For full biographical listings, see the Martindale-Hubbell Law Directory

RATNER & PRESTIA, A PROFESSIONAL CORPORATION (AV)

Suite 400, 500 North Gulph Road, P.O. Box 980, 19482
Telephone: 610-265-6666
Telex: 846169
Telecopy: 610-265-8935

Paul F. Prestia
Allan Ratner
Andrew L. Ney
Kenneth N. Nigon
Kevin R. Casey
Guy T. Donatiello
James Charles Simmons
Viviana Amzel (Not admitted in PA)

Benjamin E. Leace
Lawrence E. Ashery
Christopher R. Lewis
Anthony L. Di Bartolomeo
Steven E Koffs
Allan M. Wheatcraft
Anthony Grillo

For full biographical listings, see the Martindale-Hubbell Law Directory

ZACHARY T. WOBENSMITH, III (AV)

86 The Commons at Valley Forge East, 1288 Valley Forge Road, P.O. Box 750, 19482-0750
Telephone: 610-935-9750
Telecopier: 610-935-0600

For full biographical listings, see the Martindale-Hubbell Law Directory

WILLOW GROVE, Montgomery Co.

JOHN W. LOGAN JR. & ASSOCIATES (AV)

Suite C-13, Executive Mews, 2300 Computer Avenue, 19090
Telephone: 215-657-6850
Fax: 215-657-0174

Gary A. Hecht — Daniel Williams

For full biographical listings, see the Martindale-Hubbell Law Directory

RHODE ISLAND

*PROVIDENCE,** Providence Co.

BARLOW & BARLOW, LTD. (AV)

1150 New London Avenue, 02920-3081
Telephone: 401-463-6830
Fax: 401-463-6835

Herbert B. Barlow, Jr.

David R. Josephs

OF COUNSEL

John A. Haug (Not admitted in RI)

Representative Clients: A. T. Cross Co.; Brown Broadcasting Servine-WBRU; Furon-Dixon Industries Corp.; H. F. Hanscom Co.; Hilsinger Corp.; Rhyme & Reason Toys, Ltd.; Johnson & Wales University; Leonard Valve Co.; Rhode Island Textile Co.; Union Wadding Co.

WM. W. RYMER (AV)

400 South Main Street, 02903
Telephone: 401-331-0181
Telecopier: 401-274-5070

For full biographical listings, see the Martindale-Hubbell Law Directory

SOUTH CAROLINA

*GREENVILLE,** Greenville Co.

RALPH BAILEY, P.A. (AV)

125 Broadus Avenue, 29601
Telephone: 803-242-5454
Fax: 803-242-3040

Ralph Bailey

Jeffrey Wayne Wheeler

For full biographical listings, see the Martindale-Hubbell Law Directory

DORITY & MANNING, P.A. (AV)

Suite 15, 700 East North at Williams, 29601
Telephone: 803-271-1592
Spartanburg Telephone: 803-582-7243
Facsimile: 803-233-7342

Julian W. Dority
Wellington M. Manning, Jr.
James M. Bagarazzi
Richard M. Moose
Mark C. Dukes
Stephen E. Bondura
Neil C. Jones

Craig N. Killen — Timothy A. Cassidy
LLoyd G. Farr

Representative Clients: Rieter Ingolstadt Spinnereimaschinenbau Aktiengesellschaft; Clemson University; Steel Heddle Manufacturing Co.; SSI Medical Services, Inc.; Beverage Air Co.; Builder Marts of America, Inc.; Meyn B.V.; Meyn, U.S.A.; Reliance Electric Co.; Jacobs Chuck Mfg. Co.

For full biographical listings, see the Martindale-Hubbell Law Directory

Greenville—Continued

HARDAWAY LAW FIRM, P.A. (AV)

1000 East North Street, 29601
Telephone: 803-233-6700
FAX: 803-233-2284
Mailing Address: P.O. Box 10107, Federal Station, Greenville, South Carolina, 29603-0107

John B. Hardaway, III
Jeffrey L. Wilson
John Bennett Mullinax
Michael A. Cicero
Steven M. Reiss

OF COUNSEL

Charles L. Schwab (Not admitted in SC)

LEGAL SUPPORT PERSONNEL

PARALEGALS

Sheryl A. Cross
Kathy J. Steading
Dorothy C. Rutledge

For full biographical listings, see the Martindale-Hubbell Law Directory

HAYNSWORTH, MARION, MCKAY & GUÉRARD, L.L.P. (AV)

Two Insignia Financial Plaza, 75 Beattie Place, P.O. Box 2048, 29602
Telephone: 803-240-3200
Telecopier: 803-240-3300
Columbia, South Carolina Office: Suite 2400 A T & T Building, 1201 Main Street, P.O. Drawer 7157, 29202
Telephone: 803-765-1818.
Telecopier: 803-765-2399.
Charleston, South Carolina Office: #2 Prioleau Street, P.O. Box 1119, 29402.
Telephone: 803-722-7606.
Telecopier: 803-723-5263.

MEMBER OF FIRM

O. G. Calhoun, Jr.

ASSOCIATE

Brent O. Clinkscale

Counsel for: Duke Power Co.; Liberty Mutual Insurance Co.; Equitable Life Assurance Society of the United States; St. Paul Insurance Group; Allstate Insurance Co.; Fluor-Daniel Corp.; Snyalloy Corporation; Greenville Hospital System.

For Complete List of Firm Personnel, See General Section

For full biographical listings, see the Martindale-Hubbell Law Directory

TENNESSEE

*CHATTANOOGA,** Hamilton Co.

ALAN RUDERMAN (AV)

806 Maclellan Building, 37402
Telephone: 615-267-6980
Fax: 615-756-0731

Reference: First American National Bank.

For full biographical listings, see the Martindale-Hubbell Law Directory

*KNOXVILLE,** Knox Co.

EGERTON, MCAFEE, ARMISTEAD & DAVIS, P.C. (AV)

500 First American National Bank Center, P.O. Box 2047, 37901
Telephone: 615-546-0500
Fax: 615-525-5293

M. W. Egerton (1897-1969)
Joseph A. McAfee (1903-1984)
William W. Davis
M. W. Egerton, Jr.
Joe M. McAfee
Lewis C. Foster, Jr.
William W. Davis, Jr.
Dan W. Holbrook
Herbert H. Slatery III
Barry K. Maxwell
Stephen A. McSween
William E. McClamroch, III

Jonathan D. Reed
Wesley L. Hatmaker

OF COUNSEL

John M. Armistead
Rockforde D. King

Representative Clients: First American National Bank of Knoxville; Home Federal Bank of Tennessee, F.S.B.; Bush Bros. & Co.; Johnson & Galyon Contractors; Baptist Hospital of East Tennessee; Revco D.S., Inc.; White Realty Corp.; Dick Broadcasting, Inc.

For full biographical listings, see the Martindale-Hubbell Law Directory

LUEDEKA, NEELY & GRAHAM, P.C. (AV)

Suite 1030 First American Center, 507 Gay Street, S.W., 37902
Telephone: 615-546-4305
Fax: 615-523-4478

(See Next Column)

Andrew S. Neely
Mark S. Graham

Robert O. Fox
W. Allen Marcontell (Not admitted in TN)
David E. LaRose (Not admitted in TN)
Richard W. Barnes
Michael E. Sellers
Edwin M. Luedeka

For full biographical listings, see the Martindale-Hubbell Law Directory

*MEMPHIS,** Shelby Co.

BAKER, DONELSON, BEARMAN & CALDWELL (AV)

20th Floor, First Tennessee Building, 165 Madison, 38103
Telephone: 901-526-2000
Telecopier: 901-577-2303
Nashville, Tennessee Office: 1700 Nashville City Center, 511 Union Street, 37219.
Telephone: 615-726-5600.
Telecopier: 615-726-0464.
Knoxville, Tennessee Office: 2200 Riverview Tower, 900 Gay Street, 37901.
Telephone: 615-549-7000.
Telecopier: 615-525-8569.
Chattanooga, Tennessee Office: 1800 Republic Centre, 633 Chestnut Street, 37450-1800.
Telephone: 615-752-4400.
Telecopier: 615-752-4410.
Huntsville, Tennessee Office: 3 Courthouse Square, 37756.
Telephone: 615-663-2321.
Telecopier: 615-663-2111.
Johnson City, Tennessee Office: Hamilton Bank Building, 207 Mockingbird Lane, 37604.
Telephone: 615-928-0181.
Telecopier: 615-928-5694; 615-928-3654; Kingsport: 615-246-6191.
Washington, D.C. Office: Market Square, 801 Pennsylvania Avenue, N.W., 20004.
Telephone: 202-508-3400.
Telecopier: 202-508-3402.

PARTNERS

Grady M. Garrison
Scott K. Haight

ASSOCIATES

William B. Clemmons, Jr.
Hollie A. Smith

For Complete List of Firm Personnel, See General Section

For full biographical listings, see the Martindale-Hubbell Law Directory

WALKER, MCKENZIE & WALKER, A PROFESSIONAL CORPORATION (AV)

6363 Poplar Avenue, Suite 434, 38119-4896
Telephone: 901-685-7428
Facsimile: 901-682-6488

John R. Walker, III
Larry W. McKenzie
Russell H. Walker

For full biographical listings, see the Martindale-Hubbell Law Directory

TEXAS

*AUSTIN,** Travis Co.

* indicates certain Bar Register subscribers whose principal office is located elsewhere in the state and who have arranged for representation as a part of the state capital listings that follow

*** ARNOLD, WHITE & DURKEE, A PROFESSIONAL CORPORATION** (AV)

1900 One American Center, 600 Congress Avenue, 78701-3248
Telephone: 512-418-3000
Facsimile: 512-474-7577
Houston, Texas Office: 750 Bering Drive, 77057-2198, P. O. Box 4433, 77210-4433.
Telephone: 713-787-1400.
Facsimile: 713-789-2679.
Telex: 79-0924.
Arlington, Virginia Office: 2001 Jefferson Davis Highway, Suite 401, 22202-3604.
Telephone: 703-415-1720.
Facsimile: 703-415-1728.
Chicago, Illinois Office: 800 Quaker Tower, 321 North Clark Street, 60610-4714.
Telephone: 312-744-0090.
Facsimile: 312-755-4489.
Minneapolis, Minnesota Office: 4850 First Bank Place, 601 Second Avenue South, 55402-4320.
Telephone: 612-321-2800.
Facsimile: 612-321-9600.

(See Next Column)

ARNOLD, WHITE & DURKEE A PROFESSIONAL CORPORATION, *Austin—Continued*

Palo Alto, California Office: Five Palo Alto Square, Suite 700, 94306-2122.
Telephone: 415-812-2929.
Facsimile: 415-812-2949.

Louis T. Pirkey
Floyd R. Nation
Willem G. Schuurman
William D. Raman
Daniel S. Hodgins
Richard J. Groos
David L. Parker
David D. Bahler
William G. Barber
Denise L. Mayfield
Barbara S. Kitchell
Michael S. Metteauer
Donald G. Jones
Amber L. Hatfield
Richard D. Egan
Shannon T. Vale
Mark B. Wilson
Brian W. Peterman
Gary J. Sertich
Mark A. Thurmon
Rose A. Hagan
Daniel J. Brennan
Robert M. O'Keefe (Not admitted in TX)
Steven L. Highlander (Not admitted in TX)
Adam V. Floyd

OF COUNSEL

Mark A. Lemley (Not admitted in TX)

For full biographical listings, see the Martindale-Hubbell Law Directory

BAKER & BOTTS, L.L.P. (AV)

1600 San Jacinto Center, 98 San Jacinto Boulevard, 78701
Telephone: 512-322-2500
Fax: 512-322-2501
Houston, Texas Office: One Shell Plaza, 910 Louisiana.
Telephone: 713-229-1234.
Dallas, Texas Office: 2001 Ross Avenue.
Telephone: 214-953-6500.
Washington, D.C. Office: The Warner, 1299 Pennsylvania Avenue, N.W.
Telephone: 202-639-7700.
New York, New York Office: 885 Third Avenue, Suite 2000.
Telephone: 212-705-5000.
Moscow, Russian Federation Office: 10 ul. Pushkinskaya, 103031.
Telephone: 7095/921-5300 (Local); 7501/929-7070 (International).

MEMBER OF FIRM

William Noble Hulsey III

ASSOCIATES

Dennis William Braswell
Ann Livingston

For Complete List of Firm Personnel, See General Section

For full biographical listings, see the Martindale-Hubbell Law Directory

SKJERVEN, MORRILL, MACPHERSON, FRANKLIN & FRIEL (AV Ⓣ)

Suite 1050, 100 Congress Street, 78701
Telephone: 512-404-3600
Telecopier: 512-404-3601
San Francisco, California Office: Suite 800, 601 California Street.
Telephone: 415-986-8383.
Telecopier: 415-982-7372.
San Jose, California Office: Suite 700, 25 Metro Drive.
Telephone: 408-283-1222.
Telecopier: 408-283-1233.

David H. Carroll (Resident)
Richard H. Skjerven

RESIDENT ASSOCIATES

Mark P. Kahler (Not admitted in TX)
Ken J. Koestner (Not admitted in TX)
Stephen A. Terrile (Not admitted in TX)
Kent B. Chambers

PATENT AGENT

Andrew C. Graham

Reference: Bank of America.

For full biographical listings, see the Martindale-Hubbell Law Directory

*DALLAS,** Dallas Co.

BAKER & BOTTS, L.L.P. (AV)

2001 Ross Avenue, 75201
Telephone: 214-953-6500
Fax: 214-953-6503
Houston, Texas Office: One Shell Plaza, 910 Louisiana.
Telephone: 713-229-1234.
Washington, D.C. Office: The Warner, 1299 Pennsylvania Avenue, N.W.
Telephone: 202-639-7700.
Austin, Texas Office: 1600 San Jacinto Center, 98 San Jacinto Boulevard.
Telephone: 512-322-2500.
New York, New York Office: 885 Third Avenue, Suite 2000.
Telephone: 212-705-5000.
Moscow, Russian Federation Office: 10 ul. Pushkinskaya, 103031.
Telephone: 7095/921-5300 (Local); 7095/929-7070.

MEMBERS OF FIRM

Jerry W. Mills
Robert M. Chiaviello, Jr.

(See Next Column)

ASSOCIATES

Thomas R. Felger
Charles S. Fish
David Norman Fogg, Sr.
Thomas A. Gigliotti
Wei Wei Jeang
Robert Hugh Johnston III
Kevin J. Meek
Richard J. Moura (Not admitted in TX)
Anthony Ernest Peterman
Barton Earl Showalter
Kelly Mahon Tullier
Robert J. Ward
David Gerald Wille

For Complete List of Firm Personnel, See General Section

For full biographical listings, see the Martindale-Hubbell Law Directory

CALHOUN & STACY (AV)

5700 NationsBank Plaza, 901 Main Street, 75202-3747
Telephone: 214-748-5000
Telecopier: 214-748-1421
Telex: 211358 CALGUMP UR

Mark Alan Calhoun
David W. Elrod
Steven D. Goldston
Parker Nelson
Roy L. Stacy

ASSOCIATES

Shannon S. Barclay
Robert A. Bragalone
Dennis D. Conder
Jane Elizabeth Diseker
Lawrence I. Fleishman
Thomas C. Jones
Katherine Johnson Knight
V. Paige Pace
Veronika Willard
Michael C. Wright

LEGAL CONSULTANT

Rees T. Bowen, III

For full biographical listings, see the Martindale-Hubbell Law Directory

HARRIS, TUCKER & HARDIN, P.C. (AV)

2100, One Galleria Tower, 75240-6604
Telephone: 214-233-5712
Telex: 288163 HTTT UR
Facsimile: Omnifax 214-934-9553

William D. Harris, Jr.
L. Dan Tucker
Roy W. Hardin
William D. Jackson
Harry J. Watson

George R. (Russ) Schultz
David W. Carstens
Kristin K. Jordan
Michael W. Piper
Craig J. Cox

For full biographical listings, see the Martindale-Hubbell Law Directory

THOMPSON & KNIGHT, A PROFESSIONAL CORPORATION (AV)

(Attorneys and Counselors)
1700 Pacific Avenue Suite 3300, 75201
Telephone: 214-969-1700
Telecopy: 214-969-1751
Cable Address: "Tomtex"
Telex: 732298
Austin, Texas Office: 1200 San Jacinto Center, 98 San Jacinto Boulevard, 78701.
Telephone: 512-469-6100.
Telecopy: 512-469-6180.
Fort Worth, Texas Office: 801 Cherry Street, Suite 1600, 76102.
Telephone: 817-347-1700.
Telecopy: 817-347-1799.
Houston, Texas Office: 1700 Texas Commerce Tower, 600 Travis, 77002.
Telephone: 713-217-2800.
Telecopy: 713-217-2828.
Monterrey, Mexico Office: Edificio Losoles PD-4, Av. Lázaro Cárdenas No. 2400 Pte., San Pedro Garza Garcia, Nuevo Léon C.P. 66220.
Telephone: (52-8) 363-0096.
Telecopy: (52-8) 363-3067.

SHAREHOLDERS

P. Jefferson Ballew
Jane Politz Brandt
Frank Finn
Bruce S. Sostek
Peter J. Thoma

For Complete List of Firm Personnel, See General Section

For full biographical listings, see the Martindale-Hubbell Law Directory

*HOUSTON,** Harris Co.

ARNOLD, WHITE & DURKEE, A PROFESSIONAL CORPORATION (AV)

750 Bering Drive (77057-2198), P.O. Box 4433, 77210-4433
Telephone: 713-787-1400
Facsimile: 713-789-2679
Telex: 79-0924
Austin, Texas Office: 1900 One American Center, 600 Congress Avenue, 78701-3248.
Telephone: 512-418-3000.
Facsimile: 512-474-7577.

(See Next Column)

ARNOLD, WHITE & DURKEE A PROFESSIONAL CORPORATION—*Continued*

Arlington, Virginia Office: 2001 Jefferson Davis Highway, Suite 401, 22202-3604.
Telephone: 703-415-1720.
Facsimile: 703-415-1728.
Chicago, Illinois Office: 800 Quaker Tower, 321 North Clark Street, 60610-4714.
Telephone: 312-744-0090.
Facsimile: 312-755-4489.
Minneapolis, Minnesota Office: 4850 First Bank Place, 601 Second Avenue South, 55402-4320.
Telephone: 612-321-2800.
Facsimile: 612-321-9600.
Palo Alto, California Office: Five Palo Alto Square, Suite 700, 94306-2122.
Telephone: 415-812-2929.
Facsimile: 415-812-2949.

Tom Arnold
Robert A. White (1929-1977)
Bill Durkee
Louis T. Pirkey (Resident, Austin, Texas Office)
John F. Lynch
Jack C. Goldstein
Rodney K. Caldwell
Stephen G. Rudisill (Resident, Chicago, Illinois Office)
Floyd R. Nation (Resident, Austin, Texas Office)
Wayne M. Harding
Clarence E. Eriksen
Charles H. De La Garza
J. Paul Williamson (Resident, Arlington, Virginia Office)
Willem G. Schuurman (Resident, Austin, Texas Office)
Travis Gordon White
James J. Elacqua
John D. Norris
William D. Raman (Resident, Austin, Texas Office)
Patricia A. Kammerer
Michael E. Macklin
Peter J. Shurn III
Stephen H. Cagle
Patricia N. Brantley (Resident, Palo Alto, California Office)
Timothy N. Trop
Thomas A. Miller
Kenneth D. Goodman
Michael L. Lynch
Craig M. Lundell
Ronald B. Coolley (Resident, Chicago, Illinois Office)
J. Bradford Leaheey (Resident, Chicago, Illinois Office)
D. C. Toedt III
Daniel S. Hodgins (Resident, Austin, Texas Office)
Richard C. Auchterlonie
Danny L. Williams
Christopher R. Benson
Richard J. Groos (Resident, Austin, Texas Office)
Glenn W. Rhodes
David L. Parker (Resident, Austin, Texas Office)
Karen Bryant Tripp
David D. Bahler (Resident, Austin, Texas Office)
Stephen D. Dellett
Douglas H. Elliott
Henry A. Petri, Jr.
Melinda L. Patterson
William G. Barber (Resident, Austin, Texas Office)
Susan Kelly Knoll
Steven P. Arnold
Denise L. Mayfield (Resident, Austin, Texas Office)
W. David Westergard
James D. Smith
Richard L. Stanley
Barbara S. Kitchell (Resident, Austin, Texas Office)
Michael S. Metteauer (Resident, Austin, Texas Office)
Terry D. Morgan
Donald G. Jones (Resident, Austin, Texas Office)
Joseph D. Lechtenberger
J. Mike Amerson
Suzanne E. Lecocke
Barry D. Blount (Resident, Chicago, Illinois Office)
Amber L. Hatfield (Resident, Austin, Texas Office)
Timothy M. Honeycutt
Kerry Kampschmidt
Keith A. Rutherford
L. Gene Spears, Jr.
Joseph A. Uradnik
Russell L. Sandidge
Richard D. Egan (Resident, Austin, Texas Office)
Michael J. Blankstein (Resident, Chicago, Illinois Office)
Julio A. Garceran (Resident, Chicago, Illinois Office)
Shannon T. Vale (Resident, Austin, Texas Office)
John C. Cain
Michael S. Dowler
Stephen E. Edwards
Jeffrey L. Garrett
Louis Brucculeri
Louis A. Riley
Mark B. Wilson (Resident, Austin, Texas Office)
Ana E. Kadala
Michael G. Fletcher
Robert J. McAughan, Jr.
Gay L. Bonorden
Nicolas G. Barzoukas
Kevin S. Kudlac
Michael E. Lee
Paul R. Kitch (Resident, Chicago, Illinois Office)
Hugh R. Kress
Brian W. Peterman (Resident, Austin, Texas Office)
Gary J. Fischman
Peter J. Chassman
Gary J. Sertich (Resident, Austin, Texas Office)
Richard J. Lutton
John T. Polasek
Robert B. Lytle
Paul R. Morico
Stephen L. Lundwall
Linda A. Stokley
Mark A. Thurmon (Resident, Austin, Texas Office)
Michelle D. Kahn (Resident, Palo Alto, California Office)
David L. Bilsker (Resident, Palo Alto, California Office)
James F. Valentine (Resident, Palo Alto, California Office)
Mark K. Dickson (Resident, Palo Alto, California Office)
Rose A. Hagan (Resident, Austin, Texas Office)
Michael J. Collins
Daniel J. Brennan (Resident, Austin, Texas, Office)
Robert M. O'Keefe (Resident, Austin, Texas, Office)
Mark A. Thomas (Resident, Chicago, Illinois Office)
Christine F. Martin (Resident, Chicago, Illinois Office)
Steven L. Highlander (Resident, Austin, Texas Office)

(See Next Column)

Adam V. Floyd (Resident, Austin, Texas Office)
Thomas C. Mavrakakis
Hoyt A. Fleming, III
Todd D. Mattingly
Janelle D. Waack

OF COUNSEL

James A. Reilly
Paul M. Janicke
David J. Healey
Mark A. Lemley (Resident, Austin, Texas, Office)
Charles S. Baker

For full biographical listings, see the Martindale-Hubbell Law Directory

BAKER & BOTTS, L.L.P. (AV)

One Shell Plaza, 910 Louisiana, 77002
Telephone: 713-229-1234
Cable Address: "Boterlove"
Fax: 713-229-1522
Washington, D.C. Office: The Warner, 1299 Pennsylvania Avenue, N.W.
Telephone: 202-639-7700.
New York, New York Office: 885 Third Avenue, Suite 2000.
Telephone: 212-705-5000.
Austin, Texas Office: 1600 San Jacinto Center, 98 San Jacinto Boulevard.
Telephone: 512-322-2500.
Dallas, Texas Office: 2001 Ross Avenue.
Telephone: 214-953-6500.
Moscow, Russian Federation Office: 10 ul. Pushkinskaya, 103031.
Telephone: 7095/921-5300 (Local); 7095/929-7070 (International).

MEMBERS OF FIRM

William C. Slusser
Scott F. Partridge
Lee Landa Kaplan
Thomas H. Adolph
Mitchell D. Lukin

ASSOCIATES

Andres M. Arismendi, Jr.
Jason D. Firth
Roger J. Fulghum
J. Timothy Headley
Pamela Lunn Hohensee
David Charles Hricik
Danita J. M. Maseles
Scott Joseph Miller
Jayme Partridge Roden
Tim T. Shen
Richard S. Siluk
Howard L. Speight
Lori D. Stiffler
C. Patrick Turley
Michael E. Wilson

For Complete List of Firm Personnel, See General Section

For full biographical listings, see the Martindale-Hubbell Law Directory

BROWNING, BUSHMAN, ANDERSON & BROOKHART, A PROFESSIONAL CORPORATION (AV)

5718 Westheimer, Suite 1800, 77057
Telephone: 713-266-5593
Facsimile: 713-266-5169

Ralph R. Browning (1905-1979)
C. James Bushman
Margaret E. Anderson
Walter R. Brookhart
William E. Johnson, Jr.
Loren G. Helmreich

Kenneth L. Nash

Representative Clients: Keystone International, Inc.; Vista Chemical Co.; Exxon Chemical Company; Baroid Corp.; NL Industries, Inc.; Coastal Corp.; Varco/Shaffer, Inc.

For full biographical listings, see the Martindale-Hubbell Law Directory

FISH & RICHARDSON P.C. (AVⓉ)

One Riverway Suite 1200, 77056
Telephone: 713-629-5070
Telecopier: 713-629-7811
Boston, Massachusetts Office: 225 Franklin Street.
Telephone: 617-542-5070.
Telecopier: 617-542-8906.
Cable Address: "Fishrich, Boston".
Telex: RCA 200154 Fishr Ur.
Washington, D.C. Office: 601 13th Street, N.W.
Telephone: 202-783-5070.
Telecopier: 202-783-2331.
Menlo Park, California Office: 2200 Sand Hill Road, Suite 100.
Telephone: 415-854-5277.
Telecopier: 415-854-0875.
Minneapolis, Minnesota Office: Fish & Richardson P.C., P.A., 2500 One Financial Plaza, 120 South Sixth Street.
Telephone: 612-335-5070.
Facsimile: 612-288-9696.

Frederick P. Fish (1855-1930)
W.K. Richardson (1859-1951)

RESIDENT MEMBERS OF FIRM

Michael O. Sutton
Alan H. Gordon
Alan D. Rosenthal

OF COUNSEL

Douglas Baldwin

(See Next Column)

FISH & RICHARDSON P.C., *Houston—Continued*

RESIDENT ASSOCIATES

Gordon G. Waggett
Albert B. Deaver, Jr.
John E. Vick, Jr.
Kenneth S. Barrow
Jon R. Trembath
Jonathan P. Osha
Sharon A. Israel

For full biographical listings, see the Martindale-Hubbell Law Directory

PRAVEL, HEWITT, KIMBALL & KRIEGER, A PROFESSIONAL CORPORATION (AV)

Tenth Floor, 1177 West Loop South, 77027
Telephone: 713-850-0909
FAX: 713-850-0165
New Orleans, Louisiana Office: 1515 Poydras Street, Suite 2300.
Telephone: 504-524-7207.
FAX: 504-524-3960.

Bernarr Roe Pravel
Albert B. Kimball, Jr.
Lester L. Hewitt
Paul E. Krieger
Charles M. Cox
Paul C. Van Slyke
Marc L. Delflache
James H. Riley II
Rita Mankovich Irani
Keith Lutsch
Richard D. Fladung
John Wilson Jones

Douglas W. Rommelmann
Gerard Alan Witte
David R. Clonts
Jan K. Simpson
Paul W. Fulbright
E. Randall Smith
Denise M. Kettelberger
Mayumi Maeda
T. Grant Ritz

OF COUNSEL

Claude E. Cooke, Jr.

LEGAL SUPPORT PERSONNEL

Dan C. Hu

For full biographical listings, see the Martindale-Hubbell Law Directory

VADEN, EICKENROHT, THOMPSON, BOULWARE & FEATHER, L.L.P. (AV)

A Registered Limited Liability Partnership
Suite 1100, One Riverway, 77056-1982
Telephone: 713-961-3525
Telex: 4997115 VETB UI
Fax: 713-961-3723

MEMBERS OF FIRM

Frank S. Vaden III, (P.C)
Marvin B. Eickenroht
Jennings B. Thompson (P.C.)
Margaret A. Boulware
John R. Feather

ASSOCIATES

Mark R. Wisner
Kent A. Rowald
Jeffrey A. Pyle
Margaret A. Kirick
Sarah T. Harris
Steven L. Christian
Frank C. Turner

For full biographical listings, see the Martindale-Hubbell Law Directory

VINSON & ELKINS L.L.P. (AV)

2300 First City Tower, 1001 Fannin, 77002-6760
Telephone: 713-758-2222
Fax: 713-758-2346
International Telex: 6868314
Cable Address: Vinelkins
Austin, Texas Office: One American Center, 600 Congress Avenue.
Telephone: 512-495-8400.
Fax: 512-495-8612.
Dallas, Texas Office: 3700 Trammell Crow Center, 2001 Ross Avenue.
Telephone: 214-220-7700.
Fax: 214-220-7716.
Washington, D.C. Office: The Willard Office Building, 1455 Pennsylvania Avenue, N.W.
Telephone: 202-639-6500.
Fax: 202-639-6604.
Cable Address: Vinelkins.
London, England Office: 47 Charles Street, Berkeley Square, London, W1X 7PB, England.
Telephone: 011 (44-171) 491-7236.
Fax: 011 (44-71) 499-5320.
Cable Address: Vinelkins London W.1.
Moscow, Russian Federation Office: 16 Alexey Tolstoy Street, Second Floor, Moscow, 103001 Russian Federation.
Telephone: 011 (70-95) 956-1995.
Telecopy: 011 (70-95) 956-1996.
Mexico City, Mexico Office: Aristóteles 77, 5°Piso, Colonia Chapultepec Polanco, 11560 Mexico, D.F.
Telephone: (52-5) 280-7828.
Fax: (52-5) 280-9223.

(See Next Column)

Singapore Office: 50 Raffles Place, #19-05 Shell Tower, 0104. U.S. Voice Mailbox: 713-758-3500.
Telephone: (65) 536-8300.
Fax: (65) 536-8311.

Steven R. Borgman
George Harvey Dunn, III
A. H. Evans
William L. LaFuze
J. Clark Martin
Peter E. Mims
W. Ronald Robins

HOUSTON OF COUNSEL

Alan R. Thiele

ASSOCIATES

Valerie S. Boutwell
W. Scott Brown
Leslie Jean Clark
Laura A. Crowe
Barry E. Engel
Kevin M. Hart
Kelly Williams Raley
Karen Tucker White

For Complete List of Firm Personnel, See General Section

For full biographical listings, see the Martindale-Hubbell Law Directory

*SAN ANTONIO,** Bexar Co.

COX & SMITH INCORPORATED (AV)

112 East Pecan Street, Suite 1800, 78205
Telephone: 210-554-5500
Telecopier: 210-226-8395

Gale R. Peterson
J. Daniel Harkins
W. Bradley Haymond (Not admitted in TX)

OF COUNSEL

W. Al Schaich

Representative Clients: Clarke American; The Dee Howard Company; Texas Tech University; Texas A & M University. Southwest Production Biomedical Research.

For Complete List of Firm Personnel, See General Section

For full biographical listings, see the Martindale-Hubbell Law Directory

MATTHEWS & BRANSCOMB, A PROFESSIONAL CORPORATION (AV)

One Alamo Center, 106 S. St. Mary's Street, Suite 800, 78205
Telephone: 210-226-4211
Facsimile: 210-226-0521
Telex: 5106009283
Cable Code: MBLAW
Austin, Texas Office: 301 Congress Avenue, Suite 2050.
Telephone: 512-305-4400.
Facsimile: 512-305-4413.
Corpus Christi, Texas Office: 802 N. Carancahua, Suite 1900.
Telephone: 512-888-9261.
Facsimile: 512-888-8504.
Eagle Pass, Texas Office: 675 Main Street.
Telephone: 210-773-6700.
Facsimile: 210-757-4045.
Uvalde, Texas Office: 200 E. Nopal #208.
Telephone: 210-278-4597.
Facsimile: 210-278-4806.
(Associated with Hall, Quintanilla & Alarcon, L.C., Laredo, Texas, under the name of Hall, Quintanilla, Alarcon, Matthews & Branscomb, P.L.L.C.)

William F. Nowlin (1902-1978)
Harper Macfarlane (1901-1980)
Lionel R. Fuller (1919-1984)
Grady Barrett (1895-1986)
William H. Nowlin (1934-1987)
Wilbur L. Matthews
Patrick H. Swearingen, Jr.
Lewis T. Tarver, Jr.
Richard E. Goldsmith
William H. Robison
John D. Fisch
Jon C. Wood
J. Joe Harris
George P. Parker, Jr.
James M. Doyle, Jr.
C. Michael Montgomery
W. Roger Wilson
Howard P. Newton
Charles J. Muller, III
John McPherson Pinckney, III
Richard C. Danysh
J. Tullos Wells
Charles J. Fitzpatrick
Marshall T. Steves, Jr.
Judith R. Blakeway
James H. Kizziar, Jr.
Frank Z. Ruttenberg
Leslie Selig Byrd
Patrick H. Autry
Farley P. Katz
Dawn Bruner Finlayson
John A. Ferguson, Jr.
Julie B. Adler Koppenheffer
Mary M. Potter
Annalyn G. Smith
Arthur G. Uhl, III
Nancy H. Stumberg
Howard D. Bye
Judy K. Jetelina
Mark A. Phariss
Merritt M. Clements
Robert Shaw-Meadow
Daniel M. Elder
Mark A. Jones
Kay L. Reamey
Timothy H. Bannwolf
Victoria M. Garcia
Anthony E. Rebollo
Steven J. Pugh
Elizabeth H. Chumney
Craig A. Arnold
Inez M. McBride
Kathleen A. Devine
Raquel G. Perez
David L. Doggett
Roberta J. Sharp
Mary Helen Medina

(See Next Column)

MATTHEWS & BRANSCOMB A PROFESSIONAL CORPORATION—*Continued*

OF COUNSEL

Francis W. Baker
Judson Wood, Jr.

Representative Clients: Coca Cola Bottling Company of the Southwest; Concord Oil Co.; Ellison Enterprises, Inc.; H. E. Butt Grocery Co.; Frank B. Hall & Co., Inc.; The Hearst Corp., San Antonio Light Division; San Antonio Gas & Electric Utilities (City Board); Southern Pacific Transportation Co.; Southwest Texas Methodist Hospital.

For full biographical listings, see the Martindale-Hubbell Law Directory

UTAH

*SALT LAKE CITY,** Salt Lake Co.

MALLINCKRODT & MALLINCKRODT (AV)

Suite 510 Newhouse Building, 10 Exchange Place, 84111
Telephone: 801-328-1624
FAX: 801-328-1627
Ogden, Utah Office: First Security Bank Building.
Telephone: 801-393-0331.

MEMBERS OF FIRM

Philip A. Mallinckrodt
Robert R. Mallinckrodt
A. Ray Osburn (Resident at Ogden, Utah)

OF COUNSEL

George H. Mortimer

Representative Clients: BSD Medical Corporation; Christensen Mining Products; Mountain Fuel Supply Co.; Wescor, Inc.

For full biographical listings, see the Martindale-Hubbell Law Directory

TRASK, BRITT & ROSSA, A PROFESSIONAL CORPORATION (AV)

525 South 300 East, P.O. Box 2550, 84110
Telephone: 801-532-1922
Telecopier: 801-531-9168
Internet: tbrlaw @ delphicom

David V. Trask
William S. Britt
Thomas J. Rossa
Laurence B. Bond
Joseph A. Walkowski
James R. Duzan
H. Dickson Burton
Allen C. Turner
Alan K. Aldous
Julie K. Morriss

LEGAL SUPPORT PERSONNEL

Susan E. Sweigert

Reference: Key Bank.

For full biographical listings, see the Martindale-Hubbell Law Directory

VAN COTT, BAGLEY, CORNWALL & MCCARTHY, A PROFESSIONAL CORPORATION (AV)

Suite 1600, 50 South Main Street, P.O. Box 45340, 84145
Telephone: 801-532-3333
Telex: 453149
Telecopier: 801-534-0058
Ogden, Utah Office: Suite 900, 2404 Washington Boulevard.
Telephone: 801-394-5783.
Park City, Utah Office: 314 Main Street, Suite 205.
Telephone: 801-649-3889.
Reno, Nevada Office: Jeppson & Lee, 100 West Liberty, Suite 990.
Telephone: 702-333-6800.

R. Stephen Marshall
Jon C. Christiansen
David L. Arrington

James D. Gilson
David E. Allen
Craig W. Dallon
Daniel P. McCarthy
Preston C. Regehr

Representative Clients: Standard Oil Company of California (and affiliated companies); FMC Corp.; Leucadia National Corp.; Key Bank of Utah; Southern Pacific Lines; Intermountain Health Care, Inc.; Huntsman Chemical Corp.; Iomega Corp.; Metropolitan Life Ins. Co.

For Complete List of Firm Personnel, See General Section

For full biographical listings, see the Martindale-Hubbell Law Directory

WORKMAN, NYDEGGER & SEELEY, A PROFESSIONAL CORPORATION (AV)

1000 Eagle Gate Tower, 60 East South Temple, 84111
Telephone: 801-533-9800
Telecopier: 801-328-1707
Telex: 453251 PATENTS SLC UD

H. Ross Workman
Rick D. Nydegger
David O. Seeley
Brent P. Lorimer
Thomas R. Vuksinick
Kent S. Burningham
Larry R. Laycock
Todd E. Zenger
Jonathan W. Richards
David R. Wright
John C. Stringham
Michael F. Krieger
Bradley K. DeSandro
John M. Guynn
Dana L. Tangren
Eric L. Maschoff

(See Next Column)

Gregory M. Taylor
Kevin B. Laurence
Gregory V. Bean
Brian C. Kunzler
Susan K. Morris

OF COUNSEL

Allen R. Jensen

For full biographical listings, see the Martindale-Hubbell Law Directory

VIRGINIA

ALEXANDRIA, (Independent City)

BURNS, DOANE, SWECKER & MATHIS (AV)

Suite 100, 699 Prince Street, 22314
Telephone: 703-836-6620
Cable Address: "Patburn"
Telex: Itt 440 580 Bdsm Ale
and Wu 901855 Bdsm Ale *Facsimile:* 703-836-2021; 703-836-7356; 703-836-3503
Mailing Address: P.O. Box 1404, 22313,
Menlo Park, California Office: 3000 Sand Hill Road, Building 4, Suite 160 94025.
Telephone: 415-854-7400.
Facsimile: 415-854-8275.

MEMBERS OF FIRM

William L. Mathis
Robert S. Swecker
Platon N. Mandros
Benton S. Duffett, Jr.
Joseph R. Magnone
Norman H. Stepno
Ronald L. Grudziecki (Admitted in District of Columbia; limited admission in Virginia)
Frederick G. Michaud, Jr.
Alan E. Kopecki
Regis E. Slutter
Samuel C. Miller, III
Ralph L. Freeland, Jr. (Menlo Park, California Office)
Robert G. Mukai
George A. Hovanec, Jr.
James A. LaBarre
E. Joseph Gess
David D. Reynolds
R. Danny Huntington
Eric H. Weisblatt
James W. Peterson (Menlo Park, California Office)
Teresa Stanek Rea (Not admitted in VA)
Robert E. Krebs (Menlo Park, California Office)
Adrienne L. White
Robert M. Schulman (Not admitted in VA)
William C. Rowland
T. Gene Dillahunty (Menlo Park, California Office)
Anthony W. Shaw
Patrick C. Keane (Not admitted in VA)
B. Jefferson Boggs, Jr.
William H. Benz (Menlo Park, California Office)
Peter K. Skiff
Richard J. McGrath
Matthew L. Schneider

COUNSEL

J. Preston Swecker (Not admitted in VA)

OF COUNSEL

Peter H. Smolka

ASSOCIATES

David J. Serbin (Not admitted in VA)
Ronni S. Malamud (Not admitted in VA)
Steven S. Payne
Charles F. Wieland III
William R. Johnson

For full biographical listings, see the Martindale-Hubbell Law Directory

*ARLINGTON,** Arlington Co.

ARNOLD, WHITE & DURKEE, A PROFESSIONAL CORPORATION (AV)

2001 Jefferson Davis Highway, Suite 401, 22202-3604
Telephone: 703-415-1720
Facsimile: 703-415-1728
Houston, Texas Office: 750 Bering Drive, 77057-2198; P.O. Box 4433, 77210-4433.
Telephone: 713-787-1400.
Facsimile: 713-789-2679.
Telex: 79-0924.
Austin, Texas Office: 1900 One American Center, 600 Congress Avenue, 78701-3248.
Telephone: 512-418-3000.
Facsimile: 512-474-7577.
Chicago, Illinois Office: 800 Quaker Tower, 321 North Clark Street, 60610-4714.
Telephone: 312-744-0090.
Facsimile: 312-755-4489.
Minneapolis, Minnesota Office: 4850 First Bank Place, 601 Second Avenue South, 55402-4320.
Telephone: 612-321-2800.
Facsimile: 612-321-9600.
Palo Alto, California Office: Five Palo Alto Square, Suite 700, 94306-2122.
Telephone: 415-812-2929.
Facsimile: 415-812-2949.

(See Next Column)

ARNOLD, WHITE & DURKEE A PROFESSIONAL CORPORATION, *Arlington—Continued*

J. Paul Williamson

For full biographical listings, see the Martindale-Hubbell Law Directory

LARSON AND TAYLOR (AV)

727 Twenty-Third Street South, 22202
Telephone: 703-920-7200
Telex: 89-2548
Facsimile: 703-892-84 28

MEMBERS OF FIRM

Roberts B. Larson (1904-1985)
Andrew E. Taylor *
Walter C. Gillis
Marvin Petry *
Thomas P. Sarro
Ross F. Hunt, Jr.
William E. Jackson (Not admitted in VA)
Douglas E. Jackson (Not admitted in VA)
Brewster B. Taylor (Not admitted in VA)
B. Aaron Schulman (Not admitted in VA)

ASSOCIATES

Linda R. Poteate
Kevin J. Dunleavy
Susan S. Morse

OF COUNSEL

E. Fulton Brylawski (P.C.) (Not admitted in VA)
Harold L. Novick (Not admitted in VA)
Gayle Parker

*Admission in Virginia limited to Patent, Trademark, Copyright and Unfair Competition Causes only.

For full biographical listings, see the Martindale-Hubbell Law Directory

LITMAN LAW OFFICES, LTD. (AV)

Suite 800-801, Crystal Square II, 1725 South Jefferson Davis Highway, 22202
Telephone: 703-412-1000; 1-800-4-PATENT
Facsimile: 703-412-7000
Internet Address: 4 patent @ access. digex. net
Mailing Address: P.O. Box 15035, Arlington (Crystal City), Virginia, 22215-0035

Walter R. Baylor
Robert N. Blackmon
William S. Goldman (Not admitted in VA)
Walter E. Kubitz
Joseph Thomas Leone
Hanno I. Rittner
G. Andrew Spencer (Not admitted in VA)
Karl I.E. Tamai (Not admitted in VA)
John R. Wenzel

PATENT AGENTS

Carl L. Benson
Ourmazd S. Ojan
George T. Ozaki
Dolph H. Torrence

For full biographical listings, see the Martindale-Hubbell Law Directory

NIXON & VANDERHYE P.C. (AV)

8th Floor, 1100 North Glebe Road, 22201
Telephone: 703-816-4000
Telex: 200797 Answerback: 200797 NIXN UR
Facsimile: 703-816-4100

Larry S. Nixon
Robert A. Vanderhye
Arthur R. Crawford
James T. Hosmer
Robert W. Faris
Michael J. Keenan
Mark E. Nusbaum
Richard G. Besha
Robert W. Adams
Bryan H. Davidson
Stanley C. Spooner
Leonard C. Mitchard (Not admitted in VA)
Robert A. Rowan
Duane M. Byers (Not admitted in VA)
Paul J. Henon (Not admitted in VA)
Jeffry H. Nelson
Donna J. Bunton (Not admitted in VA)
John R. Lastova (Not admitted in VA)
H. Warren Burnam, Jr.
Thomas E. Byrne (Not admitted in VA)
Mary J. Wilson (Not admitted in VA)
J. Scott Davidson (Not admitted in VA)
Ralph Falcone

For full biographical listings, see the Martindale-Hubbell Law Directory

SHAPIRO AND SHAPIRO (AV)

Suite 1701, 1100 Wilson Boulevard, 22209
Telephone: 703-276-0700
Cable Address: "Harnel"
Telex: 440166
Telecopier: 703-528-2457

MEMBERS OF FIRM

Arthur Shapiro (1900-1961)
Harry G. Shapiro (1912-1979)
Nelson H. Shapiro *
Ronald E. Shapiro
Mitchell W. Shapiro

(See Next Column)

*Admission in Virginia limited to Patent, Trademark, Copyright and Unfair Competition Causes only.

For full biographical listings, see the Martindale-Hubbell Law Directory

LAW OFFICES OF L.S. VAN LANDINGHAM, JR. (AV)

Suite 507, 2001 Jefferson Davis Highway, 22202
Telephone: 703-979-4244
Facsimile: 703-415-1244

For full biographical listings, see the Martindale-Hubbell Law Directory

FALLS CHURCH, (Independent City)

BIRCH, STEWART, KOLASCH & BIRCH (AV)

8110 Gatehouse Road, Suite 500 East, P.O. Box 747, 22040-0747
Telephone: 703-205-8000
Cable Address: "Stekol" Falls Church, Va.
Telex: 248345
Telecopier Facsimile: 703-205-8050

MEMBERS OF FIRM

Terrell C. Birch *
Raymond C. Stewart
Joseph A. Kolasch
Anthony L. Birch *
James M. Slattery
Donald C. Kolasch *
Bernard L. Sweeney (Not admitted in VA)
Michael K. Mutter
Charles Gorenstein *
Gerald M. Murphy, Jr.
Leonard R. Svensson
Terry L. Clark
Andrew D. Meikle
Marc S. Weiner
Joe M. Muncy
Andrew F. Reish

ASSOCIATES

Robert J. Kenney
C. Joseph Faraci
Barbara A. Fisher
John W. Bailey
Donald J. Daley
John A. Castellano, III
Thomas W. Steinberg (Not admitted in VA)
Blossom E. Loo (Not admitted in VA)
Charles E. Cohen
Bruce D. Gray
Mark R. Buscher
Gary D. Yacura

OF COUNSEL

Herbert M. Birch (Not admitted in VA)
William L. Gates (Not admitted in VA)
Elliot A. Goldberg (Not admitted in VA)
Paul M. Craig, Jr. (Not admitted in VA)

Reference: NationsBank, N.A., Falls Church, Virginia.
*Admission in Virginia limited to Patent, Trademark, Copyright and Unfair Competition Causes only

For full biographical listings, see the Martindale-Hubbell Law Directory

MCLEAN, Fairfax Co.

SIXBEY, FRIEDMAN, LEEDOM & FERGUSON, P.C. (AV)

Suite 600, 2010 Corporate Ridge, 22102
Telephone: 703-790-9110
Telecopier: 703-883-0370
Arlington, Virginia Office: 2001 Jefferson Davis Highway.
Telephone: 703-415-0416.
Telecopier: 703-415-0417.

Daniel W. Sixbey (Not admitted in VA)
Stuart J. Friedman (Not admitted in VA)
Charles M. Leedom, Jr. *
Gerald J. Ferguson, Jr. *
David S. Safran
Thomas W. Cole *
Donald R. Studebaker (Not admitted in VA)
Evan R. Smith
Jeffrey L. Costellia

Joan Kux Lawrence
Tim Leonard Brackett, Jr.
Eric J. Robinson

*Admission in Virginia limited to Patent, Trademark, Copyright and Unfair Competition Causes only.

For full biographical listings, see the Martindale-Hubbell Law Directory

WASHINGTON

*SEATTLE,** King Co.

CHRISTENSEN, O'CONNOR, JOHNSON & KINDNESS (AV)

1420 Fifth Avenue, Suite 2800, 98101-2347
Telephone: 206-682-8100
Cable Address: "Patentable"
Telex: 4938023
Telecopier: 206-224-0779

(See Next Column)

CHRISTENSEN, O'CONNOR, JOHNSON & KINDNESS—*Continued*

MEMBERS OF FIRM

Orland M. Christensen (1920-1984)
Michael G. Toner (1943-1992)
Bruce E. O'Connor
Lee E. Johnson
Gary S. Kindness
James W. Anable
James R. Uhlir
Jerald E. Nagae
Thomas F. Broderick
Dennis K. Shelton
Frederick Ross Boundy
KiSong Kim Lang-Caditz
Jeffrey M. Sakoi
Ward Brown
Robert J. Carlson
Shaukat A. Karjeker (Not admitted in WA)

OF COUNSEL

Paul L. Gardner

ASSOCIATES

Faye L. Mattson
Thomas D. Theisen
Diana V. Blakney
Marcia S. Kelbon
Rodney C. Tullett
Ronald O. Zink
Stacy Quan
Steven P. Berreth
Chun M. Ng
Darren J. Jones
Brian P. Furrer
Stephen C. Bishop
Maria L. Culic
Julie A. Christian
David A. Lowe

LEGAL SUPPORT PERSONNEL

Gary Tomlinson (Executive Director)

Representative Clients: Aldus Corporation; The Boeing Company; Fred Hutchinson Cancer Research Center; Icicle Seafoods, Inc.; K-2 Corporation; Nalley's Fine Foods; Nintendo of America, Inc.; Seattle-First National Bank; University of Washington; Westin Hotel Company.

For full biographical listings, see the Martindale-Hubbell Law Directory

WISCONSIN

*MADISON,** Dane Co.

DEWITT ROSS & STEVENS, S.C. (AV)

Manchester Place, 2 East Mifflin Street, Suite 600, 53703
Telephone: 608-255-8891
Facsimile: 608-252-9243
West Madison Office: 8000 Excelsior Drive, Suite 401, Madison, WI 53717.
Telephone: 608-831-2100.
Telecopier: 608-831-2106.

Charles S. Sara (Resident)

Craig A. Fieschko

Representative Clients: Wisconsin Alumni Research Foundation; Promega Corporation; Wisconsin Milk Marketing Board; Cancer Immuno-Biology Laboratory; Marshfield Clinic; DMV USA, Inc.; PDQ Food Stores, Inc.; PostalSoft, Inc.; Strandex Corporation; Larex International, Inc.

For Complete List of Firm Personnel, See General Section

For full biographical listings, see the Martindale-Hubbell Law Directory

LATHROP & CLARK (AV)

Suite 1000, 122 West Washington Avenue, P.O. Box 1507, 53701-1507
Telephone: 608-257-7766
Fax: 608-257-1507
Poynette, Wisconsin Office: 111 North Main Street, P.O. Box 128.
Telephone: 608-635-4324.
FAX: 608-635-4690.
Lodi, Wisconsin Office: 108 Lodi Street, P.O. Box 256.
Telephone: 608-592-3877.
FAX: 608-592-5844.
Belleville, Wisconsin Office: 27 West Main.
Telephone: 608-424-3404.

MEMBERS OF FIRM

Theodore J. Long
David R. J. Stiennon

ASSOCIATE

Patrick J. G. Stiennon

Representative Clients: Cuna Mutual Insurance Group; American Family Mutual Insurance; Sheldons's, Inc.; TriEnda Corp.; Hughes Co., Inc.; Lyco Manufacturing, Inc.; Placon Corp.; Highsmith Inc.; Auto Glass Specialists, Inc.

For Complete List of Firm Personnel, See General Section

For full biographical listings, see the Martindale-Hubbell Law Directory

STROUD, STROUD, WILLINK, THOMPSON & HOWARD (AV)

25 West Main Street, Suite 300, P.O. Box 2236, 53701
Telephone: 608-257-2281
FAX: 608-257-7643

(See Next Column)

MEMBERS OF FIRM

Mark S. Zimmer
Teresa J. Welch
Grady J. Frenchick

ASSOCIATE

Margaret M. Liss

Patent Council For: Lunar Corp.; Alza Corp.; Promega Corp.; Lake Region Manufacturing Co., Inc.; Surgidev Corp.; China Bicycle Co., Ltd.; Midwestern Bio-Ag Products and Services, Inc.

For Complete List of Firm Personnel, See General Section

For full biographical listings, see the Martindale-Hubbell Law Directory

*MILWAUKEE,** Milwaukee Co.

ANDRUS, SCEALES, STARKE & SAWALL (AV)

100 East Wisconsin Avenue, Suite 1100, 53202-4178
Telephone: 414-271-7590
Telex: 26-832 ANDSTARK MIL
Telefax: 414-271-5770

MEMBERS OF FIRM

Elwin A. Andrus (1939-1982)
Merl E. Sceales (1941-1987)
Glenn O. Starke
Eugene R. Sawall
Daniel D. Fetterley
George H. Solveson
Gary A. Essmann
Thomas M. Wozny
Michael E. Taken
Joseph J. Jochman, Jr.
Andrew S. McConnell

ASSOCIATES

Peter C. Stomma
Edward R. Williams, Jr.
Timothy J. Ziolkowski
Mimi Claudine Thebert

LEGAL SUPPORT PERSONNEL

William L. Falk (Patent Agent)

Patent Counsel for: Briggs & Stratton Corp.; Johnson Controls, Inc.; Kolmar Laboratories, Inc.; Research Products Corp., Madison, Wis.; Overly Inc., Neenah, Wis.; Kelly Co.; Nelson Industries, Stoughton, Wis.; Green Bay Packaging, Inc., Green Bay.

For full biographical listings, see the Martindale-Hubbell Law Directory

MICHAEL, BEST & FRIEDRICH (AV)

100 East Wisconsin Avenue, 53202-4108
Telephone: 414-271-6560
Telecopier: 414-277-0656
Cable Address: "Mibef"
Madison, Wisconsin Office: One South Pinckney Street, Firstar Plaza, P.O. Box 1806, 53701-1806.
Telephone: 608-257-3501.
Telecopier: 283-2275.
Chicago, Illinois Office: 135 South LaSalle Street, Suite 1610, 60603-4391.
Telephone: 312-845-5800.
Telecopier: 312-845-5828.
Affiliated Law Firm: Edward D. Heffernan, Penthouse One, 1019 19th Street, N.W., Washington, D.C. 20036.
Telephone: 202-331-7444.

PARTNERS

Joseph A. Gemignani
Robert E. Clemency
Andrew O. Riteris
Glenn A. Busé
David B. Smith
Michael E. Husmann
Toni Lee Bonney
Fred Wiviott
David R. Price
Robert S. Beiser (Resident Partner, Chicago, Illinois Office)

OF COUNSEL

Bayard H. Michael

ASSOCIATES

Dyann L. Bumpke
Timothy M. Kelley
Kenneth D. Wahlin
Thomas A. Miller
Billie Jean Strandt
Jeffrey D. Hunt

For Complete List of Firm Personnel, See General Section

For full biographical listings, see the Martindale-Hubbell Law Directory

QUARLES & BRADY (AV)

411 East Wisconsin Avenue, 53202-4497
Telephone: 414-277-5000
Cable Address: "Lawdock"
Fax: 414-271-3552.
TWX: 910-262-3426
Madison, Wisconsin Office: Firstar Plaza, One South Pinckney Street, P.O. Box 2113.
Telephone: 608-251-5000.
Fax: 608-251-9166.
West Palm Beach, Florida Office: 222 Lakeview Avenue, 4th Floor.
Telephone: 407-653-5000.
Fax: 407-653-5333.
Naples, Florida Office: Barnett Center, 4501 Tamiami Trail North.
Telephone: 813-262-5959.
Fax: 813-434-4999.

(See Next Column)

QUARLES & BRADY, *Milwaukee—Continued*

Phoenix, Arizona Office: One Camelback Building, One East Camelback Road, Suite 400.
Telephone: 602-230-5500.
Fax: 602-230-5598.

MEMBERS OF FIRM
(ALPHABETICALLY BY YEAR OF ADMISSION TO BAR)

Allan W. Leiser
Thad F. Kryshak
Thomas W. Ehrmann
Thomas O. Kloehn
J. Rodman Steele, Jr. (Resident, West Palm Beach, Florida Office)
Barry E. Sammons
Michael J. McGovern
Robert L. Titley
George E. Haas
Nicholas J. Seay (Resident, Madison Office)
Carl R. Schwartz
Glenn Spencer Bacal (Resident, Phoenix, Arizona Office)
John D. Franzini
Marta S. Levine
Gregory A. Nelson (Resident, West Palm Beach, Florida Office)

ASSOCIATES

Neil E. Hamilton
Keith M. Baxter
Kenneth J. Hansen (Resident, Madison Office)
Anthony A. Tomaselli (Resident, Madison Office)
Jean C. Baker
Robert J. Sacco (Resident, West Palm Beach, Florida Office)
Bennett Berson (Resident, Madison, Wisconsin Office)
Sean D. Garrison (Resident, Phoenix, Arizona Office)
Michael A. Jaskolski
David G. Ryser

For Complete List of Firm Personnel, See General Section

For full biographical listings, see the Martindale-Hubbell Law Directory

REINHART, BOERNER, VAN DEUREN, NORRIS & RIESELBACH, S.C. (AV)

1000 North Water Street, P.O. Box 92900, 53202-0900
Telephone: 414-298-1000
Facsimile: 414-298-8097
Denver, Colorado Office: One Norwest Center, 1700 Lincoln Street, Suite 3725.
Telephone: 303-831-0909.
Fax: 303-831-4805.
Madison, Wisconsin Office: 7617 Mineral Point Road, 53701-2020.
Telephone: 608-283-7900.
Fax: 608-283-7919.
Washington, D.C. Office: 601 Pennsylvania Avenue, N.W., North Building, Suite 750.
Telephone: 202-393-3636.
Fax: 202-393-0796.

Michael D. Rechtin
Philip P. Mann

Rodney D. DeKruif
Peter W. Becker
Gerald L. Fellows

For Complete List of Firm Personnel, See General Section

For full biographical listings, see the Martindale-Hubbell Law Directory

WHEELER & KROMHOLZ (AV)

10400 West North Avenue, Suite 450, 53226
Telephone: 414-258-1213; 1-800-686-9333 (In Wisconsin)
Facsimile: 414-258-1545

Allan B. Wheeler
Joseph A. Kromholz

John M. Manion
S. Lawrence Wheeler (1921-1972)
Joseph P. House, Jr. (1949-1979)
Arthur L. Morsell (Retired)

For full biographical listings, see the Martindale-Hubbell Law Directory

CANADA ALBERTA

*EDMONTON,** Edmonton Jud. Dist.

EMERY JAMIESON (AV)

1700 Oxford Tower, Edmonton Centre, 10235 - 101 Street, T5J 3G1
Telephone: 403-426-5220
Telecopier: 403-420-6277

MEMBERS OF FIRM

Howard T. Emery, Q.C. (1899-1990)
Sydney A. Bercov, Q.C.
Henry B. Martin, Q.C.
W. Paul Sharek
Phyllis A. Smith, Q.C.
John H. Jamieson, Q.C. (Retired)
L. Wayne Drewry, Q.C.
Richard B. Drewry
Robert W. Thompson
Andrew R. Hudson

(See Next Column)

MEMBERS OF FIRM (Continued)

Gordon D. Sustrik
Michael J. Penny
Rex M. Nielsen
Susan L. Bercov
Terrence N. Kuharchuk
Murray F. Tait
Shirley A. McNeilly
G. Bruce Comba
Donna Carson Read
Bruce F. Hughson
Helen Garwasiuk
Robert D. McDonald

ASSOCIATES

Ellen S. Ticoll
Jeffrey K. Friesen
Blair E. Maxston
Frederica L. Schutz
Donald V. Tomkins
Earl J. Evaniew
Edward T. Yoo
Janet N. Alexander-Smith
Claire M. Klassen
Jennifer Kaufman-Shaw
Regina M. Corrigan

Reference: Canadian Imperial Bank of Commerce.

For full biographical listings, see the Martindale-Hubbell Law Directory

CANADA BRITISH COLUMBIA

*VANCOUVER,** Vancouver Co.

CLARK, WILSON (AV)

Suite 800 - 885 West Georgia Street, V6C 3H1
Telephone: 604-687-5700
Telecopier: 604-687-6314
Associated with: Eiko General Law Office, Osaka, Japan.
Telephone: (06) 365-1251.
Fax: (06) 365-1252.

MEMBERS OF FIRM

David W. Buchanan, Q.C.
David W. Donohoe
William C. Helgason
David J. Cowan
Robert J. Lesperance
Neil P. Melliship

ASSOCIATE

Mark Ming-Jen Yang

Representative Clients: Hongkong Bank of Canada; Shell Canada Limited.
Reference: Hongkong Bank of Canada.

For full biographical listings, see the Martindale-Hubbell Law Directory

CANADA ONTARIO

*OTTAWA,** Regional Munic. of Ottawa-Carleton

BARRIGAR MOSS HAMMOND MCGRUDER CASSAN & MACLEAN (AV)

81 Metcalfe Street, 7th Floor, K1P 6K7
Telephone: 613-238-6404
Telecopier: 613-230-8755
Affiliated Offices also in Mississauga, Ontario and Vancouver, British Columbia.

MEMBERS OF FIRM

David J. McGruder
Lynn S. Cassan
P. Scott Maclean

For full biographical listings, see the Martindale-Hubbell Law Directory

BENNETT JONES VERCHERE (AV)

Suite 1800, 350 Alberta Street, P.O. Box 25, K1R 1A4
Telephone: (613) 230-4935
Facsimile: (613) 230-3836
Calgary, Alberta Office: 4500 Bankers Hall East. 855-2nd Street S.W.
Telephone: (403) 298-3100.
Facsimile: (403) 265-7219.
Edmonton, Alberta Office: 1000, 10035-105 Street.
Telephone: (403) 421-8133.
Facsimile: (403) 421-7951.
Toronto, Ontario Office: 3400 1 First Canadian Place, P.O. Box 130.
Telephone: (416) 863-1200.
Facsimile: (416) 863-1716.
Montreal, Quebec Office: Suite 1600, 1 Place Ville Marie.
Telephone: (514) 871-1200.
Facsimile: (514) 871-8115.

RESIDENT MEMBER OF FIRM

George Edward Fisk

For Complete List of Firm Personnel, See General Section

For full biographical listings, see the Martindale-Hubbell Law Directory

Ottawa—Continued

MACERA & JARZYNA (AV)

81 Metcalfe Street, 11th & 12th Floor, P.O. Box 2088, Station D, K1P 5W3
Telephone: 613-238-8173
Facsimile: 613-235-2508

John S. Macera
Andrew K. Jarzyna
J. Kevin Carton
Gary K. Arkin
Elizabeth G. Elliott
Linda M. Wright
Philip B. Kerr

ASSOCIATE

Solomon M.W. Gold

TRADEMARK AGENT

James R. Palmer

For full biographical listings, see the Martindale-Hubbell Law Directory

OSLER, HOSKIN & HARCOURT (AV)

Barristers & Solicitors
Patent and Trade-Mark Agents
Suite 1500, 50 O'Connor Street, K1P 6L2
Telephone: 613-235-7234
FAX: 613-235-2867
Toronto, Ontario Office: 1 First Canadian Place, P.O. Box 50, M5X 1B8.
Telephone: 416-362-2111.
FAX: 416-862-6666.
New York, N.Y. Office: Osler Renault* - Suite 3217, 200 Park Avenue, 10166-0193.
Telephone: 212-867-5800.
Fax: 212-867-5802.
London, England Office: Osler Renault* - 20 Little Britain, London, EC1A 7DH.
Telephone: 071-606-0777.
FAX: 071-606-0222.
Paris, France Office: Osler Renault* - 4 rue Bayard, 75008.
Telephone: 33-1.42.89.00.54.
Fax: 33-1.42.89.51.60.
Hong Kong Office: Osler Renault* - Suite 1708, One Pacific Place. 88 Queensway.
Telephone: 011-852-2877-3933.
Fax: 011-852-2877-0866.
Singapore Office: Osler Renault* - 65 Chulia Street, #40-05 OCBC Centre, Singapore 0104.
Telephone: (65) 538-2077.
Fax: (65) 538-2977.
** Osler Renault is an international partnership of Osler, Hoskin & Harcourt and Ogilvy Renault.*

MEMBERS OF FIRM

Kent H.E. Plumley
Glen A. Bloom
David W. Aitken
Donna G. White

ASSOCIATE

Diane E. Cornish

RETIRED PARTNER

James G. Fogo

PATENT AGENT

James R. Keneford

TRADE-MARK LAW CLERK

Marion Bailey

For Complete List of Firm Personnel, See General Section
For full biographical listings, see the Martindale-Hubbell Law Directory

SHAPIRO, COHEN, ANDREWS, FINLAYSON (AV)

112 Kent Street, P.O. Box 3440, Station D, K1P 6P1
Telephone: 613-232-5300
Telecopier: 613-563-9231
Cable Address: "Shapiro" Ottawa

MEMBERS OF FIRM

Jonathan C. Cohen
Michael D. Andrews
Adele Finlayson

ASSOCIATES

Susan D. Beaubien
Hollie E. Elder
John D. Harris

LEGAL SUPPORT PERSONNEL

PATENT AGENTS

Robert A. Wilkes
Robert G. Hendry
Karen Stauss

TRADEMARK AGENTS

Mary H. Cardillo
Christine St. Denis
Mary Jane Lemenchick
Theresa M. Corneau
Gladys A. Tibbo

For full biographical listings, see the Martindale-Hubbell Law Directory

SMART & BIGGAR (AV)

Suite 900, 55 Metcalfe Street, P.O. Box 2999, Station D, K1P 5Y6
Telephone: 613-232-2486
Telex: 053-3731
Facsimile: 613-232-8440
Toronto, Ontario Office: Suite 2300, 439 University Avenue, M5G 1Y8.
Telephone: 416-593-5514.
Facsimile: 416-591-1690.
Telex: 053-3731.
Montreal, Quebec Office: Suite 601, 4 Place Ville Marie, H3B 2E7.
Telephone: 514-954-1500.
Facsimile: 514-954-1396.
Telex: 053-3731.
Vancouver, British Columbia Office: Suite 1010, 510 Burrard Street, V6C 3A8.
Telephone: 604-682-7295.
Facsimile: 604-682-0274.
Telex: 053-3731.

MEMBERS OF FIRM

James D. Kokonis, Q.C.
Peter L. Beck
Alan R. Campbell
Robert D. Gould
Raymond Trudeau
**(Not admitted in ON)
Joy D. Morrow
Gunars A. Gaikis *
Michael D. Manson
Glen B. Tremblay
James A. Devenny, Q.C.
Nicholas H. Fyfe, Q.C.
A. David Morrow
John R. Morrissey *
Thomas R. Kelly
John Bochnovic
François Guay
**(Not admitted in ON)
Keltie R. Sim *
Mark K. Evans *

ASSOCIATES

Donald F. Phenix
J. Christopher Robinson ***
Louis Carbonneau
**(Not admitted in ON)
Annie Robitaille
**(Not admitted in ON)
Martin Langlois
**(Not admitted in ON)
Ronald D. Faggetter *
Paul Smith ***
Alistair G. Simpson *
Brian P. Isaac
Jeffrey W. Astle *
Steven B. Garland
Sally J. Daub *
Peter R. Wilcox *
Robert A. Kennedy

COUNSEL

Donald A. Hill
Immanuel Goldsmith, Q.C. *

PATENT & TRADEMARK AGENTS

C. Vance Marston
Geoffrey C. Clark ***
James McGraw
Michael E. Wheeler
Tokuo Hirama
David L.T. Conn
Hugh O'Gorman
William H. James ***
A. Dennis Armstrong
John Paxton
Stephan P. Georgiev **
Neil S. Clark ***
Micheline L. Gravelle

*Toronto Office
**Montreal Office
***Vancouver Office

For full biographical listings, see the Martindale-Hubbell Law Directory

*TORONTO,** Regional Munic. of York

BERESKIN & PARR (AV)

Box 401, 40 King Street, West, M5H 3Y2
Telephone: 416-364-7311
Cable Address: "Arnbee" Toronto
Telex: 06-23115
Telecopier: 416-361-1398

MEMBERS AND ASSOCIATES

Daniel R. Bereskin, Q.C.
H. Roger Hart
Cynthia Rowden
Timothy J. Sinnott
Robert B. Storey
Linda M. Kurdydyk
Jill Diane Jarvis-Tonus
Robin L. Coster
Amalia Trister
William B. Vass
Jill M. Holmes
Mark L. Robbins
Richard J. Parr
C. Lloyd Sarginson
Gregory A. Piasetzki
Jill W. Bradbury
James T. Nenniger
Philip C. Mendes da Costa
Michael E. Charles
Shona S. McDiarmid
Jonathan G. Colombo
David M. Reive
Marie Lussier
Justine Wiebe

PATENT AND TRADEMARK AGENTS

David W. R. Langton
Marie E. Manza
H. Samuel Frost
Terry Edwards
Jane Sarjeant

For full biographical listings, see the Martindale-Hubbell Law Directory

Toronto—Continued

BORDEN & ELLIOT (AV)

Barristers & Solicitors
Scotia Plaza, 40 King Street West, M5H 3Y4
Telephone: 416-367-6000
Telecopier: 416-367-6749
Internet: @ borden.com
A Member of the national association of Borden DuMoulin Howard Gervais, comprising Borden & Elliot in Toronto, Ontario, Russell & DuMoulin in Vancouver, British Columbia, Howard, Mackie in Calgary, Alberta and Mackenzie Gervais in Montréal, Québec. Borden DuMoulin Howard Gervais also operates an office in London, England.

MEMBER AND ASSOCIATES

Gordon J. Zimmerman

For Complete List of Firm Personnel, See General Section

For full biographical listings, see the Martindale-Hubbell Law Directory

DEETH WILLIAMS WALL (AV)

National Bank Building, 150 York Street, Suite 400, M5H 3S5
Telephone: 416-941-9440
Facsimile: 416-941-9443

MEMBERS OF FIRM

Douglas N. Deeth
Amy-Lynne Williams
Gervas W. Wall
A. Marijo Coates
Victor V. Butsky
Eileen M. McMahon
Michael Erdle

For full biographical listings, see the Martindale-Hubbell Law Directory

DIMOCK & ASSOCIATES (AV)

20 Queen Street West, Suite 3202, P.O. Box 102, M5H 3R3
Telephone: 416-971-7202
Fax: 416-971-6638

Ronald E. Dimock

ASSOCIATES

Bruce W. Stratton
Dino P. Clarizio
Michelle L. Wassenaar

For full biographical listings, see the Martindale-Hubbell Law Directory

OSLER, HOSKIN & HARCOURT (AV)

Barristers & Solicitors
Patent and Trade-Mark Agents
1 First Canadian Place, P.O. Box 50, M5X 1B8
Telephone: 416-362-2111
FAX: 416-862-6666
Ottawa, Ontario Office: Suite 1500, 50 O'Connor Street, K1P 6L2.
Telephone: 613-235-7234.
FAX: 613-235-2867.
New York, N.Y. Office: Osler Renault* - Suite 3217, 200 Park Avenue, 10166-0193.
Telephone: 212-867-5800.
Fax: 212-867-5802.
London, England Office: Osler Renault* - 20 Little Britain, London EC1A 7DH.
Telephone: 071-606-0777.
FAX: 071-606-0222.
Paris, France Office: Osler Renault* - 4, rue Bayard, 75008.
Telephone: 33-1.42.89.00.54.
Fax: 33-1.42.89.51.60.
Hong Kong Office: Osler Renault* - Suite 1708, One Pacific Place. 88 Queensway.
Telephone: 011-852-2877-3933.
Fax: 011-852-2877-0866.
Singapore Office: Osler Renault* - 65 Chulia Street, #40-05 OCBC Centre, Singapore 0104.
Telephone: (65) 538-2077.
Fax: (65) 538-2977.
**Osler Renault is an international partnership of Osler, Hoskin & Harcourt and Ogilvy Renault.*

MEMBERS OF FIRM

Kent H.E. Plumley (Resident in Ottawa, Ontario)
Brian G. Morgan
Marilyn M.M. Field-Marsham
W. Lee Webster
David W. Aitken (Resident in Ottawa, Ontario)
John M.M. Roland, Q.C.
Frank Zaid
Glen A. Bloom (Resident in Ottawa, Ontario)
Valerie A. E. Dyer
Donna G. White (Resident in Ottawa, Ontario)
G. Lee Muirhead

ASSOCIATES

Diane E. Cornish (Resident in Ottawa, Ontario)
Rodger Madden
John C. Cotter
Deborah A. Glendinning
Kelly L. Moffatt
Jodi M. Nieman

RETIRED PARTNER

James G. Fogo

(See Next Column)

PATENT AGENT

James R. Keneford (Resident in Ottawa, Ontario)

TRADE-MARK LAW CLERK

Marion Bailey (Resident in Ottawa, Ontario)

For Complete List of Firm Personnel, See General Section

For full biographical listings, see the Martindale-Hubbell Law Directory

ROGERS & MILNE (AV)

42nd Floor, 1 First Canadian Place, P.O. Box 84, M5X 1B1
Telephone: 416-863-4369
Fax: 416-863-4592

MEMBERS OF FIRM

David Rogers, Q.C.
Peter Milne

For full biographical listings, see the Martindale-Hubbell Law Directory

SIM, HUGHES, ASHTON & MCKAY (AV)

Suite 701, 330 University Avenue, M5G 1R7
Telephone: 416-595-1155
Cable Address: "Simbas" Toronto
Telex: 065-24567
Telecopier: 416-595-1163

Donald F. Sim, Q.C. (1927-1986)
Kenneth D. McKay
Timothy M. Lowman
Roger T. Hughes, Q.C.
Toni B. Polson Ashton
Donald M. Cameron
Stephen M. Lane
Arthur B. Renaud

ASSOCIATES

John N. Allport
Patricia A. Rae
R. Scott MacKendrick

PATENT AND TRADEMARK AGENTS

Peter W. McBurney
John H. Woodley
Brenda L. Boardman
Stephen J. Perry
Michael I. Stewart
Thomas T. Rieder
John R. S. Orange
Warren J. Galloway

For full biographical listings, see the Martindale-Hubbell Law Directory

SMART & BIGGAR (AV)

Suite 2300, 439 University Avenue, M5G 1Y8
Telephone: 416-593-5514
Telex: 053-3731;
Facsimile: 416-591-1690
Ottawa, Ontario Office: Suite 900, 55 Metcalfe Street, P.O. Box 2999, Station D, K1P 5Y6.
Telephone: 613-232-2486.
Telex: 053-3731.
Facsimile: 613-232-8440.
Montreal, Quebec Office: Suite 601, 4 Place Ville Marie, H3B 2E7.
Telephone: 514-954-1500.
Telex: 053-3731.
Facsimile: 514-954-1396.
Vancouver, British Columbia Office: Suite 1010, 510 Burrard Street, V6C 3A8.
Telephone: 604-682-7295.
Facsimile: 604-682-0274.
Telex: 053-3731.

MEMBERS OF FIRM

John R. Morrissey (Resident)
Keltie R. Sim (Resident)
Gunars A. Gaikis (Resident)
Mark K. Evans (Resident)

ASSOCIATES

Ronald D. Faggetter (Resident)
Jeffrey W. Astle (Resident)
Alistair G. Simpson (Resident)
Sally J. Daub (Resident)
Peter R. Wilcox (Resident)

COUNSEL

Immanuel Goldsmith, Q.C. (Resident)

For full biographical listings, see the Martindale-Hubbell Law Directory

CANADA QUEBEC

*MONTREAL,** Montreal Dist.

MENDELSOHN ROSENTZVEIG SHACTER (AV)

1000 Sherbrooke Street West, 27th Floor, H3A 3G4
Telephone: 514-987-5000
Telex: 05-27284 Colorlaw
Telecopier: 514-987-1213

(See Next Column)

MENDELSOHN ROSENTZVEIG SHACTER—*Continued*

MEMBERS OF FIRM AND ASSOCIATES

S. Leon Mendelsohn, Q.C.
Leo Rosentzveig, Q.C.
Manuel Shacter, Q.C.
Jack C. Shayne
William Levitt
Arthur A. Garvis
Max Mendelsohn
Edward E. Aronoff
L. Michael Blumenstein
Monroe A. Charlap
Earl S. Cohen
William Fraiberg
Michael Garonce
Philip S. Garonce, Q.C.
Donald M. Devine
Richard S. Uditsky
Boris P. Stein
Joel Weitzman
Ian R. Rudnikoff
Marc I. Leiter
L. B. Erdle
Frank Zylberberg
Fredric L. Carsley
David L. Rosentzveig
Jules Brossard
Michael Ludwick
Catherine Muraz
Judith G. Shenker
Judie K. Jokinen
Gilles Seguin
Martin Desrosiers
Jean Carrière

ASSOCIATES

Alain Breault
Joelle Sebag
Sharyn W. Gore
Louis Frédérick Côté
Hillel D. Frankel
Sandra Abitan
Dominique Lafleur
Linda Schachter
Roberto Buffone
Emmanuelle Saucier
Arnold Cohen
Isabelle Papillon
Lorne Beiles
Aaron Makovka
Céline Tessier

For full biographical listings, see the Martindale-Hubbell Law Directory

---

SMART & BIGGAR (AV)

Suite 601, 4 Place Ville Marie, H3B 2E7
Telephone: 514-954-1500
Facsimile: 514-954-1396;
Telex: 053-3731
Ottawa, Ontario Office: Suite 900, 55 Metcalfe Street, P.O. Box 2999, Station D, K1P 5Y6.
Telephone: 613-232-2486.
Telex: 053-3731.
Facsimile: 613-232-8440.
Toronto, Ontario Office: Suite 2300, 439 University Avenue, M5G 1Y8.
Telephone: 416-593-5514.
Telex: 053-3731.
Facsimile: 416-591-1690.
Vancouver, British Columbia Office: Suite 1010, 510 Burrard Street, V6C 3A8.
Telephone: 604-682-7295.
Facsimile: 604-682-0274.
Telex: 053-3731.

MEMBERS OF FIRM

Raymond Trudeau (Resident)
François Guay (Resident)

ASSOCIATES

Louis Carbonneau (Resident)
Annie Robitaille (Resident)
Martin Langlois (Resident)

PATENT & TRADEMARK AGENT

Stephan P. Georgiev (Resident)

For full biographical listings, see the Martindale-Hubbell Law Directory

PERSONAL INJURY LAW

ALABAMA

ALEXANDER CITY, Tallapoosa Co.

MORRIS, HAYNES, INGRAM & HORNSBY (AV)

101 Madison Street, P.O. Box 1449, 35010
Telephone: 205-329-2000
Fax: 205-329-2015

Larry W. Morris
Randall Stark Haynes
Kenneth F. Ingram, Jr.
Clay Hornsby

OF COUNSEL

John F. Dillon, IV
Jennie Lee Kelley

Representative Clients: First National Bank; City of Alexander City; Town of Wadley; Russell Corp.
Approved Attorneys for: Lawyers Title Insurance Corp.; Mississippi Valley Title Insurance Co.

For full biographical listings, see the Martindale-Hubbell Law Directory

*BIRMINGHAM,** Jefferson Co.

BALCH & BINGHAM (AV)

1710 Sixth Avenue North, P.O. Box 306, 35201
Telephone: 205-251-8100
Facsimile: 205-226-8798
Other Birmingham, Alabama Office: 1901 Sixth Avenue North, 35203.
Telephone: 205-251-8100.
Facsimile: 205-226-8799.
Montgomery, Alabama Office: The Winter Building, 2 Dexter Avenue, 36101.
Telephone: 205-834-6500.
Facsimile: 205-269-3115.
Huntsville, Alabama Office: Suite 810, 200 West Court Square, 35801.
Telephone: 205-551-0171.
Facsimile: 205-551-0174.
Washington, D.C. Office: Suite 800, 1101 Connecticut Avenue, N.W., 20036.
Telephone: 202-296-0387.
Facsimile: 202-452-8180.

MEMBERS OF FIRM

John P. Scott, Jr.
S. Allen Baker, Jr.
Steven F. Casey
James A. Bradford
Alan T. Rogers

ASSOCIATE

Michael D. Freeman

Counsel for: Alabama Power Co.; Blue Cross and Blue Shield of Alabama; The Boeing Company; Brasfield & Gorrie, Inc.; Compass Bancshares, Inc.; Harbert Corp.; Kimberly-Clark Corp.; Southern Company Services, Inc.; Southern Research Institute; Vesta Insurance Group, Inc.

For Complete List of Firm Personnel, See General Section

For full biographical listings, see the Martindale-Hubbell Law Directory

BRADLEY, ARANT, ROSE & WHITE (AV)

1400 Park Place Tower, 2001 Park Place, 35203
Telephone: 205-521-8000
Telex: 494-1324
Facsimile: 205-251-8611, 251-8665, 252-0264
Facsimile (Southtrust Office): 205-251-9915
Huntsville, Alabama Office: 200 Clinton Avenue West, Suite 900.
Telephone: 205-517-5100.
Facsimile: 205-533-5069.

MEMBERS OF FIRM

John H. Morrow
Hobart A. McWhorter, Jr.
Gary C. Huckaby (Resident, Huntsville Office)
James W. Gewin
Brittin Turner Coleman
E. Cutter Hughes, Jr. (Resident, Huntsville Office)
Walter J. Sears, III
Joseph B. Mays, Jr.
Scott M. Phelps
Norman Jetmundsen, Jr.
Joseph S. Bird, III
John D. Watson, III
Michael D. McKibben
David Glenn Hymer
G. Rick Hall (Resident, Huntsville Office)
Sid J. Trant
Stewart M. Cox

(See Next Column)

ASSOCIATES

Philip J. Carroll III
John E. Goodman
T. Michael Brown
Michael S. Denniston
Warne S. Heath (Resident, Huntsville Office)
Kenneth M. Perry

For Complete List of Firm Personnel, See General Section

For full biographical listings, see the Martindale-Hubbell Law Directory

BURGE & WETTERMARK, P.C. (AV)

2300 SouthTrust Tower, 420 North 20th Street, 35203-3204
Telephone: 205-251-9729; 800-633-3733
Fax: 205-323-0512
Atlanta, Georgia Office: One Atlantic Center, Suite 3250.
Telephone: 505-875-2500; 800-749-8687.
Fax: 404-875-5807.

Frank O. Burge, Jr.
James H. Wettermark
F. Tucker Burge
Courtney Burge Brown
Claire B. Morgan
Michael J. Warshauer (Not admitted in AL)

Monroe D. Barber, Jr.
Van Kirk McCombs, II
James R. Holland, II (Not admitted in AL)

References: AmSouth Bank; First Alabama Bank, Birmingham, Alabama.

For full biographical listings, see the Martindale-Hubbell Law Directory

HARDIN & HAWKINS (AV)

A Partnership including a Professional Corporation
2201 Arlington Avenue, 35205
Telephone: 205-930-6900
1-800-368-1960
Telecopier: 205-930-6910
Mailing Address: P.O. Box 55705, 35255-5705

Edward L. Hardin, Jr. (P.C.)
Kevin John Hawkins

ASSOCIATES

Belinda Masdon Kimble
W. Lee Gresham, III
Jill T. Karle

OF COUNSEL

Hubert A. Grissom, Jr.

For full biographical listings, see the Martindale-Hubbell Law Directory

RICHARD S. JAFFE, P.C. (AV)

1905 Fourteenth Avenue South, 35205
Telephone: 205-930-9800
Telecopier: 205-930-9809

Richard S. Jaffe

Stephen A. Strickland
Dennis Wayne Jacobs

For full biographical listings, see the Martindale-Hubbell Law Directory

LIGHTFOOT, FRANKLIN, WHITE & LUCAS (AV)

300 Financial Center, 505 20th Street North, 35203-2706
Telephone: 205-581-0700
Facsimile: 205-581-0799

MEMBERS OF FIRM

Warren B. Lightfoot
Samuel H. Franklin
Jere F. White, Jr.
William R. Lucas, Jr.
Mac M. Moorer
John M. Johnson
M. Christian King
E. Glenn Waldrop, Jr.
Adam K. Peck
Harlan I. Prater, IV

ASSOCIATES

Michael L. Bell
William S. Cox, III
William H. King, III
Sabrina A. Simon
Madeline H. Haikala
Sarah Bruce Jackson
William H. Brooks
S. Douglas Williams, Jr.
J. Banks Sewell, III
Lee M. Hollis
Kim A. Craddock
Wynn M. Shuford
John P. Dulin, Jr.

Counsel for: AT&T; Ford Motor Co.; Emerson Electric Co.; Monsanto Co.; Chrysler Corp.; Unocal Corp.; The Upjohn Co.; Bristol-Myers Squibb Co.; The Goodyear Tire & Rubber Co.; Mitsubishi Motor Sales of America, Inc.

For full biographical listings, see the Martindale-Hubbell Law Directory

PITTMAN, HOOKS, MARSH, DUTTON & HOLLIS, P.C. (AV)

1100 Park Place Tower, 35203
Telephone: 205-322-8880
Telecopier: 205-328-2711

(See Next Column)

PITTMAN, HOOKS, MARSH, DUTTON & HOLLIS P.C., *Birmingham—Continued*

W. Lee Pittman
Kenneth W. Hooks
David H. Marsh
Tom Dutton
L. Andrew Hollis, Jr.
Jeffrey C. Kirby
Ralph Bohanan, Jr.
Nat Bryan

Jeffrey C. Rickard
Susan J. Silvernail
Nici F. Williams
Chris T. Hellums
Adam P. Morel

OF COUNSEL

James H. Davis (Not admitted in AL)
Myra B. Staggs

For full biographical listings, see the Martindale-Hubbell Law Directory

PRITCHARD, MCCALL & JONES (AV)

800 Financial Center, 35203
Telephone: 205-328-9190

MEMBERS OF FIRM

William S. Pritchard (1890-1967)
Alexander W. Jones (1914-1988)
William S. Pritchard, Jr.
Madison W. O'Kelley, Jr.
Julian P. Hardy, Jr.
Alexander W. Jones, Jr.
F. Hilton-Green Tomlinson
James G. Henderson
William S. Pritchard, III

ASSOCIATES

Michael L. McKerley
Robert Bond Higgins
Nina Michele LaFleur
Mary W. Burge

Representative Clients: First National Bank of Columbiana; Central State Bank of Calera; Buffalo Rock-Pepsi-Cola Bottling Co.; Gillis Advertising, Inc.; Liberty Mutual Insurance Co.; Reliance Insurance Company; SouthTrust Bank, N.A.; Bromberg & Company, Inc.; Farmers Furniture Company; First Commercial Bank.

For full biographical listings, see the Martindale-Hubbell Law Directory

REDDEN, MILLS & CLARK (AV)

940 First Alabama Bank Building, 35203
Telephone: 205-322-0457
Fax: 205-322-8481

MEMBERS OF FIRM

L. Drew Redden
William H. Mills
William N. Clark
Gerald L. Miller
Stephen W. Shaw

ASSOCIATES

Maxwell H. Pulliam, Jr.
Joseph H. Hilley

References: SouthTrust Bank; First Alabama Bank.

For full biographical listings, see the Martindale-Hubbell Law Directory

SPAIN, GILLON, GROOMS, BLAN & NETTLES (AV)

The Zinszer Building, 2117 2nd Avenue North, 35203
Telephone: 205-328-4100
Telecopier: 205-324-8866

MEMBERS OF FIRM

Allwin E. Horn, III
Eugene P. Stutts
Alton B. Parker, Jr.
James A. Kee, Jr.

General Counsel for: Liberty National Life Insurance Co.; United States Fidelity & Guaranty Co.; Piggly Wiggly Alabama Distributing Co.; AmSouth Mortgage Co., Inc.; Alabama Insurance Guaranty Association; Alabama Life and Disability Insurance Guaranty Association; Alabama Insurance Underwriters Association.
Counsel for: The Prudential Insurance Company of America; Government Employees Insurance Co.; Massachusetts Mutual Life Insurance Co.

For Complete List of Firm Personnel, See General Section

For full biographical listings, see the Martindale-Hubbell Law Directory

STARNES & ATCHISON (AV)

100 Brookwood Place, P.O. Box 598512, 35259-8512
Telephone: 205-868-6000
Telecopier: 205-868-6099

MEMBERS OF FIRM

W. Stancil Starnes
W. Michael Atchison
William Anthony Davis, III
Michael A. Florie
J. Bentley Owens, III
Walter William Bates
Robert P. Mackenzie, III
Jeffrey E. Friedman

ASSOCIATES

Joe L. Leak
Mark W. Macoy

Representative Clients: Aetna Casualty & Surety Company; Harbert Construction Co.; AMI Brookwood Medical Center; International Playtex, Inc.; Kawasaki Motors Corp.; Honda North America, Inc.; Roadway, Inc.; Cigna Corp.; Travelers Ins. Co.; United States Fidelity and Guaranty Co.

For full biographical listings, see the Martindale-Hubbell Law Directory

*DOTHAN,** Houston Co.

FARMER, PRICE, HORNSBY & WEATHERFORD (AV)

115 West Adams Street, Drawer 2228, 36301
Telephone: 334-793-2424
Fax: 334-793-6624

MEMBERS OF FIRM

J. Hubert Farmer (1896-1976)
Edward M. Price, Jr.
Ernest H. Hornsby
Joel W. Weatherford
D. Lewis Terry, Jr.
Elizabeth B. Glasgow

Representative Clients: AmSouth Bank, N.A.; Pea River Electric Cooperative; Hollis & Spann, Inc.; Faulkner Construction Co., Inc.; Burnham Shoes, Inc.; Quality Inn Carousel; Sheraton Inn, Holiday Inn-Ozark, Holiday Inn-Crestview, Inn South-Montgomery; Personnel Resources, Inc.; Lowe's; Acme Roofing & Sheetmetal Co., Inc.

For full biographical listings, see the Martindale-Hubbell Law Directory

*FLORENCE,** Lauderdale Co.

POTTS & YOUNG (AV)

107 East College Street, 35630
Telephone: 205-764-7142
Fax: 205-764-7717

OF COUNSEL

Doyle R. Young (Retired)
Robert L. Potts

MEMBERS OF FIRM

Frank V. Potts
Frank B. Potts

ASSOCIATES

Robert W. Beasley
Debra H. Coble
Mark A. Sanderson

Representative Clients: E. A. Nelson Co., Inc.; Nelco, Inc.; Lauderdale County Board of Education; American Abrasive Air & Service Co., Inc.; Diversified Products, Inc.; BIG DELI STORES, Inc.; Spry Funeral Homes of Russellville, Sheffield & Florence; Americans United for the Separation of Church & State; Colbert County Community Economic Development Corp.
Reference: Bank Independent.

For full biographical listings, see the Martindale-Hubbell Law Directory

SELF & SELF (AV)

408 West Dr. Hicks Boulevard, P.O. Box 1062, 35631
Telephone: 205-767-2570; 1-800-336-2574
Fax: 205 767-2632

MEMBERS OF FIRM

Henry (Hank) H. Self, Jr.
Gilbert P. Self

OF COUNSEL

Barry Mansell

Reference: Bank Independent; AmSouth Bank; Central Bank of the South.

For full biographical listings, see the Martindale-Hubbell Law Directory

*FORT PAYNE,** De Kalb Co.

SCRUGGS, JORDAN & DODD, P.A. (AV)

207 Alabama Avenue, South, P.O. Box 1109, 35967
Telephone: 205-845-5932
Fax: 205-845-4325

William D. Scruggs, Jr.
Robert K. Jordan
David Dodd
E. Allen Dodd, Jr.

Representative Clients: State Farm Insurance Company; Allstate Insurance Co., Inc.; USF&G Insurance Co.; Nucor, Inc.; Ladd Engineering, Inc.; ALABAMA Band; First Federal Savings & Loan Association of Dekalb County; Fritz Structural Steel, Inc.; Williamson Oil Co., Inc.

For full biographical listings, see the Martindale-Hubbell Law Directory

*HAMILTON,** Marion Co.

FITE, DAVIS, ATKINSON, GUYTON & BENTLEY, P.C. (AV)

Court Square, P.O. Box 157, 35570-0157
Telephone: 205-921-7878; 921-4464
Fax: 205-921-9717
Winfield, Alabama Office: Highway 43 South. P.O. Box 1080.
Telephone: 205-487-4848.
Fax: 205-487-4890.

Rankin Fite (1916-1980)
James K. Davis
William H. Atkinson
William T. Atkinson
Jerry F. Guyton
John H. Bentley

Representative Clients: First State Bank of Lamar County; City of Winfield.

For full biographical listings, see the Martindale-Hubbell Law Directory

*HUNTSVILLE,** Madison Co.

BERRY, ABLES, TATUM, LITTLE & BAXTER, P.C. (AV)

Legal Building, 315 Franklin Street, S.E., P.O. Box 165, 35804-0165
Telephone: 205-533-3740
Facsimile: 205-533-3751

William H. Blanton (1889-1973)
Joe M. Berry
L. Bruce Ables
James T. Tatum, Jr.
Loyd H. Little, Jr.
James T. Baxter, III
Thomas E. Parker, Jr.
Bill G. Hall

Representative Clients: AmSouth Bank, N.A.; First Alabama Bank; General Shale Products Co.; The Hartz Corp.; Litton Industries, Inc.; Farmers Tractor Co.; Colonial Bank; Farm Credit Bank of Texas; Resolution Trust Corp.
Reference: First Alabama Bank.

For full biographical listings, see the Martindale-Hubbell Law Directory

BRADLEY, ARANT, ROSE & WHITE (AV)

200 Clinton Avenue West, Suite 900, 35801
Telephone: 205-517-5100
Facsimile: 205-533-5069
Birmingham, Alabama Office: 1400 Park Place Tower, 2001 Park Place.
Telephone: 205-521-8000.
Telex: 494-1324.
Facsimile: 205-251-8611, 251-8665, 252-0264. Facsimile (Southtrust Office): 205-251-9915.

RESIDENT PARTNERS

Gary C. Huckaby
E. Cutter Hughes, Jr.
Patrick H. Graves, Jr.
G. Rick Hall

RESIDENT ASSOCIATES

Warne S. Heath
H. Knox McMillan
Frank M. Caprio

For Complete List of Firm Personnel, See General Section

For full biographical listings, see the Martindale-Hubbell Law Directory

HORNSBY, WATSON & MEGINNISS (AV)

1110 Gleneagles Drive, 35801
Telephone: 205-650-5500
Fax: 205-650-5504

Ralph W. Hornsby
S. A. "Bud" Watson, Jr.
David H. Meginniss
Ralph W. Hornsby, Jr.

For full biographical listings, see the Martindale-Hubbell Law Directory

WATSON, GAMMONS & FEES, P.C. (AV)

200 Clinton Avenue, N.W., Suite 800, P.O. Box 46, 35804
Telephone: 205-536-7423
Telecopier: 205-536-2689

Herman Watson, Jr.
Robert C. Gammons
Michael L. Fees
Joseph A. Jimmerson
J. Barton Warren
Charles H. Pullen
Billie B. Line, Jr.

OF COUNSEL

George K. Williams

LEGAL SUPPORT PERSONNEL

James W. Lowery, Jr. (Administrator)

For full biographical listings, see the Martindale-Hubbell Law Directory

*MOBILE,** Mobile Co.

BRISKMAN & BINION, P.C. (AV)

205 Church Street, P.O. Box 43, 36601
Telephone: 334-433-7600
Fax: 334-433-4485

Donald M. Briskman
Mack B. Binion

Donna Ward Black
Alex F. Lankford, IV
Christ N. Coumanis

A List of Representative Clients will be furnished upon request.
References: First Alabama Bank; AmSouth Bank, N.A.; Southtrust Bank of Mobile.

For full biographical listings, see the Martindale-Hubbell Law Directory

BRYANT, BLACKSHER & LESTER (AV)

Suite 1107 Riverview Plaza Office Tower, 63 South Royal Street, Drawer 1465, 36633
Telephone: 334-432-4671
Telecopier: 334-433-6393
Fairhope, Alabama Office: 21 S. Section Street 36532.
Telephone: 205-990-8998.
Telecopier: 205-990-9878.

(See Next Column)

MEMBERS OF FIRM

Thomas E. Bryant, Jr.
Wesley H. Blacksher
F. Martin Lester, Jr.
Woodrow Eugene Howard, III
Theodore L. Greenspan
Carole W. Delchamps
Deidre W. Lee

For full biographical listings, see the Martindale-Hubbell Law Directory

BURNS, CUNNINGHAM & MACKEY, P.C. (AV)

50 St. Emanuel Street, P.O. Box 1583, 36633
Telephone: 334-432-0612

Peter F. Burns
William M. Cunningham, Jr.
Peter S. Mackey

Max Cassady

For full biographical listings, see the Martindale-Hubbell Law Directory

CUNNINGHAM, BOUNDS, YANCE, CROWDER & BROWN (AV)

1601 Dauphin Street, P.O. Box 66705, 36660
Telephone: 334-471-6191
Fax: 334-479-1031

Richard Bounds
James A. Yance
John T. Crowder, Jr.
Robert T. Cunningham, Jr.
Joseph M. Brown, Jr.
Gregory B. Breedlove
Andrew T. Citrin
Michael A. Worel

David G. Wirtes, Jr.
Randolph B. Walton
Toby D. Brown
Mitchell K. Shelly

OF COUNSEL

Robert T. Cunningham
Valentino D. B. Mazzia

For full biographical listings, see the Martindale-Hubbell Law Directory

DIAMOND, HASSER & FROST (AV)

1325 Dauphin Street, P.O. Drawer 40600, 36640
Telephone: 334-432-3362
Fax: 334-432-3367

MEMBERS OF FIRM

Ross Diamond, Jr. (1919-1978)
Ross M. Diamond, III
James E. Hasser, Jr.
James H. Frost

References: First Alabama Bank, Mobile; AM South Bank, Mobile.

For full biographical listings, see the Martindale-Hubbell Law Directory

FINKBOHNER AND LAWLER (AV)

169 Dauphin Street Suite 300, P.O. Box 3085, 36652
Telephone: 334-438-5871
Fax: 334-432-8052

MEMBERS OF FIRM

George W. Finkbohner, Jr.
John L. Lawler
George W. Finkbohner, III
Royce A. Ray, III

For full biographical listings, see the Martindale-Hubbell Law Directory

HELMSING, LYONS, SIMS & LEACH, P.C. (AV)

The Laclede Building, 150 Government Street, P.O. Box 2767, 36652
Telephone: 334-432-5521
Telecopy: 334-432-0633

Larry U. Sims
Champ Lyons, Jr.
Frederick G. Helmsing
John N. Leach, Jr.
Warren C. Herlong, Jr.
James B. Newman
Robert H. Rouse
Charles H. Dodson, Jr.
Sandy Grisham Robinson
Richard E. Davis
Joseph P. H. Babington
John J. Crowley, Jr.
Joseph D. Steadman

Todd S. Strohmeyer
William R. Lancaster
Robin Kilpatrick Fincher

For full biographical listings, see the Martindale-Hubbell Law Directory

RICHARDSON, DANIELL, SPEAR & UPTON, P.C. (AV)

Suite 400, 1110 Montlimar Drive, P.O. Box 16428, 36616
Telephone: 334-344-8181
Fax: 334-344-6629

John D. Richardson
David F. Daniell
Mark E. Spear
Mark J. Upton
Gary Randall Spear

James Lynn Perry

For full biographical listings, see the Martindale-Hubbell Law Directory

*MONTGOMERY,** Montgomery Co.

BEASLEY, WILSON, ALLEN, MAIN & CROW, P.C. (AV)

218 Commerce Street, P.O. Box 4160, 36103-4160
Telephone: 334-269-2343
Fax: 334-269-2371

Jere Locke Beasley
J. Greg Allen
Michael J. Crow

W. Daniel "Dee" Miles, III
Robert L. Pittman
Rhon E. Jones

For full biographical listings, see the Martindale-Hubbell Law Directory

ALASKA

*ANCHORAGE,** Third Judicial District

YOUNG, SANDERS & FELDMAN, INC. (AV)

Suite 400, 500 L Street, 99501
Telephone: 907-272-3538
Telecopier: 907-274-0819

Joseph L. Young
Eric T. Sanders
Jeffrey M. Feldman
Kristen Young

Reference: Key Bank of Alaska.

For full biographical listings, see the Martindale-Hubbell Law Directory

ARIZONA

CASA GRANDE, Pinal Co.

FITZGIBBONS LAW OFFICES (AV)

Suite E, 711 East Cottonwood Lane, P.O. Box 11208, 85230-1208
Telephone: 602-426-3824
Fax: 602-426-9355

David A. Fitzgibbons

ASSOCIATES

David A. Fitzgibbons, III
Denis M. Fitzgibbons

For Complete List of Firm Personnel, See General Section

For full biographical listings, see the Martindale-Hubbell Law Directory

COTTONWOOD, Yavapai Co.

RON L. LEE (AV)

547 South Main Street, 86326
Telephone: 602-634-2273
Fax: 602-634-0506
Flagstaff, Arizona Office: 114 North San Francisco, Suite 1, 86001.
Telephone: 602-774-8777.

For full biographical listings, see the Martindale-Hubbell Law Directory

*FLAGSTAFF,** Coconino Co.

ASPEY, WATKINS & DIESEL (AV)

123 North San Francisco, 86001
Telephone: 602-774-1478
Facsimile: 602-774-1043
Sedona, Arizona Office: 120 Soldier Pass Road.
Telephone: 602-282-5955.
Facsimile: 602-282-5962.
Page, Arizona Office: 904 North Navajo.
Telephone: 602-645-9694.
Winslow, Arizona Office: 205 North Williamson.
Telephone: 602-289-5963.
Cottonwood, Arizona Office: 905 Cove Parkway, Unite 201.
Telephone: 602-639-1881.

MEMBERS OF FIRM

Frederick M. Fritz Aspey
Harold L. Watkins
Louis M. Diesel
Bruce S. Griffen
Donald H. Bayles, Jr.
Kaign N. Christy
John J. Dempsey

Zachary Markham
James E. Ledbetter
Whitney Cunningham
Holly S. Karris

(See Next Column)

LEGAL SUPPORT PERSONNEL

Deborah D. Roberts (Legal Assistant)
C. Denece Pruett (Legal Assistant)
Dominic M. Marino, Jr, (Paralegal Assistant)

Representative Clients: Farmer's Insurance Company of Arizona; Kelley-Moore Paint Co.; Pepsi-Cola Bottling Company of Northern Arizona; Bill Luke's Chrysler-Plymouth, Inc.; First American Title Insurance Company ; Transamerica Title Insurance Co.; Page Electric Utility; Comprehensive Access Health Plan, Inc.
Reference: First Interstate Bank-Arizona, N.A., Flagstaff, Arizona.

For full biographical listings, see the Martindale-Hubbell Law Directory

MANGUM, WALL, STOOPS & WARDEN, P.L.L.C. (AV)

222 East Birch Avenue, P.O. Box 10, 86002
Telephone: 602-779-6951
Fax: 602-773-1312

H. Karl Mangum (1908-1993)

OF COUNSEL

Douglas J. Wall
Robert W. Warden

MEMBERS OF FIRM

Daniel J. Stoops
A. Dean Pickett
Stephen K. Smith
Melinda L. Garrahan
Jon W. Thompson

ASSOCIATES

Kathleen O'Brien
David W. Rozema
Corbin Vandemoer

Representative Clients: Northern Arizona University; Flagstaff Unified School District; Museum of Northern Arizona; City of Sedona; Arizona School Board Association.
Local Counsel for: Bank of America-Arizona; Arizona Public Service; U.S-.A.A.; State Farm Fire & Casualty Ins. Co.; Hartford Ins. Co.

For Complete List of Firm Personnel, See General Section

For full biographical listings, see the Martindale-Hubbell Law Directory

LAKE HAVASU CITY, Mohave Co.

WACHTEL, BIEHN & MALM (AV)

Suite A, 2240 McCulloch Boulevard, 86403
Telephone: 602-855-5115
Fax: 602-855-5211

MEMBERS OF FIRM

Denis R. Malm
Rex L. Martin

For Complete List of Firm Personnel, See General Section

For full biographical listings, see the Martindale-Hubbell Law Directory

MESA, Maricopa Co.

SKOUSEN, SKOUSEN, GULBRANDSEN & PATIENCE, P.C. (AV)

414 East Southern Avenue, 85204
Telephone: 602-833-8800
FAX: 602-833-7146

William J. Skousen
Richard E. Skousen
Richard M. Gulbrandsen
Steve Patience
Michael J. Skousen
Mark G. Setlow
Curtis M. Bergen
Michael R. Golder

References: First Interstate Bank, Mesa, Arizona; United Bank of Arizona, Mesa, Arizona.

For full biographical listings, see the Martindale-Hubbell Law Directory

*PHOENIX,** Maricopa Co.

BEGAM, LEWIS, MARKS, WOLFE & DASSE A PROFESSIONAL ASSOCIATION OF LAWYERS (AV)

111 West Monroe Street, Suite 1400, 85003-1787
Telephone: 602-254-6071
Fax: 602-252-0042

Robert G. Begam
Frank Lewis
Stanley J. Marks
Elliot G. Wolfe
Thomas F. Dasse
Cora Perez
Kelly J. McDonald
Daniel J. Adelman
Lisa Kurtz
Dena Rosen Epstein

Reference: National Bank of Arizona.

For full biographical listings, see the Martindale-Hubbell Law Directory

BESS & DYSART, P.C. (AV)

7210 North 16th Street, 82020-5201
Telephone: 602-331-4600
Telecopier: 602-331-8600

(See Next Column)

BESS & DYSART P.C.—*Continued*

Leon D. Bess
Robert L. Dysart
Donald R. Kunz
Timothy R. Hyland
William M. Demlong
Connie Totorica Gould

For full biographical listings, see the Martindale-Hubbell Law Directory

BONNETT, FAIRBOURN, FRIEDMAN, HIENTON, MINER & FRY, P.C. (AV)

4041 North Central Avenue Suite 1100, 85012
Telephone: 602-274-1100
Fax: 602-274-1199

William G. Fairbourn
Robert J. Spurlock
C. Kevin Dykstra

For full biographical listings, see the Martindale-Hubbell Law Directory

MICHAEL E. BRADFORD (AV)

4131 North 24th Street Building C Suite 201, 85016
Telephone: 602-955-0088
FAX: 602-955-6445

LEGAL SUPPORT PERSONNEL
Sandra M. Bryant
OF COUNSEL
Jerry Steele

For full biographical listings, see the Martindale-Hubbell Law Directory

CHARLES M. BREWER, LTD. (AV)

5500 North 24th Street, P.O. Box 10720, 85064
Telephone: 602-381-8787
Fax: 602-381-1152

Charles M. Brewer

Mark S. O'Connor

For full biographical listings, see the Martindale-Hubbell Law Directory

BURCH & CRACCHIOLO, P.A. (AV)

702 East Osborn Road, Suite 200, 85014
Telephone: 602-274-7611
Fax: 602-234-0341
Mailing Address: P.O. Box 16882, Phoenix, AZ, 85011

Daniel Cracchiolo
Brian Kaven
Ian Neale
Linda A. Finnegan
Daniel R. Malinski
Jess A. Lorona

Theodore (Todd) Julian

Representative Clients: Bashas' Inc.; Farmers Insurance Group; U-Haul International, Inc.

For Complete List of Firm Personnel, See General Section

For full biographical listings, see the Martindale-Hubbell Law Directory

CRONIN & STANEWICH (AV)

One Columbus Plaza, 3636 North Central Avenue, Suite 560, 85012
Telephone: 602-222-4646

MEMBERS OF FIRM

Robert S. Cronin, Jr.
Robert B. Stanewich

For full biographical listings, see the Martindale-Hubbell Law Directory

JAMES P. CUNNINGHAM, P.C. (AV)

330 North Second Avenue, 85003
Telephone: 602-257-1750
Fax: 602-252-3436

James P. Cunningham
Matthew B. Cunningham

For full biographical listings, see the Martindale-Hubbell Law Directory

DEBUS & KAZAN, LTD. (AV)

335 East Palm Lane, 85004
Telephone: 602-257-8900
Fax: 602-257-0723

Larry L. Debus
Lawrence Ian Kazan

Tracey Westerhausen

References: Firstar Metropolitan Bank; Citibank, Arizona.

For full biographical listings, see the Martindale-Hubbell Law Directory

FENNEMORE CRAIG, A PROFESSIONAL CORPORATION (AV)

Two North Central, Suite 2200, 85004
Telephone: 602-257-8700
Fax: 602-257-8527
Scottsdale, Arizona Office: 6263 North Scottsdale Road, Suite 290, 85250.
Telephone: 602-257-5400.
Fax: 602-945-4932.
Tucson, Arizona Office: One South Church Avenue, Suite 1030, 85701.
Telephone: 602-624-9312.
Fax: 602-882-7383.

John D. Everroad
F. Pendleton Gaines, III
Roger T. Hargrove
William L. Thorpe
Graeme E. M. Hancock
Kaye L. McCarthy
Scott M. Finical
William T. Burghart
Andrew M. Federhar
Christopher P. Staring

Debra L. Runbeck
Jean Marie Sullivan
Ann-Martha Andrews
Marc H. Lamber

Representative Clients: ASARCO Incorporated; AT&T Communications; Bridgestone/Firestone, Inc.; Catellus Development Corp.; Citibank (Arizona); First Interstate Bank of Arizona; GIANT Industries; Phelps Dodge Corporation; The Atchison, Topeka & Santa Fe Railway, Co.; US WEST Communications.

For Complete List of Firm Personnel, See General Section

For full biographical listings, see the Martindale-Hubbell Law Directory

FRIEDL, RICHTER & BURI (AV)

Suite 200, 1440 East Washington Street, 85034
Telephone: 602-495-1000
Fax: 602-271-4733

MEMBERS OF FIRM

William J. Friedl
Charles E. Buri
William E. Moore

For full biographical listings, see the Martindale-Hubbell Law Directory

GOLDSTEIN, KINGSLEY & MCGRODER, LTD. A PROFESSIONAL CORPORATION (AV)

Professional Arts Building, 1110 East McDowell Road, 85006-2678
Telephone: 602-254-5581
Fax: 602-258-7390
Other Phoenix Office: 2200 East Camelback Road, Suite 221, 85016-3456.
Telephone: 602-957-1500.
Telecopier: 602-956-9294.

Philip T. Goldstein
Pamela L. Kingsley
Patrick J. McGroder, III
(East Camelback Road Office)
Kathleen Delarosa
Suzanne P. Clarke

For full biographical listings, see the Martindale-Hubbell Law Directory

STUART GOLDSTEIN (AV)

2702 North Third Street, 85004
Telephone: 602-279-1666
Telecopier: 602-285-1907

Stuart W. Goldstein

Reference: First Interstate Bank, Park Central Office, Phoenix.

For full biographical listings, see the Martindale-Hubbell Law Directory

JOHN PHILIP GRACE, P.C. (AV)

4500 North 32nd Street, Suite 100, 85018
Telephone: 602-954-0464

John Philip Grace

For full biographical listings, see the Martindale-Hubbell Law Directory

HARRIS & PALUMBO, A PROFESSIONAL CORPORATION (AV)

361 East Coronado, Suite 101, P.O. Box 13568, 85002-3568
Telephone: 602-271-9344
Fax: 602-252-2099

Anthony J. Palumbo
John David Harris
Kevin W. Keenan
Gene M. Cullan
Frank I. Powers
Shawn M. Cunningham

For full biographical listings, see the Martindale-Hubbell Law Directory

JENNINGS, STROUSS AND SALMON, P.L.C. (AV)

A Professional Limited Liability Company
One Renaissance Square, Two North Central, 85004-2393
Telephone: 602-262-5911
Fax: 602-253-3255

(See Next Column)

JENNINGS, STROUSS AND SALMON P.L.C., *Phoenix—Continued*

W. Michael Flood
Gary L. Stuart
Gerald W. Alston
John A. Micheaels
Barry E. Lewin
Jay A. Fradkin
Michael R. Palumbo
H. Christian Bode
Jon D. Schneider
Frederick M. Cummings
Michael J. O'Connor
Katherine M. Cooper
Matthew D. Kleifield

J. Matthew Powell
James D. Shook
Jennifer M. Bligh
K. Thomas Slack
Kim D. Steinmetz

For Complete List of Firm Personnel, See General Section

For full biographical listings, see the Martindale-Hubbell Law Directory

MARK & PEARLSTEIN, P.A. (AV)

Suite 150 The Brookstone, 2025 North Third Street, 85004
Telephone: 602-257-0200

Leonard J. Mark
Lynn M. Pearlstein, Mr.

OF COUNSEL

Stephen G. Campbell

For full biographical listings, see the Martindale-Hubbell Law Directory

TERRENCE J. MCGILLICUDDY, P.C. (AV)

5080 North 40th Street, Suite 335, 85018
Telephone: 602-957-1960
800-957-1960
Fax: 602-957-7015

Terrence J. McGillicuddy

For full biographical listings, see the Martindale-Hubbell Law Directory

MEYER, HENDRICKS, VICTOR, OSBORN & MALEDON, A PROFESSIONAL ASSOCIATION (AV)

2929 North Central Avenue Suite 2100, 85012-2794
Telephone: 602-640-9000
Facsimile: (24 Hrs.) 602-640-9050
Mailing Address: P.O. Box 33449, 85067-3449,

Ed Hendricks
R. Douglas Dalton
Diane M. Johnsen
Mark D. Samson
David K. Duncan

Reference: Bank One Arizona, NA.

For Complete List of Firm Personnel, See General Section

For full biographical listings, see the Martindale-Hubbell Law Directory

MILLER & MILLER, LTD. (AV)

Suite 2250, 3200 North Central Avenue, 85012
Telephone: 602-266-8440
Fax: 602-266-8453

Murray Miller
Richard K. Miller
Robert M. Miller
Marcus Westervelt

For full biographical listings, see the Martindale-Hubbell Law Directory

ROBBINS & GREEN, A PROFESSIONAL ASSOCIATION (AV)

1800 CitiBank Tower, 3300 North Central Avenue, 85012-9826
Telephone: 602-248-7600
Fax: 602-266-5369

Philip A. Robbins
Richard W. Abbuhl
Wayne A. Smith
Joe M. Romley
Edmund F. Richardson
William H. Sandweg III
Jack N. Rudel
Jeffrey P. Boshes
Brian Imbornoni
Janet B. Hutchison
Bradley J. Stevens
Ronald G. Wilson
Dwayne Ross
Alfred W. Ricciardi
K. Leonard Judson
Dorothy Baran
Austin D. Potenza, II
Sarah McGiffert
Michael S. Green
Kenneth A. Hodson
Daniel L. Brown

For full biographical listings, see the Martindale-Hubbell Law Directory

LAW OFFICES OF RAYMOND J. SLOMSKI, P.C. (AV)

2901 North Central Avenue, Suite 1150, 85012
Telephone: 602-230-8777
Fax: 602-230-8707

Raymond J. Slomski

Kevin L. Beckwith
James M. Abernethy

(See Next Column)

LEGAL SUPPORT PERSONNEL

PARALEGAL

Patti A. Hibbeler

For full biographical listings, see the Martindale-Hubbell Law Directory

LAW OFFICES OF RICHARD L. STROHM, P.C. (AV)

2901 North Central Avenue Suite 200, 85012
Telephone: 602-285-5097
Telecopier: 602-285-5198

Richard L. Strohm

Representative Clients: State of Arizona; University of Arizona Medical Center; Ryder Truck Rental; The Trammell Crow Companies; Producer's Network; Sean Young.

For full biographical listings, see the Martindale-Hubbell Law Directory

TOLES & ASSOCIATES, P.C. (AV)

1010 East Jefferson Street, 85034
Telephone: 602-253-1010

M. Jeremy Toles

Richard M. Gerry
Rosann K. Johnson
Karyn E. Klausner
M. L. (Les) Weatherly, Jr.

OF COUNSEL

Barbara A. Jarvis

For full biographical listings, see the Martindale-Hubbell Law Directory

*PRESCOTT,** Yavapai Co.

MURPHY, LUTEY, SCHMITT & BECK (AV)

Elks Building, 117 East Gurley Street, 86301
Telephone: 602-445-6860
Fax: 602-445-6488
Yuma, Arizona Office: Valley Professional Plaza. 1763 West Twenty-Fourth Street, Suite 200.
Telephone: 602-726-0314.
Fax: 602-341-1079.

MEMBERS OF FIRM

Thelton D. Beck
Michael R. Murphy
Selmer D. Lutey

ASSOCIATES

Dan A. Wilson
Bruce E. Rosenberg

OF COUNSEL

Keith F. Quail

Northern Arizona Counsel for: State Farm Mutual Automobile Insurance Co.; Transamerica Title Insurance Co.; Allstate Insurance Co.
Local Counsel for: Bank One Arizona, N.A.; General Motors Corp.
Representative Clients: Chino Valley Irrigation District; Prescott College; Galpin Ford, Inc.; Yavapai Medical Center, P.C.

For Complete List of Firm Personnel, See General Section

For full biographical listings, see the Martindale-Hubbell Law Directory

SCOTTSDALE, Maricopa Co.

CARMICHAEL & TILKER (AV)

(An Association of Attorneys including a Professional Corporation)
6740 East Camelback Road Suite 100, 85251
Telephone: 602-949-7676
Fax: 602-945-2149

David H. Carmichael
James A. Tilker (P.C.)

For full biographical listings, see the Martindale-Hubbell Law Directory

JEFFREY A. MATZ A PROFESSIONAL CORPORATION (AV Ⓣ)

6711 East Camelback Road, Suite 8, 85251
Telephone: 602-955-0900
Fax: 602-955-1885

Jeffrey A. Matz (Not admitted in AZ)

*TUCSON,** Pima Co.

COREY & FARRELL, P.C. (AV)

Suite 830, Norwest Tower, One South Church Avenue, 85701-1620
Telephone: 602-882-4994
Telefax: 602-884-7757

Barry M. Corey

Representative Clients: Amphitheater Public School District; Civil Service Commission of the City of Tucson; La Quinta Homes, Inc.; Pima County Merit System Commission; DANKA-Uni-Copy Corp.; Introspect Health Care Corp.

For full biographical listings, see the Martindale-Hubbell Law Directory

Tucson—Continued

JACK A. ETTINGER, P.C. (AV)

4301 East 5th Street, Suite 201, 85711
Telephone: 602-795-3516
Facsimile: 602-323-1080

Jack A. Ettinger — Cynthia D. Ettinger

Reference: First Interstate Bank of Arizona, N.A. (Downtown Branch, Tucson).

For full biographical listings, see the Martindale-Hubbell Law Directory

HARALSON, KINERK & MOREY, P.C. (AV)

82 South Stone Avenue, 85701
Telephone: 602-792-4330
Fax: 602-623-9568

Bob Barber (1903-1978)
Dale Haralson
Burton J. Kinerk
Carter Morey

Kenneth Lee
R. Douglas Holt
Gregory G. Wasley
Daniel C. Gloria
Linda S. Sherrill
Colleen L. Kinerk

Reference: The National Bank of Arizona.

For full biographical listings, see the Martindale-Hubbell Law Directory

HEALY AND BEAL, P.C. (AV)

5255 E. Williams Circle Suite 6000-West Tower, 85711
Telephone: 602-790-6200
Fax: 602-790-1619

William T. Healy — Robert L. Beal
William D. Nelson

Dora Fitzpatrick

References: Bank of America; Merrill Lynch.

For full biographical listings, see the Martindale-Hubbell Law Directory

RONALD D. MERCALDO, LTD. (AV)

376 South Stone Avenue, 85701
Telephone: 602-624-1400
FAX: 602-624-1955

Ronald D. Mercaldo

Lucile D. Sherman — Anthony J. Wiggins

Reference: Arizona Bank.

For full biographical listings, see the Martindale-Hubbell Law Directory

MILLER, PITT & MCANALLY, P.C. (AV)

111 South Church Avenue, 85701-1680
Telephone: 602-792-3836
Telecopier: 602-624-5080
Nogales, Arizona Office: 272 West View Point, 85621.
Telephone: 602-281-1361.
Correspondent Office: Lizarraga, Robles, Savinon & Tapia, S.C. Boulevard Hidalgo 64, Colonia Centenario. CP 83000 Hermosillo, Sonora, Mexico.
Telephone: (62) 17-27-28, 12-79-89, 13-47-10, 12-79-18, 13-33-25, 12-77-70.

Barry N. Akin (1939-1988)
Janice A. Wezelman
Philip J. Hall
Grace McIlvain
Thomas G. Cotter
Armando Rivera
Gus Aragón, Jr.

Denneen L. Peterson — Jonathan Reich
Carole A. Summers

OF COUNSEL

Richard L. McAnally

Representative Clients available upon request.

For Complete List of Firm Personnel, See General Section

For full biographical listings, see the Martindale-Hubbell Law Directory

MURPHY, GOERING, ROBERTS & BERKMAN, P.C. (AV)

Suite 302, 1840 East River Road, 85718
Telephone: 602-577-9300
FAX: 602-577-0848

James M. Murphy
Thomas M. Murphy
Scott Goering
Howard T. Roberts, Jr.
David L. Berkman
William L. Rubin
Carmine A. Brogna

(See Next Column)

Representative Clients: Roman Catholic Church Diocese of Tucson; Fireman's Fund Insurance; Safeco Insurance; Royal Insurance; Sentry Insurance; INA; Carondelet Health Services, Inc.; County of Pima; State Farm Insurance.
Reference: Bank One.

For full biographical listings, see the Martindale-Hubbell Law Directory

SAMET & GAGE, P.C. (AV)

717 North Sixth Avenue, 85705
Telephone: 602-624-8595
Fax: 602-623-4560

Dee-Dee Samet — Arthur V. Gage

Reference: Bank of Arizona; Security Pacific Bank.

For full biographical listings, see the Martindale-Hubbell Law Directory

SHULTZ & ROLLINS, LTD. (AV)

St. Philip's Plaza, 4280 North Campbell Avenue, Suite 214, 85718-6580
Telephone: 602-577-7777

Silas H. Shultz — Michael F. Rollins

Gerald T. Barton

For full biographical listings, see the Martindale-Hubbell Law Directory

STOMPOLY, STROUD, GIDDINGS & GLICKSMAN, P.C. (AV)

1820 Citibank Tower, One South Church Avenue, 85702
Telephone: 602-628-8300
Telefax: 602-628-9948
Mailing Address: P.O. Box 190, Tucson, AZ, 85702-0190

John G. Stompoly — Elliot A. Glicksman
George Erickson

For Complete List of Firm Personnel, See General Section

For full biographical listings, see the Martindale-Hubbell Law Directory

STRICKLAND & O'HAIR, P.C. (AV)

4400 E. Broadway, Suite 700, 85711-3517
Telephone: 602-795-8727
Fax: 602-795-5649

William E. Strickland — William E. Strickland, Jr.
Jennele Morris O'Hair

Representative Clients: AkChin Indian Community; City of Sierra Vista; City of Benson; Golf 36 Corp.; Town of Mammoth; Town of Patagonia; Fertilizer Company of Arizona, Inc.; Gila Valley Irrigation District; Franklin Irrigation District; City of Globe.
Reference: Bank One (formerly Valley National Bank).

ARKANSAS

*FAYETTEVILLE,** Washington Co.

ODOM, ELLIOTT, WINBURN AND WATSON (AV)

No. 1 East Mountain Street, P.O. Drawer 1868, 72702
Telephone: 501-442-7575
FAX: 501-442-9008

MEMBERS OF FIRM

Bobby Lee Odom
Don R. Elliott, Jr.
Russell B. Winburn
Jason L. Watson

J. Timothy Smith — Conrad T. Odom
Timothy J. Myers

Reference: Bank of Fayetteville, Fayetteville, Arkansas.

For full biographical listings, see the Martindale-Hubbell Law Directory

*LITTLE ROCK,** Pulaski Co.

ANDERSON & KILPATRICK (AV)

The First Commercial Building, 400 West Capitol Avenue, Suite 2640, 72201
Telephone: 501-372-1887
Fax: 501-372-7706

MEMBERS OF FIRM

Overton S. Anderson, II
Joseph E. Kilpatrick, Jr.
Michael E. Aud
Aylmer Gene Williams
Randy P. Murphy
Frances E. Scroggins

ASSOCIATES

Mariam T. Hopkins — Michael P. Vanderford

For full biographical listings, see the Martindale-Hubbell Law Directory

Little Rock—Continued

DODDS, KIDD, RYAN & MOORE (AV)
313 West Second Street, 72201
Telephone: 501-375-9901
FAX: 501-376-0387

MEMBERS OF FIRM

J. B. Dodds (1909-1964)
J. L. Kidd, Jr.
Donald S. Ryan
Judson C. Kidd
Richard N. Moore, Jr.
Charles Gregory Alagood

ASSOCIATE

Robert T. James

Reference: First National Bank in Little Rock.

For full biographical listings, see the Martindale-Hubbell Law Directory

DUNCAN & RAINWATER TRIAL LAWYERS A PROFESSIONAL ASSOCIATION (AV)
Suite 500 Three Financial Centre, 900 South Shackleford, P.O. Box 25938, 72221-5938
Telephone: 501-228-7600
FAX: 501-228-7664

Phillip J. Duncan (P.A.)
Michael R. Rainwater (P.A.)
Robert A. Russell, Jr.
Neil Ray Chamberlin

For full biographical listings, see the Martindale-Hubbell Law Directory

GARY EUBANKS & ASSOCIATES, P.A. (AV)
708 West Second Street, 72201
Telephone: 501-372-0266

Gary L. Eubanks
Hugh F. Spinks

Darryl E. (Chip) Baker
William Gary Holt
James G. Schulze
T. Michael Lee
Herman W. Eubanks

For full biographical listings, see the Martindale-Hubbell Law Directory

FRIDAY, ELDREDGE & CLARK (AV)
A Partnership including Professional Associations
Formerly, Smith, Williams, Friday, Eldredge & Clark
2000 First Commercial Building, 400 West Capitol, 72201-3493
Telephone: 501-376-2011
Telecopier: 501-376-2147; 376-6369

MEMBERS OF FIRM

Robert V. Light (P.A.)
William H. Sutton (P.A.)
Frederick S. Ursery (P.A.)
John Dewey Watson (P.A.)
J. Phillip Malcom (P.A.)
James M. Simpson, Jr., (P.A.)
Donald H. Bacon (P.A.)
Barry E. Coplin (P.A.)
Elizabeth J. Robben (P.A.)
Laura Hensley Smith (P.A.)
William Mell Griffin III, (P.A.)
Kevin A. Crass (P.A.)
William A. Waddell, Jr., (P.A.)
Tab Turner (P.A.)
Calvin J. Hall (P.A.)
Scott J. Lancaster (P.A.)
James C. Baker (P.A.)
H. Charles Gschwend, Jr., (P.A.)
Scott H. Tucker (P.A.)
Guy Alton Wade (P.A.)

ASSOCIATES

J. Michael Pickens
Tonia P. Jones
David D. Wilson
Gregory D. Taylor
Fran C. Hickman
Betty J. Demory

Counsel for: Union Pacific System; St. Paul Insurance Co.; Liberty Mutual Insurance Co.; Cigna Property & Casualty Co.; Arkansas Power & Light Co.; Dillard Department Stores, Inc.; First Commercial Corp.; Browning Arms Co.; Phillips Petroleum Co.; Aetna Casualty & Surety Co.

For Complete List of Firm Personnel, See General Section

For full biographical listings, see the Martindale-Hubbell Law Directory

HUCKABAY, MUNSON, ROWLETT & TILLEY, P.A. (AV)
First Commercial Building, Suite 1900, 400 West Capitol, 72201
Telephone: 501-374-6535
FAX: 501-374-5906

Mike Huckabay
Bruce E. Munson
Beverly A. Rowlett
James W. Tilley
John E. Moore
Tim Boone
Rick Runnells
Sarah Ann Presson

Lizabeth Lookadoo
Valerie Denton
Edward T. Oglesby
D. Michael Huckabay, Jr.
Carol Lockard Worley
Mark S. Breeding
Elizabeth Fletcher Rogers
Jeffrey A. Weber

Representative Clients: Allstate Insurance Company; American International Group; American Medical International; Farmers Insurance Group; General Electric Company; Nationwide Insurance Company; Safeco Insurance Company; State Farm Mutual Automobile Insurance Company; State Farm Fire and Casualty Company; United States Fidelity and Guaranty Company.

(See Next Column)

For full biographical listings, see the Martindale-Hubbell Law Directory

ROSE LAW FIRM, A PROFESSIONAL ASSOCIATION (AV)
120 East Fourth Street, 72201
Telephone: 501-375-9131
Telecopy: 501-375-1309

Phillip Carroll
Kenneth Robert Shemin
Jerry C. Jones
David L. Williams
Richard T. Donovan
James H. Druff
Jess Askew, III
Amy Lee Stewart

Representative Clients: Kemper Insurance Group; Bridgestone/Firestone, Inc.; Aluminum Company of America; Baxter Healthcare Corporation; J.A. Riggs Tractor Co.; General American Transportation Co.

For Complete List of Firm Personnel, See General Section

For full biographical listings, see the Martindale-Hubbell Law Directory

CALIFORNIA

APTOS, Santa Cruz Co.

DENNIS J. KEHOE A LAW CORPORATION (AV)
311 Bonita Drive, 95003
Telephone: 408-662-8444
Fax: 408-662-0227

Dennis J. Kehoe

For full biographical listings, see the Martindale-Hubbell Law Directory

RUMMONDS, WILLIAMS & MAIR (AV)
311 Bonita Drive, P.O. Box 1870, 95001
Telephone: 408-688-2911
Sacramento, California Office: 6991 Garden Highway. 95837.
Telephone: 916-927-4610.

MEMBERS OF FIRM

James S. Rummonds
Sally Ann Williams

OF COUNSEL

Peter K. Mair
Patrick J. Waltz (Resident, Sacramento Office)

For full biographical listings, see the Martindale-Hubbell Law Directory

*BAKERSFIELD,** Kern Co.

KLEIN, WEGIS, DENATALE, GOLDNER & MUIR (AV)
A Partnership including Professional Corporations
(Formerly Di Giorgio, Davis, Klein, Wegis, Duggan & Friedman)
ARCO Tower, 4550 California Avenue, Second Floor, P.O. Box 11172, 93389-1172
Telephone: 805-395-1000
Telecopier: 805-326-0418
Santa Ana, California Office: Park Tower Building #610, 200 W. Santa Ana Boulevard, 92701.
Telephone: 714-285-0711.
Fax: 714-285-9003.

MEMBERS OF FIRM

Anthony J. Klein (Inc.)
Ralph B. Wegis (Inc.)
Gregory A. Muir

Representative Clients: Bank of America; Great Western Bank; Mojave Pipeline Co.; Transamerican Title Insurance Co.; Dean Whittier Reynolds, Inc.; California Republic Bank; San Joaquin Bank; Nahama & Weagant Energy Co.; Freymiller Trucking, Inc.; Westinghouse Electric Co.

For Complete List of Firm Personnel, See General Section

For full biographical listings, see the Martindale-Hubbell Law Directory

LAW OFFICES OF YOUNG WOOLDRIDGE (AV)
1800 30th Street, Fourth Floor, 93301
Telephone: 805-327-9661
Facsimile: 805-327-1087

MEMBERS OF FIRM

Joseph Wooldridge
A. Cameron Paulden (1927-1984)
Robert J. Self
G. Neil Farr
Michael R. Young
Ernest A. Conant
Steve W. Nichols
Larry R. Cox
Scott K. Kuney
Michael A. Kaia

ASSOCIATES

Russell B. Hicks
Vickie Y. Wheeler

(See Next Column)

LAW OFFICES OF YOUNG WOOLDRIDGE—*Continued*

OF COUNSEL

John B. Young
Edward M. Carpenter

Representative Clients: Arvin-Edison Water Storage District; Motor City Truck Sales and Service.
References: Wells Fargo Bank; First Interstate Bank; California Republic Bank.

For Complete List of Firm Personnel, See General Section

For full biographical listings, see the Martindale-Hubbell Law Directory

BERKELEY, Alameda Co.

GILLIN, JACOBSON, ELLIS, LARSEN & DOYLE (AV)

Seventh Floor, 2030 Addison Street, P.O. Box 523, 94701-0523
Telephone: 510-841-7820
Fax: 510-848-0266
San Francisco Office: One Sutter Street, 10th Floor.
Telephone: 415-986-4777.

Andrew R. Gillin
Ralph L. Jacobson
Luke Ellis
James Paul Larsen
Richard P. Doyle, Jr.
Susan Hunt
Mitchell S. Rosenfeld

For full biographical listings, see the Martindale-Hubbell Law Directory

BEVERLY HILLS, Los Angeles Co.

DALE S. GRIBOW A PROFESSIONAL CORPORATION (AV)

9777 Wilshire Boulevard, Suite 918, 90212
Telephone: 310-275-4525
Southern California: 1-800-ATORNEY
Fax: 310-275-1016
Palm Desert, California Office: 184 Kiva Drive. 92260.
Telephone: 619-341-4411.
Fax: 619-773-3636.

Dale S. Gribow

Harold R. Freudenheim
Wendy Rossi
Dennis H. Boothe

For full biographical listings, see the Martindale-Hubbell Law Directory

PAUL L. KRENTZMAN (AV)

Penthouse, 9454 Wilshire Boulevard, 90210
Telephone: 310-274-5466

Reference: World Trade Bank, Beverly Hills.

For full biographical listings, see the Martindale-Hubbell Law Directory

COSTA MESA, Orange Co.

LAW OFFICES OF W. DOUGLAS EASTON (AV)

3200 Park Center Drive, Suite 1000, 92626
Telephone: 714-850-4590
Fax: 714-850-4500

Anderson L. Washburn

For full biographical listings, see the Martindale-Hubbell Law Directory

*FRESNO,** Fresno Co.

LANG, RICHERT & PATCH, A PROFESSIONAL CORPORATION (AV)

Fig Garden Financial Center, 5200 North Palm Avenue, 4th Floor, P.O. Box 40012, 93755
Telephone: 209-228-6700
Fax: 209-228-6727

Frank H. Lang
William T. Richert (1937-1993)
Robert L. Patch, II
Val W. Saldaña
Douglas E. Noll
Michael T. Hertz
Victoria J. Salisch
Bradley A. Silva
David R. Jenkins
Charles Trudrung Taylor
Mark L. Creede
Peter N. Zeitler
Charles L. Doerksen

Randall C. Nelson
Barbara A. McAuliffe
Laurie Quigley Cardot
Douglas E. Griffin
Nabil E. Zumout

References: Wells Fargo Bank (Fresno Main Office); First Interstate Bank (Fresno Main Office).

For full biographical listings, see the Martindale-Hubbell Law Directory

MILES, SEARS & EANNI, A PROFESSIONAL CORPORATION (AV)

2844 Fresno Street, P.O. Box 1432, 93716
Telephone: 209-486-5200
Fax: 209-486-5240

Wm. M. Miles (1909-1991)
Robert E. Sears (1918-1992)
Carmen A. Eanni
Richard C. Watters
Gerald J. Maglio
William J. Seiler
Douglas L. Gordon

For full biographical listings, see the Martindale-Hubbell Law Directory

GLENDALE, Los Angeles Co.

FLANAGAN, BOOTH, UNGER & MOSES (AV)

1156 North Brand Boulevard, 91202-2582
Telephone: 818-244-8694
Fax: 818-244-1852
Santa Ana, California Office: 1851 East First Street, Suite 805. 92705.
Telephone: 714-835-2607.
Fax: 714-835-4825.

MEMBERS OF FIRM

J. Michael Flanagan
Douglas M. Booth
Charles J. Unger
J. Barry Moses

ASSOCIATES

Michael T. Danis
James A. Grover

For full biographical listings, see the Martindale-Hubbell Law Directory

LA JOLLA, San Diego Co.

MAURER LAW FIRM (AV)

7825 Fay Avenue, Suite 200, 92037
Telephone: 619-456-5570
Fax: 619-551-8919

Charles D. Maurer, Jr.

For full biographical listings, see the Martindale-Hubbell Law Directory

LARKSPUR, Marin Co.

KATZ, BIERER & BRADY, INC. (AV)

101 Larkspur Landing Circle, Suite 223, 94939
Telephone: 415-925-1600
FAX: 415-925-0940

Richard L. Katz
Joel D. Bierer
Steven J. Brady

OF COUNSEL

Alvin J. Schifrin

For full biographical listings, see the Martindale-Hubbell Law Directory

WEINBERG, HOFFMAN & CASEY (AV)

A Partnership including a Professional Corporation
700 Larkspur Landing Circle, Suite 280, 94939
Telephone: 415-461-9666
Fax: 415-461-9681

Ivan Weinberg
Joseph Hoffman
A. Michael Casey

For full biographical listings, see the Martindale-Hubbell Law Directory

LONG BEACH, Los Angeles Co.

BENNETT & KISTNER (AV)

301 East Ocean Boulevard, Suite 800, 90802
Telephone: 310-435-6675
Fax: 310-437-8375
Riverside, California Office: 3403 Tenth Street, Suite 605. 92501-3676.
Telephone: 909-341-9360.
Fax: 909-341-9362.

Charles J. Bennett
Wayne T. Kistner

ASSOCIATES

Richard R. Bradbury
Mary A. Estante (Resident, Riverside Office)
Todd R. Becker
Karen H. Beckman (Resident, Riverside Office)

Representative Clients: The Hertz Corporation; Thrifty Oil Co.; Golden West Refining Co.; Standard Brands Paint Co.; Mattel, Inc.; Di Salvo Trucking Co.; County of Riverside; Southern California Rapid Transit District.
Reference: First Interstate Bank of California, The Market Place Office, Long Beach, California.

For full biographical listings, see the Martindale-Hubbell Law Directory

Long Beach—Continued

BURNS, AMMIRATO, PALUMBO, MILAM & BARONIAN, A PROFESSIONAL LAW CORPORATION (AV)

One World Trade Center, Suite 1200, 90831-1200
Telephone: 310-436-8338; 714-952-1047
Fax: 310-432-6049
Pasadena, California Office: 65 North Raymond Avenue, 2nd Floor.
Telephone: 818-796-5053; 213-258-8282.
Fax: 818-792-3078.

Vincent A. Ammirato

Thomas L. Halliwell
Robert Gary Mendoza
Joseph F. O'Hara
Michael P. Vicencia
Michael E. Wenzel

For full biographical listings, see the Martindale-Hubbell Law Directory

STOLPMAN, KRISSMAN, ELBER, MANDEL & KATZMAN (AV)

A Partnership including Professional Corporations
Nineteenth Floor, 111 West Ocean Boulevard, 90802-4649
Telephone: 310-435-8300
Telecopier: 310-435-8304
Los Angeles (Westwood) Office: Suite 1800, 10880 Wilshire Boulevard.
Telephone: 213-470-8011.

MEMBERS OF FIRM

Thomas G. Stolpman (Inc.)
Leonard H. Mandel (Inc.)
Bernard Katzman (Inc.)
Joel Krissman
Mary Nielsen Abbott
Donna Silver
Dennis M. Elber

ASSOCIATES

Edwin Silver
Lynne Rasmussen
Marilyn S. Heise
Elaine Mandel

OF COUNSEL

Richard L. McWilliams (Inc.)

For full biographical listings, see the Martindale-Hubbell Law Directory

THIELEN AND BURKE, A PROFESSIONAL CORPORATION (AV)

3233 East Broadway, 90803
Telephone: 310-439-0991
FAX: 310-438-8211

Joseph E. Thielen
Sean M. Burke

References furnished upon request.

For full biographical listings, see the Martindale-Hubbell Law Directory

LOS ALTOS, Santa Clara Co.

NELSON, PERLOV & LEE, A PROFESSIONAL CORPORATION (AV)

339 South San Antonio Road, 94022
Telephone: 415-941-6161
Fax: 415-949-0695

Thomas F. Nelson
Florence T. Perlov (Retired)
Mark S. Lee
Kim James
Patricia M. Leary
Mary Acquesta
John T. Maxwell

For full biographical listings, see the Martindale-Hubbell Law Directory

*LOS ANGELES,** Los Angeles Co.

AGNEW & BRUSAVICH

(See Torrance)

MATTHEW B. F. BIREN & ASSOCIATES (AV)

815 Moraga Drive, 90049-1633
Telephone: 310-476-3031; 381-5609
FAX: 310-471-3165

Marc J. Katzman
Kimberly A. Miller
Debra J. Tauger
Michael L. Justice
Edmont T. Barrett

Reference: First Los Angeles Bank (Century City, Los Angeles, Branch).

For full biographical listings, see the Martindale-Hubbell Law Directory

WILLIAM J. GARGARO, JR. A PROFESSIONAL CORPORATION (AV)

Suite 1800, 2049 Century Park East, 90067
Telephone: 310-552-0633
FAX: 310-552-9760

William J. Gargaro, Jr.

Reference: First Interstate Bank of California.

For full biographical listings, see the Martindale-Hubbell Law Directory

HAMRICK, GARROTTO, BRISKIN & PENE, A PROFESSIONAL CORPORATION (AV)

3580 Wilshire Boulevard, 10th Floor, 90010
Telephone: 213-252-0041
Fax: 213-386-5414
Long Beach, California Office: 300 Oceangate, Suite 600.
Telephone: 310-435-4553.
Fax: 310-435-6442.

Robert S. Hamrick (A P.C.)
Greg W. Garrotto
Jeffrey F. Briskin (Resident, Long Branch Office)
Katherine B. Pene
John J. Latzanich, II

Craig A. McDougall (Resident, Long Beach Office)
Marla (Beth) Shah
Terry Porvin
Jana L. Gordon
Peter E. Garrell (Resident, Long Beach Office)
Roman Y. Nykolyshyn
Lori M. Levine
Nancy J. Lemkin (Resident, Long Beach Office)
Norman Goldman
Maureen A. McKinley
Linda L. Hamlin (Resident, Long Beach Office)

For full biographical listings, see the Martindale-Hubbell Law Directory

LAW OFFICES OF DAVID M. HARNEY (AV)

Suite 1300 Figueroa Plaza, 201 North Figueroa Street, 90012-2636
Telephone: 213-482-0881
Fax: 213-250-4042

SPECIAL COUNSEL

Thomas Kallay

ASSOCIATES

Carl A. McMahan
Julie A. Harney
David T. Harney
Andrew J. Nocas
Vincent McGowan
Peter J. Polos
Thomas A. Schultz
Christopher P. Leyel
Jeffrey B. Smith
Robert H. Pourvali
C. Michael Alder
Daniel S. Glaser

OF COUNSEL

Gert K. Hirschberg

Reference: Bank of America.

For full biographical listings, see the Martindale-Hubbell Law Directory

HAWKINS, SCHNABEL, LINDAHL & BECK (AV)

660 South Figueroa Street, Suite 1500, 90017
Telephone: 213-488-3900
Telecopier: 213-486-9883
Cable Address: "Haslin"

MEMBERS OF FIRM

Roger E. Hawkins
Laurence H. Schnabel
George M. Lindahl
Jon P. Kardassakis
William E. Keitel

For full biographical listings, see the Martindale-Hubbell Law Directory

KANANACK, MURGATROYD, BAUM & HEDLUND, A PROFESSIONAL CORPORATION (AV)

Suite 650, 12100 Wilshire Boulevard, 90025
Telephone: 310-207-3233; 800-827-0087
Facsimile: 310-820-7444
Washington, D.C. Office: 1250 24th Street, N.W., Suite 300.
Telephone: 202-466-0513; 800-827-0097.
Facsimile: 202-466-0527.

Michael L. Baum
Paul J. Hedlund
Robert E. Guilford
J. Clark Aristei
William J. Downey III

OF COUNSEL

Michael J. Kananack
George W. Murgatroyd III

John A. Greaves
Cara L. Belle (Not admitted in CA)
Denise K. Tomaiko
Robert F. Foss

Reference: Union Bank.

For full biographical listings, see the Martindale-Hubbell Law Directory

KUSSMAN & WHITEHILL (AV)

A Partnership including a Professional Corporation
Suite 1470, 10866 Wilshire Boulevard, 90024
Telephone: 310-474-4411
Fax: 310-474-6530

Russell S. Kussman (A Professional Corporation)
Michael H. Whitehill

(See Next Column)

KUSSMAN & WHITEHILL—*Continued*

Steven G. Mehta

For full biographical listings, see the Martindale-Hubbell Law Directory

LA FOLLETTE, JOHNSON, DE HAAS, FESLER & AMES, A PROFESSIONAL CORPORATION (AV)

865 South Figueroa Street, Suite 3100, 90017-5443
Telephone: 213-426-3600
Fax: 213-426-3650
San Francisco, California Office: 50 California Street, Suite 3350.
Telephone: 415-433-7610.
Telecopier: 415-392-7541.
Santa Ana, California Office: 2677 North Main Street, Suite 901.
Telephone: 714-558-7008.
Telecopier: 714-972-0379.
Riverside, California Office: 3403 Tenth Street, Suite 820.
Telephone: 714-275-9192.
Fax: 714-275-9249.

John T. La Follette (1922-1990)
Daren T. Johnson
Louis H. De Haas
Donald C. Fesler
Dennis K. Ames (Resident, Santa Ana Office)
Alfred W. Gerisch, Jr.
Brian W. Birnie
Peter J. Zomber
Robert E. Kelly, Jr.
Leon A. Zallen
G. Kelley Reid, Jr. (Resident, San Francisco Office)
Dennis J. Sinclitico
Christopher C. Cannon (Resident, Santa Ana Office)
Dorothy B. Reyes
Steven R. Odell (Santa Ana and Riverside Offices)
Christopher L. Thomas (Santa Ana and Riverside Offices)
Robert K. Warford (Resident, Riverside Office)
John L. Supple (Resident, San Francisco Office)
Vincent D. Lapointe
Steven J. Joffe
Mark M. Stewart
Bradley J. McGirr (Resident, Santa Ana Office)
Sydney La Branche Merritt

Peter R. Bing
Larry P. Nathenson
Donald R. Beck (Resident, Santa Ana Office)
Donna R. Evans
David J. Ozeran
Mark B. Guterman
Terry A. Woodward (Resident, Santa Ana Office)
Stephen C. Dreher (Resident, Santa Ana Office)
Tatiana M. Schultz (Resident, San Francisco Office)
Peter E. Theophilos (Resident, San Francisco Office)
Deborah A. Cowley
Thomas S. Alch
Kenton E. Moore
Kent T. Brandmeyer
Garry O. Moses
Jeffery R. Erickson (Resident, Riverside Office)
Michael J. O'Connor
Elizabeth Anne Scherer (Resident, Santa Ana Office)
Hugh R. Burns
Stephen K. Hiura
James G. Wold
Eileen S. Lemmon (Resident, Riverside, Office)
David M. Wright
Larry E. White (Resident, Riverside Office)
Laurie Miyamoto Johnson
David James Reinard
Michelle Louise McCoy
Duane A. Newton (Resident, Riverside Office)
Adriaan F. van der Capellen (Resident, Santa Ana Office)
William T. Gray (Resident, Santa Ana Office)
Thomas J. Lo (Resident, Santa Ana Office)
Daniel D. Sorenson (Resident, Riverside Office)
Joanne Rosendin (Resident, San Francisco Office)
Henry P. Canvel (Resident, San Francisco Office)
Peter D. Busciglio (Resident, Santa Ana Office)
Mark S. Rader (Resident, Riverside Office)
Jay B. Lake
Erin L. Muellenberg (Resident, Riverside Office)
Phyllis M. Winston (Resident, Riverside Office)
John Calfee Mulvana (Resident, Santa Ana Office)
David L. Bell
Brian T. Chu (Resident, Santa Ana Office)
John Hammond
Laurent C. Vonderweidt
David Peim
Daniel V. Kohls (Resident, San Francisco Office)
Joel E. D. Odou
Robert T. Bergsten
Marcelo A. D'Asero
Natasha M. Riggs
Henry M. Su
Richard K. Kay
Annette A. Apperson

A list of References will be furnished upon request.

For full biographical listings, see the Martindale-Hubbell Law Directory

JOSÉ Y. LAUCHENGCO, JR. (AV)

3545 Wilshire Boulevard, Suite 247, 90010
Telephone: 213-380-9897

For full biographical listings, see the Martindale-Hubbell Law Directory

LEBOVITS & DAVID, A PROFESSIONAL CORPORATION (AV)

Suite 3100, Two Century Plaza, 2049 Century Park East, 90067
Telephone: 310-277-0200
FAX: 310-552-1028

(See Next Column)

Moses Lebovits
Deborah A. David

OF COUNSEL
Joseph J. M. Lange

Reference: City National Bank (Main Office - Beverly Hills).

For full biographical listings, see the Martindale-Hubbell Law Directory

ROBERT D. WALKER A PROFESSIONAL CORPORATION (AV)

Suite 1208, One Park Plaza, 3250 Wilshire Boulevard, 90010-1606
Telephone: 213-382-8010
Fax: 213-388-1033

Robert D. Walker

Delia Flores
René M. Faucher

Reference: Bank of America (Los Angeles Main Office)

For full biographical listings, see the Martindale-Hubbell Law Directory

MENLO PARK, San Mateo Co.

O'REILLY & COLLINS, A PROFESSIONAL CORPORATION (AV)

2500 Sand Hill Road, Suite 201, 94025
Telephone: 415-854-7700
Fax: 415-854-8350

Terry O'Reilly
James P. Collins

James P. Tessier

For full biographical listings, see the Martindale-Hubbell Law Directory

LAW OFFICES OF JOHN C. SHAFFER, JR. A PROFESSIONAL LAW CORPORATION (AV)

750 Menlo Avenue, Suite 250, 94025
Telephone: 415-324-0622
Fax: 415-321-0198

John C. Shaffer, Jr.
Douglas N. Thomason

For full biographical listings, see the Martindale-Hubbell Law Directory

MISSION VIEJO, Orange Co.

ROBINSON, PHILLIPS & CALCAGNIE, A PROFESSIONAL CORPORATION (AV)

Incorporated 1986
26722 Plaza Street, Suite 230, 92690
Telephone: 714-582-6901
Fax: 714-582-3923
San Diego, California Office: 110 Laurel Street.
Telephone: 619-338-4060.
FAX: 619-338-0423.

Mark P. Robinson, Jr.
Gordon G. Phillips, Jr.
Kevin F. Calcagnie

Allan F. Davis
Susan Lee Guinn
Jeoffrey L. Robinson

For full biographical listings, see the Martindale-Hubbell Law Directory

NEWPORT BEACH, Orange Co.

DONALD PETERS A LAW CORPORATION (AV)

1300 Dove Street, Suite 200, 92660
Telephone: 714-955-3818
Fax: 714-955-1341

Donald Peters

For full biographical listings, see the Martindale-Hubbell Law Directory

LAW OFFICES OF THEODORE S. WENTWORTH (AV)

4631 Teller Avenue, Suite 100, 92660
Telephone: 714-752-7711
Fax: 714-752-8339
Temecula, California Office: 41530 Enterprise Circle South. Suite 206.
Telephone: 909-695-1888.
Fax: 909-694-4093.

Theodore S. Wentworth

Nancy Morse Knight
William M. Delli Paoli

Reference: First Interstate Bank, Airport Branch, Newport Beach, Calif.

For full biographical listings, see the Martindale-Hubbell Law Directory

*OAKLAND,** Alameda Co.

HAIMS, JOHNSON, MACGOWAN & MCINERNEY (AV)

490 Grand Avenue, 94610
Telephone: 510-835-0500
Facsimile: 510-835-2833

MEMBERS OF FIRM

Arnold B. Haims
Gary R. Johnson
Clyde L. MacGowan
Thomas McInerney
Lawrence A. Baker
Randy M. Marmor
John K. Kirby
Robert J. Frassetto
Caroline N. Valentino

ASSOCIATES

Joseph Y. Ahn
Edward D. Baldwin
Kathleen B. Boehm
Marc P. Bouret
Anne M. Michaels
Dianne D. Peebles
Michelle D. Perry
Edward C. Schroeder, Jr.

For full biographical listings, see the Martindale-Hubbell Law Directory

KAZAN, MCCLAIN, EDISES, SIMON & ABRAMS, A PROFESSIONAL LAW CORPORATION (AV)

Suite 300, 171 Twelfth Street, 94607
Telephone: 510-465-7728; 893-7211
TDD: (510) 763-8808
Fax: 510-835-4913
Internet: Kazan@kmes.com

Steven Kazan
David M. McClain
Aaron H. Simon
Denise Abrams

Francis E. Fernandez
Anne M. Landwehr
Dianna J. Lyons
Frances C. Schreiberg
Simona A. Farrise

LEGAL SUPPORT PERSONNEL

Elizabeth C. Johnson (Director of Administration and Finance)

Reference: Union Bank (Oakland Main Branch).

For full biographical listings, see the Martindale-Hubbell Law Directory

VAN BLOIS & KNOWLES (AV)

Suite 2245 Ordway Building, One Kaiser Plaza, 94612
Telephone: 510-444-1906
Contra Costa County 510-947-1055
Fax: 510-444-1294
Livermore, California Office: 2109 Fourth Street.
Telephone: 510-455-0193.

MEMBERS OF FIRM

R. Lewis Van Blois
Thomas C. Knowles
Ellen R. Schwartz
Richard J. Baskin

For full biographical listings, see the Martindale-Hubbell Law Directory

PALM SPRINGS, Riverside Co.

REGAR & PARKINSON (AV)

255 North El Cielo, Suite 200, 92262-6974
Telephone: 619-327-1516
Fax: 619-327-3291

MEMBERS OF FIRM

Barry Regar
James W. Parkinson

ASSOCIATE

Sigrid R. Hilkey

For full biographical listings, see the Martindale-Hubbell Law Directory

PASADENA, Los Angeles Co.

BURNS, AMMIRATO, PALUMBO, MILAM & BARONIAN, A PROFESSIONAL LAW CORPORATION (AV)

65 North Raymond Avenue, 2nd Floor, 91103-3919
Telephone: 818-796-5053; 213-258-8282
Fax: 818-792-3078
Long Beach, California Office: One World Trade Center, Suite 1200.
Telephone: 310-436-8338; 714-952-1047.
Fax: 310-432-6049.

Michael A. Burns
Bruce Palumbo
Jeffrey L. Milam
Robert H. Baronian
Steven J. Banner

Normand A. Ayotte
Colleen Clark
Vincent F. De Marzo
William D. Dodson
Valerie Julien-Peto
Susan E. Luhring
Grace C. Mori

Reference: First Los Angeles Bank.

For full biographical listings, see the Martindale-Hubbell Law Directory

COLLINS, COLLINS, MUIR & TRAVER (AV)

Successor to Collins & Collins
Suite 300, 265 North Euclid, 91101
Telephone: 818-793-1163
Los Angeles: 213-681-2773
FAX: 818-793-5982

MEMBERS OF FIRM

James E. Collins (1910-1987)
John J. Collins
Samuel J. Muir
Robert J. Traver

ASSOCIATES

John B. Foss
Frank J. D'Oro
Paul L. Rupard
Brian K. Stewart
Robert H. Stellwagen, Jr.
Tomas A. Guterres
Karen B. Sharp
Amina R. Merritt
Christine E. Drage

For full biographical listings, see the Martindale-Hubbell Law Directory

FRANSCELL, STRICKLAND, ROBERTS & LAWRENCE, A PROFESSIONAL CORPORATION (AV)

Penthouse, 225 South Lake Avenue, 91101-3005
Telephone: 818-304-7830; 213-684-7830; 800-303-5503 (CA Only)
Fax: 818-795-7460
Santa Ana, California Office: Suite 800, 401 Civic Center Drive West.
Telephone: 714-543-6511.
Fax: 714-543-6711.
Riverside, California Office: Suite 670, 3801 University Avenue.
Telephone: 909-686-1000.
Fax: 909-686-2565.

George J. Franscell
Tracy Strickland (Resident, Santa Ana Office)
Barbara E. Roberts (Resident, Riverside Office)
David D. Lawrence
Carol Ann Rohr
Scott D. MacLatchie
W. Charles Bradley (Resident, Riverside Office)
S. Frank Harrell (Resident, Santa Ana Office)
Conrad R. Clark (Resident, Riverside Office)
Jeri Tabback Thompson
Olaf W. Hedberg (Resident, Santa Ana Office)
Spencer Krieger
Jack D. Hoskins

For full biographical listings, see the Martindale-Hubbell Law Directory

KEVIN MEENAN (AV)

790 East Colorado Boulevard Ninth Floor Penthouse, 91101-2105
Telephone: 818-398-0000
FAX: 818-585-0999

For full biographical listings, see the Martindale-Hubbell Law Directory

GEORGE E. MOORE A PROFESSIONAL LAW CORPORATION (AV)

Wells Fargo Building, 350 West Colorado Boulevard Suite 400, 91105-1894
Telephone: 818-440-1111
Fax: 818-440-9456

George E. Moore

For full biographical listings, see the Martindale-Hubbell Law Directory

*REDDING,** Shasta Co.

TOCHER & BOECKMAN (AV)

1903 Park Marina Drive, P.O. Box 994565, 96099-4565
Telephone: 916-244-2525
Fax: 916-244-4941

MEMBERS OF FIRM

G. Neil Tocher
Bradley L. Boeckman

For full biographical listings, see the Martindale-Hubbell Law Directory

*SACRAMENTO,** Sacramento Co.

CAULFIELD, DAVIES & DONAHUE (AV)

3500 American River Drive, 1st Floor, 95864
Telephone: 916-487-7700
Fairfield, California Office: Fairfield West Plaza, 1455 Oliver Road, Suite 130.
Telephone: 707-426-0223.

MEMBERS OF FIRM

Richard Hyland Caulfield
Robert E. Davies
James R. Donahue
Bruce E. Leonard
Michael M. McKone
Douglas L. Smith

ASSOCIATES

David N. Tedesco
Matthew Paul Donahue
Brian C. Haydon
Paul R. Ramsey

For full biographical listings, see the Martindale-Hubbell Law Directory

Sacramento—Continued

DREYER, BABICH, BUCCOLA & CALLAHAM (AV)

715 University Avenue, 95825
Telephone: 916-920-2111
Fax: 916-920-5687

MEMBERS OF FIRM

Roger A. Dreyer
Joseph J. Babich
Robert A. Buccola
William C. Callaham

Craig C. Sheffer
Stephen F. Davids
Dianna L. Albini
John W. Jefferson
Leland J. Aiken

For full biographical listings, see the Martindale-Hubbell Law Directory

FRIEDMAN AND COLLARD, PROFESSIONAL CORPORATIONS (AV)

Suite 300, 7750 College Town Drive, 95826
Telephone: 916-381-9011
Telecopier: 916-381-7048

Morton L. Friedman
William H. Collard
Peter J. Stubbs
Douglas R. Thorn
C. Brooks Cutter
John Panneton
Samuel D. Hale
Eric J. Ratinoff

For full biographical listings, see the Martindale-Hubbell Law Directory

THOMAS F. LYTLE (AV)

Court Plaza Building, 901 H Street, Suite 609, 95814
Telephone: 916-442-0701
Fax: 916-442-0780

For full biographical listings, see the Martindale-Hubbell Law Directory

MASON & THOMAS (AV)

2151 River Plaza Drive, Suite 100, P.O. Box 868, 95812-0868
Telephone: 916-567-8211
Fax: 916-567-8212

MEMBERS OF FIRM

Stephen A. Mason
Bradley S. Thomas
Robert L. Moore

ASSOCIATES

Douglas W. Brown
Robert G. Kruse
David S. Yost
Patrick J. Hehir
Kevin L. Elder
Tina L. Izen

OF COUNSEL

John D. Stumbos, Jr.

For full biographical listings, see the Martindale-Hubbell Law Directory

MATHENY, POIDMORE & SEARS (AV)

2100 Northrop Avenue, Building 1200, P.O. Box 13711, 95853-4711
Telephone: 916-929-9271
Fax: 916-929-2458

MEMBERS OF FIRM

Henry G. Matheny (1933-1984)
Anthony J. Poidmore
Douglas A. Sears
Richard S. Linkert
James C. Damir
Michael A. Bishop
Ernest A. Long
Joann Georgallis
Kent M. Luckey

ASSOCIATES

Matthew C. Jaime
Jill P. Telfer
Robert B. Berrigan
Daryl M. Thomas
Ronald E. Enabnit
Cathy A. Reynolds
Byron D. Damiani, Jr.
Catherine Kennedy

OF COUNSEL

A. Laurel Bennett

LEGAL SUPPORT PERSONNEL

PARALEGALS

Karen D. Fisher
Fran Studer
Lynell Rae Steed
Jennifer Bachman
David Austin Boucher

For full biographical listings, see the Martindale-Hubbell Law Directory

*SAN BERNARDINO,** San Bernardino Co.

KASSEL & KASSEL (AV)

A Group of Independent Law Offices
Suite 207, Wells Fargo Bank Building, 334 West Third Street, 92401
Telephone: 909-884-6455
Fax: 909-884-8032

Philip Kassel
Gregory H. Kassel

References: Wells Fargo Bank; Bank of America; Bank of San Bernardino.

For full biographical listings, see the Martindale-Hubbell Law Directory

MAC LACHLAN, BURFORD & ARIAS, A LAW CORPORATION (AV)

560 East Hospitality Lane, Fourth Floor, 92408
Telephone: 909-885-4491
Fax: 909-888-6866
Rancho Cucamonga, California Office: 8280 Utica Avenue, Suite 200. 909-989-4481.
Palm Springs, California Office: 255 North El Cielo Road, Suite 470. 619-320-5761.
Victorville, California Office: 14011 Park Avenue, Suite 410. 619-243-7933.

Bruce D. Mac Lachlan
Ronald A. Burford
Joseph Arias
Michael W. Mugg
Dennis G. Popka
Leigh O. Harper (Resident, Palm Springs Office)
Clifford R. Cunningham (Resident, Rancho Cucamonga Office)
Dennis R. Stout
Sharon K. Burchett (Resident, Rancho Cucamonga Office)
Christopher D. Lockwood
Vernon C. Lauridsen (Resident, Rancho Cucamonga Office)
John G. Evans (Resident, Palm Springs Office)
Richard R. Hegner (Resident, Victorville Office)
Dennis J. Mahoney
Kathleen M. Keefe
Toni R. Fullerton
Mark R. Harris
Diana J. Carloni (Resident, Victorville Office)
Jean M. Landry
Frank M. Loo

Representative Clients: Aetna Life & Casualty; Automobile Club of Southern California; California State Automobile Association; City of San Bernardino; Reliance Insurance; Republic Insurance; Southern Pacific Transportation Co.; State Farm Fire and Casualty Co.; State Farm Mutual Automobile Insurance Co.; County of San Bernardino.

For full biographical listings, see the Martindale-Hubbell Law Directory

WILLIAM D. SHAPIRO (AV)

432 North Arrowhead Avenue, 92401
Telephone: 909-888-0102
Fax: 909-884-1767

For full biographical listings, see the Martindale-Hubbell Law Directory

RONALD G. SKIPPER (AV)

Suite 305, First American Title Building, 323 West Court Street, 92401
Telephone: 909-888-5791
Fax: 909-888-5794

Representative Clients: California Teachers Assn.; Hanniger and White Insurance; Art Scholl Aviation, Inc.; San Bernardino Teachers Assn.

For full biographical listings, see the Martindale-Hubbell Law Directory

*SAN DIEGO,** San Diego Co.

GEORGE P. ANDREOS A PROFESSIONAL LAW CORPORATION (AV)

Suite 1400 First National Bank Building, 401 West "A" Street, 92101
Telephone: 619-233-1077
Fax: 619-236-1518

George P. Andreos

For full biographical listings, see the Martindale-Hubbell Law Directory

BOUDREAU & TRENTACOSTA, A PROFESSIONAL LAW CORPORATION (AV)

401 West "A" Street, Suite 1850, 92101-9773
Telephone: 619-238-1553
Fax: 619-238-8181

Steven M. Boudreau
Robert J. Trentacosta

Jon R. Williams

For full biographical listings, see the Martindale-Hubbell Law Directory

CASEY, GERRY, CASEY, WESTBROOK, REED & SCHENK (AV)

A Partnership including Professional Law Corporations
110 Laurel Street, 92101
Telephone: 619-238-1811
Fax: 619-544-9232

MEMBERS OF FIRM

David S. Casey (A Professional Law Corporation)
Richard F. Gerry (A Professional Law Corporation)
David S. Casey, Jr.
T. Michael Reed
Frederick Schenk

ASSOCIATES

Robert J. Francavilla
Gayle Meryl Blatt
Thomas D. Penfield
Michael P. Montgomery
Suzanne C. Etpison
Bonnie E. Kane

Reference: San Diego Trust & Savings Bank.

For full biographical listings, see the Martindale-Hubbell Law Directory

San Diego—Continued

DOUGHERTY & HILDRE (AV)

2550 Fifth Avenue, Suite 600, 92103-5624
Telephone: 619-232-9131
Telefax: 619-232-7317

William O. Dougherty
Donald F. Hildre
Daniel H. Cargnelutti
Fred M. Dudek
Mona H. Freedman

For full biographical listings, see the Martindale-Hubbell Law Directory

HAASIS, POPE & CORRELL, A PROFESSIONAL CORPORATION (AV)

550 West "C" Street, 9th Floor, 92101-3509
Telephone: 619-236-9933
Fax: 619-236-8961
Voice Mail: 619-236-8955

Steven R. Haasis
A. Mark Pope
Harvey C. Berger
Denis Long

Michael J. Wijas
Nelson J. Goodin
Steven B. Bitter

Representative Clients: Aetna Insurance Co.; American States Insurance Co.; Chubb-Pacific; Great American West; Maryland Casualty; Ohio Casualty Co.; Scottsdale Insurance Co.; St. Paul Fire & Marine Insurance Co.; State Farm Fire and Casualty; United States Automobile Association.

For full biographical listings, see the Martindale-Hubbell Law Directory

MCCLELLAN & ASSOCIATES, A PROFESSIONAL CORPORATION (AV)

1144 State Street, 92101
Telephone: 619-231-0505
Fax: 619-544-0540

Craig R. McClellan

LaMar B. Brown
Andrew Phillip Greenfield

For full biographical listings, see the Martindale-Hubbell Law Directory

OLINS, FOERSTER & HAYES (AV)

A Partnership including Professional Corporations
2214 Second Avenue, 92101
Telephone: 619-238-1601
Fax: 619-238-1613

MEMBERS OF FIRM

Douglas F. Olins (A P.C.)
Barrett J. Foerster (A P.C.)
Dennis J. Hayes

ASSOCIATE

Julia Houchin Guroff

For full biographical listings, see the Martindale-Hubbell Law Directory

*SAN FRANCISCO,** San Francisco Co.

BOSTWICK & TEHIN (AV)

A Partnership including Professional Corporations
Bank of America Center, 555 California Street, 33rd Floor, 94104-1609
Telephone: 415-421-5500
Fax: 415-421-8144
Honolulu, Hawaii Office: Suite 900, 333 Queen Street.
Telephone: 808-536-7771.

MEMBERS OF FIRM

James S. Bostwick (Professional Corporation)
Nikolai Tehin (Professional Corporation)
Pamela J. Stevens

ASSOCIATES

James J. O'Donnell
Sara A. Smith
Baron J. Drexel

For full biographical listings, see the Martindale-Hubbell Law Directory

CARTWRIGHT, SLOBODIN, BOKELMAN, BOROWSKY, WARTNICK, MOORE & HARRIS, INC. (AV)

101 California Street, Suite 2600, 94111
Telephone: 415-433-0440
Telecopier: 415-391-5845

(See Next Column)

Robert E. Cartwright (1925-1988)
Jack L. Slobodin
Robert U. Bokelman
Philip Borowsky
Harry F. Wartnick
Michael B. Moore
Lee S. Harris
Robert E. Cartwright, Jr.
Mary E. Alexander
Stephen M. Tigerman
Madelyn J. Chaber
Steven M. Harowitz
Jani Iwamoto
Jan A. Gruen

Dennis Kruszynski
Richard Kirk Cannon
Anglia Benjamin-Dorward
Christopher M. Windle
Iris W. Fein
Audrey A. Smith
Richard M. Lebedeff
Steven M. Kesten
Niromi L. Wijewantha
Stephen J. Akerley
Brian P. Ring
Koorosh Afshari
Lucy Bedolla Ansel
Paul McDonald Myers

For full biographical listings, see the Martindale-Hubbell Law Directory

JOHN GARDENAL A PROFESSIONAL CORPORATION (AV)

Suite 800 Cathedral Hill Office Building, 1255 Post Street, 94109
Telephone: 415-771-2700
FAX: 415-771-2072

John Gardenal

For full biographical listings, see the Martindale-Hubbell Law Directory

ROBERT A. HARLEM, INC. & ASSOCIATES A PROFESSIONAL CORPORATION (AV)

120 Montgomery Street, Suite 2410, 94104
Telephone: 415-981-1801
Fax: 415-981-5815

Robert A. Harlem

B. Mark Fong

OF COUNSEL

Patricia Knight
Jack Miller

For full biographical listings, see the Martindale-Hubbell Law Directory

MOLLIGAN, COX & MOYER, A PROFESSIONAL CORPORATION (AV)

703 Market Street, Suite 1800, 94103
Telephone: 415-543-9464
Fax: 415-777-1828

Ingemar E. Hoberg (1903-1971)
John H. Finger (1913-1991)
Phillip E. Brown (Retired)
Peter N. Molligan
Stephen T. Cox
David W. Moyer

John C. Hentschel
Guy D. Loranger
Nicholas J. Piediscazzi

OF COUNSEL

Kenneth W. Rosenthal
Barbara A. Zuras

For full biographical listings, see the Martindale-Hubbell Law Directory

M. GERALD SCHWARTZBACH (AV)

901 Market Street, Suite 230, 94103
Telephone: 415-777-3828
Fax: 415-777-3584

For full biographical listings, see the Martindale-Hubbell Law Directory

WALKER & DURHAM (AV)

50 Francisco Street, Suite 160, 94133
Telephone: 415-986-3339
Fax: 415-986-1618

Walter H. Walker, III
Dane J. Durham

ASSOCIATE

Richard J. Ryan

For full biographical listings, see the Martindale-Hubbell Law Directory

WALKUP, MELODIA, KELLY & ECHEVERRIA, A PROFESSIONAL CORPORATION (AV)

30th Floor, 650 California Street, 94108
Telephone: 415-981-7210
Fax: 415-391-6965

Bruce Walkup
Paul V. Melodia
Daniel J. Kelly
John Echeverria
Richard B. Goethals, Jr.
Ronald H. Wecht
Michael A. Kelly
Kevin L. Domecus
Jeffrey P. Holl
Daniel Dell'Osso

(See Next Column)

WALKUP, MELODIA, KELLY & ECHEVERRIA A PROFESSIONAL CORPORATION—*Continued*

Mary E. Elliot
Richard H. Schoenberger
Cynthia F. Newton
Ann M. Richardson
Erik Brunkal
Michael J. Recupero

OF COUNSEL

John D. Link
Wesley Sokolosky

Reference: Bank of California, San Francisco Main Office, 400 California Street, San Francisco, Calif. 94104.

For full biographical listings, see the Martindale-Hubbell Law Directory

*SAN JOSE,** Santa Clara Co.

THE ALEXANDER LAW FIRM (AV)

55 South Market Street, Suite 1080, 95113
Telephone: 408-289-1776
Fax: 408-287-1776
Cincinnati, Ohio Office: 1300 Mercantile Library Building, 414 Walnut Street.
Telephone: 513-723-1776.
Fax: 513-421-1776.

Richard Alexander

ASSOCIATES

Mark P. Rapazzini
Jeffrey W. Rickard
Michael T. Alexander (Resident, Cincinnati, Ohio Office)
M. Elizabeth Graham
Jotham S. Stein

For full biographical listings, see the Martindale-Hubbell Law Directory

THE BOCCARDO LAW FIRM (AV)

Eleventh Floor, 111 West St. John Street, 95115
Telephone: 408-298-5678
Fax: 408-298-7503

MEMBERS OF FIRM

James F. Boccardo
John W. McDonald
Brian N. Lawther
John C. Stein
Richard L. Bowers
Russell L. Moore, Jr.

ASSOCIATES

Stephen Foster
David P. Moyles
Byron C. Foster
Victor F. Stefan
Robert W. Thayer
G. Matthew Fick
Charles A. Browning
Diego F. MacWilliam
Stephen A. Roberts

For full biographical listings, see the Martindale-Hubbell Law Directory

JAN CHAMPION (AV)

4 North Second Street, Suite 860, 95113
Telephone: 408-286-5550
Fax: 408-286-5597

For full biographical listings, see the Martindale-Hubbell Law Directory

COLLINS & SCHLOTHAUER (AV)

An Association of Attorneys including a Professional Corporation
60 South Market Street, Suite 1100, 95113-2369
Telephone: 408-298-5161
Fax: 408-297-5766

Mark Scott Collins (Inc.)
Steven J. Plas
David N. Poll
Linda L. Duiven
Michael P. Dunn
Jovita Prestoza

Representative Clients: Unigard Insurance; Farmers Insurance Co.; Fire Insurance Exchange; National American Insurance Co.; American Hardware Mutual Insurance; ABAG (Association of Bay Area Governmental Entities).

For full biographical listings, see the Martindale-Hubbell Law Directory

HAWKINS, BLICK & FITZPATRICK (AV)

96 North Third Street, Suite 300, 95112
Telephone: 408-280-7111
Fax: 408-292-7868
Palo Alto, California Office: 418 Florence Street.
Telephone: 415-321-5656.
Fax: 415-326-9636.

MEMBERS OF FIRM

Charles F. Hawkins
Stephen L. Blick
Michael J. Fitzpatrick

For full biographical listings, see the Martindale-Hubbell Law Directory

LICCARDO, ROSSI, STURGES & MCNEIL, A PROFESSIONAL LAW CORPORATION (AV)

1960 The Alameda, Suite 200, 95126
Telephone: 408-244-4570
Fax: 408-244-3294
Oakland, California Office: 1999 Harrison, Suite 1300.
Telephone: 415-834-2206.
Fax: 415-832-4432.

Salvador A. Liccardo
Ronald R. Rossi
Robert S. Sturges
R. Donald McNeil
David M. Hamerslough
Susan R. Reischl
Craig Needham
Gregory D. Hull
Martha Louise Caron
Cynthia L. Chase
Dann B. Jones
Laura Liccardo

Robert C. Colyar
William J. Purdy, III
Jeffery Lopez
Peter N. Brewer
Wes Wagnon
Richard B. Gullen
Deborah T. Bjonerud
Paul Salvatore Liccardo

For full biographical listings, see the Martindale-Hubbell Law Directory

DAVID MALNICK A PROFESSIONAL CORPORATION (AV)

10 Almaden Boulevard Tenth Floor, 95113-2233
Telephone: 408-292-5900
Fax: 408-292-5995

David E. Malnick

LEGAL SUPPORT PERSONNEL

Barbara Miller

For full biographical listings, see the Martindale-Hubbell Law Directory

RUOCCO, SAUCEDO & CORSIGLIA, A LAW CORPORATION (AV)

RiverPark Towers, Suite 600, 333 West San Carlos Street, 95110
Telephone: 408-289-1417
Fax: 408-289-8127

Norman W. Saucedo
Bradley M. Corsiglia

For full biographical listings, see the Martindale-Hubbell Law Directory

SHEA & SHEA, A PROFESSIONAL LAW CORPORATION (AV)

The James Square Building, 255 North Market Street, Suite 190, 95110
Telephone: 408-292-2434
Fax: 408-292-1264

Michael M. Shea
Michael M. Shea, Jr.

Beth C. Watkins

For full biographical listings, see the Martindale-Hubbell Law Directory

SAN MARINO, Los Angeles Co.

JACK K. CONWAY (AV)

2460 Huntington Drive, 91108-2643
Telephone: 818-285-4333
Fax: 818-285-1526

For full biographical listings, see the Martindale-Hubbell Law Directory

SAN MATEO, San Mateo Co.

ANDERLINI, GUHEEN, FINKELSTEIN, EMERICK & MCSWEENEY, A PROFESSIONAL CORPORATION (AV)

400 South El Camino Real, Suite 700, 94402
Telephone: 415-348-0102
Fax: 415-348-0962

P. Terry Anderlini
John J. Guheen
David G. Finkelstein
Merrill G. Emerick
Brian J. McSweeney

A. James Scholz
John P. Antonakos
Paul J. Smoot
Jennifer Gustafson

OF COUNSEL

Daniel J. Monaco (Inc.)

A list of Representative Clients will be furnished upon request.

For full biographical listings, see the Martindale-Hubbell Law Directory

*SANTA ANA,** Orange Co.

LAW OFFICES OF WYLIE A. AITKEN A LAW CORPORATION (AV)

3 Imperial Promenade, Suite 800, P.O. Box 2555, 92707-0555
Telephone: 714-434-1424
Fax: 714-434-3600

Wylie A. Aitken

(See Next Column)

LAW OFFICES OF WYLIE A. AITKEN A LAW CORPORATION, *Santa Ana—Continued*

David P. Crandall
Richard A. Cohn
Darren O'Leary Aitken
Annee M. Della Donna

Reference: Bank of America/Costa Mesa.

For full biographical listings, see the Martindale-Hubbell Law Directory

HAIGHT, BROWN & BONESTEEL (AV)

A Partnership including Professional Corporations
Suite 900, 5 Hutton Centre Drive, 92707
Telephone: 714-754-1100
Telecopier: 714-754-0826
Santa Monica, California Office: 1620 26th Street, Suite 4000 North, P.O. Box 680.
Telephone: 310-449-6000.
Telecopier: 310-829-5117.
Telex: 705837.
Riverside, California Office: 3750 University Avenue, Suite 650.
Telephone: 909-341-8300.
Fax: 909-341-8309.

RESIDENT MEMBERS

Ronald C. Kline (A Professional Corporation)
Bruce L. Cleeland
Jay T. Thompson

ASSOCIATES

Paul N. Jacobs
Laura M. Knox (Resident)
Jeffrey S. Gerardo (Resident)

Counsel for: Orange County: Aetna Casualty and Surety Co.; Zurich-American Insurance Cos.; Industrial Indemnity Co.; Professional Liability Claims Managers; Maryland Casualty Insurance Co.; Royal Insurance Company of America.

For Complete List of Firm Personnel, See General Section

For full biographical listings, see the Martindale-Hubbell Law Directory

HUNT, COLAW & ADAMS, INC. (AV)

615 Civic Center Drive West, Suite 300, 92701
Telephone: 714-558-9000
Fax: 714-558-0152

Vernon W. Hunt, Jr.
Thierry Patrick Colaw
John C. Adams, III
Ralph G. Martinez

Reference: Wells Fargo Bank.

For full biographical listings, see the Martindale-Hubbell Law Directory

*SANTA CRUZ,** Santa Cruz Co.

ATCHISON, ANDERSON, HURLEY & BARISONE, A PROFESSIONAL CORPORATION (AV)

333 Church Street, 95060
Telephone: 408-423-8383
Fax: 408-423-9401
Salinas, California Office: 137 Central Avenue, Suite 6. 93901.
Telephone: 408-755-7833.
Fax: 408-753-0293.

Rodney R. Atchison
Neal R. Anderson (1947-1986)
Vincent P. Hurley
John G. Barisone

Justin B. Lighty
Mitchell A. Jackman
David Y. Imai
Anthony P. Condotti
Mary C. Logan

Counsel for: City of Santa Cruz.

For full biographical listings, see the Martindale-Hubbell Law Directory

DUNLAP, BURDICK AND McCORMACK, A PROFESSIONAL LAW CORPORATION (AV)

121 Jewell Street, 95060
Telephone: 408-426-7040
FAX: 408-426-1095

Michael E. Dunlap
Paul P. Burdick

OF COUNSEL

Sandra C. McCormack

For full biographical listings, see the Martindale-Hubbell Law Directory

SANTA MONICA, Los Angeles Co.

DICKSON, CARLSON & CAMPILLO (AV)

120 Broadway, Suite 300, P.O. Box 2122, 90407-2122
Telephone: 310-451-2273
Telecopier: 310-451-9071

(See Next Column)

Robert L. Dickson
Jeffery J. Carlson
Ralph A. Campillo
William B. Fitzgerald
Hall R. Marston
Debra E. Pole
Roxanne M. Wilson
David J. Fleming
George E. Berry
Charles R. Messer
Kathryn C. Grogman
Mark S. Geraghty
William A. Hanssen
Mario Horwitz
Frederick J. Ufkes
Aylene M. Geringer
Daniel D. Rodarte

Karen S. Bril
Mark C. Riedel
Stephen H. Turner
Brian A. Cardoza
Pamela J. Yates
Robert C. Bohner
Deborah A. Lee-Germain
Jean A. Hobart
Thomas M. Madruga
James K. Lee

For Complete List of Firm Personnel, See General Section

For full biographical listings, see the Martindale-Hubbell Law Directory

FOGEL, FELDMAN, OSTROV, RINGLER & KLEVENS, A LAW CORPORATION (AV)

1620 26th Street, Suite 100 South, 90404-4040
Telephone: 310-453-6711
Fax: 310-828-2191

Daniel Fogel (1923-1991)
Lester G. Ostrov
Larry R. Feldman
Joel N. Klevens
Robert M. Turner
Jerome L. Ringler
Richard L. Rosett
Jon H. Levenstein

Gerald J. Miller
Stephen D. Rothschild
Leighanne Lake
Thomas H. Peters

OF COUNSEL

Carol S. May

Reference: Republic Bank of California, Beverly Hills, California.

For full biographical listings, see the Martindale-Hubbell Law Directory

GREENE, BROILLET, TAYLOR & WHEELER (AV)

100 Wilshire Boulevard, 21st Floor, 90401
Telephone: 310-576-1200

Bruce A. Broillet
Browne Greene
John C. Taylor
Timothy J. Wheeler
Brian J. Panish

Frank J. O'Kane Jr.
Mark T. Quigley
Christine D. Spagnoli
Scott H. Carr
Geoffrey S. Wells
Adam K. Shea

For full biographical listings, see the Martindale-Hubbell Law Directory

HAIGHT, BROWN & BONESTEEL (AV)

A Partnership including Professional Corporations
1620 26th Street, Suite 4000 North, P.O. Box 680, 90404
Telephone: 310-449-6000
Telecopier: 310-829-5117
Telex: 705837
Santa Ana, California Office: Suite 900, 5 Hutton Centre Drive.
Telephone: 714-754-1100.
Telecopier: 714-754-0826.
Riverside, California Office: 3750 University Avenue, Suite 650.
Telephone: 909-341-8300.
Fax: 909-341-8309.
San Francisco, California Office: Suite 300, 201 Sansome Street.
Telephone: 415-986-7700.
Fax: 415-986-6945.

MEMBERS OF FIRM

William K. Koska (A Professional Corporation)
Peter Q. Ezzell (A Professional Corporation)
William G. Baumgaertner (A Professional Corporation)
Peter A. Dubrawski
J. R. Seashore
Kevin R. Crisp
Lee Marshall
Steven E. Moyer
Frank Kendo Berfield (Resident, San Francisco Office)
Kenneth G. Anderson
William O. Martin, Jr.

ASSOCIATES

Ted J. Duffy
David C. McGovern
Lisa K. Sepe
Alicia E. Taylor
Elizabeth A. Livesay
S. Christian Stouder
Michael J. Sipos
Nancy W. Carman
Michael H. Gottschlich
Stacey R. Konkoff

For Complete List of Firm Personnel, See General Section

For full biographical listings, see the Martindale-Hubbell Law Directory

Santa Monica—Continued

J. MICHAEL KELLY & ASSOCIATES A PROFESSIONAL CORPORATION (AV)

201 Santa Monica Boulevard, 5th Floor, 90401
Telephone: 310-393-0236

J. Michael Kelly

For full biographical listings, see the Martindale-Hubbell Law Directory

*SANTA ROSA,** Sonoma Co.

BELDEN, ABBEY, WEITZENBERG & KELLY, A PROFESSIONAL CORPORATION (AV)

1105 North Dutton Avenue, P.O. Box 1566, 95402
Telephone: 707-542-5050
Telecopier: 707-542-2589

W. Barton Weitzenberg

Wayne R. Wolski

Representative Clients: Exchange Bank of Santa Rosa; Westamerica Bank; North Bay Title Co.; Northwestern Title Security Co.; Geyser Peak Winery; Arrowood Vineyards & Winery; Hansel Ford; Santa Rosa City School District.

For Complete List of Firm Personnel, See General Section

For full biographical listings, see the Martindale-Hubbell Law Directory

SAUSALITO, Marin Co.

WILLIAM C. GORDON A PROFESSIONAL CORPORATION (AV)

116 Caldonia Street, 94965
Telephone: 415-331-0200
Fax: 415-331-0252

William C. Gordon

For full biographical listings, see the Martindale-Hubbell Law Directory

SHERMAN OAKS, Los Angeles Co.

RICHARD B. WOLFE (AV)

Suite 712, 15233 Ventura Boulevard, 91403
Telephone: 818-501-1414; 213-872-3224

TORRANCE, Los Angeles Co.

AGNEW & BRUSAVICH (AV)

20355 Hawthorne Boulevard, 90503
Telephone: 310-793-1400
Facsimile: 310-793-1499

Gerald E. Agnew, Jr. — Bruce M. Brusavich

ASSOCIATES

Kevin N. Donnelly — Susan E. Hargrove
Fred M. Adelman — Joyce A. Bellucci

LEGAL SUPPORT PERSONNEL

PARALEGALS

Lisa M. O'Brien — Ivy J. Kee

For full biographical listings, see the Martindale-Hubbell Law Directory

OWEN A. SILVERMAN, INC. A PROFESSIONAL CORPORATION (AV)

23224 Crenshaw Boulevard, 90505
Telephone: 310-530-3990; 213-775-8421
Fax: 310-530-5523
Tempe, Arizona Office: 310 East Bluebell Lane.
Telephone: 602-947-7834.
Telephone: 602-941-3755.

Owen A. Silverman

Steven R. Berardino — Joseph T. Threston, III
Earl M. Hyman — Samuel K. Silverman

Reference: Pacific Heritage Bank, Torrance.

For full biographical listings, see the Martindale-Hubbell Law Directory

*VENTURA,** Ventura Co.

LAW OFFICES OF FREDERICK H. BYSSHE, JR. (AV)

10 South California Street, 93001
Telephone: 805-648-3224
Fax: 805-653-0267

Terence Geoghegan

For full biographical listings, see the Martindale-Hubbell Law Directory

ELLISON, HINKLE & BAYER, A PROFESSIONAL LAW CORPORATION (AV)

5550 Telegraph Road, P.O. Box 6130, 93006
Telephone: 805-656-4223
Fax: 805-656-4924

David R. Ellison — Thomas L. Hinkle
Robert J. Bayer

For full biographical listings, see the Martindale-Hubbell Law Directory

COLORADO

ARVADA, Jefferson Co.

THE ELLIOTT LAW OFFICES (AV)

7884 Ralston Road, 80002
Telephone: 303-424-5319
Fax: 303-424-6130

James E. Elliott, Jr. — Mark D. Elliott

LEGAL SUPPORT PERSONNEL

James R. Elliott

Reference: Vectra Bank of Lakewood, N.A.

For full biographical listings, see the Martindale-Hubbell Law Directory

*ASPEN,** Pitkin Co.

FREEMAN & JENNER, P.C. (AV⊤)

215 South Monarch Street, Suite 202, 81611
Telephone: 303-925-3400
FAX: 303-925-4043
Bethesda, Maryland Office: 3 Bethesda Metro Center, Suite 1410.
Telephone: 301-907-7747.
FAX: 301-907-9877.
Washington, D.C. Office: 1000 16th Street, N.W., Suite 300.
Telephone: 301-907-7747.

Martin H. Freeman

AURORA, Arapahoe & Adams Cos.

LEWIS W. DYMOND, JR. A PROFESSIONAL CORPORATION (AV)

Suite 212, 13900 East Harvard Avenue, 80014
Telephone: 303-695-8700
Fax: 303-696-0923

Lewis W. Dymond, Jr.

Reference: Norwest Bank of Aurora-City Center.

For full biographical listings, see the Martindale-Hubbell Law Directory

*BOULDER,** Boulder Co.

COOK & LEE, P.C. (AV)

Canyonside Office Park, 100 Arapahoe Avenue, Suite 9, 80302-5862
Telephone: 303-444-9700
Fax: 303-444-9691
Denver, Colorado Office: Sherman Street Plaza, 1888 Sherman Street, Suite 375, 80203-1158.
Telephone: 303-831-8008.

Stephen H. Cook — Larry D. Lee

Patti L. Holt — Daniel E. Bronstein

For full biographical listings, see the Martindale-Hubbell Law Directory

McCORMICK AND CHRISTOPH (AV)

1406 Pearl Street, Suite 200, 80302
Telephone: 303-443-2281
Fax: 303-443-2862

MEMBERS OF FIRM

G. Paul McCormick — James R. Christoph

For full biographical listings, see the Martindale-Hubbell Law Directory

MILLER, HALE AND HARRISON (AV)

2305 Broadway, 80304
Telephone: 303-449-2830
Fax: 303-449-2198

MEMBERS OF FIRM

Robert Bruce Miller — Daniel C. Hale
David B. Harrison

ASSOCIATE

Joan Clifford

Reference: Norwest Bank.

For full biographical listings, see the Martindale-Hubbell Law Directory

Boulder—Continued

PURVIS, GRAY, SCHUETZE & GORDON (AV)

The Exeter Building, Suite 501, 1050 Walnut Street, 80302
Telephone: 303-442-3366
Fax: 303-440-3688
Denver, Colorado Office: 303 East 17th Avenue, Suite 700.
Telephone: 303-860-1888.

MEMBERS OF FIRM

William R. Gray | Robert A. Schuetze
John A. Purvis | Glen F. Gordon

For full biographical listings, see the Martindale-Hubbell Law Directory

WILLIAMS & TRINE, P.C. (AV)

1435 Arapahoe Avenue, 80302-6390
Telephone: 303-442-0173
Fax: 303-443-7677

William A. Trine | J. Conard Metcalf
Joel H. Greenstein (1933-1984) | Mari C. Bush
Michael A. Patrick

OF COUNSEL

Charles E. Williams

Reference: Norwest Bank of Boulder.

For full biographical listings, see the Martindale-Hubbell Law Directory

*COLORADO SPRINGS,** El Paso Co.

CROSS, GADDIS, KIN, HERD & KELLY, P.C. (AV)

118 South Wahsatch, 80903
Telephone: 719-471-3848
Fax: 719-471-0317

Thomas R. Cross | David L. Quicksall (1950-1991)
Larry R. Gaddis | Thomas J. Herd
James W. Kin | Debra L. Kelly

OF COUNSEL

James B. Turner

Reference: Norwest Bank of Colorado Springs.

For full biographical listings, see the Martindale-Hubbell Law Directory

MELAT, PRESSMAN, EZELL & HIGBIE (AV)

711 South Tejon Street, 80903-4041
Telephone: 719-475-0304
Fax: 719-475-0242

MEMBERS OF FIRM

Justin R. Melat | E. Steven Ezell
Glenn S. Pressman | Alanson Higbie

ASSOCIATES

Robert J. Frank | Rebecca A. Lorenz

OF COUNSEL

Bernard R. Baker

References: Colorado Springs National Bank; Colorado Bank-Exchange.

RETHERFORD, MULLEN, JOHNSON & BRUCE (AV)

A Partnership including Professional Corporations
415 South Sahwatch, P.O. Box 1580, 80901
Telephone: 719-475-2014
Fax: 719-630-1267
Pueblo, Colorado Office: Suite 510, 201 West 8th Street, 81003.
Telephone: 719-543-7181.
Fax: 719-543-5650.

MEMBERS OF FIRM

Jerry A. Retherford | Anthony A. Johnson (P.C.)
J. Stephen Mullen (P.C.) | Thomas J. Barton (P.C.)

For Complete List of Firm Personnel, See General Section

For full biographical listings, see the Martindale-Hubbell Law Directory

SEARS, ANDERSON & SWANSON, P.C. (AV)

The Holly Sugar Building, Suite 1250 2 North Cascade Avenue, 80903
Telephone: 719-471-1984
FAX: 719-577-4356
Denver, Colorado Office: 3900 East Mexico Avenue, Denver Centerpoint, Suite 810.
Telephone: 303-759-1963.
Fax: 303-759-2760.

Lance M. Sears | Victoria C. Swanson
Leland P. Anderson (Resident, Denver, Colorado)

(See Next Column)

OF COUNSEL

Stephanie H. Yukawa

Reference: Norwest Bank of Colorado Springs, N.A.

For full biographical listings, see the Martindale-Hubbell Law Directory

J. GREGORY WALTA, P.C. (AV)

Suite 101 - Cascade Station, 620 South Cascade Avenue, 80903-4039
Telephone: 719-578-8888
FAX: 719-578-8931

J. Gregory Walta | Celeste Lisanne Crizer Gerber

Reference: Norwest Bank of Colorado Springs.

For full biographical listings, see the Martindale-Hubbell Law Directory

THE WILLS LAW FIRM (AV)

Holly Sugar Building, 2 North Cascade Avenue, Suite 1000, 80903-1651
Telephone: 719-633-8500
Telecopier: 719-471-7750

MEMBERS OF FIRM

Lee R. Wills | Wm. Andrew Wills, II

For full biographical listings, see the Martindale-Hubbell Law Directory

*DENVER,** Denver Co.

BRAGG & BAKER, P.C. (AV)

Dominion Plaza, North Tower, Suite 1700N, 600 17th Street, 80202
Telephone: 303-571-4030
Fax: 303-893-9146

Douglas E. Bragg | John T. Baker

Richard E. Werner

OF COUNSEL

John W. Hornbeck

For full biographical listings, see the Martindale-Hubbell Law Directory

COOK & LEE, P.C. (AV)

Sherman Street Plaza, 1888 Sherman Street, Suite 375, 80203-1158
Telephone: 303-831-8008
Fax: 303-860-1844
Boulder, Colorado Office: Canyonside Office Park, 100 Arapahoe Avenue, Suite 9, 80302-5862.
Telephone: 303-444-9700.
Fax: 303-444-9691.

Stephen H. Cook | Larry D. Lee

Patti L. Holt | Daniel E. Bronstein

For full biographical listings, see the Martindale-Hubbell Law Directory

FEDER, MORRIS, TAMBLYN & GOLDSTEIN, P.C. (AV)

150 Blake Street Building, 1441 Eighteenth Street, 80202
Telephone: 303-292-1441
FAX: 303-292-1126

Harold A. Feder | Leonard M. Goldstein

Reference: Guaranty Bank & Trust Co., Denver, Colorado.

For full biographical listings, see the Martindale-Hubbell Law Directory

MYERS, HOPPIN, BRADLEY AND DEVITT, P.C. (AV)

Suite 420, 4704 Harlan Street, 80212
Telephone: 303-433-8527
Fax: 303-433-8219

Frederick J. Myers | Jon T. Bradley
Charles T. Hoppin | Jerald J. Devitt

Gregg W. Fraser

OF COUNSEL

Kent E. Hanson

Reference: Bank One Lakeside Banking Center.

For full biographical listings, see the Martindale-Hubbell Law Directory

PURVIS, GRAY, SCHUETZE & GORDON (AV)

303 East 17th Avenue, Suite 700, 80203
Telephone: 303-860-1888
Boulder, Colorado Office: The Exeter Building, Suite 501, 1050 Walnut Street.
Telephone: 303-442-3366.
Fax: 303-440-3688.

(See Next Column)

PURVIS, GRAY, SCHUETZE & GORDON—*Continued*

MEMBERS OF FIRM

William R. Gray — Robert A. Schuetze
John A. Purvis — Glen F. Gordon

For full biographical listings, see the Martindale-Hubbell Law Directory

SCHADEN, LAMPERT & LAMPERT (AV)

1610 Emerson Street, 80218-1412
Telephone: 303-832-2771
Broomfield, Colorado Office: 11870 Airport Way, 80021.
Telephone: 303-465-3663.
Birmingham, Michigan Office: Schaden, Wilson and Katzman. 800 N. Woodward Avenue, Suite 102.
Telephone: 313-258-4800.

MEMBERS OF FIRM

Richard F. Schaden (Resident, Broomfield Office) — Bruce A. Lampert
Brian J. Lampert

ASSOCIATES

Kathleen M. Schaden (Resident, Boulder Office) — Susanna L. Meissner-Cutler
Patricia M. Jarzobski

For full biographical listings, see the Martindale-Hubbell Law Directory

SPRINGER & STEINBERG, A PROFESSIONAL CORPORATION (AV)

Suite 1500, 1600 Broadway, 80202
Telephone: 303-861-2800
Fax: 303-832-7116

Jeffrey A. Springer — Harvey A. Steinberg

Reference: Norwest Bank of Denver.

For full biographical listings, see the Martindale-Hubbell Law Directory

ENGLEWOOD, Arapahoe Co.

SALMON, GODSMAN & NICHOLSON, PROFESSIONAL CORPORATION (AV)

Salmon Law Building, (I-25 at East Belleview) 7450 East Progress Place, 80111
Telephone: 303-771-9900
Toll Free in Colorado: 1-800-547-9055
Fax: 303-773-6843
Breckenridge, Colorado Office: Briar Rose House, 213 Briar Rose Lane.
Telephone: 1-800-547-9055

John G. Salmon — William P. Godsman
P. Randolph Nicholson

Francine R. Salazar — Penelope Clor

For full biographical listings, see the Martindale-Hubbell Law Directory

THOMAS J. TOMAZIN, P.C. (AV)

Suite 200, 5655 South Yosemite, 80111
Telephone: 303-771-1900
FAX: 303-793-0923

Thomas J. Tomazin

Reference: Key Bank.

For full biographical listings, see the Martindale-Hubbell Law Directory

LAKEWOOD, Jefferson Co.

BUSCH AND COHEN, P.C. (AV)

Suite A-130, 12600 West Colfax Avenue, 80215
Telephone: 303-232-0362
Fax: 303-232-1125

Robert G. Busch — Michael A. Cohen

For full biographical listings, see the Martindale-Hubbell Law Directory

PLAUT LIPSTEIN MORTIMER PC (AV)

Suite C-400, 12600 West Colfax Avenue, 80215
Telephone: 303-232-5151
Fax: 303-232-5161
Denver, Colorado Office: 2750 Lincoln Center. 1660 Lincoln Street, 80264.
Telephone: 303-232-5154.

Frank Plaut — Evan S. Lipstein
Charles E. Mortimer, Jr.

For full biographical listings, see the Martindale-Hubbell Law Directory

POLIDORI, GEROME, FRANKLIN AND JACOBSON (AV)

Suite 300, 550 South Wadsworth Boulevard, 80226
Telephone: 303-936-3300
Fax: 303-936-0125

(See Next Column)

Gary L. Polidori — Dennis J. Jacobson

For Complete List of Firm Personnel, See General Section

For full biographical listings, see the Martindale-Hubbell Law Directory

*LAMAR,** Prowers Co.

JOHN GEHLHAUSEN, P.C. (AV)

200 South Fifth Street, Drawer 1079, 81052
Telephone: 719-336-9071
Fax: Available Upon Request

John Gehlhausen

Darla Scranton Specht

For full biographical listings, see the Martindale-Hubbell Law Directory

CONNECTICUT

*BRIDGEPORT,** Fairfield Co.

MEEHAN & MEEHAN (AV)

76 Lyon Terrace, 06604
Telephone: 203-333-1888
Fax: 203-331-0107

Richard T. Meehan, Sr. — Richard T. Meehan, Jr.
Edward J. Gavin

For full biographical listings, see the Martindale-Hubbell Law Directory

WILLIAMS, COONEY & SHEEHY (AV)

One Lafayette Circle, 06604
Telephone: 203-331-0888
Telecopier: 203-331-0896

MEMBERS OF FIRM

Ronald D. Williams
Robert J. Cooney
Edward Maum Sheehy
Peter D. Clark
Peter J. Dauk
Dion W. Moore
Ronald D. Williams, Jr.
Francis A. Smith, Jr. (1951-1989)

Lawrence F. Reilly — Michael P. Bowler
Michael Cuff Deakin

Representative Clients: Aetna Life & Casualty Co.; Nationwide Insurance Co.; Connecticut Medical Insurance Co.; ; Zimmer Manufacturing Co.; Textron-Lycoming; The Stop & Shop Companies, Inc.; Shawmut Bank Connecticut, N.A.; Allied Van Lines, Inc.; Podiatary Insurance Company of America; Town of Easton, Conn.

For full biographical listings, see the Martindale-Hubbell Law Directory

CHESHIRE, New Haven Co.

DODD, LESSACK, RANANDO & DALTON, L.L.C. (AV)

700 West Johnson Avenue, Suite 305, 06410
Telephone: 203-272-1883
FAX: 203-272-2077

MEMBERS OF FIRM

Edward T. Dodd, Jr. — Paul S. Ranando
Ross T. Lessack — Mary-Margaret Dalton
Charles F. Senich

Jack Senich

For full biographical listings, see the Martindale-Hubbell Law Directory

GROTON, New London Co.

O'BRIEN, SHAFNER, STUART, KELLY & MORRIS, P.C. (AV)

475 Bridge Street, P.O. Drawer 929, 06340
Telephone: 203-445-2463
Fax: 203-445-4539
Norwich, Connecticut Office: 2 Courthouse Square.
Telephone: 203-889-3855.
Fax: 203-886-6352.

John C. O'Brien
Matthew Shafner
Peter F. Stuart
Carolyn P. Kelly
Granville R. Morris
Frank N. Eppinger
Mark E. Block (Resident at Norwich Office)
Raymond T. Trebisacci
Mark W. Oberlatz
Lloyd L. Langhammer
Susan B. Pochal

(See Next Column)

O'BRIEN, SHAFNER, STUART, KELLY & MORRIS P.C., *Groton—Continued*

Nathan J. Shafner
Richard J. Pascal
Daniel R. Cunningham
Amy M. Stone
Thomas W. Teixeira, II
Eric M. Janney
Stephen M. Reck

For full biographical listings, see the Martindale-Hubbell Law Directory

*HARTFORD,** Hartford Co.

JACKSON, O'KEEFE AND PHELAN (AV)

36 Russ Street, 06106-1571
Telephone: 203-278-4040
Fax: 203-527-2500
West Hartford, Connecticut Office: 62 LaSalle Road.
Telephone: 203-521-7500.
Fax: 203-561-5399.
Bethlehem, Connecticut Office: 423 Munger Lane.
Telephone: 203-266-5255.

MEMBERS OF FIRM

Jay W. Jackson
Andrew J. O'Keefe
Denise Martino Phelan
Matthew J. O'Keefe
Peter K. O'Keefe
Philip R. Dunn, Jr.
Michael J. Walsh
Anna M. Carbonaro
Denise Rodosevich

OF COUNSEL

Maureen Sullivan Dinnan

Representative Clients: Aetna Casualty & Surety Co.; ITT Hartford; Liberty Mutual Insurance Co.; Connecticut Medical Insurance Co.

For full biographical listings, see the Martindale-Hubbell Law Directory

KENNY, BRIMMER, MELLEY & MAHONEY (AV)

5 Grand Street, 06106
Telephone: 203-527-4226
FAX: 203-527-0214

Joseph P. Kenny (1920-1993)

MEMBERS OF FIRM

Leslie R. Brimmer
William J. Melley, III
Richard C. Mahoney

ASSOCIATES

Anita M. Varunes
Dennis F. McCarthy
Maurice M. O'Shea
Beverly Johns

For full biographical listings, see the Martindale-Hubbell Law Directory

REGNIER, TAYLOR, CURRAN & EDDY (AV)

CityPlace, 06103-4402
Telephone: 203-249-9121
FAX: 203-527-4343

MEMBERS OF FIRM

J. Ronald Regnier (1906-1987)
Robert F. Taylor (1930-1994)
Edmund T. Curran
Ralph G. Eddy
Jack D. Miller

ASSOCIATES

Lawrence L. Connelli
A. Patrick Alcarez
Robert B. McLaughlin
Sandra L. Connelli
A. Alan Sheffy
Robert A. Byers
Jay F. Huntington
John D. Palermo
Frederick M. O'Brien
Keith Mccabe
Margaret H. Ralphs

Representative Clients: Atlantic Mutual Insurance Co.; Government Employees Insurance Co.; Hartford Accident & Indemnity Co.; Hartford Fire Insurance Co.; Pioneer Co-operative Fire; United Services Automobile Assn.

For full biographical listings, see the Martindale-Hubbell Law Directory

RISCASSI AND DAVIS, P.C. (AV)

131 Oak Street, P.O. Box 260550, 06126-0550
Telephone: 203-522-1196
FAX: 203-246-5847

Leon RisCassi (1908-1986)
William R. Davis

James D. Bartolini
Andrew S. Groher
Michael C. Jainchill
John J. Houlihan, Jr.
David W. Cooney
Eugene K. Swain
Kathryn Calibey
Douglas W. Hammond
Everett Howard Madin, Jr.
Paul M. Iannaccone

For full biographical listings, see the Martindale-Hubbell Law Directory

MILFORD, New Haven Co.

HURWITZ & SAGARIN, P.C. (AV)

147 North Broad Street, P.O. Box 112, 06460
Telephone: 203-877-8000
Fax: 203-878-9800

(See Next Column)

Lewis A. Hurwitz
J. Daniel Sagarin
Christine M. Gonillo
Elias A. Alexiades

For Complete List of Firm Personnel, See General Section

For full biographical listings, see the Martindale-Hubbell Law Directory

*NEW HAVEN,** New Haven Co.

JACOBS & JACOBS (AV)

555 Long Wharf Drive, Suite 13A, 06511
Telephone: 203-777-2300
Fax: 203-787-5628

MEMBERS OF FIRM

Israel J. Jacobs (1918-1963)
Stanley A. Jacobs
Bruce D. Jacobs
Irene Prosky Jacobs
Carol Wolven

Reference: Connecticut National Bank.

For full biographical listings, see the Martindale-Hubbell Law Directory

PAUL A. SCHOLDER ATTORNEY AT LAW, P.C. (AV)

2 Whitney Avenue, P.O. Box 1722, 06507
Telephone: 203-777-7218
Fax: 203-772-2672

Paul A. Scholder

John J. Morgan

References: Peoples Bank; Lafayette American Bank.

For full biographical listings, see the Martindale-Hubbell Law Directory

SHAY, SLOCUM & DEWEY (AV)

234 Church Street, P.O. Box 1921, 06509
Telephone: 203-772-3600
Fax: 203-787-4581

MEMBERS OF FIRM

Edward N. Shay
Shaun M. Slocum
Earl F. Dewey, II

ASSOCIATE

Kathryn J. Coassin

Representative Clients: Hartford Accident and Indemnity Co.; United Services Automobile Association; Commercial Union Insurance Co.; Atlantic Mutual Insurance Co.; Northbrook Insurance Co.; Safeco Insurance Co.; Andover Insurance Co.; National Interstate Transportation Insurance Specialists; First Financial Insurance Co.; Burlington Insurance Group.

For full biographical listings, see the Martindale-Hubbell Law Directory

LAW OFFICES OF JOHN R. WILLIAMS (AV)

51 Elm Street, 06510
Telephone: 203-562-9931
Fax: 203-776-9494

ASSOCIATES

Diane Polan
Katrena Engstrom
Norman A. Pattis
Denise A. Bailey-Garris

Reference: Founders Bank.

For full biographical listings, see the Martindale-Hubbell Law Directory

NEW LONDON, New London Co.

FAULKNER & BOYCE, P.C. (AV)

216 Broad Street, P.O. Box 66, 06320
Telephone: 203-442-9900
Fax: 203-443-6428

MEMBERS OF FIRM

Dale Patrick Faulkner
Thomas W. Boyce, Jr.
Humbert J. Polito, Jr.

ASSOCIATES

Lucia M. Mercurio
Michael J. Quinn
Jane Richardson
Nicholas W. Burlingham

Reference: Shawmut Bank Connecticut.

For full biographical listings, see the Martindale-Hubbell Law Directory

REARDON & NAZZARO, P.C. (AV)

160 Hempstead Street, Drawer 1430, 06320
Telephone: 203-442-0444
Telecopier: 203-444-6445

Robert I. Reardon, Jr.
John J. Nazzaro
Maryann Diaz

Angelo A. Ziotas
Stephen J. MacKinnon

(See Next Column)

REARDON & NAZZARO P.C.—*Continued*

LEGAL SUPPORT PERSONNEL

Bette B. Beam (Legal Administrator)
Carolyn B. Dickey (Paralegal)
Kelly G. MacDonald (Paralegal)
Jillene B. Mattern (Paralegal)

For full biographical listings, see the Martindale-Hubbell Law Directory

STAMFORD, Fairfield Co.

MORGAN P. AMES (AV)

1977 Shippan Avenue, 06902
Telephone: 203-324-3933

For full biographical listings, see the Martindale-Hubbell Law Directory

CASPER & DE TOLEDO (AV)

600 Summer Street, 06901-1418
Telephone: 203-325-8600
Fax: 203-323-5970

Stewart M. Casper
Victoria de Toledo

ASSOCIATES

Renée Mayerson Cannella
Daniel S. Fabricant

For full biographical listings, see the Martindale-Hubbell Law Directory

PIAZZA, MELMED & BERKOWITZ (AV)

112 Prospect Street, P.O. Box 15390, 06901
Telephone: 203-348-2465
FAX: 203-964-9509

MEMBERS OF FIRM

Anthony A. Piazza
Julian K. Melmed
Russell J. Berkowitz

Alan Scott Pickel
Wesley M. Malowitz

For full biographical listings, see the Martindale-Hubbell Law Directory

SILVER, GOLUB & TEITELL (AV)

184 Atlantic Street, P.O. Box 389, 06904
Telephone: 203-325-4491
FAX: 203-325-3769

MEMBERS OF FIRM

Richard A. Silver
David S. Golub
Ernest F. Teitell
Elaine T. Silver

John D. Josel
Mario DiNatale
Jonathan M. Levine
Marilyn J. Ramos
Jack Zaremski (Not admitted in CT)

For Complete List of Firm Personnel, See General Section

For full biographical listings, see the Martindale-Hubbell Law Directory

WOFSEY, ROSEN, KWESKIN & KURIANSKY (AV)

600 Summer Street, 06901
Telephone: 203-327-2300
FAX: 203-967-9273

MEMBERS OF FIRM

Abraham Wofsey (1915-1944)
Michael Wofsey (1927-1951)
David M. Rosen (1926-1967)
Julius B. Kuriansky (1910-1992)
Monroe Silverman
Emanuel Margolis
Howard C. Kaplan
Anthony R. Lorenzo
Edward M. Kweskin
David M. Cohen
Marshall Goldberg
Stephen A. Finn
Judith Rosenberg
Robert L. Teicher
Mark H. Henderson

Steven D. Grushkin

OF COUNSEL

Saul Kwartin
Sydney C. Kweskin (Retired)

ASSOCIATES

Brian Bandler
John J.L. Chober
Steven M. Frederick
Eric M. Higgins
James A. Lenes
Valerie E. Maze
Maurice K. Segall
Randall M. Skigen
Gregory J. Williams

Representative Clients: Benenson Realty; Cellular Information Systems, Inc.; Gateway Bank; Hartford Provision Company; Louis Dreyfus Corp.; Norwalk Federation of Teachers; Patient Care, Inc.; People's Bank; Ridgeway Shopping Center and Stamford Housing Authority.

For full biographical listings, see the Martindale-Hubbell Law Directory

STRATFORD, Fairfield Co.

COUSINS AND JOHNSON (AV)

2563 Main Street, 06497
Telephone: 203-386-1433
Fax: 203-386-9714

MEMBERS OF FIRM

Donald C. Cousins
Norma S. Johnson
Albert E. Desrosiers
Michael A. Wolak, III

ASSOCIATES

Steven H. Cousins
Andrew V. O'Shea

Approved Attorneys for: Chicago Title Insurance Co.; Lawyers Title Insurance Corp.

For full biographical listings, see the Martindale-Hubbell Law Directory

WALLINGFORD, New Haven Co.

GERALD E. FARRELL, P.C. (AV)

375 Center Street, P.O. Box 369, 06492
Telephone: 203-269-7756
Fax: 203-269-1927

Gerald E. Farrell

Gerald E. Farrell, Jr.
Ann Farrell Leslie
Brian J. Leslie

References: Dime Savings Bank of Wallingford; Shawmut Bank (Wallingford Office).

For full biographical listings, see the Martindale-Hubbell Law Directory

WATERBURY, New Haven Co.

TINLEY, NASTRI & RENEHAN (AV)

161 North Main Street, 06702
Telephone: 203-596-9030
Fax: 203-596-9036

Jeffrey J. Tinley
Robert Nastri, Jr.
Richard P. Renehan
Mary Piscatelli Brigham
William T. Blake, Jr.

Representative Clients: Center Capital Corporation; Citizens Fidelity Bank & Trust Co.; Gar-San Corporation; General Electric Capital Commercial Automotive Finance Inc.; Mahler Financial Group Inc.; Mobil Oil Corporation; St. Mary's Hospital; Teikyo Post University.

For full biographical listings, see the Martindale-Hubbell Law Directory

WESTPORT, Fairfield Co.

LAWRENCE W. KANAGA (AV)

830 Post Road East, 06880-5291
Telephone: 203-221-0696
Fax: 203-226-6866

For full biographical listings, see the Martindale-Hubbell Law Directory

LAW OFFICES OF PAUL J. PACIFICO (AV)

12 Avery Place, Second Floor, 06880
Telephone: 203-221-8066
Fax: 203-221-8076

LEGAL SUPPORT PERSONNEL

Karen L. Kosinski

For full biographical listings, see the Martindale-Hubbell Law Directory

RUTKIN AND EFFRON, P.C. (AV)

323 Riverside Avenue, P.O. Box 295, 06881
Telephone: 203-227-7301
Fax: 222-9295
New Haven, Connecticut Office: 201 Orange Street.
Telephone: 203-498-1887.
Fax: 203-772-0124.

Arnold H. Rutkin
Ellen J. Effron

Sarah S. Oldham

OF COUNSEL

Kathleen A. Hogan

For full biographical listings, see the Martindale-Hubbell Law Directory

DELAWARE

*WILMINGTON,** New Castle Co.

CASARINO, CHRISTMAN & SHALK (AV)

Suite 1220, 222 Delaware Avenue, P.O. Box 1276, 19899
Telephone: 302-594-4500
Telecopier: 302-594-4509

MEMBERS OF FIRM

Stephen P. Casarino
Colin M. Shalk
Beth H. Christman

Donald M. Ransom
Kenneth M. Doss

For full biographical listings, see the Martindale-Hubbell Law Directory

DALEY, ERISMAN & VAN OGTROP (AV)

1224 King Street, 19801
Telephone: 302-658-4000
FAX: 302-652-8975
Newark, Delaware Office: 206 East Delaware Avenue.
Telephone: 302-368-0133.
FAX: 302-368-4587.

MEMBERS OF FIRM

Robert E. Daley
James A. Erisman
Piet H. van Ogtrop

References: Wilmington Trust Company; Beneficial National Bank.

For full biographical listings, see the Martindale-Hubbell Law Directory

KIMMEL, WEISS & CARTER, P.A. (AV)

12th Floor, 913 Market Street, P.O. Box 272, 19899-0272
Telephone: 302-571-0800

Morton Richard Kimmel
Michael Weiss
Edward B. Carter, Jr.

Thomas J. Roman
Michael D. Bednash
William Peltz
Matthew M. Bartkowski

Reference: Wilmington Trust Co.; Delaware Trust Co.

For full biographical listings, see the Martindale-Hubbell Law Directory

EUGENE J. MAURER, JR., P.A. (AV)

1201-A King Street, 19801
Telephone: 302-652-7900
Fax: 302-652-2173

Eugene J. Maurer, Jr.
Marilou A. Szymanski

For full biographical listings, see the Martindale-Hubbell Law Directory

POTTER ANDERSON & CORROON (AV)

350 Delaware Trust Building, P.O. Box 951, 19899-0951
Telephone: 302-658-6771
FAX: 658-1192; 655-1190; 655-1199

MEMBERS OF FIRM

Daniel F. Wolcott, Jr.
Somers S. Price, Jr.
Kathleen Furey McDonough

ASSOCIATES

David L. Baumberger
Lewis C. Ledyard, III

Representative Clients: Conrail; National Railroad Passenger Corp.; General Motors Corp.; Chrysler Corp.; U.S. Mineral Products Co.; Boise Cascade Corp.; Mentor Corp.; Harley Davidson; Ford-New Holland, Inc.

For Complete List of Firm Personnel, See General Section

For full biographical listings, see the Martindale-Hubbell Law Directory

SMITH, KATZENSTEIN & FURLOW (AV)

1220 Market Building, P.O. Box 410, 19899
Telephone: 302-652-8400
FAX: 302-652-8405

MEMBERS OF FIRM

Robert J. Katzenstein
Susan L. Parker
Vicki A. Hagel

Kathleen M. Miller

For Complete List of Firm Personnel, See General Section

For full biographical listings, see the Martindale-Hubbell Law Directory

TRZUSKOWSKI, KIPP, KELLEHER & PEARCE, P.A. (AV)

1020 North Bancroft Parkway, P.O. Box 429, 19899-0429
Telephone: 302-571-1782
Fax: 302-571-1638

(See Next Column)

Francis J. Trzuskowski
Robert K. Pearce
James F. Kipp
Edward F. Kafader
Daniel F. Kelleher
Francis J. Schanne

For full biographical listings, see the Martindale-Hubbell Law Directory

TYBOUT, REDFEARN & PELL (AV)

Suite 1100, PNC Bank Building, 300 Delaware Avenue, P.O. Box 2092, 19899
Telephone: 302-658-6901
FAX: 658-4018

F. Alton Tybout
Anne L. Naczi
B. Wilson Redfearn
Nancy E. Chrissinger
Richard W. Pell
David G. Culley

ASSOCIATES

Sherry Ruggiero Fallon
Michael I. Silverman
Sean A. Dolan
Bernadette M. Plaza
Elizabeth Daniello Maron
Joel R. Brown
Francis X. Nardo
John J. Klusman, Jr.
Todd M. Finchler

Representative Clients: CIGNA Ins., Co.; Liberty Mutual Ins., Co.; Hartford Ins., Co.; Universal Underwriters; PHICO; State of Delaware; GAB Business Services Inc.; State Farm Ins., Co.; Alliance of American Insurers; Insurance Guarantee Assn.

For full biographical listings, see the Martindale-Hubbell Law Directory

DISTRICT OF COLUMBIA

WASHINGTON, D.C. Co.

THE ABELSON LAW FIRM (AV)

Suite 300, 1000 Sixteenth Street, N.W., 20036
Telephone: 202-331-0600
Fax: 202-429-9088

Michael A. Abelson

For full biographical listings, see the Martindale-Hubbell Law Directory

ANDERSON & QUINN (AV)

1220 L Street, N.W., Suite 540, 20005
Telephone: 202-371-1245
Rockville, Maryland Office: Adams Law Center, 25 Wood Lane.
Telephone: 301-762-3303.
FAX: 301-762-3776.

MEMBERS OF FIRM

Charles C. Collins (1900-1973)
Francis X. Quinn
Robert E. Anderson (Retired)
William Ray Scanlin
Donald P. Maiberger

ASSOCIATE

Richard L. Butler

Representative Clients: C & P Telephone; Commercial Union Insurance Cos.; Allstate Insurance Co.; State Farm Mutual Automobile Insurance Co.; Northbrook Insurance Cos.; Travelers Insurance Co.; National General Insurance Co.; American International Adjustment Co.; Marriott Corp.

For Complete List of Firm Personnel, See General Section

For full biographical listings, see the Martindale-Hubbell Law Directory

BRAULT, GRAHAM, SCOTT & BRAULT (AV)

1906 Sunderland Place, N.W., 20036
Telephone: 202-785-1200
Fax: 202-785-4301
Rockville, Maryland Office: 101 South Washington Street.
Telephone: 301-424-1060.
FAX: 301-424-7991.
Arlington, Virginia Office: Suite 1201, 2300 North Clarendon Boulevard, Courthouse Plaza.
Telephone: 703-522-1781.

OF COUNSEL

Laurence T. Scott

MEMBERS OF FIRM

Denver H. Graham (1922-1987)
Daniel L. Shea (Resident, Rockville, Maryland Office)
Albert E. Brault (Retired)
Albert D. Brault (Resident, Rockville, Maryland Office)
Keith M. Bonner
M. Kathleen Parker (Resident, Rockville, Maryland Office)
Leo A. Roth, Jr.
James S. Wilson (Resident, Rockville, Maryland Office)
Regina Ann Casey (Resident, Rockville, Maryland Office)
Ronald G. Guziak (Resident, Rockville, Maryland Office)
James M. Brault (Resident, Rockville, Maryland Office)

(See Next Column)

BRAULT, GRAHAM, SCOTT & BRAULT—*Continued*

ASSOCIATES

David G. Mulquin (Not admitted in DC; Resident, Rockville, Maryland Office)
Sanford A. Friedman
Holly D. Shupert (Not admitted in DC; Resident, Rockville, Maryland Office)
Eric A. Spacek
Joan F. Brault (Resident, Rockville, Maryland Office)

Representative Clients: American Oil Co.; Crum & Forster Group; Fireman's Fund American Insurance Cos.; Kemper Group; Reliance Insurance Cos.; Safeco Group; Government Employees Insurance Co.; Medical Mutual Society of Maryland; Legal Mutual Liability Insurance Society of Maryland.

For Complete List of Firm Personnel, See General Section

For full biographical listings, see the Martindale-Hubbell Law Directory

FORET & THOMPSON (AV)

1275 K Street, N.W., Suite 1101, 20005
Telephone: 202-408-4700
Facsimile: 202-408-4708

MEMBERS OF FIRM

L. Palmer Foret
Mark R. Thompson

ASSOCIATE

Craig L. Davitian

For full biographical listings, see the Martindale-Hubbell Law Directory

KANANACK, MURGATROYD, BAUM & HEDLUND, A PROFESSIONAL CORPORATION (AV)

1250 24th Street, N.W., Suite 300, 20037
Telephone: 202-466-0513; 800-827-0097
Fax: 202-466-0527
Los Angeles, California Office: Suite 650, 12100 Wilshire Boulevard.
Telephones: 310-207-3233; 800-827-0087.
Facsimile: 310-820-7444.

Cara L. Belle

For full biographical listings, see the Martindale-Hubbell Law Directory

KOONZ, MCKENNEY, JOHNSON & REGAN, P.C. (AV)

Suite 840, 2020 K Street, N.W., 20006
Telephone: 202-659-5500
Fax: 202-785-3719
Greenbelt, Maryland Office: 6411 Ivy Lane, Suite 204.
Telephone: 301-345-5700.
Fax: 301-474-5578.
Falls Church, Virginia Office: Koonz, McKenney, Johnson & DePaolis, P.C. Suite 400, George Mason Square, 103 W. Broad Street.
Telephone: 703-237-9300.
Fax: 703-533-5974.

Joseph H. Koonz, Jr.
Carolyn McKenney
Roger C. Johnson
Patrick M. Regan
Peter C. DePaolis (Resident at Falls Church, Virginia Office)
Mark J. Brice
William P. Lightfoot, Jr.
Christopher K. Mangold (Resident at Greenbelt, Maryland Office)
Robert V. Clark, Jr. (Resident at Greenbelt, Maryland Office)
Marc Fiedler
Lisa R. Riggs
Kenneth D. Bynum (Resident, Falls Church, Virginia Office)

Karen A. Crist (Resident at Falls Church, Virginia Office)
John P. Zanelotti (Resident at Greenbelt, Maryland Office)
Paulette E. Chapman
David M. Schloss
Dean C. Kremer (Resident, Greenbelt, Maryland Office)
Victor E. Long
Keith W. Donahoe
Jonathan E. Halperin
William A. Musto (Not admitted in DC; Resident at Falls Church, Virginia Office)
Salvatore J. Zambri
Julie H. Heiden (Not admitted in DC; Resident at Falls Church, Virginia Office)
Sha-Ron M. Grayson-Kelsey
Juan E. Milanés

OF COUNSEL

Harold E. Brazil

For full biographical listings, see the Martindale-Hubbell Law Directory

PAULSON, NACE & NORWIND (AV)

1814 N Street, N.W., 20036
Telephone: 202-463-1999
Fax: 202-223-6824

MEMBERS OF FIRM

Richard S. Paulson (1928-1986)
Barry J. Nace
Edward L. Norwind

(See Next Column)

ASSOCIATES

John S. Lopatto, III
Mark R. Lightfoot

OF COUNSEL

Irving R. M. Panzer

For full biographical listings, see the Martindale-Hubbell Law Directory

FLORIDA

*BARTOW,** Polk Co.

FROST, O'TOOLE & SAUNDERS, P.A. (AV)

395 South Central Avenue, P.O. Box 2188, 33830
Telephone: 813-533-0314; 800-533-0967
Telecopier: 813-533-8985

John W. Frost, II
Neal L. O'Toole
Thomas C. Saunders
Richard E. "Rick" Dantzler
Robert A. Carr
Robert H. Van Hart
James R. Franklin
John Marc Tamayo

Reference: Community National Bank, Bartow.

For full biographical listings, see the Martindale-Hubbell Law Directory

BOCA RATON, Palm Beach Co.

CARTER & CONNOLLY, P.A. (AV)

Suite 312, 1200 North Federal Highway, 33432
Telephone: 407-368-9900

John Edward Carter
Andrew James Connolly

OF COUNSEL

Robert T. Carlile

For full biographical listings, see the Martindale-Hubbell Law Directory

KAUFFMAN & SCHWARTZ, P.A. (AV)

Crocker Plaza, Suite 301, 5355 Town Center Road, 33486
Telephone: 407-394-7600
Fax: 407-394-0891

Alan C. Kauffman
Harvey A. Nussbaum
Thomas G. Pye
Robert M. Schwartz

Thomas U. Graner
Rick S. Felberbaum (Not admitted in FL)
Seth I. Cohen

OF COUNSEL

David M. Beckerman

For full biographical listings, see the Martindale-Hubbell Law Directory

WEISS & HANDLER, P.A. (AV)

Suite 218A, One Boca Place, 2255 Glades Road, 33431-7313
Telephone: 407-997-9995
Broward: 305-421-5101
Palm Beach: 407-734-8008
Telecopier: 407-997-5280

Howard I. Weiss
Henry B. Handler
Donald Feldman
Walter M. Cooperstein
Carol A. Kartagener
Bruce A. Harris
David K. Friedman
William M. Franz
Mia Lucas

OF COUNSEL

Malcolm L. Stein (Not admitted in FL)
Raoul Lionel Felder (Not admitted in FL)

For full biographical listings, see the Martindale-Hubbell Law Directory

*BRADENTON,** Manatee Co.

MULOCK, COLEMAN & THOMPSON, P.A. (AV)

519 13th Street West, 34205
Telephone: 813-748-2104
Fax: 813-748-6588

Edwin T. Mulock
Larry K. Coleman
W. Wade Thompson

LEGAL SUPPORT PERSONNEL

Nancy A. Martin (Certified Legal Assistant)

Representative Clients: Clerk of Circuit Court of Manatee County; The Bradenton Herald; Belk-Lindsey Department Stores; Bill Graham Ford Co.; Walgreen Co.
Approved Attorneys for: Attorneys' Title Insurance Fund.

For full biographical listings, see the Martindale-Hubbell Law Directory

*CLEARWATER,** Pinellas Co.

JOHN D. FERNANDEZ, P.A. (AV)

918 Drew Street, 34615
Telephone: 813-461-4441

John D. Fernandez

Pamela Cole Bell

For full biographical listings, see the Martindale-Hubbell Law Directory

CRYSTAL RIVER, Citrus Co.

BEST & ANDERSON, P.A. (AV)

7655 West Gulf to Lake Highway, Suite 6, 34429
Telephone: 904-795-1107
Orlando, Florida Office: 20 North Orange Avenue, Suite 505.
Telephone: 407-425-2985.

David R. Best
George H. "Dutch" Anderson, III

Mark S. Walker
G. Clay Morris
Perry M. Nardi
Lawrence I. Hauser

For full biographical listings, see the Martindale-Hubbell Law Directory

*DADE CITY,** Pasco Co.

GREENFELDER, MANDER, HANSON, MURPHY & DWYER (AV)

14217 Third Street, 33525
Telephone: 904-567-0411
Fax: 904-567-7758

MEMBERS OF FIRM

Albert R. Mander, III
T. Philip Hanson, Jr.

For full biographical listings, see the Martindale-Hubbell Law Directory

DAYTONA BEACH, Volusia Co.

LAW OFFICE OF PAUL A. BERNARDINI (AV)

464 South Ridgewood Avenue, P.O. Drawer 2200, 32115-2200
Telephone: 904-258-3453; 800-899-3453

ASSOCIATES

J. David Kerce
Ryan L. Butler

Reference: Sun Bank of Volusia County.

For full biographical listings, see the Martindale-Hubbell Law Directory

CHANFRAU & CHANFRAU (AV)

A Partnership of Professional Associations
701 North Peninsula Drive, P.O. Box 265880, 32126-5880
Telephone: 904-258-7313
Telecopier: 904-238-1464

W. M. Chanfrau (P.A.)
Philip J. Chanfrau, Jr., (P.A.)

For full biographical listings, see the Martindale-Hubbell Law Directory

SMITH, SCHODER, ROUSE & BOUCK, P.A. (AV)

605 South Ridgewood Avenue, 32014
Telephone: 904-255-0505
FAX: 904-252-4794
Other Daytona Beach Office: 214 Loomis Avenue.
Telephone: 904-255-6711.

James W. Smith
Robert K. Rouse, Jr.

For full biographical listings, see the Martindale-Hubbell Law Directory

*FORT LAUDERDALE,** Broward Co.

BYRD & MURPHY (AV)

Suite 200N Justice Building, 524 South Andrews Avenue, 33301
Telephone: 305-463-1423
FAX: 305-463-5428

MEMBERS OF FIRM

Thomas E. Byrd
James O. Murphy, Jr.

Approved Attorneys for: Attorneys' Title Insurance Fund.

For Complete List of Firm Personnel, See General Section

For full biographical listings, see the Martindale-Hubbell Law Directory

E. HUGH CHAPPELL JR., P.A. (AV)

420 Northeast 3rd Street, 33301
Telephone: 305-467-2727
Fax: 305-523-3240

(See Next Column)

E. Hugh Chappell, Jr.

Reference: Sun Bank/Broward, N.A.

For full biographical listings, see the Martindale-Hubbell Law Directory

CONRAD, SCHERER, JAMES & JENNE (AV)

A Partnership of Professional Associations
Eighth Floor, 633 South Federal Highway, P.O. Box 14723, 33302
Telephone: 305-462-5500
Facsimile: 305-463-9244
Miami, Florida Office: 2180 Southwest 12th Avenue, P.O. Box 450888, 33245-0888.
Telephone: 305-856-9920.
Facsimile: 305-856-4546.

MEMBERS OF FIRM

William R. Scherer, Jr., (P.A.)
Gary S. Genovese (P.A.)
Gordon James, III, (P.A.)
Valerie Shea (P.A.)
Kenneth C. Jenne, II (P.A.)
William V. Carcioppolo (P.A.)

OF COUNSEL

Rex Conrad

ASSOCIATES

Linda Rae Spaulding
Kimberly A. Kisslan
Lynn Futch Cooney
Reid A. Cocalis
Albert L. Frevola, Jr.

Local Counsel for: American Home Assurance Group; Caterpillar Tractor Co.; Division of Risk Management, State of Florida; Florida East Coast Railway; Fort Motor Co.; Liberty Mutual Insurance Co.; Ryder Truck Lines; Unigard Insurance Group.
Approved Attorneys for: Attorneys' Title Insurance Fund.
Reference: Barnett Bank of Fort Lauderdale.

For Complete List of Firm Personnel, See General Section

For full biographical listings, see the Martindale-Hubbell Law Directory

COONEY, HALICZER, MATTSON, LANCE, BLACKBURN, PETTIS & RICHARDS, P.A. (AV)

301 East Las Olas Boulevard, P.O. Box 14546, 33302
Telephone: Telephone: 305-779-1900
WATS: 1-800-745-3864
Telecopier: 305-779-1910

David F. Cooney
Kenneth E. White
James S. Haliczer
Kieran O'Connor
Michael C. Mattson
Lorna E. Brown-Burton
Victor Lance
Bruce Michael Trybus
Ace J. Blackburn, Jr.
Pamela R. Kittrell
Eugene K. Pettis
Lawrence E. Brownstein
John H. Richards
Christopher D. Malin
Amy B. Talisman

For full biographical listings, see the Martindale-Hubbell Law Directory

ESLER PETRIE & SALKIN, P.A. (AV)

Suite 300 The Advocate Building, 315 S.E. Seventh Street, 33301
Telephone: 305-764-5400
FAX: 305-764-5408

Gary A. Esler
C. Daniel Petrie, Jr.
Sonya L. Salkin

Laurie S. Moss

Representative Clients: The Chubb Group of Insurance Cos.; Fireman's Fund Insurance Co.; State of Florida-Department of Risk Management; Marriott Corp.; Gregson Furniture Industries, Inc.; Loewenstein, Inc.; Richfield Hotel Management, Inc.; Mobile America Insurance Group, Inc.; Colonial Penn Insurance Co.
References: Capital Bank.

For full biographical listings, see the Martindale-Hubbell Law Directory

FERRERO & MIDDLEBROOKS, P.A. (AV)

Sixth Floor Blackstone Building, 707 Southeast Third Avenue, P.O. Box 14604, 33302
Telephone: 305-462-4500
Miami: 949-2784
Telecopier: 305-462-6597

Ray Ferrero, Jr.
Ed Middlebrooks

Michael J. Carbo
Todd Middlebrooks

Reference: Barnett Bank of Broward County.

For full biographical listings, see the Martindale-Hubbell Law Directory

Fort Lauderdale—Continued

GUNTHER & WHITAKER, P.A. (AV)

Fifth Floor The Legal Center, 888 Southeast Third Avenue, P.O. Box 14608, 33302
Telephone: 305-523-5885
FAX: 305-760-9531

Dieter K. Gunther
Robert Hunt Schwartz
Alan B. Whitaker, Jr.
Jack T. Frost
Scott C. Burgess

Representative Clients: State Farm Mutual Automobile Insurance Co.; United States Fidelity Guaranty Co.; Home Insurance Co.; Cincinnati Insurance Companies; City of Fort Lauderdale; City of Plantation; City of Pompano Beach; Government Employees Insurance Company.

For full biographical listings, see the Martindale-Hubbell Law Directory

HEINRICH GORDON BATCHELDER HARGROVE & WEIHE (AV)

A Partnership including Professional Associations
500 East Broward Boulevard, Suite 1000, 33394-3092
Telephone: 305-527-2800
Telecopier: 305-524-9481

MEMBERS OF FIRM

Mark R. Boyd
Eugene L. Heinrich (P.A.)
Richard G. Gordon (P.A.)
Jeffrey A. O'Keefe

ASSOCIATES

Kandice L. Kilkelly
Kenneth W. Waterway
Jodi R. Stone
Eric M. Zivitz

OF COUNSEL

Gilbert E. Theissen

Representative Clients: Aetna Life Insurance Company; Allstate Insurance Company; Amerisure Companies; The BellSouth Companies; Blackfin Yacht Corporation, Inc.; First Westinghouse Equities Corporation; Schindler Elevator Corporation; Sears, Roebuck and Co.; Westinghouse Electric Corporation.

For Complete List of Firm Personnel, See General Section

For full biographical listings, see the Martindale-Hubbell Law Directory

KRUPNICK CAMPBELL MALONE ROSELLI BUSER & SLAMA, P.A. (AV)

700 Southeast 3rd Avenue, 33316
Telephone: 305-763-8181
FAX: 305-763-8292

Jon E. Krupnick
Thomas E. Buser
Walter G. Campbell, Jr.
Joseph J. Slama
Kevin A. Malone
Kelly D. Hancock
Richard J. Roselli
Lisa A. McNelis

Kelley Badger Gelb
Scott S. Liberman
Elaine P. Krupnick
Robert J. McKee
Adria E. Quintela

Reference: Citizens and Southern Bank.

For full biographical listings, see the Martindale-Hubbell Law Directory

LAW OFFICES PRINCE, GLICK & MCFARLANE, P.A. (AV)

1112 Southeast 3rd Avenue, 33316
Telephone: Broward: 305-525-1112
Dade: 305-940-6414
FAX: 305-462-1243

Charles M. Prince
Joseph Glick
William J. McFarlane, III

For full biographical listings, see the Martindale-Hubbell Law Directory

PURDY AND FLYNN (AV)

One East Broward Boulevard, 7th Floor, 33303
Telephone: 305-356-0008

H. Mark Purdy
Rose Ann Flynn

OF COUNSEL

Michael S. Insler

For full biographical listings, see the Martindale-Hubbell Law Directory

WEAVER & WEAVER, P.A. (AV)

500 Southeast Sixth Street, P.O. Box 14663, 33302-4663
Telephone: 305-763-2511
Miami: 305-944-4452
West Palm Beach: 407-655-6012
FAX: 305-764-3590

Ben J. Weaver
Dianne Jay Weaver

For full biographical listings, see the Martindale-Hubbell Law Directory

*FORT MYERS,** Lee Co.

BURKERT & HART (AV)

2205 McGregor Boulevard, P.O. Box 2485, 33902
Telephone: 813-337-4800
Fax: 813-337-5920
Naples Office: 4077 Tamiami Trail, North, Suite D204.
Telephone: 813-649-4800.
Fax: 813-337-5920.

MEMBERS OF FIRM

Kim Patrick Hart
Peter C. Burkert

For full biographical listings, see the Martindale-Hubbell Law Directory

GARVIN & TRIPP, A PROFESSIONAL ASSOCIATION (AV)

2532 East First Street, P.O. Drawer 2040, 33902
Telephone: 813-334-1824
FAX: 813-334-6848

Jeffrey R. Garvin
Theodore L. Tripp, Jr.

Andrew Scott Epstein

Reference: Northern Trust Bank, Fort Myers, Florida.

For full biographical listings, see the Martindale-Hubbell Law Directory

GOLDBERG, GOLDSTEIN & BUCKLEY, P.A. (AV)

1515 Broadway, P.O. Box 2366, 33901-2366
Telephone: 813-334-1146
Fax: 813-334-3039
Naples, Florida Office: 2150 Goodlette Road, Suite 105, Parkway Financial Center, 33940.
Telephone: 813-262-4888.
Fax: 813-262-8716.
Port Charlotte, Florida Office: Emerald Square, Suite 1, 2852 Tamiami Trail, 33952.
Telephone: 813-624-2393.
Fax: 813-624-2155.
Cape Coral, Florida Office: 2330 S.E. 16th Place.
Telephone: 813-574-5575.
Fax: 813-574-9213.
Lehigh Acres, Florida Office: 1458 Lee Boulevard, Lee Boulevard Shopping Center, 33936.
Telephone: 813-368-6101.
Fax: 813-368-2461.
South Fort Myers, Florida Office: Horizon Plaza, 16050 South Tamiami Trail, Suites 101 and 102, 33908.
Telephone: 813-433-6777.
Fax: 813-433-0578.
Bonita Springs, Florida Office: 3431 Bonita Beach Road, Suite 208, 33923.
Telephone: 813-495-0003.
Fax: 813-495-0564.

Morton A. Goldberg
Richard Lee Purtz
Ray Goldstein
Martin G. Arnowitz
Stephen W. Buckley
George J. Mitar
Harvey B. Goldberg
Steven P. Kushner
John B. Cechman
Michael J. Ciccarone
J. Jeffrey Rice
Terry S. Nelson
Mark A. Steinberg
William L. Welker
David R. Linn
Jay Cooper
Donna L. Schnorr
Jonathan D. Conant
Mark P. Smith
Raymond L. Racila
Luis E. Insignares

Approved Attorneys for: Attorneys' Title Insurance Fund; Chicago Title Insurance Co.; American Pioneer Title Insurance Company; Stewart Title Guaranty Co.; First American Title Insurance Company.

For Complete List of Firm Personnel, See General Section

For full biographical listings, see the Martindale-Hubbell Law Directory

HENDERSON, FRANKLIN, STARNES & HOLT, PROFESSIONAL ASSOCIATION (AV)

1715 Monroe Street, P.O. Box 280, 33902-0280
Telephone: 813-334-4121
Telecopier: 813-332-4494

Albert M. Frierson
Bruce M. Stanley
Stephen L. Helgemo
Daniel W. Sheppard
John A. Noland
Jack E. Lundy
Gerald W. Pierce
Steven G. Koeppel
J. Terrence Porter
Douglas B. Szabo
Michael J. Corso
Andrew L. Ringers, Jr.
Vicki L. Sproat
John F. Potanovic, Jr.
John W. Lewis
Robert C. Shearman
Craig Ferrante
Kevin D. Cooper
James L. Nulman
Jeffrey D. Kottkamp
Harold N. Hume, Jr.
Gregory D. Whitworth

(See Next Column)

HENDERSON, FRANKLIN, STARNES & HOLT PROFESSIONAL ASSOCIATION, *Fort Myers—Continued*

Representative Clients: Aetna Life & Casualty Group; CIGNA Group; CSX Transportation, Inc.; Fireman's Fund Insurance Cos.; Barnett Bank of Lee County, N.A.; Northern Trust Bank of Florida, N.A.; The Hartford Insurance Group; Travelers Group; United Telephone Company of Florida.

For Complete List of Firm Personnel, See General Section

For full biographical listings, see the Martindale-Hubbell Law Directory

*FORT PIERCE,** St. Lucie Co.

NEILL GRIFFIN JEFFRIES & LLOYD, CHARTERED (AV)

311 South Second Street, P.O. Box 1270, 34954
Telephone: 407-464-8200
Fax: 407-464-2566

Michael Jeffries
J. Stephen Tierney, III
Richard V. Neill, Jr.

Local Counsel for: Sun Bank Treasure Coast, N.A., (Commercial and Trust Departments); St. Paul Fire and Marine Insurance Co.; Chubb Group of Insurances Co.; Becker Holding Corp.
Approved Attorneys for: Attorneys' Title Insurance Fund; Commonwealth Land Title Insurance Co.
Reference: Sun Bank Treasure Coast, N.A., Fort Pierce, Florida (Commercial and Trust Departments).

For full biographical listings, see the Martindale-Hubbell Law Directory

*JACKSONVILLE,** Duval Co.

HOWELL O'NEAL & JOHNSON (AV)

The Greenleaf Building, Suite 1100, 200 Laura Street, 32202
Telephone: 904-353-0024
Fax: 904-353-0061

Charles Cook Howell, III
Michael S. O'Neal
Bradley R. Johnson

Representative Clients: Albertson's, Inc.; Chrysler Corp.; Crum & Forster Commercial Insurance; Dresser Industries; Hertz Equipment Rental Co.; ITT Hartford; McDonald's Restaurants of Florida, Inc.; Tokio Marine Claim Service; Transus, Inc.; University of Florida, J. Hillis Miller Health Center.

For full biographical listings, see the Martindale-Hubbell Law Directory

LILES, GAVIN & COSTANTINO (AV)

One Enterprise Center, Suite 1500, 225 Water Street, 32202
Telephone: 904-634-1100
Fax: 904-634-1234

Rutledge R. Liles
R. Kyle Gavin
R. Scott Costantino
F. Bay Neal III

For full biographical listings, see the Martindale-Hubbell Law Directory

PAJCIC & PAJCIC, P.A. (AV)

3100 Independent Square, 32202
Telephone: 904-358-8881
Fax: 904-354-1180

Gary Pajcic
Stephen J. Pajcic, III
Katherine Brown
Robert J. Link
Alan Chipperfield
Lee T. Griffin
Christine A. Clark

Reference: Barnett Bank of Jacksonville, N.A.

For full biographical listings, see the Martindale-Hubbell Law Directory

TYGART AND SCHULER, P.A. (AV)

103 Barnett Regency Tower, 9550 Regency Square Boulevard, 32225-8164
Telephone: 904-721-0744
Facsimile: 904-721-5080

S. Thompson Tygart, Jr.
Carl Scott Schuler

Representative Client: Allstate Insurance Co.
Reference: Barnett Bank of Regency.

For full biographical listings, see the Martindale-Hubbell Law Directory

*MIAMI,** Dade Co.

CLARKE & SILVERGLATE, PROFESSIONAL ASSOCIATION (AV)

100 North Biscayne Boulevard, Suite 2401, 33132
Telephone: 305-377-0700
Fax: 305-377-3001

Mercer K. Clarke
Spencer H. Silverglate
Kelly Anne Luther

For full biographical listings, see the Martindale-Hubbell Law Directory

COLSON, HICKS, EIDSON, COLSON, MATTHEWS & GAMBA (AV)

Floor 47 First Union Financial Center, 200 South Biscayne Boulevard, 33131-2351
Telephone: 305-373-5400

MEMBERS OF FIRM

Bill Colson
William M. Hicks
Mike Eidson
Dean C. Colson
Joseph M. Matthews
Tomas F. Gamba
Tony Korvick
Enid Duany Mendoza

Reference: Northern Trust Bank of Florida.

For Complete List of Firm Personnel, See General Section

For full biographical listings, see the Martindale-Hubbell Law Directory

DEUTSCH & BLUMBERG, P.A. (AV)

Suite 2802 New World Tower, 100 North Biscayne Boulevard, 33132
Telephone: 305-358-6329
Fax: 305-358-9304

Steven K. Deutsch
Edward R. Blumberg
Louis Thaler

For full biographical listings, see the Martindale-Hubbell Law Directory

HALL AND O'BRIEN, P.A. (AV)

Penthouse, 1428 Brickell Avenue, 33131
Telephone: 305-374-5030
Fax: 305-374-5033

Andrew C. Hall
Richard F. O'Brien, III

Leana Marie Vastine
Christopher M. David

For full biographical listings, see the Martindale-Hubbell Law Directory

HARDY, BISSETT & LIPTON, P.A. (AV)

501 Northeast First Avenue, 33132
Telephone: 305-358-6200
Broward: 305-462-6377
Fax: 305-577-8230
Boca Raton, Florida Office: 2201 Corporate Boulevard, N.W., Suite 205.
Telephone: 407-998-9202.
Telecopier: 407-998-9693.

G. Jack Hardy
G. William Bissett
Stephen N. Lipton (Resident, Boca Raton Office)

Howard K. Cherna
Lee Philip Teichner
Matthew Kennedy
H. Dane Mottlau

Representative Clients: International Paper Co.; Masonite Corp.; Bridgestone/Firestone Inc.; American International Underwriters; American International Group, Inc.; Pennsylvania National Insurance Cos.; Crown Equipment Corp.; The Coleman Co., Inc.; Interamerican Car Rental, Inc.; York International Corp.

For full biographical listings, see the Martindale-Hubbell Law Directory

THOMAS W. MCALILEY, P.A. (AV)

3260 Miami Center, 201 South Biscayne Boulevard, 33131
Telephone: 305-373-6551
Telecopier: 305-358-3404

Thomas W. McAliley

For full biographical listings, see the Martindale-Hubbell Law Directory

NICKLAUS, VALLE, CRAIG & WICKS (AV)

15th Floor New World Tower, 100 North Biscayne Boulevard, 33132
Telephone: 305-358-2888
Facsimile: 305-358-5501
Fort Lauderdale, Florida Office: Suite 101N, Justice Building, 524 South Andrews Avenue, 33301.
Telephone: 305-523-1858.
Facsimile: 305-523-8068.

MEMBERS OF FIRM

Edward R. Nicklaus
Laurence F. Valle
Lawrance B. Craig, III
William R. Wicks, III
James W. McCready, III
Michael W. Whitaker

ASSOCIATES

Richard D. Settler
Kevin M. Fitzmaurice
Timothy Maze Hartley
Keith S. Grybowski
Patricia Blanco
Michael J. Lynott

For full biographical listings, see the Martindale-Hubbell Law Directory

Miami—Continued

PODHURST, ORSECK, JOSEFSBERG, EATON, MEADOW, OLIN & PERWIN, P.A. (AV)

Suite 800 City National Bank Building, 25 West Flagler Street, 33130-1780
Telephone: 305-358-2800; Fort Lauderdale: 305-463-4346
Fax: 305-358-2382

Aaron Podhurst
Robert Orseck (1934-1978)
Robert C. Josefsberg
Joel D. Eaton
Barry L. Meadow
Michael S. Olin
Joel S. Perwin
Steven C. Marks
Victor M. Diaz, Jr.
Katherine W. Ezell

Karen B. Podhurst

OF COUNSEL

Walter H. Beckham, Jr.

Reference: City National Bank of Miami; United National Bank of Miami.

For full biographical listings, see the Martindale-Hubbell Law Directory

SAMS, MARTIN & LISTER, P.A. (AV)

The Atrium, Suite 200, 1500 San Remo Avenue (Coral Gables), 33146
Telephone: 305-666-3181
Fax: 305-666-5867
Fort Lauderdale, Florida Office: Sams, Spier, Hoffman and Hastings, P.A., 500 Southeast Sixth Street, Suite 101, 33301.
Telephone: 305-467-3181.
Fax: 305-523-5462.
Jacksonville, Florida Office: Sams, Spier, Hoffman and Hastings, P.A., 1301 Gulf Life Drive, Suite 2010, 32207.
Telephone: 904-399-5546.
Fax: 904-354-0182.

Murray Sams, Jr.
Timothy M. Martin
David P. Lister

Julianne K. Lara

For full biographical listings, see the Martindale-Hubbell Law Directory

LELAND E. STANSELL, JR., P.A. (AV)

903 Biscayne Building, 19 West Flagler Street, 33130
Telephone: 305-374-5911

ASSOCIATE

Charles L. Balli

For full biographical listings, see the Martindale-Hubbell Law Directory

*NAPLES,** Collier Co.

HARDT & STEWART (AV)

Suite 705 Sun Bank Building, 801 Laurel Oak Drive, 33963
Telephone: 813-598-2900
Fax: 813-598-3785

MEMBERS OF FIRM

Frederick R. Hardt
Joseph D. Stewart
John D. Kehoe

References: Northern Trust Bank of Florida/Naples, N.A.; U.S. Trust Company of Florida; Sun Bank/Naples, N.A.

For full biographical listings, see the Martindale-Hubbell Law Directory

NEW PORT RICHEY, Pasco Co.

ROBERTS, SOJKA & DORAN, P.A. (AV)

5841 Main Street, 34652
Telephone: 813-847-1103
West Palm Beach, Florida Office: Gary W. Roberts, P.A. Lawyers, 1675 Palm Beach Lakes Boulevard, Seventh Floor, P.O. Drawer 4175, 33402.
Telephone: 407-686-1800.
Fax: 407-686-1533.

Gary W. Roberts
Cindy A. Sojka
J. Stephen Doran

For full biographical listings, see the Martindale-Hubbell Law Directory

NORTH PALM BEACH, Palm Beach Co.

LAW OFFICES OF PATRICK C. MASSA, P.A. (AV)

11891 U.S. Highway One, Suite 110, 33408-2864
Telephone: 407-694-1800
Facsimile: 407-694-1833

Patrick C. Massa

For full biographical listings, see the Martindale-Hubbell Law Directory

ORANGE PARK, Clay Co.

HEAD, SMITH, METCALF, AGUILAR, MOSS & SIERON, P.A. (AV)

1329A Kingsley Avenue, P.O. Box 855, 32073
Telephone: 904-264-6000
Fax: 904-264-9223

Robert J. Head, Jr.
Larry Smith
Frank B. Metcalf
Robert Aguilar
John B. Moss
Mark A. Sieron

Holly Fulton Perritt

For full biographical listings, see the Martindale-Hubbell Law Directory

*ORLANDO,** Orange Co.

BEST & ANDERSON, P.A. (AV)

20 North Orange Avenue, Suite 505, 32801
Telephone: 407-425-2985
Crystal River, Florida Office: 7655 West Gulf to Lake Highway, Suite 6.
Telephone: 904-795-1107.

David R. Best
George H. "Dutch" Anderson, III

Mark S. Walker
Perry M. Nardi
Jeffrey B. Sexton
G. Clay Morris
Lawrence I. Hauser

For full biographical listings, see the Martindale-Hubbell Law Directory

CUNNINGHAM & MORGAN, PROFESSIONAL ASSOCIATION (AV)

330 East Central Boulevard, 32801
Telephone: 407-425-2000
Fax: 407-843-8274

James Owen Cunningham
Mary Ann Morgan

Joseph E. Boatwright, Jr.

For full biographical listings, see the Martindale-Hubbell Law Directory

LAW OFFICES OF JACK F. (JAY) DURIE, JR. (AV)

1000 East Robinson Street, 32801
Telephone: 407-841-6000; 1-800-940-0442
Fax: 407-841-2425

Jack F. (Jay) Durie, Jr.

ASSOCIATE

Jean Marie Steedley

For full biographical listings, see the Martindale-Hubbell Law Directory

MAHER, GIBSON AND GUILEY A PROFESSIONAL ASSOCIATION OF LAWYERS (AV)

Suite 200, 90 East Livingston Street, 32801
Telephone: 407-839-0866
Fax: 407-425-7958

Michael Maher
Patricia M. Gibson
David D. Guiley

Steven R. Maher
Robin M. Orosz
Monique M. Edwards

OF COUNSEL

John Edward Jones (P.A.)

LEGAL SUPPORT PERSONNEL

INSURANCE CLAIM COORDINATOR

Charles R. Simpson

For full biographical listings, see the Martindale-Hubbell Law Directory

MARTINEZ & DALTON, PROFESSIONAL ASSOCIATION (AV)

719 Vassar Street, 32804
Telephone: 407-425-0712
Fax: 407-425-1856

Mel R. Martinez
Roy B. Dalton, Jr.
Robert H. Dellecker
Brian T. Wilson

Yvonne M. Yegge
Leticia Marques

For full biographical listings, see the Martindale-Hubbell Law Directory

Orlando—Continued

McDonough, O'Dell, Wieland & Williams (AV)

19 East Central Boulevard, P.O. Drawer 1991, 32802
Telephone: 407-425-7577
Fax: 407-423-0234

John R. McDonough
Donald L. O'Dell
William J. Wieland
Donald N. Williams
Michael J. Krakar
A. Scott Toney
Nicholas a. Shannin

For full biographical listings, see the Martindale-Hubbell Law Directory

Parrish, Bailey & Morsch, P.A. (AV)

116 America Street, 32801
Telephone: 407-849-1776

Sidney H. Parrish
Michael K. Bailey
Mark V. Morsch

Jay M. Fisher
Donald A. Myers, Jr.

For full biographical listings, see the Martindale-Hubbell Law Directory

Irby G. Pugh (AV)

218 Annie Street, 32806
Telephone: 407-843-5840

Reference: Schofield Corporation; Kingsland Investments.

For full biographical listings, see the Martindale-Hubbell Law Directory

PALM BEACH GARDENS, Palm Beach Co.

Mathison & Mathison (AV)

A Partnership of Professional Associations
PGA Concourse Building, 5606 PGA Boulevard, Suite 211, 33418
Telephone: 407-624-2001
Telecopier: 407-624-0036
West Palm Beach, Office: Centre Park Plaza, 1400 Centre Park Boulevard, 33401-7412.
Telephone: 407-471-4144.
Fax: 407-471-3988.

MEMBERS OF FIRM

Carl M. Mathison, Jr., (P.A.)
Stephen S. Mathison (P.A.)

ASSOCIATE

Frederic T. DeHon, Jr., (P.A.)

For full biographical listings, see the Martindale-Hubbell Law Directory

Slawson & Glick (AV)

Harbour Financial Center, 2401 PGA Boulevard, Suite 140, 33410
Telephone: 407-625-6260
Facsimile: 407-625-6269
Boca Raton, Florida Office: The Plaza, Suite 801, 5355 Town Center Road.
Telephone: 407-391-4900.
Facsimile: 407-368-9274.

Richard W. Slawson (P.A.)
Brian J. Glick (P.A.)
Fred A. Cunningham
Patrick St. George Cousins

For full biographical listings, see the Martindale-Hubbell Law Directory

PLANTATION, Broward Co.

Fenster and Faerber, Professional Association (AV)

Suite 307, The Gulfstream Building, 8751 West Broward Boulevard, 33324
Telephone: 305-473-1500; Miami: 305-949-9998
Mailing Address: P.O. Box 16688, 33318

Jeffrey M. Fenster
Jesse S. Faerber
Stacie L. Cohen

OF COUNSEL

Elizabeth Anne Beavers

For full biographical listings, see the Martindale-Hubbell Law Directory

ST. PETERSBURG, Pinellas Co.

Chambers, Salzman & Bannon, Professional Association (AV)

520 Fourth Street North, 33701
Telephone: 813-896-2167
Fax: 813-822-8981

Joseph H. Chambers
Barry M. Salzman
Rick G. Bannon
Joseph W. Chambers
Jeffrey K. Chambers

Reference: C & S National Bank of St. Petersburg.

For full biographical listings, see the Martindale-Hubbell Law Directory

Williams, Brasfield, Wertz, Fuller, Goldman, Freeman & Lovell, P.A. (AV)

2553 First Avenue, North, P.O. Box 12349, 33733-2349
Telephone: 813-327-2258, Tampa: 813-224-0430
Fax: 813-328-1340

John W. Williams
J. Scott Brasfield
Larry W. Wertz
Jeffrey R. Fuller
Carl A. Goldman
Stuart J. Freeman
Maron E. "Ron" Lovell
Billie Ann O'Hern
Karen A. Dean
D. Keith Thomas
Robert A. Santa Lucia

For full biographical listings, see the Martindale-Hubbell Law Directory

*STUART,** Martin Co.

Lewis, Berger & Ferraro (AV)

A Partnership of Professional Associations
3601 East Ocean Boulevard, Suite 201 (Sewall's Point), 34996
Telephone: 407-221-0600
FAX: 407-220-0640
Other Stuart, Florida Office: 1115 East Ocean Boulevard. Telephone 407-286-7861. Fax 407-288-2013.
Port St. Lucie, Florida Office: 1531 S.E. Port St. Lucie Boulevard.
Telephone: 407-335-1996.
FAX: 407-335-1998.

Bruce D. Berger (P.A.)
Russell J. Ferraro, Jr. (P.A.)
J. D. Lewis, III (P.A.)

Danie V. La Guerre (P.A.)
Michael J. Mortell (P.A.)
Sharon E. Lever

LEGAL SUPPORT PERSONNEL

Dorthea M. Duncan

For full biographical listings, see the Martindale-Hubbell Law Directory

McCarthy, Summers, Bobko, McKey & Bonan, P.A. (AV)

2081 East Ocean Boulevard, Suite 2-A, 34996
Telephone: 407-286-1700
FAX: 407-283-1803

Terence P. McCarthy
Robert P. Summers
Noel A. Bobko
John D. McKey, Jr.
W. Martin Bonan

Representative Clients: American Bank of Martin County; First National Bank and Trust Company of the Treasure Coast; Great Western Bank; Hydratech Utilities; Lost Lake at Hobe Sound; Taylor Creek Marina, Inc.; GBS Excavating, Inc.; Seaboard Savings Bank; The Stuart News; Gary Player Design Group.

For full biographical listings, see the Martindale-Hubbell Law Directory

*TALLAHASSEE,** Leon Co.

Davis & Taff (AV)

210 East College Avenue, Suite 200, P.O. Box 37190, 32315-7190
Telephone: 904-222-6026
Telecopier: 904-224-1039

MEMBERS OF FIRM

Ken Davis
Angus Broward Taff, Jr.

For full biographical listings, see the Martindale-Hubbell Law Directory

Fonvielle & Hinkle (AV)

3375-A Capital Circle Northeast, 32308
Telephone: 904-422-7773
Fax: 904-422-3449

MEMBERS OF FIRM

C. David Fonvielle
Donald M. Hinkle
Halley B. Lewis, III

For full biographical listings, see the Martindale-Hubbell Law Directory

McFarlain, Wiley, Cassedy & Jones, Professional Association (AV)

215 South Monroe Street, Suite 600, P.O. Box 2174, 32316-2174
Telephone: 904-222-2107
Telecopier: 904-222-8475

Richard C. McFarlain
William B. Wiley
Marshall R. Cassedy
Douglas P. Jones
Charles A. Stampelos
Linda McMullen
H. Darrell White, Jr.
Christopher Barkas

Harold R. Mardenborough, Jr.
Katherine Hairston LaRosa
J. Robert Griffin

(See Next Column)

McFarlain, Wiley, Cassedy & Jones Professional Association—*Continued*

OF COUNSEL

Betty J. Steffens

For full biographical listings, see the Martindale-Hubbell Law Directory

Wadsworth & Davis (AV)

Suite 1, 203 North Gadsden Street, P.O. Box 10529, 32302-2529
Telephone: 904-224-9037
FAX: 904-561-6119

MEMBERS OF FIRM

Murray M. Wadsworth William H. Davis

ASSOCIATE

James J. Dean

Reference: Capital City First National Bank.

For full biographical listings, see the Martindale-Hubbell Law Directory

*TAMPA,** Hillsborough Co.

Cunningham Law Group, P.A. (AV)

100 Ashley Drive, South, Suite 100, 33602
Telephone: 813-228-0505
Telefax: 813-229-7982

Anthony W. Cunningham Donald G. Greiwe
James D. Clark

For full biographical listings, see the Martindale-Hubbell Law Directory

Patrick H. Dekle, P.A. (AV)

808 Landmark Building, 412 Madison Street, 33602-4640
Telephone: 813-223-2300

Patrick H. Dekle

For full biographical listings, see the Martindale-Hubbell Law Directory

Fuentes and Kreischer (AV)

1407 West Busch Boulevard, 33612
Telephone: 813-933-6647
Fax: 813-932-8588

MEMBERS OF FIRM

Lawrence E. Fuentes Albert C. Kreischer, Jr.

OF COUNSEL

W. Andrew Hamilton

Reference: Northside Bank of Tampa.

For full biographical listings, see the Martindale-Hubbell Law Directory

William P. Levens (AV)

1907 West Kennedy Boulevard, 33606
Telephone: 813-251-5775

For full biographical listings, see the Martindale-Hubbell Law Directory

Levine, Hirsch, Segall & Northcutt, P.A. (AV)

First Union Center, 100 South Ashley Drive, Suite 1600, P.O. Box 3429, 33601-3429
Telephone: 813-229-6585
Telecopier: 813-229-7210

Arnold D. Levine Stephen L. Segall
Richard A. Hirsch Stevan T. Northcutt

Edward M. Brennan

Representative Clients: Bank Societe Generale (Paris and Stockholm); Payment Systems for Credit Unions, Inc.

For full biographical listings, see the Martindale-Hubbell Law Directory

Pippinger, Tropp & Matassini, P.A. (AV)

101 East Kennedy Boulevard, Suite 3305, 33602
Telephone: 813-225-1611

Richard G. Pippinger Robert A. Tropp
Nicholas M. Matassini

For full biographical listings, see the Martindale-Hubbell Law Directory

Charles F. Sansone (AV)

Suite 200, 701 North Franklin Street, 33602
Telephone: 813-223-9282
FAX: 813-229-0595

For full biographical listings, see the Martindale-Hubbell Law Directory

Wagner, Vaughan & McLaughlin, P.A. (AV)

708 Jackson Street (Corner of Jefferson), and 601 Bayshore Boulevard, Suite 910, 33602
Telephone: 813-223-7421; 813-225-4000
FAX: 813-221-0254; 813-225-4010

Bill Wagner (Resident, Bayshore Boulevard Office) Roger A. Vaughan, Jr.
John J. McLaughlin

Alan F. Wagner (Resident, Bayshore Boulevard Office) Denise E. Vaughan
Ruth Whetstone Wagner (Resident, Bayshore Boulevard Office) Weldon "Web" Earl Brennan (Resident, Bayshore Boulevard Office)
Bob Vaughan

For full biographical listings, see the Martindale-Hubbell Law Directory

Yerrid, Knopik & Valenzuela, P.A. (AV)

Barnett Plaza, Suite 2160, 101 East Kennedy Boulevard, 33602
Telephone: 813-222-8222
FAX: 813-222-8224

C. Steven Yerrid Christopher S. Knopik
Henry E. Valenzuela

Matthew S. Mudano

For full biographical listings, see the Martindale-Hubbell Law Directory

VENICE, Sarasota Co.

Snyder, Groner & Schieb (AV)

A Partnership including Professional Associations
355 West Venice Avenue, 34285
Telephone: 813-485-9626; 800-260-9626
Telecopier: 813-485-8163
Sarasota, Florida Office: 2033 Main Street, Suite 403.
Telephone: 813-951-1333; 800-448-0721.
Telecopier: 813-953-9685.

W. Russell Snyder (P.A.) Scott A. Schieb
Richard W. Groner W. Andrew Clayton, Jr.
Stanley M. Krawetz

Reference: Community National Bank of Sarasota

For full biographical listings, see the Martindale-Hubbell Law Directory

*VERO BEACH,** Indian River Co.

Clem, Polackwich & Vocelle (AV)

A Partnership including Professional Associations
Univest Building-Suite 501, 2770 North Indian River Boulevard, 32960
Telephone: 407-562-8111
Fax: 407-562-2870

MEMBERS OF FIRM

Chester Clem (P.A.) Louis B. Vocelle, Jr., (P.A.)
Alan S. Polackwich, Sr. (P.A.) James A. Taylor, III

ASSOCIATE

Paul Richard Berg

OF COUNSEL

Robert Golden

References: Barnett Bank of The Treasure Coast; Beach Bank of Vero Beach; Indian River National Bank; Riverside National Bank of Florida.

For full biographical listings, see the Martindale-Hubbell Law Directory

*WEST PALM BEACH,** Palm Beach Co.

Babbitt, Hazouri and Johnson, P.A. (AV)

1801 Australian Avenue South, Suite 200, P.O. Drawer 024426, 33402
Telephone: 407-684-2500
Fax: 407-684-6308

Theodore Babbitt Fred A. Hazouri
Joseph R. Johnson

For full biographical listings, see the Martindale-Hubbell Law Directory

Lawrence U. L. Chandler (AV)

1555 Palm Beach Lakes Boulevard, Suite 1520
Telephone: 407-478-1478
Fax: 407-478-1498

For full biographical listings, see the Martindale-Hubbell Law Directory

Farish, Farish & Romani (AV)

316 Banyan Boulevard, P.O. Box 4118, 33402
Telephone: 407-659-3500
Fax: 407-655-3158

(See Next Column)

FARISH, FARISH & ROMANI, *West Palm Beach—Continued*

MEMBERS OF FIRM

Joseph D. Farish (1892-1977)
Joseph D. Farish, Jr.
Robert V. Romani

ASSOCIATES

S. Emory Rogers
Peter Bassaline
Keith R. Taylor

LEGAL SUPPORT PERSONNEL

Ken P. Beelner

References: 1st Union Bank; Clewiston National Bank; Barnett Bank of Palm Beach County.

For full biographical listings, see the Martindale-Hubbell Law Directory

FREEMAN & ROSS, P.A. (AV)

811 North Olive Avenue, 33401-3709
Telephone: 407-655-6025
Fax: 407-655-5759
Palatka Office: 415 St. Johns Avenue.
Telephone: 904-325-6239.
Fax: 904-329-9626.

Terry N. Freeman
Robert C. Ross

OF COUNSEL

Henry P. Ruffolo

LEGAL SUPPORT PERSONNEL

Debra J. McPherson
E.I. "Chuck" Engelking

For full biographical listings, see the Martindale-Hubbell Law Directory

THOMAS E. KINGCADE PROFESSIONAL ASSOCIATION (AV)

209 South Olive Avenue, 33401
Telephone: 407-659-7300
FAX: 407-655-1593

Thomas E. Kingcade

William W. Booth

For full biographical listings, see the Martindale-Hubbell Law Directory

LIGGIO & LUCKMAN (AV)

213 Southern Boulevard, 33405
Telephone: 407-833-6604
Fax: 407-833-0870

MEMBERS OF FIRM

Jeffrey M. Liggio
Eric H. Luckman

LEGAL SUPPORT PERSONNEL

Yara B. Vega (Paralegal)

For full biographical listings, see the Martindale-Hubbell Law Directory

LYTAL & REITER (AV)

A Partnership including Professional Associations
Tenth Floor, 515 North Flagler Drive, 33401
Telephone: 407-655-1990
Fax: 407-832-2932
Mailing Address: P.O. Box 4056, 33402

Lake Lytal, Jr. (P.A.)
Joseph J. Reiter (P.A.)
Mark W. Clark
Tracy R. Sharpe

Donald R. Fountain, Jr.
Rafael J. Roca
William S. Williams
Michael J. Overbeck
Yvette Trelles Murray
Kevin C. Smith
Gerald T. McCarthy

Reference: United National Bank.

For full biographical listings, see the Martindale-Hubbell Law Directory

MATHISON & MATHISON (AV)

A Partnership of Professional Associations
Centre Park Plaza, 1400 Centre Park Boulevard, 33401-7412
Telephone: 407-471-4144
FAX: 407-471-3988
Palm Beach Gardens, Office: 5606 P.G.A Boulevard, Suite 211, 33418.
Telephone: 407-624-2001.
FAX: 407-624-0036.

MEMBERS OF FIRM

Carl M. Mathison, Jr., (P.A.)
Stephen S. Mathison (P.A.)

ASSOCIATE

Frederic T. DeHon, Jr., (P.A.)

Reference: Flagler National Bank.

For full biographical listings, see the Martindale-Hubbell Law Directory

RICCI, HUBBARD & LEOPOLD ATTORNEYS AT LAW, P.A. (AV)

United National Bank Building, 1645 Palm Beach Lakes Boulevard, P.O. Box 2946, 33402
Telephone: 407-684-6500
Fax: 407-697-2383

Edward M. Ricci
James R. Hubbard
Theodore J. Leopold
Theresa A. DiPaola
Scott C. Murray

LEGAL SUPPORT PERSONNEL

Robert V. Pautsch (Automotive Engineer)
Janice C. Develle (Paralegal)
Lisa B. Simone (Paralegal)
Joseph L. Vaccaro (Paralegal)
Linda J. Hermans (Paralegal)

For full biographical listings, see the Martindale-Hubbell Law Directory

GARY W. ROBERTS, P.A., LAWYERS (AV)

1675 Palm Beach Lakes Boulevard, Seventh Floor P.O. Drawer 4178, 33401
Telephone: 407-686-1800
FAX: 407-686-1533
New Port Richey, Florida Office: Roberts, Sojka & Doran, P.A., 5841 Main Street, 34652.
Telephone: 813-847-1103.

Gary W. Roberts
Cindy A. Sojka

For full biographical listings, see the Martindale-Hubbell Law Directory

ROTH, DUNCAN & LABARGA, P.A. (AV)

Northbridge Centre, Suite 325, 515 North Flagler Drive, 33401
Telephone: 407-655-5529
Telecopier: 407-655-7818
Mailing Address: P.O. Box 770, 33402

David Roth
Douglas Duncan
Jorge Labarga

For full biographical listings, see the Martindale-Hubbell Law Directory

SEARCY DENNEY SCAROLA BARNHART & SHIPLEY, PROFESSIONAL ASSOCIATION (AV)

2139 Palm Beach Lakes Boulevard, P.O. Drawer 3626, 33402-3626
Telephone: 407-686-6300
800-780-8607
Fax: 407-478-0754

Christian D. Searcy, Sr.
Earl L. Denney, Jr.
John Scarola
F. Gregory Barnhart
John A. Shipley
Lois J. Frankel
David K. Kelley, Jr.
Lawrence J. Block, Jr.
C. Calvin Warriner, III
William A. Norton
David J. Sales

James N. Nance
Katherine Ann Martinez
T. Michael Kennedy
Todd S. Stewart
Christopher K. Speed

LEGAL SUPPORT PERSONNEL

Deane L. Cady (Paralegal/Investigator)
James E. Cook (Paralegal/Investigator)
Emilio Diamantis (Paralegal/Investigator)
David W. Gilmore (Paralegal/Investigator)
John C. Hopkins (Paralegal/Investigator)
Thaddeus E. Kulesa (Paralegal/Investigator)
J. Peter Love (Paralegal/Investigator)
Marjorie A. Morgan (Paralegal)
Joel C. Padgett (Paralegal/Investigator)
William H. Seabold (Paralegal/Investigator)
Kathleen Simon (Paralegal)
Steve M. Smith (Paralegal/Investigator)
Judson Whitehorn (Paralegal/Investigator)
Marcia Yarnell Dodson (Not admitted in FL; Law Clerk)
Kelly Lynn Hopkins (Paralegal/Investigator)
Frank Cotton (Paralegal/Investigator)

For full biographical listings, see the Martindale-Hubbell Law Directory

WAGNER, NUGENT, JOHNSON & MCAFEE, P.A. (AV)

Commerce Pointe, Suite 450, 1818 South Australian Avenue, P.O. Box 3466, 33402
Telephone: 407-686-5200; 1-800-899-5200
FAX: 407-686-6710

Ward Wagner, Jr.
Robert R. Johnson
Helen Wagner McAfee
William J. McAfee
Julia A. Wagner

Michael G. Bodik

OF COUNSEL

Charles A. Nugent, Jr.

References: Sunbank/South Florida, N.A.; Fidelity Federal Savings & Loan Association of West Palm Beach.

For full biographical listings, see the Martindale-Hubbell Law Directory

GEORGIA

*ALBANY,** Dougherty Co.

CANNON, MEYER VON BREMEN & MEIER (AV)

2417 Westgate Drive, P.O. Box 70909, 31708-0909
Telephone: 912-435-1470
Telefax: 912-888-2156

MEMBERS OF FIRM

William E. Cannon, Jr.
John A. Meier, II
Michael S. Meyer von Bremen
Timothy O. Davis

For full biographical listings, see the Martindale-Hubbell Law Directory

*AMERICUS,** Sumter Co.

OXFORD, McKELVEY & JONES, P.C. (AV)

Old Fire Hall, 109 North Lee Street, P.O. Box J, 31709-0298
Telephone: 912-924-6108
FAX: 912-924-0935

Charles Oliver Oxford
Howard S. McKelvey, Jr.
Randolph B. Jones, Jr.

Representative Client: Reeves Construction Co.

For full biographical listings, see the Martindale-Hubbell Law Directory

*ATLANTA,** Fulton Co.

BEDFORD, KIRSCHNER AND VENKER, P.C. (AV)

Suite 450, 600 West Peachtree Street, N.W., 30308
Telephone: 404-872-6646

T. Jackson Bedford, Jr.
Andrew R. Kirschner
Thomas J. Venker

For full biographical listings, see the Martindale-Hubbell Law Directory

BELTRAN & ASSOCIATES (AV)

One Atlantic Center, Suite 3095, 1201 West Peachtree Street, 30309
Telephone: 404-892-3100
Facsimile: 404-892-1222

Frank J. Beltran
Simone R. Siex
Ralph Perales

Reference: NationsBank.

For full biographical listings, see the Martindale-Hubbell Law Directory

BIRD, BALLARD & STILL (AV)

14 Seventeenth Street, Suite 5, P.O. Box 7009, 30357
Telephone: 404-873-4696
Fax: 404-872-3745

William Q. Bird
William L. Ballard
Edward R. Still
John G. Mabrey
Kevin B. Carlock

For full biographical listings, see the Martindale-Hubbell Law Directory

BLACKWOOD & MATTHEWS (AV)

Monarch Plaza, 3414 Peachtree Road Suite 660, 30326
Telephone: 404-237-5050
Toll Free: 800-776-0098
Fax: 404-233-3910

B. Randall Blackwood
John D. Steel
James B. Matthews, III
John B. Briggs
H. Craig Stafford

For full biographical listings, see the Martindale-Hubbell Law Directory

DAVID WM. BOONE, P.C. (AV)

3155 Roswell Road Suite 100, The Cotton Exchange, 30305
Telephone: 404-239-0305
FAX: 404-239-0520

David William Boone

Leigh McCranie Smith

For full biographical listings, see the Martindale-Hubbell Law Directory

R. DAVID BOTTS (AV)

152 Nassau Street, N.W., 30303
Telephone: 404-688-5500
FAX: 404-688-6463

For full biographical listings, see the Martindale-Hubbell Law Directory

BUTLER, WOOTEN, OVERBY & CHEELEY (AV)

2719 Buford Highway, 30324
Telephone: 404-321-1700
WATS 1-800-242-2962
FAX: 404-321-1713
Columbus, Georgia Office: 1500 Second Avenue, P.O. Box 2766.
Telephone: 706-322-1990; National Wats: 1-800-233-4086.
FAX: 706-323-2962.

MEMBERS OF FIRM

James E. Butler, Jr.
Robert D. Cheeley
Joel O. Wooten, Jr.
Albert M. Pearson, III
C. Frederick Overby
George W. Fryhofer, III

ASSOCIATES

Peter J. Daughtery
Lee Tarte
J. Frank Myers, III
Jason L. Crawford
Patrick A. Dawson
Keith A. Pittman

Reference: Columbus Bank and Trust, Columbus, Ga.

For full biographical listings, see the Martindale-Hubbell Law Directory

CARR & KESSLER (AV)

An Association of Attorneys, Not a Partnership
3379 Peachtree Road, N.E., Suite 980, 30326
Telephone: 404-233-5008
FAX: 404-233-4713

James C. Carr, Jr.
Kathleen Kessler

For full biographical listings, see the Martindale-Hubbell Law Directory

CHAMBERS, MABRY, McCLELLAND & BROOKS (AV)

Tenth Floor, 2200 Century Parkway, N.E., 30345
Telephone: 404-325-4800
FAX: 404-325-0596
Lawrenceville, Georgia Office: Suite 377, 175 Gwinnett Drive.
Telephone: 404-339-7660.
FAX: 404-339-7060.

MEMBERS OF FIRM

Eugene P. Chambers, Jr.
Genevieve L. Frazier
E. Speer Mabry, III
Virginia Jane Reed
Walter B. McClelland
Jan Philip Cohen
Wilbur C. Brooks
James T. Budd
Lawrence J. Hogan (Resident at Lawrenceville Office)
Douglas F. Aholt
John C. Stivarius, Jr.
Rex D. Smith
Robert M. Darroch
Clyde E. Rickard, III
Cynthia J. Becker
Edwin L. Hamilton

ASSOCIATES

Benjamin T. Hughes
Vincent A. Toreno
F. Scott Young
Dale C. Ray, Jr.
Beth L. Singletary
Sandra G. Kirk
DeeAnn Boatright Waller
R. Michael Malcom
C. Gregory Ragsdale (Resident at Lawrenceville Office)
Michael E. Hardin

OF COUNSEL

H. A. Stephens, Jr.

Representative Clients: Allstate Insurance Co.; The Security Mutual Insurance Company of New York; National Automobile Insurance Co.

For full biographical listings, see the Martindale-Hubbell Law Directory

EDGAR L. CROSSETT, III, P.C. (AV)

5447 Roswell Road, Suite 200, 30342
Telephone: 404-843-1640
Telecopier: 404-847-0602

Edgar L. Crossett, III

For full biographical listings, see the Martindale-Hubbell Law Directory

DENNIS, CORRY, PORTER & GRAY (AV)

3300 One Atlanta Plaza, 950 East Paces Ferry Road, P.O. Box 18640, 30326
Telephone: 404-240-6900
Wats: 800-735-0838
Fax: 404-240-6909
Telex: 4611041

MEMBERS OF FIRM

Robert E. Corry, Jr.
William E. Gray, II
R. Clay Porter
James S. Strawinski
Grant B. Smith

(See Next Column)

DENNIS, CORRY, PORTER & GRAY, *Atlanta—Continued*

OF COUNSEL

Douglas Dennis

ASSOCIATES

Frederick D. Evans, III
Virginia M. Greer
Robert G. Ballard
Matthew J. Jewell
Pamela Jean Gray
Ronald G. Polly, Jr.
Thomas D. Trask
J. Steven Fisher
Stephanie F. Goff
Alison Roberts Solomon
Robert David Schoen
Brian DeVoe Rogers

Representative Clients: Farmers Insurance Group; Roadway Services, Inc.

For full biographical listings, see the Martindale-Hubbell Law Directory

DWYER & WHITE (AV)

A Partnership including a Professional Corporation
Suite 700, 2100 Riveredge Parkway, 30328-4654
Telephone: 404-956-1984
FAX: 404-956-1381

MEMBERS

J. Matthew Dwyer, Jr. (P.C.)
William Woods White

ASSOCIATES

Anne Woolf Sapp
Carmen D. Smith
Carmen S. Mills

For full biographical listings, see the Martindale-Hubbell Law Directory

EICHELBERGER & PERROTTA (AV)

The Hurt Building, 50 Hurt Plaza, Suite 902, 30303
Telephone: 404-524-1957
Telecopier: 404-577-9490

MEMBERS OF FIRM

James A. Eichelberger
Theodore B. Eichelberger
Joseph D. Perrotta

For full biographical listings, see the Martindale-Hubbell Law Directory

ENGLAND & McKNIGHT (AV)

Suite 410 River Ridge, 9040 Roswell Road, 30350
Telephone: 404-641-6010
FAX: 404-641-6003

MEMBERS OF FIRM

J. Melvin England
Robert H. McKnight, Jr.

Reference: Bank South, N.A.

For full biographical listings, see the Martindale-Hubbell Law Directory

GARLAND, SAMUEL & LOEB, P.C. (AV)

3151 Maple Drive, N.E., 30305
Telephone: 404-262-2225
FAX: 404-365-5041

Edward T. M. Garland
Donald F. Samuel
Robin N. Loeb
Patrick J. Geheren

For full biographical listings, see the Martindale-Hubbell Law Directory

GOLDNER, SOMMERS, SCRUDDER & BASS (AV)

2839 Paces Ferry Road, Suite 800, 30339-3774
Telephone: 404-436-4777
Facsimile: 404-436-8777

Stephen L. Goldner
Henry E. Scrudder, Jr.

For Complete List of Firm Personnel, See General Section

For full biographical listings, see the Martindale-Hubbell Law Directory

HART & McINTYRE (AV)

Promenade Two Suite 3775, 1230 Peachtree Street, N.E., 30309
Telephone: 800-521-3775 (Nationwide); 404-876-3775
Fax: 404-873-3799

MEMBERS OF FIRM

George W. Hart
John C. McIntyre, Jr.
Bonnie M. Wharton

Reference: BankSouth.

For full biographical listings, see the Martindale-Hubbell Law Directory

HILL AND BLEIBERG (AV)

Suite 200, 47 Perimeter Center East, 30346
Telephone: 404-394-7800
Fax: 404-394-7802

MEMBERS OF FIRM

Robert P. Bleiberg
Gary Hill

For full biographical listings, see the Martindale-Hubbell Law Directory

HOLT, NEY, ZATCOFF & WASSERMAN (AV)

A Partnership including Professional Corporations
100 Galleria Parkway, Suite 600, 30339
Telephone: 404-956-9600
Facsimile Number: 404-956-1490

MEMBERS OF FIRM

Robert G. Holt (P.C.)
James M. Ney (P.C.)
Sanford H. Zatcoff (P.C.)
Michael G. Wasserman (P.C.)
J. Scott Jacobson
Charles D. Vaughn
Stephen C. Greenberg
Richard P. Vornholt
Barbara J. Schneider

ASSOCIATES

Brian P. Cain
David S. O'Quinn
Jay Frank Castle

Representative Clients: AmeriHealth, Inc.; Citibank, N.A.; Cummins South, Inc.; First American Title Insurance Co.; First National Bank of Chicago; First Union National Bank of Georgia; Georgia Scientific & Technical Research Foundation; NationsBank of Georgia, N.A.; Safety-Kleen Corp.; Trammell Crow Residential.

For full biographical listings, see the Martindale-Hubbell Law Directory

JOHNSON & WARD (AV)

2100 The Equitable Building, 100 Peachtree Street N.W., 30303-1962
Telephone: 404-524-5626
Facsimile: 404-524-1769

MEMBERS OF FIRM

Clark H. McGehee
John C. Dabney, Jr.
William D. deGolian
D. Lake Rumsey, Jr.

For full biographical listings, see the Martindale-Hubbell Law Directory

THOMAS WILLIAM MALONE (AV)

Two Ravinia Drive Suite 300, 30346
Telephone: 404-390-7550
Fax: 404-390-7560

Lawrence J. Pond
J. Hoyt Young

References: Trust Company Bank, Atlanta, Georgia; Trust Company Bank of South Georgia.

For full biographical listings, see the Martindale-Hubbell Law Directory

LAW OFFICES OF J. WAYNE PIERCE, P.A. (AV)

Two Paces West, Suite 1700 4000 Cumberland Parkway, 30339
Telephone: 404-435-0500
Telecopier: 404-435-0362

J. Wayne Pierce

Dargan Scott Cole
Thomas L. Schaefer

For full biographical listings, see the Martindale-Hubbell Law Directory

POPE, McGLAMRY, KILPATRICK & MORRISON (AV)

A Partnership including Professional Corporations
83 Walton Street, N.W., P.O. Box 1733, 30303
Telephone: 404-523-7706;
Phenix City, Alabama: 205-298-7354
Columbus, Georgia Office: 318 11th Street, 2nd Floor, P.O. Box 2128, 31902-2128.
Telephone: 706-324-0050.

MEMBERS OF FIRM

C. Neal Pope (P.C.)
Max R. McGlamry (P.C.) (Resident, Columbus, Georgia Office)
Paul V. Kilpatrick, Jr. (Resident, Columbus, Georgia Office)
R. Timothy Morrison
Michael L. McGlamry
Earle F. Lasseter
William J. Cornwell
Jay F. Hirsch
Daniel W. Sigelman
Wade H. Tomlinson, III
William Usher Norwood, III

RESIDENT ASSOCIATE

C. Elizabeth Pope

Reference: Columbus Bank & Trust Co.

For full biographical listings, see the Martindale-Hubbell Law Directory

REYNOLDS & McARTHUR (AV)

A Partnership including a Professional Corporation
Suite 1010, One Buckhead Plaza, 3060 Peachtree Road, N.W., 30305
Telephone: 404-240-0265
Fax: 404-262-3557
Macon, Georgia Office: 850 Walnut Street.
Telephone: 912-741-6000.
Fax: 912-742-0750.

(See Next Column)

REYNOLDS & MCARTHUR—*Continued*

Asheville, North Carolina Office: The Jackson Building, 22 South Pack Square, Suite 1200.
Telephone: 704-254-8523.
Fax: 704-254-3038.

MEMBERS OF FIRM

W. Carl Reynolds (P.C.)
Katherine L. McArthur
Steve Ray Warren
(Not admitted in GA)
Charles M. Cork, III
O. Wendell Horne, III
Bradley J. Survant
Laura D. Hogue

For full biographical listings, see the Martindale-Hubbell Law Directory

ANDREW M. SCHERFFIUS, P.C. (AV)

3166 Mathieson Drive, P.O. Box 53299, 30355
Telephone: 404-261-3562; 1-800-521-2867
Fax: 404-841-0861

Andrew M. Scherffius

Tamara McDowell Ayres

For full biographical listings, see the Martindale-Hubbell Law Directory

KENNETH L. SHIGLEY (AV)

5180 Roswell Road, N.W., 30342-2208
Telephone: 404-252-1108
Fax: 404-303-4924

For full biographical listings, see the Martindale-Hubbell Law Directory

SULLIVAN, HALL, BOOTH & SMITH, A PROFESSIONAL CORPORATION (AV)

One Midtown Plaza, 1360 Peachtree Street, N.E., Suite 800, 30309
Telephone: 404-870-8000
FAX: 404-870-8020

Terrance C. Sullivan
John E. Hall, Jr.
Alexander H. Booth
Rush S. Smith, Jr.
Henry D. Green, Jr.
Jack G. Slover, Jr.
Timothy H. Bendin
Michael A. Pannier
Brynda Sue Rodriguez
Roger S. Sumrall

David V. Johnson
Jeffrey T. Wise
Eleanor L. Martel
A. Spencer McManes, Jr.
David G. Goodchild, Jr.
Robert L. Shannon, Jr.
T. Andrew Graham
Earnest Redwine
Melanie P. Simon
(Not admitted in GA)

Reference: Wachovia Bank of Georgia.

For full biographical listings, see the Martindale-Hubbell Law Directory

THOMAS, KENNEDY, SAMPSON & PATTERSON (AV)

1600 Bank South Building, 55 Marietta Street, N.W., 30303
Telephone: 404-688-4503
Telecopier: 404-681-2950

MEMBERS OF FIRM

John Loren Kennedy
(1942-1994)
Thomas G. Sampson
P. Andrew Patterson
Myra H. Dixon
R. David Ware
Patrise M. Perkins-Hooker
Jeffrey E. Tompkins

ASSOCIATES

Rosalind T. Drakeford
Regina E. McMillan
Melynee C. Leftridge
La'Sean M. Zilton

For full biographical listings, see the Martindale-Hubbell Law Directory

*BLAKELY,** Early Co.

WILLIAM S. STONE, P.C. (AV)

Stone Building, 107 College Street, P.O. Box 70, 31723
Telephone: 912-723-3045
FAX: 912-723-4834

William S. Stone
William Lowrey Stone
(1894-1970)

Thomas E. Sasser, III
Kevin R. Dean
T. Craig Earnest

For full biographical listings, see the Martindale-Hubbell Law Directory

*BRUNSWICK,** Glynn Co.

LISSNER, KILLIAN, CUNNINGHAM AND BOYD (AV)

506 Monk Street, P.O. Box 1795, 31521
Telephone: 912-265-5063; 1-800-339-5063 (S.E. Georgia only)
Fax: 912-265-1209

OF COUNSEL

Jack J. Lissner, Jr.

(See Next Column)

MEMBERS OF FIRM

Robert P. Killian
Robert M. Cunningham
Roy J. Boyd, Jr.
Darrell Lee Burrow

Representative Clients: Barnett Bank; Brunswick Nissan, Inc.; Century Communications; Goldome Credit Corp.; 1st Franklin Finance; Alpha Motor Sales, Inc.

For full biographical listings, see the Martindale-Hubbell Law Directory

*CEDARTOWN,** Polk Co.

MUNDY & GAMMAGE, P.C. (AV)

216 Main Street, P.O. Box 930, 30125-0930
Telephone: 706-748-3870
706-688-9416 (Atlanta)
Fax: 706-748-2489
Rome, Georgia Office: The Carnegie Building, 607 Broad Street.
Telephone: 706-290-5180.

Emil Lamar Gammage, Jr.
William D. Sparks
(Mrs.) Gerry E. Holmes
George E. Mundy
Miles L. Gammage
John S. Husser
B. Jean Crane
Kelly A. Benedict

For full biographical listings, see the Martindale-Hubbell Law Directory

*COLUMBUS,** Muscogee Co.

BRINKLEY AND BRINKLEY (AV)

Suite 901 Corporate Center, 233 12th Street, P.O. Box 2016, 31902-2016
Telephone: 706-576-5322
FAX: 706-324-3766

MEMBERS OF FIRM

Jack Thomas Brinkley
Jack T. Brinkley, Jr.

Reference: Columbus Bank & Trust Co.

For full biographical listings, see the Martindale-Hubbell Law Directory

BUTLER, WOOTEN, OVERBY & CHEELEY (AV)

1500 Second Avenue, P.O. Box 2766, 31902
Telephone: 706-322-1990;
National Wats: 1-800-233-4086
FAX: 706-323-2962
Atlanta, Georgia Office: 2719 Buford Highway, 30324.
Telephone: 404-321-1700.
FAX: 404-321-1713. Wats Line: 1-800-242-2962.

MEMBERS OF FIRM

James E. Butler, Jr.
Joel O. Wooten, Jr.
C. Frederick Overby
Robert D. Cheeley
Albert M. Pearson, III
George W. Fryhofer, III

ASSOCIATES

Peter J. Daughtery
J. Frank Myers, III
Patrick A. Dawson
Lee Tarte
Jason L. Crawford
Keith A. Pittman

For full biographical listings, see the Martindale-Hubbell Law Directory

POPE, MCGLAMRY, KILPATRICK & MORRISON (AV)

A Partnership including Professional Corporations
318 11th Street, 2nd Floor, P.O. Box 2128, 31902-2128
Telephone: 706-324-0050;
Phenix City, Alabama: 205-298-7354
Atlanta, Georgia Office: 83 Walton Street, N.W., P.O. Box 1733, 30303.
Telephone: 404-523-7706.

MEMBERS OF FIRM

C. Neal Pope (P.C.)
Max R. McGlamry (P.C.)
(Resident)
Paul V. Kilpatrick, Jr.
(Resident)
R. Timothy Morrison (Resident, Atlanta, Georgia Office)
Michael L. McGlamry
Earle F. Lasseter
William J. Cornwell
Jay F. Hirsch
Daniel W. Sigelman
Wade H. Tomlinson, III
(Resident, Atlanta Office)
William Usher Norwood, III
(Resident, Atlanta Office)

RESIDENT ASSOCIATES

Joan S. Redmond
Teresa Pike Majors

Reference: Columbus Bank & Trust Co.

For full biographical listings, see the Martindale-Hubbell Law Directory

TAYLOR, HARP & CALLIER (AV)

Suite 900 The Corporate Center, P.O. Box 2645, 31902-2645
Telephone: 706-323-7711
National WATS: 1-800-422-3352
Fax: 706-323-7544

MEMBERS OF FIRM

J. Sherrod Taylor
J. Anderson Harp
Jefferson C. Callier

For full biographical listings, see the Martindale-Hubbell Law Directory

*DECATUR,** De Kalb Co.

HYATT & HYATT, P.C. (AV)

Suite 201, Trust Building, 545 North McDonough Street, 30030
Telephone: 404-377-3635
Fax: 404-377-8304

Charles H. Hyatt (Retired) John M. Hyatt

For full biographical listings, see the Martindale-Hubbell Law Directory

PARKERSON & SHELFER (AV)

715 First Union Decatur Building, 250 East Ponce De Leon Avenue, 30030
Telephone: 404-377-8143
Telecopier: 404-373-6829

MEMBERS OF FIRM

William S. Shelfer (1900-1975) I. J. Parkerson
William S. Shelfer, Jr.

Reference: Nations Bank of Georgia.

For full biographical listings, see the Martindale-Hubbell Law Directory

*JONESBORO,** Clayton Co.

DRIEBE & DRIEBE, P.C. (AV)

6 Courthouse Way, P.O. Box 975, 30237
Telephone: 404-478-8894
FAX: 404-478-9606
Atlanta, Georgia Office: 152 Nassau Street, N.W.
Telephone: 404-688-5500.

Charles J. Driebe Charles J. Driebe, Jr.
J. Ron Stegall

Approved Attorneys for: First American Title Insurance Co.; Attorney's Title Guaranty Fund.
Representative Clients: Atlanta International Records, Inc.; Henry County Airport, Inc.; Clayton News/Daily; Atlanta Beach Sports & Entertainment Park, Inc.

For full biographical listings, see the Martindale-Hubbell Law Directory

*MACON,** Bibb Co.

CHAMBLESS, HIGDON & CARSON (AV)

Suite 200 Ambrose Baber Building, 577 Walnut Street, P.O. Box 246, 31298-5399
Telephone: 912-745-1181
Telecopier: 912-746-9479

MEMBERS OF FIRM

Joseph H. Davis
Joseph H. Chambless
David B. Higdon
James F. Carson, Jr.
Thomas F. Richardson
Mary Mendel Katz
Emmitte H. Griggs
Marc T. Treadwell

ASSOCIATES

Kim H. Stroup Christopher Balch
Jon Christopher Wolfe

Local Counsel for: Atlanta Gas Light Co.; First Union National Bank of Georgia; Security National Bank.

For full biographical listings, see the Martindale-Hubbell Law Directory

HALL, BLOCH, GARLAND & MEYER (AV)

1500 Charter Medical Building, P.O. Box 5088, 31213-3199
Telephone: 912-745-1625
Telecopier: 912-741-8822

MEMBERS OF FIRM

F. Kennedy Hall
Benjamin M. Garland
J. Steven Stewart
Mark E. Toth

ASSOCIATE

Todd C. Brooks

For Complete List of Firm Personnel, See General Section

For full biographical listings, see the Martindale-Hubbell Law Directory

O'NEAL, BROWN & SIZEMORE, A PROFESSIONAL CORPORATION (AV)

Suite 1001, American Federal Building, 544 Mulberry Street, 31201
Telephone: 912-742-8981
Telecopier: 912-743-5035
Atlanta, Georgia Office: Suite 2600, One Atlanta Plaza, 950 East Paces Ferry Road, N.E.
Telephone: 404-237-6701.
Telecopier: 404-233-1267.

(See Next Column)

H. T. O'Neal, Jr. (1924-1983) Manley F. Brown
Lamar W. Sizemore, Jr.

For Complete List of Firm Personnel, See General Section

For full biographical listings, see the Martindale-Hubbell Law Directory

REYNOLDS & MCARTHUR (AV)

A Partnership including a Professional Corporation
850 Walnut Street, 31201
Telephone: 912-741-6000
Fax: 912-742-0750
Atlanta, Georgia Office: Suite 1010, One Buckhead Plaza, 3060 Peachtree Road, N.W.
Telephone: 404-240-0265.
Fax: 404-262-3557.
Asheville, North Carolina Office: The Jackson Building, 22 South Pack Square, Suite 1200.
Telephone: 704-254-8523.
Fax: 704-254-3038.

MEMBERS OF FIRM

W. Carl Reynolds (P.C.)
Katherine L. McArthur
Steve Ray Warren (Not admitted in GA)
Charles M. Cork, III
O. Wendell Horne, III
Bradley J. Survant
Laura D. Hogue

For full biographical listings, see the Martindale-Hubbell Law Directory

SELL & MELTON (AV)

A Partnership including a Professional Corporation
14th Floor, Charter Medical Building, P.O. Box 229, 31297-2899
Telephone: 912-746-8521
Telecopier: 912-745-6426

Mitchel P. House, Jr.
Doye E. Green
John A. Draughon
Russell M. Boston (P.C.)

General Counsel for: Macon Telegraph Publishing Co. (The Macon Telegraph); Macon-Bibb County Hospital Authority; County of Bibb; County of Twiggs; Smith & Sons Foods, Inc. (S & S Cafeterias); Macon Bibb County Industrial Authority; Burgess Pigment Co.

For Complete List of Firm Personnel, See General Section

For full biographical listings, see the Martindale-Hubbell Law Directory

MANCHESTER, Meriwether Co.

TYRON C. ELLIOTT (AV)

Old Post Office Building, 133 Main Street, P.O. Drawer 389, 31816
Telephone: 706-846-8438
FAX: 706-846-8754

References: Farmers and Merchants Bank of Manchester; Woodbury Banking Company.

For full biographical listings, see the Martindale-Hubbell Law Directory

*MARIETTA,** Cobb Co.

AWTREY AND PARKER, P.C. (AV)

211 Roswell Street, P.O. Box 997, 30061
Telephone: 404-424-8000
Fax: 404-424-1594

L. M. Awtrey, Jr. (1915-1986)
George L. Dozier, Jr.
Harvey D. Harkness
Mike Harrison
Dana L. Jackel
Donald A. Mangerie (1924-1988)
Michael L. Marsh
Barbara H. Martin
A. Sidney Parker
Toby B. Prodgers
J. Lynn Rainey
Annette M. Risse (Mrs.)
Robert B. Silliman

Gregg A. Landau Lisa G. Gunn
Alan H. Sheldon

OF COUNSEL

Allan J. Hall J. Ben Moore
S. Alan Schlact

General Counsel for: Kennesaw Finance Co.; Cobb Electric Membership Corporation; Development Authority of Cobb County.
Local Counsel for: Coats & Clark; Bell South Mobility; Lockheed-Georgia Corp.; Post Properties, Inc.; CSX Transportation, Inc.

For full biographical listings, see the Martindale-Hubbell Law Directory

BARNES, BROWNING, TANKSLEY & CASURELLA (AV)

Suite 225, 166 Anderson Street, 30060
Telephone: 404-424-1500
Fax: 404-424-1740

(See Next Column)

BARNES, BROWNING, TANKSLEY & CASURELLA—*Continued*

MEMBERS OF FIRM

Roy E. Barnes
Thomas J. Browning
Charles B. Tanksley
Thomas J. Casurella (1956-1989)
Jerry A. Landers, Jr.
Jeffrey G. Casurella
Benny C. Priest

OF COUNSEL

George T. Smith
Howard D. Rothbloom

For full biographical listings, see the Martindale-Hubbell Law Directory

STEVEN L. BEARD, P.C. (AV)

324 Cherokee Street, 30060
Telephone: 404-422-2642
FAX: 404-422-8954

Steven L. Beard

Susan Pipkin Lisenby

For full biographical listings, see the Martindale-Hubbell Law Directory

DOWNEY & CLEVELAND (AV)

288 Washington Avenue, 30060
Telephone: 404-422-3233
Fax: 404-423-4199

OF COUNSEL

Lynn A. Downey

MEMBERS OF FIRM

Joseph C. Parker
Y. Kevin Williams
Russell B. Davis
G. Lee Welborn

ASSOCIATES

Rodney S. Shockley
W. Curtis Anderson

Representative Clients: Allstate Insurance Co.; St. Paul Insurance Cos.; Georgia Farm Bureau Mutual Insurance Co.; State Farm Insurance Cos.; Cotton States Mutual Insurance Co.; Colonial Insurance Co. of California; Ed Voyles Oldsmobile, Honda and Chrysler-Plymouth; Chuck Clancy Ford; City of Acworth; Lockheed Aeronautical Systems Company, a Division of Lockheed Corporation.

For Complete List of Firm Personnel, See General Section

For full biographical listings, see the Martindale-Hubbell Law Directory

*SAVANNAH,** Chatham Co.

JONES, BOYKIN & ASSOCIATES, PROFESSIONAL CORPORATION (AV)

701 Abercorn Street, 31401
Telephone: 912-236-6161

John Wright Jones
Noble L. Boykin, Jr.
H. Gregory Fowler
Harold J. Cronk
Charles W. Snyder
Robert K. Hardeman
Gilbert L. Stacy

References: Trust Company Bank of Savannah.

For full biographical listings, see the Martindale-Hubbell Law Directory

HAWAII

*HONOLULU,** Honolulu Co.

ASHFORD & NAKAMURA (AV)

2910 Pacific Tower, 1001 Bishop Street, 96813
Telephone: 808-528-0444
Telex: 723-8158
Telecopier: (808) 533-0761
Cable Address: Justlaw

George W. Ashford, Jr.
Lee T. Nakamura

Ann C. Kemp
Francis T. O'Brien

Representative Clients: Baker Industries, Inc.; Burns International Security Services; Clark Equipment Co.; Great Lakes Chemical Corporation; California Union Insurance Co.; Fireman's Fund Insurance Companies; Great American Insurance Companies; Guaranty National Companies; Horace Mann Insurance Company; Marine Office of America Corp.

For full biographical listings, see the Martindale-Hubbell Law Directory

AYABE, CHONG, NISHIMOTO, SIA & NAKAMURA (AV)

A Partnership including a Professional Corporation
3000 Grosvenor Center, 737 Bishop Street, 96813
Telephone: 808-537-6119
Telecopier: 808-526-3491

MEMBERS OF FIRM

Sidney K. Ayabe (P.C.)
John S. Nishimoto
Richard Nakamura
Jeffrey H. K. Sia
Francis M. Nakamoto
Calvin E. Young
Diane W. Wong
Rodney S. Nishida
Patricia T. Fujii
Rhonda Nishimura
Gail M. Kang

Ann H. Aratani
Ronald M. Shigekane
Robin R. Horner
Daria Ann Loy
Virgil B. Prieto

Representative Clients: Travelers Insurance Co.; St. Paul Fire and Marine Insurance Co.; The Employers Group of Insurance Companies; TIG Insurance Co.; Pacific Insurance Co.; Hartford Accident and Indemnity Co.; Continental Casualty Co.; First Insurance Company of Hawaii, Ltd.

For Complete List of Firm Personnel, See General Section

For full biographical listings, see the Martindale-Hubbell Law Directory

CRONIN, FRIED, SEKIYA, KEKINA & FAIRBANKS ATTORNEYS AT LAW, A LAW CORPORATION (AV)

1900 Davies Pacific Center, 841 Bishop Street, 96813
Telephone: 808-524-1433
FAX: 808-536-2073

Paul F. Cronin
L. Richard Fried, Jr.
Gerald Y. Sekiya
Wayne K. Kekina
David L. Fairbanks
John D. Thomas, Jr.
Stuart A. Kaneko
Bert S. Sakuda
Allen K. Williams
Keith K. H. Young

Patrick W. Border
Gregory L. Lui-Kwan
Patrick F. McTernan
Irene M. Nakano

For full biographical listings, see the Martindale-Hubbell Law Directory

IAN L. MATTOCH (AV)

Suite 1835 Grosvenor Center, 737 Bishop Street, 96813
Telephone: 808-523-2451
Cable Address: "Illnoncarb"
Fax: 808-531-2652
Hilo, Hawaii Office: 688 Kinoole Street, Suite 202, 96720.
Telephone: 808-969-3302.
Fax: 808-961-5599.
Kailua Kona Office: Hualalai Center, Suite D-211, 75-170 Hualalai Road.
Telephone: 808-326-1516.
Fax: 808-326-7416.

William Copulos
Kelly Kotada
Rodger I. Hoffman (Resident Kailua Kona Office)
Virgil James Wilson, III

OF COUNSEL

Walter Davis

Reference: First Hawaiian Bank.

For full biographical listings, see the Martindale-Hubbell Law Directory

DENNIS W. POTTS ATTORNEY AT LAW, A LAW CORPORATION (AV)

2770 Pacific Tower, 1001 Bishop Street, 96813
Telephone: 808-537-4575
Fax: 808-599-3524

Dennis W. Potts

For full biographical listings, see the Martindale-Hubbell Law Directory

PRICE OKAMOTO HIMENO & LUM ATTORNEYS AT LAW, A LAW CORPORATION (AV)

Suite 728, Ocean View Center, 707 Richards Street, 96813
Telephone: 808-538-1113
FAX: 808-533-0549

Warren Price, III
Kenneth T. Okamoto
Sharon R. Himeno
Bettina W. J. Lum
Terence S. Yamamoto

John H. Yuen

OF COUNSEL

Stuart M. Cowan

For full biographical listings, see the Martindale-Hubbell Law Directory

Honolulu—Continued

LAW OFFICE OF KENNETH S. ROBBINS ATTORNEY AT LAW, A LAW CORPORATION (AV)

Suite 2220 Davies Pacific Center, 841 Bishop Street, 96813
Telephone: 808-524-2355
Fax: 808-526-0290

Kenneth S. Robbins

Vincent A. Rhodes
Shinken Naitoh

For full biographical listings, see the Martindale-Hubbell Law Directory

DAVID C. SCHUTTER & ASSOCIATES (AV)

Suite 300 Ocean View Center, 707 Richards Street, 96813
Telephone: 808-524-4600
Facsimile: 808-521-2870

ASSOCIATES

Emlyn H. Higa
Karen Kightlinger
Paul V. Smith
James R. Veary
Mitchell S. Wong
Gary M. Levitt

For full biographical listings, see the Martindale-Hubbell Law Directory

WEINBERG & BELL ATTORNEYS AT LAW, A LAW CORPORATION (AV)

Suite 1200, 1164 Bishop Street, 96813
Telephone: 808-523-9477
FAX: 808-521-4681

Jan M. Weinberg
Roy J. Bell, III

For full biographical listings, see the Martindale-Hubbell Law Directory

MICHAEL J. Y. WONG (AV)

2222 Central Pacific Plaza, 220 South King Street, 96813
Telephone: 808-536-1855
Fax: 808-536-1857

ASSOCIATE

R. Malia Taum

For full biographical listings, see the Martindale-Hubbell Law Directory

*WAILUKU,** Maui Co.

ROST & GEIGER (AV)

610 One Main Plaza, 2200 Main Street, 96793
Telephone: 808-244-9044
FAX: 808-242-4195

Richard L. Rost
James W. Geiger

For full biographical listings, see the Martindale-Hubbell Law Directory

ILLINOIS

AURORA, Kane Co.

MURPHY, HUPP, FOOTE, MIELKE AND KINNALLY (AV)

North Island Center, P.O. Box 5030, 60507
Telephone: 708-844-0056
FAX: 708-844-1905

MEMBERS OF FIRM

William C. Murphy
Robert B. Hupp
Robert M. Foote
Craig S. Mielke
Patrick M. Kinnally
Paul G. Krentz
Joseph C. Loran
Gerald K. Hodge

Timothy D. O'Neil
Thomas U. Hipp

OF COUNSEL

Robert T. Olson

Representative Clients: American Telephone & Telegraph Co.; Fox Valley Park District; Lyon Metal Products; Kane County Forest Preserve District; Hollywood Casino; Employers Mutual Insurance Co.; Forty-Eight Insulations, Inc.; UNR Asbestos Disease Trust; Richards-Wilcox Co.; National Bank & Trust Company of Syracuse.

For full biographical listings, see the Martindale-Hubbell Law Directory

*BELLEVILLE,** St. Clair Co.

KUEHN, TRENTMAN & O'GARA (AV)

2027 West Main Street, 62223
Telephone: 618-277-6646; 398-6648
Fax: 618-277-6649

(See Next Column)

MEMBERS OF FIRM

Clyde L. Kuehn
Brian K. Trentman
John J. O'Gara, Jr.

Reference: Bank of Belleville, Belleville, Illinois.

For full biographical listings, see the Martindale-Hubbell Law Directory

GEORGE RIPPLINGER & ASSOCIATES (AV)

2215 West Main Street, 62223
Telephone: 618-234-2440; 800-733-8333
Telecopier: 618-234-6728
St. Louis, Missouri Office: 4144 Lindell Boulevard.

George R. Ripplinger, Jr.

ASSOCIATES

Thomas L. Zimmer
Lisa M. Pennock

A list of Representative Clients provided on request.
Reference: First National Bank of Belleville, Illinois.

For full biographical listings, see the Martindale-Hubbell Law Directory

*CHICAGO,** Cook Co.

ANESI, OZMON & RODIN, LTD. (AV)

161 North Clark Street, 21st Floor, 60601
Telephone: 312-372-3822
Fax: 312-372-3833

Nat P. Ozmon
Charles E. Anesi
Richard A. Lewin (1925-1985)
Curt N. Rodin
Mark Novak
Arnold G. Rubin
Richard L. Rumsey
Bruce M. Kohen
Richard A. Kimnach
Joseph J. Miroballi
Douglas A. Colby
David J. Comeau
James J. Morici, Jr.
Alain Leval
Stephen S. Phalen
Marc A. Taxman
Scott H. Rudin
John A. Salzeider
David Figlioli
Martin J. Lucas
Christopher J. Dallavo
Daniel V. O'Connor
Micaela M. Cassidy
John M. Popelka
Telly C. Nakos
Michelle Dekalb
Mark Murnane

OF COUNSEL

Noel C. Lindenmuth
Irving D. Fasman

For full biographical listings, see the Martindale-Hubbell Law Directory

BERMAN AND TRACHTMAN, P.C. (AV)

Suite 2215, 100 North La Salle Street, 60602
Telephone: 312-726-0531
Fax: 312-726-4928

Michael H. Berman
Steven B. Trachtman

Joy C. Airaudi

For full biographical listings, see the Martindale-Hubbell Law Directory

CHARLES A. BOYLE & ASSOCIATES, LTD. (AV)

29 South La Salle Street, Suite 345, 60603
Telephone: 312-346-4944
FAX: 312-368-1061

Charles A. Boyle

Mary C. Sweeney
Marc A. Korman

Reference: Northern Trust of Chicago.

For full biographical listings, see the Martindale-Hubbell Law Directory

CORBOY • DEMETRIO • CLIFFORD, P.C. (AV)

33 North Dearborn Street 21st Floor, 60602
Telephone: 312-346-3191
FAX: 312-346-5562
TDD: 312-236-3191

Philip H. Corboy
Thomas A. Demetrio
Robert A. Clifford
Philip Harnett Corboy, Jr.

Robert J. Bingle
Kevin G. Burke
Michael K. Demetrio
Kevin P. Durkin
Keith A. Hebeisen
Francis Patrick Murphy
Susan J. Schwartz

Thomas F. Boleky
Richard F. Burke, Jr.
Susan A. Capra
Patricia J. Carlson
Timothy J. Cavanagh
Barry R. Chafetz
G. Grant Dixon III
Mary E. Doherty
J. Matthew Dudley
Shawn S. Kasserman
Jeffrey J. Kroll
Michael G. Mahoney

(See Next Column)

CORBOY • DEMETRIO • CLIFFORD P.C.—*Continued*

Michael K. Muldoon
Margaret M. Power
Thomas K. Prindable
Richard L. Pullano
Michael Flinn Roe
Robert P. Walsh, Jr.
Edward G. Willer
David C. Wise

OF COUNSEL

Robert P. Sheridan
Phillip Taxman

Reference: The American National Bank & Trust Company, Chicago, Illinois.

For full biographical listings, see the Martindale-Hubbell Law Directory

EPSTEIN, ZAIDEMAN & ESRIG, P.C. (AV)

120 South Riverside Plaza, Suite 1150, 60606
Telephone: 312-207-0005
Fax: 312-207-1332

Robert J. Zaideman
Jerry A. Esrig

Elizabeth A. Kaveny

For full biographical listings, see the Martindale-Hubbell Law Directory

GESSLER, FLYNN, FLEISCHMANN, HUGHES & SOCOL, LTD. (AV)

Three First National Plaza, Suite 2200, 60602
Telephone: 312-580-0100
Telecopy: 312-580-1994

Mark S. Dym
Michael J. Flaherty
Thomas J. Fleischmann
Terence E. Flynn
George W. Gessler
John K. Hughes
William P. Jones
Peter M. Katsaros
Mark A. LaRose
Terence J. Moran
Matthew J. Piers
David J. Pritchard
Kalman D. Resnick
Jonathan A. Rothstein
Donna Kaner Socol

Eric Berg
Benjamin P. Beringer
Anjali Dayal
Ruth M. Dunning
Jennifer Fischer
Charles J. Holley
Laura C. Liu
Kimberley Marsh
Alex W. Miller
Paul A. Reasoner
Michael P. Simkus
Marci S. Sperling
Maria L. Venturo
Vanessa J. Weathersby
Mark B. Weiner
Charles H. Winterstein

OF COUNSEL

James T. Derico, Jr.
Susan R. Gzesh
Foster Marshall, Jr.

For full biographical listings, see the Martindale-Hubbell Law Directory

JOHN PATRICK HEALY (AV)

29 South La Salle - Suite 640, 60603
Telephone: 312-332-7950
FAX: 312-782-4502

ASSOCIATE

Sheryl E. Healy

For full biographical listings, see the Martindale-Hubbell Law Directory

PETER D. KASDIN, LTD. (AV)

Suite 1960, 135 South La Salle Street, 60603
Telephone: 312-630-1990
Facsimile: 312-630-1103

Peter D. Kasdin

David W. Hepplewhite
Regina Picone Etherton
Meredith H. Emerson

OF COUNSEL

David W. Horan

For full biographical listings, see the Martindale-Hubbell Law Directory

KENNETH C. MILLER, LTD. (AV)

33 North Dearborn Street, Suite 1930, 60602
Telephone: 312-236-8634
Telecopier: 312-236-1882

Kenneth C. Miller
James W. O'Connor
Joy L. Sparling

For full biographical listings, see the Martindale-Hubbell Law Directory

BERNARD R. NEVORAL AND ASSOCIATES LTD. (AV)

150 North Wacker Drive, Suite 2450, 60606
Telephone: 312 263-7058
FAX: 312-263-4566

Bernard R. Nevoral

(See Next Column)

Paul W. Pasche
John L. Malevitis
Maurice E. Dusky

For full biographical listings, see the Martindale-Hubbell Law Directory

STEPHEN M. PASSEN, LTD. (AV)

Suite 2900, 120 North La Salle Street, 60602
Telephone: 312-236-5878
Facsimile: 312-236-1162

Stephen M. Passen

David G. Susler

For full biographical listings, see the Martindale-Hubbell Law Directory

PAVALON & GIFFORD (AV)

Two North La Salle Street, Suite 1600, 60602
Telephone: 312-419-7400
FAX: 312-419-7408
Rockford, Illinois Office: 501 Seventh Street, Suite 501, 61104.
Telephone: 815-968-5100.

MEMBERS OF FIRM

Eugene I. Pavalon
Geoffrey L. Gifford
Gary K. Laatsch
Frank C. Marino

Kathleen A. Russell
Jodi L. Habush
Richard S. Goode

OF COUNSEL

Henry Phillip Gruss

For full biographical listings, see the Martindale-Hubbell Law Directory

POWER ROGERS & SMITH, P.C. (AV)

35 West Wacker Drive, Suite 3700, 60601
Telephone: 312-236-9381
Fax: 312-236-0920

Joseph A. Power, Jr.
Larry R. Rogers
Todd A. Smith
Thomas G. Siracusa
Paul L. Salzetta
Thomas M. Power

Larry R. Rogers, Jr.
Ruth M. Degnan

For full biographical listings, see the Martindale-Hubbell Law Directory

SCHAFFENEGGER, WATSON & PETERSON, LTD. (AV)

Suite 3504, One East Wacker Drive, 60601-1802
Telephone: 312-527-5566
Fax: 312-527-5540

J. V. Schaffenegger (1914-1986)
Jack L. Watson
Donald G. Peterson
Jay Scott Nelson
Michael A. Strom

James L. McKnight

Reference: American National Bank & Trust Co.

For full biographical listings, see the Martindale-Hubbell Law Directory

LAW OFFICES DENNIS T. SCHOEN, P.C. (AV)

Suite 663, 221 North La Salle Street, 60601
Telephone: 312-558-9143
Facsimile: 312-558-5426

Dennis T. Schoen

Michael J. Brennan
Todd R. Mcquiston

For full biographical listings, see the Martindale-Hubbell Law Directory

JOHN B. SCHWARTZ & ASSOCIATES (AV)

Suite 408, Thirty-Nine South La Salle Street, 60603
Telephone: 312-332-1586
Fax: 312-332-7009

ASSOCIATES

Stephen J. Caron
David J. Spira

OF COUNSEL

Thomas W. Duda

For full biographical listings, see the Martindale-Hubbell Law Directory

JOHN C. WUNSCH, P.C. (AV)

77 West Washington Street, Suite 1420, 60602
Telephone: 312-855-0705
Fax: 312-236-2573

(See Next Column)

JOHN C. WUNSCH, P.C., *Chicago—Continued*

John C. Wunsch

Reference: The Northern Trust Co.

For full biographical listings, see the Martindale-Hubbell Law Directory

*EDWARDSVILLE,** Madison Co.

CARLSON WENDLER & ASSOCIATES, P.C. (AV)

90 Edwardsville Professional Park, P.O. Box 527, 62025
Telephone: 618-656-0066
Fax: 618-656-0009
Kansas City, Missouri Office: 8900 Ward Parkway, Suite 200.
Telephone: 816-822-2700.

Jon G. Carlson | Brian M. Wendler

Daniel Jay Cohen | Charles W. Armbruster, III

OF COUNSEL

Jonathan Isbell | James T. Williamson

For full biographical listings, see the Martindale-Hubbell Law Directory

ELGIN, Cook & Kane Cos.

JUERGENSMEYER, STRAIN AND ASSOCIATES (AV)

707-A Davis Road (I-90 Frontage Road), 60123-1346
Telephone: 708-695-9800
FAX: 708-695-9818
Chicago, Illinois Office: One North La Salle Street, Suite 2200.
Telephone: 312-332-1114.

John E. Juergensmeyer | Judson L. Strain

ASSOCIATES

Richard P. Bingham | Neil Michael Bruce Rowe
Leena Soni

OF COUNSEL

Thomas M. Hartwell

For full biographical listings, see the Martindale-Hubbell Law Directory

*JOLIET,** Will Co.

MCKEOWN, FITZGERALD, ZOLLNER, BUCK, HUTCHISON & RUTTLE (AV)

2455 Glenwood Avenue, 60435
Telephone: 815-729-4800
FAX: 815-729-4711
Frankfort, Illinois Office: 28 Kansas Street.
Telephone: 815-469-2176.
FAX: 815-469-0295.

MEMBERS OF FIRM

Charles J. McKeown (1908-1985)
Paul O. McKeown (1913-1982)
Richard T. Buck (1936-1992)
Joseph C. Fitzgerald
Max E. Zollner
Douglas P. Hutchison
David L. Ruttle
Theodore J. Jarz
Douglas J. McKeown
Timothy J. Rathbun
James B. Harvey
Kenneth A. Grey
Michael R. Lucas

ASSOCIATES

Christopher N. Wise | Frank S. Cservenyak, Jr.
Gary S. Mueller | William P Mullarkey
Arthur J. Wilhelmi

OF COUNSEL

Stewart C. Hutchison

Representative Clients: Caterpillar Tractor Co.; First National Bank of Lockport; Homart Development Co.; First Midwest Bank, N.A.; Silver Cross Hospital; Joliet Township High School District; Villages of: Plainfield and Mokena; Southwest Agency for Risk Management; Joliet Junior College Foundation; Health Service Systems, Inc.

For full biographical listings, see the Martindale-Hubbell Law Directory

SPESIA, AYERS, ARDAUGH & WUNDERLICH (AV)

Two Rialto Square, 116 North Chicago Street, Suite 200, 60431
Telephone: 815-726-4311
FAX: 815-726-6828

MEMBERS OF FIRM

Douglas F. Spesia | John R. Ardaugh
E. Kent Ayers | Gary L. Wunderlich

ASSOCIATES

Dinah Lennon Archambeault | John C. Roth
Edward J. Schoen, Jr.

(See Next Column)

OF COUNSEL

Ralph C. Murphy | Kenneth E. Timm
Arthur T. Lennon (1923-1988)

Counsel For: Commonwealth Edison Co.; Illinois Bell Telephone Co.; Country Mutual Insurance Co.; Northern Illinois Gas Co.; Metropolitan Life Insurance Co.; Indiana Consolidated Insurance Cos.; A.N.R. Pipeline Co.; Amoco Chemical Corp.; Village of New Lenox; Peoples Gas Light & Coke Company.

For full biographical listings, see the Martindale-Hubbell Law Directory

*MARION,** Williamson Co.

HARRIS, LAMBERT, HOWERTON & DORRIS (AV)

300 West Main Street, P.O. Box 1005, 62959
Telephone: 618-993-2616
Fax: 618-997-1845

MEMBERS OF FIRM

Ralph W. Harris (1904-1982) | Robert H. Howerton
Richard Gordon Lambert | Douglas N. Dorris

ASSOCIATE

Eric Kirkpatrick

For full biographical listings, see the Martindale-Hubbell Law Directory

*OTTAWA,** La Salle Co.

MYERS, DAUGHERITY, BERRY & O'CONOR, LTD. (AV)

130 East Madison Street, 61350
Telephone: 815-434-6206
Fax: 815-434-6203
Streator, Illinois Office: 7 North Point Drive.
Telephone: 815-672-3116.
Fax: 815-672-0738.

Eugene P. Daugherity | Richard J. Berry

Representative Clients: Auto Owners Insurance, Co.; Union Bank; First National Bank of Ottawa, Illinois; Union Bancorp Inc.; First State Bank; United States Fidelity & Guaranty Co.; St. Mary's Hospital; General Casualty Insurance, Co.

For Complete List of Firm Personnel, See General Section

For full biographical listings, see the Martindale-Hubbell Law Directory

PERU, La Salle Co.

ANTHONY C. RACCUGLIA & ASSOCIATES (AV)

1200 Maple Drive, 61354
Telephone: 815-223-0230
Ottawa, Illinois Office: 633 La Salle Street.
Telephone: 815-434-2003.

ASSOCIATES

James A. McPhedran | Louis L. Bertrand

References: La Salle National Bank; Citizens First National Bank of Peru, Illinois.

For full biographical listings, see the Martindale-Hubbell Law Directory

*WAUKEGAN,** Lake Co.

DIVER, GRACH, QUADE & MASINI (AV)

First Federal Savings and Loan Building, 111 North County Street, 60085
Telephone: 708-662-8611
FAX: 708-662-2960

MEMBERS OF FIRM

Clarence W. Diver (1883-1962) | David R. Quade
Thomas W. Diver | Robert J. Masini
Brian S. Grach | Sarah P. Lessman

Heidi J. Aavang | Donna-Jo Rodden Vorderstrasse

A list of Representative Clients will be furnished upon request.
Reference: First Midwest Bank of Waukegan.

For full biographical listings, see the Martindale-Hubbell Law Directory

LAW OFFICES OF PATRICK A. SALVI, P.C. (AV)

218 North Utica Street, 60085
Telephone: 708-249-1227
Telefax: 708-249-0138

Patrick A. Salvi

Michael P. Schostok | Terrence S. Carden, III
Megan E. Chadwick | Dorothy Lupton Moran
John Andrew Kornak

OF COUNSEL

Bernard E. Grysen

References: First Midwest Bank, Waukegan, Illinois; Northern Trust Bank, Lake Forest, Illinois.

For full biographical listings, see the Martindale-Hubbell Law Directory

WEST FRANKFORT, Franklin Co.

SAM C. MITCHELL & ASSOCIATES (AV)

115 1/2 East Main Street, P.O. Box 280, 62896
Telephone: 618-932-2772; 937-2662
Telecopier: 618-932-3456

Sam C. Mitchell

ASSOCIATE

Bruce D. Irish

For full biographical listings, see the Martindale-Hubbell Law Directory

*WHEATON,** Du Page Co.

DONOVAN & ROBERTS, P.C. (AV)

104 East Roosevelt Road, Suite 202, P.O. Box 417, 60189-0417
Telephone: 708-668-4211
Fax: 708-668-2076

Keith E. Roberts, Sr.
Keith E. (Chuck) Roberts, Jr.
Robert R. Verchota
James J. Konetski

Marie F. Leach
Mark J. Lyons
Andrew L. Dryjanski
Robert M. Skutt
Robert J. Lentz
Rosemarie Calandra

For full biographical listings, see the Martindale-Hubbell Law Directory

SCHROEDER & HRUBY, LTD. (AV)

2100 Manchester Road, Suite 1015, P.O. Box 230, 60189
Telephone: 708-462-1400
Facsimile: 708-462-1665

Carl F. Schroeder
Ralph R. Hruby

Reference: West Suburban Bank.

For full biographical listings, see the Martindale-Hubbell Law Directory

INDIANA

*BLOOMINGTON,** Monroe Co.

BUNGER & ROBERTSON (AV)

226 South College Square, P.O. Box 910, 47402-0910
Telephone: 812-332-9295
Fax: 812-331-8808

MEMBERS OF FIRM

Len E. Bunger, Jr. (1921-1993)
Don M. Robertson
Thomas Bunger
Joseph D. O'Connor III
James L. Whitlatch
Samuel R. Ardery

ASSOCIATES

Margaret M. Frisbie
William J. Beggs
John W. Richards

OF COUNSEL

Philip C. Hill

Representative Clients: Aetna Insurance Companies; Bloomington Hospital; Commercial Union Group; Indiana Insurance Co.; Liberty Mutual Insurance; Medical Protective Co.; Monroe County Community School Corp.; Professional Golf Car, Inc.; Prudential Insurance Company of America; State Farm Automobile Insurance Co.

For full biographical listings, see the Martindale-Hubbell Law Directory

KELLEY, BELCHER & BROWN, A PROFESSIONAL CORPORATION (AV)

301 West Seventh Street, P.O. Box 3250, 47402-3250
Telephone: 812-336-9963
Telecopier: 812-336-4588

William H. Kelley
Thomas J. Belcher
Barry Spencer Brown

Shannon L. Robinson
Darla Sue Brown

For full biographical listings, see the Martindale-Hubbell Law Directory

CARMEL, Hamilton Co.

COOTS, HENKE & WHEELER, PROFESSIONAL CORPORATION (AV)

255 East Carmel Drive, 46032
Telephone: 317-844-4693
Fax: 317-573-5385

E. Davis Coots
Steven H. Henke
James K. Wheeler
Jeffrey O. Meunier
Jeffrey S. Zipes
Elizabeth I. Van Tassel

For Complete List of Firm Personnel, See General Section

For full biographical listings, see the Martindale-Hubbell Law Directory

CLARKSVILLE, Clark Co.

HANGER, ENGEBRETSON, MAYER & VOGT (AV)

501 Eastern Boulevard, 47129
Telephone: 812-288-1235
Louisville, Kentucky: 502-584-5800
Fax: 812-288-1240

MEMBERS OF FIRM

William F. Engebretson
John M. Mayer, Jr.
Samuel H. Vogt, Jr.
Steven K. Palmquist

ASSOCIATES

Cara Wells Stigger
Susan Wagner Hynes
Kerstin Ann Schuhmann

Representative Clients: First Federal Savings and Loan Association of Clark County; Ticor Title Insurance Company; Old Republic National Title Insurance Company.
Approved Attorneys for: Commonwealth Land Title Insurance Co.
Reference: First Federal Savings and Loan Association of Clark County; PNC Bank Indiana, Inc.

For Complete List of Firm Personnel, See General Section

For full biographical listings, see the Martindale-Hubbell Law Directory

ELKHART, Elkhart Co.

CHESTER, PFAFF & BROTHERSON (AV)

317 West Franklin Street, P.O. Box 507, 46515-0507
Telephone: 219-294-5421
Telecopier: 219-522-1476

ASSOCIATE

Robert C. Whippo

For Complete List of Firm Personnel, See General Section

For full biographical listings, see the Martindale-Hubbell Law Directory

THORNE, GRODNIK, RANSEL, DUNCAN, BYRON & HOSTETLER (AV)

228 West High Street, 46516-3176
Telephone: 219-294-7473
FAX: 219-294-5390
Mishawaka, Indiana Office: 310 Valley American Bank and Trust Building, 310 West McKinley Avenue. P.O. Box 1210.
Telephone: 219-256-5660.
FAX: 219-674-6835.

MEMBERS OF FIRM

William A. Thorne
Charles H. Grodnik
J. Richard Ransel
Glenn L. Duncan
James R. Byron
Steven L. Hostetler

ASSOCIATES

James H. Milstone
Michael A. Trippel

OF COUNSEL

F. Richard Kramer
Joseph C. Zakas

Counsel for: Witmer-McNease Music Co., Inc.; Valley American Bank and Trust Co., Mishawaka, Indiana.

For Complete List of Firm Personnel, See General Section

For full biographical listings, see the Martindale-Hubbell Law Directory

*EVANSVILLE,** Vanderburgh Co.

BERGER AND BERGER (AV)

313 Main Street, 47708-1485
Telephone: 812-425-8101;
Indiana Only: 800-622-3604;
Outside Indiana: 800-327-0182
Fax: 812-421-5909

MEMBERS OF FIRM

Sydney L. Berger (1917-1988)
Charles L. Berger
Sheila M. Corcoran
Mark W. Rietman
Robert J. Pigman

(See Next Column)

BERGER AND BERGER, *Evansville—Continued*

References: Citizens National Bank of Evansville; Old National Bank in Evansville.

For full biographical listings, see the Martindale-Hubbell Law Directory

GERLING LAW OFFICES, PROFESSIONAL CORPORATION (AV)

519 Main Street Walkway, P.O. Box 3203, 47731
Telephone: 812-423-5251
Fax: 812-423-9928

Gary L. Gerling
Daniel J. McGinn
Edward B. Anderson
David G. Hatfield
Christian M. Lenn
Barbara S. Barrett
Gayle Gerling Pettinga

For full biographical listings, see the Martindale-Hubbell Law Directory

LOCKYEAR & KORNBLUM (AV)

555 Sycamore Street, P.O. Box 3515, 47734
Telephone: 812-422-1199
Fax: 812-426-0799

MEMBERS OF FIRM

Theodore Lockyear
James A. Kornblum

Reference: Citizens National Bank.

For full biographical listings, see the Martindale-Hubbell Law Directory

*FORT WAYNE,** Allen Co.

ROBY & HOOD (AV)

Standard Federal Plaza, Suite 520, 200 East Main, 46802
Telephone: 219-423-3366
Fax: 219-423-3367
Anderson, Indiana Office: One Citizens Plaza, Suite 305.
Telephone: 317-642-2402.

MEMBERS OF FIRM

Daniel A. Roby
G. Stanley Hood
Kathryn J. Roudebush
Thomas A. Manges

ASSOCIATE

Theodore T. Storer

References: Norwest Bank; NBD Bank.

For full biographical listings, see the Martindale-Hubbell Law Directory

HAMMOND, Lake Co.

RUMAN, CLEMENTS, TOBIN & HOLUB, P.C. (AV)

5261 Hohman Avenue, 46320
Telephone: 219-933-7600
Fax: 219-931-7116

Saul I. Ruman
Thomas A. Clements
William H. Tobin
David W. Holub
David M. Hamacher
Kevin W. Marshall
Lynn Morrow Malkowski
Jennifer Kalas
William E. Dittrich

OF COUNSEL

James E. Mahoney

References: Calumet National Bank; Mercantile National Bank.

For full biographical listings, see the Martindale-Hubbell Law Directory

*INDIANAPOLIS,** Marion Co.

CONOUR • DOEHRMAN (AV)

Suite 1725, One Indiana Square, 46204
Telephone: 317-269-3550
Fax: 317-269-3564

MEMBERS OF FIRM

William F. Conour
Thomas C. Doehrman

ASSOCIATES

Rex E. Baker
Daniel S. Chamberlain
Daniel J. Mages

LEGAL SUPPORT PERSONNEL

Linda S. Carmichael (Legal Administrator)
Stacey M. Merchant
Paula M. Roseman (Legal Assistant)
Kimberly N. Beasley (Legal Assistant)
Sarah E. Stites

For full biographical listings, see the Martindale-Hubbell Law Directory

HOLLAND & HOLLAND (AV)

Two Market Square Center, Suite 1011, 251 East Ohio Street, 46204
Telephone: 317-637-4400
Fax: Available Upon Request

C. Warren Holland
Michael W. Holland

ASSOCIATE

Gretchen Holland Elling

OF COUNSEL

Charles G. Reeder

Reference: The Indiana National Bank.

For full biographical listings, see the Martindale-Hubbell Law Directory

ICE MILLER DONADIO & RYAN (AV)

One American Square Box 82001, 46282-0002
Telephone: 317-236-2100
Fax: 317-236-2219

MEMBERS OF FIRM

James R. Fisher
Cory Brundage
Debra Hanley Miller
Michael D. Marine

ASSOCIATE

Donald M. Snemis

For Complete List of Firm Personnel, See General Section

For full biographical listings, see the Martindale-Hubbell Law Directory

LOCKE REYNOLDS BOYD & WEISELL (AV)

1000 Capital Center South, 201 North Illinois Street, 46204
Telephone: 317-237-3800
Telecopier: 317-237-3900

Hugh E. Reynolds, Jr.
Lloyd H. Milliken, Jr.
William V. Hutchens
David S. Allen
David M. Haskett
Michael A. Bergin
David T. Kasper
Steven J. Strawbridge
Thomas L. Davis
Robert A. Fanning
Randall R. Riggs
Alan S. Brown
Mark J. Roberts
Kevin Charles Murray
Julia M. Blackwell
Richard A. Huser
Thomas J. Campbell
Diane L. Parsons
Burton M. Harris
Thomas W. Farlow
Karl M. Koons, III
James Dimos

Stephen L. Vaughan
Kristen K. Rollison
Thomas R. Schultz
Todd J. Kaiser
Eric A. Riegner
Kevin C. Schiferl
Ariane Schallwig Johnson
Peter H. Pogue
John H. Daerr
Robert W. Wright
Robert T. Dassow
Jeffrey J. Mortier
Mary A. Schopper
Susan E. Cline
Dirk Wallsmith
Jerrilyn Powers Ramsey
Katherine Coble Dassow
Lisa A. McCallum
Kathryn Weymouth Williams
Mary Margaret Ruth Feldhake

OF COUNSEL

William H. Vobach
Robert C. Riddell

Representative Clients: American Honda Motor Co., Inc.; Associated Aviation Underwriters; Center for Claims Resolution; CNA Insurance Cos.; Citizens Insurance Co.; General Motors Corp.; Nationwide Insurance Co.; Siemens Corp.; St. Francis Hospital.

For Complete List of Firm Personnel, See General Section

For full biographical listings, see the Martindale-Hubbell Law Directory

MILLER MULLER MENDELSON & KENNEDY (AV)

8900 Keystone Crossing Suite 1250, 46240
Telephone: 317-574-4500
1-800-394-3094
Fax: 317-574-4501

MEMBERS OF FIRM

Michael S. Miller
John Muller
Tilden Mendelson
Timothy J. Kennedy
Faith L. Pottschmidt

For full biographical listings, see the Martindale-Hubbell Law Directory

MITCHELL HURST JACOBS & DICK (AV)

152 East Washington Street, 46204
Telephone: 317-636-0808
1-800-636-0808
Fax: 317-633-7680

MEMBERS OF FIRM

Marvin H. Mitchell
William W. Hurst
Samuel L. Jacobs
Richard J. Dick
Marshall S. Hanley
Steven K. Huffer
Robert W. Strohmeyer, Jr.

ASSOCIATES

Danielle A. Takla
John M. Reames
Michael T. McNelis
Michael P. Kilkenny

LEGAL SUPPORT PERSONNEL

L. Kathleen Hughes Brown, R.N.

General Counsel for: Premium Optical Co.; Calderon Bros. Vending Machines, Inc.; Grocers Supply Co., Inc.; Power Train Services, Inc.; Frank E. Irish, Inc.; Bedding Liquidators; Galyan's Trading Co.; Harcourt Management Co., Inc.; Kosene & Kosene Mgt. & Dev. Co., Inc.; Hasten Bancorp.

For full biographical listings, see the Martindale-Hubbell Law Directory

Indianapolis—Continued

NORRIS, CHOPLIN & SCHROEDER (AV)

Ninth Floor, 101 West Ohio Street, 46204-1906
Telephone: 317-269-9330
FAX: 317-269-9338

MEMBERS OF FIRM

Richard L. Norris
John M. Choplin, II
Peter A. Schroeder
Bruce L. Kamplain
Raymond L. Faust
Mary Jo Hunter Wedding

ASSOCIATES

Ellen White Quigley
Kyle A. Jones
Peter Peck-Koh Ho
Nelson A. Nettles
Andrew C. Chapman

OF COUNSEL

James D. Matthews

Reference: The Indiana National Bank.

For full biographical listings, see the Martindale-Hubbell Law Directory

PARDIECK, GILL & VARGO, A PROFESSIONAL CORPORATION (AV)

The Old Bailey Building, 244 North College Avenue, 46202
Telephone: 317-639-3321
FAX: 317-639-3318
Seymour, Indiana Office: 100 North Chestnut Street. P.O. Box 608.
Telephone: 812-523-8686.

Roger L. Pardieck
W. Brent Gill
John F. Vargo

Thomas L. Landwerlen
Janet O. Vargo
Robert C. Rothkopf

For full biographical listings, see the Martindale-Hubbell Law Directory

PRICE & BARKER (AV)

The Hammond Block Building, 301 Massachusetts Avenue, 46204
Telephone: 317-633-8787
Telecopier: 317-633-8797

PARTNERS

Henry J. Price
Robert G. Barker
Mary Arlien Findling
Jennifer L. Graham
Jerry A. Garau
Mary J. Hoeller

ASSOCIATES

H. Dean Bowman
Melissa A. Clark
Stephanie L. Franco
Barbara J. Germano
Larry R. Jackson

For full biographical listings, see the Martindale-Hubbell Law Directory

TOWNSEND, HOVDE & MONTROSS (AV)

230 East Ohio Street, 46204
Telephone: 317-264-4444
FAX: 317-264-2080

F. Boyd Hovde
John F. Townsend, Jr.
W. Scott Montross
Frederick R. Hovde

OF COUNSEL

John F. Townsend

Reference: The Indiana National Bank of Indianapolis.

For full biographical listings, see the Martindale-Hubbell Law Directory

TOWNSEND & TOWNSEND (AV)

151 East Market Street, 46204
Telephone: 317-631-7777; 800-272-5720
FAX: 317-686-4449
Roscommon, Michigan Office: 603 Lake Street.
Telephone: 517-821-9114.

Earl C. Townsend, Jr.
Earl C. Townsend, III

For full biographical listings, see the Martindale-Hubbell Law Directory

WILSON, KEHOE & WININGHAM (AV)

2859 North Meridian, 46208
Telephone: 317-920-6400
Fax: 317-920-6405

MEMBERS OF FIRM

Harry A. Wilson, Jr.
D. Bruce Kehoe
William E. Winingham, Jr.

ASSOCIATES

John A. Payton
Ralph E. Dowling

(See Next Column)

OF COUNSEL

Robert E. Lehman

Reference: The Indiana National Bank.

For full biographical listings, see the Martindale-Hubbell Law Directory

YARLING, ROBINSON, HAMMEL & LAMB (AV)

151 North Delaware, Suite 1535, P.O. Box 44128, 46204
Telephone: 317-262-8800
Fax: 317-262-3046

MEMBERS OF FIRM

Richard W. Yarling
Charles F. Robinson, Jr.
John W. Hammel
Linda Y. Hammel
Edgar H. Lamb
Douglas E. Rogers
Mark S. Gray

Representative Clients: Allstate Insurance Co.; American Family Mutual Insurance Company; Chrysler Credit Corporation; Fleet Financenter; General Motors Acceptance Corporation; Household Finance Corporation; Monroe Guaranty Insurance Company; Northbrook Property & Casualty Company; Pafco General Insurance Company; Security Pacific Finance Corporation.

For full biographical listings, see the Martindale-Hubbell Law Directory

YOSHA, LADENDORF & TODD (AV)

2220 North Meridian Street, 46208
Telephone: 317-925-9200
FAX: 317-923-5759

MEMBERS OF FIRM

Louis Buddy Yosha
William Levy
Mark C. Ladendorf
Teresa L. Todd

ASSOCIATE

David C. Krahulik

OF COUNSEL

Irwin J. Prince
Irving L. Fink
Theodore F. Smith, Jr.

References: NBD Indiana; Bank One, Indianapolis.

For full biographical listings, see the Martindale-Hubbell Law Directory

YOUNG & RILEY (AV)

277 East 12th Street, 46202
Telephone: 317-639-2000
Fax: 317-639-2005

Thomas J. Young
William N. Riley

For full biographical listings, see the Martindale-Hubbell Law Directory

*KOKOMO,** Howard Co.

BAYLIFF, HARRIGAN, CORD & MAUGANS, P.C. (AV)

The Security Building, 123 North Buckeye, P.O. Box 2249, 46904-2249
Telephone: 317-459-3941
Fax: 317-459-3974

Edgar W. Bayliff
Daniel J. Harrigan
C. Michael Cord
J. Conrad Maugans

Mark A. Scott

Reference: Society National Bank, Indiana; First Federal Savings Bank of Kokomo, Indiana.

For full biographical listings, see the Martindale-Hubbell Law Directory

*LAFAYETTE,** Tippecanoe Co.

BALL, EGGLESTON, BUMBLEBURG & MCBRIDE (AV)

810 Bank One Building, P.O. Box 1535, 47902
Telephone: 317-742-9046
Fax: 317-742-1966

Cable G. Ball (1904-1981)
Owen Crook (1908-1977)
Warren N. Eggleston (1923-1991)

MEMBERS OF FIRM

Joseph T. Bumbleburg
John K. McBride
Jack L. Walkey
Michael J. Stapleton
Jeffrey J. Newell
James T. Hodson
Brian Wade Walker

ASSOCIATES

Cheryl M. Knodle
Randy J. Williams
Norman G. Printer

Representative Clients: Available Upon Request.

For full biographical listings, see the Martindale-Hubbell Law Directory

HANNA, GERDE & BURNS (AV)

Fifth Floor Bank & Trust Building, P.O. Box 1098, 47902
Telephone: 317-742-5005

(See Next Column)

HANNA, GERDE & BURNS, *Lafayette—Continued*

Charles H. Robertson (1902-1982)

MEMBERS OF FIRM

George L. Hanna | Cy Gerde
Eric H. Burns

Reference: Lafayette Bank & Trust Co.

For full biographical listings, see the Martindale-Hubbell Law Directory

HOFFMAN, LUHMAN & BUSCH (AV)

300 Main Street, Suite 700, P.O. Box 99, 47902
Telephone: 317-423-5404
Fax: 317-742-6448

MEMBERS OF FIRM

J. Frederick Hoffman | David W. Luhman
Thomas H. Busch

References: Lafayette Bank & Trust Co., Lafayette, Indiana; Farmers & Merchants Bank, Rochester, Indiana; Lafayette Savings Bank, Lafayette, Indiana.

For Complete List of Firm Personnel, See General Section

For full biographical listings, see the Martindale-Hubbell Law Directory

MERRILLVILLE, Lake Co.

SPANGLER, JENNINGS & DOUGHERTY, P.C. (AV)

8396 Mississippi Street, 46410-6398
Telephone: 219-769-2323
Facsimile: 219-769-5007
Valparaiso, Indiana Office: 150 Lincolnway, Suite 3001.
Telephone: 219-462-6151.
FAX: 219-477-4935.

Harry J. Jennings
Samuel J. Furlin
Richard A. Mayer
Jay A. Charon
John P. McQuillan
Samuel J. Bernardi, Jr. (Valparaiso Office)
Jon F. Schmoll
Robert D. Hawk
David J. Hanson
Robert P. Kennedy
James T. McNiece
Daniel A. Gioia
James D. McQuillan
David L. Abel, II
Harold G. Hagberg
Theresa Lazar Springmann

Gregory J. Tonner
Robert D. Brown
Robert J. Dignam
David R. Phillips
Feisal Amin Istrabadi
Anthony F. Tavitas
Lloyd P. Mullen
Kisti Good Risse
Jeff J. Shaw

Representative Clients: Allstate Insurance Cos.; Bank One, Merriville, N.A.; First National Bank of Valparaiso; Ford Motor Credit Co.; Inland Steel Co.; Munster Calumet Shopping Center; School Town of Munster; St. Paul Insurance Cos.; State Farm Cos.; Volkswagen of America.

For Complete List of Firm Personnel, See General Section

For full biographical listings, see the Martindale-Hubbell Law Directory

MISHAWAKA, St. Joseph Co.

SCHINDLER AND OLSON (AV)

122 South Mill Street, P.O. Box 100, 46544
Telephone: 219-259-5461
Fax: 219-259-5462

MEMBERS OF FIRM

John W. Schindler, Jr. | James J. Olson

A List of Representative Clients Will Be Furnished Upon Request.
Reference: 1st Source Bank of Mishawaka.

For Complete List of Firm Personnel, See General Section

For full biographical listings, see the Martindale-Hubbell Law Directory

MUNSTER, Lake Co.

LAW OFFICES OF TIMOTHY F. KELLY (AV)

Suite 2A, 9250 Columbia Avenue, 46321
Telephone: 219-836-4062
Telecopier: 219-836-0167

MEMBERS OF FIRM

Timothy F. Kelly | Karl K. Vanzo

ASSOCIATE

Harvey Karlovac

For Complete List of Firm Personnel, See General Section

For full biographical listings, see the Martindale-Hubbell Law Directory

*NEW ALBANY,** Floyd Co.

DAVID V. SCOTT (AV)

409 Bank Street, P.O. Box 785, 47150
Telephone: 812-945-9151

Reference: PNC Bank, Indiana.

For full biographical listings, see the Martindale-Hubbell Law Directory

*NOBLESVILLE,** Hamilton Co.

CHURCH, CHURCH, HITTLE & ANTRIM (AV)

938 Conner Street, P.O. Box 10, 46060-0010
Telephone: 317-773-2190
Telecopier: 317-773-5320

MEMBERS OF FIRM

Manson E. Church
Douglas D. Church
Jack G. Hittle
J. Michael Antrim
Martin E. Risacher
Bruce M. Bittner

ASSOCIATES

Brian J. Zaiger | David Joseph Barker
Leslie Craig Henderzahs

OF COUNSEL

Gary D. Beerbower

Representative Clients: Noblesville Schools; Westfield-Washington Schools; Indiana School Finance Corp.; Community Bank; Metrobank; Towns of Westfield, Fishers and Noblesville; Reynolds Farm Equipment Co.; Weihe Engineering.

For full biographical listings, see the Martindale-Hubbell Law Directory

SEYMOUR, Jackson Co.

PARDIECK, GILL & VARGO, A PROFESSIONAL CORPORATION (AV)

100 North Chestnut Street, P.O. Box 608, 47274
Telephone: 812-523-8686
FAX: 812-522-4199
Indianapolis, Indiana Office: The Old Bailey Building, 244 North College Avenue.
Telephone: 317-639-3321.

Roger L. Pardieck | W. Brent Gill

Bruce A. MacTavish

OF COUNSEL

Barbara Stevens

References: Home Federal Savings Bank, Seymour, Indiana.

For full biographical listings, see the Martindale-Hubbell Law Directory

*SOUTH BEND,** St. Joseph Co.

HARDIG, LEE AND GROVES, PROFESSIONAL ASSOCIATION (AV)

Suite 502, First Bank Building, 205 West Jefferson Boulevard, 46601
Telephone: 219-232-5923
Fax: 219-232-5942

Edward W. Hardig | Robert D. Lee
James F. Groves

William T. Webb

Representative Client: South Bend-Mishawaka New Car Dealers Assn.
Reference: First Interstate Bank of South Bend.

For full biographical listings, see the Martindale-Hubbell Law Directory

EDWARD N. KALAMAROS & ASSOCIATES PROFESSIONAL CORPORATION (AV)

129 North Michigan Avenue, P.O. Box 4156, 46634
Telephone: 219-232-4801
Telecopier: 219-232-9736

Edward N. Kalamaros
Timothy J. Walsh
Thomas F. Cohen
Joseph M. Forte
Robert Deane Woods
Peter J. Agostino
Patrick J. Hinkle
Bernard E. Edwards
Philip E. Kalamaros
Sally P. Norton
Kevin W. Kearney
Lynn E. Arnold

Representative Clients: Liberty Mutual Insurance Co.; Employers Mutual of Wausau; Fireman's Fund American Insurance Group; St. Paul Insurance Companies; U.S.F. & G.; Cincinnati Insurance Co.; Kemper Group; Continental Loss Adjusting Services, Inc.; Orion Group.

For full biographical listings, see the Martindale-Hubbell Law Directory

ROWE, FOLEY & GARDNER (AV)

Suite 900 Society Bank Building, 46601
Telephone: 219-233-8200

(See Next Column)

ROWE, FOLEY & GARDNER—*Continued*

R. Kent Rowe
R. Kent Rowe, III
Edmond W. Foley
Martin J. Gardner

ASSOCIATES

Gregory J. Haines
Timothy J. Maher
Lee Korzan
Steven D. Groth
Evan S. Roberts
William James O'Mahony

For full biographical listings, see the Martindale-Hubbell Law Directory

*TERRE HAUTE,** Vigo Co.

MCGLONE LAW OFFICE (AV)

702 Sycamore Building, 47807
Telephone: 812-234-7796
Fax: 812-232-2464

MEMBERS OF FIRM

Gerald H. McGlone
James A. McGlone
Daniel J. McGlone

Reference: Merchants National Bank.

For full biographical listings, see the Martindale-Hubbell Law Directory

*VALPARAISO,** Porter Co.

BLACHLY, TABOR, BOZIK & HARTMAN (AV)

Suite 401 Indiana Federal Building, 46383
Telephone: 219-464-1041

MEMBERS OF FIRM

Glenn J. Tabor
Duane W. Hartman
David L. DeBoer
Thomas F. Macke

ASSOCIATE

Roger A. Weitgenant

Reference: First National Bank.

For Complete List of Firm Personnel, See General Section

For full biographical listings, see the Martindale-Hubbell Law Directory

DOUGLAS, ALEXA, KOEPPEN & HURLEY (AV)

14 Indiana Avenue, P.O. Box 209, 46384-0209
Telephone: 219-462-2126
Fax: 219-477-4408

MEMBERS OF FIRM

Herbert K. Douglas
William E. Alexa
R. Bradley Koeppen
Brian J. Hurley

ASSOCIATE

Mark A. Gland

OF COUNSEL

George W. Douglas
Leo J. Clifford

Attorneys for: Urschel Laboratories, Inc.; Northern Indiana Public Service Co.; Midwest Steel Division, National Steel; McGill Manufacturing Co., Inc.; Park District, City of Valparaiso.

For full biographical listings, see the Martindale-Hubbell Law Directory

LAW OFFICES OF JAMES V. TSOUTSOURIS (AV)

Five Lincolnway, 46383
Telephone: 219-462-4148
Fax: 219-477-4932

ASSOCIATES

Joann Tsoutsouris
G. Anthony Bertig
John Edward Martin
Lori L. Ferngren

A list of Representative Clients and References will be furnished upon request.

For full biographical listings, see the Martindale-Hubbell Law Directory

IOWA

CEDAR FALLS, Black Hawk Co.

REDFERN, MASON, DIETER, LARSEN & MOORE (AV)

315 Clay Street, P.O. Box 627, 50613
Telephone: 319-277-6830
Facsimile: 319-277-3531

MEMBERS OF FIRM

David R. Mason
Robert J. Dieter
John C. Larsen
Steven D. Moore
Donald B. Redfern
Mark W. Fransdal
Mark S. Rolinger

(See Next Column)

ASSOCIATE

Susan Bernau Staudt

Representative Clients: Norwest Bank Iowa; The National Bank of Waterloo; Don R. Havens Co.; Control-O-fax Corp.; Cedar Falls Community School District; University of Northern Iowa Foundation; United States Fidelity and Guaranty Co.; The Travelers Insurance Cos.; Fireman's Fund Insurance Companies.

For Complete List of Firm Personnel, See General Section

For full biographical listings, see the Martindale-Hubbell Law Directory

*CEDAR RAPIDS,** Linn Co.

TOM RILEY LAW FIRM, P.C. (AV)

4040 First Avenue N.E., P.O. Box 998, 52406-0998
Telephone: 319-363-4040
FAX: 319-363-9789
Iowa City, Iowa Office: 1220 Highway 6 West.
Telephone: 319-351-4996.
Burlington, Iowa Office: First National Bank Building, Second Floor, Main and Jefferson Streets, P.O. Box 1114.
Telephone: 319-753-5111.

Tom Riley
Peter C. Riley
T. Todd Becker
Mark E. Liabo
Hugh G. Albrecht
Sara Riley Brown
Charles C. Brown, Jr.
Thomas J. Currie
James E. Bennett
Gerald J. Kucera
Martin A. Diaz
Nestor Lobodiak
Susan A. Diehl
Michael E. Sheehy
Andrew B. Prosser
Elmer M. Jones

OF COUNSEL

Edward W. Dailey

A list of Representative Clients will be furnished upon request.

For full biographical listings, see the Martindale-Hubbell Law Directory

*COUNCIL BLUFFS,** Pottawattamie Co.

PERKINS, SACKS, HANNAN, REILLY AND PETERSEN (AV)

215 South Main Street, P.O. Box 1016, 51502-1016
Telephone: 712-328-1575
Fax: 712-328-1562

MEMBERS OF FIRM

Proctor R. Perkins (Retired)
Kenneth Sacks (Retired)
C. R. Hannan
Michael G. Reilly
Deborah L. Petersen

ASSOCIATE

Kellie Rae Taylor

References: First National Bank; Firstar Bank of Council Bluffs; State Bank and Trust.

For full biographical listings, see the Martindale-Hubbell Law Directory

*DES MOINES,** Polk Co.

ROXANNE B. CONLIN AND ASSOCIATES, P.C. (AV)

The Plaza, 300 Walnut Street - Suite 5, 50309-2239
Telephone: 515-282-3333
Fax: 515-282-0318

Roxanne B. Conlin

For full biographical listings, see the Martindale-Hubbell Law Directory

NICHOLAS CRITELLI ASSOCIATES, P.C. (AV)

Suite 500, 317 Sixth Avenue, 50309-4128
Telephone: 515-243-3122
Telecopier: (FAX) 515-243-3121
London, England Office: 11 Stone Buildings, Lincoln's Inn.
Telephone: 011-44-71-404-5055.
FAX: 011-44-71-405-1551.

Nick Critelli, Jr.
Lylea Dodson Critelli
Connie L. Diekema
Joseph B. Saluri

References: Boatmen's Bank of Des Moines, N.A.; Iowa State Bar Association.

For full biographical listings, see the Martindale-Hubbell Law Directory

THE JAMES LAW FIRM, P.C. (AV)

630 Equitable Building, 50309
Telephone: 515-246-8484
Fax: 515-246-8767

Dwight W. James
Frederick W. James
Michael J. Carroll
Scott L. Bandstra

Reference: Norwest Bank.

For full biographical listings, see the Martindale-Hubbell Law Directory

Des Moines—Continued

PATTERSON, LORENTZEN, DUFFIELD, TIMMONS, IRISH, BECKER & ORDWAY (AV)

729 Insurance Exchange Building, 50309
Telephone: 515-283-2147
Fax: 515-283-1002

MEMBERS OF FIRM

G. O. Patterson (1914-1982)
James A. Lorentzen
Theodore T. Duffield
William E. Timmons
Roy M. Irish
Gary D. Ordway
Robin L. Hermann
Harry Perkins, III
Michael F. Lacey, Jr.
Jeffrey A. Boehlert
Douglas A. Haag
Charles E. Cutler
Ronald M. Rankin
Michael D. Huppert
William A. Wickett

ASSOCIATES

Jeffrey A. Baker
Janice M. Herfkens
Coreen K. Bezdicek
Scott S. Bellis

OF COUNSEL

F. H. Becker

Representative Clients: Allied Mutual Insurance Company; CNA Insurance Company; Chubb Insurance Group; Continental Western Insurance Co.; Farmers Insurance Group; Farmland Insurance Company; Grinnell Mutual Reinsurance Company; Hawkeye Security Insurance Company; Iowa Insurance Institute, St. Paul Fire & Marine Insurance Company.

For Complete List of Firm Personnel, See General Section

For full biographical listings, see the Martindale-Hubbell Law Directory

THE ROSENBERG LAW FIRM (AV)

1010 Insurance Exchange Building, 505 Fifth Avenue, 50309
Telephone: 515-243-7600

MEMBERS OF FIRM

Raymond Rosenberg
Paul H. Rosenberg

ASSOCIATES

Dean A. Stowers
Brent D. Rosenberg

Reference: Firstar Bank, Des Moines, Iowa.

For full biographical listings, see the Martindale-Hubbell Law Directory

WASKER, DORR, WIMMER & MARCOUILLER, P.C. (AV)

801 Grand Avenue, Suite 3100, 50309-8036
Telephone: 515-283-1801
Facsimile: 515-283-1802

Fred L. Dorr

Jennifer Ann Tyler
Matthew D. Kern

For Complete List of Firm Personnel, See General Section

For full biographical listings, see the Martindale-Hubbell Law Directory

*KEOKUK,** Lee Co.

LAW OFFICES OF JAMES P. HOFFMAN (AV)

Middle Road, P.O. Box 1087, 52632-1087
Telephone: 319-524-4441

For full biographical listings, see the Martindale-Hubbell Law Directory

KANSAS

*KANSAS CITY,** Wyandotte Co.

McANANY, VAN CLEAVE & PHILLIPS, P.A. (AV)

Fourth Floor, 707 Minnesota Avenue, P.O. Box 1300, 66117
Telephone: 913-371-3838
Facsimile: 913-371-4722
Lenexa, Kansas Office: Suite 200, 11900 West 87th Street Parkway.
Telephone: 913-888-9000.
Facsimile: 913-888-7049.
Kansas City, Missouri Office: Suite 304, 819 Walnut Street.
Telephone: 816-556-9417.

John J. Jurcyk, Jr.
Robert D. Benham
Clifford T. Mueller (Resident, Lenexa Office)
Patrick D. McAnany (Resident, Lenexa Office)
Frank D. Menghini
David M. Druten (Resident, Lenexa Office)
William P. Coates, Jr. (Resident, Lenexa Office)
Robert F. Rowe, Jr. (Resident, Lenexa Office)
Douglas M. Greenwald
Daniel F. Church
Terri L. Savely Bezek

(See Next Column)

Reference: UMB Commercial National Bank.

For Complete List of Firm Personnel, See General Section

For full biographical listings, see the Martindale-Hubbell Law Directory

OVERLAND PARK, Johnson Co.

SHAMBERG, JOHNSON, BERGMAN & MORRIS, CHARTERED (AV)

Suite 355, 4551 West 107th Street, 66207
Telephone: 913-642-0600
Fax: 913-642-9629
Kansas City, Kansas Office: Suite 860, New Brotherhood Building, 8th and State Streets.
Telephone: 913-281-1900.
Kansas City, Missouri Office: Suite 205, Scarritt Arcade Building, 819 Walnut.
Telephone: 816-556-9431.

Lynn R. Johnson
Victor A. Bergman
David R. Morris
John M. Parisi

Steven G. Brown
John E. Rogers
Steve N. Six
Anthony L. DeWitt (Not admitted in KS)
Patrick A. Hamilton

OF COUNSEL

John E. Shamberg

For full biographical listings, see the Martindale-Hubbell Law Directory

*TOPEKA,** Shawnee Co.

DAVIS, UNREIN, HUMMER, McCALLISTER & BUCK (AV)

100 East Ninth Street, Third Floor, P.O. Box 3575, 66601-3575
Telephone: 913-354-1100
Fax: 913-354-1113

MEMBERS OF FIRM

Byron M. Gray (1901-1986)
Maurice D. Freidberg (1902-1965)
Charles L. Davis, Jr. (1921-1992)
Michael J. Unrein
J. Franklin Hummer
Mark A. Buck
James B. Biggs
Christopher M. Rohrer
Brenda L. Head

OF COUNSEL

Gary D. McCallister

For full biographical listings, see the Martindale-Hubbell Law Directory

FISHER, PATTERSON, SAYLER & SMITH (AV)

534 Kansas Avenue, Suite 400, 66603-3463
Telephone: 913-232-7761
Fax: 913-232-6604
Overland Park, Kansas Office: Suite 210, 11050 Roe Street. 66211.
Telephone: 913-339-6757.
Fax: 913-339-6187.

MEMBERS OF FIRM

Donald Patterson
Charles Keith Sayler
Edwin Dudley Smith (Resident, Overland Park Office)
Larry G. Pepperdine
James P. Nordstrom
Justice B. King
J. Steven Pigg
Steve R. Fabert
Ronald J. Laskowski
Michael K. Seck (Resident, Overland Park Office)
David P. Madden (Resident, Overland Park Office)
Steven K. Johnson

ASSOCIATES

Kristine A. Larscheid
Michael L. Bennett
Kurt A. Level (Resident, Overland Park Office)
Betty J. Mick

OF COUNSEL

David H. Fisher

Representative Clients: Gage Shopping Center, Inc.; Fireman's Fund-American Insurance Cos.; United States Fidelity and Guaranty Co.; Hartford Insurance Group.; The Procter & Gamble Company; American Cyanamid Company; Commercial Union Insurance Companies; Kansas Fire & Casualty Co.; National Casualty/Scottsdale Insurance Co.

For full biographical listings, see the Martindale-Hubbell Law Directory

PALMER & LOWRY (AV)

Suite 102 Columbian Building, 112 West Sixth, 66603-3862
Telephone: 913-233-1836
Fax: 913-233-3703

MEMBERS OF FIRM

Jerry R. Palmer
Kirk W. Lowry

ASSOCIATE

L J Leatherman

References: Commerce State Bank; Merchants National Bank.

For full biographical listings, see the Martindale-Hubbell Law Directory

Topeka—Continued

WRIGHT, HENSON, SOMERS, SEBELIUS, CLARK & BAKER (AV)

Commerce Bank Building, 100 Southeast Ninth Street, 2nd Floor, P.O. Box 3555, 66601-3555
Telephone: 913-232-2200
FAX: 913-232-3344

MEMBERS OF FIRM

Thomas E. Wright
K. Gary Sebelius

ASSOCIATES

Catherine A. Walter
Evelyn Zabel Wilson

For Complete List of Firm Personnel, See General Section

For full biographical listings, see the Martindale-Hubbell Law Directory

*WICHITA,** Sedgwick Co.

DEPEW & GILLEN (AV)

151 North Main, Suite 700, 67202-1408
Telephone: 316-265-9621
Facsimile: 316-265-3819

MEMBERS OF FIRM

Spencer L. Depew
Dennis L. Gillen
Jack Scott McInteer
David W. Nickel
Nicholas S. Daily
David E. Rogers
Charles Christian Steincamp

For full biographical listings, see the Martindale-Hubbell Law Directory

FOULSTON & SIEFKIN (AV)

(Formerly Foulston, Siefkin, Powers & Eberhardt)
700 Fourth Financial Center, Broadway at Douglas, 67202
Telephone: 316-267-6371
Facsimile: 316-267-6345
Topeka, Kansas Office: 1515 Bank IV Tower, 534 Kansas Avenue. 66603.
Telephone: 913-233-3600.
FAX: 913-233-1610.
Member: Lex Mundi, A Global Association of Independent Firms

MEMBERS OF FIRM

Mikel L. Stout
Darrell L. Warta
Jay F. Fowler
Amy S. Lemley
Craig W. West

For Complete List of Firm Personnel, See General Section

For full biographical listings, see the Martindale-Hubbell Law Directory

YOUNG, BOGLE, McCAUSLAND, WELLS & CLARK, P.A. (AV)

106 West Douglas, Suite 923, 67202
Telephone: 316-265-7841
Facsimile: 316-265-3956

Glenn D. Young, Jr.
Jerry D. Bogle
Paul S. McCausland
William A. Wells
Kenneth M. Clark

Representative Clients: Horace Mann Ins. Co.; Deere & Co.; Bridgestone/-Firestone, Inc.; Massey-Ferguson, Inc.; Sears Roebuck & Co.; GAF Corp. (asbestos litigation).

For Complete List of Firm Personnel, See General Section

For full biographical listings, see the Martindale-Hubbell Law Directory

KENTUCKY

*BOWLING GREEN,** Warren Co.

CAMPBELL, KERRICK & GRISE (AV)

1025 State Street, P.O. Box 9547, 42102-9547
Telephone: 502-782-8160
FAX: 502-782-5856

MEMBERS OF FIRM

Joe Bill Campbell
Thomas N. Kerrick
John R. Grise
Gregory N. Stivers
H. Brent Brennenstuhl
Deborah Tomes Wilkins

ASSOCIATES

H. Harris Pepper, Jr.
Lanna Martin Kilgore
Laura Hagan

Representative Clients: Dollar General Corp.; Greenview Hospital; Hospital Corporation of America; Hardin Memorial Hospital; Monarch Environmental, Inc.; Mid-South Management Group, Inc.; Western Kentucky University; Service One Credit Union; Trans Financial Bank; TKR Cable.

For full biographical listings, see the Martindale-Hubbell Law Directory

ENGLISH, LUCAS, PRIEST & OWSLEY (AV)

1101 College Street, P.O. Box 770, 42102-0770
Telephone: 502-781-6500
Telecopier: 502-782-7782

MEMBERS OF FIRM

Whayne C. Priest, Jr.
Kurt W. Maier
Charles E. English, Jr.

For Complete List of Firm Personnel, See General Section

For full biographical listings, see the Martindale-Hubbell Law Directory

HARLIN & PARKER, P.S.C. (AV)

519 East Tenth Street, P.O. Box 390, 42102-0390
Telephone: 502-842-5611
Telefax: 502-842-2607
Smiths Grove, Kentucky Office: Old Farmers Bank Building.
Telephone: 502-563-4701.

William Jerry Parker
Max B. Harlin, III
James D. Harris, Jr.
Michael K. Bishop

Insurance Clients: Allstate Insurance Co.; CNA Insurance Companies; Maryland Casualty Co.
Railroad and Utilities Clients: District Attorneys for South Central Bell Telephone Co.; CSX Transportation, Inc.
Representative Clients: Sears Roebuck & Company; Honda Motor Co.; Kawasaki Motors Corp. U.S.A.
Local Counsel for: General Motors Corp.; Ford Motor Co.; Chrysler Corp.

For Complete List of Firm Personnel, See General Section

For full biographical listings, see the Martindale-Hubbell Law Directory

RUDLOFF, GOLDEN & EVANS (AV)

553 East Main Street, 42101-2256
Telephone: 502-781-7754; 781-7762

MEMBERS OF FIRM

William J. Rudloff
J. Dale Golden
R. Brian Evans

Reference: National City Bank, Bowling Green, Ky.

For full biographical listings, see the Martindale-Hubbell Law Directory

COVINGTON, Kenton Co.

ADAMS, BROOKING, STEPNER, WOLTERMANN & DUSING (AV)

421 Garrard Street, P.O. Box 861, 41012
Telephone: 606-291-7270
FAX: 606-291-7902
Florence, Kentucky Office: 8100 Burlington Pike, Suite 400, 41042.
Telephone: 606-371-6220.
FAX: 606-371-8341.

Charles S. Adams (1906-1971)
John R. S. Brooking
Donald L. Stepner
James G. Woltermann (Resident at Florence Office)
Gerald F. Dusing (Resident at Florence Office)
Michael M. Sketch (Resident at Florence Office)
Dennis R. Williams (Resident at Florence Office)
James R. Kruer
Jeffrey C. Mando

ASSOCIATES

Marc D. Dietz (Resident at Florence Office)
Gregory S. Shumate
John S. "Brook" Brooking (Resident at Florence Office)
Stacey L. Graus
Lori A. Schlarman (Resident, Florence Office)
Paul J. Darpel (Resident, Florence Office)
Chandra S. Baldwin (Not admitted in KY)

Representative Clients: CSX Transportation; Balluff, Inc., Wampler, Inc., Kisters, Inc., Krauss-Maffei, Inc., A group of German companies; State Automobile Mutual Insurance Co.; Chevron of California; Great American Insurance Co.; Grange Mutual Insurance Co.; Meridian Mutual Insurance Co.; Fifth-Third Bank of Northern Ky.; Northern Kentucky University.

For full biographical listings, see the Martindale-Hubbell Law Directory

ROBERT C. CETRULO, P.S.C. (AV)

The Cetrulo Building, 620 Washington Street, 41011
Telephone: 606-491-6200
FAX: 606-491-6201

Robert C. Cetrulo

Reference: Star Bank, Covington, Kentucky.

For full biographical listings, see the Martindale-Hubbell Law Directory

Covington—Continued

GREENEBAUM DOLL & McDONALD (AV)

A Partnership including Professional Service Corporations
50 East Rivercenter Boulevard, P.O. Box 2050, 41012-2050
Telephone: 606-655-4200
Telecopier: 606-655-4239
Louisville, Kentucky Office: 3300 National City Tower.
Telephone: 502-589-4200.
Fax: 502-587-3695.
Lexington, Kentucky Office: 1400 Vine Center Tower.
Telephone: 606-231-8500.
Fax: 606-255-2742.
Cincinnati, Ohio Office: 832 Main Street.
Telephone: 513-421-8087.
Fax: 513-421-8089.

MEMBERS OF FIRM

Wm. T. Robinson, III
Hiram Ely, III
Roger N. Braden (Resident)

ASSOCIATES

J. Kevin King
Sheryl E. Heeter

Representative Clients: Aetna Life Insurance Co.; ANDALEX Resources, Inc.; Ashland Oil, Inc.; A T & T Communications, Inc.; Bethlehem Steel Corp.; Brown-Forman Corp.; Citizens Fidelity Bank & Trust Co.; Humana, Inc.; KFC National Cooperative Advertising Program, Inc.
*A Professional Service Corporation

For Complete List of Firm Personnel, See General Section

For full biographical listings, see the Martindale-Hubbell Law Directory

ROBERT E. SANDERS AND ASSOCIATES, P.S.C. (AV)

The Charles H. Fisk House, 1017 Russell Street, 41011
Telephone: 606-491-3000
FAX: 606-655-4642

Robert E. Sanders

Julie Lippert Duncan

LEGAL SUPPORT PERSONNEL

Shirley L. Sanders
Harry E. Holtkamp
Sandra A. Head
Joseph E. Schmiade, Sr.

For full biographical listings, see the Martindale-Hubbell Law Directory

FLORENCE, Boone Co.

ADAMS, BROOKING, STEPNER, WOLTERMANN & DUSING (AV)

8100 Burlington Pike, Suite 400, 41042-0576
Telephone: 606-371-6220
FAX: 606-371-8341
Covington, Kentucky Office: 421 Garrard Street.
Telephone: 606-291-7270.
FAX: 606-291-7902.

Donald L. Stepner
James G. Woltermann (Resident)
Gerald F. Dusing (Resident)
Michael M. Sketch (Resident)
Dennis R. Williams (Resident)
Jeffrey C. Mando

ASSOCIATES

Marc D. Dietz (Resident)
John S. "Brook" Brooking (Resident)
Lori A. Schlarman
Paul J. Darpel

Representative Clients: CSX Transportation; State Automobile Mutual Insurance Co.; Standard Oil Co. (Ky.); Great American Insurance Co.; Grange Mutual Insurance Co.; Meridian Mutual Insurance Co.; Fifth-Third Bank of Boone County; Northern Kentucky University.

For full biographical listings, see the Martindale-Hubbell Law Directory

*FRANKLIN,** Simpson Co.

STEERS & STEERS, P.S.C. (AV)

211 South College Street, P.O. Box 447, 42135-0447
Telephone: 502-586-4466
Telecopier: 502-586-4467

Roy L. Steers (1917-1980)
R. Lee Steers, Jr.

William Scott Crabtree
Gregory R. Vincent

Reference: Simpson County Bank.

For full biographical listings, see the Martindale-Hubbell Law Directory

*HINDMAN,** Knott Co.

WEINBERG, CAMPBELL, SLONE & SLONE, P.S.C. (AV)

Main Street, P.O. Box 727, 41822
Telephone: 606-785-5048; 785-5049
FAX: 606-785-3021

(See Next Column)

William R. Weinberg
Jerry Wayne Slone
Randy A. Campbell
Randy G. Slone

References: Bank of Hindman; Thacker & Grigsby Telephone Co.

For full biographical listings, see the Martindale-Hubbell Law Directory

*LEXINGTON,** Fayette Co.

LANDRUM & SHOUSE (AV)

106 West Vine Street, P.O. Box 951, 40588-0951
Telephone: 606-255-2424
Facsimile: 606-233-0308
Louisville, Kentucky Office: 400 West Market Street, Suite 1550, 40202.
Telephone: 502-589-7616.
Facsimile: 502-589-2119.

MEMBERS OF FIRM

John H. Burrus
George P. Parker (Resident, Louisville Office)
Thomas M. Cooper
William C. Shouse
Pierce W. Hamblin
Mark L. Moseley
Leslie Patterson Vose
John R. Martin, Jr. (Resident, Louisville Office)
James W. Smirz
Larry C. Deener
Sandra Mendez Dawahare
Mark J. Hinkel
Delores Hill Pregliasco (Resident, Louisville Office)
Benjamin Cowgill, Jr.
John Garry McNeill
Jack E. Toliver
Michael J. O'Connell (Resident, Louisville Office)
R. Kent Westberry (Resident, Louisville Office)
J. Denis Ogburn (Resident, Louisville Office)
Jane Durkin Samuel

ASSOCIATES

Stephen D. Milner
Stephen R. Chappell
David G. Hazlett (Resident, Louisville Office)
Charles E. Christian
Thomas E. Roma, Jr. (Resident, Louisville Office)
Virginia W. Gregg
Timothy D. Martin (Resident, Louisville Office)
Douglas L. Hoots
Dave Whalin (Resident, Louisville Office)
G. Bruce Stigger (Resident, Louisville Office)
Daniel E. Murner
Courtney T. Baxter (Resident, Louisville Office)
Julie A. Butcher
Frank M. Jenkins, III

OF COUNSEL

Weldon Shouse
Frank J. Dougherty, Jr. (Resident, Louisville Office)

District Attorneys: CSX Transportation, Inc.
Special Trial Counsel: Ford Motor Co. and Affiliates (Eastern Kentucky); Clark Equipment Co.
Representative Clients: The Continental Insurance Cos.; U.S. Insurance Group; U.S. Fidelity & Guaranty Co.; Ohio Casualty Insurance Co.; CIGNA; Royal Insurance Cos.

For Complete List of Firm Personnel, See General Section

For full biographical listings, see the Martindale-Hubbell Law Directory

PETER PERLMAN LAW OFFICES, P.S.C. (AV)

388 South Broadway, 40508
Telephone: 606-253-3919
FAX: 606-259-0493

Peter Perlman

Bryce D. Franklin, Jr.
Pamela D. Perlman

For full biographical listings, see the Martindale-Hubbell Law Directory

PIPER, WELLMAN & BOWERS (AV)

200 North Upper Street, 40507
Telephone: 606-231-1012
FAX: 606-231-7367

MEMBERS OF FIRM

George C. Piper
Dean T. Wellman
Barbara J. Bowers

ASSOCIATE

Johann F. Herklotz

For Complete List of Firm Personnel, See General Section

For full biographical listings, see the Martindale-Hubbell Law Directory

ROBERTS & SMITH (AV)

167 West Main Street Suite 200, 40507
Telephone: 606-233-1104

MEMBERS OF FIRM

Larry S. Roberts
Kenneth W. Smith

For full biographical listings, see the Martindale-Hubbell Law Directory

Lexington—Continued

SAVAGE, GARMER & ELLIOTT, P.S.C. (AV)

Opera House Office Building, 141 North Broadway, 40507
Telephone: 606-254-9351
Fax: 606-233-9769

Joe C. Savage
William R. Garmer
Robert L. Elliott

For full biographical listings, see the Martindale-Hubbell Law Directory

STURGILL, TURNER & TRUITT (AV)

155 East Main Street, 40507
Telephone: 606-255-8581
Fax: 606-231-0851

MEMBERS OF FIRM

Gardner L. Turner
Stephen L. Barker
Donald P. Moloney, II
Phillip M. Moloney
Douglas L. McSwain

For Complete List of Firm Personnel, See General Section

For full biographical listings, see the Martindale-Hubbell Law Directory

*LOUISVILLE,** Jefferson Co.

FRANKLIN AND HANCE, P.S.C. (AV)

The Speed House, 505 West Ormsby Avenue, 40203
Telephone: 502-637-6000
Fax: 502-637-1413

Larry B. Franklin
Michael R. Hance

David B. Gray

Reference: First National Bank.

For full biographical listings, see the Martindale-Hubbell Law Directory

GREENEBAUM DOLL & MCDONALD (AV)

A Partnership including Professional Service Corporations
3300 National City Tower, 40202
Telephone: 502-589-4200
Fax: 502-587-3695
Lexington, Kentucky Office: 1400 Vine Center Tower.
Telephone: 606-231-8500.
Fax: 606-255-2742.
Covington, Kentucky Office: 50 East River Center Boulevard, P.O. Box 2050.
Telephone: 606-655-4200.
Fax: 606-655-4239.
Cincinnati, Ohio Office: 832 Main Street.
Telephone: 513-421-8087.
Fax: 513-421-8089.

Wm. T. Robinson, III
James G. LeMaster (Resident at Lexington, Kentucky)
Hiram Ely, III
Roger N. Braden (Resident at Covington, Kentucky)
Mark T. Hayden (Resident at Lexington, Kentucky)

ASSOCIATES

J. Kevin King (Lexington and Covington, Kentucky and Cincinnati, Ohio)
Angela McCormick Bisig
Benjamin D. Crocker (Resident, Lexington Office)
Sheryl E. Heeter (Covington and Cincinnati Offices)

Representative Clients: Aetna Life Insurance Co.; ANDALEX Resources, Inc.; Ashland Oil, Inc.; A T & T Communications, Inc.; Bethlehem Steel Corp.; Brown-Forman Corp.; Humana, Inc.; Kentucky Kingdom, Inc.; KFC National Cooperative Advertising Program, Inc.
*A Professional Service Corporation

For Complete List of Firm Personnel, See General Section

For full biographical listings, see the Martindale-Hubbell Law Directory

FRANK E. HADDAD, JR. (AV)

Kentucky Home Life Building, 239 South Fifth Street, Fifth Floor, 40202
Telephone: 502-583-4881
Fax: 502-589-1058

Reference: Citizens Fidelity Bank & Trust Co.

For full biographical listings, see the Martindale-Hubbell Law Directory

LANDRUM & SHOUSE (AV)

400 West Market Street Suite 1550, 40202
Telephone: 502-589-7616
Facsimile: 502-589-2119
Lexington, Kentucky Office: 106 West Vine Street, P.O. Box 951.
Telephone: 606-255-2424.
Facsimile: 606-233-0308.

(See Next Column)

RESIDENT MEMBERS OF THE FIRM

George P. Parker
John R. Martin, Jr.
Delores Hill Pregliasco
Michael J. O'Connell
R. Kent Westberry
J. Denis Ogburn

RESIDENT ASSOCIATES

David G. Hazlett
Thomas E. Roma, Jr.
Timothy D. Martin
Dave Whalin
G. Bruce Stigger
Courtney T. Baxter
D. Sean Nilsen

OF COUNSEL

Frank J. Dougherty, Jr.

For full biographical listings, see the Martindale-Hubbell Law Directory

MIDDLETON & REUTLINGER, P.S.C. (AV)

2500 Brown and Williamson Tower, 40202-3410
Telephone: 502-584-1135
Fax: 502-561-0442
Jeffersonville, Indiana Office: 605 Watt Street, 47130.
Telephone: 812-282-4886.

O. Grant Bruton
Charles G. Middleton, III
Charles D. Greenwell
John W. Bilby
Timothy P. O'Mara
Stewart L. Prather
G. Kennedy Hall, Jr.
Mark S. Fenzel
Kathiejane Oehler
David J. Kellerman

Julie A. Gregory
Dennis D. Murrell
Augustus S. Herbert

Counsel for: Chevron USA; Liberty National Bank; Logan Aluminum, Inc.; Louisville Gas & Electric Co.; MCI Telecommunications Corp.; Metropolitan Life Insurance Co.; Kosmos Cement Co.; Porcelain Metal Corp.; The Home Insurance Co.; The Kroger Co.; Demars Haka Development, Inc.

For Complete List of Firm Personnel, See General Section

For full biographical listings, see the Martindale-Hubbell Law Directory

OLDFATHER & MORRIS (AV)

One Mezzanine The Morrissey Building, 304 West Liberty Street, 40202
Telephone: 502-589-5500
Fax: 502-589-5338

Ann B. Oldfather
Douglas H. Morris, II
William F. McMurry
James Barrett
Teresa A. Talbott

For full biographical listings, see the Martindale-Hubbell Law Directory

W. R. (PAT) PATTERSON, JR. (AV)

Suite 408, 310 West Liberty Street, 40202
Telephone: 502-583-1122
FAX: 502-583-3520

For full biographical listings, see the Martindale-Hubbell Law Directory

RUBIN HAYS & FOLEY (AV)

First Trust Centre 200 South Fifth Street, 40202
Telephone: 502-569-7550
Telecopier: 502-569-7555

MEMBERS OF FIRM

Wm. Carl Fust
Harry Lee Meyer
David W. Gray
Irvin D. Foley
Joseph R. Gathright, Jr.
Lisa Koch Bryant
Sharon C. Hardy
Charles S. Musson
W. Randall Jones
K. Gail Russell

ASSOCIATE

Christian L. Juckett

OF COUNSEL

James E. Fahey
Newman T. Guthrie

Representative Clients: J.C. Bradford & Co., Inc.; J.J.B. Hilliard, W.L. Lyons, Inc.; Huntington National Bank; Liberty National Bank and Trust Company; National City Bank; PNC Bank; Prudential Bache & Co., Inc.; Prudential Securities, Inc.; Society Bank; Stock Yards Bank and Trust Co.

For full biographical listings, see the Martindale-Hubbell Law Directory

SEILLER & HANDMAKER (AV)

2200 Meidinger Tower, 40202
Telephone: 502-584-7400
Telecopier: 502-583-2100
Paris, Kentucky Office: Seiller, Handmaker & Blevins, P.S.C., 1431 South Main Street.
Telephone: 606-987-3980.
Telecopier: 606-987-3982.
New Albany, Indiana Office: 204 Pearl Street, Suite 200.
Telephone: 812-948-8307.
Telecopier: 812-948-8383.

Edward F. Seiller (1897-1990)

(See Next Column)

SEILLER & HANDMAKER, *Louisville—Continued*

MEMBERS OF FIRM

Stuart Allen Handmaker
Bill V. Seiller
David M. Cantor
Neil C. Bordy
Kyle Anne Citrynell
Maury D. Kommor
Cynthia Compton Stone

ASSOCIATES

Glenn A. Cohen
Pamela M. Greenwell
Tomi Anne Blevins Pulliam (Resident, Paris Office)
Linda Scholle Cowan
Mary Zeller Wing Ceridan
Michael C. Bratcher
John E. Brengle
Patrick R. Holland, II
Edwin Jon Wolfe
Donna F. Townsend
William C. Robinson

OF COUNSEL

Robert S. Frey

For full biographical listings, see the Martindale-Hubbell Law Directory

WEISS & FREDERICK (AV)

1425 Citizens Plaza, 40202
Telephone: 502-583-1000
FAX: 502-583-4478

MEMBERS OF FIRM

Gary M. Weiss
Carl D. Frederick
Howard H. Swartz
Janice M. Weiss

OF COUNSEL

Henry M. Burt

For full biographical listings, see the Martindale-Hubbell Law Directory

LOWMANSVILLE, Lawrence Co.

MARCUM & TRIPLETT (AV)

U.S. 23, P.O. Box 178, 41232
Telephone: 606-297-6403
Telecopier: 606-297-6405

MEMBERS OF FIRM

Leo A. Marcum
John R. Triplett

Reference: Inez Deposit Bank, Inez, Kentucky.

For full biographical listings, see the Martindale-Hubbell Law Directory

*OWENSBORO,** Daviess Co.

RUMMAGE, KAMUF, YEWELL, PACE & CONDON (AV)

Great Financial Federal Building, 322 Frederica Street, 42301
Telephone: 502-685-3901
FAX: 502-926-2005

MEMBERS OF FIRM

William E. Rummage
Charles J. Kamuf
David L. Yewell
Patrick D. Pace
David C. Condon

Representative Clients: Owensboro Municipal Utilities Commission; Lincoln Service Corp.; Hancock County Planning Commission; Daviess County Board of Education; Barmet Aluminum Corp.; Owensboro Sewer Commission; TICOR Title Insurance Co.; Chicago Title Insurance Co.; Owensboro Riverport Authority; Housing Authority of Owensboro.

For Complete List of Firm Personnel, See General Section

For full biographical listings, see the Martindale-Hubbell Law Directory

LAW OFFICES OF CHARLES S. WIBLE, P.S.C. (AV)

324 St. Ann Street, P.O. Box 936, 42301
Telephone: 502-926-3377
1-800-737-3377
FAX: 502-683-0408

Charles S. Wible

Jeffrey T. Sampson

References: Central Bank & Trust Co.; Citizens State Bank; Owensboro National Bank.

For full biographical listings, see the Martindale-Hubbell Law Directory

*RICHMOND,** Madison Co.

COY, GILBERT & GILBERT (AV)

212 North Second Street, 40475
Telephone: 606-623-3877
Fax: 606-624-5435

MEMBERS OF FIRM

Charles R. Coy
James T. Gilbert
Sandra A. Bolin

For Complete List of Firm Personnel, See General Section

For full biographical listings, see the Martindale-Hubbell Law Directory

*VANCEBURG,** Lewis Co.

STANLEY AND BERTRAM (AV)

P.O. Box 40, 41179-0040
Telephone: 606-796-3024; 796-3025
Fax: 606-796-2113

MEMBERS OF FIRM

Avery L. Stanley
Thomas M. Bertram, II
Anita Esham Stanley

A list of Representative Clients will be furnished upon request.

For full biographical listings, see the Martindale-Hubbell Law Directory

LOUISIANA

*BATON ROUGE,** East Baton Rouge Parish

JAMES F. ABADIE (AV)

Court Plaza, Suite 205, 10500 Coursey Boulevard, 70816
Telephone: 504-295-1234
Telecopier: 504-295-1292

For full biographical listings, see the Martindale-Hubbell Law Directory

GEORGE AND GEORGE, LTD., A PROFESSIONAL LAW CORPORATION (AV)

8110 Summa Avenue, 70809
Telephone: 504-769-3064
Fax: 504-766-9974
Toll Free Numbers: 1-800-654-2335
Nationwide: 1-800-843-5702

James A. George

Reference: Hibernia National Bank of Baton Rouge.

For full biographical listings, see the Martindale-Hubbell Law Directory

BERT K. ROBINSON (AV)

10357 Old Hammond Highway, 70816-8261
Telephone: 504-924-0296
Fax: 504-924-5288

ASSOCIATE

Johanna R. Landreneau

OF COUNSEL

Charles C. Holbrook

For full biographical listings, see the Martindale-Hubbell Law Directory

SEALE, SMITH, ZUBER & BARNETTE (AV)

Two United Plaza, Suite 200, 8550 United Plaza Boulevard, 70809
Telephone: 504-924-1600
Telecopier: 504-924-6100

Armbrust Gordon Seale (1913-1989)
Robert W. Smith (1922-1989)
Donald S. Zuber
Kenneth E. Barnette
William C. Kaufman III
John W. L. Swanner
James H. Morgan III
Ronald A. Seale
Brent E. Kinchen
Charles K. Watts
Myron A. Walker, Jr.
Daniel A. Reed
Kenner O. Miller, Jr.
William C. Rowe, Jr.
Lawrence R. Anderson, Jr.

ASSOCIATES

Richard T. Reed
Barbara G. Chatelain
Anthony J. Russo, Jr.
Catherine S. Nobile

Representative Clients: Farmers Insurance Group; St. Paul Fire and Marine Insurance Company; United Services Automobile Association; General Motors Acceptance Corporation.
Reference: City National Bank, Baton Rouge, Louisiana.

For full biographical listings, see the Martindale-Hubbell Law Directory

*LAFAYETTE,** Lafayette Parish

DOMENGEAUX, WRIGHT, MOROUX & ROY, A PROFESSIONAL LAW CORPORATION (AV)

556 Jefferson Street, Suite 500, P.O. Box 3668, 70502-3668
Telephone: 318-233-3033; 1-800-375-3106
Fax: 318-232-8213
Hammond, Louisiana Office: Magnolia Plaza, Suite K, 1007 West Thomas Street, P. O. Box 1558.
Telephone: 504-542-4963; 1-800-423-1160.

(See Next Column)

DOMENGEAUX, WRIGHT, MOROUX & ROY A PROFESSIONAL LAW CORPORATION—*Continued*

James Domengeaux (1907-1988)
Anthony D. Moroux (1948-1993)
Bob F. Wright (A Professional Law Corporation)
James Parkerson Roy (A Professional Law Corporation)
Robert K. Tracy (A Professional Law Corporation)
Thomas R. Edwards (A Professional Law Corporation)
Frank Edwards (Resident, Hammond Office)
James Wattigny
James H. Domengeaux
R. Hamilton Davis
Gilbert Hennigan Dozier
Carla Marie Perron
Tyron D. Picard

OF COUNSEL

Jerome E. Domengeaux

Reference: Mid-South National Bank; Advocate Financial, L.L.C.

For full biographical listings, see the Martindale-Hubbell Law Directory

RICHARD R. KENNEDY A PROFESSIONAL LAW CORPORATION (AV)

309 Polk Street, P.O. Box 3243, 70502-3243
Telephone: 318-232-1934
Fax: 318-232-9720

Richard R. Kennedy

For full biographical listings, see the Martindale-Hubbell Law Directory

*LAKE CHARLES,** Calcasieu Parish

PLAUCHÉ SMITH & NIESET, A PROFESSIONAL LAW CORPORATION (AV)

1123 Pithon Street, P.O. Drawer 1705, 70602
Telephone: 318-436-0522
Facsimile: 318-436-9637

S. W. Plauché (1889-1952)
S. W. Plauché, Jr. (1915-1966)
A. Lane Plauché
Allen L. Smith, Jr.
James R. Nieset
Frank M. Walker, Jr.
Michael J. McNulty, III
Jeffrey M. Cole
Andrew R. Johnson, IV
Charles V. Musso, Jr.
Christopher P. Ieyoub
H. David Vaughan, II
Rebecca S. Young
Stephanie A. Landry

Representative Clients: CIGNA; CNA Insurance Cos.; Commercial Union Insurance Cos.; Crum & Forster; General Motors Corp.; Reliance Insurance Cos.; Royal Insurance Group; State Farm; U.S. Insurance Group.

For full biographical listings, see the Martindale-Hubbell Law Directory

*MONROE,** Ouachita Parish

MCLEOD, VERLANDER, EADE & VERLANDER (AV)

A Partnership including Professional Law Corporations
1900 North 18th Street, Suite 610, P.O. Box 2270, 71207-2270
Telephone: 318-325-7000
Telecopier: 318-324-0580

MEMBERS OF FIRM

Robert P. McLeod (P.L.C.)
David E. Verlander, III (P.L.C.)
Ellen R. Eade
Paul J. Verlander
Rick W. Duplissey
Pamela G. Nathan

For full biographical listings, see the Martindale-Hubbell Law Directory

*NEW ORLEANS,** Orleans Parish

CAPITELLI & WICKER (AV)

2950 Energy Centre, 1100 Poydras Street, 70163-2950
Telephone: 504-582-2425
FAX: 504-582-2422

Ralph Capitelli
T. Carey Wicker, III
Paul Michael Elvir, Jr.

OF COUNSEL

Terry Q. Alarcon

For full biographical listings, see the Martindale-Hubbell Law Directory

GAINSBURGH, BENJAMIN, FALLON, DAVID & ATES (AV)

A Partnership including Professional Law Corporations
2800 Energy Centre, 1100 Poydras, 70163-2800
Telephone: 504-522-2304
Telecopier: 504-528-9973

OF COUNSEL

Samuel C. Gainsburgh (P.L.C.)

(See Next Column)

MEMBERS OF FIRM

Jack C. Benjamin (P.L.C.)
Eldon E. Fallon (P.L.C.)
Robert J. David
George S. Meyer (1939-1977)
J. Robert Ates (P.L.C.)
Gerald E. Meunier
Nick F. Noriea, Jr.
Irving J. Warshauer
Stevan C. Dittman
Madeleine M. Landrieu

ASSOCIATES

Darryl M. Phillips
Andrew A. Lemmon
Michael G. Calogero

For full biographical listings, see the Martindale-Hubbell Law Directory

DARLEEN M. JACOBS A PROFESSIONAL LAW CORPORATION (AV)

823 St. Louis Street, 70112
Telephone: 504-522-3287; 522-0155
Cable Address: "Darjac."

Darleen M. Jacobs
Honorable S. Sanford Levy (1902-1989)

For full biographical listings, see the Martindale-Hubbell Law Directory

MURRAY LAW FIRM (AV)

Suite 2550, LL&E Tower, 909 Poydras Street, 70112
Telephone: 504-525-8100
Fax: 504-584-5249
1-800-467-8100

Stephen B. Murray
Patricia R. Murray

Charles R. Ward, Jr.
Joseph A. Race
Perry Michael Nicosia

For full biographical listings, see the Martindale-Hubbell Law Directory

SLATER LAW FIRM, A PROFESSIONAL CORPORATION (AV)

650 Poydras Street Suite 2400, 70130-6101
Telephone: 504-523-7333
Fax: 504-528-1080

Benjamin R. Slater, Jr.
Benjamin R. Slater, III
Mark E. Van Horn
Kevin M. Wheeler

Anne Elise Brown
Donald J. Miester, Jr.

OF COUNSEL

Michael O. Waguespack

Representative Clients: Norfolk Southern Corporation; The Quaker Oats Company; Electric Mutual Liability Insurance Company; Diversified Foods and Seasonings.

For full biographical listings, see the Martindale-Hubbell Law Directory

*SHREVEPORT,** Caddo Parish

TROY E. BAIN (AV)

1540 Irving Place, 71101
Telephone: 318-221-0076
Fax: 318-227-8290

Reference: Commercial National Bank of Shreveport.

For full biographical listings, see the Martindale-Hubbell Law Directory

BODENHEIMER, JONES, KLOTZ & SIMMONS (AV)

509 Milam Street, 71101
Telephone: 318-221-1507
Fax: 318-221-4560

MEMBERS OF FIRM

G. M. Bodenheimer, Jr.
Harry D. Simmons
James P. Bodenheimer

ASSOCIATE

David A. Szwak

For full biographical listings, see the Martindale-Hubbell Law Directory

SOCKRIDER, BOLIN & ANGLIN, A PROFESSIONAL LAW CORPORATION (AV)

327 Crockett Street, 71101
Telephone: 318-221-5503
Fax: 318-221-3849

John R. Pleasant (1905-1983)
H. F. Sockrider, Jr.
James E. Bolin, Jr.
D. Rex Anglin
Gregory H. Batte

For full biographical listings, see the Martindale-Hubbell Law Directory

Shreveport—Continued

WIENER, WEISS, MADISON & HOWELL, A PROFESSIONAL CORPORATION (AV)

333 Texas Street, Suite 2350, P.O. Box 21990, 71120-1990
Telephone: 318-226-9100
Fax: 318-424-5128

James Fleet Howell
James R. Madison
Katherine Clark Hennessey
Jeffrey W. Weiss
R. Joseph Naus

Representative Clients: Pioneer Bank & Trust Co.; Ford Motor Credit Corp.; CNA Insurance Companies; International Paper Companies; Louisiana Homebuilders Association Self Insurers Fund; LSU-Shreveport; Sealy Realty, Inc.; Palmer Petroleum, Inc.; Brookshire Grocery Company (Louisiana); Northwest Louisiana Production Credit Association.

For Complete List of Firm Personnel, See General Section

For full biographical listings, see the Martindale-Hubbell Law Directory

MAINE

*AUGUSTA,** Kennebec Co.

* indicates certain Bar Register subscribers whose principal office is located elsewhere in the state and who have arranged for representation as a part of the state capital listings that follow

*** PIERCE, ATWOOD, SCRIBNER, ALLEN, SMITH & LANCASTER (AV)**

77 Winthrop Street, 04330
Telephone: 207-622-6311
Fax: 207-623-9367
Portland, Maine Office: One Monument Square.
Telephone: 207-773-6411.
Camden, Maine Office: 36 Chestnut Street, P.O. Box 780.
Telephone: 207-236-4333.

MEMBERS OF FIRM

Malcolm L. Lyons
John C. Nivison

ASSOCIATES

Daniel J. Stevens
Benjamin P. Townsend

For Complete List of Firm Personnel, See General Section

For full biographical listings, see the Martindale-Hubbell Law Directory

*BANGOR,** Penobscot Co.

EATON, PEABODY, BRADFORD & VEAGUE, P.A. (AV)

Fleet Center-Exchange Street, P.O. Box 1210, 04402-1210
Telephone: 207-947-0111
Telecopier: 207-942-3040
Augusta, Maine Office: 2 Central Plaza.
Telephone: 207-622-3747.
Telecopier: 207-622-9732.
Brunswick, Maine Office: 167 Park Row.
Telephone: 207-729-1144.
Telecopier: 207-729-1140.
Camden, Maine Office: 7-9 Washington Street.
Telephone: 207-236-3325.
Telecopier: 207-236-8611.
Dover-Foxcroft, Maine Office: 30 East Main Street.
Telephone: 207-564-8378.
Telecopier: 207-564-7059.

Thomas M. Brown
Bernard J. Kubetz
Douglas M. Smith (Resident, Dover-Foxcroft and Augusta Offices)
Stephen G. Morrell (Resident, Brunswick Office)
Glen L. Porter
Gordon H. S. Scott (Resident, Augusta Office)
William B. Devoe
Paul L. Gibbons (Resident, Camden Office)

John M. Monahan (Resident, Dover-Foxcroft Office)
Jonathan B. Huntington (Resident, Dover-Foxcroft Office)
Judy A.S. Metcalf (Resident, Brunswick Office)
Thad B. Zmistowski

A List of Representative Clients available upon request.

For Complete List of Firm Personnel, See General Section

For full biographical listings, see the Martindale-Hubbell Law Directory

VAFIADES, BROUNTAS & KOMINSKY (AV)

Key Plaza, 23 Water Street, P.O. Box 919, 04402-0919
Telephone: 207-947-6915
Telecopier: 207-941-0863

(See Next Column)

MEMBERS OF FIRM

Nicholas P. Brountas
Susan R. Kominsky
Marvin H. Glazier
Eugene C. Coughlin, III

OF COUNSEL

Lewis V. Vafiades

For Complete List of Firm Personnel, See General Section

For full biographical listings, see the Martindale-Hubbell Law Directory

BAR HARBOR, Hancock Co.

FENTON, CHAPMAN, FENTON, SMITH & KANE, P.A. (AV)

109 Main Street, P.O. Box B, 04609
Telephone: 207-288-3331
FAX: 207-288-9326

Douglas B. Chapman
Nathaniel R. Fenton
Chadbourn H. Smith

Reference: Bar Harbor Banking and Trust Co.

For Complete List of Firm Personnel, See General Section

For full biographical listings, see the Martindale-Hubbell Law Directory

*BATH,** Sagadahoc Co.

CONLEY, HALEY & O'NEIL (AV)

Thirty Front Street, 04530
Telephone: 207-443-5576
Telefax: 207-443-6665

J. Michael Conley
Arlyn H. Weeks
Laura M. O'Hanlon

Representative Clients: Bath Iron Works Corporation; Central Maine Power Company; Saco Defense, Inc.; Sugarloaf Mountain Corporation.
References: Casco Northern Bank, N.A.; First Federal Savings & Loan Association of Bath; Shawmut Bank.

For Complete List of Firm Personnel, See General Section

For full biographical listings, see the Martindale-Hubbell Law Directory

BRIDGTON, Cumberland Co.

BERMAN & SIMMONS, P.A. (AV)

Route 302, Portland Street, 04009
Telephone: 207-647-3125
Fax: 207-647-3134
Lewiston, Maine Office: 129 Lisbon Street, P.O. Box 961, 04243-0961.
Telephone: 207-784-3576.
Fax: 207-784-7699.
Portland, Maine Office: 178 Middle Street.
Telephone: 207-774-5277.
Fax: 207-774-0166.
South Paris, Maine Office: 4 Western Avenue.
Telephone: 207-743- 8775.
Fax: 207-743-8559.

C. Martin Berman
Julian L. Sweet
David W. Grund

For full biographical listings, see the Martindale-Hubbell Law Directory

LEWISTON, Androscoggin Co.

BERMAN & SIMMONS, P.A. (AV)

129 Lisbon Street, P.O. Box 961, 04243-0961
Telephone: 207-784-3576
Fax: 207-784-7699
Portland, Maine Office: 178 Middle Street.
Telephone: 207-774-5277.
Fax: 207-774-0166.
South Paris, Maine Office: 4 Western Avenue.
Telephone: 207-743- 8775.
Fax: 207-743-8559.
Bridgton, Maine Office: Route 302, Portland Street.
Telephone: 207-647-3125.
Fax: 207-647-3134.

C. Martin Berman
Jack H. Simmons
John E. Sedgewick
William D. Robitzek
Julian L. Sweet
Jeffrey Rosenblatt
Paul F. Macri
Jeffrey A. Thaler
Steven D. Silin
Valerie Stanfill
Tyler N. Kolle
Glenn S. Eddy
David J. Van Dyke
David W. Grund
Daniel G. Kagan
Joy C. Cantrell
Ivy L. Frignoca

For full biographical listings, see the Martindale-Hubbell Law Directory

*PORTLAND,** Cumberland Co.

HERBERT H. BENNETT AND ASSOCIATES, P.A. (AV)

Suite 300, 121 Middle Street, P.O. Box 7799, 04112-7799
Telephone: 207-773-4775
Telecopier: 207-774-2366

Herbert H. Bennett (1928-1992)
Peter Bennett
Jeffrey Bennett
Frederick B. Finberg
Melinda J. Caterine
Hilary A. Rapkin

Counsel for: Associated Grocers of New England; Casco Northern Bank, N.A.; Coca Cola Bottling Company of Northern New England, Inc.; Northern Utilities/Bay State Gas; Pratt & Whitney (Division of United Technologies); Primerica Financial Services; Sprague Energy (C.H. Sprague & Son); Perrier Group of America, Inc.; Lepage Bakeries, Inc. (Country Kitchen); Table Talk Pies, Inc.; Texaco, Inc.

For full biographical listings, see the Martindale-Hubbell Law Directory

BERMAN & SIMMONS, P.A. (AV)

178 Middle Street, 04101
Telephone: 207-774-5277
Fax: 207-774-0166
Lewiston, Maine Office: 129 Lisbon Street.
Telephone: 207-784-3576.
Fax: 207-784-7699.
South Paris, Maine Office: 4 Western Avenue.
Telephone: 207-743-8775.
Fax: 207-743-8559.
Bridgton, Maine Office: Route 302, Portland Street.
Telephone: 207-647-3125.
Fax: 207-647-3134.

William D. Robitzek

For full biographical listings, see the Martindale-Hubbell Law Directory

CHILDS, EMERSON, RUNDLETT, FIFIELD & CHILDS (AV)

257 Deering Avenue, 04103
Telephone: 207-773-0275
Fax: 207-772-6723

Dana W. Childs
Richard S. Emerson, Jr.
Ellsworth T. Rundlett, III
Dwight A. Fifield
William H. Childs

For full biographical listings, see the Martindale-Hubbell Law Directory

FRIEDMAN & BABCOCK (AV)

Suite 400, Six City Center, P.O. Box 4726, 04112-4726
Telephone: 207-761-0900
Telecopier: 207-761-0186

MEMBERS OF FIRM

Harold J. Friedman
Ernest J. Babcock
Martha C. Gaythwaite
Gregory W. Powell
Thomas A. Cox
Karen Frink Wolf
Jennifer S. Begel
Laurence H. Leavitt

ASSOCIATES

Theodore H. Irwin, Jr.
Lee H. Bals
Michelle A. Landmann
Arthur J. Lamothe
Brian L. Champion
Laurie B. Perzley
Elizabeth A. Germani
Tracey G. Burton
Jonathan Marc Dunitz
Lori A. Desjardins

For full biographical listings, see the Martindale-Hubbell Law Directory

PIERCE, ATWOOD, SCRIBNER, ALLEN, SMITH & LANCASTER (AV)

One Monument Square, 04101
Telephone: 207-773-6411
Fax: 207-773-3419
Augusta, Maine Office: 77 Winthrop Street.
Telephone: 207-622-6311.
Camden, Maine Office: 36 Chestnut Street, P.O. Box 780.
Telephone: 207-236-4333.

MEMBERS OF FIRM

Ralph I. Lancaster, Jr.
Peter W. Culley
Daniel M. Snow
John C. Nivison (Resident, Augusta Office)
John J. Aromando
David E. Barry

ASSOCIATES

Stephen G. Grygiel
Gisele M. Nadeau
Daniel J. Stevens (Resident, Augusta Office)

For Complete List of Firm Personnel, See General Section

For full biographical listings, see the Martindale-Hubbell Law Directory

SMITH ELLIOTT SMITH & GARMEY, P.A. (AV)

100 Commercial Street, Suite 304, 04101
Telephone: 207-774-3199
Telefax: 207-774-2235
Kennebunk, Maine Office: Route One South, P.O. Box 980.
Telephone: 207-985-4464.
Telefax: 207-985-3946.
Saco, Maine Office: 199 Main Street, P.O. Box 1179.
Telephone: 207-282-1527.
Telefax: 207-283-4412. Sanford
Telephone: 207-324-1560. Wells
Telephone: 207-464-0970.

Randall E. Smith
Terrence D. Garmey
Richard P. Romeo
Robert H. Furbish
Michael J. Waxman

Reference: Casco Northern Bank, N.A. (Saco Branch); Saco & Biddeford Savings Institution.

For full biographical listings, see the Martindale-Hubbell Law Directory

THOMPSON & BOWIE (AV)

Three Canal Plaza, P.O. Box 4630, 04112
Telephone: 207-774-2500
Telecopier: 207-774-3591

MEMBERS OF FIRM

Roy E. Thompson, Jr.
James M. Bowie
Daniel R. Mawhinney
Rebecca H. Farnum
Glenn H. Robinson
Frank W. DeLong, III
Michael E. Saucier
Mark V. Franco

ASSOCIATES

Elizabeth G. Knox
Cathy S. Roberts
Paul C. Catsos

For full biographical listings, see the Martindale-Hubbell Law Directory

SACO, York Co.

SMITH ELLIOTT SMITH & GARMEY, P.A. (AV)

199 Main Street, P.O. Box 1179, 04072
Telephone: 207-282-1527
Telefax: 207-283-4412
Sanford Telephone: 207-324-1560
Portland Telephone: 207-774-3199
Wells Telephone: 207-646-0970
Kennebunk, Maine Office: Route One South, P.O. Box 980.
Telephone: 207-985-4464.
Telefax: 207-985-3946.
Portland, Maine Office: 100 Commercial Street, Suite 304.
Telephone: 207-774-3199.
Telefax: 207-774-2235.

Randall E. Smith
Charles W. Smith, Jr.
Peter W. Schroeter
John H. O'Neil, Jr.
Harry B. Center, II
Michael J. Waxman

References: Casco Northern Bank, N.A. (Saco Branch); Saco & Biddeford Savings Institution.

For Complete List of Firm Personnel, See General Section

For full biographical listings, see the Martindale-Hubbell Law Directory

*SKOWHEGAN,** Somerset Co.

WRIGHT & MILLS, P.A. (AV)

218 Water Street, P.O. Box 9, 04976
Telephone: 207-474-3324
Telefax: 207-474-3609

Carl R. Wright
S. Peter Mills, III
Paul P. Sumberg
Kenneth A. Lexier
Dale F. Thistle

Representative Clients: Design Professionals Insurance Company, New Jersey; Solon Manufacturing Company, Solon, Maine; Kleinschmidt Associates-Engineers, Pittsfield, Maine; Acheron Engineering, Newport, Maine; E.W. Littlefield-Contractors, Hartland, Maine; WBRC-Architects, Bangor, Maine.

For full biographical listings, see the Martindale-Hubbell Law Directory

*SOUTH PARIS,** Oxford Co.

BERMAN & SIMMONS, P.A. (AV)

4 Western Avenue, 04281
Telephone: 207-743-8775
Fax: 207-743-8559
Lewiston, Maine Office: 129 Lisbon Street, P.O. Box 961.
Telephone: 207-284-3576.
Fax: 207-784-7699.

(See Next Column)

BERMAN & SIMMONS P.A., *South Paris—Continued*

Portland, Maine Office: 178 Middle Street.
Telephone: 207-774-5277.
Fax: 207-774-0166.
Bridgton, Maine Office: Route 302, Portland Street.
Telephone: 207-647-3125.
Fax: 207-647-3134.

Jack H. Simmons
Glenn S. Eddy

For full biographical listings, see the Martindale-Hubbell Law Directory

MARYLAND

*BALTIMORE,** (Independent City)

ISRAELSON, SALSBURY, CLEMENTS & BEKMAN (AV)

300 West Pratt Street, Suite 450, 21201
Telephone: 410-539-6633
FAX: 410-625-9554

MEMBERS OF FIRM

Stuart Marshall Salsbury
Daniel M. Clements
Paul D. Bekman
Matthew Zimmerman
Laurence A. Marder

Suzanne K. Farace
Scott R. Scherr
Carol J. Glover

COUNSEL TO THE FIRM

Max R. Israelson

OF COUNSEL

Samuel Omar Jackson, Jr. (Semi-Retired)

For full biographical listings, see the Martindale-Hubbell Law Directory

JANET & STRAUSBERG (AV)

A Partnership of Professional Associations
Executive Centre at Hooks Lane, 8 Reservoir Circle, Suite 200, 21208
Telephone: 410-653-3200
Fax: 410-653-9030

MEMBERS OF FIRM

Howard A. Janet (P.A.)
Gary I. Strausberg (P.A.)

ASSOCIATES

Wayne M. Willoughby
Randal D. Getz
Zev T. Gershon
Sammie Lee Mouton

For full biographical listings, see the Martindale-Hubbell Law Directory

ROBINETTE, DUGAN & JAKUBOWSKI, P.A. (AV)

The Robinette-Dugan Building, 801 St. Paul Street, 21202
Telephone: 410-659-6700
FAX: 410-752-0456

Gilbert H. Robinette
Ruth A. Jakubowski
Henry E. Dugan, Jr.
Bruce J. Babij

Pamela S. Foresman
George S. Tolley, III

OF COUNSEL

Marian V. Fleming

For full biographical listings, see the Martindale-Hubbell Law Directory

ROLLINS, SMALKIN, RICHARDS & MACKIE (AV)

401 North Charles Street, 21201
Telephone: 410-727-2443
Fax: 410-727-8390

MEMBERS OF FIRM

H. Beale Rollins (1898-1985)
John F. Linsenmeyer
Samuel S. Smalkin (1906-1982)
Thomas C. Gentner
T. Benjamin Weston (1913-1980)
Glenn W. Trimmer
Thomas G. Andrew (1910-1973)
Patrick G. Cullen
Edward C. Mackie
James P. O'Meara
Dennis J. Sullivan

ASSOCIATES

Francis B. Buckley
Ralph E. Wilson III
Elaine R. Wilford
Kenneth G. Macleay
Paul G. Donoghue
Donna Lynn Kolakowski-Hollen

OF COUNSEL

Raymond A. Richards (Retired)
Hartman J. Miller

For full biographical listings, see the Martindale-Hubbell Law Directory

SCHOCHOR, FEDERICO AND STATON, P.A. (AV)

The Paulton, 1211 St. Paul Street, 21202
Telephone: 410-234-1000
FAX: 410-234-1010
Washington D.C. Office: 777 North Capitol Street, N.E., Suite 910.
Telephone: 202-408-3300.
Fax: 202-408-3304.

Jonathan Schochor
Philip C. Federico
Kerry D. Staton

Louis G. Close, III
Diane M. Littlepage
Christopher P. Kennedy

For full biographical listings, see the Martindale-Hubbell Law Directory

VENABLE, BAETJER AND HOWARD (AV)

A Partnership including Professional Corporations
1800 Mercantile Bank & Trust Building, 2 Hopkins Plaza, 21201
Telephone: 410-244-7400
Washington, D.C. Office: Venable, Baetjer, Howard & Civiletti. Suite 1000, 1201 New York Avenue, N.W.
Telephone: 202-962-4800.
McLean, Virginia Office: Suite 400, 2010 Corporate Ridge.
Telephone: 703-760-1600.
Rockville, Maryland Office: Suite 500, One Church Street, P. O. Box 1906.
Telephone: 301-217-5600.
Towson, Maryland Office: 210 Allegheny Avenue, P. O. Box 5517.
Telephone: 410-494-6200.

MEMBERS OF FIRM

Roger W. Titus (Resident, Rockville, Maryland Office)
Douglas D. Connah, Jr. (P.C.) (Also at Washington, D.C. Office)
John H. Zink, III (Resident, Towson, Maryland Office)
Bruce E. Titus (Resident, McLean, Virginia Office)
William D. Dolan, III (P.C.) (Not admitted in MD; Resident, McLean, Virginia Office)
Paul T. Glasgow (Resident, Rockville, Maryland Office)
Joseph C. Wich, Jr. (Resident, Towson, Maryland Office)
Susan K. Gauvey (Also at Towson, Maryland Office)
James K. Archibald (Also at Washington, D.C. and Towson, Maryland Offices)
Jeffrey A. Dunn (also at Washington, D.C. Office)
George F. Pappas (Also at Washington, D.C. Office)
James L. Shea (Also at Washington, D.C. Office)
Amy Berman Jackson (Not admitted in MD; Resident, Washington, D.C. Office)
William D. Quarles (Also at Washington, D.C. and Towson, Maryland Offices)
C. Carey Deeley, Jr. (Also at Towson, Maryland Office)
Kathleen Gallogly Cox (Resident, Towson, Maryland Office)
Christopher R. Mellott
Cynthia M. Hahn (Resident, Towson, Maryland Office)
M. King Hill, III (Resident, Towson, Maryland Office)
James A. Dunbar (Also at Washington, D.C. Office)
David J. Heubeck
Herbert G. Smith, II (Not admitted in MD; Resident, McLean, Virginia Office)

ASSOCIATES

Paul D. Barker, Jr.
Daniel William China
Marina Lolley Dame (Resident, Towson, Maryland Office)
J. Van L. Dorsey (Resident, Towson, Maryland Office)
Fred Joseph Federici, III (Resident, Washington, D.C. Office)
David W. Goewey (Not admitted in MD; Resident, Washington, D.C. Office)
E. Anne Hamel
Gregory L. Laubach (Resident, Rockville, Maryland Office)
Vicki Margolis
Christine M. McAnney (Not admitted in MD; Resident, McLean, Virginia Office)
John A. McCauley
Timothy J. McEvoy
John T. Prisbe
Michael W. Robinson (Not admitted in MD; Resident, McLean, Virginia Office)
Terri L. Turner

For Complete List of Firm Personnel, See General Section

For full biographical listings, see the Martindale-Hubbell Law Directory

VERDERAIME & DU BOIS, P.A. (AV)

1231 North Calvert Street, 21202
Telephone: 410-752-8888
FAX: 301-752-0425

Robert C. Verderaime
William D. Kurtz
A. Harold Du Bois
Elizabeth Jesukiewicz Frey
Neil J. Bixler

Reference: Maryland National Bank, Baltimore, Maryland.

For full biographical listings, see the Martindale-Hubbell Law Directory

Baltimore—Continued

ROBIN PAGE WEST (AV)

110 St. Paul Street, Suite 301, 21202
Telephone: 410-244-0400
Fax: 410-244-0402

For full biographical listings, see the Martindale-Hubbell Law Directory

*BEL AIR,** Harford Co.

STARK & KEENAN, A PROFESSIONAL ASSOCIATION (AV)

30 Office Street, 21014
Telephone: 410-838-5522
Baltimore: 410-879-2222
Fax: 410-879-0688

Elwood V. Stark, Jr.
Charles B. Keenan, Jr.
Thomas E. Marshall
Edwin G. Carson
Judith C. H. Cline
Gregory A. Szoka
Robert S. Lynch

Claire Prin Blomquist
Kimberly Kahoe Muenter
Paul W. Ishak

For full biographical listings, see the Martindale-Hubbell Law Directory

BETHESDA, Montgomery Co.

FREEMAN & JENNER, P.C. (AV)

3 Bethesda Metro Center, Suite 1410, 20814
Telephone: 301-907-7747
FAX: 301-907-9877
Washington, D.C. Office: 1000 16th Street, N.W., Suite 300.
Telephone: 301-907-7747.
Aspen, Colorado Office: 215 South Monarch Street, Suite 202.
Telephone: 303-925-3400.
FAX: 303-925-4043.

Martin H. Freeman
Robert K. Jenner

Barbara E. Hirsch
Mark Allan Freeman

Reference: Crestar Bank of Maryland.

For full biographical listings, see the Martindale-Hubbell Law Directory

*ROCKVILLE,** Montgomery Co.

ANDERSON & QUINN (AV)

The Adams Law Center, 25 Wood Lane, 20850
Telephone: 301-762-3303
FAX: 301-762-3776
Washington, D.C. Office: 1220 L Street, N.W., Suite 540.
Telephone: 202-371-1245.

MEMBERS OF FIRM

Charles C. Collins (1900-1973)
Robert E. Anderson (Not admitted in MD; Retired)
Francis X. Quinn
William Ray Scanlin (Resident, Washington, D.C. Office)
Donald P. Maiberger
Robert P. Scanlon (Resident, Washington, D.C. Office)
James G. Healy

ASSOCIATES

John A. Rego
Richard L. Butler (Resident, Washington, D.C. Office)
Marie M. Gavigan (Mrs.)
Donald J. Urgo, Jr.
Laura A. Garufi

Representative Clients: C & P Telephone; Commercial Union Insurance Cos.; Allstate Insurance Co.; State Farm Mutual Automobile Insurance Co.; Liberty Mutual Insurance Co.; Northbrook Insurance Cos.; Travelers Insurance Co.; National General Insurance Co.; American International Adjustment Co.; Marriott Corp.

For Complete List of Firm Personnel, See General Section

For full biographical listings, see the Martindale-Hubbell Law Directory

ARMSTRONG, DONOHUE & CEPPOS, CHARTERED (AV)

Suite 101, 204 Monroe Street, 20850
Telephone: 301-251-0440
Telecopier: 301-279-5929

Larry A. Ceppos
H. Patrick Donohue
H. Kenneth Armstrong
Benjamin S. Vaughan
John C. Monahan

Kirk S. Burgee
Oya S. Oner
Pamela Barrow Kincheloe
Maura J. Condon
Richard S. Schrager
Sharon A. Marcial

For full biographical listings, see the Martindale-Hubbell Law Directory

BRAULT, GRAHAM, SCOTT & BRAULT (AV)

101 South Washington Street, 20850
Telephone: 301-424-1060
Fax: 301-424-7991
Washington, D.C. Office: 1906 Sunderland Place, N.W.
Telephone: 202-785-1200.
FAX: 202-785-4301.
Arlington, Virginia Office: Suite 1201, 2300 North Clarendon Boulevard, Courthouse Plaza.
Telephone: 703-522-1781.

OF COUNSEL

Laurence T. Scott

MEMBERS OF FIRM

Denver H. Graham (1922-1987)
Albert E. Brault (Retired)
Albert D. Brault (Resident)
Leo A. Roth, Jr.
James S. Wilson (Resident)
Ronald G. Guziak (Resident)
Daniel L. Shea (Resident)
Keith M. Bonner
M. Kathleen Parker (Resident)
Regina Ann Casey (Resident)
James M. Brault (Resident)

ASSOCIATES

David G. Mulquin (Resident)
Sanford A. Friedman
Holly D. Shupert (Resident)
Eric A. Spacek (Not admitted in MD)
Joan F. Brault (Resident)

Representative Clients: American Oil Co.; Crum & Forster Group; Fireman's Fund American Insurance Cos.; Kemper Group; Reliance Insurance Cos.; Safeco Group; Government Employees Insurance Co.; Medical Mutual Insurance Society of Maryland; Legal Mutual Liability Insurance Society of Maryland.

For Complete List of Firm Personnel, See General Section

For full biographical listings, see the Martindale-Hubbell Law Directory

PAULSON, NACE, NORWIND & SELLINGER (AV)

31 Wood Lane, 20850
Telephone: 301-294-8060
Washington, D.C. Office: 1814 N Street, N.W.
Telephone: 202-463-1999.
Fax: 202-223-6824.

John J. Sellinger

For full biographical listings, see the Martindale-Hubbell Law Directory

SHADOAN AND MICHAEL (AV)

108 Park Avenue, 20850
Telephone: 301-762-5150

MEMBERS OF FIRM

George W. Shadoan
Robert R. Michael

ASSOCIATE

David J. Kaminow

Reference: Crestar Bank, N.A.

For full biographical listings, see the Martindale-Hubbell Law Directory

STEIN, SPERLING, BENNETT, DE JONG, DRISCOLL, GREENFEIG & METRO, P.A. (AV)

25 West Middle Lane, 20850
Telephone: 301-340-2020; 800-435-5230
Telecopier: 301-340-8217

David C. Driscoll, Jr.
Stuart S. Greenfeig
Donald N. Sperling
Paul T. Stein

Fred A. Balkin

For Complete List of Firm Personnel, See General Section

For full biographical listings, see the Martindale-Hubbell Law Directory

*TOWSON,** Baltimore Co.

NOLAN, PLUMHOFF & WILLIAMS, CHARTERED (AV)

Suite 700 Court Towers, 210 West Pennsylvania Avenue, 21204
Telephone: 410-823-7800
Fax: 410-296-2765

Stephen J. Nolan
Robert L. Hanley, Jr.
Robert E. Cahill, Jr.
J. Joseph Curran, III

Representative Clients: Injured Plaintiffs and Workers; Bituminous Insurance Companies; Carolina Freight Carriers Corporation; Keystone Insurance Company; Maryland Automobile Insurance Fund; Principal Casualty Insurance Company.

For Complete List of Firm Personnel, See General Section

For full biographical listings, see the Martindale-Hubbell Law Directory

Towson—Continued

VENABLE, BAETJER AND HOWARD (AV)

A Partnership including Professional Corporations
210 Allegheny Avenue, P.O. Box 5517, 21204
Telephone: 410-494-6200
FAX: 410-821-0147
Baltimore, Maryland Office: 1800 Mercantile Bank & Trust Building, 2 Hopkins Plaza.
Telephone: 410-244-7400.
Washington, D.C. Office: Venable, Baetjer, Howard & Civiletti. Suite 1000, 1201 New York Avenue, N.W.
Telephone: 202-962-4800.
McLean, Virginia Office: Suite 400, 2010 Corporate Ridge.
Telephone: 703-760-1600.
Rockville, Maryland Office: Suite 500, One Church Street, P. O. Box 1906.
Telephone: 301-217-5600.

PARTNERS

John H. Zink, III
Joseph C. Wich, Jr.
Susan K. Gauvey (Also at Baltimore, Maryland Office)
James K. Archibald (Also at Baltimore, Maryland and Washington, D.C. Offices)
William D. Quarles (Also at Washington, D.C. Office)
C. Carey Deeley, Jr. (Also at Baltimore, Maryland Office)
Kathleen Gallogly Cox
Cynthia M. Hahn
M. King Hill, III

ASSOCIATES

Marina Lolley Dame
J. Van L. Dorsey
Mary-Dulany James

For Complete List of Firm Personnel, See General Section

For full biographical listings, see the Martindale-Hubbell Law Directory

MASSACHUSETTS

*BOSTON,** Suffolk Co.

BARRON & STADFELD, P.C. (AV)

Two Center Plaza, 02108
Telephone: 617-723-9800
Telecopier: 617-523-8359
Hyannis, Massachusetts Office: 258 Winter Street.
Telephone: 617-778-6622.

Bernard A. Dwork
Enid M. Starr
Edward E. Kelly
David P. Dwork
Robert J. Hoffer
Rosemary Purtell

Christine Ann Gardner

For Complete List of Firm Personnel, See General Section

For full biographical listings, see the Martindale-Hubbell Law Directory

DENNIS J. CURRAN (AV)

One State Street, Suite 410, 02109
Telephone: 617-742-3010
Fax: 617-742-1799

For full biographical listings, see the Martindale-Hubbell Law Directory

PALMER & DODGE (AV)

(Storey Thorndike Palmer & Dodge)
One Beacon Street, 02108
Telephone: 617-573-0100
Telecopier: 617-227-4420
Telex: 951104
Cable Address: "Storeydike," Boston

MEMBERS OF FIRM

Jeffrey F. Jones
Francis C. Lynch
Craig E. Stewart

For Complete List of Firm Personnel, See General Section

For full biographical listings, see the Martindale-Hubbell Law Directory

SHAPIRO & ASSOCIATES (AV)

One Beacon Street, 24th Floor, 02108
Telephone: 617-227-8100

Daniel B. Shapiro

ASSOCIATE

Michael A. Mc Kinnon

Representative Clients: NLC Insurance Companies; Trust Insurance Co.; Liberty Mutual Insurance Co.

For full biographical listings, see the Martindale-Hubbell Law Directory

SHERBURNE, POWERS & NEEDHAM, P.C. (AV)

One Beacon Street, 02108
Telephone: 617-523-2700
Fax: 617-523-6850

William D. Weeks
John T. Collins
Allan J. Landau
John L. Daly
Stephen A. Hopkins
Alan I. Falk
C. Thomas Swaim
James Pollock
William V. Tripp III
Stephen S. Young
William F. Machen
W. Robert Allison
Jacob C. Diemert
Philip J. Notopoulos
Richard J. Hindlian
Paul E. Troy
Harold W. Potter, Jr.
Dale R. Johnson
Philip S. Lapatin
Pamela A. Duckworth
Mark Schonfeld
James D. Smeallie
Paul Killeen
Gordon P. Katz
Joseph B. Darby, III
Richard M Yanofsky
James E. McDermott
Robert V. Lizza
Miriam Goldstein Altman
John J. Monaghan
Margaret J. Palladino
Mark C. Michalowski
David Scott Sloan
M. Chrysa Long
Lawrence D. Bradley
Miriam J. McKendall

Cynthia A. Brown
Cynthia M. Hern
Dianne R. Phillips
Paul M. James
Theodore F. Hanselman
Joshua C. Krumholz
Ieuan G. Mahony
Kenneth L. Harvey
Christopher J. Trombetta
Edwin F. Landers, Jr.
Amy J. Mastrobattista
William Howard McCarthy, Jr.
Douglas W. Clapp
Tamara E. Goulston
Nicholas J. Psyhogeos

COUNSEL

Haig Der Manuelian
Mason M. Taber, Jr.
Karl J. Hirshman
Benjamin Volinski
Kenneth P. Brier

OF COUNSEL

John Barr Dolan

For full biographical listings, see the Martindale-Hubbell Law Directory

SUGARMAN AND SUGARMAN, P.C. (AV)

One Beacon Street, 02108
Telephone: 617-542-1000
Telecopier: 617-542-1359

Nathan Fink (1920-1974)
Paul R. Sugarman
Neil Sugarman
W. Thomas Smith
Steven L. Hoffman
Robert W. Casby
Kerry Paul Choi
Valerie A. Yarashus
Charlotte E. Glinka

Jodi M. Petrucelli
Darin Michael Colucci
Kimberly Ellen Nelson Winter
Marianne Camille LeBlanc

For full biographical listings, see the Martindale-Hubbell Law Directory

SWARTZ & SWARTZ (AV)

10 Marshall Street, 02108
Telephone: 617-742-1900
Fax: 617-367-7193

Edward M. Swartz
Alan L. Cantor
Joseph A. Swartz
Victor A. Denaro
Joan E. Swartz
James A. Swartz
Robert S. Berger
Harold David Levine

OF COUNSEL

Fredric A. Swartz

For full biographical listings, see the Martindale-Hubbell Law Directory

WITMER & THUOTTE (AV)

One Joy Street, 02108
Telephone: 617-248-0550
Telefax: 617-248-0607

Ronald A. Witmer
Robert W. Thuotte

ASSOCIATE

Lynn C. Rooney

For full biographical listings, see the Martindale-Hubbell Law Directory

BROCKTON, Plymouth Co.

VINCENT P. CAHALANE, P.C. (AV)

478 Torrey Street, 02401
Telephone: 508-588-1222
Fax: 508-584-4748

Vincent P. Cahalane
Robert J. Zullas
Julie A. Cahalane

(See Next Column)

VINCENT P. CAHALANE, P.C.—*Continued*

LEGAL SUPPORT PERSONNEL

PARALEGALS

Joan C. Cahalane
Kristopher S. Stefani

For full biographical listings, see the Martindale-Hubbell Law Directory

FITCHBURG, Worcester Co.

O'CONNOR AND RYAN, P.C. (AV)

61 Academy Street, 01420
Telephone: 508-345-4166
Fax: 508-343-8416

John M. O'Connor
Edward P. Ryan, Jr.
John Markham O'Connor

For full biographical listings, see the Martindale-Hubbell Law Directory

LOWELL, Middlesex Co.

MACARONIS LAW FIRM (AV)

Nine Central Street, Second Floor, 01852
Telephone: 508-453-3252
Fax: 508-454-5959

Nicholas Macaronis
Steven Holmes Bowen
Christopher W. Kita
William S. Swartz
Michael L. Tyner
Robert B. Tolins

For full biographical listings, see the Martindale-Hubbell Law Directory

*SPRINGFIELD,** Hampden Co.

ELY & KING (AV)

One Financial Plaza, 1350 Main Street, 01103
Telephone: 413-781-1920
Telecopier: 413-733-3360

MEMBERS OF FIRM

Joseph Buell Ely (1905-1956)
Raymond T. King (1919-1971)
Frederick M. Kingsbury (1924-1968)
Hugh J. Corcoran (1938-1992)
Richard S. Milstein
Donald A. Beaudry
Richard F. Faille
Leland B. Seabury
Gregory A. Schmidt
Pamela Manson
Anthony T. Rice
Russell J. Mawdsley

ASSOCIATE

Donna M. Brown

Representative Clients: Hartford Accident & Indemnity Co.; Albert Steiger Cos.; Shawmut Bank N.A.; Springfield Institution for Savings; St. Paul Fire & Marine Insurance Co.; The Rouse Co.; Tighe & Bond, Inc.; Northeast Utilities.

For full biographical listings, see the Martindale-Hubbell Law Directory

KEYES AND DONNELLAN, P.C. (AV)

Northeast Savings Bank Building, 1243 Main Street, 01103
Telephone: 413-781-6540
Fax: 413-739-3502

Daniel M. Keyes, Jr.
Edward L. Donnellan
Deborah A. Bloom
Michael K. Manning
Melinda M. Phelps
Dennis R. Anti

Kevin C. Giordano
Kathleen E. Sheehan
Mark D. Sullivan
John M. Payne, Jr.

For full biographical listings, see the Martindale-Hubbell Law Directory

MORIARTY, DONOGHUE & LEJA, P.C. (AV)

1331 Main Street, 01103
Telephone: 413-737-4319
Fax: 413-732-8767

James P. Moriarty (1878-1973)
Thomas J. Donoghue
Edward V. Leja
Patricia A. Barbalunga

Robert F. Connelly
John B. Stewart
Bernard Romani, III

Local Counsel for: Insurance Company of North America; United Community Insurance Company; Transamerica Insurance Co.; Preferred Mutual Insurance Co.; Utica Mutual Insurance Co.; Spalding & Evenflo Cos. Inc.; St. Paul Insurance Co.; Cigna Insurance Co.; Ina Pro; Ford Motor Co.

For full biographical listings, see the Martindale-Hubbell Law Directory

WESTBOROUGH, Worcester Co.

GREENWALD, GREENWALD & POWERS (AV)

33 Lyman Street, 01581-1404
Telephone: 508-366-6094
Fax: 508-366-6159
Milford, Massachusetts Office: 409 Fortune Boulevard, Granite Park.
Telephone: 508-478-8611.
Fax: 508-634-3959; 478-5937.

Alan Greenwald
Steven A. Greenwald
John D. Powers
Jacqueline Nastro Hathaway
Sarah Orlov
Stephen A. Gould
Patricia J. Flynn
Stefani Jill Saitow
Sean W. Melville

For full biographical listings, see the Martindale-Hubbell Law Directory

*WORCESTER,** Worcester Co.

FULLER, ROSENBERG, PALMER & BELIVEAU (AV)

14 Harvard Street, P.O. Box 764, 01613
Telephone: 508-755-5225
Telecopier: 508-757-1039

MEMBERS OF FIRM

Albert E. Fuller
Kenneth F. Rosenberg
Peter A. Palmer
Thomas W. Beliveau

ASSOCIATES

Robert W. Towle
Julie Bednarz Russell
Timothy O. Ribley
Mark W. Murphy
Lisa R. Bertonazzi
Mark C. Darling
William J. Mason
Antoinette J. Yitchinsky
Michael I. Mutter
Brian F. Welsh
John J. Finn

For full biographical listings, see the Martindale-Hubbell Law Directory

MICHIGAN

*ANN ARBOR,** Washtenaw Co.

BLASKE AND BLASKE (AV)

320 North Main, Suite 303, 48104
Telephone: 313-747-7055
Battle Creek, Michigan Office: 1509 Comerica Building, 25 West Michigan Mall.
Telephone: 616-964-9491.

Edmund R. Blaske (1911-1982)
Thomas H. Blaske
E. Robert Blaske

Reference: Comerica Bank-Battle Creek.

For full biographical listings, see the Martindale-Hubbell Law Directory

DAVIS AND FAJEN, P.C. (AV)

Suite 400, 320 North Main Street, 48104
Telephone: 313-995-0066
Facsimile: 313-995-0184
Grand Haven, Michigan Office: Davis, Fajen & Miller. Harbourfront Place, 41 Washington Street, Suite 260.
Telephone: 616-846-9875.
Facsimile: 616-846-4920.

Peter A. Davis
James A. Fajen
Nelson P. Miller
Richard B. Bailey
Catherine G. Tennant

Reference: First of America Bank-Ann Arbor.

For full biographical listings, see the Martindale-Hubbell Law Directory

HURBIS, CMEJREK & CLINTON (AV)

Fifth Floor, City Center Building, 48104
Telephone: 313-761-8358
Fax: 313-761-3134

Charles J. Hurbis
James R. Cmejrek
Mary F. Clinton

Robert Lipnik

Representative Clients: General Motors Corp.; ITT Hartford; Insurance Company of North America; The University of Michigan; North Oakland Medical Center; City of Pontiac; Sears Roebuck and Co.; Montgomery Ward and Co., Inc.; Sedjwick-James, Inc.; Michigan State Accident Fund.

For full biographical listings, see the Martindale-Hubbell Law Directory

Ann Arbor—Continued

O'BRIEN AND O'BRIEN (AV)

300 North Fifth Avenue, 48104
Telephone: 313-996-0550
Fax: 313-996-5555

MEMBERS OF FIRM

Thomas C. O'Brien — Darlene A. O'Brien

OF COUNSEL

Francis L. O'Brien (1907-1991)

Reference: Society Bank.

For full biographical listings, see the Martindale-Hubbell Law Directory

BATTLE CREEK, Calhoun Co.

BLASKE AND BLASKE (AV)

1509 Comerica Building, 25 West Michigan Mall, 49017
Telephone: 616-964-9491
Ann Arbor, Michigan Office: 320 North Main, Suite 303.
Telephone: 313-747-7055.

Edmund R. Blaske (1911-1982) — E. Robert Blaske
Thomas H. Blaske

Reference: Comerica Bank-Battle Creek.

For full biographical listings, see the Martindale-Hubbell Law Directory

*BIG RAPIDS,** Mecosta Co.

WALZ & WARBA, P.C. (AV)

115 Ives, 49307
Telephone: 616-796-5887
Fax: 616-796-5949
Traverse City, Michigan Office: 13983 West Bayshore Drive.
Telephone: 616-947-0313.
Fax: 616-947-8811.

Kenneth P. Walz — Mark J. Warba

For full biographical listings, see the Martindale-Hubbell Law Directory

BIRMINGHAM, Oakland Co.

CARSON FISCHER, P.L.C. (AV)

Third Floor, 300 East Maple Road, 48009-6317
Telephone: 810-644-4840
Facsimile: 810-644-1832

Robert M. Carson — Kathleen A. Stibich
Anne Cole Pierce — George M. Head

For full biographical listings, see the Martindale-Hubbell Law Directory

GOREN & GOREN, P.C. (AV)

Suite 470, 30400 Telegraph Road, 48025
Telephone: 810-540-3100

Robert Goren — Steven E. Goren

Reference: Michigan National Bank-Oakland.

KORNEY & HELDT (AV)

30700 Telegraph Road, Suite 1551, 48025
Telephone: 810-646-1050
Fax: 810-646-1054

J. Douglas Korney — Jeffrey A. Heldt

For full biographical listings, see the Martindale-Hubbell Law Directory

MICHAEL B. SERLING, P.C. (AV)

280 North Woodward Avenue, Suite 406, 48009
Telephone: 810-647-6966

Michael B. Serling

Russell R. Beaudoen

Reference: Comerica Bank, Birmingham, MI.

For full biographical listings, see the Martindale-Hubbell Law Directory

BLOOMFIELD HILLS, Oakland Co.

BAUM & ASSOCIATES (AV)

200 East Long Lake Road Suite 180, 48304
Telephone: 810-647-6890

Martin S. Baum

ASSOCIATE

Margo S. Horwitz

For full biographical listings, see the Martindale-Hubbell Law Directory

FEENEY KELLETT & WIENNER, PROFESSIONAL CORPORATION (AV)

950 N. Hunter Boulevard, Third Floor, 48304-3927
Telephone: 810-258-1580
Fax: 810-258-0421

James P. Feeney — David N. Goltz
S. Thomas Wienner — G. Gregory Schuetz
Peter M. Kellett — Tracy D. Knox
Cheryl A. Bush — (Not admitted in MI)
Linda M. Galante — Patrick G. Seyferth
Deborah F. Collins — Mark A. Fisher

For full biographical listings, see the Martindale-Hubbell Law Directory

GOOGASIAN, HOPKINS, HOHAUSER & FORHAN, P.C. (AV)

6895 Telegraph Road, 48301-3138
Telephone: 810-540-3333
Fax: 810-540-7213

George A. Googasian — Craig G. Forhan
Stephen J. Hopkins — Craig Weber
Michael S. Hohauser — Steven G. Googasian

For full biographical listings, see the Martindale-Hubbell Law Directory

DAVID D. PATTON & ASSOCIATES, P.C. (AV)

100 Bloomfield Hills Parkway, Suite 110, 48304
Telephone: 810-258-6020
Fax: 810-258-6052

David D. Patton

Ellen Bartman Jannette — Patricia C. White
James A. Reynolds, Jr. — David H. Patton (1912-1993)

For full biographical listings, see the Martindale-Hubbell Law Directory

PORTNOY, PIDGEON & ROTH, P.C. (AV)

3883 Telegraph, Suite 103, 48302
Telephone: 810-647-4242
Fax: 810-647-8251

Bernard N. Portnoy — Robert P. Roth
James M. Pidgeon — Marc S. Berlin
Berton K. May

For full biographical listings, see the Martindale-Hubbell Law Directory

*DETROIT,** Wayne Co.

BAUM & ASSOCIATES

(See Bloomfield Hills)

COTICCHIO, ZOTTER, SULLIVAN, MOLTER, SKUPIN & TURNER, PROFESSIONAL CORPORATION (AV)

155 West Congress, Suite 300, 48226
Telephone: 313-961-0425

George W. Coticchio — Charles G. Skupin
Walter J. Zotter — James Howard Turner
Timothy J. Sullivan — Stephen A. Coticchio
Ronald A. Molter — Joseph F. Lucas
Donald N. Payne, II

For full biographical listings, see the Martindale-Hubbell Law Directory

DENARDIS, MCCANDLESS & MULLER, P.C. (AV)

800 Buhl Building, 48226-3602
Telephone: 313-963-9050
Fax: 313-963-4553

Ronald F. DeNardis — Mark F. Miller
William McCandless — Lawrence M. Hintz
Gregory J. Muller — Michael D. Dolenga

For full biographical listings, see the Martindale-Hubbell Law Directory

DYKEMA GOSSETT (AV)

400 Renaissance Center, 48243-1668
Telephone: 313-568-6800
Cable Address: "Dyke-Detroit"
Telex: 23-0121
Fax: 313-568-6594
Ann Arbor, Michigan Office: 315 East Eisenhower Parkway, Suite 100, 48108-3306.
Telephone: 313-747-7660.
Fax: 313-747-7696.
Bloomfield Hills, Michigan Office: 1577 North Woodward Avenue, Suite 300, 48304-2820.
Telephone: 810-540-0700.
Fax: 810-540-0763.

(See Next Column)

DYKEMA GOSSETT—*Continued*

Grand Rapids, Michigan Office: 200 Oldtown Riverfront Building, 248 Louis Campau Promenade, N.W., 49503-2668.
Telephone: 616-776-7500.
Fax: 616-776-7573.
Lansing, Michigan Office: 800 Michigan National Tower, 48933-1707.
Telephone: 517-374-9100.
Fax: 517-374-9191.
Washington, D.C. Office: Franklin Square, Suite 300 West Tower, 1300 I Street, N.W., 20005-3306.
Telephone: 202-522-8600.
Fax: 202-522-8669.
Chicago, Illinois Office: Three First National Plaza, Suite 1400, 70 W. Madison, 60602-4270.
Telephone: 312-214-3380.
Fax: 312-214-3441.

MEMBERS OF FIRM

Ted T. Amsden
Susan Artinian
Joseph C. Basta
Richard B. Baxter (Resident at Grand Rapids Office)
William J. Brennan (Resident at Grand Rapids Office)
James M. Cameron, Jr. (Resident at Ann Arbor Office)
Laurence D. Connor
Michael P. Cooney
John B. Curcio (Resident at Lansing Office)
J. Terrance Dillon (Resident at Grand Rapids Office)
John A. Ferroli (Resident at Grand Rapids Office)
Robert J. Franzinger
Dennis M. Haffey (Resident at Bloomfield Hills Office)
Mark E. Hauck
E. Edward Hood (Resident at Ann Arbor Office)
Kathryn J. Humphrey
Craig L. John (Resident at Bloomfield Hills Office)
Sharon M. Kelly (Resident at Ann Arbor Office)
Gregory M. Kopacz
J. Thomas Lenga
Bonnie L. Mayfield
Richard J. McClear
Derek I. Meier
Jack C. Radcliffe, Jr. (Resident at Ann Arbor Office)
Jonathan D. Rowe (Resident at Ann Arbor Office)
Mary Elizabeth Royce (Resident at Bloomfield Hills Office)
Suzanne Sahakian
Daniel J. Scully, Jr.
Lori M. Silsbury (Resident at Lansing Office)
Mark H. Sutton (Resident at Bloomfield Hills Office)
Stephen D. Winter
Daniel G. Wyllie

OF COUNSEL

Donald E. Shely

RETIRED PARTNER

Robert N. Hammond (Resident at Grand Rapids Office)

ASSOCIATES

Michael J. Brown (Resident at Lansing Office)
Margaret A. Costello
Cheryl Anne Fletcher
Lee S. Fruman
Kevin P. Fularczyk
Margaret M. Gillis
Zora E. Johnson
Bryan D. Marcus
Mark W. Osler
Paul W. Ritsema (Resident at Grand Rapids Office)
James R. Saalfeld (Resident at Grand Rapids Office)
Rosemary G. Schikora
John F. Smart (Resident at Grand Rapids Office)
Thomas R. Stevick (Resident at Ann Arbor Office)

For Complete List of Firm Personnel, See General Section

For full biographical listings, see the Martindale-Hubbell Law Directory

EAMES, WILCOX, MASTEJ, BRYANT, SWIFT & RIDDELL (AV)

1400 Buhl Building, 48226-3602
Telephone: 313-963-3750
Facsimile: 313-963-8485

MEMBERS OF FIRM

Leonard A. Wilcox, Jr.
Ronald J. Mastej
John W. Bryant
Jerry R. Swift
Neill T. Riddell
Elizabeth Roberto
Kevin N. Summers

ASSOCIATE

Keith M. Aretha

OF COUNSEL

Rex Eames
Robert E. Gesell
William B. McIntyre, Jr.

Representative Clients: ABF Freight System, Inc.; Chrysler Credit Corp.; City Transfer Co.; Engineered Heat Treat, Inc.; Fetz Engineering Co.; I E & E Industries, Inc.; Schneider Transport; Tank Carrier Employers Association of Michigan; TNT Transport Group, Inc.; Waste Management of Michigan.

For full biographical listings, see the Martindale-Hubbell Law Directory

EGGENBERGER, EGGENBERGER, MCKINNEY, WEBER & HOFMEISTER, P.C. (AV)

42nd Floor Penobscot Building, 48226
Telephone: 313-961-9722

(See Next Column)

William J. Eggenberger (1900-1984)
William D. Eggenberger
Robert E. Eggenberger
John P. McKinney
Stephen L. Weber
Paul D. Hofmeister

R. Scott Mills
Mary T. Humbert
James B. Eggenberger

Representative Clients: Central National Insurance Group of Omaha; Great Central Insurance Co.; Preferred Risk Mutual Insurance Company of Des Moines, Iowa; State Automobile and Casualty Underwriters; State Farm Fire and Casualty Co.
Reference: Comerica Bank-Detroit.

For full biographical listings, see the Martindale-Hubbell Law Directory

HOUGHTON, POTTER, SWEENEY & BRENNER, A PROFESSIONAL CORPORATION (AV)

The Guardian Building, 500 Griswold Street, Suite 3300, 48226-3806
Telephone: 313-964-0050
Facsimile: 313-964-4005

William C. Potter, Jr.

LEGAL SUPPORT PERSONNEL

LEGAL ASSISTANTS

Ann E. Adams
Janet C. Driver

Representative Clients: Bell Sports, Inc.

For full biographical listings, see the Martindale-Hubbell Law Directory

KITCH, DRUTCHAS, WAGNER & KENNEY, P.C. (AV)

One Woodward, Tenth Floor, 48226-3412
Telephone: 313-965-7900
Fax: 313-965-7403
Lansing, Michigan Office: 120 Washington Square, North, Suite 805, One Michigan Avenue, 48933-1609.
Telephone: 517-372-6430.
Fax: 517-372-0441.
Macomb County Office: Towne Square Development, 10 South Main Street, Suite 301, Mount Clemens, 48043-7903.
Telephone: 810-463-9770.
Fax: 810-463-8994.
Toledo, Ohio Office: 405 Madison Avenue, Suite 1500, 43604-1235.
Telephone: 419-243-4006.
Fax: 419-243-7333.
Troy, Michigan Office: 3001 West Big Beaver Road, Suite 200, 48084-3103.
Telephone: 810-637-3500.
Fax: 810-637-6630.
Ann Arbor, Michigan Office: 303 Detroit Street, Suite 400, P.O. Box 8610, 48107-8610.
Telephone: 313-994-7600.
Fax: 313-994-7626.

Richard A. Kitch
Ronald E. Wagner
Jeremiah J. Kenney (Managing Principal)
Ralph F. Valitutti, Jr.
Richard R. DeNardis
Mona K. Majzoub
Harry J. Sherbrook
Anthony G. Arnone
Mark D. Willmarth (Principal)
Charles W. Fisher
Clyde M. Metzger, III (Principal, Ann Arbor Office)
Thomas J. Foley
Victor J. Abela (Principal, Troy Office)
Jeffrey H. Chilton
James H. Hughesian
John P. Ryan (Principal, Lansing Office)
William D. Chaklos
Steve N. Cheolas (Principal, Macomb County Office)
Richard S. Baron
Susan Healy Zitterman
William Vertes (Principal, Lansing Office)
William A. Tanoury (Principal, Ann Arbor Office)
R. Michael O'Boyle (Associate Principal, Troy Office)
John J. Ramar
John Stephen Wasung (Principal, Toledo, Ohio Office)
Bruce R. Shaw
Karen Bernard Berkery (Associate Principal)
Susan M. Ramage (Associate Principal, Lansing Office)
Pamela Hobbs
Daniel R. Corbet
Brian R. Garves
Daniel R. Shirey
Daniel J. Niemann (Associate Principal, Ann Arbor Office)
John M. Sier (Associate Principal)
Philip Cwagenberg (Troy Office)
William P. O'Leary
David M. Kraus
Verlin R. Nafziger
Robert A. Fehniger (Macomb County Office)
Christopher P. Dinverno
Kenneth M. Essad
Steven Waclawski
Ronald S. Bowling
Sara Mae Gerbitz
Linda M. Garbarino
Antonio Mauti
Lawrence David Rosenstock
Thomas R. Shimmel
Susan Marie Beutel
Carole S. Empey (Ann Arbor Office)
Debra S. Hirsch (Lansing Office)
David R. Nauts
Carol Ann Tarnowsky (Troy Office)
Richard T. Counsman
Karen Ann Smyth
Mark A. Wisniewski
Julia Kelly McNelis

(See Next Column)

KITCH, DRUTCHAS, WAGNER & KENNEY P.C., *Detroit—Continued*

J. Mark Trimble (Toledo, Ohio Office)
Sharon A. DeWaele
Dean A. Etsios
Michael K. McCoy
Stephen R. Brzezinski
Kent Riesen (Toledo, Ohio Office)
Joseph P. McGill
Paula M. Burgess (Toledo, Ohio Office)
Lisa M. Iulianelli
Fred J. Fresard
Matthew M. Walton (Mount Clemens Office)
Barbara A. Martin
Carol S. Allis (Ann Arbor Office)
Terese L. Farhat
Richard P. Cuneo
Kim J. Sveska

For Complete List of Firm Personnel, See General Section

For full biographical listings, see the Martindale-Hubbell Law Directory

LOPATIN, MILLER, FREEDMAN, BLUESTONE, HERSKOVIC & HEILMANN, A PROFESSIONAL CORPORATION (AV)

1301 East Jefferson, 48207
Telephone: 313-259-7800

Albert Lopatin
Sheldon L. Miller
Stuart G. Freedman
Saul Bluestone
Maurice Herskovic
Michael G. Heilmann

Michael A. Gantz (1939-1990)
David F. Dickinson
Richard E. Shaw
Ronald Robinson
Jeffrey A. Danzig
B. J. Belcoure
David R. Berndt
Stephen I. Kaufman
Jeffrey S. Cook
Robert J. Boyd, III
Patrick M. Horan
Richard R. Mannausa
Alan Wittenberg

OF COUNSEL

Harry Okrent (1912-1990)
Lee R. Franklin (Ms.)
Bernard L. Humphrey

For full biographical listings, see the Martindale-Hubbell Law Directory

MILLER, CANFIELD, PADDOCK AND STONE, P.L.C. (AV)

A Professional Limited Liability Company
Founded in 1852 by Sidney Davy Miller
150 West Jefferson, Suite 2500, 48226-4415
Telephone: 313-963-6420
Fax: 313-496-7500
Cable Address: "Stem Detroit"
Detroit, Michigan Office: 150 West Jefferson, Suite 2500, 48226-4415.
Telephone: 313-963-6420.
Fax: 313-496-7500.
Cable Address: "Stem Detroit."
Ann Arbor, Michigan Office: 101 North Main Street, 7th Floor, 48104-1400.
Telephone: 313-663-2445.
Fax: 313-747-7147.
Bloomfield Hills, Michigan Office: Suite 100, Pinehurst Office Center, 1400 North Woodward, 48303-2014.
Telephone: 313-645-5000.
Fax: 313-645-1917.
Grand Rapids, Michigan Office: 1200 Campau Square Plaza, 99 Monroe, N.W., 49503-2639.
Telephone: 616-454-8656.
Fax: 616-776-6322.
Howell, Michigan Office: 121 South Barnard Street, Suite 4, 48843-2305.
Telephone: 517-546-7600.
Telecopier: 517-546-6974.
Kalamazoo, Michigan Office: 444 West Michigan Avenue, 49007-3752.
Telephone: 616-381-7030.
Fax: 616-382-0244.
Lansing, Michigan Office: One Michigan Avenue, Suite 900, 48933-1609.
Telephone: 517-487-2070.
Fax: 517-374-6304.
Monroe, Michigan Office: The Executive Centre, 214 East Elm Avenue, 48161-2682.
Telephone: 313-243-2000.
Fax: 313-243-0901.
Washington, D.C. Office: 1225 Nineteenth Street, N.W., Suite 400. 20036.
Telephone: 202-429-5575; 785-0600.
Fax: 202-331-1118; 785-1234.
Pensacola, Florida Office: 25 West Cedar, 32501.
Telephone: 904-469-1088.
Fax: 904-432-0677.
St. Petersburg, Florida Office: 100 Second Avenue S., Suite 7045, 33701.
Telephone: 813-982-6000.
Fax: 813-892-6002.
Gdansk, Poland Office: Suite 322, Dom Technika Building, Ul. Rajska 6, 80-850.
Telephone: 011-485-831-2808.
Fax: 011-485-831-4719.
Warsaw, Poland Office: Ul. Marszalkowska 82, Suite 561, 00-517.
Telephone: 011-482-623-6457 and 6458.
Fax: 011-482-623-6459.

(See Next Column)

MEMBERS OF FIRM

Charles E. Ritter (Kalamazoo Office)
Thomas G. Parachini
W. Mack Faison
Leland D. Barringer
Ryan H. Haywood
Ronald E. Baylor (Kalamazoo Office)
Stephen J. Ott
Robert D. VanderLaan (Grand Rapids Office)
Pamela Chapman Enslen (Kalamazoo Office)
Richard F. X. Urisko

SENIOR ATTORNEY

Irene Bruce Hathaway

ASSOCIATES

Brian J. Doren
Robert J. Haddad
Erich H. Hintzen
Brian S. Westenberg
Brian K. Telfair

Representative Firm Clients: Chrysler Corp.; Comerica, Inc.; City of Detroit, Mich.; Detroit Tigers, Inc.; First of Michigan; Fretter, Inc.; Ford Motor Co.; Ford Motor Credit Co.; Great Lakes Bancorp; Henry Ford Hospital.

For Complete List of Firm Personnel, See General Section

For full biographical listings, see the Martindale-Hubbell Law Directory

PRATHER & ASSOCIATES, P.C. (AV)

3800 Penobscot Building, 48226-4220
Telephone: 313-962-7722
Facsimile: 313-962-2653

Kenneth E. Prather

Jan Rewers McMillan

For full biographical listings, see the Martindale-Hubbell Law Directory

ROSEN & LOVELL, P.C. (AV)

Penobscot Building, 645 Griswold Street, Suite 3080, 48226-4224
Telephone: 313-961-7510
Fax: 313-961-2905

Paul A. Rosen
Joan Lovell

For full biographical listings, see the Martindale-Hubbell Law Directory

SCHUREMAN, FRAKES, GLASS & WULFMEIER (AV)

440 East Congress, Fourth Floor, 48226
Telephone: 313-961-1500
Telecopier: 313-961-1087
Harbor Springs, Michigan Office: One Spring Street Sq., 49740.
Telephone: 616-526-1145.
Telecopier: 616-526-9343.

MEMBERS OF FIRM

Jeptha W. Schureman
John C. Frakes, Jr.
Charles F. Glass
LeRoy H. Wulfmeier, III
Cheryl L. Chandler
David M. Ottenwess

ASSOCIATES

Daniel J. Dulworth
John J. Moran
Paul A. Salyers
Erane C. Washington

Reference: Comerica.

For full biographical listings, see the Martindale-Hubbell Law Directory

VANDEVEER GARZIA, PROFESSIONAL CORPORATION (AV)

Suite 1600, 333 West Fort Street, 48226
Telephone: 313-961-4880
Fax: 313-961-3822
Oakland County Office: 220 Park Street, Suite 300, Birmingham, Michigan.
Telephone: 810-645-0100.
Fax: 810-645-2430.
Macomb County Office: 50 Crocker Boulevard, Mount Clemens, Michigan.
Telephone: 810-468-4880.
Fax: 810-465-7159.
Kent County Office: 510 Grand Plaza Place, 220 Lyon Square, Grand Rapids, Michigan.
Telephone: 616-366-8600.
Fax: 616-786-9095.
Holland, Michigan Office: 1121 Ottawa Beach Road, Suite 140.
Telephone: 616-399-8600.
Fax: 616-786-9095.

Thomas P. Rockwell
James A. Sullivan
Michael M. Hathaway
John J. Lynch, III (Resident, Oakland County Office)
Thomas M. Peters
James K. Thome (Resident, Oakland County Office)
Cecil F. Boyle, Jr. (Resident, Oakland County Office)
Ronald L. Cornell (Resident, Macomb County Office)
William J. Heaphy (Kent County and Holland Offices)
Gary Alan Miller
William L. Kiriazis

(See Next Column)

VANDEVEER GARZIA PROFESSIONAL CORPORATION—*Continued*

Cynthia E. Merry
Dennis B. Cotter
Daniel P. Steele
Shelley K. Miller (Resident, Oakland County Office)
Terrance P. Lynch

OF COUNSEL

John M. Heaphy
Roy C. Hebert

For Complete List of Firm Personnel, See General Section

For full biographical listings, see the Martindale-Hubbell Law Directory

ZEFF AND ZEFF, P.C. (AV)

The Zeff Building, 607 Shelby, 48226
Telephone: 313-962-3825
Fax: 313-962-6007

Louis Zeff (1896-1966)
A. Robert Zeff

Sheryl L. Berenbaum
Paul Broschay
Edward J. Kreski

For full biographical listings, see the Martindale-Hubbell Law Directory

EAST LANSING, Ingham Co.

FARHAT, STORY & KRAUS, P.C. (AV)

Beacon Place, 4572 South Hagadorn Road, Suite 3, 48823
Telephone: 517-351-3700
Fax: 517-332-4122

Leo A. Farhat
James E. Burns (1925-1979)
Monte R. Story
Richard C. Kraus
Max R. Hoffman Jr.
Chris A. Bergstrom
Kitty L. Groh
Charles R. Toy
David M. Platt

Lawrence P. Schweitzer
Jeffrey J. Short
Kathy A. Breedlove
Thomas L. Sparks

Reference: Capitol National Bank.

For full biographical listings, see the Martindale-Hubbell Law Directory

FARMINGTON HILLS, Oakland Co.

KAUFMAN AND PAYTON (AV)

200 Northwestern Financial Center, 30833 Northwestern Highway, 48334
Telephone: 810-626-5000
Telefacsimile: 810-626-2843
Grand Rapids, Michigan Office: 420 Trust Building.
Telephone: 616-459-4200.
Fax: 616-459-4929.
Traverse City, Michigan Office: 122 West State Street.
Telephone: 616-947-4050.
Fax: 616-947-7321.

Alan Jay Kaufman
Donald L. Payton
Kenneth C. Letherwood
Stephen R. Levine
Thomas L. Vitu
Ralph C. Chapa, Jr.
Raymond I. Foley, II
Jeffrey K. Van Hattum
Leo D. Neville

For full biographical listings, see the Martindale-Hubbell Law Directory

*FLINT,** Genesee Co.

BELTZ & ASSOCIATES (AV)

444 Church Street, 48502
Telephone: 810-767-5421
Fax: 810-767-5369

C. Robert Beltz

ASSOCIATE

Charles D. Riley

For full biographical listings, see the Martindale-Hubbell Law Directory

MACDONALD, FITZGERALD, MACDONALD & SIMON, P.C. (AV)

200 McKinnon Building, 48502
Telephone: 810-232-3184; 234-2204
Fax: 810-232-9632

Robert J. MacDonald (1914-1987)
John J. FitzGerald
R. Duncan MacDonald
Timothy J. Simon
Timothy J. MacDonald

References: Michigan National Bank; Genesee Merchants Bank & Trust Co.

For full biographical listings, see the Martindale-Hubbell Law Directory

WINEGARDEN, SHEDD, HALEY, LINDHOLM & ROBERTSON (AV)

501 Citizens Bank Building, 48502-1983
Telephone: 810-767-3600
Telecopier: 810-767-8776

(See Next Column)

MEMBERS OF FIRM

William C. Shedd
Dennis M. Haley
John T. Lindholm
Donald H. Robertson
L. David Lawson
John R. Tucker

ASSOCIATES

Alan F. Himelhoch
Suellen J. Parker
Damion Frasier
Peter T. Mooney

OF COUNSEL

Howard R. Grossman

Representative Clients: Citizens Commercial and Savings Bank; R. L. White Development Corporation; Interstate Traffic Consultants (Intracon) Inc.; Downtown Development Authority of Flint; Young Olds-Cadillac, Inc.; First American Title Insurance Co.; Sorensen Gross Construction Co.; Genesee County; Insight, Inc.; Modern Industries, Inc.

For Complete List of Firm Personnel, See General Section

For full biographical listings, see the Martindale-Hubbell Law Directory

GRAND BLANC, Genesee Co.

EDWIN W. JAKEWAY (AV)

G-8161 South Saginaw Avenue, 48439
Telephone: 810-694-1211; 694-1212
Fax: 810-694-2178

ASSOCIATE

Michael J. Kelly

LEGAL SUPPORT PERSONNEL

Ruth C. DeMaria

LAW CLERKS

Morgan H. Jakeway
Craig E. Jakeway

Reference: Citizens Commercial and Savings Bank.

For full biographical listings, see the Martindale-Hubbell Law Directory

*GRAND RAPIDS,** Kent Co.

BREMER, WADE, NELSON, LOHR & COREY (AV)

600 Three Mile Road, N.W., 49504-1601
Telephone: 616-784-4434
Fax: 616-784-7322

MEMBERS OF FIRM

William M. Bremer
Michael D. Wade
Phillip J. Nelson
James H. Lohr
Michael J. Corey

ASSOCIATES

Michael S. Dantuma
J. Mark Cooney
Cheryl L. Bart
Barbara L. Olafsson

LEGAL SUPPORT PERSONNEL

Kathleen A. Fitzpatrick

For full biographical listings, see the Martindale-Hubbell Law Directory

BUCHANAN & BOS (AV)

300 Ottawa N.W., Suite 800, 49503
Telephone: 616-458-1224
Fax: 616-458-0608

MEMBERS OF FIRM

John C. Buchanan
Carole D. Bos
Bradley K. Glazier
Lee T. Silver

ASSOCIATES

Raymond S. Kent
Jane M. Beckering
Richard A. Stevens
Susan Wilson Keener
Gwen E. Buday
Anne M. Frye
Brian K. Lawson
Nancy K. Haynes

For full biographical listings, see the Martindale-Hubbell Law Directory

CLARY, NANTZ, WOOD, HOFFIUS, RANKIN & COOPER (AV)

500 Calder Plaza, 250 Monroe Avenue, N.W., 49503-2244
Telephone: 616-459-9487
Telecopier: 616-459-5121

MEMBERS OF FIRM

Robert L. DeJong
Stanley J. Stek
Mark R. Smith

Representative Clients: United Bank of Michigan; D&W Food Centers, Inc.; FMB First Michigan Bank-Grand Rapids; Goodrich Theatres & Radio, Inc.; S. Abraham & Sons, Inc.; Garb-Ko, Inc., d/b/a 7-Eleven; Weather Shield Mfg., Inc.; JET Electronics & Technology, Inc.; Westinghouse Credit Corp.

For Complete List of Firm Personnel, See General Section

For full biographical listings, see the Martindale-Hubbell Law Directory

Grand Rapids—Continued

De Groot, Keller & Vincent (AV)

300 Michigan Trust Building, 49503
Telephone: 616-459-6251
Fax: 616-459-6352

MEMBERS OF FIRM

Murray B. De Groot
Brian D. Vincent

For full biographical listings, see the Martindale-Hubbell Law Directory

Farr & Oosterhouse (AV)

Suite 400, Ledyard Building, 125 Ottawa Avenue, N.W., 49503
Telephone: 616-459-3355
Fax: 616-235-3350

MEMBERS OF FIRM

William S. Farr
Kenneth R. Oosterhouse
Joel E. Krissoff
John R. Oostema
Charles E. Chamberlain, Jr.

ASSOCIATE

Michelene B. Pattee

For full biographical listings, see the Martindale-Hubbell Law Directory

Gruel, Mills, Nims and Pylman (AV)

50 Monroe Place, Suite 700 West, 49503
Telephone: 616-235-5500
Fax: 616-235-5550

MEMBERS OF FIRM

Grant J. Gruel
William F. Mills
J. Clarke Nims
Norman H. Pylman, II
Scott R. Melton
Brion J. Brooks
Thomas R. Behm
J. Paul Janes

Representative Clients: Aquinas College; Bell Helmet Co.; Blodgett Memorial Medical Center; Butterworth Hospital; Chem Central, Inc.; Cook Pump Co.; Grove, Inc.; NBDC; Heim Corp.

For full biographical listings, see the Martindale-Hubbell Law Directory

Linsey, Strain & Worsfold, P.C. (AV)

1200 Michigan National Bank Building, 77 Monroe Center, N.W., 49503
Telephone: 616-456-1661
Fax: 616-456-5027

Dale M. Strain
Alan R. Smith
Patrick D. Murphy
Larry D. Vander Wal
David J. Buter
Peter D. Bosch

Joseph P. Vander Veen
William D. Howard
Kurt R. Killman

For full biographical listings, see the Martindale-Hubbell Law Directory

Miller, Canfield, Paddock and Stone, P.L.C. (AV)

A Professional Limited Liability Company
Founded in 1852 by Sidney Davy Miller
1200 Campau Square Plaza, 99 Monroe, N.W., P.O. Box 329, 49503-2639
Telephone: 616-454-8656
Fax: 616-776-6322
Detroit, Michigan Office: 150 West Jefferson, Suite 2500, 48226-4415.
Telephone: 313-963-6420.
Fax: 313-496-7500.
Cable Address: "Stem Detroit."
Ann Arbor, Michigan Office: 101 North Main Street, 7th Floor, 48104-1400.
Telephone: 313-663-2445.
Fax: 313-747-7147.
Bloomfield Hills, Michigan Office: Suite 100, Pinehurst Office Center, 1400 North Woodward, 48303-2014.
Telephone: 313-645-5000.
Fax: 313-645-1917.
Howell, Michigan Office: 121 South Barnard Street, Suite 4, 48843-2305.
Telephone: 517-546-7600.
Telecopier: 517-546-6974.
Kalamazoo, Michigan Office: 444 West Michigan Avenue, 49007-3752.
Telephone: 616-381-7030.
Fax: 616-382-0244.
Lansing, Michigan Office: One Michigan Avenue, Suite 900, 48933-1609.
Telephone: 517-487-2070.
Fax: 517-374-6304.
Monroe, Michigan Office: The Executive Centre, 214 East Elm Avenue, 48161-2682.
Telephone: 313-243-2000.
Fax: 313-243-0901.
Washington, D.C. Office: 1225 Nineteenth Street, N.W., Suite 400. 20036.
Telephone: 202-429-5575; 785-0600;
Fax: 202-331-1118; 785-1234.
Pensacola, Florida Office: 25 West Cedar 32501.
Telephone: 904-469-1088.
Fax: 904-432-0677.

(See Next Column)

St. Petersburg Florida Office: 100 Second Avenue S., Suite 7045, 33701.
Telephone: 813-982-6000.
Fax: 813-892-6002.
Gdansk, Poland Office: Suite 322, Dom Technika Building, Ul. Rajska 6, 80-850.
Telephone: 011-485-831-2808.
Fax: 011-485-831-4719.
Warsaw, Poland Office: Ul. Marszalkowska 82, Suite 561, 00-517.
Telephone: 011-482-623-6457 and 6458.
Fax: 011-482-623-6459.

MEMBER OF FIRM

Robert D. VanderLaan (Resident)

Representative Firm Clients: Chrysler Corp.; Comerica, Inc.; City of Detroit, Mich.; Detroit Tigers, Inc.; First of Michigan; Fretter, Inc.; Ford Motor Co.; Ford Motor Credit Co.; Great Lakes Bancorp; Henry Ford Hospital.

For Complete List of Firm Personnel, See General Section

For full biographical listings, see the Martindale-Hubbell Law Directory

Roberts, Betz & Bloss, P.C. (AV)

555 Riverfront Plaza Building, 55 Campau, 49503
Telephone: 616-235-9955
Telecopier: 616-235-0404

Michael J. Roberts
Michael W. Betz
David J. Bloss
Gregory A. Block
Michael T. Small
Ralph M. Reisinger
Elena C. Cardenas
Henry S. Emrich

For full biographical listings, see the Martindale-Hubbell Law Directory

HANCOCK, Houghton Co.

Wisti & Jaaskelainen, P.C. (AV)

101 Quincy Street, 49930
Telephone: 906-482-5220
Iron Mountain, Michigan Office: 623 Stephenson Avenue.
Telephone: 906-779-1280.
Marquette, Michigan Office: 117 South Front Street.
Telephone: 906-228-8204.

Andrew H. Wisti
Mark Wisti
Daniel J. Wisti

David M. Gemignani

OF COUNSEL

Gordon J. Jaaskelainen

References: Superior National Bank & Trust Company of Hancock, Michigan; Houghton National Bank, Houghton, Michigan.

For full biographical listings, see the Martindale-Hubbell Law Directory

*KALAMAZOO,** Kalamazoo Co.

Deming, Hughey, Lewis, Allen & Chapman, P.C. (AV)

800 Old Kent Bank Building, 49007
Telephone: 616-349-6601
Fax: 616-349-3831

Ned W. Deming
Richard M. Hughey
Dean S. Lewis
W. Fred Allen, Jr.
Ross E. Chapman
Winfield J. Hollander
John A. Scott
Bruce W. Martin (Resident)
Daniel L. Conklin
William A. Redmond
Stephen M. Denenfeld
Thomas C. Richardson
Gregory G. St. Arnauld
Roger G. Allen (Retired)
Anne McGregor Fries
Amy J. Glass
Richard M. Hughey, Jr.
Richard J. Bosch
Thomas P. Lewis
Christopher T. Haenicke

LEGAL SUPPORT PERSONNEL

Dorothy B. Kelly

For full biographical listings, see the Martindale-Hubbell Law Directory

Miller, Canfield, Paddock and Stone, P.L.C. (AV)

A Professional Limited Liability Company
Founded in 1852 by Sidney Davy Miller
444 West Michigan Avenue, 49007-3752
Telephone: 616-381-7030
Fax: 616-382-0244
Detroit, Michigan Office: 150 West Jefferson, Suite 2500, 48226-4415.
Telephone: 313-963-6420.
Fax: 313-496-7500.
Cable Address: "Stem Detroit."
Ann Arbor, Michigan Office: 101 North Main Street, 7th Floor, 48104-1400.
Telephone: 313-663-2445.
Fax: 313-747-7147.

(See Next Column)

MILLER, CANFIELD, PADDOCK AND STONE P.L.C.—*Continued*

Bloomfield Hills, Michigan Office: Suite 100, Pinehurst Office Center, 1400 North Woodward, 48303-2014.
Telephone: 313-645-5000.
Fax: 313-645-1917.
Grand Rapids, Michigan Office: 1200 Campau Square Plaza, 99 Monroe, N.W., 49503-2639.
Telephone: 616-454-8656.
Fax: 616-776-6322.
Howell, Michigan Office: 121 South Barnard Street, Suite 4, 48843-2305.
Telephone: 517-546-7600.
Telecopier: 517-546-6974.
Lansing, Michigan Office: One Michigan Avenue, Suite 900, 48933-1609.
Telephone: 517-487-2070.
Fax: 517-374-6304.
Monroe, Michigan Office: The Executive Centre, 214 East Elm Avenue, 48161-2682.
Telephone: 313-243-2000.
Fax: 313-243-0901.
Washington, D.C. Office: 1225 Nineteenth Street, N.W., Suite 400. 20036.
Telephone: 202-429-5575; 785-0600.
Fax: 202-331-1118; 785-1234.
Pensacola, Florida Office: 25 West Cedar, 32501.
Telephone: 904-469-1088.
Fax: 904-432-0677.
St. Petersburg, Florida Office: 100 Second Avenue S., Suite 7045,33701.
Telephone: 813-982-6000.
Fax: 813-892-6002.
Gdansk, Poland Office: Suite 322, Dom Technika Building, Ul. Rajska 6, 80-850.
Telephone: 011-485-831-2808.
Fax: 011-485-831-4719.
Warsaw, Poland Office: Ul. Marszalkowska 82, Suite 561, 00-517.
Telephone: 011-482-623-6457 and 6458.
Fax: 011-482-623-6459.

MEMBERS OF FIRM

Charles E. Ritter (Resident)
Ronald E. Baylor (Resident)
Pamela Chapman Enslen (Resident)

Representative Firm Clients: Chrysler Corp.; Comerica, Inc.; City of Detroit, Mich.; Detroit Tigers, Inc.; First of Michigan; Fretter, Inc.; Ford Motor Co.; Ford Motor Credit Co.; Great Lakes Bancorp; Henry Ford Hospital.

For Complete List of Firm Personnel, See General Section

For full biographical listings, see the Martindale-Hubbell Law Directory

LANSING, Ingham Co.

CHURCH, KRITSELIS, WYBLE & ROBINSON, P.C. (AV)

3939 Capital City Boulevard, 48906-9962
Telephone: 517-323-4770

William N. Kritselis
J. Richard Robinson
James T. Heos
David S. Mittleman

D. Michael Dudley
Catherine Groll
James M. Hofer

For full biographical listings, see the Martindale-Hubbell Law Directory

DENFIELD, TIMMER, JAMO & O'LEARY (AV)

521 Seymour Avenue, 48933
Telephone: 517-371-3500
Fax: 517-371-4514

George H. Denfield
James A. Timmer
James S. Jamo
James S. O'Leary
Kathleen A. Lopilato

Representative Clients: Auto-Owners Insurance Co.; National Indemnity Insurance Co.; Travelers Insurance Co.; Ohio Farmers Insurance Co.; Bankers Life & Casualty Co.; Western Casualty & Surety Co.; Indiana Insurance Group; Western Surety Co.; Michigan Municipal League; Preston Trucking.

For full biographical listings, see the Martindale-Hubbell Law Directory

DUNNINGS & FRAWLEY, P.C. (AV)

Duncan Building, 530 South Pine Street, 48933-2299
Telephone: 517-487-8222
Fax: 517-487-2026

Stuart J. Dunnings, Jr.
John J. Frawley

Stuart J. Dunnings, III
Steven D. Dunnings

For full biographical listings, see the Martindale-Hubbell Law Directory

FOSTER, SWIFT, COLLINS & SMITH, P.C. (AV)

313 South Washington Square, 48933-2193
Telephone: 517-371-8100
Telecopier: 517-371-8200
Farmington Hills, Michigan Office: 32300 Northwestern Highway, Suite 230.
Telephone: 810-851-7500.
Fax: 810-851-7504.

John L. Collins
William R. Schulz
David H. Aldrich
Scott A. Storey
Charles E. Barbieri
Scott L. Mandel
Michael D. Sanders
Frank A. Fleischmann
Kevin T. McGraw
Matthew W. Collins

LEGAL SUPPORT PERSONNEL

LEGAL ASSISTANTS

Laurie A. Delaney
Nancy O'Shea
Theresa G. Solberg

General Counsel for: First American Bank-Central; Story, Inc.; Michigan Milk Producers Assn.; Edward W. Sparrow Hospital; St. Lawrence Hospital; Demmer Corp.; Michigan Financial Corp.
Local Counsel for: Shell Oil Co.; Michigan-Mutual Insurance Co.; Century Cellunet.

For Complete List of Firm Personnel, See General Section

For full biographical listings, see the Martindale-Hubbell Law Directory

STREET & GRUA (AV)

2401 East Grand River, 48912
Telephone: 517-487-8300
Fax: 517-487-8306

MEMBERS OF FIRM

Victor C. Anderson (1904-1981)
Cassius E. Street, Jr.
Remo Mark Grua

Representative Clients: Applegate Insulation Manufacturing; General Aviation, Inc.; Classic Aircraft Corp.; General White GMC; Old Kent Bank of Lansing.
References: First of America-Central; Old Kent Bank of Lansing, N.A.

For full biographical listings, see the Martindale-Hubbell Law Directory

*MOUNT CLEMENS,** Macomb Co.

MARTIN, BACON & MARTIN, P.C. (AV)

44 First Street, 48043
Telephone: 810-979-6500
Fax: 810-468-7016

James N. Martin
John G. Bacon
Jonathan E. Martin
Paul R. VanTol
Michael R. Janes
Kevin L. Moffatt
John W. Crimando
Victor T. Van Camp

Deborah S. Forster

Reference: First National Bank of Mt. Clemens.

For full biographical listings, see the Martindale-Hubbell Law Directory

*MOUNT PLEASANT,** Isabella Co.

GRAY, SOWLE & IACCO, A PROFESSIONAL CORPORATION (AV)

600 East Broadway, 48858
Telephone: 517-772-5932
Fax: 517-773-0538

Loren E. Gray
Donald N. Sowle
Daniel A. Iacco

References: Isabella Bank & Trust; First of American of Mount Pleasant.

For full biographical listings, see the Martindale-Hubbell Law Directory

PLYMOUTH, Wayne Co.

DRAUGELIS & ASHTON (AV)

843 Penniman Avenue, 48170-1690
Telephone: 313-453-4044
Clawson, Michigan Office: 380 North Main Street.
Telephone: 313-810-7704.

MEMBERS OF FIRM

Edward F. Draugelis
John A. Ashton
Donald S. Scully
Richard T. Haynes
Lamberto DiStefano
David T. Rogers

ASSOCIATES

Debra Clancy
Dawn E. Clancy
Joseph R. Conte
Timothy M. O'Connor
Steven O. Ashton
Floyd C. Virant
Taras P. Jarema
Deborah A. Tonelli
Timothy M. McKercher
Anne K. Mayer
Sally S. Stauffer
Robert D. Wilkins
Darlene M. Germaine
Joel B. Ashton

For full biographical listings, see the Martindale-Hubbell Law Directory

*PONTIAC,** Oakland Co.

BOOTH, PATTERSON, LEE, NEED & ADKISON, P.C. (AV)

1090 West Huron Street, 48328
Telephone: 810-681-1200
FAX: 810-681-1754

Douglas W. Booth (1918-1992)
Calvin E. Patterson (1913-1987)
Parvin Lee, Jr.
J. Timothy Patterson
David J. Lee
Gregory K. Need
Phillip G. Adkison
Martin L. Kimmel
Allan T. Motzny
Ann DeCaminada Christ
Kathryn Niazy Nichols

For full biographical listings, see the Martindale-Hubbell Law Directory

*SAGINAW,** Saginaw Co.

BRAUN KENDRICK FINKBEINER (AV)

8th Floor Second National Bank Building, 48607
Telephone: 517-753-3461
Telecopier: 517-753-3951
Bay City, Michigan Office: 201 Phoenix Building, P.O. Box 2039.
Telephone: 517-895-8505.
Telecopier: 517-895-8437.

MEMBERS OF FIRM

Harold J. Blanchet, Jr.
Craig W. Horn

Representative Clients: The Dow Chemical Co.; General Motors Corp.; Lobdell Emery Manufacturing Co.; Merrill, Lynch, Inc.; Saginaw General Hospital; Saginaw News; The Wickes Foundation.

For Complete List of Firm Personnel, See General Section

For full biographical listings, see the Martindale-Hubbell Law Directory

*SAULT STE. MARIE,** Chippewa Co.

MOHER & CANNELLO, P.C. (AV)

150 Water Street, P.O. Box 538, 49783
Telephone: 906-632-3397
FAX: 906-632-0479
Newberry, Michigan Office: 200 East John.
Telephone: 906-293-3600.

Thomas G. Moher
Steven J. Cannello
Timothy S. Moher

For full biographical listings, see the Martindale-Hubbell Law Directory

SOUTHFIELD, Oakland Co.

FIEGER, FIEGER & SCHWARTZ, A PROFESSIONAL CORPORATION (AV)

19390 West Ten Mile Road, 48075-2463
Telephone: 810-355-5555
FAX: 810-355-5148

Bernard J. Fieger (1922-1988)
Geoffrey N. Fieger
Michael Alan Schwartz
Dennis Fuller
Pamela A. Hamway
Dean W. Amburn
Ronald S. Glaser
Gary S. Fields
Todd J. Weglarz

OF COUNSEL

Barry Fayne
Stephen L. Witenoff
Beverly Hires Brode

For full biographical listings, see the Martindale-Hubbell Law Directory

GORDON, CUTLER AND HOFFMAN, P.C. (AV)

18411 West Twelve Mile Road, 48076
Telephone: 810-443-1500

Arnold M. Gordon
Joel L. Hoffman
Donald M. Cutler
Michael H. Cutler
John M. Callahan

Reference: Michigan National Bank-Oakland.

HIGHLAND & ZANETTI (AV)

Suite 205, 24445 Northwestern Highway, 48075
Telephone: 810-352-9580

John N. Highland
J. R. Zanetti, Jr.
R. Michael John

Duncan Hall Brown
Joseph M. LaBella
James S. Meyerand

For full biographical listings, see the Martindale-Hubbell Law Directory

PEARLMAN, PIANIN & SCHAEFER (AV)

3000 Town Center, Suite 1050, 48075
Telephone: 810-350-1111
Facsimile: 810-350-1317

MEMBERS OF FIRM

Arvin J. Pearlman
Michael Pianin
Jeffrey E. Schaefer
Marilyn J. Lubbers
Sheryl R. Lederman
James M. Cull

For full biographical listings, see the Martindale-Hubbell Law Directory

PROVIZER, LICHTENSTEIN & PHILLIPS, P.C. (AV)

4000 Town Center, Suite 1800, 48075
Telephone: 810-352-9080
Facsimile: 810-352-1491
Los Angeles, California Office: Provizer, Lichtenstein, Phillips & Cleary, P.C. 1801 Century Park East, Suite 2400.
Telephone: 310-552-0581.
New York, N.Y. Office: Provizer, Lichtenstein, Phillips & Madon, P.C. 21 E. 40th Street, Suite 1601.
Telephone: 800-288-9080.
Fax: 212-481-6424.

Harold M. Provizer
David S. Lichtenstein
Randall E. Phillips
Marilyn A. Madorsky
David M. Moss
Evan A. Zagoria
Deborah Molitz
Constance S. Hall
Noel F. Beck
William J. Selinsky
Jeffrey S. Weisswasser
Robert I. Brown
Eric J. Smith
Elizabeth A. Foley
Arnold M. Fink
Marc Mulder
Attilio V. Colella

For full biographical listings, see the Martindale-Hubbell Law Directory

SCHWARTZ & JALKANEN, P.C. (AV)

Suite 200, 24400 Northwestern Highway, 48075
Telephone: 810-352-2555
Facsimile: 810-352-5963

Melvin R. Schwartz
Arthur W. Jalkanen
Karl Eric Hannum

Anne Loridas Randall
Deborah L. Laura
Lisa M. Green

For full biographical listings, see the Martindale-Hubbell Law Directory

SOMMERS, SCHWARTZ, SILVER & SCHWARTZ, P.C. (AV)

2000 Town Center, Suite 900, 48075
Telephone: 810-355-0300
Telecopier: 810-746-4001
Plymouth, Michigan Office: 747 South Main Street.
Telephone: 313-455-4250.

Stanley S. Schwartz
Jeffrey N. Shillman
Jeremy L. Winer
David R. Getto
Norman D. Tucker
Robert H. Darling
Paul W. Hines
Stephen N. Leuchtman
Richard D. Fox
Frank Mafrice
Richard L. Groffsky
David J. Winter
B. A. Tyler
Michael J. Cunningham
James D. Ledbetter
Matthew G. Curtis
Helen K. Joyner
John L. Runco
Susanne Pryce
David J. Shea
Anne M. Schoepfle
Gary D. Dodds
Kenneth T. Watkins
James A. Carlin

OF COUNSEL

Howard Silver

General Counsel for: City of Taylor; Foodland Distributors; C.A. Muer Corporation; Vlasic & Company; Nederlander Corporation; Woodland Physicians; Midwest Health Centers, P.C.
Representative Clients: Crum & Forster Insurance Company; City of Pontiac; Michigan National Bank; Perry Drugs.

For Complete List of Firm Personnel, See General Section

For full biographical listings, see the Martindale-Hubbell Law Directory

*TRAVERSE CITY,** Grand Traverse Co.

MURCHIE, CALCUTT & BOYNTON (AV)

109 East Front Street, Suite 300, 49684
Telephone: 616-947-7190
Fax: 616-947-4341

Robert B. Murchie (1894-1975)
Harry Calcutt
Jack E. Boynton
William B. Calcutt
Mark A. Burnheimer
Dawn M. Rogers

(See Next Column)

MURCHIE, CALCUTT & BOYNTON—*Continued*

ASSOCIATES

George W. Hyde, III
Ralph J. Dilley (Not admitted in MI)

General Counsel for: Old Kent Bank-Grand Traverse; Northwestern Savings Bank & Trust; Central-State Bancorp; Traverse City Record Eagle; WPNB-7 & WTOM-4; Emergency Consultants, Inc.; National Guardian Risk Retention Group, Inc.; Farmers Mutual Insurance Co.; Environmental Solutions, Inc.
Local Counsel For: Consumers Power Co.

For full biographical listings, see the Martindale-Hubbell Law Directory

THOMPSON, PARSONS & O'NEIL (AV)

309 East Front Street, P.O. Box 429, 49685
Telephone: 616-929-9700; 1-800-678-1307
Fax: 616-929-7262

MEMBERS OF FIRM

George R. Thompson
Grant W. Parsons
Daniel P. O'Neil

William J. Brooks

For full biographical listings, see the Martindale-Hubbell Law Directory

WALTON, SMITH, PHILLIPS & DIXON, P.C. (AV)

216 Cass Street, P.O. Box 549, 49685
Telephone: 616-947-7410
Fax: 616-947-5112

Geoff G. Smith
L. Kent Walton
Thomas L. Phillips

OF COUNSEL

David S. Dixon

Representative Clients: The Travelers Insurance Cos.; Farm Bureau Insurance Group; First Of America-Northern Michigan; State Farm Insurance;
Reference: First of America-Northern Michigan.

For full biographical listings, see the Martindale-Hubbell Law Directory

WALZ & WARBA, P.C. (AV)

13983 West Bayshore Drive, 49684
Telephone: 616-947-0313
Fax: 616-947-8811
Big Rapids, Michigan Office: 115 Ives.
Telephone: 616-796-5887.
Fax: 616-796-5949.

Kenneth P. Walz
Mark J. Warba

References: Mutual Savings Bank, FSB; Chemical Bank Central of Big Rapids; Old Kent Bank & Trust of Big Rapids.

For full biographical listings, see the Martindale-Hubbell Law Directory

TROY, Oakland Co.

HOLAHAN, MALLOY, MAYBAUGH & MONNICH (AV)

Suite 100, 2690 Crooks Road, 48084-4700
Telephone: 810-362-4747
Fax: 810-362-4779
East Tawas, Michigan Office: 910 East Bay Street.
Telephone: 517-362-4747.
Fax: 517-362-7331.

MEMBERS OF FIRM

J. Michael Malloy, III
John R. Monnich
James D. Maybaugh
David L. Delie, Jr.
William J. Kliffel

OF COUNSEL

Thomas H. O'Connor
Maureen Holahan (Retired; Resident, East Tawas Office)

For full biographical listings, see the Martindale-Hubbell Law Directory

HUTSON, SAWYER, CHAPMAN & REILLY (AV)

292 Town Center Drive, 48084-1799
Telephone: 810-689-5700
Fax: 810-689-5741

MEMBERS OF FIRM

Thomas G. Sawyer
Ronald A. Chapman
Michael W. Hutson
Michael J. Reilly

References: First of America Bank; Michigan National Bank.

For full biographical listings, see the Martindale-Hubbell Law Directory

POLING, MCGAW & POLING, P.C. (AV)

Suite 275, 5435 Corporate Drive, 48098
Telephone: 810-641-0500
Telecopier: 810-641-0506

(See Next Column)

Benson T. Buck (1926-1989)
David W. Moore
Richard B. Poling
Gregory C. Hamilton
D. Douglas McGaw
Veronica B. Winter
Richard B. Poling, Jr.
James R. Parker

OF COUNSEL

Ralph S. Moore

Representative Clients: County of Oakland; City of Troy; United States Fidelity & Guaranty Co.; Sentry Insurance Co.; Admiral Insurance; DeMaria Construction Co.; Leo Corporation; Aetna Casualty and Surety Co.; Concord Design; Pneumo-Abex.

For full biographical listings, see the Martindale-Hubbell Law Directory

STEPHEN K. VALENTINE, JR., P.C. (AV)

600 Columbia Center, 201 West Big Beaver Road, 48084
Telephone: 810-851-3010
West Bloomfield, Michigan Office: Suite 400, 5767 West Maple Road.
Telephone: 810-851-3010.

Stephen K. Valentine, Jr.

For full biographical listings, see the Martindale-Hubbell Law Directory

WEST BLOOMFIELD, Oakland Co.

STEPHEN K. VALENTINE, JR., P.C. (AV)

5767 West Maple Road, Suite 400, 48322
Telephone: 810-851-3010
Troy, Michigan Office: 600 Columbia Center. 201 West Big Beaver Road.
Telephone: 810-851-3010.

Stephen K. Valentine, Jr.

OF COUNSEL

Philip G. Meyer

For full biographical listings, see the Martindale-Hubbell Law Directory

MINNESOTA

*DULUTH,** St. Louis Co.

BROWN, ANDREW, HALLENBECK, SIGNORELLI & ZALLAR, P.A. (AV)

300 Alworth Building, 55802
Telephone: 218-722-1764
FAX: 218-722-6137

Gerald J. Brown
Mark T. Signorelli
Thomas F. Andrew
Robert J. Zallar
Terry C. Hallenbeck
James C. Boos

For full biographical listings, see the Martindale-Hubbell Law Directory

FRYBERGER, BUCHANAN, SMITH & FREDERICK, P.A. (AV)

700 Lonsdale Building, 302 West Superior Street, 55802
Telephone: 218-722-0861
Fax: 218-722-9568
St. Paul Office: Capitol Center, 386 N. Wabasha.
Telephone: 612-221-1044.

Bruce Buchanan
Neal J. Hessen
Nick Smith
Joseph J. Mihalek
Harold A. Frederick
Shawn M. Dunlevy
Dexter A. Larsen
Anne Lewis
James H. Stewart
David R. Oberstar
Robert E. Toftey
Abbot G. Apter
Michael K. Donovan
Michael Cowles
Martha M. Markusen

Daniel D. Maddy
Teresa M. O'Toole
Stephanie A. Ball
Dean R. Borgh
Paul B. Kilgore
James F. Voegeli (Resident, St. Paul Office)
Mary Frances Skala
Rolf A. Lindberg (Resident, St. Paul Office)
James A. Lund
Mark D. Britton (Resident, St. Paul Office)
Kevin T. Walli (Resident, St. Paul Office)
Judith A. Zollar
Kevin J. Dunlevy (Resident, St. Paul Office)

OF COUNSEL

Herschel B. Fryberger, Jr.

Representative Clients: North Shore Bank of Commerce; General Motors Acceptance Corp.; Western Lake Superior Sanitary District; City of Duluth; First Bank Minnesota (N.A.); Norwest Bank Minnesota North N.A.; Airport State Bank; Park State Bank; M & I First National Bank of Superior; St. Lukes Hospital Duluth.

For full biographical listings, see the Martindale-Hubbell Law Directory

EDEN VALLEY, Meeker Co.

JOHN H. BRADSHAW (AV)

P.O. Box 559, 55329
Telephone: 612-453-6645
FAX: 612-453-6649

ASSOCIATE

Michael A. Bryant

For full biographical listings, see the Martindale-Hubbell Law Directory

*HALLOCK,** Kittson Co.

BRINK, SOBOLIK, SEVERSON, VROOM & MALM, P.A. (AV)

217 South Birch Avenue, P.O. Box 790, 56728
Telephone: 218-843-3686
FAX: 218-843-2724

Dennis M. Sobolik
Robert K. Severson
Ronald C. Vroom
Roger C. Malm
Robert M. Albrecht
Blake S. Sobolik

Representative Clients: Northwestern State Bank, Hallock, Minn.; Karlstad State Bank, Karlstad, Minn.; Argyle State Bank, Argyle, Minn.; City of Hallock; American Federal Savings & Loan Assn.; State Farm Insurance Co.; Minnesota Rice Growers, Inc.

For Complete List of Firm Personnel, See General Section

For full biographical listings, see the Martindale-Hubbell Law Directory

*HASTINGS,** Dakota Co.

SIEBEN, POLK, LAVERDIERE, JONES & HAWN, A PROFESSIONAL ASSOCIATION (AV)

999 Westview Drive, 55033
Telephone: 612-437-3148
Fax: 612-437-2732
St. Paul, Minnesota Office: Galtier Plaza, Suite 550, Box 45, 175 Fifth Street East.
Telephone: 612-222-4146.
Fax: 612-223-8279.

Michael R. Sieben
Michael S. Polk
Harvey N. Jones
Richard A. LaVerdiere
Steven D. Hawn (Resident, St. Paul Office)

Thomas R. Longfellow (Resident, St. Paul Office)
Bernie M. Dusich
Mark J. Fellman (Resident, St. Paul Office)
Michael R. Strom
John P. Sieben (Resident, St. Paul Office)
Scott J. Hertogs
Sara M. Hulse

For full biographical listings, see the Martindale-Hubbell Law Directory

*MINNEAPOLIS,** Hennepin Co.

ARNOLD & McDOWELL (AV)

5881 Cedar Lake Road, 55416-1492
Telephone: 612-545-9000
Minnesota Wats Line: 800-343-4545
Fax: 612-545-1793
Princeton, Minnesota Office: 501 South Fourth Street.
Telephone: 612-389-2214.
Hutchinson, Minnesota Office: 101 Park Place.
Telephone: 612-587-7575.

MEMBERS OF FIRM

David B. Arnold
Gary D. McDowell
G. Barry Anderson
Steven S. Hoge

ASSOCIATE

Richard G. McGee

For Complete List of Firm Personnel, See General Section

For full biographical listings, see the Martindale-Hubbell Law Directory

ARTHUR, CHAPMAN, McDONOUGH, KETTERING & SMETAK, P.A. (AV)

500 Young Quinlan Building, 81 South Ninth Street, 55402
Telephone: 612-339-3500
Fax: 612-339-7655

Lindsay G. Arthur, Jr.
John T. Chapman
Michael P. McDonough
Robert W. Kettering, Jr.
Theodore J. Smetak
Donna D. Geck
Patrick C. Cronan
Thomas A. Pearson
Colby B. Lund
Michael R. Quinlivan
Sally J. Ferguson
James S. Pikala
Jeremiah P. Gallivan
Katherine L. MacKinnon
Blake W. Duerre
Karen Melling van Vliet
Richard C. Nelson
Eugene C. Shermoen, Jr.

(See Next Column)

Paul J. Rocheford
Lee J. Keller
Gregory J. Johnson
Paula Duggan Vraa
Joseph W. Waller

Representative Clients: American International Group; American States; Bristol Myers-Squibb, Inc.; Continental Insurance Co.; General Casualty; Home Insurance Co.; Metropolitan Property & Liability Insurance Co.; Navistar International; Safeco Insurance Co.; USAA.

For Complete List of Firm Personnel, See General Section

For full biographical listings, see the Martindale-Hubbell Law Directory

AUSTIN & ABRAMS, A PROFESSIONAL ASSOCIATION (AV)

700 Northstar West, 55402
Telephone: 612-332-4273; 800-659-2679
FAX: 612-342-2107

Robert M. Austin
Jerome B. Abrams
Paul R. Smith
Lauris Heyerdahl
Keith J. Goar
Paul V. Kieffer
Timothy J. Wilson

Representative Clients: Hawkeye Security Ins. Co.; CNA Insurance; Employer's Mutual Ins. Co.

For Complete List of Firm Personnel, See General Section

For full biographical listings, see the Martindale-Hubbell Law Directory

BASSFORD, LOCKHART, TRUESDELL & BRIGGS, P.A. (AV)

(Formerly Richards, Montgomery, Cobb & Bassford, P.A.)
3550 Multifoods Tower, 55402-3787
Telephone: 612-333-3000
Telecopier: 612-333-8829

Fred B. Snyder (1859-1951)
Edward C. Gale (1862-1943)
Frank A. Janes (1908-1959)
Nathan A. Cobb, Sr. (1905-1976)
Bergmann Richards (1888-1978)
Edmund T. Montgomery (1904-1987)
Charles A. Bassford (1914-1990)
Greer E. Lockhart
Lynn G. Truesdell
Jerome C. Briggs
Frederick E. Finch
John M. Degnan
Lewis A. Remele, Jr.
Kevin P. Keenan
James O. Redman
Rebecca Egge Moos
John M. Anderson
Charles E. Lundberg
Gregory P. Bulinski
Donna J. Blazevic
Mary E. Steenson
Mark P. Hodkinson
Thomas J. Niemiec
Andrew L. Marshall
Michael A. Klutho
Kathryn H. Davis
Gregory W. Deckert

Kevin P. Hickey
John P. Buckley
Bradley J. Betlach
Mark Whitmore
Christopher R. Morris
Kelly Christensen

Representative Clients: Chubb/Pacific Indemnity Group; Greyhound Lines, Inc.; John Hancock Mutual Life Insurance Co.; Medical Protective Co.; Metropolitan Life Insurance Co.; The Travelers Insurance Cos.; The St. Paul Insurance Cos.

For full biographical listings, see the Martindale-Hubbell Law Directory

BROSNAHAN, JOSEPH, LOCKHART & SUGGS (AV)

700 Pillsbury Center, 200 South Sixth Street, 55402
Telephone: 612-339-9930
Fax: 612-373-3207

Roger P. Brosnahan
Jane E. Joseph
Kristin Nering Lockhart
David L. Suggs

For full biographical listings, see the Martindale-Hubbell Law Directory

FRED BURSTEIN & ASSOCIATES, P.A. (AV)

5450 Norwest Center, 90 South Seventh Street, 55402
Telephone: 612-339-6561
Fax: 612-337-5572

Fred Burstein

Dylan J. McFarland
Eric J. Olsen

Reference: Firstar Bank of Minnesota, N.A.

For full biographical listings, see the Martindale-Hubbell Law Directory

CHESTNUT & BROOKS, PROFESSIONAL ASSOCIATION (AV)

3700 Piper Jaffray Tower, 222 South Ninth Street, 55402
Telephone: 612-339-7300
Fax: 612-336-2940
Suburban Office: 4661 Highway 61, NorthStar Bank Building, Suite 204, White Bear Lake, Minnesota, 55110.
Telephone: 612-653-0990.

(See Next Column)

CHESTNUT & BROOKS PROFESSIONAL ASSOCIATION—*Continued*

Jack L. Chestnut
Richard C. Jones (1926-1969)
Karl L. Cambronne
Cort C. Holten
Craig A. Erickson
Dennis B. Johnson (Resident, White Bear Lake Office)
Alan B. Demmer

Janet Waller
Robert A. LaFleur
Jeanette A. Frederickson
Stuart C. Bear
Sandra J. McGoldrick-Kendall
Jeffrey D. Bores
Timothy P. McCarthy

Representative Clients: Minnesota Mining and Manufacturing Co.; Minnesota Judges Assn.

For full biographical listings, see the Martindale-Hubbell Law Directory

COX & GOUDY (AV)

600A Butler Square, 100 North Sixth Street, 55403-1592
Telephone: 612-338-1414
Fax: 612-338-6754

MEMBERS OF FIRM

Charles A. Cox
Craig A. Goudy
Charles A. Cox, III

For full biographical listings, see the Martindale-Hubbell Law Directory

DUNKLEY, BENNETT & CHRISTENSEN, P.A. (AV)

Suite 700, 701 Fourth Avenue South, 55415
Telephone: 612-339-1290
FAX: 612-339-9545

Robert P. Christensen
John Harper, III
Thomas J. Hunziker
James E. Betz
Terrance J. Wagener

For full biographical listings, see the Martindale-Hubbell Law Directory

FETTERLY & GORDON, P.A. (AV)

808 Nicollet Mall, Suite 800, 55402
Telephone: 612-333-2003
Fax: 612-333-5950

James L. Fetterly
Gary J. Gordon
Keith A. Hanson

Stephen G. Lickteig
Diane B. Bratvold
Timothy J. Fetterly

Reference: National City Bank.

For full biographical listings, see the Martindale-Hubbell Law Directory

WILLIAM D. FOSTER & ASSOCIATES (AV)

2124 Dupont Avenue South, 55405
Telephone: 612-897-0749
Fax: 612-879-0059

ASSOCIATES

Janet M. McCutcheon
Miaja L. Gunewitz

For full biographical listings, see the Martindale-Hubbell Law Directory

GILMORE, AAFEDT, FORDE, ANDERSON & GRAY, P.A. (AV)

150 South Fifth Street, Suite 3100, 55402
Telephone: 612-339-8965
Fax: 612-349-6839

Curtis C. Gilmore (Retired)
John R. de Lambert (Retired)
Michael D. Aafedt
Michael Forde
Donald W. Anderson
James R. Gray
Jay T. Hartman
Roderick C. Cosgriff
Janet Monson
Steven C. Gilmore
Mary Marvin Hager

Peter M. Banovetz
Robin D. Simpson
Kirk C. Thompson
Kathy A. Endres
Miriam P. Rykken
Janet Scheel Stellpflug
Lawrence C. Miller
Adam S. Wolkoff
David J. Klaiman
David Brian Kempston
Charles S. Bierman
Sheryl A. Zaworski
Kathryn M. Hipp

Representative Clients: Aetna Casualty and Surety Company; CIGNA Companies; Crawford Risk Management Service; Kemper Insurance Group; Liberty Mutual Insurance Group; Sentry Insurance Company; St. Paul Companies; United States Fidelity and Guaranty; U.S. Insurance Group/Crum and Forster Commercial Insurance; Western National Insurance Group.

For full biographical listings, see the Martindale-Hubbell Law Directory

HUNEGS, STONE, KOENIG & DOLAN, P.A. (AV)

565 Northstar East, 608 Second Avenue South, 55402
Telephone: 612-339-4511; 800-328-4340
Fax: 612-339-5150

William H. DeParcq (1905-1988)
Richard Gene Hunegs
Robert N. Stone
Ralph E. Koenig
Robert T. Dolan

Frances S. P. Li
Lawrence Alan Thomas

Reference: First Bank of Minneapolis.

For full biographical listings, see the Martindale-Hubbell Law Directory

HVASS, WEISMAN & KING, CHARTERED (AV)

Suite 450, 100 South Fifth Street, 55402
Telephone: 612-333-0201
FAX: 612-342-2606

Charles T. Hvass (Retired)
Si Weisman (1912-1992)
Robert J. King
Frank J. Brixius
Richard A. Williams, Jr.
Charles T. Hvass, Jr.
Robert J. King, Jr.
Michael W. Unger

John E. Daly
John M. Dornik
Mark T. Porter

For full biographical listings, see the Martindale-Hubbell Law Directory

MESHBESHER & SPENCE, LTD. (AV)

1616 Park Avenue, 55404
Telephone: 612-339-9121
Fax: 612-339-9188
St. Paul, Minnesota Office: World Trade Center.
Telephone: 612-227-0799.
St. Cloud, Minnesota Office: 400 Zapp Bank Plaza.
Telephone: 612-656-0484.

Kenneth Meshbesher
Ronald I. Meshbesher
Russell M. Spence (Resident, St. Paul Office)
James H. Gilbert
John P. Clifford
Dennis R. Johnson
Jack Nordby
Paul W. Bergstrom (Resident, St. Paul Office)
Patrick K. Horan (Resident, St. Paul Office)
Daniel J. Boivin
Michael C. Snyder
James A. Wellner
John P. Sheehy
Mark D. Streed
Randall Spence
Howard I. Bass
Daniel C. Guerrero
Katherine S. Flom
Pamela R. Finney
Jeffrey P. Oistad (Resident, St. Cloud Office)
Daniel E. Meshbesher

For Complete List of Firm Personnel, See General Section

For full biographical listings, see the Martindale-Hubbell Law Directory

RAMBOW & AWSUMB, P.A. (AV)

Suite 102, 7901 Xerxes Avenue South, 55431-1253
Telephone: 612-888-9595
Fax: 612-888-9589

Robert A. Awsumb
Paul R. Rambow

For full biographical listings, see the Martindale-Hubbell Law Directory

SIEBEN, GROSE, VON HOLTUM, MCCOY & CAREY, LTD. (AV)

900 Midwest Plaza East, 800 Marquette Avenue, 55402
Telephone: 612-333-4500
Fairfax, Minnesota Office: 117 South Park Street.
Telephone: 507-426-8211.
Duluth, Minnesota Office: 220 Missabe Building.
Telephone: 218-722-6848. Toll Free (Minnesota): 800-422-0612.

Harry A. Sieben, Jr.
John W. Carey
Mark R. Kosieradzki
Raymond R. Peterson
James P. Carey
David W. H. Jorstad
William O. Bongard
Arthur C. Kosieradzki
Susan M. Holden

Douglas E. Schmidt
Willard L. Wentzel, Jr.
John B. Wolfe, Jr.

For full biographical listings, see the Martindale-Hubbell Law Directory

*ST. PAUL,** Ramsey Co.

BANNIGAN & KELLY, P.A. (AV)

Suite 1750, North Central Life Tower, 445 Minnesota Street, 55101
Telephone: 612-224-3781
FAX: 612-223-8019

(See Next Column)

BANNIGAN & KELLY P.A., *St. Paul—Continued*

John F. Bannigan, Jr.
Patrick J. Kelly
James J. Hanton
Janet M. Wilebski
John W. Quarnstrom

For full biographical listings, see the Martindale-Hubbell Law Directory

COLLINS, BUCKLEY, SAUNTRY AND HAUGH (AV)

West 1100 First National Bank Building, 332 Minnesota Street, 55101
Telephone: 612-227-0611
Telecopier: 612-227-0758

MEMBERS OF FIRM

Eugene D. Buckley
Theodore J. Collins
Michael J. Sauntry
William E. Haugh, Jr.
Mark W. Gehan, Jr.
Patrick T. Tierney
Thomas J. Germscheid
John R. Schulz
Thomas R. O'Connell
Dan C. O'Connell
Christine L. Stroemer
Sarah J. Batzli

ASSOCIATES

Bonnie J. Bennett
Thomas E. McEllistrem

Reference: First National Bank of St. Paul.

For full biographical listings, see the Martindale-Hubbell Law Directory

GOFF, KAPLAN & WOLF, PROFESSIONAL ASSOCIATION (AV)

900 Capital Centre, 386 North Wabasha, 55102
Telephone: 612-222-6341
Fax: 612-222-6346

Howard L. Kaplan

Karen J. Kingsley

For full biographical listings, see the Martindale-Hubbell Law Directory

JARDINE, LOGAN & O'BRIEN (AV)

2100 Piper Jaffray Plaza, 444 Cedar Street, 55101
Telephone: 612-290-6500
Fax: 612-223-5070

MEMBERS OF FIRM

Donald M. Jardine
John R. O'Brien
Gerald M. Linnihan
Alan R. Vanasek
John M. Kennedy, Jr.
Eugene J. Flick
Charles E. Gillin
James J. Galman
Pierre N. Regnier
Mark A. Fonken
Gregory G. Heacox
George W. Kuehner
James A. Jardine
Patti J. Skoglund
Sean E. Hade
Gregg A. Johnson
Timothy S. Crom
Lawrence M. Rocheford

ASSOCIATES

Thomas M. Countryman
James G. Golembeck
Kerry C. Koep
David J. Hoekstra
James K. Helling
Thomas A. Harder
Marsha E. Devine
Leonard J. Schweich
Kimberly K. Hobert
Katherine E. Sprague
Michael A. Rayer
Marlene S. Garvis
Mary Patricia Rowe
Karen R. Cote
Randall S. Lane
Jane Lanoue Binzak
Nathan W. Hart
Joseph E. Flynn
Ronald R. Envall
William R. Hauck

Representative Clients: American Hardware Mutual Insurance Co.; Ohio-Casualty Group; Farmers Insurance Group; Maryland-Casualty Co; CIGNA; Federated Insurance Co.; American International Group; Lumbermen's Underwriting Alliance; Dodson Insurance Group; Safeco Insurance Co.

For Complete List of Firm Personnel, See General Section

For full biographical listings, see the Martindale-Hubbell Law Directory

*WILLMAR,** Kandiyohi Co.

SCHNEIDER LAW FIRM, A PROFESSIONAL ASSOCIATION (AV)

706 South First Street, P.O. Box 776, 56201
Telephone: 612-235-1850
WATS: 800-840-1850
Fax: 612-235-3611

Ronald H. Schneider (P.A.)

Reference: First Bank Willmar.

For full biographical listings, see the Martindale-Hubbell Law Directory

MISSISSIPPI

*ASHLAND,** Benton Co.

FARESE, FARESE & FARESE, P.A. (AV)

122 Church Street, P.O. Box 98, 38603
Telephone: 601-224-6211
Fax: 601-224-3229

John B. Farese
John Booth Farese
Steven E. Farese
C. Collier Carlton, Jr.
Anthony L. Farese
Linda S. Laher
Robert Q. Whitwell
David Reid Wamble

For full biographical listings, see the Martindale-Hubbell Law Directory

BILOXI, Harrison Co.

MINOR AND GUICE (AV)

A Partnership including a Professional Association
160 Main Street, Drawer 1388, 39533
Telephone: 601-374-5151
FAX: 601-374-6630

Paul S. Minor (P.A.)
Judy M. Guice

Mark D. Lumpkin
Michael Bruffey

For full biographical listings, see the Martindale-Hubbell Law Directory

PAGE, MANNINO & PERESICH (AV)

759 Vieux Marché Mall, P.O. Drawer 289, 39530
Telephone: 601-374-2100
Telecopier: 601-432-5539
Jackson, Mississippi Office: One LeFleurs Square, 4735 Old Canton Road, P.O. Box 12159.
Telephone: 601-364-1100.
Telecopier: 601-364-1118.
Gulfport, Mississippi Office: Markham Building, 2301 - 14th Street, Suite 600, Drawer 660.
Telephone: 601-863-8861.
Telecopier: 601-863-8871.

MEMBERS OF FIRM

Lyle M. Page
Frederick J. Mannino
Ronald G. Peresich
Michael B. McDermott
Stephen G. Peresich
Jess H. Dickinson
Tere Richardson Steel
David S. Raines
Michael P. Collins
Randolph Cook Wood
Mary A. Nichols
Joseph Henry Ros
Thomas William Busby
Michael E. Whitehead
Katharine Malley Samson
Douglas J. Wise

Representative Clients: United States Fidelity & Guaranty Co.; St. Paul Fire & Marine Insurance Co.; Crawford & Co.; Anheuser-Busch Corp.
General Counsel for: Peoples Bank of Biloxi, Mississippi; Biloxi Regional Medical Center; Bank of Mississippi (Gulf Coast Division).

For full biographical listings, see the Martindale-Hubbell Law Directory

*CLARKSDALE,** Coahoma Co.

CHAPMAN, LEWIS & SWAN (AV)

501 First Street, P.O. Box 428, 38614
Telephone: 601-627-4105
FAX: 601-627-4171

Ralph E. Chapman
Richard B. Lewis
Dana J. Swan

For full biographical listings, see the Martindale-Hubbell Law Directory

*GREENVILLE,** Washington Co.

DYER, DYER, JONES & DANIELS, A PROFESSIONAL ASSOCIATION (AV)

149 North Edison Street, 38701
Telephone: 601-378-2626; 378-2627
Telecopier: 601-378-2672

Howard Dyer (1915-1986)
Howard Dyer, III
Gaines S. Dyer
J. Rabun Jones, Jr.
John H. Daniels, III

For full biographical listings, see the Martindale-Hubbell Law Directory

*GULFPORT,** Harrison Co.

BOYCE HOLLEMAN A PROFESSIONAL CORPORATION (AV)

1913 15th Street, P.O. Drawer 1030, 39502
Telephone: 601-863-3142
Telecopier: 601-863-9829

Boyce Holleman

(See Next Column)

BOYCE HOLLEMAN A PROFESSIONAL CORPORATION—*Continued*

Michael B. Holleman
Timothy C. Holleman
Leslie Dean Holleman
David J. White

References: Hancock Bank, Gulfport; Merchants Bank & Trust Co., Gulfport; Bank of Wiggins, Wiggins, Mississippi.

For full biographical listings, see the Martindale-Hubbell Law Directory

PAGE, MANNINO & PERESICH (AV)

Markham Building, 2301 14th Street, Suite 600, Drawer 660, 39501-2095
Telephone: 601-863-8861
Telecopier: 601-863-8871
Biloxi, Mississippi Office: 759 Vieux MarchéMall, P.O. Drawer 289.
Telephone: 601-374-2100.
Telecopier: 601-432-5539.
Jackson, Mississippi Office: One Lefleurs Square, 4735 Old Canton Road, P.O. Box 12159.
Telephone: 601-364-1100.
Telecopier: 601-364-1118.

MEMBERS OF FIRM

Lyle M. Page
Frederick J. Mannino
Ronald G. Peresich
Michael B. McDermott
Stephen G. Peresich
Jess H. Dickinson
Tere Richardson Steel
David S. Raines
Michael P. Collins
Randolph Cook Wood
Mary A. Nichols
Joseph Henry Ros
Thomas William Busby
Michael E. Whitehead
Katharine Malley Samson
Douglas J. Wise

Representative Clients: United States Fidelity & Guaranty Co.; St. Paul Fire & Marine Insurance Co.; Crawford & Co.; Anheuser-Busch Corp.
General Counsel for: Peoples Bank of Biloxi, Mississippi; Biloxi Regional Medical Center; Bank of Mississippi (Gulf Coast Division).

For full biographical listings, see the Martindale-Hubbell Law Directory

*JACKSON,** Hinds Co.

ALLRED & DONALDSON (AV)

101 West Capitol Street, Suite 300, P.O. Box 3828, 39207-3828
Telephone: 601-948-2086
Telefax: 601-948-2175

MEMBERS OF FIRM

Michael S. Allred
John I. Donaldson

ASSOCIATES

Stephen M. Maloney
Kathleen H. Eiler

For full biographical listings, see the Martindale-Hubbell Law Directory

FERRELL & HUBBARD (AV)

Ferrell & Hubbard Building, 405 Tombigbee Street, P.O. Box 24448, 39225-4448
Telephone: 601-969-4700
Telecopier: 601-354-5548

MEMBERS OF FIRM

Wayne E. Ferrell, Jr.
Dale Hubbard
Karla J. Pierce

References: Deposit Guaranty National Bank; First National Bank of Vicksburg; Trustmark National Bank.

For full biographical listings, see the Martindale-Hubbell Law Directory

MCNAMARA, KELLY & WELSH (AV)

4273 I-55 North, Suite 200, 39206
Telephone: 601-362-6700
Telecopier: 601-362-4888

MEMBERS OF FIRM

J. Leray (Ray) McNamara
Ann H. Kelly
Jennifer L. Welsh

Representative Clients: Deposit Guaranty National Bank; Sears, Roebuck and Co.; Wal-Mart Stores, Inc.; Chubb and Son, Inc.; Kawasaki Motors Corp., U.S.A.; Medical Assurance Company of Mississippi; Mississippi Hospital Association.
References: Deposit Guaranty National Bank; Sunburst Bank.

For full biographical listings, see the Martindale-Hubbell Law Directory

PAGE, MANNINO & PERESICH (AV)

One LeFleurs Square, 4735 Old Canton Road, P.O. Box 12159, 39236-2159
Telephone: 601-364-1100
Telecopier: 601-364-1118
Biloxi, Mississippi Office: 759 Vieux MarchéMall, P.O. Drawer 289.
Telephone: 601-374-2100.
Telecopier: 601-432-5539.

(See Next Column)

Gulfport, Mississippi Office: Markham Building, 2301 - 14th Street, Suite 600, P.O. Drawer 660.
Telephone: 601-863-8861.
Telecopier: 601-863-8871.

MEMBERS OF FIRM

Lyle M. Page
Frederick J. Mannino
Ronald G. Peresich
Michael B. McDermott
Stephen G. Peresich
Jess H. Dickinson
Tere Richardson Steel
David S. Raines
Michael P. Collins
Randolph Cook Wood
Mary A. Nichols
Joseph Henry Ros
Thomas William Busby
Michael E. Whitehead
Katharine Malley Samson
Douglas J. Wise
(Not admitted in MS)

Representative Clients: United States Fidelity & Guaranty Co.; St. Paul Fire & Marine Insurance Co.; Crawford & Co.; Anheuser-Busch Corp.
General Counsel for: Peoples Bank of Biloxi, Mississippi; Biloxi Regional Medical Center; Bank of Mississippi (Gulf Coast Division).

For full biographical listings, see the Martindale-Hubbell Law Directory

PRICE & ZIRULNIK (AV)

Suite 1150 Capital Towers, 125 South Congress Street, P.O. Box 3439, 39207-3439
Telephone: 601-353-3000
Telecopier: 601-353-3007

John H. Price, Jr.
Barry S. Zirulnik

ASSOCIATE

William G. Cheney, Jr.

Representative Clients: Yellow Freight System, Inc.; Mississippi Dairy Products Association, Inc.; LuVel Dairy Products, Inc.; Mississippi Farm Bureau Federation; Mississippi Department of Transportation; Mississippi High School Activities Association, Inc.; Variety Wholesalers, Inc.; Mississippi Bankers Association; Metal Rolling, Inc.

For full biographical listings, see the Martindale-Hubbell Law Directory

WATKINS & EAGER (AV)

Suite 300 The Emporium Building, P.O. Box 650, 39205
Telephone: 601-948-6470
Facsimile: (601) 354-3623

OF COUNSEL

Thomas M. Murphree, Jr.

MEMBERS OF FIRM

James A. Becker, Jr.
Michael W. Ulmer
Steven D. Orlansky
David L. Ayers
Michael O. Gwin

Representative Clients: Caterpillar Tractor Co.; Ford Motor Co.; Goodyear Tire & Rubber; Michelin Tire Corp.; Sterling Winthrop Inc.; Toyota Motor Sales, U.S.A., Inc.

For Complete List of Firm Personnel, See General Section

For full biographical listings, see the Martindale-Hubbell Law Directory

*MERIDIAN,** Lauderdale Co.

HAMILTON & LINDER (AV)

2713 Seventh Street, P.O. Box 2146, 39302-2146
Telephone: 601-693-5548
FAX: 601-693-2949

MEMBERS OF FIRM

Joe Clay Hamilton
David H. Linder

For full biographical listings, see the Martindale-Hubbell Law Directory

*NEW ALBANY,** Union Co.

TALMADGE D. LITTLEJOHN (AV)

108 East Main Street, P.O. Box 869, 38652
Telephone: 601-534-6835; 534-6215
FAX: 601-534-6215

References: First National Bank, New Albany, Miss.; Bank of New Albany.

For full biographical listings, see the Martindale-Hubbell Law Directory

*PASCAGOULA,** Jackson Co.

COLINGO, WILLIAMS, HEIDELBERG, STEINBERGER & MCELHANEY, P.A. (AV)

711 Delmas Avenue, P.O. Box 1407, 39568-0240
Telephone: 601-762-8021
FAX: 601-762-7589

Joe R. Colingo
Roy C. Williams
James H. Heidelberg
Karl R. Steinberger
Michael J. McElhaney, Jr.
James H. Colmer, Jr.
Robert W. Wilkinson
Brett K. Williams

(See Next Column)

COLINGO, WILLIAMS, HEIDELBERG, STEINBERGER & MCELHANEY P.A., *Pascagoula—Continued*

Carol S. Noblitt — Stephen Walker Burrow
Karen N. Haarala — Scott D. Smith
Gina L. Bardwell

LEGAL SUPPORT PERSONNEL

Harry H. Carpenter

Representative Clients: International Paper Co.; R.J. Reynolds; Westinghouse Corp.; St. Paul Fire & Marine Ins. Co.; Kemper Group; Singing River Hospital System.

For full biographical listings, see the Martindale-Hubbell Law Directory

*POPLARVILLE,** Pearl River Co.

WILLIAMS, WILLIAMS AND MONTGOMERY, P.A. (AV)

109 Erlanger Street, P.O. Box 113, 39470
Telephone: 601-795-4572
FAX: 601-795-8382
Picayune, Mississippi Office: 900 Highway 11 South, P.O. Box 1058.
Telephone: 601-798-0480.
FAX: 601-798-5481.

E. B. Williams (1890-1976) — Joseph H. Montgomery
E. B. Williams, Jr. (1917-1990) — E. Bragg Williams, III
Lampton O'Neal Williams — L. O'Neal Williams, Jr.

Michael E. Patten — Anne M. Parker

Representative Clients: Hancock Bank, Bank of Commerce Branch; Wesley's Fertilizer Plant, Inc.; Wesley Oil and Gas Co., Inc.; Garrett Industries, Inc.; Bass Pecan Co., Lumberton, Miss.; Joe N. Miles & Sons Lumber Co., Inc., Lumberton and Silver Creek, Miss. and Bogalusa, La.
Reference: Hancock Bank, Bank of Commerce Branch, Poplarville, Mississippi.

For full biographical listings, see the Martindale-Hubbell Law Directory

MISSOURI

*INDEPENDENCE,** Jackson Co.

JAMES & BIAGIOLI, P.C. (AV)

123 West Kansas, 64050
Telephone: 816-836-5500
FAX: 816-836-2273

Jimmie D. James — John A. Biagioli

Mary Ellen Bigge — Jonathan C. Lourenco
Douglas A. Hick

OF COUNSEL

David G. Sperry

References: Noland Road Bank; Boatmen's Bank; Bank of Grain Valley.

KANSAS CITY, Jackson, Clay & Platte Cos.

BARTIMUS, KAVANAUGH & FRICKLETON, A PROFESSIONAL CORPORATION (AV)

23rd Floor City Center Square, 1100 Main Street, 64105
Telephone: 816-842-2300
FAX: 816-421-2111

James R. Bartimus — James P. Frickleton
Paul F. Kavanaugh — Kirk R. Presley

OF COUNSEL

Max W. Foust

LEGAL SUPPORT PERSONNEL

LEGAL ASSISTANTS

Janet L. Smith-Lierman — Stephanie Lang
Tammy J. Gilliams — Laura M. Burbach
Arnella R. McNichols

For full biographical listings, see the Martindale-Hubbell Law Directory

HANOVER & TURNER (AV)

700 Commerce Trust Building, 922 Walnut Street, 64106
Telephone: 816-221-2888
Fax: 816-221-4453

MEMBERS OF FIRM

Hollis H. Hanover — John E. Turner

For full biographical listings, see the Martindale-Hubbell Law Directory

REDFEARN & BROWN, A PROFESSIONAL CORPORATION (AV)

Suite 814, 1125 Grand Avenue, 64106
Telephone: 816-421-5301
FAX: 816-421-3785

Paul L. Redfearn — Daniel R. Brown

For full biographical listings, see the Martindale-Hubbell Law Directory

LAKE OZARK, Miller & Camden Cos.

THOMAS E. LORAINE, P.C. (AV)

2840 Bagnell Dam Boulevard, 65049
Telephone: 314-365-3035
Fax: 314-365-3044

Thomas E. Loraine — Dale M. Weppner

For full biographical listings, see the Martindale-Hubbell Law Directory

ST. LOUIS, (Independent City)

LAW OFFICES THOMAS M. BURKE, P.C. (AV)

1007 Olive Street - 3rd Floor, 63101
Telephone: 314-241-8200
Telecopier: 314-621-6941

Thomas M. Burke

For full biographical listings, see the Martindale-Hubbell Law Directory

THE JOHN J. FRANK PARTNERSHIP (AV)

Suite 850 The Boatmen's Tower, 100 North Broadway, 63102
Telephone: 314-421-2811
Fax: 314-421-3121

John J. Frank — Mary Coffey
Toni Griesbach — Joseph A. Frank
Kris Bryant

For full biographical listings, see the Martindale-Hubbell Law Directory

GREENBERG & PLEBAN (AV)

100 South Fourth Street, Suite 600, 63102
Telephone: 314-241-4141
Telecopier: 314-241-1038

Burton M. Greenberg — C. John Pleban

ASSOCIATES

Karen A. Greenberg — George A. Kiser
Michael J. Schaller

OF COUNSEL

Sarah Shelledy Pleban

Reference: Boatmen's National Bank.

For full biographical listings, see the Martindale-Hubbell Law Directory

THE HULLVERSON LAW FIRM (AV)

Suite 1550, 1010 Market Street, 63101-2091
Telephone: 314-421-2313
Fax: 314-421-2341

Everett Hullverson (1897-1975) — Philip C. Denton
James E. Hullverson — Gretchen Godar Myers
Thomas C. Hullverson — Richard R. Kordenbrock
Stephen H. Ringkamp — Spencer E. Farris
James E. Hullverson, Jr. — Mark J. Becker

For full biographical listings, see the Martindale-Hubbell Law Directory

PADBERG, MCSWEENEY, SLATER & MERZ, A PROFESSIONAL CORPORATION (AV)

Suite 800, 1015 Locust Street, 63101
Telephone: 314-621-3787
Telecopier: 314-621-7396

Godfrey P. Padberg — R. J. Slater
Edward P. McSweeney — Charles L. Merz

Richard J. Burke, Jr. — Anthony J. Soukenik
Matthew J. Padberg — Thomas C. Simon
James P. Leonard — Mary K. Munroe
Marty Daesch

For full biographical listings, see the Martindale-Hubbell Law Directory

DAVID J. RAUSCHER, P.C. (AV)

8112 Maryland Avenue Suite 205, 63105-3700
Telephone: 314-721-2220
Fax: 314-721-2746

David J. Rauscher

(See Next Column)

DAVID J. RAUSCHER, P.C.—*Continued*

Kathleen L. Rauscher

For full biographical listings, see the Martindale-Hubbell Law Directory

SCHLICHTER, BOGARD & DENTON (AV)

Suite 900, 100 South Fourth Street, 63102
Telephone: 314-621-6115
Fax: 314-621-7151
Fairview Heights, Illinois Office: 333 Salem Place, Suite 260. Telephone 618-632-3329.

MEMBERS OF FIRM

Jerome J. Schlichter
Robert S. Bogard
Roger C. Denton

ASSOCIATES

Steven L. Groves
Steven J. Stolze
Hal Goldsmith

For full biographical listings, see the Martindale-Hubbell Law Directory

SINDEL & SINDEL, P.C. (AV)

Suite 301, 8008 Carondelet, 63105
Telephone: 314-721-6040
Telecopier: 314-721-8545

Charles D. Sindel

Christopher P. Cox

For full biographical listings, see the Martindale-Hubbell Law Directory

WITTNER, POGER, ROSENBLUM & SPEWAK, P.C. (AV)

Suite 400, 7700 Bonhomme Avenue, 63105
Telephone: 314-862-3535
Fax: 314-862-5741

Gerald M. Poger
Howard A. Wittner
N. Scott Rosenblum
Steven B. Spewak
David S. Spewak
Jean H. Maylack

Ramona L. Marten
Jane M. Carriker
Gary M. Siegel
Barbara Greenberg
Vanessa C. Antoniou
Joseph L. Green

For full biographical listings, see the Martindale-Hubbell Law Directory

MONTANA

*BILLINGS,** Yellowstone Co.

CROWLEY, HAUGHEY, HANSON, TOOLE & DIETRICH (AV)

500 Transwestern II, 490 North 31st Street, P.O. Box 2529, 59103
Telephone: 406-252-3441
Fax: 406-259-4159
Helena, Montana Office: IBM Building, 100 North Park Avenue, Suite 300, 59601.
Telephone: 406-449-4165.
Fax: 406-449-5149.

OF COUNSEL

Bruce R. Toole
Neil S. Keefer

MEMBERS OF FIRM

George C. Dalthorp
Herbert I. Pierce, III
Ronald R. Lodders
Charles R. Cashmore
Lawrence B. Cozzens
Carolyn S. Ostby
Steven J. Lehman
Donald L. Harris
William J. Mattix
Peter F. Habein
Jon T. Dyre
Bruce A. Fredrickson
Janice L. Rehberg
Joe C. Maynard, Jr.

ASSOCIATES

Steven Robert Milch
Leonard H. Smith
Neil G. Westesen
Robert T. Bell

Representative Clients: Crawford & Co.; Farmers Insurance Group; St. Paul Insurance Cos.; The Doctor's Co.; The Home Insurance Cos.; Montana State Compensation Insurance Fund.

For Complete List of Firm Personnel, See General Section

For full biographical listings, see the Martindale-Hubbell Law Directory

EDWARDS LAW FIRM (AV)

1601 Lewis Avenue, Suite 206, P.O. Box 20039, 59104
Telephone: 406-256-8155
Fax: 406-256-8159
Toll Free: 1-800-556-8155

(See Next Column)

MEMBERS OF FIRM

A. Clifford Edwards
Kevin M. Funyak
Charles P. Myers
Roger W. Frickle

For full biographical listings, see the Martindale-Hubbell Law Directory

*BOZEMAN,** Gallatin Co.

KIRWAN & BARRETT, P.C. (AV)

215 West Mendenhall, P.O. Box 1348, 59771-1348
Telephone: 406-586-1553
Fax: 406-586-8971

Peter M. Kirwan
Stephen M. Barrett

Tom W. Stonecipher

For full biographical listings, see the Martindale-Hubbell Law Directory

*GREAT FALLS,** Cascade Co.

CONKLIN, NYBO, LEVEQUE & MURPHY, P.C. (AV)

Suite 203, 9 Third Street North, P.O. Box 2049, 59403-2049
Telephone: 406-727-9270
Fax: 406-761-1406

William Conklin
L. D. Nybo
E. Lee LeVeque
Thomas J. Murphy
Allen P. Lanning

Jeffrey T. McAllister
Evan F. Danno

Reference: Norwest Bank of Great Falls.

For full biographical listings, see the Martindale-Hubbell Law Directory

NEBRASKA

*LINCOLN,** Lancaster Co.

ERICKSON & SEDERSTROM, P.C. (AV)

Suite 400, Cornhusker Plaza, 301 South 13th Street, 68508
Telephone: 402-476-1000
Fax: 402-476-6167
Omaha, Nebraska Office: Regency Westpointe, 10330 Regency Parkway Drive.
Telephone: 402-397-2200.
Fax: 402-390-7137.

Charles Thone
Charles D. Humble
Alan M. Wood
Douglas L. Curry
Mark M. Schorr
Linda W. Rohman
David C. Mussman

Representative Clients: California Public Employees Retirement Plan (CALPERS); Chase Manhattan Leasing Co.; Albertson's, Inc.; Baker's Supermarkets, Inc.; Osco Drug, Inc.; Lincoln General Hospital; Martin Luther Home; Lincoln Electric System.

For full biographical listings, see the Martindale-Hubbell Law Directory

NORFOLK, Madison Co.

DOMINA & COPPLE, P.C. (AV)

2425 Taylor Avenue, P.O. Box 78, 68702-0078
Telephone: 402-371-4300
Fax: 402-371-0790
Omaha, Nebraska Office: 1065 North 115th Street, Suite 150.
Telephone: 402-493-4100.
FAX: 402-493-9782.

David A. Domina
David E. Copple

Kathleen K. Rockey
James G. Kube
David H. Ptak
Steven D. Sunde

For full biographical listings, see the Martindale-Hubbell Law Directory

*OMAHA,** Douglas Co.

DWYER, POHREN, WOOD, HEAVEY, GRIMM, GOODALL & LAZER (AV)

A Partnership including Professional Corporations
Suite 400, 8712 West Dodge Road, 68114
Telephone: 402-392-0101
Telefax: 402-392-1011

(See Next Column)

DWYER, POHREN, WOOD, HEAVEY, GRIMM, GOODALL & LAZER, *Omaha—Continued*

MEMBERS OF FIRM

Robert V. Dwyer, Jr.
Edward F. Pohren
W. Eric Wood (P.C.)
Michael W. Heavey (P.C.)
Andrew E. Grimm
Mark L. Goodall
Michael L. Lazer
James D. Loerts
Lisa A. Sarver
Shawn M. Ilg

Representative Clients: K-Products, Inc.; Deutsche Credit Corp.; Purina Mills, Inc.; Bishop Clarkson Memorial Hospital, Omaha, Nebraska; Nebraska Hospital Association; Strategic Air Command Federal Credit Union; Heller Financial, Inc.; Fordmotor Credit Company; National Medical Enterprises, Inc.; CETAC Technologies, Inc.

For full biographical listings, see the Martindale-Hubbell Law Directory

ERICKSON & SEDERSTROM, P.C. (AV)

Regency Westpointe, 10330 Regency Parkway Drive, 68114
Telephone: 402-397-2200
Fax: 402-390-7137
Lincoln, Nebraska Office: Suite 400, Cornhusker Plaza, 301 South 13th Street.
Telephone: 402-476-1000.
Fax: 402-476-6167.

Lewis R. Leigh
Ray R. Simon
Donald H. Erickson
Daniel D. Koukol
Wm. E. Morrow, Jr.
Soren S. Jensen
Daniel B. Kinnamon
Joel Davis
Virgil K. Johnson
Charles V. Sederstrom, Jr.
Michael C. Washburn
John C. Brownrigg
Thomas J. Culhane
Richard J. Gilloon
Samuel Earle Clark
Gary L. Hoffman
J Russell Derr
Jerald L. Rauterkus
Mark Peterson
Sherry L. Hubert
Lane D. Edenburn

OF COUNSEL

Leo Eisenstatt
Roland J. Santoni
Michael A. Fortune
Anne O. Fortune

Representative Clients: Nebraska State Bank of Omaha; Berkshire Hathaway, Inc.; Bozell, Inc.; IBP, Inc.; Quaker Oats Co.; United A-G Cooperative, Inc.; Immanuel Medical Center; Cornhusker Casualty Co.; Hartford Accident & Indemnity Co.; Mortgage Guaranty Insurance Corp. (MGIC).

For Complete List of Firm Personnel, See General Section

For full biographical listings, see the Martindale-Hubbell Law Directory

NEVADA

*LAS VEGAS,** Clark Co.

ALBRIGHT, STODDARD, WARNICK & ALBRIGHT, A PROFESSIONAL CORPORATION (AV)

Quail Park I, Building D-4, 801 South Rancho Drive, 89106
Telephone: 702-384-7111
FAX: 702-384-0605

G. Vern Albright
William H. Stoddard
Whitney B. Warnick
G. Mark Albright

Michael W. Brimley
Gavin C. Jangard
D. Chris Albright

Representative Clients: Tokio Marine and Fire Ins. Co.; INAPRO, a CIGNA Co.; Nevada Ready Mix; North American Health Care, Inc. (Nursing Home); Royal Insurance; First Security Bank of Utah; Nevada Community Bank; Nationwide Insurance Co.; Liberty Mutual Insurance; CB Commercial.

For full biographical listings, see the Martindale-Hubbell Law Directory

CROCKETT & MYERS, LTD. A PROFESSIONAL CORPORATION (AV)

700 South Third Street, 89101
Telephone: 702-382-6711
Fax: 702-384-8102

J. R. Crockett, Jr.
Richard W. Myers
James V. Lavelle III
Eleissa C. Lavelle
Michael P. Villani

Laura E. Wunsch Stubberud

Reference: Sun State Bank.

For full biographical listings, see the Martindale-Hubbell Law Directory

GALATZ, EARL & BULLA (AV)

710 South Fourth Street, 89101
Telephone: 702-386-0000
Fax: 702-384-0394

Neil G. Galatz
Allan R. Earl
Bonnie A. Bulla

For full biographical listings, see the Martindale-Hubbell Law Directory

GOODMAN & CHESNOFF, A PROFESSIONAL CORPORATION (AV)

520 South Fourth Street, 89101-6593
Telephone: 702-384-5563
Fax: 702-598-1425

Oscar B. Goodman
David Z. Chesnoff
Eckley M. Keach

OF COUNSEL

Stephen Stein

For full biographical listings, see the Martindale-Hubbell Law Directory

GREENMAN, GOLDBERG, RABY & MARTINEZ, PROFESSIONAL CORPORATION (AV)

601 South Ninth Street, 89101-7012
Telephone: 702-384-1616
FAX: 702-384-2990

John A. Greenman
Aubrey Goldberg
Paul E. Raby
Gabriel A. Martinez

Eduardo G. San Miguel
Daniel S. Simon

Representative Client: Las Vegas Metropolitan Police Protective Assn.

For full biographical listings, see the Martindale-Hubbell Law Directory

JOLLEY, URGA, WIRTH & WOODBURY (AV)

Suite 800 Bank of America Plaza, 300 South Fourth Street, 89101
Telephone: 702-385-5161
Telecopier: 702-382-6814
Boulder City, Nevada Office: Suite 105, 1000 Nevada Highway.
Telephone: 702-293-3674.

MEMBERS OF FIRM

R. Gardner Jolley
Bruce L. Woodbury
Jay Earl Smith

ASSOCIATES

Troy E. Peyton
John T. Steffen

For Complete List of Firm Personnel, See General Section

For full biographical listings, see the Martindale-Hubbell Law Directory

GARY LOGAN (AV)

Third Floor, First Interstate Bank Building, 302 East Carson Avenue, 89101
Telephone: 702-385-9900
Telecopier: 702-382-4800

OF COUNSEL

Richard I. Feinberg

References: Bank of America-Nevada; The Chase Manhattan Bank, N.A.

For full biographical listings, see the Martindale-Hubbell Law Directory

VANNAH COSTELLO HOWARD & CANEPA (AV)

A Partnership including a Professional Corporation
Greystone, 1850 East Flamingo, Suite 236, 89119
Telephone: 702-369-4161
Fax: 702-369-0104

MEMBERS OF FIRM

Robert D. Vannah (Chartered)
Nathan M. Costello
James W. Howard, Jr.
Scott K. Canepa

ASSOCIATE

Jerry A. Wiese

Representative Clients: Prudential Property and Casualty Insurance Co.; USF&G Co.; CNA; OUM Group Insurance Co.; American Golf Corp.; Reliance Insurance Co.

For full biographical listings, see the Martindale-Hubbell Law Directory

*RENO,** Washoe Co.

CALVIN R. X. DUNLAP (AV)

537 Ralston Street, P.O. Box 3689, 89505
Telephone: 702-323-7790
FAX: 702-323-5454

Reference: Valley Bank (Wells Ave. Branch).

For full biographical listings, see the Martindale-Hubbell Law Directory

Reno—Continued

ERICKSON, THORPE & SWAINSTON, LTD. (AV)

601 S. Arlington Avenue, P.O. Box 3559, 89505
Telephone: 702-786-3930
Fax: 702-786-4160

Roger L. Erickson
Donald A. Thorpe
George W. Swainston
William G. Cobb
James L. Lundemo
Gary A. Cardinal
Thomas Peter Beko
John A. Aberasturi

Representative Clients: Albertson's, Inc.; Allstate Insurance Co.; Avis Rent-A-Car System; Chrysler Corp.; Firestone Tire and Rubber Co.; Industrial Indemnity Co.; Airport Authority of Washoe County; Dow Corning; Bank of America Nevada.

For full biographical listings, see the Martindale-Hubbell Law Directory

NEW HAMPSHIRE

*CONCORD,** Merrimack Co.

ORR & RENO, PROFESSIONAL ASSOCIATION (AV)

One Eagle Square, P.O. Box 3550, 03302-3550
Telephone: 603-224-2381
Fax: 603-224-2318

Ronald L. Snow
Richard B. Couser
William L. Chapman

Representative Clients: Beach Aircraft Corporation; Chubb Life America; Fleet Bank; Dartmouth-Hitchcock Medical Center; EnergyNorth, Inc.; National Grange Mutual Co.; New England College; New England Electric System Co.; Newspapers of New England, Inc.; St. Paul's School.

For Complete List of Firm Personnel, See General Section

For full biographical listings, see the Martindale-Hubbell Law Directory

*LACONIA,** Belknap Co.

NORMANDIN, CHENEY & O'NEIL (AV)

Normandin Square, 213 Union Avenue, P.O. Box 575, 03247-0575
Telephone: 603-524-4380

MEMBERS OF FIRM

A. Gerard O'Neil
A.G. O'Neil, Jr.
James F. LaFrance

Counsel for: Laconia Savings Bank; Lakes Region Mental Health Center; Laconia Airport Authority; Community TV Corp.; Central New Hampshire Realty, Inc.; All Metals Industries, Inc.; Lakes Region Anesthesiology, P.A.; Cormier Corp.; Scotia Technology; Vemaline Products.

For Complete List of Firm Personnel, See General Section

For full biographical listings, see the Martindale-Hubbell Law Directory

*MANCHESTER,** Hillsborough Co.

ABRAMSON, REIS AND BROWN (AV)

1819 Elm Street, 03104
Telephone: 603-647-0300
Fax: 603-666-4227
Nashua, New Hampshire Office: 11 Concord Street.
Telephone: 603-886-0308.

MEMBERS OF FIRM

Stanley M. Brown
Kenneth C. Brown
Randolph J. Reis
Mark A. Abramson
Kevin F. Dugan

For full biographical listings, see the Martindale-Hubbell Law Directory

BOUCHARD & MALLORY, P.A. (AV)

100 Middle Street, 03101
Telephone: 603-623-7222
Fax: 603-623-8953

Kenneth G. Bouchard
Mark L. Mallory

Paul B. Kleinman
Blake M. Sutton
Susan A. Vaillancourt
Christine Friedman
Robert S. Stephen

For full biographical listings, see the Martindale-Hubbell Law Directory

NEW JERSEY

BURLINGTON, Burlington Co.

SMITH, GOLDSTEIN & MAGRAM, A PROFESSIONAL CORPORATION (AV)

415 High Street, P.O. Box 603, 08016-0603
Telephone: 609-386-2633
Fax: 609-386-8674

Louis A. Smith
Jeffrey N. Goldstein
Edward J. Magram

Elizabeth D. Berenato

Reference: First Fidelity Bank of South Jersey, Burlington, New Jersey.

For full biographical listings, see the Martindale-Hubbell Law Directory

CALDWELL, Essex Co.

JOHNSON, GALLAGHER, BURGIO & MARTIN (AV)

Johnson & Gallagher, 1959-1978
Johnson, Gallagher & Burgio, 1978-1991
Johnson, Gallagher, Burgio & Martin, 1992-
10 Forest Avenue, P.O. Box 407, 07006
Telephone: 201-226-6682
Fax: 201-226-1605

MEMBERS OF FIRM

James J. Gallagher (1923-1985)
Austin B. Johnson, Jr.
John E. Burgio
Kathleen G. Martin

OF COUNSEL

Stanley G. Bedford

Counsel for: Luce, Schwab & Kase, Inc.
Representative Clients: Carolina Freight Carriers Corp.; Merchants Insurance Group; Cardinal Freight Carriers; Risk Management Claim Services, Inc.; Ranger Transportation, Inc.; Gemini Transportation Services, Inc.; Poole Truck Lines, Inc.
Reference: Midlantic National Bank (Caldwell Office).

For full biographical listings, see the Martindale-Hubbell Law Directory

CHATHAM, Morris Co.

O'CONNOR & RHATICAN, A PROFESSIONAL CORPORATION (AV)

383 Main Street, 07928
Telephone: 201-635-2210
FAX: 201-635-2622

Gerald B. O'Connor
Peter E. Rhatican
Vivian Demas

Paul A. O'Connor, III

OF COUNSEL

Patricia J. Cooney

For full biographical listings, see the Martindale-Hubbell Law Directory

CHERRY HILL, Camden Co.

GARRIGLE & PALM (AV)

Suite 204, 1415 State Highway 70 East, 08034
Telephone: 609-427-9300
Fax: 609-427-9590

MEMBERS OF FIRM

William A. Garrigle
John M. Palm

ASSOCIATES

Harold H. Thomasson
Paul F Kulinski
James J. Law
Eleanore A. Rogalski

Representative Clients: Crum & Forster Group; Kemper Insurance Group; Atlantic Mutual Group; American Hardware Mutual; National General Insurance Co.; Transamerica Group; State Farm Fire Insurance Co.; Progressive Insurance Co.; United Southern Insurance Co.; New Jersey Market Transition Facility and Joint Underwriting Association.

For full biographical listings, see the Martindale-Hubbell Law Directory

MONTANO, SUMMERS, MULLEN, MANUEL, OWENS AND GREGORIO, A PROFESSIONAL CORPORATION (AV)

Two Executive Campus, Suite 400, Route 70 and Cuthbert Boulevard, 08002
Telephone: 609-665-9400
Fax: 609-665-0006
Northfield, New Jersey Office: The Executive Plaza, 2111 New Road, Suite 105.
Telephone: 609-383-8900.
Philadelphia, Pennsylvania Office: 1700 Market Street - Suite 2628.
Telephone: 215-732-3900.

(See Next Column)

MONTANO, SUMMERS, MULLEN, MANUEL, OWENS AND GREGORIO A PROFESSIONAL CORPORATION, *Cherry Hill—Continued*

Carl Kisselman (1899-1975)
James A. Mullen, Jr.
G. Wesley Manuel, Jr.
F. Herbert Owens, III
Carl J. Gregorio
Gary L. Jakob
Lawrence D. Lally
Paul F. Gilligan, Jr.
David D. Duffin
Michael G. B. David

Craig W. Summers
Mary C. Brennan
James A. Nolan, Jr.
Alfred J. Quasti, Jr.
Robert H. Ayik
Stephen D. Holtzman (Resident, Northfield Office)
Arthur E. Donnelly, III
Bruce C. Truesdale
Ronald S. Collins, Jr.
Matthew P. Lyons
William J. Rudnik (Resident, Northfield Office)

OF COUNSEL

Arthur Montano
William W. Summers

Local Counsel for: Indemnity Insurance Company of North America; Royal Group; General Motors Corp.
Reference: Midlantic National Bank, Cherry Hill, New Jersey.

For full biographical listings, see the Martindale-Hubbell Law Directory

CRANFORD, Union Co.

McCREEDY AND COX (AV)

Second Floor, Six Commerce Drive, 07016-3509
Telephone: 908-709-0400
Fax: 908-709-0405

MEMBERS OF FIRM

Edwin J. McCreedy
Robert F. Cox

ASSOCIATE

Patrick J. Hermesmann

Reference: United Counties Trust Co.

For full biographical listings, see the Martindale-Hubbell Law Directory

FLORHAM PARK, Morris Co.

HACK, PIRO, O'DAY, MERKLINGER, WALLACE & McKENNA, P.A. (AV)

30 Columbia Turnpike, P.O. Box 941, 07932-0941
Telephone: 201-301-6500
Fax: 201-301-0094

David L. Hack
Peter A. Piro
William J. O'Day
M. Richard Merklinger
Joseph V. Wallace
Peter T. Melnyk
Patrick M. Sages

Bonny G. Rafel
Darlene D. Steinhart
Robert G. Alencewicz
John T. West
Scott D. Samansky
John J. Petrizzo
William F. Murphy
Thomas M. Madden

Representative Clients: Aetna Life & Casualty Co.; Avis Rent-a-Car Systems; Eastman Kodak Co.; State Farm Insurance Cos.; Trans World Airlines, Inc.; Travelers Insurance Co.; Westinghouse Electric Co.; Weyerhauser Co.

For Complete List of Firm Personnel, See General Section

For full biographical listings, see the Martindale-Hubbell Law Directory

*HACKENSACK,** Bergen Co.

BRESLIN AND BRESLIN, P.A. (AV)

41 Main Street, 07601
Telephone: 201-342-4014; 342-4015
Fax: 201-342-0068; 201-342-3077

Charles Rodgers
E. Carter Corriston
Donald A. Caminiti

Michael T. Fitzpatrick
Angelo A. Bello
Terrence J. Corriston
Kevin C. Corriston
Karen Boe Gatlin
Lawrence Farber
E. Carter Corriston, Jr.

Representative Clients: Bergen County Housing Authority; Phillips Fuel Co.; Prudential Insurance Co.; Rent Leveling Board of Township of North Bergen; Housing Authority of Passaic.
Reference: United Jersey Bank.

For Complete List of Firm Personnel, See General Section

For full biographical listings, see the Martindale-Hubbell Law Directory

CUCCIO AND CUCCIO (AV)

45 Essex Street, 07601
Telephone: 201-487-7411
Fax: 201-487-6574
Mailing Address: P.O. Box 2223, South Hackensack, New Jersey, 07606

(See Next Column)

MEMBERS OF FIRM

Frank J. Cuccio
Emil S. Cuccio

ASSOCIATE

Pamela Beth Keitz

Representative Clients: TCI of Northern New Jersey; Huffman Koos, Inc.; The Actors Fund of America; Blue Circle-Raia, Inc.; Zimpro, Inc., Division of Sterling Drug; Honig Chemical and Processing Corp.; Napp Technologies, Inc.; River Terrace Gardens Assoc.; Franklin Lakes P.B.A. Local 150.

For full biographical listings, see the Martindale-Hubbell Law Directory

HARWOOD LLOYD (AV)

130 Main Street, 07601
Telephone: 201-487-1080
Facsimile: 487-4758; 487-8410
East Brunswick, New Jersey Office: Two Tower Center, 10th Floor.
Telephone: 908-214-1010.
Facsimile: 908-214-1818.
Ridgewood, New Jersey Office: 41 Oak Street.
Telephone: 201-447-1422.
Facsimile: 201-447-1926.

MEMBERS OF FIRM

Victor C. Harwood, III
Frank V. D. Lloyd
Brian J. Coyle
Michael B. Oropollo
Richard J. Ryan
Leonard P. Rosa
John D. Allen, III
Frank Holahan
Russell A. Pepe
Gregory J. Irwin
Anthony M. Carlino
Thomas B. Hanrahan
Brian R. Ade
Brian C. Gallagher
Bernadette N. Gordon
Edward Zampino
Jonathan Bubrow

OF COUNSEL

David F. McBride
Theodore W. Trautwein
August Schedler
Francis V. D. Lloyd (1896-1974)
John W. Griggs (1929-1980)
Charles C. Shenier (1905-1970)
Emil M. Wulster (1907-1978)
Daniel Gilady (1927-1975)
George A. Brown (1913-1986)

Local Counsel for: Aetna Casualty & Surety Co.; Allstate Insurance Co.; Midlantic National Bank/North; United Jersey Bank; Gulf Oil Corp.; Volvo North America Corp.; Kemper Group.

For Complete List of Firm Personnel, See General Section

For full biographical listings, see the Martindale-Hubbell Law Directory

HEIN, SMITH, BEREZIN, MALOOF & ROGERS (AV)

Court Plaza East, 19 Main Street, 07601-7023
Telephone: 201-487-7400
Telecopier: 201-487-4228

MEMBERS OF FIRM

Robert J. Maloof
Allan H. Rogers
Robert L. Baum
Lawrence H. Jacobs

ASSOCIATES

John L. Shanahan
Ellen W. Smith
Carla H. Madnick
Marian H. Speid

Representative Clients: Aetna Insurance Co.; Commercial Union of New York; Employers of Wausau; Great American Insurance Cos.; Hanover Insurance Co.; Health Care Insurance Co.; Merchants Mutual Insurance Co.; St. Paul Fire & Marine Insurance Co.; U.S. Fidelity & Guaranty Co.
Reference: United Jersey Bank.

For Complete List of Firm Personnel, See General Section

For full biographical listings, see the Martindale-Hubbell Law Directory

HACKETTSTOWN, Warren Co.

MULLIGAN & MULLIGAN (AV)

480 Highway 517, P.O. Box 211, 07840
Telephone: 908-852-0202
Fax: 908-852-0626

MEMBERS OF FIRM

William G. Mulligan (1906-1991)
Elinor Patterson Mulligan
Amy O'Connor

ASSOCIATE

Richard D. Fifield

For full biographical listings, see the Martindale-Hubbell Law Directory

LIVINGSTON, Essex Co.

PHILIP M. LUSTBADER & DAVID LUSTBADER A PROFESSIONAL CORPORATION (AV)

615 West Mount Pleasant Avenue, 07039
Telephone: 201-740-1000
Fax: 201-740-1520

Philip M. Lustbader
David Lustbader

(See Next Column)

PHILIP M. LUSTBADER & DAVID LUSTBADER A PROFESSIONAL CORPORATION—*Continued*

John N. Holly
John L. Riordan, Jr.

OF COUNSEL

Robert J. McKenna

For full biographical listings, see the Martindale-Hubbell Law Directory

MORGAN, MELHUISH, MONAGHAN, ARVIDSON, ABRUTYN & LISOWSKI (AV)

(Formerly Schneider and Morgan)
651 West Mount Pleasant Avenue, 07039
Telephone: 201-994-2500
Fax: 201-994-3375
New York, N.Y. Office: 39 Broadway, 35th Floor.
Telephone: 212-809-1111.
Fax: 212-509-3422.

MEMBERS OF FIRM

Jacob Schneider (1910-1949)
Louis Schneider (1921-1965)
Henry G. Morgan
James L. Melhuish
Robert E. Monaghan
William F. Perry
Richard E. Arvidson
John I. Lisowski
Elliott Abrutyn
Jeffrey M. Kadish
Paul A. Tripodo
John J. Agostini
Robert J. Aste
Mary Adele Hornish
Richard E. Snyder
David M. Welt
Michael A. Sicola
Joseph DeDonato
Robert A. Assuncao

Richard Micliz
Roger C. Schechter
Richard J. Hull
Leonard C. Leicht
Nina Lynn Caroselli
Anthony M. Santoro, Jr.
Robert J. Machi
Michael H. Cohen
Timothy K. Saia
Mary Ellen Scalera
Robert G. Klinck
Linda G. O'Connell

OF COUNSEL

Vincent J. Cirlin

Represent: The Home Insurance Co.; The Insurance Company of North American Cos.; General Accident Fire & Life Assurance Corp., Ltd.; Zurich Insurance Co.; Trans America Insurance Group; Allstate Insurance Co.; Penn Mutual Insurance Co.; State Farm Insurance; Ohio Casualty Co.; American Mutual Liability Insurance Co.

For Complete List of Firm Personnel, See General Section

For full biographical listings, see the Martindale-Hubbell Law Directory

MILLBURN, Essex Co.

KUTTNER LAW OFFICES (AV)

24 Lackawanna Plaza, P.O. Box 745, 07041-0745
Telephone: 201-467-8300
Fax: 201-467-4333

Bernard A. Kuttner
Robert D. Kuttner

Reference: Summit Bank, Millburn, New Jersey.

For full biographical listings, see the Martindale-Hubbell Law Directory

MCDERMOTT & MCGEE (AV)

64 Main Street, P.O. Box 192, 07041-0192
Telephone: 201-467-8080
FAX: 201-467-0012

MEMBERS OF FIRM

John L. McDermott
John P. McGee
Richard P. Maggi
Thomas A. Wester
Richard A. Tango
Frank P. Leanza
John L. McDermott, Jr.

ASSOCIATES

Lawrence G. Tosi
David J. Dickinson
A. Charles Lorenzo
Robert A. McDermott
Kevin John McGee

OF COUNSEL

Daniel K. Van Dorn

Representative Clients: Allstate Insurance Co.; American Hardware Mutual Insurance Co.; Argonaut Insurance Cos.; Continental Insurance Cos.; Commercial Union Insurance Cos.; General Accident Group; Maryland-American General Group; Zurich-American Insurance Co.; P.C.M. Intermediaries, Ltd.; The Hanover Insurance Cos.

For full biographical listings, see the Martindale-Hubbell Law Directory

MONTVALE, Bergen Co.

BEATTIE PADOVANO (AV)

50 Chestnut Ridge Road, P.O. Box 244, 07645-0244
Telephone: 201-573-1810
Fax: (DEX) 201-573-9736

MEMBERS OF FIRM

James R. Beattie
Ralph J. Padovano
Roger W. Breslin, Jr.
Brian R. Martinotti

ASSOCIATES

Brenda J. McAdoo
Susan Calabrese

Reference: United Jersey Bank.

For Complete List of Firm Personnel, See General Section

For full biographical listings, see the Martindale-Hubbell Law Directory

MOORESTOWN, Burlington Co.

CHIERICI & WRIGHT, A PROFESSIONAL CORPORATION (AV)

Blason Campus - III, 509 South Lenola Road Building Six, 08057-1561
Telephone: 609-234-6300
Fax: 609-234-9490

Donald R. Chierici, Jr.
David B. Wright
Elizabeth Coleman Chierici
Julie C. Smith
Sheri Nelson Oliano
Jaunice M. Canning
Rhonda J. Eiger
Michael A. Foresta
Linda M. Novosel

For full biographical listings, see the Martindale-Hubbell Law Directory

*MORRISTOWN,** Morris Co.

MASKALERIS & ASSOCIATES (AV)

30 Court Street, 07960
Telephone: 201-267-0222
Newark, New Jersey Office: Federal Square Station, P.O. Box 20207.
Telephone: 201-622-4300.
Far Hills, New Jersey Office: Route 202 Station Plaza.
Telephone: 201-234-0600.
New York, New York Office: 123 Bank Street.
Telephone: 212-724-8669.
Athens, Greece Office: Stadio 28, Fourth Floor.
Telephone: 322-6790.

Stephen N. Maskaleris

ASSOCIATES

Peter C. Ioannou
Christopher P. Luongo

For full biographical listings, see the Martindale-Hubbell Law Directory

PORZIO, BROMBERG & NEWMAN, A PROFESSIONAL CORPORATION (AV)

163 Madison Avenue, 07962-1997
Telephone: 201-538-4006
Facsimile: 201-538-5146
New York, New York Office: 655 Third Avenue, 10017-5617.
Telephone: 212-986-0600.
Facsimile: 212-986-6491.

Myron J. Bromberg
D. Jeffrey Campbell
Thomas R. Chesson
Roy Alan Cohen
Alexander J. Drago (Resident, New York Office)
Lauren E. Handler
Anita Hotchkiss
Kenneth R. Meyer

COUNSEL

Stewart A. Cunningham
Charles E. Erway, III

Maura E. Blau
Howard P. Davis
Christopher P. DePhillips
Garineh S. Dovletian
Peter A. Drucker
Frank Fazio
Karen A. Kaplan
Vanessa M. Kelly
Jonathan M. Korn
William A. Krais
Jonathan R. Kuhlman
Coleen McCaffery
Jay R. McDaniel
Nancy Gail Minikes
Dean M. Monti (Resident Associate, New York Office)
Randi N. Pomerantz
Robert T. Quackenboss
Cynthia D. Richardson
Gregory J. Schwartz
Diane M. Siana
Charles J. Stoia
Janet A. Sullivan
Morna L. Sweeney
Stephen L. Willis

Representative Clients: American Cyanamid Co.; American Home Products Corp.; ASARCO Inc.; Ayerst Laboratories; Johnson & Johnson; Pfizer Inc.; Warner-Lambert Co.

For Complete List of Firm Personnel, See General Section

For full biographical listings, see the Martindale-Hubbell Law Directory

Morristown—Continued

STEPHEN S. WEINSTEIN A PROFESSIONAL CORPORATION (AV)

20 Park Place, Suite 301, 07960
Telephone: 201-267-5200
FAX: 201-538-1779

Stephen S. Weinstein

Gail S. Boertzel
Peter N. Gilbreth
William A. Johnson
Melissa H. Luce

For full biographical listings, see the Martindale-Hubbell Law Directory

*NEWARK,** Essex Co.

BROWN & BROWN, P.C. (AV)

One Gateway Center, Fifth Floor, 07102
Telephone: 201-622-1846
Fax: 201-622-2223
Jersey City, New Jersey Office:
Telephone: 201-656-2381.

Raymond A. Brown
Raymond M. Brown

Reference: National Westminster Bank, NJ.

For full biographical listings, see the Martindale-Hubbell Law Directory

CARPENTER, BENNETT & MORRISSEY (AV)

(Formerly Carpenter, Gilmour & Dwyer)
Three Gateway Center, 17th Floor, 100 Mulberry Street, 07102-4079
Telephone: 201-622-7711
New York City: 212-943-6530
Telex: 139405
Telecopier: 201-622-5314
EasyLink: 62827845
ABA/net: CARPENTERB

MEMBERS OF FIRM

John C. Heavey
John E. Keale
Rudy B. Coleman
Rosemary J. Bruno
William A. Carpenter, Jr.
Thomas F. McGuane
Joseph D. Rasnek
Robert M. Goodman
Lynn D. Healy
Robert L. Heugle, Jr.
Thomas M. Moore

ASSOCIATES

Jane A. Rigby
Joel L. Botwick
Michelle M. Hydrusko
Matthew Q. Berge
C. Brian Kornbrek
Deborah L. Neilan
John M. O'Connor

Representative Clients: General Motors Corp.; E. I. du Pont de Nemours and Company; Texaco Inc.; AT&T; Litton Industries; ITT Corp.; International Flavors & Fragrances Inc.; New Jersey Hospital Association; Prudential Insurance Company of America; United Jersey Bank.

For Complete List of Firm Personnel, See General Section

For full biographical listings, see the Martindale-Hubbell Law Directory

GOLDSTEIN TILL & LITE (AV)

Suite 800, 744 Broad Street, 07102-3803
Telephone: 201-623-3000
FAX: 201-623-0858
Telex: 262320 USA UR

MEMBERS OF FIRM

Andrew J. Goldstein
Peter W. Till
Allyn Z. Lite
Joseph J. DePalma

Nancy Lem
Amy M. Riel
Richard T. Luzzi
Denise L. Panicucci
Robin May Messing
Michael E. Patunas
Donna Lavista Schwartz

For full biographical listings, see the Martindale-Hubbell Law Directory

MCCARTER & ENGLISH (AV)

Four Gateway Center, 100 Mulberry Street, P.O. Box 652, 07101-0652
Telephone: 201-622-4444
Telecopier: 201-624-7070
Cable Address: "McCarter" Newark
Cherry Hill, New Jersey Office: 1810 Chapel Avenue West.
Telephone: 609-662-8444.
Telecopier: 609-662-6203.
New York, New York Office: Suite 1519, One World Trade Center.
Telephone: 212-466-9018.
Telecopier: 212-432-6568.
Boca Raton, Florida Office: 2255 Glades Road, Suite 319-A.
Telephone: 407-994-6262.
Telecopier: 407-241-0798.
Wilmington, Delaware Office: Mellon Bank Center, 919 Market Street.
Telephone: 302-654-8010.
Telecopier: 302-654-0795.

(See Next Column)

MEMBERS OF FIRM

John E. Flaherty
James H. Keale

COUNSEL

Joseph F. Falgiani

For Complete List of Firm Personnel, See General Section

For full biographical listings, see the Martindale-Hubbell Law Directory

MEDVIN & ELBERG (AV)

One Gateway Center, 16th Floor, 07102
Telephone: 201-642-1300
Fax: 201-642-8613

MEMBERS OF FIRM

Philip Elberg
Alan Y. Medvin

Robert A. Jones
Edna Y. Baugh

For full biographical listings, see the Martindale-Hubbell Law Directory

SILLS CUMMIS ZUCKERMAN RADIN TISCHMAN EPSTEIN & GROSS, A PROFESSIONAL CORPORATION (AV)

One Riverfront Plaza, 07102-5400
Telephone: 201-643-7000
Fax: 201-643-6500
Telex: 820630 Sillsbeck Nwk
Atlantic City, New Jersey Office: 17 Gordon's Alley.
Telephone: 609-344-2800.
New York, N.Y. Office: 250 Park Avenue.
Telephone: 212-643-7000.

Barry M. Epstein
Jeffrey Barton Cahn
Marc S. Klein
James D. Toll (Resident at Atlantic City, N.J. Office)
Alan J. Cohen (Resident at Atlantic City, N.J. Office)

Steven R. Rowland
Eric D. Mann (Resident at Atlantic City, N.J. Office)
Beth S. Rose
Scott N. Rubin
Bennet Susser
N. Lynne Hughes (Resident at Atlantic City Office)

For Complete List of Firm Personnel, See General Section

For full biographical listings, see the Martindale-Hubbell Law Directory

LAW OFFICES OF IRA J. ZARIN (AV)

One Gateway Center, Suite 1612, 07102
Telephone: 201-622-3533
Telecopier: 201-622-1338

ASSOCIATE

Jeffrey E. Strauss

For full biographical listings, see the Martindale-Hubbell Law Directory

*NEW BRUNSWICK,** Middlesex Co.

LUTZ, SHAFRANSKI, GORMAN AND MAHONEY, P.A. (AV)

77 Livingston Avenue, P.O. Box 596, 08903
Telephone: 908-249-0444
Fax: 908-249-0834

Francis J. Lutz
James A. Shafranski
John R. Gorman
John L. Mahoney

Reference: National Westminster Bank.

For full biographical listings, see the Martindale-Hubbell Law Directory

NORTH BRUNSWICK, Middlesex Co.

BUSCH AND BUSCH (AV)

215 North Center Drive, Commerce Center - U.S. #1 South, P.O. Box 7448, 08902-7448
Telephone: 908-821-2300
Telecopier: 908-821-5588

OF COUNSEL

Henry Busch

MEMBERS OF FIRM

Lewis D. Busch (1901-1986)
Malcolm R. Busch
Ronald J. Busch
Bertram E. Busch
Mark N. Busch
Leonard R. Busch
Steven F. Satz

Donald J. Sears
Kenneth A. Levine

Representative Clients: Littman Jewelers; Middlesex County Mosquito Extermination Commission; Utica Mutual Insurance Co.; New Brunswick Tomorrow; Township of East Brunswick; Minnesota Mutual Life Insurance Co.; Township of Monroe, Board of Education.

For full biographical listings, see the Martindale-Hubbell Law Directory

PHILLIPSBURG, Warren Co.

JOHN J. COYLE, JR., P.C. (AV)

Memorial Parkway at 2nd Street, P.O. Box 5270, 08865
Telephone: 908-454-3300
Telecopier: 908-454-9367

John J. Coyle, Jr.

James S. DeBosh

Reference: Phillipsburg National Bank.

For full biographical listings, see the Martindale-Hubbell Law Directory

PRINCETON, Mercer Co.

PELLETTIERI, RABSTEIN AND ALTMAN (AV)

100 Nassau Park Boulevard Suite 111, 08540
Telephone: 609-520-0900
Fax: 609-452-8796
Mount Holly, New Jersey Office: Tarnsfield & Woodlane Roads.
Telephone: 609-267-3390.

MEMBERS OF FIRM

George Pellettieri (1903-1980)
Richard M. Altman
Ira C. Miller
John A. Hartmann, III
Andrew M. Rockman
Bruce P. Miller
Edward Slaughter, Jr.
Anne P. McHugh
Neal S. Solomon
Gary E. Adams
Mel Narol
E. Elizabeth Sweetser
Arthur Penn
Thomas R. Smith
George Louis Pellettieri (1961-1973)

ASSOCIATES

Christine McHugh
James Lazzaro
Jed S. Kadish
Martin S. Pappaterra
Daniel S. Sweetser
Lydia Fabbro Keephart
Kenneth W. Lozier
John K. Semler, Jr.
Nicole J. Huckerby
Elyse Genek
Mark K. Smith

OF COUNSEL

Ruth Rabstein

For full biographical listings, see the Martindale-Hubbell Law Directory

RED BANK, Monmouth Co.

PHILIP G. AUERBACH A PROFESSIONAL CORPORATION (AV)

231 Maple Avenue, P.O. Box Y, 07701
Telephone: 908-842-6660

Philip G. Auerbach

Edward A. Genz
John J. Ryan

For full biographical listings, see the Martindale-Hubbell Law Directory

ROSELAND, Essex Co.

BRACH, EICHLER, ROSENBERG, SILVER, BERNSTEIN, HAMMER & GLADSTONE, A PROFESSIONAL CORPORATION (AV)

101 Eisenhower Parkway, 07068
Telephone: 201-228-5700
Telecopier: 201-228-7852

Alan H. Bernstein
Charles X. Gormally
Alan S. Pralgever

David J. Klein
Thomas M. Badenhausen
David S. Bernstein
Regina A. McGuire
Carl J. Soranno

OF COUNSEL

Lance A. Posner

Representative Clients: Ohio Casualty Insurance Group; New Jersey Neurological Assn.; Saint Barnabas Medical Center; Union Hospital; Radiological Society of New Jersey; Mercer Medical Center.

For Complete List of Firm Personnel, See General Section

For full biographical listings, see the Martindale-Hubbell Law Directory

*SOMERVILLE,** Somerset Co.

OZZARD WHARTON, A PROFESSIONAL PARTNERSHIP (AV)

75-77 North Bridge Street, P.O. Box 938, 08876
Telephone: 908-526-0700
Telecopier: 908-526-2246

William E. Ozzard
Victor A. Rizzolo
George A. Mauro, Jr.

(See Next Column)

Arthur D. Fialk
Kam S. Minhas
Frederick H. Allen, III
Wendy L. Wiebalk

Representative Clients: American Cyanamid; New Jersey Manufacturers Insurance Co.; Travelers Insurance Co.; Porter Hayden, General Accident Insurance Company; Hanover Insurance Company; Minnesota Mining & Manufacturing Co.

For Complete List of Firm Personnel, See General Section

For full biographical listings, see the Martindale-Hubbell Law Directory

SCHACHTER, TROMBADORE, OFFEN, STANTON & PAVICS, A PROFESSIONAL CORPORATION (AV)

45 East High Street, P.O. Box 520, 08876-0520
Telephone: 908-722-5700
Fax: 908-722-8853

Richard J. Schachter
John J. Trombadore
Stephen M. Offen
Michael J. Stanton
Thomas A. Pavics

William D. Alden
Mary Ann Bauer
Timothy P. McKeown

LEGAL SUPPORT PERSONNEL

Joan V. Shaw (Office Manager)

References: Summit Bank; First National Bank of Central Jersey; New Jersey Savings Bank.

For full biographical listings, see the Martindale-Hubbell Law Directory

SPRINGFIELD, Union Co.

JAVERBAUM WURGAFT & HICKS (AV)

Park Place Legal Center, 959 South Springfield Avenue, 07081-3555
Telephone: 201-379-4200
Fax: 201-379-7872
Newark, New Jersey Office: 233 Lafayette Street, 07105.
Telephone: 201-623-8754.

Kenneth S. Javerbaum
Jack Wurgaft
Robert G. Hicks

Anthony P. Valenti
Karen Lee
John M. Pinho

For full biographical listings, see the Martindale-Hubbell Law Directory

SUMMIT, Union Co.

HAGGERTY, DONOHUE & MONAGHAN, A PROFESSIONAL ASSOCIATION (AV)

One Springfield Avenue, 07901
Telephone: 908-277-2600
Fax: 908-273-1641

James C. Haggerty
George J. Donohue
Walter E. Monaghan

Rose Ann Haggerty
Thomas J. Haggerty
Alfred F. Carolonza, Jr.
William A. Wenzel
Mahlon H. Ortman
Michael A. Conway
James C. Haggerty, Jr.

OF COUNSEL

Joseph D. Haggerty

Representative Clients: American International Group; Chubb/Pacific Indemnity Co.; Crawford & Co.; Crum & Forster; Hertz Corp.; Jefferson Insurance Group; Material Damage Adjustment Corp.; New Jersey Manufacturers; New Jersey Property Liability Guaranty Association; Royal Insurance Co.

For Complete List of Firm Personnel, See General Section

For full biographical listings, see the Martindale-Hubbell Law Directory

*TRENTON,** Mercer Co.

DEVLIN, CITTADINO & SHAW, P.C. (AV)

3131 Princeton Pike, Building 1-A, 08648
Telephone: 609-896-2222
Fax: 609-896-2279

Robert A. Shaw (1964-1992)
John W. Devlin
Benjamin N. Cittadino

John G. Devlin

Reference: United Jersey Bank.

For full biographical listings, see the Martindale-Hubbell Law Directory

VINELAND, Cumberland Co.

JAY H. GREENBLATT & ASSOCIATES A PROFESSIONAL CORPORATION (AV)
200 North Eighth Street, P.O. Box 883, 08360-0883
Telephone: 609-691-0424
Facsimile: 609-696-1010

M. Joseph Greenblatt (1896-1992)
Jay H. Greenblatt

Bonnie L. Laube
Nicholas Kiernіesky
Charles S. Epstein
John M. Amorison

Counsel for: Newcomb Medical Center; Ware's Van & Storage Co., Inc.
Local Counsel for: A. O. Smith Corp.; Vik Brothers Insurance Group; Chance Industries, Inc.; Coca Cola Bottlers' Association; Fireman's Fund Insurance Co.; Ford Motor Co.; Thermadyne Industries; The West Bend Company.

For full biographical listings, see the Martindale-Hubbell Law Directory

JOSEPH D. O'NEILL A PROFESSIONAL CORPORATION (AV)
30 West Chestnut Avenue, P.O. Box 847, 08360
Telephone: 609-692-2400
Telecopier: 609-696-9036

Joseph D. O'Neill

Charles I. Coant
James T. Dugan
Amber Sharp Pallante

For full biographical listings, see the Martindale-Hubbell Law Directory

WAYNE, Passaic Co.

DEYOE, HEISSENBUTTEL & MATTIA (AV)
401 Hamburg Turnpike, P.O. Box 2449, 07474-2449
Telephone: 201-595-6300
Fax: 201-595-0146; 201-595-9262

MEMBERS OF FIRM

Charles P. DeYoe (1923-1973)
Wood M. DeYoe
Frederick C. Heissenbuttel
Philip F. Mattia
Gary R. Matano
Scott B. Piekarsky

ASSOCIATES

Anne Hutton
Glenn Z. Poosikian
Jo Ann G. Durr
Frank D. Samperi
Frank A. Campana
John E. Clarke
Jason T. Shafron
Maura Waters Brady

LEGAL SUPPORT PERSONNEL

Marilyn Moore (Office Manager)

Representative Clients: INA/Aetna Insurance Co. (Cigna); Medical Inter-Insurance Companies; Hanover-Amgro, Inc.; Maryland Casualty Co.; Ohio Casualty Insurance Co.; Motor Club of America; Selected Insurance Co.

For full biographical listings, see the Martindale-Hubbell Law Directory

WEST ORANGE, Essex Co.

ZUCKER, FACHER AND ZUCKER, A PROFESSIONAL CORPORATION (AV)
100 Executive Drive, Third Floor, 07052
Telephone: 201-736-0444
Fax: 201-736-4011

Morris R. Zucker
Irwin L. Facher
Roger C. Wilson
Paul J. Soderman

Judy L. Berberian
Brian Edward Tierney
James Kevin Haney

State Counsel for: Hobart; Becor Western.
Local Counsel for: United States Fidelity & Guaranty Co.; Kemper Insurance Group; Chubb & Son.

For full biographical listings, see the Martindale-Hubbell Law Directory

NEW MEXICO

*ALBUQUERQUE,** Bernalillo Co.

CARPENTER & CHÁVEZ, LTD. (AV)
1600 University Boulevard, N.E., Suite B, 87102-1711
Telephone: 505-243-1336
Facsimile: 505-243-1339

(See Next Column)

William H. Carpenter
Edward L. Chávez
David J. Stout

Reference: First Security Bank, Albuquerque, New Mexico.

For full biographical listings, see the Martindale-Hubbell Law Directory

THE FARLOW LAW FIRM (AV)
Suite 1020, 6501 Americas Parkway, NE, 87110
Telephone: 505-883-4975
Fax: 505-883-4992

LeRoi Farlow
Suzanne Guest
Marianne L. Bowers

Representative Clients: Allstate Insurance Co.; Commercial Insurance Co.; Sentry Insurance Co.; National Farmers Union Insurance Co.; Preferred Risk Mutual Insurance Co.; Guaranty National Insurance Co.
Reference: Bank of New Mexico.

For full biographical listings, see the Martindale-Hubbell Law Directory

RODEY, DICKASON, SLOAN, AKIN & ROBB, P.A. (AV)
Albuquerque Plaza, Suite 2200, 201 Third Street, N.W., P.O. Box 1888, 87103-1888
Telephone: 505-765-5900
Fax: 505-768-7395
Santa Fe, New Mexico Office: Suite 101 Marcy Plaza, 123 East Marcy Street, P.O. Box 1357, 87504-1357.
Telephone: 505-984-0100.
Fax: 505-989-9542.

James C. Ritchie
Joseph J. Mullins
Robert G. McCorkle
Mark C. Meiering
Travis R. Collier
W. Mark Mowery (Resident, Santa Fe Office)
Patrick M. Shay
Ellen G. Thorne
Tracy E. McGee
Charles E. Stuckey
Charles Kipps Purcell
Andrew G. Schultz
John M. Brant
Susan S. Throckmorton
Angela M. Martinez
R. Nelson Franse
Paul R. Koller

Charles J. Vigil
Sheryl S. Mahaney
Mark L. Allen

For Complete List of Firm Personnel, See General Section

For full biographical listings, see the Martindale-Hubbell Law Directory

SHEEHAN, SHEEHAN & STELZNER, P.A. (AV)
Suite 300, 707 Broadway, N.E., P.O. Box 271, 87103
Telephone: 505-247-0411
Fax: 505-842-8890

Craig T. Erickson
Juan L. Flores
Kim A. Griffith
Philip P. Larragoite
Susan C. Little
Maria O'Brien
Judith D. Schrandt
Timothy M. Sheehan
Luis G. Stelzner
Elizabeth Newlin Taylor
Robert P. Warburton

OF COUNSEL

Briggs F. Cheney
Charles T. DuMars
Thomas J. Horan
Pat Sheehan

For full biographical listings, see the Martindale-Hubbell Law Directory

*ROSWELL,** Chaves Co.

HINKLE, COX, EATON, COFFIELD & HENSLEY (AV)
Suite 700, United Bank Plaza, P.O. Box 10, 88202
Telephone: 505-622-6510
FAX: 505-623-9332
Midland, Texas Office: 6 Desta Drive, Suite 2800, P.O. Box 3580, 79705.
Telephone: 915-683-4691.
FAX: 915-683-6518.
Amarillo, Texas Office: 1700 Bank One Center, P.O. Box 9238, 79105-9238.
Telephone: 806-372-5569.
FAX: 806-372-9761.
Santa Fe, New Mexico Office: 218 Montezuma, P.O. Box 2068, 87504.
Telephone: 505-982-4554.
FAX: 505-982-8623.
Albuquerque, New Mexico Office: Suite 800, 500 Marquette, N.W., P.O. Box 2043, 87103.
Telephone: 505-768-1500.
FAX: 505-768-1529.
Austin, Texas Office: 401 West 15th Street, Suite 800, 78701.
Telephone: 512-476-7137.
FAX: 512-476-5431.
Associated Office: Hoffman & Stephens, P.C., 401 West 15th Street, Suite 800, 78701.
Telephone: 512-476-5434.
Fax: 512-476-5431.

(See Next Column)

HINKLE, COX, EATON, COFFIELD & HENSLEY—*Continued*

RESIDENT PARTNERS

Harold L. Hensley, Jr. · Albert L. Pitts
Stuart D. Shanor · Thomas D. Haines, Jr.
Richard E. Olson · Rebecca Nichols Johnson
William Paul Johnson

Representative Clients: ARCO; Exxon; Pennzoil; Phillips Petroleum Co.; Southwestern Public Service Co.; Texaco; Transwestern Pipeline Co.; United New Mexico Bank at Roswell.

For full biographical listings, see the Martindale-Hubbell Law Directory

*SANTA FE,** Santa Fe Co.

PATRICK A. CASEY, P.A. (AV)

1421 Luisa Street, Suite Q, P.O. Box 2436, 87504
Telephone: 505-982-3639
Fax: 505-989-9181

Patrick A. Casey

David C. Ruyle

References: First Interstate Bank of Santa Fe; Sunwest Bank.

For full biographical listings, see the Martindale-Hubbell Law Directory

STEVEN G. FARBER (AV)

409 Hillside Avenue, P.O. Box 2473, 87504-2473
Telephone: 505-988-9725

For full biographical listings, see the Martindale-Hubbell Law Directory

HINKLE, COX, EATON, COFFIELD & HENSLEY (AV)

218 Montezuma, P.O. Box 2068, 87504
Telephone: 505-982-4554
FAX: 505-982-8623
Roswell, New Mexico Office: Suite 700 United Bank Plaza, P.O. Box 10, 88202.
Telephone: 505-622-6510.
FAX: 505-623-9332.
Midland, Texas Office: 6 Desta Drive, Suite 2800, P.O. Box 3580, 79705.
Telephone: 915-683-4691.
FAX: 915-683-6518.
Amarillo, Texas Office: 1700 Bank One Center, P.O. Box 9238, 79105-9238.
Telephone: 806-372-5569.
FAX: 806-372-9761.
Albuquerque, New Mexico Office: Suite 800, 500 Marquette, N.W., P.O. Box 2043, 87103.
Telephone: 505-768-1500.
FAX: 505-768-1529.
Austin, Texas Office: 401 West 15th Street, Suite 800, 78701.
Telephone: 512-476-7137.
FAX: 512-476-5431.
Associated Office: Hoffman & Stephens, P.C., 401 West 15th Street, Suite 800, 78701.
Telephone: 512-476-5434.
Fax: 512-476-5431.

RESIDENT PARTNERS

Jeffrey L. Fornaciari · Thomas M. Hnasko

Representative Clients: Federated Insurance; New Mexico Self-Insurers Fund; State of New Mexico; W.R. Grace and Co.

For full biographical listings, see the Martindale-Hubbell Law Directory

ROTH, VAN AMBERG, GROSS, ROGERS & ORTIZ (AV)

347 East Palace Avenue, P.O. Box 1447, 87501
Telephone: 505-983-7319; 988-8979
Fax: 505-983-7508

F. Joel Roth · Michael P. Gross
Ronald J. Van Amberg · Carl Bryant Rogers
Raymond Z. Ortiz

Reference: First Interstate Bank.

For full biographical listings, see the Martindale-Hubbell Law Directory

NEW YORK

*ALBANY,** Albany Co.

ISEMAN, CUNNINGHAM, RIESTER & HYDE (AV)

9 Thurlow Terrace, 12203
Telephone: 518-462-3000
Telecopier: 518-462-4199

(See Next Column)

MEMBERS OF FIRM

Frederick C. Riester · Robert Hall Iseman
Michael J. Cunningham · Carol Ann Hyde
Michael J. McNeil

Brian M. Culnan · Linda J. Clark

For full biographical listings, see the Martindale-Hubbell Law Directory

ROCHE CORRIGAN McCOY & BUSH (AV)

The Wilem Van Zandt Building, 36 South Pearl Street, 12207
Telephone: 518-436-9370

MEMBERS OF FIRM

Robert P. Roche · Joseph M. McCoy
Peter J. Corrigan · Scott W. Bush

Reference: 1st American Bank, Albany.

For full biographical listings, see the Martindale-Hubbell Law Directory

ROWLEY, FORREST, O'DONNELL & HITE, P.C. (AV)

90 State Street Suite 729, 12207-1715
Telephone: 518-434-6187
Fax: 518-434-1287

Richard R. Rowley · Robert S. Hite
Thomas J. Forrest · John H. Beaumont
Brian J. O'Donnell · Mark S. Pelersi
David C. Rowley

James J. Seaman · Richard W. Bader
David P. Miranda · Daniel W. Coffey
Kevin S. Casey · Thomas D. Spain

OF COUNSEL

Rush W. Stehlin

Reference: Norstar Bank.

For full biographical listings, see the Martindale-Hubbell Law Directory

THORN AND GERSHON (AV)

5 Wembley Court, New Karner Road, P.O. Box 15054, 12212
Telephone: 518-464-6770
Fax: 518-464-6778

MEMBERS OF FIRM

Richard M. Gershon · Jeffrey J. Tymann
Arthur H. Thorn · Maureen Sullivan Bonanni
Robin Bartlett Phelan

ASSOCIATES

Murry S. Brower · Sheila Toborg
Noreen J. Eaton · John C. Garvey
Paul J. Catone · Paul D. Jureller
Nancy Nicholson Bogan · Mario D. Cometti
Robert S. Bruschini

OF COUNSEL

Robert F. Doran

For full biographical listings, see the Martindale-Hubbell Law Directory

*BRONX,** Bronx Co.

MAXWELL S. PFEIFER (AV)

714 East 241st Street, 10470
Telephone: 718-325-5000
Fax: 718-324-0333
Hallandale, Florida Office: 1920 East Hallandale Beach Boulevard, Suite 606.
Telephone: 305-454-1550.

ASSOCIATES

Steven E. Millon · Robert S. Summer

OF COUNSEL

Hon. Alexander A. Dellecese · Sandra Krevitsky Janin
Anthony J. Hatab

LEGAL SUPPORT PERSONNEL

Jay S. Zwerling

For full biographical listings, see the Martindale-Hubbell Law Directory

*BUFFALO,** Erie Co.

J. MICHAEL HAYES (AV)

69 Delaware Avenue, Suite 1201, 14202
Telephone: 716-852-2027
Fax: 716-852-0711

ASSOCIATE

R. Colin Campbell

For full biographical listings, see the Martindale-Hubbell Law Directory

Buffalo—Continued

KOREN, BERTELL & HOEY (AV)

Suite 1820 Liberty Building, 14202
Telephone: 716-856-3631
Fax: 716-856-5457

MEMBERS OF FIRM

M. Robert Koren (1920-1992)
Benjamin J. Hoey
John T. Bertell
Bruce Kevin Koren

ASSOCIATES

Marc J. Hopkins
Richard J. Lutzel

For full biographical listings, see the Martindale-Hubbell Law Directory

---

RENALDO, MYERS, REGAN & PALUMBO, P.C. (AV)

69 Delaware Avenue, 14202
Telephone: 716-853-1865
Fax: 716-852-1872
Williamsville, New York Office: 350 Essjay Road.
Telephone: 716-631-5157.

Anthony J. Renaldo
William J. Regan
James I. Myers
Jeffery D. Palumbo
James Ian Miller

Rachel Anne Roth
Mark J. Longo
Marla DePan Brown
Thomas F. Keefe

References: Manufacturers & Traders Trust Co. (Main Office); Marine Midland Bank.

For full biographical listings, see the Martindale-Hubbell Law Directory

---

ROSENTHAL, SIEGEL, MUENKEL & WOLF (AV)

300 Main Street, 14202
Telephone: 716-854-1300
FAX: 716-842-6354
Amherst, New York Office: Pierce Arrow Plaza, 390 Evans Street.
Telephone: 716-634-8720.

MEMBERS OF FIRM

Jay N. Rosenthal
Joseph P. Muenkel
David Alan Siegel
J. Michael Wolf

ASSOCIATES

Keith I. Kadish
Linda M. DiPasquale
Frank J. Frascogna
Carol R. Rosenthal
Mary E. Virginia
David E. Rosenthal
Robert A. Fiordaliso
Amy Murphy
Roslyn Sierci Sackel

LEGAL SUPPORT PERSONNEL

Patricia E. Lipka

For full biographical listings, see the Martindale-Hubbell Law Directory

---

LAW OFFICES OF LOUIS H. SIEGEL (AV)

602 Chemical Bank Building, 69 Delaware Avenue, 14202
Telephone: 716-854-2626
Facsimile: 716-854-2629

Reference: Fleet Bank.

For full biographical listings, see the Martindale-Hubbell Law Directory

---

SMITH, KELLER, MINER & O'SHEA (AV)

69 Delaware Avenue Suite 1212, 14202-3891
Telephone: 716-855-3611
Fax: 716-855-3250

MEMBERS OF FIRM

Terry D. Smith
Philip J. O'Shea, Jr.
Robert E. Keller
Deborah Bergeron O'Shea
R. Charles Miner
Carrie L. Smith

For full biographical listings, see the Martindale-Hubbell Law Directory

---

GARDEN CITY, Nassau Co.

GALLAGHER GOSSEEN & FALLER (AV)

1010 Franklin Avenue, Suite 400, 11530-2927
Telephone: 516-742-2500
Fax: 516-742-2516
Cable: COMPROAIR
New York, New York Office: 350 Fifth Avenue.
Telephone: 212-947-5800.
FAX: 212-967-4965.

MEMBERS OF FIRM

James A. Gallagher, Jr.
Alan D. Kaplan
Robert A. Faller
Michael J. Crowley
William E. Vita

(See Next Column)

ASSOCIATES

David H. Arnsten
Jeanne M. Gonsalves-Lloyd
William A. Bales, Jr.
Brian P. Morrissey
Jennifer Greenberg
Robert A. Sparer (Resident, New York City Office)

OF COUNSEL

Edward M. O'Brien (Resident, New York City Office)
Peter F. Vetro
Daniel F. Hayes
John P. Coogan

For Complete List of Firm Personnel, See General Section

For full biographical listings, see the Martindale-Hubbell Law Directory

---

SAWYER, DAVIS & HALPERN (AV)

600 Old Country Road, 11530
Telephone: 516-222-4567
Telecopier: 516-222-4585

MEMBER OF FIRM

James Sawyer

ASSOCIATE

Adam C. Demetri

For Complete List of Firm Personnel, See General Section

For full biographical listings, see the Martindale-Hubbell Law Directory

---

HAVERSTRAW, Rockland Co.

MILLER & MILLER, P.C. (AV)

90 New Main Street, P.O. Box 360, 10927
Telephone: 914-429-5371

Samuel Miller
Daniel Miller

Phyllis Weinstein Shandler

For full biographical listings, see the Martindale-Hubbell Law Directory

---

HUNTINGTON, Suffolk Co.

GOLDSTEIN & RUBINTON, P.C. (AV)

18 West Carver Street, 11743
Telephone: 516-421-9051
Telefax: 516-421-9122

Arthur Goldstein
Ronald L. Goldstein
Peter D. Rubinton
S. Russ Di Fazio

References: Chemical Bank; New York Trust Co.; Town of Huntingdon.

For full biographical listings, see the Martindale-Hubbell Law Directory

---

*ITHACA,** Tompkins Co.

WIGGINS & MASSON (AV)

308 North Tioga Street, P.O. Box 399, 14851
Telephone: 607-272-0479
Telecopier: 607-273-0502

MEMBERS OF FIRM

Walter J. Wiggins
Robin Abrahamson Masson

ASSOCIATE

Eileen M. McGlinchey Fahey

Approved Attorneys for: Ticor Title Guaranty Corp.
References: Tompkins County Trust Co.; Citizens Savings Bank.

For full biographical listings, see the Martindale-Hubbell Law Directory

---

MELVILLE, Suffolk Co.

GANDIN, SCHOTSKY & RAPPAPORT, P.C. (AV)

445 Broad Hollow Road, 11747
Telephone: 516-293-2300
Fax: 516-293-2918

Michael I. Gandin
Arnold M. Schotsky
Charles J. Rappaport
Michael R. Greene
Michael G. Glass

Margery Weinroth
Robert A. Katz
Kevin E. Balfe
Robert A. Isler
Michael S. Levine
Edmond C. Chakmakian

For full biographical listings, see the Martindale-Hubbell Law Directory

---

*MINEOLA,** Nassau Co.

SHAYNE, DACHS, STANISCI, CORKER & SAUER (AV)

250 Old Country Road, 11501
Telephone: 516-747-1100
Telecopier: 516-747-1185

(See Next Column)

SHAYNE, DACHS, STANISCI, CORKER & SAUER—*Continued*

MEMBERS OF FIRM

Moe Levine (1968-1974)
Neil T. Shayne
Norman H. Dachs
Thomas W. Stanisci
W. Russell Corker
Brian J. Sauer
Kenneth J. Landau
Jonathan A. Dachs

Naomi R. Nathan

For full biographical listings, see the Martindale-Hubbell Law Directory

*NEW YORK,** New York Co.

BAUMAN & KUNKIS, P.C. (AV)

225 West 34th Street, 10122
Telephone: 212-564-3555
Fax: 212-564-2841

Bert Bauman
Roger M. Kunkis
Rose Marie Cavera

For full biographical listings, see the Martindale-Hubbell Law Directory

COSTELLO, SHEA & GAFFNEY (AV)

One Battery Park Plaza, 10004
Telephone: 212-483-9600
Fax: 212-344-7680

MEMBERS OF FIRM

Joseph M. Costello
Mortimer C. Shea
Frederick N. Gaffney
Steven E. Garry
William A. Goldstein
Donald J. Scialabba
Paul E. Blutman
Alan T. Blutman

ASSOCIATES

Robert R. Arena
Edward S. Benson
J Mcgarry Costello
Mario J. DiRe
Leo V. Duval, III
Cathy Ann Gallagher
Jozef K. Goscilo
Adam Charles Kandell
Timothy M. McCann
Kevin B. McHugh
Samuel Mark Mizrahi
Margaret Sullivan O'Connell
Manuel Ortega
John F. Parker
Neil B. Ptashnik
David Schrager
Lydia P. Shure
David N. Zane
Craig F. Wilson
Brian G. Winter

OF COUNSEL

James F. Corcoran

For full biographical listings, see the Martindale-Hubbell Law Directory

DEBLASIO & ALTON, P.C. (AV)

Woolworth Building, 233 Broadway, 10279
Telephone: 212-732-2620
Fax: 212-571-2045

Peter E. DeBlasio
Walter G. Alton, Jr.
Steven A. Epstein
Rhoda Grossberg Faller
Stephen S. La Rocca

For full biographical listings, see the Martindale-Hubbell Law Directory

DANIEL DONNELLY (AV)

521 Fifth Avenue Suite 1740, 10175
Telephone: 212-757-6454
Garrison, New York Office: Garrison's Landing, P.O. Box 253. 10524.
Telephone: 914-424-3877.
Facsimile: 914-424-3968

For full biographical listings, see the Martindale-Hubbell Law Directory

EVANS, ORR, LAFFAN, TORRES & DEMAGGIO, P.C. (AV)

225 Broadway, Suite 1405, 10007-3001
Telephone: 212-267-1800
FAX: 212-964-0958
Long Island Office: 25 Jackson Avenue, Syosset, 11791.
Telephone: 516-364-0300.

Walter G. Evans (1886-1981)
William F. Laffan, Jr.
Frank Torres
David DeMaggio

Seymour I. Yanofsky
Eugene Guarneri
Angelantonio Bianchi
Cari E. Pepkin
Maura V. Laffan
Christian A. Rofrano
Paula T. Amsterdam
Donald G. Derrico
Patricia Ann Cavagnaro
Thomas P. Ryan, Jr.
Lambert C Sheng
Richard Fama

OF COUNSEL

Steven DeMaggio

OF COUNSEL EMERITUS

Alexander Orr, Jr.
Alfred V. Norton, Jr.
Edward J. Pacelli

(See Next Column)

LEGAL SUPPORT PERSONNEL
PARALEGALS

Alicia Carrano
Susan Dunphy
Damian L. Calemmo
Diana L. Cohen

For full biographical listings, see the Martindale-Hubbell Law Directory

GAIR, GAIR, CONASON, STEIGMAN & MACKAUF (AV)

80 Pine Street, 10005
Telephone: 212-943-1090

MEMBERS OF FIRM

Robert L. Conason
Herbert H. Hirschhorn
Seymour Boyers
Herman Schmertz
Ernest R. Steigman
Stephen H. Mackauf
Warren J. Willinger
Ronald Berson
Jerome I. Katz
David G. Miller
Candice Singer Ram
Jeffrey B. Bloom
Anthony H. Gair
Mary Nicholls
Gayle F. Bertoldo
Vincent F. Maher
Robert E. Godosky
Rick S. Conason
Ben B. Rubinowitz

COUNSEL

Harriet E. Gair

For full biographical listings, see the Martindale-Hubbell Law Directory

GANZ, HOLLINGER & TOWE (AV)

1394 Third Avenue, 10021
Telephone: 212-517-5500; 838-9600
Cable Address: "Ganzlaw New York"
Telex: 852970 GANZLAW NYK
FAX: 212-772-2720; 772-2216

David L. Ganz
Jerrietta R. Hollinger
Teri Noel Towe

ASSOCIATE

Nancy A. Torres (Not admitted in NY)

For full biographical listings, see the Martindale-Hubbell Law Directory

GINSBERG & BROOME (AV)

225 Broadway, Suite 3105, 10007
Telephone: 212-227-4225

Robert M. Ginsberg
Alvin H. Broome

ASSOCIATE

Michael Finkelstein

For full biographical listings, see the Martindale-Hubbell Law Directory

JULIEN & SCHLESINGER, P.C. (AV)

150 William Street, 19th Floor, 10038
Telephone: 212-962-8020

Alfred S. Julien (1910-1989)
Stuart A. Schlesinger
Denise Mortner Kranz
Ira M. Newman
David B. Turret

OF COUNSEL

Louis Fusco, Jr.

Mary Elizabeth Burns
Richard A. Robbins
Michael J. Taub
Marla L. Schiff
Alvin Craig Gordon
Adam Schlesinger
Robert J. Epstein

For full biographical listings, see the Martindale-Hubbell Law Directory

KOPFF, NARDELLI & DOPF (AV)

440 Ninth Avenue, 10001
Telephone: 212-244-2999
Telecopier: 212-643-0862

MEMBERS OF FIRM

Peter C. Kopff
Camillo Nardelli (1936-1987)
Glenn W. Dopf
Scott F. Morgan
Charles K. Faillace
Joseph R. Cammarosano
Victoria A. Lombardi
Michael L. Manci
Martin B. Adams

ASSOCIATES

Eugene A. Ward
Mary E. Pearson
Joseph T. Belevich
Catherine R. Richter
Susan D. Noble
John A. Orbon
Denise D. Sapanara
Ronnie Michelle Grill
Richard J. Valent
Edward J. Arevalo
Edward A. Flores
Peter S. Williams
Tara K. Curcillo
Jonathan Adam Judd

Representative Clients: Aetna Casualty and Surety Co.; American International Group; Citicorp, U.S.A.; County of Nassau, State of New York; Franklin Hospital Medical Center; Guarantee National Insurance Co.;

(See Next Column)

KOPFF, NARDELLI & DOPF, *New York—Continued*

Lenox Hill Hospital; The May Department Stores Co.; Medical Inter-Insurance Exchange of New Jersey; Medical Liability Mutual Insurance Co.

For full biographical listings, see the Martindale-Hubbell Law Directory

LITMAN, ASCHE, LUPKIN, GIOIELLA & BASSIN (AV)

45 Broadway Atrium, 10006
Telephone: 212-809-4500
Telecopier: GP II, III (212) 509-8403

MEMBERS OF FIRM

Richard M. Asche
Jack T. Litman
Stanley N. Lupkin
Russell M. Gioiella
Steven Jay Bassin

ASSOCIATES

Mary Lou Chatterton
Frederick L. Sosinsky

OF COUNSEL

Alan C. Rothfeld
Ronald S. Pohl

For full biographical listings, see the Martindale-Hubbell Law Directory

STEVEN E. NORTH, P.C. (AV)

148 East 74th Street, 10021
Telephone: 212-861-5000
Telecopier: 212-861-4055

Steven E. North

For full biographical listings, see the Martindale-Hubbell Law Directory

QUELLER & FISHER (AV)

A Law Partnership including Professional Corporations
110 Wall Street, 10005-3851
Telephone: 212-422-3600
Cable Address: "Quelfish, New York"
Facsimile: 212-422-2828

MEMBERS OF FIRM

Fred Queller (P.C.)
Bertram D. Fisher (P.C.)
Walter F. Benson

ASSOCIATES

Ira Bartfield
Marshall Schmeizer
Kevin S. McDonald
Phillip P. Nikolis
Edmund L. Rothschild
Dorothy S. Morrill
David P. Horowitz
Glenn Verchick
Ira Fogelgaren
Frances I. Beaupierre (Not admitted in NY)

For full biographical listings, see the Martindale-Hubbell Law Directory

JEFFREY SAMEL & ASSOCIATES (AV)

120 Broadway, Suite 1755, 10271
Telephone: 212-587-9690
Fax: 212-587-9673

ASSOCIATES

Robert G. Spevack
Dorothy T. Zeman
Ricardo Rengifo
James H. O'Hare
David M. Samel
David S. Gary

OF COUNSEL

Richard A. Soberman

Representative Clients: New York City Transit Authority; New York City Housing Authority; Empire Insurance Co.; National General Insurance Co.; Federal Express Corp.; Shell Oil Corp.; American Building Maintenance Corp.

For full biographical listings, see the Martindale-Hubbell Law Directory

SCHNEIDER, KLEINICK, WEITZ, DAMASHEK, GODOSKY & GENTILE (AV)

233 Broadway, Fifth Floor, 10279-0003
Telephone: 212-553-9000
Fax: 212-804-0820

Ivan S. Schneider
Arnold L. Kleinick
Harvey Weitz
Philip M. Damashek
Richard Godosky
Anthony P. Gentile
Gregory J. Cannata
Robert B. Jackson
Brian J. Shoot

Richard B. Ancowitz
Jeffrey R. Brecker
Scott A. Buxbaum
Dawn S. DeWeil
Steven M. Fink
Steven Gold
Keith H. Gross
Wilma Guzman
Leslie Debra Kelmachter
Keith A. Kleinick
Matthew R. Kreinces
Ruth Frances Leve
Gerard Anthony Lucciola
Grace Carreras McCallen
Charles J. Nolet, Jr.
Harlan Platz

(See Next Column)

Lloyd M. Roberts
Paul Bryan Schneider
Perry D. Silver
Clifford J. Stern
Paul B. Weitz

For full biographical listings, see the Martindale-Hubbell Law Directory

SIMONSON HESS & LEIBOWITZ, P.C. (AV)

15 Maiden Lane, 10038
Telephone: 212-233-5000

Paul Simonson
Alan B. Leibowitz
Steven L. Hess

Nancy S. Stuzin
Kathleen Marie O'Neill
Jennifer Levine

For full biographical listings, see the Martindale-Hubbell Law Directory

WHITE, FLEISCHNER & FINO (AV)

195 Broadway, 10007
Telephone: 212-227-6292
Telex: 645255
Telecopier: 212-227-7812
Westfield, New Jersey Office: 215 North Avenue, West.
Telephone: 908-654-6266.
Telecopier: 908-654-3686.
London, England Office: Plantation House. 31/35 Fenchurch S. EC3M 3DX.
Telephone: 071-375-2037.
Telecopier: 071-375-2039.

MEMBERS OF FIRM

Allan P. White
Benjamin A. Fleischner
Paul A. Fino, Jr.
Robert G. Schenker
Marcia J. Lynn
Marisa Goetz

ASSOCIATES

Patti F. Potash
Mitchell R. Friedman
Mitchell L. Shadowitz
Debra E. Ruderman
David I. Blee
Sandra L. Bonder
Michael J. Asta
Stephanie M. Holzback
Mark R. Osherow
Virginia L. McGrane
Beth A. Goldklang
Sean Upton
Wendy K. Carrano
Nancy D. Lyness
Randy Scott Faust
Elizabeth C. Mirisola
Sheri E. Holland

LEGAL SUPPORT PERSONNEL

Darien Anderson (Paralegal)
Helen Wasey (Claims Consultant)

For full biographical listings, see the Martindale-Hubbell Law Directory

NYACK, Rockland Co.

MACCARTNEY, MACCARTNEY, KERRIGAN & MACCARTNEY (AV)

MacCartney Building, 13 North Broadway, P.O. Box 350, 10960
Telephone: 914-358-0074
Fax: 914-358-0793

MEMBERS OF FIRM

Harold Y. MacCartney (1901-1988)
Harold Y. MacCartney, Jr.
John D. MacCartney
William K. Kerrigan

ASSOCIATES

Christopher J. Walsh
Stephen M. Honan
Brigitte M. Gulliver
Phyllis A. Ingram
David Castagna
Harold Y. MacCartney, III
Anthony J. Mamo
Reginald H. Rutishauser

Local Trial Counsel for: Associated Mutual Insurance Co.; The Andover Cos.; County of Orange; Government Employees Insurance Co.; Maryland Casualty Co.; North American Specialty Insurance Co.; Orange and Rockland Utilities, Inc.; Preferred Mutual Insurance Co.; Utica Fire Insurance Co.

For full biographical listings, see the Martindale-Hubbell Law Directory

ONEONTA, Otsego Co.

LAW OFFICE OF JOHN SCARZAFAVA (AV)

48 Dietz Street, Suite C, 13820-5107
Telephone: 607-432-9341
Fax: 607-432-1986

John F. Scarzafava

ASSOCIATE

Elizabeth Ellen Little

Reference: Key Bank.

For full biographical listings, see the Martindale-Hubbell Law Directory

RHINEBECK, Dutchess Co.

STEVEN M. MELLEY (AV)

22 East Market Street, 12572
Telephone: 914-876-4057
Fax: 914-876-5745

Representative Client: First National Bank of Rhinebeck.

For full biographical listings, see the Martindale-Hubbell Law Directory

*ROCHESTER,** Monroe Co.

ROBERT J. MICHAEL (AV)

39 State Street, Suite 420, 14614
Telephone: 716-232-3460
Fax: 716-232-4583

OF COUNSEL

Mark H. Tiernan

Reference: Chemical Bank.

For full biographical listings, see the Martindale-Hubbell Law Directory

ROME, Oneida Co.

PAUL L. PILECKAS (AV)

Professional Building, 217 N. Washington Street, 13440
Telephone: 315-339-3020
Utica: 315-724-6381

Representative Clients: Don Davidson Motors, Inc.; Maple Lane Farms, Inc.; Cataldo Ready Mix, Inc.; Cataldo Bros., Inc.

For full biographical listings, see the Martindale-Hubbell Law Directory

SMITHTOWN, Suffolk Co.

GRESHIN, ZIEGLER & PRUZANSKY (AV)

199 East Main Street, P.O. Box 829, 11787
Telephone: 516-265-2550
Telecopier: 516-265-2832

Benjamin Greshin
Joel J. Ziegler
Joshua M. Pruzansky

ASSOCIATE

Joanne Skiadas

For full biographical listings, see the Martindale-Hubbell Law Directory

STANFORDVILLE, Dutchess Co.

WILLIAM E. STANTON (AV)

Village Centre, Route 82, P.O. Box 370, 12581
Telephone: 914-868-7514
FAX: 914-868-7761

Representative Clients: Dupont de Nemours & Co.; Millbrook School; Hanover Insurance Co.; New York Telephone Co.
Reference: Fishkill National Bank.

For full biographical listings, see the Martindale-Hubbell Law Directory

*STATEN ISLAND,** Richmond Co.

SIMONSON & COHEN, P.C. (AV)

4060 Amboy Road, 10308
Telephone: 718-948-2100
Telecopier: 718-356-2379

Sidney O. Simonson (1911-1986)
Robert M. Cohen
Daniel Cohen
James R. Cohen

Michael Adler
Lawrence J. Lorczak

For full biographical listings, see the Martindale-Hubbell Law Directory

*SYRACUSE,** Onondaga Co.

BOND, SCHOENECK & KING (AV)

18th Floor One Lincoln Center, 13202-1355
Telephone: 315-422-0121
Fax: 315-422-3598
Albany, New York Office: 111 Washington Avenue.
Telephone: 518-462-7421.
Fax: 518-462-7441.
Boca Raton, Florida Office: 5355 Town Center Road, Suite 1002.
Telephone: 407-368-1212.
Fax: 407-338-9955.
Naples, Florida Office: 1167 Third Street South.
Telephone: 813-262-6812.
Fax: 813-262-6908.
Oswego, New York Office: 130 East Second Street.
Telephone: 315-343-9116.
Fax: 315-343-1231.

(See Next Column)

Overland Park, Kansas Office: 7500 College Boulevard, Suite 910.
Telephone: 913-345-8001.
Fax: 913-345-9017.

MEMBERS OF FIRM

S. Paul Battaglia
Thomas D. Keleher
John D. Allen
John G. McGowan
Thomas E. Myers
Deborah H. Karalunas
Thomas R. Smith
Jonathan B. Fellows

General Counsel for: Syracuse University; Unity Mutual Life Insurance Co.; Manufacturers Association of Central New York.
Regional or Special Counsel for: Newhouse Broadcasting Corp. (WSYR, AM-FM); Syracuse Herald-Post Standard Newspapers.; Miller Brewing Co.; Allied Corp.; General Electric Co.; National Grange.

For Complete List of Firm Personnel, See General Section

For full biographical listings, see the Martindale-Hubbell Law Directory

GREENE AND REID (AV)

Brighton Hill, 892 Brighton Avenue, 13205
Telephone: 315-492-9665
FAX: 315-492-9741
Toll Free: 800-688-8189
Newark, New York Office: 124 Church Street.
Telephone: 315-331-5633.
Sackets Harbor, New York Office: 101 East Main Street.
Telephone: 315-646-2500.

MEMBERS OF FIRM

Arthur M. Greene
James E. Reid

LEGAL SUPPORT PERSONNEL

John M. Hogan
Polly Spring

Reference: Merchants National Bank & Trust Company of Syracuse.

For full biographical listings, see the Martindale-Hubbell Law Directory

HARTNETT LAW OFFICE (AV)

The Syracuse Building, Suite 208, 224 Harrison Street, 13202
Telephone: 315-478-5791
FAX: 315-478-0106

Robert W. Hartnett
Peter M. Hartnett

Reference: Chase Manhattan.

For full biographical listings, see the Martindale-Hubbell Law Directory

*UTICA,** Oneida Co.

DURR AND KEINZ (AV)

The Paul Building, 209 Elizabeth Street, 13501
Telephone: 315-735-6185
FAX: 315-797-5521

MEMBERS OF FIRM

Robert W. Durr (1927-1973)
Donald E. Keinz

Reference: Fleet Bank.

For full biographical listings, see the Martindale-Hubbell Law Directory

JULIAN & PERTZ, P.C. (AV)

1629 Oneida Street, 13501
Telephone: 315-797-5610
FAX: 315-797-7403

Robert F. Julian
Richard Pertz

Mildred E. Pelrine

LEGAL SUPPORT PERSONNEL

Tracey A. Wilkinson-Synakowski (Legal Assistant/Paralegal)
Barbara A. Grabski (Paralegal/Legal Assistant)
Nadine J. Fitch (Paralegal)

For full biographical listings, see the Martindale-Hubbell Law Directory

*WHITE PLAINS,** Westchester Co.

CERUSSI & SPRING, A PROFESSIONAL CORPORATION (AV)

One North Lexington Avenue, 10601-1700
Telephone: 914-948-1200
Cable Address: Cerspringlaw Whiteplainsnewyork
Facsimile: 914-948-1579
Greenwich, Connecticut Office: 66 Field Point Road.
Telephone: 203-661-4000.
Facsimile: 203-661-1197.

Michael A. Cerussi, Jr.
Joseph A. D'Avanzo
Ronald G. Crispi
Arthur J. Spring

(See Next Column)

CERUSSI & SPRING A PROFESSIONAL CORPORATION, *White Plains—Continued*

Thomas F. Cerussi
Denise M. Cossu
Kathleen A. DePalma
Mark C. Dillon
Michael P. Fitzgerald
Matthew K. Flanagan
Thomas A. Hayes, Jr.
Anne E. Kershaw
Steven R. Lau
John J.A.M. Loveless
Curt D. Marshall
Maria J. Morreale
Owen S. Mudge, Jr.
Jeffrey C. Nagle
(Not admitted in NY)
William J. Rizzo
Mary E. Toop
Gina M. Von Oehsen

For full biographical listings, see the Martindale-Hubbell Law Directory

CLARK, GAGLIARDI & MILLER, P.C. (AV)

Inns of Court Building, 99 Court Street, 10601
Telephone: 914-946-8900
Telecopier: 914-946-8960
New York, New York Office: Suite 2525, 230 Park Avenue.
Telephone: 914-926-8900.

Robert Y. Clark (1881-1961)
Frank M. Gagliardi (1886-1980)
Joseph F. Gagliardi (1911-1992)
Henry G. Miller
Lawrence T. D'Aloise, Jr.
Lucille A. Fontana
Robert J. Frisenda

Angela Morcone Giannini
Padraic D. Lee
Denise Liotta DeMarzo

OF COUNSEL

Morton B. Silberman

For full biographical listings, see the Martindale-Hubbell Law Directory

KEEGAN, KEEGAN & ASSOCIATES, P.C. (AV)

81 Main Street, 10601
Telephone: 914-949-7227
Telecopier: 914-681-0933

John W. Keegan
Raymond J. Keegan

John W. Keegan, Jr.
Barry R. Strutt
Michael D. Kessler

For full biographical listings, see the Martindale-Hubbell Law Directory

WILSON, BAVE, CONBOY, COZZA & COUZENS, P.C. (AV)

Two William Street, 10601
Telephone: 914-686-9010
Telecopier: 914-686-0873

William H. Bave (1919-1991)
Donald C. Wilson (1917-1994)
R. Kevin Conboy
William H. Bave, Jr.
Michael J. Cozza
John C. Couzens, Jr.
Michele A. Fournier
Joseph T. Jednak
Patricia Bave-Planell
Kevin D. Odell
Leo T. McGrath
Alexandra C. Karamitsos

LEGAL SUPPORT PERSONNEL

PARALEGAL

John R. Pearsall

Representative Clients: Royal Insurance; Kemper Insurance Co.; State Farm Mutual Automobile Insurance Co.; Continental National American Group; Utica Mutual Insurance Co.; Jefferson Insurance Co.; Nationwide Insurance Co.; Medical Liability Mutual Insurance Co.

For full biographical listings, see the Martindale-Hubbell Law Directory

NORTH CAROLINA

*ASHEVILLE,** Buncombe Co.

ELMORE & ELMORE, P.A. (AV)

53 North Market Street, 28801
Telephone: 704-253-1492
Fax: 704-253-9648

Bruce A. Elmore
Bruce A. Elmore, Jr.

Reed G. Williams

For full biographical listings, see the Martindale-Hubbell Law Directory

REYNOLDS & MCARTHUR (AV Ⓣ)

A Partnership including a Professional Corporation
The Jackson Building, 22 South Pack Square Suite 1200, 28801
Telephone: 704-254-8523
Fax: 704-254-3038
Macon, Georgia Office: 850 Walnut Street.
Telephone: 912-741-6000.
Fax: 912-742-0750.
Atlanta, Georgia Office: Suite 1080, One Buckhead Plaza, 3060 Peachtree Road, N.W.
Telephone: 404-240-0265.
Fax: 404-262-3557.

MEMBERS OF FIRM

W. Carl Reynolds (P.C.)
(Not admitted in NC)
Katherine L. McArthur
Charles M. Cork, III
(Not admitted in NC)
O. Wendell Horne, III
(Not admitted in NC)
Bradley J. Survant
(Not admitted in NC)
Steve Ray Warren

For full biographical listings, see the Martindale-Hubbell Law Directory

*BEAUFORT,** Carteret Co.

DAVIS, MURRELLE & LUMSDEN, P.A. (AV)

Beaufort Professional Center, 412 Front Street, P.O. Box 819, 28516
Telephone: 919-728-4080
FAX: 919-728-3235

Edward L. Murrelle
Treve B. Lumsden

Janet M. Lyles

OF COUNSEL

Warren J. Davis

Representative Clients: NationsBank; Cooperative Bank for Savings; Zapata Haynie Corp.; Roman Catholic Diocese of Raleigh for Carteret County; International Longshoreman's Association Local 1807; Town of Cedar Point; John Yancey Corp.; Morehead City Export Terminal, Inc.; Morehead City Docking Masters Assoc., Inc.; Crow Hill Farms, Inc.

For full biographical listings, see the Martindale-Hubbell Law Directory

CHAPEL HILL, Orange Co.

BERNHOLZ & HERMAN (AV)

Suite 300, The Center, 1506 East Franklin Street, 27514
Telephone: 919-929-7151
Fax: 919-929-3892

MEMBERS OF FIRM

Steven A. Bernholz
Roger B. Bernholz
G. Nicholas Herman

OF COUNSEL

J. Austin Lybrand, IV

For full biographical listings, see the Martindale-Hubbell Law Directory

LONG & LONG (AV)

116 Mallette Street, 27516
Telephone: 919-929-0408
Fax: 919-929-6819

MEMBERS OF FIRM

Lunsford Long
Florence J. Long

For full biographical listings, see the Martindale-Hubbell Law Directory

NORTHEN, BLUE, ROOKS, THIBAUT, ANDERSON & WOODS, L.L.P. (AV)

Suite 550, 100 Europa Center, P.O. Box 2208, 27515-2208
Telephone: 919-968-4441
Facsimile: 919-942-6603

MEMBERS OF FIRM

John A. Northen
J. William Blue, Jr.
David M. Rooks, III
Charles H. Thibaut
Charles T. L. Anderson
Jo Ann Ragazzo Woods
Carol J. Holcomb

ASSOCIATES

James C. Stanford
Gregory Herman-Giddens
Cheryl Y. Capron

References: Central Carolina Bank; The Village Bank; Investors Title Insurance Co.; First Union National Bank; Centura Bank; United Carolina Bank; BB&T; Balbirer & Coleman, CPA's.

For full biographical listings, see the Martindale-Hubbell Law Directory

*CHARLOTTE,** Mecklenburg Co.

BAILEY, PATTERSON, CADDELL, HART & BAILEY, P.A. (AV)

Suite 502, Cameron Brown Building, 301 South McDowell Street, 28204
Telephone: 704-333-8612
FAX: 704-333-5279

(See Next Column)

BAILEY, PATTERSON, CADDELL, HART & BAILEY P.A.—*Continued*

Allen A. Bailey
Michael A. Bailey
William J. Patterson
H. Morris Caddell, Jr.
Walter L. Hart, IV

Richard A. Culler
Emery E. Milliken
David C. Cordes
Martha L. Ramsay
Thomas D. Thompson

For full biographical listings, see the Martindale-Hubbell Law Directory

CAUDLE & SPEARS, P.A. (AV)

2600 Interstate Tower, 121 West Trade Street, 28202
Telephone: 704-377-1200
Telecopier: 704-338-5858

Lloyd C. Caudle
Harold C. Spears
Thad A. Throneburg
Patrick Jenkins
L. Cameron Caudle, Jr.
Nancy E. Walker
Timothy T. Leach
John A. Folmar
Sean M. Phelan
Jeffrey L. Helms

Counsel for: Bituminous Casualty Corp.; Baumann Springs A.G.; The A. G. Boone Co.; Consolidated Freightways; Employers Mutual Casualty Co.; Metromont Materials; Otis Elevator Co.; N.C. Farm Bureau Mutual Insurance Co.; Toyoda Textile Machinery, Inc.; U. S. Bottlers Machinery Co.

For full biographical listings, see the Martindale-Hubbell Law Directory

TIM L. HARRIS AND ASSOCIATES (AV)

4000 Tuckaseegee Road, 28208
Telephone: 704-392-4111
Fax: 704-391-1905
Gastonia, North Carolina Office: 223 West Main Avenue, P.O. Box 249.
Telephone: 704-864-3409.
Fax: 704-853-1040.

MEMBER OF FIRM

Tim L. Harris
Jerry Neil Ragan

ASSOCIATES

T. Scott White
William K. Goldfarb
Stephen M. Coe (Resident)

For full biographical listings, see the Martindale-Hubbell Law Directory

*DURHAM,** Durham Co.

GLENN, MILLS & FISHER, P.A. (AV)

Suite 709, South Bank Building, 400 West Main Street, P.O. Drawer 3865, 27702-3865
Telephone: 919-683-2135
FAX: 919-688-9339

Robert B. Glenn, Jr.
William S. Mills
Stewart W. Fisher

For full biographical listings, see the Martindale-Hubbell Law Directory

*FAYETTEVILLE,** Cumberland Co.

BERRY & BYRD (AV)

The Sedberry - Holmes House Courthouse Plaza, 232 Person Street, Drawer 2797, 28302-2797
Telephone: 910-323-2555
FAX: 910-323-9694

MEMBERS OF FIRM

H. Dolph Berry
Wade E. Byrd

Representative Clients: Thomas Investment, Inc.; Bill Ellis Realtors; Harleysville Insurance Co.; Falcon Children's Home; Town of Falcon; Avco Mortgage and Acceptance Services; Nations Bank, N.A.; New East Bank of Cape Fear.
References: Nations Bank, N.A.; New East Bank of Cape Fear.

For full biographical listings, see the Martindale-Hubbell Law Directory

*GASTONIA,** Gaston Co.

TIM L. HARRIS AND ASSOCIATES (AV)

223 West Main Avenue, P.O. Box 249, 28053-0249
Telephone: 704-864-3409
Fax: 704-853-1040
Charlotte, North Carolina Office: 4000 Tuckaseegee Road.
Telephone: 704-392-4111.

MEMBERS OF FIRM

Tim L. Harris
Jerry Neil Ragan

ASSOCIATES

T. Scott White
Russell L. Needell
William K. Goldfarb
Stephen M. Coe

For full biographical listings, see the Martindale-Hubbell Law Directory

*GREENSBORO,** Guilford Co.

VANCE BARRON, JR. (AV)

301 South Greene Street, Suite 310, 27401
Telephone: 910-274-4782
FAX: 910-379-8592
Mailing Address: P.O. Box 2370, Greensboro, NC, 27402-2370

For full biographical listings, see the Martindale-Hubbell Law Directory

GREESON, GRIFFIN & ASSOCIATES (AV)

400 West Market Street, Suite 300, P.O. Box 2460, 27402
Telephone: 910-370-4800
Fax: 910-370-0305

Harold F. Greeson
Mark F. Griffin

Christopher C. Kessler
George Podgorny, Jr.

For full biographical listings, see the Martindale-Hubbell Law Directory

HENSON HENSON BAYLISS & SUE (AV)

1610 First Union Tower, P.O. Box 3525, 27402
Telephone: 910-275-0587
Facsimile: 910-273-2585

MEMBERS OF FIRM

Perry C. Henson
Perry C. Henson, Jr.
Jack B. Bayliss, Jr.
Gary K. Sue
Walter K. Burton

ASSOCIATES

Daniel L. Deuterman
Brian A. Buchanan
Miriam S. Forbis
David K. Williams, Jr.

Representative Clients: Allstate Insurance Co.; The Home Indemnity Company; Kmart Corporation; Nationwide Mutual Insurance Co.; N.C. Farm Bureau Mutual Ins. Co.; Old Dominion Freight Line; Wausau Insurance Company.

For full biographical listings, see the Martindale-Hubbell Law Directory

MCNAIRY, CLIFFORD & CLENDENIN (AV)

127 North Greene Street, Suite 300, 27401
Telephone: 910-378-1212
FAX: 910-333-9820

MEMBER OF FIRM

Harry H. Clendenin, III

For full biographical listings, see the Martindale-Hubbell Law Directory

*GREENVILLE,** Pitt Co.

MARVIN K. BLOUNT, JR. (AV)

400 West First Street, P.O. Drawer 58, 27835-0058
Telephone: 919-752-6000
FAX: 919-752-2174

ASSOCIATES

Joseph T. Edwards
James F. Hopf
Sharron R. Edwards

Reference: Branch Banking & Trust Co., Greenville, N.C.

For full biographical listings, see the Martindale-Hubbell Law Directory

*HILLSBOROUGH,** Orange Co.

COLEMAN, GLEDHILL & HARGRAVE, P.C. (AV)

129 East Tryon Street, P.O. Drawer 1529, 27278
Telephone: 919-732-2196
FAX: 919-732-7997

Alonzo B. Coleman, Jr.
Geoffrey E. Gledhill
Douglas Hargrave

Kim K. Steffan
Janet B. Dutton
Douglas P. Thoren

For full biographical listings, see the Martindale-Hubbell Law Directory

MOREHEAD CITY, Carteret Co.

BENNETT, MCCONKEY, THOMPSON & MARQUARDT, P.A. (AV)

1007 Shepard Street, P.O. Drawer 189, 28557
Telephone: 919-726-4114
FAX: 919-726-7975

Thomas S. Bennett
Samuel A. McConkey, Jr.
James W. Thompson, III
Dennis M. Marquardt

Approved Attorneys For: Lawyers Title Insurance Corp.
Reference: First Citizens Bank & Trust Co.

For full biographical listings, see the Martindale-Hubbell Law Directory

*RALEIGH,** Wake Co.

BAILEY & DIXON (AV)

2500 Two Hannover Square, 434 Fayetteville Street Mall, P.O. Box 1351, 27602
Telephone: 919-828-0731
Facsimile: 919-828-6592

MEMBERS OF FIRM

Ralph McDonald
Gary S. Parsons
Carson Carmichael, III
Dorothy V. Kibler
Alan J. Miles
Patricia P. Kerner
Cathleen M. Plaut
David S. Coats

OF COUNSEL

J. Ruffin Bailey
Wright T. Dixon, Jr.
James H. Walker (1920-1994)
David M. Britt

ASSOCIATES

Marcus B. Liles, III
Renee C. Riggsbee
Denise Stanford Haskell
Kenyann G. Brown
Christopher L. Mewborn
Sylvia Stanley Wood

Representative Clients: Employers Casualty Co.; North Carolina League of Municipalities Risk Management Services; Lawyers Mutual Liability Insurance Company of North Carolina; Aetna Life and Casualty Insurance Company; Nationwide Insurance Company; Liberty Mutual Insurance Co.; Erie Insurance Company; Jefferson-Pilot Fire and Casualty Co.; ITT Hartford Insurance Group; Scottsdale Insurance Co.

For full biographical listings, see the Martindale-Hubbell Law Directory

BLANCHARD, TWIGGS, ABRAMS & STRICKLAND, P.A. (AV)

First Union Capitol Center, 150 Fayetteville Street Mall, 11th Floor, P.O. Drawer 30, 27602
Telephone: 919-828-4357
FAX: 919-833-7924

Howard F. Twiggs
Douglas B. Abrams
Donald R. Strickland
Jerome P. Trehy, Jr.

Margaret Smith Abrams
Robert O. Jenkins
Karen M. Rabenau

OF COUNSEL

Charles F. Blanchard
Donald H. Beskind

For full biographical listings, see the Martindale-Hubbell Law Directory

BURNS, DAY & PRESNELL, P.A. (AV)

Suite 560, 2626 Glenwood Avenue, P.O. Box 10867, 27605
Telephone: 919-782-1441
Fax: 919-782-2311

David W. Boone
James M. Day
Daniel C. Higgins
Greg L. Hinshaw
Lacy M. Presnell III
Susan F. Vick

OF COUNSEL

F. Kent Burns

For full biographical listings, see the Martindale-Hubbell Law Directory

CRANFILL, SUMNER & HARTZOG (AV)

Hillsborough Place, 225 Hillsborough Street, Suite 300, P.O. Box 27808, 27611
Telephone: 919-828-5100
Fax: 919-828-2277
Charlotte, North Carolina Office: 212 North McDowell Street, Suite 200.
Telephone: 704-332-8300.
Fax: 704-377-8880.

MEMBERS OF FIRM

Paul L. Cranfill
Robert W. Sumner
Dan M. Hartzog
Alene M. Mercer
Richard T. Boyette
David D. Ward
Patricia L. Holland
David H. Batten
H. Lee Evans, Jr.
C. D. Taylor Pace
Samuel H. Poole, Jr. (Resident, Charlotte Office)
Susan K. Burkhart
Buxton S. Copeland
P. Collins Barwick, III
Robert H. Griffin

ASSOCIATES

Kari L. Russwurm
David A. Rhoades
Sheila M. Bossier
M. Andrew Avram (Resident, Charlotte Office)
Brady W. Wells
Anthony T. Lathrop (Resident at Charlotte Office)
Gregory M. Kash
Joseph B. Chambliss, Jr.
Scott J. Lasso
W. Scott Fuller
Nicholas Peter Valaoras (Resident, Charlotte Office)
Robin H. Terry
William J. Garrity (Resident, Charlotte Office)
Edward C. LeCarpentier, III

Representative Clients: Continental Insurance Companies; Great American Insurance Group; Hartford Accident & Indemnity Co.; Liberty Mutual Insurance Co.

(See Next Column)

For full biographical listings, see the Martindale-Hubbell Law Directory

FULLER, BECTON, BILLINGS, SLIFKIN & BELL, P.A. (AV)

4020 Westchase Boulevard Suite 575, 27607
Telephone: 919-755-1068
FAX: 919-828-7543

James C. Fuller, Jr.
Charles L. Becton
James G. Billings
Anne R. Slifkin

Asa L. Bell, Jr.
Maria J. Mangano
Michele L. Flowers

For full biographical listings, see the Martindale-Hubbell Law Directory

JOHNNY S. GASKINS (AV)

150 Fayetteville Street Suite 2700, 27601
Telephone: 919-831-8717
Facsimile: 919-831-4755

For full biographical listings, see the Martindale-Hubbell Law Directory

HOWARD, FROM, STALLINGS & HUTSON, P.A. (AV)

Suite 400, 4000 WestChase Boulevard, P.O. Box 12347, 27607
Telephone: 919-833-2983
Fax: 919-834-3481
New Bern, North Carolina Office: 405 Middle Street, P.O. Box 975.
Telephones: 919-633-3006; 800-822-4182.
FAX: 919-633-3097.

Edward Cader Howard
I. Allan From
Joseph H. Stallings
John N. Hutson, Jr.
William M. Black, Jr.
Beth Ferebee Atkins (Resident, New Bern Office)
Catherine C. McLamb
Peggy S. Vincent
B. Joan Davis
Charles H. Livaudais, Jr.
Kory J. Goldsmith
Scott A. Miskimon
Lewis E. Lamb III

Representative Client: Branch Banking and Trust Co.

For full biographical listings, see the Martindale-Hubbell Law Directory

PATTERSON, DILTHEY, CLAY & BRYSON, L.L.P. (AV)

4020 WestChase Boulevard, Suite 550, 27607
Telephone: 919-821-4020
Fax: 919-829-0055
Wilmington, North Carolina Office: 116 Princess Street.
Telephone: 910-762-6544.
Fax: 910-762-4241.

MEMBERS OF FIRM

Grady S. Patterson, Jr. (Retired)
Ronald C. Dilthey
Robert M. Clay
E. C. Bryson, Jr.
Richard Bruce Conely, Sr.
Reid Russell
Stuart L. Egerton (Resident, Wilmington Office)
Mark E. Anderson

ASSOCIATES

Donna Renfrow Rutala
Kathleen M. Millikan
Phillip J. Anthony
G. Lawrence Reeves, Jr.
Jonathan E. Hall
Erle E. Peacock, Jr.
Charles George

Representative Clients: Continental Insurance Companies; Great American Insurance Group; Hartford Accident & Indemnity Co.; Liberty Mutual Insurance Co.

For full biographical listings, see the Martindale-Hubbell Law Directory

PIPKIN & KNOTT, L.L.P. (AV)

100 East Six Forks Road, Suite 308, 27609-7752
Telephone: 919-783-5900
Telecopier: 919-783-9650

MEMBERS OF FIRM

Ashmead P. Pipkin
Joe T. Knott, III
Michael Wood Clark

For full biographical listings, see the Martindale-Hubbell Law Directory

PHILIP O. REDWINE, P.A. (AV)

Capital Club Building, 16 West Martin Street, Suite 700, P.O. Box 1030, 27601
Telephone: 919-831-1312
Telecopier: 919-831-1327

Philip O. Redwine

For full biographical listings, see the Martindale-Hubbell Law Directory

WALLACE, CREECH, SARDA & ZAYTOUN, L.L.P. (AV)

Suite 390, 3605 Glenwood Avenue, P.O. Box 12065, 27605
Telephone: 919-782-9322
Fax: 919-782-8113

(See Next Column)

WALLACE, CREECH, SARDA & ZAYTOUN L.L.P.—*Continued*

MEMBERS OF FIRM

John R. Wallace
Paul P. Creech
Peter J. Sarda
Robert E. Zaytoun
Richard P. Nordan
Richard T. Fountain, III

ASSOCIATE

Patricia Wilson Medynski

Representative Clients: United Carolina Bank; Wachovia Bank of N.C., N.A.; Professional Mail Services, Inc.; Triangle Rent A Car, Inc.; Telamon Corp.; Planning & Design Associates, P.A.; Consolidated Administrators, Inc.; KMart Corp.; Novopharm, Ltd., an Ontario Corporation; National Security Service, Inc.

For full biographical listings, see the Martindale-Hubbell Law Directory

*SMITHFIELD,** Johnston Co.

ARMSTRONG & ARMSTRONG, P.A. (AV)

P.O. Box 27, 27577-4352
Telephone: 919-934-1575
FAX: 919-934-1846

L. Lamar Armstrong, Jr.
Angela D. Matney

For full biographical listings, see the Martindale-Hubbell Law Directory

*WILMINGTON,** New Hanover Co.

BOYLE, CARTER & GAINES (AV)

720 Market Street, 28401
Telephone: 910-762-2468
FAX: 910-762-9652

MEMBERS OF FIRM

Karen Paden Boyle
Lori A. Gaines

For full biographical listings, see the Martindale-Hubbell Law Directory

YOW, CULBRETH & FOX (AV)

102 North Fifth Avenue, P.O. Drawer 479, 28401
Telephone: 910-762-2421
FAX: 910-251-9247

MEMBERS OF FIRM

Edgar L. Yow (1902-1983)
Cicero P. Yow (1914-1990)
Lionel L. Yow
Stephen E. Culbreth
Douglas A. Fox
Jerry A. Mannen, Jr.

OF COUNSEL

William Allen Cobb

Representative Client: General Motors Acceptance Corp.
References: Central Carolina Bank; First Union National Bank; NCNB National Bank of North Carolina; Southern National Bank; United Carolina Bank.

For full biographical listings, see the Martindale-Hubbell Law Directory

ZIMMER AND ZIMMER, L.L.P. (AV)

111 Princess Street, P.O. Box 2628, 28402
Telephone: 910-763-4669
Telecopier: 910-762-1999

MEMBERS OF FIRM

Herbert J. Zimmer
Jeffrey Lee Zimmer
Melinda Haynie Crouch
Maura A. McCaughey

Reference: Centura Bank; Wachovia Bank of North Carolina, N.A.

For full biographical listings, see the Martindale-Hubbell Law Directory

*WINSTON-SALEM,** Forsyth Co.

WHITE AND CRUMPLER (AV)

11 West Fourth Street, 27101
Telephone: 910-725-1304
FAX: 910-761-8845

MEMBERS OF FIRM

James G. White (1924-1974)
Fred G. Crumpler, Jr.
G. Edgar Parker
David B. Freedman
Dudley A. Witt

ASSOCIATES

Joan E. Brodish
Teresa Hier

OF COUNSEL

Frank M. Armstrong (1900-1979)
Barbara C. Westmoreland
Clyde C. Randolph, Jr.

Reference: Wachovia Bank and Trust Co., N.A., Winston-Salem, North Carolina.

For full biographical listings, see the Martindale-Hubbell Law Directory

NORTH DAKOTA

*BISMARCK,** Burleigh Co.

FLECK, MATHER & STRUTZ, LTD. (AV)

Sixth Floor, Norwest Bank Building, 400 East Broadway, P.O. Box 2798, 58502
Telephone: 701-223-6585
Telecopier: 701-222-4853

William A. Strutz
Gary R. Wolberg
Steven A. Storslee
Robert J. Udland
Curtis L. Wike
Charles S. Miller, Jr.
DeeNelle Louise Ruud

Representative Clients: ITT Hartford; American International Group; CNA Insurance Cos.; PHICO Insurance Co.; North Dakota Insurance Reserve Fund; Continental Insurance Co.; Employers Mutual Insurance Cos.; Firemen's Fund; National Farmers Union; Royal Insurance Co.

For Complete List of Firm Personnel, See General Section

For full biographical listings, see the Martindale-Hubbell Law Directory

PETERSON, SCHMITZ, MOENCH & SCHMIDT, A PROFESSIONAL CORPORATION (AV)

Second Floor, Suite 200, 116 North Fourth Street, P.O. Box 2076, 58502-2076
Telephone: 701-224-0400
Fax: 701-224-0399

David L. Peterson
Orell D. Schmitz
Dale W. Moench
William D. Schmidt

OF COUNSEL

Gerald Glaser

LEGAL SUPPORT PERSONNEL

Vicki J. Kunz
Traci L. Albers

For full biographical listings, see the Martindale-Hubbell Law Directory

*FARGO,** Cass Co.

CONMY, FESTE, BOSSART, HUBBARD & CORWIN, LTD. (AV)

400 Norwest Center, Fourth Street and Main Avenue, 58126
Telephone: 701-293-9911
Fax: 701-293-3133

Charles A. Feste
David R. Bossart
Paul M. Hubbard
Wickham Corwin
Kim E. Brust
Lauris N. Molbert
Michael M. Thomas
Robert J. Schultz
Nancy J. Morris
Jiming Zhu

OF COUNSEL

E. T. Conmy, Jr.

State Counsel for: Metropolitan Life Insurance Company.
Representative Clients: Ford Motor Credit Co.; Norwest Corporation Region VII Banks (North Dakota & Minnesota West); U.S. Gypsum Co.
Insurance: American Hardware Insurance Group; Great American Insurance Companies; The Maryland.

For full biographical listings, see the Martindale-Hubbell Law Directory

LEE HAGEN LAW OFFICE, LTD. (AV)

902 28th Street South, P.O. Box 3143, 58108-3143
Telephone: 701-293-8425
FAX: 701-293-0834

Leland F. Hagen

H. Patrick Weir, Jr.
Paul D. Johnson

Reference: Norwest Bank, Fargo.

For full biographical listings, see the Martindale-Hubbell Law Directory

MARING LAW OFFICE, P.C. (AV)

1220 Main Avenue, Suite 105, P.O. Box 2103, 58107-2103
Telephone: 701-237-5297
Fax: 701-235-2268

Mary Muehlen Maring
Michael J. Williams
David S. Maring

For full biographical listings, see the Martindale-Hubbell Law Directory

NILLES, HANSEN & DAVIES, LTD. (AV)

1800 Radisson Tower, P.O. Box 2626, 58108
Telephone: 701-237-5544

(See Next Column)

NILLES, HANSEN & DAVIES LTD., *Fargo—Continued*

Donald R. Hansen
Stephen W. Plambeck
Leo F. J. Wilking

For Complete List of Firm Personnel, See General Section

For full biographical listings, see the Martindale-Hubbell Law Directory

VOGEL, BRANTNER, KELLY, KNUTSON, WEIR & BYE, LTD. (AV)

502 First Avenue North, P.O. Box 1389, 58107
Telephone: 701-237-6983
Facsimile: 701-237-0847

John D. Kelly
Carlton J. Hunke
Mart Daniel Vogel
Harlan G. Fuglesten
Pamela J. Hermes
W. Todd Haggart
Lori J. Beck
Bruce Douglas Quick
Charles Alan Stock

Representative Clients: American Family Insurance Group; CIGNA Companies; CNA Insurance Company; Dakota Fire Insurance Company; Home Insurance Company; Midwest Medical Insurance Company; Milbank State Automobile Insurance Company; National Farmers Union Insurance Company; Phico Insurance Company; St. Paul Insurance Companies.

For Complete List of Firm Personnel, See General Section

For full biographical listings, see the Martindale-Hubbell Law Directory

OHIO

*BOWLING GREEN,** Wood Co.

SPITLER, VOGTSBERGER & HUFFMAN (AV)

131 East Court Street, 43402-2495
Telephone: 419-352-2535
FAX: 419-353-8728
Rossford, Ohio Office: 932 Dixie Highway.
Telephone: 419-666-7130.

MEMBERS OF FIRM

Emmett V. Spitler
Daniel T. Spitler
Robert E. Spitler
Thomas H. Vogtsberger
Rex H. Huffman
Diane Rausch Huffman

Representative Clients: First Federal Savings & Loan Association of Wood County; Prudential Insurance Company of America; The Mutual Benefit Life Insurance Co.; John Hancock Mutual Life Insurance Co.; Equitable Life Assurance Society of the U.S.; Minnesota Mutual Life Insurance Co.

For full biographical listings, see the Martindale-Hubbell Law Directory

*CINCINNATI,** Hamilton Co.

ALTMAN & CALARDO CO. A LEGAL PROFESSIONAL ASSOCIATION (AV)

Suite 1006, 414 Walnut Street, 45202
Telephone: 513-721-2180
Fax: 513-721-2299

D. David Altman
Stephen P. Calardo

Amy J. Leonard
Kevin P. Braig

For full biographical listings, see the Martindale-Hubbell Law Directory

JAMES J. CHALFIE CO., L.P.A. (AV)

36 East Seventh Street, Suite 1600, 45202
Telephone: 513-381-8616
FAX: 513-381-8619

James J. Chalfie

For Complete List of Firm Personnel, See General Section

For full biographical listings, see the Martindale-Hubbell Law Directory

DINSMORE & SHOHL (AV)

1900 Chemed Center, 255 East Fifth Street, 45202-3172
Telephone: 513-977-8200
FAX: 513-977-8141
Florence, Kentucky Office: Turfway Ridge Office Park, 7300 Turfway Road, Suite 430 41042-1355.
Telephone: 606-283-0515.
FAX: 606-283-6017.
Dayton, Ohio Office: 500 Courthouse Plaza, S.W., 10 N. Ludlow Street, 45402-1834.
Telephone: 513-228-8012.
FAX: 513-461-2543.

(See Next Column)

Columbus, Ohio Office: NBD Bank Building, Suite 330, 175 South Third Street, 43215-5134.
Telephone: 614-224-7887.
FAX: 614-224-7882.

MEMBERS OF FIRM

Gordon C. Greene
Michael D. Eagen
Deborah R. Lydon
Nancy J. Gill
Stephen K. Shaw
Lawrence A. Flemer
K. C. Green

ASSOCIATES

Andrew C. Osterbrock
Frederick M. Erny
Steven H. Ray
Stephen M. Rosenberger
John J. Hoffmann (Resident, Dayton, Ohio Office)
Michael L. Squillace (Resident, Columbus, Ohio Office)
Thomas A. Prewitt (Resident, Florence, Kentucky Office)
Nancy Korb Griffiths
Ann Collins Hindman
Michael E. Finucane
William A. Dickhaut
Christopher L. Riegler (Resident, Dayton, Ohio Office)

For Complete List of Firm Personnel, See General Section

For full biographical listings, see the Martindale-Hubbell Law Directory

HERMANIES, MAJOR, CASTELLI & GOODMAN (AV)

Suite 740-Cincinnati Club Building, 30 Garfield Place, 45202-4396
Telephone: 513-621-2345
Fax: 513-621-2519

MEMBERS OF FIRM

John H. Hermanies
Ronald D. Major
Anthony D. Castelli
Richard Lanahan Goodman
Mark Allen Ferestad

References: Southern Ohio Bank; First National Bank of Cincinnati; The PNC Bank.

For full biographical listings, see the Martindale-Hubbell Law Directory

KEPLEY, MACCONNELL & EYRICH A LEGAL PROFESSIONAL ASSOCIATION (AV)

Formerly Clark & Eyrich
2200 Ameritrust Center, 525 Vine Street, 45202
Telephone: 513-241-5540; 621-1045
FAX: 513-241-8111; 621-0038

Stephen T. MacConnell
Augustine Giglio
Wm. Eric Minamyer

Representative Clients and References furnished upon request.

For full biographical listings, see the Martindale-Hubbell Law Directory

RICHARD D. LAWRENCE AND ASSOCIATES CO., L.P.A. (AV)

Suite 2020, CBLD Building, 36 East Seventh Street, 45202
Telephone: 513-651-4130
FAX: Available upon request

Richard D. Lawrence
James B. McGrath, Jr.

Jill Gustafson

For full biographical listings, see the Martindale-Hubbell Law Directory

REISENFELD & STATMAN (AV)

Auburn Barrister House, 2355 Auburn Avenue, 45219
Telephone: 513-381-6810
FAX: 513-381-0255

Sylvan P. Reisenfeld
Alan J. Statman

John L. Day, Jr.
Melisa J. Richter
Bradley A. Reisenfeld
Rosemary E. Scollard
John Schmidt

For full biographical listings, see the Martindale-Hubbell Law Directory

GATES T. RICHARDS (AV)

3807 Carew Tower, 441 Vine Street, 45202
Telephone: 513-621-1991

Reference: First National Bank, Cincinnati, Ohio.

For full biographical listings, see the Martindale-Hubbell Law Directory

SANTEN & HUGHES A LEGAL PROFESSIONAL ASSOCIATION (AV)

Suite 3100, 312 Walnut Street, 45202
Telephone: 513-721-4450
FAX: 513-721-7644; 721-0109

(See Next Column)

SANTEN & HUGHES A LEGAL PROFESSIONAL ASSOCIATION—*Continued*

William E. Santen
John D. Holschuh, Jr.
William E. Santen, Jr.
David M. Kothman

LEGAL SUPPORT PERSONNEL

Karen W. Crane (Corporate Paralegal)
Deborah M. McKinney (Trust/Estate Paralegal)
Karen L. Jansen (Litigation Paralegal)
Bobbie S. Ebbers (Paralegal)

For Complete List of Firm Personnel, See General Section

For full biographical listings, see the Martindale-Hubbell Law Directory

LAW OFFICES OF JOSEPH W. SHEA III (AV)

36 East 7th Street, Suite 2650, 45202-4459
Telephone: 513-621-8333
Telecopier: 513-651-3272

ASSOCIATE

Shirley A. Coffey

LEGAL SUPPORT PERSONNEL

NURSE - LEGAL ASSISTANT

Marianne E. Alf

For full biographical listings, see the Martindale-Hubbell Law Directory

WAITE, SCHNEIDER, BAYLESS & CHESLEY CO., L.P.A. (AV)

1513 Central Trust Tower, Fourth and Vine Streets, 45202
Telephone: 513-621-0267
Fax: 513-381-2375; 621-0262

Stanley M. Chesley

Thomas F. Rehme
Fay E. Stilz
Louise M. Roselle
D. Arthur Rabourn
Jerome L. Skinner
Janet G. Abaray
Paul M. De Marco
Terrence L. Goodman
Sherrill P. Hondorf
Colleen M. Hegge
Dianna Pendleton
Randy F. Fox
Glenn D. Feagan
Theresa L. Groh
Theodore N. Berry

For full biographical listings, see the Martindale-Hubbell Law Directory

*CLEVELAND,** Cuyahoga Co.

FRIEDMAN, DOMIANO & SMITH CO., L.P.A. (AV)

Sixth Floor, Standard Building, 44113-1701
Telephone: 216-621-0070
Fax: 216-621-3231
Naples, Florida Office: 800 Laurel Oak Drive, Suite 200, Pelican Bay, 33963.
Telephone: 813-642-0252.

Jeffrey H. Friedman
Joseph C. Domiano
M. David Smith
Lisa M. Gerlack

Lillian V. Blageff
Stephen S. Vanek

For full biographical listings, see the Martindale-Hubbell Law Directory

GREENE & MCQUILLAN CO. L.P.A. (AV)

1801 Bond Court Building, 44114-1585
Telephone: 216-687-0900
Telecopier: 216-687-0651

William Martin Greene
Jean M. McQuillan

For full biographical listings, see the Martindale-Hubbell Law Directory

HERMANN, CAHN & SCHNEIDER (AV)

Suite 500, 1301 East Ninth Street, 44114
Telephone: 216-781-5515
Facsimile: 216-781-1030

MEMBER OF FIRM

Kent B. Schneider

For full biographical listings, see the Martindale-Hubbell Law Directory

JANIK & DUNN (AV)

400 Park Plaza Building, 1111 Chester Avenue, 44114
Telephone: 216-781-9700
Fax: 216-781-1250
Brea, California Office: 2601 Saturn Street, Suite 300.
Telephone: 714-572-1101.
Fax: 714-572-1103.

MEMBERS OF FIRM

Steven G. Janik
Theodore M. Dunn, Jr.

(See Next Column)

ASSOCIATES

Myra Staresina
David L. Mast

For full biographical listings, see the Martindale-Hubbell Law Directory

NURENBERG, PLEVIN, HELLER & MCCARTHY CO., L.P.A. (AV)

1370 Ontario Street First Floor, 44113-1792
Telephone: 216-621-2300
FAX: 216-771-2242

A. H. Dudnik (1905-1963)
S. F. Komito (1902-1984)
Marshall I. Nurenberg
Leon M. Plevin
Maurice L. Heller
John J. McCarthy
Thomas Mester
Harlan M. Gordon
Andrew P. Krembs
Anne L. Kilbane
David M. Paris
Richard C. Alkire
Richard L. Demsey
Joel Levin
Jamie R. Lebovitz
William S. Jacobson

Dean C. Nieding
Jeffrey A. Leikin
Robin J. Peterson
Robert S. Zeller
James T. Schumacher
Ellen M. McCarthy
J. Charles Ruiz-Bueno
Sandra J. Rosenthal
Kathleen St. John
Jessica F. Kahn

Reference: Society Key Corp.

For full biographical listings, see the Martindale-Hubbell Law Directory

RUBENSTEIN, NOVAK, EINBUND, PAVLIK & CELEBREZZE (AV)

Suite 270, Skylight Office Tower Tower City Center, 44113-1498
Telephone: 216-781-8700
Telecopier: 216-781-9227

MEMBERS OF FIRM

William J. Novak
Lewis Einbund

For full biographical listings, see the Martindale-Hubbell Law Directory

TIMOTHY A. SHIMKO & ASSOCIATES A LEGAL PROFESSIONAL ASSOCIATION (AV)

2010 Huntington Building, 925 Euclid Avenue, 44115
Telephone: 216-241-8300
Fax: 216-241-2702

Timothy A. Shimko

Janet I. Stich
Theresa A. Tarchinski
Ronald K. Starkey
Frank E. Piscitelli, Jr.

OF COUNSEL

Frank B. Mazzone

Reference: National City Bank, Cleveland.

For full biographical listings, see the Martindale-Hubbell Law Directory

ZIEGLER, METZGER & MILLER (AV)

2020 Huntington Building, 44115-1407
Telephone: 216-781-5470
FAX: 216-781-0714

MEMBER OF FIRM

Timothy M. Bittel

ASSOCIATES

Christopher W. Siemen
Jeffrey L. Koberg
William E. Karnatz, Jr

For Complete List of Firm Personnel, See General Section

For full biographical listings, see the Martindale-Hubbell Law Directory

*COLUMBUS,** Franklin Co.

BERRY & SHOEMAKER (AV)

42 East Gay Street, Suite 1515, 43215
Telephone: 614-464-0100
Portsmouth Telephone: 614-354-4838
Fax: 614-464-4033
Portsmouth, Ohio Office: 703 National City Bank Building, 45662.
Telephone: 614-354-4838.
Chillicothe, Ohio Office: 63 N. Paint Street, 45601.
Telephone: 614-775-8941.

MEMBERS OF FIRM

John F. Berry
Kevin L. Shoemaker
D. Lewis Clark, Jr.

OF COUNSEL

Brenda S. Shoemaker

For full biographical listings, see the Martindale-Hubbell Law Directory

Columbus—Continued

J. BOYD BINNING (AV)

592 South Third Street, 43215
Telephone: 614-224-1979
Facsimile: 614-224-1984

For full biographical listings, see the Martindale-Hubbell Law Directory

---

BUTLER, CINCIONE, DICUCCIO & DRITZ (AV)

Suite 700 LeVeque Lincoln Tower, 50 West Broad Street, 43215
Telephone: 614-221-3151
Fax: 614-221-8196

MEMBERS OF FIRM

Robert A. Butler
Alphonse P. Cincione
N. Gerald DiCuccio
Stanley B. Dritz
David B. Barnhart

Matthew P. Cincione
Gail M. Zalimeni

References: National City Bank, Columbus, Ohio; Bank One, Columbus, Ohio.

For full biographical listings, see the Martindale-Hubbell Law Directory

---

CLARK, PERDUE, ROBERTS & SCOTT CO., L.P.A. (AV)

471 East Broad Street Suite 1400, 43215
Telephone: 614-469-1400
Fax: 614-469-0900

Dale K. Perdue
Paul O. Scott
Douglas S. Roberts
Edward L. Clark
Glen R. Pritchard
Robert W. Kerpsack, Jr.
D. Andrew List
Brian W. Palmer

For full biographical listings, see the Martindale-Hubbell Law Directory

---

CLOPPERT, PORTMAN, SAUTER, LATANICK & FOLEY (AV)

225 East Broad Street, 43215-3709
Telephone: 614-461-4455
Fax: 614-461-0072
Portsmouth, Ohio Office: 812 6th Street.
Telephone: 614-354-2553.
Fax: 614-353-5293.

MEMBERS OF FIRM

Mark A. Foley
Frederick G. Cloppert, Jr.
Frederic A. Portman
David G. Latanick
Robert W. Sauter
Robert L. Washburn, Jr.
Walter J. Gerhardstein
Michael J. Hunter
Russell E. Carnahan
Grant D. Shoub
Susan Hayest Kozlowski
Charles J. Smith

William J. Steele
Nancy E. Leech
Debra D. Paxson

LEGAL SUPPORT PERSONNEL

Victoria L. Wythe

Reference: Bank One of Columbus, N.A.

For full biographical listings, see the Martindale-Hubbell Law Directory

---

MICHAEL F. COLLEY CO., L.P.A. (AV)

Hoster & High Building, 536 South High Street, 43215-5674
Telephone: 614-228-6453
Fax: 614-228-7122

Michael F. Colley

David I. Shroyer
Daniel N. Abraham
Elizabeth Schorpp Burkett
Jennifer K. Thivener
Thomas F. Martello, Jr.

OF COUNSEL

Marvin Sloin
David K. Frank

Reference: Bank One of Columbus, NA.

For full biographical listings, see the Martindale-Hubbell Law Directory

---

DENMEAD & MALONEY (AV)

37 West Broad Street, Suite 1150, 43215-4189
Telephone: 614-228-5271
Telecopier: 614-228-7624

Craig Denmead
Kevin M. Maloney
Deborah A. Bonarrigo

OF COUNSEL

Mark A. Hutson

For full biographical listings, see the Martindale-Hubbell Law Directory

TIMOTHY D. GERRITY (AV)

50 West Broad Street, 43215
Telephone: 614-464-2211

For full biographical listings, see the Martindale-Hubbell Law Directory

---

LAMKIN, VAN EMAN, TRIMBLE, BEALS & ROURKE (AV)

Suite 200, 500 South Front Street, 43215-5671
Telephone: 614-224-8187
Fax: 614-224-4943

MEMBERS OF FIRM

William W. Lamkin
Timothy L. Van Eman
Thomas W. Trimble
David A. Beals
Michael J. Rourke

ASSOCIATE

Kathy A. Dougherty

Reference: Huntington National Bank.

For full biographical listings, see the Martindale-Hubbell Law Directory

---

MCCARTHY, PALMER, VOLKEMA, BOYD & THOMAS A LEGAL PROFESSIONAL ASSOCIATION (AV)

140 East Town Street, Suite 1100, 43215
Telephone: Telephone: 614-221-4400
Telecopier: 614-221-6010

Dennis M. McCarthy
Robert Gray Palmer
Daniel R. Volkema
Jeffrey D. Boyd
Warner M. Thomas, Jr.

Craig P. Scott

COUNSEL

Russell H. Volkema
Stanton G. Darling, II

Reference: Huntington National Bank.

For full biographical listings, see the Martindale-Hubbell Law Directory

---

RAY, TODARO & ALTON CO., L.P.A. (AV)

175 South Third Street, Suite 350, 43215-5100
Telephone: 614-221-7791
Fax: 614-221-8957

Frank A. Ray
John M. Alton
Frank E. Todaro

Gregory W. Kirstein

For full biographical listings, see the Martindale-Hubbell Law Directory

---

SCHERNER & HANSON (AV)

130 Northwoods Boulevard, 43235-4725
Telephone: 614-431-7200
Fax: 614-431-7262
Delaware, Ohio Office: 5300 David Road.
Telephone: 614-595-3366.

Hans Scherner
Robert E. Hanson

For full biographical listings, see the Martindale-Hubbell Law Directory

---

TYACK, BLACKMORE & LISTON CO., L.P.A. (AV)

536 South High Street, 43215
Telephone: 614-221-1341
Fax: 614-228-0253

Thomas M. Tyack
Margaret L. Blackmore
Jefferson E. Liston

Angela F. Albert

References: Huntington National Bank; Bank One of Columbus, NA.

For full biographical listings, see the Martindale-Hubbell Law Directory

---

WOLSKE & BLUE A LEGAL PROFESSIONAL ASSOCIATION (AV)

580 South High Street, 43215-5672
Telephone: 614-228-6969
Cincinnati, Ohio Office: The Society Bank Center, 36 East Seventh Street, Suite 2120.
Telephone: 513-579-1181.

Walter J. Wolske, Jr.
Jason A. Blue
Gerald S. Leeseberg
Michael S. Miller

Anne M. Valentine
William Mann
David B. Shaver
Douglas J. Blue
Maryellen C. Spirito
Sarah Meirson

Reference: Bank One of Columbus, N.A.

For full biographical listings, see the Martindale-Hubbell Law Directory

*DAYTON,** Montgomery Co.

CREW, BUCHANAN & LOWE (AV)

Formerly Cowden, Pfarrer, Crew & Becker
2580 Kettering Tower, 45423-2580
Telephone: 513-223-6211
Facsimile: 513-223-7631

MEMBERS OF FIRM

Charles A. Craighead (1857-1926)
Robert E. Cowden (1886-1954)
Robert E. Cowden, Jr. (1910-1968)
Charles P. Pfarrer (1905-1984)
Philip Rohrer Becker (1905-1989)
Charles D. Lowe
Jeffrey A. Swillinger

ASSOCIATES

R. Anne Shale
Dana K. Cole

For Complete List of Firm Personnel, See General Section

For full biographical listings, see the Martindale-Hubbell Law Directory

DYER, GAROFALO, MANN & SCHULTZ A LEGAL PROFESSIONAL ASSOCIATION (AV)

The Barclay Building at 1st and Main Street, 137 North Main Street, 45402
Telephone: 513-223-8888
Fax: 513-223-0127
Springfield, Ohio Office: 1714 Valley Loop Road, 45504.
Telephone: 513-324-1440.

Michael E. Dyer
Carmine M. Garofalo
Douglas A. Mann
Ronald E. Schultz

Jean M. Steigerwald
Douglas A. Hess
James M. Thorson, Jr.
Gilbert B. Switala Jr.
Kimberly Harshbarger
Sigurd R. Peterson, Jr.
Diane E. Hanson

For full biographical listings, see the Martindale-Hubbell Law Directory

E. S. GALLON & ASSOCIATES (AV)

1100 Miami Valley Tower, 40 West Fourth Street, 45402
Telephone: 513-461-3694
Fax: 513-461-7840
Cincinnati, Ohio Office: The Kroger Building, 1014 Vine Street, Suite 1925.
Telephone: 513-721-1139.
Fax: 513-621-2768.

MEMBERS OF FIRM

David M. Deutsch
Patrick W. Allen
James D. Dennis

ASSOCIATE

David R. Salyer

For full biographical listings, see the Martindale-Hubbell Law Directory

*ELYRIA,** Lorain Co.

SPIKE & MECKLER (AV)

1551 West River Street North, 44035
Telephone: 216-324-5353
Fax: 216-324-6529

MEMBERS OF FIRM

Allen S. Spike
Stephen G. Meckler
Douglas M. Brill

For full biographical listings, see the Martindale-Hubbell Law Directory

*FINDLAY,** Hancock Co.

BERNARD K. BAUER CO., L.P.A. (AV)

410 West Sandusky Street, Suite One, P.O. Box 932, 45839
Telephone: 419-423-2673
FAX: 419-423-2127

Bernard K. Bauer

For full biographical listings, see the Martindale-Hubbell Law Directory

FRANKLIN, Warren Co.

RUPPERT, BRONSON, CHICARELLI & SMITH CO., L.P.A. (AV)

1063 East Second Street, P.O. Box 369, 45005
Telephone: 513-746-2832
Fax: 513-746-2855
Springboro, Ohio Office: 610 North Main, P.O. Box 186.
Telephone: 513-748-1314.

(See Next Column)

James D. Ruppert
Barbara J. Bronson
David A. Chicarelli
Rupert E. Ruppert
John D. Smith
Timothy N. Tepe

Ronald W. Ruppert
Deborah Bailey
Donna K. Czechowski
Michael J. D'Amico

For full biographical listings, see the Martindale-Hubbell Law Directory

*GALLIPOLIS,** Gallia Co.

HALLIDAY, SHEETS & SAUNDERS (AV)

19 Locust Street, P.O. Box 325, 45631
Telephone: 614-446-1652
Fax: 614-446-6382

MEMBERS OF FIRM

John E. Halliday
Warren F. Sheets
Brent A. Saunders
Mark E. Sheets

Representative Clients: Ohio Valley Bank; Radio Station WJEH; Evans Enterprises, Inc.; O'Dell Lumber Co.; Riverside Motors, Inc.
Approved Attorneys for: Lawyers Title Insurance Corp.

For full biographical listings, see the Martindale-Hubbell Law Directory

*IRONTON,** Lawrence Co.

SPEARS & SPEARS (AV)

122 South Fourth Street, 45638
Telephone: 614-532-5815; 614-532-6913

MEMBERS OF FIRM

Harold D. Spears
David R. Spears

References: Star Bank; National City Bank.

For full biographical listings, see the Martindale-Hubbell Law Directory

*LANCASTER,** Fairfield Co.

STEBELTON, ARANDA & SNIDER A LEGAL PROFESSIONAL ASSOCIATION (AV)

One North Broad Street, P.O. Box 130, 43130
Telephone: 614-654-4141;
Columbus Direct Line: 614-837-1212;
1-800-543-Laws
Fax: 614-654-2521

Gerald L. Stebelton
James C. Aranda
Rick L. Snider
John M. Snider

Sandra W. Davis
Jason A. Price

LEGAL SUPPORT PERSONNEL

Sandra J. Steinhauser
Rose M. Sels
Sandra K. Hillyard
Michelle K. Garlinger

For full biographical listings, see the Martindale-Hubbell Law Directory

*MARYSVILLE,** Union Co.

CANNIZZARO, FRASER & BRIDGES (AV)

302 South Main Street, 43040
Telephone: 513-644-9125

MEMBERS OF FIRM

John F. Cannizzaro
Don W. Fraser
Robert L. Bridges

*SPRINGFIELD,** Clark Co.

COLE ACTON HARMON DUNN A LEGAL PROFESSIONAL ASSOCIATION (AV)

Riverbend Condominiums, 333 North Limestone Street, P.O. Box 1687, 45501
Telephone: 513-322-0891
Fax: 513-322-9931

John M. Cole (1879-1960)
Abe Gardner (1903-1964)
Fred M. Cole (1909-1975)
George W. Cole (1914-1982)
Robert C. Acton (1924-1987)
James A. Harmon
Edward W. Dunn
Charles P. Crabill
Barry P. Reich
William C. Hicks
Phyllis S. Nedelman
Joseph A. Dunn

Representative Clients: Society National Bank; National City Bank; Huntington National Bank; Navistar International; Springfield Newspapers, Inc.; Fulmer Supermarkets, Inc.; Chakeres Theatres Inc.; Springfield Metropolitan Housing Authority; Prudential Insurance Company of America; Springfield Area Chamber of Commerce.

For full biographical listings, see the Martindale-Hubbell Law Directory

SWANTON, Fulton Co.

The McQuades Co., L.P.A. (AV)

Lincoln at Broadway, P.O. Box 237, 43558
Telephone: 419-826-0055
Fax: 419-825-3871
Archbold, Ohio Office: 200 N. Defiance Street.
Telephone: 419-445-3755.
Whitehouse, Ohio Office: 6632 Providence Street.
Telephone: 419-877-0746.

Daniel P. McQuade
Colin J. McQuade

Alan J. Lehenbauer

OF COUNSEL

Richard B. McQuade

For full biographical listings, see the Martindale-Hubbell Law Directory

*TOLEDO,** Lucas Co.

James D. Caruso (AV)

405 Madison Avenue, Suite 2300, 43604-1207
Telephone: 419-248-2300
Fax: 419-242-1605

For full biographical listings, see the Martindale-Hubbell Law Directory

Connelly, Soutar & Jackson (AV)

405 Madison Avenue Suite 1600, 43604
Telephone: 419-243-2100
Fax: 419-243-7119

MEMBERS OF FIRM

David M. Soutar (1937-1981)
William M. Connelly
Reginald S. Jackson, Jr.
Steven R. Smith
Steven P. Collier
Kevin E. Joyce
Anthony P. Georgetti
Michael A. Bonfiglio

ASSOCIATES

Thomas G. Mackin
Beverly J. Cox
Janine T. Avila
Sarah Steele Riordan (Not admitted in OH)

OF COUNSEL

Gerald P. Openlander

For full biographical listings, see the Martindale-Hubbell Law Directory

Lackey, Nusbaum, Harris, Reny & Torzewski A Legal Professional Association (AV)

Two Maritime Plaza Third Floor, 43604
Telephone: 419-243-1105
Fax: 419-243-8953

Jay Harris
D. Michael Reny

References: Fifth Third Bank; Society Bank.

For full biographical listings, see the Martindale-Hubbell Law Directory

Ritter, Robinson, McCready & James (AV)

1850 National City Bank Building, 405 Madison Avenue, 43624
Telephone: 419-241-3213
Detroit, Michigan: 313-422-1610
FAX: 419-241-4925

MEMBERS OF FIRM

William S. McCready
Timothy C. James

Counsel for: Chrysler Corp.; Rubini Motors, Inc.; Ohio Casualty Insurance Co.; National Mutual Insurance Co.; Celina Mutual Insurance Co.; Westfield Insurance Co.; Northwestern National Insurance Co.; Midwestern Insurance Co.; United Ohio Insurance Co.; Toledo Auto Electric Co.

For Complete List of Firm Personnel, See General Section

For full biographical listings, see the Martindale-Hubbell Law Directory

Schnorf & Schnorf Co., L.P.A. A Professional Corporation (AV)

1400 National City Bank Building, 405 Madison Avenue, 43604
Telephone: 419-248-2646
Facsimile: 419-248-2889

David M. Schnorf
Christopher F. Parker

Local Counsel for: Universal Underwriters Group; Cincinnati Insurance Company; Blue Cross and Blue Shield Mutual of Ohio; Bankers Multiple Line Insurance Company; National City Bank, Northwest
Representative Clients: American Federation of Teachers, AFL-CIO; Ohio Federation of Teachers, AFL-CIO; Toledo Federation of Teachers, AFL-CIO; Thomas R. Hart Associates, Inc.

(See Next Column)

For Complete List of Firm Personnel, See General Section

For full biographical listings, see the Martindale-Hubbell Law Directory

OKLAHOMA

*LAWTON,** Comanche Co.

Ashton, Ashton, Wisener and Munkacsy, Inc. (AV)

711 "C" Avenue, 73501
Telephone: 405-357-2010
FAX: 405-357-2017

Alfred J. Ashton, Jr.
Mark A. Ashton
Thomas W. Wisener
John Munkacsy

Representative Clients: Felton-Dean Pontiac-Oldsmobile-GMC; Ted Horton (Architect); R & H Implement Co.; City of Indiahoma; Park View Nursing Home, Inc., Walters, Oklahoma; Beulah Jones Realty; Sawyer, Liester & Stabler, Inc. (CPAs); Security Bank & Trust Co., Lawton, Oklahoma; Wichita National Life Insurance Company; Shiflett Transport Services, Inc.

For full biographical listings, see the Martindale-Hubbell Law Directory

*OKLAHOMA CITY,** Oklahoma Co.

Abel, Musser, Sokolosky, Mares, Haubrich, Burch & Kouri (AV)

Suite 600, One Leadership Square, 211 North Robinson, 73102
Telephone: 405-239-7046
Fax: 405-272-1090

Ed Abel
Sidney A. Musser, Jr.
Jerry D. Sokolosky
Lynn B. Mares
Greg Haubrich
Derek K. Burch
Harry J. (Trey) Kouri, III

ASSOCIATES

Kenneth G. Cole
Daniel Pines Markoff
Melvin R. Singleterry
Kelly S. Bishop
Kelly A. George
Gregory J. Ryan

OF COUNSEL

Arthur R. Angel
James A. Ikard
Warner E. Lovell, Jr.
Leo H. Whinery

For full biographical listings, see the Martindale-Hubbell Law Directory

Abowitz, Welch and Rhodes (AV)

Tenth Floor 15 North Robinson, P.O. Box 1937, 73101
Telephone: 405-236-4645
Telecopier: 405-239-2843

MEMBERS OF FIRM

Murray E. Abowitz
Mort G. Welch
Sarah Jackson Rhodes

Lisa Luschen Gilbert
Denis P. Rischard
Norman Lemonik
Janice M. Dansby

Representative Clients: Jefferson Insurance Company of New York; Admiral Insurance Co.; Liberty Mutual Insurance Company; Mazda Distributors (West), Inc.; National Farmers Union Insurance Company; Oklahoma Farmers Union Mutual Insurance Company; Trinity Universal Insurance Co.

For full biographical listings, see the Martindale-Hubbell Law Directory

Gary L. Brooks (AV)

6303 Waterford Boulevard, Suite 220, 73118-1122
Telephone: 405-840-1066
Fax: 405-843-8446
Dayton, Ohio Office: First National Plaza, Suite 1700, 45402.
Telephone: 513-224-3400.
Fax: 513-228-0331.

ASSOCIATE

Ann Jarrard

For full biographical listings, see the Martindale-Hubbell Law Directory

Durland & Durland (AV)

300 Bank IV Tower, 1601 Northwest Expressway, 73118
Telephone: 405-840-0060
FAX: 405-842-8547

Jack R. Durland, Jr.
Harvey L. Harmon, Jr.
Kathleen Garewal

OF COUNSEL

Jack R. Durland
Robert D. Allen

For full biographical listings, see the Martindale-Hubbell Law Directory

Oklahoma City—Continued

FOLIART, HUFF, OTTAWAY & CALDWELL, A PROFESSIONAL CORPORATION (AV)

20th Floor, First National Center, 120 North Robinson, 73102
Telephone: 405-232-4633
FAX: 405-232-3462

James D. Foliart
Glen D. Huff
Larry D. Ottaway
M. Dan Caldwell
Monty B. Bottom
Michael C. Felty

Susan A. Short
David A. Branscum
Timothy M. Melton
Darrell W. Downs
David K. McPhail
Kevin E. McCarty
Michael T. Maloan
Jeffrey R. Atkins

For full biographical listings, see the Martindale-Hubbell Law Directory

HOLLOWAY, DOBSON, HUDSON, BACHMAN, ALDEN, JENNINGS, ROBERTSON & HOLLOWAY, A PROFESSIONAL CORPORATION (AV)

Suite 900 One Leadership Square 211 North Robinson, 73102-7102
Telephone: 405-235-8593
Fax: 405-235-1707

Page Dobson
Ronald R. Hudson
Gary C. Bachman
Charles F. Alden, III
James A. Jennings, III
Vicki Robertson
Dan L. Holloway
Don M. Vaught
John R. Denneny
Rodney L. Cook
J. William Archibald
Mark E. Duvall
James R. Baker

Lu Ann Stout
Stephen D. Bachman
Elizabeth J. Bradford
Angela D. Chancellor

OF COUNSEL

Russell B. Holloway

Representing: Associated Aviation Underwriters; Chubb Group of Insurance Cos.; Continental Insurance Cos; General Motors Corp.

For full biographical listings, see the Martindale-Hubbell Law Directory

HUGHES, WHITE, ADAMS & GRANT (AV)

The Paragon, 5801 North Broadway Extension, Suite 302, 73118-7438
Telephone: 405-848-0111
FAX: 405-848-3507

Carl D. Hughes
Joe E. White, Jr.
Richard S. Adams
Michael E. Grant

For Complete List of Firm Personnel, See General Section

For full biographical listings, see the Martindale-Hubbell Law Directory

McCAFFREY & TAWWATER (AV)

Bank of Oklahoma Plaza, Suite 1100 201 Robert S. Kerr Avenue, 73102
Telephone: 405-235-2900
Fax: 405-235-4932
Other Oklahoma City, Oklahoma Offices: Suite 1950, One Leadership Square, 211 North Robinson.

MEMBERS OF FIRM

George J. McCaffrey
Larry A. Tawwater

ASSOCIATES

Robert M. Behlen
Charles L. Cashion
Jo Lynn Slama
Gloria E. Trout
Loren F. Gibson
David Little
Steven R. Davis
Piper E. Mills

For full biographical listings, see the Martindale-Hubbell Law Directory

MILLS & WHITTEN, A PROFESSIONAL CORPORATION (AV)

Suite 500, One Leadership Square 211 North Robinson, 73102
Telephone: 405-239-2500
Fax: 405-235-4655

Earl D. Mills
Reggie N. Whitten
Robert B. Mills
W. Wayne Mills
Bill M. Roberts

Steve L. Lawson
Barbara K. Buratti
Kathryn D. Mansell
Glynis C. Edgar
Kent R. McGuire
Donald R. Martin, Jr.
Kay L. Hargrave
Brian E. Dittrich
Douglas A. Terry

Representative Clients: Biomet, Inc.; Crum & Forster Commercial Ins. Co.; Mid-Continent Casualty Co.; Oklahoma Farm Bureau Mutual Ins. Co.; The St. Paul Insurance Companies; OML Municipal Assurance Group; Great West Casualty; Houston General Ins. Co.; National American Ins. Co.; Progressive Casualty; Titan Indemnity.

(See Next Column)

For full biographical listings, see the Martindale-Hubbell Law Directory

OLDFIELD & COKER (AV)

4808 North Classen Boulevard, 73118
Telephone: 405-840-0555
Fax: 405-840-4808

MEMBERS OF FIRM

John S. Oldfield, Jr.
Michael G. Coker

ASSOCIATES

Rose M. J. Sloan
Matthew J. Graves

Representative Clients: CNA Insurance; Bunte Candies, Inc.; Nationwide Insurance Co.; Fine Candy Co.
Reference: Liberty Bank & Trust Co., Oklahoma City, Okla.

For full biographical listings, see the Martindale-Hubbell Law Directory

*SHAWNEE,** Pottawatomie Co.

THE WEST LAW FIRM (AV)

124 West Highland, 74801
Telephone: 405-275-0040
Fax: 405-275-0052
Meeker, Oklahoma Office: 613 West Main; P.O. Box 310.
Telephone: 405-279-3524.

Terry W. West
Bradley C. West
James David Cawthon
James D. Berry (Resident, Meeker, Oklahoma Office)
Wayne L. Johnson

For full biographical listings, see the Martindale-Hubbell Law Directory

*TULSA,** Tulsa Co.

ATKINSON, HASKINS, NELLIS, BOUDREAUX, HOLEMAN, PHIPPS & BRITTINGHAM (AV)

A Partnership including Professional Corporations
1500 ParkCentre, 525 South Main Street, 74103
Telephone: 918-582-8877
Fax: 918-585-8096

PARTNERS

Michael P. Atkinson, P.C.
Walter D. Haskins, P.C.
Gregory D. Nellis, P.C.
Paul T. Boudreaux, P.C.
Daniel E. Holeman, P.C.
K. Clark Phipps
Galen Lee Brittingham, P.C.
John S. Gladd

ASSOCIATES

Martha J. Phillips
Marthanda J. Beckworth
Ann E. Allison
William A. Fiasco
Owen T. Evans
Mark W. Maguire
Jon D. Starr
Michael R. Annis
James N. Edmonds
David A. Russell
Kirsten E. Pace

OF COUNSEL

Joseph F. Glass

Representative Clients: Allstate Insurance Co.; Crum & Forester Insurance Co.; Hartford Insurance Company; National American Insurance Co.; Federated Insurance Co.; Guaranty National Insurance Co.; Liberty Mutual Insurance Co.; Physicians Liability Insurance Co.; State Farm Mutual Automobile Insurance Co.; United States Aviation Underwriters.

For full biographical listings, see the Martindale-Hubbell Law Directory

BEST, SHARP, HOLDEN, SHERIDAN, BEST & SULLIVAN, A PROFESSIONAL CORPORATION (AV)

Oneok Plaza, 100 W. 5th, Suite 808, 74103-4225
Telephone: 918-582-1234
Fax: 918-585-9447

Joseph M. Best
Joseph A. Sharp
Steven E. Holden
John H. T. Sheridan
Timothy G. Best
Daniel S. Sullivan
Steven K. Bunting
Amy Kempfert

Karen M. Grundy
Timothy E. Tipton
Philip M. Best
Malinda S. Matlock
Catherine L. Campbell
Terry S. O'Donnell
Mark Thomas Steele
Jennifer Ellen Mustain
Douglas E. Stall
Malcom D. Smith, Jr.
Bobby L. Latham, Jr.

OF COUNSEL

William E. Patten

For full biographical listings, see the Martindale-Hubbell Law Directory

LIPE, GREEN, PASCHAL, TRUMP & BRAGG, A PROFESSIONAL CORPORATION (AV)

3700 First National Tower, 15 East Fifth Street, Suite 3700, 74103-4344
Telephone: 918-599-9400
Fax: 918-599-9404

(See Next Column)

LIPE, GREEN, PASCHAL, TRUMP & BRAGG A PROFESSIONAL CORPORATION, *Tulsa—Continued*

Larry B. Lipe
James E. Green, Jr.
Richard A. Paschal
Timothy T. Trump
Patricia Dunmire Bragg

Melodie Freeman-Burney
Mark E. Dreyer
Constance L. Young
Leah Lowder Mills

For full biographical listings, see the Martindale-Hubbell Law Directory

SNEED, LANG, ADAMS & BARNETT, A PROFESSIONAL CORPORATION (AV)

2300 Williams Center Tower II, Two West Second Street, 74103
Telephone: 918-583-3145
Telecopier: 918-582-0410

James C. Lang
D. Faith Orlowski
Brian S. Gaskill
G. Steven Stidham
Stephen R. McNamara
Thomas E. Black, Jr.
Robbie Emery Burke
C. Raymond Patton, Jr.
Frederick K. Slicker
Richard D. Black
John D. Russell
Jeffrey S. Swyers

OF COUNSEL

James L. Sneed
O. Edwin Adams
Howard G. Barnett, Jr.

Representative Clients: Amoco Production Company; Continental Bank; Deloitte & Touche; Enron Corporation; Halliburton Energy Services; Helmerich & Payne, Inc.; Lehman Brothers, Inc.; Shell Oil Company; Smith Barney, Inc.; State Farm Mutual Automobile Insurance Company.

For full biographical listings, see the Martindale-Hubbell Law Directory

UNGERMAN & IOLA (AV)

Riverbridge Office Park, 1323 East 71st Street, Suite 300, P.O. Box 701917, 74170-1917
Telephone: 918-495-0550
Fax: 918-495-0561

MEMBERS OF FIRM

Irvine E. Ungerman (1908-1980)
Maynard I. Ungerman
Mark H. Iola

ASSOCIATE

Randall L. Iola

Representative Client: Northeastern Oklahoma Building and Construction Trades Council.

For full biographical listings, see the Martindale-Hubbell Law Directory

OREGON

*EUGENE,** Lane Co.

TED CARP (AV)

1852 Willamette Street, 97401
Telephone: 503-345-8751
Fax: 503-345-8753

For full biographical listings, see the Martindale-Hubbell Law Directory

*GRANTS PASS,** Josephine Co.

MYRICK, SEAGRAVES, ADAMS & DAVIS (AV)

600 N.W. Fifth Street, 97526
Telephone: 503-476-6627
Fax: 503-476-7048

MEMBERS OF FIRM

Donald H. Coulter (Retired)
Charles H. Seagraves, Jr.
Lynn Michael Myrick
Richard D. Adams
John E. Davis
Holly A. Preslar

Reference: United States National Bank of Oregon.

For full biographical listings, see the Martindale-Hubbell Law Directory

*NEWPORT,** Lincoln Co.

BARTON AND STREVER, P.C. (AV)

214 South West Coast Highway, P.O. Box 870, 97365
Telephone: 503-265-5377
Fax: 503-265-5614

William A. Barton
Kevin K. Strever

(See Next Column)

LEGAL SUPPORT PERSONNEL

Greg A. Estep

References: National Security Bank; Bank of Newport.

For full biographical listings, see the Martindale-Hubbell Law Directory

*OREGON CITY,** Clackamas Co.

DONALD B. BOWERMAN (AV)

1001 Molalla Avenue, Suite 208, P.O. Box 88, 97045
Telephone: 503-650-0700
FAX: 503-650-0053

ASSOCIATE

Jonathan N. Neff

OF COUNSEL

Roderick A. Boutin

For full biographical listings, see the Martindale-Hubbell Law Directory

*PORTLAND,** Multnomah Co.

LABARRE & ASSOCIATES, P.C. (AV)

Suite 1212, 900 S.W. Fifth Avenue, 97204-1268
Telephone: 503-228-3511
FAX: 503-273-8658

Jerome E. LaBarre

Dayna Ellen Peck

OF COUNSEL

Robert A. Russell

For full biographical listings, see the Martindale-Hubbell Law Directory

O'DONNELL, RAMIS, CREW, CORRIGAN & BACHRACH (AV)

Ballow & Wright Building, 1727 N.W. Hoyt Street, 97209
Telephone: 503-222-4402
FAX: 503-243-2944
Clackamas County Office: Suite 202, 181 N. Grant, Canby.
Telephone: 503-266-1149.

MEMBERS OF FIRM

Mark P. O'Donnell
Timothy V. Ramis
Stephen F. Crew
Charles E. Corrigan
Jeff H. Bachrach

SPECIAL COUNSEL

James M. Coleman

ASSOCIATES

Pamela J. Beery
Mark L. Busch
Gary Firestone
G. Frank Hammond
William A. Monahan
William J. Stalnaker
Ty K. Wyman

LEGAL SUPPORT PERSONNEL

Margaret M. Daly
Mary C. Meyers
Laurel L. Ramsey
G. William Selzer
Dawna S. Shattuck (Legal Assistant)

For full biographical listings, see the Martindale-Hubbell Law Directory

PENNSYLVANIA

*ALLENTOWN,** Lehigh Co.

RICHARD J. MAKOUL (AV)

461 Linden Street, 18102
Telephone: 610-433-4233
FAX: 610-776-7221

For full biographical listings, see the Martindale-Hubbell Law Directory

*CARLISLE,** Cumberland Co.

DOUGLAS, DOUGLAS & DOUGLAS (AV)

27 West High Street, 17013-0261
Telephone: 717-243-1790
Fax: 717-243-8955

MEMBERS OF FIRM

George F. Douglas, Jr.
William P. Douglas
George F. Douglas, III

Representative Client: State Farm Insurance Cos.

For full biographical listings, see the Martindale-Hubbell Law Directory

*DOYLESTOWN,** Bucks Co.

WILLIAM L. GOLDMAN (AV)

90 East State Street, P.O. Box 1989, 18901
Telephone: 215-348-2605
Fax: 215-348-5247
Levittown, Pennsylvania Office: One Stonybrook Drive, P.O. Box 38.
Telephone: 215-945-8700.

ASSOCIATES

William L. Goldman, Jr.
Patricia Handy Cooley
John D. Conroy
Donna M. McKillop
J. Todd Savarese

Representative Clients: Sinkler, Inc., Southampton, Pennsylvania; Fraternal Order of Police Lodge #53, State Police Lodge; Bucks County Federation of Sportsmen's Club.

For full biographical listings, see the Martindale-Hubbell Law Directory

*EASTON,** Northampton Co.

FOX, OLDT & BROWN (AV)

Suite 508, First Fidelity Bank Building, Six South Third Street, Center Square, 18042
Telephone: 610-258-6111
Fax: 610-253-4532

MEMBERS OF FIRM

Charles L. Oldt
Robert C. Brown, Jr.

Counsel for: Merchants Bank, N.A.; Easton Cemetery; Travelers Insurance Co.

For full biographical listings, see the Martindale-Hubbell Law Directory

GUS MILIDES (AV)

654 Wolf Avenue, 18042
Telephone: 610-258-0433

ASSOCIATE

Beth Ann Milides

For full biographical listings, see the Martindale-Hubbell Law Directory

*ERIE,** Erie Co.

CONNER & RILEY (AV)

The Bell Telephone Building, 17 West 10th Street, 16501
Telephone: 814-453-3343
Fax: 814-454-6713

MEMBERS OF FIRM

Andrew J. Conner
Steven E. "Tim" Riley, Jr.

For full biographical listings, see the Martindale-Hubbell Law Directory

*HARRISBURG,** Dauphin Co.

ANGINO & ROVNER, P.C. (AV)

4503 North Front Street, 17110-1799
Telephone: 717-238-6791
Fax: 717-238-5610

Richard C. Angino
Neil J. Rovner

Joseph M. Melillo
David S. Wisneski
Terry S. Hyman
Nijole C. Olson
David L. Lutz
Michael J. Navitsky
Michael E. Kosik
Robin J. Marzella
Pamela G. Shuman
Lawrence F. Barone
Catherine M. Mahady-Smith
Dawn L. Jennings
Richard A. Sadlock
Stephen R. Pedersen

References: Harrisburg Credit Exchange; Hamilton Bank.

For full biographical listings, see the Martindale-Hubbell Law Directory

BUCHANAN INGERSOLL, PROFESSIONAL CORPORATION (AV)

Vartan Parc, 30 North Third Street, 17101
Telephone: 717-237-4800
Telecopier: 717-233-0852
Pittsburgh, Pennsylvania Office: 5800 USX Tower, 600 Grant Street.
Telephone: 412-562-8800.
Philadelphia, Pennsylvania Office: Two Logan Square, Twelfth Floor, 18th & Arch Streets.
Telephone: 215-665-8700.
Tampa, Florida Office: 101 East Kennedy Boulevard, Suite 1030.
Telephone: 813-222-8180.
North Miami Beach, Florida Office: 19495 Biscayne Boulevard.
Telephone: 305-933-5600.
Lexington, Kentucky Office: 1210 Vine Center Office Tower, 333 West Vine Street.
Telephone: 606-225-5333.
Princeton, New Jersey Office: Buchanan Ingersoll, A Partnership, College Centre, 500 College Road East.
Telephone: 609-452-2666.

(See Next Column)

Andrew S. Gordon

For Complete List of Firm Personnel, See General Section

For full biographical listings, see the Martindale-Hubbell Law Directory

GOLDBERG, KATZMAN & SHIPMAN, P.C. (AV)

320 Market Street - Strawberry Square, P.O. Box 1268, 17108-1268
Telephone: 717-234-4161
Telecopier: 717-234-6808; 717-234-6810

F. Lee Shipman
John A. Statler
Thomas E. Brenner
April L. Strang-Kutay
James M. Sheehan
Guy H. Brooks
Jefferson J. Shipman

Karen S. Feuchtenberger

Reference: Fulton Bank.

For Complete List of Firm Personnel, See General Section

For full biographical listings, see the Martindale-Hubbell Law Directory

HEPFORD, SWARTZ & MORGAN (AV)

111 North Front Street, P.O. Box 889, 17108-0889
Telephone: 717-234-4121
Fax: 717-232-6802
Lewistown, Pennsylvania Office: 12 South Main Street, P.O. Box 867.
Telephone: 717-248-3913.

MEMBERS OF FIRM

H. Joseph Hepford
Sandra L. Meilton
Lee C. Swartz
Stephen M. Greecher, Jr.
James G. Morgan, Jr.
Dennis R. Sheaffer

COUNSEL

Stanley H. Siegel (Resident, Lewistown Office)

ASSOCIATES

Richard A. Estacio
Michael H. Park
Andrew K. Stutzman

For full biographical listings, see the Martindale-Hubbell Law Directory

JOSEPH A. KLEIN A PROFESSIONAL CORPORATION (AV)

100 Chestnut Street, Suite 210, P.O. Box 1152, 17108
Telephone: 717-233-0132
Fax: 717-233-2516

Joseph A. Klein
Mark S. Silver

For full biographical listings, see the Martindale-Hubbell Law Directory

MANCKE, WAGNER, HERSHEY AND TULLY (AV)

2233 North Front Street, 17110
Telephone: 717-234-7051
Fax: 717-234-7080

MEMBERS OF FIRM

John B. Mancke
David E. Hershey
P. Richard Wagner
William T. Tully

ASSOCIATE

David R. Breschi

For full biographical listings, see the Martindale-Hubbell Law Directory

METZGER, WICKERSHAM, KNAUSS & ERB (AV)

Mellon Bank Building, 111 Market Street, P.O. Box 93, 17108-0093
Telephone: 717-238-8187
Telefax: 717-234-9478
Other Harrisburg, Pennsylvania Office: 4813 Jonestown Road, P.O. Box 93, 17108.
Telephone: 717-652-7020.

MEMBERS OF FIRM

Maurice R. Metzger (1918-1980)
Robert E. Yetter
F. Brewster Wickersham (1918-1974)
James F. Carl
Robert P. Reed
Edward E. Knauss, III (Retired)
Edward E. Knauss, IV
Christian S. Erb, Jr.
Jered L. Hock
Karl R. Hildabrand

ASSOCIATES

Richard B. Druby
Steven P. Miner
Clark DeVere

Representative Clients: Allstate Insurance Co.; Chubb Group of Insurance Companies; Fireman's Fund American Insurance Group; Liberty Mutual Insurance Co.; Continental Insurance Co.; Crum & Forster.

For full biographical listings, see the Martindale-Hubbell Law Directory

Harrisburg—Continued

SCHMIDT & RONCA, P.C. (AV)

209 State Street, 17101
Telephone: 717-232-6300
Fax: 717-232-6467

Charles E. Schmidt, Jr.
Gerard C. Kramer
James R. Ronca
Scott B. Cooper

For full biographical listings, see the Martindale-Hubbell Law Directory

*LANCASTER,** Lancaster Co.

MIKUS LAW ASSOCIATES (AV)

408 West Chestnut Street, 17603
Telephone: 717-299-4840; 299-4575
FAX: 717-299-6869

Kent D. Mikus

Peter I. Hahn
David B. Diffenbach
Michael P. McDonald

LEGAL SUPPORT PERSONNEL

Sharon R. Fasnacht (Medical Paralegal)
Donna L. Simpson (Litigation Paralegal)
Barbara M. Shirk (Medical Paralegal)

For full biographical listings, see the Martindale-Hubbell Law Directory

JOSEPH F. RODA, P.C. (AV)

301 Cipher Building, 36 East King Street, 17602
Telephone: 717-397-1700
Fax: 717-397-3669

Joseph F. Roda

Ronald C. Messmann
Gail A. Weber
Robin A. Jabour

For full biographical listings, see the Martindale-Hubbell Law Directory

LANSDALE, Montgomery Co.

PEARLSTINE/SALKIN ASSOCIATES (AV)

1250 South Broad Street Suite 1000, P.O. Box 431, 19446
Telephone: 215-699-6000
Fax: 215-699-0231

MEMBERS OF FIRM

Philip Salkin
F. Craig La Rocca
Ronald E. Robinson
Jeffrey T. Sultanik
Barry Cooperberg
Neal R. Pearlstine
Frederick C. Horn
Wendy G. Rothstein
Marc B. Davis
Alan L. Eisen
William R. Wanger
Glenn D. Fox

Wilhelm L. Gruszecki
James R. Hall
Brian E. Subers
Michael S. Paul
Mark S. Cappuccio
David J. Draganosky
Lawrence P. Kempner

For full biographical listings, see the Martindale-Hubbell Law Directory

RUBIN, GLICKMAN AND STEINBERG, A PROFESSIONAL CORPORATION (AV)

2605 North Broad Street, P.O. Box 1277, 19446
Telephone: 215-822-7575; 855-5500; 800-358-9367
Facsimile: 215-822-1713

Irwin S. Rubin
Gregory R. Gifford
Jay C. Glickman
Amy S. Newman
Marc Robert Steinberg
Lewis Goodman
Toby Lynn Dickman
Kathleen M. O'Brien
Steven M. Koloski

Reference: Union National Bank and Trust Company of Souderton.

For full biographical listings, see the Martindale-Hubbell Law Directory

*MEDIA,** Delaware Co.

CRAMP, D'IORIO, MCCONCHIE AND FORBES, P.C. (AV)

215 North Olive Street, P.O. Box 568, 19063
Telephone: 610-565-1700
Fax: 610-566-0379

Ralph B. D'Iorio
Joseph W. Kauffman
George J. McConchie
David G. Blake
Andrew J. Forbes
Gary C. Bender
Guy N. Paolino

Alexander D. DiSanti
Frances Marie Piccoli

(See Next Column)

OF COUNSEL

John F. Cramp

Local Counsel for: Bell Atlantic.
Trial Counsel for: Insurance Company of North America (CIGNA); Commercial Union Insurance Co.; State Farm Insurance Co.; Continental Casualty Co.; Fireman's Fund American Insurance Group; Pennsylvania Manufacturers Assn. (PMA); U.S. Fidelity & Guaranty Co.; United Services Automobile Association.
General Counsel for: Williamson School.

For full biographical listings, see the Martindale-Hubbell Law Directory

DIORIO & FALZONE (AV)

Front and Plum Streets, P.O. Box 1789, 19063
Telephone: 610-565-5700
FAX: 610-891-0652

MEMBERS OF FIRM

Robert M. DiOrio
Raymond J. Falzone, Jr.

ASSOCIATE

Christopher R. Mattox

For full biographical listings, see the Martindale-Hubbell Law Directory

HARRIS & SMITH (AV)

211 West State Street, 19063
Telephone: 610-565-5300
Fax: 610-565-7292

MEMBER OF FIRM

G. Guy Smith

ASSOCIATES

Susan E. Murray
Russell F. Daly

OF COUNSEL

Edgar Y. Harris
Theresa Hagenbach White

For full biographical listings, see the Martindale-Hubbell Law Directory

KASSAB ARCHBOLD JACKSON & O'BRIEN (AV)

Lawyers-Title Building, 214 North Jackson Street, P.O. Box 626, 19063
Telephone: 610-565-3800
Telecopier: 610-892-6888
Wilmington, Delaware Office: 1326 King Street.
Telephone: 302-656-3393.
Fax: 302-656-1993.
Wildwood, New Jersey Office: 5201 New Jersey Avenue.
Telephone: 609-522-6559.

MEMBERS OF FIRM

Edward Kassab
Joseph Patrick O'Brien
William C. Archbold, Jr.
Richard A. Stanko
Robert James Jackson
Roy T. J. Stegena

OF COUNSEL

Matthew J. Ryan
John W. Nilon, Jr.

ASSOCIATES

Kevin William Gibson
George C. McFarland, Jr.
Cynthia Kassab Larosa
Jill E. Aversa
Marc S. Stein
Pamela A. La Torre
Terrance A. Kline
Kenneth D. Kynett

Representative Clients furnished upon request.

For full biographical listings, see the Martindale-Hubbell Law Directory

RICHARD, DISANTI, HAMILTON & GALLAGHER, A PROFESSIONAL CORPORATION (AV)

25 West Second Street, P.O. Box 900, 19063
Telephone: 610-565-4600
Fax: 610-566-8257

Howard Richard
Leonard V. Tenaglia
John M. Gallagher, Jr.
Joseph W. Chupein, Jr.

Kevin Robert Marciano

For Complete List of Firm Personnel, See General Section

For full biographical listings, see the Martindale-Hubbell Law Directory

SCHWARTZ & SCHWARTZ (AV)

The Appleton Building, 341 West State Street, 19063
Telephone: 610-892-9500
FAX: 610-566-5000

Marc Schwartz
Michael R. Schwartz

Representative Clients: Numerous Plantiffs. Defense: Preferred Risk Insurance Co.; Midwest Mutual Insurance Co.; Empire Blue Cross Blue Sheild; Blue Cross and Blue Shield of Minnesota.

For full biographical listings, see the Martindale-Hubbell Law Directory

*NORRISTOWN,** Montgomery Co.

LINDLEY M. COWPERTHWAIT, JR., P.C. (AV)

17 East Airy Street, 19401
Telephone: 610-277-6622
Fax: 610-277-6601
Cherry Hill, New Jersey Office: 1040 North Kings Highway, Suite 600, 08034.
Telephone: 609-482-8600.

Lindley M. Cowperthwait, Jr. Adam D. Zucker

For full biographical listings, see the Martindale-Hubbell Law Directory

GERBER & GERBER (AV)

Suite 500, One Montgomery Plaza, 19401
Telephone: 610-279-6700
Fax: 610-279-7126

MEMBERS OF FIRM

Morris Gerber A. Richard Gerber

ASSOCIATE

Parke H. Ulrich

For full biographical listings, see the Martindale-Hubbell Law Directory

MANNING, KINKEAD, BROOKS & BRADBURY, A PROFESSIONAL CORPORATION (AV)

412 DeKalb Street, 19404-0231
Telephone: 610-279-1800
Fax: 610-279-8682

Franklin L. Wright (1880-1965)
William Perry Manning, Jr.
William H. Kinkead, III
William H. Bradbury, III

Cheri D. Andrews

Counsel for: The Philadelphia National Bank; John Deere Co.; The Rouse Co.; Consolidated Rail Corp.; Bethlehem Steel Co.; Royal Globe Insurance Co.; Nationwide Mutual Insurance Co.

For full biographical listings, see the Martindale-Hubbell Law Directory

MURPHY & OLIVER, P.C. (AV)

43 East Marshall Street, 19401-4869
Telephone: 610-272-4222; 643-5900
Fax: 610-272-2549
Mount Laurel, New Jersey Office: 1288 State Highway 73, Suite 120, 08054.
Telephone: 609-234-1495.

James J. Oliver Frank P. Murphy

Joseph M. Hoeffel III
Carla E. Connor
Barbara A. Barnes
Paul C. Cipriano, Jr.

For full biographical listings, see the Martindale-Hubbell Law Directory

RAYMOND M. VICTOR, P.C. (AV)

616 DeKalb Street, 19401
Telephone: 610-272-5253
Fax: 610-272-7422

Raymond M. Victor Dolores Victor

For full biographical listings, see the Martindale-Hubbell Law Directory

*PHILADELPHIA,** Philadelphia Co.

ANAPOL, SCHWARTZ, WEISS AND COHAN, A PROFESSIONAL CORPORATION (AV)

1900 Delancey Place, 19103
Telephone: 215-735-1130
Fax: 215-735-2024
Bristol, Pennsylvania Office: 1811 Farragut Avenue.
Telephone: 215-785-3400.
Cherry Hill, New Jersey Office: 402 Park Boulevard.
Telephone: 1-609-427-9229.

Alan Schwartz
Paul R. Anapol
Richard B. Schwartz
Sol H. Weiss
Stanton Dubin
Lawrence R. Cohan
Joel D. Feldman
Howard J. Levin
Bernard W. Smalley
Margaret A. Barry
Stephen J. Pokiniewski, Jr.
Nancy L. Goldstein
Sidney M. Grobman

Colleen M. Hickey
Nathaniel E.P. Ehrlich
Nelson Levin
Thomas R. Anapol
Lisa R. Schwartz
Paul A. Czech

(See Next Column)

LEGAL SUPPORT PERSONNEL

Joanne N. Borders (Legal Assistant)

Reference: Meridian Bank, Philadelphia, Pennsylvania.

For full biographical listings, see the Martindale-Hubbell Law Directory

MARVIN I. BARISH LAW OFFICES A PROFESSIONAL CORPORATION (AV)

625 Walnut Street, Suite 801, 19106-3308
Telephone: 215-923-8900; 800-233-7101
Cable Address: "Marsbar-Philadelphia"
Fax: 215-351-0593

Marvin I. Barish

Robert J. Meyers
Stacey E. Barish
Timothy Garvey

For full biographical listings, see the Martindale-Hubbell Law Directory

CLIFFORD B. COHN (AV)

1919 Walnut Street, 19103
Telephone: 215-665-1800
Fax: 215-665-8434

For full biographical listings, see the Martindale-Hubbell Law Directory

COZEN AND O'CONNOR, A PROFESSIONAL CORPORATION (AV)

1900 Market Street, 19103
Telephone: 215-665-2000
800-523-2900
Telecopier: 215-665-2013
Charlotte, North Carolina Office: One First Union Plaza, 28202.
Telephones: 704-376-3400; 800-762-3575.
Telecopier: 704-334-3351.
Columbia, South Carolina Office: Suite 200 The Palmetto Center, 1426 Main Street.
Telephones: 803-799-3900; 800-338-1117.
Telecopier: 803-254-7233.
Dallas, Texas Office: Suite 4100, NationsBank Plaza, 901 Main Street.
Telephones: 214-761-6700; 800-448-1207.
Telecopier: 214-761-6788.
New York, N.Y. Office: 45 Broadway Atrium.
Telephones: 212-509-9400; 800-437-9400.
Telecopier: 212-509-9492.
San Diego, California Office: Suite 1610, 501 West Broadway.
Telephones: 619-234-1700; 800-782-3366.
Telecopier: 619-234-7831.
Seattle, Washington Office: Suite 5200, Washington Mutual Tower, 1201 Third Avenue.
Telephones: 206-340-1000; 800-423-1950.
Telecopier: 206-621-8783.
Westmont, New Jersey Office: 316 Haddon Avenue.
Telephones: 609-854-4900; 800-523-2900.
Telecopier: 609-854-1782.

FIRM MEMBERS IN PHILADELPHIA

Christopher C. Fallon, Jr. A. Richard Bailey
Gerald J. Dugan

Representative Clients: Available upon request.

For Complete List of Firm Personnel, See General Section

For full biographical listings, see the Martindale-Hubbell Law Directory

KATHLEEN L. DAERR-BANNON (AV)

Suite 300, 1211 Chestnut Street, 19107-4113
Telephone: 215-563-9300
Fax: 215-563-3337

Reference: Provident National Bank.

For full biographical listings, see the Martindale-Hubbell Law Directory

DRANOFF-PERLSTEIN ASSOCIATES (AV)

1604 Spruce Street, 19103
Telephone: 215-732-3333; 800-732-4878
Fax: 215-732-8059
Exton, Pennsylvania Office: The Commons at Lincoln Center, 117 John Robert Thomas Drive.
Telephone: 215-524-9200.
Hamlin, Pennsylvania Office: P.O. Box 788, 18427-0788.
Telephone: 717-689-4878.

Steven M. Dranoff Paul Mark Perlstein

ASSOCIATE

Robert J. Foster

For full biographical listings, see the Martindale-Hubbell Law Directory

Philadelphia—Continued

FORCENO & HANNON (AV)

Suite 1000, The Bourse, 111 S. Independence Mall East, 19106-2574
Telephone: 215-732-1630; 800-222-3352 in U.S.
Fax: 215-923-8507

MEMBERS OF FIRM

Raymond P. Forceno
Gregory John Hannon

Thomas J. Joyce, III
Donald J. Richmond

For full biographical listings, see the Martindale-Hubbell Law Directory

GALLAGHER, REILLY AND LACHAT, P.C. (AV)

Suite 1300, 2000 Market Street, 19103
Telephone: 215-299-3000
FAX: 215-299-3010
Pennsauken, New Jersey Office: Kevon Office Center, Suite 130, 2500 McClellan Boulevard, 08109.
Telephone: 609-663-8200.

Stanley S. Frazee, Jr.
Paul F. X. Gallagher
Thomas F. Reilly
Frederick T. Lachat, Jr.
Richard K. Hohn
James Emerson Egbert
Stephen A. Scheuerle
Elizabeth F. Walker

David Scott Morgan
Wilfred T. Mills, Jr.
Maureen Rowan
Charles L. McNabb
Thomas O'Neill
Laurence I. Gross
Sean F. Kennedy
Milica Novakovic
John A. Livingood, Jr.

SPECIAL COUNSEL

Dolores Rocco Kulp

For full biographical listings, see the Martindale-Hubbell Law Directory

GAY & CHACKER, A PROFESSIONAL CORPORATION (AV)

1731 Spring Garden Street, 19130-3893
Telephone: 215-567-7955
Fax: 215-567-6809
Northeast Philadelphia Office: 12018 Bustleton Avenue.
Telephone: 215-698-9300.
Fax: 215-698-2816.
Collingswood, New Jersey Office: 601 Haddon Executive Center, 601 Haddon Avenue.
Telephone: 609-854-0780.
King of Prussia, Pennsylvania Office: 707 West DeKalb Pike.
Telephone: 610-337-8700.

Andrew G. Gay
Edward F. Chacker
Neil I. Mittin

Daniel J. Siegel
Leanne L. Litwin

For full biographical listings, see the Martindale-Hubbell Law Directory

GREENSPAN, BERK & GABER, P.C. (AV)

Suite 805, 1420-22 Chestnut Street, 19102-2505
Telephone: 215-569-0130
Fax: 215-569-1737

Mitchell S. Greenspan
Todd M. Berk
Andrew H. Gaber

For full biographical listings, see the Martindale-Hubbell Law Directory

KELLEY, JASONS, MCGUIRE & SPINELLI (AV)

Suite 1300, 1234 Market Street, 19107-3713
Telephone: 215-854-0658
Fax: 215-854-8434
Cherry Hill, New Jersey Office: 1230 Brace Road, 08034.
Telephone: 609-429-8956.
Wilmington, Delaware Office: 1220 Market Building, P.O. Box 194, 19899.
Telephone: 302-652-8560.
Fax: 302-652-8405.

MEMBERS OF FIRM

John Patrick Kelley
Catherine N. Jasons
Joseph W. McGuire
Armand J. Della Porta, Jr.
Christopher N. Santoro
Robert N. Spinelli
Thomas P. Hanna
Thomas J. Johanson
Michael L. Turner

ASSOCIATES

Kelly J. Sasso (Resident, Wilmington, Delaware Office)
Richard L. Walker, II
Bernard E. Kueny, III
Timothy McGowan
Neal C. Glenn

OF COUNSEL

Joseph P. Green
Matthew D. Blum, M.D.
W. Matthew Reber

For full biographical listings, see the Martindale-Hubbell Law Directory

KOPS AND FENNER, P.C. (AV)

210 West Washington Square, 19106
Telephone: 215-625-9999
FAX: 215-440-9475

Stanley P. Kops
Diane Fenner
Gershon D. Greenblatt
Michael I. McDermott
Marc S. Henzel

For full biographical listings, see the Martindale-Hubbell Law Directory

ALFRED MARROLETTI AND ASSOCIATES (AV)

The Graham Building-Suite 1504, One Penn Square West 30 S. 15th Street, 19102
Telephone: 215-563-0400

ASSOCIATES

Jacob N. Snyder
Joseph A. Marroletti

For full biographical listings, see the Martindale-Hubbell Law Directory

MCALLISTER & GALLAGHER, P.C. (AV)

Suite 1100, 1760 Market Street, 19103
Telephone: 215-963-1555
Fax: 215-963-9104

John M. McAllister
John J. Gallagher

Michael S. Henry
Laura L. Carberry
Elizabeth McHugh

For full biographical listings, see the Martindale-Hubbell Law Directory

JOHN P. MCKELLIGOTT (AV)

Centre Square East, Suite 1200, 1500 Market Street, 19102
Telephone: 215-557-8201; 610-622-7530
Fax: 610-622-7592
Lansdowne, Pennsylvania Office: 107 Gladstone Road.

For full biographical listings, see the Martindale-Hubbell Law Directory

NEMEROFF, ROBERTS & SAFFREN, A PROFESSIONAL CORPORATION (AV)

260 South Broad Street, 19102
Telephone: 215-790-9750
Elkins Park, Pennsylvania Office: Suite 104, 7848 Old York Road.
Telephone: 215-635-8980.

Milton A. Nemeroff
Lawrence J. Roberts
Kenneth S. Saffren

For full biographical listings, see the Martindale-Hubbell Law Directory

OMINSKY, WELSH & STEINBERG, P.C. (AV)

1760 Market Street, 10th Floor, 19103-4129
Telephone: 215-568-4500
Fax: 215-751-9005
Bridgeport, Pennsylvania Office: 408 East Fourth Street.
Telephone: 215-270-9600.
FAX: 215-270-9990.

Albert Ominsky
Barney B. Welsh
Lennard B. Steinberg
David M. Giles
Joseph L. Messa, Jr.
Mark W. Tanner
Glenn F. Gilman

OF COUNSEL

Jack A. Meyerson
Joel I. Fishbein
Thomas W. Sheridan

RAYNES, MCCARTY, BINDER, ROSS & MUNDY (AV)

1845 Walnut Street, 20th Floor, 19103
Telephone: 215-568-6190
Fax: 215-988-0618
Cable Address: "RAYMAC"
Haddon Heights, New Jersey Office: 116 White Horse Pike, 08035.
Telephone: 609-854-1556.

MEMBERS OF FIRM

Arthur G. Raynes
John J. McCarty
David F. Binder
James F. Mundy
Robert M. Ross
Eugene D. McGurk, Jr.
A. Roy DeCaro
Germaine Ingram (On Leave)
Harold I. Goodman
Harry M. Roth
Nathan B. Ploener
Mark C. Cavanaugh
Frank C. DePasquale, Jr.
Nancy R. Dubow

For full biographical listings, see the Martindale-Hubbell Law Directory

ROSENTHAL AND WEISBERG, P.C. (AV)

Two Logan Square Suite 1565, 18th & Arch Streets, 19103
Telephone: 215-656-4100
Fax: 215-656-4119

(See Next Column)

ROSENTHAL AND WEISBERG P.C.—*Continued*

Brian D. Rosenthal — Michael Stuart Weisberg

Neil T. Murray — Jeffrey A. Nerenberg

For full biographical listings, see the Martindale-Hubbell Law Directory

RUSH & SEIKEN, P.C. (AV)

Suite 1600, 1845 Walnut Street, 19103
Telephone: 215-567-4100

Philip H. Rush, P.C. — Jeffry M. Seiken

Judith M. Sonnenblick

For full biographical listings, see the Martindale-Hubbell Law Directory

SAMUEL AND BALLARD, A PROFESSIONAL CORPORATION (AV)

225 South 15th Street, Suite 1700, 19102
Telephone: 215-893-9990

Ralph David Samuel — Alice W. Ballard

OF COUNSEL

Babette Josephs

Shari Reed — Lynn Malmgren

For full biographical listings, see the Martindale-Hubbell Law Directory

SHRAGER, McDAID, LOFTUS, FLUM & SPIVEY (AV)

32nd Floor, Two Commerce Square, 2001 Market Street, 19103
Telephone: 215-568-7771
Fax: 215-568-7495
Voorhees, New Jersey Office: 502 Haddonfield-Berlin Road.
Telephone: 609-354-9116.

MEMBERS OF FIRM

David S. Shrager — Joanna Hamill Flum
Edward B. McDaid — Wayne R. Spivey
William A. Loftus — Michael S. Bloom

David Stein

For full biographical listings, see the Martindale-Hubbell Law Directory

SARAH M. THOMPSON (AV)

1710 Spruce Street, 19103
Telephone: 215-790-4568
Fax: 215-735-2211

For full biographical listings, see the Martindale-Hubbell Law Directory

*PITTSBURGH,** Allegheny Co.

ADERSON, FRANK & STEINER, A PROFESSIONAL CORPORATION (AV)

2320 Grant Building, 15219
Telephone: 412-263-0500
Fax: 412-263-0565

Mark S. Frank — Richard H. Malmstrom

For full biographical listings, see the Martindale-Hubbell Law Directory

BALZARINI, CAREY & WATSON (AV)

3303 Grant Building, 15219
Telephone: 412-471-1200
Fax: 412-471-8326

MEMBERS OF FIRM

Edward J. Balzarini — David J. Watson
Francis J. Carey — Michael Balzarini
Edward J. Balzarini, Jr. — Joseph S. Bielecki

For full biographical listings, see the Martindale-Hubbell Law Directory

BERGER KAPETAN MEYERS ROSEN LOUIK & RAIZMAN, P.C. (AV)

Suite 200 The Frick Building, 15219-6003
Telephone: 412-281-4200
Fax: 412-281-3262

Daniel M. Berger — Michael Louik
Alex N. Kapetan — Dorothy L. Raizman
Jerry I. Meyers — Susan E. Mahood
Neil R. Rosen — Andrew L. Horvath

For full biographical listings, see the Martindale-Hubbell Law Directory

BUCHANAN INGERSOLL, PROFESSIONAL CORPORATION (AV)

5800 USX Tower, 600 Grant Street, 15219
Telephone: 412-562-8800
Telecopier: 412-562-1041
Philadelphia, Pennsylvania Office: Two Logan Square, Twelfth Floor, 18th & Arch Streets.
Telephone: 215-665-8700.
Harrisburg, Pennsylvania Office: Vartan Parc, 30 North Third Street.
Telephone: 717-237-4800.
Tampa, Florida Office: 101 East Kennedy Boulevard, Suite 1030.
Telephone: 813-222-8180.
North Miami Beach, Florida Office: 19495 Biscayne Boulevard.
Telephone: 305-933-5600.
Lexington, Kentucky Office: 1210 Vine Center Office Tower, 333 West Vine Street.
Telephone: 606-225-5333.
Princeton, New Jersey Office: Buchanan Ingersoll, A Partnership, College Centre, 500 College Road East.
Telephone: 609-452-2666.

Paul D. Kruper — Stanley Yorsz

For Complete List of Firm Personnel, See General Section

For full biographical listings, see the Martindale-Hubbell Law Directory

JOHN A. CAPUTO & ASSOCIATES (AV)

Fifth Floor, Three Gateway Center, 15222
Telephone: 412-391-4990

Allan Meyers Cox — Bernard C. Caputo

For full biographical listings, see the Martindale-Hubbell Law Directory

ROBERT A. COHEN (AV)

819 Frick Building, 15219
Telephone: 412-261-9700

For full biographical listings, see the Martindale-Hubbell Law Directory

EVANS, IVORY P.C. (AV)

1311 Frick Building, 15219
Telephone: 412-471-3740
Fax: 412-471-3457

Paul E. Moses — Robin S. Wertkin
Thomas Hollander — Dennis M. Morgenstern
J. Bradley Kearns

For full biographical listings, see the Martindale-Hubbell Law Directory

EVANS, PORTNOY & QUINN (AV)

36th Floor, One Oxford Centre, 301 Grant Street, 15219-6401
Telephone: 412-765-3800
Fax: 412-765-3747

Charles E. Evans — Irving M. Portnoy
John E. Quinn

ASSOCIATES

Anita Amato Scaglione — Herbert B. Cohen
Mark E. Milsop

For full biographical listings, see the Martindale-Hubbell Law Directory

FECZKO AND SEYMOUR (AV)

520 Grant Building, 15219
Telephone: 412-261-4970
Fax: Available upon Request
Bethel Park, Pennsylvania Office: 3400 South Park Road.
Telephone: 412-833-5554.

MEMBERS OF FIRM

Albert G. Feczko, Jr. — Michael J. Seymour

ASSOCIATES

Mark F. Bennett — Michael D. Seymour

Reference: Pittsburgh National Bank.

For full biographical listings, see the Martindale-Hubbell Law Directory

FELDSTEIN GRINBERG STEIN & McKEE, A PROFESSIONAL CORPORATION (AV)

428 Boulevard of the Allies, 15219
Telephone: 412-471-0677
Fax: 412-263-6129
Elizabeth, Pennsylvania Office: 400 Second Street.
Telephone: 412-384-6111.
Wexford, Pennsylvania Office: 12300 Perry Highway.
Telephone: 412-935-5540.

Jay H. Feldstein — Gary M. Lang

(See Next Column)

FELDSTEIN GRINBERG STEIN & MCKEE A PROFESSIONAL CORPORATION, *Pittsburgh—Continued*

Craig L. Fishman
Joseph L. Orszulak, II

For full biographical listings, see the Martindale-Hubbell Law Directory

GACA, MATIS & HAMILTON, A PROFESSIONAL CORPORATION (AV)

300 Four PPG Place, 15222-5404
Telephone: 412-338-4750
Fax: 412-338-4742

Giles J. Gaca
Thomas A. Matis
Mark R. Hamilton
John W. Jordan, IV
Alan S. Baum
Thomas P. McGinnis
Bernard R. Rizza
Jeffrey A. Ramaley
Stephen J. Dalesio
John Timothy Hinton, Jr.
Shawn Lynne Reed

LEGAL SUPPORT PERSONNEL

PARALEGALS

Tina M. Shanafelt
Jill M. Peterson

For full biographical listings, see the Martindale-Hubbell Law Directory

GAITENS, TUCCERI & NICHOLAS, A PROFESSIONAL CORPORATION (AV)

519 Court Place, 15219
Telephone: 412-391-6920
Fax: 412-391-1189

Larry P. Gaitens
Vincent A. Tucceri
Romel L. Nicholas

Reference: Pittsburgh National Bank.

For Complete List of Firm Personnel, See General Section

For full biographical listings, see the Martindale-Hubbell Law Directory

HAROLD GONDELMAN (AV)

The 38th Floor, One Oxford Centre, 15219
Telephone: 412-263-1833

For full biographical listings, see the Martindale-Hubbell Law Directory

WILLIAM W. GUTHRIE & ASSOCIATES A PROFESSIONAL CORPORATION (AV)

416 Frick Building, 437 Grant Street, 15219
Telephone: 412-562-0556
Fax: 412-562-5920

William W. Guthrie

Reference: Pittsburgh National Bank (Potter Office).

For full biographical listings, see the Martindale-Hubbell Law Directory

KIGER MESSER & ALPERN (AV)

1404 Grant Building, 15219
Telephone: 412-281-7200
Fax: 412-765-0440

MEMBERS OF FIRM

Jerome W. Kiger
Howard F. Messer
Charles H. Alpern

ASSOCIATE

Alice Warner Shumlas

For Complete List of Firm Personnel, See General Section

For full biographical listings, see the Martindale-Hubbell Law Directory

KING & KING (AV)

Twenty Chatham Square, 15219
Telephone: 412-391-1200
Fax: 412-391-7082

Peter J. King
Linda A. King

Approved Attorneys for: First American Title Insurance Company.

For full biographical listings, see the Martindale-Hubbell Law Directory

LITMAN LITMAN HARRIS & BROWN, P.C. (AV)

3600 One Oxford Centre, 15219
Telephone: 412-456-2000
Fax: 412-456-2020

(See Next Column)

S. David Litman, P.C.
Roslyn M. Litman
Stephen J. Harris
David R. Brown
Martha S. Helmreich
Lester G. Nauhaus
Daniel L. Chunko
Mark F. Flaherty
Joseph Leibowicz
Robert J. O'Hara, III

For full biographical listings, see the Martindale-Hubbell Law Directory

MARCUS & SHAPIRA (AV)

35th Floor, One Oxford Centre, 301 Grant Street, 15219-6401
Telephone: 412-471-3490
Telecopier: 412-391-8758

MEMBERS OF FIRM

Bernard D. Marcus
Daniel H. Shapira
George P. Slesinger
Robert L. Allman, II
Estelle F. Comay
Susan Gromis Flynn
Darlene M. Nowak
Glenn M. Olcerst
Elly Heller-Toig
Sylvester A. Beozzo

OF COUNSEL

John M. Burkoff

SPECIAL COUNSEL

Jane Campbell Moriarty

ASSOCIATES

Scott D. Livingston
Robert M. Barnes
Stephen S. Zubrow
David B. Rodes
Lori E. McMaster
Melody A. Pollock
James F. Rosenberg
Amy M. Gottlieb

For full biographical listings, see the Martindale-Hubbell Law Directory

WILLIAM W. MCVAY (AV)

Suite 530, 2559 Washington Road, 15241
Telephone: 412-854-3250

ASSOCIATES

William W. McVay, III
James M. McVay, II

Legal Counsel for: United Transportation Union.

For full biographical listings, see the Martindale-Hubbell Law Directory

MERCER & MERCER (AV)

1218 Frick Building, 15219
Telephone: 412-281-2728
FAX: 412-281-2248

H. Fred Mercer (1904-1939)
H. Fred Mercer, III

Gina M. Campisano
Amy B. Kubisiak

OF COUNSEL

H. Fred Mercer

Reference: Pittsburgh National Bank.

For full biographical listings, see the Martindale-Hubbell Law Directory

PIETRAGALLO, BOSICK & GORDON (AV)

The Thirty-Eighth Floor, One Oxford Centre, 15219
Telephone: 412-263-2000
Facsimile: 412-261-5295

MEMBERS OF FIRM

William Pietragallo, II
Joseph J. Bosick
Mark Gordon
John E. Hall
Spencer D. Hirshberg
Robert J. Behling
Lawrence J. Baldasare
William S. Smith
Francis E. Pipak, Jr.
LuAnn Haley
Paul K. Vey
Nora Barry Fischer
Thomas J. Sweeney, Jr.
Daniel D. Harshman
Robert E. Dapper, Jr.
David H. Dille

ASSOCIATES

Robert H. Gustine
Harry J. Klucher
Robert R. Leight
Christopher L. Wildfire
Heather S. Heidelbaugh
Eric K. Falk
James G. Orie
Stacey F. Vernallis
Mark F. Haak
Pamela G. Cochenour
William W. Schrimpf, Sr.
Michael P. Sosso
Vincent A Coppola
Clem C. Trischler, Jr.
Anthony G. Sanchez
Kenneth T. Newman
C. Peter Hitson
Raymond G. McLaughlin
David Paul Franklin
Brian S. Kane
Linda M. Gillen
Robert J. Colville
Brian K. Parker
Sean B. Epstein
Lisa P. McQuarrie

COUNSEL

Harold Gondelman
Alfred S. Pelaez

For full biographical listings, see the Martindale-Hubbell Law Directory

Pittsburgh—Continued

SCOTT, VOGRIN, RIESTER & JAMIOLKOWSKI, A PROFESSIONAL CORPORATION (AV)

1510 Frick Building, 15219
Telephone: 412-261-0905
Fax: 412-261-3090
Shaler Township, Pennsylvania Office: 1330 Evergreen Avenue, Pittsburgh, 15209.
Telephone: 412-261-0905.
Sewickley, Pennsylvania Office: Osborne Plaza, Suite 603, 1106 Ohio River Boulevard, 15143.
Telephone: 412-261-0905.

Richard S. Scott
Alexander J. Jamiolkowski

Margaret Mary Egan

For full biographical listings, see the Martindale-Hubbell Law Directory

SWENSEN PERER & JOHNSON (AV)

Two PNC Plaza, Suite 2710, 15222
Telephone: 412-281-1970
Fax: 412-281-2808
Erie, Pennsylvania Office: 209 Court House Commons.
Telephone: 814-456-0489.

MEMBERS OF FIRM

Jan C. Swensen
Alan H. Perer
J. Alan Johnson
Peter B. Skeel
David M. Landay
John W. McCandless (Resident Partner, Erie, Pennsylvania Office)

ASSOCIATES

John Carl Bogut, Jr.
David A. Schroeder (Resident Associate, Erie, Pennsylvania Office)
John J. Edson, V
Anthony J. Sciarrino
George M. Kontos

For full biographical listings, see the Martindale-Hubbell Law Directory

TARASI & JOHNSON, P.C. (AV)

510 Third Avenue, 15219
Telephone: 412-391-7135
Fax: 412-471-2673

Louis M. Tarasi, Jr.
David E. Johnson

John A. Adamczyk
Elizabeth Tarasi Stevenson
Jean A. Kell
Matthew A. Hartley

For full biographical listings, see the Martindale-Hubbell Law Directory

WIMER LAW OFFICES, P.C. (AV)

Two Fox Chapel Place, 1326 Freeport Road, 15238
Telephone: 412-967-9111
Fax: 412-967-0178

Matthew R. Wimer

PUNXSUTAWNEY, Jefferson Co.

LORENZO & KULAKOWSKI, P.C. (AV)

410 West Mahoning Street, 15767
Telephone: 814-938-6390

Nicholas F. Lorenzo, Jr.
George D. Kulakowski

Nicholas A. Gianvito

For full biographical listings, see the Martindale-Hubbell Law Directory

*SCRANTON,** Lackawanna Co.

FOLEY, MCLANE, NEALON, FOLEY & MCDONALD (AV)

Linden Plaza, 600 Linden Street, P.O. Box 1108, 18501-1108
Telephone: 717-342-8194
Fax: 717-342-4658
Stroudsburg, Pennsylvania Office: 26 North Sixth Street.
Telephone: 717-424-1757.
Fax: 717-424-2764.

Thomas J. Foley, Jr.
John T. McLane
Terrence R. Nealon
Michael J. Foley
Michael J. McDonald
Thomas J. Foley, III (Resident, Stroudsburg Office)
Kevin P. Foley
Malcolm L. MacGregor
M. Colleen Foley Canovas

For full biographical listings, see the Martindale-Hubbell Law Directory

KREDER, BROOKS, HAILSTONE & LUDWIG (AV)

Suite 200, 220 Penn Avenue, 18503
Telephone: 717-346-7922
Telecopier: 717-346-3715

(See Next Column)

Cody H. Brooks
Andrew Hailstone
Lawrence M. Ludwig
Lucille Marsh
Michael J. Donohue
David K. Brown
J. Frederick Rohrbeck
James J. Wilson
Richard G. Reed
Stephen William Saunders

ASSOCIATES

Ann Lavelle Powell
Linda Dwyer Cleary
Barbara Sardella
Alyce Hailstone Farrell
Robert B. Farrell
David A. Aikens, Jr.

OF COUNSEL

Joseph C. Kreder
Willard M. Henkelman
James Edson O'Connell

Counsel for: Consolidated Rail Corp.; PNC Bank; U.S. Fidelity & Guaranty Co.; Nationwide Insurance Co.; Liberty Mutual Insurance Co.; Citizens Savings Assn.; NEP Supershooters, Inc.

For full biographical listings, see the Martindale-Hubbell Law Directory

LENAHAN & DEMPSEY, A PROFESSIONAL CORPORATION (AV)

116 North Washington Avenue, 18503-0234
Telephone: 717-346-2097
Fax: 717-346-1174
Mailing Address: P.O. Box 234, Scranton, Pennsylvania, 18501-0234

John R. Lenahan, Sr.
William J. Dempsey
John R. Lenahan, Jr.
Joseph P. Lenahan
Kathleen A. Lenahan
David E. Heisler
Timothy G. Lenahan
Matthew D. Dempsey

Marianne J. Gilmartin
Alan P. Schoen
Brian J. Lenahan
Diane Hepford Lenahan
George E. Mehalchick
Brian Yeager
Thomas R. Daniels
Myles P. McAliney
Terrence E. Dempsey
Carmina M. Rinkunas
Thomas R. Chesnick
William M. Blaum
Christine S. Mayernick
Patricia Corbett

Representative Insurance Clients: Allstate Insurance Co.; America Security Insurance Co.; Metropolitan Casualty Insurance Co.; Statesman Insurance Group; Foremost Insurance Co.; Aetna Insurance Co.; Pennsylvania National Insurance Group; Kemper Insurance Group; American Mutual Insurance Cos.; American States Insurance, Co.

For full biographical listings, see the Martindale-Hubbell Law Directory

MUNLEY, MATTISE, KELLY & CARTWRIGHT (AV)

205 Madison Avenue, P.O. Box 1066, 18503
Telephone: 717-346-7401
Fax: 717-346-3452

MEMBERS OF FIRM

Robert W. Munley
Nicholas S. Mattise
P. Timothy Kelly
Marion Munley
Matthew A. Cartwright
J. Christopher Munley

Reference: First National Bank of Jermyn.

For full biographical listings, see the Martindale-Hubbell Law Directory

*STROUDSBURG,** Monroe Co.

GEORGE W. WESTERVELT, JR. (AV)

304 Park Avenue, P.O. Box 549, 18360-0549
Telephone: 717-421-6100
FAX: 717-421-8027

John C. Prevoznik
Jonathan Mark

Reference: First Eastern Bank, N.A.

For full biographical listings, see the Martindale-Hubbell Law Directory

*WELLSBORO,** Tioga Co.

SPENCER, GLEASON, HEBE & RAGUE (AV)

17 Central Avenue, P.O. Box 507, 16901
Telephone: 717-724-1832
FAX: 717-724-7610

MEMBERS OF FIRM

Warren H. Spencer (1921-1991)
Gary M. Gleason
William A. Hebe
James T. Rague

ASSOCIATE

Jeffrey S. Loomis

References: Citizens & Northern Bank; Commonwealth Bank & Trust Co.

For full biographical listings, see the Martindale-Hubbell Law Directory

*WEST CHESTER,** Chester Co.

BUCKLEY, NAGLE, GENTRY, McGUIRE & MORRIS (AV)

304 North High Street, P.O. Box 133, 19380
Telephone: 610-436-4400
Telecopier: 610-436-8305
Thorndale, Pennsylvania Office: 3532 East Lincoln Highway.
Telephone: 215-383-5666.

MEMBERS OF FIRM

C. Barry Buckley
Ronald C. Nagle
W. Richard Gentry
Stephen P. McGuire
Anthony Morris
John J. Teti, Jr.
Jeffrey R. Sommer
Isabel M. Albuquerque

OF COUNSEL

R. Curtis Schroder

For full biographical listings, see the Martindale-Hubbell Law Directory

DUFFY & GREEN (AV)

10 North Church Street, Suite 307, 19380
Telephone: 610-692-0500
FAX: 610-430-6668

MEMBERS OF FIRM

John J. Duffy
Joseph P. Green, Jr.

ASSOCIATES

Richard E. Meanix
P.J. Redmond

For full biographical listings, see the Martindale-Hubbell Law Directory

LAMB, WINDLE & McERLANE, P.C. (AV)

24 East Market Street, P.O. Box 565, 19381-0565
Telephone: 610-430-8000
Telecopier: 610-692-0877

COUNSEL

Theodore O. Rogers

William H. Lamb
Susan Windle Rogers
James E. McErlane
E. Craig Kalemjian
James C. Sargent, Jr.
John D. Snyder
William P. Mahon
Guy A. Donatelli
Vincent M. Pompo
James J. McEntee III

Tracy Blake DeVlieger
P. Andrew Schaum
Lawrence J. Persick
Thomas K. Schindler
Daniel A. Loewenstern
Thomas F. Oeste
John W. Pauciulo
Andrea B. Pettine
John J. Cunningham

Representative Clients: Chester County; First Financial Savings Bank, PaSA; Bank of Chester County; Jefferson Bank; Downingtown Area and Great Valley School Districts; Philadelphia Electric Company; Central and Western Chester County Industrial Development Authority; Valley Forge Sewer Authority; Manito Title Insurance Company.

For full biographical listings, see the Martindale-Hubbell Law Directory

MACELREE, HARVEY, GALLAGHER, FEATHERMAN & SEBASTIAN, LTD. (AV)

17 West Miner Street, P.O. Box 660, 19381-0660
Telephone: 610-436-0100
Fax: 610-430-7885
Kennett Square, Pennsylvania Office: 211 E. State Street, P. O. Box 363.
Telephone 215-444-3180.
Fax: 215-444-3270.
Spring City, Pennsylvania Office: 3694 Schuylkill Road.
Telephone: 215-948-5700.

Lawrence E. MacElree
Dominic T. Marrone
William J. Gallagher
John A. Featherman, III
Randy L. Sebastian
Terry W. Knox
Michael G. Louis
Randall C. Schauer
Stacey W. McConnell
Frederick P. Kramer, II
John F. McKenna
C. Douglas Parvin
Harry J. DiDonato
Lance J. Nelson
Bernadette M. Walsh
Linda C. Tice
Joseph F. Harvey (1921-1985)
J. Barton Rettew, Jr. (1901-1981)
Richard Reifsnyder (1928-1974)

For full biographical listings, see the Martindale-Hubbell Law Directory

*WILKES-BARRE,** Luzerne Co.

HOURIGAN, KLUGER, SPOHRER & QUINN, A PROFESSIONAL CORPORATION (AV)

700 Mellon Bank Center, 8 West Market Street, 18701-1867
Telephone: 717-825-9401
FAX: 717-829-3460
Scranton, Pennsylvania Office: Suite 200, 434 Lackawanna Avenue.
Telephone: 717-346-8414.

(See Next Column)

Allentown, Pennsylvania Office: Sovereign Building, 609 Hamilton Mall.
Telephone: 610-437-1584.
Hazelton, Pennsylvania Office: CAN DO Building, One South Church Street.
Telephone: 717-455-5141.

Joseph A. Quinn, Jr.
Eugene D. Sperazza
Melissa A. Scartelli
Fred T. Howe
Jacqueline Musto Carroll
Daniel J. Distasio, Jr.
Joseph M. Campolieto (Resident, Scranton Office)

Representative Client: Aetna Casualty & Surety Co.

For Complete List of Firm Personnel, See General Section

For full biographical listings, see the Martindale-Hubbell Law Directory

*WILLIAMSPORT,** Lycoming Co.

MITCHELL, MITCHELL, GRAY & GALLAGHER, A PROFESSIONAL CORPORATION (AV)

10 West Third Street, 17701
Telephone: 717-323-8404
Fax: 717-323-8585

C. Edward S. Mitchell
Richard A. Gray
Robert A. Gallagher
Gary L. Weber

Bret J. Southard
Eric R. Linhardt

OF COUNSEL

Jacob Neafie Mitchell

For full biographical listings, see the Martindale-Hubbell Law Directory

RIEDERS, TRAVIS, MUSSINA, HUMPHREY & HARRIS (AV)

161 West Third Street, P.O. Box 215, 17703-0215
Telephone: 717-323-8711
1-800-326-9259
Fax: 717-323-4192

MEMBERS OF FIRM

Gary T. Harris
John M. Humphrey
Malcolm S. Mussina
Clifford A. Rieders
Ronald C. Travis
Thomas Waffenschmidt
C. Scott Waters

ASSOCIATES

Robert H. Vesely
Jeffrey C. Dohrmann
James Michael Wiley

LEGAL SUPPORT PERSONNEL

Kimberly A. Paulhamus

Representative Clients: Jersey Shore State Bank; Gamble Twp.; Crown American Corp.; Fowler Motors, Inc.; Twin Hills oldsmobile, Inc.; Brady Twp.; Cascade Twp.; Cogan House Twp.; Susquehana Twp.; Upper Fairfield Twp.; Borough of Picture Rocks.

For full biographical listings, see the Martindale-Hubbell Law Directory

RHODE ISLAND

MIDDLETOWN, Newport Co.

JOSEPH R. PALUMBO, JR. (AV)

294 Valley Road, 02842
Telephone: 401-846-5200
Telecopier: 401-848-0984

For full biographical listings, see the Martindale-Hubbell Law Directory

*PROVIDENCE,** Providence Co.

CHISHOLM AND FELDMAN (AV)

1410 Hospital Trust Tower, 02903
Telephone: 401-331-6300
Telecopier: 401-421-3185

MEMBERS OF FIRM

Vincent J. Chisholm
Howard L. Feldman

ASSOCIATES

Nancy M. Feldman
Denise Aiken-Salandria
Robert V. Chisholm

For full biographical listings, see the Martindale-Hubbell Law Directory

DECOF & GRIMM, A PROFESSIONAL CORPORATION (AV)

One Smith Hill, 02903
Telephone: 401-272-1110
Facsimile: 401-351-6641
Newport, Rhode Island Office: 130 Bellevue Avenue, 02840.
Telephone: 401-848-5700.
Facsimile: 401-847-3391.

(See Next Column)

DECOF & GRIMM A PROFESSIONAL CORPORATION—*Continued*

Leonard Decof
E. Paul Grimm
Mark B. Decof
John S. Foley
Vincent T. Cannon
Donna M. Di Donato
David Morowitz
Daniel J. Schatz
Howard B. Klein
Suzanne M. McGrath
Peri Ann Aptaker
(Not admitted in RI)
Christine M. Renda
(Not admitted in RI)

OF COUNSEL

Arthur I. Fixler

For full biographical listings, see the Martindale-Hubbell Law Directory

MARTIN K. DONOVAN (AV)

Second Floor, One Park Row, 02903
Telephone: 401-831-2500
Facsimile: 401-751-7830

Reference: Fleet National Bank.

For full biographical listings, see the Martindale-Hubbell Law Directory

GIDLEY, SARLI & MARUSAK (AV)

Greater Providence Bank Building, 170 Westminster Street, 02903
Telephone: 401-274-6644
Telecopier: 401-331-9304

MEMBERS OF FIRM

Thomas D. Gidley
Michael G. Sarli
James P. Marusak
Mark C. Hadden

ASSOCIATES

Michael R. DeLuca
Linn Foster Freedman
Denise M. Lombardo
William L. Wheatley
Stuart D. Hallagan III

LEGAL SUPPORT PERSONNEL

Elaine M. Noren
Mary Repoza Caplette
Darlene E. Kotkofski

For full biographical listings, see the Martindale-Hubbell Law Directory

HODOSH, SPINELLA & ANGELONE (AV)

128 Dorrance Street, Shakespeare Hall, Suite 450, P.O. Box 1516, 02901-1516
Telephone: 401-274-0200
Fax: 401-274-7538

Thomas C. Angelone
Hugh L. Moore, Jr.
Kevin M. Cain

ASSOCIATE

John R. Izzo

Reference: Fleet National Bank.

For Complete List of Firm Personnel, See General Section

For full biographical listings, see the Martindale-Hubbell Law Directory

VINCENT D. MORGERA (AV)

One Old Stone Square, 02903-7104
Telephone: 401-456-0300
Telecopier: 401-456-0303

For full biographical listings, see the Martindale-Hubbell Law Directory

VOGEL, SOULS & WOODBINE (AV)

312 South Main Street, 02903
Telephone: 401-454-5350

MEMBERS OF FIRM

Netti C. Vogel
Donald A. Woodbine
James M. Souls

For full biographical listings, see the Martindale-Hubbell Law Directory

WARWICK, Kent Co.

KIRSHENBAUM LAW ASSOCIATES (AV)

67 Jefferson Boulevard, 02888-1053
Telephone: 401-467-5300
Fax: 401-461-4464

MEMBERS OF FIRM

Allen M. Kirshenbaum
Carolyn R. Barone
Lauri S. Medwin
Evan M. Kirshenbaum

For full biographical listings, see the Martindale-Hubbell Law Directory

WESTERLY, Washington Co.

ADAMO & NEWMAN (AV)

42 Granite Street, 02891
Telephone: 401-596-7795
Telecopier: 401-596-9000

MEMBERS OF FIRM

John Joseph Adamo
Edward H. Newman

OF COUNSEL

George A. Comolli

LEGAL SUPPORT PERSONNEL

Susan E. Bookataub

For full biographical listings, see the Martindale-Hubbell Law Directory

SOUTH CAROLINA

*AIKEN,** Aiken Co.

BODENHEIMER, BUSBEE, HUNTER & GRIFFITH (AV)

147 Newberry Street, N.W., P.O. Drawer 2009, 29802
Telephone: 803-648-3255
Telefax: 803-648-3278

MEMBERS OF FIRM

John T. Bodenheimer
John M. Hunter, Jr.
M. Anderson Griffith

For Complete List of Firm Personnel, See General Section

For full biographical listings, see the Martindale-Hubbell Law Directory

HENDERSON & SALLEY (AV)

111 Park Avenue, Southwest, P.O. Box 517, 29802-0517
Telephone: 803-648-4213
Fax: 803-648-2601

MEMBERS OF FIRM

Julian B. Salley, Jr.
Michael K. Farmer
William H. Tucker
James D. Nance

ASSOCIATE

Amy Patterson Shumpert

Attorneys for: NationsBank South Carolina (N.A.); South Carolina Electric & Gas Co.; The Graniteville Co.; Maryland Casualty Co.; Southern Bell Telephone & Telegraph Co.; Owens Corning Fiberglass Corp.; City of Aiken; United Merchants & Manufacturers, Inc.; Allstate Insurance Co.

For full biographical listings, see the Martindale-Hubbell Law Directory

JOHNSON, JOHNSON, WHITTLE, SNELGROVE & WEEKS, P.A. (AV)

117 Pendleton Street, N.W., P.O. Box 2619, 29802-2619
Telephone: 803-649-5338
FAX: 803-641-4517

B. Henderson Johnson, Jr.
Barry H. Johnson
James E. Whittle, Jr.
Vicki Johnson Snelgrove
John W. (Bill) Weeks
Paige Weeks Johnson
Todd J. Johnson

For full biographical listings, see the Martindale-Hubbell Law Directory

*CHARLESTON,** Charleston Co.

HOOD LAW FIRM (AV)

172 Meeting Street, P.O. Box 1508, 29402
Telephone: 803-577-4435
FAX: 803-722-1630

MEMBERS OF FIRM

Robert H. Hood
Louis P. Herns
G. Mark Phillips
Carl Everette Pierce, II
John K. Blincow, Jr.

James G. Kennedy
James Dowell Gandy, III
William R. Hearn, Jr.
Joseph C. Wilson, IV
Dixon F. Pearce, III
Margaret Allison Snead
Barbara Wynne Showers
Christine L. Companion
Hugh Willcox Buyck
Jerry A. Smith
Allan Poe Sloan, III
Todd W. Smyth

For full biographical listings, see the Martindale-Hubbell Law Directory

ROSEN, ROSEN & HAGOOD, P.A. (AV)

134 Meeting Street, Suite 200, P.O. Box 893, 29402
Telephone: 803-577-6726

(See Next Column)

ROSEN, ROSEN & HAGOOD P.A., *Charleston—Continued*

Morris D. Rosen
Richard S. Rosen
Susan Corner Rosen

Peter Brandt Shelbourne
Alexander B. Cash
Daniel F. Blanchard, III

Reference: NationsBank of South Carolina, N.A.

For Complete List of Firm Personnel, See General Section

For full biographical listings, see the Martindale-Hubbell Law Directory

SOLOMON, KAHN, BUDMAN & STRICKER (AV)

39 Broad Street, P.O. Drawer P, 29402
Telephone: 803-577-7182
Telecopier: 803-722-0485

A. Bernard Solomon
Ellis I. Kahn
Donald J. Budman
Michael A. Stricker

ASSOCIATE

Justin S. Kahn

Local Counsel for: Lawyers Title Insurance Corp.

For full biographical listings, see the Martindale-Hubbell Law Directory

*COLUMBIA,** Richland Co.

FINKEL, GOLDBERG, SHEFTMAN & ALTMAN, P.A. (AV)

Suite 1800, 1201 Main Street, P.O. Box 1799, 29202
Telephone: 803-765-2935
Fax: 803-252-0786
Charleston, South Carolina Office: 12 Exchange Street, P.O. Box 225.
Telephone: 803-577-5460.
Fax: 803-577-5135.

Gerald M. Finkel
Harry L. Goldberg
Howard S. Sheftman

Representative Clients: Hewitt-Robins; 1st Union National Bank; Banc One Mortgage Co.; Motorola Communications & Electronics Corp.

For full biographical listings, see the Martindale-Hubbell Law Directory

FURR AND HENSHAW (AV)

A Partnership of Professional Corporations
1534 Blanding Street, 29201
Telephone: 803-252-4050
Fax: 803-254-7513
Myrtle Beach, South Carolina Office: 1900 Oak Street, P.O. Box 2909.
Telephone: 803-626-7621.
FAX: 803-448-6445.

O. Fayrell Furr, Jr. (P.C.)
Charles L. Henshaw, Jr. (P.C.)

Karolan Furr Ohanesian (Resident, Myrtle Beach Office)

Reference: Anchor Bank, Myrtle Beach, S.C.

For full biographical listings, see the Martindale-Hubbell Law Directory

GLENN, IRVIN, MURPHY, GRAY & STEPP (AV)

Southern National Bank Building, Suite 390, 1901 Assembly Street, P.O. Box 1550, 29202-1550
Telephone: 803-765-1100
Telecopy: 803-765-0755

MEMBERS OF FIRM

Wilmot B. Irvin
Peter L. Murphy

Blaney A. Coskrey, III
Robert A. Culpepper

Reference: Southern National.

For Complete List of Firm Personnel, See General Section

For full biographical listings, see the Martindale-Hubbell Law Directory

RICHARDSON, PLOWDEN, GRIER AND HOWSER, P.A. (AV)

1600 Marion Street, P.O. Drawer 7788, 29202
Telephone: 803-771-4400
Telecopy: 803-779-0016
Myrtle Beach, South Carolina Office: Southern National Bank Building, Suite 202, 601 21st Avenue North, P.O. Box 3646, 29578.
Telephone: 803-448-1008.
FAX: 803-448-1533.

Donald V. Richardson, III
Charles N. Plowden, Jr.
F. Barron Grier, III
R. Davis Howser
Charles E. Carpenter, Jr.
Michael A. Pulliam
George C. Beighley
William H. Hensel
Leslie A. Cotter, Jr.
James P. Newman, Jr.

(See Next Column)

Deborah Harrison Sheffield
Douglas C. Baxter
William G. Besley
Mary L. Sowell League

Representative Clients: Insurance: CNA Insurance Co.; The Hartford; Kemper Insurance Co.; Pennsylvania National Mutual Casualty Insurance Co.; Wausau Insurance Cos.; The Reudlinger Cos.

For Complete List of Firm Personnel, See General Section

For full biographical listings, see the Martindale-Hubbell Law Directory

ROBINSON, MCFADDEN & MOORE, P.C. (AV)

Fifteen Hundred NationsBank Plaza, 1901 Main Street, P.O. Box 944, 29202
Telephone: 803-779-8900
Telecopier: 803-252-0724

David W. Robinson, Sr. (1869-1935)
R. Hoke Robinson (1916-1977)
J. Means McFadden (1901-1990)
David W. Robinson (1899-1989)
David W. Robinson, II
D. Reece Williams, III
John S. Taylor, Jr.
James M. Brailsford, III
Daniel T. Brailsford
Frank R. Ellerbe, III
Thomas W. Bunch, II
J. Kershaw Spong
D. Clay Robinson
Jacquelyn Lee Bartley
E. Meredith Manning
R. William Metzger, Jr.
Kevin K. Bell
Annemarie B. Mathews

OF COUNSEL

Thomas T. Moore

Representative Clients: NationsBank; Chemical Financial Corp.; Transcontinental Gas Pipe Line Corp.; The Equitable Life Insurance Society of the U.S.; Metropolitan Life Insurance Co.; Firestone Tire & Rubber Co.; Mutual Life Insurance Company of New York.; South Carolina Insurance Reserve Fund; South Carolina Insurance Co.

For full biographical listings, see the Martindale-Hubbell Law Directory

TURNER, PADGET, GRAHAM & LANEY, P.A. (AV)

Seventeenth Floor, 1901 Main Street, P.O. Box 1473, 29202
Telephone: 803-254-2200
Telecopy: 803-799-3957
Florence, South Carolina Office: Fourth Floor, 1831 West Evans Street, P.O. Box 5478, 29501.
Telephone: 803-662-9008.
Telecopy: 803-667-0828.

Nathaniel A. Turner (1897-1959)
Edward W. Laney, III (1930-1980)
Harrell M. Graham (Retired)
George E. Lewis
Ronald E. Boston
Edwin P. Martin
Carl B. Epps, III
W. Duvall Spruill
Charles E. Hill
Thomas C. Salane
Danny C. Crowe
R. Wayne Byrd (Resident, Florence, SC, Office)
W. Hugh McAngus
John S. Wilkerson, III (Resident, Florence, SC, Office)
Steven W. Ouzts
Michael S. Church
Timothy D. St. Clair
Laura Callaway Hart
John E. Cuttino
Arthur E. Justice, Jr. (Resident, Florence, SC, Office)
Edward W. Laney, IV
Elbert S. Dorn
J. Russell Goudelock, II

OF COUNSEL

Henry Fletcher Padget, Jr.
Hugh M. Claytor (Resident, Florence, SC, Office)
James R. Courie

J. Kenneth Carter, Jr.

Representative Clients: Independent Life & Accident Insurance Co.; Ford Motor Co.; Insurance Company of North America; Navistar International Corp.; Winn-Dixie Stores, Inc.; Allstate Insurance Co.; Continental Insurance Co.; Atlantic Soft Drink Co.; National Council on Compensation Insurance.

For Complete List of Firm Personnel, See General Section

For full biographical listings, see the Martindale-Hubbell Law Directory

WOODWARD, LEVENTIS, UNGER, DAVES, HERNDON AND COTHRAN (AV)

(Formerly Woodward, Leventis, Unger, Herndon and Cothran)
1300 Sumter, P.O. Box 12399, 29211
Telephone: 803-799-9772
Fax: 803-779-3256

MEMBERS OF FIRM

James C. Leventis
Richard M. Unger
Gary R. Daves
Warren R. Herndon, Jr.
Darra Williamson Cothran

ASSOCIATE

Frances G. Smith

(See Next Column)

WOODWARD, LEVENTIS, UNGER, DAVES, HERNDON AND COTHRAN—*Continued*

OF COUNSEL

Edward M. Woodward, Sr. Gwendelyn Geidel
James S. Guignard

General Counsel for: The Columbia College.

For full biographical listings, see the Martindale-Hubbell Law Directory

*GREENVILLE,** Greenville Co.

FEW & FEW, P.A. (AV)

850 Wade Hampton Boulevard, P.O. Box 10085, Fed. Station, 29603
Telephone: 803-232-6456
Fax: 803-370-0671

J. Kendall Few John C. Few

For full biographical listings, see the Martindale-Hubbell Law Directory

PARHAM & SMITH (AV)

Suite 200 Falls Place, 531 South Main, 29601
Telephone: 803-235-5692; 242-9008

MEMBERS OF FIRM

Michael Parham Barney O. Smith, Jr.

For full biographical listings, see the Martindale-Hubbell Law Directory

MYRTLE BEACH, Horry Co.

STEVENS, STEVENS & THOMAS, P.C. (AV)

1215 48th Avenue North, 29577-2468
Telephone: 803-449-9675
Fax: 803-497-2262
Loris, South Carolina Office: 3341 Broad Street.
Telephone: 803-756-7652.
Fax: 803-756-3785.

James P. Stevens, Jr. (Resident, Loris Office) J. Jackson Thomas

Angela T. Jordan (Resident Loris Office)

OF COUNSEL

James P. Stevens

For full biographical listings, see the Martindale-Hubbell Law Directory

*SPARTANBURG,** Spartanburg Co.

HARRISON & HAYES (AV)

200 Library Street, Second Floor, P.O. Box 5367, 29304
Telephone: 803-542-2990
Fax: 803-542-2994

Benjamin C. Harrison J. Mark Hayes, II

For full biographical listings, see the Martindale-Hubbell Law Directory

*WALHALLA,** Oconee Co.

LARRY C. BRANDT, P.A. (AV)

205 West Main Street, P.O. Drawer 738, 29691
Telephone: 803-638-5406
803-638-7873

Larry C. Brandt

D. Bradley Jordan J. Bruce Schumpert

LEGAL SUPPORT PERSONNEL

Debra C. Miller

For full biographical listings, see the Martindale-Hubbell Law Directory

SOUTH DAKOTA

*SIOUX FALLS,** Minnehaha Co.

DAVENPORT, EVANS, HURWITZ & SMITH (AV)

513 South Main Avenue, P.O. Box 1030, 57101-1030
Telephone: 605-336-2880
Telecopier: 605-335-3639

MEMBERS OF FIRM

Edwin E. Evans Rick W. Orr
Michael L. Luce Timothy M. Gebhart
Michael J. Schaffer Susan Jansa Brunick
Thomas M. Frankman Roberto A. Lange

Counsel for: American Society of Composers, Authors and Publishers (A.S.C.A.P.); Burlington Northern, Inc.; Continental Insurance Cos.; The First National Bank in Sioux Falls; Ford Motor Credit Co.; General Motors Corp.; The St. Paul Cos.; The Travelers.

(See Next Column)

For Complete List of Firm Personnel, See General Section

For full biographical listings, see the Martindale-Hubbell Law Directory

NASSER LAW OFFICES, P.C. (AV)

101 South Main Avenue, Suite 613, 57102-1126
Telephone: 605-335-0001
FAX: 605-335-6269

N. Dean Nasser, Jr.

Reference: Western Bank.

For full biographical listings, see the Martindale-Hubbell Law Directory

TENNESSEE

*CHATTANOOGA,** Hamilton Co.

CAMPBELL & CAMPBELL (AV)

1200 James Building, 37402
Telephone: 615-266-1108
Fax: 615-266-8222

MEMBERS OF FIRM

Paul Campbell (1885-1974) Michael Ross Campbell
Paul Campbell, Jr. Paul Campbell, III
Douglas M. Campbell

ASSOCIATE

Odile M. Farrell

OF COUNSEL

James C. Lee (P.C.)

Representative Clients: Tennessee Farmers Mutual Insurance Co.; Pennsylvania National Mutual Casualty Insurance Co.; Amerisure Cos.; National Grange Mutual Insurance Co.

For full biographical listings, see the Martindale-Hubbell Law Directory

FOSTER, FOSTER, ALLEN & DURRENCE (AV)

Formerly Hall, Haynes & Foster
Suite 515 Pioneer Bank Building, 37402
Telephone: 615-266-1141
Telecopier: 615-266-4618

MEMBERS OF FIRM

George Lane Foster Craig R. Allen
William M. Foster Phillip M. Durrence, Jr.

ASSOCIATES

David J. Ward Clayton M. Whittaker
John M. Hull

LEGAL SUPPORT PERSONNEL

Peggy Sue Bates

Division Counsel for: Alabama Great Southern Railroad Co.; C.N.O. & T.P. Railway Co.
Attorneys for: CNA/Insurance; U.S.P. & G. Co.; The Firestone Tire & Rubber Co.; Exxon, Corp.; Murphy Oil Corp.; Chicago Title Insurance Co.; City of East Ridge; Jim Walter Homes; Raymond James & Associates; Morgan Keegan & Co.

For full biographical listings, see the Martindale-Hubbell Law Directory

NELSON, MCMAHAN, PARKER & NOBLETT (AV)

(An Association of Attorneys)
400 Pioneer Bank Building, 37402
Telephone: 615-756-2291
Telecopier: 615-756-0737

Randall L. Nelson Phillip A. Noblett
Michael A. McMahan Douglas M. Cox
Wm. Shelley Parker, Jr. Kenneth O. Fritz
Rosalind H. Reid-Houser

OF COUNSEL

Joe E. Manuel

For full biographical listings, see the Martindale-Hubbell Law Directory

O'NEAL, WALKER & BOEHM (AV)

An Association including a Professional Corporation
808 Maclellan Building, 37402
Telephone: 615-756-5111

Thomas H. O'Neal (P.C.) J. Taylor Walker
Jeffrey D. Boehm

Counsel for: American Consumers, Inc. (Shop-Rite).

For full biographical listings, see the Martindale-Hubbell Law Directory

Chattanooga—Continued

STOPHEL & STOPHEL, P.C. (AV)

500 Tallan Building, Two Union Square, 37402-2571
Telephone: 615-756-2333
Fax: 615-266-5032

Richard W. Bethea, Jr.
W. Lee Maddux
W. Jeffrey Hollingsworth
Arthur P. Brock

Ronald D. Gorsline
Stephen S. Duggins
William R. Dearing
Lisa A. Yacuzzo

Representative Clients: Browning-Ferris Industries, Inc.; Astec Industries, Inc.

For Complete List of Firm Personnel, See General Section

For full biographical listings, see the Martindale-Hubbell Law Directory

SUMMERS, McCREA & WYATT, P.C. (AV)

500 Lindsay Street, 37402
Telephone: 615-265-2385
Fax: 615-266-5211

Jerry H. Summers
Sandra K. McCrea
Thomas L. Wyatt
Jeffrey W. Rufolo

For full biographical listings, see the Martindale-Hubbell Law Directory

WEILL & WEILL (AV)

Eleventh Floor, Chubb Life Building, 37402
Telephone: 615-756-5900
Telecopier: 615-756-5909

MEMBERS OF FIRM

Harry Weill
Flossie Weill
James S. Dreaden
Wilfred Shawn Clelland

ASSOCIATES

James Rayburn Kennamer
Brian Kopet

For full biographical listings, see the Martindale-Hubbell Law Directory

*CLARKSVILLE,** Montgomery Co.

RUNYON AND RUNYON (AV)

Main Street at Third, P.O. Box 1023, 37041-1023
Telephone: 615-647-3377

MEMBER OF FIRM

Frank J. Runyon

Representative Clients: Clarksville Department of Electricity; St. Paul Insurance Co.; The Trane Co.; Aetna Life & Casualty Co.
Reference: First Union Bank, Clarksville.

For full biographical listings, see the Martindale-Hubbell Law Directory

*CLINTON,** Anderson Co.

RIDENOUR, RIDENOUR & FOX (AV)

108 South Main Street, 37716
Telephone: 615-457-0755
FAX: 615-457-4878

MEMBERS OF FIRM

Roger L. Ridenour
Ronald H. Ridenour
Bruce D. Fox

ASSOCIATES

Philip R. Crye, Jr.
Lea Ellen Ridenour

For full biographical listings, see the Martindale-Hubbell Law Directory

*DYERSBURG,** Dyer Co.

PALMER LAW FIRM (AV)

116 West Court Street, P.O. Box 746, 38024
Telephone: 901-285-7382
Fax: 901-286-6537

MEMBERS OF FIRM

E. T. "Rocky" Palmer (1907-1986)
John W. Palmer
H. Tod Taylor

For full biographical listings, see the Martindale-Hubbell Law Directory

*GREENEVILLE,** Greene Co.

KING & KING (AV)

124 South Main Street, 37743
Telephone: 615-639-6881

MEMBERS OF FIRM

Kyle K. King
K. Kidwell King, Jr.

For full biographical listings, see the Martindale-Hubbell Law Directory

*JACKSON,** Madison Co.

RAINEY, KIZER, BUTLER, REVIERE & BELL (AV)

105 Highland Avenue South, P.O. Box 1147, 38302-1147
Telephone: 901-423-2414
Telecopier: 901-423-1386

MEMBERS OF FIRM

Thomas H. Rainey
Jerry D. Kizer, Jr.
Clinton V. Butler, Jr.
Russell E. Reviere
John D. Burleson
Gregory D. Jordan
Robert O. Binkley, Jr.

ASSOCIATES

R. Dale Thomas
Mitchell Glenn Tollison
Marty R. Phillips
Stephen P. Miller
Milton D. Conder, Jr.

Representative Clients: First Tennessee Bank, Jackson, Tennessee; CIGNA Insurance Co.; State Farm Mutual Automobile Insurance Co.; Auto-Owners Insurance Co.; USF&G; CNA Group; Royal Insurance Co.; Great American Insurance Co.; ITT-Hartford; Union Planters National Bank.

For Complete List of Firm Personnel, See General Section

For full biographical listings, see the Martindale-Hubbell Law Directory

*KNOXVILLE,** Knox Co.

BUTLER, VINES AND BABB (AV)

Suite 810, First American Center, P.O. Box 2649, 37901-2649
Telephone: 615-637-3531
Fax: 615-637-3385

MEMBERS OF FIRM

Warren Butler
William D. Vines, III
Dennis L. Babb
Martin L. Ellis
Ronald C. Koksal
James C. Wright
Bruce A. Anderson
Gregory Kevin Hardin
Steven Boyd Johnson
Edward U. Babb

ASSOCIATES

John W. Butler
Vonda M. Laughlin
Gregory F. Vines
Scarlett May

LEGAL SUPPORT PERSONNEL

PARALEGALS

Virginia H. Carver
Susie DeLozier
Dena K. Martin

Reference: First American Bank.

For full biographical listings, see the Martindale-Hubbell Law Directory

GILREATH & ASSOCIATES (AV)

550 Main Avenue, Suite 600, P.O. Box 1270, 37901
Telephone: 615-637-2442
FAX: 615-971-4116
Nashville, Tennessee Office: Sidney W. Gilreath, 2828 Stouffer Tower, 611 Commerce Street.
Telephone: 615-256-3388.

Sidney W. Gilreath

ASSOCIATES

Meridith C. Bond
Donna Keene Holt
Richard Baker, Jr.
Mark W. Strange
Paul Kaufman
Richard L. Duncan

LEGAL SUPPORT PERSONNEL

Janie Turpin (Paralegal)
Janet L. Tucker (Paralegal)
Pamela Smith Wise (Legal Assistant to Senior Partner)
Susan Stogner (Legal Assistant to Senior Partner)
Bryan L. Capps (Legal Administrator)

Reference: Third National Bank.
Representative Client: Transportation Communications International Union.

For full biographical listings, see the Martindale-Hubbell Law Directory

PRYOR, FLYNN, PRIEST & HARBER (AV)

Suite 600 Two Centre Square, 625 Gay Street, P.O. Box 870, 37901
Telephone: 615-522-4191
Telecopier: 615-522-0910

Robert E. Pryor
Frank L. Flynn, Jr.
Timothy A. Priest
John K. Harber

ASSOCIATES

Mark E. Floyd
Donald R. Coffey
M. Christopher Coffey

References: Third National Bank; First National Bank.

For full biographical listings, see the Martindale-Hubbell Law Directory

RAINWATER, HUMBLE & VOWELL (AV)

2037 Plaza Tower, P.O. Box 2775, 37901
Telephone: 615-525-0321
Fax: 615-525-2431

(See Next Column)

RAINWATER, HUMBLE & VOWELL—*Continued*

MEMBERS OF FIRM

J. Earl Rainwater
J. Randolph Humble
Donald K. Vowell

Representative Clients: Acme Construction, Inc.; Curtis Construction Co., Inc.; Knoxville Pediatric Associates, P.C.; National Gas Distributors, Inc.; Neel's Wholesale Produce Co., Inc.; Oldham Insurance Inc.; Sherrod Electric Co., Inc.; Towe Iron Works, Inc.; Wm. S. Trimble Co., Inc.

For full biographical listings, see the Martindale-Hubbell Law Directory

*MEMPHIS,** Shelby Co.

ARMSTRONG ALLEN PREWITT GENTRY JOHNSTON & HOLMES (AV)

80 Monroe Avenue Suite 700, 38103
Telephone: 901-523-8211
Telecopier: 901-524-4936
Jackson, Missipi Office: 1350 One Jackson Place, 188 East Capitol Street.
Telephone: 601-948-8020.
Telecopier: 601-948-8389.

MEMBERS OF FIRM

Thomas R. Prewitt
Stephen P. Hale

For Complete List of Firm Personnel, See General Section

For full biographical listings, see the Martindale-Hubbell Law Directory

JAMES S. COX & ASSOCIATES (AV)

60 North Third Street, 38103
Telephone: 901-575-2040
Telecopier: 901-575-2077

ASSOCIATES

Gary K. Morrell
David A.E. Lumb
Russell Fowler
Todd B. Murrah
Sherry S. Fernandez

For full biographical listings, see the Martindale-Hubbell Law Directory

THOMASON, HENDRIX, HARVEY, JOHNSON & MITCHELL (AV)

Twenty-Ninth Floor, One Commerce Square, 38103
Telephone: 901-525-8721
Telecopier: 901-525-6722

MEMBERS OF FIRM

John J. Thomason
Michael L. Robb

For Complete List of Firm Personnel, See General Section

For full biographical listings, see the Martindale-Hubbell Law Directory

*MURFREESBORO,** Rutherford Co.

WALDRON AND FANN (AV)

202 West Main Street, 37130
Telephone: 615-890-7365
Telecopier: 615-848-1658

MEMBERS OF FIRM

R. Steven Waldron
Terry A. Fann

For full biographical listings, see the Martindale-Hubbell Law Directory

*NASHVILLE,** Davidson Co.

WHITE & REASOR (AV)

3305 West End Avenue, 37203
Telephone: 615-383-3345
Facsimile: 615-383-5534; 615-383-9390

MEMBERS OF FIRM

David J. White, Jr.
John M. Baird
Charles B. Reasor, Jr.
Dudley M. West
Barrett B. Sutton, Jr.
Van P. East, III
Steven L. West

For full biographical listings, see the Martindale-Hubbell Law Directory

*TRENTON,** Gibson Co.

HARRELL AND HARRELL (AV)

Court Square, 38382
Telephone: 901-855-1351; 855-1352
Fax: 901-855-1212

MEMBERS OF FIRM

Limmie Lee Harrell
Limmie Lee Harrell, Jr.

Representative Clients: Trenton Gin Co., Trenton, Tenn.; State Auto Mutual Insurance Co.; Gibson County Special School District, Trenton, Tenn.; Bank of Commerce, Trenton, Tenn.; PDQ Transportation Co., Humboldt, Tenn.; Special School District, Trenton, Tenn.
Reference: The Bank of Commerce, Trenton.

For full biographical listings, see the Martindale-Hubbell Law Directory

TEXAS

*ABILENE,** Taylor Co.

NORVELL & ASSOCIATES, A PROFESSIONAL CORPORATION (AV)

744 Hickory Street, 79601
Telephone: 915-676-1617
Fax: 915-676-4421

James D. Norvell

Thomas G. McIlhany

LEGAL SUPPORT PERSONNEL

Margaret Roberts
Debora Sanger
David A. LeBleu
Thomas L. Brewster, Jr.

Reference: Security State Bank.

For full biographical listings, see the Martindale-Hubbell Law Directory

*AMARILLO,** Potter Co.

GARNER, LOVELL & STEIN, P.C. (AV)

Amarillo National Plaza Two, 500 South Taylor, Suite 1200, 79101-2442
Telephone: 806-379-7111
Telecopier: 806-379-7176

Robert E. Garner
Samuel Lee Stein
John H. Lovell
Brian T. Cartwright
Joe L. Lovell
Tim D. Newsom

Representative Clients: Panhandle Capitol Corporation; Friona Industries, Inc.; Amarillo National Bank; Caviness Packing Co.

For full biographical listings, see the Martindale-Hubbell Law Directory

*AUSTIN,** Travis Co.

GIBBINS, WINCKLER & HARVEY, L.L.P. (AV)

500 West 13th Street, P.O. Box 1452, 78767
Telephone: 512-474-2441

Bob Gibbins
Jay L. Winckler
Jay Harvey

ASSOCIATES

Steven Gibbins
Wayne Prosperi
Susan P. Russell
Neil M. Bonavita

Reference: Nationsbank, Austin.

For full biographical listings, see the Martindale-Hubbell Law Directory

LONG, BURNER, PARKS & SEALY, A PROFESSIONAL CORPORATION (AV)

301 Congress, Suite 800, P.O. Box 2212, 78768-2212
Telephone: 512-474-1587
Fax: 512-322-0301

Tom Long (1922-1989)
Wendy Kendall Schaefer
Clay Cotten (1916-1991)
Elisabeth (Betty) DeLargy
Burnie Burner
James W. (Woody) Butler
Larry Parks
Christopher A. McClellan
Earl W. (Rusty) Sealy
Paula A. Jones
Jane G. Noble
M. Scott Holter

For full biographical listings, see the Martindale-Hubbell Law Directory

LUDLUM & LUDLUM (AV)

Second Floor The Enterprise Plaza, 13915 Burnet Road at Wells Branch Parkway, 78728
Telephone: 512-255-4000
Cable Address: "Ludlum"
Telecopier: 512-244-7000

FIRM FOUNDER

James N. Ludlum (Retired 1987)

MEMBERS OF FIRM

James Ludlum, Jr.
Anthony G. Brocato, Jr
Catherine L. Kyle
M. Winfield Atkins, IV

Representative Clients: American Hardware Insurance Group; American International Group; American International Underwriters, Inc.; Go Pro Underwriters, Inc.; National Casualty Company; New Hampshire Insurance Group; North American Specialty Insurance Group; United National Insurance Group.

For full biographical listings, see the Martindale-Hubbell Law Directory

Austin—Continued

MITHOFF & JACKS, L.L.P. (AV)

Suite 1010, Franklin Plaza, 111 Congress Avenue, 78701
Telephone: 512-478-4422
Telecopier: 512-478-5015
Houston, Texas Office: Penthouse, 3450, One Allen Center.
Telephone: 713-654-1122.

Tommy Jacks
Richard Warren Mithoff
James L. Wright

Mark George Einfalt

For full biographical listings, see the Martindale-Hubbell Law Directory

MULLEN, MACINNES & REDDING (AV)

812 San Antonio, 6th Floor, 78701
Telephone: 512-477-6813
Fax: 512-477-7573
San Antonio, Texas Office: 434 South Main Street, Suite 208.
Telephone: 210-271-3791.
Fax: 210-271-7718.

MEMBERS OF FIRM

Pat Mullen
Robert A. MacInnes
James E. "Buck" Redding (1938-1992)
Jerri L. Ward
Gregory A. Whigham
Sam Lively

ASSOCIATES

Mark H. Siefken
Alicia A. Wilde
Karl Tiger Hanner
V. Jay Youngblood
Robert D. Wilkes
Elena N. Cablao
Connie Lynn Hawkins
Bradley P. Bengtson

For full biographical listings, see the Martindale-Hubbell Law Directory

SPIVEY, GRIGG, KELLY & KNISELY, P.C. (AV)

48 East Avenue, Suite 100, 78701-4320
Telephone: 512-474-6061
Fax: 512-474-1605

Broadus A. Spivey
Dicky Grigg
Patrick Michael Kelly
Paul E. Knisely

Tom P. Prehoditch
Rick Leeper

Reference: Texas Commerce Bank.

For full biographical listings, see the Martindale-Hubbell Law Directory

LAW OFFICES OF MICHAEL A. WASH (AV)

32nd Floor, One American Center, 600 Congress Avenue, 78701
Telephone: 512-480-9494
Facsimile: 512-480-9976

ASSOCIATE

Michael M. Probus, Jr.

For full biographical listings, see the Martindale-Hubbell Law Directory

*BEAUMONT,** Jefferson Co.

LAW OFFICES OF GILBERT T. ADAMS A PROFESSIONAL CORPORATION (AV)

1855 Calder Avenue, P.O. Box 3688, 77704-3688
Telephone: 409-835-3000
Telecopier: 409-832-6162

Gilbert T. Adams (1905-1984)
Gilbert T. Adams, Jr.

Curtis L. Soileau
Earl B. Stover, III
Jesse L. English, III
Theme Sue Linh
Cheryl A. Schultz
Gilbert Timbrell Adams, III

For full biographical listings, see the Martindale-Hubbell Law Directory

DRYDEN, GROSSHEIM & SUTTON (AV)

Suite 915, Goodhue Building, 77701
Telephone: 409-838-6208, 835-5955, 835-4527

MEMBERS OF FIRM

Woodson E. Dryden
Robert C. Grossheim
Brian Sutton

Fern V. Jacobs

References: Texas Commerce Bank, Beaumont; Allied Union Bank.

For full biographical listings, see the Martindale-Hubbell Law Directory

GERMER & GERTZ, L.L.P. (AV)

805 Park Street, P.O. Box 3728, 77704
Telephone: 409-838-2080
Fax: 409-838-4050

MEMBERS OF FIRM

Lawrence L. Germer
Paul W. Gertz

ASSOCIATES

Karen R. Bennett
Larry J. Simmons, Jr.
Catherine P. Waites

For full biographical listings, see the Martindale-Hubbell Law Directory

REAUD, MORGAN & QUINN (AV)

801 Laurel, 77701
Telephone: 409-838-1000
Fax: 409-833-8236

MEMBERS OF FIRM

Wayne A. Reaud
Glen W. Morgan
Cris Quinn
Richard J. Clarkson
Bob Wortham

ASSOCIATES

Larry W. Thorpe
Keith F. Ellis
Suzanne Maltais

For full biographical listings, see the Martindale-Hubbell Law Directory

WELLER, GREEN, MCGOWN & TOUPS, L.L.P. (AV)

5th Floor, Petroleum Tower, 550 Fannin Street, P.O. Box 350, 77704
Telephone: 409-838-0101
Telecopy: 409-838-6780

George A. Weller (1911-1986)
Edward H. Green
Michael R. McGown
Mitchell A. Toups
Raymond Lyn Stevens

John R. Dolezal
E. Hart Green, Jr.
Nicholas S. Baldo
Gene M. Zona Jones
Michael R. Walzel
B. Adam Terrell
Steven R. Thomas
Steven C. Toups
Michael K. Rose
Ellen G. Reynard
Christine M. Simoneaux (Not admitted in TX)

Representative Clients: Fireman's Fund Insurance Companies; Liberty Mutual Insurance Co.

For full biographical listings, see the Martindale-Hubbell Law Directory

*CORPUS CHRISTI,** Nueces Co.

EDWARDS, TERRY, BAIAMONTE & EDWARDS (AV)

802 North Carancahua, Suite 1400 (78470), P.O. Drawer 480, 78403-0480
Telephone: 512-883-0971
Toll Free: 1-800-475-0971
Fax: 512-883-7221

MEMBERS OF FIRM

William R. Edwards
Michael G. Terry
Terry Edwards Baiamonte
William R. Edwards, III
Angelina Beltran

For full biographical listings, see the Martindale-Hubbell Law Directory

JOHNSON & TOWER (AV)

611 South Tancahua Street, 78401
Telephone: 512-888-4411

John L. Johnson
Danny Tower

Reference: Citizens Bank of Corpus Christi.

RANGEL & CHRISS (AV)

719 South Shoreline Boulevard, Suite 500, P.O. Box 880, 78403
Telephone: 512-883-8555
Facsimile: 512-883-9187

MEMBERS OF FIRM

Jorge C. Rangel
William J. Chriss

ASSOCIATE

Augustin Rivera, Jr.

For full biographical listings, see the Martindale-Hubbell Law Directory

*DALLAS,** Dallas Co.

BAKER & BOTTS, L.L.P. (AV)

2001 Ross Avenue, 75201
Telephone: 214-953-6500
Fax: 214-953-6503
Houston, Texas Office: One Shell Plaza, 910 Louisiana.
Telephone: 713-229-1234.
Washington, D.C. Office: The Warner, 1299 Pennsylvania Avenue, N.W.
Telephone: 202-639-7700.

(See Next Column)

BAKER & BOTTS L.L.P.—*Continued*

Austin, Texas Office: 1600 San Jacinto Center, 98 San Jacinto Boulevard.
Telephone: 512-322-2500.
New York, New York Office: 885 Third Avenue, Suite 2000.
Telephone: 212-705-5000.
Moscow, Russian Federation Office: 10 ul. Pushkinskaya, 103031.
Telephone: 7095/921-5300 (Local); 7095/929-7070.

MEMBERS OF FIRM

Larry D. Carlson
Earl B. Austin
Peter A. Moir

ASSOCIATES

Jeffrey Joseph Cox
Harold Harvey Hunter
Margaret N. McGann
James Kemp Sawers
Lynn S. Switzer
Jeffrey M. Tillotson

For Complete List of Firm Personnel, See General Section

For full biographical listings, see the Martindale-Hubbell Law Directory

BARBER, HART & O'DELL, L.L.P. (AV)

4310 Gaston Avenue, 75246-1398
Telephone: 214-821-8840
Fax: 214-821-3834

James C. Barber
David G. Hart
David M. O'Dell

For full biographical listings, see the Martindale-Hubbell Law Directory

LAW OFFICES OF FRANK L. BRANSON, P.C. (AV)

18th Floor, Highland Park Place, 4514 Cole Avenue, 75205
Telephone: 214-522-0200;
Metro: 817-263-7452
Fax: 214-521-5485

Frank L. Branson
Debbie D. Branson
George A. Quesada, Jr.
Jerry M. White
J. Stephen King
Christopher A. Payne
Michael L. Parham
Joel M. Fineberg

OF COUNSEL

Ted Z. Robertson
J. Hadley Edgar, Jr.

For full biographical listings, see the Martindale-Hubbell Law Directory

CALHOUN & STACY (AV)

5700 NationsBank Plaza, 901 Main Street, 75202-3747
Telephone: 214-748-5000
Telecopier: 214-748-1421
Telex: 211358 CALGUMP UR

Mark Alan Calhoun
David W. Elrod
Steven D. Goldston
Parker Nelson
Roy L. Stacy

ASSOCIATES

Shannon S. Barclay
Robert A. Bragalone
Dennis D. Conder
Jane Elizabeth Diseker
Lawrence I. Fleishman
Thomas C. Jones
Katherine Johnson Knight
V. Paige Pace
Veronika Willard
Michael C. Wright

LEGAL CONSULTANT

Rees T. Bowen, III

For full biographical listings, see the Martindale-Hubbell Law Directory

HAROLD J. COOPER (AV)

714 Jackson Street, Suite 110, 75202
Telephone: 214-748-0133
FAX: 214-748-0314

For full biographical listings, see the Martindale-Hubbell Law Directory

HULEN FORD (AV)

Two Hillcrest Green, Suite 910, 12720 Hillcrest Road, 75230
Telephone: 214-980-4494
800-547-4757

For full biographical listings, see the Martindale-Hubbell Law Directory

WILLIAM M. HAYNER & ASSOCIATES (AV)

2522 McKinney Avenue, Suite 102, 75201
Telephone: 214-871-2500
Fax: 214-871-7387

ASSOCIATES

Anne P. Stark
William M. Hayner, Jr

For full biographical listings, see the Martindale-Hubbell Law Directory

LAW OFFICES OF ALAN K. LAUFMAN, J.D., M.D. A PROFESSIONAL CORPORATION (AV)

Suite 1000 Turtle Creek Centre, 3811 Turtle Creek Boulevard, 75219
Telephone: 214-559-3300
Fax: 214-526-1150

Alan K. Laufman

For full biographical listings, see the Martindale-Hubbell Law Directory

MISKO, HOWIE & SWEENEY (AV)

Turtle Creek Centre, Suite 1900, 3811 Turtle Creek Boulevard, 75219
Telephone: 214-443-8000
Fax: 214-443-8000

Fred Misko, Jr.
John R. Howie
Paula Sweeney

ASSOCIATES

Charles S. Siegel
James L. Mitchell, Jr.
Raymond A. Williams, III
Christopher D. Jones
Bryan D. Pope

For full biographical listings, see the Martindale-Hubbell Law Directory

GEORGE A. OTSTOTT & ASSOCIATES A PROFESSIONAL CORPORATION (AV)

3611 Fairmount, 75219
Telephone: 214-522-9999
Terrell, Texas Office: 304 East Wheeler.
Telephone: 214-563-2222.
Jefferson, Texas Office: 117 West Lafayette Street.
Telephone: 903-665-3300.
Denton, Texas Office: 1010 Dallas Drive.
Telephone: 817-383-8080.
Greenville, Texas Office: 2718 Wesley.
Telephone: 903-454-4444.
Waxahachie, Texas Office: 303 South Elm Street.
Telephone: 214-937-3000.

George A. Otstott

Jerry D. Andrews
Jean A. Robb
David Townsend

For full biographical listings, see the Martindale-Hubbell Law Directory

THE LAW FIRM OF C.L. MIKE SCHMIDT, P.C. (AV)

3102 Oak Lawn, Suite 730, LB 158, 75219
Telephone: 214-521-4898
Toll Free No. 1-800-677-4898
Fax: 214-521-9995

C. L. Mike Schmidt

Ronald D. Wren
Michael E. Schmidt

For full biographical listings, see the Martindale-Hubbell Law Directory

LAW OFFICES OF WINDLE TURLEY, P.C. (AV)

1000 University Tower, 6440 North Central Expressway, 75206
Telephone: 214-691-4025
Telefax: 214-361-5802
Telex: 734049

Windle Turley
Linda Turley
Thomas J. Stutz
Michael P. Metcalf
David Rodriguez Weiner
Susan Allen
Robert L. Greening
Tahira Khan Merritt
Michael G. Sawicki
Mary Elizabeth Robertson
David A. Surratt
Martin J. Hoffman
Barbara J. Elias-Perciful
Hal Parker
R. Christopher Cowan

For full biographical listings, see the Martindale-Hubbell Law Directory

*DENTON,** Denton Co.

WOOD, SPRINGER & LYLE, A PROFESSIONAL CORPORATION (AV)

513 West Oak, 76201
Telephone: 817-387-0404
Fax: 817-566-6673

R. William Wood
J. Jeffrey Springer
Frank G. Lyle
C. Jane La Rue
Grace A. Weatherly

For full biographical listings, see the Martindale-Hubbell Law Directory

*EL PASO,** El Paso Co.

ARMSTRONG & STRAHAN, A PROFESSIONAL CORPORATION (AV)

6028 Surety Drive, Suite 105, 79905
Telephone: 915-566-5529
Fax: 915-779-6827

Dan L. Armstrong Jeffery V. Strahan

For full biographical listings, see the Martindale-Hubbell Law Directory

CHARLES A. DEASON, JR. (AV)

1141 East Rio Grande, 79902-1371
Telephone: 915-544-1371
Fax: 915-544-2013

For full biographical listings, see the Martindale-Hubbell Law Directory

DUDLEY, DUDLEY, WINDLE & STEVENS (AV)

2501 North Mesa, Suite 200, 79902
Telephone: 915-544-3090
Fax: 915-542-2651

MEMBERS OF FIRM

William C. (Pat) Dudley
Paul W. Dudley
Wayne Windle
J. Monty Stevens
Lawrence M. Jordan
J. Malcolm Harris

ASSOCIATES

John C. Steinberger
Steven R. Hatch
Mary W. Craig
Boyd W. Naylor
Albert G. "Al" Weisenberger
Bonnie L. Jones
Jaime A. Villalobos
Regina B. Arditti

Representative Clients: Allstate Insurance Co.; A.I.G. Group; Argonaut Insurance Co.; Chubb Group of Insurance Companies; CNA Insurance Co.; Continental Loss Adjusting; Crawford & Company.

For full biographical listings, see the Martindale-Hubbell Law Directory

JOSEPH A. MORGAN (AV)

4100 Rio Bravo, Suite 207, 79902
Telephone: 915-542-1881
Fax: 915-533-2517

OF COUNSEL

Ralph E. Harris

Reference: The Bank of El Paso.

For full biographical listings, see the Martindale-Hubbell Law Directory

*FORT WORTH,** Tarrant Co.

RUSSELL, TURNER, LAIRD & JONES, L.L.P. (AV)

One Colonial Place, 2400 Scott Avenue, 76103-2200
Telephone: 817-531-3000; 1-800-448-2889
Fax: 817-535-3046
Dallas, Texas Office: Williams Square, Central Tower, Suite 700, 5215 North O'Connor Boulevard, Las Colinas Urban Center.
Telephone: 214-444-0444; 1-800-448-2889.

Wm. Greg Russell
Randall E. Turner
Steven C. Laird
Gregory G. Jones

For full biographical listings, see the Martindale-Hubbell Law Directory

*HALLETTSVILLE,** Lavaca Co.

SCHWARTZ & SCHWARTZ (AV)

North LaGrange Street, P.O. Box 385, 77964
Telephone: 512-798-3668

MEMBERS OF FIRM

Armond G. Schwartz Marcus F. Schwartz

For full biographical listings, see the Martindale-Hubbell Law Directory

*HOUSTON,** Harris Co.

BAKER & BOTTS, L.L.P. (AV)

One Shell Plaza, 910 Louisiana, 77002
Telephone: 713-229-1234
Cable Address: "Boterlove"
Fax: 713-229-1522
Washington, D.C. Office: The Warner, 1299 Pennsylvania Avenue, N.W.
Telephone: 202-639-7700.
New York, New York Office: 885 Third Avenue, Suite 2000.
Telephone: 212-705-5000.
Austin, Texas Office: 1600 San Jacinto Center, 98 San Jacinto Boulevard.
Telephone: 512-322-2500.
Dallas, Texas Office: 2001 Ross Avenue.
Telephone: 214-953-6500.
Moscow, Russian Federation Office: 10 ul. Pushkinskaya, 103031.
Telephone: 7095/921-5300 (Local); 7095/929-7070 (International).

(See Next Column)

MEMBERS OF FIRM

Finis E. Cowan
Lee Landa Kaplan
Michael S. Goldberg
David R. Poage
R. Paul Yetter
Ronald C. Lewis

ASSOCIATES

Thomas R. Ajamie
Cesar Enrique Arreaza
Travis James Sales
Suzanne H. Stenson

For Complete List of Firm Personnel, See General Section

For full biographical listings, see the Martindale-Hubbell Law Directory

BENNETT, BROOCKS, BAKER & LANGE, L.L.P. (AV)

1700 Neils Esperson Building, 808 Travis, 77002
Telephone: 713-222-1434

Robert S. Bennett

Stephen R. Reeves

For full biographical listings, see the Martindale-Hubbell Law Directory

CRAWFORD & MCKINNEY (AV)

550 Westcott, Suite 590, 77007
Telephone: 713-869-1500
Fax: 713-880-4638

MEMBERS OF FIRM

Stanley W. Crawford R. L. Pete McKinney

For full biographical listings, see the Martindale-Hubbell Law Directory

FLOYD, TAYLOR & RILEY, L.L.P. (AV)

Suite 3440, Three Houston Center, 1301 McKinney, 77010
Telephone: 713-646-1000
Fax: 713-646-1036

MEMBERS OF FIRM

Robert C. Floyd
Warren R. Taylor
Timothy D. Riley
Diana Kay Ball
Britton B. Harris

Terri S. Harris
Ralph E. Burnham
Gary Martin Jewell
Patrick W. O'Briant

For full biographical listings, see the Martindale-Hubbell Law Directory

HARDY & JOHNS (AV)

500 Two Houston Center, 909 Fannin at McKinney, 77010
Telephone: 713-222-0381
Fax: 713-759-9650
Bay City, Texas Office: 2042 Avenue F.
Telephone: 409-245-3797.
Texas City, Texas Office: 3020 Palmer Highway.
Telephone: 409-945-0606.

G. P. Hardy, Jr. (1913-1988)
G. P. Hardy, III
Gail Johns

ASSOCIATES

Timothy M. Purcell
Mark G. Cypert
Gwen E. Richard
Patricia Haylon
Melissa Wolin

OF COUNSEL

Billie Pirner Garde

Reference: Bay City Bank & Trust.

For full biographical listings, see the Martindale-Hubbell Law Directory

KRIST, GUNN, WELLER, NEUMANN & MORRISON, L.L.P. (AV)

17555 El Camino Real (Clear Lake City), 77058
Telephone: 713-283-8500
Fax: 713-488-3489

MEMBERS OF FIRM

Ronald D. Krist
Jerry W. Gunn
Harvill E. Weller, Jr.
William G. Neumann, Jr.
Richard R. Morrison, III
David A. Slaughter
Kevin D. Krist
Perry O. Barber Jr. (1938-1992)

Scott C. Krist
Todd C. Benson

Reference: Nations Bank, Houston, Texas.

For full biographical listings, see the Martindale-Hubbell Law Directory

LORANCE & THOMPSON, A PROFESSIONAL CORPORATION (AV)

303 Jackson Hill, 77007
Telephone: 713-868-5560
Fax: 713-864-4671; 868-1605
Phoenix, Arizona Office: 2525 East Camelback Road, Suite 230, 85016.
Telephone: 602-224-4000.
Fax: 602-224-4098.

(See Next Column)

LORANCE & THOMPSON A PROFESSIONAL CORPORATION—*Continued*

San Diego, California Office: 555 West Beech Street, Suite 222, 92101.
Telephone: 800-899-1844.

Larry D. Thompson
Wayne Adams
Frank B. Stahl, Jr.
William K. Luyties
Clifford A. Lawrence, Jr.
Walter F. (Trey) Williams, III
David O. Cluck
Phillip C. Summers
David F. Webb
Richard H. Martin
Vicki F. Brann
Ronald E. Hood
Gwen W. Dobrowski
Mark D. Flanagan
F. Barham Lewis

David W. Prasifka
Gregory D. Solcher
John A. Culberson
George Eric Van Noy
James E. Simmons
John H. Thomisee, Jr.
Tracey R. Burridge
Douglas A. Haldane
Geoffrey C. Guill
Diane M. Guariglia
Kelly B. Lea
Tracey Landrum Foster
Ronnie B. Arnold
Teresa A. Carver
Terrance D. Dill, Jr.
J. Wayne Little
William T. Sebesta
Richard N. Moore
Matthew R. Pearson

OF COUNSEL

John Holman Barr
Shannon P. Davis
Alexis J. Gomez

Representative Clients: Allstate Insurance Co.; The Hartford Insurance Group.

For full biographical listings, see the Martindale-Hubbell Law Directory

MCFALL, SHERWOOD & SHEEHY, A PROFESSIONAL CORPORATION (AV)

2500 Two Houston Center, 909 Fannin Street, 77010-1003
Telephone: 713-951-1000
Telecopier: 713-951-1199

Donald B. McFall
Thomas P. Sartwelle
William A. Sherwood
Richard A. Sheehy
Kent C. Sullivan
David B. Weinstein
D. Wayne Clawater
John S. Serpe
Kenneth R. Breitbeil
Shelley Rogers
Joseph A. Garnett
R. Edward Perkins
Raymond A. Neuer

Caroline E. Baker
Lauren Beck
David Brill
John M. Davidson
Robert R. Debes, Jr.
Eugene R. Egdorf
John H. Ferguson IV
Jeffrey R. Gilbert
M. Randall Jones
Christopher J. Lowman
James J. Maher
David J. McTaggart
David W. Medack
Catherine A. Mezick
Matthew G. Pletcher
Martin S. Schexnayder
David R. Tippetts
James W. K. Wilde

OF COUNSEL

Gay C. Brinson, Jr.
Edward S. Hubbard
Paul B. Radelat

Representative Clients: Dresser Industries, Inc.; The Procter & Gamble Co.; Channel Two Television; St. Paul Fire & Marine Insurance Co.; Texas Lawyers' Insurance Exchange; U.S. Aviation Underwriters; Dow Corning Corp.; Columbia Hospital Corp.; Farm & Home Savings Association.

For Complete List of Firm Personnel, See General Section

For full biographical listings, see the Martindale-Hubbell Law Directory

PERDUE & CLORE, L.L.P. (AV)

2727 Allen Parkway, Suite 800, 77019
Telephone: 713-520-2500

Jim M. Perdue
Mark D. Clore

ASSOCIATES

Joann V. Bennett
Jo Emma Arechiga
John Walter Lewis

For full biographical listings, see the Martindale-Hubbell Law Directory

REYNOLDS & SYDOW, L.L.P. (AV)

One Riverway, Suite 1950, 77056
Telephone: 713-840-9600
Fax: 713-840-9605

Michael D. Sydow
Kelli McDonald Sydow
Paula S. Elliott
Kay K. Morgan

OF COUNSEL

Joe H. Reynolds

For full biographical listings, see the Martindale-Hubbell Law Directory

DON R. RIDDLE, P.C. (AV)

6810 FM 1960 West, Suite 200, 77069
Telephone: 713-893-4567
FAX: 713-893-1827

Don R. Riddle

For full biographical listings, see the Martindale-Hubbell Law Directory

*LUFKIN,** Angelina Co.

LAW OFFICES OF GEORGE CHANDLER (AV)

207 East Frank Street, P.O. Box 340, 75901
Telephone: 409-632-7778
Fax: 409-632-1304

George E. Chandler

ASSOCIATES

John T. Fleming
Reich O'Hara Chandler
William Jeffrey Paradowski

OF COUNSEL

L. Brent Farney

For full biographical listings, see the Martindale-Hubbell Law Directory

*MIDLAND,** Midland Co.

LESLIE G. MCLAUGHLIN (AV)

1209 West Texas Avenue, 79701
Telephone: 915-687-1331
Fax: 915-687-1336

For full biographical listings, see the Martindale-Hubbell Law Directory

*SAN ANGELO,** Tom Green Co.

WEBB, STOKES & SPARKS (AV)

314 West Harris Avenue, P.O. Box 1271, 76902
Telephone: 915-653-6866
Telecopier: 915-655-1250

MEMBERS OF FIRM

Aubrey D. Stokes (1921-1990)
Tom Webb
Sam D. Sparks
Max Parker
Guy D. Choate
Mary Noel Golder

References: First National Bank of Mertzon; The First National Bank of Abilene, Texas; New First City.

For full biographical listings, see the Martindale-Hubbell Law Directory

*SAN ANTONIO,** Bexar Co.

BRANTON & HALL, P.C. (AV)

737 Travis Park Plaza Building, 711 Navarro Street, Suite 737, 78205
Telephone: 210-224-4474
Fax: 210-224-1928

James L. Branton
James A. Hall

Carol P. Lomax
Brian C. Steward
Marc A. Notzon

OF COUNSEL

Richard Clayton Trotter
Franklin S. Spears

For full biographical listings, see the Martindale-Hubbell Law Directory

HORNBUCKLE & CLARK, P.C. (AV)

Greatview Office Center, Suite 100, 8207 Callaghan Road, 78230-4736
Telephone: 210-344-7995
Telecopier: 210-344-7996

William E. Hornbuckle
Ronald L. Clark

For full biographical listings, see the Martindale-Hubbell Law Directory

TINSMAN & HOUSER, INC. (AV)

One Riverwalk Place, 14th Floor, 700 North St. Mary's Street, 78205
Telephone: 210-225-3121
Texas Wats: 1-800-292-9999
Fax: 210-225-6235

Richard Tinsman
Franklin D. Houser
Margaret M. Maisel
David G. Jayne
Robert C. Scott
Daniel J. T. Sciano
Rey Perez
Bernard Wm. Fischman
Sharon L. Cook
Christopher Pettit
Ronald J. Salazar
Sue Dodson

For full biographical listings, see the Martindale-Hubbell Law Directory

TEXARKANA, Bowie Co.

PATTON, HALTOM, ROBERTS, MCWILLIAMS & GREER, L.L.P. (AV)

A Registered Limited Liability Partnership including Professional Corporations
700 Texarkana National Bank Building, P.O. Box 1928, 75504-1928
Telephone: 903-794-3341
Fax: 903-792-6542; 903-792-0448

James N. Haltom (P.C.)
George L. McWilliams (P.C.)
John B. Greer, III, (P.C.)
William G. Bullock

ASSOCIATES

Kristi Ingold McCasland
Caroline Malone
Ralph K. Burgess
Johanna Elizabeth Haltom Salter (1960-1993)

Representative Clients: Allstate Insurance Co.; Aetna Casualty & Surety Co.; Royal Insurance Group; Continental Insurance Group; Ranger/Pan American Insurance Cos.; The Hanover Insurance Group; American Mutual Liability Insurance Co.; American Hardware Mutual Insurance Co.; Kemper Insurance Co.; Texarkana National Bancshares, Inc.

For Complete List of Firm Personnel, See General Section

For full biographical listings, see the Martindale-Hubbell Law Directory

LAW OFFICES OF DAMON YOUNG (AV)

4122 Texas Boulevard, P.O. Box 1897, 75504
Telephone: 501-774-3206; 903-794-1303
Facsimile: 903-792-5098

ASSOCIATES

Thomas H. Holcombe
Tera Futrell Kesterson

For full biographical listings, see the Martindale-Hubbell Law Directory

*TYLER,** Smith Co.

BAILEY, NEGEM & PATTERSON, L.L.P. (AV)

440 South Vine Street, 75702
Telephone: 903-595-4466
Fax: 903-593-3266

Blake Bailey
Jimmy M. Negem
Mike Patterson
Mary Strand

For full biographical listings, see the Martindale-Hubbell Law Directory

*VICTORIA,** Victoria Co.

HARTMAN, LAPHAM & SMITH, L.L.P. (AV)

Limited Liability Partnership including a Professional Corporation
201 South Main Street, P.O. Drawer D, 77902-1079
Telephone: 512-578-0271
Fax: 512-578-1402

MEMBERS OF FIRM

Arthur L. Lapham
David Atmar Smith (P.C.)
Joyce Zarosky Heller
Scott Kimball, III
Boniface S. Gbalazeh

OF COUNSEL

Wayne L. Hartman

For full biographical listings, see the Martindale-Hubbell Law Directory

*WACO,** McLennan Co.

JIM MEYER & ASSOCIATES, P.C. (AV)

4734 West Waco Drive, P.O. Box 21957, 76710
Telephone: 817-772-9255
Fax: 817-776-9110

Jim Meyer

Matthew E. Johnson

For full biographical listings, see the Martindale-Hubbell Law Directory

*WICHITA FALLS,** Wichita Co.

MORRISON & SHELTON, A PROFESSIONAL CORPORATION (AV)

City National Building, 807 Eighth Street, Suite 1010, 76301-3319
Telephone: 817-322-2929
Telecopier: 817-322-7463

Lonny D. Morrison
Stephen R. Shelton

For full biographical listings, see the Martindale-Hubbell Law Directory

UTAH

*PROVO,** Utah Co.

HOWARD, LEWIS & PETERSEN, P.C. (AV)

Delphi Building, 120 East 300 North Street, P.O. Box 778, 84603
Telephone: 801-373-6345
Fax: 801-377-4991

Jackson Howard
Don R. Petersen
Craig M. Snyder
John L. Valentine
D. David Lambert
Fred D. Howard
Leslie W. Slaugh

Richard W. Daynes
Phillip E. Lowry
Kenneth Parkinson

OF COUNSEL

S. Rex Lewis

LEGAL SUPPORT PERSONNEL

Mary Jackson
John O. Sump
Ray Winger

For full biographical listings, see the Martindale-Hubbell Law Directory

*SALT LAKE CITY,** Salt Lake Co.

JOEL M. ALLRED, P.C. (AV)

McIntyre Building, 68 South Main Street, 84101
Telephone: 801-531-8300
Fax: 801-363-2420

Joel M. Allred

For full biographical listings, see the Martindale-Hubbell Law Directory

CALLISTER, NEBEKER & MCCULLOUGH, A PROFESSIONAL CORPORATION (AV)

800 Kennecott Building, 84133
Telephone: 801-530-7300
Telecopier: 801-364-9127

Gary R. Howe
James R. Black
P. Bryan Fishburn

Representative Client: Workers Compensation Fund of Utah.

For Complete List of Firm Personnel, See General Section

For full biographical listings, see the Martindale-Hubbell Law Directory

KIPP AND CHRISTIAN, P.C. (AV)

175 East 400 South 330 City Centre I, 84111
Telephone: 801-521-3773
Fax: 801-359-9004

Carman E. Kipp
D. Gary Christian
J. Anthony Eyre
William W. Barrett
Gregory J. Sanders
Heinz J. Mahler
Michael F. Skolnick
Shawn McGarry
Kirk G. Gibbs
Sandra L. Steinvoort

Representative Clients: United States Fidelity & Guaranty Co.; E & O Professionals; Home Insurance Company; Montgomery Elevator; National Farmers Union Ins. Co.; Republic Financial Services, Inc.; Utah Medical Insurance Association (UMIA); Utah State Bar; Crum & Forster.

For Complete List of Firm Personnel, See General Section

For full biographical listings, see the Martindale-Hubbell Law Directory

KIRTON & MCCONKIE, A PROFESSIONAL CORPORATION (AV)

1800 Eagle Gate Tower, 60 East South Temple, 84111
Telephone: 801-328-3600
Telecopier: 801-321-4893

Wilford W. Kirton, Jr.
Oscar W. McConkie, Jr.
Raymond W. Gee
Anthony I. Bentley, Jr.
J. Douglas Mitchell
Richard R. Neslen
Myron L. Sorensen
Robert W. Edwards
B. Lloyd Poelman
Raeburn G. Kennard
Jerry W. Dearinger
R. Bruce Findlay
Charles W. Dahlquist, II
M. Karlynn Hinman
Robert P. Lunt
Brinton R. Burbidge
Gregory S. Bell
Lee Ford Hunter
Larry R. White
William H. Wingo
David M. McConkie
Read R. Hellewell
Rolf H. Berger
Oscar W. McConkie, III
Marc Nick Mascaro
Lorin C. Barker
David M. Wahlquist
Robert S. Prince
Wallace O. Felsted
Merrill F. Nelson
Paul H. Matthews
Fred D. Essig
Clark B. Fetzer
Samuel D. McVey

(See Next Column)

KIRTON & MCCONKIE A PROFESSIONAL CORPORATION—*Continued*

Blake T. Ostler
Daniel Bay Gibbons
Gregory M. Simonsen
Von G. Keetch
Patrick Hendrickson
Stuart F. Weed
Thomas D. Walk
James E. Ellsworth
Daniel V. Goodsell
David J. Hardy
Randy T. Austin

For Complete List of Firm Personnel, See General Section

For full biographical listings, see the Martindale-Hubbell Law Directory

MORGAN & HANSEN (AV)

Kearns Building, Eighth Floor, 136 South Main Street, 84101
Telephone: 801-531-7888
Telefax: 801-531-9732

MEMBERS OF FIRM

Stephen G. Morgan
Darwin C. Hansen
John C. Hansen
Cynthia K.C. Meyer
Mitchel T. Rice
Joseph E. Minnock
Eric C. Singleton

OF COUNSEL

Dennis R. James

Representative Clients: Albertson's Inc.; Smith Food and Drug Centers, Inc.; Colorado Casualty; Farmers Insurance Group; SCL Airport Authority; St. Paul Fire and Marine Insurance Co.; State Farm Fire and Casualty; State Farm Mutual Automobile Insurance Co.; Utah Farm Bureau Insurance Co.; Utah Local Government's Insurance Trust.

For full biographical listings, see the Martindale-Hubbell Law Directory

PARSONS BEHLE & LATIMER, A PROFESSIONAL CORPORATION (AV)

One Utah Center, 201 South Main Street, Suite 1800, P.O. Box 45898, 84145-0898
Telephone: 801-532-1234
Telecopy: 801-536-6111

Gordon L. Roberts
Charles H. Thronson
Francis M. Wikstrom
Chris Wangsgard
Spencer E. Austin
John B. Wilson
Daniel W. Hindert
Michael L. Larsen
Derek Langton
Mark S. Webber
J. Michael Bailey
Elizabeth S. Conley
William J. Evans

For full biographical listings, see the Martindale-Hubbell Law Directory

VAN COTT, BAGLEY, CORNWALL & MCCARTHY, A PROFESSIONAL CORPORATION (AV)

Suite 1600, 50 South Main Street, P.O. Box 45340, 84145
Telephone: 801-532-3333
Telex: 453149
Telecopier: 801-534-0058
Ogden, Utah Office: Suite 900, 2404 Washington Boulevard.
Telephone: 801-394-5783.
Park City, Utah Office: 314 Main Street, Suite 205.
Telephone: 801-649-3889.
Reno, Nevada Office: Jeppson & Lee, 100 West Liberty, Suite 990.
Telephone: 702-333-6800.

E. Scott Savage
Michael F. Richman
Jeffrey E. Nelson
Donald L. Dalton
Casey K. McGarvey
Bryon J. Benevento

OF COUNSEL

James P. Cowley

Michael T. Roberts (Resident, Ogden, Utah Office)

For Complete List of Firm Personnel, See General Section

For full biographical listings, see the Martindale-Hubbell Law Directory

VERMONT

BRATTLEBORO, Windham Co.

CRISPE & CRISPE (AV)

114 Main Street, P.O. Box 556, 05302
Telephone: 802-254-4441
Fax: 802-254-4482

A. Luke Crispe (1911-1992)
Lawrin P. Crispe

ASSOCIATE

Kristen Swartwout

Representative Clients: Mutual of New York; The Stratton Corp.; Liberty Mutual Insurance Co.; DeWitt Beverage Co.

(See Next Column)

For full biographical listings, see the Martindale-Hubbell Law Directory

*BURLINGTON,** Chittenden Co.

LISMAN & LISMAN, A PROFESSIONAL CORPORATION (AV)

84 Pine Street, P.O. Box 728, 05402-0728
Telephone: 802-864-5756
Fax: 802-864-3629

Carl H. Lisman
Allen D. Webster
Mary G. Kirkpatrick
E. William Leckerling, III
Douglas K. Riley

Judith Lillian Dillon
Richard W. Kozlowski

OF COUNSEL

Bernard Lisman
Louis Lisman

For full biographical listings, see the Martindale-Hubbell Law Directory

MANCHESTER LAW OFFICES, PROFESSIONAL CORPORATION (AV)

One Lawson Lane, P.O. Box 1459, 05402-1459
Telephone: 802-658-7444
Fax: 802-658-2078

Robert E. Manchester
Patricia S. Orr

LEGAL SUPPORT PERSONNEL

LEGAL NURSE CONSULTANTS

Tina L Mulvey
Rosemeryl S. Harple
Maureen P. Tremblay

For full biographical listings, see the Martindale-Hubbell Law Directory

SYLVESTER & MALEY, INC. (AV)

78 Pine Street, P.O. Box 1053, 05402-1053
Telephone: 802-864-5722
Fax: 802-658-6124

Alan F. Sylvester
John P. Maley
Michael S. Brow

Geoffrey M. Fitzgerald
Amy E. Sylvester

For full biographical listings, see the Martindale-Hubbell Law Directory

*MIDDLEBURY,** Addison Co.

CONLEY & FOOTE (AV)

11 South Pleasant Street, P.O. Drawer 391, 05753
Telephone: 802-388-4061
Fax: 802-388-0210

MEMBERS OF FIRM

John T. Conley (1900-1971)
Ralph A. Foote
Charity A. Downs
D. Michael Mathes
Richard P. Foote
Janet P. Shaw

For full biographical listings, see the Martindale-Hubbell Law Directory

*RUTLAND,** Rutland Co.

CARROLL, GEORGE & PRATT (AV)

64 & 66 North Main Street, P.O. Box 280, 05702-0280
Telephone: 802-775-7141
Telecopier: 802-775-6483
Woodstock, Vermont Office: The Mill - Route #4 E., P.O. Box 388, 05091.
Telephone: 802-457-1000.
Telecopier: 802-457-1874.

MEMBERS OF FIRM

Henry G. Smith (1938-1974)
James P. Carroll
Alan B. George
Robert S. Pratt
Neal C. Vreeland
Jon S. Readnour
Timothy U. Martin
Randall F. Mayhew (Resident Partner, Woodstock Office)
Richard S. Smith
Judy Godnick Barone
John J. Kennelly

ASSOCIATES

Thomas A. Zonay
Jeffrey P. White
Susan Boyle Ford (Resident, Woodstock Office)
Charles C. Humpstone

For full biographical listings, see the Martindale-Hubbell Law Directory

DAVID L. CLEARY ASSOCIATES A PROFESSIONAL CORPORATION (AV)

110 Merchants Row, P.O. Box 6740, 05702-6740
Telephone: 802-775-8800
Telefax: 802-775-8809

David L. Cleary

(See Next Column)

DAVID L. CLEARY ASSOCIATES A PROFESSIONAL CORPORATION, *Rutland—Continued*

Kaveh S. Shahi
Ellen J. Abbott
George A. Holoch, Jr.
Thomas P. Aicher
Karen S. Heald

For full biographical listings, see the Martindale-Hubbell Law Directory

MILLER & FAIGNANT, A PROFESSIONAL CORPORATION (AV)

36 Merchants Row, P.O. Box 6688, 05702-6688
Telephone: 802-775-2521
Fax: 802-775-8274

Lawrence Miller
John Paul Faignant

Barbara R. Blackman
Christopher J. Whelton

LEGAL SUPPORT PERSONNEL

Cynthia L. Bonvouloir
Marie T. Fabian

Representative Clients: Travelers Insurance Co.; Government Employees Insurance Co.; Utica Mutual Insurance Co.; Universal Underwriters Insurance Co.
Reference: Travelers Insurance Co.

For full biographical listings, see the Martindale-Hubbell Law Directory

VIRGINIA

*ABINGDON,** Washington Co.

TATE, LOWE & ROWLETT, P.C. (AV)

205 West Main Street, 24210
Telephone: 703-628-5185
Telecopier: 703-628-5045

Mary Lynn Tate
Fredrick A. Rowlett
C. Randall Lowe
Terrence Shea Cook

Representative Clients: Island Creek Coal Co.; Jewell Resources, Inc.; Pikeville National Bank; Charter Federal Savings Bank; Rapoca Energy Co.
Approved Attorneys for: Lawyers Title Insurance Co.; Safeco Title Insurance Co.; Nations Bank; First Virginia Bank; Bank of Marion; Central Fidelity Bank.

For full biographical listings, see the Martindale-Hubbell Law Directory

YEARY & ASSOCIATES, P.C. (AV)

161 East Main Street, P.O. Box 1685, 24210
Telephone: 703-628-9107
Telecopier: 703-628-1998

Emmitt F. Yeary

W. Hobart Robinson
Kathleen Calvert Yeary

LEGAL SUPPORT PERSONNEL

Michael A. Bragg (Legal Assistant)

Representative Clients: Abingdon Nursing Homes, Inc.; D.S. Buck, Inc.; East Gate Drug Stores of Abingdon, Inc.; Abingdon Printing, Inc.; ERA Anderson & Associates; Southwest Virginia Research & Development Corp.
Approved Attorneys for: Lawyers Title Insurance Co.; First Bank & Trust Co.; First Virginia Bank; Chicago Title Insurance Co.

For full biographical listings, see the Martindale-Hubbell Law Directory

ALEXANDRIA, (Independent City)

STEPHEN R. PICKARD, P.C. (AV)

115 Oronoco Street, P.O. Box 1685, 22313-1685
Telephone: 703-836-3505

Stephen R. Pickard

For full biographical listings, see the Martindale-Hubbell Law Directory

*ARLINGTON,** Arlington Co.

WILLIAM E. ARTZ A PROFESSIONAL CORPORATION (AV)

1010 Rosslyn Metro Center, 1700 North Moore Street, 22209
Telephone: 703-243-3500
Facsimile: 703-524-8770

William E. Artz

Dominique D. Michel

For full biographical listings, see the Martindale-Hubbell Law Directory

BEAN, KINNEY & KORMAN, A PROFESSIONAL CORPORATION (AV)

2000 North 14th Street, Suite 100, 22201
Telephone: 703-525-4000
Facsimile: 703-525-2207

James W. Korman
James Bruce Davis
Jonathan C. Kinney
James R. Schroll
Frederick R. Taylor
Carol Schrier-Polak
Leo S. Fisher
Joseph P. Corish

OF COUNSEL

L. Lee Bean (1916-1989)
Marilyn Tebor Shaw
Clifford A. Dougherty
David B. Kinney (Emeritus)
Barbara S. Kinosky

J. Carlton Howard, Jr.
Jennifer A. Brust
Marbeth M. Spreyer
Karen L. Keyes
Charles E. Curran
Eric H. D. Sahl
Dannon G. Williams

Counsel for: Nations Bank, N.A.
Reference: Nations Bank, N.A.

For full biographical listings, see the Martindale-Hubbell Law Directory

SCHWARTZ AND ELLIS, LTD. (AV)

6950 North Fairfax Drive, 22213
Telephone: 703-532-9300
Telex: 892320
Facsimile: 703-534-0329

John P. Ellis

John S. Petrillo

References: First Virginia Bank; Signet Bank; First Union National Bank.

For full biographical listings, see the Martindale-Hubbell Law Directory

GEORGE D. VAROUTSOS (AV)

6045 Wilson Boulevard Suite 300, 22205
Telephone: 703-532-6900
Fax: 703-532-6351

ASSOCIATE

Elise R. Lapidus

OF COUNSEL

Paul G. Varoutsos
Louis Koutoulakos

For full biographical listings, see the Martindale-Hubbell Law Directory

DANVILLE, (Independent City)

CARTER, CRAIG, BASS, BLAIR & KUSHNER, P.C. (AV)

126 South Union Street, P.O. Box 601, 24543
Telephone: 804-792-9311
Fax: 804-792-4373

OF COUNSEL

Charles E. Carter

Stuart L. Craig
D. Thomas Blair
Stephen G. Bass
Samuel A. Kushner, Jr.

Reference: Signet Bank (Danville).

For full biographical listings, see the Martindale-Hubbell Law Directory

*FAIRFAX,** (Ind. City; Seat of Fairfax Co.)

HALL, MARKLE, SICKELS & FUDALA, P.C. (AV)

4010 University Drive, Suite 200, 22030
Telephone: 703-591-8600
Telecopier: 703-591-7053

Robert T. Hall
David J. Fudala
G. Donald Markle
James T. Bacon
Charles W. Sickels
Warner F. Young, III

Holly Parkhurst Lear
Laurie A. Amell
Howard R. Philips

OF COUNSEL

Guy O. Farley, Jr.

For full biographical listings, see the Martindale-Hubbell Law Directory

RUST, RUST & SILVER, A PROFESSIONAL CORPORATION (AV)

4103 Chain Bridge Road Fourth Floor, P.O. Box 460, 22030
Telephone: 703-591-7000
Telecopier: 703-591-7336

John H. Rust, Jr.
Glenn H. Silver
C. Thomas Brown

James E. Kane
Paulo E. Franco, Jr.
Andrew W. White

(See Next Column)

RUST, RUST & SILVER A PROFESSIONAL CORPORATION—*Continued*

RETIRED, EMERITUS

John H. Rust, Sr. (Retired)

Representative Clients: Crestar Bank; Commonwealth Land Title Insurance Co.; Patriot National Bank; Century Graphics Corp.

For full biographical listings, see the Martindale-Hubbell Law Directory

*HALIFAX,** Halifax Co.

JAMES E. EDMUNDS (AV)

Court Square, P.O. Box 157, 24558
Telephone: 804-476-6202; 476-6578

References: First Federal Savings & Loan Assn., South Boston; Crestar Bank, South Boston.

For full biographical listings, see the Martindale-Hubbell Law Directory

*LEESBURG,** Loudoun Co.

HANES, SEVILA, SAUNDERS & MCCAHILL, A PROFESSIONAL CORPORATION (AV)

30 North King Street, P.O. Box 678, 22075
Telephone: 703-777-5700
Metro: 471-9800; Fax: 703-771-4161

William B. Hanes
Robert E. Sevila
Richard R. Saunders, Jr.
Burke F. McCahill
Douglas L. Fleming, Jr.
Jon D. Huddleston
Craig E. White

For full biographical listings, see the Martindale-Hubbell Law Directory

LYNCHBURG, (Independent City)

JOSEPH R. JOHNSON, JR. & ASSOCIATES (AV)

9th Floor, Allied Arts Building, 725 Church Street, P.O. Box 717, 24505
Telephone: 804-845-4541
Fax: 804-845-4134

Travis Harry Witt
P. Scott De Bruin

For full biographical listings, see the Martindale-Hubbell Law Directory

*MANASSAS,** Prince William Co.

J. EDWARD MCGOLRICK, JR., P.C. (AV)

9257 Lee Avenue, 22110
Telephone: 703-361-1110
Metro: 703-631-2262
Fax: 703-631-1186

J. Edward McGolrick, Jr.

*MARTINSVILLE,** (Ind. City; Seat of Henry Co.)

DOUGLAS K. FRITH & ASSOCIATES, P.C. (AV)

(Member, Commonwealth Law Group, Ltd.)
58 West Church Street, P.O. Box 591, 24114
Telephone: 703-632-7137
FAX: 703-632-3988

Douglas K. Frith

General Counsel for: Frith Construction Co., Inc.; Koger/Air Corp.; Prillaman & Pace, Inc.; Radio Station WHEE; Fuller & Gray Tire Co., Inc.; Millard's Machinery, Inc.
Representative Client: Hartford Accident & Indemnity.

For full biographical listings, see the Martindale-Hubbell Law Directory

EBB H. WILLIAMS, III, P.C. (AV)

First Federal Savings & Loan of Martinsville Building, 25 West Church Street, P.O. Box 1009, 24114
Telephone: 703-638-3967
Fax: 703-638-1848

Ebb H. Williams, III

Counsel For: Hairston Home For Adults, Inc.; Nationwide Homes, Inc.; American Standard Building Systems, Inc.

For full biographical listings, see the Martindale-Hubbell Law Directory

MCLEAN, Fairfax Co.

JOHNSON & ROCHE (AV)

8355 Greensboro Drive, Tysons Corner, 22102
Telephone: 703-821-3740

(See Next Column)

MEMBERS OF FIRM

Robert A. Johnson
Brien A. Roche
Jon E. Shields

References: Nations Bank; First Virginia Bank; Signet Bank.

For full biographical listings, see the Martindale-Hubbell Law Directory

NEWPORT NEWS, (Independent City)

PHILLIPS M. DOWDING (AV)

12335 Warwick Boulevard, 23606
Telephone: 804-595-0338
FAX: 804-595-3979

Representative Clients: The Aetna Casualty & Surety Co.; The Hartford Insurance Group; Security Group; Utica Mutual Insurance Co.; Riverside Hospital; PENTRAN; CIGNA Insurance Group; Selective Insurance Group; Commercial Union; Moore Group, Inc.

For full biographical listings, see the Martindale-Hubbell Law Directory

NORFOLK, (Independent City)

GOLDBLATT, LIPKIN & COHEN, P.C. (AV)

Suite 300, 415 St. Paul's Boulevard, P.O. Box 3505, 23514
Telephone: 804-627-6225
Telefax: 804-622-3698

Paul M. Lipkin
Robert S. Cohen
Steven M. Legum
Mary G. Commander
Beril M. Abraham
Larry W. Shelton

Approved Attorneys for: Lawyers Title Insurance Corp.

For full biographical listings, see the Martindale-Hubbell Law Directory

THOMAS J. HARLAN, JR., P.C. (AV)

1200 Dominion Tower, 999 Waterside Drive, 23510
Telephone: 804-625-8300
FAX: 804-625-3714

Thomas J. Harlan, Jr.

John M. Flora
Kevin M. Thompson (Not admitted in VA)

LEGAL SUPPORT PERSONNEL

Mary Hayse Grant Wareing (Paralegal)
Barry Wade Vanderhoof (Paralegal)

Reference: Commerce Bank.

For full biographical listings, see the Martindale-Hubbell Law Directory

PAYNE, GATES, FARTHING & RADD, P.C. (AV)

15th Floor, Dominion Tower, 23510
Telephone: 804-640-1500

Charles E. Payne
Ronald M. Gates
Philip R. Farthing
Anthony F. Radd
Reid H. Ervin
Mark R. Skolrood
Craig L. Mytelka
Todd Joseph Preti

For full biographical listings, see the Martindale-Hubbell Law Directory

RABINOWITZ, RAFAL, SWARTZ, TALIAFERRO & GILBERT, P.C. (AV)

Wainwright Building, Suite 700, 229 West Bute Street, P.O. Box 3332, 23514
Telephone: 804-622-3931; 623-6674
FAX: 804-626-1003

Franklin A. Swartz
William L. Taliaferro, Jr.
Oscar L. Gilbert

Calvin R. Depew, Jr.

For full biographical listings, see the Martindale-Hubbell Law Directory

SACKS, SACKS & IMPREVENTO (AV)

Suite 501 Town Point Center, 150 Boush Street, P.O. Box 3874, 23514
Telephone: 804-623-2753
FAX: 804-640-7170

Herman A. Sacks (1886-1983)
Stanley E. Sacks
Andrew M. Sacks
Michael F. Imprevento

For full biographical listings, see the Martindale-Hubbell Law Directory

TAVSS, FLETCHER, EARLEY & KING, P.C. (AV)

Suite 100, Two Commercial Place, 23510
Telephone: 804-625-1214
Fax: 804-622-7295
Mailing Address: P.O. Box 3747, 23514

(See Next Column)

TAVSS, FLETCHER, EARLEY & KING P.C., *Norfolk—Continued*

Richard J. Tavss
Mark L. Earley
John R. Fletcher
Ray W. King
Besianne Tavss Shilling

LEGAL SUPPORT PERSONNEL

Maurice J. O'Connor

Reference: Bank of the Commonwealth.

For full biographical listings, see the Martindale-Hubbell Law Directory

PETERSBURG, (Independent City)

CUTHBERT LAW OFFICES, A PROFESSIONAL CORPORATION (AV)

220 North Sycamore Street, 23803
Telephone: 804-733-3100

Charles H. Cuthbert, Jr.

Margaret Cuthbert Broaddus

For full biographical listings, see the Martindale-Hubbell Law Directory

PORTSMOUTH, (Independent City)

BANGEL, BANGEL & BANGEL (AV)

505 Court Street, P.O. Box 760, 23705-0760
Telephone: 804-397-3471
Telecopier: 804-393-3736

MEMBERS OF FIRM

A. A. Bangel (1893-1978)
Stanley J. Bangel (1925-1992)
Herbert K. Bangel
Keith H. Bangel
Michael J. Blachman
John W. Eppler
J. Darrell Foster
Edward H. McNew, Jr.

ASSOCIATES

Burle U. Stromberg
Lawrence W. I'Anson, III

For full biographical listings, see the Martindale-Hubbell Law Directory

MOODY, STROPLE & KLOEPPEL, LTD. (AV)

300 Commerce Bank Building, 500 Crawford Street, P.O. Box 1138, 23705-1138
Telephone: 804-393-4093
FAX: 804-397-7257

Willard J. Moody, Sr.
Raymond H. Strople
Byron P. Kloeppel
Willard J. Moody, Jr.
Robert A. Small
John C. Bittrick
John E. Basilone
Stephen E. Heretick
Joseph J. Perez
Thomas F. Burris, III
Kevin P. Bilms
Richard Wright West
Joseph T. McFadden, Jr.
Stan Murphy
Fred D. Smith, Jr.

Reference: Commerce Bank.

For full biographical listings, see the Martindale-Hubbell Law Directory

RADFORD, (Independent City)

STONE, HARRISON, TURK & SHOWALTER, P.C. (AV)

Tyler Office Plaza, 1902 Downey Street, P.O. Box 2968, 24143-2968
Telephone: 703-639-9056
Telecopier: 703-731-4665

Edwin C. Stone
Clifford L. Harrison
James C. Turk, Jr.
Josiah T. Showalter, Jr.
Margaret E. Stone

Representative Clients: St. Albans Psychiatric Hospital; Radford Community Hospital; Inland Motor Corp.; The K-C Corp.; Meadowgold Dairies; Lynchburg Foundry; Hartford Accident and Indemnity Co.; Cigna Insurance Cos.; Hercules, Inc.; Norfolk Southern Corp.

For full biographical listings, see the Martindale-Hubbell Law Directory

*RICHMOND,** (Ind. City; Seat of Henrico Co.)

DUANE AND SHANNON, P.C. (AV)

10 East Franklin Street, 23219
Telephone: 804-644-7400
Fax: 804-649-8329

Harley W. Duane, III
James C. Shannon
B. Craig Dunkum
David L. Hauck
Arnold B. Snukals
William V. Riggenbach
Carl R. Schwertz

Martha P. Smith

For full biographical listings, see the Martindale-Hubbell Law Directory

LEVIT & MANN (AV)

419 North Boulevard, 23220
Telephone: 804-355-7766
Fax: 804-358-4018

MEMBERS OF FIRM

Jay J. Levit
John B. Mann

For full biographical listings, see the Martindale-Hubbell Law Directory

ROANOKE, (Independent City)

MUNDY, ROGERS & FRITH (AV)

Third Street and Woods Avenue, S.W., P.O. Box 2240, 24009
Telephone: 703-982-2900
FAX: 703-982-1362

MEMBERS OF FIRM

G. Marshall Mundy
Frank W. Rogers, III
T. Daniel Frith, III
Cheryl Watson Smith

Reference: First Union.

For full biographical listings, see the Martindale-Hubbell Law Directory

SUFFOLK, (Independent City)

GLASSCOCK, GARDY AND SAVAGE (AV)

4th Floor National Bank Building, P.O. Box 1876, 23434
Telephone: 804-539-3474
FAX: 804-925-1419

MEMBERS OF FIRM

J. Samuel Glasscock
Jeffrey L. Gardy
William R. Savage, III

Representative Clients: Seaboard Railway System; Planters Peanuts (Division of Nabisco); Norfolk Southern Railway Co.; Nationwide Mutual Insurance Co.; State Farm Mutual Automobile Insurance Co.; Virginia Power Co.; Virginia Farm Bureau Mutual Insurance Co.; Suffolk Redevelopment and Housing Authority.
Approved Attorneys for: Lawyers Title Insurance Corp.

*TAZEWELL,** Tazewell Co.

GALUMBECK SIMMONS AND REASOR (AV)

104 West Main Street, P.O. Box 561, 24651
Telephone: 703-988-9436; 988-6561
Telecopier: 703-988-2921

MEMBERS OF FIRM

Robert M. Galumbeck
Deanis L. Simmons
Jackson E. Reasor, Jr.

References: Lawyers Title Insurance; Bank of Tazewell County.

For full biographical listings, see the Martindale-Hubbell Law Directory

VIRGINIA BEACH, (Independent City)

BRYDGES & MAHAN (AV)

Professional Building, 1369 Laskin Road, 23451
Telephone: 804-428-6021
FAX: 804-491-7634

MEMBERS OF FIRM

Richard G. Brydges
Stephen C. Mahan

Reference: Sovran Bank.
Approved Mediator/Arbitrator For: United States Arbitration and Mediation, Inc.; Arbitration Associates, Inc.

For full biographical listings, see the Martindale-Hubbell Law Directory

WASHINGTON

BAINBRIDGE ISLAND, Kitsap Co.

MORROW & OTOROWSKI (AV)

298 Winslow Way West, 98110
Telephone: 206-842-1000
Facsimile: 206-842-0797
Mercer Island, Washington Office: 2955 80th Avenue S.E., Suite 103, 98010.
Telephone: 206-236-4000.
Fax: 206-236-6100.

MEMBERS OF FIRM

Albert Morrow (Resident, Mercer Island Office)
Christopher L. Otorowski

ASSOCIATE

Jennifer A. Kowalski

For full biographical listings, see the Martindale-Hubbell Law Directory

BELLEVUE, King Co.

Patrick H. LePley (AV)

4122 128th Avenue, S.E., Suite 301, 98006
Telephone: 206-641-5353
Fax: 206-747-0611

Reference: Sea-First (Factoria).

For full biographical listings, see the Martindale-Hubbell Law Directory

*BELLINGHAM,** Whatcom Co.

Brett & Daugert (AV)

300 North Commercial, P.O. Box 5008, 98227
Telephone: 360-733-0212
FAX: 360-647-1902

MEMBERS OF FIRM

Dean R. Brett
Timothy C. Farris

ASSOCIATE

Breean Lawrence Beggs

References: Security Pacific Bank Washington (Bellingham Branch); Key Bank.

For Complete List of Firm Personnel, See General Section

For full biographical listings, see the Martindale-Hubbell Law Directory

FEDERAL WAY, King Co.

Bruce Clement (AV)

31919 1st Avenue, South, 98003
Telephone: 206-661-3111

MOSES LAKE, Grant Co.

Calbom & Schwab, P.S.C. (AV)

1042 West Ivy Avenue, P.O. Drawer 1429, 98837
Telephone: 509-765-1851
Toll Free: 1-800-497-1755
Fax: 509-766-2727
Wenatchee & Kennewick
Wenatchee, Washington Office: 819 N. Miller.
Telephone: 509-662-5677.
Kennewick, Washington Office: 201 North Edison, Suite 245.
Telephone: 509-736-0866.

G. Joe Schwab
John E. Calbom (Retired)

David L. Lybbert
Kathleen G. Kilcullen

LEGAL SUPPORT PERSONNEL

PARALEGALS

Gary Edwards
Joy Province
Jeff Parkinson
Philip J. Ammons
Jane V. King
Gracie Ortiz
Jeffrey Schwab

Reference: Seattle-First National Bank, Moses Lake Branch.

For full biographical listings, see the Martindale-Hubbell Law Directory

*MOUNT VERNON,** Skagit Co.

Welts & Welts (AV)

R. V. Welts Building, 311 Myrtle Street, P.O. Box 1108, 98273
Telephone: 206-336-5141
Fax: 206-336-3048

R.V. Welts (1914-1978)
Richard O. Welts (1933-1973)
David A. Welts

For full biographical listings, see the Martindale-Hubbell Law Directory

*OLYMPIA,** Thurston Co.

Bean & Gentry (AV)

Columbia Square, 320 North Columbia, P.O. Box 2317, 98507
Telephone: 206-943-8040
Fax: 206-786-6943

MEMBERS OF FIRM

Stephen J. Bean
Fred D. Gentry

ASSOCIATES

Mary G. Gentry
Cecilia Marie Clynch

Reference: Key Bank of Puget Sound.

For full biographical listings, see the Martindale-Hubbell Law Directory

*PORT ANGELES,** Clallam Co.

Williams Law Office (AV)

804 South Oak Street, 98362
Telephone: 206-457-1139
FAX: 206-457-1176

Gary Williams

ASSOCIATE

Deborah Nelson Willis

For full biographical listings, see the Martindale-Hubbell Law Directory

POULSBO, Kitsap Co.

Tolman • Kirk (AV)

18925 Front N.E., P.O. Box 851, 98370
Telephone: 206-779-5561
FAX: 206-779-2516

MEMBERS OF FIRM

Jeffrey L. Tolman
Michael A. Kirk

For full biographical listings, see the Martindale-Hubbell Law Directory

*SEATTLE,** King Co.

Aaby, Putnam, Albo & Causey A Professional Services Corporation (AV)

401 Second Avenue South, 303 Court in the Square, 98104
Telephone: 206-292-8627
Fax: 206-292-8196
Bellingham, Washington Office: 1402 F Street.
Telephone: 206-676-5225.
Fax: 206-676-9247.
Olympia, Washington Office: 915 East Legion Way.
Telephone: 206-754-7707.
Fax: 206-754-4474.

John Aaby (Resident, Bellingham Office)
Kim R. Putnam (Resident, Olympia Office)
Joseph A. Albo
James C. Causey, Jr.
Wayne Lieb (Resident, Olympia Office)
Gerry R. Zmolek (Resident, Bellingham Office)
Judith M. Proller (Resident, Bellingham Office)
Eugene A. Studer
Michael J. Heatherly (Resident, Bellingham Office)
Kip Wayerski (Resident, Bellingham Office)

For full biographical listings, see the Martindale-Hubbell Law Directory

Law Offices of Lembhard G. Howell, P.S. (AV)

Arctic Building, Penthouse Suite, 700 Third Avenue, 98104
Telephone: 206-623-5296
Cable Address: "Old Seattle"

Lembhard G. Howell

For full biographical listings, see the Martindale-Hubbell Law Directory

*SPOKANE,** Spokane Co.

Chase, Hayes & Kalamon, P.S. (AV)

1000 Seafirst Financial Center, 99201
Telephone: 509-456-0333
FAX: 509-838-9826

Richard E. Hayes

Gervais Ward McAuliffe III

Representative Clients: American States Insurance; Reliance Insurance ; U.S-.A.A.; Empire Fire & Marine Insurance Co.; Farmers Insurance Group; State Farm Insurance Co.

For Complete List of Firm Personnel, See General Section

For full biographical listings, see the Martindale-Hubbell Law Directory

*TACOMA,** Pierce Co.

Messina Bufalini Bulzomi (AV)

5316 Orchard Street West, 98467
Telephone: 206-472-6000; 1-800-992-9LAW
Fax: 206-475-7886

MEMBERS OF FIRM

John L. Messina
David A. Bufalini
Stephen L. Bulzomi

ASSOCIATES

Virginia L. De Costa
John R. Christensen

OF COUNSEL

Richard I. Gustafson

For full biographical listings, see the Martindale-Hubbell Law Directory

*YAKIMA,** Yakima Co.

ABEYTA-NELSON P.C. (AV)

1102 West Yakima Avenue, 98902-3029
Telephone: 509-575-1588
Fax: 509-457-8426

Terry P. Abeyta
Rodney K. Nelson
Derek L. Sutton

Reference: West One Bank.

For full biographical listings, see the Martindale-Hubbell Law Directory

WEST VIRGINIA

*CHARLESTON,** Kanawha Co.

CICCARELLO, DEL GIUDICE & LAFON (AV)

Suite 100, 1219 Virginia Street, East, 25301
Telephone: 304-343-4440
Telecopier: 304-343-4464

MEMBERS OF FIRM

Arthur T. Ciccarello
Michael J. Del Giudice
Timothy J. LaFon

For full biographical listings, see the Martindale-Hubbell Law Directory

GOODWIN & GOODWIN (AV)

1500 One Valley Square, 25301
Telephone: 304-346-7000
Fax: 304-344-9692
Ripley, West Virginia Office: 500 Church Street, P.O. Box 349.
Telephone: 304-372-2651.
Parkersburg, West Virginia Office: 201 Third Street, Town Square.
Telephone: 304-485-2345.
Fax: 304-485-3459.

MEMBERS OF FIRM

Joseph R. Goodwin
Richard E. Rowe
Richard D. Owen

Representative Clients: Bucyrus-Erie Co.; CSX Corp.; Eastern American Energy Corp.; The Eureka Pipe Line Company.

For Complete List of Firm Personnel, See General Section

For full biographical listings, see the Martindale-Hubbell Law Directory

HUNT, LEES, FARRELL & KESSLER (AV)

7 Players Club Drive, P.O. Box 2506, 25329-2506
Telephone: 304-344-9651
Telecopier: 304-343-1916
Huntington, West Virginia Office: Prichard Building, 601 Ninth Street, P.O. Box 2191, 25722.
Telephone: 304-529-1999.
Martinsburg, West Virginia Office: 1012 B Winchester Avenue. P.O. Box 579. 25401.
Telephone: 304-267-3100.

MEMBERS OF FIRM

James B. Lees, Jr.
John A. Kessler
Joseph M. Farrell, Jr. (Resident, Huntington Office)

ASSOCIATES

James A. McKowen
Meikka A. Cutlip (Resident, Huntington Office)
Jeffrey T. Jones
Marion Eugene Ray
Sharon M. Fedorochko
Mark Jenkinson (Resident, Martinsburg Office)

OF COUNSEL

L. Alvin Hunt

For full biographical listings, see the Martindale-Hubbell Law Directory

MASINTER & LACY (AV)

Suite 1401 Bank One Center, 707 Virginia Street East, 25301
Telephone: 304-344-3532
Fax: 304-346-2306

Allan H. Masinter
Gerald R. Lacy

For full biographical listings, see the Martindale-Hubbell Law Directory

MASTERS & TAYLOR, L.C. (AV)

Fourth Floor - Peoples Building, 179 Summers Street, 25301
Telephone: 304-342-3106

Marvin W. Masters
Robert A. Taylor

(See Next Column)

Laurie Garrigan McKowen
Richard A. Monahan
Kathleen T. Pettigrew
David L. Stuart

References: One Valley Bank; Parkersburg Inn (Holiday Inn, Parkersburg).

For full biographical listings, see the Martindale-Hubbell Law Directory

*CLARKSBURG,** Harrison Co.

JOHNSON, SIMMERMAN & BROUGHTON, L.C. (AV)

Suite 210, Goff Building, P.O. Box 150, 26301
Telephone: 304-624-6555
Telecopier: 304-623-4933

Charles G. Johnson
Frank E. Simmerman, Jr.
Marcia Allen Broughton

For full biographical listings, see the Martindale-Hubbell Law Directory

WEST & JONES (AV)

360 Washington Avenue, P.O. Box 2348, 26302
Telephone: 304-624-5501
FAX: 304-624-4454

MEMBERS OF FIRM

James C. West, Jr.
John S. Kaull
Jerald E. Jones
Lewis A. Clark

ASSOCIATES

Kathryn K. Allen
Norman T. Farley

Reference: The Union National Bank of West Virginia.

For Complete List of Firm Personnel, See General Section

For full biographical listings, see the Martindale-Hubbell Law Directory

*MADISON,** Boone Co.

SHAFFER AND SHAFFER (AV)

330 State Street, P.O. Box 38, 25130
Telephone: 304-369-0511
Fax: 304-369-5431
Charleston, West Virginia Office: 1710 Bank One Center, P.O. Box 3973.
Telephone: 304-344-8716.
Fax: 304-342-1105.

MEMBER OF FIRM

Norman W. White

Representative Clients: Bank One, West Virginia, N.A., Boone; Armco Inc.; Westmoreland Coal Co.; State Farm Mutual Insurance Cos.; Nationwide Insurance Co.

For Complete List of Firm Personnel, See General Section

For full biographical listings, see the Martindale-Hubbell Law Directory

*PRINCETON,** Mercer Co.

GIBSON & ASSOCIATES (AV)

1345 Mercer Street, 24740
Telephone: 304-425-8276
800-742-3545

MEMBER OF FIRM

Michael F. Gibson

ASSOCIATES

Derrick Ward Lefler
Bill Huffman
Kelly R. Charnock

LEGAL SUPPORT PERSONNEL

SOCIAL SECURITY PARALEGALS

Nancy Belcher

PERSONAL INJURY PARALEGALS

Kathy Richards

WORKERS COMPENSATION PARALEGAL

Carol Hylton

MEDICAL NEGLIGENCE PARALEGAL

Deborah Fye

For full biographical listings, see the Martindale-Hubbell Law Directory

SANDERS, AUSTIN, SWOPE & FLANIGAN (AV)

Hunter Park, 320 Courthouse Road, 24740
Telephone: 304-425-8125
FAX: 304-425-4155

MEMBERS OF FIRM

Hartley Sanders (1879-1952)
William H. Sanders, III
Lane O. Austin
William B. Flanigan
Derek C. Swope
Gregory S. Prudich

ASSOCIATES

S. Paige Burress
Omar J. Aboulhosn

(See Next Column)

SANDERS, AUSTIN, SWOPE & FLANIGAN—*Continued*

OF COUNSEL

William H. Sanders, II

References: First Community Bank-Princeton; One Valley Bank-Princeton.

For full biographical listings, see the Martindale-Hubbell Law Directory

*WHEELING,** Ohio Co.

BACHMANN, HESS, BACHMANN & GARDEN (AV)

1226 Chapline Street, P.O. Box 351, 26003
Telephone: 304-233-3511
Fax: 304-233-3199

MEMBERS OF FIRM

Carl G. Bachmann (1890-1980)
Lester C. Hess (1903-1971)
John B. Garden (1925-1994)
Gilbert S. Bachmann
Lester C. Hess, Jr.
John L. Allen
R. Noel Foreman
Paul T. Tucker
George E. McLaughlin
Jeffrey R. Miller
Suzanne Quinn
Anthony Ira Werner

ASSOCIATES

Rhonda L. Wade
Jeffrey A. Grove
Elizabeth A. Abraham
Samuel H. Foreman

For full biographical listings, see the Martindale-Hubbell Law Directory

GOMPERS, BUCH, McCARTHY & McCLURE (AV)

Suite 302, Board of Trade Building, 26003
Telephone: 304-233-2450
Fax: 304-233-3656

MEMBERS OF FIRM

William J. Gompers (1887-1957)
Joseph A. Gompers
Harry L. Buch
T. Carroll McCarthy, Jr.
James T. McClure
John E. Gompers

For full biographical listings, see the Martindale-Hubbell Law Directory

SCHRADER, RECHT, BYRD, COMPANION & GURLEY (AV)

1000 Hawley Building, 1025 Main Street, P.O. Box 6336, 26003
Telephone: 304-233-3390
Fax: 304-233-2769
Martins Ferry, Ohio Office: 205 North Fifth Street, P.O. Box 309.
Telephone: 614-633-8976.
Fax: 614-633-0400.

PARTNERS

Henry S. Schrader (Retired)
Arthur M. Recht
Ray A. Byrd
James F. Companion
Terence M. Gurley
Frank X. Duff
Teresa Rieman-Camilletti
Yolonda G. Lambert
Patrick S. Casey
Sandra M. Chapman
Daniel P. Fry (Resident, Martins Ferry, Ohio Office)
James P. Mazzone

ASSOCIATES

Sandra K. Law
D. Kevin Coleman
Denise A. Jebbia
Edythe A. Nash
Robert G. McCoid
Denise D. Klug
Thomas E. Johnston

OF COUNSEL

James A. Byrum, Jr.

General Counsel: WesBanco Bank-Elm Grove.
Representative Clients: CIGNA Property and Casualty Cos.; Columbia Gas Transmission Corp.; Commercial Union Assurance Co.; Hazlett, Burt & Watson, Inc.; Stone & Thomas Department Stores; Transamerica Commercial Finance Corp.; Wheeling-Pittsburgh Steel Corp.

For full biographical listings, see the Martindale-Hubbell Law Directory

WISCONSIN

*APPLETON,** Outagamie Co.

MENN, NELSON, SHARRATT, TEETAERT & BEISENSTEIN, LTD. (AV)

(Formerly, Fulton, Menn & Nehs, Ltd.)
222 North Oneida Street, P.O. Box 785, 54912-0785
Telephone: 414-731-6631
FAX: 414-734-0981

(See Next Column)

Homer H. Benton (1886-1957)
Alfred C. Bosser (1890-1965)
Franklin L. Nehs (1922-1979)
David L. Fulton (1911-1985)
Glenn L. Sharratt (Retired)
John B. Menn
Peter S. Nelson
John R. Teetaert
Joseph J. Beisenstein
Mark R. Feldmann
Joseph A. Bielinski
Jonathan M. Menn
Douglas D. Hahn
Keith W. Kostecke
Robert N. Duimstra

LEGAL SUPPORT PERSONNEL

Kathy J. Krause

Representative Clients: Insurance: Allstate Insurance Co.; General Casualty Company of Wisconsin; Hartford Insurance Group; Liberty Mutual Insurance Co.; St. Paul Insurance Cos.; Travelers Insurance Co. Corporate: Bank One Appleton, NA; Kimberly Clark Corp; Time Warner Entertainment Company LP.

For full biographical listings, see the Martindale-Hubbell Law Directory

MURPHY, GILLICK, WICHT & PRACHTHAUSER (AV)

54 Park Place, 54915
Telephone: 414-730-0200
Appleton: 1-800-942-2882
Milwaukee, Wisconsin Office: Suite 1200, 330 East Kilbourn Avenue.
Telephone: 414-271-1011. Milwaukee: 1-800-942-2880. South Office: Edgewood Bank Building, 4811 South 76th Street.
Telephone: 414-281-5700.
North Office: Northridge Bank Building, 9001 North 76th Street.
Telephone: 414-354-5051.
Brookfield, Wisconsin Office: Brookfield Lakes Corporate Center, 300 North Corporate Drive (180th Street & Blue Mound Road).
Telephone: 414-792-0888.

Anthony W. Welhouse (Resident)

For full biographical listings, see the Martindale-Hubbell Law Directory

*LA CROSSE,** La Crosse Co.

WILLIAM SKEMP LAW FIRM, S.C. (AV)

505 King Street, Suite 209, 54601
Telephone: 608-791-2500
Facsimile: 608-791-2510

William P. Skemp
William G. Skemp

For full biographical listings, see the Martindale-Hubbell Law Directory

LAKE GENEVA, Walworth Co.

BRADEN & OLSON (AV)

716 Wisconsin Street, P.O. Box 940, 53147
Telephone: 414-248-6636
Fax: 414-248-2901

Berwyn B. Braden
John O. Olson

Michael J. Rielly
Kurt T. Van Buskirk
Christine Tomas (Not admitted in WI)

For full biographical listings, see the Martindale-Hubbell Law Directory

*MADISON,** Dane Co.

AXLEY BRYNELSON (AV)

(Formerly Brynelson, Herrick, Bucaida, Dorschel & Armstrong Including the former Easton & Assoc., S.C.)
2 East Mifflin Street, P.O. Box 1767, 53701-1767
Telephone: 608-257-5661
Fax: 608-257-5444

MEMBERS OF FIRM

Frank J. Bucaida
Bradley D. Armstrong
John H. Schmid, Jr.
Timothy D. Fenner
John C. Mitby
Daniel T. Hardy
John Walsh
Bruce L. Harms
David Easton
Curtis C. Swanson
Michael S. Anderson
Patricia M. Gibeault
Michael J. Westcott
Larry K. Libman
Richard E. Petershack
Steven A. Brezinski
Steven M. Streck
Joy L. O'Grosky

ASSOCIATES

Arthur E. Kurtz
Edith F. Merila
Michael J. Modl
Sabin S. Peterson

OF COUNSEL

Ralph E. Axley
Floyd A. Brynelson
James C. Herrick
Griffin G. Dorschel

For Complete List of Firm Personnel, See General Section

For full biographical listings, see the Martindale-Hubbell Law Directory

Madison—Continued

BOARDMAN, SUHR, CURRY & FIELD (AV)

One South Pinckney Street, Suite 410, P.O. Box 927, 53701-0927
Telephone: 608-257-9521
FAX: 608-283-1709

MEMBERS OF FIRM

Henry A. Field, Jr.
Kenneth T. McCormick, Jr.
Bradway A. Liddle, Jr.
Claude J. Covelli
Paul R. Norman
Mark W. Pernitz
Michael P. May
Richard J. Delacenserie
James E. Bartzen
Steven C. Zach
Amanda J. Kaiser
Catherine M. Rottier
Mark J. Steichen
Madelyn D. Leopold

Representative Clients: CUNA Mutual Insurance Group; Liberty Mutual Insurance Co.; Madison Newspapers, Inc.; Oscar Mayer Foods Corp.; State Farm Insurance Co.; Wausau Insurance Cos.; Wisconsin Bankers Assn.

For Complete List of Firm Personnel, See General Section

For full biographical listings, see the Martindale-Hubbell Law Directory

HABUSH, HABUSH, DAVIS & ROTTIER, S.C. (AV)

Suite 500, 217 South Hamilton Street, 53703
Telephone: 608-255-6663
Fax: 608-255-0745
Milwaukee, Wisconsin Office: Suite 2200, First Wisconsin Center, 777 East Wisconsin Avenue.
Telephone: 414-271-0900.
FAX: 414-271-6854.
Appleton, Wisconsin Office: Appleton Center, 100 West Lawrence Street.
Telephone: 414-738-0900.
FAX: 414-738-7785.
Wausau, Wisconsin Office: 401 Fifth Street.
Telephone: 715-842-4444.
FAX: 715-845-8898.
Racine, Wisconsin Office: Durand Place, 5439 Durand Avenue, Suite 220.
Telephone: 414-554-6200.
FAX: 414-554-7166.
Waukesha, Wisconsin Office: Stone Ridge I, N14 W23755 Stone Ridge Drive, Suite 225.
Telephone: 414-523-4700.
Rhinelander, Wisconsin Office: 26 South Brown Street.
Telephone: 715-369-5959.
FAX: 715-369-5961.

Robert L. Habush
Daniel A. Rottier (Resident)
James R. Jansen (Resident)
Susan R. Steingass (Resident)
P. Jeffrey Archibald (Resident)
Nicholas J. McNamara (Resident)

For full biographical listings, see the Martindale-Hubbell Law Directory

LAFOLLETTE & SINYKIN (AV)

One East Main, Suite 500, 53703
Telephone: 608-257-3911
Fax: 608-257-0609
Mailing Address: P.O. Box 2719, 53701-2719
Sauk City, Wisconsin Office: 603 Water Street.
Telephone: 608-643-2408.
Stoughton, Wisconsin Office: 113 East Main Street, P.O. Box 191.
Telephone: 608-873-9464.
Fax: 608-873-0781.

MEMBERS OF FIRM

Philip F. LaFollette (1897-1965)
Gordon Sinykin (1910-1991)
James E. Doyle (1915-1987)
Earl H. Munson
Christopher J. Wilcox
Howard A. Sweet
Thomas A. Hoffner
David E. McFarlane
Linda M. Clifford
Jeffrey J. Kassel
Noreen J. Parrett
Eugenia G. Carter

OF COUNSEL

William E. Chritton (Resident, Stoughton Office)
Daniel Sinykin
Frank M. Tuerkheimer

Reference: M&I Madison Bank.

For Complete List of Firm Personnel, See General Section

For full biographical listings, see the Martindale-Hubbell Law Directory

LAWTON & CATES, S.C. (AV)

214 West Mifflin Street, 53703-2594
Telephone: 608-256-9031
Fax: 608-256-4670

John C. Carlson
James A. Olson
James W. Gardner
Kent I. Carnell

Reference: Bank One, Madison.

For full biographical listings, see the Martindale-Hubbell Law Directory

*MILWAUKEE,** Milwaukee Co.

CANNON & DUNPHY, S.C. (AV)

100 East Wisconsin Avenue Suite 1040, 53202
Telephone: 414-782-2700
Facsimile: 414-796-5800
Brookfield, Wisconsin Office: 595 North Barker Road, P.O. Box 1750.
Telephone: 414-782-2700.
Facsimile: 414-796-5800. (Mailing Address)

William M. Cannon
Patrick O. Dunphy
Lynn R. Laufenberg
Mark L. Thomsen

Raymond E. Schrank, II

For full biographical listings, see the Martindale-Hubbell Law Directory

HABUSH, HABUSH, DAVIS & ROTTIER, S.C. (AV)

Suite 2200 First Wisconsin Center, 777 East Wisconsin Avenue, 53202
Telephone: 414-271-0900
Fax: 414-271-6854
Madison, Wisconsin Office: Suite 500, 217 South Hamilton Street.
Telephone: 608-255-6663.
FAX: 608-255-0745.
Appleton, Wisconsin Office: Appleton Center, 100 West Lawrence Street.
Telephone: 414-738-0900.
FAX: 414-738-7785.
Wausau, Wisconsin Office: 401 Fifth Street.
Telephone: 715-842-4444.
FAX: 715-845-8898.
Racine, Wisconsin Office: Durand Place, 5439 Durand Avenue, Suite 220.
Telephone: 414-554-6200.
FAX: 414-554-7166.
Waukesha, Wisconsin Office: Stone Ridge I, N14 W23755 Stone Ridge Drive, Suite 225.
Telephone: 414-523-4700.
Rhinelander, Wisconsin Office: 26 South Brown Street.
Telephone: 715-369-5959.
FAX: 715-369-5961.

Robert L. Habush
Jesse J. Habush (1930-1983)
Howard A. Davis
Charles F. Stierman
Mark S. Young
Donald H. Slavik
Catherine T. Tully
Virginia M. Antoine
Laurence J. Fehring
Marcia L. Grinder
Colleen B. Beaman
Kathy L. Davis

For full biographical listings, see the Martindale-Hubbell Law Directory

KERSTEN & MCKINNON, S.C. (AV)

231 West Wisconsin Avenue, Suite 1200, 53203
Telephone: 414-271-0054
Fax: 414-271-7131

Charles J. Kersten (1925-1972)
J. P. McKinnon (1943-1973)
Arlo McKinnon
E. Campion Kersten
George P. Kersten
Kenan J. Kersten
Dyan Evans Barbeau
Leslie Van Buskirk

Sheila M. Hanrahan

For full biographical listings, see the Martindale-Hubbell Law Directory

MURPHY, GILLICK, WICHT & PRACHTHAUSER (AV)

Suite 1200, 330 East Kilbourn Avenue, 53202
Telephone: 414-271-1011
Milwaukee: 1-800-942-2880
South Office: Edgewood Bank Building, 4811 South 76th Street.
Telephone: 414-281-5700.
North Office: Northridge Bank Building, 9001 North 76th Street.
Telephone: 414-354-5051.
Appleton, Wisconsin Office: 54 Park Place.
Telephone: 414-730-0200. Appleton: 1-800-942-2882.
Brookfield, Wisconsin Office: Brookfield Lakes Corporate Center, 300 North Corporate Drive (180th Street and Blue Mound Road).
Telephone: 414-792-0888.

MEMBERS OF FIRM

James J. Murphy
Michael H. Gillick
Dennis H. Wicht
Don C. Prachthauser
Anthony W. Welhouse (Resident, Appleton Office)
George F. Graf (Resident, Brookfield Office)
Patrick J. Gillick
Melita M. Biese
Kevin J. Kukor

ASSOCIATES

Keith R. Stachowiak
John J. Laffey
Thadd J. Llaurado
Mark D. Baus
Erika T. Flierl
Sandra K. Graf

OF COUNSEL

M. Josef Zimmermann

For full biographical listings, see the Martindale-Hubbell Law Directory

Milwaukee—Continued

Reinhart, Boerner, Van Deuren, Norris & Rieselbach, S.C. (AV)
1000 North Water Street, P.O. Box 92900, 53202-0900
Telephone: 414-298-1000
Facsimile: 414-298-8097
Denver, Colorado Office: One Norwest Center, 1700 Lincoln Street, Suite 3725.
Telephone: 303-831-0909.
Fax: 303-831-4805.
Madison, Wisconsin Office: 7617 Mineral Point Road, 53701-2020.
Telephone: 608-283-7900.
Fax: 608-283-7919.
Washington, D.C. Office: 601 Pennsylvania Avenue, N.W., North Building, Suite 750.
Telephone: 202-393-3636.
Fax: 202-393-0796.

Paul V. Lucke
William R. Steinmetz
Stephen T. Jacobs
Scott W. Hansen
Richard P. Carr
Anne Willis Reed
Francis W. Deisinger
Steven P. Bogart

R. Timothy Muth
Anne Morgan Hlavacka
Kathleen S. Donius
Christine L. Thierfelder
David J. Sisson
Patrick J. Hodan
Katherine McConahay Nealon
Colleen D. Ball
Dean E. Mabie
Geri Krupp-Gordon
Daniel J. La Fave
David G. Hanson

For Complete List of Firm Personnel, See General Section

For full biographical listings, see the Martindale-Hubbell Law Directory

Slattery, Hausman & Hoefle, Ltd. (AV)
The Milwaukee Center, Suite 1800, 111 East Kilbourn Avenue, 53202
Telephone: 414-271-4555
Facsimile: 414-271-9045

Robert A. Slattery
C. Michael Hausman
Paul R. Hoefle

Alan E. Gesler
Steven J. Snedeker

For full biographical listings, see the Martindale-Hubbell Law Directory

Warshafsky, Rotter, Tarnoff, Reinhardt & Bloch, S.C. (AV)
839 North Jefferson Street, 53202-3796
Telephone: 414-276-4970
Fax: 414-276-5533

Ted M. Warshafsky
Gerald J. Bloch
Randall E. Reinhardt
Merton N. Rotter
Michael I. Tarnoff
Werner A. Reis
Victor C. Harding
Robert P. Goldstein
David M. Skoglind
Frank T. Crivello II
Paul H. Chanan

For full biographical listings, see the Martindale-Hubbell Law Directory

NEW RICHMOND, St. Croix Co.

Doar, Drill & Skow, S.C. (AV)
103 North Knowles Avenue, 54017
Telephone: 715-246-2211
Fax: 715-246-4405
Baldwin, Wisconsin Office: Office Park.
Telephone: 715-684-3227.

W.T. Doar (1882-1952)
James A. Drill
Thomas D. Bell

OF COUNSEL

W. T. Doar, Jr.

Lisa M. Drill
Matthew Alan Biegert
Michael J. Brose

Counsel for: Bank of New Richmond; Polk County Bank, Centuria, Wis.

For full biographical listings, see the Martindale-Hubbell Law Directory

*OSHKOSH,** Winnebago Co.

Curtis Wilde & Neal Law Offices (AV)
1010 West 20th Avenue, P.O. Box 2845, 54903-2845
Telephone: 414-233-1010
Markesan, Wisconsin Office: 10 East Water Street.
Telephone: 414-398-2314.

George W. Curtis
William R. Wilde
John A. Neal

(See Next Column)

Scott C. Woldt

Reference: Valley Bank.

For full biographical listings, see the Martindale-Hubbell Law Directory

*WAUKESHA,** Waukesha Co.

Cramer, Multhauf & Hammes (AV)
1601 East Racine Avenue, P.O. Box 558, 53187
Telephone: 414-542-4278
Telecopier: 414-542-4270

MEMBERS OF FIRM

James W. Hammes
Peter J. Plaushines

ASSOCIATES

Kathryn Sawyer Gutenkunst
Timothy J. Andringa

Reference: Waukesha State Bank.

For Complete List of Firm Personnel, See General Section

For full biographical listings, see the Martindale-Hubbell Law Directory

*WAUSAU,** Marathon Co.

Jerome A. Maeder Law Offices, S.C. (AV)
602 Jackson Street, P.O. Box 1626, 54401
Telephone: 715-842-2281
FAX: 715-842-1046

Jerome A. Maeder

Vincent A. Maeder
William D. Mansell
Robert J. Gray

For full biographical listings, see the Martindale-Hubbell Law Directory

WYOMING

*CASPER,** Natrona Co.

Duncan & Kofakis (AV)
Suite 325, Key Bank Building, 300 South Wolcott Street, 82601
Telephone: 307-265-0934
Fax: 307-237-0718

Hugh M. Duncan

For full biographical listings, see the Martindale-Hubbell Law Directory

James Richard McCarty, P.C. (AV)
The Ormsby Mansion, 536 South Center Street, 82601-3195
Telephone: 307-237-1568
FAX: 307-237-1570

James Richard McCarty

For full biographical listings, see the Martindale-Hubbell Law Directory

Schwartz, Bon, Walker & Studer (AV)
141 South Center, Suite 505, 82601
Telephone: 307-235-6681
Fax: 307-234-5099

William T. Schwartz
William S. Bon
Cameron S. Walker
Judith A. W. Studer

ASSOCIATES

Patrick T. Holscher
Peter J. Young
Kathleen J. Doyle

Representative Clients: Key Bank of Casper; Equitable Life Assurance Society; ANR Production; Union Carbide Corp.; Hill Top Shopping Center; Exxon Co., U.S.A.; Armco Steel Corp.; USF&G; American Insurance Cos.

For full biographical listings, see the Martindale-Hubbell Law Directory

*CHEYENNE,** Laramie Co.

Hickey, Mackey, Evans, Walker & Stewart (AV)
1712 Carey Avenue, P.O. Drawer 467, 82003
Telephone: 307-634-1525
Telecopier: 307-638-7335

MEMBERS OF FIRM

Paul J. Hickey
Terry W. Mackey
David F. Evans
John M. Walker
Mark R. Stewart III
Richard D. Tim Bush

A List of Representative Clients will be furnished upon request.
Reference: Norwest Bank, Cheyenne, N.A.

For full biographical listings, see the Martindale-Hubbell Law Directory

*JACKSON,** Teton Co.

King and King (AV)

Suite 201 Centennial Building, 610 West Broadway, P.O. Box 40, 83001
Telephone: 307-733-2904
Fax: 307-733-1058

MEMBERS OF FIRM

Floyd R. King
Bret F. King

Reference: Key Bank, N.A., Jackson, Wyoming.

For full biographical listings, see the Martindale-Hubbell Law Directory

Spence, Moriarity & Schuster (AV)

15 South Jackson Street, P.O. Box 548, 83001
Telephone: 307-733-7290
Fax: 307-733-5248
Cheyenne, Wyoming Office: Suite 302 Pioneer Center, 2424 Pioneer Avenue, P.O. Box 1006.
Telephone: 307-635-1533.
Fax: 307-635-1539.

MEMBERS OF FIRM

Gerry L. Spence
Edward P. Moriarity
Robert P. Schuster
Gary L. Shockey
J. Douglas McCalla
Roy A. Jacobson, Jr.

ASSOCIATES

Glen G. Debroder
Kent W. Spence
Robert A. Krause
Heather Noble

Reference: First Interstate Bank, Casper, Wyoming.

For Complete List of Firm Personnel, See General Section

For full biographical listings, see the Martindale-Hubbell Law Directory

ROCK SPRINGS, Sweetwater Co.

Honaker, Hampton & Newman (AV)

214 Winston Drive, P.O. Box 1000, 82902
Telephone: 307-382-6443
Fax: 307-382-7866

MEMBERS OF FIRM

Richard H. Honaker
David A. Hampton
Michael D. Newman

LEGAL SUPPORT PERSONNEL

Julee Dreben
Kaye Fabritz-Tyler
Benjamin Allison

References: American National Bank of Rock Springs; Rock Springs National Bank; United Steelworkers of America, Local Nos. 13214 and 15320; Firefighters Local No. 1499; Rock Springs Police Protection Association.

For full biographical listings, see the Martindale-Hubbell Law Directory

PUERTO RICO

SAN JUAN, San Juan Dist.

Indiano, Williams & Weinstein-Bacal

Hato Rey Tower, 21st Floor, 268 Muñoz Rivera Avenue (Hato Rey), 00918
Telephone: 809-754-2323; 763-0485
Fax: 809-766-3366
St. Thomas, Virgin Islands Office: Stuart A. Weinstein-Bacal, P.O. Box 9820, Charlotte Amalie, 00801.
Telephone: 809-776-2500.
Telecopier: 809-779-6918.

MEMBERS OF FIRM

Stuart A. Weinstein-Bacal
David C. Indiano
Jeffrey M. Williams

ASSOCIATES

Javier A. Morales Ramos
Madeline Garcia-Rodriguez

For full biographical listings, see the Martindale-Hubbell Law Directory

Jiménez, Graffam & Lausell

Formerly Jiménez & Fusté
Suite 505, Midtown Building, 421 Muñoz Rivera Avenue, Hato Rey, P.O. Box 366104, 00936-6104
Telephone: 809-767-1030; 767-1000; 767-1061; 767-1064
Telefax: 809-751-4068;
Cable: "Nezte"; RCA
Telex: 325-2730

(See Next Column)

MEMBERS OF FIRM

Nicolás Jiménez
William A. Graffam
Steven C. Lausell
J. Ramón Rivera-Morales
José Juan Torres-Escalera
Raquel M. Dulzaides
Manuel San Juan

ASSOCIATES

Manolo T. Rodríguez-Bird
Patricia Garrity
Carlos E. Bayrón
Isabel J. Vélez-Serrano
Edgardo A. Vega-López
Alexandra M. Serracante-Cadilla
Luis Saldaña-Roman

Representative Clients: McAllister Brothers; The United Kingdom Steamship P & I Association; The Britannia Steamship Insurance Association; The West of England Ship Owners Mutual Insurance Association; Assurance Foreningen Skuld; The Standard Steamship Owners' P & I Association.

For full biographical listings, see the Martindale-Hubbell Law Directory

VIRGIN ISLANDS

*CHARLOTTE AMALIE, ST. THOMAS,** St. Thomas

Grunert Stout Bruch & Moore

24-25 Kongensgade, P.O. Box 1030, 00804
Telephone: 809-774-1320
Fax: 809-774-7839

MEMBERS OF FIRM

John E. Stout
Susan Bruch Moorehead
Treston E. Moore

ASSOCIATES

Maryleen Thomas
Richard F. Taylor
H. Kevin Mart (Not admitted in VI)

OF COUNSEL

William L. Blum

For full biographical listings, see the Martindale-Hubbell Law Directory

CANADA
ALBERTA

*EDMONTON,** Edmonton Jud. Dist.

Parlee McLaws (AV)

15th Floor Manulife Place, 10180 101st Street, T5J 4K1
Telephone: 403-423-8500
Telecopier: 403-423-2870
Calgary, Alberta Office: 3400, Western Canadian Place, 707 - 8th Avenue, S.W.
Telephone: 403-294-7000.
Telecopier: 403-265-8263.

MEMBERS OF FIRM

C. H. Kerr, Q.C.
M. D. MacDonald
K. F. Bailey, Q.C.
R. B. Davison, Q.C.
F. R. Haldane
P. E. J. Curran
D. G. Finlay
J. K. McFadyen
R. C. Secord
D. L. Kennedy
D. C. Rolf
D. F. Pawlowski
A. A. Garber
R. P. James
D. C. Wintermute
J. L. Cairns
R. A. Newton, Q.C.
T. A. Cockrall, Q.C.
H. D. Montemurro
F. J. Niziol
R. W. Wilson
I. L. MacLachlan
R. O. Langley
R. G. McBean
J. T. Neilson
E. G. Rice
J. F. McGinnis
J. H. H. Hockin
G. W. Jaycock
M. J. K. Nikel
B. J. Curial
S. L. May
M. S. Poretti

ASSOCIATES

C. R. Head
A.W. Slemko
L. H. Hamdon
K.A. Smith
K. D. Fallis-Howell
D. S. Tam
J.W. McClure
F.H. Belzil
R.A. Renz
J.G. Paulson
K. E. Buss
B. L. Andriachuk
P. E. S. J. Kennedy
R. Feraco
R.J. Billingsley
N.B.R. Thompson
P. A. Shenher
I. C. Johnson
K.G. Koshman
D.D. Dubrule
G. T. Lund
W.D. Johnston
G. E. Flemming
K. P. Nayyer

For full biographical listings, see the Martindale-Hubbell Law Directory

CANADA
BRITISH COLUMBIA

*VANCOUVER,** Vancouver Co.

RUSSELL & DuMOULIN (AV)

2100-1075 West Georgia Street, V6E 3G2
Telephone: 604-631-3131
Fax: 604-631-3232
A Member of the national association of Borden DuMoulin Howard Gervais, comprising Russell & DuMoulin, Vancouver, British Columbia; Howard Mackie, Calgary, Alberta; Borden & Elliot, Toronto, Ontario; Mackenzie Gervais, Montreal, Quebec and Borden DuMoulin Howard Gervais, London, England.
Strategic Alliance with Perkins Coie with offices in Seattle, Spokane and Bellevue, Washington; Portland, Oregon; Anchorage, Alaska; Los Angeles, California; Washington, D.C.; Hong Kong and Taipei, Taiwan.
Represented in Hong Kong by Vincent T.K. Cheung, Yap & Co.

MEMBER OF FIRM

William T. Morley

Representative Clients: Alcan Smelters & Chemicals Ltd.; The Bank of Nova Scotia; Canada Trust Co.; The Canada Life Assurance Co.; Forest Industrial Relations Ltd.; Honda Canada Inc.; IBM Canada Ltd.; Macmillan Bloedel Ltd.; Nissho Iwai Canada Ltd.; The Toronto-Dominion Bank.

For Complete List of Firm Personnel, See General Section

For full biographical listings, see the Martindale-Hubbell Law Directory

CANADA
MANITOBA

*WINNIPEG,** Eastern Jud. Dist.

AIKINS, MACAULAY & THORVALDSON (AV)

Thirtieth Floor, Commodity Exchange Tower, 360 Main Street, R3C 4G1
Telephone: 204-957-0050
Fax: 204-957-0840

MEMBERS OF FIRM

Michael J. Mercury, Q.C.
Cyril G. Labman
Rod E. Stephenson, Q.C.
Knox B. Foster, Q.C.
Colin R. MacArthur, Q.C.
Eleanor R. Dawson, Q.C.

Counsel for: Air Canada; Bank of Montreal; Boeing of Canada; Canada Safeway Limited; Canadian Medical Protective Association; Federal Industries Ltd.; The Great West Life Assurance Company; John Labatt Limited; Winnipeg Free Press; Winnipeg Jets.

For Complete List of Firm Personnel, See General Section

For full biographical listings, see the Martindale-Hubbell Law Directory

CANADA
NEW BRUNSWICK

*SAINT JOHN,** Saint John Co.

CLARK, DRUMMIE & COMPANY (AV)

40 Wellington Row, P.O. Box 6850 Station "A", E2L 4S3
Telephone: 506-633-3800
Telecopier (Automatic): 506-633-3811

MEMBERS OF FIRM

Barry R. Morrison, Q.C.
W. Andrew LeMesurier
Timothy M. Hopkins
Norman J. Bossé
William B. Richards
Peter H. MacPhail

Reference: Royal Bank of Canada.

For Complete List of Firm Personnel, See General Section

For full biographical listings, see the Martindale-Hubbell Law Directory

CANADA
NOVA SCOTIA

*HALIFAX,** Halifax Co.

McINNES COOPER & ROBERTSON (AV)

1601 Lower Water Street, P.O. Box 730, B3J 2V1
Telephone: 902-425-6500
Fax: 902-425-6350
St. John's, Newfoundland Office: Suite 602, Scotia Centre, 235 Water Street, P.O. Box 547. A1C, 5K8.
Telephone: 709-726-9500.
Fax: 709-726-9550.

David A. Graves
Deborah K. Smith
Eric LeDrew

Attorneys for: Bank of Nova Scotia; Imperial Oil, Limited; Frank B. Hall & Co., Inc. (New York); American Steamship Owners Protection & Indemnity Association, Inc.; Coca-Cola, Ltd.; Scott Worldwide Inc.; Hong Kong Bank of Canada.

For Complete List of Firm Personnel, See General Section

For full biographical listings, see the Martindale-Hubbell Law Directory

CANADA
ONTARIO

KITCHENER, Regional Munic. of Waterloo

GIFFEN, LEE, WAGNER, MORLEY & GARBUTT (AV)

50 Queen Street North, P.O. Box 2396, N2H 6M3
Telephone: 519-578-4150
Fax: 519-578-8740

MEMBERS OF FIRM

Jeffrey J. Mansfield (1955-1991)
J. Peter Giffen, Q.C.
Bruce L. Lee
J. Scott Morley
Brian R. Wagner
Philip A. Garbutt

ASSOCIATES

Edward J. Vanderkloet
Keith C. Masterman
Daniel J. Fife
Jeffrey W. Boich

For full biographical listings, see the Martindale-Hubbell Law Directory

*TORONTO,** Regional Munic. of York

BORDEN & ELLIOT (AV)

Barristers & Solicitors
Scotia Plaza, 40 King Street West, M5H 3Y4
Telephone: 416-367-6000
Telecopier: 416-367-6749
Internet: @ borden.com
A Member of the national association of Borden DuMoulin Howard Gervais, comprising Borden & Elliot in Toronto, Ontario, Russell & DuMoulin in Vancouver, British Columbia, Howard, Mackie in Calgary, Alberta and Mackenzie Gervais in Montréal, Québec. Borden DuMoulin Howard Gervais also operates an office in London, England.

MEMBER AND ASSOCIATES

Edward A. Ayers, Q.C.

For Complete List of Firm Personnel, See General Section

For full biographical listings, see the Martindale-Hubbell Law Directory

CANADA
PRINCE EDWARD ISLAND

*CHARLOTTETOWN,** Queen's Co.

CAMPBELL, LEA, MICHAEL, McCONNELL & PIGOT (AV)

15 Queen Street, P.O. Box 429, C1A 7K7
Telephone: 902-566-3400
Telecopier: 902-566-9266

MEMBERS OF FIRM

Paul D. Michael, Q.C.
M. Jane Ralling
Robert A. McConnell
Kenneth L. Godfrey

General Counsel in Prince Edward Island for: Canadian Imperial Bank of Commerce; Maritime Electric Co., Ltd.; Michelin Tires (Canada) Ltd.; Newsco Investments Ltd. (Dundas Farms); Queen Elizabeth Hospital Inc.; Imperial Oil Limited; General Motors of Canada; Co-op Atlantic; Liberty Mutual; Employers Reinsurance Group.

(See Next Column)

CAMPBELL, LEA, MICHAEL, MCCONNELL & PIGOT, *Charlottetown—Continued*

For Complete List of Firm Personnel, See General Section

For full biographical listings, see the Martindale-Hubbell Law Directory

CANADA
QUEBEC

*MONTREAL,** Montreal Dist.

MCMASTER MEIGHEN (AV)

A General Partnership
7th Floor, 630 René-Lévesque Boulevard West, H3B 4H7
Telephone: 514-879-1212
Telecopier: 514-878-0605
Cable Address: "Cammerall"
Telex: "Cammerall MTL" 05-268637
Affiliated with Fraser & Beatty in Toronto, North York, Ottawa and Vancouver.

MEMBERS OF FIRM

Alex K. Paterson, O.C., O.Q., Q.C.
Alexis P. Bergeron
Michel A. Pinsonnault
Marc Duchesne
Robert J. Torralbo
Yvan Houle
John G. Murphy
Valérie Beaudin
Jacques Brien
Colin K. Irving
Daniel Ayotte
Diane Quenneville
Richard R. Provost
Jacques Gauthier
Douglas C. Mitchell
Luc Béliveau
Kurt A. Johnson

For Complete List of Firm Personnel, See General Section

For full biographical listings, see the Martindale-Hubbell Law Directory

PROBATE AND ESTATE PLANNING LAW

ALABAMA

*BIRMINGHAM,** Jefferson Co.

BALCH & BINGHAM (AV)
1710 Sixth Avenue North, P.O. Box 306, 35201
Telephone: 205-251-8100
Facsimile: 205-226-8798
Other Birmingham, Alabama Office: 1901 Sixth Avenue North, 35203.
Telephone: 205-251-8100.
Facsimile: 205-226-8799.
Montgomery, Alabama Office: The Winter Building, 2 Dexter Avenue, 36101.
Telephone: 205-834-6500.
Facsimile: 205-269-3115.
Huntsville, Alabama Office: Suite 810, 200 West Court Square, 35801.
Telephone: 205-551-0171.
Facsimile: 205-551-0174.
Washington, D.C. Office: Suite 800, 1101 Connecticut Avenue, N.W., 20036.
Telephone: 202-296-0387.
Facsimile: 202-452-8180.

MEMBERS OF FIRM

A. Key Foster, Jr. William E. Shanks, Jr.

ASSOCIATE

Phillip Anthony Nichols

Counsel for: Alabama Power Co.; Blue Cross and Blue Shield of Alabama; The Boeing Company; Brasfield & Gorrie, Inc.; Compass Bancshares, Inc.; Harbert Corp.; Kimberly-Clark Corp.; Southern Company Services, Inc.; Southern Research Institute; Vesta Insurance Group, Inc.

For Complete List of Firm Personnel, See General Section

For full biographical listings, see the Martindale-Hubbell Law Directory

BERKOWITZ, LEFKOVITS, ISOM & KUSHNER, A PROFESSIONAL CORPORATION (AV)
1600 SouthTrust Tower, 420 North Twentieth Street, 35203
Telephone: 205-328-0480
Telecopier: 205-322-8007

Arnold K. Lefkovits Anne W. Mitchell
Harold B. Kushner Thomas O. Kolb

Andrew J. Potts

For Complete List of Firm Personnel, See General Section

For full biographical listings, see the Martindale-Hubbell Law Directory

BRADLEY, ARANT, ROSE & WHITE (AV)
1400 Park Place Tower, 2001 Park Place, 35203
Telephone: 205-521-8000
Telex: 494-1324
Facsimile: 205-251-8611, 251-8665, 252-0264
Facsimile (Southtrust Office): 205-251-9915
Huntsville, Alabama Office: 200 Clinton Avenue West, Suite 900.
Telephone: 205-517-5100.
Facsimile: 205-533-5069.

MEMBERS OF FIRM

John N. Wrinkle Charles A. J. Beavers, Jr.
William L. Hinds, Jr. Ralph Howard Yeilding

ASSOCIATE

Jennifer Byers McLeod

For Complete List of Firm Personnel, See General Section

For full biographical listings, see the Martindale-Hubbell Law Directory

BURR & FORMAN (AV)
3000 SouthTrust Tower, 420 North 20th Street, 35203
Telephone: 205-251-3000
Telecopier: 205-458-5100
Huntsville, Alabama Office: Suite 204, Regency Center, 400 Meridian Street.
Telephone: 205-551-0010.

(See Next Column)

MEMBERS OF FIRM

Paul O. Woodall Bruce A. Rawls
A. Brand Walton Marvin Glenn Perry, Jr.

ASSOCIATE

Warren C. Matthews

For Complete List of Firm Personnel, See General Section

For full biographical listings, see the Martindale-Hubbell Law Directory

CORLEY, MONCUS & WARD, P.C. (AV)
Suite 650, 2100 SouthBridge Parkway, 35209
Telephone: 205-879-5959
Telecopier: 205-879-5859

Claude McCain Moncus Gene W. Gray, Jr.

For Complete List of Firm Personnel, See General Section

For full biographical listings, see the Martindale-Hubbell Law Directory

PRITCHARD, MCCALL & JONES (AV)
800 Financial Center, 35203
Telephone: 205-328-9190

MEMBERS OF FIRM

William S. Pritchard (1890-1967) Julian P. Hardy, Jr.
Alexander W. Jones (1914-1988) Alexander W. Jones, Jr.
William S. Pritchard, Jr. F. Hilton-Green Tomlinson
Madison W. O'Kelley, Jr. James G. Henderson
William S. Pritchard, III

ASSOCIATES

Michael L. McKerley Nina Michele LaFleur
Robert Bond Higgins Mary W. Burge

Representative Clients: First National Bank of Columbiana; Central State Bank of Calera; Buffalo Rock-Pepsi-Cola Bottling Co.; Gillis Advertising, Inc.; Liberty Mutual Insurance Co.; Reliance Insurance Company; South-Trust Bank, N.A.; Bromberg & Company, Inc.; Farmers Furniture Company; First Commercial Bank.

For full biographical listings, see the Martindale-Hubbell Law Directory

SIROTE & PERMUTT, P.C. (AV)
2222 Arlington Avenue, South, P.O. Box 55727, 35255
Telephone: 205-933-7111
Facsimile: 205-930-5301
Huntsville, Alabama Office: 200 Clinton Avenue, N.W., Suite 1000.
Telephone: 205-536-1711.
Facsimile: 205-534-9650.
Mobile, Alabama Office: One St. Louis Centre, Suite 1000.
Telephone: 205-432-1671.
Facsimile: 205-434-0196.
Montgomery, Alabama Office: Colonial Commerce Center, Suite 305 One Commerce Street.
Telephone: 205-261-3400.
Facsimile: 205-261-3434.
Tuscaloosa, Alabama Office: 2216 14th Street.
Telephone: 205-752-2089.

Harold I. Apolinsky Judith F. Todd
Melinda McEachern Mathews Dale B. Stone
Candace Lee Hemphill

Representative Clients: International Business Machines (IBM); General Motors Corp.; Colonial Bank; Bruno's, Inc.; University of Alabama Hospitals; Westinghouse Electric Corp.; First Alabama Bank; Monsanto Chemical Company; South Central Bell; Prudential Insurance Company; American Home Products, Inc.; Minnesota Mining and Manufacturing, Inc. (3M).

For Complete List of Firm Personnel, See General Section

For full biographical listings, see the Martindale-Hubbell Law Directory

SPAIN, GILLON, GROOMS, BLAN & NETTLES (AV)
The Zinszer Building, 2117 2nd Avenue North, 35203
Telephone: 205-328-4100
Telecopier: 205-324-8866

MEMBERS OF FIRM

John P. McKleroy, Jr. J. Birch Bowdre
Samuel H. Frazier Glenn E. Estess, Jr.
J. Sanford Mullins, III

General Counsel for: Liberty National Life Insurance Co.; United States Fidelity & Guaranty Co.; Piggly Wiggly Alabama Distributing Co.; AmSouth Mortgage Co., Inc.; Alabama Insurance Guaranty Association; Alabama Life and Disability Insurance Guaranty Association; Alabama Insurance Underwriters Association.
Counsel for: The Prudential Insurance Company of America; Government Employees Insurance Co.; Massachusetts Mutual Life Insurance Co.

For Complete List of Firm Personnel, See General Section

For full biographical listings, see the Martindale-Hubbell Law Directory

*FLORENCE,** Lauderdale Co.

KELLER & PITTS (AV)

212 South Cedar Street, P.O. Box 933, 35631
Telephone: 205-764-5822
Fax: 205-767-6360

MEMBERS OF FIRM

Jesse A. Keller
Conrad C. Pitts
Peter L. Paine

Counsel for: The American Road Insurance Co.; Lambert Transfer Co.

For full biographical listings, see the Martindale-Hubbell Law Directory

*HUNTSVILLE,** Madison Co.

BERRY, ABLES, TATUM, LITTLE & BAXTER, P.C. (AV)

Legal Building, 315 Franklin Street, S.E., P.O. Box 165, 35804-0165
Telephone: 205-533-3740
Facsimile: 205-533-3751

William H. Blanton (1889-1973)
Joe M. Berry
L. Bruce Ables
James T. Tatum, Jr.
Loyd H. Little, Jr.
James T. Baxter, III
Thomas E. Parker, Jr.
Bill G. Hall

Representative Clients: AmSouth Bank, N.A.; First Alabama Bank; General Shale Products Co.; The Hartz Corp.; Litton Industries, Inc.; Farmers Tractor Co.; Colonial Bank; Farm Credit Bank of Texas; Resolution Trust Corp.
Reference: First Alabama Bank.

For full biographical listings, see the Martindale-Hubbell Law Directory

BRADLEY, ARANT, ROSE & WHITE (AV)

200 Clinton Avenue West, Suite 900, 35801
Telephone: 205-517-5100
Facsimile: 205-533-5069
Birmingham, Alabama Office: 1400 Park Place Tower, 2001 Park Place.
Telephone: 205-521-8000.
Telex: 494-1324.
Facsimile: 205-251-8611, 251-8665, 252-0264. Facsimile (Southtrust Office): 205-251-9915.

RESIDENT PARTNERS

Robert Sellers Smith
Scott E. Ludwig

For Complete List of Firm Personnel, See General Section

For full biographical listings, see the Martindale-Hubbell Law Directory

BURR & FORMAN (AV)

Suite 204, Regency Center, 400 Meridian Street, 35801
Telephone: 205-551-0010
Birmingham, Alabama Office: 3000 SouthTrust Tower, 420 North 20th Street.
Telephone: 205-251-3000.
Telecopier: 205-458-5100.

RESIDENT PARTNER

S. Dagnal Rowe

For full biographical listings, see the Martindale-Hubbell Law Directory

SIROTE & PERMUTT, P.C. (AV)

Suite 1000, 200 Clinton Avenue, N.W., 35801
Telephone: 205-536-1711
Facsimile: 205-534-9650
Birmingham, Alabama Office: 2222 Arlington Avenue, South, P.O. Box 55727.
Telephone: 205-933-7111.
Facsimile: 205-930-5301.
Mobile, Alabama Office: One St. Louis Centre, Suite 1000.
Telephone: 205-432-1671.
Facsimile: 205-434-0196.
Montgomery, Alabama Office: Colonial Commerce Center, Suite 305, One Commerce Street.
Telephone: 205-261-3400.
Facsimile: 205-261-3434.
Tuscaloosa, Alabama Office: 2216 14th Street.
Telephone: 205-752-2089.

George W. Royer, Jr.
Christine Sampson Hinson

For Complete List of Firm Personnel, See General Section

For full biographical listings, see the Martindale-Hubbell Law Directory

*JASPER,** Walker Co.

O'REAR & O'REAR (AV)

Suite B Bankhead-Byars Building, 1816 Third Avenue, P.O. Box 191, 35502-0191
Telephone: 205-387-2196
Fax: 205-387-2190

(See Next Column)

MEMBERS OF FIRM

Caine O'Rear, Jr.
Griff O'Rear
Mark A. McWhorter

Reference: First National Bank of Jasper.

For full biographical listings, see the Martindale-Hubbell Law Directory

*MOBILE,** Mobile Co.

BRYANT, BLACKSHER & LESTER (AV)

Suite 1107 Riverview Plaza Office Tower, 63 South Royal Street, Drawer 1465, 36633
Telephone: 334-432-4671
Telecopier: 334-433-6393
Fairhope, Alabama Office: 21 S. Section Street 36532.
Telephone: 205-990-8998.
Telecopier: 205-990-9878.

MEMBERS OF FIRM

Thomas E. Bryant, Jr.
Wesley H. Blacksher
F. Martin Lester, Jr.
Woodrow Eugene Howard, III
Theodore L. Greenspan
Carole W. Delchamps
Deidre W. Lee

For full biographical listings, see the Martindale-Hubbell Law Directory

JOHNSTONE, ADAMS, BAILEY, GORDON AND HARRIS (AV)

Royal St. Francis Building, 104 St. Francis Street, P.O. Box 1988, 36633
Telephone: 334-432-7682
Facsimile: 334-432-2800
Telex: 782040

MEMBERS OF FIRM

Charles B. Bailey, Jr.
E. Watson Smith
R. Gregory Watts

ASSOCIATES

Robert S. Frost
C. William Rasure, Jr.

General Counsel for: First Alabama Bank, Mobile; Infirmary Health System/Mobile Infirmary Medical Center/Rotary Rehabilitation Hospital (Multi-Hospital System).
Counsel for: Oil and Gas: Exxon Corp. Business and Corporate: Bell South Telecommunications, Inc.; Aluminum Co. of America; Michelin Tire Corp.; Metropolitan Life Insurance Co.; The Travelers Insurance Cos. Marine: The West of England Ship Owners Mutual Protection and Indemnity Association (Luxembourg); The Standard Steamship Owners' Protection and Indemnity Association (Bermuda) Ltd.

For Complete List of Firm Personnel, See General Section

For full biographical listings, see the Martindale-Hubbell Law Directory

LYONS, PIPES & COOK, P.C. (AV)

2 North Royal Street, P.O. Box 2727, 36652-2727
Telephone: 334-432-4481
Cable Address: "Lysea"
Telecopier: 334-433-1820

Thomas F. Garth
R. Mark Kirkpatrick
John C. Bell

General Counsel: Inchcape Shipping Services.
Counsel: The Hertz Corp.; McKenzie Tank Lines, Inc.; SCNO Barge Lines, Inc.; Scott Paper Co.; Shell Oil Corp.
Trial Counsel: Aetna Life & Casualty Co.; Chubb Group of Insurance Companies.

For Complete List of Firm Personnel, See General Section

For full biographical listings, see the Martindale-Hubbell Law Directory

SIROTE & PERMUTT, P.C. (AV)

One St. Louis Centre, Suite 1000, P.O. Drawer 2025, 36652-2025
Telephone: 334-432-1671
Facsimile: 334-434-0196
Birmingham, Alabama Office: 2222 Arlington Avenue, South, P.O. Box 55727.
Telephone: 205-933-7111.
Facsimile: 205-930-5301.
Huntsville, Alabama Office: 200 Clinton Avenue, N.W., Suite 1000.
Telephone: 205-536-1711.
Facsimile: 205-534-9650.
Montgomery, Alabama Office: Colonial Commerce Center, Suite 305, One Commerce Street.
Telephone: 205-261-3400.
Facsimile: 205-261-3434.
Tuscaloosa, Alabama Office: 2216 14th Street.
Telephone: 205-752-2089.

William H. McDermott
Shirley Mahan Justice

For Complete List of Firm Personnel, See General Section

For full biographical listings, see the Martindale-Hubbell Law Directory

*MONTGOMERY,** Montgomery Co.

* indicates certain Bar Register subscribers whose principal office is located elsewhere in the state and who have arranged for representation as a part of the state capital listings that follow

*** BALCH & BINGHAM** (AV)

The Winter Building, 2 Dexter Avenue, P.O. Box 78, 36101
Telephone: 334-834-6500
Facsimile: 334-269-3115
Birmingham, Alabama Offices: 1710 Sixth Avenue North, 35203.
Telephone: 205-251-8100.
Facsimile: 205-226-8798. 1901 Sixth Avenue North, 35203.
Telephone: 205-251-8100.
Facsimile: 205-226-8799.
Huntsville, Alabama Office: Suite 810, 200 West Court Square, 35801.
Telephone: 205-551-0171.
Facsimile: 205-551-0174.
Washington, D.C. Office: Suite 800, 1101 Connecticut Avenue, N.W., 20036.
Telephone: 202-296-0387.
Facsimile: 202-452-8180.

RESIDENT MEMBER OF FIRM
Malcolm N. Carmichael
RESIDENT ASSOCIATES

Patricia Anne Hamilton
James Ernest Bridges, III

Counsel for: Alabama Power Co.; Blue Cross and Blue Shield of Alabama; The Boeing Company; Brasfield & Gorrie, Inc.; Compass Bancshares, Inc.; Harbert Corp.; Kimberly-Clark Corp.; Southern Company Services, Inc.; Southern Research Institute; Vesta Insurance Group, Inc.

For Complete List of Firm Personnel, See General Section

For full biographical listings, see the Martindale-Hubbell Law Directory

CAPELL, HOWARD, KNABE & COBBS, P.A. (AV)

57 Adams Avenue, P.O. Box 2069, 36102-2069
Telephone: 334-241-8000

Jack L. Capell
Fontaine M. Howard (1908-1985)
Walter J. Knabe (1898-1979)
Edward E. Cobbs (1909-1982)
L. Lister Hill (1936-1993)
Herman H. Hamilton, Jr.
Rufus M. King
Robert S. Richard
John B. Scott, Jr.
John F. Andrews
James M. Scott
Thomas S. Lawson, Jr.
John L. Capell, III
William D. Coleman
William K. Martin
Bruce J. Downey III
Henry C. Barnett, Jr.
Palmer Smith Lehman
Richard F. Allen
Neal H. Acker
Henry H. Hutchinson
Shapard D. Ashley
D. Kyle Johnson
J. Lister Hubbard
James N. Walter, Jr.
James H. McLemore
H. Dean Mooty, Jr.
Jim B. Grant, Jr.
Wyeth Holt Speir, III
Chad S. Wachter
Ellen M. Hastings
Debra Deames Spain
William Rufus King
C. Clay Torbert, III

OF COUNSEL
Timothy Sullivan

For full biographical listings, see the Martindale-Hubbell Law Directory

CAPOUANO, WAMPOLD, PRESTWOOD & SANSONE, P.A. (AV)

350 Adams Avenue, P.O. Box 1910, 36102-1910
Telephone: 334-264-6401
Fax: 334-834-4954

Leon M. Capouano
Alvin T. Prestwood
Jerome D. Smith
Ellis D. Hanan
Joseph P. Borg
Joseph W. Warren

OF COUNSEL
Charles H. Wampold, Jr.

Thomas B. Klinner
Linda Smith Webb
James M. Sizemore, Jr.

Counsel for: First Alabama Bank of Montgomery, N.A.; Union Bank and Trust Co.; Real Estate Financing, Inc.; SouthTrust Bank; AmSouth Bank; Central Bank; City Federal Savings & Loan Assoc.; Colonial Mortgage Co.; Lomas & Nettleton; First Bank of Linden.

For full biographical listings, see the Martindale-Hubbell Law Directory

SIROTE & PERMUTT, P.C. (AV)

Colonial Commerce Center, Suite 305, One Commerce Street, 36104
Telephone: 334-261-3400
Facsimile: 334-261-3434
Birmingham, Alabama Office: 2222 Arlington Avenue, South, P.O. Box 55727.
Telephone: 205-933-7111.
Facsimile: 205-930-5301.

(See Next Column)

Huntsville, Alabama Office: 200 Clinton Avenue, N.W., Suite 1000.
Telephone: 205-536-1711.
Facsimile: 205-534-9650.
Mobile, Alabama Office: One St. Louis Centre, Suite 1000.
Telephone: 205-432-1671.
Facsimile: 205-434-0196.
Tuscaloosa, Alabama Office: 2216 14th Street.
Telephone: 205-752-2089.

Jeff Kohn
Charles Middleton

For Complete List of Firm Personnel, See General Section

For full biographical listings, see the Martindale-Hubbell Law Directory

ARIZONA

CASA GRANDE, Pinal Co.

FITZGIBBONS LAW OFFICES (AV)

Suite E, 711 East Cottonwood Lane, P.O. Box 11208, 85230-1208
Telephone: 602-426-3824
Fax: 602-426-9355

David A. Fitzgibbons

For Complete List of Firm Personnel, See General Section

For full biographical listings, see the Martindale-Hubbell Law Directory

*FLAGSTAFF,** Coconino Co.

ASPEY, WATKINS & DIESEL (AV)

123 North San Francisco, 86001
Telephone: 602-774-1478
Facsimile: 602-774-1043
Sedona, Arizona Office: 120 Soldier Pass Road.
Telephone: 602-282-5955.
Facsimile: 602-282-5962.
Page, Arizona Office: 904 North Navajo.
Telephone: 602-645-9694.
Winslow, Arizona Office: 205 North Williamson.
Telephone: 602-289-5963.
Cottonwood, Arizona Office: 905 Cove Parkway, Unite 201.
Telephone: 602-639-1881.

MEMBERS OF FIRM

Frederick M. Fritz Aspey
Harold L. Watkins
Louis M. Diesel
Bruce S. Griffen
Donald H. Bayles, Jr.
Kaign N. Christy
John J. Dempsey

Zachary Markham
James E. Ledbetter
Whitney Cunningham
Holly S. Karris

LEGAL SUPPORT PERSONNEL

Deborah D. Roberts (Legal Assistant)
C. Denece Pruett (Legal Assistant)
Dominic M. Marino, Jr, (Paralegal Assistant)

Representative Clients: Farmer's Insurance Company of Arizona; Kelley-Moore Paint Co.; Pepsi-Cola Bottling Company of Northern Arizona; Bill Luke's Chrysler-Plymouth, Inc.; First American Title Insurance Company ; Transamerica Title Insurance Co.; Page Electric Utility; Comprehensive Access Health Plan, Inc.
Reference: First Interstate Bank-Arizona, N.A., Flagstaff, Arizona.

For full biographical listings, see the Martindale-Hubbell Law Directory

MANGUM, WALL, STOOPS & WARDEN, P.L.L.C. (AV)

222 East Birch Avenue, P.O. Box 10, 86002
Telephone: 602-779-6951
Fax: 602-773-1312

OF COUNSEL
Douglas J. Wall
MEMBER OF FIRM
A. Dean Pickett
ASSOCIATE
Corbin Vandemoer

Representative Clients: Valley National Bank of Arizona; First Interstate Bank of Arizona; Nordstrom & Associates, CPA's.

For Complete List of Firm Personnel, See General Section

For full biographical listings, see the Martindale-Hubbell Law Directory

LAKE HAVASU CITY, Mohave Co.

WACHTEL, BIEHN & MALM (AV)

Suite A, 2240 McCulloch Boulevard, 86403
Telephone: 602-855-5115
Fax: 602-855-5211

MEMBERS OF FIRM

Don Biehn
Steven A. Biehn

For Complete List of Firm Personnel, See General Section

For full biographical listings, see the Martindale-Hubbell Law Directory

*PHOENIX,** Maricopa Co.

BURCH & CRACCHIOLO, P.A. (AV)

702 East Osborn Road, Suite 200, 85014
Telephone: 602-274-7611
Fax: 602-234-0341
Mailing Address: P.O. Box 16882, Phoenix, AZ, 85011

Daniel Cracchiolo
Guadalupe Iniguez

Thomas A. Longfellow

Representative Clients: Bashas' Inc.; Farmers Insurance Group; U-Haul International, Inc.

For Complete List of Firm Personnel, See General Section

For full biographical listings, see the Martindale-Hubbell Law Directory

A. JERRY BUSBY, P.C. (AV)

Suite 150, 5070 North 40th Street, 85018
Telephone: 602-957-0071
Fax: 602-957-0460

A. Jerry Busby

Representative Clients: The Circle K Corp.; Sun World Corp.
Reference: Bank of Scottsdale.

For full biographical listings, see the Martindale-Hubbell Law Directory

EHMANN & HILLER, P.C. (AV)

Suite 350, 4722 North 24th Street, 85016
Telephone: 602-956-5050
Telecopier: 602-468-9775

Anthony V. Ehmann
Neil H. Hiller
John G. Pattullo
John F. Daniels, III

OF COUNSEL

Thomas G. Georgiou

References: Valley National Bank of Arizona (Trust Department); First Interstate Bank of Arizona, N.A. (Trust Department); M & I Thunderbird Bank.

For full biographical listings, see the Martindale-Hubbell Law Directory

FENNEMORE CRAIG, A PROFESSIONAL CORPORATION (AV)

Two North Central, Suite 2200, 85004
Telephone: 602-257-8700
Fax: 602-257-8527
Scottsdale, Arizona Office: 6263 North Scottsdale Road, Suite 290, 85250.
Telephone: 602-257-5400.
Fax: 602-945-4932.
Tucson, Arizona Office: One South Church Avenue, Suite 1030, 85701.
Telephone: 602-624-9312.
Fax: 602-882-7383.

Neal Kurn
Louis F. Comus, Jr.
Rita A. Eisenfeld

Karen A. Curosh
Brenda K. Church
Stephen A. Good

Representative Clients: ASARCO Incorporated; AT&T Communications; Bridgestone/Firestone, Inc.; Catellus Development Corp.; Citibank (Arizona); First Interstate Bank of Arizona; GIANT Industries; Phelps Dodge Corporation; The Atchison, Topeka & Santa Fe Railway, Co.; US WEST Communications.

For Complete List of Firm Personnel, See General Section

For full biographical listings, see the Martindale-Hubbell Law Directory

GOODSON & MANLEY, P.C. (AV)

The Brookstone Building, 2025 North 3rd Street, Suite 200, 85004-1471
Telephone: 602-252-5110
Fax: 602-257-1883

(See Next Column)

John F. Goodson
Colleen C. Manley
Richard E. Durfee, Jr.
Joel M. Klinge

A list of Representative Clients will be furnished upon request.
Reference: Caliber (Arizona).

For full biographical listings, see the Martindale-Hubbell Law Directory

JENNINGS, STROUSS AND SALMON, P.L.C. (AV)

A Professional Limited Liability Company
One Renaissance Square, Two North Central, 85004-2393
Telephone: 602-262-5911
Fax: 602-253-3255

John R. Christian
Richard L. Lassen
I. Douglas Dunipace
K. Thomas Finke
John R. Becker

For Complete List of Firm Personnel, See General Section

For full biographical listings, see the Martindale-Hubbell Law Directory

MCCABE, O'DONNELL & WRIGHT, A PROFESSIONAL ASSOCIATION (AV)

Suite 2000, 300 East Osborn, 85012
Telephone: 602-264-0800
Telecopier: 602-274-0146

Joseph I. McCabe
Kathleen M. O'Donnell

References: First Interstate Bank of Arizona, N.A., Trust Department.

For Complete List of Firm Personnel, See General Section

For full biographical listings, see the Martindale-Hubbell Law Directory

THOMAS J. SHUMARD (AV)

3550 North Central Avenue, Suite 1407, 85012
Telephone: 602-234-2247
Fax: 602-274-0103

For full biographical listings, see the Martindale-Hubbell Law Directory

SNELL & WILMER (AV)

One Arizona Center, 85004-0001
Telephone: 602-382-6000
Fax: 602-382-6070
Tucson, Arizona Office: 1500 Norwest Tower, One South Church Avenue 85701-1612.
Telephone: 602-882-1200.
Fax: 602-884-1294.
Orange County Office: 1920 Main Street, Suite 1200, P.O. Box 19601, Irvine, California, 92714.
Telephone: 714-253-2700.
Fax: 714-955-2507.
Salt Lake City, Utah Office: Broadway Centre, 111 East Broadway, Suite 900, 84111.
Telephone: 801-237-1900.
Fax: 801-237-1950.

OF COUNSEL

James D. Bruner

MEMBERS OF FIRM

Joseph T. Melczer, III
Thomas R. Hoecker

For Complete List of Firm Personnel, See General Section

For full biographical listings, see the Martindale-Hubbell Law Directory

*PRESCOTT,** Yavapai Co.

FAVOUR, MOORE, WILHELMSEN & SCHUYLER, A PROFESSIONAL ASSOCIATION (AV)

1580 Plaza West Drive, P.O. Box 1391, 86302
Telephone: 602-445-2444
Fax: 602-771-0450

John B. Schuyler, Jr.
Mark M. Moore
David K. Wilhelmsen
Lance B. Payette
Clifford G. Cozier

OF COUNSEL

John M. Favour
Richard G. Kleindienst

References: Bank of America; Northern Trust Bank of Arizona; Valley National Bank of Arizona; Citibank (Arizona); First Interstate Bank of Arizona; M & I Marshall & Ilsley Trust Company of Arizona.

For full biographical listings, see the Martindale-Hubbell Law Directory

SCOTTSDALE, Maricopa Co.

LOWRY, CLEMENTS & POWELL, P.C. (AV)

The Security Pacific Bank Building, 6900 East Camelback Road Suite 1040, 85251
Telephone: 602-949-8998
Fax: 602-949-1987

Edward F. Lowry, Jr. William W. Clements
John Powell

OF COUNSEL

Robert L. Bluemle

For full biographical listings, see the Martindale-Hubbell Law Directory

ROSEPINK & ESTES (AV)

7373 North Scottsdale Road Suite D102, 85253
Telephone: 602-443-1280
Fax: 602-443-3664

Robert J. Rosepink David J. Estes

ASSOCIATE

Lynn F. Chandler

References: Bank of America, Arizona; Biltmore Investors Bank; Chase Trust Company of Arizona; First Interstate Bank of Arizona, N.A.; Firstar Metropolitan Bank & Trust; M & I Marshall & Ilsley Trust Co. of Arizona; Northern Trust Bank of Arizona.

For full biographical listings, see the Martindale-Hubbell Law Directory

SPARKS & SILER, P.C. (AV)

7503 First Street, 85251-4573
Telephone: 602-949-1339
Fax: 602-949-7587

E. Dennis Siler

References: Bank One, Arizona, Trust Department; Northern Trust Bank of Arizona, N.A.; First Interstate Bank of Arizona; Bank of America, Arizona, Trust Department.

For full biographical listings, see the Martindale-Hubbell Law Directory

GUY C. WILSON (AV)

Gainey Ranch Financial Center, Suite 130, 7373 East Doubletree Ranch Road, 85258
Telephone: 602-483-7455
Fax: 602-483-7457

For full biographical listings, see the Martindale-Hubbell Law Directory

SUN CITY, Maricopa Co.

O'CONNOR, CAVANAGH, ANDERSON, WESTOVER, KILLINGSWORTH & BESHEARS, A PROFESSIONAL ASSOCIATION (AV)

13250 North Del Webb Boulevard, Suite B, 85351-3053
Telephone: 602-263-2808
FAX: 602-933-3100
Phoenix, Arizona Office: One East Camelback Road, Suite 1100, 85012.
Telephone: 602-263-2400.
FAX: 602-263-2900.
Tucson, Arizona Office: Suite 2200, One South Church Avenue, 85701.
Telephone: 602-882-8912.
FAX: 602-624-9564.
Nogales, Arizona Office: 1827 North Mastick Way, 85621.
Telephone: 602-761-4215.
FAX: 602-761-3505.

William C. Wahl, Jr.

For full biographical listings, see the Martindale-Hubbell Law Directory

*TUCSON,** Pima Co.

BOGUTZ & GORDON, P.C. (AV)

1730 East River Road, Suite 107, 85718
Telephone: 602-577-1611
Fax: 602-577-0342

Allan D. Bogutz Brian C. Bjorndahl

For full biographical listings, see the Martindale-Hubbell Law Directory

COREY & FARRELL, P.C. (AV)

Suite 830, Norwest Tower, One South Church Avenue, 85701-1620
Telephone: 602-882-4994
Telefax: 602-884-7757

(See Next Column)

Barry M. Corey Patrick J. Farrell

Representative Clients: Amphitheater Public School District; Civil Service Commission of the City of Tucson; La Quinta Homes, Inc.; Pima County Merit System Commission; DANKA-Uni-Copy Corp.; Introspect Health Care Corp.

For full biographical listings, see the Martindale-Hubbell Law Directory

PETER T. GIANAS, P.C. (AV)

4400 East Broadway, Suite 800, 85711
Telephone: 602-795-6630
Fax: 602-327-1922

Peter T. Gianas

For full biographical listings, see the Martindale-Hubbell Law Directory

HAWLEY, NYSTEDT & FLETCHER, P.C. (AV)

Old Farm Executive Park, 6075 East Grant Road, P.O. Box 31657, 85751-1657
Telephone: 602-886-3166
FAX: 602-886-5280

Gerald G. Hawley Bradley Jon Nystedt
Gary L. Fletcher

Reference: Northern Trust Bank of Arizona.

For full biographical listings, see the Martindale-Hubbell Law Directory

MUNGER AND MUNGER, P.L.C. (AV)

333 N. Wilmot, Suite 300, 85711
Telephone: 602-721-1900
Fax: 602-747-1550
Northwest Tucson Office: 6700 N. Oracle Road, Suite 411, Tucson 85704.
Telephone: 602-797-7173.
Fax: 602-797-7178.

John F. Munger Clark W. Munger (Resident, Northwest Tucson Office)

Philip Kimble Martin P. Janello
Karen S. Haller Susan Gaylord Willis
Mark Edward Chadwick

Representative Clients: Richmond American Homes, Inc.; Jones Intercable; The Nature Conservancy; Property Tax Appeals, Inc.; Photon Sciences; Tucson Greyhound Park; Tucson Realty and Trust; Associated Dermatologists; Arizona State Radiology; Allied Waste Industries, Inc.

For full biographical listings, see the Martindale-Hubbell Law Directory

O'CONNELL & NEWMAN (AV)

A Partnership of Professional Corporations
Suite 100, 1840 East River Road, 85718
Telephone: 602-577-8880
Telefax: 602-577-0687

Daniel H. O'Connell (P.C.) Douglas J. Newman (P.C.)

Rosanne F. Lapan

Representative Clients: Empire West Cos.; Southwest Energy, Inc.; El Dorado Internal Medicine, P.C.; Pima Heart Associates, P.C.
Reference: Bank of America.

For full biographical listings, see the Martindale-Hubbell Law Directory

LAW OFFICES OF SLOSSER & HUDGINS, P.L.C. (AV)

Suite 125, 3573 East Sunrise Drive, 85718
Telephone: 602-529-3280
Fax: 602-529-1047

Paul D. Slosser Richard S. Hudgins

Caryn I. Tate

For full biographical listings, see the Martindale-Hubbell Law Directory

STOMPOLY, STROUD, GIDDINGS & GLICKSMAN, P.C. (AV)

1820 Citibank Tower, One South Church Avenue, 85702
Telephone: 602-628-8300
Telefax: 602-628-9948
Mailing Address: P.O. Box 190, Tucson, AZ, 85702-0190

John G. Stompoly James L. Stroud
Charles E. Giddings

For Complete List of Firm Personnel, See General Section
For full biographical listings, see the Martindale-Hubbell Law Directory

ARKANSAS

*BENTONVILLE,** Benton Co.

GOCIO, DOSSEY & REEVES (AV)

104 South Main Street, P.O. Box 588, 72712
Telephone: 501-273-3324
Fax: 501-273-3435

MEMBERS OF FIRM

Charles L. Gocio
Jerry B. Dossey
Samuel M. Reeves

Representative Client: Decatur State Bank.
Approved Attorneys for: Chicago Title Insurance Co.; St. Paul Title Insurance Co.

For full biographical listings, see the Martindale-Hubbell Law Directory

*LITTLE ROCK,** Pulaski Co.

ARNOLD, GROBMYER & HALEY, A PROFESSIONAL ASSOCIATION (AV)

875 Union National Plaza, 124 West Capitol Avenue, P.O. Box 70, 72203
Telephone: 501-376-1171
Fax: 501-375-3548

John H. Haley
Charles D. McDaniel
Joe A. Polk
Beth Ann Long

For Complete List of Firm Personnel, See General Section

For full biographical listings, see the Martindale-Hubbell Law Directory

HOOVER & STOREY (AV)

111 Center Street, 11th Floor, 72201-4445
Telephone: 501-376-8500
Facsimile: 501-372-3255

MEMBERS OF FIRM

Paul W. Hoover, Jr.
O. H. Storey, III
John Kooistra, III
Lawrence Joseph Brady
William P. Dougherty
Max C. Mehlburger
Joyce Bradley Babin
Herbert W. Kell, Jr.
Letty McAdams

For full biographical listings, see the Martindale-Hubbell Law Directory

ROSE LAW FIRM, A PROFESSIONAL ASSOCIATION (AV)

120 East Fourth Street, 72201
Telephone: 501-375-9131
Telecopy: 501-375-1309

W. Dane Clay
W. Wilson Jones
William E. Bishop
C. Brantly Buck
Ronald M. Clark
David A. Smith

COUNSEL

J. Gaston Williamson

James L. Harris
Clay H. Davis
Bryant K. Cranford

Representative Clients: Acxiom Corporation; Arkansas Association of Bank Holding Cos.; Winthrop Rockefeller Foundation; Stephens, Inc.; TCBY Enterprises, Inc.; Tyson Foods, Inc.; Wal-Mart Stores, Inc.; Worthen Banking Corp.

For Complete List of Firm Personnel, See General Section

For full biographical listings, see the Martindale-Hubbell Law Directory

WALKER & BLACK (AV)

1000 West Third Street, P.O. Box 591, 72203-0591
Telephone: 501-376-2382
Fax: 501-376-3352

MEMBERS OF FIRM

W. J. Walker
Kendell R. Black

Reference: First Commercial Bank.

For full biographical listings, see the Martindale-Hubbell Law Directory

CALIFORNIA

ARCADIA, Los Angeles Co.

HELMS, HANRAHAN & MYERS (AV)

Suite 685 Towne Centre Building, 150 North Santa Anita Avenue, 91006
Telephone: 818-445-1177

(See Next Column)

James R. Helms, Jr.
James J. Hanrahan
Sterling E. Myers

LEGAL SUPPORT PERSONNEL

PARALEGALS

Michelle L. Upp
Josephine Phillips

Reference: Bank of America National Trust & Savings Assn. (Arcadia Branch).

For full biographical listings, see the Martindale-Hubbell Law Directory

*BAKERSFIELD,** Kern Co.

BUNKER, SAGHATELIAN & GIBBS (AV)

A Law Partnership
2821 "H" Street, 93301-1913
Telephone: 805-634-1144
Telecopier: 805-327-1923

Bruce F. Bunker
Tommi R. Saghatelian
Steven G. Gibbs

ASSOCIATE

Timothy L. Kleier

For full biographical listings, see the Martindale-Hubbell Law Directory

ELDON R. HUGIE A PROFESSIONAL CORPORATION (AV)

Suite 100, 1405 Commercial Way, 93309
Telephone: 805-328-0200
Telecopier: 805-328-0204

Eldon R. Hugie

Representative Clients: Tri-Fanucchi Farms, Inc.; Aquaculture Enterprises; Kern College Land Co.
References: Community First Bank (Bakersfield Main Branch).

For full biographical listings, see the Martindale-Hubbell Law Directory

KLEIN, WEGIS, DENATALE, GOLDNER & MUIR (AV)

A Partnership including Professional Corporations
(Formerly Di Giorgio, Davis, Klein, Wegis, Duggan & Friedman)
ARCO Tower, 4550 California Avenue, Second Floor, P.O. Box 11172, 93389-1172
Telephone: 805-395-1000
Telecopier: 805-326-0418
Santa Ana, California Office: Park Tower Building #610, 200 W. Santa Ana Boulevard, 92701.
Telephone: 714-285-0711.
Fax: 714-285-9003.

MEMBERS OF FIRM

Anthony J. Klein (Inc.)
Claude P. Kimball

ASSOCIATES

Carol J. Kern
Kevin C. Findley
Michael E. Hugie

Representative Clients: Bank of America; Great Western Bank; Mojave Pipeline Co.; Transamerican Title Insurance Co.; Dean Whittier Reynolds, Inc.; California Republic Bank; San Joaquin Bank; Nahama & Weagant Energy Co.; Freymiller Trucking, Inc.; Westinghouse Electric Co.

For Complete List of Firm Personnel, See General Section

For full biographical listings, see the Martindale-Hubbell Law Directory

BEVERLY HILLS, Los Angeles Co.

ERVIN, COHEN & JESSUP (AV)

A Partnership including Professional Corporations
9401 Wilshire Boulevard, 90212-2974
Telephone: 310-273-6333
Facsimile: 310-859-2325

MEMBERS OF FIRM

W. Edgar Jessup, Jr.
Melvin S. Spears
Marvin H. Lewis
Harold J. Delevie (P.C.)
Reeve E. Chudd

Reference: Bank of California, N.A. (Beverly Hills).

For Complete List of Firm Personnel, See General Section

For full biographical listings, see the Martindale-Hubbell Law Directory

HOCHMAN, SALKIN AND DEROY, A PROFESSIONAL CORPORATION (AV)

9150 Wilshire Boulevard Suite 300, 90212-3414
Telephone: 310-281-3200; 273-1181
Fax: 310-859-1430

Bruce I. Hochman
Avram Salkin
Charles Rettig
Dennis Perez
Steven R. Toscher

(See Next Column)

HOCHMAN, SALKIN AND DEROY A PROFESSIONAL CORPORATION—*Continued*

OF COUNSEL

George DeRoy James V. Looby

Michael W. Popoff Joanna J. Tulio

Reference: Bank of California.

For full biographical listings, see the Martindale-Hubbell Law Directory

SAMUEL D. INGHAM, III (AV)

Suite 830, 8383 Wilshire Boulevard, 90211
Telephone: 213-651-5980
FAX: 213-651-5725

For full biographical listings, see the Martindale-Hubbell Law Directory

SMITH & SMITH (AV)

121 South Beverly Drive, 90212
Telephone: 310-275-5132
Los Angeles: 213-272-7807

David S. Smith Lee S. Smith

For full biographical listings, see the Martindale-Hubbell Law Directory

TURNER, GERSTENFELD, WILK, TIGERMAN & YOUNG (AV)

Formerly, Turner, Gerstenfeld & Wilk. . . est. 1972
Suite 510, 8383 Wilshire Boulevard, 90211
Telephone: 213-653-3900
Facsimile: 213-653-3021

MEMBERS OF FIRM

Gerald F. Gerstenfeld Bert Z. Tigerman
Linda Wight Mazur

For Complete List of Firm Personnel, See General Section

For full biographical listings, see the Martindale-Hubbell Law Directory

BURBANK, Los Angeles Co.

ALVIN N. LOSKAMP A LAW CORPORATION (AV)

290 East Verdugo Avenue, Suite 103, 91502
Telephone: 818-846-9000
Fax: 818-843-1441

Alvin N. Loskamp

References: Wells Fargo Bank, Glenoaks Branch, Burbank; Highland Savings & Loan, Burbank.

For full biographical listings, see the Martindale-Hubbell Law Directory

CARLSBAD, San Diego Co.

LODGE & HELLER (AV)

A Partnership including a Professional Corporation
1901 Camino Vida Roble, Suite 110, 92008
Telephone: 619-931-9700
Fax: 619-931-1155
Pauma Valley, California Office: The Pauma Building, Suite 403, 16160 Highway 76, P.O. Box 600.
Telephone: 619-749-3199.

MEMBERS OF FIRM

Eric T. Lodge (P.C.) Richard A. Heller

William R. Baber

For full biographical listings, see the Martindale-Hubbell Law Directory

CARMEL, Monterey Co.

IAN D. MCPHAIL A PROFESSIONAL CORPORATION (AV)

Villa Carmel, Suite 4, Mission at Fourth, P.O. Box 2734, 93921
Telephone: 408-625-4135
Telecopier: 408-625-4155
Santa Cruz, California Office: 331 Soquel Avenue, 95062.
Telephone: 408-427-2363.
Telecopier: 408-427-0511.

Ian D. McPhail

References: Comerica Bank; Home Savings; Coast Commercial Bank.

For full biographical listings, see the Martindale-Hubbell Law Directory

COSTA MESA, Orange Co.

BALFOUR MACDONALD TALBOT MIJUSKOVIC & OLMSTED, A PROFESSIONAL CORPORATION (AV)

Suite 720, 611 Anton Boulevard, 92626
Telephone: 714-546-2400
Fax: 714-546-5008

James B. MacDonald

For Complete List of Firm Personnel, See General Section

For full biographical listings, see the Martindale-Hubbell Law Directory

RUTAN & TUCKER (AV)

A Partnership including Professional Corporations
611 Anton Boulevard, Suite 1400, P.O. Box 1950, 92626
Telephone: 714-641-5100; 213-625-7586
Telecopier: 714-546-9035

MEMBER OF FIRM

Paul Frederic Marx

OF COUNSEL

David J. Garibaldi, III

For Complete List of Firm Personnel, See General Section

For full biographical listings, see the Martindale-Hubbell Law Directory

ENCINO, Los Angeles Co.

MARINO & DALLINGER (AV)

An Association including a Professional Corporation
17835 Ventura Boulevard, Suite 209, 91316
Telephone: 818-774-3636
FAX: 818-774-3635

Timothy G. Dallinger J. Anthony Marino (A Professional Corporation)

For full biographical listings, see the Martindale-Hubbell Law Directory

ESCONDIDO, San Diego Co.

DOROTHY A. COLE (AV)

Town View Professional Centre, 215 South Hickory Street, Suite 224, 92025-4361
Telephone: 619-745-6313

For full biographical listings, see the Martindale-Hubbell Law Directory

*EUREKA,** Humboldt Co.

HARLAND LAW FIRM (AV)

622 H Street, 95501
Telephone: 707-444-9281
Fax: 707-445-2961
Fortuna, California Office: 954 Main Street.
Telephone: 707-725-4426.
Fax: 707-725-5738.
Crescent City, California Office: 1225 Marshall Street, Suite 6.
Telephone: 707-465-3894.
Fax: 707-465-4255.

MEMBERS OF FIRM

Gerald R. Harland Thomas J. Becker
Richard A. Smith William T. Kay, Jr.
David C. Moore John W. Warren
Geri Anne Johnson

ASSOCIATES

Christine A. Doehle (Resident Associate, Crescent City Office) Julia S. Gold

For full biographical listings, see the Martindale-Hubbell Law Directory

*FRESNO,** Fresno Co.

DOWLING, MAGARIAN, AARON & HEYMAN, INCORPORATED (AV)

Suite 200, 6051 North Fresno Street, 93710
Telephone: 209-432-4500
Fax: 209-432-4590

Michael D. Dowling William J. Keeler, Jr.
Richard M. Aaron John C. Ganahl

Mark D. Magarian

OF COUNSEL

Donald J. Magarian Morris M. Sherr

Reference: Wells Fargo Bank (Main).

(See Next Column)

DOWLING, MAGARIAN, AARON & HEYMAN INCORPORATED, *Fresno—Continued*

For Complete List of Firm Personnel, See General Section

For full biographical listings, see the Martindale-Hubbell Law Directory

PARICHAN, RENBERG, CROSSMAN & HARVEY, LAW CORPORATION (AV)

Suite 130, 2350 West Shaw Avenue, P.O. Box 9950, 93794-0950
Telephone: 209-431-6300
FAX: 209-432-1018

Harold A. Parichan
Charles L. Renberg
Richard C. Crossman
Ima Jean Harvey
Stephen T. Knudsen
Larry C. Gollmer
Robert G. Eliason
Steven M. McQuillan
Peter S. Bradley

Deborah A. Coe
Maureen P. Holford
Karen L. Lynch
Michael L. Renberg
Brady Kyle McGuinness

Reference: Bank of America, Commercial Banking Office, Fresno, California.

For full biographical listings, see the Martindale-Hubbell Law Directory

FULLERTON, Orange Co.

MARK SCOTT ROBERTS AND ASSOCIATES A PROFESSIONAL LAW CORPORATION (AV)

Suite 107, 285 East Imperial Highway, 92635
Telephone: 714-870-6050
Fax: 714-680-0906

Mark Scott Roberts

For full biographical listings, see the Martindale-Hubbell Law Directory

GLENDALE, Los Angeles Co.

GREENWALD, HOFFMAN & MEYER (AV)

500 North Brand Boulevard, Suite 920, 91203-1904
Telephone: 818-507-8100; 213-381-1131
Fax: 818-507-8484

MEMBERS OF FIRM

Guy Preston Greenwald, Jr. (1914-1984)
Donald M. Hoffman
Lawrence F. Meyer
Raul M. Montes

ASSOCIATE

Jeanne Burns-Haindel

References: Bank of America (Los Angeles and Pasadena Trust Offices); Northern Trust of California (Headquarters Office); Bank of America (Glendale Main Branch); Sanwa Bank (Glendale Office).

For full biographical listings, see the Martindale-Hubbell Law Directory

INDIAN WELLS, Riverside Co.

ROEMER & HARNIK (AV)

45-025 Manitou Drive at Highway 111, 92210
Telephone: 619-360-2400
Fax: 619-360-1211

Richard I. Roemer
Brian S. Harnik

For full biographical listings, see the Martindale-Hubbell Law Directory

IRVINE, Orange Co.

PIVO & HALBREICH (AV)

1920 Main Street, Suite 800, 92714
Telephone: 714-253-2000; 213-688-7311

Kenneth R. Pivo
Eva S. Halbreich
Richard O. Schwartz

ASSOCIATE

Mona Z. Hanna

Representative Clients: Harbor Regional Center; Developmental Disabilities Regional Center; South Central Los Angeles Regional Center; North Los Angeles County Regional Center; Far Northern Regional Center; Kern Regional Center and Related Entities.

For full biographical listings, see the Martindale-Hubbell Law Directory

LAGUNA BEACH, Orange Co.

WILLIAM M. WILCOXEN (AV)

Suite A, 801 Glenneyre, 92651
Telephone: 714-494-7565
FAX: 714-494-7567

Reference: Bank of America (Laguna Beach Branch).

LAGUNA HILLS, Orange Co.

NANCY BOXLEY TEPPER A PROFESSIONAL CORPORATION (AV)

24031 El Toro Road, Suite 130, 92653
Telephone: 714-830-6660
Fax: 714-830-6123

Nancy Boxley Tepper

For full biographical listings, see the Martindale-Hubbell Law Directory

LA JOLLA, San Diego Co.

FERGUSON, NEWBURN & WESTON, A PROFESSIONAL CORPORATION (AV)

Suite 260, 7777 Fay Avenue, 92037
Telephone: 619-454-4233
Facsimile: 619-454-3052

Keith M. Ferguson (1903-1965)
John L. Newburn (Retired, 1989)
William E. Ferguson
David Weston

References: Union Bank (La Jolla Office); Scripps Bank (La Jolla Office).

For full biographical listings, see the Martindale-Hubbell Law Directory

LANCASTER, Los Angeles Co.

MARK E. THOMPSON A PROFESSIONAL CORPORATION (AV)

857 West Lancaster Boulevard, 93534
Telephone: 805-945-5868
Fax: 805-723-7089

Mark E. Thompson

Cynthia R. Pollock

Reference: Antelope Valley Bank, Lancaster, California.

For full biographical listings, see the Martindale-Hubbell Law Directory

LOS ALTOS, Santa Clara Co.

MALOVOS & KONEVICH (AV)

Los Altos Plaza, 5150 El Camino Real, Suite A-22, 94022
Telephone: 415-988-9700
Facsimile: 415-988-9639

Marian Malovos Konevich
Robert W. Konevich

RETIRED FOUNDING PARTNER

Kenneth R. Malovos

References: Bank of America, Mountain View, California Branch; First Interstate Bank, Mountain View and Los Altos, California Branches.

For full biographical listings, see the Martindale-Hubbell Law Directory

*LOS ANGELES,** Los Angeles Co.

EDNA R.S. ALVAREZ (AV)

10850 Wilshire Boulevard, Fourth Floor, 90024-4318
Telephone: 310-475-5837
Fax: 310-474-6926

For full biographical listings, see the Martindale-Hubbell Law Directory

ANTIN & TAYLOR (AV)

1875 Century Park East, Suite 700, 90067
Telephone: 310-788-2733
Fax: 310-788-0754

MEMBERS OF FIRM

Michael Antin
Michael L. Taylor

For full biographical listings, see the Martindale-Hubbell Law Directory

JOHN A. CALFAS A PROFESSIONAL CORPORATION (AV)

Suite 1920, 11601 Wilshire Boulevard, 90025
Telephone: 310-477-1920
FAX: 310-477-7132

John A. Calfas

For full biographical listings, see the Martindale-Hubbell Law Directory

Los Angeles—Continued

Clark & Trevithick, A Professional Corporation (AV)
800 Wilshire Boulevard, 12th Floor, 90017
Telephone: 213-629-5700
Telecopier: 213-624-9441

Kevin P. Fiore Dean I. Friedman

References: Wells Fargo Bank (Los Angeles Main Office); National Bank of California.

For Complete List of Firm Personnel, See General Section

For full biographical listings, see the Martindale-Hubbell Law Directory

Creutz and Creutz (AV)
206 Brentwood Square Building, 11661 San Vicente Boulevard, 90049
Telephone: 310-826-3545; 213-879-0339

Gregory M. Creutz (1892-1966) Mary G. Creutz

Reference: Union Bank, Brentwood Branch.

For full biographical listings, see the Martindale-Hubbell Law Directory

Darling, Hall & Rae (AV)
777 South Figueroa, 34th Floor, 90017
Telephone: 213-627-8104
FAX: 213-627-7795

MEMBERS OF FIRM

Hugh W. Darling (1901-1986)
Edward S. Shattuck (1901-1965)
George Gaylord Gute (1922-1981)
Donald Keith Hall (1918-1984)
Matthew S. Rae, Jr.
Richard L. Stack
John L. Flowers

Reference: Bank of America NT & SA (Wilshire & Grand Office, Los Angeles, California).

For full biographical listings, see the Martindale-Hubbell Law Directory

Demetriou, Del Guercio, Springer & Moyer (AV)
801 South Grand Avenue, 10th Floor, 90017
Telephone: 213-624-8407
Telecopy: 213-624-0174

MEMBERS OF FIRM

Ronald J. Del Guercio Angela Shanahan

Reference: Bank of America, L.A. Main Office, Los Angeles, Calif.

For full biographical listings, see the Martindale-Hubbell Law Directory

Goldman & Kagon, Law Corporation (AV)
1801 Century Park East, Suite 2222, 90067
Telephone: 310-552-1707
Telex: 701076
Cable: GOKALAW
Telecopier: 310-552-7938

Kenneth L. Goldman

Christopher B. Fagan

For Complete List of Firm Personnel, See General Section

For full biographical listings, see the Martindale-Hubbell Law Directory

Greenberg, Glusker, Fields, Claman & Machtinger (AV)
20th Floor, 1900 Avenue of the Stars (Century City), 90067
Telephone: 310-553-3610
Fax: 310-553-0687

MEMBERS OF FIRM

Jon J. Gallo
Robert E. Bennett, Jr.
Martin H. Webster
Arnold D. Kahn

Reference: Wells Fargo Bank, 1800 Century Park East, Los Angeles, CA 90067.

For Complete List of Firm Personnel, See General Section

For full biographical listings, see the Martindale-Hubbell Law Directory

Hanna and Morton (AV)
A Partnership including Professional Corporations
Seventeenth Floor, Wilshire-Grand Building, 600 Wilshire Boulevard, 90017
Telephone: 213-628-7131

MEMBERS OF FIRM

Gregory R. Ryan Glenn Lorin Krinsky

OF COUNSEL

William N. Greene

For Complete List of Firm Personnel, See General Section

For full biographical listings, see the Martindale-Hubbell Law Directory

Holley & Galen (AV)
800 South Figueroa, Suite 1100, 90017
Telephone: 213-629-1880
Fax: 213-895-0363

MEMBERS OF FIRM

Albert J. Galen (Retired)
W. Michael Johnson
Richard E. Llewellyn, II
A. Steven Brown

ASSOCIATES

Debra Burchard Coffeen Charles A. Jordan

For Complete List of Firm Personnel, See General Section

For full biographical listings, see the Martindale-Hubbell Law Directory

Kindel & Anderson (AV)
A Partnership including Professional Corporations
Twenty-Ninth Floor, 555 South Flower Street, 90071
Telephone: 213-680-2222
Cable Address: "Kayanda"
Telex: 67-7497
FAX: 213-688-7564
Irvine, California Office: 5 Park Plaza, Suite 1000.
Telephone: 714-752-0777.
Woodland Hills, California Office: Suite 244, 5959 Topanga Canyon Boulevard.
Telephone: 818-712-0036.
San Francisco, California Office: 580 California Street, 15th Floor.
Telephone: 415-398-0110.

MEMBER OF FIRM

Thomas Curtiss, Jr.

ASSOCIATE

Maryann S. Meggelin

For Complete List of Firm Personnel, See General Section

For full biographical listings, see the Martindale-Hubbell Law Directory

Loeb and Loeb (AV)
A Partnership including Professional Corporations
Suite 1800, 1000 Wilshire Boulevard, 90017-2475
Telephone: 213-688-3400
Telecopier: 213-688-3460; 688-3461; 688-3462
Century City, California Office: Suite 2200, 10100 Santa Monica Boulevard, Los Angeles, 90067-4164.
Telephone: 310-282-2000.
Telecopier: 310-282-2191; 282-2192.
New York, N.Y. Office: 345 Park Avenue, 10154-0037.
Telephone: 212-407-4000.
Facsimile: 212-407-4990.
Nashville, Tennessee Office: 45 Music Square West, 37203-3205.
Telephone: 615-749-8300;
Facsimile: 615-749-8308.
Rome, Italy Office: Piazza Digione 1, 00197.
Telephone: 011-396-808-8456.
Telecopier: 011-396-674-8223.

MEMBERS OF FIRM

Andrew S. Garb (A P.C.)
Abraham S. Guterman (New York City Office)
Jerome L. Levine (New York City Office)
Jeffrey M. Loeb
Stanford K. Rubin (A P.C.) (Century City Office)
William P. Wasserman (A P.C.)
Bruce J. Wexler (New York City Office)

OF COUNSEL

James R. Birnberg
Arthur A. Segall (New York City Office)
Alan D. Shulman
Bernard M. Silbert (Century City Office)
Harvey L. Silbert (Century City Office)
John S. Warren (A P.C.)

For Complete List of Firm Personnel, See General Section

For full biographical listings, see the Martindale-Hubbell Law Directory

Minton, Minton and Rand (AV)
510 West Sixth Street, 90014
Telephone: 213-624-9394
Fax: 213-624-9323

MEMBERS OF FIRM

Carl W. Minton (1902-1974) Carl Minton
David E. Rand

Reference: Bank of America National Trust & Savings Assn. (Seventh & Flower Office, Los Angeles, Calif.).

For full biographical listings, see the Martindale-Hubbell Law Directory

Los Angeles—Continued

MITCHELL, SILBERBERG & KNUPP (AV)

A Partnership of Professional Corporations
11377 West Olympic Boulevard, 90064
Telephone: 310-312-2000
Cable Address: "Silmitch"
Telex: 69-1347
Telecopier: 310-312-3200

MEMBER OF FIRM

Allan B. Cutrow (A Professional Corporation)

OF COUNSEL

Stanley I. Arenberg (A Professional Corporation)
Jeffrey B. Wheeler

Reference: First Interstate Bank of California (Headquarters, Los Angeles, California).

For Complete List of Firm Personnel, See General Section

For full biographical listings, see the Martindale-Hubbell Law Directory

FLOYD H. NORRIS (AV)

Suite 405 Norris Building, 714 South Hill Street, 90014
Telephone: 213-624-4088
FAX: 213-624-4080

References: Bank of America; Wells Fargo.

For full biographical listings, see the Martindale-Hubbell Law Directory

POPKOFF & STERN (AV)

501 Shatto Place, Suite 100, 90020-1792
Telephone: 213-389-1358; 389-2174
Fax: 213-380-4154
Palm Springs, California Office: 225 South Civic Drive, Suite 212, 92262.
Telephone: 619-322-8041.

MEMBERS OF FIRM

Burton R. Popkoff
Gary N. Stern

Representative Clients: Fred Glaser Insurance Associates, Inc.; Don Odessky, Inc., Market Research.

ROSS, SACKS & GLAZIER (AV)

Suite 3900 300 South Grand Avenue, 90071
Telephone: 213-617-2950
Fax: 213-617-9350

MEMBERS OF FIRM

Bruce S. Ross
Kenneth M. Glazier
Robert N. Sacks

ASSOCIATES

Jana W. Bray
Terrence M. Franklin
Deborah J. Cantrell
Margaret G. Lodise

COUNSEL

Jeryll S. Cohen

For full biographical listings, see the Martindale-Hubbell Law Directory

WILLIAMS & NENNEY (AV)

(An Association of Attorneys)
11520 San Vicente Boulevard, P.O. Box 49696, 90049
Telephone: 310-826-3551
Fax: 310-826-2367

Milton J. Nenney
Donald A. Williams

References of Milton J. Nenney: First Interstate Bank; Bank of America.
References of Donald A. Williams: First Interstate Bank; Sanwa Bank.

For full biographical listings, see the Martindale-Hubbell Law Directory

STUART D. ZIMRING (AV)

12650 Riverside Drive (North Hollywood), 91607-3492
Telephone: 818-755-4848
Fax: 818-508-0181

ASSOCIATE

Dena L. Mesler

Representative Clients: TransWorld Bank; American Cyanamid; Cytec Aerospace Inc.; Huntington Palisades Property Owners Association; Riviera Estates Homeowner's Association; Buff, Smith & Hensman Architects, Inc.

For full biographical listings, see the Martindale-Hubbell Law Directory

LOS GATOS, Santa Clara Co.

MASON J. SACKS, INC. A PROFESSIONAL LAW CORPORATION (AV)

Suite 101, 16615 Lark Avenue, 95030
Telephone: 408-358-4400
Fax: 408-358-2487

(See Next Column)

Mason J. Sacks

For full biographical listings, see the Martindale-Hubbell Law Directory

LOS OSOS, San Luis Obispo Co.

GEORGE, GALLO & SULLIVAN, A LAW CORPORATION (AV)

2238 Bayview Heights Drive, P.O. Box 6129, 93402
Telephone: 805-528-3351
Cable: SLOLAW
Telecopier: 805-528-5598
San Luis Obispo, California Office: 694 Santa Rosa, P.O. Box 12710.
Telephone: 805-544-3351.
Facsimile: 805-528-5598.

J. K. George

Anne C. Cyr

Reference: Mid State Bank, Los Osos, California.

For full biographical listings, see the Martindale-Hubbell Law Directory

MANHATTAN BEACH, Los Angeles Co.

STEINBERG, FOSTER & BARNESS (AV)

1334 Park View Avenue, Suite 100, 90266
Telephone: 310-546-5838
Telecopier: 310-546-5630

MEMBERS OF FIRM

Alex Steinberg
Douglas B. Foster
Daniel I. Barness

ASSOCIATE

William R. (Randy) Kirkpatrick

References: Home Bank; Imperial Bank; Citizens Commerical Trust & Savings Bank; Bank of America.

For full biographical listings, see the Martindale-Hubbell Law Directory

MENLO PARK, San Mateo Co.

ROBIN D. FAISANT (AV)

1550 El Camino Real, Suite 220, 94025
Telephone: 415-328-6333
Telecopier: 415-324-1031

For full biographical listings, see the Martindale-Hubbell Law Directory

*MODESTO,** Stanislaus Co.

BRUNN & FLYNN, A PROFESSIONAL CORPORATION (AV)

928 12th Street, P.O. Box 3366, 95353
Telephone: 209-521-2133
Fax: 209-521-7584

Charles K. Brunn

Reference: Pacific Valley Bank.

For full biographical listings, see the Martindale-Hubbell Law Directory

MOUNTAIN VIEW, Santa Clara Co.

SCHNEIDER, LUCE, QUILLINAN & MORGAN (AV)

A Partnership including a Professional Corporation
444 Castro Street, Suite 900, 94041-2073
Telephone: 415-969-4000
FAX: 415-969-6953

MEMBERS OF FIRM

Michael E. Schneider (A P.C.)
James V. Quillinan
James G. Luce
Michael R. Morgan

ASSOCIATES

Richard Posilippo
Melissa C. Johnson

For full biographical listings, see the Martindale-Hubbell Law Directory

NEWPORT BEACH, Orange Co.

PETER C. BRADFORD (AV)

Suite 1250, 610 Newport Center Drive, 92660
Telephone: 714-640-1800
FAX: 714-721-9923

References: Wells Fargo Bank; Bank of America.

For full biographical listings, see the Martindale-Hubbell Law Directory

COLLEEN M. CLAIRE (AV)

Suite 1, 3800 Pacific Coast Highway (Corona Del Mar), 92625
Telephone: 714-675-0755
Fax: 714-675-7536

For full biographical listings, see the Martindale-Hubbell Law Directory

Newport Beach—Continued

JOHN C. LAUTSCH A PROFESSIONAL CORPORATION (AV)

4220 Von Karman, Suite 120, 92660
Telephone: 714-955-9095
Telefax: 714-955-2978

John C. Lautsch

Kurt E. English

For full biographical listings, see the Martindale-Hubbell Law Directory

MILLAR, HODGES & BEMIS (AV)

One Newport Place, Suite 900, 1301 Dove Street, 92660-2448
Telephone: 714-752-7722
FAX: 714-752-6131

MEMBERS OF FIRM

Richard W. Millar, Jr.
Kenneth R. Hodges
Larry R. Bemis

ASSOCIATE

David A. St.Clair

Reference: Manufacturers Bank, Newport Beach, California.

For full biographical listings, see the Martindale-Hubbell Law Directory

EDWARD H. STONE, P.C. (AV)

270 Newport Center Drive, 92660-7535
Telephone: 714-640-2812
Fax: 714-640-9951

Edward H. Stone

For full biographical listings, see the Martindale-Hubbell Law Directory

MICHAEL V. VOLLMER (AV)

4340 Campus Drive, Suite 100, 92660-1892
Telephone: 714-852-0833
Fax: 714-852-8731

References: Bank of America NT&SA (Costa Mesa, California); First American Trust Company (Newport Beach, California); First Interstate Bank (Newport Beach, California).

For full biographical listings, see the Martindale-Hubbell Law Directory

NORTH HOLLYWOOD, Los Angeles Co.

CLARKE & LEARY (AV)

4605 Lankershim Boulevard #721, 91602
Telephone: 818-769-5000
Fax: 818-763-2487

Thomas W. Clarke

F. BENTLEY MOONEY, JR. A LAW CORPORATION (AV)

4605 Lankershim Boulevard, Suite 718, 91602
Telephone: 818-769-4221
213-877-3902
FAX: 818-769-5002

F. Bentley Mooney, Jr.

For full biographical listings, see the Martindale-Hubbell Law Directory

*OAKLAND,** Alameda Co.

HARDIN, COOK, LOPER, ENGEL & BERGEZ (AV)

1999 Harrison Street, 18th Floor, 94612-3541
Telephone: 510-444-3131
Telecopier: 510-839-7940

MEMBERS OF FIRM

John C. Loper
George S. Peyton, Jr.
Barrie Engel
Sandra F. Wagner
Linda C. Roodhouse

Representative Clients: Firemans Fund Insurance Cos.; City of Piedmont; The Dow Chemical Co.; Nissan Motor Corp.; Subaru of America; Weyerhauser Co.; Bay Area Rapid Transit District; Diamond Shamrock; Home Indemnity Co.; Rhone-Poulenc.

For Complete List of Firm Personnel, See General Section

For full biographical listings, see the Martindale-Hubbell Law Directory

NEAL & ASSOCIATES (AV)

Montclair Village, 6200 Antioch Street, Suite 202, P.O. Box 13314, 500, 94661-0314
Telephone: 510-339-0233
FAX: 510-339-6672

Howard D. Neal

(See Next Column)

Frank J. Gilbert
Steven S. Miyake

For full biographical listings, see the Martindale-Hubbell Law Directory

ONTARIO, San Bernardino Co.

JOHN SCHESSLER (AV)

218 West E Street, 91762
Telephone: 909-986-2095
Fax: 909-391-0058

Reference: First Interstate Bank (Ontario, California).

For full biographical listings, see the Martindale-Hubbell Law Directory

PALM SPRINGS, Riverside Co.

SCHLECHT, SHEVLIN & SHOENBERGER, A LAW CORPORATION (AV)

Suite 100, 801 East Tahquitz Canyon Way, P.O. Box 2744, 92263-2744
Telephone: 619-320-7161
Facsimile: 619-323-1758; 619-325-4623

James M. Schlecht
John C. Shevlin

Representative Clients: Outdoor Resorts of America; The Escrow Connection; Wells Fargo Bank; Canyon Country Club; Waste Management Co.

For Complete List of Firm Personnel, See General Section

For full biographical listings, see the Martindale-Hubbell Law Directory

PALO ALTO, Santa Clara Co.

FINCH, MONTGOMERY & WRIGHT (AV)

350 Cambridge Avenue, Suite 175, 94306
Telephone: 415-327-0888

MEMBERS OF FIRM

Toby F. Montgomery
Barbara P. Wright
Nathan C. Finch (1909-1990)

For full biographical listings, see the Martindale-Hubbell Law Directory

JOHN E. MILLER (AV)

250 Cambridge Avenue, Suite 102, 94306-1504
Telephone: 415-321-8886
Fax: 415-321-8998

ASSOCIATES

Annalisa C Wood
Laura L. Reynolds

Reference: Bank of the West.

For full biographical listings, see the Martindale-Hubbell Law Directory

PASADENA, Los Angeles Co.

LAGERLOF, SENECAL, BRADLEY & SWIFT (AV)

301 North Lake Avenue, 10th Floor, 91101-4107
Telephone: 818-793-9400
FAX: 818-793-5900

MEMBERS OF FIRM

Joseph J. Burris (1913-1980)
Stanley C. Lagerlof
H. Melvin Swift, Jr.
H. Jess Senecal
Jack T. Swafford
John F. Bradley
Timothy J. Gosney
William F. Kruse
Thomas S. Bunn, III
Andrew D. Turner
Rebecca J. Thyne

ASSOCIATES

Paul M. Norman
John F. Machtinger
James D. Ciampa
Ellen M. Burkhart

LEGAL SUPPORT PERSONNEL

Ronald E. Hagler

Representative Clients: Anchor Glass Container Corporation; Bethlehem Steel Corp.; Orthopaedic Hospital; Palmdale Water District; Public Water Agencies Group; Walnut Valley Water District.
Special Counsel: City of Redondo Beach, Calif.; Ventura Port Dist., Calif.

For full biographical listings, see the Martindale-Hubbell Law Directory

MARTIN & HUDSON (AV)

Suite 320, 350 West Colorado Boulevard, 91105
Telephone: 818-793-8500
Telecopier: 818-793-8779

MEMBERS OF FIRM

Robert B. Martin, Jr.
Boyd D. Hudson

For full biographical listings, see the Martindale-Hubbell Law Directory

Pasadena—Continued

RICHARD F. MILLER A PROFESSIONAL CORPORATION (AV)

Suite 511, 199 South Los Robles Avenue, 91101
Telephone: 213-681-5400; 818-584-1400
Telecopier: 818-584-1447

Richard F. Miller

For full biographical listings, see the Martindale-Hubbell Law Directory

ALAN R. TALT (AV)

Suite 710, 790 East Colorado Boulevard, 91101
Telephone: 818-356-0853
Telecopier: 818-356-0731

Reference: Northern Trust of California.

For full biographical listings, see the Martindale-Hubbell Law Directory

TAYLOR KUPFER SUMMERS & RHODES (AV)

301 East Colorado Boulevard, Suite 407, 91101
Telephone: 818-304-0953; 213-624-7877
Fax: 818-795-6375

MEMBERS OF FIRM

John D. Taylor
Robert C. Summers
Stephen F. Peters

COUNSEL

Kenneth O. Rhodes

Reference: Citizens Bank (Pasadena).

For Complete List of Firm Personnel, See General Section

For full biographical listings, see the Martindale-Hubbell Law Directory

PLEASANTON, Alameda Co.

JAMES J. PHILLIPS A PROFESSIONAL CORPORATION (AV)

4900 Hopyard Road, Suite 260, 94588
Telephone: 510-463-1980
Hayward, California Office: 1331 B Street, Suite 4.
Telephone: 510-886-2120.

James J. Phillips

References: Community First National Bank; Wells Fargo Bank; Com Core Realty.

For full biographical listings, see the Martindale-Hubbell Law Directory

*SACRAMENTO,** Sacramento Co.

WILKE, FLEURY, HOFFELT, GOULD & BIRNEY (AV)

A Partnership including Professional Corporations
400 Capitol Mall, Suite 2200, 95814-4408
Telephone: 916-441-2430
Telefax: 916-442-6664
Mailing Address: P.O. Box 15559, 95852-0559

MEMBERS OF FIRM

Richard H. Hoffelt (Inc.)
William A. Gould, Jr., (Inc.)
Philip R. Birney (Inc.)
Thomas G. Redmon (Inc.)
Scott L. Gassaway
Donald Rex Heckman II (Inc.)
Alan G. Perkins
Bradley N. Webb
Ernest James Krtil
Robert R. Mirkin
Matthew W. Powell
Mark L. Andrews
Stephen K. Marmaduke
David A. Frenznick
John R. Valencia
Angus M. MacLeod

ASSOCIATES

Paul A. Dorris
Kelli M. Kennaday
Tracy S. Hendrickson
Joseph G. De Angelis
Jennifer L. Kennedy
Anthony J. DeCristoforo
Rachel N. Kook
Alicia F. From
Michael Polis
Matthew J. Smith
Wayne L. Ordos

OF COUNSEL

Sherman C. Wilke
Anita Seipp Marmaduke
Benjamin G. Davidian

Representative Clients: NOR-CAL Mutual Insurance Co.; California Optometric Assn.; KPMG Peat Marwick; Glaxo, Inc.

For full biographical listings, see the Martindale-Hubbell Law Directory

*SAN BERNARDINO,** San Bernardino Co.

GRESHAM, VARNER, SAVAGE, NOLAN & TILDEN (AV)

Suite 300, 600 North Arrowhead Avenue, 92401
Telephone: 909-884-2171
Fax: 909-888-2120
Victorville, California Office: 14011 Park Avenue, Suite 140.
Telephone: 619-243-2889.
Fax: 619-243-3057.

(See Next Column)

Riverside, California Office: 3737 Main Street, Suite 420.
Telephone: 714-274-7777.
Fax: 714-274-7770.

MEMBER OF FIRM

Philip M. Savage, III

ASSOCIATE

Daryl H. Carlson

Representative Clients: Kaiser Resources, Inc.; Southern California Edison Co.; General Telephone Company of California; Southern California Gas Co.; General Motors Corp.; Pfizer Inc.; San Bernardino Valley, Pomona Valley, Covina-San Gabriel; Azusa-Glendora Boards of Realtors.

For Complete List of Firm Personnel, See General Section

For full biographical listings, see the Martindale-Hubbell Law Directory

WILSON, BORROR, DUNN, SCOTT & DAVIS (AV)

Suite 307, The Bank of California Building, 255 North D Street, P.O. Box 540, 92401
Telephone: 909-884-8855
Fax: 909-884-5161

MEMBERS OF FIRM

Fred A. Wilson (1886-1973)
Wm. H. Wilson (1915-1981)
Caywood J. Borror
James R. Dunn
Richard L. Scott
Thomas M. Davis
Keith D. Davis

ASSOCIATES

Timothy P. Prince
Sarah L. Overton

Representative Clients: Travelers Insurance Co.; Rockwell International; Westinghouse Air Brake Co.; Goodyear Tire and Rubber Co.; Home Insurance Co.; Cities of: Redlands, Chino, Colton, San Bernardino and Upland; The Canadian Insurance Co.

For full biographical listings, see the Martindale-Hubbell Law Directory

SAN CARLOS, San Mateo Co.

RICHARD W. HENSON (AV)

909 Laurel Street, 94070
Telephone: 415-591-7352
Fax: 415-591-9239

For full biographical listings, see the Martindale-Hubbell Law Directory

*SAN DIEGO,** San Diego Co.

GARRISON R. ARMSTRONG LAW CORPORATION (AV)

Suite 1300, 401 West A Street, 92101-7988
Telephone: 619-232-1811

Garrison R. Armstrong

For full biographical listings, see the Martindale-Hubbell Law Directory

DAVID L. HICKSON (AV)

8910 University Center Lane Suite 230, 92122
Telephone: 619-457-1100
Facsimile: 619-457-0109

For full biographical listings, see the Martindale-Hubbell Law Directory

HILLYER & IRWIN, A PROFESSIONAL CORPORATION (AV)

550 West C Street, 16th Floor, 92101
Telephone: 619-234-6121
Telecopier: 619-595-1313

Kent W. Hildreth
Colin W. Wied

For full biographical listings, see the Martindale-Hubbell Law Directory

LINDLEY, LAZAR & SCALES, A PROFESSIONAL CORPORATION (AV)

One America Plaza, 600 West Broadway, Suite 1400, 92101-3302
Telephone: 619-234-9181
Fax: 619-234-8475

William E. Johns
Stephen F. Treadgold
Raymond L. Heidemann
Elise Streicher Rogerson

OF COUNSEL

Maurice T. Watson
Philip P. Martin, Jr.

For Complete List of Firm Personnel, See General Section

For full biographical listings, see the Martindale-Hubbell Law Directory

San Diego—Continued

MILLER, MONSON & PESHEL (AV)

A Partnership of Professional Law Corporations
501 West Broadway, Suite 700, 92101
Telephone: 619-239-7777
Fax Telephone: 619-238-8808
Cable Address: "Sandylaw"

Ralph Gano Miller
Thomas M. Monson
Mary J. Peshel
Philip R. Fredricksen
Timothy C. Polacek
Susan L. Horner
Adam K. Ratner
Charles R. Kimmel

OF COUNSEL

Richard Glasner

References: California First Bank; First Interstate Bank.

For full biographical listings, see the Martindale-Hubbell Law Directory

WALTERS & WARD, A PROFESSIONAL CORPORATION (AV)

Lakeview Professional Building, Rancho Bernardo, 11665 Avena Place, Suite 203, 92128-2403
Telephone: 619-485-9045; 566-1480
FAX: 619-485-0398

R. Michael Walters
Diane K. Ward

Robert N. Gary
Julie Ann Bowler

For full biographical listings, see the Martindale-Hubbell Law Directory

WEINTRAUB & ASSOCIATES, A PROFESSIONAL LAW CORPORATION (AV)

The Plaza La Jolla Village, 4320 La Jolla Village Drive, Suite 270, 92122-1233
Telephone: 619-535-1444
FAX: 619-535-1447

Richard A. Weintraub
Mark T. Mauerman

OF COUNSEL

Marvin D. Brody (Not admitted in CA)

For full biographical listings, see the Martindale-Hubbell Law Directory

WINGERT, GREBING, ANELLO & BRUBAKER (AV)

A Partnership including Professional Corporations
One America Plaza, Seventh Floor, 600 West Broadway, 92101-3370
Telephone: 619-232-8151
Facsimile: 619-232-4665

MEMBERS OF FIRM

John R. Wingert (A Professional Corporation)
Charles R. Grebing (A Professional Corporation)
Michael M. Anello (A Professional Corporation)
Alan K. Brubaker (A Professional Corporation)
Norman A. Ryan
James Goodwin
Robert M. Caietti
Eileen Mulligan Marks
Christopher W. Todd
Robert L. Johnson
Douglas J. Simpson
Shawn D. Morris
Robert M. Juskie

ASSOCIATES

Julie E. Saake
Michael Sullivan
John S. Addams
Carolyn P. Gallinghouse
Michael S. Burke
Kimberly I. Cary
Terie M. Theis
James P. Broder
James J. Brown, Jr.
Sara A. Henry
Sarah F. Burke
Beverly A. Kalasky
Craig Gross

OF COUNSEL

William L. Todd, Jr.

Representative Clients: California Casualty Insurance Co.; Farmers Insurance Group; The Ohio Casualty Group; United Services Automobile Assn.; Transamerica Insurance Group; United States Fidelity & Guaranty Co.

For full biographical listings, see the Martindale-Hubbell Law Directory

*SAN FRANCISCO,** San Francisco Co.

ADVICE & COUNSEL INCORPORATED (AV Ⓣ)

300 Montgomery Street, Suite 435, 94104-1906
Telephone: 415-955-5700
Fax: 415-955-5715
E-Mail: WILLTRUST@aol.com
San Diego, California Office: Suite 105, 2204 Garnet Avenue, 92109.
Telephone: 619-490-2800.
Fax: 619-490-2908.

Gerry H. Goldsholle
Daniel Gordon Le Vine

For full biographical listings, see the Martindale-Hubbell Law Directory

AVERY & ASSOCIATES (AV)

49 Geary Street, Suite 202, 94108-5727
Telephone: 415-954-4800
Fax: 415-954-4810

Luther J. Avery

ASSOCIATE

Mark J. Avery

LEGAL SUPPORT PERSONNEL

Matthew S. Avery

For full biographical listings, see the Martindale-Hubbell Law Directory

LAW OFFICES OF GARY D. BERGER (AV)

One Sansome Street, 19th Floor, 94104
Telephone: 415-731-2268
Fax: 415-239-5147

For full biographical listings, see the Martindale-Hubbell Law Directory

FELDMAN, WALDMAN & KLINE, A PROFESSIONAL CORPORATION (AV)

2700 Russ Building, 235 Montgomery Street, 94104
Telephone: 415-981-1300
Telex: 650-223-3204
Fax: 415-394-0121
Stockton, California Office: Sperry Building, 146-148 West Weber Avenue.
Telephone: 209-943-2004.
Fax: 209-943-0905.

Murry J. Waldman
Leland R. Selna, Jr.
Michael L. Korbholz
Howard M. Wexler
Patricia S. Mar
Kenneth W. Jones
Paul J. Dion
Vern S. Bothwell
L. J. Chris Martiniak
Kenneth A. Freed
Martha Jeanne Shaver (Resident, Stockton Office)
Robert Cedric Goodman
Steven K. Denebeim
Laura Grad
William F. Adams
William M. Smith
Elizabeth A. Thompson
Julie A. Jones
David L. Kanel

Abram S. Feuerstein
John R. Capron
Ted S. Storey
A. Todd Berman
Laura J. Dawson

OF COUNSEL

Richard L. Jaeger
Malcolm Leader-Picone
Gerald A. Sherwin (Resident, Stockton Office)

For full biographical listings, see the Martindale-Hubbell Law Directory

SCHINDLER & MEYER, PROFESSIONAL CORPORATION (AV)

Bank of Canton Building, 555 Montgomery Street, 15th Floor, 94111
Telephone: 415-421-0855
Fax: 415-421-6736

Richard A. Schindler
Anne W. Meyer

References: Civic Bank of Commerce; Bank of America.

For full biographical listings, see the Martindale-Hubbell Law Directory

SUCHERMAN & COLLINS (AV)

Suite 1750, 88 Kearny Street, 94108
Telephone: 415-956-5554
Fax: 415-781-4367

Lowell H. Sucherman
Carroll J. Collins III

ASSOCIATE

Michelene Insalaco

For full biographical listings, see the Martindale-Hubbell Law Directory

VOGL & MEREDITH (AV)

456 Montgomery Street, 20th Floor, 94104
Telephone: 415-398-0200
Facsimile: 415-398-2820

Samuel E. Meredith
David R. Vogl
Bryan A. Marmesh
John P. Walovich
Jean N. Yeh
Janet Brayer
Thomas S. Clifton (Resident)

George C. Leal

For full biographical listings, see the Martindale-Hubbell Law Directory

*SAN JOSE,** Santa Clara Co.

Ferrari, Alvarez, Olsen & Ottoboni, A Professional Corporation (AV)

333 West Santa Clara Street, Suite 700, 95113
Telephone: 408-280-0535
Fax: 408-280-0151
Palo Alto, California Office: 550 Hamilton Avenue.
Telephone: 415-327-3233.

Clarence J. Ferrari, Jr.
Kent E. Olsen
John M. Ottoboni
Richard S. Bebb
James J. Eller
Robert C. Danneskiold
Terence M. Kane
Emma Peña Madrid
John P. Thurau
Roger D. Wintle
Christopher E. Cobey

Michael D. Brayton
Lisa Intrieri Caputo
Jil Dalesandro
Gregory R. Dietrich
J. Timothy Maximoff
Joseph W. Mell, Jr.
George P. Mulcaire
Eleanor C. Schuermann
Melva M. Vollersen

OF COUNSEL

Edward M. Alvarez

For full biographical listings, see the Martindale-Hubbell Law Directory

Owen G. Fiore (AV)

Bank of America Building, 101 Park Center Plaza, Suite 1150, 95113
Telephone: 408-293-3616
Facsimile: 408-293-0430

John F. Ramsbacher
Leslie J. Daniels

For full biographical listings, see the Martindale-Hubbell Law Directory

Liccardo, Rossi, Sturges & McNeil, A Professional Law Corporation (AV)

1960 The Alameda, Suite 200, 95126
Telephone: 408-244-4570
Fax: 408-244-3294
Oakland, California Office: 1999 Harrison, Suite 1300.
Telephone: 415-834-2206.
Fax: 415-832-4432.

Salvador A. Liccardo
Ronald R. Rossi
Robert S. Sturges
R. Donald McNeil
David M. Hamerslough
Susan R. Reischl
Craig Needham
Gregory D. Hull
Martha Louise Caron
Cynthia L. Chase
Dann B. Jones
Laura Liccardo

Robert C. Colyar
William J. Purdy, III
Jeffery Lopez
Peter N. Brewer
Wes Wagnon
Richard B. Gullen
Deborah T. Bjonerud
Paul Salvatore Liccardo

For full biographical listings, see the Martindale-Hubbell Law Directory

*SAN LUIS OBISPO,** San Luis Obispo Co.

George, Gallo & Sullivan, A Law Corporation (AV)

694 Santa Rosa, P.O. Box 12710, 93406
Telephone: 805-544-3351
Facsimile: 805-528-5598
Los Osos, California Office: 2238 Bayview Heights Drive, P.O. Box 6129.
Telephone: 805-528-3351.
Telecopier: 805-528-5598.

J. K. George

Anne C. Cyr

Reference: Mid State Bank, Los Osos, California.

For full biographical listings, see the Martindale-Hubbell Law Directory

SAN MATEO, San Mateo Co.

Anderlini, Guheen, Finkelstein, Emerick & McSweeney, A Professional Corporation (AV)

400 South El Camino Real, Suite 700, 94402
Telephone: 415-348-0102
Fax: 415-348-0962

P. Terry Anderlini
John J. Guheen
David G. Finkelstein
Merrill G. Emerick
Brian J. McSweeney

(See Next Column)

A. James Scholz
John P. Antonakos
Paul J. Smoot
Jennifer Gustafson

OF COUNSEL

Daniel J. Monaco (Inc.)

A list of Representative Clients will be furnished upon request.

For full biographical listings, see the Martindale-Hubbell Law Directory

Basye & Golden (AV)

520 South El Camino Real, Suite 700, 94402
Telephone: 415-342-2500
Fax: 415-342-9560

MEMBERS OF FIRM

Paul E. Basye (1901-1991)
John P. Golden

For full biographical listings, see the Martindale-Hubbell Law Directory

*SANTA ANA,** Orange Co.

Portigal, Hammerton & Allen (AV)

Suite 100 El Rancho Plaza, 2021 East 4th Street, 92705
Telephone: 714-558-6991
Fax: 714-558-0638
Temecula, California Office: 27349 Jefferson Avenue, Suite 204.
Telephone: 714-694-8622.
Fax: 714-699-8571.

MEMBERS OF FIRM

H. Allan Portigal (1919-1986)
James R. Hammerton
Barry L. Allen
Michael A. Portigal (Resident, Temecula Office)
Ken W. Nielsen
Timothy J. Donahue

ASSOCIATES

Thomas D. Mullings, Jr.
Debra E. Allen

Representative Clients: State Farm Insurance Cos.; Ohio Casualty Insurance Co.; County of Orange; Orange Coast Community College District.

For full biographical listings, see the Martindale-Hubbell Law Directory

*SANTA CRUZ,** Santa Cruz Co.

Atchison, Anderson, Hurley & Barisone, A Professional Corporation (AV)

333 Church Street, 95060
Telephone: 408-423-8383
Fax: 408-423-9401
Salinas, California Office: 137 Central Avenue, Suite 6. 93901.
Telephone: 408-755-7833.
Fax: 408-753-0293.

Rodney R. Atchison
Neal R. Anderson (1947-1986)
Vincent P. Hurley
John G. Barisone

Justin B. Lighty
Mitchell A. Jackman
David Y. Imai
Anthony P. Condotti
Mary C. Logan

Counsel for: City of Santa Cruz.

For full biographical listings, see the Martindale-Hubbell Law Directory

SANTA MONICA, Los Angeles Co.

Jakle and Hromadka (AV)

A Partnership including a Professional Corporation
3201 Wilshire Boulevard, Suite 301, 90403
Telephone: 310-582-2200
Facsimile: 310-453-3314

John B. Jakle
Donald J. Hromadka (P.C.)

References: Century Federal Savings & Loan, Santa Monica; Santa Monica Bank.

For full biographical listings, see the Martindale-Hubbell Law Directory

*SANTA ROSA,** Sonoma Co.

Belden, Abbey, Weitzenberg & Kelly, A Professional Corporation (AV)

1105 North Dutton Avenue, P.O. Box 1566, 95402
Telephone: 707-542-5050
Telecopier: 707-542-2589

Thomas P. Kelly, Jr.

Representative Clients: Exchange Bank of Santa Rosa; Westamerica Bank; North Bay Title Co.; Northwestern Title Security Co.; Geyser Peak Winery; Arrowood Vineyards & Winery; Hansel Ford; Santa Rosa City School District.

For Complete List of Firm Personnel, See General Section

For full biographical listings, see the Martindale-Hubbell Law Directory

*STOCKTON,** San Joaquin Co.

Richard W. Konig (AV)

6702 Inglewood Avenue, Suite A, 95207-3872
Telephone: 209-474-1251

TORRANCE, Los Angeles Co.

Finer, Kim & Stearns (AV)

An Association of Professional Corporations
City National Bank Building, 3424 Carson Street, Suite 500, 90503
Telephone: 310-214-1477
Telecopier: 310-214-0764

W. A. Finer (A Professional Corporation)

Mark Andrew Hooper

LEGAL SUPPORT PERSONNEL

Marcia E. Talbert

For Complete List of Firm Personnel, See General Section

For full biographical listings, see the Martindale-Hubbell Law Directory

Christopher M. Moore & Associates A Law Corporation (AV)

Suite 490 Union Bank Tower, 21515 Hawthorne Boulevard, 90503
Telephone: 310-540-8855
Fax: 310-316-1307

Christopher M. Moore

Rebecca Lee Tomlinson Schroff

For full biographical listings, see the Martindale-Hubbell Law Directory

UNIVERSAL CITY, Los Angeles Co.

David W. Fleming, P.C. (AV)

10 Universal City Plaza, Suite 2570, 91608
Telephone: 818-753-8141
Fax: 818-753-5657

David W. Fleming

For full biographical listings, see the Martindale-Hubbell Law Directory

UPLAND, San Bernardino Co.

Vinnedge, Gafney & Gladson, Inc. (AV)

255 West Foothill Boulevard, Suite 210, 91786
Telephone: 909-931-0879
Fax: 909-931-9219

George W. Vinnedge
Thomas J. Gafney
Linda J. Gladson

LEGAL SUPPORT PERSONNEL

Linda A. Gooding (Probate Assistant)
Sandra L. Lukens (Paralegal)

Representative Client: First Trust Bank, Ontario, Calif.

For full biographical listings, see the Martindale-Hubbell Law Directory

*VENTURA,** Ventura Co.

Taylor McCord, A Law Corporation (AV)

721 East Main Street, P.O. Box 1477, 93002
Telephone: 805-648-4700
Fax: 805-653-6124

Richard L. Taylor
Robert L. McCord, Jr.
Ellen G. Conroy
David L. Praver

Patrick Cherry
Susan D. Siple

For full biographical listings, see the Martindale-Hubbell Law Directory

VISTA, San Diego Co.

Ernest L. Hunt, Jr. (AV)

630 Alta Vista Drive, Suite 103, P.O. Box 640, 92085-0640
Telephone: 619-726-3839
Fax: 619-726-5491

For full biographical listings, see the Martindale-Hubbell Law Directory

WALNUT CREEK, Contra Costa Co.

Stewart, Stewart & O'Neil (AV)

1908 Tice Valley Boulevard Rossmoor Shopping Center, 94595
Telephone: 510-932-8000
Fax: 510-932-4681

Thomas N. Stewart, Jr.
Jeannine O'Neil

For full biographical listings, see the Martindale-Hubbell Law Directory

WHITTIER, Los Angeles Co.

Bewley, Lassleben & Miller (AV)

A Law Partnership including Professional Corporations
Suite 510 Whittier Square, 13215 East Penn Street, 90602
Telephone: 310-698-9771; 723-8062; 714-994-5131
Telecopier: 310-696-6357

MEMBERS OF FIRM

Thomas W. Bewley (1903-1986)
William M. Lassleben, Jr. (A Professional Corporation)
Edward L. Miller (A Professional Corporation)
J. Terrence Mooschekian
Richard A. Hayes (A Professional Corporation)
Ernie Zachary Park (A Professional Corporation)
Robert H. Dewberry (A Professional Corporation)
Richard L. Dewberry (A Professional Corporation)
Jeffrey S. Baird
Kevin P. Duthoy
Joseph A. Vinatieri
Jason C. Demille

Representative Clients: Quaker City Federal Savings & Loan Assn.; Whittier College; Presbyterian Intercommunity Hospital; Bank of Whittier; Circuit Systems, Inc.; Lockhart Industries, Inc.; Subdivided Land, Inc.; United Ad-Label Co., Inc.
References: Bank of America National Trust & Savings Assn. (Whittier Main Office); Southern California Bank.

For Complete List of Firm Personnel, See General Section

For full biographical listings, see the Martindale-Hubbell Law Directory

WOODLAND HILLS, Los Angeles Co.

Walleck, Shane, Stanard & Blender (AV)

5959 Topanga Canyon Boulevard, Suite 200, 91367
Telephone: 818-346-1333
Fax: 818-702-8939

MEMBERS OF FIRM

David L. Shane
David L. Blender
Gary N. Schwartz

Representative Clients: San Fernando Valley Board of Realtors; Keffco, Inc.; Fuller-Jeffrey Broadcasting; Lynn Simay-Key Centers, Inc.; DA/PRO Rubber, Inc.; Pinnacle Estate Properties, Inc.; Comet Electric, Inc.; Wausau Insurance Company; Western States Imports Co., Inc.; California Coast Escrow, Inc.

For full biographical listings, see the Martindale-Hubbell Law Directory

COLORADO

AURORA, Arapahoe & Adams Cos.

David W. Kirch (AV)

14001 East Iliff Avenue, Suite 318, 80014
Telephone: 303-671-7726
Fax: 303-671-7679

Representative Clients: The Rocky Mountain District Lutheran Church-Missouri Synod; Midwest Chemical and Supply; Plaza III Townhome Association.

For full biographical listings, see the Martindale-Hubbell Law Directory

*BOULDER,** Boulder Co.

Doty & Shapiro, P.C. (AV)

1720 Fourteenth Street, Suite 100, 80302-6353
Telephone: 303-443-3234
Telecopier: 303-443-3438

H. McGregor Doty, II
Mark R. Shapiro

For full biographical listings, see the Martindale-Hubbell Law Directory

*COLORADO SPRINGS,** El Paso Co.

Wilton W. Cogswell, III (AV)

Suite 1020, Alamo Corporate Center, 102 South Tejon, 80903
Telephone: 719-473-1448
Facsimile: 719-473-1449

(See Next Column)

WILTON W. COGSWELL III, *Colorado Springs—Continued*

OF COUNSEL

Wilton W. Cogswell, IV

For full biographical listings, see the Martindale-Hubbell Law Directory

CROSS, GADDIS, KIN, HERD & KELLY, P.C. (AV)

118 South Wahsatch, 80903
Telephone: 719-471-3848
Fax: 719-471-0317

Thomas R. Cross
Larry R. Gaddis
James W. Kin
David L. Quicksall (1950-1991)
Thomas J. Herd
Debra L. Kelly

OF COUNSEL

James B. Turner

Reference: Norwest Bank of Colorado Springs.

For full biographical listings, see the Martindale-Hubbell Law Directory

DANIEL P. EDWARDS, P.C. (AV)

Suite 310, 128 South Tejon, 80903
Telephone: 719-634-6620
Fax: 719-634-3142

Daniel P. Edwards

For full biographical listings, see the Martindale-Hubbell Law Directory

KRUSE & LYNCH, P.C. (AV)

Suite 1050, 2 North Cascade, 80903
Telephone: 719-473-9911
FAX: 719-471-7750

Clifton B. Kruse, Jr.
Franklin E. Lynch

Reference: Bank One, Colorado Springs, N.A.

For full biographical listings, see the Martindale-Hubbell Law Directory

JAMES A. WEIR (AV)

Suite 510 Alamo Corporate Center, 102 South Tejon, 80903
Telephone: 719-473-9906
FAX: 719-578-8869

References: Bank One; Colorado National Bank/Exchange.

For full biographical listings, see the Martindale-Hubbell Law Directory

*CRAIG,** Moffat Co.

WILLIAM V. LAWRENCE (AV)

510 Breeze Street, P.O. Box 1131, 81626
Telephone: 303-824-4730

Reference: Bank One of Craig.

For full biographical listings, see the Martindale-Hubbell Law Directory

*DENVER,** Denver Co.

HARRY L. ARKIN & ASSOCIATES (AV)

Suite 2750 Lincoln Center, 1660 Lincoln Street, 80264
Telephone: 303-863-8400
Telefax: 303-832-4703
London, England Office: Verulam Chambers, Peer House, 8-14 Verulam Street, WCIX 8LZ.
Telephone: 071 813-2400.
Fax: 071 405-3870.

ASSOCIATE

Simon L. Krauss

For full biographical listings, see the Martindale-Hubbell Law Directory

ATLASS PROFESSIONAL CORPORATION (AV)

2100 East Fourteenth Avenue, 80206
Telephone: 303-377-0707
Fax: 303-321-2655

Theodore B. Atlass

Carol Buchanan Lay

OF COUNSEL

John DeBruyn

For full biographical listings, see the Martindale-Hubbell Law Directory

ROBERT L. BARTHOLIC (AV)

Suite 600, 1600 Broadway, 80202
Telephone: 303-830-0500
Fax: 303-860-7855

(See Next Column)

OF COUNSEL

Clarence L. Bartholic

Approved Attorney for: Mid-South Title Insurance Corp; Lawyers Title Insurance Co.
Representative Clients: Anschutz Corp.; Denver and Rio Grande Western Railroad Co.; Johnson Anderson Mortgage Co.; Arco Environmental Affairs; Burlington Northern Railroad Co. and Subsidiaries; American Association of Private Railroad Car Owners, Inc.
References: Colorado National Bank; Colorado State Bank.

For full biographical listings, see the Martindale-Hubbell Law Directory

JOHN DEBRUYN LAW OFFICES (AV)

2100 East Fourteenth Avenue, 80206
Telephone: 303-377-0707
Telecopier: 303-321-2655
(Also Of Counsel to Atlass Professional Corporation)

OF COUNSEL

Theodore B. Atlass

For full biographical listings, see the Martindale-Hubbell Law Directory

MICHAEL R. DICE AND COMPANY, L.L.C. (AV)

Suite 600, 3300 East First Avenue, 80206
Telephone: 303-321-6872
Fax: 303-321-3196
Downtown Denver Office: Suite 2750 Lincoln Center, 1660 Lincoln Street, 80264.
Telephone: 303-832-1225.
Lakewood, Colorado Office: Suite C-400, 12600 West Colfax Avenue, 80215.
Telephone: 303-232-5151.

Michael R. Dice

Tom A. Hemry
Ronald K. Ledgerwood
Julia Griffith McVey

OF COUNSEL

Thomas A. Faulkner

SPECIAL COUNSEL

Robert C. Leher

For full biographical listings, see the Martindale-Hubbell Law Directory

ENGEL & RUDMAN, P.C. (AV)

The Quadrant, 5445 DTC Parkway, Suite 1025 (Englewood), 80111
Telephone: 303-741-1111
Fax: 303-694-4028

Barry S. Engel
Ronald L. Rudman

David L. Lockwood

For full biographical listings, see the Martindale-Hubbell Law Directory

FEDER, MORRIS, TAMBLYN & GOLDSTEIN, P.C. (AV)

150 Blake Street Building, 1441 Eighteenth Street, 80202
Telephone: 303-292-1441
FAX: 303-292-1126

John B. Carraher
Barbara Salomon

Reference: Guaranty Bank & Trust Co., Denver, Colorado.

For full biographical listings, see the Martindale-Hubbell Law Directory

GODDARD & GODDARD, P.C. (AV)

Suite 203, 1900 Wazee Street, 80202
Telephone: 303-292-3228
Fax: 303-292-1956

Susan B. Goddard
Jo Anna Goddard

Representative Clients: Cogent Systems, Inc.; Colorado Yule Marble, Co.; Corporate Finance Associates.

For full biographical listings, see the Martindale-Hubbell Law Directory

HOLME ROBERTS & OWEN LLC (AV)

Suite 4100, 1700 Lincoln, 80203
Telephone: 303-861-7000
Telex: 45-4460
Telecopier: 303-866-0200
Boulder, Colorado Office: Suite 400, 1401 Pearl Street.
Telephone: 303-444-5955.
Telecopier: 303-444-1063.
Colorado Springs, Colorado Office: Suite 1300, 90 South Cascade Avenue.
Telephone: 719-473-3800.
Telecopier: 719-633-1518.
Salt Lake City, Utah Office: Suite 1100, 111 East Broadway.
Telephone: 801-521-5800.
Telecopier: 801-521-9639.

(See Next Column)

HOLME ROBERTS & OWEN LLC—*Continued*

London, England Office: 4th Floor, Mellier House, 26a Albemarle Street.
Telephone: 44-171-499-8776.
Telecopier: 44-171-499-7769.
Moscow, Russia Office: 14 Krivokolenny Pr., Suite 30, 101000.
Telephone: 095-925-7816.
Telecopier: 095-923-2726.

MEMBERS OF FIRM

James E. Bye
Judson W. Detrick
William S. Huff
Donald J. Hopkins
Steve L. Gaines (Colorado Springs Office)
Douglas A. Pluss
McKay Marsden (Salt Lake City Office)
Stephanie M. Tuthill
Sharon A. Higgins (Colorado Springs Office)

ASSOCIATES

Steven C. Bednar (Salt Lake City Office)
Charles B. Bruce, Jr.
Michelle M. Rose-Hughes

For Complete List of Firm Personnel, See General Section

For full biographical listings, see the Martindale-Hubbell Law Directory

MYER, SWANSON & ADAMS, P.C. (AV)

The Colorado State Bank Building, 1600 Broadway, Suite 1850, 80202-4918
Telephone: 303-866-9800
Facsimile: 303-866-9818

Rendle Myer
Allan B. Adams
Robert K. Swanson
Thomas J. Wolf

Kevin M. Brady

OF COUNSEL

Robert Swanson
Fred E. Neef (1910-1986)

Representative Clients: The Oppenheimer Funds; Daily Cash Accumulation Fund; The Centennial Trusts; Mile High Chapter of American Red Cross; Master Lease; Heartland Management Company; Kan-Build of Colorado, Inc.
Reference: The Colorado State Bank of Denver.

For full biographical listings, see the Martindale-Hubbell Law Directory

MYERS, HOPPIN, BRADLEY AND DEVITT, P.C. (AV)

Suite 420, 4704 Harlan Street, 80212
Telephone: 303-433-8527
Fax: 303-433-8219

Frederick J. Myers
Charles T. Hoppin
Jon T. Bradley
Jerald J. Devitt

Gregg W. Fraser

OF COUNSEL

Kent E. Hanson

Reference: Bank One Lakeside Banking Center.

For full biographical listings, see the Martindale-Hubbell Law Directory

SHERMAN & HOWARD L.L.C. (AV)

Attorneys at Law
633 Seventeenth Street, Suite 3000, 80202
Telephone: 303-297-2900
Telecopier: 303-298-0940
Colorado Springs, Colorado Office: Suite 1500, 90 South Cascade Avenue, 80903.
Telephone: 719-475-2440.
Las Vegas, Nevada Office: Swendseid & Stern a member in Sherman & Howard L.L.C., 317 Sixth Street, 89101.
Telephone: 702-387-6073.
Reno, Nevada Office: Swendseid & Stern, a member in Sherman & Howard L.L.C., 50 West Liberty Street, Suite 660, 89501.
Telephone: 702-323-1980.

Douglas M. Cain
Duane F. Wurzer
David Thomas III

COUNSEL

William P. Cantwell

Carol V. Berger
Katherine F. Beckes

Representative Clients: AT&T Corp.; Eastmen Kodak Co.; Hathaway Corp.; Newmont Gold Corp.

For Complete List of Firm Personnel, See General Section

For full biographical listings, see the Martindale-Hubbell Law Directory

WADE ASH WOODS HILL & FARLEY, P.C. (AV)

Suite 400, 360 South Monroe Street, 80209
Telephone: 303-322-8943
Fax: 303-320-7501

(See Next Column)

James R. Wade
Walter B. Ash
James W. Hill
J. Michael Farley
Steven R. Warden
Constance H. Block

David M. Swank

OF COUNSEL

Lucius E. Woods (Retired)

Representative Clients: American Cancer Society (Colorado Division); Clayton College Foundation; Colorado National Bank of Denver (Trust Department); Drive Train Industries, Inc.; Investment Trust Co.; Kalcevic Farms, Inc.; Affiliated National Bank - Englewood (Trust Department); University of Colorado Foundation; Drive Train Industries.

For full biographical listings, see the Martindale-Hubbell Law Directory

ZISMAN AND INGRAHAM, P.C. (AV)

Suite 250, 3773 Cherry Creek Drive North, 80209
Telephone: 303-320-0023
Fax: 303-320-0034

Sanford Zisman
James F. Ingraham

For full biographical listings, see the Martindale-Hubbell Law Directory

*DURANGO,** La Plata Co.

SHAND, MCLACHLAN & NEWBOLD, P.C. (AV)

124 East Ninth Street, P.O. Drawer I, 81302-2790
Telephone: 303-247-3091
Fax: 303-247-3100

E. Bentley Hamilton (1918-1981)
J. Douglas Shand
Michael E. McLachlan
Keith Newbold

David A. Bode
A. Michael Chapman (Resident)
Sheryl Rogers

For full biographical listings, see the Martindale-Hubbell Law Directory

*GREELEY,** Weld Co.

BREGA & WINTERS, P.C. (AV)

1100 Tenth Street, Suite 402, 80631
Telephone: 303-352-4805
Fax: 303-352-6547
Denver, Colorado Office: One United Bank Center. 1700 Lincoln Street, Suite 2222 Street.
Telephone: 303-866-9400.
FAX: 303-861-9109.

Jerry D. Winters
Pamela A. Shaddock

Bradley D. Laue

For full biographical listings, see the Martindale-Hubbell Law Directory

LAKEWOOD, Jefferson Co.

POLIDORI, GEROME, FRANKLIN AND JACOBSON (AV)

Suite 300, 550 South Wadsworth Boulevard, 80226
Telephone: 303-936-3300
Fax: 303-936-0125

R. Jerold Gerome

Representative Client: Colorado National Bank.

For Complete List of Firm Personnel, See General Section

For full biographical listings, see the Martindale-Hubbell Law Directory

*WRAY,** Yuma Co.

CALLAHAN & CALLAHAN (AV)

312 Main Street, P.O. Box 445, 80758
Telephone: 303-332-4858
Fax: 303-332-4859

Thomas J. Callahan

ASSOCIATE

Anne N. Callahan

OF COUNSEL

Joseph T. Callahan

Attorney For: FHA Authorized Home Loan Attorney; First Pioneer National Bank of Wray; Arikaree Ground Water Management District.
Reference: First Pioneer National Bank of Wray.

CONNECTICUT

CHESHIRE, New Haven Co.

WINTERS & FORTE (AV)

Waverly Professional Park, 315 Highland Avenue, Suite 102, P.O. Box 844, 06410
Telephone: 203-272-2927
Fax: 203-271-1222

MEMBERS OF FIRM

David Wayne Winters
Michael C. Forte

A List of Representative Clients will be furnished upon request.
Re ferences: Bank of Boston, Connecticut; Centerbank; American National Bank.

For full biographical listings, see the Martindale-Hubbell Law Directory

GREENWICH, Fairfield Co.

ALBERT, WARD & JOHNSON, P.C. (AV)

125 Mason Street, P.O. Box 1668, 06836
Telephone: 203-661-8600
Telecopier: 203-661-8051

OF COUNSEL

David Albert

Tom S. Ward, Jr.
Scott R. Johnson
Jane D. Hogeman
Howard R. Wolfe

Christopher A. Kristoff

For full biographical listings, see the Martindale-Hubbell Law Directory

IVEY, BARNUM & O'MARA (AV)

Meridian Building, 170 Mason Street, P.O. Box 1689, 06830
Telephone: 203-661-6000
Telecopier: 203-661-9462

MEMBERS OF FIRM

Michael J. Allen
Robert C. Barnum, Jr.
Edward D. Cosden, Jr.
James W. Cuminale
Wilmot L. Harris, Jr.
William I. Haslun, II
Edward T. Krumeich, Jr.
Donat C. Marchand
Miles F. McDonald, Jr.
Edwin J. O'Mara, Jr.
Remy A. Rodas
Gregory A. Saum
Lorraine Slavin

ASSOCIATES

Juerg A. Heim
Melissa Townsend Klauberg
Nicole Barrett Lecher
Alan S. Rubenstein

OF COUNSEL

Philip R. McKnight

For full biographical listings, see the Martindale-Hubbell Law Directory

*HARTFORD,** Hartford Co.

COPP & BERALL (AV)

55 Farmington Avenue, Suite 703, 06105
Telephone: 203-249-5261
Fax: 203-947-6382

MEMBERS OF FIRM

Frank S. Berall
Mark H. Neikrie
Suzanne Brown Walsh

OF COUNSEL

Belton A. Copp

References: Fleet Bank, N.A.; Connecticut National Bank; Union Trust Co.; Bank of Boston.

For full biographical listings, see the Martindale-Hubbell Law Directory

GORDON, MUIR AND FOLEY (AV)

Hartford Square North, Ten Columbus Boulevard, 06106-1944
Telephone: 203-525-5361
Telecopier: 203-525-4849

MEMBERS OF FIRM

William S. Gordon, Jr. (1946-1956)
George Muir (1939-1976)
Edward J. Foley (1955-1983)
Peter C. Schwartz
John J. Reid
John H. Goodrich, Jr.
R. Bradley Wolfe
Jon Stephen Berk
William J. Gallitto
Gerald R. Swirsky
Robert J. O'Brien
Philip J. O'Connor
Kenneth G. Williams
Chester J. Bukowski
Mary Ann Santacroce

(See Next Column)

ASSOCIATES

J. Lawrence Price
Mary Anne Alicia Charron
James G. Kelly
Kevin F. Morin
Claudia A. Baio
Patrick T. Treacy
Andrew J. Hern
Eileen Geel
Christopher L. Slack
Renee W. Dwyer
David B. Heintz

OF COUNSEL

Stephen M. Riley

Reference: Fleet Bank.

For full biographical listings, see the Martindale-Hubbell Law Directory

SHIPMAN & GOODWIN (AV)

One American Row, 06103
Telephone: 203-251-5000
Telecopier: 203-251-5099
Lakeville, Connecticut Office: Porter Street.
Telephone: 203-435-2539.
Stamford, Connecticut Office: Three Landmark Square.
Telephone: 203-359-4544.

MEMBERS OF FIRM

Stuyvesant K. Bearns (Lakeville Office)
James T. Betts
Coleman H. Casey

ASSOCIATES

Stephen K. Gellman
Donna A. Muschell

COUNSEL

Warren S. Randall
William H. Wood, Jr.
Robert Ewing

For Complete List of Firm Personnel, See General Section

For full biographical listings, see the Martindale-Hubbell Law Directory

SOROKIN SOROKIN GROSS HYDE & WILLIAMS P.C. (AV)

One Corporate Center, 06103
Telephone: 203-525-6645
Fax: 203-522-1781
Simsbury, Connecticut Office: 730 Hopmeadow Street.
Telephone: 203-651-9348.
Rocky Hill, Connecticut Office: 2360 Main Street.
Telephone: 203-563-9305.
Fax: 203-529-6931.
Glastonbury, Connecticut Office: 124 Hebron Avenue.
Telephone: 203-659-8801.

Richard G. Convicer
Charles R. Moore, Jr.
Lewis Rabinovitz
Barrie K. Wetstone

OF COUNSEL

Ethel Silver Sorokin

For Complete List of Firm Personnel, See General Section

For full biographical listings, see the Martindale-Hubbell Law Directory

*NEW HAVEN,** New Haven Co.

BERGMAN, HOROWITZ & REYNOLDS, P.C. (AV)

157 Church Street, 19th Floor, P.O. Box 426, 06502
Telephone: 203-789-1320
FAX: 203-785-8127
New York, New York Office: 499 Park Avenue, 26th Floor.
Telephone: 212-582-3580.

Stanley N. Bergman
Robert H. Horowitz
David L. Reynolds
Kenneth N. Musen
William C. G. Swift, Jr.
Richard J. Klein
James Russell Brockway
Bruce I. Judelson
David A. Ringold
Kathryn Harner Smith
Donald S. Hendel
Joy M. Miyasaki
Paul M. Roy

Louis R. Piscatelli
James G. Dattaro
Edward A. Renn
Anthony L. Galvagna
Frederick A. Thomas

For Complete List of Firm Personnel, See General Section

For full biographical listings, see the Martindale-Hubbell Law Directory

NEW LONDON, New London Co.

WALLER, SMITH & PALMER, P.C. (AV)

52 Eugene O'Neill Drive, P.O. Box 88, 06320
Telephone: 203-442-0367
Telecopier: 203-447-9915
Old Lyme, Connecticut Office: 103-A Halls Road.
Telephone: 203-434-8063.

(See Next Column)

WALLER, SMITH & PALMER P.C.—*Continued*

Birdsey G. Palmer (Retired)
William W. Miner
Robert P. Anderson, Jr.
Robert W. Marrion
Hughes Griffis
Edward B. O'Connell
Frederick B. Gahagan
Linda D. Loucony
Mary E. Driscoll
William E. Wellette

Tracy M. Collins
Donna Richer Skaats
David P. Condon
Valerie Ann Votto
Charles C. Anderson

OF COUNSEL

Suzanne Donnelly Kitchings

General Counsel for: Colotone Group.
Counsel for: Union Trust Co.; Coastal Savings Bank; Cash Home Center, Inc.
Local Counsel for: Metropolitan Insurance Co.; Connecticut General Life Insurance Co.

For Complete List of Firm Personnel, See General Section

For full biographical listings, see the Martindale-Hubbell Law Directory

ORANGE, New Haven Co.

SCHINE & JULIANELLE, P.C. (AV)

Suite 28, 477 Boston Post Road, P.O. Box 905, 06477-3548
Telephone: 203-795-3563
FAX: 203-799-9655
Westport, Connecticut Office: Suite 100, 830 Post Road East.
Telephone: 203-226-6861.
FAX: 203-226-6866.

Leonard A. Schine (1943-1982)
Robert L. Julianelle

Mary D. Mix
Patrick W. Frazier, Jr.
Natale V. Di Natale

OF COUNSEL

Lawrence W. Kanaga

Representative Client: Sacred Heart University.

For full biographical listings, see the Martindale-Hubbell Law Directory

SOUTHPORT, Fairfield Co.

BRODY AND OBER, P.C. (AV)

135 Rennell Drive, 06490
Telephone: 203-259-7405
Fax: 203-255-8572

Charles S. Brody (1894-1976)
Seth O. L. Brody
Stanley B. Garrell
Frank F. Ober
S. Giles Payne
William J. Britt
James M. Thorburn
Barbara S. Miller
Ronald B. Noren

Stephen L. Lichtman
Diane F. Martucci
Richard W. Mather

For full biographical listings, see the Martindale-Hubbell Law Directory

STAMFORD, Fairfield Co.

WOFSEY, ROSEN, KWESKIN & KURIANSKY (AV)

600 Summer Street, 06901
Telephone: 203-327-2300
FAX: 203-967-9273

MEMBERS OF FIRM

Abraham Wofsey (1915-1944)
Michael Wofsey (1927-1951)
David M. Rosen (1926-1967)
Julius B. Kuriansky (1910-1992)
Monroe Silverman
Emanuel Margolis
Howard C. Kaplan
Anthony R. Lorenzo
Edward M. Kweskin
David M. Cohen
Marshall Goldberg
Stephen A. Finn
Judith Rosenberg
Robert L. Teicher
Mark H. Henderson

Steven D. Grushkin

OF COUNSEL

Saul Kwartin
Sydney C. Kweskin (Retired)

ASSOCIATES

Brian Bandler
John J.L. Chober
Steven M. Frederick
Eric M. Higgins
James A. Lenes
Valerie E. Maze
Maurice K. Segall
Randall M. Skigen
Gregory J. Williams

Representative Clients: Benenson Realty; Cellular Information Systems, Inc.; Gateway Bank; Hartford Provision Company; Louis Dreyfus Corp.; Norwalk Federation of Teachers; Patient Care, Inc.; People's Bank; Ridgeway Shopping Center and Stamford Housing Authority.

(See Next Column)

For full biographical listings, see the Martindale-Hubbell Law Directory

TRUMBULL, Fairfield Co.

BRAUNSTEIN AND TODISCO, PROFESSIONAL CORPORATION (AV)

Brinsmade Building, 965 White Plains Road, 06611
Telephone: 203-452-9700
Telecopier: 203-459-0004

Samuel L. Braunstein
Amy E. Todisco
Jonathan J. Klein

References: The Bank of Boston-Connecticut; UST Bank Connecticut.

For full biographical listings, see the Martindale-Hubbell Law Directory

WEST HARTFORD, Hartford Co.

BERMAN, BOURNS & CURRIE (AV)

970 Farmington Avenue, P.O. Box 271837, 06127-1837
Telephone: 203-232-4471
Fax: 203-523-4605

MEMBERS OF FIRM

John A. Berman
Courtney B. Bourns
John K. Currie

ASSOCIATES

Robert B. Fawber
Mary Beth Anderson

For full biographical listings, see the Martindale-Hubbell Law Directory

WESTPORT, Fairfield Co.

BLAZZARD, GRODD & HASENAUER, P.C. (AV)

943 Post Road East, P.O. Box 5108, 06881
Telephone: 203-226-7866
Telecopier: 203-454-4855

Norse N. Blazzard
Leslie E. Grodd
Judith A. Hasenauer
William E. Hasenauer
Raymond A. O'Hara, III

Lynn Korman Stone

For full biographical listings, see the Martindale-Hubbell Law Directory

STUART A. MCKEEVER (AV)

155 Post Road, East, 06880
Telephone: 203-227-4756
Fax: 203-454-2031

Reference: Fleet Bank.

For full biographical listings, see the Martindale-Hubbell Law Directory

WILLIAM L. SCHEFFLER (AV(T))

315 Post Road West, 06880
Telephone: 203-226-6600; 212-795-7800
Telecopier: 203-227-1873

For full biographical listings, see the Martindale-Hubbell Law Directory

RONALD L. SHEIMAN (AV)

1804 Post Road East, 06880
Telephone: 203-259-0599
Telex: 238198 TLXAUR
Telecopier: 203-255-2570

For full biographical listings, see the Martindale-Hubbell Law Directory

TIROLA & HERRING (AV)

1221 Post Road East, P.O. Box 631, 06881
Telephone: 203-226-8926
Fax: 203-226-9500
New York, New York Office: Suite 4E, 10 Sheridan Square.
Telephone: 212-463-9642.

MEMBERS OF FIRM

Vincent S. Tirola
Charles Fredericks, Jr.
Elizabeth C. Seeley
Buddy O. H. Herring

Dan Shaban
Marc J. Grenier

OF COUNSEL

Edward Kanowitz
C. Michael Carter
Alan D. Lieberson

Reference: The Westport Bank and Trust Co.

For full biographical listings, see the Martindale-Hubbell Law Directory

WAKE, SEE, DIMES & BRYNICZKA (AV)

27 Imperial Avenue, P.O. Box 777, 06881
Telephone: 203-227-9545
Telecopier: 203-226-1641

(See Next Column)

WAKE, SEE, DIMES & BRYNICZKA, *Westport—Continued*

MEMBERS OF FIRM

Hereward Wake (1905-1977)
Edgar T. See
Edwin K. Dimes
Jacob P. Bryniczka
Amy L. Y. Day
Ira W. Bloom
Ernest Michael Dichele
Jonathan A. Flatow

ASSOCIATES

Douglas E. LoMonte
Rosamond A. Koether

OF COUNSEL

Richard S. Gibbons

General Counsel for: L.H. Gault & Son, Inc.; M.B.I., Inc.; The Danbury Mint; Beta Shim, Co.; Easton Press; Coverbind Corp.; D.L. Ryan Companies, Ltd.;
Approved Attorneys for: Lawyers Title Insurance Corporation of Richmond, Va.; Chicago Title Insurance Co.; Old Republic National Title Insurance Co.

For full biographical listings, see the Martindale-Hubbell Law Directory

DELAWARE

*WILMINGTON,** New Castle Co.

CONNOLLY, BOVE, LODGE & HUTZ (AV)

1220 Market Street, P.O. Box 2207, 19899-2207
Telephone: 302-658-9141
Telecopier: 302-658-5614
Cable Address: "Artcon"
Telex: 83-5477

James M. Mulligan, Jr.
Richard David Levin
Charles J. Durante
Anne Love Barnett
(Not admitted in DE)

For Complete List of Firm Personnel, See General Section

For full biographical listings, see the Martindale-Hubbell Law Directory

DALEY, ERISMAN & VAN OGTROP (AV)

1224 King Street, 19801
Telephone: 302-658-4000
FAX: 302-652-8975
Newark, Delaware Office: 206 East Delaware Avenue.
Telephone: 302-368-0133.
FAX: 302-368-4587.

MEMBERS OF FIRM

Robert E. Daley
James A. Erisman
Piet H. van Ogtrop

References: Wilmington Trust Company; Beneficial National Bank.

For full biographical listings, see the Martindale-Hubbell Law Directory

POTTER ANDERSON & CORROON (AV)

350 Delaware Trust Building, P.O. Box 951, 19899-0951
Telephone: 302-658-6771
FAX: 658-1192; 655-1190; 655-1199

MEMBERS OF FIRM

Leonard S. Togman
David J. Garrett

ASSOCIATE

Scott E. Waxman

Representative Clients: Delaware Trust Capital Management, Inc.

For Complete List of Firm Personnel, See General Section

For full biographical listings, see the Martindale-Hubbell Law Directory

SCHLUSSER, REIVER, HUGHES & SISK (AV)

1700 West 14th Street, 19806
Telephone: 302-655-8181
Fax: 302-655-8190

MEMBERS OF FIRM

Robert E. Schlusser
Joanna Reiver
Mark D. Sisk
Bryan E. Keenan
Brian P. Glancy

OF COUNSEL

Thomas G. Hughes

ASSOCIATES

Theresa P. Wilson
(Not admitted in DE)
John A. Ciccarone

For full biographical listings, see the Martindale-Hubbell Law Directory

WILLIAMS, HERSHMAN & WISLER, P.A. (AV)

Suite 600, One Commerce Center, Twelfth and Orange Streets, P.O. Box 511, 19899-0511
Telephone: 302-575-0873
Telecopier: 302-575-1642

David Nicol Williams
Douglas M. Hershman
Jeffrey C. Wisler
Barbara Snapp Danberg
F. Peter Conaty, Jr.

References: Wilmington Trust Co.; PNC Bank.

For full biographical listings, see the Martindale-Hubbell Law Directory

DISTRICT OF COLUMBIA

WASHINGTON, D.C. Co.

* indicates certain Bar Register subscribers, in cities of comparable size and importance, who maintain an additional office in Washington, D.C. and who have arranged for representation as a part of the Washington, D.C. listings that follow

THE LAW OFFICES OF SHELTON M. BINSTOCK (AV)

1140 Connecticut Avenue, N.W., Suite 703, 20036
Telephone: 202-785-1111
Telecopier: 202-293-1471

David B. Torchinsky

For full biographical listings, see the Martindale-Hubbell Law Directory

CAPLIN & DRYSDALE, CHARTERED (AV)

One Thomas Circle, N.W., 20005
Telephone: 202-862-5000
Cable Address: "Capdale"
Telex: 904001 CAPL UR WSH
Fax: 202-429-3301
New York, N.Y. Office: 399 Park Avenue.
Telephone: 212-319-7125.
Fax: 212-644-6755.

Mortimer M. Caplin
Robert A. Klayman
Ralph A. Muoio
Elihu Inselbuch
(Resident, New York Office)
Ronald B. Lewis
Richard W. Skillman
Patricia G. Lewis
Bernard S. Bailor
Stafford Smiley
Sally A. Regal
Julie W. Davis
Carl S. Kravitz
Robert A. Boisture
Charles T. Plambeck
Beth Shapiro Kaufman
Craig A. Sharon
James E. Salles
Paul G. Cellupica
Michael Doran
(Not admitted in DC)
Dorothy L. Foley
Matthew W. Frank
Elizabeth M. Sellers
(Not admitted in DC)
Douglas D. Drysdale
Thomas A. Troyer
David N. Webster
H. David Rosenbloom
Peter Van N. Lockwood
Cono R. Namorato
Daniel B. Rosenbaum
Richard E. Timbie
Graeme W. Bush
Albert G. Lauber, Jr.
Scott D. Michel
Kent A. Mason
Trevor W. Swett III
James Sottile, IV
Harry J. Hicks, III
C. Sanders McNew
(Resident, New York Office)
Ann C. McMillan
Catherine E. Livingston
Christian R. Pastore
(Resident, New York Office)
Nathan D. Finch
Jessica L. Goldstein

OF COUNSEL

Robert H. Elliott, Jr.
Milton Cerny
Myron C. Baum
Vivian L. Cavalieri

For full biographical listings, see the Martindale-Hubbell Law Directory

CROSS, MURPHY, SMUCK & HOUSTON (AV)

1350 Connecticut Avenue, N.W., Suite 300, 20036
Telephone: 202-393-8668
Telecopier: 202-833-2351

MEMBERS OF FIRM

John W. Cross (1902-1971)
James Russell Murphy
(1905-1986)
John C. Smuck
Stuart E. Houston

Reference: Crestar Bank, N.A.

For full biographical listings, see the Martindale-Hubbell Law Directory

Washington—Continued

THE FALK LAW FIRM A PROFESSIONAL LIMITED COMPANY (AV)

Suite 260 One Westin Center, 2445 M Street, N.W., 20037
Telephone: 202-833-8700
Telecopier: 202-872-1725

James H. Falk, Sr.
James H. Falk, Jr.
John M. Falk
Rose Burks Emery (Not admitted in DC)
Robert K. Tompkins (Not admitted in DC)

OF COUNSEL

Pierre E. Murphy

For full biographical listings, see the Martindale-Hubbell Law Directory

IVINS, PHILLIPS & BARKER, CHARTERED (AV)

Suite 600, 1700 Pennsylvania Avenue, N.W., 20006
Telephone: 202-393-7600
Fax: 202-347-4256

Jay W. Glasmann
Joseph E. McAndrews
H. Stewart Dunn, Jr.
Carroll J. Savage
Eric R. Fox
William L. Sollee
Carol K. Nickel
Leslie Jay Schneider
Robert H. Wellen
William R. Reiter
Kevin P. O'Brien
Michael F. Solomon
Daniel B. Stone
Patrick J. Smith
Michael R. Huffstetler
Laurie E. Keenan
Peter M. Daub

Jeffrey E. Moeller
Lee Meyer
Steven H. Witmer
Patricia G. Copeland
Rosina B. Barker
Claude B. Stansbury
John Bailey

For full biographical listings, see the Martindale-Hubbell Law Directory

JOHN A. KENDRICK (AV)

The Kendrick Building, 233 Massachusetts Avenue, N.E., 20002
Telephone: 202-544-3131
Fax: 202-547-4897

SUTHERLAND, ASBILL & BRENNAN (AV)

1275 Pennsylvania Avenue, N.W., 20004-2404
Telephone: 202-383-0100
Cable Address: "Sutab Wash"
Telex: 89-501
Facsimile: 202-637-3593
Atlanta, Georgia Office: 999 Peachtree Street, N. E., 30309-3996.
Telephone: 404-853-8000.
New York, N.Y. Office: 1270 Avenue of the Americas, 10020-1700.
Telephone: 212-332-3000.
Austin, Texas Office: 111 Congress Avenue, 23rd Floor, 78701-4079.
Telephone: 512-469-3350.

Lloyd Leva Plaine

For Complete List of Firm Personnel, See General Section

For full biographical listings, see the Martindale-Hubbell Law Directory

* **THOMPSON, HINE AND FLORY** (AV)

1920 N Street, N.W., 20036-1601
Telephone: 202-331-8800
Fax: 202-331-8330
Telex: 904173
Cable Address: "Caglaw"
Akron, Ohio Office: 50 S. Main Street, Suite 502, 44308-1828.
Telephone: 216-376-8090.
Fax: 216-376-8386.
Cincinnati, Ohio Office: 312 Walnut Street, 14th Floor, 45202-4029.
Telephone: 513-352-6700.
Fax: 513-241-4771.
Telex: 938003.
Cleveland, Ohio Office: 1100 National City Bank Building, 629 Euclid Avenue, 44114.
Telephone: 216-566-5500.
Fax: 216-566-5583.
Telex: 980217. Cable Address "Thomflor".
Columbus, Ohio Office: One Columbus, 10 West Broad Street, 43215-34353.
Telephone: 614-469-3200.
Fax: 614-469-3361.
Dayton, Ohio Office: 2000 Courthouse Plaza, N.E., 45402-1706.
Telephone: 513-443-6600.
Fax: 513-443-6637, 513-443-6635.
Palm Beach, Florida Office: 125 Worth Avenue, 33480-4466.
Telephone: 407-833-5900.
Fax: 407-833-5951.

(See Next Column)

Brussels, Belgium Office: Rue Des Chevaliers, Ridderstraat 14 - B.10, B-1050.
Telephone: 011-32-2-511-9326.
Fax: 011-32-2-513-9206.

MEMBER OF FIRM

Michael Wm. Sacks

For Complete List of Firm Personnel, See General Section

For full biographical listings, see the Martindale-Hubbell Law Directory

ZUCKERMAN, SPAEDER, GOLDSTEIN, TAYLOR & KOLKER (AV)

1201 Connecticut Avenue, N.W., 20036
Telephone: 202-778-1800
Fax: 202-822-8106
Miami, Florida Office: Zuckerman, Spaeder, Taylor & Evans. Suite 900, Miami Center, 201 South Biscayne Boulevard.
Telephones: 305-358-5000; 305-579-0110; Broward County: 305-523-0277.
Fax: 305-579-9749.
Ft. Lauderdale, Florida Office: Zuckerman, Spaeder, Taylor & Evans. One East Broward Boulevard, Suite 700.
Telephone: 305-356-0463.
Fax: 305-356-0406.
Baltimore, Maryland Office: Zuckerman, Spaeder, Goldstein, Taylor & Better. Suite 2440, 100 East Pratt Street.
Telephone: 410-332-0444.
Fax: 410-659-0436.
Tampa, Florida Office: Zuckerman, Spaeder, Taylor & Evans. 101 East Kennedy Boulevard, Suite 3140.
Telephone: 813-221-1010.
Fax: 813-223-7961.
New York, N.Y. Office: 1114 Avenue of the Americas, 45th Floor, Grace Building.
Telephone: 212-479-6500.
Fax: 212-479-6512.

MEMBERS OF FIRM

Arthur K. Mason
Eric F. Facer

ASSOCIATES

Ellen K. Fishbein
Maria A. Stamoulas
Loren Bendall

Reference: Sovran Bank/DC National.

For full biographical listings, see the Martindale-Hubbell Law Directory

FLORIDA

BOCA RATON, Palm Beach Co.

CARTER & CONNOLLY, P.A. (AV)

Suite 312, 1200 North Federal Highway, 33432
Telephone: 407-368-9900

John Edward Carter
Andrew James Connolly

OF COUNSEL

Robert T. Carlile

For full biographical listings, see the Martindale-Hubbell Law Directory

DICKENSON, MURDOCH, REX AND SLOAN, CHARTERED (AV)

Suite 410 Compson Financial Center, 980 North Federal Highway, 33432
Telephone: 407-391-1900
Facsimile: 407-391-1933

David B. Dickenson
Richard A. Murdoch
Robert H. Rex
Barbara A. Sloan
Barbara K. Olson

For full biographical listings, see the Martindale-Hubbell Law Directory

KAUFFMAN & SCHWARTZ, P.A. (AV)

Crocker Plaza, Suite 301, 5355 Town Center Road, 33486
Telephone: 407-394-7600
Fax: 407-394-0891

Alan C. Kauffman
Harvey A. Nussbaum
Thomas G. Pye
Robert M. Schwartz

Thomas U. Graner
Rick S. Felberbaum (Not admitted in FL)
Seth I. Cohen

OF COUNSEL

David M. Beckerman

For full biographical listings, see the Martindale-Hubbell Law Directory

Boca Raton—Continued

OSBORNE, OSBORNE & DECLAIRE, P.A. (AV)

Suite 100 Via Mizner Financial Plaza, 798 South Federal Highway, P.O. Drawer 40, 33429-9974
Telephone: 407-395-1000
Fax: 407-368-6930

Ray C. Osborne — R. Brady Osborne, Jr.
George F. deClaire

Approved Attorneys for: First Union National Bank of Florida, N.A.; SunBank/South Florida, N.A.; Northern Trust Bank of Florida; Boca Bank, a Florida Banking Corp.

For full biographical listings, see the Martindale-Hubbell Law Directory

SCHROEDER & LARCHE, P.A. (AV)

One Boca Place, Suite 319-A, 2255 Glades Road, 33431-7313
Telephone: 407-241-0300
Broward: 305-421-0878
Telecopier: 407-241-0798

Michael A. Schroeder — W. Lawrence Larche

Alan Pellingra

For full biographical listings, see the Martindale-Hubbell Law Directory

BOYNTON BEACH, Palm Beach Co.

ROBERT M. ARLEN, P.A. (AV)

Suite 200, 1501 Corporate Drive, 33426
Telephone: 407-734-9977
Broward Line: 305-781-7822
Telefax: 407-734-7511

Robert M. Arlen

For full biographical listings, see the Martindale-Hubbell Law Directory

*BRADENTON,** Manatee Co.

GRIMES, GOEBEL, GRIMES & HAWKINS, P.A. (AV)

The Professional Building, 1023 Manatee Avenue West, P.O. Box 1550, 34206
Telephone: 813-748-0151
Fax: 813-748-0158

William C. Grimes

John F. Jewell

Counsel for: First Commercial Bank of Manatee County; First Federal Savings & Loan Association of Florida; Schroeder-Manatee, Inc.
Approved Attorneys for: Chicago Title Insurance Co.; Attorneys' Title Insurance Fund; American Pioneer Title Insurance Co.

For Complete List of Firm Personnel, See General Section

For full biographical listings, see the Martindale-Hubbell Law Directory

*CLEARWATER,** Pinellas Co.

H. H. BASKIN, JR. P.A. (AV)

703 Court Street, 34616
Telephone: 813-441-4550
Fax: 813-461-2919

H. H. Baskin, Jr.

For full biographical listings, see the Martindale-Hubbell Law Directory

RICHARDS, GILKEY, FITE, SLAUGHTER, PRATESI & WARD, P.A. (AV)

Richards Building, 1253 Park Street, 34616
Telephone: 813-443-3281
Fax: 813-446-3741
Port Richey, Florida Office: 8410 U.S. Highway 19, Suite 104. 34668.
Telephone: 813-841-7833.
Fax: 813-847-6742.

John D. Fite — John E. Slaughter, Jr.
Cynthia I. Rice

OF COUNSEL

William W. Gilkey — William M. MacKenzie

Representative Clients: USR Realty Development Division of USX Corp.; Pall Corp; Orange Bank; Rutland's Florida Gulf Bank; First Union National Bank of Florida; Park Group Companies of America; Donald Roebling Trusts; Calvin P. Vary Trust; Morton F. Plant Hospital Trust; Madison Savings and Loan Assn.

For Complete List of Firm Personnel, See General Section

For full biographical listings, see the Martindale-Hubbell Law Directory

CHARLES F. ROBINSON (AV)

410 South Lincoln Avenue, 34616-5826
Telephone: 813-441-4516
Fax: 813-447-7578

ASSOCIATE

Linda R. Chamberlain

For full biographical listings, see the Martindale-Hubbell Law Directory

CORAL GABLES, Dade Co.

HENDRICKS & HENDRICKS (AV)

310 Alhambra Circle, 33134
Telephone: 305-445-3692

MEMBERS OF FIRM

R. A. Hendricks (1868-1963) — B. E. Hendricks (1904-1978)
Robert A. Hendricks

For full biographical listings, see the Martindale-Hubbell Law Directory

DAVIE, Broward Co.

WILLIAM A. SNYDER (AV)

7931 S.W. 45th Street, 33328
Telephone: Broward: 305-475-1139
Dade: 305-940-5397

For full biographical listings, see the Martindale-Hubbell Law Directory

DELRAY BEACH, Palm Beach Co.

DEVITT & THISTLE, P.A. (AV)

30 Southeast 4th Avenue, 33483
Telephone: 407-276-7436

Rhea Whitley (1903-1968) — Fred B. Devitt, Jr.
Calhoun Y. Byrd (1900-1985) — J. Jeffrey Thistle
Fred B. Devitt, III

Approved Attorneys for: Attorneys' Title Insurance Fund.
References: Sun Bank/South Florida, N.A.; Barnett Banks Trust Co., N.A.

For full biographical listings, see the Martindale-Hubbell Law Directory

MACMILLAN & STANLEY (AV)

MacMillan Building, 29 North East Fourth Avenue, 33483
Telephone: 407-276-6363; 276-5284

Carol MacMillan Stanley — Neil E. MacMillan (Retired)

Approved Attorneys for: Attorneys' Title Insurance Fund.
References: Barnett Banks Trust Company, N.A.; Sun Bank/South Florida, N.A.

For full biographical listings, see the Martindale-Hubbell Law Directory

H. CASSEDY SUMRALL, JR. PROFESSIONAL ASSOCIATION (AV)

54 Northeast Fourth Avenue, 33483
Telephone: 407-272-7040

H. Cassedy Sumrall, Jr.

Reference: Sun Bank/of Palm Beach County, Delray Beach, Florida.

For full biographical listings, see the Martindale-Hubbell Law Directory

DESTIN, Okaloosa Co.

J. JEROME MILLER (AV)

Suite 3, 415 Mountain Drive, 32541
Telephone: 904-837-3860
Fax: 904-837-6158

Lamar A. Conerly, Jr.

For full biographical listings, see the Martindale-Hubbell Law Directory

*FORT LAUDERDALE,** Broward Co.

FRIEDRICH & FRIEDRICH, P.A. (AV)

Sun Bank Building, Fifth Floor, 2626 East Oakland Park Boulevard, 33306
Telephone: 305-564-1245
Fax: 305-563-5079

J. Peter Friedrich — J. Peter Friedrich, Jr.

Approved Attorneys for: Northern Trust Bank of Florida; SunBank of S. Florida, NA.

For full biographical listings, see the Martindale-Hubbell Law Directory

Fort Lauderdale—Continued

THEODORE H. FULTON, JR. (AV)

321 Southeast 15th Avenue, 33303
Telephone: 305-467-2000
Telecopier: 305-467-2306

For full biographical listings, see the Martindale-Hubbell Law Directory

WILLIAM A. ZEIHER, P.A. (AV)

2780 East Oakland Park Boulevard, 33306
Telephone: 305-561-8205
FAX: 305-561-8208

William A. Zeiher

Representative Client: National Oil & Gas, Inc.
Approved Attorney for: Attorneys' Title Insurance Fund.

For full biographical listings, see the Martindale-Hubbell Law Directory

*FORT MYERS,** Lee Co.

AVERY, WHIGHAM & WINESETT, P.A. (AV)

Corner of First and Hendry Streets, 2248 First Street, P.O. Drawer 610, 33902-0610
Telephone: 813-334-7040
FAX: 813-334-6258

Richard W. Winesett
Sherra Winesett
Dennis L. Avery
James M. Costello

For full biographical listings, see the Martindale-Hubbell Law Directory

HENDERSON, FRANKLIN, STARNES & HOLT, PROFESSIONAL ASSOCIATION (AV)

1715 Monroe Street, P.O. Box 280, 33902-0280
Telephone: 813-334-4121
Telecopier: 813-332-4494

Ernest H. Hatch, Jr.

Representative Clients: Aetna Life & Casualty Group; CIGNA Group; CSX Transportation, Inc.; Fireman's Fund Insurance Cos.; Barnett Bank of Lee County, N.A.; Northern Trust Bank of Florida, N.A.; The Hartford Insurance Group; Travelers Group; United Telephone Company of Florida.

For Complete List of Firm Personnel, See General Section

For full biographical listings, see the Martindale-Hubbell Law Directory

*FORT PIERCE,** St. Lucie Co.

MELVILLE & FOWLER, P.A. (AV)

Laurel Professional Park, 2940 South 25th Street, 34981
Telephone: 407-464-7900
FAX: 407-464-8220

Harold G. Melville
Michael D. Fowler

David N. Sowerby
Richard M. Carnell, Jr.

OF COUNSEL

Charles R. P. Brown

For full biographical listings, see the Martindale-Hubbell Law Directory

*JACKSONVILLE,** Duval Co.

JEAN C. COKER, P.A. (AV)

Suite 160 Barnett Plaza, 6622 Southpoint Drive South, 32216
Telephone: 904-296-1100
Fax: 904-296-1200
Jacksonville Beach, Florida Office: 2320 South 3rd Street, 32250.
Telephone: 904-246-2009.

Jean C. Coker

LEGAL SUPPORT PERSONNEL

Diana M. Len
Lisa D. Ray (Estate Planning Paralegal)

References: Barnett Banks Trust Company, National Association; First Union National Bank of Florida.

For full biographical listings, see the Martindale-Hubbell Law Directory

JUPITER, Palm Beach Co.

JOSEPH C. KEMPE PROFESSIONAL ASSOCIATION (AV)

Attorneys and Counselors at Law
American Plaza, Suite 400, 1070 East Indiantown Road, 33477-5111
Telephone: 407-747-7300
FAX: 407-747-7722
Stuart, Florida Office: Royal Palm Financial Center II, Suite 200, 789 South Federal Highway.
Telephone: 407-223-0700.
Fax: 407-223-0707.
Vero Beach, Florida Office: Suite B, 664 Azalea Lane.
Telephone: 407-562-4022.
Fax: 407-234-1422.

Joseph C. Kempe

(See Next Column)

David Pratt
Lesley Hogan

OF COUNSEL

Ann L. Vano

For full biographical listings, see the Martindale-Hubbell Law Directory

*KISSIMMEE,** Osceola Co.

POHL & BROWN, P.A.

(See Winter Park)

LAKE WORTH, Palm Beach Co.

ALTMAN & GREER (AV)

219 North Dixie Highway, 33460
Telephone: 407-588-3311
Fax: 407-588-3315

MEMBERS OF FIRM

Zell H. Altman
Bruce G. Greer

ASSOCIATE

Thomas H. Dougherty

For full biographical listings, see the Martindale-Hubbell Law Directory

MAITLAND, Orange Co.

DITTMER, WOHLUST & WILKINS, P.A. (AV)

Suite 100, 230 Lookout Place, P.O. Box 941690, 32794-1690
Telephone: 407-539-0009
Fax: 407-539-1995

Terrance H. Dittmer
G. Charles Wohlust
Robert C. Wilkins, Jr.

For full biographical listings, see the Martindale-Hubbell Law Directory

MELBOURNE, Brevard Co.

KRASNY AND DETTMER (AV)

A Partnership of Professional Associations
780 South Apollo Boulevard, P.O. Box 428, 32902-0428
Telephone: 407-723-5646
Telecopier: 407-768-1147

Myron S. (Mike) Krasny (P.A.)
Dale A. Dettmer (P.A.)

Scott Krasny

Representative Client: Security National Bank.

For full biographical listings, see the Martindale-Hubbell Law Directory

*MIAMI,** Dade Co.

BREIER AND SEIF, P.A. (AV)

1320 South Dixie Highway (Coral Gables), 33146-2986
Telephone: 305-667-0046; 667-0065
Telecopier: 305-667-3071

Robert G. Breier
Evan D. Seif

For full biographical listings, see the Martindale-Hubbell Law Directory

MERSHON, SAWYER, JOHNSTON, DUNWODY & COLE (AV)

A Partnership including Professional Associations
Suite 4500 First Union Financial Center, 200 South Biscayne Boulevard, 33131-2387
Telephone: 305-358-5100
Cable Address: "Mercole"
Telex: 515705
Fax: 305-376-8654
Naples, Florida Office: Pelican Bay Corporate Centre, Suite 501, 5551 Ridgewood Drive.
Telephone: 813-598-1055.
Fax: 813-598-1868.
West Palm Beach, Florida Office: 777 South Flagler Drive, Suite 900.
Telephone: 407-659-5990.
Fax: 407-659-6313.
Key West, Florida Office: 3132 North Side Drive, Suite 102.
Telephone: 305-296-1774.
Fax: 305-296-1715
London, England Office: Blake Lodge, Bridge Lane, London SW11 3AD, England.
Telephone: 44-71-978-7748.
Fax: 44-71-350-0156.

MEMBERS OF FIRM

Robert D. W. Landon, II, (P.A.)
William M. Pearson (P.A.)
Ronald L. Fick (P.A.) (Resident, West Palm Beach Office)
John J. Grundhauser

(See Next Column)

MERSHON, SAWYER, JOHNSTON, DUNWODY & COLE, *Miami—Continued*

OF COUNSEL

Atwood Dunwody Robert A. White (P.A.)

ASSOCIATES

Mitchell E. Silverstein Jonna Stukel Brown

Representative Clients: Arvida/JMB Partners; Bankers Trust Co.; Biscayne Kennel Club, Inc.; The Chase Manhattan Bank, N.A.; Lennar Corp.; Reynolds Metals Co.; United States Sugar Corp.; University of Miami.

For Complete List of Firm Personnel, See General Section

For full biographical listings, see the Martindale-Hubbell Law Directory

SPARBER, KOSNITZKY, TRUXTON, DE LA GUARDIA SPRATT & BROOKS, P.A. (AV)

1401 Brickell Avenue Suite 700, 33131
Telephone: Dade: 305-379-7200; Broward: 305-760-9133
Fax: 305-379-0800

Byron L. Sparber

Jorge A. Gonzalez Thomas O. Wells
Deborah R. Mayo

For Complete List of Firm Personnel, See General Section

For full biographical listings, see the Martindale-Hubbell Law Directory

TESCHER CHAVES HOCHMAN RUBIN & MULLER, P.A. (AV)

One Datran Center-Penthouse I, 9100 South Dadeland Boulevard, 33156
Telephone: 305-670-0444
Broward: 800-782-6392
Fax: 305-670-0734
Ft. Lauderdale, Florida Office: Trade Centre South. 100 W. Cypress Creek Road, Suite 900. 33309.
Telephone: Miami: 305-938-4555; 800-938-938-4555.
Fax: 305-935-9555.

Robert A. Chaves Charles E. Muller, II
Deborah Plaks Hochman Charles D. Rubin
Donald R. Tescher

OF COUNSEL

Dale A. Heckerling

For full biographical listings, see the Martindale-Hubbell Law Directory

*NAPLES,** Collier Co.

GOODMAN BREEN LILE & GOLDMAN (AV)

3033 Riviera Drive, Suite 106, 33940
Telephone: 813-649-7778
Fax: 813-649-7780
Marco Island, Florida Office: 950 North Collier Boulevard.
Telephone: 813-642-4441.
Bonita Springs, Florida Office: Bonita Bay Executive Center, Suite 211, 3451 Bonita Bay Boulevard, 33923.
Telephone: 912-947-8244.

Dorothy M. Breen Kenneth D. Goodman
Robert W. Goldman Laird A. Lile

For full biographical listings, see the Martindale-Hubbell Law Directory

MYERS KRAUSE & STEVENS, CHARTERED (AV)

5811 Pelican Bay Boulevard, Suite 600, 33963
Telephone: 813-598-1221
Fax: 813-598-3499

William H. Myers Andrew J. Krause
William K. Stevens

Richard S. Franklin Robert J. Stommel
David P. Browne Jeffrey J. Beihoff
Johnine R. Hays

References: Barnett Banks Trust Co., N.A.; NBD Trust Company of Florida N.A.; Northern Trust Bank of Florida, N.A.; Sun Bank Southwest Florida

For full biographical listings, see the Martindale-Hubbell Law Directory

PARKS, BENNETT & STEWART (AV)

Parks Building, 865 Fifth Avenue South, 33940
Telephone: 941-262-0400
Fax: 941-261-8646

Benjamin G. Parks Richard K. Bennett
Deborah A. Stewart

For full biographical listings, see the Martindale-Hubbell Law Directory

DENNIS R. WHITE, P.A. (AV)

Suite 300, Fifth Third Bank Building, 4099 Tamiami Trail North, 33940-3598
Telephone: 813-261-4700
Facsimile: 813-261-4721; Internet: drw @ whitelaw.com

Dennis R. White

For full biographical listings, see the Martindale-Hubbell Law Directory

NORTH MIAMI BEACH, Dade Co.

BUCHANAN INGERSOLL, PROFESSIONAL CORPORATION (AV)

One Turnberry Place, 19495 Biscayne Boulevard, 33180
Telephone: 305-933-5600
Telecopier: 305-933-2350
Pittsburgh, Pennsylvania Office: 5800 USX Tower, 600 Grant Street.
Telephone: 412-562-8800.
Philadelphia, Pennsylvania Office: Two Logan Square, Twelfth Floor, 18th & Arch Streets.
Telephone: 215-665-8700.
Harrisburg, Pennsylvania Office: Vartan Parc, 30 North Third Street.
Telephone: 717-237-4800.
Tampa, Florida Office: Suite 1030, 101 East Kennedy Boulevard.
Telephone: 813-222-8180.
Princeton, New Jersey Office: Buchanan Ingersoll, A Partnership, College Centre, 500 College Road East.
Telephone: 609-452-2666.
Lexington, Kentucky Office: Suite 600, PNC Bank Plaza, 200 West Vine Street.
Telephone: 606-225-5333.

Barry A. Nelson

For Complete List of Firm Personnel, See General Section

For full biographical listings, see the Martindale-Hubbell Law Directory

WILLIAM J. SEGAL, P.A. (AV)

20801 Biscayne Boulevard, Suite 304, 33180
Telephone: 305-682-1110
Telefax: 305-682-1800

William J. Segal

For full biographical listings, see the Martindale-Hubbell Law Directory

ORANGE PARK, Clay Co.

HEAD, SMITH, METCALF, AGUILAR, MOSS & SIERON, P.A. (AV)

1329A Kingsley Avenue, P.O. Box 855, 32073
Telephone: 904-264-6000
Fax: 904-264-9223

Robert J. Head, Jr. Robert Aguilar
Larry Smith John B. Moss
Frank B. Metcalf Mark A. Sieron

Holly Fulton Perritt

For full biographical listings, see the Martindale-Hubbell Law Directory

*ORLANDO,** Orange Co.

DAVID C. BRENNAN (AV)

201 East Pine Street Suite 1402, P.O. Box 2706, 32802-2706
Telephone: 407-422-8630
Fax: 407-422-8306

For full biographical listings, see the Martindale-Hubbell Law Directory

POHL & BROWN, P.A.

(See Winter Park)

CRAIG B. WARD, P.A. (AV)

Suite 501, 105 East Robinson Street, 32801
Telephone: 407-839-0222
Fax: 407-839-0577

Craig B. Ward

OF COUNSEL

Charles D. Miner

For full biographical listings, see the Martindale-Hubbell Law Directory

Orlando—Continued

WINDERWEEDLE, HAINES, WARD & WOODMAN, P.A. (AV)

Barnett Bank Center, 390 North Orange Avenue, P.O. Box 1391, 32802-1391
Telephone: 407-423-4246
Telecopier: 407-423-7014
Winter Park, Florida Office: Barnett Bank Building 250 Park Avenue, South, P.O. Box 880.
Telephone: 407-644-6312.
Telecopier: 407-645-3728.

Harold A. Ward, III — William A. Walker II

References: Barnett Bank of Central Florida, N.A., Orlando, Florida; Security National Bank; United American Bank; Seminole National Bank; Georgia Pacific Corp.; USX Corp.

For Complete List of Firm Personnel, See General Section

For full biographical listings, see the Martindale-Hubbell Law Directory

PALM BEACH, Palm Beach Co.

BAUGHER, METTLER & SHELTON (AV)

340 Royal Poinciana Plaza, P.O. Box 109, 33480
Telephone: 407-833-9631
Fax: 407-655-2835

MEMBERS OF FIRM

Thomas M. Mettler — John W. Shelton

ASSOCIATES

Francis X. J. Lynch — Pamela A. Markley

Reference: First National Bank in Palm Beach.

For full biographical listings, see the Martindale-Hubbell Law Directory

LOUIS LEIBOVIT (AV)

350 Royal Palm Way, 33480
Telephone: 407-655-6588

Approved Attorney for: Attorneys' Title Insurance Fund.
Reference: Barnett Bank (Palm Beach Branch Office).

For full biographical listings, see the Martindale-Hubbell Law Directory

MINTMIRE & ASSOCIATES (AV)

265 Sunrise Avenue, Suite 204, 33480
Telephone: 407-832-5696
Fax: 407-659-5371

Donald F. Mintmire

ASSOCIATES

Jeffrey A. Shaffer — Timothy D. Friedman

OF COUNSEL

Paul Safran, Jr.

For full biographical listings, see the Martindale-Hubbell Law Directory

MURPHY, REID & PILOTTE, P.A. (AV)

340 Royal Palm Way, 33480
Telephone: 407-655-4060
Facsimile: 407-832-5436
Vero Beach, Florida Office: Plantation Plaza, 6606-20th Street, P.O. Drawer M.
Telephone: 407-567-6480.
Facsimile: 407-562-0220.

Eugene W. Murphy, Jr. — Frank T. Pilotte

For Complete List of Firm Personnel, See General Section

For full biographical listings, see the Martindale-Hubbell Law Directory

*SARASOTA,** Sarasota Co.

ABEL, BAND, RUSSELL, COLLIER, PITCHFORD & GORDON, CHARTERED (AV)

Barnett Bank Center, 240 South Pineapple Avenue, P.O. Box 49948, 34230-6948
Telephone: 813-366-6660
FAX: 813-366-3999
Fort Myers, Florida Office: The Tidewater Building, 1375 Jackson Street, Suite 201, 33901.
Telephone: 813-337-0062.
FAX: 813-337-0406.
Venice, Florida Office: Suite 199, 333 South Tamiami Trail, 34285.
Telephone: 813-485-8200.
Fax: 813-488-9436.

(See Next Column)

David S. Band — Anthony J. Abate
Jeffrey S. Russell — Steven J. Chase
Ronald L. Collier — Kathryn Angell Carr
Malcolm J. Pitchford — Michael S. Taaffe
Cheryl Lasris Gordon — Mark W. McFall
Jan Walters Pitchford

OF COUNSEL

Harvey J. Abel — Johnson S. Savary

Saralyn Abel — Jane M. Kennedy
Douglas M. Bales — Christine Edwards Lamia
Gregory S. Band — Bradley D. Magee
John A. Garner — George H. Mazzarantani
Mark D. Hildreth — Philip C. Zimmerman

References: Barnett Bank of Southwest Florida; Sun Bank/Gulf Coast.

For full biographical listings, see the Martindale-Hubbell Law Directory

BURKET, SMITH, BOWMAN & GEORGE (AV)

22 South Tuttle Avenue-Suite 3, 34237
Telephone: 813-366-5510
Fax: 813-951-0839

MEMBERS OF FIRM

John F. Burket (1875-1947) — David G. Bowman
John F. Burket, Jr. (1915-1984) — Eugene O. George

OF COUNSEL

V. Morris Smith

General Counsel for: Bay Village of Sarasota, Inc. (Life Care Facility); Southern Grocery Co.; Florida Ladder Co.; Siesta Key Utilities Authority, Inc. (S.K.U.A.); Ludwig-Walpole Co. (General Insurance).

For full biographical listings, see the Martindale-Hubbell Law Directory

ROBERT A. KIMBROUGH (AV)

1530 Cross Street, 34236-7015
Telephone: 813-951-1234
FAX: 813-952-1530

Approved Attorney for: Attorneys Title Insurance Fund.
References: NationsBank; Northern Trust Bank of Florida, N.A.; First Union National Bank of Florida; Barnett Bank.

For full biographical listings, see the Martindale-Hubbell Law Directory

LYONS & BEAUDRY, P.A. (AV)

Suite 1111, Ellis Building, 1605 Main Street, 34236
Telephone: 813-366-3282
Fax: 813-954-1484

Robert W. Beaudry (1929-1991) — John J. Lyons

Carol Whitcher Wood — R. Craig Harrison

Reference: Nations Bank.

For full biographical listings, see the Martindale-Hubbell Law Directory

NAMACK, CLARK & KEENEY (AV)

A Partnership of Professional Associations
1800 Second Street, Suite 920 and 758, 34236
Telephone: 813-365-5996 and 366-4141
Fax: 813-364-9805 and 954-4762

William H. Namack, III — James C. Clark
James D. Keeney

Lisa Kane DeVitto

For full biographical listings, see the Martindale-Hubbell Law Directory

DAVID S. WATSON CHARTERED (AV)

1605 Main Street, Suite 612, 34236
Telephone: 813-366-8891
FAX: 813-366-1806

David S. Watson

OF COUNSEL

Richard W. Cooney

For full biographical listings, see the Martindale-Hubbell Law Directory

WILLIAMS, PARKER, HARRISON, DIETZ & GETZEN, PROFESSIONAL ASSOCIATION (AV)

1550 Ringling Boulevard, 34230-3258
Telephone: 813-366-4800
Telecopier: 813-366-5109
Mailing Address: P.O. Box 3258, Sarasota, Florida, 34230-3258

(See Next Column)

WILLIAMS, PARKER, HARRISON, DIETZ & GETZEN PROFESSIONAL ASSOCIATION, *Sarasota—Continued*

William T. Harrison, Jr.
George A. Dietz
Monte K. Marshall
James L. Ritchey
Hugh McPheeters, Jr.
William G. Lambrecht
John T. Berteau
John V. Cannon, III
Charles D. Bailey, Jr.
J. Michael Hartenstine
Michele Boardman Grimes
James L. Turner
William M. Seider
Elizabeth C. Marshall
Robert W. Benjamin
Frank Strelec
David A. Wallace
Terri Jayne Salt
Jeffrey A. Grebe
John Leslie Moore
Mark A. Schwartz
Linda R. Getzen

OF COUNSEL

William E. Getzen
Elvin W. Phillips

Counsel for: Sarasota-Manatee Airport Authority; Sarasota County Public Hospital Board; William G. & Marie Selby Foundation; Taylor Woodrow Homes Ltd.; The School Board of Sarasota County.
Local Counsel for: NationsBank of Florida; Arvida/JMB Partners.

For Complete List of Firm Personnel, See General Section

For full biographical listings, see the Martindale-Hubbell Law Directory

WILSON, JOHNSON & JAFFER, P.A. (AV)

27 South Orange Avenue, P.O. Box 1298, 34230-1298
Telephone: 813-955-5800
FAX: 813-955-7353

Clyde H. Wilson (1908-1994)
Robert M. Johnson
Clyde H. Wilson, Jr.
John S. Jaffer

James M. Kunick

For full biographical listings, see the Martindale-Hubbell Law Directory

*STUART,** Martin Co.

BRODIE & PAWLUC (AV)

Royal Palm Financial Center Shawmut National Building, 819 South Federal Highway, Suite 106, P.O. Box 2690, 34995
Telephone: 407-221-0110
Facsimile: 407-221-0113

Lawrence P. Brodie
Sonia M. Pawluc

For full biographical listings, see the Martindale-Hubbell Law Directory

JOSEPH C. KEMPE PROFESSIONAL ASSOCIATION (AV)

Attorneys and Counselors at Law
Royal Palm Financial Center II, Suite 200, 789 South Federal Highway, 34994
Telephone: 407-223-0700
FAX: 407-223-0707
Jupiter, Florida Office: American Plaza, Suite 400, 1070 East Indiantown Road. Telephone 407-747-7300.
Fax: 407-747-7722.
Vero Beach, Florida Office: 664 Azalea Lane, Suite B.
Telephone: 407-562-4022.
Fax: 407-234-1422.

Joseph C. Kempe

For full biographical listings, see the Martindale-Hubbell Law Directory

OUGHTERSON, OUGHTERSON, PREWITT & SUNDHEIM, P.A. (AV)

310 Southwest Ocean Boulevard, 34994-2007
Telephone: 407-287-0660
FAX: 407-287-0422

T. T. Oughterson (1904-1983)
Wm. A. Oughterson
John E. Prewitt
Frederick G. Sundheim, Jr.

Counsel for: The Hobe Sound Co.; Martin County Taxpayers Assn.; The Jupiter Island Club.
Local Counsel for: Chase Federal Bank.
Approved Attorneys for: Attorneys' Title Insurance Fund; Chicago Title Insurance Co.; Commonwealth Land Title Insurance Co.

For full biographical listings, see the Martindale-Hubbell Law Directory

*TALLAHASSEE,** Leon Co.

MARK FREUND, P.A. (AV)

227 North Bronough Street, Suite 1101, P.O. Box 10171, 32302
Telephone: 904-681-0066
FAX: 904-681-3798

Mark Freund

(See Next Column)

Laura Beth Faragasso

Representative Client: Abbey Color, Inc.; Cedar Concepts Corp.; Florida Commerce Federal Credit Union; Pride Resorts, Ltd.; Pride Resorts - Panama City Beach, Ltd.; Sport-Craft, Inc.; Tallahassee State Bank Corp.; Celwal Concepts Corp.
Reference: Tallahassee State Bank.

For full biographical listings, see the Martindale-Hubbell Law Directory

*TAMPA,** Hillsborough Co.

LYNWOOD F. ARNOLD, JR. (AV)

2011 West Cleveland Street Suite F, P.O. Box 3357, 33601-3357
Telephone: 813-251-8111
Facsimile: 813-251-9225

For full biographical listings, see the Martindale-Hubbell Law Directory

FUENTES AND KREISCHER (AV)

1407 West Busch Boulevard, 33612
Telephone: 813-933-6647
Fax: 813-932-8588

MEMBERS OF FIRM

Lawrence E. Fuentes
Albert C. Kreischer, Jr.

OF COUNSEL

W. Andrew Hamilton

Reference: Northside Bank of Tampa.

For full biographical listings, see the Martindale-Hubbell Law Directory

GOLD, RESNICK & SEGALL, P.A. (AV)

704 West Bay Street, 33606
Telephone: 813-254-2071
FAX: (813) 251-0616

Aaron J. Gold
Eddy R. Resnick
Larry M. Segall

Nancy J. Cass

Reference: Barnett Bank of Tampa.

For full biographical listings, see the Martindale-Hubbell Law Directory

KALISH & WARD, PROFESSIONAL ASSOCIATION (AV)

4100 Barnett Plaza, 101 East Kennedy Boulevard, P.O. Box 71, 33601-0071
Telephone: 813-222-8700
Facsimile: 813-222-8701

William Kalish
Alton C. Ward
Richard A. Schlosser
Roger J. Rovell
Michael A. Bedke
William T. Harrison, III
Thomas P. McNamara
Robert Reid Haney
Charles H. Carver
Kelley A. Bosecker

For full biographical listings, see the Martindale-Hubbell Law Directory

LANGFORD, HILL & TRYBUS, P.A. (AV)

Suite 800, Bayshore Place, 601 Bayshore Boulevard, 33606
Telephone: 813-251-5533
Telecopier: 813-251-1900
Wats: 1-800-277-2005

E. C. Langford
Edward A. Hill
Ronald H. Trybus
Ronald G. Hock
Catherine M. Catlin
Debra M. Kubicsek
William B. Smith

Fredrique B. Boire
Muriel Desloovere
Kevin H. O'Neill
Vicki L. Page
Frederick T. Reeves
Barbara A. Sinsley
Stephens B. Woodrough (Not admitted in FL)
Anthony G. Woodward

Representative Clients: Affiliated of Florida, Inc.; American Federation Insurance Co.; Armor Insurance; Bank of Tampa; Central Bank of Tampa; Cintas Corp.; Container Corporation of America; CU Financial Services; Farm Stores, Inc.; First Union Home Equity Bank.

For full biographical listings, see the Martindale-Hubbell Law Directory

*VERO BEACH,** Indian River Co.

JOSEPH C. KEMPE PROFESSIONAL ASSOCIATION (AV)

Attorneys and Counselors at Law
664 Azalea Lane, Suite B, 32963
Telephone: 407-562-4022
Fax: 407-234-1442
Jupiter, Florida Office: 1070 E. Indiantown Rd.
Telephone: 407-747-7300.
Fax: 407-747-7722.
Stuart, Florida Office: 789 S. Federal Highway, Suite 200.
Telephone: 407-223-0700.
Fax: 407-223-0707.

Joseph C. Kempe David Pratt

For full biographical listings, see the Martindale-Hubbell Law Directory

E. STEVEN LAUER, P.A. (AV)

612 Beachland Boulevard, 32963
Telephone: 407-234-4200
FAX: 407-234-4249

E. Steven Lauer

OF COUNSEL

Hiram Manning

For full biographical listings, see the Martindale-Hubbell Law Directory

JOHN H. SUTHERLAND, P.A. (AV)

Schlitt Professional Plaza, 321-21st Street, 32960
Telephone: 407-567-5191
FAX: 407-567-9401

John H. Sutherland

Alexander Glenn Sutherland

General Counsel for: Greene Citrus Management, Inc.; Orange Avenue Citrus Growers Association, Inc.

For full biographical listings, see the Martindale-Hubbell Law Directory

*WEST PALM BEACH,** Palm Beach Co.

AUGUST, COMITER, KULUNAS & SCHEPPS, P.A. (AV)

250 Australian Avenue South Suite 1100, 33401
Telephone: 407-835-9600
Fax: 407-835-9602
Washington, D.C. Office: 501 School Street, Suite 700.
Telephone: 202-646-5160.

Jerald David August
Richard B. Comiter
Joseph J. Kulunas
Mitchell D. Schepps

For full biographical listings, see the Martindale-Hubbell Law Directory

REID MOORE, JR. (AV)

The Midway Law Building, 836 Belvedere Road, 33405
Telephone: 407-655-0400
FAX: 407-655-6695

For full biographical listings, see the Martindale-Hubbell Law Directory

PRESSLY & PRESSLY, P.A. (AV)

Esperante, Suite 910, 222 Lakeview Avenue, 33401-6112
Telephone: 407-659-4040
FAX: 407-655-6006

James G. Pressly, Jr. David S. Pressly
Trent S. Kiziah

For full biographical listings, see the Martindale-Hubbell Law Directory

ELLIOT S. SHAW, P.A. (AV)

Centurion Plaza, 1601 Forum Place, Suite 1212, 33401
Telephone: 407-687-9000
FAX: 407-687-5339

Elliot S. Shaw

Peter S. Roumbos

For full biographical listings, see the Martindale-Hubbell Law Directory

JAMES E. WEBER, P.A. (AV)

Suite 502 The Flagler Center, 501 South Flagler Drive, 33401
Telephone: 407-832-2266
Fax: 407-833-3816

James E. Weber

For full biographical listings, see the Martindale-Hubbell Law Directory

WINTER PARK, Orange Co.

FREDERICK W. PEIRSOL (AV)

280 West Canton Avenue, Suite 305, 32789
Telephone: 407-647-6363
Fax: 407-647-6378

LEGAL SUPPORT PERSONNEL

Susan Koser (Legal Assistant)

Reference: Trust Dept., Sun Bank, N.A., Winter Park & Orlando, Florida.

POHL & BROWN, P.A. (AV)

280 West Canton Avenue, Suite 410, P.O. Box 3208, 32789
Telephone: 407-647-7645; 407-647-POHL
Telefax: 407-647-2314

Frank L. Pohl
Usher L. Brown
Houston E. Short
Dwight I. Cool
William W. Pouzar
Mary B. Van Leuven

OF COUNSEL

Frederick W. Peirsol

Representative Clients: Orange County Comptroller; Osceola County; School Board of Osceola County, Florida; Osceola Tourist Development Council; NationsBank of Florida, N.A.; SunBank, N.A.; The Bank of Winter Park; Bekins Moving and Storage Co., Inc.; Champion Boats, Inc.; KeyCom Telephone Systems, Inc.

For full biographical listings, see the Martindale-Hubbell Law Directory

WINDERWEEDLE, HAINES, WARD & WOODMAN, P.A. (AV)

Barnett Bank Building, 250 Park Avenue, South, P.O. Box 880, 32790-0880
Telephone: 407-644-6312
Telecopier: 407-645-3728
Orlando, Florida Office: Barnett Bank Center, 390 North Orange Avenue, P.O. Box 1391.
Telephone: 407-423-4246.
Telecopier: 407-423-7014.

Harold A. Ward, III
John D. Haines
William A. Walker II
C. Brent McCaghren
Randolph J. Rush
W. Graham White

References: Barnett Bank of Central Florida, N.A., Orlando, Florida; Security National Bank; United American Bank; Seminole National Bank; Georgia Pacific Corp.; USX Corp.

For Complete List of Firm Personnel, See General Section

For full biographical listings, see the Martindale-Hubbell Law Directory

GEORGIA

*ATLANTA,** Fulton Co.

FRANCIS M. BIRD, JR. (AV)

50 Hurt Plaza, Suite 730, 30303
Telephone: 404-525-0885
Fax: 404-523-2806

OF COUNSEL

Pamela L. Tremayne

For full biographical listings, see the Martindale-Hubbell Law Directory

BIVENS, HOFFMAN & FOWLER (AV)

A Partnership of Professional Corporations
5040 Roswell Road, N.E., 30342
Telephone: 404-256-6464
FAX: 404-256-1422

MEMBERS OF FIRM

Clifford G. Hoffman (P.C.) Michael C. Fowler (P.C.)

For full biographical listings, see the Martindale-Hubbell Law Directory

CHAMBERS, MABRY, McCLELLAND & BROOKS (AV)

Tenth Floor, 2200 Century Parkway, N.E., 30345
Telephone: 404-325-4800
FAX: 404-325-0596
Lawrenceville, Georgia Office: Suite 377, 175 Gwinnett Drive.
Telephone: 404-339-7660.
FAX: 404-339-7060.

MEMBERS OF FIRM

E. Speer Mabry, III
Lawrence J. Hogan (Resident at Lawrenceville Office)
Edwin L. Hamilton

(See Next Column)

CHAMBERS, MABRY, MCCLELLAND & BROOKS, *Atlanta—Continued*

ASSOCIATE

R. Michael Malcom

Representative Clients: Allstate Insurance Co.; The Security Mutual Insurance Company of New York; National Automobile Insurance Co.

For full biographical listings, see the Martindale-Hubbell Law Directory

FRANKEL, HARDWICK, TANENBAUM & FINK, P.C. (AV)

359 East Paces Ferry Road, N.E., 30305
Telephone: 404-266-2930
Fax: 404-231-3362

Neal J. Fink

Stephen E. Parker

For Complete List of Firm Personnel, See General Section

For full biographical listings, see the Martindale-Hubbell Law Directory

LONG ALDRIDGE & NORMAN (AV)

A Partnership including Professional Corporations
One Peachtree Center, Suite 5300, 303 Peachtree Street, 30308
Telephone: 404-527-4000
Telecopier: 404-527-4198
Washington, D.C. Office: Suite 950, 1615 L Street, 20036.
Telephone: 202-223-7033.
Telecopier: 202-223-7013.

MEMBERS OF FIRM

W. Stell Huie | Ann Distler Salo

ASSOCIATE

Melissa P. Walker

For Complete List of Firm Personnel, See General Section

For full biographical listings, see the Martindale-Hubbell Law Directory

MCLAIN & MERRITT, P.C. (AV)

3340 Peachtree Road, Suite 1250, 30326-1075
Telephone: 404-266-9171
Telecopier: 404-262-7531

James P. McLain | Julie Childs

Approved Attorneys for: Lawyers Title Insurance Corporation.

For full biographical listings, see the Martindale-Hubbell Law Directory

SUTHERLAND, ASBILL & BRENNAN (AV)

999 Peachtree Street, N.E., 30309-3996
Telephone: 404-853-8000
Facsimile: 404-853-8806
Washington, D.C. Office: 1275 Pennsylvania Avenue, N.W., 20004-2404.
Telephone: 202-383-0100.
New York, N.Y. Office: 1270 Avenue of the Americas, 10020-1700.
Telephone: 212-332-3000.
Austin, Texas Office: 111 Congress Avenue, 23rd Floor, 78701-4079.
Telephone: 512-469-3350.

Michael J. Egan | Charles D. Hurt, Jr.
Herbert R. Elsas | Larry J. White

Representative Clients: Trust Company Bank of Georgia; C & S/Sovran Trust Company (Georgia), N.A.; Wachovia Bank of Georgia, N.A.; First Union National Bank of Georgia.

For Complete List of Firm Personnel, See General Section

For full biographical listings, see the Martindale-Hubbell Law Directory

*AUGUSTA,** Richmond Co.

WARLICK, TRITT & STEBBINS (AV)

15th Floor, First Union Bank Building, 30901
Telephone: 706-722-7543
Fax: 706-722-1822
Columbia County Office: 119 Davis Road, Martinez, Georgia 30907.
Telephone: 706-860-7595.
Fax: 705-860-7597.

MEMBERS OF FIRM

William Byrd Warlick | E. L. Clark Speese
Roy D. Tritt (Resident, Martinez Office) | Michael W. Terry
Charles C. Stebbins, III | D. Scott Broyles
 | Ross S. Snellings

C. Gregory Bryan

OF COUNSEL

Richard E. Miley

For full biographical listings, see the Martindale-Hubbell Law Directory

*COLUMBUS,** Muscogee Co.

BRINKLEY AND BRINKLEY (AV)

Suite 901 Corporate Center, 233 12th Street, P.O. Box 2016, 31902-2016
Telephone: 706-576-5322
FAX: 706-324-3766

MEMBERS OF FIRM

Jack Thomas Brinkley | Jack T. Brinkley, Jr.

Reference: Columbus Bank & Trust Co.

For full biographical listings, see the Martindale-Hubbell Law Directory

DAVIDSON, CALHOUN & MILLER, P.C. (AV)

The Joseph House, 828 Broadway, P.O. Box 2828, 31902-2828
Telephone: 706-327-2552
Telecopier: 706-323-5838

J. Quentin Davidson, Jr. | Charles W. Miller

David A. Buehler

For Complete List of Firm Personnel, See General Section

For full biographical listings, see the Martindale-Hubbell Law Directory

HATCHER, STUBBS, LAND, HOLLIS & ROTHSCHILD (AV)

Suite 500 The Corporate Center, 233 12th Street, P.O. Box 2707, 31902-2707
Telephone: 706-324-0201
Telecopier: 706-322-7747

MEMBERS OF FIRM

Alan F. Rothschild | George W. Mize, Jr.
Charles T. Staples | John M. Tanzine, III

Alan F. Rothschild, Jr.

ASSOCIATE

Mote W. Andrews III

General Counsel for: Trust Company Bank of Columbus, N.A.; TOM'S Foods Inc.; Burnham Service Corp.; Kinnett Dairies, Inc.; St. Francis Hospital, Inc.; Bill Heard Enterprises, Inc.
Local Counsel for: First Union National Bank of Georgia; Equitable Life Assurance Society of the United States; Prudential Insurance Company of America; Metropolitan Life Insurance Co.

For Complete List of Firm Personnel, See General Section

For full biographical listings, see the Martindale-Hubbell Law Directory

*GRIFFIN,** Spalding Co.

JOHN M. COGBURN, JR. (AV)

115 North Sixth Street, P.O. Box 907, 30224
Telephone: 404-228-2148
Telecopier: 404-228-5018
McDonough, Georgia Office: Suite 300E, First Community Bank Building, 12 North Cedar Street.
Telephone: 404-954-9004.
Fax: 404-228-5018.

ASSOCIATE

R. Michelle Denton

Representative Clients: Griffin-Spalding County Hospital Authority; Allstar Knitwear Co., Inc. (Textiles); Atlanta Tees, Inc. (Sportswear Distribution); Industrial Refrigeration Enterprises, Inc. (Refrigeration Engineers and Contractors); Spauchus Associates, Inc. (Chemical Engineering Consultants).

For full biographical listings, see the Martindale-Hubbell Law Directory

*MARIETTA,** Cobb Co.

AWTREY AND PARKER, P.C. (AV)

211 Roswell Street, P.O. Box 997, 30061
Telephone: 404-424-8000
Fax: 404-424-1594

L. M. Awtrey, Jr. (1915-1986) | Michael L. Marsh
George L. Dozier, Jr. | Barbara H. Martin
Harvey D. Harkness | A. Sidney Parker
Mike Harrison | Toby B. Prodgers
Dana L. Jackel | J. Lynn Rainey
Donald A. Mangerie (1924-1988) | Annette M. Risse (Mrs.)

Robert B. Silliman

Gregg A. Landau | Lisa G. Gunn

Alan H. Sheldon

OF COUNSEL

Allan J. Hall | J. Ben Moore

S. Alan Schlact

General Counsel for: Kennesaw Finance Co.; Cobb Electric Membership Corporation; Development Authority of Cobb County.
Local Counsel for: Coats & Clark; Bell South Mobility; Lockheed-Georgia Corp.; Post Properties, Inc.; CSX Transportation, Inc.

(See Next Column)

AWTREY AND PARKER P.C.—*Continued*

For full biographical listings, see the Martindale-Hubbell Law Directory

W. R. ROBERTSON, III (AV)

244 Roswell Street, Suite 600, 30060-2000
Telephone: 404-422-0200
Fax: 404-424-1322

For full biographical listings, see the Martindale-Hubbell Law Directory

*SAVANNAH,** Chatham Co.

SILVERS AND SIMPSON, PROFESSIONAL CORPORATION (AV)

Suite 102, AmeriBank Plaza, 7393 Hodgson Memorial Drive, 31406
Telephone: 912-925-7200
Facsimile: 912-925-0100

Mark M. Silvers, Jr.
K. Russell Simpson

Katherine Lynn Levy

For full biographical listings, see the Martindale-Hubbell Law Directory

HAWAII

*HONOLULU,** Honolulu Co.

CADES SCHUTTE FLEMING & WRIGHT (AV)

Formerly Smith, Wild, Beebe & Cades
1000 Bishop Street, P.O. Box 939, 96808
Telephone: 808-521-9200
Telex: 7238589
Telecopier: 808-531-8738
Affiliated Law Firm: Udom-Prok Associates Law Offices, 105/36 Tharinee Mansion, Borom Raj Chananee Road Bangkoknoi, Bangkok, Thailand, 10700.
Telephone: 011 660 435-4146.
Kailua-Kona, Hawaii Office: Hualalai Center, Suite B-303, 75-170 Hualalai Road.
Telephone: 808-329-5811.
Telecopier: 808-326-1175.

MEMBERS OF FIRM

Robert B. Bunn
David C. Larsen
Rhonda L. Griswold

ASSOCIATE

Eric S.T. Young

Counsel for: Amfac, Inc.; First Hawaiian Bank; Bishop Trust Co., Ltd.; Alexander & Baldwin, Inc.; Theo. H. Davies & Co., Ltd.; C. Brewer & Company, Ltd.; Bank of America, FSB.

For Complete List of Firm Personnel, See General Section

For full biographical listings, see the Martindale-Hubbell Law Directory

FOLEY MAEHARA NIP & CHANG (AV)

2700 Grosvenor Center, 737 Bishop Street, 96813
Telephone: 808-526-3011
Telecopier: 808-523-1171, 808-526-0121, 808-533-4814

MEMBERS OF FIRM

Thomas M. Foley
Eric T. Maehara
Renton L. K. Nip
Wesley Y. S. Chang
Carl Tom
Edward R. Brooks
Arlene S. Kishi
Susan M. Ichinose
Robert F. Miller
Christian P. Porter

ASSOCIATES

Paula W. Chong
Lenore H. Lee
Leanne A. N. Nikaido
Jordan D. Wagner
Donna H. Yamamoto
Mark J. Bernardin
Jenny K. T. Wakayama

OF COUNSEL

Elizabeth A. Ivey

References: First Hawaiian Bank; Bank of Honolulu; Bank of Hawaii.

For full biographical listings, see the Martindale-Hubbell Law Directory

GERSON GREKIN WYNHOFF & THIELEN ATTORNEYS AT LAW, A LAW CORPORATION (AV)

Suite 780 Pacific Tower, 1001 Bishop Street, 96813
Telephone: 808-524-4800
Telecopier: 808-537-1420

(*See Next Column*)

Kathleen M. Douglas
Mervyn S. Gerson
Nancy Nissen Grekin
Matthew F. Kadish
Jody Lynn Kea
Cynthia Thielen
William J. Wynhoff

For full biographical listings, see the Martindale-Hubbell Law Directory

ELLIOT H. LODEN ATTORNEY AT LAW, A LAW CORPORATION (AV)

2990 Grosvenor Center, 737 Bishop Street, 96813
Telephone: 808-524-8099
FAX: 808-526-0968
Wailuku, Maui, Hawaii Office: 2158 Main Street, Suite 105.
Telephone: 808-242-9292.

Elliot H. Loden

References: First Hawaiian Bank.

For full biographical listings, see the Martindale-Hubbell Law Directory

IDAHO

*BOISE,** Ada Co.

HALL, FARLEY, OBERRECHT & BLANTON (AV)

Key Financial Center, 702 West Idaho Street, Suite 700, P.O. Box 1271, 83701-1271
Telephone: 208-336-0404
Facsimile: 208-336-5193

Richard E. Hall
Donald J. Farley
Phillip S. Oberrecht
Raymond D. Powers
Candy Wagahoff Dale
Robert B. Luce
J. Kevin West
Bart W. Harwood

J. Charles Blanton
John J. Burke
Steven J. Hippler
Thorpe P. Orton
Ronald S. Best (Not admitted in ID)

References: Boise State University; Farm Bureau Mutual Insurance Company of Idaho; Medical Insurance Exchange of California; The St. Paul Cos.

For full biographical listings, see the Martindale-Hubbell Law Directory

MARTIN, CHAPMAN, SCHILD & LASSAW, CHARTERED (AV)

Suite 100, 476 North 12th Street, P.O. Box 2898, 83701
Telephone: 208-343-6485
Fax: 208-343-9819
Sun Valley, Idaho Office: P.O. Box 744.
Telephone: 208-788-2876.
Fax: 208-788-2818.
Twin Falls, Idaho Office: 834 Falls Avenue, Suite 1020A.
Telephone: 208-734-9629.

John S. Chapman

References: West One Bank, Idaho, N.A. (formerly Idaho First National Bank); First Security Bank of Idaho, N.A.

For Complete List of Firm Personnel, See General Section

For full biographical listings, see the Martindale-Hubbell Law Directory

*POCATELLO,** Bannock Co.

MERRILL & MERRILL, CHARTERED (AV)

Key Bank Building, P.O. Box 991, 83204
Telephone: 208-232-2286
Fax: 208-232-2499

Wesley F. Merrill
Dave R. Gallafent
N. Randy Smith

For Complete List of Firm Personnel, See General Section

For full biographical listings, see the Martindale-Hubbell Law Directory

SUN VALLEY, Blaine Co.

MARTIN, CHAPMAN, SCHILD & LASSAW, CHARTERED (AV)

P.O. Box 744, 83303
Telephone: 208-788-2876
Fax: 208-788-2818
Boise, Idaho Office: Suite 100, 476 North 12th Street, P.O. Box 2989.
Telephone: 208-343-6485.
Fax: 208-343-9819.
Twin Falls, Idaho Office: 834 Falls Avenue, Suite 1020A.
Telephone: 208-734-9629.

John S. Chapman

References: First Security Bank of Idaho, N.A.; West One Bank, Idaho, N.A. (formerly Idaho First National Bank).

(*See Next Column*)

MARTIN, CHAPMAN, SCHILD & LASSAW CHARTERED, *Sun Valley—Continued*

For full biographical listings, see the Martindale-Hubbell Law Directory

ILLINOIS

*CARMI,** White Co.

CONGER & ELLIOTT, PROF. CORP. (AV)

Farm Bureau Building, 62821
Telephone: 618-382-4187
Fax: 618-384-2452

Chauncey S. Conger (Deceased)
Ivan A. Elliott (Deceased)
Ivan A. Elliott, Jr.
Robert Michael Drone
Gregory K. Stewart

Representative Clients: First National Bank of Carmi; State Farm Insurance Co.; Country Mutual Insurance Co.; Prudential Insurance Co.; Community Unit School District No. 3; Central Illinois Public Service Co.; Carmi Township Hospital; Egyptian Health Department; Commonwealth Edison.

For full biographical listings, see the Martindale-Hubbell Law Directory

*CHICAGO,** Cook Co.

ARONBERG GOLDGEHN DAVIS & GARMISA (AV)

Suite 3000 One IBM Plaza, 60611-3633
Telephone: 312-828-9600
Telecopier: 312-828-9635

MEMBERS OF FIRM

James S. Jarvis
Ned S. Robertson

For Complete List of Firm Personnel, See General Section

For full biographical listings, see the Martindale-Hubbell Law Directory

CHUHAK & TECSON, P.C. (AV)

225 West Washington Street, Suite 1300, 60606
Telephone: 312-444-9300
FAX: 312-444-9027

Thomas S. Chuhak
Joseph A. Tecson
John Laurence Kienlen
Barry A. Feinberg
Albert L. Grasso
Andrew P. Tecson
Donald J. Russ, Jr.
Edwin I. Josephson
Cary S. Fleischer
Stephen M. Margolin
John P. Fadden
Dennis A. Ferraro
Ricky L. Hammond
Arnold E. Karolewski
James W. Naisbitt
Alan R. Dolinko
Don M. Sowers, Jr.

John P. Adams
Thomas F. Bennington, Jr.
Barbara Chuhak Bernau
Barbara A. Cronin
John M. Foley
Stephen A. Glickman
Jeffrey A. Kerensky
Karen S. Kogachi
Raymond S. Makowski
John F. Mahoney
Michael B. McVickar
Laurie A. Pegler
Shawn P. Ryan
Stacy E. Singer
Mitchell D. Weinstein
Michael D. Weis

OF COUNSEL

Lawrence E. Glick
Joseph O. Rubinelli

LEGAL SUPPORT PERSONNEL

William J. Kreft

For full biographical listings, see the Martindale-Hubbell Law Directory

COWEN, CROWLEY & NORD, P.C. (AV)

Xerox Centre, 55 West Monroe Street, Suite 500, 60603
Telephone: 312-641-0060
Fax: 312-641-6959

Donald C. Nord

For full biographical listings, see the Martindale-Hubbell Law Directory

DEUTSCH, LEVY & ENGEL, CHARTERED (AV)

Suite 1700, 225 West Washington Street, 60606
Telephone: 312-346-1460
Boynton, Beach Florida Office: 3C Westgate Lane.
Telephone: 407-737-6003.
Wheaton, Illinois Office: Suite B2, 620 West Roosevelt Road.
Telephone: 312-665-9112.

Frank R. Cohen
Jerry I. Rudman

(See Next Column)

David I. Addis
Martin P. Ryan

For Complete List of Firm Personnel, See General Section

For full biographical listings, see the Martindale-Hubbell Law Directory

HOOGENDOORN, TALBOT, DAVIDS, GODFREY & MILLIGAN (AV)

122 South Michigan Avenue Suite 1220, 60603-6107
Telephone: 312-786-2250
FAX: 312-786-0708

MEMBERS OF FIRM

Case Hoogendoorn
Thomas J. Godfrey, Jr.
Francis J. Milligan, Jr.
Brian L. Dobben
Edward N. Tiesenga

For full biographical listings, see the Martindale-Hubbell Law Directory

MCBRIDE BAKER & COLES (AV)

500 West Madison Street 40th Floor, 60661
Telephone: 312-715-5700
Cable Address: "Chilaw"
Telex: 270258
Telecopier: 312-993-9350

MEMBERS OF FIRM

Andrew R. Gelman
Sidney C. Kleinman
Robert I. Schwimmer
David Shayne

OF COUNSEL

Robert O. Case

ASSOCIATE

Steven R. Lifson

For Complete List of Firm Personnel, See General Section

For full biographical listings, see the Martindale-Hubbell Law Directory

WILSON & MCILVAINE (AV)

500 West Madison, Suite 3700, 60661-2511
Telephone: 312-715-5000
Telecopier: 312-715-5155

PARTNERS

Walter W. Bell
Thomas E. Chomicz
Jerry D. Jones
Sarah M. Linsley
Thomas A. Polachek
Janice E. Rodgers

ASSOCIATES

Patrick J. Bitterman
Alison L. Paul

For Complete List of Firm Personnel, See General Section

For full biographical listings, see the Martindale-Hubbell Law Directory

*DECATUR,** Macon Co.

TENNEY & TENNEY (AV)

1264 First of America Center, P.O. Box 355, 62525
Telephone: 217-423-1800
Fax: 217-423-0524

MEMBERS OF FIRM

Harold F. Tenney
Carl J. Tenney

Representative Client: The Travelers Insurance Companies: Design Professional Insurance Company (DPIC Companies); Shelter Insurance Companies; Right Recreation, Inc.; Lucas Meyer, Inc. (lecithin products); Miles Chevrolet, Inc.; Crown Oldsmobile-Toyota, Inc.; Bob Brady Dodge, Inc.; Sims Lumber Company; Heinkel's Packing Co., Inc.

For full biographical listings, see the Martindale-Hubbell Law Directory

*GENEVA,** Kane Co.

SMITH, LANDMEIER & SKAAR, P.C. (AV)

15 North Second Street, 60134
Telephone: 708-232-2880
Fax: 708-232-2889

Howard E. Smith, Jr.
Allen L. Landmeier
James D. Skaar

Brian W. Baugh
Vincent J. Elders

References: Firstar Bank, Geneva, N.A., Geneva, Illinois; State Bank of Geneva, Geneva, Illinois.

For full biographical listings, see the Martindale-Hubbell Law Directory

*JOLIET,** Will Co.

McKeown, Fitzgerald, Zollner, Buck, Hutchison & Ruttle (AV)

2455 Glenwood Avenue, 60435
Telephone: 815-729-4800
FAX: 815-729-4711
Frankfort, Illinois Office: 28 Kansas Street.
Telephone: 815-469-2176.
FAX: 815-469-0295.

MEMBERS OF FIRM

Charles J. McKeown (1908-1985)
Paul O. McKeown (1913-1982)
Richard T. Buck (1936-1992)
Joseph C. Fitzgerald
Max E. Zollner
Douglas P. Hutchison
David L. Ruttle
Theodore J. Jarz
Douglas J. McKeown
Timothy J. Rathbun
James B. Harvey
Kenneth A. Grey
Michael R. Lucas

ASSOCIATES

Christopher N. Wise
Gary S. Mueller
Frank S. Cservenyak, Jr.
William P Mullarkey
Arthur J. Wilhelmi

OF COUNSEL

Stewart C. Hutchison

Representative Clients: Caterpillar Tractor Co.; First National Bank of Lockport; Homart Development Co.; First Midwest Bank, N.A.; Silver Cross Hospital; Joliet Township High School District; Villages of: Plainfield and Mokena; Southwest Agency for Risk Management; Joliet Junior College Foundation; Health Service Systems, Inc.

For full biographical listings, see the Martindale-Hubbell Law Directory

*PEORIA,** Peoria Co.

Jerold I. Horn (AV)

124 S.W. Adams Street, 61602-1320
Telephone: 309-676-2778
Fax: 309-676-2779

References: First of America Bank, Illinois, N.A.

For full biographical listings, see the Martindale-Hubbell Law Directory

*PONTIAC,** Livingston Co.

Johnson & Taylor (AV)

Formerly Ortman, Johnson & Taylor
109 North Mill Street, 61764
Telephone: 815-844-7151
FAX: 815-844-7539

MEMBERS OF FIRM

F. A. Ortman (1882-1955)
John A. Taylor
Taylor F. Johnson

OF COUNSEL

J. Kenneth Johnson

Attorneys for: Illinois Central Gulf Railroad; Flanagan State Bank; Villages of Flanagan, Long Point and Emington; Flanagan Unit 4 School District; Flanagan-Graymont and Long Point Fire Districts; Arco Pipe Line Co.

For full biographical listings, see the Martindale-Hubbell Law Directory

*ROCKFORD,** Winnebago Co.

Conde, Stoner & Killoren (AV)

120 West State Street, Suite 400, 61101
Telephone: 815-987-4000
FAX: 815-987-9889
Rochelle, Illinois Office: 400 Maymart Drive, 61068.
Telephone: 815-562-2677.

MEMBERS OF FIRM

Dale F. Conde
Clifford E. Stoner
Thomas A. Killoren
Thomas A. Bueschel
Robert A. Calgaro

James M. Hess
Alan H. Cooper
Kimberly Baker Timmerwilke

OF COUNSEL

Clifford A. Pedderson
Lisle W. Menzimer

References: Rockford School District; Central Commodities Limited; Medical Protective Co.; Wausau Insurance Companies; Caronia Corp.; National Medical Enterprises; Professional Risk Management, Inc.; Krause, Inc.; First of America, North Central N.A.

For full biographical listings, see the Martindale-Hubbell Law Directory

*ROCK ISLAND,** Rock Island Co.

Nepple, Van Der Kamp & Flynn, P.C. (AV)

Suite 202 American Bank Building, 1600 Fourth Avenue, P.O. Box 5408, 61204-5408
Telephone: 309-786-5700
Telecopier: 309-786-5745
Muscatine, Iowa Office: 216 Sycamore Street, P.O. Box 386, 52761-0386.
Telephone: 319-264-6840.

Roy W. Van Der Kamp
James A. Nepple
Patrick J. Flynn

Milissa M. Knudsen

LEGAL SUPPORT PERSONNEL

Steven D. Perkins

Representative Clients: First of America Bank - Quad Cities, N.A.; Northwest Bank and Trust Company; Brenton First National Bank; Bituminous Insurance Companies; Shive-Hattery Engineers and Architects, Inc.; Ruhl & Ruhl, Inc.; Stanley Consultants, Inc. and affiliates; The Stanley Foundation; Stanley Employee Stock Ownership Plan; Valley Construction Company.

For full biographical listings, see the Martindale-Hubbell Law Directory

INDIANA

*BLOOMINGTON,** Monroe Co.

Bunger & Robertson (AV)

226 South College Square, P.O. Box 910, 47402-0910
Telephone: 812-332-9295
Fax: 812-331-8808

MEMBERS OF FIRM

Len E. Bunger, Jr. (1921-1993)
Don M. Robertson
Thomas Bunger

Representative Clients: Aetna Insurance Companies; Bloomington Hospital; Commercial Union Group; Indiana Insurance Co.; Liberty Mutual Insurance; Medical Protective Co.; Monroe County Community School Corp.; Professional Golf Car, Inc.; Prudential Insurance Company of America; State Farm Automobile Insurance Co.

For Complete List of Firm Personnel, See General Section

For full biographical listings, see the Martindale-Hubbell Law Directory

CARMEL, Hamilton Co.

Coots, Henke & Wheeler, Professional Corporation (AV)

255 East Carmel Drive, 46032
Telephone: 317-844-4693
Fax: 317-573-5385

E. Davis Coots
Steven H. Henke
T. Jay Curts

For Complete List of Firm Personnel, See General Section

For full biographical listings, see the Martindale-Hubbell Law Directory

Knowles & Associates (AV)

811 South Range Line Road, 46032
Telephone: 317-848-4360
Telecopier: 317-848-4363

William W. Knowles

Pamela Y. Rhine
D. Brandon Johnston

For full biographical listings, see the Martindale-Hubbell Law Directory

CLARKSVILLE, Clark Co.

Hanger, Engebretson, Mayer & Vogt (AV)

501 Eastern Boulevard, 47129
Telephone: 812-288-1235
Louisville, Kentucky: 502-584-5800
Fax: 812-288-1240

MEMBERS OF FIRM

John M. Mayer, Jr.
Samuel H. Vogt, Jr.

ASSOCIATE

Susan Wagner Hynes

Representative Clients: First Federal Savings and Loan Association of Clark County; Ticor Title Insurance Company; Old Republic National Title Insurance Company.

(See Next Column)

HANGER, ENGEBRETSON, MAYER & VOGT, *Clarksville—Continued*

Approved Attorneys for: Commonwealth Land Title Insurance Co.
Reference: First Federal Savings and Loan Association of Clark County; PNC Bank Indiana, Inc.

For Complete List of Firm Personnel, See General Section

For full biographical listings, see the Martindale-Hubbell Law Directory

*COLUMBIA CITY,** Whitley Co.

GATES & GATES (AV)

Gates & Gates is over 100 years old.
216 West Van Buren Street, P.O. Box 251, 46725-0251
Telephone: 219-244-5175
Fax: Available Upon Request

MEMBER OF FIRM

Benton E. Gates, Jr.

ASSOCIATE

Richard W. Gates

Attorneys For: Holmes & Co., Inc.; LML Corp.; NBD; Prudential Insurance Co.; American States Insurance Co.; Farm Credit Service.

For full biographical listings, see the Martindale-Hubbell Law Directory

*COLUMBUS,** Bartholomew Co.

SHARPNACK, BIGLEY, DAVID & RUMPLE (AV)

321 Washington Street, P.O. Box 310, 47202-0310
Telephone: 812-372-1553
Fax: 812-372-1567

MEMBERS OF FIRM

Thomas C. Bigley, Jr.
John R. Rumple
Jeffrey S. Washburn

Representative Clients: Irwin Union Bank and Trust Co.; PSI Energy, Inc.; State Farm Mutual Insurance Cos.; American States Insurance Co.; Home News Enterprises; Cummins Federal Credit Union; Richards Elevator, Inc.

For Complete List of Firm Personnel, See General Section

For full biographical listings, see the Martindale-Hubbell Law Directory

ELKHART, Elkhart Co.

CHESTER, PFAFF & BROTHERSON (AV)

317 West Franklin Street, P.O. Box 507, 46515-0507
Telephone: 219-294-5421
Telecopier: 219-522-1476

MEMBERS OF FIRM

Robert A. Pfaff
James R. Brotherson
Glenn E. Killoren

OF COUNSEL

Willard H. Chester

For Complete List of Firm Personnel, See General Section

For full biographical listings, see the Martindale-Hubbell Law Directory

THORNE, GRODNIK, RANSEL, DUNCAN, BYRON & HOSTETLER (AV)

228 West High Street, 46516-3176
Telephone: 219-294-7473
FAX: 219-294-5390
Mishawaka, Indiana Office: 310 Valley American Bank and Trust Building, 310 West McKinley Avenue. P.O. Box 1210.
Telephone: 219-256-5660.
FAX: 219-674-6835.

MEMBERS OF FIRM

William A. Thorne
Charles H. Grodnik
J. Richard Ransel
Glenn L. Duncan
James R. Byron
Steven L. Hostetler

ASSOCIATES

James H. Milstone
Michael A. Trippel

OF COUNSEL

F. Richard Kramer
Joseph C. Zakas

Counsel for: Witmer-McNease Music Co., Inc.; Valley American Bank and Trust Co., Mishawaka, Indiana.

For Complete List of Firm Personnel, See General Section

For full biographical listings, see the Martindale-Hubbell Law Directory

*EVANSVILLE,** Vanderburgh Co.

LAW OFFICES OF RANDALL K. CRAIG (AV)

Reed Building Suite 5, 2709 Washington Avenue, 47714
Telephone: 812-477-3337
Telefax: 812-477-3658

For full biographical listings, see the Martindale-Hubbell Law Directory

FINE & HATFIELD (AV)

520 N.W. Second Street, P.O. Box 779, 47705-0779
Telephone: 812-425-3592
Telecopier: 812-421-4269

MEMBERS OF FIRM

James E. Marchand
Thomas R. Fitzsimmons
Stephen S. Lavallo

ASSOCIATES

Shannon Scholz Frank
William H. Mullis
Debra S. McGowan

For Complete List of Firm Personnel, See General Section

For full biographical listings, see the Martindale-Hubbell Law Directory

STATHAM, JOHNSON & McCRAY (AV)

215 North West Martin Luther King Jr. Boulevard, P.O. Box 3567, 47734-3567
Telephone: 812-425-5223
Facsimile: 812-421-4238

MEMBER OF FIRM

R. Eugene Johnson

ASSOCIATE

Thomas P. Norton

For Complete List of Firm Personnel, See General Section

For full biographical listings, see the Martindale-Hubbell Law Directory

JACK A. STONE (AV)

1400 Old National Bank Building, 47708
Telephone: 812-423-2045
Fax: Available Upon Request

For full biographical listings, see the Martindale-Hubbell Law Directory

*FORT WAYNE,** Allen Co.

HELMKE, BEAMS, BOYER & WAGNER (AV)

300 Metro Building, Berry & Harrison Streets, 46802-2242
Telephone: 219-422-7422
Telecopier: 219-422-6764

MEMBERS OF FIRM

Walter E. Helmke (1901-1976)
Walter P. Helmke
R. David Boyer
Robert A. Wagner
J. Timothy McCaulay
Daniel J. Borgmann

ASSOCIATE

Trina Glusenkamp Gould

OF COUNSEL

Glen J. Beams
John G. Reiber

Representative Clients: Aalco Distributing Co., Inc.; Brotherhood Mutual Insurance Co.; Fremont Community Schools; Teco, Inc.; Air-O-Mat, Inc.; Leo Distributors, Inc.

For full biographical listings, see the Martindale-Hubbell Law Directory

SHAMBAUGH, KAST, BECK & WILLIAMS (AV)

600 Standard Federal Plaza, 46802-2405
Telephone: 219-423-1430
FAX: 219-422-9038

MEMBERS OF FIRM

Michael H. Kast (Semi-Active)
Stephen J. Williams
Edward E. Beck
Daniel E. Serban
John B. Powell
Timothy L. Claxton
James D. Streit

Counsel for: Hagerman Construction Corp.; Rogers Markets, Inc.; K & H Realty Corp.; Olive B. Cole Foundation; M. E. Raker Foundation, Inc.; Associates Financial Services Co., of Indiana, Inc.; Professional Federal Credit Union; Fort Wayne Education Association; American Ambassador Casualty Company; CBT Credit Services, Inc.

For Complete List of Firm Personnel, See General Section

For full biographical listings, see the Martindale-Hubbell Law Directory

*FOWLER,** Benton Co.

WILLIAM B. WEIST (AV)

Weist Building, P.O. Box 101, 47944
Telephone: 317-884-1840
Fax: Available Upon Request

ASSOCIATE

Rex W. Kepner

References: Fowler State Bank, Fowler, Indiana; Farmers and Merchants Bank, Boswell, Indiana.

For full biographical listings, see the Martindale-Hubbell Law Directory

GREENWOOD, Johnson Co.

VAN VALER WILLIAMS & HEWITT (AV)

Suite 400 National City Bank Building, 300 South Madison Avenue, P.O. Box 405, 46142
Telephone: 317-888-1121
Fax: 317-887-4069

MEMBERS OF FIRM

Joe N. Van Valer
Jon E. Williams
Brian C. Hewitt

ASSOCIATES

J. Lee Robbins
John M. White
William M. Waltz
Kim Van Valer Shilts
Mark E. Need

For full biographical listings, see the Martindale-Hubbell Law Directory

*INDIANAPOLIS,** Marion Co.

BACKER & BACKER, A PROFESSIONAL CORPORATION (AV)

101 West Ohio Street, Suite 1500, 46204
Telephone: 317-684-3000
Telecopier: 317-684-3004

Herbert J. Backer
Stephen A. Backer
David J. Backer

Reference: Bank One, Indianapolis.

For full biographical listings, see the Martindale-Hubbell Law Directory

BOBERSCHMIDT, MILLER, O'BRYAN, TURNER & ABBOTT, A PROFESSIONAL ASSOCIATION (AV)

Bank One Center/Circle, 111 Monument Circle, Suite 302, 46204-5169
Telephone: 317-632-5892
Telecopier: 317-686-3423

Philip F. Boberschmidt
Berton W. O'Bryan
Jerald L. Miller
L. Craig Turner

A List of Representative Clients will be furnished upon request.

For Complete List of Firm Personnel, See General Section

For full biographical listings, see the Martindale-Hubbell Law Directory

COATES, HATFIELD, CALKINS & WELLNITZ (AV)

One Indiana Square, Suite 2335, 46204
Telephone: 317-637-2577
800-542-9516
Fax: Available Upon Request

MEMBERS OF FIRM

Ben F. Hatfield, Jr.
R. Ronald Calkins
Craig O. Wellnitz

Representative Clients: Bank One, Indianapolis; NBD National Bank; National City Bank.

For full biographical listings, see the Martindale-Hubbell Law Directory

DALE & EKE, PROFESSIONAL CORPORATION (AV)

Suite 400, 9100 Keystone Crossing, 46240
Telephone: 317-844-7400
FAX: 317-574-9426

William J. Dale, Jr.
Karen A. Hosack
Joseph W. Eke
A. Robert Lasich
Deborah J. Caruso
Dawn Michelle Snow
Catherine Chambers Kennedy
Janet S. Ellis

For full biographical listings, see the Martindale-Hubbell Law Directory

HALL, RENDER, KILLIAN, HEATH & LYMAN, PROFESSIONAL CORPORATION (AV)

Suite 2000, One American Square Box 82064, 46282
Telephone: 317-633-4884
Telecopier: 317-633-4878
North Office: Suite 820, 8402 Harcourt Road, 46260.
Telephone: 317-871-6222.

William S. Hall
Jeffrey Peek
R. Terry Heath
Douglas P. Long
Fred J. Bachmann

For Complete List of Firm Personnel, See General Section

For full biographical listings, see the Martindale-Hubbell Law Directory

ICE MILLER DONADIO & RYAN (AV)

One American Square Box 82001, 46282-0002
Telephone: 317-236-2100
Fax: 317-236-2219

(See Next Column)

MEMBERS OF FIRM

Gordon D. Wishard
Lisa Stone Sciscoe

For Complete List of Firm Personnel, See General Section

For full biographical listings, see the Martindale-Hubbell Law Directory

JOHNSON, HALL AND LAWHEAD, PROFESSIONAL CORPORATION (AV)

Suite 940, 8900 Keystone Crossing, 46240-2162
Telephone: 317-848-5808
FAX: 317-574-3429

G. Weldon Johnson
Richard M. Hall
Lawrence E. Lawhead

Gregory L. Padgett
Annette T. Brogden

For full biographical listings, see the Martindale-Hubbell Law Directory

KROGER, GARDIS & REGAS (AV)

111 Monument Circle, Suite 900, 46204-3059
Telephone: 317-692-9000
Telecopier: 317-264-6832

MEMBERS OF FIRM

James G. Lauck
Brian C. Bosma

ASSOCIATE

Marcia E. Roan

Representative Clients: Beneficial Finance Company of America; National City Bank.

For full biographical listings, see the Martindale-Hubbell Law Directory

ROBERT A. LICHTENAUER (AV)

Suite 110, 8140 Knue Road, 46250
Telephone: 317-845-1988

For full biographical listings, see the Martindale-Hubbell Law Directory

MCCLURE, MCCLURE & KAMMEN (AV)

235 North Delaware, 46204
Telephone: 317-236-0400
Telecopier: 317-236-0404

MEMBERS OF FIRM

David E. McClure
Richard Kammen

Reference: Indiana National Bank.

For full biographical listings, see the Martindale-Hubbell Law Directory

*KOKOMO,** Howard Co.

FELL, MCGARVEY, TRAURING & WILSON (AV)

515 West Sycamore Street, P.O. Box 958, 46903-0958
Telephone: 317-457-9321
Telecopier: 317-452-0882

MEMBERS OF FIRM

John E. Fell, Jr.
Eugene J. McGarvey, Jr.

Representative Clients: Big R Stores; First National Bank, Kokomo; Haynes International, Inc.; Hospital Authority of the City of Kokomo; Kokomo City Hall Building Corp.; PPG Industries, Inc.; Star Building Supply, Inc.; Mervis Industries, Inc.; G-W Invader, Inc.; Taylor Community School Corp.
References: First National Bank; Society Bank of Howard County.

For Complete List of Firm Personnel, See General Section

For full biographical listings, see the Martindale-Hubbell Law Directory

*LAFAYETTE,** Tippecanoe Co.

MAYFIELD AND BROOKS (AV)

322 Main Street, P.O. Box 650, 47902
Telephone: 317-423-5454
FAX: 317-742-8666

Thomas L. Brooks

Representative Clients: DeFouw Chevrolet, Inc.; Kendrick Buick-Cadillac, Inc.; Century 21 Bouwkamp Agency; Lafayette Real Estate Marketing Corp.; Smith Office Equipment, Inc.; American Vending Corp.; Sun Industries, Inc.; National Attorneys' Title Insurance Fund, Inc.
Reference: NBD Bank, N.A.

For Complete List of Firm Personnel, See General Section

MISHAWAKA, St. Joseph Co.

SCHINDLER AND OLSON (AV)

122 South Mill Street, P.O. Box 100, 46544
Telephone: 219-259-5461
Fax: 219-259-5462

(See Next Column)

SCHINDLER AND OLSON, *Mishawaka—Continued*

MEMBERS OF FIRM

John W. Schindler, Jr. James J. Olson

A List of Representative Clients Will Be Furnished Upon Request.
Reference: 1st Source Bank of Mishawaka.

For Complete List of Firm Personnel, See General Section

For full biographical listings, see the Martindale-Hubbell Law Directory

*MUNCIE,** Delaware Co.

SHIREY, EDWARDS & GLASS (AV)

Century Building, Suite Four, 330 East Main Street, 47305
Telephone: 317-288-0207

MEMBERS OF FIRM

Wayne A. Shirey Joseph G. Edwards

ASSOCIATE

David B. Roesner

Reference: American National Bank & Trust Co.

For Complete List of Firm Personnel, See General Section

For full biographical listings, see the Martindale-Hubbell Law Directory

MUNSTER, Lake Co.

PINKERTON AND FRIEDMAN, PROFESSIONAL CORPORATION (AV)

The Fairmont, 9245 Calumet Avenue Suite 201, 46321
Telephone: 219-836-3050
Fax: 219-836-2955

Kirk A. Pinkerton Jeffrey F. Gunning
Stuart J. Friedman Gail Oosterhof

For full biographical listings, see the Martindale-Hubbell Law Directory

*TERRE HAUTE,** Vigo Co.

COX, ZWERNER, GAMBILL & SULLIVAN (AV)

511 Wabash Avenue, P.O. Box 1625, 47808-1625
Telephone: 812-232-6003
Fax: 812-232-6567

MEMBERS OF FIRM

Ernest J. Zwerner (1918-1980) David W. Sullivan
Benjamin G. Cox (1915-1988) Robert L. Gowdy
Gilbert W. Gambill, Jr. Louis F. Britton
James E. Sullivan Robert D. Hepburn
Benjamin G. Cox, Jr. Carroll D. Smeltzer
Jeffry A. Lind

ASSOCIATE

Ronald E. Jumps

Counsel for: Terre Haute First National Bank; Farmers Insurance Group; Indiana-American Water Co.; Indiana State University; Merchants National Bank of Terre Haute; Rose-Hulman Institute of Technology; Tribune-Star Publishing Co., Inc.; Weston Paper & Manufacturing Co.

For full biographical listings, see the Martindale-Hubbell Law Directory

WILKINSON, GOELLER, MODESITT, WILKINSON & DRUMMY (AV)

333 Ohio Street, P.O. Box 800, 47808-0800
Telephone: 812-232-4311
Fax: 812-235-5107

MEMBERS OF FIRM

Myrl O. Wilkinson Kelvin L. Roots
David H. Goeller John C. Wall
Raymond H. Modesitt William M. Olah
B. Curtis Wilkinson Craig M. McKee
Scott M. Kyrouac

Representative Corporate Clients: Merchants National Bank; Owens Corning Fiberglass; CSX, Inc.; General Housewares Corp.; MAB Paints; Chicago Title Insurance Co.; Terre Haute Board of Realtors; Union Hospital; Associated Physicians and Surgeons Clinic, Inc.; PSI Energy, Inc.

For Complete List of Firm Personnel, See General Section

For full biographical listings, see the Martindale-Hubbell Law Directory

*VALPARAISO,** Porter Co.

BLACHLY, TABOR, BOZIK & HARTMAN (AV)

Suite 401 Indiana Federal Building, 46383
Telephone: 219-464-1041

MEMBERS OF FIRM

Quentin A. Blachly David L. Hollenbeck
Glenn J. Tabor David L. DeBoer
James S. Bozik Thomas F. Macke
Duane W. Hartman Randall J. Zromkoski
Richard J. Rupcich

(See Next Column)

ASSOCIATE

Roger A. Weitgenant

Reference: First National Bank.

For Complete List of Firm Personnel, See General Section

For full biographical listings, see the Martindale-Hubbell Law Directory

DOUGLAS, ALEXA, KOEPPEN & HURLEY (AV)

14 Indiana Avenue, P.O. Box 209, 46384-0209
Telephone: 219-462-2126
Fax: 219-477-4408

MEMBERS OF FIRM

Herbert K. Douglas R. Bradley Koeppen
William E. Alexa Brian J. Hurley

ASSOCIATE

Mark A. Gland

OF COUNSEL

George W. Douglas Leo J. Clifford

Attorneys for: Urschel Laboratories, Inc.; Northern Indiana Public Service Co.; Midwest Steel Division, National Steel; McGill Manufacturing Co., Inc.; Park District, City of Valparaiso.

For full biographical listings, see the Martindale-Hubbell Law Directory

*WARSAW,** Kosciusko Co.

HARRIS & HARRIS (AV)

222 North Buffalo Street, 46580
Telephone: 219-267-2111
Fax: 219-268-2277

Philip J. Harris Stephen P. Harris
Marcus Kosins, Jr.

Representative Clients: Mutual Federal Savings Bank; Akron Foundry, Inc.; Bertsch Food Service Co.; Carey Realty, Inc.; Miller & Sons Structures, Inc.; Patona Bay Boat Service; Sun Metal Products, Inc.; Warsaw Plating Works, Inc.; Union Tool Corp.; U.C.C. Coffee Company (Japan).

For full biographical listings, see the Martindale-Hubbell Law Directory

LEMON, REED, ARMEY, HEARN & LEININGER (AV)

210 North Buffalo Street, P.O. Box 770, 46581-0770
Telephone: 219-268-9111
Telecopier: 219-267-8647

MEMBERS OF FIRM

Thomas R. Lemon Michael E. Armey
Rex L. Reed R. Steven Hearn
Daniel K. Leininger

ASSOCIATE

Jane L. Kauffman

OF COUNSEL

Robert L. Rasor

Representative Clients: Lake City Bank; Zimmer Inc.; The Dalton Foundries, Inc.; Grace Schools, Inc.; Kosciusko Community Hospital, Inc.

For Complete List of Firm Personnel, See General Section

For full biographical listings, see the Martindale-Hubbell Law Directory

IOWA

CEDAR FALLS, Black Hawk Co.

REDFERN, MASON, DIETER, LARSEN & MOORE (AV)

315 Clay Street, P.O. Box 627, 50613
Telephone: 319-277-6830
Facsimile: 319-277-3531

MEMBERS OF FIRM

LeRoy H. Redfern Steven D. Moore
David R. Mason Donald B. Redfern
Robert J. Dieter Mark W. Fransdal
John C. Larsen Mark S. Rolinger

ASSOCIATE

Susan Bernau Staudt

Representative Clients: Norwest Bank Iowa; The National Bank of Waterloo; Don R. Havens Co.; Control-O-fax Corp.; Cedar Falls Community School District; University of Northern Iowa Foundation; United States Fidelity and Guaranty Co.; The Travelers Insurance Cos.; Fireman's Fund Insurance Companies.

For Complete List of Firm Personnel, See General Section

For full biographical listings, see the Martindale-Hubbell Law Directory

*CEDAR RAPIDS,** Linn Co.

SHUTTLEWORTH & INGERSOLL, P.C. (AV)

500 Firstar Bank Building, P.O. Box 2107, 52406-2107
Telephone: 319-365-9461
Fax: 319-365-8443

Thomas M. Collins
Michael O. McDermott
Gary J. Streit
Carroll J. Reasoner
William P. Prowell
William S. Hochstetler

Dean D. Carrington

OF COUNSEL

W. R. Shuttleworth

Representative Clients: Firstar Bank Cedar Rapids, N.A.; First National Bank of Cedar Rapids; Norwest Bank Iowa, N.A.

For Complete List of Firm Personnel, See General Section

For full biographical listings, see the Martindale-Hubbell Law Directory

SIMMONS, PERRINE, ALBRIGHT & ELLWOOD, L.L.P. (AV)

A Partnership including a Professional Corporation
115 Third Street S.E. Suite 1200, 52401
Telephone: 319-366-7641
Telecopier: 319-366-1917 (I,II,III)

PARTNERS

Darrel A. Morf
Dean R. Einck
David W. Kubicek

For Complete List of Firm Personnel, See General Section

For full biographical listings, see the Martindale-Hubbell Law Directory

*COUNCIL BLUFFS,** Pottawattamie Co.

SMITH PETERSON LAW FIRM (AV)

35 Main Place, Suite 300, P.O. Box 249, 51502
Telephone: 712-328-1833
Fax: 712-328-8320
Omaha, Nebraska Office: 9290 West Dodge Road, Suite 205.
Telephone: 402-397-8500.
Fax: 402-397-5519.

MEMBERS OF FIRM

Raymond A. Smith (1892-1977)
John LeRoy Peterson (1895-1969)
Harold T. Beckman
Robert J. Laubenthal
Richard A. Heininger
Lawrence J. Beckman
Gregory G. Barntsen
W. Curtis Hewett
Steven H. Krohn
Randy R. Ewing
Joseph D. Thornton

ASSOCIATES

Trent D. Reinert (Not admitted in IA)
T. J. Pattermann

Representative Clients: Aetna Life and Casualty Co.; Employers Mutual Co.; First National Bank of Council Bluffs; IMT Insurance Co.; Monsanto Co.; United Fire & Casualty Co.; U.S. Fidelity and Guaranty.

For full biographical listings, see the Martindale-Hubbell Law Directory

*DES MOINES,** Polk Co.

CONNOLLY, O'MALLEY, LILLIS, HANSEN & OLSON (AV)

820 Liberty Building, 6th & Grand Avenue, 50309
Telephone: 515-243-8157
Fax: 515-243-3919

MEMBERS OF FIRM

William J. Lillis
Russell J. Hansen
Michael W. O'Malley
Eugene E. Olson
Peter S. Cannon
Streetar Cameron
Douglas A. Fulton
Daniel L. Manning

ASSOCIATE

Christopher R. Pose

OF COUNSEL

John Connolly, III

A list of Representative Clients will be furnished upon request.
References will be furnished upon request.

For full biographical listings, see the Martindale-Hubbell Law Directory

DICKINSON, MACKAMAN, TYLER & HAGEN, P.C. (AV)

Suite 1600 Hub Tower, 699 Walnut Street, 50309-3986
Telephone: 515-244-2600
Telecopier: 515-246-4550

(See Next Column)

L. J. Dickinson (1873-1968)
L. Call Dickinson (1905-1974)
Addison M. Parker (Retired)
John H. Raife (Retired)
Robert B. Throckmorton (Retired)
Helen C. Adams
Brent R. Appel
Barbara G. Barrett
John W. Blyth
L. Call Dickinson, Jr.
Jeanine M. Freeman
David J. Grace
Craig F. Graziano
Howard O. Hagen
J. Russell Hixson
Paul E. Horvath
F. Richard Lyford
John R. Mackaman
Richard A. Malm
James W. O'Brien
Arthur F. Owens
Rebecca Boyd Parrott
David M. Repp
Robert C. Rouwenhorst
Russell L. Samson
David S. Steward
Philip E. Stoffregen
Francis (Frank) J. Stork
Jon P. Sullivan
Celeste L. Tito (Not admitted in IA)
Paul R. Tyler
John K. Vernon
J. Marc Ward
Linda S. Weindruch

OF COUNSEL

Robert E. Mannheimer

Representative Clients: Archer-Daniels-Midland Co.; Board of Water Works Trustees, Des Moines, Iowa; Merchants Bonding Co. (Mutual); Norwest Bank, N.A.

For full biographical listings, see the Martindale-Hubbell Law Directory

GREFE & SIDNEY (AV)

2222 Grand Avenue, P.O. Box 10434, 50306
Telephone: 515-245-4300
Fax: 515-245-4452

MEMBERS OF FIRM

Rolland E. Grefe
Thomas W. Carpenter
Robert C. Thomson
Craig S. Shannon

Representative Clients: Easter Stores; Freeman Decorating Co.; Iowa-Nebraska Farm Equipment Association, Inc.; Pella Corp.; State Farm Mutual Insurance Companies of Bloomington, Ill.; Liberty Mutual Insurance Co.; United States Fidelity and Guaranty Co.; Koehring Co.

For Complete List of Firm Personnel, See General Section

For full biographical listings, see the Martindale-Hubbell Law Directory

SHEARER, TEMPLER, PINGEL & KAPLAN, A PROFESSIONAL CORPORATION (AV)

Suite 437 3737 Woodland Avenue (West Des Moines, 50266), P.O. Box 1991, 50309
Telephone: 515-225-3737
Fax: 515-225-9510

Ronni F. Begleiter
Thomas M. Cunningham
Jeffrey L. Goodman
Ronald M. Kaplan
Lawrence L. Marcucci
Mark L. McManigal
John R. Perkins
G. Brian Pingel
Leon R. Shearer
Brenton D. Soderstrum
Jeffrey D. Stone
David G. Stork
John A. Templer, Jr.
Ann M. Ver Heul

For Complete List of Firm Personnel, See General Section

For full biographical listings, see the Martindale-Hubbell Law Directory

*MASON CITY,** Cerro Gordo Co.

WINSTON, REUBER & BYRNE, LAWYERS, A PROFESSIONAL CORPORATION (AV)

119 Second Street, N.W., 50401
Telephone: 515-423-1913
FAX: 515-423-8998

Harold R. Winston
John H. Reuber
Michael G. Byrne

Representative Clients: Libbey-Owens Ford Glass Co.; Goodyear Tire and Rubber; Skelly Oil; United Guernsey Co-op; Norwest Bank; First Interstate Bank of Mason City.

For full biographical listings, see the Martindale-Hubbell Law Directory

*SIOUX CITY,** Woodbury Co.

SHULL, COSGROVE, HELLIGE, DU BRAY & LUNDBERG (AV)

700 Frances Building, 505 Fifth Street, P.O. Box 1828, 51102
Telephone: 712-255-4444
Telecopier: 712-255-4465

MEMBERS OF FIRM

James M. Cosgrove
Michael R. Hellige
F. Joseph Du Bray
Paul D. Lundberg
M. James Daley
Robert F. Meis
Scott A. Hindman
James W. Radig
Christopher K. Miller

(See Next Column)

SHULL, COSGROVE, HELLIGE, DU BRAY & LUNDBERG, *Sioux City—Continued*

OF COUNSEL
D. Carlton Shull

Representative Clients: Burlington Northern Inc.; Employers Mutual Cos.; Ford Motor Co.; The Hartford; Liberty Mutual Insurance Co.; Prince Manufacturing Corp.; Sioux City Journal; The Travelers; Western Iowa Tech Community College.

For full biographical listings, see the Martindale-Hubbell Law Directory

KANSAS

PRAIRIE VILLAGE, Johnson Co.

HOLMAN, MCCOLLUM & HANSEN, P.C. (AV⊕)

9400 Mission Road Suite 205, 66206
Telephone: 913-648-7272
Fax: 913-383-9596
Kansas City, Missouri Office: 644 West 57th Terrace.
Telephone: 816-333-8522.
Fax: 913-383-9596.

Joseph Y. Holman
Frank B. W. McCollum
Eric L. Hansen
Dana L. Parks
Nancy Merrill Wilson
Amy L. Brown
E. John Edwards III (Not admitted in KS)
Katherine E. Rich

For full biographical listings, see the Martindale-Hubbell Law Directory

*TOPEKA,** Shawnee Co.

GOODELL, STRATTON, EDMONDS & PALMER (AV)

515 South Kansas Avenue, 66603-3999
Telephone: 913-233-0593
Telecopier: 913-233-8870

MEMBERS OF FIRM

Gerald L. Goodell
H. Philip Elwood
Gerald J. Letourneau

Local Counsel for: Farm Bureau Mutual Insurance Co.; Metropolitan Life Insurance Co.; St. Paul Fire & Marine Insurance Co.
General Counsel for: American Home Life Insurance Co.; Columbian National Title Insurance Co.; The Menninger Foundation; Stauffer Communications, Inc.; Kansas Association of Realtors; Kansas Medical Society; Kansas Hospital Association.

For Complete List of Firm Personnel, See General Section

For full biographical listings, see the Martindale-Hubbell Law Directory

*WICHITA,** Sedgwick Co.

FLEESON, GOOING, COULSON & KITCH, L.L.C. (AV)

125 North Market Street, Suite 1600, P.O. Box 997, 67201-0997
Telephone: 316-267-7361
Telecopier: 316-267-1754

Willard B. Thompson
Mark F. Anderson
Timothy P. O'Sullivan
Edward J. Healy
Linda K. Constable

John R. Gerdes
Joan M. Bowen

Attorneys for: Bank IV, Wichita, N.A; Intrust Bank, N.A.; Wichita Eagle and Beacon Publishing Co., Inc.; Southwest Kansas Royalty Owners Assn.; Liberty Mutual Insurance Co.; Grant Thornton; The Law Company; Vulcan Materials Co.; The Wichita State University Board of Trustees.

For Complete List of Firm Personnel, See General Section

For full biographical listings, see the Martindale-Hubbell Law Directory

FOULSTON & SIEFKIN (AV)

(Formerly Foulston, Siefkin, Powers & Eberhardt)
700 Fourth Financial Center, Broadway at Douglas, 67202
Telephone: 316-267-6371
Facsimile: 316-267-6345
Topeka, Kansas Office: 1515 Bank IV Tower, 534 Kansas Avenue. 66603.
Telephone: 913-233-3600.
FAX: 913-233-1610.
Member: Lex Mundi, A Global Association of Independent Firms

MEMBERS OF FIRM

Richard C. Harris
Stanley G. Andeel
Jim H. Goering

For Complete List of Firm Personnel, See General Section

For full biographical listings, see the Martindale-Hubbell Law Directory

YOUNG, BOGLE, MCCAUSLAND, WELLS & CLARK, P.A. (AV)

106 West Douglas, Suite 923, 67202
Telephone: 316-265-7841
Facsimile: 316-265-3956

Jerry D. Bogle
William A. Wells
Patrick C. Blanchard

References provided upon request.

For Complete List of Firm Personnel, See General Section

For full biographical listings, see the Martindale-Hubbell Law Directory

KENTUCKY

ASHLAND, Boyd Co.

VANANTWERP, MONGE, JONES & EDWARDS (AV)

1544 Winchester Avenue Fifth Floor, P.O. Box 1111, 41105-1111
Telephone: 606-329-2929
Fax: 606-329-0490
Ironton, Ohio Office: Cooper & VanAntwerp, A Legal Professional Association, 407 Center Street.
Telephone: 614-532-4366.

MEMBERS OF FIRM

Howard VanAntwerp, III
Gregory Lee Monge
William H. Jones, Jr.
Carl D. Edwards, Jr.
Kimberly Scott McCann

ASSOCIATES

Matthew J. Wixsom
William Mitchell Hall
James D. Keffer
Stephen S. Burchett

Representative Clients: Armco; Bank of Ashland; Calgon Carbon Corp.; King's Daughters' Hospital; Allstate Insurance Co.; Kemper Insurance Group; Commercial Union Cos.; The Mayo Coal Cos.; Maryland Casualty Co.; Merck & Co.

For full biographical listings, see the Martindale-Hubbell Law Directory

*BOWLING GREEN,** Warren Co.

CAMPBELL, KERRICK & GRISE (AV)

1025 State Street, P.O. Box 9547, 42102-9547
Telephone: 502-782-8160
FAX: 502-782-5856

MEMBERS OF FIRM

Joe Bill Campbell
Thomas N. Kerrick
John R. Grise
Gregory N. Stivers
H. Brent Brennenstuhl
Deborah Tomes Wilkins

ASSOCIATES

H. Harris Pepper, Jr.
Lanna Martin Kilgore
Laura Hagan

Representative Clients: Dollar General Corp.; Greenview Hospital; Hospital Corporation of America; Hardin Memorial Hospital; Monarch Environmental, Inc.; Mid-South Management Group, Inc.; Western Kentucky University; Service One Credit Union; Trans Financial Bank; TKR Cable.

For full biographical listings, see the Martindale-Hubbell Law Directory

CATRON, KILGORE & BEGLEY (AV)

918 State Street, P.O. Box 280, 42102-0280
Telephone: 502-842-1050
Fax: 502-842-4720

Stephen B. Catron
J. Patrick Kilgore
Ernest Edward Begley, II

For full biographical listings, see the Martindale-Hubbell Law Directory

ENGLISH, LUCAS, PRIEST & OWSLEY (AV)

1101 College Street, P.O. Box 770, 42102-0770
Telephone: 502-781-6500
Telecopier: 502-782-7782

MEMBERS OF FIRM

Charles E. English
James H. Lucas
Whayne C. Priest, Jr.
Keith M. Carwell
Wade T. Markham, II

ASSOCIATE

Vance Cook

For Complete List of Firm Personnel, See General Section

For full biographical listings, see the Martindale-Hubbell Law Directory

Bowling Green—Continued

HARLIN & PARKER, P.S.C. (AV)

519 East Tenth Street, P.O. Box 390, 42102-0390
Telephone: 502-842-5611
Telefax: 502-842-2607
Smiths Grove, Kentucky Office: Old Farmers Bank Building.
Telephone: 502-563-4701.

William Jerry Parker — James David Bryant

Insurance Clients: Allstate Insurance Co.; American Hardware Mutual Insurance Co.; American International Group; CNA Insurance Companies; Government Employees Insurance Co.; Meridian Mutual Insurance Co.
Railroad and Utilities Clients: District Attorneys for South Central Bell Telephone Co.; CSX Transportation, Inc.
Local Counsel for: General Motors Corp.; Ford Motor Corp.; Chrysler Corp.

For Complete List of Firm Personnel, See General Section

For full biographical listings, see the Martindale-Hubbell Law Directory

*CARROLLTON,** Carroll Co.

SHEPHERD & MONK (AV)

115 Fifth Street, P.O. Box 246, 41008
Telephone: 502-732-4281
FAX: 502-732-9279

James W. Shepherd — James C. Monk

Counsel for: Star Bank, N.A., Carrollton, Kentucky.
Local Counsel for: Dow Corning Corp.

For full biographical listings, see the Martindale-Hubbell Law Directory

*CATLETTSBURG,** Boyd Co.

ADKINS & ADKINS (AV)

Adkins Building, 2813 Louisa Street, P.O. Box 653, 41129
Telephone: 606-739-4151
Fax: Available Upon Request

James E. Adkins — James E. Adkins, II

General Counsel for: Catlettsburg Federal Savings & Loan Assn.; Kentucky-Farmers Bank.
Local Counsel for: Federal National Mortgage Assn.
Approved Attorneys for: Farmers Home Administration.

COVINGTON, Kenton Co.

ADAMS, BROOKING, STEPNER, WOLTERMANN & DUSING (AV)

421 Garrard Street, P.O. Box 861, 41012
Telephone: 606-291-7270
FAX: 606-291-7902
Florence, Kentucky Office: 8100 Burlington Pike, Suite 400, 41042.
Telephone: 606-371-6220.
FAX: 606-371-8341.

Charles S. Adams (1906-1971)
John R. S. Brooking
Donald L. Stepner
James G. Woltermann (Resident at Florence Office)
Gerald F. Dusing (Resident at Florence Office)
Michael M. Sketch (Resident at Florence Office)
Dennis R. Williams (Resident at Florence Office)
James R. Kruer
Jeffrey C. Mando

ASSOCIATES

Marc D. Dietz (Resident at Florence Office)
Gregory S. Shumate
John S. "Brook" Brooking (Resident at Florence Office)
Stacey L. Graus
Lori A. Schlarman (Resident, Florence Office)
Paul J. Darpel (Resident, Florence Office)
Chandra S. Baldwin (Not admitted in KY)

Representative Clients: CSX Transportation; Balluff, Inc., Wampler, Inc., Kisters, Inc., Krauss-Maffei, Inc., A group of German companies; State Automobile Mutual Insurance Co.; Chevron of California; Great American Insurance Co.; Grange Mutual Insurance Co.; Meridian Mutual Insurance Co.; Fifth-Third Bank of Northern Ky.; Northern Kentucky University.

For full biographical listings, see the Martindale-Hubbell Law Directory

KLETTE AND KLETTE (AV)

250 Grandview Drive, Suite 250, Ft. Mitchell, 41017-5610
Telephone: 606-344-9966
Fax: 606-344-9900
Cincinnati, Ohio Office: 3905 Brigadoon Drive, 45255.
Telephone: 513-421-6699.

MEMBERS OF FIRM

John H. Klette, Jr. — V. Ruth Klette
Debra S. Fox

LEGAL SUPPORT PERSONNEL

Evelyn Richard (Paralegal)

General Counsel for: The Northern Kentucky Motor Club; First Federal Savings & Loan Association of Covington.

(See Next Column)

For full biographical listings, see the Martindale-Hubbell Law Directory

TALIAFERRO AND MEHLING (AV)

1005 Madison Avenue, P.O. Box 468, 41012-0468
Telephone: 606-291-9900
Fax: 606-291-3014

MEMBERS OF FIRM

Philip Taliaferro, III — Christopher J. Mehling

ASSOCIATES

Lucinda C. Shirooni
C. Houston Ebert
Alice G. Keys
J. David Brittingham

OF COUNSEL

Robert W. Carran — Norbert J. Bischoff

For full biographical listings, see the Martindale-Hubbell Law Directory

FLORENCE, Boone Co.

ADAMS, BROOKING, STEPNER, WOLTERMANN & DUSING (AV)

8100 Burlington Pike, Suite 400, 41042-0576
Telephone: 606-371-6220
FAX: 606-371-8341
Covington, Kentucky Office: 421 Garrard Street.
Telephone: 606-291-7270.
FAX: 606-291-7902.

Donald L. Stepner
James G. Woltermann (Resident)
Gerald F. Dusing (Resident)
Michael M. Sketch (Resident)
Dennis R. Williams (Resident)
Jeffrey C. Mando

ASSOCIATES

Marc D. Dietz (Resident)
John S. "Brook" Brooking (Resident)
Lori A. Schlarman
Paul J. Darpel

Representative Clients: CSX Transportation; State Automobile Mutual Insurance Co.; Standard Oil Co. (Ky.); Great American Insurance Co.; Grange Mutual Insurance Co.; Meridian Mutual Insurance Co.; Fifth-Third Bank of Boone County; Northern Kentucky University.

For full biographical listings, see the Martindale-Hubbell Law Directory

*GEORGETOWN,** Scott Co.

BRADLEY & BRADLEY (AV)

Bradley Building, 102 West Main Street, 40324
Telephone: 502-863-1464

MEMBERS OF FIRM

Victor A. Bradley, Sr. (1885-1969)
J. Craig Bradley, Sr. (1881-1961)
Victor A. Bradley, Jr. (1913-1984)
J. Craig Bradley, Jr.
Clay M. Brock
James B. Wooten, Jr.

Vice Division Counsel: Cincinnati, New Orleans & Texas Pacific Railway.
Assistant Division Counsel for: Southern Railway System.
Attorneys for: Louisville & Nashville Railroad Co.; Kentucky Utilities Co.; First National Bank & Trust Co.; Farmers Bank & Trust Company of Georgetown, Ky.; The Chesapeake & Ohio Railroad Co.; South Central Bell Telephone Co.; Georgetown College; State Farm Mutual Insurance Co.

For full biographical listings, see the Martindale-Hubbell Law Directory

E. DURWARD WELDON (AV)

217 East Main Street, 40324
Telephone: 502-863-1285

Approved Attorney For: Lawyers Title Insurance Corporation of Richmond, Virginia; Louisville Title Division of Commonwealth Land Title Insurance Co. (Binder Agent); The Equitable Life Assurance Society of the United States.

For full biographical listings, see the Martindale-Hubbell Law Directory

*LEXINGTON,** Fayette Co.

BROCK, BROCK & BAGBY (AV)

190 Market Street, P.O. Box 1630, 40592-1630
Telephone: 606-255-7795
Fax: 606-255-6198

MEMBERS OF FIRM

Walter L. Brock, Jr.
Daniel N. Brock
Glen S. Bagby
J. Robert Lyons, Jr.
Beverly Benton Polk

ASSOCIATE

Bruce A. Rector

LEGAL SUPPORT PERSONNEL

PARALEGALS

Pamela H. Brown — Freda Greer Grubbs

For full biographical listings, see the Martindale-Hubbell Law Directory

Lexington—Continued

GREENEBAUM DOLL & MCDONALD (AV)

A Partnership including Professional Service Corporations
1400 Vine Center Tower, 40508
Telephone: 606-231-8500
Telecopier: 606-255-2742
Telex: 213029
Louisville, Kentucky Office: 3300 National City Tower.
Telephone: 502-589-4200.
Fax: 502-587-3695.
Covington, Kentucky Office: 50 East River Center Boulevard, P.O. Box 2050.
Telephone: 606-655-4200.
Fax: 606-655-4239.
Cincinnati, Ohio Office: 832 Main Street.
Telephone: 513-421-8087.
Fax: 513-421-8089.

MEMBERS OF FIRM

A. Robert Doll *
Job D. Turner, III (Resident)
John R. Cummins
Henry C. T. Richmond, III

Representative Clients: Aetna Life Insurance Co.; ANDALEX Resources, Inc.; Ashland Oil, Inc.; AT&T Communications, Inc.; Bethlehem Steel Corp.; Brown-Forman Corp.; Columbia Gas & Transmission Co.; Commonwealth Aluminum Corp.; Consolidation Coal Co.; Costain Coal, Inc.
*A Professional Service Corporation

For Complete List of Firm Personnel, See General Section

For full biographical listings, see the Martindale-Hubbell Law Directory

LANDRUM & SHOUSE (AV)

106 West Vine Street, P.O. Box 951, 40588-0951
Telephone: 606-255-2424
Facsimile: 606-233-0308
Louisville, Kentucky Office: 400 West Market Street, Suite 1550, 40202.
Telephone: 502-589-7616.
Facsimile: 502-589-2119.

MEMBERS OF FIRM

John H. Burrus
William C. Shouse
Mark L. Moseley

ASSOCIATE

Charles E. Christian

District Attorneys: CSX Transportation, Inc.
Special Trial Counsel: Ford Motor Co. and Affiliates (Eastern Kentucky); Clark Equipment Co.
Representative Clients: The Continental Insurance Cos.; U.S. Insurance Group; U.S. Fidelity & Guaranty Co.; Ohio Casualty Insurance Co.; CIGNA; Royal Insurance Cos.

For Complete List of Firm Personnel, See General Section

For full biographical listings, see the Martindale-Hubbell Law Directory

STOLL, KEENON & PARK (AV)

201 E. Main Street, Suite 1000, 40507-1380
Telephone: 606-231-3000
Telecopier: 606-253-1093; 606-253-1027
Frankfort, Kentucky Office: 326 West Main Street.
Telephone: 502-875-6000.
Telecopier: 502-875-6008.
Louisville, Kentucky Office: 400 West Market Street, Suite 2650, 40202.
Telephone: 502-568-9100.
Telecopier: 502-568-6340.

MEMBERS OF FIRM

William T. Bishop, III
Douglas P. Romaine

ASSOCIATE

Roger W. Madden

For Complete List of Firm Personnel, See General Section

For full biographical listings, see the Martindale-Hubbell Law Directory

STURGILL, TURNER & TRUITT (AV)

155 East Main Street, 40507
Telephone: 606-255-8581
Fax: 606-231-0851

MEMBERS OF FIRM

Gardner L. Turner
Ann D. Sturgill

For Complete List of Firm Personnel, See General Section

For full biographical listings, see the Martindale-Hubbell Law Directory

*LOUISVILLE,** Jefferson Co.

CONLIFFE, SANDMANN & SULLIVAN (AV)

621 West Main Street, 40202
Telephone: 502-587-7711
Telecopier: 502-587-7756
Other Louisville Office: 4169 Westport Road, Suite 111, 40207.
Telephone: 502-896-2966.
Jeffersonville, Indiana Office: 141 E. Spring Street, 47150.
Telephone: 812-949-7711.

Charles I. Sandmann (1936-1992)

MEMBERS OF FIRM

I. G. Spencer, Jr.
Steven J. Kriegshaber
Karl N. Victor, Jr.
Edwin J. Lowry, Jr.
Michael E. Conliffe
Olivia Morris Fuchs
Richard M. Sullivan
James A. Babbitz
Sam Deeb
Kenneth A. Bohnert
Jack R. Underwood, Jr.
James T. Mitchell
E. Bruce Neikirk
Wm. Dennis Sims
Victoria Ann Ogden
Edward F. Busch
Robert A. Donald, III
Laura J. Ensor
Sally Hardin Lambert
Richard B. Taylor
John R. Broadway

OF COUNSEL

Allen P. Dodd, III
Alan R. Miller

For full biographical listings, see the Martindale-Hubbell Law Directory

GREENEBAUM DOLL & MCDONALD (AV)

A Partnership including Professional Service Corporations
3300 National City Tower, 40202
Telephone: 502-589-4200
Fax: 502-587-3695
Lexington, Kentucky Office: 1400 Vine Center Tower.
Telephone: 606-231-8500.
Fax: 606-255-2742.
Covington, Kentucky Office: 50 East River Center Boulevard, P.O. Box 2050.
Telephone: 606-655-4200.
Fax: 606-655-4239.
Cincinnati, Ohio Office: 832 Main Street.
Telephone: 513-421-8087.
Fax: 513-421-8089.

A. Robert Doll *
Henry C. T. Richmond, III
John R. Cummins
William L. Montague (Covington, Kentucky and Cincinnati, Ohio Offices)
Job D. Turner, III (Resident at Lexington, Kentucky)

ASSOCIATES

Mark H. Oppenheimer
John S. Lueken

OF COUNSEL

Martin S. Weinberg

Representative Clients: Aetna Life Insurance Co.; ANDALEX Resources, Inc.; Ashland Oil, Inc.; A T & T Communications, Inc.; Bethlehem Steel Corp.; Brown-Forman Corp.; Humana, Inc.; Kentucky Kingdom, Inc.; KFC National Cooperative Advertising Program, Inc.
*A Professional Service Corporation

For Complete List of Firm Personnel, See General Section

For full biographical listings, see the Martindale-Hubbell Law Directory

LAWRENCE AND LAWRENCE (AV)

Suite 300, 200 South Seventh Street, 40202
Telephone: 502-583-4484
Fax: 502-583-4486

William W. Lawrence

Reference: Citizens Fidelity Bank and Trust Co.

For full biographical listings, see the Martindale-Hubbell Law Directory

HENRY B. MANN (AV)

22nd Floor Citizens Plaza, 40202
Telephone: 502-587-6544

References: Liberty National Bank & Trust; PNC Bank, Kentucky; Bank of Louisville; National City Bank, Kentucky.

For full biographical listings, see the Martindale-Hubbell Law Directory

MIDDLETON & REUTLINGER, P.S.C. (AV)

2500 Brown and Williamson Tower, 40202-3410
Telephone: 502-584-1135
Fax: 502-561-0442
Jeffersonville, Indiana Office: 605 Watt Street, 47130.
Telephone: 812-282-4886.

(See Next Column)

MIDDLETON & REUTLINGER P.S.C.—*Continued*

Ian Y. Henderson
Charles G. Middleton, III
Brooks Alexander
Kipley J. McNally

Karen M. Campbell

Counsel for: Chevron USA; Liberty National Bank; Logan Aluminum, Inc.; Louisville Gas & Electric Co.; MCI Telecommunications Corp.; Metropolitan Life Insurance Co.; Kosmos Cement Co.; Porcelain Metal Corp.; The Home Insurance Co.; The Kroger Co.; Demars Haka Development, Inc.

For Complete List of Firm Personnel, See General Section

For full biographical listings, see the Martindale-Hubbell Law Directory

OGDEN NEWELL & WELCH (AV)

1200 One Riverfront Plaza, 40202-2973
Telephone: 502-582-1601
Fax: 502-581-9564

MEMBERS OF FIRM

Joseph C. Oldham
James L. Coorssen
Robert E. Thieman
Turney P. Berry

Counsel for: KU Energy Corp.; Kentucky Utilities Co.; Brown-Forman Corp.; B.F. Goodrich Co.; J.J.B. Hilliard, W.L. Lyons, Inc.; Interlock Industries, Inc.; Liberty National Bank; United Medical Corp.; Bank of Louisville.

For Complete List of Firm Personnel, See General Section

For full biographical listings, see the Martindale-Hubbell Law Directory

RUBIN HAYS & FOLEY (AV)

First Trust Centre 200 South Fifth Street, 40202
Telephone: 502-569-7550
Telecopier: 502-569-7555

MEMBERS OF FIRM

Wm. Carl Fust
Harry Lee Meyer
David W. Gray
Irvin D. Foley
Joseph R. Gathright, Jr.
Lisa Koch Bryant
Sharon C. Hardy
Charles S. Musson
W. Randall Jones
K. Gail Russell

ASSOCIATE

Christian L. Juckett

OF COUNSEL

James E. Fahey
Newman T. Guthrie

Representative Clients: J.C. Bradford & Co., Inc.; J.J.B. Hilliard, W.L. Lyons, Inc.; Huntington National Bank; Liberty National Bank and Trust Company; National City Bank; PNC Bank; Prudential Bache & Co., Inc.; Prudential Securities, Inc.; Society Bank; Stock Yards Bank and Trust Co.

For full biographical listings, see the Martindale-Hubbell Law Directory

WEBER & ROSE PROFESSIONAL SERVICE CORPORATION (AV)

2700 Providian Center, 400 West Market Street, 40202
Telephone: 502-589-2200
Fax: 502-589-3400
Jeffersonville, Indiana Office: 432 East Court Avenue.
Telephone: 812-288-4372.

L. R. Curtis (1880-1968)
Shelton R. Weber
C. Alex Rose
Michael W. McGrath, Jr.
Wesley P. Adams, Jr.
Russell H. Saunders
James M. Gary
A. Andrew Draut
R. Hite Nally
Martin A. Arnett
Edward J. Smith

Bruce D. Atherton
Patrick W. Gault
Karen L. Keith

Counsel for: The Enro Shirt Co.

For full biographical listings, see the Martindale-Hubbell Law Directory

*MOREHEAD,** Rowan Co.

DEHNER & ELLIS (AV)

206 East Main Street, 40351
Telephone: 606-783-1504
FAX: 606-784-2744

Truman L. Dehner
John J. Ellis

For full biographical listings, see the Martindale-Hubbell Law Directory

*OWENSBORO,** Daviess Co.

CONNOR, NEAL & STEVENSON (AV)

613 Frederica Street, 42301
Telephone: 502-926-9911
Fax: 502-686-7905

(See Next Column)

MEMBERS OF FIRM

Sidney A. Neal (1927-1987)
Jack A. Connor
Thomas E. Neal
John W. Stevenson
James A. Wethington, II

ASSOCIATE

William A. Mitchell

Representative Client: Grange Mutual Casualty Co.
Approved Attorneys for: Farmers Home Administration.

For full biographical listings, see the Martindale-Hubbell Law Directory

WILSON, JOHNSON & PRESSER (AV)

418 West Third Street, 42301
Telephone: 502-926-1717
FAX: 502-926-1722

MEMBERS OF FIRM

R. Allen Wilson
E. Louis Johnson
Ronald L. Presser

For full biographical listings, see the Martindale-Hubbell Law Directory

WILSON, WILSON & PLAIN (AV)

414 Masonic Building, 42301
Telephone: 502-926-2525
Telecopier: 502-683-3812

MEMBERS OF FIRM

George S. Wilson, Jr. (1902-1966)
William L. Wilson (1912-1993)
George S. Wilson, III
R. Scott Plain
William L. Wilson, Jr.
Thomas S. Poteat
R. Scott Plain, Jr.

Representative Clients: Liberty National Bank, Owensboro, Ky.; Owensboro Board of Education; Owensboro River Sand & Gravel Co.; The Prudential Ins. Co.; Kentucky Farm Bureau Mutual Insurance Co.; Baskin Robbins; Motorist Mutual Insurance Co.; Yager Materials, Inc.
Approved Attorneys for: Louisville Title Division of Commonwealth Land Title Insurance Co.

For full biographical listings, see the Martindale-Hubbell Law Directory

*OWINGSVILLE,** Bath Co.

BYRON & ROBERTS (AV)

112 Court Street, 40360
Telephone: 606-674-2911

MEMBERS OF FIRM

Roger A. Byron
Winifred Byron Roberts

General Counsel for: Farmers Bank, Owingsville, Kentucky.
Local Counsel for: Delta Natural Gas Co.
Approved Attorney for: Lawyers Title Insurance Corp.

For full biographical listings, see the Martindale-Hubbell Law Directory

*VANCEBURG,** Lewis Co.

STANLEY AND BERTRAM (AV)

P.O. Box 40, 41179-0040
Telephone: 606-796-3024; 796-3025
Fax: 606-796-2113

MEMBERS OF FIRM

Avery L. Stanley
Thomas M. Bertram, II
Anita Esham Stanley

A list of Representative Clients will be furnished upon request.

For full biographical listings, see the Martindale-Hubbell Law Directory

LOUISIANA

*BATON ROUGE,** East Baton Rouge Parish

KANTROW, SPAHT, WEAVER & BLITZER, A PROFESSIONAL LAW CORPORATION (AV)

Suite 300, City Plaza, 445 North Boulevard, P.O. Box 2997, 70821-2997
Telephone: 504-383-4703
Fax: 504-343-0630; 343-0637

Byron R. Kantrow
Carlos G. Spaht
Geraldine B. Weaver
Sidney M. Blitzer, Jr.
Paul H. Spaht
Lee C. Kantrow
John C. Miller
Vincent P. Fornias
David S. Rubin
Diane L. Crochet
Richard F. Zimmerman, Jr.
Bob D. Tucker
Martin E. Golden
Joseph A. Schittone, Jr.

(See Next Column)

KANTROW, SPAHT, WEAVER & BLITZER A PROFESSIONAL LAW CORPORATION, *Baton Rouge—Continued*

S. Layne Lee
J. Michael Robinson, Jr.
Connell L. Archey
Richard D. Moreno
Randal J. Robert

Representative Clients: CNA Insurance Cos.; Federal Deposit Insurance Corp.; Hartford Insurance Group; Air Products and Chemicals, Inc.; CF Industries, Inc.; AT&T; United Companies Financial Corp.

For full biographical listings, see the Martindale-Hubbell Law Directory

KEAN, MILLER, HAWTHORNE, D'ARMOND, MCCOWAN & JARMAN, L.L.P. (AV)

22nd Floor, One American Place, P.O. Box 3513, 70821
Telephone: 504-387-0999
Fax: 504-388-9133
New Orleans, Louisiana Office: Energy Centre, Suite 1470, 1100 Poydras Street.
Telephone: 504-585-3050.
Fax: 504-585-3051.

MEMBERS OF FIRM

Ben R. Miller, Jr.
Robert A. Hawthorne, Jr.
Carey J. Messina
Isaac M. Gregorie, Jr.
Todd A. Rossi

Mary Dougherty Jackson

SPECIAL COUNSEL

Gerald Le Van

For Complete List of Firm Personnel, See General Section

For full biographical listings, see the Martindale-Hubbell Law Directory

BERT K. ROBINSON (AV)

10357 Old Hammond Highway, 70816-8261
Telephone: 504-924-0296
Fax: 504-924-5288

ASSOCIATE

Johanna R. Landreneau

OF COUNSEL

Charles C. Holbrook

For full biographical listings, see the Martindale-Hubbell Law Directory

*HOMER,** Claiborne Parish

SHAW AND SHAW, A PROFESSIONAL LAW CORPORATION (AV)

522 East Main Street, P.O. Box 420, 71040
Telephone: 318-927-6149

William M. Shaw

Reference: Homer National Bank.

*LAKE CHARLES,** Calcasieu Parish

JONES, TÊTE, NOLEN, HANCHEY, SWIFT & SPEARS, L.L.P. (AV)

First Federal Building, P.O. Box 910, 70602
Telephone: 318-439-8315
Telefax: 436-5606; 433-5536

MEMBERS OF FIRM

Sam H. Jones (1897-1978)
William R. Tête
William M. Nolen
James C. Hanchey
Carl H. Hanchey
William B. Swift
Kenneth R. Spears
Edward J. Fonti
Charles N. Harper
Gregory W. Belfour
Robert J. Tête
Yul D. Lorio

OF COUNSEL

John A. Patin
Edward D. Myrick

ASSOCIATES

Lilynn A. Cutrer
Lydia Ann Guillory-Lee
Clint David Bischoff

General Counsel for: First Federal Savings & Loan Association of Lake Charles; Beauregard Electric Cooperative, Inc.
Representative Clients: Atlantic Richfield Company; CITGO Petroleum Corp.; Conoco Inc.; HIMONT U.S.A., Inc.; ITT Hartford; Olin Corporation; OXY USA Inc.; Premier Bank, National Association; W.R. Grace & Co.

For full biographical listings, see the Martindale-Hubbell Law Directory

METAIRIE, Jefferson Parish

KIEFER & RUDMAN, A PROFESSIONAL LAW CORPORATION (AV)

One Galleria Boulevard, Suite 1212, 70001
Telephone: 504-838-2250
Telefax: 504-838-2251
New Orleans, Louisiana Office: One Seine Court, Suite 112.
Telephone: 504-368-2220.
Fax: 504-368-2278.

John B. Kiefer
Laurence D. Rudman
Roger B. Jacobs
Bruce M. Danner
Philip Schoen Brooks
Harry L. Cahill, III
Terri Bankston Stirling
Pierre V. Miller II
Gregory G. Faia
Scott B. Kiefer

References: First National Bank of Commerce; First National Bank of Commerce of Jefferson Parish; Hibernia National Bank; Jefferson Guaranty Bank; Whitney National Bank of New Orleans.

For full biographical listings, see the Martindale-Hubbell Law Directory

WEIR AND WALLEY (AV)

2721 Division Street, 70002-7084
Telephone: 504-455-7264
Fax: 504-455-7266

MEMBERS OF FIRM

Andrew M. Weir
James M. Walley

References: the Whitney National Bank; First National Bank of Commerce.

For full biographical listings, see the Martindale-Hubbell Law Directory

*SHREVEPORT,** Caddo Parish

BARLOW AND HARDTNER L.C. (AV)

Tenth Floor, Louisiana Tower, 401 Edwards Street, 71101-3289
Telephone: 318-227-1131
Telecopier: 318-227-1141
Mailing Address: P.O. Box 8, Shreveport, Louisiana, 71161-0008

Quintin T. Hardtner, III
Stephen E. Ramey

OF COUNSEL

Cecil E. Ramey, Jr.
Paula Hazelrig Hickman

Representative Clients: Kelley Oil Corporation; NorAm Energy Corp. (formerly Arkla, Inc.); Central and South West; Panhandle Eastern Corp.; Pennzoil Producing Co.; Johnson Controls, Inc.; Ashland Oil, Inc.; Southwestern Electric Power Company; Brammer Engineering, Inc.; General Electric Co.

For Complete List of Firm Personnel, See General Section

For full biographical listings, see the Martindale-Hubbell Law Directory

BODENHEIMER, JONES, KLOTZ & SIMMONS (AV)

509 Milam Street, 71101
Telephone: 318-221-1507
Fax: 318-221-4560

MEMBERS OF FIRM

J. W. Jones
David B. Klotz
C. Gary Mitchell

For full biographical listings, see the Martindale-Hubbell Law Directory

COOK, YANCEY, KING & GALLOWAY, A PROFESSIONAL LAW CORPORATION (AV)

1700 Commercial National Tower, 333 Texas Street, P.O. Box 22260, 71120-2260
Telephone: 318-221-6277
Telecopier: 318-227-2606

Sidney B. Galloway
Stephen R. Yancey II
James H. Campbell
J. Benjamin Warren, Jr.
William C. Kalmbach, III

A list of representative clients will be furnished upon request.

For Complete List of Firm Personnel, See General Section

For full biographical listings, see the Martindale-Hubbell Law Directory

WIENER, WEISS, MADISON & HOWELL, A PROFESSIONAL CORPORATION (AV)

333 Texas Street, Suite 2350, P.O. Box 21990, 71120-1990
Telephone: 318-226-9100
Fax: 318-424-5128

Donald P. Weiss
John M. Madison, Jr.
Lawrence Russo, III
Allen P. Jones
Donald B. Wiener

Representative Clients: Pioneer Bank & Trust Co.; Ford Motor Credit Corp.; CNA Insurance Companies; International Paper Companies; Louisiana Homebuilders Association Self Insurers Fund; LSU-Shreveport; Sealy Re-

(See Next Column)

WIENER, WEISS, MADISON & HOWELL A PROFESSIONAL CORPORATION—*Continued*

alty, Inc.; Palmer Petroleum, Inc.; Brookshire Grocery Company (Louisiana); Northwest Louisiana Production Credit Association.

For Complete List of Firm Personnel, See General Section

For full biographical listings, see the Martindale-Hubbell Law Directory

*WINNFIELD,** Winn Parish

SIMMONS AND DERR (AV)

Simmons Building, Church Street, P.O. Box 525, 71483
Telephone: 318-628-3951

MEMBERS OF FIRM

Kermit M. Simmons   Jacque D. Derr

Reference: Bank of Winnfield & Trust Co.

For full biographical listings, see the Martindale-Hubbell Law Directory

MAINE

*BANGOR,** Penobscot Co.

EATON, PEABODY, BRADFORD & VEAGUE, P.A. (AV)

Fleet Center-Exchange Street, P.O. Box 1210, 04402-1210
Telephone: 207-947-0111
Telecopier: 207-942-3040
Augusta, Maine Office: 2 Central Plaza.
Telephone: 207-622-3747.
Telecopier: 207-622-9732.
Brunswick, Maine Office: 167 Park Row.
Telephone: 207-729-1144.
Telecopier: 207-729-1140.
Camden, Maine Office: 7-9 Washington Street.
Telephone: 207-236-3325.
Telecopier: 207-236-8611.
Dover-Foxcroft, Maine Office: 30 East Main Street.
Telephone: 207-564-8378.
Telecopier: 207-564-7059.

John W. Conti
Calvin E. True
Clarissa B. Edelston
Douglas M. Smith (Resident, Dover-Foxcroft and Augusta Offices)

OF COUNSEL

Donald A. Spear (Resident, Brunswick Office)

R. Lee Ivy   David W. Kesner

A List of Representative Clients available upon request.

For Complete List of Firm Personnel, See General Section

For full biographical listings, see the Martindale-Hubbell Law Directory

CAMDEN, Knox Co.

PIERCE, ATWOOD, SCRIBNER, ALLEN, SMITH & LANCASTER (AV)

36 Chestnut Street, P.O. Box 780, 04843
Telephone: 207-236-4333
Fax: 207-236-6247
Portland, Maine Office: One Monument Square.
Telephone: 207-773-6411.
Augusta, Maine Office: 77 Winthrop Street.
Telephone: 207-622-6311.

MEMBERS OF FIRM

Richard A. McKittrick   Peter G. Warren

For full biographical listings, see the Martindale-Hubbell Law Directory

KENNEBUNK, York Co.

REAGAN, ADAMS & CADIGAN (AV)

Eleven Main Street, P.O. Box 709, 04043
Telephone: 207-985-7181
Telecopier: 207-985-7003

MEMBERS OF FIRM

Thomas J. Reagan
Wayne T. Adams
Christopher Reagan
Paul W. Cadigan

Counsel for: Kennebunk Savings Bank.

For full biographical listings, see the Martindale-Hubbell Law Directory

*PORTLAND,** Cumberland Co.

McCANDLESS & HUNT (AV)

57 Exchange Street, 04101
Telephone: 207-772-4100
Telecopier: 207-772-1300

MEMBERS OF FIRM

Eileen M. L. Epstein
David E. Hunt
Elizabeth T. McCandless

ASSOCIATE

Dennis J. O'Donovan

For full biographical listings, see the Martindale-Hubbell Law Directory

PIERCE, ATWOOD, SCRIBNER, ALLEN, SMITH & LANCASTER (AV)

One Monument Square, 04101
Telephone: 207-773-6411
Fax: 207-773-3419
Augusta, Maine Office: 77 Winthrop Street.
Telephone: 207-622-6311.
Camden, Maine Office: 36 Chestnut Street, P.O. Box 780.
Telephone: 207-236-4333.

MEMBERS OF FIRM

Fred C. Scribner, Jr. (1908-1994)
Sigrid E. Tompkins
William C. Smith
Warren E. Winslow, Jr. (Resident, Augusta Office)
Everett P. Ingalls
Richard A. McKittrick (Resident, Camden Office)
Michael R. Currie
Peter G. Warren (Resident, Camden Office)

ASSOCIATES

Barbara K. Wheaton   Mary McQuillen

For Complete List of Firm Personnel, See General Section

For full biographical listings, see the Martindale-Hubbell Law Directory

PRETI, FLAHERTY, BELIVEAU & PACHIOS (AV)

443 Congress Street, P.O. Box 11410, 04104-7410
Telephone: 207-791-3000
Telecopier: 207-791-3111
Augusta, Maine Office: 45 Memorial Circle, P.O. Box 1058, 04332-1058.
Telephone: 207-623-5300.
Telecopier: 207-623-2914.
Rumford, Maine Office: 150 Congress Street, P.O. Drawer L, 04276-2035.
Telephone: 207-364-4593.
Telecopier: 207-369-9421.

MEMBERS OF FIRM

Albert J. Beliveau, Jr. (Rumford Office)
Estelle A. Lavoie
Michael L. Sheehan

OF COUNSEL

Robert F. Preti   Robert W. Smith

For Complete List of Firm Personnel, See General Section

For full biographical listings, see the Martindale-Hubbell Law Directory

MARYLAND

*BALTIMORE,** (Independent City)

HYLTON & GONZALES (AV)

Suite 418 Equitable Building, 10 North Calvert Street, 21202
Telephone: 410-547-0900
Telecopier: 410-625-1560

MEMBER OF FIRM

Louise Michaux Gonzales

For Complete List of Firm Personnel, See General Section

For full biographical listings, see the Martindale-Hubbell Law Directory

McKENNEY, THOMSEN AND BURKE (AV)

Suite 400, One North Charles Street, 21201
Telephone: 410-539-2595
FAX: 410-783-0710
Washington, D.C. Office: Suite 500, 1225 Eye Street, N.W.
Telephone: 202-682-4741.
FAX: 202-547-3713.

OF COUNSEL

W. Gibbs McKenney

MEMBERS OF FIRM

George E. Thomsen
Paul E. Burke, Jr.
Roszel C. Thomsen, II

(See Next Column)

McKenney, Thomsen and Burke, *Baltimore—Continued*

ASSOCIATES

Hedley A. Clark
Patrick Kennedy

References: NationsBank; Mercantile-Safe Deposit & Trust Co.; Carroll County Bank and Trust Co.

For full biographical listings, see the Martindale-Hubbell Law Directory

Venable, Baetjer and Howard (AV)

A Partnership including Professional Corporations
1800 Mercantile Bank & Trust Building, 2 Hopkins Plaza, 21201
Telephone: 410-244-7400
Washington, D.C. Office: Venable, Baetjer, Howard & Civiletti. Suite 1000, 1201 New York Avenue, N.W.
Telephone: 202-962-4800.
McLean, Virginia Office: Suite 400, 2010 Corporate Ridge.
Telephone: 703-760-1600.
Rockville, Maryland Office: Suite 500, One Church Street, P. O. Box 1906.
Telephone: 301-217-5600.
Towson, Maryland Office: 210 Allegheny Avenue, P. O. Box 5517.
Telephone: 410-494-6200.

MEMBERS OF FIRM

Jacques T. Schlenger (P.C.)
David D. Downes (Resident, Towson, Maryland Office)
John Henry Lewin, Jr. (P.C.)
Roger W. Titus (Resident, Rockville, Maryland Office)
Douglas D. Connah, Jr. (P.C.) (Also at Washington, D.C. Office)
Robert E. Madden (Not admitted in MD; also at Washington, D.C. and McLean, Virginia Offices)
Alexander I. Lewis, III (P.C.) (Also at Towson, Maryland Office)
Paul T. Glasgow (Resident, Rockville, Maryland Office)
Joseph C. Wich, Jr. (Resident, Towson, Maryland Office)
Jeffrey J. Radowich
Nell B. Strachan
L. Paige Marvel
James K. Archibald (Also at Washington, D.C. and Towson, Maryland Offices)
Christopher R. Mellott
M. King Hill, III (Resident, Towson, Maryland Office)
James A. Dunbar (Also at Washington, D.C. Office)
Robert L. Waldman
David J. Heubeck

OF COUNSEL

Robert M. Thomas (P.C.)
Robert R. Bair (P.C.)
Emried D. Cole, Jr.

ASSOCIATES

John P. Edgar
Jeffrey K. Gonya
Lisa H. Rice Hayes

For Complete List of Firm Personnel, See General Section

For full biographical listings, see the Martindale-Hubbell Law Directory

*BEL AIR,** Harford Co.

Stark & Keenan, A Professional Association (AV)

30 Office Street, 21014
Telephone: 410-838-5522
Baltimore: 410-879-2222
Fax: 410-879-0688

Elwood V. Stark, Jr.
Charles B. Keenan, Jr.
Thomas E. Marshall
Edwin G. Carson
Judith C. H. Cline
Gregory A. Szoka
Robert S. Lynch

Claire Prin Blomquist
Kimberly Kahoe Muenter
Paul W. Ishak

For full biographical listings, see the Martindale-Hubbell Law Directory

GREENBELT, Prince Georges Co.

Stanley S. Pickett (AV)

Suite 414 Capital Office Park, 6411 Ivy Lane, 20770
Telephone: 301-513-0613

Stanley Sinclair Pickett

ASSOCIATE

Gordon J. Brumback

Representative Clients: B.F. Saul Co.; McDonald and Eudy Printers, Inc.; Condominium Management, Inc.; Long & Foster Realtors; Mitron Systems Corp.; Coldwell Banker; Eastern Property Group, Inc.; Glenanden Housing Authority; Koones & Montgomery, Inc.; Trans America Management, Inc.

For full biographical listings, see the Martindale-Hubbell Law Directory

*ROCKVILLE,** Montgomery Co.

Katz, Frome and Bleecker, P.A. (AV)

6116 Executive Boulevard, Suite 200, 20852
Telephone: 301-230-5800
Facsimile: 301-230-5830

(See Next Column)

Steven M. Katz
Morton J. Frome
Lorin H. Bleecker
Gail B. Landau

Susan J. Rubin
Marilyn J. Brasier
Leslie Anne Sullivan
Seth B. Popkin
Richard O'Connor
Stanley A. Snyder

OF COUNSEL

Philip F. Finelli, Jr.

For full biographical listings, see the Martindale-Hubbell Law Directory

Stein, Sperling, Bennett, De Jong, Driscoll, Greenfeig & Metro, P.A. (AV)

25 West Middle Lane, 20850
Telephone: 301-340-2020; 800-435-5230
Telecopier: 301-340-8217

David S. De Jong
Ann G. Jakabcin

For Complete List of Firm Personnel, See General Section

For full biographical listings, see the Martindale-Hubbell Law Directory

SILVER SPRING, Montgomery Co.

Dena C. Feeney, P.A. (AV)

Suite 220, 1010 Wayne Avenue, 20910
Telephone: 301-587-2240
Fax: 301-589-5412

Dena C. Feeney

Mary Frances Rhodes

For full biographical listings, see the Martindale-Hubbell Law Directory

*TOWSON,** Baltimore Co.

Venable, Baetjer and Howard (AV)

A Partnership including Professional Corporations
210 Allegheny Avenue, P.O. Box 5517, 21204
Telephone: 410-494-6200
FAX: 410-821-0147
Baltimore, Maryland Office: 1800 Mercantile Bank & Trust Building, 2 Hopkins Plaza.
Telephone: 410-244-7400.
Washington, D.C. Office: Venable, Baetjer, Howard & Civiletti. Suite 1000, 1201 New York Avenue, N.W.
Telephone: 202-962-4800.
McLean, Virginia Office: Suite 400, 2010 Corporate Ridge.
Telephone: 703-760-1600.
Rockville, Maryland Office: Suite 500, One Church Street, P. O. Box 1906.
Telephone: 301-217-5600.

PARTNERS

David D. Downes
Alexander I. Lewis, III (P.C.) (Also at Baltimore, Maryland Office)
Joseph C. Wich, Jr.
James K. Archibald (Also at Baltimore, Maryland and Washington, D.C. Offices)
M. King Hill, III

For Complete List of Firm Personnel, See General Section

For full biographical listings, see the Martindale-Hubbell Law Directory

MASSACHUSETTS

AMESBURY, Essex Co.

Hamel, Deshaies & Gagliardi (AV)

Five Market Square, P.O. Box 198, 01913
Telephone: 508-388-3558
Telecopier: 508-388-0441

MEMBERS OF FIRM

Richard P. Hamel
Robert J. Deshaies
Paul J. Gagliardi

ASSOCIATES

H. Scott Haskell
Peter R. Ayer, Jr.
Roger D. Turgeon
Charles E. Schissel

Representative Clients: Essex County Gas Co., Amesbury, MA; First and Ocean National Bank, Newburyport, MA; Amesbury Co-Operative Bank, Amesbury, MA.
Approved Attorneys for: Chicago Title Insurance; Old Republic Title Insurance Co.

For full biographical listings, see the Martindale-Hubbell Law Directory

ARLINGTON, Middlesex Co.

GRANNAN & MALOY, P.C. (AV)

Suite 408, 22 Mill Street, 02174
Telephone: 617-646-3200

William J. Grannan
Paul F. Maloy

For full biographical listings, see the Martindale-Hubbell Law Directory

*BOSTON,** Suffolk Co.

CUDDY BIXBY (AV)

One Financial Center, 02111
Telephone: 617-348-3600
Telecopier: 617-348-3643
Wellesley, Massachusetts Office: 60 Walnut Street.
Telephone: 617-235-1034.

Francis X. Cuddy (Retired)
Wayne E. Hartwell
Brian D. Bixby
Anthony M. Ambriano
William E. Kelly
Paul G. Boylan
Robert A. Vigoda
Paul J. Murphy
Alexander L. Cataldo
Duncan S. Payne
Stephen T. Kunian
Arthur P. Menard
Joseph H. Walsh
Michael J. Owens
Robert J. O'Regan
Andrew R. Menard
David F. Hendren
Glenn B. Asch
Timothy E. McAllister
William R. Moriarty
Kevin P. Sweeney
Denise I. Murphy

For full biographical listings, see the Martindale-Hubbell Law Directory

HEMENWAY & BARNES (AV)

60 State Street, 02109
Telephone: 617-227-7940
Fax: 617-227-0781

MEMBERS OF FIRM

George H. Kidder
David H. Morse
Roy A. Hammer
Lawrence T. Perera
George T. Shaw
Timothy F. Fidgeon
Michael J. Puzo
Deborah J. Hall
Kurt F. Somerville

For Complete List of Firm Personnel, See General Section

For full biographical listings, see the Martindale-Hubbell Law Directory

PALMER & DODGE (AV)

(Storey Thorndike Palmer & Dodge)
One Beacon Street, 02108
Telephone: 617-573-0100
Telecopier: 617-227-4420
Telex: 951104
Cable Address: "Storeydike," Boston

MEMBERS OF FIRM

Lawrence B. Cohen
Casimir de Rham, Jr.
Laurie J. Hall
Eric F. Menoyo
Arthur B. Page
R. Robert Woodburn, Jr.
Jackson W. Wright, Jr.

COUNSEL

Pamela M. Veasy

OF COUNSEL

Mary G. Sullivan

For Complete List of Firm Personnel, See General Section

For full biographical listings, see the Martindale-Hubbell Law Directory

RACKEMANN, SAWYER & BREWSTER, PROFESSIONAL CORPORATION (AV)

One Financial Center, 02111
Telephone: 617-542-2300
Telecopier: 617-542-7437

William B. Tyler
George V. Anastas
Henry H. Thayer
Stephen Carr Anderson
Albert M. Fortier, Jr.
Michael F. O'Connell
Stuart T. Freeland
Raymond J. Brassard
Alan B. Rubenstein
Martin R. Healy
James R. Shea, Jr.
Brian M. Hurley
Janet M. Smith
Peter Friedenberg
Richard S. Novak
J. David Leslie
Alexander H. Spaulding
Sanford M. Matathia
Anne P. Zebrowski

OF COUNSEL

Albert B. Wolfe
August R. Meyer
Richard H. Lovell

COUNSEL

Ronald S. Duby
Ross J. Hamlin

(See Next Column)

Margaret L. Hayes
Daniel J. Ossoff
Mary B. Freeley
Gordon M. Orloff
Donald R. Pinto, Jr.
Lucy West Behymer
Richard J. Gallogly
Melissa Langer Ellis
James A. Wachta
Susan Dempsey Baer
Daniel J. Bailey, III
Michael S. Giaimo
Maura E. Murphy
Mary L. Gallant
Peter A. Alpert
Lauren D. Armstrong
Robert B. Foster
Elizabeth A. Gibbons

For full biographical listings, see the Martindale-Hubbell Law Directory

SHERBURNE, POWERS & NEEDHAM, P.C. (AV)

One Beacon Street, 02108
Telephone: 617-523-2700
Fax: 617-523-6850

William D. Weeks
John T. Collins
Allan J. Landau
John L. Daly
Stephen A. Hopkins
Alan I. Falk
C. Thomas Swaim
James Pollock
William V. Tripp III
Stephen S. Young
William F. Machen
W. Robert Allison
Jacob C. Diemert
Philip J. Notopoulos
Richard J. Hindlian
Paul E. Troy
Harold W. Potter, Jr.
Dale R. Johnson
Philip S. Lapatin
Pamela A. Duckworth
Mark Schonfeld
James D. Smeallie
Paul Killeen
Gordon P. Katz
Joseph B. Darby, III
Richard M Yanofsky
James E. McDermott
Robert V. Lizza
Miriam Goldstein Altman
John J. Monaghan
Margaret J. Palladino
Mark C. Michalowski
David Scott Sloan
M. Chrysa Long
Lawrence D. Bradley
Miriam J. McKendall

Cynthia A. Brown
Cynthia M. Hern
Dianne R. Phillips
Paul M. James
Theodore F. Hanselman
Joshua C. Krumholz
Ieuan G. Mahony
Kenneth L. Harvey
Christopher J. Trombetta
Edwin F. Landers, Jr.
Amy J. Mastrobattista
William Howard McCarthy, Jr.
Douglas W. Clapp
Tamara E. Goulston
Nicholas J. Psyhogeos

COUNSEL

Haig Der Manuelian
Mason M. Taber, Jr.
Karl J. Hirshman
Benjamin Volinski
Kenneth P. Brier

OF COUNSEL

John Barr Dolan

For full biographical listings, see the Martindale-Hubbell Law Directory

WARNER & STACKPOLE (AV)

75 State Street, 02109
Telephone: 617-951-9000
Cable Address: "Warstack"
Telecopier: 617-951-9151
Telex: 940139

MEMBERS OF FIRM

Gordon M. Stevenson, Jr.
Elizabeth F. Potter
Patricia R. Hurley

ASSOCIATES

Kevin M. Meuse
Stephanie L. Dadaian

COUNSEL

David W. Lewis, Jr.

OF COUNSEL

Endicott Smith

For Complete List of Firm Personnel, See General Section

For full biographical listings, see the Martindale-Hubbell Law Directory

MERVIN M. WILF, LTD. (AV)

300 Commonwealth Avenue, 02115
Telephone: 617-437-7981
Philadelphia, Pennsylvania Office: 3200 Mellon Bank Center. 1735 Market Street.
Telephone: 215-575-7650. 568-4842.
Facsimile: 215-575-7652.

Mervin M. Wilf

A list of Representative Clients and References will be furnished upon request.

For full biographical listings, see the Martindale-Hubbell Law Directory

*CAMBRIDGE,** Middlesex Co.

JOHN J. ROCHE & ASSOCIATES (AV)

One Cambridge Center, Suite 405, 02142
Telephone: 617-621-3100
TELECOPIER: 617-621-3140

ASSOCIATE

Thomas J. Furlong, Jr.

For full biographical listings, see the Martindale-Hubbell Law Directory

FRANKLIN, Norfolk Co.

GILMORE, REES & CARLSON, P.C. (AV)

1000 Franklin Village Drive, 02038
Telephone: 508-520-2200
Telecopier: 508-520-2217
Wellesley, Massachusetts Office: 20 Walnut Street, 02181.
Telephone: 617-431-9788.
Fax: 617-431-1957.

Daniel J. Gilmore
Christopher T. Carlson
Bruce J. Bettigole

OF COUNSEL

William J. Rees

Michael P. Doherty
Craig A. Ciechanowski
Katherine A. Botelho
Jane Fisher Carlson
James H. Goldsmith

For full biographical listings, see the Martindale-Hubbell Law Directory

HYANNIS, Barnstable Co.

HADDLETON & COLLINS, P.C. (AV)

251 South Street, P.O. Box 1298, 02601
Telephone: 508-771-3132
Fax: 508-790-3760
Wellesley, Massachusetts Office: One Washington Street.
Telephone: 617-237-6059.

Russell E. Haddleton
Joyce M. Collins

Pamela Woodcock-White

For full biographical listings, see the Martindale-Hubbell Law Directory

*SPRINGFIELD,** Hampden Co.

GABERMAN & PARISH, P.C. (AV)

32 Hampden Street, 01103
Telephone: 413-781-5066
Fax: 413-732-5439

Richard M. Gaberman
Ronda G. Parish

Richard D. Keough

OF COUNSEL

Leonard Judelson

For full biographical listings, see the Martindale-Hubbell Law Directory

WESTON, Middlesex Co.

BOYD & BOYD, P.C. (AV)

Riverside Office Park, 13 Riverside Road, Suite 201, 02193
Telephone: 617 899-7100
FAX: 617-899-4007
Centerville, Massachusetts Office: Center Place, 1550 Route 28, Suite 4, 02632.
Telephone: 508-775-7800.

F. Keats Boyd, Jr.
F. Keats Boyd, III

For full biographical listings, see the Martindale-Hubbell Law Directory

MICHIGAN

*ANN ARBOR,** Washtenaw Co.

BODMAN, LONGLEY & DAHLING (AV)

110 Miller, Suite 300, 48104
Telephone: 313-761-3780
Fax: 313-930-2494
Detroit, Michigan Office: 34th Floor, 100 Renaissance Center.
Telephone: 313-259-7777.
Troy, Michigan Office: Suite 2020, 755 West Big Beaver Road.
Telephone: 810-362-2110.

(See Next Column)

Northern Michigan Office: 229 Court Street, P.O. Box 405, Cheboygan.
Telephone: 616-627-4351.

RESIDENT PARTNERS

Mark W. Griffin
Harvey W. Berman
Thomas A. Roach
Jerold Lax
Randolph S. Perry
Susan M. Kornfield

RESIDENT COUNSEL

John S. Dobson
Patricia D. White

RESIDENT ASSOCIATES

Sandra L. Sorini
Stephen K. Postema
Lydia Pallas Loren

For full biographical listings, see the Martindale-Hubbell Law Directory

HOOPER, HATHAWAY, PRICE, BEUCHE & WALLACE (AV)

126 South Main Street, 48104
Telephone: 313-662-4426
Fax: 313-662-9559

Alan E. Price

Representative Clients: Chem-Trend, Inc.; Dundee Cement Co.; Ervin Industries, Inc.; First Martin Corp.; Group 243 Design, Inc.; Honeywell; Microwave Sensors, Inc.; Shearson Lehman Hutton; O'Neal Construction Co.; Pittsfield Products, Inc.

For Complete List of Firm Personnel, See General Section

For full biographical listings, see the Martindale-Hubbell Law Directory

MILLER, CANFIELD, PADDOCK AND STONE, P.L.C. (AV)

A Professional Limited Liability Company
Founded in 1852 by Sidney Davy Miller
101 North Main Street, Seventh Floor, 48104-1400
Telephone: 313-663-2445
Fax: 313-747-7147
Detroit, Michigan Office: 150 West Jefferson, Suite 2500, 48226-4415.
Telephone: 313-963-6420.
Fax: 313-496-7500.
Cable Address: "Stem Detroit."
Bloomfield Hills, Michigan Office: Suite 100, Pinehurst Office Center, 1400 North Woodward, 48303-2014.
Telephone: 313-645-5000.
Fax: 313-645-1917.
Grand Rapids, Michigan Office: 1200 Campau Square Plaza, 99 Monroe, N.W., 49503-2639.
Telephone: 616-454-8656.
Fax: 616-776-6322.
Howell, Michigan Office: 121 South Barnard Street, Suite 4, 48843-2305.
Telephone: 517-546-7600.
Telecopier: 517-546-6974.
Kalamazoo, Michigan Office: 444 West Michigan Avenue, 49007-3752.
Telephone: 616-381-7030.
Fax: 616-382-0244.
Lansing, Michigan Office: One Michigan Avenue, Suite 900, 48933-1609.
Telephone: 517-487-2070.
Fax: 517-374-6304.
Monroe, Michigan Office: The Executive Centre, 214 East Elm Avenue, 48161-2682.
Telephone: 313-243-2000.
Fax: 313-243-0901.
Washington, D.C. Office: 1225 Nineteenth Street, N.W., Suite 400. 20036.
Telephone: 202-429-5575; 785-0600.
Fax: 202-331-1118; 785-1234.
Pensacola, Florida Office: 25 West Cedar, 32501.
Telephone: 904-469-1088.
Fax: 904-432-0677.
St. Petersburg, Florida Office: 100 Second Avenue S., Suite 7045, 33701.
Telephone: 813-982-6000.
Fax: 813-892-6002.
Gdansk, Poland Office: Suite 322, Dom Technika Building, Ul. Rajska 6, 80-850.
Telephone: 011-485-831-2808.
Fax: 011-485-831-4719.
Warsaw, Poland Office: Ul. Marszalkowska 82, Suite 561, 00-517.
Telephone: 011-482-623-6457 and 6458.
Fax: 011-482-623-6459.

RESIDENT PARTNER

Robert E. Gilbert

SENIOR ATTORNEY

Ronald D. Gardner

Representative Firm Clients: Chrysler Corp.; Comerica, Inc.; City of Detroit, Mich.; Detroit Tigers, Inc.; First of Michigan; Fretter, Inc.; Ford Motor Co.; Ford Motor Credit Co.; Great Lakes Bancorp; Henry Ford Hospital.

For Complete List of Firm Personnel, See General Section

For full biographical listings, see the Martindale-Hubbell Law Directory

Ann Arbor—Continued

PEAR SPERLING EGGAN & MUSKOVITZ, P.C. (AV)

Domino's Farms, 24 Frank Lloyd Wright Drive, 48105
Telephone: 313-665-4441
Fax: 313-665-8788
Ypsilanti, Michigan Offices: 5 South Washington Street.
Telephone: 313-483-3626 and 2164 Bellevue at Washtenaw.
Telephone: 313-483-7177.

Edwin L. Pear — Andrew M. Eggan

For Complete List of Firm Personnel; See General Section

For full biographical listings, see the Martindale-Hubbell Law Directory

BINGHAM FARMS, Oakland Co.

MEISNER AND HODGDON, P.C. (AV)

Suite 467, 30200 Telegraph Road, 48025-4506
Telephone: 810-644-4433
Fax: 810-644-2941

Robert M. Meisner — Samuel K. Hodgdon

Reference: Comerica Bank.

For full biographical listings, see the Martindale-Hubbell Law Directory

BIRMINGHAM, Oakland Co.

CARSON FISCHER, P.L.C. (AV)

Third Floor, 300 East Maple Road, 48009-6317
Telephone: 810-644-4840
Facsimile: 810-644-1832

Robert M. Carson — William C. Edmunds

For full biographical listings, see the Martindale-Hubbell Law Directory

MACDONALD AND GOREN, P.C. (AV)

Suite 200, 260 East Brown Street, 48009
Telephone: 810-645-5940
Fax: 810-645-2490

Harold C. MacDonald — David D. Marsh
Kalman G. Goren — Glenn G. Ross
Cindy Rhodes Victor — Miriam Blanks-Smart
Amy L. Glenn — John T. Klees

Representative Clients: Bay Corrugated Container, Inc.; Miles Fox Company; Orlandi Gear Company, Inc.; Bing Steel, Inc.; Superb Manufacturing, Inc.; Spring Engineering, Inc.; Adrian Steel Company; Southfield Radiology Associates, P.C.; Blockbuster Entertainment Corporation; E.N.U.F. Internationale, Inc.

For full biographical listings, see the Martindale-Hubbell Law Directory

WEINGARDEN & HAUER, P.C. (AV)

30100 Telegraph Road, Suite 221, 48025
Telephone: 810-258-0800
Telecopier: 810-258-2750

Larry A. Weingarden

Reference: Security Bank & Trust.

For full biographical listings, see the Martindale-Hubbell Law Directory

WILLIAMS, SCHAEFER, RUBY & WILLIAMS, PROFESSIONAL CORPORATION (AV)

Suite 300, 380 North Woodward Avenue, 48009
Telephone: 810-642-0333
Telecopy: 810-642-0856

James A. Williams — Richard D. Rattner
Edward L. Ruby — James J. Williams
R. Jamison Williams, Jr. — Lisa Symula-Nahikian

For full biographical listings, see the Martindale-Hubbell Law Directory

BLOOMFIELD HILLS, Oakland Co.

MEYER, KIRK, SNYDER & SAFFORD (AV)

Suite 100, 100 West Long Lake Road, 48304
Telephone: 810-647-5111
Telecopier: 810-647-6079
Detroit, Michigan Office: 2500 Penobscot Building.
Telephone: 313-961-1261.

George H. Meyer — Ralph R. Safford
John M. Kirk — Donald H. Baker, Jr.
George E. Snyder — Patrick K. Rode

ASSOCIATES

Christopher F. Clark — Boyd C. Farnam
Debra S. Meier

(See Next Column)

OF COUNSEL

Mark R. Solomon

Representative Clients: Chemical Waste Management; Ervin Advertising; The Michigan and S.E. Michigan McDonald's Operators Assn.; The Southland Corp. (7-Eleven Food Stores); Stauffer Chemical Co.; Techpoint, Inc.

For full biographical listings, see the Martindale-Hubbell Law Directory

STROBL AND MANOOGIAN, P.C. (AV)

300 East Long Lake Road, Suite 200, 48304-2376
Telephone: 810-645-0306
Facsimile: 810-645-2690

John Sharp — James A. Rocchio

Sara S. Lisznyai — Robert F. Boesiger

For Complete List of Firm Personnel, See General Section

For full biographical listings, see the Martindale-Hubbell Law Directory

*DETROIT,** Wayne Co.

ABBOTT, NICHOLSON, QUILTER, ESSHAKI & YOUNGBLOOD, P.C. (AV)

19th Floor, One Woodward Avenue, 48226
Telephone: 313-963-2500
Telecopier: 313-963-7882

C. Richard Abbott — James B. Perry
John R. Nicholson — Carl F. Jarboe
Thomas R. Quilter III — Jay A. Kennedy
Gene J. Esshaki — Timothy A. Stoepker
John F. Youngblood — Timothy J. Kramer
Donald E. Conley — Norbert T. Madison, Jr.
William D. Gilbride, Jr.

Mary P. Nelson — Anne D. Warren Bagno
Michael R. Blum — Mark E. Mueller
Thomas Ferguson Hatch — Eric J. Girdler

OF COUNSEL

Thomas C. Shumaker — Roy R. Hunsinger

For full biographical listings, see the Martindale-Hubbell Law Directory

BODMAN, LONGLEY & DAHLING (AV)

34th Floor 100 Renaissance Center, 48243
Telephone: 313-259-7777
Fax: 313-393-7579
Troy, Michigan Office: Suite 2020, 755 West Big Beaver Road.
Telephone: 810-362-2110.
Ann Arbor, Michigan Office: 110 Miller, Suite 300.
Telephone: 313-761-3780.
Northern Michigan Office: 229 Court Street, P.O. Box 405, Cheboygan.
Telephone: 616-627-4351.

MEMBERS OF FIRM

George D. Miller, Jr. — R. Craig Hupp
Kenneth R. Lango (Troy Office) — Patrick C. Cauley
David M. Hempstead — David P. Larsen

COUNSEL

John S. Dobson (Ann Arbor Office)

ASSOCIATE

Barnett Jay Colvin

Representative Clients: Abitibi Price Group; Archdiocese of Detroit; Comerica Bank; The Detroit Lions, Inc.; Ford Estates; General Motors Corporation; Charles Steward Mott Foundation; Norfolk Southern Corporation; Panhandle Eastern Corporation; State Farm Mutual Automobile Insurance Company.

For Complete List of Firm Personnel, See General Section

For full biographical listings, see the Martindale-Hubbell Law Directory

BUTZEL LONG, A PROFESSIONAL CORPORATION (AV)

Suite 900, 150 West Jefferson, 48226
Telephone: 313-225-7000
Telecopier: 313-225-7080
Birmingham, Michigan Office: Suite 200, 32270 Telegraph Road.
Telephone: 810-258-1616.
Telecopier: 810-258-1439.
Lansing, Michigan Office: 118 West Ottawa Street.
Telephone: 517-372-6622.
Telecopier: 517-372-6672.
Ann Arbor, Michigan Office: Suite 400, 121 West Washington.
Telephone: 313-995-3110.
Telecopier: 313-995-1777.
Grosse Pointe Farms, Michigan Office: Suite 260, 21 Kercheval.
Telephone: 313-886-5446.
Telecopier: 313-886-2114.

(See Next Column)

BUTZEL LONG A PROFESSIONAL CORPORATION, *Detroit—Continued*

Paul L. Triemstra (Birmingham)
T. Gordon Scupholm II (Birmingham)
David W. Sommerfeld (Birmingham, Grosse Pointe Farms and Ann Arbor)
Michael D. Guzick
Gary J. Abraham (Birmingham)

OF COUNSEL

William A. Penner, Jr.
Robin S. Phillips (Ann Arbor)

Katherine B. Albrecht (Birmingham)
Robert P. Perry (Birmingham)

For Complete List of Firm Personnel, See General Section

For full biographical listings, see the Martindale-Hubbell Law Directory

CLARK, KLEIN & BEAUMONT (AV)

1600 First Federal Building, 1001 Woodward Avenue, 48226
Telephone: 313-965-8300
Facsimile: 313-962-4348
Bloomfield Hills Office: 1533 North Woodward Avenue, Suite 220, 48304.
Telephone: 810-258-2900.
Facsimile: 810-258-2949.

MEMBERS OF FIRM

Douglas J. Rasmussen
Thomas S. Nowinski
Curtis J. Mann (Resident Bloomfield Hills, Michigan Office)
Michael G. Cumming
J. Thomas MacFarlane
Andrea M. Kanski

ASSOCIATES

Robin D. Ferriby
Jennifer Crawford

Representative Clients: BASF; Booth Communications, Inc.; The Budd Co.; Coopers & Lybrand; Dow Corning Corp.; First Federal of Michigan; The Home Depot, Inc.; The Prudential Insurance Companies of America; R.P. Scherer Corp.; Trammell Crow Company.

For Complete List of Firm Personnel, See General Section

For full biographical listings, see the Martindale-Hubbell Law Directory

DICKINSON, WRIGHT, MOON, VAN DUSEN & FREEMAN (AV)

500 Woodward Avenue, Suite 4000, 48226-3425
Telephone: 313-223-3500
Facsimile: 313-223-3598
Bloomfield Hills, Michigan Office: 525 North Woodward Avenue, Suite 2000.
Telephone: 810-433-7200.
Facsimile: 810-433-7274.
Grand Rapids, Michigan Office: 200 Ottawa Avenue, N.W., Suite 900.
Telephone: 616-458-1300.
Facsimile: 616-458-6753.
Lansing, Michigan Office: Suite 200, 215 South Washington Square.
Telephone: 517-371-1730.
Facsimile: 517-487-4700.
Washington, D.C. Office: Suite 800, 1901 L Street, N.W.
Telephone: 202-457-0160.
Facsimile: 202-659-1559.
Chicago, Illinois Office: 225 West Washington, Suite 400.
Telephone: 312-220-0300.
Facsimile: 312-220-0021.
Warsaw, Poland Office: 46 Wilcza Street, 4th Floor, 00-679.
Telephone: (48-22) 299-241.
Facsimile: (48-2) 628-4107. Komertel Satellite Phone: (48-39) 121-510.

MEMBERS OF FIRM

Robert V. Peterson (Bloomfield Hills Office)
Peter S. Sheldon (Lansing Office)
Joyce Q. Lower (Bloomfield Hills Office)
David L. Turner
John H. Norris (Bloomfield Hills Office)
Henry M. Grix
Cynthia A. Moore (Bloomfield Hills Office)

OF COUNSEL

Douglas L. Mann (Bloomfield Hills Office)

For Complete List of Firm Personnel, See General Section

For full biographical listings, see the Martindale-Hubbell Law Directory

EAMES, WILCOX, MASTEJ, BRYANT, SWIFT & RIDDELL (AV)

1400 Buhl Building, 48226-3602
Telephone: 313-963-3750
Facsimile: 313-963-8485

MEMBERS OF FIRM

Leonard A. Wilcox, Jr.
Ronald J. Mastej
John W. Bryant
Jerry R. Swift
Neill T. Riddell
Elizabeth Roberto
Kevin N. Summers

ASSOCIATE

Keith M. Aretha

(See Next Column)

OF COUNSEL

Rex Eames
Robert E. Gesell
William B. McIntyre, Jr.

Representative Clients: ABF Freight System, Inc.; Chrysler Credit Corp.; City Transfer Co.; Engineered Heat Treat, Inc.; Fetz Engineering Co.; I E & E Industries, Inc.; Schneider Transport; Tank Carrier Employers Association of Michigan; TNT Transport Group, Inc.; Waste Management of Michigan.

For full biographical listings, see the Martindale-Hubbell Law Directory

FOSTER, MEADOWS & BALLARD, P.C. (AV)

3200 Penobscot Building, 48226
Telephone: 313-961-3234
Cable Address: "Foster"
Telex: 23-5823
Facsimile: 313-961-6184

Sparkman D. Foster (1897-1967)
John L. Foster
Charles R. Hrdlicka
Paul D. Galea
Richard A. Dietz
Robert H. Fortunate
Robert G. Lahiff
Camille A. Raffa-Dietz

Michael J. Liddane
Paul A. Kettunen

OF COUNSEL

John F. Langs
John A. Mundell, Jr.

Counsel for: Air Canada; Canadian National Railways; Grand Trunk Western Railroad; Alexander and Alexander; Shand Morahan; Utica Mutual.
Admiralty Counsel for: Ford Motor; Bob Lo Co.

For full biographical listings, see the Martindale-Hubbell Law Directory

HOUGHTON, POTTER, SWEENEY & BRENNER, A PROFESSIONAL CORPORATION (AV)

The Guardian Building, 500 Griswold Street, Suite 3300, 48226-3806
Telephone: 313-964-0050
Facsimile: 313-964-4005

Thomas F. Sweeney

LEGAL SUPPORT PERSONNEL

LEGAL ASSISTANTS

Ann E. Adams
Janet C. Driver

For full biographical listings, see the Martindale-Hubbell Law Directory

JAFFE, RAITT, HEUER & WEISS, PROFESSIONAL CORPORATION (AV)

One Woodward Avenue, Suite 2400, 48226
Telephone: 313-961-8380
Telecopier: 313-961-8358
Cable Address: "Jafsni"
Southfield, Michigan Office: Travelers Tower, Suite 1520.
Telephone: 313-961-8380.
Monroe, Michigan Office: 212 East Front Street, Suite 3.
Telephone: 313-241-6470.
Telefacsimile: 313-241-3849.

Penny L. Carolan
Joel S. Golden

Derek S. Adolf
Lesley A. Gaber

See General Practice Section for List of Representative Clients.

For Complete List of Firm Personnel, See General Section

For full biographical listings, see the Martindale-Hubbell Law Directory

JOSLYN KEYDEL & WALLACE (AV)

A Partnership of Professional Corporations
211 West Fort Street, Suite 2211, 48226-3270
Telephone: 313-964-4181
Fax: 313-964-4996

MEMBERS OF FIRM

Lee E. Joslyn (1864-1936)
Lee E. Joslyn, Jr. (1895-1955)
Alan W. Joslyn (1899-1990)
Frederick R. Keydel (P.C.)
Harvey B. Wallace II (P.C.)
Robert B. Joslyn (P.C.)

ASSOCIATES

Patrice M. Ticknor
Michael D. Whitty

LEGAL SUPPORT PERSONNEL

William J. Johnson

PARALEGALS

Diane C. Simpson
Kathryn A. Keefer
D. Louise Cowan
Ruth G. Spector

References: NBD Bank, N.A.; Comerica Bank.

For full biographical listings, see the Martindale-Hubbell Law Directory

Detroit—Continued

Keller, Thoma, Schwarze, Schwarze, DuBay & Katz, P.C. (AV)

440 E. Congress, 5th Floor, 48226
Telephone: 313-965-7610
Bloomfield Hills, Michigan Office: Suite 122, 100 West Long Lake Road.
Telephone: 313-647-3114.

James R. Miller — Anthony J. Heckemeyer

Counsel for: Livonia Public Schools; Ludington News Co., Inc.
Representative Clients: Borg-Warner Corp.; E & L Transport Co.; The Kroger Co.; Holnam, Inc.
Public Employer Clients: City of Farmington Hills; City of Flint; City of Grosse Pointe Woods; Saginaw Public Schools.

For Complete List of Firm Personnel, See General Section

For full biographical listings, see the Martindale-Hubbell Law Directory

Kerr, Russell and Weber (AV)

One Detroit Center, 500 Woodward Avenue, Suite 2500, 48226-3406
Telephone: 313-961-0200
Telecopier: 313-961-0388
Bloomfield Hills, Michigan Office: 3883 Telegraph Road.
Telephone: 810-649-5990.
East Lansing, Michigan Office: 1301 North Hagadorn Road.
Telephone: 517-336-6767.

Curtis J. DeRoo — Mark J. Stasa
Michael D. Gibson — Jeffrey A. Brantley
George J. Christopoulos — Richard C. Buslepp
Paul M. Shirilla — Daniel J. Schulte

For Complete List of Firm Personnel, See General Section

For full biographical listings, see the Martindale-Hubbell Law Directory

Miller, Canfield, Paddock and Stone, P.L.C. (AV)

A Professional Limited Liability Company
Founded in 1852 by Sidney Davy Miller
150 West Jefferson, Suite 2500, 48226-4415
Telephone: 313-963-6420
Fax: 313-496-7500
Cable Address: "Stem Detroit"
Detroit, Michigan Office: 150 West Jefferson, Suite 2500, 48226-4415.
Telephone: 313-963-6420.
Fax: 313-496-7500.
Cable Address: "Stem Detroit."
Ann Arbor, Michigan Office: 101 North Main Street, 7th Floor, 48104-1400.
Telephone: 313-663-2445.
Fax: 313-747-7147.
Bloomfield Hills, Michigan Office: Suite 100, Pinehurst Office Center, 1400 North Woodward, 48303-2014.
Telephone: 313-645-5000.
Fax: 313-645-1917.
Grand Rapids, Michigan Office: 1200 Campau Square Plaza, 99 Monroe, N.W., 49503-2639.
Telephone: 616-454-8656.
Fax: 616-776-6322.
Howell, Michigan Office: 121 South Barnard Street, Suite 4, 48843-2305.
Telephone: 517-546-7600.
Telecopier: 517-546-6974.
Kalamazoo, Michigan Office: 444 West Michigan Avenue, 49007-3752.
Telephone: 616-381-7030.
Fax: 616-382-0244.
Lansing, Michigan Office: One Michigan Avenue, Suite 900, 48933-1609.
Telephone: 517-487-2070.
Fax: 517-374-6304.
Monroe, Michigan Office: The Executive Centre, 214 East Elm Avenue, 48161-2682.
Telephone: 313-243-2000.
Fax: 313-243-0901.
Washington, D.C. Office: 1225 Nineteenth Street, N.W., Suite 400. 20036.
Telephone: 202-429-5575; 785-0600.
Fax: 202-331-1118; 785-1234.
Pensacola, Florida Office: 25 West Cedar, 32501.
Telephone: 904-469-1088.
Fax: 904-432-0677.
St. Petersburg, Florida Office: 100 Second Avenue S., Suite 7045, 33701.
Telephone: 813-982-6000.
Fax: 813-892-6002.
Gdansk, Poland Office: Suite 322, Dom Technika Building, UI. Rajska 6, 80-850.
Telephone: 011-485-831-2808.
Fax: 011-485-831-4719.
Warsaw, Poland Office: UI. Marszalkowska 82, Suite 561, 00-517.
Telephone: 011-482-623-6457 and 6458.
Fax: 011-482-623-6459.

(See Next Column)

MEMBERS OF FIRM

Lawrence A. King (P.C.) (Bloomfield Hills Office) — James W. Williams (Bloomfield Hills Office)
George E. Parker, III — Gregory V. Di Censo (Bloomfield Hills Office)
Kenneth E. Konop (Bloomfield Hills Office)

OF COUNSEL

William G. Butler — Peter P. Thurber
John A. Gilray, Jr., (P.C.) (Bloomfield Hills Office)

SENIOR ATTORNEYS

Michael J. Taylor (Grand Rapids Office) — Ronald D. Gardner (Ann Arbor Office)

ASSOCIATES

Kathryn L. Ossian — Dawn M. Schluter (Bloomfield Hills Office)

Representative Firm Clients: Chrysler Corp.; Comerica, Inc.; City of Detroit, Mich.; Detroit Tigers, Inc.; First of Michigan; Fretter, Inc.; Ford Motor Co.; Ford Motor Credit Co.; Great Lakes Bancorp; Henry Ford Hospital.

For Complete List of Firm Personnel, See General Section

For full biographical listings, see the Martindale-Hubbell Law Directory

R.H. Pytell & Associates, P.C. (AV)

18580 Mack Avenue, 48236
Telephone: 313-343-9200
Fax: 313-343-0207

R. H. Pytell — Henry C. Pytell (1903-1988)
Paul E. Varchetti

OF COUNSEL

Lewis M. Slater

For full biographical listings, see the Martindale-Hubbell Law Directory

David M. Thoms & Associates, P.C. (AV)

400 Renaissance Center, Suite 950, 48243
Telephone: 313-259-6333
Facsimile: 313-259-7037
Bloomfield Hills, Office: 1500 Woodward Avenue, Suite 100.
Telephone: 313-259-6333.
Fax: 313-259-7037.
Grosse Pointe Office: 377 Fisher Road.
Telephone: 313-259-6333.
Fax: 313-259-7037.

David M. Thoms

Audrey R. Holley — Duane B. Brown

OF COUNSEL

Allan G. Meganck — Thomas V. Trainer

Representative Clients: Avion Concepts, Inc.; Fowler Agency Corp.; Gibbs World Wide Wines, Inc.; deBary Travel, Inc.; North Management, Inc.; St. Jude Children's Research Hospital.
References: Comerica Bank-Detroit, National Bank of Detroit.

For full biographical listings, see the Martindale-Hubbell Law Directory

Timmis & Inman (AV)

300 Talon Centre, 48207
Telephone: 313-396-4200
Telecopier: 313-396-4228

MEMBERS OF FIRM

Michael T. Timmis — Wayne C. Inman
Richard L. Levin

ASSOCIATES

George M. Malis — Kevin S. Kendall
Mark Robert Adams — John P. Kanan

Representative Clients: Stylecraft Printing Company; Stylerite Label Corporation; Retail Resources, Inc.; Deneb Robotics, Inc.; Peabody Management, Inc.; Ferndale Honda, Inc,; Applied Process, Inc.; Insilco Corporation; Variety Foods, Inc.; Certain Underwriters at Lloyds of London.

For Complete List of Firm Personnel, See General Section

For full biographical listings, see the Martindale-Hubbell Law Directory

EAST LANSING, Ingham Co.

Farhat, Story & Kraus, P.C. (AV)

Beacon Place, 4572 South Hagadorn Road, Suite 3, 48823
Telephone: 517-351-3700
Fax: 517-332-4122

(See Next Column)

FARHAT, STORY & KRAUS P.C., *East Lansing—Continued*

Leo A. Farhat
James E. Burns (1925-1979)
Monte R. Story
Richard C. Kraus
Max R. Hoffman Jr.
Chris A. Bergstrom
Kitty L. Groh
Charles R. Toy
David M. Platt

Lawrence P. Schweitzer
Jeffrey J. Short
Kathy A. Breedlove
Thomas L. Sparks

Representative Clients: Big L. Corp.; Michigan Automotive Wholesalers Association; Hartman-Fabco, Inc.; Lansing Electric Motors, Inc.; Mike Miller Lincoln Mercury; The John E. Fetzer Trust; The Ferris Foundation, Meijer Foundation.
Reference: Capitol National Bank.

For full biographical listings, see the Martindale-Hubbell Law Directory

FARMINGTON HILLS, Oakland Co.

DAGUANNO AND ACCETTURA (AV)

Arboretum Office Park, 34705 West Twelve Mile Road, Suite 311, 48331
Telephone: 810-489-1444
Fax: 810-489-1453

MEMBERS OF FIRM

Richard Daguanno
P. Mark Accettura

ASSOCIATES

Robert J. Constan
Harry P. Bugeja

OF COUNSEL

John A. Zick
Robert E. Miller

References: Comerica Bank; Michigan Chamber of Commerce.

For full biographical listings, see the Martindale-Hubbell Law Directory

HOROWITZ & GUDEMAN, P.C. (AV)

31700 Middlebelt, 48334
Telephone: 810-855-6020
Facsimile: 810-855-6025

Marvin I. Horowitz
Edward J. Gudeman

For full biographical listings, see the Martindale-Hubbell Law Directory

KAUFMAN AND PAYTON (AV)

200 Northwestern Financial Center, 30833 Northwestern Highway, 48334
Telephone: 810-626-5000
Telefacsimile: 810-626-2843
Grand Rapids, Michigan Office: 420 Trust Building.
Telephone: 616-459-4200.
Fax: 616-459-4929.
Traverse City, Michigan Office: 122 West State Street.
Telephone: 616-947-4050.
Fax: 616-947-7321.

Alan Jay Kaufman
Donald L. Payton
Kenneth C. Letherwood
Stephen R. Levine
Thomas L. Vitu
Ralph C. Chapa, Jr.
Raymond I. Foley, II
Jeffrey K. Van Hattum
Leo D. Neville

For full biographical listings, see the Martindale-Hubbell Law Directory

*FLINT,** Genesee Co.

HICKS, SCHMIDLIN & BANCROFT, P.C. (AV)

2300 Austin Parkway, Suite 120, 48507
Telephone: 810-232-5038
Fax: 810-232-5538

L. James Hicks
Randall R. Schmidlin
Robert H. Bancroft
Carolyn S. Pringle
David J. Ledermann

Representative Clients: Atlas Technologies, Inc.; J. Austin Oil Company; Flint Plumbers and Pipefitting Pension Fund; Genesys Regional Medical Center-Wheelock Memorial Campus; Harding Mott Foundation; The Harvey and Elizabeth Mackey Foundation; Industrial Mutual Association of Flint; McLaren Regional Medical Center;
References: Citizens Commercial & Savings Bank; NBD Bank, N.A.

For full biographical listings, see the Martindale-Hubbell Law Directory

WINEGARDEN, SHEDD, HALEY, LINDHOLM & ROBERTSON (AV)

501 Citizens Bank Building, 48502-1983
Telephone: 810-767-3600
Telecopier: 810-767-8776

MEMBERS OF FIRM

William C. Shedd
Dennis M. Haley
John T. Lindholm
Donald H. Robertson
L. David Lawson
John R. Tucker

(See Next Column)

ASSOCIATES

Alan F. Himelhoch
Suellen J. Parker
Damion Frasier
Peter T. Mooney

OF COUNSEL

Howard R. Grossman

Representative Clients: Citizens Commercial and Savings Bank; R. L. White Development Corporation; Interstate Traffic Consultants (Intracon) Inc.; Downtown Development Authority of Flint; Young Olds-Cadillac, Inc.; First American Title Insurance Co.; Sorensen Gross Construction Co.; Genesee County; Insight, Inc.; Modern Industries, Inc.

For Complete List of Firm Personnel, See General Section

For full biographical listings, see the Martindale-Hubbell Law Directory

*GRAND RAPIDS,** Kent Co.

VARNUM, RIDDERING, SCHMIDT & HOWLETT (AV)

Bridgewater Place, P.O. Box 352, 49501-0352
Telephone: 616-336-6000
800-262-0011
Facsimile: 616-336-7000
Telex: 1561593 VARN
Lansing, Michigan Office: The Victor Center, Suite 810, 210 North Washington Square, 48933.
Telephone: 517-482-6237.
Facsimile: 517-482-6937.
Kalamazoo, Michigan Office: 350 East Michigan Avenue, 49007.
Telephone: 616-382-2300.
Facsimile: 616-382-2382.
Grand Haven, Michigan Office: 321 Washington Street, P.O. Box 288, 49417.
Telephone: 616-846-7100.
Facsimile: 616-846-7101.
Battle Creek, Michigan Office: 4950 West Dickman Road, Suite B-1, 49015.
Telephone: 616-962-7144.
Detroit, Michigan Office: 440 East Congress, Fourth Floor, 48226.
Telephone: 313-961-1600.
Facsimile: 313-961-1636.

OF COUNSEL

Gordon B. Boozer

MEMBERS OF FIRM

Hilary F. Snell
John C. Carlyle (Resident at Grand Haven Office)
Thomas T. Huff (Resident at Kalamazoo Office)
Dirk Hoffius
Fredric A. Sytsma
Marilyn A. Lankfer
Jeffrey W. Beswick (Resident at Grand Haven Office)

ASSOCIATES

Thomas G. Kyros
Pamela J. Tyler

For Complete List of Firm Personnel, See General Section

For full biographical listings, see the Martindale-Hubbell Law Directory

WHEELER UPHAM, A PROFESSIONAL CORPORATION (AV)

Second Floor, Trust Building, 40 Pearl Street, N.W., 49503
Telephone: 616-459-7100
Fax: 616-459-6366

Gordon B. Wheeler (1904-1986)
Buford A. Upham (Retired)
Robert H. Gillette
Geoffrey L. Gillis
John M. Roels
Gary A. Maximiuk
Timothy J. Orlebeke
Kenneth E. Tiews
Jack L. Hoffman
Janet C. Baxter
Peter Kladder, III
James M. Shade
Thomas A. Kuiper

Counsel for: Travelers Insurance Co.; Prudential Insurance Co. of America; Farmers Insurance Group; Metropolitan Life Insurance Co.; Conrail Trans.; Monsanto Co.; Firestone Tire & Rubber Co.; Navistar, Inc.; Medtronic, Inc.; Westdale Better Homes and Gardens.

For full biographical listings, see the Martindale-Hubbell Law Directory

GROSSE POINTE WOODS, Wayne Co.

JON B. GANDELOT, P.C. (AV)

19251 Mack Avenue, 48236
Telephone: 313-885-9100
Facsimile: 313-885-9152

Jon B. Gandelot

For full biographical listings, see the Martindale-Hubbell Law Directory

*HOWELL,** Livingston Co.

PETER B. VAN WINKLE, P.C. (AV)

105 East Grand River, 48843
Telephone: 517-546-2680

(See Next Column)

PETER B. VAN WINKLE, P.C.—*Continued*

William P. Van Winkle (1858-1920)
Don W. Van Winkle (1887-1971)
Charles K. Van Winkle (Retired)
Peter B. Van Winkle

Reference: First National Bank in Howell, Howell, Mich.

For full biographical listings, see the Martindale-Hubbell Law Directory

*KALAMAZOO,** Kalamazoo Co.

DEMING, HUGHEY, LEWIS, ALLEN & CHAPMAN, P.C. (AV)

800 Old Kent Bank Building, 49007
Telephone: 616-349-6601
Fax: 616-349-3831

Ned W. Deming
Richard M. Hughey
Dean S. Lewis
W. Fred Allen, Jr.
Ross E. Chapman
Winfield J. Hollander
John A. Scott
Bruce W. Martin (Resident)
Daniel L. Conklin
William A. Redmond
Stephen M. Denenfeld
Thomas C. Richardson
Gregory G. St. Arnauld
Roger G. Allen (Retired)
Anne McGregor Fries
Amy J. Glass
Richard M. Hughey, Jr.
Richard J. Bosch
Thomas P. Lewis
Christopher T. Haenicke

LEGAL SUPPORT PERSONNEL

Dorothy B. Kelly

For full biographical listings, see the Martindale-Hubbell Law Directory

DIETRICH, ZODY, HOWARD & VANDERROEST, P.C. (AV)

834 King Highway, Suite 110, 49001
Telephone: 616-344-9236
Fax: 616-344-0412

G. Philip Dietrich
Richard J. Howard
James W. Smith
James E. VanderRoest
Brenda Wheeler Zody

Barbara S. Weintraub

For full biographical listings, see the Martindale-Hubbell Law Directory

EARLY, LENNON, PETERS & CROCKER, P.C. (AV)

900 Comerica Building, 49007-4752
Telephone: 616-381-8844
Fax: 616-349-8525

George H. Lennon, III
Gordon C. Miller
Robert M. Taylor

Attorneys for: General Motors Corp.; Wal-Mart Stores; Borgess Medical Center; Aetna Insurance: Kemper Group; Medical Protective Co.; Zurich Insurance; AAA; Liberty Mutual; Home Insurance.

For Complete List of Firm Personnel, See General Section

For full biographical listings, see the Martindale-Hubbell Law Directory

KREIS, ENDERLE, CALLANDER & HUDGINS, A PROFESSIONAL CORPORATION (AV)

One Moorsbridge, 49002
Telephone: 616-324-3000
Telecopier: 616-324-3010

Russell A. Kreis
C. Reid Hudgins III
Robert B. Borsos
Daniel P. Mc Glinn

For Complete List of Firm Personnel, See General Section

For full biographical listings, see the Martindale-Hubbell Law Directory

MILLER, CANFIELD, PADDOCK AND STONE, P.L.C. (AV)

A Professional Limited Liability Company
Founded in 1852 by Sidney Davy Miller
444 West Michigan Avenue, 49007-3752
Telephone: 616-381-7030
Fax: 616-382-0244
Detroit, Michigan Office: 150 West Jefferson, Suite 2500, 48226-4415.
Telephone: 313-963-6420.
Fax: 313-496-7500.
Cable Address: "Stem Detroit."
Ann Arbor, Michigan Office: 101 North Main Street, 7th Floor, 48104-1400.
Telephone: 313-663-2445.
Fax: 313-747-7147.
Bloomfield Hills, Michigan Office: Suite 100, Pinehurst Office Center, 1400 North Woodward, 48303-2014.
Telephone: 313-645-5000.
Fax: 313-645-1917.

(See Next Column)

Grand Rapids, Michigan Office: 1200 Campau Square Plaza, 99 Monroe, N.W., 49503-2639.
Telephone: 616-454-8656.
Fax: 616-776-6322.
Howell, Michigan Office: 121 South Barnard Street, Suite 4, 48843-2305.
Telephone: 517-546-7600.
Telecopier: 517-546-6974.
Lansing, Michigan Office: One Michigan Avenue, Suite 900, 48933-1609.
Telephone: 517-487-2070.
Fax: 517-374-6304.
Monroe, Michigan Office: The Executive Centre, 214 East Elm Avenue, 48161-2682.
Telephone: 313-243-2000.
Fax: 313-243-0901.
Washington, D.C. Office: 1225 Nineteenth Street, N.W., Suite 400. 20036.
Telephone: 202-429-5575; 785-0600.
Fax: 202-331-1118; 785-1234.
Pensacola, Florida Office: 25 West Cedar, 32501.
Telephone: 904-469-1088.
Fax: 904-432-0677.
St. Petersburg, Florida Office: 100 Second Avenue S., Suite 7045,33701.
Telephone: 813-982-6000.
Fax: 813-892-6002.
Gdansk, Poland Office: Suite 322, Dom Technika Building, Ul. Rajska 6, 80-850.
Telephone: 011-485-831-2808.
Fax: 011-485-831-4719.
Warsaw, Poland Office: Ul. Marszalkowska 82, Suite 561, 00-517.
Telephone: 011-482-623-6457 and 6458.
Fax: 011-482-623-6459.

MEMBER OF FIRM

Eric V. Brown, Jr. (Resident)

Representative Firm Clients: Chrysler Corp.; Comerica, Inc.; City of Detroit, Mich.; Detroit Tigers, Inc.; First of Michigan; Fretter, Inc.; Ford Motor Co.; Ford Motor Credit Co.; Great Lakes Bancorp; Henry Ford Hospital.

For Complete List of Firm Personnel, See General Section

For full biographical listings, see the Martindale-Hubbell Law Directory

LANSING, Ingham Co.

FOSTER, SWIFT, COLLINS & SMITH, P.C. (AV)

313 South Washington Square, 48933-2193
Telephone: 517-371-8100
Telecopier: 517-371-8200
Farmington Hills, Michigan Office: 32300 Northwestern Highway, Suite 230.
Telephone: 810-851-7500.
Fax: 810-851-7504.

Allan J. Claypool
Charles A. Janssen
Louis K. Nigg
Patricia A. Calore

LEGAL SUPPORT PERSONNEL

LEGAL ASSISTANTS

Sandra L. De Santis
Kelly A. LaGrave
Constance G. Powis

General Counsel for: First American Bank-Central; Story, Inc.; Michigan Milk Producers Assn.; Edward W. Sparrow Hospital; St. Lawrence Hospital; Demmer Corp.; Michigan Financial Corp.
Local Counsel for: Shell Oil Co.; Michigan-Mutual Insurance Co.; Century Cellunet.

For Complete List of Firm Personnel, See General Section

For full biographical listings, see the Martindale-Hubbell Law Directory

FRASER TREBILCOCK DAVIS & FOSTER, P.C. (AV)

1000 Michigan National Tower, 48933
Telephone: 517-482-5800
Fax: 517-482-0887
Okemos, Michigan Office: 2188 Commons Parkway.
Telephone: 517-349-1300.
Fax: 517-349-0922.

Joe C. Foster, Jr.
Everett R. Zack
Richard C. Lowe

John E. Bos
Nancy L. Little
Sharon A. Bruner

Counsel for: Bank One, East Lansing; Comerica Bank; First of America Bank-Central; Michigan National Bank; Old Kent Bank.

For Complete List of Firm Personnel, See General Section

For full biographical listings, see the Martindale-Hubbell Law Directory

Lansing—Continued

MILLER, CANFIELD, PADDOCK AND STONE, P.L.C. (AV)

A Professional Limited Liability Company
Founded in 1852 by Sidney Davy Miller
Suite 900, One Michigan Avenue, 48933-1609
Telephone: 517-487-2070
Fax: 517-374-6304
Detroit, Michigan Office: 150 West Jefferson, Suite 2500, 48226-4415.
Telephone: 313-963-6420.
Fax: 313-496-7500.
Cable Address: "Stem Detroit."
Ann Arbor, Michigan Office: 101 North Main Street, 7th Floor, 48104-1400.
Telephone: 313-663-2445.
Fax: 313-747-7147.
Bloomfield Hills, Michigan Office: Suite 100, Pinehurst Office Center, 1400 North Woodward, 48303-2014.
Telephone: 313-645-5000.
Fax: 313-645-1917.
Grand Rapids, Michigan Office: 1200 Campau Square Plaza, 99 Monroe, N.W., 49503-2639.
Telephone: 616-454-8656.
Fax: 616-776-6322.
Howell, Michigan Office: 121 South Barnard Street, Suite 4, 48843-2305.
Telephone: 517-546-7600.
Telecopier: 517-546-6974.
Kalamazoo, Michigan Office: 444 West Michigan Avenue, 49007-3752.
Telephone: 616-381-7030.
Fax: 616-382-0244.
Monroe, Michigan Office: The Executive Centre, 214 East Elm Avenue, 48161-2682.
Telephone: 313-243-2000.
Fax: 313-243-0901.
Washington, D.C. Office: 1225 Nineteenth Street, N.W., Suite 400. 20036.
Telephone: 202-429-5575; 785-0600.
Fax: 202-331-1118; 785-1234.
Pensacola, Florida Office: 25 West Cedar, 32501.
Telephone: 904-469-1088.
Fax: 904-432-0677.
St. Petersburg Office: 100 Second Avenue S., Suite 7045, 33701.
Telephone: 813-982-6000.
Fax: 813-892-6002.
Gdansk, Poland Office: Suite 322, Dom Technika Building, Ul. Rajska 6, 80-850.
Telephone: 011-485-831-2808.
Fax: 011-485-831-4719.
Warsaw, Poland Office: Ul. Marszalkowska 82, Suite 561, 00-517.
Telephone: 011-482-623-6457 and 6458.
Fax: 011-482-623-6459.

MEMBER OF FIRM

Michael R. Atkins (Resident)

Representative Firm Clients: Chrysler Corp.; Comerica, Inc.; City of Detroit, Mich.; Detroit Tigers, Inc.; First of Michigan; Fretter, Inc.; Ford Motor Co.; Ford Motor Credit Co.; Great Lakes Bancorp; Henry Ford Hospital.

For Complete List of Firm Personnel, See General Section

For full biographical listings, see the Martindale-Hubbell Law Directory

*MONROE,** Monroe Co.

BRAUNLICH, RUSSOW & BRAUNLICH, A PROFESSIONAL CORPORATION (AV)

111 South Macomb Street, 48161
Telephone: 313-241-8300
Fax: 313-241-7715

William J. Braunlich, Jr. (1924-1992)
Thomas P. Russow
William H. Braunlich

Philip A. Costello
Patricia M. Poupard
Ann L. Nickel
Marie C. Kennedy
Susan J. Mehregan
Robert Wetzel
Michael G. Roehrig

LEGAL SUPPORT PERSONNEL

Ruth G. Flint

Representative Clients: State Farm Mutual Insurance Co.; Auto Club Insurance Assn.; Farm Bureau Insurance Co.; Home Mutual Insurance Co.; Cincinnati Insurance Co.; Board of Road Commissioners, Monroe County; Port of Monroe; Monroe County Community College; City of Luna Pier; City of Petersburg.

For full biographical listings, see the Martindale-Hubbell Law Directory

*PONTIAC,** Oakland Co.

BOOTH, PATTERSON, LEE, NEED & ADKISON, P.C. (AV)

1090 West Huron Street, 48328
Telephone: 810-681-1200
FAX: 810-681-1754

(See Next Column)

Douglas W. Booth (1918-1992)
Calvin E. Patterson (1913-1987)
Parvin Lee, Jr.
J. Timothy Patterson
David J. Lee
Gregory K. Need
Phillip G. Adkison
Martin L. Kimmel
Allan T. Motzny
Ann DeCaminada Christ
Kathryn Niazy Nichols

For full biographical listings, see the Martindale-Hubbell Law Directory

STERLING, SCHILLING & THORBURN, P.C. (AV)

1400 NBD Building, 48342
Telephone: 810-334-4544
Fax: 810-334-1021

Robert P. Sauer (1906-1974)
J. Robert Sterling
Ronald F. Schilling
Bruce J. Thorburn

Reference: First of America, O.M.

For full biographical listings, see the Martindale-Hubbell Law Directory

*SAGINAW,** Saginaw Co.

BRAUN KENDRICK FINKBEINER (AV)

8th Floor Second National Bank Building, 48607
Telephone: 517-753-3461
Telecopier: 517-753-3951
Bay City, Michigan Office: 201 Phoenix Building, P.O. Box 2039.
Telephone: 517-895-8505.
Telecopier: 517-895-8437.

MEMBERS OF FIRM

J. Richard Kendrick
James V. Finkbeiner
Hugo E. Braun, Jr.
Michael H. Allen
Thomas R. Luplow

ASSOCIATE

Carolyn Pollock Cary

BAY CITY, MICHIGAN OFFICE

Gregory T. Demers

Representative Clients: The Dow Chemical Co.; General Motors Corp.; Lobdell Emery Manufacturing Co.; Merrill, Lynch, Inc.; Saginaw General Hospital; Saginaw News; The Wickes Foundation.

For Complete List of Firm Personnel, See General Section

For full biographical listings, see the Martindale-Hubbell Law Directory

*ST. JOSEPH,** Berrien Co.

FISHER LAW OFFICE (AV)

Law & Title Building, P.O. Box 83, 49085
Telephone: 616-983-5511
Telecopier: 616-893-5571

Vance A. Fisher

For full biographical listings, see the Martindale-Hubbell Law Directory

TROFF, PETZKE & AMMESON (AV)

Law and Title Building, 811 Ship Street, P.O. Box 67, 49085
Telephone: 616-983-0161
Facsimile: 616-983-0166

MEMBERS OF FIRM

Theodore E. Troff
Roger A. Petzke
Charles F. Ammeson

ASSOCIATES

Bennett S. Schwartz
Daniel G. Lambrecht
Deborah L. Berecz

Representative Clients: Auto Owners Insurance Co.; CSX Transportation, Inc.; NBD Bank, N.A.

For full biographical listings, see the Martindale-Hubbell Law Directory

SOUTHFIELD, Oakland Co.

ROBERT B. LABE, P.C. (AV)

260 Franklin Center, 29100 Northwestern Highway, 48034
Telephone: 810-354-3100
Telecopier: 810-351-0487

Robert B. Labe

Reference: NBD Bank, N.A.

For full biographical listings, see the Martindale-Hubbell Law Directory

MADDIN, HAUSER, WARTELL, ROTH, HELLER & PESSES, P.C. (AV)

Third Floor Essex Center, 28400 Northwestern Highway, P.O. Box 215, 48037
Telephone: 810-354-4030, 355-5200
Telefax: 810-354-1422

(See Next Column)

MADDIN, HAUSER, WARTELL, ROTH, HELLER & PESSES P.C.—*Continued*

Milton M. Maddin (1902-1984)
Michael W. Maddin
Mark R. Hauser
C. Robert Wartell
Richard J. Maddin
Richard F. Roth
Harvey R. Heller
Ian D. Pesses
Michael S. Leib
Robert D. Kaplow
William E. Sigler
Stewart C. W. Weiner
Charles M. Lax
Stuart M. Bordman
Steven D. Sallen
Joseph M. Fazio

Gregory J. Gamalski
Julie Chenot Mayer
Nathaniel H. Simpson
Ronald A. Sollish
Lisa Schatz Broder
Mark H. Fink
Brian J. Simmons
Gayle L. Landrum
Gary E. Perlmuter
Lowell D. Salesin
Jeffrey B. Hollander

Reference: Comerica Bank.

For full biographical listings, see the Martindale-Hubbell Law Directory

MAY AND MAY, PROFESSIONAL CORPORATION (AV)

3000 Town Center, Suite 2600, 48075
Telephone: 810-358-3800
Fax: 810-358-1627
Detroit, Michigan Office: 5510 Woodward Avenue.
Telephone: 810-358-3800.

Alan A. May

Lawrence G. Snyder
Laura M. Kystad
Penny L. Deitch

For full biographical listings, see the Martindale-Hubbell Law Directory

RUBENSTEIN PLOTKIN, PROFESSIONAL CORPORATION (AV)

2000 Town Center, Suite 2700, 48075-1318
Telephone: 810-354-3200
FAX: 810-354-3106

Edward L. Haroutunian
Burton E. Isaacs
Jeffrey B. Levine
Marcus Plotkin
Erwin A. Rubenstein
Robert W. Siegel
Allan D. Sobel
David B. Walters
Mark E. Wilson
Neil Zales

Eric Joel Gould
Casimir J. Swastek

OF COUNSEL

Murray Yolles

For full biographical listings, see the Martindale-Hubbell Law Directory

SOMMERS, SCHWARTZ, SILVER & SCHWARTZ, P.C. (AV)

2000 Town Center, Suite 900, 48075
Telephone: 810-355-0300
Telecopier: 810-746-4001
Plymouth, Michigan Office: 747 South Main Street.
Telephone: 313-455-4250.

Paul Groffsky
Victor A. Coen
Tracy L. Allen

OF COUNSEL

H. Rollin Allen

General Counsel for: City of Taylor; Foodland Distributors; C.A. Muer Corporation; Vlasic & Company; Nederlander Corporation; Woodland Physicians; Midwest Health Centers, P.C.
Representative Clients: Crum & Forster Insurance Company; City of Pontiac; Michigan National Bank; Perry Drugs.

For Complete List of Firm Personnel, See General Section

For full biographical listings, see the Martindale-Hubbell Law Directory

TROY, Oakland Co.

HOLAHAN, MALLOY, MAYBAUGH & MONNICH (AV)

Suite 100, 2690 Crooks Road, 48084-4700
Telephone: 810-362-4747
Fax: 810-362-4779
East Tawas, Michigan Office: 910 East Bay Street.
Telephone: 517-362-4747.
Fax: 517-362-7331.

MEMBERS OF FIRM

J. Michael Malloy, III
James D. Maybaugh
John R. Monnich
David L. Delie, Jr.
William J. Kliffel

(See Next Column)

OF COUNSEL

Thomas H. O'Connor
Maureen Holahan (Retired; Resident, East Tawas Office)

Representative Clients: Johnson & Higgens; Employers Reinsurance; Chubb Companies; American States Insurance Co.; Travelers Insurance; Pontiac Osteopathic Hospital; Michigan Health Care Corporation.

For full biographical listings, see the Martindale-Hubbell Law Directory

KEYWELL AND ROSENFELD (AV)

Suite 600, 2301 West Big Beaver Road, 48084
Telephone: 810-649-3200
Fax: 810-649-0454

MEMBERS OF FIRM

Gary A. Goldberg
Norman E. Greenfield
Lucy R. Benham
Jerrold M. Bigelman

ASSOCIATE

Kelly M. Hayes

Reference: National Bank of Detroit.

For full biographical listings, see the Martindale-Hubbell Law Directory

POLING, MCGAW & POLING, P.C. (AV)

Suite 275, 5435 Corporate Drive, 48098
Telephone: 810-641-0500
Telecopier: 810-641-0506

Benson T. Buck (1926-1989)
Richard B. Poling
D. Douglas McGaw
Richard B. Poling, Jr.
David W. Moore
Gregory C. Hamilton
Veronica B. Winter
James R. Parker

OF COUNSEL

Ralph S. Moore

Representative Clients: County of Oakland; City of Troy; United States Fidelity & Guaranty Co.; Sentry Insurance Co.; Admiral Insurance; DeMaria Construction Co.; Leo Corporation; Aetna Casualty and Surety Co.; Concord Design; Pneumo-Abex.

For full biographical listings, see the Martindale-Hubbell Law Directory

YPSILANTI, Washtenaw Co.

PEAR SPERLING EGGAN & MUSKOVITZ, P.C. (AV)

5 South Washington Street, 48197
Telephone: 313-483-3626
Fax: 313-483-1107
Ann Arbor, Michigan Office: Domino's Farms, 24 Frank Lloyd Wright Drive.
Telephone: 313-665-4441
Other Ypsilanti, Michigan Office: 2164 Bellevue at Washtenaw.
Telephone: 313-483-7177.

Lawrence W. Sperling
Andrew M. Eggan
Thomas E. Daniels
Helen Conklin Vick

Counsel for: Domino's Pizza, Inc.; Bank One, Ypsilanti, N.A.; Townsend and Bottum, Inc.; Ann Arbor Housing Commission; The Credit Bureau of Ypsilanti; City of Ypsilanti (Labor Counsel); Michigan Municipal Worker's Compensation; Self-Insurance Fund.
Approved Attorneys for: Lawyers Title Insurance Corp.

For full biographical listings, see the Martindale-Hubbell Law Directory

MINNESOTA

*DULUTH,** St. Louis Co.

BROWN, ANDREW, HALLENBECK, SIGNORELLI & ZALLAR, P.A. (AV)

300 Alworth Building, 55802
Telephone: 218-722-1764
FAX: 218-722-6137

Gerald J. Brown
Thomas F. Andrew
Terry C. Hallenbeck
Mark T. Signorelli
Robert J. Zallar
James C. Boos

For full biographical listings, see the Martindale-Hubbell Law Directory

HANFT, FRIDE, O'BRIEN, HARRIES, SWELBAR & BURNS, P.A. (AV)

1000 First Bank Place, 130 West Superior Street, 55802-2094
Telephone: 218-722-4766
Fax: 218-720-4920

(See Next Column)

HANFT, FRIDE, O'BRIEN, HARRIES, SWELBAR & BURNS P.A., *Duluth—Continued*

Gilbert W. Harries　　Richard R. Burns

For Complete List of Firm Personnel, See General Section

For full biographical listings, see the Martindale-Hubbell Law Directory

*MANKATO,** Blue Earth Co.

JOHNSON, ANDERSON & ZELLMER (AV)

600 South Second Street, P.O. Box 637, 56001
Telephone: 507-387-4002
FAX: 507-345-5001

MEMBERS OF FIRM

C. A. (Gus) Johnson, II　　Randy J. Zellmer
Jerome T. Anderson　　Suzette E. Johnson

For full biographical listings, see the Martindale-Hubbell Law Directory

*MINNEAPOLIS,** Hennepin Co.

ABDO AND ABDO, P.A. (AV)

710 Northstar West, 625 Marquette Avenue, 55402
Telephone: 612-333-1526
Fax: 612-342-2608

Robert P. Abdo　　Keith J. Broady
Steven R. Hedges　　Kenneth J. Abdo
Timothy C. Matson

Representative Clients: ADT Security Systems, Inc.; Cold Spring Brewing Co., Cold Spring, Minn.

For Complete List of Firm Personnel, See General Section

For full biographical listings, see the Martindale-Hubbell Law Directory

FRED BURSTEIN & ASSOCIATES, P.A. (AV)

5450 Norwest Center, 90 South Seventh Street, 55402
Telephone: 612-339-6561
Fax: 612-337-5572

Fred Burstein

Dylan J. McFarland　　Eric J. Olsen

Reference: Firstar Bank of Minnesota, N.A.

For full biographical listings, see the Martindale-Hubbell Law Directory

LOVETT & SMITH, LTD. (AV)

100 South Fifth Street, Suite 2250, 55402
Telephone: 612-339-4567

Thomas G. Lovett, Jr.　　Glenn L. Smith
Larry B. Ricke

For full biographical listings, see the Martindale-Hubbell Law Directory

MANSFIELD & TANICK, P.A. (AV)

International Centre, 900 Second Avenue South, 15th Floor, 55402
Telephone: 612-339-4295
Fax: 612-339-3161

Seymour J. Mansfield　　Teresa J. Ayling
Marshall H. Tanick　　Sholly A. Blustin
Earl H. Cohen　　Catherine M. Klimek
Robert A. Johnson　　Phillip J. Trobaugh
Richard J. Fuller

OF COUNSEL

Daniel S. Kleinberger

For full biographical listings, see the Martindale-Hubbell Law Directory

MISSISSIPPI

*ABERDEEN,** Monroe Co.

HOLCOMB, DUNBAR, CONNELL, CHAFFIN & WILLARD, A PROFESSIONAL ASSOCIATION (AV)

109 1/2 West Commerce Street, P.O. Box 866, 39730
Telephone: 601-369-8800
Facsimile: 601-369-9404
Jackson, Mississippi Office: 111 East Capitol Street, Suite 290, P.O. Box 2990, 39207-2990.
Telephone: 601-948-0048.
Facsimile: 601-948-0050.

(See Next Column)

Clarksdale, Mississippi Office: 152 Delta Avenue, P.O. Box 368, 38614.
Telephone: 601-627-2241.
Facsimile: 601-627-9788.
Oxford, Mississippi Office: 1217 Jackson Avenue, P.O. Drawer 707, 38655.
Telephone: 601-234-8775.
Facsimile: 601-234-8638.
Southhaven, Mississippi Office: Suite 1, 8727 Northwest Drive, P.O. Box 190, 38671.
Telephone: 601-342-6806.
Facsimile: 601-342-6792.

Jack F. Dunbar　　Barry C. Blackburn

OF COUNSEL

Ralph E. Pogue

For Complete List of Firm Personnel, See General Section

For full biographical listings, see the Martindale-Hubbell Law Directory

BILOXI, Harrison Co.

RUSHING & GUICE (AV)

683 Water Street, P.O. Box 1925, 39533-1925
Telephone: 601-374-2313
Telecopier: 601-374-8155

MEMBERS OF FIRM

Charles L. Rushing (1881-1923)　　William L. Guice (1887-1971)
William Lee Guice III

OF COUNSEL

Jacob D. Guice

ASSOCIATES

Edgar F. Maier　　R. Scott Wells

LEGAL SUPPORT PERSONNEL

Antonia Strong

For full biographical listings, see the Martindale-Hubbell Law Directory

*CLARKSDALE,** Coahoma Co.

HOLCOMB, DUNBAR, CONNELL, CHAFFIN & WILLARD, A PROFESSIONAL ASSOCIATION (AV)

152 Delta Avenue, P.O. Box 368, 38614
Telephone: 601-627-2241
Facsimile: 601-627-9788
Jackson, Mississippi Office: 111 East Capitol Street, Suite 290, P.O. Box 2990, 39207-2990.
Telephone: 601-948-0048.
Facsimile: 601-948-0050.
Aberdeen, Mississippi Office: 109 1/2 West Commerce Street, P.O. Box 866, 39730.
Telephone: 601-369-8800.
Facsimile: 601-369-9404.
Oxford, Mississippi Office: 1217 Jackson Avenue, P.O. Drawer 707, 38655.
Telephone: 601-234-8775.
Facsimile: 601-234-8638.
Southaven, Mississippi Office: Suite 1, 8727 Northwest Drive, 38671.
Telephone: 601-342-6806.
Facsimile: 601-342-6792.

William M. Chaffin　　Barry C. Blackburn

OF COUNSEL

Edward P. Connell

For Complete List of Firm Personnel, See General Section

For full biographical listings, see the Martindale-Hubbell Law Directory

*GREENWOOD,** Leflore Co.

FLOYD M. MELTON, JR. (AV)

107 1/2 E. Market, P.O. Box 534, 38930
Telephone: 601-453-8016
Fax: 601-453-0145

For full biographical listings, see the Martindale-Hubbell Law Directory

*GULFPORT,** Harrison Co.

FRANKE, RAINEY & SALLOUM (AV)

2605 14th Street, P.O. Drawer 460, 39502
Telephone: 601-868-7070
Telecopier: 601-868-7090

MEMBERS OF FIRM

Paul M. Franke, Jr.　　Paul B. Howell
William M. Rainey　　Ronald T. Russell
Richard P. Salloum　　Fredrick B. Feeney, II
Traci M. Castille

(See Next Column)

FRANKE, RAINEY & SALLOUM—*Continued*

ASSOCIATES

Kaleel G. Salloum, Jr.
Ruth E. Bennett
Donald P. Moore
Roland F. Samson, III
Jeffrey S. Bruni
Stefan G. Bourn

For full biographical listings, see the Martindale-Hubbell Law Directory

HOPKINS, DODSON, CRAWLEY, BAGWELL, UPSHAW & PERSONS (AV)

2701 24th Avenue, P.O. Box 1510, 39502-1510
Telephone: 601-864-2200
Mississippi & USA Wats: 1-800-421-3629
Fax: 601-868-9358; 601-863-4227

MEMBERS OF FIRM

Alben N. Hopkins
Lisa P. Dodson
Timothy D. Crawley
Douglas Bagwell
Jessica Sibley Upshaw
James B. Persons

ASSOCIATES

Perre M. Cabell
Christopher Anthony Davis
James Robert Reeves, Jr.
Ottis B. Crocker, III
Kaye Johnson Persons (Not admitted in MS)
Matthew G. Mestayer
Regina A. Lightsey
Mary Benton-Shaw (Not admitted in MS)
K. Douglas Lee (Not admitted in MS)
Thomas A. Waller
M. Amanda Baucum (Not admitted in MS)

LEGAL SUPPORT PERSONNEL

PARALEGALS

Cherri Nickoles
Penny W. West
Jennifer Susan Regan
Justina M. Tillman
Jayme L. Evans
Tracey L. Owen
Marcia P. Henry
Anne B. Parks

Representative Clients: Avondale Shipyards; Employers Insurance of Wausau; Fireman's Fund Insurance Company; General Cable Company; Hartford Insurance Company and Its Affiliates; Insurance Company of North America; Libery Mutual Group; Reliance Insurance; USX Corporation.

For full biographical listings, see the Martindale-Hubbell Law Directory

MEADOWS, RILEY, KOENENN AND TEEL, P.A. (AV)

1720 23rd Avenue, P.O. Box 550, 39502
Telephone: 601-864-4511
Telecopier: 601-868-2178

Joseph R. Meadows
Donnie D. Riley
Alfred R. Koenenn
Walter W. Teel
Jerry D. Riley
Karen J. Young

Representative Clients: Bubba Oustalat Lincoln Mercury, Inc.; Lee Tractor Co. of Mississippi.
Reference: Hancock Bank.

For full biographical listings, see the Martindale-Hubbell Law Directory

*JACKSON,** Hinds Co.

DRISDALE & LINDSTROM, P.A. (AV Ⓣ)

302 Banner Hall, 4465 I-55 North, P.O. Box 13329, 39236-3329
Telephone: 601-982-5599
Telecopier: 601-982-3005
MS Wats 1-800-710-7833

John K. Drisdale, Jr.
Eric E. Lindstrom, Jr.

For full biographical listings, see the Martindale-Hubbell Law Directory

HOLCOMB, DUNBAR, CONNELL, CHAFFIN & WILLARD, A PROFESSIONAL ASSOCIATION (AV)

111 East Capitol Street, Suite 290, P.O. Box 2990, 39207-2990
Telephone: 601-948-0048
Facsimile: 601-948-0050
Clarksdale, Mississippi Office: 152 Delta Avenue, P.O. Box 368, 38614.
Telephone: 601-627-2241.
Facsimile: 601-627-9788.
Aberdeen, Mississippi Office: 109 1/2 West Commerce Street, P.O. Box 866, 39730.
Telephone: 601-369-8800.
Facsimile: 601-369-9404.
Oxford, Mississippi Office: 1217 Jackson Avenue, P.O. Drawer 707, 38655.
Telephone: 601-234-8775.
Facsimile: 601-234-8638.
Southaven, Mississippi Office: Suite 1, 8727 Northwest Drive, P.O. Box 190, 38671.
Telephone: 601-342-6806.
Facsimile: 601-342-6792.

Jack F. Dunbar
C. Michael Pumphrey
Barry C. Blackburn

(See Next Column)

OF COUNSEL

Edward P. Connell

For Complete List of Firm Personnel, See General Section

For full biographical listings, see the Martindale-Hubbell Law Directory

MCDAVID, NOBLIN & WEST (AV)

Suite 1000, Security Centre North, 200 South Lamar Street, 39201
Telephone: 601-948-3305
Telecopier: 601-354-4789

MEMBERS OF FIRM

John Land McDavid
William C. Noblin, Jr.
W. Eric West
John Sanford McDavid
John C. Robertson

OF COUNSEL

Lowell F. Stephens

For full biographical listings, see the Martindale-Hubbell Law Directory

WISE CARTER CHILD & CARAWAY, PROFESSIONAL ASSOCIATION (AV)

600 Heritage Building, 401 East Capitol Street, P.O. Box 651, 39205
Telephone: 601-968-5500
FAX: 601-968-5519

Louis H. Watson
W. McDonald Nichols

For Complete List of Firm Personnel, See General Section

For full biographical listings, see the Martindale-Hubbell Law Directory

*OXFORD,** Lafayette Co.

HOLCOMB, DUNBAR, CONNELL, CHAFFIN & WILLARD, A PROFESSIONAL ASSOCIATION (AV)

1217 Jackson Avenue P.O. Drawer 707, 38655
Telephone: 601-234-8775
Facsimile: 601-234-8638
Jackson, Mississippi Office: 111 East Capitol Street, Suite 290. P.O. Box 2990, 39207-2990.
Telephone: 601-948-0048.
Facsimile: 601-948-0050.
Clarksdale, Mississippi Office: 152 Delta Avenue, P.O. Box 368, 38614.
Telephone: 601-627-2241.
Facsimile: 601-627-9788.
Aberdeen, Mississippi Office: 109 1/2 West Commerce Street, P.O. Box 866, 39730.
Telephone: 601-369-8800.
Facsimile: 601-369-9404.
Southaven, Mississippi Office: Suite 1, 8727 Northwest Drive, P.O. Box 190, 38671.
Telephone: 601-342-6806.
Facsimile: 601-342-6792.

Jack F. Dunbar
Barry C. Blackburn

OF COUNSEL

Edward P. Connell

For Complete List of Firm Personnel, See General Section

For full biographical listings, see the Martindale-Hubbell Law Directory

SOUTHAVEN, De Soto Co.

HOLCOMB, DUNBAR, CONNELL, CHAFFIN & WILLARD, A PROFESSIONAL ASSOCIATION (AV)

Suite 1, 8727 Northwest Drive, P.O. Box 190, 38671
Telephone: 601-342-6806
Facsimile: 601-342-6792
Jackson, Mississippi Office: 111 East Capitol Street, Suite 290, P.O. Box 2990, 39207-2990.
Telephone: 601-948-0048.
Facsimile: 601-948-0050.
Clarksdale, Mississippi Office: 152 Delta Avenue, P.O. Box 368, 38614.
Telephone: 601-627-2241.
Facsimile: 601-627-9788.
Aberdeen, Mississippi Office: 109 1/2 West Commerce Street, P.O. Box 866, 39730.
Telephone: 601-369-8800.
Facsimile: 601-369-9404.
Oxford, Mississippi Office: 1217 Jackson Avenue, P.O. Drawer 707, 38655.
Telephone: 601-234-8775.
Facsimile: 601-234-8638.

William M. Chaffin
Barry C. Blackburn

OF COUNSEL

Edward P. Connell

For Complete List of Firm Personnel, See General Section

For full biographical listings, see the Martindale-Hubbell Law Directory

Southaven—Continued

TAYLOR, JONES, ALEXANDER, SORRELL & MCFALL, LTD. (AV)

961 State Line Road, West, P.O. Box 188, 38671
Telephone: 601-342-1300
Telecopier: 601-342-1312

Ronald L. Taylor
Jack R. Jones, III
Keith M. Alexander
Mark K. Sorrell
George McFall

Approved Attorneys for: Mississippi Valley Title Insurance Co.; First American Title, Insurance.
Reference: Sunburst Bank, Southaven, Miss.

For full biographical listings, see the Martindale-Hubbell Law Directory

*TUPELO,** Lee Co.

HOLLAND, RAY & UPCHURCH, P.A. (AV)

322 Jefferson Street, P.O. Drawer 409, 38802
Telephone: 601-842-1721
Facsimile: 601-844-6413

Sam E. Lumpkin (1908-1964)
Ralph L. Holland
James Hugh Ray
Robert K. Upchurch
W. Reed Hillen, III
Thomas A. Wicker

Michael D. Tapscott

Representative Clients: The Travelers; Continental Casualty Co.; South Central Bell Telephone Co.; The Greyhound Corp.; Mississippi Valley Gas Co.; Bryan-Rogers, Inc.; The Housing Authority of the City of Tupelo; Action Industries, Inc.; American Cable Systems, Inc.; American Funeral Assurance Co.

For full biographical listings, see the Martindale-Hubbell Law Directory

MISSOURI

KANSAS CITY, Jackson, Clay & Platte Cos.

SWANSON, MIDGLEY, GANGWERE, KITCHIN & MCLARNEY, L.L.C. (AV)

1500 Commerce Trust Building, 922 Walnut, 64106-1848
Telephone: 816-842-6100
Overland Park, Kansas Office: The NCAA Building, Suite 350, 6201 College Boulevard.
Telephone: 816-842-6100.

George H. Gangwere, Jr.
John J. Kitchin
James H. McLarney
Rodney V. Hipp

Counsel for: General Electric Co.; Chrysler Corp.; Conoco, Inc.; Yellow Freight System, Inc.; The Prudential Insurance Co. of America; Metropolitan Life Insurance Co.; National Collegiate Athletic Assn.; Land Title Insurance Co.; Safeway Stores, Inc.; The Lee Apparel Co.

For Complete List of Firm Personnel, See General Section

For full biographical listings, see the Martindale-Hubbell Law Directory

LEE'S SUMMIT, Jackson Co.

CARL CHINNERY & ASSOCIATES, P.C. (AV)

200 South Douglas, 64063
Telephone: 816-525-2050

Carl L. Chinnery

Nancy E. Blackwell

OF COUNSEL

Elizabeth Unger Carlyle

LEGAL SUPPORT PERSONNEL

PARALEGALS

Jean Wehner Chinnery
Janice Sue Hancock
Elaine K. Hanrahan
Alicia Hodges
Susan Breitenbach

For full biographical listings, see the Martindale-Hubbell Law Directory

*MEXICO,** Audrain Co.

SEIGFREID, RUNGE, LEONATTI, POHLMEYER & SEIGFREID, P.C. (AV)

123 East Jackson Street, 65265
Telephone: 314-581-2211
Telecopier: 314-581-6577

(See Next Column)

Michael J. Pohlmeyer

Counsel for: Commerce Bank N.A.; Aetna Casualty & Surety Co.; State Farm Mutual Insurance Cos.; National Refractories and Minerals Corp.; City of Mexico, Mo.; Central Electric Co.; U. S. Fidelity & Guaranty Co; Audrain Medical Center.

For Complete List of Firm Personnel, See General Section

For full biographical listings, see the Martindale-Hubbell Law Directory

ST. LOUIS, (Independent City)

JEROME R. MANDELSTAMM (AV)

Suite 1600, 1010 Market Street, 63101
Telephone: 314-621-2261

For full biographical listings, see the Martindale-Hubbell Law Directory

THOMPSON & MITCHELL (AV)

One Mercantile Center, Suite 3300, 63101
Telephone: 314-231-7676
Telecopier: 314-342-1717
Belleville, Illinois Office: 525 West Main Street.
Telephone: 618-277-4700; 314-271-1800.
Telecopier: 618-236-3434.
St. Charles, Missouri Office: 200 North Third Street.
Telephone: 314-946-7717.
Telecopier: 314-946-4938.
Washington, D.C. Office: 700 14th Street, N.W., Suite 900.
Telephone: 202-508-1000.
Telecopier: 202-508-1010.

MEMBERS OF FIRM

Joseph P. Logan
Thomas R. Corbett
James G. Blase
Harris A. Maynord

ASSOCIATES

Mark J. Drish
Lorna L. Frahm
Katherine G. Knapp
Jane M. Moul

Representative Clients: Chrysler Corp.; Enterprise Rent-A-Car Company; Magna Banks; Mallinckrodt, Inc.; Maritz, Inc.; Mercantile Bancorporation, Inc.; Monsanto Company; PaineWebber Incorporated; Peabody Coal Co.; Union Pacific Railroad Company.

For Complete List of Firm Personnel, See General Section

For full biographical listings, see the Martindale-Hubbell Law Directory

MONTANA

*BILLINGS,** Yellowstone Co.

CROWLEY, HAUGHEY, HANSON, TOOLE & DIETRICH (AV)

500 Transwestern II, 490 North 31st Street, P.O. Box 2529, 59103
Telephone: 406-252-3441
Fax: 406-259-4159
Helena, Montana Office: IBM Building, 100 North Park Avenue, Suite 300, 59601.
Telephone: 406-449-4165.
Fax: 406-449-5149.

MEMBERS OF FIRM

John M. Dietrich
Myles J. Thomas
David L. Johnson
James P. Sites
Daniel N. McLean
Robert G. Michelotti, Jr.
Eric K. Anderson

ASSOCIATE

Scott M. Heard

Representative Clients: First Interstate Bank of Commerce, Trust Department.

For Complete List of Firm Personnel, See General Section

For full biographical listings, see the Martindale-Hubbell Law Directory

*BOZEMAN,** Gallatin Co.

KIRWAN & BARRETT, P.C. (AV)

215 West Mendenhall, P.O. Box 1348, 59771-1348
Telephone: 406-586-1553
Fax: 406-586-8971

Janice K. Whetstone
Stephen M. Barrett

Tom W. Stonecipher

For full biographical listings, see the Martindale-Hubbell Law Directory

NEBRASKA

*BROKEN BOW,** Custer Co.

SCHAPER & STEFFENS (AV)

345 South 10th Avenue, P.O. Box 586, 68822
Telephone: 308-872-6481
Fax: 308-872-6385

MEMBERS OF FIRM

William C. Schaper (1890-1977) Carlos E. Schaper
William Vern Steffens

General Counsel for: Custer Federal Savings & Loan Assn., Broken Bow; United Nebraska Bank, Broken Bow, Nebraska; Security State Bank, Ansley.
Local Counsel for: Federated Mutual Implement and Hardware Insurance Co.; Shield of Shelter Insurance Co.; John Hancock Mutual Life Insurance Co.; Prudential Life Insurance Co.; Massey-Ferguson, Inc.; F.D.I.C.; Resolution Trust Corporation.

For full biographical listings, see the Martindale-Hubbell Law Directory

*GRAND ISLAND,** Hall Co.

THE LEGAL PROFESSIONAL CORPORATION OF TRACY & McQUILLAN (AV)

706 West Koenig Street, 68801-6556
Telephone: 308-382-5154
Fax: 308-382-3242

Howard E. Tracy Michael J. McQuillan

For full biographical listings, see the Martindale-Hubbell Law Directory

*LINCOLN,** Lancaster Co.

BARLOW, JOHNSON, FLODMAN, SUTTER, GUENZEL & ESKE (AV)

1227 Lincoln Mall, P.O. Box 81686, 68501-1686
Telephone: 402-475-4240
Fax: 402-475-0329

MEMBER OF FIRM

Steven E. Guenzel

Special Counsel: Nebraska Public Power District.
Representative Clients: Allied Group; Chubb/Pacific Indemnity Group; Citizens State Bank, Polk, Nebraska; Crum & Foster; Federated Rural Electric Insurance Corp.; Runza Drive-Inns of America; United States Fidelity & Guaranty Co.; Viking Insurance Company of Wisconsin.

For Complete List of Firm Personnel, See General Section

For full biographical listings, see the Martindale-Hubbell Law Directory

ERICKSON & SEDERSTROM, P.C. (AV)

Suite 400, Cornhusker Plaza, 301 South 13th Street, 68508
Telephone: 402-476-1000
Fax: 402-476-6167
Omaha, Nebraska Office: Regency Westpointe, 10330 Regency Parkway Drive.
Telephone: 402-397-2200.
Fax: 402-390-7137.

Charles Thone
Charles D. Humble
Alan M. Wood
Douglas L. Curry
Mark M. Schorr
Linda W. Rohman
David C. Mussman

Representative Clients: California Public Employees Retirement Plan (CALPERS); Chase Manhattan Leasing Co.; Albertson's, Inc.; Baker's Supermarkets, Inc.; Osco Drug, Inc.; Lincoln General Hospital; Martin Luther Home; Lincoln Electric System.

For full biographical listings, see the Martindale-Hubbell Law Directory

SCUDDER LAW FIRM, P.C. (AV)

Second Floor, 411 South 13th Street, P.O. Box 81277, 68508
Telephone: 402-435-3223
Fax: 402-435-4239

Beverly Evans Grenier
Christine C. Schwartzkopf Schroff
Earl H. Scudder, Jr.
Mark A. Scudder

For full biographical listings, see the Martindale-Hubbell Law Directory

*OMAHA,** Douglas Co.

ERICKSON & SEDERSTROM, P.C. (AV)

Regency Westpointe, 10330 Regency Parkway Drive, 68114
Telephone: 402-397-2200
Fax: 402-390-7137
Lincoln, Nebraska Office: Suite 400, Cornhusker Plaza, 301 South 13th Street.
Telephone: 402-476-1000.
Fax: 402-476-6167.

Lewis R. Leigh
Ray R. Simon
Donald H. Erickson
Daniel D. Koukol
Wm. E. Morrow, Jr.
Soren S. Jensen
Daniel B. Kinnamon
Joel Davis
Virgil K. Johnson
Charles V. Sederstrom, Jr.
Michael C. Washburn
John C. Brownrigg
Thomas J. Culhane
Richard J. Gilloon
Samuel Earle Clark
Gary L. Hoffman
J Russell Derr
Mark Peterson
Sherry L. Hubert
Lane D. Edenburn

OF COUNSEL

Leo Eisenstatt
Roland J. Santoni
Michael A. Fortune
Anne O. Fortune

Representative Clients: Nebraska State Bank of Omaha; Berkshire Hathaway, Inc.; Bozell, Inc.; IBP, Inc.; Quaker Oats Co.; United A-G Cooperative, Inc.; Immanuel Medical Center; Cornhusker Casualty Co.; Hartford Accident & Indemnity Co.; Mortgage Guaranty Insurance Corp. (MGIC).

For Complete List of Firm Personnel, See General Section

For full biographical listings, see the Martindale-Hubbell Law Directory

LAUGHLIN, PETERSON & LANG (AV)

11306 Davenport Street, 68154
Telephone: 402-330-1900
Fax: 402-330-0936

MEMBERS OF FIRM

Mark L. Laughlin Robert F. Peterson
James E. Lang

Representative Clients: Andersen Electric Co.; General Electric Capital Corp.; Sears, Roebuck & Co.; Dodge Land Co.; Security Mutual Life Insurance Co. of Lincoln, NE; Century Development Co.

For full biographical listings, see the Martindale-Hubbell Law Directory

NEVADA

*ELKO,** Elko Co.

WILSON AND BARROWS, LTD. (AV)

442 Court Street, P.O. Box 389, 89801
Telephone: 702-738-7271
FAX: 702-738-5041

Richard G. Barrows

Representative Clients: Petan Company of Nevada, Inc. (Cattle); Idaho Power Co.; Upper Humbolt Water Users Assn.; Salmon River Cattlemen's Assn.; El Aero Services, Inc.; Red Lion Casino; Club 93 Casino; Elko County School District; Casino Express Airlines.

For Complete List of Firm Personnel, See General Section

For full biographical listings, see the Martindale-Hubbell Law Directory

*LAS VEGAS,** Clark Co.

JEROME L. BLUT CHARTERED (AV)

Suite B, 550 East Charleston Boulevard, 89104
Telephone: 702-382-8840
FAX: 702-383-8452

Jerome L. Blut

References: First Interstate Bank of Nevada; Nevada State Bank.

For full biographical listings, see the Martindale-Hubbell Law Directory

CROCKETT & MYERS, LTD. A PROFESSIONAL CORPORATION (AV)

700 South Third Street, 89101
Telephone: 702-382-6711
Fax: 702-384-8102

J. R. Crockett, Jr.
Richard W. Myers
James V. Lavelle III
Eleissa C. Lavelle
Michael P. Villani

(See Next Column)

CROCKETT & MYERS LTD. A PROFESSIONAL CORPORATION, *Las Vegas—Continued*

Laura E. Wunsch Stubberud

Reference: Sun State Bank.

For full biographical listings, see the Martindale-Hubbell Law Directory

HALE, LANE, PEEK, DENNISON AND HOWARD (AV)

Suite 800, Nevada Financial Center, 2300 West Sahara Avenue, Box 8, 89102
Telephone: 702-362-5118
Fax: 702-365-6940
Reno, Nevada Office: Porsche Building, 100 West Liberty Street, Tenth Floor, P.O. Box 3237.
Telephone: 702-786-7900.
Telefax: 702-786-6179.

MEMBERS OF FIRM

Steve Lane
Marilyn L. Skender

ASSOCIATE

James L. Kelly

For Complete List of Firm Personnel, See General Section

For full biographical listings, see the Martindale-Hubbell Law Directory

JOLLEY, URGA, WIRTH & WOODBURY (AV)

Suite 800 Bank of America Plaza, 300 South Fourth Street, 89101
Telephone: 702-385-5161
Telecopier: 702-382-6814
Boulder City, Nevada Office: Suite 105, 1000 Nevada Highway.
Telephone: 702-293-3674.

MEMBERS OF FIRM

R. Gardner Jolley
Bruce L. Woodbury
Kathryn Elizabeth Stryker

ASSOCIATE

Craig M. Murphy

Representative Clients: First Interstate Bank of Nevada; Nevada State Bank; Citicorp National Services, Inc.; Continental National Bank; First Nationwide Bank; PriMerit Bank.

For Complete List of Firm Personnel, See General Section

For full biographical listings, see the Martindale-Hubbell Law Directory

MCDONALD, CARANO, WILSON, MCCUNE, BERGIN, FRANKOVICH & HICKS (AV)

Suite 1000, 2300 West Sahara Avenue, 89102
Telephone: 702-873-4100
Telecopier: 702-873-9966
Reno, Nevada Office: 241 Ridge Street.
Telephone: 702-322-0635.
Telecopier: 702-786-9532.

MEMBER OF FIRM

Robert E. Armstrong

ASSOCIATE

Scott A. Swain (Resident)

Representative Clients: AT&T Communications of Nevada; Bally Gaming, Inc.; Boomtown, Inc.; Boyd Gaming Corporation; First Interstate Bank of Nevada; Jackpot Enterprises, Inc.; Primadonna Resorts, Inc.; Shaver Construction.

For Complete List of Firm Personnel, See General Section

For full biographical listings, see the Martindale-Hubbell Law Directory

MONSEY & ANDREWS (AV)

3900 Paradise Road, Suite 283, 89109
Telephone: 702-732-9897
Facsimile: 702-732-9667
Boulder City, Nevada Office: 402 Nevada Highway.
Telephone: 702-294-1112.
Facsimile: 294-0235.

MEMBERS OF FIRM

Earl Monsey
B. G. Andrews (Resident, Boulder City, Nevada)

Representative Clients: Chrysler Capital Corp.; Jack Matthews Realty; Mortgage Loans America; United Pacific Insurance Co.; Planet Insurance Co.; Reliance Insurance Co.; KNPR Nevada Public Radio Corporation; Agassi Enterprises; World Savings; The Walt Disney Co.

For full biographical listings, see the Martindale-Hubbell Law Directory

JOHN D. O'BRIEN, LTD. (AV)

1409 Bank of America Plaza, 300 South Fourth Street, 89101
Telephone: 702-382-5222
Fax: 702-382-0540

(See Next Column)

John D. O'Brien

For full biographical listings, see the Martindale-Hubbell Law Directory

OSHINS & GIBBONS (AV)

Suite G-46, 501 South Rancho Drive, 89106
Telephone: 702-386-1935
Fax: 702-386-6823
Santa Ana, California Office: Oshins & Inouye, 3 Imperial Promenade, Suite 11 D.
Telephone: 714-850-4828.

MEMBERS OF FIRM

Richard A. Oshins
Mark W. Gibbons

OF COUNSEL

Edward S. Inouye (Not admitted in NV)

For full biographical listings, see the Martindale-Hubbell Law Directory

WOODBURN AND WEDGE (AV)

Suite 620 Bank of America Plaza, 300 South Fourth Street, 89101
Telephone: 702-387-1000
Reno, Nevada Office: 16th Floor, First Interstate Bank Building. P.O. Box 2311.
Telephone: 702-688-3000.
Telecopier: 702-688-3088.

MEMBERS OF FIRM

Virgil H. Wedge
Michael E. Kearney
James J. Halley
Lynne K. Jones

Representative Clients: Atlantic Richfield Co.; Sierra Pacific Power Co.; The Union Pacific Railroad Co.; Western Union Telegraph Co.; Cyprus Minerals Corp.; The Roman Catholic Bishop of Reno, A Corporation Sole.

For full biographical listings, see the Martindale-Hubbell Law Directory

*RENO,** Washoe Co.

HALE, LANE, PEEK, DENNISON AND HOWARD (AV)

Porsche Building, 100 West Liberty Street, Tenth Floor, P.O. Box 3237, 89501
Telephone: 702-786-7900
Telefax: 702-786-6179
Las Vegas, Nevada Office: Suite 800, Nevada Financial Center, 2300 West Sahara Avenue, Box 8.
Telephone: 702-362-5118.
Fax: 702-365-6940.

MEMBERS OF FIRM

Steve Lane
Marilyn L. Skender

ASSOCIATE

James L. Kelly

For Complete List of Firm Personnel, See General Section

For full biographical listings, see the Martindale-Hubbell Law Directory

MCDONALD, CARANO, WILSON, MCCUNE, BERGIN, FRANKOVICH & HICKS (AV)

241 Ridge Street, 89505
Telephone: 702-322-0635
Telecopier: 702-786-9532
Las Vegas, Nevada Office: Suite 1000, 2300 West Sahara Avenue.
Telephone: 702-873-4100.
Telecopier: 702-873-9966.

MEMBERS OF FIRM

Robert E. Armstrong
John B. Galvin

ASSOCIATES

Scott A. Swain (Resident, Las Vegas Office)
David F. Grove

Representative Clients: AT&T Communications of Nevada; Associated General Contractors of America; Eldorado Hotel & Casino; First Interstate Bank of Nevada; Intermountain Federal Land Bank Association; James Hardie (USA), Inc.; Primadonna Resorts, Inc.; Scolari's Warehouse Markets; Shaver Construction; Time Oil Company (Nevada Counsel).

For Complete List of Firm Personnel, See General Section

For full biographical listings, see the Martindale-Hubbell Law Directory

WOODBURN AND WEDGE (AV)

16th Floor, First Interstate Bank Building, One East First Street, P.O. Box 2311, 89505
Telephone: 702-688-3000
Telecopier: 702-688-3088
Las Vegas, Nevada Office: Suite 620 Bank of American Plaza, 300 South Court Street.
Telephone: 702-387-1000.

(See Next Column)

WOODBURN AND WEDGE—*Continued*

MEMBERS OF FIRM

Virgil H. Wedge
James J. Halley
Michael E. Kearney
Lynne K. Jones

Representative Clients: Atlantic Richfield Co.; Sierra Pacific Power Co.; The Union Pacific Railroad Co.; Western Union Telegraph Co.; Bank of America; Cyprus Minerals Corp.; The Roman Catholic Bishop of Reno, A Corporation Sole.

For full biographical listings, see the Martindale-Hubbell Law Directory

NEW HAMPSHIRE

CAMPTON, Grafton Co.

LAW OFFICES OF RUSSELL E. CARLISLE, P.A. (AV)

Campton Common, Route 49 at Route 175, P.O. Box 327, 03223
Telephone: 603-726-7524
FAX: 603-726-4673

Russell E. Carlisle

For full biographical listings, see the Martindale-Hubbell Law Directory

*CONCORD,** Merrimack Co.

ORR & RENO, PROFESSIONAL ASSOCIATION (AV)

One Eagle Square, P.O. Box 3550, 03302-3550
Telephone: 603-224-2381
Fax: 603-224-2318

Charles F. Leahy
Mary Susan Leahy

Representative Clients: Beach Aircraft Corporation; Chubb Life America; Fleet Bank; Dartmouth-Hitchcock Medical Center; EnergyNorth, Inc.; National Grange Mutual Co.; New England College; New England Electric System Co.; Newspapers of New England, Inc.; St. Paul's School.

For Complete List of Firm Personnel, See General Section

For full biographical listings, see the Martindale-Hubbell Law Directory

RANSMEIER & SPELLMAN, PROFESSIONAL CORPORATION (AV)

One Capitol Street, P.O. Box 600, 03302-0600
Telephone: 603-228-0477
Telecopier: 603-224-2780

Joseph S. Ransmeier
John C. Ransmeier
Jeffrey J. Zellers

Thomas N. Masland
Lisa L. Biklen

For Complete List of Firm Personnel, See General Section

For full biographical listings, see the Martindale-Hubbell Law Directory

HAMPTON, Rockingham Co.

CASASSA AND RYAN (AV)

459 Lafayette Road, 03842
Telephone: 603-926-6336
Fax: 603-926-4127

MEMBERS OF FIRM

H. Alfred Casassa
John J. Ryan
Peter J. Saari
Kenneth D. Murphy
Robert A. Casassa

ASSOCIATES

Faye R. Goldberg
Daniel R. Hartley

General Counsel: Foss Manufacturing Company.
Representative Clients: Town of Hampton Falls; Town of North Hampton; Rye Beach Village District; Hampton School District; Susan Conway Enterprises; Clipper Nursing Homes; Wal-Mart Inc.

For full biographical listings, see the Martindale-Hubbell Law Directory

*KEENE,** Cheshire Co.

BELL, FALK & NORTON, P.A. (AV)

8 Middle Street, P.O. Box F, 03431
Telephone: 603-352-5950
FAX: 603-352-5930

Ernest L. Bell, Jr. (1925-1961)
Ernest L. Bell
Arnold R. Falk
John C. Norton

William James Robinson

For full biographical listings, see the Martindale-Hubbell Law Directory

*LACONIA,** Belknap Co.

NORMANDIN, CHENEY & O'NEIL (AV)

Normandin Square, 213 Union Avenue, P.O. Box 575, 03247-0575
Telephone: 603-524-4380

MEMBERS OF FIRM

Paul L. Normandin
John D. O'Shea, Jr.
Robert A. Dietz

ASSOCIATE

Susanne M. Strong

Counsel for: Laconia Savings Bank; Lakes Region Mental Health Center; Laconia Airport Authority; Community TV Corp.; Central New Hampshire Realty, Inc.; All Metals Industries, Inc.; Lakes Region Anesthesiology, P.A.; Cormier Corp.; Scotia Technology; Vemaline Products.

For Complete List of Firm Personnel, See General Section

For full biographical listings, see the Martindale-Hubbell Law Directory

NEW JERSEY

ATLANTIC CITY, Atlantic Co.

LEVINE, STALLER, SKLAR, CHAN & BRODSKY, P.A. (AV)

3030 Atlantic Avenue, 08401
Telephone: 609-348-1300
Telecopier: 609-345-2473

Lee A. Levine
Alan C. Staller
Arthur E. Sklar
Paul T. Chan
Lawrence A. Brodsky
Brian J. Cullen
Benjamin Zeltner

Arthur M. Brown
Scott J. Mitnick

Representative Clients: A. G. Edwards & Sons, Inc.; Atlantic Plastic Containers Inc.; The Michaels Development Co., Inc.; Nawas International Travel Services, Inc.; Trump Casino Hotels - Atlantic City, NJ; Interstate Realty Management Company.

For full biographical listings, see the Martindale-Hubbell Law Directory

CALDWELL, Essex Co.

BRANDLEY AND KLEPPE (AV)

13 Smull Avenue, P.O. Box 33, 07006
Telephone: 201-226-0526
Fax: 201-226-1947

MEMBERS OF FIRM

Walter G. Brandley (1887-1965)
David F. Brandley
Andrew W. Kleppe

Counsel for: West Essex Savings Bank, Caldwell, New Jersey.

For full biographical listings, see the Martindale-Hubbell Law Directory

FLORHAM PARK, Morris Co.

GEDNEY, SEAMAN & HILGENDORFF (AV)

248 Columbia Turnpike, P.O. Box 166, 07932-0166
Telephone: 201-377-9120
Fax: 201-377-9126
Morristown, New Jersey Office: 15 James Street.
Telephone: 201-539-3088.
Fax: 201-539-0163

MEMBERS OF FIRM

Stanley L. Gedney, Jr. (1889-1977)
Bradford C. Seaman (1898-1986)
Hugo A. Hilgendorff, Jr. (1914-1991)
Hugo A. Hilgendorff, III

ASSOCIATES

Peter B. Hilgendorff
George B. Wright

For full biographical listings, see the Martindale-Hubbell Law Directory

HACK, PIRO, O'DAY, MERKLINGER, WALLACE & MCKENNA, P.A. (AV)

30 Columbia Turnpike, P.O. Box 941, 07932-0941
Telephone: 201-301-6500
Fax: 201-301-0094

David L. Hack
John M. McKenna

(See Next Column)

HACK, PIRO, O'DAY, MERKLINGER, WALLACE & MCKENNA P.A., *Florham Park—Continued*

Angela J. Mendelsohn
Michelle M. Monte
John F. Lanahan
Rosemarie Deehan Berard

Representative Clients: Cenlar Federal Savings Bank; County Mortgage Company, Inc.; First Fidelity Bank, N.A., N.J.; Citicorp Mortgage, Inc.; Travelers Insurance Co.; State Farm Insurance Companies; Aetna Life & Casualty Co.

For Complete List of Firm Personnel, See General Section

For full biographical listings, see the Martindale-Hubbell Law Directory

*HACKENSACK,** Bergen Co.

DEENER, FEINGOLD & STERN, A PROFESSIONAL CORPORATION (AV)

2 University Plaza, Suite 602, 07601
Telephone: 201-343-8788
Fax: 201-343-4640

Jerome A. Deener
Cal R. Feingold
Robert A. Stern

Debra T. Hirsch
David M. Edelblum
Anthony M. Vizzoni
James J. Costello, Jr. (Not admitted in NJ)

References: United Jersey Bank; Midlantic Bank; Midland Bank and Trust Co. (Trust Department); Fidelity Bank; Hudson United Bank.

For full biographical listings, see the Martindale-Hubbell Law Directory

DUNN, PASHMAN, SPONZILLI, SWICK & FINNERTY (AV)

411 Hackensack Avenue, 07601
Telephone: 201-489-1500; 845-4000
Fax: 201-489-1512

COUNSEL

Morris Pashman
Murray L. Cole
Paul D. Rosenberg

MEMBERS OF FIRM

Joseph Dunn
Louis Pashman
John E. Finnerty
Edward G. Sponzilli
Daniel A. Swick
Robert E. Rochford
Warren S. Robins

ASSOCIATES

Nicholas F. Pellitta
Laura S. Kirsch
Danya A. Grunyk
Richard P. Jacobson
Jeffrey M. Shapiro
Deborah L. Ustas
Mark E. Lichtblau
Edward B. Stevenson
Stephen F. Roth

References: United Jersey Bank; Valley National Bank.

For full biographical listings, see the Martindale-Hubbell Law Directory

HEIN, SMITH, BEREZIN, MALOOF & ROGERS (AV)

Court Plaza East, 19 Main Street, 07601-7023
Telephone: 201-487-7400
Telecopier: 201-487-4228

MEMBER OF FIRM

Alan A. Davidson

OF COUNSEL

Seymour A. Smith

For Complete List of Firm Personnel, See General Section

For full biographical listings, see the Martindale-Hubbell Law Directory

LITWIN & HOLSINGER (AV)

Two University Plaza, 07601
Telephone: 201-487-9000
Telecopier: 201-487-9070

MEMBERS OF FIRM

John R. Holsinger
Gerald H. Litwin

OF COUNSEL

Bernard J. Koster (Not admitted in NJ)

For full biographical listings, see the Martindale-Hubbell Law Directory

MAHWAH, Bergen Co.

ARNOLD E. REITER (AV)

2 North Bayard Lane, P.O. Box 915, 07430
Telephone: 201-818-2333
Fax: 201-825-1509
Affiliated Office: Estate Plan Institute, Inc., Suffern, New York, 75 Montebello Road.
Telephone: 914-357-2215.
Fax: 914-357-4437.

Representative Clients: AST Development Corp.; Gary Goldberg & Co.
Reference: Bank of New York/National Community Bank.

MILLBURN, Essex Co.

KUTTNER LAW OFFICES (AV)

24 Lackawanna Plaza, P.O. Box 745, 07041-0745
Telephone: 201-467-8300
Fax: 201-467-4333

Bernard A. Kuttner
Robert D. Kuttner

Reference: Summit Bank, Millburn, New Jersey.

For full biographical listings, see the Martindale-Hubbell Law Directory

MONTCLAIR, Essex Co.

BOOTH, BATE, GRIECO AND BRIODY (AV)

Formerly Boyd, Dodd, Keer & Booth
31 Park Street, 07042
Telephone: 201-744-1900

John A. Booth (1901-1984)

MEMBERS OF FIRM

David S. Bate
Gloria E. Grieco
Thomas M. Briody

Counsel for: Annin & Co.; Borough of Essex Fells, New Jersey; The Florence and John Schumann Foundation; The International Foundation.

For full biographical listings, see the Martindale-Hubbell Law Directory

MOORESTOWN, Burlington Co.

BRANDT, HAUGHEY, PENBERTHY, LEWIS, HYLAND & CLAYPOOLE, A PROFESSIONAL CORPORATION (AV)

240 West State Highway 38, P.O. Box 1002, 08057-0949
Telephone: 609-235-1111
Telecopier: 609-722-0357

S. David Brandt
Gerald E. Haughey
Edward A. Penberthy
Robert S. Lewis
William F. Hyland, Jr.
Susan L. Claypoole
Patrick F. McAndrew
Thomas J. DiPilla, Jr.
Steven A. Aboloff
Eileen K. Fahey

Representative Clients: City of Camden (Tax Matters); Davis Enterprises; Deptford Mall, Inc.; McDonald's Corp.; Mobil Oil Corp.; Chemical Bank; Continental Title Insurance Co.; Texaco; The Radner/Canuso Partnership.

For full biographical listings, see the Martindale-Hubbell Law Directory

*MORRISTOWN,** Morris Co.

PITNEY, HARDIN, KIPP & SZUCH (AV)

Park Avenue at Morris County, P.O. Box 1945, 07962-1945
Telephone: 201-966-6300
New York City: 212-926-0331
Telex: 642014
Telecopier: 201-966-1550

MEMBERS OF FIRM

James C. Pitney
Robert C. Neff
Richard Kahn
Mary Lou Parker
Kevin J. O'Donnell

COUNSEL

Jane H. Hardin

ASSOCIATES

Charles P. Abraham
L. Allison Garde
Sally A. Roll

Representative Clients: AlliedSignal Inc.; AT&T; Base Ten Systems, Inc.; Exxon Corp.; Ford Motor Co.; Midlantic National Bank; Sony Electronics, Inc.; Union Carbide Corp.; United Parcel Services, Inc.; Warner-Lambert Co.

For Complete List of Firm Personnel, See General Section

For full biographical listings, see the Martindale-Hubbell Law Directory

*NEWARK,** Essex Co.

CARPENTER, BENNETT & MORRISSEY (AV)

(Formerly Carpenter, Gilmour & Dwyer)
Three Gateway Center, 17th Floor, 100 Mulberry Street, 07102-4079
Telephone: 201-622-7711
New York City: 212-943-6530
Telex: 139405
Telecopier: 201-622-5314
EasyLink: 62827845
ABA/net: CARPENTERB

MEMBERS OF FIRM

Laurence Reich
Edward F. Day, Jr.
Francis X. O'Brien
John D. Goldsmith

OF COUNSEL

Warren Lloyd Lewis

ASSOCIATES

Hans G. Polak
Kevin F. Murphy
Dawn M. Felipe

Representative Clients: General Motors Corp.; E. I. du Pont de Nemours and Company; Texaco Inc.; AT&T; Litton Industries; ITT Corp.; International Flavors & Fragrances Inc.; New Jersey Hospital Association; Prudential Insurance Company of America; United Jersey Bank.

For Complete List of Firm Personnel, See General Section

For full biographical listings, see the Martindale-Hubbell Law Directory

FOX AND FOX (AV)

570 Broad Street, 07102
Telephone: 201-622-3624
Telecopier: 201-622-6220

MEMBERS OF FIRM

David I. Fox
Martin Kesselhaut
Arthur D. Grossman
Dennis J. Alessi
Paul I. Rosenberg
Gabriel H. Halpern
Kenneth H. Fast
Steven A. Holt
Nancy C. McDonald

OF COUNSEL

Jacob Fox (1898-1992)
Robert J. Rohrberger
Martin S. Fox
Robert S. Catapano-Friedman

ASSOCIATES

Robert P. Donovan
Katherine J. Welsh
Stacey B. Rosenberg
Craig S. Gumpel
Susan R. Fox
Brett Alison Rosenberg
Virginia S. Ryan
Alfred V. Acquaviva
Ronnie Ann Powell
Anthony F. Vitiello

For full biographical listings, see the Martindale-Hubbell Law Directory

LEVY, EHRLICH & KRONENBERG, A PROFESSIONAL CORPORATION (AV)

60 Park Place, 07102
Telephone: 201-643-0040
Telecopier: 201-596-1781
Hackensack, New Jersey Office: 1 University Plaza, Suite 501, 07601.
Telephone: 301-342-4445.

Ira A. Levy
Arthur Kronenberg
Alan Ehrlich
John J. Petriello
David L. Eisbrouch

Representative Clients: Panasonic Co.; Transamerica; General Electric.
Reference: First Fidelity Bank.

For Complete List of Firm Personnel, See General Section

For full biographical listings, see the Martindale-Hubbell Law Directory

McCARTER & ENGLISH (AV)

Four Gateway Center, 100 Mulberry Street, P.O. Box 652, 07101-0652
Telephone: 201-622-4444
Telecopier: 201-624-7070
Cable Address: "McCarter" Newark
Cherry Hill, New Jersey Office: 1810 Chapel Avenue West.
Telephone: 609-662-8444.
Telecopier: 609-662-6203.
New York, New York Office: Suite 1519, One World Trade Center.
Telephone: 212-466-9018.
Telecopier: 212-432-6568.
Boca Raton, Florida Office: 2255 Glades Road, Suite 319-A.
Telephone: 407-994-6262.
Telecopier: 407-241-0798.
Wilmington, Delaware Office: Mellon Bank Center, 919 Market Street.
Telephone: 302-654-8010.
Telecopier: 302-654-0795.

MEMBERS OF FIRM

Rodney N. Houghton
David A. Ludgin
Myrna L. Wigod

(See Next Column)

OF COUNSEL

Peter C. Aslanides

COUNSEL

Beth Yingling

For Complete List of Firm Personnel, See General Section

For full biographical listings, see the Martindale-Hubbell Law Directory

MEYNER AND LANDIS (AV)

One Gateway Center, Suite 2500, 07102-5311
Telephone: 201-624-2800
Fax: 201-624-0356

MEMBERS OF FIRM

Edwin C. Landis, Jr.
Anthony F. Siliato
Jeffrey L. Reiner
Francis R. Perkins
John N. Malyska
Geralyn A. Boccher
William J. Fiore
Howard O. Thompson
Robert B. Meyner (1908-1990)

ASSOCIATES

Kathryn Schatz Koles
Maureen K Higgins
Linda Townley Snyder
Richard A. Haws
William H. Schmidt, Jr.
Michael J. Palumbo
Scott T. McCleary
Theodore E. Lorenz

For full biographical listings, see the Martindale-Hubbell Law Directory

SILLS CUMMIS ZUCKERMAN RADIN TISCHMAN EPSTEIN & GROSS, A PROFESSIONAL CORPORATION (AV)

One Riverfront Plaza, 07102-5400
Telephone: 201-643-7000
Fax: 201-643-6500
Telex: 820630 Sillsbeck Nwk
Atlantic City, New Jersey Office: 17 Gordon's Alley.
Telephone: 609-344-2800.
New York, N.Y. Office: 250 Park Avenue.
Telephone: 212-643-7000.

Herbert L. Zuckerman
Robert J. Alter
Simon Levin
Allan C. Bell
Alan E. Sherman
Richard J. Sapinski

Nathan E. Arnell
Jay A. Soled

OF COUNSEL

David Beck
Dena L. Wolf

Representative Clients: First Fidelity Bank; NatWest.

For Complete List of Firm Personnel, See General Section

For full biographical listings, see the Martindale-Hubbell Law Directory

NORTH BRUNSWICK, Middlesex Co.

BORRUS, GOLDIN, FOLEY, VIGNUOLO, HYMAN & STAHL, A PROFESSIONAL CORPORATION (AV)

2875 U.S. Highway 1, Route 1 & Finnigans Lane, P.O. Box 1963, 08902
Telephone: 908-422-1000
Fax: 908-422-1016

Jack Borrus
James F. Clarkin III
Martin S. Goldin
Anthony M. Campisano
David M. Foley
Aphrodite C. Koscelansky
Anthony B. Vignuolo
Robert C. Nisenson
Jeffrey M. Hyman
Michael L. Marcus
James E. Stahl
Eileen Mary Foley
Rosalind Westlake

OF COUNSEL

Gerald T. Foley (1903-1976)

Representative Clients: United Jersey Bank/Franklin State; R. J. Reynolds Tobacco Co.; N.J. Aluminum Co.; K. Hovnanian Enterprises, Inc.; Chicago Title Insurance Co.; Transamerica Title Insurance Co.

For full biographical listings, see the Martindale-Hubbell Law Directory

NUTLEY, Essex Co.

FRANCIS J. COSTENBADER (AV)

391 Franklin Avenue, P.O. Box 107, 07110
Telephone: 201-661-5000
Fax: 201-661-0513

Scott Rumana

Representative Clients: Consumer Value Stores (CVS); Melville Corp.; Melville Realty Corp.; Linens 'N Things, Inc.; This End Up Furniture Co., Inc.

For full biographical listings, see the Martindale-Hubbell Law Directory

PARSIPPANY, Morris Co.

HUGH B. MCCLUSKEY (AV)

General Motors Building, Suite 285, 9 Sylvan Way, 07054
Telephone: 201-326-8887; 326-8862
Telefax: 201-326-9479

ASSOCIATE

William G. Harris

For full biographical listings, see the Martindale-Hubbell Law Directory

PRINCETON, Mercer Co.

MCCARTHY AND SCHATZMAN, P.A. (AV)

228 Alexander Street, P.O. Box 2329, 08543-2329
Telephone: 609-924-1199
Fax: 609-683-5251

John F. McCarthy, Jr.
John F. McCarthy, III
Richard Schatzman
Michael A. Spero
G. Christopher Baker
Barbara Strapp Nelson
W. Scott Stoner

James A. Endicott
Angelo J. Onofri

Representative Clients: Trustees of Princeton University; The Linpro Co.; United Jersey Bank; Chemical Bank, New Jersey, N.A.; Carnegie Center Associates; Merrill Lynch Pierce Fenner & Smith, Inc.; Prudential Insurance Co.

For full biographical listings, see the Martindale-Hubbell Law Directory

RAMSEY, Bergen Co.

DONALD C. OHNEGIAN (AV)

88 West Main Street, P.O. Box 360, 07446
Telephone: 201-327-7000
Telefax: 201-327-6651

ASSOCIATE

Diane K. Gaylinn

Representative Clients: Upon Request.

For full biographical listings, see the Martindale-Hubbell Law Directory

WEBER, MUTH & WEBER (AV)

One Cherry Lane, P.O. Box 912, 07446-0912
Telephone: 201-327-5000
Telecopier: 201-327-6848

MEMBER OF FIRM

Walter W. Weber, Jr.

ASSOCIATE

Cynthia A. Kasica

For Complete List of Firm Personnel, See General Section

For full biographical listings, see the Martindale-Hubbell Law Directory

ROSELAND, Essex Co.

GOLDMAN, JACOBSON, KRAMER, FRADKIN & STARR, A PROFESSIONAL CORPORATION (AV)

(Formerly Starr, Weinberg and Fradkin A Professional Corporation)
101 Eisenhower Parkway, P.O. Box 610, 07068
Telephone: 201-228-5888
Telecopier: 201-228-4606

Edwin Fradkin
Scott D. Jacobson
Bruce E. Goldman
Elliot I. Kramer
Andrew P. Fradkin

For full biographical listings, see the Martindale-Hubbell Law Directory

MARK LEVIN (AV)

5 Becker Farm Road, 4th Floor, 07068
Telephone: 201-740-9299

For full biographical listings, see the Martindale-Hubbell Law Directory

ORLOFF, LOWENBACH, STIFELMAN & SIEGEL, A PROFESSIONAL CORPORATION (AV)

101 Eisenhower Parkway, 07068
Telephone: 201-622-6200
Telecopier: 201-622-3073

Joel D. Siegel
Alan F. Kornstein
Frank L. Stifelman
Susan Medinets Holzman

(See Next Column)

James A. Mohoney
Valerie Jacobson Kelleher

For Complete List of Firm Personnel, See General Section

For full biographical listings, see the Martindale-Hubbell Law Directory

*SOMERVILLE,** Somerset Co.

OZZARD WHARTON, A PROFESSIONAL PARTNERSHIP (AV)

75-77 North Bridge Street, P.O. Box 938, 08876
Telephone: 908-526-0700
Telecopier: 908-526-2246

William E. Ozzard
William B. Savo
Edward M. Hogan

Ellen M. Gillespie
Suzette Nanovic Berrios

OF COUNSEL

A. Arthur Davis, 3rd
Louis A. Imfeld
John H. Beekman, Jr.

Representative Clients: American Cyanamid; Science Management Corp.; Mack Development Co.; New Jersey Savings Bank; Summit Bank; Somerset Valley Bank.

For Complete List of Firm Personnel, See General Section

For full biographical listings, see the Martindale-Hubbell Law Directory

SPRINGFIELD, Union Co.

JARDINE & PAGANO, A PROFESSIONAL CORPORATION (AV)

11 Cleveland Place, 07081
Telephone: 201-467-1620
Fax: 201-467-5562

Thomas V. Jardine
Joseph R. Pagano

For full biographical listings, see the Martindale-Hubbell Law Directory

SUMMIT, Union Co.

BOURNE, NOLL & KENYON, A PROFESSIONAL CORPORATION (AV)

382 Springfield Avenue, 07901
Telephone: 908-277-2200
Telecopier: 908-277-6808

Donald Bourne (1903-1987)
Kenneth R. Johanson
Edward T. Kenyon
Martin Rubashkin
Cary R. Hardy
David G. White
Charles R. Berman
Roger Mehner
James R. Ottobre

OF COUNSEL

Robert B. Bourne
Clyde M. Noll (Retired)

Lauren K. Harris
Michael O'B. Boldt
Jaime A. O'Brien
Christopher D. Boyman
Ellyn A. Draikiwicz
Paul Ramirez
Dean T. Bennett
Timothy A. Kalas
Craig M. Lessner
Robert F. Moriarty
Mary E. Scrupski

For full biographical listings, see the Martindale-Hubbell Law Directory

COOPER ROSE & ENGLISH (AV)

480 Morris Avenue, 07901-1527
Telephone: 908-273-1212
Fax: 908-273-8922
Rumson, New Jersey Office: 20 Bingham Avenue. 07760.
Telephone: 908-741-7777.
Fax: 908-758-1879.

MEMBERS OF FIRM

John W. Cooper
Arthur H. Garvin, III
Frederick W. Rose
Peter M. Burke
Jerry Fitzgerald English
Gary F. Danis
Joseph E. Imbriaco
John J. DeLaney, Jr.
Roger S. Clapp
David G. Hardin

OF COUNSEL

Harrison F. Durand
Russell T. Kerby, Jr.
Ronald J. Tell

ASSOCIATES

Fredi L. Pearlmutter
J. Andrew Kinsey
Kristi Bragg
Jonathan S. Chester
Stephen R. Geller
Daniel Jon Kleinman
Peter W. Ulicny
Holly English
Thomas J. Sateary
Margaret R. Kalas
Gianfranco A. Pietrafesa
Mary T. Zdanowicz
Donna M. Russo
Robert A. Meyers
Richard F. Iglar

(See Next Column)

COOPER ROSE & ENGLISH—*Continued*

Counsel for: Ciba-Geigy Corp.; Witco Corp.; New Jersey American Water Co.; Mikropul Corp.; AT&T Bell Laboratories; Aircast.

For full biographical listings, see the Martindale-Hubbell Law Directory

*TRENTON,** Mercer Co.

SCHRAGGER, LAVINE & NAGY, A PROFESSIONAL CORPORATION (AV)

The Atrium at Lawrence, 133 Franklin Corner Road (Lawrenceville), 08648
Telephone: 609-896-9777
Fax: 609-895-1373

Alan S. Lavine
Bruce M. Schragger
Raymond L. Nagy
James A. Schragger
Jonathan S. Robinson

OF COUNSEL

Henry C. Schragger
A. Jerome Moore

Representative Clients: Sears, Roebuck & Co.; New Jersey Manufacturers Insurance Co.; Mercer County Community College; Mercer Mutual Insurance Co..

For full biographical listings, see the Martindale-Hubbell Law Directory

WESTFIELD, Union Co.

BUTTERMORE, MULLEN, JEREMIAH AND PHILLIPS (AV)

445 East Broad Street, P.O. Box 2189, 07091
Telephone: 908-232-0292
Telecopier: 908-232-3277

MEMBERS OF FIRM

Grant M. Buttermore
Susan N. Mullen
William S. Jeremiah, II
John C. Phillips
Georgette E. David

Reference: First Fidelity Bank, N.A., New Jersey.

For Complete List of Firm Personnel, See General Section

For full biographical listings, see the Martindale-Hubbell Law Directory

WEST ORANGE, Essex Co.

GOLDBERG, MUFSON & SPAR, A PROFESSIONAL CORPORATION (AV)

200 Executive Drive, 07052
Telephone: 201-736-0100
Telecopier: 201-736-0961

Leonard M. Goldberg
Ann Mufson
Michael R. Spar
Kenneth J. Isaacson
Eric W. Olson

OF COUNSEL

Jerome E. Sharfman

For full biographical listings, see the Martindale-Hubbell Law Directory

MELVIN J. WALLERSTEIN, P.A. (AV)

200 Executive Drive Suite 100, 07052
Telephone: 201-731-2500
Fax: 201-731-0163

Melvin J. Wallerstein

LEGAL SUPPORT PERSONNEL
LEGAL ADMINISTRATOR

Charlotte M. Burns

For full biographical listings, see the Martindale-Hubbell Law Directory

WOODBRIDGE, Middlesex Co.

WILENTZ, GOLDMAN & SPITZER, A PROFESSIONAL CORPORATION (AV)

90 Woodbridge Center Drive Suite 900, Box 10, 07095
Telephone: 908-636-8000
Telecopier: 908-855-6117
Eatontown, New Jersey Office: Meridian Center I, Two Industrial Way West, 07724.
Telephone: 908-493-1000.
Telecopier: 908-493-8387.
New York, New York Office: Wall Street Plaza, 88 Pine Street, 9th Floor, 10005.
Telephone: 212-267-3091.
Telecopier: 212-267-3828.

Richard F. Lert
Stuart T. Cox, Jr.

(See Next Column)

Elizabeth Connolly Dell

Representative Clients: Amerada Hess Corp.; Chevron, U.S.A. Inc.; Cumberland Farms, Inc.; Middlesex County Utilities Co.; New Jersey Automobile Dealers Assn.; Co-Steel Raritan; The Rouse Co.

For Complete List of Firm Personnel, See General Section

For full biographical listings, see the Martindale-Hubbell Law Directory

NEW MEXICO

*ALBUQUERQUE,** Bernalillo Co.

CAMPBELL, PICA, OLSON & SEEGMILLER (AV)

6565 Americas Parkway, N.E., Suite 800, P.O. Box 35459, 87176
Telephone: 505-883-9110
Fax: 505-884-3882

MEMBERS OF FIRM

Lewis O. Campbell
Nicholas R. Pica
David C. Olson
Douglas Seegmiller

ASSOCIATES

Brad Vaughn
Roger A. Stansbury
Philip Craig Snyder
Arthur J. G. Lacerte, Jr.
Jeffrey C. Gilmore

For full biographical listings, see the Martindale-Hubbell Law Directory

MILLER, STRATVERT, TORGERSON & SCHLENKER, P.A. (AV)

500 Marquette Avenue, N.W., Suite 1100, P.O. Box 25687, 87102
Telephone: 505-842-1950
Facsimile: 505-243-4408
Farmington, New Mexico Office: Suite 300, 300 West Arrington. P.O. Box 869.
Telephone: 505-326-4521.
Facsimile: 505-325-5474.
Las Cruces, New Mexico Office: Suite 300, 277 East Amador. P.O. Drawer 1231.
Telephone: 505-523-2481.
Facsimile: 505-526-2215.
Santa Fe, New Mexico Office: 125 Lincoln Avenue, Suite 221. P.O. Box 1986.
Telephone: 505-989-9614.
Facsimile: 505-989-9857.

Ranne B. Miller
Alan C. Torgerson
Kendall O. Schlenker
Alice Tomlinson Lorenz
Gregory W. Chase
Alan Konrad
Margo J. McCormick
Lyman G. Sandy
Stephen M. Williams
Stephan M. Vidmar
Robert C. Gutierrez
Seth V. Bingham (Resident at Farmington Office)
Michael H. Hoses
James B. Collins (Resident at Farmington Office)
Timothy Ray Briggs
Walter R. Parr (Resident at Santa Fe Office)
Rudolph A. Lucero
Daniel E. Ramczyk
Dean G. Constantine
Deborah A. Solove
Gary L. Gordon
Lawrence R. White (Resident at Las Cruces Office)
Sharon P. Gross
Virginia Anderman
Marte D. Lightstone
Bradford K. Goodwin
John R. Funk (Resident at Las Cruces Office)
J. Scott Hall (Resident at Santa Fe Office)
Thomas R. Mack
Michael J. Happe (Resident at Farmington Office)
Denise Barela Shepherd
Nancy Augustus
Jill Burtram
Terri L. Sauer
Joel T. Newton (Resident at Las Cruces Office)
Judith K. Nakamura
Thomas M. Domme
David H. Thomas, III
C. Brian Charlton

COUNSEL

William K. Stratvert
Paul W. Robinson

Clair Growney; Richard M. Krannawitter Trust; Ticor Title Insurance Co.

For Complete List of Firm Personnel, See General Section

For full biographical listings, see the Martindale-Hubbell Law Directory

RODEY, DICKASON, SLOAN, AKIN & ROBB, P.A. (AV)

Albuquerque Plaza, Suite 2200, 201 Third Street, N.W., P.O. Box 1888, 87103-1888
Telephone: 505-765-5900
Fax: 505-768-7395
Santa Fe, New Mexico Office: Suite 101 Marcy Plaza, 123 East Marcy Street, P.O. Box 1357, 87504-1357.
Telephone: 505-984-0100.
Fax: 505-989-9542.

(See Next Column)

RODEY, DICKASON, SLOAN, AKIN & ROBB P.A., *Albuquerque—Continued*

Robert M. St. John
Patricia M. Taylor

COUNSEL

Jeffrey W. Loubet

For Complete List of Firm Personnel, See General Section

For full biographical listings, see the Martindale-Hubbell Law Directory

*CLOVIS,** Curry Co.

TATUM & McDOWELL (AV)

Suite D, Sagebrush Professional Office Complex, 921 East 21st Street, P.O. Drawer 1270, 88101
Telephone: 505-762-7756
Fax: 505-769-1606

MEMBER OF FIRM

Edwin B. Tatum

Representative Clients: High Plains Federal Credit Union; Sunwest Bank of Clovis, N.A.; Citizens Bank of Clovis; American Cattle Feeders, Inc.; Retirement Ranch, Inc.; Curry County Abstract Co.
References: Sunwest Bank of Clovis, N.A.; Citizens Bank of Clovis.

For Complete List of Firm Personnel, See General Section

For full biographical listings, see the Martindale-Hubbell Law Directory

*LAS CRUCES,** Dona Ana Co.

WEINBRENNER, RICHARDS, PAULOWSKY & RAMIREZ, P.A. (AV)

8th Floor, First National Tower, P.O. Drawer O, 88004-1719
Telephone: 505-524-8624
Fax: 505-524-4252

Ralph Wm. Richards
Michael T. Murphy
Fred Schiller

General Counsel for: Stahmann Farms, Inc.; First National Bank of Dona Ana County.
Representative Clients: American General Cos.; Hartford Group; CNA Insurance; Fireman's Fund; United States Fidelity & Guaranty Co.; Travelers Insurance Co.; General Accident Group.

For Complete List of Firm Personnel, See General Section

For full biographical listings, see the Martindale-Hubbell Law Directory

*SANTA FE,** Santa Fe Co.

CATRON, CATRON & SAWTELL, A PROFESSIONAL ASSOCIATION (AV)

2006 Botulph Road, P.O. Box 788, 87504-0788
Telephone: 505-982-1947
Telecopier: 505-986-1013

Thomas B. Catron III
John S. Catron
William A. Sawtell, Jr.
Fletcher R. Catron
W. Anthony Sawtell
Forrest S. Smith

LEGAL SUPPORT PERSONNEL

Peggy L. Feldt (Certified Public Accountant)

Attorneys for: Santa Fe Board of Education; American Express Co.; The Santa Fe Opera; Sunwest Bank of Santa Fe; VNS Health Services, Inc.

For Complete List of Firm Personnel, See General Section

For full biographical listings, see the Martindale-Hubbell Law Directory

ROSE, KOHL & DAVENPORT, LTD. (AV)

1516 Paseo De Peralta, 87501
Telephone: 505-982-0080
Fax: 505-982-0081

Filmore E. Rose
Bruce R. Kohl
Beth R. Davenport
Robert J. Dodds, III
Marie A. Cioth (Not admitted in NM)

Reference: The First National Bank of Santa Fe.

For full biographical listings, see the Martindale-Hubbell Law Directory

SCHEUER, YOST & PATTERSON, A PROFESSIONAL CORPORATION (AV)

125 Lincoln Avenue, Suite 223, P.O. Drawer 9570, 87504
Telephone: 505-982-9911
Fax: 505-982-1621

Ralph H. Scheuer
Mel E. Yost
John N. Patterson
Holly A. Hart
Roger L. Prucino
Elizabeth A. Jaffe
Tracy Erin Conner
Ruth M. Fuess

(See Next Column)

OF COUNSEL

Melvin T. Yost

Representative Clients: Cyprus-AMAX, Inc.; Century Bank, FSB; School of American Research; GEIGO; Los Alamos National Bank; Rocky Mountain Bankcard System; St. John's College; Sun Loan Companies; Territorial Abstract & Title Co.; Tosco Corporation.

For full biographical listings, see the Martindale-Hubbell Law Directory

WHITE, KOCH, KELLY & McCARTHY, A PROFESSIONAL ASSOCIATION (AV)

433 Paseo De Peralta, P.O. Box 787, 87504-0787
Telephone: 505-982-4374
ABA/NET: 1154
Fax: 505-982-0350; 984-8631

William Booker Kelly
John F. McCarthy, Jr.
Benjamin J. Phillips
David F. Cunningham
Albert V. Gonzales
Janet Clow
Kevin V. Reilly
Charles W. N. Thompson, Jr.
M. Karen Kilgore
Sandra J. Brinck

SPECIAL COUNSEL

Paul L. Bloom

Aaron J. Wolf
Carolyn R. Glick

Representative Clients: Southern Pacific Transportation Co.; Nationwide Insurance Co.; Risk Management Division of New Mexico General Services Department; Alliance of American Insurers; Santa Fe Community College; First American Title Insurance Co.; Century Bank; Public Service Company of New Mexico; AT&SF Railway Co.; Gallager Bassett.

For full biographical listings, see the Martindale-Hubbell Law Directory

NEW YORK

*ALBANY,** Albany Co.

KOHN, BOOKSTEIN & KARP, P.C. (AV)

Ninety State Street Suite 929, 12207-1888
Telephone: 518-449-8810
Fax: 518-449-1029

Edward L. Bookstein
Eugene M. Karp
Richard A. Kohn

James Blendell
Amy S. O'Connor

OF COUNSEL

Irving I. Waxman
Karen Martino Valle

Representative Clients: Adirondack Transit Lines, Inc.; Amfast Corp.; Simmons Fastener Corp.; Tagsons Papers, Inc.; Thermo Products, Inc.

For Complete List of Firm Personnel, See General Section

For full biographical listings, see the Martindale-Hubbell Law Directory

NANCY M. SILLS (AV)

Suite 200, Wall Street Center, 450 New Karner Road, 12205-3822
Telephone: 518-869-6227
Fax: 518-869-0572
(Also Of Counsel to Lemery & Reid, A Professional Corporation)

For full biographical listings, see the Martindale-Hubbell Law Directory

*BROOKLYN,** Kings Co.

CULLEN AND DYKMAN (AV)

177 Montague Street, 11201
Telephone: 718-855-9000
Telecopier: 718-855-4282
Garden City, New York Office: Garden City Center, 100 Quentin Roosevelt Boulevard.
Telephone: 516-357-3700.
Telecopier: 516-357-3792.
Washington, D.C. Office: 1225 Nineteenth Street, N.W., Suite 320.
Telephone: 202-223-8890.
Telecopier: 202-457-1405.
Newark, New Jersey Office: One Riverfront Plaza, Suite 1410.
Telephone: 201-622-1545.
Telecopier: 201-622-4563.

MEMBER OF FIRM

Paul A. Golinski

For Complete List of Firm Personnel, See General Section

For full biographical listings, see the Martindale-Hubbell Law Directory

*BUFFALO,** Erie Co.

ALBRECHT, MAGUIRE, HEFFERN & GREGG, P.C. (AV)

2100 Main Place Tower, 14202
Telephone: 716-853-1521
Fax: 716-852-2609

James M. Beardsley

For Complete List of Firm Personnel, See General Section

For full biographical listings, see the Martindale-Hubbell Law Directory

HURWITZ & FINE, P.C. (AV)

1300 Liberty Building, 14202-3613
Telephone: 716-849-8900
Telecopier: 716-855-0874

Robert P. Fine
Lawrence C. Franco

David P. Lazenski

For Complete List of Firm Personnel, See General Section

For full biographical listings, see the Martindale-Hubbell Law Directory

EAST MEADOW, Nassau Co.

CERTILMAN BALIN ADLER & HYMAN, LLP (AV)

90 Merrick Avenue, 11554
Telephone: 516-296-7000
Telecopier: 516-296-7111

MEMBERS OF FIRM

Ira J. Adler
Dale Allinson
Herbert M. Balin
Bruce J. Bergman
Michael D. Brofman
Morton L. Certilman
Murray Greenberg
David Z. Herman
Richard Herzbach
M. Allan Hyman
Bernard Hyman
Donna-Marie Korth
Steven J. Kuperschmid
Thomas J. McNamara
Fred S. Skolnik
Louis Soloway
Harold Somer
Howard M. Stein
Brian K. Ziegler

OF COUNSEL

Daniel S. Cohan
Norman J. Levy
Marilyn Price

ASSOCIATES

Howard B. Busch
Scott M. Gerber
Jodi S. Hoffman
Glenn Kleinbaum
Michael C. Manniello
Jaspreet S. Mayall
Stacey R. Miller
Lawrence S. Novak
Kim J. Radbell

For full biographical listings, see the Martindale-Hubbell Law Directory

GARDEN CITY, Nassau Co.

ALBANESE, ALBANESE & FIORE LLP (AV)

1050 Franklin Avenue, 5th Floor, 11530
Telephone: 516-248-7000

MEMBER OF FIRM

Joseph R. Albanese

ASSOCIATES

Richard H. Ferriggi
Laura Paglia Sikorski
Vincent A. Albanese

COUNSEL

Theodore D. Hoffmann

LEGAL SUPPORT PERSONNEL

Linda Cristando

References: Apple Bank for Savings; Bank of New York; North Fork Bank; First American Title Insurance Company; American Title Insurance Company; Greater Jamaica Development Corp.; United Nations Plaza Tower Associates, Ltd.; Fidelity National Title Insurance Company of New York.

For Complete List of Firm Personnel, See General Section

For full biographical listings, see the Martindale-Hubbell Law Directory

SAWYER, DAVIS & HALPERN (AV)

600 Old Country Road, 11530
Telephone: 516-222-4567
Telecopier: 516-222-4585

MEMBER OF FIRM

Jay Davis

(See Next Column)

ASSOCIATE

Ralph W. Lee

For Complete List of Firm Personnel, See General Section

For full biographical listings, see the Martindale-Hubbell Law Directory

HUNTINGTON, Suffolk Co.

SMYTH & LACK (AV)

202 East Main Street, 11743
Telephone: 516-271-7500
Telecopier: 516-271-7504

MEMBERS OF FIRM

Vincent A. Smyth
James J. Lack

ASSOCIATES

Thomas P. Solferino
Dana M. Barberis
Stephen I. Witdorchic

Reference: Chemical Bank.

For full biographical listings, see the Martindale-Hubbell Law Directory

KATONAH, Westchester Co.

COVEY, ROBERTS, BUCHANAN & LONERGAN (AV)

Village Commons East, 200 Katonah Avenue, 10536
Telephone: 914-232-5161
Telecopier: 914-232-0574
North Palm Beach, Florida Office: Crystal Tree Plaza, 1201 U.S. No. 1, Suite 240.
Telephone: 407-622-8151.
Telecopier: 407-627-0225.

Edwin B. Covey (1908-1975)
George Hunter Roberts
Jeffrey D. Buchanan (1943-1994)
William R. Lonergan, Jr.

OF COUNSEL

Arthur R. Covey

Representative Clients: New York State Electric & Gas Co.; Katonah-Lewisboro Schools; Goldens Bridge Fire District; Katonah Fire District.
Reference: Chase Bank/NBW.

For full biographical listings, see the Martindale-Hubbell Law Directory

MASPETH, Queens Co.

EDWARD M. MCGOWAN (AV)

68-15 Borden Avenue, 11378
Telephone: 718-651-7360
Telecopier: 718-446-0796

For full biographical listings, see the Martindale-Hubbell Law Directory

MELVILLE, Suffolk Co.

SPANTON, PARSOFF & SIEGEL, P.C. (AV)

425 Broad Hollow Road, Route 110, 11747
Telephone: 516-777-3200
Fax: 516-777-3204
New York, N.Y. Office: 790 Madison Avenue, 10021.
Telephone: 212-717-5948.

Donald M. Spanton
Neil M. Parsoff
Lawrence A. Siegel

Pamela G. Weiss

OF COUNSEL

Murray D. Schwartz

For full biographical listings, see the Martindale-Hubbell Law Directory

*MINEOLA,** Nassau Co.

HASKEL, HAND & LANCASTER (AV)

170 Old Country Road, 11501-4366
Telephone: 516-294-0500
Fax: 516-294-5006

MEMBERS OF FIRM

Jules J. Haskel
Stephen B. Hand
William W. Lancaster, III

For full biographical listings, see the Martindale-Hubbell Law Directory

*NEW CITY,** Rockland Co.

FREEMAN & LOFTUS (AV)

4 Laurel Road, P.O. Box 629, 10956-0629
Telephone: 914-634-0888
Fax: 914-634-9312

MEMBERS OF FIRM

James J. Freeman, Jr.
Patrick J. Loftus

(See Next Column)

FREEMAN & LOFTUS, *New City—Continued*

OF COUNSEL

James H. Bowers
Ira M. Emanuel
Albert J. Kaiser

For full biographical listings, see the Martindale-Hubbell Law Directory

*NEW YORK,** New York Co.

MITCHELL B. BOOTH (AV)

City Spire, 156 West 56th Street, 10019
Telephone: 212-977-9500
Telecopier: 212-459-8947
Cable Address: "Boothlaws"

For full biographical listings, see the Martindale-Hubbell Law Directory

CAPLIN & DRYSDALE, CHARTERED (AV)

399 Park Avenue, 10022
Telephone: 212-319-7125
Fax: 212-644-6755
Washington, D.C. Office: One Thomas Circle, N.W.
Telephone: 202-862-5000.
Fax: 202-429-3301.

Elihu Inselbuch
C. Sanders McNew
Christian R. Pastore

For full biographical listings, see the Martindale-Hubbell Law Directory

LOEB AND LOEB (AV)

A Partnership including Professional Corporations
345 Park Avenue, 10154-0037
Telephone: 212-407-4000
Facsimile: 212-407-4990
Los Angeles, California Office: Suite 1800, 1000 Wilshire Boulevard, 90017-2475.
Telephone: 213-688-3400.
Cable Address: "Loband LSA".
Telecopier: 213-688-3460; 688-3461; 688-3462.
Century City (Los Angeles), California Office: Suite 2200, 10100 Santa Monica Boulevard, Los Angeles, 90067-4164.
Telephone: 310-282-2000.
Telecopier: 310-282-2191; 282-2192.
Nashville, Tennessee Office: 45 Music Square West, 37203-3205.
Telephone: 615-749-8300.
Facsimile: 615-749-8308.
Rome, Italy Office: Piazza Digione 1, 00197.
Telephone: 011-396-808-8456.
Telecopier: 011-396-674-8223.

MEMBERS OF FIRM

Abraham S. Guterman
Jerome L. Levine
Fredric M. Sanders
Bruce J. Wexler

OF COUNSEL

Arthur A. Segall

For Complete List of Firm Personnel, See General Section

For full biographical listings, see the Martindale-Hubbell Law Directory

OTTERBOURG, STEINDLER, HOUSTON & ROSEN, P.C. (AV)

230 Park Avenue, 10169
Telephone: 212-661-9100
Cable Address: "Otlerton";
Telecopier: 212-682-6104
Telex: 960916

Eugene V. Kokot

COUNSEL

Lawrence B. Milling

For Complete List of Firm Personnel, See General Section

For full biographical listings, see the Martindale-Hubbell Law Directory

PARKER CHAPIN FLATTAU & KLIMPL, L.L.P. (AV)

1211 Avenue of the Americas, 10036
Telephone: 212-704-6000
Telecopier: 212-704-6288
Cable Address: "Lawpark"
Telex: 640347
Great Neck, New York Office: 175 Great Neck Road.
Telephone: 516-482-4422.
Telecopier: 516-482-4469.

MEMBER OF FIRM

Carol F. Burger

SENIOR COUNSEL

Seymour Levine

(See Next Column)

ASSOCIATE

Susan E. Greenwald

For Complete List of Firm Personnel, See General Section

For full biographical listings, see the Martindale-Hubbell Law Directory

PRERAU & TEITELL

(See White Plains)

SHACK & SIEGEL, P.C. (AV)

530 Fifth Avenue, 10036
Telephone: 212-782-0700
Fax: 212-730-1964

Charles F. Crames
Pamela E. Flaherty
Paul S. Goodman
Ronald S. Katz
Donald D. Shack
Jeffrey N. Siegel
Jeffrey B. Stone

Paul A. Lucido
Steven M. Lutt
Ruby S. Teich
Keith D. Wellner
Adam F. Wergeles (Not admitted in NY)

For full biographical listings, see the Martindale-Hubbell Law Directory

*POUGHKEEPSIE,** Dutchess Co.

TEAHAN & CONSTANTINO (AV)

325 South Road, 12601
Telephone: 914-452-1834
Fax: 914-452-1421
New York, New York Office: 380 Lexington Avenue.
Telephone: 212-986-3925.
Fax: 212-599-2332.
Albany, New York Office: 99 Pine Street, 12207.
Telephone: 518-426-9203.
Fax: 518-426-4655.

MEMBERS OF FIRM

Vincent L. Teahan
James P. Constantino

OF COUNSEL

Gina A. Gulotty

For full biographical listings, see the Martindale-Hubbell Law Directory

*ROCHESTER,** Monroe Co.

HARRIS & CHESWORTH (AV)

1820 East Avenue, 14607
Telephone: 716-242-2400
Fax: 716-242-2424

MEMBERS OF FIRM

Wayne M. Harris
Donald O. Chesworth
Edward M. O'Brien

ASSOCIATES

David J. Gutmann
Michael A. Damia
David Mayer
Timothy P. Blodgett

SPECIAL COUNSEL

Melvin Bressler

For full biographical listings, see the Martindale-Hubbell Law Directory

ROME, Oneida Co.

GRIFFITH LAW OFFICES (AV)

225 North Washington Street, 13440
Telephone: 315-336-6500
Fax: 315-336-6628

Emlyn I. Griffith
James R. Griffith

Representative Clients: Camroden Associates, Inc.; C & H Plastics, Inc.; D & H Asphalt Co., Inc.; H-P Farmers Cooperative; Knowledge Systems Concepts, Inc.; Pohl Feedway, Inc.; Statewide Funding Corp; Stonehedge Nursing Home.
Approved Attorneys for: The Title Guarantee Co.

For full biographical listings, see the Martindale-Hubbell Law Directory

SMITHTOWN, Suffolk Co.

GRESHIN, ZIEGLER & PRUZANSKY (AV)

199 East Main Street, P.O. Box 829, 11787
Telephone: 516-265-2550
Telecopier: 516-265-2832

Benjamin Greshin
Joel J. Ziegler
Joshua M. Pruzansky

ASSOCIATE

Joanne Skiadas

For full biographical listings, see the Martindale-Hubbell Law Directory

*STATEN ISLAND,** Richmond Co.

SIMONSON & COHEN, P.C. (AV)

4060 Amboy Road, 10308
Telephone: 718-948-2100
Telecopier: 718-356-2379

Sidney O. Simonson (1911-1986) Robert M. Cohen
Daniel Cohen James R. Cohen

Michael Adler Lawrence J. Lorczak

For full biographical listings, see the Martindale-Hubbell Law Directory

*UTICA,** Oneida Co.

GROBEN, GILROY, OSTER & SAUNDERS (AV)

Formerly Groben, Liddy, Cardamone & Gilroy
Suite 1013-1027, 185 Genesee Street, 13503
Telephone: 315-724-4166
FAX: 315-797-1944

MEMBERS OF FIRM

Gilbert R. Hughes (1889-1977) Robert Groben
Joseph J. Cardamone, Jr. (1918-1979) James H. Gilroy, Jr.
Stanley J. Kowal, Jr.
John M. Liddy (1910-1987) James C. Oster
Joseph E. F. Saunders

ASSOCIATES

Claudia Tenney Cleary Nathan M. Hayes

Counsel for: Marine Midland Bank, N.A.; Norstar Bank of Upstate N.Y.; The Homestead Savings (FA); United Parcel Service, Inc.; Reliance Insurance Cos.; Prudential Insurance Co.

For full biographical listings, see the Martindale-Hubbell Law Directory

*WHITE PLAINS,** Westchester Co.

DANZIGER & MARKHOFF (AV)

A Partnership including a Professional Corporation
Centroplex-123 Main Street, 10601
Telephone: 914-948-1556
Telecopier: 914-948-1706

Joel Danziger Ira Langer (P.C.)
Harris Markhoff Scott M. Sherman
Joshua S. Levine

Anita L. Pomerance Susan I. Porter
Robert B. Danziger Susan B. Slater-Jansen
Michael Markhoff Katherine R. Steiner

LEGAL SUPPORT PERSONNEL

ENROLLED ACTUARIES

William Martin Miller Aileen T. Palazzo

COUNSEL

Irwin N. Rubin

References: Chase Manhattan Bank, White Plains, N.Y. (Trust Dept.); Bank of New York County Trust Region; Lazard Freres & Co.

For full biographical listings, see the Martindale-Hubbell Law Directory

KENT, HAZZARD, JAEGER, GREER, WILSON & FAY (AV)

50 Main Street, 10606
Telephone: 914-948-4700
Telecopier: 914-948-4721

MEMBERS OF FIRM

Ralph S. Kent (1878-1949) Lawrence F. Fay
Lawrence S. Hazzard (1900-1958) Robert D. Hazzard
Gregory C. Freeman
William J. Greer (1920-1994) Robert G. O'Donnell
Mizell Wilson, Jr. Katharine Wilson Conroy
John R. Dinin

OF COUNSEL

Malcolm Wilson Otto C. Jaeger
Edward J. Freeman George Beisheim, Jr.
Peter F. Blasi

Representative Clients: The Bank of New York.
References: Bank of New York; Peoples Westchester Savings Bank.

For full biographical listings, see the Martindale-Hubbell Law Directory

KURZMAN & EISENBERG (AV)

One North Broadway, 10601
Telephone: 914-285-9800
Fax: 914-285-9855
New York, N.Y. Office: 99 Park Avenue.
Telephone: 212-671-1322.

(See Next Column)

Hollywood, Florida Office: 2021 Tyler Street.
Telephone: 305-921-5500.

MEMBERS OF FIRM

Robert G. Kurzman Joel S. Lever
Sam Eisenberg Jack S. Older
Lee Harrison Corbin Alan John Rein
Robert L. Ecker Fred D. Weinstein

OF COUNSEL

Richard A. Danzig R. Mark Goodman
Stephen R. Levy

For full biographical listings, see the Martindale-Hubbell Law Directory

O'CONNOR, MCGUINNESS, CONTE, DOYLE, OLESON & COLLINS (AV)

One Barker Avenue, 10601
Telephone: 914-948-4500
Telecopier: 914-948-0645

MEMBERS OF FIRM

Dennis L. O'Connor (1913-1989) J. Peter Collins
Rocco Conte Richard C. Oleson
Dennis T. Doyle Dennis L. O'Connor, Jr.
William S. Oleson William R. Watson
Kevin M. Loftus

ASSOCIATES

Craig P. Curcio Andrew F. Pisanelli
Louis K. Szarka Montgomery Lee Effinger
Mary Pat Burke Dara A. Ruderman
Patricia Lacy Philomena Basuk
Pamela R. Millian Debora J. Dillon
Daniel M. Miller

OF COUNSEL

Eugene J. McGuinness Russell J. Hauck

Attorneys for: Insurance Company of North America; Allstate Insurance Co.; Continental Insurance Group; Government Employers Insurance Co.; Merchants Mutual Insurance Co.; Prudential Insurance Co.; Consolidated Rail Corp.; Medical Liability Mutual Insurance Co.; Colonial Penn Insurance Co.

For full biographical listings, see the Martindale-Hubbell Law Directory

PRERAU & TEITELL (AV)

50 Main Street, 10606
Telephone: 914-682-9300
Cable Address: "Humanitas"
Telecopier: 914-682-1521

MEMBERS OF FIRM

Sydney Prerau (1900-1968) Conrad Teitell
Philip T. Temple

ASSOCIATES

Gail D. Resnikoff Andrea H. Semenuk

For full biographical listings, see the Martindale-Hubbell Law Directory

SMITH, RANSCHT, CONNORS, MUTINO, NORDELL & SIRIGNANO, P.C. (AV)

235 Main Street, 10601
Telephone: 914-946-8800
Telecopier: 914-946-8861
Cable Address: "Smiran" White Plains, New York
Greenwich, Connecticut Office: P.O. Box 4847, 06830-0605.
Telephone: 203-622-6660.

Peter T. Manos (1923-1991) Peter J. Mutino
James P. Connors, Jr. Michael Nordell
William F. Ranscht, Jr. George A. Sirignano, Jr.

OF COUNSEL

Gary E. Bashian James M. Pollock
Anthony J. Enea

Counsel for: The Corham Artificial Flower Co.; Universal Builders Supply, Inc.; Kalman Floor Co., Inc.; The Walter Karl Companies.

For full biographical listings, see the Martindale-Hubbell Law Directory

WOODBURY, Nassau Co.

STEBEL & PASELTINER, P.C. (AV)

7600 Jericho Turnpike, 11797
Telephone: 516-496-8117
Telecopier: 516-496-8112

Bernard Stebel David E. Paseltiner

Mindy K. Smolevitz Steven M. Gelfman

COUNSEL

Edwin H. Baker Mitchell G. Mandell
Alan M. Pollack Lori Samet Schwarz
Michael E. Greene Scott A. Sommer

(See Next Column)

STEBEL & PASELTINER P.C., *Woodbury—Continued*

References: Chemical Bank; Fleet Bank.

For full biographical listings, see the Martindale-Hubbell Law Directory

NORTH CAROLINA

*ASHEBORO,** Randolph Co.

JOHN N. OGBURN, JR. (AV)

Suite 201, Triad Bank Building, 261 North Fayetteville Street, Drawer 4067, 27204-4067
Telephone: 910-629-3345
Facsimile: 910-629-1882

Representative Clients: Bossong Mill, Inc.; Asheboro Hosiery Mill; Shaw Furniture Galleries; City of Randleman; Vestal Motors; Mid-State Motors; Weeks Construction Co.; The North Carolina One-Call Center; Triad Bank; Hospice of Randolph, Inc.

For full biographical listings, see the Martindale-Hubbell Law Directory

*CHARLOTTE,** Mecklenburg Co.

LINDSEY AND SCHRIMSHER, P.A. (AV)

2316 Randolph Road, 28207
Telephone: 704-333-2141
Fax: 704-376-2562

Robert L. Lindsey, Jr.
Frank L. Schrimsher
B. Scott Schrimsher

Representative Clients: American General Finance; C.I.T. Group/Sales Financing, Inc.; Crestar Bank; Crestar Mortgage; Wachovia Bank of North Carolina, N.A.; Central Carolina Bank & Trust Co.; NationsBanc Financial Services; Lawyers Title Insurance Corp.; First Union Home Equity Corp.; Sunshine Mortgage Corp.; ContiMortgage Corp.

For full biographical listings, see the Martindale-Hubbell Law Directory

*DURHAM,** Durham Co.

WILLIAM V. MCPHERSON, JR. (AV)

Suite 806 University Tower 3100 Tower Boulevard, 27707
Telephone: 919-493-0584
Facsimile: 919-493-0856

For full biographical listings, see the Martindale-Hubbell Law Directory

*GREENSBORO,** Guilford Co.

FORMAN, MARTH, BLACK & ANGLE, P.A. (AV)

235 North Greene Street, P.O. Drawer 2020, 27402-2020
Telephone: 910-378-0172; 272-5591
FAX: 910-378-0015

Richard C. Forman
T. Keith Black
Paul E. Marth
Robert B. Angle, Jr.
Jeffrey S. Iddings

Reference: Wachovia Bank & Trust Co., N.A.; Triad Bank.

For full biographical listings, see the Martindale-Hubbell Law Directory

FRASSINETI AND GLOVER (AV)

Suite 403, 201 West Market Street, P.O. Drawer 1799, 27402
Telephone: 910-273-9794
FAX: 910-273-1570

Jordan J. Frassineti (Retired)
Durant M. Glover

A list of Representative Clients and Approved Attorneys For will be Furnished upon Request.

For full biographical listings, see the Martindale-Hubbell Law Directory

MOREHEAD CITY, Carteret Co.

BENNETT, MCCONKEY, THOMPSON & MARQUARDT, P.A. (AV)

1007 Shepard Street, P.O. Drawer 189, 28557
Telephone: 919-726-4114
FAX: 919-726-7975

Thomas S. Bennett
James W. Thompson, III
Samuel A. McConkey, Jr.
Dennis M. Marquardt

Approved Attorneys For: Lawyers Title Insurance Corp.
Reference: First Citizens Bank & Trust Co.

For full biographical listings, see the Martindale-Hubbell Law Directory

*WINSTON-SALEM,** Forsyth Co.

CRAIGE, BRAWLEY, LIIPFERT, WALKER & SEARCY (AV)

500 West Fourth Street, Suite 200, P.O. Box 1666, 27102-1666
Telephone: 910-725-0583
FAX: 910-725-4677
Kernersville, North Carolina Office: Suite E, 516 East Mountain Street.
Telephone: 919-993-6912.
Telecopy: 919-993-6908.

MEMBERS OF FIRM

Cowles Liipfert
Diane Brock Oser
William W. Walker
George Wilson Martin, Jr.
Philip E. Searcy
Warren E. Kasper

ASSOCIATE

B. Bailey Liipfert, III

Approved Attorneys for: Lawyers Title Insurance Corp.; Chicago Title Insurance Co.; Commonwealth Land Title Insurance Co.; First American Title Insurance Co.; Jefferson-Pilot Title Insurance Co.

For Complete List of Firm Personnel, See General Section

For full biographical listings, see the Martindale-Hubbell Law Directory

WOMBLE CARLYLE SANDRIDGE & RICE (AV)

A Professional Limited Liability Company
1600 Southern National Financial Center, P.O. Drawer 84, 27102
Telephone: 910-721-3600
Telecopy: 910-721-3660
Telex: 806498
Charlotte, North Carolina Office: 3300 One First Union Center, 301 South College Street.
Telephone: 704-331-4900.
Telecopy: 704-331-4955.
Telex: 853609.
Raleigh, North Carolina Office: 2100 First Union Capitol Center, 150 Fayetteville Street Mall, P.O. Box 831.
Telephone: 919-755-2100.
Telecopy: 919-755-2150.
Telex: 806498.
Atlanta, Georgia Office: One Ninety One Peachtree Tower, 191 Peachtree Street, N.E., Suite 3250.
Telephone: 404-614-2580.
Fax: 404-614-2595.

MEMBERS OF FIRM

Elizabeth L. Quick
George A. Ragland

ASSOCIATE

Jean Taylor Adams

Representative Clients: Brad Ragan, Inc.; Brenner Companies; Food Lion, Inc.; Hanes Companies, Inc.; North Carolina Baptist Hospitals, Inc.; R.J. Reynolds Tobacco Company; Summit Communications Group, Inc.; Thomasville Furniture Industries, Inc.; Wachovia Corporation; Wake Forest University.

For Complete List of Firm Personnel, See General Section

For full biographical listings, see the Martindale-Hubbell Law Directory

NORTH DAKOTA

*BISMARCK,** Burleigh Co.

TSCHIDER & SMITH (AV)

A Partnership including Professional Corporations
Professional Building - Suite 200, 418 East Rosser Avenue, 58501
Telephone: 701-258-4000
Fax: 701-258-4001

MEMBERS OF FIRM

Morris A. Tschider (P.C.)
Sean O. Smith (P.C.)
David A. Tschider

Representative Clients: Agri Bank, FCB; Farm Credit Services of Mandan, FLCA; Farm Credit Services of Mandan, P.C.A.; Twin City Implement, Inc.; First Bank Bismarck; N.D. Independent Insurance Agents; Western Steel & Plumbing; Froelich Oil Co.; Bismarck Eagles.

For full biographical listings, see the Martindale-Hubbell Law Directory

*FARGO,** Cass Co.

CONMY, FESTE, BOSSART, HUBBARD & CORWIN, LTD. (AV)

400 Norwest Center, Fourth Street and Main Avenue, 58126
Telephone: 701-293-9911
Fax: 701-293-3133

(See Next Column)

CONMY, FESTE, BOSSART, HUBBARD & CORWIN LTD.—*Continued*

Charles A. Feste
David R. Bossart
Paul M. Hubbard
Wickham Corwin
Kim E. Brust
Lauris N. Molbert
Michael M. Thomas
Robert J. Schultz
Nancy J. Morris
Jiming Zhu

OF COUNSEL

E. T. Conmy, Jr.

State Counsel for: Metropolitan Life Insurance Company.
Representative Clients: Ford Motor Credit Co.; Norwest Corporation Region VII Banks (North Dakota & Minnesota West); U.S. Gypsum Co.
Insurance: American Hardware Insurance Group; Great American Insurance Companies; The Maryland.

For full biographical listings, see the Martindale-Hubbell Law Directory

NILLES, HANSEN & DAVIES, LTD. (AV)

1800 Radisson Tower, P.O. Box 2626, 58108
Telephone: 701-237-5544

Timothy Q. Davies
Russell F. Freeman
Gregory B. Selbo

Representative Client: First Trust Company of North Dakota.

For Complete List of Firm Personnel, See General Section

For full biographical listings, see the Martindale-Hubbell Law Directory

VOGEL, BRANTNER, KELLY, KNUTSON, WEIR & BYE, LTD. (AV)

502 First Avenue North, P.O. Box 1389, 58107
Telephone: 701-237-6983
Facsimile: 701-237-0847

C. Nicholas Vogel

For Complete List of Firm Personnel, See General Section

For full biographical listings, see the Martindale-Hubbell Law Directory

*MINOT,** Ward Co.

MCGEE, HANKLA, BACKES & WHEELER, P.C. (AV)

Suite 305 Norwest Center, 15 Second Avenue Southwest, P.O. Box 998, 58702-0998
Telephone: 701-852-2544
Fax: 701-838-4724

Richard H. McGee (1918-1992)
Walfrid B. Hankla
Orlin W. Backes
Robert A. Wheeler
Donald L. Peterson
Richard H. McGee, II
Collin P. Dobrovolny
Brian W. Hankla
Robert J. Hovland
Jon W. Backes

LEGAL SUPPORT PERSONNEL

Janice M. Eslinger
Jane K. Hutchison
Ardella M. Burtman
Michelle Erdmann

For full biographical listings, see the Martindale-Hubbell Law Directory

WEST FARGO, Cass Co.

OHNSTAD TWICHELL, P.C. (AV)

901 13th Avenue East, P.O. Box 458, 58078-0458
Telephone: 701-282-3249
FAX: 701-282-0825
Hillsboro, North Dakota Office: West Caledonia Avenue, P.O. Box 220.
Telephone: 701-436-5700.
FAX: 701-436-4025.
Mayville, North Dakota Office: 12 Third Street, S.E., P.O. Box 547.
Telephone: 701-786-3251.
FAX: 701-786-4243.
Fargo, North Dakota Office: 15 Broadway, Suite 202.
Telephone: 701-280-5801.
Fax: 701-280-5803.

Robert E. Rosenvold

Representative Clients: First National Bank North Dakota; Quality Boneless Beef; City of West Fargo; Bond Counsel for Cities of Fargo, Jamestown, West Fargo and Valley City; Insurance Company of North America; Reliance Insurance Co.; The Continental Insurance Cos.; Underwriters Adjusting Co.; Industrial Indemnity Co.; Integrity Insurance Co.

For Complete List of Firm Personnel, See General Section

For full biographical listings, see the Martindale-Hubbell Law Directory

OHIO

*AKRON,** Summit Co.

DANIEL G. LAPORTE AND ASSOCIATES (AV)

3250 West Market Street Suite 306, 44333-3321
Telephone: 216-836-5544
Fax: 216-836-2064

ASSOCIATE

Christopher M. Van Devere

For full biographical listings, see the Martindale-Hubbell Law Directory

*CHILLICOTHE,** Ross Co.

CUTRIGHT & CUTRIGHT (AV)

72 West Second Street, 45601
Telephone: 614-772-5595
Fax: 614-773-9261

MEMBERS OF FIRM

James M. Cutright
James K. Cutright

Representative Clients: Citizens National Bank; Chivaho Federal Credit Union; Fifth Third Bank of Southern Ohio; Rockhold, Brown & Co. Bank; Litter Industries; Scioto Valley Mental Health Center; Paint Valley Adamms Board.
Approved Attorneys for: Lawyers Title Insurance Co.; Ohio Bar Title Insurance Co.; Chicago Title Insurance Co., Inc.

For full biographical listings, see the Martindale-Hubbell Law Directory

*CINCINNATI,** Hamilton Co.

BARRETT & WEBER A LEGAL PROFESSIONAL ASSOCIATION (AV)

400 Atlas Building, 524 Walnut Street, 45202-3114
Telephone: 513-721-2120
Facsimile: 513-721-2139

H. Patrick Weber

For full biographical listings, see the Martindale-Hubbell Law Directory

BENJAMIN, YOCUM & HEATHER (AV)

1500 Central Trust Tower, 5 West 4th Street, 45202-3681
Telephone: 513-721-5672
FAX: 513-721-5910

MEMBERS OF FIRM

John A. Benjamin
Thomas R. Yocum
Timothy P. Heather
Michael J. Bergmann
Anthony J. Iaciofano

ASSOCIATES

Lisa Marie Bitter
Jeffrey Paul McSherry

For full biographical listings, see the Martindale-Hubbell Law Directory

JAMES J. CHALFIE CO., L.P.A. (AV)

36 East Seventh Street, Suite 1600, 45202
Telephone: 513-381-8616
FAX: 513-381-8619

James J. Chalfie

For Complete List of Firm Personnel, See General Section

For full biographical listings, see the Martindale-Hubbell Law Directory

DINSMORE & SHOHL (AV)

1900 Chemed Center, 255 East Fifth Street, 45202-3172
Telephone: 513-977-8200
FAX: 513-977-8141
Florence, Kentucky Office: Turfway Ridge Office Park, 7300 Turfway Road, Suite 430 41042-1355.
Telephone: 606-283-0515.
FAX: 606-283-6017.
Dayton, Ohio Office: 500 Courthouse Plaza, S.W., 10 N. Ludlow Street, 45402-1834.
Telephone: 513-228-8012.
FAX: 513-461-2543.
Columbus, Ohio Office: NBD Bank Building, Suite 330, 175 South Third Street, 43215-5134.
Telephone: 614-224-7887.
FAX: 614-224-7882.

MEMBERS OF FIRM

Jerome H. Kearns
Wiley Dinsmore
J. Michael Cooney
Edward J. Buechel (Resident, Florence, Kentucky Office)
C. Christopher Muth

(See Next Column)

DINSMORE & SHOHL, *Cincinnati—Continued*

ASSOCIATES

Timothy A. Tepe
Bonnie G. Camden

For Complete List of Firm Personnel, See General Section

For full biographical listings, see the Martindale-Hubbell Law Directory

---

DREW, WARD, GRAF, COOGAN & GOEDDEL A LEGAL PROFESSIONAL ASSOCIATION (AV)

24th Floor, Central Trust Tower, 4th and Vine Streets, 45202
Telephone: 513-621-8210
Telecopier: 513-621-5444

Richard H. Ward
William R. Graf
James H. Coogan
Frederic L. Goeddel
E. Beth Farrell

OF COUNSEL

George Raymond Drew
Albert C. Eiselein, Jr.

Representative Clients: AAA Cincinnati; Deaconess Hospital; Stevenson Photo Color Co.
Reference: Star Bank, N.A.

For full biographical listings, see the Martindale-Hubbell Law Directory

---

EICHEL & KRONE CO., L.P.A. (AV)

508 Atlas Bank Building, 524 Walnut Street, 45202
Telephone: 513-241-1234
Fax: 513-241-2731

Lawrence E. Eichel (1908-1981)
Paul W. Krone
Bruce A. Krone

References: Star Bank N.A.; PNC Bank N.A.

For full biographical listings, see the Martindale-Hubbell Law Directory

---

KATZ, TELLER, BRANT & HILD A LEGAL PROFESSIONAL ASSOCIATION (AV)

2400 Chemed Center, 255 East Fifth Street, 45202-4724
Telephone: 513-721-4532
Telecopier: 513-721-7120

Reuven J. Katz
Jerome S. Teller
Joseph A. Brant
Guy M. Hild
Robert A. Pitcairn, Jr.
Robert E. Brant
Ronald J. Goret
Stephen C. Kisling
Andrew R. Berger
Mark J. Jahnke
William F. Russo
John R. Gierl
Bruce A. Hunter
Gregory E. Land
Bradley G. Haas
Daniel P. Utt
Brent G. Houk
Cynthia Loren Gibson
Suzanne Prieur Land
Tedd H. Friedman

Representative Clients: Eagle Picher Industries, Inc.; F & C International, Inc.; Jewish Hospitals of Cincinnati; Johnny Bench; Texo Corporation; University of Cincinnati Medical Associates, Inc.

For full biographical listings, see the Martindale-Hubbell Law Directory

---

KLAINE, WILEY, HOFFMANN & MEURER A LEGAL PROFESSIONAL ASSOCIATION (AV)

Suite 1850, 105 East Fourth Street, 45202-4080
Telephone: 513-241-0202
Fax: 513-241-9322

Donald L. Wiley
James P. Minutolo

For Complete List of Firm Personnel, See General Section

For full biographical listings, see the Martindale-Hubbell Law Directory

---

PORTER & PORTER (AV)

2100 Central Trust Tower, 45202
Telephone: 513-621-3993
Fax: 513-621-1746

MEMBERS OF FIRM

Robert C. Porter (1890-1954)
Robert C. Porter, Jr.
Robert C. Porter, III

Representative Client: Paul Homes, Inc.

For full biographical listings, see the Martindale-Hubbell Law Directory

---

SANTEN & HUGHES A LEGAL PROFESSIONAL ASSOCIATION (AV)

Suite 3100, 312 Walnut Street, 45202
Telephone: 513-721-4450
FAX: 513-721-7644; 721-0109

(See Next Column)

Harry H. Santen
Charles M. Meyer
Charles E. Reynolds
James P. Wersching
R. Mark Addy
Charles J. Kubicki, Jr.

LEGAL SUPPORT PERSONNEL

Karen W. Crane (Corporate Paralegal)
Deborah M. McKinney (Trust/Estate Paralegal)
Karen L. Jansen (Litigation Paralegal)
Bobbie S. Ebbers (Paralegal)

For Complete List of Firm Personnel, See General Section

For full biographical listings, see the Martindale-Hubbell Law Directory

---

SCHWARTZ, MANES & RUBY A LEGAL PROFESSIONAL ASSOCIATION (AV)

2900 Carew Tower, 441 Vine Street, 45202
Telephone: 513-579-1414
Telecopier: 513-579-1418

Richard M. Schwartz
Dennis L. Manes
Stanley L. Ruby
Thomas J. Breed
Debbe A. Levin

For Complete List of Firm Personnel, See General Section

For full biographical listings, see the Martindale-Hubbell Law Directory

---

THOMPSON, HINE AND FLORY (AV)

312 Walnut Street, 14th Floor, 45202-4029
Telephone: 513-352-6700
Fax: 513-241-4771;
Telex: 938003
Akron, Ohio Office: 50 S. Main Street, Suite 502, 44308-1828.
Telephone: 216-376-8090.
Fax: 216-376-8386.
Cleveland, Ohio Office: 1100 National City Bank Building, 629 Euclid Avenue, 44114-3070.
Telephone: 216-566-5500.
Fax: 216-556-5583.
Telex: 980217.
Cable Address: "Thomflor".
Columbus, Ohio Office: One Columbus, 10 West Broad Street, 43215-3435.
Telephone: 614-469-3200.
Fax: 614-469-3361.
Dayton, Ohio Office: 2000 Courthouse Plaza, N.E., 45402-1706.
Telephone: 513-443-6600.
Fax: 513-443-6637; 443-6635.
Palm Beach, Florida Office: 125 Worth Avenue, 33480-4466.
Telephone: 407-833-5900.
Fax: 407-833-5951.
Washington, D.C. Office: 1920 N Street, N.W., 20036-1601.
Telephone: 202-331-8800.
Fax: 202-331-8330.
Telex: 904173.
Cable Address: "Caglaw".
Brussels, Belgium Office: Rue des Chevaliers / Ridderstraat 14 - B.10, B - 1050.
Telephone: 011(32-2) 511-9326.
Fax: 011(-32-2) 513-9206.

MEMBERS OF FIRM

William T. Bahlman, Jr.
Mary J. Healy
Richard J. Ruebel

For Complete List of Firm Personnel, See General Section

For full biographical listings, see the Martindale-Hubbell Law Directory

---

*CIRCLEVILLE,** Pickaway Co.

HUFFER AND HUFFER CO., L.P.A. (AV)

203 South Scioto Street, P.O. Box 464, 43113
Telephone: 614-474-2179
Fax: 614-477-1778

Robert H. Huffer
Roy H. Huffer, Jr.

Representative Client: PPG Industries.

For full biographical listings, see the Martindale-Hubbell Law Directory

---

*CLEVELAND,** Cuyahoga Co.

BAKER & HOSTETLER (AV)

3200 National City Center, 1900 East Ninth Street, 44114-3485
Telephone: 216-621-0200
Telecopier: 216-696-0740
TWX: 810 421 8375
RCA Telex: 215032
In Columbus, Ohio: Capitol Square, Suite 2100, 65 East State Street.
Telephone: 614-228-1541.
In Denver, Colorado: 303 East 17th Avenue, Suite 1100.
Telephone: 303-861-0600.
In Houston, Texas: 1000 Louisiana, Suite 2000.
Telephone: 713-751-1600.

(See Next Column)

BAKER & HOSTETLER—*Continued*

In Long Beach, California: 300 Oceangate, Suite 620.
Telephone: 310-432-2827.
In Los Angeles, California: 600 Wilshire Boulevard.
Telephone: 213-624-2400.
In Orlando, Florida: SunBank Center, Suite 2300, 200 South Orange Avenue.
Telephone: 407-649-4000.
In Washington, D. C.: Washington Square, Suite 1100, 1050 Connecticut Avenue, N.W.
Telephone: 202-861-1500.
In College Park, Maryland: 9658 Baltimore Boulevard, Suite 206.
Telephone: 301-441-2781.
In Alexandria, Virginia: 437 North Lee Street.
Telephone: 703-549-1294.
In San Francisco, California: One Sansome Street, Suite 2000.
Telephone: 415-951-4705.

PARTNERS

Oakley V. Andrews, Robert M. Brucken, Calvin B. Kirchick, Robert K. Lease, Kevin G. Robertson

ASSOCIATES

Jane T. Haylor, Stacey S. Staub

For Complete List of Firm Personnel, See General Section

For full biographical listings, see the Martindale-Hubbell Law Directory

KADISH & BENDER A LEGAL PROFESSIONAL ASSOCIATION (AV)

2112 East Ohio Building, 44114
Telephone: 216-696-3030
Telecopier: 216-696-3492

Stephen L. Kadish, J. Timothy Bender, Kevin M. Hinkel, David G. Weibel

Aaron H. Bulloff, Joseph P. Alexander, David G. Lambert, William A. Duncan, Mary Beth Duffy, James H. Rownd

For full biographical listings, see the Martindale-Hubbell Law Directory

SEELEY, SAVIDGE AND AUSSEM A LEGAL PROFESSIONAL ASSOCIATION (AV)

800 Bank One Center, 600 Superior Avenue, East, 44114-2655
Telephone: 216-566-8200
Cable Address: "See Sau"
Fax-Telecopier: 216-566-0213
Elyria, Ohio Office: 538 Broad Street.
Telephone: 216-236-8158.

James S. Aussem, Gary A. Ebert

OF COUNSEL

Edmund W. Rothschild, William M. Fumich, Jr.

References: Society National Bank; AmeriTrust.

For Complete List of Firm Personnel, See General Section

For full biographical listings, see the Martindale-Hubbell Law Directory

SPIETH, BELL, MCCURDY & NEWELL CO., L.P.A. (AV)

2000 Huntington Building, 925 Euclid Avenue, 44115-1496
Telephone: 216-696-4700
Telecopier: 216-696-6569; 216-696-2706; 216-696-1052

Lincoln Reavis, James R. Bright

Representative Clients: Cleveland Cavaliers; Nationwide Advertising Services, Inc.; Independent Steel Co.; Baldwin Wallace College; The Tool-Die Engineering Company.
Representative Labor Relations Clients (Management Only): Parker Hannifin Corp.; Reliance Electric Co.; Brush Wellman Co.

For Complete List of Firm Personnel, See General Section

For full biographical listings, see the Martindale-Hubbell Law Directory

THOMPSON, HINE AND FLORY (AV)

1100 National City Bank Building, 629 Euclid Avenue, 44114-3070
Telephone: 216-566-5500
Fax: 216-566-5583
Telex: 980217
Cable Address: "Thomflor"
Akron, Ohio Office: 50 S. Main Street, Suite 502, 44308-1828.
Telephone: 216-376-8090.
Fax: 216-376-8386.
Cincinnati, Ohio Office: 312 Walnut Street, 14th Floor, 45202-4029.
Telephone: 513-352-6700.
Fax: 513-241-4771.
Telex: 938003.

(See Next Column)

Columbus, Ohio Office: One Columbus, 10 West Broad Street, 43215-3435.
Telephone: 614-469-3200.
Fax: 614-469-3361.
Dayton, Ohio Office: 2000 Courthouse Plaza, N.E., 45402-1706.
Telephone: 513-443-6600.
Fax: 513-443-6637; 443-6635.
Palm Beach, Florida Office: 125 Worth Avenue, Suite 117, 33480-4466.
Telephone: 407-833-5900.
Fax: 407-833-5951.
Washington, D.C. Office: 1920 N Street, N.W., 20036-1601.
Telephone: 202-331-8800.
Fax: 202-331-8330.
Telex: 904173.
Cable Address: "Caglaw".
Brussels, Belgium Office: Rue des Chevaliers, Ridderstraat 14 - B.10, B - 1050.
Telephone: 011(32-2) 511-9326.
Fax: 011(32-2) 513-9206.

MEMBERS OF FIRM

Malvin E. Bank, Nancy H. Canary (In Palm Beach, Florida and Cleveland, Ohio) (Partner-in-Charge in Palm Beach, Florida), Andrew L. Fabens, Robert B. Ford, Oliver C. Henkel, Jr., Ralph P. Higgins, Jr., William C. Trier, Jr., Thomas M. Turner

STAFF ATTORNEY

Laura C. Gockel

For Complete List of Firm Personnel, See General Section

For full biographical listings, see the Martindale-Hubbell Law Directory

ZIEGLER, METZGER & MILLER (AV)

2020 Huntington Building, 44115-1407
Telephone: 216-781-5470
FAX: 216-781-0714

MEMBERS OF FIRM

William L. Ziegler, Robert L. Metzger, William L. Spring, Richard T. Spotz, Jr.

ASSOCIATE

Joseph W. Kampman

LEGAL SUPPORT PERSONNEL

P. Thomas Austin (Consultant), Cynthia Moore (Tax Accountant)

For Complete List of Firm Personnel, See General Section

For full biographical listings, see the Martindale-Hubbell Law Directory

*COLUMBUS,** Franklin Co.

* indicates certain Bar Register subscribers whose principal office is located elsewhere in the state and who have arranged for representation as a part of the state capital listings that follow

EMENS, KEGLER, BROWN, HILL & RITTER (AV)

Capitol Square Suite 1800, 65 East State Street, 43215-4294
Telephone: 614-462-5400
Telecopier: 614-464-2634
Cable Address: "Law EKBHR"
Telex: 246671

John F. Allevato, Edward C. Hertenstein, Charles J. Kegler, John B. Tingley, R. Douglas Wrightsel

Mary Ten Eyck Taylor

For Complete List of Firm Personnel, See General Section

For full biographical listings, see the Martindale-Hubbell Law Directory

*** THOMPSON, HINE AND FLORY (AV)**

One Columbus, 10 West Broad Street, 43215-3435
Telephone: 614-469-3200
Fax: 614-469-3361
Akron, Ohio Office: 50 S. Main Street, Suite 502, 44308-1828.
Telephone: 216-376-8090.
Fax: 216-376-8386.
Cincinnati, Ohio Office: 312 Walnut Street, 14th Floor, 45202-4029.
Telephone: 513-352-6700.
Fax: 513-241-4771.
Telex: 938003.
Cleveland, Ohio Office: 1100 National City Bank Building, 629 Euclid Avenue, 44114-3070.
Telephone: 216-566-5500.
Fax: 216-556-5583.
Telex: 980217.
Cable Address: "Thomflor".
Dayton, Ohio Office: 2000 Courthouse Plaza, N.E., 45402-1706.
Telephone: 513-443-6600.
Fax: 513-443-6637; 443-6635.

(See Next Column)

THOMPSON, HINE AND FLORY, *Columbus—Continued*

Palm Beach, Florida Office: 125 Worth Avenue, 33480-4466.
Telephone: 407-833-5900.
Fax: 407-833-5951.
Washington, D.C. Office: 1920 N Street, N.W., 20036-1601.
Telephone: 202-331-8800.
Fax: 202-331-8330.
Telex: 904173.
Cable Address: "Caglaw".
Brussels, Belgium Office: Rue des Chevaliers / Ridderstraat 14 - B.10, B - 1050.
Telephone: 011(32-2) 511-9326.
Fax: 011(32-2) 513-9206.

MEMBER OF FIRM

Thomas J. Bonasera

For Complete List of Firm Personnel, See General Section

For full biographical listings, see the Martindale-Hubbell Law Directory

*DAYTON,** Montgomery Co.

ALTICK & CORWIN (AV)

1700 One Dayton Centre, One South Main Street, 45402
Telephone: 513-223-1201
Fax: 513-223-5100

MEMBERS OF FIRM

Robert N. Farquhar
Marshall D. Ruchman
R. Paul Perkins, Jr.
Thomas R. Noland
Thomas M. Baggott
Robert B. Berner
Dennis J. Adkins
Richard A. Boucher
Philip B. Herron
Deborah J. Adler

OF COUNSEL

Raymond J. Pikna, Jr.

ASSOCIATE

Donald K. Scott

RETIRED

Robert B. Brumbaugh
Robert K. Corwin
Ronald H. McDonnell, Jr.

Representative Clients: City of Beavercreek; City of Centerville; The Miami Conservancy District; Miami Valley Cable Council; Woodland Cemetery Assn.

For Complete List of Firm Personnel, See General Section

For full biographical listings, see the Martindale-Hubbell Law Directory

LOUIS & FROELICH A LEGAL PROFESSIONAL ASSOCIATION (AV)

1812 Kettering Tower, 45423
Telephone: 513-226-1776
FAX: 513-226-1945
Trotwood, Ohio Office: 101 East Main Street.
Telephone: 513-226-1776.

Herbert M. Louis
Jeffrey A. Winwood

James I. Weprin

Reference: Society Bank, N.A. of Dayton, Ohio.

For Complete List of Firm Personnel, See General Section

For full biographical listings, see the Martindale-Hubbell Law Directory

STOECKLEIN, KOVERMAN & SMITH (AV)

1300 Hulman Building, 45402
Telephone: 513-222-6926
Fax: 513-222-6901

Robert J. Stoecklein (1917-1990)
John R. Koverman, Jr.
Patrick K. Smith
James E. Fox

For full biographical listings, see the Martindale-Hubbell Law Directory

THOMPSON, HINE AND FLORY (AV)

2000 Courthouse Plaza, N.E., 45402-1706
Telephone: 513-443-6600
Fax: 513-443-6637; 443-6635
Akron, Ohio Office: 50 S. Main Street, Suite 502, 44308-1828.
Telephone: 216-376-8090.
Fax: 216-376-8386.
Cincinnati, Ohio Office: 312 Walnut Street, 14th Floor, 45202-4029.
Telephone: 513-352-6700.
Fax: 513-241-4771.
Telex: 938003.

(See Next Column)

Cleveland, Ohio Office: 1100 National City Bank Building, 629 Euclid Avenue, 44114-3070.
Telephone: 216-566-5500.
Fax: 216-556-5583.
Telex: 980217.
Cable Address: "Thomflor".
Columbus, Ohio Office: One Columbus, 10 West Broad Street, 43215-3435.
Telephone: 614-469-3200.
Fax: 614-469-3361.
Palm Beach, Florida Office: 125 Worth Avenue, 33480-4466.
Telephone: 407-833-5900.
Fax: 407-833-5951.
Washington, D.C. Office: 1920 N Street, N.W., 20036-1601.
Telephone: 202-331-8800.
Fax: 202-331-8330.
Telex: 904173.
Cable Address: "Caglaw".
Brussels, Belgium Office: Rue des Chevaliers / Ridderstraat 14 - B.10, B - 1050.
Telephone: 011(32-2) 511-9326.
Fax: 011(32-2) 513-9206.

MEMBERS OF FIRM

Richard F. Carlile
Crofford J. Macklin, Jr.

ASSOCIATE

Mark A. Conway

For Complete List of Firm Personnel, See General Section

For full biographical listings, see the Martindale-Hubbell Law Directory

TYE & TYE (AV)

Suite 120, 2600 Far Hills Avenue, 45419
Telephone: 513-298-7078
Telecopier: 513-298-3104

MEMBERS OF FIRM

Rose R. Tye
Timothy N. Tye

References: The First National Bank; Bank One, Dayton N.A.

For full biographical listings, see the Martindale-Hubbell Law Directory

*EATON,** Preble Co.

BENNETT & BENNETT (AV)

Bennett Law Building, 200 West Main Street, 45320
Telephone: 513-456-4100
Fax: 513-456-5100

MEMBERS OF FIRM

Lloyd B. Bennett (1909-1983)
Herd L. Bennett
Gray W. Bennett

Representative Clients: The National Hummel Foundation and Museum; Star Bank of Preble County, Ohio; Eaton National Bank & Trust Co.; First National Bank of Southwestern Ohio; Brookville National Bank; Farm Credit Services of Mid-America; Miller's Super Markets, Inc.; Northedge Shopping Center, Inc.; Herman M. Brubaker Registered Holstein Cattle; The Eaton Foundation.

For Complete List of Firm Personnel, See General Section

For full biographical listings, see the Martindale-Hubbell Law Directory

*IRONTON,** Lawrence Co.

COLLIER & COLLIER (AV)

411 Center Street, 45638
Telephone: 614-532-8034
Fax: 614-533-3457

MEMBERS OF FIRM

James Collier (1893-1973)
J. B. Collier
J. B. Collier, Jr.

For full biographical listings, see the Martindale-Hubbell Law Directory

SPEARS & SPEARS (AV)

122 South Fourth Street, 45638
Telephone: 614-532-5815; 614-532-6913

MEMBERS OF FIRM

Harold D. Spears
David R. Spears

References: Star Bank; National City Bank.

For full biographical listings, see the Martindale-Hubbell Law Directory

MAUMEE, Lucas Co.

WEBER & STERLING (AV)

1721 Indian Wood Circle, Suite 1, 43537-4008
Telephone: 419-893-3360
Fax: 419-893-7146

MEMBERS OF FIRM

Edward F. Weber
Robert V. Sterling
Dennis P. Williams

(See Next Column)

WEBER & STERLING—*Continued*

ASSOCIATE

John D. DiSalle

Representative Clients: Toledo Community Foundation; Toledo Museum of Art; Society Bank & Trust.
References: The Fifth Third Bank of Northwestern Ohio, N.A.; National City Bank, Northwest.

For full biographical listings, see the Martindale-Hubbell Law Directory

PERRYSBURG, Wood Co.

LEATHERMAN, WITZLER, DOMBEY & HART (AV)

353 Elm Street, 43551
Telephone: 419-874-3536
Fax: 419-874-3899

MEMBERS OF FIRM

Wayne M. Leatherman
James H. Hart
Earl N. Witzler
Timothy J. Brown
Philip L. Dombey
T. Hamilton Noll
Kay L. Howard

Representative Clients: Cook Insurance Agency, Inc.; Craig Transportation Co.; Ed Schmidt Pontiac, Inc.; Perrysburg Board of Education; Perrysburg Township Trustees; Service Travel Co.; Toledo Impression Co. (Dies & Molds); Village of Holland; 577 Foundation.

For full biographical listings, see the Martindale-Hubbell Law Directory

*PORTSMOUTH,** Scioto Co.

C. CLAYTON JOHNSON CO. A LEGAL PROFESSIONAL ASSOCIATION (AV)

400 Bank One Plaza, P.O. Box 1505, 45662
Telephone: 614-354-4200
Telecopier: 614-353-2413

C. Clayton Johnson

Stephen L. Oliver

OF COUNSEL

Robert Kurt McCurdy

Representative Clients: Bank One, Portsmouth, N.A.; OSCO Industries, Inc.; Citizens Deposit Bank and Trust; First National Bank of Lewis County, Kentucky; Home Federal Savings and Loan; McDonalds Corp.; National Maintenance & Repair, Inc.; McGinnis, Inc.
Approved Attorney for: Lawyers Title Insurance Co.

For full biographical listings, see the Martindale-Hubbell Law Directory

*SPRINGFIELD,** Clark Co.

GORMAN, VESKAUF, HENSON & WINEBERG (AV)

4 West Main Street Suite 723, 45502
Telephone: 513-325-7058
Fax: 513-325-9914

MEMBERS OF FIRM

James M. Gorman (1916-1994)
Douglas A. Henson
Thomas J. Veskauf
Robert A. Wineberg
W. D. Shane Latham

ASSOCIATES

Thomas W. Kendo, Jr.
Daniel D. Carey

OF COUNSEL

George M. Winwood

Representative Clients: Liberty Mutual Insurance Co.; Security National Bank & Trust Co.; New Carlisle Federal Savings & Loan Assn.; Sweet Manufacturing Co.
Reference: Security National Bank and Trust Co.

For full biographical listings, see the Martindale-Hubbell Law Directory

*TOLEDO,** Lucas Co.

DOYLE, LEWIS & WARNER (AV)

202 North Erie Street, P.O. Box 2168, 43603
Telephone: 419-248-1500
Fax: 419-248-2002

MEMBERS OF FIRM

Steven Timonere
Michael E. Hyrne
Richard F. Ellenberger
John A. Borell
Michael A. Bruno

ASSOCIATE

Kevin A. Pituch

(See Next Column)

OF COUNSEL

Harold A. James
John R. Wanick

Counsel for: Consolidated Rail Corp.; The Lakefront Dock & Railroad Terminal Co.; Prudential Insurance Co. of America; Equitable Life Assurance Society of the U.S.; Metropolitan Life Insurance Co.; Greyhound Lines; Fireman's Fund Insurance Cos.

For Complete List of Firm Personnel, See General Section

For full biographical listings, see the Martindale-Hubbell Law Directory

EASTMAN & SMITH (AV)

One Seagate, Twenty-Fourth Floor, 43604
Telephone: 419-241-6000
Telecopier: 419-247-1777
Columbus, Ohio Office: 65 East State Street, Suite 1000, 43215.
Telephone: 614-460-3556.
Telecopier: 614-228-5371.

MEMBERS OF FIRM

Frank D. Jacobs
Morton Bobowick
John H. Boggs

ASSOCIATES

Lori B. Hart
David A. Dennis
David C. Krock

OF COUNSEL

Gerald P. Moran

For Complete List of Firm Personnel, See General Section

For full biographical listings, see the Martindale-Hubbell Law Directory

FREDERICKSON & HEINTSCHEL, CO., L.P.A. (AV)

1313 Fifth Third Center, 608 Madison Avenue, 43604
Telephone: 419-242-5100
FAX: 419-242-5556

Craig F. Frederickson
Thomas W. Heintschel

Douglas W. King

For full biographical listings, see the Martindale-Hubbell Law Directory

FULLER & HENRY (AV)

One Seagate Suite 1700, P.O. Box 2088, 43603-2088
Telephone: 419-247-2500
Telecopier: 419-247-2665
Port Clinton, Ohio Office: 125 Jefferson.
Telephone: 419-734-2153.
Telecopier: 419-732-8246.
Columbus, Ohio Office: 2210 Huntington Center, 41 South High Street.
Telephone: 614-228-6611.
Telecopier: 614-228-6623.

MEMBERS OF FIRM

Raymond G. Esch
James M. Morton, Jr.
Glenn L. Rambo

Counsel for: Building Industry Association of Northwest Ohio, Inc.; Catawba-Cleveland Development Corp.; Chrysler Corp.; Chubb Group of Insurance Cos.; E. I. DuPont De Nemours & Co.; The Ohio Bell Telephone Co.; Owens-Illinois, Inc.; Phillips Petroleum Co.; The Toledo Edison Co.

For Complete List of Firm Personnel, See General Section

For full biographical listings, see the Martindale-Hubbell Law Directory

RITTER, ROBINSON, MCCREADY & JAMES (AV)

1850 National City Bank Building, 405 Madison Avenue, 43624
Telephone: 419-241-3213
Detroit, Michigan: 313-422-1610
FAX: 419-241-4925

MEMBER OF FIRM

William S. McCready

Representative Clients: Ohio Casualty Insurance Co.; National Mutual Insurance Co.; Celina Mutual Insurance Co.; Westfield Insurance Co.; Northwestern National Insurance Co.; Midwestern Insurance Co.; United Ohio Insurance Co.

For Complete List of Firm Personnel, See General Section

For full biographical listings, see the Martindale-Hubbell Law Directory

STOCKWELL & COOPERMAN A LEGAL PROFESSIONAL ASSOCIATION (AV)

Suite 1610, One SeaGate, 43604
Telephone: 419-247-1500
Telecopier: 419-247-1575

John P. Stockwell
Ronald M. Cooperman
Katherine Raup O'Connell

(See Next Column)

STOCKWELL & COOPERMAN A LEGAL PROFESSIONAL ASSOCIATION, *Toledo—Continued*

Scott T. Janson

Reference: Fifth Third Bank, Toledo, Ohio.

For full biographical listings, see the Martindale-Hubbell Law Directory

WATKINS, BATES & CAREY (AV)

1200 Fifth Third Center, 608 Madison Avenue, 43604-1157
Telephone: 419-241-2100
Telecopier: 419-241-1960

MEMBERS OF FIRM

William F. Bates
Gary O. Sommer
Thomas C. Gess

Counsel for: Goerlich Family Foundation, Inc.; The Judson Palmer Home; Zenith Foundation, Inc.; Joseph L. Wolcott Scholarship Fund; C.C. Whitmore Trust Estate.

For Complete List of Firm Personnel, See General Section

For full biographical listings, see the Martindale-Hubbell Law Directory

WELLSTON, Jackson Co.

OTHS & HEISER (AV)

Sixteen East Broadway, P.O. Box 309, 45692-0309
Telephone: 614-384-2111
Fax: 614-384-5632

MEMBERS OF FIRM

Joseph A. Oths
Lawrence A. Heiser

ASSOCIATES

Christopher J. Regan
Robert R. Miller

Representative Clients: The First National Bank; The Milton Banking Co.; Farm Credit Services of Mid-America, ACA.
Approved Attorneys for: TransOhio Title Co.; Louisville Title Division of Commonwealth Land Title Insurance Co.

For full biographical listings, see the Martindale-Hubbell Law Directory

*WILMINGTON,** Clinton Co.

BUCKLEY, MILLER & WRIGHT (AV)

145 North South Street, P.O. Box 311, 45177
Telephone: 513-382-0946
Fax: 513-382-1361
Sabina, Ohio Office: 34 North Howard Street.
Telephone: 513-584-4663.

MEMBERS OF FIRM

Frederick J. Buckley
Jeffrey L. Wright
James P. Miller
Karen Buckley
John P. Miller

Representative Clients: The Wilmington Savings Bank; Wilmington College; Sabina Farmers Exchange; The Sabina Bank; Community Improvement Corporation of Wilmington.
Approved Attorneys for: Lawyers Title Insurance Corp. (Title Agent); The Ohio Bar Title Insurance Co. (Title Agent).

For full biographical listings, see the Martindale-Hubbell Law Directory

OKLAHOMA

BLACKWELL, Kay Co.

JAMES R. RODGERS (AV)

Security Bank Building, P.O. Box 514, 74631
Telephone: 405-363-3684
Fax: 405-363-1063

William W. Rodgers (1907-1979)

Attorney for: Security Bank and Trust Co., Blackwell, Oklahoma; Electron Corp.; Blackwell Board of Education.

For full biographical listings, see the Martindale-Hubbell Law Directory

*DUNCAN,** Stephens Co.

LEACH, SULLIVAN, SULLIVAN & WATKINS (AV)

921 Main Street, P.O. Box 160, 73534
Telephone: 405-255-8260
Telecopier: 405-255-5587

MEMBERS OF FIRM

William O. Leach (1919-1990)
Michael P. Sullivan
Paul D. Sullivan
Kent P. Sullivan
Patrick D. Sullivan
Jay B. Watkins

(See Next Column)

Representative Clients: The Oklahoma National Bank; Citizens' Bank, Velma, Oklahoma; Universal Fidelity Life Insurance Co.; Duncan Regional Hospital, Inc.; Leffler Construction Co.

For Complete List of Firm Personnel, See General Section

For full biographical listings, see the Martindale-Hubbell Law Directory

*KINGFISHER,** Kingfisher Co.

BEALL & JOHNSON LAW OFFICE, INC. (AV)

215 North Main Street, P.O. Box 298, 73750-0298
Telephone: 405-375-3188
Fax: 405-375-3308

James P. Beall
Cloise E. Johnson, Jr.

General Counsel For: Kingfisher Bank and Trust Co.; Kingfisher Bancorp, Inc.
Representative Clients: Oppel Bros., Inc. (construction and farms); Boeckman Ford, Inc.; Kingfisher Newspapers, Inc. Francis Trust (land development); Okarche Development, Inc.; G.E.B., Inc. (real estate); Felta Yost Trust; Kingfisher County Rural Water Districts; Farmers Cooperative Supply; Kingfisher Educational Foundation, Inc.; Kingfisher Community Trust; Oklahoma Seed Co.

For full biographical listings, see the Martindale-Hubbell Law Directory

LAVERNE, Harper Co.

G. W. ARMOR (AV)

103 West Main Street, P.O. Box 267, 73848
Telephone: 405-921-3335
FAX: 405-921-5720

*OKLAHOMA CITY,** Oklahoma Co.

ANDREWS DAVIS LEGG BIXLER MILSTEN & PRICE, A PROFESSIONAL CORPORATION (AV)

500 West Main, 73102
Telephone: 405-272-9241
FAX: 405-235-8786

James F. Davis
Richard B. Kells, Jr.
Mark H. Price

Lynn O. Holloman

For Complete List of Firm Personnel, See General Section

For full biographical listings, see the Martindale-Hubbell Law Directory

LESLIE L. CONNER, JR. (AV)

6801 North Broadway Extension, Suite 205, 73116-9037
Telephone: 405-843-1404
Fax: 405-843-1495

For full biographical listings, see the Martindale-Hubbell Law Directory

FULLER, TUBB & POMEROY (AV)

800 Bank of Oklahoma Plaza, 201 Robert S. Kerr Avenue, 73102-4292
Telephone: 405-235-2575
Fax: 405-232-8384

MEMBERS OF FIRM

G. M. Fuller
Jerry Tubb
L. David Pomeroy
Joe Heaton
Michael A. Bickford
Terry Stokes

Representative Clients: French Petroleum Corp.; Independent Insurance Agents of Oklahoma, Inc.; LTV Energy Products Co.; Northwestern National Life Insurance Co.; Purina Mills, Inc.; Sequa Corp.; Halliburton Oil Producing Co.; Chemical Bank/Chemical Financial Corporation; Pitney Bowes, Inc.; Norwest Banks.

For Complete List of Firm Personnel, See General Section

For full biographical listings, see the Martindale-Hubbell Law Directory

HARTZOG CONGER & CASON, A PROFESSIONAL CORPORATION (AV)

1600 Bank of Oklahoma Plaza, 73102
Telephone: 405-235-7000
Facsimile: 405-235-7329

Larry D. Hartzog
J. William Conger
Len Cason
James C. Prince
Alan Newman
Steven C. Davis
Valerie K. Couch
Mark D. Dickey
Joseph P. Hogsett
John D. Robertson
Kurt M. Rupert
Laura Haag McConnell

Susan B. Shields
Ryan S. Wilson
Melanie J. Jester
Armand Paliotta
Julia Watson
J. Leslie LaReau

(See Next Column)

HARTZOG CONGER & CASON A PROFESSIONAL CORPORATION—*Continued*

OF COUNSEL
Kent F. Frates

For full biographical listings, see the Martindale-Hubbell Law Directory

THE LAW OFFICES OF HEMRY & HEMRY, P.C. (AV)

621 N. Robinson, Second Floor, P.O. Box 2207, 73101
Telephone: 405-235-3571
FAX: 405-235-0944

Jerry L. Hemry
Kenneth M. Hemry

OF COUNSEL

Jerome E. Hemry
Tom A. Hemry (Not admitted in OK)

William P. McDoniel

Counsel for: American General Life Insurance Company of Oklahoma; Lippert Bros. Construction Co; Oklahoma Land Title Association.

For full biographical listings, see the Martindale-Hubbell Law Directory

*PERRY,** Noble Co.

HARVEY D. YOST II (AV)

623 Delaware Street, P.O. Box 874, 73077-0874
Telephone: 405-336-5511
Facsimile: 405-336-3554

ASSOCIATE
Donna Occhipinti Yost

For full biographical listings, see the Martindale-Hubbell Law Directory

*TULSA,** Tulsa Co.

GABLE & GOTWALS (AV)

2000 Bank IV Center, 15 West Sixth Street, 74119-5447
Telephone: 918-582-9201
Facsimile: 918-586-8383

Teresa B. Adwan
Pamela S. Anderson
John R. Barker
David L. Bryant
Gene C. Buzzard
Dennis Clarke Cameron
Timothy A. Carney
Renee DeMoss
Elsie C. Draper
Sidney G. Dunagan
Theodore Q. Eliot
Richard W. Gable
Jeffrey Don Hassell
Patricia Ledvina Himes
Oliver S. Howard
Richard D. Koljack, Jr.
J. Daniel Morgan
Joseph W. Morris
Elizabeth R. Muratet
Richard B. Noulles
Ronald N. Ricketts
John Henry Rule
M. Benjamin Singletary
James M. Sturdivant
Patrick O. Waddel
Michael D. Hall
David Edward Keglovits
Stephen W. Lake
Kari S. McKee
Terry D. Ragsdale
Jeffrey C. Rambach

OF COUNSEL

G. Ellis Gable
Charles P. Gotwals, Jr.

For full biographical listings, see the Martindale-Hubbell Law Directory

JAMES, POTTS AND WULFERS (AV)

Suite 705, 320 South Boston Avenue, 74103-3712
Telephone: 918-584-0881
FAX: 918-584-4521

MEMBERS OF FIRM

David F. James
Thomas G. Potts
David W. Wulfers

For full biographical listings, see the Martindale-Hubbell Law Directory

JOHNSON, ALLEN, JONES & DORNBLASER (AV)

900 Petroleum Club Building, 601 South Boulder, 74119
Telephone: 918-584-6644
FAX: 918-584-6645

MEMBERS OF FIRM

Mark H. Allen
W. Thomas Coffman
Kenneth E. Dornblaser
John B. Johnson, Jr.
C. Robert Jones
Richard D. Jones
Randy R. Shorb

ASSOCIATE
Frances F. Hillsman

For full biographical listings, see the Martindale-Hubbell Law Directory

JOYCE AND POLLARD (AV)

Suite 300, 515 South Main Mall, 74103
Telephone: 918-585-2751
Fax: 918-582-9308

MEMBERS OF FIRM

J. C. Joyce
Dwayne C. Pollard
Ted J. Nelson
Sheila M. Bradley
John C. Joyce

A list of Representative Clients furnished upon request.

For full biographical listings, see the Martindale-Hubbell Law Directory

MCDOUGAL, EVANS & BENNETT, P.C. (AV)

406 South Boulder, Suite 610, 74103-3825
Telephone: 918-583-6754
FAX: 918-592-5568

M. M. McDougal
Julie A. Evans
Claudia N. Bennett

For full biographical listings, see the Martindale-Hubbell Law Directory

J. BARLOW NELSON, INC. (AV)

Suite 805 Utica Tower Building, 1924 South Utica Avenue, 74104-5468
Telephone: 918-743-6101
Fax: 918-743-6103

J. Barlow Nelson

Reference: F & M Bank & Trust Co.

For full biographical listings, see the Martindale-Hubbell Law Directory

RISELING & ASSOCIATES, A PROFESSIONAL CORPORATION (AV)

Inverness Park, 2510 E. 21st Street, 74114
Telephone: 918-747-0111
Fax: 918-747-0776
Bartlesville Office: 501 E. Frank Philips Boulevard, Suite 201.
Telephone: 918-336-0600

Ted M. Riseling

Reference: F & M Bank.

For full biographical listings, see the Martindale-Hubbell Law Directory

SNEED, LANG, ADAMS & BARNETT, A PROFESSIONAL CORPORATION (AV)

2300 Williams Center Tower II, Two West Second Street, 74103
Telephone: 918-583-3145
Telecopier: 918-582-0410

James C. Lang
D. Faith Orlowski
Brian S. Gaskill
G. Steven Stidham
Stephen R. McNamara
Thomas E. Black, Jr.
Robbie Emery Burke
C. Raymond Patton, Jr.
Frederick K. Slicker
Richard D. Black
John D. Russell
Jeffrey S. Swyers

OF COUNSEL

James L. Sneed
O. Edwin Adams
Howard G. Barnett, Jr.

Representative Clients: Amoco Production Company; Continental Bank; Deloitte & Touche; Enron Corporation; Halliburton Energy Services; Helmerich & Payne, Inc.; Lehman Brothers, Inc.; Shell Oil Company; Smith Barney, Inc.; State Farm Mutual Automobile Insurance Company.

For full biographical listings, see the Martindale-Hubbell Law Directory

OREGON

*PORTLAND,** Multnomah Co.

CABLE HUSTON BENEDICT HAAGENSEN & FERRIS (AV)

1001 S.W. Fifth Avenue, Suite 2000, 97204
Telephone: 503-224-3092
Facsimile: 503-224-3176
Corvallis, Oregon Office: 566 N.W. Van Buren, 97339.
Telephone: 503-754-7477.
Facsimile: 503-754-0051.
Seattle, Washington Office: Cable Haagensen Benedict Lybeck & McElroy. 3080 Washington Mutual Tower, 1201 Third Avenue, 98101.
Telephone: 206-654-4160.
Facsimile: 206-654-4161.

MEMBER OF FIRM
Robert T. Huston

(See Next Column)

CABLE HUSTON BENEDICT HAAGENSEN & FERRIS, *Portland—Continued*

OF COUNSEL

David K. McAdams

Representative Clients: Bank of Tokyo, Ltd.; Chemical Waste Management, Inc.; Clatskanie People's Utility District; Community Pacific Broadcasting Company L.P.; Eugene Water & Electric Board; The Hongkong and Shangai Banking Corporation Limited; Manufacturing Management, Inc.; Rhône-Poulenc, Inc.; SimmCo Properties, Inc.; Waste Management, Inc.

For full biographical listings, see the Martindale-Hubbell Law Directory

GRENLEY, ROTENBERG EVANS & BRAGG, P.C. (AV)

30th Floor, Pacwest Center, 1211 S.W. Fifth Avenue, 97204
Telephone: 503-241-0570
Facsimile: 503-241-0914

Gary I. Grenley
Stan N. Rotenberg
Lawrence Evans
Michael J. Bragg
Steven D. Adler
Michael S. Evans
Michael C. Zusman
Jeffrey C. Bodie

OF COUNSEL

Sol Siegel
Robert C. Laskowski
Norman A. Rickles

Ann M. Lane

Reference: Key Bank of Oregon.

For full biographical listings, see the Martindale-Hubbell Law Directory

HAGEN, DYE, HIRSCHY & DILORENZO, P.C. (AV)

19th Floor Benj. Franklin Plaza, One S.W. Columbia Street, 97258-2087
Telephone: 503-222-1812
FAX: 503-274-7979

Joseph T. Hagen
Jeffrey L. Dye
John A. Hirschy
John A. DiLorenzo, Jr.
Dana R. Taylor
Mark A. Golding
Kenneth A. Williams

Blanche I. Sommers
Timothy J. Wachter
Annie T. Buell
Adam S. Rittenberg
Michael E. Farnell
John D. Parsons

LEGAL SUPPORT PERSONNEL

Carol A. R. Wong
Flora L. Wade

For full biographical listings, see the Martindale-Hubbell Law Directory

SUSSMAN SHANK WAPNICK CAPLAN & STILES (AV)

1000 S.W. Broadway Suite 1400, 97205
Telephone: 503-227-1111
Telecopier: 503-248-0130

ASSOCIATE

William S. Manne

SPECIAL COUNSEL

Aaron Jay Besen
John E. McCormick

For Complete List of Firm Personnel, See General Section

For full biographical listings, see the Martindale-Hubbell Law Directory

PENNSYLVANIA

*ALLENTOWN,** Lehigh Co.

NOONAN & PROKUP (AV)

526 Walnut Street, 18101
Telephone: 610-433-5211
Fax: 610-433-5219

MEMBERS OF FIRM

Charles T. Noonan
Thomas K. Noonan
Michael Prokup
Linda S. Noonan
Susan M. Noonan

OF COUNSEL

Karl Y. Donecker

For full biographical listings, see the Martindale-Hubbell Law Directory

TALLMAN, HUDDERS & SORRENTINO, P.C. (AV)

Suite 301 The Paragon Centre, 1611 Pond Road, 18104
Telephone: 610-391-1800
Fax: 610-391-1805

(See Next Column)

Robert G. Tallman
John R. Hudders
William H. Fitzgerald
Thomas C. Sadler, Jr.
Oldrich Foucek, III
Matthew R. Sorrentino
Timothy J. Siegfried
Dolores A. Laputka
Scott B. Allinson

Sherri L. Palopoli
David Andrew Williams
Mary C. Crocker
Scott R. Lipson
Theodore J. Zeller, III

OF COUNSEL

Harold Caplan
Paul J. Schoff

For full biographical listings, see the Martindale-Hubbell Law Directory

BRYN MAWR, Montgomery Co.

MURPHY AND MURPHY (AV)

801 Old Lancaster Road, 19010
Telephone: 610-519-0400
Fax: 610-519-0104
Trenton, New Jersey Office: Suite A 311 White Horse Avenue.
Telephone: 609-581-8559.

L. Francis Murphy
Francis J. Murphy
Michael T. Murphy

For full biographical listings, see the Martindale-Hubbell Law Directory

SHEA AND SHEA (AV)

11 Elliott Avenue, 19010
Telephone: 610-527-4000
Fax: 610-527-5919

MEMBERS OF FIRM

John G. Shea
Phyllis McCormick Shea
Michael S. Dinney

Reference: The Bryn Mawr Trust Co., Bryn Mawr, Pennsylvania.

For full biographical listings, see the Martindale-Hubbell Law Directory

*DOYLESTOWN,** Bucks Co.

GATHRIGHT AND LEONARD (AV)

Suite 102, Landmark Building, 105 Clinton Street, 18901
Telephone: 215-340-7900
Fax: 215-340-9307

MEMBERS OF FIRM

Howard T. Gathright
Nicholas A. Leonard

LEGAL SUPPORT PERSONNEL

Lynn A. Leonard (Paralegal)

Reference: Bank & Trust Company of Old York Road.

For full biographical listings, see the Martindale-Hubbell Law Directory

*EASTON,** Northampton Co.

HERSTER, NEWTON & MURPHY (AV)

127 North Fourth Street, P.O. Box 1087, 18042
Telephone: 610-258-6219

MEMBERS OF FIRM

Andrew L. Herster, Jr.
Henry R. Newton
William K. Murphy

General Counsel For: Valley Federal Savings & Loan Assn.; Lafayette Bank; Easton Printing Co.; Northampton Community College; Eisenhardt Mills, Inc.; Delaware Wood Products, Inc.; Panuccio Construction, Inc.
References: Merchants Bank, N.A.; Lafayette Bank; Valley Federal Savings and Loan.

*GREENSBURG,** Westmoreland Co.

WALTHOUR AND GARLAND (AV)

Park Building, 121 North Main Street, 15601
Telephone: 412-834-4900

MEMBERS OF FIRM

Christ. C. Walthour, Jr.
Robert Wm. Garland
Holly G. Garland

Representative Clients: Peoples National Gas Co.; Baltimore & Ohio Railroad; Old Guard Insurance Company; Manor National Bank.
References: Manor National Bank; Southwest National Bank of Pennsylvania.

For full biographical listings, see the Martindale-Hubbell Law Directory

*HARRISBURG,** Dauphin Co.

BUCHANAN INGERSOLL, PROFESSIONAL CORPORATION (AV)

Vartan Parc, 30 North Third Street, 17101
Telephone: 717-237-4800
Telecopier: 717-233-0852
Pittsburgh, Pennsylvania Office: 5800 USX Tower, 600 Grant Street.
Telephone: 412-562-8800.
Philadelphia, Pennsylvania Office: Two Logan Square, Twelfth Floor, 18th & Arch Streets.
Telephone: 215-665-8700.
Tampa, Florida Office: 101 East Kennedy Boulevard, Suite 1030.
Telephone: 813-222-8180.
North Miami Beach, Florida Office: 19495 Biscayne Boulevard.
Telephone: 305-933-5600.
Lexington, Kentucky Office: 1210 Vine Center Office Tower, 333 West Vine Street.
Telephone: 606-225-5333.
Princeton, New Jersey Office: Buchanan Ingersoll, A Partnership, College Centre, 500 College Road East.
Telephone: 609-452-2666.

Bradley J. Gunnison — Gerald K. Morrison

COUNSEL

Evelyn S. Harris

For Complete List of Firm Personnel, See General Section

For full biographical listings, see the Martindale-Hubbell Law Directory

GOLDBERG, KATZMAN & SHIPMAN, P.C. (AV)

320 Market Street - Strawberry Square, P.O. Box 1268, 17108-1268
Telephone: 717-234-4161
Telecopier: 717-234-6808; 717-234-6810

Ronald M. Katzman — Neil Hendershot

Arnold B. Kogan

Reference: Fulton Bank.

For Complete List of Firm Personnel, See General Section

For full biographical listings, see the Martindale-Hubbell Law Directory

HEPFORD, SWARTZ & MORGAN (AV)

111 North Front Street, P.O. Box 889, 17108-0889
Telephone: 717-234-4121
Fax: 717-232-6802
Lewistown, Pennsylvania Office: 12 South Main Street, P.O. Box 867.
Telephone: 717-248-3913.

MEMBERS OF FIRM

H. Joseph Hepford — Sandra L. Meilton
Lee C. Swartz — Stephen M. Greecher, Jr.
James G. Morgan, Jr. — Dennis R. Sheaffer

COUNSEL

Stanley H. Siegel (Resident, Lewistown Office)

ASSOCIATES

Richard A. Estacio — Michael H. Park
Andrew K. Stutzman

For full biographical listings, see the Martindale-Hubbell Law Directory

MCNEES, WALLACE & NURICK (AV)

100 Pine Street, P.O. Box 1166, 17108
Telephone: 717-232-8000
Fax: 717-237-5300

MEMBERS OF FIRM

Richard R. Lefever — David M. Watts, Jr.
Richard W. Stevenson — Neal S. West

ASSOCIATES

Peter F. Kriete — Sharon R. Paxton
Chuong H. Pham

For Complete List of Firm Personnel, See General Section

For full biographical listings, see the Martindale-Hubbell Law Directory

METZGER, WICKERSHAM, KNAUSS & ERB (AV)

Mellon Bank Building, 111 Market Street, P.O. Box 93, 17108-0093
Telephone: 717-238-8187
Telefax: 717-234-9478
Other Harrisburg, Pennsylvania Office: 4813 Jonestown Road, P.O. Box 93, 17108.
Telephone: 717-652-7020.

(See Next Column)

MEMBERS OF FIRM

Maurice R. Metzger (1918-1980) — Robert E. Yetter
F. Brewster Wickersham (1918-1974) — James F. Carl
Robert P. Reed
Edward E. Knauss, III (Retired) — Edward E. Knauss, IV
Christian S. Erb, Jr. — Jered L. Hock
Karl R. Hildabrand

ASSOCIATES

Richard B. Druby — Steven P. Miner
Clark DeVere

Representative Clients: Allstate Insurance Co.; Chubb Group of Insurance Companies; Fireman's Fund American Insurance Group; Liberty Mutual Insurance Co.; Continental Insurance Co.; Crum & Forster.

For full biographical listings, see the Martindale-Hubbell Law Directory

NAUMAN, SMITH, SHISSLER & HALL (AV)

Eighteenth Floor, 200 North Third Street, P.O. Box 840, 17108-0840
Telephone: 717-236-3010
Telefax: 717-234-1925

MEMBERS OF FIRM

David C. Eaton — John C. Sullivan
Spencer G. Nauman, Jr. — J. Stephen Feinour
Craig J. Staudenmaier

ASSOCIATES

Benjamin Charles Dunlap, Jr. — Stephen J. Keene

OF COUNSEL

Ralph W. Boyles, Jr.

Representative Clients: The W.O. Hickok Mfg. Co.; Mellon Bank, N.A.; PNC Bank, N.A.; Enders Insurance Associates; Patriot-News Co.; The Greater Harrisburg Foundation; GHF, Inc.; Commonwealth Community Foundations (PA).

For full biographical listings, see the Martindale-Hubbell Law Directory

HAVERFORD, Montgomery & Delaware Cos.

BENJAMIN S. OHRENSTEIN (AV)

354 West Lancaster Avenue, Suite 212, 19041
Telephone: 610-649-1268; 215-473-6900
Fax: 610-642-6553

For full biographical listings, see the Martindale-Hubbell Law Directory

LANSDALE, Montgomery Co.

PEARLSTINE/SALKIN ASSOCIATES (AV)

1250 South Broad Street Suite 1000, P.O. Box 431, 19446
Telephone: 215-699-6000
Fax: 215-699-0231

MEMBERS OF FIRM

Philip Salkin — F. Craig La Rocca
Ronald E. Robinson — Jeffrey T. Sultanik
Barry Cooperberg — Neal R. Pearlstine
Frederick C. Horn — Wendy G. Rothstein
Marc B. Davis — Alan L. Eisen
William R. Wanger — Glenn D. Fox

Wilhelm L. Gruszecki — James R. Hall
Brian E. Subers — Michael S. Paul
Mark S. Cappuccio — David J. Draganosky
Lawrence P. Kempner

For full biographical listings, see the Martindale-Hubbell Law Directory

RUBIN, GLICKMAN AND STEINBERG, A PROFESSIONAL CORPORATION (AV)

2605 North Broad Street, P.O. Box 1277, 19446
Telephone: 215-822-7575; 855-5500; 800-358-9367
Facsimile: 215-822-1713

Irwin S. Rubin — Gregory R. Gifford
Jay C. Glickman — Amy S. Newman
Marc Robert Steinberg — Lewis Goodman
Toby Lynn Dickman — Kathleen M. O'Brien
Steven M. Koloski

Reference: Union National Bank and Trust Company of Souderton.

For full biographical listings, see the Martindale-Hubbell Law Directory

*MEDIA,** Delaware Co.

BEATTY, YOUNG, OTIS & LINCKE (AV)

300 West State Street, Suite 200, P.O. Box 901, 19063-0901
Telephone: 610-565-8800
Fax: 610-565-8127

MEMBERS OF FIRM

Lewis B. Beatty, Jr. — David J. Otis
William P. Lincke

(See Next Column)

BEATTY, YOUNG, OTIS & LINCKE, *Media—Continued*

ASSOCIATES

Natalie M. Habert
Carol E. Tucci
Peter W. Dicce
Katherine J. Dickinson (Not admitted in PA)

OF COUNSEL

Robert C. Grasberger
Joseph R. Young (1921-1993)

Representative Clients: Suburban Federal Savings Bank; Elwyn Inc.; Delaware County School Employees Health and Welfare Trust.

For full biographical listings, see the Martindale-Hubbell Law Directory

FRONEFIELD AND DE FURIA (AV)

107 West Third Street, P.O. Box 647, 19063
Telephone: 610-565-3100
Fax: 610-565-2349

MEMBERS OF FIRM

Frank I. Ginsburg
John R. Larkin
Rosemary C. McMunigal
J. Joseph Herring, Jr.
F. Martin Duus
Bruce A. Irvine
Charles F. Knapp
Leo A. Hackett
Francis T. Sbandi

ASSOCIATES

David C. Corujo
Jane E. Mcnerney
Donna Lynn Coyne

OF COUNSEL

Albert E. Holl, Jr.

For full biographical listings, see the Martindale-Hubbell Law Directory

KASSAB ARCHBOLD JACKSON & O'BRIEN (AV)

Lawyers-Title Building, 214 North Jackson Street, P.O. Box 626, 19063
Telephone: 610-565-3800
Telecopier: 610-892-6888
Wilmington, Delaware Office: 1326 King Street.
Telephone: 302-656-3393.
Fax: 302-656-1993.
Wildwood, New Jersey Office: 5201 New Jersey Avenue.
Telephone: 609-522-6559.

MEMBERS OF FIRM

Edward Kassab
Joseph Patrick O'Brien
William C. Archbold, Jr.
Richard A. Stanko
Robert James Jackson
Roy T. J. Stegena

OF COUNSEL

Matthew J. Ryan
John W. Nilon, Jr.

ASSOCIATES

Kevin William Gibson
George C. McFarland, Jr.
Cynthia Kassab Larosa
Jill E. Aversa
Marc S. Stein
Pamela A. La Torre
Terrance A. Kline
Kenneth D. Kynett

Representative Clients furnished upon request.

For full biographical listings, see the Martindale-Hubbell Law Directory

*NORRISTOWN,** Montgomery Co.

DONALD F. COPELAND (AV)

One Meeting House Place, 19401
Telephone: 610-279-3700
Fax: 610-272-2242

For full biographical listings, see the Martindale-Hubbell Law Directory

MANNING, KINKEAD, BROOKS & BRADBURY, A PROFESSIONAL CORPORATION (AV)

412 DeKalb Street, 19404-0231
Telephone: 610-279-1800
Fax: 610-279-8682

Franklin L. Wright (1880-1965)
William H. Kinkead, III
William Perry Manning, Jr.
William H. Bradbury, III

Cheri D. Andrews

Counsel for: The Philadelphia National Bank; John Deere Co.; The Rouse Co.; Consolidated Rail Corp.; Bethlehem Steel Co.; Royal Globe Insurance Co.; Nationwide Mutual Insurance Co.

For full biographical listings, see the Martindale-Hubbell Law Directory

*PHILADELPHIA,** Philadelphia Co.

ASTOR WEISS KAPLAN & ROSENBLUM (AV)

The Bellevue, 6th Floor, Broad Street at Walnut, 19102
Telephone: 215-790-0100
Fax: 215-790-0509
Bala Cynwyd, Pennsylvania Office: Suite 100, Three Bala Plaza West, P.O. Box 1665.
Telephone: 610-667-8660.
Fax: 610-667-2783.
Cherry Hill, New Jersey Office: Woodland Falls Corporate Park, 210 Lake Drive East, Suite 201.
Telephone: 609-795-1113.
Fax: 609-795-7413.

MEMBERS OF FIRM

Paul C. Astor
David S. Mandel
Alvin M. Weiss (1936-1976)
David Gutin (Resident at Bala Cynwyd Office)
G. David Rosenblum
Arthur H. Kaplan
Joseph B. Finlay, Jr.
Barbara Oaks Silver
Howard K. Goldstein
Richard H. Martin
Steven W. Smith
Allen B. Dubroff
Gerald J. Schorr
David S. Workman
Jean M. Biesecker (Resident, Bala Cynwyd Office)

ASSOCIATES

Carol L. Vassallo
Marc S. Zamsky
Thomas J. Maiorino
Janet G. Felgoise (Resident, Bala Cynwyd Office)
John R. Poeta
Bradley J. Begelman
Jacqueline G. Segal (Resident, Bala Cynwyd Office)
Andrew S. Kessler

SPECIAL COUNSEL

Neil Hurowitz (Resident, Bala Cynwyd Office)

OF COUNSEL

Erwin L. Pincus
Edward W. Silver
Lloyd Zane Remick

For full biographical listings, see the Martindale-Hubbell Law Directory

BALLARD SPAHR ANDREWS & INGERSOLL (AV)

1735 Market Street, 51st Floor, 19103-7599
Telephone: 215-665-8500
Fax: 215-864-8999
Denver, Colorado Office: Seventeenth Street Plaza Building, Suite 2300, 1225 17th Street.
Telephone: 303-292-2400.
Fax: 303-296-3956.
Kaunas, Lithuania Office: Donelaicio g., 71-2, Kaunas 3000.
Telephone: (370-7) 20 56 66.
Fax: (370-7) 20 56 91.
Salt Lake City, Utah Office: One Utah Center, Suite 1200, 201 South Main Street.
Telephone: 801-531-3000.
Fax: 801-531-3001.
Washington, D.C. Office: Suite 900 East, 555 13th Street, N.W.
Telephone: 202-383-8800.
Fax: 202-383-8877; 383-8893.
Baltimore, Maryland Office: 300 East Lombard Street. 19th Floor.
Telephone: 410-528-5600.
Fax: 410-528-5650.
Camden, New Jersey Office: 800 Hudson Square, 5th Floor.
Telephone: 609-541-5577.
Fax: 609-541-8272.

Bruce L. Castor
Mary G. Lawler
Benjamin R. Neilson
Regina O'Brien Thomas

COUNSEL

Marilyn C. Sanborne

Ann T. Loftus
James F. Mannion

For Complete List of Firm Personnel, See General Section

For full biographical listings, see the Martindale-Hubbell Law Directory

LESLIE J. CARSON, JR. (AV)

42 South 15th Street, Suite 1150, 19102
Telephone: 215-568-1980
Fax: 215-568-6882

For full biographical listings, see the Martindale-Hubbell Law Directory

D'ANGELO AND EURELL (AV)

Twenty-Second Floor, Land Title Building, 19110
Telephone: 215-564-5022
Fax: 215-557-7651

(See Next Column)

D'ANGELO AND EURELL—*Continued*

MEMBERS OF FIRM

George A. D'Angelo
John B. Eurell
David S. D'Angelo

For full biographical listings, see the Martindale-Hubbell Law Directory

RICHARD H. KNOX (AV)

2226 Land Title Building, 19110
Telephone: 215-563-4613
Fax: 215-557-7651

For full biographical listings, see the Martindale-Hubbell Law Directory

JAMES M. ORMAN (AV)

3000 Mellon Bank Center, 1735 Market Street, 19103
Telephone: 215-575-7630
Fax: 215-575-7640
(Also Of Counsel to Marjory Stone, Wilmington, Delaware and Marion, Satzberg, Trichon & Kogan, P.C.)

For full biographical listings, see the Martindale-Hubbell Law Directory

STRONG, STEVENS, BRISCOE & HAMILTON, P.C. (AV)

4000 Bell Atlantic Tower, 1717 Arch Street, 19103
Telephone: 215-563-5900
Fax: 215-563-2982
Blue Bell, Pennsylvania Office: 640 Sentry Parkway, First Floor.
Telephone: 215-832-5900.
Fax: 215-832-5914.

George V. Strong, Jr.
Richard K. Stevens, Jr.
James H. Stevens
Jack C. Briscoe
Jeffrey F. Janoski
Emory A. Wyant, Jr.
Thomas R. Kellogg
Ronald W. Fenstermacher, Jr.
Ralf W. Greenwood, Jr.
Mary K. Lemmon

COUNSEL

Samuel L. Sagendorph

For full biographical listings, see the Martindale-Hubbell Law Directory

GERALD S. SUSMAN & ASSOCIATES, P.C. (AV)

Suite 432 Benjamin Franklin Business Center, 834 Chestnut Street, 19107
Telephone: 215-440-7500
Fax: 215-440-0188
Cable: Taxlaw
Boca Raton, Florida Office: 1200 N. Federal Highway.
Telephone: 407-368-1888.
West Palm Beach, Florida Office: 1800 S. Australian Boulevard, Suite 205.

Gerald S. Susman

Richard J. Cohen

For full biographical listings, see the Martindale-Hubbell Law Directory

MERVIN M. WILF, LTD. (AV)

3200 Mellon Bank Center, 1735 Market Street, 19103
Telephone: 215-575-7650; 568-4842
Facsimile: 215-575-7652
Boston, Massachusetts Office: 300 Commonwealth Avenue, 02115.
Telephone: 617-437-7981.

Mervin M. Wilf

A list of Representative Clients and References will be furnished upon request.

For full biographical listings, see the Martindale-Hubbell Law Directory

*PITTSBURGH,** Allegheny Co.

ADERSON, FRANK & STEINER, A PROFESSIONAL CORPORATION (AV)

2320 Grant Building, 15219
Telephone: 412-263-0500
Fax: 412-263-0565

Sanford M. Aderson
Edward A. Witt
Nancy L. Rackoff
Bruce F. Rudoy

For full biographical listings, see the Martindale-Hubbell Law Directory

BUCHANAN INGERSOLL, PROFESSIONAL CORPORATION (AV)

5800 USX Tower, 600 Grant Street, 15219
Telephone: 412-562-8800
Telecopier: 412-562-1041
Philadelphia, Pennsylvania Office: Two Logan Square, Twelfth Floor, 18th & Arch Streets.
Telephone: 215-665-8700.
Harrisburg, Pennsylvania Office: Vartan Parc, 30 North Third Street.
Telephone: 717-237-4800.

(See Next Column)

Tampa, Florida Office: 101 East Kennedy Boulevard, Suite 1030.
Telephone: 813-222-8180.
North Miami Beach, Florida Office: 19495 Biscayne Boulevard.
Telephone: 305-933-5600.
Lexington, Kentucky Office: 1210 Vine Center Office Tower, 333 West Vine Street.
Telephone: 606-225-5333.
Princeton, New Jersey Office: Buchanan Ingersoll, A Partnership, College Centre, 500 College Road East.
Telephone: 609-452-2666.

R. Michael Daniel
Christopher F. Farrell
Robert Y. Kopf, Jr.
Lawrence J. Kuremsky
Francis A. Muracca, II
K. Sidney Neuman
Larry E. Phillips
Jonathan M. Schmerling

R. Douglas DeNardo
Samuel J. Goncz

OF COUNSEL

Jack G. Armstrong

For Complete List of Firm Personnel, See General Section

For full biographical listings, see the Martindale-Hubbell Law Directory

DICKIE, MCCAMEY & CHILCOTE, A PROFESSIONAL CORPORATION (AV)

Suite 400, Two PPG Place, 15222-5402
Telephone: 412-281-7272
Fax: 412-392-5367
Wheeling, West Virginia Office: Suite 2002, 1233 Main Street, 26003-2839.
Telephone: 304-233-1022.
Facsimile: 304-233-1026.

Thomas P. Lutz
William Campbell Ries

Jean McCree Simmonds
John C. Carlos

For Complete List of Firm Personnel, See General Section

For full biographical listings, see the Martindale-Hubbell Law Directory

FECZKO AND SEYMOUR (AV)

520 Grant Building, 15219
Telephone: 412-261-4970
Fax: Available upon Request
Bethel Park, Pennsylvania Office: 3400 South Park Road.
Telephone: 412-833-5554.

MEMBERS OF FIRM

Albert G. Feczko, Jr.
Michael J. Seymour

ASSOCIATES

Mark F. Bennett
Michael D. Seymour

Reference: Pittsburgh National Bank.

For full biographical listings, see the Martindale-Hubbell Law Directory

HOUSTON, HOUSTON & DONNELLY (AV)

2510 Centre City Tower, 650 Smithfield Street, 15222
Telephone: 412-471-5828
FAX: 412-471-0736

MEMBERS OF FIRM

William McC. Houston
Fred Chalmers Houston, Jr.
John F. Meck

ASSOCIATES

Mario Santilli, Jr.
Theodore M. Hammer

Representative Clients: Federated Investors; Federated Investors Group of Mutual Funds; Iron City Sash & Door Co.; The Park Mansions; A. Stucki Co.; Sewickley Valley Hospital Authority.

For Complete List of Firm Personnel, See General Section

For full biographical listings, see the Martindale-Hubbell Law Directory

MARCUS & SHAPIRA (AV)

35th Floor, One Oxford Centre, 301 Grant Street, 15219-6401
Telephone: 412-471-3490
Telecopier: 412-391-8758

MEMBERS OF FIRM

Bernard D. Marcus
Daniel H. Shapira
George P. Slesinger
Robert L. Allman, II
Estelle F. Comay
Susan Gromis Flynn
Darlene M. Nowak
Glenn M. Olcerst
Elly Heller-Toig
Sylvester A. Beozzo

OF COUNSEL

John M. Burkoff

SPECIAL COUNSEL

Jane Campbell Moriarty

(See Next Column)

MARCUS & SHAPIRA, *Pittsburgh—Continued*

ASSOCIATES

Scott D. Livingston
Robert M. Barnes
Stephen S. Zubrow
David B. Rodes
Lori E. McMaster
Melody A. Pollock
James F. Rosenberg
Amy M. Gottlieb

For full biographical listings, see the Martindale-Hubbell Law Directory

McCANN, GARLAND, RIDALL & BURKE (AV)

Suite 4000, 309 Smithfield Street, 15222
Telephone: 412-566-1818
Fax: 412-566-1817

MEMBERS OF FIRM

Edmund W. Ridall, Jr.
Edward C. Wachter, Jr.

ASSOCIATE

Thea G. Evankovich

For Complete List of Firm Personnel, See General Section

For full biographical listings, see the Martindale-Hubbell Law Directory

SCOTT, VOGRIN, RIESTER & JAMIOLKOWSKI, A PROFESSIONAL CORPORATION (AV)

1510 Frick Building, 15219
Telephone: 412-261-0905
Fax: 412-261-3090
Shaler Township, Pennsylvania Office: 1330 Evergreen Avenue, Pittsburgh, 15209.
Telephone: 412-261-0905.
Sewickley, Pennsylvania Office: Osborne Plaza, Suite 603, 1106 Ohio River Boulevard, 15143.
Telephone: 412-261-0905.

Richard S. Scott

For full biographical listings, see the Martindale-Hubbell Law Directory

TENER, VAN KIRK, WOLF & MOORE (AV)

407 Oliver Building, 15222-2368
Telephone: 412-281-5580

MEMBERS OF FIRM

Alexander C. Tener (1888-1965)
J. R. Van Kirk (1890-1966)
William R. Balph (1908-1979)
Lester K. Wolf
Martin L. Moore, Jr.
Robert B. Shust
Robert B. Wolf
Timothy F. Burke, Jr.
Thomas J. Kessinger

Reference: Pittsburgh National Bank.

For full biographical listings, see the Martindale-Hubbell Law Directory

THORP, REED & ARMSTRONG (AV)

One Riverfront Center, 15222
Telephone: 412-394-7711
Fax: 412-394-2555

MEMBERS OF FIRM

John W. Eichleay, Jr.
James K. Goldberg
Keith H. West

For Complete List of Firm Personnel, See General Section

For full biographical listings, see the Martindale-Hubbell Law Directory

TUCKER ARENSBERG, P.C. (AV)

1500 One PPG Place, 15222
Telephone: 412-566-1212
Telex: 902914
Fax: 412-594-5619
Harrisburg, Pennsylvania Office: 116 Pine Street.
Telephone: 717-238-2007.
Fax: 717-238-2242.
Pittsburgh Airport Area Office: Airport Professional Office Center, 1150 Thorn Run Road Ext., Moon Township, Pennsylvania, 15108.
Telephone: 412-262-3730.
Fax: 412-262-2576.

Charles F. C. Arensberg (1879-1974)
Frank R. S. Kaplan (1886-1957)
Donald L. Very (1933-1979)
Linda A. Acheson
W. Theodore Brooks
Matthew J. Carl
Richard W. Cramer
J. Kent Culley
Donald P. Eriksen
Paul F. Fagan
Gary J. Gushard
William T. Harvey
Joel M. Helmrich
Gary P. Hunt
Raymond M. Komichak
Jeffrey J. Leech
Beverly Weiss Manne
Garland H. McAdoo, Jr.
John M. McElroy
Robert L. McTiernan
John B. Montgomery
Stanley V. Ostrow
William A. Penrod
Daniel J. Perry
Henry S. Pool

(See Next Column)

Richard B. Tucker, III
Bradley S. Tupi
Charles J. Vater
Gary E. Wieczorek
G. Ashley Woolridge

Donald E. Ambrose
Robin K. Capozzi
Diane Hernon Chavis
Toni L. DiGiacobbe
Donna M. Donaher
John E. Graf
Mark L. Heleen
David P. Hvizdos
Timothy S. Johnson
Joni L. Landy
Jonathan S. McAnney
G. Ross Rhodes
Christopher J. Richardson
Eric M. Schumann
Steven H. Seel
Steven B. Silverman
Michael J. Tobak, III
Homer L. Walton

HARRISBURG OFFICE

J. Kent Culley

John G. Di Leonardo

SPECIAL COUNSEL

Richard S. Crone
Elliott W. Finkel
Michael J. Laffey
John P. Papuga
William J. Staley
Richard B. Tucker, Jr.

For full biographical listings, see the Martindale-Hubbell Law Directory

WELLER, WICKS & WALLACE, PROFESSIONAL CORPORATION (AV)

1800 Benedum-Trees Building, 15222
Telephone: 412-471-1751
Fax: 412-471-8117

John S. Weller (1866-1944)
John O. Wicks (1880-1947)
C. L. Wallace (1885-1953)
Henry A. Bergstrom (1911-1993)
J. Murray Egan
Donald W. Shaffer
Henry A. Bergstrom, Jr.
Thomas A. Woodward

Reference: Pittsburgh National Bank.

For full biographical listings, see the Martindale-Hubbell Law Directory

WITTLIN GOLDSTON & CAPUTO, P.C. (AV)

213 Smithfield Street, Suite 200, 15222
Telephone: 412-261-4200
Telecopier: 412-261-9137

Charles E. Wittlin
Linda Leebov Goldston
John H. Iannucci
Sharon W. Perelman

For Complete List of Firm Personnel, See General Section

For full biographical listings, see the Martindale-Hubbell Law Directory

*READING,** Berks Co.

MOGEL, SPEIDEL, BOBB & KERSHNER, A PROFESSIONAL CORPORATION (AV)

520 Walnut Street, P.O. Box 8581, 19603-8581
Telephone: 610-376-1515
Telecopier: 610-372-8710

George B. Balmer (1902-1969)
George A. Kershner (1907-1969)
Carl F. Mogel (1919-1994)
Donald K. Bobb
Edwin H. Kershner
Frederick R. Mogel
Samuel R. Fry II
Kathleen A. B. Kovach
Michael L. Mixell
George M. Lutz
Stephen H. Price
Kathryn K. Harenza

OF COUNSEL

Harry W. Speidel
Henry A. Gass

Representative Clients: Great Valley Savings Bank; Clover Farms Dairy Co.; National Penn Bank; Meridian Leasing, Inc.; Ducharme, McMillen & Associates; Edwards Business Machines, Inc.; Greater Berks Development Fund; Union Township, Berks County, Pennsylvania.

For full biographical listings, see the Martindale-Hubbell Law Directory

ROSEMONT, Montgomery & Delaware Cos.

JACK ARTHUR KIRBY (AV)

1516 County Line Road, 19010
Telephone: 610-527-1366

For full biographical listings, see the Martindale-Hubbell Law Directory

SELINSGROVE, Snyder Co.

MOORE & CRAVITZ (AV)

719 North Market Street, 17870
Telephone: 717-374-8138
FAX: 717-374-7558

MEMBERS OF FIRM

John R. Moore
Robert M. Cravitz

(See Next Column)

MOORE & CRAVITZ—*Continued*

ASSOCIATE

Jonathan A. Moore

For full biographical listings, see the Martindale-Hubbell Law Directory

*STROUDSBURG,** Monroe Co.

HANNA, YOUNG, UPRIGHT & PAZUHANICH (AV)

800 Main Street, 18360
Telephone: 717-424-9400; 646-2486
Fax: 717-424-9426

MEMBERS OF FIRM

Jerry F. Hanna
Kirby G. Upright
Alan Price Young
Mark P. Pazuhanich

ASSOCIATES

Janet K. Catina
Thomas V. Casale
Nicholas Joseph Masington, III
Ann Marie T. Nasek

For full biographical listings, see the Martindale-Hubbell Law Directory

SWARTHMORE, Delaware Co.

ROBERT A. DETWEILER (AV)

11 Amherst Avenue, 19081
Telephone: 610-328-9900; 328-9901

Representative Clients: State Farm Insurance Cos.; Westinghouse Electric Corp.
Reference: Meridian Bank.

*WASHINGTON,** Washington Co.

GREENLEE, DERRICO, POSA & RODGERS (AV)

325 Washington Trust Building, 15301
Telephone: 412-225-7660; Pittsburgh: 412-344-9400
Fax: 412-228-1704

MEMBERS OF FIRM

Patrick C. Derrico
Paul P. Posa
John Allan Rodgers

For full biographical listings, see the Martindale-Hubbell Law Directory

PEACOCK, KELLER, YOHE, DAY & ECKER (AV)

East Beau Building, 70 East Beau Street, 15301
Telephone: 412-222-4520
Telefax: 412-222-3318 ABA/NET ABA 34517
Waynesburg, Pennsylvania Office: 102 East High Street.
Telephone: 412-627-8331.
Telefax: 412-627-8025.

MEMBERS OF FIRM

Kenneth L. Baker
Richard J. Amrhein

SENIOR COUNSEL

Davis G. Yohe

Representative Clients: Consolidation Coal Co.; Monongahela Valley Hospital, Inc.; Nationwide Insurance Co.; Family Health Council, Inc.; Cal-Ed Federal Credit Union; Marianna & Scenery Hill Telephone Co.; Maternal & Family Health Services, Inc.; Pennsylvania Hospital Insurance Company.

For Complete List of Firm Personnel, See General Section

For full biographical listings, see the Martindale-Hubbell Law Directory

*WELLSBORO,** Tioga Co.

COX, COX & STOKES, P.C. (AV)

19 Central Avenue, 16901
Telephone: 717-724-1444
Telecopier: 717-724-6633
Westfield, Pennsylvania Office: 144 Church Street.
Telephone: 814-376-2203.

Robert F. Cox, Sr.
Robert F. Cox, Jr.
William R. Stokes, II

Annette Doleski Maza

Reference: Commonwealth Bank

OWLETT, LEWIS & GINN, P.C. (AV)

One Charles Street, P.O. Box 878, 16901
Telephone: 717-723-1000
Fax: 717-724-6822
Elkland, Pennsylvania Office: 102 East Main Street.
Telephone: 814-258-5148.
Knoxville, Pennsylvania Office: 106 East Main Street.
Telephone: 814-326-4161.

(See Next Column)

Edwin A. Glover
Edward H. Owlett, III
Edward H. Owlett
Raymond E. Ginn, Jr.
Thomas M. Owlett

Bruce L. Vickery
Judith DeMeester Nichols

OF COUNSEL

John Dean Lewis

Reference: Citizens and Northern Bank.

For full biographical listings, see the Martindale-Hubbell Law Directory

*WEST CHESTER,** Chester Co.

JOHN E. GOOD (AV)

331 West Miner Street, 19382
Telephone: 610-436-6565

Reference: First National Bank of West Chester.

For full biographical listings, see the Martindale-Hubbell Law Directory

LAMB, WINDLE & MCERLANE, P.C. (AV)

24 East Market Street, P.O. Box 565, 19381-0565
Telephone: 610-430-8000
Telecopier: 610-692-0877

COUNSEL

Theodore O. Rogers

William H. Lamb
John D. Snyder
Susan Windle Rogers
William P. Mahon
James E. McErlane
Guy A. Donatelli
E. Craig Kalemjian
Vincent M. Pompo
James C. Sargent, Jr.
James J. McEntee III

Tracy Blake DeVlieger
Daniel A. Loewenstern
P. Andrew Schaum
Thomas F. Oeste
Lawrence J. Persick
John W. Pauciulo
Thomas K. Schindler
Andrea B. Pettine
John J. Cunningham

Representative Clients: Chester County; First Financial Savings Bank, PaSA; Bank of Chester County; Jefferson Bank; Downingtown Area and Great Valley School Districts; Philadelphia Electric Company; Central and Western Chester County Industrial Development Authority; Valley Forge Sewer Authority; Manito Title Insurance Company.

For full biographical listings, see the Martindale-Hubbell Law Directory

ROBERT S. SUPPLEE, P.C. (AV)

Washington Building, Suite A, 109 East Evans Street, 19380
Telephone: 610-344-9560
Fax: 610-344-9829

Robert S. Supplee

For full biographical listings, see the Martindale-Hubbell Law Directory

*WILKES-BARRE,** Luzerne Co.

GALLAGHER, BRENNAN & GILL (AV)

220 Pierce Street, 18701-4641
Telephone: 717-288-8255
Telecopier: 717-288-7005

MEMBERS OF FIRM

Joseph F. Gallagher (1912-1989)
John J. Gill, Jr.
Thomas P. Brennan
Christine E. McLaughlin

OF COUNSEL

Cecilia Meighan

Approved Attorneys for: Commonwealth Land Title Insurance Co.
Representative Clients: PNC Bank, National Association; Mercy Hospital, Wilkes Barre, Pennsylvania; Guaranty Bank.

For full biographical listings, see the Martindale-Hubbell Law Directory

HOURIGAN, KLUGER, SPOHRER & QUINN, A PROFESSIONAL CORPORATION (AV)

700 Mellon Bank Center, 8 West Market Street, 18701-1867
Telephone: 717-825-9401
FAX: 717-829-3460
Scranton, Pennsylvania Office: Suite 200, 434 Lackawanna Avenue.
Telephone: 717-346-8414.
Allentown, Pennsylvania Office: Sovereign Building, 609 Hamilton Mall.
Telephone: 610-437-1584.
Hazelton, Pennsylvania Office: CAN DO Building, One South Church Street.
Telephone: 717-455-5141.

(See Next Column)

HOURIGAN, KLUGER, SPOHRER & QUINN A PROFESSIONAL CORPORATION, *Wilkes-Barre—Continued*

Allan M. Kluger
Richard M. Goldberg
Richard S. Bishop (Resident, Scranton Office)
Terrence J. Herron (Resident, Hazelton Office)
Joseph E. Kluger
Christina A. Morrison

Representative Client: Aetna Casualty & Surety Co.

For Complete List of Firm Personnel, See General Section

For full biographical listings, see the Martindale-Hubbell Law Directory

ROSENN, JENKINS & GREENWALD (AV)

15 South Franklin Street, 18711-0075
Telephone: 717-826-5600
Fax: 717-826-5640

MEMBERS OF FIRM

Harry R. Hiscox
Murray Ufberg
Alan S. Hollander
David B. Hiscox
Gerard M. Musto, Jr.

ASSOCIATE

Carolyn Carr Rhoden

Representative Clients: Allstate Insurance Co.; C-TEC Corporation; Chicago Title Insurance Co.; Franklin First Savings Bank; The Geisinger Medical Center; Guard Insurance Group; The Mays Department Stores Company; Student LoanMarketing Association (Sallie Mae); Subaru of America, Inc.

For Complete List of Firm Personnel, See General Section

For full biographical listings, see the Martindale-Hubbell Law Directory

*WILLIAMSPORT,** Lycoming Co.

CANDOR, YOUNGMAN, GIBSON AND GAULT (AV)

25 West Third Street, 8th Floor, 17701
Telephone: 717-322-6144
Fax: 717-322-8935

John G. Candor (1879-1971)

OF COUNSEL

John C. Youngman
Harry R. Gibson
John C. Gault

MEMBER OF FIRM

John C. Youngman, Jr.

Local Counsel for: Bell Telephone Co. of Pa.; Allstate; Gulf Insurance Co.; Hartford Life Insurance Co.; Household Finance; Motorist Insurance Co.; National Grange Insurance Co.; Northwestern Life Insurance; Metropolitan Life Insurance Co.; Security Mutual Life Insurance.

For full biographical listings, see the Martindale-Hubbell Law Directory

MURPHY, BUTTERFIELD, HOLLAND & PRICE, P.C. (AV)

442 William Street, 17701
Telephone: 717-326-6505
Fax: 717-326-0437

Bertram S. Murphy
Jonathan E. Butterfield
Fred A. Holland
George R. Price, Jr.

Reference: Commonwealth Bank.

For full biographical listings, see the Martindale-Hubbell Law Directory

RHODE ISLAND

CRANSTON, Providence Co.

TAFT & MCSALLY (AV)

21 Garden City Drive, P.O. Box 20130, 02920
Telephone: 401-946-3800
Fax: 401-943-8859

MEMBERS OF FIRM

James L. Taft (1901-1959)
Bernard F. McSally (1928-1978)
James L. Taft, Jr.

ASSOCIATES

Sarah Taft-Carter
John V. McGreen
Robert D. Murray
David H. Ferrara
Eleanor W. Taft

LEGAL SUPPORT PERSONNEL

Mary T. Rochford

Representative Clients: General Motors Corp.; General Motors Acceptance Corp.; Chrysler Credit Corp.; Providence Gas Co.; Fleet National Bank; Fleet Mortgage; Citizens Savings Bank; Rhode Island Hospital Trust National Bank; Town of Narragansett, Rhode Island (Bond Counsel); Brown Broadcasting Service, Inc.

(See Next Column)

For full biographical listings, see the Martindale-Hubbell Law Directory

*PROVIDENCE,** Providence Co.

HIGGINS & SLATTERY (AV)

Greater Providence Bank Building, 170 Westminster Street, Suite 1100, 02903
Telephone: 401-751-3600
Telecopier: 401-751-4648

MEMBERS OF FIRM

James A. Higgins (1902-1985)
John H. Slattery (1948-1962)
John A. Baglini
Robert J. Dumouchel
John A. McQueeney
Joseph W. Baglini

ASSOCIATE

Jessica L. Papazian-Ross

OF COUNSEL

Eugene V. Higgins

Representative Clients: General Accident Group; John Hancock Property & Casualty Insurance Co.; Prudential Property & Casualty Insurance Co.; Ryder Truck; USAA Rental,Inc.; Wausau Insurance Cos. .
Reference: Fleet National Bank.

For full biographical listings, see the Martindale-Hubbell Law Directory

LISA & SOUSA, LTD. (AV)

5 Benefit Street, 02904
Telephone: 401-274-0600
Fax: 401-421-6117

Carl B. Lisa
Louis A. Sousa

OF COUNSEL

Robert G. Branca, Jr.

References: Citizens Savings Bank; Fleet National Bank; Rhode Island Hospital Trust National Bank.

For full biographical listings, see the Martindale-Hubbell Law Directory

WESTERLY, Washington Co.

THORNTON, THORNTON & THOMSEN (AV)

43 Broad Street, P.O. Box 531, 02891-0531
Telephone: 401-596-4953
Telecopier: 401-596-6659

MEMBERS OF FIRM

William B. Thornton
Matthew H. Thomsen

ASSOCIATES

Marc J. Soss
Pasquale A. Cavaliere (Not admitted in RI)

COUNSEL

James D. Thornton
Chaplin B. Barnes

Approved Attorneys for: Lawyers Title Insurance Corporation of Richmond, Virginia.
Reference: The Washington Trust Co.

For full biographical listings, see the Martindale-Hubbell Law Directory

URSO, LIGUORI AND URSO (AV)

85 Beach Street, P.O. Box 1277, 02891
Telephone: 401-596-7751
Telecopier: 401-596-7963

MEMBERS OF FIRM

Natale Louis Urso
Thomas J. Liguori, Jr.
M. Linda Urso

General Counsel for: National Education Association Rhode Island; Westerly Broadcasting Co.
Approved Attorneys for: Lawyers Title Insurance Corporation of Richmond, Virginia.
Reference: Fleet National Bank.

For full biographical listings, see the Martindale-Hubbell Law Directory

SOUTH CAROLINA

*CHARLESTON,** Charleston Co.

EVANS, CARTER, KUNES & BENNETT, P.A. (AV)

151 Meeting Street, Suite 415, P.O. Box 369, 29402-0369
Telephone: 803-577-2300
Telefax: 803-577-2055

George C. Evans
T. Heyward Carter, Jr.
Robert M. Kunes
Edward G. R. Bennett

(See Next Column)

EVANS, CARTER, KUNES & BENNETT P.A.—*Continued*

Charlotte Nancie Quick

For full biographical listings, see the Martindale-Hubbell Law Directory

ROSEN, ROSEN & HAGOOD, P.A. (AV)

134 Meeting Street, Suite 200, P.O. Box 893, 29402
Telephone: 803-577-6726

Morris D. Rosen | Irvin G. Condon

Reference: NationsBank of South Carolina, N.A.

For Complete List of Firm Personnel, See General Section

For full biographical listings, see the Martindale-Hubbell Law Directory

*COLUMBIA,** Richland Co.

SHERRILL AND ROGERS, PC (AV)

1441 Main Street, 10th Floor, P.O. Box 100200, 29202-3200
Telephone: 803-771-7900
Fax: 803-254-6305

Franchelle Cole Millender | Albert L. Moses

W. Alex Weatherly, Jr.

For Complete List of Firm Personnel, See General Section

For full biographical listings, see the Martindale-Hubbell Law Directory

*GREENVILLE,** Greenville Co.

JAMES R. GILREATH, P.A. (AV)

110 Lavinia Avenue, P.O. Box 2147, 29602
Telephone: 803-242-4727
Telecopier: 803-232-4395

James R. Gilreath

Stephen G. Potts

For full biographical listings, see the Martindale-Hubbell Law Directory

HAYNSWORTH, MARION, MCKAY & GUÉRARD, L.L.P. (AV)

Two Insignia Financial Plaza, 75 Beattie Place, P.O. Box 2048, 29602
Telephone: 803-240-3200
Telecopier: 803-240-3300
Columbia, South Carolina Office: Suite 2400 A T & T Building, 1201 Main Street, P.O. Drawer 7157, 29202
Telephone: 803-765-1818.
Telecopier: 803-765-2399.
Charleston, South Carolina Office: #2 Prioleau Street, P.O. Box 1119, 29402.
Telephone: 803-722-7606.
Telecopier: 803-723-5263.

MEMBER OF FIRM
David L. McMurray
ASSOCIATE
Arthur Frazier McLean, III

For Complete List of Firm Personnel, See General Section

For full biographical listings, see the Martindale-Hubbell Law Directory

MERLINE & THOMAS, P.A. (AV)

665 North Academy Street, P.O. Box 10796, 29603
Telephone: 803-242-4080
Fax: 803-242-5758

David A. Merline | David A. Merline, Jr.
John R. Thomas | Keith G. Meacham

For full biographical listings, see the Martindale-Hubbell Law Directory

CHARLES M. STUART, JR. (AV)

Suite F 862 South Pleasantburg Drive, 29607
Telephone: 803-232-5411
FAX: 803-232-5179

For full biographical listings, see the Martindale-Hubbell Law Directory

WYCHE, BURGESS, FREEMAN & PARHAM, PROFESSIONAL ASSOCIATION (AV)

44 East Camperdown Way, P.O. Box 728, 29602-0728
Telephone: 803-242-8200
Telecopier: 803-235-8900

(See Next Column)

Cary H. Hall, Jr. | Lesley R. Moore

Counsel for: Multimedia, Inc.; Delta Woodside Industries, Inc.; Milliken & Company; Ryan's Family Steak Houses, Inc.; St. Francis Hospital; Span-America Medical Systems, Inc.; Carolina First Bank; KEMET Electronics Corp.; Builder Marts of America, Inc.; One Price Clothing, Inc.

For Complete List of Firm Personnel, See General Section

For full biographical listings, see the Martindale-Hubbell Law Directory

HILTON HEAD ISLAND, Beaufort Co.

BETHEA, JORDAN & GRIFFIN, P.A. (AV)

Suite 400, Shelter Cove Executive Park, 23-B Shelter Cove Lane, P.O. Drawer 3, 29938-5666
Telephone: 803-785-2171
Fax: 803-686-5991

William L. Bethea, Jr. | Joseph R. Barker
Michael L. M. Jordan | Stephen S. Bird
Cary S. Griffin | Marty D. Propst

Stephen E. Carter | William R. Phipps
Michael E. Cofield | David J. Tigges (Not admitted in SC)
Robert Deeb
Keith M. Parrella (Not admitted in SC)

OF COUNSEL

John C. West | John C. West, Jr. (P.A.)

For full biographical listings, see the Martindale-Hubbell Law Directory

RUTH & MACNEILLE, PROFESSIONAL ASSOCIATION (AV)

The Anchor Bank Building, 11 Pope Avenue, 29938
Telephone: 803-785-4251
Telex: 988944
Telecopier: 803-686-5404

William A. Ruth

References: NationsBank of South Carolina, N.A.; Anchor Bank; South Carolina National Bank; Chicago Title Insurance Corp.; First American Title Insurance Co.

For full biographical listings, see the Martindale-Hubbell Law Directory

SOUTH DAKOTA

*BELLE FOURCHE,** Butte Co.

BENNETT, MAIN & FREDERICKSON, A PROFESSIONAL CORPORATION (AV)

618 State Street, 57717-1489
Telephone: 605-892-2011
Fax: 605-892-4084

OF COUNSEL
Donn Bennett

Representative Clients: Royal Bank of Canada; Bank of Montreal; Security Pacific National Bank; Pioneer Bank and Trust; Norwest Bank South Dakota.

For Complete List of Firm Personnel, See General Section

For full biographical listings, see the Martindale-Hubbell Law Directory

*BROOKINGS,** Brookings Co.

LEWAYNE M. ERICKSON, P.C. (AV)

517 Sixth Street, 57006-1436
Telephone: 605-692-6158
Fax: 605-692-7734

Lewayne M. Erickson

For full biographical listings, see the Martindale-Hubbell Law Directory

*SIOUX FALLS,** Minnehaha Co.

JOHN L. WILDS (AV)

Third Floor, 300 North Dakota Avenue, 57102-0332
Telephone: 605-332-1822
Telecopier: 605-332-0340
Representative Clients: Metropolitan Federal Bank; Mid-Coastal Transportation; J & L Harley-Davidson; KSFY (ABC) TV; R & L Supply, Ltd.; Hillyard Floor Care Supply; Enviro Safe Air; UAW Legal Services; Super America Group, Inc.

For full biographical listings, see the Martindale-Hubbell Law Directory

TENNESSEE

*CHATTANOOGA,** Hamilton Co.

CHAMBLISS & BAHNER (AV)

1000 Tallan Building, Two Union Square, 37402-2500
Telephone: 615-756-3000
Fax: 615-265-9574

MEMBERS OF FIRM

Kirk Snouffer
Martin L. Pierce
Dana B. Perry

ASSOCIATES

George H. Suzich
Lori L. Smith

OF COUNSEL

Joe V. W. Gaston

For Complete List of Firm Personnel, See General Section

For full biographical listings, see the Martindale-Hubbell Law Directory

GEARHISER, PETERS & HORTON (AV)

320 McCallie Avenue, 37402-2007
Telephone: 615-756-5171
Fax: 615-266-1605

MEMBERS OF FIRM

Charles J. Gearhiser
R. Wayne Peters
William H. Horton
Roy C. Maddox, Jr.
Robert L. Lockaby, Jr.
Ralph E. Tallant, Jr.
Terry Atkin Cavett
Sam D. Elliott
Lane C. Avery
Michael A. Anderson
Wade K. Cannon

ASSOCIATE

Robin L. Miller

References: First Tennessee Bank; Pioneer Bank.

For full biographical listings, see the Martindale-Hubbell Law Directory

GRANT, KONVALINKA & HARRISON, PROFESSIONAL CORPORATION (AV)

Ninth Floor, Republic Centre, 633 Chestnut Street, 37450
Telephone: 615-756-8400
Fax: 615-756-6518

John R. Anderson
Mathew D. Brownfield
Harry R. Cash
J. Wayne Cropp
Pamela McNutt Fleenor
H. Wayne Grant
David E. Harrison
David Christopher Higney
John P. Konvalinka
Susan Kerr Lee
Carole Yard Lynch
Fredrick H. L. McClure
J. Scott McDearman
Tonya Kennedy McIntosh
Michael D. Randles
Thomas E. Smith
Donald W. Strickland
Rebekah Harris Whitaker

OF COUNSEL

Stephen R. Beckham
Maurice R. Bowen, Jr.

For full biographical listings, see the Martindale-Hubbell Law Directory

HUGH F. KENDALL, ATTORNEY, P.C. (AV)

Suite 305, Victorian Gardens, 6918 Shallowford Road, 37421-1783
Telephone: 615-499-9863
Telecopier: 615-894-0682

Hugh F. Kendall

For full biographical listings, see the Martindale-Hubbell Law Directory

SHUMACKER & THOMPSON (AV)

Suite 500, First Tennessee Building, 701 Market Street, 37402-4800
Telephone: 615-265-2214
Telecopier: 615-266-1842
Branch Office: Suite 103, One Park Place, 6148 Lee Highway, Chattanooga, Tennessee, 37421-2900.
Telephone: 615-855-1814.
Telecopier: 615-899-1278.

MEMBERS OF FIRM

Albert W. Secor
Alan L. Cates
Stanley W. Hildebrand

For Complete List of Firm Personnel, See General Section

For full biographical listings, see the Martindale-Hubbell Law Directory

SPEARS, MOORE, REBMAN & WILLIAMS (AV)

8th Floor Blue Cross Building, 801 Pine Street, 37402
Telephone: 615-756-7000
Facsimile: 615-756-4801

(See Next Column)

MEMBERS OF FIRM

William L. Taylor, Jr.
Randy Chennault
David E. Fowler

Counsel for: Pioneer Bank; Chattanooga Gas Co.; South Central Bell Telephone Co.; Tennessee-American Water Co.; Blue Cross and Blue Shield of Tennessee; State Farm Mutual Automobile Insurance Cos.; Nationwide Insurance Co.; Siskin Steel & Supply Co., Inc.; CSX Transportation, Inc.; The McCallie School; Mueller Co.

For Complete List of Firm Personnel, See General Section

For full biographical listings, see the Martindale-Hubbell Law Directory

STOPHEL & STOPHEL, P.C. (AV)

500 Tallan Building, Two Union Square, 37402-2571
Telephone: 615-756-2333
Fax: 615-266-5032

John C. Stophel
Glenn C. Stophel
Barton C. Burns
Wayne E. Thomas
Donald E. Morton

For Complete List of Firm Personnel, See General Section

For full biographical listings, see the Martindale-Hubbell Law Directory

*CLARKSVILLE,** Montgomery Co.

RUNYON AND RUNYON (AV)

Main Street at Third, P.O. Box 1023, 37041-1023
Telephone: 615-647-3377

MEMBER OF FIRM

Frank J. Runyon

Representative Clients: Clarksville Department of Electricity; St. Paul Insurance Co.; The Trane Co.; Aetna Life & Casualty Co.
Reference: First Union Bank, Clarksville.

For full biographical listings, see the Martindale-Hubbell Law Directory

KINGSPORT, Sullivan Co.

MOORE, STOUT, WADDELL & LEDFORD (AV)

238 Broad Street, P.O. Box 1345, 37662
Telephone: 615-246-2344
Fax: 615-246-2210

MEMBERS OF FIRM

W. Gorman Waddell
William S. Lewis

Representative Clients: First Virginia Banks, Inc.; Tri City Bank & Trust Company; First Tennessee Bank, National Association.

For Complete List of Firm Personnel, See General Section

For full biographical listings, see the Martindale-Hubbell Law Directory

*KNOXVILLE,** Knox Co.

EGERTON, MCAFEE, ARMISTEAD & DAVIS, P.C. (AV)

500 First American National Bank Center, P.O. Box 2047, 37901
Telephone: 615-546-0500
Fax: 615-525-5293

William W. Davis
M. W. Egerton, Jr.
Joe M. McAfee
Lewis C. Foster, Jr.
Dan W. Holbrook

Jonathan D. Reed

Representative Clients: First American Trust Company; Home Federal Bank of Tennessee, F.S.B.; Bush Bros. & Co.; East Tennessee Baptist Hospital; Baptist Hospital of East Tennessee; Carson Newman College; East Tennessee Foundation; Knoxville Symphony Society.

For Complete List of Firm Personnel, See General Section

For full biographical listings, see the Martindale-Hubbell Law Directory

RAINWATER, HUMBLE & VOWELL (AV)

2037 Plaza Tower, P.O. Box 2775, 37901
Telephone: 615-525-0321
Fax: 615-525-2431

MEMBERS OF FIRM

J. Earl Rainwater
J. Randolph Humble
Donald K. Vowell

Representative Clients: Acme Construction, Inc.; Curtis Construction Co., Inc.; Knoxville Pediatric Associates, P.C.; National Gas Distributors, Inc.; Neel's Wholesale Produce Co., Inc.; Oldham Insurance Inc.; Sherrod Electric Co., Inc.; Towe Iron Works, Inc.; Wm. S. Trimble Co., Inc.

For full biographical listings, see the Martindale-Hubbell Law Directory

*MEMPHIS,** Shelby Co.

ARMSTRONG ALLEN PREWITT GENTRY JOHNSTON & HOLMES (AV)

80 Monroe Avenue Suite 700, 38103
Telephone: 901-523-8211
Telecopier: 901-524-4936
Jackson, Missipi Office: 1350 One Jackson Place, 188 East Capitol Street.
Telephone: 601-948-8020.
Telecopier: 601-948-8389.

MEMBERS OF FIRM

Newton P. Allen
Joseph Brent Walker
James Rogers Hall, Jr.

For Complete List of Firm Personnel, See General Section

For full biographical listings, see the Martindale-Hubbell Law Directory

THE BOGATIN LAW FIRM (AV)

A Partnership including Professional Corporations
(Formerly Bogatin Lawson & Chiapella)
860 Ridge Lake Boulevard, Suite 360, 38120
Telephone: 901-767-1234
Telecopier: 901-767-2803 & 901-767-4010

MEMBERS OF FIRM

G. Patrick Arnoult
Irvin Bogatin (P.C.)
H. Stephen Brown
Susan Callison (P.C.)
Tillman C. Carroll
Matthew P. Cavitch
John André Chiapella (P.C.)
David J. Cocke
Russell J. Hensley
Arlie C. Hooper
Charles M. Key
William H. Lawson, Jr., (P.C.)
David C. Porteous
Arthur E. Quinn
Thaddeus S. Rodda, Jr., (P.C.)

ASSOCIATES

Robert F. Beckmann
James Q. Carr, II
C. William Denton, Jr.
Thomas M. Federico (Not admitted in TN)
James S. King
John F. Murrah

For full biographical listings, see the Martindale-Hubbell Law Directory

CAUSEY, CAYWOOD, TAYLOR & McMANUS (AV)

Suite 2400, 100 North Main Building, 38103
Telephone: 901-526-0206
Telecopier: 901-525-1540

MEMBERS OF FIRM

James D. Causey
David E. Caywood
Daniel Loyd Taylor
John E. McManus
Darrell D. Blanton
Craid B. Flood
Jean E. Markowitz
Amy R. Fulton
Marc E. Reisman
James H. Taylor III
David Shepherd Walker

For full biographical listings, see the Martindale-Hubbell Law Directory

SCHNEIDER & SIEGEL, P.C. (AV)

5170 Sanderlin Road Suite 200, 38117
Telephone: 901-685-3131
Telecopy: 901-683-0875

Harry Schneider
Arleen L. Siegel

For full biographical listings, see the Martindale-Hubbell Law Directory

THOMASON, HENDRIX, HARVEY, JOHNSON & MITCHELL (AV)

Twenty-Ninth Floor, One Commerce Square, 38103
Telephone: 901-525-8721
Telecopier: 901-525-6722

MEMBERS OF FIRM

Roy W. Hendrix, Jr.
Cheryl Rumage Estes
J. Martin Regan, Jr.

For Complete List of Firm Personnel, See General Section

For full biographical listings, see the Martindale-Hubbell Law Directory

*NASHVILLE,** Davidson Co.

ADAMS & WHITEAKER, P.C. (AV)

444 James Robertson Parkway, 37219
Telephone: 615-726-0900
Telecopier: 615-256-3634

Alfred T. Adams (1898-1982)
Alfred T. Adams, Jr.
R. C. Whiteaker, Jr.

(See Next Column)

Worrick G. Robinson, IV

Representative Clients: BellSouth Advertising & Publishing Corp.; Gale, Smith & Company, Inc.; BellSouth Telecommunications, Inc.; Enco Materials, Inc.
References: Sovran Bank; First American Bank, N.A.

For full biographical listings, see the Martindale-Hubbell Law Directory

HOLTON & HOWARD, A PROFESSIONAL CORPORATION (AV)

424 Church Street, Suite 2700, 37219
Telephone: 615-256-3338
Telecopier: 615-244-2104

Richard D. Holton
Bryan Howard

William E. Blackstone
Scott E. Swartz
K. Coleman Westbrook, Jr.

Reference: Third National Bank in Nashville.

For full biographical listings, see the Martindale-Hubbell Law Directory

MANIER, HEROD, HOLLABAUGH & SMITH, A PROFESSIONAL CORPORATION (AV)

First Union Tower 2200 One Nashville Place, 150 Fourth Avenue North, 37219-2494
Telephone: 615-244-0030
Telecopier: 615-242-4203

Will R. Manier, Jr. (1885-1953)
Larkin E. Crouch (1882-1948)
Vincent L. Fuqua, Jr. (1930-1974)
J. Olin White (1907-1982)
Miller Manier (1897-1986)
William Edward Herod (1917-1992)
Lewis B. Hollabaugh
Don L. Smith
James M. Doran, Jr.
Stephen E. Cox
J. Michael Franks
Randall C. Ferguson
Terry L. Hill
James David Leckrone
Robert C. Evans
Tommy C. Estes
B. Gail Reese
Michael E. Evans
Laurence M. Papel
John M. Gillum
Gregory L. Cashion
Sam H. Poteet, Jr.
Samuel Arthur Butts III
David J. Deming
Mark S. LeVan
Richard McCallister Smith
Mary Paty Lynn Jetton
H. Rowan Leathers III
Jefferson C. Orr
William L. Penny

Lawrence B. Hammet II
John H. Rowland
Susan C. West
John E. Quinn
John F. Floyd
Paul L. Sprader
Lela M. Hollabaugh
J. Steven Kirkham
T. Richard Travis
Stephanie M. Jennings
Jerry W. Taylor
C. Benton Patton
Kenneth A. Weber
Phillip Robert Newman
Brett A. Oeser

General Counsel for: McKinnon Bridge Co., Inc.

For full biographical listings, see the Martindale-Hubbell Law Directory

TEXAS

*AMARILLO,** Potter Co.

HINKLE, COX, EATON, COFFIELD & HENSLEY (AV)

1700 Bank One Center, P.O. Box 9238, 79105-9238
Telephone: 806-372-5569
FAX: 806-372-9761
Roswell, New Mexico Office: 700 United Bank Plaza, P. O. Box 10, 88202.
Telephone: 505-622-6510.
FAX: 505-623-9332.
Midland, Texas Office: 6 Desta Drive, Suite 2800, P.O. Box 3580, 79702.
Telephone: 915-683-4691.
FAX: 915-683-6518.
Santa Fe, New Mexico Office: 218 Montezuma, P.O. Box 2068, 87504.
Telephone: 505-982-4554.
FAX: 505-982-8623.
Albuquerque, New Mexico Office: Suite 800, 500 Marquette, N.W., P.O. Box 2043, 87102.
Telephone: 505-768-1500.
FAX: 505-768-1529.
Austin, Texas Office: 401 West 15th Street, Suite 800, 78701.
Telephone: 512-476-7137.
FAX: 512-476-5431.
Associated Office: Hoffman & Stephens, P.C., 401 West 15th Street, Suite 800, 78701.
Telephone: 512-476-5434. Fax; 512-476-5431.

(See Next Column)

HINKLE, COX, EATON, COFFIELD & HENSLEY, *Amarillo—Continued*

RESIDENT PARTNERS

William F. Countiss
W. H. Brian, Jr.
Thomas E. Hood

Representative Clients: Amarillo National Bank; Bank One, Texas, N.A.; Boatmen's First National Bank of Amarillo.

For full biographical listings, see the Martindale-Hubbell Law Directory

*AUSTIN,** Travis Co.

DAVIS & DAVIS, P.C. (AV)

Arboretum Plaza One, 9th Floor, 9442 Capitol of Texas Highway, P.O. Box 1588, 78767
Telephone: 512-343-6248
Fax: 512-343-0121

C. Dean Davis
Fred E. Davis
Alexis J. Fuller, Jr.
Francis A. (Tony) Bradley
Ruth Russell-Schafer

Bill Cline, Jr.
Brian Gregory Jackson

For Complete List of Firm Personnel, See General Section

For full biographical listings, see the Martindale-Hubbell Law Directory

IKARD & GOLDEN, P.C. (AV)

823 Congress Avenue, Suite 910, P.O. Box 684367, 78768-4367
Telephone: 512-472-6695
Fax: 512-472-3669

Frank N. Ikard, Jr.
Alvin J. Golden

Glenn M. Karisch

For full biographical listings, see the Martindale-Hubbell Law Directory

JOHN MCDUFF, P.C. A PROFESSIONAL CORPORATION (AV)

100 Congress Avenue Suite 1817, 78701
Telephone: 512-469-6360
Fax: 512-469-5505

John McDuff

For full biographical listings, see the Martindale-Hubbell Law Directory

J. SCOTT MORRIS, P.C. (AV)

701 Brazos, Suite 500, 78701
Telephone: 512-320-9039
Facsimile: 512-320-5821

J. Scott Morris

For full biographical listings, see the Martindale-Hubbell Law Directory

OSBORNE, LOWE, HELMAN & SMITH, L.L.P. (AV)

301 Congress Avenue Suite 1900, 78701
Telephone: 512-469-7700
FAX: 512-469-7711

MEMBERS OF FIRM

Duncan Elliott Osborne
Hugh S. Lowe
Stephen Jody Helman
Paula Y. Smith
Key Collie
William C. Pollard
Jack E. Owen, Jr.
Derry Wayne Swanger
Leslie C. Giordani
Elizabeth Gibson Deleery

For full biographical listings, see the Martindale-Hubbell Law Directory

SAEGERT, ANGENEND & AUGUSTINE, P.C. (AV)

1145 West Fifth Street, Suite 300, 78703
Telephone: 512-474-6521
Fax: 512-477-4512

Jerry C. Saegert
Paul D. Angenend
John C. Augustine
Mark D. Swanson
John R. Whisenhunt (1949-1994)
Harrell Glenn Hall, Jr.
Wendall Corrigan
Rebecca K. Knapik
Walter C. Guebert
Paul Vincent Mouer

For full biographical listings, see the Martindale-Hubbell Law Directory

*CORPUS CHRISTI,** Nueces Co.

MATTHEWS & BRANSCOMB, A PROFESSIONAL CORPORATION (AV)

802 North Carancahua, Suite 1900, 78470-0700
Telephone: 512-888-9261
Facsimile: 512-888-8504
Austin, Texas Office: 301 Congress Avenue, Suite 2050.
Telephone: 512-305-4400.
Facsimile: 512-305-4413.

(See Next Column)

San Antonio, Texas Office: One Alamo Center, 106 S. St. Mary's Street, Suite 800.
Telephone: 210-226-4211.
Facsimile: 210-226-0521.
Telex: 51060009283. Cable Code: MBLAW.
Eagle Pass, Texas Office: 675 Main Street.
Telephone: 210-773-6700.
Facsimile: 210-757-4045.
Uvalde, Texas Office: 200 E. Nopal #208.
Telephone: 210-278-4597.
Facsimile: 210-278-4806.
(Associated with Hall, Quintanilla & Alarcon, L.C., Laredo, Texas, under the name of Hall, Quintanilla, Alarcon, Matthews & Branscomb, P.L.L.C.).

G. Ray Miller, Jr.
Michael W. Stukenberg
Scott L. Sherman

For Complete List of Firm Personnel, See General Section

For full biographical listings, see the Martindale-Hubbell Law Directory

*DALLAS,** Dallas Co.

JOSEPH E. ASHMORE, JR., P.C. (AV)

Regency Plaza, 3710 Rawlins, Suite 1210, LB 84, 75219-4217
Telephone: 214-559-7202
Fax: 214-520-1550

Joseph E. Ashmore, Jr.

C. Gregory Shamoun
W. Charles Campbell
L. James Ashmore
Howard J. Klatsky

OF COUNSEL

B. Garfield Haynes
Mark S. Michael

For Complete List of Firm Personnel, See General Section

For full biographical listings, see the Martindale-Hubbell Law Directory

HAROLD B. BERMAN (AV)

8333 Douglas Avenue, Suite 1200, 75225
Telephone: 214-369-7779
Fax: 214-691-2691

For full biographical listings, see the Martindale-Hubbell Law Directory

CALHOUN & STACY (AV)

5700 NationsBank Plaza, 901 Main Street, 75202-3747
Telephone: 214-748-5000
Telecopier: 214-748-1421
Telex: 211358 CALGUMP UR

Mark Alan Calhoun
David W. Elrod
Steven D. Goldston
Parker Nelson
Roy L. Stacy

ASSOCIATES

Shannon S. Barclay
Robert A. Bragalone
Dennis D. Conder
Jane Elizabeth Diseker
Lawrence I. Fleishman
Thomas C. Jones
Katherine Johnson Knight
V. Paige Pace
Veronika Willard
Michael C. Wright

LEGAL CONSULTANT

Rees T. Bowen, III

For full biographical listings, see the Martindale-Hubbell Law Directory

GODWIN & CARLTON, A PROFESSIONAL CORPORATION (AV)

Suite 3300, 901 Main Street, 75202-3714
Telephone: 214-939-4400
Telecopier: 214-760-7332
Monterrey, Mexico Correspondent: Quintero y Quintero Abogodos. Martin De Zalva 840-3 Sur Esquinna Con Hidalgo.
Telephone: 44-07-74, 44-07-80, 44-06-56, 44-06-28.
Fax: 83-40-34-54.

James G. Vetter, Jr.
Bob J. Shelton
William F. Pyne

For Complete List of Firm Personnel, See General Section

For full biographical listings, see the Martindale-Hubbell Law Directory

HUGHES & LUCE, L.L.P. (AV)

A Registered Limited Liability Partnership including Professional Corporations
1717 Main Street, Suite 2800, 75201
Telephone: 214-939-5500
Fax: 214-939-6100
Telex: 730836
Austin, Texas Office: 111 Congress, Suite 900.
Telephone: 512-482-6800.
Fax: 512-482-6859.

(See Next Column)

HUGHES & LUCE L.L.P.—*Continued*

Houston, Texas Office: Three Allen Center, 333 Clay Street, Suite 3800.
Telephone: 713-754-5200.
Fax: 713-754-5206.
Fort Worth, Texas Office: 2421 Westport Parkway, Suite 500A.
Telephone: 817-439-3000.
Fax: 817-439-4222.

MEMBERS OF FIRM

Kathryn G. Henkel
Vester T. Hughes, Jr.

ASSOCIATE

Elizabeth R. Turner

STAFF ATTORNEY

Michael L. Kaufman

For Complete List of Firm Personnel, See General Section

For full biographical listings, see the Martindale-Hubbell Law Directory

NOVAKOV, DAVIDSON & FLYNN, A PROFESSIONAL CORPORATION (AV)

2000 St. Paul Place, 750 North St. Paul, 75201-3286
Telephone: 214-922-9221
Telecopy: 214-969-7557

Daniel P. Novakov

For Complete List of Firm Personnel, See General Section

For full biographical listings, see the Martindale-Hubbell Law Directory

PALMER, ALLEN & MCTAGGART, L.L.P. (AV)

A Partnership including Professional Corporations
1900 St. Paul Place, 750 North St. Paul Street, 75201
Telephone: 214-969-0069
Telecopy: 214-720-0104
Austin, Texas Office: 6505 Lohmann's Crossing (Lago Vista).
Telephone: 512-267-1993. Mailing Address: P.O. Box 4345, Lago Vista, Texas, 78645.

Steven G. Palmer (P.C.)
Joe B. Allen III
Robert D. McTaggart (P.C.)
Guy Myrph Foote, Jr., (P.C.)
Brian G. Dicus (P.C.)

OF COUNSEL

Robert S. Leithiser (P.C.)
Dick P. Wood, Jr., (P.C.)

For full biographical listings, see the Martindale-Hubbell Law Directory

THOMPSON & KNIGHT, A PROFESSIONAL CORPORATION (AV)

(Attorneys and Counselors)
1700 Pacific Avenue Suite 3300, 75201
Telephone: 214-969-1700
Telecopy: 214-969-1751
Cable Address: "Tomtex"
Telex: 732298
Austin, Texas Office: 1200 San Jacinto Center, 98 San Jacinto Boulevard, 78701.
Telephone: 512-469-6100.
Telecopy: 512-469-6180.
Fort Worth, Texas Office: 801 Cherry Street, Suite 1600, 76102.
Telephone: 817-347-1700.
Telecopy: 817-347-1799.
Houston, Texas Office: 1700 Texas Commerce Tower, 600 Travis, 77002.
Telephone: 713-217-2800.
Telecopy: 713-217-2828.
Monterrey, Mexico Office: Edificio Losoles PD-4, Av. Lázaro Cárdenas No. 2400 Pte., San Pedro Garza Garcia, Nuevo Léon C.P. 66220.
Telephone: (52-8) 363-0096.
Telecopy: (52-8) 363-3067.

SHAREHOLDERS

Margaret S. Alford
Barbara B. Ferguson
John Michael Holt
P. Mike McCullough
Rust E. Reid
James Y. Robb III

ASSOCIATES

D'Ana Howard Mikeska
William R. Mureiko

OF COUNSEL

Terry L. Simmons

For Complete List of Firm Personnel, See General Section

For full biographical listings, see the Martindale-Hubbell Law Directory

*DENTON,** Denton Co.

PHILIPS AND HOPKINS, P.C. (AV)

P.O. Box 2027, 76202-2027
Telephone: 817-566-7010
Facsimile: 817-898-0502

(See Next Column)

Gerald W. Cobb
T. Miller Davidge, Jr.
Robert N. Eames
William P. Philips, Jr.
Gray W. Shelton
Randolph W. Stout

OF COUNSEL

George Hopkins

Chris Raesz
Leigh Hilton
Barry D. Irwin

Representative Clients: North Texas Savings & Loan Assn., Denton, Texas; First State Bank of Texas, Denton, Texas; Sanger Bank, Sanger, Texas; BankOne, Texas, N.A.; Texas Bank, Denton, Texas; Dentex Title Co., Denton, Texas.

For full biographical listings, see the Martindale-Hubbell Law Directory

*EL PASO,** El Paso Co.

GUEVARA, REBE, BAUMANN, COLDWELL & GARAY (AV)

Suite A-201, 4171 North Mesa, P.O. Box 2009, 79950
Telephone: 915-544-6646, 544-6647
Fax: 915-544-8305

MEMBERS OF FIRM

Andrew R. Guevara
Sal Rebe
James E. Baumann
Colbert N. Coldwell
Juan Carlos Garay
Lane C. Reedman

Representative Clients: Mutual Building and Loan Association, Las Cruces, New Mexico; Beneficial Texas, Inc.; Dean Witter Reynolds, Inc.; Meca Homes, Inc.; Romney Implement, Inc.; Sam Corp. (Construction); Truck Enterprises, Inc.; Farm Fresh Product, Inc.; Truck Cab Fabrication, Inc.

For full biographical listings, see the Martindale-Hubbell Law Directory

MOUNCE & GALATZAN, A PROFESSIONAL CORPORATION (AV)

7th Floor, Texas Commerce Bank Building, 79901-1334
Telephone: 915-532-3911
Fax: 915-541-1597

William T. Kirk

Representative Clients: Natural Gas Co.; Texas Commerce Bank, El Paso; El Paso Independent School District; Commercial Union Assurance Cos.; State Farm Mutual Automobile Insurance Co.; Employers Insurance of Texas; Greater El Paso Association of Realtors.

For Complete List of Firm Personnel, See General Section

For full biographical listings, see the Martindale-Hubbell Law Directory

*FORT WORTH,** Tarrant Co.

JOHN W. CRUMLEY, P.C. (AV)

210 University Centre 1, 1300 South University Drive, 76107-5734
Telephone: 817-334-0291
Fax: 817-334-0775

John W. Crumley

For full biographical listings, see the Martindale-Hubbell Law Directory

H. ELDRIDGE DICKEY, JR. (AV)

Sundance Courtyard, 115 West Second Street, Suite 204, 76102
Telephone: 817-336-3006
FAX: 817-336-3211

For full biographical listings, see the Martindale-Hubbell Law Directory

HAROLD S. SPARKS III (AV)

Suite 2602 Bank One Building, 500 Throckmorton Street, 76102-3813
Telephone: 817-335-8353
Telecopier: 817-332-1701

For full biographical listings, see the Martindale-Hubbell Law Directory

THOMPSON & KNIGHT, A PROFESSIONAL CORPORATION (AV)

(Attorneys and Counselors)
801 Cherry Street, Suite 1600, 76102
Telephone: 817-347-1700
Telecopy: 817-347-1799
Dallas, Texas Office: 1700 Pacific Avenue, Suite 3300, 75201.
Telephone: 214-969-1700.
Telecopy: 214-969-1751.
Cable Address: "Tomtex."
Telex: 732298.
Austin, Texas Office: 1200 San Jacinto Center, 98 San Jacinto Boulevard, 78701.
Telephone: 512-469-6100.
Telecopy: 512-469-6180.
Houston, Texas Office: 1700 Texas Commerce Tower, 600 Travis, 77002.
Telephone: 713-217-2800.
Telecopy: 713-217-2828; 713-2882.

(See Next Column)

THOMPSON & KNIGHT A PROFESSIONAL CORPORATION, *Fort Worth—Continued*

Monterrey, Mexico Office: Edificio Losoles PD-4, Av. Lázaro Cárdenas No. 2400 Pte., San Pedro Garza Garcia, Nuevo Léon C.P. 66220.
Telephone: (52-8) 363-0096.
Telecopy: (52-8) 363-3067.

SHAREHOLDERS

R Gordon Appleman

For Complete List of Firm Personnel, See General Section

For full biographical listings, see the Martindale-Hubbell Law Directory

FRISCO, Collin & Denton Cos.

WINIKATES & WINIKATES (AV)

Prosper State Bank Building, P.O. Box 249, 75034-0249
Telephone: 214-335-1122
Fax: 214-335-1125

MEMBERS OF FIRM

Charles J. Winikates
Charles J. Winikates, Jr.
Regina W. Mentesana

OF COUNSEL

Frances A. Fazio

For full biographical listings, see the Martindale-Hubbell Law Directory

*GRAHAM,** Young Co.

MONTGOMERY & PEAVY, L.L.P. (AV)

First National Bank Building, P.O. Drawer 1300, 76450
Telephone: 817-549-7400
Telecopier: 817-549-7402

Elton M. Montgomery
Stanley H. Peavy, III

LEGAL SUPPORT PERSONNEL

Sue Herring

For full biographical listings, see the Martindale-Hubbell Law Directory

*GREENVILLE,** Hunt Co.

MORGAN AND GOTCHER (AV)

2610-A Stonewall Street, P.O. Box 556, 75403-0556
Telephone: 903-455-3183
Dallas Telephone: 214-226-1474
Fax: 903-454-4654

J. Harris Morgan
Holly H. Gotcher

Representative Clients: Huffines Enterprises; Greenville Independent School District; International Cassettes, Inc.; Universal Health Services, Inc.; Hunt County Appraisal District; Bank One Greenville; Citizens Bank of Royce City.

For full biographical listings, see the Martindale-Hubbell Law Directory

*HOUSTON,** Harris Co.

BAKER & BOTTS, L.L.P. (AV)

One Shell Plaza, 910 Louisiana, 77002
Telephone: 713-229-1234
Cable Address: "Boterlove"
Fax: 713-229-1522
Washington, D.C. Office: The Warner, 1299 Pennsylvania Avenue, N.W.
Telephone: 202-639-7700.
New York, New York Office: 885 Third Avenue, Suite 2000.
Telephone: 212-705-5000.
Austin, Texas Office: 1600 San Jacinto Center, 98 San Jacinto Boulevard.
Telephone: 512-322-2500.
Dallas, Texas Office: 2001 Ross Avenue.
Telephone: 214-953-6500.
Moscow, Russian Federation Office: 10 ul. Pushkinskaya, 103031.
Telephone: 7095/921-5300 (Local); 7095/929-7070 (International).

MEMBERS OF FIRM

Harold L. Metts
Ronald W. Kesterson
S. Stacy Eastland
Robert M. Weylandt
John W. Porter

ASSOCIATES

Margaret W. Brown
J. Kristine Dubiel
Laura K. Devitt
Carol M. Reumont

For Complete List of Firm Personnel, See General Section

For full biographical listings, see the Martindale-Hubbell Law Directory

BAYLESS & STOKES (AV)

2931 Ferndale Street, P.O. Box 22678, 77227-2678
Telephone: 713-522-2224
Fax: 713-522-2218

(See Next Column)

Bobbie G. Bayless
Dalia Browning Stokes

For full biographical listings, see the Martindale-Hubbell Law Directory

THOMAS E. BERRY & ASSOCIATES (AV)

225 Houston Club Building, 811 Rusk Avenue, 77002-2811
Telephone: 713-223-8061
Fax: 713-223-4638

Betty B. Moser
Anne Hardiman
Gary M. Howell

For full biographical listings, see the Martindale-Hubbell Law Directory

GREGG & MIESZKUC, P.C. (AV)

17044 El Camino Real (Clear Lake City), 77058-2686
Telephone: 713-488-8680
Facsimile: 713-488-8531

Dick H. Gregg, Jr.
Polly P. Lewis
Marilyn Mieszkuc
Charles A. Daughtry

Elizabeth E. Scott
Dick H. Gregg, III

For full biographical listings, see the Martindale-Hubbell Law Directory

*LUBBOCK,** Lubbock Co.

CRENSHAW, DUPREE & MILAM, L.L.P. (AV)

Norwest Center, P.O. Box 1499, 79408-1499
Telephone: 806-762-5281
Fax: 806-762-3510

John Crews
Jack McCutchin, Jr.

For Complete List of Firm Personnel, See General Section

For full biographical listings, see the Martindale-Hubbell Law Directory

MCALLEN, Hidalgo Co.

WILKINS & SLUSHER (AV)

800 First City Bank Tower, P.O. Box 3609, 78501
Telephone: 210-682-4551
Fax: 210-682-4554

MEMBERS OF FIRM

Tom Wilkins
Boone Slusher

ASSOCIATE

Brian Howell

Representative Clients: L.G. Community Exchange (Cattleman's Exchange); Romain Orchards, Inc.; Rio National Bank, McAllen, Texas; The Border Bank, Hidalgo, Texas; Beauregard Groves, Inc.; Rio Grande Railcar, Inc.; Skloss Farms, Inc.
References: First State Bank & Trust Company of Mission, Texas; Texas State Bank, McAllen, Texas.

For full biographical listings, see the Martindale-Hubbell Law Directory

*SAN ANTONIO,** Bexar Co.

JOHN E. BAKKE III (AV)

The Fountainhead, 8200 Robert F. McDermott Freeway, Suite 820, 78230
Telephone: 210-341-9371
FAX: 210-340-5637

For full biographical listings, see the Martindale-Hubbell Law Directory

CROMAN • GIBBS • SCHWARTZMAN (AV)

A Partnership including Professional Corporations
5717 Northwest Parkway, 78249
Telephone: 210-691-2999
Fax: 210-691-1939

Earl L. Croman (P.C.)
Larry W. Gibbs (P.C.)
Mark A. Schwartzman

For full biographical listings, see the Martindale-Hubbell Law Directory

SCHOENBAUM, CURPHY & SCANLAN, P.C. (AV)

NationsBank Plaza, Suite 1775, 300 Convent Street, 78205-3744
Telephone: 210-224-4491
Fax: 210-224-7983

Stanley Schoenbaum
Alfred G. Holcomb
R. James Curphy
Banks M. Smith
William Scanlan, Jr.
R. Bradley Oxford
Darin N. Digby

(See Next Column)

SCHOENBAUM, CURPHY & SCANLAN P.C.—*Continued*

Patricia Flora Sitchler
Emily Harrison Liljenwall
Susan L. Saeger

For full biographical listings, see the Martindale-Hubbell Law Directory

TEXARKANA, Bowie Co.

PATTON, HALTOM, ROBERTS, MCWILLIAMS & GREER, L.L.P. (AV)

A Registered Limited Liability Partnership including Professional Corporations
700 Texarkana National Bank Building, P.O. Box 1928, 75504-1928
Telephone: 903-794-3341
Fax: 903-792-6542; 903-792-0448

William B. Roberts
Fred R. Norton, Jr.

Representative Clients: Allstate Insurance Co.; Aetna Casualty & Surety Co.; Royal Insurance Group; Continental Insurance Group; Ranger/Pan American Insurance Cos.; The Hanover Insurance Group; American Mutual Liability Insurance Co.; American Hardware Mutual Insurance Co.; Kemper Insurance Co.; Texarkana National Bancshares, Inc.

For Complete List of Firm Personnel, See General Section

For full biographical listings, see the Martindale-Hubbell Law Directory

*TYLER,** Smith Co.

ROBERT M. BANDY, P.C. (AV)

NationsBank Plaza Tower, Suite 1122, 75702-7252
Telephone: 903-592-7333
800-374-2263
FAX: 903-592-7751
Dallas, Texas Office: University Tower, Suite 314, 6440 North Central Expressway.
Telephone: 214-480-8220.
Longview, Texas Office: 703 N. Green, 75606.
Telephone: 903-757-7506.
Fax: 903-592-7751.

Robert M. Bandy

William H. Lively, Jr.

For full biographical listings, see the Martindale-Hubbell Law Directory

UTAH

*SALT LAKE CITY,** Salt Lake Co.

CALLISTER, NEBEKER & MCCULLOUGH, A PROFESSIONAL CORPORATION (AV)

800 Kennecott Building, 84133
Telephone: 801-530-7300
Telecopier: 801-364-9127

Charles M. Bennett
Craig F. McCullough

Douglas K. Cummings

Representative Clients: Zions First National Bank Trust Department.

For Complete List of Firm Personnel, See General Section

For full biographical listings, see the Martindale-Hubbell Law Directory

KIRTON & MCCONKIE, A PROFESSIONAL CORPORATION (AV)

1800 Eagle Gate Tower, 60 East South Temple, 84111
Telephone: 801-328-3600
Telecopier: 801-321-4893

Lorin C. Barker
Fred D. Essig

For Complete List of Firm Personnel, See General Section

For full biographical listings, see the Martindale-Hubbell Law Directory

STRONG & HANNI, A PROFESSIONAL CORPORATION (AV)

Sixth Floor Boston Building, 9 Exchange Place, 84111
Telephone: 801-532-7080
Fax: 801-596-1508

(See Next Column)

Gordon R. Strong (1909-1969)
Glenn C. Hanni
Henry E. Heath
Philip R. Fishler
Roger H. Bullock
Robert A. Burton
R. Scott Williams
Dennis M. Astill (Managing Partner)
S. Baird Morgan
Stuart H. Schultz
Paul M. Belnap
Stephen J. Trayner
Joseph J. Joyce
Bradley Wm. Bowen

Robert L. Janicki
Elizabeth L. Willey
Peter H. Christensen
H. Burt Ringwood
David R. Nielson
Adam Trupp
Catherine M. Larson

Representative Clients: State Farm Mutual Automobile Insurance Co.; Standard Accident Insurance Co.; United Services Automobile Assn.; Western Casualty & Surety Co.; Government Employees Insurance Co.; Guaranty Mutual Life Co.

For full biographical listings, see the Martindale-Hubbell Law Directory

VAN COTT, BAGLEY, CORNWALL & MCCARTHY, A PROFESSIONAL CORPORATION (AV)

Suite 1600, 50 South Main Street, P.O. Box 45340, 84145
Telephone: 801-532-3333
Telex: 453149
Telecopier: 801-534-0058
Ogden, Utah Office: Suite 900, 2404 Washington Boulevard.
Telephone: 801-394-5783.
Park City, Utah Office: 314 Main Street, Suite 205.
Telephone: 801-649-3889.
Reno, Nevada Office: Jeppson & Lee, 100 West Liberty, Suite 990.
Telephone: 702-333-6800.

David E. Salisbury
Stephen D. Swindle
Alan F. Mecham
J. Keith Adams
Richard C. Skeen
Steven D. Woodland
Richard H. Johnson, II
S. Robert Bradley
Gregory N. Barrick
Douglas A. Taggart (Resident, Ogden, Utah Office)

Susan Pierce Lawrence
David E. Sloan

For Complete List of Firm Personnel, See General Section

For full biographical listings, see the Martindale-Hubbell Law Directory

VERMONT

BARRE, Washington Co.

OTTERMAN & ALLEN, P.C. (AV)

188 Washington Street, P.O. Box 473, 05641
Telephone: 802-479-2552

Harvey B. Otterman, Jr.
O. Fay Allen, Jr. (Retired)
David A. Otterman

Andrea L. Gallitano

Representative Clients: Shawmut Bank of Boston N. A.; Towns of Fairlee, Orange, West Fairlee, Groton, Topsham, Hardwick.

For full biographical listings, see the Martindale-Hubbell Law Directory

BRATTLEBORO, Windham Co.

KRISTENSEN, CUMMINGS & MURTHA, P.C. (AV)

5 Grove Street, P.O. Box 677, 05302-0677
Telephone: 802-254-8733
FAX: 802-254-8860

John G. Kristensen
Charles R. Cummings
J. Garvan Murtha

Stephen R. Phillips
Richard C. Carroll
Joseph C. Galanes

LEGAL SUPPORT PERSONNEL

Mary Louise Nelson (Paralegal)

For full biographical listings, see the Martindale-Hubbell Law Directory

WEBER, PERRA & WILSON, P.C. (AV)

16 Linden Street, P.O. Box 558, 05302
Telephone: 802-257-7161
Fax: 802-257-0572

(See Next Column)

WEBER, PERRA & WILSON P.C., *Brattleboro—Continued*

Raymond P. Perra   Lucy W. McVitty

For Complete List of Firm Personnel, See General Section

For full biographical listings, see the Martindale-Hubbell Law Directory

*BURLINGTON,** Chittenden Co.

GRAVEL AND SHEA, A PROFESSIONAL CORPORATION (AV)

Corporate Plaza, 76 St. Paul Street, P.O. Box 369, 05402-0369
Telephone: 802-658-0220
Fax: 802-658-1456

Charles T. Shea   Stephen R. Crampton
William G. Post, Jr.

Stephen P. Magowan

OF COUNSEL

Clarke A. Gravel

SPECIAL COUNSEL

Norman Williams

For Complete List of Firm Personnel, See General Section

For full biographical listings, see the Martindale-Hubbell Law Directory

LISMAN & LISMAN, A PROFESSIONAL CORPORATION (AV)

84 Pine Street, P.O. Box 728, 05402-0728
Telephone: 802-864-5756
Fax: 802-864-3629

Carl H. Lisman   Mary G. Kirkpatrick
Allen D. Webster   E. William Leckerling, III
Douglas K. Riley

Judith Lillian Dillon   Richard W. Kozlowski

OF COUNSEL

Bernard Lisman   Louis Lisman

For full biographical listings, see the Martindale-Hubbell Law Directory

ESSEX JUNCTION, Chittenden Co.

KOLVOORD, OVERTON AND WILSON (AV)

3 Main Street, 05452
Telephone: 802-878-3346
FAX: 802-879-0964

Philip A. Kolvoord   Gregg H. Wilson
Alan D. Overton   Michael D. Danley

ASSOCIATES

Herbert J. Downing   Carol N. Angus
Daniel L. Overton

Representative Clients: The Howard Bank; Chittenden Bank; S. T. Griswold & Co., Inc. (Construction); Aquatec, Inc. (Environmental Studies); Burlington Savings Bank; Champlain Water District (Regional Water Municipality); Town of Essex School District; Town of Jericho; International Business Machines (IBM Corp.).

*MIDDLEBURY,** Addison Co.

CONLEY & FOOTE (AV)

11 South Pleasant Street, P.O. Drawer 391, 05753
Telephone: 802-388-4061
Fax: 802-388-0210

MEMBERS OF FIRM

John T. Conley (1900-1971)   D. Michael Mathes
Ralph A. Foote   Richard P. Foote
Charity A. Downs   Janet P. Shaw

For full biographical listings, see the Martindale-Hubbell Law Directory

*RUTLAND,** Rutland Co.

CARROLL, GEORGE & PRATT (AV)

64 & 66 North Main Street, P.O. Box 280, 05702-0280
Telephone: 802-775-7141
Telecopier: 802-775-6483
Woodstock, Vermont Office: The Mill - Route #4 E., P.O. Box 388, 05091.
Telephone: 802-457-1000.
Telecopier: 802-457-1874.

MEMBERS OF FIRM

Henry G. Smith (1938-1974)   Timothy U. Martin
James P. Carroll   Randall F. Mayhew (Resident Partner, Woodstock Office)
Alan B. George   Richard S. Smith
Robert S. Pratt   Judy Godnick Barone
Neal C. Vreeland   John J. Kennelly
Jon S. Readnour

(See Next Column)

ASSOCIATES

Thomas A. Zonay   Susan Boyle Ford (Resident, Woodstock Office)
Jeffrey P. White
Charles C. Humpstone

For full biographical listings, see the Martindale-Hubbell Law Directory

CHRISTOPHER A. WEBBER, JR. (AV)

92 Allen Street, P.O. Box 189, 05702
Telephone: 802-775-6255
Fax: 802-775-6367

For full biographical listings, see the Martindale-Hubbell Law Directory

VIRGINIA

ALEXANDRIA, (Independent City)

GRAD, LOGAN & KLEWANS, P.C. (AV)

112 North Columbus Street, P.O. Box 1417-A44, 22313
Telephone: 703-548-8400
Facsimile: 703-836-6289

John D. Grad   Michael P. Logan
Samuel N. Klewans

Sean C. E. McDonough   Claire R. Pettrone
David A. Damiani

OF COUNSEL

Jeanne F. Franklin

For full biographical listings, see the Martindale-Hubbell Law Directory

E. MICHAEL PATURIS (AV)

Lee Street Square, 431 North Lee Street, 22314-2301
Telephone: 703-836-2501
Facsimile: 703-836-4487

For full biographical listings, see the Martindale-Hubbell Law Directory

*ARLINGTON,** Arlington Co.

KEN MCFARLANE SMITH, P.C. (AV)

5235 Wilson Boulevard, 22205-1113
Telephone: 703-522-1350
FAX: 703-522-0129

Ken McFarlane Smith

Joseph P. Engler

LEGAL SUPPORT PERSONNEL

Marcia K. Gavin

For full biographical listings, see the Martindale-Hubbell Law Directory

BLACKSBURG, Montgomery Co.

GILMER, SADLER, INGRAM, SUTHERLAND & HUTTON (AV)

201 West Roanoke Street, P.O. Box 908, 24063-0908
Telephone: 703-552-1061
Telecopier: 703-552-8227
Pulaski, Virginia Office: Midtown Professional Building, 65 East Main Street, P.O. Box 878.
Telephone: 703-980-1360; 703-639-0027.
Telecopier: 703-980-5264.

MEMBERS OF FIRM

James L. Hutton   John J. Gill
Todd G. Patrick   Gary C. Hancock
Howard C. Gilmer, Jr. (1906-1975)   Jackson M. Bruce
Michael J. Barbour
Roby K. Sutherland (1909-1975)   Deborah Wood Dobbins
Philip M. Sadler (1915-1994)   Debra Fitzgerald-O'Connell
Robert J. Ingram   Scott A. Rose
Thomas J. McCarthy, Jr.   Timothy Edmond Kirtner

OF COUNSEL

James R. Montgomery

Representative Clients: Appalachian Power Co.; Magnox, Inc.; Liberty Mutual Insurance Co.; Norfolk Southern Railway Co.; Pulaski Furniture Corp.; NationsBank; Travelers Insurance Co.; Charles Lunsford Sons & Associates; Corning Glass Works.

For full biographical listings, see the Martindale-Hubbell Law Directory

*CHARLOTTESVILLE,** (Ind. City; Seat of Albemarle Co.)

ROBERT M. MUSSELMAN & ASSOCIATES (AV)

413 7th Street, N.E., P.O. Box 254, 22902
Telephone: 804-977-4500
Fax: 804-293-5727

ASSOCIATES

Carolyn C. Musselman
Douglas E. Little
Rose Marie Downs
Matthew A. Fass

For full biographical listings, see the Martindale-Hubbell Law Directory

RICHMOND AND FISHBURNE (AV)

Queen Charlotte Square, 214 East High Street, P.O. Box 559, 22902
Telephone: 804-977-8590
Telefax: 804-296-9861

MEMBERS OF FIRM

Joseph W. Richmond, Jr.
Wendall L. Winn, Jr.
Thomas G. Nolan

Representative Clients: Budget-Rent-A-Car; Charlottesville Area Association of Realtors; Fireman's Fund; Horace Mann Insurance Co.; Martha Jefferson Hospital; Nationwide Insurance Co.; Norfolk-Southern Corp.; State Farm Insurance Co.; USAA; Virginia Farm Bureau Insurance Services.

For Complete List of Firm Personnel, See General Section

For full biographical listings, see the Martindale-Hubbell Law Directory

SLAUGHTER & REDINGER, P.C. (AV)

Lewis and Clark Square, 250 West Main Street, Suite 300, P.O. Box 2964, 22902
Telephone: 804-295-8300
FAX: 804-295-3390

Edward R. Slaughter, Jr.
Craig T. Redinger
David Z. Izakowitz
Jane C. Clarke
Caroline Nunley Barber

Patrick J. Nettesheim (Not admitted in VA)

OF COUNSEL

Neill H. Alford, Jr.

For full biographical listings, see the Martindale-Hubbell Law Directory

*RICHMOND,** (Ind. City; Seat of Henrico Co.)

FLORANCE, GORDON AND BROWN, A PROFESSIONAL CORPORATION (AV)

800 Mutual Building, 909 East Main Street, 23219
Telephone: 804-697-5100
Facsimile: 804-697-5159

Richard Florance (1902-1980)
Walker Florance (1909-1983)
James W. Gordon, Jr. (Retired)
Delmar L. Brown
Fred J. Bernhardt, Jr.
William H. Hoofnagle, III
Hamill D. "Skip" Jones, Jr.
Cary A. Ralston
Robert J. Kloeti
Conard B. Mattox, III
Kathleen N. Scott

Christopher S. Dillon
Kimberlee Harris Ramsey
Farhad Aghdami
Bryan W. Horn
Roger Gallup Bowers

Reference: Crestar Bank.

For full biographical listings, see the Martindale-Hubbell Law Directory

THOMPSON, SMITHERS, NEWMAN & WADE (AV)

5911 West Broad Street, P.O. Box 6357, 23230
Telephone: 804-288-4007
Telecopier: 804-282-5379

MEMBERS OF FIRM

Harry L. Thompson
William S. Smithers, Jr.
Nathaniel S. Newman
Winfrey T. Wade
R. Paul Childress, Jr.
Kimberly Smithers Wright
R. Ferrell Newman
Anton J. Stelly
Robert S. Carter

ASSOCIATES

James C. Bodie
Paul D. Georgiadis
Suzanne Elizabeth Wade
Glenn S. Phelps

Approved Attorneys for: Lawyers Title Insurance Corp.

For full biographical listings, see the Martindale-Hubbell Law Directory

WILLIAMS, MULLEN, CHRISTIAN & DOBBINS, A PROFESSIONAL CORPORATION (AV)

Two James Center, 1021 East Cary Street, P.O. Box 1320, 23210-1320
Telephone: 804-643-1991
Fax: 804-783-6456
Glen Allen, Virginia Office: 4401 Waterfront Drive, Suite 140.
Telephone: 804-965-9168.
Fax: 804-965-0955.
Washington, D.C. Office: 1575 Eye Street, N.W.
Telephone: 202-289-6200.
Fax: 202-289-4126.

David D. Addison
Charles L. Cabell
C. Richard Davis
Robert L. Musick, Jr.
Craig L. Rascoe
Derek L. Smith
Julious P. Smith, Jr.
Fielding L. Williams, Jr.
Russell Alton Wright

For Complete List of Firm Personnel, See General Section

For full biographical listings, see the Martindale-Hubbell Law Directory

ROANOKE, (Independent City)

BERSCH & RHODES, P.C. (AV)

640 Crestar Plaza, P.O. Box 1529, 24007
Telephone: 703-345-7400
Facsimile: 703-345-7353

Robert S. Bersch
Harry S. Rhodes

William C. Leach
Scott A. Butler

For full biographical listings, see the Martindale-Hubbell Law Directory

VIENNA, Fairfax Co.

BORING, PARROTT & PILGER, P.C. (AV)

307 Maple Avenue West, Suite D, 22180-4368
Telephone: 703-281-2161
FAX: 703-281-9464

James L. Boring
M. Bruce Hirshorn

Representative Clients: Balmar, Inc.; Hewlett-Packard Co.; Toshiba America Information Systems, Inc.; King Wholesale, Inc.; FSM Leasing, Inc.; KDI Sylvan Pools, Inc.; Brobst International, Inc.; Telematics, Inc.; Northern Virginia Surgical Associates, P.C.; Rainbow Industries, Inc.

For full biographical listings, see the Martindale-Hubbell Law Directory

PETERSON & BASHA, P.C. (AV)

Tysons Square Office Park, 8214-C Old Courthouse Road, 22182-3855
Telephone: 703-442-3890
Fax: 703-448-1834

Gary G. Peterson
Leigh-Alexandra Basha

Alison K. Markell
Cynthia L. Gausvik
Ki Jun Sung

OF COUNSEL

Daniel J. O'Connell

For full biographical listings, see the Martindale-Hubbell Law Directory

*WARRENTON,** Fauquier Co.

ROBIN C. GULICK, P.C. (AV)

70 Main Street Suite 52, P.O. Box 880, 22186
Telephone: 703-347-3022
Fax: 703-347-9711

Robin C. Gulick
William W. Carson, Jr.

General Counsel for: Jefferson Savings & Loan.
References: Fauquier National Bank; The Peoples National Bank.

For full biographical listings, see the Martindale-Hubbell Law Directory

WASHINGTON

BELLEVUE, King Co.

DONALD D. FLEMING, P.S. (AV)

800 Bellevue Way, N.E., Suite 300, 98004
Telephone: 206-637-3001
FAX: 206-453-9062

Donald D. Fleming

For full biographical listings, see the Martindale-Hubbell Law Directory

MOSES LAKE, Grant Co.

DANO * MILLER * RIES (AV)

100 East Broadway, P.O. Box 1159, 98837
Telephone: 509-765-9285
FAX: 509-766-0087
Othello, Washington Office: 705 East Hemlock, P.O. Box 494.
Telephone: 509-488-2601.
Fax: 509-488-2703.

OF COUNSEL

Harrison K. Dano

MEMBERS OF FIRM

Brian J. Dano
Garth L. Dano
Brian H. Miller (Resident at Othello Office)
Harry E. Ries
Christopher F. Ries

Representative Clients: El Oro Cattle Co.; Sunfresh Potato; Irrigators, Inc.; Quincy Livestock Market; Nexus Ag Chemical, Inc.; Evergreen Implement, Inc.

For full biographical listings, see the Martindale-Hubbell Law Directory

POULSBO, Kitsap Co.

TOLMAN • KIRK (AV)

18925 Front N.E., P.O. Box 851, 98370
Telephone: 206-779-5561
FAX: 206-779-2516

MEMBERS OF FIRM

Jeffrey L. Tolman
Michael A. Kirk

For full biographical listings, see the Martindale-Hubbell Law Directory

*SEATTLE,** King Co.

BRUCE R. MOEN (AV)

2929 Westin Building, 2001 Sixth Avenue, 98121-2578
Telephone: 206-441-1156
Fax: 206-441-6727

For full biographical listings, see the Martindale-Hubbell Law Directory

STOKES, EITELBACH & LAWRENCE, P.S. (AV)

800 Fifth Avenue, Suite 4000, 98104-3199
Telephone: 206-626-6000
Fax: 206-464-1496

Douglas C. Lawrence
Sandra Lynn Perkins

Lora L. Brown

For full biographical listings, see the Martindale-Hubbell Law Directory

*SPOKANE,** Spokane Co.

CHASE, HAYES & KALAMON, P.S. (AV)

1000 Seafirst Financial Center, 99201
Telephone: 509-456-0333
FAX: 509-838-9826

Roger F. Chase
Hedley W. Greene

Nancy A. Pohlman
Brent T. Stanyer
Gerald Kobluk

OF COUNSEL

W. Kenneth Jones

Representative Clients: Albertson's Inc.; Key Tronic Corp.; Volvo of America, Inc.; Security Management; Familian Northwest; Tidyman's Inc.; Farmers Insurance Group; Sacred Heart Medical Center; Farm Credit Bank of Spokane.

For Complete List of Firm Personnel, See General Section

For full biographical listings, see the Martindale-Hubbell Law Directory

WEST VIRGINIA

*CHARLESTON,** Kanawha Co.

BIBBY & GOOD (AV)

808 Security Building, P.O. Box 2106, 25328-2106
Telephone: 304-343-5531

(See Next Column)

James A. Bibby, Jr.
Albert F. Good

Representative Clients: Delta Dental Plan of West Virginia, Inc.; Eastern Energy Investments, Inc.; First Big Mountain Mining Co.; Matlack, Inc.; Middle Atlantic Conference; Stowers & Sons Trucking Co.; West Virginia Dental Assn.
Approved Attorneys for: Lawyers Title Insurance Corp.

JACKSON & KELLY (AV)

1600 Laidley Tower, P.O. Box 553, 25322
Telephone: 304-340-1000
Fax: 304-340-1130
Martinsburg, West Virginia Office: 300 Foxcroft Avenue, P.O. Box 1068.
Telephone: 304-263-8800.
Morgantown, West Virginia Office: 6000 Hampton Center, P.O. Box 619.
Telephone: 304-599-3000.
New Martinsville, West Virginia Office: 256 Russell Avenue, P.O. Box 68.
Telephone: 304-455-1751.
Charles Town, West Virginia Office: 700 East Washington Street, P.O. Box 983.
Telephone: 304-728-6088.
Clarksburg, West Virginia Office: 203 Main Street, P.O. Box 1587.
Telephone: 304-623-3002.
Lexington, Kentucky Office: 175 East Main Street, Suite 500, P.O. Box 2150.
Telephone: 606-255-9500.
Washington, D. C. Office: 2401 Pennsylvania Avenue, N.W., Suite 400.
Telephone: 202-973-0200.
Denver, Colorado Office: Suite 2710, 1660 Lincoln Street.
Telephone: 303-837-0003.

MEMBERS OF FIRM

J. S. Francis (New Martinsville, West Virginia Office)
Louis S. Southworth, II
Thomas G. Freeman, II
Jeffrey J. Yost (Resident, Lexington, Kentucky Office)
David Layva (Martinsburg and Charles Town, West Virginia Offices)

ASSOCIATES

Eric H. London (Resident, Morgantown Office)
Anthony J. Ferrise
John G. Byrd
Patience A. Alexander

For Complete List of Firm Personnel, See General Section

For full biographical listings, see the Martindale-Hubbell Law Directory

PAYNE, LOEB & RAY (AV)

1210 One Valley Square, 25301
Telephone: 304-342-1141
Fax: 304-342-0691

MEMBERS OF FIRM

Charles W. Loeb
Christopher J. Winton

Counsel for: One Valley Bank, N.A.; Outdoor Advertising Association of West Virginia; Trojan Steel Co.; Thomas, Field & Co.; Kanawha Village Apartments, Inc.; Guyan Machinery Co.

For Complete List of Firm Personnel, See General Section

For full biographical listings, see the Martindale-Hubbell Law Directory

*CLARKSBURG,** Harrison Co.

JOHNSON, SIMMERMAN & BROUGHTON, L.C. (AV)

Suite 210, Goff Building, P.O. Box 150, 26301
Telephone: 304-624-6555
Telecopier: 304-623-4933

Charles G. Johnson
Frank E. Simmerman, Jr.
Marcia Allen Broughton

For full biographical listings, see the Martindale-Hubbell Law Directory

MCNEER, HIGHLAND & MCMUNN (AV)

Empire Building, P.O. Drawer 2040, 26301
Telephone: 304-623-6636
Facsimile: 304-623-3035
Morgantown Office: McNeer, Highland & McMunn, Baker & Armistead, 168 Chancery Row. P.O. Box 1615.
Telephone: 304-292-8473.
Fax: 304-292-1528.
Martinsburg, Office: 1446-1 Edwin Miller Boulevard. P.O. Box 2509.
Telephone: 304-264-4621.
Fax: 304-264-8623.

MEMBERS OF FIRM

C. David McMunn
J. Cecil Jarvis
James A. Varner
George B. Armistead (Resident, Morgantown Office)
Catherine D. Munster
Robert W. Trumble (Resident, Martinsburg Office)
Dennis M. Shreve
Geraldine S. Roberts
Harold M. Sklar
Jeffrey S. Bolyard
Steven R. Bratke
Michael J. Novotny (Resident, Martinsburg Office)

(See Next Column)

McNeer, Highland & McMunn—*Continued*

OF COUNSEL

James E. McNeer — Cecil B. Highland, Jr.
William L. Fury

Representative Clients: One Valley Bank of Clarksburg, National Association; Bruceton Bank; Harrison County Bank; Nationwide Mutual Insurance Cos.; Clarksburg Publishing Co.; C.I.T. Financial Services; State Automobile Mutual Insurance Co.; United Hospital Center, Inc.; West Virginia Coals, Inc.; Swanson Plating Company.

For Complete List of Firm Personnel, See General Section

For full biographical listings, see the Martindale-Hubbell Law Directory

*HUNTINGTON,** Cabell & Wayne Cos.

Frazier & Oxley, L.C. (AV)

The St. James, 401 Tenth Street Mezzanine Level, P.O. Box 2808, 25727
Telephone: 304-697-4370
FAX: Available upon request

William M. Frazier — Leon K. Oxley
W. Michael Frazier

References: The Old National Bank; Commerce Bank, Huntington, N.A.

For full biographical listings, see the Martindale-Hubbell Law Directory

*WHEELING,** Ohio Co.

Seibert, Kasserman, Farnsworth, Gillenwater, Glauser, Richardson & Curtis, L.C. (AV)

1217 Chapline Street, P.O. Box 311, 26003
Telephone: 304-233-1220
Fax: 304-233-4813

Carl B. Galbraith (1903-1972)
George H. Seibert, Jr. (1913-1986)
Ronald W. Kasserman
Sue Seibert Farnsworth
James E. Seibert
Elba Gillenwater, Jr.
M. Jane Glauser
Randolf E. Richardson
Ronald William Kasserman
Linda Weatherholt Curtis
Donald A. Nickerson, Jr.

Representative Clients: Ohio Valley Medical Center, Inc.; Ohio Valley Window Co.; The Travelers Cos.
Reference: United National Bank - Wheeling, W. Va.

For full biographical listings, see the Martindale-Hubbell Law Directory

WISCONSIN

*APPLETON,** Outagamie Co.

Menn, Nelson, Sharratt, Teetaert & Beisenstein, Ltd. (AV)

(Formerly, Fulton, Menn & Nehs, Ltd.)
222 North Oneida Street, P.O. Box 785, 54912-0785
Telephone: 414-731-6631
FAX: 414-734-0981

Homer H. Benton (1886-1957)
Alfred C. Bosser (1890-1965)
Franklin L. Nehs (1922-1979)
David L. Fulton (1911-1985)
Glenn L. Sharratt (Retired)
John B. Menn
Peter S. Nelson
John R. Teetaert
Joseph J. Beisenstein
Mark R. Feldmann
Joseph A. Bielinski
Jonathan M. Menn
Douglas D. Hahn
Keith W. Kostecke
Robert N. Duimstra

LEGAL SUPPORT PERSONNEL

Kathy J. Krause

Representative Clients: Bank One Wisconsin Trust Company, NA; Valley Trust Company; Norwest Bank Wisconsin, NA; Associated Bank, NA; Firstar Trust Company.

For full biographical listings, see the Martindale-Hubbell Law Directory

LAKE GENEVA, Walworth Co.

Braden & Olson (AV)

716 Wisconsin Street, P.O. Box 940, 53147
Telephone: 414-248-6636
Fax: 414-248-2901

Berwyn B. Braden — John O. Olson

Michael J. Rielly
Kurt T. Van Buskirk
Christine Tomas (Not admitted in WI)

For full biographical listings, see the Martindale-Hubbell Law Directory

*MADISON,** Dane Co.

Balisle & Roberson, S.C. (AV)

217 South Hamilton, Suite 302, P.O. Box 870, 53701-0870
Telephone: 608-259-8702
Fax: 608-259-0807

Linda S. Balisle — Linda Roberson
Rachel L. L. Caplan

LEGAL SUPPORT PERSONNEL

Diana K. Fleming

For full biographical listings, see the Martindale-Hubbell Law Directory

Stroud, Stroud, Willink, Thompson & Howard (AV)

25 West Main Street, Suite 300, P.O. Box 2236, 53701
Telephone: 608-257-2281
FAX: 608-257-7643

MEMBERS OF FIRM

Seward Ritchey Stroud — Robert R. Stroud
C. Vernon Howard — Carolyn A. Hegge
Mark S. Zimmer

OF COUNSEL

Donald R. Stroud — Dale R. Thompson

General Counsel for: Appleton Mills; University of Wisconsin Foundation; Temperature Systems, Inc.; Wisconsin Farm Bureau Federation; Anchor Savings and Loan Assn.; The Wisconsin Cheeseman, Inc.; J.H. Findorff & Son, Inc.; Edward Kraemer & Sons, Inc.; Hilldale Shopping Center; American T.V. & Appliance of Madison, Inc.

For Complete List of Firm Personnel, See General Section

For full biographical listings, see the Martindale-Hubbell Law Directory

*MILWAUKEE,** Milwaukee Co.

Davis & Kuelthau, S.C. (AV)

111 East Kilbourn Avenue, Suite 1400, 53202-6613
Telephone: 414-276-0200
Facsimile: 414-276-9369
Cable Address: "Shiplaw"

Dianne S. Cauble — Robert E. Kuelthau
Perry H. Friesler — John G. Vergeront

Maurice D. Jones

For full biographical listings, see the Martindale-Hubbell Law Directory

Gibbs, Roper, Loots & Williams, S.C. (AV)

735 North Water Street, 53202
Telephone: 414-273-7000
Fax: 414-273-7897

Wayne J. Roper — Thomas P. Guszkowski
Robert J. Loots — Brent E. Gregory
George A. Evans, Jr. — Catherine Mode Eastham

For Complete List of Firm Personnel, See General Section

For full biographical listings, see the Martindale-Hubbell Law Directory

Meissner & Tierney, S.C. (AV)

The Milwaukee Center, 111 East Kilbourn Avenue, 19th Floor, 53202-6622
Telephone: 414-273-1300
Facsimile: 414-273-5840

Paul F. Meissner — Todd J. Mitchell
Joseph E. Tierney III — Thomas J. Nichols
Randal J. Brotherhood

Catherine M. Priebe Hertzberg

For full biographical listings, see the Martindale-Hubbell Law Directory

Quarles & Brady (AV)

411 East Wisconsin Avenue, 53202-4497
Telephone: 414-277-5000
Cable Address: "Lawdock"
Fax: 414-271-3552.
TWX: 910-262-3426
Madison, Wisconsin Office: Firstar Plaza, One South Pinckney Street, P.O. Box 2113.
Telephone: 608-251-5000.
Fax: 608-251-9166.
West Palm Beach, Florida Office: 222 Lakeview Avenue, 4th Floor.
Telephone: 407-653-5000.
Fax: 407-653-5333.

(See Next Column)

QUARLES & BRADY, *Milwaukee—Continued*

Naples, Florida Office: Barnett Center, 4501 Tamiami Trail North.
Telephone: 813-262-5959.
Fax: 813-434-4999.
Phoenix, Arizona Office: One Camelback Building, One East Camelback Road, Suite 400.
Telephone: 602-230-5500.
Fax: 602-230-5598.

MEMBERS OF FIRM

(ALPHABETICALLY BY YEAR OF ADMISSION TO BAR)

John S. Sammond (Resident, West Palm Beach, Florida Office)
David L. MacGregor
Jackson M. Bruce, Jr.
Jeremy C. Shea (Resident, Madison Office)
Donald S. Taitelman
Peter J. Lettenberger
Henry J. Loos
David L. Kinnamon
Anthony W. Asmuth, III
Thomas E. Maloney (Resident, Naples, Florida Office)
Steven R. Duback
James F. Daly
John H. Lhost
Charles W. Littell (Resident, West Palm Beach, Florida Office)
John T. Bannen
William D. McEachern (Resident, West Palm Beach, Florida Office)
Paul J. Tilleman
Kimberly Leach Johnson (Resident, Naples, Florida Office)
Kathleen A. Gray

OF COUNSEL

A. William Asmuth, Jr.
Dale L. Sorden

ASSOCIATES

Lynn Frances Chandler (Resident, Naples, Florida Office)
Sally C. Merrell
Jeffrey L. Elverman
Chris K. Gawart
Laurene M. Brooks
Elizabeth A. Dougherty (Resident, West Palm Beach, Florida Office)

For Complete List of Firm Personnel, See General Section

For full biographical listings, see the Martindale-Hubbell Law Directory

REINHART, BOERNER, VAN DEUREN, NORRIS & RIESELBACH, S.C. (AV)

1000 North Water Street, P.O. Box 92900, 53202-0900
Telephone: 414-298-1000
Facsimile: 414-298-8097
Denver, Colorado Office: One Norwest Center, 1700 Lincoln Street, Suite 3725.
Telephone: 303-831-0909.
Fax: 303-831-4805.
Madison, Wisconsin Office: 7617 Mineral Point Road, 53701-2020.
Telephone: 608-283-7900.
Fax: 608-283-7919.
Washington, D.C. Office: 601 Pennsylvania Avenue, N.W., North Building, Suite 750.
Telephone: 202-393-3636.
Fax: 202-393-0796.

Arthur F. Lubke, Jr.
Frederic G. Friedman
John A. Herbers
Michael R. Smith

Paul L. Winter (Not admitted in WI)
Jennifer R. D'Amato

LEGAL SUPPORT PERSONNEL

Dianne Ostrowski
Deanna Shimko-Herman

Representative Clients: Bank One Wisconsin Trust Co.; First Wisconsin Trust Co.; M&I Marshall & Illsley Trust Co.; First Bank--Milwaukee Trust Dept.; Valley Trust Co.

For Complete List of Firm Personnel, See General Section

For full biographical listings, see the Martindale-Hubbell Law Directory

*WAUKESHA,** Waukesha Co.

CRAMER, MULTHAUF & HAMMES (AV)

1601 East Racine Avenue, P.O. Box 558, 53187
Telephone: 414-542-4278
Telecopier: 414-542-4270

MEMBERS OF FIRM

John E. Multhauf
John M. Remmers

Reference: Waukesha State Bank.

For Complete List of Firm Personnel, See General Section

For full biographical listings, see the Martindale-Hubbell Law Directory

WYOMING

*BUFFALO,** Johnson Co.

OMOHUNDRO, PALMERLEE AND DURRANT (AV)

An Association of Attorneys
130 South Main Street, 82834
Telephone: 307-684-2207
Telecopier: 307-684-9364
Gillette, Wyoming Office: East Entrance, Suite 700, 201 West Lakeway Road.
Telephone: 307-682-7826.

William D. Omohundro (P.C.)
David F. Palmerlee
Sean P. Durrant

For full biographical listings, see the Martindale-Hubbell Law Directory

*CASPER,** Natrona Co.

BROWN & DREW (AV)

Casper Business Center, Suite 800, 123 West First Street, 82601-2486
Telephone: 307-234-1000
800-877-6755
Telefax: 307-265-8025

MEMBERS OF FIRM

Morris R. Massey
Harry B. Durham, III
W. Thomas Sullins, II
John A. Warnick
Thomas F. Reese

ASSOCIATES

Carol Warnick
Drew A. Perkins

Attorneys for: First Interstate Bank of Wyoming, N.A.; Norwest Bank Wyoming, N.A.; The CIT Group/Industrial Financing; Aetna Casualty & Surety Co.; The Doctor's Co.; MEDMARC; WOTCO, Inc.; Chevron USA; Kerr-McGee Corp.; Chicago and NorthWestern Transportation Company.

For Complete List of Firm Personnel, See General Section

For full biographical listings, see the Martindale-Hubbell Law Directory

*CODY,** Park Co.

SIMPSON, KEPLER & EDWARDS (AV)

1135 14th Street, P.O. Box 490, 82414
Telephone: 307-527-7891
FAX: 307-527-7897

MEMBERS OF FIRM

Milward L. Simpson (1897-1993)
Charles G. Kepler
William L. Simpson
Colin M. Simpson
Chris D. Edwards

References: Key Bank-Cody; Shoshone-First National Bank; Jackson State Bank.

For full biographical listings, see the Martindale-Hubbell Law Directory

CANADA
ALBERTA

*CALGARY,** Calgary Jud. Dist.

BENNETT JONES VERCHERE (AV)

4500 Bankers Hall East, 855-2nd Street S.W., T2P 4K7
Telephone: (403) 298-3100
Facsimile: (403) 265-7219
Edmonton, Alberta Office: 1000, 10035-105 Street.
Telephone: (403) 421-8133.
Facsimile: (403) 421-7951.
Toronto, Ontario Office: 3400 1 First Canadian Place. P.O. Box 130.
Telephone: (416) 863-1200.
Facsimile: (416) 863-1716.
Ottawa, Ontario Office: Suite 1800. 350 Alberta Street, Box 25, K1R 1A4.
Telephone: (613) 230-4935.
Facsimile: (613) 230-3836.
Montreal, Quebec Office: Suite 1600, 1 Place Ville Marie.
Telephone: (514) 871-1200.
Facsimile: (514) 871-8115.

MEMBER OF FIRM

John C. Armstrong, Q.C.

For Complete List of Firm Personnel, See General Section

For full biographical listings, see the Martindale-Hubbell Law Directory

*EDMONTON,** Edmonton Jud. Dist.

LUCAS BOWKER & WHITE (AV)

Esso Tower - Scotia Place, 1201-10060 Jasper Avenue, T5J 4E5
Telephone: 403-426-5330
Telecopier: 403-428-1066

MEMBERS OF FIRM

Cecilia I. Johnstone, Q.C.
Kent H. Davidson
Alan R. Gray
David J. Stam
Donald J. Wilson

ASSOCIATE

Annette E. Koski

Reference: Canadian Imperial Bank of Commerce.

For Complete List of Firm Personnel, See General Section

For full biographical listings, see the Martindale-Hubbell Law Directory

PARLEE McLAWS (AV)

15th Floor Manulife Place, 10180 101st Street, T5J 4K1
Telephone: 403-423-8500
Telecopier: 403-423-2870
Calgary, Alberta Office: 3400, Western Canadian Place, 707 - 8th Avenue, S.W.
Telephone: 403-294-7000.
Telecopier: 403-265-8263.

MEMBERS OF FIRM

C. H. Kerr, Q.C.
M. D. MacDonald
K. F. Bailey, Q.C.
R. B. Davison, Q.C.
F. R. Haldane
P. E. J. Curran
D. G. Finlay
J. K. McFadyen
R. C. Secord
D. L. Kennedy
D. C. Rolf
D. F. Pawlowski
A. A. Garber
R. P. James
D. C. Wintermute
J. L. Cairns
R. A. Newton, Q.C.
T. A. Cockrall, Q.C.
H. D. Montemurro
F. J. Niziol
R. W. Wilson
I. L. MacLachlan
R. O. Langley
R. G. McBean
J. T. Neilson
E. G. Rice
J. F. McGinnis
J. H. H. Hockin
G. W. Jaycock
M. J. K. Nikel
B. J. Curial
S. L. May
M. S. Poretti

ASSOCIATES

C. R. Head
A.W. Slemko
L. H. Hamdon
K.A. Smith
K. D. Fallis-Howell
D. S. Tam
J.W. McClure
F.H. Belzil
R.A. Renz
J.G. Paulson
K. E. Buss
B. L. Andriachuk
P. E. S. J. Kennedy
R. Feraco
R.J. Billingsley
N.B.R. Thompson
P. A. Shenher
I. C. Johnson
K.G. Koshman
D.D. Dubrule
G. T. Lund
W.D. Johnston
G. E. Flemming
K. P. Nayyer

For full biographical listings, see the Martindale-Hubbell Law Directory

CANADA BRITISH COLUMBIA

*VANCOUVER,** Vancouver Co.

RUSSELL & DuMOULIN (AV)

2100-1075 West Georgia Street, V6E 3G2
Telephone: 604-631-3131
Fax: 604-631-3232
A Member of the national association of Borden DuMoulin Howard Gervais, comprising Russell & DuMoulin, Vancouver, British Columbia; Howard Mackie, Calgary, Alberta; Borden & Elliot, Toronto, Ontario; Mackenzie Gervais, Montreal, Quebec and Borden DuMoulin Howard Gervais, London, England.
Strategic Alliance with Perkins Coie with offices in Seattle, Spokane and Bellevue, Washington; Portland, Oregon; Anchorage, Alaska; Los Angeles, California; Washington, D.C.; Hong Kong and Taipei, Taiwan.
Represented in Hong Kong by Vincent T.K. Cheung, Yap & Co.

MEMBERS OF FIRM

Leopold Amighetti, Q.C.
James G. Carphin

Representative Clients: Alcan Smelters & Chemicals Ltd.; The Bank of Nova Scotia; Canada Trust Co.; The Canada Life Assurance Co.; Forest Industrial Relations Ltd.; Honda Canada Inc.; IBM Canada Ltd.; Macmillan Bloedel Ltd.; Nissho Iwai Canada Ltd.; The Toronto-Dominion Bank.

(See Next Column)

For Complete List of Firm Personnel, See General Section

For full biographical listings, see the Martindale-Hubbell Law Directory

CANADA MANITOBA

*WINNIPEG,** Eastern Jud. Dist.

AIKINS, MACAULAY & THORVALDSON (AV)

Thirtieth Floor, Commodity Exchange Tower, 360 Main Street, R3C 4G1
Telephone: 204-957-0050
Fax: 204-957-0840

MEMBERS OF FIRM

A. Lorne Campbell, O.C., C.D., Q.C., LL.D.
Joel A. Weinstein
S. Jane Evans, Q.C.
Herbert J. Peters
Anita R. Wortzman
Andrew C. Tough
Robert G. Smellie, Q.C.
E. Bruce Parker
Frank Lavitt
Lisa M. Collins
Carmele N. Peter
Robert L. Tyler

Counsel for: Air Canada; Bank of Montreal; Boeing of Canada; Canada Safeway Limited; Canadian Medical Protective Association; Federal Industries Ltd.; The Great West Life Assurance Company; John Labatt Limited; Winnipeg Free Press; Winnipeg Jets.

For Complete List of Firm Personnel, See General Section

For full biographical listings, see the Martindale-Hubbell Law Directory

CANADA NEW BRUNSWICK

*SAINT JOHN,** Saint John Co.

CLARK, DRUMMIE & COMPANY (AV)

40 Wellington Row, P.O. Box 6850 Station "A", E2L 4S3
Telephone: 506-633-3800
Telecopier (Automatic): 506-633-3811

MEMBERS OF FIRM

Donald F. MacGowan, Q.C.
Sherrie R. Boyd
Donald J. Higgins

Reference: Royal Bank of Canada.

For Complete List of Firm Personnel, See General Section

For full biographical listings, see the Martindale-Hubbell Law Directory

CANADA NOVA SCOTIA

*HALIFAX,** Halifax Co.

McINNES COOPER & ROBERTSON (AV)

1601 Lower Water Street, P.O. Box 730, B3J 2V1
Telephone: 902-425-6500
Fax: 902-425-6350
St. John's, Newfoundland Office: Suite 602, Scotia Centre, 235 Water Street, P.O. Box 547. A1C, 5K8.
Telephone: 709-726-9500.
Fax: 709-726-9550.

Lawrence J. Hayes, Q.C.
Linda Lee Oland
George T. H. Cooper, Q.C.
Peter M. S. Bryson
Karen Oldfield

ASSOCIATE

Bernard F. Miller

Attorneys for: Bank of Nova Scotia; Imperial Oil, Limited; Frank B. Hall & Co., Inc. (New York); American Steamship Owners Protection & Indemnity Association, Inc.; Coca-Cola, Ltd.; Scott Worldwide Inc.; Hong Kong Bank of Canada.

For Complete List of Firm Personnel, See General Section

For full biographical listings, see the Martindale-Hubbell Law Directory

CANADA
ONTARIO

KITCHENER, Regional Munic. of Waterloo

GIFFEN, LEE, WAGNER, MORLEY & GARBUTT (AV)

50 Queen Street North, P.O. Box 2396, N2H 6M3
Telephone: 519-578-4150
Fax: 519-578-8740

MEMBERS OF FIRM

Jeffrey J. Mansfield (1955-1991)
J. Peter Giffen, Q.C.
Bruce L. Lee
J. Scott Morley
Brian R. Wagner
Philip A. Garbutt

ASSOCIATES

Edward J. Vanderkloet
Keith C. Masterman
Daniel J. Fife
Jeffrey W. Boich

For full biographical listings, see the Martindale-Hubbell Law Directory

*TORONTO,** Regional Munic. of York

BORDEN & ELLIOT (AV)

Barristers & Solicitors
Scotia Plaza, 40 King Street West, M5H 3Y4
Telephone: 416-367-6000
Telecopier: 416-367-6749
Internet: @ borden.com
A Member of the national association of Borden DuMoulin Howard Gervais, comprising Borden & Elliot in Toronto, Ontario, Russell & DuMoulin in Vancouver, British Columbia, Howard, Mackie in Calgary, Alberta and Mackenzie Gervais in Montréal, Québec. Borden DuMoulin Howard Gervais also operates an office in London, England.

MEMBER AND ASSOCIATES

W. Douglas R. Beamish

For Complete List of Firm Personnel, See General Section

For full biographical listings, see the Martindale-Hubbell Law Directory

CANADA
QUEBEC

*MONTREAL,** Montreal Dist.

MCMASTER MEIGHEN (AV)

A General Partnership
7th Floor, 630 René-Lévesque Boulevard West, H3B 4H7
Telephone: 514-879-1212
Telecopier: 514-878-0605
Cable Address: "Cammerall"
Telex: "Cammerall MTL" 05-268637
Affiliated with Fraser & Beatty in Toronto, North York, Ottawa and Vancouver.

MEMBERS OF FIRM

William E. Stavert
Michael S. McAuley
Paul R. Marchand
Marc L. Weinstein
Elana Weissbach

For Complete List of Firm Personnel, See General Section

For full biographical listings, see the Martindale-Hubbell Law Directory

CANADA
SASKATCHEWAN

*REGINA,** Regina Jud. Centre

MCDOUGALL, READY (AV)

700 Royal Bank Building, 2010-11th Avenue, S4P 0J3
Telephone: 306-757-1641
Telecopier: 306-359-0785
Saskatoon, Saskatchewan, Canada Office: 301 - 111 2nd Avenue South.
Telephone: 306-653-1641.
Telecopier: 306-665-8511.

MEMBERS OF FIRM

William F. Ready, Q.C.
Elmer Youck
Robert N. Millar
Wayne L. Bernakevitch
Pamela J. Lothian

Penny Overby (Resident, Saskatoon Office)

Representative Clients: Royal Bank of Canada; Imperial Oil, Ltd.; John Deere Limited; Ford Motor Company of Canada, Ltd.; Chrysler Canada Ltd.; General Motors of Canada Limited; Phoenix of London Group; University of Regina.

For Complete List of Firm Personnel, See General Section

For full biographical listings, see the Martindale-Hubbell Law Directory

*SASKATOON,** Saskatoon Jud. Centre

MCKERCHER, MCKERCHER & WHITMORE (AV)

374 Third Avenue, South, S7K 1M5
Telephone: 306-653-2000
Fax: 306-244-7335
Regina, Saskatchewan Office: 1000 - 1783 Hamilton Street.
Telephone: 306-352-7661.
Fax: 306-781-7113.

MEMBERS OF FIRM

D. S. McKercher, Q.C.
Thomas G. (Casey) Davis

ASSOCIATES

L. J. Korchin
Caroline M. K. Gorsalitz
J. Denis Bonthoux

Representative Clients: The Royal Bank of Canada; Cominco Ltd.; Saskatoon City Hospital; London Life Insurance Co.; The University of Saskatchewan; Gulf Oil Canada, Ltd.; Chicago Title Insurance Co.

For Complete List of Firm Personnel, See General Section

For full biographical listings, see the Martindale-Hubbell Law Directory

PRODUCT LIABILITY LAW

ALABAMA

ALEXANDER CITY, Tallapoosa Co.

MORRIS, HAYNES, INGRAM & HORNSBY (AV)
101 Madison Street, P.O. Box 1449, 35010
Telephone: 205-329-2000
Fax: 205-329-2015

Larry W. Morris
Randall Stark Haynes
Kenneth F. Ingram, Jr.
Clay Hornsby

OF COUNSEL

John F. Dillon, IV
Jennie Lee Kelley

Representative Clients: First National Bank; City of Alexander City; Town of Wadley; Russell Corp.
Approved Attorneys for: Lawyers Title Insurance Corp.; Mississippi Valley Title Insurance Co.

For full biographical listings, see the Martindale-Hubbell Law Directory

*BIRMINGHAM,** Jefferson Co.

PITTMAN, HOOKS, MARSH, DUTTON & HOLLIS, P.C. (AV)
1100 Park Place Tower, 35203
Telephone: 205-322-8880
Telecopier: 205-328-2711

W. Lee Pittman
Kenneth W. Hooks
David H. Marsh
Tom Dutton
L. Andrew Hollis, Jr.
Jeffrey C. Kirby
Ralph Bohanan, Jr.
Nat Bryan

Jeffrey C. Rickard
Susan J. Silvernail
Nici F. Williams
Chris T. Hellums
Adam P. Morel

OF COUNSEL

James H. Davis (Not admitted in AL)
Myra B. Staggs

For full biographical listings, see the Martindale-Hubbell Law Directory

PRITCHARD, McCALL & JONES (AV)
800 Financial Center, 35203
Telephone: 205-328-9190

MEMBERS OF FIRM

William S. Pritchard (1890-1967)
Alexander W. Jones (1914-1988)
William S. Pritchard, Jr.
Madison W. O'Kelley, Jr.
Julian P. Hardy, Jr.
Alexander W. Jones, Jr.
F. Hilton-Green Tomlinson
James G. Henderson
William S. Pritchard, III

ASSOCIATES

Michael L. McKerley
Robert Bond Higgins
Nina Michele LaFleur
Mary W. Burge

Representative Clients: First National Bank of Columbiana; Central State Bank of Calera; Buffalo Rock-Pepsi-Cola Bottling Co.; Gillis Advertising, Inc.; Liberty Mutual Insurance Co.; Reliance Insurance Company; SouthTrust Bank, N.A.; Bromberg & Company, Inc.; Farmers Furniture Company; First Commercial Bank.

For full biographical listings, see the Martindale-Hubbell Law Directory

*FLORENCE,** Lauderdale Co.

JONES, TROUSDALE & THOMPSON (AV)
115 Helton Court, Suite B, 35630
Telephone: 205-767-0333
Telefax: 205-767-0331

MEMBERS OF FIRM

Robert E. Jones, III
Preston S. Trousdale, Jr.
R. Waylon Thompson

For full biographical listings, see the Martindale-Hubbell Law Directory

POTTS & YOUNG (AV)
107 East College Street, 35630
Telephone: 205-764-7142
Fax: 205-764-7717

(See Next Column)

OF COUNSEL

Doyle R. Young (Retired)
Robert L. Potts

MEMBERS OF FIRM

Frank V. Potts
Frank B. Potts

ASSOCIATES

Robert W. Beasley
Debra H. Coble
Mark A. Sanderson

Representative Clients: E. A. Nelson Co., Inc.; Nelco, Inc.; Lauderdale County Board of Education; American Abrasive Air & Service Co., Inc.; Diversified Products, Inc.; BIG DELI STORES, Inc.; Spry Funeral Homes of Russellville, Sheffield & Florence; Americans United for the Separation of Church & State; Colbert County Community Economic Development Corp.
Reference: Bank Independent.

For full biographical listings, see the Martindale-Hubbell Law Directory

*HUNTSVILLE,** Madison Co.

HORNSBY, WATSON & MEGINNISS (AV)
1110 Gleneagles Drive, 35801
Telephone: 205-650-5500
Fax: 205-650-5504

Ralph W. Hornsby
S. A. "Bud" Watson, Jr.
David H. Meginniss
Ralph W. Hornsby, Jr.

For full biographical listings, see the Martindale-Hubbell Law Directory

WATSON, GAMMONS & FEES, P.C. (AV)
200 Clinton Avenue, N.W., Suite 800, P.O. Box 46, 35804
Telephone: 205-536-7423
Telecopier: 205-536-2689

Herman Watson, Jr.
Robert C. Gammons
Michael L. Fees
Joseph A. Jimmerson
J. Barton Warren
Charles H. Pullen
Billie B. Line, Jr.

OF COUNSEL

George K. Williams

LEGAL SUPPORT PERSONNEL

James W. Lowery, Jr. (Administrator)

For full biographical listings, see the Martindale-Hubbell Law Directory

*MOBILE,** Mobile Co.

BURNS, CUNNINGHAM & MACKEY, P.C. (AV)
50 St. Emanuel Street, P.O. Box 1583, 36633
Telephone: 334-432-0612

Peter F. Burns
William M. Cunningham, Jr.
Peter S. Mackey

Max Cassady

For full biographical listings, see the Martindale-Hubbell Law Directory

CUNNINGHAM, BOUNDS, YANCE, CROWDER & BROWN (AV)
1601 Dauphin Street, P.O. Box 66705, 36660
Telephone: 334-471-6191
Fax: 334-479-1031

Richard Bounds
James A. Yance
John T. Crowder, Jr.
Robert T. Cunningham, Jr.
Joseph M. Brown, Jr.
Gregory B. Breedlove
Andrew T. Citrin
Michael A. Worel

David G. Wirtes, Jr.
Randolph B. Walton
Toby D. Brown
Mitchell K. Shelly

OF COUNSEL

Robert T. Cunningham
Valentino D. B. Mazzia

References: First Alabama Bank; AmSouth Bank, N.A.

For full biographical listings, see the Martindale-Hubbell Law Directory

DIAMOND, HASSER & FROST (AV)
1325 Dauphin Street, P.O. Drawer 40600, 36640
Telephone: 334-432-3362
Fax: 334-432-3367

MEMBERS OF FIRM

Ross Diamond, Jr. (1919-1978)
Ross M. Diamond, III
James E. Hasser, Jr.
James H. Frost

References: First Alabama Bank, Mobile; AM South Bank, Mobile.

For full biographical listings, see the Martindale-Hubbell Law Directory

Mobile—Continued

FINKBOHNER AND LAWLER (AV)

169 Dauphin Street Suite 300, P.O. Box 3085, 36652
Telephone: 334-438-5871
Fax: 334-432-8052

MEMBERS OF FIRM

George W. Finkbohner, Jr. — George W. Finkbohner, III
John L. Lawler — Royce A. Ray, III

For full biographical listings, see the Martindale-Hubbell Law Directory

HAND, ARENDALL, BEDSOLE, GREAVES & JOHNSTON (AV)

3000 First National Bank Building, P.O. Box 123, Drawer C, 36601
Telephone: 334-432-5511
Fax: 334-694-6375
Washington, D.C. Office: 410 First Street, S.E., Suite 300. 20003.
Telephone: 202-863-0053.
Fax: 202-863-0096.

MEMBERS OF FIRM

Paul W. Brock — George M. Walker
Louis E. Braswell — M. Mallory Mantiply
Michael D. Knight — Henry A. Callaway, III
Edward S. Sledge, III — P. Russel Myles
Walter T. Gilmer, Jr.

General Counsel for: The Bank of Mobile; Delchamps, Inc.; The Mobile Press Register, Inc.; Mobile Asphalt Company; Gulf Telephone Company; Folmar & Associates; Mobile Community Foundation; Gulf Lumber Company; Scotch Lumber Company; Mobile Pulley & Machine Works, Inc.; Pennsylvania Shipbuilding Co.

For Complete List of Firm Personnel, See General Section

For full biographical listings, see the Martindale-Hubbell Law Directory

LYONS, PIPES & COOK, P.C. (AV)

2 North Royal Street, P.O. Box 2727, 36652-2727
Telephone: 334-432-4481
Cable Address: "Lysea"
Telecopier: 334-433-1820

Joseph H. Lyons (1874-1957) — Charles L. Miller, Jr.
Sam W. Pipes, III (1916-1982) — W. David Johnson, Jr.
Walter M. Cook (1915-1988) — Joseph J. Minus, Jr.
G. Sage Lyons — Caroline C. McCarthy
Wesley Pipes — William E. Shreve, Jr.
Norton W. Brooker, Jr. — R. Mark Kirkpatrick
Cooper C. Thurber — Kenneth A. Nixon
Marion A. Quina, Jr. — Dan S. Cushing
Thomas F. Garth — Allen E. Graham
Claude D. Boone — Michael C. Niemeyer
Walter M. Cook, Jr. — John C. Bell
John Patrick Courtney, III — Richard D. Morrison
Reggie Copeland, Jr. — M. Warren Butler
Christopher Lee George

General Counsel: Inchcape Shipping Services.
Counsel: The Hertz Corp.; McKenzie Tank Lines, Inc.; SCNO Barge Lines, Inc.; Scott Paper Co.; Shell Oil Corp.
Trial Counsel: Aetna Life & Casualty Co.; Chubb Group of Insurance Companies.

For full biographical listings, see the Martindale-Hubbell Law Directory

*MONTGOMERY,** Montgomery Co.

BEASLEY, WILSON, ALLEN, MAIN & CROW, P.C. (AV)

218 Commerce Street, P.O. Box 4160, 36103-4160
Telephone: 334-269-2343
Fax: 334-269-2371

Jere Locke Beasley — Frank M. Wilson
J. Greg Allen

Blaine C. Stevens — J. Cole Portis
Julia Anne Beasley

For full biographical listings, see the Martindale-Hubbell Law Directory

ALASKA

*ANCHORAGE,** Third Judicial District

LLOYD V. ANDERSON (AV)

370 Oceanview Drive, 99515
Telephone: 907-345-2024
Telecopier: 907-345-6384

For full biographical listings, see the Martindale-Hubbell Law Directory

YOUNG, SANDERS & FELDMAN, INC. (AV)

Suite 400, 500 L Street, 99501
Telephone: 907-272-3538
Telecopier: 907-274-0819

Joseph L. Young — Jeffrey M. Feldman
Eric T. Sanders — Kristen Young

Reference: Key Bank of Alaska.

For full biographical listings, see the Martindale-Hubbell Law Directory

ARIZONA

*PHOENIX,** Maricopa Co.

BEGAM, LEWIS, MARKS, WOLFE & DASSE A PROFESSIONAL ASSOCIATION OF LAWYERS (AV)

111 West Monroe Street, Suite 1400, 85003-1787
Telephone: 602-254-6071
Fax: 602-252-0042

Robert G. Begam — Cora Perez
Frank Lewis — Kelly J. McDonald
Stanley J. Marks — Daniel J. Adelman
Elliot G. Wolfe — Lisa Kurtz
Thomas F. Dasse — Dena Rosen Epstein

Reference: National Bank of Arizona.

For full biographical listings, see the Martindale-Hubbell Law Directory

BROWN & BAIN, A PROFESSIONAL ASSOCIATION (AV)

2901 North Central Avenue, P.O. Box 400, 85001-0400
Telephone: 602-351-8000
Cable: TWX 910-951-0646
Telecopier: 602-351-8516
Palo Alto, California Affiliated Office: Brown & Bain, 600 Hansen Way.
Telephone: 415-856-9411.
Telecopier: 415-856-6061.
Tucson, Arizona Affiliated Office: Brown & Bain, A Professional Association. One South Church Avenue, Nineteenth Floor, P.O. Box 2265.
Telephone: 602-798-7900
Telecopier: 602-798-7945.

C. Randall Bain — Howard Ross Cabot
John A. Buttrick — Joel W. Nomkin
Charles S. Price

Christopher J. Raboin

For Complete List of Firm Personnel, See General Section

For full biographical listings, see the Martindale-Hubbell Law Directory

BURCH & CRACCHIOLO, P.A. (AV)

702 East Osborn Road, Suite 200, 85014
Telephone: 602-274-7611
Fax: 602-234-0341
Mailing Address: P.O. Box 16882, Phoenix, AZ, 85011

Ian Neale — Linda A. Finnegan

Representative Clients: Bashas' Inc.; Farmers Insurance Group; U-Haul International, Inc.

For Complete List of Firm Personnel, See General Section

For full biographical listings, see the Martindale-Hubbell Law Directory

O'CONNOR, CAVANAGH, ANDERSON, WESTOVER, KILLINGSWORTH & BESHEARS, A PROFESSIONAL ASSOCIATION (AV)

One East Camelback Road, Suite 1100, 85012-1656
Telephone: 602-263-2400
FAX: 602-263-2900
Sun City, Arizona Office: 13250 North Del Webb Boulevard, Suite B, 85351.
Telephone: 602-263-2808.
FAX: 602-933-3100.
Tucson, Arizona Office: Suite 2200, One South Church Avenue, 85701.
Telephone: 602-882-8912.
FAX: 602-624-9564.
Nogales, Arizona Office: 1827 North Mastick Way, 85621.
Telephone: 602-761-4215.
FAX: 602-761-3505.

(See Next Column)

O'CONNOR, CAVANAGH, ANDERSON, WESTOVER, KILLINGSWORTH & BESHEARS A PROFESSIONAL ASSOCIATION—*Continued*

Ralph E. Hunsaker
Thomas A. McGuire, Jr.
George H. Mitchell
Richard J. Woods
Steven D. Smith
Michael W. Carnahan
Carol N. Cure
Scott A. Salmon
David L. Kurtz
Paul J. Giancola
Lisa M. Sommer

Robert W. Blesch

Ashley D. Adams
Janet M. Walsh
Mark D. Dillon
Kent S. Berk

Representative Clients: Fleetwood Enterprises; Johnson & Johnson; Clorox; Abbott Laboratories; Keller Industries; Black & Decker Corp.; Arizona Elevator, Inc.

For Complete List of Firm Personnel, See General Section

For full biographical listings, see the Martindale-Hubbell Law Directory

SCOTTSDALE, Maricopa Co.

JEFFREY A. MATZ A PROFESSIONAL CORPORATION (AV(T))

6711 East Camelback Road, Suite 8, 85251
Telephone: 602-955-0900
Fax: 602-955-1885

Jeffrey A. Matz (Not admitted in AZ)

*TUCSON,** Pima Co.

O'CONNOR, CAVANAGH, ANDERSON, WESTOVER, KILLINGSWORTH & BESHEARS, A PROFESSIONAL ASSOCIATION (AV)

Suite 2200 One South Church Avenue, 85701-1621
Telephone: 602-882-8912
FAX: 602-624-9564
Phoenix, Arizona Office: One East Camelback Road, Suite 1100, 85012.
Telephone: 602-263-2400.
FAX: 602-263-2900.
Sun City, Arizona Office: 13250 North Del Webb Boulevard, Suite B, 85351.
Telephone: 602-263-2808.
FAX: 602-933-3100.
Nogales, Arizona Office: 1827 North Mastick Way, 85621.
Telephone: 602-761-4215.
FAX: 602-761-3505.

Ted A. Schmidt
Peter Akmajian

Amy M. Samberg
James D. Campbell

Representative Client: Jeffco, Inc.
Reference: Citibank.

For Complete List of Firm Personnel, See General Section

For full biographical listings, see the Martindale-Hubbell Law Directory

ARKANSAS

WEST MEMPHIS, Crittenden Co.

RIEVES & MAYTON (AV)

304 East Broadway, P.O. Box 1359, 72303
Telephone: 501-735-3420
Telecopier: 501-735-4678

MEMBERS OF FIRM

Elton A. Rieves, Jr. (1909-1984)
Elton A. Rieves, III
Michael R. Mayton
Elton A. Rieves, IV

ASSOCIATES

Martin W. Bowen
William J. Stanley

For full biographical listings, see the Martindale-Hubbell Law Directory

CALIFORNIA

BEVERLY HILLS, Los Angeles Co.

DANA B. TASCHNER, P.C. (AV(T))

9454 Wilshire Boulevard, Suite 550, 90212-2915
Telephone: 310-592-2600
Fax: 310-592-2640
Dallas, Texas Office: 350 St. Paul Street. 75201.
Liechtenstein Associated Office: DDr. Proksch & Partner. ITA P&A Bürotel Building. Landstrasse 161-163. FL 9494 Schaan.
Telephone: 41 75 2332303, 2322614, 2324121.
Facsimile: 41 75 2323562, 2324133, 2329181.
Telex: 899520 ita fl E-Mail:100415,1733 @ compuserve.com

Dana B. Taschner

OF COUNSEL

Reinhard J. Proksch (Not admitted in CA)

For full biographical listings, see the Martindale-Hubbell Law Directory

LARKSPUR, Marin Co.

WEINBERG, HOFFMAN & CASEY (AV)

A Partnership including a Professional Corporation
700 Larkspur Landing Circle, Suite 280, 94939
Telephone: 415-461-9666
Fax: 415-461-9681

Ivan Weinberg
Joseph Hoffman
A. Michael Casey

For full biographical listings, see the Martindale-Hubbell Law Directory

LONG BEACH, Los Angeles Co.

BENNETT & KISTNER (AV)

301 East Ocean Boulevard, Suite 800, 90802
Telephone: 310-435-6675
Fax: 310-437-8375
Riverside, California Office: 3403 Tenth Street, Suite 605. 92501-3676.
Telephone: 909-341-9360.
Fax: 909-341-9362.

Charles J. Bennett
Wayne T. Kistner

ASSOCIATES

Richard R. Bradbury
Mary A. Estante (Resident, Riverside Office)
Todd R. Becker
Karen H. Beckman (Resident, Riverside Office)

Representative Clients: The Hertz Corporation; Thrifty Oil Co.; Golden West Refining Co.; Standard Brands Paint Co.; Mattel, Inc.; Di Salvo Trucking Co.; County of Riverside; Southern California Rapid Transit District.
Reference: First Interstate Bank of California, The Market Place Office, Long Beach, California.

For full biographical listings, see the Martindale-Hubbell Law Directory

STOLPMAN, KRISSMAN, ELBER, MANDEL & KATZMAN (AV)

A Partnership including Professional Corporations
Nineteenth Floor, 111 West Ocean Boulevard, 90802-4649
Telephone: 310-435-8300
Telecopier: 310-435-8304
Los Angeles (Westwood) Office: Suite 1800, 10880 Wilshire Boulevard.
Telephone: 213-470-8011.

MEMBERS OF FIRM

Thomas G. Stolpman (Inc.)
Leonard H. Mandel (Inc.)
Bernard Katzman (Inc.)
Joel Krissman
Mary Nielsen Abbott
Donna Silver
Dennis M. Elber

ASSOCIATES

Edwin Silver
Lynne Rasmussen
Marilyn S. Heise
Elaine Mandel

OF COUNSEL

Richard L. McWilliams (Inc.)

For full biographical listings, see the Martindale-Hubbell Law Directory

*LOS ANGELES,** Los Angeles Co.

MATTHEW B. F. BIREN & ASSOCIATES (AV)

815 Moraga Drive, 90049-1633
Telephone: 310-476-3031; 381-5609
FAX: 310-471-3165

Marc J. Katzman
Kimberly A. Miller
Debra J. Tauger
Michael L. Justice
Edmont T. Barrett

(See Next Column)

MATTHEW B. F. BIREN & ASSOCIATES, *Los Angeles—Continued*

Reference: First Los Angeles Bank (Century City, Los Angeles, Branch).

For full biographical listings, see the Martindale-Hubbell Law Directory

---

CLARK & TREVITHICK, A PROFESSIONAL CORPORATION (AV)

800 Wilshire Boulevard, 12th Floor, 90017
Telephone: 213-629-5700
Telecopier: 213-624-9441

Philip W. Bartenetti
Dolores Cordell
Vincent Tricarico
Leonard Brazil
Arturo Santana Jr.
Kerry T. Ryan

References: Wells Fargo Bank (Los Angeles Main Office); National Bank of California.

For Complete List of Firm Personnel, See General Section

For full biographical listings, see the Martindale-Hubbell Law Directory

---

WILLIAM J. GARGARO, JR. A PROFESSIONAL CORPORATION (AV)

Suite 1800, 2049 Century Park East, 90067
Telephone: 310-552-0633
FAX: 310-552-9760

William J. Gargaro, Jr.

Reference: First Interstate Bank of California.

For full biographical listings, see the Martindale-Hubbell Law Directory

---

HAWKINS, SCHNABEL, LINDAHL & BECK (AV)

660 South Figueroa Street, Suite 1500, 90017
Telephone: 213-488-3900
Telecopier: 213-486-9883
Cable Address: "Haslin"

MEMBERS OF FIRM

Roger E. Hawkins
Laurence H. Schnabel
George M. Lindahl
Jon P. Kardassakis
William E. Keitel

For full biographical listings, see the Martindale-Hubbell Law Directory

---

KOSLOV & CADY (AV)

Suite 650 Roosevelt Building, 727 West Seventh Street, 90017
Telephone: 213-629-2647
FAX: 213-689-9628

MEMBERS OF FIRM

John Koslov
Eurus Cady

ASSOCIATES

Judy L. McKelvey
Melina J. Burns
William P. Medlen

For full biographical listings, see the Martindale-Hubbell Law Directory

---

LA FOLLETTE, JOHNSON, DE HAAS, FESLER & AMES, A PROFESSIONAL CORPORATION (AV)

865 South Figueroa Street, Suite 3100, 90017-5443
Telephone: 213-426-3600
Fax: 213-426-3650
San Francisco, California Office: 50 California Street, Suite 3350.
Telephone: 415-433-7610.
Telecopier: 415-392-7541.
Santa Ana, California Office: 2677 North Main Street, Suite 901.
Telephone: 714-558-7008.
Telecopier: 714-972-0379.
Riverside, California Office: 3403 Tenth Street, Suite 820.
Telephone: 714-275-9192.
Fax: 714-275-9249.

John T. La Follette (1922-1990)
Daren T. Johnson
Louis H. De Haas
Donald C. Fesler
Dennis K. Ames (Resident, Santa Ana Office)
Alfred W. Gerisch, Jr.
Brian W. Birnie
Peter J. Zomber
Robert E. Kelly, Jr.
Leon A. Zallen
G. Kelley Reid, Jr. (Resident, San Francisco Office)
Dennis J. Sinclitico
Christopher C. Cannon (Resident, Santa Ana Office)
Dorothy B. Reyes
Steven R. Odell (Santa Ana and Riverside Offices)
Christopher L. Thomas (Santa Ana and Riverside Offices)
Robert K. Warford (Resident, Riverside Office)
John L. Supple (Resident, San Francisco Office)
Vincent D. Lapointe
Steven J. Joffe
Mark M. Stewart
Bradley J. McGirr (Resident, Santa Ana Office)
Sydney La Branche Merritt

(See Next Column)

Peter R. Bing
Larry P. Nathenson
Donald R. Beck (Resident, Santa Ana Office)
Donna R. Evans
David J. Ozeran
Mark B. Guterman
Terry A. Woodward (Resident, Santa Ana Office)
Stephen C. Dreher (Resident, Santa Ana Office)
Tatiana M. Schultz (Resident, San Francisco Office)
Peter E. Theophilos (Resident, San Francisco Office)
Deborah A. Cowley
Thomas S. Alch
Kenton E. Moore
Kent T. Brandmeyer
Garry O. Moses
Jeffery R. Erickson (Resident, Riverside Office)
Michael J. O'Connor
Elizabeth Anne Scherer (Resident, Santa Ana Office)
Hugh R. Burns
Stephen K. Hiura
James G. Wold
Eileen S. Lemmon (Resident, Riverside, Office)
David M. Wright
Larry E. White (Resident, Riverside Office)
Laurie Miyamoto Johnson
David James Reinard
Michelle Louise McCoy
Duane A. Newton (Resident, Riverside Office)
Adriaan F. van der Capellen (Resident, Santa Ana Office)
William T. Gray (Resident, Santa Ana Office)
Thomas J. Lo (Resident, Santa Ana Office)
Daniel D. Sorenson (Resident, Riverside Office)
Joanne Rosendin (Resident, San Francisco Office)
Henry P. Canvel (Resident, San Francisco Office)
Peter D. Busciglio (Resident, Santa Ana Office)
Mark S. Rader (Resident, Riverside Office)
Jay B. Lake
Erin L. Muellenberg (Resident, Riverside Office)
Phyllis M. Winston (Resident, Riverside Office)
John Calfee Mulvana (Resident, Santa Ana Office)
David L. Bell
Brian T. Chu (Resident, Santa Ana Office)
John Hammond
Laurent C. Vonderweidt
David Peim
Daniel V. Kohls (Resident, San Francisco Office)
Joel E. D. Odou
Robert T. Bergsten
Marcelo A. D'Asero
Natasha M. Riggs
Henry M. Su
Richard K. Kay
Annette A. Apperson

A list of References will be furnished upon request.

For full biographical listings, see the Martindale-Hubbell Law Directory

---

LANE POWELL SPEARS LUBERSKY (AV)

A Partnership including Professional Corporations
333 South Hope Street, Suite 2400, 90071
Telephone: 213-680-1010
FAX: 213-680-1784
Other Offices at: Seattle, Mount Vernon and Olympia, Washington; Anchorage, Alaska; San Francisco, California; Portland, Oregon; London, England

MEMBERS OF FIRM

John J. Geary, Jr.
Kathryn R. Janssen
Laurence F. Janssen
Lawrence P. Riff

ASSOCIATES

Benjamin M. Chin
Celeste V. De Petris
Ruth D. Kahn
Jay E. Smith

Chevron Corp.; Exxon Company, U.S.A.; Shell Oil Co.; Monsanto Co.; Ashland Chemical Co.; Unocal Corp.; Texaco, Inc.; Mobil Oil Corp.; ARCO Chemical Co.; The Dow Chemical Co.

For full biographical listings, see the Martindale-Hubbell Law Directory

MENLO PARK, San Mateo Co.

O'REILLY & COLLINS, A PROFESSIONAL CORPORATION (AV)

2500 Sand Hill Road, Suite 201, 94025
Telephone: 415-854-7700
Fax: 415-854-8350

Terry O'Reilly
James P. Collins

James P. Tessier

For full biographical listings, see the Martindale-Hubbell Law Directory

*OAKLAND,** Alameda Co.

HAIMS, JOHNSON, MACGOWAN & MCINERNEY (AV)

490 Grand Avenue, 94610
Telephone: 510-835-0500
Facsimile: 510-835-2833

MEMBERS OF FIRM

Arnold B. Haims
Gary R. Johnson
Clyde L. MacGowan
Thomas McInerney
Lawrence A. Baker
Randy M. Marmor
John K. Kirby
Robert J. Frassetto
Caroline N. Valentino

(See Next Column)

HAIMS, JOHNSON, MACGOWAN & MCINERNEY—*Continued*

ASSOCIATES

Joseph Y. Ahn
Edward D. Baldwin
Kathleen B. Boehm
Marc P. Bouret
Anne M. Michaels
Dianne D. Peebles
Michelle D. Perry
Edward C. Schroeder, Jr.

For full biographical listings, see the Martindale-Hubbell Law Directory

PALM SPRINGS, Riverside Co.

REGAR & PARKINSON (AV)

255 North El Cielo, Suite 200, 92262-6974
Telephone: 619-327-1516
Fax: 619-327-3291

MEMBERS OF FIRM

Barry Regar
James W. Parkinson

ASSOCIATE

Sigrid R. Hilkey

For full biographical listings, see the Martindale-Hubbell Law Directory

*SACRAMENTO,** Sacramento Co.

CAULFIELD, DAVIES & DONAHUE (AV)

3500 American River Drive, 1st Floor, 95864
Telephone: 916-487-7700
Fairfield, California Office: Fairfield West Plaza, 1455 Oliver Road, Suite 130.
Telephone: 707-426-0223.

MEMBERS OF FIRM

Richard Hyland Caulfield
Robert E. Davies
James R. Donahue
Bruce E. Leonard
Michael M. McKone
Douglas L. Smith

ASSOCIATES

David N. Tedesco
Matthew Paul Donahue
Brian C. Haydon
Paul R. Ramsey

For full biographical listings, see the Martindale-Hubbell Law Directory

DREYER, BABICH, BUCCOLA & CALLAHAM (AV)

715 University Avenue, 95825
Telephone: 916-920-2111
Fax: 916-920-5687

MEMBERS OF FIRM

Roger A. Dreyer
Joseph J. Babich
Robert A. Buccola
William C. Callaham

Craig C. Sheffer
Stephen F. Davids
Dianna L. Albini
John W. Jefferson
Leland J. Aiken

For full biographical listings, see the Martindale-Hubbell Law Directory

JOHNSON, SCHACHTER, LEWIS & COLLINS, A PROFESSIONAL CORPORATION (AV)

701 University Avenue, Suite 150, 95825
Telephone: 916-921-5800
Telecopier: 916-921-0247
Walnut Creek, California Office: 500 Ygnacio Valley Road #490.
Telephone: 510-947-0100.
Fax: 510-947-0111.
Chico, California Office: 515 Wall Street.
Telephone: 916-895-1623.

Robert H. Johnson
Alesa M. Schachter
Luther R. Lewis
Kim H. Collins

George W. Holt
Timothy P. Dailey
James B. Walker
R. James Miller

OF COUNSEL

Ford R. Smith
Carolyn M. Wood
Susanne M. Shelley
James W. Rushford

Representative Clients: Fireman's Fund Insurance Cos; GAB Business Services; Jonsson Communications Corp.; McClatchy Newspapers and Broadcasting; State Farm Fire & Casualty Co.; State Farm Mutual Automobile Insurance Co.
Reference: Business & Professional Bank, Sacramento.

For full biographical listings, see the Martindale-Hubbell Law Directory

SCHUERING ZIMMERMAN SCULLY & NOLEN (AV)

400 University Avenue, 95825
Telephone: 916-567-0400
Fax: 916-568-0400

(See Next Column)

MEMBERS OF FIRM

Leo H. Schuering, Jr.
Robert H. Zimmerman
Steven T. Scully
Rhudolph Nolen, Jr.
Thomas J. Doyle
Lawrence S. Giardina
Anthony D. Lauria

Keith D. Chidlaw
Regina A. Favors
Raymond R. Gates
Scott A. Linn
Donna W. Low
Dominique A. Pollara
Theodore D. Poppinga
Janet Marie Richmond
John J. Sillis

For full biographical listings, see the Martindale-Hubbell Law Directory

*SAN BERNARDINO,** San Bernardino Co.

MAC LACHLAN, BURFORD & ARIAS, A LAW CORPORATION (AV)

560 East Hospitality Lane, Fourth Floor, 92408
Telephone: 909-885-4491
Fax: 909-888-6866
Rancho Cucamonga, California Office: 8280 Utica Avenue, Suite 200. 909-989-4481.
Palm Springs, California Office: 255 North El Cielo Road, Suite 470. 619-320-5761.
Victorville, California Office: 14011 Park Avenue, Suite 410. 619-243-7933.

Bruce D. Mac Lachlan
Ronald A. Burford
Joseph Arias
Michael W. Mugg
Dennis G. Popka
Leigh O. Harper (Resident, Palm Springs Office)
Clifford R. Cunningham (Resident, Rancho Cucamonga Office)
Dennis R. Stout
Sharon K. Burchett (Resident, Rancho Cucamonga Office)
Christopher D. Lockwood
Vernon C. Lauridsen (Resident, Rancho Cucamonga Office)
John G. Evans (Resident, Palm Springs Office)
Richard R. Hegner (Resident, Victorville Office)
Dennis J. Mahoney
Kathleen M. Keefe
Toni R. Fullerton
Mark R. Harris
Diana J. Carloni (Resident, Victorville Office)
Jean M. Landry
Frank M. Loo

Representative Clients: Aetna Life & Casualty; Automobile Club of Southern California; California State Automobile Association; City of San Bernardino; Reliance Insurance; Republic Insurance; Southern Pacific Transportation Co.; State Farm Fire and Casualty Co.; State Farm Mutual Automobile Insurance Co.; County of San Bernardino.

For full biographical listings, see the Martindale-Hubbell Law Directory

*SAN DIEGO,** San Diego Co.

DOUGHERTY & HILDRE (AV)

2550 Fifth Avenue, Suite 600, 92103-5624
Telephone: 619-232-9131
Telefax: 619-232-7317

William O. Dougherty
Donald F. Hildre
Daniel H. Cargnelutti
Fred M. Dudek
Mona H. Freedman

For full biographical listings, see the Martindale-Hubbell Law Directory

HUGHES & NUNN (AV)

A Partnership including a Professional Corporation
450 "B" Street, Suite 2000, 92101
Telephone: 619-231-1661
Telecopier: 619-236-9271

MEMBERS OF FIRM

William D. Hughes (A Professional Corporation)
Randall M. Nunn
Scott D. Schabacker

ASSOCIATES

Lucia Rivas
E. Kenneth Purviance
Regan Furcolo

For full biographical listings, see the Martindale-Hubbell Law Directory

MCCLELLAN & ASSOCIATES, A PROFESSIONAL CORPORATION (AV)

1144 State Street, 92101
Telephone: 619-231-0505
Fax: 619-544-0540

Craig R. McClellan

LaMar B. Brown
Andrew Phillip Greenfield

For full biographical listings, see the Martindale-Hubbell Law Directory

San Diego—Continued

NEIL, DYMOTT, PERKINS, BROWN & FRANK, A PROFESSIONAL CORPORATION (AV)

1010 Second Avenue, Suite 2500, 92101-4959
Telephone: 619-238-1712
Fax: 619-238-1562

Michael I. Neil | Roger G. Perkins
Thomas M. Dymott | Tim S. McClain

Reference: 1st Interstate Bank - San Diego.

For full biographical listings, see the Martindale-Hubbell Law Directory

*SAN FRANCISCO,** San Francisco Co.

BOSTWICK & TEHIN (AV)

A Partnership including Professional Corporations
Bank of America Center, 555 California Street, 33rd Floor, 94104-1609
Telephone: 415-421-5500
Fax: 415-421-8144
Honolulu, Hawaii Office: Suite 900, 333 Queen Street.
Telephone: 808-536-7771.

MEMBERS OF FIRM

James S. Bostwick (Professional Corporation) | Nikolai Tehin (Professional Corporation)
Pamela J. Stevens

ASSOCIATES

James J. O'Donnell | Sara A. Smith
Baron J. Drexel

For full biographical listings, see the Martindale-Hubbell Law Directory

JOHN GARDENAL A PROFESSIONAL CORPORATION (AV)

Suite 800 Cathedral Hill Office Building, 1255 Post Street, 94109
Telephone: 415-771-2700
FAX: 415-771-2072

John Gardenal

For full biographical listings, see the Martindale-Hubbell Law Directory

ROBERT A. HARLEM, INC. & ASSOCIATES A PROFESSIONAL CORPORATION (AV)

120 Montgomery Street, Suite 2410, 94104
Telephone: 415-981-1801
Fax: 415-981-5815

Robert A. Harlem

B. Mark Fong

OF COUNSEL

Patricia Knight | Jack Miller

For full biographical listings, see the Martindale-Hubbell Law Directory

LIEFF, CABRASER & HEIMANN (AV)

Embarcadero Center West, 30th Floor, 275 Battery Street, 94111
Telephone: 415-956-1000
Telecopier: 415-956-1008

Robert L. Lieff | Karen E. Karpen
Elizabeth J. Cabraser | Michael F. Ram
Richard M. Heimann | William M. Audet
William Bernstein | Joseph R. Saveri
William B. Hirsch | Steven E. Fineman
James M. Finberg | Donald C. Arbitblit
Robert J. Nelson

Kristine E. Bailey | Jacqueline E. Mottek
Suzanne A. Barr | Kimberly W. Pate
Kelly M. Dermody | Melanie M. Piech
Deborah A. Kemp | Morris A. Ratner
Anthony K. Lee | Rhonda L. Woo

For full biographical listings, see the Martindale-Hubbell Law Directory

MOLLIGAN, COX & MOYER, A PROFESSIONAL CORPORATION (AV)

703 Market Street, Suite 1800, 94103
Telephone: 415-543-9464
Fax: 415-777-1828

Ingemar E. Hoberg (1903-1971) | Peter N. Molligan
John H. Finger (1913-1991) | Stephen T. Cox
Phillip E. Brown (Retired) | David W. Moyer

John C. Hentschel | Guy D. Loranger
Nicholas J. Piediscazzi

(See Next Column)

OF COUNSEL

Kenneth W. Rosenthal | Barbara A. Zuras

For full biographical listings, see the Martindale-Hubbell Law Directory

O'CONNOR, COHN, DILLON & BARR, A LAW CORPORATION (AV)

The Folger Coffee Building, 101 Howard Street, Fifth Floor, 94105-1619
Telephone: 415-281-8888
Fax: 415-281-8890

Joseph T. O'Connor (Deceased, 1959) | Janet L. Grove
Harold H. Cohn (1910-1992) | Mark Oium
James L. Dillon | Jerald W. F. Jamison
Duncan Barr | Lisa T. Ungerer
| Joel C. Lamp
Michael J. FitzSimons

Thomas G. Manning | Deems A. Fishman
Susan Reifel Goins | Jeanine M. Donohue
Dexter B. Louie | Karen K. Smith
Deborah L. Panter | Daniel J. Herp
Marirose Piciucco | James A. Beltzer
Keith Reyen | (Not admitted in CA)

For full biographical listings, see the Martindale-Hubbell Law Directory

SARRAIL, LYNCH & HALL (AV)

44 Montgomery Street, 34th Floor, 94104
Telephone: 415-398-2404
Fax: 415-391-9076

Stephen W. Hall (1955-1993) | Linda J. Lynch
James A. Sarrail | Bruce C. F. McArthur

Michael J. Ruggles | Jonathan S. Larsen
David Y. Wong | Susan A. Byron
Todd M. Barnett | Ernest D. Faitos
Frances H. Yoshimura

LEGAL SUPPORT PERSONNEL

Cynthia R. Benzerara

For full biographical listings, see the Martindale-Hubbell Law Directory

SCADDEN, HAMILTON & RYAN (AV)

580 California Street, Suite 1400, 94104
Telephone: 415-362-5116
Facsimile: 415-362-4214

James G. Scadden | Robert P. Hamilton
Robert J. Ryan

James P. Cunningham | Julie M. Sinclair
James F. Hetherington | Charles O. Thompson
Eileen Santana Wright

For full biographical listings, see the Martindale-Hubbell Law Directory

WALKUP, MELODIA, KELLY & ECHEVERRIA, A PROFESSIONAL CORPORATION (AV)

30th Floor, 650 California Street, 94108
Telephone: 415-981-7210
Fax: 415-391-6965

Bruce Walkup | Ronald H. Wecht
Paul V. Melodia | Michael A. Kelly
Daniel J. Kelly | Kevin L. Domecus
John Echeverria | Jeffrey P. Holl
Richard B. Goethals, Jr. | Daniel Dell'Osso

Mary E. Elliot | Ann M. Richardson
Richard H. Schoenberger | Erik Brunkal
Cynthia F. Newton | Michael J. Recupero

OF COUNSEL

John D. Link | Wesley Sokolosky

Reference: Bank of California, San Francisco Main Office, 400 California Street, San Francisco, Calif. 94104.

For full biographical listings, see the Martindale-Hubbell Law Directory

*SAN JOSE,** Santa Clara Co.

THE ALEXANDER LAW FIRM (AV)

55 South Market Street, Suite 1080, 95113
Telephone: 408-289-1776
Fax: 408-287-1776
Cincinnati, Ohio Office: 1300 Mercantile Library Building, 414 Walnut Street.
Telephone: 513-723-1776.
Fax: 513-421-1776.

(See Next Column)

THE ALEXANDER LAW FIRM—*Continued*

Richard Alexander

ASSOCIATES

Mark P. Rapazzini
Jeffrey W. Rickard
Michael T. Alexander (Resident, Cincinnati, Ohio Office)
M. Elizabeth Graham
Jotham S. Stein

For full biographical listings, see the Martindale-Hubbell Law Directory

THE BOCCARDO LAW FIRM (AV)

Eleventh Floor, 111 West St. John Street, 95115
Telephone: 408-298-5678
Fax: 408-298-7503

MEMBERS OF FIRM

James F. Boccardo
John W. McDonald
Brian N. Lawther
John C. Stein
Richard L. Bowers
Russell L. Moore, Jr.

ASSOCIATES

Stephen Foster
David P. Moyles
Byron C. Foster
Victor F. Stefan
Robert W. Thayer
G. Matthew Fick
Charles A. Browning
Diego F. MacWilliam
Stephen A. Roberts

For full biographical listings, see the Martindale-Hubbell Law Directory

ROHLFF, HOWIE & FRISCHHOLZ (AV)

150 Almaden Boulevard Suite 400, 95113
Telephone: 408-286-1100
Fax: 408-286-5285

MEMBERS OF FIRM

Yale W. Rohlff
Robert G. Howie
Barbara J. Frischholz
Nancy L. Peterson
Michael A. Penfield
James S. Gottesman
Donn Waslif

For full biographical listings, see the Martindale-Hubbell Law Directory

*SANTA ANA,** Orange Co.

CASSIDY, WARNER, BROWN, COMBS & THURBER, A PROFESSIONAL CORPORATION (AV)

600 West Santa Ana Boulevard, Suite 700, 92701
Telephone: 714-835-9431
Fax: 714-835-5264

Alvin M. Cassidy
B. Kent Warner
Joe R. Brown
A. Bennett Combs
David K. Thurber
Timothy X. Lane
Bruce A. Winstead

Lloyd W. Felver
John A. Monkvic
David C. Olson
Dale L. Pomerantz
Glen A. Stebens
Robert E. Tarozzi

For full biographical listings, see the Martindale-Hubbell Law Directory

*SANTA CRUZ,** Santa Cruz Co.

DUNLAP, BURDICK AND McCORMACK, A PROFESSIONAL LAW CORPORATION (AV)

121 Jewell Street, 95060
Telephone: 408-426-7040
FAX: 408-426-1095

Michael E. Dunlap
Paul P. Burdick

OF COUNSEL

Sandra C. McCormack

For full biographical listings, see the Martindale-Hubbell Law Directory

WALNUT CREEK, Contra Costa Co.

ANDERSON, GALLOWAY & LUCCHESE, A PROFESSIONAL CORPORATION (AV)

1676 North California Boulevard, Suite 500, 94596-4183
Telephone: 510-943-6383
Facsimile: 510-943-7542

Robert L. Anderson
George Patrick Galloway
David R. Lucchese
Martin J. Everson
Thomas J. Donnelly
Ralph J. Smith
James M. Nelson
Scott E. Murray
Henry E. Needham
Stephen F. Lucey
David A. Depolo
Karen A. Sparks
Stephen J. Brooks
James J. Zenere

(See Next Column)

Joseph S. Picchi
Coleen L. Welch
Deborah C. Moritz-Farr
Marc G. Cowden
Lauren E. Tate
Erin C. Ruddy
Lea K. McMahan

For full biographical listings, see the Martindale-Hubbell Law Directory

COLORADO

*DENVER,** Denver Co.

SCHADEN, LAMPERT & LAMPERT (AV)

1610 Emerson Street, 80218-1412
Telephone: 303-832-2771
Broomfield, Colorado Office: 11870 Airport Way, 80021.
Telephone: 303-465-3663.
Birmingham, Michigan Office: Schaden, Wilson and Katzman. 800 N. Woodward Avenue, Suite 102.
Telephone: 313-258-4800.

MEMBERS OF FIRM

Richard F. Schaden (Resident, Broomfield Office)
Bruce A. Lampert
Brian J. Lampert

ASSOCIATES

Kathleen M. Schaden (Resident, Boulder Office)
Susanna L. Meissner-Cutler
Patricia M. Jarzobski

For full biographical listings, see the Martindale-Hubbell Law Directory

WHITE AND STEELE, PROFESSIONAL CORPORATION (AV)

1225 17th Street, Suite 2800, 80202
Telephone: 303-296-2828
Telecopier: 303-296-3131
Cheyenne, Wyoming Office: 1912 Capital Avenue, Suite 404, 82003.
Telephone: 307-778-4160.

Lowell White (1897-1983)
Walter A. Steele
R. Eric Peterson
Stephen K. Gerdes
Michael W. Anderson
James M. Dieterich
Glendon L. Laird
John M. Lebsack
Stephen G. Sparr
John P. Craver
David J. Nowak
Sandra Spencer
John M. Palmeri
Frederick W. Klann
William F. Campbell, Jr.
Richard M. Kaudy
Peter W. Rietz
Kurt A. Horton
Stewart J. Rourke
Allan Singer
Michael J. Daugherty
Robert R. Carlson

Thomas B. Quinn
George A. Codding, III
Christopher P. Kenney
June Baker
Robert H. D. Coate
Monty L. Barnett
Joseph R. King

OF COUNSEL

Fred L. Witsell

Colorado Tort Counsel for: Goodyear Tire and Rubber Co.; The Dow Chemical Co.; Celotex.
Insurance Clients: Allied Insurance Co.; CNA; Kemper Insurance Group; Massachusetts Mutual Life Insurance Co.; U.S.A.A.; Underwriters at Lloyds; Farmers Insurance Group.

For Complete List of Firm Personnel, See General Section

For full biographical listings, see the Martindale-Hubbell Law Directory

CONNECTICUT

*BRIDGEPORT,** Fairfield Co.

WILLIAMS, COONEY & SHEEHY (AV)

One Lafayette Circle, 06604
Telephone: 203-331-0888
Telecopier: 203-331-0896

MEMBERS OF FIRM

Ronald D. Williams
Robert J. Cooney
Edward Maum Sheehy
Peter D. Clark
Peter J. Dauk
Dion W. Moore
Ronald D. Williams, Jr.
Francis A. Smith, Jr. (1951-1989)

Lawrence F. Reilly
Michael P. Bowler
Michael Cuff Deakin

Representative Clients: Aetna Life & Casualty Co.; Nationwide Insurance Co.; The Travelers; Zimmer Manufacturing Co.; Textron-Lycoming: The Stop & Shop Companies, Inc.; Shawmut Bank Connecticut, N.A.; Utica Mutual Insurance Co.; Royal Insurance; General Star Indemnity Company.

For full biographical listings, see the Martindale-Hubbell Law Directory

NEW LONDON, New London Co.

Reardon & Nazzaro, P.C. (AV)

160 Hempstead Street, Drawer 1430, 06320
Telephone: 203-442-0444
Telecopier: 203-444-6445

Robert I. Reardon, Jr.
John J. Nazzaro
Maryann Diaz

Angelo A. Ziotas
Stephen J. MacKinnon

LEGAL SUPPORT PERSONNEL

Bette B. Beam (Legal Administrator)
Carolyn B. Dickey (Paralegal)
Kelly G. MacDonald (Paralegal)
Jillene B. Mattern (Paralegal)

For full biographical listings, see the Martindale-Hubbell Law Directory

STAMFORD, Fairfield Co.

Silver, Golub & Teitell (AV)

184 Atlantic Street, P.O. Box 389, 06904
Telephone: 203-325-4491
FAX: 203-325-3769

MEMBERS OF FIRM

Richard A. Silver
Ernest F. Teitell
David S. Golub
Patricia M. Haugh (1942-1988)
Elaine T. Silver

John D. Josel
Marilyn J. Ramos
Mario DiNatale
Jack Zaremski (Not admitted in CT)
Jonathan M. Levine

For full biographical listings, see the Martindale-Hubbell Law Directory

DELAWARE

*WILMINGTON,** New Castle Co.

Burt & Burt (AV)

Suite 1700 Mellon Bank Center, 919 Market Street, 19801
Telephone: 302-429-9430
Fax: 302-429-9427

Warren B. Burt
David H. Burt

Richard D. Abrams
Michael F. Duggan

For full biographical listings, see the Martindale-Hubbell Law Directory

Smith, Katzenstein & Furlow (AV)

1220 Market Building, P.O. Box 410, 19899
Telephone: 302-652-8400
FAX: 302-652-8405

MEMBERS OF FIRM

Robert J. Katzenstein
Vicki A. Hagel

For Complete List of Firm Personnel, See General Section

For full biographical listings, see the Martindale-Hubbell Law Directory

Tybout, Redfearn & Pell (AV)

Suite 1100, PNC Bank Building, 300 Delaware Avenue, P.O. Box 2092, 19899
Telephone: 302-658-6901
FAX: 658-4018

F. Alton Tybout
Anne L. Naczi
B. Wilson Redfearn
Nancy E. Chrissinger
Richard W. Pell
David G. Culley

ASSOCIATES

Sherry Ruggiero Fallon
Michael I. Silverman
Sean A. Dolan
Bernadette M. Plaza
Elizabeth Daniello Maron
Joel R. Brown
Francis X. Nardo
John J. Klusman, Jr.
Todd M. Finchler

Representative Clients: CIGNA Ins., Co.; Liberty Mutual Ins., Co.; Hartford Ins., Co.; Universal Underwriters; PHICO; State of Delaware; GAB Business Services Inc.; State Farm Ins., Co.; Alliance of American Insurers; Insurance Guarantee Assn.

For full biographical listings, see the Martindale-Hubbell Law Directory

DISTRICT OF COLUMBIA

WASHINGTON, D.C. Co.

* indicates certain Bar Register subscribers, in cities of comparable size and importance, who maintain an additional office in Washington, D.C. and who have arranged for representation as a part of the Washington, D.C. listings that follow

Kenneth R. Feinberg & Associates (AV)

1120 20th Street, N.W. Suite 740 South, 20036
Telephone: 202-371-1110
Fax: 202-962-9290
New York, N.Y. Office: 780 3rd Avenue, Suite 2202.
Telephone: 212-527-9600.
Fax: 212-527-9611.

ASSOCIATES

Deborah E. Greenspan
Peter H. Woodin (Not admitted in DC)
Michael K. Rozen (Not admitted in DC)

For full biographical listings, see the Martindale-Hubbell Law Directory

*** Venable, Baetjer, Howard & Civiletti (AV)**

A Partnership including Professional Corporations
Suite 1000, 1201 New York Avenue, N.W., 20005
Telephone: 202-962-4800
Fax: 202-962-8300
Baltimore, Maryland Office: Venable, Baetjer and Howard, 1800 Mercantile Bank & Trust Building, 2 Hopkins Plaza.
Telephone: 410-244-7400.
McLean, Virginia Office: Venable, Baetjer and Howard, Suite 400, 2010 Corporate Ridge.
Telephone: 703-760-1600.
Rockville, Maryland Office: Venable, Baetjer and Howard, Suite 500, One Church Street, P. O. Box 1906.
Telephone: 301-217-5600.
Towson, Maryland Office: Venable, Baetjer and Howard, 210 Allegheny Avenue, P. O. Box 5517.
Telephone: 410-494-6200.

MEMBERS OF FIRM

Benjamin R. Civiletti (P.C.) (Also at Baltimore and Towson, Maryland Offices)
Douglas D. Connah, Jr. (P.C.) (Also at Baltimore, Maryland Office)
James K. Archibald (Also at Baltimore and Towson, Maryland Offices)
Jeffrey A. Dunn (Also at Baltimore, Maryland Office)
George F. Pappas (Also at Baltimore, Maryland Office)
James L. Shea (Not admitted in DC; also at Baltimore, Maryland Office)
Gary M. Hnath

ASSOCIATES

Fred Joseph Federici, III
David W. Goewey

For Complete List of Firm Personnel, See General Section

For full biographical listings, see the Martindale-Hubbell Law Directory

FLORIDA

DAYTONA BEACH, Volusia Co.

Eubank, Hassell & Lewis (AV)

Suite 301, 149 South Ridgewood Avenue, P.O. Box 2229, 32015-2229
Telephone: 904-238-1357
Telecopier: 904-258-7406

MEMBERS OF FIRM

James O. Eubank, II
F. Bradley Hassell
Lester A. Lewis

ASSOCIATES

Jennifer M. Dehn
Timothy A. Traster
Alfred Truesdell
Joseph D. Tessitore

For full biographical listings, see the Martindale-Hubbell Law Directory

*MIAMI,** Dade Co.

Clarke & Silverglate, Professional Association (AV)

100 North Biscayne Boulevard, Suite 2401, 33132
Telephone: 305-377-0700
Fax: 305-377-3001

(See Next Column)

CLARKE & SILVERGLATE PROFESSIONAL ASSOCIATION—*Continued*

Mercer K. Clarke — Spencer H. Silverglate
Kelly Anne Luther

For full biographical listings, see the Martindale-Hubbell Law Directory

DEUTSCH & BLUMBERG, P.A. (AV)

Suite 2802 New World Tower, 100 North Biscayne Boulevard, 33132
Telephone: 305-358-6329
Fax: 305-358-9304

Steven K. Deutsch — Edward R. Blumberg
Louis Thaler

For full biographical listings, see the Martindale-Hubbell Law Directory

HADDAD, JOSEPHS, JACK, GAEBE & MARKARIAN (AV)

1493 Sunset Drive (Coral Gables), P.O. Box 345118, 33114
Telephone: Dade County: 305-666-6006
Broward County: 305-463-6699
Telecopier: 305-662-9931

MEMBERS OF FIRM

Gil Haddad — Lewis N. Jack, Jr.
Michael R. Josephs — John S. Gaebe
David K. Markarian

ASSOCIATES

Amarillys E. Garcia-Perez — Elisabeth M. McClosky

For full biographical listings, see the Martindale-Hubbell Law Directory

HARDY, BISSETT & LIPTON, P.A. (AV)

501 Northeast First Avenue, 33132
Telephone: 305-358-6200
Broward: 305-462-6377
Fax: 305-577-8230
Boca Raton, Florida Office: 2201 Corporate Boulevard, N.W., Suite 205.
Telephone: 407-998-9202.
Telecopier: 407-998-9693.

G. Jack Hardy — Stephen N. Lipton
G. William Bissett — (Resident, Boca Raton Office)

Howard K. Cherna — Matthew Kennedy
Lee Philip Teichner — H. Dane Mottlau

Representative Clients: International Paper Co.; Masonite Corp.; Bridgestone/Firestone Inc.; American International Underwriters; American International Group, Inc.; Pennsylvania National Insurance Cos.; Crown Equipment Corp.; The Coleman Co., Inc.; Interamerican Car Rental, Inc.; York International Corp.

For full biographical listings, see the Martindale-Hubbell Law Directory

NICKLAUS, VALLE, CRAIG & WICKS (AV)

15th Floor New World Tower, 100 North Biscayne Boulevard, 33132
Telephone: 305-358-2888
Facsimile: 305-358-5501
Fort Lauderdale, Florida Office: Suite 101N, Justice Building, 524 South Andrews Avenue, 33301.
Telephone: 305-523-1858.
Facsimile: 305-523-8068.

MEMBERS OF FIRM

Edward R. Nicklaus — William R. Wicks, III
Laurence F. Valle — James W. McCready, III
Lawrance B. Craig, III — Michael W. Whitaker

ASSOCIATES

Richard D. Settler — Keith S. Grybowski
Kevin M. Fitzmaurice — Patricia Blanco
Timothy Maze Hartley — Michael J. Lynott

For full biographical listings, see the Martindale-Hubbell Law Directory

LELAND E. STANSELL, JR., P.A. (AV)

903 Biscayne Building, 19 West Flagler Street, 33130
Telephone: 305-374-5911

ASSOCIATE

Charles L. Balli

For full biographical listings, see the Martindale-Hubbell Law Directory

*ORLANDO,** Orange Co.

MAHER, GIBSON AND GUILEY A PROFESSIONAL ASSOCIATION OF LAWYERS (AV)

Suite 200, 90 East Livingston Street, 32801
Telephone: 407-839-0866
Fax: 407-425-7958

(See Next Column)

Michael Maher — Patricia M. Gibson
David D. Guiley

Steven R. Maher — Robin M. Orosz
Monique M. Edwards

OF COUNSEL

John Edward Jones (P.A.)

LEGAL SUPPORT PERSONNEL

INSURANCE CLAIM COORDINATOR

Charles R. Simpson

For full biographical listings, see the Martindale-Hubbell Law Directory

MARTINEZ & DALTON, PROFESSIONAL ASSOCIATION (AV)

719 Vassar Street, 32804
Telephone: 407-425-0712
Fax: 407-425-1856

Mel R. Martinez — Robert H. Dellecker
Roy B. Dalton, Jr. — Brian T. Wilson

Yvonne M. Yegge — Leticia Marques

For full biographical listings, see the Martindale-Hubbell Law Directory

PARRISH, BAILEY & MORSCH, P.A. (AV)

116 America Street, 32801
Telephone: 407-849-1776

Sidney H. Parrish — Michael K. Bailey
Mark V. Morsch

Jay M. Fisher — Donald A. Myers, Jr.

For full biographical listings, see the Martindale-Hubbell Law Directory

*PENSACOLA,** Escambia Co.

FULLER, JOHNSON & FARRELL, P.A. (AV)

Quayside Quarters, 700 South Palafox, Suite 300, P.O. Box 12219, 32581
Telephone: 904-434-8845
Fax: 904-432-6667
Tallahassee, Florida Office: 111 North Calhoun Street, P.O. Box 1739, 32302-1739.
Telephone: 904-224-4663.
Fax: 904-561-8839.

Belinda Barnes deKozan (Resident) — Michael W. Kehoe (Resident)
Alan R. Horky (Resident)

Representative Clients: American Motors Corp.; Amoco Oil Co.; Black & Decker (U.S.), Inc.; Ford Motor Co.; Hitachi Power Tools USA, Ltd.; Hoffman-LaRoche, Inc.; Montgomery Ward and Company, Inc.; Robeson Industrial Corp.; Ryder Truck Lines, Inc.; Squibb, Inc.

For full biographical listings, see the Martindale-Hubbell Law Directory

B. RICHARD YOUNG, P.A. (AV)

309B South Palafox Place, 32501
Telephone: 904-432-2222
Fax: 904-432-1444

B. Richard Young

For full biographical listings, see the Martindale-Hubbell Law Directory

*TALLAHASSEE,** Leon Co.

COLLINS & TRUETT, P.A. (AV)

2804 Remington Green Circle, Suite 4, Post Office Drawer 12429, 32317-2429
Telephone: 904-386-6060
Telecopier: 904-385-8220

Richard B. Collins — Gary A. Shipman

Brett Q. Lucas (Resident) — C. Timothy Gray
Dawn D. Caloca — Rogelio Fontela
Joseph E. Brooks — Charles N. Cleland, Jr.
Clifford W. Rainey

OF COUNSEL

Edgar C. Booth — James A. Dixon, Jr.

Representative Clients: Agency Rent-A-Car; Agricultural Excess and Surplus Insurance Co.; AIG Life Insurance Co.; Alliance Insurance Group; Allstate Insurance Co.; American Empire Surplus Lines Insurance Co.; American International Underwriters Inc.; Atlanta Casualty Insurance Co.; Avis Rent-A-Car; Bankers and Shippers Insurance Co.

For full biographical listings, see the Martindale-Hubbell Law Directory

Tallahassee—Continued

FONVIELLE & HINKLE (AV)

3375-A Capital Circle Northeast, 32308
Telephone: 904-422-7773
Fax: 904-422-3449

MEMBERS OF FIRM

C. David Fonvielle | Donald M. Hinkle
Halley B. Lewis, III

For full biographical listings, see the Martindale-Hubbell Law Directory

FULLER, JOHNSON & FARRELL, P.A. (AV)

111 North Calhoun Street, P.O. Box 1739, 32302-1739
Telephone: 904-224-4663
Fax: 904-561-8839
Pensacola, Florida Office: Quayside Quarters, 700 South Palafox, Suite 300, P.O. Box 12219, 32581.
Telephone: 904-434-8845.
FAX: 904-432-6667.

Ben A. Andrews
Jeannette M. Andrews
Marjorie M. Cain
M. Elizabeth Chesser
Robert C. Crabtree
Patrick J. Farrell, Jr.
S. William Fuller, Jr.
Beverly H. Heckler
Alan R. Horky (Resident, Pensacola Office)
Fred M. Johnson
Michael W. Kehoe (Resident, Pensacola Office)
J. Craig Knox
Belinda Barnes deKozan (Resident, Pensacola Office)
William R. Mabile, III
P. Scott Mitchell
Steven Michael Puritz
Cynthia D. Simmons
Michael J. Thomas
Robert W. Ritsch
Sidney M. McCrackin

Representative Clients: Aetna Life & Casualty; American Continental Insurance Company; American International Group; American States Insurance Company; Amoco Oil Company; Anesthesiologists' Professional Assurance Trust; Black & Decker (U.S.), Inc.; Bruno's, Inc.; CIGNA Companies; Coca-Cola Enterprises, Inc.

For full biographical listings, see the Martindale-Hubbell Law Directory

MCFARLAIN, WILEY, CASSEDY & JONES, PROFESSIONAL ASSOCIATION (AV)

215 South Monroe Street, Suite 600, P.O. Box 2174, 32316-2174
Telephone: 904-222-2107
Telecopier: 904-222-8475

Richard C. McFarlain
William B. Wiley
Marshall R. Cassedy
Douglas P. Jones
Charles A. Stampelos
Linda McMullen
H. Darrell White, Jr.
Christopher Barkas

Harold R. Mardenborough, Jr.
Katherine Hairston LaRosa
J. Robert Griffin

OF COUNSEL

Betty J. Steffens

For full biographical listings, see the Martindale-Hubbell Law Directory

*TAMPA,** Hillsborough Co.

MICHAEL C. ADDISON (AV)

Suite 2175, 100 North Tampa Street, 33602-5145
Telephone: 813-223-2000
Facsimile: 813-228-6000
Mailing Address: P.O. Box 2175, Tampa, Florida, 33601-2175

For full biographical listings, see the Martindale-Hubbell Law Directory

CUNNINGHAM LAW GROUP, P.A. (AV)

100 Ashley Drive, South, Suite 100, 33602
Telephone: 813-228-0505
Telefax: 813-229-7982

Anthony W. Cunningham | Donald G. Greiwe
James D. Clark

For full biographical listings, see the Martindale-Hubbell Law Directory

GUNN, OGDEN & SULLIVAN, PROFESSIONAL ASSOCIATION (AV)

201 East Kennedy Boulevard, Suite 1850, P.O. Box 1006, 33601
Telephone: 813-223-5111
FAX: 813-229-2336

Timon V. Sullivan | Randy J. Ogden
Lee D. Gunn, IV

(See Next Column)

Bradley J. Goewert
Andrea L. Hairelson
Michael F. Hancock
Brian Thompson
Charles E. Mckeon
Kelly K. Griffin
Daneil M. McAuliffe

For full biographical listings, see the Martindale-Hubbell Law Directory

RYWANT, ALVAREZ, JONES & RUSSO, PROFESSIONAL ASSOCIATION (AV)

Suite 500 Perry Paint & Glass Building, 109 North Brush Street, P.O. Box 3283, 33601
Telephone: 813-229-7007
Fax: 813-223-6544
Ocala, Florida Office: 3300 S.W. 34th Avenue, Suite 124C, 32674.
Telephone: 904-237-8810.
FAX: 904-237-2022.

Manuel J. Alvarez
Jill M. Deziel
Darrell D. Dirks
Matthew D. Emerson
John A.C. Guyton, III
Gregory D. Jones
Burke G. Lopez
Kerry C. McGuinn, Jr.
Andrew F. Russo
Michael S. Rywant
Scott M. Whitley
James R. Wilson
Susan M. Zwiesler

LEGAL SUPPORT PERSONNEL

Traci D. Tew
Bradley Hugh Holt
Stephanie Dickinson Neal (Paralegal)

Representative Clients: Peerless Insurance Co.; Gulf Insurance Group; Employers Casualty Co.; Landmark Insurance Co.

For full biographical listings, see the Martindale-Hubbell Law Directory

CHARLES F. SANSONE (AV)

Suite 200, 701 North Franklin Street, 33602
Telephone: 813-223-9282
FAX: 813-229-0595

For full biographical listings, see the Martindale-Hubbell Law Directory

WAGNER, VAUGHAN & MCLAUGHLIN, P.A. (AV)

708 Jackson Street (Corner of Jefferson), and 601 Bayshore Boulevard, Suite 910, 33602
Telephone: 813-223-7421; 813-225-4000
FAX: 813-221-0254; 813-225-4010

Bill Wagner (Resident, Bayshore Boulevard Office)
Roger A. Vaughan, Jr.
John J. McLaughlin

Alan F. Wagner (Resident, Bayshore Boulevard Office)
Ruth Whetstone Wagner (Resident, Bayshore Boulevard Office)
Denise E. Vaughan
Weldon "Web" Earl Brennan (Resident, Bayshore Boulevard Office)
Bob Vaughan

For full biographical listings, see the Martindale-Hubbell Law Directory

YERRID, KNOPIK & VALENZUELA, P.A. (AV)

Barnett Plaza, Suite 2160, 101 East Kennedy Boulevard, 33602
Telephone: 813-222-8222
FAX: 813-222-8224

C. Steven Yerrid

For full biographical listings, see the Martindale-Hubbell Law Directory

*WEST PALM BEACH,** Palm Beach Co.

LYTAL & REITER (AV)

A Partnership including Professional Associations
Tenth Floor, 515 North Flagler Drive, 33401
Telephone: 407-655-1990
Fax: 407-832-2932
Mailing Address: P.O. Box 4056, 33402

Lake Lytal, Jr. (P.A.)
Joseph J. Reiter (P.A.)
Mark W. Clark
Tracy R. Sharpe

Donald R. Fountain, Jr.
Rafael J. Roca
William S. Williams
Michael J. Overbeck
Yvette Trelles Murray
Kevin C. Smith
Gerald T. McCarthy

Reference: United National Bank.

For full biographical listings, see the Martindale-Hubbell Law Directory

SEARCY DENNEY SCAROLA BARNHART & SHIPLEY, PROFESSIONAL ASSOCIATION (AV)

2139 Palm Beach Lakes Boulevard, P.O. Drawer 3626, 33402-3626
Telephone: 407-686-6300
800-780-8607
Fax: 407-478-0754

Christian D. Searcy, Sr.
Earl L. Denney, Jr.
John Scarola
F. Gregory Barnhart
John A. Shipley
Lois J. Frankel
David K. Kelley, Jr.
Lawrence J. Block, Jr.
C. Calvin Warriner, III
William A. Norton
David J. Sales

(See Next Column)

SEARCY DENNEY SCAROLA BARNHART & SHIPLEY PROFESSIONAL ASSOCIATION—*Continued*

James N. Nance
T. Michael Kennedy
Katherine Ann Martinez
Todd S. Stewart
Christopher K. Speed

LEGAL SUPPORT PERSONNEL

Deane L. Cady (Paralegal/Investigator)
Joel C. Padgett (Paralegal/Investigator)
James E. Cook (Paralegal/Investigator)
William H. Seabold (Paralegal/Investigator)
Emilio Diamantis (Paralegal/Investigator)
Kathleen Simon (Paralegal)
David W. Gilmore (Paralegal/Investigator)
Steve M. Smith (Paralegal/Investigator)
John C. Hopkins (Paralegal/Investigator)
Judson Whitehorn (Paralegal/Investigator)
Thaddeus E. Kulesa (Paralegal/Investigator)
Marcia Yarnell Dodson (Not admitted in FL; Law Clerk)
J. Peter Love (Paralegal/Investigator)
Kelly Lynn Hopkins (Paralegal/Investigator)
Marjorie A. Morgan (Paralegal)
Frank Cotton (Paralegal/Investigator)

For full biographical listings, see the Martindale-Hubbell Law Directory

GEORGIA

*ATLANTA,** Fulton Co.

BIRD, BALLARD & STILL (AV)

14 Seventeenth Street, Suite 5, P.O. Box 7009, 30357
Telephone: 404-873-4696
Fax: 404-872-3745

William Q. Bird
William L. Ballard
Edward R. Still
John G. Mabrey
Kevin B. Carlock

For full biographical listings, see the Martindale-Hubbell Law Directory

BLACKWOOD & MATTHEWS (AV)

Monarch Plaza, 3414 Peachtree Road Suite 660, 30326
Telephone: 404-237-5050
Toll Free: 800-776-0098
Fax: 404-233-3910

B. Randall Blackwood
James B. Matthews, III
John D. Steel

For full biographical listings, see the Martindale-Hubbell Law Directory

CHAMBERS, MABRY, MCCLELLAND & BROOKS (AV)

Tenth Floor, 2200 Century Parkway, N.E., 30345
Telephone: 404-325-4800
FAX: 404-325-0596
Lawrenceville, Georgia Office: Suite 377, 175 Gwinnett Drive.
Telephone: 404-339-7660.
FAX: 404-339-7060.

MEMBERS OF FIRM

Rex D. Smith
Cynthia J. Becker

ASSOCIATE

DeeAnn Boatright Waller

Representative Clients: Allstate Insurance Co.; The Security Mutual Insurance Company of New York; National Automobile Insurance Co.

For full biographical listings, see the Martindale-Hubbell Law Directory

ENGLAND & MCKNIGHT (AV)

Suite 410 River Ridge, 9040 Roswell Road, 30350
Telephone: 404-641-6010
FAX: 404-641-6003

MEMBERS OF FIRM

J. Melvin England
Robert H. McKnight, Jr.

Reference: Bank South, N.A.

For full biographical listings, see the Martindale-Hubbell Law Directory

FREEMAN & HAWKINS (AV)

4000 One Peachtree Center, 303 Peachtree Street, N.E., 30308-3243
Telephone: 404-614-7400
Fax: 404-614-750
CompuServe address: 73541,1626
Internet address: 73451.1626@compuserve.com

(See Next Column)

MEMBERS OF FIRM

Joe C. Freeman, Jr.
H. Lane Young, II
Albert H. Parnell
Julia Bennett Jagger
A. Timothy Jones
Stephen M. Lore
Michael J. Goldman
Lawrence J. Myers

ASSOCIATES

Ollie M. Harton
Michael E. Hutchins
Kristine Berry Morain

Representative Clients: The Coca-Cola Co.; Eli Lilly & Co.; Atlantic Richfield; Ericsson Radio Systems, Inc.; American Suzuki Motor Co.; Baxter Corp.; MEDMARC.

For Complete List of Firm Personnel, See General Section

For full biographical listings, see the Martindale-Hubbell Law Directory

GARLAND, SAMUEL & LOEB, P.C. (AV)

3151 Maple Drive, N.E., 30305
Telephone: 404-262-2225
FAX: 404-365-5041

Edward T. M. Garland
Robin N. Loeb
Donald F. Samuel
Patrick J. Geheren

For full biographical listings, see the Martindale-Hubbell Law Directory

GOLDNER, SOMMERS, SCRUDDER & BASS (AV)

2839 Paces Ferry Road, Suite 800, 30339-3774
Telephone: 404-436-4777
Facsimile: 404-436-8777

Stephen L. Goldner
Glenn S. Bass
Henry E. Scrudder, Jr.
C. G. Jester, Jr.

For Complete List of Firm Personnel, See General Section

For full biographical listings, see the Martindale-Hubbell Law Directory

HILL AND BLEIBERG (AV)

Suite 200, 47 Perimeter Center East, 30346
Telephone: 404-394-7800
Fax: 404-394-7802

MEMBERS OF FIRM

Robert P. Bleiberg
Gary Hill

For full biographical listings, see the Martindale-Hubbell Law Directory

JOHNSON & WARD (AV)

2100 The Equitable Building, 100 Peachtree Street N.W., 30303-1962
Telephone: 404-524-5626
Facsimile: 404-524-1769

MEMBERS OF FIRM

William C. Lanham
Clark H. McGehee

For full biographical listings, see the Martindale-Hubbell Law Directory

MILLS & MORAITAKIS (AV)

Resurgens Plaza, Suite 2515 945 East Paces Ferry Road, Northeast, 30326
Telephone: 404-261-0016
Facsimile: 404-261-0024

Roger Mills
Nicholas C. Moraitakis
Glenn E. Kushel

For full biographical listings, see the Martindale-Hubbell Law Directory

SAMUEL P. PIERCE, JR., P.C. (AV)

One Buckhead Plaza, Suite 850, 3060 Peachtree Road, N.W., 30305
Telephone: 404-364-2890
FAX: 404-240-0232

Samuel P. Pierce, Jr.

For full biographical listings, see the Martindale-Hubbell Law Directory

REYNOLDS & MCARTHUR (AV)

A Partnership including a Professional Corporation
Suite 1010, One Buckhead Plaza, 3060 Peachtree Road, N.W., 30305
Telephone: 404-240-0265
Fax: 404-262-3557
Macon, Georgia Office: 850 Walnut Street.
Telephone: 912-741-6000.
Fax: 912-742-0750.
Asheville, North Carolina Office: The Jackson Building, 22 South Pack Square, Suite 1200.
Telephone: 704-254-8523.
Fax: 704-254-3038.

(See Next Column)

REYNOLDS & MCARTHUR, *Atlanta—Continued*

MEMBERS OF FIRM

W. Carl Reynolds (P.C.)
Katherine L. McArthur
Steve Ray Warren
(Not admitted in GA)
Charles M. Cork, III
Bradley J. Survant
Laura D. Hogue

For full biographical listings, see the Martindale-Hubbell Law Directory

KENNETH L. SHIGLEY (AV)

5180 Roswell Road, N.W., 30342-2208
Telephone: 404-252-1108
Fax: 404-303-4924

For full biographical listings, see the Martindale-Hubbell Law Directory

SULLIVAN, HALL, BOOTH & SMITH, A PROFESSIONAL CORPORATION (AV)

One Midtown Plaza, 1360 Peachtree Street, N.E., Suite 800, 30309
Telephone: 404-870-8000
FAX: 404-870-8020

Terrance C. Sullivan
John E. Hall, Jr.
Alexander H. Booth
Rush S. Smith, Jr.
Henry D. Green, Jr.
Jack G. Slover, Jr.
Timothy H. Bendin
Michael A. Pannier
Brynda Sue Rodriguez
Roger S. Sumrall

David V. Johnson
Jeffrey T. Wise
Eleanor L. Martel
A. Spencer McManes, Jr.
David G. Goodchild, Jr.
Robert L. Shannon, Jr.
T. Andrew Graham
Earnest Redwine
Melanie P. Simon
(Not admitted in GA)

Reference: Wachovia Bank of Georgia.

For full biographical listings, see the Martindale-Hubbell Law Directory

THOMAS, KENNEDY, SAMPSON & PATTERSON (AV)

1600 Bank South Building, 55 Marietta Street, N.W., 30303
Telephone: 404-688-4503
Telecopier: 404-681-2950

MEMBERS OF FIRM

John Loren Kennedy
(1942-1994)
Thomas G. Sampson
P. Andrew Patterson
Myra H. Dixon
R. David Ware
Patrise M. Perkins-Hooker
Jeffrey E. Tompkins

ASSOCIATES

Rosalind T. Drakeford
Regina E. McMillan
Melynee C. Leftridge
La'Sean M. Zilton

For full biographical listings, see the Martindale-Hubbell Law Directory

*MACON,** Bibb Co.

CHAMBLESS, HIGDON & CARSON (AV)

Suite 200 Ambrose Baber Building, 577 Walnut Street, P.O. Box 246, 31298-5399
Telephone: 912-745-1181
Telecopier: 912-746-9479

MEMBERS OF FIRM

Joseph H. Davis
Joseph H. Chambless
David B. Higdon
James F. Carson, Jr.
Thomas F. Richardson
Mary Mendel Katz
Emmitte H. Griggs
Marc T. Treadwell

ASSOCIATES

Kim H. Stroup
Christopher Balch
Jon Christopher Wolfe

Local Counsel for: Atlanta Gas Light Co.; First Union National Bank of Georgia; Security National Bank.

For full biographical listings, see the Martindale-Hubbell Law Directory

REYNOLDS & MCARTHUR (AV)

A Partnership including a Professional Corporation
850 Walnut Street, 31201
Telephone: 912-741-6000
Fax: 912-742-0750
Atlanta, Georgia Office: Suite 1010, One Buckhead Plaza, 3060 Peachtree Road, N.W.
Telephone: 404-240-0265.
Fax: 404-262-3557.
Asheville, North Carolina Office: The Jackson Building, 22 South Pack Square, Suite 1200.
Telephone: 704-254-8523.
Fax: 704-254-3038.

(See Next Column)

MEMBERS OF FIRM

W. Carl Reynolds (P.C.)
Katherine L. McArthur
Steve Ray Warren
(Not admitted in GA)
Charles M. Cork, III
O. Wendell Horne, III
Bradley J. Survant
Laura D. Hogue

For full biographical listings, see the Martindale-Hubbell Law Directory

*MARIETTA,** Cobb Co.

BARNES, BROWNING, TANKSLEY & CASURELLA (AV)

Suite 225, 166 Anderson Street, 30060
Telephone: 404-424-1500
Fax: 404-424-1740

MEMBERS OF FIRM

Roy E. Barnes
Charles B. Tanksley
Jerry A. Landers, Jr.
Jeffrey G. Casurella

For full biographical listings, see the Martindale-Hubbell Law Directory

*SAVANNAH,** Chatham Co.

FORBES & BOWMAN (AV)

Park South D-14, 7505 Waters Avenue, P.O. Box 13929, 31416-0929
Telephone: 912-352-1190
FAX: 912-352-1471

Morton G. Forbes
Catherine M. Bowman
John A. Foster
Isabel M. Pauley

For full biographical listings, see the Martindale-Hubbell Law Directory

PAINTER, RATTERREE & BART (AV)

The Commerce Building, 222 West Oglethorpe Avenue, Suite 401, P.O. Box 9946, 31412
Telephone: 912-233-9700
FAX: 912-233-2281

Paul W. Painter, Jr.
R. Clay Ratterree
Randall K. Bart
James L. Elliott
Sarah Brown Akins
Robert H. Stansfield

For full biographical listings, see the Martindale-Hubbell Law Directory

HAWAII

*HONOLULU,** Honolulu Co.

ASHFORD & NAKAMURA (AV)

2910 Pacific Tower, 1001 Bishop Street, 96813
Telephone: 808-528-0444
Telex: 723-8158
Telecopier: (808) 533-0761
Cable Address: Justlaw

George W. Ashford, Jr.
Lee T. Nakamura

Ann C. Kemp
Francis T. O'Brien

Representative Clients: Baker Industries, Inc.; Burns International Security Services; Clark Equipment Co.; Great Lakes Chemical Corporation; California Union Insurance Co.; Fireman's Fund Insurance Companies; Great American Insurance Companies; Guaranty National Companies; Horace Mann Insurance Company; Marine Office of America Corp.

For full biographical listings, see the Martindale-Hubbell Law Directory

LAW OFFICES OF STUART M. COWAN (AV)

Ocean View Center, 707 Richards Street, Suite 728, 96813
Telephone: 808-533-1767
Fax: 808-533-0549
Kaneohe, Hawaii Office: Suite 202, 47-653 Kamehameha Highway.
Telephone: 808-533-1767.
Fax: 808-239-9175.

Reference: 1st Hawaiian Bank.

For full biographical listings, see the Martindale-Hubbell Law Directory

CRONIN, FRIED, SEKIYA, KEKINA & FAIRBANKS ATTORNEYS AT LAW, A LAW CORPORATION (AV)

1900 Davies Pacific Center, 841 Bishop Street, 96813
Telephone: 808-524-1433
FAX: 808-536-2073

Paul F. Cronin
L. Richard Fried, Jr.
Gerald Y. Sekiya
Wayne K. Kekina
David L. Fairbanks
John D. Thomas, Jr.
Stuart A. Kaneko
Bert S. Sakuda
Allen K. Williams
Keith K. H. Young

(See Next Column)

CRONIN, FRIED, SEKIYA, KEKINA & FAIRBANKS ATTORNEYS AT LAW, A LAW CORPORATION—*Continued*

Patrick W. Border
Patrick F. McTernan
Gregory L. Lui-Kwan
Irene M. Nakano

For full biographical listings, see the Martindale-Hubbell Law Directory

LAW OFFICE OF KENNETH S. ROBBINS ATTORNEY AT LAW, A LAW CORPORATION (AV)

Suite 2220 Davies Pacific Center, 841 Bishop Street, 96813
Telephone: 808-524-2355
Fax: 808-526-0290

Kenneth S. Robbins

Vincent A. Rhodes
Shinken Naitoh

For full biographical listings, see the Martindale-Hubbell Law Directory

ILLINOIS

*CHICAGO,** Cook Co.

DOWD & DOWD, LTD. (AV)

Suite 1000, 55 West Wacker Drive, 60601
Telephone: 312-704-4400
Telecopier: 312-704-4500

Joseph V. Dowd
Kenneth Gurber
Michael E. Dowd
Robert C. Yelton III
Patrick C. Dowd

S. Robert Depke
Donald G. Machalinski
Robert J. Golden
John M. McAndrews
Kevin J. Kane
Martha A. Niles
Jeffrey Edward Kehl
Michael G. Patrizio
Joseph J. Leonard
Patrick J. Ruberry
Ronald J. Lukes
Anthony R. Rutkowski
Karen W. Worsek

LEGAL SUPPORT PERSONNEL

Carrie J. Julian
Jill A. Weiseman

OF COUNSEL

Guenther Ahlf
Joel S. Ostrow

Reference: Central National Bank in Chicago.

For full biographical listings, see the Martindale-Hubbell Law Directory

EPSTEIN, ZAIDEMAN & ESRIG, P.C. (AV)

120 South Riverside Plaza, Suite 1150, 60606
Telephone: 312-207-0005
Fax: 312-207-1332

James R. Epstein
Robert J. Zaideman
Jerry A. Esrig

Jeffrey L. Whitcomb
Elizabeth A. Kaveny
David R. Nordwall

OF COUNSEL

Donald W. Aaronson

For full biographical listings, see the Martindale-Hubbell Law Directory

KENNETH C. MILLER, LTD. (AV)

33 North Dearborn Street, Suite 1930, 60602
Telephone: 312-236-8634
Telecopier: 312-236-1882

Kenneth C. Miller
James W. O'Connor
Joy L. Sparling

For full biographical listings, see the Martindale-Hubbell Law Directory

BERNARD R. NEVORAL AND ASSOCIATES LTD. (AV)

150 North Wacker Drive, Suite 2450, 60606
Telephone: 312 263-7058
FAX: 312-263-4566

Bernard R. Nevoral

Paul W. Pasche
John L. Malevitis
Maurice E. Dusky

For full biographical listings, see the Martindale-Hubbell Law Directory

SCHAFFENEGGER, WATSON & PETERSON, LTD. (AV)

Suite 3504, One East Wacker Drive, 60601-1802
Telephone: 312-527-5566
Fax: 312-527-5540

J. V. Schaffenegger (1914-1986)
Donald G. Peterson
Jack L. Watson
Jay Scott Nelson
Michael A. Strom

James L. McKnight

Reference: American National Bank & Trust Co.

For full biographical listings, see the Martindale-Hubbell Law Directory

SCHOEN & SMITH, LTD. (AV)

30 North La Salle Street, Suite 1500, 60602
Telephone: 312-726-5151
FAX: 312-726-0884

Lee J. Schoen
David M. Smith
Thomas W. Starck

Randall Smith
Thomas P. Mangan
Steven Christophell
Mary J. Duffy
Susan Fox Gillis

For full biographical listings, see the Martindale-Hubbell Law Directory

SWANSON, MARTIN & BELL (AV)

One IBM Plaza, Suite 2900, 60611
Telephone: 312-321-9100
Fax: 312-321-0990
Wheaton, Illinois Office: 605 East Roosevelt Road.
Telephone: 708-653-2266.
Fax: 708-653-2292.

MEMBERS OF FIRM

Lenard C. Swanson
Lawrence Helms
Kevin T. Martin
Joseph P. Switzer
Brian W. Bell
George F. Fitzpatrick, Jr.
Stanley V. Boychuck
David E. Kawala
Kay L. Schichtel
Bruce S. Terlep
David J. Cahill (Resident, Wheaton Office)

ASSOCIATES

Kevin V. Boyle
Robert J. Meyer
Matthew D. Jacboson
Sheryl A. Pethers
Joseph P. Kincaid
Barbara N. Petrungaro
Patricia S. Kocour
Aaron T. Shepley
William Blake Weiler

For full biographical listings, see the Martindale-Hubbell Law Directory

PERU, La Salle Co.

ANTHONY C. RACCUGLIA & ASSOCIATES (AV)

1200 Maple Drive, 61354
Telephone: 815-223-0230
Ottawa, Illinois Office: 633 La Salle Street.
Telephone: 815-434-2003.

ASSOCIATES

James A. McPhedran
Louis L. Bertrand

References: La Salle National Bank; Citizens First National Bank of Peru, Illinois.

For full biographical listings, see the Martindale-Hubbell Law Directory

INDIANA

*BLOOMINGTON,** Monroe Co.

KELLEY, BELCHER & BROWN, A PROFESSIONAL CORPORATION (AV)

301 West Seventh Street, P.O. Box 3250, 47402-3250
Telephone: 812-336-9963
Telecopier: 812-336-4588

William H. Kelley
Thomas J. Belcher
Barry Spencer Brown

Shannon L. Robinson
Darla Sue Brown

For full biographical listings, see the Martindale-Hubbell Law Directory

*EVANSVILLE,** Vanderburgh Co.

FINE & HATFIELD (AV)

520 N.W. Second Street, P.O. Box 779, 47705-0779
Telephone: 812-425-3592
Telecopier: 812-421-4269

MEMBERS OF FIRM

Thomas H. Bryan
Danny E. Glass
D. Timothy Born

ASSOCIATE

William H. Mullis

For Complete List of Firm Personnel, See General Section

For full biographical listings, see the Martindale-Hubbell Law Directory

STATHAM, JOHNSON & McCRAY (AV)

215 North West Martin Luther King Jr. Boulevard, P.O. Box 3567, 47734-3567
Telephone: 812-425-5223
Facsimile: 812-421-4238

MEMBERS OF FIRM

William E. Statham
Stephen Hensleigh Thomas
Michael McCray
Gerald F. Allega
Douglas V. Jessen

ASSOCIATES

Brent Alan Raibley
Bryan S. Rudisill

Representative Clients: American Family Insurance Group; American States Insurance; Hartford Insurance Group; Indiana Insurance Company; Meridian Mutual Insurance; Pennsylvania Hospital Insurance Company; Royal Insurance; St. Paul Insurance Cos.; Shelter Insurance Companies; U.S. Insurance Group.

For Complete List of Firm Personnel, See General Section

For full biographical listings, see the Martindale-Hubbell Law Directory

*INDIANAPOLIS,** Marion Co.

LEWIS & WAGNER (AV)

500 Place, 501 Indiana Avenue, Suite 200, 46202-3199
Telephone: 317-237-0500
Fax: 317-630-2790

Robert F. Wagner
Thomas C. Hays
John C. Trimble
R. Robert Stommel
William Owen Harrington

For full biographical listings, see the Martindale-Hubbell Law Directory

LOCKE REYNOLDS BOYD & WEISELL (AV)

1000 Capital Center South, 201 North Illinois Street, 46204
Telephone: 317-237-3800
Telecopier: 317-237-3900

Hugh E. Reynolds, Jr.
Steven J. Strawbridge
Lloyd H. Milliken, Jr.
Randall R. Riggs
William V. Hutchens
Richard A. Huser
Michael A. Bergin
Thomas J. Campbell
Burton M. Harris

Stephen L. Vaughan
Ariane Schallwig Johnson
Eric A. Riegner
Robert T. Dassow
Nicholas C. Pappas

OF COUNSEL

William H. Vobach

Allied Signal Inc.; American Honda Motor Co., Inc.; American Suzuki Motor Corporation; Black & Decker (U.S.) Inc.; Emerson Electric Company; General Motors Corporation; New United Motor Manufacturing; Siemens Medical Systems, Inc.; Toyota Motor Sales, U.S.A., Inc.; White Consolidated Industries, Inc.

For Complete List of Firm Personnel, See General Section

For full biographical listings, see the Martindale-Hubbell Law Directory

MILLER MULLER MENDELSON & KENNEDY (AV)

8900 Keystone Crossing Suite 1250, 46240
Telephone: 317-574-4500
1-800-394-3094
Fax: 317-574-4501

MEMBERS OF FIRM

Michael S. Miller
John Muller
Timothy J. Kennedy

For full biographical listings, see the Martindale-Hubbell Law Directory

MITCHELL HURST JACOBS & DICK (AV)

152 East Washington Street, 46204
Telephone: 317-636-0808
1-800-636-0808
Fax: 317-633-7680

MEMBERS OF FIRM

Marvin H. Mitchell
Richard J. Dick
William W. Hurst
Marshall S. Hanley
Samuel L. Jacobs
Steven K. Huffer
Robert W. Strohmeyer, Jr.

ASSOCIATES

Danielle A. Takla
Michael T. McNelis
John M. Reames
Michael P. Kilkenny

LEGAL SUPPORT PERSONNEL

L. Kathleen Hughes Brown, R.N.

General Counsel for: Premium Optical Co.; Calderon Bros. Vending Machines, Inc.; Grocers Supply Co., Inc.; Power Train Services, Inc.; Frank E. Irish, Inc.; Bedding Liquidators; Galyan's Trading Co.; Harcourt Management Co., Inc.; Kosene & Kosene Mgt. & Dev. Co., Inc.; Hasten Bancorp.

For full biographical listings, see the Martindale-Hubbell Law Directory

OSBORN HINER & LISHER P.C. (AV)

Suite 380, One Woodfield, 8330 Woodfield Crossing Boulevard, 46240
Telephone: 317-469-2100
Fax: 317-469-9011

John R. Hiner (1920-1986)
John L. Lisher

Donald G. Orzeske
Donald K. Broad

OF COUNSEL

William M. Osborn
Edward A. Straith-Miller
Janet K. Storer

For full biographical listings, see the Martindale-Hubbell Law Directory

PARDIECK, GILL & VARGO, A PROFESSIONAL CORPORATION (AV)

The Old Bailey Building, 244 North College Avenue, 46202
Telephone: 317-639-3321
FAX: 317-639-3318
Seymour, Indiana Office: 100 North Chestnut Street. P.O. Box 608.
Telephone: 812-523-8686.

Roger L. Pardieck
W. Brent Gill
John F. Vargo

Thomas L. Landwerlen
Janet O. Vargo
Robert C. Rothkopf

For full biographical listings, see the Martindale-Hubbell Law Directory

PRICE & BARKER (AV)

The Hammond Block Building, 301 Massachusetts Avenue, 46204
Telephone: 317-633-8787
Telecopier: 317-633-8797

PARTNERS

Henry J. Price
Jerry A. Garau
Robert G. Barker
Mary J. Hoeller

For full biographical listings, see the Martindale-Hubbell Law Directory

TOWNSEND, HOVDE & MONTROSS (AV)

230 East Ohio Street, 46204
Telephone: 317-264-4444
FAX: 317-264-2080

F. Boyd Hovde
W. Scott Montross
John F. Townsend, Jr.
Frederick R. Hovde

OF COUNSEL

John F. Townsend

Reference: The Indiana National Bank of Indianapolis.

For full biographical listings, see the Martindale-Hubbell Law Directory

WILSON, KEHOE & WININGHAM (AV)

2859 North Meridian, 46208
Telephone: 317-920-6400
Fax: 317-920-6405

MEMBERS OF FIRM

Harry A. Wilson, Jr.
D. Bruce Kehoe
William E. Winingham, Jr.

ASSOCIATES

John A. Payton
Ralph E. Dowling

(See Next Column)

WILSON, KEHOE & WININGHAM—*Continued*

OF COUNSEL

Robert E. Lehman

Reference: The Indiana National Bank.

For full biographical listings, see the Martindale-Hubbell Law Directory

YOSHA, LADENDORF & TODD (AV)

2220 North Meridian Street, 46208
Telephone: 317-925-9200
FAX: 317-923-5759

MEMBERS OF FIRM

Louis Buddy Yosha
Mark C. Ladendorf
William Levy
Teresa L. Todd

ASSOCIATE

David C. Krahulik

OF COUNSEL

Irwin J. Prince
Irving L. Fink
Theodore F. Smith, Jr.

References: NBD Indiana; Bank One, Indianapolis.

For full biographical listings, see the Martindale-Hubbell Law Directory

YOUNG & RILEY (AV)

277 East 12th Street, 46202
Telephone: 317-639-2000
Fax: 317-639-2005

Thomas J. Young
William N. Riley

For full biographical listings, see the Martindale-Hubbell Law Directory

*LA PORTE,** La Porte Co.

NEWBY, LEWIS, KAMINSKI & JONES (AV)

916 Lincoln Way, 46350
Telephone: 219-362-1577
Direct Line Michigan City: 219-879-6300
Fax: 219-362-2106
Mailing Address: P.O. Box 1816, La Porte, Indiana, 46352-1816

MEMBERS OF FIRM

John E. Newby (1916-1990)
Edward L. Volk
Daniel E. Lewis, Jr.
Mark L. Phillips
Gene M. Jones
Martin W. Kus
John W. Newby
Marsha Schatz Volk
Perry F. Stump, Jr.
Mark A. Lienhoop
James W. Kaminski

ASSOCIATES

John F. Lake
Christine A. Sulewski
William S. Kaminski
David P. Jones

SENIOR COUNSEL

Leon R. Kaminski

OF COUNSEL

Daniel E. Lewis

Counsel for: U. S. F. & G. Co.; State Farm Mutual Insurance Co.; Auto Owners Insurance Co.; La Porte Bank & Trust Co.; Liberty Mutual Insurance Co.; Sullair Corp.; La Porte Community School Corp.; United Farm Bureau Mutual Insurance Co.; Physicians Insurance of Indiana.

For full biographical listings, see the Martindale-Hubbell Law Directory

MERRILLVILLE, Lake Co.

HOEPPNER WAGNER AND EVANS (AV)

Twin Towers, Suite 606 South, 1000 East 80th Place, 46410
Telephone: 219-769-6552; 465-0432
FAX: 219-738-2349
Valparaiso, Indiana Office: 103 East Lincolnway, P.O. Box 2357.
Telephone: 219-464-4961; 769-8995.
Fax: 219-465-0603.

RESIDENT MEMBER

F. Joseph Jaskowiak

RESIDENT ASSOCIATES

James L. Clement, Jr.
J. Brian Hittinger

For full biographical listings, see the Martindale-Hubbell Law Directory

MUNSTER, Lake Co.

LAW OFFICES OF TIMOTHY F. KELLY (AV)

Suite 2A, 9250 Columbia Avenue, 46321
Telephone: 219-836-4062
Telecopier: 219-836-0167

MEMBERS OF FIRM

Timothy F. Kelly
Karl K. Vanzo

ASSOCIATES

Harvey Karlovac
Douglas George Amber

(See Next Column)

LEGAL SUPPORT PERSONNEL
LEGAL ASSISTANTS

Kristen Cook Faso
Kathleen E. Peek

For full biographical listings, see the Martindale-Hubbell Law Directory

*NEW ALBANY,** Floyd Co.

DAVID V. SCOTT (AV)

409 Bank Street, P.O. Box 785, 47150
Telephone: 812-945-9151

Reference: PNC Bank, Indiana.

For full biographical listings, see the Martindale-Hubbell Law Directory

SEYMOUR, Jackson Co.

PARDIECK, GILL & VARGO, A PROFESSIONAL CORPORATION (AV)

100 North Chestnut Street, P.O. Box 608, 47274
Telephone: 812-523-8686
FAX: 812-522-4199
Indianapolis, Indiana Office: The Old Bailey Building, 244 North College Avenue.
Telephone: 317-639-3321.

Roger L. Pardieck
W. Brent Gill

Bruce A. MacTavish

OF COUNSEL

Barbara Stevens

References: Home Federal Savings Bank, Seymour, Indiana.

For full biographical listings, see the Martindale-Hubbell Law Directory

*SOUTH BEND,** St. Joseph Co.

HARDIG, LEE AND GROVES, PROFESSIONAL ASSOCIATION (AV)

Suite 502, First Bank Building, 205 West Jefferson Boulevard, 46601
Telephone: 219-232-5923
Fax: 219-232-5942

Edward W. Hardig
Robert D. Lee
James F. Groves

William T. Webb

Representative Client: South Bend-Mishawaka New Car Dealers Assn.
Reference: First Interstate Bank of South Bend.

For full biographical listings, see the Martindale-Hubbell Law Directory

EDWARD N. KALAMAROS & ASSOCIATES PROFESSIONAL CORPORATION (AV)

129 North Michigan Avenue, P.O. Box 4156, 46634
Telephone: 219-232-4801
Telecopier: 219-232-9736

Edward N. Kalamaros
Patrick J. Hinkle
Timothy J. Walsh
Bernard E. Edwards
Thomas F. Cohen
Philip E. Kalamaros
Joseph M. Forte
Sally P. Norton
Robert Deane Woods
Kevin W. Kearney
Peter J. Agostino
Lynn E. Arnold

Representative Clients: Liberty Mutual Insurance Co.; Employers Mutual of Wausau; Fireman's Fund American Insurance Group; St. Paul Insurance Companies; U.S.F. & G.; Cincinnati Insurance Co.; Kemper Group; Continental Loss Adjusting Services, Inc.; Orion Group.

For full biographical listings, see the Martindale-Hubbell Law Directory

ROWE, FOLEY & GARDNER (AV)

Suite 900 Society Bank Building, 46601
Telephone: 219-233-8200

R. Kent Rowe
Edmond W. Foley
R. Kent Rowe, III
Martin J. Gardner

ASSOCIATES

Gregory J. Haines
Steven D. Groth
Timothy J. Maher
Evan S. Roberts
Lee Korzan
William James O'Mahony

For full biographical listings, see the Martindale-Hubbell Law Directory

*TERRE HAUTE,** Vigo Co.

MCGLONE LAW OFFICE (AV)

702 Sycamore Building, 47807
Telephone: 812-234-7796
Fax: 812-232-2464

(See Next Column)

McGlone Law Office, *Terre Haute—Continued*

MEMBERS OF FIRM

Gerald H. McGlone
James A. McGlone
Daniel J. McGlone

Reference: Merchants National Bank.

For full biographical listings, see the Martindale-Hubbell Law Directory

Wilkinson, Goeller, Modesitt, Wilkinson & Drummy (AV)

333 Ohio Street, P.O. Box 800, 47808-0800
Telephone: 812-232-4311
Fax: 812-235-5107

MEMBERS OF FIRM

Raymond H. Modesitt
William W. Drummy
Scott M. Kyrouac

Representative Corporate Clients: Merchants National Bank; Owens Corning Fiberglass; CSX, Inc.; General Housewares Corp.; MAB Paints; Chicago Title Insurance Co.; Terre Haute Board of Realtors; Union Hospital; Associated Physicians and Surgeons Clinic, Inc.; PSI Energy, Inc.

For Complete List of Firm Personnel, See General Section

For full biographical listings, see the Martindale-Hubbell Law Directory

*VALPARAISO,** Porter Co.

Hoeppner Wagner and Evans (AV)

103 East Lincolnway, P.O. Box 2357, 46384-2357
Telephone: 219-464-4961; 769-8995
Fax: 219-465-0603
Merrillville, Indiana Office: Twin Towers, Suite 606 South, 1000 East 80th Place.
Telephone: 219-769-6552. Porter County: 219-465-0432.
Fax: 219-738-2349.

RETIRED

Delmar R. Hoeppner (Retired)

MEMBERS OF FIRM

William H. Wagner
Larry G. Evans
William F. Satterlee, III
Gordon A. Etzler
John E. Hughes
Morris A. Sunkel
James A. Cheslek
James L. Jorgensen
Ronald P. Kuker
Richard A. Browne
F. Joseph Jaskowiak (Resident, Merrillville Office)
Richard M. Davis
Mark E. Schmidtke

ASSOCIATES

Todd A. Leeth
Michael P. Blaize
Mary Jill Sisson
Heidi B. Jark
James L. Clement, Jr. (Resident, Merrillville Office)
Jonathan R. Hanson
Robert L. Clark
J. Brian Hittinger
Lauren K. Kroeger
Jeffrey W. Clymer

Attorneys for: Bethlehem Steel Corp.; Chester, Inc.; Hunt-Wesson Foods, Inc.; NBD Gainer; Owens-Corning Fiberglas Corp.; Valparaiso University; State Farm Insurance; Allstate Insurance Co.

For full biographical listings, see the Martindale-Hubbell Law Directory

KANSAS

OVERLAND PARK, Johnson Co.

Fisher, Patterson, Sayler & Smith (AV)

Suite 210, 11050 Roe Street, 66211
Telephone: 913-339-6757
FAX: 913-339-6187
Topeka, Kansas Office: 534 Kansas Avenue, Suite 400. 66603-3463.
Telephone: 913-232-7761.
Fax: 913-232-6604.

MEMBERS OF FIRM

Edwin Dudley Smith (Resident)
Michael K. Seck (Resident)
David P. Madden (Resident)

ASSOCIATE

Kurt A. Level (Resident)

For full biographical listings, see the Martindale-Hubbell Law Directory

Risjord & James (AV)

Suite 100, 10680 Barkley, 66212
Telephone: 913-381-5151
Fax: 913-381-2569

MEMBERS OF FIRM

John C. Risjord
Randy W. James

(See Next Column)

ASSOCIATE

Aaron N. Woods

For full biographical listings, see the Martindale-Hubbell Law Directory

Shamberg, Johnson, Bergman & Morris, Chartered (AV)

Suite 355, 4551 West 107th Street, 66207
Telephone: 913-642-0600
Fax: 913-642-9629
Kansas City, Kansas Office: Suite 860, New Brotherhood Building, 8th and State Streets.
Telephone: 913-281-1900.
Kansas City, Missouri Office: Suite 205, Scarritt Arcade Building, 819 Walnut.
Telephone: 816-556-9431.

Lynn R. Johnson
Victor A. Bergman
David R. Morris
John M. Parisi

Steven G. Brown
John E. Rogers
Steve N. Six
Anthony L. DeWitt (Not admitted in KS)
Patrick A. Hamilton

OF COUNSEL

John E. Shamberg

For full biographical listings, see the Martindale-Hubbell Law Directory

KENTUCKY

*BOWLING GREEN,** Warren Co.

Bell, Orr, Ayers & Moore, P.S.C. (AV)

1010 College Street, P.O. Box 738, 42102-0738
Telephone: 502-781-8111
Telecopier: 502-781-9027

Reginald L. Ayers
Timothy L. Mauldin
Barton D. Darrell
Timothy L. Edelen

General Counsel for: First American National Bank of Kentucky; Farm Credit Services of Mid-America, ACA.; Houchens Industries, Inc. (Food Markets and Shopping Centers); Warren County Board of Education; Bowling Green Municipal Utilities.
Representative Clients: Chicago Title Insurance Co.; Commonwealth Land Title Insurance Co.; Kentucky Farm Bureau Mutual Insurance Co.; Martin Automotive Group; Home Insurance Group.

For Complete List of Firm Personnel, See General Section

For full biographical listings, see the Martindale-Hubbell Law Directory

Campbell, Kerrick & Grise (AV)

1025 State Street, P.O. Box 9547, 42102-9547
Telephone: 502-782-8160
FAX: 502-782-5856

MEMBERS OF FIRM

Joe Bill Campbell
Thomas N. Kerrick
John R. Grise
Gregory N. Stivers
H. Brent Brennenstuhl
Deborah Tomes Wilkins

ASSOCIATES

H. Harris Pepper, Jr.
Lanna Martin Kilgore
Laura Hagan

Representative Clients: Dollar General Corp.; Greenview Hospital; Hospital Corporation of America; Hardin Memorial Hospital; Monarch Environmental, Inc.; Mid-South Management Group, Inc.; Western Kentucky University; Service One Credit Union; Trans Financial Bank; TKR Cable.

For full biographical listings, see the Martindale-Hubbell Law Directory

Harlin & Parker, P.S.C. (AV)

519 East Tenth Street, P.O. Box 390, 42102-0390
Telephone: 502-842-5611
Telefax: 502-842-2607
Smiths Grove, Kentucky Office: Old Farmers Bank Building.
Telephone: 502-563-4701.

William Jerry Parker
Max B. Harlin, III
James D. Harris, Jr.
Michael K. Bishop

Insurance Clients: Allstate Insurance Co.; CNA Insurance Co.; Maryland Casualty Co.
Railroad and Utilities Clients: District Attorneys for South Central Bell Telephone Co.; CSX Transportation, Inc.
Representative Clients: Honda Motor Co.; Kawasaki Motors Corp U.S.A.; Deere & Co.
Local Counsel for: General Motors Corp.; News Publishing Co.

For Complete List of Firm Personnel, See General Section

For full biographical listings, see the Martindale-Hubbell Law Directory

COVINGTON, Kenton Co.

ROBERT E. SANDERS AND ASSOCIATES, P.S.C. (AV)

The Charles H. Fisk House, 1017 Russell Street, 41011
Telephone: 606-491-3000
FAX: 606-655-4642

Robert E. Sanders

Julie Lippert Duncan

LEGAL SUPPORT PERSONNEL

Shirley L. Sanders
Sandra A. Head
Harry E. Holtkamp
Joseph E. Schmiade, Sr.

For full biographical listings, see the Martindale-Hubbell Law Directory

*HINDMAN,** Knott Co.

WEINBERG, CAMPBELL, SLONE & SLONE, P.S.C. (AV)

Main Street, P.O. Box 727, 41822
Telephone: 606-785-5048; 785-5049
FAX: 606-785-3021

William R. Weinberg
Randy A. Campbell
Jerry Wayne Slone
Randy G. Slone

References: Bank of Hindman; Thacker & Grigsby Telephone Co.

For full biographical listings, see the Martindale-Hubbell Law Directory

*LONDON,** Laurel Co.

FARMER, KELLEY & FARMER (AV)

502 West Fifth Street, Drawer 490, 40743
Telephone: 606-878-7640
Fax: 606-878-2364
Lexington Office: 121 Prosperous Place, Suite 13 B, 40509-1834.
Telephone: 606: 263-2567.
Facsimile: 606: 263-2567.

MEMBERS OF FIRM

F. Preston Farmer
John F. Kelley, Jr.
Michael P. Farmer

ASSOCIATES

Martha L. Brown
Jeffrey T. Weaver

References: The First National Bank; Cumberland Valley National Bank & Trust Company of London, Ky.; London Bank & Trust Co.

For full biographical listings, see the Martindale-Hubbell Law Directory

*LOUISVILLE,** Jefferson Co.

OGDEN NEWELL & WELCH (AV)

1200 One Riverfront Plaza, 40202-2973
Telephone: 502-582-1601
Fax: 502-581-9564

MEMBERS OF FIRM

John T. Ballantine
Stephen F. Schuster
Scott T. Wendelsdorf
David A. Harris
D. Brian Rattliff

ASSOCIATES

Douglas C. Ballantine
Tracy S. Prewitt
Jennifer J. Hall

Counsel for: Commercial Union Insurance Company; First Oak Brook Corporate Syndicate; Winston Industries; Dell Computer Corporation.

For Complete List of Firm Personnel, See General Section

For full biographical listings, see the Martindale-Hubbell Law Directory

OLDFATHER & MORRIS (AV)

One Mezzanine The Morrissey Building, 304 West Liberty Street, 40202
Telephone: 502-589-5500
Fax: 502-589-5338

Ann B. Oldfather
Douglas H. Morris, II
William F. McMurry
James Barrett
Teresa A. Talbott

For full biographical listings, see the Martindale-Hubbell Law Directory

WOODWARD, HOBSON & FULTON (AV)

2500 National City Tower, 101 South Fifth Street, 40202
Telephone: 502-581-8000
Fax: 502-581-8111
Lexington, Kentucky Office: National City Plaza, 301 East Main Street, Suite 650.
Telephone: 606-244-7100.
Telecopier: 606-244-7111.

(See Next Column)

MEMBERS OF FIRM

William D. Grubbs
Lionel A. Hawse (Resident, Lexington, Kentucky Office)
Harry K. Herren
David R. Monohan
Will H. Fulton
Bradley R. Hume
Richard H. C. Clay
Mary Jo Wetzel
Gregory L. Smith
Gregory A. Bölzle
Elizabeth Ullmer Mendel
Jann B. Logsdon

ASSOCIATES

David T. Schaefer
I. Johan Trengove
D. Craig York
Sandra Tremper O'Brien
Christopher R. Cashen (Resident, Lexington, Kentucky Office)
L. Jay Gilbert

OF COUNSEL

Fielden Woodward

Representative Clients: General Motors Corp.; Fischer Packing Co.; Ralston Purina Co.; Sears, Roebuck & Co.; Greyhound Lines; Liberty Mutual Insurance Co.; Kitchen Kompact; Sts. Mary & Elizabeth; Kemper Insurance Co.

For Complete List of Firm Personnel, See General Section

For full biographical listings, see the Martindale-Hubbell Law Directory

LOUISIANA

*BATON ROUGE,** East Baton Rouge Parish

BERT K. ROBINSON (AV)

10357 Old Hammond Highway, 70816-8261
Telephone: 504-924-0296
Fax: 504-924-5288

ASSOCIATE

Johanna R. Landreneau

OF COUNSEL

Charles C. Holbrook

For full biographical listings, see the Martindale-Hubbell Law Directory

WATSON, BLANCHE, WILSON & POSNER (AV)

505 North Boulevard, P.O. Drawer 2995, 70821-2995
Telephone: 504-387-5511
Fax: 504-387-5972
Other Baton Rouge, Louisiana Office: 4000 South Sherwood Forest Boulevard, Suite 504.
Telephone: 504-291-5280.
Fax: 504-293-8075.

Peter T. Dazzio
Felix R. Weill
William E. Scott, III
P. Chauvin Wilkinson, Jr.
Randall L. Champagne

ASSOCIATES

P. Scott Jolly
Raymond A. Daigle, Jr.

Representative Clients: BP Chemicals, Inc.; Nutri/System, Inc.; Baton Rouge General Medical Center; Woman's Hospital; American International Group.

For Complete List of Firm Personnel, See General Section

For full biographical listings, see the Martindale-Hubbell Law Directory

*LAFAYETTE,** Lafayette Parish

DOMENGEAUX, WRIGHT, MOROUX & ROY, A PROFESSIONAL LAW CORPORATION (AV)

556 Jefferson Street, Suite 500, P.O. Box 3668, 70502-3668
Telephone: 318-233-3033; 1-800-375-3106
Fax: 318-232-8213
Hammond, Louisiana Office: Magnolia Plaza, Suite K, 1007 West Thomas Street, P. O. Box 1558.
Telephone: 504-542-4963; 1-800-423-1160.

James Domengeaux (1907-1988)
Anthony D. Moroux (1948-1993)
Bob F. Wright (A Professional Law Corporation)
James Parkerson Roy (A Professional Law Corporation)
Robert K. Tracy (A Professional Law Corporation)
Thomas R. Edwards (A Professional Law Corporation)
Frank Edwards (Resident, Hammond Office)
James Wattigny
James H. Domengeaux
R. Hamilton Davis
Gilbert Hennigan Dozier
Carla Marie Perron
Tyron D. Picard

OF COUNSEL

Jerome E. Domengeaux

Reference: Mid-South National Bank; Advocate Financial, L.L.C.

For full biographical listings, see the Martindale-Hubbell Law Directory

Lafayette—Continued

Hill & Beyer, A Professional Law Corporation (AV)

101 LaRue France, Suite 502, P.O. Box 53006, 70505-3006
Telephone: 318-232-9733
Fax: 1-318-237-2566

John K. Hill, Jr.
Bret C. Beyer
David R. Rabalais
Lisa C. McCowen
Eugene P. Matherne
Robert B. Purser
Erin J. Sherburne
Harold Adam Lawrence

For full biographical listings, see the Martindale-Hubbell Law Directory

Roy, Bivins, Judice & Henke, A Professional Law Corporation (AV)

600 Jefferson Street, Suite 800, P.O. Drawer Z, 70502
Telephone: 318-233-7430
Telecopier: 318-233-8403
Telex: 9102505130

Harmon F. Roy
John A. Bivins
Ronald J. Judice
Kenneth M. Henke
W. Alan Lilley
Philip E. Roberts
Patrick M. Wartelle

Representative Clients: Employers Insurance of Wausau; Louisiana Medical Mutual Ins. Co.; C.N.A.; Aetna Casualty & Surety; Zurich Ins. Co.; Our Lady of Lourdes Regional Medical Center, Inc.; St Paul Fire & Marine Ins. Co.; First Financial Insurance Company.

For full biographical listings, see the Martindale-Hubbell Law Directory

*NEW ORLEANS,** Orleans Parish

Pulaski, Gieger & Laborde, A Professional Law Corporation (AV)

Suite 4800, One Shell Square, 701 Poydras Street, 70139
Telephone: 504-561-0400
Telecopier: 504-561-1011

Michael T. Pulaski (P.C.)
Ernest P. Gieger, Jr., (P.C.)
Kenneth H. Laborde
Robert W. Maxwell
Keith W. McDaniel
Sharon D. Smith
Gary G. Hebert
Leo R. McAloon, III
J. Jeffrey Raborn
James E. Swinnen
Gina S. Montgomery
Diana L. Tonagel
Katherine B. Hardy
Mary Beth Meyer

For full biographical listings, see the Martindale-Hubbell Law Directory

Slater Law Firm, A Professional Corporation (AV)

650 Poydras Street Suite 2400, 70130-6101
Telephone: 504-523-7333
Fax: 504-528-1080

Benjamin R. Slater, Jr.
Benjamin R. Slater, III
Mark E. Van Horn
Kevin M. Wheeler

Anne Elise Brown
Donald J. Miester, Jr.

OF COUNSEL

Michael O. Waguespack

Representative Clients: Anheuser-Busch, Inc.; The Quaker Oats Company; Electric Mutual Liability Insurance Company; Diversified Foods and Seasonings.

For full biographical listings, see the Martindale-Hubbell Law Directory

*OPELOUSAS,** St. Landry Parish

Dauzat, Falgoust, Caviness, Bienvenu & Stipe (AV)

510 S. Court Street, P.O. Box 1450, 70571
Telephone: 318-942-5811
Fax: 318-948-9512

MEMBERS OF FIRM

Jimmy L. Dauzat
Jerry J. Falgoust
Peter F. Caviness
Steven J. Bienvenu
Jeigh L. Stipe

For full biographical listings, see the Martindale-Hubbell Law Directory

*SHREVEPORT,** Caddo Parish

Barlow and Hardtner L.C. (AV)

Tenth Floor, Louisiana Tower, 401 Edwards Street, 71101-3289
Telephone: 318-227-1131
Telecopier: 318-227-1141
Mailing Address: P.O. Box 8, Shreveport, Louisiana, 71161-0008

Joseph L. Shea, Jr.
Michael B. Donald

Representative Clients: Ashland Oil, Inc.; Beaird Industries, Inc.; Kelley Oil Corporation; NorAm Energy Corp. (formerly Arkla, Inc.); Central and South West; Panhandle Eastern Corp.; Pennzoil Producing Co.; Johnson Controls, Inc.; Ashland Oil, Inc.; Southwestern Electric Power Company.

(See Next Column)

For Complete List of Firm Personnel, See General Section

For full biographical listings, see the Martindale-Hubbell Law Directory

MAINE

*AUGUSTA,** Kennebec Co.

* indicates certain Bar Register subscribers whose principal office is located elsewhere in the state and who have arranged for representation as a part of the state capital listings that follow

*** Pierce, Atwood, Scribner, Allen, Smith & Lancaster** (AV)

77 Winthrop Street, 04330
Telephone: 207-622-6311
Fax: 207-623-9367
Portland, Maine Office: One Monument Square.
Telephone: 207-773-6411.
Camden, Maine Office: 36 Chestnut Street, P.O. Box 780.
Telephone: 207-236-4333.

MEMBERS OF FIRM

Malcolm L. Lyons
Michael D. Seitzinger
John C. Nivison

ASSOCIATE

Daniel J. Stevens

For Complete List of Firm Personnel, See General Section

For full biographical listings, see the Martindale-Hubbell Law Directory

LEWISTON, Androscoggin Co.

Berman & Simmons, P.A. (AV)

129 Lisbon Street, P.O. Box 961, 04243-0961
Telephone: 207-784-3576
Fax: 207-784-7699
Portland, Maine Office: 178 Middle Street.
Telephone: 207-774-5277.
Fax: 207-774-0166.
South Paris, Maine Office: 4 Western Avenue.
Telephone: 207-743- 8775.
Fax: 207-743-8559.
Bridgton, Maine Office: Route 302, Portland Street.
Telephone: 207-647-3125.
Fax: 207-647-3134.

C. Martin Berman
Jack H. Simmons
John E. Sedgewick
William D. Robitzek
Julian L. Sweet
Jeffrey Rosenblatt
Paul F. Macri
Jeffrey A. Thaler
Steven D. Silin
Valerie Stanfill
Tyler N. Kolle
Glenn S. Eddy
David J. Van Dyke
David W. Grund
Daniel G. Kagan
Joy C. Cantrell
Ivy L. Frignoca

For full biographical listings, see the Martindale-Hubbell Law Directory

*PORTLAND,** Cumberland Co.

Amerling & Burns, A Professional Association (AV)

193 Middle Street, 04101
Telephone: 207-775-3581
Facsimile: 207-775-3814
Affiliated St. Croix Office: Coon & Sanford, P.O. Box 25918, Six Chandlers's Wharf, Suite 202, 00824-0918.

W. John Amerling
George F. Burns
David P. Ray
John R. Coon
Arnold C. Macdonald
Mary DeLano
Joanne F. Cole
A. Robert Ruesch

OF COUNSEL

Bruce M. Jervis

Representative Clients: H.E. Sargent, Inc. (construction); Merrill Trust; J.M. Huber, Inc.; Jackson Laboratories; Hague International (engineering); Aetna Life & Casualty Co.; The Hartford; Great American Insurance Co.; Wausau Insurance Co.

For full biographical listings, see the Martindale-Hubbell Law Directory

Friedman & Babcock (AV)

Suite 400, Six City Center, P.O. Box 4726, 04112-4726
Telephone: 207-761-0900
Telecopier: 207-761-0186

(See Next Column)

FRIEDMAN & BABCOCK—*Continued*

MEMBERS OF FIRM

Harold J. Friedman
Ernest J. Babcock
Martha C. Gaythwaite
Gregory W. Powell
Thomas A. Cox
Karen Frink Wolf
Jennifer S. Begel
Laurence H. Leavitt

ASSOCIATES

Theodore H. Irwin, Jr.
Lee H. Bals
Michelle A. Landmann
Arthur J. Lamothe
Brian L. Champion
Laurie B. Perzley
Elizabeth A. Germani
Tracey G. Burton
Jonathan Marc Dunitz
Lori A. Desjardins

For full biographical listings, see the Martindale-Hubbell Law Directory

RICHARDSON & TROUBH, A PROFESSIONAL CORPORATION (AV)

465 Congress Street, P.O. Box 9732, 04104-5032
Telephone: 207-774-5821
Telecopier: 207-761-2056
Bangor, Maine Office: Richardson Troubh & Badger, A Professional Corporation, 82 Columbia Street.
Telephone: 207-945-5900.
Telecopier: 207-945-0758.

Harrison L. Richardson
William B. Troubh
Edwin A. Heisler
John S. Whitman
Robert J. Piampiano
Richard J. Kelly
Wendell G. Large
Frederick J. Badger, Jr. (Resident, Bangor Office)
Kevin M. Gillis
Michael P. Boyd
Thomas E. Getchell
John W. Chapman
Michael Richards
William K. McKinley
Elizabeth G. Stouder
Barri Bloom
Daniel F. Gilligan
Paul S. Bulger
Ann M. Murray (Resident, Bangor Maine)

Frederick F. Costlow (Resident, Bangor Office)
John B. Lucy (Resident, Bangor Office)
M. Thomasine Burke
John G. Richardson
Kevin G. Anderson
Anne H. Cressey
Daniel R. Felkel
Thomas R. McKeon

Representative Clients: Fireman's Fund American Insurance Companies; Ford Motor Company; Great American Insurance Co.; CIGNA; Kemper Insurance Group; Liberty Mutual Insurance Co.; Norfolk & Dedham Mutual Fire Insurance Co.; Security Insurance Group; Scott Paper Co.; United Parcel Service.

For Complete List of Firm Personnel, See General Section

For full biographical listings, see the Martindale-Hubbell Law Directory

THOMPSON & BOWIE (AV)

Three Canal Plaza, P.O. Box 4630, 04112
Telephone: 207-774-2500
Telecopier: 207-774-3591

MEMBERS OF FIRM

Roy E. Thompson, Jr.
James M. Bowie
Daniel R. Mawhinney
Rebecca H. Farnum
Glenn H. Robinson
Frank W. DeLong, III
Michael E. Saucier
Mark V. Franco

ASSOCIATES

Elizabeth G. Knox
Cathy S. Roberts
Paul C. Catsos

For full biographical listings, see the Martindale-Hubbell Law Directory

MARYLAND

*BALTIMORE,** (Independent City)

ISRAELSON, SALSBURY, CLEMENTS & BEKMAN (AV)

300 West Pratt Street, Suite 450, 21201
Telephone: 410-539-6633
FAX: 410-625-9554

MEMBERS OF FIRM

Stuart Marshall Salsbury
Paul D. Bekman
Daniel M. Clements
Matthew Zimmerman
Laurence A. Marder

Suzanne K. Farace
Scott R. Scherr
Carol J. Glover

COUNSEL TO THE FIRM

Max R. Israelson

(See Next Column)

OF COUNSEL

Samuel Omar Jackson, Jr. (Semi-Retired)

For full biographical listings, see the Martindale-Hubbell Law Directory

JANET & STRAUSBERG (AV)

A Partnership of Professional Associations
Executive Centre at Hooks Lane, 8 Reservoir Circle, Suite 200, 21208
Telephone: 410-653-3200
Fax: 410-653-9030

MEMBERS OF FIRM

Howard A. Janet (P.A.)
Gary I. Strausberg (P.A.)

ASSOCIATES

Wayne M. Willoughby
Zev T. Gershon
Randal D. Getz
Sammie Lee Mouton

For full biographical listings, see the Martindale-Hubbell Law Directory

VENABLE, BAETJER AND HOWARD (AV)

A Partnership including Professional Corporations
1800 Mercantile Bank & Trust Building, 2 Hopkins Plaza, 21201
Telephone: 410-244-7400
Washington, D.C. Office: Venable, Baetjer, Howard & Civiletti. Suite 1000, 1201 New York Avenue, N.W.
Telephone: 202-962-4800.
McLean, Virginia Office: Suite 400, 2010 Corporate Ridge.
Telephone: 703-760-1600.
Rockville, Maryland Office: Suite 500, One Church Street, P. O. Box 1906.
Telephone: 301-217-5600.
Towson, Maryland Office: 210 Allegheny Avenue, P. O. Box 5517.
Telephone: 410-494-6200.

MEMBERS OF FIRM

Benjamin R. Civiletti (P.C.) (Also at Washington, D.C. and Towson, Maryland Offices)
George Cochran Doub (P.C.)
Roger W. Titus (Resident, Rockville, Maryland Office)
Robert G. Smith (P.C.)
Douglas D. Connah, Jr. (P.C.) (Also at Washington, D.C. Office)
John H. Zink, III (Resident, Towson, Maryland Office)
Paul F. Strain (P.C.)
Joseph C. Wich, Jr. (Resident, Towson, Maryland Office)
Nell B. Strachan
Susan K. Gauvey (Also at Towson, Maryland Office)
James K. Archibald (Also at Washington, D.C. and Towson, Maryland Offices)
Jeffrey A. Dunn (also at Washington, D.C. Office)
George F. Pappas (Also at Washington, D.C. Office)
James L. Shea (Also at Washington, D.C. Office)
Elizabeth C. Honeywell
C. Carey Deeley, Jr. (Also at Towson, Maryland Office)
Kathleen Gallogly Cox (Resident, Towson, Maryland Office)
Christopher R. Mellott
M. King Hill, III (Resident, Towson, Maryland Office)
David J. Heubeck
Gary M. Hnath (Resident, Washington, D.C. Office)

ASSOCIATES

Paul D. Barker, Jr.
J. Van L. Dorsey (Resident, Towson, Maryland Office)
Fred Joseph Federici, III (Resident, Washington, D.C. Office)
David W. Goewey (Not admitted in MD; Resident, Washington, D.C. Office)
Maria F. Howell
Mary-Dulany James (Resident, Towson, Maryland Office)
Gregory L. Laubach (Resident, Rockville, Maryland Office)
Vicki Margolis
Christine M. McAnney (Not admitted in MD; Resident, McLean, Virginia Office)
John A. McCauley
Mitchell Y. Mirviss
John T. Prisbe
Michael W. Robinson (Not admitted in MD; Resident, McLean, Virginia Office)
Robert A. Schwinger

For Complete List of Firm Personnel, See General Section

For full biographical listings, see the Martindale-Hubbell Law Directory

ROBIN PAGE WEST (AV)

110 St. Paul Street, Suite 301, 21202
Telephone: 410-244-0400
Fax: 410-244-0402

For full biographical listings, see the Martindale-Hubbell Law Directory

*LA PLATA,** Charles Co.

DAVID NEWMAN & ASSOCIATES, P.C. (AV)

Centennial Square, P.O. Box 2728, 20646-2728
Telephone: 301-934-6100; 202-842-8400
Facsimile: 301-934-5782

David B. Newman, Jr.

Suzin C. Bailey

(See Next Column)

DAVID NEWMAN & ASSOCIATES, P.C., *La Plata—Continued*

LEGAL SUPPORT PERSONNEL

TECHNICAL ADVISORS

Dr. Christopher J. Newman
Dr. Amy Hauck Newman

For full biographical listings, see the Martindale-Hubbell Law Directory

*ROCKVILLE,** Montgomery Co.

SHADOAN AND MICHAEL (AV)

108 Park Avenue, 20850
Telephone: 301-762-5150

MEMBERS OF FIRM

George W. Shadoan
Robert R. Michael

ASSOCIATE

David J. Kaminow

Reference: Crestar Bank, N.A.

For full biographical listings, see the Martindale-Hubbell Law Directory

*TOWSON,** Baltimore Co.

HOWELL, GATELY, WHITNEY & CARTER (AV)

401 Washington Avenue, Twelfth Floor, 21204
Telephone: 410-583-8000
FAX: 410-583-8031

MEMBERS OF FIRM

H. Thomas Howell
William F. Gately
Benjamin R. Goertemiller
Daniel W. Whitney
David A. Carter
William R. Levasseur

ASSOCIATES

Una M. Perez
John S. Bainbridge, Jr.
George D. Bogris
Wendy A. Lassen
Kathleen D. Leslie

For full biographical listings, see the Martindale-Hubbell Law Directory

VENABLE, BAETJER AND HOWARD (AV)

A Partnership including Professional Corporations
210 Allegheny Avenue, P.O. Box 5517, 21204
Telephone: 410-494-6200
FAX: 410-821-0147
Baltimore, Maryland Office: 1800 Mercantile Bank & Trust Building, 2 Hopkins Plaza.
Telephone: 410-244-7400.
Washington, D.C. Office: Venable, Baetjer, Howard & Civiletti. Suite 1000, 1201 New York Avenue, N.W.
Telephone: 202-962-4800.
McLean, Virginia Office: Suite 400, 2010 Corporate Ridge.
Telephone: 703-760-1600.
Rockville, Maryland Office: Suite 500, One Church Street, P. O. Box 1906.
Telephone: 301-217-5600.

PARTNERS

Benjamin R. Civiletti (P.C.) (Also at Washington, D.C. and Baltimore, Maryland Offices)
John H. Zink, III
Joseph C. Wich, Jr.
Susan K. Gauvey (Also at Baltimore, Maryland Office)
James K. Archibald (Also at Baltimore, Maryland and Washington, D.C. Offices)
C. Carey Deeley, Jr. (Also at Baltimore, Maryland Office)
Kathleen Gallogly Cox
M. King Hill, III

ASSOCIATES

J. Van L. Dorsey
Mary-Dulany James

For Complete List of Firm Personnel, See General Section

For full biographical listings, see the Martindale-Hubbell Law Directory

MASSACHUSETTS

*BOSTON,** Suffolk Co.

HANIFY & KING, PROFESSIONAL CORPORATION (AV)

One Federal Street, 02110-2007
Telephone: 617-423-0400
Telefax: 617-423-0498

James Coyne King
John D. Hanify
Harold B. Murphy
David Lee Evans
Daniel J. Lyne
Donald F. Farrell, Jr.
Barbara Wegener Pfirrman
Gerard P. Richer
Timothy P. O'Neill

(See Next Column)

Gordon M. Jones, III
Kara L. Thornton
Jean A. Musiker
Ann M. Chiacchieri
Melissa J. Cassedy
Kara M. Lucciola
Philip C. Silverman
Michael R. Perry
Jeffrey S. Cedrone
Charles A. Dale, III
Joseph F. Cortellini
Hiram N. Pan
Amy Conroy
Michael S. Bloom
Andrew G. Lizotte
Peter D. Lee
Martin F. Gaynor, III

For full biographical listings, see the Martindale-Hubbell Law Directory

SWARTZ & SWARTZ (AV)

10 Marshall Street, 02108
Telephone: 617-742-1900
Fax: 617-367-7193

Edward M. Swartz
Alan L. Cantor
Joseph A. Swartz
Victor A. Denaro
Joan E. Swartz
James A. Swartz
Robert S. Berger
Harold David Levine

OF COUNSEL

Fredric A. Swartz

For full biographical listings, see the Martindale-Hubbell Law Directory

WARNER & STACKPOLE (AV)

75 State Street, 02109
Telephone: 617-951-9000
Cable Address: "Warstack"
Telecopier: 617-951-9151
Telex: 940139

MEMBERS OF FIRM

Samuel Adams
Joseph J. Leghorn
Ralph T. Lepore, III
Antoinette D. Hubbard
Michael DeMarco

ASSOCIATES

Charlene D. Andros
Robert A. Whitney
Peter T. Wechsler
Ellen S. Rosenberg
Alexis L. Smith
Daniel E. Rosenfeld

COUNSEL

Andrew F. Lane

For Complete List of Firm Personnel, See General Section

For full biographical listings, see the Martindale-Hubbell Law Directory

BROCKTON, Plymouth Co.

VINCENT P. CAHALANE, P.C. (AV)

478 Torrey Street, 02401
Telephone: 508-588-1222
Fax: 508-584-4748

Vincent P. Cahalane
Robert J. Zullas
Julie A. Cahalane

LEGAL SUPPORT PERSONNEL

PARALEGALS

Joan C. Cahalane
Kristopher S. Stefani

For full biographical listings, see the Martindale-Hubbell Law Directory

*SPRINGFIELD,** Hampden Co.

ELY & KING (AV)

One Financial Plaza, 1350 Main Street, 01103
Telephone: 413-781-1920
Telecopier: 413-733-3360

MEMBERS OF FIRM

Joseph Buell Ely (1905-1956)
Raymond T. King (1919-1971)
Frederick M. Kingsbury (1924-1968)
Hugh J. Corcoran (1938-1992)
Richard S. Milstein
Donald A. Beaudry
Richard F. Faille
Leland B. Seabury
Gregory A. Schmidt
Pamela Manson
Anthony T. Rice
Russell J. Mawdsley

ASSOCIATE

Donna M. Brown

Representative Clients: Hartford Accident & Indemnity Co.; Albert Steiger Cos.; Shawmut Bank N.A.; Springfield Institution for Savings; St. Paul Fire & Marine Insurance Co.; The Rouse Co.; Tighe & Bond, Inc.; Northeast Utilities.

For full biographical listings, see the Martindale-Hubbell Law Directory

*WORCESTER,** Worcester Co.

FULLER, ROSENBERG, PALMER & BELIVEAU (AV)

14 Harvard Street, P.O. Box 764, 01613
Telephone: 508-755-5225
Telecopier: 508-757-1039

MEMBERS OF FIRM

Albert E. Fuller
Peter A. Palmer
Kenneth F. Rosenberg
Thomas W. Beliveau

ASSOCIATES

Robert W. Towle
Mark C. Darling
Julie Bednarz Russell
William J. Mason
Timothy O. Ribley
Antoinette J. Yitchinsky
Mark W. Murphy
Michael I. Mutter
Lisa R. Bertonazzi
Brian F. Welsh
John J. Finn

For full biographical listings, see the Martindale-Hubbell Law Directory

MICHIGAN

*ANN ARBOR,** Washtenaw Co.

DAVIS AND FAJEN, P.C. (AV)

Suite 400, 320 North Main Street, 48104
Telephone: 313-995-0066
Facsimile: 313-995-0184
Grand Haven, Michigan Office: Davis, Fajen & Miller. Harbourfront Place, 41 Washington Street, Suite 260.
Telephone: 616-846-9875.
Facsimile: 616-846-4920.

Peter A. Davis
Nelson P. Miller
James A. Fajen
Richard B. Bailey
Catherine G. Tennant

Reference: First of America Bank-Ann Arbor.

For full biographical listings, see the Martindale-Hubbell Law Directory

HURBIS, CMEJREK & CLINTON (AV)

Fifth Floor, City Center Building, 48104
Telephone: 313-761-8358
Fax: 313-761-3134

Charles J. Hurbis
James R. Cmejrek
Mary F. Clinton

Robert Lipnik

Representative Clients: General Motors Corp.; ITT Hartford; Insurance Company of North America; The University of Michigan; North Oakland Medical Center; City of Pontiac; Sears Roebuck and Co.; Montgomery Ward and Co., Inc.; Sedjwick-James, Inc.; Michigan State Accident Fund.

For full biographical listings, see the Martindale-Hubbell Law Directory

BLOOMFIELD HILLS, Oakland Co.

BAUM & ASSOCIATES (AV)

200 East Long Lake Road Suite 180, 48304
Telephone: 810-647-6890

Martin S. Baum

ASSOCIATE

Margo S. Horwitz

For full biographical listings, see the Martindale-Hubbell Law Directory

FEENEY KELLETT & WIENNER, PROFESSIONAL CORPORATION (AV)

950 N. Hunter Boulevard, Third Floor, 48304-3927
Telephone: 810-258-1580
Fax: 810-258-0421

James P. Feeney
David N. Goltz
S. Thomas Wienner
G. Gregory Schuetz
Peter M. Kellett
Tracy D. Knox (Not admitted in MI)
Cheryl A. Bush
Patrick G. Seyferth
Linda M. Galante
Mark A. Fisher
Deborah F. Collins

For full biographical listings, see the Martindale-Hubbell Law Directory

PORTNOY, PIDGEON & ROTH, P.C. (AV)

3883 Telegraph, Suite 103, 48302
Telephone: 810-647-4242
Fax: 810-647-8251

(See Next Column)

Bernard N. Portnoy
Robert P. Roth

For full biographical listings, see the Martindale-Hubbell Law Directory

*DETROIT,** Wayne Co.

BODMAN, LONGLEY & DAHLING (AV)

34th Floor 100 Renaissance Center, 48243
Telephone: 313-259-7777
Fax: 313-393-7579
Troy, Michigan Office: Suite 2020, 755 West Big Beaver Road.
Telephone: 810-362-2110.
Ann Arbor, Michigan Office: 110 Miller, Suite 300.
Telephone: 313-761-3780.
Northern Michigan Office: 229 Court Street, P.O. Box 405, Cheboygan.
Telephone: 616-627-4351.

MEMBERS OF FIRM

Henry E. Bodman (1874-1963)
Clifford B. Longley (1888-1954)
Louis F. Dahling (1892-1992)
Pierre V. Heftler
Richard D. Rohr
Theodore Souris
Joseph A. Sullivan
Carson C. Grunewald
Walter O. Koch (Troy Office)
Alfred C. Wortley, Jr.
Michael B. Lewiston
George D. Miller, Jr.
Mark W. Griffin (Ann Arbor Office)
Thomas A. Roach (Ann Arbor Office)
Kenneth R. Lango (Troy Office)
James T. Heimbuch
Herold McC. Deason
James A. Smith
James R. Buschmann
George G. Kemsley
Joseph N. Brown
David M. Hempstead
Joseph J. Kochanek
Randolph S. Perry (Ann Arbor Office)
James J. Walsh
David G. Chardavoyne
David W. Hipp
Robert G. Brower
Larry R. Shulman
Charles N. Raimi
Terrence B. Larkin (Troy Office)
Thomas Van Dusen (Troy Office)
Fredrick J. Dindoffer
Robert J. Diehl, Jr.
John C. Cashen (Troy Office)
James C. Conboy, Jr. (Northern Michigan Office)
Lloyd C. Fell (Northern Michigan Office)
F. Thomas Lewand
Michael A. Stack (Northern Michigan Office)
Kathleen A. Lieder (Northern Michigan Office)
Karen L. Piper
Martha Bedsole Goodloe (Troy Office)
Harvey W. Berman (Ann Arbor Office)
Barbara Bowman Bluford
R. Craig Hupp
Lawrence P. Hanson (Northern Michigan Office)
Christopher J. Dine (Troy Office)
Henry N. Carnaby (Troy Office)
Jerold Lax (Ann Arbor Office)
Linda J. Throne (Northern Michigan Office)
Diane L. Akers
Ralph E. McDowell
Susan M. Kornfield (Ann Arbor Office)
Stephen I. Greenhalgh
Kathleen O'Callaghan Hickey
Patrick C. Cauley
Dennis J. Levasseur
David P. Larsen
Gail Pabarue Bennett (Troy Office)
Kay E. Malaney (Troy Office)

COUNSEL

Robert A. Nitschke
John S. Dobson (Ann Arbor Office)
Lewis A. Rockwell
Patricia D. White (Ann Arbor Office)

ASSOCIATES

Gary D. Reeves (Troy Office)
Joseph W. Girardot
Barnett Jay Colvin
David W. Barton (Northern Michigan Office)
Susan E. Conboy (Northern Michigan Office)
Sandra L. Sorini (Ann Arbor Office)
Stephen K. Postema (Ann Arbor Office)
Bonnie S. Sherr
Lisa M. Panourgias
R. Carl Lanfear
Louise-Annette Marcotty
William L. Hoey
Laurie A. Allen (Troy Office)
Marc M. Bakst
A. Craig Klomparens (Northern Michigan Office)
Kim M. Williams
David P. Rea
Jodee Fishman Raines
Nicholas P. Scavone, Jr.
Lydia Pallas Loren (Ann Arbor Office)
Robert C. Skramstad
Deanna L. Dixon
Arthur F. deVaux (Troy Office)

Representative Clients: Abitibi Price Group; Archdiocese of Detroit; Comerica Bank; The Detroit Lions, Inc.; Ford Estates; General Motors Corporation; Charles Stewart Mott Foundation; Norfolk Southern Corporation; Panhandle Eastern Corporation; State Farm Mutual Automobile Insurance Company.

For full biographical listings, see the Martindale-Hubbell Law Directory

BUTZEL LONG, A PROFESSIONAL CORPORATION (AV)

Suite 900, 150 West Jefferson, 48226
Telephone: 313-225-7000
Telecopier: 313-225-7080
Birmingham, Michigan Office: Suite 200, 32270 Telegraph Road.
Telephone: 810-258-1616.
Telecopier: 810-258-1439.

(See Next Column)

BUTZEL LONG A PROFESSIONAL CORPORATION, *Detroit—Continued*

Lansing, Michigan Office: 118 West Ottawa Street.
Telephone: 517-372-6622.
Telecopier: 517-372-6672.
Ann Arbor, Michigan Office: Suite 400, 121 West Washington.
Telephone: 313-995-3110.
Telecopier: 313-995-1777.
Grosse Pointe Farms, Michigan Office: Suite 260, 21 Kercheval.
Telephone: 313-886-5446.
Telecopier: 313-886-2114.

Xhafer Orhan
Edward M. Kronk
Daniel P. Malone
James E. Wynne
Jack J. Mazzara
Bruce L. Sendek
Lynn Abraham Sheehy

William D. Vanderhoef
Robert E. Norton II

Representative Clients: Bridgestone/Firestone, Inc.; The Detroit News, Inc.; Detroit Diesel Corp.; Kelly Services; Kelsey Hayes Co.; Merrill Lynch & Co., Inc.; Stroh Brewery Co.; Takata Corp.; United Parcel Services of America, Inc.; The University of Michigan.

For Complete List of Firm Personnel, See General Section

For full biographical listings, see the Martindale-Hubbell Law Directory

CLARK, KLEIN & BEAUMONT (AV)

1600 First Federal Building, 1001 Woodward Avenue, 48226
Telephone: 313-965-8300
Facsimile: 313-962-4348
Bloomfield Hills Office: 1533 North Woodward Avenue, Suite 220, 48304.
Telephone: 810-258-2900.
Facsimile: 810-258-2949.

MEMBERS OF FIRM

Dennis G. Bonucchi
James E. Baiers
Jonathan T. Walton, Jr.
Michael J. Sullivan
Cynthia L.M. Johnson

ASSOCIATE

Katrina I. Crawley

Representative Clients: The Budd Co.; Dow Corning Corporation; Kaiser Aluminum and Chemical Co.

For Complete List of Firm Personnel, See General Section

For full biographical listings, see the Martindale-Hubbell Law Directory

DENARDIS, MCCANDLESS & MULLER, P.C. (AV)

800 Buhl Building, 48226-3602
Telephone: 313-963-9050
Fax: 313-963-4553

Ronald F. DeNardis
William McCandless
Gregory J. Muller
Mark F. Miller
Lawrence M. Hintz
Michael D. Dolenga

For full biographical listings, see the Martindale-Hubbell Law Directory

DICKINSON, WRIGHT, MOON, VAN DUSEN & FREEMAN (AV)

500 Woodward Avenue, Suite 4000, 48226-3425
Telephone: 313-223-3500
Facsimile: 313-223-3598
Bloomfield Hills, Michigan Office: 525 North Woodward Avenue, Suite 2000.
Telephone: 810-433-7200.
Facsimile: 810-433-7274.
Grand Rapids, Michigan Office: 200 Ottawa Avenue, N.W., Suite 900.
Telephone: 616-458-1300.
Facsimile: 616-458-6753.
Lansing, Michigan Office: Suite 200, 215 South Washington Square.
Telephone: 517-371-1730.
Facsimile: 517-487-4700.
Washington, D.C. Office: Suite 800, 1901 L Street, N.W.
Telephone: 202-457-0160.
Facsimile: 202-659-1559.
Chicago, Illinois Office: 225 West Washington, Suite 400.
Telephone: 312-220-0300.
Facsimile: 312-220-0021.
Warsaw, Poland Office: 46 Wilcza Street, 4th Floor, 00-679.
Telephone: (48-22) 299-241.
Facsimile: (48-2) 628-4107. Komertel Satellite Phone: (48-39) 121-510.

MEMBERS OF FIRM

John E. S. Scott
Robert S. Krause
Michael Gary Vartanian
Richard L. Braun, II
Richard A. Glaser
(Grand Rapids Office)
Richard W. Paul
Richard L. Caretti
Margaret A. Coughlin
Thomas J. Manganello
Robert E. Kinchen
Richard A. Wilhelm
Barbara Hughes Erard
Kenneth T. Brooks
(Lansing Office)
Kathleen A. Lang
Brian K. Cullin
Thomas G. McNeill
Cynthia M. York

(See Next Column)

ASSOCIATES

Andrew S. Doctoroff
Sandra J. LeFevre
Linda S. McAlpine
Marian Keidan Seltzer
Rock A. Wood
(Grand Rapids Office)

For Complete List of Firm Personnel, See General Section

For full biographical listings, see the Martindale-Hubbell Law Directory

FOSTER, MEADOWS & BALLARD, P.C. (AV)

3200 Penobscot Building, 48226
Telephone: 313-961-3234
Cable Address: "Foster"
Telex: 23-5823
Facsimile: 313-961-6184

Sparkman D. Foster (1897-1967)
John L. Foster
Charles R. Hrdlicka
Paul D. Galea
Richard A. Dietz
Robert H. Fortunate
Robert G. Lahiff
Camille A. Raffa-Dietz

Michael J. Liddane
Paul A. Kettunen

OF COUNSEL

John F. Langs
John A. Mundell, Jr.

Counsel for: Air Canada; Canadian National Railways; Grand Trunk Western Railroad; Alexander and Alexander; Shand Morahan; Utica Mutual.
Admiralty Counsel for: Ford Motor; Bob Lo Co.

For full biographical listings, see the Martindale-Hubbell Law Directory

HAYDUK, ANDREWS & HYPNAR, P.C. (AV)

444 Penobscot Building, 48226
Telephone: 313-962-4500
Fax: 313-964-6577

Mark S. Hayduk
Robin K. Andrews
Mark A. Hypnar
Paul J. Ellison
Sean Angus McPhillips
Robert J. Heimbuch

Representative Clients: Farmers Insurance Group; GameTime, Inc.; Admiral Insurance Co.; Safeco Insurance Cos.; Heritage Ins. Alexis; LMI; Meijer, Inc.; Condon & Forsyth; Pinkerton's Inc.

For full biographical listings, see the Martindale-Hubbell Law Directory

LUPO, KOCZKUR & PETRELLA, P.C. (AV)

1000 First National Building, 48226
Telephone: 313-964-0110
Fax: 313-964-3711

Dane A. Lupo
Paul S. Koczkur
Marisa C. Petrella
Bradley S. Mitseff
Sandra M. Vozza
Dehai Tao
Michael P. Fresard

For full biographical listings, see the Martindale-Hubbell Law Directory

ROSEN & LOVELL, P.C. (AV)

Penobscot Building, 645 Griswold Street, Suite 3080, 48226-4224
Telephone: 313-961-7510
Fax: 313-961-2905

Paul A. Rosen
Joan Lovell

For full biographical listings, see the Martindale-Hubbell Law Directory

JOSEPH C. SMITH, P.C. (AV)

600 Renaissance Center Suite 1500, 48243
Telephone: 313-567-8300
Fax: 313-567-0892

Joseph C. Smith

For full biographical listings, see the Martindale-Hubbell Law Directory

FARMINGTON HILLS, Oakland Co.

KAUFMAN AND PAYTON (AV)

200 Northwestern Financial Center, 30833 Northwestern Highway, 48334
Telephone: 810-626-5000
Telefacsimile: 810-626-2843
Grand Rapids, Michigan Office: 420 Trust Building.
Telephone: 616-459-4200.
Fax: 616-459-4929.
Traverse City, Michigan Office: 122 West State Street.
Telephone: 616-947-4050.
Fax: 616-947-7321.

(See Next Column)

KAUFMAN AND PAYTON—*Continued*

Alan Jay Kaufman
Donald L. Payton
Kenneth C. Letherwood
Stephen R. Levine
Thomas L. Vitu
Ralph C. Chapa, Jr.
Raymond I. Foley, II
Jeffrey K. Van Hattum
Leo D. Neville

For full biographical listings, see the Martindale-Hubbell Law Directory

STILL, NEMIER, TOLARI & LANDRY, P.C. (AV)

37000 Grand River, Suite 300, 48335
Telephone: 810-476-6900
Fax: 810-476-6564

William R. Still
Craig L. Nemier
Jeffrey L. Tolari
David B. Landry
Mark R. Johnson
Rik Mazzeo
Catherine L. West
Michelle E. Mathieu
Christopher A. Todd
Thomas S. McLeod
Victoria W. Ryan

OF COUNSEL

Terry E. Pietryga
Veeder Ann Willey

For full biographical listings, see the Martindale-Hubbell Law Directory

*FLINT,** Genesee Co.

BELTZ & ASSOCIATES (AV)

444 Church Street, 48502
Telephone: 810-767-5421
Fax: 810-767-5369

C. Robert Beltz

ASSOCIATE

Charles D. Riley

For full biographical listings, see the Martindale-Hubbell Law Directory

GROVES, DECKER & WYATT, PROFESSIONAL CORPORATION (AV)

2357 Stone Bridge Drive, 48532
Telephone: 810-732-6920
Fax: 810-732-9015
East Lansing, Michigan Office: 2760 East Lansing Drive, Suite 4.
Telephone: 517-332-7715.
Facsimile: 517-332-4405.

Harvey R. Groves
Lee A. Decker
George H. Wyatt III
William L. Meuleman III
Thomas J. Ruth
Cameron D. Reddy

Representative Clients: American International Group; Ameritech; Crawford & Co.; Kmart Corp.; Sherwin-Williams Co.; Sumitomo Fire and Marine Insurance co.; Weyerhauser Co.; Zurich Insurance Co.

For full biographical listings, see the Martindale-Hubbell Law Directory

MACDONALD, FITZGERALD, MACDONALD & SIMON, P.C. (AV)

200 McKinnon Building, 48502
Telephone: 810-232-3184; 234-2204
Fax: 810-232-9632

Robert J. MacDonald (1914-1987)
John J. FitzGerald
R. Duncan MacDonald
Timothy J. Simon
Timothy J. MacDonald

References: Michigan National Bank; Genesee Merchants Bank & Trust Co.

For full biographical listings, see the Martindale-Hubbell Law Directory

*GRAND RAPIDS,** Kent Co.

BUCHANAN & BOS (AV)

300 Ottawa N.W., Suite 800, 49503
Telephone: 616-458-1224
Fax: 616-458-0608

MEMBERS OF FIRM

John C. Buchanan
Carole D. Bos
Bradley K. Glazier
Lee T. Silver

ASSOCIATES

Raymond S. Kent
Jane M. Beckering
Richard A. Stevens
Susan Wilson Keener
Gwen E. Buday
Anne M. Frye
Brian K. Lawson
Nancy K. Haynes

For full biographical listings, see the Martindale-Hubbell Law Directory

CHOLETTE, PERKINS & BUCHANAN (AV)

900 Campau Square Plaza Building, 99 Monroe Avenue, N.W., 49503
Telephone: 616-774-2131
Fax: 616-774-7016

(See Next Column)

MEMBERS OF FIRM

Calvin R. Danhof
Frederick W. Bleakley
Reynolds A. Brander, Jr.
Bruce M. Bieneman
William J. Warren
Donald C. Exelby
Thomas H. Cypher
William A. Brengle
Alfred J. Parent
Charles H. Worsfold
Michael P. McCasey
Marc A. Kidder
Michael C. Mysliwiec
Evan L. MacFarlane
John A. Quinn
Albert J. Engel, III
Stephen C. Oldstrom
William E. McDonald, Jr.
Mark E. Fatum
Richard K. Grover, Jr.
David J. DeGraw

ASSOCIATES

Kenneth L. Block
William J. Yob
Robert E. Attmore
Martin W. Buschle
Miles J. Murphy, III
Martha P. Forman
Kathrine M. West
Robert A. Kamp

Counsel for: Aetna Casualty & Surety Co.; Argonaut Insurance Co.; Auto-Owners Insurance Co.; Employers Mutual; Liberty Mutual Insurance Co.; Sentry Group; State Farm Insurance; Eastern Aviation and Marine Underwriters; Home Insurance Co.; Nationwide Insurance.

For Complete List of Firm Personnel, See General Section

For full biographical listings, see the Martindale-Hubbell Law Directory

WHEELER UPHAM, A PROFESSIONAL CORPORATION (AV)

Second Floor, Trust Building, 40 Pearl Street, N.W., 49503
Telephone: 616-459-7100
Fax: 616-459-6366

Gordon B. Wheeler (1904-1986)
Buford A. Upham (Retired)
Robert H. Gillette
Geoffrey L. Gillis
John M. Roels
Gary A. Maximiuk
Timothy J. Orlebeke
Kenneth E. Tiews
Jack L. Hoffman
Janet C. Baxter
Peter Kladder, III
James M. Shade
Thomas A. Kuiper

Counsel for: Travelers Insurance Co.; Prudential Insurance Co. of America; Farmers Insurance Group; Metropolitan Life Insurance Co.; Conrail Trans.; Monsanto Co.; Firestone Tire & Rubber Co.; Navistar, Inc.; Medtronic, Inc.; Westdale Better Homes and Gardens.

For full biographical listings, see the Martindale-Hubbell Law Directory

LANSING, Ingham Co.

CHURCH, KRITSELIS, WYBLE & ROBINSON, P.C. (AV)

3939 Capital City Boulevard, 48906-9962
Telephone: 517-323-4770

William N. Kritselis
J. Richard Robinson
James T. Heos
David S. Mittleman

D. Michael Dudley
Catherine Groll
James M. Hofer

For full biographical listings, see the Martindale-Hubbell Law Directory

FRASER TREBILCOCK DAVIS & FOSTER, P.C. (AV)

1000 Michigan National Tower, 48933
Telephone: 517-482-5800
Fax: 517-482-0887
Okemos, Michigan Office: 2188 Commons Parkway.
Telephone: 517-349-1300.
Fax: 517-349-0922.

Joe C. Foster, Jr.
Eugene Townsend (1926-1982)
Ronald R. Pentecost
Donald A. Hines
Peter L. Dunlap
Everett R. Zack
Douglas J. Austin
Robert W. Stocker, II
Michael E. Cavanaugh
John J. Loose
David E. S. Marvin
Stephen L. Burlingame
C. Mark Hoover
Darrell A. Lindman
Ronald R. Sutton
Iris K. Socolofsky-Linder
Brett Jon Bean
Richard C. Lowe
Gary C. Rogers
Mark A. Bush
Michael H. Perry
Brandon W. Zuk
David D. Waddell
Thomas J. Waters

John E. Bos
Michael C. Levine
Mark R. Fox
Nancy L. Little
Sharon A. Bruner
Michael S. Ashton
Michael James Reilly
Michelyn E. Pastuer
Patrick K. Thornton
Charyn K. Hain
Brian D. Herrington
Michael J. Laramie
Marcy R. Meyer

(See Next Column)

FRASER TREBILCOCK DAVIS & FOSTER P.C., *Lansing—Continued*

OF COUNSEL

Archie C. Fraser
Everett R. Trebilcock
James R. Davis

Counsel for: Auto Club Insurance Assn. (ACIA); Auto Owners Insurance Co.; City of Mackinac Island; Federal Insurance Co.; General Motors Corp.; Grand Trunk Ry. Co.; Prudential Insurance Company of America; State Farm Automobile Insurance Co.

For full biographical listings, see the Martindale-Hubbell Law Directory

RAYMOND JOSEPH (AV)

1602 Michigan National Tower, 48933
Telephone: 517-372-4410
Fax: 517-372-2137

OF COUNSEL

George R. Sidwell (1899-1983)
Michael Bowman
Bruce C. Blanton

Representative Clients: Ashland Oil, Inc.; Complete Auto Transit, Inc.; Employers Insurance of Wausau; Evans Products Co.; Grain Dealers Mutl.; Harbor Insurance Co.; Interstate Motor Freight System; Lansing Symphony Assn., Inc.; RCA Service Co.; West American Insurance Co.

For full biographical listings, see the Martindale-Hubbell Law Directory

*MOUNT CLEMENS,** Macomb Co.

MARTIN, BACON & MARTIN, P.C. (AV)

44 First Street, 48043
Telephone: 810-979-6500
Fax: 810-468-7016

James N. Martin
John G. Bacon
Jonathan E. Martin
Paul R. VanTol
Michael R. Janes
Kevin L. Moffatt
John W. Crimando
Victor T. Van Camp

Deborah S. Forster

Reference: First National Bank of Mt. Clemens.

For full biographical listings, see the Martindale-Hubbell Law Directory

SOUTHFIELD, Oakland Co.

GORDON, CUTLER AND HOFFMAN, P.C. (AV)

18411 West Twelve Mile Road, 48076
Telephone: 810-443-1500

Arnold M. Gordon
Joel L. Hoffman
Donald M. Cutler
John M. Callahan

Reference: Michigan National Bank-Oakland.

HIGHLAND & ZANETTI (AV)

Suite 205, 24445 Northwestern Highway, 48075
Telephone: 810-352-9580

John N. Highland
J. R. Zanetti, Jr.
R. Michael John

Duncan Hall Brown
Joseph M. LaBella
James S. Meyerand

For full biographical listings, see the Martindale-Hubbell Law Directory

SCHWARTZ & JALKANEN, P.C. (AV)

Suite 200, 24400 Northwestern Highway, 48075
Telephone: 810-352-2555
Facsimile: 810-352-5963

Melvin R. Schwartz
Arthur W. Jalkanen
Karl Eric Hannum

Anne Loridas Randall
Deborah L. Laura
Lisa M. Green

For full biographical listings, see the Martindale-Hubbell Law Directory

SOMMERS, SCHWARTZ, SILVER & SCHWARTZ, P.C. (AV)

2000 Town Center, Suite 900, 48075
Telephone: 810-355-0300
Telecopier: 810-746-4001
Plymouth, Michigan Office: 747 South Main Street.
Telephone: 313-455-4250.

Leonard B. Schwartz
Robert H. Darling
James J. Vlasic
Joseph E. Grinnan
B. A. Tyler

General Counsel for: City of Taylor; Foodland Distributors; C.A. Muer Corporation; Vlasic & Company; Nederlander Corporation; Woodland Physicians; Midwest Health Centers, P.C.

(See Next Column)

Representative Clients: Crum & Forster Insurance Company; City of Pontiac; Michigan National Bank; Perry Drugs.

For Complete List of Firm Personnel, See General Section

For full biographical listings, see the Martindale-Hubbell Law Directory

*TRAVERSE CITY,** Grand Traverse Co.

THOMPSON, PARSONS & O'NEIL (AV)

309 East Front Street, P.O. Box 429, 49685
Telephone: 616-929-9700; 1-800-678-1307
Fax: 616-929-7262

MEMBERS OF FIRM

George R. Thompson
Grant W. Parsons
Daniel P. O'Neil

William J. Brooks

For full biographical listings, see the Martindale-Hubbell Law Directory

MINNESOTA

*MINNEAPOLIS,** Hennepin Co.

BOWMAN AND BROOKE (AV)

Suite 2600 Fifth Street Towers, 150 South Fifth Street, 55402
Telephone: 612-339-8682
Fax: 612-672-3200
Phoenix, Arizona Office: Phoenix Plaza, Suite 1700, 2929 North Central Avenue.
Telephone: 602-248-0899.
Fax: 602-248-0947.
Detroit, Michigan Office: 1800 Fisher Building, 3011 West Grand Boulevard.
Telephone: 313-871-3000.
Fax: 313-871-3006.
San Jose, California Office: Suite 1150, 160 West Santa Clara Street.
Telephone: 408-279-5393.
Fax: 408-279-5845.
Torrance, California Office: Suite 1000, 19191 South Vermont Avenue.
Telephone: 310-768-3068.
Fax: 310-719-1019.

MEMBERS OF FIRM

Richard A. Bowman
John Q. McShane
David R. Kelly
David W. Graves, Jr.
George W. Soule
Hildy Bowbeer
Kent B. Hanson
Wayne D. Struble
Thomas B. Heffelfinger
Matthew J. Valitchka, II
Kenneth Ross
Robert E. Pederson (Not admitted in MN)
Robert K. Miller
Marcia M. Kull
Mickey W. Greene
Cynthia J. Atsatt
Lezlie Ott Marek
James W. Halbrooks, Jr.
Mary E. Bolkcom
Timothy J. Mattson

ASSOCIATES

Daniel C. Adams
Kim M. Schmid
David N. Lutz
Sheryl A. Bjork
John D. Sear
Anton J. van der Merwe
Steven L. Reitenour
Cortney G. Sylvester
Darin D. Smith
Bard D. Borkon
C. Paul Carver
Jacqueline M. Moen

OF COUNSEL

Michael G. Fiergola (Not admitted in MN)

For full biographical listings, see the Martindale-Hubbell Law Directory

COSGROVE, FLYNN & GASKINS (AV)

29th Floor, Metropolitan Centre, 333 South Seventh Street, 55402
Telephone: 612-333-9500
Fax: 612-333-9579

MEMBERS OF FIRM

Hugh J. Cosgrove
George W. Flynn
Steve Gaskins
Robert J. Terhaar
Jeannine L. Lee
Douglas R. Archibald
Barbara Jean D'Aquila
Susan D. Hall
Steven J. Pfefferle
Thomas Klosowski

ASSOCIATES

Randall J. Pattee
Bradley J. Ayers
Hal A. Shillingstad
David A. Wikoff
Gary D. Ansel
Laurie A. Willard
Sarah L. Brew
Lisa R. Griebel
Thomas F. Ascher
Lynn M. Meyer
Scott M. Rusert
Jennifer F. Rosemark
Anthony J. Kane

For full biographical listings, see the Martindale-Hubbell Law Directory

Minneapolis—Continued

GILMORE, AAFEDT, FORDE, ANDERSON & GRAY, P.A. (AV)

150 South Fifth Street, Suite 3100, 55402
Telephone: 612-339-8965
Fax: 612-349-6839

Curtis C. Gilmore (Retired)
John R. de Lambert (Retired)
Michael D. Aafedt
Michael Forde
Donald W. Anderson
James R. Gray
Jay T. Hartman
Roderick C. Cosgriff
Janet Monson
Steven C. Gilmore
Mary Marvin Hager

Peter M. Banovetz
Robin D. Simpson
Kirk C. Thompson
Kathy A. Endres
Miriam P. Rykken
Janet Scheel Stellpflug
Lawrence C. Miller
Adam S. Wolkoff
David J. Klaiman
David Brian Kempston
Charles S. Bierman
Sheryl A. Zaworski
Kathryn M. Hipp

Representative Client: General Casualty/Reliance.

For full biographical listings, see the Martindale-Hubbell Law Directory

HVASS, WEISMAN & KING, CHARTERED (AV)

Suite 450, 100 South Fifth Street, 55402
Telephone: 612-333-0201
FAX: 612-342-2606

Charles T. Hvass (Retired)
Si Weisman (1912-1992)
Robert J. King
Frank J. Brixius
Richard A. Williams, Jr.
Charles T. Hvass, Jr.
Robert J. King, Jr.
Michael W. Unger

John E. Daly
John M. Dornik
Mark T. Porter

For full biographical listings, see the Martindale-Hubbell Law Directory

*WILLMAR,** Kandiyohi Co.

SCHNEIDER LAW FIRM, A PROFESSIONAL ASSOCIATION (AV)

706 South First Street, P.O. Box 776, 56201
Telephone: 612-235-1850
WATS: 800-840-1850
Fax: 612-235-3611

Ronald H. Schneider (P.A.)

Reference: First Bank Willmar.

For full biographical listings, see the Martindale-Hubbell Law Directory

MISSISSIPPI

BILOXI, Harrison Co.

BROWN & WATT, P.A. (AV)

115 Main Street, P.O. Box 1377, 39533-1377
Telephone: 601-374-2999
Telecopier: 601-435-7090
Pascagoula, Mississippi Office: 3112 Canty Street, P.O. Box 2220.
Telephone: 601-762-0035.
Fax: 601-762-0299.

Raymond L. Brown
W. Lee Watt
Patrick R. Buchanan
William M. Edwards
A. Kelly Sessoms, III
R. Bradley Prewitt
Alan K. Sudduth

General Counsel For: Mississippi Export Railroad Co.; Pascagoula Municipal Separate School District.
Representative Clients: United States Fidelity & Guaranty Co.; The Travelers Companies; The Home Insurance Co.; CSX Transportation, Inc.; Blue Cross-Blue Shield of Mississippi; Burlington Insurance Co.; Continental Insurance; Deere & Company.

For full biographical listings, see the Martindale-Hubbell Law Directory

MINOR AND GUICE (AV)

A Partnership including a Professional Association
160 Main Street, Drawer 1388, 39533
Telephone: 601-374-5151
FAX: 601-374-6630

Paul S. Minor (P.A.)
Judy M. Guice

(See Next Column)

Mark D. Lumpkin
Michael Bruffey

For full biographical listings, see the Martindale-Hubbell Law Directory

PAGE, MANNINO & PERESICH (AV)

759 Vieux Marché Mall, P.O. Drawer 289, 39530
Telephone: 601-374-2100
Telecopier: 601-432-5539
Jackson, Mississippi Office: One LeFleurs Square, 4735 Old Canton Road, P.O. Box 12159.
Telephone: 601-364-1100.
Telecopier: 601-364-1118.
Gulfport, Mississippi Office: Markham Building, 2301 - 14th Street, Suite 600, Drawer 660.
Telephone: 601-863-8861.
Telecopier: 601-863-8871.

MEMBERS OF FIRM

Lyle M. Page
Frederick J. Mannino
Ronald G. Peresich
Michael B. McDermott
Stephen G. Peresich
Jess H. Dickinson
Tere Richardson Steel
David S. Raines
Michael P. Collins
Randolph Cook Wood
Mary A. Nichols
Joseph Henry Ros
Thomas William Busby
Michael E. Whitehead
Katharine Malley Samson
Douglas J. Wise

Representative Clients: United States Fidelity & Guaranty Co.; St. Paul Fire & Marine Insurance Co.; Crawford & Co.; Anheuser-Busch Corp.
General Counsel for: Peoples Bank of Biloxi, Mississippi; Biloxi Regional Medical Center; Bank of Mississippi (Gulf Coast Division).

For full biographical listings, see the Martindale-Hubbell Law Directory

*GULFPORT,** Harrison Co.

DUKES, DUKES, KEATING AND FANECA, P.A. (AV)

2308 East Beach Boulevard, P.O. Drawer W, 39501
Telephone: 601-868-1111
FAX: 601-863-2886

William F. Dukes
Walter W. Dukes
Cy Faneca

David Charles Goff

For full biographical listings, see the Martindale-Hubbell Law Directory

PAGE, MANNINO & PERESICH (AV)

Markham Building, 2301 14th Street, Suite 600, Drawer 660, 39501-2095
Telephone: 601-863-8861
Telecopier: 601-863-8871
Biloxi, Mississippi Office: 759 Vieux MarchéMall, P.O. Drawer 289.
Telephone: 601-374-2100.
Telecopier: 601-432-5539.
Jackson, Mississippi Office: One Lefleurs Square, 4735 Old Canton Road, P.O. Box 12159.
Telephone: 601-364-1100.
Telecopier: 601-364-1118.

MEMBERS OF FIRM

Lyle M. Page
Frederick J. Mannino
Ronald G. Peresich
Michael B. McDermott
Stephen G. Peresich
Jess H. Dickinson
Tere Richardson Steel
David S. Raines
Michael P. Collins
Randolph Cook Wood
Mary A. Nichols
Joseph Henry Ros
Thomas William Busby
Michael E. Whitehead
Katharine Malley Samson
Douglas J. Wise

Representative Clients: United States Fidelity & Guaranty Co.; St. Paul Fire & Marine Insurance Co.; Crawford & Co.; Anheuser-Busch Corp.
General Counsel for: Peoples Bank of Biloxi, Mississippi; Biloxi Regional Medical Center; Bank of Mississippi (Gulf Coast Division).

For full biographical listings, see the Martindale-Hubbell Law Directory

*JACKSON,** Hinds Co.

ALLRED & DONALDSON (AV)

101 West Capitol Street, Suite 300, P.O. Box 3828, 39207-3828
Telephone: 601-948-2086
Telefax: 601-948-2175

MEMBERS OF FIRM

Michael S. Allred
John I. Donaldson

ASSOCIATES

Stephen M. Maloney
Kathleen H. Eiler

For full biographical listings, see the Martindale-Hubbell Law Directory

Jackson—Continued

PAGE, MANNINO & PERESICH (AV)

One LeFleurs Square, 4735 Old Canton Road, P.O. Box 12159, 39236-2159
Telephone: 601-364-1100
Telecopier: 601-364-1118
Biloxi, Mississippi Office: 759 Vieux MarchéMall, P.O. Drawer 289.
Telephone: 601-374-2100.
Telecopier: 601-432-5539.
Gulfport, Mississippi Office: Markham Building, 2301 - 14th Street, Suite 600, P.O. Drawer 660.
Telephone: 601-863-8861.
Telecopier: 601-863-8871.

MEMBERS OF FIRM

Lyle M. Page
Frederick J. Mannino
Ronald G. Peresich
Michael B. McDermott
Stephen G. Peresich
Jess H. Dickinson
Tere Richardson Steel
David S. Raines
Michael P. Collins
Randolph Cook Wood
Mary A. Nichols
Joseph Henry Ros
Thomas William Busby
Michael E. Whitehead
Katharine Malley Samson
Douglas J. Wise (Not admitted in MS)

Representative Clients: United States Fidelity & Guaranty Co.; St. Paul Fire & Marine Insurance Co.; Crawford & Co.; Anheuser-Busch Corp.
General Counsel for: Peoples Bank of Biloxi, Mississippi; Biloxi Regional Medical Center; Bank of Mississippi (Gulf Coast Division).

For full biographical listings, see the Martindale-Hubbell Law Directory

*OXFORD,** Lafayette Co.

FREELAND & FREELAND (AV)

1013 Jackson Avenue, P.O. Box 269, 38655
Telephone: 601-234-3414
Telecopier: 601-234-0604

MEMBERS OF FIRM

T. H. Freeland, III
T. H. Freeland, IV
J. Hale Freeland

ASSOCIATE

Paul W. Crutcher

Representative Clients: The Ohio Casualty Group; Crum & Forester.

For full biographical listings, see the Martindale-Hubbell Law Directory

*PASCAGOULA,** Jackson Co.

BROWN & WATT, P.A. (AV)

3112 Canty Street, P.O. Box 2220, 39569-2220
Telephone: 601-762-0035
Telecopier: 601-762-0299
Biloxi, Mississippi Office: 115 Main Street, P.O. Box 1377.
Telephone: 601-374-2999.
Fax: 601-435-7090.

Raymond L. Brown
W. Lee Watt
Patrick R. Buchanan
William M. Edwards
A. Kelly Sessoms, III
R. Bradley Prewitt
Alan K. Sudduth

General Counsel For: Mississippi Export Railroad Co.; Pascagoula Municipal Separate School District.
Representative Clients: United States Fidelity & Guaranty Co.; The Travelers Companies; The Home Insurance Co.; CSX Transportation, Inc.; Blue Cross-Blue Shield of Mississippi; Burlington Insurance Co.; Continental Insurance; Deere & Company.

For full biographical listings, see the Martindale-Hubbell Law Directory

MISSOURI

KANSAS CITY, Jackson, Clay & Platte Cos.

BARTIMUS, KAVANAUGH & FRICKLETON, A PROFESSIONAL CORPORATION (AV)

23rd Floor City Center Square, 1100 Main Street, 64105
Telephone: 816-842-2300
FAX: 816-421-2111

James R. Bartimus
Paul F. Kavanaugh
James P. Frickleton
Kirk R. Presley

OF COUNSEL

Max W. Foust

(See Next Column)

LEGAL SUPPORT PERSONNEL

LEGAL ASSISTANTS

Janet L. Smith-Lierman
Tammy J. Gilliams
Stephanie Lang
Laura M. Burbach
Arnella R. McNichols

For full biographical listings, see the Martindale-Hubbell Law Directory

HANOVER & TURNER (AV)

700 Commerce Trust Building, 922 Walnut Street, 64106
Telephone: 816-221-2888
Fax: 816-221-4453

MEMBERS OF FIRM

Hollis H. Hanover
John E. Turner

For full biographical listings, see the Martindale-Hubbell Law Directory

REDFEARN & BROWN, A PROFESSIONAL CORPORATION (AV)

Suite 814, 1125 Grand Avenue, 64106
Telephone: 816-421-5301
FAX: 816-421-3785

Paul L. Redfearn
Daniel R. Brown

For full biographical listings, see the Martindale-Hubbell Law Directory

LAKE OZARK, Miller & Camden Cos.

THOMAS E. LORAINE, P.C. (AV)

2840 Bagnell Dam Boulevard, 65049
Telephone: 314-365-3035
Fax: 314-365-3044

Thomas E. Loraine
Dale M. Weppner

For full biographical listings, see the Martindale-Hubbell Law Directory

ST. LOUIS, (Independent City)

GREENBERG & PLEBAN (AV)

100 South Fourth Street, Suite 600, 63102
Telephone: 314-241-4141
Telecopier: 314-241-1038

Burton M. Greenberg
C. John Pleban

ASSOCIATES

Karen A. Greenberg
George A. Kiser
Michael J. Schaller

OF COUNSEL

Sarah Shelledy Pleban

Reference: Boatmen's National Bank.

For full biographical listings, see the Martindale-Hubbell Law Directory

PADBERG, MCSWEENEY, SLATER & MERZ, A PROFESSIONAL CORPORATION (AV)

Suite 800, 1015 Locust Street, 63101
Telephone: 314-621-3787
Telecopier: 314-621-7396

Godfrey P. Padberg
Edward P. McSweeney
R. J. Slater
Charles L. Merz

Richard J. Burke, Jr.
Matthew J. Padberg
James P. Leonard
Anthony J. Soukenik
Thomas C. Simon
Mary K. Munroe
Marty Daesch

For full biographical listings, see the Martindale-Hubbell Law Directory

MONTANA

*BILLINGS,** Yellowstone Co.

CROWLEY, HAUGHEY, HANSON, TOOLE & DIETRICH (AV)

500 Transwestern II, 490 North 31st Street, P.O. Box 2529, 59103
Telephone: 406-252-3441
Fax: 406-259-4159
Helena, Montana Office: IBM Building, 100 North Park Avenue, Suite 300, 59601.
Telephone: 406-449-4165.
Fax: 406-449-5149.

OF COUNSEL

Bruce R. Toole

(See Next Column)

CROWLEY, HAUGHEY, HANSON, TOOLE & DIETRICH—*Continued*

MEMBERS OF FIRM

George C. Dalthorp
Ronald R. Lodders
Charles R. Cashmore
Christopher Mangen, Jr.
Bruce A. Fredrickson

ASSOCIATE

Leonard H. Smith

Representative Clients: Montana Power Co.; First Interstate Bank of Commerce; MDU Resources Group, Inc.; Chevron U.S.A., Inc.; Noranda Minerals Corp.; United Parcel Service.
Insurance Clients: Farmers Insurance Group; New York Life Insurance Co.

For Complete List of Firm Personnel, See General Section

For full biographical listings, see the Martindale-Hubbell Law Directory

NEVADA

*LAS VEGAS,** Clark Co.

MORRIS BRIGNONE & PICKERING (AV)

1203 Bank of America Plaza, 300 South Fourth Street, 89101
Telephone: 702-474-9400
Facsimile: 702-474-9422
Reno, Nevada Office: Wiegand Center, 165 West Liberty, #100, 89501.
Telephone: 702-322-7777.
Facsimile: 702-322-7791.

MEMBERS OF FIRM

Steve Morris
Mary Kristina Pickering

ASSOCIATES

Mark A. Hutchison
Ann Lyter Thomas

For full biographical listings, see the Martindale-Hubbell Law Directory

VANNAH COSTELLO HOWARD & CANEPA (AV)

A Partnership including a Professional Corporation
Greystone, 1850 East Flamingo, Suite 236, 89119
Telephone: 702-369-4161
Fax: 702-369-0104

MEMBERS OF FIRM

Robert D. Vannah (Chartered)
Nathan M. Costello
James W. Howard, Jr.
Scott K. Canepa

ASSOCIATE

Jerry A. Wiese

Representative Clients: Prudential Property and Casualty Insurance Co.; USF&G Co.; CNA; OUM Group Insurance Co.; American Golf Corp.; Reliance Insurance Co.

For full biographical listings, see the Martindale-Hubbell Law Directory

NEW HAMPSHIRE

*CONCORD,** Merrimack Co.

RANSMEIER & SPELLMAN, PROFESSIONAL CORPORATION (AV)

One Capitol Street, P.O. Box 600, 03302-0600
Telephone: 603-228-0477
Telecopier: 603-224-2780

Lawrence E. Spellman
Lawrence S. Smith
Michael Lenehan
Steven E. Hengen
Garry R. Lane
Charles P. Bauer

R. Stevenson Upton
R. Matthew Cairns
Carol J. Holahan
John T. Alexander

For Complete List of Firm Personnel, See General Section

For full biographical listings, see the Martindale-Hubbell Law Directory

*LACONIA,** Belknap Co.

NORMANDIN, CHENEY & O'NEIL (AV)

Normandin Square, 213 Union Avenue, P.O. Box 575, 03247-0575
Telephone: 603-524-4380

MEMBERS OF FIRM

A. Gerard O'Neil
A.G. O'Neil, Jr.

(See Next Column)

ASSOCIATE

Duncan J. Farmer

Counsel for: Laconia Savings Bank; Lakes Region Mental Health Center; Laconia Airport Authority; Community TV Corp.; Central New Hampshire Realty, Inc.; All Metals Industries, Inc.; Lakes Region Anesthesiology, P.A.; Cormier Corp.; Scotia Technology; Vemaline Products.

For Complete List of Firm Personnel, See General Section

For full biographical listings, see the Martindale-Hubbell Law Directory

*MANCHESTER,** Hillsborough Co.

BOUCHARD & MALLORY, P.A. (AV)

100 Middle Street, 03101
Telephone: 603-623-7222
Fax: 603-623-8953

Kenneth G. Bouchard
Mark L. Mallory

Paul B. Kleinman
Blake M. Sutton
Susan A. Vaillancourt
Christine Friedman
Robert S. Stephen

For full biographical listings, see the Martindale-Hubbell Law Directory

NEW JERSEY

CALDWELL, Essex Co.

JOHNSON, GALLAGHER, BURGIO & MARTIN (AV)

Johnson & Gallagher, 1959-1978
Johnson, Gallagher & Burgio, 1978-1991
Johnson, Gallagher, Burgio & Martin, 1992-
10 Forest Avenue, P.O. Box 407, 07006
Telephone: 201-226-6682
Fax: 201-226-1605

MEMBERS OF FIRM

James J. Gallagher (1923-1985)
Austin B. Johnson, Jr.
John E. Burgio
Kathleen G. Martin

OF COUNSEL

Stanley G. Bedford

Counsel for: Luce, Schwab & Kase, Inc.
Representative Clients: Carolina Freight Carriers Corp.; Merchants Insurance Group; Cardinal Freight Carriers; Risk Management Claim Services, Inc.; Ranger Transportation, Inc.; Gemini Transportation Services, Inc.; Poole Truck Lines, Inc.
Reference: Midlantic National Bank (Caldwell Office).

For full biographical listings, see the Martindale-Hubbell Law Directory

CRANFORD, Union Co.

MCCREEDY AND COX (AV)

Second Floor, Six Commerce Drive, 07016-3509
Telephone: 908-709-0400
Fax: 908-709-0405

MEMBERS OF FIRM

Edwin J. McCreedy
Robert F. Cox

ASSOCIATE

Patrick J. Hermesmann

Reference: United Counties Trust Co.

For full biographical listings, see the Martindale-Hubbell Law Directory

FLORHAM PARK, Morris Co.

HACK, PIRO, O'DAY, MERKLINGER, WALLACE & MCKENNA, P.A. (AV)

30 Columbia Turnpike, P.O. Box 941, 07932-0941
Telephone: 201-301-6500
Fax: 201-301-0094

Peter A. Piro
William J. O'Day
M. Richard Merklinger
Peter T. Melnyk
Patrick M. Sages

Bonny G. Rafel
Robert G. Alencewicz
Douglas J. Olcott
John J. Petrizzo
William F. Murphy

Representative Clients: Aetna Life & Casualty Co.; Avis Rent-a-Car Systems; Eastman Kodak Co.; State Farm Insurance Cos.; Travelers Insurance Co.; Westinghouse Electric Co.; Weyerhauser Co.

For Complete List of Firm Personnel, See General Section

For full biographical listings, see the Martindale-Hubbell Law Directory

MOORESTOWN, Burlington Co.

CHIERICI & WRIGHT, A PROFESSIONAL CORPORATION (AV)
Blason Campus - III, 509 South Lenola Road Building Six, 08057-1561
Telephone: 609-234-6300
Fax: 609-234-9490

Donald R. Chierici, Jr.
David B. Wright
Elizabeth Coleman Chierici
Julie C. Smith
Sheri Nelson Oliano
Jaunice M. Canning
Rhonda J. Eiger
Michael A. Foresta
Linda M. Novosel

For full biographical listings, see the Martindale-Hubbell Law Directory

*MORRISTOWN,** Morris Co.

MASKALERIS & ASSOCIATES (AV)
30 Court Street, 07960
Telephone: 201-267-0222
Newark, New Jersey Office: Federal Square Station, P.O. Box 20207.
Telephone: 201-622-4300.
Far Hills, New Jersey Office: Route 202 Station Plaza.
Telephone: 201-234-0600.
New York, New York Office: 123 Bank Street.
Telephone: 212-724-8669.
Athens, Greece Office: Stadio 28, Fourth Floor.
Telephone: 322-6790.

Stephen N. Maskaleris

ASSOCIATES

Peter C. Ioannou
Christopher P. Luongo

For full biographical listings, see the Martindale-Hubbell Law Directory

STEPHEN S. WEINSTEIN A PROFESSIONAL CORPORATION (AV)
20 Park Place, Suite 301, 07960
Telephone: 201-267-5200
FAX: 201-538-1779

Stephen S. Weinstein

Gail S. Boertzel
Peter N. Gilbreth
William A. Johnson
Melissa H. Luce

For full biographical listings, see the Martindale-Hubbell Law Directory

*NEWARK,** Essex Co.

LAW OFFICES OF IRA J. ZARIN (AV)
One Gateway Center, Suite 1612, 07102
Telephone: 201-622-3533
Telecopier: 201-622-1338

ASSOCIATE

Jeffrey E. Strauss

For full biographical listings, see the Martindale-Hubbell Law Directory

PHILLIPSBURG, Warren Co.

JOHN J. COYLE, JR., P.C. (AV)
Memorial Parkway at 2nd Street, P.O. Box 5270, 08865
Telephone: 908-454-3300
Telecopier: 908-454-9367

John J. Coyle, Jr.

James S. DeBosh

Reference: Phillipsburg National Bank.

For full biographical listings, see the Martindale-Hubbell Law Directory

RED BANK, Monmouth Co.

PHILIP G. AUERBACH A PROFESSIONAL CORPORATION (AV)
231 Maple Avenue, P.O. Box Y, 07701
Telephone: 908-842-6660

Philip G. Auerbach

Edward A. Genz
John J. Ryan

For full biographical listings, see the Martindale-Hubbell Law Directory

SPRINGFIELD, Union Co.

BUMGARDNER, HARDIN & ELLIS, A PROFESSIONAL CORPORATION (AV)
673 Morris Avenue, 07081
Telephone: 201-564-6500
Fax: 201-564-6527; 201-912-9847

(See Next Column)

William R. Bumgardner
George R. Hardin
Roger G. Ellis
Robert L. Polifroni
Janet L. Poletto
Mark S. Kundla
John F. McKeon
M. Christie Wise
James R. Greene
John Samuel Favate

Laurie A. Villano
Nicea J. D'Annunzio
Patricia L. Noll
Kieran P. Hughes
Nicholas J. Lombardi
Russel V. Mancino
Edward M. Suarez, Jr.
Patrick J. Clare
Charles T. McCook, Jr.
Marybeth Scriven
Anna Marie Strand
Edward Walsh
Jeffrey A. Oshin
Janice G. Meola
Ethan Jesse Sheffet
Cheryl A. McAvaddy
Francine M. Chillemi
Leona C. McFadden
Mark A. Edwards
Jennifer Zima
Jared P. Kingsley
Michael A. Swimmer
Charles M. Fisher
Joseph A. DeFuria
John G. Kilbride
Deborah J. Metzger-Mulvey
Elizabeth E. Groisser
Joseph R. Lowicky
Tracy C. Forsyth
Michael J. Rant
Emmanuel Abongwa

Representative Clients: Volvo North American Corp.; Allen Bradley Co.; Allstate Insurance Co.; Black & Decker (U.S.), Inc.; Detrex Chemical Co.; Lincoln Electric Co.; Niagra Machine and Tool Co.; Sea Ray Boats, Inc.; Suburban Propane Co., Inc.; Toys 'R' Us, Inc.

For full biographical listings, see the Martindale-Hubbell Law Directory

JAVERBAUM WURGAFT & HICKS (AV)
Park Place Legal Center, 959 South Springfield Avenue, 07081-3555
Telephone: 201-379-4200
Fax: 201-379-7872
Newark, New Jersey Office: 233 Lafayette Street, 07105.
Telephone: 201-623-8754.

Kenneth S. Javerbaum
Jack Wurgaft
Robert G. Hicks

Anthony P. Valenti
Karen Lee
John M. Pinho

For full biographical listings, see the Martindale-Hubbell Law Directory

MCDONOUGH, KORN & EICHHORN, A PROFESSIONAL CORPORATION (AV)
Park Place Legal Center, 959 South Springfield Avenue, P.O. Box 712, 07081-0712
Telephone: 201-912-9099
Fax: 201-912-8604

Peter L. Korn
R. Scott Eichhorn
James R. Korn
William S. Mezzomo

Timothy J. Jaeger
Dona Feeney
Karen M. Lerner
Wilfred P. Coronato
Gail R. Arkin
Nancy Crosta Landale
Christopher K. Costa

OF COUNSEL

Robert P. McDonough

Representative Client: Meeker Sharkey & MacBean.
Reference: United Counties Trust Company.

For full biographical listings, see the Martindale-Hubbell Law Directory

SUMMIT, Union Co.

HAGGERTY, DONOHUE & MONAGHAN, A PROFESSIONAL ASSOCIATION (AV)
One Springfield Avenue, 07901
Telephone: 908-277-2600
Fax: 908-273-1641

James C. Haggerty
George J. Donohue
Walter E. Monaghan

Rose Ann Haggerty
Thomas J. Haggerty
Alfred F. Carolonza, Jr.
William A. Wenzel
Mahlon H. Ortman
Michael A. Conway
James C. Haggerty, Jr.

OF COUNSEL

Joseph D. Haggerty

Representative Clients: American International Group; Chubb/Pacific Indemnity Co.; Crawford & Co.; Crum & Forster; Hertz Corp.; Jefferson Insurance Group; Material Damage Adjustment Corp.; New Jersey Manufacturers; New Jersey Property Liability Guaranty Association; Royal Insurance Co.

(See Next Column)

HAGGERTY, DONOHUE & MONAGHAN A PROFESSIONAL ASSOCIATION—*Continued*

For Complete List of Firm Personnel, See General Section

For full biographical listings, see the Martindale-Hubbell Law Directory

*TRENTON,** Mercer Co.

NEEDELL & MCGLONE, A PROFESSIONAL CORPORATION (AV)

Quakerbridge Commons, 2681 Quakerbridge Road, 08619-1625
Telephone: 609-584-7700
Fax: 609-584-0123

Stanley H. Needell — Patricia Hart McGlone

Michael W. Krutman — Barbara Brosnan
Anthony P. Castellani — Douglas R. D'Antonio

For full biographical listings, see the Martindale-Hubbell Law Directory

WAYNE, Passaic Co.

DEYOE, HEISSENBUTTEL & MATTIA (AV)

401 Hamburg Turnpike, P.O. Box 2449, 07474-2449
Telephone: 201-595-6300
Fax: 201-595-0146; 201-595-9262

MEMBERS OF FIRM

Charles P. DeYoe (1923-1973) — Philip F. Mattia
Wood M. DeYoe — Gary R. Matano
Frederick C. Heissenbuttel — Scott B. Piekarsky

ASSOCIATES

Anne Hutton — Frank A. Campana
Glenn Z. Poosikian — John E. Clarke
Jo Ann G. Durr — Jason T. Shafron
Frank D. Samperi — Maura Waters Brady

LEGAL SUPPORT PERSONNEL

Marilyn Moore (Office Manager)

Representative Clients: INA/Aetna Insurance Co. (Cigna); Medical Inter-Insurance Companies; Hanover-Amgro, Inc.; Maryland Casualty Co.; Ohio Casualty Insurance Co.; Motor Club of America; Selected Insurance Co.

For full biographical listings, see the Martindale-Hubbell Law Directory

WESTWOOD, Bergen Co.

LAW OFFICES OF ROBERT J. MCGUIRL (AV)

345 Kinderkamack Road, Suite B, 07675
Telephone: 201-358-0800
Fax: 201-358-9434

ASSOCIATE

Vera Egan

LEGAL SUPPORT PERSONNEL

Ramiro A. Andrade — Keyvan Rabbani

For full biographical listings, see the Martindale-Hubbell Law Directory

NEW MEXICO

*ALBUQUERQUE,** Bernalillo Co.

CARPENTER & CHÁVEZ, LTD. (AV)

1600 University Boulevard, N.E., Suite B, 87102-1711
Telephone: 505-243-1336
Facsimile: 505-243-1339

William H. Carpenter — Edward L. Chávez
David J. Stout

Reference: First Security Bank, Albuquerque, New Mexico.

For full biographical listings, see the Martindale-Hubbell Law Directory

RODEY, DICKASON, SLOAN, AKIN & ROBB, P.A. (AV)

Albuquerque Plaza, Suite 2200, 201 Third Street, N.W., P.O. Box 1888, 87103-1888
Telephone: 505-765-5900
Fax: 505-768-7395
Santa Fe, New Mexico Office: Suite 101 Marcy Plaza, 123 East Marcy Street, P.O. Box 1357, 87504-1357.
Telephone: 505-984-0100.
Fax: 505-989-9542.

James C. Ritchie — W. Robert Lasater, Jr.
Joseph J. Mullins — Mark C. Meiering
Robert G. McCorkle — Travis R. Collier
Bruce Hall — W. Mark Mowery (Resident, Santa Fe Office)
Jonathan W. Hewes

(See Next Column)

Patrick M. Shay — John M. Brant
Ellen G. Thorne — Scott D. Gordon
Tracy E. McGee — Susan S. Throckmorton
Charles E. Stuckey — Angela M. Martinez
Charles Kipps Purcell — R. Nelson Franse
Paul R. Koller

Sheryl S. Mahaney — Thomas L. Stahl
Mark L. Allen — Susan K. Barger

For Complete List of Firm Personnel, See General Section

For full biographical listings, see the Martindale-Hubbell Law Directory

NEW YORK

*BRONX,** Bronx Co.

MAXWELL S. PFEIFER (AV)

714 East 241st Street, 10470
Telephone: 718-325-5000
Fax: 718-324-0333
Hallandale, Florida Office: 1920 East Hallandale Beach Boulevard, Suite 606.
Telephone: 305-454-1550.

ASSOCIATES

Steven E. Millon — Robert S. Summer

OF COUNSEL

Hon. Alexander A. Dellecese — Sandra Krevitsky Janin
Anthony J. Hatab

LEGAL SUPPORT PERSONNEL

Jay S. Zwerling

For full biographical listings, see the Martindale-Hubbell Law Directory

GARDEN CITY, Nassau Co.

GALLAGHER GOSSEEN & FALLER (AV)

1010 Franklin Avenue, Suite 400, 11530-2927
Telephone: 516-742-2500
Fax: 516-742-2516
Cable: COMPROAIR
New York, New York Office: 350 Fifth Avenue.
Telephone: 212-947-5800.
FAX: 212-967-4965.

MEMBERS OF FIRM

James A. Gallagher, Jr. — Robert A. Faller
Robert I. Gosseen (Resident, New York City Office) — Alan D. Kaplan
Michael J. Crowley
William E. Vita

ASSOCIATES

David H. Arnsten — Brian P. Morrissey
William A. Bales, Jr. — Leslie A. Rosenstein
Jennifer Greenberg — Robert A. Sparer (Resident, New York City Office)
Jeanne M. Gonsalves-Lloyd

OF COUNSEL

Edward M. O'Brien (Resident, New York City Office) — Peter F. Vetro
Daniel F. Hayes
John P. Coogan

For full biographical listings, see the Martindale-Hubbell Law Directory

L'ABBATE, BALKAN, COLAVITA & CONTINI, L.L.P. (AV)

1050 Franklin Avenue, 11530
Telephone: 516-294-8844
Telecopier: 516-294-8202; 742-6563

MEMBERS OF FIRM

Donald R. L'Abbate — Richard P. Byrne
Kenneth J. Balkan — Ronald C. Burke
Anthony P. Colavita — Harry Makris
Peter L. Contini — Marie Ann Hoenings
Monte E. Sokol — Jane M. Myers
Douglas L. Pintauro — Dean L. Milber
James Plousadis

OF COUNSEL

Paula M. Gart

ASSOCIATES

Anna M. DiLonardo — Joseph A. Barra
David B. Kosakoff — Stephane Jasmin
Lewis A. Bartell — Lawrence A. Kushnick
Ralph A. Catalano — Diane H. Miller
Gay B. Levine — Barbara Jean Romaine
Victoria Roberts Drogin — Joseph V. Cambareri
Douglas R. Halstrom — Christine Andreoli

(See Next Column)

L'ABBATE, BALKAN, COLAVITA & CONTINI L.L.P., *Garden City—Continued*

A list of References and Representative Clients will be furnished upon request.

For full biographical listings, see the Martindale-Hubbell Law Directory

HAUPPAUGE, Suffolk Co.

ERIC H. HOLTZMAN (AV)

330 Vanderbilt Motor Parkway, P.O. Box 11005, 11788-0903
Telephone: 516-435-8800
Fax: 516-435-8832

Richard E. Trachtenberg

Reference: European-American Bank & Trust Co.

For full biographical listings, see the Martindale-Hubbell Law Directory

MELVILLE, Suffolk Co.

GANDIN, SCHOTSKY & RAPPAPORT, P.C. (AV)

445 Broad Hollow Road, 11747
Telephone: 516-293-2300
Fax: 516-293-2918

Michael I. Gandin
Arnold M. Schotsky
Charles J. Rappaport
Michael R. Greene
Michael G. Glass

Margery Weinroth
Robert A. Katz
Kevin E. Balfe
Robert A. Isler
Michael S. Levine
Edmond C. Chakmakian

For full biographical listings, see the Martindale-Hubbell Law Directory

*MINEOLA,** Nassau Co.

DOMINIC J. CORNELLA ASSOCIATES, P.C. (AV)

1539 Franklin Avenue, 11501
Telephone: 516-294-1400
Fax: 516-294-1453
New York, N.Y. Office: 80 Beekman Street, 10038.
Telephone: 212-732-4042.
Fax: 212-964-3676.

Dominic J. Cornella

For full biographical listings, see the Martindale-Hubbell Law Directory

*NEW YORK,** New York Co.

DANIEL DONNELLY (AV)

521 Fifth Avenue Suite 1740, 10175
Telephone: 212-757-6454
Garrison, New York Office: Garrison's Landing, P.O. Box 253. 10524.
Telephone: 914-424-3877.
Facsimile: 914-424-3968

For full biographical listings, see the Martindale-Hubbell Law Directory

JOHNSTON & MCSHANE, P.C. (AV)

Graybar Building, 420 Lexington Avenue, 10170
Telephone: 212-972-5252
Facsimile: 212-697-2737

William R. Johnston
Bruce W. McShane
Peter F. Breheny

Dennis W. Grogan
Andrew Ross
Arthur J. Smith
Robert D. Donahue
Kenneth E. Moffett, Jr.
James M. Carman

OF COUNSEL

Charles A. Miller, II (Not admitted in NY)

For full biographical listings, see the Martindale-Hubbell Law Directory

JULIEN & SCHLESINGER, P.C. (AV)

150 William Street, 19th Floor, 10038
Telephone: 212-962-8020

Alfred S. Julien (1910-1989)
Denise Mortner Kranz
Stuart A. Schlesinger
Ira M. Newman
David B. Turret

OF COUNSEL

Louis Fusco, Jr.

(See Next Column)

Mary Elizabeth Burns
Marla L. Schiff
Richard A. Robbins
Alvin Craig Gordon
Michael J. Taub
Adam Schlesinger
Robert J. Epstein

For full biographical listings, see the Martindale-Hubbell Law Directory

LAVIN, COLEMAN, FINARELLI & GRAY (AV Ⓣ)

780 Third Avenue Suite 1401, 10017
Telephone: 212-319-6898
Fax: 212-319-6932
Philadelphia, Pennsylvania Office: 12th Floor, Penn Mutual Tower, 510 Walnut Street.
Telephone: 215-627-0303.
Fax: 215-627-2551.
Mount Laurel, New Jersey Office: 10000 Midlantic Drive, Suite 300 West.
Telephone: 609-778-5544.
Fax: 609-778-3383.

William J. Ricci (Not admitted in NY)
Joseph A. McGinley
Edward A. Gray (Not admitted in NY)
Michael D. Brophy

John Kieran Daly
Steven R. Kramer
Joseph F. Dunne

For full biographical listings, see the Martindale-Hubbell Law Directory

LONDON FISCHER (AV)

375 Park Avenue, 10152
Telephone: 212-888-3636
Facsimile: 212-888-3974

MEMBERS OF FIRM

Bernard London
John W. Manning
James L. Fischer
Daniel Zemann, Jr.
John E. Sparling

ASSOCIATES

Richard S. Endres
John P. Bruen
Nicholas Kalfa
Christina M. Ambrosio
Evan D. Lieberman
William C. Nanis
Amy M. Kramer
Michael P. Mezzacappa
Robert S. Sunshine
Douglas W. Hammond
Robert M. Vecchione
Michael S. Leavy
Robert L. Honig

For full biographical listings, see the Martindale-Hubbell Law Directory

PARKER CHAPIN FLATTAU & KLIMPL, L.L.P. (AV)

1211 Avenue of the Americas, 10036
Telephone: 212-704-6000
Telecopier: 212-704-6288
Cable Address: "Lawpark"
Telex: 640347
Great Neck, New York Office: 175 Great Neck Road.
Telephone: 516-482-4422.
Telecopier: 516-482-4469.

MEMBER OF FIRM

Jesse J. Graham, II

For Complete List of Firm Personnel, See General Section

For full biographical listings, see the Martindale-Hubbell Law Directory

JEFFREY SAMEL & ASSOCIATES (AV)

120 Broadway, Suite 1755, 10271
Telephone: 212-587-9690
Fax: 212-587-9673

ASSOCIATES

Robert G. Spevack
James H. O'Hare
Dorothy T. Zeman
David M. Samel
Ricardo Rengifo
David S. Gary

OF COUNSEL

Richard A. Soberman

Representative Clients: New York City Transit Authority; New York City Housing Authority; Empire Insurance Co.; National General Insurance Co.; Federal Express Corp.; Shell Oil Corp.; American Building Maintenance Corp.; Morbark Industries.

For full biographical listings, see the Martindale-Hubbell Law Directory

SHEFT & SHEFT (AV)

909 Third Avenue, 10022
Telephone: 212-688-7788
Telecopier: 212-355-7373
Jersey City, New Jersey Office: Harborside Financial Center, Suite 704 Plaza Three.
Telephone: 201-332-2233.
Telecopier: 201-435-9177.

(See Next Column)

SHEFT & SHEFT—*Continued*

Leonard A. Sheft
Peter I. Sheft
Norman J. Golub (Resident, Jersey City, New Jersey Office)
Marjorie Heyman Mintzer
Marian S. Hertz
Leonard G. Kamlet

COUNSEL

Gerald A. Greenberger (Resident, Jersey City, New Jersey Office)

David Holmes (Resident, Jersey City, New Jersey Office)
Phillip C. Landrigan
Thomas J. Leonard
Myra Needleman
Howard K. Fishman
Mary C. Bennett
Jeffrey S. Leonard (Resident, Jersey City, New Jersey Office)
Stacy B. Parker
Edward Hayum
Daniel H. Hecht
Jerrald J. Hochman
James M. Dennis
Frank V. Kelly
Ellen G. Margolis
Guy J. Levasseur
Joseph F. Arkins
Jordan Sklar
Herbert L. Lazar
Maria E. Cannon (Resident, Jersey City, New Jersey Office)

For full biographical listings, see the Martindale-Hubbell Law Directory

WHITE, FLEISCHNER & FINO (AV)

195 Broadway, 10007
Telephone: 212-227-6292
Telex: 645255
Telecopier: 212-227-7812
Westfield, New Jersey Office: 215 North Avenue, West.
Telephone: 908-654-6266.
Telecopier: 908-654-3686.
London, England Office: Plantation House. 31/35 Fenchurch S. EC3M 3DX.
Telephone: 071-375-2037.
Telecopier: 071-375-2039.

MEMBERS OF FIRM

Allan P. White
Benjamin A. Fleischner
Paul A. Fino, Jr.
Robert G. Schenker
Marcia J. Lynn
Marisa Goetz

ASSOCIATES

Patti F. Potash
Mitchell R. Friedman
Mitchell L. Shadowitz
Debra E. Ruderman
David I. Blee
Sandra L. Bonder
Michael J. Asta
Stephanie M. Holzback
Mark R. Osherow
Virginia L. McGrane
Beth A. Goldklang
Sean Upton
Wendy K. Carrano
Nancy D. Lyness
Randy Scott Faust
Elizabeth C. Mirisola
Sheri E. Holland

LEGAL SUPPORT PERSONNEL

Darien Anderson (Paralegal)
Helen Wasey (Claims Consultant)

For full biographical listings, see the Martindale-Hubbell Law Directory

ONEONTA, Otsego Co.

LAW OFFICE OF JOHN SCARZAFAVA (AV)

48 Dietz Street, Suite C, 13820-5107
Telephone: 607-432-9341
Fax: 607-432-1986

John F. Scarzafava

ASSOCIATE

Elizabeth Ellen Little

Reference: Key Bank.

For full biographical listings, see the Martindale-Hubbell Law Directory

*ROCHESTER,** Monroe Co.

ROBERT J. MICHAEL (AV)

39 State Street, Suite 420, 14614
Telephone: 716-232-3460
Fax: 716-232-4583

OF COUNSEL

Mark H. Tiernan

Reference: Chemical Bank.

For full biographical listings, see the Martindale-Hubbell Law Directory

STANFORDVILLE, Dutchess Co.

WILLIAM E. STANTON (AV)

Village Centre, Route 82, P.O. Box 370, 12581
Telephone: 914-868-7514
FAX: 914-868-7761

Representative Clients: Dupont de Nemours & Co.; Millbrook School; Hanover Insurance Co.; New York Telephone Co.
Reference: Fishkill National Bank.

For full biographical listings, see the Martindale-Hubbell Law Directory

*STATEN ISLAND,** Richmond Co.

SIMONSON & COHEN, P.C. (AV)

4060 Amboy Road, 10308
Telephone: 718-948-2100
Telecopier: 718-356-2379

Sidney O. Simonson (1911-1986)
Daniel Cohen
Robert M. Cohen
James R. Cohen

Michael Adler
Lawrence J. Lorczak

For full biographical listings, see the Martindale-Hubbell Law Directory

NORTH CAROLINA

*ASHEVILLE,** Buncombe Co.

REYNOLDS & McARTHUR (AV Ⓣ)

A Partnership including a Professional Corporation
The Jackson Building, 22 South Pack Square Suite 1200, 28801
Telephone: 704-254-8523
Fax: 704-254-3038
Macon, Georgia Office: 850 Walnut Street.
Telephone: 912-741-6000.
Fax: 912-742-0750.
Atlanta, Georgia Office: Suite 1080, One Buckhead Plaza, 3060 Peachtree Road, N.W.
Telephone: 404-240-0265.
Fax: 404-262-3557.

MEMBERS OF FIRM

W. Carl Reynolds (P.C.) (Not admitted in NC)
Katherine L. McArthur
Charles M. Cork, III (Not admitted in NC)
O. Wendell Horne, III (Not admitted in NC)
Bradley J. Survant (Not admitted in NC)
Steve Ray Warren

For full biographical listings, see the Martindale-Hubbell Law Directory

*RALEIGH,** Wake Co.

BLANCHARD, TWIGGS, ABRAMS & STRICKLAND, P.A. (AV)

First Union Capitol Center, 150 Fayetteville Street Mall, 11th Floor, P.O. Drawer 30, 27602
Telephone: 919-828-4357
FAX: 919-833-7924

Howard F. Twiggs
Douglas B. Abrams
Donald R. Strickland
Jerome P. Trehy, Jr.

Margaret Smith Abrams
Robert O. Jenkins
Karen M. Rabenau

OF COUNSEL

Charles F. Blanchard
Donald H. Beskind

For full biographical listings, see the Martindale-Hubbell Law Directory

*WINSTON-SALEM,** Forsyth Co.

WOMBLE CARLYLE SANDRIDGE & RICE (AV)

A Professional Limited Liability Company
1600 Southern National Financial Center, P.O. Drawer 84, 27102
Telephone: 910-721-3600
Telecopy: 910-721-3660
Telex: 806498
Charlotte, North Carolina Office: 3300 One First Union Center, 301 South College Street.
Telephone: 704-331-4900.
Telecopy: 704-331-4955.
Telex: 853609.
Raleigh, North Carolina Office: 2100 First Union Capitol Center, 150 Fayetteville Street Mall, P.O. Box 831.
Telephone: 919-755-2100.
Telecopy: 919-755-2150.
Telex: 806498.

(See Next Column)

WOMBLE CARLYLE SANDRIDGE & RICE, *Winston-Salem—Continued*

Atlanta, Georgia Office: One Ninety One Peachtree Tower, 191 Peachtree Street, N.E., Suite 3250.
Telephone: 404-614-2580.
Fax: 404-614-2595.

MEMBERS OF FIRM

Reid C. Adams, Jr.
Conrad C. Baldwin, Jr.
Samuel Fraley Bost
R. Michael Leonard
Alexander S. Nicholas
Erna A. Patrick
Thomas D. Schroeder
William F. Womble, Jr.

ASSOCIATES

Dawn Jordan
Jonathan B. Mason
J. Keith Tart
F. Bruce Williams

Representative Clients: Brad Ragan, Inc.; Brenner Companies; Food Lion, Inc.; Hanes Companies, Inc.; North Carolina Baptist Hospitals, Inc.; R.J. Reynolds Tobacco Company; Summit Communications Group, Inc.; Thomasville Furniture Industries, Inc.; Wachovia Corporation; Wake Forest University.

For Complete List of Firm Personnel, See General Section

For full biographical listings, see the Martindale-Hubbell Law Directory

NORTH DAKOTA

*BISMARCK,** Burleigh Co.

PEARCE AND DURICK (AV)

314 East Thayer Avenue, P.O. Box 400, 58502
Telephone: 701-223-2890
Fax: 701-223-7865

MEMBERS OF FIRM

Patrick W. Durick
B. Timothy Durick
Christine A. Hogan
Joel W. Gilbertson
Jerome C. Kettleson
Larry L. Boschee

ASSOCIATE

Stephen D. Easton

Representative Clients: American Insurance Assn.; Cigna-INA Insurance Co.; Deere & Co.; Federal Deposit Insurance Corp.; Ford Motor Co.; General Motors Corp.; MDU Resources Group, Inc.; Northwest Airlines; Royal Insurance Co.; Travelers Insurance Co.

For Complete List of Firm Personnel, See General Section

For full biographical listings, see the Martindale-Hubbell Law Directory

PETERSON, SCHMITZ, MOENCH & SCHMIDT, A PROFESSIONAL CORPORATION (AV)

Second Floor, Suite 200, 116 North Fourth Street, P.O. Box 2076, 58502-2076
Telephone: 701-224-0400
Fax: 701-224-0399

David L. Peterson
Orell D. Schmitz
Dale W. Moench
William D. Schmidt

OF COUNSEL

Gerald Glaser

LEGAL SUPPORT PERSONNEL

Vicki J. Kunz
Traci L. Albers

For full biographical listings, see the Martindale-Hubbell Law Directory

OHIO

*CINCINNATI,** Hamilton Co.

DINSMORE & SHOHL (AV)

1900 Chemed Center, 255 East Fifth Street, 45202-3172
Telephone: 513-977-8200
FAX: 513-977-8141
Florence, Kentucky Office: Turfway Ridge Office Park, 7300 Turfway Road, Suite 430 41042-1355.
Telephone: 606-283-0515.
FAX: 606-283-6017.
Dayton, Ohio Office: 500 Courthouse Plaza, S.W., 10 N. Ludlow Street, 45402-1834.
Telephone: 513-228-8012.
FAX: 513-461-2543.
Columbus, Ohio Office: NBD Bank Building, Suite 330, 175 South Third Street, 43215-5134.
Telephone: 614-224-7887.
FAX: 614-224-7882.

(See Next Column)

MEMBERS OF FIRM

Thomas S. Calder
John W. Beatty
John M. Kunst, Jr.
Frank C. Woodside, III
Gordon C. Greene
Harry L. Riggs, Jr. (Resident, Florence, Kentucky Office)
Nancy A. Lawson
Deborah R. Lydon
John E. Jevicky
Nancy J. Gill
Stephen K. Shaw
Lawrence A. Flemer
Robert R. Furnier
Neal D. Baker
K. C. Green
M. Gabrielle Hils

ASSOCIATES

Richard J. Mitchell, Jr.
Marlene M. Evans
Melissa A. Fetters
Louis D. Proietti
Frederick N. Hamilton
Michael J. Suffern
Jeffrey L. Stec
Nancy Korb Griffiths
Michael E. Finucane

For Complete List of Firm Personnel, See General Section

For full biographical listings, see the Martindale-Hubbell Law Directory

LAW OFFICES OF JOSEPH W. SHEA III (AV)

36 East 7th Street, Suite 2650, 45202-4459
Telephone: 513-621-8333
Telecopier: 513-651-3272

ASSOCIATE

Shirley A. Coffey

LEGAL SUPPORT PERSONNEL

NURSE - LEGAL ASSISTANT

Marianne E. Alf

For full biographical listings, see the Martindale-Hubbell Law Directory

WAITE, SCHNEIDER, BAYLESS & CHESLEY CO., L.P.A. (AV)

1513 Central Trust Tower, Fourth and Vine Streets, 45202
Telephone: 513-621-0267
Fax: 513-381-2375; 621-0262

Stanley M. Chesley

Thomas F. Rehme
Fay E. Stilz
Louise M. Roselle
Dwight Tillery
D. Arthur Rabourn
Jerome L. Skinner
Janet G. Abaray
Paul M. De Marco
Terrence L. Goodman
Sherrill P. Hondorf
Colleen M. Hegge
Dianna Pendleton
Randy F. Fox
Glenn D. Feagan
Theresa L. Groh
Theodore N. Berry
Jane H. Walker
Renée Infante
Allen P. Grunes

OF COUNSEL

Jos. E. Rosen
James F. Keller

For full biographical listings, see the Martindale-Hubbell Law Directory

*CLEVELAND,** Cuyahoga Co.

FRIEDMAN, DOMIANO & SMITH CO., L.P.A. (AV)

Sixth Floor, Standard Building, 44113-1701
Telephone: 216-621-0070
Fax: 216-621-3231
Naples, Florida Office: 800 Laurel Oak Drive, Suite 200, Pelican Bay, 33963.
Telephone: 813-642-0252.

Jeffrey H. Friedman
Joseph C. Domiano
M. David Smith
Lisa M. Gerlack

Lillian V. Blageff
Stephen S. Vanek

For full biographical listings, see the Martindale-Hubbell Law Directory

HERMANN, CAHN & SCHNEIDER (AV)

Suite 500, 1301 East Ninth Street, 44114
Telephone: 216-781-5515
Facsimile: 216-781-1030

MEMBER OF FIRM

Gary D. Hermann

For full biographical listings, see the Martindale-Hubbell Law Directory

JANIK & DUNN (AV)

400 Park Plaza Building, 1111 Chester Avenue, 44114
Telephone: 216-781-9700
Fax: 216-781-1250
Brea, California Office: 2601 Saturn Street, Suite 300.
Telephone: 714-572-1101.
Fax: 714-572-1103.

MEMBERS OF FIRM

Steven G. Janik
Theodore M. Dunn, Jr.

(See Next Column)

JANIK & DUNN—*Continued*

ASSOCIATES

Myra Staresina   David L. Mast

For full biographical listings, see the Martindale-Hubbell Law Directory

KELLER AND CURTIN CO., L.P.A. (AV)

Suite 330 The Hanna Building, 44115-1901
Telephone: 216-566-7100
Telecopier: 216-566-5430
Akron, Ohio Office: 2304 First National Tower, 44308-1419.
Telephone: 216-376-7245.
Telecopier: 216-376-8128.

Stanley S. Keller   Walter H. Krohngold
G. Michael Curtin   James M. Johnson

Joseph G. Ritzler   Phillip A. Kuri

Reference: Bank One, Cleveland.

For full biographical listings, see the Martindale-Hubbell Law Directory

MEYERS, HENTEMANN, SCHNEIDER & REA CO., L.P.A. (AV)

21st Floor, Superior Building, 815 Superior Avenue, N.E., 44114
Telephone: 216-241-3435
Telecopier: 216-241-6568
Elyria, Ohio Office: 301 Fifth Street, 44035.
Telephone: 216-323-6920.

John S. Rea   Henry A. Hentemann
Joseph G. Schneider   Richard C. Talbert
Thomas L. Brunn

Representative Clients: State Farm Mutual Insurance Co.; Travelers Insurance Co.; J.C. Penney Insurance, formerly Educator & Executive Insurance Co.; Lloyds Underwriters, London, England; Preferred Risk Mutual Insurance Co.; American Suzuki Motor Corp.; Detroit Automobile Inter-Insurance Exchange; Electrical Mutual; Automation Plastics, Inc.; Environmental Structures, Inc.

For Complete List of Firm Personnel, See General Section

For full biographical listings, see the Martindale-Hubbell Law Directory

RUBENSTEIN, NOVAK, EINBUND, PAVLIK & CELEBREZZE (AV)

Suite 270, Skylight Office Tower Tower City Center, 44113-1498
Telephone: 216-781-8700
Telecopier: 216-781-9227

MEMBER OF FIRM

Lewis Einbund

For full biographical listings, see the Martindale-Hubbell Law Directory

TIMOTHY A. SHIMKO & ASSOCIATES A LEGAL PROFESSIONAL ASSOCIATION (AV)

2010 Huntington Building, 925 Euclid Avenue, 44115
Telephone: 216-241-8300
Fax: 216-241-2702

Timothy A. Shimko

Janet I. Stich   Ronald K. Starkey
Theresa A. Tarchinski   Frank E. Piscitelli, Jr.

OF COUNSEL

Frank B. Mazzone

Reference: National City Bank, Cleveland.

For full biographical listings, see the Martindale-Hubbell Law Directory

SMITH, MARSHALL AND WEAVER (AV)

500 National City East Sixth Building, 1965 East Sixth Street, 44114
Telephone: 216-781-4994
Telecopier: 216-781-9448

MEMBERS OF FIRM

Philip J. Weaver, Jr.   Frederick P. Vergon, Jr.
T. Charles Cooper

Representative Clients: American States Insurance Co.; Fireman's Fund Insurance Co.; Hartford Insurance Group; State Automobile Mutual Insurance Co.

For full biographical listings, see the Martindale-Hubbell Law Directory

*COLUMBUS,** Franklin Co.

CLARK, PERDUE, ROBERTS & SCOTT CO., L.P.A. (AV)

471 East Broad Street Suite 1400, 43215
Telephone: 614-469-1400
Fax: 614-469-0900

(See Next Column)

Dale K. Perdue   Glen R. Pritchard
Paul O. Scott   Robert W. Kerpsack, Jr.
Douglas S. Roberts   D. Andrew List
Edward L. Clark   Brian W. Palmer

For full biographical listings, see the Martindale-Hubbell Law Directory

MICHAEL F. COLLEY CO., L.P.A. (AV)

Hoster & High Building, 536 South High Street, 43215-5674
Telephone: 614-228-6453
Fax: 614-228-7122

Michael F. Colley

David I. Shroyer   Elizabeth Schorpp Burkett
Daniel N. Abraham   Jennifer K. Thivener
Thomas F. Martello, Jr.

OF COUNSEL

Marvin Sloin   David K. Frank

Reference: Bank One of Columbus, NA.

For full biographical listings, see the Martindale-Hubbell Law Directory

LAMKIN, VAN EMAN, TRIMBLE, BEALS & ROURKE (AV)

Suite 200, 500 South Front Street, 43215-5671
Telephone: 614-224-8187
Fax: 614-224-4943

MEMBERS OF FIRM

William W. Lamkin   Thomas W. Trimble
Timothy L. Van Eman   David A. Beals
Michael J. Rourke

ASSOCIATE

Kathy A. Dougherty

Reference: Huntington National Bank.

For full biographical listings, see the Martindale-Hubbell Law Directory

MCCARTHY, PALMER, VOLKEMA, BOYD & THOMAS A LEGAL PROFESSIONAL ASSOCIATION (AV)

140 East Town Street, Suite 1100, 43215
Telephone: Telephone: 614-221-4400
Telecopier: 614-221-6010

Dennis M. McCarthy   Daniel R. Volkema
Robert Gray Palmer   Jeffrey D. Boyd
Warner M. Thomas, Jr.

Craig P. Scott

COUNSEL

Russell H. Volkema   Stanton G. Darling, II

Reference: Huntington National Bank.

For full biographical listings, see the Martindale-Hubbell Law Directory

RAY, TODARO & ALTON CO., L.P.A. (AV)

175 South Third Street, Suite 350, 43215-5100
Telephone: 614-221-7791
Fax: 614-221-8957

Frank A. Ray   John M. Alton
Frank E. Todaro

Gregory W. Kirstein

For full biographical listings, see the Martindale-Hubbell Law Directory

*DAYTON,** Montgomery Co.

FREUND, FREEZE & ARNOLD A LEGAL PROFESSIONAL ASSOCIATION (AV)

Suite 1800 One Dayton Centre, One South Main Street, 45402-2017
Telephone: 513-222-2424
Telecopier: 513-222-5369
Cincinnati, Ohio Office: Suite 2110 Carew Tower, 441 Vine Street, 45202-4157.
Telephone: 513-287-8400.
FAX: 513-287-8403.

Neil F. Freund   Christopher W. Carrigg
Stephen V. Freeze   Scott F. McDaniel
Gordon D. Arnold   Lisa A. Hesse
Patrick J. Janis   Gregory J. Berberich
Jane M. Lynch   Mary E. Lentz
Francis S. McDaniel   Thomas B. Bruns
Stephen C. Findley   Shawn M. Blatt
Robert N. Snyder   Matthew K. Fox

(See Next Column)

FREUND, FREEZE & ARNOLD A LEGAL PROFESSIONAL ASSOCIATION, *Dayton—Continued*

Fredric L. Young
Philip D. Mervis
Thomas P. Glass
Lori S. Kibby
August T. Janszen

Local Counsel for: Auto-Owners Insurance Co.; CNA Insurance Co.; Crum and Foster Underwriters; Employers Reinsurance Corp.; Farmers Insurance Group; Lloyds of London; Medical Protective; Midwestern Group; State Farm Mutual Automobile Insurance Co.; The Travelers Insurance Co.
Special Trial Counsel for: City of Dayton.

For full biographical listings, see the Martindale-Hubbell Law Directory

*ELYRIA,** Lorain Co.

ERIC H. ZAGRANS (AV)

474 Overbrook Road, 44035-3623
Telephone: 216-365-5400
Facsimile: 216-365-5100

For full biographical listings, see the Martindale-Hubbell Law Directory

*TOLEDO,** Lucas Co.

ROBERT M. ANSPACH ASSOCIATES (AV)

Suite 2100, 405 Madison Avenue, 43604-1236
Telephone: 419-246-5757
FAX: 419-321-6979

Robert M. Anspach
Stephen R. Serraino
Catherine G. Hoolahan
Mark D. Meeks
J. Roy Nunn
Paul F. Burtis

ASSOCIATES

Barry Y. Freeman
L. Nathalie Hiemstra

For full biographical listings, see the Martindale-Hubbell Law Directory

BUNDA STUTZ & DEWITT (AV)

One SeaGate, Suite 650, 43604
Telephone: 419-247-2777
Telecopier: 419-247-2727

MEMBERS OF FIRM

Robert A. Bunda
Barbara J. Stutz
Theresa R. DeWitt

ASSOCIATES

Anne Y. Koester
John C. Stewart
Richard A. Papurt
Yvonne D. Powell

Representative Clients: AC and S, Inc.; Acme Steel Co.; B.F. Goodrich Co.; Conoco, Inc.; Ethyl Corp.; Gustafson, Inc.

For full biographical listings, see the Martindale-Hubbell Law Directory

OKLAHOMA

*OKLAHOMA CITY,** Oklahoma Co.

GARY L. BROOKS (AV)

6303 Waterford Boulevard, Suite 220, 73118-1122
Telephone: 405-840-1066
Fax: 405-843-8446
Dayton, Ohio Office: First National Plaza, Suite 1700, 45402.
Telephone: 513-224-3400.
Fax: 513-228-0331.

ASSOCIATE

Ann Jarrard

For full biographical listings, see the Martindale-Hubbell Law Directory

PIERCE COUCH HENDRICKSON BAYSINGER & GREEN (AV)

1109 North Francis, P.O. Box 26350, 73126
Telephone: 405-235-1611
Fax: 405-235-2904
Tulsa, Oklahoma Office: Suite 6110, 5555 East 71St. Street, 74136.
Telephone: 918-493-4944.
Fax: 918-493-6196.

MEMBERS OF FIRM

Gerald P. Green
Stephen L. Olson
D. Lynn Babb
John Roger Hurt
Curtis L. Smith

ASSOCIATES

Kathleen J. Adler
John Christopher Condren
Scott A. Law
G. Calvin Sharpe

(See Next Column)

OF COUNSEL

Kevin T. Gassaway (Resident, Tulsa Office)

Piper Aircraft Corp.; U.S. Aviation Underwriters; Sears, Roebuck & Company; Oklahoma Natural Gas; Well-Tech Corp.; White Consolidated Industries; Overhead Door Corp.; Cessna Aircraft Corp.; Chamberlaim Manufacturing; Duchoissis Industries.

For Complete List of Firm Personnel, See General Section

For full biographical listings, see the Martindale-Hubbell Law Directory

*TULSA,** Tulsa Co.

SECREST, HILL & FOLLUO (AV)

7134 South Yale, Suite 900, 74136-6342
Telephone: 918-494-5905
Fax: 918-494-2847

MEMBERS OF FIRM

James K. Secrest, II
W. Michael Hill
Dan S. Folluo

Dan W. Ernst
Melvin C. Weiman
Edward John Main
Roger N. Butler, Jr.
Andrew B. Morsman
Bob D. James
Douglas M. Borochoff

For full biographical listings, see the Martindale-Hubbell Law Directory

PENNSYLVANIA

*EASTON,** Northampton Co.

GUS MILIDES (AV)

654 Wolf Avenue, 18042
Telephone: 610-258-0433

ASSOCIATE

Beth Ann Milides

For full biographical listings, see the Martindale-Hubbell Law Directory

ELKINS PARK, Montgomery Co.

MONAGHAN & GOLD, P.C. (AV)

7837 Old York Road, 19027
Telephone: 215-782-1800
Fax: 215-782-1010

John F. X. Monaghan, Jr.
Alan Steven Gold

Brian E. Appel
Murray R. Glickman
Barbara Malett Weitz
Tanya M. Sweet

FORT WASHINGTON, Montgomery Co.

DALLER GREENBERG & DIETRICH (AV)

Valley Green Corporate Center, 7111 Valley Green Road, 19034
Telephone: 215-836-1100
Facsimile: 215-836-2845
Haddon Heights, New Jersey Office: 2 White Horse Pike.
Telephone: 609-547-9068.
Telecopier: 609-547-2391.

Morton F. Daller
Edward A. Greenberg
Gerhard P. Dietrich
Charles E. Pugh
Eileen M. Johnson
Dennis R. Callahan
Nancy P. Horn
A. M. Laszlo
Tracy Canuso Nugent (Resident, Haddon Heights, New Jersey Office)
Catherine N. Walto

For full biographical listings, see the Martindale-Hubbell Law Directory

*HARRISBURG,** Dauphin Co.

ANGINO & ROVNER, P.C. (AV)

4503 North Front Street, 17110-1799
Telephone: 717-238-6791
Fax: 717-238-5610

Richard C. Angino
Neil J. Rovner

Joseph M. Melillo
Terry S. Hyman
David L. Lutz
Michael E. Kosik
Pamela G. Shuman
Catherine M. Mahady-Smith
Richard A. Sadlock
David S. Wisneski
Nijole C. Olson
Michael J. Navitsky
Robin J. Marzella
Lawrence F. Barone
Dawn L. Jennings
Stephen R. Pedersen

(See Next Column)

ANGINO & ROVNER P.C.—*Continued*

References: Harrisburg Credit Exchange; Hamilton Bank.

For full biographical listings, see the Martindale-Hubbell Law Directory

GOLDBERG, KATZMAN & SHIPMAN, P.C. (AV)

320 Market Street - Strawberry Square, P.O. Box 1268, 17108-1268
Telephone: 717-234-4161
Telecopier: 717-234-6808; 717-234-6810

F. Lee Shipman
Thomas E. Brenner
James M. Sheehan
John A. Statler
April L. Strang-Kutay
Guy H. Brooks
Jefferson J. Shipman

Karen S. Feuchtenberger

Representative Clients: Atlantic Mutual Companies; Cincinnati Insurance Co.; Pennsylvania National Insurance Co.; Fulton Bank.

For Complete List of Firm Personnel, See General Section

For full biographical listings, see the Martindale-Hubbell Law Directory

HEPFORD, SWARTZ & MORGAN (AV)

111 North Front Street, P.O. Box 889, 17108-0889
Telephone: 717-234-4121
Fax: 717-232-6802
Lewistown, Pennsylvania Office: 12 South Main Street, P.O. Box 867.
Telephone: 717-248-3913.

MEMBERS OF FIRM

H. Joseph Hepford
Lee C. Swartz
James G. Morgan, Jr.
Sandra L. Meilton
Stephen M. Greecher, Jr.
Dennis R. Sheaffer

COUNSEL

Stanley H. Siegel (Resident, Lewistown Office)

ASSOCIATES

Richard A. Estacio
Michael H. Park
Andrew K. Stutzman

For full biographical listings, see the Martindale-Hubbell Law Directory

METZGER, WICKERSHAM, KNAUSS & ERB (AV)

Mellon Bank Building, 111 Market Street, P.O. Box 93, 17108-0093
Telephone: 717-238-8187
Telefax: 717-234-9478
Other Harrisburg, Pennsylvania Office: 4813 Jonestown Road, P.O. Box 93, 17108.
Telephone: 717-652-7020.

MEMBERS OF FIRM

Maurice R. Metzger (1918-1980)
F. Brewster Wickersham (1918-1974)
Edward E. Knauss, III (Retired)
Christian S. Erb, Jr.
Robert E. Yetter
James F. Carl
Robert P. Reed
Edward E. Knauss, IV
Jered L. Hock
Karl R. Hildabrand

ASSOCIATES

Richard B. Druby
Steven P. Miner
Clark DeVere

Representative Clients: Allstate Insurance Co.; Chubb Group of Insurance Companies; Fireman's Fund American Insurance Group; Liberty Mutual Insurance Co.; Continental Insurance Co.; Crum & Forster.

For full biographical listings, see the Martindale-Hubbell Law Directory

*LANCASTER,** Lancaster Co.

ATLEE & HALL (AV)

8 North Queen Street, P.O. Box 449, 17603
Telephone: 717-393-9596
FAX: 717-393-2138

MEMBERS OF FIRM

William A. Atlee, Jr.
Thomas W. Hall

ASSOCIATES

Steven D. Costello
Dan M. Brookhart
Jan S. Barnett
Terri L. Ackerman

For full biographical listings, see the Martindale-Hubbell Law Directory

LANSDALE, Montgomery Co.

PEARLSTINE/SALKIN ASSOCIATES (AV)

1250 South Broad Street Suite 1000, P.O. Box 431, 19446
Telephone: 215-699-6000
Fax: 215-699-0231

(See Next Column)

MEMBERS OF FIRM

Philip Salkin
Ronald E. Robinson
Barry Cooperberg
Frederick C. Horn
Marc B. Davis
William R. Wanger
F. Craig La Rocca
Jeffrey T. Sultanik
Neal R. Pearlstine
Wendy G. Rothstein
Alan L. Eisen
Glenn D. Fox

Wilhelm L. Gruszecki
Brian E. Subers
Mark S. Cappuccio
James R. Hall
Michael S. Paul
David J. Draganosky
Lawrence P. Kempner

For full biographical listings, see the Martindale-Hubbell Law Directory

*MEDIA,** Delaware Co.

KASSAB ARCHBOLD JACKSON & O'BRIEN (AV)

Lawyers-Title Building, 214 North Jackson Street, P.O. Box 626, 19063
Telephone: 610-565-3800
Telecopier: 610-892-6888
Wilmington, Delaware Office: 1326 King Street.
Telephone: 302-656-3393.
Fax: 302-656-1993.
Wildwood, New Jersey Office: 5201 New Jersey Avenue.
Telephone: 609-522-6559.

MEMBERS OF FIRM

Edward Kassab
William C. Archbold, Jr.
Robert James Jackson
Joseph Patrick O'Brien
Richard A. Stanko
Roy T. J. Stegena

OF COUNSEL

Matthew J. Ryan
John W. Nilon, Jr.

ASSOCIATES

Kevin William Gibson
Cynthia Kassab Larosa
Marc S. Stein
Terrance A. Kline
George C. McFarland, Jr.
Jill E. Aversa
Pamela A. La Torre
Kenneth D. Kynett

Representative Clients furnished upon request.

For full biographical listings, see the Martindale-Hubbell Law Directory

*NORRISTOWN,** Montgomery Co.

LINDLEY M. COWPERTHWAIT, JR., P.C. (AV)

17 East Airy Street, 19401
Telephone: 610-277-6622
Fax: 610-277-6601
Cherry Hill, New Jersey Office: 1040 North Kings Highway, Suite 600, 08034.
Telephone: 609-482-8600.

Lindley M. Cowperthwait, Jr.
Adam D. Zucker

For full biographical listings, see the Martindale-Hubbell Law Directory

RAYMOND M. VICTOR, P.C. (AV)

616 DeKalb Street, 19401
Telephone: 610-272-5253
Fax: 610-272-7422

Raymond M. Victor
Dolores Victor

For full biographical listings, see the Martindale-Hubbell Law Directory

*PHILADELPHIA,** Philadelphia Co.

FORCENO & HANNON (AV)

Suite 1000, The Bourse, 111 S. Independence Mall East, 19106-2574
Telephone: 215-732-1630; 800-222-3352 in U.S.
Fax: 215-923-8507

MEMBERS OF FIRM

Raymond P. Forceno
Gregory John Hannon

Thomas J. Joyce, III
Donald J. Richmond

For full biographical listings, see the Martindale-Hubbell Law Directory

GALLAGHER, REILLY AND LACHAT, P.C. (AV)

Suite 1300, 2000 Market Street, 19103
Telephone: 215-299-3000
FAX: 215-299-3010
Pennsauken, New Jersey Office: Kevon Office Center, Suite 130, 2500 McClellan Boulevard, 08109.
Telephone: 609-663-8200.

Stanley S. Frazee, Jr.
Paul F. X. Gallagher
Thomas F. Reilly
Frederick T. Lachat, Jr.
Richard K. Hohn
James Emerson Egbert
Stephen A. Scheuerle
Elizabeth F. Walker

(See Next Column)

GALLAGHER, REILLY AND LACHAT P.C., *Philadelphia—Continued*

David Scott Morgan
Wilfred T. Mills, Jr.
Maureen Rowan
Charles L. McNabb
Thomas O'Neill
Laurence I. Gross
Sean F. Kennedy
Milica Novakovic
John A. Livingood, Jr.

SPECIAL COUNSEL

Dolores Rocco Kulp

For full biographical listings, see the Martindale-Hubbell Law Directory

GOLDFEIN & JOSEPH, A PROFESSIONAL CORPORATION (AV)

17th Floor, Packard Building, 111 South 15th Street, 19102-2695
Telephone: 215-977-9800
Fax: 215-988-0062
Princeton, New Jersey Office: Princeton Metro Center, Suite 115, 5 Vaughn Drive.
Telephone: 609-520-0400.
Fax: 609-520-1450.
Wilmington, Delaware Office: PNC Bank Center, Suite 1212, P.O. Box 2206, 222 Delaware Avenue.
Telephone: 302-656-3301.
Fax: 302-656-0643.

Edward B. Joseph
Fredric L. Goldfein
E. Chandler Hosmer, III
Ellen Brown Furman
Leslie Anne Miller
David C. Weinberg
James Patrick Hadden
Bernard L. Levinthal
Gary H. Kaplan (Resident, Wilmington, Delaware Office)
Roseann Lynn Brenner
Elissa J. Kahn

John A. Turlik
Susan Burton Stadtmauer
David M. Katzenstein (Resident, Princeton, New Jersey Office)
Scott I. Fegley
William J. Weiss
Michael A. Billotti (Not admitted in PA; Resident, Princeton, New Jersey Office)
Lawrence E. Currier
Robert P. Coleman
Robert T. Connor
Ann B. Cairns
Frederick A. Kiegel
Janet E. Golup
Ted Martin Berg (Resident, Wilmington, Delaware Office)

OF COUNSEL

Charles B. Burr, II

For full biographical listings, see the Martindale-Hubbell Law Directory

KELLEY, JASONS, MCGUIRE & SPINELLI (AV)

Suite 1300, 1234 Market Street, 19107-3713
Telephone: 215-854-0658
Fax: 215-854-8434
Cherry Hill, New Jersey Office: 1230 Brace Road, 08034.
Telephone: 609-429-8956.
Wilmington, Delaware Office: 1220 Market Building, P.O. Box 194, 19899.
Telephone: 302-652-8560.
Fax: 302-652-8405.

MEMBERS OF FIRM

John Patrick Kelley
Catherine N. Jasons
Joseph W. McGuire
Armand J. Della Porta, Jr.
Christopher N. Santoro
Robert N. Spinelli
Thomas P. Hanna
Thomas J. Johanson
Michael L. Turner

ASSOCIATES

Kelly J. Sasso (Resident, Wilmington, Delaware Office)
Richard L. Walker, II
Bernard E. Kueny, III
Timothy McGowan
Neal C. Glenn

OF COUNSEL

Joseph P. Green
Matthew D. Blum, M.D.
W. Matthew Reber

For full biographical listings, see the Martindale-Hubbell Law Directory

LAVIN, COLEMAN, FINARELLI & GRAY (AV)

12th Floor Penn Mutual Tower, 510 Walnut Street, 19106
Telephone: 215-627-0303
Fax: 215-627-2551
Mount Laurel, New Jersey Office: 10000 Midlantic Drive, Suite 300 West.
Telephone: 609-778-5544.
Fax: 609-778-3383.
New York, New York Office: 780 Third Avenue, Suite 1401.
Telephone: 212-319-6898.
Fax: 212-319-6932.

George J. Lavin, Jr.
Thomas Finarelli
William V. Coleman
Francis F. Quinn
Joseph E. O'Neil
Francis P. Burns, III
William J. Ricci
Edward A. Gray
Basil A. DiSipio
Wayne A. Graver
James Weiner
Frederick W. Rom
Gerard Cedrone
Robert Szwajkos

(See Next Column)

Mary Grace Maley
Christine O. Boyd
Michael D. Brophy
Joseph A. McGinley
Polly N. Phillippi

John J. Bateman
Stephen M. Beaudoin
Ronald W. Boak
Denise L. Carroll
Henry Michael Clinton
John J. Coughlin, IV
John Kieran Daly (Not admitted in PA)
Michael T. Droogan, Jr.
Joseph F. Dunne (Not admitted in PA)
B. Lynn Enderby
Louis Giansante
Francis J. Grey, Jr.
Mitchell Gruner
Robert J. Hafner
Eugene Hamill
Sandra Hourahan
Ernest H. Hutchinson, III
Regina A. Jones
Bridget A. Kelleher
Michael P. Kinkopf
Steven R. Kramer (Not admitted in PA)
Ellen Hatch Kueny
George J. Lavin, III
Peter W. Lee
Robert J. Martin
Karen Howard Matthews
William C. Mead, Jr.
Stephen E. Moore
Jane Elizabeth Nagle
Peter M. Newman
John J. O'Donnell
LeaNora J. Patterson
Jo E. Peifer
Michael J. Quinn
Mary D. Rafferty
Susan Ellyn Satkowski
William E. Staas, III
Fiona J. Van Dych
Thomas J. Wagner
Anne E. Walters
Maribeth Bohs Wechsler
Richard B. Wickersham, Jr.

For full biographical listings, see the Martindale-Hubbell Law Directory

LEVIN, FISHBEIN, SEDRAN & BERMAN (AV)

Suite 600, 320 Walnut Street, 19106
Telephone: 215-592-1500
Fax: 215-592-4663

MEMBERS OF FIRM

Arnold Levin
Michael D. Fishbein
Howard J. Sedran
Laurence S. Berman
Frederick S. Longer

Robert M. Unterberger
Craig D. Ginsburg
Jonathan Shub
Cheryl R. Brown Hill
Roberta Shaner

For full biographical listings, see the Martindale-Hubbell Law Directory

MANTA AND WELGE (AV)

A Partnership of Professional Corporations
One Commerce Square, 37th Floor, 2005 Market Street, 19103
Telephone: 215-851-6600
Telecopy: 215-851-6644
Allentown, Pennsylvania Office: Suite 115 Commerce Plaza, 5050 Tilghman Street.
Telephone: 215-395-7499.
Fax: 215-398-7878.
Princeton, New Jersey Office: 101 Carnegie Center, Suite 215. P.O. Box 5306.
Telephone: 609-452-8833.
Fax: 609-452-9109.
Cherry Hill, New Jersey Office: Suite 600, 1040 North King Highway.
Telephone: 609-795-7611.
Fax: 609-795-7612.

MEMBERS OF FIRM

Joseph G. Manta
Mark A. Welge
William R. Hourican
Albert L. Piccerilli
John C. Sullivan
Joel Schneider
Joseph M. Cincotta
James V. Bielunas
Richard S. Mannella
Joanne M. Walker
Francis McGill Hadden
Walter A. Stewart

OF COUNSEL

Albert J. Bartosic

Peter F. Rosenthal
Susan Simpson-Brown
Gregory S. Thomas
Andrea L. Smith
Anton G. Marzano
Margaret E. Wenke
Wendy F. Tucker
Jacqueline Borock
David G. C. Arnold
Karen C. Buck
Laurie A. Carroll
Mark J. Manta
David S. Florig
Stephen F. Brock
Geoffrey J. Alexander
Wendy R. S. O'Connor
Kathleen K. Kerns
Fernando Santiago
Peter L. Frattarelli
Holly C. Dobrosky

For full biographical listings, see the Martindale-Hubbell Law Directory

MCKISSOCK & HOFFMAN, P.C. (AV)

1700 Market Street, Suite 3000, 19103
Telephone: 215-246-2100
Fax: 215-246-2144
Mount Holly, New Jersey Office: 211 High Street.
Telephone: 609-267-1006.

(See Next Column)

McKissock & Hoffman P.C.—*Continued*

Doylestown, Pennsylvania Office: 77 North Broad Street, Second Floor.
Telephone: 215-345-4501.
Harrisburg, Pennsylvania Office: 127 State Street.
Telephone: 717-234-0103.

J. Bruce McKissock
Peter J. Hoffman
Richard L. McMonigle
Jill Baratz Clarke
Marybeth Stanton Christiansen
Catherine Hill Kunda
Bryant Craig Black (Resident, Harrisburg, Office)
John M. Willis
John J. McGrath
Debra Schwaderer Dunne
Donald J. Brooks, Jr.
William J. Mundy
Elizabeth E. Davies
Christopher Thomson
Kathleen M. Kenna
K. Reed Haywood
Sara J. Thomson
Maureen P. Fitzgerald
Veronica E. Noonan
Kathleen M. Sholette
Patricia D. Shippee

For full biographical listings, see the Martindale-Hubbell Law Directory

Perry, Fialkowski & Perry (AV)

Suite 1802 One Penn Square West, 19102
Telephone: 215-561-4110
Fax: 215-981-1472
Clementon, New Jersey Office: 180 White Horse Pike.
Telephone: 609-627-1005.

MEMBERS OF FIRM

David Perry
Anne E. Fialkowski
Sherryl R. Perry
Marcia F. Rosenbaum

For full biographical listings, see the Martindale-Hubbell Law Directory

Sweeney, Sheehan & Spencer, A Professional Corporation (AV)

19th Floor, 1515 Market Street, 19102
Telephone: 215-563-9811
Fax: 215-557-0999
Voorhees, New Jersey Office: 120 Fairview Avenue.
Telephone: 609-428-8088.
Fax: 609-428-9765.

George D. Sheehan (1911-1985)
Donald J. P. Sweeney
M. Landon Spencer
George D. Sheehan, Jr.
Walter S. Jenkins
Thomas L. Delevie
Dennis L. Platt
Robert B. Goodyear
Warren E. Voter
Guy Mercogliano
Andrew Siegeltuch
Barbara A. O'Connell
Gregory J. Sharkey

Suzanne M. O'Brien
Bayard H. Graf
Racheal De Cicco
Harold E. Viletto
Robyn Farrell McGrath
J. David Outtrim
Robert Thompson Veon
J. Michael Kunsch
Victoria L. Rees

For full biographical listings, see the Martindale-Hubbell Law Directory

Sarah M. Thompson (AV)

1710 Spruce Street, 19103
Telephone: 215-790-4568
Fax: 215-735-2211

For full biographical listings, see the Martindale-Hubbell Law Directory

Wilbraham, Lawler & Buba, A Professional Corporation (AV)

The Curtis Center, Suite 450, 601 Walnut Street, 19106-3304
Telephone: 215-923-0133
Fax: 215-923-0471
Haddonfield, New Jersey Office: 24 Kings Highway West. 08033-2122.
Telephone: 609-795-4422.
Fax: 609-795-4699.

Edward J. Wilbraham
Robert B. Lawler
Barbara J. Buba
Mark A. Stevens
Michael J. Block
Kim Hollaender

Mary S. Cook
Pamela B. Hinton
Garry B. Hutchinson
James W. McCartney

For full biographical listings, see the Martindale-Hubbell Law Directory

*PITTSBURGH,** Allegheny Co.

Aderson, Frank & Steiner, A Professional Corporation (AV)

2320 Grant Building, 15219
Telephone: 412-263-0500
Fax: 412-263-0565

(See Next Column)

Mark S. Frank
Richard H. Malmstrom

For full biographical listings, see the Martindale-Hubbell Law Directory

Berger Kapetan Meyers Rosen Louik & Raizman, P.C. (AV)

Suite 200 The Frick Building, 15219-6003
Telephone: 412-281-4200
Fax: 412-281-3262

Daniel M. Berger
Neil R. Rosen
Michael Louik
Susan E. Mahood
Andrew L. Horvath

For full biographical listings, see the Martindale-Hubbell Law Directory

John A. Caputo & Associates (AV)

Fifth Floor, Three Gateway Center, 15222
Telephone: 412-391-4990

Allan Meyers Cox
Bernard C. Caputo

For full biographical listings, see the Martindale-Hubbell Law Directory

Robert A. Cohen (AV)

819 Frick Building, 15219
Telephone: 412-261-9700

For full biographical listings, see the Martindale-Hubbell Law Directory

William W. Guthrie & Associates A Professional Corporation (AV)

416 Frick Building, 437 Grant Street, 15219
Telephone: 412-562-0556
Fax: 412-562-5920

William W. Guthrie

Reference: Pittsburgh National Bank (Potter Office).

For full biographical listings, see the Martindale-Hubbell Law Directory

Heintzman, Warren & Wise (AV)

The 35th Floor, Gulf Tower, 707 Grant Street, 15219
Telephone: 412-394-7810
Fax: 412-263-5222

MEMBERS OF FIRM

Michael D. Heintzman
Charles S. Warren
Roger L. Wise

ASSOCIATES

Jeanine L. Fonner
Joseph R. Schaper
Kenneth F. Klanica
Diane K. Wohlfarth

For full biographical listings, see the Martindale-Hubbell Law Directory

Kiger Messer & Alpern (AV)

1404 Grant Building, 15219
Telephone: 412-281-7200
Fax: 412-765-0440

MEMBERS OF FIRM

Jerome W. Kiger
Howard F. Messer
Charles H. Alpern

For Complete List of Firm Personnel, See General Section

For full biographical listings, see the Martindale-Hubbell Law Directory

Richard J. Mills & Associates (AV)

200 Benedum Trees Building, 223 Fourth Avenue, 15222-1713
Telephone: 412-471-2442
Fax: 412-471-2456

Richard J. Mills

Austin P. Henry

For full biographical listings, see the Martindale-Hubbell Law Directory

Swensen Perer & Johnson (AV)

Two PNC Plaza, Suite 2710, 15222
Telephone: 412-281-1970
Fax: 412-281-2808
Erie, Pennsylvania Office: 209 Court House Commons.
Telephone: 814-456-0489.

MEMBERS OF FIRM

Jan C. Swensen
Alan H. Perer
J. Alan Johnson
Peter B. Skeel
David M. Landay
John W. McCandless (Resident Partner, Erie, Pennsylvania Office)

(See Next Column)

SWENSEN PERER & JOHNSON, *Pittsburgh—Continued*

ASSOCIATES

John Carl Bogut, Jr.
David A. Schroeder (Resident Associate, Erie, Pennsylvania Office)
John J. Edson, V
Anthony J. Sciarrino
George M. Kontos

For full biographical listings, see the Martindale-Hubbell Law Directory

THORP, REED & ARMSTRONG (AV)

One Riverfront Center, 15222
Telephone: 412-394-7711
Fax: 412-394-2555

MEMBERS OF FIRM

Michael R. Bucci, Jr.
G. Daniel Carney
Scott E. Henderson
Julie A. Maloney
Randolph T. Struk
William M. Wycoff
C. James Zeszutek

ASSOCIATES

Kimberly A. Brown
Donald M. Lund

For Complete List of Firm Personnel, See General Section

For full biographical listings, see the Martindale-Hubbell Law Directory

*SCRANTON,** Lackawanna Co.

KREDER, BROOKS, HAILSTONE & LUDWIG (AV)

Suite 200, 220 Penn Avenue, 18503
Telephone: 717-346-7922
Telecopier: 717-346-3715

Cody H. Brooks
Andrew Hailstone
Lawrence M. Ludwig
Lucille Marsh
Michael J. Donohue
David K. Brown
J. Frederick Rohrbeck
James J. Wilson
Richard G. Reed
Stephen William Saunders

ASSOCIATES

Ann Lavelle Powell
Linda Dwyer Cleary
Barbara Sardella
Alyce Hailstone Farrell
Robert B. Farrell
David A. Aikens, Jr.

OF COUNSEL

Joseph C. Kreder
Willard M. Henkelman
James Edson O'Connell

Counsel for: Consolidated Rail Corp.; PNC Bank; U.S. Fidelity & Guaranty Co.; Nationwide Insurance Co.; Liberty Mutual Insurance Co.; Citizens Savings Assn.; NEP Supershooters, Inc.

For full biographical listings, see the Martindale-Hubbell Law Directory

*WILLIAMSPORT,** Lycoming Co.

MITCHELL, MITCHELL, GRAY & GALLAGHER, A PROFESSIONAL CORPORATION (AV)

10 West Third Street, 17701
Telephone: 717-323-8404
Fax: 717-323-8585

C. Edward S. Mitchell
Richard A. Gray
Robert A. Gallagher
Gary L. Weber

Bret J. Southard
Eric R. Linhardt

OF COUNSEL

Jacob Neafie Mitchell

For full biographical listings, see the Martindale-Hubbell Law Directory

RIEDERS, TRAVIS, MUSSINA, HUMPHREY & HARRIS (AV)

161 West Third Street, P.O. Box 215, 17703-0215
Telephone: 717-323-8711
1-800-326-9259
Fax: 717-323-4192

MEMBERS OF FIRM

Gary T. Harris
John M. Humphrey
Malcolm S. Mussina
Clifford A. Rieders
Ronald C. Travis
Thomas Waffenschmidt
C. Scott Waters

ASSOCIATES

Robert H. Vesely
Jeffrey C. Dohrmann
James Michael Wiley

LEGAL SUPPORT PERSONNEL

Kimberly A. Paulhamus

Representative Clients: Jersey Shore State Bank; Gamble Twp.; Crown American Corp.; Fowler Motors, Inc.; Twin Hills oldsmobile, Inc.; Brady Twp.; Cascade Twp.; Cogan House Twp.; Susquehana Twp.; Upper Fairfield Twp.; Borough of Picture Rocks.

For full biographical listings, see the Martindale-Hubbell Law Directory

RHODE ISLAND

*PROVIDENCE,** Providence Co.

VINCENT D. MORGERA (AV)

One Old Stone Square, 02903-7104
Telephone: 401-456-0300
Telecopier: 401-456-0303

For full biographical listings, see the Martindale-Hubbell Law Directory

SOUTH CAROLINA

*BEAUFORT,** Beaufort Co.

DAVIS, TUPPER, GRIMSLEY & SEELHOFF (AV)

611 Bay Street, P.O. Box 2055, 29901-2055
Telephone: 803-524-1116
Facsimile: 803-524-1463

MEMBERS OF FIRM

Hutson S. Davis, Jr.
Ralph E. Tupper
James A. Grimsley, III
Scott A. Seelhoff
Erin D. Dean

For full biographical listings, see the Martindale-Hubbell Law Directory

*CHARLESTON,** Charleston Co.

HAYNSWORTH, MARION, MCKAY & GUÉRARD, L.L.P (AV)

#2 Prioleau Street, P.O. Box 1119, 29402
Telephone: 803-722-7606
Telecopier: 803-723-5263
Columbia, South Carolina Office: Suite 2400 AT&T Building, 1201 Main Street, P.O. Drawer 7157, 29202.
Telephone: 803-765-1818.
Telecopier: 803-765-2399.
Greenville, South Carolina Office: Two Insignia Financial Plaza, 75 Beattie Place, P.O. Box 2048, 29602.
Telephone: 803-240-3200.
Telecopier: 803-240-3300.

MEMBERS OF FIRM

William C. Cleveland
J. Paul Trouche

ASSOCIATE

Meredith Grier Buyck

Counsel for: Bank of South Carolina; Baker Hospital; Healthsources of South Carolina; Allstate Insurance Co.; CSX Corporation; Lloyd's Underwriters; Coward-Hund Construction Co.; South Carolina Public Service Authority; South Carolina Jobs - Economic Development Authority; City of Hanahan.

For Complete List of Firm Personnel, See General Section

For full biographical listings, see the Martindale-Hubbell Law Directory

HOOD LAW FIRM (AV)

172 Meeting Street, P.O. Box 1508, 29402
Telephone: 803-577-4435
FAX: 803-722-1630

MEMBERS OF FIRM

Robert H. Hood
Louis P. Herns
G. Mark Phillips
Carl Everette Pierce, II
John K. Blincow, Jr.

James G. Kennedy
James Dowell Gandy, III
William R. Hearn, Jr.
Joseph C. Wilson, IV
Dixon F. Pearce, III
Margaret Allison Snead
Barbara Wynne Showers
Christine L. Companion
Hugh Willcox Buyck
Jerry A. Smith
Allan Poe Sloan, III
Todd W. Smyth

For full biographical listings, see the Martindale-Hubbell Law Directory

*COLUMBIA,** Richland Co.

***** indicates certain Bar Register subscribers whose principal office is located elsewhere in the state and who have arranged for representation as a part of the state capital listings that follow

BARNES, ALFORD, STORK & JOHNSON, L.L.P. (AV)

1613 Main Street, P.O. Box 8448, 29202
Telephone: 803-799-1111
Telefax: 803-254-1335

(See Next Column)

BARNES, ALFORD, STORK & JOHNSON L.L.P.—*Continued*

James W. Alford Robert E. Salane
Richard C. Thomas

Representative Clients: First Union National Bank of South Carolina; Aetna Casualty and Surety Co.; Kline Iron & Steel Co.

For Complete List of Firm Personnel, See General Section

For full biographical listings, see the Martindale-Hubbell Law Directory

BOWERS ORR & ROBERTSON (AV)

Suite 1100, 1401 Main Street, P.O. Box 7307, 29202
Telephone: 803-252-0494
Telefax: 803-252-1068

MEMBER OF FIRM

Glenn Bowers

For full biographical listings, see the Martindale-Hubbell Law Directory

GLENN, IRVIN, MURPHY, GRAY & STEPP (AV)

Southern National Bank Building, Suite 390, 1901 Assembly Street, P.O. Box 1550, 29202-1550
Telephone: 803-765-1100
Telecopy: 803-765-0755

MEMBERS OF FIRM

Wilmot B. Irvin Peter L. Murphy
Elizabeth G. Howard

Blaney A. Coskrey, III

Reference: Southern National.

For Complete List of Firm Personnel, See General Section

For full biographical listings, see the Martindale-Hubbell Law Directory

*** HAYNSWORTH, MARION, MCKAY & GUÉRARD, L.L.P.** (AV)

Suite 2400 A T & T Building, 1201 Main Street, P.O. Drawer 7157, 29202
Telephone: 803-765-1818
Telecopier: 803-765-2399
Greenville, South Carolina Office: Two Insignia Financial Plaza, 75 Beattie Place, P.O. Box 2048, 29602.
Telephone: 803-240-3200.
Telecopier: 803-240-3300.
Charleston, South Carolina Office: #2 Prioleau Street, P.O. Box 1119, 29402.
Telephone: 803-722-7606.
Telecopier: 803-723-5263.

MEMBER OF FIRM

William P. Simpson

ASSOCIATES

Stephen F. McKinney Boyd B. Nicholson, Jr.
Edward Wade Mullins, III

Counsel for: The B. F. Goodrich Company; Bausch & Lomb, Inc.; General Motors; Ford Motor Company; Stone Manufacturing Co.; Dunlop Slazenger Corp.; Caterpillar Corporation; E. I. DuPont Corp.; Gerber Childrenswear, Inc.; Steel Heddle Mfg. Co.

For Complete List of Firm Personnel, See General Section

For full biographical listings, see the Martindale-Hubbell Law Directory

MCKAY, MCKAY, HENRY & FOSTER, P.A. (AV)

1325 Laurel Street, P.O. Box 7217, 29202
Telephone: 803-256-4645
FAX: 803-765-1839

Douglas McKay, Jr. Angela L. Henry
Julius W. McKay, II Ruskin C. Foster

Representative Clients: Americlaim Adjustment Corp.; Amoco Oil Company; Britanco Underwriters, Inc.; Browning-Ferris Industries, Inc.; Homestead Insurance Co.; Pennsylvania Manufacturers' Association Ins. Co. (PMA); Schneider National Carriers; South Carolina Division of General Services-Insurance Reserve Fund (IRF); South Carolina Medical Malpractice Joint Underwriting Assn. (JUA); Underwriters Laboratories, Inc.

For Complete List of Firm Personnel, See General Section

For full biographical listings, see the Martindale-Hubbell Law Directory

ERNEST J. NAUFUL, JR., P.C. (AV)

1330 Lady Street Suite 615, P.O. Box 5907, 29250
Telephone: 803-256-4045
Facsimile: 803-254-0776

Ernest J. Nauful, Jr.

For full biographical listings, see the Martindale-Hubbell Law Directory

RICHARDSON, PLOWDEN, GRIER AND HOWSER, P.A. (AV)

1600 Marion Street, P.O. Drawer 7788, 29202
Telephone: 803-771-4400
Telecopy: 803-779-0016
Myrtle Beach, South Carolina Office: Southern National Bank Building, Suite 202, 601 21st Avenue North, P.O. Box 3646, 29578.
Telephone: 803-448-1008.
FAX: 803-448-1533.

F. Barron Grier, III Michael A. Pulliam
R. Davis Howser William H. Hensel
Leslie A. Cotter, Jr.

Douglas C. Baxter Benjamin D. McCoy
Anne Macon Flynn

Representative Clients: Insurance: CNA Insurance Co.; The Hartford; Kemper Insurance Co.; Pennsylvania National Mutual Casualty Insurance Co.; Wausau Insurance Cos.; The Reudlinger Cos.; Sumitomo Marine Claims Services (USA); Honda North America, Inc.; Yamaha Motor Corp. (USA).

For Complete List of Firm Personnel, See General Section

For full biographical listings, see the Martindale-Hubbell Law Directory

*GREENVILLE,** Greenville Co.

FEW & FEW, P.A. (AV)

850 Wade Hampton Boulevard, P.O. Box 10085, Fed. Station, 29603
Telephone: 803-232-6456
Fax: 803-370-0671

J. Kendall Few John C. Few

For full biographical listings, see the Martindale-Hubbell Law Directory

HAYNSWORTH, MARION, MCKAY & GUÉRARD, L.L.P. (AV)

Two Insignia Financial Plaza, 75 Beattie Place, P.O. Box 2048, 29602
Telephone: 803-240-3200
Telecopier: 803-240-3300
Columbia, South Carolina Office: Suite 2400 A T & T Building, 1201 Main Street, P.O. Drawer 7157, 29202
Telephone: 803-765-1818.
Telecopier: 803-765-2399.
Charleston, South Carolina Office: #2 Prioleau Street, P.O. Box 1119, 29402.
Telephone: 803-722-7606.
Telecopier: 803-723-5263.

MEMBERS OF FIRM

Donald L. Ferguson W. Francis Marion, Jr.
G. Dewey Oxner, Jr. John B. McLeod
James B. Pressly, Jr. Edwin Brown Parkinson, Jr.
H. Donald Sellers Floyd Matlock Elliott
Ellis M. Johnston, II Moffatt Grier McDonald

ASSOCIATES

Amy Miller Snyder Brent O. Clinkscale
Eric Keith Englebardt Harry L. Phillips, Jr.
James Derrick Quattlebaum Julie Kaye Hackworth
William David Conner

Representative Clients: State Industries; Wausau Insurance Co.; Prudential Property & Casualty; Owens Corning Fiberglas; Anheuser Bush.

For Complete List of Firm Personnel, See General Section

For full biographical listings, see the Martindale-Hubbell Law Directory

*WALHALLA,** Oconee Co.

LARRY C. BRANDT, P.A. (AV)

205 West Main Street, P.O. Drawer 738, 29691
Telephone: 803-638-5406
803-638-7873

Larry C. Brandt

D. Bradley Jordan J. Bruce Schumpert

LEGAL SUPPORT PERSONNEL

Debra C. Miller

For full biographical listings, see the Martindale-Hubbell Law Directory

TENNESSEE

*CHATTANOOGA,** Hamilton Co.

FLEISSNER, COOPER, MARCUS & QUINN (AV)

800 Vine Street, 37403
Telephone: 615-756-3595
Telecopier: 615-266-5455

(See Next Column)

FLEISSNER, COOPER, MARCUS & QUINN, *Chattanooga—Continued*

Phillip A. Fleissner
Gary A. Cooper
H. Richard Marcus
J. Bartlett Quinn
Robert L. Widerkehr, Jr.

ASSOCIATE

Cynthia D. Hall

For full biographical listings, see the Martindale-Hubbell Law Directory

*KNOXVILLE,** Knox Co.

HODGES, DOUGHTY AND CARSON (AV)

617 Main Street, P.O. Box 869, 37901-0869
Telephone: 615-546-9611
Telecopier: 615-544-2014

MEMBERS OF FIRM

J. H. Hodges (1896-1983)
J. H. Doughty (1903-1987)
Richard L. Carson (1912-1980)
John P. Davis, Jr. (1923-1977)
Robert R. Campbell
David E. Smith
John W. Wheeler
Dalton L. Townsend
Douglas L. Dutton
William F. Alley, Jr.
Roy L. Aaron
Dean B. Farmer
David Wedekind
Julia Saunders Howard
Albert J. Harb
Edward G. White, II
Thomas H. Dickenson
J. William Coley
J. Michael Haynes
T. Kenan Smith
Wayne A. Kline

ASSOCIATES

James M. Cornelius, Jr.
W. Tyler Chastain

OF COUNSEL

Jonathan H. Burnett

Representative Clients: General Motors Corp.; Sears, Roebuck and Co.; Navistar International; Martin Marietta Energy Systems; Union Carbide Corp.; NationsBank of Tennessee; K-Mart Corporation; Aetna Life and Casualty Group; Fireman's Fund American Insurance Company; Safeco Insurance Group.

For full biographical listings, see the Martindale-Hubbell Law Directory

PRYOR, FLYNN, PRIEST & HARBER (AV)

Suite 600 Two Centre Square, 625 Gay Street, P.O. Box 870, 37901
Telephone: 615-522-4191
Telecopier: 615-522-0910

Robert E. Pryor
Frank L. Flynn, Jr.
Timothy A. Priest
John K. Harber

ASSOCIATES

Mark E. Floyd
Donald R. Coffey
M. Christopher Coffey

References: Third National Bank; First National Bank.

For full biographical listings, see the Martindale-Hubbell Law Directory

RAINWATER, HUMBLE & VOWELL (AV)

2037 Plaza Tower, P.O. Box 2775, 37901
Telephone: 615-525-0321
Fax: 615-525-2431

MEMBERS OF FIRM

J. Earl Rainwater
J. Randolph Humble
Donald K. Vowell

Representative Clients: Acme Construction, Inc.; Curtis Construction Co., Inc.; Knoxville Pediatric Associates, P.C.; National Gas Distributors, Inc.; Neel's Wholesale Produce Co., Inc.; Oldham Insurance Inc.; Sherrod Electric Co., Inc.; Towe Iron Works, Inc.; Wm. S. Trimble Co., Inc.

For full biographical listings, see the Martindale-Hubbell Law Directory

WATSON, HOLLOW & REEVES (AV)

1700 Plaza Tower, P.O. Box 131, 37901
Telephone: 615-522-3803
Telecopier: 615-525-2514

MEMBERS OF FIRM

Robert Harmon Watson, Jr.
Richard L. Hollow
Pamela L. Reeves
Jon G. Roach
John C. Duffy
John T. Batson, Jr.
Earl Jerome Melson

ASSOCIATES

Arthur Franklin Knight, III
Robert W. Willingham

For full biographical listings, see the Martindale-Hubbell Law Directory

*MEMPHIS,** Shelby Co.

GLASSMAN, JETER, EDWARDS & WADE, P.C. (AV)

26 North Second Street Building, 38103
Telephone: 901-527-4673
Telecopier: 901-521-0940
Lexington, Tennessee Office: 85 East Church.
Telephone: 901-968-2561.

Richard Glassman
William M. Jeter
Tim Edwards
B. J. Wade
John Barry Burgess
Carl K. Wyatt, Jr.
Nicholas E. Bragorgos
Ben W. Keesee
Lucinda S. Murray
Robert A. Cox
Lori J. Keen
James F. Horner, Jr.

For full biographical listings, see the Martindale-Hubbell Law Directory

*NASHVILLE,** Davidson Co.

MANIER, HEROD, HOLLABAUGH & SMITH, A PROFESSIONAL CORPORATION (AV)

First Union Tower 2200 One Nashville Place, 150 Fourth Avenue North, 37219-2494
Telephone: 615-244-0030
Telecopier: 615-242-4203

Will R. Manier, Jr. (1885-1953)
Larkin E. Crouch (1882-1948)
Vincent L. Fuqua, Jr. (1930-1974)
J. Olin White (1907-1982)
Miller Manier (1897-1986)
William Edward Herod (1917-1992)
Lewis B. Hollabaugh
Don L. Smith
James M. Doran, Jr.
Stephen E. Cox
J. Michael Franks
Randall C. Ferguson
Terry L. Hill
James David Leckrone
Robert C. Evans
Tommy C. Estes
B. Gail Reese
Michael E. Evans
Laurence M. Papel
John M. Gillum
Gregory L. Cashion
Sam H. Poteet, Jr.
Samuel Arthur Butts III
David J. Deming
Mark S. LeVan
Richard McCallister Smith
Mary Paty Lynn Jetton
H. Rowan Leathers III
Jefferson C. Orr
William L. Penny

Lawrence B. Hammet II
John H. Rowland
Susan C. West
John E. Quinn
John F. Floyd
Paul L. Sprader
Lela M. Hollabaugh
J. Steven Kirkham
T. Richard Travis
Stephanie M. Jennings
Jerry W. Taylor
C. Benton Patton
Kenneth A. Weber
Phillip Robert Newman
Brett A. Oeser

General Counsel for: McKinnon Bridge Co., Inc.

For full biographical listings, see the Martindale-Hubbell Law Directory

TEXAS

*AMARILLO,** Potter Co.

HINKLE, COX, EATON, COFFIELD & HENSLEY (AV)

1700 Bank One Center, P.O. Box 9238, 79105-9238
Telephone: 806-372-5569
FAX: 806-372-9761
Roswell, New Mexico Office: 700 United Bank Plaza, P. O. Box 10, 88202.
Telephone: 505-622-6510.
FAX: 505-623-9332.
Midland, Texas Office: 6 Desta Drive, Suite 2800, P.O. Box 3580, 79702.
Telephone: 915-683-4691.
FAX: 915-683-6518.
Santa Fe, New Mexico Office: 218 Montezuma, P.O. Box 2068, 87504.
Telephone: 505-982-4554.
FAX: 505-982-8623.
Albuquerque, New Mexico Office: Suite 800, 500 Marquette, N.W., P.O. Box 2043, 87102.
Telephone: 505-768-1500.
FAX: 505-768-1529.
Austin, Texas Office: 401 West 15th Street, Suite 800, 78701.
Telephone: 512-476-7137.
FAX: 512-476-5431.
Associated Office: Hoffman & Stephens, P.C., 401 West 15th Street, Suite 800, 78701.
Telephone: 512-476-5434. Fax; 512-476-5431.

RESIDENT PARTNERS

Richard R. Wilfong
John C. Chambers
Russell J. Bailey
David M. Russell

Representative Clients: Federated Insurance; General Motors Corp.

For full biographical listings, see the Martindale-Hubbell Law Directory

*BEAUMONT,** Jefferson Co.

Reaud, Morgan & Quinn (AV)

801 Laurel, 77701
Telephone: 409-838-1000
Fax: 409-833-8236

MEMBERS OF FIRM

Wayne A. Reaud
Glen W. Morgan
Cris Quinn
Richard J. Clarkson
Bob Wortham

ASSOCIATES

Larry W. Thorpe
Keith F. Ellis
Suzanne Maltais

For full biographical listings, see the Martindale-Hubbell Law Directory

*CORPUS CHRISTI,** Nueces Co.

Dunn & Weathered, P.C. (AV)

611 South Upper Broadway, 78401
Telephone: 512-883-1594
FAX: 512-883-1599

David J. Dunn
Frank E. Weathered
John A. Smith, III
Mark DeKoch

OF COUNSEL

L. Nelson Hall

Reference: Citizens Bank.

For full biographical listings, see the Martindale-Hubbell Law Directory

*DALLAS,** Dallas Co.

Calhoun & Stacy (AV)

5700 NationsBank Plaza, 901 Main Street, 75202-3747
Telephone: 214-748-5000
Telecopier: 214-748-1421
Telex: 211358 CALGUMP UR

Mark Alan Calhoun
David W. Elrod
Steven D. Goldston
Parker Nelson
Roy L. Stacy

ASSOCIATES

Shannon S. Barclay
Robert A. Bragalone
Dennis D. Conder
Jane Elizabeth Diseker
Lawrence I. Fleishman
Thomas C. Jones
Katherine Johnson Knight
V. Paige Pace
Veronika Willard
Michael C. Wright

LEGAL CONSULTANT

Rees T. Bowen, III

For full biographical listings, see the Martindale-Hubbell Law Directory

Law Offices of Alan K. Laufman, J.D., M.D. A Professional Corporation (AV)

Suite 1000 Turtle Creek Centre, 3811 Turtle Creek Boulevard, 75219
Telephone: 214-559-3300
Fax: 214-526-1150

Alan K. Laufman

For full biographical listings, see the Martindale-Hubbell Law Directory

Misko, Howie & Sweeney (AV)

Turtle Creek Centre, Suite 1900, 3811 Turtle Creek Boulevard, 75219
Telephone: 214-443-8000
Fax: 214-443-8000

Fred Misko, Jr.
John R. Howie
Paula Sweeney

ASSOCIATES

Charles S. Siegel
James L. Mitchell, Jr.
Raymond A. Williams, III
Christopher D. Jones
Bryan D. Pope

For full biographical listings, see the Martindale-Hubbell Law Directory

George A. Otstott & Associates A Professional Corporation (AV)

3611 Fairmount, 75219
Telephone: 214-522-9999
Terrell, Texas Office: 304 East Wheeler.
Telephone: 214-563-2222.
Jefferson, Texas Office: 117 West Lafayette Street.
Telephone: 903-665-3300.
Denton, Texas Office: 1010 Dallas Drive.
Telephone: 817-383-8080.
Greenville, Texas Office: 2718 Wesley.
Telephone: 903-454-4444.

(See Next Column)

Waxahachie, Texas Office: 303 South Elm Street.
Telephone: 214-937-3000.

George A. Otstott

Jerry D. Andrews
Jean A. Robb
David Townsend

For full biographical listings, see the Martindale-Hubbell Law Directory

*FORT WORTH,** Tarrant Co.

Brockermeyer & Associates (AV)

1024 North Main, P.O. Box 4160, 76164-0160
Telephone: 817-625-8833
Fax: 817-625-9840

Kae L. Brockermeyer

For full biographical listings, see the Martindale-Hubbell Law Directory

Russell, Turner, Laird & Jones, L.L.P. (AV)

One Colonial Place, 2400 Scott Avenue, 76103-2200
Telephone: 817-531-3000; 1-800-448-2889
Fax: 817-535-3046
Dallas, Texas Office: Williams Square, Central Tower, Suite 700, 5215 North O'Connor Boulevard, Las Colinas Urban Center.
Telephone: 214-444-0444; 1-800-448-2889.

Wm. Greg Russell
Randall E. Turner
Steven C. Laird
Gregory G. Jones

For full biographical listings, see the Martindale-Hubbell Law Directory

*HOUSTON,** Harris Co.

Funderburk & Funderburk, L.L.P. (AV)

1080 Riviana Building, 2777 Allen Parkway, 77019
Telephone: 713-526-1801

MEMBERS OF FIRM

Weldon W. Funderburk
Larry B. Funderburk
Don Karotkin
Howard R. King
H. Dwayne Newton
John P. Cahill, Jr.
James A. Newsom
Ryan A. Beason
Cynthia L. Jones

ASSOCIATES

Thomas L. Cougill
Mark J. Courtois
J. Gregory Guy Funderburk
John L. Engvall, Jr.
David W. Funderburk
Brittian A. Featherston
Jeffrey Pierce Fultz

Representative Client: American States Insurance Co.; Citgo Petroleum Corporation; CNA Insurance; Texas Medical Liability Insurance Underwriting Association (JUA); Kemper National; Lawyers Surety Corporation; Maryland Insurance; The Medical Protective Company; The Mundy Companies; Waste Management, Inc.

For full biographical listings, see the Martindale-Hubbell Law Directory

Lorance & Thompson, A Professional Corporation (AV)

303 Jackson Hill, 77007
Telephone: 713-868-5560
Fax: 713-864-4671; 868-1605
Phoenix, Arizona Office: 2525 East Camelback Road, Suite 230, 85016.
Telephone: 602-224-4000.
Fax: 602-224-4098.
San Diego, California Office: 555 West Beech Street, Suite 222, 92101.
Telephone: 800-899-1844.

Larry D. Thompson
Wayne Adams
Frank B. Stahl, Jr.
William K. Luyties
Clifford A. Lawrence, Jr.
Walter F. (Trey) Williams, III
David O. Cluck
Phillip C. Summers
David F. Webb
Richard H. Martin
Vicki F. Brann
Ronald E. Hood
Gwen W. Dobrowski
Mark D. Flanagan
F. Barham Lewis

David W. Prasifka
Gregory D. Solcher
John A. Culberson
George Eric Van Noy
James E. Simmons
John H. Thomisee, Jr.
Tracey R. Burridge
Douglas A. Haldane
Geoffrey C. Guill
Diane M. Guariglia
Kelly B. Lea
Tracey Landrum Foster
Ronnie B. Arnold
Teresa A. Carver
Terrance D. Dill, Jr.
J. Wayne Little
William T. Sebesta
Richard N. Moore
Matthew R. Pearson

OF COUNSEL

John Holman Barr
Shannon P. Davis
Alexis J. Gomez

Representative Clients: Allstate Insurance Co.; The Hartford Insurance Group.

(See Next Column)

LORANCE & THOMPSON A PROFESSIONAL CORPORATION, *Houston—Continued*

For full biographical listings, see the Martindale-Hubbell Law Directory

*SAN ANTONIO,** Bexar Co.

TINSMAN & HOUSER, INC. (AV)

One Riverwalk Place, 14th Floor, 700 North St. Mary's Street, 78205
Telephone: 210-225-3121
Texas Wats: 1-800-292-9999
Fax: 210-225-6235

Richard Tinsman
Franklin D. Houser
Margaret M. Maisel
David G. Jayne
Robert C. Scott
Daniel J. T. Sciano
Rey Perez
Bernard Wm. Fischman
Sharon L. Cook
Christopher Pettit
Ronald J. Salazar
Sue Dodson

For full biographical listings, see the Martindale-Hubbell Law Directory

UTAH

*SALT LAKE CITY,** Salt Lake Co.

STRONG & HANNI, A PROFESSIONAL CORPORATION (AV)

Sixth Floor Boston Building, 9 Exchange Place, 84111
Telephone: 801-532-7080
Fax: 801-596-1508

Gordon R. Strong (1909-1969)
Glenn C. Hanni
Henry E. Heath
Philip R. Fishler
Roger H. Bullock
Robert A. Burton
R. Scott Williams
Dennis M. Astill (Managing Partner)
S. Baird Morgan
Stuart H. Schultz
Paul M. Belnap
Stephen J. Trayner
Joseph J. Joyce
Bradley Wm. Bowen

Robert L. Janicki
Elizabeth L. Willey
Peter H. Christensen
H. Burt Ringwood
David R. Nielson
Adam Trupp
Catherine M. Larson

Representative Clients: State Farm Mutual Automobile Insurance Co.; Standard Accident Insurance Co.; United Services Automobile Assn.; Western Casualty & Surety Co.; Government Employees Insurance Co.; Guaranty Mutual Life Co.

For full biographical listings, see the Martindale-Hubbell Law Directory

VERMONT

*RUTLAND,** Rutland Co.

DAVID L. CLEARY ASSOCIATES A PROFESSIONAL CORPORATION (AV)

110 Merchants Row, P.O. Box 6740, 05702-6740
Telephone: 802-775-8800
Telefax: 802-775-8809

David L. Cleary

Kaveh S. Shahi
George A. Holoch, Jr.
Ellen J. Abbott
Thomas P. Aicher
Karen S. Heald

For full biographical listings, see the Martindale-Hubbell Law Directory

HULL, WEBBER & REIS (AV)

(Formerly Dick, Hackel & Hull)
60 North Main Street, P.O. Box 890, 05702-0890
Telephone: 802-775-2361
Fax: 802-775-0739

Donald H. Hackel (1925-1985)
John B. Webber
Robert K. Reis
John C. Holler
Lisa L. Chalidze

ASSOCIATES

Phyllis R. McCoy
Karen Abatiell Kalter

OF COUNSEL

Richard A. Hull (P.C.)
Steven D. Vogl

Representative Clients: Aetna Insurance Co.; Great American Insurance Cos.; Deere & Co.; Arctco, Inc.

(See Next Column)

For full biographical listings, see the Martindale-Hubbell Law Directory

MILLER & FAIGNANT, A PROFESSIONAL CORPORATION (AV)

36 Merchants Row, P.O. Box 6688, 05702-6688
Telephone: 802-775-2521
Fax: 802-775-8274

Lawrence Miller
John Paul Faignant

Barbara R. Blackman
Christopher J. Whelton

LEGAL SUPPORT PERSONNEL

Cynthia L. Bonvouloir
Marie T. Fabian

Representative Clients: Travelers Insurance Co.; Government Employees Insurance Co.; Utica Mutual Insurance Co.; Universal Underwriters Insurance Co.
Reference: Travelers Insurance Co.

For full biographical listings, see the Martindale-Hubbell Law Directory

WASHINGTON

*SEATTLE,** King Co.

BETTS, PATTERSON & MINES, P.S. (AV)

800 Financial Center, 1215 Fourth Avenue, 98161-1090
Telephone: 206-292-9988
Fax: 206-343-7053

Michael Mines
William P. Fite
Livingston Wernecke
Christopher W. Tompkins
Kenneth S. McEwan
Steven Goldstein
David L. Hennings
Charles W. Davis
S. Karen Bamberger
Susan C. Hacker

OF COUNSEL

Mark M. Miller
Martin T. Collier

Samual S. Chapin
Glenn S. Draper

Representative Clients: A.O. Smith Corp.; American Medical Systems, Inc.; Chrysler Corporation; Coachman Industries, Inc.; Cooper Industries, Inc.; Crum & Forster Insurance Company; Fleetwood Enterprises, Inc.; Great Lakes Chemical Corp.; Howmedica, Inc.; Minnesota Mining and Manufacturing Company; Pfizer, Inc.

For full biographical listings, see the Martindale-Hubbell Law Directory

WEST VIRGINIA

*PRINCETON,** Mercer Co.

GIBSON & ASSOCIATES (AV)

1345 Mercer Street, 24740
Telephone: 304-425-8276
800-742-3545

MEMBER OF FIRM

Michael F. Gibson

ASSOCIATES

Derrick Ward Lefler
Bill Huffman
Kelly R. Charnock

LEGAL SUPPORT PERSONNEL

SOCIAL SECURITY PARALEGALS

Nancy Belcher

PERSONAL INJURY PARALEGALS

Kathy Richards

WORKERS COMPENSATION PARALEGAL

Carol Hylton

MEDICAL NEGLIGENCE PARALEGAL

Deborah Fye

For full biographical listings, see the Martindale-Hubbell Law Directory

SANDERS, AUSTIN, SWOPE & FLANIGAN (AV)

Hunter Park, 320 Courthouse Road, 24740
Telephone: 304-425-8125
FAX: 304-425-4155

MEMBERS OF FIRM

Hartley Sanders (1879-1952)
Lane O. Austin
Derek C. Swope
William H. Sanders, III
William B. Flanigan
Gregory S. Prudich

(See Next Column)

SANDERS, AUSTIN, SWOPE & FLANIGAN—*Continued*

ASSOCIATES

S. Paige Burress
Omar J. Aboulhosn

OF COUNSEL

William H. Sanders, II

References: First Community Bank-Princeton; One Valley Bank-Princeton.

For full biographical listings, see the Martindale-Hubbell Law Directory

WISCONSIN

*MILWAUKEE,** Milwaukee Co.

QUARLES & BRADY (AV)

411 East Wisconsin Avenue, 53202-4497
Telephone: 414-277-5000
Cable Address: "Lawdock"
Fax: 414-271-3552.
TWX: 910-262-3426
Madison, Wisconsin Office: Firstar Plaza, One South Pinckney Street, P.O. Box 2113.
Telephone: 608-251-5000.
Fax: 608-251-9166.
West Palm Beach, Florida Office: 222 Lakeview Avenue, 4th Floor.
Telephone: 407-653-5000.
Fax: 407-653-5333.
Naples, Florida Office: Barnett Center, 4501 Tamiami Trail North.
Telephone: 813-262-5959.
Fax: 813-434-4999.
Phoenix, Arizona Office: One Camelback Building, One East Camelback Road, Suite 400.
Telephone: 602-230-5500.
Fax: 602-230-5598.

MEMBERS OF FIRM
(ALPHABETICALLY BY YEAR OF ADMISSION TO BAR)

Michael L. Zaleski (Resident, Madison Office)
Frank J. Daily
Patrick W. Schmidt
Eric J. Van Vugt
John A. Rothstein
David B. Bartel
Nancy Meissner Kennedy
Michael J. Gonring
Mark A. Kircher

ASSOCIATES

Francis H. LoCoco
Margaret C. Kelsey
Mitchell S. Moser

For Complete List of Firm Personnel, See General Section

For full biographical listings, see the Martindale-Hubbell Law Directory

CANADA
BRITISH COLUMBIA

*VANCOUVER,** Vancouver Co.

CAMP CHURCH & ASSOCIATES (AV)

4th Floor, The Randall Building, 555 West Georgia Street, V6B 1Z5
Telephone: 604-689-7555
Fax: 604-689-7554

MEMBERS OF FIRM

J.J. Camp, Q.C.
David P. Church

Giuseppe (Joe) Fiorante
Andrew J. Pearson
Sharon D. Matthews

For full biographical listings, see the Martindale-Hubbell Law Directory

CANADA
ONTARIO

KITCHENER, Regional Munic. of Waterloo

GIFFEN, LEE, WAGNER, MORLEY & GARBUTT (AV)

50 Queen Street North, P.O. Box 2396, N2H 6M3
Telephone: 519-578-4150
Fax: 519-578-8740

MEMBERS OF FIRM

Jeffrey J. Mansfield (1955-1991)
J. Peter Giffen, Q.C.
Bruce L. Lee
J. Scott Morley
Brian R. Wagner
Philip A. Garbutt

ASSOCIATES

Edward J. Vanderkloet
Keith C. Masterman
Daniel J. Fife
Jeffrey W. Boich

For full biographical listings, see the Martindale-Hubbell Law Directory

CANADA
SASKATCHEWAN

*REGINA,** Regina Jud. Centre

McDOUGALL, READY (AV)

700 Royal Bank Building, 2010-11th Avenue, S4P 0J3
Telephone: 306-757-1641
Telecopier: 306-359-0785
Saskatoon, Saskatchewan, Canada Office: 301 - 111 2nd Avenue South.
Telephone: 306-653-1641.
Telecopier: 306-665-8511.

MEMBERS OF FIRM

Gordon J. Kuski, Q.C.
Kenneth A. Ready
Aaron A. Fox
Brian M. Banilevic
Pamela J. Lothian
Walter J. Matkowski (Resident, Saskatoon Office)
Susan B. Barber

Kevin A. Lang
Brent D. Barilla (Resident, Saskatoon Office)

Representative Clients: Ford Motor Co. of Canada; Chrysler Canada Ltd.; General Motors of Canada.

For Complete List of Firm Personnel, See General Section

For full biographical listings, see the Martindale-Hubbell Law Directory

PUBLIC UTILITIES LAW

ALABAMA

*MONTGOMERY,** Montgomery Co.

Parker, Brantley & Wilkerson, P.C. (AV)
323 Adams Avenue, P.O. Box 4992, 36103-4992
Telephone: 334-265-1500
Fax: 334-265-0319

Edward B. Parker, II
Mark D. Wilkerson
Paul A. Brantley
Leah Snell Stephens
Darla T. Furman

Representative Clients: Federated Rural Electric Insurance Corp.; Alabama Emergency Room Administrative Services, P.C.
Reference: SouthTrust Bank, N.A.

For full biographical listings, see the Martindale-Hubbell Law Directory

ARIZONA

*PHOENIX,** Maricopa Co.

Brown & Bain, A Professional Association (AV)
2901 North Central Avenue, P.O. Box 400, 85001-0400
Telephone: 602-351-8000
Cable: TWX 910-951-0646
Telecopier: 602-351-8516
Palo Alto, California Affiliated Office: Brown & Bain, 600 Hansen Way.
Telephone: 415-856-9411.
Telecopier: 415-856-6061.
Tucson, Arizona Affiliated Office: Brown & Bain, A Professional Association. One South Church Avenue, Nineteenth Floor, P.O. Box 2265.
Telephone: 602-798-7900
Telecopier: 602-798-7945.

Philip R. Higdon (Resident at Tucson Office)
Stephen E. Lee
Joseph E. Mais
Cynthia Y. McCoy
Michael F. McNulty (Resident at Tucson Office)
Joseph W. Mott
Joel W. Nomkin
Michael W. Patten
Lex J. Smith
Scott M. Theobald
Charles Van Cott
George C. Wallach

N. Todd Leishman
Daniel G. Martin

For Complete List of Firm Personnel, See General Section

For full biographical listings, see the Martindale-Hubbell Law Directory

COLORADO

*DENVER,** Denver Co.

Holme Roberts & Owen LLC (AV)
Suite 4100, 1700 Lincoln, 80203
Telephone: 303-861-7000
Telex: 45-4460
Telecopier: 303-866-0200
Boulder, Colorado Office: Suite 400, 1401 Pearl Street.
Telephone: 303-444-5955.
Telecopier: 303-444-1063.
Colorado Springs, Colorado Office: Suite 1300, 90 South Cascade Avenue.
Telephone: 719-473-3800.
Telecopier: 719-633-1518.
Salt Lake City, Utah Office: Suite 1100, 111 East Broadway.
Telephone: 801-521-5800.
Telecopier: 801-521-9639.
London, England Office: 4th Floor, Mellier House, 26a Albemarle Street.
Telephone: 44-171-499-8776.
Telecopier: 44-171-499-7769.
Moscow, Russia Office: 14 Krivokolenny Pr., Suite 30, 101000.
Telephone: 095-925-7816.
Telecopier: 095-923-2726.

(See Next Column)

MEMBERS OF FIRM

Raymond L. Petros
Richard A. Johnson (Boulder Office)

SPECIAL COUNSEL

Thomas F. Dixon

ASSOCIATE

Steven J. Bushong (Boulder Office)

For Complete List of Firm Personnel, See General Section

For full biographical listings, see the Martindale-Hubbell Law Directory

White and Steele, Professional Corporation (AV)
1225 17th Street, Suite 2800, 80202
Telephone: 303-296-2828
Telecopier: 303-296-3131
Cheyenne, Wyoming Office: 1912 Capital Avenue, Suite 404, 82003.
Telephone: 307-778-4160.

Michael W. Anderson
Kurt A. Horton
John M. Palmeri
Robert R. Carlson

OF COUNSEL

Fred L. Witsell

Colorado Tort Counsel for: Goodyear Tire and Rubber Co.; The Dow Chemical Co.; Celotex.
Insurance Clients: Allied Insurance Co.; CNA; Kemper Insurance Group; Massachusetts Mutual Life Insurance Co.; U.S.A.A.; Underwriters at Lloyds; Farmers Insurance Group.

For Complete List of Firm Personnel, See General Section

For full biographical listings, see the Martindale-Hubbell Law Directory

DISTRICT OF COLUMBIA

WASHINGTON, D.C. Co.

Brickfield, Burchette & Ritts, P.C. (AV)
8th Floor, West Tower, 1025 Thomas Jefferson Street, N.W., 20007-0805
Telephone: 202-342-0800
Fax: 202-342-0807
Austin, Texas Office: Suite 1050, 1005 Congress Avenue.
Telephone: 512-472-1081.

Peter J. P. Brickfield
William H. Burchette
Mark C. Davis (Not admitted in DC; Resident, Austin, Texas Office)
Daniel C. Kaufman
Michael E. Kaufmann
Peter J. Mattheis
Michael N. McCarty
Frederick H. Ritts
Fernando Rodriguez (Not admitted in DC; Resident, Austin, Texas Office)
Christine C. Ryan
Garrett A. Stone

COUNSEL

Philip L. Chabot, Jr.
Foster De Reitzes
Robert L. McCarty
A. Hewitt Rose

Lisa A. Cottle (Not admitted in DC)
Vincent P. Duane
Julie B. Greenisen (Not admitted in DC)
Stephen J. Karina (Not admitted in DC)
Sandra E. Rizzo
Sonnet C. Schmidt (Not admitted in DC)

LEGAL SUPPORT PERSONNEL

Jean Levicki

For full biographical listings, see the Martindale-Hubbell Law Directory

Bruder, Gentile & Marcoux (AV)
1100 New York Avenue, N.W., Suite 510 East, 20005-3934
Telephone: 202-783-1350
Telecopiers: 202-737-9117; 347-2644

MEMBERS OF FIRM

George F. Bruder
Carmen L. Gentile
Albert R. Simonds, Jr.
J. Michel Marcoux
David E. Goroff
Gary E. Guy
James H. McGrew
Thomas L. Blackburn
Arlene Pianko Groner

For full biographical listings, see the Martindale-Hubbell Law Directory

Travis & Gooch (AV)
Suite 301, 1275 Pennsylvania Avenue, N.W., 20004
Telephone: 202-508-9000
Fax: 202-508-9033
Houston, Texas Office: Suite 1270, 800 Gessner, 77024.
Telephone: 713-973-6377.
Fax: 713-973-6379.

(See Next Column)

TRAVIS & GOOCH, *Washington—Continued*

MEMBERS OF FIRM

R. Gordon Gooch
Edmunds Travis, Jr. (Not admitted in DC; Resident, Houston, Texas Office)
Jon L. Brunenkant
Katherine B. Edwards
Mark R. Haskell
Dena Eve Wiggins

ASSOCIATE

Glenn Benson (Not admitted in DC)

For full biographical listings, see the Martindale-Hubbell Law Directory

FLORIDA

*TALLAHASSEE,** Leon Co.

COLLINS & TRUETT, P.A. (AV)

2804 Remington Green Circle, Suite 4, Post Office Drawer 12429, 32317-2429
Telephone: 904-386-6060
Telecopier: 904-385-8220

Richard B. Collins
Gary A. Shipman

Brett Q. Lucas (Resident)
Dawn D. Caloca
Joseph E. Brooks
C. Timothy Gray
Rogelio Fontela
Charles N. Cleland, Jr.
Clifford W. Rainey

OF COUNSEL

Edgar C. Booth
James A. Dixon, Jr.

Representative Clients: Agency Rent-A-Car; Agricultural Excess and Surplus Insurance Co.; AIG Life Insurance Co.; Alliance Insurance Group; Allstate Insurance Co.; American Empire Surplus Lines Insurance Co.; American International Underwriters Inc.; Atlanta Casualty Insurance Co.; Avis Rent-A-Car; Bankers and Shippers Insurance Co.

For full biographical listings, see the Martindale-Hubbell Law Directory

GATLIN, WOODS, CARLSON & COWDERY (AV)

A Partnership including a Professional Corporation
The Mahan Station, 1709-D Mahan Drive, 32308
Telephone: 904-877-7191
Telecopier: 904-877-9031

MEMBERS OF FIRM

B. Kenneth Gatlin (P.A.)
Thomas F. Woods
John D. Carlson
Kathryn G. W. Cowdery

ASSOCIATE

Wayne L. Schiefelbein

For full biographical listings, see the Martindale-Hubbell Law Directory

ROSE, SUNDSTROM & BENTLEY (AV)

A Partnership including Professional Associations
2548 Blairstone Pines Drive, P.O. Box 1567, 32302-1567
Telephone: 904-877-6555
Telecopier: 904-656-4029

MEMBERS OF FIRM

Chris H. Bentley (P.A.)
F. Marshall Deterding
Martin S. Friedman (P.A.)
John R. Jenkins
Robert M. C. Rose (P.A.)
William E. Sundstrom (P.A.)
John L. Wharton

Representative Clients: Aloha Utilities, Inc.; East Central Florida Services, Inc.; Hydratech Utilities, Inc.; Orange-Osceola Utilities, Inc.; North Fort Myers Utility, Inc.; Utility Board of the City of Key West; Rotonda West Utilities Corp.; Jax Utilities Management, Inc.

For full biographical listings, see the Martindale-Hubbell Law Directory

GEORGIA

*ATLANTA,** Fulton Co.

LONG ALDRIDGE & NORMAN (AV)

A Partnership including Professional Corporations
One Peachtree Center, Suite 5300, 303 Peachtree Street, 30308
Telephone: 404-527-4000
Telecopier: 404-527-4198
Washington, D.C. Office: Suite 950, 1615 L Street, 20036.
Telephone: 202-223-7033.
Telecopier: 202-223-7013.

(See Next Column)

MEMBERS OF FIRM

Douglas L. Beresford (Resident, Washington, D.C. Office)
Gordon D. Giffin
John E. Holtzinger, Jr. (Resident, Washington, D.C. Office)
Albert G. Norman, Jr.
Jacolyn A. Simmons (Resident, Washington, D.C. Office)
John T. Stough, Jr. (Resident, Washington, D.C. Office)
Robert I. White (Resident, Washington, D.C. Office)

ASSOCIATES

L. Craig Dowdy
Kevin M. Downey (Resident, Washington, D.C. Office)
Kyle Michel (Resident, Washington, D.C. Office)
Joel D. Newton (Resident, Washington, D.C. Office)

OF COUNSEL

Nancy A. White (Resident, Washington, D.C. Office)

For Complete List of Firm Personnel, See General Section

For full biographical listings, see the Martindale-Hubbell Law Directory

*CARROLLTON,** Carroll Co.

TISINGER, TISINGER, VANCE & GREER, A PROFESSIONAL CORPORATION (AV)

100 Wagon Yard Plaza, P.O. Box 2069, 30117
Telephone: 404-834-4467
FAX: 404-834-5426

Richard G. Tisinger
C. David Mecklin, Jr.
Steven T. Minor

Representative Clients: Carroll Electric Membership Corporation; Excelsior Electric Membership Corporation; Georgia Electric Membership Corporation; Oglethorpe Power Corporation.

For Complete List of Firm Personnel, See General Section

For full biographical listings, see the Martindale-Hubbell Law Directory

IDAHO

*POCATELLO,** Bannock Co.

MERRILL & MERRILL, CHARTERED (AV)

Key Bank Building, P.O. Box 991, 83204
Telephone: 208-232-2286
Fax: 208-232-2499

Wesley F. Merrill
Stephen S. Dunn

Representative Client: Utah Power & Light Co. (PacifiCorp).

For Complete List of Firm Personnel, See General Section

For full biographical listings, see the Martindale-Hubbell Law Directory

ILLINOIS

*CHICAGO,** Cook Co.

SAUNDERS & MONROE (AV)

Suite 4201, 205 North Michigan Avenue, 60601
Telephone: 312-946-9000
Facsimile: 312-946-0528

MEMBERS OF FIRM

George L. Saunders, Jr.
Lee A. Monroe
Thomas F. Bush, Jr.
Matthew E. Van Tine

Thomas A. Doyle
Christina J. Norton
Gwen A. Niedbalski

For full biographical listings, see the Martindale-Hubbell Law Directory

INDIANA

*INDIANAPOLIS,** Marion Co.

BOSE MCKINNEY & EVANS (AV)

2700 First Indiana Plaza, 135 North Pennsylvania Street, 46204
Telephone: 317-684-5000
Facsimile: 317-684-5173
Indianapolis North Office: Suite 1201, 8888 Keystone Crossing, 46240.
Telephone: 317-574-3700.
Facsimile: 317-574-3716.

(See Next Column)

BOSE MCKINNEY & EVANS—*Continued*

MEMBER OF FIRM

L. Parvin Price

ASSOCIATE

Robert K. Johnson

OF COUNSEL

Peter Lynn Goerges

Representative Clients: Community Natural Gas Co.; German Township Water District; Gibson County Solid Waste DIstrict; Midwest Natural Gas Co.; Smith Cogeneration of Indiana.

For Complete List of Firm Personnel, See General Section

For full biographical listings, see the Martindale-Hubbell Law Directory

KENTUCKY

*LOUISVILLE,** Jefferson Co.

OGDEN NEWELL & WELCH (AV)

1200 One Riverfront Plaza, 40202-2973
Telephone: 502-582-1601
Fax: 502-581-9564

MEMBERS OF FIRM

Richard F. Newell
Walter Lapp Sales
Kendrick R. Riggs

ASSOCIATES

John Wade Hendricks
James G. Campbell
Allyson K. Sturgeon

Counsel for: KU Energy Corp.; Kentucky Utilities Co.; Virginia Electric and Power Company; Indiana Municipal Power Agency; Illinois Municipal Electric Agency; West Oldham Utilities Company; Electric Energy Inc.

For Complete List of Firm Personnel, See General Section

For full biographical listings, see the Martindale-Hubbell Law Directory

LOUISIANA

*BATON ROUGE,** East Baton Rouge Parish

KEAN, MILLER, HAWTHORNE, D'ARMOND, MCCOWAN & JARMAN, L.L.P. (AV)

22nd Floor, One American Place, P.O. Box 3513, 70821
Telephone: 504-387-0999
Fax: 504-388-9133
New Orleans, Louisiana Office: Energy Centre, Suite 1470, 1100 Poydras Street.
Telephone: 504-585-3050.
Fax: 504-585-3051.

MEMBERS OF FIRM

G. William Jarman
Katherine W. King

James Randy Young

Representative Clients: MCI Telecommunications Corporation, Washington, D.C.; Louisiana Energy Users Group.

For Complete List of Firm Personnel, See General Section

For full biographical listings, see the Martindale-Hubbell Law Directory

*LAFAYETTE,** Lafayette Parish

ROY, BIVINS, JUDICE & HENKE, A PROFESSIONAL LAW CORPORATION (AV)

600 Jefferson Street, Suite 800, P.O. Drawer Z, 70502
Telephone: 318-233-7430
Telecopier: 318-233-8403
Telex: 9102505130

Ronald J. Judice

Representative Clients: Employers Insurance of Wausau; Louisiana Medical Mutual Ins. Co.; C.N.A.; Aetna Casualty & Surety; Zurich Ins. Co.; Our Lady of Lourdes Regional Medical Center, Inc.; St Paul Fire & Marine Ins. Co.; First Financial Insurance Company.

For Complete List of Firm Personnel, See General Section

For full biographical listings, see the Martindale-Hubbell Law Directory

*SHREVEPORT,** Caddo Parish

BARLOW AND HARDTNER L.C. (AV)

Tenth Floor, Louisiana Tower, 401 Edwards Street, 71101-3289
Telephone: 318-227-1131
Telecopier: 318-227-1141
Mailing Address: P.O. Box 8, Shreveport, Louisiana, 71161-0008

Ray A. Barlow
Malcolm S. Murchison
David R. Taggart
Clair F. White
Philip E. Downer, III
Michael B. Donald

Representative Clients: Central Louisiana Electric Co., Inc.; Central and South West; Louisiana Intrastate Gas Corp.; NorAm Energy Corp. (formerly Arkla, Inc.); NorAm Gas Transmission Company; Southwestern Electric Power Company; Kelley Oil Corporation; Panhandle Eastern Corp.; Pennzoil Producing Co.; Johnson Controls, Inc.

For Complete List of Firm Personnel, See General Section

For full biographical listings, see the Martindale-Hubbell Law Directory

WILKINSON, CARMODY & GILLIAM (AV)

1700 Beck Building, 400 Travis Street, P.O. Box 1707, 71166
Telephone: 318-221-4196
Telecopier: 318-221-3705

MEMBERS OF FIRM

John D. Wilkinson (1867-1929)
William Scott Wilkinson (1895-1985)
Arthur R. Carmody, Jr.
Bobby S. Gilliam
Mark E. Gilliam
Penny D. Sellers
Brian D. Landry

Representative Clients: Farmers Insurance Group; Home Federal Savings & Loan Association of Shreveport; The Kansas City Southern Railway Co.; KTAL-TV; Lincoln National Life Insurance Co.; Mobil Oil Co.; Schumpert Medical Center; Sears, Roebuck & Co.; Southern Pacific Transportation Co.; Southwestern Electric Power Co.

For full biographical listings, see the Martindale-Hubbell Law Directory

MAINE

*BATH,** Sagadahoc Co.

CONLEY, HALEY & O'NEIL (AV)

Thirty Front Street, 04530
Telephone: 207-443-5576
Telefax: 207-443-6665

Mark L. Haley

Representative Clients: Bath Iron Works Corporation; Central Maine Power Company; Saco Defense, Inc.; Sugarloaf Mountain Corporation.
References: Casco Northern Bank, N.A.; First Federal Savings & Loan Association of Bath; Shawmut Bank.

For Complete List of Firm Personnel, See General Section

For full biographical listings, see the Martindale-Hubbell Law Directory

*PORTLAND,** Cumberland Co.

PIERCE, ATWOOD, SCRIBNER, ALLEN, SMITH & LANCASTER (AV)

One Monument Square, 04101
Telephone: 207-773-6411
Fax: 207-773-3419
Augusta, Maine Office: 77 Winthrop Street.
Telephone: 207-622-6311.
Camden, Maine Office: 36 Chestnut Street, P.O. Box 780.
Telephone: 207-236-4333.

MEMBERS OF FIRM

Gerald M. Amero
John W. Gulliver
Kevin F. Gordon

ASSOCIATE

David Allen Brenningmeyer

For Complete List of Firm Personnel, See General Section

For full biographical listings, see the Martindale-Hubbell Law Directory

MASSACHUSETTS

*BOSTON,** Suffolk Co.

RICH, MAY, BILODEAU & FLAHERTY, P.C. (AV)

The Old South Building, 294 Washington Street, 02108-4675
Telephone: 617-482-1360
FAX: 617-556-3889

John F. Rich (1908-1987)
Thomas H. Bilodeau (1915-1987)
Gerald May
Harold B. Dondis
Walter L. Landergan, Jr.
Edwin J. Carr
Arthur F. Flaherty
Franklin M. Hundley
Michael F. Donlan
Joseph F. Sullivan, Jr.
Owen P. Maher
Nicolas A. Kensington
Daniel T. Clark
Gerald V. May, Jr.
Eric J. Krathwohl
Michael J. McHugh
James M. Behnke
James M. Avery
Stephen M. Kane
Mark C. O'Connor
Walter A. Wright, III
Emmett E. Lyne

Nicholas F. Kourtis
James T. Finnigan
Carol E. Kazmer
Robert P. Snell

For full biographical listings, see the Martindale-Hubbell Law Directory

MISSOURI

KANSAS CITY, Jackson, Clay & Platte Cos.

SPRADLEY & RIESMEYER, A PROFESSIONAL CORPORATION (AV)

Boatmen's Center Suite 1900, 920 Main Street, 64105
Telephone: 816-474-6006
Telecopier: 816-474-1803

Ronald C. Spradley
Frederick H. Riesmeyer, II
Douglas D. Silvius

J. Dale Youngs
Derron D. Gunderman

OF COUNSEL

Robert M. Landman

LEGAL SUPPORT PERSONNEL

SENIOR LEGAL ASSISTANTS

Staci Holcom
Keenan J. Barker

For full biographical listings, see the Martindale-Hubbell Law Directory

MONTANA

*BILLINGS,** Yellowstone Co.

CROWLEY, HAUGHEY, HANSON, TOOLE & DIETRICH (AV)

500 Transwestern II, 490 North 31st Street, P.O. Box 2529, 59103
Telephone: 406-252-3441
Fax: 406-259-4159
Helena, Montana Office: IBM Building, 100 North Park Avenue, Suite 300, 59601.
Telephone: 406-449-4165.
Fax: 406-449-5149.

OF COUNSEL

Bruce R. Toole

MEMBERS OF FIRM

Louis R. Moore
Carolyn S. Ostby
Michael E. Webster
Jon T. Dyre

Representative Clients: Montana Power Co.; First Interstate Bank of Commerce; MDU Resources Group, Inc.; Chevron U.S.A., Inc.; Noranda Minerals Corp.; United Parcel Service.
Insurance Clients: Farmers Insurance Group; New York Life Insurance Co.

For Complete List of Firm Personnel, See General Section

For full biographical listings, see the Martindale-Hubbell Law Directory

NEW HAMPSHIRE

*CONCORD,** Merrimack Co.

RATH, YOUNG, PIGNATELLI AND OYER, P.A. (AV)

Two Capital Plaza, P.O. Box 854, 03302-0854
Telephone: 603-226-2600
Telecopier: 603-226-2700; 228-2294
Nashua, New Hampshire Office: The Glass Tower, 20 Trafalgar Square.
Telephone: 603-889-9952.
Telecopier: 603-595-7489.

Thomas D. Rath
Sherilyn Burnett Young
Michael A. Pignatelli
Eve H. Oyer
Ann McLane Kuster
David M. Howe
William F. J. Ardinger
M. Curtis Whittaker
Andrew W. Serell
Brian T. Tucker
Constance P. Powers
Andrew J. Harmon
Charles George Willing, Jr.
Diane Murphy Quinlan
Elise S. Feldman
Ian D. Hecker

LEGAL SUPPORT PERSONNEL

Eugene A. Savage
Lindsey Dalton

For full biographical listings, see the Martindale-Hubbell Law Directory

NEW JERSEY

CHERRY HILL, Camden Co.

DAVIS, REBERKENNY & ABRAMOWITZ, A PROFESSIONAL CORPORATION (AV)

(Formerly Starr, Summerill & Davis and Hyland, Davis & Reberkenny, P.A. and Davis & Reberkenny, A Professional Corporation)
499 Cooper Landing Road, P.O. Box 5459, 08002
Telephone: 609-667-6000
Telecopier: 609-667-7434

Edward A. Kondracki
Ira G. Megdal
William D. Lavery, Jr.
David R. Oberlander

OF COUNSEL

William C. Davis

For full biographical listings, see the Martindale-Hubbell Law Directory

ELMWOOD PARK, Bergen Co.

ANDORA, PALMISANO & GEANEY, A PROFESSIONAL CORPORATION (AV)

303 Molnar Drive, P.O. Box 431, 07407-0431
Telephone: 201-791-0100
Fax: 201-791-8922

Anthony D. Andora
John P. Palmisano
John F. Geaney, Jr.
Vincent A. Siano
Joseph M. Andresini
Patrick J. Spina
Melissa A. Muilenburg
Joseph A. Venti

Representative Client: Hackensack Water Co.

For full biographical listings, see the Martindale-Hubbell Law Directory

NEW MEXICO

*ALBUQUERQUE,** Bernalillo Co.

RODEY, DICKASON, SLOAN, AKIN & ROBB, P.A. (AV)

Albuquerque Plaza, Suite 2200, 201 Third Street, N.W., P.O. Box 1888, 87103-1888
Telephone: 505-765-5900
Fax: 505-768-7395
Santa Fe, New Mexico Office: Suite 101 Marcy Plaza, 123 East Marcy Street, P.O. Box 1357, 87504-1357.
Telephone: 505-984-0100.
Fax: 505-989-9542.

John D. Robb
Mark K. Adams

For Complete List of Firm Personnel, See General Section

For full biographical listings, see the Martindale-Hubbell Law Directory

NEW YORK

*NEW YORK,** New York Co.

SEHAM SEHAM MELTZ & PETERSEN (AV)

380 Madison Avenue, Suite 17, 10017-2513
Telephone: 212-557-9577

Martin C. Seham Scott C. Petersen

For full biographical listings, see the Martindale-Hubbell Law Directory

OHIO

*CINCINNATI,** Hamilton Co.

BOEHM, KURTZ & LOWRY (AV)

Suite 2110, 36 East Seventh Street, 45202
Telephone: 513-421-2255
Telecopier: 513-421-2764

MEMBERS OF FIRM

David F. Boehm Michael L. Kurtz
John P. Lowry

For full biographical listings, see the Martindale-Hubbell Law Directory

KEPLEY, MACCONNELL & EYRICH A LEGAL PROFESSIONAL ASSOCIATION (AV)

Formerly Clark & Eyrich
2200 Ameritrust Center, 525 Vine Street, 45202
Telephone: 513-241-5540; 621-1045
FAX: 513-241-8111; 621-0038

F. Bruce Abel James J. Ryan

Representative Clients and References furnished upon request.

For full biographical listings, see the Martindale-Hubbell Law Directory

WAITE, SCHNEIDER, BAYLESS & CHESLEY CO., L.P.A. (AV)

1513 Central Trust Tower, Fourth and Vine Streets, 45202
Telephone: 513-621-0267
Fax: 513-381-2375; 621-0262

Stanley M. Chesley

Thomas F. Rehme
Fay E. Stilz
Louise M. Roselle
Dwight Tillery
D. Arthur Rabourn
Jerome L. Skinner
Janet G. Abaray
Paul M. De Marco
Terrence L. Goodman
Sherrill P. Hondorf
Colleen M. Hegge
Dianna Pendleton
Randy F. Fox
Glenn D. Feagan
Theresa L. Groh
Theodore N. Berry
Jane H. Walker
Renée Infante
Allen P. Grunes

OF COUNSEL

Jos. E. Rosen James F. Keller

For full biographical listings, see the Martindale-Hubbell Law Directory

OKLAHOMA

*OKLAHOMA CITY,** Oklahoma Co.

RAINEY, ROSS, RICE & BINNS (AV)

735 First National Center West, 73102-7405
Telephone: 405-235-1356
Telecopier: 405-235-2340

MEMBERS OF FIRM

Hugh D. Rice
H. D. Binns, Jr.
Rodney L. Cook
Roberta Browning Fields

General Attorneys for Oklahoma: Santa Fe Pacific Corp.; Santa Fe Railway System.
Oklahoma Counsel for: Oklahoma Gas & Electric Co.
Attorneys for: Agristor Credit Corp.; AT&T Communications; Boatmen's First National Bank of Oklahoma; The Circle K Corp.; Continental Air Lines; Dover Elevator Co.; Dover Industries Acceptance, Inc.

For Complete List of Firm Personnel, See General Section

For full biographical listings, see the Martindale-Hubbell Law Directory

PENNSYLVANIA

*PHILADELPHIA,** Philadelphia Co.

LOUIS J. CARTER (AV)

7300 City Line Avenue, 19151-2291
Telephone: 215-879-8665
FAX: 215- 877-0955

For full biographical listings, see the Martindale-Hubbell Law Directory

MCALLISTER & GALLAGHER, P.C. (AV)

Suite 1100, 1760 Market Street, 19103
Telephone: 215-963-1555
Fax: 215-963-9104

John M. McAllister John J. Gallagher

Michael S. Henry Laura L. Carberry
Elizabeth McHugh

For full biographical listings, see the Martindale-Hubbell Law Directory

DAVID V. STIVISON (AV)

870 North 30th Street, 19130-1104
Telephone: 215-763-2809

Representative Clients: Weatherline, Inc., St. Louis, Missouri; Philadelphia Suburban Water Co., Bryn Mawr, Pennsylvania.

For full biographical listings, see the Martindale-Hubbell Law Directory

*READING,** Berks Co.

RYAN, RUSSELL, OGDEN & SELTZER (AV)

1100 Berkshire Boulevard, P.O. Box 6219, 19610-0219
Telephone: 610-372-4761
Fax: 610-372-4177

Samuel B. Russell Alan Michael Seltzer
W. Edwin Ogden Harold J. Ryan (1896-1972)
John S. McConaghy (1907-1981)

ASSOCIATES

Jeffrey A. Franklin Janet E. Arnold

For full biographical listings, see the Martindale-Hubbell Law Directory

SOUTH CAROLINA

*CHARLESTON,** Charleston Co.

HAYNSWORTH, MARION, MCKAY & GUÉRARD, L.L.P (AV)

#2 Prioleau Street, P.O. Box 1119, 29402
Telephone: 803-722-7606
Telecopier: 803-723-5263
Columbia, South Carolina Office: Suite 2400 AT&T Building, 1201 Main Street, P.O. Drawer 7157, 29202.
Telephone: 803-765-1818.
Telecopier: 803-765-2399.
Greenville, South Carolina Office: Two Insignia Financial Plaza, 75 Beattie Place, P.O. Box 2048, 29602.
Telephone: 803-240-3200.
Telecopier: 803-240-3300.

MEMBER OF FIRM

J. Paul Trouche

Counsel for: Westinghouse Savannah River Project; South Carolina Public Service Authority; Duke Power Company; Santee Cooper Electric Cooperative.

For Complete List of Firm Personnel, See General Section

For full biographical listings, see the Martindale-Hubbell Law Directory

*COLUMBIA,** Richland Co.

* indicates certain Bar Register subscribers whose principal office is located elsewhere in the state and who have arranged for representation as a part of the state capital listings that follow

*** HAYNSWORTH, MARION, MCKAY & GUÉRARD, L.L.P.** (AV)

Suite 2400 A T & T Building, 1201 Main Street, P.O. Drawer 7157, 29202
Telephone: 803-765-1818
Telecopier: 803-765-2399
Greenville, South Carolina Office: Two Insignia Financial Plaza, 75 Beattie Place, P.O. Box 2048, 29602.
Telephone: 803-240-3200.
Telecopier: 803-240-3300.
Charleston, South Carolina Office: #2 Prioleau Street, P.O. Box 1119, 29402.
Telephone: 803-722-7606.
Telecopier: 803-723-5263.

MEMBERS OF FIRM

William P. Simpson
Samuel W. Howell, IV
Gary W. Morris

ASSOCIATE

Edward G. Kluiters

Counsel for: Duke Power Co.; South Carolina Jobs - Economic Development Authority; The State of South Carolina; Business Development Corp. of South Carolina; Santee Cooper Electric Cooperative; Cooper River Park and Playground Commission; John Deer Industrial Development, Inc.; School District of Richland County.

For Complete List of Firm Personnel, See General Section

For full biographical listings, see the Martindale-Hubbell Law Directory

*GREENVILLE,** Greenville Co.

HAYNSWORTH, MARION, MCKAY & GUÉRARD, L.L.P. (AV)

Two Insignia Financial Plaza, 75 Beattie Place, P.O. Box 2048, 29602
Telephone: 803-240-3200
Telecopier: 803-240-3300
Columbia, South Carolina Office: Suite 2400 A T & T Building, 1201 Main Street, P.O. Drawer 7157, 29202
Telephone: 803-765-1818.
Telecopier: 803-765-2399.
Charleston, South Carolina Office: #2 Prioleau Street, P.O. Box 1119, 29402.
Telephone: 803-722-7606.
Telecopier: 803-723-5263.

MEMBER OF FIRM

Donald L. Ferguson

Counsel for: Duke Power Co.; Liberty Mutual Insurance Co.; Equitable Life Assurance Society of the United States; St. Paul Insurance Group; Allstate Insurance Co.; Fluor-Daniel Corp.; Snyalloy Corporation; Greenville Hospital System.

For Complete List of Firm Personnel, See General Section

For full biographical listings, see the Martindale-Hubbell Law Directory

TENNESSEE

*KNOXVILLE,** Knox Co.

WAGNER, MYERS & SANGER, A PROFESSIONAL CORPORATION (AV)

1801 Plaza Tower, P.O. Box 1308, 37929
Telephone: 615-525-4600
Fax: 615-524-5731

Sam F. Fowler, Jr.
Herbert S. Sanger, Jr.
John R. Seymour
Charles W. Van Beke
Charles A. Wagner III
William C. Myers, Jr.
M. Douglas Campbell, Jr.

Joseph N. Clarke, Jr.
Ronald D. Garland
Robert E. Hyde
Barbara D. Boulton

Representative Clients: Carolina Power & Light Co.; Cullman Electric Cooperative; Diversified Energy, Inc.; Fort Sanders Health Systems; Gatliff Coal Company; Martin Marietta Energy Systems, Inc.; NorthAmerican Rayon Corp.; Regal Cinemas, Inc.; Roddy Vending; Skyline Coal Company.

For full biographical listings, see the Martindale-Hubbell Law Directory

TEXAS

*AMARILLO,** Potter Co.

HINKLE, COX, EATON, COFFIELD & HENSLEY (AV)

1700 Bank One Center, P.O. Box 9238, 79105-9238
Telephone: 806-372-5569
FAX: 806-372-9761
Roswell, New Mexico Office: 700 United Bank Plaza, P. O. Box 10, 88202.
Telephone: 505-622-6510.
FAX: 505-623-9332.
Midland, Texas Office: 6 Desta Drive, Suite 2800, P.O. Box 3580, 79702.
Telephone: 915-683-4691.
FAX: 915-683-6518.
Santa Fe, New Mexico Office: 218 Montezuma, P.O. Box 2068, 87504.
Telephone: 505-982-4554.
FAX: 505-982-8623.
Albuquerque, New Mexico Office: Suite 800, 500 Marquette, N.W., P.O. Box 2043, 87102.
Telephone: 505-768-1500.
FAX: 505-768-1529.
Austin, Texas Office: 401 West 15th Street, Suite 800, 78701.
Telephone: 512-476-7137.
FAX: 512-476-5431.
Associated Office: Hoffman & Stephens, P.C., 401 West 15th Street, Suite 800, 78701.
Telephone: 512-476-5434. Fax; 512-476-5431.

RESIDENT PARTNERS

Paul W. Eaton
Richard R. Wilfong
Jerry F. Shackelford
Jeffrey W. Hellberg

Representative Clients: Aerion Industries, Inc.; Amarillo Diagnostic Clinic; Amarillo Federal Credit Union; Amarillo Health Facilities Corp.; Amarillo National Bank; Chrysler Management Corp.; Conoco, Inc.; Federated Insurance; First Interstate Management Co.; Flowers Cattle Co.; Southwestern Public Service Co.

For full biographical listings, see the Martindale-Hubbell Law Directory

*EL PASO,** El Paso Co.

DIAMOND RASH GORDON & JACKSON, P.C. (AV)

300 East Main Drive, 7th Floor, 79901
Telephone: 915-533-2277
Fax: 915-545-4623

Tom Diamond
Alan V. Rash
Norman J. Gordon
Ronald L. Jackson
John R. Batoon
Robert J. Truhill

Russell D. Leachman

Representative Clients: City of El Paso; El Paso Housing Finance Corp.; City of El Paso Industrial Development Authority; Ysleta del sur Pueblo Indian Tribe; Alabama and Coushatta Indian Tribe of Texas; Metropolitan Life Insurance Company; De Bruyn, Cooper, Maldonada Advertising, Inc.

For full biographical listings, see the Martindale-Hubbell Law Directory

*HOUSTON,** Harris Co.

ALSUP BEVIS & PETTY (AV)

333 Clay Suite 4930, 77098
Telephone: 713-739-1313
Fax: 713-739-7095

Richard C. Alsup
Randall F. Bevis
Andrew H. Petty

ASSOCIATE

Michael J. Short

For full biographical listings, see the Martindale-Hubbell Law Directory

UTAH

*SALT LAKE CITY,** Salt Lake Co.

VAN COTT, BAGLEY, CORNWALL & MCCARTHY, A PROFESSIONAL CORPORATION (AV)

Suite 1600, 50 South Main Street, P.O. Box 45340, 84145
Telephone: 801-532-3333
Telex: 453149
Telecopier: 801-534-0058
Ogden, Utah Office: Suite 900, 2404 Washington Boulevard.
Telephone: 801-394-5783.
Park City, Utah Office: 314 Main Street, Suite 205.
Telephone: 801-649-3889.
Reno, Nevada Office: Jeppson & Lee, 100 West Liberty, Suite 990.
Telephone: 702-333-6800.

(See Next Column)

VAN COTT, BAGLEY, CORNWALL & MCCARTHY A PROFESSIONAL CORPORATION—*Continued*

John T. Nielsen
Matthew F. McNulty, III

Representative Clients: Standard Oil Company of California (and affiliated companies); FMC Corp.; Leucadia National Corp.; Key Bank of Utah; Southern Pacific Lines; Intermountain Health Care, Inc.; Huntsman Chemical Corp.; Iomega Corp.; Metropolitan Life Ins. Co.

For Complete List of Firm Personnel, See General Section

For full biographical listings, see the Martindale-Hubbell Law Directory

VERMONT

*BURLINGTON,** Chittenden Co.

BURAK & ANDERSON (AV)

Executive Square, 346 Shelburne Street, P.O. Box 64700, 05406-4700
Telephone: 802-862-0500
Telecopier: 802-862-8176

MEMBERS OF FIRM

Michael L. Burak
Jon Anderson

For Complete List of Firm Personnel, See General Section

For full biographical listings, see the Martindale-Hubbell Law Directory

WEST VIRGINIA

*CHARLESTON,** Kanawha Co.

JACKSON & KELLY (AV)

1600 Laidley Tower, P.O. Box 553, 25322
Telephone: 304-340-1000
Fax: 304-340-1130
Martinsburg, West Virginia Office: 300 Foxcroft Avenue, P.O. Box 1068.
Telephone: 304-263-8800.
Morgantown, West Virginia Office: 6000 Hampton Center, P.O. Box 619.
Telephone: 304-599-3000.
New Martinsville, West Virginia Office: 256 Russell Avenue, P.O. Box 68.
Telephone: 304-455-1751.
Charles Town, West Virginia Office: 700 East Washington Street, P.O. Box 983.
Telephone: 304-728-6088.
Clarksburg, West Virginia Office: 203 Main Street, P.O. Box 1587.
Telephone: 304-623-3002.
Lexington, Kentucky Office: 175 East Main Street, Suite 500, P.O. Box 2150.
Telephone: 606-255-9500.
Washington, D. C. Office: 2401 Pennsylvania Avenue, N.W., Suite 400.
Telephone: 202-973-0200.
Denver, Colorado Office: Suite 2710, 1660 Lincoln Street.
Telephone: 303-837-0003.

MEMBERS OF FIRM

James Knight Brown
Michael A. Albert
Jeffrey J. Yost (Resident, Lexington, Kentucky Office)
Samme L. Gee
John Philip Melick

Representative Clients: West Virginia-American Water Co.; Citizens Utilities Co.; Cabot Oil and Gas of West Virginia; S & S Grading, Inc. (Eastern Environmental); Monongalia Power Co.; West Virginia Power Gas Service Co. (Utils Corp United); GTE South; Southwestern Bell Mobile Systems, Inc.; Virginia Electric & Power Co.; Contel Cellular.

For Complete List of Firm Personnel, See General Section

For full biographical listings, see the Martindale-Hubbell Law Directory

WISCONSIN

*MILWAUKEE,** Milwaukee Co.

QUARLES & BRADY (AV)

411 East Wisconsin Avenue, 53202-4497
Telephone: 414-277-5000
Cable Address: "Lawdock"
Fax: 414-271-3552.
TWX: 910-262-3426
Madison, Wisconsin Office: Firstar Plaza, One South Pinckney Street, P.O. Box 2113.
Telephone: 608-251-5000.
Fax: 608-251-9166.
West Palm Beach, Florida Office: 222 Lakeview Avenue, 4th Floor.
Telephone: 407-653-5000.
Fax: 407-653-5333.
Naples, Florida Office: Barnett Center, 4501 Tamiami Trail North.
Telephone: 813-262-5959.
Fax: 813-434-4999.
Phoenix, Arizona Office: One Camelback Building, One East Camelback Road, Suite 400.
Telephone: 602-230-5500.
Fax: 602-230-5598.

MEMBERS OF FIRM
(ALPHABETICALLY BY YEAR OF ADMISSION TO BAR)

Robert H. Diaz, Jr.
Larry J. Martin

ASSOCIATES

Erica M. Eisinger (Resident, Madison Office)
Christopher H. Kallaher

For Complete List of Firm Personnel, See General Section

For full biographical listings, see the Martindale-Hubbell Law Directory

WYOMING

*CASPER,** Natrona Co.

BROWN & DREW (AV)

Casper Business Center, Suite 800, 123 West First Street, 82601-2486
Telephone: 307-234-1000
800-877-6755
Telefax: 307-265-8025

MEMBERS OF FIRM

Morris R. Massey
Donn J. McCall
Thomas F. Reese
Russell M. Blood
J. Kenneth Barbe

ASSOCIATES

Jon B. Huss
Courtney Robert Kepler

Attorneys for: KN Energy, Inc. and subsidiaries; Chicago and NorthWestern Transportation Company.

For Complete List of Firm Personnel, See General Section

For full biographical listings, see the Martindale-Hubbell Law Directory

CANADA
ALBERTA

*CALGARY,** Calgary Jud. Dist.

BENNETT JONES VERCHERE (AV)

4500 Bankers Hall East, 855-2nd Street S.W., T2P 4K7
Telephone: (403) 298-3100
Facsimile: (403) 265-7219
Edmonton, Alberta Office: 1000, 10035-105 Street.
Telephone: (403) 421-8133.
Facsimile: (403) 421-7951.
Toronto, Ontario Office: 3400 1 First Canadian Place. P.O. Box 130.
Telephone: (416) 863-1200.
Facsimile: (416) 863-1716.
Ottawa, Ontario Office: Suite 1800. 350 Alberta Street, Box 25, K1R 1A4.
Telephone: (613) 230-4935.
Facsimile: (613) 230-3836.
Montreal, Quebec Office: Suite 1600, 1 Place Ville Marie.
Telephone: (514) 871-1200.
Facsimile: (514) 871-8115.

(See Next Column)

BENNETT JONES VERCHERE, *Calgary—Continued*

MEMBER OF FIRM

William L. Britton, Q.C.

For Complete List of Firm Personnel, See General Section

For full biographical listings, see the Martindale-Hubbell Law Directory

*EDMONTON,** Edmonton Jud. Dist.

PARLEE MCLAWS (AV)

15th Floor Manulife Place, 10180 101st Street, T5J 4K1
Telephone: 403-423-8500
Telecopier: 403-423-2870
Calgary, Alberta Office: 3400, Western Canadian Place, 707 - 8th Avenue, S.W.
Telephone: 403-294-7000.
Telecopier: 403-265-8263.

MEMBERS OF FIRM

C. H. Kerr, Q.C.
M. D. MacDonald
K. F. Bailey, Q.C.
R. B. Davison, Q.C.
F. R. Haldane
P. E. J. Curran
D. G. Finlay
J. K. McFadyen
R. C. Secord
D. L. Kennedy
D. C. Rolf
D. F. Pawlowski
A. A. Garber
R. P. James
D. C. Wintermute
J. L. Cairns
R. A. Newton, Q.C.
T. A. Cockrall, Q.C.
H. D. Montemurro
F. J. Niziol
R. W. Wilson
I. L. MacLachlan
R. O. Langley
R. G. McBean
J. T. Neilson
E. G. Rice
J. F. McGinnis
J. H. H. Hockin
G. W. Jaycock
M. J. K. Nikel
B. J. Curial
S. L. May
M. S. Poretti

ASSOCIATES

C. R. Head
A.W. Slemko
L. H. Hamdon
K.A. Smith
K. D. Fallis-Howell
D. S. Tam
J.W. McClure
F.H. Belzil
R.A. Renz
J.G. Paulson
K. E. Buss
B. L. Andriachuk
P. E. S. J. Kennedy
R. Feraco
R.J. Billingsley
N.B.R. Thompson
P. A. Shenher
I. C. Johnson
K.G. Koshman
D.D. Dubrule
G. T. Lund
W.D. Johnston
G. E. Flemming
K. P. Nayyer

For full biographical listings, see the Martindale-Hubbell Law Directory

REAL ESTATE LAW

ALABAMA

*BIRMINGHAM,** Jefferson Co.

BALCH & BINGHAM (AV)

1710 Sixth Avenue North, P.O. Box 306, 35201
Telephone: 205-251-8100
Facsimile: 205-226-8798
Other Birmingham, Alabama Office: 1901 Sixth Avenue North, 35203.
Telephone: 205-251-8100.
Facsimile: 205-226-8799.
Montgomery, Alabama Office: The Winter Building, 2 Dexter Avenue, 36101.
Telephone: 205-834-6500.
Facsimile: 205-269-3115.
Huntsville, Alabama Office: Suite 810, 200 West Court Square, 35801.
Telephone: 205-551-0171.
Facsimile: 205-551-0174.
Washington, D.C. Office: Suite 800, 1101 Connecticut Avenue, N.W., 20036.
Telephone: 202-296-0387.
Facsimile: 202-452-8180.

MEMBERS OF FIRM

H. Hampton Boles
Randolph H. Lanier
Steven F. Casey

SENIOR ATTORNEY

Virginia S. Boliek

ASSOCIATE

Felton W. Smith

Counsel for: Alabama Power Co.; Blue Cross and Blue Shield of Alabama; Brasfield & Gorrie, Inc.; Colonial Properties, Inc.; Compass Bancshares, Inc.; Harbert Corp.; Kimberly-Clark Corp.; Southern Research Institute; The Equitable Life Assurance Society of the United States; Vesta Insurance Group, Inc.

For Complete List of Firm Personnel, See General Section

For full biographical listings, see the Martindale-Hubbell Law Directory

BERKOWITZ, LEFKOVITS, ISOM & KUSHNER, A PROFESSIONAL CORPORATION (AV)

1600 SouthTrust Tower, 420 North Twentieth Street, 35203
Telephone: 205-328-0480
Telecopier: 205-322-8007

Arnold K. Lefkovits
William R. Sylvester
Chervis Isom
David L. Silverstein
Denise W. Killebrew

Representative Clients: Alabama Waste Services, Inc.; Bayer Properties, Inc.; Crest Realty Co.; Daniel Realty Corp.; Eason, Eyster & Sandner; Engel Realty Co., Inc.; McDonald's Corp.; Parisian, Inc.; Books-A-Million.

For Complete List of Firm Personnel, See General Section

For full biographical listings, see the Martindale-Hubbell Law Directory

BRADLEY, ARANT, ROSE & WHITE (AV)

1400 Park Place Tower, 2001 Park Place, 35203
Telephone: 205-521-8000
Telex: 494-1324
Facsimile: 205-251-8611, 251-8665, 252-0264
Facsimile (Southtrust Office): 205-251-9915
Huntsville, Alabama Office: 200 Clinton Avenue West, Suite 900.
Telephone: 205-517-5100.
Facsimile: 205-533-5069.

MEMBERS OF FIRM

J. Robert Fleenor
Lant B. Davis
Robert C. Walthall
Bobby C. Underwood
Charles A. J. Beavers, Jr.
John E. Hagefstration, Jr.
Axel Bolvig III

ASSOCIATE

Frank C. Galloway, III

Counsel for: SouthTrust Bank of Alabama, National Association; Energen, Corporation; Blount, Inc.; Torchmark Corp.; Russell Corp.; Coca-Cola Bottling Company United, Inc.; Ford Motor Co.; Walter Industries, Inc.; The Birmingham Post Co. (Post-Herald); The New York Times Co.

(See Next Column)

For Complete List of Firm Personnel, See General Section

For full biographical listings, see the Martindale-Hubbell Law Directory

BURR & FORMAN (AV)

3000 SouthTrust Tower, 420 North 20th Street, 35203
Telephone: 205-251-3000
Telecopier: 205-458-5100
Huntsville, Alabama Office: Suite 204, Regency Center, 400 Meridian Street.
Telephone: 205-551-0010.

MEMBERS OF FIRM

J. Fred Powell
Dwight L. Mixson, Jr.
Joseph G. Stewart
Carol H. Stewart
John F. DeBuys, Jr.
Deborah P. Fisher
Jack P. Stephenson, Jr.
Gail Livingston Mills
Eric L. Carlton
W. Benjamin Johnson

ASSOCIATES

Jeffrey T. Baker
Jill Verdeyen Deer

For Complete List of Firm Personnel, See General Section

For full biographical listings, see the Martindale-Hubbell Law Directory

CORLEY, MONCUS & WARD, P.C. (AV)

Suite 650, 2100 SouthBridge Parkway, 35209
Telephone: 205-879-5959
Telecopier: 205-879-5859

Claude McCain Moncus
Gene W. Gray, Jr.
W. Lewis Garrison, Jr.

For Complete List of Firm Personnel, See General Section

For full biographical listings, see the Martindale-Hubbell Law Directory

DOMINICK, FLETCHER, YEILDING, WOOD & LLOYD, P.A. (AV)

2121 Highland Avenue, 35205
Telephone: 205-939-0033

Frank Dominick
Walter Fletcher
Mary P. Thornton

Counsel for: Citizens Federal Savings Bank; St. Vincent's Hospital; Castle Mortgage Corporation; Thornton Construction Company, Inc.; Collateral Mortgage Corp.

For Complete List of Firm Personnel, See General Section

For full biographical listings, see the Martindale-Hubbell Law Directory

GORHAM, STEWART, KENDRICK, BRYANT & BATTLE, P.C. (AV)

2101 6th Avenue North, Suite 700, 35203
Telephone: 205-254-3216, 251-9166
Telecopier: 205-324-3802

William J. Bryant

OF COUNSEL

John T. Natter

Representative Clients: Jefferson County Personnel Board; Birmingham-Jefferson Civic Center Authority; The Water Works and Sewer Board of the City of Birmingham; City of Homewood; American Federation of Government Employees Local #1945; City of Pelham; Town of Kimberly; Alabama Tire Dealers Assn.; Southern States Body Shop Assn.

For Complete List of Firm Personnel, See General Section

For full biographical listings, see the Martindale-Hubbell Law Directory

PRITCHARD, MCCALL & JONES (AV)

800 Financial Center, 35203
Telephone: 205-328-9190

MEMBERS OF FIRM

William S. Pritchard (1890-1967)
Julian P. Hardy, Jr.
Alexander W. Jones (1914-1988)
Alexander W. Jones, Jr.
William S. Pritchard, Jr.
F. Hilton-Green Tomlinson
Madison W. O'Kelley, Jr.
James G. Henderson
William S. Pritchard, III

ASSOCIATES

Michael L. McKerley
Nina Michele LaFleur
Robert Bond Higgins
Mary W. Burge

Representative Clients: First National Bank of Columbiana; Central State Bank of Calera; Buffalo Rock-Pepsi-Cola Bottling Co.; Gillis Advertising, Inc.; Liberty Mutual Insurance Co.; Reliance Insurance Company; SouthTrust Bank, N.A.; Bromberg & Company, Inc.; Farmers Furniture Company; First Commercial Bank.

For full biographical listings, see the Martindale-Hubbell Law Directory

Birmingham—Continued

Sirote & Permutt, P.C. (AV)

2222 Arlington Avenue, South, P.O. Box 55727, 35255
Telephone: 205-933-7111
Facsimile: 205-930-5301
Huntsville, Alabama Office: 200 Clinton Avenue, N.W., Suite 1000.
Telephone: 205-536-1711.
Facsimile: 205-534-9650.
Mobile, Alabama Office: One St. Louis Centre, Suite 1000.
Telephone: 205-432-1671.
Facsimile: 205-434-0196.
Montgomery, Alabama Office: Colonial Commerce Center, Suite 305 One Commerce Street.
Telephone: 205-261-3400.
Facsimile: 205-261-3434.
Tuscaloosa, Alabama Office: 2216 14th Street.
Telephone: 205-752-2089.

Jerry E. Held
Maurice L. Shevin
Steven A. Brickman
Thomas A. Ansley
J. Scott Sims

Representative Clients: International Business Machines (IBM); General Motors Corp.; Colonial Bank; Bruno's, Inc.; University of Alabama Hospitals; Westinghouse Electric Corp.; First Alabama Bank; Monsanto Chemical Company; South Central Bell; Prudential Insurance Company; American Home Products, Inc.; Minnesota Mining and Manufacturing, Inc. (3M).

For Complete List of Firm Personnel, See General Section

For full biographical listings, see the Martindale-Hubbell Law Directory

Spain, Gillon, Grooms, Blan & Nettles (AV)

The Zinszer Building, 2117 2nd Avenue North, 35203
Telephone: 205-328-4100
Telecopier: 205-324-8866

MEMBERS OF FIRM

John P. McKleroy, Jr.
Samuel H. Frazier
Harold H. Goings

General Counsel for: Liberty National Life Insurance Co.; United States Fidelity & Guaranty Co.; Piggly Wiggly Alabama Distributing Co.; AmSouth Mortgage Co., Inc.; Alabama Insurance Guaranty Association; Alabama Life and Disability Insurance Guaranty Association; Alabama Insurance Underwriters Association.
Counsel for: The Prudential Insurance Company of America; Government Employees Insurance Co.; Massachusetts Mutual Life Insurance Co.

For Complete List of Firm Personnel, See General Section

For full biographical listings, see the Martindale-Hubbell Law Directory

EUFAULA, Barbour Co.

William V. Neville, Jr. (AV)

302 East Broad Street, P.O. Box 337, 36072-0337
Telephone: 334-687-5183
Fax: 334-687-6602

For full biographical listings, see the Martindale-Hubbell Law Directory

*GUNTERSVILLE,** Marshall Co.

Wright and Wright, A Professional Corporation (AV)

Worth Street, P.O. Box 70, 35976-0070
Telephone: 205-582-3721; 582-8590; 582-8411
Fax: 205-582-3733

T. Harvey Wright (1890-1972)
Harvey J. Wright
Wade K. Wright

Approved Attorneys for: Commonwealth Land Title Insurance Co.; Lawyers Title Insurance Corp.

*HUNTSVILLE,** Madison Co.

Berry, Ables, Tatum, Little & Baxter, P.C. (AV)

Legal Building, 315 Franklin Street, S.E., P.O. Box 165, 35804-0165
Telephone: 205-533-3740
Facsimile: 205-533-3751

William H. Blanton (1889-1973)
Joe M. Berry
L. Bruce Ables
James T. Tatum, Jr.
Loyd H. Little, Jr.
James T. Baxter, III
Thomas E. Parker, Jr.
Bill G. Hall

Representative Clients: AmSouth Bank, N.A.; First Alabama Bank; General Shale Products Co.; The Hartz Corp.; Litton Industries, Inc.; Farmers Tractor Co.; Colonial Bank; Farm Credit Bank of Texas; Resolution Trust Corp.
Reference: First Alabama Bank.

For full biographical listings, see the Martindale-Hubbell Law Directory

Bradley, Arant, Rose & White (AV)

200 Clinton Avenue West, Suite 900, 35801
Telephone: 205-517-5100
Facsimile: 205-533-5069
Birmingham, Alabama Office: 1400 Park Place Tower, 2001 Park Place.
Telephone: 205-521-8000.
Telex: 494-1324.
Facsimile: 205-251-8611, 251-8665, 252-0264. Facsimile (Southtrust Office): 205-251-9915.

RESIDENT PARTNER

Patrick H. Graves, Jr.

For Complete List of Firm Personnel, See General Section

For full biographical listings, see the Martindale-Hubbell Law Directory

Burr & Forman (AV)

Suite 204, Regency Center, 400 Meridian Street, 35801
Telephone: 205-551-0010
Birmingham, Alabama Office: 3000 SouthTrust Tower, 420 North 20th Street.
Telephone: 205-251-3000.
Telecopier: 205-458-5100.

RESIDENT PARTNER

L. Tennent Lee, III

For full biographical listings, see the Martindale-Hubbell Law Directory

Sirote & Permutt, P.C. (AV)

Suite 1000, 200 Clinton Avenue, N.W., 35801
Telephone: 205-536-1711
Facsimile: 205-534-9650
Birmingham, Alabama Office: 2222 Arlington Avenue, South, P.O. Box 55727.
Telephone: 205-933-7111.
Facsimile: 205-930-5301.
Mobile, Alabama Office: One St. Louis Centre, Suite 1000.
Telephone: 205-432-1671.
Facsimile: 205-434-0196.
Montgomery, Alabama Office: Colonial Commerce Center, Suite 305, One Commerce Street.
Telephone: 205-261-3400.
Facsimile: 205-261-3434.
Tuscaloosa, Alabama Office: 2216 14th Street.
Telephone: 205-752-2089.

Julian D. Butler
Joe H. Ritch

For Complete List of Firm Personnel, See General Section

For full biographical listings, see the Martindale-Hubbell Law Directory

Stephens, Millirons, Harrison & Williams, P.C. (AV)

333 Franklin Street, P.O. Box 307, 35801
Telephone: 205-533-7711
Telecopier: 205-536-9388

Arthur M. Stephens
Paul L. Millirons
James G. Harrison
Bruce E. Williams
Vicki Ann Bell

Attorneys for: Lomas Mortgage USA, Inc.; AmSouth Mortgage Co., Inc.

For full biographical listings, see the Martindale-Hubbell Law Directory

Watson, Gammons & Fees, P.C. (AV)

200 Clinton Avenue, N.W., Suite 800, P.O. Box 46, 35804
Telephone: 205-536-7423
Telecopier: 205-536-2689

Herman Watson, Jr.
Robert C. Gammons
Michael L. Fees
Joseph A. Jimmerson
J. Barton Warren
Charles H. Pullen
Billie B. Line, Jr.

OF COUNSEL

George K. Williams

LEGAL SUPPORT PERSONNEL

James W. Lowery, Jr. (Administrator)

For full biographical listings, see the Martindale-Hubbell Law Directory

*JASPER,** Walker Co.

O'Rear & O'Rear (AV)

Suite B Bankhead-Byars Building, 1816 Third Avenue, P.O. Box 191, 35502-0191
Telephone: 205-387-2196
Fax: 205-387-2190

(See Next Column)

O'REAR & O'REAR—*Continued*

MEMBERS OF FIRM

Caine O'Rear, Jr. Griff O'Rear
Mark A. McWhorter

Reference: First National Bank of Jasper.

For full biographical listings, see the Martindale-Hubbell Law Directory

*MOBILE,** Mobile Co.

JOHNSTONE, ADAMS, BAILEY, GORDON AND HARRIS (AV)

Royal St. Francis Building, 104 St. Francis Street, P.O. Box 1988, 36633
Telephone: 334-432-7682
Facsimile: 334-432-2800
Telex: 782040

MEMBER OF FIRM

I. David Cherniak

ASSOCIATES

Robert S. Frost C. William Rasure, Jr.

General Counsel for: First Alabama Bank, Mobile; Infirmary Health System/Mobile Infirmary Medical Center/Rotary Rehabilitation Hospital (Multi-Hospital System).
Counsel for: Oil and Gas: Exxon Corp. Business and Corporate: Bell South Telecommunications, Inc.; Aluminum Co. of America; Michelin Tire Corp.; Metropolitan Life Insurance Co.; The Travelers Insurance Cos. Marine: The West of England Ship Owners Mutual Protection and Indemnity Association (Luxembourg); The Standard Steamship Owners' Protection and Indemnity Association (Bermuda) Ltd.

For Complete List of Firm Personnel, See General Section

For full biographical listings, see the Martindale-Hubbell Law Directory

LYONS, PIPES & COOK, P.C. (AV)

2 North Royal Street, P.O. Box 2727, 36652-2727
Telephone: 334-432-4481
Cable Address: "Lysea"
Telecopier: 334-433-1820

Norton W. Brooker, Jr.
Marion A. Quina, Jr.
Thomas F. Garth
W. David Johnson, Jr.
R. Mark Kirkpatrick
John C. Bell

Representative Clients: James Graham Brown Foundation; Browning-Ferris Industries of Alabama, Inc.; Champion International Corporation; Inchcape Shipping Services, Inc.; SouthTrust Bank of Mobile.

For Complete List of Firm Personnel, See General Section

For full biographical listings, see the Martindale-Hubbell Law Directory

PIERCE, CARR & ALFORD, P.C. (AV)

Suite 900 Montlimar Place Office Building, 1110 Montlimar Drive, P.O. Box 16046, 36616
Telephone: 334-344-5151
FAX: 334-344-9696

Donald F. Pierce
Davis Carr
Helen Johnson Alford
Goodman G. Ledyard
Forrest S. Latta
H. William Wasden
Andrew C. Clausen

James W. Lampkin II
John Chas. S. Pierce
Pamela Kirkwood Millsaps
Mignon Mestayer DeLashmet
Rachel D. Sanders
C. William Daniels, Jr.

Representative Clients: Grove Worldwide; Beloit Corp.; Koehring Cranes & Excavators; Winnebago; Toyota Motor Sales Corp.; Blue Cross and Blue Shield; Charter Medical Corp.; Connecticut Mutual Life Ins. Co.; Nationwide Insurance Cos.

For full biographical listings, see the Martindale-Hubbell Law Directory

SIROTE & PERMUTT, P.C. (AV)

One St. Louis Centre, Suite 1000, P.O. Drawer 2025, 36652-2025
Telephone: 334-432-1671
Facsimile: 334-434-0196
Birmingham, Alabama Office: 2222 Arlington Avenue, South, P.O. Box 55727.
Telephone: 205-933-7111.
Facsimile: 205-930-5301.
Huntsville, Alabama Office: 200 Clinton Avenue, N.W., Suite 1000.
Telephone: 205-536-1711.
Facsimile: 205-534-9650.
Montgomery, Alabama Office: Colonial Commerce Center, Suite 305, One Commerce Street.
Telephone: 205-261-3400.
Facsimile: 205-261-3434.
Tuscaloosa, Alabama Office: 2216 14th Street.
Telephone: 205-752-2089.

(See Next Column)

William H. McDermott
Gordon O. Tanner
Shirley Mahan Justice
Joseph P. Jones, Jr.

For Complete List of Firm Personnel, See General Section

For full biographical listings, see the Martindale-Hubbell Law Directory

*MONTGOMERY,** Montgomery Co.

* indicates certain Bar Register subscribers whose principal office is located elsewhere in the state and who have arranged for representation as a part of the state capital listings that follow

* BALCH & BINGHAM (AV)

The Winter Building, 2 Dexter Avenue, P.O. Box 78, 36101
Telephone: 334-834-6500
Facsimile: 334-269-3115
Birmingham, Alabama Offices: 1710 Sixth Avenue North, 35203.
Telephone: 205-251-8100.
Facsimile: 205-226-8798. 1901 Sixth Avenue North, 35203.
Telephone: 205-251-8100.
Facsimile: 205-226-8799.
Huntsville, Alabama Office: Suite 810, 200 West Court Square, 35801.
Telephone: 205-551-0171.
Facsimile: 205-551-0174.
Washington, D.C. Office: Suite 800, 1101 Connecticut Avenue, N.W., 20036.
Telephone: 202-296-0387.
Facsimile: 202-452-8180.

RESIDENT MEMBERS OF FIRM

John S. Bowman Warren H. Goodwyn

Counsel for: Alabama Power Co.; Blue Cross and Blue Shield of Alabama; Brasfield & Gorrie, Inc.; Colonial Properties, Inc.; Compass Bancshares, Inc.; Harbert Corp.; Kimberly-Clark Corp.; Southern Research Institute; The Equitable Life Assurance Society of the United States; Vesta Insurance Group, Inc.

For Complete List of Firm Personnel, See General Section

For full biographical listings, see the Martindale-Hubbell Law Directory

CAPELL, HOWARD, KNABE & COBBS, P.A. (AV)

57 Adams Avenue, P.O. Box 2069, 36102-2069
Telephone: 334-241-8000

Jack L. Capell
Fontaine M. Howard (1908-1985)
Walter J. Knabe (1898-1979)
Edward E. Cobbs (1909-1982)
L. Lister Hill (1936-1993)
Herman H. Hamilton, Jr.
Rufus M. King
Robert S. Richard
John B. Scott, Jr.
John F. Andrews
James M. Scott
Thomas S. Lawson, Jr.
John L. Capell, III
William D. Coleman
William K. Martin
Bruce J. Downey III
Henry C. Barnett, Jr.
Palmer Smith Lehman
Richard F. Allen
Neal H. Acker
Henry H. Hutchinson
Shapard D. Ashley
D. Kyle Johnson
J. Lister Hubbard
James N. Walter, Jr.
James H. McLemore
H. Dean Mooty, Jr.
Jim B. Grant, Jr.
Wyeth Holt Speir, III
Chad S. Wachter
Ellen M. Hastings
Debra Deames Spain
William Rufus King
C. Clay Torbert, III

OF COUNSEL

Timothy Sullivan

For full biographical listings, see the Martindale-Hubbell Law Directory

CAPOUANO, WAMPOLD, PRESTWOOD & SANSONE, P.A. (AV)

350 Adams Avenue, P.O. Box 1910, 36102-1910
Telephone: 334-264-6401
Fax: 334-834-4954

Leon M. Capouano
Alvin T. Prestwood
Jerome D. Smith
Ellis D. Hanan
Joseph P. Borg
Joseph W. Warren

OF COUNSEL

Charles H. Wampold, Jr.

Thomas B. Klinner Linda Smith Webb
James M. Sizemore, Jr.

Counsel for: First Alabama Bank of Montgomery, N.A.; Union Bank and Trust Co.; Real Estate Financing, Inc.; SouthTrust Bank; AmSouth Bank; Central Bank; City Federal Savings & Loan Assoc.; Colonial Mortgage Co.; Lomas & Nettleton; First Bank of Linden.

For full biographical listings, see the Martindale-Hubbell Law Directory

Montgomery—Continued

KAUFMAN & ROTHFEDER, P.C. (AV)

2740 Zelda Road Post Office Drawer 4540, 36103-4540
Telephone: 334-244-1111
Fax: 334-244-1969

Samuel Kaufman
Richardson B. McKenzie, III
George W. Thomas
William B. Sellers

Counsel for: Russell Corp.; Sanders Lead Co., Inc.; Waste Management of North America, Inc.

For full biographical listings, see the Martindale-Hubbell Law Directory

ALASKA

*ANCHORAGE,** Third Judicial District

FRANCIS J. NOSEK, JR. A PROFESSIONAL CORPORATION (AV)

310 K Street, Suite 601, 99501
Telephone: 907-274-2602
Telefax: 907-258-2001
Compuserve No.: 720102420

Francis J. Nosek, Jr.

Reference: First National Bank of Anchorage.

For full biographical listings, see the Martindale-Hubbell Law Directory

WOHLFORTH, ARGETSINGER, JOHNSON & BRECHT, A PROFESSIONAL CORPORATION (AV)

900 West 5th Avenue, Suite 600, 99501
Telephone: 907-276-6401
Telecopier: 907-276-5093

Peter Argetsinger
Julius J. Brecht
Robert M. Johnson
Thomas F. Klinkner
James A. Sarafin
Kenneth E. Vassar
Eric E. Wohlforth

Cynthia Lea Cartledge
Carol L. Giles
Bradley E. Meyen

For full biographical listings, see the Martindale-Hubbell Law Directory

ARIZONA

*FLAGSTAFF,** Coconino Co.

ASPEY, WATKINS & DIESEL (AV)

123 North San Francisco, 86001
Telephone: 602-774-1478
Facsimile: 602-774-1043
Sedona, Arizona Office: 120 Soldier Pass Road.
Telephone: 602-282-5955.
Facsimile: 602-282-5962.
Page, Arizona Office: 904 North Navajo.
Telephone: 602-645-9694.
Winslow, Arizona Office: 205 North Williamson.
Telephone: 602-289-5963.
Cottonwood, Arizona Office: 905 Cove Parkway, Unite 201.
Telephone: 602-639-1881.

MEMBERS OF FIRM

Frederick M. Fritz Aspey
Harold L. Watkins
Louis M. Diesel
Bruce S. Griffen
Donald H. Bayles, Jr.
Kaign N. Christy
John J. Dempsey

Zachary Markham
James E. Ledbetter
Whitney Cunningham
Holly S. Karris

LEGAL SUPPORT PERSONNEL

Deborah D. Roberts (Legal Assistant)
C. Denece Pruett (Legal Assistant)
Dominic M. Marino, Jr, (Paralegal Assistant)

Representative Clients: Farmer's Insurance Company of Arizona; Kelley-Moore Paint Co.; Pepsi-Cola Bottling Company of Northern Arizona; Bill Luke's Chrysler-Plymouth, Inc.; First American Title Insurance Company ; Transamerica Title Insurance Co.; Page Electric Utility; Comprehensive Access Health Plan, Inc.
Reference: First Interstate Bank-Arizona, N.A., Flagstaff, Arizona.

For full biographical listings, see the Martindale-Hubbell Law Directory

*NOGALES,** Santa Cruz Co.

O'CONNOR, CAVANAGH, ANDERSON, WESTOVER, KILLINGSWORTH & BESHEARS, A PROFESSIONAL ASSOCIATION (AV)

1827 North Mastick Way, 85621
Telephone: 602-761-4215
FAX: 602-761-3505
Phoenix, Arizona Office: One East Camelback Road, Suite 1100, 85012.
Telephone: 602-263-2400.
FAX: 602-263-2900.
Tucson, Arizona Office: Suite 2200, One South Church Avenue, 85701.
Telephone: 602-882-8912.
FAX: 602-624-9564.
Sun City, Arizona Office: 13250 North Del Webb Boulevard, Suite B, 85351.
Telephone: 602-263-2808.
FAX: 602-933-3100.

Hector G. Arana
Kimberly A. Howard Arana

OF COUNSEL

James D. Robinson

Representative Clients: Omega Produce Co.; Frank's Distributing, Inc.; City of Nogales; Collectron of Ariz., Inc.; James K. Wilson Produce Co.; Agricola Bon, S. de R.L. de C.V.; Angel Demerutis E.; Rene Carrillo C.; Arturo Lomeli; Theojary Crisantes E.

For full biographical listings, see the Martindale-Hubbell Law Directory

*PHOENIX,** Maricopa Co.

APKER, APKER, HAGGARD & KURTZ, P.C. (AV)

2111 East Highland Avenue, Suite 230, 85016
Telephone: 602-381-0085
Telecopier: 602-956-3457

Burton M. Apker
Jerry L. Haggard
David B. Apker
Gerrie Apker Kurtz

Cynthia M. Chandley
Kevin M. Moran

Representative Clients: ASARCO Incorporated; Douglas Land Corp.; Frito-Lay, Inc.; Lawyers Title Insurance Corp.; Nevada Power Company; The North West Life Assurance Co.; Phelps Dodge Corporation; Santa Fe Pacific Gold Corporation; Santa Fe Pacific Industrials; Western Federal Savings & Loan Assn.

For full biographical listings, see the Martindale-Hubbell Law Directory

BONN, LUSCHER, PADDEN & WILKINS, CHARTERED (AV)

805 North Second Street, 85004
Telephone: 602-254-5557
Fax: 602-254-0656

Paul V. Bonn
Brian A. Luscher
Jeff C. Padden
Randall D. Wilkins

For full biographical listings, see the Martindale-Hubbell Law Directory

BROWN & BAIN, A PROFESSIONAL ASSOCIATION (AV)

2901 North Central Avenue, P.O. Box 400, 85001-0400
Telephone: 602-351-8000
Cable: TWX 910-951-0646
Telecopier: 602-351-8516
Palo Alto, California Affiliated Office: Brown & Bain, 600 Hansen Way.
Telephone: 415-856-9411.
Telecopier: 415-856-6061.
Tucson, Arizona Affiliated Office: Brown & Bain, A Professional Association. One South Church Avenue, Nineteenth Floor, P.O. Box 2265.
Telephone: 602-798-7900
Telecopier: 602-798-7945.

Richard Calvin Cooledge
Kyle B. Hettinger
Michael F. McNulty (Resident at Tucson Office)
Sarah R. Simmons (Resident at Tucson Office)
Scott M. Theobald
Charles Van Cott
George C. Wallach

For Complete List of Firm Personnel, See General Section

For full biographical listings, see the Martindale-Hubbell Law Directory

BURCH & CRACCHIOLO, P.A. (AV)

702 East Osborn Road, Suite 200, 85014
Telephone: 602-274-7611
Fax: 602-234-0341
Mailing Address: P.O. Box 16882, Phoenix, AZ, 85011

(See Next Column)

BURCH & CRACCHIOLO P.A.—*Continued*

Jack D. Klausner
Guadalupe Iniguez
Daryl Manhart
Edwin C. Bull
Andrew Abraham
Clare H. Abel
Ralph D. Harris

Marvin Davis
David M. Villadolid
J. Brent Welker

Representative Clients: Bashas' Inc.; Farmers Insurance Group; U-Haul International, Inc.

For Complete List of Firm Personnel, See General Section

For full biographical listings, see the Martindale-Hubbell Law Directory

CARMICHAEL & POWELL, PROFESSIONAL CORPORATION (AV)

7301 North 16th Street, 85020-5224
Telephone: 602-861-0777
Facsimile: 602-870-0296

Ronald W. Carmichael
Donald W. Powell
Laurence B. Stevens
Sid A. Horwitz

Stephen Manes
Craig A. Raby
Brian A. Hatch
Richard C. Gramlich

Representative Clients: Home Builders Association of Central Arizona: Ryland Homes.

For full biographical listings, see the Martindale-Hubbell Law Directory

COHEN AND COTTON, A PROFESSIONAL CORPORATION (AV)

One Arizona Center, Suite 400, 400 East Van Buren Street, 85004
Telephone: 602-252-8400
FAX: 602-252-5339

Ronald Jay Cohen
John H. Cotton
Laura Hartigan Kennedy
Daniel G. Dowd
David W. Smith
Scott L. Long
Paula M. DeMore
Darlene M. Wauro
Joshua R. Woodard
Samantha Gail Masters-Brown
Robert N. Mann
John Maston O'Neal

Representative Clients: Amex Life Assurance Co.; Coopers & Lybrand; Del Webb Corp.; Fireman's Fund; Grubb & Ellis Realty Co.; Talley Industries, Inc.; U-Haul International, Inc.; United States Fidelity and Guaranty Co.; Accuvanc Mortgage Co.; Express America Mortgage Co.

For full biographical listings, see the Martindale-Hubbell Law Directory

DUSHOFF MCCALL, A PROFESSIONAL CORPORATION (AV)

Two Renaissance Square, 40 North Central, 14th Floor, 85004
Telephone: 602-254-3800
Fax: 602-258-2551

Jay Dushoff
Jack E. McCall
Michael J. McGivern
Denise J. Henslee
Jean Weaver Rice
Janice Sloan Feinberg Massey

OF COUNSEL
Dawn Stoll Zeitlin (P.C.)

LEGAL SUPPORT PERSONNEL
Thomas M. Flynn

For full biographical listings, see the Martindale-Hubbell Law Directory

FENNEMORE CRAIG, A PROFESSIONAL CORPORATION (AV)

Two North Central, Suite 2200, 85004
Telephone: 602-257-8700
Fax: 602-257-8527
Scottsdale, Arizona Office: 6263 North Scottsdale Road, Suite 290, 85250.
Telephone: 602-257-5400.
Fax: 602-945-4932.
Tucson, Arizona Office: One South Church Avenue, Suite 1030, 85701.
Telephone: 602-624-9312.
Fax: 602-882-7383.

Edward C. LeBeau
William T. Boutell, Jr.
Robert P. Robinson
Philip A. Edlund
Ronald L. Ballard
Stephen M. Savage
William L. Kurtz
Mark A. Nesvig
James R. Huntwork
George T. Cole
Leland M. Jones
Charles M. King
Michael V. Mulchay
Margaret R. Gallogly
Peter M. Gerstman
Lesa J. Storey

Darren J. McCleve
Christopher W. Zaharis

Representative Clients: ASARCO Incorporated; AT&T Communications; Bridgestone/Firestone, Inc.; Catellus Development Corp.; Citibank (Arizona); First Interstate Bank of Arizona; GIANT Industries; Phelps Dodge Corporation; The Atchison, Topeka & Santa Fe Railway, Co.; US WEST Communications.

(See Next Column)

For Complete List of Firm Personnel, See General Section

For full biographical listings, see the Martindale-Hubbell Law Directory

GAMMAGE & BURNHAM (AV)

One Renaissance Square, Two North Central Avenue, Suite 1800, 85004
Telephone: 602-256-0566
Fax: 602-256-4475

MEMBERS OF FIRM

Grady Gammage, Jr.
Shawn E. Tobin
Thomas J. McDonald
Jeffrey J. Miller

Representative Clients: W.M. Grace Development; Viehmann, Martin & Associates; Evans-Withycombe, Inc.; Opus Southwest; Kaufman & Broad of Arizona, Inc.

For Complete List of Firm Personnel, See General Section

For full biographical listings, see the Martindale-Hubbell Law Directory

JOHN C. HOVER, P.C. (AV)

2901 North Central Avenue, Suite 1150, 85012
Telephone: 602-230-8777
Fax: 602-230-8707

John C. Hover

LEGAL SUPPORT PERSONNEL
PARALEGAL
Diana G. Weeks

Representative Clients: First National Bank of Arizona; Bank of Hawaii; Buckeye Irrigation Co.; Linkletter-Perris Partnership.

For full biographical listings, see the Martindale-Hubbell Law Directory

JENNINGS, STROUSS AND SALMON, P.L.C. (AV)

A Professional Limited Liability Company
One Renaissance Square, Two North Central, 85004-2393
Telephone: 602-262-5911
Fax: 602-253-3255

John R. Christian
Gary G. Keltner
Lee E. Esch
Douglas G. Zimmerman
Philip J. MacDonnell
Donald J. Oppenheim
Diane K. Geimer
Gerrit M. Steenblik
Carol A. Cluff
George Esahak-Gage
Robert E. Coltin

Brett L Hopper
Stephanie McRae

For Complete List of Firm Personnel, See General Section

For full biographical listings, see the Martindale-Hubbell Law Directory

JOHN S. LANCY & ASSOCIATES A PROFESSIONAL CORPORATION (AV)

Suite 600, 2425 East Camelback Road, 85016
Telephone: 602-381-6555
Fax: 602-381-6560

John S. Lancy
Steven W. Bienstock

For full biographical listings, see the Martindale-Hubbell Law Directory

LEWIS AND ROCA (AV)

A Partnership including Professional Corporations
40 North Central Avenue, 85004-4429
Telephone: 602-262-5311
Fax: 602-262-5747
Tucson, Arizona Office: One South Church Avenue, Suite 700.
Telephone: 602-622-2090.
Fax: 602-622-3088.

MEMBERS OF FIRM

S. L. Schorr (Resident, Tucson Office)
Douglas R. Chandler
D. Randall Stokes
Kenneth Van Winkle, Jr.

ASSOCIATES

Lynn Robbins Wagner
Thel W. Casper

OF COUNSEL
Lyman A. Manser

Representative Clients: ANF Property Holdings; Bank One, Arizona, NA; Gosnell Builders Corp.; Phoenix Memorial Hospital; The Prudential Insurance Company of America; UDC Homes, Inc.

For Complete List of Firm Personnel, See General Section

For full biographical listings, see the Martindale-Hubbell Law Directory

Phoenix—Continued

Linzer, Lang & Ditsch, P.C. (AV)

3242 North Sixteenth Street, 85016
Telephone: 602-956-2525
Fax: 602-241-9885

Stephen P. Linzer

For full biographical listings, see the Martindale-Hubbell Law Directory

MacLean & Jacques, Ltd. (AV)

Suite 202, 40 East Virginia, 85004
Telephone: 602-263-5771
FAX: 602-279-5569

John H. MacLean (1932-1992)
Raoul T. Jacques

Cary T. Inabinet
Macre S. Inabinet

For full biographical listings, see the Martindale-Hubbell Law Directory

McCabe, O'Donnell & Wright, A Professional Association (AV)

Suite 2000, 300 East Osborn, 85012
Telephone: 602-264-0800
Telecopier: 602-274-0146

Joseph I. McCabe
Kathleen M. O'Donnell
Jerry W. Lawson
Jeffrey A. Ekbom

For Complete List of Firm Personnel, See General Section

For full biographical listings, see the Martindale-Hubbell Law Directory

Meyer, Hendricks, Victor, Osborn & Maledon, A Professional Association (AV)

2929 North Central Avenue Suite 2100, 85012-2794
Telephone: 602-640-9000
Facsimile: (24 Hrs.) 602-640-9050
Mailing Address: P.O. Box 33449, 85067-3449,

Paul J. Meyer
David Victor
Jones Osborn II
Jeffrey L. Sellers
Jay I. Moyes
Gary A. Gotto
William M. Hardin
Michelle M. Matiski
Jeffrey C. Zimmerman
Lucia Fakonas Howard
Robert V. Kerrick
Thayne Lowe

Laurie B. Shough

Reference: Bank One Arizona, NA.

For Complete List of Firm Personnel, See General Section

For full biographical listings, see the Martindale-Hubbell Law Directory

O'Connor, Cavanagh, Anderson, Westover, Killingsworth & Beshears, A Professional Association (AV)

One East Camelback Road, Suite 1100, 85012-1656
Telephone: 602-263-2400
FAX: 602-263-2900
Sun City, Arizona Office: 13250 North Del Webb Boulevard, Suite B, 85351.
Telephone: 602-263-2808.
FAX: 602-933-3100.
Tucson, Arizona Office: Suite 2200, One South Church Avenue, 85701.
Telephone: 602-882-8912.
FAX: 602-624-9564.
Nogales, Arizona Office: 1827 North Mastick Way, 85621.
Telephone: 602-761-4215.
FAX: 602-761-3505.

Gerald L. Jacobs
Mayor Shanken
K. David Lindner
Michael E. Woolf
Scott A. Rose
Steven L. Lisker
Glenn M. Feldman
Daniel W. Peters
Neil D. Biskind
David L. Lansky

Robert H. Nagle

Representative Clients: Del Webb Corporation; The Dial Corp; Mobile Land Development Corporation; Johnson Wax Development Corporation; Citibank, N.A.; Shimizu Corporation; Connecticut General Life Insurance Company of America; Bankers Trust Company; The Equitable Life Assurance Society of the United States; Ameritech Pension Trust.

For Complete List of Firm Personnel, See General Section

For full biographical listings, see the Martindale-Hubbell Law Directory

Ridenour, Swenson, Cleere & Evans, P.C. (AV)

302 North First Avenue, Suite 900, 85003
Telephone: 602-254-2143
Fax: 602-254-8670

William G. Ridenour
Gerard R. Cleere
William D. Fearnow
Natalie P. Garth

Kurt A. Peterson

Representative Clients: American Arbitration Assn.; Arizona Agricultural Credit Assn.; Biltmore Investors Bank; Citibank (Arizona); Federal Home Life Insurance Co.; First West Bank; Guarantee Mutual Life Co.; Indianapolis Life Insurance Co.; Kahler Corp.; Marriott Corp.

For full biographical listings, see the Martindale-Hubbell Law Directory

Robbins & Green, A Professional Association (AV)

1800 CitiBank Tower, 3300 North Central Avenue, 85012-9826
Telephone: 602-248-7600
Fax: 602-266-5369

Wayne A. Smith
Joe M. Romley
Edmund F. Richardson
Jack N. Rudel
Jeffrey P. Boshes
Janet B. Hutchison
Alfred W. Ricciardi
Dorothy Baran

For Complete List of Firm Personnel, See General Section

For full biographical listings, see the Martindale-Hubbell Law Directory

Snell & Wilmer (AV)

One Arizona Center, 85004-0001
Telephone: 602-382-6000
Fax: 602-382-6070
Tucson, Arizona Office: 1500 Norwest Tower, One South Church Avenue 85701-1612.
Telephone: 602-882-1200.
Fax: 602-884-1294.
Orange County Office: 1920 Main Street, Suite 1200, P.O. Box 19601, Irvine, California, 92714.
Telephone: 714-253-2700.
Fax: 714-955-2507.
Salt Lake City, Utah Office: Broadway Centre, 111 East Broadway, Suite 900, 84111.
Telephone: 801-237-1900.
Fax: 801-237-1950.

MEMBERS OF FIRM

Richard K. Mallery
Jay D. Wiley
Joyce Kline Wright
Robert C. Bates
Peter G. Santin
Jody Kathleen Pokorski
Shawn M. McLeran

ASSOCIATE

Robert C. Venberg

Representative Clients: American Newland Associates; Arizona Public Service; AZTAR Corp.; The Hewson Co.; Markland Properties, Inc.; Perini Land & Development Co.; SunCor Development Co.; The Symington Co.; Toyota Motor Corp.; Bank One, Arizona, NA.

For Complete List of Firm Personnel, See General Section

For full biographical listings, see the Martindale-Hubbell Law Directory

Streich Lang, A Professional Association (AV)

Renaissance One, Two N. Central Avenue, 85004-2391
Telephone: 602-229-5200
Fax: 602-229-5690
Tucson, Arizona Office: One S. Church Avenue, Suite 1700.
Telephone: 602-770-8700.
Fax: 602-623-2518.
Las Vegas, Nevada Affiliated Office: Dawson & Associates, 3800 Howard Hughes Parkway, Suite 1500.
Telephone: 702-792-2727.
Fax: 702-792-2676.
Los Angeles, California Office: 444 S. Flower Street, Suite 1530.
Telephone: 213-896-0484.

Steven A. Betts
Diane M. Haller
R. Neil Irwin
Thomas J. Lang
Bruce B. May
Preston J. Steenhoek
Kent W. Stevens

OF COUNSEL

Matthew Mehr

David L. Johnson
Kevin J. Morris

Representative Clients: BetaWest Properties, Inc.; CBS Properties, Inc.; First Interstate Bank of Arizona, N.A.; Jaren Corp.; Koll Company; Merrill Lynch Realty, Inc.; Phelps Dodge Corp.; Rouse Company; Suncor Development Co.; Valley National Bank of Arizona.

For Complete List of Firm Personnel, See General Section

For full biographical listings, see the Martindale-Hubbell Law Directory

*PRESCOTT,** Yavapai Co.

FAVOUR, MOORE, WILHELMSEN & SCHUYLER, A PROFESSIONAL ASSOCIATION (AV)

1580 Plaza West Drive, P.O. Box 1391, 86302
Telephone: 602-445-2444
Fax: 602-771-0450

John B. Schuyler, Jr. | David K. Wilhelmsen
Mark M. Moore | Lance B. Payette
Clifford G. Cozier

OF COUNSEL

John M. Favour | Richard G. Kleindienst

Representative Clients: Yavapai Title Co.; Hidden Valley Ranch; Glenn Straub Appraisers, Inc.; Lawyers Title Insurance Co.; Bullwacker Associates; The Ranch at Prescott Homeowner's Assn.; Sedona Brokers Ginny Hays Realty, Inc.; Village of Oak Creek Assn.

For full biographical listings, see the Martindale-Hubbell Law Directory

SCOTTSDALE, Maricopa Co.

FENNEMORE CRAIG, A PROFESSIONAL CORPORATION (AV)

6263 North Scottsdale Road, Suite 290, 85250
Telephone: 602-257-5400
Fax: 602-945-4932
TWX: 910-950-4608
Phoenix, Arizona Office: Two North Central Avenue, Suite 2200, 85004.
Telephone: 602-257-8700.
Fax: 602-257-8527.
Tucson, Arizona Office: One South Church Avenue, Suite 1030, 85701.
Telephone: 602-624-9312.
Fax: 602-882-7383.

Edward C. LeBeau | Philip A. Edlund
George T. Cole

Representative Clients: ASARCO Incorporated; AT&T Communications; Bridgestone/Firestone, Inc.; Catellus Development Corp.; Cyprus Amax Mineral Co.; First Interstate Bank of Arizona; GFC Financial Corp.; GIANT Industries; PETsMART, Inc.; Phelps Dodge Corporation.

For full biographical listings, see the Martindale-Hubbell Law Directory

PESKIND HYMSON & GOLDSTEIN, P.C. (AV)

14595 North Scottsdale Road, Suite 14, 85254
Telephone: 602-991-9077
Fax: 602-443-8854

E. J. Peskind | Irving Hymson

Bradley S. Braun

OF COUNSEL

Marilee Miller Clarke

For full biographical listings, see the Martindale-Hubbell Law Directory

SPARKS & SILER, P.C. (AV)

7503 First Street, 85251-4573
Telephone: 602-949-1339
Fax: 602-949-7587

Joe P. Sparks | E. Dennis Siler

Kevin T. Tehan | John H. Ryley

References: Bank One, Arizona, Trust Department; Northern Trust Bank of Arizona, N.A.; First Interstate Bank of Arizona; Bank of America, Arizona, Trust Department.

For full biographical listings, see the Martindale-Hubbell Law Directory

GUY C. WILSON (AV)

Gainey Ranch Financial Center, Suite 130, 7373 East Doubletree Ranch Road, 85258
Telephone: 602-483-7455
Fax: 602-483-7457

For full biographical listings, see the Martindale-Hubbell Law Directory

*TUCSON,** Pima Co.

CHANDLER, TULLAR, UDALL & REDHAIR (AV)

1700 Bank of America Plaza, 33 North Stone Avenue, 85701
Telephone: 602-623-4353
Telefax: 602-792-3426

(See Next Column)

MEMBERS OF FIRM

Thomas Chandler | Edwin M. Gaines, Jr.
D. B. Udall | Dwight M. Whitley, Jr.
Jack Redhair | E. Hardy Smith
Joe F. Tarver, Jr. | John J. Brady
Steven Weatherspoon | Christopher J. Smith
S. Jon Trachta | Charles V. Harrington
Bruce G. MacDonald

ASSOCIATES

Margaret A. Barton | Mark Fredenberg
Joel T. Ireland | Mariann T. Shinoskie
Kurt Kroese

Representative Clients: Arizona Electric Cooperative Power, Inc.; Atlantic Richfield Co.; Northwestern Mutual Life Insurance; Preferred Risk Life Insurance Co.; Citizen Auto Stage; Starpass Properties.

For full biographical listings, see the Martindale-Hubbell Law Directory

COREY & FARRELL, P.C. (AV)

Suite 830, Norwest Tower, One South Church Avenue, 85701-1620
Telephone: 602-882-4994
Telefax: 602-884-7757

Patrick J. Farrell | Barrett L. Kime

Representative Clients: Amphitheater Public School District; Civil Service Commission of the City of Tucson; La Quinta Homes, Inc.; Pima County Merit System Commission; DANKA-Uni-Copy Corp.; Introspect Health Care Corp.

For full biographical listings, see the Martindale-Hubbell Law Directory

LAW OFFICES OF GEORGE J. FEULNER, P.C. (AV)

262 N. Main, 85701-8220
Telephone: 602-622-4866
Fax: 602-624-7034

George J. Feulner

For full biographical listings, see the Martindale-Hubbell Law Directory

PETER T. GIANAS, P.C. (AV)

4400 East Broadway, Suite 800, 85711
Telephone: 602-795-6630
Fax: 602-327-1922

Peter T. Gianas

For full biographical listings, see the Martindale-Hubbell Law Directory

LEONARD FELKER ALTFELD & BATTAILE, P.C. (AV)

250 North Meyer Avenue, P.O. Box 191, 85702-0191
Telephone: 602-622-7733
Fax: 602-622-7967

David J. Leonard | Judith B. Leonard
Sidney L. Felker | Denise Ann Faulk
Clifford B. Altfeld | Donna M. Aversa
John F. Battaile III | Lynne M. Schwartz
Edward O. Comitz

For full biographical listings, see the Martindale-Hubbell Law Directory

LEWIS AND ROCA (AV)

A Partnership including Professional Corporations
One South Church Avenue Suite 700, 85701-1620
Telephone: 602-622-2090
Fax: 602-622-3088
Phoenix, Arizona Office: 40 North Central Avenue.
Telephone: 602-262-5311.
Fax: 602-262-5747.

RESIDENT MEMBERS

S. L. Schorr | Andrew Daru Schorr
Frank S. Bangs, Jr. | Lewis D. Schorr

Representative Clients: Aetna Life Insurance Company; Capin Mercantile Corporation; Citibank (Arizona); The Hartford; Heron Financial Corporation; Pacific Mutual Life Insurance Company; Perini Land & Development Company; City of Scottsdale.

For full biographical listings, see the Martindale-Hubbell Law Directory

MUNGER AND MUNGER, P.L.C. (AV)

333 N. Wilmot, Suite 300, 85711
Telephone: 602-721-1900
Fax: 602-747-1550
Northwest Tucson Office: 6700 N. Oracle Road, Suite 411, Tucson 85704.
Telephone: 602-797-7173.
Fax: 602-797-7178.

John F. Munger | Clark W. Munger (Resident, Northwest Tucson Office)

(See Next Column)

MUNGER AND MUNGER P.L.C., *Tucson—Continued*

Philip Kimble, Martin P. Janello
Karen S. Haller, Susan Gaylord Willis
Mark Edward Chadwick

Representative Clients: Richmond American Homes, Inc.; Jones Intercable; The Nature Conservancy; Property Tax Appeals, Inc.; Photon Sciences; Tucson Greyhound Park; Tucson Realty and Trust; Associated Dermatologists; Arizona State Radiology; Allied Waste Industries, Inc.

For full biographical listings, see the Martindale-Hubbell Law Directory

O'CONNOR, CAVANAGH, ANDERSON, WESTOVER, KILLINGSWORTH & BESHEARS, A PROFESSIONAL ASSOCIATION (AV)

Suite 2200 One South Church Avenue, 85701-1621
Telephone: 602-882-8912
FAX: 602-624-9564
Phoenix, Arizona Office: One East Camelback Road, Suite 1100, 85012.
Telephone: 602-263-2400.
FAX: 602-263-2900.
Sun City, Arizona Office: 13250 North Del Webb Boulevard, Suite B, 85351.
Telephone: 602-263-2808.
FAX: 602-933-3100.
Nogales, Arizona Office: 1827 North Mastick Way, 85621.
Telephone: 602-761-4215.
FAX: 602-761-3505.

Thomas M. Pace

Drue A. Morgan-Birch

Gregory E. Good

Representative Client: Jeffco, Inc.
Reference: Citibank.

For Complete List of Firm Personnel, See General Section

For full biographical listings, see the Martindale-Hubbell Law Directory

RAVEN, KIRSCHNER & NORELL, P.C. (AV)

Suite 1600, One South Church Avenue, 85701-1612
Telephone: 602-628-8700
Telefax: 602-798-5200

Benis E. Bernstein, Mark B. Raven
Bradley G.A. Cloud, S. Leonard Scheff
Andrew Oldland Norell, Stephen A. Thomas

Representative Clients: Pace American Bonding Company; Citibank (Arizona); Continental Medical Systems, Inc.; El Paso Natural Gas Co.; Norwest Bank Arizona; El Rio-Santa Cruz Neighborhood Health Center, Inc.; Resolution Trust Corp.; Sierra Vista Community Hospital; Southern Arizona Rehabilitation Hospital; Ford Motor Credit.

For Complete List of Firm Personnel, See General Section

For full biographical listings, see the Martindale-Hubbell Law Directory

SNELL & WILMER (AV)

1500 Norwest Tower, One South Church Avenue, 85701-1612
Telephone: 602-882-1200
Fax: 602-884-1294
Phoenix, Arizona Office: One Arizona Center, 85004-0001.
Telephone: 602-382-6000.
Fax: 602-382-6070.
Orange County Office: 1920 Main Street, Suite 1200, P.O. Box 19601, Irvine, California, 92714.
Telephone: 714-253-2700
Fax: 714-955-2507.
Salt Lake City, Utah Office: Broadway Centre, 111 East Broadway, Suite 900, 84111.
Telephone: 801-237-1900.
Fax: 801-237-1950.

MEMBERS OF FIRM

Michael S. Milroy, Marc G. Simon

Representative Clients: The Estes Company; Perini Land and Development Company; Ramada, Inc. (now AZTAR Corporation); Rosehaugh/Montleigh Associates; The Symington Company; Talley Industries; Toyota Technical Center, Inc.; Tucson Airport Authority; Bank One, Arizona, NA.; Zev Bufman Sports, Entertainment and Facility Development Group.

For full biographical listings, see the Martindale-Hubbell Law Directory

WATERFALL, ECONOMIDIS, CALDWELL, HANSHAW & VILLAMANA, P.C. (AV)

Suite 800, Williams Centre, 5210 East Williams Circle, 85711
Telephone: 602-790-5828
Telecopier: 602-745-1279

(See Next Column)

A. Alan Hanshaw, Steven M. Cox
Hugh M. Caldwell, Jr., Cary Sandman
Robert L. Villamana, Jane L. Eikleberry
John C. Rambow

Robert C. Craff, Cynthia Ley Anson

Representative Clients: National Bank of Arizona; First Interstate Bank of Arizona; Federal Deposit Insurance Corp.; Magma Copper Co.; Pioneer Title Co.; Chicago Title Insurance Co.; Broadway Realty & Trust; Tucson Realty & Trust.

For Complete List of Firm Personnel, See General Section

For full biographical listings, see the Martindale-Hubbell Law Directory

*YUMA,** Yuma Co.

BYRNE & BENESCH, P.C. (AV)

230 W. Morrison Street, P.O. Box 6446, 85364
Telephone: 602-782-1805
Fax: 602-782-1808

Peter C. Byrne (1916-1994), William S. Dieckhoff
Wayne C. Benesch, Pamela Walsma

For full biographical listings, see the Martindale-Hubbell Law Directory

ARKANSAS

*LITTLE ROCK,** Pulaski Co.

ARNOLD, GROBMYER & HALEY, A PROFESSIONAL ASSOCIATION (AV)

875 Union National Plaza, 124 West Capitol Avenue, P.O. Box 70, 72203
Telephone: 501-376-1171
Fax: 501-375-3548

Benjamin F. Arnold, Joe A. Polk
John H. Haley, Richard L. Ramsay
Robert R. Ross

For Complete List of Firm Personnel, See General Section

For full biographical listings, see the Martindale-Hubbell Law Directory

RICHARD C. DOWNING, P.A. (AV)

Lafayette Building, Suite 750, 523 South Louisiana, 72201
Telephone: 501-372-2066
FAX: 501-376-6420

Richard C. Downing

For full biographical listings, see the Martindale-Hubbell Law Directory

HOOVER & STOREY (AV)

111 Center Street, 11th Floor, 72201-4445
Telephone: 501-376-8500
Facsimile: 501-372-3255

MEMBERS OF FIRM

Paul W. Hoover, Jr., William P. Dougherty
O. H. Storey, III, Max C. Mehlburger
John Kooistra, III, Joyce Bradley Babin
Lawrence Joseph Brady, Herbert W. Kell, Jr.
Letty McAdams

For full biographical listings, see the Martindale-Hubbell Law Directory

WILLIAM L. OWEN (AV)

The Fones House, 902 West Second, P.O. Box 989, 72203
Telephone: 501-372-1655
Fax: 501-372-7884

For full biographical listings, see the Martindale-Hubbell Law Directory

ROSE LAW FIRM, A PROFESSIONAL ASSOCIATION (AV)

120 East Fourth Street, 72201
Telephone: 501-375-9131
Telecopy: 501-375-1309

George E. Campbell, Kevin R. Burns
Herbert C. Rule, III, John T. Hardin
Garland J. Garrett, Stephen N. Joiner
Thomas P. Thrash, Brian Rosenthal
J. Scott Schallhorn

Steven D. Durand, Stephen E. Snider

Representative Clients: Beverly Enterprises; The Equitable Life Assurance Society of the United States; John Hancock Mutual Life Insurance Co.; Harvest Foods, Inc.; Massachusetts Mutual Life Assurance Co.; Panhandle East-

(See Next Column)

ROSE LAW FIRM A PROFESSIONAL ASSOCIATION—*Continued*

ern Corp.; Tramell Crow Companies; Tyson Foods, Inc.; Worthen Banking Corp.

For Complete List of Firm Personnel, See General Section

For full biographical listings, see the Martindale-Hubbell Law Directory

WRIGHT & BONDS (AV)

Centre Place Suite 900, 212 Center Street, 72201
Telephone: 501-376-2500
Fax: 501-376-7826

MEMBERS OF FIRM

Edward L. Wright
Barbara P. Bonds

For full biographical listings, see the Martindale-Hubbell Law Directory

CALIFORNIA

*BAKERSFIELD,** Kern Co.

ELDON R. HUGIE A PROFESSIONAL CORPORATION (AV)

Suite 100, 1405 Commercial Way, 93309
Telephone: 805-328-0200
Telecopier: 805-328-0204

Eldon R. Hugie

Representative Clients: Tri-Fanucchi Farms, Inc.; Aquaculture Enterprises; Kern College Land Co.
References: Community First Bank (Bakersfield Main Branch).

For full biographical listings, see the Martindale-Hubbell Law Directory

KLEIN, WEGIS, DENATALE, GOLDNER & MUIR (AV)

A Partnership including Professional Corporations
(Formerly Di Giorgio, Davis, Klein, Wegis, Duggan & Friedman)
ARCO Tower, 4550 California Avenue, Second Floor, P.O. Box 11172, 93389-1172
Telephone: 805-395-1000
Telecopier: 805-326-0418
Santa Ana, California Office: Park Tower Building #610, 200 W. Santa Ana Boulevard, 92701.
Telephone: 714-285-0711.
Fax: 714-285-9003.

MEMBERS OF FIRM

Anthony J. Klein (Inc.)
Barry L. Goldner
Thomas V. DeNatale, Jr.
David J. Cooper
Claude P. Kimball

Representative Clients: World Title Company; Transamerica Title Insurance Company; The Prudential America West.

For Complete List of Firm Personnel, See General Section

For full biographical listings, see the Martindale-Hubbell Law Directory

KUHS, PARKER & STANTON (AV)

Suite 200, 1200 Truxtun Avenue, P.O. Box 2205, 93303
Telephone: 805-322-4004
FAX: 805-322-2906

William C. Kuhs
James R. Parker, Jr.
David B. Stanton

Lorraine G. Adams
John P. Doering, III
Robert G. Kuhs

Reference: First Interstate Bank (Bakersfield Main Branch).

For full biographical listings, see the Martindale-Hubbell Law Directory

BEVERLY HILLS, Los Angeles Co.

SCHWARTZ, WISOT & RODOV, A PROFESSIONAL LAW CORPORATION (AV)

Suite 315, 315 South Beverly Drive, 90212
Telephone: 310-277-2323
Fax: 310-556-2308

Bruce Edward Schwartz
Valerie Wisot
Valentina Rodov

Reference: Home Savings of America (Century City Office, Los Angeles, California)

For full biographical listings, see the Martindale-Hubbell Law Directory

TURNER, GERSTENFELD, WILK, TIGERMAN & YOUNG (AV)

Formerly, Turner, Gerstenfeld & Wilk. . . est. 1972
Suite 510, 8383 Wilshire Boulevard, 90211
Telephone: 213-653-3900
Facsimile: 213-653-3021

MEMBERS OF FIRM

Rubin M. Turner
Bert Z. Tigerman
Gerald F. Gerstenfeld
Steven E. Young
Barry R. Wilk
Edward Friedman
Linda Wight Mazur

ASSOCIATES

Joan R. Isaacs
Dortha Larene Pyles

For Complete List of Firm Personnel, See General Section

For full biographical listings, see the Martindale-Hubbell Law Directory

CARLSBAD, San Diego Co.

WEIL & WRIGHT (AV)

1921 Palomar Oaks Way, Suite 301, 92008
Telephone: 619-438-1214
Telefax: 619-438-2666

Paul M. Weil
James T. Reed, Jr.
Archie T. Wright III
David A. Ebersole

For full biographical listings, see the Martindale-Hubbell Law Directory

COSTA MESA, Orange Co.

BALFOUR MACDONALD TALBOT MIJUSKOVIC & OLMSTED, A PROFESSIONAL CORPORATION (AV)

Suite 720, 611 Anton Boulevard, 92626
Telephone: 714-546-2400
Fax: 714-546-5008

M. D. Talbot

For Complete List of Firm Personnel, See General Section

For full biographical listings, see the Martindale-Hubbell Law Directory

COULOMBE KOTTKE & KING, A PROFESSIONAL CORPORATION (AV)

Comerica Bank Tower, 611 Anton Boulevard, Suite 1260, P.O. Box 2410, 92628-2410
Telephone: 714-540-1234
Fax: 714-754-0808; 714-754-0707

Ronald B. Coulombe
Jon S. Kottke
Raymond King

COUNSEL

Mary J. Swanson
Roy B. Woolsey

LEGAL SUPPORT PERSONNEL

PARALEGALS

Karen M. Carrillo
Laura A. Bieser
Vicky M. Pearson

LEGAL ADMINISTRATOR

Sheila O. Elpern

For full biographical listings, see the Martindale-Hubbell Law Directory

DRUMMY KING & WHITE, A PROFESSIONAL CORPORATION (AV)

3200 Park Center Drive, Suite 1000, 92626
Telephone: 714-850-1800
Fax: 714-850-4500

Stephen C. Drummy
Leroy M. Gire
John P. King, Jr.
Jeffrey M. Richard
Alan I. White
Lisa A. Stepanski
Charles W. Parret
Geoffrey S. Payne
Michael G. Joerger
James L. Vandeberg

Mark R. Beckington
Kenneth W. Curtis
Douglas F. Rubino
Alan A. Greenberg
Lawrence M. Burek
Robert M. De Feo
Leigh Otsuka

For full biographical listings, see the Martindale-Hubbell Law Directory

RUTAN & TUCKER (AV)

A Partnership including Professional Corporations
611 Anton Boulevard, Suite 1400, P.O. Box 1950, 92626
Telephone: 714-641-5100; 213-625-7586
Telecopier: 714-546-9035

(See Next Column)

RUTAN & TUCKER, *Costa Mesa—Continued*

MEMBERS OF FIRM

James R. Moore (P.C.)
William R. Biel
Richard A. Curnutt
Michael W. Immell
Richard P. Sims
Jeffrey M. Oderman (P.C.)
Marcia A. Forsyth
Anne Nelson Lanphar
Randall M. Babbush
Mary M. Green
Lori Sarner Smith
Kim D. Thompson

For Complete List of Firm Personnel, See General Section

For full biographical listings, see the Martindale-Hubbell Law Directory

EL MONTE, Los Angeles Co.

MICHAEL B. MONTGOMERY A LAW CORPORATION (AV)

10501 Valley Boulevard, Suite 121, 91731
Telephone: 818-452-1222
Fax: 818-452-8323

Michael B. Montgomery

Reference: Bank of America (San Marino Branch).

For full biographical listings, see the Martindale-Hubbell Law Directory

ENCINO, Los Angeles Co.

AARONSON & AARONSON (AV)

16133 Ventura Boulevard, Suite 1080, 91436
Telephone: 818-783-3858; 818-783-0444
Fax: 818-783-3873; 818-783-3825

MEMBERS OF FIRM

Edward D. Aaronson
Arthur Aaronson

ASSOCIATE

Steven J. Berman

For full biographical listings, see the Martindale-Hubbell Law Directory

MARINO & DALLINGER (AV)

An Association including a Professional Corporation
17835 Ventura Boulevard, Suite 209, 91316
Telephone: 818-774-3636
FAX: 818-774-3635

Timothy G. Dallinger
J. Anthony Marino (A Professional Corporation)

For full biographical listings, see the Martindale-Hubbell Law Directory

*FRESNO,** Fresno Co.

DOWLING, MAGARIAN, AARON & HEYMAN, INCORPORATED (AV)

Suite 200, 6051 North Fresno Street, 93710
Telephone: 209-432-4500
Fax: 209-432-4590

Michael D. Dowling
Richard M. Aaron
Bruce S. Fraser
John C. Ganahl
Sheila M. Smith

Christopher A. Brown

OF COUNSEL

Morris M. Sherr

Reference: Wells Fargo Bank (Main).

For Complete List of Firm Personnel, See General Section

For full biographical listings, see the Martindale-Hubbell Law Directory

KIMBLE, MACMICHAEL & UPTON, A PROFESSIONAL CORPORATION (AV)

Fig Garden Financial Center, 5260 North Palm Avenue, Suite 221, P.O. Box 9489, 93792-9489
Telephone: 209-435-5500
Telecopier: 209-435-1500

Joseph C. Kimble (1910-1972)
Thomas A. MacMichael (1920-1990)
Jon Wallace Upton
Robert E. Bergin
Jeffrey G. Boswell
Steven D. McGee
Robert E. Ward
John P. Eleazarian
Robert H. Scribner
Michael E. Moss
David D. Doyle
Mark D. Miller
Michael F. Tatham
W. Richard Lee
D. Tyler Tharpe
Sylvia Halkousis Coyle

(See Next Column)

Michael J. Jurkovich
S. Brett Sutton
Douglas V. Thornton
Robert William Branch
Brian N. Folland
Christopher L. Wanger
Elise M. Krause
Donald J. Pool
Susan King Hatmaker

For full biographical listings, see the Martindale-Hubbell Law Directory

LANG, RICHERT & PATCH, A PROFESSIONAL CORPORATION (AV)

Fig Garden Financial Center, 5200 North Palm Avenue, 4th Floor, P.O. Box 40012, 93755
Telephone: 209-228-6700
Fax: 209-228-6727

Frank H. Lang
William T. Richert (1937-1993)
Robert L. Patch, II
Val W. Saldaña
Douglas E. Noll
Michael T. Hertz
Victoria J. Salisch
Bradley A. Silva
David R. Jenkins
Charles Trudrung Taylor
Mark L. Creede
Peter N. Zeitler
Charles L. Doerksen

Randall C. Nelson
Barbara A. McAuliffe
Laurie Quigley Cardot
Douglas E. Griffin
Nabil E. Zumout

References: Wells Fargo Bank (Fresno Main Office); First Interstate Bank (Fresno Main Office).

For full biographical listings, see the Martindale-Hubbell Law Directory

GLENDALE, Los Angeles Co.

LASKIN & GRAHAM (AV)

Suite 840, 800 North Brand Boulevard, 91203
Telephone: 213-665-6955; 818-547-4800; 714-957-3031
Telecopier: 818-547-3100

MEMBERS OF FIRM

Arnold K. Graham
Susan L. Vaage
John S. Peterson
Michael Anthony Cisneros
Gregson M. Perry
Lynn I. Ibara
Jason L. Glovinsky

OF COUNSEL

Richard Laskin

For full biographical listings, see the Martindale-Hubbell Law Directory

O'ROURKE, ALLAN & FONG (AV)

3rd Floor, 104 North Belmont, P.O. Box 10220, 91209-3220
Telephone: 818-247-4303
Fax: 818-247-1451

MEMBERS OF FIRM

Denis M. O'Rourke
Joan H. Allan
Roderick D. Fong

ASSOCIATE

Robert G. Mindess

Reference: Verdugo Banking Company (Glendale, California); Community Bank (Glendale, California).

For full biographical listings, see the Martindale-Hubbell Law Directory

INDIAN WELLS, Riverside Co.

ROEMER & HARNIK (AV)

45-025 Manitou Drive at Highway 111, 92210
Telephone: 619-360-2400
Fax: 619-360-1211

Richard I. Roemer
Brian S. Harnik

For full biographical listings, see the Martindale-Hubbell Law Directory

IRVINE, Orange Co.

LAW OFFICES OF WILLIAM C. HOLZWARTH (AV)

2600 Michelson Drive, Suite 780, 92715
Telephone: 714-851-0550
Fax: 714-252-1514

William C. Holzwarth (P.C.)

For full biographical listings, see the Martindale-Hubbell Law Directory

PARILLA, MILITZOK & SHEDDEN (AV)

Suite 1250, 1 Park Plaza, 92714
Telephone: 714-263-1010
Telecopier: 714-263-1693

(See Next Column)

PARILLA, MILITZOK & SHEDDEN—*Continued*

MEMBERS OF FIRM

Bradley N. Garber
Paul H. Parilla
Steven Militzok
Rhea S. Shedden

ASSOCIATES

Marc Ettinger
William A. Kozub

For full biographical listings, see the Martindale-Hubbell Law Directory

WATT, TIEDER & HOFFAR (AV(T))

3 Park Plaza, Suite 1530, 92714
Telephone: 714-852-6700
Telecopier: 714-261-0771
McLean Virginia Office: 7929 Westpark Drive, Suite 400,
Telephone: 703-749-1000.
Telex: 248797 WATTR.
Telecopier: 703-893-8029.
Washington, D.C. Office: 601 Pennsylvania Avenue, N.W. Suite 900,
Telephone: 202-462-4697.

MEMBERS OF FIRM

John B. Tieder, Jr. (Not admitted in CA)
Robert M. Fitzgerald (Not admitted in CA)
Michael G. Long

ASSOCIATE

Christopher P. Pappas

For full biographical listings, see the Martindale-Hubbell Law Directory

LA JOLLA, San Diego Co.

LAW OFFICES OF MAURILE C. TREMBLAY A PROFESSIONAL CORPORATION (AV)

4180 La Jolla Village Drive, Suite 210, 92037
Telephone: 619-558-3030
FAX: 619-558-2502

Maurile C. Tremblay

Mark D. Estle
Ted A. Connor

OF COUNSEL

David R. Endres

For full biographical listings, see the Martindale-Hubbell Law Directory

LONG BEACH, Los Angeles Co.

CAMERON, MADDEN, PEARLSON, GALE & SELLARS (AV)

One World Trade Center Suite 1600, 90831-1600
Telephone: 310-436-3888
Telecopier: 310-437-1967

MEMBERS OF THE FIRM

Timothy C. Cameron
Patrick T. Madden
Charles M. Gale
Paul R. Pearlson
James D. Sellars

ASSOCIATE

Lillian D. Salinger

For full biographical listings, see the Martindale-Hubbell Law Directory

TAUBMAN, SIMPSON, YOUNG & SULENTOR (AV)

Suite 700 Home Savings Building, 249 East Ocean Boulevard, P.O. Box 22670, 90801
Telephone: 310-436-9201
FAX: 310-590-9695

E. C. Denio (1864-1952)
Richard G. Wilson (1928-1993)
Geo. A. Hart (1881-1967)
Roger W. Young
Geo. P. Taubman, Jr. (1897-1970)
William J. Sulentor
Peter M. Williams
Matthew C. Simpson (1900-1988)
Scott R. Magee
Valerie K. de Martino
Maria M. Rohaidy

Attorneys for: Bixby Land Co.; Renick Cadillac, Inc.; Oil Operators Incorporated.
Local Counsel: Crown Cork & Seal Co., Inc.

For full biographical listings, see the Martindale-Hubbell Law Directory

LOS ALTOS, Santa Clara Co.

MALOVOS & KONEVICH (AV)

Los Altos Plaza, 5150 El Camino Real, Suite A-22, 94022
Telephone: 415-988-9700
Facsimile: 415-988-9639

Marian Malovos Konevich
Robert W. Konevich

(See Next Column)

RETIRED FOUNDING PARTNER

Kenneth R. Malovos

References: Bank of America, Mountain View, California Branch; First Interstate Bank, Mountain View and Los Altos, California Branches.

For full biographical listings, see the Martindale-Hubbell Law Directory

*LOS ANGELES,** Los Angeles Co.

ADAMS, DUQUE & HAZELTINE (AV)

A Partnership including Professional Corporations
777 South Figueroa Street, Tenth Floor, 90017
Telephone: 213-620-1240
FAX: 213-896-5500
San Francisco, California Office: 500 Washington Street.
Telephone: 415-982-1240.
FAX: 415-982-0130.

MEMBERS OF FIRM

Bruce A. Beckman
R. Stephen Doan
Dale A. Welke
Charles D. Schoor
Kimler G. Casteel
J. Timothy Scott
Marc Barrett Leh

ASSOCIATE

Maura B. O'Connor

For Complete List of Firm Personnel, See General Section

For full biographical listings, see the Martindale-Hubbell Law Directory

ARGUE PEARSON HARBISON & MYERS (AV)

A Partnership including a Professional Corporation
801 South Flower Street Suite 500, 90017-4699
Telephone: 213-622-3100
Telecopier: 213-622-7575

MEMBERS OF FIRM

Louis W. Myers (1943-1993)
Jerry K. Staub
John C. Argue
Douglas F. Galanter
Don M. Pearson (A Professional Corporation)
Anthony M. Vienna
Philip J. Kaplan
Stephen F. Harbison
Todd Daniel Beld
William A. Jones
Richard G. Rasmussen

ASSOCIATES

Thomas Schalow
Patricia Venegas
Scott Chaplan

For full biographical listings, see the Martindale-Hubbell Law Directory

BAKER & HOSTETLER (AV)

600 Wilshire Boulevard, 90017-3212
Telephone: 213-624-2400
FAX: 213-975-1740
In Cleveland, Ohio, 3200 National City Center, 1900 East Ninth Street.
Telephone: 216-621-0200.
In Columbus, Ohio, Capitol Square, Suite 2100, 65 East State Street.
Telephone: 614-228-1541.
In Denver, Colorado, 303 East 17th Avenue, Suite 1100. Telephone: 303-861-0600.
In Houston, Texas, 1000 Louisiana, Suite 2000. Telephone: 713-236-0020.
In Long Beach, California: 300 Oceangate, Suite 620.
Telephone: 310-432-2827.
In Orlando, Florida, SunBank Center, Suite 2300, 200 South Orange Avenue. Telephone: 407-649-4000.
In Washington, D. C., Washington Square, Suite 1100, 1050 Connecticut Avenue, N. W. Telephone: 202-861-1500.
In College Park, Maryland, 9658 Baltimore Boulevard, Suite 206.
Telephone: 301-441-2781.
In Alexandria, Virginia, 437 North Lee Street. Telephone: 703-549-1294.
In San Francisco, California: One Sansome Street, Suite 2000.
Telephone: 415-951-4705.

PARTNERS

Byron Hayes, Jr.
Thomas G. Roberts
David C. Sampson

For Complete List of Firm Personnel, See General Section

For full biographical listings, see the Martindale-Hubbell Law Directory

BERGMAN & WEDNER, INC. (AV)

Suite 900, 10880 Wilshire Boulevard, 90024
Telephone: 310-470-6110
Fax: Available on Request

Gregory M. Bergman
Mark E. Fingerman
Gregory A. Wedner
Alan Harvey Mittelman
Robert M. Mason III

Kristi Anne Sjoholm-Sierchio
John V. Tamborelli
Keith A. Robinson
Blithe Ann Smith
John P. Dacey
Adrienne Elizabeth Nash
Lisa S. Shukiar

(See Next Column)

BERGMAN & WEDNER INC., *Los Angeles—Continued*

OF COUNSEL

Lloyd A. Bergman (1923-1994) William L. Battles
Jacob A. Wedner

SPECIAL COUNSEL

Richard V. Godino

For full biographical listings, see the Martindale-Hubbell Law Directory

LAW OFFICES OF DAVID B. BLOOM A PROFESSIONAL CORPORATION (AV)

3325 Wilshire Boulevard, Ninth Floor, 90010
Telephone: 213-938-5248; 384-4088
Telecopier: 213-385-2009

David B. Bloom

Stephen S. Monroe (A Professional Corporation)
Raphael A. Rosemblat
James E. Adler
Bonni S. Mantovani
Martin A. Cooper
Roy A. Levun
Cherie S. Raidy
Jonathan Udell
Susan Carole Jay
Edward Idell
Sandra Kamenir
Steven Wayne Lazarus
Andrew Edward Briseno
Harold C. Klaskin
Shelley M. Gould
B. Eric Nelson
John C. Notti
Peter O. Israel
Anthony V. Seferian

For full biographical listings, see the Martindale-Hubbell Law Directory

BODKIN, MCCARTHY, SARGENT & SMITH (AV)

Fifty-First Floor, First Interstate Bank Building, 707 Wilshire Boulevard, 90017
Telephone: 213-620-1000
Facsimile: 213-623-5224
Cable Address: "Bolindy"

MEMBERS OF FIRM

Henry G. Bodkin, Jr.
J. Thomas McCarthy
Edward B. Smith, III
Gordon F. Sausser
Michael A. Branconier
Robert H. Berkes
Donna D. Melby
Barbara S. Hodous
James F. Boyle

Reference: First Interstate Bank (Los Angeles Main Office, Los Angeles, California).

For Complete List of Firm Personnel, See General Section

For full biographical listings, see the Martindale-Hubbell Law Directory

BUCHALTER, NEMER, FIELDS & YOUNGER, A PROFESSIONAL CORPORATION (AV)

24th Floor, 601 South Figueroa Street, 90017
Telephone: 213-891-0700
Fax: 213-896-0400
Cable Address: "Buchnem"
Telex: 68-7485
New York, New York Office: 19th Floor, 237 Park Avenue.
Telephone: 212-490-8600.
Fax: 212-490-6022.
San Francisco, California Office: 29th Floor, 333 Market Street.
Telephone: 415-227-0900.
Fax: 415-227-0770.
San Jose, California Office: 12th Floor, 50 West San Fernando Street.
Telephone: 408-298-0350.
Fax: 408-298-7683.
Newport Beach, California Office: Suite 300, 620 Newport Center Drive.
Telephone: 714-760-1121.
Fax: 714-720-0182.
Century City, California Office: Suite 2400, 1801 Century Park East.
Telephone: 213-891-0700.
Fax: 310-551-0233.

Kevin M. Brandt
Richard S. Angel
Bryan Mashian

Kenneth W. Swenson
Dean Stackel
Mary LePique Dickson
Shirley Sheau-Lih Lu
Thomas M. Walker
Nicolas M. Kublicki

References: City National Bank; Wells Fargo Bank; Metrobank.

For Complete List of Firm Personnel, See General Section

For full biographical listings, see the Martindale-Hubbell Law Directory

CLARK & TREVITHICK, A PROFESSIONAL CORPORATION (AV)

800 Wilshire Boulevard, 12th Floor, 90017
Telephone: 213-629-5700
Telecopier: 213-624-9441

(See Next Column)

Donald P. Clark
Alexander C. McGilvray, Jr.
Kevin P. Fiore
James S. Arico

OF COUNSEL

John A. Tucker, Jr.

References: Wells Fargo Bank (Los Angeles Main Office); National Bank of California.

For Complete List of Firm Personnel, See General Section

For full biographical listings, see the Martindale-Hubbell Law Directory

PAUL N. CRANE (AV)

Suite 1400, 10920 Wilshire Boulevard, 90024
Telephone: 310-208-0055
FAX: 310-208-4801

For full biographical listings, see the Martindale-Hubbell Law Directory

DARLING, HALL & RAE (AV)

777 South Figueroa, 34th Floor, 90017
Telephone: 213-627-8104
FAX: 213-627-7795

MEMBERS OF FIRM

Hugh W. Darling (1901-1986)
Edward S. Shattuck (1901-1965)
George Gaylord Gute (1922-1981)
Donald Keith Hall (1918-1984)
Matthew S. Rae, Jr.
Richard L. Stack
John L. Flowers

Reference: Bank of America NT & SA (Wilshire & Grand Office, Los Angeles, California).

For full biographical listings, see the Martindale-Hubbell Law Directory

DEMETRIOU, DEL GUERCIO, SPRINGER & MOYER (AV)

801 South Grand Avenue, 10th Floor, 90017
Telephone: 213-624-8407
Telecopy: 213-624-0174

MEMBERS OF FIRM

Ronald J. Del Guercio
Jeffrey Z. B. Springer
Stephen A. Del Guercio
Regina Liudzius Cobb

Reference: Bank of America, L.A. Main Office, Los Angeles, Calif.

For full biographical listings, see the Martindale-Hubbell Law Directory

EZER & WILLIAMSON (AV)

(Formerly Rich & Ezer)
1888 Century Park East, Suite 2020 (Century City), 90067-1706
Telephone: 310-277-7747
Telecopier: 310-277-2576

Mitchel J. Ezer
Richard E. Williamson

OF COUNSEL

John Cramer
Kelli G. Hawley

Renee Ellen Ezer

For full biographical listings, see the Martindale-Hubbell Law Directory

FRIED, BIRD & CRUMPACKER, A PROFESSIONAL CORPORATION (AV)

10100 Santa Monica Boulevard, Suite 300, 90067-6031
Telephone: 310-551-7400
Facsimile: 310-556-4487

Jack Fried
Brian James Bird
David W. Crumpacker, Jr.
Nikki Wolontis
David M. Schachter

David K. Johnson

For full biographical listings, see the Martindale-Hubbell Law Directory

GOLDMAN, GORDON & LIPSTONE (AV)

Suite 1920, 1801 Century Park East, 90067
Telephone: 310-277-7171
FAX: 310-277-1547

MEMBERS OF FIRM

A. S. Goldman (1895-1966)
Leonard A. Goldman
Robert P. Gordon
Ronald K. Lipstone

ASSOCIATE

Jerry A. Jacobson

References: Bank of America, Fourth and Spring Branch, Los Angeles; Bank of America, Wilshire-San Vincente Branch, Beverly Hills.

For full biographical listings, see the Martindale-Hubbell Law Directory

Los Angeles—Continued

Earle Gary Goodman (AV)

Suite 1400, 10940 Wilshire Boulevard, 90024
Telephone: 310-208-5330
Fax: 310-208-5770

Reference: Bank of America, Westwood Village Office.

For full biographical listings, see the Martindale-Hubbell Law Directory

Halstead, Baker & Olson (AV)

Suite 500, 1000 Wilshire Boulevard, 90017
Telephone: 213-622-0200
Telecopier: 213-623-3836

MEMBERS OF FIRM

Harry M. Halstead
Sheldon S. Baker
Eric Olson
John J. Jacobson
Charles L. LeCroy, III
William C. Hansen
Arsen Danielian

ASSOCIATES

Michael S. Simon
Andrea L. Esterson
Donald J. Gary, Jr.

For full biographical listings, see the Martindale-Hubbell Law Directory

Hanna and Morton (AV)

A Partnership including Professional Corporations
Seventeenth Floor, Wilshire-Grand Building, 600 Wilshire Boulevard, 90017
Telephone: 213-628-7131

MEMBERS OF FIRM

Gregory R. Ryan
James P. Modisette

ASSOCIATE

Michael P. Wippler

For Complete List of Firm Personnel, See General Section

For full biographical listings, see the Martindale-Hubbell Law Directory

Loeb and Loeb (AV)

A Partnership including Professional Corporations
Suite 1800, 1000 Wilshire Boulevard, 90017-2475
Telephone: 213-688-3400
Telecopier: 213-688-3460; 688-3461; 688-3462
Century City, California Office: Suite 2200, 10100 Santa Monica Boulevard, Los Angeles, 90067-4164.
Telephone: 310-282-2000.
Telecopier: 310-282-2191; 282-2192.
New York, N.Y. Office: 345 Park Avenue, 10154-0037.
Telephone: 212-407-4000.
Facsimile: 212-407-4990.
Nashville, Tennessee Office: 45 Music Square West, 37203-3205.
Telephone: 615-749-8300;
Facsimile: 615-749-8308.
Rome, Italy Office: Piazza Digione 1, 00197.
Telephone: 011-396-808-8456.
Telecopier: 011-396-674-8223.

MEMBERS OF FIRM

Michael D. Beck (New York City Office)
Maribeth A. Borthwick (Century City Office)
Frank E. Feder (A P.C.) (Century City and New York Offices)
David C. Fischer (New York City Office)
Kenneth D. Freeman (New York City Office)
James D. Friedman
Joseph P. Heffernan (A P.C.)
James C. Hughes
Gerald D. Kleinman (A P.C.) (Century City Office)
Michael Langs
Andrew E. Lippmann (New York City Office)
Susan V. Noonoo

For Complete List of Firm Personnel, See General Section

For full biographical listings, see the Martindale-Hubbell Law Directory

Minton, Minton and Rand (AV)

510 West Sixth Street, 90014
Telephone: 213-624-9394
Fax: 213-624-9323

MEMBERS OF FIRM

Carl W. Minton (1902-1974)
Carl Minton
David E. Rand

Reference: Bank of America National Trust & Savings Assn. (Seventh & Flower Office, Los Angeles, Calif.).

For full biographical listings, see the Martindale-Hubbell Law Directory

O'Melveny & Myers (AV)

400 South Hope Street, 90071-2899
Telephone: 213-669-6000
Cable Address: "Moms"
Facsimile: 213-669-6407
Century City, California Office: 1999 Avenue of the Stars, 7th Floor, 90067-6035.
Telephone: 310-553-6700.
Facsimile: 310-246-6779.
Newport Beach, California Office: 610 Newport Center Drive, Suite 1700, 92660.
Telephone: 714-760-9600.
Cable Address: "Moms".
Facsimile: 714-669-6994.
San Francisco, California Office: Embarcadero Center West Tower, 275 Battery Street, Suite 2600, 94111.
Telephone: 415-984-8700.
Facsimile: 415-984-8701.
New York, N.Y. Office: Citicorp Center, 153 East 53rd Street, 54th Floor, 10022-4611.
Telephone: 212-326-2000.
Facsimile: 212-326-2061.
Washington, D.C. Office: 555 13th Street, N.W., Suite 500 West, 20004-1109.
Telephone: 202-383-5300.
Cable Address: "Moms".
Facsimile: 202-383-5414.
Newark, New Jersey Office: One Gateway Center, 7th Floor, 07102.
Telephone: 201-639-8600.
Facsimile: 201-639-8630.
London, England Office: 10 Finsbury Square, London, EC2A 1LA.
Telephone: 011-44-171-256 8451.
Facsimile: 011-44-171-638-8205.
Tokyo, Japan Office: Sanbancho KB-6 Building, 6 Sanbancho, Chiyoda-ku, Tokyo 102, Japan.
Telephone: 011-81-3-3239-2800.
Facsimile: 011-81-3-3239-2432.
Hong Kong Office: 1104 Lippo Tower, Lippo Centre, 89 Queensway, Central Hong Kong.
Telephone: 011-852-523-8266.
Facsimile: 011-852-522-1760.

MEMBERS OF FIRM

Francis J. Burgweger, Jr. (New York, N.Y. Office)
David W. Cartwright (Century City Office)
Theresa A. Cerezola (Not admitted in CA; New York, N.Y. Office)
William N. Cooney
Stephen A. Cowan (San Francisco Office)
Steven L. Edwards (Newport Beach Office)
Patricia Frobes (Newport Beach and Los Angeles Offices)
Peter T. Healy (San Francisco Office)
Howard M. Heitner
Jack B. Hicks III
Edward W. Hieronymus
Robert S. Insolia (Not admitted in CA; New York, N.Y. Office)
James H. Kinney (Century City Office)
Lowell C. Martindale, Jr. (Newport Beach Office)
Mitchell B. Menzer
Scott A. Meyerhoff (Newport Beach Office)
Paul E. Mosley (Newport Beach Office)
F. Thomas Muller, Jr.
Gregg Oppenheimer
Laurence G. Preble (New York, N.Y. Office)
Frank L. Rugani (Newport Beach Office)
Gregory B. Thorpe
Jacqueline A. Weiss (Not admitted in CA; New York, N.Y. Office)

OF COUNSEL

Owen Olpin

SPECIAL COUNSEL

Joseph L. Coleman (Newport Beach Office)
David G. Estes (San Francisco Office)
M. Manuel Fishman (San Francisco Office)
Peter C. Kelley (Century City Office)
John Charles Maddux (San Francisco Office)
Pamela Lynne Westhoff

ASSOCIATES

Robert H. Bienstock (Not admitted in CA; New York, N.Y. Office)
Brandon F.R. Bradkin
Deborah J. Brown (Century City Office)
Cynthia Jeann Christian
Robin L. Gohlke
Lisa Maree Campbell Gooden (Century City Office)
Edward C. Hagerott, Jr. (San Francisco Office)
Maria Snyder Hardy (Century City Office)
Richard J. Holmstrom (Not admitted in CA; New York, N.Y. Office)
Sandra Segal Ikuta
Teresa L. Johnson
David S. Kitchen
Malcolm M. Kratzer (Not admitted in CA; New York, N. Y. Office)
Karen M. Lower
Dennis J. Martin (New York, N.Y. Office)
Joseph G. McHugh
Ann Catherine Menard

(See Next Column)

O'MELVENY & MYERS, *Los Angeles—Continued*

ASSOCIATES (Continued)

Maureen O'Connor (Not admitted in CA; New York, N.Y. Office)
Dean Pappas (Century City Office)
Mark A. Robertson (Century City Office)
Kelby Van Patten (Newport Beach Office)
Michael A. Williamson
Dean A. Willis

For Complete List of Firm Personnel, See General Section

For full biographical listings, see the Martindale-Hubbell Law Directory

ROSENFELD & WOLFF, A PROFESSIONAL CORPORATION (AV)

2049 Century Park East, Suite 600, 90067
Telephone: 310-556-1221
Fax: 310-556-0401

Morton M. Rosenfeld
Steven G. Wolff
Alan D. Aronson

Yelena Yeruhim

For full biographical listings, see the Martindale-Hubbell Law Directory

SCHWARTZ, STEINSAPIR, DOHRMANN & SOMMERS (AV)

Suite 1820, 3580 Wilshire Boulevard, 90010
Telephone: 213-487-5700
Fax: 213-487-5548

MEMBERS OF FIRM

Laurence D. Steinsapir
Robert M. Dohrmann
Richard D. Sommers
Stuart Libicki

For full biographical listings, see the Martindale-Hubbell Law Directory

SHEPPARD, MULLIN, RICHTER & HAMPTON (AV)

A Partnership including Professional Corporations
Forty-Eighth Floor, 333 South Hope Street, 90071-1406
Telephone: 213-620-1780
Telecopier: 213-620-1398
Cable Address: "Sheplaw"
Telex: 19-4424
Orange County, California Office: Seventh Floor, 4695 MacArthur Court, Newport Beach.
Telephone: 714-752-6400.
Telecopier: 714-851-0739.
Telex: 19-4424.
San Francisco, California Office: Seventeenth Floor, Four Embarcadero Center.
Telephone: 415-434-9100.
Telecopier: 415-434-3947.
Telex: 19-4424.
San Diego, California Office: Nineteenth Floor, 501 West Broadway.
Telephone: 619-338-6500.
Telecopier: 619-234-3815.
Telex: 19-4424.

MEMBERS OF FIRM

Domenic C. Drago (San Diego Office)
James Blythe Hodge * (San Francisco Office)
Brent R. Liljestrom (Orange County Office)
James A. Lonergan
Christopher B. Neils (San Diego Office)
Mark L. Nelson
Mark T. Okuma
Jack H. Rubens
Thomas R. Sheppard *
John R. Simon * (Orange County Office)
L. Kirk Wallace
Robert E. Williams

SPECIAL COUNSEL

Steven C. Nock (Orange County Office)

ASSOCIATES

Gene R. Clark (Orange County Office)
Susan Morton Derian
Paula A. Hobson
Frank W. Iaffaldano
Christopher J. Kearns (San Diego Office)
Jay T. Kinn
Kelly Kinnon
Randy J. Myricks
Patricia V. Ostiller
Steven A. Ross
Craig M. Schmitz
Lisa H. Sturzenegger

*Professional Corporation

For Complete List of Firm Personnel, See General Section

For full biographical listings, see the Martindale-Hubbell Law Directory

SHERWOOD AND HARDGROVE (AV)

A Partnership including a Professional Corporation
Suite 240, 11990 San Vicente Boulevard, 90049-5004
Telephone: 310-826-2625
FAX: 310-826-6055

Don C. Sherwood (P.C.)
Kenneth M. Hardgrove

(See Next Column)

ASSOCIATES

Charles G. Brackins
Nancy C. Brown
Janet I. Ray
Timothy S. Plum
Chet A. Cramin
Darlene R. Willmot
Pamela J. Paluga

For full biographical listings, see the Martindale-Hubbell Law Directory

MANHATTAN BEACH, Los Angeles Co.

RICHARD W. LYMAN, JR. (AV)

1601 North Sepulveda Boulevard Box 194, 90266-5133
Telephone: 310-546-7607
Fax: 310-546-7608

For full biographical listings, see the Martindale-Hubbell Law Directory

STEINBERG, FOSTER & BARNESS (AV)

1334 Park View Avenue, Suite 100, 90266
Telephone: 310-546-5838
Telecopier: 310-546-5630

MEMBERS OF FIRM

Alex Steinberg
Douglas B. Foster
Daniel I. Barness

ASSOCIATE

William R. (Randy) Kirkpatrick

References: Home Bank; Imperial Bank; Citizens Commerical Trust & Savings Bank; Bank of America.

For full biographical listings, see the Martindale-Hubbell Law Directory

*MODESTO,** Stanislaus Co.

RICHARD DOUGLAS BREW A PROFESSIONAL LAW CORPORATION (AV)

Suite 350 / Judge Frank C. Damrell Building, 1601 I Street, 95354-1110
Telephone: 209-572-3157
Telefax: 209-572-4641

Richard Douglas Brew

For full biographical listings, see the Martindale-Hubbell Law Directory

BRUNN & FLYNN, A PROFESSIONAL CORPORATION (AV)

928 12th Street, P.O. Box 3366, 95353
Telephone: 209-521-2133
Fax: 209-521-7584

Charles K. Brunn
Timothy T. Flynn
Gerald E. Brunn
Roger S. Matzkind

Reference: Pacific Valley Bank.

For full biographical listings, see the Martindale-Hubbell Law Directory

MONTEREY, Monterey Co.

MURPHY, THOMPSON & GUNTER, A PROFESSIONAL LAW PARTNERSHIP (AV)

580 Calle Principal, 93940-2818
Telephone: 408-646-1221
Fax: 408-646-0953

Ralph W. Thompson, III
Roy C. Gunter, III

For full biographical listings, see the Martindale-Hubbell Law Directory

MOUNTAIN VIEW, Santa Clara Co.

SCHNEIDER, LUCE, QUILLINAN & MORGAN (AV)

A Partnership including a Professional Corporation
444 Castro Street, Suite 900, 94041-2073
Telephone: 415-969-4000
FAX: 415-969-6953

MEMBERS OF FIRM

Michael E. Schneider (A P.C.)
James G. Luce
James V. Quillinan
Michael R. Morgan

ASSOCIATES

Richard Posilippo
Melissa C. Johnson

For full biographical listings, see the Martindale-Hubbell Law Directory

NEWPORT BEACH, Orange Co.

CALL, CLAYTON & JENSEN, A PROFESSIONAL CORPORATION (AV)

Suite 700, 610 Newport Center Drive, 92660
Telephone: 714-760-8711
FAX: 714-759-3637

(See Next Column)

CALL, CLAYTON & JENSEN A PROFESSIONAL CORPORATION—*Continued*

Wayne W. Call
L. Whitney Clayton, III
Troy L. Tate
Seth L. Liebman
Jay W. Deverich

Michael R. Overly
Maryam Shokrai
James A. Durant

For full biographical listings, see the Martindale-Hubbell Law Directory

DAVIS, PUNELLI, KEATHLEY & WILLARD (AV)

610 Newport Center Drive, Suite 1000, P.O. Box 7920, 92658-7920
Telephone: 714-640-0700
Telecopier: 714-640-0714
San Diego, California Office: 4370 La Jolla Village Drive, Suite 300.
Telephone: 619-558-2581.

MEMBERS OF FIRM

Robert E. Willard
S. Eric Davis
Frank Punelli, Jr.
H. James Keathley
Leonard R. Sager
Eric G. Anderson
Katherine D. O'Brian

OF COUNSEL

Lewis K. Uhler

For full biographical listings, see the Martindale-Hubbell Law Directory

*OAKLAND,** Alameda Co.

GRAVES, ALLEN, CORNELIUS & CELESTRE (AV)

2101 Webster Street, Suite 1590, P.O. Box 30817, 94604-6917
Telephone: 510-839-8777
Telecopier: 510-839-5192
Lafayette, California Office: 3650 Mount Diablo Boulevard, Suite 180, 94549.
Telephone: 510-283-9977.
FAX: 510-283-5192.

Jeffrey Allen
Bruce A. Cornelius (Resident)
W. Michael Celestre

For full biographical listings, see the Martindale-Hubbell Law Directory

ORANGE, Orange Co.

WALSWORTH, FRANKLIN & BEVINS (AV)

1 City Boulevard West, Suite 308, 92668
Telephone: 714-634-2522
LAW-FAX: 714-634-0686
San Francisco, California Office: 580 California Street, Suite 1335.
Telephone: 415-781-7072.
Fax: 415-391-6258.

Jeffrey P. Walsworth
Ferdie F. Franklin
Ronald H. Bevins, Jr.
Michael T. McCall
Noel Edlin (Resident, San Francisco Office)
Lawrence E. Duffy, Jr.
Sheldon J. Fleming
J. Wayne Allen
James A. Anton
Ingrid K. Campagne (Resident, San Francisco Office)
Robert M. Channel (Resident, San Francisco Office)
Nicholas A. Cipiti
Sharon L. Clisham (Resident, San Francisco Office)
David W. Epps (Resident, San Francisco Office)
Richard M. Hills (Resident, San Francisco Office)
Sandra G. Kennedy
Randall J. Lee (Resident, San Francisco Office)
Kimberly K. Mays
Bruce A. Nelson (Resident, San Francisco Office)
Kevin Pegan
Allan W. Ruggles
Jonathan M. Slipp
Cyrian B. Tabuena (Resident, San Francisco Office)
John L. Trunko
Houston M. Watson, II
Mary A. Watson

For full biographical listings, see the Martindale-Hubbell Law Directory

OXNARD, Ventura Co.

ENGLAND, WHITFIELD, SCHRÖEDER & TREDWAY (AV)

6th Floor, Union Bank Tower, 300 Esplanade Drive, 93030
Telephone: 805-485-9627
Ventura: 647-8237
Southern California Toll Free: 800-255-3485
Fax: 805-983-0297
Thousand Oaks, California Office: Rolling Oaks Office Center. 351 Rolling Oaks Drive.
Telephone: Southern California Toll Free: 800-255-3485.

MEMBERS OF FIRM

Theodore J. England
Anson M. Whitfield
Robert W. Schröeder
David W. Tredway
Robert A. McSorley
Stuart A. Comis
Mitchel B. Kahn
Mark A. Nelson
Eric J. Kananen
Mary E. Schröeder
Oscar C. Gonzalez
Steven K. Perrin

(See Next Column)

ASSOCIATES

William J. Kesatie
Melissa E. Cohen
Terry R. Bailey
Andrew S. Hughes
Madison M. Christian
Kurt Edward Kananen
William W. Webb
Jeremy J. F. Gray
Melodee A. Yee
Robert David Schwartz
Linda Kathryn Ash
Carla Jean Ortega

Representative Clients: Seneca Resources Corp. (oil & gas); Cal-Sun Produce Co.; Waste Management of California, Inc; Dah Chong Hong (Honda, Toyota, Mazda, Lexus, Accura, Saturn automobile dealerships); Willamette Industries; Oxnard Harbor Association of Realtors; Port of Hueneme; Conejo Valley Association of Realtors; Power-One, Inc.

For full biographical listings, see the Martindale-Hubbell Law Directory

PALM DESERT, Riverside Co.

CRANDALL & TRAVER (AV)

43-645 Monterey Avenue, Suite D, 92260
Telephone: 619-346-7557
Telecopier: 619-773-3589

Lynn D. Crandall
Walter J.R. Traver

Lisa A. Garvin
Elizabeth Olivier
Toni Eggebraaten
Kimberly G. Oleson

Reference: Eldorado Bank, Palm Desert Office.

For full biographical listings, see the Martindale-Hubbell Law Directory

PALM SPRINGS, Riverside Co.

SCHLECHT, SHEVLIN & SHOENBERGER, A LAW CORPORATION (AV)

Suite 100, 801 East Tahquitz Canyon Way, P.O. Box 2744, 92263-2744
Telephone: 619-320-7161
Facsimile: 619-323-1758; 619-325-4623

James M. Schlecht
Daniel T. Johnson
Bonnie Garland Guss

Representative Clients: Outdoor Resorts of America; The Escrow Connection; Wells Fargo Bank; Canyon Country Club; Waste Management Co.

For Complete List of Firm Personnel, See General Section

For full biographical listings, see the Martindale-Hubbell Law Directory

PALO ALTO, Santa Clara Co.

HANNA & VAN ATTA (AV)

A Partnership of Professional Corporations
525 University Avenue, Suite 705, 94301
Telephone: 415-321-5700
Fax: 415-321-5639

John Paul Hanna
David M. Van Atta

Representative Clients: Calprop Corp; Citation Homes; Dividend Development Corp.; Haseko (California), Inc.; Hayman Homes; Kaufman and Broad; Lincoln Property Co.; Shea Homes.

For full biographical listings, see the Martindale-Hubbell Law Directory

PASADENA, Los Angeles Co.

BARKER & ASSOCIATES, A PROFESSIONAL CORPORATION (AV)

301 East Colorado Boulevard Suite 200, 91101-1977
Telephone: 818-578-1970; 213-617-3112
Facsimile: 818-578-0768

Lee Barker
Steven G. Harman
Timothy M. Howett
Kelly G. Richardson
John J. Isaza
Blaine Jay Wanke

Reference: Union Bank.

For full biographical listings, see the Martindale-Hubbell Law Directory

LAGERLOF, SENECAL, BRADLEY & SWIFT (AV)

301 North Lake Avenue, 10th Floor, 91101-4107
Telephone: 818-793-9400
FAX: 818-793-5900

MEMBERS OF FIRM

Joseph J. Burris (1913-1980)
Stanley C. Lagerlof
H. Melvin Swift, Jr.
H. Jess Senecal
Jack T. Swafford
John F. Bradley
Timothy J. Gosney
William F. Kruse
Thomas S. Bunn, III
Andrew D. Turner
Rebecca J. Thyne

ASSOCIATES

Paul M. Norman
John F. Machtinger
James D. Ciampa
Ellen M. Burkhart

(See Next Column)

LAGERLOF, SENECAL, BRADLEY & SWIFT, *Pasadena—Continued*

LEGAL SUPPORT PERSONNEL

Ronald E. Hagler

Representative Clients: Anchor Glass Container Corporation; Bethlehem Steel Corp.; Orthopaedic Hospital; Palmdale Water District; Public Water Agencies Group; Walnut Valley Water District.
Special Counsel: City of Redondo Beach, Calif.; Ventura Port Dist., Calif.

For full biographical listings, see the Martindale-Hubbell Law Directory

TAYLOR KUPFER SUMMERS & RHODES (AV)

301 East Colorado Boulevard, Suite 407, 91101
Telephone: 818-304-0953; 213-624-7877
Fax: 818-795-6375

MEMBERS OF FIRM

John D. Taylor
Robert C. Summers
Stephen F. Peters

COUNSEL

Kenneth O. Rhodes

Reference: Citizens Bank (Pasadena).

For Complete List of Firm Personnel, See General Section

For full biographical listings, see the Martindale-Hubbell Law Directory

PLEASANTON, Alameda Co.

GEOFFREY C. ETNIRE (AV)

4900 Hopyard Road, Suite 260, 94588
Telephone: 510-734-9950
Fax: 510-734-9170

For full biographical listings, see the Martindale-Hubbell Law Directory

*SACRAMENTO,** Sacramento Co.

HANSEN, BOYD, CULHANE & WATSON (AV)

A Partnership including Professional Corporations
Central City Centre, 1331 Twenty-First Street, 95814
Telephone: 916-444-2550
Telecopier: 916-444-2358

Hartley T. Hansen (Inc.)
Kevin R. Culhane (Inc.)
David E. Boyd
Lawrence R. Watson
John J. Rueda
James J. Banks

OF COUNSEL

Betsy S. Kimball

Lorraine M. Pavlovich
Thomas L. Riordan
D. Jeffery Grimes
Joseph Zuber
James O. Moses

For full biographical listings, see the Martindale-Hubbell Law Directory

MATHENY, POIDMORE & SEARS (AV)

2100 Northrop Avenue, Building 1200, P.O. Box 13711, 95853-4711
Telephone: 916-929-9271
Fax: 916-929-2458

MEMBERS OF FIRM

Henry G. Matheny (1933-1984)
Anthony J. Poidmore
Douglas A. Sears
Richard S. Linkert
James C. Damir
Michael A. Bishop
Ernest A. Long
Joann Georgallis
Kent M. Luckey

ASSOCIATES

Matthew C. Jaime
Jill P. Telfer
Robert B. Berrigan
Daryl M. Thomas
Ronald E. Enabnit
Cathy A. Reynolds
Byron D. Damiani, Jr.
Catherine Kennedy

OF COUNSEL

A. Laurel Bennett

LEGAL SUPPORT PERSONNEL

PARALEGALS

Karen D. Fisher
Fran Studer
Lynell Rae Steed
Jennifer Bachman
David Austin Boucher

For full biographical listings, see the Martindale-Hubbell Law Directory

THE LAW OFFICE OF DONALD R. PERSON (AV)

7919 Folsom Boulevard, Suite 215, 95826
Telephone: 916-381-3262
Telecopier: 916-381-6321

Representative Clients: Camray Construction, Inc.; Camray Development and Construction Co., Inc.; Lodi Athletic Clubs; Minnesota Mining and Manufacturing Co.; Rio Del Oro Racquet Club; Sacramento Capitals Team Tennis; Spare Time, Inc.

(See Next Column)

For full biographical listings, see the Martindale-Hubbell Law Directory

WILKE, FLEURY, HOFFELT, GOULD & BIRNEY (AV)

A Partnership including Professional Corporations
400 Capitol Mall, Suite 2200, 95814-4408
Telephone: 916-441-2430
Telefax: 916-442-6664
Mailing Address: P.O. Box 15559, 95852-0559

MEMBERS OF FIRM

Richard H. Hoffelt (Inc.)
William A. Gould, Jr., (Inc.)
Philip R. Birney (Inc.)
Thomas G. Redmon (Inc.)
Scott L. Gassaway
Donald Rex Heckman II (Inc.)
Alan G. Perkins
Bradley N. Webb
Ernest James Krtil
Robert R. Mirkin
Matthew W. Powell
Mark L. Andrews
Stephen K. Marmaduke
David A. Frenznick
John R. Valencia
Angus M. MacLeod

ASSOCIATES

Paul A. Dorris
Kelli M. Kennaday
Tracy S. Hendrickson
Joseph G. De Angelis
Jennifer L. Kennedy
Anthony J. DeCristoforo
Rachel N. Kook
Alicia F. From
Michael Polis
Matthew J. Smith
Wayne L. Ordos

OF COUNSEL

Sherman C. Wilke
Anita Seipp Marmaduke
Benjamin G. Davidian

Representative Clients: NOR-CAL Mutual Insurance Co.; California Optometric Assn.; KPMG Peat Marwick; Glaxo, Inc.

For full biographical listings, see the Martindale-Hubbell Law Directory

*SAN BERNARDINO,** San Bernardino Co.

GRESHAM, VARNER, SAVAGE, NOLAN & TILDEN (AV)

Suite 300, 600 North Arrowhead Avenue, 92401
Telephone: 909-884-2171
Fax: 909-888-2120
Victorville, California Office: 14011 Park Avenue, Suite 140.
Telephone: 619-243-2889.
Fax: 619-243-3057.
Riverside, California Office: 3737 Main Street, Suite 420.
Telephone: 714-274-7777.
Fax: 714-274-7770.

MEMBERS OF FIRM

Bruce D. Varner
Mark A. Ostoich
Thomas N. Jacobson
Robert W. Ritter, Jr.
Ernest E. Riffenburgh
Michael Duane Davis (Resident, Victorville Office)

Representative Clients: Kaiser Resources, Inc.; Southern California Edison Co.; General Telephone Company of California; Southern California Gas Co.; General Motors Corp.; San Bernardino Valley, Pomona Valley, Covina-San Gabriel, Azusa-Glendora Boards of Realtors.

For Complete List of Firm Personnel, See General Section

For full biographical listings, see the Martindale-Hubbell Law Directory

*SAN DIEGO,** San Diego Co.

DETISCH, CHRISTENSEN & WOOD (AV)

444 West C Street, Suite 200, 92101
Telephone: 619-236-9343
Fax: 619-236-8307

MEMBERS OF FIRM

Charles B. Christensen
Donald W. Detisch
John W. Wood

ASSOCIATE

Lydia L. Brashear

For full biographical listings, see the Martindale-Hubbell Law Directory

FERRIS & BRITTON, A PROFESSIONAL CORPORATION (AV)

1600 First National Bank Center, 401 West A Street, 92101
Telephone: 619-233-3131
Fax: 619-232-9316

Alfred G. Ferris
Harry J. Proctor
Gary T. Moyer

Representative Clients: Allstate Insurance Co.; Cox Communications, Inc.; Enterprise Rent-a-Car; Exxon; Immuno Pharmaceutics, Inc.; Invitrogen Corporation; Teleport Communications Group; Southwest Airlines; Times-Mirror Cable Television.

For Complete List of Firm Personnel, See General Section

For full biographical listings, see the Martindale-Hubbell Law Directory

San Diego—Continued

HILLYER & IRWIN, A PROFESSIONAL CORPORATION (AV)

550 West C Street, 16th Floor, 92101
Telephone: 619-234-6121
Telecopier: 619-595-1313

Henry J. Klinker | Gary S. Hardke
James E. Drummond | Robert J. Hanna
John C. O'Neill

For full biographical listings, see the Martindale-Hubbell Law Directory

HOVEY, KIRBY, THORNTON & HAHN, A PROFESSIONAL CORPORATION (AV)

101 West Broadway, Suite 1100, 92101-8297
Telephone: 619-685-4000
Fax: 619-685-4004

Gregg B. Hovey | Cynthia K. Thornton
Dean T. Kirby, Jr. | M. Leslie Hovey
Jane Hahn

For full biographical listings, see the Martindale-Hubbell Law Directory

HYDE AND CANOFF (AV)

401 West "A" Street, Suite 1200, 92101
Telephone: 619-696-6911
Telecopier: 619-696-6919

MEMBERS OF FIRM

Laurel Lee Hyde | Karen H. Canoff

Representative Clients: HomeFed Bank; San Diego Trust & Savings Bank; Union Bank; The Resolution Trust Corp.; American Pacific Builders & Contractors; The Hahn Company; The Regents of the University of California; San Diego Gas and Electric Co.; The San Diego Metropolitan Transit Development Board; Kmart Corporation.

For full biographical listings, see the Martindale-Hubbell Law Directory

LINDLEY, LAZAR & SCALES, A PROFESSIONAL CORPORATION (AV)

One America Plaza, 600 West Broadway, Suite 1400, 92101-3302
Telephone: 619-234-9181
Fax: 619-234-8475

Luke R. Corbett | Stephen F. Treadgold
John M. Seitman | James Henry Fox
Robert M. McLeod | R. Gordon Huckins
William E. Johns | Kenneth C. Jones

Representative Clients: Westana Builders-Developers; Chicago Title Insurance Company; Palomar Savings & Loan Association; George Wimpey, Inc.; Shapell Industries, Inc.; Pointe Builders.

For Complete List of Firm Personnel, See General Section

For full biographical listings, see the Martindale-Hubbell Law Directory

LUCE, FORWARD, HAMILTON & SCRIPPS (AV)

A Partnership including Professional Corporations
600 West Broadway, Suite 2600, 92101
Telephone: 619-236-1414
Fax: 619-232-8311
La Jolla, California Office: 4275 Executive Square, Suite 800, 92037.
Telephone: 619-535-2639.
Fax: 619-453-2812.
Los Angeles, California Office: 777 South Figueroa, 36th Floor, 90017.
Telephone: 213-892-4992.
Fax: 213-892-7731.
San Francisco, California Office: 100 Bush Street, 20th Floor, 94104.
Telephone: 415-395-7900.
Fax: 415-395-7949.
New York, N.Y. Office: Citicorp Center, 153 East 53rd Street, 26th Floor, 10022.
Telephone: 212-754-1414.
Fax: 212-644-9727.

MEMBERS OF FIRM

Steven S. Wall | Nancy T. Scull
Thomas M. Murray | Thomas A. May
Ronald W. Rouse | Stephen T. Toohill
Charles L. Hellerich | Robert D. Buell
Craig K. Beam | Marjorie J. Floyd
Robert J. Bell | Valentine S. Hoy, VIII
Mark Hagarty | Timothy R. Pestotnik

ASSOCIATES

Christopher K. Barnette | Bruce D. Lundstrom
David M. Hymer | Edward L. Bushor
Jeffrey A. Chine | Pamela S. Ewers
Roger C. Haerr | Michael L. Branch
Lynne D. Kaelin

(See Next Column)

For Complete List of Firm Personnel, See General Section

For full biographical listings, see the Martindale-Hubbell Law Directory

PROCOPIO, CORY, HARGREAVES AND SAVITCH (AV)

2100 Union Bank Building, 530 B Street, 92101
Telephone: 619-238-1900
Telecopier: 619-235-0398

A. T. Procopio (1900-1974) | John H. Barrett (Retired)
Harry Hargreaves (Retired) | Dennis H. McKee (Retired)
Gerald E. Olson (Retired)

MEMBERS OF FIRM

Alec L. Cory | Robert G. Russell, Jr.
Emmanuel Savitch | Kelly M. Edwards
Todd E. Leigh | Craig P. Sapin
Robert J. Berton | Eric B. Shwisberg

ASSOCIATE

Matthew W. Argue

Representative Clients: Union Bank; Daley Corporation; Associated General Contractors; Lomas Santa Fe Cos.; McGrath Development, Inc.; National Realty Advisors; Inland Industries; California State Teachers Retirement System; Koll Co.

For Complete List of Firm Personnel, See General Section

For full biographical listings, see the Martindale-Hubbell Law Directory

ARTHUR M. WILCOX, JR. (AV)

Koll Center, 501 West Broadway, Suite 1600, 92101
Telephone: 619-696-6788
Fax: 619-696-8685

For full biographical listings, see the Martindale-Hubbell Law Directory

*SAN FRANCISCO,** San Francisco Co.

ADAMS, DUQUE & HAZELTINE (AV)

A Partnership including Professional Corporations
500 Washington Street, 94111
Telephone: 415-982-1240
FAX: 415-982-0130
Los Angeles, California Office: 777 South Figueroa Street, Tenth Floor.
Telephone: 213-620-1240.
FAX: 213-896-5500.

MEMBER OF FIRM

George G. Weickhardt

OF COUNSEL

Barrie Cowan

For Complete List of Firm Personnel, See General Section

For full biographical listings, see the Martindale-Hubbell Law Directory

BERG, ZIEGLER, ANDERSON & PARKER (AV)

4 Embarcadero Center, Suite 1400, 94111
Telephone: 415-397-6000
Telecopier: 415-397-9449
Portland, Oregon Office: 1211 S.W. Fifth Avenue, Suite 2900, 97204.
Telephone: 503-245-0989.
Telecopier: 503-228-5799.

MEMBERS OF FIRM

James M. Berg | Robert Ted Parker
William J. Ziegler, Jr. | David B. Franklin
Robert L. Anderson | David L. Monetta
Ivan M. Gold

Douglas A. Applegate | Jeffrey B. Kirschenbaum
F. Gale Connor | Jennifer S. Malloy
Mark W. Epstein | Patrick J. O'Brien
Michael A. Gardiner | Luis V. Garcia
Jill Meier Garvey (Resident, Portland, Oregon Office)

PARALEGALS

David A. Dunbar | Sharon L. Gostlin
Diane E. Gresham | Lizabeth N. Uhlmann

For full biographical listings, see the Martindale-Hubbell Law Directory

ALLAN M. BERLAND (AV)

601 California Street, Suite 206, 94108
Telephone: 415-397-6711

For full biographical listings, see the Martindale-Hubbell Law Directory

BICKEL & ASSOCIATES (AV)

Four Embarcadero Center, Suite 3440, 94111
Telephone: 415-433-1200
Fax: 415-433-2985

(See Next Column)

BICKEL & ASSOCIATES, *San Francisco—Continued*

Branden E. Bickel

ASSOCIATE

Dawn A. Silberstein

For full biographical listings, see the Martindale-Hubbell Law Directory

EWELL & LEVY (AV)

351 California Street, 94104-2501
Telephone: 415-788-6600
Fax: 415-433-7311

Arthur D. Levy
Gary Ewell

OF COUNSEL

Scott H. Miller
Theresa R. Owens

For full biographical listings, see the Martindale-Hubbell Law Directory

FELDMAN, WALDMAN & KLINE, A PROFESSIONAL CORPORATION (AV)

2700 Russ Building, 235 Montgomery Street, 94104
Telephone: 415-981-1300
Telex: 650-223-3204
Fax: 415-394-0121
Stockton, California Office: Sperry Building, 146-148 West Weber Avenue.
Telephone: 209-943-2004.
Fax: 209-943-0905.

Murry J. Waldman
Leland R. Selna, Jr.
Michael L. Korbholz
Howard M. Wexler
Patricia S. Mar
Kenneth W. Jones
Paul J. Dion
Vern S. Bothwell
L. J. Chris Martiniak
Kenneth A. Freed
Martha Jeanne Shaver (Resident, Stockton Office)
Robert Cedric Goodman
Steven K. Denebeim
Laura Grad
William F. Adams
William M. Smith
Elizabeth A. Thompson
Julie A. Jones
David L. Kanel

Abram S. Feuerstein
John R. Capron
Ted S. Storey
A. Todd Berman
Laura J. Dawson

OF COUNSEL

Richard L. Jaeger
Malcolm Leader-Picone
Gerald A. Sherwin (Resident, Stockton Office)

For full biographical listings, see the Martindale-Hubbell Law Directory

GRIFFINGER, FREED, HEINEMANN, COOK & FOREMAN (AV)

24th Floor, Steuart Street Tower, One Market Plaza, 94105
Telephone: 415-243-0300
Telecopier: 415-777-9366

MEMBERS OF FIRM

Theodore A. Griffinger, Jr.
Michael S. Freed
Peter M. Heinemann
Karen A. Cook
Stewart H. Foreman
Jonathan A. Funk
Peter S. Fishman

Dwight L. Monson
Eileen Trujillo
Robert L. Wishner
Marie C. Bendy
Eric C. Starr
Jonathan Polland

LEGAL SUPPORT PERSONNEL

LEGAL ADMINISTRATOR

Kathleen H. Hartley

PARALEGALS

Jeanne Diettinger
Jean Mahony
Irene E. Bernasconi
Janet L. Johnston

Representative Client: Smith Barney, Harris Upham Co., Inc.
Reference: Bank of America (Main Office).

For full biographical listings, see the Martindale-Hubbell Law Directory

DEAN W. MCPHEE (AV)

100 Pine Street, 21st Floor, 94111
Telephone: 415-398-8220
Telecopier: 415-421-0320

For full biographical listings, see the Martindale-Hubbell Law Directory

MURPHY, PEARSON, BRADLEY & FEENEY, A PROFESSIONAL CORPORATION (AV)

88 Kearny Street, 11th Floor, 94108
Telephone: 415-788-1900
Telecopier: 415-393-8087
Sacramento, California Office: Suite 200, 3600 American River Drive, 95864.
Telephone: 916-483-6074.
Telecopier: 916-483-6088.

James A. Murphy
Arthur V. Pearson
Michael P. Bradley
John H. Feeney
Gregory A. Bastian (Resident, Sacramento Office)
Timothy J. Halloran
Karen M. Goodman (Resident, Sacramento Office)
Mark S. Perelman
Mark Ellis (Resident, Sacramento Office)
William S. Kronenberg

Peter L. Isola
Gregg Anthony Thornton
Anne F. Marchant
Antoinette Waters Farrell
Tomislav (Tom) Peraic
Douglas L. Johnson (Resident, Sacramento Office)
Michael K. Pazdernik (Resident, Sacramento Office)
Reed R. Johnson (Resident, Sacramento Office)
Alexander J. Berline
Alec Hunter Boyd
Amy Bisson Holloway (Resident, Sacramento Office)
Peter W. Thompson (Resident, Sacramento Office)
Gregory S. Maple
Rita K. Johnson
Jane L. O'Hara Gamp
Joseph E. Addiego, III
Kevin T. Burton (Resident at Sacramento, California Office)
Stacy Marie Howard (Resident, Sacramento Office)

LEGAL SUPPORT PERSONNEL

Wilfred A. Fregeau

For full biographical listings, see the Martindale-Hubbell Law Directory

STUBBS, HITTIG & LEONE, A PROFESSIONAL CORPORATION (AV)

Suite 818, Fox Plaza, 1390 Market Street, 94102-5399
Telephone: 415-861-8200
Telecopier: 415-861-6700

Gregory E. Stubbs
H. Christopher Hittig
Louis A. Leone

For full biographical listings, see the Martindale-Hubbell Law Directory

LAW FIRM OF ROBERT A. SUSK (AV)

101 California Street, Suite 3550, 94111-5847
Telephone: 415-982-3950
Fax: 415-982-6143

Robert A. Susk
Leslie J. Mann
Phillip H. Kalsched

For full biographical listings, see the Martindale-Hubbell Law Directory

*SAN JOSE,** Santa Clara Co.

FERRARI, ALVAREZ, OLSEN & OTTOBONI, A PROFESSIONAL CORPORATION (AV)

333 West Santa Clara Street, Suite 700, 95113
Telephone: 408-280-0535
Fax: 408-280-0151
Palo Alto, California Office: 550 Hamilton Avenue.
Telephone: 415-327-3233.

Clarence J. Ferrari, Jr.
Kent E. Olsen
John M. Ottoboni
Richard S. Bebb
James J. Eller
Robert C. Danneskiold
Terence M. Kane
Emma Peña Madrid
John P. Thurau
Roger D. Wintle
Christopher E. Cobey

Michael D. Brayton
Lisa Intrieri Caputo
Jil Dalesandro
Gregory R. Dietrich
J. Timothy Maximoff
Joseph W. Mell, Jr.
George P. Mulcaire
Eleanor C. Schuermann
Melva M. Vollersen

OF COUNSEL

Edward M. Alvarez

For full biographical listings, see the Martindale-Hubbell Law Directory

LICCARDO, ROSSI, STURGES & MCNEIL, A PROFESSIONAL LAW CORPORATION (AV)

1960 The Alameda, Suite 200, 95126
Telephone: 408-244-4570
Fax: 408-244-3294
Oakland, California Office: 1999 Harrison, Suite 1300.
Telephone: 415-834-2206.
Fax: 415-832-4432.

(See Next Column)

Liccardo, Rossi, Sturges & McNeil A Professional Law Corporation—*Continued*

Salvador A. Liccardo	Craig Needham
Ronald R. Rossi	Gregory D. Hull
Robert S. Sturges	Martha Louise Caron
R. Donald McNeil	Cynthia L. Chase
David M. Hamerslough	Dann B. Jones
Susan R. Reischl	Laura Liccardo

Robert C. Colyar	Wes Wagnon
William J. Purdy, III	Richard B. Gullen
Jeffery Lopez	Deborah T. Bjonerud
Peter N. Brewer	Paul Salvatore Liccardo

For full biographical listings, see the Martindale-Hubbell Law Directory

SAN MATEO, San Mateo Co.

Anderlini, Guheen, Finkelstein, Emerick & McSweeney, A Professional Corporation (AV)

400 South El Camino Real, Suite 700, 94402
Telephone: 415-348-0102
Fax: 415-348-0962

P. Terry Anderlini	David G. Finkelstein
John J. Guheen	Merrill G. Emerick

Brian J. McSweeney

A. James Scholz	Paul J. Smoot
John P. Antonakos	Jennifer Gustafson

OF COUNSEL

Daniel J. Monaco (Inc.)

A list of Representative Clients will be furnished upon request.

For full biographical listings, see the Martindale-Hubbell Law Directory

*SANTA ANA,** Orange Co.

Lancaster & Associates (AV)

313 North Birch Street, P.O. Box 22021, 92701-2021
Telephone: 714-836-1411
Fax: 714-836-9930

Michael J. Lancaster

ASSOCIATE

Dieter Zacher

For full biographical listings, see the Martindale-Hubbell Law Directory

Sperling & Pergande (AV)

3 Hutton Centre, Suite 670, 92707
Telephone: 714-540-8500
Facsimile: 714-540-2599

MEMBERS OF FIRM

Dean P. Sperling	K. William Pergande

For full biographical listings, see the Martindale-Hubbell Law Directory

*SANTA CRUZ,** Santa Cruz Co.

Atchison, Anderson, Hurley & Barisone, A Professional Corporation (AV)

333 Church Street, 95060
Telephone: 408-423-8383
Fax: 408-423-9401
Salinas, California Office: 137 Central Avenue, Suite 6. 93901.
Telephone: 408-755-7833.
Fax: 408-753-0293.

Rodney R. Atchison	Vincent P. Hurley
Neal R. Anderson (1947-1986)	John G. Barisone

Justin B. Lighty	David Y. Imai
Mitchell A. Jackman	Anthony P. Condotti

Mary C. Logan

Counsel for: City of Santa Cruz.

For full biographical listings, see the Martindale-Hubbell Law Directory

Dunlap, Burdick and McCormack, A Professional Law Corporation (AV)

121 Jewell Street, 95060
Telephone: 408-426-7040
FAX: 408-426-1095

Michael E. Dunlap	Paul P. Burdick

OF COUNSEL

Sandra C. McCormack

For full biographical listings, see the Martindale-Hubbell Law Directory

SANTA MONICA, Los Angeles Co.

Sacks & Zweig (AV)

A Partnership of Professional Corporations
100 Wilshire Building, Suite 1300, 100 Wilshire Boulevard, 90401
Telephone: 310-451-3113
Facsimile: 310-451-0089

Lee Sacks	Michael K. Zweig

Filomena E. Meyer

OF COUNSEL

Dennis Holahan

For full biographical listings, see the Martindale-Hubbell Law Directory

Steinberg, Nutter & Brent, Law Corporation (AV)

501 Colorado Avenue, Suite 300, 90401
Telephone: 310-451-9714
Telecopier: 310-451-0929

Peter T. Steinberg	Guy B. Nutter

Paul M. Brent

James M. Buck

Reference: Santa Monica Bank.

For full biographical listings, see the Martindale-Hubbell Law Directory

*SANTA ROSA,** Sonoma Co.

Belden, Abbey, Weitzenberg & Kelly, A Professional Corporation (AV)

1105 North Dutton Avenue, P.O. Box 1566, 95402
Telephone: 707-542-5050
Telecopier: 707-542-2589

Thomas P. Kelly, Jr.	Richard W. Abbey

Candace H. Shirley

Lewis R. Warren	Peter J. Walls

Representative Clients: Exchange Bank of Santa Rosa; Westamerica Bank; North Bay Title Co.; Northwestern Title Security Co.; Geyser Peak Winery; Hansel Ford; Santa Rosa City School District.

For Complete List of Firm Personnel, See General Section

For full biographical listings, see the Martindale-Hubbell Law Directory

Clement, Fitzpatrick & Kenworthy, Incorporated (AV)

3333 Mendocino Avenue, P.O. Box 1494, 95402
Telephone: 707-523-1181
Telecopier: 707-546-1360

Clayton E. Clement	Peter C. De Golia
Paul J. Fitzpatrick	Anthony Cohen
K. Randall Kenworthy	Stephen K. Butler

Christopher W. Silva

References: Exchange Bank; Sonoma National Bank.

For full biographical listings, see the Martindale-Hubbell Law Directory

TORRANCE, Los Angeles Co.

Finer, Kim & Stearns (AV)

An Association of Professional Corporations
City National Bank Building, 3424 Carson Street, Suite 500, 90503
Telephone: 310-214-1477
Telecopier: 310-214-0764

Harry J. Kim (A Professional Corporation)	W. A. Finer (A Professional Corporation)

Robert David Ciaccio	Robert B. Parsons

Mark Andrew Hooper

OF COUNSEL

Bennett A. Rheingold	Ryan E. Stearns

LEGAL SUPPORT PERSONNEL

Marcia E. Talbert

For full biographical listings, see the Martindale-Hubbell Law Directory

VISTA, San Diego Co.

Ernest L. Hunt, Jr. (AV)

630 Alta Vista Drive, Suite 103, P.O. Box 640, 92085-0640
Telephone: 619-726-3839
Fax: 619-726-5491

For full biographical listings, see the Martindale-Hubbell Law Directory

WALNUT CREEK, Contra Costa Co.

Field, Baker & Richardson (AV)

Peri Executive Centre, 2033 North Main Street, Suite 900, 94596-3729
Telephone: 510-934-7700
Telecopier: 510-934-6090

MEMBERS

Robert C. Field
R. Gordon Baker, Jr.
Robert W. Richardson
Alan J. Wilhelmy

ASSOCIATE

Emelyn Jewett Carothers

Reference: Civic Bank of Commerce (Walnut Creek Regional Office).

For full biographical listings, see the Martindale-Hubbell Law Directory

Jackl & Katzen (AV)

2033 North Main Street, Suite 700, 94596
Telephone: 510-932-8500
Fax: 510-932-1961

MEMBERS OF FIRM

V. James Jackl
Linda R. Katzen

Christopher J. Joy
David W. Walters
James M. Sitkin
Andrew N. Contopoulos
David A. Schuricht

For full biographical listings, see the Martindale-Hubbell Law Directory

McNamara, Houston, Dodge, McClure & Ney (AV)

1211 Newell Avenue, Second Floor, P.O. Box 5288, 94596-1288
Telephone: 510-939-5330
Facsimile: 510-939-0203
Fairfield, California Office: 639 Kentucky Street, Suite 110.
Telephone: 707-427-3998.
Fax: 707-427-0268.

MEMBERS OF FIRM

William K. Houston, Jr.
Richard E. Dodge
Douglas C. McClure
Michael J. Ney
Thomas G. Beatty
Robert M. Slattery
Thomas E. Pfalzer
William J. Diffenderfer (Resident, Fairfield Office)
Linda J. Seifert
Guy D. Borges (Resident at Fairfield Office)
Raymond L. MacKay
Roger J. Brothers

ASSOCIATES

Dianne Kremen Colville
Stuart C. Gilliam
Ricardo A. Martinez
R. Dewey Wheeler
Ellen H. Nolting
Kim E. McBride
Jane Luciano
Lisa R. Roberts
Martin J. Ambacher
Janet Sirlin Roberts (Resident, Fairfield Office)
Denise Billups-Slone
Natalie A. Meyer
Kathleen A. Nelson (Resident at Fairfield Office)
Jeffrey D. Hosking
Todd M. Green
Brendan J. Dooley
Jon A. Turigliatto
Brett M. Witter
Joseph E. Finkel
Edward M. Callaghan
Michael K. Walton (Resident, Fairfield Office)
John Wesley Smith
Donald A. Odell
Jenifer Kuhn

OF COUNSEL

Daniel J. McNamara

Representative Clients: Allstate Insurance Co.; Canadian Indemnity Co.; Chubb Group of Insurance Cos.; Kaiser-Permanente Medical Group; Medical Insurance Exchange of California; California State Automobile Assn.; Farmers Insurance Group.

For full biographical listings, see the Martindale-Hubbell Law Directory

WOODLAND HILLS, Los Angeles Co.

Feldman, Karp & Feldman, A Professional Corporation (AV)

5959 Topanga Canyon Boulevard, Suite 275, 91367
Telephone: 818-992-0357
Facsimile: 818-992-0537

Deborah L. Feldman
David I. Karp
Yacoba Ann Feldman

Douglas A. Bordner

LEGAL SUPPORT PERSONNEL

Debra Kay "BJ" Philben (Paralegal)

For full biographical listings, see the Martindale-Hubbell Law Directory

Walleck, Shane, Stanard & Blender (AV)

5959 Topanga Canyon Boulevard, Suite 200, 91367
Telephone: 818-346-1333
Fax: 818-702-8939

MEMBERS OF FIRM

David L. Shane
Roger L. Stanard
David L. Blender
Stephen A. DiGiuseppe

Representative Clients: San Fernando Valley Board of Realtors; Keffco, Inc.; Fuller-Jeffrey Broadcasting; Lynn Simay-Key Centers, Inc.; DA/PRO Rubber, Inc.; Pinnacle Estate Properties, Inc.; Comet Electric, Inc.; Wausau Insurance Company; Western States Imports Co., Inc.; California Coast Escrow, Inc.

For full biographical listings, see the Martindale-Hubbell Law Directory

COLORADO

*ASPEN,** Pitkin Co.

Austin, Peirce & Smith, P.C. (AV)

Suite 205, 600 East Hopkins Avenue, 81611
Telephone: 303-925-2600
FAX: 303-925-4720

Ronald D. Austin
Frederick F. Peirce
Thomas Fenton Smith

Rhonda J. Bazil

Counsel for: Clark's Market; Coates, Reid & Waldron Realtors; Crystal Palace Corp.; Snowmass Shopping Center; Coldwell Banker; William Poss & Assoc., Architects; Snowmass Resort Association; Real Estate Affiliates, Inc.; Raleigh Enterprises.

For full biographical listings, see the Martindale-Hubbell Law Directory

J. Nicholas McGrath, P.C. (AV)

Suite 203, 600 East Hopkins Avenue, 81611
Telephone: 303-925-2612
Telecopier: 303-925-4402

J. Nicholas McGrath

Cynthia C. Tester
Susan W. Laatsch (Not admitted in CO)

Representative Clients: Alpine Surveys, Inc.; Aspen Alps Condominium Assn.; Aspen Center for Physics; Gant Condominium Assn.; Hotel Jerome Associates, Ltd. Partners; Redstone Investments, Inc. (Cleveholm Castle).

For full biographical listings, see the Martindale-Hubbell Law Directory

*CASTLE ROCK,** Douglas Co.

Folkestad, Kokish & Fazekas, P.C. (AV)

316 Wilcox Street, 80104-2495
Telephone: 303-688-3045
FAX: 303-688-3189

James B. Folkestad
John Kokish
Ernest F. Fazekas, II

Susan B. Shoemaker
Douglas E. Saunders

Representative Clients: Bank of Douglas County; Johnson & Sons Construction, Inc.; B & W Construction Co.; Proto Construction & Paving, Inc.; Grimm Construction Co.; Ashcroft Homes of Denver LLC.
References: Bank of Douglas County; First National Bank of Castle Rock; First Bank of Castle Rock; Colorado National Bank.

For full biographical listings, see the Martindale-Hubbell Law Directory

*COLORADO SPRINGS,** El Paso Co.

Cross, Gaddis, Kin, Herd & Kelly, P.C. (AV)

118 South Wahsatch, 80903
Telephone: 719-471-3848
Fax: 719-471-0317

Thomas R. Cross
Larry R. Gaddis
James W. Kin
David L. Quicksall (1950-1991)
Thomas J. Herd
Debra L. Kelly

OF COUNSEL

James B. Turner

Reference: Norwest Bank of Colorado Springs.

For full biographical listings, see the Martindale-Hubbell Law Directory

Colorado Springs—Continued

DANIEL P. EDWARDS, P.C. (AV)
Suite 310, 128 South Tejon, 80903
Telephone: 719-634-6620
Fax: 719-634-3142

Daniel P. Edwards

Representative Clients: Marth Taylor and Associates, Inc.; Martin Properties, Inc.; Phoenix Partners, LLC; Realtec Associates; WP Development Company.

For full biographical listings, see the Martindale-Hubbell Law Directory

FLYNN MCKENNA & WRIGHT, LIMITED LIABILITY COMPANY (AV)
20 Boulder Crescent, 80903
Telephone: 719-578-8444
Fax: 719-578-8836

James T. Flynn
R. Tim McKenna
Bruce M. Wright

Michael C. Potarf

Representative Clients: Peregrine Joint Venture; Nor'wood Development, Inc.; Vintage Development, Inc.; The Woziwodski Group (Consulting Architects); Wal-Mart Stores; Comito Custom Homes, Inc.; Colorado Springs Savings and Loan Association; Chase Manhattan of Colorado, Inc.

For full biographical listings, see the Martindale-Hubbell Law Directory

JAMES A. WEIR (AV)
Suite 510 Alamo Corporate Center, 102 South Tejon, 80903
Telephone: 719-473-9906
FAX: 719-578-8869

References: Bank One; Colorado National Bank/Exchange.

For full biographical listings, see the Martindale-Hubbell Law Directory

*DENVER,** Denver Co.

ROBERT L. BARTHOLIC (AV)
Suite 600, 1600 Broadway, 80202
Telephone: 303-830-0500
Fax: 303-860-7855

OF COUNSEL
Clarence L. Bartholic

Approved Attorney for: Mid-South Title Insurance Corp; Lawyers Title Insurance Co.
Representative Clients: Anschutz Corp.; Denver and Rio Grande Western Railroad Co.; Johnson Anderson Mortgage Co.; Arco Environmental Affairs; Burlington Northern Railroad Co. and Subsidiaries; American Association of Private Railroad Car Owners, Inc.
References: Colorado National Bank; Colorado State Bank.

For full biographical listings, see the Martindale-Hubbell Law Directory

BEARMAN TALESNICK & CLOWDUS, PROFESSIONAL CORPORATION (AV)
1200 Seventeenth Street, Suite 2600, 80202-5826
Telephone: 303-572-6500
Facsimile: 303-572-6511

W. Michael Clowdus
Martha S. Nachman

SPECIAL COUNSEL
Andrea Bloom

Representative Clients: Keystone Resorts Management, Inc.; Metropolitan Mortgage; Preferred Equities Corporation; The Christie Lodge; Vacation Internationale, Inc.; Rosewood Property Company.

For full biographical listings, see the Martindale-Hubbell Law Directory

BROWNSTEIN HYATT FARBER & STRICKLAND, P.C. (AV)
Twenty-Second Floor, 410 Seventeenth Street, 80202-4437
Telephone: 303-534-6335
Telecopier: 303-623-1956

Norman Brownstein
Steven W. Farber
Edward N. Barad
John R. Call
Ronald B. Merrill
Lynda A. McNeive
Laura Jean Christman
Wayne H. Hykan
Bruce A. James

OF COUNSEL
Jack N. Hyatt
Ann B. Riley
Susan F. Hammerman

Robert Kaufmann
Jay F. Kamlet
Ana Lazo Tenzer
David M. Brown
Gregory A. Vallin
Jill E. Murray
Howard J. Pollack (Not admitted in CO)

(See Next Column)

Representative Clients: Metropolitan Life Insurance Co. of America; Nomura Asset Capital Corporation; Omnivest International, Inc.; Property Trust of America; The Prudential Insurance Co. of America; SunAmerica, Inc.; Trammell Crow Company; The Travelers Insurance Company; U.S. Home Corporation; Vail Associates, Inc.

For Complete List of Firm Personnel, See General Section

For full biographical listings, see the Martindale-Hubbell Law Directory

CARPENTER & KLATSKIN, P.C. (AV)
1500 Denver Club Building, 518 Seventeenth Street, 80202
Telephone: 303-534-6315
Telecopier: 303-534-0514

Willis V. Carpenter
Andrew S. Klatskin

Max A. Minnig, Jr.

LEGAL SUPPORT PERSONNEL
PARALEGAL
Holly S. Hoxeng

Reference: Colorado State Bank.

For full biographical listings, see the Martindale-Hubbell Law Directory

JON B. CLARKE, P.C. (AV)
Two DTC, Suite 150, 5290 DTC Parkway (Englewood), 80111-2721
Telephone: 303-779-0600
Fax: 303-850-7115

Jon B. Clarke

For full biographical listings, see the Martindale-Hubbell Law Directory

GLEN B. CLARK, JR., P.C. (AV)
Mile High Center, 1700 Broadway, Suite 1217, 80290
Telephone: 303-832-3000
Fax: 303-832-3044

Glen B. Clark, Jr.

Representative Clients: Citadel Bank, Colorado Springs; Cyclo Manufacturing Co.; Camp Coast to Coast, Inc.; Charter Bank & Trust, Inc.; Corporate Air, Inc.; Vacation Matrix, Inc.

For full biographical listings, see the Martindale-Hubbell Law Directory

DAVIS & WEINSTEIN (AV)
Suite 2600, 1600 Broadway, 80202
Telephone: 303-861-4166
Fax: 303-861-2976

MEMBERS OF FIRM
Wendy W. Davis
Jo Ann Weinstein

Reference: The Women's Bank, N.A., Denver, Colo.

For full biographical listings, see the Martindale-Hubbell Law Directory

DUCKER, DEWEY & SEAWELL, P.C. (AV)
One Civic Center Plaza, Suite 1500, 1560 Broadway, 80202
Telephone: 303-861-2828
Telecopier: 303-861-4017
Frisco, Colorado Office: 179 Willow Lane, Suite A, P.O. Box 870, 80443.
Telephone: 303-668-3776. Direct Dial from Denver: 674-1783.

Bruce Ducker
Stephen Gurko (Resident, Frisco Office)
Michael J. Kelly
Robert C. Montgomery
Thomas C. Seawell
L. Bruce Nelson
Christopher J. Walsh

OF COUNSEL
Charles F. Dewey

For full biographical listings, see the Martindale-Hubbell Law Directory

DUFFORD & BROWN, P.C. (AV)
1700 Broadway, Suite 1700, 80290-1701
Telephone: 303-861-8013
Facsimile: 303-832-3804

Thomas G. Brown
Beverly J. Quail
Randall J. Feuerstein
S. Kirk Ingebretsen
Edward D. White

Representative Clients: CF&I Steel, L.P.; Teachers Insurance and Annuity Association; IDS Life Insurance Company; G.T. Land Colorado, Inc.; Hall and Hall Mortgage Corporation; Hill Samuel Bank Limited; Lincoln National Life Insurance Company; Reorganized CF&I Steel Corp.; Winding Brook Corporation.

For Complete List of Firm Personnel, See General Section

For full biographical listings, see the Martindale-Hubbell Law Directory

Denver—Continued

FAIRFIELD AND WOODS, P.C. (AV)

One Norwest Center, Suite 2400, 1700 Lincoln Street, 80203-4524
Telephone: 303-830-2400
Telecopier: 303-830-1033

Peter F. Breitenstein
Charlton H. Carpenter
Howard Holme
Robert S. Slosky
James L. Stone
Michael M. McKinstry
Jac K. Sperling
Robert L. Loeb, Jr.
Daniel R. Frost
Stephen W. Seifert
Mary Jo Gross
Robert A. Holmes
John J. Silver
Thomas P. Kearns
Rocco A. Dodson
Mary E. Moser
Christine K. Truitt
Brent T. Johnson
Craig A. Umbaugh
Stephen H. Leonhardt
Caroline C. Fuller
John M. Frew
Gregory C. Smith
John M. Tanner
Neil T. Duggan

OF COUNSEL

George C. Keely (Retired)

Douglas J. Becker
Brent A. Waite
Thomas M. Pierce
Suzanne R. Kalutkiewicz
Philip J. Roselli
Mary Sommerville Welch
Lisa A. D'Ambrosia (Not admitted in CO)
Jacalyn W. Peter
David L. Joeris

Representative Clients: ACX Technologies, Inc.; Bank of America; Bank of Montreal; Colorado Bankers Association; Copper Mountain, Inc.; Crown Life Insurance Company; Denver Metropolitan Major League Baseball Stadium District; The Denver Nuggets Limited Partnership; East West Partners; John Hancock Mutual Life Insurance Company; Norwest Bank Colorado, N.A.; Prime Retail, Inc.; Simpson Housing Corporation; Sun Life Assurance Company of Canada.

For full biographical listings, see the Martindale-Hubbell Law Directory

---

HOLLAND & HART (AV)

Suite 2900, 555 Seventeenth Street, P.O. Box 8749, 80201
Telephone: 303-295-8000
Cable Address: "Holhart Denver"
Telecopier: 303-295-8261
TWX: 910-931-0568
Denver Tech Center, Colorado Office: Suite 1050, 4601 DTC Boulevard.
Telephone: 303-290-1600.
Telecopier: 303-290-1606.
Aspen, Colorado Office: 600 East Main Street.
Telephone: 303-925-3476.
Telecopier: 303-925-9367.
Boulder, Colorado Office: Suite 500, 1050 Walnut.
Telephone: 303-473-2700.
Telecopier: 303-473-2720.
Colorado Springs, Colorado Office: Suite 1000, 90 S. Cascade Avenue.
Telephone: 719-475-7730.
Telex: 82077 SHHTLX.
Telecopier: 719-634-2461.
Washington, D.C. Office: Suite 310, 1001 Pennsylvania Avenue, N.W.
Telephone: 202-638-5500.
Telecopier: 202-737-8998.
Boise, Idaho Office: Suite 1400, West One Plaza, 101 South Capitol Boulevard, P.O. Box 2527.
Telephone: 208-342-5000.
Telecopier: 208-343-8869.
Billings, Montana Office: Suite 1500, First Interstate Center, 401 North 31st Street, P.O. Box 639.
Telephone: 406-252-2166.
Telecopier: 406-252-1669.
Salt Lake City, Utah Office: Suite 880, 111 East Broadway.
Telephone: 801-578-6000.
FAX: 801-578-6010.
Cheyenne, Wyoming Office: Holland & Hart, A Partnership including Professional Corporations, Suite 500, 2020 Carey Avenue, P.O. Box 1347.
Telephone: 307-778-4200.
Telecopier: 307-778-8175.
Jackson, Wyoming Office: Holland & Hart, A Partnership including Professional Corporations, Suite 2, 175 South King Street, P.O. Box 68.
Telephone: 307-739-9741.
Telecopier: 307-739-9744.

MEMBERS OF FIRM

James E. Hegarty
James P. Lindsay
Dennis M. Jackson
Richard M. Koon
Michael D. Martin
Jesse B. Heath, Jr.
Elizabeth A. Sharrer

OF COUNSEL

Charles E. Pear, Jr.
Howard R. Tallman

ASSOCIATES

J. Kevin Bridston
Lynn A. Cleveland
Daniel J. Glivar
Shari R. Lefkoff
Rufus C. Taylor, Jr.

(See Next Column)

ASPEN, COLORADO RESIDENT PARTNERS

Charles T. Brandt
Arthur C. Daily

ASPEN, COLORADO OF COUNSEL

Thomas J. Todd

COLORADO SPRINGS, COLORADO PARTNERS

Ronald M. Martin
Ronald A. Lehmann (Resident)
Edward H. Flitton (Resident)
Gary R. Burghart (Resident)

BOISE, IDAHO RESIDENT PARTNERS

J. Frederick Mack
Larry E. Prince

BOISE, IDAHO RESIDENT ASSOCIATE

Sandra L. Clapp

BILLINGS, MONTANA PARTNERS

Donald W. Quander
David R. Chisholm

CHEYENNE, WYOMING PARTNERS

Jack D. Palma, II (P.C.)
Lawrence J. Wolfe (P.C.)

CHEYENNE, WYOMING OF COUNSEL

Teresa Burkett Buffington

CHEYENNE, WYOMING RESIDENT ASSOCIATE

James R. Belcher

JACKSON, WYOMING RESIDENT PARTNER

John L. Gallinger (P.C.)

JACKSON RESIDENT OF COUNSEL

Stephen R. Duerr

RESIDENT ASSOCIATE

Brian T. Hansen

For Complete List of Firm Personnel, See General Section

For full biographical listings, see the Martindale-Hubbell Law Directory

---

HOLME ROBERTS & OWEN LLC (AV)

Suite 4100, 1700 Lincoln, 80203
Telephone: 303-861-7000
Telex: 45-4460
Telecopier: 303-866-0200
Boulder, Colorado Office: Suite 400, 1401 Pearl Street.
Telephone: 303-444-5955.
Telecopier: 303-444-1063.
Colorado Springs, Colorado Office: Suite 1300, 90 South Cascade Avenue.
Telephone: 719-473-3800.
Telecopier: 719-633-1518.
Salt Lake City, Utah Office: Suite 1100, 111 East Broadway.
Telephone: 801-521-5800.
Telecopier: 801-521-9639.
London, England Office: 4th Floor, Mellier House, 26a Albemarle Street.
Telephone: 44-171-499-8776.
Telecopier: 44-171-499-7769.
Moscow, Russia Office: 14 Krivokolenny Pr., Suite 30, 101000.
Telephone: 095-925-7816.
Telecopier: 095-923-2726.

MEMBERS OF FIRM

Richard G. Wohlgenant
G. Kevin Conwick
Bruce L. Likoff
David D. Kleinkopf
Jill K. Rood (Boulder Office)
Robert H. Bach
Paul V. Timmins

ASSOCIATES

Paul V. Franke
Lisa A. Hawkins
Kevin H. Kelley
David E. Tenzer (Boulder Office)
Christopher T. Toll

For Complete List of Firm Personnel, See General Section

For full biographical listings, see the Martindale-Hubbell Law Directory

---

KARSH AND FULTON, PROFESSIONAL CORPORATION (AV)

Suite 710, 950 South Cherry Street, 80222
Telephone: 303-759-9669
Fax: 303-782-0902

Alan E. Karsh
Larry C. Fulton
Fred Gabler
J. Terry Wiggins
Seymour Joseph

Antonio T. Ciccarelli

Representative Clients: Marcus and Millichap; Fidelity National Title Insurance; American Title Insurance Co.; TransAmerica Title Insurance Company; The Travelers Insurance Company; Colorado Land Source, Ltd.; Zeff Properties; Lawyers Title Insurance Corp.; Commonwealth Land Title Insurance Corp.; First American Title Insurance Company.

For full biographical listings, see the Martindale-Hubbell Law Directory

---

LOHF, SHAIMAN & JACOBS, P.C. (AV)

900 Cherry Tower, 950 South Cherry Street, 80222
Telephone: 303-753-9000
Telecopier: 303-753-9997

(See Next Column)

LOHF, SHAIMAN & JACOBS P.C.—*Continued*

Charles H. Jacobs Lynn S. Jordan
Robert Shaiman

Reference: Professional Bank.

For full biographical listings, see the Martindale-Hubbell Law Directory

LAW OFFICES OF NANCY D. MILLER, P.C. (AV)

1600 Broadway, Suite 2112, 80202
Telephone: 303-861-4404
Telecopier: 303-861-4133

Nancy D. Miller

Marianne Marshall Tims

OF COUNSEL

Sheila H. Meer (P.C.)

For full biographical listings, see the Martindale-Hubbell Law Directory

OPPERMAN & ASSOCIATES, P.C. (AV)

Suite 410 Kittredge Building, 511 16th Street, 80202
Telephone: 303-623-1970
Telecopier: 303-893-9328

Marlin D. Opperman

William M. Schell Timothy L. Goddard
Douglas S. Widlund

Representative Clients: Denver Urban Renewal Authority; City of Denver, Denver International Airport; City of Boulder, Colo.; City of Westminster, Colo.; City of Telluride, Colorado; City of Central City, Colorado; American Society of Farm Managers and Rural Appraisers, Inc.; City of Thornton.
Reference: Colorado National Bank.

For full biographical listings, see the Martindale-Hubbell Law Directory

*DURANGO,** La Plata Co.

FRANK J. ANESI (AV)

Suite 220, 835 East Second Avenue, P.O. Box 2185, 81302
Telephone: 303-247-9246
Fax: 303-259-2793

References: First National Bank of Durango; Burns Bank, Durango.

For full biographical listings, see the Martindale-Hubbell Law Directory

SHAND, MCLACHLAN & NEWBOLD, P.C. (AV)

124 East Ninth Street, P.O. Drawer I, 81302-2790
Telephone: 303-247-3091
Fax: 303-247-3100

E. Bentley Hamilton (1918-1981) Michael E. McLachlan
J. Douglas Shand Keith Newbold

David A. Bode A. Michael Chapman (Resident)
Sheryl Rogers

For full biographical listings, see the Martindale-Hubbell Law Directory

ENGLEWOOD, Arapahoe Co.

BANTA, HOYT, GREENE & EVERALL, P.C. (AV)

Suite 555, 6300 South Syracuse Way, 80111
Telephone: 303-220-8000
Fax: 303-220-0153

Richard J. Banta Charles A. Kuechenmeister
Jane S. Brautigam

John L. Palmquist

OF COUNSEL

Craig E. Wagner

Representative Clients: American Institute of Timber Construction; Cherry Creek School District No. 5; City of Greenwood Village; Colorado School District Self Insurance Pool; Intermountain Rural Electric Association; Kiewit Western Co.; Littleton Public Schools; National Union Fire Insurance Co. (local); Southgate Sanitation and Water Districts.

For Complete List of Firm Personnel, See General Section

For full biographical listings, see the Martindale-Hubbell Law Directory

*FORT COLLINS,** Larimer Co.

FISCHER, HOWARD & FRANCIS (AV)

Suite 900, 125 South Howes, P.O. Box 506, 80522
Telephone: 303-482-4710
Fax: 303-482-4729

(See Next Column)

MEMBERS OF FIRM

Gene E. Fischer Stephen E. Howard
Steven G. Francis

Approved Attorneys for: Attorney's Title Guaranty Fund, Inc.
Reference: First National Bank of Fort Collins, N.A.

For full biographical listings, see the Martindale-Hubbell Law Directory

*GOLDEN,** Jefferson Co.

BRADLEY, CAMPBELL, CARNEY & MADSEN, PROFESSIONAL CORPORATION (AV)

1717 Washington Avenue, 80401-1994
Telephone: 303-278-3300
Fax: 303-278-3379

Ronald K. Reeves Bryant S. Messner

Counsel for: Adolph Coors Co.; Coors Brewing Co.; Evergreen National Bank, Evergreen, Colorado; Coors Ceramics Co.; Clear Creek National Bank, Georgetown, Colorado; ASARCO, Inc.; Morrison-Knudsen; Westinghouse Electric Corp.
Local Counsel for: Public Service Company of Colorado.
Reference: Colorado National Bank, Denver, Colorado.

For Complete List of Firm Personnel, See General Section

For full biographical listings, see the Martindale-Hubbell Law Directory

HOLLEY, ALBERTSON & POLK, P.C. (AV)

Suite 100, 1667 Cole Boulevard, 80401
Telephone: 303-233-7838
Fax: 303-233-2860

George Alan Holley Scott D. Albertson
Dennis B. Polk

Eric E. Torgersen Thomas A. Walsh
Howard R. Stone

Reference: First Bank of Wheat Ridge.

For full biographical listings, see the Martindale-Hubbell Law Directory

*GREELEY,** Weld Co.

BREGA & WINTERS, P.C. (AV)

1100 Tenth Street, Suite 402, 80631
Telephone: 303-352-4805
Fax: 303-352-6547
Denver, Colorado Office: One United Bank Center. 1700 Lincoln Street, Suite 2222 Street.
Telephone: 303-866-9400.
FAX: 303-861-9109.

Jerry D. Winters Pamela A. Shaddock

Bradley D. Laue

For full biographical listings, see the Martindale-Hubbell Law Directory

VAIL, Eagle Co.

DUNN, ABPLANALP & CHRISTENSEN, P.C. (AV)

Suite 300 Vail National Bank Building, 108 South Frontage Road West, 81657-5087
Telephone: 303-476-0300
Telecopier: 303-476-4765

John W. Dunn Arthur A. Abplanalp, Jr.

Representative Clients: Towns of Avon, Minturn and Red Cliff, Colorado.

For Complete List of Firm Personnel, See General Section

For full biographical listings, see the Martindale-Hubbell Law Directory

OTTO, PORTERFIELD & POST (AV)

0020 Eagle Road, P.O. Box 3149, 81658-3149
Telephone: 303-949-5380
Denver Direct Line: 303-623-5926
Fax: 303-845-9135

Frederick S. Otto Wendell B. Porterfield, Jr.
William J. Post

Reference: 1st Bank of Vail; Vail Bank.

For full biographical listings, see the Martindale-Hubbell Law Directory

CONNECTICUT

*BRIDGEPORT,** Fairfield Co.

ELSTEIN AND ELSTEIN, P.C. (AV)

Suite 400 1087 Broad Street, 06604-4231
Telephone: 203-367-4421
Telecopier: 203-366-8615

Henry Elstein — Bruce L. Elstein

For full biographical listings, see the Martindale-Hubbell Law Directory

GREENWICH, Fairfield Co.

ALBERT, WARD & JOHNSON, P.C. (AV)

125 Mason Street, P.O. Box 1668, 06836
Telephone: 203-661-8600
Telecopier: 203-661-8051

OF COUNSEL
David Albert

Tom S. Ward, Jr. — Jane D. Hogeman
Scott R. Johnson — Howard R. Wolfe

Christopher A. Kristoff

For full biographical listings, see the Martindale-Hubbell Law Directory

IVEY, BARNUM & O'MARA (AV)

Meridian Building, 170 Mason Street, P.O. Box 1689, 06830
Telephone: 203-661-6000
Telecopier: 203-661-9462

MEMBERS OF FIRM

Michael J. Allen — Edward T. Krumeich, Jr.
Robert C. Barnum, Jr. — Donat C. Marchand
Edward D. Cosden, Jr. — Miles F. McDonald, Jr.
James W. Cuminale — Edwin J. O'Mara, Jr.
Wilmot L. Harris, Jr. — Remy A. Rodas
William I. Haslun, II — Gregory A. Saum
Lorraine Slavin

ASSOCIATES

Juerg A. Heim — Nicole Barrett Lecher
Melissa Townsend Klauberg — Alan S. Rubenstein

OF COUNSEL
Philip R. McKnight

For full biographical listings, see the Martindale-Hubbell Law Directory

*HARTFORD,** Hartford Co.

GORDON, MUIR AND FOLEY (AV)

Hartford Square North, Ten Columbus Boulevard, 06106-1944
Telephone: 203-525-5361
Telecopier: 203-525-4849

MEMBERS OF FIRM

William S. Gordon, Jr. (1946-1956) — Jon Stephen Berk
George Muir (1939-1976) — William J. Gallitto
Edward J. Foley (1955-1983) — Gerald R. Swirsky
Peter C. Schwartz — Robert J. O'Brien
John J. Reid — Philip J. O'Connor
John H. Goodrich, Jr. — Kenneth G. Williams
R. Bradley Wolfe — Chester J. Bukowski
Mary Ann Santacroce

ASSOCIATES

J. Lawrence Price — Patrick T. Treacy
Mary Anne Alicia Charron — Andrew J. Hern
James G. Kelly — Eileen Geel
Kevin F. Morin — Christopher L. Slack
Claudia A. Baio — Renee W. Dwyer
David B. Heintz

OF COUNSEL
Stephen M. Riley

Reference: Fleet Bank.

For full biographical listings, see the Martindale-Hubbell Law Directory

LEVIN & D'AGOSTINO (AV)

One State Street, 06103
Telephone: 203-527-0400
Telecopier: 203-249-7500

MEMBERS OF FIRM

Michael R. Levin — Nancy DuBois Wright
John B. D'Agostino — Walter E. Paulekas
Paul W. Ford — Eugene N. Axelrod

(See Next Column)

ASSOCIATES

Peter Menting — William J. Egan
Lawrence A. Dvorin — David A. Hill, Jr.
Margaret A. McCue

For full biographical listings, see the Martindale-Hubbell Law Directory

SOROKIN SOROKIN GROSS HYDE & WILLIAMS P.C. (AV)

One Corporate Center, 06103
Telephone: 203-525-6645
Fax: 203-522-1781
Simsbury, Connecticut Office: 730 Hopmeadow Street.
Telephone: 203-651-9348.
Rocky Hill, Connecticut Office: 2360 Main Street.
Telephone: 203-563-9305.
Fax: 203-529-6931.
Glastonbury, Connecticut Office: 124 Hebron Avenue.
Telephone: 203-659-8801.

James G. Dowling, Jr. — Amelia M. Rugland
Richard D. Tulisano (Resident, Rocky Hill Office)

For Complete List of Firm Personnel, See General Section

For full biographical listings, see the Martindale-Hubbell Law Directory

MILFORD, New Haven Co.

HARLOW, ADAMS & FRIEDMAN, P.C. (AV)

300 Bic Drive, 06460-3508
Telephone: 203-878-0661
Fax: 203-878-9568

William D. Harlow (1921-1988) — Dana Eric Friedman
George W. Adams, III — Theodore H. Shumaker
Stephen P. Wright

Eric R. Gaynor — Joseph A. Kubic

For full biographical listings, see the Martindale-Hubbell Law Directory

*NEW HAVEN,** New Haven Co.

BERGMAN, HOROWITZ & REYNOLDS, P.C. (AV)

157 Church Street, 19th Floor, P.O. Box 426, 06502
Telephone: 203-789-1320
FAX: 203-785-8127
New York, New York Office: 499 Park Avenue, 26th Floor.
Telephone: 212-582-3580.

Melvin Ditman

David M. Spinner — Jeremy A. Mellitz
Richard M. Porter

For Complete List of Firm Personnel, See General Section

For full biographical listings, see the Martindale-Hubbell Law Directory

BRENNER, SALTZMAN & WALLMAN (AV)

A Partnership including Professional Corporations
271 Whitney Avenue, P.O. Box 1746, 06507-1746
Telephone: 203-772-2600
Facsimile: 203-562-2098

Newton D. Brenner (P.C.) — Donald W. Anderson (P.C.)
Stephen L. Saltzman (P.C.) — Carol N. Theodore (P.C.)
Marc A. Wallman (P.C.) — Samuel M. Hurwitz
David R. Schaefer (P.C.) — Wayne A. Martino, P.C.
Stuart Jay Mandel (P.C.) — M. Anne Peters
Kenneth Rosenthal

Peter K. Marsh — Brian P. Daniels
Alice Jo Mick — John R. Bashaw
George Brencher, IV

For full biographical listings, see the Martindale-Hubbell Law Directory

GORMAN & ENRIGHT P.C. (AV)

59 Elm Street, P.O. Box 1961, 06509
Telephone: 203-865-1382
Telecopier: 203-776-7250

John R. Gorman — Brian G. Enright

Patricia King

References: Bank of Boston Connecticut; Bank of New Haven.

For full biographical listings, see the Martindale-Hubbell Law Directory

New Haven—Continued

SACHS, BERMAN & SHURE, SKLARZ & GALLANT, P.C. (AV)

Granite Square 700 State Street, P.O. Box 1960, 06509-1960
Telephone: 203-782-3000
Telex: ESL 62239500
Telecopier: 203-777-3347

Arthur S. Sachs
Howard D. Komisar
Daniel N. Hoffnung

Representative Client: Fusco Corp.

For Complete List of Firm Personnel, See General Section

For full biographical listings, see the Martindale-Hubbell Law Directory

SUSMAN, DUFFY & SEGALOFF, P.C. (AV)

55 Whitney Avenue, 06510-1300
Telephone: 203-624-9830
Telecopier: 203-562-8430
Mailing Address: P.O. Box 1684, New Haven, Connecticut, 06507-1684

Allen H. Duffy (1931-1986)
Michael Susman
James H. Segaloff
David A. Reif
Joseph E. Faughnan
Susan W. Wolfson
Laura M. Sklaver
Andrew R. Lubin
James J. Perito
Matthew C. Susman
Thomas E. Katon

Charles J. Filardi, Jr.
Jennifer L. Schancupp
Donna Decker Morris
Peter G. Kruzynski
Joshua W. Cohen

OF COUNSEL

Diana C. Ballard

For full biographical listings, see the Martindale-Hubbell Law Directory

NEW LONDON, New London Co.

PAVETTI & FREEMAN (AV)

Court House Square Building, 83 Huntington Street, P.O. Box 829, 06320
Telephone: 203-442-9409
Telecopier: 203-443-0264

MEMBERS OF FIRM

Francis J. Pavetti
Jane W. Freeman

For full biographical listings, see the Martindale-Hubbell Law Directory

WALLER, SMITH & PALMER, P.C. (AV)

52 Eugene O'Neill Drive, P.O. Box 88, 06320
Telephone: 203-442-0367
Telecopier: 203-447-9915
Old Lyme, Connecticut Office: 103-A Halls Road.
Telephone: 203-434-8063.

William W. Miner
Robert P. Anderson, Jr.
Robert W. Marrion
Hughes Griffis
Edward B. O'Connell
Frederick B. Gahagan
Linda D. Loucony
Mary E. Driscoll
William E. Wellette

Tracy M. Collins
Donna Richer Skaats

OF COUNSEL

Suzanne Donnelly Kitchings

General Counsel for: Colotone Group.
Counsel for: Union Trust Co.; Coastal Savings Bank; Cash Home Center, Inc.
Local Counsel for: Metropolitan Insurance Co.; Connecticut General Life Insurance Co.

For Complete List of Firm Personnel, See General Section

For full biographical listings, see the Martindale-Hubbell Law Directory

NORWALK, Fairfield Co.

LEV, SPALTER & BERLIN, P.C. (AV)

535 Connecticut Avenue, 06854
Telephone: 203-838-8500
Telecopier: 203-854-1652

Bruce L. Lev
Susan B. Spalter
Duane L. Berlin

Donna M. Lattarulo
Eric J. Dale

Reference: Fleet Bank, N.A.

For full biographical listings, see the Martindale-Hubbell Law Directory

SOUTHPORT, Fairfield Co.

BRODY AND OBER, P.C. (AV)

135 Rennell Drive, 06490
Telephone: 203-259-7405
Fax: 203-255-8572

Charles S. Brody (1894-1976)
Seth O. L. Brody
Stanley B. Garrell
Frank F. Ober
S. Giles Payne
William J. Britt
James M. Thorburn
Barbara S. Miller
Ronald B. Noren

Stephen L. Lichtman
Diane F. Martucci
Richard W. Mather

For full biographical listings, see the Martindale-Hubbell Law Directory

STAMFORD, Fairfield Co.

CHAPMAN & FENNELL (AV)

Three Landmark Square, 06901
Telephone: 203-353-8000
Telecopier: 203-353-8799
New York, New York Office: 330 Madison Avenue.
Telephone: 212-687-3600.
Washington, D.C. Office: 2000 L Street, N.W., Suite 200.
Telephone: 202-822-9351.

MEMBERS OF FIRM

John Haven Chapman
Philip M. Chiappone (Resident, New York, N.Y. Office)
Darrell K. Fennell (Resident, New York, N.Y. Office)
Peter S. Gummo
D. Seeley Hubbard
Eric S. Kamisher (Resident, New York, N.Y. Office)
Brian E. Moran
Victor L. Zimmermann, Jr.

ASSOCIATE

Barton Meyerhoff (Not admitted in CT)

OF COUNSEL

Kevin T. Hoffman
Carol E. Meltzer (Resident, New York, N.Y. Office)
Brainard S. Patton
E. Gabriel Perle (Not admitted in CT)
Victor J. Toth (Resident, Washington, D.C. Office)
Michael Winger (Resident, New York, N.Y. Office)

For full biographical listings, see the Martindale-Hubbell Law Directory

WEST HARTFORD, Hartford Co.

BERMAN, BOURNS & CURRIE (AV)

970 Farmington Avenue, P.O. Box 271837, 06127-1837
Telephone: 203-232-4471
Fax: 203-523-4605

MEMBERS OF FIRM

John A. Berman
Courtney B. Bourns
John K. Currie

ASSOCIATES

Robert B. Fawber
Mary Beth Anderson

For full biographical listings, see the Martindale-Hubbell Law Directory

WESTPORT, Fairfield Co.

STUART A. MCKEEVER (AV)

155 Post Road, East, 06880
Telephone: 203-227-4756
Fax: 203-454-2031

Reference: Fleet Bank.

For full biographical listings, see the Martindale-Hubbell Law Directory

WILLIAM L. SCHEFFLER (AV Ⓣ)

315 Post Road West, 06880
Telephone: 203-226-6600; 212-795-7800
Telecopier: 203-227-1873

For full biographical listings, see the Martindale-Hubbell Law Directory

TIROLA & HERRING (AV)

1221 Post Road East, P.O. Box 631, 06881
Telephone: 203-226-8926
Fax: 203-226-9500
New York, New York Office: Suite 4E, 10 Sheridan Square.
Telephone: 212-463-9642.

MEMBERS OF FIRM

Vincent S. Tirola
Charles Fredericks, Jr.
Elizabeth C. Seeley
Buddy O. H. Herring

Dan Shaban
Marc J. Grenier

(See Next Column)

TIROLA & HERRING, *Westport—Continued*

OF COUNSEL

Edward Kanowitz | C. Michael Carter
Alan D. Lieberson

Reference: The Westport Bank and Trust Co.

For full biographical listings, see the Martindale-Hubbell Law Directory

DELAWARE

*DOVER,** Kent Co.

PARKOWSKI, NOBLE & GUERKE, PROFESSIONAL ASSOCIATION (AV)

116 West Water Street, P.O. Box 598, 19903
Telephone: 302-678-3262
Telecopier: 302-678-9415

F. Michael Parkowski
John W. Noble
I. Barry Guerke
Clay T. Jester
Jeremy W. Homer
John C. Andrade
Jonathan Eisenberg
Donald R. Kinsley

Dana J. Schaefer

OF COUNSEL

George F. Gardner, III

Representative Clients: Delaware Solid Waste Authority; Cabe Associates (Consulting Engineers).
Approved Attorneys for: Ticor Title Insurance Co.
Reference: First National Bank of Wyoming.

For full biographical listings, see the Martindale-Hubbell Law Directory

*WILMINGTON,** New Castle Co.

DALEY, ERISMAN & VAN OGTROP (AV)

1224 King Street, 19801
Telephone: 302-658-4000
FAX: 302-652-8975
Newark, Delaware Office: 206 East Delaware Avenue.
Telephone: 302-368-0133.
FAX: 302-368-4587.

MEMBERS OF FIRM

Robert E. Daley
James A. Erisman
Piet H. van Ogtrop

References: Wilmington Trust Company; Beneficial National Bank.

For full biographical listings, see the Martindale-Hubbell Law Directory

WILLIAMS, HERSHMAN & WISLER, P.A. (AV)

Suite 600, One Commerce Center, Twelfth and Orange Streets, P.O. Box 511, 19899-0511
Telephone: 302-575-0873
Telecopier: 302-575-1642

David Nicol Williams
Douglas M. Hershman
Jeffrey C. Wisler
Barbara Snapp Danberg
F. Peter Conaty, Jr.

References: Wilmington Trust Co.; PNC Bank.

For full biographical listings, see the Martindale-Hubbell Law Directory

DISTRICT OF COLUMBIA

WASHINGTON, D.C. Co.

* indicates certain Bar Register subscribers, in cities of comparable size and importance, who maintain an additional office in Washington, D.C. and who have arranged for representation as a part of the Washington, D.C. listings that follow

*** FRIED, FRANK, HARRIS, SHRIVER & JACOBSON** (AV)

A Partnership including Professional Corporations
Suite 800, 1001 Pennsylvania Avenue, N.W., 20004-2505
Telephone: 202-639-7000
Cable Address: "Steric Washington"
Telex: 892406
Telecopy Rapifax: 202-639-7008
Zap Mail: 202-338-0110
New York, New York Office: One New York Plaza.
Telephone: 212-859-8000.
Cable Address: "Steric New York." W.U. Int.
Telex: 620223. W.U. Int.
Telex: 662119. W.U. Domestic: 128173.
Telecopier: 212-859-4000 (Dex 6200).
Los Angeles, California Office: 725 South Figueroa Street.
Telephone: 213- 689-5800.
London, England Office: 4 Chiswell Street, London EC1Y 4UP.
Telephone: 011-44-171-972-9600.
Fax: 011-44-171-972-9602.
Paris, France Office: 7, Rue Royale, 75008.
Telephone: (+331) 40-17-04-04.
Fax: (+331) 40-17-08-30.

WASHINGTON, D.C. PARTNERS

T. J. Anthony, Jr. | Leonard A. Zax

ASSOCIATE

Michele E. Foster

For Complete List of Firm Personnel, See General Section

For full biographical listings, see the Martindale-Hubbell Law Directory

INGERSOLL AND BLOCH, CHARTERED (AV)

1401 Sixteenth Street, N.W., 20036
Telephone: 202-232-1015
Fax: 202-232-4757

William B. Ingersoll
Stuart Marshall Bloch
Larry M. Berkow
Susan G. Braden
Robert M. Chasnow
Philip A. Gorelick
Neal Goldfarb
Sung Park Reynolds
Reuben B. Robertson, III
Jeffrey B. Stern
Susan Lee Voss
Mel S. Weinberger

For full biographical listings, see the Martindale-Hubbell Law Directory

SHAWN, MANN & NIEDERMAYER, L.L.P. (AV)

1850 M Street, N.W., Suite 280, 20036-5803
Telephone: 202-331-7900
Fax: 202-331-0726

MEMBERS OF FIRM

Roy I. Niedermayer | Eshel Bar-Adon

For full biographical listings, see the Martindale-Hubbell Law Directory

SUTHERLAND, ASBILL & BRENNAN (AV)

1275 Pennsylvania Avenue, N.W., 20004-2404
Telephone: 202-383-0100
Cable Address: "Sutab Wash"
Telex: 89-501
Facsimile: 202-637-3593
Atlanta, Georgia Office: 999 Peachtree Street, N. E., 30309-3996.
Telephone: 404-853-8000.
New York, N.Y. Office: 1270 Avenue of the Americas, 10020-1700.
Telephone: 212-332-3000.
Austin, Texas Office: 111 Congress Avenue, 23rd Floor, 78701-4079.
Telephone: 512-469-3350.

David Schwinger

For Complete List of Firm Personnel, See General Section

For full biographical listings, see the Martindale-Hubbell Law Directory

Washington—Continued

✱ THOMPSON, HINE AND FLORY (AV)

1920 N Street, N.W., 20036-1601
Telephone: 202-331-8800
Fax: 202-331-8330
Telex: 904173
Cable Address: "Caglaw"
Akron, Ohio Office: 50 S. Main Street, Suite 502, 44308-1828.
Telephone: 216-376-8090.
Fax: 216-376-8386.
Cincinnati, Ohio Office: 312 Walnut Street, 14th Floor, 45202-4029.
Telephone: 513-352-6700.
Fax: 513-241-4771.
Telex: 938003.
Cleveland, Ohio Office: 1100 National City Bank Building, 629 Euclid Avenue, 44114.
Telephone: 216-566-5500.
Fax: 216-566-5583.
Telex: 980217. Cable Address "Thomflor".
Columbus, Ohio Office: One Columbus, 10 West Broad Street, 43215-34353.
Telephone: 614-469-3200.
Fax: 614-469-3361.
Dayton, Ohio Office: 2000 Courthouse Plaza, N.E., 45402-1706.
Telephone: 513-443-6600.
Fax: 513-443-6637, 513-443-6635.
Palm Beach, Florida Office: 125 Worth Avenue, 33480-4466.
Telephone: 407-833-5900.
Fax: 407-833-5951.
Brussels, Belgium Office: Rue Des Chevaliers, Ridderstraat 14 - B.10, B-1050.
Telephone: 011-32-2-511-9326.
Fax: 011-32-2-513-9206.

MEMBERS OF FIRM

Roberta B. Aronson
Alfred M. Goldberg
William R. Naeher
Louis Pohoryles
Robert V. Staton

ASSOCIATE

Lisa Sullivan Franzen

OF COUNSEL

William E. Constable
Glenn D. Simpson

For Complete List of Firm Personnel, See General Section

For full biographical listings, see the Martindale-Hubbell Law Directory

✱ VENABLE, BAETJER, HOWARD & CIVILETTI (AV)

A Partnership including Professional Corporations
Suite 1000, 1201 New York Avenue, N.W., 20005
Telephone: 202-962-4800
Fax: 202-962-8300
Baltimore, Maryland Office: Venable, Baetjer and Howard, 1800 Mercantile Bank & Trust Building, 2 Hopkins Plaza.
Telephone: 410-244-7400.
McLean, Virginia Office: Venable, Baetjer and Howard, Suite 400, 2010 Corporate Ridge.
Telephone: 703-760-1600.
Rockville, Maryland Office: Venable, Baetjer and Howard, Suite 500, One Church Street, P. O. Box 1906.
Telephone: 301-217-5600.
Towson, Maryland Office: Venable, Baetjer and Howard, 210 Allegheny Avenue, P. O. Box 5517.
Telephone: 410-494-6200.

MEMBERS OF FIRM

Benjamin R. Civiletti (P.C.) (Also at Baltimore and Towson, Maryland Offices)
Jan K. Guben (Not admitted in DC; Also at Baltimore, Maryland Office)
Thomas J. Madden
Robert E. Madden (Also at Baltimore, Maryland and McLean, Virginia Offices)
John G. Milliken (Also at McLean, Virginia Office)
Joel Z. Silver
Thomas B. Hudson (Also at Baltimore, Maryland Office)
James K. Archibald (Also at Baltimore and Towson, Maryland Offices)
George F. Pappas (Also at Baltimore, Maryland Office)
William D. Quarles (Also at Towson, Maryland Office)
James A. Dunbar (Also at Baltimore, Maryland Office)
Joel J. Goldberg (Also at McLean, Virginia Office)
Paul A. Serini (Not admitted in DC; Also at Baltimore, Maryland Office)

For Complete List of Firm Personnel, See General Section

For full biographical listings, see the Martindale-Hubbell Law Directory

WATT, TIEDER & HOFFAR (AV)

601 Pennsylvania Avenue, N.W., Suite 900, 20004
Telephone: 202-462-4697
Telecopier: 703-893-8029
McLean Virginia Office: 7929 Westpark Drive, Suite 400,
Telephone: 703-749-1000.
Telecopier: 703-893-8029.

(See Next Column)

Irvine California Office: 3 Park Plaza, Suite 1530.
Telephone: 714-852-6700.

MEMBERS OF FIRM

John B. Tieder, Jr.
Robert K. Cox
David C. Romm

For full biographical listings, see the Martindale-Hubbell Law Directory

WILKES, ARTIS, HEDRICK & LANE, CHARTERED (AV)

Suite 1100, 1666 K Street, N.W., 20006-2897
Telephone: 202-457-7800
Cable Address: "Wilan, Washington, D.C."
Annapolis, Maryland Office: Suite 400, 47 State Circle.
Telephone: 410-263-7800.
Bethesda, Maryland Office: Suite 800, 3 Bethesda Metro Center.
Telephone: 301-654-7800.
Fairfax, Virginia Office: Suite 600, 11320 Random Hills Road.
Telephone: 703-385-8000.
Greenbelt, Maryland Office: Suite 410, 6305 Ivy Lane.
Telephone: 301-345-7700.

James C. Wilkes (1899-1968)
James E. Artis (1907-1978)
David M. Bond
Charles A. Camalier, III
Jerald S. Cohn
Christopher H. Collins
James P. Downey (Resident, Fairfax, Virginia Office)
Maureen Ellen Dwyer
John T. Epting
Jonathan L. Farmer
Nancy G. Fax (Resident, Bethesda, Maryland Office)
Stanley J. Fineman
Norman M. Glasgow
Norman M. Glasgow, Jr.
Robert L. Gorham
Robert R. Harris (Bethesda & Greenbelt, Maryland Office)
Allen Jones, Jr.
Eric S. Kassoff (Resident, Bethesda, Maryland Office)
John D. Lane
Albert L. Ledgard, Jr.
J. Carter McKaig
Robert X. Perry, Jr.
Allison Carney Prince
John E. Prominski, Jr.
Whayne S. Quin
Richard K. Reed (Not admitted in DC)
Louis P. Robbins
Frank W. Stearns (Resident at Fairfax, Virginia Office)
Dana Brewington Stebbins
Lois J. Vermillion
Joseph B. Whitebread, Jr.
David L. Winstead
Ramsey L. Woodworth

Matthew G. Ahrens (Resident, Bethesda, Maryland Office)
Ilene Baxt Campbell (Resident, Fairfax, Virginia Office)
Carlos J. Deupi
Katherine Watson Downs
Timothy Dugan (Resident, Bethesda, Maryland Office)
David A. Fuss
Robert M. Gurss
Patricia Ann Harris (Resident, Bethesda, Maryland Office)
Daniel G. Lloyd (Not admitted in DC)
Gail Prentiss Miller (Resident, Fairfax, Virginia Office)
Mark S. Randall
Karin M. Ryan
David H. Saffern
Stuart A. Turow

LEGAL SUPPORT PERSONNEL

DIRECTOR OF ZONING SERVICES

Steven E. Sher

URBAN PLANNERS

Lori B. Langford (Fairfax, Virginia Office)
Richard S. Nero, Jr.

ARCHITECTURAL HISTORIANS

Anne H. Adams
Mary Carolyn Brown

LEGAL ASSISTANTS

Elizabeth A. Agre
Carol R. Albert
Cynthia T. Fitzpatrick (Fairfax, Virginia Office)
Anne Moore Golden (Bethesda, Maryland Office)
Karen G. Gregory
Diana Herndon
Sharon L. Hopkins (Bethesda, Maryland Office)
Victor R. Larsen
Carol J. Mayfield (Fairfax, Virginia Office)
Jennifer A. Mitchell
Debra L. Randall
Johnette D. Roberts
Joan D. Schmith (Bethesda, Maryland Office)
Linda F. Wells (Fairfax, Virginia Office)
Freda Y. Zamer-Hobar

For full biographical listings, see the Martindale-Hubbell Law Directory

FLORIDA

BOCA RATON, Palm Beach Co.

DICKENSON, MURDOCH, REX AND SLOAN, CHARTERED (AV)

Suite 410 Compson Financial Center, 980 North Federal Highway, 33432
Telephone: 407-391-1900
Facsimile: 407-391-1933

(See Next Column)

DICKENSON, MURDOCH, REX AND SLOAN CHARTERED, *Boca Raton—Continued*

David B. Dickenson
Richard A. Murdoch
Robert H. Rex
Barbara A. Sloan
Barbara K. Olson

For full biographical listings, see the Martindale-Hubbell Law Directory

JOEL H. FELDMAN, P.A. (AV)

Suite 207, Tower D, Sanctuary Centre, 4800 North Federal Highway, 33431
Telephone: 407-392-4400
Fax: 407-392-1521

Joel H. Feldman

For full biographical listings, see the Martindale-Hubbell Law Directory

KAUFFMAN & SCHWARTZ, P.A. (AV)

Crocker Plaza, Suite 301, 5355 Town Center Road, 33486
Telephone: 407-394-7600
Fax: 407-394-0891

Alan C. Kauffman
Harvey A. Nussbaum
Thomas G. Pye
Robert M. Schwartz

Thomas U. Graner
Rick S. Felberbaum (Not admitted in FL)
Seth I. Cohen

OF COUNSEL

David M. Beckerman

For full biographical listings, see the Martindale-Hubbell Law Directory

SCHROEDER & LARCHE, P.A. (AV)

One Boca Place, Suite 319-A, 2255 Glades Road, 33431-7313
Telephone: 407-241-0300
Broward: 305-421-0878
Telecopier: 407-241-0798

Michael A. Schroeder
W. Lawrence Larche

Alan Pellingra

For full biographical listings, see the Martindale-Hubbell Law Directory

WEISS & HANDLER, P.A. (AV)

Suite 218A, One Boca Place, 2255 Glades Road, 33431-7313
Telephone: 407-997-9995
Broward: 305-421-5101
Palm Beach: 407-734-8008
Telecopier: 407-997-5280

Howard I. Weiss
Henry B. Handler
Donald Feldman
Walter M. Cooperstein
Carol A. Kartagener
Bruce A. Harris
David K. Friedman
William M. Franz
Mia Lucas

OF COUNSEL

Malcolm L. Stein (Not admitted in FL)
Raoul Lionel Felder (Not admitted in FL)

For full biographical listings, see the Martindale-Hubbell Law Directory

*BRADENTON,** Manatee Co.

GRIMES, GOEBEL, GRIMES & HAWKINS, P.A. (AV)

The Professional Building, 1023 Manatee Avenue West, P.O. Box 1550, 34206
Telephone: 813-748-0151
Fax: 813-748-0158

William C. Grimes
Caleb J. Grimes
Leslie Horton Gladfelter

Representative Clients: Schroeder Manatee, Inc.; Pursley, Inc.; Old Hyde Park Village Center, Ltd.; Creekwood Investors.

For Complete List of Firm Personnel, See General Section

For full biographical listings, see the Martindale-Hubbell Law Directory

*CLEARWATER,** Pinellas Co.

LARSON & BOBENHAUSEN, PROFESSIONAL ASSOCIATION (AV)

16120 U.S. Highway 19 North, Suite 210, P.O. Box 17620, 34622-0620
Telephone: 813-535-5594
Telecopier: 813-535-4266

(See Next Column)

Roger A. Larson
Gale M. Bobenhausen
Scott Torrie
Camille J. Iurillo

Representative Clients: First Union National Bank of Florida; AmSouth Bank of Florida; Barnett Bank of Pasco County; Barnett Banks, Inc.; SunBank of Tampa Bay, N.A.; Rutenberg Housing Corp.

For full biographical listings, see the Martindale-Hubbell Law Directory

RICHARDS, GILKEY, FITE, SLAUGHTER, PRATESI & WARD, P.A. (AV)

Richards Building, 1253 Park Street, 34616
Telephone: 813-443-3281
Fax: 813-446-3741
Port Richey, Florida Office: 8410 U.S. Highway 19, Suite 104. 34668.
Telephone: 813-841-7833.
Fax: 813-847-6742.

Emil G. Pratesi
R. Carlton Ward

OF COUNSEL

William W. Gilkey

Representative Clients: USR Realty Development Division of USX Corp.; Pall Corp; Orange Bank; Rutland's Florida Gulf Bank; First Union National Bank of Florida; Park Group Companies of America; Donald Roebling Trusts; Calvin P. Vary Trust; Morton F. Plant Hospital Trust; Madison Savings and Loan Assn.

For Complete List of Firm Personnel, See General Section

For full biographical listings, see the Martindale-Hubbell Law Directory

DELRAY BEACH, Palm Beach Co.

H. CASSEDY SUMRALL, JR. PROFESSIONAL ASSOCIATION (AV)

54 Northeast Fourth Avenue, 33483
Telephone: 407-272-7040

H. Cassedy Sumrall, Jr.

Reference: Sun Bank/of Palm Beach County, Delray Beach, Florida.

For full biographical listings, see the Martindale-Hubbell Law Directory

*FORT LAUDERDALE,** Broward Co.

BERGER, SHAPIRO & DAVIS, P.A. (AV)

Suite 400, 100 N.E. 3rd Avenue, 33301
Telephone: 305-525-9900
Fax: 305-523-2872

James L. Berger
Mitchell W. Berger
James B. Davis
Manuel Kushner
Leonard K. Samuels
Laz L. Schneider

Thomas L. Abrams
Melissa P. Anderson
Lawrence C. Callaway, III
Nick Jovanovich
Robert B. Judd
Brent L. Moody
Terri E. Tuchman

OF COUNSEL

Franklin H. Caplan
Kenneth W. Shapiro

For full biographical listings, see the Martindale-Hubbell Law Directory

BRINKLEY, MCNERNEY, MORGAN, SOLOMON & TATUM (AV)

Suite 1800, New River Center, 200 East Las Olas Boulevard, P.O. Box 522, 33301-2209
Telephone: Broward: 305-522-2200
Miami: 305-945-1145
Facsimile: 305-522-9123

MEMBERS OF FIRM

W. Michael Brinkley
Michael J. McNerney
Philip J. Morgan
Harris K. Solomon
Thomas R. Tatum
Amy R. Reeck
Stephen L. Ziegler
Kenneth E. Keechl

ASSOCIATES

Donald J. Lunny, Jr.
Christopher M. Trapani
Pamela C. Keller
Kenneth J. Joyce

OF COUNSEL

John R. Tatum (Retired)

Approved Attorneys for: Attorneys' Title Insurance Fund; Chicago Title Insurance Co.; Commonwealth Land Title Insurance Co.; First American Title Insurance Co.

For full biographical listings, see the Martindale-Hubbell Law Directory

CLARK & SCHOLNIK (AV)

A Partnership of Professional Associations
California Federal Tower, 2400 East Commercial Boulevard, Suite 820, 33308
Telephone: 305-776-3800
Telecopier: 305-776-3825

(See Next Column)

CLARK & SCHOLNIK—*Continued*

MEMBER OF FIRM

Thomas M. Clark (P.A.)

Representative Clients: SunBank/South Florida, N.A.; Midland Federal Savings and Loan Association; Metmor Financial, Inc.; Haymarket Cooperative Bank; Colorado Federal Savings Bank; Bluebonnett Savings Bank, F.S.B.

For Complete List of Firm Personnel, See General Section

For full biographical listings, see the Martindale-Hubbell Law Directory

HEINRICH GORDON BATCHELDER HARGROVE & WEIHE (AV)

A Partnership including Professional Associations
500 East Broward Boulevard, Suite 1000, 33394-3092
Telephone: 305-527-2800
Telecopier: 305-524-9481

MEMBER OF FIRM

Drake M. Batchelder

Representative Clients: Aetna Life Insurance Company; Berkshire Life Insurance Company; Draper & Kramer, Inc.; First Union National Bank of Florida; First Westinghouse Equities Corporation; Gregory Properties, Inc.; Latimer & Buck of Florida, Inc.; Life Insurance Company of Georgia; Massachusetts Mutual Life Insurance Company; Westinghouse Credit Corporation.

For Complete List of Firm Personnel, See General Section

For full biographical listings, see the Martindale-Hubbell Law Directory

WILLIAM A. ZEIHER, P.A. (AV)

2780 East Oakland Park Boulevard, 33306
Telephone: 305-561-8205
FAX: 305-561-8208

William A. Zeiher

Representative Client: National Oil & Gas, Inc.
Approved Attorney for: Attorneys' Title Insurance Fund.

For full biographical listings, see the Martindale-Hubbell Law Directory

*FORT MYERS,** Lee Co.

AVERY, WHIGHAM & WINESETT, P.A. (AV)

Corner of First and Hendry Streets, 2248 First Street, P.O. Drawer 610, 33902-0610
Telephone: 813-334-7040
FAX: 813-334-6258

Richard W. Winesett
Dwight A. Whigham
Robert A. Winesett
James M. Costello

For full biographical listings, see the Martindale-Hubbell Law Directory

HENDERSON, FRANKLIN, STARNES & HOLT, PROFESSIONAL ASSOCIATION (AV)

1715 Monroe Street, P.O. Box 280, 33902-0280
Telephone: 813-334-4121
Telecopier: 813-332-4494

Ronald W. Smalley
Denis H. Noah
Russell P. Schropp
Charles J. Basinait
Thomas H. Gunderson
David K. Fowler

Representative Clients: Aetna Life & Casualty Group; CIGNA Group; CSX Transportation, Inc.; Fireman's Fund Insurance Cos.; Barnett Bank of Lee County, N.A.; Northern Trust Bank of Florida, N.A.; The Hartford Insurance Group; Travelers Group; United Telephone Company of Florida.

For Complete List of Firm Personnel, See General Section

For full biographical listings, see the Martindale-Hubbell Law Directory

LAW OFFICES OF LLOYD G. HENDRY, P.A. (AV)

Society First Federal Center, 2201 Second Street, Suite 502, P.O. Box 1509, 33902
Telephone: 813-332-7123
Fax: 813-332-5147

Lloyd G. Hendry
Mary Hendry Sonne
Harry O. Hendry

For full biographical listings, see the Martindale-Hubbell Law Directory

SMOOT ADAMS EDWARDS & GREEN, P.A. (AV)

One University Park Suite 600, 12800 University Drive, P.O. Box 60259, 33906-6259
Telephone: 813-489-1776
(800) 226-1777 (in Florida)
Fax: 813-489-2444

(See Next Column)

J. Tom Smoot, Jr.
Hal Adams
Bruce D. Green
Steven I. Winer
Mark R. Komray
Thomas P. Clark

Lynne E. Denneler
Clayton W. Crevasse
M. Brian Cheffer
Robert S. Forman
Thomas M. Howell
Plutarco M. Villalobos

For Complete List of Firm Personnel, See General Section

For full biographical listings, see the Martindale-Hubbell Law Directory

*FORT PIERCE,** St. Lucie Co.

GONANO & HARRELL, CHARTERED (AV)

Riverside National Bank Building, 1600 South Federal Highway, Suite 200, 34950-5194
Telephone: 407-464-1032
FAX: 407-464-0282

Douglas E. Gonano
Daniel B. Harrell

David F. Hanley
John J. Campione

General Counsel: School Board of St. Lucie County; Reserve Community Development District; St. Lucie West Services District.
Representative Clients: Armellini Industries, Inc.; East Coast Lumber & Supply Co.; Riverside National Bank of Florida; Superior Title Services, Inc.
Approved Attorneys for: Attorneys' Title Insurance Fund; Commonwealth Land Title Insurance Co.
References: Riverside National Bank of Florida; Sun Bank/Treasure Coast, N.A.

For full biographical listings, see the Martindale-Hubbell Law Directory

NEILL GRIFFIN JEFFRIES & LLOYD, CHARTERED (AV)

311 South Second Street, P.O. Box 1270, 34954
Telephone: 407-464-8200
Fax: 407-464-2566

Chester B. Griffin
Robert M. Lloyd
J. Stephen Tierney, III
Richard V. Neill, Jr.

Local Counsel for: Sun Bank Treasure Coast, N.A., (Commercial and Trust Departments); St. Paul Fire and Marine Insurance Co.; Chubb Group of Insurances Co.; Becker Holding Corp.
Approved Attorneys for: Attorneys' Title Insurance Fund; Commonwealth Land Title Insurance Co.
Reference: Sun Bank Treasure Coast, N.A., Fort Pierce, Florida (Commercial and Trust Departments).

For full biographical listings, see the Martindale-Hubbell Law Directory

*JACKSONVILLE,** Duval Co.

DONAHOO, DONAHOO & BALL, P.A. (AV)

(Incorporated in 1981)
2925 Barnett Center, 50 North Laura Street, 32202
Telephone: 904-354-8080
Fax: 904-791-9563

John W. Donahoo (1907-1993)
Thomas M. Donahoo
Haywood M. Ball
William B. McMenamy
Bruce D. Johnson

For full biographical listings, see the Martindale-Hubbell Law Directory

*KISSIMMEE,** Osceola Co.

POHL & BROWN, P.A.

(See Winter Park)

LAKELAND, Polk Co.

HAHN, MCCLURG, WATSON, GRIFFITH & BUSH, P.A. (AV)

101 South Florida Avenue, P.O. Box 38, 33802
Telephone: 813-688-7747
Telecopier: 813-683-4582

James P. Hahn
E.V. McClurg
Stephen C. Watson
John R. Griffith
Philip H. Bush

OF COUNSEL

J. Tom Watson

Special Counsel: Peoples Bank of Lakeland; First Federal of Florida; Publix Super Markets, Inc.
Approved Attorneys For: Attorneys' Title Insurance Fund; American Title Insurance Co.; Title & Trust Company of Florida; Federal Land Bank of Columbia, Columbia, S.C.
Reference: Peoples Bank of Lakeland.

For full biographical listings, see the Martindale-Hubbell Law Directory

Lakeland—Continued

PETERSON, MYERS, CRAIG, CREWS, BRANDON & PUTERBAUGH, P.A. (AV)

100 East Main Street, P.O. Box 24628, 33802-4628
Telephone: 813-683-6511; 676-6934
Telecopier: 813-682-8031
Lake Wales, Florida Office: 130 East Central Avenue, P.O. Box 1079.
Telephones: 813-676-7611; 683-8942.
Winter Haven, Florida Office: Suite 300, 141 5th Street, N.W., P.O. Drawer 7608.
Telephone: 813-294-3360

Jack P. Brandon
Beach A Brooks, Jr.
J. Davis Connor
Roy A. Craig, Jr.
Jacob C. Dykxhoorn
Dennis P. Johnson
Kevin C. Knowlton
Douglas A. Lockwood, III
Corneal B. Myers
Cornelius B. Myers, III
Robert E. Puterbaugh
Abel A. Putnam
Thomas B. Putnam, Jr.
Deborah A. Ruster
Stephen R. Senn
Andrea Teves Smith
Kerry M. Wilson

General Counsel For: Barnett Bank of Polk County.
Representative Clients: Mutual Wholesale Co.; Sun Bank/Mid-Florida, N.A.; Chase Commercial Corp.; Barnett Banks, Inc.; Ben Hill Griffin, Inc.; Alcoma Association, Inc.
Approved Attorneys For: Equitable Life Assurance Society of the United States; Federal Land Bank of Columbia, S.C.; Attorneys' Title Insurance Fund.

For full biographical listings, see the Martindale-Hubbell Law Directory

LAKE WALES, Polk Co.

PETERSON, MYERS, CRAIG, CREWS, BRANDON & PUTERBAUGH, P.A. (AV)

130 East Central Avenue, P.O. Box 1079, 33853
Telephone: 813-676-7611; 683-8942
Telecopier: 813-676-0643
Lakeland, Florida Office: 100 East Main Street, P.O. Box 24628.
Telephones: 813-683-6511; 676-6934.
Winter Haven, Florida Office: Suite 300, 141 5th Street, N.W., P.O. Drawer 7608.
Telephone: 813-294-3360.

Jack P. Brandon
Beach A Brooks, Jr.
Beach A Brooks, Jr.
J. Davis Connor
Roy A. Craig, Jr.
Jacob C. Dykxhoorn
Dennis P. Johnson
Kevin C. Knowlton
Douglas A. Lockwood, III
Corneal B. Myers
Cornelius B. Myers, III
Robert E. Puterbaugh
Robert E. Puterbaugh
Abel A. Putnam
Thomas B. Putnam, Jr.
Deborah A. Ruster
Stephen R. Senn
Andrea Teves Smith
Kerry M. Wilson

General Counsel for: Barnett Bank of Polk County.
Representative Clients: Mutual Wholesale Co.; Sun Bank/Mid-Florida, N.A.; Chase Commercial Corp.; Barnett Banks, Inc.; Ben Hill Griffin, Inc.; Alcoma Association, Inc.
Approved Attorneys for: Equitable Life Assurance Society of the United States; Federal Land Bank of Columbia, S.C.; Attorneys' Title Insurance Fund.

For full biographical listings, see the Martindale-Hubbell Law Directory

LAKE WORTH, Palm Beach Co.

ALTMAN & GREER (AV)

219 North Dixie Highway, 33460
Telephone: 407-588-3311
Fax: 407-588-3315

MEMBERS OF FIRM

Zell H. Altman
Bruce G. Greer

ASSOCIATE

Thomas H. Dougherty

For full biographical listings, see the Martindale-Hubbell Law Directory

MELBOURNE, Brevard Co.

GLEASON, BARLOW & BOHNE, P.A. (AV)

121-123 Fifth Avenue (Indialantic), P.O. Box 3648, 32903
Telephone: 407-723-5121
Fax: 407-984-5426

William H. Gleason
T. Mitchell Barlow, Jr. (Resident)
Karl W. Bohne, Jr.

Reference: First Union National Bank of Florida, Melbourne, Florida.

For full biographical listings, see the Martindale-Hubbell Law Directory

KRASNY AND DETTMER (AV)

A Partnership of Professional Associations
780 South Apollo Boulevard, P.O. Box 428, 32902-0428
Telephone: 407-723-5646
Telecopier: 407-768-1147

Myron S. (Mike) Krasny (P.A.)
Dale A. Dettmer (P.A.)
Scott Krasny

Representative Client: Security National Bank.

For full biographical listings, see the Martindale-Hubbell Law Directory

*MIAMI,** Dade Co.

PAUL G. FLETCHER, P.A. (AV)

Suite 200 Barnett Bank Building, 1500 South Dixie Highway (Coral Gables), 33146
Telephone: 305-661-6125
FAX: 305-661-6197

Paul G. Fletcher

For full biographical listings, see the Martindale-Hubbell Law Directory

MERSHON, SAWYER, JOHNSTON, DUNWODY & COLE (AV)

A Partnership including Professional Associations
Suite 4500 First Union Financial Center, 200 South Biscayne Boulevard, 33131-2387
Telephone: 305-358-5100
Cable Address: "Mercole"
Telex: 515705
Fax: 305-376-8654
Naples, Florida Office: Pelican Bay Corporate Centre, Suite 501, 5551 Ridgewood Drive.
Telephone: 813-598-1055.
Fax: 813-598-1868.
West Palm Beach, Florida Office: 777 South Flagler Drive, Suite 900.
Telephone: 407-659-5990.
Fax: 407-659-6313.
Key West, Florida Office: 3132 North Side Drive, Suite 102.
Telephone: 305-296-1774.
Fax: 305-296-1715
London, England Office: Blake Lodge, Bridge Lane, London SW11 3AD, England.
Telephone: 44-71-978-7748.
Fax: 44-71-350-0156.

MEMBERS OF FIRM

Osmond C. Howe, Jr., (P.A.)
Brian P. Tague
Richard C. Grant (P.A.) (Resident, Naples Office)
Russell T. Kamradt (Resident, West Palm Beach Office)
Jose E. Castro (P.A.)
Richard M. Bezold
Thomas E. Streit (Resident, West Palm Beach Office)
Marjie C. Nealon (P.A.)
Michael T. Lynott (P.A.)
John F. Halula

OF COUNSEL

Jeri A. Poller

ASSOCIATE

G. Helen Athan (Resident, Naples Office)

Representative Clients: Arvida/JMB Partners; Bankers Trust Co.; Biscayne Kennel Club, Inc.; The Chase Manhattan Bank, N.A.; Lennar Corp.; Reynolds Metals Co.; United States Sugar Corp.; University of Miami.

For Complete List of Firm Personnel, See General Section

For full biographical listings, see the Martindale-Hubbell Law Directory

PATTERSON, CLAUSSEN, SANTOS & HUME (AV)

A Partnership of Professional Associations
18th Floor, Courthouse Tower, 44 West Flagler Street, 33130-1808
Telephone: 305-350-9000
Fax: 305-372-3940

John H. Patterson (P.A.)

OF COUNSEL

James H. Sweeny, III (P.A.)

For Complete List of Firm Personnel, See General Section

For full biographical listings, see the Martindale-Hubbell Law Directory

SHAPO, FREEDMAN & FLETCHER, P.A. (AV)

First Union Financial Center, 47th Floor, 200 South Biscayne Boulevard, 33131
Telephone: 305-358-4440
Telefax: 305-358-0521

Ronald A. Shapo
David A. Freedman
Patricia Kimball Fletcher

(See Next Column)

SHAPO, FREEDMAN & FLETCHER P.A.—*Continued*

Howard Allen Cohen
Luis E. Rojas
Richard Daniel Friess
Geoffrey T. Kirk

For full biographical listings, see the Martindale-Hubbell Law Directory

SIEGFRIED, RIVERA, LERNER, DE LA TORRE & PETERSEN, P.A. (AV)

Suite 1102, 201 Alhambra Circle (Coral Gables), 33134
Telephone: 305-442-3334
Fax: 305-443-3292
Fort Lauderdale Office: One Financial Plaza, Suite 2012, 33394.
Telephone: 305-832-0766.
Fax: 305-764-1759.

Steven M. Siegfried
Oscar R. Rivera
Lisa A. Lerner
Helio De La Torre
Byron G. Petersen (Resident, Fort Lauderdale Office)
Peter H. Edwards

Maria Victoria Arias
Daniel Davis
James F. Harrington
Elisabeth D. Kozlow
H. Hugh Mc Connell
Alberto Nouel Moris
Samuel A. Persaud

Reference: Southeast First National Bank of Miami.

For full biographical listings, see the Martindale-Hubbell Law Directory

SPARBER, KOSNITZKY, TRUXTON, DE LA GUARDIA SPRATT & BROOKS, P.A. (AV)

1401 Brickell Avenue Suite 700, 33131
Telephone: Dade: 305-379-7200; Broward: 305-760-9133
Fax: 305-379-0800

Gregg S. Truxton

Diana L. Grub

For Complete List of Firm Personnel, See General Section

For full biographical listings, see the Martindale-Hubbell Law Directory

STEARNS WEAVER MILLER WEISSLER ALHADEFF & SITTERSON, P.A. (AV)

Suite 2200 Museum Tower, 150 West Flagler Street, 33130
Telephone: 305-789-3200
FAX: 305-789-3395
Tampa, Florida Office: Suite 2200 Landmark Centre, 401 East Jackson Street.
Telephone: 813-223-4800.
Fort Lauderdale, Florida Office: 200 East Broward Boulevard, Suite 1900.
Telephone: 305-462-9500.

E. Richard Alhadeff
Louise Jacowitz Allen
Stuart D. Ames
Thomas P. Angelo (Resident, Fort Lauderdale Office)
Lawrence J. Bailin (Resident, Tampa Office)
Patrick A. Barry (Resident, Fort Lauderdale Office)
Lisa K. Bennett (Resident, Fort Lauderdale Office)
Susan Fleming Bennett (Resident, Tampa Office)
Mark J. Bernet (Resident, Tampa Office)
Claire Bailey Carraway (Resident, Tampa Office)
Seth T. Craine (Resident, Tampa Office)
Piero Luciano Desiderio (Resident, Fort Lauderdale Office)
Mark P. Dikeman
Sharon Quinn Dixon
Alan H. Fein
Owen S. Freed
Dean M. Freitag
Robert E. Gallagher, Jr.
Alice R. Huneycutt (Resident, Tampa Office)
Theodore A. Jewell
Elizabeth J. Keeler
Teddy D. Klinghoffer
Robert T. Kofman
Thomas A. Lash (Resident, Tampa Office)
Joy Spillis Lundeen
Brian J. McDonough
Francisco J. Menendez
Antonio R. Menendez
Alison W. Miller
Vicki Lynn Monroe
Harold D. Moorefield, Jr.
John N. Muratides (Resident, Tampa Office)
John K. Olson (Resident, Tampa Office)
Robert C. Owens
Patricia A. Redmond
Carl D. Roston
Steven D. Rubin
Mark A. Schneider
Curtis H. Sitterson
Mark D. Solov
Eugene E. Stearns
Bradford Swing
Dennis R. Turner
Ronald L. Weaver (Resident, Tampa Office)
Robert I. Weissler
Patricia G. Welles
Martin B. Woods (Resident, Fort Lauderdale Office)

(See Next Column)

Shawn M. Bayne (Resident, Fort Lauderdale Office)
Lisa Berg
Hans C. Beyer (Resident, Tampa Office)
Dawn A. Carapella (Resident, Tampa Office)
Christina Maria Diaz
Robert I. Finvarb
Patricia K. Green
Marilyn D. Greenblatt
Richard B. Jackson
Aimee C. Jimenez
Cheryl A. Kaplan
Michael I. Keyes
Vernon L. Lewis
Kevin Bruce Love
Adam Coatsworth Mishcon
Elizabeth G. Rice (Resident, Tampa Office)
Glenn M. Rissman
Claudia J. Saenz
Richard E. Schatz
Robert P. Shantz (Resident, Tampa Office)
Martin S. Simkovic
Ronni D. Solomon
Jo Claire Spear (Resident, Tampa Office)
Gail Marie Stage (Resident, Fort Lauderdale Office)
Annette Torres
Barbara L. Wilhite

OF COUNSEL

Stephen A. Bennett

For full biographical listings, see the Martindale-Hubbell Law Directory

STUZIN AND CAMNER, PROFESSIONAL ASSOCIATION (AV)

25th Floor, 1221 Brickell Avenue, 33131-3260
Telephone: 305-577-0600

Charles B. Stuzin
Alfred R. Camner
Stanley A. Beiley
Marsha D. Bilzin
David S. Garbett
Nina S. Gordon
Barry D. Hunter
Nikki J. Nedbor
Neale J. Poller

Lisa R. Carstarphen
Maria E. Chang
Barry P. Gruher
Gustavo D. Llerena
Sherry D. McMillan
Roger A. Preziosi

OF COUNSEL

Anne Shari Camner

References: Citizens Federal Bank; City National Bank of Miami; Barnett Bank of South Florida, N.A.

For full biographical listings, see the Martindale-Hubbell Law Directory

WILLIAM C. SUSSMAN, P.A. (AV)

Suite 311, 1570 Madruga Avenue (Coral Gables), 33146
Telephone: 305-662-1991
Telefax: 305-661-6692

William C. Sussman

For full biographical listings, see the Martindale-Hubbell Law Directory

ZIEGLER & GINSBURG, P.A. (AV)

370 Minorca Avenue, Suite 21 (Coral Gables), 33134
Telephone: 305-444-5676
Facsimile: 305-444-3937

Stuart Harvey Ziegler
Edwin M. Ginsburg

For full biographical listings, see the Martindale-Hubbell Law Directory

ZUCKERMAN, SPAEDER, TAYLOR & EVANS (AV)

Miami Center, 201 South Biscayne Boulevard, Suite 900, 33131
Telephone: 305-358-5000; 305-579-0110
Broward County: 305-523-0277
Fax: 305-579-9749
Tampa, Florida Office: 101 East Kennedy Boulevard, Suite 3140.
Telephone: 813-221-1010.
Fax: 813-223-7961.
Ft. Lauderdale, Florida Office: One East Broward Boulevard, Suite 700.
Telephone: 305-356-0463.
Fax: 305-356-0406.
Washington, D.C. Office: Zuckerman, Spaeder, Goldstein, Taylor & Kolker, 1201 Connecticut Avenue, N.W.
Telephone: 202-778-1800.
Fax: 202-822-8106.
Baltimore, Maryland Office: Zuckerman, Spaeder, Goldstein, Taylor & Better, Suite 2440, 100 East Pratt Street.
Telephone: 410-332-0444.
Fax: 410-659-0436.
New York, N.Y. Office: Zuckerman, Spaeder, Goldstein, Taylor & Kolker, 1114 Avenue of the Americas, 45th Floor, Grace Building.
Telephone: 212-479-6500.
Fax: 212-479-6512.

MEMBERS OF FIRM

Ronald B. Ravikoff (Resident)
Michael Steven Greene
Edward C. Berkowitz (Resident, Washington D.C. Office)
Peter R. Kolker (Resident, Washington, D.C. Office)
Anthony Thompson (Resident, Washington, D.C. Office)
Marshall S. Wolff (Resident, Washington D.C. Office)

(See Next Column)

ZUCKERMAN, SPAEDER, TAYLOR & EVANS, *Miami—Continued*

ASSOCIATES

Jeffrey P. Agron
Jill M. Granat
Rebeca Sanchez-Roig

For full biographical listings, see the Martindale-Hubbell Law Directory

*NAPLES,** Collier Co.

MYERS KRAUSE & STEVENS, CHARTERED (AV)

5811 Pelican Bay Boulevard, Suite 600, 33963
Telephone: 813-598-1221
Fax: 813-598-3499

William H. Myers
Andrew J. Krause
William K. Stevens

Richard S. Franklin
Robert J. Stommel
David P. Browne
Jeffrey J. Beihoff
Johnine R. Hays

References: Barnett Banks Trust Co., N.A.; NBD Trust Company of Florida N.A.; Northern Trust Bank of Florida, N.A.; Sun Bank Southwest Florida

For full biographical listings, see the Martindale-Hubbell Law Directory

PARKS, BENNETT & STEWART (AV)

Parks Building, 865 Fifth Avenue South, 33940
Telephone: 941-262-0400
Fax: 941-261-8646

Benjamin G. Parks
Richard K. Bennett
Deborah A. Stewart

For full biographical listings, see the Martindale-Hubbell Law Directory

VEGA, BROWN, STANLEY, MARTIN & ZELMAN, P.A. (AV)

2660 Airport Road, South, 33962
Telephone: 813-774-3333
Fax: 813-774-6420

John F. Stanley

OF COUNSEL

Thomas R. Brown

Representative Clients: Lely Development; John Remington; Quail Creek.

For Complete List of Firm Personnel, See General Section

For full biographical listings, see the Martindale-Hubbell Law Directory

NEW PORT RICHEY, Pasco Co.

MARTIN, FIGURSKI & HARRILL (AV)

A Partnership of Professional Associations
Suite B-1, 8406 Massachusetts Avenue, P.O. Box 786, 34653
Telephone: 813-842-8439
Clearwater, Florida Office: 28059 U.S. Highway 19, Suite 202.
Telephone: 813-796-3259.
Fax: 813-796-3598.

MEMBERS OF FIRM

Daniel N. Martin (P.A.)
Gerald A. Figurski (P.A.)
James Benjamin Harrill (P.A.)

Representative Clients: Regency Communities, Inc., formerly Minieri Communities of Florida, Inc.; Greene Builders, Inc.; Mobil Oil Corp.; Barnett Bank of Pasco County; Hospital Corporation of America; U.S. Home Corp.
Approved Attorneys For: Attorneys' Title Insurance Fund; First American Title Insurance Co.; Commonwealth Land Title Insurance Company.
Reference: Barnett Bank of Pasco County.

For full biographical listings, see the Martindale-Hubbell Law Directory

NORTH MIAMI, Dade Co.

KLEIN AND ASSOCIATES, P.A. (AV)

901 Northeast 125th Street, 33161
Telephone: 305-891-6100
Fax: 305-891-6104

Ronald G. Klein

For full biographical listings, see the Martindale-Hubbell Law Directory

NORTH MIAMI BEACH, Dade Co.

BUCHANAN INGERSOLL, PROFESSIONAL CORPORATION (AV)

One Turnberry Place, 19495 Biscayne Boulevard, 33180
Telephone: 305-933-5600
Telecopier: 305-933-2350
Pittsburgh, Pennsylvania Office: 5800 USX Tower, 600 Grant Street.
Telephone: 412-562-8800.
Philadelphia, Pennsylvania Office: Two Logan Square, Twelfth Floor, 18th & Arch Streets.
Telephone: 215-665-8700.

(See Next Column)

Harrisburg, Pennsylvania Office: Vartan Parc, 30 North Third Street.
Telephone: 717-237-4800.
Tampa, Florida Office: Suite 1030, 101 East Kennedy Boulevard.
Telephone: 813-222-8180.
Princeton, New Jersey Office: Buchanan Ingersoll, A Partnership, College Centre, 500 College Road East.
Telephone: 609-452-2666.
Lexington, Kentucky Office: Suite 600, PNC Bank Plaza, 200 West Vine Street.
Telephone: 606-225-5333.

Dennis J. Eisinger

Andrea B. Mackson
Richard N. Schermer

For Complete List of Firm Personnel, See General Section

For full biographical listings, see the Martindale-Hubbell Law Directory

WILLIAM J. SEGAL, P.A. (AV)

20801 Biscayne Boulevard, Suite 304, 33180
Telephone: 305-682-1110
Telefax: 305-682-1800

William J. Segal

Representative Clients: Safari Limited; Garci Plastics, Inc.; Commonwealth Distributors; City Cellular and Uniforms, Inc.
Title Agent For: Attorneys Title Insurance Fund; First American Title Insurance Co.

For full biographical listings, see the Martindale-Hubbell Law Directory

ORANGE PARK, Clay Co.

HEAD, SMITH, METCALF, AGUILAR, MOSS & SIERON, P.A. (AV)

1329A Kingsley Avenue, P.O. Box 855, 32073
Telephone: 904-264-6000
Fax: 904-264-9223

Robert J. Head, Jr.
Robert Aguilar
Larry Smith
John B. Moss
Frank B. Metcalf
Mark A. Sieron

Holly Fulton Perritt

For full biographical listings, see the Martindale-Hubbell Law Directory

*ORLANDO,** Orange Co.

BAKER & HOSTETLER (AV)

SunBank Center, Suite 2300, 200 South Orange Avenue, 32802-3432
Telephone: 407-649-4000
In Cleveland, Ohio: 3200 National City Center, 1900 East Ninth Street.
Telephone: 216-621-0200.
In Columbus, Ohio: Capitol Square, Suite 2100, 65 East State Street.
Telephone: 614-228-1541.
In Denver, Colorado: 303 East 17th Avenue, Suite 1100.
Telephone: 303-861-0600.
In Houston, Texas: 1000 Louisiana, Suite 2000.
Telephone: 713-751-1600.
In Long Beach, California: 300 Oceangate, Suite 620.
Telephone: 310-432-2827.
In Los Angeles, California: 600 Wilshire Boulevard.
Telephone: 213-624-2400.
In Washington, D.C.: Washington Square, Suite 1100, 1050 Connecticut Avenue, N.W., Suite 1100.
Telephone: 202-861-1500.
In College Park, Maryland: 9658 Baltimore Boulevard, Suite 206.
Telephone: 301-441-2781.
In Alexandria, Virginia: 437 North Lee Street.
Telephone: 703-549-1294.
In San Francisco, California: One Sansome Street, Suite 2000.
Telephone: 415-951-4705.

MEMBER OF FIRM IN ORLANDO, FLORIDA

G. Thomas Ball (Managing Partner-Orlando Office)

PARTNERS

Stephen E. Cook
Max F. Morris
Richard T. Fulton
Rosemary O'Shea
Robert J. Webb

ASSOCIATES

Elise L. Bloom
Kurt P. Gruber
Jacqueline Bozzuto
Brian T. Lower
Andrew T. Marcus

For Complete List of Firm Personnel, See General Section

For full biographical listings, see the Martindale-Hubbell Law Directory

Orlando—Continued

FIXEL & MAGUIRE, P.A. (AV)

1250 Eola Park Centre, 200 East Robinson Street, 32801
Telephone: 407-841-0443
Fax: 407-841-9850
Tallahassee, Florida Office: 211 South Gadsden Street, 32301.
Telephone: 904-681-1800.
Fax: 904-681-9017.

Joe W. Fixel — Raymer F. Maguire, III

Representative Clients: Condemnees: Allen Morris Co.; Franklin Carriage Gate Shopping Center, Ltd.; Miccosukee Village Shopping Center, Ltd.; Nick Nicholas Ford, Inc.; Weaver Oil Co.; United Fuel Corp.; Majik Market Convenience Stores.
Condemnors: Collier County Board of County Commissioners; Hillsborough County Board of County Commissioners.
Reference: Barnett Bank.

For full biographical listings, see the Martindale-Hubbell Law Directory

HONIGMAN MILLER SCHWARTZ AND COHN (AV)

A Partnership including Professional Corporations
390 North Orange Avenue, Suite 1300, 32801-1632
Telephone: 407-648-0300
Telecopier: 407-648-1155
West Palm Beach, Florida Office: Suite 800 Esperante Building, 222 Lakeview Avenue.
Telephone: 407-838-4500.
Tampa, Florida Office: 2700 Landmark Centre, 401 E. Jackson Street.
Telephone: 813-221-6600.
Detroit, Michigan Office: 2290 First National Building.
Telephone: 313-256-7800.
Lansing, Michigan Office: 222 North Washington Square, Suite 400.
Telephone: 517-484-8282.
Houston, Texas Office: 3100 First Interstate Bank Plaza, 1000 Louisiana.
Telephone: 713-650-2600.
Los Angeles, California Office: Watt Plaza, Suite 2200, 1875 Century Park East.
Telephone: 310-789-3800.
Fax: 310-789-3814.

MEMBERS

Wendy Anderson (P.A.) — Michael J. Grindstaff (P.A.)
J. Lindsay Builder, Jr., (P.A.) — Michael J. Sullivan (P.A.)

ASSOCIATES

Suzanne M. Amaducci — Orlando L. Evora
Roseanna J. Lee

For Complete List of Firm Personnel, See General Section

For full biographical listings, see the Martindale-Hubbell Law Directory

POHL & BROWN, P.A.

(See Winter Park)

RUSSELL & HULL, P.A. (AV)

537 North Magnolia Avenue, P.O. Box 2751, 32802
Telephone: 407-422-1234

Rodney Laird Russell — Norman L. Hull

Reference: First Union National Bank, N.A.

For full biographical listings, see the Martindale-Hubbell Law Directory

CRAIG B. WARD, P.A. (AV)

Suite 501, 105 East Robinson Street, 32801
Telephone: 407-839-0222
Fax: 407-839-0577

Craig B. Ward

OF COUNSEL

Charles D. Miner

For full biographical listings, see the Martindale-Hubbell Law Directory

WINDERWEEDLE, HAINES, WARD & WOODMAN, P.A. (AV)

Barnett Bank Center, 390 North Orange Avenue, P.O. Box 1391, 32802-1391
Telephone: 407-423-4246
Telecopier: 407-423-7014
Winter Park, Florida Office: Barnett Bank Building 250 Park Avenue, South, P.O. Box 880.
Telephone: 407-644-6312.
Telecopier: 407-645-3728.

Victor E. Woodman — Joseph Penn Carolan, III
William A. Walker II — Dykes C. Everett
John H. Dyer, Jr.

Approved Attorneys For: Attorneys Title Insurance Fund, Inc.; Chicago Title Insurance Co.; Commonwealth Land Title Insurance Co.

(See Next Column)

Counsel for: Barnett Bank of Central Florida, N.A.
Representative Clients: Security National Bank; Whispering Waters Apartments.

For Complete List of Firm Personnel, See General Section

For full biographical listings, see the Martindale-Hubbell Law Directory

PALM BEACH, Palm Beach Co.

BAUGHER, METTLER & SHELTON (AV)

340 Royal Poinciana Plaza, P.O. Box 109, 33480
Telephone: 407-833-9631
Fax: 407-655-2835

MEMBERS OF FIRM

Thomas M. Mettler — John W. Shelton

ASSOCIATES

Francis X. J. Lynch — Pamela A. Markley

Reference: First National Bank in Palm Beach.

For full biographical listings, see the Martindale-Hubbell Law Directory

LOUIS LEIBOVIT (AV)

350 Royal Palm Way, 33480
Telephone: 407-655-6588

Approved Attorney for: Attorneys' Title Insurance Fund.
Reference: Barnett Bank (Palm Beach Branch Office).

For full biographical listings, see the Martindale-Hubbell Law Directory

MURPHY, REID & PILOTTE, P.A. (AV)

340 Royal Palm Way, 33480
Telephone: 407-655-4060
Facsimile: 407-832-5436
Vero Beach, Florida Office: Plantation Plaza, 6606-20th Street, P.O. Drawer M.
Telephone: 407-567-6480.
Facsimile: 407-562-0220.

Eugene W. Murphy, Jr.

For Complete List of Firm Personnel, See General Section

For full biographical listings, see the Martindale-Hubbell Law Directory

ST. PETERSBURG, Pinellas Co.

CARTER, STEIN, SCHAAF & TOWZEY (AV)

270 First Avenue South, Suite 300, 33701-4306
Telephone: 813-894-4333
Fax: 813-894-0175

Victoria Hunt Carter — Gary M. Schaaf
Henry A. Stein — Phyllis J. Towzey

For full biographical listings, see the Martindale-Hubbell Law Directory

*SARASOTA,** Sarasota Co.

LYONS & BEAUDRY, P.A. (AV)

Suite 1111, Ellis Building, 1605 Main Street, 34236
Telephone: 813-366-3282
Fax: 813-954-1484

Robert W. Beaudry (1929-1991) — John J. Lyons

Carol Whitcher Wood — R. Craig Harrison

Reference: Nations Bank.

For full biographical listings, see the Martindale-Hubbell Law Directory

WILLIAMS, PARKER, HARRISON, DIETZ & GETZEN, PROFESSIONAL ASSOCIATION (AV)

1550 Ringling Boulevard, 34230-3258
Telephone: 813-366-4800
Telecopier: 813-366-5109
Mailing Address: P.O. Box 3258, Sarasota, Florida, 34230-3258

William T. Harrison, Jr. — James L. Turner
George A. Dietz — William M. Seider
Monte K. Marshall — Elizabeth C. Marshall
James L. Ritchey — Robert W. Benjamin
Hugh McPheeters, Jr. — Frank Strelec
William G. Lambrecht — David A. Wallace
John T. Berteau — Terri Jayne Salt
John V. Cannon, III — Jeffrey A. Grebe
Charles D. Bailey, Jr. — John Leslie Moore
J. Michael Hartenstine — Mark A. Schwartz
Michele Boardman Grimes — Morgan R. Bentley

(See Next Column)

WILLIAMS, PARKER, HARRISON, DIETZ & GETZEN PROFESSIONAL ASSOCIATION, *Sarasota—Continued*

OF COUNSEL

Frazer F. Hilder
William E. Getzen
Elvin W. Phillips

Counsel for: Sarasota-Manatee Airport Authority; Sarasota County Public Hospital Board; William G. & Marie Selby Foundation; Taylor Woodrow Homes Ltd.; The School Board of Sarasota County.
Local Counsel for: NationsBank of Florida; Arvida/JMB Partners.

For Complete List of Firm Personnel, See General Section

For full biographical listings, see the Martindale-Hubbell Law Directory

WILSON, JOHNSON & JAFFER, P.A. (AV)

27 South Orange Avenue, P.O. Box 1298, 34230-1298
Telephone: 813-955-5800
FAX: 813-955-7353

Clyde H. Wilson (1908-1994)
Clyde H. Wilson, Jr.
Robert M. Johnson
John S. Jaffer

James M. Kunick

For full biographical listings, see the Martindale-Hubbell Law Directory

*STUART,** Martin Co.

MCCARTHY, SUMMERS, BOBKO, MCKEY & BONAN, P.A. (AV)

2081 East Ocean Boulevard, Suite 2-A, 34996
Telephone: 407-286-1700
FAX: 407-283-1803

Terence P. McCarthy
Noel A. Bobko
Robert P. Summers
John D. McKey, Jr.
W. Martin Bonan

Representative Clients: American Bank of Martin County; First National Bank and Trust Company of the Treasure Coast; Great Western Bank; Hydratech Utilities; Lost Lake at Hobe Sound; Taylor Creek Marina, Inc.; GBS Excavating, Inc.; Seaboard Savings Bank; The Stuart News; Gary Player Design Group.

For full biographical listings, see the Martindale-Hubbell Law Directory

*TALLAHASSEE,** Leon Co.

COLLINS & TRUETT, P.A. (AV)

2804 Remington Green Circle, Suite 4, Post Office Drawer 12429, 32317-2429
Telephone: 904-386-6060
Telecopier: 904-385-8220

Richard B. Collins
Gary A. Shipman

Brett Q. Lucas (Resident)
C. Timothy Gray
Dawn D. Caloca
Rogelio Fontela
Joseph E. Brooks
Charles N. Cleland, Jr.
Clifford W. Rainey

OF COUNSEL

Edgar C. Booth
James A. Dixon, Jr.

Representative Clients: Agency Rent-A-Car; Agricultural Excess and Surplus Insurance Co.; AIG Life Insurance Co.; Alliance Insurance Group; Allstate Insurance Co.; American Empire Surplus Lines Insurance Co.; American International Underwriters Inc.; Atlanta Casualty Insurance Co.; Avis Rent-A-Car; Bankers and Shippers Insurance Co.

For full biographical listings, see the Martindale-Hubbell Law Directory

NOVEY & MENDELSON (AV)

851 East Park Avenue, P.O. Box 1855, 32302-1855
Telephone: 904-224-2000
FAX: 904-222-4951

Jerome M. Novey
Robert D. Mendelson
Kristin Adamson

For full biographical listings, see the Martindale-Hubbell Law Directory

ROSE, SUNDSTROM & BENTLEY (AV)

A Partnership including Professional Associations
2548 Blairstone Pines Drive, P.O. Box 1567, 32302-1567
Telephone: 904-877-6555
Telecopier: 904-656-4029

MEMBERS OF FIRM

Chris H. Bentley (P.A.)
Martin S. Friedman (P.A.)

Representative Clients: Aloha Utilities, Inc.; Bonita Springs Utility, Inc.; Clay County, Florida; First American Title Insurance Company; North Fort Myers Utility, Inc.; Orange-Osceola Utilities, Inc.; Wise Realty Company.
Reference: Barnett Bank, Tallahassee.

For full biographical listings, see the Martindale-Hubbell Law Directory

*TAMPA,** Hillsborough Co.

LYNWOOD F. ARNOLD, JR. (AV)

2011 West Cleveland Street Suite F, P.O. Box 3357, 33601-3357
Telephone: 813-251-8111
Facsimile: 813-251-9225

For full biographical listings, see the Martindale-Hubbell Law Directory

FUENTES AND KREISCHER (AV)

1407 West Busch Boulevard, 33612
Telephone: 813-933-6647
Fax: 813-932-8588

MEMBERS OF FIRM

Lawrence E. Fuentes
Albert C. Kreischer, Jr.

OF COUNSEL

W. Andrew Hamilton

Reference: Northside Bank of Tampa.

For full biographical listings, see the Martindale-Hubbell Law Directory

GARCIA & FIELDS, P.A. (AV)

Suite 2560 Barnett Plaza, 101 East Kennedy Boulevard, 33602
Telephone: 813-222-8500
FAX: 813-222-8520

Joseph Garcia
Lesley J. Friedsam
Robert W. Fields
Victor D. Ines
Hugo C. Edberg

Reference: Barnett Bank of Tampa.

For full biographical listings, see the Martindale-Hubbell Law Directory

GOLD, RESNICK & SEGALL, P.A. (AV)

704 West Bay Street, 33606
Telephone: 813-254-2071
FAX: (813) 251-0616

Aaron J. Gold
Eddy R. Resnick
Larry M. Segall

Nancy J. Cass

Reference: Barnett Bank of Tampa.

For full biographical listings, see the Martindale-Hubbell Law Directory

HILL, WARD & HENDERSON, A PROFESSIONAL ASSOCIATION (AV)

101 East Kennedy Boulevard, Suite 3700, P.O. Box 2231, 33601
Telephone: 813-221-3900
FAX: 813-221-2900

Thomas W. Black
Andrew J. Lubrano
Martin L. Garcia
Douglas P. McClurg
Thomas N. Henderson, III
Brett J. Preston
Benjamin H. Hill, III
R. James Robbins, Jr.
John L. Holcomb
W. Lawrence Smith
Stephen M. Hudoba
Jeanne Trudeau Tate
Timothy A. Hunt
David R. Tyrrell
David T. Knight
Dennis P. Waggoner
David E. Ward, Jr.

Marie A. Borland
Pamela Schmitt Herman
Phillip S. Dingle
Jonathan P. Jennewein
S. Katherine Frazier
Jeffrey D. Murphy
Troy A. Fuhrman
Karen E. Ross
Robert B. Gough, III
Seth M. Schimmel
John B. Grandoff III
D. Keith Wickenden

Representative Clients: Allstate Insurance Co.; Aetna Casualty and Surety Co.; Bridgestone/Firestone, Inc.; Busch Entertainment Corp.; Cargill Fertilizer, Inc.; Chrysler Motors Corp.; City of Tampa; Citibank, N.A; Ch2M Hill; Fidelity and Deposit Company of Maryland.

For full biographical listings, see the Martindale-Hubbell Law Directory

KALISH & WARD, PROFESSIONAL ASSOCIATION (AV)

4100 Barnett Plaza, 101 East Kennedy Boulevard, P.O. Box 71, 33601-0071
Telephone: 813-222-8700
Facsimile: 813-222-8701

William Kalish
William T. Harrison, III
Alton C. Ward
Thomas P. McNamara
Richard A. Schlosser
Robert Reid Haney
Roger J. Rovell
Charles H. Carver
Michael A. Bedke
Kelley A. Bosecker

For full biographical listings, see the Martindale-Hubbell Law Directory

Tampa—Continued

LANGFORD, HILL & TRYBUS, P.A. (AV)

Suite 800, Bayshore Place, 601 Bayshore Boulevard, 33606
Telephone: 813-251-5533
Telecopier: 813-251-1900
Wats: 1-800-277-2005

E. C. Langford
Edward A. Hill
Ronald H. Trybus
Ronald G. Hock
Catherine M. Catlin
Debra M. Kubicsek
William B. Smith

Fredrique B. Boire
Muriel Desloovere
Kevin H. O'Neill
Vicki L. Page
Frederick T. Reeves
Barbara A. Sinsley
Stephens B. Woodrough (Not admitted in FL)
Anthony G. Woodward

Representative Clients: Affiliated of Florida, Inc.; American Federation Insurance Co.; Armor Insurance; Bank of Tampa; Central Bank of Tampa; Cintas Corp.; Container Corporation of America; CU Financial Services; Farm Stores, Inc.; First Union Home Equity Bank.

For full biographical listings, see the Martindale-Hubbell Law Directory

JOSEPH M. PANIELLO (AV)

Suite 2720 One Tampa City Center, 201 North Franklin Street, P.O. Box 2347, 33601
Telephone: 813-228-7004
FAX: 813-221-2418

J. Mackie Paniello

ASSOCIATES

Gregory T. Hall
Clay A. Holtsinger

Representative Clients: J. I. Kislak Mortgage Corp.; Corinthian Mortgage Corp.; Knutson Mortgage Corp.; GE Capital Asset Mgt. Corp.; Margaretten & Company, Inc.; Source One Mortgage Services Corp.; Eastern Savings; Banc Plus Mortgage Co.
Approved Attorney for: Attorney's Title Insurance Fund.

For full biographical listings, see the Martindale-Hubbell Law Directory

RYDBERG, GOLDSTEIN & BOLVES, P.A. (AV)

Suite 200, 500 East Kennedy Boulevard, 33602
Telephone: 813-229-3900
Telecopier: 813-229-6101

Marsha Griffin Rydberg
Bruce S. Goldstein
Brian A. Bolves
Robert E. V. Kelley, Jr.
Homer Duvall, III
Richard Thomas Petitt
Donald Alan Workman
David M. Corry
Leenetta Blanton
Peter Baker
Jeffery R. Ward
Roy J. Ford, Jr.
John J. Dingfelder

For full biographical listings, see the Martindale-Hubbell Law Directory

SMITH, WILLIAMS & BOWLES, P.A. (AV)

Old Hyde Park, 712 South Oregon Avenue, 33606
Telephone: 813-253-5400
Fax: 813-254-3459
Orlando, Florida Office: Smith, Williams & Humphries, P.A., Southeast Bank Building, Suite 700, 201 East Pine Street.
Telephone: 407-849-5151.
St. Cloud, Florida Office: 1700-13th Street, Suite 2, 34769.
Telephone: 407-892-5545.

David Lisle Smith
Gregory L. Williams
Margaret E. Bowles
Jana P. Andrews
Jeffrey A. Aman
J. Gregory Humphries (Resident, Orlando Office)
James A. Muench
Dale K. Bohner
Neal A. Sivyer
Robert L. Harding (Resident, Orlando Office)
Daniel William King
Rebecca H. Forest (Resident, Orlando Office)

For full biographical listings, see the Martindale-Hubbell Law Directory

ZUCKERMAN, SPAEDER, TAYLOR & EVANS (AV)

101 East Kennedy Boulevard, Suite 3140, 33602
Telephone: 813-221-1010
Fax: 813-223-7961
Miami, Florida Office: Suite 900, Miami Center, 201 South Biscayne Boulevard.
Telephones: 305-358-5000; 305-579-0110; Broward County: 305-523-0277.
Fax: 305-579-9749.
Ft. Lauderdale, Florida Office: One East Broward Boulevard, Suite 700.
Telephone: 305-356-0463.
Fax: 305-356-0406.
Washington, D.C. Office: Zuckerman, Spaeder, Goldstein, Taylor & Kolker, 1201 Connecticut Avenue, N.W.
Telephone: 202-778-1800.
Fax: 202-822-8106.

(See Next Column)

Baltimore, Maryland Office: Zuckerman, Spaeder, Goldstein, Taylor & Better, Suite 2440, 100 East Pratt Street.
Telephone: 410-332-0444.
Fax: 410-659-0436.
New York, N.Y. Office: Zuckerman, Spaeder, Goldstein, Taylor & Kolker, 1114 Avenue of the Americas, 45th Floor, Grace Building.
Telephone: 212-479-6500.
Fax: 212-479-6512.

MEMBERS OF FIRM

Ronald B. Ravikoff (Resident, Miami, Florida Office)
Michael Steven Greene (Resident, Miami, Florida Office)

ASSOCIATES

Jeffrey P. Agron (Resident, Miami, Florida Office)
Jill M. Granat (Resident, Miami, Florida Office)
Rebeca Sanchez-Roig (Resident, Miami, Florida Office)

For full biographical listings, see the Martindale-Hubbell Law Directory

*VERO BEACH,** Indian River Co.

CLEM, POLACKWICH & VOCELLE (AV)

A Partnership including Professional Associations
Univest Building-Suite 501, 2770 North Indian River Boulevard, 32960
Telephone: 407-562-8111
Fax: 407-562-2870

MEMBERS OF FIRM

Chester Clem (P.A.)
Alan S. Polackwich, Sr. (P.A.)
Louis B. Vocelle, Jr., (P.A.)
James A. Taylor, III

ASSOCIATE

Paul Richard Berg

OF COUNSEL

Robert Golden

References: Barnett Bank of The Treasure Coast; Beach Bank of Vero Beach; Indian River National Bank; Riverside National Bank of Florida.

For full biographical listings, see the Martindale-Hubbell Law Directory

COLLINS, BROWN & CALDWELL, CHARTERED (AV)

756 Beachland Boulevard, P.O. Box 3686, 32964
Telephone: 407-231-4343
FAX: 407-234-5213

George G. Collins, Jr.
Calvin B. Brown
William W. Caldwell
Bruce D. Barkett
Bradley W. Rossway
Michael J. Garavaglia
John E. Moore, III

Reference: First Union Bank of Indian River County, Vero Beach, Florida.

For full biographical listings, see the Martindale-Hubbell Law Directory

JOHN H. SUTHERLAND, P.A. (AV)

Schlitt Professional Plaza, 321-21st Street, 32960
Telephone: 407-567-5191
FAX: 407-567-9401

John H. Sutherland

Alexander Glenn Sutherland

General Counsel for: Greene Citrus Management, Inc.; Orange Avenue Citrus Growers Association, Inc.

For full biographical listings, see the Martindale-Hubbell Law Directory

*WEST PALM BEACH,** Palm Beach Co.

HONIGMAN MILLER SCHWARTZ AND COHN (AV)

A Partnership including Professional Corporations
Suite 800 Esperante Building, 222 Lakeview Avenue, 33401-6112
Telephone: 407-838-4500
Telecopier: 407-832-3036; 832-2645
Tampa, Florida Office: 2700 Landmark Centre, 401 E. Jackson Street.
Telephone: 813-221-6600.
Orlando, Florida Office: 390 North Orange Avenue, Suite 1300.
Telephone: 407-648-0300.
Detroit, Michigan Office: 2290 First National Building.
Telephone: 313-256-7800.
Lansing, Michigan Office: 222 North Washington Square, Suite 400.
Telephone: 517-484-8282.
Houston, Texas: 3100 First Interstate Bank Plaza, 1000 Louisiana.
Telephone: 713-650-2600.
Los Angeles, California Office: Watt Plaza, Suite 2200, 1875 Century Park East.
Telephone: 310-789-3800.
Fax: 310-789-3814.

(See Next Column)

HONIGMAN MILLER SCHWARTZ AND COHN, *West Palm Beach—Continued*

MEMBERS

Carl Angeloff (P.A.)
Neil W. Platock
Steven R. Parson (P.A.)
Donald H. Reed, Jr.
Marvin S. Rosen (P.A.)

For Complete List of Firm Personnel, See General Section

For full biographical listings, see the Martindale-Hubbell Law Directory

PRESSLY & PRESSLY, P.A. (AV)

Esperante, Suite 910, 222 Lakeview Avenue, 33401-6112
Telephone: 407-659-4040
FAX: 407-655-6006

James G. Pressly, Jr.
David S. Pressly
Trent S. Kiziah

For full biographical listings, see the Martindale-Hubbell Law Directory

WINTER HAVEN, Polk Co.

PETERSON, MYERS, CRAIG, CREWS, BRANDON & PUTERBAUGH, P.A. (AV)

Suite 300, 141 5th Street N.W., P.O. Drawer 7608, 33883-7608
Telephone: 813-294-3360
Lake Wales, Florida Office: 130 East Central Avenue, P.O. Box 1079.
Telephones: 813-676-7611; 683-8942.
Lakeland, Florida Office: 100 East Main Street, P.O. Box 24628.
Telephones: 813-683-6511; 676-6934.

Jack P. Brandon
Beach A Brooks, Jr.
J. Davis Connor
Michael S. Craig
Roy A. Craig, Jr.
Jacob C. Dykxhoorn
Dennis P. Johnson
Kevin C. Knowlton
Douglas A. Lockwood, III
Corneal B. Myers
Cornelius B. Myers, III
Robert E. Puterbaugh
Abel A. Putnam
Thomas B. Putnam, Jr.
Deborah A. Ruster
Stephen R. Senn
Andrea Teves Smith
Kerry M. Wilson

General Counsel for: Barnett Bank of Polk County.
Representative Clients: Mutual Wholesale Co.; Sun Bank/Mid-Florida, N.A.; Chase Commercial Corp.; Barnett Banks, Inc.; Ben Hill Griffin, Inc.; Alcoma Association, Inc.
Approved Attorneys for: Attorneys' Title Insurance Fund; Federal Land Bank, Columbia, South Carolina; Equitable Life Assurance Society of the United States.

For full biographical listings, see the Martindale-Hubbell Law Directory

WINTER PARK, Orange Co.

GRAHAM, CLARK, JONES, PRATT & MARKS (AV)

Third Floor, NationsBank Building, 369 North New York Avenue, P.O. Drawer 1690, 32790
Telephone: 407-647-4455
Telefax: 407-740-7063
Orlando, Florida Office: 111 North Orlando Avenue, Suite 1075, 32801.
Telephone: 407-648-5740.

MEMBERS OF FIRM

Jesse E. Graham
Scott D. Clark
Frederick W. Jones
James R. Pratt
Howard S. Marks
Geoffrey D. Withers
J. Gary Miller
John L. DiMasi
Mary W. Christian
Laura L. Jacobs
Jesse E. Graham, Jr.

Approved Attorneys for: Chicago Title Insurance Co.
Reference: NationsBank of Florida.

For full biographical listings, see the Martindale-Hubbell Law Directory

POHL & BROWN, P.A. (AV)

280 West Canton Avenue, Suite 410, P.O. Box 3208, 32789
Telephone: 407-647-7645; 407-647-POHL
Telefax: 407-647-2314

Frank L. Pohl
Usher L. Brown
Houston E. Short
Dwight I. Cool
William W. Pouzar
Mary B. Van Leuven

OF COUNSEL

Frederick W. Peirsol

Representative Clients: Orange County Comptroller; Osceola County; School Board of Osceola County, Florida; Osceola Tourist Development Council; NationsBank of Florida, N.A.; SunBank, N.A.; The Bank of Winter Park; Bekins Moving and Storage Co., Inc.; Champion Boats, Inc.; KeyCom Telephone Systems, Inc.

For full biographical listings, see the Martindale-Hubbell Law Directory

WINDERWEEDLE, HAINES, WARD & WOODMAN, P.A. (AV)

Barnett Bank Building, 250 Park Avenue, South, P.O. Box 880, 32790-0880
Telephone: 407-644-6312
Telecopier: 407-645-3728
Orlando, Florida Office: Barnett Bank Center, 390 North Orange Avenue, P.O. Box 1391.
Telephone: 407-423-4246.
Telecopier: 407-423-7014.

Victor E. Woodman
John D. Haines
C. Brent McCaghren
Randolph J. Rush
Gregory L. Holzhauer

Approved Attorneys For: Attorneys Title Insurance Fund, Inc.; Chicago Title Insurance Co.; Commonwealth Land Title Insurance Co.
Counsel for: Barnett Bank of Central Florida, N.A.
Representative Clients: Security National Bank; Whispering Waters Apartments.

For Complete List of Firm Personnel, See General Section

For full biographical listings, see the Martindale-Hubbell Law Directory

GEORGIA

*ALBANY,** Dougherty Co.

CANNON, MEYER VON BREMEN & MEIER (AV)

2417 Westgate Drive, P.O. Box 70909, 31708-0909
Telephone: 912-435-1470
Telefax: 912-888-2156

MEMBERS OF FIRM

William E. Cannon, Jr.
Michael S. Meyer von Bremen
John A. Meier, II
Timothy O. Davis

For full biographical listings, see the Martindale-Hubbell Law Directory

*AMERICUS,** Sumter Co.

OXFORD, MCKELVEY & JONES, P.C. (AV)

Old Fire Hall, 109 North Lee Street, P.O. Box J, 31709-0298
Telephone: 912-924-6108
FAX: 912-924-0935

Charles Oliver Oxford
Howard S. McKelvey, Jr.
Randolph B. Jones, Jr.

Representative Client: Reeves Construction Co.

For full biographical listings, see the Martindale-Hubbell Law Directory

*ATLANTA,** Fulton Co.

ALEMBIK, FINE & CALLNER, P.A. (AV)

Marquis One Tower, Fourth Floor, 245 Peachtree Center Avenue, N.E., 30303
Telephone: 404-688-8800
Telecopier: 404-420-7191

Michael D. Alembik (1936-1993)
Lowell S. Fine
Bruce W. Callner
Kathy L. Portnoy
Ronald T. Gold
G. Michael Banick
Mark E. Bergeson
Russell P. Love

Z. Ileana Martinez
Kevin S. Green
Susan M. Lieppe
T. Kevin Mooney
Bruce R. Steinfeld
Janet Lichiello Franchi

For full biographical listings, see the Martindale-Hubbell Law Directory

ALSTON & BIRD (AV)

A Partnership including Professional Corporations
One Atlantic Center, 1201 West Peachtree Street, 30309-3424
Telephone: 404-881-7000
Telecopier: 404-881-7777
Cable Address: AMGRAM GA
Telex: 54-2996
Easylink: 62985848
Washington, D.C. Office: 700 Thirteenth Street, Suite 350 20005-3960.
Telephone: 202-508-3300.
Telecopier: 202-508-3333.

MEMBERS OF FIRM

Ralph Williams, Jr.
Walter W. Mitchell
Rawson Foreman
A. James Elliott (P.C.)
Joseph V. Myers, Jr.
James F. Nellis, Jr.
T. Michael Tennant
Michael R. Davis
Christopher Glenn Sawyer
Charles A. Brake, Jr.
Albert E. Bender, Jr.
Timothy J. Pakenham
William R. Klapp, Jr.
Mark C. Rusche
Marci P. Schmerler

(See Next Column)

ALSTON & BIRD—*Continued*

ASSOCIATES

Leon Adams, Jr.	James G. Farris, Jr.
Christina K. Braisted	Jeff A. Israel
Glenda G. Bugg	Jennifer Greer McCrory
Douglas E. Cloud	Blair G. Schlossberg
Sarah V. Elliott	Joseph P. L. Snyder

OF COUNSEL

Robert L. Foreman, Jr.	Richard A. Allison

Representative Clients: A. G. Spanos Development, Inc.; Anheuser-Busch Companies; New York Life Insurance Co.; Prudential Insurance Company of America; The Equitable Life Assurance Society of the United States; The Rouse Company.

For Complete List of Firm Personnel, See General Section

For full biographical listings, see the Martindale-Hubbell Law Directory

ALTMAN, KRITZER & LEVICK, P.C. (AV)

Powers Ferry Landing, Suite 224, 6400 Powers Ferry Road, N.W., 30339
Telephone: 404-955-3555
Telecopier: 404-952-7821, 955-2866, 955-0038, 955-3697
Schaumburg, Illinois Affiliate: Altman, Kritzer & Levick, Ltd., Suite 400, 1101 Perimeter Drive, 60173.
Telephone: 708-240-0340.
FAX: 708-240-0344.

Allen D. Altman	Elizabeth H. Hutchins
Craig H. Kritzer	Theodore H. Sandler
Mark J. Levick	Frank Slover
D. Charles Houk	Kenneth A. Shapiro
Charles L. Wood	Linda L. West
Ephraim Spielman	Steven A. Pepper
Emily Sanford Bair	George A. Mattingly
Benno G. Rothschild, Jr.	W. Daniel Hicks, Jr.

COUNSEL

Richard P. Rubenoff	Robert D. Simons
Martin N. Goldsmith	Peter M. Hartman
Susan E. Stoffer	William R. Ham

Duane D. Sitar	Gregory A. Jacobs
Debra L. Thompson	Andrew R. Bauman
Lori E. Kilberg	Lawrence H. Freiman
Richard W. Probert	Ian L. Levin

LEGAL SUPPORT PERSONNEL

Cynthia A. Groszkiewicz	Rebecca G. Middleton

Representative Clients: Atlantic Southeast Airlines, Inc.; Ingles Markets, Inc.; The Home Depot, Inc.; Pacesetter Steel Service, Inc.; Homart Development Co.

For full biographical listings, see the Martindale-Hubbell Law Directory

COHEN/DAVID & ASSOCIATES, P.C. (AV)

6000 Lake Forrest Drive, N.W. 100 Century Springs West, 30328-5902
Telephone: 404-256-7802
Fax: 404-255-0137
Tucker, Georgia Office: Suite 104, Building 12, 2193 Northlake Parkway, 30084.
Telephone: 404-493-8445.
Fax: 404-493-1831.
Roswell, Georgia Office: Suite 400, 1172 Grimes Bridge Road, 30075.
Telephone: 404-998-8100.
Fax: 404-998-6804.

Bruce P. Cohen	Glenn F. Sherman
John H. David, Jr. (Resident, Roswell Office)	Jacquelyn S. Rago (Resident, Tucker Office)

OF COUNSEL

Loyd Justin Cohen (Not admitted in GA)

For full biographical listings, see the Martindale-Hubbell Law Directory

DAVID G. CROCKETT, P.C. (AV)

1000 Equitable Building, 100 Peachtree Street, N.W., 30303
Telephone: 404-522-4280
Telecopier: 404-589-9891

David G. Crockett

Approved Attorney for: Chicago Title Insurance Co.
Reference: NationsBank, N.A.

For full biographical listings, see the Martindale-Hubbell Law Directory

DAVIS, MATTHEWS & QUIGLEY, P.C. (AV)

Fourteenth Floor, Lenox Towers II, 3400 Peachtree Road, 30326
Telephone: 404-261-3900
Telecopier: 404-261-0159

(See Next Column)

Ron L. Quigley	J. Michael Harrison

Approved Attorneys for: Lawyers Title Insurance Corp.

For Complete List of Firm Personnel, See General Section

For full biographical listings, see the Martindale-Hubbell Law Directory

FRANKEL, HARDWICK, TANENBAUM & FINK, P.C. (AV)

359 East Paces Ferry Road, N.E., 30305
Telephone: 404-266-2930
Fax: 404-231-3362

Pearce D. Hardwick	Barbara A. Lincoln

Representative Clients: Commercial Bank of Georgia; First Capital Bank; Metro Bank; The Money Store Investment Corp.; Mountain National Bank; SouthTrust Bank of Georgia, N.A.; The Venture Construction Company.

For Complete List of Firm Personnel, See General Section

For full biographical listings, see the Martindale-Hubbell Law Directory

GLASS, MCCULLOUGH, SHERRILL & HARROLD (AV)

1409 Peachtree Street, N.E., 30309
Telephone: 404-885-1500
Telecopier: 404-892-1801
Buckhead Office: Monarch Plaza, 3414 Peachtree Road, N.E., Suite 450, Atlanta, Georgia, 30326-1162.
Telephone: 404-885-1500.
Telecopier: 404-231-1978.
Washington, D.C. Office: 1155 15th Street, N.W., Suite 400, Washington, D.C., 20005.
Telephone: 202-785-8118.
Telecopier: 202-785-0128.

MEMBERS OF FIRM

Peter B. Glass	Kenneth R. McCullough
William D. Brunstad	James H. Kaminer, Jr.
Luther C. Curtis	Jerry A. Shaifer

Robert M. Trusty

For Complete List of Firm Personnel, See General Section

For full biographical listings, see the Martindale-Hubbell Law Directory

HOLT, NEY, ZATCOFF & WASSERMAN (AV)

A Partnership including Professional Corporations
100 Galleria Parkway, Suite 600, 30339
Telephone: 404-956-9600
Facsimile Number: 404-956-1490

MEMBERS OF FIRM

Robert G. Holt (P.C.)	Sanford H. Zatcoff (P.C.)
James M. Ney (P.C.)	Richard P. Vornholt

ASSOCIATE

Brian P. Cain

Representative Clients: Abrams Properties, Inc.; Citicorp Real Estate, Inc.; Childress Klein Properties, Inc.; Confederation Life Insurance Co.; Trammell Crow Residential; First American Title Insurance Co.; Metric Realty; Old Republic National Title Insurance Co.; Roberts Properties, Inc.; Sterling Trust.

For Complete List of Firm Personnel, See General Section

For full biographical listings, see the Martindale-Hubbell Law Directory

LONG ALDRIDGE & NORMAN (AV)

A Partnership including Professional Corporations
One Peachtree Center, Suite 5300, 303 Peachtree Street, 30308
Telephone: 404-527-4000
Telecopier: 404-527-4198
Washington, D.C. Office: Suite 950, 1615 L Street, 20036.
Telephone: 202-223-7033.
Telecopier: 202-223-7013.

MEMBERS OF FIRM

Clyde E. Click	Robert D. Hancock, Jr.
James A. Fleming	William F. Stevens

William F. Timmons

ASSOCIATES

James L. Barkin	Brooke Hume Pendleton
Thomas J. Flanigan	Janice Nathanson Smith
W. Gregory Null	Wendy A. Strassner

For Complete List of Firm Personnel, See General Section

For full biographical listings, see the Martindale-Hubbell Law Directory

MACEY, WILENSKY, COHEN, WITTNER & KESSLER (AV)

Suite 700 Carnegie Building, 133 Carnegie Way, Northwest, 30303
Telephone: 404-584-1200
Telecopier: 404-681-4355
Other Atlanta, Georgia Office: 5784 Lake Forrest Drive, Suite 214, 30328.

(See Next Column)

MACEY, WILENSKY, COHEN, WITTNER & KESSLER, *Atlanta—Continued*

MEMBERS OF FIRM

Morris W. Macey
Frank B. Wilensky
M. Todd Westfall

ASSOCIATE

Pamela Gronauer Hill

For Complete List of Firm Personnel, See General Section

For full biographical listings, see the Martindale-Hubbell Law Directory

RAMSAY & CALLOWAY (AV)

56 Perimeter Center East, N.E., Suite 400, 30346-2283
Telephone: 404-698-7960
Telecopier: 404-698-7990
Hilton Head, South Carolina Office: Suite 300 Professional Building.
Telephone: 803-686-4006.
Telecopier: 803-686-4494.

MEMBERS OF FIRM

Ernest C. Ramsay
S. Marcus Calloway
N. H. Purvis
Richard J. Beam, Jr.
J. D. Benson
J. F. Mixson, III

ASSOCIATES

Donald J. Schliessmann, Jr.
Christy B. Cash
Christine A. Hofmann (Resident, Hilton Head, South Carolina Office)

Reference: NationsBank.

For full biographical listings, see the Martindale-Hubbell Law Directory

SCHREEDER, WHEELER & FLINT (AV)

1600 Candler Building, 127 Peachtree Street, N.E., 30303-1845
Telephone: 404-681-3450
Telecopy: 404-681-1046

MEMBERS OF FIRM

Charles L. Schreeder, III
Warren O. Wheeler
Samuel F. Boyte
Mark W. Forsling
Leo Rose III

ASSOCIATES

Clifford A. Barshay
Laura R. Champion

Reference: Fidelity National Bank; Wachovia Bank of Georgia, NA.

For full biographical listings, see the Martindale-Hubbell Law Directory

SUTHERLAND, ASBILL & BRENNAN (AV)

999 Peachtree Street, N.E., 30309-3996
Telephone: 404-853-8000
Facsimile: 404-853-8806
Washington, D.C. Office: 1275 Pennsylvania Avenue, N.W., 20004-2404.
Telephone: 202-383-0100.
New York, N.Y. Office: 1270 Avenue of the Americas, 10020-1700.
Telephone: 212-332-3000.
Austin, Texas Office: 111 Congress Avenue, 23rd Floor, 78701-4079.
Telephone: 512-469-3350.

Alfred G. Adams, Jr.
H. Edward Hales, Jr.
J. Patton Hyman, III
James Bruce Jordan
William R. Patterson
James R. Paulk, Jr.
Haynes R. Roberts
Barbara S. Rudisill

For Complete List of Firm Personnel, See General Section

For full biographical listings, see the Martindale-Hubbell Law Directory

THOMAS, KENNEDY, SAMPSON & PATTERSON (AV)

1600 Bank South Building, 55 Marietta Street, N.W., 30303
Telephone: 404-688-4503
Telecopier: 404-681-2950

MEMBERS OF FIRM

John Loren Kennedy (1942-1994)
Thomas G. Sampson
P. Andrew Patterson
Myra H. Dixon
R. David Ware
Patrise M. Perkins-Hooker
Jeffrey E. Tompkins

ASSOCIATES

Rosalind T. Drakeford
Regina E. McMillan
Melynee C. Leftridge
La'Sean M. Zilton

For full biographical listings, see the Martindale-Hubbell Law Directory

VINCENT, CHOREY, TAYLOR & FEIL, A PROFESSIONAL CORPORATION (AV)

Suite 1700, The Lenox Building, 3399 Peachtree Road, N.E., 30326
Telephone: 404-841-3200
Telex: 650 298-1749
Telecopier: 404-841-3221

(See Next Column)

Richard H. Vincent
Eric D. Ranney
Susan Shivers Fink

M. Suellen Henderson
Gregory P. Youra
Philip M. Rees

For Complete List of Firm Personnel, See General Section

For full biographical listings, see the Martindale-Hubbell Law Directory

*AUGUSTA,** Richmond Co.

CAPERS, DUNBAR, SANDERS & BRUCKNER (AV)

Fifteenth Floor, First Union Bank Building, 30901-1454
Telephone: 706-722-7542
Telecopier: 706-724-7776

MEMBERS OF FIRM

John D. Capers
Paul H. Dunbar, III
E. Frederick Sanders
Ziva P. Bruckner

ASSOCIATE

Carl P. Dowling

For full biographical listings, see the Martindale-Hubbell Law Directory

HULL, TOWILL, NORMAN & BARRETT, A PROFESSIONAL CORPORATION (AV)

Seventh Floor, Trust Company Bank Building, P.O. Box 1564, 30903-1564
Telephone: 706-722-4481
Fax: 706-722-9779

James M. Hull (1885-1975)
George B. Barrett (1894-1942)
Julian J. Willingham (1887-1963)
John Bell Towill (1907-1991)
Robert C. Norman (Retired, 1991)
W. Hale Barrett
Lawton Jordan, Jr.
Patrick J. Rice
Douglas D. Batchelor, Jr.
David E. Hudson
Neal W. Dickert
John W. Gibson
William F. Hammond
Mark S. Burgreen
George R. Hall
James B. Ellington
F. Michael Taylor

Robert A. Mullins
William J. Keogh, III
Edward J. Tarver
J. Noel Schweers, III
Michael S. Carlson
Ralph Emerson Hanna, III
Susan D. Barrett
Timothy Moses

Counsel for: Trust Company Bank of Augusta, N.A.; Georgia Federal Bank, FSB, Augusta Division; Southeastern Newspapers Corp.; Georgia Power Co.; Southern Bell Telephone & Telegraph Co.; St. Joseph Hospital, Augusta, Georgia, Inc.; Norfolk Southern Corp.; Merry Land & Investment Co., Inc.; Housing Authority of the City of Augusta; Georgia Press Association.

For full biographical listings, see the Martindale-Hubbell Law Directory

*CARROLLTON,** Carroll Co.

TISINGER, TISINGER, VANCE & GREER, A PROFESSIONAL CORPORATION (AV)

100 Wagon Yard Plaza, P.O. Box 2069, 30117
Telephone: 404-834-4467
FAX: 404-834-5426

Richard G. Tisinger
Phillip D. Wilkins
Stacey L. Blackmon

Representative Clients: Carrollton Federal Bank-Federal Savings Bank; Fairfield Communities, Inc.; William Hilton Parkway Retail Associates.

For Complete List of Firm Personnel, See General Section

For full biographical listings, see the Martindale-Hubbell Law Directory

*COLUMBUS,** Muscogee Co.

HATCHER, STUBBS, LAND, HOLLIS & ROTHSCHILD (AV)

Suite 500 The Corporate Center, 233 12th Street, P.O. Box 2707, 31902-2707
Telephone: 706-324-0201
Telecopier: 706-322-7747

MEMBERS OF FIRM

Albert W. Stubbs
Alan F. Rothschild
William B. Hardegree
Morton A. Harris
J. Barrington Vaught
Charles T. Staples
James E. Humes, II
Joseph L. Waldrep
Robert C. Martin, Jr.
George W. Mize, Jr.
John M. Tanzine, III
Alan F. Rothschild, Jr.
William C. Pound

(See Next Column)

HATCHER, STUBBS, LAND, HOLLIS & ROTHSCHILD—*Continued*

ASSOCIATES

Mote W. Andrews III
C. Morris Mullin
Theodore Darryl (Ted) Morgan

General Counsel for: Trust Company Bank of Columbus, N.A.; TOM'S Foods Inc.; Muscogee County Board of Education; The Jordan Co.; Flournoy Development Corp.; St. Francis Hospital, Inc.; Bill Heard Enterprises, Inc.
Assistant Division Counsel for: Norfolk Southern Corp.
Local Counsel for: First Union National Bank of Georgia.

For Complete List of Firm Personnel, See General Section

For full biographical listings, see the Martindale-Hubbell Law Directory

*DECATUR,** De Kalb Co.

SIMMONS, WARREN & SZCZECKO, PROFESSIONAL ASSOCIATION (AV)

315 West Ponce de Leon Avenue, Suite 850, 30030
Telephone: 404-378-1711
Fax: 404-377-6101

Wesley B. Warren, Jr.
William C. McFee, Jr.

Representative Clients: David Hocker & Associates (Shopping Center Development); Julian LeCraw & Company (Real Estate); Royal Oldsmobile,; Cotter & Co.; Atlanta Neurosurgical Associates, P.A.; Villager Lodge, Inc.; Troncalli Motors, Inc.

For Complete List of Firm Personnel, See General Section

For full biographical listings, see the Martindale-Hubbell Law Directory

*GAINESVILLE,** Hall Co.

SMITH, GILLIAM AND WILLIAMS (AV)

200 Old Coca-Cola Building, 301 Green Street, N.W., P.O. Box 1098, 30503
Telephone: 404-536-3381
Fax: 404-531-1491

MEMBERS OF FIRM

R. Wilson Smith, Jr. (1906-1983)
John H. Smith
Steven P. Gilliam
Jerry A. Williams
Kelly Anne Miles
Bradley J. Patten

ASSOCIATES

M. Tyler Smith
Scott Arthur Ball

General Counsel for: Gainesville Industrial Electric Co.; Georgia Mutual Insurance Co.; L & R Farms; H. Wilson Manufacturing Co.; Goforth Electrical Supply; North Georgia Petroleum Co.; Gibbs Management Group, Inc.

For full biographical listings, see the Martindale-Hubbell Law Directory

*GRIFFIN,** Spalding Co.

JOHN M. COGBURN, JR. (AV)

115 North Sixth Street, P.O. Box 907, 30224
Telephone: 404-228-2148
Telecopier: 404-228-5018
McDonough, Georgia Office: Suite 300E, First Community Bank Building, 12 North Cedar Street.
Telephone: 404-954-9004.
Fax: 404-228-5018.

ASSOCIATE

R. Michelle Denton

Representative Clients: Griffin-Spalding County Hospital Authority; Allstar Knitwear Co., Inc. (Textiles); Atlanta Tees, Inc. (Sportswear Distribution); Industrial Refrigeration Enterprises, Inc. (Refrigeration Engineers and Contractors); Spauchus Associates, Inc. (Chemical Engineering Consultants).

For full biographical listings, see the Martindale-Hubbell Law Directory

CUMMING, CUMMING & ESARY (AV)

322 South Sixth Street, P.O. Box 577, 30224
Telephone: 706-227-3746
Fax: 706-227-3891

MEMBERS OF FIRM

D. R. Cumming (1888-1970)
Joseph R. Cumming (1906-1990)
W. Barron Cumming
Sidney R. Esary

Counsel for: First National Bank of Griffin; United Bank of Griffin; Dundee Mills, Inc.; Rushton Cotton Mills.
Local Counsel for: Thomaston Cotton Mills.
Approved Attorneys for: Lawyers Title Insurance Corp.; Chicago Title Insurance Co.; Title Insurance Company of Minnesota.

For full biographical listings, see the Martindale-Hubbell Law Directory

*HARTWELL,** Hart Co.

WALTER JAMES GORDON (AV)

Gordon Building, P.O. Box 870, 30643
Telephone: 706-376-5418
FAX: 706-376-5416

ASSOCIATE

Eleanor Patat Cotton

LEGAL SUPPORT PERSONNEL

Flo W. Brown

References: NationsBank of Georgia, N.A.; The Bank of Hartwell; Athens First Bank & Trust Company.

For full biographical listings, see the Martindale-Hubbell Law Directory

*MARIETTA,** Cobb Co.

MOORE & ROGERS (AV)

192 Anderson Street, P.O. Box 3305, 30060
Telephone: 404-429-1499
Telecopier: 404-429-8631

MEMBERS OF FIRM

John H. Moore
G. Phillip Beggs
Eldon L. Basham

ASSOCIATES

Sarah L. Bargo
Sara J. Murphree

Representative Clients: Traton Corp.; Oakleigh Development Corp.
Approved Attorneys For: Chicago Title Insurance Co.; First American Title Insurance Co.; Lawyers Title Insurance Corp.; Ticor Title Insurance Company of California.
References: Charter Bank and Trust Co.; First Alliance Bank.

For full biographical listings, see the Martindale-Hubbell Law Directory

SCHAAF & HODGES (AV)

An Association of Sole Practitioners
Suite 202, 1853 Piedmont Road, 30066
Telephone: 404-971-4312
Fax: 404-971-5106

Michael L. Schaaf
R.E. Hodges, Jr.

OF COUNSEL

James R. Gee

Reference: Wachovia Bank.

For full biographical listings, see the Martindale-Hubbell Law Directory

*MCDONOUGH,** Henry Co.

SMITH, WELCH & STUDDARD (AV)

41 Keys Ferry Street, P.O. Box 31, 30253
Telephone: 404-957-3937
Fax: 404-957-9165
Stockbridge, Georgia Office: 1231-A Eagle's Landing Parkway.
Telephone: 404-389-4864.
FAX: 404-389-5157.

MEMBERS OF FIRM

Ernest M. Smith (1911-1992)
A. J. Welch, Jr.
Ben W. Studdard, III
J. Mark Brittain (Resident, Stockbridge Office)

ASSOCIATES

Patrick D. Jaugstetter
E. Gilmore Maxwell
J.V. Dell, Jr. (Resident, Stockbridge Office)

Representative Clients: Alliance Corp.; Atlanta Motor Speedway, Inc.; Bellamy-Strickland Chevrolet, Inc.; Ceramic and Metal Coatings Corp.; City of Hampton; City of Locust Grove; City of Stockbridge.

For full biographical listings, see the Martindale-Hubbell Law Directory

*NEWNAN,** Coweta Co.

GLOVER & DAVIS, P.A. (AV)

10 Brown Street, P.O. Box 1038, 30264
Telephone: 404-253-4330;
Atlanta: 404-463-1100
Fax: 404-251-7152
Peachtree City, Georgia Office: Suite 130, 200 Westpark Drive.
Telephone: 404-487-5834.
Fax: 404-487-3492.

J. Littleton Glover, Jr.
Alan W. Jackson
Randy E. Connell
W. Robert Hancock, Jr. (Resident, Peachtree Office)
Felicia Odom Smith (Resident, Peachtree Office)

Representative Clients: Newnan Savings Bank; Pike Transfer Co.; Batson-Cook Company, General Corporate and Construction Divisions; Coweta County, Georgia.

(See Next Column)

GLOVER & DAVIS P.A., *Newnan—Continued*

Local Counsel for: International Latex Corp.; First Union National Bank of Georgia; West Georgia Farm Credit, ACA.

For Complete List of Firm Personnel, See General Section

For full biographical listings, see the Martindale-Hubbell Law Directory

ROSENZWEIG, JONES & MACNABB, P.C. (AV)

32 South Court Square, P.O. Box 220, 30264
Telephone: 404-253-3282;
(Atlanta) 404-577-5376
FAX: 404-251-7262

Sidney Pope Jones, Jr.

Charles C. Witcher

Approved Attorneys for: Lawyers Title Insurance Corp.; Commonwealth Land Title Insurance Co.; St. Paul Title Insurance Co.; Chicago Title Insurance Co.

For Complete List of Firm Personnel, See General Section

For full biographical listings, see the Martindale-Hubbell Law Directory

*SAVANNAH,** Chatham Co.

INGLESBY, FALLIGANT, HORNE, COURINGTON & NASH, A PROFESSIONAL CORPORATION (AV)

300 Bull Street, Suite 302, P.O. Box 1368, 31402-1368
Telephone: 912-232-7000
Telecopier: 912-232-7300

Sam P. Inglesby, Jr.
J. Daniel Falligant
Kathleen Horne
Dorothy W. Courington, II
Thomas A. Nash, Jr.
Dolly Chisholm

Representative Clients: NationsBank of Georgia, N.A.; Intermarine USA; Rotary Corp.; Atlanta Gas Light Co.; Ford Motor Credit Co.; Independent Insurance Agents of Savannah, Inc.; Savannah Christian Preparatory School.

For full biographical listings, see the Martindale-Hubbell Law Directory

HAWAII

*HONOLULU,** Honolulu Co.

AYABE, CHONG, NISHIMOTO, SIA & NAKAMURA (AV)

A Partnership including a Professional Corporation
3000 Grosvenor Center, 737 Bishop Street, 96813
Telephone: 808-537-6119
Telecopier: 808-526-3491

MEMBERS OF FIRM

Sidney K. Ayabe (P.C.)
Jeffrey H. K. Sia
Rodney S. Nishida
Gail M. Kang

Representative Clients: Travelers Insurance Co.; St. Paul Fire and Marine Insurance Co.; The Employers Group of Insurance Companies; TIG Insurance Co.; Pacific Insurance Co.; Hartford Accident and Indemnity Co.; Continental Casualty Co.; First Insurance Company of Hawaii, Ltd.

For Complete List of Firm Personnel, See General Section

For full biographical listings, see the Martindale-Hubbell Law Directory

CADES SCHUTTE FLEMING & WRIGHT (AV)

Formerly Smith, Wild, Beebe & Cades
1000 Bishop Street, P.O. Box 939, 96808
Telephone: 808-521-9200
Telex: 7238589
Telecopier: 808-531-8738
Affiliated Law Firm: Udom-Prok Associates Law Offices, 105/36 Tharinee Mansion, Borom Raj Chananee Road Bangkoknoi, Bangkok, Thailand, 10700.
Telephone: 011 660 435-4146.
Kailua-Kona, Hawaii Office: Hualalai Center, Suite B-303, 75-170 Hualalai Road.
Telephone: 808-329-5811.
Telecopier: 808-326-1175.

MEMBERS OF FIRM

Robert B. Bunn
Douglas E. Prior
Donald E. Scearce
Richard A. Hicks
Bernice Littman
Nicholas C. Dreher
Mark A. Hazlett
Philip J. Leas
Larry T. Takumi
Cary S. Matsushige
Gino L. Gabrio
Martin E. Hsia
Gail M. Tamashiro
Grace Nihei Kido
Donna Y. L. Leong

(See Next Column)

ASSOCIATES

Jeffrey D. Watts
Marjorie A. Lau
Laurie A. Kuribayashi
James H. Ashford
Michele M. Sunahara
Nani Lee (Resident, Kona Office)
Carlito P. Caliboso
Karen Wong
Jeffrey K. Natori
Dean T. Yamamoto

OF COUNSEL

Harold S. Wright

Counsel for: Amfac, Inc.; First Hawaiian Bank; Bishop Trust Co., Ltd.; Alexander & Baldwin, Inc.; Theo. H. Davies & Co., Ltd.; C. Brewer & Company, Ltd.; Bank of America, FSB; Kamehameha Schools/Bernice Pauahi Bishop Estate.

For Complete List of Firm Personnel, See General Section

For full biographical listings, see the Martindale-Hubbell Law Directory

DWYER IMANAKA SCHRAFF KUDO MEYER & FUJIMOTO ATTORNEYS AT LAW, A LAW CORPORATION (AV)

1800 Pioneer Plaza, 900 Fort Street Mall, 96813
Telephone: 808-524-8000
Telecopier: 808-526-1419
Mailing Address: P.O. Box 2727, 96803

John R. Dwyer, Jr.
Mitchell A. Imanaka
Paul A. Schraff
Benjamin A. Kudo (Atty. at Law, A Law Corp.)
William G. Meyer, III
Wesley M. Fujimoto
Ronald Van Grant
Jon M. H. Pang
Blake W. Bushnell
Kenn N. Kojima

Adelbert Green
Richard T. Asato, Jr.
Scott W. Settle
Darcie S. Yoshinaga
Tracy Timothy Woo
Lawrence I. Kawasaki
Douglas H. Inouye
Christine A. Low

OF COUNSEL

Randall Y. Iwase

For full biographical listings, see the Martindale-Hubbell Law Directory

FOLEY MAEHARA NIP & CHANG (AV)

2700 Grosvenor Center, 737 Bishop Street, 96813
Telephone: 808-526-3011
Telecopier: 808-523-1171, 808-526-0121, 808-533-4814

MEMBERS OF FIRM

Thomas M. Foley
Eric T. Maehara
Renton L. K. Nip
Wesley Y. S. Chang
Carl Tom
Edward R. Brooks
Arlene S. Kishi
Susan M. Ichinose
Robert F. Miller
Christian P. Porter

ASSOCIATES

Paula W. Chong
Lenore H. Lee
Leanne A. N. Nikaido
Jordan D. Wagner
Donna H. Yamamoto
Mark J. Bernardin
Jenny K. T. Wakayama

OF COUNSEL

Elizabeth A. Ivey

References: First Hawaiian Bank; Bank of Honolulu; Bank of Hawaii.

For full biographical listings, see the Martindale-Hubbell Law Directory

KOBAYASHI, SUGITA & GODA (AV)

A Partnership including Professional Corporations
8th Floor, Hawaii Tower, 745 Fort Street, 96813
Telephone: 808-539-8700
Telecopier: 808-539-8799
Telex: 6502396585 MCI
MCI Mail: 23 96585
ABA/Net: ABA2281

OF COUNSEL

Bert T. Kobayashi, Sr.

Reference: First Hawaiian Bank.

For Complete List of Firm Personnel, See General Section

For full biographical listings, see the Martindale-Hubbell Law Directory

MCCORRISTON MIHO MILLER MUKAI (AV)

Five Waterfront Plaza, 4th Floor, 500 Ala Moana Boulevard, 96813
Telephone: 808-529-7300
Facsimile: 808-524-8293
Cable: Attorneys, Honolulu

(See Next Column)

McCorriston Miho Miller Mukai—*Continued*

MEMBERS OF FIRM

Jon T. Miho
Clifford J. Miller
Michael D. Tom
Calvert G. Chipchase, III
D. Scott MacKinnon
Kenneth B. Marcus
Kenneth G. K. Hoo
Patrick K. Lau
David N. Kuriyama
Eric T. Kawatani
Keith K. Suzuka
Randal Keiji Nagatani

ASSOCIATES

Sharon H. Nishi
Andrew W. Char
Randall F. Sakumoto
Lynn M. Petry
Alexander R. Jampel
Leslie H. Kondo
Peter J. Hamasaki
Darren Patrick Conley

For Complete List of Firm Personnel, See General Section

For full biographical listings, see the Martindale-Hubbell Law Directory

Pitluck & Kido (AV)

701 Bishop Street, 96813
Telephone: 808-523-5030
Telecopier: 808-545-4015

MEMBERS OF FIRM

Wayne Marshall Pitluck
Alan Takashi Kido
Dana Kiyomi Nalani Sato

James Mauliola Keaka Stone, Jr.
Margaret Ann Leong

Reference: Bank of Hawaii.

For full biographical listings, see the Martindale-Hubbell Law Directory

Price Okamoto Himeno & Lum Attorneys at Law, A Law Corporation (AV)

Suite 728, Ocean View Center, 707 Richards Street, 96813
Telephone: 808-538-1113
FAX: 808-533-0549

Warren Price, III
Kenneth T. Okamoto
Sharon R. Himeno
Bettina W. J. Lum
Terence S. Yamamoto

John H. Yuen

OF COUNSEL

Stuart M. Cowan

For full biographical listings, see the Martindale-Hubbell Law Directory

IDAHO

*BOISE,** Ada Co.

Wilson, Carnahan & McColl, Chartered (AV)

420 Washington Street, P.O. Box 1544, 83701
Telephone: 208-345-9100
FAX: 208-384-0442

Jeffrey M. Wilson
Debrha Jo Carnahan
Brian F. McColl
Stephanie Jo Williams

Representative Clients: A & J Construction, Inc.; Pure-gro Company; Transamerica Commercial Finance Corp.; John H. Crowther, Inc.; Jess W. Swan Insurance Agency; Higgins and Rutledge Insurance Co., Inc.; Communication Workers of America, Local # 8103.

For full biographical listings, see the Martindale-Hubbell Law Directory

KETCHUM, Blaine Co.

James L. Kennedy, Jr. (AV)

340 Second Street East, P.O. Box 2165, 83340
Telephone: 208-726-8255

Reference: First Interstate Bank of Idaho, N.A. (Ketchum-Sun Valley Branch); First Security Bank of Idaho, N.A. (Ketchum Branch)

For full biographical listings, see the Martindale-Hubbell Law Directory

*POCATELLO,** Bannock Co.

Merrill & Merrill, Chartered (AV)

Key Bank Building, P.O. Box 991, 83204
Telephone: 208-232-2286
Fax: 208-232-2499

Dave R. Gallafent

Representative Client: Lawyers Title Insurance Co.

(See Next Column)

For Complete List of Firm Personnel, See General Section

For full biographical listings, see the Martindale-Hubbell Law Directory

*TWIN FALLS,** Twin Falls Co.

Rosholt, Robertson & Tucker, Chartered (AV)

142 Third Avenue North, P.O. Box 1906, 83303-1906
Telephone: 208-734-0700
Fax: 208-736-0041
Boise, Idaho Office: Suite 600, 1221 W. Idaho, P.O. Box 2139.
Telephone: 208-336-0700.
Fax: 208-344-6034.

John A. Rosholt
J. Evan Robertson
Gary D. Slette

Timothy J. Stover

For full biographical listings, see the Martindale-Hubbell Law Directory

ILLINOIS

*CHICAGO,** Cook Co.

Aronberg Goldgehn Davis & Garmisa (AV)

Suite 3000 One IBM Plaza, 60611-3633
Telephone: 312-828-9600
Telecopier: 312-828-9635

MEMBERS OF FIRM

Ronald J. Aronberg
Steven P. Davis
William J. Garmisa
Robert N. Sodikoff
Ned S. Robertson

ASSOCIATE

David H. Sachs

For Complete List of Firm Personnel, See General Section

For full biographical listings, see the Martindale-Hubbell Law Directory

Bailey, Borlack, Nadelhoffer & Carroll (AV)

Suite 2000, 135 South La Salle Street, 60603
Telephone: 312-629-2700
Telecopier: 312-629-0174

Robert C. Bailey
Alan R. Borlack
Clement J. Carroll, Jr.
Sarah K. Nadelhoffer
Eric G. Grossman

For full biographical listings, see the Martindale-Hubbell Law Directory

Bell, Boyd & Lloyd (AV)

Three First National Plaza Suite 3300, 70 West Madison Street, 60602
Telephone: 312-372-1121
FAX: 312-372-2098
Washington, D.C. Office: 1615 L Street, N.W.
Telephone: 202-466-6300.
FAX: 202-463-0678.

MEMBERS OF FIRM

Gregory R. Andre
Robert J. Best
Terrence E. Budny
Lawrence C. Eppley
Sanford R. Gail
D. Scott Hargadon
Thomas Z. Hayward, Jr.
Thomas C. Homburger
Lawrence M. Mages
Matthew K. Phillips
David M. Saltiel

OF COUNSEL

Stanton H. Berlin
John C. York

ASSOCIATES

Michelle D, Bowers
Kathryn A. Finn
Brian P. Gallagher

For Complete List of Firm Personnel, See General Section

For full biographical listings, see the Martindale-Hubbell Law Directory

Deutsch, Levy & Engel, Chartered (AV)

Suite 1700, 225 West Washington Street, 60606
Telephone: 312-346-1460
Boynton, Beach Florida Office: 3C Westgate Lane.
Telephone: 407-737-6003.
Wheaton, Illinois Office: Suite B2, 620 West Roosevelt Road.
Telephone: 312-665-9112.

Marshall D. Krolick
Barry R. Katz
Kenneth W. Funk

For Complete List of Firm Personnel, See General Section

For full biographical listings, see the Martindale-Hubbell Law Directory

Chicago—Continued

GOLDBERG, KOHN, BELL, BLACK, ROSENBLOOM & MORITZ, LTD. (AV)

Suite 3700, 55 East Monroe Street, 60603
Telephone: 312-201-4000
Telecopier: 312-332-2196

Stephen B. Bell
Karen Ruth Bieber
Dennis B. Black
Philip M. Blackman
Denise B. Caplan
David L. Dranoff
Wayne S. Gilmartin
Robert J. Goldberg
Robert M. Heinrich
Gerald L. Jenkins
Michael D. Karpeles
Frederic R. Klein
Richard M. Kohn
David M. Mason
William C. Meyers
Terry F. Moritz
James B. Rosenbloom
Gary N. Ruben
Daniel P. Shapiro
Alan P. Solow
Carole K. Towne
Kenneth S. Ulrich
Gary T. Zussman

Oscar L. Alcantara
Joel F. Brown
Steven J. Callistein
Bruce M. Chanen
David J. Chizewer
Frederick H. Cohen
Michael C. Davis
Bruce A. Frank
Michael B. Gray
Randall L. Klein
Steven A. Levy
Karla L. Liffmann
William R. Loesch
Michael B. Manuel
Nora A. Naughton
Kim Slotky Reich
Michael J. Small
Douglas P. Taber
Heidi A. Wagman
Joanna C. Wagner

COUNSEL

Jeanne Boxer Ettelson

For full biographical listings, see the Martindale-Hubbell Law Directory

GORDON & EINSTEIN, LTD. (AV)

224 East Ontario, 60611
Telephone: 312-280-7766
Telecopier: 312-280-9599

Raymond P. Gordon
Jean M. Einstein

LEGAL SUPPORT PERSONNEL

Laura A. Kozicki

For full biographical listings, see the Martindale-Hubbell Law Directory

HOOGENDOORN, TALBOT, DAVIDS, GODFREY & MILLIGAN (AV)

122 South Michigan Avenue Suite 1220, 60603-6107
Telephone: 312-786-2250
FAX: 312-786-0708

MEMBERS OF FIRM

Earl A. Talbot
Edward N. Tiesenga
Richard D. Boonstra

For full biographical listings, see the Martindale-Hubbell Law Directory

LEVENFELD, EISENBERG, JANGER, GLASSBERG, SAMOTNY & HALPER (AV)

21st Floor, 33 West Monroe Street, 60603
Telephone: 312-346-8380
Facsimile: 346-8434
Cable Address: "Taxlaw"

MEMBER OF FIRM

Marc Z. Samotny

For full biographical listings, see the Martindale-Hubbell Law Directory

MCBRIDE BAKER & COLES (AV)

500 West Madison Street 40th Floor, 60661
Telephone: 312-715-5700
Cable Address: "Chilaw"
Telex: 270258
Telecopier: 312-993-9350

MEMBERS OF FIRM

David Ackerman
Francis L. Keldermans
Thomas J. Kinasz
Sidney C. Kleinman
David S. Mann
Elias N. Matsakis
Robert I. Schwimmer
Michael L. Weissman

OF COUNSEL

Robert O. Case

ASSOCIATES

Adam E. Berman
Thomas R. Stilp

For Complete List of Firm Personnel, See General Section

For full biographical listings, see the Martindale-Hubbell Law Directory

EARL L. NEAL & ASSOCIATES (AV)

Suite 1700, 111 West Washington Street, 60602
Telephone: 312-641-7144
Fax: 312-641-5137

Earl Langdon Neal

ASSOCIATES

Michael D. Leroy
Anne L. Fredd
Richard F. Friedman
Terrance Lee Diamond
Langdon D. Neal
Roxanne M. Ward
D. Rainell Rains
Francine D. Lynch
Grady B. Murdock, Jr.
Valda D. Staton
Jeanette Sublett

OF COUNSEL

George N. Leighton
Earl J. Barnes

For full biographical listings, see the Martindale-Hubbell Law Directory

O'BRIEN, O'ROURKE & HOGAN (AV)

135 South La Salle Street, 60603
Telephone: 312-372-1462
Fax: 312-372-8029
Orlando, Florida Office: Moye, O'Brien, O'Rourke, Hogan & Pickert, 201 East Pine Street, Suite 710.
Telephone: 407-843-3341.

MEMBERS OF FIRM

William J. Cotter
W. Craig Fowler
Michael A. Gilman
Frederic G. Hogan
Gregory R. Meeder

For full biographical listings, see the Martindale-Hubbell Law Directory

PRETZEL & STOUFFER, CHARTERED (AV)

One South Wacker Drive Suite 2500, 60606-4673
Telephone: 312-346-1973
FAX: 312-346-8242; 346-8060

James P. Moran
Robert D. Tuerk

Representative Clients: Allstate Insurance Co.; St. Paul Insurance Companies.

For Complete List of Firm Personnel, See General Section

For full biographical listings, see the Martindale-Hubbell Law Directory

WATT & SAWYIER (AV)

Amalgamated Bank Annex Building, 55 West Van Buren Street, Suite 500, 60605
Telephone: 312-663-1440
Telecopier: 312-663-1410

MEMBER OF FIRM

Michael T. Sawyier

Representative Clients: First National Bank of Chicago; Chicago Title & Trust Company; North Carolina Mutual Life Insurance Company (Durham, North Carolina); Supreme Life Insurance Company of America; Illinois/Service Federal Savings and Loan Association of Chicago; Sonicraft, Inc.; Universal Casket Company (Cassopolis, Michigan).

For full biographical listings, see the Martindale-Hubbell Law Directory

WILSON & MCILVAINE (AV)

500 West Madison, Suite 3700, 60661-2511
Telephone: 312-715-5000
Telecopier: 312-715-5155

PARTNERS

C. John Anderson
Cynthia A. Bergmann
Richard P. Blessen
Michael F. Csar
Douglas R. Hoffman
Peter A. Sarasek
Stephanie B. Shellenback

ASSOCIATE

Marie K. Eitrheim

OF COUNSEL

Frank A. Reichelderfer

For Complete List of Firm Personnel, See General Section

For full biographical listings, see the Martindale-Hubbell Law Directory

*JOLIET,** Will Co.

HERSCHBACH, TRACY, JOHNSON, BERTANI & WILSON (AV)

Two Rialto Square, 116 North Chicago Street, Sixth Floor, 60431
Telephone: 815-723-8500
Fax: 815-727-4846

(See Next Column)

HERSCHBACH, TRACY, JOHNSON, BERTANI & WILSON—*Continued*

Wayne R. Johnson
Thomas R. Wilson
Richard H. Teas
George F. Mahoney, III
Michael W. Hansen
Raymond E. Meader
A. Michael Wojtak
Kenneth A. Carlson
David J. Silverman
Roger D. Rickmon
John S. Gallo
Thomas R. Osterberger

OF COUNSEL

Donald J. Tracy
Louis R. Bertani
John L. O'Brien

General Counsel For: First National Bancorp.; First National Bank of Joliet; Southwest Suburban Bank; Bank of Lockport.
Representative Clients: Chicago Title Insurance Co.; Vulcan Materials Company; Dow Chemical, U.S.A.; Marathon Oil Co.; Crosfield Chemicals, Inc.; Waste Management, Inc.

For Complete List of Firm Personnel, See General Section

For full biographical listings, see the Martindale-Hubbell Law Directory

LA SALLE, La Salle Co.

HERBOLSHEIMER, LANNON, HENSON, DUNCAN AND REAGAN, P.C. (AV)

State Bank Building, Suite 400, 654 First Street, P.O. Box 539, 61301
Telephone: 815-223-0111
FAX: 815-223-5829
Ottawa, Illinois Office: 200 First Federal Savings Bank Building. Ottawa, IL 61350.

George L. Herbolsheimer (1911-1992)
R. James Lannon, Jr.
T. Donald Henson
John S. Duncan, III
Michael T. Reagan (Resident, Ottawa Office)
Douglas A. Gift
Gary R. Eiten

Karen C. Eiten
Jonathan F. Brandt
Michael C. Jansz (Resident, Ottawa Office)
Jill W. Broderick
Murl Tod Melton

Attorneys for: Aetna Insurance Group; St. Paul Fire and Marine Insurance Co.; State Farm Insurance Co.; The La Salle National Bank; La Salle State Bank; The Daily News Tribune Company, La Salle; Eureka Savings and Loan Assn.; Illinois Valley Community Hospital; Community Hospital of Ottawa; Commonwealth Edison, Co.

For full biographical listings, see the Martindale-Hubbell Law Directory

*MOUNT VERNON,** Jefferson Co.

LAW OFFICE OF TERRY SHARP, P.C. (AV)

1115 Harrison Street, P.O. Box 906, 62864
Telephone: 618-242-0246
Fax: 618-242-1170
Benton, Illinois Office: 105 North Main Street.
Telephone: 618-435-5109.
FAX: 618-242-1170.

Terrell Lee Sharp

Marcus H. Herbert

For full biographical listings, see the Martindale-Hubbell Law Directory

*SPRINGFIELD,** Sangamon Co.

MOHAN, ALEWELT, PRILLAMAN & ADAMI (AV)

First of America Center, Suite 325, 1 North Old Capitol Plaza, 62701-1323
Telephone: 217-528-2517
Telecopier: 217-528-2553

MEMBER

Edward J. Alewelt

Representative Clients: Andrews Environmental Engineering, Inc.; B & W Land Co.; Browning-Ferris Industries of Illinois, Inc.; Carlinville Area Hospital; Evans Construction Co.; Federal Deposit Insurance Corp.; McLaughlin Manufacturing Co.; Park Realty.

For Complete List of Firm Personnel, See General Section

For full biographical listings, see the Martindale-Hubbell Law Directory

INDIANA

*BLOOMINGTON,** Monroe Co.

BUNGER & ROBERTSON (AV)

226 South College Square, P.O. Box 910, 47402-0910
Telephone: 812-332-9295
Fax: 812-331-8808

MEMBERS OF FIRM

Len E. Bunger, Jr. (1921-1993)
Don M. Robertson
Thomas Bunger

ASSOCIATES

William J. Beggs
John W. Richards

OF COUNSEL

Philip C. Hill

Representative Clients: Aetna Insurance Companies; Bloomington Hospital; Commercial Union Group; Indiana Insurance Co.; Liberty Mutual Insurance; Medical Protective Co.; Monroe County Community School Corp.; Professional Golf Car, Inc.; Prudential Insurance Company of America; State Farm Automobile Insurance Co.

For Complete List of Firm Personnel, See General Section

For full biographical listings, see the Martindale-Hubbell Law Directory

CARMEL, Hamilton Co.

COOTS, HENKE & WHEELER, PROFESSIONAL CORPORATION (AV)

255 East Carmel Drive, 46032
Telephone: 317-844-4693
Fax: 317-573-5385

E. Davis Coots
Steven H. Henke
Jeffrey O. Meunier
James E. Zoccola

Representative Clients: Century 21-Scheetz Co., Inc.; Radnor Corp.; Landmark Development; AmeriFab, Inc.; Hokanson Companies, Inc.; Safco Development Corp.

For Complete List of Firm Personnel, See General Section

For full biographical listings, see the Martindale-Hubbell Law Directory

CLARKSVILLE, Clark Co.

HANGER, ENGEBRETSON, MAYER & VOGT (AV)

501 Eastern Boulevard, 47129
Telephone: 812-288-1235
Louisville, Kentucky: 502-584-5800
Fax: 812-288-1240

MEMBERS OF FIRM

William F. Engebretson
Samuel H. Vogt, Jr.
Steven K. Palmquist

ASSOCIATE

Susan Wagner Hynes

Representative Clients: First Federal Savings and Loan Association of Clark County; Ticor Title Insurance Company; Old Republic National Title Insurance Company.
Approved Attorneys for: Commonwealth Land Title Insurance Co.
Reference: First Federal Savings and Loan Association of Clark County; PNC Bank Indiana, Inc.

For Complete List of Firm Personnel, See General Section

For full biographical listings, see the Martindale-Hubbell Law Directory

*COLUMBIA CITY,** Whitley Co.

GATES & GATES (AV)

Gates & Gates is over 100 years old.
216 West Van Buren Street, P.O. Box 251, 46725-0251
Telephone: 219-244-5175
Fax: Available Upon Request

MEMBER OF FIRM

Benton E. Gates, Jr.

ASSOCIATE

Richard W. Gates

Attorneys For: Holmes & Co., Inc.; LML Corp.; NBD; Prudential Insurance Co.; American States Insurance Co.; Farm Credit Services.

For full biographical listings, see the Martindale-Hubbell Law Directory

ELKHART, Elkhart Co.

CHESTER, PFAFF & BROTHERSON (AV)

317 West Franklin Street, P.O. Box 507, 46515-0507
Telephone: 219-294-5421
Telecopier: 219-522-1476

(See Next Column)

CHESTER, PFAFF & BROTHERSON, *Elkhart—Continued*

MEMBERS OF FIRM

Robert A. Pfaff — James R. Brotherson

ASSOCIATE

Robert C. Whippo

For Complete List of Firm Personnel, See General Section

For full biographical listings, see the Martindale-Hubbell Law Directory

THORNE, GRODNIK, RANSEL, DUNCAN, BYRON & HOSTETLER (AV)

228 West High Street, 46516-3176
Telephone: 219-294-7473
FAX: 219-294-5390
Mishawaka, Indiana Office: 310 Valley American Bank and Trust Building, 310 West McKinley Avenue. P.O. Box 1210.
Telephone: 219-256-5660.
FAX: 219-674-6835.

MEMBERS OF FIRM

William A. Thorne — Glenn L. Duncan
Charles H. Grodnik — James R. Byron
J. Richard Ransel — Steven L. Hostetler

ASSOCIATES

James H. Milstone — Michael A. Trippel

OF COUNSEL

F. Richard Kramer — Joseph C. Zakas

Counsel for: Witmer-McNease Music Co., Inc.; Valley American Bank and Trust Co., Mishawaka, Indiana.

For Complete List of Firm Personnel, See General Section

For full biographical listings, see the Martindale-Hubbell Law Directory

*EVANSVILLE,** Vanderburgh Co.

BOWERS, HARRISON, KENT & MILLER (AV)

25 N.W. Riverside Drive, P.O. Box 1287, 47706-1287
Telephone: 812-426-1231
Fax: 812-464-3676

MEMBERS OF FIRM

Joseph H. Harrison — Gregory A. Kahre
Timothy J. Hubert

ASSOCIATES

Cedric Hustace — William O. Williams, II

OF COUNSEL

K. Wayne Kent

Representative Clients: Citizens Realty and Insurance, Inc.; General Growth Properties; Regency Associates, Ltd.; National Attorney's Title Assurance Fund, Inc.; Shell Mining Company; Commonwealth Land Title Insurance Company.

For Complete List of Firm Personnel, See General Section

For full biographical listings, see the Martindale-Hubbell Law Directory

FINE & HATFIELD (AV)

520 N.W. Second Street, P.O. Box 779, 47705-0779
Telephone: 812-425-3592
Telecopier: 812-421-4269

MEMBERS OF FIRM

James E. Marchand — Stephen S. Lavallo

For Complete List of Firm Personnel, See General Section

For full biographical listings, see the Martindale-Hubbell Law Directory

KAHN, DEES, DONOVAN & KAHN (AV)

P.O. Box 3646, 47735-3646
Telephone: 812-423-3183
Fax: 812-423-3841

MEMBERS OF FIRM

Alan N. Shovers — G. Michael Schopmeyer
Jeffrey K. Helfrich

ASSOCIATE

Kent A. Brasseale, II

Representative Clients: Advance Transportation Company; D. Patrick, Inc.; Deaconess Hospital, Inc.; Keller-Crescent Co., Inc.; Kempf Group Inc.; O'-Daniel-Ranes, Inc.; Red Spot Paint & Varnish Co., Inc.; Rehabilitation Development Services, Inc.; J.H. Rudolph & Company, Inc.; J.E. Shekell, Inc.

For Complete List of Firm Personnel, See General Section

For full biographical listings, see the Martindale-Hubbell Law Directory

STATHAM, JOHNSON & McCRAY (AV)

215 North West Martin Luther King Jr. Boulevard, P.O. Box 3567, 47734-3567
Telephone: 812-425-5223
Facsimile: 812-421-4238

MEMBERS OF FIRM

R. Eugene Johnson — Thomas J. Kimpel
Donald J. Fuchs

ASSOCIATES

Thomas P. Norton — Keith E. Rounder

Representative Clients: City of Evansville, Indiana; Elberfeld State Bank; ERA Steve Thompson Realty, Inc.; Evansville Federal Savings Bank; Fleet Mortgage Corp.; NBD Bank, N.A.; NBD Mortgage Company; Precedent Financial Corporation; First Indiana Bank; United Companies Lending Corp.

For Complete List of Firm Personnel, See General Section

For full biographical listings, see the Martindale-Hubbell Law Directory

WRIGHT, EVANS AND DALY (AV)

425 Main Street, 47708
Telephone: 812-424-3300
Fax: 812-421-5588

MEMBERS OF FIRM

Claude B. Lynn (Retired) — Gerald H. Evans
Donald R. Wright — R. Lawrence Daly

ASSOCIATES

Christopher L. Lucas — Keith M. Wallace

Representative Clients: Bosecker Construction Company; Castle Contracting Co., Inc.; Evansville Apartments, Inc.; Homehunters of Greater Evansville, Inc.; Huegel Realty, Inc.; Indian Woods Apartments, Ltd.; Indiana Realty Fund, Ltd.; Magnum Construction, Inc.; Mills-Wallace and Associates, Inc. Design Professionals; K & R Development Company.

For full biographical listings, see the Martindale-Hubbell Law Directory

GREENWOOD, Johnson Co.

VAN VALER WILLIAMS & HEWITT (AV)

Suite 400 National City Bank Building, 300 South Madison Avenue, P.O. Box 405, 46142
Telephone: 317-888-1121
Fax: 317-887-4069

MEMBERS OF FIRM

Joe N. Van Valer — Jon E. Williams
Brian C. Hewitt

ASSOCIATES

J. Lee Robbins — John M. White
William M. Waltz — Kim Van Valer Shilts
Mark E. Need

For full biographical listings, see the Martindale-Hubbell Law Directory

*INDIANAPOLIS,** Marion Co.

BACKER & BACKER, A PROFESSIONAL CORPORATION (AV)

101 West Ohio Street, Suite 1500, 46204
Telephone: 317-684-3000
Telecopier: 317-684-3004

Herbert J. Backer — Stephen A. Backer
David J. Backer

Reference: Bank One, Indianapolis.

For full biographical listings, see the Martindale-Hubbell Law Directory

BAKER & DANIELS (AV)

300 North Meridian Street, 46204
Telephone: 317-237-0300
FAX: 317-237-1000
Fort Wayne, Indiana Office: 2400 Fort Wayne National Bank Building.
Telephone: 219-424-8000.
South Bend, Indiana Office: First Bank Building, 205 West Jefferson Boulevard.
Telephone: 219-234-4149.
Elkhart, Indiana Office: 301 South Main Street, Suite 307,
Telephone: 219-296-6000.
Washington, D.C. Office: 1701 K Street, N.W., Suite 400.
Telephone: 202-785-1565.

MEMBERS OF FIRM

William F. Landers, Jr. — Harry F. McNaught, Jr.
Rory O'Bryan — George W. Somers
Mary Katherine Lisher — Karl P. Haas
Thomas A. Vogtner — Joseph M. Scimia

ASSOCIATES

Andrew Z. Soshnick — Mark E. Wright

(See Next Column)

BAKER & DANIELS—*Continued*

LEGAL SUPPORT PERSONNEL

Eugene Valanzano

Representative Clients: Associated Insurance Companies, Inc.; Bank One, Indianapolis, N.A.; Borg-Warner Corp.; City of Indianapolis; Cummins Engine Co.; Eli Lilly and Company; General Motors Corp.; Indiana Bell; Indianapolis Public Schools; United Airlines.

For Complete List of Firm Personnel, See General Section

For full biographical listings, see the Martindale-Hubbell Law Directory

BOSE MCKINNEY & EVANS (AV)

2700 First Indiana Plaza, 135 North Pennsylvania Street, 46204
Telephone: 317-684-5000
Facsimile: 317-684-5173
Indianapolis North Office: Suite 1201, 8888 Keystone Crossing, 46240.
Telephone: 317-574-3700.
Facsimile: 317-574-3716.

MEMBERS OF FIRM

Wayne C. Ponader
Philip A. Nicely
Thomas M. Johnston
David L. Wills
Linda E. Coletta
James C. Carlino
Elizabeth Theobald Young
Michael A. Trentadue

ASSOCIATES

Natalie J. Stucky
Tammy K. Haney
Robert C. Sproule

Representative Clients: Duke Realty Investments, Inc.; ; Aaron Y. Cohen; Carlstedt Dickman, Inc.; Citimark Development Cos.; Centex Homes; Ryland Homes; H. Emerson Young; HMI, Inc.; Skinner & Broadbent; The Inland Group, Inc.; The Travelers Insurance Co.

For Complete List of Firm Personnel, See General Section

For full biographical listings, see the Martindale-Hubbell Law Directory

CLARK, QUINN, MOSES & CLARK (AV)

One Indiana Square, Suite 2200, 46204-2011
Telephone: 317-637-1321
Fax: 317-687-2344

MEMBERS OF FIRM

Thomas Michael Quinn
J. Murray Clark
Matthew R. Clark

ASSOCIATES

Michael D. Keele
Cameron F. Clark

Representative Clients: Justus; The Shorewood Corporation; Marina Limited Partnership; Lafarge Corporation; Meijer Realty, Inc.; Lowe's; Kite Development; U-Stor Self Storage Warehouses; Mechanic's Laundry; Davis Homes.

For full biographical listings, see the Martindale-Hubbell Law Directory

DALE & EKE, PROFESSIONAL CORPORATION (AV)

Suite 400, 9100 Keystone Crossing, 46240
Telephone: 317-844-7400
FAX: 317-574-9426

William J. Dale, Jr.
Joseph W. Eke
Deborah J. Caruso
Catherine Chambers Kennedy
A. Robert Lasich
Dawn Michelle Snow

For full biographical listings, see the Martindale-Hubbell Law Directory

FEIWELL & ASSOCIATES (AV)

251 North Illinois Street, Suite 1700, P.O. Box 44141, 46204
Telephone: 317-237-2727
Facsimile: 317-237-2722

Murray J. Feiwell

ASSOCIATES

Douglas J. Hannoy
Lisa Kay Decker

Representative Clients: Lomas Mortgage USA, Inc.; Standard Federal Savings Bank; NBD Mortgage Company; Source One Mortgage Services Corp.; United Companies Lending Corp.; Ford Consumer Finance Company, Inc.; GMAC Mortgage Corp.; Barclays American Mortgage Corporation; Associates Financial Services; Margarretten & Company, Inc.

For full biographical listings, see the Martindale-Hubbell Law Directory

GOODIN & KRAEGE (AV)

8888 Keystone Crossing Suite 820, 46240-4616
Telephone: 317-843-2606
FAX: 317-574-3095

James A. Goodin
Richard C. Kraege
Jon C. Abernathy
Amy Loraine White
Patrick L. Miller
James W. Johnson, III

(See Next Column)

OF COUNSEL

Wilson S. Stober

Representative Clients: Allstate Insurance Companies; American National Property and Casualty Co.; Bituminous Insurance Company; Builder's Square; Commercial Union Insurance Companies; Continental Loss Adjusting Service; Construction Associates, Inc.; Continental Western Insurance Company; Economy Fire & Casualty; General Casualty Companies.

For full biographical listings, see the Martindale-Hubbell Law Directory

HACKMAN MCCLARNON HULETT & CRACRAFT (AV)

2400 One Indiana Square, 46204
Telephone: 317-636-5401
Facsimile: 317-686-3288

MEMBERS OF FIRM

James R. McClarnon
Marvin L. Hackman
Robert S. Hulett
Michael B. Cracraft
Timothy K. Ryan
Philip B. McKiernan
Vicki L. Anderson

ASSOCIATES

Jane A. Phillips
Jeffrey G. Jackson
Thomas F. Bedsole
Thomas A. Dickey

OF COUNSEL

John D. Cochran, Jr.
Mark S. Alderfer

Representative Clients: F.C. Tucker Co., Inc.; Texas Eastern Products Pipeline Co.; The State Life Insurance Co.; NBD Bank, N.A.; Met Life International Real Estate Partners Limited Partnership; Manufacturers Life Insurance Company.

For full biographical listings, see the Martindale-Hubbell Law Directory

HUGHES AND HUGHES (AV)

(Not a Partnership)
Two Meridian Plaza, Suite 202, 10401 North Meridian Street, 46290
Telephone: 317-573-2255
Telecopier: 317-573-2266

David B. Hughes
Gary D. Sallee

For full biographical listings, see the Martindale-Hubbell Law Directory

ICE MILLER DONADIO & RYAN (AV)

One American Square Box 82001, 46282-0002
Telephone: 317-236-2100
Fax: 317-236-2219

MEMBERS OF FIRM

John A. Grayson
Charles E. Wilson
Phillip L. Bayt
Zeff A. Weiss

SENIOR COUNSEL

Timothy W. Sullivan

OF COUNSEL

James B. Burroughs
Mark D. Grant

ASSOCIATES

Dodd Joseph Gray
Heather K. Olinger

Representative Clients: The Sexton Cos.; DeMars Haka Development, Inc.; Citicorp Real Estate, Inc.; Bank of America; Kimco Realty Corp.; Heitman Properties; Consolidated Products, Inc.; Westinghouse Credit Corp.; Federated Department Stores; Ford Motor Credit Co.

For Complete List of Firm Personnel, See General Section

For full biographical listings, see the Martindale-Hubbell Law Directory

JOHNSON, SMITH, DENSBORN, WRIGHT & HEATH (AV)

One Indiana Square Suite 1800, 46204
Telephone: 317-634-9777
Telecopier: 317-636-9061

MEMBERS OF FIRM

John F. Joyce (1948-1994)
Wayne O. Adams, III
Thomas A. Barnard
David J. Carr
Peter D. Cleveland
David R. Day
Donald K. Densborn
Thomas N. Eckerle
Mark W. Ford
G. Ronald Heath
Robert B. Hebert
John David Hoover
Andrew W. Hull
Dennis A. Johnson
Richard L. Johnson
Michael J. Kaye
John R. Kirkwood
David Williams Russell
James T. Smith
David E. Wright

ASSOCIATES

Robert C. Wolf (1949-1993)
Carolyn H. Andretti
David G. Blachly
Robert T. Buday
Jeffrey S. Cohen
Patricia L. Marshall
David D. Robinson
Ronald G. Sentman
Sally Franklin Zweig

(See Next Column)

JOHNSON, SMITH, DENSBORN, WRIGHT & HEATH, *Indianapolis—Continued*

OF COUNSEL

Earl Auberry (1923-1989)
Bruce W. Claycombe
Paul D. Gresk
William T. Lawrence
Mark A. Palmer
Catherine A. Singleton

For Complete List of Firm Personnel, See General Section

For full biographical listings, see the Martindale-Hubbell Law Directory

KROGER, GARDIS & REGAS (AV)

111 Monument Circle, Suite 900, 46204-3059
Telephone: 317-692-9000
Telecopier: 317-264-6832

MEMBERS OF FIRM

James A. Knauer
James G. Lauck

ASSOCIATE

Steven R. Schafer

LEGAL SUPPORT PERSONNEL

PARALEGALS

Debra K. Nix

Representative Clients: City of Indianapolis; Marion County Treasurer; First of America Bank; Society National Bank; Consumer Finance Co.; Household Finance Corp.; NBD Bank; Bank One; Beneficial Mortgage.

For full biographical listings, see the Martindale-Hubbell Law Directory

MITCHELL HURST JACOBS & DICK (AV)

152 East Washington Street, 46204
Telephone: 317-636-0808
1-800-636-0808
Fax: 317-633-7680

MEMBERS OF FIRM

Marvin H. Mitchell
William W. Hurst
Samuel L. Jacobs
Richard J. Dick
Marshall S. Hanley
Steven K. Huffer
Robert W. Strohmeyer, Jr.

ASSOCIATES

Danielle A. Takla
John M. Reames
Michael T. McNelis
Michael P. Kilkenny

LEGAL SUPPORT PERSONNEL

L. Kathleen Hughes Brown, R.N.

General Counsel for: Premium Optical Co.; Calderon Bros. Vending Machines, Inc.; Grocers Supply Co., Inc.; Power Train Services, Inc.; Frank E. Irish, Inc.; Bedding Liquidators; Galyan's Trading Co.; Harcourt Management Co., Inc.; Kosene & Kosene Mgt. & Dev. Co., Inc.; Hasten Bancorp.

For full biographical listings, see the Martindale-Hubbell Law Directory

SOMMER & BARNARD, ATTORNEYS AT LAW, PC (AV)

4000 Bank One Tower, 111 Monument Circle, P.O. Box 44363, 46244-0363
Telephone: 317-630-4000
FAX: 317-236-9802
North Office: 8900 Keystone Crossing, Suite 1046, Indianapolis, Indiana, 46240-2134.
Telephone: 317-630-4000.
FAX: 317-844-4780.

Julianne S. Lis-Milam

OF COUNSEL

Glenn Scolnik

Representative Clients: Comerica Bank; Excel Industries; Federal Express; New York Life; Renault Automation; Reppert International; Kimball International; Monsanto; TRW, Inc.

For Complete List of Firm Personnel, See General Section

For full biographical listings, see the Martindale-Hubbell Law Directory

STARK DONINGER & SMITH (AV)

Suite 700, 50 South Meridian Street, 46204
Telephone: 317-638-2400
Fax: 317-633-6618; 633-6619

MEMBERS OF FIRM

John C. Stark
Bruce E. Smith
John W. Van Buskirk
Richard W. Dyar
Patricia Seasor Bailey
Brian J. Tuohy
Mark A. Bailey
Lewis E. Willis, Jr.

ASSOCIATES

Neil E. Lucas
Richard B. Kaufman
Patrick J. Dietrick

(See Next Column)

COUNSEL

Clarence H. Doninger
Gregory S. Fehribach
John F. Hoehner
Robert D. Maas
William K. Byrum

Representative Clients: American Consulting Engineers, Inc.; Ost Enterprises; The C.P. Morgan Co.; Nationwide Life Insurance Co.; Trinity Homes, Inc.

For full biographical listings, see the Martindale-Hubbell Law Directory

*KOKOMO,** Howard Co.

FELL, McGARVEY, TRAURING & WILSON (AV)

515 West Sycamore Street, P.O. Box 958, 46903-0958
Telephone: 317-457-9321
Telecopier: 317-452-0882

MEMBERS OF FIRM

John E. Fell, Jr.
Eugene J. McGarvey, Jr.

Representative Clients: Big R Stores; First National Bank, Kokomo; Haynes International, Inc.; Hospital Authority of the City of Kokomo; Kokomo City Hall Building Corp.; PPG Industries, Inc.; Star Building Supply, Inc.; Mervis Industries, Inc.; G-W Invader, Inc.; Taylor Community School Corp.
References: First National Bank; Society Bank of Howard County.

For Complete List of Firm Personnel, See General Section

For full biographical listings, see the Martindale-Hubbell Law Directory

MERRILLVILLE, Lake Co.

BURKE, MURPHY, COSTANZA & CUPPY (AV)

Suite 600 8585 Broadway, 46410
Telephone: 219-769-1313
Telecopier: 219-769-6806
East Chicago, Indiana Office: First National Bank Building. 720 W. Chicago Avenue.
Telephone: 219-397-2401.
Telecopier: 219-397-0506.
Palm Harbor, Florida Office: Suite 280, 33920 U.S. Highway 19 North.
Telephone: 813-787-7799.
Telecopier: 813-787-7237.

MEMBERS OF FIRM

Edward L. Burke
Gerald K. Hrebec
George W. Carberry
Demetri J. Retson

Representative Clients: NBD Gainer Bank; Gough & Lesch Development Corporation; Whiteco Industries; The Prime Group; Great Lakes Industrial Center; Focus Group; City of East Chicago Department of Redevelopment; Capital and Regional Properties.

For Complete List of Firm Personnel, See General Section

For full biographical listings, see the Martindale-Hubbell Law Directory

HODGES & DAVIS, P.C. (AV)

5525 Broadway, 46410
Telephone: 219-981-2557
Fax: 219-980-7090
Portage, Indiana Office: 6508 U.S. Highway 6.
Telephone: 219-762-9129.
Fax: 219-762-2826.

Clyde D. Compton
William B. Davis
Earle F. Hites
R. Lawrence Steele
Gregory A. Sobkowski
Bonnie C. Coleman
Jill M. Madajczyk
Laura B. Brown
David H. Kreider

OF COUNSEL

Edward J. Hussey

Representative Clients: Lake Mortgage Co., Inc.; McDonald's Corporation; Walgreen Co.; Century 21 Heritage Realtors; D.G. Real Estate, Inc.

For Complete List of Firm Personnel, See General Section

For full biographical listings, see the Martindale-Hubbell Law Directory

MISHAWAKA, St. Joseph Co.

SCHINDLER AND OLSON (AV)

122 South Mill Street, P.O. Box 100, 46544
Telephone: 219-259-5461
Fax: 219-259-5462

MEMBERS OF FIRM

John W. Schindler, Jr.
James J. Olson

Representative Clients: Penn-Harris-Madison School Corp.; All Star Realty Co.; School City of Mishawaka; Edward Rose & Sons.
Reference: 1st Source Bank of Mishawaka.

For Complete List of Firm Personnel, See General Section

For full biographical listings, see the Martindale-Hubbell Law Directory

PORTAGE, Porter Co.

HODGES & DAVIS, P.C. (AV)
6508 U.S. Highway 6, 46368
Telephone: 219-762-9129
Fax: 219-762-2826
Merrillville, Indiana Office: 5525 Broadway.
Telephone: 219-981-2557.
Fax: 219-980-7090.

Clyde D. Compton
R. Lawrence Steele
Earle F. Hites
Gregory A. Sobkowski
Bonnie C. Coleman

Representative Clients: Porter County Plan Commission; McDonald's Corporation; Walgreen Co.; Century 21 Heritage Realtors; D.G. Real Estate, Inc.; Lake Mortgage Co., Inc.

For full biographical listings, see the Martindale-Hubbell Law Directory

*PRINCETON,** Gibson Co.

HALL, PARTENHEIMER & KINKLE (AV)
219 North Hart Street, P.O. Box 313, 47670
Telephone: 812-386-0050
FAX: 812-385-2575

MEMBERS OF FIRM

Verner P. Partenheimer
J. Robert Kinkle
R. Scott Partenheimer

Representative Clients: Interlake Inc.; Gibson County Bank; Old Ben Coal Co.
Approved Attorneys for: Lawyers Title Insurance; Ticor Title Insurance.

For full biographical listings, see the Martindale-Hubbell Law Directory

*SOUTH BEND,** St. Joseph Co.

JONES, OBENCHAIN, FORD, PANKOW, LEWIS & WOODS (AV)
1800 Valley American Bank Building, P.O. Box 4577, 46634
Telephone: 219-233-1194
Fax: 233-8957; 233-9675

Vitus G. Jones (1879-1951)
Francis Jones (1907-1988)
Roland Obenchain (1890-1961)
Roland Obenchain (Retired)
Milton A. Johnson (Retired)

MEMBERS OF FIRM

James H. Pankow
Robert W. Mysliwiec
Thomas F. Lewis, Jr.
Robert M. Edwards, Jr.
Timothy W. Woods
John B. Ford
John R. Obenchain
Mark J. Phillipoff
John W. Van Laere

ASSOCIATES

Patrick D. Murphy
Edward P. Benchik
Wendell G. Davis, Jr.

OF COUNSEL

G. Burt Ford

Attorneys For: Jack Hickey Homes; Portage Realty; Saint Joseph's Medical Center; The Equitable Life Assurance Society of the United States; Panzica Construction Co.

For full biographical listings, see the Martindale-Hubbell Law Directory

*TERRE HAUTE,** Vigo Co.

COX, ZWERNER, GAMBILL & SULLIVAN (AV)
511 Wabash Avenue, P.O. Box 1625, 47808-1625
Telephone: 812-232-6003
Fax: 812-232-6567

MEMBERS OF FIRM

Ernest J. Zwerner (1918-1980)
David W. Sullivan
Benjamin G. Cox (1915-1988)
Robert L. Gowdy
Gilbert W. Gambill, Jr.
Louis F. Britton
James E. Sullivan
Robert D. Hepburn
Benjamin G. Cox, Jr.
Carroll D. Smeltzer
Jeffry A. Lind

ASSOCIATE

Ronald E. Jumps

Counsel for: Terre Haute First National Bank; Farmers Insurance Group; Indiana-American Water Co.; Indiana State University; Merchants National Bank of Terre Haute; Rose-Hulman Institute of Technology; Tribune-Star Publishing Co., Inc.; Weston Paper & Manufacturing Co.

For full biographical listings, see the Martindale-Hubbell Law Directory

*VALPARAISO,** Porter Co.

BLACHLY, TABOR, BOZIK & HARTMAN (AV)
Suite 401 Indiana Federal Building, 46383
Telephone: 219-464-1041

(See Next Column)

MEMBERS OF FIRM

Quentin A. Blachly
David L. Hollenbeck
Glenn J. Tabor
David L. DeBoer
James S. Bozik
Thomas F. Macke
Duane W. Hartman
Randall J. Zromkoski
Richard J. Rupcich

ASSOCIATE

Roger A. Weitgenant

Reference: First National Bank.

For Complete List of Firm Personnel, See General Section

For full biographical listings, see the Martindale-Hubbell Law Directory

DOUGLAS, ALEXA, KOEPPEN & HURLEY (AV)
14 Indiana Avenue, P.O. Box 209, 46384-0209
Telephone: 219-462-2126
Fax: 219-477-4408

MEMBERS OF FIRM

Herbert K. Douglas
R. Bradley Koeppen
William E. Alexa
Brian J. Hurley

ASSOCIATE

Mark A. Gland

OF COUNSEL

George W. Douglas
Leo J. Clifford

Attorneys for: Urschel Laboratories, Inc.; Northern Indiana Public Service Co.; Midwest Steel Division, National Steel; McGill Manufacturing Co., Inc.; Park District, City of Valparaiso.

For full biographical listings, see the Martindale-Hubbell Law Directory

IOWA

CEDAR FALLS, Black Hawk Co.

REDFERN, MASON, DIETER, LARSEN & MOORE (AV)
315 Clay Street, P.O. Box 627, 50613
Telephone: 319-277-6830
Facsimile: 319-277-3531

MEMBERS OF FIRM

LeRoy H. Redfern
Steven D. Moore
David R. Mason
Donald B. Redfern
Robert J. Dieter
Mark W. Fransdal
John C. Larsen
Mark S. Rolinger

ASSOCIATE

Susan Bernau Staudt

Representative Clients: Norwest Bank Iowa; The National Bank of Waterloo; Don R. Havens Co.; Control-O-fax Corp.; Cedar Falls Community School District; University of Northern Iowa Foundation; United States Fidelity and Guaranty Co.; The Travelers Insurance Cos.; Fireman's Fund Insurance Companies.

For Complete List of Firm Personnel, See General Section

For full biographical listings, see the Martindale-Hubbell Law Directory

*CEDAR RAPIDS,** Linn Co.

SHUTTLEWORTH & INGERSOLL, P.C. (AV)
500 Firstar Bank Building, P.O. Box 2107, 52406-2107
Telephone: 319-365-9461
Fax: 319-365-8443

James C. Nemmers
Thomas P. Peffer
Michael O. McDermott
William P. Prowell
Carroll J. Reasoner
William S. Hochstetler

LeeAnn M. Ferry
Dean D. Carrington

OF COUNSEL

W. R. Shuttleworth

COUNSEL

Joan Lipsky
Theodore J. Collins

Representative Clients: Amana Society; Archer-Daniels-Midland Co.; Cargill, Inc.; Cedar River Paper Company; Firstar Bank Cedar Rapids, N.A.; Lawyers Title Insurance Company; Met-Coil Systems Corporation; PMX Industries, Inc.; Ryan Construction Company; Shive-Hattery Engineers & Architects, Inc.

For Complete List of Firm Personnel, See General Section

For full biographical listings, see the Martindale-Hubbell Law Directory

Cedar Rapids—Continued

SIMMONS, PERRINE, ALBRIGHT & ELLWOOD, L.L.P. (AV)

A Partnership including a Professional Corporation
115 Third Street S.E. Suite 1200, 52401
Telephone: 319-366-7641
Telecopier: 319-366-1917 (I,II,III)

PARTNERS

Dennis J. McMenimen
David W. Kubicek
Linda M. Kirsch

Representative Clients: Amana Refrigeration, Inc.; Norwest Bank Iowa, N.A.; Sheaffer Pen; Weyerhaeuser Co.; Grand Wood Area Education Agency; Howard R. Green Co.; Varied Investments, Inc.; Norand Corp.; Universal Gym Equipment Co.; Hall Foundation.

For Complete List of Firm Personnel, See General Section

For full biographical listings, see the Martindale-Hubbell Law Directory

*COUNCIL BLUFFS,** Pottawattamie Co.

SMITH PETERSON LAW FIRM (AV)

35 Main Place, Suite 300, P.O. Box 249, 51502
Telephone: 712-328-1833
Fax: 712-328-8320
Omaha, Nebraska Office: 9290 West Dodge Road, Suite 205.
Telephone: 402-397-8500.
Fax: 402-397-5519.

MEMBERS OF FIRM

Raymond A. Smith (1892-1977)
John LeRoy Peterson (1895-1969)
Harold T. Beckman
Robert J. Laubenthal
Richard A. Heininger
Lawrence J. Beckman
Gregory G. Barntsen
W. Curtis Hewett
Steven H. Krohn
Randy R. Ewing
Joseph D. Thornton

ASSOCIATES

Trent D. Reinert (Not admitted in IA)
T. J. Pattermann

Representative Clients: Aetna Life and Casualty Co.; Employers Mutual Co.; First National Bank of Council Bluffs; IMT Insurance Co.; Monsanto Co.; United Fire & Casualty Co.; U.S. Fidelity and Guaranty.

For full biographical listings, see the Martindale-Hubbell Law Directory

*DES MOINES,** Polk Co.

CONNOLLY, O'MALLEY, LILLIS, HANSEN & OLSON (AV)

820 Liberty Building, 6th & Grand Avenue, 50309
Telephone: 515-243-8157
Fax: 515-243-3919

MEMBERS OF FIRM

William J. Lillis
Russell J. Hansen
Michael W. O'Malley
Eugene E. Olson
Streetar Cameron

ASSOCIATE

Christopher R. Pose

A list of Representative Clients will be furnished upon request.
References will be furnished upon request.

For Complete List of Firm Personnel, See General Section

For full biographical listings, see the Martindale-Hubbell Law Directory

DICKINSON, MACKAMAN, TYLER & HAGEN, P.C. (AV)

Suite 1600 Hub Tower, 699 Walnut Street, 50309-3986
Telephone: 515-244-2600
Telecopier: 515-246-4550

L. J. Dickinson (1873-1968)
L. Call Dickinson (1905-1974)
Addison M. Parker (Retired)
John H. Raife (Retired)
Robert B. Throckmorton (Retired)
Helen C. Adams
Brent R. Appel
Barbara G. Barrett
John W. Blyth
L. Call Dickinson, Jr.
Jeanine M. Freeman
David J. Grace
Craig F. Graziano
Howard O. Hagen
J. Russell Hixson
Paul E. Horvath
F. Richard Lyford
John R. Mackaman
Richard A. Malm
James W. O'Brien
Arthur F. Owens
Rebecca Boyd Parrott
David M. Repp
Robert C. Rouwenhorst
Russell L. Samson
David S. Steward
Philip E. Stoffregen
Francis (Frank) J. Stork
Jon P. Sullivan
Celeste L. Tito (Not admitted in IA)
Paul R. Tyler
John K. Vernon
J. Marc Ward
Linda S. Weindruch

(See Next Column)

OF COUNSEL

Robert E. Mannheimer

Representative Clients: Archer-Daniels-Midland Co.; Board of Water Works Trustees, Des Moines, Iowa; Merchants Bonding Co. (Mutual); Norwest Bank, N.A.

For full biographical listings, see the Martindale-Hubbell Law Directory

WASKER, DORR, WIMMER & MARCOUILLER, P.C. (AV)

801 Grand Avenue, Suite 3100, 50309-8036
Telephone: 515-283-1801
Facsimile: 515-283-1802

Charles F. Wasker
Fred L. Dorr
D. Mark Marcouiller

Robert A. Sims
David A. Bolte
Jennifer Ann Tyler
Matthew D. Kern

For Complete List of Firm Personnel, See General Section

For full biographical listings, see the Martindale-Hubbell Law Directory

*MASON CITY,** Cerro Gordo Co.

WINSTON, REUBER & BYRNE, LAWYERS, A PROFESSIONAL CORPORATION (AV)

119 Second Street, N.W., 50401
Telephone: 515-423-1913
FAX: 515-423-8998

Harold R. Winston
John H. Reuber
Michael G. Byrne

Representative Clients: Libbey-Owens Ford Glass Co.; Goodyear Tire and Rubber; Skelly Oil; United Guernsey Co-op; Norwest Bank; First Interstate Bank of Mason City.

For full biographical listings, see the Martindale-Hubbell Law Directory

*WATERLOO,** Black Hawk Co.

SWISHER & COHRT (AV)

528 West Fourth Street, P.O. Box 1200, 50704
Telephone: 319-232-6555
FAX: 319-232-4835

MEMBERS OF FIRM

Benjamin F. Swisher (1878-1959)
L. J. Cohrt (1898-1974)
Charles F. Swisher (1919-1986)
Eldon R. McCann
Steven A. Weidner
Larry J. Cohrt
J. Douglas Oberman
Stephen J. Powell
Jim D. DeKoster
Jeffrey J. Greenwood
Samuel C. Anderson
Robert C. Griffin
Kevin R. Rogers

ASSOCIATES

Beth E. Hansen
Mark F. Conway
Natalie Williams Burr

Firm is Counsel for: Koehring Corp.; Clay Equipment; Chamberlain Manufacturing Co.; Waterloo Courier.
Local Counsel for: Allied Group; John Deere Insurance; Liberty Mutual Insurance Co.

For full biographical listings, see the Martindale-Hubbell Law Directory

KANSAS

*WICHITA,** Sedgwick Co.

FOULSTON & SIEFKIN (AV)

(Formerly Foulston, Siefkin, Powers & Eberhardt)
700 Fourth Financial Center, Broadway at Douglas, 67202
Telephone: 316-267-6371
Facsimile: 316-267-6345
Topeka, Kansas Office: 1515 Bank IV Tower, 534 Kansas Avenue. 66603.
Telephone: 913-233-3600.
FAX: 913-233-1610.
Member: Lex Mundi, A Global Association of Independent Firms

MEMBERS OF FIRM

Phillip S. Frick
James D. Oliver
Larry G. Rapp
Gary E. Knight

For Complete List of Firm Personnel, See General Section

For full biographical listings, see the Martindale-Hubbell Law Directory

Wichita—Continued

YOUNG, BOGLE, MCCAUSLAND, WELLS & CLARK, P.A. (AV)
106 West Douglas, Suite 923, 67202
Telephone: 316-265-7841
Facsimile: 316-265-3956

William A. Wells
Kenneth M. Clark
Patrick C. Blanchard

Representative Clients: Equitable AgriBusiness, Inc.; 1st Nationwide Bank; Transamerica Financial Corp.; Citicorp., N.A.; Security Pacific Business Credit.

For Complete List of Firm Personnel, See General Section

For full biographical listings, see the Martindale-Hubbell Law Directory

KENTUCKY

ASHLAND, Boyd Co.

HOLBROOK & PITT (AV)
200 Home Federal Building, 1500 Carter Avenue, 41101
Telephone: 606-324-5136
Fax: 606-329-8998

Charles R. Holbrook, Jr. (1909-1993)
Charles R. Holbrook III
Ernest M. Pitt, Jr.
Anna Holmes Ruth

References: First American Bank; Third National Bank; Bank of Ashland.

For full biographical listings, see the Martindale-Hubbell Law Directory

VANANTWERP, MONGE, JONES & EDWARDS (AV)
1544 Winchester Avenue Fifth Floor, P.O. Box 1111, 41105-1111
Telephone: 606-329-2929
Fax: 606-329-0490
Ironton, Ohio Office: Cooper & VanAntwerp, A Legal Professional Association, 407 Center Street.
Telephone: 614-532-4366.

MEMBERS OF FIRM

Howard VanAntwerp, III
William H. Jones, Jr.
Gregory Lee Monge
Carl D. Edwards, Jr.
Kimberly Scott McCann

ASSOCIATES

Matthew J. Wixsom
James D. Keffer
William Mitchell Hall
Stephen S. Burchett

Representative Clients: Armco; Bank of Ashland; Calgon Carbon Corp.; King's Daughters' Hospital; Allstate Insurance Co.; Kemper Insurance Group; Commercial Union Cos.; The Mayo Coal Cos.; Maryland Casualty Co.; Merck & Co.

For full biographical listings, see the Martindale-Hubbell Law Directory

*BOWLING GREEN,** Warren Co.

CAMPBELL, KERRICK & GRISE (AV)
1025 State Street, P.O. Box 9547, 42102-9547
Telephone: 502-782-8160
FAX: 502-782-5856

MEMBERS OF FIRM

Joe Bill Campbell
Gregory N. Stivers
Thomas N. Kerrick
H. Brent Brennenstuhl
John R. Grise
Deborah Tomes Wilkins

ASSOCIATES

H. Harris Pepper, Jr.
Lanna Martin Kilgore
Laura Hagan

Representative Clients: Bowling Green Bank & Trust, N.A.; Service One Credit Union; Meyer Mortgage Co.; Huntington Mortgage Corp.; TransFinancial Bank; American National Bank; Century 21-Buddy Adams & Associates, Inc.; First Federal Savings and Loan Association.

For full biographical listings, see the Martindale-Hubbell Law Directory

CATRON, KILGORE & BEGLEY (AV)
918 State Street, P.O. Box 280, 42102-0280
Telephone: 502-842-1050
Fax: 502-842-4720

Stephen B. Catron
J. Patrick Kilgore
Ernest Edward Begley, II

Representative Clients: City-County Planning Commission of Warren County; Chicago Title Insurance Company; Commonwealth Land Title Insurance Company; Bowling Green Bank & Trust Company, N.A.; Trans Financial Bank, N.A.; Convention Center Authority; Bowling Green-Warren County Industrial Park Authority, Inc.; Camping World, Inc.; International Paper Company; National Corvette Museum.

(See Next Column)

For full biographical listings, see the Martindale-Hubbell Law Directory

ENGLISH, LUCAS, PRIEST & OWSLEY (AV)
1101 College Street, P.O. Box 770, 42102-0770
Telephone: 502-781-6500
Telecopier: 502-782-7782

MEMBERS OF FIRM

Charles E. English
Whayne C. Priest, Jr.
Keith M. Carwell

General Counsel for: Warren Rural Electric Cooperative Corporation; Trans Financial Bank, N.A.
Representative Clients: Commercial Union Insurance Cos.; Kemper Insurance Group; St. Paul Insurance Co.; Desa International; Sumitomo Electric Systems, Inc.
Agent For: First American Title Insurance Company; Chicago Title Insurance Company.
Approved Attorneys For: Commonwealth Land Title Insurance Co.

For Complete List of Firm Personnel, See General Section

For full biographical listings, see the Martindale-Hubbell Law Directory

HARLIN & PARKER, P.S.C. (AV)
519 East Tenth Street, P.O. Box 390, 42102-0390
Telephone: 502-842-5611
Telefax: 502-842-2607
Smiths Grove, Kentucky Office: Old Farmers Bank Building.
Telephone: 502-563-4701.

William Jerry Parker
Michael K. Bishop
Jerry A. Burns
Mark D. Alcott (Resident, Smith Grove Office)
Scott Charles Marks

Railroad and Utilities: District Attorney for South Central Bell Telephone Co.; CSX Transportation, Inc.
Local Counsel For: General Motors Corp.; Ford Motor Co.; Chrysler Corp.
Approved Attorneys For: Commonwealth Land Title Insurance Co.
Representative Clients: Jim Walker Homes, Inc.; American General Insurance Group; American Diversified Development Co. (Bowling Green Mall); Equitable Life Assurance Society of the United States.

For Complete List of Firm Personnel, See General Section

For full biographical listings, see the Martindale-Hubbell Law Directory

*CATLETTSBURG,** Boyd Co.

ADKINS & ADKINS (AV)
Adkins Building, 2813 Louisa Street, P.O. Box 653, 41129
Telephone: 606-739-4151
Fax: Available Upon Request

James E. Adkins
James E. Adkins, II

General Counsel for: Catlettsburg Federal Savings & Loan Assn.; Kentucky-Farmers Bank.
Local Counsel for: Federal National Mortgage Assn.
Approved Attorneys for: Farmers Home Administration.

COVINGTON, Kenton Co.

KLETTE AND KLETTE (AV)
250 Grandview Drive, Suite 250, Ft. Mitchell, 41017-5610
Telephone: 606-344-9966
Fax: 606-344-9900
Cincinnati, Ohio Office: 3905 Brigadoon Drive, 45255.
Telephone: 513-421-6699.

MEMBERS OF FIRM

John H. Klette, Jr.
V. Ruth Klette
Debra S. Fox

LEGAL SUPPORT PERSONNEL

Evelyn Richard (Paralegal)

General Counsel for: The Northern Kentucky Motor Club; First Federal Savings & Loan Association of Covington.

For full biographical listings, see the Martindale-Hubbell Law Directory

TALIAFERRO AND MEHLING (AV)
1005 Madison Avenue, P.O. Box 468, 41012-0468
Telephone: 606-291-9900
Fax: 606-291-3014

MEMBERS OF FIRM

Philip Taliaferro, III
Christopher J. Mehling

ASSOCIATES

Lucinda C. Shirooni
Alice G. Keys
C. Houston Ebert
J. David Brittingham

OF COUNSEL

Robert W. Carran
Norbert J. Bischoff

For full biographical listings, see the Martindale-Hubbell Law Directory

*FRANKFORT,** Franklin Co.

William M. Johnson (AV)

Suite 3, Sower Building, 219 St. Clair Street, 40601
Telephone: 502-223-2322
FAX: 502-223-2666

ASSOCIATE

Geoffrey B. Greenawalt

Reference: Farmers Bank & Capital Trust Co.

For full biographical listings, see the Martindale-Hubbell Law Directory

*GEORGETOWN,** Scott Co.

E. Durward Weldon (AV)

217 East Main Street, 40324
Telephone: 502-863-1285

Approved Attorney For: Lawyers Title Insurance Corporation of Richmond, Virginia; Louisville Title Division of Commonwealth Land Title Insurance Co. (Binder Agent); The Equitable Life Assurance Society of the United States.

For full biographical listings, see the Martindale-Hubbell Law Directory

*GLASGOW,** Barren Co.

Garmon & Goodman (AV)

139 North Public Square, P.O. Box 663, 42142-0663
Telephone: 502-651-8812
Telecopier: 502-651-8846

MEMBERS OF FIRM

Larry D. Garmon
Charles A. Goodman III

Approved Attorneys for: Commonwealth Land Title Insurance Co. (agent); Chicago Title Insurance Co.
References: Trans Financial Bank, N.A., Glasgow, Ky; The New Farmers National Bank of Glasgow; South Central Bank of Barren County, Inc., Glasgow, Ky.; Farm Credit Services of Mid-America, ACA; Farmers Home Administration; Commonwealth Relocation Services.

For full biographical listings, see the Martindale-Hubbell Law Directory

Herbert & Herbert (AV)

135 North Public Square, P.O. Box 1000, 42141
Telephone: 502-651-9000
FAX: 502-651-3317

MEMBERS OF FIRM

H. Jefferson Herbert, Jr.
Betty Reece Herbert

Representative Clients: South Central Bank, South Broadway, Glasgow, Kentucky; Resort Financial Services, Inc., Park City, Kentucky; Commonwealth Land Title Insurance Co., Louisville, Kentucky; Pan-Osten Co.

For full biographical listings, see the Martindale-Hubbell Law Directory

*HENDERSON,** Henderson Co.

King, Deep and Branaman (AV)

127 North Main Street, P.O. Box 43, 42420
Telephone: 502-827-1852
FAX: 502-826-7729

MEMBERS OF FIRM

Leo King (1893-1982)
William M. Deep (1920-1990)
William Branaman
Harry L. Mathison, Jr.
W. Mitchell Deep, Jr.
H. Randall Redding
Dorin E. Luck

ASSOCIATES

Leslie M. Newman
Robert Khuon Wiederstein
Greg L. Gager

Counsel for: Har-Ken Oil Co.; Equitable Resources Corp.; Farm Credit Services; Ohio Valley National Bank; Commonwealth Land Title Insurance Co.; Able Energy Co.; Lamar Properties; Hercules Petroleum.

For full biographical listings, see the Martindale-Hubbell Law Directory

*LEXINGTON,** Fayette Co.

Fowler, Measle & Bell (AV)

Kincaid Towers, 300 West Vine Street, Suite 650, 40507-1660
Telephone: 606-252-6700
Fax: 606-255-3735

MEMBERS OF FIRM

Guy R. Colson
John E. Hinkel, Jr.
Robert S. Ryan
Michael W. Troutman

Representative Clients: Bank One, Lexington, NA; Citizens Union Bank of Shelbyville; PNC Bank, Kentucky, Inc.; National City Bank & Trust Co.; Fifth Third Bank; Fifth Third Leasing; Liberty National Bank; Union Bank, CA.

(See Next Column)

For Complete List of Firm Personnel, See General Section

For full biographical listings, see the Martindale-Hubbell Law Directory

Geralds, Moloney & Jones (AV)

259 West Short Street, 40507
Telephone: 606-255-7946

R. P. Moloney (1902-1963)
Donald P. Moloney (1921-1972)
Richard P. Moloney (1929-1972)
Oscar H. Geralds, Jr.
Michael R. Moloney
Ernest H. Jones, II
Billy W. Sherrow
John P. Schrader
E. Douglas Stephan
Robert L. Swisher
John G. Rice
Frances Geralds Rohlfing
Kathryn Ann Walton
Gail Luhn Pyle

Representative Clients: Aetna Life and Casualty Co.; Allstate Insurance Co.; State Farm Mutual Automobile Insurance Co.; Nationwide Insurance Co.
Reference: Commerce National Bank.

For full biographical listings, see the Martindale-Hubbell Law Directory

Greenebaum Doll & McDonald (AV)

A Partnership including Professional Service Corporations
1400 Vine Center Tower, 40508
Telephone: 606-231-8500
Telecopier: 606-255-2742
Telex: 213029
Louisville, Kentucky Office: 3300 National City Tower.
Telephone: 502-589-4200.
Fax: 502-587-3695.
Covington, Kentucky Office: 50 East River Center Boulevard, P.O. Box 2050.
Telephone: 606-655-4200.
Fax: 606-655-4239.
Cincinnati, Ohio Office: 832 Main Street.
Telephone: 513-421-8087.
Fax: 513-421-8089.

MEMBERS OF FIRM

Michael M. Fleishman *
Eric L. Ison
Robert C. Stilz, Jr. (Resident)
Job D. Turner, III (Resident)
John V. Wharton (Resident)
Peggy B. Lyndrup
Nicholas R. Glancy
Susan J. Hoffmann (Resident)
Stephen W. Switzer (Resident)

ASSOCIATE

Gregory R. Schaaf (Resident)

Representative Clients: Aetna Life Insurance Co.; ANDALEX Resources, Inc.; Ashland Oil, Inc.; AT&T Communications, Inc.; Bethlehem Steel Corp.; Brown-Forman Corp.; Columbia Gas & Transmission Co.; Commonwealth Aluminum Corp.; Consolidation Coal Co.; Costain Coal, Inc.
*A Professional Service Corporation

For Complete List of Firm Personnel, See General Section

For full biographical listings, see the Martindale-Hubbell Law Directory

Landrum & Shouse (AV)

106 West Vine Street, P.O. Box 951, 40588-0951
Telephone: 606-255-2424
Facsimile: 606-233-0308
Louisville, Kentucky Office: 400 West Market Street, Suite 1550, 40202.
Telephone: 502-589-7616.
Facsimile: 502-589-2119.

MEMBERS OF FIRM

John H. Burrus
William C. Shouse
Mark L. Moseley

District Attorneys: CSX Transportation, Inc.
Special Trial Counsel: Ford Motor Co. and Affiliates (Eastern Kentucky); Clark Equipment Co.
Representative Clients: The Continental Insurance Cos.; U.S. Insurance Group; U.S. Fidelity & Guaranty Co.; Ohio Casualty Insurance Co.; CIGNA; Royal Insurance Cos.

For Complete List of Firm Personnel, See General Section

For full biographical listings, see the Martindale-Hubbell Law Directory

Martin, Ockerman & Brabant (AV)

200 North Upper Street, 40507
Telephone: 606-254-4401

MEMBERS OF FIRM

Hogan Yancey (1881-1960)
William B. Martin (1895-1975)
Thomas C. Brabant
Foster Ockerman, Jr.
Madeleine B. Eldred

OF COUNSEL

Foster Ockerman

Counsel for: Lexington Federal Savings Bank; Good Samaritan Hospital; Newmarket Bloodstock Agency, Ltd.; Equity Property and Development Co.; Park Communications of KY (WTVQ); AAA Blue Grass/Kentucky; Good Samaritan Foundation.

(See Next Column)

MARTIN, OCKERMAN & BRABANT—*Continued*

Reference: Bank One, Lexington, N.A.

For full biographical listings, see the Martindale-Hubbell Law Directory

STOLL, KEENON & PARK (AV)

201 E. Main Street, Suite 1000, 40507-1380
Telephone: 606-231-3000
Telecopier: 606-253-1093; 606-253-1027
Frankfort, Kentucky Office: 326 West Main Street.
Telephone: 502-875-6000.
Telecopier: 502-875-6008.
Louisville, Kentucky Office: 400 West Market Street, Suite 2650, 40202.
Telephone: 502-568-9100.
Telecopier: 502-568-6340.

MEMBERS OF FIRM

William M. Lear, Jr.
Gary W. Barr
Frank L. Wilford
Robert W. Kellerman
Rena Gardner Wiseman
Dan M. Rose

ASSOCIATES

Richard A. Nunnelley
Paul C. Harnice

Representative Clients: Ball Homes; R.J. Reynolds Tobacco Co.; McDonalds Corp.; Kentucky River Coal Corp.; Super America, Inc.

For Complete List of Firm Personnel, See General Section

For full biographical listings, see the Martindale-Hubbell Law Directory

STURGILL, TURNER & TRUITT (AV)

155 East Main Street, 40507
Telephone: 606-255-8581
Fax: 606-231-0851

MEMBERS OF FIRM

Gardner L. Turner
Ann D. Sturgill
Phillip M. Moloney
Kevin G. Henry

For Complete List of Firm Personnel, See General Section

For full biographical listings, see the Martindale-Hubbell Law Directory

*LOUISVILLE,** Jefferson Co.

GREENEBAUM DOLL & MCDONALD (AV)

A Partnership including Professional Service Corporations
3300 National City Tower, 40202
Telephone: 502-589-4200
Fax: 502-587-3695
Lexington, Kentucky Office: 1400 Vine Center Tower.
Telephone: 606-231-8500.
Fax: 606-255-2742.
Covington, Kentucky Office: 50 East River Center Boulevard, P.O. Box 2050.
Telephone: 606-655-4200.
Fax: 606-655-4239.
Cincinnati, Ohio Office: 832 Main Street.
Telephone: 513-421-8087.
Fax: 513-421-8089.

Michael G. Shaikun *
Michael M. Fleishman *
Eric L. Ison
John H. Stites, III
Robert C. Stilz, Jr. (Resident at Lexington, Kentucky)
Mark S. Ament *
Job D. Turner, III (Resident at Lexington, Kentucky)
John V. Wharton (Resident at Lexington, Kentucky)
Peggy B. Lyndrup
Nicholas R. Glancy (Lexington and Covington, Kentucky)
Tandy C. Patrick
Susan J. Hoffmann (Resident at Lexington, Kentucky)
Jeffrey A. McKenzie
Stephen W. Switzer (Resident at Lexington, Kentucky)

ASSOCIATES

J. Mark Grundy
Gregory R. Schaaf (Resident at Lexington, Kentucky)

OF COUNSEL

Edward B. Weinberg *

Representative Clients: NTS Corp.; The Webb Cos.; The Mace Rich Co.; Kessler Cos.; Paragon Group; Rally's, Inc.; Andalex Resources.
*A Professional Service Corporation

For Complete List of Firm Personnel, See General Section

For full biographical listings, see the Martindale-Hubbell Law Directory

HENRY B. MANN (AV)

22nd Floor Citizens Plaza, 40202
Telephone: 502-587-6544

References: Liberty National Bank & Trust; PNC Bank, Kentucky; Bank of Louisville; National City Bank, Kentucky.

For full biographical listings, see the Martindale-Hubbell Law Directory

MAPOTHER & MAPOTHER (AV)

801 West Jefferson Street, 40202
Telephone: 502-587-5400
Fax: 502-587-5444
Lexington, Kentucky Office: 177 North Upper Street.
Telephone: 606-253-0003.
Fax: 606-255-3961.
Stanton, Kentucky Office: 209 Main Street.
Telephone: 606-663-9037.
Jeffersonville, Indiana Office: 505 East Seventh Street.
Telephone: 812-288-5059.
Fax: 502-587-5444.
Cincinnati, Ohio Office: Kroger Building, Suite 2220, 1014 Vine Street.
Telephone: 513-381-4888.
Fax: 513-381-3117.
Huntington, West Virginia Office: Morris Building, Suite 401, 845 Fourth Avenue.
Telephone: 304-525-1185.
Fax: 304-529-3764.
Evansville, Indiana Office: 329 Main Street.
Telephone: 812-421-9108.
Fax: 812-421-9109.

MEMBERS OF FIRM

Thomas C. Mapother (1907-1986)
William R. Mapother
Thomas L. Canary, Jr. (Resident, Lexington Office)
Elizabeth Lee Thompson (Resident, Lexington Office)
Charles M. Friedman

Brian P. Conaty
Andrea Fried Neichter
Kathryn Pry Coryell (Resident, Jeffersonville, Indiana Office)
Roberta S. Dunlap (Resident, Evansville, Indiana Office)
Terry Risner (Resident, Cincinnati, Ohio Office)
Lee W. Grace
Dean A. Langdon
T. Lawson McSwain, II
Charles Brent Robbins (Resident, Lexington Office)

Representative Clients: General Electric Capital Corp.; Ford Motor Credit Co.; General Motors Acceptance Corp.; Associates Commercial Corp.; Cuna Mutual Insurance Society; Bank One; National City Bank; PNC Bank BancOhio National Bank.

For full biographical listings, see the Martindale-Hubbell Law Directory

MORRIS, GARLOVE, WATERMAN & JOHNSON (AV)

Established 1925 as Morris and Garlove.
Suite 1000, One Riverfront Plaza, 40202-2959
Telephone: 502-589-3200
Fax: 502-589-3219

Irwin G. Waterman
Joseph H. Cohen
Alan N. Linker
Robert V. Waterman
Louis I. Waterman

Representative Clients: Dixie Associates Shopping Centers; McMahan Group Shopping Centers; Roth Realty Co.

For Complete List of Firm Personnel, See General Section

For full biographical listings, see the Martindale-Hubbell Law Directory

MULLOY, WALZ, WETTERER, FORE & SCHWARTZ (AV)

First Trust Centre, Suite 700N, 200 South Fifth Street, 40202
Telephone: 502-589-5250
Fax: 502-589-1637

MEMBERS OF FIRM

William P. Mulloy
Karl M. Walz
William S. Wetterer, Jr.
F. Larkin Fore
Dan T. Schwartz
B. Mark Mulloy
Mary Anne Wetterer Watkins
William S. Wetterer, III
Bryan J. Dillon
J. Gregory Clare
Ronda Hartlage
T. Lee Sisney

OF COUNSEL

Stephen H. Miller

Reference: American States Insurance Co.; Crawford & Company; Paragon Group, Inc.; Queens Group; Southeastern Dairies, Inc.; Ticor Title Co.; First National Bank of Louisville; Stockyards Bank; Arrow Electric Co.

For full biographical listings, see the Martindale-Hubbell Law Directory

OGDEN NEWELL & WELCH (AV)

1200 One Riverfront Plaza, 40202-2973
Telephone: 502-582-1601
Fax: 502-581-9564

MEMBERS OF FIRM

Joseph C. Oldham
John G. Treitz, Jr.
Ernest W. Williams
Lisa Ann Vogt

(See Next Column)

OGDEN NEWELL & WELCH, *Louisville—Continued*

ASSOCIATES

John Wade Hendricks
James G. Campbell
Teresa C. Buchheit
Thomas E. Rutledge

Counsel for: KU Energy Corp.; Kentucky Utilities Co.; Brown-Forman Corp.; B. F. Goodrich Co.; Brown & Williamson Tobacco Corp.; J.J.B. Hilliard, W.L. Lyons, Inc.; Interlock Industries, Inc.; Akzo Coatings, Inc.; United Medical Corp.; Bank of Louisville.

For Complete List of Firm Personnel, See General Section

For full biographical listings, see the Martindale-Hubbell Law Directory

RUBIN HAYS & FOLEY (AV)

First Trust Centre 200 South Fifth Street, 40202
Telephone: 502-569-7550
Telecopier: 502-569-7555

MEMBERS OF FIRM

Wm. Carl Fust
Harry Lee Meyer
David W. Gray
Irvin D. Foley
Joseph R. Gathright, Jr.
Lisa Koch Bryant
Sharon C. Hardy
Charles S. Musson
W. Randall Jones
K. Gail Russell

ASSOCIATE

Christian L. Juckett

OF COUNSEL

James E. Fahey
Newman T. Guthrie

Representative Clients: J.C. Bradford & Co., Inc.; J.J.B. Hilliard, W.L. Lyons, Inc.; Huntington National Bank; Liberty National Bank and Trust Company; National City Bank; PNC Bank; Prudential Bache & Co., Inc.; Prudential Securities, Inc.; Society Bank; Stock Yards Bank and Trust Co.

For full biographical listings, see the Martindale-Hubbell Law Directory

TAUSTINE, POST, SOTSKY, BERMAN, FINEMAN & KOHN (AV)

8th Floor Marion E. Taylor Building, 40202
Telephone: 502-589-5760
Telecopier: 502-584-5927

MEMBERS OF FIRM

Hugo Taustine (1899-1987)
Edward M. Post (1929-1986)
Marvin M. Sotsky
Jerome D. Berman
Joseph E. Fineman
Robert A. Kohn
Alex Berman
H. Philip Grossman
Stanley W. Whetzel, Jr.
Maria A. Fernandez

ASSOCIATE

Sandra Sotsky Harrison

OF COUNSEL

W. David Shearer, Jr.
David A. Friedman
Martin R. Snyder
Jerald R. Steinberg (Also Practicing individually as Steinberg & Steinberg)
Craig I. Lustig

For full biographical listings, see the Martindale-Hubbell Law Directory

*OWENSBORO,** Daviess Co.

CONNOR, NEAL & STEVENSON (AV)

613 Frederica Street, 42301
Telephone: 502-926-9911
Fax: 502-686-7905

MEMBERS OF FIRM

Sidney A. Neal (1927-1987)
Jack A. Connor
Thomas E. Neal
John W. Stevenson
James A. Wethington, II

ASSOCIATE

William A. Mitchell

Representative Client: Grange Mutual Casualty Co.
Approved Attorneys for: Farmers Home Administration.

For full biographical listings, see the Martindale-Hubbell Law Directory

LOVETT & LAMAR (AV)

208 West Third Street, 42303-4121
Telephone: 502-926-3000
FAX: 502-685-2625

MEMBERS OF FIRM

Wells T. Lovett
Charles L. Lamar
John T. Lovett
Marty G. Jacobs

Representative Clients: Beaver Dam Deposit Bank; Central Bank & Trust Co.; Emmick Oil Co.; Farm Credit Services of Mid-America ACA: Farmers Home Administration; Taylor Brothers Farm; Whitaker-Stavis Construction Co.; Cumberland Federal Savings Bank.

For full biographical listings, see the Martindale-Hubbell Law Directory

RUMMAGE, KAMUF, YEWELL, PACE & CONDON (AV)

Great Financial Federal Building, 322 Frederica Street, 42301
Telephone: 502-685-3901
FAX: 502-926-2005

MEMBERS OF FIRM

William E. Rummage
Charles J. Kamuf

Representative Clients: Owensboro Municipal Utilities Commission; Lincoln Service Corp.; Hancock County Planning Commission; Daviess County Board of Education; Barmet Aluminum Corp.; Owensboro Sewer Commission; TICOR Title Insurance Co.; Chicago Title Insurance Co.; Owensboro Riverport Authority; Housing Authority of Owensboro.

For Complete List of Firm Personnel, See General Section

For full biographical listings, see the Martindale-Hubbell Law Directory

*OWINGSVILLE,** Bath Co.

BYRON & ROBERTS (AV)

112 Court Street, 40360
Telephone: 606-674-2911

MEMBERS OF FIRM

Roger A. Byron
Winifred Byron Roberts

General Counsel for: Farmers Bank, Owingsville, Kentucky.
Local Counsel for: Delta Natural Gas Co.
Approved Attorney for: Lawyers Title Insurance Corp.

For full biographical listings, see the Martindale-Hubbell Law Directory

*RICHMOND,** Madison Co.

COY, GILBERT & GILBERT (AV)

212 North Second Street, 40475
Telephone: 606-623-3877
Fax: 606-624-5435

MEMBERS OF FIRM

Charles R. Coy
James T. Gilbert
Jerry W. Gilbert
Sandra A. Bolin

ASSOCIATE

Mark A. Shepherd

Approved Attorneys For: Lawyers Title Insurance Co.; Commonwealth Land Title Ins.
General Counsel: Peoples Bank and Trust Co. of Madison County.

For full biographical listings, see the Martindale-Hubbell Law Directory

*WILLIAMSTOWN,** Grant Co.

THRELKELD & THRELKELD, P.S.C. (AV)

144 N. Main Street, P.O. Box 277, 41097
Telephone: 606-824-3302
FAX: 606-824-3303

William F. Threlkeld
John Brent Threlkeld

Title Attorney for: Eagle Bank.
Approved Attorneys for: Lawyers Title Insurance Corp.; Chicago Title Insurance Co.; Commonwealth Land Title Insurance Co.

For full biographical listings, see the Martindale-Hubbell Law Directory

LOUISIANA

*BATON ROUGE,** East Baton Rouge Parish

KANTROW, SPAHT, WEAVER & BLITZER, A PROFESSIONAL LAW CORPORATION (AV)

Suite 300, City Plaza, 445 North Boulevard, P.O. Box 2997, 70821-2997
Telephone: 504-383-4703
Fax: 504-343-0630; 343-0637

Byron R. Kantrow
Carlos G. Spaht
Geraldine B. Weaver
Sidney M. Blitzer, Jr.
Paul H. Spaht
Lee C. Kantrow
John C. Miller
Vincent P. Fornias
David S. Rubin
Diane L. Crochet
Richard F. Zimmerman, Jr.
Bob D. Tucker
Martin E. Golden
Joseph A. Schittone, Jr.

S. Layne Lee
J. Michael Robinson, Jr.
Connell L. Archey
Richard D. Moreno
Randal J. Robert

Representative Clients: CNA Insurance Cos.; Federal Deposit Insurance Corp.; Hartford Insurance Group; Air Products and Chemicals, Inc.; CF Industries, Inc.; AT&T; United Companies Financial Corp.

For full biographical listings, see the Martindale-Hubbell Law Directory

Baton Rouge—Continued

KIZER, HOOD & MORGAN, L.L.P. (AV)

A Partnership including a Professional Corporation
748 Main Street, 70802-5526
Telephone: 504-387-3121
Fax: 504-387-5611

Roland C. Kizer (1899-1988)
Roland C. Kizer, Jr., (Ltd., A Law Corporation)
Ralph E. Hood
J. Donald Morgan
Walter N. O'Roark, III
Stacy G. Butler

Representative Clients: Hibernia National Bank; Premier Bank, National Association; The Dime Savings Bank of New York, FSB; G.E. Capital Asset Management Corp.; Bankers Systems, Inc.; United Companies Lending Corporation; Rabenhorst Life Insurance Co.; General Equipment, Inc. d/b/a Scott General; Old South Builders, Inc.; P.P.R., Inc.

For full biographical listings, see the Martindale-Hubbell Law Directory

JAMES K. MCCAY (AV)

10500 Coursey Boulevard, Suite 305, 70816-4039
Telephone: 504-292-9470
Fax: 504-295-1073

For full biographical listings, see the Martindale-Hubbell Law Directory

*LAFAYETTE,** Lafayette Parish

MANGHAM, DAVIS AND OGLESBEE (AV)

Suite 1400 First National Bank Towers, 600 Jefferson Street, P.O. Box 93110, 70509-3110
Telephone: 318-233-6200
Fax: 318-233-6521

Michael R. Mangham
Louis R. Davis
Michael G. Oglesbee
Herman E. Garner, Jr.

ASSOCIATES

Dawn Mayeux Fuqua
Lisa Hanchey Sevier

SPECIAL COUNSEL

Michael J. O'Shee

OF COUNSEL

George W. Hardy, III
Robert E. Rowe

Reference: The First National Bank of Lafayette, Lafayette, Louisiana.

For full biographical listings, see the Martindale-Hubbell Law Directory

*LAKE CHARLES,** Calcasieu Parish

BERGSTEDT & MOUNT (AV)

Second Floor, Magnolia Life Building, P.O. Drawer 3004, 70602-3004
Telephone: 318-433-3004
Facsimile: 318-433-8080

MEMBERS OF FIRM

Thomas M. Bergstedt
Benjamin W. Mount

ASSOCIATES

Van C. Seneca
Thomas J. Gayle
Gregory P. Marceaux

OF COUNSEL

Charles S. Ware

Representative Clients: Armstrong World Industries; Ashland Oil Co.; CIGNA Property & Casualty Companies; Homequity; Lake Area Medical Center; Leach Company; Olin Corporation; Terra Corporation; Town of Iowa; R. D. Werner Company.

For Complete List of Firm Personnel, See General Section

For full biographical listings, see the Martindale-Hubbell Law Directory

METAIRIE, Jefferson Parish

KIEFER & RUDMAN, A PROFESSIONAL LAW CORPORATION (AV)

One Galleria Boulevard, Suite 1212, 70001
Telephone: 504-838-2250
Telefax: 504-838-2251
New Orleans, Louisiana Office: One Seine Court, Suite 112.
Telephone: 504-368-2220.
Fax: 504-368-2278.

John B. Kiefer
Laurence D. Rudman
Roger B. Jacobs
Bruce M. Danner
Philip Schoen Brooks
Harry L. Cahill, III
Terri Bankston Stirling
Pierre V. Miller II
Gregory G. Faia
Scott B. Kiefer

References: First National Bank of Commerce; First National Bank of Commerce of Jefferson Parish; Hibernia National Bank; Jefferson Guaranty Bank; Whitney National Bank of New Orleans.

For full biographical listings, see the Martindale-Hubbell Law Directory

*NEW ORLEANS,** Orleans Parish

MIDDLEBERG, RIDDLE & GIANNA (AV)

31st Floor, Place St. Charles, 201 St. Charles Avenue, 70170-3100
Telephone: 504-525-7200
Telecopier: 504-581-5983
Dallas, Texas Office: 2323 Bryan Street, Suite 1600.
Telephone: 214-220-6300;
Telecopier: 214-220-2785.
Austin, Texas Office: 901 South Mopac Expressway.
Telephone: 512-329-3012.

MEMBERS OF FIRM

Ira Joel Middleberg
Michael Lee Riddle (Resident, Dallas, Texas)
Dominic J. Gianna

Paul J. Mirabile
John D. Person
Alan Dean Weinberger
Evelyn Foley Pugh
L. Marlene Quarles
Ronald J. Vega
Edward T. Suffern, Jr.
Gary S. Brown
Tina S. Clark
E. Ralph Lupin
A.J. Herbert, III
Cynthia A. Langston
Marshall Joseph Simien, Jr.
Wade P. Webster
Brian G. Meissner
William M. Blackston
A. Elizabeth Tarver
Maria N. Rabieh

For full biographical listings, see the Martindale-Hubbell Law Directory

*OPELOUSAS,** St. Landry Parish

DAUZAT, FALGOUST, CAVINESS, BIENVENU & STIPE (AV)

510 S. Court Street, P.O. Box 1450, 70571
Telephone: 318-942-5811
Fax: 318-948-9512

MEMBERS OF FIRM

Jimmy L. Dauzat
Jerry J. Falgoust
Peter F. Caviness
Steven J. Bienvenu
Jeigh L. Stipe

For full biographical listings, see the Martindale-Hubbell Law Directory

*SHREVEPORT,** Caddo Parish

BARLOW AND HARDTNER L.C. (AV)

Tenth Floor, Louisiana Tower, 401 Edwards Street, 71101-3289
Telephone: 318-227-1131
Telecopier: 318-227-1141
Mailing Address: P.O. Box 8, Shreveport, Louisiana, 71161-0008

Ray A. Barlow
Malcolm S. Murchison
Stephen E. Ramey
Philip E. Downer, III
Jay A. Greenleaf

Representative Clients: AmCom General Corporation; The Brinkmann Corporation; General Electric Co.; Kelley Oil Corporation; NorAm Energy Corp. (formerly Arkla, Inc.); Central and South West; Panhandle Eastern Corp.; Pennzoil Producing Co.; Johnson Controls, Inc.; Ashland Oil, Inc.

For Complete List of Firm Personnel, See General Section

For full biographical listings, see the Martindale-Hubbell Law Directory

BODENHEIMER, JONES, KLOTZ & SIMMONS (AV)

509 Milam Street, 71101
Telephone: 318-221-1507
Fax: 318-221-4560

MEMBERS OF FIRM

J. W. Jones
C. Gary Mitchell

For full biographical listings, see the Martindale-Hubbell Law Directory

COOK, YANCEY, KING & GALLOWAY, A PROFESSIONAL LAW CORPORATION (AV)

1700 Commercial National Tower, 333 Texas Street, P.O. Box 22260, 71120-2260
Telephone: 318-221-6277
Telecopier: 318-227-2606

Stephen R. Yancey II
J. William Fleming
James H. Campbell
Frank M. Dodson

A list of representative clients will be furnished upon request.

For Complete List of Firm Personnel, See General Section

For full biographical listings, see the Martindale-Hubbell Law Directory

WEEMS, WRIGHT, SCHIMPF, HAYTER & CARMOUCHE, A PROFESSIONAL LAW CORPORATION (AV)

912 Kings Highway, 71104
Telephone: 318-222-2100
Telecopier: 318-227-0136

(See Next Column)

Weems, Wright, Schimpf, Hayter & Carmouche A Professional Law Corporation, *Shreveport—Continued*

Ronald R. Weems | Kenneth P. Wright
John W. Pou

John C. Geyer

Representative Clients: First American Title Insurance Company; Lawyer's Title Insurance Company; Hibernia National Bank; Barksdale Federal Credit Union; Farm Credit Bank of Texas; Georgia-Pacific Corporation; Louisiana Title Company; Patterson Insurance.

For full biographical listings, see the Martindale-Hubbell Law Directory

*WINNFIELD,** Winn Parish

Simmons and Derr (AV)

Simmons Building, Church Street, P.O. Box 525, 71483
Telephone: 318-628-3951

MEMBERS OF FIRM

Kermit M. Simmons | Jacque D. Derr

Reference: Bank of Winnfield & Trust Co.

For full biographical listings, see the Martindale-Hubbell Law Directory

MAINE

*BANGOR,** Penobscot Co.

Eaton, Peabody, Bradford & Veague, P.A. (AV)

Fleet Center-Exchange Street, P.O. Box 1210, 04402-1210
Telephone: 207-947-0111
Telecopier: 207-942-3040
Augusta, Maine Office: 2 Central Plaza.
Telephone: 207-622-3747.
Telecopier: 207-622-9732.
Brunswick, Maine Office: 167 Park Row.
Telephone: 207-729-1144.
Telecopier: 207-729-1140.
Camden, Maine Office: 7-9 Washington Street.
Telephone: 207-236-3325.
Telecopier: 207-236-8611.
Dover-Foxcroft, Maine Office: 30 East Main Street.
Telephone: 207-564-8378.
Telecopier: 207-564-7059.

John W. Conti
Robert J. Eaton
Edward D. Leonard, III
Douglas M. Smith (Resident, Dover-Foxcroft and Augusta Offices)
Martin L. Wilk (Resident, Brunswick Office)
John A. Cunningham (Resident, Brunswick Office)
Karen A. Huber
Terry W. Calderwood (Resident, Camden Office)
Paul L. Gibbons (Resident, Camden Office)

OF COUNSEL

Donald A. Spear (Resident, Brunswick Office)

John M. Monahan (Resident, Dover-Foxcroft Office)
Jonathan B. Huntington (Resident, Dover-Foxcroft Office)
Lorena R. Rush

A List of Representative Clients available upon request.

For Complete List of Firm Personnel, See General Section

For full biographical listings, see the Martindale-Hubbell Law Directory

Gross, Minsky, Mogul & Singal, P.A. (AV)

Key Plaza, 23 Water Street, P.O. Box 917, 04402-0917
Telephone: 207-942-4644
Telecopier: 207-942-3699
Ellsworth, Maine Office: 26 State Street.
Telephone: 207-667-4611.
Telecopier: 207-667-6206.

Jules L. Mogul (1930-1994)
Norman Minsky
George Z. Singal
Louis H. Kornreich
George C. Schelling
Edward W. Gould
Steven J. Mogul
James R. Wholly

Wayne P. Libhart (Resident, Ellsworth, Maine Office)
Daniel A. Pileggi
Philip K. Clarke
Christopher R. Largay (Resident, Ellsworth Office)
Hans G. Huessy
William B. Entwisle
Sandra L. Rothera

(See Next Column)

OF COUNSEL

Edward I. Gross

Approved Attorneys For: First American Title Insurance Co.; New York TRW Title Insurance, Inc.
Agent For: First American Title Insurance Co.; New York TRW Title Insurance Co.

For full biographical listings, see the Martindale-Hubbell Law Directory

Vafiades, Brountas & Kominsky (AV)

Key Plaza, 23 Water Street, P.O. Box 919, 04402-0919
Telephone: 207-947-6915
Telecopier: 207-941-0863

MEMBERS OF FIRM

Nicholas P. Brountas | Marvin H. Glazier

Approved Attorneys For: Chicago Title Insurance Co.; Lawyers Title Insurance Corp.; New York TRW; Title Insurance, Inc.

For Complete List of Firm Personnel, See General Section

For full biographical listings, see the Martindale-Hubbell Law Directory

BAR HARBOR, Hancock Co.

Fenton, Chapman, Fenton, Smith & Kane, P.A. (AV)

109 Main Street, P.O. Box B, 04609
Telephone: 207-288-3331
FAX: 207-288-9326

William Fenton
Douglas B. Chapman
Nathaniel R. Fenton
Chadbourn H. Smith

Margaret A. Timothy

Reference: Bar Harbor Banking and Trust Co.

For Complete List of Firm Personnel, See General Section

For full biographical listings, see the Martindale-Hubbell Law Directory

CAMDEN, Knox Co.

Pierce, Atwood, Scribner, Allen, Smith & Lancaster (AV)

36 Chestnut Street, P.O. Box 780, 04843
Telephone: 207-236-4333
Fax: 207-236-6247
Portland, Maine Office: One Monument Square.
Telephone: 207-773-6411.
Augusta, Maine Office: 77 Winthrop Street.
Telephone: 207-622-6311.

MEMBERS OF FIRM

Richard A. McKittrick | Peter G. Warren

For full biographical listings, see the Martindale-Hubbell Law Directory

KENNEBUNK, York Co.

Reagan, Adams & Cadigan (AV)

Eleven Main Street, P.O. Box 709, 04043
Telephone: 207-985-7181
Telecopier: 207-985-7003

MEMBERS OF FIRM

Thomas J. Reagan
Wayne T. Adams
Christopher Reagan
Paul W. Cadigan

Counsel for: Kennebunk Savings Bank.

For full biographical listings, see the Martindale-Hubbell Law Directory

*PORTLAND,** Cumberland Co.

Jensen Baird Gardner & Henry (AV)

Ten Free Street, P.O. Box 4510, 04112
Telephone: 207-775-7271
Telecopier: 207-775-7935
York County Office: 419 Alfred Street, Biddeford, Maine.
Telephone: 207-282-5107.
Telecopier: 207-282-6301.

MEMBERS OF FIRM

John D. Bradford (Resident, York County Office)
Walter E. Webber
Kenneth M. Cole, III
David J. Jones (Resident, York County Office)
Ralph W. Austin (Resident, York County Office)
Ronald A. Epstein
Leslie E. Lowry, III

Representative Clients: General Motors Acceptance Corp.; York Mutual Insurance Co.; Knutson Mortgage Corp.; Maine Mall; Key Bank of Maine.

For Complete List of Firm Personnel, See General Section

For full biographical listings, see the Martindale-Hubbell Law Directory

Portland—Continued

PIERCE, ATWOOD, SCRIBNER, ALLEN, SMITH & LANCASTER (AV)

One Monument Square, 04101
Telephone: 207-773-6411
Fax: 207-773-3419
Augusta, Maine Office: 77 Winthrop Street.
Telephone: 207-622-6311.
Camden, Maine Office: 36 Chestnut Street, P.O. Box 780.
Telephone: 207-236-4333.

MEMBERS OF FIRM

Richard A. McKittrick (Resident, Camden Office)
Peter G. Warren (Resident, Camden Office)
Dennis C. Keeler
Elaine S. Falender

ASSOCIATES

Jennie L. Clegg
Nancy V. Savage
Pamela C. Morris

STAFF ATTORNEY

Judith A. Fletcher Woodbury

For Complete List of Firm Personnel, See General Section

For full biographical listings, see the Martindale-Hubbell Law Directory

PRETI, FLAHERTY, BELIVEAU & PACHIOS (AV)

443 Congress Street, P.O. Box 11410, 04104-7410
Telephone: 207-791-3000
Telecopier: 207-791-3111
Augusta, Maine Office: 45 Memorial Circle, P.O. Box 1058, 04332-1058.
Telephone: 207-623-5300.
Telecopier: 207-623-2914.
Rumford, Maine Office: 150 Congress Street, P.O. Drawer L, 04276-2035.
Telephone: 207-364-4593.
Telecopier: 207-369-9421.

MEMBERS OF FIRM

Michael J. Gentile (Augusta Office)
Richard H. Spencer, Jr.
Eric P. Stauffer
James C. Pitney, Jr. (Augusta Office)
Dennis C. Sbrega
Estelle A. Lavoie
Susan E. LoGiudice
Michael L. Sheehan

ASSOCIATES

Jeanne T. Cohn-Connor
Marilyn E. Mistretta

Representative Clients: Guy Gannett Publishing Co.; Key Bank of Maine; RECOLL Management Corp.; Patten Corporation of Maine; Fleet Bank of Maine; Liberty Group.

For Complete List of Firm Personnel, See General Section

For full biographical listings, see the Martindale-Hubbell Law Directory

YORK, York Co.

ERWIN, OTT, CLARK & CAMPBELL (AV)

16A Woodbridge Road, P.O. Box 545, 03909
Telephone: 207-363-5208
Facsimile: 207-363-5322

MEMBERS OF FIRM

Frank E. Hancock (1923-1988)
James S. Erwin
John P. Campbell
David N. Ott
Jeffery J. Clark

For full biographical listings, see the Martindale-Hubbell Law Directory

MARYLAND

*ANNAPOLIS,** Anne Arundel Co.

BENJAMIN MICHAELSON, JR., P.A. (AV)

275 West Street, Suite 60, 21401
Telephone: 410-267-8178
Baltimore: 410-269-6966
Washington, D.C.: 301-261-2889
Fax: 410-267-8072

Benjamin Michaelson, Jr.

Karen J. Elliott

Representative Clients: Annapolis Federal Savings Bank; Maryland Service Corp.

For full biographical listings, see the Martindale-Hubbell Law Directory

P. JAMES UNDERWOOD (AV)

9A Maryland Avenue, P.O. Box 2335, 21404
Telephone: 410-268-4247

Representative Clients: R D K & W Joint Venture; Kaufmann Limited Partnership; W K D & R Real Estate Company; Elanne Corporation.

*BALTIMORE,** (Independent City)

BALLARD SPAHR ANDREWS & INGERSOLL (AV)

300 East Lombard Street, 19th Floor, 21202-3268
Telephone: 410-528-5600
Fax: 410-528-5650
Philadelphia, Pennsylvania Office: 1735 Market Street, 51st Floor.
Telephone: 215-665-8500.
Fax: 215-864-8999.
Denver, Colorado Office: Seventeenth Street Plaza Building, Suite 2300, 1225 17th Street.
Telephone: 303-292-2400.
Fax: 303-296-3956.
Salt Lake City, Utah Office: One Utah Center, 201 South Main Street, Suite 1200.
Telephone: 801-531-3000.
Fax: 801-531-3001.
Washington, D.C. Office: Suite 900 East, 555 13th Street, N.W.
Telephone: 202-383-8800.
Fax: 202-383-8877; 383-8893.
Camden, New Jersey Office: 800 Hudson Square, 5th Floor.
Telephone: 609-541-5577.
Fax: 609-541-8272.

Ronald P. Fish
Morton P. Fisher, Jr.
James C. Oliver
Gregory Reed
Jane Ennis Sheehan
Raymond G. Truitt
Fred Wolf, III

R. Kelvin Antill
Jill Reynolds Seidman

For full biographical listings, see the Martindale-Hubbell Law Directory

GALLAGHER, EVELIUS & JONES (AV)

Park Charles Suite 400, 218 North Charles Street, 21201
Telephone: 410-727-7702
Telecopier: 410-837-3079

MEMBERS OF FIRM

Francis X. Gallagher (1928-1972)
C. Edward Jones (Retired)
John C. Evelius
Richard O. Berndt
Thomas N. Biddison, Jr.
Robert R. Kern, Jr.
Saul E. Gilstein
Thomas B. Lewis
Bonnie Abrams Travieso
Stephen A. Goldberg
Linda H. Jones
Christopher J. Fritz
David E. Raderman
Peter E. Keith
Nita L. Schultz
Michael W. Skojec
Kathryn Kelley Hoskins
Mark P. Keener

ASSOCIATES

Kevin J. Davidson
Eileen M. Lunga
Lori A. Nicolle
Thomas C. Dame
Mary Catherine Collins Gaver
Julie Ellen Squire
Matthew W. Oakey

LEGAL ASSISTANTS

Patricia C. Quayle
Jeanmarie McGlynn
Iris T. Hooker
Cheryl J. Reinke

Representative Clients: Roman Catholic Archdiocese of Baltimore; Shelter Corporation of Canada; Bozzuto & Associates, Inc.; The Enterprise Foundation; Mercy Medical Center, Inc.; First National Bank of Maryland.

For full biographical listings, see the Martindale-Hubbell Law Directory

GORDON, FEINBLATT, ROTHMAN, HOFFBERGER & HOLLANDER (AV)

The Garrett Building, 233 East Redwood Street, 21202
Telephone: 410-576-4000
Telex: 908041 BAL

MEMBERS OF FIRM

David H. Fishman (Chairman)
Thomas J. Doud, Jr.
Timothy D. A. Chriss
Neil J. Schechter

ASSOCIATES

Seth M. Rotenberg
Edward N. Kane, Jr.

For Complete List of Firm Personnel, See General Section

For full biographical listings, see the Martindale-Hubbell Law Directory

Baltimore—Continued

VENABLE, BAETJER AND HOWARD (AV)

A Partnership including Professional Corporations
1800 Mercantile Bank & Trust Building, 2 Hopkins Plaza, 21201
Telephone: 410-244-7400
Washington, D.C. Office: Venable, Baetjer, Howard & Civiletti. Suite 1000, 1201 New York Avenue, N.W.
Telephone: 202-962-4800.
McLean, Virginia Office: Suite 400, 2010 Corporate Ridge.
Telephone: 703-760-1600.
Rockville, Maryland Office: Suite 500, One Church Street, P. O. Box 1906.
Telephone: 301-217-5600.
Towson, Maryland Office: 210 Allegheny Avenue, P. O. Box 5517.
Telephone: 410-494-6200.

MEMBERS OF FIRM

Russell Ronald Reno, Jr. (P.C.)
Thomas P. Perkins, III (P.C.)
James A. Cole
Benjamin R. Civiletti (P.C.) (Also at Washington, D.C. and Towson, Maryland Offices)
John B. Howard (Resident, Towson, Maryland Office)
David D. Downes (Resident, Towson, Maryland Office)
Roger W. Titus (Resident, Rockville, Maryland Office)
Daniel O'C. Tracy, Jr. (Also at Rockville, Maryland Office)
Jan K. Guben (Also at Washington, D. C Office)
James D. Wright (P.C.)
David T. Stitt (Not admitted in MD; Resident, McLean, Virginia Office)
Robert E. Madden (Not admitted in MD; also at Washington, D.C. and McLean, Virginia Offices)
John H. Zink, III (Resident, Towson, Maryland Office)
John G. Milliken (Not admitted in MD; Also at Washington, D.C. and McLean, Virginia Offices)
Bruce E. Titus (Resident, McLean, Virginia Office)
Joel Z. Silver (Not admitted in MD; Resident, Washington, D.C. Office)
Paul T. Glasgow (Resident, Rockville, Maryland Office)
Joseph C. Wich, Jr. (Resident, Towson, Maryland Office)
Sondra Harans Block (Resident, Rockville, Maryland Office)
Thomas B. Hudson (Also at Washington, D.C. Office)
David G. Lane (Resident, McLean, Virginia Office)
James K. Archibald (Also at Washington, D.C. and Towson, Maryland Offices)
F. Dudley Staples, Jr. (Also at Towson, Maryland Office)
Edward L. Wender (P.C.)
George F. Pappas (Also at Washington, D.C. Office)
Nathaniel E. Jones, Jr.
Ellen F. Dyke (Not admitted in MD; Resident, McLean, Virginia Office)
William D. Quarles (Also at Washington, D.C. and Towson, Maryland Offices)
Cynthia M. Hahn (Resident, Towson, Maryland Office)
James A. Dunbar (Also at Washington, D.C. Office)
Robert A. Hoffman (Resident, Towson, Maryland Office)
J. Michael Brennan (Resident, Towson, Maryland Office)
Joel J. Goldberg (Not admitted in MD; Washington, D.C. and McLean, Virginia Offices)
Paul A. Serini (Also at Washington, D.C. Office)
Kevin L. Shepherd
Michael H. Davis (Resident, Towson, Maryland Office)

OF COUNSEL

Judith A. Armold
Mary T. Flynn (Not admitted in MD; Resident, McLean, Virginia Office)

ASSOCIATES

Courtney G. Capute
Christine J. Collins
J. Van L. Dorsey (Resident, Towson, Maryland Office)
Mary-Dulany James (Resident, Towson, Maryland Office)
Paula Titus Laboy (Resident, Rockville, Maryland Office)
Patricia A. Malone (Resident, Towson, Maryland Office)
Vicki Margolis
John T. Prisbe
Michael W. Robinson (Not admitted in MD; Resident, McLean, Virginia Office)
G. Page Wingert (Resident, Towson, Maryland Office)

For Complete List of Firm Personnel, See General Section

For full biographical listings, see the Martindale-Hubbell Law Directory

*BEL AIR,** Harford Co.

STARK & KEENAN, A PROFESSIONAL ASSOCIATION (AV)

30 Office Street, 21014
Telephone: 410-838-5522
Baltimore: 410-879-2222
Fax: 410-879-0688

Elwood V. Stark, Jr.
Charles B. Keenan, Jr.
Thomas E. Marshall
Edwin G. Carson
Judith C. H. Cline
Gregory A. Szoka
Robert S. Lynch

Claire Prin Blomquist
Kimberly Kahoe Muenter
Paul W. Ishak

For full biographical listings, see the Martindale-Hubbell Law Directory

GREENBELT, Prince Georges Co.

STANLEY S. PICKETT (AV)

Suite 414 Capitol Office Park, 6411 Ivy Lane, 20770
Telephone: 301-513-0613

Stanley Sinclair Pickett

ASSOCIATE

Gordon J. Brumback

Representative Clients: B.F. Saul Co.; McDonald and Eudy Printers, Inc.; Condominium Management, Inc.; Long & Foster Realtors; Mitron Systems Corp.; Coldwell Banker; Eastern Property Group, Inc.; Glenanden Housing Authority; Koones & Montgomery, Inc.; Trans America Management, Inc.

For full biographical listings, see the Martindale-Hubbell Law Directory

*ROCKVILLE,** Montgomery Co.

CHEN, WALSH, TECLER & MCCABE (AV)

Suite 300, 200-A Monroe Street, 20850
Telephone: 301-279-9500
FAX: 301-294-5195

MEMBERS OF FIRM

William James Chen, Jr.
John Burgess Walsh, Jr.
Kenneth B. Tecler
John F. McCabe, Jr.

For full biographical listings, see the Martindale-Hubbell Law Directory

STEIN, SPERLING, BENNETT, DE JONG, DRISCOLL, GREENFEIG & METRO, P.A. (AV)

25 West Middle Lane, 20850
Telephone: 301-340-2020; 800-435-5230
Telecopier: 301-340-8217

Jack A. Garson
Donald N. Sperling

Beth H. McIntosh
Ann H. Sablosky

For Complete List of Firm Personnel, See General Section

For full biographical listings, see the Martindale-Hubbell Law Directory

SEABROOK, Prince Georges Co.

FOSSETT & BRUGGER, CHARTERED (AV)

The Aerospace Building, 10210 Greenbelt Road, 20706
Telephone: 301-794-6900
Telecopy: 301-794-7638
La Plata, Maryland Office: 105 LaGrange Avenue, P.O. Box F.
Telephone: 301-934-4200. Washington Line: 301-753-9600.
FAX: 301-870-2884.

George A. Brugger
Clarence L. Fossett
Jonathan I. Kipnis
Nancy L. Slepicka
Diane O. Leasure
Midgett S. Parker, Jr.
William M. Shipp
John C. Fredrickson
Lorraine J. Webb (Resident, La Plata Office)
Michael A. Faerber
Michael F. Canning, Jr.
Harold Gregory Martin
Mary A. Liano

Representative Clients: Banyan Management Corp.; Capital Office Park; Coscan Washington, Inc.; Citizens Bank & Trust Company of Maryland; Greenhorne & O'Mara, Inc.; Kettler Brothers; Michael T. Rose Cos.; The Mutual Life Insurance Company of New York; Richmond-American Homes; Winchester Homes, Inc.

For Complete List of Firm Personnel, See General Section

For full biographical listings, see the Martindale-Hubbell Law Directory

SILVER SPRING, Montgomery Co.

ALEXANDER, GEBHARDT, APONTE & MARKS, L.L.C. (AV)

Lee Plaza-Suite 805, 8601 Georgia Avenue, 20910
Telephone: 301-589-2222
Facsimile: 301-589-2523
Washington, D.C. Office: 1314 Nineteenth Street, N.W., 20036.
Telephone: 202-835-1555.
New York, New York Office: 330 Madison Avenue, 36th Floor.
Telephone: 212-808-0008.
Fax: 212-599-1028.

Koteles Alexander (Not admitted in MD)
S. Ricardo Narvaiz (Not admitted in MD)

David B. Johnson

Reference: Riggs National Bank of Washington, D.C.

For full biographical listings, see the Martindale-Hubbell Law Directory

*TOWSON,** Baltimore Co.

VENABLE, BAETJER AND HOWARD (AV)

A Partnership including Professional Corporations
210 Allegheny Avenue, P.O. Box 5517, 21204
Telephone: 410-494-6200
FAX: 410-821-0147
Baltimore, Maryland Office: 1800 Mercantile Bank & Trust Building, 2 Hopkins Plaza.
Telephone: 410-244-7400.
Washington, D.C. Office: Venable, Baetjer, Howard & Civiletti. Suite 1000, 1201 New York Avenue, N.W.
Telephone: 202-962-4800.
McLean, Virginia Office: Suite 400, 2010 Corporate Ridge.
Telephone: 703-760-1600.
Rockville, Maryland Office: Suite 500, One Church Street, P. O. Box 1906.
Telephone: 301-217-5600.

PARTNERS

Benjamin R. Civiletti (P.C.) (Also at Washington, D.C. and Baltimore, Maryland Offices)
John B. Howard
David D. Downes
John H. Zink, III
Joseph C. Wich, Jr.
James K. Archibald (Also at Baltimore, Maryland and Washington, D.C. Offices)
F. Dudley Staples, Jr. (Also at Baltimore, Maryland Office)
William D. Quarles (Also at Washington, D.C. Office)
Cynthia M. Hahn
Robert A. Hoffman
J. Michael Brennan
Michael H. Davis

ASSOCIATES

J. Van L. Dorsey
Mary-Dulany James
Patricia A. Malone
G. Page Wingert

For Complete List of Firm Personnel, See General Section

For full biographical listings, see the Martindale-Hubbell Law Directory

MASSACHUSETTS

ARLINGTON, Middlesex Co.

GRANNAN & MALOY, P.C. (AV)

Suite 408, 22 Mill Street, 02174
Telephone: 617-646-3200

William J. Grannan
Paul F. Maloy

For full biographical listings, see the Martindale-Hubbell Law Directory

*BOSTON,** Suffolk Co.

BARRON & STADFELD, P.C. (AV)

Two Center Plaza, 02108
Telephone: 617-723-9800
Telecopier: 617-523-8359
Hyannis, Massachusetts Office: 258 Winter Street.
Telephone: 617-778-6622.

Thomas V. Bennett
Julie Taylor Moran
Joseph G. Butler

Donna M. Pisciotta

For Complete List of Firm Personnel, See General Section

For full biographical listings, see the Martindale-Hubbell Law Directory

PALMER & DODGE (AV)

(Storey Thorndike Palmer & Dodge)
One Beacon Street, 02108
Telephone: 617-573-0100
Telecopier: 617-227-4420
Telex: 951104
Cable Address: "Storeydike," Boston

MEMBERS OF FIRM

Raymond M. Murphy
John E. Rattigan, Jr.
David E. Rideout
David R. Rodgers
Thomas G. Schnorr
James M. Whalen

For Complete List of Firm Personnel, See General Section

For full biographical listings, see the Martindale-Hubbell Law Directory

RACKEMANN, SAWYER & BREWSTER, PROFESSIONAL CORPORATION (AV)

One Financial Center, 02111
Telephone: 617-542-2300
Telecopier: 617-542-7437

(See Next Column)

William B. Tyler
George V. Anastas
Henry H. Thayer
Stephen Carr Anderson
Albert M. Fortier, Jr.
Michael F. O'Connell
Stuart T. Freeland
Raymond J. Brassard
Alan B. Rubenstein
Martin R. Healy
James R. Shea, Jr.
Brian M. Hurley
Janet M. Smith
Peter Friedenberg
Richard S. Novak
J. David Leslie
Alexander H. Spaulding
Sanford M. Matathia
Anne P. Zebrowski

OF COUNSEL

Albert B. Wolfe
August R. Meyer
Richard H. Lovell

COUNSEL

Ronald S. Duby
Ross J. Hamlin

Margaret L. Hayes
Daniel J. Ossoff
Mary B. Freeley
Gordon M. Orloff
Donald R. Pinto, Jr.
Lucy West Behymer
Richard J. Gallogly
Melissa Langer Ellis
James A. Wachta
Susan Dempsey Baer
Daniel J. Bailey, III
Michael S. Giaimo
Maura E. Murphy
Mary L. Gallant
Peter A. Alpert
Lauren D. Armstrong
Robert B. Foster
Elizabeth A. Gibbons

For full biographical listings, see the Martindale-Hubbell Law Directory

RICH, MAY, BILODEAU & FLAHERTY, P.C. (AV)

The Old South Building, 294 Washington Street, 02108-4675
Telephone: 617-482-1360
FAX: 617-556-3889

John F. Rich (1908-1987)
Thomas H. Bilodeau (1915-1987)
Gerald May
Harold B. Dondis
Walter L. Landergan, Jr.
Edwin J. Carr
Arthur F. Flaherty
Franklin M. Hundley
Michael F. Donlan
Joseph F. Sullivan, Jr.
Owen P. Maher
Nicolas A. Kensington
Daniel T. Clark
Gerald V. May, Jr.
Eric J. Krathwohl
Michael J. McHugh
James M. Behnke
James M. Avery
Stephen M. Kane
Mark C. O'Connor
Walter A. Wright, III
Emmett E. Lyne

Nicholas F. Kourtis
James T. Finnigan
Carol E. Kazmer
Robert P. Snell

For full biographical listings, see the Martindale-Hubbell Law Directory

RUBIN AND RUDMAN (AV)

50 Rowes Wharf, 02110
Telephone: 617-330-7000
Telecopier: 617-439-9556

Howard Rubin
Milton Bordwin
Myrna Putziger
Harold Stahler
Raymond M. Kwasnick
Jonathan D. Canter
James H. Greene

Robert J. Mack
David C. Fixler

For Complete List of Firm Personnel, See General Section

For full biographical listings, see the Martindale-Hubbell Law Directory

SHERBURNE, POWERS & NEEDHAM, P.C. (AV)

One Beacon Street, 02108
Telephone: 617-523-2700
Fax: 617-523-6850

William D. Weeks
John T. Collins
Allan J. Landau
John L. Daly
Stephen A. Hopkins
Alan I. Falk
C. Thomas Swaim
James Pollock
William V. Tripp III
Stephen S. Young
William F. Machen
W. Robert Allison
Jacob C. Diemert
Philip J. Notopoulos
Richard J. Hindlian
Paul E. Troy
Harold W. Potter, Jr.
Dale R. Johnson
Philip S. Lapatin
Pamela A. Duckworth
Mark Schonfeld
James D. Smeallie
Paul Killeen
Gordon P. Katz
Joseph B. Darby, III
Richard M Yanofsky
James E. McDermott
Robert V. Lizza
Miriam Goldstein Altman
John J. Monaghan
Margaret J. Palladino
Mark C. Michalowski
David Scott Sloan
M. Chrysa Long
Lawrence D. Bradley
Miriam J. McKendall

(See Next Column)

SHERBURNE, POWERS & NEEDHAM P.C., *Boston—Continued*

Cynthia A. Brown
Cynthia M. Hern
Dianne R. Phillips
Paul M. James
Theodore F. Hanselman
Joshua C. Krumholz
Ieuan G. Mahony
Kenneth L. Harvey
Christopher J. Trombetta
Edwin F. Landers, Jr.
Amy J. Mastrobattista
William Howard McCarthy, Jr.
Douglas W. Clapp
Tamara E. Goulston
Nicholas J. Psyhogeos

COUNSEL

Haig Der Manuelian
Mason M. Taber, Jr.
Karl J. Hirshman
Benjamin Volinski
Kenneth P. Brier

OF COUNSEL

John Barr Dolan

For full biographical listings, see the Martindale-Hubbell Law Directory

SHERIN AND LODGEN (AV)

100 Summer Street, 02110
Telephone: 617-426-5720
Telecopier: 617-542-5186
Los Angeles, California Office: 11300 W. Olympic Boulevard, Suite 700.
Telephone: 310-914-7891.
Fax: 310-552-5327.
Nashua New Hampshire Office: One Indian Head Plaza.
Telephone: 603-595-4511.
Fax: 603-595-4968.
Providence, Rhode Island Office: 55 Pine Street.
Telephone: 401-274-8060.

MEMBERS OF FIRM

Arthur L. Sherin (1946-1964)
George E. Lodgen (1946-1971)
Morton B. Brown
George Waldstein
John M. Reed
Robert J. Muldoon, Jr.
Alette E. Reed
Edward M. Bloom
Thomas J. Raftery
Joshua M. Alper
Gary M. Markoff
Bryan G. Killian
David A. Guberman
Kenneth R. Berman
Frank J. Bailey
Thomas P. Gorman
Dorothy Nelson Stookey
Mark A. Nowak
Ronald W. Ruth
Steven D. Eimert
Daniel B. Winslow
Barbara A. O'Donnell
Brian C. Levey
A. Neil Hartzell
Kenneth J. Mickiewicz
Craig M. Brown
Andrew Royce
Daniel O. Gaquin
Thomas A. Hippler
Rhonda B. Parker
John J. Slater, III (Resident)

ASSOCIATES

Joanna E. Scannell
Nereyda Garcia
John C. La Liberte
Karen Elise Berman
Margaret H. Leeson
Joseph M. Kerwin
Christopher A. Kenney
David Benfield
Michael C. Giardiello

OF COUNSEL

Paul Melrose
Michael S. Strauss

LEGAL SUPPORT PERSONNEL

Marilyn Stewart

For full biographical listings, see the Martindale-Hubbell Law Directory

SIMONDS, WINSLOW, WILLIS & ABBOTT, A PROFESSIONAL ASSOCIATION (AV)

50 Congress Street, 02109
Telephone: 617-523-5520
Fax: 617-523-4619

William S. Abbott
William L. Eaton
Marc A. Elfman
Robert S. Gulick
Peter R. Johnson
Brenda G. Levy
Robert Torrence Morrison
Hugh V. A. Starkey
Dudley H. Willis
Byron E. Woodman, Jr.
John L. Worden III
Edward J. Wynne III

For full biographical listings, see the Martindale-Hubbell Law Directory

WARNER & STACKPOLE (AV)

75 State Street, 02109
Telephone: 617-951-9000
Cable Address: "Warstack"
Telecopier: 617-951-9151
Telex: 940139

MEMBERS OF FIRM

Stanley V. Ragalevsky
Michael A. Leon
Leon J. Lombardi
James G. Ward
Paul C. Bauer

ASSOCIATES

Richard R. Loewy
John T. Smolak

(See Next Column)

COUNSEL

Howard A. Levine

For Complete List of Firm Personnel, See General Section

For full biographical listings, see the Martindale-Hubbell Law Directory

*CAMBRIDGE,** Middlesex Co.

WILLIAM M. O'BRIEN (AV)

Suite 216, 186 Alewife Brook Parkway, 02138
Telephone: 617-661-2600
Fax: 617-864-0654

For full biographical listings, see the Martindale-Hubbell Law Directory

CONCORD, Middlesex Co.

LAW OFFICE OF HENRY J. DANE (AV)

37 Main Street, P.O. Box 540, 01742
Telephone: 508-369-8333
Fax: 508-369-3106
Cable Address: Danelaw

ASSOCIATE

Trevor A. Haydon, Jr.

OF COUNSEL

Mark D. Shuman

For full biographical listings, see the Martindale-Hubbell Law Directory

FRANKLIN, Norfolk Co.

ROCHE AND MURPHY (AV)

Franklin Office Park West, 38 Pond Street, Suite 308, P.O. Box 267, 02038
Telephone: 508-528-8300
FAX: 508-528-8889

MEMBERS OF FIRM

Neil J. Roche
Paul G. Murphy

ASSOCIATE

John J. Roche

For full biographical listings, see the Martindale-Hubbell Law Directory

*NORTHAMPTON,** Hampshire Co.

BOWEN & SIEGEL (AV)

40 Center Street, 01060
Telephone: 413-584-3384
Fax: 413-584-0139

MEMBERS OF FIRM

Kenneth B. Bowen
Andrew J. Siegel

Local Counsel for: Southern New England Farm Credit, ACA.
Town Counsel for: Town of Williamsburg.

For full biographical listings, see the Martindale-Hubbell Law Directory

*SPRINGFIELD,** Hampden Co.

ELY & KING (AV)

One Financial Plaza, 1350 Main Street, 01103
Telephone: 413-781-1920
Telecopier: 413-733-3360

MEMBERS OF FIRM

Joseph Buell Ely (1905-1956)
Raymond T. King (1919-1971)
Frederick M. Kingsbury (1924-1968)
Hugh J. Corcoran (1938-1992)
Richard S. Milstein
Donald A. Beaudry
Richard F. Faille
Leland B. Seabury
Gregory A. Schmidt
Pamela Manson
Anthony T. Rice
Russell J. Mawdsley

ASSOCIATE

Donna M. Brown

Representative Clients: Hartford Accident & Indemnity Co.; Albert Steiger Cos.; Shawmut Bank N.A.; Springfield Institution for Savings; St. Paul Fire & Marine Insurance Co.; The Rouse Co.; Tighe & Bond, Inc.; Northeast Utilities.

For full biographical listings, see the Martindale-Hubbell Law Directory

GABERMAN & PARISH, P.C. (AV)

32 Hampden Street, 01103
Telephone: 413-781-5066
Fax: 413-732-5439

Richard M. Gaberman
Ronda G. Parish

Richard D. Keough

(See Next Column)

GABERMAN & PARISH P.C.—*Continued*

OF COUNSEL

Leonard Judelson

For full biographical listings, see the Martindale-Hubbell Law Directory

HENDEL, COLLINS & NEWTON, P.C. (AV)

101 State Street, 01103
Telephone: 413-734-6411
Fax: 413-734-8069

Philip J. Hendel
Joseph B. Collins
Carla W. Newton

Joseph H. Reinhardt
Henry E. Geberth, Jr.
Jonathan R. Goldsmith
George I. Roumeliotis

Representative Clients: Springfield Institution for Savings; Shawmut Bank, N.A.; United Cooperative Bank.
Approved Attorneys for: First American Title Insurance Co.; Commonwealth Land Title Ins. Co.
Reference: Shawmut Bank, N.A.

For full biographical listings, see the Martindale-Hubbell Law Directory

SUDBURY, Middlesex Co.

COURNOYER & ASSOCIATES, P.C. (AV)

321 Boston Post Road, 01776
Telephone: 508-443-5599; 800-696-0517
Facsimile: 508-443-9499

Gerald S. Cournoyer, Jr.

Melinda M. Berman
Robin B. Plunkett

For full biographical listings, see the Martindale-Hubbell Law Directory

WESTBOROUGH, Worcester Co.

GREENWALD, GREENWALD & POWERS (AV)

33 Lyman Street, 01581-1404
Telephone: 508-366-6094
Fax: 508-366-6159
Milford, Massachusetts Office: 409 Fortune Boulevard, Granite Park.
Telephone: 508-478-8611.
Fax: 508-634-3959; 478-5937.

Alan Greenwald
Sarah Orlov
Steven A. Greenwald
Stephen A. Gould
John D. Powers
Patricia J. Flynn
Jacqueline Nastro Hathaway
Stefani Jill Saitow
Sean W. Melville

For full biographical listings, see the Martindale-Hubbell Law Directory

MICHIGAN

*ADRIAN,** Lenawee Co.

WALKER, WATTS, JACKSON & MCFARLAND (AV)

160 North Winter Street, 49221
Telephone: 517-265-8138
Fax: 517-265-8286

MEMBERS OF FIRM

William H. Walker
Mark A. Jackson
Prosser M. Watts, Jr.
Michael McFarland

Attorneys for: Adrian State Bank; Bank of Lenawee; Consumers Power Co.; Norfolk & Western Railway Co.; Citizens Gas Fuel Co.; Auto Owners Insurance Co.; Amerisure Co.; Citizens Mutual Liability; State Farm Mutual Insurance Co.; Tower Insurance Co.; Blissfield Manufacturing Co.

For full biographical listings, see the Martindale-Hubbell Law Directory

*ANN ARBOR,** Washtenaw Co.

BODMAN, LONGLEY & DAHLING (AV)

110 Miller, Suite 300, 48104
Telephone: 313-761-3780
Fax: 313-930-2494
Detroit, Michigan Office: 34th Floor, 100 Renaissance Center.
Telephone: 313-259-7777.
Troy, Michigan Office: Suite 2020, 755 West Big Beaver Road.
Telephone: 810-362-2110.
Northern Michigan Office: 229 Court Street, P.O. Box 405, Cheboygan.
Telephone: 616-627-4351.

(See Next Column)

RESIDENT PARTNERS

Mark W. Griffin
Harvey W. Berman
Thomas A. Roach
Jerold Lax
Randolph S. Perry
Susan M. Kornfield

RESIDENT COUNSEL

John S. Dobson
Patricia D. White

RESIDENT ASSOCIATES

Sandra L. Sorini
Stephen K. Postema
Lydia Pallas Loren

For full biographical listings, see the Martindale-Hubbell Law Directory

CONLIN, MCKENNEY & PHILBRICK, P.C. (AV)

700 City Center Building, 48104-1994
Telephone: 313-761-9000
Fax: 313-761-9001

Edward F. Conlin (1902-1953)
Robert M. Brimacombe
John W. Conlin (1904-1972)
David S. Swartz
Albert J. Parker (1901-1970)
James A. Schriemer
Chris L. McKenney
Elizabeth M. Petoskey
Karl R. Frankena
Bradley J. MeLampy
Allen J. Philbrick
Joseph W. Phillips
Phillip J. Bowen
William M. Sweet
Richard E. Conlin
Lori A. Buiteweg
Michael D. Highfield
Douglas G. McClure
Bruce N. Elliott
Thomas B. Bourque
Neil J. Juliar
Marjorie M. Dixon
Bonnie H. Keen

OF COUNSEL

John W. Conlin

Representative Clients: Fingerle Lumber Co.; Ann Arbor Area Board of Realtors; Borders, Inc.; Society Bank, Michigan; Auto-Owners Insurance Co.; Wolverine Title Co.
Approved Attorneys for: American Title Insurance Co.; Ticor Title Insurance Co.

For full biographical listings, see the Martindale-Hubbell Law Directory

HOOPER, HATHAWAY, PRICE, BEUCHE & WALLACE (AV)

126 South Main Street, 48104
Telephone: 313-662-4426
Fax: 313-662-9559

Joseph C. Hooper (1899-1980)
Gregory A. Spaly
Alan E. Price
Robert W. Southard
James R. Beuche
William J. Stapleton
Bruce T. Wallace
Bruce C. Conybeare, Jr.
Charles W. Borgsdorf
Anthony P. Patti
Mark R. Daane
Marcia J. Major

OF COUNSEL

James A. Evashevski
Roderick K. Daane

Representative Clients: Chem-Trend, Inc.; Dundee Cement Co.; Ervin Industries, Inc.; First Martin Corp.; Group 243 Design, Inc.; Honeywell; Microwave Sensors, Inc.; Shearson Lehman Hutton; O'Neal Construction Co.; Pittsfield Products, Inc.

For Complete List of Firm Personnel, See General Section

For full biographical listings, see the Martindale-Hubbell Law Directory

MILLER, CANFIELD, PADDOCK AND STONE, P.L.C. (AV)

A Professional Limited Liability Company
Founded in 1852 by Sidney Davy Miller
101 North Main Street, Seventh Floor, 48104-1400
Telephone: 313-663-2445
Fax: 313-747-7147
Detroit, Michigan Office: 150 West Jefferson, Suite 2500, 48226-4415.
Telephone: 313-963-6420.
Fax: 313-496-7500.
Cable Address: "Stem Detroit."
Bloomfield Hills, Michigan Office: Suite 100, Pinehurst Office Center, 1400 North Woodward, 48303-2014.
Telephone: 313-645-5000.
Fax: 313-645-1917.
Grand Rapids, Michigan Office: 1200 Campau Square Plaza, 99 Monroe, N.W., 49503-2639.
Telephone: 616-454-8656.
Fax: 616-776-6322.
Howell, Michigan Office: 121 South Barnard Street, Suite 4, 48843-2305.
Telephone: 517-546-7600.
Telecopier: 517-546-6974.
Kalamazoo, Michigan Office: 444 West Michigan Avenue, 49007-3752.
Telephone: 616-381-7030.
Fax: 616-382-0244.
Lansing, Michigan Office: One Michigan Avenue, Suite 900, 48933-1609.
Telephone: 517-487-2070.
Fax: 517-374-6304.

(See Next Column)

MILLER, CANFIELD, PADDOCK AND STONE P.L.C., *Ann Arbor—Continued*

Monroe, Michigan Office: The Executive Centre, 214 East Elm Avenue, 48161-2682.
Telephone: 313-243-2000.
Fax: 313-243-0901.
Washington, D.C. Office: 1225 Nineteenth Street, N.W., Suite 400. 20036.
Telephone: 202-429-5575; 785-0600.
Fax: 202-331-1118; 785-1234.
Pensacola, Florida Office: 25 West Cedar, 32501.
Telephone: 904-469-1088.
Fax: 904-432-0677.
St. Petersburg, Florida Office: 100 Second Avenue S., Suite 7045, 33701.
Telephone: 813-982-6000.
Fax: 813-892-6002.
Gdansk, Poland Office: Suite 322, Dom Technika Building, Ul. Rajska 6, 80-850.
Telephone: 011-485-831-2808.
Fax: 011-485-831-4719.
Warsaw, Poland Office: Ul. Marszalkowska 82, Suite 561, 00-517.
Telephone: 011-482-623-6457 and 6458.
Fax: 011-482-623-6459.

RESIDENT PARTNERS

Robert E. Gilbert — Gary A. Bruder

Representative Firm Clients: Chrysler Corp.; Comerica, Inc.; City of Detroit, Mich.; Detroit Tigers, Inc.; First of Michigan; Fretter, Inc.; Ford Motor Co.; Ford Motor Credit Co.; Great Lakes Bancorp; Henry Ford Hospital.

For Complete List of Firm Personnel, See General Section

For full biographical listings, see the Martindale-Hubbell Law Directory

PEAR SPERLING EGGAN & MUSKOVITZ, P.C. (AV)

Domino's Farms, 24 Frank Lloyd Wright Drive, 48105
Telephone: 313-665-4441
Fax: 313-665-8788
Ypsilanti, Michigan Offices: 5 South Washington Street.
Telephone: 313-483-3626 and 2164 Bellevue at Washtenaw.
Telephone: 313-483-7177.

Edwin L. Pear — Thomas E. Daniels
Andrew M. Eggan — Joel F. Graziani
Paul R. Fransway

Counsel For: Domino's Pizza, Inc.; Victory Lane Quick Oil Change, Inc.; Bank One, Ypsilanti, N.A.; Ann Arbor Housing Commission.

For Complete List of Firm Personnel, See General Section

For full biographical listings, see the Martindale-Hubbell Law Directory

*BAY CITY,** Bay Co.

BRAUN KENDRICK FINKBEINER (AV)

201 Phoenix Building, P.O. Box 2039, 48708
Telephone: 517-895-8505
Telecopier: 517-895-8437
Saginaw, Michigan Office: 8th Floor Second National Bank Building.
Telephone: 517-753-3461.
Telecopier: 517-753-3951.

MEMBERS OF FIRM

Ralph J. Isackson — Frank M. Quinn
Patrick D. Neering — Gregory E. Meter
George F. Gronewold, Jr. — Daniel S. Opperman
Gregory T. Demers

Representative Clients: APV Chemical Machinery, Inc.; Bay Health Systems; Berger and Co.; Catholic Federal Credit Union; Charter Township of Bridgeport; City of Saginaw; City of Vassar; City of Zilwaukee; Corporate Service; Cox Cable.

For Complete List of Firm Personnel, See General Section

For full biographical listings, see the Martindale-Hubbell Law Directory

BINGHAM FARMS, Oakland Co.

MEISNER AND HODGDON, P.C. (AV)

Suite 467, 30200 Telegraph Road, 48025-4506
Telephone: 810-644-4433
Fax: 810-644-2941

Robert M. Meisner — Samuel K. Hodgdon

Reference: Comerica Bank.

For full biographical listings, see the Martindale-Hubbell Law Directory

SOTIROFF ABRAMCZYK & RAUSS, P.C. (AV)

30400 Telegraph Road, Suite 444, 48025-4541
Telephone: 810-642-6000
Facsimile: 810-642-9001

(See Next Column)

Philip Sotiroff — Lawrence A. Tower
Lawrence R. Abramczyk — Robert B. Goldi
Dennis M. Rauss — Keith A. Sotiroff
Edward S. Toth

OF COUNSEL

John N. Kaspers

For full biographical listings, see the Martindale-Hubbell Law Directory

BIRMINGHAM, Oakland Co.

LOUIS J. BURNETT, P.C. (AV)

555 South Woodward, Suite 755, 48009-6782
Telephone: 810-642-4345
Fax: 810-642-2005

Louis J. Burnett

Reference: Comerica, Detroit, Michigan.

For full biographical listings, see the Martindale-Hubbell Law Directory

CARSON FISCHER, P.L.C. (AV)

Third Floor, 300 East Maple Road, 48009-6317
Telephone: 810-644-4840
Facsimile: 810-644-1832

Robert M. Carson — William C. Edmunds
Peter L. Wanger — Todd M. Fink

For full biographical listings, see the Martindale-Hubbell Law Directory

MACDONALD AND GOREN, P.C. (AV)

Suite 200, 260 East Brown Street, 48009
Telephone: 810-645-5940
Fax: 810-645-2490

Harold C. MacDonald — David D. Marsh
Kalman G. Goren — Glenn G. Ross
Cindy Rhodes Victor — Miriam Blanks-Smart
Amy L. Glenn — John T. Klees

Representative Clients: Bay Corrugated Container, Inc.; Miles Fox Company; Orlandi Gear Company, Inc.; Bing Steel, Inc.; Superb Manufacturing, Inc.; Spring Engineering, Inc.; Adrian Steel Company; Southfield Radiology Associates, P.C.; Blockbuster Entertainment Corporation; E.N.U.F. Internationale, Inc.

For full biographical listings, see the Martindale-Hubbell Law Directory

SIMPSON & BERRY, P.C. (AV)

260 East Brown, Suite 300, 48009
Telephone: 810-647-0200
Telecopier: 810-647-2776

Daniel F. Berry — Philip J. Goodman
Clark G. Doughty — James A. Simpson
Katheryne L. Zelenock

LEGAL SUPPORT PERSONNEL

Dwight Noble Baker, Jr.

Representative Clients: Anthony S. Brown Development Co., Inc.; Automation Services Equipment, Inc.; Brown Tire Co.; Chenoweth Construction Co.; Detroit Public Schools; Hall Financial Group; Trizec Properties, Inc.; Premier Construction Company; Dart Properties.

For full biographical listings, see the Martindale-Hubbell Law Directory

WILLIAMS, SCHAEFER, RUBY & WILLIAMS, PROFESSIONAL CORPORATION (AV)

Suite 300, 380 North Woodward Avenue, 48009
Telephone: 810-642-0333
Telecopy: 810-642-0856

James A. Williams — Richard D. Rattner
Edward L. Ruby — William E. Hosler, III

Representative Clients: Amoco Oil Company; Beachum & Roeser Development Corporation; Biltmore Properties; Frankel Development Company; Jonna Construction Corporation; Lawyers Title Insurance Corp.; Michigan National Bank; Morgan-Mitsubishi Development Corporation; Sunderland Development Corporation; Western Development Company.

For full biographical listings, see the Martindale-Hubbell Law Directory

BLOOMFIELD HILLS, Oakland Co.

JON H. BERKEY, P.C. (AV)

1760 South Telegraph Road, Suite 300, 48302-0183
Telephone: 810-332-2100

Jon H. Berkey

Anthony A. Yezbick

For full biographical listings, see the Martindale-Hubbell Law Directory

Bloomfield Hills—Continued

CLARK, KLEIN & BEAUMONT (AV)

1533 North Woodward Avenue, Suite 220, 48304
Telephone: 810-258-2900
Facsmile: 810-258-2949
Detroit, Michigan Office: 1600 First Federal Building. 1001 Woodward Avenue.
Telephone: 313-965-8300.
Facsimile: 313-962-4348.

MEMBERS OF FIRM

Michael D. Mulcahy — Edward C. Dawda

ASSOCIATE

Todd A. Schafer

Representative Clients: Home Depot, Inc.; The Rouse Company; Metropolitan Life Insurance Company; The Prudential Insurance Company of America; The Provident Companies; Wal-Mart Stores, Inc.; Aegon Realty Investors; J.E. Robert Company; Trammell Crow Company and CB Commercial Inc.

For Complete List of Firm Personnel, See General Section

For full biographical listings, see the Martindale-Hubbell Law Directory

HOWARD & HOWARD ATTORNEYS, P.C. (AV)

The Pinehurst Office Center, Suite 101, 1400 North Woodward Avenue, 48304-2856
Telephone: 810-645-1483
Telecopier: 810-645-1568
Kalamazoo, Michigan Office: The Kalamazoo Building, Suite 400, 107 West Michigan Avenue.
Telephone: 616-382-1483.
Telecopier: 616-382-1568.
Lansing, Michigan Office: The Phoenix Building, Suite 500, 222 Washington Square, North.
Telephone: 517-485-1483.
Telecopier: 517-485-1568.
Peoria, Illinois Office: Howard & Howard, P.C., The Creve Coeur Building, Suite 200, 321 Liberty Street.
Telephone: 309-672-1483.
Telecopier: 309-672-1568.

Robert L. Biederman — Paul Green

Representative Clients: For Representative Client list, see General Practice, Bloomfield Hills, MI.

For Complete List of Firm Personnel, See General Section

For full biographical listings, see the Martindale-Hubbell Law Directory

MAY, SIMPSON & STROTE, A PROFESSIONAL CORPORATION (AV)

100 West Long Lake Road Suite 200, P.O. Box 541, 48303-0541
Telephone: 810-646-9500

Richard H. May — Steven M. Raymond
Thomas C. Simpson — John A. Forrest
Ronald P. Strote — David K. McDonnell

Steven F. Alexsy — Marilynn K. Arnold
Michele A. Lerner

Representative Clients: Aamco Transmission; American Annuity Life Insurance; Container Corporation of America; Citicorp Financial Center; Century 21 Real Estate Corp.; First American Title; Financial Guardian Insurance; NBD Bank, N.A.; Oak Hills Mortgage Corp.; Ziebart International Corp.

For full biographical listings, see the Martindale-Hubbell Law Directory

MEYER, KIRK, SNYDER & SAFFORD (AV)

Suite 100, 100 West Long Lake Road, 48304
Telephone: 810-647-5111
Telecopier: 810-647-6079
Detroit, Michigan Office: 2500 Penobscot Building.
Telephone: 313-961-1261.

George H. Meyer — Ralph R. Safford
John M. Kirk — Donald H. Baker, Jr.
George E. Snyder — Patrick K. Rode

ASSOCIATES

Christopher F. Clark — Boyd C. Farnam
Debra S. Meier

OF COUNSEL

Mark R. Solomon

Representative Clients: Chemical Waste Management; Ervin Advertising; The Michigan and S.E. Michigan McDonald's Operators Assn.; The Southland Corp. (7-Eleven Food Stores); Stauffer Chemical Co.; Techpoint, Inc.

For full biographical listings, see the Martindale-Hubbell Law Directory

STROBL AND MANOOGIAN, P.C. (AV)

300 East Long Lake Road, Suite 200, 48304-2376
Telephone: 810-645-0306
Facsimile: 810-645-2690

Thomas J. Strobl — Brian C. Manoogian
John Sharp

James T. Dunn

Representative Clients: Comerica Bank; Masco Corporation; Midwest Guaranty Bank.

For Complete List of Firm Personnel, See General Section

For full biographical listings, see the Martindale-Hubbell Law Directory

---

*DETROIT,** Wayne Co.

ABBOTT, NICHOLSON, QUILTER, ESSHAKI & YOUNGBLOOD, P.C. (AV)

19th Floor, One Woodward Avenue, 48226
Telephone: 313-963-2500
Telecopier: 313-963-7882

C. Richard Abbott — James B. Perry
John R. Nicholson — Carl F. Jarboe
Thomas R. Quilter III — Jay A. Kennedy
Gene J. Esshaki — Timothy A. Stoepker
John F. Youngblood — Timothy J. Kramer
Donald E. Conley — Norbert T. Madison, Jr.
William D. Gilbride, Jr.

Mary P. Nelson — Anne D. Warren Bagno
Michael R. Blum — Mark E. Mueller
Thomas Ferguson Hatch — Eric J. Girdler

OF COUNSEL

Thomas C. Shumaker — Roy R. Hunsinger

For full biographical listings, see the Martindale-Hubbell Law Directory

BARRIS, SOTT, DENN & DRIKER, P.L.L.C. (AV)

211 West Fort Street, Fifteenth Floor, 48226-3281
Telephone: 313-965-9725
Telecopier: 313-965-2493
313-965-5398

MEMBERS OF FIRM

Donald E. Barris — Robert E. Kass
Herbert Sott — Daniel M. Share
David L. Denn — Elaine Fieldman
Eugene Driker — Morley Witus
William G. Barris — John A. Libby
Sharon M. Woods — James S. Fontichiaro
Stephen E. Glazek — Daniel J. LaCombe

COUNSEL

Leon S. Cohan

OF COUNSEL

Stanley M. Weingarden — Robert E. Epstein

ASSOCIATES

Dennis M. Barnes — Thomas F. Cavalier
Gary Schwarcz — Bonita R. Gardner
Matthew J. Boettcher — C. David Bargamian
Barry R. Powers — Michael J. Reynolds
John Christopher Clark

Representative Clients: Avis Rent A CarSystem, Inc.; Borman's, Inc.; Consumers Power Co.; County of Wayne, Michigan; Ford Motor Co.; The Great Atlantic & Pacific Tea Company, Inc.; Henry Ford Health System; Michigan Consolidated Gas Co.; NBD Bank, N.A.; Textron, Inc.

For full biographical listings, see the Martindale-Hubbell Law Directory

BIERI & BERNSTEIN (AV)

400 Renaissance Center, 35th Floor, 48243
Telephone: 313-567-4200
Fax: 313-567-2705

MEMBERS OF FIRM

James C. Bieri — Melvin S. Bernstein

For full biographical listings, see the Martindale-Hubbell Law Directory

BODMAN, LONGLEY & DAHLING (AV)

34th Floor 100 Renaissance Center, 48243
Telephone: 313-259-7777
Fax: 313-393-7579
Troy, Michigan Office: Suite 2020, 755 West Big Beaver Road.
Telephone: 810-362-2110.
Ann Arbor, Michigan Office: 110 Miller, Suite 300.
Telephone: 313-761-3780.
Northern Michigan Office: 229 Court Street, P.O. Box 405, Cheboygan.
Telephone: 616-627-4351.

(See Next Column)

BODMAN, LONGLEY & DAHLING, *Detroit—Continued*

MEMBERS OF FIRM

Alfred C. Wortley, Jr.
Michael B. Lewiston
Mark W. Griffin (Ann Arbor Office)
David W. Hipp
Larry R. Shulman
Michael A. Stack (Northern Michigan Office)
Harvey W. Berman (Ann Arbor Office)

Representative Clients: Abitibi Price Group; Archdiocese of Detroit; Comerica Bank; The Detroit Lions, Inc.; Ford Estates; General Motors Corporation; Charles Stewart Mott Foundation; Norfolk Southern Corporation; Panhandle Eastern Corporation; State Farm Mutual Automobile Insurance Company.

For Complete List of Firm Personnel, See General Section

For full biographical listings, see the Martindale-Hubbell Law Directory

BUTZEL LONG, A PROFESSIONAL CORPORATION (AV)

Suite 900, 150 West Jefferson, 48226
Telephone: 313-225-7000
Telecopier: 313-225-7080
Birmingham, Michigan Office: Suite 200, 32270 Telegraph Road.
Telephone: 810-258-1616.
Telecopier: 810-258-1439.
Lansing, Michigan Office: 118 West Ottawa Street.
Telephone: 517-372-6622.
Telecopier: 517-372-6672.
Ann Arbor, Michigan Office: Suite 400, 121 West Washington.
Telephone: 313-995-3110.
Telecopier: 313-995-1777.
Grosse Pointe Farms, Michigan Office: Suite 260, 21 Kercheval.
Telephone: 313-886-5446.
Telecopier: 313-886-2114.

Stephen A. Bromberg (Birmingham)
Allan Nachman (Birmingham)
George H. Zinn, Jr.
Edward D. Gold (Birmingham)
Jack D. Shumate
Leonard F. Charla
T. Gordon Scupholm II (Birmingham)
David W. Berry (Birmingham)
Carl Rashid, Jr.
D. Stewart Green (Birmingham)
Gordon W. Didier
Peter D. Holmes
Alan S. Levine
Darlene M. Domanik
Brian P. Henry (Birmingham and Lansing)

OF COUNSEL

Erwin S. Simon

Anthony J. Saulino, Jr. (Birmingham)
Clara DeMatteis Mager
Patrick A. Karbowski (Birmingham)
Ronald E. Reynolds
Susan Klein Friedlaender (Birmingham)

Representative Clients: Capital Cities/ABC, Inc.; William Beaumont Hospital; Besser Co.; Blue Cross/Blue Shield of Michigan; Bridgestone/Firestone, Inc.; C.B.S, Inc.; Central Michigan University; Chrysler Motor Corp.; The Detroit News; Dow Chemical Co.

For Complete List of Firm Personnel, See General Section

For full biographical listings, see the Martindale-Hubbell Law Directory

CLARK, KLEIN & BEAUMONT (AV)

1600 First Federal Building, 1001 Woodward Avenue, 48226
Telephone: 313-965-8300
Facsimile: 313-962-4348
Bloomfield Hills Office: 1533 North Woodward Avenue, Suite 220, 48304.
Telephone: 810-258-2900.
Facsimile: 810-258-2949.

MEMBERS OF FIRM

William B. Dunn
Michael D. Mulcahy (Resident Bloomfield Hills, Michigan Office)
Edward C. Dawda (Resident Bloomfield Hills, Michigan Office)
Timothy M. Koltun

ASSOCIATES

Judith Greenstone Miller
David A. Foster
Todd A. Schafer (Resident, Bloomfield Hills, Michigan Office)

Representative Clients: Home Depot, Inc.; The Rouse Company; Metropolitan Life Insurance Company; The Prudential Insurance Company of America; The Provident Companies; Wal-Mart Stores, Inc.; Aegon Realty Investors; J.E. Robert Company; Trammell Crow Company and CB Commercial Inc.

For Complete List of Firm Personnel, See General Section

For full biographical listings, see the Martindale-Hubbell Law Directory

DICKINSON, WRIGHT, MOON, VAN DUSEN & FREEMAN (AV)

500 Woodward Avenue, Suite 4000, 48226-3425
Telephone: 313-223-3500
Facsimile: 313-223-3598
Bloomfield Hills, Michigan Office: 525 North Woodward Avenue, Suite 2000.
Telephone: 810-433-7200.
Facsimile: 810-433-7274.
Grand Rapids, Michigan Office: 200 Ottawa Avenue, N.W., Suite 900.
Telephone: 616-458-1300.
Facsimile: 616-458-6753.
Lansing, Michigan Office: Suite 200, 215 South Washington Square.
Telephone: 517-371-1730.
Facsimile: 517-487-4700.
Washington, D.C. Office: Suite 800, 1901 L Street, N.W.
Telephone: 202-457-0160.
Facsimile: 202-659-1559.
Chicago, Illinois Office: 225 West Washington, Suite 400.
Telephone: 312-220-0300.
Facsimile: 312-220-0021.
Warsaw, Poland Office: 46 Wilcza Street, 4th Floor, 00-679.
Telephone: (48-22) 299-241.
Facsimile: (48-2) 628-4107. Komertel Satellite Phone: (48-39) 121-510.

MEMBERS OF FIRM

Russell A. McNair, Jr.
James N. Candler, Jr.
C. Beth DunCombe
James M. Tervo (Chicago, Illinois Office)
William T. Burgess
Danna Marie Kozerski

ASSOCIATE

Diane G. Schwartz

Representative Clients: Federal-Mogul Corp.; Florists' Transworld Delivery Assn.; GMF Robotics Corp.; Kmart Corp.; Kuhlman Corp.; Michigan Consolidated Gas Co.; NBD Bank, N.A.

For Complete List of Firm Personnel, See General Section

For full biographical listings, see the Martindale-Hubbell Law Directory

DYKEMA GOSSETT (AV)

400 Renaissance Center, 48243-1668
Telephone: 313-568-6800
Cable Address: "Dyke-Detroit"
Telex: 23-0121
Fax: 313-568-6594
Ann Arbor, Michigan Office: 315 East Eisenhower Parkway, Suite 100, 48108-3306.
Telephone: 313-747-7660.
Fax: 313-747-7696.
Bloomfield Hills, Michigan Office: 1577 North Woodward Avenue, Suite 300, 48304-2820.
Telephone: 810-540-0700.
Fax: 810-540-0763.
Grand Rapids, Michigan Office: 200 Oldtown Riverfront Building, 248 Louis Campau Promenade, N.W., 49503-2668.
Telephone: 616-776-7500.
Fax: 616-776-7573.
Lansing, Michigan Office: 800 Michigan National Tower, 48933-1707.
Telephone: 517-374-9100.
Fax: 517-374-9191.
Washington, D.C. Office: Franklin Square, Suite 300 West Tower, 1300 I Street, N.W., 20005-3306.
Telephone: 202-522-8600.
Fax: 202-522-8669.
Chicago, Illinois Office: Three First National Plaza, Suite 1400, 70 W. Madison, 60602-4270.
Telephone: 312-214-3380.
Fax: 312-214-3441.

MEMBERS OF FIRM

David E. Doran (Resident at Grand Rapids Office)
Fred J. Fechheimer (Resident at Bloomfield Hills Office)
Dennis M. Gannan (Resident at Bloomfield Hills Office)
Alan M. Greene (Resident at Bloomfield Hills Office)
Michael A. Lesha
Sandra Lea Meyer
William T. Myers (Resident at Bloomfield Hills Office)
Robert L. Nelson (Resident at Grand Rapids Office)
Brian J. Page (Resident at Grand Rapids Office)
Cameron H. Piggott
Richard E. Rabbideau
Wilfred A. Steiner, Jr.

OF COUNSEL

Mary Steck Kershner

RETIRED PARTNER

James W. Draper

ASSOCIATES

Daniel J. Brondyk (Resident at Grand Rapids Office)
Sean M. Carty
Susan Allene Kovach
Howard N. Luckoff (Resident at Bloomfield Hills Office)
Catherine Kim Shierk (Resident at Bloomfield Hills Office)

For Complete List of Firm Personnel, See General Section

For full biographical listings, see the Martindale-Hubbell Law Directory

Detroit—Continued

FILDEW, HINKS, MILLER, TODD & WANGEN (AV)

3600 Penobscot Building, 48226-4291
Telephone: 313-961-9700
Telecopier: 313-961-0754

MEMBERS OF FIRM

Stanley L. Fildew (1896-1978)
Frank T. Hinks (1887-1974)
Richard E. Hinks (1916-1990)
John H. Fildew
Alan C. Miller
Charles D. Todd III
Randall S. Wangen
Mary Jane Ruffley
Robert D. Welchli
William P. Thorpe
Colleen A. Kramer
Stephen J. Pokoj

ASSOCIATES

Charles S. Kennedy, III
Gerald M. Swiacki

References: First of America Bank-Detroit, N.A.; Comerica Bank-Detroit; National Bank of Detroit.

For full biographical listings, see the Martindale-Hubbell Law Directory

FOSTER, MEADOWS & BALLARD, P.C. (AV)

3200 Penobscot Building, 48226
Telephone: 313-961-3234
Cable Address: "Foster"
Telex: 23-5823
Facsimile: 313-961-6184

Sparkman D. Foster (1897-1967)
John L. Foster
Charles R. Hrdlicka
Paul D. Galea
Richard A. Dietz
Robert H. Fortunate
Robert G. Lahiff
Camille A. Raffa-Dietz

Michael J. Liddane
Paul A. Kettunen

OF COUNSEL

John F. Langs
John A. Mundell, Jr.

Counsel for: Air Canada; Canadian National Railways; Grand Trunk Western Railroad; Alexander and Alexander; Shand Morahan; Utica Mutual.
Admiralty Counsel for: Ford Motor; Bob Lo Co.

For full biographical listings, see the Martindale-Hubbell Law Directory

HAISCH & BOYDA (AV)

100 Renaissance Center, Suite 1750, 48243
Telephone: 313-259-4370
Facsimile: 313-259-6487

Anthony A. Haisch
John M. Boyda

ASSOCIATE

Donald C. Wheaton, Jr.

Representative Clients: AT&T Corp.; AT&T Universal Card Services Corp.; Amoco Corp.; North American Philips Corp.; Empire Blue Cross & Blue Shield; Lyon Financial Services, Inc.; Schwans' Sales Enterprises; Marshalls, Inc.; Access America Inc.; Grant Industries, Inc.

For full biographical listings, see the Martindale-Hubbell Law Directory

HONIGMAN MILLER SCHWARTZ AND COHN (AV)

A Partnership including Professional Corporations
2290 First National Building, 48226
Telephone: 313-256-7800
Telecopier: 313-962-0176
Telex: 235705
Lansing, Michigan Office: Phoenix Building, 222 North Washington Square, Suite 400.
Telephone: 517-484-8282.
West Palm Beach, Florida Office: Suite 800 Esperante Building, 222 Lakeview Avenue.
Telephone: 407-838-4500.
Tampa, Florida Office: 2700 Landmark Centre, 401 E. Jackson Street.
Telephone: 813-221-6600.
Orlando, Florida Office: 390 North Orange Avenue, Suite 1300.
Telephone: 407-648-0300.
Houston, Texas Office: 3100 First Interstate Bank Plaza, 1000 Louisiana.
Telephone: 713-650-2600.
Los Angeles, California Office: McNeill Plaza, Suite 820, 15260 Ventura Boulevard, 91403.
Telephone: 818-784-2900.

MEMBERS OF FIRM

Joel S. Adelman
John E. Amerman
Elizabeth A. Baergen
C. Leslie Banas
Thomas J. Beale
Maurice S. Binkow
Jonathan R. Borenstein
Richard J. Burstein
Therese Byrnes
Gregory J. DeMars
Frederick J. Frank
H. Alan Gocha
Margaret E. Greene
Carl W. Herstein
Alan M. Hurvitz
Norman Hyman
Edward F. Kickham
Kevin M. Kohls
Jeffrey R. Kravitz
Denise J. Lewis

(See Next Column)

MEMBERS OF FIRM (Continued)

Lawrence D. McLaughlin
Mitchell R. Meisner
Nancy M. Omichinski
J. Adam Rothstein
Phyllis G. Rozof
Roberta R. Russ
Jerome M. Salle
Laurence J. Schiff
Edward R. Schonberg
Michael B. Shapiro
Randall P. Whately
William C. Whitbeck (Lansing, Michigan Office)
Sheldon P. Winkelman
William J. Zousmer

ASSOCIATES

Daniel M. Halprin
Samina R. Hurst

OF COUNSEL

Milton J. Miller
Rodman N. Myers
Jason L. Honigman (1904-1990)
Irwin I. Cohn (1896-1984)

RESIDENT IN WEST PALM BEACH, FLORIDA OFFICE

MEMBERS

Carl Angeloff (P.A.)
Steven R. Parson (P.A.)
Neil W. Platock
Donald H. Reed, Jr.
Marvin S. Rosen (P.A.)

RESIDENT IN TAMPA, FLORIDA OFFICE

MEMBERS

Maria Maistrellis
James B. Soble (P.A.)

RESIDENT IN ORLANDO, FLORIDA OFFICE

MEMBERS

Wendy Anderson (P.A.)
J. Lindsay Builder, Jr., (P.A.)
Donald J. Curotto (P.A.)
Michael J. Grindstaff (P.A.)
Michael J. Sullivan (P.A.)

ASSOCIATES

Suzanne M. Amaducci
Orlando J. Evora

General Counsel for: Arbor Drugs Inc.; The Detroit Free Press; The Detroit Medical Center; Handleman Co.; PHM Corporation (Pulte Home Corp.); William C. Roney & Co.
Local or Special Counsel for: American Society of Composers, Authors and Publishers (ASCAP); AutoAlliance International Inc. (formerly Mazda Motor Manufacturing (USA) Corporation); NBD Bank, N.A.; The Taubman Company, Inc.

For Complete List of Firm Personnel, See General Section

For full biographical listings, see the Martindale-Hubbell Law Directory

HOUGHTON, POTTER, SWEENEY & BRENNER, A PROFESSIONAL CORPORATION (AV)

The Guardian Building, 500 Griswold Street, Suite 3300, 48226-3806
Telephone: 313-964-0050
Facsimile: 313-964-4005

Thomas F. Sweeney
Robert R. Maxwell

LEGAL SUPPORT PERSONNEL

LEGAL ASSISTANTS

Ann E. Adams
Janet C. Driver

For full biographical listings, see the Martindale-Hubbell Law Directory

JAFFE, RAITT, HEUER & WEISS, PROFESSIONAL CORPORATION (AV)

One Woodward Avenue, Suite 2400, 48226
Telephone: 313-961-8380
Telecopier: 313-961-8358
Cable Address: "Jafsni"
Southfield,Michigan Office: Travelers Tower, Suite 1520.
Telephone: 313-961-8380.
Monroe, Michigan Office: 212 East Front Street, Suite 3.
Telephone: 313-241-6470.
Telefacsimile: 313-241-3849.

Gail A. Anderson
Robert S. Bolton
Penny L. Carolan
Jeffrey L. Forman
Joel S. Golden
Blair B. Hysni
Ira J. Jaffe
Robin H. Krueger
Mark P. Krysinski
Joel J. Morris
Cecil G. Raitt
Mark D. Rubenfire
Lawrence R. Shoffner
Arthur A. Weiss
Richard A. Zussman

Lesley A. Gaber
Gerald F. Reinhart
Jeffrey M. Weiss

OF COUNSEL

Nathan L. Milstein

See General Practice Section of List of Representative Clients.

For Complete List of Firm Personnel, See General Section

For full biographical listings, see the Martindale-Hubbell Law Directory

Detroit—Continued

KERR, RUSSELL AND WEBER (AV)

One Detroit Center, 500 Woodward Avenue, Suite 2500, 48226-3406
Telephone: 313-961-0200
Telecopier: 313-961-0388
Bloomfield Hills, Michigan Office: 3883 Telegraph Road.
Telephone: 810-649-5990.
East Lansing, Michigan Office: 1301 North Hagadorn Road.
Telephone: 517-336-6767.

Richard D. Weber
Robert Royal Nix, II
Michael B. Lewis
Curtis J. DeRoo
Michael D. Gibson
James R. Case
George J. Christopoulos
Kurt R. Vilders
James R. Cambridge
Mark M. Cunningham
Mark J. Stasa
David E. Sims
Dennis A. Martin
Richard C. Buslepp
Eric I. Lark
James E. DeLine
Daniel J. Schulte
John D. Gatti

For Complete List of Firm Personnel, See General Section

For full biographical listings, see the Martindale-Hubbell Law Directory

LEWIS, WHITE & CLAY, A PROFESSIONAL CORPORATION (AV)

1300 First National Building, 660 Woodward Avenue, 48226-3531
Telephone: 313-961-2550
Washington, D.C. Office: 1250 Connecticut Avenue, N.W., Suite 630, 20036.
Telephone: 202-835-0616.
Fax: 202-833-3316.

David Baker Lewis
Richard Thomas White
Eric Lee Clay
Reuben A. Munday
Ulysses Whittaker Boykin
S. Allen Early, III
Carl F. Stafford
Helen Francine Strong
Derrick P. Mayes
Frank E. Barbee
Camille Stearns Miller
Melvin J. Hollowell, Jr.
Michael T. Raymond
Jacqueline H. Sellers
Thomas R. Paxton
Kathleen Miles (Resident, Washington, D.C. Office)
David N. Zacks

Karen Kendrick Brown (Resident, Washington, D.C. Office)
J. Taylor Teasdale
Wade Harper McCree
Tyrone A. Powell
Blair A. Person
Susan D. Hoffman
Stephon E. Johnson
John J. Walsh
Andrea L. Powell
Teresa N. Gueyser
Hans J. Massaquoi, Jr.
Werten F. W. Bellamy, Jr. (Resident, Washington, D.C. Office)
Akin O. Akindele
Regina P. Freelon-Solomon
Calita L. Elston
Nancy C. Borland
Terrence Randall Haugabook
Lynn R. Westfall
Lance W. Mason

OF COUNSEL

Otis M. Smith (1922-1994)
Inez Smith Reid (Resident, Washington, D.C. Office)

Representative Clients: Omnicare Health Plan; Aetna Life & Casualty Co.; Chrysler Motors Corp.; Chrysler Financial Corp.; MCI Communications Corp.; City of Detroit; City of Detroit Building Authority; City of Detroit Downtown Development Authority; Consolidated Rail Corp. (Conrail); Equitable Life Assurance Society of the United States.

For full biographical listings, see the Martindale-Hubbell Law Directory

MAGER, MERCER, SCOTT & ALBER, P.C. (AV)

2400 First National Building, 48226
Telephone: 313-965-1700
Facsimile: 313-965-3690
Macomb County Office: 18285 Ten Mile Road, Suite 100, Roseville, Michigan.
Telephone: 810-771-1100.

George J. Mager, Jr.
Phillip G. Alber
Lawrence M. Scott (Resident at Roseville Office)
George D. Mercer
Raymond C. McVeigh
Michael R. Alberty
Bruce H. Hoffman
Jeffrey M. Frank
Michael A. Schwartz

Representative Clients: ABB Flakt, Inc.; American States Insurance Co.; CEI Industries; Central Venture Corp.; CIGNA; Construction Management, Inc.

For full biographical listings, see the Martindale-Hubbell Law Directory

MILLER, CANFIELD, PADDOCK AND STONE, P.L.C. (AV)

A Professional Limited Liability Company
Founded in 1852 by Sidney Davy Miller
150 West Jefferson, Suite 2500, 48226-4415
Telephone: 313-963-6420
Fax: 313-496-7500
Cable Address: "Stem Detroit"
Detroit, Michigan Office: 150 West Jefferson, Suite 2500, 48226-4415.
Telephone: 313-963-6420.
Fax: 313-496-7500.
Cable Address: "Stem Detroit."
Ann Arbor, Michigan Office: 101 North Main Street, 7th Floor, 48104-1400.
Telephone: 313-663-2445.
Fax: 313-747-7147.
Bloomfield Hills, Michigan Office: Suite 100, Pinehurst Office Center, 1400 North Woodward, 48303-2014.
Telephone: 313-645-5000.
Fax: 313-645-1917.
Grand Rapids, Michigan Office: 1200 Campau Square Plaza, 99 Monroe, N.W., 49503-2639.
Telephone: 616-454-8656.
Fax: 616-776-6322.
Howell, Michigan Office: 121 South Barnard Street, Suite 4, 48843-2305.
Telephone: 517-546-7600.
Telecopier: 517-546-6974.
Kalamazoo, Michigan Office: 444 West Michigan Avenue, 49007-3752.
Telephone: 616-381-7030.
Fax: 616-382-0244.
Lansing, Michigan Office: One Michigan Avenue, Suite 900, 48933-1609.
Telephone: 517-487-2070.
Fax: 517-374-6304.
Monroe, Michigan Office: The Executive Centre, 214 East Elm Avenue, 48161-2682.
Telephone: 313-243-2000.
Fax: 313-243-0901.
Washington, D.C. Office: 1225 Nineteenth Street, N.W., Suite 400. 20036.
Telephone: 202-429-5575; 785-0600.
Fax: 202-331-1118; 785-1234.
Pensacola, Florida Office: 25 West Cedar, 32501.
Telephone: 904-469-1088.
Fax: 904-432-0677.
St. Petersburg, Florida Office: 100 Second Avenue S., Suite 7045, 33701.
Telephone: 813-982-6000.
Fax: 813-892-6002.
Gdansk, Poland Office: Suite 322, Dom Technika Building, UI. Rajska 6, 80-850.
Telephone: 011-485-831-2808.
Fax: 011-485-831-4719.
Warsaw, Poland Office: UI. Marszalkowska 82, Suite 561, 00-517.
Telephone: 011-482-623-6457 and 6458.
Fax: 011-482-623-6459.

MEMBERS OF FIRM

Allen Schwartz
Robert E. Gilbert (Ann Arbor Office)
Mark E. Schlussel
Stephen G. Palms
Frank L. Andrews (Detroit and Bloomfield Hills Offices)
Gary A. Bruder (Ann Arbor Office)
Michael A. Limauro

OF COUNSEL

Anne H. Hiemstra

SENIOR ATTORNEY

David J. Hasper (Grand Rapids Office)

ASSOCIATES

Ilana A. Stein Ben-Ze'ev
L. Jeffrey Zauberman

Representative Firm Clients: Chrysler Corp.; Comerica, Inc.; City of Detroit, Mich.; Detroit Tigers, Inc.; First of Michigan; Fretter, Inc.; Ford Motor Co.; Ford Motor Credit Co.; Great Lakes Bancorp; Henry Ford Hospital.

For Complete List of Firm Personnel, See General Section

For full biographical listings, see the Martindale-Hubbell Law Directory

SHAHEEN, JACOBS & ROSS, P.C. (AV)

585 East Larned, Suite 200, 48226-4316
Telephone: 313-963-1301
Telecopier: 313-963-7123

Joseph Shaheen (1920-1984)
Michael A. Jacobs (1949-1992)
Steven P. Ross
Michael J. Thomas
Leslie Kujawski Carr
Margaret Conti Schmidt

OF COUNSEL

Mark A. Armitage, P.C.

For full biographical listings, see the Martindale-Hubbell Law Directory

TIMMIS & INMAN (AV)

300 Talon Centre, 48207
Telephone: 313-396-4200
Telecopier: 313-396-4228

(See Next Column)

TIMMIS & INMAN—*Continued*

MEMBERS OF FIRM

Michael T. Timmis
Wayne C. Inman
Charles W. Royer
Henry J. Brennan, III
Richard M. Miettinen
Lisa R. Gorman

ASSOCIATES

Bradley J. Knickerbocker
Kevin S. Kendall
John P. Kanan

Representative Clients: Talon, Inc.; Talon Development Associates, Inc.; F & M Distributors, Inc.; Franks Nursery & Crafts; Chateau Estates and/or CP Limited Partnership.

For Complete List of Firm Personnel, See General Section

For full biographical listings, see the Martindale-Hubbell Law Directory

EAST LANSING, Ingham Co.

FARHAT, STORY & KRAUS, P.C. (AV)

Beacon Place, 4572 South Hagadorn Road, Suite 3, 48823
Telephone: 517-351-3700
Fax: 517-332-4122

Leo A. Farhat
James E. Burns (1925-1979)
Monte R. Story
Richard C. Kraus
Max R. Hoffman Jr.
Chris A. Bergstrom
Kitty L. Groh
Charles R. Toy
David M. Platt

Lawrence P. Schweitzer
Jeffrey J. Short
Kathy A. Breedlove
Thomas L. Sparks

Representative Clients: Big L. Corp.; Michigan Automotive Wholesalers Association; Hartman-Fabco, Inc.; Lansing Electric Motors, Inc.; Mike Miller Lincoln Mercury; Edward Rose Realty, Inc.
Reference: Capitol National Bank.

For full biographical listings, see the Martindale-Hubbell Law Directory

*ESCANABA,** Delta Co.

BUTCH, QUINN, ROSEMURGY, JARDIS, BUSH, BURKHART & STROM, P.C. (AV)

816 Ludington Street, 49829
Telephone: 906-786-4422
Fax: 906-786-5128
Gladstone, Michigan Office: 201 First National Bank Building.
Telephone: 906-428-3123.
Marquette, Michigan Office: 300 South Front Street.
Telephone: 906-228-4440.
Iron Mountain, Michigan Office: 500 South Stephenson Avenue.
Telephone: 906-774-4460.
Marinette, Wisconsin Office: 2008 Ella Court.
Telephone: 715-732-4154.

Thomas L. Butch
Michael B. Quinn
Peter W. Strom
James E. Soderberg
JoJean A. Miller

Representative Clients: Upper Peninsula Association of Realtors; Coldwell Banker Pro Realty; American Dream Realty, Inc.; Century 21 Lakewood Real Estate; State Wide Real Estate Services, Inc.; Alpine Realty; American Title Insurance Co.

For Complete List of Firm Personnel, See General Section

For full biographical listings, see the Martindale-Hubbell Law Directory

FARMINGTON HILLS, Oakland Co.

HOROWITZ & GUDEMAN, P.C. (AV)

31700 Middlebelt, 48334
Telephone: 810-855-6020
Facsimile: 810-855-6025

Marvin I. Horowitz
Edward J. Gudeman

For full biographical listings, see the Martindale-Hubbell Law Directory

KAUFMAN AND PAYTON (AV)

200 Northwestern Financial Center, 30833 Northwestern Highway, 48334
Telephone: 810-626-5000
Telefacsimile: 810-626-2843
Grand Rapids, Michigan Office: 420 Trust Building.
Telephone: 616-459-4200.
Fax: 616-459-4929.
Traverse City, Michigan Office: 122 West State Street.
Telephone: 616-947-4050.
Fax: 616-947-7321.

(See Next Column)

Alan Jay Kaufman
Donald L. Payton
Kenneth C. Letherwood
Stephen R. Levine
Thomas L. Vitu
Ralph C. Chapa, Jr.
Raymond I. Foley, II
Jeffrey K. Van Hattum
Leo D. Neville

For full biographical listings, see the Martindale-Hubbell Law Directory

TILCHIN, HALL & DIEDRICH, P.C. (AV)

31731 Northwestern Highway, Suite 106, 48334
Telephone: 810-855-0995
Facsimile: 810-855-0850

Asher N. Tilchin
Steven E. Hall
Robert S. Diedrich

OF COUNSEL

Barbara Klarman
Younghea Lee

References: Comerica Bank; Lawyers Title Insurance Corp.; Philip F. Greco Title Co.

For full biographical listings, see the Martindale-Hubbell Law Directory

*FLINT,** Genesee Co.

WINEGARDEN, SHEDD, HALEY, LINDHOLM & ROBERTSON (AV)

501 Citizens Bank Building, 48502-1983
Telephone: 810-767-3600
Telecopier: 810-767-8776

MEMBERS OF FIRM

William C. Shedd
Dennis M. Haley
John T. Lindholm
Donald H. Robertson
L. David Lawson
John R. Tucker

ASSOCIATES

Alan F. Himelhoch
Suellen J. Parker
Damion Frasier
Peter T. Mooney

OF COUNSEL

Howard R. Grossman

Representative Clients: Citizens Commercial and Savings Bank; R.L. White Development Corporation; Interstate Traffic Consultants (Intracon) Inc.; Downtown Development Authority of Flint; Young Olds-Cadillac, Inc.; First American Title Insurance Co.; Sorensen Gross Construction Co.; Genesee County; Insight, Inc..; Flint Counsel, National Bank of Detroit.

For Complete List of Firm Personnel, See General Section

For full biographical listings, see the Martindale-Hubbell Law Directory

*GRAND RAPIDS,** Kent Co.

BORRE, PETERSON, FOWLER & REENS, P.C. (AV)

The Philo C. Fuller House, 44 Lafayette, N.E., P.O. Box 1767, 49501-1767
Telephone: 616-459-1971
FAX: 616-459-2393

Glen V. Borre
James B. Peterson
Ben A. Fowler
William C. Reens
Frank H. Johnson
Mark D. Sevald
William R. Vander Sluis

Reference: Old Kent Bank & Trust Co.

For Complete List of Firm Personnel, See General Section

For full biographical listings, see the Martindale-Hubbell Law Directory

CLARY, NANTZ, WOOD, HOFFIUS, RANKIN & COOPER (AV)

500 Calder Plaza, 250 Monroe Avenue, N.W., 49503-2244
Telephone: 616-459-9487
Telecopier: 616-459-5121

MEMBERS OF FIRM

Leonard M. Hoffius
Richard A. Wendt

OF COUNSEL

Richard J. Rankin, Jr.

Representative Clients: Central States Property Management, Inc.; DenUyl Investment Co.; Hutchens Co.; Investment Real Estate & Securities Corp.; John F. Gilmore Developments; Market Development Corp.; United Development Corp.

For Complete List of Firm Personnel, See General Section

For full biographical listings, see the Martindale-Hubbell Law Directory

DAY & SAWDEY, A PROFESSIONAL CORPORATION (AV)

200 Monroe Avenue, Suite 500, 49503-2217
Telephone: 616-774-8121
Telefax: 616-774-0168

(See Next Column)

DAY & SAWDEY A PROFESSIONAL CORPORATION, *Grand Rapids—Continued*

George B. Kingston (1889-1965) | James B. Frakie
John R. Porter (1915-1975) | Larry A. Ver Merris
Charles E. Day, Jr. | John Boyko, Jr.
Robert W. Sawdey | Jonathan F. Thoits
William A. Hubble | John T. Piggins
C. Mark Stoppels | Thomas A. DeMeester

John G. Grzybek | Theodore E. Czarnecki

Representative Clients: American National Bank & Trust Company of Chicago; C.M.S. - North America, Inc.; Chemical Bank; National Westminster Bank; Old Kent Bank and Trust Co.

For full biographical listings, see the Martindale-Hubbell Law Directory

MCSHANE & BOWIE (AV)

540 Old Kent Building, P.O. Box 360, 49503-2481
Telephone: 616-774-0641
Fax: 616-774-2366

MEMBERS OF FIRM

Thomas C. Shearer | Gary G. Love
David L. Smith | John R. Grant
William H. Bowie | Dan M. Challa
Keith P. Walker | John F. Shape
Terry J. Mroz | Wayne P. Bryan
Michael W. Donovan

OF COUNSEL

Jack M. Bowie

ASSOCIATES

Denise D. Twinney | Miri L. Goldman

Representative Clients: West Side Federal Savings & Loan Assn.; Hartger & Willard Mortgage Associates, Inc.

For Complete List of Firm Personnel, See General Section

For full biographical listings, see the Martindale-Hubbell Law Directory

RUSSELL & BATCHELOR (AV)

Suite 411-S Waters Building, 161 Ottawa Avenue, N.W., 49503
Telephone: 616-774-8422
Fax: 616-774-0326

MEMBERS OF FIRM

Walter J. Russell | James W. Batchelor

Representative Clients: First National Acceptance Company; Trust Corp.; Chicago Title; Cowger & Miller Mortgage Co.; Federal National Mortgage Association; Dept. of Veterans Affairs; Waterfield Mortgage Company; Chrysler First Financial; Equitable Real Estate; Eastover Savings Bank.

For full biographical listings, see the Martindale-Hubbell Law Directory

TOLLEY, VANDENBOSCH & WALTON, P.C. (AV)

5650 Foremost Drive, S.E., 49546
Telephone: 616-942-8090
Facsimile: 616-942-4677

Peter R. Tolley | Michael C. Walton
Lynwood P. VandenBosch | James B. Doezema

For full biographical listings, see the Martindale-Hubbell Law Directory

VARNUM, RIDDERING, SCHMIDT & HOWLETT (AV)

Bridgewater Place, P.O. Box 352, 49501-0352
Telephone: 616-336-6000
800-262-0011
Facsimile: 616-336-7000
Telex: 1561593 VARN
Lansing, Michigan Office: The Victor Center, Suite 810, 210 North Washington Square, 48933.
Telephone: 517-482-6237.
Facsimile: 517-482-6937.
Kalamazoo, Michigan Office: 350 East Michigan Avenue, 49007.
Telephone: 616-382-2300.
Facsimile: 616-382-2382.
Grand Haven, Michigan Office: 321 Washington Street, P.O. Box 288, 49417.
Telephone: 616-846-7100.
Facsimile: 616-846-7101.
Battle Creek, Michigan Office: 4950 West Dickman Road, Suite B-1, 49015.
Telephone: 616-962-7144.
Detroit, Michigan Office: 440 East Congress, Fourth Floor, 48226.
Telephone: 313-961-1600.
Facsimile: 313-961-1636.

(See Next Column)

MEMBERS OF FIRM

William K. Van't Hof | Mark C. Hanisch
Nyal D. Deems | Jonathan W. Anderson

Counsel for: The Homestead Resort; A.C. Geenen Construction, Inc.; United Development Co.; Federal Home Loan Mortgage Corp.; Heartwell Mortgage Corp.; Patten Corp.; Chicago Title Insurance; First Michigan Bank Corp.; Michigan National Bank; Transamerica Title Insurance.

For Complete List of Firm Personnel, See General Section

For full biographical listings, see the Martindale-Hubbell Law Directory

WARNER, NORCROSS & JUDD (AV)

900 Old Kent Building, 111 Lyon Street, N.W., 49503-2489
Telephone: 616-752-2000
Fax: 616-752-2500
Muskegon, Michigan Office: 400 Terrace Plaza, P.O. Box 900.
Telephone: 616-727-2600.
Fax: 616-727-2699.
Holland, Michigan Office: Curtis Center, Suite 300, 170 College Avenue.
Telephone: 616-396-9800.
Fax: 616-396-3656.

MEMBERS OF FIRM

Thomas R. Winquist | Jeffrey O. Birkhold
John H. Logie | John G. Cameron, Jr.
James H. Breay | Richard E. Cassard
Ernest M. Sharpe | William W. Hall
Hugh H. Makens | Sue O. Conway
Richard A. Durell | Michael H. Schubert (Resident at Muskegon Office)
Thomas H. Thornhill (Resident at Muskegon Office)

Representative Clients: Bil Mar Foods; Steelcase Inc.; Haworth, Inc.; Guardsman Products, Inc.; Kessell Foods; Old Kent Financial Corporation; The Zondervan Corporation; Kysor Industrial Corporation; Whirlpool Corporation; Foremost Corporation of America.

For Complete List of Firm Personnel, See General Section

For full biographical listings, see the Martindale-Hubbell Law Directory

WHEELER UPHAM, A PROFESSIONAL CORPORATION (AV)

Second Floor, Trust Building, 40 Pearl Street, N.W., 49503
Telephone: 616-459-7100
Fax: 616-459-6366

Gordon B. Wheeler (1904-1986) | Timothy J. Orlebeke
Buford A. Upham (Retired) | Kenneth E. Tiews
Robert H. Gillette | Jack L. Hoffman
Geoffrey L. Gillis | Janet C. Baxter
John M. Roels | Peter Kladder, III
Gary A. Maximiuk | James M. Shade
Thomas A. Kuiper

Counsel for: Travelers Insurance Co.; Prudential Insurance Co. of America; Farmers Insurance Group; Metropolitan Life Insurance Co.; Conrail Trans.; Monsanto Co.; Firestone Tire & Rubber Co.; Navistar, Inc.; Medtronic, Inc.; Westdale Better Homes and Gardens.

For full biographical listings, see the Martindale-Hubbell Law Directory

*HOWELL,** Livingston Co.

PETER B. VAN WINKLE, P.C. (AV)

105 East Grand River, 48843
Telephone: 517-546-2680

William P. Van Winkle (1858-1920) | Don W. Van Winkle (1887-1971)
Charles K. Van Winkle (Retired)
Peter B. Van Winkle

Reference: First National Bank in Howell, Howell, Mich.

For full biographical listings, see the Martindale-Hubbell Law Directory

*KALAMAZOO,** Kalamazoo Co.

DEMING, HUGHEY, LEWIS, ALLEN & CHAPMAN, P.C. (AV)

800 Old Kent Bank Building, 49007
Telephone: 616-349-6601
Fax: 616-349-3831

Ned W. Deming | Stephen M. Denenfeld
Richard M. Hughey | Thomas C. Richardson
Dean S. Lewis | Gregory G. St. Arnauld
W. Fred Allen, Jr. | Roger G. Allen (Retired)
Ross E. Chapman | Anne McGregor Fries
Winfield J. Hollander | Amy J. Glass
John A. Scott | Richard M. Hughey, Jr.
Bruce W. Martin (Resident) | Richard J. Bosch
Daniel L. Conklin | Thomas P. Lewis
William A. Redmond | Christopher T. Haenicke

(See Next Column)

DEMING, HUGHEY, LEWIS, ALLEN & CHAPMAN P.C.—*Continued*

LEGAL SUPPORT PERSONNEL

Dorothy B. Kelly

General Counsel for: The Old Kent Bank of Kalamazoo; Gilmore Brothers, Inc.; Root Spring Scraper Co.; Kalamazoo County Road Commission; Loftenberg Educational Scholarship Trust; Farm Credit Services of West Michigan; Irving S. Gilmore Foundation; National Meals on Wheels Foundation; Irving S. Gilmore International Keyboard Festival.

For full biographical listings, see the Martindale-Hubbell Law Directory

EARLY, LENNON, PETERS & CROCKER, P.C. (AV)

900 Comerica Building, 49007-4752
Telephone: 616-381-8844
Fax: 616-349-8525

James E. Beck
Lawrence M. Brenton
Blake D. Crocker
Robert M. Taylor
Patrick D. Crocker
Andrew J. Vorbrich

OF COUNSEL

Vincent T. Early

Attorneys for: General Motors Corp.; Wal-Mart Stores; Borgess Medical Center; Aetna Insurance: Kemper Group; Medical Protective Co.; Zurich Insurance; AAA; Liberty Mutual; Home Insurance.

For Complete List of Firm Personnel, See General Section

For full biographical listings, see the Martindale-Hubbell Law Directory

KREIS, ENDERLE, CALLANDER & HUDGINS, A PROFESSIONAL CORPORATION (AV)

One Moorsbridge, 49002
Telephone: 616-324-3000
Telecopier: 616-324-3010

Russell A. Kreis
Alan G. Enderle
C. Reid Hudgins III

For Complete List of Firm Personnel, See General Section

For full biographical listings, see the Martindale-Hubbell Law Directory

MILLER, CANFIELD, PADDOCK AND STONE, P.L.C. (AV)

A Professional Limited Liability Company
Founded in 1852 by Sidney Davy Miller
444 West Michigan Avenue, 49007-3752
Telephone: 616-381-7030
Fax: 616-382-0244
Detroit, Michigan Office: 150 West Jefferson, Suite 2500, 48226-4415.
Telephone: 313-963-6420.
Fax: 313-496-7500.
Cable Address: "Stem Detroit."
Ann Arbor, Michigan Office: 101 North Main Street, 7th Floor, 48104-1400.
Telephone: 313-663-2445.
Fax: 313-747-7147.
Bloomfield Hills, Michigan Office: Suite 100, Pinehurst Office Center, 1400 North Woodward, 48303-2014.
Telephone: 313-645-5000.
Fax: 313-645-1917.
Grand Rapids, Michigan Office: 1200 Campau Square Plaza, 99 Monroe, N.W., 49503-2639.
Telephone: 616-454-8656.
Fax: 616-776-6322.
Howell, Michigan Office: 121 South Barnard Street, Suite 4, 48843-2305.
Telephone: 517-546-7600.
Telecopier: 517-546-6974.
Lansing, Michigan Office: One Michigan Avenue, Suite 900, 48933-1609.
Telephone: 517-487-2070.
Fax: 517-374-6304.
Monroe, Michigan Office: The Executive Centre, 214 East Elm Avenue, 48161-2682.
Telephone: 313-243-2000.
Fax: 313-243-0901.
Washington, D.C. Office: 1225 Nineteenth Street, N.W., Suite 400. 20036.
Telephone: 202-429-5575; 785-0600.
Fax: 202-331-1118; 785-1234.
Pensacola, Florida Office: 25 West Cedar, 32501.
Telephone: 904-469-1088.
Fax: 904-432-0677.
St. Petersburg, Florida Office: 100 Second Avenue S., Suite 7045,33701.
Telephone: 813-982-6000.
Fax: 813-892-6002.
Gdansk, Poland Office: Suite 322, Dom Technika Building, UI. Rajska 6, 80-850.
Telephone: 011-485-831-2808.
Fax: 011-485-831-4719.
Warsaw, Poland Office: UI. Marszalkowska 82, Suite 561, 00-517.
Telephone: 011-482-623-6457 and 6458.
Fax: 011-482-623-6459.

(See Next Column)

MEMBER OF FIRM

Eric V. Brown, Jr. (Resident)

Representative Firm Clients: Chrysler Corp.; Comerica, Inc.; City of Detroit, Mich.; Detroit Tigers, Inc.; First of Michigan; Fretter, Inc.; Ford Motor Co.; Ford Motor Credit Co.; Great Lakes Bancorp; Henry Ford Hospital.

For Complete List of Firm Personnel, See General Section

For full biographical listings, see the Martindale-Hubbell Law Directory

LANSING, Ingham Co.

* indicates certain Bar Register subscribers whose principal office is located elsewhere in the state and who have arranged for representation as a part of the state capital listings that follow

CHURCH, KRITSELIS, WYBLE & ROBINSON, P.C. (AV)

3939 Capital City Boulevard, 48906-9962
Telephone: 517-323-4770

William N. Kritselis
J. Richard Robinson
D. Michael Dudley
James T. Heos
David S. Mittleman
Catherine Groll
James M. Hofer

For full biographical listings, see the Martindale-Hubbell Law Directory

FOSTER, SWIFT, COLLINS & SMITH, P.C. (AV)

313 South Washington Square, 48933-2193
Telephone: 517-371-8100
Telecopier: 517-371-8200
Farmington Hills, Michigan Office: 32300 Northwestern Highway, Suite 230.
Telephone: 810-851-7500.
Fax: 810-851-7504.

Thomas G. McGurrin, Jr.
Robert J. McCullen
Steven L. Owen
Brent A. Titus
Brian G. Goodenough

LEGAL SUPPORT PERSONNEL

LEGAL ASSISTANTS

Kelly A. LaGrave

General Counsel: First of America Bank - Central; Michigan Milk Producers Assn.; Story, Inc.; Edward W. Sparrow Hospital; St. Lawrence Hospital; Michigan Financial Corp.; The State Journal; Peninsular Products; Demmer Corp.

For Complete List of Firm Personnel, See General Section

For full biographical listings, see the Martindale-Hubbell Law Directory

FRASER TREBILCOCK DAVIS & FOSTER, P.C. (AV)

1000 Michigan National Tower, 48933
Telephone: 517-482-5800
Fax: 517-482-0887
Okemos, Michigan Office: 2188 Commons Parkway.
Telephone: 517-349-1300.
Fax: 517-349-0922.

Douglas J. Austin
Stephen L. Burlingame

Counsel for: Banc One Mortgage Company; Chanberg Construction Company; Delta Mills Estate Homeowners Association; Fleet Mortgage Co.; Frandorson Properties; Heron Creek Builders; Matin Commercial Properties.

For Complete List of Firm Personnel, See General Section

For full biographical listings, see the Martindale-Hubbell Law Directory

* **HONIGMAN MILLER SCHWARTZ AND COHN** (AV)

A Partnership including Professional Corporations
222 North Washington Square, Suite 400, 48933
Telephone: 517-484-8282
Telecopier: 517-484-8286
Detroit, Michigan Office: 2290 First National Building.
Telephone: 313-256-7800.
West Palm Beach, Florida Office: Suite 800 Esperante Building, 222 Lakeview Avenue.
Telephone: 407-838-4500.
Tampa, Florida Office: Suite 350 One Harbour Place, 777 South Harbour Island Boulevard.
Telephone: 813-221-6600.
Orlando, Florida Office: 390 North Orange Avenue, Suite 1300.
Telephone: 407-648-0300.
Houston, Texas Office: 3100 First Interstate Bank Plaza, 1000 Louisiana.
Telephone: 713-650-2600.
Los Angeles, California Office: McNeill Plaza, Suite 820, 15260 Ventura Boulevard, 91403.
Telephone: 818-784-2900.

(See Next Column)

HONIGMAN MILLER SCHWARTZ AND COHN, *Lansing—Continued*

MEMBERS

Gary A. Trepod William C. Whitbeck

For Complete List of Firm Personnel, See General Section

For full biographical listings, see the Martindale-Hubbell Law Directory

HOWARD & HOWARD ATTORNEYS, P.C. (AV)

The Phoenix Building, Suite 500, 222 Washington Square, North, 48933-1817
Telephone: 517-485-1483
Telecopier: 517-485-1568
Kalamazoo, Michigan Office: The Kalamazoo Building, Suite 400, 107 West Michigan Avenue.
Telephone: 616-382-1483.
Telecopier: 616-382-1568.
Bloomfield Hills, Michigan Office: The Pinehurst Office Center, Suite 101, 1400 North Woodward Avenue.
Telephone: 810-645-1483.
Telecopier: 810-645-1568.
Peoria, Illinois Office: Howard & Howard, P.C., The Creve Coeur Building, Suite 200, 321 Liberty Street.
Telephone: 309-672-1483.
Telecopier: 309-672-1568.

Todd D. Chamberlain Patrick D. Hanes

Representative Clients: For Representative Client list, see General Practice, Lansing, MI.

For Complete List of Firm Personnel, See General Section

For full biographical listings, see the Martindale-Hubbell Law Directory

MILLER, CANFIELD, PADDOCK AND STONE, P.L.C. (AV)

A Professional Limited Liability Company
Founded in 1852 by Sidney Davy Miller
Suite 900, One Michigan Avenue, 48933-1609
Telephone: 517-487-2070
Fax: 517-374-6304
Detroit, Michigan Office: 150 West Jefferson, Suite 2500, 48226-4415.
Telephone: 313-963-6420.
Fax: 313-496-7500.
Cable Address: "Stem Detroit."
Ann Arbor, Michigan Office: 101 North Main Street, 7th Floor, 48104-1400.
Telephone: 313-663-2445.
Fax: 313-747-7147.
Bloomfield Hills, Michigan Office: Suite 100, Pinehurst Office Center, 1400 North Woodward, 48303-2014.
Telephone: 313-645-5000.
Fax: 313-645-1917.
Grand Rapids, Michigan Office: 1200 Campau Square Plaza, 99 Monroe, N.W., 49503-2639.
Telephone: 616-454-8656.
Fax: 616-776-6322.
Howell, Michigan Office: 121 South Barnard Street, Suite 4, 48843-2305.
Telephone: 517-546-7600.
Telecopier: 517-546-6974.
Kalamazoo, Michigan Office: 444 West Michigan Avenue, 49007-3752.
Telephone: 616-381-7030.
Fax: 616-382-0244.
Monroe, Michigan Office: The Executive Centre, 214 East Elm Avenue, 48161-2682.
Telephone: 313-243-2000.
Fax: 313-243-0901.
Washington, D.C. Office: 1225 Nineteenth Street, N.W., Suite 400. 20036.
Telephone: 202-429-5575; 785-0600.
Fax: 202-331-1118; 785-1234.
Pensacola, Florida Office: 25 West Cedar, 32501.
Telephone: 904-469-1088.
Fax: 904-432-0677.
St. Petersburg Office: 100 Second Avenue S., Suite 7045, 33701.
Telephone: 813-982-6000.
Fax: 813-892-6002.
Gdansk, Poland Office: Suite 322, Dom Technika Building, Ul. Rajska 6, 80-850.
Telephone: 011-485-831-2808.
Fax: 011-485-831-4719.
Warsaw, Poland Office: Ul. Marszalkowska 82, Suite 561, 00-517.
Telephone: 011-482-623-6457 and 6458.
Fax: 011-482-623-6459.

MEMBER OF FIRM

William J. Danhof (Resident)

Representative Firm Clients: Chrysler Corp.; Comerica, Inc.; City of Detroit, Mich.; Detroit Tigers, Inc.; First of Michigan; Fretter, Inc.; Ford Motor Co.; Ford Motor Credit Co.; Great Lakes Bancorp; Henry Ford Hospital.

For Complete List of Firm Personnel, See General Section

For full biographical listings, see the Martindale-Hubbell Law Directory

STREET & GRUA (AV)

2401 East Grand River, 48912
Telephone: 517-487-8300
Fax: 517-487-8306

MEMBERS OF FIRM

Victor C. Anderson (1904-1981) Cassius E. Street, Jr.
Remo Mark Grua

Representative Clients: Applegate Insulation Manufacturing; General Aviation, Inc.; Classic Aircraft Corp.; General White GMC; Old Kent Bank of Lansing.
References: First of America-Central; Old Kent Bank of Lansing, N.A.

For full biographical listings, see the Martindale-Hubbell Law Directory

*MIDLAND,** Midland Co.

CURRIE & KENDALL, P.C. (AV)

6024 Eastman Avenue, P.O. Box 1846, 48641-1846
Telephone: 517-839-0300
Fax: 517-832-0077

Gilbert A. Currie (1882-1960) Daniel J. Cline
James A. Kendall Peter A. Poznak
William C. Collins Julia A. Close
Thomas L. Ludington Peter J. Kendall
Ramon F. Rolf, Jr. Jeffrey N. Dyer

OF COUNSEL

Gilbert A. Currie I. Frank Harlow
William D. Schuette

LEGAL SUPPORT PERSONNEL

Barbara J. Byron

Counsel for: Chemical Financial Corp.; Chemical Bank & Trust Co.; Saginaw Valley State University; Northwood University; The Midland Foundation; Elsa U. Pardee Foundation; Rollin M. Gerstacker Foundation; Charles J. Strosacker Foundation.

For full biographical listings, see the Martindale-Hubbell Law Directory

*MUSKEGON,** Muskegon Co.

PARMENTER O'TOOLE (AV)

175 West Apple Street, P.O. Box 786, 49443-0786
Telephone: 616-722-1621
Telecopier: 616-728-2206; 722-7866

MEMBERS OF FIRM

G. Thomas Johnson John M. Briggs, III
Eric J. Fauri Robert D. Eklund
Christopher L. Kelly

OF COUNSEL

Robert L. Forsythe Thomas J. O'Toole

General Counsel for: FMB Lumberman's Bank; AmeriBank Federal Savings Bank; City of Muskegon; Quality Tool & Stamping Co., Inc.; Radiology Muskegon, P.C.
Local Counsel for: General Electric Capital Corp.; Paine-Webber; Teledyne Industries, Inc. (Continental Motors Division); Westinghouse Electric Corporation (Knoll Group).

For Complete List of Firm Personnel, See General Section

For full biographical listings, see the Martindale-Hubbell Law Directory

PLYMOUTH, Wayne Co.

SEMPLINER, THOMAS AND BOAK (AV)

711 West Ann Arbor Trail, 48170
Telephone: 313-453-6220, 455-4560

MEMBERS OF FIRM

William Sempliner (1908-1985) John E. Thomas
Stephen H. Boak

ASSOCIATES

Mark D. Lang Tracy S. Thomas

OF COUNSEL

Robert P. Tiplady

For full biographical listings, see the Martindale-Hubbell Law Directory

*PONTIAC,** Oakland Co.

BOOTH, PATTERSON, LEE, NEED & ADKISON, P.C. (AV)

1090 West Huron Street, 48328
Telephone: 810-681-1200
FAX: 810-681-1754

(See Next Column)

BOOTH, PATTERSON, LEE, NEED & ADKISON P.C.—*Continued*

Douglas W. Booth (1918-1992)
Calvin E. Patterson (1913-1987)
Parvin Lee, Jr.
J. Timothy Patterson
David J. Lee
Gregory K. Need
Phillip G. Adkison
Martin L. Kimmel
Allan T. Motzny
Ann DeCaminada Christ
Kathryn Niazy Nichols

For full biographical listings, see the Martindale-Hubbell Law Directory

STERLING, SCHILLING & THORBURN, P.C. (AV)

1400 NBD Building, 48342
Telephone: 810-334-4544
Fax: 810-334-1021

Robert P. Sauer (1906-1974)
J. Robert Sterling
Ronald F. Schilling
Bruce J. Thorburn

Reference: First of America, O.M.

For full biographical listings, see the Martindale-Hubbell Law Directory

*SAGINAW,** Saginaw Co.

BRAUN KENDRICK FINKBEINER (AV)

8th Floor Second National Bank Building, 48607
Telephone: 517-753-3461
Telecopier: 517-753-3951
Bay City, Michigan Office: 201 Phoenix Building, P.O. Box 2039.
Telephone: 517-895-8505.
Telecopier: 517-895-8437.

MEMBERS OF FIRM

J. Richard Kendrick
James V. Finkbeiner
Hugo E. Braun, Jr.
C. Patrick Kaltenbach
Thomas R. Luplow
Brian F. Bauer

ASSOCIATE

Carolyn Pollock Cary

Representative Clients: The Dow Chemical Co.; General Motors Corp.; Lobdell Emery Manufacturing Co.; Merrill, Lynch, Inc.; Saginaw General Hospital; Saginaw News; The Wickes Foundation.

For Complete List of Firm Personnel, See General Section

For full biographical listings, see the Martindale-Hubbell Law Directory

*ST. JOSEPH,** Berrien Co.

TROFF, PETZKE & AMMESON (AV)

Law and Title Building, 811 Ship Street, P.O. Box 67, 49085
Telephone: 616-983-0161
Facsimile: 616-983-0166

MEMBERS OF FIRM

Theodore E. Troff
Roger A. Petzke
Charles F. Ammeson

ASSOCIATES

Bennett S. Schwartz
Daniel G. Lambrecht
Deborah L. Berecz

Representative Clients: Auto Owners Insurance Co.; CSX Transportation, Inc.; NBD Bank, N.A.

For full biographical listings, see the Martindale-Hubbell Law Directory

SOUTHFIELD, Oakland Co.

MADDIN, HAUSER, WARTELL, ROTH, HELLER & PESSES, P.C. (AV)

Third Floor Essex Center, 28400 Northwestern Highway, P.O. Box 215, 48037
Telephone: 810-354-4030, 355-5200
Telefax: 810-354-1422

Milton M. Maddin (1902-1984)
Michael W. Maddin
Mark R. Hauser
C. Robert Wartell
Richard J. Maddin
Richard F. Roth
Harvey R. Heller
Ian D. Pesses
Michael S. Leib
Robert D. Kaplow
William E. Sigler
Stewart C. W. Weiner
Charles M. Lax
Stuart M. Bordman
Steven D. Sallen
Joseph M. Fazio

Gregory J. Gamalski
Julie Chenot Mayer
Nathaniel H. Simpson
Ronald A. Sollish
Lisa Schatz Broder
Mark H. Fink
Brian J. Simmons
Gayle L. Landrum
Gary E. Perlmuter
Lowell D. Salesin
Jeffrey B. Hollander

Reference: Comerica Bank.

For full biographical listings, see the Martindale-Hubbell Law Directory

MASON, STEINHARDT, JACOBS & PERLMAN, PROFESSIONAL CORPORATION (AV)

Suite 1500, 4000 Town Center, 48075-1415
Telephone: 810-358-2090
Fax: 810-358-3599

John E. Jacobs
Michael B. Perlman
Richard A. Barr
Jeannine F. Gleeson-Smith

Carolyn J. Crawford
Diane Flagg Goldstein

Representative Clients: Citibank, N.A.; City of Dearborn; DeMattia Development Co.; Forest City Enterprises; Michigan Wholesale Drug Assn.; Mortgage Bankers Association of Michigan; Nationwide Insurance Co.; City of Taylor; Union Labor Life Insurance Co.; Yellow Freight Systems, Inc.

For Complete List of Firm Personnel, See General Section

For full biographical listings, see the Martindale-Hubbell Law Directory

SOMMERS, SCHWARTZ, SILVER & SCHWARTZ, P.C. (AV)

2000 Town Center, Suite 900, 48075
Telephone: 810-355-0300
Telecopier: 810-746-4001
Plymouth, Michigan Office: 747 South Main Street.
Telephone: 313-455-4250.

Steven J. Schwartz
Donald R. Epstein
Gary A. Taback
David M. Black
Jon J. Birnkrant
Joseph H. Bourgon

OF COUNSEL

Norman Samuel Sommers

General Counsel for: Michigan National Bank; Madison National Bank; Bank Hapoalim, B.M.; Beal Bank, S.A.; C.A. Muer Corporation; Kojaian Properties, Inc.; Vlasic & Company; Allstate Management Company; Foodland Distributors; Nederlander Corporation.

For Complete List of Firm Personnel, See General Section

For full biographical listings, see the Martindale-Hubbell Law Directory

*TRAVERSE CITY,** Grand Traverse Co.

MURCHIE, CALCUTT & BOYNTON (AV)

109 East Front Street, Suite 300, 49684
Telephone: 616-947-7190
Fax: 616-947-4341

Robert B. Murchie (1894-1975)
Harry Calcutt
Jack E. Boynton
William B. Calcutt
Mark A. Burnheimer
Dawn M. Rogers

ASSOCIATES

George W. Hyde, III
Ralph J. Dilley (Not admitted in MI)

General Counsel for: Old Kent Bank-Grand Traverse; Northwestern Savings Bank & Trust; Central-State Bancorp; Traverse City Record Eagle; WPNB-7 & WTOM-4; Emergency Consultants, Inc.; National Guardian Risk Retention Group, Inc.; Farmers Mutual Insurance Co.; Environmental Solutions, Inc.
Local Counsel For: Consumers Power Co.

For full biographical listings, see the Martindale-Hubbell Law Directory

TROY, Oakland Co.

HUTSON, SAWYER, CHAPMAN & REILLY (AV)

292 Town Center Drive, 48084-1799
Telephone: 810-689-5700
Fax: 810-689-5741

MEMBERS OF FIRM

Thomas G. Sawyer
Michael W. Hutson
Ronald A. Chapman
Michael J. Reilly

Representative Clients: Advanced Friction Materials Co.; Birmingham Chrysler-Plymouth Co.; Design Fabrications, Inc.; Oakland County Medical Society; Randolph Tool; Renaissance Health Care, Inc.; Smith & Schmidt Associates, Inc.; Vilican-Leman & Associates, Inc.
References: First of America Bank; Michigan National Bank.

For full biographical listings, see the Martindale-Hubbell Law Directory

JACOB & WEINGARTEN, PROFESSIONAL CORPORATION (AV)

2301 West Big Beaver Road, Suite 777, 48084
Telephone: 810-649-1900
Facsimile: 810-649-2920
West Palm Beach, Florida Office: 1555 Palm Beach Lake Boulevard, Suite 1510, 33401.
Telephone: 407-640-5600.
Facsimile: 407-683-0799.

(See Next Column)

JACOB & WEINGARTEN PROFESSIONAL CORPORATION, *Troy—Continued*

Joel G. Jacob
Harry M. Eisenberg
Peter A. Nathan (Resident, West Palm Beach, Florida Office)
Steven P. Schubiner
Carole Crosby
Frank J. Badach (Not admitted in MI)
Phillip J. Neuman
Vicky S. Wood
Michael B. Peterman

Representative Clients: Cardinal Capital Partners, Inc.; Dean Witter Realty, Inc.; Franklin Group, Inc.; New Center Company; Sunburst Properties, Inc.

For full biographical listings, see the Martindale-Hubbell Law Directory

POLING, MCGAW & POLING, P.C. (AV)

Suite 275, 5435 Corporate Drive, 48098
Telephone: 810-641-0500
Telecopier: 810-641-0506

Benson T. Buck (1926-1989)
Richard B. Poling
D. Douglas McGaw
Richard B. Poling, Jr.
David W. Moore
Gregory C. Hamilton
Veronica B. Winter

Representative Clients: County of Oakland; City of Troy; United States Fidelity & Guaranty Co.; Sentry Insurance Co.; Admital Insurance; DeMaria Construction Co.; Leo Corporation; Aetna Casualty and Surety Co.; Concord Design; Pneumo-Abex.

For full biographical listings, see the Martindale-Hubbell Law Directory

WEST BLOOMFIELD, Oakland Co.

STEPHEN K. VALENTINE, JR., P.C. (AV)

5767 West Maple Road, Suite 400, 48322
Telephone: 810-851-3010
Troy, Michigan Office: 600 Columbia Center. 201 West Big Beaver Road.
Telephone: 810-851-3010.

Stephen K. Valentine, Jr.

OF COUNSEL

Philip G. Meyer

For full biographical listings, see the Martindale-Hubbell Law Directory

MINNESOTA

*AUSTIN,** Mower Co.

HOVERSTEN, STROM, JOHNSON & RYSAVY (AV)

807 West Oakland Avenue, 55912
Telephone: 507-433-3483
Fax: 507-433-7889

MEMBERS OF FIRM

Kermit F. Hoversten
Craig W. Johnson
Donald E. Rysavy
David V. Hoversten
John S. Beckmann
Fred W. Wellmann
Steven J Hovey

ASSOCIATE

Mary Carroll Leahy

OF COUNSEL

Kenneth M. Strom

Representative Clients: Hartford Insurance Co.; Allied Insurance Group; Travelers Insurance; American States Insurance; Royal Milbank Insurance; Prudential Insurance Co.; Independent School District 756; St. Olaf Hospital; Austin Medical Clinic; Norwest Bank, Austin.

For Complete List of Firm Personnel, See General Section

For full biographical listings, see the Martindale-Hubbell Law Directory

*DULUTH,** St. Louis Co.

CRASSWELLER, MAGIE, ANDRESEN, HAAG & PACIOTTI, P.A. (AV)

1000 Alworth Building, P.O. Box 745, 55801
Telephone: 218-722-1411
Telecopier: 218-720-6817

Donald B. Crassweller
Robert H. Magie, III
Charles H. Andresen
Michael W. Haag
James P. Paciotti
Sandra E. Butterworth
Brian R. McCarthy
Bryan N. Anderson
Robert C. Barnes
Kurt D. Larson
Gerald T. Anderson

(See Next Column)

COUNSEL

John M. Donovan
Robert K. McCarthy (1915-1986)

Representative Clients: Inland Steel Co.; Allstate Insurance Co.; Liberty Mutual Insurance Co; State Farm Insurance Cos.; Great Lakes Gas Transmission Co.; Lakehead Pipe Line Co.; Trans-Canada Gas Pipeline, Ltd.

For full biographical listings, see the Martindale-Hubbell Law Directory

HALVERSON, WATTERS, BYE, DOWNS, REYELTS & BATEMAN, LTD. (AV)

700 Providence Building, 55802
Telephone: 218-727-6833
FAX: 218-727-4632

W. D. Watters

Sonia M. Sturdevant
Aaron Bransky

Representative Clients: Duluth Teachers Credit Union; Duluth, Winnipeg & Pacific Railway; I. Reiss & Sons.

For Complete List of Firm Personnel, See General Section

For full biographical listings, see the Martindale-Hubbell Law Directory

*MINNEAPOLIS,** Hennepin Co.

ABDO AND ABDO, P.A. (AV)

710 Northstar West, 625 Marquette Avenue, 55402
Telephone: 612-333-1526
Fax: 612-342-2608

Robert P. Abdo
Steven R. Hedges
Keith J. Broady
Kenneth J. Abdo
Timothy C. Matson

Representative Clients: ADT Security Systems, Inc.; Cold Spring Brewing Co., Cold Spring, Minn.

For Complete List of Firm Personnel, See General Section

For full biographical listings, see the Martindale-Hubbell Law Directory

ARNOLD & MCDOWELL (AV)

5881 Cedar Lake Road, 55416-1492
Telephone: 612-545-9000
Minnesota Wats Line: 800-343-4545
Fax: 612-545-1793
Princeton, Minnesota Office: 501 South Fourth Street.
Telephone: 612-389-2214.
Hutchinson, Minnesota Office: 101 Park Place.
Telephone: 612-587-7575.

MEMBERS OF FIRM

David B. Arnold
Gary D. McDowell
Steven A. Anderson
Paul D. Dove

ASSOCIATE

Gina M. Brandt

For Complete List of Firm Personnel, See General Section

For full biographical listings, see the Martindale-Hubbell Law Directory

BENNETT, INGVALDSON & COATY, P.A. (AV)

Suite 1640, 8500 Normandale Lake Boulevard, 55437
Telephone: 612-921-8350
Telecopier: 612-921-8351

Robert Bennett
Eric W. Ingvaldson
Michael P. Coaty

For full biographical listings, see the Martindale-Hubbell Law Directory

BRENNER & GLASSMAN, LTD. A PROFESSIONAL ASSOCIATION (AV)

Suite 170, 2001 Killebrew Drive, 55425-1822
Telephone: 612-854-7600
Telecopier: 612-854-0502

Louis W. Brenner, Sr.
Richard A. Glassman

William D. Turkula
Michael J. Orme
Thomas W. Larkin

OF COUNSEL

John J. Todd

For full biographical listings, see the Martindale-Hubbell Law Directory

FRED BURSTEIN & ASSOCIATES, P.A. (AV)

5450 Norwest Center, 90 South Seventh Street, 55402
Telephone: 612-339-6561
Fax: 612-337-5572

(See Next Column)

FRED BURSTEIN & ASSOCIATES, P.A.—*Continued*

Fred Burstein

Dylan J. McFarland
Eric J. Olsen

Reference: Firstar Bank of Minnesota, N.A.

For full biographical listings, see the Martindale-Hubbell Law Directory

STEPHEN J. DAVIS (AV)

1601 West 22nd Street, 55405
Telephone: 612-377-0300
Fax: 612-377-8821

LEGAL SUPPORT PERSONNEL
Margaret M. Boisvert

For full biographical listings, see the Martindale-Hubbell Law Directory

FROMMELT & EIDE, LTD. (AV)

580 International Centre, 900 Second Avenue South, 55402
Telephone: 612-332-2200; 800-332-2296
FAX: 612-342-2761

Roger H. Frommelt
David B. Eide
John R. Dorgan
Randy J. Sparling
James W. Rude
Jean M. Davis
Fredrick R. Krietzman
Douglas M. Ramler

For full biographical listings, see the Martindale-Hubbell Law Directory

LOMMEN, NELSON, COLE & STAGEBERG, P.A. (AV)

1800 IDS Center, 80 South 8th Street, 55402
Telephone: 612-339-8131
Fax: 612-339-8064
Hudson, Wisconsin Office: Grandview Professional Building, 400 South Second Street, Suite 210.
Telephones: 715-386-8217 and 612-436-8085.

W. Wyman Smith (1914-1994)
John P. Lommen (1927-1988)
Michael P. Shroyer (1953-1993)
Leonard T. Juster
Alvin S. Malmon
Ronald L. Haskvitz
Phillip A. Cole
Roger V. Stageberg
Glenn R. Kessel
Thomas R. Jacobson (Resident, Hudson, Wisconsin Office)
John M. Giblin
John R. McBride
J. Christopher Cuneo
Thomas F. Dougherty
Stacey A. DeKalb
Kay N. Hunt
Richard L. Plagens
Ehrich L. Koch
Margie R. Bodas
James M. Lockhart
Stephen C. Rathke
James C. Searls
Linc S. Deter
Paul L. Dinger
Sherri D. Ulland
Reid R. Lindquist

Jill G. Doescher
James R. Johnson (Resident, Hudson, Wisconsin Office)
Terrance W. Moore
Lynn M. Starkovich
Marc A. Johannsen
Angela W. Allen
Adam Levitsky
Barry A. O'Neil
Mary I. King
Sheila A. Bjorklund

OF COUNSEL
V. Owen Nelson
Henry H. Feikema

Representative Clients: Mutual Service Insurance Co.; Employers Mutual Companies; Economy Fire and Casualty Co.

For full biographical listings, see the Martindale-Hubbell Law Directory

ROBERT MERRILL ROSENBERG, P.A. (AV)

Suite 2500 One Financial Plaza, 120 South Sixth Street, 55402-1826
Telephone: 612-349-5290
Facsimile: 612-349-9962

Robert Merrill Rosenberg

For full biographical listings, see the Martindale-Hubbell Law Directory

SMITH, GENDLER, SHIELL, SHEFF & FORD, P.A. (AV)

3350 First Bank Place, 601 Second Avenue South, 55402
Telephone: 612-332-1000
Facsimile: 612-332-3836

Benjamin J. Smith
John M. Gendler
Douglas J. Shiell
Harold H. Sheff
Margaret A. Ford

For full biographical listings, see the Martindale-Hubbell Law Directory

ZAMANSKY PROFESSIONAL ASSOCIATION (AV)

4924 IDS Tower, 55402
Telephone: 612-340-9720
Fax: 612-340-9662
St. Paul, Minnesota Office: 6 West 5th Street.
Telephone: 612-297-6400.

Ronald A. Zamansky

Scott A. Weaver
Glen F. Meyer

Reference: Norwest Bank Minneapolis.

For full biographical listings, see the Martindale-Hubbell Law Directory

*MOORHEAD,** Clay Co.

DOSLAND, NORDHOUGEN, LILLEHAUG & JOHNSON, P.A. (AV)

Suite 203 American Bank Moorhead Building, 730 Center Avenue, P.O. Box 100, 56561-0100
Telephone: 218-233-2744
Fax: 218-233-1570

C. A. Nye (1886-1910)
C. G. Dosland (1898-1945)
G. L. Dosland (1927-1983)
W. B. Dosland (1954-1990)
John P. Dosland
Curtis A. Nordhougen
Duane A. Lillehaug
Joel D. Johnson
Bruce Romanick

General Counsel For: American Crystal Sugar Co.; American Bank Moorhead, Moorhead, Minnesota.
Representative Clients: Auto Owners Insurance Co.; Wausau Insurance Cos.; Gethsemane Episcopal Cathedral; Swift-Eckrich, Inc.; Barrett Mobile Home Transport, Inc.; Moorhead Economic Development Authority; Eventide.
Reference: American Bank Moorhead, Moorhead, Minnesota.

For full biographical listings, see the Martindale-Hubbell Law Directory

MISSISSIPPI

BILOXI, Harrison Co.

RUSHING & GUICE (AV)

683 Water Street, P.O. Box 1925, 39533-1925
Telephone: 601-374-2313
Telecopier: 601-374-8155

MEMBERS OF FIRM
Charles L. Rushing (1881-1923)
William L. Guice (1887-1971)
William Lee Guice III

OF COUNSEL
Jacob D. Guice

ASSOCIATES
Edgar F. Maier
R. Scott Wells

LEGAL SUPPORT PERSONNEL
Antonia Strong

For full biographical listings, see the Martindale-Hubbell Law Directory

*CLARKSDALE,** Coahoma Co.

ROSS, HUNT, SPELL & ROSS, A PROFESSIONAL ASSOCIATION (AV)

123 Court Street, P.O. Box 1196, 38614
Telephone: 601-627-5251
Telecopier No.: 601-627-5254
Clinton, Mississippi Office: 203 Monroe Street.
Telephone: 601-924-2655.

Tom T. Ross (1903-1993)
David R. Hunt
Tom T. Ross, Jr.

Representative Client: Beech Aircraft Corp., Wichita, Kansas.

For Complete List of Firm Personnel, See General Section

For full biographical listings, see the Martindale-Hubbell Law Directory

*GREENWOOD,** Leflore Co.

JOHN P. HENSON (AV)

105 West Market Street, P.O. Box 494, 38930
Telephone: 601-453-6227
Telefax: 601-453-6228

For full biographical listings, see the Martindale-Hubbell Law Directory

*GULFPORT,** Harrison Co.

DUKES, DUKES, KEATING AND FANECA, P.A. (AV)

2308 East Beach Boulevard, P.O. Drawer W, 39501
Telephone: 601-868-1111
FAX: 601-863-2886

Hugh D. Keating
Cy Faneca
William H. Pettey, Jr.

Nick B. Roberts, Jr.

For full biographical listings, see the Martindale-Hubbell Law Directory

FRANKE, RAINEY & SALLOUM (AV)

2605 14th Street, P.O. Drawer 460, 39502
Telephone: 601-868-7070
Telecopier: 601-868-7090

MEMBERS OF FIRM

Paul M. Franke, Jr.
William M. Rainey
Richard P. Salloum
Paul B. Howell
Ronald T. Russell
Fredrick B. Feeney, II
Traci M. Castille

ASSOCIATES

Kaleel G. Salloum, Jr.
Ruth E. Bennett
Donald P. Moore
Roland F. Samson, III
Jeffrey S. Bruni
Stefan G. Bourn

For full biographical listings, see the Martindale-Hubbell Law Directory

MEADOWS, RILEY, KOENENN AND TEEL, P.A. (AV)

1720 23rd Avenue, P.O. Box 550, 39502
Telephone: 601-864-4511
Telecopier: 601-868-2178

Joseph R. Meadows
Donnie D. Riley
Alfred R. Koenenn
Walter W. Teel
Jerry D. Riley
Karen J. Young

Representative Clients: Bubba Oustalat Lincoln Mercury, Inc.; Lee Tractor Co. of Mississippi.
Reference: Hancock Bank.

For full biographical listings, see the Martindale-Hubbell Law Directory

*JACKSON,** Hinds Co.

MCDAVID, NOBLIN & WEST (AV)

Suite 1000, Security Centre North, 200 South Lamar Street, 39201
Telephone: 601-948-3305
Telecopier: 601-354-4789

MEMBERS OF FIRM

John Land McDavid
William C. Noblin, Jr.
W. Eric West
John Sanford McDavid
John C. Robertson

OF COUNSEL

Lowell F. Stephens

For full biographical listings, see the Martindale-Hubbell Law Directory

*NEW ALBANY,** Union Co.

TALMADGE D. LITTLEJOHN (AV)

108 East Main Street, P.O. Box 869, 38652
Telephone: 601-534-6835; 534-6215
FAX: 601-534-6215

References: First National Bank, New Albany, Miss.; Bank of New Albany.

For full biographical listings, see the Martindale-Hubbell Law Directory

*OXFORD,** Lafayette Co.

FREELAND & FREELAND (AV)

1013 Jackson Avenue, P.O. Box 269, 38655
Telephone: 601-234-3414
Telecopier: 601-234-0604

MEMBERS OF FIRM

T. H. Freeland, III
T. H. Freeland, IV
J. Hale Freeland

ASSOCIATE

Paul W. Crutcher

Representative Clients: The Ohio Casualty Group; Crum & Forester.

For full biographical listings, see the Martindale-Hubbell Law Directory

SOUTHAVEN, De Soto Co.

BRIDGFORTH & BUNTIN (AV)

1607 State Line Road, P.O. Box 241, 38671
Telephone: 601-393-4450
Fax: 601-342-5646

MEMBERS OF FIRM

Dudley B. Bridgforth, Jr.
Taylor D. Buntin, III

For full biographical listings, see the Martindale-Hubbell Law Directory

TAYLOR, JONES, ALEXANDER, SORRELL & MCFALL, LTD. (AV)

961 State Line Road, West, P.O. Box 188, 38671
Telephone: 601-342-1300
Telecopier: 601-342-1312

Ronald L. Taylor
Jack R. Jones, III
Keith M. Alexander
Mark K. Sorrell
George McFall

Approved Attorneys for: Mississippi Valley Title Insurance Co.; First American Title, Insurance.
Reference: Sunburst Bank, Southaven, Miss.

For full biographical listings, see the Martindale-Hubbell Law Directory

*TUPELO,** Lee Co.

HOLLAND, RAY & UPCHURCH, P.A. (AV)

322 Jefferson Street, P.O. Drawer 409, 38802
Telephone: 601-842-1721
Facsimile: 601-844-6413

Sam E. Lumpkin (1908-1964)
Ralph L. Holland
James Hugh Ray
Robert K. Upchurch
W. Reed Hillen, III
Thomas A. Wicker

Michael D. Tapscott

Representative Clients: The Travelers; Continental Casualty Co.; South Central Bell Telephone Co.; The Greyhound Corp.; Mississippi Valley Gas Co.; Bryan-Rogers, Inc.; The Housing Authority of the City of Tupelo; Action Industries, Inc.; American Cable Systems, Inc.; American Funeral Assurance Co.

For full biographical listings, see the Martindale-Hubbell Law Directory

MISSOURI

KANSAS CITY, Jackson, Clay & Platte Cos.

SHERWIN L. EPSTEIN & ASSOCIATES (AV)

Suite 1700, 1006 Grand Avenue, 64106
Telephone: 816-421-6200
FAX: 816-421-6201

John W. Roe

ASSOCIATE

Mark H. Epstein

LEGAL SUPPORT PERSONNEL

Amy L. Edwards
Christine Marie Leete

For full biographical listings, see the Martindale-Hubbell Law Directory

DETLEF G. LEHNARDT (AV Ⓣ)

911 Main Street, Suite 1322, 64105
Telephone: 816-221-2440
Facsimile: 816-221-5665
New York, New York Office: 90 Park Avenue, 17th Floor.
Telephone: 212-972-4263.
Facsimile: 212-972-4264.

LEGAL SUPPORT PERSONNEL

Stephen K. Lehnardt

For full biographical listings, see the Martindale-Hubbell Law Directory

SWANSON, MIDGLEY, GANGWERE, KITCHIN & MCLARNEY, L.L.C. (AV)

1500 Commerce Trust Building, 922 Walnut, 64106-1848
Telephone: 816-842-6100
Overland Park, Kansas Office: The NCAA Building, Suite 350, 6201 College Boulevard.
Telephone: 816-842-6100.

George H. Gangwere, Jr.
John J. Kitchin
James H. McLarney
Robert W. McKinley
Richard N. Bien

(See Next Column)

SWANSON, MIDGLEY, GANGWERE, KITCHIN & MCLARNEY L.L.C.—*Continued*

Counsel for: General Electric Co.; Chrysler Corp.; Yellow Freight System, Inc.; The Prudential Insurance Co. of America; Metropolitan Life Insurance Co.; National Collegiate Athletic Assn.; Safeway Stores, Inc.; The Lee Apparel Co.; Property Reserve, Inc.; Beneficial Development Co.

For Complete List of Firm Personnel, See General Section

For full biographical listings, see the Martindale-Hubbell Law Directory

LAKE OZARK, Miller & Camden Cos.

THOMAS E. LORAINE, P.C. (AV)

2840 Bagnell Dam Boulevard, 65049
Telephone: 314-365-3035
Fax: 314-365-3044

Thomas E. Loraine
Dale M. Weppner

For full biographical listings, see the Martindale-Hubbell Law Directory

LEE'S SUMMIT, Jackson Co.

CARL CHINNERY & ASSOCIATES, P.C. (AV)

200 South Douglas, 64063
Telephone: 816-525-2050

Carl L. Chinnery

Nancy E. Blackwell

OF COUNSEL

Elizabeth Unger Carlyle

LEGAL SUPPORT PERSONNEL

PARALEGALS

Jean Wehner Chinnery
Janice Sue Hancock
Elaine K. Hanrahan
Alicia Hodges
Susan Breitenbach

For full biographical listings, see the Martindale-Hubbell Law Directory

ST. LOUIS, (Independent City)

JEROME R. MANDELSTAMM (AV)

Suite 1600, 1010 Market Street, 63101
Telephone: 314-621-2261

For full biographical listings, see the Martindale-Hubbell Law Directory

PADBERG, MCSWEENEY, SLATER & MERZ, A PROFESSIONAL CORPORATION (AV)

Suite 800, 1015 Locust Street, 63101
Telephone: 314-621-3787
Telecopier: 314-621-7396

Godfrey P. Padberg
Edward P. McSweeney
R. J. Slater
Charles L. Merz

Richard J. Burke, Jr.
Matthew J. Padberg
James P. Leonard
Anthony J. Soukenik
Thomas C. Simon
Mary K. Munroe
Marty Daesch

For full biographical listings, see the Martindale-Hubbell Law Directory

PEPER, MARTIN, JENSEN, MAICHEL AND HETLAGE (AV)

720 Olive Street, Twenty-Fourth Floor, 63101
Telephone: 314-421-3850
Fax: 314-621-4834
Fort Myers, Florida Office: 2080 McGregor Boulevard, Third Floor.
Telephone: 813-337-3850.
Fax: 813-337-0970.
Punta Gorda, Florida Office: 1625 West Marion Avenue, Suite 2.
Telephone: 813-637-1955.
Fax: 813-637-8485.
Naples, Florida Office: 850 Park Shore Drive, Suite 202.
Telephone: 813-261-6525.
Fax: 813-649-1805.
Belleville, Illinois Office: 720 West Main Street, Suite 140.
Telephone: 618-234-9574.
Fax: 618-234-9846.

MEMBERS OF FIRM

Richard A. Hetlage
Robert O. Hetlage
J. Neil Huber, Jr.
John W. Brickler
James E. Moore, III (At Punta Gorda, Florida Office)
Deborah I. Conrad
Kenneth A. Jones (At Fort Myers, Punta Gorda and Naples, Florida Offices)
Beverly Grady (At Fort Myers and Punta Gorda, Florida Offices)
Craig S. Biesterfeld

(See Next Column)

MEMBERS OF FIRM (Continued)

Kathleen T. Mueller
G. Carson McEachern (At Fort Myers and Naples, Florida Offices)
John P. McNearney

ASSOCIATES

Lisa J. Browman
Daniel J. Lett
Laura K. W. Rebbe
David L. Schlapbach
Ellen L. Theroff
Geri L. Waksler (At Fort Myers and Punta Gorda, Florida Offices)

For Complete List of Firm Personnel, See General Section

For full biographical listings, see the Martindale-Hubbell Law Directory

STONE, LEYTON & GERSHMAN, A PROFESSIONAL CORPORATION (AV)

7733 Forsyth Boulevard, Suite 500, 63105
Telephone: 314-721-7011
Telefax: 314-721-8660

Steven M. Stone
Steven H. Leyton
Jeffrey S. Gershman
Lynn G. Carey
Suzanne L. Zatlin
Thomas P. Rosenfeld
Paul J. Puricelli

Mary H. Moorkamp

OF COUNSEL

Sidney L. Stone

For full biographical listings, see the Martindale-Hubbell Law Directory

MONTANA

*BILLINGS,** Yellowstone Co.

CROWLEY, HAUGHEY, HANSON, TOOLE & DIETRICH (AV)

500 Transwestern II, 490 North 31st Street, P.O. Box 2529, 59103
Telephone: 406-252-3441
Fax: 406-259-4159
Helena, Montana Office: IBM Building, 100 North Park Avenue, Suite 300, 59601.
Telephone: 406-449-4165.
Fax: 406-449-5149.

MEMBERS OF FIRM

John M. Dietrich
Gareld F. Krieg
Arthur F. Lamey, Jr.
Myles J. Thomas
Terry B. Cosgrove
Allan L. Karell
Laura A. Mitchell
Daniel N. McLean
Robert G. Michelotti, Jr.
John R. Alexander
William D. Lamdin, III
Michael S. Dockery
Malcolm H. Goodrich
Mary Scrim
Eric K. Anderson
Renee L. Coppock

ASSOCIATES

John R. Lee
Scott M. Heard
Michael S. Lahr

Representative Clients: Aetna; Metropolitan Life Insurance Co.; Mutual Life Insurance Co., N.Y.; Equitable Life Assurance Society of the United States; Turner Enterprises, Inc.

For Complete List of Firm Personnel, See General Section

For full biographical listings, see the Martindale-Hubbell Law Directory

*BOZEMAN,** Gallatin Co.

KIRWAN & BARRETT, P.C. (AV)

215 West Mendenhall, P.O. Box 1348, 59771-1348
Telephone: 406-586-1553
Fax: 406-586-8971

Peter M. Kirwan
Stephen M. Barrett

Tom W. Stonecipher

For full biographical listings, see the Martindale-Hubbell Law Directory

*KALISPELL,** Flathead Co.

HASH, O'BRIEN & BARTLETT (AV)

Plaza West, 136 First Avenue, West, P.O. Box 1178, 59901
Telephone: 406-755-6919
Fax: 406-755-6911

(See Next Column)

HASH, O'BRIEN & BARTLETT, *Kalispell—Continued*

MEMBERS OF FIRM

Charles L. Hash
James C. Bartlett
Kenneth E. O'Brien
C. Mark Hash

General Counsel for: Glacier Bank F.S.B.; Budget Finance; Flathead County Title Co.
Representative Clients: Western Surety Co.; Liberty Mutual Insurance Co.; Allstate Insurance Co.; Hillsteads Department Store; Montana Brokers, Inc.
Reference: Glacier Bank F.S.B.

For full biographical listings, see the Martindale-Hubbell Law Directory

*MISSOULA,** Missoula Co.

KNIGHT, MACLAY & MASAR (AV)

The Florence, Suite 300, 111 North Higgins Avenue, P.O. Box 8957, 59807-8957
Telephone: 406-721-5440
Fax: 406-721-8644

MEMBERS OF FIRM

Robert M. Knight
Helena S. Maclay
James J. Masar

ASSOCIATE

Andrew C. Dana

Representative Clients: Zenchiku Land and Livestock, Inc.; Heart Bar Heart Ranch; Monture Hereford Ranch; Rocking Chair Ranch; The Nature Conservancy; Bank of Montana; Pioneer Federal Savings & Loan; Flint Creek Valley Bank; First American Title Insurance Co.; Old Republic National Title Insurance Co.

For full biographical listings, see the Martindale-Hubbell Law Directory

NEBRASKA

*BROKEN BOW,** Custer Co.

SCHAPER & STEFFENS (AV)

345 South 10th Avenue, P.O. Box 586, 68822
Telephone: 308-872-6481
Fax: 308-872-6385

MEMBERS OF FIRM

William C. Schaper (1890-1977)
Carlos E. Schaper
William Vern Steffens

General Counsel for: Custer Federal Savings & Loan Assn., Broken Bow; United Nebraska Bank, Broken Bow, Nebraska; Security State Bank, Ansley.
Local Counsel for: Federated Mutual Implement and Hardware Insurance Co.; Shield of Shelter Insurance Co.; John Hancock Mutual Life Insurance Co.; Prudential Life Insurance Co.; Massey-Ferguson, Inc.; F.D.I.C.; Resolution Trust Corporation.

For full biographical listings, see the Martindale-Hubbell Law Directory

*LINCOLN,** Lancaster Co.

SCUDDER LAW FIRM, P.C. (AV)

Second Floor, 411 South 13th Street, P.O. Box 81277, 68508
Telephone: 402-435-3223
Fax: 402-435-4239

Beverly Evans Grenier
Earl H. Scudder, Jr.
Christine C. Schwartzkopf Schroff
Mark A. Scudder

For full biographical listings, see the Martindale-Hubbell Law Directory

*OMAHA,** Douglas Co.

FRASER, STRYKER, VAUGHN, MEUSEY, OLSON, BOYER & BLOCH, P.C. (AV)

500 Energy Plaza, 409 South 17th Street, 68102
Telephone: 402-341-6000
Telecopier: 402-341-8290

Thomas F. Flaherty
Robert W. Rieke

For Complete List of Firm Personnel, See General Section

For full biographical listings, see the Martindale-Hubbell Law Directory

LAUGHLIN, PETERSON & LANG (AV)

11306 Davenport Street, 68154
Telephone: 402-330-1900
Fax: 402-330-0936

(See Next Column)

MEMBERS OF FIRM

Mark L. Laughlin
Robert F. Peterson
James E. Lang

Representative Clients: Andersen Electric Co.; General Electric Capital Corp.; Sears, Roebuck & Co.; Dodge Land Co.; Security Mutual Life Insurance Co. of Lincoln, NE; Century Development Co.

For full biographical listings, see the Martindale-Hubbell Law Directory

NEVADA

*ELKO,** Elko Co.

WILSON AND BARROWS, LTD. (AV)

442 Court Street, P.O. Box 389, 89801
Telephone: 702-738-7271
FAX: 702-738-5041

Richard G. Barrows

Representative Clients: Club 93 Casino; Red Lion Casino.

For Complete List of Firm Personnel, See General Section

For full biographical listings, see the Martindale-Hubbell Law Directory

*LAS VEGAS,** Clark Co.

ALBRIGHT, STODDARD, WARNICK & ALBRIGHT, A PROFESSIONAL CORPORATION (AV)

Quail Park I, Building D-4, 801 South Rancho Drive, 89106
Telephone: 702-384-7111
FAX: 702-384-0605

G. Vern Albright
Whitney B. Warnick
William H. Stoddard
G. Mark Albright

Michael W. Brimley
Gavin C. Jangard
D. Chris Albright

Representative Clients: Tokio Marine and Fire Ins. Co.; INAPRO, a CIGNA Co.; Nevada Ready Mix; North American Health Care, Inc. (Nursing Home); Royal Insurance; First Security Bank of Utah; Nevada Community Bank; Nationwide Insurance Co.; Liberty Mutual Insurance; CB Commercial.

For full biographical listings, see the Martindale-Hubbell Law Directory

ALVERSON, TAYLOR, MORTENSEN & NELSON (AV)

3821 W. Charleston Boulevard, 89102
Telephone: 702-384-7000
FAX: 702-385-7000

MEMBERS OF FIRM

J. Bruce Alverson
Erven T. Nelson
Eric K. Taylor
LeAnn Sanders
David J. Mortensen
David R. Clayson

ASSOCIATES

Milton J. Eichacker
Kenneth M. Marias
Douglas D. Gerrard
Jeffrey H. Ballin
Marie Ellerton
Jeffrey W. Daly
James H. Randall
Kenneth R. Ivory
Peter Dubowsky
Edward D. Boyack
Hayley B. Chambers
Sandra Smagac
Michael D. Stevenson
Jill M. Chase
Cookie Lea Olshein
Francis F. Lin

LEGAL SUPPORT PERSONNEL

PARALEGALS

Marsha Diaz
Linda Rosepiler
Mary Anne Murray
Julie A. Tolman

Representative Clients: Falcon Development Corporation; Trophy Homes; Lebud Enterprises; Overseas Chinese Bank Corporation; RMJ Development, Inc.; Frontier Bonding and Surety Corp.; Citibank Corporation; First Interstate Bank.

For full biographical listings, see the Martindale-Hubbell Law Directory

DEANER, DEANER, SCANN, CURTAS & MALAN (AV)

Suite 300, 720 South Fourth Street, 89101
Telephone: 702-382-6911
Fax: 702-386-6048

MEMBERS OF FIRM

Charles W. Deaner
John A. Curtas
J. Douglas Deaner (1944-1990)
Douglas R. Malan

Representative Client: California Federal Bank.
Reference: Nevada State Bank.

(See Next Column)

DEANER, DEANER, SCANN, CURTAS & MALAN—*Continued*

For Complete List of Firm Personnel, See General Section

For full biographical listings, see the Martindale-Hubbell Law Directory

GOOLD, PATTERSON, DEVORE & RONDEAU (AV)

905 Bank of America Plaza, 300 South Fourth Street, 89101
Telephone: 702-386-0038
Telecopier: 702-385-2484

Barry Stephen Goold
Thomas J. DeVore
Jeffrey D. Patterson
Thomas Rondeau

ASSOCIATES

Wilbur M. Roadhouse
Bryan K. Day
Kathryn S. Wonders

Representative Clients: Gateway Development Group; Hanshaw Partnership; Jack Tarr Development; Meridian Point Properties, Inc.; NationsBank; Pacific Cellular; Plaster Development Co.; RS Development; U.S.A. Capital Land Fund.
Reference: Bank of America.

For full biographical listings, see the Martindale-Hubbell Law Directory

HALE, LANE, PEEK, DENNISON AND HOWARD (AV)

Suite 800, Nevada Financial Center, 2300 West Sahara Avenue, Box 8, 89102
Telephone: 702-362-5118
Fax: 702-365-6940
Reno, Nevada Office: Porsche Building, 100 West Liberty Street, Tenth Floor, P.O. Box 3237.
Telephone: 702-786-7900.
Telefax: 702-786-6179.

MEMBERS OF FIRM

Steve Lane
R. Craig Howard
J. Stephen Peek
Stephen V. Novacek
Karen D. Dennison
William C. Davis, Jr.
Patricia J. Curtis

Representative Clients: Lenders: U.S. Bank of Nevada; First Western Bank; Sun State Bank; PriMerit Bank; Allstate Life Insurance Company. Title Companies: Chicago Title Insurance Co.; Commonwealth Land Title Insurance Co. Construction and Development: Lake at Las Vegas Joint Venture; Western Water Development Co.; Falcon Development Corp.

For Complete List of Firm Personnel, See General Section

For full biographical listings, see the Martindale-Hubbell Law Directory

JOLLEY, URGA, WIRTH & WOODBURY (AV)

Suite 800 Bank of America Plaza, 300 South Fourth Street, 89101
Telephone: 702-385-5161
Telecopier: 702-382-6814
Boulder City, Nevada Office: Suite 105, 1000 Nevada Highway.
Telephone: 702-293-3674.

MEMBERS OF FIRM

R. Gardner Jolley
Roger A. Wirth
William R. Urga
J. Douglas Driggs, Jr.

ASSOCIATE

Allen D. Emmel

Representative Clients: First Interstate Bank of Nevada; Nevada State Bank; Citicorp National Services, Inc.; Chicago Title Insurance Co.; National Title Company; Fidelity National Title; Melvin Simon & Associates, Inc.; Continental National Bank; First Nationwide Bank; PriMerit Bank.

For Complete List of Firm Personnel, See General Section

For full biographical listings, see the Martindale-Hubbell Law Directory

JONES, JONES, CLOSE & BROWN, CHARTERED (AV)

Suite 700, Bank of America Plaza, 300 South Fourth Street, 89101-6026
Telephone: 702-385-4202
Telecopier: 702-384-2276
Reno, Nevada Office: 290 South Arlington.
Telephone: 702-322-3811.
Telecopier: 702-348-0886.

Michael E. Buckley
Douglas G. Crosby
Stephen M. Rice

Representative Clients: Bank of America-Nevada; First Interstate Bank of Nevada; Lawyers Title; Chrysler Credit Corporation; Western Acceptance Corporation; Southern Farm Bureau; Life Insurance Company; Federal Deposit Insurance Corporation; Resolution Trust Corporation; Southwest Gas Corporation.

For Complete List of Firm Personnel, See General Section

For full biographical listings, see the Martindale-Hubbell Law Directory

LEAVITT, SULLY & RIVERS (AV)

An Association of Professional Corporations
601 East Bridger Avenue, 89101
Telephone: 702-382-5111
Telecopier: 702-382-2892

K. Michael Leavitt (Chartered)
W. Leslie Sully, Jr. (Chartered)
David J. Rivers, II (Chartered)

For full biographical listings, see the Martindale-Hubbell Law Directory

LIONEL SAWYER & COLLINS (AV)

1700 Bank of America Plaza, 300 South Fourth Street, 89101
Telephone: 702-383-8888
Fax: 702-383-8845
Reno, Nevada Office: Suite 1100, Bank of America Plaza, 50 West Liberty Street.
Telephone: 702-788-8666.
Fax: 702-788-8682.

MEMBERS OF FIRM

Jeffrey P. Zucker
Colleen A. Dolan (Resident, Reno Office)
David C. Whittemore
Gary Wayne Duhon (Resident, Reno Office)
Mark H. Goldstein
Paul D. Bancroft (Resident, Reno Office)

ASSOCIATES

Carl D. Savely
Bryan M. Williams
Layne J. Butt
Jeffrey D. Baustert
Mark Lemmons
Sandra D. Turner
Mark A. McIntire
Daniel Clay McGuire
Lynn S. Fulstone
Christopher R. Coley (Resident, Reno Office)
E.A. Rosenfeld

Representative Clients: Caesars Palace; Dermody Properties; First City Properties, Inc.; Hilton Hotels Corp.; Howard Hughes Properties; Lewis Homes of Nevada; MGM Grand, Inc.; Pacific Properties & Development Corporation; ITT Sheraton Corporation; Lake at Las Vegas.

For Complete List of Firm Personnel, See General Section

For full biographical listings, see the Martindale-Hubbell Law Directory

MILES & TIERNEY (AV)

3170 West Sahara Avenue Suite D-11, 89102
Telephone: 702-252-7120
FAX: 702-252-0916

MEMBERS OF FIRM

Charles H. Miles, Jr.
Keith J. Tierney

For full biographical listings, see the Martindale-Hubbell Law Directory

MONSEY & ANDREWS (AV)

3900 Paradise Road, Suite 283, 89109
Telephone: 702-732-9897
Facsimile: 702-732-9667
Boulder City, Nevada Office: 402 Nevada Highway.
Telephone: 702-294-1112.
Facsimile: 294-0235.

MEMBERS OF FIRM

Earl Monsey
B. G. Andrews (Resident, Boulder City, Nevada)

Representative Clients: Chrysler Capital Corp.; Jack Matthews Realty; Mortgage Loans America; United Pacific Insurance Co.; Planet Insurance Co.; Reliance Insurance Co.; KNPR Nevada Public Radio Corporation; Agassi Enterprises; World Savings; The Walt Disney Co.

For full biographical listings, see the Martindale-Hubbell Law Directory

PICO & MITCHELL (AV)

2000 South Eastern Avenue, 89104
Telephone: 702-457-9099
FAX: 702-457-8451

MEMBERS OF FIRM

James F. Pico
Bert O. Mitchell
Christy Brad Escobar

ASSOCIATES

James R. Rosenberger
Cory Hilton
Gary L. Myers
Lawrence Davidson
E. Breen Arntz
Thomas A. Ericsson
Robert W. Cottle
Linda M. Graham

Representative Clients: Home Insurance Co.; State Farm Mutual Insurance Co.; Industrial Indemnity Ins. Co.; Great American Insurance Co.; Argonaut Insurance Cos.; Clark County Medical Society; Rose de Lima Hospital; Fairway Chevrolet; American States Insurance Co.; Hartford Ins.

For full biographical listings, see the Martindale-Hubbell Law Directory

Las Vegas—Continued

SCHRECK, JONES, BERNHARD, WOLOSON & GODFREY, CHARTERED (AV)

600 East Charleston Boulevard, 89104
Telephone: 702-382-2101
Fax: 702-382-8135

Frank A. Schreck	Lance C. Earl
Leslie Terry Jones	Thomas R. Canham
Peter C. Bernhard	Sean T. McGowan
Kenneth A. Woloson	Dawn M. Cica
John A. Godfrey	F. Edward Mulholland, II
David D. Johnson	Todd L. Bice
James R. Chamberlain	James J. Pisanelli
Michelle L. Morgando	Ellen L. Schulhofer

John M. McManus

OF COUNSEL

Howard W. Cannon

For full biographical listings, see the Martindale-Hubbell Law Directory

WOODBURN AND WEDGE (AV)

Suite 620 Bank of America Plaza, 300 South Fourth Street, 89101
Telephone: 702-387-1000
Reno, Nevada Office: 16th Floor, First Interstate Bank Building. P.O. Box 2311.
Telephone: 702-688-3000.
Telecopier: 702-688-3088.

MEMBER OF FIRM

Casey Woodburn Vlautin

ASSOCIATES

David G. Johnson	Gregg P. Barnard

Representative Clients: Atlantic Richfield Co.; Sierra Pacific Power Co.; The Union Pacific Railroad Co.; Western Union Telegraph Co.; Cyprus Minerals Corp.; The Roman Catholic Bishop of Reno, A Corporation Sole.

For full biographical listings, see the Martindale-Hubbell Law Directory

*RENO,** Washoe Co.

HALE, LANE, PEEK, DENNISON AND HOWARD (AV)

Porsche Building, 100 West Liberty Street, Tenth Floor, P.O. Box 3237, 89501
Telephone: 702-786-7900
Telefax: 702-786-6179
Las Vegas, Nevada Office: Suite 800, Nevada Financial Center, 2300 West Sahara Avenue, Box 8.
Telephone: 702-362-5118.
Fax: 702-365-6940.

MEMBERS OF FIRM

Steve Lane	R. Craig Howard
J. Stephen Peek	Stephen V. Novacek
Karen D. Dennison	William C. Davis, Jr.

Representative Clients: Lenders: U.S. Bank of Nevada; First Western Bank; Home Federal Bank, Savings Bank; First Interstate Bank of Nevada; Pioneer Citizens Bank of Nevada. Title Companies: Chicago Title Insurance Co. Shopping Centers: Moana West Shopping Center. Construction and Development: Caughlin Ranch; McKenzie Construction, Inc.; Western Water Development Co.

For Complete List of Firm Personnel, See General Section

For full biographical listings, see the Martindale-Hubbell Law Directory

MCDONALD, CARANO, WILSON, MCCUNE, BERGIN, FRANKOVICH & HICKS (AV)

241 Ridge Street, 89505
Telephone: 702-322-0635
Telecopier: 702-786-9532
Las Vegas, Nevada Office: Suite 1000, 2300 West Sahara Avenue.
Telephone: 702-873-4100.
Telecopier: 702-873-9966.

MEMBERS OF FIRM

John J. McCune	Leo P. Bergin, III

John J. Frankovich

ASSOCIATES

Valerie Cooke Skau	David F. Grove
Andrew P. Gordon (Resident, Las Vegas Office)	

Representative Clients: Boomtown, Inc.; Eldorado Hotel & Casino; Intermountain Federal Land Bank Association (Nevada Counsel); Jackpot Enterprises, Inc.; James Hardie (USA), Inc.; Pioneer Citizens Bank of Nevada; Primadonna Resorts.

For Complete List of Firm Personnel, See General Section

For full biographical listings, see the Martindale-Hubbell Law Directory

VARGAS & BARTLETT (AV)

201 West Liberty Street, P.O. Box 281, 89504
Telephone: 702-786-5000
Cable Address: "Varbadix"
Fax: 702-786-1177

MEMBERS OF FIRM

George L. Vargas (1909-1985)	John P. Sande, III
John C. Bartlett (1910-1982)	William J. Raggio
James P. Logan (1920-1984)	Linda A. Bowman
Louis Mead Dixon (1919-1993)	C. Thomas Burton, Jr.

Clinton E. Wooster

ASSOCIATES

Jeffrey J. Whitehead	Michael G. Alonso

For Complete List of Firm Personnel, See General Section

For full biographical listings, see the Martindale-Hubbell Law Directory

WOODBURN AND WEDGE (AV)

16th Floor, First Interstate Bank Building, One East First Street, P.O. Box 2311, 89505
Telephone: 702-688-3000
Telecopier: 702-688-3088
Las Vegas, Nevada Office: Suite 620 Bank of American Plaza, 300 South Court Street.
Telephone: 702-387-1000.

MEMBERS OF FIRM

Casey Woodburn Vlautin	Kirk S. Schumacher

ASSOCIATE

Gregg P. Barnard

Representative Clients: Atlantic Richfield Co.; Sierra Pacific Power Co.; The Union Pacific Railroad Co.; Western Union Telegraph Co.; Bank of America; Cyprus Minerals Corp.; The Roman Catholic Bishop of Reno, A Corporation Sole.

For full biographical listings, see the Martindale-Hubbell Law Directory

NEW HAMPSHIRE

*CONCORD,** Merrimack Co.

ORR & RENO, PROFESSIONAL ASSOCIATION (AV)

One Eagle Square, P.O. Box 3550, 03302-3550
Telephone: 603-224-2381
Fax: 603-224-2318

Mary Susan Leahy

Representative Clients: Beach Aircraft Corporation; Chubb Life America; Fleet Bank; Dartmouth-Hitchcock Medical Center; EnergyNorth, Inc.; National Grange Mutual Co.; New England College; New England Electric System Co.; Newspapers of New England, Inc.; St. Paul's School.

For Complete List of Firm Personnel, See General Section

For full biographical listings, see the Martindale-Hubbell Law Directory

*EXETER,** Rockingham Co.

HOLLAND, DONOVAN, BECKETT & HERMANS, PROFESSIONAL ASSOCIATION (AV)

151 Water Street, P.O. Box 1090, 03833
Telephone: 603-772-5956
Fax: 603-778-1434

John W. Perkins (1902-1973)	Robert B. Donovan
Everett P. Holland (1915-1993)	William H. M. Beckett

Stephen G. Hermans

Ronald G. Sutherland

For full biographical listings, see the Martindale-Hubbell Law Directory

*LACONIA,** Belknap Co.

NORMANDIN, CHENEY & O'NEIL (AV)

Normandin Square, 213 Union Avenue, P.O. Box 575, 03247-0575
Telephone: 603-524-4380

MEMBERS OF FIRM

Paul L. Normandin	John D. O'Shea, Jr.

Robert A. Dietz

Counsel for: Laconia Savings Bank; Lakes Region Mental Health Center; Laconia Airport Authority; Community TV Corp.; Central New Hampshire Realty, Inc.; All Metals Industries, Inc.; Lakes Region Anesthesiology, P.A.; Cormier Corp.; Scotia Technology; Vemaline Products.

For Complete List of Firm Personnel, See General Section

For full biographical listings, see the Martindale-Hubbell Law Directory

NEW JERSEY

ATLANTIC CITY, Atlantic Co.

Levine, Staller, Sklar, Chan & Brodsky, P.A. (AV)
3030 Atlantic Avenue, 08401
Telephone: 609-348-1300
Telecopier: 609-345-2473

Lee A. Levine
Alan C. Staller
Arthur E. Sklar
Paul T. Chan
Lawrence A. Brodsky
Brian J. Cullen
Benjamin Zeltner

Arthur M. Brown
Scott J. Mitnick

Representative Clients: A. G. Edwards & Sons, Inc.; Atlantic Plastic Containers Inc.; The Michaels Development Co., Inc.; Nawas International Travel Services, Inc.; Trump Casino Hotels - Atlantic City, NJ; Interstate Realty Management Company.

For full biographical listings, see the Martindale-Hubbell Law Directory

BERNARDSVILLE, Somerset Co.

Shain, Schaffer & Rafanello, A Professional Corporation (AV)
150 Morristown Road, 07924
Telephone: 908-953-9300
Fax: 908-953-2969

Joel L. Shain
Marguerite M. Schaffer
Richard A. Rafanello
Jeffrey A. Donner
Joyce Wilkins Pollison
Todd R. Staretz

OF COUNSEL
Elliott L. Katz

For full biographical listings, see the Martindale-Hubbell Law Directory

CLIFTON, Passaic Co.

Celentano, Stadtmauer & Walentowicz (AV)
1035 Route 46 East, P.O. Box 2594, 07015-2594
Telephone: 201-778-1771
Telecopier: 201-778-4136

MEMBERS OF FIRM
John A. Celentano, Jr.
Arnold L. Stadtmauer
Henry Walentowicz

Ellen M. Seigerman

Representative Clients: Jefferson National Bank (N.A.); Clifton Savings Bank, S.L.A.; The General Hospital Center at Passaic (commercial); Passaic Boys Club; Smith Sondy Asphalt Construction Co., Inc.; Boro Lumber Co., Inc.; Castle Arms Condominium; ADX Copy Corp.; Country Club Towers.
References: Jefferson National Bank (N.A.), Passaic, New Jersey; Commonwealth Land Title Insurance Co., Paterson, New Jersey.

For full biographical listings, see the Martindale-Hubbell Law Directory

*FLEMINGTON,** Hunterdon Co.

Large, Scammell & Danziger, A Professional Corporation (AV)
117 Main Street, 08822
Telephone: 908-782-5313
Fax: 908-782-4816

Robert F. Danziger
C. Gregory Watts
Richard L. Tice
Kenneth J. Skowronek
Joseph H. Mulherin

Christine Naples Little
OF COUNSEL
Edwin K. Large, Jr.
Scott Scammell, II (1918-1984)

Representative Clients: Agway, Inc.; Algonquin Gas Transmission Co.; E. I. duPont; Flemington National Bank and Trust Company; Prestige State Bank; Summit Bank.

For full biographical listings, see the Martindale-Hubbell Law Directory

FLORHAM PARK, Morris Co.

Hack, Piro, O'Day, Merklinger, Wallace & McKenna, P.A. (AV)
30 Columbia Turnpike, P.O. Box 941, 07932-0941
Telephone: 201-301-6500
Fax: 201-301-0094

(See Next Column)

David L. Hack
John M. McKenna

Angela J. Mendelsohn
Michelle M. Monte
John F. Lanahan
Rosemarie Deehan Berard

Representative Clients: Cenlar Federal Savings Bank; County Mortgage Company, Inc.; First Fidelity Bank, N.A., N.J.; Citicorp Mortgage, Inc.; Travelers Insurance Co.; State Farm Insurance Companies; Aetna Life & Casualty Co.

For Complete List of Firm Personnel, See General Section

For full biographical listings, see the Martindale-Hubbell Law Directory

*HACKENSACK,** Bergen Co.

Breslin and Breslin, P.A. (AV)
41 Main Street, 07601
Telephone: 201-342-4014; 342-4015
Fax: 201-342-0068; 201-342-3077

John J. Breslin, Jr. (1899-1987)
James A. Breslin, Sr. (1900-1980)
Charles Rodgers
E. Carter Corriston
Donald A. Caminiti

Michael T. Fitzpatrick
Angelo A. Bello
Terrence J. Corriston
Kevin C. Corriston
Karen Boe Gatlin
Lawrence Farber
E. Carter Corriston, Jr.

Representative Clients: Bergen County Housing Authority; Phillips Fuel Co.; Prudential Insurance Co.; Rent Leveling Board of Township of North Bergen; Housing Authority of Passaic.
Reference: United Jersey Bank.

For Complete List of Firm Personnel, See General Section

For full biographical listings, see the Martindale-Hubbell Law Directory

Dunn, Pashman, Sponzilli, Swick & Finnerty (AV)
411 Hackensack Avenue, 07601
Telephone: 201-489-1500; 845-4000
Fax: 201-489-1512

COUNSEL
Morris Pashman
Murray L. Cole
Paul D. Rosenberg

MEMBERS OF FIRM
Joseph Dunn
Louis Pashman
John E. Finnerty
Edward G. Sponzilli
Daniel A. Swick
Robert E. Rochford
Warren S. Robins

ASSOCIATES
Nicholas F. Pellitta
Laura S. Kirsch
Danya A. Grunyk
Richard P. Jacobson
Jeffrey M. Shapiro
Deborah L. Ustas
Mark E. Lichtblau
Edward B. Stevenson
Stephen F. Roth

References: United Jersey Bank; Valley National Bank.

For full biographical listings, see the Martindale-Hubbell Law Directory

Hein, Smith, Berezin, Maloof & Rogers (AV)
Court Plaza East, 19 Main Street, 07601-7023
Telephone: 201-487-7400
Telecopier: 201-487-4228

MEMBER OF FIRM
Alan A. Davidson
OF COUNSEL
Seymour A. Smith

For Complete List of Firm Personnel, See General Section

For full biographical listings, see the Martindale-Hubbell Law Directory

Stephen H. Roth (AV)
62 Summit Avenue, 07601
Telephone: 201-489-3737
Fax: 201-489-0557

ASSOCIATE
Michele M. De Santis

Reference: Citizens First National Bank.

For full biographical listings, see the Martindale-Hubbell Law Directory

Shapiro & Shapiro (AV)
Continental Plaza II, 411 Hackensack Avenue, 07601
Telephone: 201-488-3900
Fax: 201-488-9481

(See Next Column)

SHAPIRO & SHAPIRO, *Hackensack—Continued*

Robert P. Shapiro — Susan W. Shapiro (1943-1990)
John P. Di Iorio

ASSOCIATES

David O. Marcus — Robert F. Green

Reference: National Community Bank.

For full biographical listings, see the Martindale-Hubbell Law Directory

SOKOL, BEHOT AND FIORENZO (AV)

39 Hudson Street, 07601
Telephone: 201-488-1300
Fax: 201-488-6541

MEMBERS OF FIRM

Leon J. Sokol — Joseph B. Fiorenzo
Joseph F. Behot, Jr. — Jeffrey A. Zenn

ASSOCIATES

Siobhan C. Spillane — Susan I. Wegner
Jeffrey M. Kahan

COUNSEL

Arthur Bergman — Alan Prigal

For full biographical listings, see the Martindale-Hubbell Law Directory

STOLDT AND HORAN, A PROFESSIONAL CORPORATION (AV)

Continental Plaza, 401 Hackensack Avenue, 07601
Telephone: 201-646-9200
Telecopier: 201-646-0167

Sydney V. Stoldt, Jr. — John D. Horan

Judith R. Levinson — Dorothy A. Kowal

For full biographical listings, see the Martindale-Hubbell Law Directory

HAWTHORNE, Passaic Co.

JEFFER, HOPKINSON, VOGEL, COOMBER & PEIFFER (AV)

(Formerly Jeffer, Walter, Tierney, DeKorte, Hopkinson & Vogel)
Law Building, 1600 Route 208N, P.O. Box 507, 07507
Telephone: 201-423-0100
Fax: 201-423-5614
Tequesta, Florida Office: 250 Tequesta Drive.
Telephone: 407-747-6000.
Fax: 407-575-9167.
New York, N.Y. Office: Suite 2206, 150 Broadway.
Telephone: 212-406-7260.

MEMBERS OF FIRM

Jerome A. Vogel — Gary D. Peiffer

ASSOCIATE

Darryl W. Siss

Counsel for: Brioschi, Inc.; Opici Wine Co.; Gas Pumpers of America Corp.; Jupiter Tequesta National Bank; Burroughs Development Corp.; Cedar Hill Developers; McBride Enterprises; Thomas Construction Co.

For Complete List of Firm Personnel, See General Section

For full biographical listings, see the Martindale-Hubbell Law Directory

KENILWORTH, Union Co.

ALDAN O. MARKSON (AV)

726 Boulevard, P.O. Box 236, 07033-0236
Telephone: 908-241-5555
Fax: 908-241-5529

Reference: United Counties Trust.

For full biographical listings, see the Martindale-Hubbell Law Directory

LIVINGSTON, Essex Co.

SKOLOFF & WOLFE (AV)

293 Eisenhower Parkway, 07039
Telephone: 201-992-0900
Fax: 201-992-0301
Morristown, New Jersey Office: 10 Park Place.
Telephone: 201-267-3511.

Saul A. Wolfe

For full biographical listings, see the Martindale-Hubbell Law Directory

MONTVALE, Bergen Co.

BEATTIE PADOVANO (AV)

50 Chestnut Ridge Road, P.O. Box 244, 07645-0244
Telephone: 201-573-1810
Fax: (DEX) 201-573-9736

(See Next Column)

MEMBERS OF FIRM

James R. Beattie — Martin W. Kafafian
Thomas W. Dunn — Adolph A. Romei

ASSOCIATE

Brenda J. McAdoo

Reference: United Jersey Bank.

For Complete List of Firm Personnel, See General Section

For full biographical listings, see the Martindale-Hubbell Law Directory

MOORESTOWN, Burlington Co.

BRANDT, HAUGHEY, PENBERTHY, LEWIS, HYLAND & CLAYPOOLE, A PROFESSIONAL CORPORATION (AV)

240 West State Highway 38, P.O. Box 1002, 08057-0949
Telephone: 609-235-1111
Telecopier: 609-722-0357

S. David Brandt — Susan L. Claypoole
Gerald E. Haughey — Patrick F. McAndrew
Edward A. Penberthy — Thomas J. DiPilla, Jr.
Robert S. Lewis — Steven A. Aboloff
William F. Hyland, Jr. — Eileen K. Fahey

Representative Clients: City of Camden (Tax Matters); Davis Enterprises; Deptford Mall, Inc.; McDonald's Corp.; Mobil Oil Corp.; Chemical Bank; Continental Title Insurance Co.; Texaco; The Radner/Canuso Partnership.

For full biographical listings, see the Martindale-Hubbell Law Directory

*MORRISTOWN,** Morris Co.

MCKIRDY AND RISKIN, A PROFESSIONAL CORPORATION (AV)

136 South Street, 07962-2379
Telephone: 201-539-8900
Fax: 201-984-5529

Edward D. McKirdy — John H. Buonocore, Jr.
Harry J. Riskin — Thomas M. Olson

For full biographical listings, see the Martindale-Hubbell Law Directory

PITNEY, HARDIN, KIPP & SZUCH (AV)

Park Avenue at Morris County, P.O. Box 1945, 07962-1945
Telephone: 201-966-6300
New York City: 212-926-0331
Telex: 642014
Telecopier: 201-966-1550

MEMBERS OF FIRM

David J. Connolly, Jr. — Glenn C. Geiger
Lawrence F. Reilly — Joel M. Rosen
Harriett Jane Olson

COUNSEL

Paul E. Flanagan — Thomas J. Malman

ASSOCIATES

Colleen R. Donovan — Deirdre E. Moore
Kathleen T. Kneis — Pamela A. Humbert

Representative Clients: AlliedSignal Inc.; AT&T; Base Ten Systems, Inc.; Exxon Corp.; Ford Motor Co.; Midlantic National Bank; Sony Electronics, Inc.; Union Carbide Corp.; United Parcel Services, Inc.; Warner-Lambert Co.

For Complete List of Firm Personnel, See General Section

For full biographical listings, see the Martindale-Hubbell Law Directory

SHANLEY & FISHER, A PROFESSIONAL CORPORATION (AV)

131 Madison Avenue, 07962-1979
Telephone: 201-285-1000
Telecopier: 1-201-285-1098
Telex: 475-4255 (I.T.T.)
Cable Address: "Shanley"
New York, N.Y. Office: 89th Floor, One World Trade Center.
Telephone: 212-321-1812.
Telecopier: 1-212-466-0569.

John Kandravy — Richard D. Prentice
Gerald W. Hull, Jr. — Robert A. Gladstone
Glenn S. Pantel — Michael Osterman

OF COUNSEL

Louis L. D'Arminio

Robert A. DelVecchio — Robert A. Klausner
Ieva I. Rogers — Michael E. Rothpletz, Jr.

For Complete List of Firm Personnel, See General Section

For full biographical listings, see the Martindale-Hubbell Law Directory

*NEWARK,** Essex Co.

CARPENTER, BENNETT & MORRISSEY (AV)

(Formerly Carpenter, Gilmour & Dwyer)
Three Gateway Center, 17th Floor, 100 Mulberry Street, 07102-4079
Telephone: 201-622-7711
New York City: 212-943-6530
Telex: 139405
Telecopier: 201-622-5314
EasyLink: 62827845
ABA/net: CARPENTERB

MEMBERS OF FIRM

Francis X. O'Brien
Edward F. Day, Jr.
John D. Goldsmith

ASSOCIATES

Hans G. Polak
Douglas S. Witte
Dawn M. Felipe

Representative Clients: General Motors Corp.; E. I. du Pont de Nemours and Company; Texaco Inc.; AT&T; Litton Industries; ITT Corp.; International Flavors & Fragrances Inc.; New Jersey Hospital Association; Prudential Insurance Company of America; United Jersey Bank.

For Complete List of Firm Personnel, See General Section

For full biographical listings, see the Martindale-Hubbell Law Directory

FOX AND FOX (AV)

570 Broad Street, 07102
Telephone: 201-622-3624
Telecopier: 201-622-6220

MEMBERS OF FIRM

David I. Fox
Arthur D. Grossman
Paul I. Rosenberg
Kenneth H. Fast
Martin Kesselhaut
Dennis J. Alessi
Gabriel H. Halpern
Steven A. Holt
Nancy C. McDonald

OF COUNSEL

Jacob Fox (1898-1992)
Martin S. Fox
Robert J. Rohrberger
Robert S. Catapano-Friedman

ASSOCIATES

Robert P. Donovan
Stacey B. Rosenberg
Susan R. Fox
Virginia S. Ryan
Ronnie Ann Powell
Katherine J. Welsh
Craig S. Gumpel
Brett Alison Rosenberg
Alfred V. Acquaviva
Anthony F. Vitiello

For full biographical listings, see the Martindale-Hubbell Law Directory

HELLRING LINDEMAN GOLDSTEIN & SIEGAL (AV)

One Gateway Center, 07102-5386
Telephone: 201-621-9020
Telecopier: 201-621-7406

Philip Lindeman, II
Michael Edelson
Charles Oransky
John A. Adler
Judah I. Elstein
Val Mandel
Sarah Jane Jelin
David N. Narciso

For Complete List of Firm Personnel, See General Section

For full biographical listings, see the Martindale-Hubbell Law Directory

McCARTER & ENGLISH (AV)

Four Gateway Center, 100 Mulberry Street, P.O. Box 652, 07101-0652
Telephone: 201-622-4444
Telecopier: 201-624-7070
Cable Address: "McCarter" Newark
Cherry Hill, New Jersey Office: 1810 Chapel Avenue West.
Telephone: 609-662-8444.
Telecopier: 609-662-6203.
New York, New York Office: Suite 1519, One World Trade Center.
Telephone: 212-466-9018.
Telecopier: 212-432-6568.
Boca Raton, Florida Office: 2255 Glades Road, Suite 319-A.
Telephone: 407-994-6262.
Telecopier: 407-241-0798.
Wilmington, Delaware Office: Mellon Bank Center, 919 Market Street.
Telephone: 302-654-8010.
Telecopier: 302-654-0795.

MEMBERS OF FIRM

George C. Witte, Jr.
Lois M. Van Deusen
Frank E. Ferruggia
Carol C. Stern
Martin F. Dowd

For Complete List of Firm Personnel, See General Section

For full biographical listings, see the Martindale-Hubbell Law Directory

MEYNER AND LANDIS (AV)

One Gateway Center, Suite 2500, 07102-5311
Telephone: 201-624-2800
Fax: 201-624-0356

MEMBERS OF FIRM

Edwin C. Landis, Jr.
Jeffrey L. Reiner
John N. Malyska
William J. Fiore
Anthony F. Siliato
Francis R. Perkins
Geralyn A. Boccher
Howard O. Thompson
Robert B. Meyner (1908-1990)

ASSOCIATES

Kathryn Schatz Koles
Linda Townley Snyder
William H. Schmidt, Jr.
Scott T. McCleary
Maureen K Higgins
Richard A. Haws
Michael J. Palumbo
Theodore E. Lorenz

For full biographical listings, see the Martindale-Hubbell Law Directory

SILLS CUMMIS ZUCKERMAN RADIN TISCHMAN EPSTEIN & GROSS, A PROFESSIONAL CORPORATION (AV)

One Riverfront Plaza, 07102-5400
Telephone: 201-643-7000
Fax: 201-643-6500
Telex: 820630 Sillsbeck Nwk
Atlantic City, New Jersey Office: 17 Gordon's Alley.
Telephone: 609-344-2800.
New York, N.Y. Office: 250 Park Avenue.
Telephone: 212-643-7000.

Stanley Tannenbaum
Jeffrey Hugh Newman
Morris Yamner
Gerald Span
Noah Bronkesh (Resident at Atlantic City, N.J. Office)
Margaret F. Black
Richard J. Schulman (Not admitted in NJ)
Bernard I. Flateman
Kathleen Gengaro
David J. Rabinowitz
Ronald C. Rak
Mark S. Olinsky

Wayne B. Heicklen (Not admitted in NJ)
Harry B. Noretsky
Steven Shapiro (Not admitted in NJ)
Ted Zangari
Robert Rosenberg

Representative Clients: Barnes and Noble Superstores; Hechinger Company; Circuit City Stores, Inc.; Rothschild Realty Inc.; Nature's Elements; Edison Brothers Stores, Inc.; Payless Shoe Source; Cousins New Market Development; Six Flags Great Adventure; Melvin Simon & Co.

For Complete List of Firm Personnel, See General Section

For full biographical listings, see the Martindale-Hubbell Law Directory

*NEW BRUNSWICK,** Middlesex Co.

HOAGLAND, LONGO, MORAN, DUNST & DOUKAS (AV)

40 Paterson Street, P.O. Box 480, 08903
Telephone: 908-545-4717
Fax: 908-545-4579

MEMBERS OF FIRM

John J. Hoagland
Michael J. Baker
Gary J. Hoagland
Thomas J. Walsh

ASSOCIATE

R. Michael Keefe

Representative Clients: K. Hovnanian Cos.; St. Peter's Medical Center; Akzo Chemicals, Inc.; McNichols Steel; Birchwood Homeowners Association; Cortland Neighborhood Condominium Association.

For Complete List of Firm Personnel, See General Section

For full biographical listings, see the Martindale-Hubbell Law Directory

NORTH BRUNSWICK, Middlesex Co.

BORRUS, GOLDIN, FOLEY, VIGNUOLO, HYMAN & STAHL, A PROFESSIONAL CORPORATION (AV)

2875 U.S. Highway 1, Route 1 & Finnigans Lane, P.O. Box 1963, 08902
Telephone: 908-422-1000
Fax: 908-422-1016

Jack Borrus
Martin S. Goldin
David M. Foley
Anthony B. Vignuolo
Jeffrey M. Hyman
James E. Stahl
James F. Clarkin III
Anthony M. Campisano
Aphrodite C. Koscelansky
Robert C. Nisenson
Michael L. Marcus
Eileen Mary Foley
Rosalind Westlake

OF COUNSEL

Gerald T. Foley (1903-1976)

Representative Clients: United Jersey Bank/Franklin State; R. J. Reynolds Tobacco Co.; N.J. Aluminum Co.; K. Hovnanian Enterprises, Inc.; Chicago Title Insurance Co.; Transamerica Title Insurance Co.

For full biographical listings, see the Martindale-Hubbell Law Directory

NUTLEY, Essex Co.

STRASSER & ASSOCIATES, A PROFESSIONAL CORPORATION (AV)

391 Franklin Avenue, P.O. Box 595, 07110-0107
Telephone: 201-661-5000
Fax: 201-661-0056
Saddle River, New Jersey Office: 70 East Allendale Road, 07458.
Telephone: 201-236-1861.
Fax: 201-236-1863.

William I. Strasser

Robert J. Bavagnoli
Stephen J. Morrone

For full biographical listings, see the Martindale-Hubbell Law Directory

PARAMUS, Bergen Co.

STERN STEIGER CROLAND, A PROFESSIONAL CORPORATION (AV)

One Mack Centre Drive, Mack Centre II, 07652
Telephone: 201-262-9400
Telecopier: 201-262-6055

Howard Stern
Joel J. Steiger
Barry I. Croland
Gerald Goldman
Donald R. Sorkow (1930-1985)
Norman Tanenbaum
Barry L. Baime
Jay Rubenstein
Frank L. Brunetti
Kenneth S. Goldrich
Bruce J. Ackerman
Thomas Loikith
John J. Stern
Stuart Reiser
William J. Heimbuch
Edward P. D'Alessio
E. Drew Britcher
Meridith J. Bronson
Valerie D. Solimano

William R. Kugelman
Mindy Michaels Roth
Neil E. Kozek
Lizabeth Sarakin
Joanne T. Nowicki
Armand Leone, Jr.
Craig P. Caggiano
Jeffrey P. Gardner
David Torchin

OF COUNSEL

Harvey R. Sorkow

Representative Clients: K Mart Corp.; Meyer Brothers Department Stores.

For full biographical listings, see the Martindale-Hubbell Law Directory

PARSIPPANY, Morris Co.

BARON, GALLAGHER, HERTZBERG & PERZLEY (AV)

Waterview Plaza, 2001 Route 46, 07054
Telephone: 201-335-7400
Telecopier: 201-335-8018

MEMBERS OF FIRM

Jack P. Baron
Jerome F. Gallagher, Jr.
Robert C. Hertzberg
Alan H. Perzley

ASSOCIATES

Kathleen Cavanaugh
Susan Burns
Philip A. Orsi
David A. Moss

For full biographical listings, see the Martindale-Hubbell Law Directory

PRINCETON, Mercer Co.

MCCARTHY AND SCHATZMAN, P.A. (AV)

228 Alexander Street, P.O. Box 2329, 08543-2329
Telephone: 609-924-1199
Fax: 609-683-5251

John F. McCarthy, Jr.
Richard Schatzman
G. Christopher Baker
John F. McCarthy, III
Michael A. Spero
Barbara Strapp Nelson
W. Scott Stoner

James A. Endicott
Angelo J. Onofri

Representative Clients: Trustees of Princeton University; The Linpro Co.; United Jersey Bank; Chemical Bank, New Jersey, N.A.; Carnegie Center Associates; Merrill Lynch Pierce Fenner & Smith, Inc.; Prudential Insurance Co.

For full biographical listings, see the Martindale-Hubbell Law Directory

MEZEY & MEZEY, A PROFESSIONAL CORPORATION (AV)

Princeton Executive Campus, P.O. Box 8439, 08543
Telephone: 609-951-0200
Fax: 609-951-8677
New Brunswick, New Jersey Office: 93 Bayard Street.
Telephone: 908-545-6011.

(See Next Column)

Louis A. Mezey (1929-1982)
Frederick C. Mezey
Deborah A. Cohen (1947-1993)

OF COUNSEL

Brandon Martin
Scott M. Russ
Kevin G. Blessing

For full biographical listings, see the Martindale-Hubbell Law Directory

RAMSEY, Bergen Co.

WEBER, MUTH & WEBER (AV)

One Cherry Lane, P.O. Box 912, 07446-0912
Telephone: 201-327-5000
Telecopier: 201-327-6848

MEMBER OF FIRM

Irwin B. Klugman

ASSOCIATES

Carole Ann Geronimo
Cynthia A. Kasica

For Complete List of Firm Personnel, See General Section

For full biographical listings, see the Martindale-Hubbell Law Directory

ROSELAND, Essex Co.

BRACH, EICHLER, ROSENBERG, SILVER, BERNSTEIN, HAMMER & GLADSTONE, A PROFESSIONAL CORPORATION (AV)

101 Eisenhower Parkway, 07068
Telephone: 201-228-5700
Telecopier: 201-228-7852

Alan R. Hammer
Bruce Kleinman
Paul F. Rosenberg
Michael I. Schneck
Harris R. Silver
Alexander J. Tafro

Alois V. Habjan
John P. Inglesino
Jill Daitch Rosenberg
Louis P. Lagios
Bruce J. Schanzer
Dennis P. Powers

OF COUNSEL

George Y. Sodowick

Representative Clients: The Kushner Cos.; ARC Properties, Inc.; Cali Associates; Eastman Construction; Bocina Development; WSR Corp.; Cirkus Real Estate; Gebroe-Hammer Associates; The Resolution Trust Corp.; Tibor Pivko & Company.

For Complete List of Firm Personnel, See General Section

For full biographical listings, see the Martindale-Hubbell Law Directory

HANNOCH WEISMAN, A PROFESSIONAL CORPORATION (AV)

4 Becker Farm Road, 07068-3788
Telephone: 201-535-5300
New York: 212-732-3262
Telecopier: 201-994-7198
Mailing Address: P.O. Box 1040, Newark, New Jersey, 07101-9819
Washington, D.C. Office: Suite 600, 1150 Seventeenth Street, N.W.
Telephone: 202-296-3432.

Sanders M. Chattman
Robert C. Epstein
Dean A. Gaver
Stuart J. Glick
Howard A. Kantrowitz
Carleton Richard Kemph
Richard M. Slotkin

Michael J. Geiger
Marie A. Latoff
Cynthia L. Warren

For Complete List of Firm Personnel, See General Section

For full biographical listings, see the Martindale-Hubbell Law Directory

POST, POLAK, GOODSELL & MACNEILL, P.A. (AV)

65 Livingston Avenue, 07068
Telephone: 201-994-1100
Telecopier: 201-994-1705
New York, New York Office: Suite 1006, 575 Madison Avenue.
Telephone: 212-486-1455.

John N. Post
Robert A. Goodsell
Paul D. Strauchler

Mark H. Peckman

For full biographical listings, see the Martindale-Hubbell Law Directory

SADDLE RIVER, Bergen Co.

STRASSER & ASSOCIATES, A PROFESSIONAL CORPORATION (AV)
70 East Allendale Rd., 07458
Telephone: 201-236-1861
Fax: 201-236-1863
Nutley, New Jersey Office: 391 Franklin Avenue, 07110-0107.
Telephone: 201-661-5000.
Fax: 201-661-0056.

William I. Strasser

SECAUCUS, Hudson Co.

ROSENBLUM, WOLF & LLOYD, A PROFESSIONAL CORPORATION (AV)
One Harmon Plaza, 07094
Telephone: 201-330-0220
Fax: 201-863-5472

Leo Rosenblum (1906-1990)
Edward G. Rosenblum
Nathan P. Wolf
John R. Lloyd

Reference: The Bank of New York, formerly National Community Bank.

For full biographical listings, see the Martindale-Hubbell Law Directory

*SOMERVILLE,** Somerset Co.

OZZARD WHARTON, A PROFESSIONAL PARTNERSHIP (AV)
75-77 North Bridge Street, P.O. Box 938, 08876
Telephone: 908-526-0700
Telecopier: 908-526-2246

William E. Ozzard
William B. Savo
Edward M. Hogan
Michael V. Camerino

Arthur D. Fialk
Ellen M. Gillespie
Michael G. Friedman
Suzette Nanovic Berrios
Lori E. Salowe

OF COUNSEL

A. Arthur Davis, 3rd
Louis A. Imfeld
John H. Beekman, Jr.
Mark F. Strauss

Representative Clients: American Cyanamid; Science Management Corp.; Mack Development Co.; New Jersey Savings Bank; Summit Bank; Neil Van Cleef Enterprises; SJP Properties; Larken Associates; The Morris Co.

For Complete List of Firm Personnel, See General Section

For full biographical listings, see the Martindale-Hubbell Law Directory

RAYMOND R. AND ANN W. TROMBADORE A PROFESSIONAL CORPORATION (AV)
33 East High Street, 08876
Telephone: 908-722-7555
Fax: 908-722-6269

Raymond R. Trombadore

Megan C. Seel

OF COUNSEL

Ann W. Trombadore

References: Summit Bank; New Jersey Savings Bank; Somerset Savings & Loan Assn.

For full biographical listings, see the Martindale-Hubbell Law Directory

SUMMIT, Union Co.

BOURNE, NOLL & KENYON, A PROFESSIONAL CORPORATION (AV)
382 Springfield Avenue, 07901
Telephone: 908-277-2200
Telecopier: 908-277-6808

Donald Bourne (1903-1987)
Edward T. Kenyon
Cary R. Hardy
Charles R. Berman
Kenneth R. Johanson
Martin Rubashkin
David G. White
Roger Mehner
James R. Ottobre

OF COUNSEL

Robert B. Bourne
Clyde M. Noll (Retired)

Lauren K. Harris
Jaime A. O'Brien
Ellyn A. Draikiwicz
Dean T. Bennett
Craig M. Lessner
Michael O'B. Boldt
Christopher D. Boyman
Paul Ramirez
Timothy A. Kalas
Robert F. Moriarty
Mary E. Scrupski

For full biographical listings, see the Martindale-Hubbell Law Directory

COOPER ROSE & ENGLISH (AV)
480 Morris Avenue, 07901-1527
Telephone: 908-273-1212
Fax: 908-273-8922
Rumson, New Jersey Office: 20 Bingham Avenue. 07760.
Telephone: 908-741-7777.
Fax: 908-758-1879.

MEMBERS OF FIRM

John W. Cooper
Frederick W. Rose
Jerry Fitzgerald English
Joseph E. Imbriaco
Roger S. Clapp
Arthur H. Garvin, III
Peter M. Burke
Gary F. Danis
John J. DeLaney, Jr.
David G. Hardin

OF COUNSEL

Harrison F. Durand
Russell T. Kerby, Jr.
Ronald J. Tell

ASSOCIATES

Fredi L. Pearlmutter
Kristi Bragg
Stephen R. Geller
Peter W. Ulicny
Thomas J. Sateary
Gianfranco A. Pietrafesa
Donna M. Russo
J. Andrew Kinsey
Jonathan S. Chester
Daniel Jon Kleinman
Holly English
Margaret R. Kalas
Mary T. Zdanowicz
Robert A. Meyers
Richard F. Iglar

Counsel for: Ciba-Geigy Corp.; Witco Corp.; New Jersey American Water Co.; Mikropul Corp.; AT&T Bell Laboratories; Aircast.

For full biographical listings, see the Martindale-Hubbell Law Directory

*TRENTON,** Mercer Co.

SCHRAGGER, LAVINE & NAGY, A PROFESSIONAL CORPORATION (AV)
The Atrium at Lawrence, 133 Franklin Corner Road (Lawrenceville), 08648
Telephone: 609-896-9777
Fax: 609-895-1373

Alan S. Lavine
Bruce M. Schragger
Raymond L. Nagy
James A. Schragger

OF COUNSEL

Henry C. Schragger
A. Jerome Moore

Representative Clients: Sears, Roebuck & Co.; New Jersey Manufacturers Insurance Co.; Mercer County Community College; Mercer Mutual Insurance Co..

For Complete List of Firm Personnel, See General Section

For full biographical listings, see the Martindale-Hubbell Law Directory

STERNS & WEINROTH (AV)
50 West State Street, Suite 1400, P.O. Box 1298, 08607-1298
Telephone: 609-392-2100
Fax: 609-392-7956
Atlantic City, New Jersey Office: 2901 Atlantic Avenue, Suite 201, 08401.
Telephone: 609-340-8300.
Fax: 609-340-8722.
Washington, D.C. Office: 1150 Seventeenth Street, N.W., Suite 600, 20036.
Telephone: 202-296-3432.

Frank J. Petrino
David M. Roskos

Brian J. Mulligan

For Complete List of Firm Personnel, See General Section

For full biographical listings, see the Martindale-Hubbell Law Directory

WAYNE, Passaic Co.

WILLIAMS, CALIRI, MILLER & OTLEY, A PROFESSIONAL CORPORATION (AV)
1428 Route 23, P.O. Box 995, 07474-0995
Telephone: 201-694-0800
Telecopier: 201-694-0302

Walter E. Williams (1904-1985)
David J. Caliri (Retired)
Richard S. Miller
Victor C. Otley, Jr.
Peter B. Eddy
William S. Robertson, III
David Golub
David C. Wigfield
Samuel G. Destito
John H. Hague
Stuart M. Geschwind
Steven A. Weisberger
Lawrence J. McDermott, Jr.
Darlene J. Pereksta
Hope M. Pomerantz
Cheryl H. Burstein
Joanne M. Sarubbi
Daniel Arent Colfax
David T. Miller

Representative Clients: Anchor Savings Bank, FSB; Federal Deposit Insurance Corporation (FDIC): The Hartford Accident and Indemnity Co.; The Ramapo Bank; Reliance Insurance Co.; Resolution Trust Corporation

(See Next Column)

WILLIAMS, CALIRI, MILLER & OTLEY A PROFESSIONAL CORPORATION, *Wayne—Continued*

(RTC); Time-Warner Communications, Inc.; New Jersey Sports and Exposition Authority.

For full biographical listings, see the Martindale-Hubbell Law Directory

WEST CALDWELL, Essex Co.

RONALD REICHSTEIN (AV)

West Caldwell Office Park, 195 Fairfield Avenue, Suite 4C, 07006
Telephone: 201-228-8818
Fax: 201-228-5730

References: National Community Bank; Chemical Bank.

For full biographical listings, see the Martindale-Hubbell Law Directory

WESTFIELD, Union Co.

LINDABURY, McCORMICK & ESTABROOK, A PROFESSIONAL CORPORATION (AV)

53 Cardinal Drive, P.O. Box 2369, 07091
Telephone: 908-233-6800
Fax: 908-233-5078

Anthony J. LaRusso
John R. Blasi
J. Ferd Convery III
James K. Estabrook
Robert S. Burney

OF COUNSEL

Kenneth L. Estabrook

Representative Clients: Chilton Memorial Hospital; Elberon Development Co.; Elizabeth General Medical Center; Kessler Institute for Rehabilitation; Messano Construction Co.; The Morey-La Rue Laundry Co.; Summit Bank; United Jersey Bank; Western Industries, Inc.

For Complete List of Firm Personnel, See General Section

For full biographical listings, see the Martindale-Hubbell Law Directory

WEST PATERSON, Passaic Co.

EVANS HAND (AV)

One Garret Mountain Plaza, Interstate 80 at Squirrelwood Road, 07424-3396
Telephone: 201-881-1100
Fax: 201-881-1369

MEMBERS OF FIRM

Douglas C. Borchard, Jr.
Charles D. LaFiura
Thomas F. Craig, II

ASSOCIATE

Lynda S. Korfmann

Representative Clients: Midlantic National Bank; The Bank of New York/ National Community Division; The Prudential Insurance Co. of America; Connecticut General Life Insurance Co.; Travelers Insurance Co.; New Jersey Manufacturers Insurance Co.; Bell Atlantic; Algonquin Gas Transmission Co.; Tenneco, Inc.; Corning Glass Works.

For Complete List of Firm Personnel, See General Section

For full biographical listings, see the Martindale-Hubbell Law Directory

WOODBRIDGE, Middlesex Co.

GREENBAUM, ROWE, SMITH, RAVIN AND DAVIS (AV)

Metro Corporate Campus I, P.O. Box 5600, 07095-0988
Telephone: 908-549-5600
Cable Address: "Greelaw"
Telecopier: 908-549-1881
ABA Net: 2 529

MEMBERS OF FIRM

Robert S. Greenbaum
Arthur M. Greenbaum
Wendell A. Smith
Robert C. Schachter
Benjamin D. Lambert, Jr.
Thomas J. Denitzio, Jr.
Kenneth T. Bills
Christine F. Li
Meryl Ann Greenhause Gonchar
Gary A. Kotler
Kerry Brian Flowers

ASSOCIATE

Marc D. Policastro

For Complete List of Firm Personnel, See General Section

For full biographical listings, see the Martindale-Hubbell Law Directory

WILENTZ, GOLDMAN & SPITZER, A PROFESSIONAL CORPORATION (AV)

90 Woodbridge Center Drive Suite 900, Box 10, 07095
Telephone: 908-636-8000
Telecopier: 908-855-6117
Eatontown, New Jersey Office: Meridian Center I, Two Industrial Way West, 07724.
Telephone: 908-493-1000.
Telecopier: 908-493-8387.
New York, New York Office: Wall Street Plaza, 88 Pine Street, 9th Floor, 10005.
Telephone: 212-267-3091.
Telecopier: 212-267-3828.

Robert A. Petito
Nicholas L. Santowasso
Vincent P. Maltese
Joseph J. Jankowski
Roy H. Tanzman
Paul T. Swanicke
Jeffrey R. Rich

LiliAnn Messina
Susanne Salzer O'Donohue
Holly Lichtenstein Goldberg
Michael R. Scinto

Representative Clients: Bankers Savings; Amerada Hess Corp.; CoreStates/-New Jersey National Bank.

For Complete List of Firm Personnel, See General Section

For full biographical listings, see the Martindale-Hubbell Law Directory

NEW MEXICO

*ALBUQUERQUE,** Bernalillo Co.

CAMPBELL, PICA, OLSON & SEEGMILLER (AV)

6565 Americas Parkway, N.E., Suite 800, P.O. Box 35459, 87176
Telephone: 505-883-9110
Fax: 505-884-3882

MEMBERS OF FIRM

Lewis O. Campbell
Nicholas R. Pica
David C. Olson
Douglas Seegmiller

ASSOCIATES

Brad Vaughn
Roger A. Stansbury
Philip Craig Snyder
Arthur J. G. Lacerte, Jr.
Jeffrey C. Gilmore

Representative Clients: Phelps Dodge Corporation; Chino Mines Company; Large Power Users Coalition; Sara Lee Corporation; New Mexico Retail Association; Compania Minera Ojos Del Salado S.A.

For full biographical listings, see the Martindale-Hubbell Law Directory

HINKLE, COX, EATON, COFFIELD & HENSLEY (AV)

Suite 800, 500 Marquette, N.W., P.O. Box 2043, 87103
Telephone: 505-768-1500
FAX: 505-768-1529
Roswell, New Mexico Office: Suite 700, United Bank Plaza, P.O. Box 10, 88202.
Telephone: 505-622-6510.
FAX: 505-623-9332.
Midland, Texas Office: 6 Desta Drive, Suite 2800, P.O. Box 3580, 79705.
Telephone: 915-683-4691.
FAX: 915-683-6518.
Amarillo, Texas Office: 1700 Bank One Center. P.O. Box 9238, 79105-9238.
Telephone: 806-372-5569.
FAX: 806-372-9761.
Santa Fe, New Mexico Office: 218 Montezuma, P.O. Box 2068, 87504.
Telephone: 505-982-4554.
FAX: 505-982-8623.
Austin, Texas Office: 401 West 15th Street, Suite 800, 78701.
Telephone: 512-476-7137.
FAX: 512-476-5431.
Associated Office: Hoffman & Stephens, P.C., 401 West 15th Street, Suite 800, 78701.
Telephone: 512-476-5434.
Fax: 512-476-5431.

Fred W. Schwendimann
Thomas E. Hood (Amarillo Office)
Margaret Carter Ludewig
S. Barry Paisner (Santa Fe Office)

ASSOCIATE

Scott A. Shuart (Amarillo Office)

Representative Clients: Anadarko Petroleum Corp.; Atlantic Richfield Co.; Bass Enterprises Production Co.; BHP Petroleum; Caroon & Black Management, Inc.; Chevron, USA, Inc.; CIGNA; City of Albuquerque; Coastal Oil & Gas Corp. Co.; Ethicon Inc., A Johnson & Johnson, Co.; Diagnostik; Conoco; Texaco; Presbyterian Healthcare Services.

(See Next Column)

HINKLE, COX, EATON, COFFIELD & HENSLEY—*Continued*

For Complete List of Firm Personnel, See General Section

For full biographical listings, see the Martindale-Hubbell Law Directory

KELLY, RAMMELKAMP, MUEHLENWEG, LUCERO & LEÓN, A PROFESSIONAL ASSOCIATION (AV)

Simms Tower, 400 Gold Avenue S.W., Suite 500, P.O. Box 25127, 87125-5127
Telephone: 505-247-8860
Fax: 505-247-8881

Henry A. Kelly
Robert J. Muehlenweg
Orlando Lucero

Representative Clients: Resolution Trust Corporation; First Bank of Grants; Bank of America, New Mexico; John L. Rust Co. (Caterpillar); Bridgers & Paxton Consulting Engineers, Inc.; Albuquerque Title Co.; Cinco Bisco Limited; Newman Newsom, Inc.; Envirco Corporation; Transamerica Partners #1.

For Complete List of Firm Personnel, See General Section

For full biographical listings, see the Martindale-Hubbell Law Directory

MILLER, STRATVERT, TORGERSON & SCHLENKER, P.A. (AV)

500 Marquette Avenue, N.W., Suite 1100, P.O. Box 25687, 87102
Telephone: 505-842-1950
Facsimile: 505-243-4408
Farmington, New Mexico Office: Suite 300, 300 West Arrington. P.O. Box 869.
Telephone: 505-326-4521.
Facsimile: 505-325-5474.
Las Cruces, New Mexico Office: Suite 300, 277 East Amador. P.O. Drawer 1231.
Telephone: 505-523-2481.
Facsimile: 505-526-2215.
Santa Fe, New Mexico Office: 125 Lincoln Avenue, Suite 221. P.O. Box 1986.
Telephone: 505-989-9614.
Facsimile: 505-989-9857.

Ranne B. Miller
Alan C. Torgerson
Kendall O. Schlenker
Alice Tomlinson Lorenz
Gregory W. Chase
Alan Konrad
Margo J. McCormick
Lyman G. Sandy
Stephen M. Williams
Stephan M. Vidmar
Robert C. Gutierrez
Seth V. Bingham (Resident at Farmington Office)
Michael H. Hoses
James B. Collins (Resident at Farmington Office)
Timothy Ray Briggs
Walter R. Parr (Resident at Santa Fe Office)
Rudolph A. Lucero
Daniel E. Ramczyk
Dean G. Constantine
Deborah A. Solove
Gary L. Gordon
Lawrence R. White (Resident at Las Cruces Office)
Sharon P. Gross
Virginia Anderman
Marte D. Lightstone
Bradford K. Goodwin
John R. Funk (Resident at Las Cruces Office)
J. Scott Hall (Resident at Santa Fe Office)
Thomas R. Mack
Michael J. Happe (Resident at Farmington Office)
Denise Barela Shepherd
Nancy Augustus
Jill Burtram
Terri L. Sauer
Joel T. Newton (Resident at Las Cruces Office)
Judith K. Nakamura
Thomas M. Domme
David H. Thomas, III
C. Brian Charlton

COUNSEL

William K. Stratvert
Paul W. Robinson

Representative Clients: Ticor Title Insurance Co.; Dona Ana Savings and Loan Assn.; Citizens Bank of Las Cruces; U.S. West Communications.

For Complete List of Firm Personnel, See General Section

For full biographical listings, see the Martindale-Hubbell Law Directory

RODEY, DICKASON, SLOAN, AKIN & ROBB, P.A. (AV)

Albuquerque Plaza, Suite 2200, 201 Third Street, N.W., P.O. Box 1888, 87103-1888
Telephone: 505-765-5900
Fax: 505-768-7395
Santa Fe, New Mexico Office: Suite 101 Marcy Plaza, 123 East Marcy Street, P.O. Box 1357, 87504-1357.
Telephone: 505-984-0100.
Fax: 505-989-9542.

Robert M. St. John
John P. Salazar
John P. Burton (Resident, Santa Fe Office)
Catherine T. Goldberg
Jo Saxton Brayer
Nancy J. Appleby
David C. Davenport, Jr. (Resident, Santa Fe Office)
James P. Fitzgerald
Mark A. Smith

(See Next Column)

Jay D. Hill

For Complete List of Firm Personnel, See General Section

For full biographical listings, see the Martindale-Hubbell Law Directory

SHEEHAN, SHEEHAN & STELZNER, P.A. (AV)

Suite 300, 707 Broadway, N.E., P.O. Box 271, 87103
Telephone: 505-247-0411
Fax: 505-842-8890

Craig T. Erickson
Juan L. Flores
Kim A. Griffith
Philip P. Larragoite
Susan C. Little
Maria O'Brien
Judith D. Schrandt
Timothy M. Sheehan
Luis G. Stelzner
Elizabeth Newlin Taylor
Robert P. Warburton

OF COUNSEL

Briggs F. Cheney
Charles T. DuMars
Thomas J. Horan
Pat Sheehan

Representative Clients: Archdiocese of Santa Fe; Britton Construction, Inc.; Brothers of the Good Shepherd; Herbert M. Denish & Associates, Inc.; Jaynes Corp.; Las Campanas de Santa Fe (A Lyle Anderson Co.); Orthopedic Associates; Partners Properties; R.D. Habiger & Associates, Inc.; Wright Mains Koester, Inc.

For full biographical listings, see the Martindale-Hubbell Law Directory

FARMINGTON, San Juan Co.

MILLER, STRATVERT, TORGERSON & SCHLENKER, P.A. (AV)

Suite 300, 300 West Arrington, P.O. Box 869, 87401
Telephone: 505-326-4521
Facsimile: 505-325-5474
Albuquerque, New Mexico Office: 500 Marquette Avenue, N.W., Suite 1100. P.O. Box 25687.
Telephone: 505-842-1950.
Facsimile: 505-243-4408.
Las Cruces, New Mexico Office: Suite 300, 277 East Amador. P.O. Drawer 1231.
Telephone: 505-523-2481.
Facsimile: 505-526-2215.
Santa Fe, New Mexico Office: 125 Lincoln Avenue, Suite 221. P.O. Box 1986.
Telephone: 505-989-9614.
Facsimile: 505-989-9857.

James B. Collins
Seth V. Bingham
Michael J. Happe

Representative Clients: St. Paul Insurance Cos.; State Farm Mutual Automobile Insurance Co.; The Travelers; United States Fidelity & Guaranty Co.; New Mexico Physicians Mutual Liability Insurance Co.; Farmers Insurance Group.

For full biographical listings, see the Martindale-Hubbell Law Directory

HOBBS, Lea Co.

GARY DON REAGAN, P.A. (AV)

501 North Linam, P.O. Box 780, 88241
Telephone: 505-397-6551
Fax: 505-393-2252

Gary Don Reagan
Mark Terrence Sánchez

Reference: United New Mexico Bank of Lea County; City of Eunice; Sunwest Bank of Hobbs, N.A.; F.D.I.C.; R.T.C.; Zia Properties; Gaff Dairy; High Lonesome Dairy.

For full biographical listings, see the Martindale-Hubbell Law Directory

*LAS CRUCES,** Dona Ana Co.

MILLER, STRATVERT, TORGERSON & SCHLENKER, P.A. (AV)

Suite 300, 277 East Amador, P.O. Drawer 1231, 88004
Telephone: 505-523-2481
Facsimile: 505-526-2215
Albuquerque, New Mexico Office: 500 Marquette Avenue, N.W., Suite 1100. P.O. Box 25687.
Telephone: 505-842-1950.
Facsimile: 505-243-4408.
Farmington, New Mexico Office: Suite 300, 300 West Arrington. P.O. Box 869.
Telephone: 505-326-4521.
Facsimile: 505-325-5474.
Santa Fe, New Mexico Office: 125 Lincoln Avenue, Suite 221. P.O. Box 1986.
Telephone: 505-989-9614.
Facsimile: 505-989-9857.

(See Next Column)

MILLER, STRATVERT, TORGERSON & SCHLENKER P.A., *Las Cruces—Continued*

Lawrence R. White
John R. Funk
Joel T. Newton

Representative Clients: St. Paul Insurance Cos.; State Farm Mutual Automobile Insurance Co.; The Travelers; United States Fidelity & Guaranty Co.; New Mexico Physicians Mutual Liability Insurance Co.; Farmers Insurance Group; U.S. West Communications; Ticor Title Insurance Co.; Dona Ana Savings and Loan Assn.; Citizens Bank of Las Cruces.

For full biographical listings, see the Martindale-Hubbell Law Directory

WEINBRENNER, RICHARDS, PAULOWSKY & RAMIREZ, P.A. (AV)

8th Floor, First National Tower, P.O. Drawer O, 88004-1719
Telephone: 505-524-8624
Fax: 505-524-4252

Ralph Wm. Richards

General Counsel for: Stahmann Farms, Inc.; First National Bank of Dona Ana County.
Representative Clients: American General Cos.; Hartford Group; CNA Insurance; Fireman's Fund; United States Fidelity & Guaranty Co.; Travelers Insurance Co.; General Accident Group.

For Complete List of Firm Personnel, See General Section

For full biographical listings, see the Martindale-Hubbell Law Directory

*SANTA FE,** Santa Fe Co.

CATRON, CATRON & SAWTELL, A PROFESSIONAL ASSOCIATION (AV)

2006 Botulph Road, P.O. Box 788, 87504-0788
Telephone: 505-982-1947
Telecopier: 505-986-1013

Thomas B. Catron III
Fletcher R. Catron
John S. Catron
W. Anthony Sawtell
William A. Sawtell, Jr.
Forrest S. Smith
Kathrin M. Kinzer-Ellington

LEGAL SUPPORT PERSONNEL

Peggy L. Feldt (Certified Public Accountant)

Attorneys for: Santa Fe Board of Education; American Express Co.; The Santa Fe Opera; Sunwest Bank of Santa Fe; VNS Health Services, Inc.; Rancho del Oso Pardo.

For Complete List of Firm Personnel, See General Section

For full biographical listings, see the Martindale-Hubbell Law Directory

HINKLE, COX, EATON, COFFIELD & HENSLEY (AV)

218 Montezuma, P.O. Box 2068, 87504
Telephone: 505-982-4554
FAX: 505-982-8623
Roswell, New Mexico Office: Suite 700 United Bank Plaza, P.O. Box 10, 88202.
Telephone: 505-622-6510.
FAX: 505-623-9332.
Midland, Texas Office: 6 Desta Drive, Suite 2800, P.O. Box 3580, 79705.
Telephone: 915-683-4691.
FAX: 915-683-6518.
Amarillo, Texas Office: 1700 Bank One Center, P.O. Box 9238, 79105-9238.
Telephone: 806-372-5569.
FAX: 806-372-9761.
Albuquerque, New Mexico Office: Suite 800, 500 Marquette, N.W., P.O. Box 2043, 87103.
Telephone: 505-768-1500.
FAX: 505-768-1529.
Austin, Texas Office: 401 West 15th Street, Suite 800, 78701.
Telephone: 512-476-7137.
FAX: 512-476-5431.
Associated Office: Hoffman & Stephens, P.C., 401 West 15th Street, Suite 800, 78701.
Telephone: 512-476-5434.
Fax: 512-476-5431.

RESIDENT PARTNERS

Conrad E. Coffield
Thomas M. Hnasko
Jeffrey L. Fornaciari
S. Barry Paisner

Representative Clients: Banded Peak Ranch; Conservation Fund; Fernandez Co., Ltd.; Love Mountain Ranch;

For full biographical listings, see the Martindale-Hubbell Law Directory

ROTH, VAN AMBERG, GROSS, ROGERS & ORTIZ (AV)

347 East Palace Avenue, P.O. Box 1447, 87501
Telephone: 505-983-7319; 988-8979
Fax: 505-983-7508

(See Next Column)

F. Joel Roth
Michael P. Gross
Ronald J. Van Amberg
Carl Bryant Rogers
Raymond Z. Ortiz

Reference: First Interstate Bank.

For full biographical listings, see the Martindale-Hubbell Law Directory

SCHEUER, YOST & PATTERSON, A PROFESSIONAL CORPORATION (AV)

125 Lincoln Avenue, Suite 223, P.O. Drawer 9570, 87504
Telephone: 505-982-9911
Fax: 505-982-1621

Ralph H. Scheuer
Roger L. Prucino
Mel E. Yost
Elizabeth A. Jaffe
John N. Patterson
Tracy Erin Conner
Holly A. Hart
Ruth M. Fuess

OF COUNSEL

Melvin T. Yost

Representative Clients: Cyprus-AMAX, Inc.; Century Bank, FSB; Los Alamos National Bank; Santa Fe Abstract, Ltd.; St. John's College; Santa Fe Housing Authority; Sun Loan Companies; Taos Development & Holding Co.; Territorial Abstract & Title Co.; Tosco Corporation.

For full biographical listings, see the Martindale-Hubbell Law Directory

WHITE, KOCH, KELLY & MCCARTHY, A PROFESSIONAL ASSOCIATION (AV)

433 Paseo De Peralta, P.O. Box 787, 87504-0787
Telephone: 505-982-4374
ABA/NET: 1154
Fax: 505-982-0350; 984-8631

William Booker Kelly
Janet Clow
John F. McCarthy, Jr.
Kevin V. Reilly
Benjamin J. Phillips
Charles W. N. Thompson, Jr.
David F. Cunningham
M. Karen Kilgore
Albert V. Gonzales
Sandra J. Brinck

SPECIAL COUNSEL

Paul L. Bloom

Aaron J. Wolf
Carolyn R. Glick

Representative Clients: Southern Pacific Transportation Co.; Nationwide Insurance Co.; Risk Management Division of New Mexico General Services Department; Alliance of American Insurers; Santa Fe Community College; First American Title Insurance Co.; Century Bank; Public Service Company of New Mexico; AT&SF Railway Co.; Gallager Bassett.

For full biographical listings, see the Martindale-Hubbell Law Directory

NEW YORK

*ALBANY,** Albany Co.

ISEMAN, CUNNINGHAM, RIESTER & HYDE (AV)

9 Thurlow Terrace, 12203
Telephone: 518-462-3000
Telecopier: 518-462-4199

MEMBERS OF FIRM

Frederick C. Riester
Robert Hall Iseman
Michael J. Cunningham
Carol Ann Hyde
Michael J. McNeil

Brian M. Culnan
Linda J. Clark

For full biographical listings, see the Martindale-Hubbell Law Directory

MOSER & MOSER (AV)

126 State Street, 12207
Telephone: 518-449-4643
New York, N.Y. Office: 50 Broadway.
Telephone: 212-344-4200.
Telecopier: 212-635-5470.
Philadelphia, Pennsylvania Office: 1822 Spring Garden Street.
Telephone: 215-564-7649.
Washington, D.C. Office: 1000 Connecticut Avenue, N.W.
Telephone: 202-857-8450.

MEMBER OF FIRM

Joel H. Moser

For full biographical listings, see the Martindale-Hubbell Law Directory

Albany—Continued

SHANLEY, SWEENEY & REILLY, P.C. (AV)

The Castle at Ten Thurlow Terrace, 12203
Telephone: 518-463-1415
Saratoga Springs, New York Office: 480 Broadway.
Telephone: 518-583-0777.
Fax: 518-583-1184.

Michael P. Shanley, Jr.
Robert L. Sweeney
J. Stephen Reilly (Resident, Saratoga Springs Office)
John L. Allen
Frank P. Milano
Gregory D. Faucher
J. Michael Naughton
Mark R. Marcantano
Patricia Hart Nessler
Lisa M. Peraza
Bonnie J. Riggi
Scott P. Olson

For full biographical listings, see the Martindale-Hubbell Law Directory

*BUFFALO,** Erie Co.

BLOCK & COLUCCI, P.C. (AV)

1250 Statler Towers, 14202
Telephone: 716-854-4080; 1-800-388-2595
Telex: 919-186
Fax: 716-854-0059
Litigation Fax: 716-854-4070
Jupiter, Florida Office: 1001 N. U.S. Highway One, Suite 400.
Telephone: 407-747-0110.
Fax: 407-743-0046.
Albany, New York Office: 12 Century Hill Drive, P.O. Box 1160, (Latham).
Telephone: 518-783-0535.
Fax: 518-783-5670.
Binghamton, New York Office: The Press Building, 19 Chenago Street.
Telephone: 607-724-3138.
Fax: 607-724-6227.
Rochester, New York Office: 30 West Broad Street, Suite 200.
Telephone: 716-454-1660.
Fax: 716-454-7134.
Syracuse, New York Office: 5786 Widewaters Parkway.
Telephone: 315-445-1272.
Fax: 315-445-9530.

Ernest L. Colucci (1909-1989)
David Simon Brown
Steven S. Brown
Anthony J. Colucci, Jr.
Anthony J. Colucci, III
Mark K. Cramer
William P. Hessney, Jr. (Resident at Albany Office)
William T. Jebb, II
Cheryl A. Short

Elpiniki M. Bechakas
Frank M. Cassara
Dennis H. Cleary
Frank V. Fontana
Marie L. Gallagher
Kathleen M. Kaczor
Scott J. Leitten
John J. Marchese
John K. McAndrew
Kathleen F. McGovern (Resident, Albany Office)
Melanie C. Mecca
Natalie A. Napierala
Margaret Logan Noonan
Michael W. Schafer
Lawrence R. Schwach
Damon H. Serota
Debra A. Spellman
Maureen Tucker
Frederick R. Xlander (Resident Binghamton Office)

OF COUNSEL

Lester H. Block
Joseph F. Crangle

SPECIAL COUNSEL

Richard D. Nadel (Not admitted in NY; Resident, Jupiter, Florida Office)

References: Manufacturers & Traders Trust Co.; Palm Beach National Bank & Trust Co.

For full biographical listings, see the Martindale-Hubbell Law Directory

CARLE PLACE, Nassau Co.

DOLLINGER, GONSKI, GROSSMAN, PERMUT & HIRSCHHORN (AV)

One Old Country Road, 11514
Telephone: 516-747-1010
Telecopier: 516-747-2494

MEMBERS OF FIRM

Matthew Dollinger
Dennis M. Gonski
Floyd G. Grossman
Michael Permut
Alan K. Hirschhorn

ASSOCIATES

Leslie Ann Foodim
Michael J. Spithogiannis
Jessica M. Seidman
Bruce N. Roberts
Alicia B. Devins
Bryan J. Holzberg
Mindy Anne Wallach
Rachel L. Hollander

Reference: Marine Midland National Bank, Carle Place, New York.

For full biographical listings, see the Martindale-Hubbell Law Directory

EAST MEADOW, Nassau Co.

CERTILMAN BALIN ADLER & HYMAN, LLP (AV)

90 Merrick Avenue, 11554
Telephone: 516-296-7000
Telecopier: 516-296-7111

MEMBERS OF FIRM

Ira J. Adler
Dale Allinson
Herbert M. Balin
Bruce J. Bergman
Michael D. Brofman
Morton L. Certilman
Murray Greenberg
David Z. Herman
Richard Herzbach
M. Allan Hyman
Bernard Hyman
Donna-Marie Korth
Steven J. Kuperschmid
Thomas J. McNamara
Fred S. Skolnik
Louis Soloway
Harold Somer
Howard M. Stein
Brian K. Ziegler

OF COUNSEL

Daniel S. Cohan
Norman J. Levy
Marilyn Price

ASSOCIATES

Howard B. Busch
Scott M. Gerber
Jodi S. Hoffman
Glenn Kleinbaum
Michael C. Manniello
Jaspreet S. Mayall
Stacey R. Miller
Lawrence S. Novak
Kim J. Radbell

For full biographical listings, see the Martindale-Hubbell Law Directory

GARDEN CITY, Nassau Co.

FISCHOFF, GELBERG & DIRECTOR (AV)

600 Old Country Road, Suite 410, 11530
Telephone: 516-228-4255
Facsimile: 516-228-4278

MEMBERS OF FIRM

Stuart P. Gelberg
Gary C. Fischoff
Michael C. Director

ASSOCIATES

Scott R. Schneider
Heath Berger

For full biographical listings, see the Martindale-Hubbell Law Directory

JASPAN, GINSBERG, SCHLESINGER, SILVERMAN & HOFFMAN (AV)

300 Garden City Plaza, 11530
Telephone: 516-746-8000
Telecopier: 516-746-0552

MEMBERS OF FIRM

Arthur W. Jaspan
Eugene S. Ginsberg
Steven R. Schlesinger
Kenneth P. Silverman
Carol M. Hoffman
Stanley A. Camhi
Eugene P. Cimini, Jr.
Holly Juster
Stephen P. Epstein
Gary F. Herbst
Allen Perlstein

For Complete List of Firm Personnel, See General Section

For full biographical listings, see the Martindale-Hubbell Law Directory

REDMOND, POLLIO & PITTONI, P.C. (AV)

1461 Franklin Avenue, 11530
Telephone: 516-248-2500
Telecopier: 516-248-2348

Benedict J. Pollio
M. John Pittoni

Mark E. Costello
Kathleen M. Galgano
Rachel Cohen Quaid
Ronald A. Pollio

For Complete List of Firm Personnel, See General Section

For full biographical listings, see the Martindale-Hubbell Law Directory

HUNTINGTON, Suffolk Co.

GOLDSTEIN & RUBINTON, P.C. (AV)

18 West Carver Street, 11743
Telephone: 516-421-9051
Telefax: 516-421-9122

Arthur Goldstein
Peter D. Rubinton
Ronald L. Goldstein
S. Russ Di Fazio

References: Chemical Bank; New York Trust Co.; Town of Huntingdon.

For full biographical listings, see the Martindale-Hubbell Law Directory

Huntington—Continued

SMYTH & LACK (AV)

202 East Main Street, 11743
Telephone: 516-271-7500
Telecopier: 516-271-7504

MEMBERS OF FIRM

Vincent A. Smyth
James J. Lack

ASSOCIATES

Thomas P. Solferino
Dana M. Barberis
Stephen I. Witdorchic

Reference: Chemical Bank.

For full biographical listings, see the Martindale-Hubbell Law Directory

MASPETH, Queens Co.

EDWARD M. MCGOWAN (AV)

68-15 Borden Avenue, 11378
Telephone: 718-651-7360
Telecopier: 718-446-0796

For full biographical listings, see the Martindale-Hubbell Law Directory

MIDDLETOWN, Orange Co.

MACVEAN, LEWIS, SHERWIN & MCDERMOTT, P.C. (AV)

34 Grove Street, P.O. Box 310, 10940
Telephone: 914-343-3000
Fax: 914-343-3866

Kenneth A. MacVean
Louis H. Sherwin
Kermit W. Lewis
Paul T. McDermott
Jeffrey D. Sherwin

George F. Roesch, III
Michael F. McCusker
Thomas P. Clarke, Jr.

OF COUNSEL

V. Frank Cline

Counsel for: Orange County Trust Co.; Middletown Savings Bank; First Federal Savings & Loan Association of Middletown; Goshen Savings Bank; Advest Bank.

For Complete List of Firm Personnel, See General Section

For full biographical listings, see the Martindale-Hubbell Law Directory

*MINEOLA,** Nassau Co.

KENNEDY & COMERFORD (AV)

200 Old Country Road, 11501
Telephone: 516-741-8818
Fax: 516-741-1703
New York, N.Y. Office: 805 Third Avenue.
Telephone: 212-750-1614.
Fax: 212-750-2885.

Bernard P. Kennedy
Michael J. Comerford

ASSOCIATE

Anne Marie Caradonna

OF COUNSEL

William J. Poisson
Patrick J. Hackett

For full biographical listings, see the Martindale-Hubbell Law Directory

KOEPPEL MARTONE LEISTMAN & HERMAN (AV)

155 First Street, 11501
Telephone: 516-747-6300
Telecopier: 516-741-5065

Bernard Sommer (1922-1992)
Michael R. Martone
Adolph Koeppel
Donald F. Leistman
Jay M. Herman

Rhoda Koeppel
Risë E. Rosen
Jamie P. Alpern
Lisa M. LaValle
Daniel J. Baker

OF COUNSEL

Joel P. Koeppel

Reference: European American Bank.

For full biographical listings, see the Martindale-Hubbell Law Directory

MOUNT KISCO, Westchester Co.

ANDERSON, BANKS, CURRAN & DONOGHUE (AV)

61 Smith Avenue, 10549
Telephone: 914-666-2161
Telecopier: 914-666-3292

(See Next Column)

MEMBERS OF FIRM

Stanley E. Anderson (1928-1965)
Lawrence W. Thomas
William F. Banks
John M. Donoghue
Stanley E. Anderson, Jr.
Gregory Keefe
Maurice F. Curran
James P. Drohan
Rochelle J. Auslander

ASSOCIATES

Barbara Banks Schwam
Daniel Petigrow
Suzanne Johnston
Stuart Waxman

OF COUNSEL

Margaret A. Clark

Representative Clients: The Centennial Life Insurance Company of America.

For full biographical listings, see the Martindale-Hubbell Law Directory

*NEW CITY,** Rockland Co.

FREEMAN & LOFTUS (AV)

4 Laurel Road, P.O. Box 629, 10956-0629
Telephone: 914-634-0888
Fax: 914-634-9312

MEMBERS OF FIRM

James J. Freeman, Jr.
Patrick J. Loftus

OF COUNSEL

James H. Bowers
Ira M. Emanuel
Albert J. Kaiser

For full biographical listings, see the Martindale-Hubbell Law Directory

GRANIK SILVERMAN SANDBERG CAMPBELL NOWICKI RESNIK HEKKER (AV)

254 South Main Street, 10956
Telephone: 914-634-8822; 800-822-1238

MEMBERS OF FIRM

Joseph F. X. Nowicki (1922-1976)
Martin L. Sandberg
Patrick M. Campbell
Robert R. Granik (1922-1994)
Kenneth H. Resnik
David W. Silverman
John M. Hekker
Ricki Hollis Berger

ASSOCIATE

Catherine T. O'Toole Lauritano

OF COUNSEL

Morrie Slifkin

For full biographical listings, see the Martindale-Hubbell Law Directory

*NEW YORK,** New York Co.

CUDDY & FEDER (AV)

60 East 42nd Street, 10168
Telephone: 212-949-6280
Telecopier: 212-949-6346
White Plains, New York Office: 90 Maple Avenue.
Telephone: 914-761-1300.
Telecopier: 914-761-5372.
Stamford, Connecticut Office: 707 Summer Street.
Telephone: 203-348-4780.
Norwalk, Connecticut Office: 4 Berkeley Street, 06850.
Telephone: 203-853-8001.
Telecopier: 203-831-8250.

MEMBER OF FIRM

Thomas R. Beirne (Resident)

For full biographical listings, see the Martindale-Hubbell Law Directory

FISHER & DONOVAN (AV)

405 Park Avenue, 10022
Telephone: 212-980-1900
Telefax: 212-223-0966

MEMBERS OF FIRM

Herbert F. Fisher
Nicholas T. Donovan

For full biographical listings, see the Martindale-Hubbell Law Directory

GANZ, HOLLINGER & TOWE (AV)

1394 Third Avenue, 10021
Telephone: 212-517-5500; 838-9600
Cable Address: "Ganzlaw New York"
Telex: 852970 GANZLAW NYK
FAX: 212-772-2720; 772-2216

David L. Ganz
Jerrietta R. Hollinger
Teri Noel Towe

ASSOCIATE

Nancy A. Torres (Not admitted in NY)

For full biographical listings, see the Martindale-Hubbell Law Directory

New York—Continued

Gilmartin, Poster & Shafto (AV)

One William Street, 10004
Telephone: 212-425-3220
Telex: 235073
Cable Address: "Lawpost"
Telecopier: (212) 425-3130

MEMBERS OF FIRM

Richard A. Bertocci
Patrick J. Gilmartin
Michael C. Lambert
Joseph A. Lenczycki, Jr.
Harold S. Poster
Robert L. Poster
Donald B. Shafto

ASSOCIATE

William K. Sheehy

For full biographical listings, see the Martindale-Hubbell Law Directory

Goetz, Fitzpatrick & Flynn (AV)

One Pennsylvania Plaza, 10119-0196
Telephone: 212-695-7455
Telecopier: 212-629-4013

MEMBERS OF FIRM

Gerard E. Fitzpatrick (1929-1985)
Peter Goetz
William B. Flynn
Thomas S. Finegan
Donald J. Carbone
Neal M. Eiseman
Thomas F. Cohen
Robert A. Sesti

ASSOCIATES

Lynn T. Daly
Jane Goetz
Robert M. McCartin
Alan Winkler

OF COUNSEL

Frank Muller
Charles H. Rosenberg
Harvey A. Wechsler

For full biographical listings, see the Martindale-Hubbell Law Directory

Goldberg, Weprin & Ustin (AV)

22nd Floor, 1501 Broadway, 10036
Telephone: 212-221-5700

MEMBERS OF FIRM

Jack Weprin
Arnold I. Mazel
Mark E. Kaufman
Iris A. Albstein

ASSOCIATES

Erik Veski
Andrew W. Albstein
Michael R. Bush
Barry E. Zweigbaum
Steven R. Uffner
Stephanie E. Paulos
Debbie Zacharia
Annmarie Kearney-Wood

OF COUNSEL

Goldie Rotenberg

Representative Clients: American Savings Bank; Merit Oil of New York, Inc.; Newmark & Co.
Reference: Chemical Bank.

For full biographical listings, see the Martindale-Hubbell Law Directory

Goldstick, Weinberger, Feldman & Grossman, P.C. (AV)

261 Madison Avenue, 10016-2389
Telephone: 212-687-3440
Telecopier: 212-818-0625

Bonnie Covey
Howard L. Grossman
Jane Rosenberg
Sonja Talesnik
Edward I. Weiner

OF COUNSEL

Eugene H. Feldman
Susan Kahan Rifkin
Sidney B. Weinberger

For full biographical listings, see the Martindale-Hubbell Law Directory

Max E. Greenberg, Trager, Toplitz & Herbst (AV)

100 Church Street, 10007
Telephone: 212-267-5700
Telecopier: 212-267-5814
West Orange, New Jersey Office: 200 Executive Drive West.
Telephone: 201-641-3110.
Fax: 201-731-0163.
Staten Island, New York Office: 1688 Victory Boulevard.
Telephone: 718-981-6335.
Fax: 718-981-6386.

MEMBERS OF FIRM

David A. Trager
George N. Toplitz
Leonard Shabasson
Todd L. Herbst
Kalvin Kamien
Mark A. Rosen
John M. Cilmi

(See Next Column)

ASSOCIATES

Regina C. Saat
Ira C. Wellen
Robert H. Schlosser
Allison Essner
Joseph G. Portela

For full biographical listings, see the Martindale-Hubbell Law Directory

Hutton Ingram Yuzek Gainen Carroll & Bertolotti (AV)

250 Park Avenue, 10177
Telephone: 212-907-9600
Facsimile: 212-907-9681

MEMBERS OF FIRM

Ernest J. Bertolotti
Daniel L. Carroll
Roger Cukras
Larry F. Gainen
G. Thompson Hutton
Samuel W. Ingram, Jr.
Paulette Kendler
Steven Mastbaum
Dean G. Yuzek
David G. Ebert
Shane O'Neill

ASSOCIATES

Warren E. Friss
Patricia Hewitt
Gail A. Buchman
Stuart A. Christie
Beth N. Green
Timish K. Hnateyko
Jeanne F. Pucci
Jane Drummey
Adam L. Sifre
Susan Ann Fennelly
Marc J. Schneider

For full biographical listings, see the Martindale-Hubbell Law Directory

Krasner & Chen (AV)

555 Madison Avenue, Suite 600, 10022
Telephone: 212-751-7100
Telefax: 212-371-4551

MEMBERS OF FIRM

Wesley Chen
Harvey I. Krasner

For full biographical listings, see the Martindale-Hubbell Law Directory

Loeb and Loeb (AV)

A Partnership including Professional Corporations
345 Park Avenue, 10154-0037
Telephone: 212-407-4000
Facsimile: 212-407-4990
Los Angeles, California Office: Suite 1800, 1000 Wilshire Boulevard, 90017-2475.
Telephone: 213-688-3400.
Cable Address: "Loband LSA".
Telecopier: 213-688-3460; 688-3461; 688-3462.
Century City (Los Angeles), California Office: Suite 2200, 10100 Santa Monica Boulevard, Los Angeles, 90067-4164.
Telephone: 310-282-2000.
Telecopier: 310-282-2191; 282-2192.
Nashville, Tennessee Office: 45 Music Square West, 37203-3205.
Telephone: 615-749-8300.
Facsimile: 615-749-8308.
Rome, Italy Office: Piazza Digione 1, 00197.
Telephone: 011-396-808-8456.
Telecopier: 011-396-674-8223.

MEMBERS OF FIRM

Michael D. Beck
Frank E. Feder (A P.C.)
Kenneth D. Freeman
Andrew E. Lippmann

For Complete List of Firm Personnel, See General Section

For full biographical listings, see the Martindale-Hubbell Law Directory

Moser & Moser (AV)

50 Broadway, 10004
Telephone: 212-344-4200
Telecopier: 212-635-5470
Albany, New York Office: 126 State Street.
Telephone: 518-449-4643.
Philadelphia, Pennsylvania Office: 1822 Spring Garden Street.
Telephone: 215-564-7649.
Washington, D.C. Office: 1000 Connecticut Avenue, N.W.
Telephone: 202-857-8450.

MEMBER OF FIRM

Joel H. Moser

For full biographical listings, see the Martindale-Hubbell Law Directory

Stephen I. Munzer & Associates, P.C. (AV)

777 Third Avenue, 10017
Telephone: 212-755-0008
Fax: 212-755-3174

Stephen I. Munzer

(See Next Column)

STEPHEN I. MUNZER & ASSOCIATES, P.C., *New York—Continued*

Craig A. Saunders — John E. Bersin

For full biographical listings, see the Martindale-Hubbell Law Directory

OTTERBOURG, STEINDLER, HOUSTON & ROSEN, P.C. (AV)

230 Park Avenue, 10169
Telephone: 212-661-9100
Cable Address: "Otlerton";
Telecopier: 212-682-6104
Telex: 960916

Kurt J. Wolff
Donald N. Gellert
William M. Silverman
Daniel Wallen
Anthony M. Piccione
Alan Kardon

COUNSEL

Stephen B. Weissman

Stephen H. Alpert

For Complete List of Firm Personnel, See General Section

For full biographical listings, see the Martindale-Hubbell Law Directory

PARKER CHAPIN FLATTAU & KLIMPL, L.L.P. (AV)

1211 Avenue of the Americas, 10036
Telephone: 212-704-6000
Telecopier: 212-704-6288
Cable Address: "Lawpark"
Telex: 640347
Great Neck, New York Office: 175 Great Neck Road.
Telephone: 516-482-4422.
Telecopier: 516-482-4469.

MEMBERS OF FIRM

Andrea Paretts Ascher
Aurora Cassirer
Will Burt Sandler

OF COUNSEL

Harvey M. Boneparth

ASSOCIATES

Susan M. Bernhardi
Miles M. Borden
Debra A. Jaret

For Complete List of Firm Personnel, See General Section

For full biographical listings, see the Martindale-Hubbell Law Directory

SHACK & SIEGEL, P.C. (AV)

530 Fifth Avenue, 10036
Telephone: 212-782-0700
Fax: 212-730-1964

Charles F. Crames
Pamela E. Flaherty
Paul S. Goodman
Ronald S. Katz
Donald D. Shack
Jeffrey N. Siegel
Jeffrey B. Stone

Paul A. Lucido
Steven M. Lutt
Ruby S. Teich
Keith D. Wellner
Adam F. Wergeles (Not admitted in NY)

For full biographical listings, see the Martindale-Hubbell Law Directory

*POUGHKEEPSIE,** Dutchess Co.

CORBALLY, GARTLAND AND RAPPLEYEA (AV)

35 Market Street, 12601
Telephone: 914-454-1110
FAX: 914-454-4857
Millbrook, New York Office: Bank of Millbrook Building, Franklin Avenue.
Telephone: 914-677-5539.
Clearwater, Florida Office: Citizens Bank Building, Suite 250, 1130 Cleveland Street.
Telephone: 813-461-3144.

MEMBERS OF FIRM

John Hackett (Died 1916)
James L. Williams (Died 1908)
Charles J. Corbally (1888-1966)
John J. Gartland, Jr.
Allan E. Rappleyea
Daniel F. Curtin
Fred W. Schaeffer
Michael G. Gartland
Jon H. Adams
Vincent L. DeBiase
Paul O. Sullivan
William F. Bogle, Jr.

ASSOCIATES

Rena Muckenhoupt O'Connor
Allan B. Rappleyea, Jr.

OF COUNSEL

Joseph F. Hawkins (1916-1986)
Milton M. Haven
Edward J. Murtaugh

Representative Clients: Hudson Valley Farm Credit, A.C.A.; St. Francis Hospital; Marist College; Merritt-Meridian Construction Corp.

(See Next Column)

Counsel for: Poughkeepsie Savings Bank, F.S.B.; Bank of New York; Farm Credit Bank of Springfield; Equitable Life Assurance Society of the United States; McCann Foundation, Inc.
Reference: Bank of New York.

For full biographical listings, see the Martindale-Hubbell Law Directory

*RIVERHEAD,** Suffolk Co.

BENJAMIN E. CARTER (AV)

220 Roanoke Avenue, P.O. Box 118, 11901
Telephone: 516-727-1666
FAX: 516-727-1710

For full biographical listings, see the Martindale-Hubbell Law Directory

*ROCHESTER,** Monroe Co.

HARRIS & CHESWORTH (AV)

1820 East Avenue, 14607
Telephone: 716-242-2400
Fax: 716-242-2424

MEMBERS OF FIRM

Wayne M. Harris
Donald O. Chesworth
Edward M. O'Brien

ASSOCIATES

David J. Gutmann
Michael A. Damia
David Mayer
Timothy P. Blodgett

SPECIAL COUNSEL

Melvin Bressler

For full biographical listings, see the Martindale-Hubbell Law Directory

HARTER, SECREST & EMERY (AV)

700 Midtown Tower, 14604-2070
Telephone: 716-232-6500
Telecopier: 716-232-2152
Naples, Florida Office: Suite 400, 800 Laurel Oak Drive.
Telephone: 813-598-4444.
Telecopier: 813-598-2781.
Albany, New York Office: One Steuben Place.
Telephone: 518-434-4377.
Telecopier: 518-449-4025.
Syracuse, New York Office: 431 East Fayette Street.
Telephone: 315-474-4000.
Telecopier: 315-474-7789.

MEMBERS OF FIRM

Lawrence R. Palvino
William D. Smith
William N. La Forte
Frank S. Hagelberg
T. Mary McDonald
Kathleen C. Passidomo (Not admitted in NY; Resident Partner, Naples, Florida Office)

OF COUNSEL

Harry M. Grace
D. Dyson Gay

SENIOR ATTORNEYS

William W. Bell
William F. Brandes, Jr. (Resident Counsel, Naples, Florida Office)

ASSOCIATES

Cathy Kaman Ryan
Dorothy H. Ferguson
C. Perry Peeples (Resident Associate, Naples, Florida Office)
Jill M. Myers
Teresa M. Roney (Resident Associate, Syracuse Office)

For Complete List of Firm Personnel, See General Section

For full biographical listings, see the Martindale-Hubbell Law Directory

*STATEN ISLAND,** Richmond Co.

SIMONSON & COHEN, P.C. (AV)

4060 Amboy Road, 10308
Telephone: 718-948-2100
Telecopier: 718-356-2379

Sidney O. Simonson (1911-1986)
Daniel Cohen
Robert M. Cohen
James R. Cohen

Michael Adler
Lawrence J. Lorczak

For full biographical listings, see the Martindale-Hubbell Law Directory

*SYRACUSE,** Onondaga Co.

GROSSMAN KINNEY DWYER & HARRIGAN, P.C. (AV)

5720 Commons Park, 13057
Telephone: 315-449-2131
Telecopier: 315-449-2905

(See Next Column)

GROSSMAN KINNEY DWYER & HARRIGAN P.C.—*Continued*

Richard D. Grossman
John P. Kinney
James F. Dwyer
C. Frank Harrigan
Robert E. Hornik, Jr.
Harris N. Lindenfeld

Ruth Moors D'Eredita
Edward P. Dunn
Joseph G. Shields

Representative Clients: County of Onondaga; County of Tompkins; Therm, Incorporated, Ithaca, New York; Village of Marcellus; Smith Barney Shearson; The Mitsubishi Bank, Limited (New York Branch); C&S Engineers, Inc.; Town of Harrietstown, New York.

For full biographical listings, see the Martindale-Hubbell Law Directory

*WHITE PLAINS,** Westchester Co.

CUDDY & FEDER (AV)

90 Maple Avenue, 10601-5196
Telephone: 914-761-1300
Telecopier: 914-761-5372; 914-761-6405
New York, N.Y. Office: 60 East 42nd Street.
Telephone: 212-949-6280.
Telecopier: 212-949-6346.
Stamford, Connecticut Office: 707 Summer Street.
Telephone: 203-348-4780.
Norwalk, Connecticut Office: 4 Berkeley Street.
Telephone: 203-853-8001.
Telecopier: 203-831-8250.

MEMBERS OF FIRM

Thomas R. Beirne (Resident, New York, N.Y. Office)
Joseph P. Carlucci
Kenneth DuBroff
Robert Feder
Andrew A. Glickson (Resident, Stamford & Norwalk, Connecticut Offices)
Joshua J. Grauer
Kenneth F. Jurist
Richard A. Katzive
Dennis C. Krieger
Barry E. Long
William S. Null
Neil T. Rimsky
Ruth Schorr Roth
Kevin G. Ryan
Chauncey L. Walker
Robert L. Wolfe
Kathleen Donelli
Lawrence J. Reiss

ASSOCIATES

Suzanne Bogdanoff
Ann Farrissey Carlson
Erica Tukel Wax

OF COUNSEL

William V. Cuddy
Daniel M. Zane

Reference: The Bank of New York County Trust Region.

For full biographical listings, see the Martindale-Hubbell Law Directory

GREENBURG & POSNER (AV)

399 Knollwood Road, 10603
Telephone: 914-948-6620
Telecopier: 914-948-0864

MEMBERS OF FIRM

Henry A. Greenburg
Martin Louis Posner
Jane Y. Posner
Steven N. Feinman

ASSOCIATE

Jessica Bacal

References: Chemical Bank; Citibank.

For full biographical listings, see the Martindale-Hubbell Law Directory

HOFFMAN, WACHTELL, KOSTER, MAIER & MANDEL (AV)

399 Knollwood Road, 10603
Telephone: 914-682-8000
FAX: 914-682-1512
New City, New York Office: 82 Maple Avenue, 10956.
Telephone: 914-634-8169.

MEMBERS OF FIRM

Lee A. Hoffman, Jr.
Marc J. Wachtell
Eric D. Koster
Lynn J. Maier
Richard G. Mandel

Representative Clients: Mount Hope Mines, Inc.; Eastern Educational Consortium; Westchester Community College; Prime Offices Systems, Inc.; Gateway Management Corp.;
Reference: Citibank, N.A. (White Plains Branch).

For full biographical listings, see the Martindale-Hubbell Law Directory

KEANE & BEANE, P.C. (AV)

One North Broadway, 10601
Telephone: 914-946-4777
Telecopier: 914-946-6868
Rye, New York Office: 49 Purchase Street.
Telephone: 914-967-3936.

(*See Next Column*)

Thomas F. Keane, Jr. (1932-1991)

Edward F. Beane
David Glasser
Ronald A. Longo
Richard L. O'Rourke
Lawrence Praga
Joel H. Sachs
Steven A. Schurkman
Judson K. Siebert

Debbie G. Jacobs
Lance H. Klein
Donna E. Frosco
Nicholas M. Ward-Willis

LEGAL SUPPORT PERSONNEL

Barbara S. Durkin
Toni Ann Huff

OF COUNSEL

Eric F. Jensen
Peter A. Borrok

For full biographical listings, see the Martindale-Hubbell Law Directory

KENT, HAZZARD, JAEGER, GREER, WILSON & FAY (AV)

50 Main Street, 10606
Telephone: 914-948-4700
Telecopier: 914-948-4721

MEMBERS OF FIRM

Ralph S. Kent (1878-1949)
Lawrence S. Hazzard (1900-1958)
William J. Greer (1920-1994)
Mizell Wilson, Jr.
Lawrence F. Fay
Robert D. Hazzard
Gregory C. Freeman
Robert G. O'Donnell
Katharine Wilson Conroy
John R. Dinin

OF COUNSEL

Malcolm Wilson
Edward J. Freeman
Otto C. Jaeger
George Beisheim, Jr.
Peter F. Blasi

Representative Clients: The Bank of New York.
References: Bank of New York; Peoples Westchester Savings Bank.

For full biographical listings, see the Martindale-Hubbell Law Directory

KURZMAN & EISENBERG (AV)

One North Broadway, 10601
Telephone: 914-285-9800
Fax: 914-285-9855
New York, N.Y. Office: 99 Park Avenue.
Telephone: 212-671-1322.
Hollywood, Florida Office: 2021 Tyler Street.
Telephone: 305-921-5500.

MEMBERS OF FIRM

Robert G. Kurzman
Sam Eisenberg
Lee Harrison Corbin
Robert L. Ecker
Joel S. Lever
Jack S. Older
Alan John Rein
Fred D. Weinstein

OF COUNSEL

Richard A. Danzig
R. Mark Goodman
Stephen R. Levy

For full biographical listings, see the Martindale-Hubbell Law Directory

WINDHAM, Greene Co.

BROWN, KELLEHER, ZWICKEL & WILHELM (AV)

Main Street, 12496
Telephone: 518-734-3800
Fax: 518-734-4226
Catskill, New York Office: 370 Main Street 12414.
Telephone: 518-943-1111.
Fax: 518-943-4549.

MEMBERS OF FIRM

Charles J. Brown
Kevin M. Kelleher
Charles Zwickel
Terry J. Wilhelm

ASSOCIATE

Carol D. Stevens

For full biographical listings, see the Martindale-Hubbell Law Directory

WOODBURY, Nassau Co.

STEBEL & PASELTINER, P.C. (AV)

7600 Jericho Turnpike, 11797
Telephone: 516-496-8117
Telecopier: 516-496-8112

Bernard Stebel
David E. Paseltiner

Mindy K. Smolevitz
Steven M. Gelfman

COUNSEL

Edwin H. Baker
Alan M. Pollack
Michael E. Greene
Mitchell G. Mandell
Lori Samet Schwarz
Scott A. Sommer

(*See Next Column*)

STEBEL & PASELTINER P.C., *Woodbury—Continued*

References: Chemical Bank; Fleet Bank.

For full biographical listings, see the Martindale-Hubbell Law Directory

NORTH CAROLINA

*BOONE,** Watauga Co.

CHARLES E. CLEMENT (AV)

756 West King Street, P.O. Drawer 32, 28607
Telephone: 704-264-6411
FAX: 704-264-5424

Representative Clients: First Union National Bank.
Approved Attorney for: Lawyers Title Insurance Corp.; Chicago Title Insurance Co.

For full biographical listings, see the Martindale-Hubbell Law Directory

*CHARLOTTE,** Mecklenburg Co.

CULP ELLIOTT & CARPENTER, P.L.L.C. (AV)

A Partnership including a Professional Association
227 West Trade Street Suite 1500, 28202-1675
Telephone: 704-372-6322
Telefax: 704-372-1474

William R. Culp, Jr., (P.A.)
W. Curtis Elliott, Jr.
John Joseph Carpenter
Margaret R. K. Leinbach
Jonathan E. Gopman
Christopher Hannum
Stefan R. Latorre

For full biographical listings, see the Martindale-Hubbell Law Directory

FENNEBRESQUE, CLARK, SWINDELL & HAY (AV)

NationsBank Corporate Center Suite 2900, 100 North Tryon Street, 28202-4011
Telephone: 704-347-3800
Facsimile: 704-347-3838

MEMBERS OF FIRM

John C. Fennebresque
Bernard B. Clark
Gary W. Swindell
Jeffrey S. Hay
Marvin L. Rogers, II
Michael L. Burt
James K.L. (Lynn) Thorneburg
Michael S. Marr
Mary B. Nutt
William W. Kohler
Jeffrey W. Glenney
Patricia F. Hosmer
Pamela L. Kopp
Deidre E. Holmes (Not admitted in NC)

LEGAL SUPPORT PERSONNEL

Laura L. Butz

For full biographical listings, see the Martindale-Hubbell Law Directory

MURCHISON & PAULSON (AV)

2400 NationsBank Plaza, 100 South Tryon Street, 28280
Telephone: 704-342-2000
Facsimile: 704-342-3701

Alton G. Murchison, III
David F. Paulson, Jr.

ASSOCIATE

Charles Phillip Wells

Representative Clients: Brightstar Studios, Ltd. (dba "Glamour Shots"); Hood, Hargett & Associates, Inc.; Yellow Cab Company of Charlotte, Inc.; Homebuilders of Charlotte, Inc.; Reflection Sound Productions, Inc.; Cames, Wiltsee & Asso., Inc. Southern Plastics Equipment, Inc.
Reference: Central Carolina Bank & Trust Co.

For full biographical listings, see the Martindale-Hubbell Law Directory

PARHAM, HELMS & HARRIS (AV)

1329 East Morehead Street, 28204
Telephone: 704-333-1105
FAX: 704-343-2471
Other Charlotte, North Carolina Office: 4421 Sharon Road, Suite 100.
Telephone: 704-366-6607.
FAX: 704-366-6973.

MEMBERS OF FIRM

Lewis H. Parham, Jr.
Neal G. Helms
Ralph C. Harris, Jr.
Robert B. Blythe
James H. Morton

ASSOCIATE

Regine Susanne Knox

(See Next Column)

OF COUNSEL

John L. Hazlehurst

Representative Clients: Marsh Associates, Inc.; Wachovia Mortgage Co.; Mady Construction Co., Inc.
Reference: NCNB National Bank of North Carolina.

For full biographical listings, see the Martindale-Hubbell Law Directory

PERRY, PATRICK, FARMER & MICHAUX, P.A. (AV)

2200 The Carillon, 227 West Trade Street, 28202
Telephone: 704-372-1120
Fax: 704-372-9635
Other Charlotte, North Carolina Office: South Park, 1901 Roxborough Road, Suite 100.
Telephone: 704-364-9695.
Fax: 704-364-9698.
Raleigh, North Carolina Office: 3716 National Drive, Suite 100.
Telephone: 919-787-8812.
Fax: 919-787-3312.

Robert E. Perry, Jr.
Bailey Patrick, Jr.
B. D. Farmer, III
Roy H. Michaux, Jr.
Richard W. Wilson
James G. Wallace
Carolyn Gilmer Hisley
Bryan W. Pittman
Laura L. Yaeger
Richard W. Moore (Resident, Raleigh Office)
J. Christopher Oates
W. Richard Jamison (Resident, Raleigh Office)
Leslie Miller Webb
David A. Raynes (Resident, Raleigh Office)
George S. Warren
David L. Huffstetler (Resident, Raleigh Office)
John H. Carmichael

Representative Clients: The Bissell Cos.; Centex Real Estate Corp.; Charlotte Pipe and Foundry Co.; The Crosland Group, Inc.; Crown Life Insurance Co.; C.D. Spangler Construction Co.; International Construction Equipment, Inc.; The Manufacturers Life Insurance Co.; M/I Schottenstein Cos., Inc.; The Ryland Group, Inc.

For full biographical listings, see the Martindale-Hubbell Law Directory

RUFF, BOND, COBB, WADE & MCNAIR, L.L.P. (AV)

2100 Two First Union Center, 301 South Tryon Street, 28282-8283
Telephone: 704-377-1634
FAX: 704-342-3308

MEMBERS OF FIRM

Thomas C. Ruff
Lyn Bond, Jr.
James O. Cobb
Hamlin L. Wade
William H. McNair
Marvin A. Bethune
Moses Luski
Francis W. Sturges
Robert S. Adden, Jr.
James H. Pickard

ASSOCIATES

George R. Jurch, III
Stephen D. Koehler

For full biographical listings, see the Martindale-Hubbell Law Directory

SMITH HELMS MULLISS & MOORE, L.L.P. (AV)

227 North Tryon Street, P.O. Box 31247, 28231
Telephone: 704-343-2000
Telecopier: 704-334-8467
Telex: 572460
Greensboro, North Carolina Office: Smith Helms Mulliss & Moore, Suite 1400 First Union Tower, 300 North Greene Street, P.O. Box 21927.
Telephone: 910-378-5200.
Telecopier: 910-379-9558.
Raleigh, North Carolina Office: 316 West Edenton Street, P.O. Box 27525.
Telephone: 919-755-8700.
Telecopier: 919-828-7938.

MEMBERS OF FIRM

Saxby M. Chaplin
Robert G. Brinkley (Also at Greensboro)
B. Palmer McArthur, Jr.
Elizabeth Whitener Goode

ASSOCIATES

Kathy L. Pilkington
Kevin M. Bringewatt

For Complete List of Firm Personnel, See General Section

For full biographical listings, see the Martindale-Hubbell Law Directory

WOMBLE CARLYLE SANDRIDGE & RICE (AV)

A Professional Limited Liability Company
3300 One First Union Center, 301 S. College Street, 28202-6025
Telephone: 704-331-4900
Telecopy: 704-331-4955
Telex: 853609
Winston-Salem, North Carolina Office: 1600 Southern National Financial Center.
Telephone: 919-721-3600.
Telecopy: 919-721-3660.
Telex: 806498.

(See Next Column)

WOMBLE CARLYLE SANDRIDGE & RICE—*Continued*

Raleigh, North Carolina Office: 2100 First Union Capitol Center, 150 Fayetteville Street Mall, P.O. Box 831.
Telephone: 919-755-2100.
Telecopy: 919-755-2150.
Telex: 806498.
Atlanta, Georgia Office: One Ninety One Peachtree Tower, 191 Peachtree Street N.E., Suite 3250.
Telephone: 404-614-2580.
Fax: 404-614-2595.

MEMBER OF FIRM

James R. Bryant, III

Representative Clients: Childress Klein Properties, Inc.; Food Lion, Inc.; Fieldcrest Cannon, Inc.; J.A. Jones Construction Company; Parkdale Mills, Inc.; Duke Power Company; Bowles Hollowell Conner & Company; ALLTEL Carolina, Inc.; Belk Store Services, Inc.; Philip Holzmann A.G.

For Complete List of Firm Personnel, See General Section

For full biographical listings, see the Martindale-Hubbell Law Directory

*GASTONIA,** Gaston Co.

WHITESIDES, ROBINSON, BLUE, WILSON & SMITH (AV)

246 West Main Avenue, P.O. Box 1115, 28053
Telephone: 704-864-5728
FAX: 704-864-6706
Belmont, North Carolina Office: Third Floor, Wachovia Building, Main Street, P.O. Box 901.
Telephone: 704-825-1079.
FAX: 704-825-7921.

MEMBERS OF FIRM

Henry M. Whitesides
Theodore Lamar Robinson, Jr.
Arthur C. Blue, III
Parks H. Wilson, Jr. (Resident, Belmont Office)
David W. Smith, III
Terry Albright Kenny

For full biographical listings, see the Martindale-Hubbell Law Directory

*GREENSBORO,** Guilford Co.

FRASSINETI AND GLOVER (AV)

Suite 403, 201 West Market Street, P.O. Drawer 1799, 27402
Telephone: 910-273-9794
FAX: 910-273-1570

Jordan J. Frassineti (Retired)
Durant M. Glover

A list of Representative Clients and Approved Attorneys For will be Furnished upon Request.

For full biographical listings, see the Martindale-Hubbell Law Directory

ISAACSON ISAACSON & GRIMES (AV)

Suite 400 NationsBank Building, 101 West Friendly Avenue, P.O. Box 1888, 27402
Telephone: 910-275-7626
FAX: 910-273-7293

MEMBERS OF FIRM

Henry H. Isaacson
Marc L. Isaacson
L. Charles Grimes

ASSOCIATE

Thomas B. Kobrin

For full biographical listings, see the Martindale-Hubbell Law Directory

SMITH HELMS MULLISS & MOORE, L.L.P. (AV)

Suite 1400 First Union Tower, 300 North Greene Street, P.O. Box 21927, 27420
Telephone: 910-378-5200
Telecopier: 910-379-9558
Charlotte, North Carolina Office: Smith Helms Mulliss & Moore, L.L.P., 227 North Tryon Street, P.O. Box 31247.
Telephone: 704-343-2000.
Telecopier: 704-334-8467.
Telex: 572460.
Raleigh, North Carolina Office: Smith Helms Mulliss & Moore, L.L.P., 316 West Edenton Street, P.O. Box 27525.
Telephone: 919-755-8700.
Telecopier: 919-828-7938.

OF COUNSEL

Jack L. Donnell

MEMBERS OF FIRM

Julius C. Smith, III
Charles E. Melvin, Jr.
Richard A. Leippe
E. Garrett Walker
Robert G. Brinkley (Also at Charlotte)
Donald C. Lampe

(See Next Column)

ASSOCIATE

William K. Edwards

For Complete List of Firm Personnel, See General Section

For full biographical listings, see the Martindale-Hubbell Law Directory

MOREHEAD CITY, Carteret Co.

BENNETT, MCCONKEY, THOMPSON & MARQUARDT, P.A. (AV)

1007 Shepard Street, P.O. Drawer 189, 28557
Telephone: 919-726-4114
FAX: 919-726-7975

Thomas S. Bennett
Samuel A. McConkey, Jr.
James W. Thompson, III
Dennis M. Marquardt

Approved Attorneys For: Lawyers Title Insurance Corp.
Reference: First Citizens Bank & Trust Co.

For full biographical listings, see the Martindale-Hubbell Law Directory

*RALEIGH,** Wake Co.

* indicates certain Bar Register subscribers whose principal office is located elsewhere in the state and who have arranged for representation as a part of the state capital listings that follow

HOWARD, FROM, STALLINGS & HUTSON, P.A. (AV)

Suite 400, 4000 WestChase Boulevard, P.O. Box 12347, 27607
Telephone: 919-833-2983
Fax: 919-834-3481
New Bern, North Carolina Office: 405 Middle Street, P.O. Box 975.
Telephones: 919-633-3006; 800-822-4182.
FAX: 919-633-3097.

Edward Cader Howard
I. Allan From
Joseph H. Stallings
John N. Hutson, Jr.
William M. Black, Jr.
Beth Ferebee Atkins (Resident, New Bern Office)
Catherine C. McLamb
Peggy S. Vincent
B. Joan Davis
Charles H. Livaudais, Jr.
Kory J. Goldsmith
Scott A. Miskimon
Lewis E. Lamb III

Representative Client: Branch Banking and Trust Co.

For full biographical listings, see the Martindale-Hubbell Law Directory

PERRY, PATRICK, FARMER & MICHAUX, P.A. (AV)

3716 National Drive, Suite 100, 27612
Telephone: 919-787-8812
Fax: 919-787-3312
Charlotte, North Carolina Office: 2200 The Carillon, 227 West Trade Street.
Telephone: 704-372-1120.
Fax: 704-372-9635.
Other Charlotte, North Carolina Office: South Park, 1901 Roxborough Road, Suite 100.
Telephone: 704-364-9695.
Fax: 704-364-9698.

Richard W. Moore (Resident)
W. Richard Jamison (Resident)
David A. Raynes (Resident)
David L. Huffstetler (Resident)

Representative Clients: The Bissell Cos.; Centex Real Estate Corp.; Charlotte Pipe and Foundry Co.; The Crosland Group, Inc.; Crown Life Insurance Co.; C.D. Spangler Construction Co.; International Construction Equipment, Inc.; The Manufacturers Life Insurance Co.; M/I Schottenstein Cos., Inc.; The Ryland Group, Inc.

For full biographical listings, see the Martindale-Hubbell Law Directory

PHILIP O. REDWINE, P.A. (AV)

Capital Club Building, 16 West Martin Street, Suite 700, P.O. Box 1030, 27601
Telephone: 919-831-1312
Telecopier: 919-831-1327

Philip O. Redwine

For full biographical listings, see the Martindale-Hubbell Law Directory

*** SMITH HELMS MULLISS & MOORE, L.L.P.** (AV)

316 West Edenton Street, P.O. Box 27525, 27611-7525
Telephone: 919-755-8700
Telecopier: 919-828-7938
Charlotte, North Carolina Office: 227 North Tryon Street, P.O. Box 31247.
Telephone: 704-343-2000.
Telecopier: 704-334-8467.
Telex: 572460.
Greensboro, North Carolina Office: Smith Helms Mulliss & Moore, Suite 1400 First Union Tower, 300 North Greene Street, P.O. Box 21927.
Telephone: 910-378-5200.
Telecopier: 910-379-9558.

MEMBERS OF FIRM

Michael G. Winters
Charles N. Anderson, Jr.

(See Next Column)

SMITH HELMS MULLISS & MOORE L.L.P., *Raleigh—Continued*

ASSOCIATE

Donna Kaye Blumberg

For Complete List of Firm Personnel, See General Section

For full biographical listings, see the Martindale-Hubbell Law Directory

*** WOMBLE CARLYLE SANDRIDGE & RICE (AV)**

A Professional Limited Liability Company
2100 First Union Capitol Center, 150 Fayetteville Street Mall, P.O. Box 831, 27602
Telephone: 919-755-2100
Telecopy: 919-755-2150
Telex: 806498
Charlotte, North Carolina Office: 3300 One First Union Center, 301 South College Street.
Telephone: 704-331-4900.
Telecopy: 704-331-4955.
Telex: 853609.
Winston-Salem, North Carolina Office: 1600 Southern National Financial Center.
Telephone: 919-721-3600.
Telecopy: 919-721-3660.
Telex: 806498.
Atlanta, Georgia Office: One Ninety One Peachtree Tower, 191 Peachtree Street N.E., Suite 3250.
Telephone: 404-614-2580.
Fax: 404-614-2595.

RESIDENT PARTNER

William Camp Matthews, Jr.

RESIDENT ASSOCIATE

Andrea Harris Fox

Representative Clients: Aetna Casualty and Surety Co., Inc.; ALSCO/AmeriMark Building Products, Inc.; Aoki Corporation America, Inc.; Empire of Carolina, Inc.; Hackney Brothers, Inc.; Lawyers Mutual Liability Insurance Company of North Carolina; Meredith College; Monk-Austin, Inc.; Regency Park Corporation; Wachovia Bank of North Carolina, N.A.

For Complete List of Firm Personnel, See General Section

For full biographical listings, see the Martindale-Hubbell Law Directory

RESEARCH TRIANGLE PARK, Durham Co.

PORTER & STEEL, PLLC (AV)

480 Beta Building, Headquarters Park, 2222 Chapel Hill-Nelson Highway, P.O. Box 13646, 27709-3646
Telephone: 919-361-4900
1-800-989-0503
Fax: 919-361-2262

W. Travis Porter
Charles L. Steel, IV
Gerald A. Tingen
Robert W. Saunders
Susan Haney Bartels

DIRECTOR OF GOVERNMENT RELATIONS

Leslie H. Bevacqua

For full biographical listings, see the Martindale-Hubbell Law Directory

*WILMINGTON,** New Hanover Co.

KAUFMAN & GREEN, L.L.P. (AV)

Sea Towers Business Center, 2002 Eastwood Road, Suite 202, 28406-0038
Telephone: 910-256-5135
FAX: 910-256-6451
Syracuse, New York Office: Hancock & Estabrook, 1500 Mony Tower I, 13221.
Telephone: 315-471-3151.
Fax: 315-471-3167.

James J. Kaufman
Michael A. Green

Approved Attorney For: The Title Company of NC, Inc.; Lawyers Title of North Carolina, Inc.; Chicago Title Insurance Co.; Security Union Title Insurance Co.; Investors Title; Commonwealth Title; Ticor Title Guarantee Co.; FMHA; Citizens Federal Bank; NCNB.; Hometown Funding, Inc.

For full biographical listings, see the Martindale-Hubbell Law Directory

*WINSTON-SALEM,** Forsyth Co.

STEPHEN G. CALAWAY (AV)

Ashley Square, 1330 Ashley Brook Lane, 27103
Telephone: 910-723-6768

References: Nations Bank of North Carolina; Southern National Bank.

For full biographical listings, see the Martindale-Hubbell Law Directory

WOMBLE CARLYLE SANDRIDGE & RICE (AV)

A Professional Limited Liability Company
1600 Southern National Financial Center, P.O. Drawer 84, 27102
Telephone: 910-721-3600
Telecopy: 910-721-3660
Telex: 806498
Charlotte, North Carolina Office: 3300 One First Union Center, 301 South College Street.
Telephone: 704-331-4900.
Telecopy: 704-331-4955.
Telex: 853609.
Raleigh, North Carolina Office: 2100 First Union Capitol Center, 150 Fayetteville Street Mall, P.O. Box 831.
Telephone: 919-755-2100.
Telecopy: 919-755-2150.
Telex: 806498.
Atlanta, Georgia Office: One Ninety One Peachtree Tower, 191 Peachtree Street, N.E., Suite 3250.
Telephone: 404-614-2580.
Fax: 404-614-2595.

MEMBERS OF FIRM

Leslie E. Browder
Dennis W. McNames
Kenneth Allen Moser

Representative Clients: Brad Ragan, Inc.; Brenner Companies; Food Lion, Inc.; Hanes Companies, Inc.; North Carolina Baptist Hospitals, Inc.; R.J. Reynolds Tobacco Company; Summit Communications Group, Inc.; Thomasville Furniture Industries, Inc.; Wachovia Corporation; Wake Forest University.

For Complete List of Firm Personnel, See General Section

For full biographical listings, see the Martindale-Hubbell Law Directory

NORTH DAKOTA

*BISMARCK,** Burleigh Co.

PEARCE AND DURICK (AV)

314 East Thayer Avenue, P.O. Box 400, 58502
Telephone: 701-223-2890
Fax: 701-223-7865

MEMBERS OF FIRM

William P. Pearce
Lawrence A. Dopson

Representative Clients: American Insurance Assn.; Cigna-INA Insurance Co.; Deere & Co.; Federal Deposit Insurance Corp.; Ford Motor Co.; General Motors Corp.; MDU Resources Group, Inc.; Northwest Airlines; Royal Insurance Co.; Travelers Insurance Co.

For Complete List of Firm Personnel, See General Section

For full biographical listings, see the Martindale-Hubbell Law Directory

*FARGO,** Cass Co.

CONMY, FESTE, BOSSART, HUBBARD & CORWIN, LTD. (AV)

400 Norwest Center, Fourth Street and Main Avenue, 58126
Telephone: 701-293-9911
Fax: 701-293-3133

Charles A. Feste
David R. Bossart
Paul M. Hubbard
Wickham Corwin
Kim E. Brust
Lauris N. Molbert
Michael M. Thomas
Robert J. Schultz
Nancy J. Morris
Jiming Zhu

OF COUNSEL

E. T. Conmy, Jr.

State Counsel for: Metropolitan Life Insurance Company.
Representative Clients: Ford Motor Credit Co.; Norwest Corporation Region VII Banks (North Dakota & Minnesota West); U.S. Gypsum Co.
Insurance: American Hardware Insurance Group; Great American Insurance Companies; The Maryland.

For full biographical listings, see the Martindale-Hubbell Law Directory

NILLES, HANSEN & DAVIES, LTD. (AV)

1800 Radisson Tower, P.O. Box 2626, 58108
Telephone: 701-237-5544

Timothy Q. Davies
Robert L. Stroup, II
Gregory B. Selbo

Representative Clients: Metropolitan Federal Bank (fsb); First Bank of North Dakota (NA); Chicago Title Insurance Company.

For Complete List of Firm Personnel, See General Section

For full biographical listings, see the Martindale-Hubbell Law Directory

Fargo—Continued

VOGEL, BRANTNER, KELLY, KNUTSON, WEIR & BYE, LTD. (AV)

502 First Avenue North, P.O. Box 1389, 58107
Telephone: 701-237-6983
Facsimile: 701-237-0847

David F. Knutson

Representative Clients: Associated General Contractors of North Dakota; Clark Equipment Co.; Dakota Hospital; Forum Communications Company; Merit Care Medical Group; Northern Improvement Co.; Dakota Clinic; Gateway Chevrolet, Inc.; West Acres Development Company; Fargo Glass & Paint Company.

For Complete List of Firm Personnel, See General Section

For full biographical listings, see the Martindale-Hubbell Law Directory

OHIO

*AKRON,** Summit Co.

DANIEL G. LAPORTE AND ASSOCIATES (AV)

3250 West Market Street Suite 306, 44333-3321
Telephone: 216-836-5544
Fax: 216-836-2064

ASSOCIATE

Christopher M. Van Devere

For full biographical listings, see the Martindale-Hubbell Law Directory

ALLIANCE, Stark Co.

GEIGER, TEEPLE, SMITH & HAHN (AV)

260 East Main Street, P.O. Box 2446, 44601
Telephone: 216-821-1430
Canton Office Phone: 216-478-4915
Fax: 216-821-2217

MEMBERS OF FIRM

Milton S. Geiger (1900-1991)
John N. Teeple
Bruce E. Smith
B. Scott Hahn
J. Michael Gatien

ASSOCIATE

Richard C. Ogline

Representative Clients: Bank One, Ohio N.A.; Citizens Banking Co.; Jerry Moore, Inc.; Damon Chemical Co.; M B Operating Co., Inc.; The American Simmental Assn.; Electronic Circuits & Design Co.; Atlas Energy Group, Inc.

For full biographical listings, see the Martindale-Hubbell Law Directory

*CANTON,** Stark Co.

LESH, CASNER & MILLER A LEGAL PROFESSIONAL ASSOCIATION (AV)

606 Belden-Whipple Building, 4150 Belden Village Street, N.W., 44718
Telephone: 216-493-0040
Fax: 216-493-4108

Kenneth L. Lesh (1913-1991)
James W. Casner
Rex W. Miller
Jacob F. Hess, Jr.
Thomas J. Lombardi
Dennis J. Fox
John S. McCall, Jr.
Timothy W. Watkins
John R. Frank

OF COUNSEL

Ronald G. Figler

For full biographical listings, see the Martindale-Hubbell Law Directory

*CINCINNATI,** Hamilton Co.

BARRETT & WEBER A LEGAL PROFESSIONAL ASSOCIATION (AV)

400 Atlas Building, 524 Walnut Street, 45202-3114
Telephone: 513-721-2120
Facsimile: 513-721-2139

C. Francis Barrett

For full biographical listings, see the Martindale-Hubbell Law Directory

CASH, CASH, EAGEN & KESSEL (AV)

1000 Tri State Building, 432 Walnut Street, 45202
Telephone: 513-621-4443
FAX: 513-621-5231

MEMBERS OF FIRM

Albert D. Cash
Michael J. Stegman

(See Next Column)

ASSOCIATE

Jeffrey G. Stagnaro

Representative Clients: Meridian Properties, Inc.; The St. James Limited Partnership; Longworth Development Corporation; ORP Properties Inc.; Klotter Builders, Inc.; TJL Investments, Inc.; Charles F. Shiels & Co., Inc.; Foxfire Properties; Future Healthcare, Inc.; State Farm Mutual Automobile Insurance Company.

For full biographical listings, see the Martindale-Hubbell Law Directory

DINSMORE & SHOHL (AV)

1900 Chemed Center, 255 East Fifth Street, 45202-3172
Telephone: 513-977-8200
FAX: 513-977-8141
Florence, Kentucky Office: Turfway Ridge Office Park, 7300 Turfway Road, Suite 430 41042-1355.
Telephone: 606-283-0515.
FAX: 606-283-6017.
Dayton, Ohio Office: 500 Courthouse Plaza, S.W., 10 N. Ludlow Street, 45402-1834.
Telephone: 513-228-8012.
FAX: 513-461-2543.
Columbus, Ohio Office: NBD Bank Building, Suite 330, 175 South Third Street, 43215-5134.
Telephone: 614-224-7887.
FAX: 614-224-7882.

MEMBERS OF FIRM

Thomas J. Sherman
Jay A. Rosenberg
Paul A. Ose
Joanne M. Schreiner
Steven H. Schreiber

ASSOCIATES

G. Franklin Miller
Christine L. McBroom
Lynn Marmer
Gregory O. Long
Jon S. Robins

For Complete List of Firm Personnel, See General Section

For full biographical listings, see the Martindale-Hubbell Law Directory

EICHEL & KRONE CO., L.P.A. (AV)

508 Atlas Bank Building, 524 Walnut Street, 45202
Telephone: 513-241-1234
Fax: 513-241-2731

Lawrence E. Eichel (1908-1981)
Paul W. Krone
Bruce A. Krone

References: Star Bank N.A.; PNC Bank N.A.

For full biographical listings, see the Martindale-Hubbell Law Directory

FROST & JACOBS (AV)

2500 PNC Center, 201 East Fifth Street, P.O. Box 5715, 45201-5715
Telephone: 513-651-6800
Cable Address: "Frostjac"
Telex: 21-4396 F & J CIN
Telecopier: 513-651-6981
Columbus, Ohio Office: One Columbus, 10 West Broad Street.
Telephone: 614-464-1211.
Telecopier: 614-464-1737.
Lexington, Kentucky Office: 1100 Vine Center Tower, 333 West Vine Street.
Telephone: 606-254-1100.
Telecopier: 606-253-2990.
Middletown, Ohio Office: 400 First National Bank Building, 2 North Main Street.
Telephone: 513-422-2001.
Telecopier: 513-422-3010.
Naples, Florida Office: 4001 Tamiami Trail North, Suite 220.
Telephone: 813-261-0582.
Telecopier: 813-261-2083.

MEMBERS OF FIRM

Lawrence H. Kyte, Jr.
Samuel McW. Scoggins
Jeffery R. Rush
E. Richard Oberschmidt
Kathleen W. Carr
Charles E. Schroer
Joseph W. Plye
W. Russell Wilson
P. Reid Lemasters
Frederick W. Kindel

ASSOCIATES

John C. Krug
Bruce G. Hopkins
David S. Bence
Matthew S. Massarelli
Susan Mechley Lucci
Bryan S. Blade (Not admitted in OH)
Stuart B. Frankel

OF COUNSEL

Kimberly K. Mauer

COLUMBUS, OHIO OFFICE
MEMBER OF FIRM

John I. Cadwallader

LEXINGTON, KENTUCKY OFFICE
MEMBER OF FIRM

Greg E. Mitchell

(See Next Column)

FROST & JACOBS, *Cincinnati—Continued*

MIDDLETOWN OFFICE
MEMBERS OF FIRM

Thomas A. Swope

SENIOR ATTORNEY

Daniel J. Picard

NAPLES, FLORIDA OFFICE
PARTNER

Roi E. Baugher, II

Representative Clients: Cincinnati Bell, Inc.; Federated Department Stores; North American Properties, Inc.; PNC Bank, Ohio, National Association; The Ryland Group, Inc.; Society National Bank; Southwest Ohio Regional Tansit Authority; Turner Construction Co.; The United States Shoe Corp.; Zaring Homes, Inc.

For Complete List of Firm Personnel, See General Section

For full biographical listings, see the Martindale-Hubbell Law Directory

GRIFFIN & FLETCHER (AV)

125 East Ninth Street, P.O. Box 926, 45201
Telephone: 513-421-1313

MEMBERS OF FIRM

Earl W. Griffin (1890-1970)
Edward P. Hackett (1922-1989)
Dale W. Griffin
John R. Fletcher
Michael C. Fletcher
Mary Ann Schenk

ASSOCIATES

James C. Bodley
Charles P. Wagner (Not admitted in OH)
William S. Sulau
Molly Michelle Knight

Representative Clients: Lawyers Title Insurance Corp.; Aegon USA Realty Advisors, Inc.; The Equitable Life Assurance Society; Fifth Third Bank; Brentwood Savings Association; Oak Hills Savings and Loan.
Reference: Fifth Third Bank, Star Bank, N.A.

For full biographical listings, see the Martindale-Hubbell Law Directory

KEATING, MUETHING & KLEKAMP (AV)

1800 Provident Tower, One East Fourth Street, 45202
Telephone: 513-579-6400
Facsimile: 513-579-6457

MEMBERS OF FIRM

Don R. Gardner
Herbert B. Weiss
Joseph L. Trauth, Jr.
Mark J. Weber
Steven R. Smith
Vivian M. Raby

ASSOCIATES

Gregory J. Tassone
Gail Glassmeyer Pryse
Kenneth P. Kreider
Jody Klekamp Stachler

OF COUNSEL

William J. Keating

Representative Clients: American Financial Corporation; BP America Inc.; Chiquita Brands International, Inc.; The Cincinnati Enquirer; Cintas Corporation; Comair Holdings, Inc.; Duke Associates; LSI Industries Inc.; Mosler Inc.; Provident Bankcorp, Inc.

For Complete List of Firm Personnel, See General Section

For full biographical listings, see the Martindale-Hubbell Law Directory

KEPLEY, MACCONNELL & EYRICH A LEGAL PROFESSIONAL ASSOCIATION (AV)

Formerly Clark & Eyrich
2200 Ameritrust Center, 525 Vine Street, 45202
Telephone: 513-241-5540; 621-1045
FAX: 513-241-8111; 621-0038

David J. Eyrich
Paul D. Rattermann

Representative Clients and References furnished upon request.

For full biographical listings, see the Martindale-Hubbell Law Directory

KLAINE, WILEY, HOFFMANN & MEURER A LEGAL PROFESSIONAL ASSOCIATION (AV)

Suite 1850, 105 East Fourth Street, 45202-4080
Telephone: 513-241-0202
Fax: 513-241-9322

Franklin A. Klaine, Jr.
Donald L. Wiley

For Complete List of Firm Personnel, See General Section

For full biographical listings, see the Martindale-Hubbell Law Directory

LERNER, SAMPSON & ROTHFUSS A LEGAL PROFESSIONAL ASSOCIATION (AV)

120 East Fourth Street, Suite 800, 45202
Telephone: 513-241-3100
FAX: 513-241-4094

Donald M. Lerner
Richard M. Rothfuss

Representative Clients: Lomas Mortgage USA, Inc.; Chemical Mortgage Co.; PNC Mortgage Co.
Reference: Star Bank NA of Cincinnati.

For full biographical listings, see the Martindale-Hubbell Law Directory

STRAUSS & TROY A LEGAL PROFESSIONAL ASSOCIATION (AV)

2100 PNC Center, 201 East Fifth Street, 45202-4186
Telephone: 513-621-2120
Telecopier: 513-241-8259
Northern Kentucky Office: Suite 1400, 50 East Rivercenter Boulevard, Covington, Kentucky, 41011.
Telephone: 513-621-8900; 513-621-2120.
Telecopier: 513-629-9444.

Mark H. Berliant
William V. Strauss
Daniel H. Demmerle, II
James G. Heldman
Martin C. Butler (Resident, Covington, Kentucky Office)
David A. Groenke
Andrew M. Shott

Anthony M. Barlow

OF COUNSEL

Nell D. Surber

Representative Clients: CSX Realty, Inc.; B.P. Oil Company; Standard Textile; Winegardner & Hammons, Inc.; Star Bank, N.A., (Ohio and Kentucky); National Amusements, Inc.; Corporex Properties, Inc.

For Complete List of Firm Personnel, See General Section

For full biographical listings, see the Martindale-Hubbell Law Directory

THOMPSON, HINE AND FLORY (AV)

312 Walnut Street, 14th Floor, 45202-4029
Telephone: 513-352-6700
Fax: 513-241-4771;
Telex: 938003
Akron, Ohio Office: 50 S. Main Street, Suite 502, 44308-1828.
Telephone: 216-376-8090.
Fax: 216-376-8386.
Cleveland, Ohio Office: 1100 National City Bank Building, 629 Euclid Avenue, 44114-3070.
Telephone: 216-566-5500.
Fax: 216-556-5583.
Telex: 980217.
Cable Address: "Thomflor".
Columbus, Ohio Office: One Columbus, 10 West Broad Street, 43215-3435.
Telephone: 614-469-3200.
Fax: 614-469-3361.
Dayton, Ohio Office: 2000 Courthouse Plaza, N.E., 45402-1706.
Telephone: 513-443-6600.
Fax: 513-443-6637; 443-6635.
Palm Beach, Florida Office: 125 Worth Avenue, 33480-4466.
Telephone: 407-833-5900.
Fax: 407-833-5951.
Washington, D.C. Office: 1920 N Street, N.W., 20036-1601.
Telephone: 202-331-8800.
Fax: 202-331-8330.
Telex: 904173.
Cable Address: "Caglaw".
Brussels, Belgium Office: Rue des Chevaliers / Ridderstraat 14 - B.10, B - 1050.
Telephone: 011(32-2) 511-9326.
Fax: 011(-32-2) 513-9206.

MEMBERS OF FIRM

Daniel O. Berger
Stephen M. King
William L. Martin, Jr.
Jacqueline K. McManus
Richard B. Tranter

ASSOCIATE

Michelle L. Pensyl

For Complete List of Firm Personnel, See General Section

For full biographical listings, see the Martindale-Hubbell Law Directory

*CLEVELAND,** Cuyahoga Co.

BAKER & HOSTETLER (AV)

3200 National City Center, 1900 East Ninth Street, 44114-3485
Telephone: 216-621-0200
Telecopier: 216-696-0740
TWX: 810 421 8375
RCA Telex: 215032
In Columbus, Ohio: Capitol Square, Suite 2100, 65 East State Street.
Telephone: 614-228-1541.

(See Next Column)

BAKER & HOSTETLER—*Continued*

In Denver, Colorado: 303 East 17th Avenue, Suite 1100.
Telephone: 303-861-0600.
In Houston, Texas: 1000 Louisiana, Suite 2000.
Telephone: 713-751-1600.
In Long Beach, California: 300 Oceangate, Suite 620.
Telephone: 310-432-2827.
In Los Angeles, California: 600 Wilshire Boulevard.
Telephone: 213-624-2400.
In Orlando, Florida: SunBank Center, Suite 2300, 200 South Orange Avenue.
Telephone: 407-649-4000.
In Washington, D. C.: Washington Square, Suite 1100, 1050 Connecticut Avenue, N.W.
Telephone: 202-861-1500.
In College Park, Maryland: 9658 Baltimore Boulevard, Suite 206.
Telephone: 301-441-2781.
In Alexandria, Virginia: 437 North Lee Street.
Telephone: 703-549-1294.
In San Francisco, California: One Sansome Street, Suite 2000.
Telephone: 415-951-4705.

PARTNERS

Paul E. Bennett
Dale A. Bradford
Arthur V.N. Brooks
Elaine A. Chotlos
Lawrence V. Lindberg
Patricia J. O'Donnell

For Complete List of Firm Personnel, See General Section

For full biographical listings, see the Martindale-Hubbell Law Directory

BERICK, PEARLMAN & MILLS A LEGAL PROFESSIONAL ASSOCIATION (AV)

1350 Eaton Center, 1111 Superior Avenue, 44114-2569
Telephone: 216-861-4900
Automatic Telecopier: 216-861-4929

James H. Berick
Samuel S. Pearlman
Osborne Mills, Jr.
Paul J. Singerman
Gary S. Desberg

COUNSEL

Joseph G. Berick

Representative Clients: Cleveland Browns Football Company, Inc.; The Equitable Life Assurance Society of the United States; The Huntington National Bank; Realty ReFund Trust; Republic Savings Bank; Retail Apparel Group, Inc.; A. Schulman, Inc.; Society National Bank; Third Federal Savings; The Town and Country Trust.

For Complete List of Firm Personnel, See General Section

For full biographical listings, see the Martindale-Hubbell Law Directory

JONES, DAY, REAVIS & POGUE (AV)

North Point, 901 Lakeside Avenue, 44114
Telephone: 216-586-3939
Cable Address: "Attorneys Cleveland"
Telex: 980389
Telecopier: 216-579-0212
In Columbus, Ohio: 1900 Huntington Center.
Telephone: 614-469-3939.
Cable Address: "Attorneys Columbus."
Telecopier: 614-461-4198.
In Atlanta, Georgia: 3500 One Peachtree Center, 303 Peachtree Street, N.E.
Telephone: 404-521-3939.
Cable Address: "Attorneys Atlanta".
Telex: 54-2711.
Telecopier: 404-581-8330.
In Brussels, Belgium: Avenue Louise 480, 7th Floor. B-1050 Brussels.
Telephone: 011-32-2-645-14-11.
Telecopier: 011-32-2-645-14-45.
In Chicago, Illinois: 77 West Wacker.
Telephone: 312-782-3939.
Telecopier: 312-782-8585.
In Dallas, Texas: 2300 Trammell Crow Center, 2001 Ross Avenue.
Telephone: 214-220-3939.
Cable Address: "Attorneys Dallas."
Telex: 730852.
Telecopier: 214-969-5100.
In Frankfurt, Germany: Triton Haus, Bockenheimer Landstrasse 42, 60323 Frankfurt am Main.
Telephone: 49-69-9726-3939.
Telecopier: 49-69-9726-3993.
In Geneva, Switzerland: 20, rue de Candolle.
Telephone: 011-41-22-320-2339.
Telecopier: 011-41-22-320-1232.
In Hong Kong: 1501 One Exchange Square, 8 Connaught Place.
Telephone: 011-852-2526-6895.
Telecopier: 011-852-2810-5787.
In Irvine, California: 2603 Main Street, Suite 900.
Telephone: 714-851-3939.
Telex: 194911 Lawyers LSA.
Telecopier: 714-553-7539.

(See Next Column)

In London, England: One Mount Street.
Telephone: 011-44-71-493-9361.
Cable Address: "Surgoe London WI."
Telecopier: 011-44-71-493-9666.
In Los Angeles, California: 555 West Fifth Street, Suite 4600.
Telephone: 213-489-3939.
Telex: 181439 UD.
Telecopier: 213-243-2539.
In New York, New York: 599 Lexington Avenue.
Telephone: 212-326-3939.
Cable Address: "JONESDAY NEWYORK."
Telex: 237013 JDRP UR.
Telecopier: 212-755-7306.
In Paris, France: 62, rue du Faubourg Saint-Honore.
Telephone: 011-33-1-44-71-3939.
Cable Address: "Surgoe Paris."
Telex: 290156 Surgoe.
Telecopier: 011-33-1-49-24-0471.
In Pittsburgh, Pennsylvania: 500 Grant Street, 31st Floor.
Telephone: 412-391-3939.
Cable Address: "Attorneys Pittsburgh".
Telecopier: 412-394-7959.
In Riyadh, Saudi Arabia: Law Offices of Saud M.A. Shawwaf, P.O. Box 2700.
Telephones: 011 (966-1) 465-6543, 011 (966-1) 464-8534 or 011 (966-1) 464-8540.
Telex: 401831 SAUCON SJ.
Telecopier: (966-1) 464-8480.
In Taipei, Taiwan: 8th Floor, Tun Hwa South Road, Section 2.
Telephone: 011 (886-2) 704-6808.
Telecopier: 011 (886-2) 704-6791.
In Tokyo, Japan: Toranomon MT Building, 4th Floor, 10-3, Toranomon 3-Chome, Minato-Ku, Tokyo 105, Japan.
Telephone: 011-81-3-3433-3939.
Telecopier: 011-81-3-5401-2725.
In Washington, D.C.: Metropolitan Square, 1450 G Street, N.W.
Telephone: 202-879-3939.
Cable Address: "Attorneys Washington."
Telex: 89-2410 ATTORNEYS WASH.
Telecopier: 202-737-2832.

MEMBERS OF FIRM

Gary W. Melsher
Irvin A. Leonard
Zachary T. Paris
Richard L. Reppert
William K. Smith

SENIOR ATTORNEYS

Randall A. Cole
Marc Alan Silverstein

ASSOCIATES

Stephen C. Mixter
William A. Herzberger
Bernadette Mihalic Mast

For Complete List of Firm Personnel, See General Section

For full biographical listings, see the Martindale-Hubbell Law Directory

KADISH & BENDER A LEGAL PROFESSIONAL ASSOCIATION (AV)

2112 East Ohio Building, 44114
Telephone: 216-696-3030
Telecopier: 216-696-3492

Stephen L. Kadish
J. Timothy Bender
Kevin M. Hinkel
David G. Weibel

Aaron H. Bulloff
Joseph P. Alexander
David G. Lambert
William A. Duncan
Mary Beth Duffy
James H. Rownd

For full biographical listings, see the Martindale-Hubbell Law Directory

KELLEY, MCCANN & LIVINGSTONE (AV)

35th Floor, BP America Building, 200 Public Square, 44114-2302
Telephone: 216-241-3141
FAX: 216-241-3707

MEMBERS OF FIRM

Fred J. Livingstone
John D. Brown
Margaret Anne Cannon
Michael D. Schenker
Bruce L. Waterhouse, Jr.

OF COUNSEL

David E. Burke

For Complete List of Firm Personnel, See General Section

For full biographical listings, see the Martindale-Hubbell Law Directory

MAYS, KARBERG & WACHTER (AV)

Suite 250, Corporate Circle, 30100 Chagrin Boulevard, 44124-5705
Telephone: 216-464-3030
FAX: 216-765-1258

(See Next Column)

MAYS, KARBERG & WACHTER, *Cleveland—Continued*

A. R. (Bud) Mays | Bruce K. Karberg
Mark I. Wachter

For full biographical listings, see the Martindale-Hubbell Law Directory

SEELEY, SAVIDGE AND AUSSEM A LEGAL PROFESSIONAL ASSOCIATION (AV)

800 Bank One Center, 600 Superior Avenue, East, 44114-2655
Telephone: 216-566-8200
Cable Address: "See Sau"
Fax-Telecopier: 216-566-0213
Elyria, Ohio Office: 538 Broad Street.
Telephone: 216-236-8158.

Gregory D. Seeley | James S. Aussem

James M. McClain (Resident, Elyria Office) | Patrick J. McIntyre

References: Society National Bank; AmeriTrust.

For Complete List of Firm Personnel, See General Section

For full biographical listings, see the Martindale-Hubbell Law Directory

SELKER & FURBER (AV)

1111 Ohio Savings Plaza, 1801 East Ninth Street, 44114
Telephone: 216-781-8686
FAX: 216-781-8688

MEMBERS OF FIRM

Eugene I. Selker | Philip C. Furber
Harlan Daniel Karp

For full biographical listings, see the Martindale-Hubbell Law Directory

SPIETH, BELL, MCCURDY & NEWELL CO., L.P.A. (AV)

2000 Huntington Building, 925 Euclid Avenue, 44115-1496
Telephone: 216-696-4700
Telecopier: 216-696-6569; 216-696-2706; 216-696-1052

Clyde E. Williams, Jr. | Frederick I. Taft
Henry E. Seibert, IV | James M. Havach
Lance B. Johnson | Kristin L. Ubersax

Representative Clients: Cleveland Cavaliers; Nationwide Advertising Services, Inc.; Independent Steel Co.; Baldwin Wallace College; The Tool-Die Engineering Company.
Representative Labor Relations Clients (Management Only): Parker Hannifin Corp.; Reliance Electric Co.; Brush Wellman Co.

For Complete List of Firm Personnel, See General Section

For full biographical listings, see the Martindale-Hubbell Law Directory

THOMPSON, HINE AND FLORY (AV)

1100 National City Bank Building, 629 Euclid Avenue, 44114-3070
Telephone: 216-566-5500
Fax: 216-566-5583
Telex: 980217
Cable Address: "Thomflor"
Akron, Ohio Office: 50 S. Main Street, Suite 502, 44308-1828.
Telephone: 216-376-8090.
Fax: 216-376-8386.
Cincinnati, Ohio Office: 312 Walnut Street, 14th Floor, 45202-4029.
Telephone: 513-352-6700.
Fax: 513-241-4771.
Telex: 938003.
Columbus, Ohio Office: One Columbus, 10 West Broad Street, 43215-3435.
Telephone: 614-469-3200.
Fax: 614-469-3361.
Dayton, Ohio Office: 2000 Courthouse Plaza, N.E., 45402-1706.
Telephone: 513-443-6600.
Fax: 513-443-6637; 443-6635.
Palm Beach, Florida Office: 125 Worth Avenue, Suite 117, 33480-4466.
Telephone: 407-833-5900.
Fax: 407-833-5951.
Washington, D.C. Office: 1920 N Street, N.W., 20036-1601.
Telephone: 202-331-8800.
Fax: 202-331-8330.
Telex: 904173.
Cable Address: "Caglaw".
Brussels, Belgium Office: Rue des Chevaliers, Ridderstraat 14 - B.10, B - 1050.
Telephone: 011(32-2) 511-9326.
Fax: 011(32-2) 513-9206.

MEMBERS OF FIRM

James B. Aronoff | Samuel R. Knezevic
Troy R. Brown | Thomas A. Mason
Douglas O. Cooper | David W. Salisbury
Dianne Smith Coscarelli | Linda A. Striefsky

(See Next Column)

ASSOCIATES

Thomas J. Coyne | Patrick J. Sweeney

For Complete List of Firm Personnel, See General Section

For full biographical listings, see the Martindale-Hubbell Law Directory

ZIEGLER, METZGER & MILLER (AV)

2020 Huntington Building, 44115-1407
Telephone: 216-781-5470
FAX: 216-781-0714

MEMBERS OF FIRM

William L. Ziegler | Mary Beth Ballard

ASSOCIATES

John E. Redeker | Christopher W. Siemen

For Complete List of Firm Personnel, See General Section

For full biographical listings, see the Martindale-Hubbell Law Directory

*COLUMBUS,** Franklin Co.

* indicates certain Bar Register subscribers whose principal office is located elsewhere in the state and who have arranged for representation as a part of the state capital listings that follow

BRICKER & ECKLER (AV)

100 South Third Street, 43215-4291
Telephone: 614-227-2300
Telecopy: 614-227-2390
Cleveland, Ohio Office: 600 Superior Avenue East, Suite 800.
Telephone: 216-771-0720. Fax 216-771-7702.

David G. Baker | David K. Conrad
John C. Rosenberger | Craig A. Haddox
Charles H. McCreary, III | L. Brent Miller

Andrew A. Folkerth

Representative Clients: Capitol South Community Urban Redevelopment Corporation; Columbus Metropolitan Library; Karrington Communities; Lawyers Title Insurance Corporation; Miller Brewing Company; Spiegel, Inc.; Trammell Crow Company (Ohio).

For Complete List of Firm Personnel, See General Section

For full biographical listings, see the Martindale-Hubbell Law Directory

CHESTER, WILLCOX AND SAXBE (AV)

17 South High Street, Suite 900, 43215-3413
Telephone: 614-221-4000
Fax: 614-221-4012

MEMBERS OF FIRM

John J. Chester | Roderick H. Willcox
J. Anthony Kington

ASSOCIATES

James J. Chester | John J. Chester, Jr.

Representative Clients: American Municipal Power-Ohio, Inc.; The Limited; Scioto Downs, Inc.; Tee Jaye's Country Place Restaurants.

For Complete List of Firm Personnel, See General Section

For full biographical listings, see the Martindale-Hubbell Law Directory

E. GEOFFREY CLAPHAM (AV)

88 East Broad Street Suite 1240, 43215
Telephone: 614-221-8686

EMENS, KEGLER, BROWN, HILL & RITTER (AV)

Capitol Square Suite 1800, 65 East State Street, 43215-4294
Telephone: 614-462-5400
Telecopier: 614-464-2634
Cable Address: "Law EKBHR"
Telex: 246671

Allen L. Handlan | Steven R. Russi
Larry J. McClatchey | Kevin L. Sykes
John B. Tingley

COUNSEL

Robert D. Marotta

James M. Groner | Gregory D. May
Richard W. Schuermann, Jr.

Representative Clients: BancOhio National Bank; State Savings Bank.

For Complete List of Firm Personnel, See General Section

For full biographical listings, see the Martindale-Hubbell Law Directory

Columbus—Continued

SMITH & HALE (AV)

(Formerly Wilson & Rector)
37 West Broad Street, 43215
Telephone: 614-221-4255

MEMBERS OF FIRM

Harrison W. Smith (1900-1978)
Harrison W. Smith, Jr.
Ben W. Hale, Jr.
Jeffrey L. Brown
Glen A. Dugger
Jackson B. Reynolds, III

For full biographical listings, see the Martindale-Hubbell Law Directory

*** THOMPSON, HINE AND FLORY (AV)**

One Columbus, 10 West Broad Street, 43215-3435
Telephone: 614-469-3200
Fax: 614-469-3361
Akron, Ohio Office: 50 S. Main Street, Suite 502, 44308-1828.
Telephone: 216-376-8090.
Fax: 216-376-8386.
Cincinnati, Ohio Office: 312 Walnut Street, 14th Floor, 45202-4029.
Telephone: 513-352-6700.
Fax: 513-241-4771.
Telex: 938003.
Cleveland, Ohio Office: 1100 National City Bank Building, 629 Euclid Avenue, 44114-3070.
Telephone: 216-566-5500.
Fax: 216-556-5583.
Telex: 980217.
Cable Address: "Thomflor".
Dayton, Ohio Office: 2000 Courthouse Plaza, N.E., 45402-1706.
Telephone: 513-443-6600.
Fax: 513-443-6637; 443-6635.
Palm Beach, Florida Office: 125 Worth Avenue, 33480-4466.
Telephone: 407-833-5900.
Fax: 407-833-5951.
Washington, D.C. Office: 1920 N Street, N.W., 20036-1601.
Telephone: 202-331-8800.
Fax: 202-331-8330.
Telex: 904173.
Cable Address: "Caglaw".
Brussels, Belgium Office: Rue des Chevaliers / Ridderstraat 14 - B.10, B - 1050.
Telephone: 011(32-2) 511-9326.
Fax: 011(32-2) 513-9206.

MEMBERS OF FIRM

Kenton L. Kuehnle
Michael T. Shannon
William A. Shenk

For Complete List of Firm Personnel, See General Section

For full biographical listings, see the Martindale-Hubbell Law Directory

VORYS, SATER, SEYMOUR AND PEASE (AV)

52 East Gay Street, P.O. Box 1008, 43216-1008
Telephone: 614-464-6400
Telex: 241348
Telecopier: 614-464-6350
Cable Address: "Vorysater"
Washington, D.C. Office: Suite 1111, 1828 L Street, N.W., 20036-5104.
Telephone: 202-467-8800.
Telex: 440693.
Telecopier: 202-467-8900.
Cleveland, Ohio Office: 2100 One Cleveland Center, 1375 East Ninth Street, 44114-1724.
Telephone: 216-479-6100.
Telecopier: 216-479-6060.
Cincinnati, Ohio Office: Suite 2100, 221 East Fourth Street, P.O. Box 0236, 45201-0236.
Telephone: 513-723-4000.
Telecopier: 513-723-4056.

MEMBERS OF FIRM

James B. Cushman
Kenneth M. Royalty
Daniel H. Schoedinger
Steven J. McCoy
Stephen R. Buchenroth
James M. Ball
Donald J. Shuller (Resident, Cincinnati, Ohio Office)
Gary E. Davis
John P. Wellner
Steven W. Mershon
J. Thomas Mason
Daniel J. Minor
Charles C. Bissinger, Jr. (Resident, Cincinnati, Ohio Office)
Webb I. Vorys
Kenneth A. Golonka, Jr.

John B. Weimer

OF COUNSEL

Richard G. Ison

Representative Client: Honda of America Mfg., Inc.
Local Counsel: Abbott Laboratories; Anheuser-Busch, Inc.; Connecticut General Life Insurance Co.; Exxon Company U.S.A.; General Motors Corp.; Navistar International Corporation; Ohio Manufacturers Assn.; Ranco Inc.; Wendy's International, Inc.

(See Next Column)

For Complete List of Firm Personnel, See General Section

For full biographical listings, see the Martindale-Hubbell Law Directory

*DAYTON,** Montgomery Co.

CREW, BUCHANAN & LOWE (AV)

Formerly Cowden, Pfarrer, Crew & Becker
2580 Kettering Tower, 45423-2580
Telephone: 513-223-6211
Facsimile: 513-223-7631

MEMBERS OF FIRM

Charles A. Craighead (1857-1926)
Robert E. Cowden (1886-1954)
Robert E. Cowden, Jr. (1910-1968)
Charles P. Pfarrer (1905-1984)
Philip Rohrer Becker (1905-1989)
Robert B. Crew
Joseph P. Buchanan

Representative Client: General Motors Corporation.

For Complete List of Firm Personnel, See General Section

For full biographical listings, see the Martindale-Hubbell Law Directory

LOUIS & FROELICH A LEGAL PROFESSIONAL ASSOCIATION (AV)

1812 Kettering Tower, 45423
Telephone: 513-226-1776
FAX: 513-226-1945
Trotwood, Ohio Office: 101 East Main Street.
Telephone: 513-226-1776.

Herbert M. Louis
Gary L. Froelich
Jeffrey E. Froelich
Jeffrey A. Winwood
Marybeth W. Rutledge

F. Ann Crossman
James I. Weprin

Reference: Society Bank, N.A. of Dayton, Ohio.

For full biographical listings, see the Martindale-Hubbell Law Directory

STOECKLEIN, KOVERMAN & SMITH (AV)

1300 Hulman Building, 45402
Telephone: 513-222-6926
Fax: 513-222-6901

Robert J. Stoecklein (1917-1990)
John R. Koverman, Jr.
Patrick K. Smith
James E. Fox

For full biographical listings, see the Martindale-Hubbell Law Directory

THOMPSON, HINE AND FLORY (AV)

2000 Courthouse Plaza, N.E., 45402-1706
Telephone: 513-443-6600
Fax: 513-443-6637; 443-6635
Akron, Ohio Office: 50 S. Main Street, Suite 502, 44308-1828.
Telephone: 216-376-8090.
Fax: 216-376-8386.
Cincinnati, Ohio Office: 312 Walnut Street, 14th Floor, 45202-4029.
Telephone: 513-352-6700.
Fax: 513-241-4771.
Telex: 938003.
Cleveland, Ohio Office: 1100 National City Bank Building, 629 Euclid Avenue, 44114-3070.
Telephone: 216-566-5500.
Fax: 216-556-5583.
Telex: 980217.
Cable Address: "Thomflor".
Columbus, Ohio Office: One Columbus, 10 West Broad Street, 43215-3435.
Telephone: 614-469-3200.
Fax: 614-469-3361.
Palm Beach, Florida Office: 125 Worth Avenue, 33480-4466.
Telephone: 407-833-5900.
Fax: 407-833-5951.
Washington, D.C. Office: 1920 N Street, N.W., 20036-1601.
Telephone: 202-331-8800.
Fax: 202-331-8330.
Telex: 904173.
Cable Address: "Caglaw".
Brussels, Belgium Office: Rue des Chevaliers / Ridderstraat 14 - B.10, B - 1050.
Telephone: 011(32-2) 511-9326.
Fax: 011(32-2) 513-9206.

MEMBERS OF FIRM

Robert M. Curry
Timothy J. Hackert
Robert J. Hadley

ASSOCIATE

Steven J. Davis

For Complete List of Firm Personnel, See General Section

For full biographical listings, see the Martindale-Hubbell Law Directory

Dayton—Continued

YOUNG & ALEXANDER CO., L.P.A. (AV)

Suite 100, 367 West Second Street, 45402
Telephone: 513-224-9291
Telecopier: 513-224-9679
Cincinnati, Ohio Office: 110 Boggs Lane, Suite 350.
Telephone: 513-326-5555.
FAX: 513-326-5550.

James M. Brennan

Counsel for: The Children's Medical Center, Dayton, Ohio; The Colonial Stair & Woodwork Co.; The Greater Dayton Area Hospital Assn.; Mike-Sell's Potato Chip Co.; Moorman Pontiac, Inc.
Local Counsel for: Colonial Penn Insurance Co.; John Hancock Mutual Life Insurance Co.; Hertz Corp.; State Farm Insurance Co.

For Complete List of Firm Personnel, See General Section

For full biographical listings, see the Martindale-Hubbell Law Directory

*IRONTON,** Lawrence Co.

COLLIER & COLLIER (AV)

411 Center Street, 45638
Telephone: 614-532-8034
Fax: 614-533-3457

MEMBERS OF FIRM

James Collier (1893-1973)
J. B. Collier
J. B. Collier, Jr.

For full biographical listings, see the Martindale-Hubbell Law Directory

SPEARS & SPEARS (AV)

122 South Fourth Street, 45638
Telephone: 614-532-5815; 614-532-6913

MEMBERS OF FIRM

Harold D. Spears
David R. Spears

References: Star Bank; National City Bank.

For full biographical listings, see the Martindale-Hubbell Law Directory

*SPRINGFIELD,** Clark Co.

COLE ACTON HARMON DUNN A LEGAL PROFESSIONAL ASSOCIATION (AV)

Riverbend Condominiums, 333 North Limestone Street, P.O. Box 1687, 45501
Telephone: 513-322-0891
Fax: 513-322-9931

John M. Cole (1879-1960)
Abe Gardner (1903-1964)
Fred M. Cole (1909-1975)
George W. Cole (1914-1982)
Robert C. Acton (1924-1987)
James A. Harmon
Edward W. Dunn
Charles P. Crabill
Barry P. Reich
William C. Hicks
Phyllis S. Nedelman
Joseph A. Dunn

Representative Clients: Society National Bank; National City Bank; Huntington National Bank; Navistar International; Springfield Newspapers, Inc.; Fulmer Supermarkets, Inc.; Chakeres Theatres Inc.; Springfield Metropolitan Housing Authority; Prudential Insurance Company of America; Springfield Area Chamber of Commerce.

For full biographical listings, see the Martindale-Hubbell Law Directory

*STEUBENVILLE,** Jefferson Co.

KINSEY, ALLEBAUGH & KING (AV)

200 Sinclair Building, P.O. Box 249, 43952
Telephone: 614-282-1900

MEMBERS OF FIRM

W. I. Kinsey (1876-1962)
Carl F. Allebaugh (1896-1970)
Robert P. King

ASSOCIATE

Robert C. Hargrave

OF COUNSEL

Adam E. Scurti
Otto A. Jack, Jr.

Solicitors for: Consolidated Rail Corporation/Penn Central Transportation Co.
Attorneys for: Ohio Power Co.; Columbia Gas Company of Ohio; Ohio Bell Telephone Co.; Ohio Edison Co.; Continental Casualty Co.; Allstate Insurance Co.; Westfield Cos.; Federal Insurance Co.; Unibank.

For full biographical listings, see the Martindale-Hubbell Law Directory

*TOLEDO,** Lucas Co.

BARKAN AND ROBON (AV)

Suite 405 Spitzer Building, 43604-1302
Telephone: 419-244-5591
FAX: 419-244-8736

MEMBERS OF FIRM

William I. Barkan
Marvin A. Robon
Russell R. Miller
A. Thomas Christensen
Paul A. Radon
Gregory R. Elder

ASSOCIATES

Cynthia Godbey Tesznar
Marshall W. Guerin

For full biographical listings, see the Martindale-Hubbell Law Directory

DOYLE, LEWIS & WARNER (AV)

202 North Erie Street, P.O. Box 2168, 43603
Telephone: 419-248-1500
Fax: 419-248-2002

MEMBERS OF FIRM

Steven Timonere
Richard F. Ellenberger
Michael E. Hyrne
John A. Borell
Michael A. Bruno

ASSOCIATE

Kevin A. Pituch

OF COUNSEL

Harold A. James
John R. Wanick

Counsel for: Consolidated Rail Corp.; The Lakefront Dock & Railroad Terminal Co.; Prudential Insurance Co. of America; Equitable Life Assurance Society of the U.S.; Metropolitan Life Insurance Co.; Greyhound Lines; Fireman's Fund Insurance Cos.

For Complete List of Firm Personnel, See General Section

For full biographical listings, see the Martindale-Hubbell Law Directory

FULLER & HENRY (AV)

One Seagate Suite 1700, P.O. Box 2088, 43603-2088
Telephone: 419-247-2500
Telecopier: 419-247-2665
Port Clinton, Ohio Office: 125 Jefferson.
Telephone: 419-734-2153.
Telecopier: 419-732-8246.
Columbus, Ohio Office: 2210 Huntington Center, 41 South High Street.
Telephone: 614-228-6611.
Telecopier: 614-228-6623.

MEMBERS OF FIRM

John W. Hilbert, II
Thomas M. George
Craig J. Van Horsten
David R. Bainbridge

COUNSEL

James W. Baehren

SENIOR ATTORNEY

Regina Reid Joseph

ASSOCIATES

John E. Mauntler
Keith H. Raker
Timothy A. Dismond
Robert E. Nagucki

Representative Clients: Libbey-Owens-Ford Co.; McMahon Ventures; Millar Elevator Service Company; Mill Stream Development; Northwest Ohio Venture Fund;Miracle Development; Vista Development; Owens-Illinois, Inc.; Toledo Edison Company; Hertz Corporation.

For Complete List of Firm Personnel, See General Section

For full biographical listings, see the Martindale-Hubbell Law Directory

JOSEPH H. PILKINGTON & CO., L.P.A. (AV)

One SeaGate, Suite 920, 43604
Telephone: 419-247-1600
Facsimile: 419-247-1602

Joseph H. Pilkington

References: Society Bank & Trust, Toledo, Ohio; Ohio Citizens Bank.

For full biographical listings, see the Martindale-Hubbell Law Directory

RITTER, ROBINSON, MCCREADY & JAMES (AV)

1850 National City Bank Building, 405 Madison Avenue, 43624
Telephone: 419-241-3213
Detroit, Michigan: 313-422-1610
FAX: 419-241-4925

MEMBER OF FIRM

William S. McCready

Counsel For: Chrysler Corp.; Rubini Motors, Inc.; Ohio Casualty Insurance Co.; National Mutual Insurance Co.; Celina Mutual Insurance Co.; Westfield Insurance Co.; Northwestern National Insurance Co.; Midwestern Insurance Co.; United Ohio Insurance Co.; Toledo Auto Electric Co.

(See Next Column)

RITTER, ROBINSON, MCCREADY & JAMES—*Continued*

For Complete List of Firm Personnel, See General Section

For full biographical listings, see the Martindale-Hubbell Law Directory

SPENGLER NATHANSON (AV)

608 Madison Avenue, Suite 1000, 43604-1169
Telephone: 419-241-2201
FAX: 419-241-8599

MEMBERS OF FIRM

David A. Katz
Ralph Bragg
Norman J. Rubinoff
David G. Wise
Louis J. Hattner
Gary D. Sikkema
Richard E. Wolff
Michael W. Bragg

Counsel for: Fifth-Third Bank of Northwestern Ohio, N.A.; Huntington Bank of Toledo; Society Bank & Trust; Seaway Food Town, Inc.; The University of Toledo; AP Parts; Toledo Lucas County Port Authority; Toledo Board of Education; Tuffy Associates Corp.

For Complete List of Firm Personnel, See General Section

For full biographical listings, see the Martindale-Hubbell Law Directory

STOCKWELL & COOPERMAN A LEGAL PROFESSIONAL ASSOCIATION (AV)

Suite 1610, One SeaGate, 43604
Telephone: 419-247-1500
Telecopier: 419-247-1575

John P. Stockwell
Ronald M. Cooperman
Katherine Raup O'Connell

Scott T. Janson

Reference: Fifth Third Bank, Toledo, Ohio.

For full biographical listings, see the Martindale-Hubbell Law Directory

WATKINS, BATES & CAREY (AV)

1200 Fifth Third Center, 608 Madison Avenue, 43604-1157
Telephone: 419-241-2100
Telecopier: 419-241-1960

MEMBERS OF FIRM

William F. Bates
Gary O. Sommer

ASSOCIATES

Gabrielle Davis
Jennifer L. Morrison

Counsel for: Flower Hospital; Fostoria Community Hospital; National City Bank; Heidtman Steel Products, Inc.; Nazar Rubber Co.

For Complete List of Firm Personnel, See General Section

For full biographical listings, see the Martindale-Hubbell Law Directory

OKLAHOMA

*KINGFISHER,** Kingfisher Co.

BEALL & JOHNSON LAW OFFICE, INC. (AV)

215 North Main Street, P.O. Box 298, 73750-0298
Telephone: 405-375-3188
Fax: 405-375-3308

James P. Beall
Cloise E. Johnson, Jr.

General Counsel For: Kingfisher Bank and Trust Co.; Kingfisher Bancorp, Inc.
Representative Clients: Oppel Bros., Inc. (construction and farms); Boeckman Ford, Inc.; Kingfisher Newspapers, Inc. Francis Trust (land development); Okarche Development, Inc.; G.E.B., Inc. (real estate); Felta Yost Trust; Kingfisher County Rural Water Districts; Farmers Cooperative Supply; Kingfisher Educational Foundation, Inc.; Kingfisher Community Trust; Oklahoma Seed Co.

For full biographical listings, see the Martindale-Hubbell Law Directory

*OKLAHOMA CITY,** Oklahoma Co.

ANDREWS DAVIS LEGG BIXLER MILSTEN & PRICE, A PROFESSIONAL CORPORATION (AV)

500 West Main, 73102
Telephone: 405-272-9241
FAX: 405-235-8786

J. Edward Barth
C. Temple Bixler
Charles C. Callaway, Jr.
Carolyn C. Cummins
Alan C. Durbin

(See Next Column)

OF COUNSEL

John P. Roberts

Representative Clients: BancFirst; Boatmen's Bank; First American Title Insurance Co.; Morgan Guaranty Trust Company of New York; Oak Tree Mortgage Co.; Securitie Benefit Life Insurance Co.; Southwest Title & Trust Co.; Stewart Title & Guaranty Co.

For Complete List of Firm Personnel, See General Section

For full biographical listings, see the Martindale-Hubbell Law Directory

DAY, EDWARDS, FEDERMAN, PROPESTER & CHRISTENSEN, P.C. (AV)

Suite 2900 First Oklahoma Tower, 210 Park Avenue, 73102-5605
Telephone: 405-239-2121
Telecopier: 405-236-1012

Bruce W. Day
Joe E. Edwards
William B. Federman
Richard P. Propester
D. Wade Christensen
J. Clay Christensen
Kent A. Gilliland
Rodney J. Heggy
Ricki Valerie Sonders
Thomas Pitchlynn Howell, IV
John C. Platt

David R. Widdoes
Lori R. Roberts
Carolyn A. Romberg

OF COUNSEL

Herbert F. (Jack) Hewett
Jeanette Cook Timmons
Joel Warren Harmon
Jane S. Eulberg
Mark A. Cohen

Representative Clients: Aetna Life Insurance Co.; Boatmen's First National Bank of Oklahoma; Borg-Warner Chemicals, Inc.; City Bank & Trust; Federal Deposit Insurance Corp.; Bank One, Oklahoma City; Haskell Lemon Construction Co.; Merrill Lynch, Pierce, Fenner & Smith, Inc.; Prudential Securities, Inc.

For full biographical listings, see the Martindale-Hubbell Law Directory

HARTZOG CONGER & CASON, A PROFESSIONAL CORPORATION (AV)

1600 Bank of Oklahoma Plaza, 73102
Telephone: 405-235-7000
Facsimile: 405-235-7329

Larry D. Hartzog
J. William Conger
Len Cason
James C. Prince
Alan Newman
Steven C. Davis
Valerie K. Couch
Mark D. Dickey
Joseph P. Hogsett
John D. Robertson
Kurt M. Rupert
Laura Haag McConnell

Susan B. Shields
Ryan S. Wilson
Melanie J. Jester
Armand Paliotta
Julia Watson
J. Leslie LaReau

OF COUNSEL

Kent F. Frates

For full biographical listings, see the Martindale-Hubbell Law Directory

THE LAW OFFICES OF HEMRY & HEMRY, P.C. (AV)

621 N. Robinson, Second Floor, P.O. Box 2207, 73101
Telephone: 405-235-3571
FAX: 405-235-0944

Jerry L. Hemry
Kenneth M. Hemry

OF COUNSEL

Jerome E. Hemry
Tom A. Hemry
(Not admitted in OK)

William P. McDoniel

Counsel for: American General Life Insurance Company of Oklahoma; Lippert Bros. Construction Co; Oklahoma Land Title Association.

For full biographical listings, see the Martindale-Hubbell Law Directory

MOCK, SCHWABE, WALDO, ELDER, REEVES & BRYANT, A PROFESSIONAL CORPORATION (AV)

Fifteenth Floor, One Leadership Square, 211 North Robinson Avenue, 73102
Telephone: 405-235-5500
Telecopy: 405-235-2875

James R. Waldo
James C. Elder

OF COUNSEL

Michael J. Hunter

Representative Clients: Equity Bank for Savings, F.A.; Farm Credit Bank of Wichita; Local Federal Bank, F.S.B.; Lincoln National Life Insurance, Co.; Massachusetts Mutual Life Insurance Co.; Metropolitan Life Insurance Co.;

(See Next Column)

MOCK, SCHWABE, WALDO, ELDER, REEVES & BRYANT A PROFESSIONAL CORPORATION, *Oklahoma City—Continued*

Texaco, Inc.; Liberty Bank & Trust Company of Oklahoma City; Trammell Crow Co.

For Complete List of Firm Personnel, See General Section

For full biographical listings, see the Martindale-Hubbell Law Directory

SELF, GIDDENS & LEES, INC. (AV)

2725 Oklahoma Tower, 210 Park Avenue, 73102-5604
Telephone: 405-232-3001
Telecopier: 405-232-5553

Jared D. Giddens
C. Ray Lees
Shannon T. Self

Thomas J. Blalock
Christopher R. Graves
W. Shane Smithton
Bryan J. Wells

For full biographical listings, see the Martindale-Hubbell Law Directory

STEPHEN A. SHERMAN & ASSOCIATES (AV)

117 Park Avenue Building, Fourth Floor, 73102
Telephone: 405-235-0707
Fax: 405-235-0712

Daniel K. Zorn

Representative Clients: Aetna Realty Investors, Inc.; CB Commercial Real Estate Management Services; Insignia Commercial Group, Inc.; Kaiser-Francis Oil Co.; Nationwide Insurance Co.; Self Insurer's Service Bureau, Inc.; Trammell Crow Co., Inc.; White Swan, Inc.

For full biographical listings, see the Martindale-Hubbell Law Directory

*PERRY,** Noble Co.

HARVEY D. YOST II (AV)

623 Delaware Street, P.O. Box 874, 73077-0874
Telephone: 405-336-5511
Facsimile: 405-336-3554

ASSOCIATE

Donna Occhipinti Yost

For full biographical listings, see the Martindale-Hubbell Law Directory

*TULSA,** Tulsa Co.

GABLE & GOTWALS (AV)

2000 Bank IV Center, 15 West Sixth Street, 74119-5447
Telephone: 918-582-9201
Facsimile: 918-586-8383

Teresa B. Adwan
Pamela S. Anderson
John R. Barker
David L. Bryant
Gene C. Buzzard
Dennis Clarke Cameron
Timothy A. Carney
Renee DeMoss
Elsie C. Draper
Sidney G. Dunagan
Theodore Q. Eliot
Richard W. Gable
Jeffrey Don Hassell
Patricia Ledvina Himes
Oliver S. Howard
Richard D. Koljack, Jr.
J. Daniel Morgan
Joseph W. Morris
Elizabeth R. Muratet
Richard B. Noulles
Ronald N. Ricketts
John Henry Rule
M. Benjamin Singletary
James M. Sturdivant
Patrick O. Waddel
Michael D. Hall
David Edward Keglovits
Stephen W. Lake
Kari S. McKee
Terry D. Ragsdale
Jeffrey C. Rambach

OF COUNSEL

G. Ellis Gable
Charles P. Gotwals, Jr.

For full biographical listings, see the Martindale-Hubbell Law Directory

JAMES, POTTS AND WULFERS (AV)

Suite 705, 320 South Boston Avenue, 74103-3712
Telephone: 918-584-0881
FAX: 918-584-4521

MEMBERS OF FIRM

David F. James
Thomas G. Potts
David W. Wulfers

For full biographical listings, see the Martindale-Hubbell Law Directory

STEPHEN A. SCHULLER INCORPORATED (AV)

1111 ParkCentre, 525 South Main Mall, 74103-4522
Telephone: 918-583-8205
Facsimile: 918-583-1226

Stephen A. Schuller

For full biographical listings, see the Martindale-Hubbell Law Directory

SNEED, LANG, ADAMS & BARNETT, A PROFESSIONAL CORPORATION (AV)

2300 Williams Center Tower II, Two West Second Street, 74103
Telephone: 918-583-3145
Telecopier: 918-582-0410

James C. Lang
D. Faith Orlowski
Brian S. Gaskill
G. Steven Stidham
Stephen R. McNamara
Thomas E. Black, Jr.
Robbie Emery Burke
C. Raymond Patton, Jr.
Frederick K. Slicker
Richard D. Black
John D. Russell
Jeffrey S. Swyers

OF COUNSEL

James L. Sneed
O. Edwin Adams
Howard G. Barnett, Jr.

Representative Clients: Amoco Production Company; Continental Bank; Deloitte & Touche; Enron Corporation; Halliburton Energy Services; Helmerich & Payne, Inc.; Lehman Brothers, Inc.; Shell Oil Company; Smith Barney, Inc.; State Farm Mutual Automobile Insurance Company.

For full biographical listings, see the Martindale-Hubbell Law Directory

OREGON

*PORTLAND,** Multnomah Co.

BLACK HELTERLINE (AV)

1200 The Bank of California Tower, 707 S.W. Washington Street, 97205
Telephone: 503-224-5560
Telecopier: 503-224-6148

MEMBERS OF FIRM

Albert J. Bannon
John M. McGuigan
David P. Roy
Steven R. Schell

ASSOCIATES

Stark Ackerman
Donald L. Krahmer, Jr.

OF COUNSEL

Robert E. Glasgow

Representative Clients: Aspen Ridge Group, Inc.; Catellus Development Corp.; Citation, Inc.; ESCO Corp.; Great American Development Co.; K-4, Inc.; Melvin Mark Properties; Rivergreen Construction, Inc.; The Sivers Cos.

For Complete List of Firm Personnel, See General Section

For full biographical listings, see the Martindale-Hubbell Law Directory

GRENLEY, ROTENBERG EVANS & BRAGG, P.C. (AV)

30th Floor, Pacwest Center, 1211 S.W. Fifth Avenue, 97204
Telephone: 503-241-0570
Facsimile: 503-241-0914

Gary I. Grenley
Stan N. Rotenberg
Lawrence Evans
Michael J. Bragg
Steven D. Adler
Michael S. Evans
Michael C. Zusman
Jeffrey C. Bodie

OF COUNSEL

Sol Siegel
Robert C. Laskowski
Norman A. Rickles

Ann M. Lane

Reference: Key Bank of Oregon.

For full biographical listings, see the Martindale-Hubbell Law Directory

HAGEN, DYE, HIRSCHY & DILORENZO, P.C. (AV)

19th Floor Benj. Franklin Plaza, One S.W. Columbia Street, 97258-2087
Telephone: 503-222-1812
FAX: 503-274-7979

Joseph T. Hagen
Jeffrey L. Dye
John A. Hirschy
John A. DiLorenzo, Jr.
Dana R. Taylor
Mark A. Golding
Kenneth A. Williams

Blanche I. Sommers
Timothy J. Wachter
Annie T. Buell
Adam S. Rittenberg
Michael E. Farnell
John D. Parsons

LEGAL SUPPORT PERSONNEL

Carol A. R. Wong
Flora L. Wade

For full biographical listings, see the Martindale-Hubbell Law Directory

Portland—Continued

HANNA, KERNS & STRADER, A PROFESSIONAL CORPORATION (AV)

300 Hoffman Columbia Plaza, 1300 S.W. Sixth Avenue, 97201
Telephone: 503-273-2700
FAX: 503-273-2712

Harry M. Hanna | Diane C. Kerns
Joseph J. Hanna, Jr. | Timothy R. Strader

Joe F. Yonek | David E. Grein

OF COUNSEL

Jonathan G. Blattmachr (Not admitted in OR)
Peter A. Casciato
Glen R. Kuykendall
Robert J. Woody (Not admitted in OR; Resident, Washington, D.C. Office)

For full biographical listings, see the Martindale-Hubbell Law Directory

JOSSELSON, POTTER & ROBERTS (AV)

53 S.W. Yamhill Street, 97204
Telephone: 503-228-1455
Facsimile: 503-228-0171

MEMBERS OF FIRM

Frank Josselson | Irving W. Potter
Leslie M. Roberts

OF COUNSEL

Lawrence R. Derr

For full biographical listings, see the Martindale-Hubbell Law Directory

O'DONNELL, RAMIS, CREW, CORRIGAN & BACHRACH (AV)

Ballow & Wright Building, 1727 N.W. Hoyt Street, 97209
Telephone: 503-222-4402
FAX: 503-243-2944
Clackamas County Office: Suite 202, 181 N. Grant, Canby.
Telephone: 503-266-1149.

MEMBERS OF FIRM

Mark P. O'Donnell | Jeff H. Bachrach

For full biographical listings, see the Martindale-Hubbell Law Directory

SUSSMAN SHANK WAPNICK CAPLAN & STILES (AV)

1000 S.W. Broadway Suite 1400, 97205
Telephone: 503-227-1111
Telecopier: 503-248-0130

MEMBERS OF FIRM

Norman Wapnick | William N. Stiles
Barry P. Caplan | John P. Davenport
Jeffrey R. Spere

ASSOCIATES

Robert L. Carlton | Gary E. Enloe

For Complete List of Firm Personnel, See General Section

For full biographical listings, see the Martindale-Hubbell Law Directory

PENNSYLVANIA

BALA CYNWYD, Montgomery Co.

KANIA, LINDNER, LASAK AND FEENEY (AV)

Suite 525, Two Bala Plaza, 19004
Telephone: 610-667-3240
Fax: 610-668-9676

Arthur J. Kania | John Lasak
Albert A. Lindner | Thomas J. Feeney, III
Robert A. Griffiths

ASSOCIATE

Michael F. Merlie

A list of Representative Clients for which the firm serves as General Counsel or Local Counsel will be supplied upon request.

For full biographical listings, see the Martindale-Hubbell Law Directory

BLUE BELL, Montgomery Co.

LESSER & KAPLIN, PROFESSIONAL CORPORATION (AV)

350 Sentry Parkway, Bldg. 640, 19422-0757
Telephone: 610-828-2900; Telecopier: 610-828-1555
Marlton, New Jersey Office: Three Greentree Centre, Suite 104, Route 73, 08053-3215.
Telephone: 609-596-2400.
Telecopier: 609-596-8185.

(See Next Column)

Lawrence R. Lesser | Anthony J. Krol
Marc B. Kaplin | Bruce J. Meloff
William K. Stewart, Jr. | Neil Andrew Stein
Bruce R. Lesser | L. Leonard Lundy

David S. Blum
Alan P. Fox (Resident, Marlton, New Jersey Office)
Patricia L. Talcott (Resident, Marlton, New Jersey Office)
Richard Mark Zucker
Jordan D. Warshaw

For full biographical listings, see the Martindale-Hubbell Law Directory

BRYN MAWR, Montgomery Co.

MURPHY AND MURPHY (AV)

801 Old Lancaster Road, 19010
Telephone: 610-519-0400
Fax: 610-519-0104
Trenton, New Jersey Office: Suite A 311 White Horse Avenue.
Telephone: 609-581-8559.

L. Francis Murphy | Francis J. Murphy
Michael T. Murphy

For full biographical listings, see the Martindale-Hubbell Law Directory

SHEA AND SHEA (AV)

11 Elliott Avenue, 19010
Telephone: 610-527-4000
Fax: 610-527-5919

MEMBERS OF FIRM

John G. Shea | Phyllis McCormick Shea
Michael S. Dinney

Reference: The Bryn Mawr Trust Co., Bryn Mawr, Pennsylvania.

For full biographical listings, see the Martindale-Hubbell Law Directory

CAMP HILL, Cumberland Co.

REAGER & ADLER, P.C. (AV)

2331 Market Street, 17011
Telephone: 717-763-1383
Fax: 717-730-7366
Harrisburg, Pennsylvania Address: P.O. Box 797 17108-0797.

Theodore A. Adler | David W. Reager

John J. McNally, III | Debra A. Denison
Susan H. Confair

Representative Clients: Homebuilders Association of Metropolitan Harrisburg; Pennsylvania Builders Association; The Homestead Group, Inc.

For full biographical listings, see the Martindale-Hubbell Law Directory

*EASTON,** Northampton Co.

HERSTER, NEWTON & MURPHY (AV)

127 North Fourth Street, P.O. Box 1087, 18042
Telephone: 610-258-6219

MEMBERS OF FIRM

Andrew L. Herster, Jr. | Henry R. Newton
William K. Murphy

General Counsel For: Valley Federal Savings & Loan Assn.; Lafayette Bank; Easton Printing Co.; Northampton Community College; Eisenhardt Mills, Inc.; Delaware Wood Products, Inc.; Panuccio Construction, Inc.
References: Merchants Bank, N.A.; Lafayette Bank; Valley Federal Savings and Loan.

*GREENSBURG,** Westmoreland Co.

DAVID J. MILLSTEIN (AV)

218 South Maple Avenue, 15601
Telephone: 412-837-3333
Fax: 412-837-8344

For full biographical listings, see the Martindale-Hubbell Law Directory

*HARRISBURG,** Dauphin Co.

BOSWELL, SNYDER, TINTNER & PICCOLA (AV)

315 North Front Street, P.O. Box 741, 17108-0741
Telephone: 717-236-9377
Telecopier: 717-236-9316

MEMBERS OF FIRM

William D. Boswell | Jeffrey R. Boswell
Donn L. Snyder | Brigid Q. Alford
Leonard Tintner | Mark R. Parthemer
Jeffrey E. Piccola | Charles J. Hartwell

(See Next Column)

BOSWELL, SNYDER, TINTNER & PICCOLA, *Harrisburg—Continued*

OF COUNSEL

Richard B. Wickersham

Representative Clients: Fine Line Homes; Federal National Mortgage Assoc.; J.W. Mumper Construction, Inc.; Fidelity National Title Insurance Company of Pennsylvania; Meridian Title Insurance Co.; Meritor Mortgage Corp. - East; Residential Warranty Corp.; Jack Gaughen Realtor.

For full biographical listings, see the Martindale-Hubbell Law Directory

BUCHANAN INGERSOLL, PROFESSIONAL CORPORATION (AV)

Vartan Parc, 30 North Third Street, 17101
Telephone: 717-237-4800
Telecopier: 717-233-0852
Pittsburgh, Pennsylvania Office: 5800 USX Tower, 600 Grant Street.
Telephone: 412-562-8800.
Philadelphia, Pennsylvania Office: Two Logan Square, Twelfth Floor, 18th & Arch Streets.
Telephone: 215-665-8700.
Tampa, Florida Office: 101 East Kennedy Boulevard, Suite 1030.
Telephone: 813-222-8180.
North Miami Beach, Florida Office: 19495 Biscayne Boulevard.
Telephone: 305-933-5600.
Lexington, Kentucky Office: 1210 Vine Center Office Tower, 333 West Vine Street.
Telephone: 606-225-5333.
Princeton, New Jersey Office: Buchanan Ingersoll, A Partnership, College Centre, 500 College Road East.
Telephone: 609-452-2666.

SENIOR ATTORNEY

Michael L. Solomon

Paul S. Romano

For Complete List of Firm Personnel, See General Section

For full biographical listings, see the Martindale-Hubbell Law Directory

GOLDBERG, KATZMAN & SHIPMAN, P.C. (AV)

320 Market Street - Strawberry Square, P.O. Box 1268, 17108-1268
Telephone: 717-234-4161
Telecopier: 717-234-6808; 717-234-6810

Ronald M. Katzman
Jesse Jay Cooper

Arnold B. Kogan

Reference: Fulton Bank.

For Complete List of Firm Personnel, See General Section

For full biographical listings, see the Martindale-Hubbell Law Directory

HEPFORD, SWARTZ & MORGAN (AV)

111 North Front Street, P.O. Box 889, 17108-0889
Telephone: 717-234-4121
Fax: 717-232-6802
Lewistown, Pennsylvania Office: 12 South Main Street, P.O. Box 867.
Telephone: 717-248-3913.

MEMBERS OF FIRM

H. Joseph Hepford
Lee C. Swartz
James G. Morgan, Jr.
Sandra L. Meilton
Stephen M. Greecher, Jr.
Dennis R. Sheaffer

COUNSEL

Stanley H. Siegel (Resident, Lewistown Office)

ASSOCIATES

Richard A. Estacio
Michael H. Park
Andrew K. Stutzman

For full biographical listings, see the Martindale-Hubbell Law Directory

JOSEPH A. KLEIN A PROFESSIONAL CORPORATION (AV)

100 Chestnut Street, Suite 210, P.O. Box 1152, 17108
Telephone: 717-233-0132
Fax: 717-233-2516

Joseph A. Klein
Mark S. Silver

For full biographical listings, see the Martindale-Hubbell Law Directory

MCNEES, WALLACE & NURICK (AV)

100 Pine Street, P.O. Box 1166, 17108
Telephone: 717-232-8000
Fax: 717-237-5300

MEMBERS OF FIRM

Robert M. Cherry
Gary A. Ritter
Steven J. Weingarten

(See Next Column)

ASSOCIATE

Bruce R. Spicer

For Complete List of Firm Personnel, See General Section

For full biographical listings, see the Martindale-Hubbell Law Directory

METTE, EVANS & WOODSIDE, A PROFESSIONAL CORPORATION (AV)

3401 North Front Street, P.O. Box 5950, 17110-0950
Telephone: 717-232-5000
Telecopier: 717-236-1816

Charles B. Zwally
Peter J. Ressler
Steven D. Snyder
Glen R. Grell
Paula J. Leicht

Guy P. Beneventano
Karen N. Connelly

Counsel for: The B. F. Goodrich Co.; Juniata Valley Financial Corp.; MCI Telecommunications Corp.; Monongahela Power Co.; The Procter and Gamble Paper Products Co.; United States Fidelity and Guaranty Co.; Community Banks; GTE Products Corp.; Commerce Bank.

For Complete List of Firm Personnel, See General Section

For full biographical listings, see the Martindale-Hubbell Law Directory

NAUMAN, SMITH, SHISSLER & HALL (AV)

Eighteenth Floor, 200 North Third Street, P.O. Box 840, 17108-0840
Telephone: 717-236-3010
Telefax: 717-234-1925

MEMBERS OF FIRM

David C. Eaton
Spencer G. Nauman, Jr.
John C. Sullivan
J. Stephen Feinour
Craig J. Staudenmaier

ASSOCIATES

Benjamin Charles Dunlap, Jr.
Stephen J. Keene

OF COUNSEL

Ralph W. Boyles, Jr.

Representative Clients: Consolidated Rail Corp.; The W.O. Hickok Mfg. Co.; Delta Dental of Pennsylvania; Mellon Bank, N.A.; PNC Bank, N.A.; General Motors Acceptance Corp.; Chrysler Credit Corp.; Dempsey's Restaurants, Inc.

For full biographical listings, see the Martindale-Hubbell Law Directory

*LANCASTER,** Lancaster Co.

APPEL & YOST (AV)

33 North Duke Street, 17602-2886
Telephone: 717-394-0521
Telecopier: 717-299-9781 ABA NET NUMBER 1556
New Holland, Pennsylvania Office: 142 East Main Street.
Telephone: 717-354-4117.
Strasburg, Pennsylvania Office: 39 East Main Street.
Telephone: 717-687-7871.
Quarryville, Pennsylvania Office: 201 East State Street.
Telephone: 717-786-3172.
Ephrata, Pennsylvania Office: 123 East Main Street, 17522.
Telephone: 717-733-2104.

MEMBERS OF FIRM

T. Roberts Appel, II
Harry B. Yost
James W. Appel
John L. Sampson
Kenneth H. Howard
William R. Wheatly
William J. Cassidy, Jr.
Greta R. Aul
Matthew G. Guntharp
Peter M. Schannauer

Julia G. Vanasse
Elaine G. Ugolnik
David W. Mersky

OF COUNSEL

Paul F. McKinsey
J. Marlin Shreiner

Counsel for: School Lane Hills, Inc.; Wickersham, Inc. (Construction & Development).

For full biographical listings, see the Martindale-Hubbell Law Directory

LANSDALE, Montgomery Co.

PEARLSTINE/SALKIN ASSOCIATES (AV)

1250 South Broad Street Suite 1000, P.O. Box 431, 19446
Telephone: 215-699-6000
Fax: 215-699-0231

MEMBERS OF FIRM

Philip Salkin
Ronald E. Robinson
Barry Cooperberg
Frederick C. Horn
Marc B. Davis
William R. Wanger
F. Craig La Rocca
Jeffrey T. Sultanik
Neal R. Pearlstine
Wendy G. Rothstein
Alan L. Eisen
Glenn D. Fox

(See Next Column)

PEARLSTINE/SALKIN ASSOCIATES—*Continued*

Wilhelm L. Gruszecki
Brian E. Subers
Mark S. Cappuccio
James R. Hall
Michael S. Paul
David J. Draganosky
Lawrence P. Kempner

For full biographical listings, see the Martindale-Hubbell Law Directory

*MEDIA,** Delaware Co.

KASSAB ARCHBOLD JACKSON & O'BRIEN (AV)

Lawyers-Title Building, 214 North Jackson Street, P.O. Box 626, 19063
Telephone: 610-565-3800
Telecopier: 610-892-6888
Wilmington, Delaware Office: 1326 King Street.
Telephone: 302-656-3393.
Fax: 302-656-1993.
Wildwood, New Jersey Office: 5201 New Jersey Avenue.
Telephone: 609-522-6559.

MEMBERS OF FIRM

Edward Kassab
William C. Archbold, Jr.
Robert James Jackson
Joseph Patrick O'Brien
Richard A. Stanko
Roy T. J. Stegena

OF COUNSEL

Matthew J. Ryan
John W. Nilon, Jr.

ASSOCIATES

Kevin William Gibson
Cynthia Kassab Larosa
Marc S. Stein
Terrance A. Kline
George C. McFarland, Jr.
Jill E. Aversa
Pamela A. La Torre
Kenneth D. Kynett

Representative Clients furnished upon request.

For full biographical listings, see the Martindale-Hubbell Law Directory

*NORRISTOWN,** Montgomery Co.

MANNING, KINKEAD, BROOKS & BRADBURY, A PROFESSIONAL CORPORATION (AV)

412 DeKalb Street, 19404-0231
Telephone: 610-279-1800
Fax: 610-279-8682

Franklin L. Wright (1880-1965)
William Perry Manning, Jr.
William H. Kinkead, III
William H. Bradbury, III

Cheri D. Andrews

Counsel for: The Philadelphia National Bank; John Deere Co.; The Rouse Co.; Consolidated Rail Corp.; Bethlehem Steel Co.; Royal Globe Insurance Co.; Nationwide Mutual Insurance Co.

For full biographical listings, see the Martindale-Hubbell Law Directory

*PHILADELPHIA,** Philadelphia Co.

ASTOR WEISS KAPLAN & ROSENBLUM (AV)

The Bellevue, 6th Floor, Broad Street at Walnut, 19102
Telephone: 215-790-0100
Fax: 215-790-0509
Bala Cynwyd, Pennsylvania Office: Suite 100, Three Bala Plaza West, P.O. Box 1665.
Telephone: 610-667-8660.
Fax: 610-667-2783.
Cherry Hill, New Jersey Office: Woodland Falls Corporate Park, 210 Lake Drive East, Suite 201.
Telephone: 609-795-1113.
Fax: 609-795-7413.

MEMBERS OF FIRM

Paul C. Astor
Alvin M. Weiss (1936-1976)
G. David Rosenblum
Arthur H. Kaplan
Barbara Oaks Silver
Richard H. Martin
Allen B. Dubroff
David S. Workman
David S. Mandel
David Gutin (Resident at Bala Cynwyd Office)
Joseph B. Finlay, Jr.
Howard K. Goldstein
Steven W. Smith
Gerald J. Schorr
Jean M. Biesecker (Resident, Bala Cynwyd Office)

ASSOCIATES

Carol L. Vassallo
Thomas J. Maiorino
John R. Poeta
Bradley J. Begelman
Andrew S. Kessler
Marc S. Zamsky
Janet G. Felgoise (Resident, Bala Cynwyd Office)
Jacqueline G. Segal (Resident, Bala Cynwyd Office)

SPECIAL COUNSEL

Neil Hurowitz (Resident, Bala Cynwyd Office)

(See Next Column)

OF COUNSEL

Erwin L. Pincus
Edward W. Silver
Lloyd Zane Remick

For full biographical listings, see the Martindale-Hubbell Law Directory

BALLARD SPAHR ANDREWS & INGERSOLL (AV)

1735 Market Street, 51st Floor, 19103-7599
Telephone: 215-665-8500
Fax: 215-864-8999
Denver, Colorado Office: Seventeenth Street Plaza Building, Suite 2300, 1225 17th Street.
Telephone: 303-292-2400.
Fax: 303-296-3956.
Kaunas, Lithuania Office: Donelaicio g., 71-2, Kaunas 3000.
Telephone: (370-7) 20 56 66.
Fax: (370-7) 20 56 91.
Salt Lake City, Utah Office: One Utah Center, Suite 1200, 201 South Main Street.
Telephone: 801-531-3000.
Fax: 801-531-3001.
Washington, D.C. Office: Suite 900 East, 555 13th Street, N.W.
Telephone: 202-383-8800.
Fax: 202-383-8877; 383-8893.
Baltimore, Maryland Office: 300 East Lombard Street. 19th Floor.
Telephone: 410-528-5600.
Fax: 410-528-5650.
Camden, New Jersey Office: 800 Hudson Square, 5th Floor.
Telephone: 609-541-5577.
Fax: 609-541-8272.

Lynn R. Axelroth
Thomas R. Eshelman
Philip B. Korb
Alan S. Ritterband
Frederic W. Clark
Gardner A. Evans
Bart I. Mellits
Michael Sklaroff

COUNSEL

Rachel Kipnes

Yvonne B. Haskins
Bradley A. Krouse
Joanne Phillips

For Complete List of Firm Personnel, See General Section

For full biographical listings, see the Martindale-Hubbell Law Directory

BUCHANAN INGERSOLL, PROFESSIONAL CORPORATION (AV)

Two Logan Square Twelfth Floor, 18th & Arch Streets, 19103
Telephone: 215-665-8700
Telecopier: 215-569-2066
Pittsburgh, Pennsylvania Office: 5800 USX Tower, 600 Grant Street.
Telephone: 412-562-8800.
Harrisburg, Pennsylvania Office: Vartan Parc, 30 North Third Street.
Telephone: 717-237-4800.
Tampa, Florida Office: 101 East Kennedy Boulevard, Suite 1030.
Telephone: 813-222-8180.
North Miami Beach, Florida Office: 19495 Biscayne Boulevard.
Telephone: 305-933-5600.
Lexington, Kentucky Office: 1210 Vine Center Office Tower, 333 West Vine Street.
Telephone: 606-225-5333.
Princeton, New Jersey Office: Buchanan Ingersoll, A Partnership, College Centre, 500 College Road East.
Telephone: 609-452-2666.

Jerome N. Kline

Nancy Sabol Frantz

For Complete List of Firm Personnel, See General Section

For full biographical listings, see the Martindale-Hubbell Law Directory

LESLIE J. CARSON, JR. (AV)

42 South 15th Street, Suite 1150, 19102
Telephone: 215-568-1980
Fax: 215-568-6882

For full biographical listings, see the Martindale-Hubbell Law Directory

LOUIS J. CARTER (AV)

7300 City Line Avenue, 19151-2291
Telephone: 215-879-8665
FAX: 215- 877-0955

For full biographical listings, see the Martindale-Hubbell Law Directory

Philadelphia—Continued

FELLHEIMER EICHEN BRAVERMAN & KASKEY, A PROFESSIONAL CORPORATION (AV)

21st Floor, One Liberty Place, 19103-7334
Telephone: 215-575-3800
FAX: 215-575-3801
Camden, New Jersey Office: 519 Federal Street, Suite 503 Parkade Building, 08103-1147.
Telephone: 609-541-5323.
Fax: 609-541-5370.

Alan S. Fellheimer
David L. Braverman
Judith Eichen Fellheimer
John E. Kaskey
Kenneth S. Goodkind
Anna Hom
Peter E. Meltzer

Barbara Anisko
Maia R. Caplan
Jeffrey L. Eichen
Michael N. Feder
Jolie G. Kahn
George F. Newton
David B. Spitofsky
W. Thomas Tither, Jr.

For Complete List of Firm Personnel, See General Section

For full biographical listings, see the Martindale-Hubbell Law Directory

FOX, ROTHSCHILD, O'BRIEN & FRANKEL (AV)

10th Floor, 2000 Market Street, 19103-3291
Telephone: 215-299-2000
Cable Address: FROF
Telecopier: 215-299-2150
Exton, Pennsylvania Office: Eagleview Corporate Center, 717 Constitution Drive, Suite 111, P.O. Box 673, 19341-0673.
Telephone: 610-458-2100.
Telecopier: 610-458-2112.
Trenton (Lawrenceville), New Jersey Office: Princeton Pike Corporate Center, 997 Lenox Drive, Building 3, 08648-2311.
Telephone: 609-896-3600.
Telecopier: 609-896-1469.

MEMBERS OF FIRM

Stanley S. Cohen
Herbert Bass
Mitchell T. Morris
Elaine N. Moranz
Jay S. Ruder (Resident, Trenton (Lawrenceville), New Jersey Office)
Philip L. Hinerman
Mary Ann Rossi (Resident, Exton, Pennsylvania Office)
Mark L. Morris
Gregory Kleiber

ASSOCIATES

Marjorie Stern Jacobs
Marc E. Needles
Janet R. Seligman
Robert W. Gundlach
Caroline Wroth O'Leary

For Complete List of Firm Personnel, See General Section

For full biographical listings, see the Martindale-Hubbell Law Directory

MIRIAM N. JACOBSON (AV)

Fifth Floor, 1528 Walnut Street, 19102
Telephone: 215-546-2400
Fax and Modem numbers upon request
Voorhees, NJ
Voorhees, New Jersey Office: 1307 White Horse Road. Building B.
Telephone: 609-770-0009.

For full biographical listings, see the Martindale-Hubbell Law Directory

KLEHR, HARRISON, HARVEY, BRANZBURG & ELLERS (AV)

1401 Walnut Street, 19102
Telephone: 215-568-6060
Fax: 215-568-6603
Cherry Hill, New Jersey Office: Colwick-Suite 200, 51 Haddonfield Road.
Telephone: 609-486-7900.
Fax: 609-486-4875.
Allentown, Pennsylvania Office: Roma Corporate Center, Suite 501, 1605 North Cedar Crest Boulevard.
Telephone: 215-432-1803.
Fax: 215-433-4031.
Wilmington, Delaware Office: 222 Delaware Avenue, Suite 1101.
Telephone: 302-426-1189.
Fax: 302-426-9193.

MEMBERS OF FIRM

Leonard M. Klehr
Robert C. Seiger, Jr.
Mark L. Alderman
Richard S. Roisman
Alan M. Rosen
Gary W. Levi (Resident, Cherry Hill, New Jersey Office)

ASSOCIATES

Marcy Newman Hart
Stephen P. Lieske

For Complete List of Firm Personnel, See General Section

For full biographical listings, see the Martindale-Hubbell Law Directory

MELVIN B. MILLER, LTD. (AV)

Suite 750 Curtis Center, 6th & Walnut Streets, 19106
Telephone: 215-923-8626
Telecopier: 215-574-9510

Melvin B. Miller

Representative Clients: Berkshire Investment Corp.; Asbell & Associates; Delaire Nursing Home, Inc.; Berkeley Heights Convalescent Center, Inc.; Hospicomm, Inc.; Metropolitan Management Corp.; First Winthrop Corporation.

For full biographical listings, see the Martindale-Hubbell Law Directory

NEMEROFF, ROBERTS & SAFFREN, A PROFESSIONAL CORPORATION (AV)

260 South Broad Street, 19102
Telephone: 215-790-9750
Elkins Park, Pennsylvania Office: Suite 104, 7848 Old York Road.
Telephone: 215-635-8980.

Milton A. Nemeroff
Lawrence J. Roberts
Kenneth S. Saffren

For full biographical listings, see the Martindale-Hubbell Law Directory

OMINSKY, WELSH & STEINBERG, P.C. (AV)

1760 Market Street, 10th Floor, 19103-4129
Telephone: 215-568-4500
Fax: 215-751-9005
Bridgeport, Pennsylvania Office: 408 East Fourth Street.
Telephone: 215-270-9600.
FAX: 215-270-9990.

Albert Ominsky
Barney B. Welsh
Lennard B. Steinberg
David M. Giles
Joseph L. Messa, Jr.
Mark W. Tanner
Glenn F. Gilman

OF COUNSEL

Jack A. Meyerson
Joel I. Fishbein
Thomas W. Sheridan

RAPPAPORT & FURMAN (AV)

105 South Twelfth Street, 19107
Telephone: 215-625-9070
Fax: 215-625-0680

MEMBERS OF FIRM

Samuel Rappaport
Harold Shaffer

OF COUNSEL

Jerome E. Furman

For full biographical listings, see the Martindale-Hubbell Law Directory

LAWRENCE S. ROSENWALD, P.C. (AV)

Suite 3901, Mellon Bank Center, 1735 Market Street, 19103-7501
Telephone: 215-994-1401
Fax: 215-994-1410

Lawrence S. Rosenwald

OF COUNSEL

Peter A. Galante
Gary M. Friedland

LEGAL SUPPORT PERSONNEL

Gretchen A. Anderson

Representative Clients: Philadelphia Redevelopment Authority; LCOR.

For full biographical listings, see the Martindale-Hubbell Law Directory

SEGRÉ & SENSER, P.C. (AV)

Suite 414, Two Penn Center Plaza, 19102
Telephone: 215-557-7800
Fax: 215-557-7880

Nina Segré
Karen L. Senser

For full biographical listings, see the Martindale-Hubbell Law Directory

STRONG, STEVENS, BRISCOE & HAMILTON, P.C. (AV)

4000 Bell Atlantic Tower, 1717 Arch Street, 19103
Telephone: 215-563-5900
Fax: 215-563-2982
Blue Bell, Pennsylvania Office: 640 Sentry Parkway, First Floor.
Telephone: 215-832-5900.
Fax: 215-832-5914.

George V. Strong, Jr.
Richard K. Stevens, Jr.
James H. Stevens
Jack C. Briscoe
Jeffrey F. Janoski
Emory A. Wyant, Jr.
Thomas R. Kellogg
Ronald W. Fenstermacher, Jr.
Ralf W. Greenwood, Jr.
Mary K. Lemmon

(See Next Column)

STRONG, STEVENS, BRISCOE & HAMILTON P.C.—*Continued*

COUNSEL

Samuel L. Sagendorph

For full biographical listings, see the Martindale-Hubbell Law Directory

*PITTSBURGH,** Allegheny Co.

BERNSTEIN AND BERNSTEIN, A PROFESSIONAL CORPORATION (AV)

1133 Penn Avenue, 15222
Telephone: 412-456-8100
Facsimile: 412-456-8135
Harrisburg, Pennsylvania Office: 204 State Street.
Telephone: 717-233-1000.
Fax: 717-233-8290.

Arthur J. Smith

Representative Clients: Integra Bank; Chase Manhattan Bank; Dollar Bank; Nations Credit.

For full biographical listings, see the Martindale-Hubbell Law Directory

BRENNAN, ROBINS & DALEY (AV)

Fort Pitt Commons, Suite 500, 445 Fort Pitt Boulevard, 15219-1322
Telephone: 412-281-0776
Fax: 412-281-2180

PARTNERS

Harvey E. Robins
Arnold M. Epstein

ASSOCIATE

Richard J. Klixbull

For full biographical listings, see the Martindale-Hubbell Law Directory

BUCHANAN INGERSOLL, PROFESSIONAL CORPORATION (AV)

5800 USX Tower, 600 Grant Street, 15219
Telephone: 412-562-8800
Telecopier: 412-562-1041
Philadelphia, Pennsylvania Office: Two Logan Square, Twelfth Floor, 18th & Arch Streets.
Telephone: 215-665-8700.
Harrisburg, Pennsylvania Office: Vartan Parc, 30 North Third Street.
Telephone: 717-237-4800.
Tampa, Florida Office: 101 East Kennedy Boulevard, Suite 1030.
Telephone: 813-222-8180.
North Miami Beach, Florida Office: 19495 Biscayne Boulevard.
Telephone: 305-933-5600.
Lexington, Kentucky Office: 1210 Vine Center Office Tower, 333 West Vine Street.
Telephone: 606-225-5333.
Princeton, New Jersey Office: Buchanan Ingersoll, A Partnership, College Centre, 500 College Road East.
Telephone: 609-452-2666.

Joseph J. Barnes
Calvin R. Harvey
Jack J. Kessler
Charles G. Knox
Rebecca L. Livingston

SENIOR ATTORNEYS

Elizabeth Kluger Cooper
Michael A. Donadee

Allison W. Berman
Nathaniel Chandler Hunter
Carrie Kochenbach
John E. Muolo

OF COUNSEL

Alexander Black

For Complete List of Firm Personnel, See General Section

For full biographical listings, see the Martindale-Hubbell Law Directory

HOLLINSHEAD, MENDELSON, BRESNAHAN & NIXON, P.C. (AV)

230 Grant Building, 15219
Telephone: 412-355-7070
Fax: 412-281-6099

E. D. Hollinshead, Jr.
Leonard M. Mendelson
William P. Bresnahan
David L. Nixon
Andrea Geraghty
Dwight D. Ferguson

For full biographical listings, see the Martindale-Hubbell Law Directory

MARCUS & SHAPIRA (AV)

35th Floor, One Oxford Centre, 301 Grant Street, 15219-6401
Telephone: 412-471-3490
Telecopier: 412-391-8758

MEMBERS OF FIRM

Bernard D. Marcus
Daniel H. Shapira
George P. Slesinger
Robert L. Allman, II
Estelle F. Comay
Susan Gromis Flynn
Darlene M. Nowak
Glenn M. Olcerst
Elly Heller-Toig
Sylvester A. Beozzo

(See Next Column)

OF COUNSEL

John M. Burkoff

SPECIAL COUNSEL

Jane Campbell Moriarty

ASSOCIATES

Scott D. Livingston
Robert M. Barnes
Stephen S. Zubrow
David B. Rodes
Lori E. McMaster
Melody A. Pollock
James F. Rosenberg
Amy M. Gottlieb

For full biographical listings, see the Martindale-Hubbell Law Directory

MARKEL, SCHAFER P.C. (AV)

1120 Grant Building, 15219
Telephone: 412-281-6488
Fax: 412-281-3226

Seymour J. Schafer
Harvey I. Goldstein
Kenneth A. Eisner
Steven D. Irwin
Jacob A. Markel (1896-1976)
Myron B. Markel (1934-1988)
Gertrude F. Markel (Retired)

OF COUNSEL

Nathan Hershey

Reference: Pittsburgh National Bank.

For full biographical listings, see the Martindale-Hubbell Law Directory

MCCANN, GARLAND, RIDALL & BURKE (AV)

Suite 4000, 309 Smithfield Street, 15222
Telephone: 412-566-1818
Fax: 412-566-1817

MEMBERS OF FIRM

G. Gray Garland, Jr.
Stephen J. Jurman

For Complete List of Firm Personnel, See General Section

For full biographical listings, see the Martindale-Hubbell Law Directory

MOLLICA, MURRAY & HOGUE (AV)

3400 Gulf Tower, 15219
Telephone: 412-263-5200
Fax: 412-263-5220

MEMBERS OF FIRM

James A. Mollica, Jr.
Dr. John E. Murray, Jr.
Jon Geoffrey Hogue
Blaine A. Lucas
Cathy Ann Chromulak
Timothy Murray
Sandra L. Lannis
William J. Moorhead, Jr.
Jeannine A. Schuster
Steven M. Nolan
Benjamin J. Viloski

For full biographical listings, see the Martindale-Hubbell Law Directory

PAPERNICK AND GEFSKY, A PROFESSIONAL CORPORATION (AV)

34th Floor, One Oxford Centre, 15219
Telephone: 412-765-2212
Fax: 412-765-3319
Additional Pittsburgh Office: Suite 235, 5700 Corporate Drive.
Telephone: 412-366-5322.
Pennsylvania Suburban Offices: Northern Pike Pavilion, Monroeville.
Telephone: 412-373-2212. 2000 Oxford Drive, Bethel Park.
Telephone: 412-831-2400.

Alan Papernick
Martyn I. Gefsky (Resident, Monroeville Office)
William G. Merchant
Robert L. Murphy
James P. Sommers
Evan M. Zanic
David E. McMaster (Resident, Monroeville Office)
Stephen M. Papernick

Melissa S. Lobos (Resident, Monroeville Office)
Brenda J. Yurick

For full biographical listings, see the Martindale-Hubbell Law Directory

PLOWMAN, SPIEGEL & LEWIS, P.C. (AV)

Grant Building, Suite 925, 15219-2201
Telephone: 412-471-8521
Fax: 412-471-4481

Jack W. Plowman
John L. Spiegel
Frank J. Kernan
Clifford L. Tuttle, Jr.
Kenneth W. Lee

Marshall J. Conn
David Raves

Reference: Pittsburgh National Bank.

For Complete List of Firm Personnel, See General Section

For full biographical listings, see the Martindale-Hubbell Law Directory

Pittsburgh—Continued

THOMSON, RHODES & COWIE, P.C. (AV)

Tenth Floor, Two Chatham Center, 15219
Telephone: 412-232-3400
Fax: 412-232-3498

Thomas D. Thomson
Glenn H. Gillette
Templeton Smith, Jr.

SPECIAL COUNSEL

John H. Morgan

For Complete List of Firm Personnel, See General Section

For full biographical listings, see the Martindale-Hubbell Law Directory

THORP, REED & ARMSTRONG (AV)

One Riverfront Center, 15222
Telephone: 412-394-7711
Fax: 412-394-2555

MEMBERS OF FIRM

James D. Chiafullo
Timothy M. Slavish

ASSOCIATES

Jeffrey J. Conn
Kimberly L. Wakim

SENIOR COUNSEL

Frank J. Gaffney

For Complete List of Firm Personnel, See General Section

For full biographical listings, see the Martindale-Hubbell Law Directory

VUONO, LAVELLE & GRAY (AV)

2310 Grant Building, 15219
Telephone: 412-471-1800
Fax: 412-471-4477

MEMBERS OF FIRM

John A. Vuono
William J. Lavelle
William A. Gray
Mark T. Vuono
Richard R. Wilson

ASSOCIATES

Dennis J. Kusturiss
Christine M. Dolfi
Peter J. Scanlon

Reference: Pittsburgh National Bank.

For full biographical listings, see the Martindale-Hubbell Law Directory

WITTLIN GOLDSTON & CAPUTO, P.C. (AV)

213 Smithfield Street, Suite 200, 15222
Telephone: 412-261-4200
Telecopier: 412-261-9137

Charles E. Wittlin
Robert Simcox Adams
Laurence R. Landis

For Complete List of Firm Personnel, See General Section

For full biographical listings, see the Martindale-Hubbell Law Directory

*SCRANTON,** Lackawanna Co.

LEVY & PREATE (AV)

507 Linden Street, Suite 600, 18503
Telephone: 717-346-3816
FAX: 717-346-5370

MEMBERS OF FIRM

J. Julius Levy (1891-1978)
Ernest D. Preate
Robert A. Preate
William T. Jones

ASSOCIATE

Howard C. Terreri

OF COUNSEL

David B. Miller
David J. Tomaine
Harold M. Kane
Tullio De Luca

For full biographical listings, see the Martindale-Hubbell Law Directory

*WASHINGTON,** Washington Co.

GREENLEE, DERRICO, POSA & RODGERS (AV)

325 Washington Trust Building, 15301
Telephone: 412-225-7660; Pittsburgh: 412-344-9400
Fax: 412-228-1704

MEMBERS OF FIRM

Gaylord W. Greenlee
Patrick C. Derrico
John Allan Rodgers

For full biographical listings, see the Martindale-Hubbell Law Directory

*WELLSBORO,** Tioga Co.

OWLETT, LEWIS & GINN, P.C. (AV)

One Charles Street, P.O. Box 878, 16901
Telephone: 717-723-1000
Fax: 717-724-6822
Elkland, Pennsylvania Office: 102 East Main Street.
Telephone: 814-258-5148.
Knoxville, Pennsylvania Office: 106 East Main Street.
Telephone: 814-326-4161.

Edwin A. Glover
Edward H. Owlett
Edward H. Owlett, III
Raymond E. Ginn, Jr.
Thomas M. Owlett

Bruce L. Vickery
Judith DeMeester Nichols

OF COUNSEL

John Dean Lewis

Reference: Citizens and Northern Bank.

For full biographical listings, see the Martindale-Hubbell Law Directory

*WEST CHESTER,** Chester Co.

BUCKLEY, NAGLE, GENTRY, McGUIRE & MORRIS (AV)

304 North High Street, P.O. Box 133, 19380
Telephone: 610-436-4400
Telecopier: 610-436-8305
Thorndale, Pennsylvania Office: 3532 East Lincoln Highway.
Telephone: 215-383-5666.

MEMBERS OF FIRM

C. Barry Buckley
Ronald C. Nagle
W. Richard Gentry
Stephen P. McGuire
Anthony Morris
John J. Teti, Jr.
Jeffrey R. Sommer
Isabel M. Albuquerque

OF COUNSEL

R. Curtis Schroder

For full biographical listings, see the Martindale-Hubbell Law Directory

CRAWFORD, WILSON, RYAN & AGULNICK, P.C. (AV)

220 West Gay Street, 19380
Telephone: 610-431-4500
Fax: 610-430-8718
Radnor, Pennsylvania Office: 252 Radnor-Chester Road, P. O. Box 8333, 19087.
Telephone: 215-688-1205.
Fax: 215-688-7802.

Ronald M. Agulnick
Fronefield Crawford, Jr.
Thomas R. Wilson
Kevin J. Ryan

John J. Mahoney
Kim Denise Morton
Steven L. Mutart
Rita Kathryn Borzillo
Patricia T. Brennan
Richard H. Morton
Patricia J. Kelly
Charles W. Tucker

Reference: First National Bank of West Chester.

For full biographical listings, see the Martindale-Hubbell Law Directory

JOHN E. GOOD (AV)

331 West Miner Street, 19382
Telephone: 610-436-6565

Reference: First National Bank of West Chester.

For full biographical listings, see the Martindale-Hubbell Law Directory

LAMB, WINDLE & McERLANE, P.C. (AV)

24 East Market Street, P.O. Box 565, 19381-0565
Telephone: 610-430-8000
Telecopier: 610-692-0877

COUNSEL

Theodore O. Rogers

William H. Lamb
Susan Windle Rogers
James E. McErlane
E. Craig Kalemjian
James C. Sargent, Jr.
John D. Snyder
William P. Mahon
Guy A. Donatelli
Vincent M. Pompo
James J. McEntee III

Tracy Blake DeVlieger
P. Andrew Schaum
Lawrence J. Persick
Thomas K. Schindler
Daniel A. Loewenstern
Thomas F. Oeste
John W. Pauciulo
Andrea B. Pettine
John J. Cunningham

Representative Clients: Chester County; First Financial Savings Bank, PaSA; Bank of Chester County; Jefferson Bank; Downingtown Area and Great Valley School Districts; Philadelphia Electric Company; Central and Western

(See Next Column)

LAMB, WINDLE & MCERLANE P.C.—*Continued*

Chester County Industrial Development Authority; Valley Forge Sewer Authority; Manito Title Insurance Company.

For full biographical listings, see the Martindale-Hubbell Law Directory

*WILKES-BARRE,** Luzerne Co.

GALLAGHER, BRENNAN & GILL (AV)

220 Pierce Street, 18701-4641
Telephone: 717-288-8255
Telecopier: 717-288-7005

MEMBERS OF FIRM

Joseph F. Gallagher (1912-1989)
Thomas P. Brennan
John J. Gill, Jr.
Christine E. McLaughlin

OF COUNSEL

Cecilia Meighan

Approved Attorneys for: Commonwealth Land Title Insurance Co.
Representative Clients: PNC Bank, National Association; Mercy Hospital, Wilkes Barre, Pennsylvania; Guaranty Bank.

For full biographical listings, see the Martindale-Hubbell Law Directory

HOURIGAN, KLUGER, SPOHRER & QUINN, A PROFESSIONAL CORPORATION (AV)

700 Mellon Bank Center, 8 West Market Street, 18701-1867
Telephone: 717-825-9401
FAX: 717-829-3460
Scranton, Pennsylvania Office: Suite 200, 434 Lackawanna Avenue.
Telephone: 717-346-8414.
Allentown, Pennsylvania Office: Sovereign Building, 609 Hamilton Mall.
Telephone: 610-437-1584.
Hazelton, Pennsylvania Office: CAN DO Building, One South Church Street.
Telephone: 717-455-5141.

Allan M. Kluger
Richard S. Bishop (Resident, Scranton Office)
Terrence J. Herron (Resident, Hazelton Office)
Jonathan A. Spohrer
Joseph E. Kluger
Joseph M. Campolieto (Resident, Scranton Office)
Christina A. Morrison

Representative Client: Aetna Casualty & Surety Co.

For Complete List of Firm Personnel, See General Section

For full biographical listings, see the Martindale-Hubbell Law Directory

ROSENN, JENKINS & GREENWALD (AV)

15 South Franklin Street, 18711-0075
Telephone: 717-826-5600
Fax: 717-826-5640

MEMBERS OF FIRM

Murray Ufberg
Joseph L. Persico
Garry S. Taroli
Lee S. Piatt
David B. Hiscox
William L. Higgs
Michael A. Shucosky
Lewis A. Sebia

ASSOCIATES

Sandra L. Richelmy
Mary Margaret Griffin
Patricia Ermel Lakhia

Representative Clients: Allstate Insurance Co.; C-TEC Corporation; Chicago Title Insurance Co.; Franklin First Savings Bank; The Geisinger Medical Center; Guard Insurance Group; The Mays Department Stores Company; Student LoanMarketing Association (Sallie Mae); Subaru of America, Inc.

For Complete List of Firm Personnel, See General Section

For full biographical listings, see the Martindale-Hubbell Law Directory

*WILLIAMSPORT,** Lycoming Co.

MCCORMICK, REEDER, NICHOLS, BAHL, KNECHT & PERSON (AV)

(Formerly McCormick, Herdic & Furst).
835 West Fourth Street, 17701
Telephone: 717-326-5131
Fax: 717-326-5529

OF COUNSEL

Henry Clay McCormick

MEMBERS OF FIRM

S. Dale Furst, Jr. (1904-1969)
Robert J. Sarno (1941-1982)
Paul W. Reeder
William E. Nichols
David R. Bahl
William L. Knecht
John E. Person, III
J. David Smith
Robert A. Eckenrode
Cynthia Ranck Person

(See Next Column)

ASSOCIATES

Joanne C. Ludwikowski
R. Matthew Patch
Sean P. Roman
Kenneth B. Young

General Counsel for: Northern Central Bank; Jersey Shore Steel Co.
Representative Clients: Pennsylvania Power & Light Co.; Consolidated Rail Corp.; Royal Insurance Co.; State Automobile Insurance Association.

For full biographical listings, see the Martindale-Hubbell Law Directory

RHODE ISLAND

*PROVIDENCE,** Providence Co.

LISA & SOUSA, LTD. (AV)

5 Benefit Street, 02904
Telephone: 401-274-0600
Fax: 401-421-6117

Carl B. Lisa
Louis A. Sousa

OF COUNSEL

Robert G. Branca, Jr.

References: Citizens Savings Bank; Fleet National Bank; Rhode Island Hospital Trust National Bank.

For full biographical listings, see the Martindale-Hubbell Law Directory

WESTERLY, Washington Co.

URSO, LIGUORI AND URSO (AV)

85 Beach Street, P.O. Box 1277, 02891
Telephone: 401-596-7751
Telecopier: 401-596-7963

MEMBERS OF FIRM

Natale Louis Urso
Thomas J. Liguori, Jr.
M. Linda Urso

General Counsel for: National Education Association Rhode Island; Westerly Broadcasting Co.
Approved Attorneys for: Lawyers Title Insurance Corporation of Richmond, Virginia.
Reference: Fleet National Bank.

For full biographical listings, see the Martindale-Hubbell Law Directory

WOONSOCKET, Providence Co.

CHARLES S. SOKOLOFF INCORPORATED (AV)

300 Plaza Center, 68 Cumberland Street, 02895
Telephone: 401 SOKOLAW (401-765-6529)
Fax: 401 SOKOFAX (401-765-6329)

Charles S. Sokoloff

Monique A. Roy

For full biographical listings, see the Martindale-Hubbell Law Directory

SOUTH CAROLINA

*AIKEN,** Aiken Co.

JOHNSON, JOHNSON, WHITTLE, SNELGROVE & WEEKS, P.A. (AV)

117 Pendleton Street, N.W., P.O. Box 2619, 29802-2619
Telephone: 803-649-5338
FAX: 803-641-4517

B. Henderson Johnson, Jr.
Barry H. Johnson
James E. Whittle, Jr.
Vicki Johnson Snelgrove
John W. (Bill) Weeks
Paige Weeks Johnson
Todd J. Johnson

For full biographical listings, see the Martindale-Hubbell Law Directory

*BEAUFORT,** Beaufort Co.

DAVIS, TUPPER, GRIMSLEY & SEELHOFF (AV)

611 Bay Street, P.O. Box 2055, 29901-2055
Telephone: 803-524-1116
Facsimile: 803-524-1463

MEMBERS OF FIRM

Hutson S. Davis, Jr.
Ralph E. Tupper
James A. Grimsley, III
Scott A. Seelhoff
Erin D. Dean

For full biographical listings, see the Martindale-Hubbell Law Directory

*CHARLESTON,** Charleston Co.

BUIST, MOORE, SMYTHE & MCGEE, P.A. (AV)

Successors to Buist, Buist, Smythe and Smythe and Moore, Mouzon and McGee.
Five Exchange Street, P.O. Box 999, 29402
Telephone: 803-722-3400
Cable Address: "Conferees"
Telex: 57-6488
Telecopier: 803-723-7398
North Charleston, South Carolina Office: Atrium Northwood Office Building, 7301 Rivers Avenue, Suite 288. Zip: 29406-2859.
Telephone: 803-797-3000.
Telecopier: 803-863-5500.

Susan M. Smythe
W. Foster Gaillard
Morris A. Ellison

Jeffrey A. Winkler
Robert H. Mozingo

OF COUNSEL
David H. Crawford

Counsel for: CSX Transportation; NationsBank; Metropolitan Life Insurance Co.; E. I. du Pont de Nemours & Co.; AIG Aviation, Inc.; Lamorte, Burns & Co., Inc.; Allstate Insurance Co.; General Dynamics Corp.; Independent Life & Accident Insurance Co.; Georgia-Pacific Corp.

For Complete List of Firm Personnel, See General Section

For full biographical listings, see the Martindale-Hubbell Law Directory

HAYNSWORTH, MARION, MCKAY & GUÉRARD, L.L.P (AV)

#2 Prioleau Street, P.O. Box 1119, 29402
Telephone: 803-722-7606
Telecopier: 803-723-5263
Columbia, South Carolina Office: Suite 2400 AT&T Building, 1201 Main Street, P.O. Drawer 7157, 29202.
Telephone: 803-765-1818.
Telecopier: 803-765-2399.
Greenville, South Carolina Office: Two Insignia Financial Plaza, 75 Beattie Place, P.O. Box 2048, 29602.
Telephone: 803-240-3200.
Telecopier: 803-240-3300.

MEMBER OF FIRM
W. E. Applegate, III

Counsel for: Bank of South Carolina; Baker Hospital; Healthsources of South Carolina; Allstate Insurance Co.; CSX Corporation; Lloyd's Underwriters; Coward-Hund Construction Co.; South Carolina Public Service Authority; South Carolina Jobs - Economic Development Authority; City of Hanahan.

For Complete List of Firm Personnel, See General Section

For full biographical listings, see the Martindale-Hubbell Law Directory

OBERMAN & OBERMAN (AV)

38 Broad Street, 29401
Telephone: 803-577-7010
Fax: 803-722-7359

MEMBERS OF FIRM
Marvin I. Oberman
Harold A. Oberman

For full biographical listings, see the Martindale-Hubbell Law Directory

SOLOMON, KAHN, BUDMAN & STRICKER (AV)

39 Broad Street, P.O. Drawer P, 29402
Telephone: 803-577-7182
Telecopier: 803-722-0485

A. Bernard Solomon
Ellis I. Kahn
Donald J. Budman
Michael A. Stricker

ASSOCIATE
Justin S. Kahn

Local Counsel for: Lawyers Title Insurance Corp.

For full biographical listings, see the Martindale-Hubbell Law Directory

WARREN & SINKLER (AV)

Suite 340 171 Church Street, P.O. Box 1254, 29402
Telephone: 803-577-0660
Fax: 803-577-6843

MEMBERS OF FIRM
G. Dana Sinkler
John H. Warren, III
Henry B. Fishburne, Jr.
Mark S. Sharpe
Elizabeth W. Settle
Elizabeth T. Thomas

For full biographical listings, see the Martindale-Hubbell Law Directory

*COLUMBIA,** Richland Co.

* indicates certain Bar Register subscribers whose principal office is located elsewhere in the state and who have arranged for representation as a part of the state capital listings that follow

ADAMS, QUACKENBUSH, HERRING & STUART, P.A. (AV)

NationsBank Plaza, 1901 Main Street, Suite 1400, P.O. Box 394, 29202
Telephone: 803-779-2650
Facsimile: 803-252-8964

T. Patton Adams
Robert G. Currin, Jr.
J. Craig Bower

Reference: Citizens and Southern National Bank.

For full biographical listings, see the Martindale-Hubbell Law Directory

BARNES, ALFORD, STORK & JOHNSON, L.L.P. (AV)

1613 Main Street, P.O. Box 8448, 29202
Telephone: 803-799-1111
Telefax: 803-254-1335

Rudolph C. Barnes
William C. Stork
David G. Wolff

Representative Clients: First Union National Bank of South Carolina; Aetna Casualty and Surety Co.; Kline Iron & Steel Co.

For Complete List of Firm Personnel, See General Section

For full biographical listings, see the Martindale-Hubbell Law Directory

BERRY, DUNBAR, DANIEL, O'CONNOR & JORDAN (AV)

A Partnership including Professional Associations
1200 Main Street, Eighth Floor, P.O. Box 11645, Capitol Station, 29211-1645
Telephone: 803-765-1030
Facsimile: 803-799-5536
Spartanburg, South Carolina Office: 112 West Daniel Morgan Avenue.
Telephone: 803-583-3975.
Atlanta, Georgia Office: 2400 Cain Tower, Peachtree Center.
Telephone: 404-588-0500.
Facsimile: 404-523-6714.

MEMBERS OF FIRM
Joe E. Berry, Jr.
Leonard R. Jordan, Jr. (P.A.)

ASSOCIATE
William O. Higgins

Approved Attorneys for: Lawyers Title Insurance Corporation of Richmond.

For Complete List of Firm Personnel, See General Section

For full biographical listings, see the Martindale-Hubbell Law Directory

* **HAYNSWORTH, MARION, MCKAY & GUÉRARD, L.L.P.** (AV)

Suite 2400 A T & T Building, 1201 Main Street, P.O. Drawer 7157, 29202
Telephone: 803-765-1818
Telecopier: 803-765-2399
Greenville, South Carolina Office: Two Insignia Financial Plaza, 75 Beattie Place, P.O. Box 2048, 29602.
Telephone: 803-240-3200.
Telecopier: 803-240-3300.
Charleston, South Carolina Office: #2 Prioleau Street, P.O. Box 1119, 29402.
Telephone: 803-722-7606.
Telecopier: 803-723-5263.

MEMBERS OF FIRM
William P. Simpson
Gary W. Morris

ASSOCIATE
Edward G. Kluiters

Counsel for: St. Paul Insurance Group; Allstate Insurance Co.; Fluor-Daniel Corp.; South Carolina Jobs - Economic Development Authority; Anheuser Busch Company; CSX Transportation; Ernst & Young, LLP; Willis Corroon of South Carolina, Inc.; Westinghouse Savannah River Co.; Wachovia Bank of South Carolina, N.A.

For Complete List of Firm Personnel, See General Section

For full biographical listings, see the Martindale-Hubbell Law Directory

ISAACS, ALLEY & HARVEY, L.L.P. (AV)

900 Elmwood Avenue, Suite 103, P.O. Box 8596, 29202-8596
Telephone: 803-252-6323
Telecopier: 803-779-5220

W. Joseph Isaacs
Steven E. Harvey

(See Next Column)

ISAACS, ALLEY & HARVEY L.L.P.—*Continued*

OF COUNSEL

George I. Alley

Representative Clients: NationsBank of South Carolina, N.A.; GATX Corporation; First Financial Corp.; Zurich-American Insurance Group; Wetterau Incorp.; Southland Log Homes, Inc.; Thompson Dental Co.; Dairymen Credit Union; Modern Exterminating, Inc.; Elizabeth Arden Co.; J.L. Todd Auction, Inc.; Continental Cards Co., Inc.; Norton-Senn Corporation; Eastern Flatbed Systems, Inc.; Valk Brokerage, Inc.; Snipes Electric, Inc.; The Loan Pros, Inc.; Palmetto Restorations, Inc.; Palmer & Cay/Carswell, Inc.; Plastitech Products, Inc.; Marek Brothers, Inc.; Ferillo & Associates, Inc.; Jacon Associates, Inc.; Blue Ridge Log Cabins, Inc.; Jones & Frank Corp.

For full biographical listings, see the Martindale-Hubbell Law Directory

QUINN, PATTERSON & WILLARD (AV)

2019 Park Street, P.O. Box 73, 29202
Telephone: 803-779-6365
Telefax: 803-779-6372

MEMBERS OF FIRM

Michael H. Quinn
Grady L. Patterson, III
Theodore DuBose Willard, Jr.

ASSOCIATE

Heidi Brown

Approved Attorneys for: Lawyers Title Insurance Corp.

For full biographical listings, see the Martindale-Hubbell Law Directory

RICHARDSON, PLOWDEN, GRIER AND HOWSER, P.A. (AV)

1600 Marion Street, P.O. Drawer 7788, 29202
Telephone: 803-771-4400
Telecopy: 803-779-0016
Myrtle Beach, South Carolina Office: Southern National Bank Building, Suite 202, 601 21st Avenue North, P.O. Box 3646, 29578.
Telephone: 803-448-1008.
FAX: 803-448-1533.

Frank E. Robinson, II
Frederick A. Crawford

For Complete List of Firm Personnel, See General Section

For full biographical listings, see the Martindale-Hubbell Law Directory

SHERRILL AND ROGERS, PC (AV)

1441 Main Street, 10th Floor, P.O. Box 100200, 29202-3200
Telephone: 803-771-7900
Fax: 803-254-6305

Carl L. Holloway, Jr.
C. Joseph Roof
Franchelle Cole Millender
William H. Townsend
Samuel C. Waters

Dean B. Bell
Cheryl H. Fisher

For Complete List of Firm Personnel, See General Section

For full biographical listings, see the Martindale-Hubbell Law Directory

WOODWARD, LEVENTIS, UNGER, DAVES, HERNDON AND COTHRAN (AV)

(Formerly Woodward, Leventis, Unger, Herndon and Cothran)
1300 Sumter, P.O. Box 12399, 29211
Telephone: 803-799-9772
Fax: 803-779-3256

MEMBERS OF FIRM

James C. Leventis
Gary R. Daves
Richard M. Unger
Warren R. Herndon, Jr.
Darra Williamson Cothran

ASSOCIATE

Frances G. Smith

OF COUNSEL

Edward M. Woodward, Sr.
Gwendelyn Geidel
James S. Guignard

General Counsel for: The Columbia College.

For full biographical listings, see the Martindale-Hubbell Law Directory

*GREENVILLE,** Greenville Co.

HAYNSWORTH, MARION, McKAY & GUÉRARD, L.L.P. (AV)

Two Insignia Financial Plaza, 75 Beattie Place, P.O. Box 2048, 29602
Telephone: 803-240-3200
Telecopier: 803-240-3300
Columbia, South Carolina Office: Suite 2400 A T & T Building, 1201 Main Street, P.O. Drawer 7157, 29202
Telephone: 803-765-1818.
Telecopier: 803-765-2399.

(See Next Column)

Charleston, South Carolina Office: #2 Prioleau Street, P.O. Box 1119, 29402.
Telephone: 803-722-7606.
Telecopier: 803-723-5263.

OF COUNSEL

Fred D. Cox, Jr.

MEMBERS OF FIRM

Maye R. Johnson, Jr.
Charles E. McDonald, Jr.
Anne S. Ellefson

ASSOCIATE

Karen Bruning Hipp

Counsel for: Duke Power Co.; Liberty Mutual Insurance Co.; Equitable Life Assurance Society of the United States; St. Paul Insurance Group; Allstate Insurance Co.; Fluor-Daniel Corp.; Snyalloy Corporation; Greenville Hospital System.

For Complete List of Firm Personnel, See General Section

For full biographical listings, see the Martindale-Hubbell Law Directory

WYCHE, BURGESS, FREEMAN & PARHAM, PROFESSIONAL ASSOCIATION (AV)

44 East Camperdown Way, P.O. Box 728, 29602-0728
Telephone: 803-242-8200
Telecopier: 803-235-8900

Larry D. Estridge
D. Allen Grumbine

Counsel for: Multimedia, Inc.; Delta Woodside Industries, Inc.; Milliken & Company; Ryan's Family Steak Houses, Inc.; St. Francis Hospital; Span-America Medical Systems, Inc.; Carolina First Bank; KEMET Electronics Corp.; Builder Marts of America, Inc.; One Price Clothing, Inc.

For Complete List of Firm Personnel, See General Section

For full biographical listings, see the Martindale-Hubbell Law Directory

MYRTLE BEACH, Horry Co.

STEVENS, STEVENS & THOMAS, P.C. (AV)

1215 48th Avenue North, 29577-2468
Telephone: 803-449-9675
Fax: 803-497-2262
Loris, South Carolina Office: 3341 Broad Street.
Telephone: 803-756-7652.
Fax: 803-756-3785.

James P. Stevens, Jr. (Resident, Loris Office)
J. Jackson Thomas

Angela T. Jordan (Resident Loris Office)

OF COUNSEL

James P. Stevens

For full biographical listings, see the Martindale-Hubbell Law Directory

SOUTH DAKOTA

*SIOUX FALLS,** Minnehaha Co.

DANFORTH, MEIERHENRY & MEIERHENRY (AV)

315 South Phillips, 57102
Telephone: 605-336-3075
Fax: 605-336-2593

George J. Danforth (1875-1952)
George J. Danforth, Jr. (1909-1991)
Mark V. Meierhenry
Todd V. Meierhenry
Sabrina Meierhenry

ASSOCIATE

David K. Mickelberg

For full biographical listings, see the Martindale-Hubbell Law Directory

DAVENPORT, EVANS, HURWITZ & SMITH (AV)

513 South Main Avenue, P.O. Box 1030, 57101-1030
Telephone: 605-336-2880
Telecopier: 605-335-3639

MEMBERS OF FIRM

Richard A. Cutler
P. Daniel Donohue
Jonathan P. Brown

ASSOCIATE

Jean H. Bender

Counsel for: American Society of Composers, Authors and Publishers (A.S.-C.A.P.); Burlington Northern, Inc.; Continental Insurance Cos.; The First National Bank in Sioux Falls; Ford Motor Credit Co.; General Motors Corp.; The St. Paul Cos.; The Travelers.

(See Next Column)

DAVENPORT, EVANS, HURWITZ & SMITH, *Sioux Falls—Continued*

For Complete List of Firm Personnel, See General Section

For full biographical listings, see the Martindale-Hubbell Law Directory

JOHN L. WILDS (AV)

Third Floor, 300 North Dakota Avenue, 57102-0332
Telephone: 605-332-1822
Telecopier: 605-332-0340

Representative Clients: Metropolitan Federal Bank; Mid-Coastal Transportation; J & L Harley-Davidson; KSFY (ABC) TV; R & L Supply, Ltd.; Hillyard Floor Care Supply; Enviro Safe Air; UAW Legal Services; Super America Group, Inc.

For full biographical listings, see the Martindale-Hubbell Law Directory

*WATERTOWN,** Codington Co.

BARTRON, WILES, RYLANCE & HOLGERSON (AV)

A Partnership including Professional Corporations
3 East Kemp Avenue, 57201-0227
Telephone: 605-886-5881
Fax: 605-886-3934

MEMBERS OF FIRM

R. Greg Bartron (P.C.)
John C. Wiles (P.C.)
Raymond D. Rylance (P.C.)
Albert H. Holgerson (P.C.)

OF COUNSEL

Donald E. Osheim (P.C.)

Representative Clients: Allied Group Insurance Co.; Brown Clinic; Farmers and Merchants Bank and Trust of Watertown; Fireman's Fund Insurance Co.; Hartford Insurance Co.; Harvest Life Insurance Co.; Home Insurance Co.; Liberty Mutual Insurance Co.; National Farmers Union Insurance Co.; First Premier Bank, Watertown.

For full biographical listings, see the Martindale-Hubbell Law Directory

TENNESSEE

*CHATTANOOGA,** Hamilton Co.

CHAMBLISS & BAHNER (AV)

1000 Tallan Building, Two Union Square, 37402-2500
Telephone: 615-756-3000
Fax: 615-265-9574

MEMBERS OF FIRM

Michael N. St. Charles
Jay A. Young

ASSOCIATES

S. Mark Turner
Lori L. Smith

General Counsel for: McKee Foods Corporation; SCT Yarns, Inc.; Stein Construction Co., Inc.; Hudson Construction Co.; Hickory Land Co.; Tommy Development Co.; Southern Realty Co.
Representative Clients: The BOC Group, Inc.; Cumberland Cove, Inc.; The Carlyle Group, Inc.; Chattanooga Association of Realtors.

For Complete List of Firm Personnel, See General Section

For full biographical listings, see the Martindale-Hubbell Law Directory

FOSTER, FOSTER, ALLEN & DURRENCE (AV)

Formerly Hall, Haynes & Foster
Suite 515 Pioneer Bank Building, 37402
Telephone: 615-266-1141
Telecopier: 615-266-4618

MEMBERS OF FIRM

George Lane Foster
William M. Foster
Craig R. Allen
Phillip M. Durrence, Jr.

ASSOCIATES

David J. Ward
Clayton M. Whittaker
John M. Hull

LEGAL SUPPORT PERSONNEL

Peggy Sue Bates

Division Counsel for: Alabama Great Southern Railroad Co.; C.N.O. & T.P. Railway Co.
Attorneys for: CNA/Insurance; U.S.P. & G. Co.; The Firestone Tire & Rubber Co.; Exxon, Corp.; Murphy Oil Corp.; Chicago Title Insurance Co.; City of East Ridge; Jim Walter Homes; Raymond James & Associates; Morgan Keegan & Co.

For full biographical listings, see the Martindale-Hubbell Law Directory

HUGH F. KENDALL, ATTORNEY, P.C. (AV)

Suite 305, Victorian Gardens, 6918 Shallowford Road, 37421-1783
Telephone: 615-499-9863
Telecopier: 615-894-0682

(See Next Column)

Hugh F. Kendall

For full biographical listings, see the Martindale-Hubbell Law Directory

SHUMACKER & THOMPSON (AV)

Suite 500, First Tennessee Building, 701 Market Street, 37402-4800
Telephone: 615-265-2214
Telecopier: 615-266-1842
Branch Office: Suite 103, One Park Place, 6148 Lee Highway, Chattanooga, Tennessee, 37421-2900.
Telephone: 615-855-1814.
Telecopier: 615-899-1278.

MEMBERS OF FIRM

Ralph Shumacker
Frank M. Thompson
W. Neil Thomas, Jr.
W. Neil Thomas, III
Ronald I. Feldman
Alan L. Cates
Ross I. Schram III
Stephen P. Parish
William Given Colvin
Harold L. North, Jr.
John K. Culpepper
Jeffery V. Curry
Everett L. Hixson, Jr.
Stanley W. Hildebrand
Phillip E. Fleenor
Donna S. Spurlock
James D. Henderson

ASSOCIATE

Char-La Cain Fowler

For Complete List of Firm Personnel, See General Section

For full biographical listings, see the Martindale-Hubbell Law Directory

STOPHEL & STOPHEL, P.C. (AV)

500 Tallan Building, Two Union Square, 37402-2571
Telephone: 615-756-2333
Fax: 615-266-5032

Glenn C. Stophel
E. Stephen Jett
Harry B. Ray
C. Douglas Williams

Brian L. Woodward
James C. Heartfield
John W. Rose

Representative Clients: Astec Industries, Inc.; McKenzie Leasing Corporation; The National Group, Inc.; Tennessee Temple University; HCA Valley Psychiatric Hospital Corporation; Chattanooga Armature Works, Inc.; Graco Children's Products, Inc.; American Manufacturing Co.; The Maclellan Foundation, Inc.; Roy H. Pack Broadcasting of Tennessee, Inc. (WDEF AM, FM & TV).

For Complete List of Firm Personnel, See General Section

For full biographical listings, see the Martindale-Hubbell Law Directory

*COLUMBIA,** Maury Co.

ROBIN S. COURTNEY (AV)

809 South Main Street, Suite 300, P.O. Box 1035, 38401
Telephone: 615-388-6031
Fax: 615-381-7317

For full biographical listings, see the Martindale-Hubbell Law Directory

*KNOXVILLE,** Knox Co.

CROLEY, DAVIDSON & HUIE (AV)

Suite 2210 Plaza Tower, 37929
Telephone: 615-523-0209
FAX: 615-523-6749

MEMBERS OF FIRM

Robert R. Croley
Ben M. Davidson
Joseph H. Huie
Carl W. Manning
Gordon Lee Ownby, Jr.
James E. Bondurant, Jr.
Jeffrey L. McCall

OF COUNSEL

Earl Holman Marsh

For full biographical listings, see the Martindale-Hubbell Law Directory

MCCAMPBELL & YOUNG, A PROFESSIONAL CORPORATION (AV)

2021 Plaza Tower, P.O. Box 550, 37901-0550
Telephone: 615-637-1440
Telecopier: 615-546-9731

Herbert H. McCampbell, Jr. (1905-1974)
F. Graham Bartlett (1920-1982)
Robert S. Young
Lindsay Young
Robert S. Marquis
Robert S. Stone
J. Christopher Kirk
Mark K. Williams

Janie C. Porter
Gregory E. Erickson
R. Scott Elmore
Tammy Kaousias
Benét S. Theiss
Allen W. Blevins

For full biographical listings, see the Martindale-Hubbell Law Directory

*MEMPHIS,** Shelby Co.

Armstrong Allen Prewitt Gentry Johnston & Holmes (AV)

80 Monroe Avenue Suite 700, 38103
Telephone: 901-523-8211
Telecopier: 901-524-4936
Jackson, Missippi Office: 1350 One Jackson Place, 188 East Capitol Street.
Telephone: 601-948-8020.
Telecopier: 601-948-8389.

MEMBERS OF FIRM

Wm. Rowlett Scott
William A. Carson, II

Sidney W. Farnsworth, III

For Complete List of Firm Personnel, See General Section

For full biographical listings, see the Martindale-Hubbell Law Directory

Hanover, Walsh, Jalenak & Blair (AV)

Fifth Floor - Falls Building, 22 North Front Street, 38103-2109
Telephone: 901-526-0621
Telecopier: 901-521-9759

MEMBERS OF FIRM

Joseph Hanover (1888-1984)
David Hanover (1899-1963)
Jay Alan Hanover
William M. Walsh
James B. Jalenak
Allen S. Blair
Michael E. Goldstein
Edward J. McKenney, Jr.
James R. Newsom, III
John Kevin Walsh
James A. Johnson, Jr.
Donald S. Holm III
Barbara B. Lapides

Jennifer A. Sevier
Christina von Cannon Burdette
Jeffrey S. Rosenblum

OF COUNSEL

Helyn L. Keith

For full biographical listings, see the Martindale-Hubbell Law Directory

Harkavy, Shainberg, Kosten & Pinstein (AV)

Oak Court Office Building, 530 Oak Court Drive, Suite 350, P.O. Box 241450, 38124-1450
Telephone: 901-761-1263
Telecopier: 901-763-3340

MEMBERS AND ASSOCIATES

Ronald M. Harkavy
Raymond M. Shainberg
Alan L. Kosten
Robert J. Pinstein
Michael D. Kaplan
Allen C. Dunstan
Neil Harkavy
Laurie A. Cooper
Jerome A. Broadhurst
Dixie White Ishee
Alan M. Harkavy

OF COUNSEL

Ira D. Pruitt, Jr.

For full biographical listings, see the Martindale-Hubbell Law Directory

Johnson, Grusin, Kee & Surprise, P.C. (AV)

780 Ridge Lake Boulevard, Suite 202, 38120
Telephone: 901-682-3450
Fax: 901-682-3590

David J. Johnson

For Complete List of Firm Personnel, See General Section

For full biographical listings, see the Martindale-Hubbell Law Directory

Waring Cox (AV)

Morgan Keegan Tower, 50 North Front Street, Suite 1300, 38103-1190
Telephone: 901-543-8000
Telecopy: 901-543-8030

MEMBERS OF FIRM

B. Douglas Earthman
Robert S. Kirk, Jr.

ASSOCIATE

Michael B. Chance

Representative Clients: Delta Life and Annuity; Fred's, Inc.; Catherine's Stores Corp.; Boyle Investment Co.; Vining-Sparks IBG.

For Complete List of Firm Personnel, See General Section

For full biographical listings, see the Martindale-Hubbell Law Directory

*NASHVILLE,** Davidson Co.

Manier, Herod, Hollabaugh & Smith, A Professional Corporation (AV)

First Union Tower 2200 One Nashville Place, 150 Fourth Avenue North, 37219-2494
Telephone: 615-244-0030
Telecopier: 615-242-4203

Will R. Manier, Jr. (1885-1953)
Larkin E. Crouch (1882-1948)
Vincent L. Fuqua, Jr. (1930-1974)
J. Olin White (1907-1982)
Miller Manier (1897-1986)
William Edward Herod (1917-1992)
Lewis B. Hollabaugh
Don L. Smith
James M. Doran, Jr.
Stephen E. Cox
J. Michael Franks
Randall C. Ferguson
Terry L. Hill
James David Leckrone
Robert C. Evans
Tommy C. Estes
B. Gail Reese
Michael E. Evans
Laurence M. Papel
John M. Gillum
Gregory L. Cashion
Sam H. Poteet, Jr.
Samuel Arthur Butts III
David J. Deming
Mark S. LeVan
Richard McCallister Smith
Mary Paty Lynn Jetton
H. Rowan Leathers III
Jefferson C. Orr
William L. Penny

Lawrence B. Hammet II
John H. Rowland
Susan C. West
John E. Quinn
John F. Floyd
Paul L. Sprader
Lela M. Hollabaugh
J. Steven Kirkham
T. Richard Travis
Stephanie M. Jennings
Jerry W. Taylor
C. Benton Patton
Kenneth A. Weber
Phillip Robert Newman
Brett A. Oeser

General Counsel for: McKinnon Bridge Co., Inc.

For full biographical listings, see the Martindale-Hubbell Law Directory

Gail P. Pigg (AV)

219 Second Avenue North, 37201
Telephone: 615-244-0001
FAX: 615-244-0003

References: Sovran Bank; First American Bank.

For full biographical listings, see the Martindale-Hubbell Law Directory

White & Reasor (AV)

3305 West End Avenue, 37203
Telephone: 615-383-3345
Facsimile: 615-383-5534; 615-383-9390

MEMBERS OF FIRM

David J. White, Jr.
Charles B. Reasor, Jr.
Barrett B. Sutton, Jr.
John M. Baird
Dudley M. West
Van P. East, III
Steven L. West

For full biographical listings, see the Martindale-Hubbell Law Directory

*SAVANNAH,** Hardin Co.

Hopper & Plunk, P.C. (AV)

404 West Main Street, P.O. Box 220, 38372
Telephone: 901-925-8076

James A. Hopper
Dennis W. Plunk

Representative Clients: United States Fidelity & Guaranty Co.; Tennessee Farmers Mutual Insurance Co.; Kemper Insurance Co.; Tennessee Municipal Insurance Pool; Savannah Electric.
References: Boatman's Bank, Savannah; The Hardin County Bank.

For Complete List of Firm Personnel, See General Section

For full biographical listings, see the Martindale-Hubbell Law Directory

TEXAS

*AUSTIN,** Travis Co.

Baker & Botts, L.L.P. (AV)

1600 San Jacinto Center, 98 San Jacinto Boulevard, 78701
Telephone: 512-322-2500
Fax: 512-322-2501
Houston, Texas Office: One Shell Plaza, 910 Louisiana.
Telephone: 713-229-1234.
Dallas, Texas Office: 2001 Ross Avenue.
Telephone: 214-953-6500.
Washington, D.C. Office: The Warner, 1299 Pennsylvania Avenue, N.W.
Telephone: 202-639-7700.

(See Next Column)

BAKER & BOTTS L.L.P., *Austin—Continued*

New York, New York Office: 885 Third Avenue, Suite 2000.
Telephone: 212-705-5000.
Moscow, Russian Federation Office: 10 ul. Pushkinskaya, 103031.
Telephone: 7095/921-5300 (Local); 7501/929-7070 (International).

MEMBERS OF FIRM

Shelley W. Austin
William F. Stutts, Jr.

ASSOCIATE

Catherine M. Del Castillo

For Complete List of Firm Personnel, See General Section

For full biographical listings, see the Martindale-Hubbell Law Directory

DAVIS & DAVIS, P.C. (AV)

Arboretum Plaza One, 9th Floor, 9442 Capitol of Texas Highway, P.O. Box 1588, 78767
Telephone: 512-343-6248
Fax: 512-343-0121

C. Dean Davis
Fred E. Davis
Alexis J. Fuller, Jr.
Francis A. (Tony) Bradley
Ruth Russell-Schafer

Bill Cline, Jr.
Brian Gregory Jackson
Kevin Wayde Morse
Mark Alan Keene
Kenda B. Dalrymple

For Complete List of Firm Personnel, See General Section

For full biographical listings, see the Martindale-Hubbell Law Directory

JOHN MCDUFF, P.C. A PROFESSIONAL CORPORATION (AV)

100 Congress Avenue Suite 1817, 78701
Telephone: 512-469-6360
Fax: 512-469-5505

John McDuff

For full biographical listings, see the Martindale-Hubbell Law Directory

MCGINNIS, LOCHRIDGE & KILGORE, L.L.P. (AV)

1300 Capitol Center, 919 Congress Avenue, 78701
Telephone: 512-495-6000
Houston, Texas Office: 3200 One Houston Center, 1221 McKinney Street.
Telephone: 713-615-8500.

MEMBERS OF FIRM

C. Morris Davis
William H. Bingham
Julian Lockwood
Michael A. Wren
William A. Rogers, Jr.
Edmond R. McCarthy, Jr.
Richard Kelley
Gregory S. Chanon

For Complete List of Firm Personnel, See General Section

For full biographical listings, see the Martindale-Hubbell Law Directory

*CORPUS CHRISTI,** Nueces Co.

FRANK G. DELANEY (AV)

Mercantile Tower, Suite 725, MT 47, 78477
Telephone: 512-888-4088
Fax: 512-884-7921

Reference: Mercantile Bank, N.A. of Corpus Christi.

For full biographical listings, see the Martindale-Hubbell Law Directory

MATTHEWS & BRANSCOMB, A PROFESSIONAL CORPORATION (AV)

802 North Carancahua, Suite 1900, 78470-0700
Telephone: 512-888-9261
Facsimile: 512-888-8504
Austin, Texas Office: 301 Congress Avenue, Suite 2050.
Telephone: 512-305-4400.
Facsimile: 512-305-4413.
San Antonio, Texas Office: One Alamo Center, 106 S. St. Mary's Street, Suite 800.
Telephone: 210-226-4211.
Facsimile: 210-226-0521.
Telex: 51060009283. Cable Code: MBLAW.
Eagle Pass, Texas Office: 675 Main Street.
Telephone: 210-773-6700.
Facsimile: 210-757-4045.
Uvalde, Texas Office: 200 E. Nopal #208.
Telephone: 210-278-4597.
Facsimile: 210-278-4806.
(Associated with Hall, Quintanilla & Alarcon, L.C., Laredo, Texas, under the name of Hall, Quintanilla, Alarcon, Matthews & Branscomb, P.L.L.C.).

(See Next Column)

Craig L. Williams

For Complete List of Firm Personnel, See General Section

For full biographical listings, see the Martindale-Hubbell Law Directory

*DALLAS,** Dallas Co.

BAKER & BOTTS, L.L.P. (AV)

2001 Ross Avenue, 75201
Telephone: 214-953-6500
Fax: 214-953-6503
Houston, Texas Office: One Shell Plaza, 910 Louisiana.
Telephone: 713-229-1234.
Washington, D.C. Office: The Warner, 1299 Pennsylvania Avenue, N.W.
Telephone: 202-639-7700.
Austin, Texas Office: 1600 San Jacinto Center, 98 San Jacinto Boulevard.
Telephone: 512-322-2500.
New York, New York Office: 885 Third Avenue, Suite 2000.
Telephone: 212-705-5000.
Moscow, Russian Federation Office: 10 ul. Pushkinskaya, 103031.
Telephone: 7095/921-5300 (Local); 7095/929-7070.

MEMBERS OF FIRM

James A. Taylor
Jonathan W. Dunlay
Patricia M. Stanton

ASSOCIATE

Julie A. Gregory

For Complete List of Firm Personnel, See General Section

For full biographical listings, see the Martindale-Hubbell Law Directory

BARRETT BURKE WILSON CASTLE DAFFIN & FRAPPIER, L.L.P. (AV)

A Limited Liability Partnership including Professional Corporations
6750 Hillcrest Plaza Drive, Suite 313, 75230
Telephone: 214-386-5040
Fax: 214-386-7673
Houston, Texas Office: 24 Greenway Plaza, Suite 2001.
Telephone: 713-621-8673.
Denver, Colorado Affiliated Office: Burke & Castle, P.C. 1099 Eighteenth Street, Suite 2200.
Telephone: 303-299-1800.
Fax: 303-299-1808.
Little Rock, Arkansas Affiliated Office: Wilson & Associates, P.A. 425 West Capitol Avenue, Suite 1500.
Telephone: 501-375-1820.
San Antonio, Texas Office: 1100 Northwest Loop 410, Suite 700. 78213.
Telephone: 512-366-8793.
Fax: 512-366-0198.

Michael C. Barrett

For full biographical listings, see the Martindale-Hubbell Law Directory

CALHOUN & STACY (AV)

5700 NationsBank Plaza, 901 Main Street, 75202-3747
Telephone: 214-748-5000
Telecopier: 214-748-1421
Telex: 211358 CALGUMP UR

Mark Alan Calhoun
David W. Elrod
Steven D. Goldston
Parker Nelson
Roy L. Stacy

ASSOCIATES

Shannon S. Barclay
Robert A. Bragalone
Dennis D. Conder
Jane Elizabeth Diseker
Lawrence I. Fleishman
Thomas C. Jones
Katherine Johnson Knight
V. Paige Pace
Veronika Willard
Michael C. Wright

LEGAL CONSULTANT

Rees T. Bowen, III

For full biographical listings, see the Martindale-Hubbell Law Directory

DENTON & AXLEY, A PROFESSIONAL CORPORATION (AV)

1600 San Jacinto Tower LB 71, 2121 San Jacinto Street, 75201
Telephone: 214-969-0100
Fax: 214-720-1998

Robert J. Axley
Michael G. Denton
Kathryn Koons Hargrove
R. Norris Lozano
Lyle McClellan
William E. Merritt
Jessica E. Schwarz-Zik
Sally Brenner Wolfish

For full biographical listings, see the Martindale-Hubbell Law Directory

GWEN M. EISENSTEIN, P.C. (AV)

One Energy Square, 4925 Greenville Avenue Suite 750, 75206
Telephone: 214-265-1233
FAX: 214-265-1332

(See Next Column)

GWEN M. EISENSTEIN, P.C.—*Continued*

Gwen M. Eisenstein

For full biographical listings, see the Martindale-Hubbell Law Directory

GODWIN & CARLTON, A PROFESSIONAL CORPORATION (AV)

Suite 3300, 901 Main Street, 75202-3714
Telephone: 214-939-4400
Telecopier: 214-760-7332
Monterrey, Mexico Correspondent: Quintero y Quintero Abogodos. Martin De Zalva 840-3 Sur Esquinna Con Hidalgo.
Telephone: 44-07-74, 44-07-80, 44-06-56, 44-06-28.
Fax: 83-40-34-54.

Thomas E. Rosen | John L. Hubble
Maurice J. Bates

Rodney L. Hubbard

For Complete List of Firm Personnel, See General Section

For full biographical listings, see the Martindale-Hubbell Law Directory

HUGHES & LUCE, L.L.P. (AV)

A Registered Limited Liability Partnership including Professional Corporations
1717 Main Street, Suite 2800, 75201
Telephone: 214-939-5500
Fax: 214-939-6100
Telex: 730836
Austin, Texas Office: 111 Congress, Suite 900.
Telephone: 512-482-6800.
Fax: 512-482-6859.
Houston, Texas Office: Three Allen Center, 333 Clay Street, Suite 3800.
Telephone: 713-754-5200.
Fax: 713-754-5206.
Fort Worth, Texas Office: 2421 Westport Parkway, Suite 500A.
Telephone: 817-439-3000.
Fax: 817-439-4222.

MEMBERS OF FIRM

Zammurad Hyatt Feroze | James A. Moomaw
Daniel K. Hennessy | David A. Newsom
Dwight A. Shupe

ASSOCIATES

Mark A. Damante | Deborah J. Eichner
David Lee Fields

For Complete List of Firm Personnel, See General Section

For full biographical listings, see the Martindale-Hubbell Law Directory

MIDDLEBERG, RIDDLE & GIANNA (AV)

2323 Bryan Street, Suite 1600, 75201
Telephone: 214-220-6300
Telecopier: 214-220-2785
New Orleans, Louisiana Office: 31st Floor, Place St. Charles, 201 St. Charles Avenue,
Telephone: 504-525-7200.
Telecopier: 504-581-5983.
Austin, Texas Office: 901 South Mopac Expressway.
Telephone: 512-329-3012.

Ira Joel Middleberg (Not admitted in TX) | Michael Lee Riddle
Dominic J. Gianna (Not admitted in TX)

Robert M. Duval | Marigny A. Lanier
Craig A. Eggleston | William Andrew Messer
John L. Genung | Carol J. Riddle
Jim Jordan | Alexandra Smith
Kay A. King | Sheryl Weisberg
Kenneth J. Lambert | Marsha L. Williams

OF COUNSEL

Richard S. Wilensky

For full biographical listings, see the Martindale-Hubbell Law Directory

NOVAKOV, DAVIDSON & FLYNN, A PROFESSIONAL CORPORATION (AV)

2000 St. Paul Place, 750 North St. Paul, 75201-3286
Telephone: 214-922-9221
Telecopy: 214-969-7557

James Kevin Flynn | Charles N. Nye

For Complete List of Firm Personnel, See General Section

For full biographical listings, see the Martindale-Hubbell Law Directory

PALMER, ALLEN & MCTAGGART, L.L.P. (AV)

A Partnership including Professional Corporations
1900 St. Paul Place, 750 North St. Paul Street, 75201
Telephone: 214-969-0069
Telecopy: 214-720-0104
Austin, Texas Office: 6505 Lohmann's Crossing (Lago Vista).
Telephone: 512-267-1993. Mailing Address: P.O. Box 4345, Lago Vista, Texas, 78645.

Steven G. Palmer (P.C.) | Robert D. McTaggart (P.C.)
Joe B. Allen III | Guy Myrph Foote, Jr., (P.C.)
Brian G. Dicus (P.C.)

OF COUNSEL

Robert S. Leithiser (P.C.) | Dick P. Wood, Jr., (P.C.)

For full biographical listings, see the Martindale-Hubbell Law Directory

SMITH, MERRIFIELD & RICHARDS, L.L.P. (AV)

4054 McKinney Avenue, Suite 310, 75204
Telephone: 214-520-0600
Fax: 214-559-3124

Thomas M. Smith | Thomas M. Richards
David A. Merrifield | Dixon Jace Reynolds

For full biographical listings, see the Martindale-Hubbell Law Directory

THOMPSON, COE, COUSINS & IRONS, L.L.P. (AV)

200 Crescent Court, Eleventh Floor, 75201-1840
Telephone: 214-871-8200 (Dallas)
512-480-8770 (Austin)
FAX: 214-871-8209

MEMBERS OF FIRM

Jon G. Petersen | Ronald D. Horner

ASSOCIATE

Bradley D. Broberg

Representative Clients: Hartford Insurance Group; Texas Automobile Insurance Service Office; Trinity Universal Insurance Company.

For Complete List of Firm Personnel, See General Section

For full biographical listings, see the Martindale-Hubbell Law Directory

THOMPSON & KNIGHT, A PROFESSIONAL CORPORATION (AV)

(Attorneys and Counselors)
1700 Pacific Avenue Suite 3300, 75201
Telephone: 214-969-1700
Telecopy: 214-969-1751
Cable Address: "Tomtex"
Telex: 732298
Austin, Texas Office: 1200 San Jacinto Center, 98 San Jacinto Boulevard, 78701.
Telephone: 512-469-6100.
Telecopy: 512-469-6180.
Fort Worth, Texas Office: 801 Cherry Street, Suite 1600, 76102.
Telephone: 817-347-1700.
Telecopy: 817-347-1799.
Houston, Texas Office: 1700 Texas Commerce Tower, 600 Travis, 77002.
Telephone: 713-217-2800.
Telecopy: 713-217-2828.
Monterrey, Mexico Office: Edificio Losoles PD-4, Av. Lázaro Cárdenas No. 2400 Pte., San Pedro Garza Garcia, Nuevo Léon C.P. 66220.
Telephone: (52-8) 363-0096.
Telecopy: (52-8) 363-3067.

SHAREHOLDERS

Hugh T. Blevins, Jr. | Geoffrey D. Osborn
Gregg C. Davis | Harry M. Roberts, Jr.
Martha Harris | James W. Rose
M. Lawrence Hicks, Jr. | Clint Shouse
Lou H. Jones | William R. Van Wagner
Beth Eileen Metty | Ben B. West
William R. Wright

ASSOCIATES

Susan D. Gillette | Mark M. Sloan
Scott V. Williams

OF COUNSEL

Julia Patterson Forrester | Cynthia S. Pladziewicz

For Complete List of Firm Personnel, See General Section

For full biographical listings, see the Martindale-Hubbell Law Directory

BRUCE E. TURNER (AV)

1515 Allianz Financial Centre, 2323 Bryan Street, L.B. 115, 75201
Telephone: 214-220-2895
Telecopier: 214-220-3105

For full biographical listings, see the Martindale-Hubbell Law Directory

*DENTON,** Denton Co.

PHILIPS AND HOPKINS, P.C. (AV)

P.O. Box 2027, 76202-2027
Telephone: 817-566-7010
Facsimile: 817-898-0502

William P. Philips, Jr.

Representative Clients: North Texas Savings & Loan Assn., Denton, Texas; First State Bank of Texas, Denton, Texas; Sanger Bank, Sanger, Texas; BankOne, Texas, N.A.; Texas Bank, Denton, Texas; Dentex Title Co., Denton, Texas.

For Complete List of Firm Personnel, See General Section

For full biographical listings, see the Martindale-Hubbell Law Directory

*FORT WORTH,** Tarrant Co.

JOHN W. CRUMLEY, P.C. (AV)

210 University Centre 1, 1300 South University Drive, 76107-5734
Telephone: 817-334-0291
Fax: 817-334-0775

John W. Crumley

For full biographical listings, see the Martindale-Hubbell Law Directory

HAROLD S. SPARKS III (AV)

Suite 2602 Bank One Building, 500 Throckmorton Street, 76102-3813
Telephone: 817-335-8353
Telecopier: 817-332-1701

For full biographical listings, see the Martindale-Hubbell Law Directory

THOMPSON & KNIGHT, A PROFESSIONAL CORPORATION (AV)

(Attorneys and Counselors)
801 Cherry Street, Suite 1600, 76102
Telephone: 817-347-1700
Telecopy: 817-347-1799
Dallas, Texas Office: 1700 Pacific Avenue, Suite 3300, 75201.
Telephone: 214-969-1700.
Telecopy: 214-969-1751.
Cable Address: "Tomtex."
Telex: 732298.
Austin, Texas Office: 1200 San Jacinto Center, 98 San Jacinto Boulevard, 78701.
Telephone: 512-469-6100.
Telecopy: 512-469-6180.
Houston, Texas Office: 1700 Texas Commerce Tower, 600 Travis, 77002.
Telephone: 713-217-2800.
Telecopy: 713-217-2828; 713-2882.
Monterrey, Mexico Office: Edificio Losoles PD-4, Av. Lázaro Cárdenas No. 2400 Pte., San Pedro Garza Garcia, Nuevo Léon C.P. 66220.
Telephone: (52-8) 363-0096.
Telecopy: (52-8) 363-3067.

ASSOCIATE

Susan E. Coleman

For Complete List of Firm Personnel, See General Section

For full biographical listings, see the Martindale-Hubbell Law Directory

*HOUSTON,** Harris Co.

BAKER & BOTTS, L.L.P. (AV)

One Shell Plaza, 910 Louisiana, 77002
Telephone: 713-229-1234
Cable Address: "Boterlove"
Fax: 713-229-1522
Washington, D.C. Office: The Warner, 1299 Pennsylvania Avenue, N.W.
Telephone: 202-639-7700.
New York, New York Office: 885 Third Avenue, Suite 2000.
Telephone: 212-705-5000.
Austin, Texas Office: 1600 San Jacinto Center, 98 San Jacinto Boulevard.
Telephone: 512-322-2500.
Dallas, Texas Office: 2001 Ross Avenue.
Telephone: 214-953-6500.
Moscow, Russian Federation Office: 10 ul. Pushkinskaya, 103031.
Telephone: 7095/921-5300 (Local); 7095/929-7070 (International).

MEMBERS OF FIRM

Wade H. Whilden
Fred H. Dunlop
Robert P. Wright
Marley Lott
Paul B. Landen

ASSOCIATES

Rosalind M. Lawton
Peter M. Oxman
James LeGrand Read
Mark S. Snell

For Complete List of Firm Personnel, See General Section

For full biographical listings, see the Martindale-Hubbell Law Directory

BILL DE LA GARZA & ASSOCIATES, P.C. (AV)

17050 El Camino, 77058-2610
Telephone: 713-486-7007
Fax: 713-486-0229

Bill De La Garza

David M. Oualline
Finis Royal
Sondra Kaighen

For full biographical listings, see the Martindale-Hubbell Law Directory

DOW, COGBURN & FRIEDMAN, P.C. (AV)

2300 Coastal Tower, Nine Greenway Plaza, 77046
Telephone: 713-626-5800
Telecopier: 713-940-6099

Harry Dow (1899-1985)
Melvin A. Dow
Edmund L. Cogburn
Bernard O. Dow
Abraham P. Friedman
Vincent L. Marino
Paul Easterwood
John M. Helms
George A. Rustay
B. Edward Williamson
Irving C. Stern
K. Gregory Erwin
Bruce W. Merwin
Kenneth H. Kates
Warren Hoffman
Barry E. Putterman
Jeff Lefkowitz
Irene Kopelman Cruden
Kay Carnley Vickers
Michael J. Mazzone
Maralene Martin
Thomas J. McCaffrey
David L. Pybus

Lauren G. Friedman
Kevin B. Crawford
Derek J. Lisk
P. Randall Crump
Tammie S. Haynes
Henry J. Blum
Scott J. Thomas
J. W. Beverly
Kevin Hanratty
Eric S. Dixon
John C. Dunne
Sanford L. Dow

OF COUNSEL

Clarence A. West

Representative Clients: Weingarten Realty Investors (Shopping Center Developers); Weiner's Stores, Inc. (Department Store); Transamerica Realty Services; Belin Developers (Residential Subdivisions).

For full biographical listings, see the Martindale-Hubbell Law Directory

WAYNE C. FOX (AV)

700 Louisiana, Suite 3990, 77002
Telephone: 713-224-0123
Fax: 713-224-7112

For full biographical listings, see the Martindale-Hubbell Law Directory

GILPIN, PAXSON & BERSCH (AV)

A Registered Limited Liability Partnership
1900 West Loop South, Suite 2000, 77027-3259
Telephone: 713-623-8800
Telecopier: 713-993-8451

MEMBERS OF FIRM

Gary M. Alletag
Timothy R. Bersch
Deborah J. Bullion
James L. Cornell, Jr.
George R. Diaz-Arrastia
Frank W. Gerold
John D. Gilpin
William T. Little
Darryl W. Malone
Michael W. McCoy
Michael J. Pappert
Stephen Paxson
Lionel M. Schooler
Mary E. Wilson
Kevin F. Risley

ASSOCIATES

Russell T. Abney
N. Terry Adams, Jr.
John W. Burchfield
Evan N. Kramer
Dale R. Mellencamp
P. Wayne Pickering
Susan M. Schwager

OF COUNSEL

Harless R. Benthul
Thomas F. Aubry

Representative Clients: Dominion Minerals Corporation; FBS Properties, Inc.; Greater Houston Builders Association; Hornberger Bros. Properties, Inc.; Life Forms, Inc.; Pulte Home Corporation; The Milestone Companies; Texas Association of Builders; Trammell Crow Company; Weekley Homes, Inc.

For full biographical listings, see the Martindale-Hubbell Law Directory

GOLDBERG BROWN, L.L.P. (AV)

5444 Westheimer, Suite 1750, 77056
Telephone: 713-871-8222
Fax: 713-871-0174

MEMBERS OF FIRM

Charles N. "Boots" Goldberg
Barry Allan Brown
Sarah Ann Powers
Charles J. Maddox, Jr.

(See Next Column)

GOLDBERG BROWN L.L.P.—*Continued*

ASSOCIATES

Stuart V. Kusin
John W. Wood
Larry L. Mayo
Barbara Kothmann Ferrer

For full biographical listings, see the Martindale-Hubbell Law Directory

GREGG & MIESZKUC, P.C. (AV)

17044 El Camino Real (Clear Lake City), 77058-2686
Telephone: 713-488-8680
Facsimile: 713-488-8531

Dick H. Gregg, Jr.
Polly P. Lewis
Marilyn Mieszkuc
Charles A. Daughtry

Elizabeth E. Scott
Dick H. Gregg, III

For full biographical listings, see the Martindale-Hubbell Law Directory

JACOBUS, BOLTZ & MELAMED (AV)

Three Riverway, Suite 1700, 77056
Telephone: 713-871-8781; 850-0090
Telecopier: 713-871-1427

MEMBERS OF FIRM

Charles J. Jacobus
Michael C. Boltz
Richard Melamed

For full biographical listings, see the Martindale-Hubbell Law Directory

LORANCE & THOMPSON, A PROFESSIONAL CORPORATION (AV)

303 Jackson Hill, 77007
Telephone: 713-868-5560
Fax: 713-864-4671; 868-1605
Phoenix, Arizona Office: 2525 East Camelback Road, Suite 230, 85016.
Telephone: 602-224-4000.
Fax: 602-224-4098.
San Diego, California Office: 555 West Beech Street, Suite 222, 92101.
Telephone: 800-899-1844.

Larry D. Thompson
Phillip C. Summers
Wayne Adams
David F. Webb
Frank B. Stahl, Jr.
Richard H. Martin
William K. Luyties
Vicki F. Brann
Clifford A. Lawrence, Jr.
Ronald E. Hood
Walter F. (Trey) Williams, III
Gwen W. Dobrowski
David O. Cluck
Mark D. Flanagan
F. Barham Lewis

David W. Prasifka
Diane M. Guariglia
Gregory D. Solcher
Kelly B. Lea
John A. Culberson
Tracey Landrum Foster
George Eric Van Noy
Ronnie B. Arnold
James E. Simmons
Teresa A. Carver
John H. Thomisee, Jr.
Terrance D. Dill, Jr.
Tracey R. Burridge
J. Wayne Little
Douglas A. Haldane
William T. Sebesta
Geoffrey C. Guill
Richard N. Moore
Matthew R. Pearson

OF COUNSEL

John Holman Barr
Shannon P. Davis
Alexis J. Gomez

Representative Clients: Allstate Insurance Co.; The Hartford Insurance Group.

For full biographical listings, see the Martindale-Hubbell Law Directory

SHAW & ASSOCIATES, A PROFESSIONAL CORPORATION (AV)

1717 St. James Place, Suite 136, 77056-3494
Telephone: 713-629-4140
Fax: 713-892-4711

Jo E. (Jed) Shaw, Jr.
James S. Robinson
Roxanne Klein Shaw
Michael G. Tapp

For full biographical listings, see the Martindale-Hubbell Law Directory

MCALLEN, Hidalgo Co.

CARDENAS, WHITIS & STEPHEN, L.L.P. (AV)

100 South Bicentennial, 78501
Telephone: 210-631-3381
Telecopier: 210-687-5542

MEMBERS OF FIRM

Ruben R. Cardenas
Robert W. Whitis

Representative Client: Texas Commerce Bank-McAllen, N.A.

For Complete List of Firm Personnel, See General Section

For full biographical listings, see the Martindale-Hubbell Law Directory

LAW OFFICE OF JOHN ROBERT KING (AV)

3409 North 10th, Suite 100, 78501
Telephone: 210-687-6294

ASSOCIATES

Robin C. Crow
Michael S. (Steve) Deck

Representative Clients: McAllen Board of Realtors; Stewart Title of Hidalgo County.

*SAN ANTONIO,** Bexar Co.

BARTON & SCHNEIDER, L.L.P. (AV)

Suite 1825, One Riverwalk Place, 700 North St. Marys, 78205
Telephone: 210-225-1655
Fax: 210-225-8999

J. Cary Barton
Raymond J. Schneider
Anthony W. Eugenio

ASSOCIATE

Martha Vanek Hardy

For full biographical listings, see the Martindale-Hubbell Law Directory

SCHOENBAUM, CURPHY & SCANLAN, P.C. (AV)

NationsBank Plaza, Suite 1775, 300 Convent Street, 78205-3744
Telephone: 210-224-4491
Fax: 210-224-7983

Stanley Schoenbaum
Alfred G. Holcomb
R. James Curphy
Banks M. Smith
William Scanlan, Jr.
R. Bradley Oxford
Darin N. Digby

Patricia Flora Sitchler
Emily Harrison Liljenwall
Susan L. Saeger

For full biographical listings, see the Martindale-Hubbell Law Directory

TEXARKANA, Bowie Co.

PATTON, HALTOM, ROBERTS, MCWILLIAMS & GREER, L.L.P. (AV)

A Registered Limited Liability Partnership including Professional Corporations
700 Texarkana National Bank Building, P.O. Box 1928, 75504-1928
Telephone: 903-794-3341
Fax: 903-792-6542; 903-792-0448

Kirk Patton (P.C.)
William B. Roberts
Donald W. Capshaw

Representative Clients: Allstate Insurance Co.; Aetna Casualty & Surety Co.; Royal Insurance Group; Continental Insurance Group; Ranger/Pan American Insurance Cos.; The Hanover Insurance Group; American Mutual Liability Insurance Co.; American Hardware Mutual Insurance Co.; Kemper Insurance Co.; Texarkana National Bancshares, Inc.

For Complete List of Firm Personnel, See General Section

For full biographical listings, see the Martindale-Hubbell Law Directory

UTAH

*SALT LAKE CITY,** Salt Lake Co.

CALLISTER, NEBEKER & MCCULLOUGH, A PROFESSIONAL CORPORATION (AV)

800 Kennecott Building, 84133
Telephone: 801-530-7300
Telecopier: 801-364-9127

Louis H. Callister
Steven E. Tyler
Dorothy C. Pleshe
Randall D Benson
John A. Beckstead
T. Richard Davis
John H. Rees

Representative Clients: Zions First National Bank; Western Farm Credit Bank; Aetna Insurance Company; Home Builders Association of Utah; Zions Mortgage Company.

For Complete List of Firm Personnel, See General Section

For full biographical listings, see the Martindale-Hubbell Law Directory

Salt Lake City—Continued

DURHAM, EVANS, JONES & PINEGAR (AV)

Key Bank Tower 50 South Main, Suite 850, 84144
Telephone: 801-538-2424
Fax: 801-363-1835
Telluride, Colorado Office: 126 West Colorado Avenue, Suite 102-C, P.O. Box 3153, 81435.
Telephone: 303-728-5775.
Fax: 303-728-5898.

Richard W. Evans
Paul M. Durham
Douglas R. Tueller (Resident, Telluride, Colorado Office)
G. Richard Hill
Pamela B. Slater (Resident, Telluride, Colorado Office)

For full biographical listings, see the Martindale-Hubbell Law Directory

JONES, WALDO, HOLBROOK & MCDONOUGH, A PROFESSIONAL CORPORATION (AV)

1500 First Interstate Plaza, 170 South Main Street, 84101
Telephone: 801-521-3200
Telecopier: 801-328-0537
Mailing Address: P.O. Box 45444, 84145-0444
St. George, Utah Office: The Tabernacle Tower Building, 249 East Tabernacle.
Telephone: 801-628-1627.
Telecopier: 801-628-5225.
Washington, D.C. Office: Suite 900, 2300 M Street, N.W.
Telephone: 202-296-5950.
Telecopier: 202-293-2509.

Harry E. McCoy, II
Steven D. Peterson
Thomas G. Bennett

OF COUNSEL

Gary A. Terry (Resident, St. George Office)

Representative Clients: Snowbird Ski & Summer Resort; Nevada Resort Properties, Ltd.; Owners Resorts & Exchange, Inc.; Salt Lake Redevelopment Agency; Salt Lake County Housing Authority; Marriott Ownership Resorts, Inc.; Hilton Grand Vacations Co.

For Complete List of Firm Personnel, See General Section

For full biographical listings, see the Martindale-Hubbell Law Directory

KIMBALL, PARR, WADDOUPS, BROWN & GEE, A PROFESSIONAL CORPORATION (AV)

Suite 1300, 185 South State Street, P.O. Box 11019, 84147
Telephone: 801-532-7840
Fax: 801-532-7750

David E. Gee
Scott W. Loveless
David K. Redd
James C. Swindler
Victor A. Taylor

OF COUNSEL

Charles L. Maak

For Complete List of Firm Personnel, See General Section

For full biographical listings, see the Martindale-Hubbell Law Directory

KIRTON & MCCONKIE, A PROFESSIONAL CORPORATION (AV)

1800 Eagle Gate Tower, 60 East South Temple, 84111
Telephone: 801-328-3600
Telecopier: 801-321-4893

Wilford W. Kirton, Jr.
Oscar W. McConkie, Jr.
Raymond W. Gee
Anthony I. Bentley, Jr.
J. Douglas Mitchell
Richard R. Neslen
Myron L. Sorensen
Robert W. Edwards
B. Lloyd Poelman
Raeburn G. Kennard
Jerry W. Dearinger
R. Bruce Findlay
Charles W. Dahlquist, II
M. Karlynn Hinman
Robert P. Lunt
Brinton R. Burbidge
Gregory S. Bell
Lee Ford Hunter
Larry R. White
William H. Wingo
David M. McConkie
Read R. Hellewell
Rolf H. Berger
Oscar W. McConkie, III
Marc Nick Mascaro
Lorin C. Barker
David M. Wahlquist
Robert S. Prince
Wallace O. Felsted
Merrill F. Nelson
Paul H. Matthews
Fred D. Essig
Clark B. Fetzer
Samuel D. McVey
Blake T. Ostler
Daniel Bay Gibbons
Gregory M. Simonsen
Von G. Keetch
Patrick Hendrickson
Stuart F. Weed
Thomas D. Walk
James E. Ellsworth
Daniel V. Goodsell
David J. Hardy
Randy T. Austin

For Complete List of Firm Personnel, See General Section

For full biographical listings, see the Martindale-Hubbell Law Directory

PARSONS BEHLE & LATIMER, A PROFESSIONAL CORPORATION (AV)

One Utah Center, 201 South Main Street, Suite 1800, P.O. Box 45898, 84145-0898
Telephone: 801-532-1234
Telecopy: 801-536-6111

J. Gordon Hansen
Robert C. Hyde
Craig B. Terry
Jonathan K. Butler
Shawn C. Ferrin
William R. Gray

Representative Clients: Hercules, Inc.; Kennecott Corporation; The Home Depot; Trammel Crow Company; Richards-Woodbury Mortgage Corporation; Wal-Mart Stores, Inc.

For full biographical listings, see the Martindale-Hubbell Law Directory

PRINCE, YEATES & GELDZAHLER (AV)

City Centre I, Suite 900, 175 East 400 South, 84111
Telephone: 801-524-1000
Fax: 801-524-1099
Park City, Utah Office: 614 Main Street, P.O. Box 38.
Telephones: 801-524-1000; 649-7440.

MEMBERS OF FIRM

Jon C. Heaton
Richard L. Blanck
C. Craig Liljenquist
J. Randall Call
David K. Broadbent
Carl W. Barton

Representative Clients: CrossLand Mortgage; Layton Construction; Sundance Ski Resort; Virginia Beach Federal Savings and Loan Association; Zions First National Bank.

For Complete List of Firm Personnel, See General Section

For full biographical listings, see the Martindale-Hubbell Law Directory

RAY, QUINNEY & NEBEKER, A PROFESSIONAL CORPORATION (AV)

Suite 400 Deseret Building, 79 South Main Street, P.O. Box 45385, 84145-0385
Telephone: 801-532-1500
Telecopier: 801-532-7543
Provo, Utah Office: 210 First Security Bank Building, 92 North University Avenue.
Telephone: 801-226-7210.
Telecopier: 801-375-8379.

Alan A. Enke
Scott Hancock Clark
Douglas Matsumori
Larry G. Moore
Ira B. Rubinfeld

Cameron M. Hancock

Representative Clients: First Security Bank of Utah, N.A.; Borden, Inc.; Southern Pacific Transportation; Utah Power & Light Co.; Travelers Insurance Co.; Greyhound Leasing & Financial; Holy Cross Hospital and Health System; Amoco Production Co.

For Complete List of Firm Personnel, See General Section

For full biographical listings, see the Martindale-Hubbell Law Directory

VAN COTT, BAGLEY, CORNWALL & MCCARTHY, A PROFESSIONAL CORPORATION (AV)

Suite 1600, 50 South Main Street, P.O. Box 45340, 84145
Telephone: 801-532-3333
Telex: 453149
Telecopier: 801-534-0058
Ogden, Utah Office: Suite 900, 2404 Washington Boulevard.
Telephone: 801-394-5783.
Park City, Utah Office: 314 Main Street, Suite 205.
Telephone: 801-649-3889.
Reno, Nevada Office: Jeppson & Lee, 100 West Liberty, Suite 990.
Telephone: 702-333-6800.

M. Scott Woodland
Stephen D. Swindle
Robert D. Merrill
Gregory P. Williams
Rand L. Cook
Thomas T. Billings
Richard H. Johnson, II
Thomas Berggren
Ervin R. Holmes
Guy P. Kroesche
Gregory N. Barrick
Timothy W. Blackburn (Resident, Ogden, Utah Office)
Douglas A. Taggart (Resident, Ogden, Utah Office)
Clark K. Taylor

OF COUNSEL

Leonard J. Lewis

For Complete List of Firm Personnel, See General Section

For full biographical listings, see the Martindale-Hubbell Law Directory

VERMONT

*BURLINGTON,** Chittenden Co.

BURAK & ANDERSON (AV)

Executive Square, 346 Shelburne Street, P.O. Box 64700, 05406-4700
Telephone: 802-862-0500
Telecopier: 802-862-8176

MEMBERS OF FIRM

Michael L. Burak
Jon Anderson

ASSOCIATES

Robert I. Goetz
Julie D. M. Sovern

For Complete List of Firm Personnel, See General Section

For full biographical listings, see the Martindale-Hubbell Law Directory

GRAVEL AND SHEA, A PROFESSIONAL CORPORATION (AV)

Corporate Plaza, 76 St. Paul Street, P.O. Box 369, 05402-0369
Telephone: 802-658-0220
Fax: 802-658-1456

Charles T. Shea
Stephen R. Crampton
James E. Knapp
John R. Ponsetto

James L. Vana

OF COUNSEL

Clarke A. Gravel

SPECIAL COUNSEL

Norman Williams

For Complete List of Firm Personnel, See General Section

For full biographical listings, see the Martindale-Hubbell Law Directory

LISMAN & LISMAN, A PROFESSIONAL CORPORATION (AV)

84 Pine Street, P.O. Box 728, 05402-0728
Telephone: 802-864-5756
Fax: 802-864-3629

Carl H. Lisman
Allen D. Webster
Mary G. Kirkpatrick
E. William Leckerling, III
Douglas K. Riley

Judith Lillian Dillon
Richard W. Kozlowski

OF COUNSEL

Bernard Lisman
Louis Lisman

For full biographical listings, see the Martindale-Hubbell Law Directory

SHEEHEY BRUE GRAY & FURLONG, PROFESSIONAL CORPORATION (AV)

119 South Winooski Avenue, P.O. Box 66, 05402
Telephone: 802-864-9891
Facsimile: 802-864-6815

William B. Gray (1942-1994)
David T. Austin
R. Jeffrey Behm
Nordahl L. Brue
Michael G. Furlong
Ralphine Newlin O'Rourke
Donald J. Rendall, Jr.
Christina Schulz
Paul D. Sheehey
Peter H. Zamore

Rebecca L. Owen

Representative Client: Green Mountain Power Corp.

For full biographical listings, see the Martindale-Hubbell Law Directory

*MIDDLEBURY,** Addison Co.

CONLEY & FOOTE (AV)

11 South Pleasant Street, P.O. Drawer 391, 05753
Telephone: 802-388-4061
Fax: 802-388-0210

MEMBERS OF FIRM

John T. Conley (1900-1971)
Ralph A. Foote
Charity A. Downs
D. Michael Mathes
Richard P. Foote
Janet P. Shaw

For full biographical listings, see the Martindale-Hubbell Law Directory

*RUTLAND,** Rutland Co.

CARROLL, GEORGE & PRATT (AV)

64 & 66 North Main Street, P.O. Box 280, 05702-0280
Telephone: 802-775-7141
Telecopier: 802-775-6483
Woodstock, Vermont Office: The Mill - Route #4 E., P.O. Box 388, 05091.
Telephone: 802-457-1000.
Telecopier: 802-457-1874.

MEMBERS OF FIRM

Henry G. Smith (1938-1974)
James P. Carroll
Alan B. George
Robert S. Pratt
Neal C. Vreeland
Jon S. Readnour
Timothy U. Martin
Randall F. Mayhew (Resident Partner, Woodstock Office)
Richard S. Smith
Judy Godnick Barone
John J. Kennelly

ASSOCIATES

Thomas A. Zonay
Jeffrey P. White
Susan Boyle Ford (Resident, Woodstock Office)
Charles C. Humpstone

For full biographical listings, see the Martindale-Hubbell Law Directory

VIRGINIA

*ABINGDON,** Washington Co.

TATE, LOWE & ROWLETT, P.C. (AV)

205 West Main Street, 24210
Telephone: 703-628-5185
Telecopier: 703-628-5045

Mary Lynn Tate
C. Randall Lowe
Fredrick A. Rowlett

Representative Clients: First Virginia Bank; Pikeville National Bank; Jewell Resources, Inc.; Rapoca Energy Co.; Charter Federal Savings Bank.
Approved Attorneys For: Lawyers Title Insurance Co.; Safeco Title Insurance; Talco Group Title Co.; Holston River Title Agency.
References: Nations Bank; Bank of Marion; Central Fidelity Bank.

For Complete List of Firm Personnel, See General Section

For full biographical listings, see the Martindale-Hubbell Law Directory

YEARY & ASSOCIATES, P.C. (AV)

161 East Main Street, P.O. Box 1685, 24210
Telephone: 703-628-9107
Telecopier: 703-628-1998

Emmitt F. Yeary

W. Hobart Robinson
Kathleen Calvert Yeary

LEGAL SUPPORT PERSONNEL

Michael A. Bragg (Legal Assistant)

Representative Clients: Abingdon Nursing Homes, Inc.; Rapoca Energy Co.; East Gate Drug Stores of Abingdon, Inc.; D.S. Buck, Inc.; McKinney Builders.
Approved Attorneys for: Lawyers Title Insurance Co.; Chicago Title Insurance Co.
References: First Bank & Trust Co., Abingdon; First Virginia Bank; NationsBank.

For full biographical listings, see the Martindale-Hubbell Law Directory

*ACCOMAC,** Accomack Co.

JON C. POULSON (AV)

23349 Cross Street, P.O. Box 478, 23301-0478
Telephone: 804-787-2620
Facsimile: 804-787-2749

For full biographical listings, see the Martindale-Hubbell Law Directory

ALEXANDRIA, (Independent City)

THOMAS, BALLENGER, VOGELMAN AND TURNER, P.C. (AV)

124 South Royal Street, 22314
Telephone: 703-836-3400
Fax: 703-836-3549

Earl G. Thomas
James D. Turner

References: First Union National Bank of Virginia; Burke & Herbert Bank & Trust Co.

For Complete List of Firm Personnel, See General Section

For full biographical listings, see the Martindale-Hubbell Law Directory

*ARLINGTON,** Arlington Co.

WALSH, COLUCCI, STACKHOUSE, EMRICH & LUBELEY, P.C. (AV)

Courthouse Plaza, Thirteenth Floor, 2200 Clarendon Boulevard, 22201
Telephone: 703-528-4700
Facsimile: 703-525-3197
Woodbridge, Virginia Office: Village Square, 13663 Office Place, Suite 201.
Telephones: 703-680-4664; 690-4647.
Facsimile: 703-690-2412.

Martin D. ("Art") Walsh
Thomas J. Colucci
Peter K. Stackhouse
Jerry K. Emrich
Michael D. Lubeley (Resident, Woodbridge Office)
Keith C. Martin
Nan E. Terpak
William A. Fogarty
David J. Bomgardner (Resident, Woodbridge Office)
Lynne J. Strobel
John E. Rinaldi (Resident, Woodbridge Office)
Sean P. McMullen
H. Mark Goetzman

OF COUNSEL

Nicholas Malinchak

For full biographical listings, see the Martindale-Hubbell Law Directory

BRISTOL, (Independent City)

WOODWARD, MILES & FLANNAGAN, P.C. (AV)

Suite 200, Executive Plaza, 510 Cumberland Street, P.O. Box 789, 24203-0789
Telephone: 703-669-0161
Telecopier: 703-669-7376

S. Bruce Jones (1892-1966)
Jno. W. Flannagan, Jr. (1885-1955)
Waldo G. Miles (1911-1973)
Wm. H. Woodward (1907-1992)
Francis W. Flannagan
John E. Kieffer
Larry B. Kirksey
Elizabeth Smith Jones
Christen W. Burkholder
Beth Osborne Skinner

Representative Clients: Lawyers Title Insurance Company; The First Bank and Trust Company; Leader Federal Bank for Savings; Charter Federal Savings Bank; United Telephone-Southeast, Inc.; First Union National Bank.

For full biographical listings, see the Martindale-Hubbell Law Directory

*CHARLOTTESVILLE,** (Ind. City; Seat of Albemarle Co.)

RICHMOND AND FISHBURNE (AV)

Queen Charlotte Square, 214 East High Street, P.O. Box 559, 22902
Telephone: 804-977-8590
Telefax: 804-296-9861

MEMBERS OF FIRM

Joseph W. Richmond, Jr.
Wendall L. Winn, Jr.

ASSOCIATE

Joseph M. Cochran

Approved Attorneys For: Lawyer's Title Insurance Corp.; Southern Title Insurance Corp.; Staunton Farm Credit, A.C.A.

For Complete List of Firm Personnel, See General Section

For full biographical listings, see the Martindale-Hubbell Law Directory

DANVILLE, (Independent City)

CARTER, CRAIG, BASS, BLAIR & KUSHNER, P.C. (AV)

126 South Union Street, P.O. Box 601, 24543
Telephone: 804-792-9311
Fax: 804-792-4373

OF COUNSEL

Charles E. Carter

Stuart L. Craig
Stephen G. Bass
D. Thomas Blair
Samuel A. Kushner, Jr.

Reference: Signet Bank (Danville).

For full biographical listings, see the Martindale-Hubbell Law Directory

*FAIRFAX,** (Ind. City; Seat of Fairfax Co.)

DIXON, SMITH & STAHL (AV)

4122 Leonard Drive, 22030
Telephone: 703-691-0770

MEMBERS OF FIRM

Richard E. Dixon
Donald G. Smith
Richard J. Stahl
Mark E. Sharp
Robert G. Culin, Jr.
James R. Hart
James E. Autry

(See Next Column)

ASSOCIATES

John L. Daugherty
Julie Hottle Day
Erica D.B. Glembocki

Reference: Sovran Bank, N.A.

For full biographical listings, see the Martindale-Hubbell Law Directory

ODIN, FELDMAN & PITTLEMAN, P.C. (AV)

9302 Lee Highway, Suite 1100, 22031
Telephone: 703-218-2100
Facsimile: 703-218-2160

David E. Feldman
Leslye S. Fenton
John W. Farrell

For Complete List of Firm Personnel, See General Section

For full biographical listings, see the Martindale-Hubbell Law Directory

RUST, RUST & SILVER, A PROFESSIONAL CORPORATION (AV)

4103 Chain Bridge Road Fourth Floor, P.O. Box 460, 22030
Telephone: 703-591-7000
Telecopier: 703-591-7336

John H. Rust, Jr.
Glenn H. Silver
C. Thomas Brown

James E. Kane
Paulo E. Franco, Jr.
Andrew W. White

RETIRED, EMERITUS

John H. Rust, Sr. (Retired)

Representative Clients: Crestar Bank; Commonwealth Land Title Insurance Co.; Patriot National Bank; Century Graphics Corp.

For full biographical listings, see the Martindale-Hubbell Law Directory

*HARRISONBURG,** (Ind. City; Seat of Rockingham Co.)

WHARTON, ALDHIZER & WEAVER, P.L.C. (AV)

100 South Mason Street, 22801
Telephone: 703-434-0316
Fax: 703-434-5502

Glenn M. Hodge
Roger D. Williams
George W. Barlow, III
G. Chris Brown

Representative Clients: F & M Bank - Broadway; First Union National Bank of Virginia; Rocco Enterprises, Inc.; Rockingham County; WLR Foods, Inc.

For Complete List of Firm Personnel, See General Section

For full biographical listings, see the Martindale-Hubbell Law Directory

*LEESBURG,** Loudoun Co.

WALSH, COLUCCI, STACKHOUSE, EMRICH & LUBELEY, P.C.

(See Arlington)

MCLEAN, Fairfax Co.

MICHAEL HORWATT & ASSOCIATES, P.C. (AV)

1501 Farm Credit Drive, Suite 3600, 22102
Telephone: 703-790-7790
Fax: 703-790-7796

Michael S. Horwatt

Charles F. Wright

OF COUNSEL

Frances A. Scibelli
Lawrence W. Koltun (Not admitted in VA)

For full biographical listings, see the Martindale-Hubbell Law Directory

VENABLE, BAETJER AND HOWARD (AV)

A Partnership including Professional Corporations
Suite 400, 2010 Corporate Ridge, 22102
Telephone: 703-760-1600
FAX: 703-821-8949
Baltimore, Maryland Office: 1800 Mercantile Bank & Trust Building, 2 Hopkins Plaza.
Telephone: 410-244-7400.
Washington, D.C. Office: Venable, Baetjer, Howard & Civiletti, Suite 1000, 1201 New York Avenue, N.W.
Telephone: 202-962-4800.
Rockville, Maryland Office: Suite 500, One Church Street, P.O. Box 1906.
Telephone: 301-217-5600.
Towson, Maryland Office: 210 Allegheny Avenue, P. O. Box 5517.
Telephone: 410-494-6200.

(See Next Column)

VENABLE, BAETJER AND HOWARD—*Continued*

MEMBERS OF FIRM

David T. Stitt
John G. Milliken (Also at Washington, D.C. Office)
Bruce E. Titus
David G. Lane
Ellen F. Dyke
Joel J. Goldberg (Also at Washington, D.C. Office)

OF COUNSEL

Mary T. Flynn

ASSOCIATE

Michael W. Robinson

For Complete List of Firm Personnel, See General Section

For full biographical listings, see the Martindale-Hubbell Law Directory

WATT, TIEDER & HOFFAR (AV)

7929 Westpark Drive, Suite 400, 22102
Telephone: 703-749-1000
Telecopier: 703-893-8029
Washington, D.C. Office: 601 Pennsylvania Ave, N.W., Suite 900.
Telephone: 202-462-4697.
Irvine California Office: 3 Park Plaza, Suite 1530.
Telephone: 714-852-6700.

MEMBERS OF FIRM

John B. Tieder, Jr.
Robert G. Watt
Julian F. Hoffar
Robert M. Fitzgerald
Robert K. Cox
William R. Chambers
David C. Romm
Charles E. Raley (Not admitted in VA)
Francis X. McCullough
Barbara G. Werther (Not admitted in VA)
Garry R. Boehlert
Thomas B. Newell
Lewis J. Baker
Benjamin T. Riddles, II
Timothy F. Brown
Richard G. Mann, Jr.
David C. Mancini
David C. Haas
Henry D. Danforth
Carter B. Reid
Donna S. McCaffrey
Mark J. Groff (Not admitted in VA)
Mark A. Sgarlata
Daniel E. Cohen
Michael G. Long (Resident, Irvine, California Office)

OF COUNSEL

Avv. Roberto Tassi
Clyde Harold Slease (Not admitted in VA)

ASSOCIATES

Thomas J. Powell
Douglas C. Proxmire
Tara L. Vautin
Edward Parrott
Steven G. Schassler
Joseph H. Bucci
Steven J. Weber
Paul A. Varela
Vivian Katsantonis
Charlie Lee
Kathleen A. Olden
Christopher P. Pappas (Resident, Irvine, California Office)
Shelly L. Ewald
Christopher J. Brasco
Jean V. Misterek
Charles W. Durant
Susan Latham Timoner
Fred A. Mendicino
Susan G. Sisskind
Robert G. Barbour
Keith C. Phillips
Marybeth Zientek Gaul
Timothy E. Heffernan (Not admitted in VA)
William Drew Mallender
James Moore Donahue
Heidi Brown Hering
Kerrin Maureen McCormick (Not admitted in VA)
Gretal J. Toker

For full biographical listings, see the Martindale-Hubbell Law Directory

NORFOLK, (Independent City)

CRENSHAW, WARE AND MARTIN, P.L.C. (AV)

Suite 1200 NationsBank Center, One Commercial Place, 23510-2111
Telephone: 804-623-3000
FAX: 804-623-5735

Francis N. Crenshaw
Guilford D. Ware
Howard W. Martin, Jr.
Timothy A. Coyle
Ann K. Sullivan
James L. Chapman, IV
John T. Midgett
Martha M. Poindexter

Melanie Fix
David H. Sump
Donald C. Schultz
Kristen L. Hodeen

Representative Clients: Contel Cellular, Inc.; Crestar Bank; First Virginia Bank of Tidewater; Norfolk Redevelopment and Housing Authority.

For full biographical listings, see the Martindale-Hubbell Law Directory

TAVSS, FLETCHER, EARLEY & KING, P.C. (AV)

Suite 100, Two Commercial Place, 23510
Telephone: 804-625-1214
Fax: 804-622-7295
Mailing Address: P.O. Box 3747, 23514

(See Next Column)

Richard J. Tavss
John R. Fletcher
Mark L. Earley
Ray W. King
Besianne Tavss Shilling

LEGAL SUPPORT PERSONNEL

Maurice J. O'Connor

Reference: Bank of the Commonwealth.

For full biographical listings, see the Martindale-Hubbell Law Directory

VANDEVENTER, BLACK, MEREDITH & MARTIN (AV)

500 World Trade Center, 23510
Telephone: 804-446-8600
Cable Address: "Hughsvan"
Telex: 823-671
Telecopier: 446-8670
North Carolina, Kitty Hawk Office: 6 Juniper Trail.
Telephone: 919-261-5055.
Fax: 919-261-8444.
London, England Office: Suite 692, Level 6, Lloyd's, 1 Lime Street.
Telephone: (071) 623-2081.
Facsimile: (071) 929-0043.
Telex: 987321.

MEMBERS OF FIRM

Geoffrey F. Birkhead
Norman W. Shearin, Jr. (Not admitted in VA; Resident, Kitty Hawk, North Carolina Office)

For Complete List of Firm Personnel, See General Section

For full biographical listings, see the Martindale-Hubbell Law Directory

WEINBERG & STEIN, A PROFESSIONAL CORPORATION (AV)

1825 Dominion Tower, P.O. Box 3789, 23514-3789
Telephone: 804-627-1066
Telecopier: 804-622-6870

Jerrold G. Weinberg
Edward S. Stein
Debra Cooney Albiston
Cecelia A. Weschler
Michael H. Wojcik

Reference: Crestar Bank.

For full biographical listings, see the Martindale-Hubbell Law Directory

*RICHMOND,** (Ind. City; Seat of Henrico Co.)

FLORANCE, GORDON AND BROWN, A PROFESSIONAL CORPORATION (AV)

800 Mutual Building, 909 East Main Street, 23219
Telephone: 804-697-5100
Facsimile: 804-697-5159

Richard Florance (1902-1980)
Walker Florance (1909-1983)
James W. Gordon, Jr. (Retired)
Delmar L. Brown
Fred J. Bernhardt, Jr.
William H. Hoofnagle, III
Hamill D. "Skip" Jones, Jr.
Cary A. Ralston
Robert J. Kloeti
Conard B. Mattox, III
Kathleen N. Scott

Christopher S. Dillon
Kimberlee Harris Ramsey
Farhad Aghdami
Bryan W. Horn
Roger Gallup Bowers

Reference: Crestar Bank.

For full biographical listings, see the Martindale-Hubbell Law Directory

THOMPSON, SMITHERS, NEWMAN & WADE (AV)

5911 West Broad Street, P.O. Box 6357, 23230
Telephone: 804-288-4007
Telecopier: 804-282-5379

MEMBERS OF FIRM

Harry L. Thompson
William S. Smithers, Jr.
Nathaniel S. Newman
Winfrey T. Wade
R. Paul Childress, Jr.
Kimberly Smithers Wright
R. Ferrell Newman
Anton J. Stelly
Robert S. Carter

ASSOCIATES

James C. Bodie
Paul D. Georgiadis
Suzanne Elizabeth Wade
Glenn S. Phelps

Approved Attorneys for: Lawyers Title Insurance Corp.

For full biographical listings, see the Martindale-Hubbell Law Directory

Richmond—Continued

Williams, Mullen, Christian & Dobbins, A Professional Corporation (AV)

Two James Center, 1021 East Cary Street, P.O. Box 1320, 23210-1320
Telephone: 804-643-1991
Fax: 804-783-6456
Glen Allen, Virginia Office: 4401 Waterfront Drive, Suite 140.
Telephone: 804-965-9168.
Fax: 804-965-0955.
Washington, D.C. Office: 1575 Eye Street, N.W.
Telephone: 202-289-6200.
Fax: 202-289-4126.

Michael C. Buseck
Charles L. Cabell
Robert E. Eicher
Hugh T. Harrison, II
A. Brooks Hock
John M. Mercer
Warren E. Nowlin (Washington, D.C. Office)
Philip deB. Rome
W. Scott Street, III
Russell Alton Wright

Andrew M. Condlin

For Complete List of Firm Personnel, See General Section

For full biographical listings, see the Martindale-Hubbell Law Directory

SPRINGFIELD, Fairfax Co.

T. William Dowdy (AV)

North Springfield Professional Center 2, 5417-E Backlick Road, P.O. Box 644, 22150-0644
Telephone: 703-750-2600
FAX: 703-750-9015

For full biographical listings, see the Martindale-Hubbell Law Directory

Madigan & Scott, Inc. (AV)

7880 Backlick Road, 22150-2288
Telephone: 703-455-1800; 451-2080
Fax: 703-451-4121
Manassas, Virginia Office: 9100 Church Street, Suite 107.
Telephone: 703-361-0185. Metro: 631-9193.
Fax: 703-631-9633.

Robert J. Madigan
Paul A. Scott
Scott H. Donovan (Resident, Manassas Office)
Mitchell Komaroff

Richard G. Hornig (1958-1994)

For full biographical listings, see the Martindale-Hubbell Law Directory

VIENNA, Fairfax Co.

Boring, Parrott & Pilger, P.C. (AV)

307 Maple Avenue West, Suite D, 22180-4368
Telephone: 703-281-2161
FAX: 703-281-9464

W. Thomas Parrott, III

Representative Clients: Balmar, Inc.; Hewlett-Packard Co.; Toshiba America Information Systems, Inc.; King Wholesale, Inc.; FSM Leasing, Inc.; KDI Sylvan Pools, Inc.; Brobst International, Inc.; Telematics, Inc.; Northern Virginia Surgical Associates, P.C.; Rainbow Industries, Inc.

For full biographical listings, see the Martindale-Hubbell Law Directory

Haight, Tramonte, Siciliano & Flask, P.C. (AV)

8221 Old Courthouse Road, Suite 300, 22182
Telephone: 703-734-4800
Facsimile: 703-442-9526

Gregory D. Haight
Vincent A. Tramonte, II
John A. Siciliano
Jon T. Flask
William J. Gorman
Sara Towery O'Hara
Steven M. Frei
Ronald K. Jaicks
David C. Hannah
Donald S. Culkin

Representative Clients: Pulte Home Corp.; Kettler Forlines, Inc.; Joe Theismann's Restaurants; McDonald's Corp.; The Business Bank.
Approved Attorneys for: Lawyers Title Insurance Co.; First American Title Insurance Co.

For full biographical listings, see the Martindale-Hubbell Law Directory

Peterson & Basha, P.C. (AV)

Tysons Square Office Park, 8214-C Old Courthouse Road, 22182-3855
Telephone: 703-442-3890
Fax: 703-448-1834

Gary G. Peterson
Leigh-Alexandra Basha

(See Next Column)

Alison K. Markell
Cynthia L. Gausvik
Ki Jun Sung

OF COUNSEL

Daniel J. O'Connell

For full biographical listings, see the Martindale-Hubbell Law Directory

WOODBRIDGE, Prince William Co.

Walsh, Colucci, Stackhouse, Emrich & Lubeley, P.C. (AV)

Village Square, 13663 Office Place, Suite 201, 22192
Telephone: 703-680-4664; 690-4647
Facsimile: 703-690-2412
Arlington, Virginia Office: Courthouse Plaza, Thirteenth Floor. 2200 Clarendon Boulevard.
Telephone: 703-528-4700.
Facsimile: 703-525-3197.

Michael D. Lubeley (Resident)
David J. Bomgardner (Resident)
John E. Rinaldi (Resident)

For full biographical listings, see the Martindale-Hubbell Law Directory

WASHINGTON

BELLEVUE, King Co.

Donald D. Fleming, P.S. (AV)

800 Bellevue Way, N.E., Suite 300, 98004
Telephone: 206-637-3001
FAX: 206-453-9062

Donald D. Fleming

For full biographical listings, see the Martindale-Hubbell Law Directory

*SEATTLE,** King Co.

Betts, Patterson & Mines, P.S. (AV)

800 Financial Center, 1215 Fourth Avenue, 98161-1090
Telephone: 206-292-9988
Fax: 206-343-7053

Bruce H. Hurst
John P. Braislin
Thomas F. Peterson

Ronald D. Allen
Stephen A. Crandall

Representative Clients: Associated Grocers; Cape Fox Corporation; Chicago Title Insurance Company; Chrysler Realty Corporation; Key Bank of Washington; Pfizer, Inc.; State Farm Insurance Companies; Stewart Title Company of Washington, Inc.; Supermarket Development Corp.

For full biographical listings, see the Martindale-Hubbell Law Directory

Buck & Gordon (AV)

902 Waterfront Place, 1011 Western Avenue, 98104-1097
Telephone: 206-382-9540
Telecopier: 206-626-0675

MEMBERS OF FIRM

William H. Block
Peter L. Buck
Brent Carson
Jay P. Derr
Joel M. Gordon
Amy L. Kosterlitz
Keith E. Moxon

ASSOCIATES

Alison D. Birmingham
Shelley E. Kneip

OF COUNSEL

Madeleine A. F. Brenner

Reference: Seafirst Bank, Seattle, Washington (Metropolitan Branch).

For full biographical listings, see the Martindale-Hubbell Law Directory

Gaitán & Cusack (AV)

30th Floor Two Union Square, 601 Union Street, 98101-2324
Telephone: 206-521-3000
Facsimile: 206-386-5259
Anchorage, Alaska Office: 425 G Street, Suite 760.
Telephone: 907-278-3001.
Facsimile: 907-278-6068.
San Francisco, California Office: 275 Battery Street, 20th Floor.
Telephone: 415-398-5562.
Fax: 415-398-4033.
Washington, D.C. Office: 2000 L Street, Suite 200.
Telephone: 202-296-4637.
Fax: 202-296-4650.

(See Next Column)

GAITÁN & CUSACK—*Continued*

MEMBERS OF FIRM

José E. Gaitán
Kenneth J. Cusack (Resident, Anchorage, Alaska Office)
William F. Knowles
Ronald L. Bozarth

OF COUNSEL

Howard K. Todd
Gary D. Gayton
Michel P. Stern (Also practicing alone, Bellevue, Washington)
Christopher A. Byrne
Patricia D. Ryan

ASSOCIATES

Mary F. O'Boyle
Bruce H. Williams
David J. Onsager
Diana T. Jimenez
Robert T. Mimbu
Cristina C. Kapela
Camilla M. Hedberg
John E. Lenker
Kathleen C. Healy

Representative Clients: Pioneer Title; Transamerica Title; National Bank of Alaska; Alaska Title Guarantee; Chemical Bank; Seafirst Bank; Rainier Bank; Horizon Bank; Household Finance; First American Title Company.

For full biographical listings, see the Martindale-Hubbell Law Directory

LANE POWELL SPEARS LUBERSKY (AV)

A Partnership including Professional Corporations
1420 Fifth Avenue, Suite 4100, 98101-2338
Telephone: 206-223-7000
Cable Address: "Embe"
Telex: 32-8808
Telecopier: 206-223-7107
Other Offices at: Mount Vernon and Olympia, Washington; Los Angeles and San Francisco, California; Anchorage, Alaska; Portland, Oregon; London, England.

MEMBERS OF FIRM

Robert R. Davis, Jr.
Charles R. Ekberg (P.S.)
David G. Johansen
Thomas F. Grohman
Scott F. Campbell
Douglas E. Wheeler
Jane Rakay Nelson

Representative Clients: C.D. Stimson, Co.; The Home Depot; Lincoln National Life Insurance Co.; The Manufacturers Life Insurance Co.; Nordstrom, Inc.; The Ohio Natural Life Insurance Co.; Resolution Trust Corp.; Seattle Mortgage Co.; Sentinel Real Estate Group; Union Pacific Railroad Co.

For Complete List of Firm Personnel, See General Section

For full biographical listings, see the Martindale-Hubbell Law Directory

JON G. SCHNEIDLER (AV)

4100 First Interstate Center, 999 Third Avenue, 98104
Telephone: 206-624-9400
Telecopier: 206-464-9559

Reference: Key Bank of Washington.

For full biographical listings, see the Martindale-Hubbell Law Directory

SHORT CRESSMAN & BURGESS (AV)

A Partnership including Professional Service Corporations
3000 First Interstate Center, 999 Third Avenue, 98104-4088
Telephone: 206-682-3333
Fax: 206-340-8856

MEMBERS OF FIRM

Robert E. Heaton
David R. Koopmans
Robert E. Hibbs (P.S.)
Christopher R. Osborn
Michael R. Garner
Thomas W. Read
Susan Thorbrogger
Stephan J. Francks
Kerry S. Bucklin

OF COUNSEL

Josef Diamond
Scott M. Missall

Representative Clients: CEM Associates; Seattle Steel, Inc.; Intrawest, U.S.A.; Puget Sound Multiple Listing Association; Century 21; Commercial Investment Brokers Association; Coldwell Bankers; Kidder Mathews & Segner; Watumull Enterprises, Ltd.

For Complete List of Firm Personnel, See General Section

For full biographical listings, see the Martindale-Hubbell Law Directory

SMITH, SMART, HANCOCK, TABLER & SCHWENSEN (AV)

3800 Columbia Seafirst Center, 701 Fifth Avenue, 98104
Telephone: 206-624-7272
Telecopier: 206-624-5581

MEMBERS OF FIRM

J. Dimmitt Smith
Douglas J. Smart
David G. Hancock
Walter S. Tabler
Joyce S. Schwensen
Karen A. Willie

(See Next Column)

ASSOCIATES

Anne B. Tiura
Paul J. Battaglia
Oskar E. Rey
Craig A. Fielden

Reference: Seattle-First National Bank; Bank of America; Chemical Bank; Clise Properties, Inc.; Gentra Capital Corporation; Puget Sound Pilots; Aid Association for Lutherans; Citicorp Mortgage, Inc.; Lutheran Brotherhood; City of Tacoma.

For full biographical listings, see the Martindale-Hubbell Law Directory

TOUSLEY BRAIN (AV)

A Partnership
56th Floor, AT&T Gateway Tower, 700 Fifth Avenue, 98104-5056
Telephone: 206-682-5600
Facsimile: 206-682-2992

Russell F. Tousley
Christopher I. Brain
Cynthia Thomas
Mary Foster Vrbanac
Vincent B. DePillis
Stephan E. Todd
Susan A. Shyne
Brian P. Ward

Representative Clients: Chicago Title Insurance Company & Affiliates; Heartland Group; Intrawest Companies; Koll Management Services, Inc.; Murray Franklyn Companies; Operating Engineers Local 302 & 612 Employees Retirement Fund; PACCAR Automotive, Inc.; Pope Resources; Trammell Crow Company; University Savings Bank.

For Complete List of Firm Personnel, See General Section

For full biographical listings, see the Martindale-Hubbell Law Directory

WEST VIRGINIA

*CHARLESTON,** Kanawha Co.

HAMB & POFFENBARGER (AV)

Bank One Center, Suite 515, P.O. Box 1671, 25301-1671
Telephone: 304-343-4128
Telecopier: 304-344-1974

MEMBERS OF FIRM

William E. Hamb
John T. Poffenbarger

ASSOCIATE

Robert W. Kiefer, Jr.

Representative Clients: Old Colony Co.; Simonton Building Products, Inc.; Storck Baking Company; Fisher-Brison Properties, Incorporated; First Empire Federal Savings & Loan Assn.; Eagle Bancorp.; SBR, Inc.; Travelers Insurance Companies; Yorel Development Co.; Bays, Inc.

For full biographical listings, see the Martindale-Hubbell Law Directory

JACKSON & KELLY (AV)

1600 Laidley Tower, P.O. Box 553, 25322
Telephone: 304-340-1000
Fax: 304-340-1130
Martinsburg, West Virginia Office: 300 Foxcroft Avenue, P.O. Box 1068.
Telephone: 304-263-8800.
Morgantown, West Virginia Office: 6000 Hampton Center, P.O. Box 619.
Telephone: 304-599-3000.
New Martinsville, West Virginia Office: 256 Russell Avenue, P.O. Box 68.
Telephone: 304-455-1751.
Charles Town, West Virginia Office: 700 East Washington Street, P.O. Box 983.
Telephone: 304-728-6088.
Clarksburg, West Virginia Office: 203 Main Street, P.O. Box 1587.
Telephone: 304-623-3002.
Lexington, Kentucky Office: 175 East Main Street, Suite 500, P.O. Box 2150.
Telephone: 606-255-9500.
Washington, D. C. Office: 2401 Pennsylvania Avenue, N.W., Suite 400.
Telephone: 202-973-0200.
Denver, Colorado Office: Suite 2710, 1660 Lincoln Street.
Telephone: 303-837-0003.

MEMBERS OF FIRM

Thomas E. Potter
Harvey Alan Siler
Barry S. Settles (Resident Lexington, Kentucky Office)
Mary Clare Eros (Martinsburg and Charles Town, West Virginia Offices)
James I. Manion (Martinsburg and Charles Town, West Virginia Offices)
W. Rodes Brown (Resident, Lexington, Kentucky Office)
Wendel B. Turner
Mark B. D'Antoni

ASSOCIATES

Brooks K. Barkwill (New Martinsville, West Virginia Office)
Eric H. London (Resident, Morgantown Office)
Dennis N. Broglio
William Prentice Young (Martinsburg and Charles Town, West Virginia Offices)
Stephen R. Kershner (Martinsburg and Charles Town, West Virginia Offices)

(See Next Column)

JACKSON & KELLY, *Charleston—Continued*

ASSOCIATES (Continued)

Mary L. Galan (Resident, Clarksburg, West Virginia Office)
James Eric Whytsell (Charles Town and Martinsburg Offices)

Representative Clients: Lawyers Title Insurance Co.; Go-Mart, Inc.; Pittston Coal Co.; Travelers Insurance Co.; Westvaco; Carbon Fuel Co.; Haddad & Associates; Pocahontas Land Corp.; McDonalds Corp.; One Valley Bancorp of West Virginia, Inc.;

For Complete List of Firm Personnel, See General Section

For full biographical listings, see the Martindale-Hubbell Law Directory

*CLARKSBURG,** Harrison Co.

WATERS, WARNER & HARRIS (AV)

Formerly Stathers & Cantrall
701 Goff Building, P.O. Box 1716, 26301
Telephone: 304-624-5571
Fax: 304-624-7228

Birk S. Stathers (1884-1945)
W. G. Stathers (1889-1970)
Arch M. Cantrall (1896-1967)
Stuart R. Waters
Boyd L. Warner
James A. Harris
Scott E. Wilson
James C. Turner
Francis L. Warder, Jr.
G. Thomas Smith
Thomas G. Dyer

ASSOCIATES

Michael J. Folio
Katherine M. Carpenter
Ernest Glen Hentschel, II
Katrina L. Gallagher

Representative Clients: Bethlehem Steel Corp.; United States Fidelity and Guaranty Co.; State Farm Insurance Companies; Davis-Weaver Funeral Home, Inc.; Dowell Schlumberger, Inc.; Fuel Resources Production and Development Company, Inc.; Grafton Coal Company; Harry Green Chevrolet, Inc.; Emax Oil Co.; Southern Steel Products Co.

For full biographical listings, see the Martindale-Hubbell Law Directory

WEST & JONES (AV)

360 Washington Avenue, P.O. Box 2348, 26302
Telephone: 304-624-5501
FAX: 304-624-4454

MEMBERS OF FIRM

James C. West, Jr.
Jerald E. Jones
Dean C. Ramsey
John S. Kaull
Lewis A. Clark

ASSOCIATES

Kathryn K. Allen
Norman T. Farley

OF COUNSEL

W. Lyle Jones

Reference: The Union National Bank of West Virginia.

For full biographical listings, see the Martindale-Hubbell Law Directory

*HUNTINGTON,** Cabell & Wayne Cos.

JENKINS, FENSTERMAKER, KRIEGER, KAYES, FARRELL & AGEE (AV)

Eleventh Floor Coal Exchange Building, P.O. Drawer 2688, 25726
Telephone: 304-523-2100
Charleston, WV 304-345-3100
Facsimile: 304-523-2347; 304-523-9279

MEMBERS OF FIRM

John E. Jenkins (1897-1961)
P. Thomas Krieger
Henry M. Kayes
Michael J. Farrell
Wesley F. Agee
Barry M. Taylor

ASSOCIATES

Suzanne McGinnis Oxley
Charlotte A. Hoffman
Robert H. Sweeney, Jr.
Patricia A. Jennings
Stephen J. Golder
William J. McGee, Jr.
Anne Maxwell McGee
Tamela J. White
Lee Murray Hall
Thomas J. Obrokta

OF COUNSEL

John E. Jenkins, Jr.
Susan B. Saxe

For full biographical listings, see the Martindale-Hubbell Law Directory

RIFE & DAUGHERTY (AV)

Suite 800, Chafin Building, 517 Ninth Street, P.O. Box 542, 25710
Telephone: 304-529-2721; 523-0131

MEMBERS OF FIRM

O. Jennings Rife
David H. Daugherty

References: Banc One West Virginia, Huntington, W. Va.; Commerce Bank of Huntington, Huntington, W. Va.

For full biographical listings, see the Martindale-Hubbell Law Directory

*LOGAN,** Logan Co.

CHARLES T. BAILEY (AV)

Suite 304, Sears Building, P.O. Box 1717, 25601
Telephone: 304-752-4121

For full biographical listings, see the Martindale-Hubbell Law Directory

*MADISON,** Boone Co.

SHAFFER AND SHAFFER (AV)

330 State Street, P.O. Box 38, 25130
Telephone: 304-369-0511
Fax: 304-369-5431
Charleston, West Virginia Office: 1710 Bank One Center, P.O. Box 3973.
Telephone: 304-344-8716.
Fax: 304-342-1105.

MEMBERS OF FIRM

Harry G. Shaffer (1885-1971)
Harry G. Shaffer, Jr. (Retired)
Richard L. Theibert
James J. MacCallum
George D. Blizzard, II
Charles S. Piccirillo
Harry G. Shaffer, III (Resident, Charleston Office)
Anthony J. Cicconi (Resident, Charleston Office)
Norman W. White

ASSOCIATES

Edward L. Bullman
Timothy L. Mayo
L. Lee Javins, II

Representative Clients: Bank One, West Virginia, N.A., Boone; Armco Inc.; Westmoreland Coal Co.; State Farm Mutual Insurance Cos.; Nationwide Insurance Co.

For full biographical listings, see the Martindale-Hubbell Law Directory

*WHEELING,** Ohio Co.

SCHRADER, RECHT, BYRD, COMPANION & GURLEY (AV)

1000 Hawley Building, 1025 Main Street, P.O. Box 6336, 26003
Telephone: 304-233-3390
Fax: 304-233-2769
Martins Ferry, Ohio Office: 205 North Fifth Street, P.O. Box 309.
Telephone: 614-633-8976.
Fax: 614-633-0400.

PARTNERS

Henry S. Schrader (Retired)
Arthur M. Recht
Ray A. Byrd
James F. Companion
Terence M. Gurley
Frank X. Duff
Teresa Rieman-Camilletti
Yolonda G. Lambert
Patrick S. Casey
Sandra M. Chapman
Daniel P. Fry (Resident, Martins Ferry, Ohio Office)
James P. Mazzone

ASSOCIATES

Sandra K. Law
D. Kevin Coleman
Denise A. Jebbia
Edythe A. Nash
Robert G. McCoid
Denise D. Klug
Thomas E. Johnston

OF COUNSEL

James A. Byrum, Jr.

General Counsel: WesBanco Bank-Elm Grove.
Representative Clients: CIGNA Property and Casualty Cos.; Columbia Gas Transmission Corp.; Commercial Union Assurance Co.; Hazlett, Burt & Watson, Inc.; Stone & Thomas Department Stores; Transamerica Commercial Finance Corp.; Wheeling-Pittsburgh Steel Corp.

For full biographical listings, see the Martindale-Hubbell Law Directory

WISCONSIN

*APPLETON,** Outagamie Co.

MENN, NELSON, SHARRATT, TEETAERT & BEISENSTEIN, LTD. (AV)

(Formerly, Fulton, Menn & Nehs, Ltd.)
222 North Oneida Street, P.O. Box 785, 54912-0785
Telephone: 414-731-6631
FAX: 414-734-0981

Homer H. Benton (1886-1957)
Alfred C. Bosser (1890-1965)
Franklin L. Nehs (1922-1979)
David L. Fulton (1911-1985)
Glenn L. Sharratt (Retired)
John B. Menn
Peter S. Nelson
John R. Teetaert
Joseph J. Beisenstein
Mark R. Feldmann
Joseph A. Bielinski
Jonathan M. Menn
Douglas D. Hahn
Keith W. Kostecke
Robert N. Duimstra

(See Next Column)

MENN, NELSON, SHARRATT, TEETAERT & BEISENSTEIN LTD.—*Continued*

LEGAL SUPPORT PERSONNEL

Kathy J. Krause

Representative Clients: Bank One Appleton, NA; Evans Title Companies Inc.; Time Warner Entertainment Company LP.

For full biographical listings, see the Martindale-Hubbell Law Directory

*EAU CLAIRE,** Eau Claire Co.

WILCOX, WILCOX, DUPLESSIE, WESTERLUND & ENRIGHT (AV)

1030 Regis Court, P.O. Box 128, 54701
Telephone: 715-832-6645
Fax: 715-832-8438

MEMBERS OF FIRM

Roy P. Wilcox (1873-1946)
Francis J. Wilcox
Roy S. Wilcox
Richard D. Duplessie
William J. Westerlund
Daniel A. Enright
John F. Wilcox

Attorneys for: Aetna Insurance Group; Medical Protective Assn.; American Surety Co.; Viking Insurance Co.; American Mutual Liability Ins. Co.; Continental Cas. Co.; Farmers Insurance Group.

For full biographical listings, see the Martindale-Hubbell Law Directory

*ELKHORN,** Walworth Co.

SWEET & REDDY, S.C. (AV)

Inns of Court Building, 114 North Church Street, 53121
Telephone: 414-723-5480
Fax: 414-723-2180

Lowell E. Sweet
David M Reddy

For full biographical listings, see the Martindale-Hubbell Law Directory

LAKE GENEVA, Walworth Co.

BRADEN & OLSON (AV)

716 Wisconsin Street, P.O. Box 940, 53147
Telephone: 414-248-6636
Fax: 414-248-2901

Berwyn B. Braden
John O. Olson

Michael J. Rielly
Kurt T. Van Buskirk
Christine Tomas (Not admitted in WI)

For full biographical listings, see the Martindale-Hubbell Law Directory

MENOMONEE FALLS, Waukesha Co.

NIEBLER, PYZYK & WAGNER (AV)

River Court Center, N95 W16975 Richfield Way, P.O. Box 444, 53052-0444
Telephone: 414-251-5330
Fax: 414-251-1823

MEMBERS OF FIRM

John H. Niebler
Robert G. Pyzyk
Robert F. Klaver, Jr.
Roy E. Wagner

ASSOCIATE

Jynine A. Strand

OF COUNSEL

Chester J. Niebler

For full biographical listings, see the Martindale-Hubbell Law Directory

*MILWAUKEE,** Milwaukee Co.

DAVIS & KUELTHAU, S.C. (AV)

111 East Kilbourn Avenue, Suite 1400, 53202-6613
Telephone: 414-276-0200
Facsimile: 414-276-9369
Cable Address: "Shiplaw"

James A. Brindley
Scott E. Fiducci
James H. Gormley, Jr.
Robert E. Kuelthau
Daniel J. Minahan

Kenneth A. Kirley
Victor A. Lazzaretti
Brett K. Miller

For full biographical listings, see the Martindale-Hubbell Law Directory

GIBBS, ROPER, LOOTS & WILLIAMS, S.C. (AV)

735 North Water Street, 53202
Telephone: 414-273-7000
Fax: 414-273-7897

Thomas R. Streifender

(See Next Column)

William R. West

For Complete List of Firm Personnel, See General Section

For full biographical listings, see the Martindale-Hubbell Law Directory

MEISSNER & TIERNEY, S.C. (AV)

The Milwaukee Center, 111 East Kilbourn Avenue, 19th Floor, 53202-6622
Telephone: 414-273-1300
Facsimile: 414-273-5840

Paul F. Meissner
Joseph E. Tierney III
Dennis L. Fisher
Todd J. Mitchell
Thomas J. Nichols
Randal J. Brotherhood
Michael J. Cohen

Eric J. Klumb
Kenneth A. Iwinski
Steven R. Glaser

OF COUNSEL

Thomas E. Whipp

For full biographical listings, see the Martindale-Hubbell Law Directory

QUARLES & BRADY (AV)

411 East Wisconsin Avenue, 53202-4497
Telephone: 414-277-5000
Cable Address: "Lawdock"
Fax: 414-271-3552.
TWX: 910-262-3426
Madison, Wisconsin Office: Firstar Plaza, One South Pinckney Street, P.O. Box 2113.
Telephone: 608-251-5000.
Fax: 608-251-9166.
West Palm Beach, Florida Office: 222 Lakeview Avenue, 4th Floor.
Telephone: 407-653-5000.
Fax: 407-653-5333.
Naples, Florida Office: Barnett Center, 4501 Tamiami Trail North.
Telephone: 813-262-5959.
Fax: 813-434-4999.
Phoenix, Arizona Office: One Camelback Building, One East Camelback Road, Suite 400.
Telephone: 602-230-5500.
Fax: 602-230-5598.

MEMBERS OF FIRM
(ALPHABETICALLY BY YEAR OF ADMISSION TO BAR)

Arthur H. Laun, Jr.
John S. Sammond (Resident, West Palm Beach, Florida Office)
James Urdan
Roger P. Paulsen
Samuel J. Recht
Jeremy C. Shea (Resident, Madison Office)
P. Robert Fannin (Resident, Phoenix, Arizona Office)
Thomas E. Maloney (Resident, Naples, Florida Office)
David L. Petersen (Resident, West Palm Beach, Florida Office)
Lawrence J. Jost
Gerald E. Connolly
F. Joseph McMackin, III (Resident, Naples, Florida Office)
Robert T. Bailes (Resident, Phoenix, Arizona Office)
John W. Daniels, Jr.
Timothy G. Hains (Resident, Naples, Florida Office)
John H. Lhost
Roger K. Spencer (Resident, Phoenix, Arizona Office)
Ann M. Murphy
John A. Rothstein
Charles H. McMullen
Leo J. Salvatori (Resident, Naples, Florida Office)
David G. Beauchamp (Resident, Phoenix, Arizona Office)
Mary N. Fertl
Daniel L. Muchow (Resident, Phoenix, Arizona Office)
Michael D. Zeka

OF COUNSEL

Richard W. Cutler
Michael E. Crane (Not admitted in WI)

ASSOCIATES

Lynn Frances Chandler (Resident, Naples, Florida Office)
William G. Shofstall (Resident, West Palm Beach, Florida Office)
Ann K. Comer
Robert S. Bornhoft (Resident, Phoenix, Arizona Office)
Kevin A. Delorey (Resident, Madison Office)
Mary Z. Horton (Not admitted in WI; Resident, Phoenix, Arizona Office)
John D. Humphreville (Resident, Naples, Florida Office)
Scott L. Langlois
Joseph E. Puchner
N. (Norrie) Daroga
Susan A. Cerbins
Kevin A. Denti (Resident, Naples, Florida Office)
Michael J. Ostermeyer

For Complete List of Firm Personnel, See General Section

For full biographical listings, see the Martindale-Hubbell Law Directory

Milwaukee—Continued

REINHART, BOERNER, VAN DEUREN, NORRIS & RIESELBACH, S.C. (AV)

1000 North Water Street, P.O. Box 92900, 53202-0900
Telephone: 414-298-1000
Facsimile: 414-298-8097
Denver, Colorado Office: One Norwest Center, 1700 Lincoln Street, Suite 3725.
Telephone: 303-831-0909.
Fax: 303-831-4805.
Madison, Wisconsin Office: 7617 Mineral Point Road, 53701-2020.
Telephone: 608-283-7900.
Fax: 608-283-7919.
Washington, D.C. Office: 601 Pennsylvania Avenue, N.W., North Building, Suite 750.
Telephone: 202-393-3636.
Fax: 202-393-0796.

Allen N. Rieselbach — Michael H. Simpson
William R. Steinmetz — Bruce T. Block
John A. Erich — Jerome M. Janzer
Joseph J. Balistreri

William T. Shroyer — David M. Sanders
William R. Cummings — Jeffrey S. Rheeling
Deborah C. Tomczyk

For Complete List of Firm Personnel, See General Section

For full biographical listings, see the Martindale-Hubbell Law Directory

*WAUKESHA,** Waukesha Co.

CRAMER, MULTHAUF & HAMMES (AV)

1601 East Racine Avenue, P.O. Box 558, 53187
Telephone: 414-542-4278
Telecopier: 414-542-4270

MEMBERS OF FIRM

John E. Multhauf — Richard R. Kobriger
Peter J. Plaushines

Representative Client: Bielinski Bros. Builders, Inc.
Reference: Waukesha State Bank.

For Complete List of Firm Personnel, See General Section

For full biographical listings, see the Martindale-Hubbell Law Directory

WYOMING

*BUFFALO,** Johnson Co.

KIRVEN & KIRVEN, P.C. (AV)

104 Fort Street, P.O. Box 640, 82834
Telephone: 307-684-2248
Fax: 307-684-2242

William J. Kirven (Retired) — Dennis M. Kirven
Timothy J. Kirven

Nancy Zerr

Representative Clients: Texaco Inc.; Wyoming Bank and Trust Co.; Buffalo Federal Savings & Loan Assn.; Reeves Concrete Products; Gordon Ranch; Independent Insurance Agents of Wyoming; Powder River Corporation Reservoir.

For full biographical listings, see the Martindale-Hubbell Law Directory

OMOHUNDRO, PALMERLEE AND DURRANT (AV)

An Association of Attorneys
130 South Main Street, 82834
Telephone: 307-684-2207
Telecopier: 307-684-9364
Gillette, Wyoming Office: East Entrance, Suite 700, 201 West Lakeway Road.
Telephone: 307-682-7826.

William D. Omohundro (P.C.) — David F. Palmerlee
Sean P. Durrant

For full biographical listings, see the Martindale-Hubbell Law Directory

*CASPER,** Natrona Co.

BROWN & DREW (AV)

Casper Business Center, Suite 800, 123 West First Street, 82601-2486
Telephone: 307-234-1000
800-877-6755
Telefax: 307-265-8025

(See Next Column)

MEMBERS OF FIRM

Morris R. Massey — Donn J. McCall
Harry B. Durham, III — Thomas F. Reese
W. Thomas Sullins, II — Russell M. Blood
J. Kenneth Barbe

ASSOCIATES

Jon B. Huss — Courtney Robert Kepler
Drew A. Perkins

OF COUNSEL

B. J. Baker

Attorneys for: First Interstate Bank of Wyoming, N.A.; Norwest Bank Wyoming, N.A.; The CIT Group/Industrial Financing; Aetna Casualty & Surety Co.; The Doctor's Co.; MEDMARC; WOTCO, Inc.; Chevron USA; Chicago and NorthWestern Transportation Company.

For Complete List of Firm Personnel, See General Section

For full biographical listings, see the Martindale-Hubbell Law Directory

PUERTO RICO

SAN JUAN, San Juan Dist.

FIDDLER, GONZÁLEZ & RODRÍGUEZ

Chase Manhattan Bank Building (Hato Rey), P.O. Box 363507, 00936-3507
Telephone: 809-753-3113
Telecopier: 809-759-3123

MEMBERS OF FIRM

Aurelio Emanuelli-Belaval — Leopoldo J. Cabassa-Sauri
Raúl J. Vilá-Sellés

Representative Clients: The Chase Manhattan Bank, N.A.; The Equitable Life Assurance Society of the U.S.; Pfizer, Inc.; Merck & Co., Inc.; American Cyanamid Co.; Metropolitan Life Insurance Co.; Bacardi Corp.; Pace Membership Warehouse, Inc.; General Electric Company, Real Estate and Construction Operation; Interstate General.

For Complete List of Firm Personnel, See General Section

For full biographical listings, see the Martindale-Hubbell Law Directory

GOLDMAN ANTONETTI & CÓRDOVA

American International Plaza Fourteenth & Fifteenth Floors, 250 Muñoz Rivera Avenue (Hato Rey), P.O. Box 70364, 00936-0364
Telephone: 809-759-8000
Telecopiers: 809-767-9333 (Main)
809-767-9177 (Litigation Department)
809-767-8660 (Labor & Corporate Law Departments)
809-767-9325 (Tax & Environmental Law Departments)

MEMBERS OF FIRM

Thelma Rivera-Miranda — Francisco J. García-García

OF COUNSEL

Francisco de Jesús-Schuck

ASSOCIATES

Mercedes M. Barreras Soler — María Patricia Lake
Jose J. Ledesma Rodriguez

Representative Clients: Banque Paribas; Matsushita Electric of Puerto Rico, Inc.; AIG Condado Hotel Partnership; Normandie Limited Partnership; Cadillac Uniforms and Linen Supply.

For Complete List of Firm Personnel, See General Section

For full biographical listings, see the Martindale-Hubbell Law Directory

GONZALEZ & BENNAZAR

Capital Center Building South Tower - 9th Floor, Arterial Hostos Avenue (Hato Rey), 00918
Telephone: 809-754-9191
Fax: 809-754-9325

MEMBERS OF FIRM

Raul E. González Díaz — A. J. Bennazar-Zequeira

Representative Clients: Wyndham Hotels; Albors Housing; Federal Deposit Insurance Corp.; BWAC International; M & M Mars; G-Tech Corporation.

For Complete List of Firm Personnel, See General Section

For full biographical listings, see the Martindale-Hubbell Law Directory

JORGE R. JIMENEZ

Suite 807 Bankers Finance Tower, 654 Muñoz Rivera Avenue (Hato Rey), 00918
Telephone: 809-763-0106
Fax: 809-763-0574

For full biographical listings, see the Martindale-Hubbell Law Directory

San Juan—Continued

MÁRTINEZ ODELL & CALABRIA

Banco Popular Center, 16th Floor, (Hato Rey), P.O. Box 190998, 00919-0998
Telephone: 809-753-8914
Facsimile: 809-753-8402; 809-759-9075; 809-764-5664

MEMBERS OF FIRM

Luis E. Lopez Correa
Fanny Auz-Patiño
Luis Morales-Steinmann
Benjamín Hernández-Nieves

ASSOCIATES

Lucé Vela Gutiérrez
Arnaldo A. Mignucci-Giannoni
Jose David Medina-Rivera
Gloria M. Sierra-Enriquez

Representative Clients: A.T. & T. Corp.; Pepsi-Cola P.R. Bottling Co.; Banco Popular de Puerto Rico; I.T.T. Financial Corp.; John H. Harland Company of Puerto Rico, Inc.; Lutron Electronics Co., Inc.; Paine Webber, Inc.; Lotus Development Corp.; Western Digital.

For Complete List of Firm Personnel, See General Section

For full biographical listings, see the Martindale-Hubbell Law Directory

MELLADO & MELLADO-VILLARREAL

Suite 202, 165 Ponce de Leon Avenue, 00918
Telephone: 809-767-2600
Telecopier: 809-767-2645

Ramon Mellado-Gonzalez
Jairo Mellado-Villarreal

Representative Clients: Advanced Cellular Systems; Procesadora De Granos De Puerto Rico, Inc.; First Federal Savings Bank; Fanesco Internacional Bank; Progreso Internacional Bank; Caribe Federal Credit; P.E.D. Food Distributors; San Juan Realty, Inc.; Coulter Biochemical; Coulter Electronics Sales; Meyers Parking System, Inc.; Magla Products Corporation; San Juan Gas Co., Inc.

For Complete List of Firm Personnel, See General Section

For full biographical listings, see the Martindale-Hubbell Law Directory

O'NEILL & BORGES

10th Floor, Chase Manhattan Bank Building (Hato Rey), 254 Muñoz Rivera Avenue, 00918-1995
Telephone: 809-764-8181
Telecopier: 809-753-8944

MEMBERS OF FIRM

Eduardo E. Franklin
Juan Agustín Rivero

ASSOCIATES

Estela I. Vallés-Acosta
Eduardo J. Negrón

Representative Clients: Citibank, N.A.; Edison Brothers Stores, Inc.; ESS-ROC Materials, Inc.; Kmart Corporation; Kumagai Caribbean, Inc.; Lehman Brothers, Inc.; Levitt Homes Puerto Rico Inc.; Marriott Ownership Resorts, Inc.; Smith Barney Shearson, Inc.; Misener Marine, Inc.; The First National Bank of Boston; Wyndham Hotels.

For Complete List of Firm Personnel, See General Section

For full biographical listings, see the Martindale-Hubbell Law Directory

VIRGIN ISLANDS

*CHRISTIANSTED, ST. CROIX,** St. Croix

JEAN-ROBERT ALFRED

46B-47 King Street, 00820
Telephone: 809-773-2156
Telecopier: 809-773-4301

COUNSEL

Jane Wells Kleeger

For full biographical listings, see the Martindale-Hubbell Law Directory

*CHARLOTTE AMALIE, ST. THOMAS,** St. Thomas

BIRCH, DE JONGH & HINDELS

Poinsettia House at Bluebeards Castle, P.O. Box 1197, 00804
Telephone: 809-774-1100
Telefax: 809-774-7300
Other St. Thomas Office: Palm Passage, Charlotte Amalie, 00802.

MEMBERS OF FIRM

Everett B. Birch (1922-1987)
John P. de Jongh
James H. Hindels

ASSOCIATE

Stanley L. de Jongh

(See Next Column)

OF COUNSEL

Richard P. Farrelly

Representative Clients: Barclays Bank PLC; The Chase Manhattan Bank, N.A.; Citibank, N.A.; Ernst & Young; Corestates First Pennsylvania Bank; FNMA/FHLMC (Regional Counsel); Westinghouse Foreign Sales Corp.; Hess Oil Virgin Islands Corp.; Peat, Marwick, V.I.

For Complete List of Firm Personnel, See General Section

For full biographical listings, see the Martindale-Hubbell Law Directory

BORNN BORNN HANDY

No. 8 Norre Gade, P.O. Box 1500, 00804
Telephone: 809-774-1400
Fax: 809-774-9607

SENIOR PARTNER

Edith L. Bornn

PARTNER

David A. Bornn

ASSOCIATE

Tregenza A. Roach

References: Bank of Nova Scotia; Banco Popular de P.R., St. Thomas, U.S. Virgin Islands.

For Complete List of Firm Personnel, See General Section

For full biographical listings, see the Martindale-Hubbell Law Directory

GRUNERT STOUT BRUCH & MOORE

24-25 Kongensgade, P.O. Box 1030, 00804
Telephone: 809-774-1320
Fax: 809-774-7839

MEMBERS OF FIRM

John E. Stout
Susan Bruch Moorehead
Treston E. Moore

ASSOCIATES

Maryleen Thomas
H. Kevin Mart (Not admitted in VI)
Richard F. Taylor

OF COUNSEL

William L. Blum

For full biographical listings, see the Martindale-Hubbell Law Directory

CANADA
ALBERTA

*CALGARY,** Calgary Jud. Dist.

BENNETT JONES VERCHERE (AV)

4500 Bankers Hall East, 855-2nd Street S.W., T2P 4K7
Telephone: (403) 298-3100
Facsimile: (403) 265-7219
Edmonton, Alberta Office: 1000, 10035-105 Street.
Telephone: (403) 421-8133.
Facsimile: (403) 421-7951.
Toronto, Ontario Office: 3400 1 First Canadian Place. P.O. Box 130.
Telephone: (416) 863-1200.
Facsimile: (416) 863-1716.
Ottawa, Ontario Office: Suite 1800. 350 Alberta Street, Box 25, K1R 1A4.
Telephone: (613) 230-4935.
Facsimile: (613) 230-3836.
Montreal, Quebec Office: Suite 1600, 1 Place Ville Marie.
Telephone: (514) 871-1200.
Facsimile: (514) 871-8115.

MEMBER OF FIRM

Garry C. Johnson, Q.C.

For Complete List of Firm Personnel, See General Section

For full biographical listings, see the Martindale-Hubbell Law Directory

*EDMONTON,** Edmonton Jud. Dist.

PARLEE MCLAWS (AV)

15th Floor Manulife Place, 10180 101st Street, T5J 4K1
Telephone: 403-423-8500
Telecopier: 403-423-2870
Calgary, Alberta Office: 3400, Western Canadian Place, 707 - 8th Avenue, S.W.
Telephone: 403-294-7000.
Telecopier: 403-265-8263.

(See Next Column)

PARLEE MCLAWS, *Edmonton—Continued*

MEMBERS OF FIRM

C. H. Kerr, Q.C.
M. D. MacDonald
K. F. Bailey, Q.C.
R. B. Davison, Q.C.
F. R. Haldane
P. E. J. Curran
D. G. Finlay
J. K. McFadyen
R. C. Secord
D. L. Kennedy
D. C. Rolf
D. F. Pawlowski
A. A. Garber
R. P. James
D. C. Wintermute
J. L. Cairns
R. A. Newton, Q.C.
T. A. Cockrall, Q.C.
H. D. Montemurro
F. J. Niziol
R. W. Wilson
I. L. MacLachlan
R. O. Langley
R. G. McBean
J. T. Neilson
E. G. Rice
J. F. McGinnis
J. H. H. Hockin
G. W. Jaycock
M. J. K. Nikel
B. J. Curial
S. L. May
M. S. Poretti

ASSOCIATES

C. R. Head
A.W. Slemko
L. H. Hamdon
K.A. Smith
K. D. Fallis-Howell
D. S. Tam
J.W. McClure
F.H. Belzil
R.A. Renz
J.G. Paulson
K. E. Buss
B. L. Andriachuk
P. E. S. J. Kennedy
R. Feraco
R.J. Billingsley
N.B.R. Thompson
P. A. Shenher
I. C. Johnson
K.G. Koshman
D.D. Dubrule
G. T. Lund
W.D. Johnston
G. E. Flemming
K. P. Nayyer

For full biographical listings, see the Martindale-Hubbell Law Directory

CANADA BRITISH COLUMBIA

*VANCOUVER,** Vancouver Co.

LADNER DOWNS (AV)

900 Waterfront Centre, 200 Burrard Street, P.O. Box 48600, V7X 1T2
Telephone: 604-687-5744
Fax: 604-687-1415
Telex: 04-507553

MEMBERS OF FIRM AND ASSOCIATES

David K. Camp
Barry D. Chase
David P. L. Mydske
John L. Sampson
Mary Jo E. Campbell
Daniel B. McIntyre
George P. Reilly
Larry R. Sandrin
Rosanna Wong

Sandra D. Lloyd
F. Randolph Smith
David C.S. Longcroft
Matthew G. Watson

Representative Clients: Marathon Realty Company Limited; Grosvenor International Holdings Ltd.; CN Real Estate; B.C. Rail; Metropolitan Life Insurance Company; Confederation Life Insurance Company; OMERS (Ontario Municipal Employees Retirement Board); Bank of Montreal; Hong Kong Bank; Fort Nelson Indian Band.

For Complete List of Firm Personnel, See General Section

For full biographical listings, see the Martindale-Hubbell Law Directory

RUSSELL & DUMOULIN (AV)

2100-1075 West Georgia Street, V6E 3G2
Telephone: 604-631-3131
Fax: 604-631-3232
A Member of the national association of Borden DuMoulin Howard Gervais, comprising Russell & DuMoulin, Vancouver, British Columbia; Howard Mackie, Calgary, Alberta; Borden & Elliot, Toronto, Ontario; Mackenzie Gervais, Montreal, Quebec and Borden DuMoulin Howard Gervais, London, England.
Strategic Alliance with Perkins Coie with offices in Seattle, Spokane and Bellevue, Washington; Portland, Oregon; Anchorage, Alaska; Los Angeles, California; Washington, D.C.; Hong Kong and Taipei, Taiwan.
Represented in Hong Kong by Vincent T.K. Cheung, Yap & Co.

MEMBER OF FIRM

Donald M. Dalik

Representative Clients: Alcan Smelters & Chemicals Ltd.; The Bank of Nova Scotia; Canada Trust Co.; The Canada Life Assurance Co.; Honda Canada Inc.; IBM Canada Ltd.; Macmillan Bloedel Ltd.; Nissho Iwai Canada Ltd.; Vancouver Port Commission; Sun Life Assurance Company of Canada.

For Complete List of Firm Personnel, See General Section

For full biographical listings, see the Martindale-Hubbell Law Directory

CANADA NEW BRUNSWICK

*SAINT JOHN,** Saint John Co.

CLARK, DRUMMIE & COMPANY (AV)

40 Wellington Row, P.O. Box 6850 Station "A", E2L 4S3
Telephone: 506-633-3800
Telecopier (Automatic): 506-633-3811

MEMBERS OF FIRM

Donald F. MacGowan, Q.C.
Sherrie R. Boyd
Willard M. Jenkins
Donald J. Higgins

Reference: Royal Bank of Canada.

For Complete List of Firm Personnel, See General Section

For full biographical listings, see the Martindale-Hubbell Law Directory

CANADA NOVA SCOTIA

*HALIFAX,** Halifax Co.

MCINNES COOPER & ROBERTSON (AV)

1601 Lower Water Street, P.O. Box 730, B3J 2V1
Telephone: 902-425-6500
Fax: 902-425-6350
St. John's, Newfoundland Office: Suite 602, Scotia Centre, 235 Water Street, P.O. Box 547. A1C, 5K8.
Telephone: 709-726-9500.
Fax: 709-726-9550.

Lawrence J. Hayes, Q.C.
Peter J. E. McDonough, Q.C.
David B. Ritcey, Q.C.
David H. Reardon, Q.C.
Linda Lee Oland

ASSOCIATES

Brenda L. Rice
Bernard F. Miller

Attorneys for: Bank of Nova Scotia; Imperial Oil, Limited; Frank B. Hall & Co., Inc. (New York); American Steamship Owners Protection & Indemnity Association, Inc.; Coca-Cola, Ltd.; Scott Worldwide Inc.; Hong Kong Bank of Canada.

For Complete List of Firm Personnel, See General Section

For full biographical listings, see the Martindale-Hubbell Law Directory

CANADA ONTARIO

*TORONTO,** Regional Munic. of York

BORDEN & ELLIOT (AV)

Barristers & Solicitors
Scotia Plaza, 40 King Street West, M5H 3Y4
Telephone: 416-367-6000
Telecopier: 416-367-6749
Internet: @ borden.com
A Member of the national association of Borden DuMoulin Howard Gervais, comprising Borden & Elliot in Toronto, Ontario, Russell & DuMoulin in Vancouver, British Columbia, Howard, Mackie in Calgary, Alberta and Mackenzie Gervais in Montréal, Québec. Borden DuMoulin Howard Gervais also operates an office in London, England.

MEMBER AND ASSOCIATES

Morton G. Gross, Q.C.

For Complete List of Firm Personnel, See General Section

For full biographical listings, see the Martindale-Hubbell Law Directory

MCDONALD & HAYDEN (AV)

One Queen Street East Suite 1500, M5C 2Y3
Telephone: 416-364-3100
Telecopier: 416-601-4100

(See Next Column)

McDonald & Hayden—*Continued*

MEMBERS OF FIRM

John G. McDonald, Q.C. (1922-1993)
Lloyd D. Cadsby, Q.C.
Peter Reginald Hayden, Q.C.
David C. Nathanson, Q.C.
Marvin D. Demone
D. H. Jack
David R. Street
Clifford M. Goldlist
Wendy C. Posluns
David H. Goldman
Mark Adilman
Matthew R. Alter
Susan A. Goodeve
Karen Crombie
John D. Brunt
Kevin Cai
Adrienne Parrotta

For full biographical listings, see the Martindale-Hubbell Law Directory

CANADA QUEBEC

*MONTREAL,** Montreal Dist.

Byers Casgrain (AV)

A Member of McMillan Bull Casgrain
Suite 3900, 1 Place Ville-Marie, H3B 4M7
Telephone: 514-878-8800
Telecopier: 514-866-2241
Cable Address: "Magee"
Telex: 05-24195

Marc Bourgeois
Robert S. Carswell
Ray E. Lawson
Céline April
Alain Roberge
Daniel Garant
Charles R. Spector
Nicole Sirois
Ronald Audette

For Complete List of Firm Personnel, See General Section

For full biographical listings, see the Martindale-Hubbell Law Directory

Chait Amyot (AV)

Suite 1900, 1 Place Ville-Marie, H3B 2C3
Telephone: 514-879-1353
Fax: 514-879-1460

MEMBERS OF FIRM

Samuel Chait, Q.C. (1904-1982)
Nathaniel H. Salomon
Nahum Gelber, Q.C.
Arthur I. Bronstein
Bernard Reis
Gordon L. Echenberg
C. Ralph Lipper
Sandor J. Klein
David H. Kauffman
Normand Amyot
Daniel Lessard
André A. Lévesque
Ronald H. Levy
David G. Masse
Ronald L. Stein
Marc J. Rubin
Carol Cohen
Louis Samuel
André Giroux
Jeffrey F. Edwards
Virginia K. H. Lam
Eric Lalanne
Pierre Brossoit
Frederica Jacobs
Benoît Larose
Martin Tétreault
Martin Joyal
Jacynthe Charpentier
Martin Langelier
Anne Milot

For full biographical listings, see the Martindale-Hubbell Law Directory

McMaster Meighen (AV)

A General Partnership
7th Floor, 630 René-Lévesque Boulevard West, H3B 4H7
Telephone: 514-879-1212
Telecopier: 514-878-0605
Cable Address: "Cammerall"
Telex: "Cammerall MTL" 05-268637
Affiliated with Fraser & Beatty in Toronto, North York, Ottawa and Vancouver.

MEMBERS OF FIRM

Hubert Senécal
Norman A. Saibil
Janet Casey
Catherine Rakush
Timothy R. Carsley
Yves A. Dubois
Pierre Trudeau
Darren E. Graham McGuire

For Complete List of Firm Personnel, See General Section

For full biographical listings, see the Martindale-Hubbell Law Directory

CANADA SASKATCHEWAN

*SASKATOON,** Saskatoon Jud. Centre

McKercher, McKercher & Whitmore (AV)

374 Third Avenue, South, S7K 1M5
Telephone: 306-653-2000
Fax: 306-244-7335
Regina, Saskatchewan Office: 1000 - 1783 Hamilton Street.
Telephone: 306-352-7661.
Fax: 306-781-7113.

MEMBERS OF FIRM

Hon. Stewart McKercher, Q.C. (1893-1977)
D. S. McKercher, Q.C.
Peter A. Whitmore, Q.C. (Resident, Regina Office)
Brian W. Wilkinson
Lorne Larson
Leslie J. Dick Batten
Daniel B. Konkin
Douglas B. Richardson
Paul D. Grant

ASSOCIATES

Caroline M. K. Gorsalitz
Gordon S. Wyant
Deric B. Karolat
J. Denis Bonthoux

For Complete List of Firm Personnel, See General Section

For full biographical listings, see the Martindale-Hubbell Law Directory

SECURITIES LAW

ALABAMA

*BIRMINGHAM,** Jefferson Co.

Balch & Bingham (AV)

1710 Sixth Avenue North, P.O. Box 306, 35201
Telephone: 205-251-8100
Facsimile: 205-226-8798
Other Birmingham, Alabama Office: 1901 Sixth Avenue North, 35203.
Telephone: 205-251-8100.
Facsimile: 205-226-8799.
Montgomery, Alabama Office: The Winter Building, 2 Dexter Avenue, 36101.
Telephone: 205-834-6500.
Facsimile: 205-269-3115.
Huntsville, Alabama Office: Suite 810, 200 West Court Square, 35801.
Telephone: 205-551-0171.
Facsimile: 205-551-0174.
Washington, D.C. Office: Suite 800, 1101 Connecticut Avenue, N.W., 20036.
Telephone: 202-296-0387.
Facsimile: 202-452-8180.

MEMBERS OF FIRM

Walter M. Beale, Jr.
James F. Hughey, Jr.
John F. Mandt
T. Kurt Miller

ASSOCIATES

Gregory S. Curran
Randall D. McClanahan

Counsel for: Alabama Power Co.; Blue Cross and Blue Shield of Alabama; The Boeing Company; Brasfield & Gorrie, Inc.; Compass Bancshares, Inc.; Harbert Corp.; Kimberly-Clark Corp.; Southern Company Services, Inc.; Southern Research Institute; Vesta Insurance Group, Inc.

For Complete List of Firm Personnel, See General Section

For full biographical listings, see the Martindale-Hubbell Law Directory

Berkowitz, Lefkovits, Isom & Kushner, A Professional Corporation (AV)

1600 SouthTrust Tower, 420 North Twentieth Street, 35203
Telephone: 205-328-0480
Telecopier: 205-322-8007

Lee H. Zell
B. G. Minisman, Jr.
W. Clark Goodwin

J. Fred Kingren

Representative Clients: AlaTenn Resources, Inc.; AlaTenn Natural Gas Co.; B.A.S.S., Inc.; Hanna Steel Co., Inc.; Liberty Trouser Co., Inc.; Parisian, Inc.; Southern Pipe & Supply Co., Inc.

For Complete List of Firm Personnel, See General Section

For full biographical listings, see the Martindale-Hubbell Law Directory

Bradley, Arant, Rose & White (AV)

1400 Park Place Tower, 2001 Park Place, 35203
Telephone: 205-521-8000
Telex: 494-1324
Facsimile: 205-251-8611, 251-8665, 252-0264
Facsimile (Southtrust Office): 205-251-9915
Huntsville, Alabama Office: 200 Clinton Avenue West, Suite 900.
Telephone: 205-517-5100.
Facsimile: 205-533-5069.

MEMBERS OF FIRM

John P. Adams
Charles Larimore Whitaker
John K. Molen
John B. Grenier
Michael R. Pennington
Michael D. McKibben

ASSOCIATES

Denson Nauls Franklin III
J. Paul Compton, Jr.
Amy McNeer Tucker
Hall B, Bryant III
Paul D. Gilbert

For Complete List of Firm Personnel, See General Section

For full biographical listings, see the Martindale-Hubbell Law Directory

Corley, Moncus & Ward, P.C. (AV)

Suite 650, 2100 SouthBridge Parkway, 35209
Telephone: 205-879-5959
Telecopier: 205-879-5859

Claude McCain Moncus
James S. Ward
Gene W. Gray, Jr.
W. Lewis Garrison, Jr.
Ezra B. Perry, Jr.
Kathryn H. Sumrall

For Complete List of Firm Personnel, See General Section

For full biographical listings, see the Martindale-Hubbell Law Directory

Johnston, Barton, Proctor, Swedlaw & Naff (AV)

2900 AmSouth/Harbert Plaza, 1901 Sixth Avenue North, 35203-2618
Telephone: 205-458-9400
Telecopier: 205-458-9500

MEMBERS OF FIRM

Harvey Deramus (1904-1970)
Alfred M. Naff (1923-1993)
James C. Barton
G. Burns Proctor, Jr.
Sydney L. Lavender
Jerome K. Lanning
Don B. Long, Jr.
Charles L. Robinson
J. William Rose, Jr.
Gilbert E. Johnston, Jr.
David P. Whiteside, Jr.
Ralph H. Smith II
James C. Barton, Jr.
Thomas E. Walker
Anne P. Wheeler
Raymond P. Fitzpatrick, Jr.
Hollinger F. Barnard
William D. Jones III
David W. Proctor
Oscar M. Price III
W. Hill Sewell
Robert S. Vance, Jr.
Richard J. Brockman
Anthony A. Joseph

OF COUNSEL

Gilbert E. Johnston
Alfred Swedlaw
Alan W. Heldman

ASSOCIATES

William K. Hancock
James P. Pewitt
Scott Wells Ford
David M. Hunt
Lee M. Pope
Haskins W. Jones
James M. Parker, Jr.
Michael H. Johnson
Russell L. Irby, III
R. Scott Clark
Helen Kathryn Downs

General Counsel for: The Birmingham News Co.
Counsel for: General Motors Corp.; General Electric Capital Corp.; Goldome Credit Corp.

For full biographical listings, see the Martindale-Hubbell Law Directory

Lightfoot, Franklin, White & Lucas (AV)

300 Financial Center, 505 20th Street North, 35203-2706
Telephone: 205-581-0700
Facsimile: 205-581-0799

MEMBERS OF FIRM

Warren B. Lightfoot
Samuel H. Franklin
Mac M. Moorer

ASSOCIATE

S. Douglas Williams, Jr.

Counsel for: AT&T; Ford Motor Co.; Emerson Electric Co.; Monsanto Co.; Chrysler Corp.; Unocal Corp.; The Upjohn Co.; Bristol-Myers Squibb Co.; The Goodyear Tire & Rubber Co.; Mitsubishi Motor Sales of America, Inc.

For full biographical listings, see the Martindale-Hubbell Law Directory

Patrick & Lacy, P.C. (AV)

1201 Financial Center, 35203
Telephone: 205-323-5665
Telecopier: 205-324-6221

J. Vernon Patrick, Jr.
Alex S. Lacy
William M. Acker, III
Elizabeth N. Pitman
Joseph A. Cartee

For full biographical listings, see the Martindale-Hubbell Law Directory

Ritchie & Rediker, P.C. (AV)

312 North 23rd Street, 35203
Telephone: 205-251-1288
Fax: 205-324-7830

Thomas A. Ritchie
J. Michael Rediker
Carolyn L. Duncan
Thomas L. Krebs
David R. Donaldson
David J. Guin

Steven P. Gregory

Representative Clients: Teachers Retirement System of Alabama; State Employees Retirement System of Alabama; Wall Street Deli, Inc.; AmSouth Bank, N.A.; SouthTrust Bank of Alabama, N.A.; Union Bank & Trust Co.; Sterne, Agee & Leach, Inc.; The South Carolina National Bank.

For full biographical listings, see the Martindale-Hubbell Law Directory

*MOBILE,** Mobile Co.

MILLER, HAMILTON, SNIDER & ODOM, L.L.C. (AV)

254-256 State Street, P.O. Box 46, 36601
Telephone: 334-432-1414
Telecopier: 334-433-4106
Montgomery, Alabama Office: Suite 802, One Commerce Street.
Telephone: 205-834-5550.
Telecopier: 205-265-4533.
Washington, D.C. Office: Miller, Hamilton, Snider, Odom & Bridgeman, L.L.C., Suite 1150, 1747 Pennsylvania Avenue, N.W.
Telephone: 202-429-9223.
Telecopier: 202-293-2068.

MEMBERS OF FIRM

Ronald A. Snider
Michael D. Waters (Resident Partner, Montgomery Office)
Jerome E. Speegle

ASSOCIATE

M. Stephen Dampier

Representative Clients: The Colonial BancGroup, Inc.; Colonial Mortgage Co.; Chase Manhattan Bank, N.A.; The Mitchell Co.; Poole Truck Line, Inc.; Brittania Airways, Ltd. (U.K.); Air Europe (Italy); K-Mart Corporation; K & B Alabama Corp.; Ford Consumer Finance Company, Inc.

For Complete List of Firm Personnel, See General Section

For full biographical listings, see the Martindale-Hubbell Law Directory

ARIZONA

*PHOENIX,** Maricopa Co.

FENNEMORE CRAIG, A PROFESSIONAL CORPORATION (AV)

Two North Central, Suite 2200, 85004
Telephone: 602-257-8700
Fax: 602-257-8527
Scottsdale, Arizona Office: 6263 North Scottsdale Road, Suite 290, 85250.
Telephone: 602-257-5400.
Fax: 602-945-4932.
Tucson, Arizona Office: One South Church Avenue, Suite 1030, 85701.
Telephone: 602-624-9312.
Fax: 602-882-7383.

F. Pendleton Gaines, III
Robert J. Hackett
Mark A. Nesvig
William L. Thorpe
Mark R. Herriot
Karen Ciupak McConnell
Janet W. Lord

W. T. Eggleston, Jr.
Karen Rettig Rogers

Representative Clients: ASARCO Incorporated; AT&T Communications; Bridgestone/Firestone, Inc.; Catellus Development Corp.; Citibank (Arizona); First Interstate Bank of Arizona; GIANT Industries; Phelps Dodge Corporation; The Atchison, Topeka & Santa Fe Railway, Co.; US WEST Communications.

For Complete List of Firm Personnel, See General Section

For full biographical listings, see the Martindale-Hubbell Law Directory

GALBUT & ASSOCIATES, A PROFESSIONAL CORPORATION (AV)

Camelback Esplanade, Suite 1020, 2425 East Camelback Road, 85016
Telephone: 602-955-1455
Fax: 602-955-1585

Martin R. Galbut
Paul A. Conant
Brian J. Schulman

For full biographical listings, see the Martindale-Hubbell Law Directory

JENNINGS, STROUSS AND SALMON, P.L.C. (AV)

A Professional Limited Liability Company
One Renaissance Square, Two North Central, 85004-2393
Telephone: 602-262-5911
Fax: 602-253-3255

I. Douglas Dunipace
David L. White
Donald J. Oppenheim
Anne L. Kleindienst

For Complete List of Firm Personnel, See General Section

For full biographical listings, see the Martindale-Hubbell Law Directory

KIMERER, LAVELLE, HAY & HOOD, P.L.C. (AV)

2715 North Third Street, 85004
Telephone: 602-279-5900
FAX: 602-264-5566

(See Next Column)

John L. Hay

For Complete List of Firm Personnel, See General Section

For full biographical listings, see the Martindale-Hubbell Law Directory

JOHN S. LANCY & ASSOCIATES A PROFESSIONAL CORPORATION (AV)

Suite 600, 2425 East Camelback Road, 85016
Telephone: 602-381-6555
Fax: 602-381-6560

John S. Lancy
Steven W. Bienstock

For full biographical listings, see the Martindale-Hubbell Law Directory

LEWIS AND ROCA (AV)

A Partnership including Professional Corporations
40 North Central Avenue, 85004-4429
Telephone: 602-262-5311
Fax: 602-262-5747
Tucson, Arizona Office: One South Church Avenue, Suite 700.
Telephone: 602-622-2090.
Fax: 602-622-3088.

MEMBERS OF FIRM

Kevin L. Olson
Scott DeWald
David M. Bixby
Bryant D. Barber

ASSOCIATES

Kevin G. Hunter
Julie M. Arvo MacKenzie

Representative Clients: MarkAir, Inc. (General Counsel); Rockford Corporation; Samaritan Health System.

For Complete List of Firm Personnel, See General Section

For full biographical listings, see the Martindale-Hubbell Law Directory

MEYER, HENDRICKS, VICTOR, OSBORN & MALEDON, A PROFESSIONAL ASSOCIATION (AV)

2929 North Central Avenue Suite 2100, 85012-2794
Telephone: 602-640-9000
Facsimile: (24 Hrs.) 602-640-9050
Mailing Address: P.O. Box 33449, 85067-3449,

David Victor
Jones Osborn II
Thomas H. Curzon
Gary A. Gotto
William M. Hardin
Michelle M. Matiski
Christopher D. Johnson
Catherine R. Hardwick

Bradley S. Paulson
Christine A. Dupnik

Reference: Bank One Arizona, NA.

For Complete List of Firm Personnel, See General Section

For full biographical listings, see the Martindale-Hubbell Law Directory

O'CONNOR, CAVANAGH, ANDERSON, WESTOVER, KILLINGSWORTH & BESHEARS, A PROFESSIONAL ASSOCIATION (AV)

One East Camelback Road, Suite 1100, 85012-1656
Telephone: 602-263-2400
FAX: 602-263-2900
Sun City, Arizona Office: 13250 North Del Webb Boulevard, Suite B, 85351.
Telephone: 602-263-2808.
FAX: 602-933-3100.
Tucson, Arizona Office: Suite 2200, One South Church Avenue, 85701.
Telephone: 602-882-8912.
FAX: 602-624-9564.
Nogales, Arizona Office: 1827 North Mastick Way, 85621.
Telephone: 602-761-4215.
FAX: 602-761-3505.

Robert S. Kant
Richard B. Stagg
Paul J. Roshka, Jr.
Jean E. Harris
Michelle S. Monserez

Jere M. Friedman (Not admitted in AZ)
Lisa R. Tsiolis

OF COUNSEL

Sara R. Ziskin

Representative Clients: SecurNet Mortgage Securities Corporation I; American Southwest Financial Corporation; Action Performance Companies; Cerprobe Corporation; Main Street and Main Incorporated; Microchip Technology Incorporated; Homeplex Mortgage Investments Corporation; ASR Investments Corporation; Three-Five Systems, Inc.; Rural/Metro Corporation.

For Complete List of Firm Personnel, See General Section

For full biographical listings, see the Martindale-Hubbell Law Directory

Phoenix—Continued

Streich Lang, A Professional Association (AV)

Renaissance One, Two N. Central Avenue, 85004-2391
Telephone: 602-229-5200
Fax: 602-229-5690
Tucson, Arizona Office: One S. Church Avenue, Suite 1700.
Telephone: 602-770-8700.
Fax: 602-623-2518.
Las Vegas, Nevada Affiliated Office: Dawson & Associates, 3800 Howard Hughes Parkway, Suite 1500.
Telephone: 702-792-2727.
Fax: 702-792-2676.
Los Angeles, California Office: 444 S. Flower Street, Suite 1530.
Telephone: 213-896-0484.

Don P. Martin
Deana S. Peck
James A. Ryan

Representative Clients: Allied-Signal Aerospace Company; America West Airlines, Inc.; Atlantic Richfield Co.; Chicago Title; First Interstate Bank of Arizona, N.A.; Magma Copper Co.; Motorola, Inc.; Phelps Dodge Development Corp.; TRW Inc.; The Travelers Companies.

For Complete List of Firm Personnel, See General Section

For full biographical listings, see the Martindale-Hubbell Law Directory

*TUCSON,** Pima Co.

O'Connor, Cavanagh, Anderson, Westover, Killingsworth & Beshears, A Professional Association (AV)

Suite 2200 One South Church Avenue, 85701-1621
Telephone: 602-882-8912
FAX: 602-624-9564
Phoenix, Arizona Office: One East Camelback Road, Suite 1100, 85012.
Telephone: 602-263-2400.
FAX: 602-263-2900.
Sun City, Arizona Office: 13250 North Del Webb Boulevard, Suite B, 85351.
Telephone: 602-263-2808.
FAX: 602-933-3100.
Nogales, Arizona Office: 1827 North Mastick Way, 85621.
Telephone: 602-761-4215.
FAX: 602-761-3505.

Thomas M. Pace
Bruce R. Heurlin

Gregory E. Good

Representative Client: Jeffco, Inc.
Reference: Citibank.

For Complete List of Firm Personnel, See General Section

For full biographical listings, see the Martindale-Hubbell Law Directory

ARKANSAS

*LITTLE ROCK,** Pulaski Co.

Allen Law Firm, A Professional Corporation (AV)

950 Centre Place, 212 Center Street, 72201
Telephone: 501-374-7100
Telecopier: 501-374-1611

H. William Allen

Sandra E. Jackson

Representative Clients: Worthen National Bank of Arkansas; Colonia Insurance Co.; Shoney's Inc.; Miller Brewing Co.; Garlock, Inc.

For full biographical listings, see the Martindale-Hubbell Law Directory

Richard C. Downing, P.A. (AV)

Lafayette Building, Suite 750, 523 South Louisiana, 72201
Telephone: 501-372-2066
FAX: 501-376-6420

Richard C. Downing

For full biographical listings, see the Martindale-Hubbell Law Directory

Friday, Eldredge & Clark (AV)

A Partnership including Professional Associations
Formerly, Smith, Williams, Friday, Eldredge & Clark
2000 First Commercial Building, 400 West Capitol, 72201-3493
Telephone: 501-376-2011
Telecopier: 501-376-2147; 376-6369

(See Next Column)

MEMBERS OF FIRM

Paul B. Benham, III, (P.A.)
Robert S. Shafer (P.A.)
Larry W. Burks (P.A.)
Thomas N. Rose (P.A.)
John Clayton Randolph (P.A.)

ASSOCIATES

Jeffrey H. Moore
Allison Graves Bazzel

Representative Clients: Arkansas Power & Light Co.; Dillard Department Stores, Inc.; Acxiom Corp.; First Commercial Corp.; Entergy Corp.; Union Pacific Railroad; Browning Arms Co.; Phillips Cos., Inc.; Liberty Mutual Ins. Co.; St. Paul Fire and Marine Ins. Co.

For Complete List of Firm Personnel, See General Section

For full biographical listings, see the Martindale-Hubbell Law Directory

Hilburn, Calhoon, Harper, Pruniski & Calhoun, Ltd. (AV)

P.O. Box 1256, 72203-1256
Telephone: 501-372-0110
FAX: 501-372-2029
North Little Rock, Arkansas Office: Eighth Floor, The Twin City Bank Building, One Riverfront Place, P.O. Box 5551, 72119.
Telephone: 501-372-0110.
FAX: 501-372-2029.

John E. Pruniski, III
Scott E. Daniel

Representative Clients: The Twin City Bank; Merrill Lynch Pierce Fenner & Smith, Inc.; Smith Barney Shearson, Inc.

For Complete List of Firm Personnel, See General Section

For full biographical listings, see the Martindale-Hubbell Law Directory

Hoover & Storey (AV)

111 Center Street, 11th Floor, 72201-4445
Telephone: 501-376-8500
Facsimile: 501-372-3255

MEMBERS OF FIRM

Paul W. Hoover, Jr.
William P. Dougherty
O. H. Storey, III
Max C. Mehlburger
John Kooistra, III
Joyce Bradley Babin
Lawrence Joseph Brady
Herbert W. Kell, Jr.
Letty McAdams

For full biographical listings, see the Martindale-Hubbell Law Directory

Ivester, Skinner & Camp, P.A. (AV)

Suite 1200, 111 Center Street, 72201
Telephone: 501-376-7788
FAX: 501-376-8536

Hermann Ivester
Laura G. Wiltshire
H. Edward Skinner
Mildred H. Hansen
Charles R. Camp
Valerie F. Boyce
Wayne B. Ball
Todd A. Lewellen
Randal B. Frazier
Stan D. Smith
Robert Keller Jackson
S. Scott Luton

For full biographical listings, see the Martindale-Hubbell Law Directory

Williams & Anderson (AV)

Twenty-Second Floor, 111 Center Street, 72201
Telephone: 501-372-0800
FAX: 501-372-6453

MEMBERS OF FIRM

Peter G. Kumpe
J. Leon Holmes

Representative Clients: Arkansas Development Finance Authority; Coregis; Dean Witter Reynolds Inc.; Entergy Power, Inc.; Little Rock Newspapers, Inc. d/b/a Arkansas Democrat-Gazette; Texaco Inc.; Roman Catholic Diocese of Little Rock; Transport Indemnity Insurance Co.; Wal-Mart Stores, Inc.

For Complete List of Firm Personnel, See General Section

For full biographical listings, see the Martindale-Hubbell Law Directory

Wright & Bonds (AV)

Centre Place Suite 900, 212 Center Street, 72201
Telephone: 501-376-2500
Fax: 501-376-7826

MEMBERS OF FIRM

Edward L. Wright
Barbara P. Bonds

For full biographical listings, see the Martindale-Hubbell Law Directory

CALIFORNIA

BEVERLY HILLS, Los Angeles Co.

ERVIN, COHEN & JESSUP (AV)

A Partnership including Professional Corporations
9401 Wilshire Boulevard, 90212-2974
Telephone: 310-273-6333
Facsimile: 310-859-2325

MEMBERS OF FIRM

W. Edgar Jessup, Jr.
Bertram K. Massing
Gary J. Freedman (P.C.)
David R. Eandi
E. A. (Stacey) Olliff III
J. Richard Griggs
Kenneth A. Luer

ASSOCIATES

Howard Z. Berman
Darcy L. Honig

For Complete List of Firm Personnel, See General Section

For full biographical listings, see the Martindale-Hubbell Law Directory

COSTA MESA, Orange Co.

COULOMBE KOTTKE & KING, A PROFESSIONAL CORPORATION (AV)

Comerica Bank Tower, 611 Anton Boulevard, Suite 1260, P.O. Box 2410, 92628-2410
Telephone: 714-540-1234
Fax: 714-754-0808; 714-754-0707

Ronald B. Coulombe
Jon S. Kottke
Raymond King

COUNSEL

Mary J. Swanson
Roy B. Woolsey

LEGAL SUPPORT PERSONNEL

PARALEGALS

Karen M. Carrillo
Laura A. Bieser
Vicky M. Pearson

LEGAL ADMINISTRATOR

Sheila O. Elpern

For full biographical listings, see the Martindale-Hubbell Law Directory

*LOS ANGELES,** Los Angeles Co.

MICHAEL A. BERTZ (AV)

Suite 2400, 1801 Century Park East, 90067
Telephone: 310-277-2811
Fax: 310-277-2914

For full biographical listings, see the Martindale-Hubbell Law Directory

JOHN A. CALFAS A PROFESSIONAL CORPORATION (AV)

Suite 1920, 11601 Wilshire Boulevard, 90025
Telephone: 310-477-1920
FAX: 310-477-7132

John A. Calfas

For full biographical listings, see the Martindale-Hubbell Law Directory

CLARK & TREVITHICK, A PROFESSIONAL CORPORATION (AV)

800 Wilshire Boulevard, 12th Floor, 90017
Telephone: 213-629-5700
Telecopier: 213-624-9441

Donald P. Clark
Alexander C. McGilvray, Jr.
Kevin P. Fiore
Michael K. Wofford
Brent A. Reinke

References: Wells Fargo Bank (Los Angeles Main Office); National Bank of California.

For Complete List of Firm Personnel, See General Section

For full biographical listings, see the Martindale-Hubbell Law Directory

CORINBLIT & SELTZER, A PROFESSIONAL CORPORATION (AV)

Suite 820 Wilshire Park Place, 3700 Wilshire Boulevard, 90010-3085
Telephone: 213-380-4200
Telecopier: 213-385-7503; 385-4560

Marc M. Seltzer

OF COUNSEL

Jack Corinblit
Earl P. Willens

(See Next Column)

Gretchen M. Nelson
Christina A. Snyder
George A. Shohet

Reference: Bank of America (Wilshire & Harvard Office).

For full biographical listings, see the Martindale-Hubbell Law Directory

GOLBERT KIMBALL & WEINER (AV)

555 South Flower Street Suite 2800, 90071
Telephone: 213-891-9641
Telecopier: 213-623-6130

Albert S. Golbert
George Kimball
Jeffrey M. Weiner

ASSOCIATES

Andrew H. Kopkin
Matthew F. Maccoby

For full biographical listings, see the Martindale-Hubbell Law Directory

MATTHIAS & BERG (AV)

Seventh Floor, 515 South Flower Street, 90071
Telephone: 213-895-4200
Telecopier: 213-895-4058

Michael R. Matthias
Jeffrey P. Berg
Stuart R. Singer
Kenneth M. H. Hoff

Representative Clients: N-Viro Recovery, Inc.; Supercart International, Inc.; Mexalit, S.A.; Allstar Inns; Chatsworth Products, Inc.; International Meta Systems, Inc.; MedGroup, Inc.; Palm Springs Golf Company, Inc.; Residential Resources, Inc.
Reference: First Professional Bank.

For full biographical listings, see the Martindale-Hubbell Law Directory

NEWPORT BEACH, Orange Co.

KRISTIN M. CANO (AV)

One Corporate Plaza, 92660
Telephone: 714-759-1505
FAX: 714-640-9535

For full biographical listings, see the Martindale-Hubbell Law Directory

*OAKLAND,** Alameda Co.

PEZZOLA & REINKE, A PROFESSIONAL CORPORATION (AV)

Suite 1300, Lake Merritt Plaza, 1999 Harrison Street, 94612
Telephone: 510-839-1350
Telecopier: 510-834-7440
San Francisco, California Office: 50 California Street, Suite 470. 94111. *Telephone:* 415-989-9710.

Stephen P. Pezzola
Donald C. Reinke
Thomas A. Maier
Thomas C. Armstrong
Bruce D. Whitley

OF COUNSEL

Robert E. Krebs

LEGAL SUPPORT PERSONNEL

Loretta H. Hintz
Mary A. Fitzpatrick

For full biographical listings, see the Martindale-Hubbell Law Directory

PALO ALTO, Santa Clara Co.

FTHENAKIS & VOLK (AV)

540 University Avenue, Suite 300, 94301
Telephone: 415-326-1397
Telecopier: 415-326-3203

MEMBERS OF FIRM

Basil P. Fthenakis
John D. Volk

ASSOCIATE

Oliver P. Colvin

For full biographical listings, see the Martindale-Hubbell Law Directory

CHRISTOPHER REAM (AV)

1717 Embarcadero Road, 94303
Telephone: 415-424-0821
Facsimile: 415-857-1288

For full biographical listings, see the Martindale-Hubbell Law Directory

*SAN DIEGO,** San Diego Co.

FERRIS & BRITTON, A PROFESSIONAL CORPORATION (AV)

1600 First National Bank Center, 401 West A Street, 92101
Telephone: 619-233-3131
Fax: 619-232-9316

(See Next Column)

FERRIS & BRITTON A PROFESSIONAL CORPORATION—*Continued*

Alfred G. Ferris | Harry J. Proctor
Pauline H. G. Getz

Representative Clients: Immuno Pharmaceutics, Inc.; Invitrogen Corporation; Ad Com Information Systems; Global Wireless Communications; Phase Metrics, Inc.; Receptors, Inc.

For Complete List of Firm Personnel, See General Section

For full biographical listings, see the Martindale-Hubbell Law Directory

WEINTRAUB & ASSOCIATES, A PROFESSIONAL LAW CORPORATION (AV)

The Plaza La Jolla Village, 4320 La Jolla Village Drive, Suite 270, 92122-1233
Telephone: 619-535-1444
FAX: 619-535-1447

Richard A. Weintraub | Mark T. Mauerman

OF COUNSEL

Marvin D. Brody (Not admitted in CA)

For full biographical listings, see the Martindale-Hubbell Law Directory

*SAN FRANCISCO,** San Francisco Co.

EWELL & LEVY (AV)

351 California Street, 94104-2501
Telephone: 415-788-6600
Fax: 415-433-7311

Arthur D. Levy | Gary Ewell

OF COUNSEL

Scott H. Miller | Theresa R. Owens

For full biographical listings, see the Martindale-Hubbell Law Directory

FLEISCHMANN & FLEISCHMANN (AV)

650 California Street, Suite 2550, 94108-2606
Telephone: 415-981-0140
FAX: 415-788-6234

MEMBERS OF FIRM

Hartly Fleischmann | Roger Justice Fleischmann

Stella J. Kim | Mark S. Molina

OF COUNSEL

Grace C. Shohet

LEGAL SUPPORT PERSONNEL

Lissa Dirrim

Representative Clients: Community Psychiatric Centers; Vivra, Inc.

For full biographical listings, see the Martindale-Hubbell Law Directory

GOLD & BENNETT, A PROFESSIONAL LAW CORPORATION (AV)

595 Market Street, Suite 2300, 94105
Telephone: 415-777-2230
Fax: 415-777-5189

Paul F. Bennett | Solomon B. Cera

George S. Trevor | Marc Rosner
Glenn MacRae Goffin | Robert A. Jigarjian
Gregory C. Moore | B. F. Pierce Gore

For full biographical listings, see the Martindale-Hubbell Law Directory

LIEFF, CABRASER & HEIMANN (AV)

Embarcadero Center West, 30th Floor, 275 Battery Street, 94111
Telephone: 415-956-1000
Telecopier: 415-956-1008

Robert L. Lieff | Karen E. Karpen
Elizabeth J. Cabraser | Michael F. Ram
Richard M. Heimann | William M. Audet
William Bernstein | Joseph R. Saveri
William B. Hirsch | Steven E. Fineman
James M. Finberg | Donald C. Arbitblit
Robert J. Nelson

Kristine E. Bailey | Jacqueline E. Mottek
Suzanne A. Barr | Kimberly W. Pate
Kelly M. Dermody | Melanie M. Piech
Deborah A. Kemp | Morris A. Ratner
Anthony K. Lee | Rhonda L. Woo

For full biographical listings, see the Martindale-Hubbell Law Directory

MANWELL & MILTON (AV)

101 California Street, 37th Floor, 94111
Telephone: 415-362-2375
Telecopier: 415-362-1010

Edmund R. Manwell | Denise B. Milton

ASSOCIATES

Mari C. Siebold | Kevin M. Walsh
Matthew M. Ogburn

For full biographical listings, see the Martindale-Hubbell Law Directory

ROSEN, BIEN & ASARO (AV)

Eighth Floor, 155 Montgomery Street, 94104
Telephone: 415-433-6830
Fax: 415-433-7104

Sanford Jay Rosen | Michael W. Bien
Andrea G. Asaro

Stephen M. Liacouras | Mary Ann Cryan (Not admitted in CA)
Hilary A. Fox | Donna Petrine
Thomas Nolan

For full biographical listings, see the Martindale-Hubbell Law Directory

SAVERI AND SAVERI, A PROFESSIONAL CORPORATION (AV)

41st Floor, Spear Street Tower, One Market Plaza, 94105-1001
Telephone: 415-243-4005
Fax: 415-243-4009

Richard Saveri | Guido Saveri

OF COUNSEL

John A. Kithas

For full biographical listings, see the Martindale-Hubbell Law Directory

TORRANCE, Los Angeles Co.

PETILLON & HANSEN (AV)

An Association of Professional Corporations
1260 Union Bank Tower, 21515 Hawthorne Boulevard, 90503
Telephone: 310-543-0500
Fax: 310-543-0550

Lee R. Petillon | Grant L. Simmons
Richard K. Hansen | Raymond J. Seto
Mark T. Hiraide

For full biographical listings, see the Martindale-Hubbell Law Directory

COLORADO

*DENVER,** Denver Co.

BEARMAN TALESNICK & CLOWDUS, PROFESSIONAL CORPORATION (AV)

1200 Seventeenth Street, Suite 2600, 80202-5826
Telephone: 303-572-6500
Facsimile: 303-572-6511

Alan L. Talesnick | Martha S. Nachman
Robert M. Bearman | Francis B. Barron

Representative Clients: Antennas America, Inc.; Barrett Resources Corporation; Chembio Diagnostic Systems, Inc.; Communications World International, Inc.; Specialized Computer Solutions, Inc.; USMX, Inc.

For full biographical listings, see the Martindale-Hubbell Law Directory

BERLINER ZISSER WALTER & GALLEGOS, P.C. (AV)

One Norwest Center, 1700 Lincoln Street, Suite 4700, 80203-4547
Telephone: 303-830-1700
Facsimile: 303-830-0863

Martin M. Berliner | David C. Roos
David A. Zisser | Larry D. Gallegos
Robert W. Walter | Molly K. Myer

OF COUNSEL

Phillip C. Gans

For full biographical listings, see the Martindale-Hubbell Law Directory

BREGA & WINTERS, P.C. (AV)

One Norwest Center, 1700 Lincoln Street, Suite 2222, 80203
Telephone: 303-866-9400
FAX: 303-861-9109
Greeley, Colorado Office: 1100 Tenth Street, Suite 402, 80631.
Telephone: 303-352-4805.
Fax: 303-352-6547.

(See Next Column)

BREGA & WINTERS P.C., *Denver—Continued*

James W. Bain	Brian A. Magoon
Thomas D. Birge	Loren L. Mall
Charles F. Brega	Pamela A. Shaddock (Resident, Greeley Office)
Robert R. Dormer	Jay John Schnell
Robert C. Kaufman	Jerry D. Winters (Resident, Greeley Office)
Ronald S. Loser	

Mark J. Appleton	Cathryn B. Mayers
Wesley B. Howard, Jr.	Carla B. Minckley
Jennifer G. Krolik	Nathan D. Simmons
Bradley D. Laue (Resident, Greeley Office)	Scott L. Terrell

OF COUNSEL

Mark Spitalnik

For full biographical listings, see the Martindale-Hubbell Law Directory

FRIEDLOB SANDERSON RASKIN PAULSON & TOURTILLOTT (AV)

A Partnership of Professional Corporations
1400 Glenarm Place, 80202-5099
Telephone: 303-571-1400
Fax: 303-595-3159; 303-595-3970

Raymond L. Friedlob	Herrick K. Lidstone, Jr.
Gerald Raskin	Mary M. Maikoetter

John W. Kellogg

For full biographical listings, see the Martindale-Hubbell Law Directory

HOLME ROBERTS & OWEN LLC (AV)

Suite 4100, 1700 Lincoln, 80203
Telephone: 303-861-7000
Telex: 45-4460
Telecopier: 303-866-0200
Boulder, Colorado Office: Suite 400, 1401 Pearl Street.
Telephone: 303-444-5955.
Telecopier: 303-444-1063.
Colorado Springs, Colorado Office: Suite 1300, 90 South Cascade Avenue.
Telephone: 719-473-3800.
Telecopier: 719-633-1518.
Salt Lake City, Utah Office: Suite 1100, 111 East Broadway.
Telephone: 801-521-5800.
Telecopier: 801-521-9639.
London, England Office: 4th Floor, Mellier House, 26a Albemarle Street.
Telephone: 44-171-499-8776.
Telecopier: 44-171-499-7769.
Moscow, Russia Office: 14 Krivokolenny Pr., Suite 30, 101000.
Telephone: 095-925-7816.
Telecopier: 095-923-2726.

MEMBERS OF FIRM

James C. Owen Jr.	Douglas R. Wright
Joseph W. Morrisey, Jr.	Francis R. Wheeler
W. Dean Salter	Martha Dugan Rehm
Thomas A. Richardson	John F. Knoeckel
Jeffrey A. Chase	Garth B. Jensen
Nick Nimmo	Wm. Kelly Nash (Salt Lake City Office)

OF COUNSEL

Harold S. Bloomenthal

ASSOCIATES

Steven A. Cohen	Paul G. Thompson
Robert J. Kaukol (Colorado Springs Office)	

For Complete List of Firm Personnel, See General Section

For full biographical listings, see the Martindale-Hubbell Law Directory

HOPPER AND KANOUFF, A PROFESSIONAL CORPORATION (AV)

Suite 200, 1610 Wynkoop Street, 80202
Telephone: 303-892-6000
Fax: 303-892-0457

George W. Hopper (1930-1986)	Dennis A. Graham
John P. Kanouff	Cameron J. Syke
Thomas S. Smith	Douglas R. Ferguson
Alan W. Peryam	Gene R. Thornton
Ward E. Terry, Jr.	James Rollin Miller, Jr.
Kim I. McCullough	Michael L. Glaser

Victor M. Morales	K. Harsha Krishnan
Randy E. Dunn	Lynne M. Hanson
Paul R. Wood	Michael D. Murphy
Annita M. Menogan	Garrett M. Tuttle
Harold R. Bruno, III	Darren J. Warner (Not admitted in CO)

(See Next Column)

OF COUNSEL

Jan B. Delbridge-Graham	Joseph P. Benkert

Reference: Colorado National Bank.

For full biographical listings, see the Martindale-Hubbell Law Directory

KRYS BOYLE GOLZ REICH FREEDMAN BEAN & SCOTT, P.C. (AV)

Dominion Plaza, Suite 2700 South Tower 600 Seventeenth Street, 80202
Telephone: 303-893-2300
Facsimile: 303-893-2882

Thomas Boyle	Stanley F. Freedman (P.C.)
Harold M. Golz	Russell K Bean
Douglas J. Reich	Jeffrey J. Scott

RETIRED COUNSEL

Joseph F. Krys

For full biographical listings, see the Martindale-Hubbell Law Directory

NETZORG & MCKEEVER, PROFESSIONAL CORPORATION (AV)

5251 DTC Parkway (Englewood) Penthouse One, 80111
Telephone: 303-770-8200
Fax: 303-770-8342

Gordon W. Netzorg	Susan Bernhardt
J. Nicholas McKeever, Jr.	Cecil E. Morris, Jr.

For full biographical listings, see the Martindale-Hubbell Law Directory

ALLEN G. REEVES, P.C. (AV)

900 Equitable Building, 730 17th Street, 80202
Telephone: 303-534-6278
Fax: 303-825-9147

Allen G. Reeves

Reference: Women's Bank.

REIMAN & ASSOCIATES, P.C. (AV)

1600 Broadway, Suite 1640, 80202
Telephone: 303-860-1500
Fax: 303-839-4380

Jeffrey Reiman

Marcie K. Bayaz	James Birch

For full biographical listings, see the Martindale-Hubbell Law Directory

CONNECTICUT

*HARTFORD,** Hartford Co.

SOROKIN SOROKIN GROSS HYDE & WILLIAMS P.C. (AV)

One Corporate Center, 06103
Telephone: 203-525-6645
Fax: 203-522-1781
Simsbury, Connecticut Office: 730 Hopmeadow Street.
Telephone: 203-651-9348.
Rocky Hill, Connecticut Office: 2360 Main Street.
Telephone: 203-563-9305.
Fax: 203-529-6931.
Glastonbury, Connecticut Office: 124 Hebron Avenue.
Telephone: 203-659-8801.

Morris W. Banks	Andrew C. Glassman

Sharon Kowal Freilich

For Complete List of Firm Personnel, See General Section

For full biographical listings, see the Martindale-Hubbell Law Directory

*NEW HAVEN,** New Haven Co.

BRENNER, SALTZMAN & WALLMAN (AV)

A Partnership including Professional Corporations
271 Whitney Avenue, P.O. Box 1746, 06507-1746
Telephone: 203-772-2600
Facsimile: 203-562-2098

Newton D. Brenner (P.C.)	Donald W. Anderson (P.C.)
Stephen L. Saltzman (P.C.)	Carol N. Theodore (P.C.)
Marc A. Wallman (P.C.)	Samuel M. Hurwitz
David R. Schaefer (P.C.)	Wayne A. Martino, P.C.
Stuart Jay Mandel (P.C.)	M. Anne Peters

Kenneth Rosenthal

(See Next Column)

BRENNER, SALTZMAN & WALLMAN—*Continued*

Peter K. Marsh
Alice Jo Mick
Brian P. Daniels
John R. Bashaw
George Brencher, IV

For full biographical listings, see the Martindale-Hubbell Law Directory

HOGAN & RINI, P.C. (AV)

Gold Building, 8th Floor 234 Church Street, 06510
Telephone: 203-787-4191
Telecopier: 203-777-4032

John W. Hogan, Jr.
Joseph L. Rini
Sue A. Cousineau

OF COUNSEL

Mark S. Cousineau

For full biographical listings, see the Martindale-Hubbell Law Directory

NORWALK, Fairfield Co.

LEV, SPALTER & BERLIN, P.C. (AV)

535 Connecticut Avenue, 06854
Telephone: 203-838-8500
Telecopier: 203-854-1652

Bruce L. Lev
Susan B. Spalter
Duane L. Berlin

Donna M. Lattarulo
Eric J. Dale

Reference: Fleet Bank, N.A.

For full biographical listings, see the Martindale-Hubbell Law Directory

STAMFORD, Fairfield Co.

CHAPMAN & FENNELL (AV)

Three Landmark Square, 06901
Telephone: 203-353-8000
Telecopier: 203-353-8799
New York, New York Office: 330 Madison Avenue.
Telephone: 212-687-3600.
Washington, D.C. Office: 2000 L Street, N.W., Suite 200.
Telephone: 202-822-9351.

MEMBERS OF FIRM

John Haven Chapman
Philip M. Chiappone (Resident, New York, N.Y. Office)
Darrell K. Fennell (Resident, New York, N.Y. Office)
Peter S. Gummo
D. Seeley Hubbard
Eric S. Kamisher (Resident, New York, N.Y. Office)
Brian E. Moran
Victor L. Zimmermann, Jr.

ASSOCIATE

Barton Meyerhoff (Not admitted in CT)

OF COUNSEL

Kevin T. Hoffman
Carol E. Meltzer (Resident, New York, N.Y. Office)
Brainard S. Patton
E. Gabriel Perle (Not admitted in CT)
Victor J. Toth (Resident, Washington, D.C. Office)
Michael Winger (Resident, New York, N.Y. Office)

For full biographical listings, see the Martindale-Hubbell Law Directory

WESTPORT, Fairfield Co.

BLAZZARD, GRODD & HASENAUER, P.C. (AV)

943 Post Road East, P.O. Box 5108, 06881
Telephone: 203-226-7866
Telecopier: 203-454-4855

Norse N. Blazzard
Leslie E. Grodd
Judith A. Hasenauer
William E. Hasenauer
Raymond A. O'Hara, III

Lynn Korman Stone

For full biographical listings, see the Martindale-Hubbell Law Directory

DELAWARE

*WILMINGTON,** New Castle Co.

MORRIS AND MORRIS (AV)

Suite 1600, 1105 North Market Street, P.O. Box 2166, 19899-2166
Telephone: 302-426-0400
Facsimile: 302-426-0406

(See Next Column)

Irving Morris
Karen L. Morris
Abraham Rappaport

ASSOCIATES

Patrick F. Morris
Liam G. B. Murphy
Jacqueline L. Jenkin (Not admitted in DE)
Seth D. Rigrodsky

For full biographical listings, see the Martindale-Hubbell Law Directory

DISTRICT OF COLUMBIA

WASHINGTON, D.C. Co.

* indicates certain Bar Register subscribers, in cities of comparable size and importance, who maintain an additional office in Washington, D.C. and who have arranged for representation as a part of the Washington, D.C. listings that follow

DE MARTINO FINKELSTEIN ROSEN & VIRGA (AV)

A Partnership including Professional Corporations
Suite 400, 1818 N Street, N.W., 20036
Telephone: 202-659-0494
Telecopier: 202-659-1290
New York, N.Y. Office: Suite 1700, 90 Broad Street.
Telephone: 212-363-2500.
Telecopier: 212-363-2723.

MEMBERS OF FIRM

Kathleen L. Cerveny (Resident)
Ralph V. De Martino (Resident)
Steven R. Finkelstein (Not admitted in DC; Resident, New York, N.Y. Office)
Jeffrey S. Rosen (Resident)
Gerard A. Virga (Not admitted in DC; Resident, New York, N.Y. Office)

Keith H. Peterson (Not admitted in DC; Resident, New York, N.Y. Office)
Victoria A. Baylin (Not admitted in DC; Resident)
Hal B. Perkins (Resident)
Lee W. Cassidy (Resident)

LEGAL SUPPORT PERSONNEL

J. Keoni Robinson (Paralegal)

For full biographical listings, see the Martindale-Hubbell Law Directory

* **LEWIS, WHITE & CLAY, A PROFESSIONAL CORPORATION** (AV)

1250 K Street, N.W., Suite 630, 20005
Telephone: 202-408-5419
Fax: 202-408-5456
Detroit, Michigan Office: 1300 First National Building, 660 Woodward Avenue.
Telephone: 313-961-2550.

Kathleen Miles (Resident)
Karen Kendrick Brown (Resident)
Werten F. W. Bellamy, Jr. (Not admitted in DC; Resident)

OF COUNSEL

Inez Smith Reid (Resident)

For full biographical listings, see the Martindale-Hubbell Law Directory

MULDOON, MURPHY & FAUCETTE (AV)

5101 Wisconsin Avenue, N.W., 20016
Telephone: 202-362-0840
Telecopier: 202-966-9409; 202-363-5068

MEMBERS OF FIRM

Joseph A. Muldoon, Jr.
George W. Murphy, Jr.
Douglas P. Faucette
John R. Hall
Thomas J. Haggerty (Not admitted in DC)
Richard V. Fitzgerald
Joseph G. Passaic, Jr.
Joseph P. Daly
John Bruno
Mary M. Jackley Sjoquist

ASSOCIATES

Leslie Murphy
Althea R. Day
Lori M. Beresford
Christina M. Gattuso (Not admitted in DC)
Ann E. Cox
Cynthia M. Krus (Not admitted in DC)
William E. Donnelly
Anne O'Connell Devereaux
Lawrence M. F. Spaccasi (Not admitted in DC)
Wendy L. Morris (Not admitted in DC)
Patricia A. Murphy (Not admitted in DC)
Kent M. Krudys
Philip G. Feigen (Not admitted in DC)
Andrew F. Campbell
Marc Paul Levy
William J.T. Strahan (Not admitted in DC)
Jeffrey Scibetta
Gwen M. Mulberry (Not admitted in DC)
Madra Michelle Alvis (Not admitted in DC)

(See Next Column)

MULDOON, MURPHY & FAUCETTE, *Washington—Continued*

OF COUNSEL

Mary V. Harcar
Lewis F. Morse
Ralph E. Frable

For full biographical listings, see the Martindale-Hubbell Law Directory

*** VENABLE, BAETJER, HOWARD & CIVILETTI (AV)**

A Partnership including Professional Corporations
Suite 1000, 1201 New York Avenue, N.W., 20005
Telephone: 202-962-4800
Fax: 202-962-8300
Baltimore, Maryland Office: Venable, Baetjer and Howard, 1800 Mercantile Bank & Trust Building, 2 Hopkins Plaza.
Telephone: 410-244-7400.
McLean, Virginia Office: Venable, Baetjer and Howard, Suite 400, 2010 Corporate Ridge.
Telephone: 703-760-1600.
Rockville, Maryland Office: Venable, Baetjer and Howard, Suite 500, One Church Street, P. O. Box 1906.
Telephone: 301-217-5600.
Towson, Maryland Office: Venable, Baetjer and Howard, 210 Allegheny Avenue, P. O. Box 5517.
Telephone: 410-494-6200.

MEMBERS OF FIRM

Benjamin R. Civiletti (P.C.) (Also at Baltimore and Towson, Maryland Offices)
Ronald R. Glancz
David J. Levenson
Joe A. Shull
Kenneth C. Bass, III (Also at McLean, Virginia Office)
Thomas B. Hudson (Also at Baltimore, Maryland Office)
James K. Archibald (Also at Baltimore and Towson, Maryland Offices)
James R. Myers
James L. Shea (Not admitted in DC; also at Baltimore, Maryland Office)
William D. Quarles (Also at Towson, Maryland Office)
Linda L. Lord
Paul A. Serini (Not admitted in DC; Also at Baltimore, Maryland Office)
Gary M. Hnath

ASSOCIATES

Donald P. Creston
David S. Darland
D. Brent Gunsalus

For Complete List of Firm Personnel, See General Section

For full biographical listings, see the Martindale-Hubbell Law Directory

WILMER, CUTLER & PICKERING (AV)

2445 M Street, N.W., 20037-1420
Telephone: 202-663-6000
Facsimile: 202-663-6363
Internet: Law@Wilmer.Com
European Offices:
4 Carlton Gardens, London, SW1Y 5AA, England. Telephone: 011 (4471) 839-4466.
Facsimile: 011 (4471) 839-3537.
Rue de la Loi 15 Wetstraat, B-1040 Brussels, Belgium. Telephone: 011 (322) 231-0903.
Facsimile: 011 (322) 230-4322.
Friedrichstrasse 95, D-10117 Berlin, Germany. Telephone: 011 (4930) 2643-3601.
Facsimile: 011 (4930) 2643-3630.

MEMBERS OF FIRM

Howard P. Willens
Arthur F. Mathews
Louis R. Cohen
Michael R. Klein
Stephen F. Black
Robert B. McCaw
John Rounsaville, Jr.
Roger M. Witten
David M. Becker
Marianne K. Smythe
Andrew B. Weissman
Bruce E. Coolidge
Andrew N. Vollmer
Charles E. Davidow
Joseph K. Brenner
Stephen M. Cutler
Eric R. Markus

COUNSEL

Jeremy N. Rubenstein

For Complete List of Firm Personnel, See General Section

For full biographical listings, see the Martindale-Hubbell Law Directory

FLORIDA

BOCA RATON, Palm Beach Co.

JIM SCUTTI, P.A. (AV)

980 North Federal Highway, Suite 434, 33432
Telephone: 407-750-1391
Telefax: 407-347-0828

(See Next Column)

Jim Scutti

Representative Clients: InnoVet, Inc.; Electronic Imagery, Inc.; Abdullatif Ali Alissa Establishment; Diabetic Supply Foundation, Inc.

For full biographical listings, see the Martindale-Hubbell Law Directory

LARGO, Pinellas Co.

FEDOR & FEDOR (AV)

Sugar Creek Professional Offices, 10225 Ulmerton Road, Suite 8-A, 34641
Telephone: 813-581-6100
Fax: 813-585-2232

MEMBERS OF FIRM

Allan J. Fedor
Franell Fedor

For full biographical listings, see the Martindale-Hubbell Law Directory

*MIAMI,** Dade Co.

SPARBER, KOSNITZKY, TRUXTON, DE LA GUARDIA SPRATT & BROOKS, P.A. (AV)

1401 Brickell Avenue Suite 700, 33131
Telephone: Dade: 305-379-7200; Broward: 305-760-9133
Fax: 305-379-0800

Oscar G. de la Guardia

For Complete List of Firm Personnel, See General Section

For full biographical listings, see the Martindale-Hubbell Law Directory

STUZIN AND CAMNER, PROFESSIONAL ASSOCIATION (AV)

25th Floor, 1221 Brickell Avenue, 33131-3260
Telephone: 305-577-0600

Charles B. Stuzin
Alfred R. Camner
Stanley A. Beiley
Marsha D. Bilzin
David S. Garbett
Nina S. Gordon
Barry D. Hunter
Nikki J. Nedbor
Neale J. Poller

Lisa R. Carstarphen
Maria E. Chang
Barry P. Gruher
Gustavo D. Llerena
Sherry D. McMillan
Roger A. Preziosi

OF COUNSEL

Anne Shari Camner

References: Citizens Federal Bank; City National Bank of Miami; Barnett Bank of South Florida, N.A.

For full biographical listings, see the Martindale-Hubbell Law Directory

*SARASOTA,** Sarasota Co.

SNYDER, GRONER & SCHIEB (AV)

A Partnership including a Professional Association
2033 Main Street, Suite 403, 34237
Telephone: 813-951-1333; 800-448-0721
Telecopier: 813-953-9685
Venice, Florida Office: 355 West Venice Avenue.
Telephone: 813-485-9626; 800-260-9626.
Telecopier: 813-485-8163.

W. Russell Snyder (P.A.)
Richard W. Groner
Scott A. Schieb
W. Andrew Clayton, Jr.
Stanley M. Krawetz

LEGAL SUPPORT PERSONNEL

Meryl Conte Clayton (Not admitted in FL; Of Counsel, Conte, Phillips & Clayton, Saddle Brook, New Jersey)

References: Community National Bank of Sarasota.

For full biographical listings, see the Martindale-Hubbell Law Directory

*TAMPA,** Hillsborough Co.

MICHAEL C. ADDISON (AV)

Suite 2175, 100 North Tampa Street, 33602-5145
Telephone: 813-223-2000
Facsimile: 813-228-6000
Mailing Address: P.O. Box 2175, Tampa, Florida, 33601-2175

For full biographical listings, see the Martindale-Hubbell Law Directory

KALISH & WARD, PROFESSIONAL ASSOCIATION (AV)

4100 Barnett Plaza, 101 East Kennedy Boulevard, P.O. Box 71, 33601-0071
Telephone: 813-222-8700
Facsimile: 813-222-8701

(See Next Column)

KALISH & WARD PROFESSIONAL ASSOCIATION—*Continued*

William Kalish
Alton C. Ward
Richard A. Schlosser
Roger J. Rovell
Michael A. Bedke
William T. Harrison, III
Thomas P. McNamara
Robert Reid Haney
Charles H. Carver
Kelley A. Bosecker

For full biographical listings, see the Martindale-Hubbell Law Directory

*WEST PALM BEACH,** Palm Beach Co.

BURT & PUCILLO (AV)

Esperanté, Suite 960, 222 Lakeview Avenue, 33401
Telephone: 407-835-9400
Telecopier: 407-835-0322

MEMBERS OF FIRM

C. Oliver Burt, III
Michael J. Pucillo

ASSOCIATES

Wendy Hope Zoberman
Andrew H. Kayton

OF COUNSEL

Carol McLean Brewer

For full biographical listings, see the Martindale-Hubbell Law Directory

GEORGIA

*ATLANTA,** Fulton Co.

ALTMAN, KRITZER & LEVICK, P.C. (AV)

Powers Ferry Landing, Suite 224, 6400 Powers Ferry Road, N.W., 30339
Telephone: 404-955-3555
Telecopier: 404-952-7821, 955-2866, 955-0038, 955-3697
Schaumburg, Illinois Affiliate: Altman, Kritzer & Levick, Ltd., Suite 400, 1101 Perimeter Drive, 60173.
Telephone: 708-240-0340.
FAX: 708-240-0344.

Allen D. Altman
Craig H. Kritzer
Mark J. Levick
D. Charles Houk
Charles L. Wood
Ephraim Spielman
Emily Sanford Bair
Benno G. Rothschild, Jr.
Elizabeth H. Hutchins
Theodore H. Sandler
Frank Slover
Kenneth A. Shapiro
Linda L. West
Steven A. Pepper
George A. Mattingly
W. Daniel Hicks, Jr.

COUNSEL

Richard P. Rubenoff
Martin N. Goldsmith
Susan E. Stoffer
Robert D. Simons
Peter M. Hartman
William R. Ham

Duane D. Sitar
Debra L. Thompson
Lori E. Kilberg
Richard W. Probert
Gregory A. Jacobs
Andrew R. Bauman
Lawrence H. Freiman
Ian L. Levin

LEGAL SUPPORT PERSONNEL

Cynthia A. Groszkiewicz
Rebecca G. Middleton

Representative Clients: Atlantic Southeast Airlines, Inc.; Ingles Markets, Inc.; The Home Depot, Inc.; Pacesetter Steel Service, Inc.; Homart Development Co.

For full biographical listings, see the Martindale-Hubbell Law Directory

LONG ALDRIDGE & NORMAN (AV)

A Partnership including Professional Corporations
One Peachtree Center, Suite 5300, 303 Peachtree Street, 30308
Telephone: 404-527-4000
Telecopier: 404-527-4198
Washington, D.C. Office: Suite 950, 1615 L Street, 20036.
Telephone: 202-223-7033.
Telecopier: 202-223-7013.

MEMBERS OF FIRM

William L. Floyd
M. Hill Jeffries, Jr.
Thomas R. B. Wardell (Not admitted in GA)

ASSOCIATES

David M. Calhoun
Janet Eifert Haury
Melanie McGee Platt
Richard R. Willis

OF COUNSEL

William J. Carney

For Complete List of Firm Personnel, See General Section

For full biographical listings, see the Martindale-Hubbell Law Directory

PARKER, HUDSON, RAINER & DOBBS (AV)

1500 Marquis Two Tower, 285 Peachtree Center Avenue, N.E., 30303
Telephone: 404-523-5300
FAX: 404-522-8409
Tallahassee, Florida Office: The Perkins House, 118 North Gadsden Street, 32301.
Telephone: 904-681-0191.
FAX: 904-681-9493.

MEMBERS OF FIRM

David G. Russell
G. Wayne Hillis, Jr.
William J. Holley, II

For full biographical listings, see the Martindale-Hubbell Law Directory

THRASHER, WHITLEY, HAMPTON & MORGAN, A PROFESSIONAL CORPORATION (AV)

Suite 2150, Five Concourse Parkway, 30328
Telephone: 404-804-8000
Telecopier: 404-804-5555

H. Grady Thrasher, III

Representative Clients: Georgia Dental Assn.; Kearney National, Inc.; Middle Bay Oil Company, Inc.; Nova Information Systems, Inc.; Perry & Co.; Smallwood, Reynold, Stewart, Stewart & Assoc., Inc.; Sunchase Holdings, Ltd.; Touch Industries, Inc.

For full biographical listings, see the Martindale-Hubbell Law Directory

IDAHO

*BOISE,** Ada Co.

EBERLE, BERLIN, KADING, TURNBOW & MCKLVEEN, CHARTERED (AV)

Capitol Park Plaza, 300 North Sixth Street, P.O. Box 1368, 83701
Telephone: 208-344-8535
Facsimile: 208-344-8542

R.M. Turnbow
Richard A. Riley
Bradley G. Andrews

Representative Clients: Piper Jaffray, Inc.; Prudential Securities Inc.; Waddell & Reed Financial Services; Edward D. Jones & Co.; Hecla Mining Corp.

For Complete List of Firm Personnel, See General Section

For full biographical listings, see the Martindale-Hubbell Law Directory

ELAM & BURKE, A PROFESSIONAL ASSOCIATION (AV)

Key Financial Center, 702 West Idaho Street, P.O. Box 1539, 83701
Telephone: 208-343-5454
Telecopier: 208-384-5844

Carl P. Burke
William J. Batt
Jeffrey A. Thomson

Representative Clients: Morrison-Knudsen, Inc.; Texas Instruments, Inc.; Prudential Securities, Inc.; Pechiney Corp.; Dow Corning Corporation; U.S. West Communications; State Farm Insurance Cos.; Sinclair Oil Company d/b/a Sun Valley Company; Farmers Insurance Group; Hecla Mining Company.

For Complete List of Firm Personnel, See General Section

For full biographical listings, see the Martindale-Hubbell Law Directory

ILLINOIS

*CHICAGO,** Cook Co.

BELL, BOYD & LLOYD (AV)

Three First National Plaza Suite 3300, 70 West Madison Street, 60602
Telephone: 312-372-1121
FAX: 312-372-2098
Washington, D.C. Office: 1615 L Street, N.W.
Telephone: 202-466-6300.
FAX: 202-463-0678.

MEMBERS OF FIRM

Cameron S. Avery
John H. Bitner
John C. Blew
William G. Brown
Steven E. Ducommun
Warren C. Haskin (Managing Partner)
Patrick J. Maloney
John T. McCarthy
Thomas J. Murphy
Janet D. Olsen
William S. Price
John Craig Walker

(See Next Column)

BELL, BOYD & LLOYD, *Chicago—Continued*

ASSOCIATES

Lynne Therese Boehringer
Timothy R.M. Bryant
G. Nicholas Bullat
Kevin J. McCarthy
D. Mark McMillan
Amy S. Powers
Stacy H. Winick

For Complete List of Firm Personnel, See General Section

For full biographical listings, see the Martindale-Hubbell Law Directory

BELLOWS AND BELLOWS, A PROFESSIONAL CORPORATION (AV)

Suite 800, 79 West Monroe Street, 60603
Telephone: 312-332-3340
Los Angeles, California Office: 601 South Figueroa Street, 27th Floor.
Telephone: 213-485-1555.

Joel J. Bellows
Laurel G. Bellows
Nicholas P. Iavarone

Rebecca J. Wing
Adam K. Hollander

For full biographical listings, see the Martindale-Hubbell Law Directory

FREEMAN, FREEMAN & SALZMAN, P.C. (AV)

Suite 3200, 401 North Michigan Avenue, 60611
Telephone: 312-222-5100
Facsimile: 312-822-0870

Lee A. Freeman
Lee A. Freeman, Jr.
Jerrold E. Salzman
John F. Kinney
James T. Malysiak
Glynna W. Freeman
Phillip L. Stern
Albert F. Ettinger
Derek J. Meyer
Scott A. Browdy
Chris S. Gair
Christopher M. Kelly (Not admitted in IL)

For full biographical listings, see the Martindale-Hubbell Law Directory

WILLIAM J. HARTE, LTD. (AV)

Suite 1100, 111 West Washington Street, 60602
Telephone: 312-726-5015
Fax: 312-641-1288

William J. Harte

Sylvia A. Sotiras
Erik D. Gruber
Stephen L. Garcia

OF COUNSEL

David J. Walker

For full biographical listings, see the Martindale-Hubbell Law Directory

LAWRENCE, KAMIN, SAUNDERS & UHLENHOP (AV)

208 South La Salle Street, Suite 1750, 60604
Telephone: 312-372-1947
Telecopier: 312-372-2389

MEMBERS OF FIRM

Paul B. Uhlenhop
Kent Lawrence
Charles J. Risch
Lawrence A. Rosen
Michael Wise

Representative Clients: Dean Witter Reynolds Inc.; TransMarket Group, Inc.; Checkers, Simon & Rosner; A.G. Edwards & Sons, Inc.; Nash Weiss & Co.; Gofen & Glossberg, Inc.; Beacon Investment Co.

For full biographical listings, see the Martindale-Hubbell Law Directory

MCBRIDE BAKER & COLES (AV)

500 West Madison Street 40th Floor, 60661
Telephone: 312-715-5700
Cable Address: "Chilaw"
Telex: 270258
Telecopier: 312-993-9350

MEMBERS OF FIRM

Michael J. Boland
William J. Cooney
Lola Miranda Hale
G. Gale Roberson, Jr.
Anne Hamblin Schiave
Robert I. Schwimmer
Thomas P. Ward

OF COUNSEL

Robert O. Case
Lawrence A. Coles, Jr.

ASSOCIATE

Jerald Holisky

For Complete List of Firm Personnel, See General Section

For full biographical listings, see the Martindale-Hubbell Law Directory

SAITLIN, PATZIK & FRANK LTD. (AV)

Suite 900, 150 South Wacker Drive, 60606
Telephone: 312-551-8300
Facsimile: 312-551-1101

Jeffrey H. Frank
Alan B. Patzik
Sheldon I. Saitlin
Robert P. Scales
Gary Irwin Walt

Steven M. Prebish
Keith A. Ross
Robert J. Wild

For full biographical listings, see the Martindale-Hubbell Law Directory

SAUNDERS & MONROE (AV)

Suite 4201, 205 North Michigan Avenue, 60601
Telephone: 312-946-9000
Facsimile: 312-946-0528

MEMBERS OF FIRM

George L. Saunders, Jr.
Lee A. Monroe
Thomas F. Bush, Jr.
Matthew E. Van Tine

Thomas A. Doyle
Christina J. Norton
Gwen A. Niedbalski

For full biographical listings, see the Martindale-Hubbell Law Directory

WILSON & MCILVAINE (AV)

500 West Madison, Suite 3700, 60661-2511
Telephone: 312-715-5000
Telecopier: 312-715-5155

PARTNERS

Robert F. Forrer
Kendall R. Meyer
Quinton F. Seamons
John P. Vail

OF COUNSEL

Charles W. Boand

For Complete List of Firm Personnel, See General Section

For full biographical listings, see the Martindale-Hubbell Law Directory

*WHEATON,** Du Page Co.

JAMES E. BECKLEY & ASSOCIATES, P.C. (AV)

520 West Roosevelt Road, 60187
Telephone: 708-668-1335
Fax: 708-668-1342

James E. Beckley

Leslie Gregory Bleifuss

Representative Clients: Bowater, Inc.; Smith-Barney; Capital Securities Investment Corp.

For full biographical listings, see the Martindale-Hubbell Law Directory

INDIANA

*INDIANAPOLIS,** Marion Co.

ICE MILLER DONADIO & RYAN (AV)

One American Square Box 82001, 46282-0002
Telephone: 317-236-2100
Fax: 317-236-2219

MEMBERS OF FIRM

Berkley W. Duck, III
Harry L. Gonso
John R. Thornburgh
Stephen J. Hackman
Elizabeth A. Smith

ASSOCIATES

Matthew C. Hook
Dean T. Burger

For Complete List of Firm Personnel, See General Section

For full biographical listings, see the Martindale-Hubbell Law Directory

JOHNSON, SMITH, DENSBORN, WRIGHT & HEATH (AV)

One Indiana Square Suite 1800, 46204
Telephone: 317-634-9777
Telecopier: 317-636-9061

MEMBERS OF FIRM

Thomas N. Eckerle
John R. Kirkwood

(See Next Column)

JOHNSON, SMITH, DENSBORN, WRIGHT & HEATH—*Continued*

ASSOCIATE

Charles M. Freeland

For Complete List of Firm Personnel, See General Section

For full biographical listings, see the Martindale-Hubbell Law Directory

LOCKE REYNOLDS BOYD & WEISELL (AV)

1000 Capital Center South, 201 North Illinois Street, 46204
Telephone: 317-237-3800
Telecopier: 317-237-3900

Stephen J. Dutton
Michael J. Schneider
Jeffrey B. Bailey

Curt W. Hidde

AmeriPool Securities Corporation; Baldwin & Lyons, Inc.; Dean Witter Reynolds, Inc.; Golden Rule Insurance Co.; Indy Connection Limousines, Inc.; The JEMCO Group, Inc.; Raffensperger Hughes & Co.; Real Silk Investments, Inc.; Thurston Springer Miller Herd & Titak, Inc.; Traub & Company, Inc.

For Complete List of Firm Personnel, See General Section

For full biographical listings, see the Martindale-Hubbell Law Directory

MCTURNAN & TURNER (AV)

2070 Market Tower, 10 West Market Street, 46204
Telephone: 317-464-8181
Telecopier: 317-464-8131

Lee B. McTurnan
Wayne C. Turner
Judy L. Woods
Jacqueline Bowman Ponder
Steven M. Badger
Matthew W. Foster

For full biographical listings, see the Martindale-Hubbell Law Directory

SOMMER & BARNARD, ATTORNEYS AT LAW, PC (AV)

4000 Bank One Tower, 111 Monument Circle, P.O. Box 44363, 46244-0363
Telephone: 317-630-4000
FAX: 317-236-9802
North Office: 8900 Keystone Crossing, Suite 1046, Indianapolis, Indiana, 46240-2134.
Telephone: 317-630-4000.
FAX: 317-844-4780.

James K. Sommer
William C. Barnard
James E. Hughes
Edward W. Harris, III
Frederick M. King
Jerald I. Ancel
Eric R. Johnson
Gordon L. Pittenger
Lynn Brundage Jongleux
Frank J. Deveau
John E. Taylor
Michael C. Terrell
Marlene Reich
Richard C. Richmond, III
Julianne S. Lis-Milam
Steven C. Shockley
Stephen B. Cherry
Robert J. Hicks
Lawrence A. Vanore
Donald C. Biggs
Debra McVicker Lynch

Gayle A. Reindl
Ann Carr Mackey
Gregory J. Seketa
Sandra L. Gosling
Edwin J. Broecker
Thomas R. DeVoe
Mary T. Doherty
William K. Boncosky

OF COUNSEL

Jerry Williams
Glenn Scolnik
Philip L. McCool
Charles E. Valliere
Verl L. Myers

Representative Clients: Comerica Bank; Excel Industries; Federal Express; Kimball International; Monsanto; Renault Automation; Repport International; TRW, Inc.

For full biographical listings, see the Martindale-Hubbell Law Directory

KANSAS

*TOPEKA,** Shawnee Co.

GOODELL, STRATTON, EDMONDS & PALMER (AV)

515 South Kansas Avenue, 66603-3999
Telephone: 913-233-0593
Telecopier: 913-233-8870

MEMBERS OF FIRM

Gerald L. Goodell
Robert E. Edmonds (Retired)
H. Philip Elwood
Gerald J. Letourneau
Michael W. Merriam
John H. Stauffer, Jr.

(See Next Column)

OF COUNSEL

Robert A. McClure

ASSOCIATE

Craig S. Kendall

Local Counsel for: Farm Bureau Mutual Insurance Co.; Metropolitan Life Insurance Co.; St. Paul Fire & Marine Insurance Co.
General Counsel for: American Home Life Insurance Co.; Columbian National Title Insurance Co.; The Menninger Foundation; Stauffer Communications, Inc.; Kansas Association of Realtors; Kansas Medical Society; Kansas Hospital Association.

For Complete List of Firm Personnel, See General Section

For full biographical listings, see the Martindale-Hubbell Law Directory

*WICHITA,** Sedgwick Co.

FOULSTON & SIEFKIN (AV)

(Formerly Foulston, Siefkin, Powers & Eberhardt)
700 Fourth Financial Center, Broadway at Douglas, 67202
Telephone: 316-267-6371
Facsimile: 316-267-6345
Topeka, Kansas Office: 1515 Bank IV Tower, 534 Kansas Avenue. 66603.
Telephone: 913-233-3600.
FAX: 913-233-1610.
Member: Lex Mundi, A Global Association of Independent Firms

MEMBERS OF FIRM

Benjamin C. Langel
James D. Oliver
William R. Wood, II

For Complete List of Firm Personnel, See General Section

For full biographical listings, see the Martindale-Hubbell Law Directory

KENTUCKY

*LEXINGTON,** Fayette Co.

STOLL, KEENON & PARK (AV)

201 E. Main Street, Suite 1000, 40507-1380
Telephone: 606-231-3000
Telecopier: 606-253-1093; 606-253-1027
Frankfort, Kentucky Office: 326 West Main Street.
Telephone: 502-875-6000.
Telecopier: 502-875-6008.
Louisville, Kentucky Office: 400 West Market Street, Suite 2650, 40202.
Telephone: 502-568-9100.
Telecopier: 502-568-6340.

MEMBERS OF FIRM

Robert M. Watt, III
Gary L. Stage
J. David Smith, Jr.
John Wesley Walters, Jr.

Representative Clients: Bank One, Lexington, NA; Farmers Capital Bank Corp.; The Tokai Bank Ltd.; Link Belt Construction Equipment Co.; General Motors Corp.; International Business Machines Corp.; Ohbayashi Corp.; R. J. Reynolds Tobacco Co.; Rockwell International Corp.; Square D Co.

For Complete List of Firm Personnel, See General Section

For full biographical listings, see the Martindale-Hubbell Law Directory

*LOUISVILLE,** Jefferson Co.

MIDDLETON & REUTLINGER, P.S.C. (AV)

2500 Brown and Williamson Tower, 40202-3410
Telephone: 502-584-1135
Fax: 502-561-0442
Jeffersonville, Indiana Office: 605 Watt Street, 47130.
Telephone: 812-282-4886.

C. Kent Hatfield
D. Randall Gibson
William Jay Hunter, Jr.
John M. Franck II

Counsel for: Chevron USA; Liberty National Bank; Logan Aluminum, Inc.; Louisville Gas & Electric Co.; MCI Telecommunications Corp.; Metropolitan Life Insurance Co.; Kosmos Cement Co.; Porcelain Metal Corp.; The Home Insurance Co.; The Kroger Co.; Demars Haka Development, Inc.

For Complete List of Firm Personnel, See General Section

For full biographical listings, see the Martindale-Hubbell Law Directory

MULLOY, WALZ, WETTERER, FORE & SCHWARTZ (AV)

First Trust Centre, Suite 700N, 200 South Fifth Street, 40202
Telephone: 502-589-5250
Fax: 502-589-1637

(See Next Column)

MULLOY, WALZ, WETTERER, FORE & SCHWARTZ, *Louisville—Continued*

MEMBERS OF FIRM

William P. Mulloy
Karl M. Walz
William S. Wetterer, Jr.
F. Larkin Fore
Dan T. Schwartz
B. Mark Mulloy
Mary Anne Wetterer Watkins
William S. Wetterer, III
Bryan J. Dillon
J. Gregory Clare
Ronda Hartlage
T. Lee Sisney

OF COUNSEL

Stephen H. Miller

Reference: American States Insurance Co.; Crawford & Company; Paragon Group, Inc.; Queens Group; Southeastern Dairies, Inc.; Ticor Title Co.; First National Bank of Louisville; Stockyards Bank; Arrow Electric Co.

For full biographical listings, see the Martindale-Hubbell Law Directory

OGDEN NEWELL & WELCH (AV)

1200 One Riverfront Plaza, 40202-2973
Telephone: 502-582-1601
Fax: 502-581-9564

MEMBERS OF FIRM

James S. Welch
Ernest W. Williams
Robert E. Thieman
James B. Martin, Jr.
Lisa Ann Vogt

ASSOCIATES

Lynn H. Wangerin
John Wade Hendricks
James G. Campbell
Thomas E. Rutledge

Counsel for: KU Energy Corp.; Kentucky Utilities Co.; Brown-Forman Corp.; B. F. Goodrich Co.; Brown & Williamson Tobacco Corp.; J.J.B. Hilliard, W.L. Lyons, Inc.; Interlock Industries, Inc.; Akzo Coatings, Inc.; United Medical Corp.; Bank of Louisville.

For Complete List of Firm Personnel, See General Section

For full biographical listings, see the Martindale-Hubbell Law Directory

PEDLEY, ROSS, ZIELKE & GORDINIER (AV)

1150 Starks Building, 455 South Fourth Avenue, 40202
Telephone: 502-589-4600
Fax: 502-584-0422

MEMBERS OF FIRM

Lawrence L. Pedley
Robert P. Ross
Laurence J. Zielke
John K. Gordinier
William W. Stodghill
Schuyler J. Olt
P. Stephen Gordinier
Frank G. Simpson, III
Charles F. Merz

OF COUNSEL

William C. Stone
J. Chester Porter

ASSOCIATES

William H. Mooney
William J. Shreffler
John H. Dwyer, Jr.

For full biographical listings, see the Martindale-Hubbell Law Directory

RUBIN HAYS & FOLEY (AV)

First Trust Centre 200 South Fifth Street, 40202
Telephone: 502-569-7550
Telecopier: 502-569-7555

MEMBERS OF FIRM

Wm. Carl Fust
Harry Lee Meyer
David W. Gray
Irvin D. Foley
Joseph R. Gathright, Jr.
Lisa Koch Bryant
Sharon C. Hardy
Charles S. Musson
W. Randall Jones
K. Gail Russell

ASSOCIATE

Christian L. Juckett

OF COUNSEL

James E. Fahey
Newman T. Guthrie

Representative Clients: J.C. Bradford & Co., Inc.; J.J.B. Hilliard, W.L. Lyons, Inc.; Huntington National Bank; Liberty National Bank and Trust Company; National City Bank; PNC Bank; Prudential Bache & Co., Inc.; Prudential Securities, Inc.; Society Bank; Stock Yards Bank and Trust Co.

For full biographical listings, see the Martindale-Hubbell Law Directory

LOUISIANA

*SHREVEPORT,** Caddo Parish

BARLOW AND HARDTNER L.C. (AV)

Tenth Floor, Louisiana Tower, 401 Edwards Street, 71101-3289
Telephone: 318-227-1131
Telecopier: 318-227-1141
Mailing Address: P.O. Box 8, Shreveport, Louisiana, 71161-0008

Ray A. Barlow
Joseph L. Shea, Jr.
David R. Taggart
Clair F. White
Michael B. Donald
Jay A. Greenleaf

Representative Clients: Kelley Oil Corporation; NorAm Energy Corp. (formerly Arkla, Inc.); Central and South West; Panhandle Eastern Corp.; Pennzoil Producing Co.; Johnson Controls, Inc.; Ashland Oil, Inc.; Southwestern Electric Power Company; Brammer Engineering, Inc.; General Electric Co.

For Complete List of Firm Personnel, See General Section

For full biographical listings, see the Martindale-Hubbell Law Directory

MARYLAND

*BALTIMORE,** (Independent City)

THOMAS & LIBOWITZ, A PROFESSIONAL ASSOCIATION (AV)

USF&G Tower, Suite 1100, 100 Light Street, 21202-1053
Telephone: 410-752-2468
Telecopier: 410-752-2046
Frederick, Maryland Office: 100 West Church Street.
Telephone: 301-698-4886.

Clinton R. Black, IV

For full biographical listings, see the Martindale-Hubbell Law Directory

VENABLE, BAETJER AND HOWARD (AV)

A Partnership including Professional Corporations
1800 Mercantile Bank & Trust Building, 2 Hopkins Plaza, 21201
Telephone: 410-244-7400
Washington, D.C. Office: Venable, Baetjer, Howard & Civiletti. Suite 1000, 1201 New York Avenue, N.W.
Telephone: 202-962-4800.
McLean, Virginia Office: Suite 400, 2010 Corporate Ridge.
Telephone: 703-760-1600.
Rockville, Maryland Office: Suite 500, One Church Street, P. O. Box 1906.
Telephone: 301-217-5600.
Towson, Maryland Office: 210 Allegheny Avenue, P. O. Box 5517.
Telephone: 410-494-6200.

MEMBERS OF FIRM

Benjamin R. Civiletti (P.C.) (Also at Washington, D.C. and Towson, Maryland Offices)
John Henry Lewin, Jr. (P.C.)
Lee M. Miller (P.C.)
Alan D. Yarbro (P.C.)
Ronald R. Glancz (Not admitted in MD; Resident, Washington, D.C. Office)
David J. Levenson (Not admitted in MD; Resident, Washington, D.C. Office)
Joe A. Shull (Resident, Washington, D.C. Office)
Kenneth C. Bass, III (Not admitted in MD; Also at Washington, D.C. and McLean, Virginia Offices)
John H. Zink, III (Resident, Towson, Maryland Office)
Joseph C. Wich, Jr. (Resident, Towson, Maryland Office)
Thomas B. Hudson (Also at Washington, D.C. Office)
Nell B. Strachan
James K. Archibald (Also at Washington, D.C. and Towson, Maryland Offices)
G. Stewart Webb, Jr.
James R. Myers (Not admitted in MD; Resident, Washington, D.C. Office)
James L. Shea (Also at Washington, D.C. Office)
William D. Quarles (Also at Washington, D.C. and Towson, Maryland Offices)
Christopher R. Mellott
Elizabeth R. Hughes
Linda L. Lord (Not admitted in MD; Resident, Washington, D.C. Office)
Paul A. Serini (Also at Washington, D.C. Office)
Ariel Vannier
Gary M. Hnath (Resident, Washington, D.C. Office)

OF COUNSEL

Arthur W. Machen, Jr. (P.C.)
Herbert R. O'Conor, Jr. (Resident, Towson, Maryland Office)

(See Next Column)

VENABLE, BAETJER AND HOWARD—*Continued*

ASSOCIATES

Christine J. Collins
Michael W. Conron
Donald P. Creston (Not admitted in MD; Resident, Washington, D.C. Office)
David S. Darland (Not admitted in MD; Resident, Washington, D.C. Office)
Francis X. Gallagher, Jr. (Not admitted in MD)
D. Brent Gunsalus (Not admitted in MD; Resident, Washington, D.C. Office)
E. Anne Hamel
Mary-Dulany James (Resident, Towson, Maryland Office)
Wingrove S. Lynton
Michael J. Muller
John T. Prisbe
Joseph C. Schmelter
J. Preston Turner

For Complete List of Firm Personnel, See General Section

For full biographical listings, see the Martindale-Hubbell Law Directory

COLUMBIA, Howard Co.

LAW OFFICES OF GUY B. MASERITZ (AV)

Hobbit's Glen, 5040 Rushlight Path, 21044
Telephone: 410-997-9400
Fax: 410-997-3116

Reference: First National Bank of Maryland.

MASSACHUSETTS

*BOSTON,** Suffolk Co.

GELB & GELB (AV)

20 Custom House Street, 02110
Telephone: 617-345-0010
Telecopier: 617-345-0009

MEMBER OF FIRM

Richard M. Gelb

For full biographical listings, see the Martindale-Hubbell Law Directory

PALMER & DODGE (AV)

(Storey Thorndike Palmer & Dodge)
One Beacon Street, 02108
Telephone: 617-573-0100
Telecopier: 617-227-4420
Telex: 951104
Cable Address: "Storeydike," Boston

MEMBER OF FIRM

Peter M. Saparoff

For Complete List of Firm Personnel, See General Section

For full biographical listings, see the Martindale-Hubbell Law Directory

RICH, MAY, BILODEAU & FLAHERTY, P.C. (AV)

The Old South Building, 294 Washington Street, 02108-4675
Telephone: 617-482-1360
FAX: 617-556-3889

John F. Rich (1908-1987)
Thomas H. Bilodeau (1915-1987)
Gerald May
Harold B. Dondis
Walter L. Landergan, Jr.
Edwin J. Carr
Arthur F. Flaherty
Franklin M. Hundley
Michael F. Donlan
Joseph F. Sullivan, Jr.
Owen P. Maher
Nicolas A. Kensington
Daniel T. Clark
Gerald V. May, Jr.
Eric J. Krathwohl
Michael J. McHugh
James M. Behnke
James M. Avery
Stephen M. Kane
Mark C. O'Connor
Walter A. Wright, III
Emmett E. Lyne

Nicholas F. Kourtis
James T. Finnigan
Carol E. Kazmer
Robert P. Snell

For full biographical listings, see the Martindale-Hubbell Law Directory

LYNNFIELD, Essex Co.

WILLIAM M. PRIFTI (AV)

220 Broadway, Suite 204, 01940
Telephone: 617-593-4525
Fax: 617-598-5222

For full biographical listings, see the Martindale-Hubbell Law Directory

MICHIGAN

*ANN ARBOR,** Washtenaw Co.

MILLER, CANFIELD, PADDOCK AND STONE, P.L.C. (AV)

A Professional Limited Liability Company
Founded in 1852 by Sidney Davy Miller
101 North Main Street, Seventh Floor, 48104-1400
Telephone: 313-663-2445
Fax: 313-747-7147
Detroit, Michigan Office: 150 West Jefferson, Suite 2500, 48226-4415.
Telephone: 313-963-6420.
Fax: 313-496-7500.
Cable Address: "Stem Detroit."
Bloomfield Hills, Michigan Office: Suite 100, Pinehurst Office Center, 1400 North Woodward, 48303-2014.
Telephone: 313-645-5000.
Fax: 313-645-1917.
Grand Rapids, Michigan Office: 1200 Campau Square Plaza, 99 Monroe, N.W., 49503-2639.
Telephone: 616-454-8656.
Fax: 616-776-6322.
Howell, Michigan Office: 121 South Barnard Street, Suite 4, 48843-2305.
Telephone: 517-546-7600.
Telecopier: 517-546-6974.
Kalamazoo, Michigan Office: 444 West Michigan Avenue, 49007-3752.
Telephone: 616-381-7030.
Fax: 616-382-0244.
Lansing, Michigan Office: One Michigan Avenue, Suite 900, 48933-1609.
Telephone: 517-487-2070.
Fax: 517-374-6304.
Monroe, Michigan Office: The Executive Centre, 214 East Elm Avenue, 48161-2682.
Telephone: 313-243-2000.
Fax: 313-243-0901.
Washington, D.C. Office: 1225 Nineteenth Street, N.W., Suite 400. 20036.
Telephone: 202-429-5575; 785-0600.
Fax: 202-331-1118; 785-1234.
Pensacola, Florida Office: 25 West Cedar, 32501.
Telephone: 904-469-1088.
Fax: 904-432-0677.
St. Petersburg, Florida Office: 100 Second Avenue S., Suite 7045, 33701.
Telephone: 813-982-6000.
Fax: 813-892-6002.
Gdansk, Poland Office: Suite 322, Dom Technika Building, Ul. Rajska 6, 80-850.
Telephone: 011-485-831-2808.
Fax: 011-485-831-4719.
Warsaw, Poland Office: Ul. Marszalkowska 82, Suite 561, 00-517.
Telephone: 011-482-623-6457 and 6458.
Fax: 011-482-623-6459.

RESIDENT PARTNER

David N. Parsigian

OF COUNSEL

Edmond F. DeVine

SENIOR ATTORNEY

Marta A. Manildi

RESIDENT ASSOCIATE

John O. Renken

Representative Firm Clients: Chrysler Corp.; Comerica, Inc.; City of Detroit, Mich.; Detroit Tigers, Inc.; First of Michigan; Fretter, Inc.; Ford Motor Co.; Ford Motor Credit Co.; Great Lakes Bancorp; Henry Ford Hospital.

For Complete List of Firm Personnel, See General Section

For full biographical listings, see the Martindale-Hubbell Law Directory

BIRMINGHAM, Oakland Co.

CARSON FISCHER, P.L.C. (AV)

Third Floor, 300 East Maple Road, 48009-6317
Telephone: 810-644-4840
Facsimile: 810-644-1832

Robert M. Carson
Peter L. Wanger

For full biographical listings, see the Martindale-Hubbell Law Directory

BLOOMFIELD HILLS, Oakland Co.

MILLER, CANFIELD, PADDOCK AND STONE, P.L.C. (AV)

A Professional Limited Liability Company
Founded in 1852 by Sidney Davy Miller
Suite 100 Pinehurst Office Center, 1400 North Woodward, P.O. Box 2014, 48303-2014
Telephone: 810-645-5000
Fax: 810-645-1917
Fax: 810-258-3036
Detroit, Michigan Office: 150 West Jefferson, Suite 2500, 48226-4415.
Telephone: 313-963-6420.
Fax: 313-496-7500.
Cable Address: "Stem Detroit."
Ann Arbor, Michigan Office: 101 North Main Street, 7th Floor, 48104-1400.
Telephone: 313-663-2445.
Fax: 313-747-7147.
Grand Rapids, Michigan Office: 1200 Campau Square Plaza, 99 Monroe, N.W., 49503-2639.
Telephone: 616-454-8656.
Fax: 616-776-6322.
Howell, Michigan Office: 121 South Barnard Street, Suite 4, 48843-2305.
Telephone: 517-546-7600.
Telecopier: 517-546-6974.
Kalamazoo, Michigan Office: 444 West Michigan Avenue, 49007-3752.
Telephone: 616-381-7030.
Fax: 616-382-0244.
Lansing, Michigan Office: One Michigan Avenue, Suite 900, 48933-1609.
Telephone: 517-487-2070.
Fax: 517-374-6304.
Monroe, Michigan Office: The Executive Centre, 214 East Elm Avenue, 48161-2682.
Telephone: 313-243-2000.
Fax: 313-243-0901.
Washington, D.C. Office: 1225 Nineteenth Street, N.W., Suite 400. 20036.
Telephone: 202-429-5575; 785-0600.
Fax: 202-331-1118; 785-1234.
Pensacola, Florida Office: 25 West Cedar, 32501.
Telephone: 904-469-1088.
Fax: 904-432-0677.
St. Petersburg, Florida Office: 100 Second Avenue S., Suite 7045, 33701.
Telephone: 813-982-6000.
Fax: 813-892-6002.
Gdansk, Poland Office: Suite 322, Dom Technika Building, Ul. Rajska 6, 80-850.
Telephone: 011-485-831-2808.
Fax: 011-485-831-4719.
Warsaw, Poland Office: Ul. Marszalkowska 82, Suite 561, 00-517.
Telephone: 011-482-623-6457 and 6458.
Fax: 011-482-623-6459.

RESIDENT MEMBERS

John A. Marxer (P.C.)
J. Kevin Trimmer
Brad B. Arbuckle

Representative Firm Clients: Chrysler Corp.; Comerica, Inc.; City of Detroit, Mich.; Detroit Tigers, Inc.; First of Michigan; Fretter, Inc.; Ford Motor Co.; Ford Motor Credit Co.; Great Lakes Bancorp; Henry Ford Hospital.

For Complete List of Firm Personnel, See General Section

For full biographical listings, see the Martindale-Hubbell Law Directory

STROBL AND MANOOGIAN, P.C. (AV)

300 East Long Lake Road, Suite 200, 48304-2376
Telephone: 810-645-0306
Facsimile: 810-645-2690

John Sharp

Representative Clients: Capitol Bancorp, Ltd.; Access Bidco; Midwest Guaranty Bank; Electronic Consumer Coupons, Inc.

For Complete List of Firm Personnel, See General Section

For full biographical listings, see the Martindale-Hubbell Law Directory

*DETROIT,** Wayne Co.

BODMAN, LONGLEY & DAHLING (AV)

34th Floor 100 Renaissance Center, 48243
Telephone: 313-259-7777
Fax: 313-393-7579
Troy, Michigan Office: Suite 2020, 755 West Big Beaver Road.
Telephone: 810-362-2110.
Ann Arbor, Michigan Office: 110 Miller, Suite 300.
Telephone: 313-761-3780.
Northern Michigan Office: 229 Court Street, P.O. Box 405, Cheboygan.
Telephone: 616-627-4351.

MEMBERS OF FIRM

Richard D. Rohr
Kenneth R. Lango (Troy Office)
James R. Buschmann
Randolph S. Perry (Ann Arbor Office)
Barbara Bowman Bluford

(See Next Column)

Representative Clients: Abitibi Price Group; Archdiocese of Detroit; Comerica Bank; The Detroit Lions, Inc.; Ford Estates; General Motors Corporation; Charles Stewart Mott Foundation; Norfolk Southern Corporation; Panhandle Eastern Corporation; State Farm Mutual Automobile Insurance Company.

For Complete List of Firm Personnel, See General Section

For full biographical listings, see the Martindale-Hubbell Law Directory

BUTZEL LONG, A PROFESSIONAL CORPORATION (AV)

Suite 900, 150 West Jefferson, 48226
Telephone: 313-225-7000
Telecopier: 313-225-7080
Birmingham, Michigan Office: Suite 200, 32270 Telegraph Road.
Telephone: 810-258-1616.
Telecopier: 810-258-1439.
Lansing, Michigan Office: 118 West Ottawa Street.
Telephone: 517-372-6622.
Telecopier: 517-372-6672.
Ann Arbor, Michigan Office: Suite 400, 121 West Washington.
Telephone: 313-995-3110.
Telecopier: 313-995-1777.
Grosse Pointe Farms, Michigan Office: Suite 260, 21 Kercheval.
Telephone: 313-886-5446.
Telecopier: 313-886-2114.

Douglas G. Graham
George H. Zinn, Jr.
Edward M. Kronk
Philip J. Kessler
Daniel P. Malone
Justin G. Klimko
Michael F. Golab
Edward M. Kalinka
Arthur Dudley II
Richard P. Saslow
Dennis K. Egan
Jack J. Mazzara
Sheldon H. Klein

Ronald E. Reynolds
Phillip C. Korovesis
Joshua A. Sherbin

Representative Clients: The Evening News Assn.; Merrill Lynch, Pierce, Fenner & Smith, Inc.; Prudential Securities, Inc.; Drexel Burnham Lambert; Bear Stearns; Paine Webber; Michigan Rivet Corp.; Jackson National Life Insurance Co.; Guardian Industries Co.

For Complete List of Firm Personnel, See General Section

For full biographical listings, see the Martindale-Hubbell Law Directory

CLARK, KLEIN & BEAUMONT (AV)

1600 First Federal Building, 1001 Woodward Avenue, 48226
Telephone: 313-965-8300
Facsimile: 313-962-4348
Bloomfield Hills Office: 1533 North Woodward Avenue, Suite 220, 48304.
Telephone: 810-258-2900.
Facsimile: 810-258-2949.

MEMBERS OF FIRM

D. Kerry Crenshaw
John F. Burns
Robert L. Weyhing, III
John J. Hern, Jr.

ASSOCIATES

Patrice A. Villani
Georgette Borrego Dulworth

Representative Clients: R.P. Scherer Company; LCI International; Hogg Group; Rouge Steel Company; Gerber Foundation; Frey Foundation; Hudson-Weber Foundation; The Delfield Company.

For Complete List of Firm Personnel, See General Section

For full biographical listings, see the Martindale-Hubbell Law Directory

JAFFE, RAITT, HEUER & WEISS, PROFESSIONAL CORPORATION (AV)

One Woodward Avenue, Suite 2400, 48226
Telephone: 313-961-8380
Telecopier: 313-961-8358
Cable Address: "Jafsni"
Southfield,Michigan Office: Travelers Tower, Suite 1520.
Telephone: 313-961-8380.
Monroe, Michigan Office: 212 East Front Street, Suite 3.
Telephone: 313-241-6470.
Telefacsimile: 313-241-3849.

Penny L. Carolan
Elliot A. Spoon
David D. Warner
Janet G. Witkowski

See General Practice Section for List of Representative Clients.

For Complete List of Firm Personnel, See General Section

For full biographical listings, see the Martindale-Hubbell Law Directory

Detroit—Continued

LEWIS, WHITE & CLAY, A PROFESSIONAL CORPORATION (AV)

1300 First National Building, 660 Woodward Avenue, 48226-3531
Telephone: 313-961-2550
Washington, D.C. Office: 1250 Connecticut Avenue, N.W., Suite 630, 20036.
Telephone: 202-835-0616.
Fax: 202-833-3316.

David Baker Lewis
Richard Thomas White
Eric Lee Clay
Reuben A. Munday
Ulysses Whittaker Boykin
S. Allen Early, III
Carl F. Stafford
Helen Francine Strong
Derrick P. Mayes
Frank E. Barbee
Camille Stearns Miller
Melvin J. Hollowell, Jr.
Michael T. Raymond
Jacqueline H. Sellers
Thomas R. Paxton
Kathleen Miles (Resident, Washington, D.C. Office)
David N. Zacks

Karen Kendrick Brown (Resident, Washington, D.C. Office)
J. Taylor Teasdale
Wade Harper McCree
Tyrone A. Powell
Blair A. Person
Susan D. Hoffman
Stephon E. Johnson
John J. Walsh
Andrea L. Powell
Teresa N. Gueyser
Hans J. Massaquoi, Jr.
Werten F. W. Bellamy, Jr. (Resident, Washington, D.C. Office)
Akin O. Akindele
Regina P. Freelon-Solomon
Calita L. Elston
Nancy C. Borland
Terrence Randall Haugabook
Lynn R. Westfall
Lance W. Mason

OF COUNSEL

Otis M. Smith (1922-1994)
Inez Smith Reid (Resident, Washington, D.C. Office)

Representative Clients: Omnicare Health Plan; Aetna Life & Casualty Co.; Chrysler Motors Corp.; Chrysler Financial Corp.; MCI Communications Corp.; City of Detroit; City of Detroit Building Authority; City of Detroit Downtown Development Authority; Consolidated Rail Corp. (Conrail); Equitable Life Assurance Society of the United States.

For full biographical listings, see the Martindale-Hubbell Law Directory

MILLER, CANFIELD, PADDOCK AND STONE, P.L.C. (AV)

A Professional Limited Liability Company
Founded in 1852 by Sidney Davy Miller
150 West Jefferson, Suite 2500, 48226-4415
Telephone: 313-963-6420
Fax: 313-496-7500
Cable Address: "Stem Detroit"
Detroit, Michigan Office: 150 West Jefferson, Suite 2500, 48226-4415.
Telephone: 313-963-6420.
Fax: 313-496-7500.
Cable Address: "Stem Detroit."
Ann Arbor, Michigan Office: 101 North Main Street, 7th Floor, 48104-1400.
Telephone: 313-663-2445.
Fax: 313-747-7147.
Bloomfield Hills, Michigan Office: Suite 100, Pinehurst Office Center, 1400 North Woodward, 48303-2014.
Telephone: 313-645-5000.
Fax: 313-645-1917.
Grand Rapids, Michigan Office: 1200 Campau Square Plaza, 99 Monroe, N.W., 49503-2639.
Telephone: 616-454-8656.
Fax: 616-776-6322.
Howell, Michigan Office: 121 South Barnard Street, Suite 4, 48843-2305.
Telephone: 517-546-7600.
Telecopier: 517-546-6974.
Kalamazoo, Michigan Office: 444 West Michigan Avenue, 49007-3752.
Telephone: 616-381-7030.
Fax: 616-382-0244.
Lansing, Michigan Office: One Michigan Avenue, Suite 900, 48933-1609.
Telephone: 517-487-2070.
Fax: 517-374-6304.
Monroe, Michigan Office: The Executive Centre, 214 East Elm Avenue, 48161-2682.
Telephone: 313-243-2000.
Fax: 313-243-0901.
Washington, D.C. Office: 1225 Nineteenth Street, N.W., Suite 400. 20036.
Telephone: 202-429-5575; 785-0600.
Fax: 202-331-1118; 785-1234.
Pensacola, Florida Office: 25 West Cedar, 32501.
Telephone: 904-469-1088.
Fax: 904-432-0677.
St. Petersburg, Florida Office: 100 Second Avenue S., Suite 7045, 33701.
Telephone: 813-982-6000.
Fax: 813-892-6002.
Gdansk, Poland Office: Suite 322, Dom Technika Building, Ul. Rajska 6, 80-850.
Telephone: 011-485-831-2808.
Fax: 011-485-831-4719.

(See Next Column)

Warsaw, Poland Office: Ul. Marszalkowska 82, Suite 561, 00-517.
Telephone: 011-482-623-6457 and 6458.
Fax: 011-482-623-6459.

MEMBERS OF FIRM

Eric V. Brown, Jr. (Kalamazoo Office)
Bruce D. Birgbauer
Carl H. von Ende
David D. Joswick (P.C.)
John A. Marxer (P.C.) (Bloomfield Hills Office)
Clarence L. Pozza, Jr.
Jerry T. Rupley
Kent E. Shafer
John R. Cook (Kalamazoo Office)
Thomas G. Appleman
Thomas H. Van Dis (Kalamazoo Office)
Stephen M. Tuuk (Grand Rapids Office)
Mark T. Boonstra
Karen Ann McCoy
Steven M. Stankewicz (Kalamazoo Office)
David N. Parsigian (Ann Arbor Office)
Jay B. Rising (Lansing Office)

SENIOR ATTORNEY

Marta A. Manildi (Ann Arbor Office)

ASSOCIATES

Thomas R. Cox
Janet R. Chrzanowski
John O. Renken (Ann Arbor and District of Columbia Offices)

Representative Firm Clients: Chrysler Corp.; Comerica, Inc.; City of Detroit, Mich.; Detroit Tigers, Inc.; First of Michigan; Fretter, Inc.; Ford Motor Co.; Ford Motor Credit Co.; Great Lakes Bancorp; Henry Ford Hospital.

For Complete List of Firm Personnel, See General Section

For full biographical listings, see the Martindale-Hubbell Law Directory

*GRAND RAPIDS,** Kent Co.

MCSHANE & BOWIE (AV)

540 Old Kent Building, P.O. Box 360, 49503-2481
Telephone: 616-774-0641
Fax: 616-774-2366

MEMBERS OF FIRM

Keith P. Walker
Gary G. Love
Dan M. Challa
Wayne P. Bryan

OF COUNSEL

Jack M. Bowie

Representative Clients: West Side Federal Savings & Loan Assn.; Hartger & Willard Mortgage Associates, Inc.

For Complete List of Firm Personnel, See General Section

For full biographical listings, see the Martindale-Hubbell Law Directory

MILLER, CANFIELD, PADDOCK AND STONE, P.L.C. (AV)

A Professional Limited Liability Company
Founded in 1852 by Sidney Davy Miller
1200 Campau Square Plaza, 99 Monroe, N.W., P.O. Box 329, 49503-2639
Telephone: 616-454-8656
Fax: 616-776-6322
Detroit, Michigan Office: 150 West Jefferson, Suite 2500, 48226-4415.
Telephone: 313-963-6420.
Fax: 313-496-7500.
Cable Address: "Stem Detroit."
Ann Arbor, Michigan Office: 101 North Main Street, 7th Floor, 48104-1400.
Telephone: 313-663-2445.
Fax: 313-747-7147.
Bloomfield Hills, Michigan Office: Suite 100, Pinehurst Office Center, 1400 North Woodward, 48303-2014.
Telephone: 313-645-5000.
Fax: 313-645-1917.
Howell, Michigan Office: 121 South Barnard Street, Suite 4, 48843-2305.
Telephone: 517-546-7600.
Telecopier: 517-546-6974.
Kalamazoo, Michigan Office: 444 West Michigan Avenue, 49007-3752.
Telephone: 616-381-7030.
Fax: 616-382-0244.
Lansing, Michigan Office: One Michigan Avenue, Suite 900, 48933-1609.
Telephone: 517-487-2070.
Fax: 517-374-6304.
Monroe, Michigan Office: The Executive Centre, 214 East Elm Avenue, 48161-2682.
Telephone: 313-243-2000.
Fax: 313-243-0901.
Washington, D.C. Office: 1225 Nineteenth Street, N.W., Suite 400. 20036.
Telephone: 202-429-5575; 785-0600;
Fax: 202-331-1118; 785-1234.
Pensacola, Florida Office: 25 West Cedar 32501.
Telephone: 904-469-1088.
Fax: 904-432-0677.
St. Petersburg Florida Office: 100 Second Avenue S., Suite 7045, 33701.
Telephone: 813-982-6000.
Fax: 813-892-6002.

(See Next Column)

MILLER, CANFIELD, PADDOCK AND STONE P.L.C., *Grand Rapids—Continued*

Gdansk, Poland Office: Suite 322, Dom Technika Building, UI. Rajska 6, 80-850.
Telephone: 011-485-831-2808.
Fax: 011-485-831-4719.
Warsaw, Poland Office: UI. Marszalkowska 82, Suite 561, 00-517.
Telephone: 011-482-623-6457 and 6458.
Fax: 011-482-623-6459.

MEMBERS OF FIRM

Thomas J. Heiden (Resident)
Stephen M. Tuuk (Resident)

Representative Firm Clients: Chrysler Corp.; Comerica, Inc.; City of Detroit, Mich.; Detroit Tigers, Inc.; First of Michigan; Fretter, Inc.; Ford Motor Co.; Ford Motor Credit Co.; Great Lakes Bancorp; Henry Ford Hospital.

For Complete List of Firm Personnel, See General Section

For full biographical listings, see the Martindale-Hubbell Law Directory

TOLLEY, VANDENBOSCH & WALTON, P.C. (AV)

5650 Foremost Drive, S.E., 49546
Telephone: 616-942-8090
Facsimile: 616-942-4677

Peter R. Tolley
Miles J. Postema

For full biographical listings, see the Martindale-Hubbell Law Directory

WARNER, NORCROSS & JUDD (AV)

900 Old Kent Building, 111 Lyon Street, N.W., 49503-2489
Telephone: 616-752-2000
Fax: 616-752-2500
Muskegon, Michigan Office: 400 Terrace Plaza, P.O. Box 900.
Telephone: 616-727-2600.
Fax: 616-727-2699.
Holland, Michigan Office: Curtis Center, Suite 300, 170 College Avenue.
Telephone: 616-396-9800.
Fax: 616-396-3656.

OF COUNSEL

Lawson E. Becker
Conrad A. Bradshaw
Harold F. Schumacher
Charles C. Lundstrom

MEMBERS OF FIRM

David A. Warner (1883-1966)
George S. Norcross (1889-1960)
Siegel W. Judd (1895-1982)
Platt W. Dockery (1906-1974)
J. M. Neath, Jr. (1928-1974)
Leonard D. Verdier, Jr. (1915-1989)
Thomas J. McNamara (1936-1989)
Phil R. Johnson (1908-1990)
Thomas R. Winquist
George L. Whitfield
Wallson G. Knack
Charles E. McCallum
Jerome M. Smith
John D. Tully
R. Malcolm Cumming
William K. Holmes
Roger M. Clark
Edward Malinzak
John H. Logie
Donald J. Veldman (Resident at Muskegon Office)
I. John Snider, II (Resident at Muskegon Office)
Jack B. Combs
Joseph F. Martin
John R. Marquis (Resident at Holland Office)
John H. Martin (Resident at Muskegon Office)
James H. Breay
Ernest M. Sharpe
Vernon P. Saper
Hugh H. Makens
Joseph M. Sweeney
Gordon R. Lewis
Robert J. Chovanec
Peter L. Gustafson
Roger H. Oetting
J. A. Cragwall, Jr.
Stephen R. Kretschman
W. Michael Van Haren
Richard A. Durell
Michael L. Robinson
Eugene E. Smary
Douglas E. Wagner
Robert W. Sikkel (Muskegon and Holland Offices)
Thomas H. Thornhill (Resident at Muskegon Office)
Jeffrey O. Birkhold
Timothy Hillegonds
Blake W. Krueger
John G. Cameron, Jr.
John H. McKendry, Jr. (Resident at Muskegon Office)
Paul T. Sorensen
Carl W. Dufendach
Stephen C. Waterbury
Rodney D. Martin
Richard E. Cassard
Alex J. DeYonker
Charles E. Burpee
John D. Dunn
William W. Hall
Bruce C. Young
Shane B. Hansen
F. William McKee
Louis C. Rabaut
Paul R. Jackson (Resident at Muskegon Office)
Douglas A. Dozeman
John V. Byl
Janet Percy Knaus
Kathleen M. Hanenburg
Tracy T. Larsen
Sue O. Conway
Steven R. Heacock
Cameron S. DeLong
Jeffrey B. Power
Scott D. Hubbard
Stephen B. Grow
Richard L. Bouma
Daniel R. Gravelyn
Robert J. Jonker
Devin S. Schindler
Michael H. Schubert (Resident at Muskegon Office)

(See Next Column)

ASSOCIATES

Valerie Pierre Simmons
James Moskal
Robert J. Buchanan
Mark K. Harder (Resident at Holland Office)
Kenneth W. Vermeulen
Mark E. Brouwer
Mark R. Lange
Jeffrey S. Battershall
Jeffrey A. Ott
Eric S. Richards
Martha Walters Atwater
Rodrick W. Lewis
Kevin G. Dougherty
Scott J. Gorsline
Melvin G. Moseley, Jr.
James J. Rabaut
James P. Enright
Timothy L. Horner
Richard D. Cornell, Jr. (Resident at Muskegon Office)
R. Paul Guerre
Loren M. Andrulis
Karen J. Vanderwerff
Susan Gell Meyers
Gordon J. Toering
Frank E. Berrodin (Resident at Muskegon Office)
Steven A. Palazzolo (Resident at Muskegon Office)
Norbert F. Kugele
Eric D. Stubenvoll
Shaun M. Murphy
Kevin P. McDowell (Resident at Holland Office)
Mark J. Wassink
Richard J. Suhrheinrich
David Paul Trummel
Dennis J. Donohue
Michael I. Kleaveland (Resident at Muskegon Office)
Elizabeth M. Topliffe
Susan N. McFee
Julie H. Sullivan
Molly E. McFarlane
William P. Dani
Andrew D. Hakken
Andrea J. Bernard
Brian S. Felton
Lori L. Gibson
Mark T. Ostrowski
Michael P. Lunt

General Counsel for: Bissell Inc.; Blodgett Memorial Medical Center; Guardsman Products, Inc.; Haworth, Inc.; Kysor Industrial Corp.; Michigan Bankers Assn.; Old Kent Financial Corp.; Steelcase Inc.; Wolverine World Wide, Inc.

For full biographical listings, see the Martindale-Hubbell Law Directory

*KALAMAZOO,** Kalamazoo Co.

MILLER, CANFIELD, PADDOCK AND STONE, P.L.C. (AV)

A Professional Limited Liability Company
Founded in 1852 by Sidney Davy Miller
444 West Michigan Avenue, 49007-3752
Telephone: 616-381-7030
Fax: 616-382-0244
Detroit, Michigan Office: 150 West Jefferson, Suite 2500, 48226-4415.
Telephone: 313-963-6420.
Fax: 313-496-7500.
Cable Address: "Stem Detroit."
Ann Arbor, Michigan Office: 101 North Main Street, 7th Floor, 48104-1400.
Telephone: 313-663-2445.
Fax: 313-747-7147.
Bloomfield Hills, Michigan Office: Suite 100, Pinehurst Office Center, 1400 North Woodward, 48303-2014.
Telephone: 313-645-5000.
Fax: 313-645-1917.
Grand Rapids, Michigan Office: 1200 Campau Square Plaza, 99 Monroe, N.W., 49503-2639.
Telephone: 616-454-8656.
Fax: 616-776-6322.
Howell, Michigan Office: 121 South Barnard Street, Suite 4, 48843-2305.
Telephone: 517-546-7600.
Telecopier: 517-546-6974.
Lansing, Michigan Office: One Michigan Avenue, Suite 900, 48933-1609.
Telephone: 517-487-2070.
Fax: 517-374-6304.
Monroe, Michigan Office: The Executive Centre, 214 East Elm Avenue, 48161-2682.
Telephone: 313-243-2000.
Fax: 313-243-0901.
Washington, D.C. Office: 1225 Nineteenth Street, N.W., Suite 400. 20036.
Telephone: 202-429-5575; 785-0600.
Fax: 202-331-1118; 785-1234.
Pensacola, Florida Office: 25 West Cedar, 32501.
Telephone: 904-469-1088.
Fax: 904-432-0677.
St. Petersburg, Florida Office: 100 Second Avenue S., Suite 7045,33701.
Telephone: 813-982-6000.
Fax: 813-892-6002.
Gdansk, Poland Office: Suite 322, Dom Technika Building, UI. Rajska 6, 80-850.
Telephone: 011-485-831-2808.
Fax: 011-485-831-4719.
Warsaw, Poland Office: UI. Marszalkowska 82, Suite 561, 00-517.
Telephone: 011-482-623-6457 and 6458.
Fax: 011-482-623-6459.

MEMBERS OF FIRM

Eric V. Brown, Jr. (Resident)
John R. Cook (Resident)
James G. Vantine, Jr. (Resident)
Thomas H. Van Dis (Resident)
Steven M. Stankewicz (Resident)

Representative Firm Clients: Chrysler Corp.; Comerica, Inc.; City of Detroit, Mich.; Detroit Tigers, Inc.; First of Michigan; Fretter, Inc.; Ford Motor Co.; Ford Motor Credit Co.; Great Lakes Bancorp; Henry Ford Hospital.

(See Next Column)

MILLER, CANFIELD, PADDOCK AND STONE P.L.C.—*Continued*

For Complete List of Firm Personnel, See General Section

For full biographical listings, see the Martindale-Hubbell Law Directory

*MONROE,** Monroe Co.

MILLER, CANFIELD, PADDOCK AND STONE, P.L.C. (AV)

A Professional Limited Liability Company
Founded in 1852 by Sidney Davy Miller
The Executive Centre, 214 East Elm Avenue, 48161-2682
Telephone: 313-243-2000
Fax: 313-243-0901
Detroit, Michigan Office: 150 West Jefferson, Suite 2500, 48226-4415.
Telephone: 313-963-6420.
Fax: 313-496-7500.
Cable Address: "Stem Detroit."
Ann Arbor, Michigan Office: 101 North Main Street, 7th Floor, 48104-1400.
Telephone: 313-663-2445.
Fax: 313-747-7147.
Bloomfield Hills, Michigan Office: Suite 100, Pinehurst Office Center, 1400 North Woodward, 48303-2014.
Telephone: 313-645-5000.
Fax: 313-645-1917.
Grand Rapids, Michigan Office: 1200 Campau Square Plaza, 99 Monroe, N.W., 49503-2639.
Telephone: 616-454-8656.
Fax: 616-776-6322.
Howell, Michigan Office: 121 South Barnard Street, Suite 4, 48843-2305.
Telephone: 517-546-7600.
Telecopier: 517-546-6974.
Kalamazoo, Michigan Office: 444 West Michigan Avenue, 49007-3752.
Telephone: 616-381-7030.
Fax: 616-382-0244.
Lansing, Michigan Office: One Michigan Avenue, Suite 900, 48933-1609.
Telephone: 517-487-2070.
Fax: 517-374-6304.
Washington, D.C. Office: 1225 Nineteenth Street, N.W., Suite 400. 20036.
Telephone: 202-429-5575; 785-0600.
Fax: 202-331-1118; 785-1234.
Pensacola, Florida Office: 25 West Cedar, 32501.
Telephone: 904-469-1088.
Fax: 904-432-0677.
St. Petersburg, Florida Office: 100 Second Avenue S., Suite 7045, 33701.
Telephone: 813-982-6000.
Fax: 813-892-6002.
Gdansk, Poland Office: Suite 322, Dom Technika Building, Ul. Rajska 6, 80-850.
Telephone: 011-485-831-2808.
Fax: 011-485-831-4719.
Warsaw, Poland Office: Ul. Marszalkowska 82, Suite 561, 00-517.
Telephone: 011-482-623-6457 and 6458.
Fax: 011-482-623-6459.

RESIDENT MEMBER
Rocque E. Lipford (P.C.)

Representative Firm Clients: Chrysler Corp.; Comerica, Inc.; City of Detroit, Mich.; Detroit Tigers, Inc.; First of Michigan; Fretter, Inc.; Ford Motor Co.; Ford Motor Credit Co.; Great Lakes Bancorp; Henry Ford Hospital.

For full biographical listings, see the Martindale-Hubbell Law Directory

MINNESOTA

*MINNEAPOLIS,** Hennepin Co.

ABDO AND ABDO, P.A. (AV)

710 Northstar West, 625 Marquette Avenue, 55402
Telephone: 612-333-1526
Fax: 612-342-2608

Robert P. Abdo
Steven R. Hedges
Keith J. Broady
Kenneth J. Abdo
Timothy C. Matson

Representative Clients: ADT Security Systems, Inc.; Cold Spring Brewing Co., Cold Spring, Minn.

For Complete List of Firm Personnel, See General Section

For full biographical listings, see the Martindale-Hubbell Law Directory

BERNICK AND LIFSON, P.A. (AV)

Suite 1200 The Colonnade, 5500 Wayzata Boulevard, 55416
Telephone: 612-546-1200
FAX: 612-546-1003

(See Next Column)

Ross A. Sussman
Neal J. Shapiro
Saul A. Bernick
Thomas D. Creighton
Scott Lifson
David K. Nightingale
Paul J. Quast

Theresa M. Kowalski
Rebecca J. Heltzer

Reference: First Bank N.A., Minneapolis, Minn.

For full biographical listings, see the Martindale-Hubbell Law Directory

FROMMELT & EIDE, LTD. (AV)

580 International Centre, 900 Second Avenue South, 55402
Telephone: 612-332-2200; 800-332-2296
FAX: 612-342-2761

Roger H. Frommelt
David B. Eide
John R. Dorgan
Randy J. Sparling
James W. Rude
Jean M. Davis
Fredrick R. Krietzman
Douglas M. Ramler

For full biographical listings, see the Martindale-Hubbell Law Directory

HENSON & EFRON, P.A. (AV)

1200 Title Insurance Building, 400 Second Avenue South, 55401
Telephone: 612-339-2500
FAX: 612-339-6364

Robert F. Henson
Stanley Efron
Wellington W. Tully, Jr.
Joseph T. Dixon, Jr.
Alan C. Eidsness
William F. Forsyth
Stuart T. Williams
Bruce C. Recher
Louis L. Ainsworth
Stephen L. Hopkins
Susan E. Vandenberg
Clark D. Opdahl

Karen S. Johnston
David Bradley Olsen
Jeffrey N. Saunders
Cheryl Hood Langel
Daniel A. Bueide
Cassandra Phillips Chaffee
John A. Mack
Scott A. Neilson
Sherilyn K. Beck

Representative Clients: Pentair, Inc.; Juran & Moody, Inc.

For full biographical listings, see the Martindale-Hubbell Law Directory

PARSINEN BOWMAN & LEVY, A PROFESSIONAL ASSOCIATION (AV)

100 South 5th Street Suite 1100, 55402
Telephone: 612-333-2111
FAX: 612-333-6798

Dennis A. Bowman
John Parsinen
Robert A. Levy
Jack A. Rosberg
John F. Bonner, III
David A. Gotlieb
Karen Ciegler Hansen
Jeffrey C. Robbins
E. Burke Hinds, III
Howard J. Rubin
David A. Orenstein
Diane L. Kroupa
Jeanne K. Stretch
John C. Levy
Joseph M. Sokolowski
Randy B. Evans
Brian R. Martens
Steven R. Katz

Rebecca McDaniel
Ann Marks Sanford
Timothy R. Ring
Robert A. Hill
W. James Vogl, Jr.
Bradley Allen Kletscher
John R. Bedosky
Roben D. Hunter
Jeffrey R. Johnson (Not admitted in MN)

OF COUNSEL
Bruce B. James

For full biographical listings, see the Martindale-Hubbell Law Directory

SALITERMAN & SIEFFERMAN LAW FIRM (AV)

Suite 1000 Northstar Center East, 608 Second Avenue South, 55402
Telephone: 612-339-1400
Fax: 612-349-2908

Richard A. Saliterman
Floyd E. Siefferman, Jr.
John R. Heine
Nicholas M. Wenner
Bretton J. Horttor

LEGAL SUPPORT PERSONNEL
Darryl R. Fenley

For full biographical listings, see the Martindale-Hubbell Law Directory

MISSOURI

ST. LOUIS, (Independent City)

MOLINE & SHOSTAK (AV)

The Berkley Building, 8015 Forsyth Boulevard, 63105
Telephone: 314-725-3200
Fax: 314-725-3275

Harry O. Moline
Burton H. Shostak
Sherri Cranmore Strand
Donald J. Mehan, Jr.
Deborah J. Westling
Michael S. Ghidina

For full biographical listings, see the Martindale-Hubbell Law Directory

MONTANA

*BILLINGS,** Yellowstone Co.

CROWLEY, HAUGHEY, HANSON, TOOLE & DIETRICH (AV)

500 Transwestern II, 490 North 31st Street, P.O. Box 2529, 59103
Telephone: 406-252-3441
Fax: 406-259-4159
Helena, Montana Office: IBM Building, 100 North Park Avenue, Suite 300, 59601.
Telephone: 406-449-4165.
Fax: 406-449-5149.

MEMBERS OF FIRM

John M. Dietrich
Allan L. Karell

Representative Clients: Montana Power Co.; First Interstate Bank of Commerce; MDU Resources Group, Inc.; Chevron U.S.A., Inc.; Noranda Minerals Corp.; United Parcel Service.
Insurance Clients: Farmers Insurance Group; New York Life Insurance Co.

For Complete List of Firm Personnel, See General Section

For full biographical listings, see the Martindale-Hubbell Law Directory

NEBRASKA

*LINCOLN,** Lancaster Co.

KNUDSEN, BERKHEIMER, RICHARDSON & ENDACOTT (AV)

1000 NBC Center, 68508
Telephone: 402-475-7011
Facsimile: 402-475-8912
Capitol Office: 1233 Lincoln Mall, Suite 202.
Telephone: 402-434-3399.
Facsimile: 402-434-3390.
Denver, Colorado Office: Suite 510, Alamo Plaza, 1401 - 17th Street.
Telephone: 303-395-4250.
Facsimile: 303-295-4243.

MEMBERS OF FIRM

Robert J. Routh
David R. Wilson

For Complete List of Firm Personnel, See General Section

For full biographical listings, see the Martindale-Hubbell Law Directory

SCUDDER LAW FIRM, P.C. (AV)

Second Floor, 411 South 13th Street, P.O. Box 81277, 68508
Telephone: 402-435-3223
Fax: 402-435-4239

Beverly Evans Grenier
Christine C. Schwartzkopf Schroff
Earl H. Scudder, Jr.
Mark A. Scudder

For full biographical listings, see the Martindale-Hubbell Law Directory

NEVADA

*LAS VEGAS,** Clark Co.

KUMMER KAEMPFER BONNER & RENSHAW (AV)

Seventh Floor, 3800 Howard Hughes Parkway, 89109
Telephone: 702-792-7000
Fax: 702-796-7181

(See Next Column)

MEMBERS OF FIRM

John C. Renshaw
Thomas F. Kummer
Christopher L. Kaempfer
Martha J. Ashcraft
Michael J. Bonner
John N. Brewer
Von S. Heinz
Gerald D. Waite
Elliott R. Eisner

OF COUNSEL

H. Gregory Nasky

ASSOCIATES

Shari Cassin Patterson
Georlen K. Spangler
Sherwood N. Cook
Daurean G. Sloan
Anthony A. Zmaila
John C. Jeppsen
P. Blake Allen
L. Joe Coppedge
David A. Barksdale
George J. Claseman
Dennis M. Prince
Jeffrey W. Ray (Not admitted in NV)
Jennifer M. Settles

For full biographical listings, see the Martindale-Hubbell Law Directory

LEAVITT, SULLY & RIVERS (AV)

An Association of Professional Corporations
601 East Bridger Avenue, 89101
Telephone: 702-382-5111
Telecopier: 702-382-2892

K. Michael Leavitt (Chartered)
W. Leslie Sully, Jr. (Chartered)
David J. Rivers, II (Chartered)

For full biographical listings, see the Martindale-Hubbell Law Directory

NEW JERSEY

*NEWARK,** Essex Co.

HELLRING LINDEMAN GOLDSTEIN & SIEGAL (AV)

One Gateway Center, 07102-5386
Telephone: 201-621-9020
Telecopier: 201-621-7406

Bernard Hellring (1916-1991)
Philip Lindeman, II
Joel D. Siegal
Jonathan L. Goldstein
James A. Scarpone
Michael Edelson
Margaret Dee Hellring
Richard D. Shapiro
Charles Oransky
Richard B. Honig
Richard K. Coplon
Robert S. Raymar
Ronny Jo Greenwald Siegal
Stephen L. Dreyfuss
John A. Adler
Judah I. Elstein
Ronnie F. Liebowitz
Bruce S. Etterman
Matthew E. Moloshok
Rachel N. Davidson
Val Mandel
Sarah Jane Jelin
Eric A. Savage
David N. Narciso
Sheryl E. Koomer

For full biographical listings, see the Martindale-Hubbell Law Directory

McMANIMON & SCOTLAND (AV)

One Gateway Center, 18th Floor, 07102-5311
Telephone: 201-622-1800
Fax: 201-622-7333; 201-622-3744
Atlantic City, New Jersey Office: 26 South Pennsylvania Avenue.
Telephone: 609-347-0040.
Fax: 609-347-0866.
Trenton, New Jersey Office: 172 West State Street.
Telephone: 609-278-1800.
Fax: 609-278-9222.
Washington, D.C. Office: 1275 Pennsylvania Avenue, N.W.
Telephone: 202-638-3100.
Fax: 202-638-4222.

MEMBERS OF FIRM

Joseph P. Baumann, Jr.
Carla J. Brundage
John V. Cavaliere
Edward F. Clark
Christopher H. Falcon
Felicia L. Garland
James R. Gregory
John B. Hall
Thomas A. Hart, Jr. (Resident, Washington, D.C. Office)
Leah C. Healey
Ronald J. Ianoale
Andrea L. Kahn
Jeffrey G. Kramer
Michael A. Lampert
Joseph J. Maraziti, Jr.
Edward J. McManimon, III
Steven P. Natko
Martin C. Rothfelder
Steven Schaars (Resident, Washington, D.C. Office)
Glenn F. Scotland
Michael A. Walker

ASSOCIATES

Carl E. Ailara, Jr.
Diane Alexander-McCabe
Leslie G. London
Cheryl A. Maier
Daniel E. McManus
Sheryl L. Newman
Steven J. Reed
Erik F. Remmler
David J. Ruitenberg
Bradford M. Stern

(See Next Column)

McManimon & Scotland—*Continued*

OF COUNSEL

John R. Armstrong
Carl H. Fogler (Not admitted in NJ)

LEGAL SUPPORT PERSONNEL

Helen Lysaght

PARALEGALS

Jane Folmer
Zulmira Donahue

References: First Fidelity Bank, N.A., New Jersey; Midlantic National Bank.

For full biographical listings, see the Martindale-Hubbell Law Directory

Saiber Schlesinger Satz & Goldstein (AV)

One Gateway Center, 13th Floor, 07102-5311
Telephone: 201-622-3333
Telecopier: 201-622-3349

MEMBERS OF FIRM

David M. Satz, Jr.
Bruce I. Goldstein
William F. Maderer
David J. D'Aloia
James H. Aibel
Sean R. Kelly
John L. Conover
Lawrence B. Mink
Michael L. Allen
Michael L. Messer
Jeffrey W. Lorell
Jeffrey M. Schwartz
David J. Satz
Joan M. Schwab
Jennine DiSomma
James H. Forte
Vincent F. Papalia

OF COUNSEL

Samuel S. Saiber
Norman E. Schlesinger

COUNSEL

Andrew Alcorn
Robin B. Horn
Randi Schillinger

ASSOCIATES

Audrey M. Weinstein
Robert B. Nussbaum
Michael J. Geraghty
Jonathan S. Davis
Paul S. DeGiulio
Diana L. Sussman
Deanna M. Beacham
Robert W. Geiger
William S. Gyves
Barry P. Kramer
Susan Rozman
Michelle Viola

LEGAL SUPPORT PERSONNEL

DIRECTOR OF FINANCE AND ADMINISTRATION

Ronald Henry

For full biographical listings, see the Martindale-Hubbell Law Directory

PARSIPPANY, Morris Co.

Kummer, Knox, Naughton & Hansbury (AV)

Lincoln Centre, 299 Cherry Hill Road, 07054
Telephone: 201-335-3900
Telecopier: 201-335-9577

MEMBERS OF FIRM

Richard E. Kummer
Stephen R. Knox
Michael J. Naughton
Stephan C. Hansbury

ASSOCIATES

Gail H. Fraser
Kurt W. Krauss
Linda M. DeVenuto

For full biographical listings, see the Martindale-Hubbell Law Directory

NEW MEXICO

*ALBUQUERQUE,** Bernalillo Co.

Rodey, Dickason, Sloan, Akin & Robb, P.A. (AV)

Albuquerque Plaza, Suite 2200, 201 Third Street, N.W., P.O. Box 1888, 87103-1888
Telephone: 505-765-5900
Fax: 505-768-7395
Santa Fe, New Mexico Office: Suite 101 Marcy Plaza, 123 East Marcy Street, P.O. Box 1357, 87504-1357.
Telephone: 505-984-0100.
Fax: 505-989-9542.

Robert G. McCorkle
John P. Burton (Resident, Santa Fe Office)
S. I. Betzer, Jr.
David C. Davenport, Jr. (Resident, Santa Fe Office)
Mark A. Smith

Representative Clients: Albuquerque Publishing Co.; ASCAP; Associated Aviation Underwriters Co.; Automobile Club Insurance Co.; Avonite, Inc.; Canal Insurance Co.; General Electric Co.; KOAT-TV; Liberty Mutual Insurance Co.; Sandia Corporation.

For Complete List of Firm Personnel, See General Section

For full biographical listings, see the Martindale-Hubbell Law Directory

*SANTA FE,** Santa Fe Co.

Rose, Kohl & Davenport, Ltd. (AV)

1516 Paseo De Peralta, 87501
Telephone: 505-982-0080
Fax: 505-982-0081

Filmore E. Rose
Bruce R. Kohl
Beth R. Davenport
Robert J. Dodds, III
Marie A. Cioth (Not admitted in NM)

Reference: The First National Bank of Santa Fe.

For full biographical listings, see the Martindale-Hubbell Law Directory

NEW YORK

EAST MEADOW, Nassau Co.

Certilman Balin Adler & Hyman, LLP (AV)

90 Merrick Avenue, 11554
Telephone: 516-296-7000
Telecopier: 516-296-7111

MEMBERS OF FIRM

Ira J. Adler
Dale Allinson
Herbert M. Balin
Bruce J. Bergman
Michael D. Brofman
Morton L. Certilman
Murray Greenberg
David Z. Herman
Richard Herzbach
M. Allan Hyman
Bernard Hyman
Donna-Marie Korth
Steven J. Kuperschmid
Thomas J. McNamara
Fred S. Skolnik
Louis Soloway
Harold Somer
Howard M. Stein
Brian K. Ziegler

OF COUNSEL

Daniel S. Cohan
Norman J. Levy
Marilyn Price

ASSOCIATES

Howard B. Busch
Scott M. Gerber
Jodi S. Hoffman
Glenn Kleinbaum
Michael C. Manniello
Jaspreet S. Mayall
Stacey R. Miller
Lawrence S. Novak
Kim J. Radbell

For full biographical listings, see the Martindale-Hubbell Law Directory

JERICHO, Nassau Co.

Blau, Kramer, Wactlar & Lieberman, P.C. (AV)

100 Jericho Quadrangle, 11753
Telephone: 516-822-4820
Telecopier: 516-822-4824

Harvey R. Blau
Edward I. Kramer
Edward S. Wactlar
Neil M. Kaufman
Lonnie Coleman

OF COUNSEL

David H. Lieberman
Stephen Seltzer
Martin S. Sussman

Reference: National Westminster Bank/U.S.A.

For full biographical listings, see the Martindale-Hubbell Law Directory

*NEW YORK,** New York Co.

Beatie, King & Abate (AV)

599 Lexington Avenue, Suite 1300, 10022
Telephone: 212-888-9000
Fax: 212-888-9664

Russel H. Beatie, Jr.
Kenneth J. King
Samuel J. Abate, Jr.

ASSOCIATES

Susan Kelty Law
Charna L. Gerstenhaber
Eric J. Gruber
Philip J. Miller
Peter S. Liaskos
W.H. Ramsay Lewis

For full biographical listings, see the Martindale-Hubbell Law Directory

Breslow & Walker (AV)

875 Third Avenue, 10022-7597
Telephone: 212-832-1930
Fax: 212-888-4955

Joel M. Walker
Howard S. Breslow
Gary T. Moomjian

(See Next Column)

BRESLOW & WALKER, *New York—Continued*

Leslie S. Luft
Brendan T. Guastella
Jennifer A. O'Hare

For full biographical listings, see the Martindale-Hubbell Law Directory

CHAPMAN & FENNELL (AV)

330 Madison Avenue, 10017
Telephone: 212-687-3600
Telex: WUI 880411 (ETOSHA NY)
Telefax: 212-972-5368
Stamford, Connecticut Office: Three Landmark Square.
Telephone: 203-353-8000.
Telefax: 203-353-8799.
Washington D.C. Office: 2000 L. Street, N.W., Suite 200.
Telephone: 202-822-9351.

MEMBERS OF FIRM

Darrell K. Fennell
Philip M. Chiappone

OF COUNSEL

Michael Winger
Carol E. Meltzer
Eric S. Kamisher

For full biographical listings, see the Martindale-Hubbell Law Directory

EMMET, MARVIN & MARTIN, LLP (AV)

120 Broadway, 10271
Telephone: 212-238-3000
Cable Address: EMMARRO
Fax: 212-238-3100
Morristown, New Jersey Office: 10 Madison Avenue.
Telephone: 201-538-5600.
Fax: 201-538-6448.

MEMBERS OF FIRM

Thomas B. Fenlon
Thomas F. Noone (P.C.)
Lawrence B. Thompson
William A. Leet
David M. Daly
Peter B. Tisne
Michael C. Johansen
Robert W. Viets
Dennis C. Fleischmann
Eric M. Reuben
Jeffrey S. Chavkin
J. Christopher Eagan
Jesse Dudley B. Kimball
Stephen P. Cerow
Ellen J. Bickal
Edward P. Zujkowski
John P. Uehlinger
Irving C. Apar
Julian A. McQuiston
Maria-Liisa Lydon
Christine B. Cesare
Patrick A. McCartney
Matthew P. D'Amico
Brian D. Obergfell

OF COUNSEL

Guy B. Capel
Bernard F. Joyce (P.C.)
Richard P. Bourgerie
George H. P. Dwight

ASSOCIATES

Eunice M. O'Neill
Joseph M. Samulski
Sean M. Carlin
Alfred W. J. Marks
Eileen Chin-Bow
John M. Ryan
Francine M. Kors
Wendy E. Kramer
James C. Hughes, IV
Patricia C. Caputo
Bennett E. Josselsohn
Stephen I. Frank
Mildred Quinones
Anthony M. Harvin
Lynn D. Barsamian
Margaret H. Walker
Robert L. Morgan
Sally Shreeves
Michael Fotios Mavrides
Matthew A. Wieland
Eric E. Schneck (Resident, Morristown Office)
Lisa B. Lerner
Elizabeth K. Somers
Steven M. Berg
Michael E. Cavanaugh
Nancy J. Cohen
Peter L. Mancini
Stephen M. Ksenak

For full biographical listings, see the Martindale-Hubbell Law Directory

FRIEDMAN & KAPLAN (AV)

875 Third Avenue, 10022-6225
Telephone: 212-833-1100
Telecopier: 212-355-6401

MEMBERS OF FIRM

Bruce S. Kaplan
Edward A. Friedman
Eric Seiler
Robert D. Kaplan
Gary D. Friedman
Andrew W. Goldwater
Lisa Gersh Hall
Robert J. Lack
Daniel M. Taitz
Hal Neier

ASSOCIATES

Philippe Adler
Marilyn Woroner Fisch
Lance J. Gotko
Matthew S. Haiken
Ellen A. Harnick
Edward Rubin
Katharine L. Sonnenberg
Cameron A. Stracher
Barry E. Warner
Marla J. Wasserman
Daniel R. Zenkel

For full biographical listings, see the Martindale-Hubbell Law Directory

GUSRAE, KAPLAN & BRUNO (AV)

120 Wall Street, 10005
Telephone: 212-269-1400

MEMBERS OF FIRM

Mark J. Astarita
Cirino M. Bruno
Melvyn J. Falis
Martin H. Kaplan
Robert Perez

ASSOCIATES

Richard A. Friedman
Bradford L. Jacobowitz
Shirley Kaplan
Thomas A. Rigilano

OF COUNSEL

David Greene
Bert L. Gusrae

For full biographical listings, see the Martindale-Hubbell Law Directory

HUTTON INGRAM YUZEK GAINEN CARROLL & BERTOLOTTI (AV)

250 Park Avenue, 10177
Telephone: 212-907-9600
Facsimile: 212-907-9681

MEMBERS OF FIRM

Ernest J. Bertolotti
Daniel L. Carroll
Roger Cukras
Larry F. Gainen
G. Thompson Hutton
Samuel W. Ingram, Jr.
Paulette Kendler
Steven Mastbaum
Dean G. Yuzek
David G. Ebert
Shane O'Neill

ASSOCIATES

Warren E. Friss
Patricia Hewitt
Gail A. Buchman
Stuart A. Christie
Beth N. Green
Timish K. Hnateyko
Jeanne F. Pucci
Jane Drummey
Adam L. Sifre
Susan Ann Fennelly
Marc J. Schneider

For full biographical listings, see the Martindale-Hubbell Law Directory

MALONEY, GERRA, MEHLMAN & KATZ (AV)

Chrysler Building, 405 Lexington Avenue, 10174
Telephone: 212-973-6900
Fax: 212-973-6097

MEMBERS OF FIRM

Ralph A. Gerra, Jr.
Melvin Katz
Thomas J. Maloney
Barry T. Mehlman

ASSOCIATES

Philip H. Sheehan, Jr.
Kenneth J. Zinghini

For full biographical listings, see the Martindale-Hubbell Law Directory

ORANS, ELSEN & LUPERT (AV)

33rd Floor, One Rockefeller Plaza, 10020
Telephone: 212-586-2211
Cable Address: "ORELSLU"
Telecopier: 212-765-3662

MEMBERS OF FIRM

Sheldon H. Elsen
Leslie A. Lupert
Gary H. Greenberg
Lawrence Solan
Robert L. Plotz

ASSOCIATES

Melissa A. Cohen
Amelia Anne Nickles
Jonathan J. Englander

For full biographical listings, see the Martindale-Hubbell Law Directory

OTTERBOURG, STEINDLER, HOUSTON & ROSEN, P.C. (AV)

230 Park Avenue, 10169
Telephone: 212-661-9100
Cable Address: "Otlerton";
Telecopier: 212-682-6104
Telex: 960916

Donald N. Gellert
Daniel Wallen
Kenneth J. Miller

Lloyd M. Green
John J. Kenny
Steven H. Weitzen
Marc E. Schneider

For Complete List of Firm Personnel, See General Section

For full biographical listings, see the Martindale-Hubbell Law Directory

New York—Continued

PARKER CHAPIN FLATTAU & KLIMPL, L.L.P. (AV)

1211 Avenue of the Americas, 10036
Telephone: 212-704-6000
Telecopier: 212-704-6288
Cable Address: "Lawpark"
Telex: 640347
Great Neck, New York Office: 175 Great Neck Road.
Telephone: 516-482-4422.
Telecopier: 516-482-4469.

MEMBERS OF FIRM

Mark Abramowitz
Lloyd Frank
Edward R. Mandell
Stephen G. Rinehart
Henry I. Rothman
Richard A. Rubin
Alvin M. Stein
Melvin Weinberg

OF COUNSEL

Philip J. Hoblin, Jr.

For Complete List of Firm Personnel, See General Section

For full biographical listings, see the Martindale-Hubbell Law Directory

PILIERO GOLDSTEIN JENKINS & HALL (AV)

292 Madison Avenue, 10017
Telephone: 212-213-8200
Fax: 212-685-2028
Carlstadt, New Jersey Office: One Palmer Terrace.
Telephone: 201-507-5157.
FAX: 201-507-5221.
Washington, D.C. Office: 888 17th Street, N.W., Suite 1100.
Telephone: 202-467-6991.
FAX: 202-467-6703.

MEMBERS OF FIRM

Edward J. Goldstein
Christopher P. Hall
Jon Mark Jenkins
Robert D. Piliero

ASSOCIATES

John William LaRocca
Juliana M. Moday
Elaine B. Michetti (Not admitted in NY)

OF COUNSEL

Ricardo J. Davila

For full biographical listings, see the Martindale-Hubbell Law Directory

SHACK & SIEGEL, P.C. (AV)

530 Fifth Avenue, 10036
Telephone: 212-782-0700
Fax: 212-730-1964

Charles F. Crames
Pamela E. Flaherty
Paul S. Goodman
Ronald S. Katz
Donald D. Shack
Jeffrey N. Siegel
Jeffrey B. Stone

Paul A. Lucido
Steven M. Lutt
Ruby S. Teich
Keith D. Wellner
Adam F. Wergeles (Not admitted in NY)

For full biographical listings, see the Martindale-Hubbell Law Directory

SIROTA & SIROTA (AV)

747 Third Avenue, 10017
Telephone: 212-759-5555

MEMBERS OF FIRM

Howard B. Sirota
Rachell Roffé Sirota
Saul Roffé

ASSOCIATE

Jenice L. Malecki

OF COUNSEL

Martin I. Cohen
Mark B. Brenner

For full biographical listings, see the Martindale-Hubbell Law Directory

*ROCHESTER,** Monroe Co.

HARTER, SECREST & EMERY (AV)

700 Midtown Tower, 14604-2070
Telephone: 716-232-6500
Telecopier: 716-232-2152
Naples, Florida Office: Suite 400, 800 Laurel Oak Drive.
Telephone: 813-598-4444.
Telecopier: 813-598-2781.
Albany, New York Office: One Steuben Place.
Telephone: 518-434-4377.
Telecopier: 518-449-4025.
Syracuse, New York Office: 431 East Fayette Street.
Telephone: 315-474-4000.
Telecopier: 315-474-7789.

(See Next Column)

MEMBERS OF FIRM

Nathan J. Robfogel
Kenneth A. Payment
James A. Locke, III
Thomas G. Smith
Fred G. Aten, Jr.
Susan Mascette Brandt
Jeffrey H. Bowen

ASSOCIATES

Susan A. Roberts
Barry S. Wisset
James M. Jenkins
Craig S. Wittlin

For Complete List of Firm Personnel, See General Section

For full biographical listings, see the Martindale-Hubbell Law Directory

*WHITE PLAINS,** Westchester Co.

GREENSPAN & GREENSPAN (AV)

34 South Broadway, 6th Floor, 10601
Telephone: 914-946-2500
Cable Address: "Gadlex"
Telecopier: 914-946-1432

MEMBERS OF FIRM

Leon J. Greenspan
Michael E. Greenspan

For full biographical listings, see the Martindale-Hubbell Law Directory

NORTH CAROLINA

*CHARLOTTE,** Mecklenburg Co.

RAYBURN, MOON & SMITH, P.A. (AV)

The Carillon, 227 West Trade Street, Suite 1200, 28202
Telephone: 704-334-0891
FAX: 704-377-1897; 704-358-8866

Albert F. Durham
Travis W. Moon
C. Richard Rayburn, Jr.
James C. Smith
W. Scott Cooper
Matthew R. Joyner
James L. Bagwell
Cynthia D. Lewis
Patricia B. Edmondson
Paul R. Baynard
Laura D. Fennell
G. Kirkland Hardymon

For full biographical listings, see the Martindale-Hubbell Law Directory

WOMBLE CARLYLE SANDRIDGE & RICE (AV)

A Professional Limited Liability Company
3300 One First Union Center, 301 S. College Street, 28202-6025
Telephone: 704-331-4900
Telecopy: 704-331-4955
Telex: 853609
Winston-Salem, North Carolina Office: 1600 Southern National Financial Center.
Telephone: 919-721-3600.
Telecopy: 919-721-3660.
Telex: 806498.
Raleigh, North Carolina Office: 2100 First Union Capitol Center, 150 Fayetteville Street Mall, P.O. Box 831.
Telephone: 919-755-2100.
Telecopy: 919-755-2150.
Telex: 806498.
Atlanta, Georgia Office: One Ninety One Peachtree Tower, 191 Peachtree Street N.E., Suite 3250.
Telephone: 404-614-2580.
Fax: 404-614-2595.

MEMBERS OF FIRM

Garza Baldwin, III
Joe B. Cogdell, Jr.
J. Carlton Fleming
Cyrus M. Johnson, Jr.
David E. Johnston
J. Alexander Salisbury

RESIDENT ASSOCIATES

David W. Dabbs
Jane Jeffries Jones
Douglas A. Mays
Scott W. Stevenson

Representative Clients: Childress Klein Properties, Inc.; Food Lion, Inc.; Fieldcrest Cannon, Inc.; J.A. Jones Construction Company; Parkdale Mills, Inc.; Duke Power Company; Bowles Hollowell Conner & Company; ALLTEL Carolina, Inc.; Belk Store Services, Inc.; Philip Holzmann A.G.

For Complete List of Firm Personnel, See General Section

For full biographical listings, see the Martindale-Hubbell Law Directory

*RALEIGH,** Wake Co.

* indicates certain Bar Register subscribers whose principal office is located elsewhere in the state and who have arranged for representation as a part of the state capital listings that follow

*** WOMBLE CARLYLE SANDRIDGE & RICE (AV)**

A Professional Limited Liability Company
2100 First Union Capitol Center, 150 Fayetteville Street Mall, P.O. Box 831, 27602
Telephone: 919-755-2100
Telecopy: 919-755-2150
Telex: 806498
Charlotte, North Carolina Office: 3300 One First Union Center, 301 South College Street.
Telephone: 704-331-4900.
Telecopy: 704-331-4955.
Telex: 853609.
Winston-Salem, North Carolina Office: 1600 Southern National Financial Center.
Telephone: 919-721-3600.
Telecopy: 919-721-3660.
Telex: 806498.
Atlanta, Georgia Office: One Ninety One Peachtree Tower, 191 Peachtree Street N.E., Suite 3250.
Telephone: 404-614-2580.
Fax: 404-614-2595.

RESIDENT PARTNER

Deborah Hylton Hartzog

RESIDENT ASSOCIATES

Jennifer E. Bennett Overton
Kathleen Nowack Worm

Representative Clients: Aetna Casualty and Surety Co., Inc.; ALSCO/AmeriMark Building Products, Inc.; Aoki Corporation America, Inc.; Empire of Carolina, Inc.; Hackney Brothers, Inc.; Lawyers Mutual Liability Insurance Company of North Carolina; Meredith College; Monk-Austin, Inc.; Regency Park Corporation; Wachovia Bank of North Carolina, N.A.

For Complete List of Firm Personnel, See General Section

For full biographical listings, see the Martindale-Hubbell Law Directory

*WINSTON-SALEM,** Forsyth Co.

WOMBLE CARLYLE SANDRIDGE & RICE (AV)

A Professional Limited Liability Company
1600 Southern National Financial Center, P.O. Drawer 84, 27102
Telephone: 910-721-3600
Telecopy: 910-721-3660
Telex: 806498
Charlotte, North Carolina Office: 3300 One First Union Center, 301 South College Street.
Telephone: 704-331-4900.
Telecopy: 704-331-4955.
Telex: 853609.
Raleigh, North Carolina Office: 2100 First Union Capitol Center, 150 Fayetteville Street Mall, P.O. Box 831.
Telephone: 919-755-2100.
Telecopy: 919-755-2150.
Telex: 806498.
Atlanta, Georgia Office: One Ninety One Peachtree Tower, 191 Peachtree Street, N.E., Suite 3250.
Telephone: 404-614-2580.
Fax: 404-614-2595.

MEMBERS OF FIRM

Zeb E. Barnhardt, Jr.
Kenneth G. Carroll
Linwood Layfield Davis
William Allison Davis, II
John L. W. Garrou
Murray C. Greason, Jr.
Jeffrey C. Howland

ASSOCIATES

Randall A. Hanson
Heather A. King
Taylor D. Ward (Not admitted in NC)

Representative Clients: Brad Ragan, Inc.; Brenner Companies; Food Lion, Inc.; Hanes Companies, Inc.; North Carolina Baptist Hospitals, Inc.; R.J. Reynolds Tobacco Company; Summit Communications Group, Inc.; Thomasville Furniture Industries, Inc.; Wachovia Corporation; Wake Forest University.

For Complete List of Firm Personnel, See General Section

For full biographical listings, see the Martindale-Hubbell Law Directory

OHIO

ALLIANCE, Stark Co.

GEIGER, TEEPLE, SMITH & HAHN (AV)

260 East Main Street, P.O. Box 2446, 44601
Telephone: 216-821-1430
Canton Office Phone: 216-478-4915
Fax: 216-821-2217

MEMBERS OF FIRM

Milton S. Geiger (1900-1991)
John N. Teeple
Bruce E. Smith
B. Scott Hahn
J. Michael Gatien

ASSOCIATE

Richard C. Ogline

Representative Clients: NYSE and NASD Arbitrations; NYSE Arbitrator; Surgery Alliance, LLC; James R. Smail Banking/Oil and Gas Production; Damon Chemical Co.; M B Operating Co., Inc.; Carnation Mall.

For full biographical listings, see the Martindale-Hubbell Law Directory

*CINCINNATI,** Hamilton Co.

BROWN, CUMMINS & BROWN CO., L.P.A. (AV)

3500 Carew Tower, 441 Vine Street, 45202
Telephone: 513-381-2121
Fax: 513-381-2125

James R. Cummins
Donald S. Mendelsohn
Amy G. Applegate
Melanie S. Corwin

Counsel for: Midwest Group of Funds; The Fairmont Fund Trust; Bartlett Funds; Countdown to Retirement Fund; PDC&J Funds.
Reference Star Bank of Cincinnati.

For full biographical listings, see the Martindale-Hubbell Law Directory

KLAINE, WILEY, HOFFMANN & MEURER A LEGAL PROFESSIONAL ASSOCIATION (AV)

Suite 1850, 105 East Fourth Street, 45202-4080
Telephone: 513-241-0202
Fax: 513-241-9322

Gary R. Hoffmann
Gregory J. Meurer
James P. Minutolo

For Complete List of Firm Personnel, See General Section

For full biographical listings, see the Martindale-Hubbell Law Directory

STRAUSS & TROY A LEGAL PROFESSIONAL ASSOCIATION (AV)

2100 PNC Center, 201 East Fifth Street, 45202-4186
Telephone: 513-621-2120
Telecopier: 513-241-8259
Northern Kentucky Office: Suite 1400, 50 East Rivercenter Boulevard, Covington, Kentucky, 41011.
Telephone: 513-621-8900; 513-621-2120.
Telecopier: 513-629-9444.

Alan Comstock Rosser
Thomas C. Rink
James G. Heldman
Ann W. Gerwin

Shawn M. Young

Representative Clients: PNC Bank, N.A. (Ohio and Kentucky); Corporex Companies, Inc.; Mercantile Stores Company, Inc.; Star Bank, N.A. (Ohio and Kentucky).

For Complete List of Firm Personnel, See General Section

For full biographical listings, see the Martindale-Hubbell Law Directory

WAITE, SCHNEIDER, BAYLESS & CHESLEY CO., L.P.A. (AV)

1513 Central Trust Tower, Fourth and Vine Streets, 45202
Telephone: 513-621-0267
Fax: 513-381-2375; 621-0262

Stanley M. Chesley

Thomas F. Rehme
Fay E. Stilz
Louise M. Roselle
Dwight Tillery
D. Arthur Rabourn
Jerome L. Skinner
Janet G. Abaray
Paul M. De Marco
Terrence L. Goodman
Sherrill P. Hondorf
Colleen M. Hegge
Dianna Pendleton
Randy F. Fox
Glenn D. Feagan
Theresa L. Groh
Theodore N. Berry
Jane H. Walker
Renée Infante
Allen P. Grunes

(See Next Column)

WAITE, SCHNEIDER, BAYLESS & CHESLEY CO. L.P.A.—*Continued*

OF COUNSEL

Jos. E. Rosen | James F. Keller

For full biographical listings, see the Martindale-Hubbell Law Directory

*CLEVELAND,** Cuyahoga Co.

BERICK, PEARLMAN & MILLS A LEGAL PROFESSIONAL ASSOCIATION (AV)

1350 Eaton Center, 1111 Superior Avenue, 44114-2569
Telephone: 216-861-4900
Automatic Telecopier: 216-861-4929

James H. Berick | Osborne Mills, Jr.
Samuel S. Pearlman | Daniel G. Berick

Laura D. Nemeth

Representative Clients: Cleveland Browns Football Company, Inc.; The Equitable Life Assurance Society of the United States; The Huntington National Bank; The Provident Bank; MBNA Corporation; Realty ReFund Trust; A. Schulman, Inc.; Society National Bank; The Town and Country Trust; The Tranzonic Companies.

For Complete List of Firm Personnel, See General Section

For full biographical listings, see the Martindale-Hubbell Law Directory

GOODMAN WEISS MILLER FREEDMAN (AV)

100 Erieview Plaza, 27th Floor, 44114-1824
Telephone: 216-696-3366
Telecopier: 216-363-5835

MEMBERS OF FIRM

Robert A. Goodman | Steven J. Miller
Ronald I. Weiss | Glenn S. Hansen
John F. Ballard | Richard S. Mitchell

Daniel D. Domozick | James E. Goodrich
Jay Faeges | Wendy N. Weigand

OF COUNSEL

Howard J. Freedman | Roger J. Weiss
Michael D. Goler

For full biographical listings, see the Martindale-Hubbell Law Directory

JANIK & DUNN (AV)

400 Park Plaza Building, 1111 Chester Avenue, 44114
Telephone: 216-781-9700
Fax: 216-781-1250
Brea, California Office: 2601 Saturn Street, Suite 300.
Telephone: 714-572-1101.
Fax: 714-572-1103.

MEMBERS OF FIRM

Steven G. Janik | Theodore M. Dunn, Jr.

ASSOCIATES

Myra Staresina | David L. Mast

For full biographical listings, see the Martindale-Hubbell Law Directory

KELLEY, MCCANN & LIVINGSTONE (AV)

35th Floor, BP America Building, 200 Public Square, 44114-2302
Telephone: 216-241-3141
FAX: 216-241-3707

MEMBERS OF FIRM

James P. Oliver | M. Patricia Oliver
Michael D. Schenker | Bruce L. Waterhouse, Jr.

ASSOCIATE

Halle Fine Terrion

For Complete List of Firm Personnel, See General Section

For full biographical listings, see the Martindale-Hubbell Law Directory

SEELEY, SAVIDGE AND AUSSEM A LEGAL PROFESSIONAL ASSOCIATION (AV)

800 Bank One Center, 600 Superior Avenue, East, 44114-2655
Telephone: 216-566-8200
Cable Address: "See Sau"
Fax-Telecopier: 216-566-0213
Elyria, Ohio Office: 538 Broad Street.
Telephone: 216-236-8158.

Gregory D. Seeley

Carter R. Dodge | Thomas E. Sharpe

References: Society National Bank; AmeriTrust.

(See Next Column)

For Complete List of Firm Personnel, See General Section

For full biographical listings, see the Martindale-Hubbell Law Directory

*DAYTON,** Montgomery Co.

SEBALY, SHILLITO & DYER (AV)

1300 Courthouse Plaza, NE, P.O. Box 220, 45402-0220
Telephone: 513-222-2500
Telefax: 513-222-6554; 222-8279
Springfield, Ohio Office: National City Bank Building, 4 West Main Street, Suite 530, P.O. Box 1346, 45501-1346.
Telephone: 513-325-7878.
Telefax: 513-325-6151.

MEMBERS OF FIRM

James A. Dyer | Jon M. Sebaly
Gale S. Finley | Beverly F. Shillito
William W. Lambert | Jeffrey B. Shulman
Michael P. Moloney | Karl R. Ulrich
Mary Lynn Readey | Robert A. Vaughn (Resident, Springfield Office)

Martin A. Beyer | Orly R. Rumberg
Daniel A. Brown | Juliana M. Spaeth
Anne L. Rhoades | Kendra F. Thompson

For full biographical listings, see the Martindale-Hubbell Law Directory

*ELYRIA,** Lorain Co.

ERIC H. ZAGRANS (AV)

474 Overbrook Road, 44035-3623
Telephone: 216-365-5400
Facsimile: 216-365-5100

For full biographical listings, see the Martindale-Hubbell Law Directory

OKLAHOMA

*OKLAHOMA CITY,** Oklahoma Co.

ABOWITZ, WELCH AND RHODES (AV)

Tenth Floor 15 North Robinson, P.O. Box 1937, 73101
Telephone: 405-236-4645
Telecopier: 405-239-2843

MEMBERS OF FIRM

Murray E. Abowitz | Mort G. Welch
Sarah Jackson Rhodes

Lisa Luschen Gilbert | Norman Lemonik
Denis P. Rischard | Janice M. Dansby

Representative Clients: Jefferson Insurance Company of New York; Admiral Insurance Co.; Liberty Mutual Insurance Company; Mazda Distributors (West), Inc.; National Farmers Union Insurance Company; Oklahoma Farmers Union Mutual Insurance Company; Trinity Universal Insurance Co.

For full biographical listings, see the Martindale-Hubbell Law Directory

ANDREWS DAVIS LEGG BIXLER MILSTEN & PRICE, A PROFESSIONAL CORPORATION (AV)

500 West Main, 73102
Telephone: 405-272-9241
FAX: 405-235-8786

Carolyn C. Cummins | D. Joe Rockett

Barry Christopher Rooker

Representative Clients: The Dwyer Group, Inc.; UNICO, Inc.; Oklahoma State Medical Assn.; Medical Arts Laboratory, Inc.; Cody Petroleum Corp.; Magic Circle Energy Corp.; Buttes Energy Co.; First Commercial Bank.

For Complete List of Firm Personnel, See General Section

For full biographical listings, see the Martindale-Hubbell Law Directory

BRITTON AND ADCOCK (AV)

Suite 670, 101 Park Avenue, 73102
Telephone: 405-239-2393
Fax: 405-232-5135

J. Michael Adcock

For full biographical listings, see the Martindale-Hubbell Law Directory

Oklahoma City—Continued

DAY, EDWARDS, FEDERMAN, PROPESTER & CHRISTENSEN, P.C. (AV)

Suite 2900 First Oklahoma Tower, 210 Park Avenue, 73102-5605
Telephone: 405-239-2121
Telecopier: 405-236-1012

Bruce W. Day
Joe E. Edwards
William B. Federman
Richard P. Propester
D. Wade Christensen
J. Clay Christensen
Kent A. Gilliland
Rodney J. Heggy
Ricki Valerie Sonders
Thomas Pitchlynn Howell, IV
John C. Platt

David R. Widdoes
Lori R. Roberts
Carolyn A. Romberg

OF COUNSEL

Herbert F. (Jack) Hewett
Jeanette Cook Timmons
Joel Warren Harmon
Jane S. Eulberg
Mark A. Cohen

Representative Clients: Aetna Life Insurance Co.; Boatmen's First National Bank of Oklahoma; Borg-Warner Chemicals, Inc.; City Bank & Trust; Federal Deposit Insurance Corp.; Bank One, Oklahoma City; Haskell Lemon Construction Co.; Merrill Lynch, Pierce, Fenner & Smith, Inc.; Prudential Securities, Inc.

For full biographical listings, see the Martindale-Hubbell Law Directory

DURLAND & DURLAND (AV)

300 Bank IV Tower, 1601 Northwest Expressway, 73118
Telephone: 405-840-0060
FAX: 405-842-8547

Jack R. Durland, Jr.
Harvey L. Harmon, Jr.
Kathleen Garewal

OF COUNSEL

Jack R. Durland
Robert D. Allen

For full biographical listings, see the Martindale-Hubbell Law Directory

HARTZOG CONGER & CASON, A PROFESSIONAL CORPORATION (AV)

1600 Bank of Oklahoma Plaza, 73102
Telephone: 405-235-7000
Facsimile: 405-235-7329

Larry D. Hartzog
J. William Conger
Len Cason
James C. Prince
Alan Newman
Steven C. Davis
Valerie K. Couch
Mark D. Dickey
Joseph P. Hogsett
John D. Robertson
Kurt M. Rupert
Laura Haag McConnell

Susan B. Shields
Ryan S. Wilson
Melanie J. Jester
Armand Paliotta
Julia Watson
J. Leslie LaReau

OF COUNSEL

Kent F. Frates

For full biographical listings, see the Martindale-Hubbell Law Directory

HASTIE AND KIRSCHNER, A PROFESSIONAL CORPORATION (AV)

3000 Oklahoma Tower, 210 Park Avenue, 73102-5604
Telephone: 405-239-6404
Telecopier: 405-239-6403

Mark H. Bennett
Mitchell D. Blackburn
George W. Dahnke
John W. Funk
John D. Hastie
Michael Paul Kirschner
Ronald L. Matlock
Kieran D. Maye, Jr.
Robert D. McCutcheon
David D. Morgan
Kiran A. Phansalkar
Irwin H. Steinhorn
John W. Swinford, Jr.
Ruston C. Welch
Monica A. Wittrock

OF COUNSEL

William S. Price

For full biographical listings, see the Martindale-Hubbell Law Directory

MOCK, SCHWABE, WALDO, ELDER, REEVES & BRYANT, A PROFESSIONAL CORPORATION (AV)

Fifteenth Floor, One Leadership Square, 211 North Robinson Avenue, 73102
Telephone: 405-235-5500
Telecopy: 405-235-2875

Randall D. Mock
Jay C. Jimerson

Representative Clients: Amoco Production Co.; Anson Companies; Liberty Bank & Turst Company of Oklahoma City; Atlantic Richfield Co.; Farm Credit Bank of Wichita; Federal Deposit Insurance Corporation; First Oklahoma Corporation; Holden Energy Corporation; Massachusetts Mutual Life Insurance Co.; Metropolitan Life Insurance Co.

For Complete List of Firm Personnel, See General Section

For full biographical listings, see the Martindale-Hubbell Law Directory

PRINGLE & PRINGLE, A PROFESSIONAL CORPORATION (AV)

1601 N.W. Expressway, Suite 2100, 73118
Telephone: 405-848-4810
Fax: 405-848-4819

Lynn A. Pringle
Laura Nan Smith Pringle
Conni L. Allen
Stephen W. Elliott
James R. Martin, Jr.

OF COUNSEL

Alvin C. Harrell
Michael P. Sullivan

Representative Clients: Bankers Systems, Inc.; Central Oklahoma Clearing House Association; The Bankers Bank; Bank of Western Oklahoma, Elk City; The Farmers Bank, Carnagie; The First National Bank and Trust Co., Chickasha; The First National Bank of Texhoma; Oklahoma Home Based Business Association; First State Bank, Idabel; Great Western Drilling Co.

For full biographical listings, see the Martindale-Hubbell Law Directory

*TULSA,** Tulsa Co.

BOONE, SMITH, DAVIS, HURST & DICKMAN, A PROFESSIONAL CORPORATION (AV)

500 Oneok Plaza, 100 West 5th Street, 74103
Telephone: 918-587-0000
Fax: 918-599-9317

Byron V. Boone (1908-1988)
Royce H. Savage (1904-1993)
L. K. Smith
Reuben Davis
J. Jerry Dickman
Frederic N. (Nick) Schneider III
William C. Kellough
J Schaad Titus
John A. Burkhardt
Paul E. Swain III
Carol A. Grissom
Kimberly Lambert Love
Teresa Meinders Burkett
Paul J. Cleary

R. Tom Hillis
Barry G. Reynolds
Laura L. Gonsalves
Scott R. Rowland
Shane Egan
Nancy Lynn Davis

OF COUNSEL

Edwin S. Hurst
Lloyd G. Minter

Representative Clients: American Airlines; Chevron U.S.A., Inc.; The F & M Bank & Trust Co.; Hillcrest Medical Center; Boatmen's First National Bank of Oklahoma; Phillips Petroleum Co.; Rockwell International; Sears, Roebuck & Co.; Thrifty Rent-A-Car Systems, Inc.; World Publishing Co.

For full biographical listings, see the Martindale-Hubbell Law Directory

CONNER & WINTERS, A PROFESSIONAL CORPORATION (AV)

15 East 5th Street, Suite 2400, 74103-4391
Telephone: 918-586-5711
Fax: 918-586-8982
Oklahoma City, Oklahoma Office: 204 North Robinson, Suite 950, 73102.
Telephone: 405-232-7711.
Facsimile: 405-232-2695.

Lynnwood R. Moore, Jr.
Robert A. Curry
Judith A. McCoy
R. Kevin Redwine
Robert J. Melgaard
P. David Newsome, Jr.

Anne B. Sublett
Phillip L. Allbritten
Greg S. Scharlau
Steven G. Heinen
John M. Matheson

For Complete List of Firm Personnel, See General Section

For full biographical listings, see the Martindale-Hubbell Law Directory

CRAWFORD, CROWE & BAINBRIDGE, P.A. (AV)

1714 First National Building, 74103
Telephone: 918-587-1128
Fax: 918-587-3975

B. Hayden Crawford
Harry M. Crowe, Jr.
Robert L. Bainbridge
Kyle B. Haskins
Eric B. Bolusky

For full biographical listings, see the Martindale-Hubbell Law Directory

DOERNER, STUART, SAUNDERS, DANIEL & ANDERSON (AV)

Suite 500, 320 South Boston Avenue, 74103-3725
Telephone: 918-582-1211
FAX: 918-591-5360

(See Next Column)

DOERNER, STUART, SAUNDERS, DANIEL & ANDERSON—*Continued*

MEMBERS OF FIRM

C. B. Stuart (1857-1936)
Erwin J. Doerner (1897-1980)
Samuel P. Daniel
William C. Anderson
Varley H. Taylor, Jr.
G. Michael Lewis
William B. Morgan
Lawrence T. Chambers, Jr.
Dallas E. Ferguson
Sam G. Bratton, II
Gary M. McDonald
H. Wayne Cooper
Kevin C. Coutant
Richard P. Hix
Lynn Paul Mattson
William F. Riggs
Lewis N. Carter
Linda Crook Martin
James Patrick McCann
Richard H. Foster
Charles S. Plumb
Leonard I. Pataki
S. Douglas Dodd
Elise Dunitz Brennan
Kathy R. Neal
John J. Carwile
Jon E. Brightmire
L. Dru McQueen
Tom Q. Ferguson

ASSOCIATES

Richard J. Eagleton
Rebecca McCarthy Fowler
Kristen L. Brightmire
Michael C. Redman
Steven K. Metcalf
Benjamin J. Chapman
R. Michael Cole
David B. Auer
Shelly L. Dalrymple
Russell W. Kroll
John R. Pinkerton
Robert A. Burk

OF COUNSEL

Dickson M. Saunders
R. Robert Huff

Representative Clients: Public Service Company of Oklahoma; Oklahoma Ordnance Works Authority; Sand Springs Home Co.; St. John Medical Center, Inc.

For full biographical listings, see the Martindale-Hubbell Law Directory

DOYLE & HARRIS, A PROFESSIONAL CORPORATION (AV)

Southern Hills Tower, 2431 East 61st Street, Suite 260, P.O. Box 1679, 74101-1679
Telephone: 918-743-1276
Fax: 918-748-8215

Stan P. Doyle
Steven M. Harris

Michael D. Davis
Douglas R. Haughey
Randall T. Duncan

Reference: Peoples State Bank.

For full biographical listings, see the Martindale-Hubbell Law Directory

FELDMAN, HALL, FRANDEN, WOODARD & FARRIS (AV)

1400 Park Centre, 525 South Main, 74103-4409
Telephone: 918-583-7129
Telecopier: 918-584-3814

MEMBERS OF FIRM

W. E. Green (1889-1977)
William S. Hall (1930-1991)
Raymond G. Feldman
Robert A. Franden
John R. Woodard, III
Joseph R. Farris
Larry G. Taylor
Victor R. Seagle
Tony M. Graham

ASSOCIATES

Jacqueline O'Neil Haglund
Jody Nathan
R. Jack Freeman
J. David Mustain
Margaret E. Dunn
Ellen Caslavka Edwards
Douglass R. Elliott
Cathy G. Stricker
R. Daniel Scroggins

Representative Clients: CIGNA; The Equitable Life Assurance Society of the United States; Browning-Ferris Industries, Inc.; American Cyanamid Co.; American Home Assurance Co.; Oklahoma Bar Professional Liability Insurance Co.; American Motors Corp.; Sunbeam Corp.; Aviation Underwriters Inc.; Progressive Casualty Insurance Co.

For full biographical listings, see the Martindale-Hubbell Law Directory

GABLE & GOTWALS (AV)

2000 Bank IV Center, 15 West Sixth Street, 74119-5447
Telephone: 918-582-9201
Facsimile: 918-586-8383

Teresa B. Adwan
Pamela S. Anderson
John R. Barker
David L. Bryant
Gene C. Buzzard
Dennis Clarke Cameron
Timothy A. Carney
Renee DeMoss
Elsie C. Draper
Sidney G. Dunagan
Theodore Q. Eliot
Richard W. Gable
Jeffrey Don Hassell
Patricia Ledvina Himes
Oliver S. Howard
Richard D. Koljack, Jr.
J. Daniel Morgan
Joseph W. Morris
Elizabeth R. Muratet
Richard B. Noulles
Ronald N. Ricketts
John Henry Rule
M. Benjamin Singletary
James M. Sturdivant
Patrick O. Waddel
Michael D. Hall

(See Next Column)

David Edward Keglovits
Stephen W. Lake
Kari S. McKee
Terry D. Ragsdale
Jeffrey C. Rambach

OF COUNSEL

G. Ellis Gable
Charles P. Gotwals, Jr.

For full biographical listings, see the Martindale-Hubbell Law Directory

HOLLIMAN, LANGHOLZ, RUNNELS, HOLDEN, FORSMAN & SELLERS, A PROFESSIONAL CORPORATION (AV)

Suite 500 Holarud Building, Ten East Third Street, 74103-3695
Telephone: 918-584-1471
FAX: 918-587-9652,
Telex: 251773 GRC UR
Oklahoma City, Oklahoma Office: Suite 160, Two Broadway Executive Park, 205 N.W. 63rd Street.
Telephone: 405-848-6999.
Fax: 405-840-3312.

Robert W. Langholz
Gail R. Runnels
David W. Holden
Michael S. Forsman
Keith F. Sellers
James D. Bryant

Matthew James Browne, III
Ann Nicholson Smith
Laurence Langholz

AFFILIATES

David L. Sobel
Roderick Oxford

OF COUNSEL

Joe M. Holliman
Ted P. Holshouser (Resident, Oklahoma City Office)

Representative Clients: The F & M Bank and Trust Company, Tulsa, Ok.; Transportation Leasing Co., Inc.; The Sterling Group, Inc.; Albert Investments; Bryan Industries, Inc.; Enserch Corp.; Kaiser-Francis Oil Co.; Family & Children's Service, Inc.; Junior League of Tulsa; Anadarko Bank and Trust Co.

For full biographical listings, see the Martindale-Hubbell Law Directory

HUFFMAN ARRINGTON KIHLE GABERINO & DUNN, A PROFESSIONAL CORPORATION (AV)

1000 ONEOK Plaza, 74103
Telephone: 918-585-8141
Telecopier: 918-588-7873
Oklahoma City Office: 2212 NW 50th Street, Suite 163.
Telephone: 405-840-4408.
Telecopier: 405-843-9090.

Donald A. Kihle
J. Clarke Kendall II
Sheppard F. Miers, Jr.

General Counsel for: ONEOK Inc.; Oklahoma Natural Gas Co.; H W Allen Co.; ONEOK Exploration Co.; Woodland Bank; ONEOK Drilling Co.; ONEOK Resources Co.; Renberg's, Inc.

For Complete List of Firm Personnel, See General Section

For full biographical listings, see the Martindale-Hubbell Law Directory

JOHNSON, ALLEN, JONES & DORNBLASER (AV)

900 Petroleum Club Building, 601 South Boulder, 74119
Telephone: 918-584-6644
FAX: 918-584-6645

MEMBERS OF FIRM

Mark H. Allen
W. Thomas Coffman
Kenneth E. Dornblaser
John B. Johnson, Jr.
C. Robert Jones
Richard D. Jones
Randy R. Shorb

ASSOCIATE

Frances F. Hillsman

For full biographical listings, see the Martindale-Hubbell Law Directory

SNEED, LANG, ADAMS & BARNETT, A PROFESSIONAL CORPORATION (AV)

2300 Williams Center Tower II, Two West Second Street, 74103
Telephone: 918-583-3145
Telecopier: 918-582-0410

James C. Lang
D. Faith Orlowski
Brian S. Gaskill
G. Steven Stidham
Stephen R. McNamara
Thomas E. Black, Jr.
Robbie Emery Burke
C. Raymond Patton, Jr.
Frederick K. Slicker
Richard D. Black
John D. Russell
Jeffrey S. Swyers

(See Next Column)

SNEED, LANG, ADAMS & BARNETT A PROFESSIONAL CORPORATION, *Tulsa—Continued*

OF COUNSEL

James L. Sneed
O. Edwin Adams
Howard G. Barnett, Jr.

Representative Clients: Amoco Production Company; Continental Bank; Deloitte & Touche; Enron Corporation; Halliburton Energy Services; Helmerich & Payne, Inc.; Lehman Brothers, Inc.; Shell Oil Company; Smith Barney, Inc.; State Farm Mutual Automobile Insurance Company.

For full biographical listings, see the Martindale-Hubbell Law Directory

OREGON

*PORTLAND,** Multnomah Co.

GRENLEY, ROTENBERG EVANS & BRAGG, P.C. (AV)

30th Floor, Pacwest Center, 1211 S.W. Fifth Avenue, 97204
Telephone: 503-241-0570
Facsimile: 503-241-0914

Gary I. Grenley
Stan N. Rotenberg
Lawrence Evans
Michael J. Bragg
Steven D. Adler
Michael S. Evans
Michael C. Zusman
Jeffrey C. Bodie

OF COUNSEL

Sol Siegel
Robert C. Laskowski
Norman A. Rickles

Ann M. Lane

Reference: Key Bank of Oregon.

For full biographical listings, see the Martindale-Hubbell Law Directory

LABARRE & ASSOCIATES, P.C. (AV)

Suite 1212, 900 S.W. Fifth Avenue, 97204-1268
Telephone: 503-228-3511
FAX: 503-273-8658

Jerome E. LaBarre

Dayna Ellen Peck

OF COUNSEL

Robert A. Russell

For full biographical listings, see the Martindale-Hubbell Law Directory

PENNSYLVANIA

*HARRISBURG,** Dauphin Co.

MCNEES, WALLACE & NURICK (AV)

100 Pine Street, P.O. Box 1166, 17108
Telephone: 717-232-8000
Fax: 717-237-5300

MEMBERS OF FIRM

W. Jeffry Jamouneau
Michael G. Jarman
Gary F. Yenkowski

For Complete List of Firm Personnel, See General Section

For full biographical listings, see the Martindale-Hubbell Law Directory

*PHILADELPHIA,** Philadelphia Co.

BARRACK, RODOS & BACINE (AV)

A Partnership including Professional Corporations
3300 Two Commerce Square, 2001 Market Street, 19103
Telephone: 215-963-0600
Telecopier: 215-963-0838
San Diego, California Office: Suite 1700, 600 West Broadway.
Telephone: 619-230-0800.
Telecopier: 619-230-1874.

Leonard Barrack (P.C.)
Gerald J. Rodos (P.C.)
Daniel E. Bacine (P.C.)
Sheldon L. Albert
Samuel R. Simon
M. Richard Komins
Edward M. Gergosian (Resident, San Diego, California Office)
Kirk B. Hulett (Resident, San Diego, California Office)
Robert Lipman
Jeffrey W. Golan
Anthony J. Bolognese
James J. Greenfield
Douglas J. Campion (Resident, San Diego, California Office)

(See Next Column)

Stephen R. Basser (Resident, San Diego, California Office)
Leslie Bornstein Molder
Robert A. Hoffman
Randal J. Rein (Resident, San Diego, California Office)
Lisa Clare Atkinson (Resident, San Diego, California Office)

For full biographical listings, see the Martindale-Hubbell Law Directory

FELLHEIMER EICHEN BRAVERMAN & KASKEY, A PROFESSIONAL CORPORATION (AV)

21st Floor, One Liberty Place, 19103-7334
Telephone: 215-575-3800
FAX: 215-575-3801
Camden, New Jersey Office: 519 Federal Street, Suite 503 Parkade Building, 08103-1147.
Telephone: 609-541-5323.
Fax: 609-541-5370.

Alan S. Fellheimer
David L. Braverman
Judith Eichen Fellheimer
John E. Kaskey
Kenneth S. Goodkind
Anna Hom
Peter E. Meltzer

Barbara Anisko
Maia R. Caplan
Jeffrey L. Eichen
Michael N. Feder
Jolie G. Kahn
George F. Newton
David B. Spitofsky
W. Thomas Tither, Jr.

For Complete List of Firm Personnel, See General Section

For full biographical listings, see the Martindale-Hubbell Law Directory

KLEHR, HARRISON, HARVEY, BRANZBURG & ELLERS (AV)

1401 Walnut Street, 19102
Telephone: 215-568-6060
Fax: 215-568-6603
Cherry Hill, New Jersey Office: Colwick-Suite 200, 51 Haddonfield Road.
Telephone: 609-486-7900.
Fax: 609-486-4875.
Allentown, Pennsylvania Office: Roma Corporate Center, Suite 501, 1605 North Cedar Crest Boulevard.
Telephone: 215-432-1803.
Fax: 215-433-4031.
Wilmington, Delaware Office: 222 Delaware Avenue, Suite 1101.
Telephone: 302-426-1189.
Fax: 302-426-9193.

MEMBERS OF FIRM

Edward S. Ellers
Stephen T. Burdumy
Richard S. Roisman
Jason M. Shargel
Brian J. Sisko

ASSOCIATES

Wayne D. Bloch
Barry J. Siegel
Todd L. Silverberg
Frederick J. Fisher
Gerald F. Stahlecker, III
William W. Matthews, III

For Complete List of Firm Personnel, See General Section

For full biographical listings, see the Martindale-Hubbell Law Directory

LEVIN, FISHBEIN, SEDRAN & BERMAN (AV)

Suite 600, 320 Walnut Street, 19106
Telephone: 215-592-1500
Fax: 215-592-4663

MEMBERS OF FIRM

Arnold Levin
Michael D. Fishbein
Howard J. Sedran
Laurence S. Berman
Frederick S. Longer

Robert M. Unterberger
Craig D. Ginsburg
Jonathan Shub
Cheryl R. Brown Hill
Roberta Shaner

For full biographical listings, see the Martindale-Hubbell Law Directory

MAGER LIEBENBERG & WHITE (AV)

Two Penn Center, Suite 415, 19102
Telephone: 215-569-6921
Telecopier: 215-569-6931

MEMBERS OF FIRM

Carol A. Mager
Roberta D. Liebenberg
Ann D. White

ASSOCIATES

Matthew D. Baxter
Brett M. L. Blyshak
Michael J. Salmanson
W. Scott Magargee
Nancy F. DuBoise

OF COUNSEL

Anna M. Durbin

For full biographical listings, see the Martindale-Hubbell Law Directory

MANN, UNGAR & SPECTOR, P.A. (AV)

1709 Spruce Street, 19103
Telephone: 215-732-3120
Fax: 215-790-1366

(See Next Column)

MANN, UNGAR & SPECTOR P.A.—*Continued*

Theodore R. Mann
Barry E. Ungar
Larry H. Spector
Janet Stern Holcombe
Marc J. Zucker
Sharon C. Weinman
Carol J. Sulcoski
John C. Ungar

For full biographical listings, see the Martindale-Hubbell Law Directory

SAVETT FRUTKIN PODELL & RYAN, P.C. (AV)

Suite 508, 320 Walnut Street, 19106
Telephone: 215-923-5400
FAX: 923-9353

Stuart H. Savett
Robert P. Frutkin
Barbara Anne Podell
Katharine M. Ryan

For full biographical listings, see the Martindale-Hubbell Law Directory

SPECTOR & ROSEMAN, A PROFESSIONAL CORPORATION (AV)

2000 Market Street, 12th Floor, 19103
Telephone: 215-864-2400
Telecopier: 215-864-2424
San Diego, California Office: 600 West Broadway, 1800 One American Plaza, 92101.
Telephone: 619-338-4514.
Telecopier: 619-231-7423.

Eugene A. Spector
Robert M. Roseman
Mark S. Goldman
Paul J. Scarlato

Jeffrey L. Kodroff
Ellen A. Gusikoff (Not admitted in PA)
Jacob A. Goldberg
Debra M. Kahn

For full biographical listings, see the Martindale-Hubbell Law Directory

*PITTSBURGH,** Allegheny Co.

COHEN & GRIGSBY, P.C. (AV)

2900 CNG Tower, 625 Liberty Avenue, 15222
Telephone: 412-394-4900
Telecopier: 412-391-3382

Charles C. Cohen

David J. Lowe
Daniel L. Wessels

Christopher J. Rayl

For Complete List of Firm Personnel, See General Section

For full biographical listings, see the Martindale-Hubbell Law Directory

DICKIE, MCCAMEY & CHILCOTE, A PROFESSIONAL CORPORATION (AV)

Suite 400, Two PPG Place, 15222-5402
Telephone: 412-281-7272
Fax: 412-392-5367
Wheeling, West Virginia Office: Suite 2002, 1233 Main Street, 26003-2839.
Telephone: 304-233-1022.
Facsimile: 304-233-1026.

Clayton A. Sweeney
Steven B. Larchuk
William Campbell Ries
George Randal Fox, III

Donald E. Evans

For Complete List of Firm Personnel, See General Section

For full biographical listings, see the Martindale-Hubbell Law Directory

KATARINCIC & SALMON (AV)

2600 CNG Tower, 625 Liberty Avenue, 15222
Telephone: 412-338-2900
Facsimile: 412-261-2212
Houston, Texas Office: First Interstate Bank Plaza, Suite 3170, 1000 Louisiana, 77002.
Telephone: 713-752-0010.
Fax: 713-752-0050.

Joseph A. Katarincic
Joseph Decker

For full biographical listings, see the Martindale-Hubbell Law Directory

MARCUS & SHAPIRA (AV)

35th Floor, One Oxford Centre, 301 Grant Street, 15219-6401
Telephone: 412-471-3490
Telecopier: 412-391-8758

MEMBER OF FIRM

Bernard D. Marcus

(See Next Column)

SPECIAL COUNSEL

Jane Campbell Moriarty

ASSOCIATE

Scott D. Livingston

For Complete List of Firm Personnel, See General Section

For full biographical listings, see the Martindale-Hubbell Law Directory

THORP, REED & ARMSTRONG (AV)

One Riverfront Center, 15222
Telephone: 412-394-7711
Fax: 412-394-2555

MEMBERS OF FIRM

Douglas E. Gilbert
Richard D. Rose
Edmund S. Ruffin, III
Joseph D. Shuman

For Complete List of Firm Personnel, See General Section

For full biographical listings, see the Martindale-Hubbell Law Directory

YUKEVICH, BLUME & ZANGRILLI (AV)

Sixth Floor, One Gateway Center, 15222
Telephone: 412-261-6777
Fax: 412-261-6789

MEMBERS OF FIRM

Michael Yukevich, Jr.
Peter K. Blume
Albert J. Zangrilli, Jr.

Mark Fischer

For full biographical listings, see the Martindale-Hubbell Law Directory

*SCRANTON,** Lackawanna Co.

LENAHAN & DEMPSEY, A PROFESSIONAL CORPORATION (AV)

116 North Washington Avenue, 18503-0234
Telephone: 717-346-2097
Fax: 717-346-1174
Mailing Address: P.O. Box 234, Scranton, Pennsylvania, 18501-0234

John R. Lenahan, Sr.
William J. Dempsey
John R. Lenahan, Jr.
Joseph P. Lenahan
Kathleen A. Lenahan
David E. Heisler
Timothy G. Lenahan
Matthew D. Dempsey

Marianne J. Gilmartin
Alan P. Schoen
Brian J. Lenahan
Diane Hepford Lenahan
George E. Mehalchick
Brian Yeager
Thomas R. Daniels
Myles P. McAliney
Terrence E. Dempsey
Carmina M. Rinkunas
Thomas R. Chesnick
William M. Blaum
Christine S. Mayernick
Patricia Corbett

Representative Insurance Clients: Allstate Insurance Co.; America Security Insurance Co.; Metropolitan Casualty Insurance Co.; Statesman Insurance Group; Foremost Insurance Co.; Aetna Insurance Co.; Pennsylvania National Insurance Group; Kemper Insurance Group; American Mutual Insurance Cos.; American States Insurance, Co.

For full biographical listings, see the Martindale-Hubbell Law Directory

WAYNE, Delaware Co.

BALDWIN RENNER & CLARK (AV)

The Woods Suite 905, 992 Old Eagle School Road, 19087
Telephone: 610-687-4664
Fax: 610-687-4640
Philadelphia, Pennsylvania Office: 1201 Chestnut Street, Tenth Floor.
Telephone: 215-563-1950.
Fax: 215-563-2014.

Frank B. Baldwin, III
Michael D. Renner
Francis X. Clark
Mara L. Stratt

For full biographical listings, see the Martindale-Hubbell Law Directory

SOUTH CAROLINA

*CHARLESTON,** Charleston Co.

HAYNSWORTH, MARION, MCKAY & GUÉRARD, L.L.P (AV)

#2 Prioleau Street, P.O. Box 1119, 29402
Telephone: 803-722-7606
Telecopier: 803-723-5263
Columbia, South Carolina Office: Suite 2400 AT&T Building, 1201 Main Street, P.O. Drawer 7157, 29202.
Telephone: 803-765-1818.
Telecopier: 803-765-2399.

(See Next Column)

HAYNSWORTH, MARION, MCKAY & GUÉRARD L.L.P, *Charleston—Continued*

Greenville, South Carolina Office: Two Insignia Financial Plaza, 75 Beattie Place, P.O. Box 2048, 29602.
Telephone: 803-240-3200.
Telecopier: 803-240-3300.

MEMBERS OF FIRM

W. E. Applegate, III
Samuel W. Howell, IV
Carol L. Clark

Representative Clients: Ernst & Young, LLP; AT&T Capital Corporation; Synalloy Corporation; Equitable Life Assurance Society of the United States; St. Paul Insurance Group; The Bank of South Carolina.

For Complete List of Firm Personnel, See General Section

For full biographical listings, see the Martindale-Hubbell Law Directory

*COLUMBIA,** Richland Co.

* indicates certain Bar Register subscribers whose principal office is located elsewhere in the state and who have arranged for representation as a part of the state capital listings that follow

*** HAYNSWORTH, MARION, MCKAY & GUÉRARD, L.L.P.** (AV)

Suite 2400 A T & T Building, 1201 Main Street, P.O. Drawer 7157, 29202
Telephone: 803-765-1818
Telecopier: 803-765-2399
Greenville, South Carolina Office: Two Insignia Financial Plaza, 75 Beattie Place, P.O. Box 2048, 29602.
Telephone: 803-240-3200.
Telecopier: 803-240-3300.
Charleston, South Carolina Office: #2 Prioleau Street, P.O. Box 1119, 29402.
Telephone: 803-722-7606.
Telecopier: 803-723-5263.

MEMBERS OF FIRM

Samuel W. Howell, IV
Gary W. Morris
Henry P. Wall

ASSOCIATE

Edward G. Kluiters

Counsel For: Ernst & Young, LLP; AT&T Capital Corporation; Synalloy Corporation; Equitable Life Assurance Society of the United States; St. Paul Insurance Group; The Bank of South Carolina.

For Complete List of Firm Personnel, See General Section

For full biographical listings, see the Martindale-Hubbell Law Directory

*GREENVILLE,** Greenville Co.

FEW & FEW, P.A. (AV)

850 Wade Hampton Boulevard, P.O. Box 10085, Fed. Station, 29603
Telephone: 803-232-6456
Fax: 803-370-0671

J. Kendall Few
John C. Few

For full biographical listings, see the Martindale-Hubbell Law Directory

HAYNSWORTH, MARION, MCKAY & GUÉRARD, L.L.P. (AV)

Two Insignia Financial Plaza, 75 Beattie Place, P.O. Box 2048, 29602
Telephone: 803-240-3200
Telecopier: 803-240-3300
Columbia, South Carolina Office: Suite 2400 A T & T Building, 1201 Main Street, P.O. Drawer 7157, 29202
Telephone: 803-765-1818.
Telecopier: 803-765-2399.
Charleston, South Carolina Office: #2 Prioleau Street, P.O. Box 1119, 29402.
Telephone: 803-722-7606.
Telecopier: 803-723-5263.

MEMBERS OF FIRM

O. G. Calhoun, Jr.
Jesse C. Belcher, Jr.
Ellis M. Johnston, II

ASSOCIATE

William David Conner

Representative Clients: Ernst & Young, LLP; AT&T Capital Corporation; Synalloy Corporation; Equitable Life Assurance Society of the United States; St. Paul Insurance Group; The Bank of South Carolina.

For Complete List of Firm Personnel, See General Section

For full biographical listings, see the Martindale-Hubbell Law Directory

WYCHE, BURGESS, FREEMAN & PARHAM, PROFESSIONAL ASSOCIATION (AV)

44 East Camperdown Way, P.O. Box 728, 29602-0728
Telephone: 803-242-8200
Telecopier: 803-235-8900

(See Next Column)

James M. Shoemaker, Jr.
Eric B. Amstutz
Carl F. Muller
Jo Watson Hackl
William P. Crawford, Jr.

Counsel for: Multimedia, Inc.; Delta Woodside Industries, Inc.; Milliken & Company; Ryan's Family Steak Houses, Inc.; St. Francis Hospital; Span-America Medical Systems, Inc.; Carolina First Bank; KEMET Electronics Corp.; Builder Marts of America, Inc.; One Price Clothing, Inc.

For Complete List of Firm Personnel, See General Section

For full biographical listings, see the Martindale-Hubbell Law Directory

TENNESSEE

*CHATTANOOGA,** Hamilton Co.

FOSTER, FOSTER, ALLEN & DURRENCE (AV)

Formerly Hall, Haynes & Foster
Suite 515 Pioneer Bank Building, 37402
Telephone: 615-266-1141
Telecopier: 615-266-4618

MEMBERS OF FIRM

George Lane Foster
Craig R. Allen
William M. Foster
Phillip M. Durrence, Jr.

ASSOCIATES

David J. Ward
Clayton M. Whittaker
John M. Hull

LEGAL SUPPORT PERSONNEL

Peggy Sue Bates

Division Counsel for: Alabama Great Southern Railroad Co.; C.N.O. & T.P. Railway Co.
Attorneys for: CNA/Insurance; U.S.P. & G. Co.; The Firestone Tire & Rubber Co.; Exxon, Corp.; Murphy Oil Corp.; Chicago Title Insurance Co.; City of East Ridge; Jim Walter Homes; Raymond James & Associates; Morgan Keegan & Co.

For full biographical listings, see the Martindale-Hubbell Law Directory

*KNOXVILLE,** Knox Co.

WAGNER, MYERS & SANGER, A PROFESSIONAL CORPORATION (AV)

1801 Plaza Tower, P.O. Box 1308, 37929
Telephone: 615-525-4600
Fax: 615-524-5731

John R. Seymour

Representative Clients: Carolina Power & Light Co.; Cullman Electric Cooperative; Diversified Energy, Inc.; Fort Sanders Health Systems; Gatliff Coal Company; Martin Marietta Energy Systems, Inc.; NorthAmerican Rayon Corp.; Regal Cinemas, Inc.; Roddy Vending; Skyline Coal Company.

For Complete List of Firm Personnel, See General Section

For full biographical listings, see the Martindale-Hubbell Law Directory

*MEMPHIS,** Shelby Co.

BOROD & KRAMER, P.C. (AV)

Brinkley Plaza, 80 Monroe Avenue, 5th Floor, P.O. Box 3504, 38173-0504
Telephone: 901-524-0200
Telecopier: 901-524-0242

Bruce S. Kramer

Sharon Lee Petty
Jeffery D. Parrish

For Complete List of Firm Personnel, See General Section

For full biographical listings, see the Martindale-Hubbell Law Directory

*NASHVILLE,** Davidson Co.

BASS, BERRY & SIMS (AV)

2700 First American Center, 37238-2700
Telephone: 615-742-6200
Telecopy: 615-742-6293
Knoxville, Tennessee Office: 1700 Riverview Tower, 900 S. Gay Street, P.O. Box 1509, 37901-1509.
Telephone: 615-521-6200.
Telecopy: 615-521-6234.

MEMBERS OF FIRM

James H. Cheek, III
George P. McGinn, Jr.
Bob F. Thompson
N. B. Forrest Shoaf
Leigh Walton
J. Gentry Barden
Samuel E. Stumpf, Jr.
Bonnie J. Roe
F. Mitchell Walker, Jr.
Howard H. Lamar, III
J. Page Davidson
Maria-Lisa Caldwell

(See Next Column)

BASS, BERRY & SIMS—*Continued*

MEMBERS OF FIRM (Continued)

Gregory T. Stevens
Maria A. Garner
R. Douglas Mefford
Leslie Stophel Maclellan
Mark S. Croft
Brenda A. Barnes
John C. Hayworth

Representative Clients: J.C. Bradford & Co.; Coventry Corp.; Dean Witter Reynolds, Inc.; Dollar General Corp.; Envoy Corp.; Gaylord Entertainment Co.; Massey Burch Investment Group, Inc.; Merrill Lynch & Co.; Service Merchandise Company, Inc.; The First Boston Corp.; Thomas Nelson, Inc.; Volunteer Capital Corp.

For full biographical listings, see the Martindale-Hubbell Law Directory

TEXAS

*AUSTIN,** Travis Co.

* indicates certain Bar Register subscribers whose principal office is located elsewhere in the state and who have arranged for representation as a part of the state capital listings that follow

*** THOMPSON & KNIGHT, A PROFESSIONAL CORPORATION** (AV)

(Attorneys and Counselors)
1200 San Jacinto Center, 98 San Jacinto Boulevard, 78701
Telephone: 512-469-6100
Telecopy: 512-469-6180
Dallas, Texas Office: 1700 Pacific Avenue, Suite 3300, 75201.
Telephone: 214-969-1700.
Telecopy: 512-969-1751.
Cable Address: "Tomtex."
Telex: 732298.
Fort Worth, Texas Office: 801 Cherry Street, Suite 1600, 76102.
Telephone: 817-347-1700.
Telecopy: 817-347-1799.
Houston, Texas Office: 1700 Texas Commerce Tower, 600 Travis, 77002.
Telephone: 713-217-2800.
Telecopy: 713-217-2828; 713-217-2882.
Monterrey, Mexico Office: Edificio Losoles PD-4, Av. Lázaro Cárdenas No. 2400 Pte., San Pedro Garza Garcia, Nuevo Léon C.P. 66220.
Telephone: (52-8) 363-0096.
Telecopy: (52-8) 363-3067.

SHAREHOLDERS

Carrie Parker Tiemann

OF COUNSEL

Richard J. Wieland

For Complete List of Firm Personnel, See General Section

For full biographical listings, see the Martindale-Hubbell Law Directory

*DALLAS,** Dallas Co.

THOMPSON & KNIGHT, A PROFESSIONAL CORPORATION (AV)

(Attorneys and Counselors)
1700 Pacific Avenue Suite 3300, 75201
Telephone: 214-969-1700
Telecopy: 214-969-1751
Cable Address: "Tomtex"
Telex: 732298
Austin, Texas Office: 1200 San Jacinto Center, 98 San Jacinto Boulevard, 78701.
Telephone: 512-469-6100.
Telecopy: 512-469-6180.
Fort Worth, Texas Office: 801 Cherry Street, Suite 1600, 76102.
Telephone: 817-347-1700.
Telecopy: 817-347-1799.
Houston, Texas Office: 1700 Texas Commerce Tower, 600 Travis, 77002.
Telephone: 713-217-2800.
Telecopy: 713-217-2828.
Monterrey, Mexico Office: Edificio Losoles PD-4, Av. Lázaro Cárdenas No. 2400 Pte., San Pedro Garza Garcia, Nuevo Léon C.P. 66220.
Telephone: (52-8) 363-0096.
Telecopy: (52-8) 363-3067.

SHAREHOLDERS

Michael L. Bengtson
Sam P. Burford, Jr.
Frederick W. Burnett, Jr.
Robert D. Campbell
Steven K. Cochran
Richard L. Covington
Joseph Dannenmaier
James L. Irish
Paul M. Johnston
Harold F. Kleinman
C. Neel Lemon III
Jack M. Little
Peter A. Lodwick
Don J. McDermett, Jr.
David E. Morrison
James R. Peacock III
Norman R. Rogers
William J. Schuerger
Kenn W. Webb
Jeffrey A. Zlotky

(See Next Column)

ASSOCIATES

Craig N. Adams
Ann Marie Bixby
David L. Emmons
Mark C. Gunnin
John F. Sterling

For Complete List of Firm Personnel, See General Section

For full biographical listings, see the Martindale-Hubbell Law Directory

*FORT WORTH,** Tarrant Co.

HAYNES AND BOONE, L.L.P. (AV)

1300 Burnett Plaza, 801 Cherry Street, 76102-4706
Telephone: 817-347-6600
Metro: 817-654-3308
Telecopy: 817-347-6650
Austin, Texas Office: 1600 One American Center, 600 Congress Avenue.
Telephone: 512-867-8400.
Telecopy: 512-867-8470.
Dallas, Texas Office: 3100 NationsBank Plaza, 901 Main Street.
Telephone: 214-651-5000. Metro: 214-263-2310.
Telecopy: 214-651-5940.
Telex: 73-0187.
Houston, Texas Office: 4300 First Interstate Bank Plaza, 1000 Louisiana Street.
Telephone: 713-547-2000.
Telecopy: 713-547-2600.
San Antonio, Texas Office: 112 East Pecan Street, Suite 1600.
Telephone: 210-978-7000.
Telecopy: 210-978-7450.
Washington, D.C. Office: 919 Eighteenth Street, N.W., Suite 800.
Telephone: 202-393-3502.
Telecopy: 202-296-8680.
Mexico City Office: Monte Pelvoux 111, 1er Piso, Col. Lomas de Chapultepec.
Telephone: 011-525-596-7390.
Telecopy: 011-525-596-7798.

MEMBERS OF FIRM

Brian D. Barnard
Keith D. Calcote
Lawrence Andrew Gaydos
William D. Greenhill
Mark C. Hill
David E. Keltner
Wade H. McMullen
John D. Penn
William D. Ratliff, III
G. Dennis Sheehan
Bettye S. Springer

OF COUNSEL

Robert M. Burnett
Michael L. Williams

ASSOCIATES

Terry S. Boone
Richard K. Casner
Matthew D. Goetz
David S. Goldberg
Kight L. Higgins
Amy Nickell Jacobs
Kathleen R. Parker (Not admitted in TX)
Lu Pham
Karen S. Precella
Craig M. Price

For full biographical listings, see the Martindale-Hubbell Law Directory

THOMPSON & KNIGHT, A PROFESSIONAL CORPORATION (AV)

(Attorneys and Counselors)
801 Cherry Street, Suite 1600, 76102
Telephone: 817-347-1700
Telecopy: 817-347-1799
Dallas, Texas Office: 1700 Pacific Avenue, Suite 3300, 75201.
Telephone: 214-969-1700.
Telecopy: 214-969-1751.
Cable Address: "Tomtex."
Telex: 732298.
Austin, Texas Office: 1200 San Jacinto Center, 98 San Jacinto Boulevard, 78701.
Telephone: 512-469-6100.
Telecopy: 512-469-6180.
Houston, Texas Office: 1700 Texas Commerce Tower, 600 Travis, 77002.
Telephone: 713-217-2800.
Telecopy: 713-217-2828; 713-2882.
Monterrey, Mexico Office: Edificio Losoles PD-4, Av. Lázaro Cárdenas No. 2400 Pte., San Pedro Garza Garcia, Nuevo Léon C.P. 66220.
Telephone: (52-8) 363-0096.
Telecopy: (52-8) 363-3067.

SHAREHOLDERS

Stephen B. Norris

For Complete List of Firm Personnel, See General Section

For full biographical listings, see the Martindale-Hubbell Law Directory

*HOUSTON,** Harris Co.

THOMPSON & KNIGHT, A PROFESSIONAL CORPORATION (AV)

(Attorneys and Counselors)
1700 Texas Commerce Tower, 600 Travis, 77002
Telephone: 713-217-2800
Telecopy: 713-217-2828; 713-217-2882
Dallas, Texas Office: 1700 Pacific Avenue, Suite 3300, 75201.
Telephone: 214-969-1700.
Telecopy: 214-969-1751.
Cable Address: "Tomtex."
Telex: 732298.
Austin, Texas Office: 1200 San Jacinto Center, 98 San Jacinto Boulevard, 78701.
Telephone: 512-469-6100.
Telecopy: 512-469-6180.
Fort Worth, Texas Office: 801 Cherry Street, Suite 1600, 76102.
Telephone: 817-347-1700.
Telecopy: 817-347-1799.
Monterrey, Mexico Office: Edificio Losoles PD-4, Av. Lázaro Cárdenas No. 2400 PTE., San Pedro Garza Garcia, Nuevo Léon C.P. 66220.
Telephone: (52-8) 363-0096.
Telecopy: (52-8) 363-3067.

SHAREHOLDERS

Mary Margaret Bearden
Daniel J. Hayes
Debbi M. Johnstone
Michael K. Pierce

For Complete List of Firm Personnel, See General Section

For full biographical listings, see the Martindale-Hubbell Law Directory

UTAH

*SALT LAKE CITY,** Salt Lake Co.

CALLISTER, NEBEKER & MCCULLOUGH, A PROFESSIONAL CORPORATION (AV)

800 Kennecott Building, 84133
Telephone: 801-530-7300
Telecopier: 801-364-9127

Louis H. Callister
Craig F. McCullough
R. Willis Orton
Damon E. Coombs

Representative Clients: Zions Bancorporation; Electro Brain International.

For Complete List of Firm Personnel, See General Section

For full biographical listings, see the Martindale-Hubbell Law Directory

PARSONS BEHLE & LATIMER, A PROFESSIONAL CORPORATION (AV)

One Utah Center, 201 South Main Street, Suite 1800, P.O. Box 45898, 84145-0898
Telephone: 801-532-1234
Telecopy: 801-536-6111

J. Gordon Hansen
Lawrence R. Barusch
William D. Holyoak
Robert C. Delahunty
Stuart A. Fredman
Scott R. Carpenter
William R. Gray

Representative Clients: Alta Gold; TheraTech, Inc.; Transworld Telecommunications, Inc.

For full biographical listings, see the Martindale-Hubbell Law Directory

VAN COTT, BAGLEY, CORNWALL & MCCARTHY, A PROFESSIONAL CORPORATION (AV)

Suite 1600, 50 South Main Street, P.O. Box 45340, 84145
Telephone: 801-532-3333
Telex: 453149
Telecopier: 801-534-0058
Ogden, Utah Office: Suite 900, 2404 Washington Boulevard.
Telephone: 801-394-5783.
Park City, Utah Office: 314 Main Street, Suite 205.
Telephone: 801-649-3889.
Reno, Nevada Office: Jeppson & Lee, 100 West Liberty, Suite 990.
Telephone: 702-333-6800.

Norman S. Johnson
Arthur B. Ralph
Brent Christensen
Wayne D. Swan

For Complete List of Firm Personnel, See General Section

For full biographical listings, see the Martindale-Hubbell Law Directory

VERMONT

*BURLINGTON,** Chittenden Co.

BURAK & ANDERSON (AV)

Executive Square, 346 Shelburne Street, P.O. Box 64700, 05406-4700
Telephone: 802-862-0500
Telecopier: 802-862-8176

MEMBERS OF FIRM

Michael L. Burak
Thomas R. Melloni

ASSOCIATE

Brian J. Sullivan

For Complete List of Firm Personnel, See General Section

For full biographical listings, see the Martindale-Hubbell Law Directory

SHEEHEY BRUE GRAY & FURLONG, PROFESSIONAL CORPORATION (AV)

119 South Winooski Avenue, P.O. Box 66, 05402
Telephone: 802-864-9891
Facsimile: 802-864-6815

William B. Gray (1942-1994)
David T. Austin
R. Jeffrey Behm
Nordahl L. Brue
Michael G. Furlong
Ralphine Newlin O'Rourke
Donald J. Rendall, Jr.
Christina Schulz
Paul D. Sheehey
Peter H. Zamore

Rebecca L. Owen

Representative Client: Green Mountain Power Corp.

For full biographical listings, see the Martindale-Hubbell Law Directory

*RUTLAND,** Rutland Co.

CARROLL, GEORGE & PRATT (AV)

64 & 66 North Main Street, P.O. Box 280, 05702-0280
Telephone: 802-775-7141
Telecopier: 802-775-6483
Woodstock, Vermont Office: The Mill - Route #4 E., P.O. Box 388, 05091.
Telephone: 802-457-1000.
Telecopier: 802-457-1874.

MEMBERS OF FIRM

Henry G. Smith (1938-1974)
James P. Carroll
Alan B. George
Robert S. Pratt
Neal C. Vreeland
Jon S. Readnour
Timothy U. Martin
Randall F. Mayhew (Resident Partner, Woodstock Office)
Richard S. Smith
Judy Godnick Barone
John J. Kennelly

ASSOCIATES

Thomas A. Zonay
Jeffrey P. White
Susan Boyle Ford (Resident, Woodstock Office)
Charles C. Humpstone

For full biographical listings, see the Martindale-Hubbell Law Directory

*ST. JOHNSBURY,** Caledonia Co.

PRIMMER & PIPER, PROFESSIONAL CORPORATION (AV)

52 Summer Street, P.O. Box 159, 05819
Telephone: 802-748-5061
Facsimile: 802-748-3976
Montpelier, Vermont Office: 44 East State Street, 05602. Box 1309.
Telephone: 802-223-2102.
Fax: 802-223-2628.

John L. Primmer
William B. Piper
Denise J. Deschenes
Jeffrey P. Johnson
Robert W. Martin, Jr.
James E. Clemons

Trevor R. Lewis
James D. Huber

For full biographical listings, see the Martindale-Hubbell Law Directory

VIRGINIA

MCLEAN, Fairfax Co.

MANDELL, LEWIS & GOLDBERG, A PROFESSIONAL CORPORATION (AV)

Tysons Executive Plaza, Suite 1075, 2000 Corporate Ridge (Tysons Corner), 22102
Telephone: 703-734-9622
Facsimile: 703-356-0005
Washington, D.C. Office: Suite 200, 4427A Wisconsin Avenue, N.W.
Telephone: 202-296-1666.
Sterling, Virginia Office: Suite 340, Pidgeon Hill Drive.
Telephone: 703-430-0828.

Steve A. Mandell
David M. Lewis
Michael L. Goldberg

Adam P. Feinberg

OF COUNSEL

Seidman & Associates, P.C., , Washington, D.C.

For full biographical listings, see the Martindale-Hubbell Law Directory

*RICHMOND,** (Ind. City; Seat of Henrico Co.)

WILLIAMS, MULLEN, CHRISTIAN & DOBBINS, A PROFESSIONAL CORPORATION (AV)

Two James Center, 1021 East Cary Street, P.O. Box 1320, 23210-1320
Telephone: 804-643-1991
Fax: 804-783-6456
Glen Allen, Virginia Office: 4401 Waterfront Drive, Suite 140.
Telephone: 804-965-9168.
Fax: 804-965-0955.
Washington, D.C. Office: 1575 Eye Street, N.W.
Telephone: 202-289-6200.
Fax: 202-289-4126.

Theodore L. Chandler, Jr.
David R. Johnson
Warren E. Nowlin (Washington, D.C. Office)
Paul G. Saunders, II
Robert E. Spicer, Jr.
Robin Robertson Starr
Wayne A. Whitham, Jr.

William L. Pitman

For Complete List of Firm Personnel, See General Section

For full biographical listings, see the Martindale-Hubbell Law Directory

WEST VIRGINIA

*CHARLESTON,** Kanawha Co.

JACKSON & KELLY (AV)

1600 Laidley Tower, P.O. Box 553, 25322
Telephone: 304-340-1000
Fax: 304-340-1130
Martinsburg, West Virginia Office: 300 Foxcroft Avenue, P.O. Box 1068.
Telephone: 304-263-8800.
Morgantown, West Virginia Office: 6000 Hampton Center, P.O. Box 619.
Telephone: 304-599-3000.
New Martinsville, West Virginia Office: 256 Russell Avenue, P.O. Box 68.
Telephone: 304-455-1751.
Charles Town, West Virginia Office: 700 East Washington Street, P.O. Box 983.
Telephone: 304-728-6088.
Clarksburg, West Virginia Office: 203 Main Street, P.O. Box 1587.
Telephone: 304-623-3002.
Lexington, Kentucky Office: 175 East Main Street, Suite 500, P.O. Box 2150.
Telephone: 606-255-9500.
Washington, D. C. Office: 2401 Pennsylvania Avenue, N.W., Suite 400.
Telephone: 202-973-0200.
Denver, Colorado Office: Suite 2710, 1660 Lincoln Street.
Telephone: 303-837-0003.

MEMBERS OF FIRM

James Knight Brown
Louis S. Southworth, II
Michael A. Albert
Charles D. Dunbar
Charles W. Loeb, Jr.

ASSOCIATE

Elizabeth Osenton Lord

Representative Clients: One Valley Bancorp of West Virginia, Inc.; Horizons Bancshares; Virginia Inn Management.

For Complete List of Firm Personnel, See General Section

For full biographical listings, see the Martindale-Hubbell Law Directory

WISCONSIN

*MILWAUKEE,** Milwaukee Co.

MEISSNER & TIERNEY, S.C. (AV)

The Milwaukee Center, 111 East Kilbourn Avenue, 19th Floor, 53202-6622
Telephone: 414-273-1300
Facsimile: 414-273-5840

Paul F. Meissner
Joseph E. Tierney III
Thomas J. Nichols
Randal J. Brotherhood

For full biographical listings, see the Martindale-Hubbell Law Directory

QUARLES & BRADY (AV)

411 East Wisconsin Avenue, 53202-4497
Telephone: 414-277-5000
Cable Address: "Lawdock"
Fax: 414-271-3552.
TWX: 910-262-3426
Madison, Wisconsin Office: Firstar Plaza, One South Pinckney Street, P.O. Box 2113.
Telephone: 608-251-5000.
Fax: 608-251-9166.
West Palm Beach, Florida Office: 222 Lakeview Avenue, 4th Floor.
Telephone: 407-653-5000.
Fax: 407-653-5333.
Naples, Florida Office: Barnett Center, 4501 Tamiami Trail North.
Telephone: 813-262-5959.
Fax: 813-434-4999.
Phoenix, Arizona Office: One Camelback Building, One East Camelback Road, Suite 400.
Telephone: 602-230-5500.
Fax: 602-230-5598.

MEMBERS OF FIRM
(ALPHABETICALLY BY YEAR OF ADMISSION TO BAR)

Harry G. Holz
John S. Holbrook, Jr. (Resident, Madison Office)
Michael L. Zaleski (Resident, Madison Office)
Jeffrey B. Bartell (Resident, Madison Office)
Conrad G. Goodkind
Bruce C. Davidson
P. Robert Moya (Resident, Phoenix, Arizona Office)
James D. Friedman
Michael H. Schaalman
Phillip E. Recht
Molly K. Martin (Resident, Madison Office)
Joseph D. Masterson
Kenneth V. Hallett
Paul M. Gales (Resident, Phoenix, Arizona Office)
Steven P. Emerick (Resident, Phoenix, Arizona Office)
Fredrick G. Lautz

OF COUNSEL

Neal E. Madisen

ASSOCIATES

Lorraine J. Koeper
John E. Dunn
Charles M. Weber
Walter J. Skipper
Deborah L. Skurulsky

For Complete List of Firm Personnel, See General Section

For full biographical listings, see the Martindale-Hubbell Law Directory

CANADA
ALBERTA

*CALGARY,** Calgary Jud. Dist.

BENNETT JONES VERCHERE (AV)

4500 Bankers Hall East, 855-2nd Street S.W., T2P 4K7
Telephone: (403) 298-3100
Facsimile: (403) 265-7219
Edmonton, Alberta Office: 1000, 10035-105 Street.
Telephone: (403) 421-8133.
Facsimile: (403) 421-7951.
Toronto, Ontario Office: 3400 1 First Canadian Place. P.O. Box 130.
Telephone: (416) 863-1200.
Facsimile: (416) 863-1716.
Ottawa, Ontario Office: Suite 1800. 350 Alberta Street, Box 25, K1R 1A4.
Telephone: (613) 230-4935.
Facsimile: (613) 230-3836.
Montreal, Quebec Office: Suite 1600, 1 Place Ville Marie.
Telephone: (514) 871-1200.
Facsimile: (514) 871-8115.

(See Next Column)

BENNETT JONES VERCHERE, *Calgary—Continued*

MEMBER OF FIRM

Walter B. O'Donoghue, Q.C.

For Complete List of Firm Personnel, See General Section

For full biographical listings, see the Martindale-Hubbell Law Directory

*EDMONTON,** Edmonton Jud. Dist.

PARLEE MCLAWS (AV)

15th Floor Manulife Place, 10180 101st Street, T5J 4K1
Telephone: 403-423-8500
Telecopier: 403-423-2870
Calgary, Alberta Office: 3400, Western Canadian Place, 707 - 8th Avenue, S.W.
Telephone: 403-294-7000.
Telecopier: 403-265-8263.

MEMBERS OF FIRM

C. H. Kerr, Q.C.
M. D. MacDonald
K. F. Bailey, Q.C.
R. B. Davison, Q.C.
F. R. Haldane
P. E. J. Curran
D. G. Finlay
J. K. McFadyen
R. C. Secord
D. L. Kennedy
D. C. Rolf
D. F. Pawlowski
A. A. Garber
R. P. James
D. C. Wintermute
J. L. Cairns
R. A. Newton, Q.C.
T. A. Cockrall, Q.C.
H. D. Montemurro
F. J. Niziol
R. W. Wilson
I. L. MacLachlan
R. O. Langley
R. G. McBean
J. T. Neilson
E. G. Rice
J. F. McGinnis
J. H. H. Hockin
G. W. Jaycock
M. J. K. Nikel
B. J. Curial
S. L. May
M. S. Poretti

ASSOCIATES

C. R. Head
A.W. Slemko
L. H. Hamdon
K.A. Smith
K. D. Fallis-Howell
D. S. Tam
J.W. McClure
F.H. Belzil
R.A. Renz
J.G. Paulson
K. E. Buss
B. L. Andriachuk
P. E. S. J. Kennedy
R. Feraco
R.J. Billingsley
N.B.R. Thompson
P. A. Shenher
I. C. Johnson
K.G. Koshman
D.D. Dubrule
G. T. Lund
W.D. Johnston
G. E. Flemming
K. P. Nayyer

For full biographical listings, see the Martindale-Hubbell Law Directory

CANADA ONTARIO

*TORONTO,** Regional Munic. of York

BORDEN & ELLIOT (AV)

Barristers & Solicitors
Scotia Plaza, 40 King Street West, M5H 3Y4
Telephone: 416-367-6000
Telecopier: 416-367-6749
Internet: @ borden.com
A Member of the national association of Borden DuMoulin Howard Gervais, comprising Borden & Elliot in Toronto, Ontario, Russell & DuMoulin in Vancouver, British Columbia, Howard, Mackie in Calgary, Alberta and Mackenzie Gervais in Montréal, Québec. Borden DuMoulin Howard Gervais also operates an office in London, England.

MEMBER AND ASSOCIATES

Paul G. Findlay

For Complete List of Firm Personnel, See General Section

For full biographical listings, see the Martindale-Hubbell Law Directory

CANADA QUEBEC

*MONTREAL,** Montreal Dist.

BYERS CASGRAIN (AV)

A Member of McMillan Bull Casgrain
Suite 3900, 1 Place Ville-Marie, H3B 4M7
Telephone: 514-878-8800
Telecopier: 514-866-2241
Cable Address: "Magee"
Telex: 05-24195

Paul F. Dingle, Q.C.
Claire Richer
David McAusland
Jean-Pierre Huard
Patrice Beaudin

For Complete List of Firm Personnel, See General Section

For full biographical listings, see the Martindale-Hubbell Law Directory

CANADA SASKATCHEWAN

*REGINA,** Regina Jud. Centre

MACPHERSON LESLIE & TYERMAN (AV)

1500-1874 Scarth Street, S4P 4E9
Telephone: 306-347-8000
Telecopier: 306-352-5250
Saskatoon, Saskatchewan Office: 1500-410 22nd Street East, S7K 5T6.
Telephone: 306-975-7100.
Telecopier: 306-975-7145.

MEMBERS OF FIRM

Carl A. P. Wagner
Donald K. Wilson
Danny R. Anderson (Resident, Saskatoon Office)
Robert B. Pletch, Q.C.
Douglas A. Ballou

For Complete List of Firm Personnel, See General Section

For full biographical listings, see the Martindale-Hubbell Law Directory

MEXICO

MONTERREY, NUEVO LEÓN,

Monterrey, Nuevo León

THOMPSON & KNIGHT, A PROFESSIONAL CORPORATION

(Attorneys and Counselors)
Edificio Losoles PD-4, Av. Lázaro Cárdenas No. 2400 PTE San Pedro Garza Garcia, Monterrey, Nuevo León 66220
Telephone: (52-8) 363-0096
Telecopy: (52-8) 363-3067
Dallas, Texas Office: 1700 Pacific Avenue, Suite 3300, 75201.
Telephone: 214-969-1700.
Telecopy: 214-969-1751.
Cable Address: "Tomtex."
Telex: 732298.
Austin, Texas Office: 1200 San Jacinto Center, 98 San Jacinto Boulevard, 78701.
Telephone: 512-469-6100.
Telecopy: 512-469-6180.
Fort Worth, Texas Office: 801 Cherry Street, Suite 1600, 76102.
Telephone: 817-347-1700.
Telecopy: 817-347-1799.
Houston, Texas Office: 1700 Texas Commerce Tower, 600 Travis, 77002.
Telephone: 713-217-2800.
Telecopy: 713-217-2828; 713-217-2882.

SHAREHOLDERS

Michael C. Titens

For Complete List of Firm Personnel, See General Section

For full biographical listings, see the Martindale-Hubbell Law Directory

TAX LAW

ALABAMA

*BIRMINGHAM,** Jefferson Co.

BALCH & BINGHAM (AV)
1710 Sixth Avenue North, P.O. Box 306, 35201
Telephone: 205-251-8100
Facsimile: 205-226-8798
Other Birmingham, Alabama Office: 1901 Sixth Avenue North, 35203.
Telephone: 205-251-8100.
Facsimile: 205-226-8799.
Montgomery, Alabama Office: The Winter Building, 2 Dexter Avenue, 36101.
Telephone: 205-834-6500.
Facsimile: 205-269-3115.
Huntsville, Alabama Office: Suite 810, 200 West Court Square, 35801.
Telephone: 205-551-0171.
Facsimile: 205-551-0174.
Washington, D.C. Office: Suite 800, 1101 Connecticut Avenue, N.W., 20036.
Telephone: 202-296-0387.
Facsimile: 202-452-8180.

MEMBERS OF FIRM

William J. Ward
William E. Shanks, Jr.
James F. Hughey, Jr.
Timothy J. Tracy
Alex B. Leath, III

ASSOCIATES

John Douglas Buchanan
Randall D. McClanahan

Counsel for: Alabama Power Co.; Blue Cross and Blue Shield of Alabama; The Boeing Company; Brasfield & Gorrie, Inc.; Compass Bancshares, Inc.; Harbert Corp.; Kimberly-Clark Corp.; Southern Company Services, Inc.; Southern Research Institute; Vesta Insurance Group, Inc.

For Complete List of Firm Personnel, See General Section

For full biographical listings, see the Martindale-Hubbell Law Directory

BERKOWITZ, LEFKOVITS, ISOM & KUSHNER, A PROFESSIONAL CORPORATION (AV)
1600 SouthTrust Tower, 420 North Twentieth Street, 35203
Telephone: 205-328-0480
Telecopier: 205-322-8007

Arnold K. Lefkovits
D. J. Simonetti
Harold B. Kushner
W. Clark Goodwin
Henry I. Frohsin
Barry S. Marks
Anne W. Mitchell
Ronald A. Levitt
William R. Sylvester
Thomas O. Kolb

Andrew J. Potts

Representative Clients: AlaTenn Resources, Inc.; AMI Brookwood Medical Center; B.A.S.S., Inc.; Eternal Word Television Network; Hanna Steel Co., Inc.; Liberty Trouser Co., Inc.; Parisian, Inc.; Southeast Health Plan, Inc.; Southern Pipe & Supply Co., Inc.

For Complete List of Firm Personnel, See General Section

For full biographical listings, see the Martindale-Hubbell Law Directory

BRADLEY, ARANT, ROSE & WHITE (AV)
1400 Park Place Tower, 2001 Park Place, 35203
Telephone: 205-521-8000
Telex: 494-1324
Facsimile: 205-251-8611, 251-8665, 252-0264
Facsimile (Southtrust Office): 205-251-9915
Huntsville, Alabama Office: 200 Clinton Avenue West, Suite 900.
Telephone: 205-517-5100.
Facsimile: 205-533-5069.

MEMBERS OF FIRM

Lee C. Bradley, Jr.
Robert G. Johnson
Edward M. Selfe
Robert C. Walthall
John N. Wrinkle
John K. Molen
Thomas Neely Carruthers, Jr.
Lant B. Davis
William L. Hinds, Jr.
John B. Grenier
Stuart Joseph Frentz

COUNSEL

Wm. Bew White, Jr.

(See Next Column)

ASSOCIATES

James S. Christie, Jr.
Stephen K. Greene
K. Wood Herren

For Complete List of Firm Personnel, See General Section

For full biographical listings, see the Martindale-Hubbell Law Directory

BURR & FORMAN (AV)
3000 SouthTrust Tower, 420 North 20th Street, 35203
Telephone: 205-251-3000
Telecopier: 205-458-5100
Huntsville, Alabama Office: Suite 204, Regency Center, 400 Meridian Street.
Telephone: 205-551-0010.

MEMBERS OF FIRM

Paul O. Woodall
Jack P. Stephenson, Jr.
Louis H. Anders, Jr.
Bruce A. Rawls
A. Brand Walton
Henry Graham Beene
Marvin Glenn Perry, Jr.

ASSOCIATE

Warren C. Matthews

For Complete List of Firm Personnel, See General Section

For full biographical listings, see the Martindale-Hubbell Law Directory

DOMINICK, FLETCHER, YEILDING, WOOD & LLOYD, P.A. (AV)
2121 Highland Avenue, 35205
Telephone: 205-939-0033

C. Fred Daniels
Brian T. Williams

Counsel for: Citizens Federal Savings Bank; St. Vincent's Hospital; Birmingham-Southern College; Castle Mortgage Corporation; Methodist Homes for the Aging; Integrated Health Services, Inc.; Amerex; Northeast Regional Medical Center.

For Complete List of Firm Personnel, See General Section

For full biographical listings, see the Martindale-Hubbell Law Directory

GORDON, SILBERMAN, WIGGINS & CHILDS, A PROFESSIONAL CORPORATION (AV)
1400 SouthTrust Tower, 420 North 20th Street, 35203
Telephone: 205-328-0640
Telecopier: 205-254-1500

Wilbur G. Silberman
Augustus J. Beck, Jr.
Bruce L. Gordon
Harvey L. Wachsman
Robert L. Wiggins, Jr.
Ray D. Gibbons
Robert F. Childs, Jr.
C. Michael Quinn
Dennis George Pantazis

Terrill W. Sanders
Linda J. Peacock
James Mendelsohn
Ann C. Robertson
Richard J. Ebbinghouse
Elizabeth Evans Courtney
Ann K. Norton
Byron R. Perkins
Paul H. Webb
Jon C. Goldfarb
Mark P. Williams
Gregory O. Wiggins
Samuel Fisher
Lee Winston
Timothy C. Gann
Jon E. Lewis
Naomi Hilton Archer
Deborah A. Mattison
Timothy D. Davis
Amelia H. Griffith
Joseph H. Calvin, III
Rocco Calamusa, Jr.

OF COUNSEL

Robert H. Loeb

For Complete List of Firm Personnel, See General Section

For full biographical listings, see the Martindale-Hubbell Law Directory

GORHAM, STEWART, KENDRICK, BRYANT & BATTLE, P.C. (AV)
2101 6th Avenue North, Suite 700, 35203
Telephone: 205-254-3216, 251-9166
Telecopier: 205-324-3802

William J. Bryant

Karen Brown Evans

Representative Clients: Jefferson County Personnel Board; Birmingham-Jefferson Civic Center Authority; The Water Works and Sewer Board of the City of Birmingham; City of Homewood; American Federation of Government Employees Local #1945; City of Pelham; Town of Kimberly; Alabama Tire Dealers Assn.; Southern States Body Shop Assn.

For Complete List of Firm Personnel, See General Section

For full biographical listings, see the Martindale-Hubbell Law Directory

Birmingham—Continued

JOHNSTON, BARTON, PROCTOR, SWEDLAW & NAFF (AV)

2900 AmSouth/Harbert Plaza, 1901 Sixth Avenue North, 35203-2618
Telephone: 205-458-9400
Telecopier: 205-458-9500

MEMBERS OF FIRM

Harvey Deramus (1904-1970) | James C. Barton, Jr.
Alfred M. Naff (1923-1993) | Thomas E. Walker
James C. Barton | Anne P. Wheeler
G. Burns Proctor, Jr. | Raymond P. Fitzpatrick, Jr.
Sydney L. Lavender | Hollinger F. Barnard
Jerome K. Lanning | William D. Jones III
Don B. Long, Jr. | David W. Proctor
Charles L. Robinson | Oscar M. Price III
J. William Rose, Jr. | W. Hill Sewell
Gilbert E. Johnston, Jr. | Robert S. Vance, Jr.
David P. Whiteside, Jr. | Richard J. Brockman
Ralph H. Smith II | Anthony A. Joseph

OF COUNSEL

Gilbert E. Johnston | Alfred Swedlaw
Alan W. Heldman

ASSOCIATES

William K. Hancock | Haskins W. Jones
James P. Pewitt | James M. Parker, Jr.
Scott Wells Ford | Michael H. Johnson
David M. Hunt | Russell L. Irby, III
Lee M. Pope | R. Scott Clark
Helen Kathryn Downs

General Counsel for: Anderson News Co.; The Baptist Medical Centers; The Birmingham News Co. (Publishers of the Birmingham News and owner of the Huntsville Times Co.); Southern Medical Association.
Counsel for: BellSouth Services, Inc.; General Motors Corp.; Jemison Inv. Co., Inc.; The Marmon Group; SouthTrust Bank of Alabama, N.A.

For full biographical listings, see the Martindale-Hubbell Law Directory

PRITCHARD, MCCALL & JONES (AV)

800 Financial Center, 35203
Telephone: 205-328-9190

MEMBERS OF FIRM

William S. Pritchard (1890-1967) | Julian P. Hardy, Jr.
Alexander W. Jones (1914-1988) | Alexander W. Jones, Jr.
William S. Pritchard, Jr. | F. Hilton-Green Tomlinson
Madison W. O'Kelley, Jr. | James G. Henderson
William S. Pritchard, III

ASSOCIATES

Michael L. McKerley | Nina Michele LaFleur
Robert Bond Higgins | Mary W. Burge

Representative Clients: First National Bank of Columbiana; Central State Bank of Calera; Buffalo Rock-Pepsi-Cola Bottling Co.; Gillis Advertising, Inc.; Liberty Mutual Insurance Co.; Reliance Insurance Company; SouthTrust Bank, N.A.; Bromberg & Company, Inc.; Farmers Furniture Company; First Commercial Bank.

For full biographical listings, see the Martindale-Hubbell Law Directory

SIROTE & PERMUTT, P.C. (AV)

2222 Arlington Avenue, South, P.O. Box 55727, 35255
Telephone: 205-933-7111
Facsimile: 205-930-5301
Huntsville, Alabama Office: 200 Clinton Avenue, N.W., Suite 1000.
Telephone: 205-536-1711.
Facsimile: 205-534-9650.
Mobile, Alabama Office: One St. Louis Centre, Suite 1000.
Telephone: 205-432-1671.
Facsimile: 205-434-0196.
Montgomery, Alabama Office: Colonial Commerce Center, Suite 305 One Commerce Street.
Telephone: 205-261-3400.
Facsimile: 205-261-3434.
Tuscaloosa, Alabama Office: 2216 14th Street.
Telephone: 205-752-2089.

James L. Permutt | John H. Cooper
E. M. Friend, Jr. | Judith F. Todd
Harold I. Apolinsky | Dale B. Stone
Joseph S. Bluestein | Timothy A. Bush
Richard J. Cohn | Joseph T. Ritchey
David M. Wooldridge | Bradley J. Sklar
Melinda McEachern Mathews | Candace Lee Hemphill
Jack B. Levy | W. Todd Carlisle

OF COUNSEL

Joseph W. Blackburn

Representative Clients: International Business Machines (IBM); General Motors Corp.; Colonial Bank; Bruno's, Inc.; University of Alabama Hospitals; Westinghouse Electric Corp.; First Alabama Bank; Monsanto Chemical Company; South Central Bell; Prudential Insurance Company; American Home Products, Inc.; Minnesota Mining and Manufacturing, Inc. (3M).

(See Next Column)

For Complete List of Firm Personnel, See General Section

For full biographical listings, see the Martindale-Hubbell Law Directory

SPAIN, GILLON, GROOMS, BLAN & NETTLES (AV)

The Zinszer Building, 2117 2nd Avenue North, 35203
Telephone: 205-328-4100
Telecopier: 205-324-8866

MEMBERS OF FIRM

John P. McKleroy, Jr. | J. Birch Bowdre
Samuel H. Frazier | Glenn E. Estess, Jr.
Paul S. Leonard

Representative Clients: Golden Enterprises, Inc.; City of Birmingham; First Federal of Alabama, Federal Savings Bank; Housing Authority of the Birmingham District; Piggly Wiggly Alabama Distributing Co., Inc.; Golden Flake Snack Foods, Inc.; First General Lending Corporation; Alabama Health Plan; All-South Subcontractors, Inc.; Smith Barney, Harris Upham and Co., Inc.

For Complete List of Firm Personnel, See General Section

For full biographical listings, see the Martindale-Hubbell Law Directory

*DOTHAN,** Houston Co.

JOHNSTON, HINESLEY, FLOWERS & CLENNEY, P.C., A PROFESSIONAL CORPORATION (AV)

291 North Oates Street, 36303
Telephone: 334-793-1115
Fax: 334-793-6603

G. David Johnston | William T. Flowers
William W. Hinesley | R. Eugene Clenney, Jr.

For full biographical listings, see the Martindale-Hubbell Law Directory

*FLORENCE,** Lauderdale Co.

KELLER & PITTS (AV)

212 South Cedar Street, P.O. Box 933, 35631
Telephone: 205-764-5822
Fax: 205-767-6360

MEMBERS OF FIRM

Jesse A. Keller | Conrad C. Pitts
Peter L. Paine

Counsel for: The American Road Insurance Co.; Lambert Transfer Co.

For full biographical listings, see the Martindale-Hubbell Law Directory

*HUNTSVILLE,** Madison Co.

BRADLEY, ARANT, ROSE & WHITE (AV)

200 Clinton Avenue West, Suite 900, 35801
Telephone: 205-517-5100
Facsimile: 205-533-5069
Birmingham, Alabama Office: 1400 Park Place Tower, 2001 Park Place.
Telephone: 205-521-8000.
Telex: 494-1324.
Facsimile: 205-251-8611, 251-8665, 252-0264. Facsimile (Southtrust Office): 205-251-9915.

RESIDENT PARTNERS

Robert Sellers Smith | Scott E. Ludwig

For Complete List of Firm Personnel, See General Section

For full biographical listings, see the Martindale-Hubbell Law Directory

SIROTE & PERMUTT, P.C. (AV)

Suite 1000, 200 Clinton Avenue, N.W., 35801
Telephone: 205-536-1711
Facsimile: 205-534-9650
Birmingham, Alabama Office: 2222 Arlington Avenue, South, P.O. Box 55727.
Telephone: 205-933-7111.
Facsimile: 205-930-5301.
Mobile, Alabama Office: One St. Louis Centre, Suite 1000.
Telephone: 205-432-1671.
Facsimile: 205-434-0196.
Montgomery, Alabama Office: Colonial Commerce Center, Suite 305, One Commerce Street.
Telephone: 205-261-3400.
Facsimile: 205-261-3434.
Tuscaloosa, Alabama Office: 2216 14th Street.
Telephone: 205-752-2089.

Joe H. Ritch | Christine Sampson Hinson

For Complete List of Firm Personnel, See General Section

For full biographical listings, see the Martindale-Hubbell Law Directory

*MOBILE,** Mobile Co.

ARMBRECHT, JACKSON, DEMOUY, CROWE, HOLMES & REEVES (AV)

1300 AmSouth Center, P.O. Box 290, 36601
Telephone: 334-432-6751
Facsimile: 334-432-6843; 433-3821

MEMBERS OF FIRM

Wm. H. Armbrecht (1908-1991)
Theodore K. Jackson (1910-1981)
Marshall J. DeMouy
Wm. H. Armbrecht, III
Rae M. Crowe
Broox G. Holmes
W. Boyd Reeves
E. B. Peebles III
William B. Harvey
Kirk C. Shaw
Norman E. Waldrop, Jr.
Conrad P. Armbrecht
Edward G. Hawkins
Grover E. Asmus II
David A. Bagwell
Douglas L. Brown
Donald C. Radcliff
Christopher I. Gruenewald
James Donald Hughes
M. Kathleen Miller
Dabney Bragg Foshee
Edward A. Dean
David E. Hudgens
Ray Morgan Thompson
James Dale Smith
Duane A. Graham
Robert J. Mullican
Wm. Steele Holman, II
Coleman F. Meador
Broox G. Holmes, Jr.

ASSOCIATES

James E. Robertson, Jr.
Scott G. Brown
Clifford C. Brady
Richard W. Franklin
Stephen Russell Copeland
Tara T. Bostick

Representative Clients: Ryan-Walsh Stevedoring Co.; Cooper Stevedoring Co., Inc.; WKRG-TV, Inc.; United States Sports Academy; Smith's Bakery, Inc.; Laurentian Capital Corp.; Taca International Airlines; Scott Paper Co.; Automation Technology, Inc.

For Complete List of Firm Personnel, See General Section

For full biographical listings, see the Martindale-Hubbell Law Directory

HAND, ARENDALL, BEDSOLE, GREAVES & JOHNSTON (AV)

3000 First National Bank Building, P.O. Box 123, Drawer C, 36601
Telephone: 334-432-5511
Fax: 334-694-6375
Washington, D.C. Office: 410 First Street, S.E., Suite 300. 20003.
Telephone: 202-863-0053.
Fax: 202-863-0096.

MEMBERS OF FIRM

Vivian G. Johnston, Jr.
J. Thomas Hines, Jr.
G. Porter Brock, Jr.
Stephen G. Crawford
Gregory L. Leatherbury, Jr.
Judith L. McMillin

For Complete List of Firm Personnel, See General Section

For full biographical listings, see the Martindale-Hubbell Law Directory

JOHNSTONE, ADAMS, BAILEY, GORDON AND HARRIS (AV)

Royal St. Francis Building, 104 St. Francis Street, P.O. Box 1988, 36633
Telephone: 334-432-7682
Facsimile: 334-432-2800
Telex: 782040

MEMBERS OF FIRM

Charles B. Bailey, Jr.
E. Watson Smith
R. Gregory Watts

ASSOCIATES

Robert S. Frost
C. William Rasure, Jr.

Representative Clients: Commonwealth Land Title Insurance Co.; Delaney Development, Inc.; Exxon Corporation; First Alabama Bank; Infirmary Health System/Mobile Infirmary Medical Center/Rotary Rehabilitation Hospital (Multi-Hospital System); International Marine and Industrial Applicators; Lerio Corporation; Mobile Paint Manufacturing Co., Inc.

For Complete List of Firm Personnel, See General Section

For full biographical listings, see the Martindale-Hubbell Law Directory

LYONS, PIPES & COOK, P.C. (AV)

2 North Royal Street, P.O. Box 2727, 36652-2727
Telephone: 334-432-4481
Cable Address: "Lysea"
Telecopier: 334-433-1820

Wesley Pipes
Thomas F. Garth
Reggie Copeland, Jr.
R. Mark Kirkpatrick
Michael C. Niemeyer

Counsel: James Graham Brown Foundation, Inc.; Florence Foundation, Inc.; McKenzie Tank Lines, Inc.; SCNO Barge Lines, Inc.; Scott Paper Co.; Shell Oil Corp.

For Complete List of Firm Personnel, See General Section

For full biographical listings, see the Martindale-Hubbell Law Directory

SIROTE & PERMUTT, P.C. (AV)

One St. Louis Centre, Suite 1000, P.O. Drawer 2025, 36652-2025
Telephone: 334-432-1671
Facsimile: 334-434-0196
Birmingham, Alabama Office: 2222 Arlington Avenue, South, P.O. Box 55727.
Telephone: 205-933-7111.
Facsimile: 205-930-5301.
Huntsville, Alabama Office: 200 Clinton Avenue, N.W., Suite 1000.
Telephone: 205-536-1711.
Facsimile: 205-534-9650.
Montgomery, Alabama Office: Colonial Commerce Center, Suite 305, One Commerce Street.
Telephone: 205-261-3400.
Facsimile: 205-261-3434.
Tuscaloosa, Alabama Office: 2216 14th Street.
Telephone: 205-752-2089.

Shirley Mahan Justice

For Complete List of Firm Personnel, See General Section

For full biographical listings, see the Martindale-Hubbell Law Directory

VICKERS, RIIS, MURRAY AND CURRAN (AV)

8th Floor, First Alabama Bank Building, P.O. Box 2568, 36652
Telephone: 334-432-9772
Fax: 334-432-9781

MEMBERS OF FIRM

J. Manson Murray
Zebulon M. P. Inge, Jr.
Ronald P. Davis

Representative Clients: Dravo Natural Resources Co.; Midstream Fuel Services; John E. Graham & Sons; McPhillips Manufacturing Co.; Spring Hill College; Steiner Shipyard, Inc.; Homeowners Marketing Services, Inc.; Marine Office of America Corp.; Cummins Alabama, Inc.; Ben M. Radcliff Contractor, Inc.

For Complete List of Firm Personnel, See General Section

For full biographical listings, see the Martindale-Hubbell Law Directory

*MONTGOMERY,** Montgomery Co.

* indicates certain Bar Register subscribers whose principal office is located elsewhere in the state and who have arranged for representation as a part of the state capital listings that follow

*** BALCH & BINGHAM (AV)**

The Winter Building, 2 Dexter Avenue, P.O. Box 78, 36101
Telephone: 334-834-6500
Facsimile: 334-269-3115
Birmingham, Alabama Offices: 1710 Sixth Avenue North, 35203.
Telephone: 205-251-8100.
Facsimile: 205-226-8798. 1901 Sixth Avenue North, 35203.
Telephone: 205-251-8100.
Facsimile: 205-226-8799.
Huntsville, Alabama Office: Suite 810, 200 West Court Square, 35801.
Telephone: 205-551-0171.
Facsimile: 205-551-0174.
Washington, D.C. Office: Suite 800, 1101 Connecticut Avenue, N.W., 20036.
Telephone: 202-296-0387.
Facsimile: 202-452-8180.

RESIDENT MEMBER OF FIRM

Malcolm N. Carmichael

RESIDENT ASSOCIATE

James Ernest Bridges, III

Counsel for: Alabama Power Co.; Blue Cross and Blue Shield of Alabama; The Boeing Company; Brasfield & Gorrie, Inc.; Compass Bancshares, Inc.; Harbert Corp.; Kimberly-Clark Corp.; Southern Company Services, Inc.; Southern Research Institute; Vesta Insurance Group, Inc.

For Complete List of Firm Personnel, See General Section

For full biographical listings, see the Martindale-Hubbell Law Directory

CAPELL, HOWARD, KNABE & COBBS, P.A. (AV)

57 Adams Avenue, P.O. Box 2069, 36102-2069
Telephone: 334-241-8000

Jack L. Capell
Fontaine M. Howard (1908-1985)
Walter J. Knabe (1898-1979)
Edward E. Cobbs (1909-1982)
L. Lister Hill (1936-1993)
Herman H. Hamilton, Jr.
Rufus M. King
Robert S. Richard
John B. Scott, Jr.
John F. Andrews
James M. Scott
Thomas S. Lawson, Jr.
John L. Capell, III
William D. Coleman
William K. Martin
Bruce J. Downey III
Henry C. Barnett, Jr.
Palmer Smith Lehman
Richard F. Allen
Neal H. Acker
Henry H. Hutchinson

(See Next Column)

CAPELL, HOWARD, KNABE & COBBS P.A., *Montgomery—Continued*

Shapard D. Ashley — Jim B. Grant, Jr.
D. Kyle Johnson — Wyeth Holt Speir, III
J. Lister Hubbard — Chad S. Wachter
James N. Walter, Jr. — Ellen M. Hastings
James H. McLemore — Debra Deames Spain
H. Dean Mooty, Jr. — William Rufus King
C. Clay Torbert, III

OF COUNSEL

Timothy Sullivan

For full biographical listings, see the Martindale-Hubbell Law Directory

CAPOUANO, WAMPOLD, PRESTWOOD & SANSONE, P.A. (AV)

350 Adams Avenue, P.O. Box 1910, 36102-1910
Telephone: 334-264-6401
Fax: 334-834-4954

Leon M. Capouano — Ellis D. Hanan
Alvin T. Prestwood — Joseph P. Borg
Jerome D. Smith — Joseph W. Warren

OF COUNSEL

Charles H. Wampold, Jr.

Thomas B. Klinner — Linda Smith Webb
James M. Sizemore, Jr.

Counsel for: First Alabama Bank of Montgomery, N.A.; Union Bank and Trust Co.; Real Estate Financing, Inc.; SouthTrust Bank; AmSouth Bank; Central Bank; City Federal Savings & Loan Assoc.; Colonial Mortgage Co.; Lomas & Nettleton; First Bank of Linden.

For full biographical listings, see the Martindale-Hubbell Law Directory

KAUFMAN & ROTHFEDER, P.C. (AV)

2740 Zelda Road Post Office Drawer 4540, 36103-4540
Telephone: 334-244-1111
Fax: 334-244-1969

Alan E. Rothfeder — Robert E. L. Gilpin
Jo Karen Parr — John Ward Weiss
Richardson B. McKenzie, III — Robert M. Ritchey
William B. Sellers

Counsel for: Russell Corp.; Sanders Lead Co., Inc.; Waste Management of North America, Inc.

For full biographical listings, see the Martindale-Hubbell Law Directory

SIROTE & PERMUTT, P.C. (AV)

Colonial Commerce Center, Suite 305, One Commerce Street, 36104
Telephone: 334-261-3400
Facsimile: 334-261-3434
Birmingham, Alabama Office: 2222 Arlington Avenue, South, P.O. Box 55727.
Telephone: 205-933-7111.
Facsimile: 205-930-5301.
Huntsville, Alabama Office: 200 Clinton Avenue, N.W., Suite 1000.
Telephone: 205-536-1711.
Facsimile: 205-534-9650.
Mobile, Alabama Office: One St. Louis Centre, Suite 1000.
Telephone: 205-432-1671.
Facsimile: 205-434-0196.
Tuscaloosa, Alabama Office: 2216 14th Street.
Telephone: 205-752-2089.

Jeff Kohn — M. Fredrick Simpler, Jr.
Charles Middleton

For Complete List of Firm Personnel, See General Section

For full biographical listings, see the Martindale-Hubbell Law Directory

*TUSCALOOSA,** Tuscaloosa Co.

PHELPS, JENKINS, GIBSON & FOWLER (AV)

1201 Greensboro Avenue, P.O. Box 020848, 35402-0848
Telephone: 205-345-5100
Fax: 205-758-4394
Fax: 205-391-6658

MEMBERS OF FIRM

Sam M. Phelps — Randolph M. Fowler
James J. Jenkins — Michael S. Burroughs
Johnson Russell Gibson, III — C. Barton Adcox
Farley A. Poellnitz

ASSOCIATES

K. Scott Stapp — Sandra C. Guin
Karen C. Welborn — Kimberly B. Glass
Stephen E. Snow

Attorneys for: Aetna Insurance Co.; Allstate Insurance Co.; Carolina Casualty Insurance Co.; Continental Insurance Cos.; Fireman's Fund-American Insurance Cos.; Great American Insurance Co.; Hanover Insurance Co.

(See Next Column)

For full biographical listings, see the Martindale-Hubbell Law Directory

ARIZONA

*NOGALES,** Santa Cruz Co.

O'CONNOR, CAVANAGH, ANDERSON, WESTOVER, KILLINGSWORTH & BESHEARS, A PROFESSIONAL ASSOCIATION (AV)

1827 North Mastick Way, 85621
Telephone: 602-761-4215
FAX: 602-761-3505
Phoenix, Arizona Office: One East Camelback Road, Suite 1100, 85012.
Telephone: 602-263-2400.
FAX: 602-263-2900.
Tucson, Arizona Office: Suite 2200, One South Church Avenue, 85701.
Telephone: 602-882-8912.
FAX: 602-624-9564.
Sun City, Arizona Office: 13250 North Del Webb Boulevard, Suite B, 85351.
Telephone: 602-263-2808.
FAX: 602-933-3100.

Hector G. Arana

Representative Clients: Omega Produce Co.; Frank's Distributing, Inc.; City of Nogales; Collectron of Ariz., Inc.; James K. Wilson Produce Co.; Agricola Bon, S. de R.L. de C.V.; Angel Demerutis E.; Rene Carrillo C.; Arturo Lomeli; Theojary Crisantes E.

For Complete List of Firm Personnel, See General Section

For full biographical listings, see the Martindale-Hubbell Law Directory

*PHOENIX,** Maricopa Co.

MARVIN D. BRODY PROFESSIONAL CORPORATION (AV)

Court Two, Suite 350, 4722 North 24th Street, 85016
Telephone: 602-956-5050
Telecopier: 602-468-9775

Marvin D. Brody

For full biographical listings, see the Martindale-Hubbell Law Directory

BURCH & CRACCHIOLO, P.A. (AV)

702 East Osborn Road, Suite 200, 85014
Telephone: 602-274-7611
Fax: 602-234-0341
Mailing Address: P.O. Box 16882, Phoenix, AZ, 85011

Stephen E. Silver — Guadalupe Iniguez
Brad S. Ostroff

Martha C. Patrick

Representative Clients: Bashas' Inc.; Farmers Insurance Group; U-Haul International, Inc.

For Complete List of Firm Personnel, See General Section

For full biographical listings, see the Martindale-Hubbell Law Directory

A. JERRY BUSBY, P.C. (AV)

Suite 150, 5070 North 40th Street, 85018
Telephone: 602-957-0071
Fax: 602-957-0460

A. Jerry Busby

Representative Clients: The Circle K Corp.; Sun World Corp.
Reference: Bank of Scottsdale.

For full biographical listings, see the Martindale-Hubbell Law Directory

EHMANN & HILLER, P.C. (AV)

Suite 350, 4722 North 24th Street, 85016
Telephone: 602-956-5050
Telecopier: 602-468-9775

Anthony V. Ehmann — John G. Pattullo
Neil H. Hiller — John F. Daniels, III

OF COUNSEL

Thomas G. Georgiou

References: Valley National Bank of Arizona (Trust Department); First Interstate Bank of Arizona, N.A. (Trust Department); M & I Thunderbird Bank.

For full biographical listings, see the Martindale-Hubbell Law Directory

Phoenix—Continued

FENNEMORE CRAIG, A PROFESSIONAL CORPORATION (AV)

Two North Central, Suite 2200, 85004
Telephone: 602-257-8700
Fax: 602-257-8527
Scottsdale, Arizona Office: 6263 North Scottsdale Road, Suite 290, 85250.
Telephone: 602-257-5400.
Fax: 602-945-4932.
Tucson, Arizona Office: One South Church Avenue, Suite 1030, 85701.
Telephone: 602-624-9312.
Fax: 602-882-7383.

James Powers
Arthur D. Ehrenreich
Neal Kurn
David T. Cox
Cynthia L. Shupe
Paul J. Mooney
Ray K. Harris
Gregg Hanks
Jim L. Wright
J. Barry Shelley

Marc L. Spitzer
Otto S. Shill, III
Stephen A. Good
Karen Rettig Rogers

Representative Clients: ASARCO Incorporated; AT&T Communications; Bridgestone/Firestone, Inc.; Catellus Development Corp.; Citibank (Arizona); First Interstate Bank of Arizona; GIANT Industries; Phelps Dodge Corporation; The Atchison, Topeka & Santa Fe Railway, Co.; US WEST Communications.

For Complete List of Firm Personnel, See General Section

For full biographical listings, see the Martindale-Hubbell Law Directory

JENNINGS, STROUSS AND SALMON, P.L.C. (AV)

A Professional Limited Liability Company
One Renaissance Square, Two North Central, 85004-2393
Telephone: 602-262-5911
Fax: 602-253-3255

John R. Christian
Richard L. Lassen
K. Thomas Finke
Ann M. Dumenil
Richard C. Onsager
Robert J. Werner
John R. Becker

For Complete List of Firm Personnel, See General Section

For full biographical listings, see the Martindale-Hubbell Law Directory

LEWIS AND ROCA (AV)

A Partnership including Professional Corporations
40 North Central Avenue, 85004-4429
Telephone: 602-262-5311
Fax: 602-262-5747
Tucson, Arizona Office: One South Church Avenue, Suite 700.
Telephone: 602-622-2090.
Fax: 602-622-3088.

MEMBERS OF FIRM

David E. Manch
Patrick Derdenger

ASSOCIATES

J. Tyler Haahr
Michael G. Galloway

OF COUNSEL

Hope Leibsohn

Representative Clients: Blood Systems, Inc.; The Frank Lloyd Wright Foundation; General Motors Corporation; MCI Telecommunications Corporation; Mervyn's Stores; Samaritan Health System; Target Stores; Unisys Corporation.

For Complete List of Firm Personnel, See General Section

For full biographical listings, see the Martindale-Hubbell Law Directory

McCABE, O'DONNELL & WRIGHT, A PROFESSIONAL ASSOCIATION (AV)

Suite 2000, 300 East Osborn, 85012
Telephone: 602-264-0800
Telecopier: 602-274-0146

Joseph I. McCabe
Kathleen M. O'Donnell

References: First Interstate Bank of Arizona, N.A., Trust Department.

For Complete List of Firm Personnel, See General Section

For full biographical listings, see the Martindale-Hubbell Law Directory

MEYER, HENDRICKS, VICTOR, OSBORN & MALEDON, A PROFESSIONAL ASSOCIATION (AV)

2929 North Central Avenue Suite 2100, 85012-2794
Telephone: 602-640-9000
Facsimile: (24 Hrs.) 602-640-9050
Mailing Address: P.O. Box 33449, 85067-3449,

(See Next Column)

Howard N. Singer
Thomas D. Proffitt
Jay S. Ruffner

CONSULTANTS

W. John Glancy (Not admitted in AZ)

Reference: Bank One Arizona, NA.

For Complete List of Firm Personnel, See General Section

For full biographical listings, see the Martindale-Hubbell Law Directory

NEWMARK IRVINE, P.A. (AV)

Suite 590 1419 North Third Street, 85004
Telephone: 602-230-8080
Fax: 602-230-0105

Stephen C. Newmark
Thomas K. Irvine

Jerry A. Fries

For full biographical listings, see the Martindale-Hubbell Law Directory

O'CONNOR, CAVANAGH, ANDERSON, WESTOVER, KILLINGSWORTH & BESHEARS, A PROFESSIONAL ASSOCIATION (AV)

One East Camelback Road, Suite 1100, 85012-1656
Telephone: 602-263-2400
FAX: 602-263-2900
Sun City, Arizona Office: 13250 North Del Webb Boulevard, Suite B, 85351.
Telephone: 602-263-2808.
FAX: 602-933-3100.
Tucson, Arizona Office: Suite 2200, One South Church Avenue, 85701.
Telephone: 602-882-8912.
FAX: 602-624-9564.
Nogales, Arizona Office: 1827 North Mastick Way, 85621.
Telephone: 602-761-4215.
FAX: 602-761-3505.

Richard C. Smith
Charles F. Myers
Peter C. Guild
Max K. Boyer

Leigh A. Kaylor

Representative Clients: Sun Health Corporation; Rural/Metro Corporation; Peabody Coal Co.; The P.G.A.; Del Webb Corporation; Hyatt Regency; Three-Five Systems, Inc.; Microchip, Inc.; Central Arizona Water Conservation District; Northern Trust Bank of Arizona.

For Complete List of Firm Personnel, See General Section

For full biographical listings, see the Martindale-Hubbell Law Directory

SNELL & WILMER (AV)

One Arizona Center, 85004-0001
Telephone: 602-382-6000
Fax: 602-382-6070
Tucson, Arizona Office: 1500 Norwest Tower, One South Church Avenue 85701-1612.
Telephone: 602-882-1200.
Fax: 602-884-1294.
Orange County Office: 1920 Main Street, Suite 1200, P.O. Box 19601, Irvine, California, 92714.
Telephone: 714-253-2700.
Fax: 714-955-2507.
Salt Lake City, Utah Office: Broadway Centre, 111 East Broadway, Suite 900, 84111.
Telephone: 801-237-1900.
Fax: 801-237-1950.

OF COUNSEL

Edward Jacobson
James D. Bruner

MEMBERS OF FIRM

Joseph T. Melczer, III
Charles A. Pulaski, Jr.
Thomas R. Hoecker
Richard D. Blau

ASSOCIATES

Timothy D. Brown
Robert R. Yoder

Representative Clients: American Continental Creditors Committee; Arizona Public Service Company; Arizona Sports Foundation; Aztar Corporation; City of Phoenix; Magma Copper Company; Palo Verde Nuclear Generating Station; Talley Industries; Tucson Airport Authority; Bank One, Arizona, NA.

For Complete List of Firm Personnel, See General Section

For full biographical listings, see the Martindale-Hubbell Law Directory

Phoenix—Continued

STREICH LANG, A PROFESSIONAL ASSOCIATION (AV)

Renaissance One, Two N. Central Avenue, 85004-2391
Telephone: 602-229-5200
Fax: 602-229-5690
Tucson, Arizona Office: One S. Church Avenue, Suite 1700.
Telephone: 602-770-8700.
Fax: 602-623-2518.
Las Vegas, Nevada Affiliated Office: Dawson & Associates, 3800 Howard Hughes Parkway, Suite 1500.
Telephone: 702-792-2727.
Fax: 702-792-2676.
Los Angeles, California Office: 444 S. Flower Street, Suite 1530.
Telephone: 213-896-0484.

Ronold P. Platner — John C. Vryhof
John A. Swain — Fred T. Witt, Jr.

Robin L. De Respino — Dawn R. Gabel
Laurel I. Wala

Representative Clients: America West Airlines, Inc.; Kroy, Inc.; Motorola, Inc.; State Farm Insurance Company; Microchip, Ltd.; Burr-Brown Corporation; CyCare Systems, Inc.; US Postal Service; Arizona Automobile Dealers Assn.; Microtest, Inc.

For Complete List of Firm Personnel, See General Section

For full biographical listings, see the Martindale-Hubbell Law Directory

SCOTTSDALE, Maricopa Co.

ROSEPINK & ESTES (AV)

7373 North Scottsdale Road Suite D102, 85253
Telephone: 602-443-1280
Fax: 602-443-3664

Robert J. Rosepink — David J. Estes

ASSOCIATE

Lynn F. Chandler

References: Bank of America, Arizona; Biltmore Investors Bank; Chase Trust Company of Arizona; First Interstate Bank of Arizona, N.A.; Firstar Metropolitan Bank & Trust; M & I Marshall & Ilsley Trust Co. of Arizona; Northern Trust Bank of Arizona.

For full biographical listings, see the Martindale-Hubbell Law Directory

GUY C. WILSON (AV)

Gainey Ranch Financial Center, Suite 130, 7373 East Doubletree Ranch Road, 85258
Telephone: 602-483-7455
Fax: 602-483-7457

For full biographical listings, see the Martindale-Hubbell Law Directory

SUN CITY, Maricopa Co.

O'CONNOR, CAVANAGH, ANDERSON, WESTOVER, KILLINGSWORTH & BESHEARS, A PROFESSIONAL ASSOCIATION (AV)

13250 North Del Webb Boulevard, Suite B, 85351-3053
Telephone: 602-263-2808
FAX: 602-933-3100
Phoenix, Arizona Office: One East Camelback Road, Suite 1100, 85012.
Telephone: 602-263-2400.
FAX: 602-263-2900.
Tucson, Arizona Office: Suite 2200, One South Church Avenue, 85701.
Telephone: 602-882-8912.
FAX: 602-624-9564.
Nogales, Arizona Office: 1827 North Mastick Way, 85621.
Telephone: 602-761-4215.
FAX: 602-761-3505.

William C. Wahl, Jr.

For full biographical listings, see the Martindale-Hubbell Law Directory

*TUCSON,** Pima Co.

GABROY, ROLLMAN & BOSSÉ, P.C. (AV)

Suite 201, 2195 E. River Road, 85718
Telephone: 602-577-1300
Telefax: 602-577-0717

Steven L. Bossé — Fred A. Farsjo

For Complete List of Firm Personnel, See General Section

For full biographical listings, see the Martindale-Hubbell Law Directory

HAWLEY, NYSTEDT & FLETCHER, P.C. (AV)

Old Farm Executive Park, 6075 East Grant Road, P.O. Box 31657, 85751-1657
Telephone: 602-886-3166
FAX: 602-886-5280

Gerald G. Hawley — Bradley Jon Nystedt
Gary L. Fletcher

Reference: Northern Trust Bank of Arizona.

For full biographical listings, see the Martindale-Hubbell Law Directory

O'CONNELL & NEWMAN (AV)

A Partnership of Professional Corporations
Suite 100, 1840 East River Road, 85718
Telephone: 602-577-8880
Telefax: 602-577-0687

Daniel H. O'Connell (P.C.) — Douglas J. Newman (P.C.)

Rosanne F. Lapan

Representative Clients: Empire West Cos.; Southwest Energy, Inc.; El Dorado Internal Medicine, P.C.; Pima Heart Associates, P.C.
Reference: Bank of America.

For full biographical listings, see the Martindale-Hubbell Law Directory

ARKANSAS

*LITTLE ROCK,** Pulaski Co.

ARNOLD, GROBMYER & HALEY, A PROFESSIONAL ASSOCIATION (AV)

875 Union National Plaza, 124 West Capitol Avenue, P.O. Box 70, 72203
Telephone: 501-376-1171
Fax: 501-375-3548

John H. Haley — Joe A. Polk
Charles D. McDaniel — Beth Ann Long

For Complete List of Firm Personnel, See General Section

For full biographical listings, see the Martindale-Hubbell Law Directory

CATLETT & YANCEY (AV)

Eighteenth Floor, The Tower Building, 72201
Telephone: 501-372-2121
FAX: 501-372-5566;
TELEX: 6503414534
Moscow, Russia Office: Bolshoi Gnezdnykovsky Pereulok 10, Suite 624, 103009.
Telephone: (7-095) 229-6930.
Fax: 229-83-32.

MEMBERS OF FIRM

H. B. Stubblefield (1907-1991) — Gregory Padgham
S. Graham Catlett — Pamela A. Belt
H. Lawrence Yancey — Evguiny V. Bureiko (Not Admitted in the United States)
John T. Root, Jr.

Representative Clients: Catlett & Co.; Citizens Fidelity Insurance Co.; Frost and Company, CPA's; General Properties, Inc.; McKay and Company Residential Realtors; Midwest Lumber Co.; Motel Sleepers, Inc.; National Home Centers, Inc.

For full biographical listings, see the Martindale-Hubbell Law Directory

FRIDAY, ELDREDGE & CLARK (AV)

A Partnership including Professional Associations
Formerly, Smith, Williams, Friday, Eldredge & Clark
2000 First Commercial Building, 400 West Capitol, 72201-3493
Telephone: 501-376-2011
Telecopier: 501-376-2147; 376-6369

MEMBERS OF FIRM

Byron M. Eiseman, Jr., (P.A.) — James M. Saxton (P.A.)
H. T. Larzelere, Jr., (P.A.) — W. Thomas Baxter (P.A.)
A. Wyckliff Nisbet, Jr., (P.A.) — Joseph B. Hurst, Jr., (P.A.)
James E. Harris (P.A.) — Walter M. Ebel, III, (P.A.)
J. Lee Brown (P.A.)

ASSOCIATES

Price C. Gardner — David M. Graf
John Ray White — Carla G. Spainhour

Counsel for: Union Pacific System; St. Paul Insurance Co.; Liberty Mutual Insurance Co.; Cigna Property & Casualty Co.; Arkansas Power & Light Co.; Dillard Department Stores, Inc.; First Commercial Corp.; Browning Arms Co.; Phillips Petroleum Co.; Aetna Casualty & Surety Co.

(See Next Column)

FRIDAY, ELDREDGE & CLARK—*Continued*

For Complete List of Firm Personnel, See General Section

For full biographical listings, see the Martindale-Hubbell Law Directory

HILBURN, CALHOON, HARPER, PRUNISKI & CALHOUN, LTD. (AV)

P.O. Box 1256, 72203-1256
Telephone: 501-372-0110
FAX: 501-372-2029
North Little Rock, Arkansas Office: Eighth Floor, The Twin City Bank Building, One Riverfront Place, P.O. Box 5551, 72119.
Telephone: 501-372-0110.
FAX: 501-372-2029.

Ken F. Calhoon | Carrold E. Ray

Michael E. Hartje, Jr. | Bruce D. Eddy

Representative Clients: The Twin City Bank; Merril Lynch Pierce Fenner & Smith, Inc.; Central Arkansas Risk Management Association; Smith Barney Shearson, Inc.

For Complete List of Firm Personnel, See General Section

For full biographical listings, see the Martindale-Hubbell Law Directory

HOOVER & STOREY (AV)

111 Center Street, 11th Floor, 72201-4445
Telephone: 501-376-8500
Facsimile: 501-372-3255

MEMBERS OF FIRM

Paul W. Hoover, Jr.
O. H. Storey, III
John Kooistra, III
Lawrence Joseph Brady
William P. Dougherty
Max C. Mehlburger
Joyce Bradley Babin
Herbert W. Kell, Jr.
Letty McAdams

For full biographical listings, see the Martindale-Hubbell Law Directory

IVESTER, SKINNER & CAMP, P.A. (AV)

Suite 1200, 111 Center Street, 72201
Telephone: 501-376-7788
FAX: 501-376-8536

Wayne B. Ball

For Complete List of Firm Personnel, See General Section

For full biographical listings, see the Martindale-Hubbell Law Directory

ROSE LAW FIRM, A PROFESSIONAL ASSOCIATION (AV)

120 East Fourth Street, 72201
Telephone: 501-375-9131
Telecopy: 501-375-1309

W. Wilson Jones
William E. Bishop
C. Brantly Buck
Ronald M. Clark
Jackson Farrow Jr.
David A. Smith

COUNSEL

J. Gaston Williamson

Counsel for: Aluminum Company of America; The Equitable Life Assurance Society of The United States; Bridgestone/Firestone, Inc.; Gannett River States Publishing Co.; General Motors Corp.; Minnesota Mining and Manufacturing Co.; The Prudential Insurance Company of America; The Winthrop Rockefeller Foundation; Tyson Foods, Inc.; Worthen Banking Corp.

For Complete List of Firm Personnel, See General Section

For full biographical listings, see the Martindale-Hubbell Law Directory

WILLIAMS & ANDERSON (AV)

Twenty-Second Floor, 111 Center Street, 72201
Telephone: 501-372-0800
FAX: 501-372-6453

MEMBERS OF FIRM

W. Jackson Williams | Rush B. Deacon

J. Cal McCastlain

Representative Clients: Arkansas Development Finance Authority; Coregis; Dean Witter Reynolds Inc.; Entergy Power, Inc.; Little Rock Newspapers, Inc. d/b/a/ Arkansas Democrat-Gazette; Texaco, Inc.; Transport Indemnity Insurance Co.; Wal-Mart Stores, Inc.

For Complete List of Firm Personnel, See General Section

For full biographical listings, see the Martindale-Hubbell Law Directory

CALIFORNIA

ANAHEIM, Orange Co.

JOANNE S. ROCKS (AV)

Suite 207C Anaheim Hills Professional Center, 6200 East Canyon Rim Road, 92807
Telephone: 714-974-2000
Fax: 714-974-2063

For full biographical listings, see the Martindale-Hubbell Law Directory

*BAKERSFIELD,** Kern Co.

BORTON, PETRINI & CONRON (AV)

The Borton, Petrini & Conron Building, 1600 Truxtun Avenue, P.O. Box 2026, 93303
Telephone: 805-322-3051
Cable: "Verdict"
Telex: 181-341
Fax: 805-322-4628
San Luis Obispo, California Office: 1065 Higuera Street, P.O. Box 927.
Telephone: 805-541-4340.
Fax: 805-541-4558.
Visalia, California Office: 206 South Mooney Boulevard, P.O. Box 1028.
Telephone: 209-627-5600.
Fax: 209-627-4309.
Fresno, California Office: T. W. Patterson Building, Suite 830, 2014 Tulare Street.
Telephone: 209-268-0117.
Fax: 209-237-7995.
Sacramento, California Office: Suite 350, 1545 River Park Drive.
Telephone: 916-920-2812.
Fax: 916-920-1514.
Santa Barbara, California Office: Suite D, 211 East Victoria Street.
Telephone: 805-564-2404.
Fax: 805-564-2176.
Los Angeles, California Office: One Wilshire Building, 624 South Grand Avenue, Suite 1100.
Telephone: 213-624-2869.
Fax: 213-489-3930.
San Diego, California Office: 610 West Ash Street, 9th Floor.
Telephone: 619-232-2424.
Fax: 619-531-0794.
Newport Beach, California Office: 4675 MacArthur Court, Suite 1150.
Telephone: 714-752-2333.
Fax: 714-752-2854.
Modesto, California Office: The Turner Building, 900 "H" Street, Suite D.
Telephone: 209-576-1701.
Fax: 209-527-9753.
San Francisco, California Office: Citicorp Center, One Sansome Street, Suite 1000.
Telephone: 415-981-4415.
Fax: 415-391-5538.
Redding, California Office: Suite 120, 457 Knollcrest Drive.
Telephone: 916-222-1530.
Fax: 916-222-4498.
San Bernardino, California Office: Suite 500, 290 North "D" Street.
Telephone: 909-381-0527.
Fax: 909-381-0658.
San Jose, California Office: 55 South Market Street, Suite 1212.
Telephone: 408-298-3997.
Fax: 408-298-3365.
Ventura, California Office: Suite 310, 1000 Hill Road.
Telephone: 805-650-9994.
Fax: 805-650-7125.
Santa Rosa, California: 50 Santa Rosa Avenue, 5th Floor.
Telephone: 707-527-9477.
FAX: 707-527-9488.

MEMBER OF FIRM

Stephen M. Dake

Representative Clients: Castle and Cooke; Wells Fargo Bank; Pacific Gas & Electric.

For Complete List of Firm Personnel, See General Section

For full biographical listings, see the Martindale-Hubbell Law Directory

ELDON R. HUGIE A PROFESSIONAL CORPORATION (AV)

Suite 100, 1405 Commercial Way, 93309
Telephone: 805-328-0200
Telecopier: 805-328-0204

Eldon R. Hugie

Representative Clients: Tri-Fanucchi Farms, Inc.; Upper Swanston Ranch; Aquaculture Enterprises; Kern College Land Co.
References: Community First Bank (Bakersfield Main Branch).

For full biographical listings, see the Martindale-Hubbell Law Directory

Bakersfield—Continued

KLEIN, WEGIS, DENATALE, GOLDNER & MUIR (AV)

A Partnership including Professional Corporations
(Formerly Di Giorgio, Davis, Klein, Wegis, Duggan & Friedman)
ARCO Tower, 4550 California Avenue, Second Floor, P.O. Box 11172, 93389-1172
Telephone: 805-395-1000
Telecopier: 805-326-0418
Santa Ana, California Office: Park Tower Building #610, 200 W. Santa Ana Boulevard, 92701.
Telephone: 714-285-0711.
Fax: 714-285-9003.

MEMBERS OF FIRM

Anthony J. Klein (Inc.) Claude P. Kimball

ASSOCIATES

Carol J. Kern Michael E. Hugie
Kevin C. Findley Stacy Henry Bowman
Kristin Anne Smith

Representative Clients: Bank of America; Great Western Bank; Mojave Pipeline Co.; Transamerican Title Insurance Co.; Dean Whittier Reynolds, Inc.; California Republic Bank; San Joaquin Bank; Nahama & Weagant Energy Co.; Freymiller Trucking, Inc.; Westinghouse Electric Co.

For Complete List of Firm Personnel, See General Section

For full biographical listings, see the Martindale-Hubbell Law Directory

BEVERLY HILLS, Los Angeles Co.

ERVIN, COHEN & JESSUP (AV)

A Partnership including Professional Corporations
9401 Wilshire Boulevard, 90212-2974
Telephone: 310-273-6333
Facsimile: 310-859-2325

MEMBERS OF FIRM

W. Edgar Jessup, Jr. Thomas A. Kirschbaum
Melvin S. Spears Joan B. Velazquez
Marvin H. Lewis Thomas F. R. Garvin
Harold J. Delevie (P.C.) Reeve E. Chudd
Gary Q. Michel (A P.C.) Philip Starr
Steven A. Roseman

ASSOCIATES

Layton L. Pace Darcy L. Honig
Paul F. Lawrence

Reference: Bank of California, N.A. (Beverly Hills).

For Complete List of Firm Personnel, See General Section

For full biographical listings, see the Martindale-Hubbell Law Directory

HOCHMAN, SALKIN AND DEROY, A PROFESSIONAL CORPORATION (AV)

9150 Wilshire Boulevard Suite 300, 90212-3414
Telephone: 310-281-3200; 273-1181
Fax: 310-859-1430

Bruce I. Hochman Charles Rettig
Avram Salkin Dennis Perez
Steven R. Toscher

OF COUNSEL

George DeRoy James V. Looby

Michael W. Popoff Joanna J. Tulio

Reference: Bank of California.

For full biographical listings, see the Martindale-Hubbell Law Directory

SAMUEL D. INGHAM, III (AV)

Suite 830, 8383 Wilshire Boulevard, 90211
Telephone: 213-651-5980
FAX: 213-651-5725

For full biographical listings, see the Martindale-Hubbell Law Directory

KAJAN AND MATHER, A PROFESSIONAL CORPORATION (AV)

Suite 805, 9777 Wilshire Boulevard, 90212
Telephone: 310-278-6080
Fax: 310-278-4805

Elliott H. Kajan Steven R. Mather

For full biographical listings, see the Martindale-Hubbell Law Directory

COSTA MESA, Orange Co.

RUTAN & TUCKER (AV)

A Partnership including Professional Corporations
611 Anton Boulevard, Suite 1400, P.O. Box 1950, 92626
Telephone: 714-641-5100; 213-625-7586
Telecopier: 714-546-9035

MEMBERS OF FIRM

Paul Frederic Marx Joseph D. Carruth
Michael D. Rubin Evridiki (Vicki) Dallas

For Complete List of Firm Personnel, See General Section

For full biographical listings, see the Martindale-Hubbell Law Directory

ESCONDIDO, San Diego Co.

GARTH O. REID, JR. A PROFESSIONAL LAW CORPORATION (AV)

319 East Second Avenue, 92025
Telephone: 619-746-6420

Garth O. Reid, Jr.

For full biographical listings, see the Martindale-Hubbell Law Directory

*FRESNO,** Fresno Co.

DOWLING, MAGARIAN, AARON & HEYMAN, INCORPORATED (AV)

Suite 200, 6051 North Fresno Street, 93710
Telephone: 209-432-4500
Fax: 209-432-4590

Michael D. Dowling William J. Keeler, Jr.
Richard M. Aaron John C. Ganahl
Bruce S. Fraser Sheila M. Smith

OF COUNSEL

Morris M. Sherr

Reference: Wells Fargo Bank (Main).

For Complete List of Firm Personnel, See General Section

For full biographical listings, see the Martindale-Hubbell Law Directory

JACKSON EMERICH PEDREIRA & NAHIGIAN, A PROFESSIONAL CORPORATION (AV)

7108 North Fresno Street, Suite 400, 93720-2938
Telephone: 209-261-0200
Facsimile: 209-261-0910

Donald A. Jackson Thomas A. Pedreira
David R. Emerich Eliot S. Nahigian
David A. Fike

John W. Phillips Nicholas A. Tarjoman
John M. Cardot Jeffrey B. Pape
David G. Hansen

Reference: Bank of California.

For full biographical listings, see the Martindale-Hubbell Law Directory

IRVINE, Orange Co.

GRECO, MOLLIS & O'HARA, A PROFESSIONAL CORPORATION (AV)

18400 Von Karman, Suite 500, 92715-1514
Telephone: 714-263-0600
Fax: 714-263-1513

Thomas A. Greco Kevin O'Hara
Ronald A. Mollis Lawrence P. Bellomo
Charles A. Mollis

LEGAL SUPPORT PERSONNEL

LEGAL ASSISTANTS

Michelle D. Hubbard Mary A. Stromgren

For full biographical listings, see the Martindale-Hubbell Law Directory

LONG BEACH, Los Angeles Co.

CAMERON, MADDEN, PEARLSON, GALE & SELLARS (AV)

One World Trade Center Suite 1600, 90831-1600
Telephone: 310-436-3888
Telecopier: 310-437-1967

MEMBERS OF THE FIRM

Timothy C. Cameron Patrick T. Madden
Charles M. Gale Paul R. Pearlson
James D. Sellars

(See Next Column)

CAMERON, MADDEN, PEARLSON, GALE & SELLARS—*Continued*

ASSOCIATE

Lillian D. Salinger

For full biographical listings, see the Martindale-Hubbell Law Directory

TAUBMAN, SIMPSON, YOUNG & SULENTOR (AV)

Suite 700 Home Savings Building, 249 East Ocean Boulevard, P.O. Box 22670, 90801
Telephone: 310-436-9201
FAX: 310-590-9695

E. C. Denio (1864-1952)
Geo. A. Hart (1881-1967)
Geo. P. Taubman, Jr. (1897-1970)
Matthew C. Simpson (1900-1988)
Richard G. Wilson (1928-1993)
Roger W. Young
William J. Sulentor
Peter M. Williams
Scott R. Magee
Valerie K. de Martino
Maria M. Rohaidy

Attorneys for: Bixby Land Co.; Renick Cadillac, Inc.; Oil Operators Incorporated.
Local Counsel: Crown Cork & Seal Co., Inc.

For full biographical listings, see the Martindale-Hubbell Law Directory

*LOS ANGELES,** Los Angeles Co.

ADAMS, DUQUE & HAZELTINE (AV)

A Partnership including Professional Corporations
777 South Figueroa Street, Tenth Floor, 90017
Telephone: 213-620-1240
FAX: 213-896-5500
San Francisco, California Office: 500 Washington Street.
Telephone: 415-982-1240.
FAX: 415-982-0130.

MEMBERS OF FIRM

Wilson B. Copes
R. Stephen Doan

For Complete List of Firm Personnel, See General Section

For full biographical listings, see the Martindale-Hubbell Law Directory

AJALAT, POLLEY & AYOOB (AV)

A Partnership including Professional Corporations
Suite 200, 643 South Olive Street, 90014
Telephone: 213-622-7400
Fax: 213-622-4738

MEMBERS OF FIRM

Charles R. Ajalat (A Professional Corporation)
Terry L. Polley (A Professional Corporation)
Richard J. Ayoob

Reference: Bank of America (Los Angeles Main Office).

For full biographical listings, see the Martindale-Hubbell Law Directory

ANTIN & TAYLOR (AV)

1875 Century Park East, Suite 700, 90067
Telephone: 310-788-2733
Fax: 310-788-0754

MEMBERS OF FIRM

Michael Antin
Michael L. Taylor

For full biographical listings, see the Martindale-Hubbell Law Directory

PAUL L. BASILE, JR. (AV)

11400 West Olympic Boulevard, 9th Floor, 90064-1565
Telephone: 310-478-2114
Fax: 310-478-0229

For full biographical listings, see the Martindale-Hubbell Law Directory

BUCHALTER, NEMER, FIELDS & YOUNGER, A PROFESSIONAL CORPORATION (AV)

24th Floor, 601 South Figueroa Street, 90017
Telephone: 213-891-0700
Fax: 213-896-0400
Cable Address: "Buchnem"
Telex: 68-7485
New York, New York Office: 19th Floor, 237 Park Avenue.
Telephone: 212-490-8600.
Fax: 212-490-6022.
San Francisco, California Office: 29th Floor, 333 Market Street.
Telephone: 415-227-0900.
Fax: 415-227-0770.
San Jose, California Office: 12th Floor, 50 West San Fernando Street.
Telephone: 408-298-0350.
Fax: 408-298-7683.

(See Next Column)

Newport Beach, California Office: Suite 300, 620 Newport Center Drive.
Telephone: 714-760-1121.
Fax: 714-720-0182.
Century City, California Office: Suite 2400, 1801 Century Park East.
Telephone: 213-891-0700.
Fax: 310-551-0233.

Terence S. Nunan
Philip J. Wolman
Gary J. Vyneman

References: City National Bank; Wells Fargo Bank; Metrobank.

For Complete List of Firm Personnel, See General Section

For full biographical listings, see the Martindale-Hubbell Law Directory

JOHN A. CALFAS A PROFESSIONAL CORPORATION (AV)

Suite 1920, 11601 Wilshire Boulevard, 90025
Telephone: 310-477-1920
FAX: 310-477-7132

John A. Calfas

For full biographical listings, see the Martindale-Hubbell Law Directory

CLARK & TREVITHICK, A PROFESSIONAL CORPORATION (AV)

800 Wilshire Boulevard, 12th Floor, 90017
Telephone: 213-629-5700
Telecopier: 213-624-9441

Kevin P. Fiore
Dean I. Friedman

References: Wells Fargo Bank (Los Angeles Main Office); National Bank of California.

For Complete List of Firm Personnel, See General Section

For full biographical listings, see the Martindale-Hubbell Law Directory

GOLBERT KIMBALL & WEINER (AV)

555 South Flower Street Suite 2800, 90071
Telephone: 213-891-9641
Telecopier: 213-623-6130

Albert S. Golbert
George Kimball
Jeffrey M. Weiner

ASSOCIATES

Andrew H. Kopkin
Matthew F. Maccoby

For full biographical listings, see the Martindale-Hubbell Law Directory

GREENBERG, GLUSKER, FIELDS, CLAMAN & MACHTINGER (AV)

20th Floor, 1900 Avenue of the Stars (Century City), 90067
Telephone: 310-553-3610
Fax: 310-553-0687

MEMBERS OF FIRM

Sidney J. Machtinger
C. Bruce Levine
Gary L. Kaplan

Reference: Wells Fargo Bank, 1800 Century Park East, Los Angeles, CA 90067.

For Complete List of Firm Personnel, See General Section

For full biographical listings, see the Martindale-Hubbell Law Directory

HALSTEAD, BAKER & OLSON (AV)

Suite 500, 1000 Wilshire Boulevard, 90017
Telephone: 213-622-0200
Telecopier: 213-623-3836

MEMBERS OF FIRM

Harry M. Halstead
Sheldon S. Baker
Eric Olson
John J. Jacobson
Charles L. LeCroy, III
William C. Hansen
Arsen Danielian

ASSOCIATES

Michael S. Simon
Andrea L. Esterson
Donald J. Gary, Jr.

For full biographical listings, see the Martindale-Hubbell Law Directory

HANNA AND MORTON (AV)

A Partnership including Professional Corporations
Seventeenth Floor, Wilshire-Grand Building, 600 Wilshire Boulevard, 90017
Telephone: 213-628-7131

MEMBER OF FIRM

Glenn Lorin Krinsky

(See Next Column)

HANNA AND MORTON, *Los Angeles—Continued*

OF COUNSEL

William N. Greene

For Complete List of Firm Personnel, See General Section

For full biographical listings, see the Martindale-Hubbell Law Directory

HILL, FARRER & BURRILL (AV)

A Partnership including Professional Corporations
35th Floor, Union Bank Square, 445 South Figueroa Street, 90071
Telephone: 213-620-0460
Fax: 213-624-4840; 488-1593

MEMBERS OF FIRM

Leon S. Angvire (P.C.) George Koide (P.C.)
Thomas F. Reed

For Complete List of Firm Personnel, See General Section

For full biographical listings, see the Martindale-Hubbell Law Directory

HOLLEY & GALEN (AV)

800 South Figueroa, Suite 1100, 90017
Telephone: 213-629-1880
Fax: 213-895-0363

MEMBERS OF FIRM

Albert J. Galen (Retired) W. Michael Johnson

For Complete List of Firm Personnel, See General Section

For full biographical listings, see the Martindale-Hubbell Law Directory

HUFSTEDLER & KAUS (AV)

A Partnership including Professional Corporations
Thirty-Ninth Floor, 355 South Grand Avenue, 90071-3101
Telephone: 213-617-7070
Fax: 213-617-6170

MEMBERS OF FIRM

Joseph L. Wyatt, Jr. Fred L. Leydorf
Dudley M. Lang

Reference: First Interstate Bank, 707 Wilshire.

For Complete List of Firm Personnel, See General Section

For full biographical listings, see the Martindale-Hubbell Law Directory

JONES, DAY, REAVIS & POGUE (AV)

555 West Fifth Street Suite 4600, 90013-1025
Telephone: 213-489-3939
Telex: 181439 UD
Telecopier: 213-243-2539
In Irvine, California: 2603 Main Street, Suite 900.
Telephone: 714-851-3939.
Telex: 194911 Lawyers LSA.
Telecopier: 714-553-7539.
In Atlanta, Georgia: 3500 One Peachtree Center, 303 Peachtree Street, N.E.
Telephone: 404-521-3939.
Cable Address: "Attorneys Atlanta".
Telex: 54-2711.
Telecopier: 404-581-8330.
In Brussels, Belgium: Avenue Louise 480, 7th Floor, B-1050 Brussels.
Telephone: 011-32-2-645-14-11.
Telecopier: 011-32-2-645-14-45.
In Chicago, Illinois: 77 West Wacker.
Telephone: 312-782-3939.
Telecopier: 312-782-8585.
In Cleveland, Ohio: North Point, 901 Lakeside Avenue.
Telephone: 216-586-3939.
Cable Address: "Attorneys Cleveland."
Telex: 980389.
Telecopier: 216-579-0212.
In Columbus, Ohio: 1900 Huntington Center.
Telephone: 614-469-3939.
Cable Address: "Attorneys Columbus."
Telecopier: 614-461-4198.
In Dallas, Texas: 2300 Trammell Crow Center, 2001 Ross Avenue.
Telephone: 214-220-3939.
Cable Address: "Attorneys Dallas."
Telex: 730852.
Telecopier: 214-969-5100.
In Frankfurt, Germany: Triton Haus, Bockenheimer Landstrasse 42, 60323 Frankfurt am Main.
Telephone: 49-69-9726-3939.
Telecopier: 49-69-9726-3993.
In Geneva, Switzerland: 20, rue de Candolle.
Telephone: 011-41-22-320-2339.
Telecopier: 011-41-22-320-1232.
In Hong Kong: 1501 One Exchange Square, 8 Connaught Place.
Telephone: 011-852-2526-6895.
Telecopier: 011-852-2810-5787.

(See Next Column)

In London England: One Mount Street.
Telephone: 011-44-71-493-9361.
Cable Address: "Surgoe London WI."
Telecopier: 011-44-71-493-9666.
In New York, New York: 599 Lexington Avenue.
Telephone: 212-326-3939.
Cable Address: "JONESDAY NEWYORK."
Telex: 237013 JDRP UR.
Telecopier: 212-755-7306.
In Paris, France: 62, rue du Faubourg Saint-Honore.
Telephone: 011-33-1-44-71-3939.
Cable Address: "Surgoe Paris."
Telex: 290156 Surgoe.
Telecopier: 011-33-1-49-24-0471.
In Pittsburgh, Pennsylvania: 500 Grant Street, 31st Floor.
Telephone: 412-391-3939.
Cable Address: "Attorneys Pittsburgh".
Telecopier: 412-394-7959.
In Riyadh, Saudi Arabia: Law Offices of Saud M.A. Shawwaf, P.O. Box 2700.
Telephones: 011 (966-1) 465-6543, 011 (966-1) 464-8534 or 011 (966-1) 464-8540.
Telex: 401831 SAUCON SJ.
Telecopier: (966-1) 464-8480.
In Taipei, Taiwan: 8th Floor, 2 Tun Hwa South Road, Section 2.
Telephone: 011 (886-2) 704-6808.
Telecopier: 011 (886-2) 704-6791.
In Tokyo, Japan: Toranomon MT Building, 4th Floor, 10-3, Toranomon 3-Chome, Minato-Ku, Tokyo 105, Japan.
Telephone: 011-81-3-3433-3939.
Telecopier: 011-81-3-5401-2725.
In Washington, D.C.: Metropolitan Square, 1450 G Street, N.W.
Telephone: 202-879-3939.
Cable Address: "Attorneys Washington."
Telex: 89-2410 ATTORNEYS WASH.
Telecopier: 202-737-2832.

MEMBERS OF FIRM IN LOS ANGELES

James F. Childs, Jr. David S. Boyce
Ronald S. Rizzo Deborah Crandall Saxe
Elwood Lui Sarah Heck Griffin

SENIOR ATTORNEY

Lynn Leversen Kambe

ASSOCIATES

Clayton J. Vreeland Catherine A. Cleveland

For Complete List of Firm Personnel, See General Section

For full biographical listings, see the Martindale-Hubbell Law Directory

KINDEL & ANDERSON (AV)

A Partnership including Professional Corporations
Twenty-Ninth Floor, 555 South Flower Street, 90071
Telephone: 213-680-2222
Cable Address: "Kayanda"
Telex: 67-7497
FAX: 213-688-7564
Irvine, California Office: 5 Park Plaza, Suite 1000.
Telephone: 714-752-0777.
Woodland Hills, California Office: Suite 244, 5959 Topanga Canyon Boulevard.
Telephone: 818-712-0036.
San Francisco, California Office: 580 California Street, 15th Floor.
Telephone: 415-398-0110.

MEMBERS OF FIRM

Joseph W. Burdett (P.C.) John E. James
Allan I. Grossman (P.C.) Gary W. Maeder
William C. Staley (P.C.)

OF COUNSEL

John W. Armagost (P.C.) Robert L. Whitmire (P.C.)

For Complete List of Firm Personnel, See General Section

For full biographical listings, see the Martindale-Hubbell Law Directory

KOPPLE & KLINGER (AV)

A Law Partnership including a Professional Corporation
2029 Century Park East, Suite 1040, 90067
Telephone: 310-553-1444
Facsimile: 310-553-7335

MEMBERS OF FIRM

Robert C. Kopple (P.C.) Leslie S. Klinger

OF COUNSEL

Richard P. Ayles

ASSOCIATE

Douglas W. Schwartz

For full biographical listings, see the Martindale-Hubbell Law Directory

Los Angeles—Continued

LOEB AND LOEB (AV)

A Partnership including Professional Corporations
Suite 1800, 1000 Wilshire Boulevard, 90017-2475
Telephone: 213-688-3400
Telecopier: 213-688-3460; 688-3461; 688-3462
Century City, California Office: Suite 2200, 10100 Santa Monica Boulevard, Los Angeles, 90067-4164.
Telephone: 310-282-2000.
Telecopier: 310-282-2191; 282-2192.
New York, N.Y. Office: 345 Park Avenue, 10154-0037.
Telephone: 212-407-4000.
Facsimile: 212-407-4990.
Nashville, Tennessee Office: 45 Music Square West, 37203-3205.
Telephone: 615-749-8300;
Facsimile: 615-749-8308.
Rome, Italy Office: Piazza Digione 1, 00197.
Telephone: 011-396-808-8456.
Telecopier: 011-396-674-8223.

MEMBERS OF FIRM

Mortimer H. Hess (1889-1968)
John Arao
Terence F. Cuff
Abraham S. Guterman (New York City Office)
Thomas N. Lawson
Fredric M. Sanders (New York City Office)
Paul A. Sczudlo
Bruce M. Stiglitz (A P.C.)
William P. Wasserman (A P.C.)
Debre Katz Weintraub
William S. Woods, II

OF COUNSEL

Arthur A. Segall (New York City Office)
John S. Warren (A P.C.)

ASSOCIATES

M. Katharine Davidson
Jay Fenster (New York City Office)
Nina J. Haller
Duane O. Kamei

For Complete List of Firm Personnel, See General Section

For full biographical listings, see the Martindale-Hubbell Law Directory

MATTHIAS & BERG (AV)

Seventh Floor, 515 South Flower Street, 90071
Telephone: 213-895-4200
Telecopier: 213-895-4058

Michael R. Matthias
Jeffrey P. Berg
Stuart R. Singer
Kenneth M. H. Hoff

Representative Clients: N-Viro Recovery, Inc.; Supercart International, Inc.; Mexalit, S.A.; Allstar Inns; Chatsworth Products, Inc.; International Meta Systems, Inc.; MedGroup, Inc.; Palm Springs Golf Company, Inc.; Residential Resources, Inc.
Reference: First Professional Bank.

For full biographical listings, see the Martindale-Hubbell Law Directory

MITCHELL, SILBERBERG & KNUPP (AV)

A Partnership of Professional Corporations
11377 West Olympic Boulevard, 90064
Telephone: 310-312-2000
Cable Address: "Silmitch"
Telex: 69-1347
Telecopier: 310-312-3200

MEMBERS OF FIRM

Allan E. Biblin (A Professional Corporation)
Eugene H. Veenhuis (A Professional Corporation)
David Wheeler Newman (A Professional Corporation)
Allan B. Cutrow (A Professional Corporation)

OF COUNSEL

Stanley I. Arenberg (A Professional Corporation)

ASSOCIATE

Reynolds T. Cafferata

Reference: First Interstate Bank of California (Headquarters, Los Angeles, California).

For Complete List of Firm Personnel, See General Section

For full biographical listings, see the Martindale-Hubbell Law Directory

MUSICK, PEELER & GARRETT (AV)

Suite 2000, One Wilshire Boulevard, 90017-3321
Telephone: 213-629-7600
Cable Address: "Peelgar"
Facsimile: 213-624-1376
San Diego, California Office: 1900 Home Savings Tower, 225 Broadway.
Telephone: 619-231-2500.
Facsimile: 619-231-1234.
San Francisco, California Office: Suite 1300, Steuart Street Tower, One Market Plaza.
Telephone: 415-281-2000.
Facsimile: 415-281-2010.

(See Next Column)

Sacramento, California Office: Suite 100, 1121 L Street.
Telephone: 916-442-1200.
Facsimile: 916-442-8644.
Fresno, California Office: 6041 North First Street.
Telephone: 209-228-1000.
Facsimile: 209-447-4670.

MEMBERS OF FIRM

J. Patrick Whaley
Edward A. Landry
William J. Bird
Brian J. Seery
Janet L. Wright (Resident at Fresno Office)
James M. Hassan
David C. Wright
Mark J. Grushkin
Susan J. Hazard

OF COUNSEL

Orene Levenson Kearn (Resident at San Francisco Office)
John F. Feldsted

ASSOCIATES

Samuel H. Stein
S. Andrew Pharies

For Complete List of Firm Personnel, See General Section

For full biographical listings, see the Martindale-Hubbell Law Directory

O'MELVENY & MYERS (AV)

400 South Hope Street, 90071-2899
Telephone: 213-669-6000
Cable Address: "Moms"
Facsimile: 213-669-6407
Century City, California Office: 1999 Avenue of the Stars, 7th Floor, 90067-6035.
Telephone: 310-553-6700.
Facsimile: 310-246-6779.
Newport Beach, California Office: 610 Newport Center Drive, Suite 1700, 92660.
Telephone: 714-760-9600.
Cable Address: "Moms".
Facsimile: 714-669-6994.
San Francisco, California Office: Embarcadero Center West Tower, 275 Battery Street, Suite 2600, 94111.
Telephone: 415-984-8700.
Facsimile: 415-984-8701.
New York, N.Y. Office: Citicorp Center, 153 East 53rd Street, 54th Floor, 10022-4611.
Telephone: 212-326-2000.
Facsimile: 212-326-2061.
Washington, D.C. Office: 555 13th Street, N.W., Suite 500 West, 20004-1109.
Telephone: 202-383-5300.
Cable Address: "Moms".
Facsimile: 202-383-5414.
Newark, New Jersey Office: One Gateway Center, 7th Floor, 07102.
Telephone: 201-639-8600.
Facsimile: 201-639-8630.
London, England Office: 10 Finsbury Square, London, EC2A 1LA.
Telephone: 011-44-171-256 8451.
Facsimile: 011-44-171-638-8205.
Tokyo, Japan Office: Sanbancho KB-6 Building, 6 Sanbancho, Chiyoda-ku, Tokyo 102, Japan.
Telephone: 011-81-3-3239-2800.
Facsimile: 011-81-3-3239-2432.
Hong Kong Office: 1104 Lippo Tower, Lippo Centre, 89 Queensway, Central Hong Kong.
Telephone: 011-852-523-8266.
Facsimile: 011-852-522-1760.

MEMBERS OF FIRM

Russell G. Allen (Newport Beach Office)
Ben E. Benjamin (Washington, D.C. Office)
Leah Margaret Bishop (Century City Office)
Robert D. Blashek, III (Century City Office)
Jerry W. Carlton (Newport Beach Office)
Robert N. Eccles (Not admitted in CA; Washington, D.C. Office)
Travis C. Gibbs
Gregory W. Goff
David E. Gordon
Pamela C. Gray
Linda Boyd Griffey
Theodore C. Hamilton (Newport Beach Office)
Philip D. Irwin
Wayne Jacobsen (Newport Beach Office)
Perry A. Lerner (New York, N.Y. Office)
Frederick A. Richman (Century City Office)
Robert A. Rizzi (Newport Beach Office)
Stuart P. Tobisman (Century City Office)
David D. Watts
Dean M. Weiner
Michael A. Wisnev

OF COUNSEL

Donald R. Spuehler
Clyde E. Tritt

SPECIAL COUNSEL

Paul C. Borden
Joseph G. Giannola (Not admitted in CA; New York, N.Y. Office)
Michael S. Lebovitz (Century City Office)
Marcy Jo Mandel

(See Next Column)

O'MELVENY & MYERS, *Los Angeles—Continued*

ASSOCIATES

W. Kirk Baker (New York, N.Y. Office)
Regina Covitt (Century City Office)
George C. Demos (Newport Beach Office)
David B. Goldman
Molly C. Hansen
Carol A. Johnston (Century City Office)
Deborah L. Kanter (Century City Office)
Scott L. Landsbaum (Washington, D.C. Office)
Edward A. Rosic, Jr. (Not admitted in CA; Washington, D.C. Office)
Robin F.P. Urban

For Complete List of Firm Personnel, See General Section

For full biographical listings, see the Martindale-Hubbell Law Directory

MARK D. PASTOR LAW CORPORATION (AV)

Suite 800, 1925 Century Park East (Century City), 90067
Telephone: 310-474-7494
Encino, California Office: Suite 345, 16830 Ventura Boulevard.
Telephone: 818-906-1900.

Mark D. Pastor

OF COUNSEL

Dennis A. Pastor

For full biographical listings, see the Martindale-Hubbell Law Directory

PILLSBURY MADISON & SUTRO (AV)

Citicorp Plaza, 725 South Figueroa Street, Suite 1200, 90017-2513
Telephone: 213-488-7100
Fax: 213-629-1033
Costa Mesa, California Office: Plaza Tower, 600 Anton Boulevard, Suite 1100, 92626.
Telephone: 714-436-6800.
Fax: 714-662-6999.
Menlo Park, California Office: 2700 Sand Hill Road, 94025.
Telephone: 415-233-4500.
Fax: 415-233-4545.
Sacramento, California Office: 400 Capitol Mall, Suite 1700, 95814.
Telephone: 916-329-4700.
Fax: 916-441-3583.
San Diego, California Office: 101 West Broadway, Suite 1800, 92101.
Telephone: 619-234-5000.
Fax: 619-236-1995.
San Francisco, California Office: 225 Bush Street, 94104.
Telephone: 415-983-1000.
Fax: 415-398-2096.
San Jose, California Office: Ten Almaden Boulevard, 95113.
Telephone: 408-947-4000.
Fax: 408-287-8341.
Washington, D. C. Office: 1667 K Street, N.W., Suite 1100, Suite 20006.
Telephone: 202-887-0300.
Fax: 202-296-7605.
New York, New York Office: One Liberty Plaza, 165 Broadway, 51st Floor.
Telephone: 212-374-1890.
Fax: 212-374-1852.
Hong Kong Office: 6/F Asia Pacific Finance Tower, Citibank Plaza, 3 Garden Road, Central.
Telephone: 011-852-509-7100.
Fax: 011-852-509-7188.
Tokyo, Japan Office: Churchill and Shimazaki, Gaiko-Jimo-Bengoshi Jimusho, 11-12, Toranomon, 5-chome Minato-ku, Tokyo 105, Japan.
Telephone: 800-729-9830; 011-81-3-5472-6561.
Fax: 011-81-3-5472-5761.

MEMBERS OF FIRM

Anthon S. Cannon, Jr.
Karl A. Schmidt
David L. Hayutin
Don R. Weigandt

For Complete List of Firm Personnel, See General Section

For full biographical listings, see the Martindale-Hubbell Law Directory

RUFUS VON THULEN RHOADES (AV)

633 West Fifth Street, 20th Floor, 90071
Telephone: 213-896-2491
Fax: 213-362-2957
Reference: City National Bank (3rd and Fairfax Branch).

For full biographical listings, see the Martindale-Hubbell Law Directory

SCHIFFMACHER, WEINSTEIN, BOLDT & RACINE, PROFESSIONAL CORPORATION (AV)

1801 Century Park East, Suite 2200, 90067-2336
Telephone: 310-203-8466
Cable Address: "Swbrtax"
Telex: 701-793
Telecopy: 310-552-7938

(See Next Column)

Mark D. Schiffmacher
David A. Weinstein
Ronald M. Boldt
Scott H. Racine
Roger G. Halfhide
David J. Camel

Reference: City National Bank (Los Angeles, Calif.).

For full biographical listings, see the Martindale-Hubbell Law Directory

SHEPPARD, MULLIN, RICHTER & HAMPTON (AV)

A Partnership including Professional Corporations
Forty-Eighth Floor, 333 South Hope Street, 90071-1406
Telephone: 213-620-1780
Telecopier: 213-620-1398
Cable Address: "Sheplaw"
Telex: 19-4424
Orange County, California Office: Seventh Floor, 4695 MacArthur Court, Newport Beach.
Telephone: 714-752-6400.
Telecopier: 714-851-0739.
Telex: 19-4424.
San Francisco, California Office: Seventeenth Floor, Four Embarcadero Center.
Telephone: 415-434-9100.
Telecopier: 415-434-3947.
Telex: 19-4424.
San Diego, California Office: Nineteenth Floor, 501 West Broadway.
Telephone: 619-338-6500.
Telecopier: 619-234-3815.
Telex: 19-4424.

MEMBERS OF FIRM

John R. Bonn (San Diego Office)
Lawrence M. Braun
Michael J. Changaris (San Diego Office)
Michael D. Fernhoff *
Randolph B. Godshall (Orange County Office)
Joseph G. Gorman, Jr. *
Robert Joe Hull *
Nancy Baldwin Reimann
Myrl R. Scott *
Thomas R. Sheppard *
John M. Temple

SPECIAL COUNSEL

Laurence K. Gould, Jr.

ASSOCIATE

Joelle Drucker

*Professional Corporation

For Complete List of Firm Personnel, See General Section

For full biographical listings, see the Martindale-Hubbell Law Directory

MOUNTAIN VIEW, Santa Clara Co.

SCHNEIDER, LUCE, QUILLINAN & MORGAN (AV)

A Partnership including a Professional Corporation
444 Castro Street, Suite 900, 94041-2073
Telephone: 415-969-4000
FAX: 415-969-6953

MEMBERS OF FIRM

Michael E. Schneider (A P.C.)
James G. Luce
James V. Quillinan
Michael R. Morgan

ASSOCIATES

Richard Posilippo
Melissa C. Johnson

For full biographical listings, see the Martindale-Hubbell Law Directory

NEWPORT BEACH, Orange Co.

ARTHUR P. GENERAUX A LAW CORPORATION (AV)

4400 MacArthur Boulevard, Suite 500, 92660-2031
Telephone: 714 955 7984

Arthur P. Generaux, Jr.

For full biographical listings, see the Martindale-Hubbell Law Directory

STEPHEN J. SCHUMACHER (AV)

4000 MacArthur Boulevard, Suite 6000, West Tower, 92660
Telephone: 714-752-9425
Telecopier: 714-752-8170
Reference: Bank of America (Irvine Industrial Branch).

For full biographical listings, see the Martindale-Hubbell Law Directory

RONALD K. VAN WERT A PROFESSIONAL CORPORATION (AV)

One Newport Place, Suite 900, 1301 Dove Street, 92660
Telephone: 714-752-7964

Ronald K. Van Wert

For full biographical listings, see the Martindale-Hubbell Law Directory

*OAKLAND,** Alameda Co.

PEZZOLA & REINKE, A PROFESSIONAL CORPORATION (AV)

Suite 1300, Lake Merritt Plaza, 1999 Harrison Street, 94612
Telephone: 510-839-1350
Telecopier: 510-834-7440
San Francisco, California Office: 50 California Street, Suite 470. 94111.
Telephone: 415-989-9710.

Stephen P. Pezzola
Donald C. Reinke
Thomas A. Maier
Thomas C. Armstrong
Bruce D. Whitley

OF COUNSEL

Robert E. Krebs

LEGAL SUPPORT PERSONNEL

Loretta H. Hintz
Mary A. Fitzpatrick

For full biographical listings, see the Martindale-Hubbell Law Directory

OXNARD, Ventura Co.

ENGLAND, WHITFIELD, SCHRÖEDER & TREDWAY (AV)

6th Floor, Union Bank Tower, 300 Esplanade Drive, 93030
Telephone: 805-485-9627
Ventura: 647-8237
Southern California Toll Free: 800-255-3485
Fax: 805-983-0297
Thousand Oaks, California Office: Rolling Oaks Office Center. 351 Rolling Oaks Drive.
Telephone: Southern California Toll Free: 800-255-3485.

MEMBERS OF FIRM

Theodore J. England
Anson M. Whitfield
Robert W. Schröeder
David W. Tredway
Robert A. McSorley
Stuart A. Comis
Mitchel B. Kahn
Mark A. Nelson
Eric J. Kananen
Mary E. Schröeder
Oscar C. Gonzalez
Steven K. Perrin

ASSOCIATES

William J. Kesatie
Melissa E. Cohen
Terry R. Bailey
Andrew S. Hughes
Madison M. Christian
Kurt Edward Kananen
William W. Webb
Jeremy J. F. Gray
Melodee A. Yee
Robert David Schwartz
Linda Kathryn Ash
Carla Jean Ortega

Representative Clients: Seneca Resources Corp. (oil & gas); Cal-Sun Produce Co.; Waste Management of California, Inc; Dah Chong Hong (Honda, Toyota, Mazda, Lexus, Accura, Saturn automobile dealerships); Willamette Industries; Oxnard Harbor Association of Realtors; Port of Hueneme; Conejo Valley Association of Realtors; Power-One, Inc.

For full biographical listings, see the Martindale-Hubbell Law Directory

PASADENA, Los Angeles Co.

MARTIN & HUDSON (AV)

Suite 320, 350 West Colorado Boulevard, 91105
Telephone: 818-793-8500
Telecopier: 818-793-8779

MEMBERS OF FIRM

Robert B. Martin, Jr.
Boyd D. Hudson

For full biographical listings, see the Martindale-Hubbell Law Directory

*SACRAMENTO,** Sacramento Co.

GARY G. PERRY (AV)

2251 Fair Oaks Boulevard, Suite 200, 95825
Telephone: 916-649-0742
Facsimile: 916-649-0010

For full biographical listings, see the Martindale-Hubbell Law Directory

WILKE, FLEURY, HOFFELT, GOULD & BIRNEY (AV)

A Partnership including Professional Corporations
400 Capitol Mall, Suite 2200, 95814-4408
Telephone: 916-441-2430
Telefax: 916-442-6664
Mailing Address: P.O. Box 15559, 95852-0559

MEMBERS OF FIRM

Richard H. Hoffelt (Inc.)
William A. Gould, Jr., (Inc.)
Philip R. Birney (Inc.)
Thomas G. Redmon (Inc.)
Scott L. Gassaway
Donald Rex Heckman II (Inc.)
Alan G. Perkins
Bradley N. Webb
Ernest James Krtil
Robert R. Mirkin
Matthew W. Powell
Mark L. Andrews
Stephen K. Marmaduke
David A. Frenznick
John R. Valencia
Angus M. MacLeod

(See Next Column)

ASSOCIATES

Paul A. Dorris
Kelli M. Kennaday
Tracy S. Hendrickson
Joseph G. De Angelis
Jennifer L. Kennedy
Anthony J. DeCristoforo
Rachel N. Kook
Alicia F. From
Michael Polis
Matthew J. Smith
Wayne L. Ordos

OF COUNSEL

Sherman C. Wilke
Anita Seipp Marmaduke
Benjamin G. Davidian

Representative Clients: NOR-CAL Mutual Insurance Co.; California Optometric Assn.; KPMG Peat Marwick; Glaxo, Inc.

For full biographical listings, see the Martindale-Hubbell Law Directory

*SAN BERNARDINO,** San Bernardino Co.

GRESHAM, VARNER, SAVAGE, NOLAN & TILDEN (AV)

Suite 300, 600 North Arrowhead Avenue, 92401
Telephone: 909-884-2171
Fax: 909-888-2120
Victorville, California Office: 14011 Park Avenue, Suite 140.
Telephone: 619-243-2889.
Fax: 619-243-3057.
Riverside, California Office: 3737 Main Street, Suite 420.
Telephone: 714-274-7777.
Fax: 714-274-7770.

MEMBERS OF FIRM

Philip M. Savage, III
John B. McCauley
Craig O. Dobler (Resident, Riverside Office)

ASSOCIATE

Michael O. Wolf (Resident, Riverside Office)

Representative Clients: Kaiser Resources, Inc.; Southern California Edison Co.; General Telephone Company of California; Southern California Gas Co.; General Motors Corp.; Stater Bros. Markets; North American Chemical Co.; TTX Company; California Portland Cement Co.; Sunwest Materials.

For Complete List of Firm Personnel, See General Section

For full biographical listings, see the Martindale-Hubbell Law Directory

*SAN DIEGO,** San Diego Co.

GARRISON R. ARMSTRONG LAW CORPORATION (AV)

Suite 1300, 401 West A Street, 92101-7988
Telephone: 619-232-1811

Garrison R. Armstrong

For full biographical listings, see the Martindale-Hubbell Law Directory

FERRIS & BRITTON, A PROFESSIONAL CORPORATION (AV)

1600 First National Bank Center, 401 West A Street, 92101
Telephone: 619-233-3131
Fax: 619-232-9316

Alfred G. Ferris
Harry J. Proctor
Tamara K. Fogg
Gary T. Moyer

Representative Clients: Allstate Insurance Co.; Cox Communications, Inc.; Enterprise Rent-a-Car; Exxon; Immuno Pharmaceutics, Inc.; Invitrogen Corporation; Teleport Communications Group; Southwest Airlines; Times-Mirror Cable Television.

For Complete List of Firm Personnel, See General Section

For full biographical listings, see the Martindale-Hubbell Law Directory

GRAY CARY WARE & FREIDENRICH, A PROFESSIONAL CORPORATION (AV)

Gray Cary Established in 1927
Ware & Freidenrich Established in 1969
401 "B" Street, Suite 1700, 92101
Telephone: 619-699-2700
Telecopier: 619-236-1048
Palo Alto, California Office: 400 Hamilton Avenue.
Telephone: 415-328-6561.
La Jolla, California Office: Suite 575, 1200 Prospect Street.
Telephone: 619-454-9101.
El Centro, California Office: 1224 State Street, P.O. Box 2890.
Telephone: 619-353-6140.

Edward V. Brennan
W. Alan Lautanen
Lawrence I. Tannenbaum

Neil P. Balmert
Janis S. Fagan
Lisa C. Merrill
Randy Munyon

Representative Clients: Ernest W. Hahn, Inc.; General Dynamics (Convair Division); Harcourt, Brace, Jovanovich; Imperial Corporation of America; La Jolla Bank & Trust; Mathew Hall, Ltd.; M. H. Golden Construction Co.; Scripps Clinic & Research Foundation; University of San Diego.

(See Next Column)

GRAY CARY WARE & FREIDENRICH A PROFESSIONAL CORPORATION, *San Diego—Continued*

For Complete List of Firm Personnel, See General Section

For full biographical listings, see the Martindale-Hubbell Law Directory

LINDLEY, LAZAR & SCALES, A PROFESSIONAL CORPORATION (AV)

One America Plaza, 600 West Broadway, Suite 1400, 92101-3302
Telephone: 619-234-9181
Fax: 619-234-8475

Raymond L. Heidemann

OF COUNSEL

Maurice T. Watson

For Complete List of Firm Personnel, See General Section

For full biographical listings, see the Martindale-Hubbell Law Directory

PAGE, POLIN, BUSCH & BOATWRIGHT, A PROFESSIONAL CORPORATION (AV)

350 West Ash Street, Suite 900, 92101-3404
Telephone: 619-231-1822
Fax: 619-231-1877
FAX: 619-231-1875

David C. Boatwright
Michael E. Busch
Robert K. Edmunds
Kathleen A. Cashman-Kramer
Richard L. Moskitis
Richard W. Page
Kenneth D. Polin
Steven G. Rowles

OF COUNSEL

Richard Edward Ball, Jr.

Rod S. Fiori
Christina B. Gamache
Dorothy A. Johnson
Theresa McCarthy
Jolene L. Parker
Deidre L. Schneider
Sandra L. Shippey

For full biographical listings, see the Martindale-Hubbell Law Directory

PROCOPIO, CORY, HARGREAVES AND SAVITCH (AV)

2100 Union Bank Building, 530 B Street, 92101
Telephone: 619-238-1900
Telecopier: 619-235-0398

MEMBERS OF FIRM

Frederick K. Kunzel
George L. Damoose
Craig P. Sapin
Robert K. Butterfield, Jr.
Michael J. Kinkelaar

Representative Clients: Union Bank; Daley Corp. (highway construction); Associated General Contractors; Magma Power Company.

For Complete List of Firm Personnel, See General Section

For full biographical listings, see the Martindale-Hubbell Law Directory

SELTZER CAPLAN WILKINS & MCMAHON, A PROFESSIONAL CORPORATION (AV)

2100 Symphony Towers, 750 B Street, 92101
Telephone: 619-685-3003
Fax: 619-685-3100

David J. Dorne
John H. Alspaugh

Representative Clients: Girard Savings Bank; W.R. Grace & Co--Conn.; McDonnell-Douglas Corp.; McMillin Communities; Philip Morris Incorporated; Taco Bell Corp.; Western Financial Savings Bank.

For Complete List of Firm Personnel, See General Section

For full biographical listings, see the Martindale-Hubbell Law Directory

LAW FIRM OF DAVID S. ZWEIG (AV)

Oceana Building, 4425 Bayard Street, Suite 200, 92109-4089
Telephone: 619-274-1818
Telefax: 619-274-8535

David S. Zweig

References: Union Bank (San Diego); Prudential Securities (San Diego); The RHB Trust Co., Ltd., Cayman Islands; Liberian Corporation Services; Mees Pierson Trust (Curacao) N.V.

For full biographical listings, see the Martindale-Hubbell Law Directory

*SAN FRANCISCO,** San Francisco Co.

AVERY & ASSOCIATES (AV)

49 Geary Street, Suite 202, 94108-5727
Telephone: 415-954-4800
Fax: 415-954-4810

Luther J. Avery

(See Next Column)

ASSOCIATE

Mark J. Avery

LEGAL SUPPORT PERSONNEL

Matthew S. Avery

For full biographical listings, see the Martindale-Hubbell Law Directory

LAWRENCE V. BROOKES (AV)

12th Floor, One California Street, 94111
Telephone: 415-986-0300
Fax: 415-982-1035

References in Tax Matters: Arkia, Shreveport, Louisiana; California State Automobile Assn., San Francisco, Calif.; Foster Enterprises, Foster City, Calif.; Willamette Industries, Portland, Oregon; H.H. Robertson Co., Pittsburg, Pa.

For full biographical listings, see the Martindale-Hubbell Law Directory

BUELL & BERNER (AV)

A Partnership of Professional Corporations
101 California Street, 22nd Floor, 94111
Telephone: 415-391-5011
Fax: 415-391-7383

MEMBERS OF FIRM

E. Rick Buell, II, (P.C.)
Curtis William Berner (P.C.)

For full biographical listings, see the Martindale-Hubbell Law Directory

FELDMAN, WALDMAN & KLINE, A PROFESSIONAL CORPORATION (AV)

2700 Russ Building, 235 Montgomery Street, 94104
Telephone: 415-981-1300
Telex: 650-223-3204
Fax: 415-394-0121
Stockton, California Office: Sperry Building, 146-148 West Weber Avenue.
Telephone: 209-943-2004.
Fax: 209-943-0905.

Murry J. Waldman
Leland R. Selna, Jr.
Michael L. Korbholz
Howard M. Wexler
Patricia S. Mar
Kenneth W. Jones
Paul J. Dion
Vern S. Bothwell
L. J. Chris Martiniak
Kenneth A. Freed
Martha Jeanne Shaver (Resident, Stockton Office)
Robert Cedric Goodman
Steven K. Denebeim
Laura Grad
William F. Adams
William M. Smith
Elizabeth A. Thompson
Julie A. Jones
David L. Kanel

Abram S. Feuerstein
John R. Capron
Ted S. Storey
A. Todd Berman
Laura J. Dawson

OF COUNSEL

Richard L. Jaeger
Malcolm Leader-Picone
Gerald A. Sherwin (Resident, Stockton Office)

For full biographical listings, see the Martindale-Hubbell Law Directory

GRIFFINGER, FREED, HEINEMANN, COOK & FOREMAN (AV)

24th Floor, Steuart Street Tower, One Market Plaza, 94105
Telephone: 415-243-0300
Telecopier: 415-777-9366

MEMBERS OF FIRM

Theodore A. Griffinger, Jr.
Michael S. Freed
Peter M. Heinemann
Karen A. Cook
Stewart H. Foreman
Jonathan A. Funk
Peter S. Fishman

Dwight L. Monson
Eileen Trujillo
Robert L. Wishner
Marie C. Bendy
Eric C. Starr
Jonathan Polland

LEGAL SUPPORT PERSONNEL

LEGAL ADMINISTRATOR

Kathleen H. Hartley

PARALEGALS

Jeanne Diettinger
Jean Mahony
Irene E. Bernasconi
Janet L. Johnston

Representative Client: Smith Barney, Harris Upham Co., Inc.
Reference: Bank of America (Main Office).

For full biographical listings, see the Martindale-Hubbell Law Directory

LOSEY & ASSOCIATES (AV)

650 California Street, 12th Floor, 94108
Telephone: 415-421-3840
Telecopier: 415-421-0737

(See Next Column)

LOSEY & ASSOCIATES—*Continued*

Michael J. Bollard (1961-1994)
F. Richard Losey

ASSOCIATES

Daniel J. Leer
Mary L. Symons
Kristin D. Wheeler

OF COUNSEL

Charles P. Teixeira
Paul Raynor Keating
Warren H. Rothman

For full biographical listings, see the Martindale-Hubbell Law Directory

SILK, ADLER & COLVIN, A LAW CORPORATION (AV)

Russ Building, Suite 1120, 235 Montgomery Street, 94104
Telephone: 415-421-7555
Fax: 415-421-0712

Thomas Silk
Gregory L. Colvin
Elizabeth Buchalter Adler
Rosemary E. Fei
Robert A. Wexler

For full biographical listings, see the Martindale-Hubbell Law Directory

TAYLOR & FAUST, A PROFESSIONAL CORPORATION (AV)

Suite 2525, One Montgomery Street, 94104
Telephone: 415-421-9535
Fax: 415-956-3231

Samuel Taylor (Retired)
Leland H. Faust
Steven B. Kravitz

For full biographical listings, see the Martindale-Hubbell Law Directory

MINOT WELD TRIPP, JR. (AV)

Two Embarcadero Center, Suite 1645, 94111
Telephone: 415-788-2412
Fax: 415-788-6125

Reference: Wells Fargo Bank.

For full biographical listings, see the Martindale-Hubbell Law Directory

*SAN JOSE,** Santa Clara Co.

FERRARI, ALVAREZ, OLSEN & OTTOBONI, A PROFESSIONAL CORPORATION (AV)

333 West Santa Clara Street, Suite 700, 95113
Telephone: 408-280-0535
Fax: 408-280-0151
Palo Alto, California Office: 550 Hamilton Avenue.
Telephone: 415-327-3233.

Clarence J. Ferrari, Jr.
Kent E. Olsen
John M. Ottoboni
Richard S. Bebb
James J. Eller
Robert C. Danneskiold
Terence M. Kane
Emma Peña Madrid
John P. Thurau
Roger D. Wintle
Christopher E. Cobey

Michael D. Brayton
Lisa Intrieri Caputo
Jil Dalesandro
Gregory R. Dietrich
J. Timothy Maximoff
Joseph W. Mell, Jr.
George P. Mulcaire
Eleanor C. Schuermann
Melva M. Vollersen

OF COUNSEL

Edward M. Alvarez

For full biographical listings, see the Martindale-Hubbell Law Directory

OWEN G. FIORE (AV)

Bank of America Building, 101 Park Center Plaza, Suite 1150, 95113
Telephone: 408-293-3616
Facsimile: 408-293-0430

John F. Ramsbacher
Leslie J. Daniels

For full biographical listings, see the Martindale-Hubbell Law Directory

SAN MATEO, San Mateo Co.

ANDERLINI, GUHEEN, FINKELSTEIN, EMERICK & MCSWEENEY, A PROFESSIONAL CORPORATION (AV)

400 South El Camino Real, Suite 700, 94402
Telephone: 415-348-0102
Fax: 415-348-0962

P. Terry Anderlini
John J. Guheen
David G. Finkelstein
Merrill G. Emerick
Brian J. McSweeney

(See Next Column)

A. James Scholz
John P. Antonakos
Paul J. Smoot
Jennifer Gustafson

OF COUNSEL

Daniel J. Monaco (Inc.)

A list of Representative Clients will be furnished upon request.

For full biographical listings, see the Martindale-Hubbell Law Directory

*SANTA BARBARA,** Santa Barbara Co.

SCHRAMM & RADDUE (AV)

15 West Carrillo Street, P.O. Box 1260, 93102
Telephone: 805-963-2044
Fax: 805-564-4181

MEMBERS OF FIRM

Edward W. Schramm (1913-1982)
Ralph C. Raddue (1906-1986)
Lawrence M. Parma (1911-1957)
Paul W. Hartloff, Jr.
Dale E. Hanst
Charles H. Jarvis
Douglas E. Schmidt
Kurt H. Pyle
Daniel A. Reicker
Weldon U. Howell, Jr.
Frederick W. Clough
Richard F. Lee
Michael E. Pfau
Edward C. Thoits

ASSOCIATES

Judith E. Koper
Marjorie F. Allen
Christine M. Sontag
Diana Jessup Lee

OF COUNSEL

Howard M. Simon

Representative Clients: Berkus Group Architects; Circon Corp.; LaArcada Investment Corp.; Michael Towbes Construction and Development Co.; Santa Barbara Bank & Trust; Santa Barbara Medical Foundation Clinic.

For Complete List of Firm Personnel, See General Section

For full biographical listings, see the Martindale-Hubbell Law Directory

VALENCIA, Los Angeles Co.

B. PAUL HUSBAND (AV)

27201 Tourney Road, Suite 200-D, 91355-1855
Telephone: 805-255-3123; 800-999-9509
Facsimile: 805-255-3435

For full biographical listings, see the Martindale-Hubbell Law Directory

WOODLAND HILLS, Los Angeles Co.

WALLECK, SHANE, STANARD & BLENDER (AV)

5959 Topanga Canyon Boulevard, Suite 200, 91367
Telephone: 818-346-1333
Fax: 818-702-8939

MEMBER OF FIRM

David L. Blender

Representative Clients: San Fernando Valley Board of Realtors; Keffco, Inc.; Fuller-Jeffrey Broadcasting; Lynn Simay-Key Centers, Inc.; DA/PRO Rubber, Inc.; Pinnacle Estate Properties, Inc.; Comet Electric, Inc.; Wausau Insurance Company; Western States Imports Co., Inc.; California Coast Escrow, Inc.

For full biographical listings, see the Martindale-Hubbell Law Directory

COLORADO

*COLORADO SPRINGS,** El Paso Co.

WILTON W. COGSWELL, III (AV)

Suite 1020, Alamo Corporate Center, 102 South Tejon, 80903
Telephone: 719-473-1448
Facsimile: 719-473-1449

OF COUNSEL

Wilton W. Cogswell, IV

For full biographical listings, see the Martindale-Hubbell Law Directory

*DENVER,** Denver Co.

ATLASS PROFESSIONAL CORPORATION (AV)

2100 East Fourteenth Avenue, 80206
Telephone: 303-377-0707
Fax: 303-321-2655

Theodore B. Atlass

Carol Buchanan Lay

(See Next Column)

ATLASS PROFESSIONAL CORPORATION, *Denver—Continued*

OF COUNSEL

John DeBruyn

For full biographical listings, see the Martindale-Hubbell Law Directory

BALLARD SPAHR ANDREWS & INGERSOLL (AV)

Seventeenth Street Plaza Building, Suite 2300, 1225 17th Street, 80202-5596
Telephone: 303-292-2400
Fax: 303-296-3956
Philadelphia, Pennsylvania Office: 1735 Market Street, 51st Floor.
Telephone: 215-665-8500.
Fax: 215-864-8999.
Kaunas, Lithuania Office: Donelaičio 71-2, Kaunas 3000.
Telephone: (370-7) 20 56 66.
Fax: (370-7) 20 56 91.
Salt Lake City, Utah Office: One Utah Center, 201 South Main Street, Suite 1200.
Telephone: 801-531-3000.
Fax: 801-531-3001.
Washington, D.C. Office: Suite 900 East, 555 13th Street, N.W.
Telephone: 202-383-8800.
Fax: 202-383-8877; 383-8893.
Baltimore, Maryland Office: 300 East Lombard Street, 19th Floor.
Telephone: 410-528-5600.
Fax: 410-528-5650.
Camden, New Jersey Office: 800 Hudson Square, 5th Floor.
Telephone: 609-541-5577.
Fax: 609-541-8272.

John L. Ruppert — Roger P. Thomasch

For Complete List of Firm Personnel, See General Section

For full biographical listings, see the Martindale-Hubbell Law Directory

BROWNSTEIN HYATT FARBER & STRICKLAND, P.C. (AV)

Twenty-Second Floor, 410 Seventeenth Street, 80202-4437
Telephone: 303-534-6335
Telecopier: 303-623-1956

Michael J. Sternick

Gregory W. Berger

Representative Clients: AMC Cancer Research Center; Coughlin & Company, Inc.; FBS Investment Services, Inc.; Hanifen, Imhoff Inc.; John Elway Auto Dealerships; Norwest Investment Services, Inc.; Pacifica Holding Company; Sentinel Trust Company; SunAmerica Inc.; U.S. Home Corporation.

For Complete List of Firm Personnel, See General Section

For full biographical listings, see the Martindale-Hubbell Law Directory

MELVIN A. COFFEE & ASSOCIATES, P.C. (AV)

Suite 336, Oneida Tower, 2121 South Oneida Street, 80224
Telephone: 303-759-0990
Fax: 303-759-0966

Melvin A. Coffee

W. Dirk Costin

Reference: Norwest Bank, Denver.

For full biographical listings, see the Martindale-Hubbell Law Directory

JOHN DEBRUYN LAW OFFICES (AV)

2100 East Fourteenth Avenue, 80206
Telephone: 303-377-0707
Telecopier: 303-321-2655

OF COUNSEL

Theodore B. Atlass

For full biographical listings, see the Martindale-Hubbell Law Directory

GUTHERY & RICKLES, P.C. (AV)

Cherry Creek Plaza II, 650 South Cherry Street Suite 1000, 80222
Telephone: 303-320-5889
Fax: 303-320-5890

Peter C. Guthery — Stephen P. Rickles
Kerrie A. Boese

Representative Clients: Colorado National Guard Foundation; Denver Firefighters Protective Association; Denver Health Care Group, P.C.; Denver Museum of Natural History Foundation; Eastern Star Center; Jimmie Heuga Center; Karsh & Hagan Advertising, Inc.; City of Thornton; United States Olympic Foundation; YMCA of the Rockies.

For full biographical listings, see the Martindale-Hubbell Law Directory

HOLLAND & HART (AV)

Suite 2900, 555 Seventeenth Street, P.O. Box 8749, 80201
Telephone: 303-295-8000
Cable Address: "Holhart Denver"
Telecopier: 303-295-8261
TWX: 910-931-0568
Denver Tech Center, Colorado Office: Suite 1050, 4601 DTC Boulevard.
Telephone: 303-290-1600.
Telecopier: 303-290-1606.
Aspen, Colorado Office: 600 East Main Street.
Telephone: 303-925-3476.
Telecopier: 303-925-9367.
Boulder, Colorado Office: Suite 500, 1050 Walnut.
Telephone: 303-473-2700.
Telecopier: 303-473-2720.
Colorado Springs, Colorado Office: Suite 1000, 90 S. Cascade Avenue.
Telephone: 719-475-7730.
Telex: 82077 SHHTLX.
Telecopier: 719-634-2461.
Washington, D.C. Office: Suite 310, 1001 Pennsylvania Avenue, N.W.
Telephone: 202-638-5500.
Telecopier: 202-737-8998.
Boise, Idaho Office: Suite 1400, West One Plaza, 101 South Capitol Boulevard, P.O. Box 2527.
Telephone: 208-342-5000.
Telecopier: 208-343-8869.
Billings, Montana Office: Suite 1500, First Interstate Center, 401 North 31st Street, P.O. Box 639.
Telephone: 406-252-2166.
Telecopier: 406-252-1669.
Salt Lake City, Utah Office: Suite 880, 111 East Broadway.
Telephone: 801-578-6000.
FAX: 801-578-6010.
Cheyenne, Wyoming Office: Holland & Hart, A Partnership including Professional Corporations, Suite 500, 2020 Carey Avenue, P.O. Box 1347.
Telephone: 307-778-4200.
Telecopier: 307-778-8175.
Jackson, Wyoming Office: Holland & Hart, A Partnership including Professional Corporations, Suite 2, 175 South King Street, P.O. Box 68.
Telephone: 307-739-9741.
Telecopier: 307-739-9744.

MEMBERS OF FIRM

Samuel P. Guyton (Retired) — Kevin S. Crandell
Frederick G. Meyer — John R. Maxfield
Mark D. Safty — Renée W. O'Rourke
David E. Crandall

OF COUNSEL

Robert R. Keatinge — Karen Sweeney

ASSOCIATES

Virginia L. Briggs — Jane Oglesby Francis
Robert P. Detrick — Heidi S. Glance
Daniel C. Doherty — Risa L. Wolf-Smith

DENVER TECH CENTER, COLORADO RESIDENT PARTNER

Robert Alan Poe

DENVER TECH CENTER RESIDENT OF COUNSEL

Mary D. Metzger

BOULDER, COLORADO PARTNER

Camron R. Kuelthau

COLORADO SPRINGS, COLORADO PARTNERS

Bruce T. Buell — Randolph M. Karsh
William K. Brown (Resident)

BOISE, IDAHO RESIDENT PARTNER

J. Frederick Mack

BOISE, IDAHO RESIDENT ASSOCIATE

Sandra L. Clapp

BILLINGS, MONTANA PARTNER

David R. Chisholm

CHEYENNE, WYOMING PARTNER

Lawrence J. Wolfe (P.C.)

SALT LAKE CITY UTAH RESIDENT PARTNER

Bruce N. Lemons

For Complete List of Firm Personnel, See General Section

For full biographical listings, see the Martindale-Hubbell Law Directory

HOLME ROBERTS & OWEN LLC (AV)

Suite 4100, 1700 Lincoln, 80203
Telephone: 303-861-7000
Telex: 45-4460
Telecopier: 303-866-0200
Boulder, Colorado Office: Suite 400, 1401 Pearl Street.
Telephone: 303-444-5955.
Telecopier: 303-444-1063.
Colorado Springs, Colorado Office: Suite 1300, 90 South Cascade Avenue.
Telephone: 719-473-3800.
Telecopier: 719-633-1518.

(See Next Column)

HOLME ROBERTS & OWEN LLC—*Continued*

Salt Lake City, Utah Office: Suite 1100, 111 East Broadway.
Telephone: 801-521-5800.
Telecopier: 801-521-9639.
London, England Office: 4th Floor, Mellier House, 26a Albemarle Street.
Telephone: 44-171-499-8776.
Telecopier: 44-171-499-7769.
Moscow, Russia Office: 14 Krivokolenny Pr., Suite 30, 101000.
Telephone: 095-925-7816.
Telecopier: 095-923-2726.

MEMBERS OF FIRM

James E. Bye
Robert J. Welter
Judson W. Detrick
David T. Mitzner
Charles A. Ramunno
William S. Huff
Donald J. Hopkins
James D. Butler
Carolyn E. Daniels
Steve L. Gaines (Colorado Springs Office)
Judith L. L. Roberts (Co-Director, Moscow Office; London Office)
R. Bruce Johnson (Salt Lake City Office)
Paul E. Smith (Boulder Office)
Douglas A. Pluss
Mark K. Buchi (Managing Member, Salt Lake City Office)
McKay Marsden (Salt Lake City Office)
David R. Child
John R. Wylie (Colorado Springs Office)
Stephanie M. Tuthill
Alan W. Cathcart (Not admitted in CO)
David J. Crapo (Salt Lake City Office)
Sharon A. Higgins (Colorado Springs Office)

ASSOCIATES

Charles B. Bruce, Jr.
John N. Raby
Michelle M. Rose-Hughes
Masahiro Max Yoshimura

For Complete List of Firm Personnel, See General Section

For full biographical listings, see the Martindale-Hubbell Law Directory

LOHF, SHAIMAN & JACOBS, P.C. (AV)

900 Cherry Tower, 950 South Cherry Street, 80222
Telephone: 303-753-9000
Telecopier: 303-753-9997

Charles H. Jacobs
Moshe Luber
Robert Shaiman

Reference: Professional Bank.

For full biographical listings, see the Martindale-Hubbell Law Directory

WILLIAM R. MCDONALD, P.C. (AV)

Suite 206, 155 South Madison, 80209-3013
Telephone: 303-321-3271
Fax: 303-320-1577

William R. McDonald

For full biographical listings, see the Martindale-Hubbell Law Directory

MYERS, HOPPIN, BRADLEY AND DEVITT, P.C. (AV)

Suite 420, 4704 Harlan Street, 80212
Telephone: 303-433-8527
Fax: 303-433-8219

Frederick J. Myers
Charles T. Hoppin
Jon T. Bradley
Jerald J. Devitt

Gregg W. Fraser

OF COUNSEL

Kent E. Hanson

Reference: Bank One Lakeside Banking Center.

For full biographical listings, see the Martindale-Hubbell Law Directory

SHERMAN & HOWARD L.L.C. (AV)

Attorneys at Law
633 Seventeenth Street, Suite 3000, 80202
Telephone: 303-297-2900
Telecopier: 303-298-0940
Colorado Springs, Colorado Office: Suite 1500, 90 South Cascade Avenue, 80903.
Telephone: 719-475-2440.
Las Vegas, Nevada Office: Swendseid & Stern a member in Sherman & Howard L.L.C., 317 Sixth Street, 89101.
Telephone: 702-387-6073.
Reno, Nevada Office: Swendseid & Stern, a member in Sherman & Howard L.L.C., 50 West Liberty Street, Suite 660, 89501.
Telephone: 702-323-1980.

Douglas M. Cain
Duane F. Wurzer
R. Michael Sanchez
David Thomas III
Cynthia C. Benson
Manuel D. Savage
Peggy Berning Knight

(See Next Column)

COUNSEL

William P. Cantwell

Carol V. Berger
Katherine F. Beckes
Kathleen A. Odle
Bridget K. Sullivan

Representative Clients: American National Insurance Co.; Central Bank of Denver, N.A.; Tele-Communications, Inc.; VICORP Restaurants, Inc.; Swedish Medical Center; Public Employees' Retirement Assoc.

For Complete List of Firm Personnel, See General Section

For full biographical listings, see the Martindale-Hubbell Law Directory

LAW OFFICES OF JOSEPH H. THIBODEAU, P.C. (AV)

Suite 209, 155 South Madison Street, 80209
Telephone: 303-320-1250
Fax: 303-320-1577

Joseph H. Thibodeau

Kandace C. Gerdes
Matthew T. Gehrke

For full biographical listings, see the Martindale-Hubbell Law Directory

ZISMAN AND INGRAHAM, P.C. (AV)

Suite 250, 3773 Cherry Creek Drive North, 80209
Telephone: 303-320-0023
Fax: 303-320-0034

Sanford Zisman
James F. Ingraham

For full biographical listings, see the Martindale-Hubbell Law Directory

CONNECTICUT

CHESHIRE, New Haven Co.

WINTERS & FORTE (AV)

Waverly Professional Park, 315 Highland Avenue, Suite 102, P.O. Box 844, 06410
Telephone: 203-272-2927
Fax: 203-271-1222

MEMBERS OF FIRM

David Wayne Winters
Michael C. Forte

A List of Representative Clients will be furnished upon request.
Re ferences: Bank of Boston, Connecticut; Centerbank; American National Bank.

For full biographical listings, see the Martindale-Hubbell Law Directory

GREENWICH, Fairfield Co.

IVEY, BARNUM & O'MARA (AV)

Meridian Building, 170 Mason Street, P.O. Box 1689, 06830
Telephone: 203-661-6000
Telecopier: 203-661-9462

MEMBERS OF FIRM

Michael J. Allen
Robert C. Barnum, Jr.
Edward D. Cosden, Jr.
James W. Cuminale
Wilmot L. Harris, Jr.
William I. Haslun, II
Edward T. Krumeich, Jr.
Donat C. Marchand
Miles F. McDonald, Jr.
Edwin J. O'Mara, Jr.
Remy A. Rodas
Gregory A. Saum
Lorraine Slavin

ASSOCIATES

Juerg A. Heim
Melissa Townsend Klauberg
Nicole Barrett Lecher
Alan S. Rubenstein

OF COUNSEL

Philip R. McKnight

For full biographical listings, see the Martindale-Hubbell Law Directory

*HARTFORD,** Hartford Co.

COPP & BERALL (AV)

55 Farmington Avenue, Suite 703, 06105
Telephone: 203-249-5261
Fax: 203-947-6382

MEMBERS OF FIRM

Frank S. Berall
Mark H. Neikrie
Suzanne Brown Walsh

OF COUNSEL

Belton A. Copp

References: Fleet Bank, N.A.; Connecticut National Bank; Union Trust Co.; Bank of Boston.

For full biographical listings, see the Martindale-Hubbell Law Directory

SIEGEL, O'CONNOR, SCHIFF & ZANGARI, P.C. (AV)

370 Asylum Street, 06103
Telephone: 203-727-8900
New Haven, Connecticut Office: 171 Orange Street, P.O. Box 906.
Telephone: 203-789-0001.

John W. Beck | Robert J. Percy
Donald W. Strickland

Representative Clients: Federal Paper Board Co., Inc.; Stanadyne, Inc.; Associated General Contractors; Yale University; Mystic Seaport, Inc.; General Motors Corp.; UNISYS Corp.

For full biographical listings, see the Martindale-Hubbell Law Directory

SOROKIN SOROKIN GROSS HYDE & WILLIAMS P.C. (AV)

One Corporate Center, 06103
Telephone: 203-525-6645
Fax: 203-522-1781
Simsbury, Connecticut Office: 730 Hopmeadow Street.
Telephone: 203-651-9348.
Rocky Hill, Connecticut Office: 2360 Main Street.
Telephone: 203-563-9305.
Fax: 203-529-6931.
Glastonbury, Connecticut Office: 124 Hebron Avenue.
Telephone: 203-659-8801.

Morris W. Banks | Charles R. Moore, Jr.
Richard G. Convicer | Barrie K. Wetstone

Sharon Kowal Freilich

For Complete List of Firm Personnel, See General Section

For full biographical listings, see the Martindale-Hubbell Law Directory

*NEW HAVEN,** New Haven Co.

BERGMAN, HOROWITZ & REYNOLDS, P.C. (AV)

157 Church Street, 19th Floor, P.O. Box 426, 06502
Telephone: 203-789-1320
FAX: 203-785-8127
New York, New York Office: 499 Park Avenue, 26th Floor.
Telephone: 212-582-3580.

Stanley N. Bergman | James Russell Brockway
Robert H. Horowitz | Bruce I. Judelson
David L. Reynolds | David A. Ringold
Kenneth N. Musen | Kathryn Harner Smith
William C. G. Swift, Jr. | Donald S. Hendel
Richard J. Klein | Joy M. Miyasaki
Paul M. Roy

Louis R. Piscatelli | Anthony L. Galvagna
James G. Dattaro | Frederick A. Thomas
Edward A. Renn | Richard M. Porter

For Complete List of Firm Personnel, See General Section

For full biographical listings, see the Martindale-Hubbell Law Directory

BRENNER, SALTZMAN & WALLMAN (AV)

A Partnership including Professional Corporations
271 Whitney Avenue, P.O. Box 1746, 06507-1746
Telephone: 203-772-2600
Facsimile: 203-562-2098

Newton D. Brenner (P.C.) | Donald W. Anderson (P.C.)
Stephen L. Saltzman (P.C.) | Carol N. Theodore (P.C.)
Marc A. Wallman (P.C.) | Samuel M. Hurwitz
David R. Schaefer (P.C.) | Wayne A. Martino, P.C.
Stuart Jay Mandel (P.C.) | M. Anne Peters
Kenneth Rosenthal

Peter K. Marsh | Brian P. Daniels
Alice Jo Mick | John R. Bashaw
George Brencher, IV

For full biographical listings, see the Martindale-Hubbell Law Directory

SACHS, BERMAN & SHURE, SKLARZ & GALLANT, P.C. (AV)

Granite Square 700 State Street, P.O. Box 1960, 06509-1960
Telephone: 203-782-3000
Telex: ESL 62239500
Telecopier: 203-777-3347

Mark G. Sklarz

Representative Clients: Starter Corporation.

(See Next Column)

For Complete List of Firm Personnel, See General Section

For full biographical listings, see the Martindale-Hubbell Law Directory

SIEGEL, O'CONNOR, SCHIFF & ZANGARI, P.C. (AV)

171 Orange Street, P.O. Box 906, 06504
Telephone: 203-789-0001
Hartford, Connecticut Office: 370 Asylum Street.
Telephone: 203-727-8900.

Gregory J. Bezz | Peter D. Hershman
Robert F. Cohn | Mario J. Zangari

Christine A. Barker

Representative Clients: Federal Paper Board Co., Inc.; Stanadyne, Inc.; Associated General Contractors; Blue Cross/Blue Shield of Connecticut; Mystic Seaport, Inc.; Hospital of St. Raphael.

For full biographical listings, see the Martindale-Hubbell Law Directory

SILVERSTEIN & OSACH, P.C. (AV)

Suite 903, 234 Church Street, P.O. Box 1727, 06507
Telephone: 203-865-0121
FAX: 203-865-0255

Nathan M. Silverstein | Ronald C. Osach
Kurt F. Zimmermann

Leonard K. Atkinson, Jr.

For full biographical listings, see the Martindale-Hubbell Law Directory

SOUTHPORT, Fairfield Co.

SEELEY & BERGLASS (AV)

3695 Post Road, P.O. Box 858, 06490
Telephone: 203-256-3250
Fax: 203-562-9365
New Haven, Connecticut Office: 121 Whitney Avenue.
Telephone: 203-562-5888.
Fax: 203-562-9365.

W. Parker Seeley, Jr. | Teresa E. Cichucki

OF COUNSEL
Leonard S. Paoletta

For full biographical listings, see the Martindale-Hubbell Law Directory

STAMFORD, Fairfield Co.

WOFSEY, ROSEN, KWESKIN & KURIANSKY (AV)

600 Summer Street, 06901
Telephone: 203-327-2300
FAX: 203-967-9273

MEMBERS OF FIRM

Abraham Wofsey (1915-1944) | Anthony R. Lorenzo
Michael Wofsey (1927-1951) | Edward M. Kweskin
David M. Rosen (1926-1967) | David M. Cohen
Julius B. Kuriansky (1910-1992) | Marshall Goldberg
Monroe Silverman | Stephen A. Finn
Emanuel Margolis | Judith Rosenberg
Howard C. Kaplan | Robert L. Teicher
Mark H. Henderson

Steven D. Grushkin

OF COUNSEL

Saul Kwartin | Sydney C. Kweskin (Retired)

ASSOCIATES

Brian Bandler | James A. Lenes
John J.L. Chober | Valerie E. Maze
Steven M. Frederick | Maurice K. Segall
Eric M. Higgins | Randall M. Skigen
Gregory J. Williams

Representative Clients: Benenson Realty; Cellular Information Systems, Inc.; Gateway Bank; Hartford Provision Company; Louis Dreyfus Corp.; Norwalk Federation of Teachers; Patient Care, Inc.; People's Bank; Ridgeway Shopping Center and Stamford Housing Authority.

For full biographical listings, see the Martindale-Hubbell Law Directory

TRUMBULL, Fairfield Co.

BRAUNSTEIN AND TODISCO, PROFESSIONAL CORPORATION (AV)

Brinsmade Building, 965 White Plains Road, 06611
Telephone: 203-452-9700
Telecopier: 203-459-0004

(See Next Column)

BRAUNSTEIN AND TODISCO PROFESSIONAL CORPORATION—*Continued*

Samuel L. Braunstein
Amy E. Todisco
Jonathan J. Klein

References: The Bank of Boston-Connecticut; UST Bank Connecticut.

For full biographical listings, see the Martindale-Hubbell Law Directory

WESTPORT, Fairfield Co.

BLAZZARD, GRODD & HASENAUER, P.C. (AV)

943 Post Road East, P.O. Box 5108, 06881
Telephone: 203-226-7866
Telecopier: 203-454-4855

Norse N. Blazzard
Leslie E. Grodd
Judith A. Hasenauer
William E. Hasenauer
Raymond A. O'Hara, III

Lynn Korman Stone

For full biographical listings, see the Martindale-Hubbell Law Directory

STUART A. MCKEEVER (AV)

155 Post Road, East, 06880
Telephone: 203-227-4756
Fax: 203-454-2031

Reference: Fleet Bank.

For full biographical listings, see the Martindale-Hubbell Law Directory

RONALD L. SHEIMAN (AV)

1804 Post Road East, 06880
Telephone: 203-259-0599
Telex: 238198 TLXAUR
Telecopier: 203-255-2570

For full biographical listings, see the Martindale-Hubbell Law Directory

WAKE, SEE, DIMES & BRYNICZKA (AV)

27 Imperial Avenue, P.O. Box 777, 06881
Telephone: 203-227-9545
Telecopier: 203-226-1641

MEMBERS OF FIRM

Hereward Wake (1905-1977)
Edgar T. See
Edwin K. Dimes
Jacob P. Bryniczka
Amy L. Y. Day
Ira W. Bloom
Ernest Michael Dichele
Jonathan A. Flatow

ASSOCIATES

Douglas E. LoMonte
Rosamond A. Koether

OF COUNSEL

Richard S. Gibbons

General Counsel for: L.H. Gault & Son, Inc.; M.B.I., Inc.; The Danbury Mint; Beta Shim, Co.; Easton Press; Coverbind Corp.; D.L. Ryan Companies, Ltd.;
Approved Attorneys for: Lawyers Title Insurance Corporation of Richmond, Va.; Chicago Title Insurance Co.; Old Republic National Title Insurance Co.

For full biographical listings, see the Martindale-Hubbell Law Directory

DELAWARE

*WILMINGTON,** New Castle Co.

MORRIS, NICHOLS, ARSHT & TUNNELL (AV)

1201 North Market Street, P.O. Box 1347, 19899-1347
Telephone: 302-658-9200
Telecopier: 302-658-3989

MEMBERS OF FIRM

Andrew B. Kirkpatrick, Jr.
Richard L. Sutton
Johannes R. Krahmer
O. Francis Biondi
Lewis S. Black, Jr.
Paul P. Welsh
William O. LaMotte, III
Douglas E. Whitney
William H. Sudell, Jr.
Martin P. Tully
Thomas Reed Hunt, Jr.
A. Gilchrist Sparks, III
Richard D. Allen
David Ley Hamilton
John F. Johnston
Walter C. Tuthill
Donald F. Parsons, Jr.
Jack B. Blumenfeld
Donald Nelson Isken
Donald E. Reid
Denison H. Hatch, Jr.
Thomas C. Grimm
Kenneth J. Nachbar
Andrew M. Johnston
Mary B. Graham
Michael Houghton
Edmond D. Johnson
Matthew B. Lehr

(See Next Column)

ASSOCIATES

John S. McDaniel
Thomas R. Pulsifer
Jon E. Abramczyk
Alan J. Stone
Louis G. Hering
Frederick H. Alexander
R. Judson Scaggs, Jr.
William M. Lafferty
Andrea L. Rocanelli
Karen Jacobs Louden
Karen L. Pascale
David G. Thunhorst
Elaine C. Reilly
Donna L. Culver
Julia Heaney
Jonathan I. Lessner
Kurt M. Heyman
Michael L. Vild
Lisa B. Baeurle
Christine M. Hansen

COUNSEL

S. Samuel Arsht
David A. Drexler
S. Maynard Turk
Hugh M. Morris (1878-1966)
Alexander L. Nichols (1906-1985)
James M. Tunnell, Jr. (1910-1986)

Representative Clients: The Coca Cola Co.; Delaware River and Bay Authority; Ford Motor Co.; J.P. Morgan Delaware; Longwood Foundation, Inc.; Rollins, Inc.; Texaco Inc.

For Complete List of Firm Personnel, See General Section

For full biographical listings, see the Martindale-Hubbell Law Directory

POTTER ANDERSON & CORROON (AV)

350 Delaware Trust Building, P.O. Box 951, 19899-0951
Telephone: 302-658-6771
FAX: 658-1192; 655-1190; 655-1199

MEMBERS OF FIRM

Leonard S. Togman
David J. Garrett
Mary E. Copper

ASSOCIATE

Scott E. Waxman

Representative Clients: Eastman Chemical Products, Inc.; Aramco Services Company; Republic New York Corporation.

For Complete List of Firm Personnel, See General Section

For full biographical listings, see the Martindale-Hubbell Law Directory

RICHARDS, LAYTON & FINGER, P.A. (AV)

One Rodney Square, P.O. Box 551, 19899
Telephone: 302-658-6541
Telecopier: 302-658-6548

Thomas P. Sweeney
Richard G. Bacon
Julian H. Baumann, Jr.
W. Donald Sparks, II

Darlene Marchesani Fasic

General Counsel for: Wilmington Trust Company; Continental-American Life Insurance Co.
Local Counsel for: General Motors Corp.; Shell Oil Co.; Aetna Group; Dean Witter Reynolds, Inc.; Gulf & Western Industries Inc..

For Complete List of Firm Personnel, See General Section

For full biographical listings, see the Martindale-Hubbell Law Directory

SCHLUSSER, REIVER, HUGHES & SISK (AV)

1700 West 14th Street, 19806
Telephone: 302-655-8181
Fax: 302-655-8190

MEMBERS OF FIRM

Robert E. Schlusser
Joanna Reiver
Mark D. Sisk
Bryan E. Keenan
Brian P. Glancy

OF COUNSEL

Thomas G. Hughes

ASSOCIATES

Theresa P. Wilson (Not admitted in DE)
John A. Ciccarone

For full biographical listings, see the Martindale-Hubbell Law Directory

WILLIAMS, HERSHMAN & WISLER, P.A. (AV)

Suite 600, One Commerce Center, Twelfth and Orange Streets, P.O. Box 511, 19899-0511
Telephone: 302-575-0873
Telecopier: 302-575-1642

David Nicol Williams
Douglas M. Hershman
Jeffrey C. Wisler
Barbara Snapp Danberg
F. Peter Conaty, Jr.

References: Wilmington Trust Co.; PNC Bank.

For full biographical listings, see the Martindale-Hubbell Law Directory

DISTRICT OF COLUMBIA

WASHINGTON, D.C. Co.

* indicates certain Bar Register subscribers, in cities of comparable size and importance, who maintain an additional office in Washington, D.C. and who have arranged for representation as a part of the Washington, D.C. listings that follow

AUGUST, COMITER, KULUNAS & SCHEPPS, P.A. (AV)

Suite 700, 501 School Street, 20024
Telephone: 202-646-5160
West Palm Beach Office: 250 Australian Avenue South, Suite 1100.
Telephone: 407-835-9600.
Fax: 407-835-9602.

Jerald David August (Not admitted in DC)

For full biographical listings, see the Martindale-Hubbell Law Directory

* **BAKER & BOTTS, L.L.P.** (AV)

A Registered Limited Liability Partnership
The Warner, 1299 Pennsylvania Avenue, N.W., 20004-2400
Telephone: 202-639-7700
Fax: 202-639-7832
Houston, Texas Office: One Shell Plaza, 910 Louisiana.
Telephone: 713-229-1234.
Austin, Texas Office: 1600 San Jacinto Center, 98 San Jacinto Boulevard.
Telephone: 512-322-2500.
Dallas, Texas Office: 2001 Ross Avenue.
Telephone: 214-953-6500.
New York, New York Office: 805 Third Avenue, Suite 2000.
Telephone: 212-705-5000.
Moscow, Russian Federation Office: 10 ul. Pushkinskaya, 103031.
Telephone: 7095/921-5300 (Local); 7501/929-7070 (International).

MEMBERS OF FIRM

O. Donaldson Chapoton (Not admitted in DC)
James A. Baker IV

ASSOCIATE

Jane Boland Keough

For Complete List of Firm Personnel, See General Section

For full biographical listings, see the Martindale-Hubbell Law Directory

BAKER & HOSTETLER (AV)

Washington Square, Suite 1100, 1050 Connecticut Avenue, N.W., 20036-5304
Telephone: 202-861-1500
In Cleveland, Ohio: 3200 National City Center, 1900 East Ninth Street.
Telephone: 216-621-0200.
In Columbus, Ohio: Capitol Square, Suite 2100, 65 East State Street.
Telephone: 614-228-1541.
In Denver, Colorado: 303 East 17th Avenue, Suite 1100.
Telephone: 303-861-0600.
In Houston, Texas: 1000 Louisiana, Suite 2000.
Telephone: 713-751-1600.
In Long Beach, California: 300 Oceangate, Suite 620.
Telephone: 310-432-2827.
In Los Angeles, California: 600 Wilshire Boulevard.
Telephone: 213-624-2400.
In Orlando, Florida: SunBank Center, Suite 2300, 200 South Orange Avenue.
Telephone: 305-841-1111.
In College Park, Maryland: 9658 Baltimore Boulevard, Suite 206.
Telephone: 301-441-2781.
In Alexandria, Virginia: 437 North Lee Street.
Telephone: 703-549-1294.
In San Francisco, California: One Sansome Street, Suite 2000.
Telephone: 415-951-4705.

PARTNERS

William F. Conroy
Kenneth J. Kies
H. Karl Zeswitz, Jr.

OF COUNSEL

Guy Vander Jagt (Not admitted in DC)

RETIRED PARTNER

Harlan Pomeroy

For Complete List of Firm Personnel, See General Section

For full biographical listings, see the Martindale-Hubbell Law Directory

* **BALLARD SPAHR ANDREWS & INGERSOLL** (AV)

Suite 900 East, 555 13th Street, N.W., 20004-1112
Telephone: 202-383-8800
Fax: 202-383-8877
Philadelphia, Pennsylvania Office: 1735 Market Street, 51st Floor.
Telephone: 215-665-8500.
Fax: 215-864-8999.

(See Next Column)

Denver, Colorado Office: Seventeenth Street Plaza Building, Suite 2300, 1225 17th Street.
Telephone: 303-292-2400.
Fax: 303-296-3956.
Kaunas, Lithuania Office: Donelaičio 71-2 Kaunas 3000.
Telephone: (370-7) 20 56 66.
Fax: (370-7) 20 56 91.
Salt Lake City, Utah Office: One Utah Center, 201 South Main Street, Suite 1200.
Telephone: 801-531-3000.
Fax: 801-531-3001.
Baltimore, Maryland Office: 300 East Lombard Street, 19th Floor.
Telephone: 410-528-5600.
Fax: 410-528-5650.
Camden, New Jersey Office: 800 Hudson Square, 5th Floor.
Telephone: 609-541-5577.
Fax: 609-541-8272.

Frederic L. Ballard, Jr.
Charles S. Henck

Linda B. Schakel

For Complete List of Firm Personnel, See General Section

For full biographical listings, see the Martindale-Hubbell Law Directory

CAPLIN & DRYSDALE, CHARTERED (AV)

One Thomas Circle, N.W., 20005
Telephone: 202-862-5000
Cable Address: "Capdale"
Telex: 904001 CAPL UR WSH
Fax: 202-429-3301
New York, N.Y. Office: 399 Park Avenue.
Telephone: 212-319-7125.
Fax: 212-644-6755.

Mortimer M. Caplin
Robert A. Klayman
Ralph A. Muoio
Elihu Inselbuch (Resident, New York Office)
Ronald B. Lewis
Richard W. Skillman
Patricia G. Lewis
Bernard S. Bailor
Stafford Smiley
Sally A. Regal
Julie W. Davis
Carl S. Kravitz
Robert A. Boisture
Charles T. Plambeck
Beth Shapiro Kaufman
Craig A. Sharon
James E. Salles
Paul G. Cellupica
Michael Doran (Not admitted in DC)
Dorothy L. Foley
Matthew W. Frank
Elizabeth M. Sellers (Not admitted in DC)
Douglas D. Drysdale
Thomas A. Troyer
David N. Webster
H. David Rosenbloom
Peter Van N. Lockwood
Cono R. Namorato
Daniel B. Rosenbaum
Richard E. Timbie
Graeme W. Bush
Albert G. Lauber, Jr.
Scott D. Michel
Kent A. Mason
Trevor W. Swett III
James Sottile, IV
Harry J. Hicks, III
C. Sanders McNew (Resident, New York Office)
Ann C. McMillan
Catherine E. Livingston
Christian R. Pastore (Resident, New York Office)
Nathan D. Finch
Jessica L. Goldstein

OF COUNSEL

Robert H. Elliott, Jr.
Milton Cerny
Myron C. Baum
Vivian L. Cavalieri

For full biographical listings, see the Martindale-Hubbell Law Directory

H. CLAYTON COOK, JR. (AV)

2828 Pennsylvania Avenue, N.W., 20007
Telephone: 202-338-8088
Rapifax: 202-338-1843
McLean, Virginia Office: 1011 Langley Hill Drive. 22101.
Telephone: 703-821-2468.
Rapifax: 703-821-2469.

For full biographical listings, see the Martindale-Hubbell Law Directory

CROSS, MURPHY, SMUCK & HOUSTON (AV)

1350 Connecticut Avenue, N.W., Suite 300, 20036
Telephone: 202-393-8668
Telecopier: 202-833-2351

MEMBERS OF FIRM

John W. Cross (1902-1971)
James Russell Murphy (1905-1986)
John C. Smuck
Stuart E. Houston

Reference: Crestar Bank, N.A.

For full biographical listings, see the Martindale-Hubbell Law Directory

Washington—Continued

DOW, LOHNES & ALBERTSON (AV)

Suite 500, 1255 Twenty-Third Street, N.W., 20037-1194
Telephone: 202-857-2500
Telecopier: (202) 857-2900
Atlanta, Georgia Office: One Ravinia Drive, Suite 1600.
Telephone: 404-901-8800.
Telecopier: (404) 901-8874.

MEMBERS OF THE FIRM

Corinne M. Antley
Richard L. Braunstein
Linda A. Fritts
Joyce Trimble Gwadz
David A. Hildebrandt
J. Michael Hines
John C. Jost
Paul R. Lang
Bernard J. Long, Jr.
Richard P. McHugh
John D. Ward

Andrea R. Biller
Alan S. Bloom
Michael A. Hepburn
Stephanie M. Loughlin
Mary McCarron McVey (Not admitted in DC)
Beth Davis Wilkinson

For Complete List of Firm Personnel, See General Section

For full biographical listings, see the Martindale-Hubbell Law Directory

*** FRIED, FRANK, HARRIS, SHRIVER & JACOBSON (AV)**

A Partnership including Professional Corporations
Suite 800, 1001 Pennsylvania Avenue, N.W., 20004-2505
Telephone: 202-639-7000
Cable Address: "Steric Washington"
Telex: 892406
Telecopy Rapifax: 202-639-7008
Zap Mail: 202-338-0110
New York, New York Office: One New York Plaza.
Telephone: 212-859-8000.
Cable Address: "Steric New York." W.U. Int.
Telex: 620223. W.U. Int.
Telex: 662119. W.U. Domestic: 128173.
Telecopier: 212-859-4000 (Dex 6200).
Los Angeles, California Office: 725 South Figueroa Street.
Telephone: 213- 689-5800.
London, England Office: 4 Chiswell Street, London EC1Y 4UP.
Telephone: 011-44-171-972-9600.
Fax: 011-44-171-972-9602.
Paris, France Office: 7, Rue Royale, 75008.
Telephone: (+331) 40-17-04-04.
Fax: (+331) 40-17-08-30.

WASHINGTON, D.C. PARTNERS

Peter V. Z. Cobb (Not admitted in DC)
Alan S. Kaden

OF COUNSEL

Martin D. Ginsburg (P.C.)

ASSOCIATES

Barry M. Faber
John D. Petro
Richard A. Wolfe

For Complete List of Firm Personnel, See General Section

For full biographical listings, see the Martindale-Hubbell Law Directory

HOGAN & HARTSON L.L.P. (AV)

Columbia Square, 555 13th Street, N.W., 20004-1109
Telephone: 202-637-5600
Telex: 89-2757
Cable Address: "Hogander Washington"
Fax: 202-637-5910
Brussels, Belgium Office: Avenue des Arts 41, 1040.
Telephone: (32.2) 505.09.11.
Fax: (32.2) 502.28.60.
London, England Office: Veritas House, 125 Finsbury Pavement, EC2A 1NQ.
Telephone: (44 171) 638.9595.
Fax: (44 171) 638.0884.
Moscow, Russia Office: 33/2 Usacheva Street, Building 3, 119048.
Telephone: (7095) 245-5190.
Fax: (7095) 245-5192.
Paris, France Office: Cabinet Wolfram: 14, rue Chauveau-Lagarde, 75008.
Telephone: (33-1) 44.71.97.00.
Fax: (33-1) 47.42.13.56.
Prague, Czech Republic Office: Opletalova 37, 110 00.
Telephone: (42-2) 2422-9009.
Fax: (42-2) 2421-5105.
Warsaw, Poland Office: Marszalkowska 6/6, 00-590.
Telephone: (48 2) 628 0201; Int'l (48) 3912 1413.
Fax: (48 2) 628 7787; Int'l (48) 3912 1511.
Baltimore, Maryland Office: 111 South Calvert Street, 16th Floor.
Telephone: 410-659-2700.
Fax: 410-539-6981.

(See Next Column)

Bethesda, Maryland Office: Two Democracy Center, Suite 720, 6903 Rockledge Drive.
Telephone: 301-493-0030.
Fax: 301-493-5169.
Colorado Springs, Colorado Office: 518 North Nevada Avenue, Suite 200.
Telephone: 719-635-5900.
Fax: 719-635-2847.
Denver, Colorado Office: One Tabor Center, Suite 1500, 1200 Seventeenth Street.
Telephone: 303-899-7300.
Fax: 303-899-7333.
McLean, Virginia Office: 8300 Greensboro Drive.
Telephone: 703-848-2600.
Fax: 703-448-7650.

MEMBERS OF FIRM

Deborah Taylor Ashford
Sara-Ann Determan
Prentiss E. Feagles
Mary L. Harmon
Robert H. Kapp
Timothy A. Lloyd
H. Todd Miller
William L. Neff
William C. Schmidt
John S. Stanton

COUNSEL

Howard S. Silver

OF COUNSEL

Seymour S. Mintz

ASSOCIATES

Donna Lady Alpi
Helene O. Cobb
Edward S. Desmarais, Jr.
Scott R. Lilienthal (Not admitted in DC)
Scott D. McClure
Lisa L. Poole
David A. Winter (Not admitted in DC)

For Complete List of Firm Personnel, See General Section

For full biographical listings, see the Martindale-Hubbell Law Directory

IVINS, PHILLIPS & BARKER, CHARTERED (AV)

Suite 600, 1700 Pennsylvania Avenue, N.W., 20006
Telephone: 202-393-7600
Fax: 202-347-4256

Jay W. Glasmann
Joseph E. McAndrews
H. Stewart Dunn, Jr.
Carroll J. Savage
Eric R. Fox
William L. Sollee
Carol K. Nickel
Leslie Jay Schneider
Robert H. Wellen
William R. Reiter
Kevin P. O'Brien
Michael F. Solomon
Daniel B. Stone
Patrick J. Smith
Michael R. Huffstetler
Laurie E. Keenan
Peter M. Daub

Jeffrey E. Moeller
Lee Meyer
Steven H. Witmer
Patricia G. Copeland
Rosina B. Barker
Claude B. Stansbury
John Bailey

For full biographical listings, see the Martindale-Hubbell Law Directory

*** JONES, DAY, REAVIS & POGUE (AV)**

Metropolitan Square, 1450 G Street, N.W., 20005-2088
Telephone: 202-879-3939
Cable Address: "Attorneys Washington"
Telex: W.U. (Domestic) 89-2410 ATTORNEYS WASH (International) 64363 ATTORNEYS WASH
Telecopier: 202-737-2832
In Atlanta, Georgia: 3500 One Peachtree Center, 303 Peachtree Street, N.E.
Telephone: 404-521-3939.
Cable Address: "Attorneys Atlanta".
Telex: 54-2711.
Telecopier: 404-581-8330.
In Brussels, Belgium: Avenue Louise 480, 7th Floor, B-1050 Brussels.
Telephone: 011-32-2-645-14-11.
Telecopier: 011-32-2-645-14-45.
In Chicago, Illinois: 77 West Wacker.
Telephone: 312-782-3939.
Telecopier: 312-782-8585.
In Cleveland, Ohio: North Point, 901 Lakeside Avenue.
Telephone: 216-586-3939.
Cable Address: "Attorneys Cleveland."
Telex: 980389.
Telecopier: 216-579-0212.
In Columbus, Ohio: 1900 Huntington Center.
Telephone: 614-469-3939.
Cable Address: "Attorneys Columbus."
Telecopier: 614-461-4198.
In Dallas, Texas: 2300 Trammell Crow Center, 2001 Ross Avenue.
Telephone: 214-220-3939.
Cable Address: "Attorneys Dallas."
Telex: 730852.
Telecopier: 214-969-5100.

(See Next Column)

JONES, DAY, REAVIS & POGUE, *Washington—Continued*

In Frankfurt, Germany: Triton Haus, Bockenheimer Landstrasse 42, 60323 Frankfurt am Main.
Telephone: 49-69-9726-3939.
Telecopier: 49-69-9726-3993.
In Geneva, Switzerland: 20, rue de Candolle.
Telephone: 011-41-22-320-2339.
Telecopier: 011-41-22-320-1232.
In Hong Kong: 1501 One Exchange Square, 8 Connaught Place.
Telephone: 011-852-2526-6895.
Telecopier: 011-852-2810-5787.
In Irvine, California: 2603 Main Street, Suite 900.
Telephone: 714-851-3939.
Telex: 194911 Lawyers LSA.
Telecopier: 714-553-7539.
In London, England: One Mount Street.
Telephone: 011-44-71-493-9361.
Cable Address: "Surgoe London WI."
Telecopier: 011-44-71-493-9666.
In Los Angeles, California: 555 West Fifth Street, Suite 4600.
Telephone: 213-489-3939.
Telex: 181439 UD.
Telecopier: 213-243-2539.
In New York, New York: 599 Lexington Avenue.
Telephone: 212-326-3939.
Cable Address: "JONESDAY NEWYORK."
Telex: 237013 JDRP UR.
Telecopier: 212-755-7306.
In Paris, France: 62, rue du Faubourg Saint-Honore.
Telephone: 011-33-1-44-71-3939.
Cable Address: "Surgoe Paris."
Telex: 290156 Surgoe.
Telecopier: 011-33-1-49-24-0471.
In Pittsburgh, Pennsylvania: 500 Grant Street, 31st Floor.
Telephone: 412-391-3939.
Cable Address: "Attorneys Pittsburgh".
Telecopier: 412-394-7959.
In Riyadh, Saudi Arabia: Law Offices of Saud M.A. Shawwaf, P.O. Box 2700.
Telephones: 011 (966-1) 465-6543, 011 (966-1) 464-8534 or 011 (966-1) 464-8540.
Telex: 401831 SAUCON SJ.
Telecopier: (966-1) 464-8480.
In Taipai, Taiwan: 8th Floor, 2 Tun Hwa South Road, Section 2.
Telephone: 011 (886-2) 704-6808.
Telecopier: 011 (886-2) 704-6791.
In Tokyo, Japan: Toranomon MT Building, 4th Floor, 10-3, Toranomon 3-Chome, Minato-Ku, Tokyo 105, Japan.
Telephone: 011-81-3-3433-3939.
Telecopier: 011-81-3-5401-2725.

MEMBERS OF FIRM IN WASHINGTON, D.C.

Joseph S. Iannucci
James T. O'Hara
Donald D. Kozusko
Lester W. Droller
Raymond J. Wiacek

ASSOCIATES

Charles V. Stewart
Candace A. Ridgway
James R. Saxenian

For Complete List of Firm Personnel, See General Section

For full biographical listings, see the Martindale-Hubbell Law Directory

* McDERMOTT, WILL & EMERY (AV)

A Partnership including Professional Corporations
1850 K Street, N.W., 20006-2296
Telephone: 202-887-8000
Telex: 253565 MILAM CGO
Facsimile: 202-778-8087
Chicago, Illinois Office: 227 West Monroe Street.
Telephone: 312-372-2000.
Telex: 253565 MILAM CGO.
Facsimile: 312-984-7700.
Boston, Massachusetts Office: 75 State Street, Suite 1700.
Telephone: 617-345-5000.
Telex: 951324 MILAM BSN.
Facsimile: 617-345-5077.
Miami, Florida Office: 201 South Biscayne Boulevard.
Telephone: 305-358-3500.
Telex: 441777 LEYES.
Facsimile: 305-347-6500.
Los Angeles, California Office: 2049 Century Park East.
Telephone: 310-277-4110.
Facsimile: 310-277-4730.
Newport Beach, California Office: 1301 Dove Street, Suite 500.
Telephone: 714-851-0633.
Facsimile: 714-851-9348.
New York, N.Y. Office: 1211 Avenue of the Americas.
Telephone: 212-768-5400.
Facsimile: 212-768-5444.

(See Next Column)

St. Petersburg, Russia Office: 2/2 Tchaikovsky Street, #517, 191187 St. Petersburg, Russia.
Telephone: (7) (812) 273-9831.
Facsimile: (7) (812) 273-9831.
Tallinn, Estonia Office: Tallinn Business Center, 6 Harju Street, EE0001 Tallinn, Estonia.
Telephone: 372 6 31-05-53.
Facsimile: 372 6 31-05-54.
Vilnius, Lithuania Office: Smetonos 6, 2600 Vilnius, Lithuania.
Telephone: 370 2 61-43-08.
Facsimile: 370 2 22-79-55.
Associated (Independent) Offices:
Brussels, Belgium: Uettwiller Grelon Lippens Dekeyser, 73 avenue Vandendriessche, 1150 Brussels, Belgium.
Telephone: (32) (2) 772-87-50.
Facsimile: (32) (2) 772-87-52.
London, England: Paisner & Co, Bouverie House, 154 Fleet Street, London EC4A 2DQ, England.
Telephone: (44) (71) 353-0299.
Facsimile: (44) (71) 583-8621.
Paris, France: Uettwiller Grelon Gout Canat & Associes, 68, boulevard de Courcelles, 75017 Paris, France.
Telephone: (33) (1) 48 88 89 00.
Facsimile: (33) (1) 48 88 05 50.

MEMBERS OF FIRM

Matthew T. Adams
James M. Boyle
Robert Feldgarden
Jennifer Britt Giannattasio (Not admitted in DC)
William L. Goldman
Mary B. Hevener
Thomas M. Ingoldsby
Gregory F. Jenner
Christopher Kliefoth
Philip A. McCarty
J. Gary McDavid
Evan M. Migdail
James A. Riedy
Stephen E. Wells
T. Raymond Williams
Jane E. Wilson

COUNSEL

Robert G. Kalik
Phoebe A. Mix
Ralph I. Petersberger

Marianna G. Dyson

*Denotes a lawyer employed by a Professional Corporation which is a member of the Firm

For Complete List of Firm Personnel, See General Section

For full biographical listings, see the Martindale-Hubbell Law Directory

MILLER & CHEVALIER, CHARTERED (AV)

655 Fifteenth Street, N.W., Suite 900, 20005-5701
Telephone: 202-626-5800
Fax: 202-628-0858

John Stephan Nolan
John Mourer Bixler
Robert L. Moore, II
Lawrence B. Gibbs (Not admitted in DC)
Phillip L. Mann
A. John Gabig
Dennis P. Bedell
Jay L. Carlson
F. Brook Voght
Frederick H. Robinson
John B. Magee
Alexander Zakupowsky, Jr.
C. Frederick Oliphant III
Ronald D. Aucutt
Thomas D. Johnston
Richard C. Stark
Catherine Tift Porter
David B. Cubeta
Thomas W. Mahoney, Jr.
Anne E. Moran
Robert E. Liles, II
Patricia J. Sweeney
J. Bradford Anwyll
F. Scott Farmer
Robert A. Katcher
Catherine Veihmeyer Hughes
Kevin L. Kenworthy
Patricia M. Lacey

COUNSEL

David W. Richmond
Numa L. Smith, Jr.
Charles T. Akre

Christopher S. Rizek
Joseph B. Kennedy
Catherine L. Creech
Jean A. Pawlow
Helen M. Hubbard (Not admitted in DC)
Susan G. Whitman
Bruce A. Cohen
Elizabeth P. Askey
Suzanne M. Papiewski
S. Kelly Myers
Elizabeth F. Judge
Rhonda Nesmith Crichlow (Not admitted in DC)
Michael E. Baillif
Carla McKitten Seebald (Not admitted in DC)

For Complete List of Firm Personnel, See General Section

For full biographical listings, see the Martindale-Hubbell Law Directory

Washington—Continued

STEPTOE & JOHNSON (AV)

1330 Connecticut Avenue, N.W., 20036
Telephone: 202-429-3000
Cable Address: "Stepjohn"
Telex: 89-2503
Telecopier: 202-429-3902
Phoenix, Arizona Office: Two Renaissance Square, 40 N. Central Avenue, Suite 2400, 85004.
Telephone: 602-257-5200.
Moscow, Russia Office: Steptoe & Johnson International Affiliate in Moscow. 25 Tsvetnoy Boulevard, Building 3 Moscow, Russia 103051.
Telephone: 011-7-501-929-9700.
Fax: 501-929-9701.

MEMBERS

James P. Holden
Matthew J. Zinn
Shirley D. Peterson
Theodore E. Rhodes
Mark J. Silverman
Arthur L. Bailey
Susan H. Serling
Blake D. Rubin
Melanie F. Nussdorf
J. Walker Johnson
Carol A. Rhees
Kevin M. Keyes

OF COUNSEL

William K. Condrell

For Complete List of Firm Personnel, See General Section

For full biographical listings, see the Martindale-Hubbell Law Directory

SUTHERLAND, ASBILL & BRENNAN (AV)

1275 Pennsylvania Avenue, N.W., 20004-2404
Telephone: 202-383-0100
Cable Address: "Sutab Wash"
Telex: 89-501
Facsimile: 202-637-3593
Atlanta, Georgia Office: 999 Peachtree Street, N. E., 30309-3996.
Telephone: 404-853-8000.
New York, N.Y. Office: 1270 Avenue of the Americas, 10020-1700.
Telephone: 212-332-3000.
Austin, Texas Office: 111 Congress Avenue, 23rd Floor, 78701-4079.
Telephone: 512-469-3350.

George H. Bostick
William W. Chip
N. Jerold Cohen
William S. Corey
James L. Dahlberg
Warren N. Davis
Thomas A. Gick
James V. Heffernan
Jerome B. Libin
Michael R. Miles
Clifford E. Muller
Gordon O. Pehrson, Jr.
Lloyd Leva Plaine
G. Garner Prillaman, Jr.
Richard J. Safranek
Bradley M. Seltzer
W. Mark Smith
Randolph W. Thrower

For Complete List of Firm Personnel, See General Section

For full biographical listings, see the Martindale-Hubbell Law Directory

VERNER, LIIPFERT, BERNHARD, MCPHERSON AND HAND, CHARTERED (AV)

901 15th Street, N.W., 20005-2301
Telephone: 202-371-6000
Cable Address: "Verlip"
Telex: 1561792 VERLIP UT
Fax: 202-371-6279
McLean, Virginia Office: Sixth Floor, 8280 Greensboro Drive, 22102.
Telephone: 703-749-6000.
Fax: 703-749-6027.
Houston, Texas Office: 2600 Texas Commerce Tower, 600 Travis, 77002.
Telephone: 713-237-9034.
Fax: 713-237-1216.

Michael D. Golden
Frederick J. Tansill
Susan O'Hearn Temkin

OF COUNSEL

Mikol S. B. Neilson

For Complete List of Firm Personnel, See General Section

For full biographical listings, see the Martindale-Hubbell Law Directory

WILLIAMS & CONNOLLY (AV)

725 Twelfth Street, N.W., 20005
Telephone: 202-434-5000

MEMBERS OF FIRM

Lewis H. Ferguson, III
James T. Fuller, III
Mary Greer Clark
Sven Erik Holmes

Lon E. Musslewhite

(See Next Column)

OF COUNSEL

Lyman G. Friedman

For Complete List of Firm Personnel, See General Section

For full biographical listings, see the Martindale-Hubbell Law Directory

WILMER, CUTLER & PICKERING (AV)

2445 M Street, N.W., 20037-1420
Telephone: 202-663-6000
Facsimile: 202-663-6363
Internet: Law@Wilmer.Com
European Offices:
4 Carlton Gardens, London, SW1Y 5AA, England. Telephone: 011 (4471) 839-4466.
Facsimile: 011 (4471) 839-3537.
Rue de la Loi 15 Wetstraat, B-1040 Brussels, Belgium. Telephone: 011 (322) 231-0903.
Facsimile: 011 (322) 230-4322.
Friedrichstrasse 95, D-10117 Berlin, Germany. Telephone: 011 (4930) 2643-3601.
Facsimile: 011 (4930) 2643-3630.

MEMBERS OF FIRM

F. David Lake, Jr.
Kenneth W. Gideon
William J. Wilkins
Terrill A. Hyde
Bryan Slone (Not admitted in DC; Resident, European Office, Berlin, Germany)

SPECIAL COUNSEL

R. Scott Kilgore

For Complete List of Firm Personnel, See General Section

For full biographical listings, see the Martindale-Hubbell Law Directory

ZUCKERMAN, SPAEDER, GOLDSTEIN, TAYLOR & KOLKER (AV)

1201 Connecticut Avenue, N.W., 20036
Telephone: 202-778-1800
Fax: 202-822-8106
Miami, Florida Office: Zuckerman, Spaeder, Taylor & Evans. Suite 900, Miami Center, 201 South Biscayne Boulevard.
Telephones: 305-358-5000; 305-579-0110; Broward County: 305-523-0277.
Fax: 305-579-9749.
Ft. Lauderdale, Florida Office: Zuckerman, Spaeder, Taylor & Evans. One East Broward Boulevard, Suite 700.
Telephone: 305-356-0463.
Fax: 305-356-0406.
Baltimore, Maryland Office: Zuckerman, Spaeder, Goldstein, Taylor & Better. Suite 2440, 100 East Pratt Street.
Telephone: 410-332-0444.
Fax: 410-659-0436.
Tampa, Florida Office: Zuckerman, Spaeder, Taylor & Evans. 101 East Kennedy Boulevard, Suite 3140.
Telephone: 813-221-1010.
Fax: 813-223-7961.
New York, N.Y. Office: 1114 Avenue of the Americas, 45th Floor, Grace Building.
Telephone: 212-479-6500.
Fax: 212-479-6512.

MEMBERS OF FIRM

Arthur K. Mason
Eric F. Facer

ASSOCIATES

Ellen K. Fishbein
Maria A. Stamoulas
Loren Bendall

Reference: Sovran Bank/DC National.

For full biographical listings, see the Martindale-Hubbell Law Directory

FLORIDA

BOCA RATON, Palm Beach Co.

RONALD T. MARTIN, P.A. (AV)

Suite 404, 7000 West Palmetto Park Road, 33433
Telephone: 407-338-4100
Fax: 407-338-9086

Ronald T. Martin

For full biographical listings, see the Martindale-Hubbell Law Directory

BOYNTON BEACH, Palm Beach Co.

ROBERT M. ARLEN, P.A. (AV)

Suite 200, 1501 Corporate Drive, 33426
Telephone: 407-734-9977
Broward Line: 305-781-7822
Telefax: 407-734-7511

(See Next Column)

ROBERT M. ARLEN, P.A., *Boynton Beach—Continued*

Robert M. Arlen

For full biographical listings, see the Martindale-Hubbell Law Directory

*BRADENTON,** Manatee Co.

GRIMES, GOEBEL, GRIMES & HAWKINS, P.A. (AV)

The Professional Building, 1023 Manatee Avenue West, P.O. Box 1550, 34206
Telephone: 813-748-0151
Fax: 813-748-0158

William C. Grimes

John F. Jewell

Counsel for: First Commercial Bank of Manatee County; First Federal Savings & Loan Association of Florida; Schroeder-Manatee, Inc.
Approved Attorneys for: Chicago Title Insurance Co.; Attorneys' Title Insurance Fund; American Pioneer Title Insurance Co.

For Complete List of Firm Personnel, See General Section

For full biographical listings, see the Martindale-Hubbell Law Directory

*FORT LAUDERDALE,** Broward Co.

BERGER, SHAPIRO & DAVIS, P.A. (AV)

Suite 400, 100 N.E. 3rd Avenue, 33301
Telephone: 305-525-9900
Fax: 305-523-2872

James L. Berger
Mitchell W. Berger
James B. Davis
Manuel Kushner
Leonard K. Samuels
Laz L. Schneider

Thomas L. Abrams
Melissa P. Anderson
Lawrence C. Callaway, III
Nick Jovanovich
Robert B. Judd
Brent L. Moody
Terri E. Tuchman

OF COUNSEL

Franklin H. Caplan
Kenneth W. Shapiro

For full biographical listings, see the Martindale-Hubbell Law Directory

LARRY V. BISHINS, P.A. (AV)

4548 North Federal Highway, 33308-5271
Telephone: Broward: 305-772-7900
Palm Beach: 407-732-5809
Facsimile: 305-772-7924
National Watts Line: 1-800-940-4TAX

Larry V. Bishins

Reference: NationsBank of Florida, N.A.

For full biographical listings, see the Martindale-Hubbell Law Directory

*FORT MYERS,** Lee Co.

HENDERSON, FRANKLIN, STARNES & HOLT, PROFESSIONAL ASSOCIATION (AV)

1715 Monroe Street, P.O. Box 280, 33902-0280
Telephone: 813-334-4121
Telecopier: 813-332-4494

William N. Horowitz
Guy E. Whitesman
James E. Kane

Representative Clients: Aetna Life & Casualty Group; CIGNA Group; CSX Transportation, Inc.; Fireman's Fund Insurance Cos.; Barnett Bank of Lee County, N.A.; Northern Trust Bank of Florida, N.A.; The Hartford Insurance Group; Travelers Group; United Telephone Company of Florida.

For Complete List of Firm Personnel, See General Section

For full biographical listings, see the Martindale-Hubbell Law Directory

SMOOT ADAMS EDWARDS & GREEN, P.A. (AV)

One University Park Suite 600, 12800 University Drive, P.O. Box 60259, 33906-6259
Telephone: 813-489-1776
(800) 226-1777 (in Florida)
Fax: 813-489-2444

J. Tom Smoot, Jr.
Hal Adams
Bruce D. Green
Steven I. Winer
Mark R. Komray
Thomas P. Clark

Lynne E. Denneler
Clayton W. Crevasse
M. Brian Cheffer
Robert S. Forman
Thomas M. Howell
Plutarco M. Villalobos
Lowell Schoenfeld

For Complete List of Firm Personnel, See General Section

For full biographical listings, see the Martindale-Hubbell Law Directory

*JACKSONVILLE,** Duval Co.

KENNETH G. ANDERSON (AV)

Suite 2540, Riverplace Tower, 1301 Riverplace Boulevard, 32207-9039
Telephone: 904-399-8000
Telecopier: 904-346-3078

ASSOCIATES

James P. Stevens
Robert G. Hicks

For full biographical listings, see the Martindale-Hubbell Law Directory

DONAHOO, DONAHOO & BALL, P.A. (AV)

(Incorporated in 1981)
2925 Barnett Center, 50 North Laura Street, 32202
Telephone: 904-354-8080
Fax: 904-791-9563

John W. Donahoo (1907-1993)
Thomas M. Donahoo
Haywood M. Ball
William B. McMenamy
Bruce D. Johnson

For full biographical listings, see the Martindale-Hubbell Law Directory

FRAZIER & FRAZIER, ATTORNEYS AT LAW, P.A. (AV)

Suite A 1515 Riverside Avenue, 32204
Telephone: 904-353-5616
Fax: 904-353-5619

William R. Frazier
W. Robinson Frazier

References: First Union National Bank of Florida; Barnett Bank of Jacksonville, N.A.; Enterprise National Bank of Jacksonville; First Guaranty Bank & Trust Co.

JUPITER, Palm Beach Co.

JOSEPH C. KEMPE PROFESSIONAL ASSOCIATION (AV)

Attorneys and Counselors at Law
American Plaza, Suite 400, 1070 East Indiantown Road, 33477-5111
Telephone: 407-747-7300
FAX: 407-747-7722
Stuart, Florida Office: Royal Palm Financial Center II, Suite 200, 789 South Federal Highway.
Telephone: 407-223-0700.
Fax: 407-223-0707.
Vero Beach, Florida Office: Suite B, 664 Azalea Lane.
Telephone: 407-562-4022.
Fax: 407-234-1422.

Joseph C. Kempe

David Pratt
Lesley Hogan

OF COUNSEL

Ann L. Vano

For full biographical listings, see the Martindale-Hubbell Law Directory

*KISSIMMEE,** Osceola Co.

POHL & BROWN, P.A.

(See Winter Park)

LAKELAND, Polk Co.

PETERSON, MYERS, CRAIG, CREWS, BRANDON & PUTERBAUGH, P.A. (AV)

100 East Main Street, P.O. Box 24628, 33802-4628
Telephone: 813-683-6511; 676-6934
Telecopier: 813-682-8031
Lake Wales, Florida Office: 130 East Central Avenue, P.O. Box 1079.
Telephones: 813-676-7611; 683-8942.
Winter Haven, Florida Office: Suite 300, 141 5th Street, N.W., P.O. Drawer 7608.
Telephone: 813-294-3360

Jack P. Brandon
Beach A Brooks, Jr.
J. Davis Connor
Roy A. Craig, Jr.
Jacob C. Dykxhoorn
Dennis P. Johnson
Kevin C. Knowlton
Douglas A. Lockwood, III
Corneal B. Myers
Cornelius B. Myers, III
Robert E. Puterbaugh
Abel A. Putnam

(See Next Column)

PETERSON, MYERS, CRAIG, CREWS, BRANDON & PUTERBAUGH P.A.—*Continued*

Thomas B. Putnam, Jr.
Deborah A. Ruster
Stephen R. Senn
Andrea Teves Smith
Kerry M. Wilson

General Counsel For: Barnett Bank of Polk County.
Representative Clients: Mutual Wholesale Co.; Sun Bank/Mid-Florida, N.A.; Chase Commercial Corp.; Barnett Banks, Inc.; Ben Hill Griffin, Inc.
Approved Attorneys For: Equitable Life Assurance Society of the United States; Federal Land Bank of Columbia, S.C.; Attorneys' Title Insurance Fund.

For full biographical listings, see the Martindale-Hubbell Law Directory

LAKE WALES, Polk Co.

PETERSON, MYERS, CRAIG, CREWS, BRANDON & PUTERBAUGH, P.A. (AV)
130 East Central Avenue, P.O. Box 1079, 33853
Telephone: 813-676-7611; 683-8942
Telecopier: 813-676-0643
Lakeland, Florida Office: 100 East Main Street, P.O. Box 24628.
Telephones: 813-683-6511; 676-6934.
Winter Haven, Florida Office: Suite 300, 141 5th Street, N.W., P.O. Drawer 7608.
Telephone: 813-294-3360.

Jack P. Brandon
Beach A Brooks, Jr.
Beach A Brooks, Jr.
J. Davis Connor
Roy A. Craig, Jr.
Jacob C. Dykxhoorn
Dennis P. Johnson
Kevin C. Knowlton
Douglas A. Lockwood, III
Corneal B. Myers
Cornelius B. Myers, III
Robert E. Puterbaugh
Robert E. Puterbaugh
Abel A. Putnam
Thomas B. Putnam, Jr.
Deborah A. Ruster
Stephen R. Senn
Andrea Teves Smith
Kerry M. Wilson

General Counsel for: Barnett Bank of Polk County.
Representative Clients: Mutual Wholesale Co.; Sun Bank/Mid-Florida, N.A.; Chase Commercial Corp.; Barnett Banks, Inc.; Ben Hill Griffin, Inc.; Alcoma Association, Inc.
Approved Attorneys for: Equitable Life Assurance Society of the United States; Federal Land Bank of Columbia, S.C.; Attorneys' Title Insurance Fund.

For full biographical listings, see the Martindale-Hubbell Law Directory

*MIAMI,** Dade Co.

BREIER AND SEIF, P.A. (AV)
1320 South Dixie Highway (Coral Gables), 33146-2986
Telephone: 305-667-0046; 667-0065
Telecopier: 305-667-3071

Robert G. Breier
Evan D. Seif

For full biographical listings, see the Martindale-Hubbell Law Directory

FOWLER, WHITE, BURNETT, HURLEY, BANICK & STRICKROOT, A PROFESSIONAL ASSOCIATION (AV)
International Place, Seventeenth Floor, 100 S.E. Second Street, 33131
Telephone: 305-358-6550
Cable Address: "Fowhite"
Telex: 6811696

Stuart H. Altman
Jonathan H. Warner

Reference: City National Bank.

For Complete List of Firm Personnel, See General Section

For full biographical listings, see the Martindale-Hubbell Law Directory

MERSHON, SAWYER, JOHNSTON, DUNWODY & COLE (AV)
A Partnership including Professional Associations
Suite 4500 First Union Financial Center, 200 South Biscayne Boulevard, 33131-2387
Telephone: 305-358-5100
Cable Address: "Mercole"
Telex: 515705
Fax: 305-376-8654
Naples, Florida Office: Pelican Bay Corporate Centre, Suite 501, 5551 Ridgewood Drive.
Telephone: 813-598-1055.
Fax: 813-598-1868.
West Palm Beach, Florida Office: 777 South Flagler Drive, Suite 900.
Telephone: 407-659-5990.
Fax: 407-659-6313.
Key West, Florida Office: 3132 North Side Drive, Suite 102.
Telephone: 305-296-1774.
Fax: 305-296-1715

(See Next Column)

London, England Office: Blake Lodge, Bridge Lane, London SW11 3AD, England.
Telephone: 44-71-978-7748.
Fax: 44-71-350-0156.

MEMBER OF FIRM

Henry H. Raattama, Jr., (P.A.)

OF COUNSEL

John D. Armstrong (1918-1992)

Representative Clients: Arvida/JMB Partners; Bankers Trust Co.; Biscayne Kennel Club, Inc.; The Chase Manhattan Bank, N.A.; Lennar Corp.; Reynolds Metals Co.; United States Sugar Corp.; University of Miami.

For Complete List of Firm Personnel, See General Section

For full biographical listings, see the Martindale-Hubbell Law Directory

SHUTTS & BOWEN (AV)
A Partnership including Professional Associations
1500 Miami Center, 201 South Biscayne Boulevard, 33131
Telephone: 305-358-6300
Cable Address: "Shuttsbo"
Telefax: 305-381-9982
Key Largo, Florida Office: Suite A206, 31 Ocean Reef Drive.
Telephone: 305-367-2881.
Orlando, Florida Office: 20 North Orange Avenue, Suite 1000.
Telephone: 407-423-3200.
Fax: 407-425-8316.
West Palm Beach, Florida Office: One Clearlake Centre, 250 Australian Avenue South, Suite 500.
Telephone: 407-835-8500.
Fax: 407-650-8530.
Amsterdam, The Netherlands Office: Shutts & Bowen, B.V., Europa Boulevard 59, 1083 AD, Amsterdam.
Telephone: (31 20) 661-0969.
Fax: (31 20) 642-1475.
London, England Office: 48 Mount Street, London W1Y 5RE.
Telephone: 4471493-4840.
Telefax: 4471493-4299.

MEMBERS OF FIRM

Robert E. Gunn (P.A.) (Resident at West Palm Beach Office)
Marvin A. Kirsner (Resident at West Palm Beach Office)
Louis Nostro
Stephen L. Perrone (P.A.)
Raul J. Salas
Rosemarie N. Sanderson Schade (P.A.) (Resident at Amsterdam, The Netherlands)
John B. White (P.A.)

ASSOCIATE

Christopher W. Boyett

OF COUNSEL

Jordan Bittel (P.A.)
Marshall J. Langer (P.A.) (Resident, London, England Office)

For Complete List of Firm Personnel, See General Section

For full biographical listings, see the Martindale-Hubbell Law Directory

SPARBER, KOSNITZKY, TRUXTON, DE LA GUARDIA SPRATT & BROOKS, P.A. (AV)
1401 Brickell Avenue Suite 700, 33131
Telephone: Dade: 305-379-7200; Broward: 305-760-9133
Fax: 305-379-0800

Byron L. Sparber
Michael Kosnitzky

Jorge A. Gonzalez
Thomas O. Wells
Deborah R. Mayo

For Complete List of Firm Personnel, See General Section

For full biographical listings, see the Martindale-Hubbell Law Directory

SPENCER AND KLEIN, PROFESSIONAL ASSOCIATION (AV)
Suite 1901, 801 Brickell Avenue, 33131
Telephone: 305-374-7700
Telecopier: 305-374-4890

Thomas R. Spencer, Jr.
Brent D. Klein

Representative Clients: America Publishing Group; Amerivend Corp.; Buen Hogar Magazine; Editorial America; Gold Star Medical Management, Inc.; Grupo Anaya, S.A.; Independent Living Care, Inc.; Lourdes Health Services, Inc.; Managed Care of America, Inc.

For Complete List of Firm Personnel, See General Section

For full biographical listings, see the Martindale-Hubbell Law Directory

Miami—Continued

TESCHER CHAVES HOCHMAN RUBIN & MULLER, P.A. (AV)

One Datran Center-Penthouse I, 9100 South Dadeland Boulevard, 33156
Telephone: 305-670-0444
Broward: 800-782-6392
Fax: 305-670-0734
Ft. Lauderdale, Florida Office: Trade Centre South. 100 W. Cypress Creek Road, Suite 900. 33309.
Telephone: Miami: 305-938-4555; 800-938-938-4555.
Fax: 305-935-9555.

Robert A. Chaves
Deborah Plaks Hochman
Charles E. Muller, II
Charles D. Rubin
Donald R. Tescher

OF COUNSEL

Dale A. Heckerling

For full biographical listings, see the Martindale-Hubbell Law Directory

THOMSON MURARO RAZOOK & HART, P.A. (AV)

17th Floor, One Southeast Third Avenue, 33131
Telephone: 305-350-7200
Telecopier: 305-374-1005

Robert E. Muraro
Richard J. Razook

Representative Clients: United States Sugar Corp.; Quotron Systems, Inc.; Bacardi; The Exotic Gardens, Inc.

For Complete List of Firm Personnel, See General Section

For full biographical listings, see the Martindale-Hubbell Law Directory

MIAMI BEACH, Dade Co.

THERREL BAISDEN & MEYER WEISS (AV)

Suite 500 Sun Bank/Miami, 1111 Lincoln Road Mall, 33139
Telephone: 305-672-1921
Telecopier: 305-674-0807

MEMBERS OF FIRM

Catchings Therrel (1890-1971)
Fred R. Baisden (1903-1971)
Baron De Hirsch Meyer (1899-1974)
Milton Weiss (1913-1980)
L. Jules Arkin
Nicholas M. Daniels
Ellen Rose
Leo Rose, Jr.
Fred R. Stanton
Richard A. Wood

ASSOCIATES

Jonathan Feuerman
Joseph B. Ryan, III (Resident, Miami, Florida Office)
Peter M. Lopez

OF COUNSEL

David Darlow
Bruce E. Lazar
Mark E. Pollack

General Counsel: Chase Federal Bank; Miami Postal Service Credit Union; Jefferson National Bank Trust Department; American Equity Site Developers.
Counsel for: City Planned Communities Corp.; Anthony Abraham Chevrolet.

For full biographical listings, see the Martindale-Hubbell Law Directory

*NAPLES,** Collier Co.

CATALANO, FISHER, GREGORY, CROWN & SULLIVAN, CHARTERED (AV)

Northern Trust Building, Suite 404, 4001 Tamiami Trail North, 33940
Telephone: 813-262-8000
Telecopier: 813-262-4372

Anthony J. Catalano
A. Alston Fisher, Jr.
C. Neil Gregory
Howard L. Crown
John L. Sullivan, Jr.

OF COUNSEL

Mark V. Silverio
William deForest Thompson

For full biographical listings, see the Martindale-Hubbell Law Directory

JAMES W. ELKINS, P.A. (AV)

Suite 303 The Fairway Building, 1000 Tamiami Trail North, 33940
Telephone: 813-263-0910
Fax: 813-263-6091

James W. Elkins

Approved Attorney for: Attorneys Title Insurance Fund.

For full biographical listings, see the Martindale-Hubbell Law Directory

VEGA, BROWN, STANLEY, MARTIN & ZELMAN, P.A. (AV)

2660 Airport Road, South, 33962
Telephone: 813-774-3333
Fax: 813-774-6420

(See Next Column)

Michael G. Moore

General Counsel for: Lely Estates; Naples Community Hospital.
Local Counsel: Fleischmann Trust; Quail Creek Developments.

For Complete List of Firm Personnel, See General Section

For full biographical listings, see the Martindale-Hubbell Law Directory

NORTH MIAMI BEACH, Dade Co.

BUCHANAN INGERSOLL, PROFESSIONAL CORPORATION (AV)

One Turnberry Place, 19495 Biscayne Boulevard, 33180
Telephone: 305-933-5600
Telecopier: 305-933-2350
Pittsburgh, Pennsylvania Office: 5800 USX Tower, 600 Grant Street.
Telephone: 412-562-8800.
Philadelphia, Pennsylvania Office: Two Logan Square, Twelfth Floor, 18th & Arch Streets.
Telephone: 215-665-8700.
Harrisburg, Pennsylvania Office: Vartan Parc, 30 North Third Street.
Telephone: 717-237-4800.
Tampa, Florida Office: Suite 1030, 101 East Kennedy Boulevard.
Telephone: 813-222-8180.
Princeton, New Jersey Office: Buchanan Ingersoll, A Partnership, College Centre, 500 College Road East.
Telephone: 609-452-2666.
Lexington, Kentucky Office: Suite 600, PNC Bank Plaza, 200 West Vine Street.
Telephone: 606-225-5333.

Barry A. Nelson

For Complete List of Firm Personnel, See General Section

For full biographical listings, see the Martindale-Hubbell Law Directory

ORANGE PARK, Clay Co.

HEAD, SMITH, METCALF, AGUILAR, MOSS & SIERON, P.A. (AV)

1329A Kingsley Avenue, P.O. Box 855, 32073
Telephone: 904-264-6000
Fax: 904-264-9223

Robert J. Head, Jr.
Larry Smith
Frank B. Metcalf
Robert Aguilar
John B. Moss
Mark A. Sieron

Holly Fulton Perritt

For full biographical listings, see the Martindale-Hubbell Law Directory

*ORLANDO,** Orange Co.

BAKER & HOSTETLER (AV)

SunBank Center, Suite 2300, 200 South Orange Avenue, 32802-3432
Telephone: 407-649-4000
In Cleveland, Ohio: 3200 National City Center, 1900 East Ninth Street.
Telephone: 216-621-0200.
In Columbus, Ohio: Capitol Square, Suite 2100, 65 East State Street.
Telephone: 614-228-1541.
In Denver, Colorado: 303 East 17th Avenue, Suite 1100.
Telephone: 303-861-0600.
In Houston, Texas: 1000 Louisiana, Suite 2000.
Telephone: 713-751-1600.
In Long Beach, California: 300 Oceangate, Suite 620.
Telephone: 310-432-2827.
In Los Angeles, California: 600 Wilshire Boulevard.
Telephone: 213-624-2400.
In Washington, D.C.: Washington Square, Suite 1100, 1050 Connecticut Avenue, N.W., Suite 1100.
Telephone: 202-861-1500.
In College Park, Maryland: 9658 Baltimore Boulevard, Suite 206.
Telephone: 301-441-2781.
In Alexandria, Virginia: 437 North Lee Street.
Telephone: 703-549-1294.
In San Francisco, California: One Sansome Street, Suite 2000.
Telephone: 415-951-4705.

PARTNER

Joel H. Sharp, Jr.

ASSOCIATE

Daniel F. Hogan (Not admitted in FL)

For Complete List of Firm Personnel, See General Section

For full biographical listings, see the Martindale-Hubbell Law Directory

Orlando—Continued

HONIGMAN MILLER SCHWARTZ AND COHN (AV)

A Partnership including Professional Corporations
390 North Orange Avenue, Suite 1300, 32801-1632
Telephone: 407-648-0300
Telecopier: 407-648-1155
West Palm Beach, Florida Office: Suite 800 Esperante Building, 222 Lakeview Avenue.
Telephone: 407-838-4500.
Tampa, Florida Office: 2700 Landmark Centre, 401 E. Jackson Street.
Telephone: 813-221-6600.
Detroit, Michigan Office: 2290 First National Building.
Telephone: 313-256-7800.
Lansing, Michigan Office: 222 North Washington Square, Suite 400.
Telephone: 517-484-8282.
Houston, Texas Office: 3100 First Interstate Bank Plaza, 1000 Louisiana.
Telephone: 713-650-2600.
Los Angeles, California Office: Watt Plaza, Suite 2200, 1875 Century Park East.
Telephone: 310-789-3800.
Fax: 310-789-3814.

MEMBER
Brad M. Tomtishen

For Complete List of Firm Personnel, See General Section

For full biographical listings, see the Martindale-Hubbell Law Directory

POHL & BROWN, P.A.

(See Winter Park)

PALM BEACH, Palm Beach Co.

BAUGHER, METTLER & SHELTON (AV)

340 Royal Poinciana Plaza, P.O. Box 109, 33480
Telephone: 407-833-9631
Fax: 407-655-2835

MEMBERS OF FIRM

Thomas M. Mettler
John W. Shelton

ASSOCIATES

Francis X. J. Lynch
Pamela A. Markley

Reference: First National Bank in Palm Beach.

For full biographical listings, see the Martindale-Hubbell Law Directory

MURPHY, REID & PILOTTE, P.A. (AV)

340 Royal Palm Way, 33480
Telephone: 407-655-4060
Facsimile: 407-832-5436
Vero Beach, Florida Office: Plantation Plaza, 6606-20th Street, P.O. Drawer M.
Telephone: 407-567-6480.
Facsimile: 407-562-0220.

Frank T. Pilotte

For Complete List of Firm Personnel, See General Section

For full biographical listings, see the Martindale-Hubbell Law Directory

*SARASOTA,** Sarasota Co.

WILLIAMS, PARKER, HARRISON, DIETZ & GETZEN, PROFESSIONAL ASSOCIATION (AV)

1550 Ringling Boulevard, 34230-3258
Telephone: 813-366-4800
Telecopier: 813-366-5109
Mailing Address: P.O. Box 3258, Sarasota, Florida, 34230-3258

William T. Harrison, Jr.
George A. Dietz
Monte K. Marshall
James L. Ritchey
Hugh McPheeters, Jr.
William G. Lambrecht
John T. Berteau
John V. Cannon, III
Charles D. Bailey, Jr.
J. Michael Hartenstine
Michele Boardman Grimes
James L. Turner
William M. Seider
Elizabeth C. Marshall
Robert W. Benjamin
Frank Strelec
David A. Wallace
Terri Jayne Salt
Jeffrey A. Grebe
John Leslie Moore
Mark A. Schwartz
Susan Barrett Jewell
Phillip D. Eck

OF COUNSEL

Frazer F. Hilder
William E. Getzen
Elvin W. Phillips

Counsel for: Sarasota-Manatee Airport Authority; Sarasota County Public Hospital Board; William G. & Marie Selby Foundation; Taylor Woodrow Homes Ltd.; The School Board of Sarasota County.
Local Counsel for: NationsBank of Florida; Arvida/JMB Partners.

(See Next Column)

For Complete List of Firm Personnel, See General Section

For full biographical listings, see the Martindale-Hubbell Law Directory

*STUART,** Martin Co.

JOSEPH C. KEMPE PROFESSIONAL ASSOCIATION (AV)

Attorneys and Counselors at Law
Royal Palm Financial Center II, Suite 200, 789 South Federal Highway, 34994
Telephone: 407-223-0700
FAX: 407-223-0707
Jupiter, Florida Office: American Plaza, Suite 400, 1070 East Indiantown Road. Telephone 407-747-7300.
Fax: 407-747-7722.
Vero Beach, Florida Office: 664 Azalea Lane, Suite B.
Telephone: 407-562-4022.
Fax: 407-234-1422.

Joseph C. Kempe

For full biographical listings, see the Martindale-Hubbell Law Directory

*TAMPA,** Hillsborough Co.

KALISH & WARD, PROFESSIONAL ASSOCIATION (AV)

4100 Barnett Plaza, 101 East Kennedy Boulevard, P.O. Box 71, 33601-0071
Telephone: 813-222-8700
Facsimile: 813-222-8701

William Kalish
Alton C. Ward
Richard A. Schlosser
Roger J. Rovell
Michael A. Bedke
William T. Harrison, III
Thomas P. McNamara
Robert Reid Haney
Charles H. Carver
Kelley A. Bosecker

For full biographical listings, see the Martindale-Hubbell Law Directory

LANGFORD, HILL & TRYBUS, P.A. (AV)

Suite 800, Bayshore Place, 601 Bayshore Boulevard, 33606
Telephone: 813-251-5533
Telecopier: 813-251-1900
Wats: 1-800-277-2005

E. C. Langford
Edward A. Hill
Ronald H. Trybus
Ronald G. Hock
Catherine M. Catlin
Debra M. Kubicsek
William B. Smith

Fredrique B. Boire
Muriel Desloovere
Kevin H. O'Neill
Vicki L. Page
Frederick T. Reeves
Barbara A. Sinsley
Stephens B. Woodrough (Not admitted in FL)
Anthony G. Woodward

Representative Clients: Affiliated of Florida, Inc.; American Federation Insurance Co.; Armor Insurance; Bank of Tampa; Central Bank of Tampa; Cintas Corp.; Container Corporation of America; CU Financial Services; Farm Stores, Inc.; First Union Home Equity Bank.

For full biographical listings, see the Martindale-Hubbell Law Directory

MANEY, DAMSKER, HARRIS & JONES, P.A. (AV)

606 Madison Street, P.O. Box 172009, 33672-0009
Telephone: 813-228-7371
Fax: 813-223-4846

David A. Maney
Karen Lynn Jones

For full biographical listings, see the Martindale-Hubbell Law Directory

*VERO BEACH,** Indian River Co.

JOSEPH C. KEMPE PROFESSIONAL ASSOCIATION (AV)

Attorneys and Counselors at Law
664 Azalea Lane, Suite B, 32963
Telephone: 407-562-4022
Fax: 407-234-1442
Jupiter, Florida Office: 1070 E. Indiantown Rd.
Telephone: 407-747-7300.
Fax: 407-747-7722.
Stuart, Florida Office: 789 S. Federal Highway, Suite 200.
Telephone: 407-223-0700.
Fax: 407-223-0707.

Joseph C. Kempe
David Pratt

For full biographical listings, see the Martindale-Hubbell Law Directory

E. STEVEN LAUER, P.A. (AV)

612 Beachland Boulevard, 32963
Telephone: 407-234-4200
FAX: 407-234-4249

(See Next Column)

E. STEVEN LAUER, P.A., *Vero Beach—Continued*

E. Steven Lauer

OF COUNSEL

Hiram Manning

For full biographical listings, see the Martindale-Hubbell Law Directory

*WEST PALM BEACH,** Palm Beach Co.

AUGUST, COMITER, KULUNAS & SCHEPPS, P.A. (AV)

250 Australian Avenue South Suite 1100, 33401
Telephone: 407-835-9600
Fax: 407-835-9602
Washington, D.C. Office: 501 School Street, Suite 700.
Telephone: 202-646-5160.

Jerald David August
Richard B. Comiter
Joseph J. Kulunas
Mitchell D. Schepps

For full biographical listings, see the Martindale-Hubbell Law Directory

JONES, FOSTER, JOHNSTON & STUBBS, P.A. (AV)

Flagler Center Tower, 505 South Flagler Drive, P.O. Box 3475, 33402-3475
Telephone: 407-659-3000
Fax: 407-832-1454

Sidney A. Stubbs, Jr.
John Blair McCracken
John C. Randolph
Herbert Adams Weaver, Jr.
Larry B. Alexander
Thornton M. Henry
Margaret L. Cooper
D. Culver Smith III (P.A.)
Allen R. Tomlinson
Peter S. Holton
Michael P. Walsh
Peter A. Sachs
Michael T. Kranz
John S. Trimper
Mark B. Kleinfeld
Andrew R. Ross
Scott Gardner Hawkins
Steven J. Rothman
Rebecca G. Doane

Joyce A. Conway
Stephen J. Aucamp
Christopher S. Duke
Scott L. McMullen
John C. Rau
Tracey Biagiotti
Edward Diaz

Counsel For: U.S. Trust Co.; NationsBank of Florida, N.A.; Island National Bank; Bankers Trust Company of Florida; Sun Bank/South Florida, N.A.; General Motors Acceptance Corp.

For full biographical listings, see the Martindale-Hubbell Law Directory

DAVID S. MEISEL, P.A. (AV)

Phillips Point, West Tower, Suite 1113, 777 South Flagler Drive, 33401
Telephone: 407-833-1833
Fax: 407-833-1556

David S. Meisel

For full biographical listings, see the Martindale-Hubbell Law Directory

ROGERS, BOWERS, DEMPSEY AND PALADINO (AV)

Flagler Center Tower, Suite 1330, 505 South Flagler Drive, 33401
Telephone: 407-655-8980
Fax: 407-655-9480

MEMBERS OF FIRM

Robert O. Rogers
David E. Bowers
W. Glenn Dempsey
Richard Paladino

For full biographical listings, see the Martindale-Hubbell Law Directory

WINTER PARK, Orange Co.

POHL & BROWN, P.A. (AV)

280 West Canton Avenue, Suite 410, P.O. Box 3208, 32789
Telephone: 407-647-7645; 407-647-POHL
Telefax: 407-647-2314

Frank L. Pohl
Usher L. Brown
Houston E. Short
Dwight I. Cool
William W. Pouzar
Mary B. Van Leuven

OF COUNSEL

Frederick W. Peirsol

Representative Clients: Orange County Comptroller; Osceola County; School Board of Osceola County, Florida; Osceola Tourist Development Council; NationsBank of Florida, N.A.; SunBank, N.A.; The Bank of Winter Park; Bekins Moving and Storage Co., Inc.; Champion Boats, Inc.; KeyCom Telephone Systems, Inc.

For full biographical listings, see the Martindale-Hubbell Law Directory

GEORGIA

*ATLANTA,** Fulton Co.

ALSTON & BIRD (AV)

A Partnership including Professional Corporations
One Atlantic Center, 1201 West Peachtree Street, 30309-3424
Telephone: 404-881-7000
Telecopier: 404-881-7777
Cable Address: AMGRAM GA
Telex: 54-2996
Easylink: 62985848
Washington, D.C. Office: 700 Thirteenth Street, Suite 350 20005-3960.
Telephone: 202-508-3300.
Telecopier: 202-508-3333.

MEMBERS OF FIRM

Frazer Durrett, Jr.
Robert G. Edge
Joe T. Taylor
Philip C. Cook
Arnold L. Feinstein
Benjamin T. White
Helene Z. Cohen
John L. Coalson, Jr.
Pinney L. Allen
James S. Hutchinson
Terence J. Greene
Gregory C. Braden
Michael T. Petrik
Timothy J. Peaden
Craig R. Pett
Sam K. Kaywood, Jr.

ASSOCIATES

Bobby L. Dexter
John R. Hickman
Ben E. Muraskin
John C. Sawyer
Karen L. Sukin

Representative Clients: Atlantic Steel Industries, Inc.; Delta Air Lines, Inc.; Genuine Parts Company; Gold Kist Inc.; National Data Corporation; NationsBank Corporation; Sears, Roebuck and Co.

For Complete List of Firm Personnel, See General Section

For full biographical listings, see the Martindale-Hubbell Law Directory

BIVENS, HOFFMAN & FOWLER (AV)

A Partnership of Professional Corporations
5040 Roswell Road, N.E., 30342
Telephone: 404-256-6464
FAX: 404-256-1422

MEMBER OF FIRM

Clifford G. Hoffman (P.C.)

For full biographical listings, see the Martindale-Hubbell Law Directory

DAVIS, MATTHEWS & QUIGLEY, P.C. (AV)

Fourteenth Floor, Lenox Towers II, 3400 Peachtree Road, 30326
Telephone: 404-261-3900
Telecopier: 404-261-0159

William M. Matthews
J. Michael Harrison
Melvin L. Drake, Jr.

Chason Lash Harrison, Jr.

Approved Attorneys for: Lawyers Title Insurance Corp.

For Complete List of Firm Personnel, See General Section

For full biographical listings, see the Martindale-Hubbell Law Directory

ROBERT W. FISHER, P.C. (AV)

The Peachtree, Suite 1700, 1355 Peachtree Street, 30309-3266
Telephone: 404-853-3500
Telecopier: 404-853-3501
Telex: 154210

Robert W. Fisher
Stephen C. Beeler
(Not admitted in GA)
John R. Jones, Jr.
David W. Drake

For full biographical listings, see the Martindale-Hubbell Law Directory

GOMEL & DAVIS (AV)

812 Peachtree Center Harris Tower, 233 Peachtree Street, N.E., 30303-1506
Telephone: 404-223-5900
Telecopier: 404-524-4755

MEMBERS OF FIRM

Walter E. Gomel
Ronald J. Davis
Jed Steven Beardsley
Gregory A. Sanderson

ASSOCIATES

David L. Watson
Timothy R. Brown
Marie K. Evans

(See Next Column)

GOMEL & DAVIS—*Continued*

OF COUNSEL

Edward O. C. Ord (Not admitted in GA)
William K. Norman (Not admitted in GA)

References: Trust Company Bank; Merrill Lynch.

For full biographical listings, see the Martindale-Hubbell Law Directory

HISHON & BURBAGE (AV)

Suite 2000 Eleven Hundred Peachtree Building, 1100 Peachtree Street, 30309
Telephone: 404-898-9880
Telecopier: 404-898-9890

MEMBERS OF FIRM

Robert H. Hishon
R. Bradley Carr

ASSOCIATE

Mike Bothwell

OF COUNSEL

James G. Killough

For Complete List of Firm Personnel, See General Section

For full biographical listings, see the Martindale-Hubbell Law Directory

HOLT, NEY, ZATCOFF & WASSERMAN (AV)

A Partnership including Professional Corporations
100 Galleria Parkway, Suite 600, 30339
Telephone: 404-956-9600
Facsimile Number: 404-956-1490

MEMBER OF FIRM

Michael G. Wasserman (P.C.)

Representative Clients: AmeriHealth, Inc.; Trammell Crow Residential; Roberts Properties, Inc.; The Sterling Group, Inc.; Novak Development Corp.

For Complete List of Firm Personnel, See General Section

For full biographical listings, see the Martindale-Hubbell Law Directory

JONES, DAY, REAVIS & POGUE (AV)

3500 One Peachtree Center, 303 Peachtree Street, N.E., 30308-3242
Telephone: 404-521-3939
Cable Address: "Attorneys Atlanta"
Telex: 54-2711
Telecopier: 404-581-8330
In Brussels, Belgium: Avenue Louise 480, 7th Floor, B-1050 Brussels.
Telephone: 011-32-2-645-14-11.
Telecopier: 011-32-2-645-14-45.
In Chicago, Illinois: 77 West Wacker.
Telephone: 312-782-3939.
Telecopier: 312-782-8585.
In Cleveland, Ohio: North Point. 901 Lakeside Avenue.
Telephone: 216-586-3939.
Cable Address: "Attorneys Cleveland".
Telex: 980389.
Telecopier: 216-579-0212.
In Columbus, Ohio: 1900 Huntington Center.
Telephone: 614-469-3939.
Cable Address: "Attorneys Columbus".
Telecopier: 614-461-4198.
In Dallas, Texas: 2300 Trammell Crow Center, 2001 Ross Avenue.
Telephone: 214-220-3939.
Cable Address: "Attorneys Dallas."
Telex: 730852.
Telecopier: 214-969-5100.
In Frankfurt, Germany: Westendstrasse 41, 60325 Frankfurt am Main.
Telephone: 011-49-69-7438-3939.
Telecopier: 011-49-69-741-1686.
In Geneva, Switzerland: 20, rue de Candolle.
Telephone: 011-41-22-320-2339.
Telecopier: 011-41-22-320-1232.
In Hong Kong: 1501 One Exchange Square, 8 Connaught Place.
Telephone: 011-852-526-6895.
Telecopier: 011-852-810-5787.
In Irvine, California: 2603 Main Street, Suite 900.
Telephone: 714-851-3939.
Telex: 194911 Lawyers LSA.
Telecopier: 714-553-7539.
In London, England: One Mount Street.
Telephone: 011-44-71-493-9361.
Cable Address: "Surgoe London WI."
Telecopier: 011-44-71-493-9666.
In Los Angeles, California: 555 West Fifth Street, Suite 4600.
Telephone: 213-489-3939.
Telex: 181439 UD.
Telecopier: 213-243-2539.
In New York, New York: 599 Lexington Avenue.
Telephone: 212-326-3939.
Cable Address: "JONESDAY NEWYORK."
Telex: 237013 JDRP UR.
Telecopier: 212-755-7306.

(See Next Column)

In Paris, France: 62, rue du Faubourg Saint-Honore.
Telephone: 011-33-1-44-71-3939.
Cable Address: "Surgoe Paris."
Telex: 290156 Surgoe.
Telecopier: 011-33-1-49-24-0471.
In Pittsburgh, Pennsylvania: 500 Grant Street, 31st Floor.
Telephone: 412-391-3939.
Cable Address: "Attorneys Pittsburgh".
Telecopier: 412-394-7959.
In Riyadh, Saudi Arabia: Law Offices of Saud M.A. Shawwaf, P.O. Box 2700.
Telephones: 011 (966-1) 465-6543, 011 (966-1) 464-8534 or 011 (966-1) 464-8540.
Telex: 401831 SAUCON SJ.
Telecopier: (966-1) 464-8480.
In Taipei, Taiwan: 7th Floor, 2 Tun Hwa South Road, Section 2.
Telephone: 011 (886-2) 704-6808 and 704-6809.
Telecopier: 011 (886-2) 704-6791.
In Tokyo, Japan: Shiroyama JT Mori Bldg., 15th Floor, 3-1, Toranomon 4-chome Minato-ku.
Telephone: 011-81-3-3433-3939.
Telecopier: 011-81-3-5401-2725.
In Washington, D.C.: Metropolitan Square, 1450 G Street, N.W.
Telephone: 202-879-3939.
Cable Address: "Attorneys Washington."
Telex: 89-2410 ATTORNEYS WASH.
Telecopier: 202-737-2832, 2-737-2832.

MEMBERS OF FIRM IN ATLANTA

James H. Landon
Milford B. Hatcher, Jr.

ASSOCIATES

Rory D. Lyons (Not admitted in GA)
Ralph R. Morrison

For Complete List of Firm Personnel, See General Section

For full biographical listings, see the Martindale-Hubbell Law Directory

LONG ALDRIDGE & NORMAN (AV)

A Partnership including Professional Corporations
One Peachtree Center, Suite 5300, 303 Peachtree Street, 30308
Telephone: 404-527-4000
Telecopier: 404-527-4198
Washington, D.C. Office: Suite 950, 1615 L Street, 20036.
Telephone: 202-223-7033.
Telecopier: 202-223-7013.

MEMBERS OF FIRM

Mark S. Lange
Ann Distler Salo
Patricia E. Tate
Charles T. Zink

ASSOCIATES

Alison M. Drummond
Melissa P. Walker

OF COUNSEL

Bruce H. Wynn

For Complete List of Firm Personnel, See General Section

For full biographical listings, see the Martindale-Hubbell Law Directory

SUTHERLAND, ASBILL & BRENNAN (AV)

999 Peachtree Street, N.E., 30309-3996
Telephone: 404-853-8000
Facsimile: 404-853-8806
Washington, D.C. Office: 1275 Pennsylvania Avenue, N.W., 20004-2404.
Telephone: 202-383-0100.
New York, N.Y. Office: 1270 Avenue of the Americas, 10020-1700.
Telephone: 212-332-3000.
Austin, Texas Office: 111 Congress Avenue, 23rd Floor, 78701-4079.
Telephone: 512-469-3350.

William H. Bradley
Reginald J. Clark
Katherine Meyers Cohen
N. Jerold Cohen
Michael J. Egan
Herbert R. Elsas
Stephen F. Gertzman
William M. Hames
James K. Hasson, Jr.
Charles D. Hurt, Jr.
Mark D. Kaufman
Bennett Lexon Kight
M. Celeste Pickron
Randolph W. Thrower
C. Christopher Trower
Larry J. White
Walter H. Wingfield

For Complete List of Firm Personnel, See General Section

For full biographical listings, see the Martindale-Hubbell Law Directory

*AUGUSTA,** Richmond Co.

WARLICK, TRITT & STEBBINS (AV)

15th Floor, First Union Bank Building, 30901
Telephone: 706-722-7543
Fax: 706-722-1822
Columbia County Office: 119 Davis Road, Martinez, Georgia 30907.
Telephone: 706-860-7595.
Fax: 705-860-7597.

(See Next Column)

WARLICK, TRITT & STEBBINS, *Augusta—Continued*

MEMBERS OF FIRM

William Byrd Warlick
Roy D. Tritt
(Resident, Martinez Office)
Charles C. Stebbins, III
E. L. Clark Speese
Michael W. Terry
D. Scott Broyles
Ross S. Snellings
C. Gregory Bryan

OF COUNSEL

Richard E. Miley

For full biographical listings, see the Martindale-Hubbell Law Directory

*COLUMBUS,** Muscogee Co.

DAVIDSON, CALHOUN & MILLER, P.C. (AV)

The Joseph House, 828 Broadway, P.O. Box 2828, 31902-2828
Telephone: 706-327-2552
Telecopier: 706-323-5838

J. Quentin Davidson, Jr.
Charles W. Miller
David A. Buehler

For Complete List of Firm Personnel, See General Section

For full biographical listings, see the Martindale-Hubbell Law Directory

HATCHER, STUBBS, LAND, HOLLIS & ROTHSCHILD (AV)

Suite 500 The Corporate Center, 233 12th Street, P.O. Box 2707, 31902-2707
Telephone: 706-324-0201
Telecopier: 706-322-7747

MEMBERS OF FIRM

Alan F. Rothschild
Charles T. Staples
John M. Tanzine, III
Alan F. Rothschild, Jr.

ASSOCIATE

Mote W. Andrews III

General Counsel for: Trust Company Bank of Columbus, N.A.; TOM'S Foods Inc.; Muscogee County Board of Education; The Jordan Co.; Flournoy Development Corp.; Bill Heard Enterprises, Inc.; St. Francis Hospital, Inc.
Local Counsel for: First Union National Bank of Georgia.

For Complete List of Firm Personnel, See General Section

For full biographical listings, see the Martindale-Hubbell Law Directory

LAYFIELD, ROTHSCHILD & MORGAN (AV)

1030 First Avenue, P.O. Box 2788, 31902-2788
Telephone: 706-324-4167
FAX: 706-324-1969

MEMBER OF FIRM

Jerome M. Rothschild

Reference: Columbus Bank and Trust Company.

For Complete List of Firm Personnel, See General Section

For full biographical listings, see the Martindale-Hubbell Law Directory

*GAINESVILLE,** Hall Co.

SMITH, GILLIAM AND WILLIAMS (AV)

200 Old Coca-Cola Building, 301 Green Street, N.W., P.O. Box 1098, 30503
Telephone: 404-536-3381
Fax: 404-531-1491

MEMBERS OF FIRM

R. Wilson Smith, Jr. (1906-1983)
John H. Smith
Steven P. Gilliam
Jerry A. Williams
Kelly Anne Miles
Bradley J. Patten

ASSOCIATES

M. Tyler Smith
Scott Arthur Ball

General Counsel for: Gainesville Industrial Electric Co.; Georgia Mutual Insurance Co.; L & R Farms; H. Wilson Manufacturing Co.; Goforth Electrical Supply; North Georgia Petroleum Co.; Gibbs Management Group, Inc.

For full biographical listings, see the Martindale-Hubbell Law Directory

*MACON,** Bibb Co.

ANDERSON, WALKER & REICHERT (AV)

Suite 404 Trust Company Bank Building, P.O. Box 6497, 31208-6497
Telephone: 912-743-8651
Telecopier: 912-743-9636

MEMBERS OF FIRM

Albert P. Reichert, Jr.
John D. Reeves

Representative Clients: Riverwood International Georgia, Inc.; Hospital Corporation of America; Pepsi-Cola Bottling Company of Macon; Radiology Associates of Macon, P.C.; Thiele Kaolin Company; Trust Company Bank of Middle Georgia, N.A.

(See Next Column)

General Insurance Clients: Liberty Mutual Insurance Co.; United States Fidelity & Guaranty Co.; Continental Insurance Cos.; Alexis, Inc.

For Complete List of Firm Personnel, See General Section

For full biographical listings, see the Martindale-Hubbell Law Directory

HALL, BLOCH, GARLAND & MEYER (AV)

1500 Charter Medical Building, P.O. Box 5088, 31213-3199
Telephone: 912-745-1625
Telecopier: 912-741-8822

MEMBER OF FIRM

J. Patrick Meyer, Jr.

ASSOCIATE

Ramsey T. Way, Jr.

For Complete List of Firm Personnel, See General Section

For full biographical listings, see the Martindale-Hubbell Law Directory

*SAVANNAH,** Chatham Co.

SILVERS AND SIMPSON, PROFESSIONAL CORPORATION (AV)

Suite 102, AmeriBank Plaza, 7393 Hodgson Memorial Drive, 31406
Telephone: 912-925-7200
Facsimile: 912-925-0100

Mark M. Silvers, Jr.
K. Russell Simpson

Katherine Lynn Levy

For full biographical listings, see the Martindale-Hubbell Law Directory

HAWAII

*HONOLULU,** Honolulu Co.

MCCORRISTON MIHO MILLER MUKAI (AV)

Five Waterfront Plaza, 4th Floor, 500 Ala Moana Boulevard, 96813
Telephone: 808-529-7300
Facsimile: 808-524-8293
Cable: Attorneys, Honolulu

COUNSEL

Michael J. O'Malley
Michael Rosenthal

OF COUNSEL

Stanley Y. Mukai

For Complete List of Firm Personnel, See General Section

For full biographical listings, see the Martindale-Hubbell Law Directory

IDAHO

*BOISE,** Ada Co.

EBERLE, BERLIN, KADING, TURNBOW & MCKLVEEN, CHARTERED (AV)

Capitol Park Plaza, 300 North Sixth Street, P.O. Box 1368, 83701
Telephone: 208-344-8535
Facsimile: 208-344-8542

William J. McKlveen
Joseph H. Uberuaga, II
Steven E. Alkire

Representative Clients: TJ International; Hecla Mining Company; Agri Beef Co.

For Complete List of Firm Personnel, See General Section

For full biographical listings, see the Martindale-Hubbell Law Directory

ELAM & BURKE, A PROFESSIONAL ASSOCIATION (AV)

Key Financial Center, 702 West Idaho Street, P.O. Box 1539, 83701
Telephone: 208-343-5454
Telecopier: 208-384-5844

Melville W. Fisher, II
Peter C. K. Marshall

Representative Clients: Morrison-Knudsen, Inc.; Texas Instruments, Inc.; Prudential Securities, Inc.; Pechiney Corp.; Dow Corning Corporation; U.S. West Communications; State Farm Insurance Cos.; Sinclair Oil Company d/b/a Sun Valley Company; Farmers Insurance Group; Hecla Mining Company.

For Complete List of Firm Personnel, See General Section

For full biographical listings, see the Martindale-Hubbell Law Directory

*POCATELLO,** Bannock Co.

MERRILL & MERRILL, CHARTERED (AV)

Key Bank Building, P.O. Box 991, 83204
Telephone: 208-232-2286
Fax: 208-232-2499

Wesley F. Merrill　　N. Randy Smith

Representative Clients: West One Bank of Idaho; Idaho State University (Financial Department); First Security Bank.

For Complete List of Firm Personnel, See General Section

For full biographical listings, see the Martindale-Hubbell Law Directory

ILLINOIS

*BELLEVILLE,** St. Clair Co.

THOMPSON & MITCHELL (AV)

525 West Main Street, 62220
Telephone: 618-277-4700; 314-271-1800
Telecopier: 618-236-3434
St. Louis, Missouri Office: One Mercantile Center, Suite 3300.
Telephone: 314-231-7676.
Telecopier: 314-342-1717.
St. Charles, Missouri Office: 200 North Third Street.
Telephone: 314-946-7717.
Telecopier: 314-946-4938.
Washington, D.C. Office: 700 14th Street, N.W., Suite 900.
Telephone: 202-508-1000.
Telecopier: 202-508-1010.

MEMBERS OF FIRM

Joseph R. Lowery
Garrett C. Reuter
Mark J. Stegman
Kurt S. Schroeder

Representative Clients: First Illinois Bank; Harcros Pigments, Inc.; Illinois-American Water Co.; Illinois Bell Telephone Co.; Magna Group, Inc.; Magna Trust Co.; Marsh Company; Memorial Hospital of Belleville; Norfolk Southern Corp.; Union Electric Co.

For Complete List of Firm Personnel, See General Section

For full biographical listings, see the Martindale-Hubbell Law Directory

*CHICAGO,** Cook Co.

BELL, BOYD & LLOYD (AV)

Three First National Plaza Suite 3300, 70 West Madison Street, 60602
Telephone: 312-372-1121
FAX: 312-372-2098
Washington, D.C. Office: 1615 L Street, N.W.
Telephone: 202-466-6300.
FAX: 202-463-0678.

MEMBERS OF FIRM

Durward J. (James) Gehring
Thomas F. Joyce
Alice S. Lonoff
Paul T. Metzger
Richard L. Sevcik
Paul A. Strasen
Anita Medina Tyson
Robert L. Wiesenthal

OF COUNSEL

Alan R. Brodie
William N. Haddad
Rollin C. Huggins, Jr.
Allen R. Smart

ASSOCIATE

Faye L. Katt

For Complete List of Firm Personnel, See General Section

For full biographical listings, see the Martindale-Hubbell Law Directory

CHAPMAN AND CUTLER (AV)

111 West Monroe Street, 60603
Telephone: 312-845-3000
TWX: 910-221-2103
Fax: 312-701-2361
Salt Lake City, Utah Office: Suite 800, Key Bank Tower, 50 South Main Street.
Telephone: 801-533-0066.
Fax: 801-533-9595.
Phoenix, Arizona Office: Suite 1100, One Renaissance Square, 2 North Central Avenue.
Telephone: 602-256-4060.
Fax: 602-256-4099.

Vincent M. Aquilino
Jeffrey D. Berry
David J. Cholst
Steven G. Frost

(See Next Column)

Bruce D. Agin
Steven D. Conlon
Alan L. Kennard
Anthony R. Rosso
Suzanne M. Russell
Tedd T. Termunde

For Complete List of Firm Personnel, See General Section

For full biographical listings, see the Martindale-Hubbell Law Directory

DEUTSCH, LEVY & ENGEL, CHARTERED (AV)

Suite 1700, 225 West Washington Street, 60606
Telephone: 312-346-1460
Boynton, Beach Florida Office: 3C Westgate Lane.
Telephone: 407-737-6003.
Wheaton, Illinois Office: Suite B2, 620 West Roosevelt Road.
Telephone: 312-665-9112.

Terry L. Engel
Frank R. Cohen
Jerry I. Rudman

David I. Addis
Martin P. Ryan

For Complete List of Firm Personnel, See General Section

For full biographical listings, see the Martindale-Hubbell Law Directory

GORDON & EINSTEIN, LTD. (AV)

224 East Ontario, 60611
Telephone: 312-280-7766
Telecopier: 312-280-9599

Raymond P. Gordon　　Jean M. Einstein

LEGAL SUPPORT PERSONNEL

Laura A. Kozicki

For full biographical listings, see the Martindale-Hubbell Law Directory

HOOGENDOORN, TALBOT, DAVIDS, GODFREY & MILLIGAN (AV)

122 South Michigan Avenue Suite 1220, 60603-6107
Telephone: 312-786-2250
FAX: 312-786-0708

MEMBERS OF FIRM

Case Hoogendoorn　　Kathryn E. Skelton

OF COUNSEL

Kathleen A. Salzer　　Raymond C. Odom

For full biographical listings, see the Martindale-Hubbell Law Directory

JONES, DAY, REAVIS & POGUE (AV)

77 West Wacker, 60601-1692
Telephone: 312-782-3939
Telecopier: 312-782-8585
In Atlanta, Georgia: 3500 One Peachtree Center, 303 Peachtree Street, N.E.
Telephone: 404-521-3939.
Cable Address: "Attorneys Atlanta".
Telex: 54-2711.
Telecopier: 404-581-8330.
In Brussels, Belgium: Avenue Louise 480, 7th Floor, B-1050 Brussels.
Telephone: 011-32-2-645-14-11.
Telecopier: 011-32-2-645-14-45.
In Cleveland, Ohio: North Point, 901 Lakeside Avenue.
Telephone: 216-586-3939.
Cable Address: "Attorneys Cleveland."
Telex: 980389.
Telecopier: 216-579-0212.
In Columbus, Ohio: 1900 Huntington Center.
Telephone: 614-469-3939.
Cable Address: "Attorneys Columbus."
Telecopier: 614-461-4198.
In Dallas, Texas: 2300 Trammell Crow Center, 2001 Ross Avenue.
Telephone: 214-220-3939.
Cable Address: "Attorneys Dallas."
Telex: 730852.
Telecopier: 214-969-5100.
In Frankfurt, Germany: Westendstrasse 41, 60325 Frankfurt am Main.
Telephone: 011-49-69-7438-3939.
Telecopier: 011-49-69-741-1686.
In Geneva, Switzerland: 20, rue de Candolle.
Telephone: 011-41-22-320-2339.
Telecopier: 011-41-22-320-1232.
In Hong Kong: 1501 One Exchange Square, 8 Connaught Place.
Telephone: 011-852-526-6895.
Telecopier: 011-852-810-5787.
In Irvine, California: 2603 Main Street, Suite 900.
Telephone: 714-851-3939.
Telex: 194911 Lawyers LSA.
Telecopier: 714-553-7539.
In London, England: One Mount Street.
Telephone: 011-44-71-493-9361.
Cable Address: "Surgoe London WI."
Telecopier: 011-44-71-493-9666.

(See Next Column)

JONES, DAY, REAVIS & POGUE, *Chicago—Continued*

In Los Angeles, California: 555 West Fifth Street, Suite 4600.
Telephone: 213-489-3939.
Telex: 181439 UD.
Telecopier: 213-243-2539.
In New York, New York: 599 Lexington Avenue.
Telephone: 212-326-3939.
Cable Address: "JONESDAY NEWYORK."
Telex: 237013 JDRP UR.
Telecopier: 212-755-7306.
In Paris, France: 62, rue du Faubourg Saint-Honore.
Telephone: 011-33-1-44-71-3939.
Cable Address: "Surgoe Paris."
Telex: 290156 Surgoe.
Telecopier: 011-33-1-49-24-0471.
In Pittsburgh, Pennsylvania: 500 Grant Street, 31st Floor.
Telephone: 412-391-3939.
Cable Address: "Attorneys Pittsburgh."
Telecopier: 412-394-7959.
In Riyadh, Saudi Arabia: Law Offices of Saud M.A. Shawwaf, P.O. Box 2700.
Telephones: 011 (966-1) 465-6543, 011 (966-1) 464-8534 or 011 (966-1) 464-8540.
Telex: 401831 SAUCON SJ.
Telecopier: (966-1) 464-8480.
In Taipei, Taiwan: 7th Floor, 2 Tun Hwa South Road, Section 2.
Telephone: 011 (886-2) 704-6808 and 704-6809.
Telecopier: 011 (886-2) 704-6791.
In Tokyo, Japan: Shiroyama JT Mori Bldg., 15th Floor, 3-1, Toranomon 4-chome, Minato-Ku.
Telephone: 011-81-3-3433-3939.
Telecopier: 011-81-3-5401-2725.
In Washington, D.C.: Metropolitan Square, 1450 G Street, N.W.
Telephone: 202-879-3939.
Cable Address: "Attorneys Washington."
Telex: 89-2410 ATTORNEYS WASH.
Telecopier: 202-737-2832.

MEMBERS OF FIRM IN CHICAGO

Ronald S. Rizzo (Not admitted in IL)
Douglas H. Walter

OF COUNSEL

William S. McKay, Jr.

ASSOCIATES

Stephanie E. Balcerzak
Joni L. Andrioff

For Complete List of Firm Personnel, See General Section

For full biographical listings, see the Martindale-Hubbell Law Directory

THE LAW OFFICES OF MARC J. LANE A PROFESSIONAL CORPORATION (AV)

Suite 2100 180 North La Salle Street, 60601-2701
Telephone: 312-372-1040
Fax: 312-346-1040

Marc J. Lane

Gregory A. Papiernik

For full biographical listings, see the Martindale-Hubbell Law Directory

MARTIN, BROWN & SULLIVAN, LTD. (AV)

321 South Plymouth Court 10th Floor, 60604
Telephone: 312-360-5000
Fax: 312-360-5026

Royal B. Martin
Steven S. Brown
Leigh D. Roadman

Daniel T. Hartnett
Michael D. Cotton

For full biographical listings, see the Martindale-Hubbell Law Directory

MCBRIDE BAKER & COLES (AV)

500 West Madison Street 40th Floor, 60661
Telephone: 312-715-5700
Cable Address: "Chilaw"
Telex: 270258
Telecopier: 312-993-9350

MEMBERS OF FIRM

David Ackerman
Andrew R. Gelman
Thomas J. Kinasz
Morgan J. Ordman
Robert I. Schwimmer
David Shayne

ASSOCIATE

Jonathan E. Strouse

For Complete List of Firm Personnel, See General Section

For full biographical listings, see the Martindale-Hubbell Law Directory

MCDERMOTT, WILL & EMERY (AV)

A Partnership including Professional Corporations
227 West Monroe Street, 60606-5096
Telephone: 312-372-2000
Telex: 253565 Milam CGO
Facsimile: 312-984-7700
Boston, Massachusetts Office: 75 State Street, Suite 1700.
Telephone: 617-345-5000.
Telex: 951324 MILAM BSN.
Facsimile: 617-345-5077.
Miami, Florida Office: 201 South Biscayne Boulevard.
Telephone: 305-358-3500.
Telex: 441777 LEYES.
Facsimile: 305-347-6500.
Washington, D.C. Office: 1850 K Street, N.W.
Telephone: 202-887-8000.
Telex: 253565 MILAM CGO.
Facsimile: 202-778-8087.
Los Angeles, California Office: 2049 Century Park East.
Telephone: 310-277-4110.
Facsimile: 310-277-4730.
Newport Beach, California Office: 1301 Dove Street, Suite 500.
Telephone: 714-851-0633.
Facsimile: 714-851-9348.
New York, N.Y. Office: 1211 Avenue of the Americas.
Telephone: 212-768-5400.
Facsimile: 212-768-5444.
St. Petersburg, Russia Office: 2/2 Tchaikovsky Street, #517, 191187 St. Petersburg, Russia.
Telephone: (7) (812) 273-9831.
Facsimile: (7) (812) 273-9831.
Tallinn, Estonia Office: Tallinn Business Center, 6 Harju Street, EE0001 Tallinn, Estonia.
Telephone: 372 6 31-05-53.
Facsimile: 372 6 31-05-54.
Vilnius, Lithuania Office: Smetonos 6, 2600 Vilnius, Lithuania.
Telephone: 370 2 61-43-08.
Facsimile: 370 2 22-79-55.
Associated (Independent) Offices:
Brussels, Belgium: Uettwiller Grelon Lippens Dekeyser, 73 avenue Vandendriessche, 1150 Brussels, Belgium.
Telephone: (32) (2) 772-87-50.
Facsimile: (32) (2) 772-87-52.
London, England: Paisner & Co, Bouverie House, 154 Fleet Street, London EC4A 2DQ, England.
Telephone: (44) (71) 353-0299.
Facsimile: (44) (71) 583-8621.
Paris, France: Uettwiller Grelon Gout Canat & Associes, 68, boulevard de Courcelles, 75017 Paris, France.
Telephone: (33) (1) 48 88 89 00.
Facsimile: (33) (1) 48 88 05 50.

MEMBERS OF FIRM

Frederick G. Acker
W. Timothy Baetz *
David A. Baker
George W. Benson
Stuart M. Berkson *
Thomas C. Borders *
Raymond E. Boyle
Alan C. Brown
William J. Butler
Stephen M. Chiles
Sophia E. Chrusciel
Paul J. Compernolle
Richard L. Dees *
Thomas H. Donohoe
David J. Duez *
John M. Eckel *
Scott Ellwood
Cecilia M. Eytalis
Michael R. Fayhee *
Jerry K. Fellows
John Edmund Gaggini *
Richard J. Garvey *
Lawrence Gerber *
Richard A. Hanson *
Don S. Harnack *
Carol A. Harrington
Mark M. Harris
Alan J. Hawksley
Quentin G. Heisler, Jr. *
John P. Hendrickson *
Charles E. Hussey II
Thomas M. Jones *
Stanley R. Kaminski, Jr.
Gary C. Karch
Melinda M. Kleehamer
Andrea S. Kramer
Jean M. Langie
Gerard M. Latus *
Wade S. Leathers
Richard T. Lorenz, Jr. *
James L. Malone III *
Edward F. Michalak
Stephen R. Miller
Lonn W. Myers *
Alan D. Nesburg *
Franklin W. Nitikman *
Alan J. Olson *
Anne M. Pachciarek
Gregory G. Palmer
William R. Pomierski
Barry J. Quirke
James M. Roche *
Joseph O. Rubinelli, Jr.
David R. Ryder
Karen A. Simonsen
Hugh F. Smart
James M. Trapp *
Lowell D. Yoder
Daniel N. Zucker

COUNSEL

M. Kevin Outterson

OF COUNSEL

James W. Ashley
Arthur E. Bryan, Jr.
Patrick J. Caraher *
Charles N. Huber
Joseph P. Mulhern
John S. Pennell
Rainer R. Weigel *

(See Next Column)

McDermott, Will & Emery—*Continued*

ASSOCIATES

Joseph S. Adams	Robert D. LoPrete
John A. Biek (Not admitted in IL)	Sandra Parker McGill
James E. Dickett	Diane M. Morgenthaler
Kevin J. Feeley	Gail H. Morse
David A. Fruchtman	Adam J. Narot
Alfonso Garcia-Mingo (Not admitted in the United States)	Susan M. Nash
Nancy S. Gerrie	Maureen A. Pastika
Susan Shaw Gleason	Carol S. Portman
Marcelo Halpern	Matthew M. Preston
Kristen E. Hazel	Elizabeth A. Rourke
Lydia R. B. Kelley	Courtney N. Stillman
	Jan E. Stone
	Wendy Merz Wells

Peggy A. Zemanick

*Denotes a lawyer employed by a Professional Corporation which is a member of the Firm.

For Complete List of Firm Personnel, See General Section

For full biographical listings, see the Martindale-Hubbell Law Directory

Pretzel & Stouffer, Chartered (AV)

One South Wacker Drive Suite 2500, 60606-4673
Telephone: 312-346-1973
FAX: 312-346-8242; 346-8060

Glen R. Bernfield — Michael D. Goodman

Representative Clients: Allstate Insurance Co.; St. Paul Insurance Companies.

For Complete List of Firm Personnel, See General Section

For full biographical listings, see the Martindale-Hubbell Law Directory

Saitlin, Patzik & Frank Ltd. (AV)

Suite 900, 150 South Wacker Drive, 60606
Telephone: 312-551-8300
Facsimile: 312-551-1101

Jeffrey H. Frank — Sheldon I. Saitlin
Alan B. Patzik — Robert P. Scales
Gary Irwin Walt

Steven M. Prebish — Keith A. Ross
Robert J. Wild

For full biographical listings, see the Martindale-Hubbell Law Directory

Sarnoff & Baccash (AV)

One North La Salle Street Suite 1701, 60602-3907
Telephone: 312-782-8310
Fax: 312-782-8635

MEMBERS OF FIRM

Michael F. Baccash — Robert M. Sarnoff

LEGAL SUPPORT PERSONNEL

REAL ESTATE APPRAISER (MAI) AND ENVIRONMENTAL ANALYST

James G. Frommeyer, III

PROPERTY TAX ADMINISTRATORS

Cheryl Gray, Property Tax Analyst — Scott Herzeg, Property Tax and Computer Systems Analyst.
Jeanine Marie Herzeg, Senior, Property Tax Analyst. — Milena K. Mesin, Property Tax Analyst.

For full biographical listings, see the Martindale-Hubbell Law Directory

Vedder, Price, Kaufman & Kammholz (AV)

A Partnership including Vedder, Price, Kaufman & Kammholz, P.C.
222 North La Salle Street, 60601-1003
Telephone: 312-609-7500
Fax: 312-609-5005
Rockford, Illinois Office: Vedder, Price, Kaufman & Kammholz, 4615 East State Street, Suite 201.
Telephone: 815-226-7700.
Washington, D.C. Office: Vedder, Price, Kaufman, Kammholz & Day, 1600 M. Street, N.W.
Telephone: 202-296-0500.
New York, New York Office: Vedder, Price, Kaufman, Kammholz & Day, 805 Third Avenue.
Telephone: 212-407-7700.

MEMBERS OF FIRM

Michael G. Beemer — Daniel T. Sherlock
William F. Walsh — Jonathan H. Bogaard

ASSOCIATE

Timothy W. O'Donnell

For Complete List of Firm Personnel, See General Section

For full biographical listings, see the Martindale-Hubbell Law Directory

*ROCKFORD,** Winnebago Co.

Conde, Stoner & Killoren (AV)

120 West State Street, Suite 400, 61101
Telephone: 815-987-4000
FAX: 815-987-9889
Rochelle, Illinois Office: 400 Maymart Drive, 61068.
Telephone: 815-562-2677.

MEMBERS OF FIRM

Dale F. Conde — Thomas A. Killoren
Clifford E. Stoner — Thomas A. Bueschel
Robert A. Calgaro

James M. Hess — Alan H. Cooper
Kimberly Baker Timmerwilke

OF COUNSEL

Clifford A. Pedderson — Lisle W. Menzimer

References: Rockford School District; Central Commodities Limited; Medical Protective Co.; Wausau Insurance Companies; Caronia Corp.; National Medical Enterprises; Professional Risk Management, Inc.; Krause, Inc.; First of America, North Central N.A.

For full biographical listings, see the Martindale-Hubbell Law Directory

Williams & McCarthy, A Professional Corporation (AV)

321 West State Street, P.O. Box 219, 61105-0219
Telephone: 815-987-8900
Fax: 815-968-0019 ABANET: ABA 5519
Oregon, Illinois Office: 607 Washington Street. P.O. Box 339.
Telephone: 815-732-2101.
Fax: 815-732-2289.

John R. Kinley — Elmer C. Rudy
John E. Pfau

Representative Clients: Anderson Industries, Inc.; Liberty Mutual Insurance Co.; Atwood Industries, Inc.; The Travelers; American Mutual Insurance Co.; Rockford Memorial Hospital; Chrysler Corp.; USF&G, West Bend.

For Complete List of Firm Personnel, See General Section

For full biographical listings, see the Martindale-Hubbell Law Directory

*ROCK ISLAND,** Rock Island Co.

Nepple, Van Der Kamp & Flynn, P.C. (AV)

Suite 202 American Bank Building, 1600 Fourth Avenue, P.O. Box 5408, 61204-5408
Telephone: 309-786-5700
Telecopier: 309-786-5745
Muscatine, Iowa Office: 216 Sycamore Street, P.O. Box 386, 52761-0386.
Telephone: 319-264-6840.

Roy W. Van Der Kamp — James A. Nepple
Patrick J. Flynn

Milissa M. Knudsen

LEGAL SUPPORT PERSONNEL

Steven D. Perkins

Representative Clients: First of America Bank - Quad Cities, N.A.; Northwest Bank and Trust Company; Brenton First National Bank; Bituminous Insurance Companies; Shive-Hattery Engineers and Architects, Inc.; Ruhl & Ruhl, Inc.; Stanley Consultants, Inc. and affiliates; The Stanley Foundation; Stanley Employee Stock Ownership Plan; Valley Construction Company.

For full biographical listings, see the Martindale-Hubbell Law Directory

*SPRINGFIELD,** Sangamon Co.

Mohan, Alewelt, Prillaman & Adami (AV)

First of America Center, Suite 325, 1 North Old Capitol Plaza, 62701-1323
Telephone: 217-528-2517
Telecopier: 217-528-2553

MEMBERS

Edward J. Alewelt — Cheryl Stickel Neal

OF COUNSEL

James T. Mohan

Representative Clients: Andrews Environmental Engineering, Inc.; B & W Land Co.; Browning-Ferris Industries of Illinois, Inc.; Carlinville Area Hospital; Evans Construction Co.; Federal Deposit Insurance Corp.; McLaughlin Manufacturing Co.; Park Realty.

For Complete List of Firm Personnel, See General Section

For full biographical listings, see the Martindale-Hubbell Law Directory

*URBANA,** Champaign Co.

WEBBER & THIES, P.C. (AV)

202 Lincoln Square, P.O. Box 189, 61801
Telephone: 217-367-1126
FAX: 217-367-3752

Richard L. Thies | Craig R. Webber
Holten D. Summers

Alan R. Singleton

For Complete List of Firm Personnel, See General Section

For full biographical listings, see the Martindale-Hubbell Law Directory

INDIANA

*EVANSVILLE,** Vanderburgh Co.

LAW OFFICES OF RANDALL K. CRAIG (AV)

Reed Building Suite 5, 2709 Washington Avenue, 47714
Telephone: 812-477-3337
Telefax: 812-477-3658

For full biographical listings, see the Martindale-Hubbell Law Directory

FINE & HATFIELD (AV)

520 N.W. Second Street, P.O. Box 779, 47705-0779
Telephone: 812-425-3592
Telecopier: 812-421-4269

MEMBERS OF FIRM

Thomas R. Fitzsimmons | Stephen S. Lavallo

ASSOCIATE

Shannon Scholz Frank

For Complete List of Firm Personnel, See General Section

For full biographical listings, see the Martindale-Hubbell Law Directory

KAHN, DEES, DONOVAN & KAHN (AV)

P.O. Box 3646, 47735-3646
Telephone: 812-423-3183
Fax: 812-423-3841

MEMBERS OF FIRM

Alan N. Shovers | John E. Hegeman
G. Michael Schopmeyer | Jeffrey K. Helfrich

ASSOCIATE

Marjorie J. Scharpf

Representative Clients: Joe W. Morgan, Inc.; Intrametco Processing, Inc.; Crescent Plastics, Inc.; Elmer Buchta Trucking, Inc.; Schuttler Music; Deaconess Hospital, Inc.; Old National Bancorp; North Park Cinemas, Inc.; Red Spot Paint & Varnish Co.

For Complete List of Firm Personnel, See General Section

For full biographical listings, see the Martindale-Hubbell Law Directory

JACK A. STONE (AV)

1400 Old National Bank Building, 47708
Telephone: 812-423-2045
Fax: Available Upon Request

For full biographical listings, see the Martindale-Hubbell Law Directory

*FORT WAYNE,** Allen Co.

SHAMBAUGH, KAST, BECK & WILLIAMS (AV)

600 Standard Federal Plaza, 46802-2405
Telephone: 219-423-1430
FAX: 219-422-9038

MEMBERS OF FIRM

Michael H. Kast (Semi-Active) | Daniel E. Serban
Stephen J. Williams | John B. Powell
Edward E. Beck | Timothy L. Claxton
James D. Streit

Counsel for: Hagerman Construction Corp.; Rogers Markets, Inc.; K & H Realty Corp.; Olive B. Cole Foundation; M. E. Raker Foundation, Inc.; Associates Financial Services Co., of Indiana, Inc.; Professional Federal Credit Union; Fort Wayne Education Association; American Ambassador Casualty Company; CBT Credit Services, Inc.

For Complete List of Firm Personnel, See General Section

For full biographical listings, see the Martindale-Hubbell Law Directory

*INDIANAPOLIS,** Marion Co.

BAKER & DANIELS (AV)

300 North Meridian Street, 46204
Telephone: 317-237-0300
FAX: 317-237-1000
Fort Wayne, Indiana Office: 2400 Fort Wayne National Bank Building.
Telephone: 219-424-8000.
South Bend, Indiana Office: First Bank Building, 205 West Jefferson Boulevard.
Telephone: 219-234-4149.
Elkhart, Indiana Office: 301 South Main Street, Suite 307,
Telephone: 219-296-6000.
Washington, D.C. Office: 1701 K Street, N.W., Suite 400.
Telephone: 202-785-1565.

MEMBERS OF FIRM

Stephen H. Paul | Francina A. Dlouhy
Donald P. Bennett | J. Daniel Ogren

ASSOCIATES

Robert M. Bond | Cynthia L. Ramsey
Brian S. Fennerty

LEGAL SUPPORT PERSONNEL

James L. Turner

Representative Clients: Associated Insurance Companies, Inc.; Bank One, Indianapolis, N.A.; Borg-Warner Corp.; City of Indianapolis; Cummins Engine Co.; Eli Lilly and Company; General Motors Corp.; Indiana Bell; Indianapolis Public Schools; United Airlines.

For Complete List of Firm Personnel, See General Section

For full biographical listings, see the Martindale-Hubbell Law Directory

BOSE MCKINNEY & EVANS (AV)

2700 First Indiana Plaza, 135 North Pennsylvania Street, 46204
Telephone: 317-684-5000
Facsimile: 317-684-5173
Indianapolis North Office: Suite 1201, 8888 Keystone Crossing, 46240.
Telephone: 317-574-3700.
Facsimile: 317-574-3716.

MEMBERS OF FIRM

Robert P. Kassing | Ronald M. Soskin
G. Pearson Smith, Jr. | R. J. McConnell

ASSOCIATE

Gary L. Chapman

Representative Clients: Association of Indiana Life Insurance Cos.; First Indiana Bank; Indiana League of Savings Institutions, Inc.; Indianapolis Life Insurance Co.; Duke Realty Investments, Inc.; Emmis Broadcasting Corp.; Young Automotive Group; USX Corp.

For Complete List of Firm Personnel, See General Section

For full biographical listings, see the Martindale-Hubbell Law Directory

DALE & EKE, PROFESSIONAL CORPORATION (AV)

Suite 400, 9100 Keystone Crossing, 46240
Telephone: 317-844-7400
FAX: 317-574-9426

William J. Dale, Jr. | Karen A. Hosack
Joseph W. Eke | Dawn Michelle Snow

For full biographical listings, see the Martindale-Hubbell Law Directory

ICE MILLER DONADIO & RYAN (AV)

One American Square Box 82001, 46282-0002
Telephone: 317-236-2100
Fax: 317-236-2219

MEMBERS OF FIRM

Donald G. Sutherland | Barton T. Sprunger
Leonard J. Betley | Gregory L. Pemberton
James D. Kemper | Steven K. Humke
Mark J. Richards

ASSOCIATES

Joseph E. Whitsett, Jr. | Brian G. Steinkamp
Catherine R. Beck | Timothy A. Brooks
Daniel S. Corsaro | Kathleen Weyher Kiefer

Counsel for: Cummins Engine Company, Inc.; Indianapolis Motor Speedway Corp.; Biomet, Inc.; Bristol-Myers Squibb Co.; Aluminum Company of America; Amax, Inc.; Community Hospitals of Indiana, Inc.; Pension Fund of the Christian Church; Thomson Consumer Electronics, Inc.; Reilly Industries, Inc.

For Complete List of Firm Personnel, See General Section

For full biographical listings, see the Martindale-Hubbell Law Directory

Indianapolis—Continued

ROBERT A. LICHTENAUER (AV)

Suite 110, 8140 Knue Road, 46250
Telephone: 317-845-1988

For full biographical listings, see the Martindale-Hubbell Law Directory

LOCKE REYNOLDS BOYD & WEISELL (AV)

1000 Capital Center South, 201 North Illinois Street, 46204
Telephone: 317-237-3800
Telecopier: 317-237-3900

James J. McGrath
Michael T. Bindner
Michael J. Schneider
Michael J. Rusnak
Peter H. Donahoe

OF COUNSEL

Jeffrey S. Dible

Counsel For: Bethlehem Steel Corp.; Caylor-Nickel Clinic, P.C.; Countrymark Cooperative, Inc.; Health & Hospital Corporation; IBM Corporation; Jefferson Smurfit Corp.; Messenger Courier Association of America; Mid-America Capital Resources, Inc. (subsidiary of IPALCO, Inc.); National Wine & Spirits Corp.; Resort Condominiums International, Inc.

For Complete List of Firm Personnel, See General Section

For full biographical listings, see the Martindale-Hubbell Law Directory

LAW OFFICES OF LINDA L. PENCE (AV)

2300 First Indiana Plaza, 135 North Pennsylvania Street, 46204
Telephone: 317-264-5555
Fax: 317-264-5564

ASSOCIATES

David J. Hensel
Anthony J. Rose
Jane Ann Himsel

LEGAL SUPPORT PERSONNEL

Penny S. Bloemker
Teresa L. Zembrycki
Rachel I. Lamb

For full biographical listings, see the Martindale-Hubbell Law Directory

MUNSTER, Lake Co.

PINKERTON AND FRIEDMAN, PROFESSIONAL CORPORATION (AV)

The Fairmont, 9245 Calumet Avenue Suite 201, 46321
Telephone: 219-836-3050
Fax: 219-836-2955

Kirk A. Pinkerton
Stuart J. Friedman
Jeffrey F. Gunning
Gail Oosterhof

For full biographical listings, see the Martindale-Hubbell Law Directory

*TERRE HAUTE,** Vigo Co.

WILKINSON, GOELLER, MODESITT, WILKINSON & DRUMMY (AV)

333 Ohio Street, P.O. Box 800, 47808-0800
Telephone: 812-232-4311
Fax: 812-235-5107

MEMBERS OF FIRM

Myrl O. Wilkinson
David H. Goeller
William M. Olah

Representative Corporate Clients: Merchants National Bank; Owens Corning Fiberglass; CSX, Inc.; General Housewares Corp.; MAB Paints; Chicago Title Insurance Co.; Terre Haute Board of Realtors; Union Hospital; Associated Physicians and Surgeons Clinic, Inc.; PSI Energy, Inc.

For Complete List of Firm Personnel, See General Section

For full biographical listings, see the Martindale-Hubbell Law Directory

IOWA

CEDAR FALLS, Black Hawk Co.

REDFERN, MASON, DIETER, LARSEN & MOORE (AV)

315 Clay Street, P.O. Box 627, 50613
Telephone: 319-277-6830
Facsimile: 319-277-3531

MEMBERS OF FIRM

LeRoy H. Redfern
David R. Mason
Robert J. Dieter
John C. Larsen
Steven D. Moore
Donald B. Redfern
Mark W. Fransdal
Mark S. Rolinger

(See Next Column)

ASSOCIATE

Susan Bernau Staudt

Representative Clients: Norwest Bank Iowa, N.A.; The National Bank of Waterloo; Sartori Memorial Hospital; Cedar Falls Utilities; University of Northern Iowa Foundation; Cedar Falls Community School District; United States Fidelity & Guaranty Co.; The Travelers Insurance Cos.; Fireman's Fund Insurance Cos.; Control-o-fax Corp.

For Complete List of Firm Personnel, See General Section

For full biographical listings, see the Martindale-Hubbell Law Directory

*CEDAR RAPIDS,** Linn Co.

SHUTTLEWORTH & INGERSOLL, P.C. (AV)

500 Firstar Bank Building, P.O. Box 2107, 52406-2107
Telephone: 319-365-9461
Fax: 319-365-8443

Michael O. McDermott
Gary J. Streit
William S. Hochstetler

Dean D. Carrington

Representative Clients: Amana Society; Archer-Daniels-Midland Co.; Coe College; Firstar Bank Cedar Rapids, N.A.; Hansen Lind Meyer, Inc.; McLeod Telecommunications Group, Inc.; Met-Coil Systems Corporation; SCI Financial Group, Inc.

For Complete List of Firm Personnel, See General Section

For full biographical listings, see the Martindale-Hubbell Law Directory

*COUNCIL BLUFFS,** Pottawattamie Co.

SMITH PETERSON LAW FIRM (AV)

35 Main Place, Suite 300, P.O. Box 249, 51502
Telephone: 712-328-1833
Fax: 712-328-8320
Omaha, Nebraska Office: 9290 West Dodge Road, Suite 205.
Telephone: 402-397-8500.
Fax: 402-397-5519.

MEMBERS OF FIRM

Raymond A. Smith (1892-1977)
John LeRoy Peterson (1895-1969)
Harold T. Beckman
Robert J. Laubenthal
Richard A. Heininger
Lawrence J. Beckman
Gregory G. Barntsen
W. Curtis Hewett
Steven H. Krohn
Randy R. Ewing
Joseph D. Thornton

ASSOCIATES

Trent D. Reinert (Not admitted in IA)
T. J. Pattermann

Representative Clients: Aetna Life and Casualty Co.; Employers Mutual Co.; First National Bank of Council Bluffs; IMT Insurance Co.; Monsanto Co.; United Fire & Casualty Co.; U.S. Fidelity and Guaranty.

For full biographical listings, see the Martindale-Hubbell Law Directory

*DES MOINES,** Polk Co.

AHLERS, COONEY, DORWEILER, HAYNIE, SMITH & ALLBEE, P.C. (AV)

100 Court Avenue, Suite 600, 50309-2231
Telephone: 515-243-7611
Fax: 515-243-2149

Ronald L. Sutphin
Mark W. Beerman

OF COUNSEL

James Evans Cooney

Representative Clients: Brownell's Inc.; Drake University; Koss Construction Co.; McDonalds Corp.; Pittsburgh-Des Moines Steel Co.; Sears, Roebuck & Co.

For Complete List of Firm Personnel, See General Section

For full biographical listings, see the Martindale-Hubbell Law Directory

DAVIS, HOCKENBERG, WINE, BROWN, KOEHN & SHORS, P.C. (AV)

The Financial Center, 666 Walnut Street, Suite 2500, 50309-3993
Telephone: 515-288-2500
Cable: Davis Law
Facsimile: 515-243-0654
Affiliated London, England Office: Vizards, Solicitors, 42 Bedford Row. London WC1R 4JL England.
Telephone: 071-405-6302.
Facsimile: 071-405-6248.

(See Next Column)

DAVIS, HOCKENBERG, WINE, BROWN, KOEHN & SHORS P.C., *Des Moines—Continued*

Donald J. Brown
Stephen W. Roberts
Michael G. Kulik
Frank J. Carroll
Bruce I. Campbell
David B. VanSickel
Nicholas H. Roby
David W. Body

For Complete List of Firm Personnel, See General Section

For full biographical listings, see the Martindale-Hubbell Law Directory

DICKINSON, MACKAMAN, TYLER & HAGEN, P.C. (AV)

Suite 1600 Hub Tower, 699 Walnut Street, 50309-3986
Telephone: 515-244-2600
Telecopier: 515-246-4550

L. J. Dickinson (1873-1968)
L. Call Dickinson (1905-1974)
Addison M. Parker (Retired)
John H. Raife (Retired)
Robert B. Throckmorton (Retired)
Helen C. Adams
Brent R. Appel
Barbara G. Barrett
John W. Blyth
L. Call Dickinson, Jr.
Jeanine M. Freeman
David J. Grace
Craig F. Graziano
Howard O. Hagen
J. Russell Hixson
Paul E. Horvath
F. Richard Lyford
John R. Mackaman
Richard A. Malm
James W. O'Brien
Arthur F. Owens
Rebecca Boyd Parrott
David M. Repp
Robert C. Rouwenhorst
Russell L. Samson
David S. Steward
Philip E. Stoffregen
Francis (Frank) J. Stork
Jon P. Sullivan
Celeste L. Tito (Not admitted in IA)
Paul R. Tyler
John K. Vernon
J. Marc Ward
Linda S. Weindruch

OF COUNSEL

Robert E. Mannheimer

Representative Clients: Archer-Daniels-Midland Co.; Board of Water Works Trustees, Des Moines, Iowa; Merchants Bonding Co. (Mutual); Norwest Bank, N.A.

For full biographical listings, see the Martindale-Hubbell Law Directory

GREFE & SIDNEY (AV)

2222 Grand Avenue, P.O. Box 10434, 50306
Telephone: 515-245-4300
Fax: 515-245-4452

MEMBERS OF FIRM

Rolland E. Grefe
Ross H. Sidney
Thomas W. Carpenter
Henry A. Harmon
Claude H. Freeman
Stephen D. Hardy
Robert C. Thomson
Craig S. Shannon
John Werner
Patrick J. McNulty
Iris J. Post
Mark W. Thomas
Guy R. Cook

ASSOCIATES

Ken A. Winjum
David C. Duncan
Andrew D. Hall
Kevin W. Techau
Stephanie L. Glenn

Representative Clients: Easter Stores; Freeman Decorating Co.; Iowa-Nebraska Farm Equipment Association, Inc.; Pella Corp.; State Farm Mutual Insurance Companies of Bloomington, Ill.; Liberty Mutual Insurance Co.; United States Fidelity and Guaranty Co.; Koehring Co.

For Complete List of Firm Personnel, See General Section

For full biographical listings, see the Martindale-Hubbell Law Directory

*SIOUX CITY,** Woodbury Co.

BERENSTEIN VRIEZELAAR MOORE MOSER & TIGGES (AV)

300 Commerce Building, P.O. Box 1557, 51102
Telephone: 712-252-3226
Fax: 712-252-4873
Dakota Dunes, South Dakota Office: One River Place, Suite 111, 600 Stevens Port Drive, 57049.
Telephone: 605-232-9464.
Fax: 712-252-4873.

MEMBERS OF FIRM

Marvin S. Berenstein
Kent Vriezelaar
Dale C. Tigges
Ray H. Edgington

Representative Clients: Aalfs Manufacturing, Inc.; Briar Cliff College; Canal Capital Corp.- Sioux City Stockyards; Firstar Bank-Sioux City, N.A.; Gateway 2000, Inc.; Metropolitan Life Insurance Co.; Metz Baking Co.; Sioux Tools, Inc.; Sisters of Mercy-Marian Health Center; Wells Dairy & Blue Bunny Ice Cream.

For Complete List of Firm Personnel, See General Section

For full biographical listings, see the Martindale-Hubbell Law Directory

KANSAS

PRAIRIE VILLAGE, Johnson Co.

HOLMAN, MCCOLLUM & HANSEN, P.C. (AV㊉)

9400 Mission Road Suite 205, 66206
Telephone: 913-648-7272
Fax: 913-383-9596
Kansas City, Missouri Office: 644 West 57th Terrace.
Telephone: 816-333-8522.
Fax: 913-383-9596.

Joseph Y. Holman
Frank B. W. McCollum
Eric L. Hansen
Dana L. Parks
Nancy Merrill Wilson
Amy L. Brown
E. John Edwards III (Not admitted in KS)
Katherine E. Rich

For full biographical listings, see the Martindale-Hubbell Law Directory

*TOPEKA,** Shawnee Co.

COFFMAN, DEFRIES & NOTHERN, A PROFESSIONAL ASSOCIATION (AV)

(Formerly Schroeder, Heeney, Groff and Coffman)
Suite 408 Capitol Tower, 400 Southwest Eight Avenue, 66603-3956
Telephone: 913-234-3461
Fax: 913-234-3363

Harold R. Schroeder (1920-1986)
Barney J. Heeney, Jr. (Retired)
James Robert Groff (Retired)
H. Hurst Coffman
S. Lucky DeFries
R. Austin Nothern

Richard Harmon
Susan J. Krehbiel

Representative Clients: Martin Tractor Co., Inc.; Radiology & Nuclear Medicine, A Professional Association; Cohen Esrey Real Estate Co.; Colgate-Palmolive Co.; Melvin Simon & Associates.

For full biographical listings, see the Martindale-Hubbell Law Directory

FOULSTON & SIEFKIN (AV)

(Formerly Foulston, Siefkin, Powers & Eberhardt)
1515 Bank IV Tower, 534 Kansas Avenue, 66603
Telephone: 913-233-3600
FAX: 913-233-1610
Wichita, Kansas Office: 700 Fourth Financial Center, Broadway at Douglas. 67202.
Telephone: 316-267-6371.
Facsimile: 316-267-6345.
Member: Lex Mundi, A Global Association of Independent Firms

MEMBERS OF FIRM

James P. Rankin
Stanley G. Andeel (Resident, Wichita Office)
Harvey R. Sorensen (Resident, Wichita Office)
Christopher M. Hurst (Resident, Wichita Office)
Eric F. Melgren (Resident, Wichita Office)

For full biographical listings, see the Martindale-Hubbell Law Directory

GOODELL, STRATTON, EDMONDS & PALMER (AV)

515 South Kansas Avenue, 66603-3999
Telephone: 913-233-0593
Telecopier: 913-233-8870

MEMBERS OF FIRM

H. Philip Elwood
Gerald J. Letourneau

OF COUNSEL

Robert A. McClure

ASSOCIATE

Craig S. Kendall

SPECIAL COUNSEL

Joseph E. McKinney

Local Counsel for: Farm Bureau Mutual Insurance Co.; Metropolitan Life Insurance Co.; St. Paul Fire & Marine Insurance Co.
General Counsel for: American Home Life Insurance Co.; Columbian National Title Insurance Co.; The Menninger Foundation; Stauffer Communications, Inc.; Kansas Association of Realtors; Kansas Medical Society; Kansas Hospital Association.

For Complete List of Firm Personnel, See General Section

For full biographical listings, see the Martindale-Hubbell Law Directory

*WICHITA,** Sedgwick Co.

BEVER, DYE, MUSTARD & BELIN (AV)

700 First National Bank Building, 106 W. Douglas, 67202-3390
Telephone: 316-263-8294
Fax: 316-263-3142

Ellis D. Bever (Retired)
James D. Dye (Retired)
Thomas D. Mustard (1909-1979)
Oscar F. Belin
Don B. Stahr
William M. Cobb
Jack D. Flesher
R. Chris Robe
Eric J. Larson
Robert M. Hughes
Gregory L. Franken
David B. Sutton
R. Eric Ireland

Representative Clients: Borton, Inc.; City Publishing Co., Inc.; First National Bank in Wichita; F.G. Holl Estate; Kansas Health Foundation; Klepper Oil Co.; Krause Plow Corp.; National Cooperative Refinery Assn.; Pickrell Drilling Co.; Vanier, Inc.

For full biographical listings, see the Martindale-Hubbell Law Directory

FLEESON, GOOING, COULSON & KITCH, L.L.C. (AV)

125 North Market Street, Suite 1600, P.O. Box 997, 67201-0997
Telephone: 316-267-7361
Telecopier: 316-267-1754

Willard B. Thompson
Timothy P. O'Sullivan
Edward J. Healy
Dixie F. Madden

John R. Gerdes

Attorneys for: Bank IV, Wichita, N.A; Intrust Bank, N.A.; Wichita Eagle and Beacon Publishing Co., Inc.; Southwest Kansas Royalty Owners Assn.; Liberty Mutual Insurance Co.; Grant Thornton; The Law Company; Vulcan Materials Co.; The Wichita State University Board of Trustees.

For Complete List of Firm Personnel, See General Section

For full biographical listings, see the Martindale-Hubbell Law Directory

FOULSTON & SIEFKIN (AV)

(Formerly Foulston, Siefkin, Powers & Eberhardt)
700 Fourth Financial Center, Broadway at Douglas, 67202
Telephone: 316-267-6371
Facsimile: 316-267-6345
Topeka, Kansas Office: 1515 Bank IV Tower, 534 Kansas Avenue. 66603.
Telephone: 913-233-3600.
FAX: 913-233-1610.
Member: Lex Mundi, A Global Association of Independent Firms

MEMBERS OF FIRM

Stanley G. Andeel
Harvey R. Sorensen
Christopher M. Hurst
James P. Rankin (Resident, Topeka Office)
Eric F. Melgren

For Complete List of Firm Personnel, See General Section

For full biographical listings, see the Martindale-Hubbell Law Directory

HINKLE, EBERHART & ELKOURI, L.L.C. (AV)

Suite 2000 Epic Center, 301 North Main Street, 67202
Telephone: 316-267-2000
Fax: 316-264-1518

David S. Elkouri
Eric S. Namee
Dan C. Peare

Connie D. Tatum

Representative Clients: Rand Graphics, Inc.; Hugoton Energy Corporation; Interex Computer Products; Capital Enterprises; Kirkpatrick & Sprecker, C.P.A.'s; Wichita Airport Authority; Beech Aircraft Corporation; Federal Farm Credit Bank; Consolidated Mftg. Inc.; Universal Lubricants.

For Complete List of Firm Personnel, See General Section

For full biographical listings, see the Martindale-Hubbell Law Directory

KENTUCKY

*BOWLING GREEN,** Warren Co.

BELL, ORR, AYERS & MOORE, P.S.C. (AV)

1010 College Street, P.O. Box 738, 42102-0738
Telephone: 502-781-8111
Telecopier: 502-781-9027

(See Next Column)

Chas. R. Bell (1891-1976)
Joe B. Orr (1914-1987)
Reginald L. Ayers
Ray B. Buckberry, Jr.
Quinten B. Marquette
George E. Strickler, Jr.
Kevin C. Brooks
Timothy L. Mauldin
Barton D. Darrell
Timothy L. Edelen

James S. Weisz

General Counsel for: First American National Bank of Kentucky; Farm Credit Services of Mid-America, ACA.; Houchens Industries, Inc. (Food Markets and Shopping Centers); Warren County Board of Education; Bowling Green Municipal Utilities.
Representative Clients: Chicago Title Insurance Co.; Commonwealth Land Title Insurance Co.; Kentucky Farm Bureau Mutual Insurance Co.; Martin Automotive Group; Home Insurance Group.

For full biographical listings, see the Martindale-Hubbell Law Directory

CATRON, KILGORE & BEGLEY (AV)

918 State Street, P.O. Box 280, 42102-0280
Telephone: 502-842-1050
Fax: 502-842-4720

Stephen B. Catron
J. Patrick Kilgore
Ernest Edward Begley, II

Representative Clients: Western Kentucky University; Bowling Green-Warren County Industrial Park Authority, Inc.

For full biographical listings, see the Martindale-Hubbell Law Directory

ENGLISH, LUCAS, PRIEST & OWSLEY (AV)

1101 College Street, P.O. Box 770, 42102-0770
Telephone: 502-781-6500
Telecopier: 502-782-7782

MEMBERS OF FIRM

Charles E. English
Wade T. Markham, II

ASSOCIATE

Vance Cook

For Complete List of Firm Personnel, See General Section

For full biographical listings, see the Martindale-Hubbell Law Directory

COVINGTON, Kenton Co.

TALIAFERRO AND MEHLING (AV)

1005 Madison Avenue, P.O. Box 468, 41012-0468
Telephone: 606-291-9900
Fax: 606-291-3014

MEMBERS OF FIRM

Philip Taliaferro, III
Christopher J. Mehling

ASSOCIATES

Lucinda C. Shirooni
C. Houston Ebert
Alice G. Keys
J. David Brittingham

OF COUNSEL

Robert W. Carran
Norbert J. Bischoff

For full biographical listings, see the Martindale-Hubbell Law Directory

*LEXINGTON,** Fayette Co.

WILLIAM R. BAGBY (AV)

1107 First National Building, 40507
Telephone: 606-254-2321

For full biographical listings, see the Martindale-Hubbell Law Directory

STOLL, KEENON & PARK (AV)

201 E. Main Street, Suite 1000, 40507-1380
Telephone: 606-231-3000
Telecopier: 606-253-1093; 606-253-1027
Frankfort, Kentucky Office: 326 West Main Street.
Telephone: 502-875-6000.
Telecopier: 502-875-6008.
Louisville, Kentucky Office: 400 West Market Street, Suite 2650, 40202.
Telephone: 502-568-9100.
Telecopier: 502-568-6340.

MEMBERS OF FIRM

William T. Bishop, III
R. David Lester
Douglas P. Romaine
Frank L. Wilford
C. Joseph Beavin
John Wesley Walters, Jr.

ASSOCIATE

Roger W. Madden

Representative Clients: A.T. Massey Coal Co., Inc.; Breeders Cup Ltd.; Claiborne Farm; Delta Airlines; Keeneland Assn., Inc.; Kentucky Thoroughbred Assn., Inc.; Mill Ridge Farm, Ltd.; Pathology & Cytology Laboratories, Inc. Peabody Coal Sales.

(See Next Column)

STOLL, KEENON & PARK, *Lexington—Continued*

For Complete List of Firm Personnel, See General Section

For full biographical listings, see the Martindale-Hubbell Law Directory

*LOUISVILLE,** Jefferson Co.

GREENEBAUM DOLL & MCDONALD (AV)

A Partnership including Professional Service Corporations
3300 National City Tower, 40202
Telephone: 502-589-4200
Fax: 502-587-3695
Lexington, Kentucky Office: 1400 Vine Center Tower.
Telephone: 606-231-8500.
Fax: 606-255-2742.
Covington, Kentucky Office: 50 East River Center Boulevard, P.O. Box 2050.
Telephone: 606-655-4200.
Fax: 606-655-4239.
Cincinnati, Ohio Office: 832 Main Street.
Telephone: 513-421-8087.
Fax: 513-421-8089.

Laramie L. Leatherman (1932-1994)
A. Robert Doll *
Thomas A. Brown
Lawrence K. Banks *
Charles Fassler
John R. Cummins
Charles J. Lavelle
William L. Montague (Covington, Kentucky and Cincinnati, Ohio Offices)
Patrick J. Welsh

ASSOCIATES

Mark F. Sommer
Damien M. Prather
John S. Lueken

OF COUNSEL

Martin S. Weinberg

Representative Clients: Ashland Oil, Inc.; Columbia/HCA Healthcare Corp.; First Kentucky National Corp.; The Gheens Foundation, Inc.; Humana, Inc.; Louisville Gas & Electric; NTS Development Co.; Texas Gas Transmission Corp.
*A Professional Service Corporation

For Complete List of Firm Personnel, See General Section

For full biographical listings, see the Martindale-Hubbell Law Directory

HIRN DOHENY REED & HARPER (AV)

A Partnership including a Professional Service Corporation
2000 Meidinger Tower, 40202
Telephone: 502-585-2450
Telecopiers: 502-585-2207; 585-2529

MEMBER OF FIRM

Gary R. Weitkamp

ASSOCIATES

Maxine E. Bizer
James Nitsche

Representative Clients: Humana, Inc.; Louisville Gas & Electric Co.; Presbyterian Church (U.S.A.).

For Complete List of Firm Personnel, See General Section

For full biographical listings, see the Martindale-Hubbell Law Directory

MIDDLETON & REUTLINGER, P.S.C. (AV)

2500 Brown and Williamson Tower, 40202-3410
Telephone: 502-584-1135
Fax: 502-561-0442
Jeffersonville, Indiana Office: 605 Watt Street, 47130.
Telephone: 812-282-4886.

Brooks Alexander
D. Randall Gibson
Kipley J. McNally
Michael R. Shumate

Representative Clients: The Kroger Co.; Campbell Tobacco Rehandling Co., Inc.; Chevron U.S.A., Inc.; Henderson Electric Co.; Cardinal Aluminum Co.; Porcelain Metal Corp.; EnTrade Corp.; Soltech, Inc.; Bluegrass Electronics, Inc.; Alexander & Alexander (SISCO).

For Complete List of Firm Personnel, See General Section

For full biographical listings, see the Martindale-Hubbell Law Directory

MORRIS, GARLOVE, WATERMAN & JOHNSON (AV)

Established 1925 as Morris and Garlove.
Suite 1000, One Riverfront Plaza, 40202-2959
Telephone: 502-589-3200
Fax: 502-589-3219

(See Next Column)

Irwin G. Waterman
Alan N. Linker
Michael T. Hymson

For Complete List of Firm Personnel, See General Section

For full biographical listings, see the Martindale-Hubbell Law Directory

OGDEN NEWELL & WELCH (AV)

1200 One Riverfront Plaza, 40202-2973
Telephone: 502-582-1601
Fax: 502-581-9564

MEMBERS OF FIRM

Joseph C. Oldham
James L. Coorssen
Robert E. Thieman
James B. Martin, Jr.
Turney P. Berry

ASSOCIATE

Lady Evelyn Booth

Counsel for: KU Energy Corp.; Kentucky Utilities Co.; Brown-Forman Corp.; B.F. Goodrich Co.; Brown & Williamson Tobacco Corp.; J.J.B. Hilliard, W.L. Lyons, Inc.; Akzo Coatings, Inc.; Bramco, Inc.; Interlock Industries, Inc.; Bank of Louisville.

For Complete List of Firm Personnel, See General Section

For full biographical listings, see the Martindale-Hubbell Law Directory

RUBIN HAYS & FOLEY (AV)

First Trust Centre 200 South Fifth Street, 40202
Telephone: 502-569-7550
Telecopier: 502-569-7555

MEMBERS OF FIRM

Wm. Carl Fust
Harry Lee Meyer
David W. Gray
Irvin D. Foley
Joseph R. Gathright, Jr.
Lisa Koch Bryant
Sharon C. Hardy
Charles S. Musson
W. Randall Jones
K. Gail Russell

ASSOCIATE

Christian L. Juckett

OF COUNSEL

James E. Fahey
Newman T. Guthrie

Representative Clients: J.C. Bradford & Co., Inc.; J.J.B. Hilliard, W.L. Lyons, Inc.; Huntington National Bank; Liberty National Bank and Trust Company; National City Bank; PNC Bank; Prudential Bache & Co., Inc.; Prudential Securities, Inc.; Society Bank; Stock Yards Bank and Trust Co.

For full biographical listings, see the Martindale-Hubbell Law Directory

TAUSTINE, POST, SOTSKY, BERMAN, FINEMAN & KOHN (AV)

8th Floor Marion E. Taylor Building, 40202
Telephone: 502-589-5760
Telecopier: 502-584-5927

MEMBERS OF FIRM

Hugo Taustine (1899-1987)
Edward M. Post (1929-1986)
Marvin M. Sotsky
Jerome D. Berman
Joseph E. Fineman
Robert A. Kohn
Alex Berman
H. Philip Grossman
Stanley W. Whetzel, Jr.
Maria A. Fernandez

ASSOCIATE

Sandra Sotsky Harrison

OF COUNSEL

W. David Shearer, Jr.
David A. Friedman
Martin R. Snyder
Jerald R. Steinberg (Also Practicing individually as Steinberg & Steinberg)
Craig I. Lustig

For full biographical listings, see the Martindale-Hubbell Law Directory

*PADUCAH,** McCracken Co.

WHITLOW, ROBERTS, HOUSTON & RUSSELL (AV)

Old National Bank Building, 300 Broadway, P.O. Box 995, 42001
Telephone: 502-443-4516
FAX: 502-443-4571

MEMBERS OF FIRM

Gary B. Houston
Randy L. Treece

Representative Clients: Peoples First National Bank & Trust Co., Paducah; First Liberty Bank, Calvert City/Benton; First National Bank, LaCenter; Salem Bank, Salem/Smithland; Bank of Murray, Murray; Paxton Media Group, Inc.; Crounse Corporation.

For Complete List of Firm Personnel, See General Section

For full biographical listings, see the Martindale-Hubbell Law Directory

LOUISIANA

*ALEXANDRIA,** Rapides Parish

GOLD, WEEMS, BRUSER, SUES & RUNDELL, A PROFESSIONAL LAW CORPORATION (AV)

2001 MacArthur Drive, P.O. Box 6118, 71307-6118
Telephone: 318-445-6471
Telecopier: 318-445-6476

Charles S. Weems, III — Kenneth O. Ortego

Representative Clients: Roy O. Martin Lumber Co., Inc.; Rapides Bank & Trust Company in Alexandria; Rapides Regional Medical Center; Aetna Casualty Group; Allstate Insurance Co.; Texas Industries, Inc.; International Paper Company; Louisiana-Pacific Corporation; Crest Industries, Inc.

For Complete List of Firm Personnel, See General Section

For full biographical listings, see the Martindale-Hubbell Law Directory

*BATON ROUGE,** East Baton Rouge Parish

KEAN, MILLER, HAWTHORNE, D'ARMOND, MCCOWAN & JARMAN, L.L.P. (AV)

22nd Floor, One American Place, P.O. Box 3513, 70821
Telephone: 504-387-0999
Fax: 504-388-9133
New Orleans, Louisiana Office: Energy Centre, Suite 1470, 1100 Poydras Street.
Telephone: 504-585-3050.
Fax: 504-585-3051.

MEMBERS OF FIRM

Ben R. Miller, Jr. — Isaac M. Gregorie, Jr.
Carey J. Messina — G. Blane Clark, Jr.
Todd A. Rossi

Representative Clients: Arcadian Corporation, Geismar, La.; Copolymer Rubber and Chemical Corporation, Baton Rouge, La.; Dow Chemical Company, Midland, Co.; Dowell Schlumberger, Houston, Texas; Georgia Gulf Corporation, Atlanta, Ga.; ICI Americas, Wilmington, Del.; The Lamar Corporation, Baton Rouge, La.; Riverwood International Corporation, West Monroe, La.; Rhone-Poulenc Basic Chemicals Company, Shelton, Ct.; Vulcan Materials Company, Birmingham, Al.

For Complete List of Firm Personnel, See General Section

For full biographical listings, see the Martindale-Hubbell Law Directory

SCHMIDT & KUEHNE, A PROFESSIONAL LAW CORPORATION (AV)

10935 Perkins Road, P.O. Box 80317, 70898
Telephone: 504-767-7093
Telecopier: 504-767-7096

Robert C. Schmidt — G. Bruce Kuehne

For full biographical listings, see the Martindale-Hubbell Law Directory

WATSON, BLANCHE, WILSON & POSNER (AV)

505 North Boulevard, P.O. Drawer 2995, 70821-2995
Telephone: 504-387-5511
Fax: 504-387-5972
Other Baton Rouge, Louisiana Office: 4000 South Sherwood Forest Boulevard, Suite 504.
Telephone: 504-291-5280.
Fax: 504-293-8075.

Harvey H. Posner — Alton J. Reine, Jr.
Robert L. Roland — Richard S. Dunn

Representative Clients: Citizens Savings and Loan Association; Community Coffee Company, Inc.; Louisiana Hospital Association; Prudential Insurance Company of America (The).

For Complete List of Firm Personnel, See General Section

For full biographical listings, see the Martindale-Hubbell Law Directory

*NEW ORLEANS,** Orleans Parish

DEUTSCH, KERRIGAN & STILES (AV)

A Partnership including Professional Law Corporations
755 Magazine Street, 70130-3672
Telephone: 504-581-5141
Cable Address: "Dekest"
Telex: 584358
Telecopier: 504-566-1201

MEMBERS OF FIRM

Harry S. Anderson (P.L.C.) — L. Paul Hood, Jr.

For Complete List of Firm Personnel, See General Section

For full biographical listings, see the Martindale-Hubbell Law Directory

THE GODFREY FIRM A PROFESSIONAL LAW CORPORATION (AV)

2500 Energy Centre, 1100 Poydras Street, 70163-2500
Telephone: 504-585-7538
Fax: 504-585-7535

Jarrell E. Godfrey, Jr. — Glenn J. Reames
Jacob S. Capraro — Paul F. Guarisco

For full biographical listings, see the Martindale-Hubbell Law Directory

MILLING, BENSON, WOODWARD, HILLYER, PIERSON & MILLER (AV)

A Partnership including Professional Law Corporations
Suite Twenty-Three Hundred, 909 Poydras Street, 70112-1017
Telephone: 504-569-7000
Cable Address: "Milling"
Telex: 58-4211
Telecopier: 504-569-7001
ABA net: 15656
MCI Mail: "Milling"
Lafayette, Louisiana Office: 101 LaRue France, Suite 200.
Telephone: 318-232-3929.
Telecopier: 318-233-4957.
Baton Rouge, Louisiana Office: Suite 402, 8555 United Plaza Blvd.
Telephone: 504-928-688.
Fax: 504-928-6881.

PARTNER EMERITUS

M. Truman Woodward, Jr., (P.C.)

MEMBERS OF FIRM

G. Henry Pierson, Jr., (P.C.) — Charles A. Snyder (P.C.)
David J. Conroy (P.C.) — Richard A. Whann (P.C.)
William C. Gambel (P.C.) — Hilton S. Bell (P.C.)
John W. Colbert (P.C.)

SPECIAL COUNSEL

J. Clifford Rogillio (P.C.)

ASSOCIATE

Julia M. Pearce

For List of Representative Clients and Complete List of Firm Personnel, See General Section.

For Complete List of Firm Personnel, See General Section

For full biographical listings, see the Martindale-Hubbell Law Directory

NESSER, KING & LEBLANC (AV)

Suite 3800 Place St. Charles, 201 St. Charles Avenue, 70170
Telephone: 504-582-3800
Telecopier: 504-582-1233

John T. Nesser, III — Patricia Ann Krebs
Henry A. King — Robert J. Burvant
Joseph E. LeBlanc, Jr. — Eric Earl Jarrell
David S. Bland — Liane K. Hinrichs

Jeffrey M. Burmaster — Elton A. Foster
Jeffrey A. Mitchell — Elizabeth S. Wheeler
Margaret M. Sledge — Robert J. Bergeron
Josh M. Kantrow — Timothy S. Madden
Elizabeth A. Meek

OF COUNSEL

Clare P. Hunter — J. Grant Coleman
George B. Jurgens, III — Len R. Brignac
George Farber, Jr.

For full biographical listings, see the Martindale-Hubbell Law Directory

PHELPS DUNBAR, L.L.P. (AV)

Texaco Center, 400 Poydras Street, 70130-3245
Telephone: 504-566-1311
Telecopier: 504-568-9130, 504-568-9007
Cable Address: "Howspencer"
Telex: 584125 WU
Telex: 6821155 WUI
Baton Rouge, Louisiana Office: Suite 701, City National Bank Building, P.O. Box 4412.
Telephone: 504-346-0285.
Telecopier: 504-381-9197.
Jackson, Mississippi Office: Suite 500, Security Centre North, 200 South Lamar Street, P.O. Box 23066.
Telephone: 601-352-2300.
Telecopier: 601-360-9777.
Tupelo, Mississippi Office: Seventh Floor, One Mississippi Plaza, P.O. Box 1220.
Telephone: 601-842-7907.
Telecopier: 601-842-3873.
Houston, Texas Office: Suite 501, 4 Houston Center, 1331 Lamar Street.
Telephone: 713-659-1386.
Telecopier: 713-659-1388.

(See Next Column)

PHELPS DUNBAR L.L.P., *New Orleans—Continued*

London, England Office: Suite 976, Level 9, Lloyd's, 1 Lime Street, London EC3M 7DQ England.
Telephone: 011-44-71-929-4765.
Telecopier: 011-44-71-929-0046.
Telex: 987321.

MEMBERS OF FIRM

F. M. Bush, III (Not admitted in LA; Jackson and Tupelo, Mississippi Offices)
C. Delbert Hosemann, Jr. (Not admitted in LA; Resident, Jackson, Mississippi Office)
Robert W. Nuzum
Glover A. Russell, Jr. (Not admitted in LA; Resident, Jackson, Mississippi Office)
Deborah Shelby Nichols (Not admitted in LA; Resident, Jackson, Mississippi Office)
David P. Webb (Not admitted in LA; Resident, Jackson, Mississippi Office)

COUNSEL

Jane E. Armstrong
Linda Bounds Sherman (Not admitted in LA; Resident, Jackson, Mississippi Office)
Gregory D. Pirkle (Not admitted in LA; Jackson and Tupelo, Mississippi Offices)

ASSOCIATES

John B. Beard (Not admitted in LA; Resident, Jackson, Mississippi Office)
John B. Landry, Jr. (Not admitted in LA; Resident, Jackson, Mississippi Office)
Stephen M. Wilson (Not admitted in LA; Jackson and Tupelo, Mississippi Offices)

Representative Clients: Bank of Mississippi; Dominion Resources, Inc.; Falco Lime, Inc.; First National Bank of Commerce; First National Bank of Jefferson Parish; Hibernia National Bank; International Business Machines Corporation; Louisiana General Services, Inc.; Pathology Laboratories, Inc. dba Puckett Labs; Rubicon Inc.

For Complete List of Firm Personnel, See General Section

For full biographical listings, see the Martindale-Hubbell Law Directory

*SHREVEPORT,** Caddo Parish

BARLOW AND HARDTNER L.C. (AV)

Tenth Floor, Louisiana Tower, 401 Edwards Street, 71101-3289
Telephone: 318-227-1131
Telecopier: 318-227-1141
Mailing Address: P.O. Box 8, Shreveport, Louisiana, 71161-0008

Quintin T. Hardtner, III
Malcolm S. Murchison
David R. Taggart

OF COUNSEL

Cecil E. Ramey, Jr.
Paula Hazelrig Hickman

Representative Clients: Kelley Oil Corporation; NorAm Energy Corp. (formerly Arkla, Inc.); Central and South West; Panhandle Eastern Corp.; Pennzoil Producing Co.; Johnson Controls, Inc.; Ashland Oil, Inc.; Southwestern Electric Power Company; Brammer Engineering, Inc.; General Electric Co.

For Complete List of Firm Personnel, See General Section

For full biographical listings, see the Martindale-Hubbell Law Directory

COOK, YANCEY, KING & GALLOWAY, A PROFESSIONAL LAW CORPORATION (AV)

1700 Commercial National Tower, 333 Texas Street, P.O. Box 22260, 71120-2260
Telephone: 318-221-6277
Telecopier: 318-227-2606

Sidney B. Galloway
J. Benjamin Warren, Jr.
William C. Kalmbach, III

Counsel For: Commercial National Bank; Wheless Industries, Inc.; American Rose Society; Falco S & D, Inc.; Crystal Oil Co.; Specialty Oil Co.; WWF Oil Corp.; Tensas Delta Land Co.

For Complete List of Firm Personnel, See General Section

For full biographical listings, see the Martindale-Hubbell Law Directory

WIENER, WEISS, MADISON & HOWELL, A PROFESSIONAL CORPORATION (AV)

333 Texas Street, Suite 2350, P.O. Box 21990, 71120-1990
Telephone: 318-226-9100
Fax: 318-424-5128

Donald P. Weiss
Allen P. Jones

Representative Clients: Pioneer Bank & Trust Co.; Ford Motor Credit Corp.; CNA Insurance Companies; International Paper Companies; Louisiana Homebuilders Association Self Insurers Fund; LSU-Shreveport; Sealy Realty, Inc.; Palmer Petroleum, Inc.; Brookshire Grocery Company (Louisiana); Northwest Louisiana Production Credit Association.

(See Next Column)

For Complete List of Firm Personnel, See General Section

For full biographical listings, see the Martindale-Hubbell Law Directory

MAINE

LEWISTON, Androscoggin Co.

BRANN & ISAACSON (AV)

184 Main Street, P.O. Box 3070, 04243-3070
Telephone: 207-786-3566
Telecopier: 207-783-9325

MEMBERS OF FIRM

Louis J. Brann (1876-1948)
Peter A. Isaacson (1895-1980)
Irving Isaacson
George S. Isaacson
Alfred C. Frawley, III
Martin I. Eisenstein
Martha E. Greene
David W. Bertoni

ASSOCIATES

Benjamin W. Lund
Peter D. Lowe
Daniel C. Stockford
Roy T. Pierce
David C. Pierson

Representative Clients: L.L. Bean, Inc.; Direct Marketing Assn.; Readers Digest Assn.; The Sharper Image; Bantam Doubleday Dell, Inc.; Supreme Slipper Manufacturing Company, Inc.; Livermore Falls Trust Co.; Dow Chemical Co.; United Egg Producers; Miller Hydro Group.

For full biographical listings, see the Martindale-Hubbell Law Directory

*PORTLAND,** Cumberland Co.

MCCANDLESS & HUNT (AV)

57 Exchange Street, 04101
Telephone: 207-772-4100
Telecopier: 207-772-1300

MEMBERS OF FIRM

Eileen M. L. Epstein
David E. Hunt
Elizabeth T. McCandless

ASSOCIATE

Dennis J. O'Donovan

For full biographical listings, see the Martindale-Hubbell Law Directory

PIERCE, ATWOOD, SCRIBNER, ALLEN, SMITH & LANCASTER (AV)

One Monument Square, 04101
Telephone: 207-773-6411
Fax: 207-773-3419
Augusta, Maine Office: 77 Winthrop Street.
Telephone: 207-622-6311.
Camden, Maine Office: 36 Chestnut Street, P.O. Box 780.
Telephone: 207-236-4333.

MEMBERS OF FIRM

Fred C. Scribner, Jr. (1908-1994)
William C. Smith
Everett P. Ingalls
James G. Good
Daniel M. Snow
Michael R. Currie
William H. Nichols

ASSOCIATES

Sarah H. Beard
Barbara K. Wheaton
Michael S. Wilson
Eric D. Altholz
Mary McQuillen
Jonathan A. Block

For Complete List of Firm Personnel, See General Section

For full biographical listings, see the Martindale-Hubbell Law Directory

PRETI, FLAHERTY, BELIVEAU & PACHIOS (AV)

443 Congress Street, P.O. Box 11410, 04104-7410
Telephone: 207-791-3000
Telecopier: 207-791-3111
Augusta, Maine Office: 45 Memorial Circle, P.O. Box 1058, 04332-1058.
Telephone: 207-623-5300.
Telecopier: 207-623-2914.
Rumford, Maine Office: 150 Congress Street, P.O. Drawer L, 04276-2035.
Telephone: 207-364-4593.
Telecopier: 207-369-9421.

MEMBERS OF FIRM

Severin M. Beliveau (Augusta Office)
James C. Pitney, Jr. (Augusta Office)
Michael L. Sheehan

ASSOCIATE

James E. Phipps

Representative Clients: IBM; IMB Credit Corp.; Bowater Inc./Great Northern Paper Inc.; UAH Hydro-Kennebec L.P.; Stratton Energy Associates; United Timber Corp.; Mount Desert Island Hospital; Maine Coast Memorial Hospital; Maine Auto Dealers Assn.; Maine Oil Dealers Assn.

(See Next Column)

PRETI, FLAHERTY, BELIVEAU & PACHIOS—*Continued*

For Complete List of Firm Personnel, See General Section

For full biographical listings, see the Martindale-Hubbell Law Directory

SOUTH PORTLAND, Cumberland Co.

VAN MEER & BELANGER, P.A. (AV)

25 Long Creek Drive, 04106
Telephone: 207-871-7500
Fax: 207-871-7505

Thomas J. Van Meer
Norman R. Belanger
D. Kelley Young
Richard N. Bryant

Betts J. Gorsky

For full biographical listings, see the Martindale-Hubbell Law Directory

MARYLAND

*BALTIMORE,** (Independent City)

McKENNEY, THOMSEN AND BURKE (AV)

Suite 400, One North Charles Street, 21201
Telephone: 410-539-2595
FAX: 410-783-0710
Washington, D.C. Office: Suite 500, 1225 Eye Street, N.W.
Telephone: 202-682-4741.
FAX: 202-547-3713.

OF COUNSEL

W. Gibbs McKenney

MEMBERS OF FIRM

George E. Thomsen
Paul E. Burke, Jr.
Roszel C. Thomsen, II

ASSOCIATES

Hedley A. Clark
Patrick Kennedy

References: NationsBank; Mercantile-Safe Deposit & Trust Co.; Carroll County Bank and Trust Co.

For full biographical listings, see the Martindale-Hubbell Law Directory

MILES & STOCKBRIDGE, A PROFESSIONAL CORPORATION (AV)

10 Light Street, 21202-1487
Telephone: 410-727-6464
Telecopier: 385-3700
Towson, Maryland Office: 600 Washington Avenue, Suite 300.
Telephone: 410-821-6565.
Telecopier: 823-8123.
Easton, Maryland Office: 101 Bay Street.
Telephone: 410-822-5280.
Telecopier: 822-5450.
Cambridge, Maryland Office: 300 Academy Street.
Telephone: 410-228-4545.
Telecopier: 228-5652.
Rockville, Maryland Office: 22 West Jefferson Street.
Telephone: 301-762-1600.
Telecopier: 762-0363.
Frederick, Maryland Office: 30 West Patrick Street.
Telephone: 301-662-5155.
Telecopier: 662-3647.
Washington, D.C. Office: 1450 G. Street, N.W., Suite 445.
Telephone: 202-737-9600.
Telecopier: 737-0097.
Fairfax, Virginia Office: Fair Oaks Plaza, 11350 Random Hills Road.
Telephone: 703-273-2440.
Telecopier: 273-4446.

Theodore W. Hirsh
Edward J. Adkins
Richard E. Levine
Harold Altscher
Timothy K. Hogan

Representative Clients: Maryland National Bank; Lloyd's of London; The Black & Decker Corp.; Aetna Life & Casualty Co.; Martin Marietta Corp.; Employers Mutual Casualty Co.; Transcontinental Gas Pipeline Corp.; Westinghouse Electric Corp.; Crum & Forster Group; NationsBank Corporation.

For Complete List of Firm Personnel, See General Section

For full biographical listings, see the Martindale-Hubbell Law Directory

PIPER & MARBURY (AV)

Charles Center South, 36 South Charles Street, 21201-3010
Telephone: 410-539-2530
FAX: 410-539-0489
Washington, D.C. Office: 1200 Nineteenth Street, N.W., 20036-2430.
Telephone: 202-861-3900.
FAX: 202-223-2085.

(See Next Column)

Easton, Maryland Office: 117 Bay Street, 21601-2703.
Telephone: 410-820-4460.
FAX: 410-820-4463.
Garrison, New York Office: Garrison Landing.
Telephone: 914-424-3711.
Fax: 914-424-3045.
New York, N.Y. Office: 31 West 52nd Street, 10019-6118.
Telephone: 212-261-2000.
FAX: 212-261-2001.
Philadelphia, Pennsylvania Office: Suite 1500, 2 Penn Center Plaza, 19102-1715.
Telephone: 215-656-3300.
FAX: 215-656-3301.
London, England Office: 14 Austin Friars, EC2N 2HE.
Telephone: 071-638-3833.
FAX: 071-638-1208.

MEMBERS OF FIRM

Stuart A. Smith (Resident, New York Office)
Lawrence M. Katz
Joseph H. Langhirt
Lee A. Sheller
Nancy Doerr O'Neil

ASSOCIATES

Stephen M. Sharkey
Jordan I. Bailowitz

For Complete List of Firm Personnel, See General Section

For full biographical listings, see the Martindale-Hubbell Law Directory

RICHARD T. STANSBURY A PROFESSIONAL ASSOCIATION (AV)

Suite 920, The B & O Building, Two North Charles Street, 21201-3754
Telephone: 410-727-6200
Facsimile: 410-385-2939
Annapolis, Maryland Office: 5th Floor, The Conte Building, 116 Defense Highway.
Telephone: 410-974-6007.
Facsimile: 410-974-6019.

Richard T. Stansbury

Sherri R. Heyman

For full biographical listings, see the Martindale-Hubbell Law Directory

VENABLE, BAETJER AND HOWARD (AV)

A Partnership including Professional Corporations
1800 Mercantile Bank & Trust Building, 2 Hopkins Plaza, 21201
Telephone: 410-244-7400
Washington, D.C. Office: Venable, Baetjer, Howard & Civiletti. Suite 1000, 1201 New York Avenue, N.W.
Telephone: 202-962-4800.
McLean, Virginia Office: Suite 400, 2010 Corporate Ridge.
Telephone: 703-760-1600.
Rockville, Maryland Office: Suite 500, One Church Street, P. O. Box 1906.
Telephone: 301-217-5600.
Towson, Maryland Office: 210 Allegheny Avenue, P. O. Box 5517.
Telephone: 410-494-6200.

MEMBERS OF FIRM

Jacques T. Schlenger (P.C.)
Neal D. Borden (Also at Washington, D.C. Office)
Daniel O'C. Tracy, Jr. (Also at Rockville, Maryland Office)
Jan K. Guben (Also at Washington, D. C Office)
Robert E. Madden (Not admitted in MD; also at Washington, D.C. and McLean, Virginia Offices)
Lars E. Anderson (Not admitted in MD; Resident, McLean, Virginia Office)
Alexander I. Lewis, III (P.C.) (Also at Towson, Maryland Office)
Michael Schatzow (Also at Washington, D.C. and Towson, Maryland Offices)
Bryson L. Cook (P.C.) (Also at Washington, D.C. Office)
Barbara E. Schlaff
L. Paige Marvel
Edward L. Wender (P.C.)
David M. Fleishman
Mitchell Kolkin
W. Robert Zinkham
Robert L. Waldman
John A. Roberts (Also at Rockville, Maryland Office)
Robert J. Bolger, Jr. (Also at Washington, D.C. Office)
Bruce H. Jurist (Also at Washington, D.C. Office)

OF COUNSEL

Robert M. Thomas (P.C.)
Robert R. Bair (P.C.)
Emried D. Cole, Jr.
Joyce K. Becker

ASSOCIATES

Michael J. Baader
John P. Edgar
Newton B. Fowler, III
Robert H. Geis, Jr.
Jeffrey K. Gonya
Lisa H. Rice Hayes
Gregory L. Laubach (Resident, Rockville, Maryland Office)
Traci H. Mundy (Not admitted in MD; Resident, Washington, D.C. Office)
Vadim A. Mzhen
Todd K. Snyder
Neal H. Strum
Linda Marotta Thomas
Robin L. Zimelman

For Complete List of Firm Personnel, See General Section

For full biographical listings, see the Martindale-Hubbell Law Directory

BETHESDA, Montgomery Co.

PALEY, ROTHMAN, GOLDSTEIN, ROSENBERG & COOPER, CHARTERED (AV)

Seventh Floor, One Bethesda Center, 4800 Hampden Lane, 20814
Telephone: 301-656-7603
Telecopier: 301-654-7354

Victor J. Rosenberg
Mark S. Rothman
Stephen H. Paley
Ronald A. Dweck
Robert H. Maclay
Steven A. Widdes
Dennis L. Sharp
Jeffrey A. Kolender

For Complete List of Firm Personnel, See General Section

For full biographical listings, see the Martindale-Hubbell Law Directory

*ROCKVILLE,** Montgomery Co.

STEIN, SPERLING, BENNETT, DE JONG, DRISCOLL, GREENFEIG & METRO, P.A. (AV)

25 West Middle Lane, 20850
Telephone: 301-340-2020; 800-435-5230
Telecopier: 301-340-8217

David S. De Jong
Ann G. Jakabcin

For Complete List of Firm Personnel, See General Section

For full biographical listings, see the Martindale-Hubbell Law Directory

SILVER SPRING, Montgomery Co.

ALEXANDER, GEBHARDT, APONTE & MARKS, L.L.C. (AV)

Lee Plaza-Suite 805, 8601 Georgia Avenue, 20910
Telephone: 301-589-2222
Facsimile: 301-589-2523
Washington, D.C. Office: 1314 Nineteenth Street, N.W., 20036.
Telephone: 202-835-1555.
New York, New York Office: 330 Madison Avenue, 36th Floor.
Telephone: 212-808-0008.
Fax: 212-599-1028.

Koteles Alexander (Not admitted in MD)

Suelyn Smith
Suzette Wynn Blackwell

Reference: Riggs National Bank of Washington, D.C.

For full biographical listings, see the Martindale-Hubbell Law Directory

MASSACHUSETTS

*BOSTON,** Suffolk Co.

BINGHAM, DANA & GOULD (AV)

150 Federal Street, 02110
Telephone: 617-951-8000
Cable Address: "Blodgham Bsn"
Telex: 275147 BDGBSN UR
Telecopy: 617-951-8736
Hartford, Connecticut Office: 100 Pearl Street.
Telephone: 203-244-3770.
Telecopy: 203-527-5188.
London, England Office: 39 Victoria Street, SWIH 0EE.
Telephone: 011-44-71-799-2646.
Telecopy: 011-44-71-799-2654.
Telex: 888179 BDGLDN G.
Cable Address: "Blodgham Ldn".
Washington, D.C. Office: 1550 M Street, N.W.
Telephone: 202-822-9320.
Telecopy: 202-833-1506.

MEMBERS OF FIRM

Donald-Bruce Abrams
John S. Brown
M. Gordon Ehrlich
William A. Hazel
Russell E. Isaia
George P. Mair
Lawrence I. Silverstein

OF COUNSEL

Hugh J. Ault
Kenneth W. Bergen
J. Patrick Dowdall

ASSOCIATE

Darcy A. Ryding

For Complete List of Firm Personnel, See General Section

For full biographical listings, see the Martindale-Hubbell Law Directory

BURNS & LEVINSON (AV)

125 Summer Street, 02110-1624
Telephone: 617-345-3000
Telecopier: 617-345-3299
Rockland, Massachusetts Office: 1001 Hingham Street.
Telephone: 617-749-1023; 982-4100.
Telecopier: 617-982-4141.

MEMBERS OF FIRM

Howard D. Medwed
Melvin A. Warshaw
Evelyn A. Haralampu

For Complete List of Firm Personnel, See General Section

For full biographical listings, see the Martindale-Hubbell Law Directory

FOLEY, HOAG & ELIOT (AV)

One Post Office Square, 02109
Telephone: 617-482-1390
Cable Address: "Foleyhoag"
Telex: 94-0693
Telecopier: 617-482-7347
Washington, D.C. Office: 1615 L Street, N.W.
Telephone: 202-775-0600.
Telecopier: 202-857-0140.

MEMBERS OF FIRM

Robert L. Birnbaum
Leonard Schneidman
Paul E. Tsongas
Louis P. Georgantas
Deborah A. Willard
John L. Burke, Jr. (Managing Partner, Washington, D.C. Office)
Stefanie D. Cantor
Bruce A. Kinn
James T. Montgomery, Jr. (Resident at Washington, D.C. Office)
Richard R. Schaul-Yoder

ASSOCIATES

Harry F. Lee
David H. Ruttenberg

For Complete List of Firm Personnel, See General Section

For full biographical listings, see the Martindale-Hubbell Law Directory

GOODWIN, PROCTER & HOAR (AV)

A Partnership including Professional Corporations
Exchange Place, 02109-2881
Telephone: 617-570-1000
Cable Address: "Goodproct, Boston"
Telex: 94-0640
Telecopier: 617-523-1231
Washington, D.C. Office: 901 Fifteenth Street, N.W., Suite 410.
Telephone: 202-414-6160.
Telecopier: 202-789-1720.
Albany, New York Office: One Steuben Place.
Telephone: 518-472-9460.
Telecopier: 518-472-9472.

MEMBERS OF FIRM

Robert B. Fraser (P.C.)
Edward L. Glazer (P.C.)
John J. Cleary (P.C.)
Diane L. Currier (P.C.)
Marian A. Tse

For Complete List of Firm Personnel, See General Section

For full biographical listings, see the Martindale-Hubbell Law Directory

PALMER & DODGE (AV)

(Storey Thorndike Palmer & Dodge)
One Beacon Street, 02108
Telephone: 617-573-0100
Telecopier: 617-227-4420
Telex: 951104
Cable Address: "Storeydike," Boston

MEMBERS OF FIRM

Neil P. Arkuss
Robert W. Buck
Ralph C. Derbyshire
Karl P. Fryzel
Malcolm E. Hindin
Robert G. Holdway
Eric F. Menoyo
Arthur B. Page
Thomas M. Spera
Jackson W. Wright, Jr.

OF COUNSEL

Robert J. McGee

For Complete List of Firm Personnel, See General Section

For full biographical listings, see the Martindale-Hubbell Law Directory

RACKEMANN, SAWYER & BREWSTER, PROFESSIONAL CORPORATION (AV)

One Financial Center, 02111
Telephone: 617-542-2300
Telecopier: 617-542-7437

(See Next Column)

RACKEMANN, SAWYER & BREWSTER PROFESSIONAL CORPORATION—*Continued*

William B. Tyler
George V. Anastas
Henry H. Thayer
Stephen Carr Anderson
Albert M. Fortier, Jr.
Michael F. O'Connell
Stuart T. Freeland
Raymond J. Brassard
Alan B. Rubenstein
Martin R. Healy
James R. Shea, Jr.
Brian M. Hurley
Janet M. Smith
Peter Friedenberg
Richard S. Novak
J. David Leslie
Alexander H. Spaulding
Sanford M. Matathia
Anne P. Zebrowski

OF COUNSEL

Albert B. Wolfe
August R. Meyer
Richard H. Lovell

COUNSEL

Ronald S. Duby
Ross J. Hamlin

Margaret L. Hayes
Daniel J. Ossoff
Mary B. Freeley
Gordon M. Orloff
Donald R. Pinto, Jr.
Lucy West Behymer
Richard J. Gallogly
Melissa Langer Ellis
James A. Wachta
Susan Dempsey Baer
Daniel J. Bailey, III
Michael S. Giaimo
Maura E. Murphy
Mary L. Gallant
Peter A. Alpert
Lauren D. Armstrong
Robert B. Foster
Elizabeth A. Gibbons

For full biographical listings, see the Martindale-Hubbell Law Directory

ROPES & GRAY (AV)

One International Place, 02110
Telephone: 617-951-7000
Fax: 617-951-7050
Washington, D.C. Office: Suite 1200, 1001 Pennsylvania Avenue, N.W.
Telephone: 202-626-3900.
Telecopy: 202-626-3961.
Providence, Rhode Island Office: 30 Kennedy Plaza.
Telephone: 401-455-4400.
Telecopy: 401-455-4401.

MEMBERS OF FIRM

David J. Blattner, Jr.
David M. Donaldson
Fred R. Becker
Ronald L. Groves
Carolyn M. Osteen
Stephen E. Shay (Not admitted in MA)
Susan A. Johnston
Eric M. Elfman
Adelbert L. Spitzer
Brett A. Robbins

ASSOCIATES

Christopher M. Leich
Raj Marphatia

OF COUNSEL

Wilson C. Piper
Harry K. Mansfield

For Complete List of Firm Personnel, See General Section

For full biographical listings, see the Martindale-Hubbell Law Directory

SHERBURNE, POWERS & NEEDHAM, P.C. (AV)

One Beacon Street, 02108
Telephone: 617-523-2700
Fax: 617-523-6850

William D. Weeks
John T. Collins
Allan J. Landau
John L. Daly
Stephen A. Hopkins
Alan I. Falk
C. Thomas Swaim
James Pollock
William V. Tripp III
Stephen S. Young
William F. Machen
W. Robert Allison
Jacob C. Diemert
Philip J. Notopoulos
Richard J. Hindlian
Paul E. Troy
Harold W. Potter, Jr.
Dale R. Johnson
Philip S. Lapatin
Pamela A. Duckworth
Mark Schonfeld
James D. Smeallie
Paul Killeen
Gordon P. Katz
Joseph B. Darby, III
Richard M Yanofsky
James E. McDermott
Robert V. Lizza
Miriam Goldstein Altman
John J. Monaghan
Margaret J. Palladino
Mark C. Michalowski
David Scott Sloan
M. Chrysa Long
Lawrence D. Bradley
Miriam J. McKendall

Cynthia A. Brown
Cynthia M. Hern
Dianne R. Phillips
Paul M. James
Theodore F. Hanselman
Joshua C. Krumholz
Ieuan G. Mahony
Kenneth L. Harvey
Christopher J. Trombetta
Edwin F. Landers, Jr.
Amy J. Mastrobattista
William Howard McCarthy, Jr.
Douglas W. Clapp
Tamara E. Goulston
Nicholas J. Psyhogeos

(See Next Column)

COUNSEL

Haig Der Manuelian
Mason M. Taber, Jr.
Karl J. Hirshman
Benjamin Volinski
Kenneth P. Brier

OF COUNSEL

John Barr Dolan

For full biographical listings, see the Martindale-Hubbell Law Directory

WARNER & STACKPOLE (AV)

75 State Street, 02109
Telephone: 617-951-9000
Cable Address: "Warstack"
Telecopier: 617-951-9151
Telex: 940139

MEMBERS OF FIRM

Stephen E. Moore
Steven L. Paul

ASSOCIATE

Jill M. Pechacek

For Complete List of Firm Personnel, See General Section

For full biographical listings, see the Martindale-Hubbell Law Directory

MERVIN M. WILF, LTD. (AV)

300 Commonwealth Avenue, 02115
Telephone: 617-437-7981
Philadelphia, Pennsylvania Office: 3200 Mellon Bank Center. 1735 Market Street.
Telephone: 215-575-7650. 568-4842.
Facsimile: 215-575-7652.

Mervin M. Wilf

A list of Representative Clients and References will be furnished upon request.

For full biographical listings, see the Martindale-Hubbell Law Directory

*SPRINGFIELD,** Hampden Co.

GABERMAN & PARISH, P.C. (AV)

32 Hampden Street, 01103
Telephone: 413-781-5066
Fax: 413-732-5439

Richard M. Gaberman
Ronda G. Parish

Richard D. Keough

OF COUNSEL

Leonard Judelson

For full biographical listings, see the Martindale-Hubbell Law Directory

MICHIGAN

*ANN ARBOR,** Washtenaw Co.

MILLER, CANFIELD, PADDOCK AND STONE, P.L.C. (AV)

A Professional Limited Liability Company
Founded in 1852 by Sidney Davy Miller
101 North Main Street, Seventh Floor, 48104-1400
Telephone: 313-663-2445
Fax: 313-747-7147
Detroit, Michigan Office: 150 West Jefferson, Suite 2500, 48226-4415.
Telephone: 313-963-6420.
Fax: 313-496-7500.
Cable Address: "Stem Detroit."
Bloomfield Hills, Michigan Office: Suite 100, Pinehurst Office Center, 1400 North Woodward, 48303-2014.
Telephone: 313-645-5000.
Fax: 313-645-1917.
Grand Rapids, Michigan Office: 1200 Campau Square Plaza, 99 Monroe, N.W., 49503-2639.
Telephone: 616-454-8656.
Fax: 616-776-6322.
Howell, Michigan Office: 121 South Barnard Street, Suite 4, 48843-2305.
Telephone: 517-546-7600.
Telecopier: 517-546-6974.
Kalamazoo, Michigan Office: 444 West Michigan Avenue, 49007-3752.
Telephone: 616-381-7030.
Fax: 616-382-0244.
Lansing, Michigan Office: One Michigan Avenue, Suite 900, 48933-1609.
Telephone: 517-487-2070.
Fax: 517-374-6304.

(See Next Column)

MILLER, CANFIELD, PADDOCK AND STONE P.L.C., *Ann Arbor—Continued*

Monroe, Michigan Office: The Executive Centre, 214 East Elm Avenue, 48161-2682.
Telephone: 313-243-2000.
Fax: 313-243-0901.
Washington, D.C. Office: 1225 Nineteenth Street, N.W., Suite 400. 20036.
Telephone: 202-429-5575; 785-0600.
Fax: 202-331-1118; 785-1234.
Pensacola, Florida Office: 25 West Cedar, 32501.
Telephone: 904-469-1088.
Fax: 904-432-0677.
St. Petersburg, Florida Office: 100 Second Avenue S., Suite 7045, 33701.
Telephone: 813-982-6000.
Fax: 813-892-6002.
Gdansk, Poland Office: Suite 322, Dom Technika Building, UI. Rajska 6, 80-850.
Telephone: 011-485-831-2808.
Fax: 011-485-831-4719.
Warsaw, Poland Office: UI. Marszalkowska 82, Suite 561, 00-517.
Telephone: 011-482-623-6457 and 6458.
Fax: 011-482-623-6459.

RESIDENT PARTNER

Robert E. Gilbert

SENIOR ATTORNEY

Ronald D. Gardner

Representative Firm Clients: Chrysler Corp.; Comerica, Inc.; City of Detroit, Mich.; Detroit Tigers, Inc.; First of Michigan; Fretter, Inc.; Ford Motor Co.; Ford Motor Credit Co.; Great Lakes Bancorp; Henry Ford Hospital.

For Complete List of Firm Personnel, See General Section

For full biographical listings, see the Martindale-Hubbell Law Directory

RALPH S. RUMSEY (AV)

121 West Washington, Suite 400, 48104
Telephone: 313-995-3110
Fax: 313-995-1777
(Also Of Counsel to Butzel Long, Ann Arbor)

For full biographical listings, see the Martindale-Hubbell Law Directory

BATTLE CREEK, Calhoun Co.

VARNUM, RIDDERING, SCHMIDT & HOWLETT (AV)

4950 West Dickman Road, Suite B-1, 49015
Telephone: 616-962-7144
Grand Rapids, Michigan Office: Bridgewater Place, P.O. Box 352, 49501-0352.
Telephone: 616-336-6000; 800-262-0011.
Facsimile: 616-336-7000.
Telex: 1561593 VARN.
Lansing, Michigan Office: The Victor Center, Suite 810, 201 North Washington Square, 48933.
Telephone: 517-482-6237.
Facsimile: 517-482-6937.
Kalamazoo, Michigan Office: 350 East Michigan Avenue, 49007.
Telephone: 616-382-2300.
Facsimile: 616-382-2382.
Grand Haven, Michigan Office: 321 Washington Street, P.O. Box 288, 49417.
Telephone: 616-846-7100.
Facsimile: 616-846-7101.
Detroit, Michigan Office: 440 East Congress, Fourth Floor, 48226.
Telephone: 313-961-1600.
Facsimile: 313-961-1636.

MEMBER OF FIRM

Carl E. Ver Beek

For full biographical listings, see the Martindale-Hubbell Law Directory

*BAY CITY,** Bay Co.

BRAUN KENDRICK FINKBEINER (AV)

201 Phoenix Building, P.O. Box 2039, 48708
Telephone: 517-895-8505
Telecopier: 517-895-8437
Saginaw, Michigan Office: 8th Floor Second National Bank Building.
Telephone: 517-753-3461.
Telecopier: 517-753-3951.

MEMBERS OF FIRM

Ralph J. Isackson
Patrick D. Neering
George F. Gronewold, Jr.
Frank M. Quinn
Gregory E. Meter
Daniel S. Opperman
Gregory T. Demers

Representative Clients: APV Chemical Machinery, Inc.; Bay Health Systems; Berger and Co.; Catholic Federal Credit Union; Charter Township of Bridgeport; City of Saginaw; City of Vassar; City of Zilwaukee; Corporate Service; Cox Cable.

(See Next Column)

For Complete List of Firm Personnel, See General Section

For full biographical listings, see the Martindale-Hubbell Law Directory

BIRMINGHAM, Oakland Co.

CARSON FISCHER, P.L.C. (AV)

Third Floor, 300 East Maple Road, 48009-6317
Telephone: 810-644-4840
Facsimile: 810-644-1832

Robert M. Carson
William C. Edmunds

For full biographical listings, see the Martindale-Hubbell Law Directory

MACDONALD AND GOREN, P.C. (AV)

Suite 200, 260 East Brown Street, 48009
Telephone: 810-645-5940
Fax: 810-645-2490

Harold C. MacDonald
Kalman G. Goren
Cindy Rhodes Victor
Amy L. Glenn
David D. Marsh
Glenn G. Ross
Miriam Blanks-Smart
John T. Klees

Representative Clients: Bay Corrugated Container, Inc.; Miles Fox Company; Orlandi Gear Company, Inc.; Bing Steel, Inc.; Superb Manufacturing, Inc.; Spring Engineering, Inc.; Adrian Steel Company; Southfield Radiology Associates, P.C.; Blockbuster Entertainment Corporation; E.N.U.F. Internationale, Inc.

For full biographical listings, see the Martindale-Hubbell Law Directory

PIERCE & PIERCE, P.C. (AV)

255 S. Woodward Avenue, Suite 205, 48009
Telephone: 810-647-0404
Fax: 810-647-0849

Robert B. Pierce
Mark C. Pierce
Paul T. Mengel

For full biographical listings, see the Martindale-Hubbell Law Directory

WEINGARDEN & HAUER, P.C. (AV)

30100 Telegraph Road, Suite 221, 48025
Telephone: 810-258-0800
Telecopier: 810-258-2750

Larry A. Weingarden

Reference: Security Bank & Trust.

For full biographical listings, see the Martindale-Hubbell Law Directory

BLOOMFIELD HILLS, Oakland Co.

CLARK, KLEIN & BEAUMONT (AV)

1533 North Woodward Avenue, Suite 220, 48304
Telephone: 810-258-2900
Facsmile: 810-258-2949
Detroit, Michigan Office: 1600 First Federal Building. 1001 Woodward Avenue.
Telephone: 313-965-8300.
Facsimile: 313-962-4348.

MEMBER OF FIRM

Curtis J. Mann

Representative Clients: Chrysler Corporation; Eagle Trailer Company; Merck & Co.; Michigan Manufacturers Association; Quaker Chemical Corporation; Rouge Steel Company; Sidley Diamond Tool Co.; Thompson Transport.

For Complete List of Firm Personnel, See General Section

For full biographical listings, see the Martindale-Hubbell Law Directory

HOWARD & HOWARD ATTORNEYS, P.C. (AV)

The Pinehurst Office Center, Suite 101, 1400 North Woodward Avenue, 48304-2856
Telephone: 810-645-1483
Telecopier: 810-645-1568
Kalamazoo, Michigan Office: The Kalamazoo Building, Suite 400, 107 West Michigan Avenue.
Telephone: 616-382-1483.
Telecopier: 616-382-1568.
Lansing, Michigan Office: The Phoenix Building, Suite 500, 222 Washington Square, North.
Telephone: 517-485-1483.
Telecopier: 517-485-1568.
Peoria, Illinois Office: Howard & Howard, P.C., The Creve Coeur Building, Suite 200, 321 Liberty Street.
Telephone: 309-672-1483.
Telecopier: 309-672-1568.

Robert L. Biederman
Mark A. Davis
John E. Young

Representative Clients: For Representative Client list, see General Practice, Bloomfield Hills, MI.

(See Next Column)

HOWARD & HOWARD ATTORNEYS P.C.—*Continued*

For Complete List of Firm Personnel, See General Section

For full biographical listings, see the Martindale-Hubbell Law Directory

STROBL AND MANOOGIAN, P.C. (AV)

300 East Long Lake Road, Suite 200, 48304-2376
Telephone: 810-645-0306
Facsimile: 810-645-2690

John Sharp
James A. Rocchio
Kieran F. Cunningham

Brian M. Gottry
Robert F. Boesiger

Representative Clients: Flat Rock Metal, Inc.; Bohn Aluminum Corporation.

For Complete List of Firm Personnel, See General Section

For full biographical listings, see the Martindale-Hubbell Law Directory

*DETROIT,** Wayne Co.

BARRIS, SOTT, DENN & DRIKER, P.L.L.C. (AV)

211 West Fort Street, Fifteenth Floor, 48226-3281
Telephone: 313-965-9725
Telecopier: 313-965-2493
313-965-5398

MEMBERS OF FIRM

Donald E. Barris
Herbert Sott
David L. Denn
Eugene Driker
William G. Barris
Sharon M. Woods
Stephen E. Glazek
Robert E. Kass
Daniel M. Share
Elaine Fieldman
Morley Witus
John A. Libby
James S. Fontichiaro
Daniel J. LaCombe

COUNSEL

Leon S. Cohan

OF COUNSEL

Stanley M. Weingarden
Robert E. Epstein

ASSOCIATES

Dennis M. Barnes
Gary Schwarcz
Matthew J. Boettcher
Barry R. Powers
Thomas F. Cavalier
Bonita R. Gardner
C. David Bargamian
Michael J. Reynolds
John Christopher Clark

Representative Clients: Avis Rent A Car System, Inc.; Borman's, Inc.; Consumers Power Co.; County of Wayne, Michigan; Ford Motor Co.; The Great Atlantic & Pacific Tea Company, Inc.; Henry Ford Health System; Michigan Consolidated Gas Co.; NBD Bank, N.A.; Textron, Inc.

For full biographical listings, see the Martindale-Hubbell Law Directory

BODMAN, LONGLEY & DAHLING (AV)

34th Floor 100 Renaissance Center, 48243
Telephone: 313-259-7777
Fax: 313-393-7579
Troy, Michigan Office: Suite 2020, 755 West Big Beaver Road.
Telephone: 810-362-2110.
Ann Arbor, Michigan Office: 110 Miller, Suite 300.
Telephone: 313-761-3780.
Northern Michigan Office: 229 Court Street, P.O. Box 405, Cheboygan.
Telephone: 616-627-4351.

MEMBERS OF FIRM

Pierre V. Heftler
George D. Miller, Jr.
David M. Hempstead
John C. Cashen (Troy Office)
Christopher J. Dine (Troy Office)
Patrick C. Cauley

Representative Clients: Abitibi Price Group; Archdiocese of Detroit; Comerica Bank; The Detroit Lions, Inc.; Ford Estates; General Motors Corporation; Charles Stewart Mott Foundation; Norfolk Southern Corporation; Panhandle Eastern Corporation; State Farm Mutual Automobile Insurance Company.

For Complete List of Firm Personnel, See General Section

For full biographical listings, see the Martindale-Hubbell Law Directory

BUTZEL LONG, A PROFESSIONAL CORPORATION (AV)

Suite 900, 150 West Jefferson, 48226
Telephone: 313-225-7000
Telecopier: 313-225-7080
Birmingham, Michigan Office: Suite 200, 32270 Telegraph Road.
Telephone: 810-258-1616.
Telecopier: 810-258-1439.
Lansing, Michigan Office: 118 West Ottawa Street.
Telephone: 517-372-6622.
Telecopier: 517-372-6672.

(See Next Column)

Ann Arbor, Michigan Office: Suite 400, 121 West Washington.
Telephone: 313-995-3110.
Telecopier: 313-995-1777.
Grosse Pointe Farms, Michigan Office: Suite 260, 21 Kercheval.
Telephone: 313-886-5446.
Telecopier: 313-886-2114.

Mark S. Smallwood
Mark R. Lezotte
James L. Hughes
Gary J. Abraham (Birmingham)

COUNSEL

Oscar H. Feldman

Representative Clients: Guardian Industries Corp.; Jackson National Life Insurance; Kajima International; Mobil Oil Corp.; The Stroth Brewery Co.; United Parcel Service of America, Inc.; The Uniroyal Goodrich Tire Co.; William Beaumont Hospital; Kelly Services; Takata Corp.

For Complete List of Firm Personnel, See General Section

For full biographical listings, see the Martindale-Hubbell Law Directory

CLARK, KLEIN & BEAUMONT (AV)

1600 First Federal Building, 1001 Woodward Avenue, 48226
Telephone: 313-965-8300
Facsimile: 313-962-4348
Bloomfield Hills Office: 1533 North Woodward Avenue, Suite 220, 48304.
Telephone: 810-258-2900.
Facsimile: 810-258-2949.

MEMBERS OF FIRM

Douglas J. Rasmussen
Robert G. Buydens
Thomas S. Nowinski
Curtis J. Mann (Resident Bloomfield Hills, Michigan Office)
Joseph A. Bonventre
Michael G. Cumming
J. Thomas MacFarlane
Edward C. Hammond
Andrea M. Kanski

ASSOCIATES

Maureen A. Darmanin
Robin D. Ferriby
Jennifer Crawford

Representative Clients: Chrysler Corporation; Eagle Trailer Company; Merck & Co.; Michigan Manufacturers Association; Quaker Chemical Corporation; Rouge Steel Company; Sidley Diamond Tool Co.; Thompson Transport.

For Complete List of Firm Personnel, See General Section

For full biographical listings, see the Martindale-Hubbell Law Directory

DICKINSON, WRIGHT, MOON, VAN DUSEN & FREEMAN (AV)

500 Woodward Avenue, Suite 4000, 48226-3425
Telephone: 313-223-3500
Facsimile: 313-223-3598
Bloomfield Hills, Michigan Office: 525 North Woodward Avenue, Suite 2000.
Telephone: 810-433-7200.
Facsimile: 810-433-7274.
Grand Rapids, Michigan Office: 200 Ottawa Avenue, N.W., Suite 900.
Telephone: 616-458-1300.
Facsimile: 616-458-6753.
Lansing, Michigan Office: Suite 200, 215 South Washington Square.
Telephone: 517-371-1730.
Facsimile: 517-487-4700.
Washington, D.C. Office: Suite 800, 1901 L Street, N.W.
Telephone: 202-457-0160.
Facsimile: 202-659-1559.
Chicago, Illinois Office: 225 West Washington, Suite 400.
Telephone: 312-220-0300.
Facsimile: 312-220-0021.
Warsaw, Poland Office: 46 Wilcza Street, 4th Floor, 00-679.
Telephone: (48-22) 299-241.
Facsimile: (48-2) 628-4107. Komertel Satellite Phone: (48-39) 121-510.

MEMBERS OF FIRM

Ward Randol, Jr. (Bloomfield Hills Office)
Peter S. Sheldon (Lansing Office)
Frank G. Pollock (Bloomfield Hills Office)
Joyce Q. Lower (Bloomfield Hills Office)
David L. Turner
Richard J. Meyers
Henry M. Grix
Thomas D. Hammerschmidt, Jr.
Deborah L. Grace (Bloomfield Hills Office)

CONSULTING PARTNER

Ernest Getz

See General Section for list of Representative Clients.

For Complete List of Firm Personnel, See General Section

For full biographical listings, see the Martindale-Hubbell Law Directory

Detroit—Continued

DYKEMA GOSSETT (AV)

400 Renaissance Center, 48243-1668
Telephone: 313-568-6800
Cable Address: "Dyke-Detroit"
Telex: 23-0121
Fax: 313-568-6594
Ann Arbor, Michigan Office: 315 East Eisenhower Parkway, Suite 100, 48108-3306.
Telephone: 313-747-7660.
Fax: 313-747-7696.
Bloomfield Hills, Michigan Office: 1577 North Woodward Avenue, Suite 300, 48304-2820.
Telephone: 810-540-0700.
Fax: 810-540-0763.
Grand Rapids, Michigan Office: 200 Oldtown Riverfront Building, 248 Louis Campau Promenade, N.W., 49503-2668.
Telephone: 616-776-7500.
Fax: 616-776-7573.
Lansing, Michigan Office: 800 Michigan National Tower, 48933-1707.
Telephone: 517-374-9100.
Fax: 517-374-9191.
Washington, D.C. Office: Franklin Square, Suite 300 West Tower, 1300 I Street, N.W., 20005-3306.
Telephone: 202-522-8600.
Fax: 202-522-8669.
Chicago, Illinois Office: Three First National Plaza, Suite 1400, 70 W. Madison, 60602-4270.
Telephone: 312-214-3380.
Fax: 312-214-3441.

MEMBERS OF FIRM

James M. Elsworth
William E. Fisher
Steven E. Grob
Raymond T. Huetteman, Jr. (Resident at Ann Arbor Office)
Margaret Adams Hunter
Louis W. Kasischke (Resident at Bloomfield Hills Office)
Stewart L. Mandell
Richard M. Matthews
Theodore H. Oldham
David M. Rosenberger (Resident at Bloomfield Hills Office)
Thomas B. Spillane, Jr. (Resident at Bloomfield Hills Office)

OF COUNSEL

Eugene A. Gargaro, Jr.

RETIRED PARTNER

E. James Gamble

ASSOCIATES

Marie R. Deveney (Resident at Ann Arbor Office)
Dennis M. Doherty
Nancy L. Farnam (Resident at Bloomfield Hills Office)
Mark C. Larson
Gina M. Torielli (Resident at Lansing Office)
Sherrill D. Wolford

For Complete List of Firm Personnel, See General Section

For full biographical listings, see the Martindale-Hubbell Law Directory

FILDEW, HINKS, MILLER, TODD & WANGEN (AV)

3600 Penobscot Building, 48226-4291
Telephone: 313-961-9700
Telecopier: 313-961-0754

MEMBERS OF FIRM

Stanley L. Fildew (1896-1978)
Frank T. Hinks (1887-1974)
Richard E. Hinks (1916-1990)
John H. Fildew
Alan C. Miller
Charles D. Todd III
Randall S. Wangen
Mary Jane Ruffley
Robert D. Welchli
William P. Thorpe
Colleen A. Kramer
Stephen J. Pokoj

ASSOCIATES

Charles S. Kennedy, III
Gerald M. Swiacki

References: First of America Bank-Detroit, N.A.; Comerica Bank-Detroit; National Bank of Detroit.

For full biographical listings, see the Martindale-Hubbell Law Directory

HONIGMAN MILLER SCHWARTZ AND COHN (AV)

A Partnership including Professional Corporations
2290 First National Building, 48226
Telephone: 313-256-7800
Telecopier: 313-962-0176
Telex: 235705
Lansing, Michigan Office: Phoenix Building, 222 North Washington Square, Suite 400.
Telephone: 517-484-8282.
West Palm Beach, Florida Office: Suite 800 Esperante Building, 222 Lakeview Avenue.
Telephone: 407-838-4500.
Tampa, Florida Office: 2700 Landmark Centre, 401 E. Jackson Street.
Telephone: 813-221-6600.
Orlando, Florida Office: 390 North Orange Avenue, Suite 1300.
Telephone: 407-648-0300.

(See Next Column)

Houston, Texas Office: 3100 First Interstate Bank Plaza, 1000 Louisiana.
Telephone: 713-650-2600.
Los Angeles, California Office: McNeill Plaza, Suite 820, 15260 Ventura Boulevard, 91403.
Telephone: 818-784-2900.

MEMBERS OF FIRM

Keith B. Braun
Roger Cook
John H. Eggertsen
Gerald M. Griffith
Jeffrey A. Hyman
Mary Jo Larson
Marguerite Munson Lentz
Mark Morton (Lansing, Michigan Office)
Charles Nida
James H. Novis
Benjamin O. Schwendener, Jr. (Lansing, Michigan Office)
Sherill Siebert
Richard S. Soble
Alan M. Valade (Lansing, Michigan Office)
Richard E. Zuckerman

ASSOCIATE

Michael J. Friedman

RESIDENT IN TAMPA, FLORIDA OFFICE

MEMBER

Brad M. Tomtishen (P.A.)

RESIDENT IN ORLANDO, FLORIDA OFFICE

MEMBERS

Thomas R. Allen (P.A.)
Brad M. Tomtishen (P.A.)

Representative Clients: See General Section.

For Complete List of Firm Personnel, See General Section

For full biographical listings, see the Martindale-Hubbell Law Directory

HOUGHTON, POTTER, SWEENEY & BRENNER, A PROFESSIONAL CORPORATION (AV)

The Guardian Building, 500 Griswold Street, Suite 3300, 48226-3806
Telephone: 313-964-0050
Facsimile: 313-964-4005

Thomas F. Sweeney

LEGAL SUPPORT PERSONNEL

LEGAL ASSISTANTS

Ann E. Adams
Janet C. Driver

For full biographical listings, see the Martindale-Hubbell Law Directory

JAFFE, RAITT, HEUER & WEISS, PROFESSIONAL CORPORATION (AV)

One Woodward Avenue, Suite 2400, 48226
Telephone: 313-961-8380
Telecopier: 313-961-8358
Cable Address: "Jafsni"
Southfield,Michigan Office: Travelers Tower, Suite 1520.
Telephone: 313-961-8380.
Monroe, Michigan Office: 212 East Front Street, Suite 3.
Telephone: 313-241-6470.
Telefacsimile: 313-241-3849.

Alexander B. Bragdon
Gary R. Glenn
Ira J. Jaffe
Robert E. Lewis
Joel J. Morris
David H. Raitt
William E. Sider
Arthur A. Weiss
Janet G. Witkowski

See General Practice Section for List of Representative Clients.

For Complete List of Firm Personnel, See General Section

For full biographical listings, see the Martindale-Hubbell Law Directory

KERR, RUSSELL AND WEBER (AV)

One Detroit Center, 500 Woodward Avenue, Suite 2500, 48226-3406
Telephone: 313-961-0200
Telecopier: 313-961-0388
Bloomfield Hills, Michigan Office: 3883 Telegraph Road.
Telephone: 810-649-5990.
East Lansing, Michigan Office: 1301 North Hagadorn Road.
Telephone: 517-336-6767.

Michael D. Gibson
George J. Christopoulos
Mark J. Stasa
Jeffrey A. Brantley
Richard C. Buslepp
Daniel J. Schulte
John D. Gatti

For Complete List of Firm Personnel, See General Section

For full biographical listings, see the Martindale-Hubbell Law Directory

Detroit—Continued

MILLER, CANFIELD, PADDOCK AND STONE, P.L.C. (AV)

A Professional Limited Liability Company
Founded in 1852 by Sidney Davy Miller
150 West Jefferson, Suite 2500, 48226-4415
Telephone: 313-963-6420
Fax: 313-496-7500
Cable Address: "Stem Detroit"
Detroit, Michigan Office: 150 West Jefferson, Suite 2500, 48226-4415.
Telephone: 313-963-6420.
Fax: 313-496-7500.
Cable Address: "Stem Detroit."
Ann Arbor, Michigan Office: 101 North Main Street, 7th Floor, 48104-1400.
Telephone: 313-663-2445.
Fax: 313-747-7147.
Bloomfield Hills, Michigan Office: Suite 100, Pinehurst Office Center, 1400 North Woodward, 48303-2014.
Telephone: 313-645-5000.
Fax: 313-645-1917.
Grand Rapids, Michigan Office: 1200 Campau Square Plaza, 99 Monroe, N.W., 49503-2639.
Telephone: 616-454-8656.
Fax: 616-776-6322.
Howell, Michigan Office: 121 South Barnard Street, Suite 4, 48843-2305.
Telephone: 517-546-7600.
Telecopier: 517-546-6974.
Kalamazoo, Michigan Office: 444 West Michigan Avenue, 49007-3752.
Telephone: 616-381-7030.
Fax: 616-382-0244.
Lansing, Michigan Office: One Michigan Avenue, Suite 900, 48933-1609.
Telephone: 517-487-2070.
Fax: 517-374-6304.
Monroe, Michigan Office: The Executive Centre, 214 East Elm Avenue, 48161-2682.
Telephone: 313-243-2000.
Fax: 313-243-0901.
Washington, D.C. Office: 1225 Nineteenth Street, N.W., Suite 400. 20036.
Telephone: 202-429-5575; 785-0600.
Fax: 202-331-1118; 785-1234.
Pensacola, Florida Office: 25 West Cedar, 32501.
Telephone: 904-469-1088.
Fax: 904-432-0677.
St. Petersburg, Florida Office: 100 Second Avenue S., Suite 7045, 33701.
Telephone: 813-982-6000.
Fax: 813-892-6002.
Gdansk, Poland Office: Suite 322, Dom Technika Building, Ul. Rajska 6, 80-850.
Telephone: 011-485-831-2808.
Fax: 011-485-831-4719.
Warsaw, Poland Office: Ul. Marszalkowska 82, Suite 561, 00-517.
Telephone: 011-482-623-6457 and 6458.
Fax: 011-482-623-6459.

MEMBERS OF FIRM

Lawrence A. King (P.C.) (Bloomfield Hills Office)
Joseph F. Maycock, Jr.
George E. Parker, III
Stevan Uzelac (P.C.)
Robert S. Ketchum
Samuel J. McKim, III, (P.C.)
Rocque E. Lipford (P.C.) (Monroe Office)
John A. Thurber (P.C.) (Bloomfield Hills Office)
Orin D. Brustad
John A. Campbell (Kalamazoo Office)
Kenneth E. Konop (Bloomfield Hills Office)
James W. Williams (Bloomfield Hills Office)
Michael R. Atkins (Lansing Office)
Jeffrey M. McHugh
Robert F. Rhoades
Gregory V. Di Censo (Bloomfield Hills Office)
Michael A. Indenbaum
Vernon Bennett III (Grand Rapids and Kalamazoo Offices)
Deborah W. Thompson

OF COUNSEL

William G. Butler
John A. Gilray, Jr., (P.C.) (Bloomfield Hills Office)
Peter P. Thurber

SENIOR ATTORNEYS

Michael J. Taylor (Grand Rapids Office)
Ronald D. Gardner (Ann Arbor Office)

ASSOCIATES

Walter A. Payne, III
Richard I. Loebl
Joanne B. Faycurry
Dawn M. Schluter (Bloomfield Hills Office)

Representative Firm Clients: Chrysler Corp.; Comerica, Inc.; City of Detroit, Mich.; Detroit Tigers, Inc.; First of Michigan; Fretter, Inc.; Ford Motor Co.; Ford Motor Credit Co.; Great Lakes Bancorp; Henry Ford Hospital.

For Complete List of Firm Personnel, See General Section

For full biographical listings, see the Martindale-Hubbell Law Directory

DAVID M. THOMS & ASSOCIATES, P.C. (AV)

400 Renaissance Center, Suite 950, 48243
Telephone: 313-259-6333
Facsimile: 313-259-7037
Bloomfield Hills, Office: 1500 Woodward Avenue, Suite 100.
Telephone: 313-259-6333.
Fax: 313-259-7037.
Grosse Pointe Office: 377 Fisher Road.
Telephone: 313-259-6333.
Fax: 313-259-7037.

David M. Thoms

Audrey R. Holley
Duane B. Brown

OF COUNSEL

Allan G. Meganck
Thomas V. Trainer

Representative Clients: Avion Concepts, Inc.; Fowler Agency Corp.; Gibbs World Wide Wines, Inc.; deBary Travel, Inc.; North Management, Inc.; St. Jude Children's Research Hospital.
References: Comerica Bank-Detroit, National Bank of Detroit.

For full biographical listings, see the Martindale-Hubbell Law Directory

TIMMIS & INMAN (AV)

300 Talon Centre, 48207
Telephone: 313-396-4200
Telecopier: 313-396-4228

MEMBERS OF FIRM

Michael T. Timmis
Wayne C. Inman
Richard L. Levin

ASSOCIATES

George M. Malis
Mark Robert Adams
John P. Kanan

Representative Client: Talon, Inc.; Chateau Properties, Inc.; F & M Distributors.

For Complete List of Firm Personnel, See General Section

For full biographical listings, see the Martindale-Hubbell Law Directory

EAST LANSING, Ingham Co.

FARHAT, STORY & KRAUS, P.C. (AV)

Beacon Place, 4572 South Hagadorn Road, Suite 3, 48823
Telephone: 517-351-3700
Fax: 517-332-4122

Leo A. Farhat
James E. Burns (1925-1979)
Monte R. Story
Richard C. Kraus
Max R. Hoffman Jr.
Chris A. Bergstrom
Kitty L. Groh
Charles R. Toy
David M. Platt

Lawrence P. Schweitzer
Jeffrey J. Short
Kathy A. Breedlove
Thomas L. Sparks

Representative Clients: Big L. Corp.; Michigan Automotive Wholesalers Association.; Hartman-Fabco, Inc.; Lansing Electric Motors, Inc.; Mike Miller Lincoln Mercury; GTE Sprint Communications Corp.; GTE Directories Services Corp.; The John E Fetzer Trust.
Reference: Capitol National Bank.

For full biographical listings, see the Martindale-Hubbell Law Directory

FARMINGTON HILLS, Oakland Co.

COUZENS, LANSKY, FEALK, ELLIS, ROEDER & LAZAR, P.C. (AV)

33533 West Twelve Mile Road, Suite 150, P.O. Box 9057, 48333-9057
Telephone: 810-489-8600
Telecopier: 810-489-4156

Jack S. Couzens, II
Donald M. Lansky
Alan C. Roeder
Alan J. Ferrara
Renard J. Kolasa
Kathryn Gilson Sussman
Jeffrey A. Levine
Stephen M. Feldman
Marc L. Prey
Lisa J. Walters
Michael P. Witzke
Cyrus Raamin Kashef
William P. Lyshak
Gregg A. Nathanson
Aaron H. Sherbin

References: Comerica Bank-Southfield;
Representative Clients: Provided upon request.

For full biographical listings, see the Martindale-Hubbell Law Directory

DAGUANNO AND ACCETTURA (AV)

Arboretum Office Park, 34705 West Twelve Mile Road, Suite 311, 48331
Telephone: 810-489-1444
Fax: 810-489-1453

MEMBERS OF FIRM

Richard Daguanno
P. Mark Accettura

(See Next Column)

DAGUANNO AND ACCETTURA, *Farmington Hills—Continued*

ASSOCIATES

Robert J. Constan — Harry P. Bugeja

OF COUNSEL

John A. Zick — Robert E. Miller

References: Comerica Bank; Michigan Chamber of Commerce.

For full biographical listings, see the Martindale-Hubbell Law Directory

*FLINT,** Genesee Co.

WINEGARDEN, SHEDD, HALEY, LINDHOLM & ROBERTSON (AV)

501 Citizens Bank Building, 48502-1983
Telephone: 810-767-3600
Telecopier: 810-767-8776

MEMBERS OF FIRM

William C. Shedd — Donald H. Robertson
Dennis M. Haley — L. David Lawson
John T. Lindholm — John R. Tucker

ASSOCIATES

Alan F. Himelhoch — Damion Frasier
Suellen J. Parker — Peter T. Mooney

OF COUNSEL

Howard R. Grossman

Representative Clients: Citizens Commercial and Savings Bank; R.L. White Development Corporation; Interstate Traffic Consultants (Intracon) Inc.; Downtown Development Authority of Flint; Young Olds-Cadillac, Inc.; First American Title Insurance Co.; Sorensen Gross Construction Co.; Genesee County; Insight, Inc.; Flint Counsel, National Bank of Detroit.

For Complete List of Firm Personnel, See General Section

For full biographical listings, see the Martindale-Hubbell Law Directory

*GRAND RAPIDS,** Kent Co.

BORRE, PETERSON, FOWLER & REENS, P.C. (AV)

The Philo C. Fuller House, 44 Lafayette, N.E., P.O. Box 1767, 49501-1767
Telephone: 616-459-1971
FAX: 616-459-2393

Glen V. Borre

Representative Clients: A.L. Truck Lines, Inc.; Chadalee Farms, Inc.; Beaver Island Boat Co.; Big Rapids Products, Inc.; Herbruck Poultry Ranch; J & H Oil Co.; Master Finish Co.; Q.S.C., Inc.; Pfeiffer Lincoln Mercy, Inc.; Van Pines, Inc.

For Complete List of Firm Personnel, See General Section

For full biographical listings, see the Martindale-Hubbell Law Directory

CLARY, NANTZ, WOOD, HOFFIUS, RANKIN & COOPER (AV)

500 Calder Plaza, 250 Monroe Avenue, N.W., 49503-2244
Telephone: 616-459-9487
Telecopier: 616-459-5121

MEMBERS OF FIRM

Leonard M. Hoffius — Stephen J. Mulder
Edward J. Inman

ASSOCIATES

Thomas J. Dempsey (Not admitted in MI) — Kathryn Kraus Nunzio

Representative Clients: United Bank of Michigan; D&W Food Centers, Inc.; FMB First Michigan Bank-Grand Rapids; Goodrich Theatres & Radio, Inc.; S. Abraham & Sons, Inc.; Garb-Ko, Inc., d/b/a 7-Eleven; Weather Shield Mfg., Inc.; JET Electronics & Technology, Inc.; Westinghouse Credit Corp.

For Complete List of Firm Personnel, See General Section

For full biographical listings, see the Martindale-Hubbell Law Directory

RUSSELL & BATCHELOR (AV)

Suite 411-S Waters Building, 161 Ottawa Avenue, N.W., 49503
Telephone: 616-774-8422
Fax: 616-774-0326

MEMBER OF FIRM

Walter J. Russell

ASSOCIATE

Lawrence W. Wilson

Representative Clients: Progressive Architects/Engineers/Planners, Inc.; Quality Brass, Inc.; Seal Craft, Inc.; Shellcast, Inc.; Victor S. Barnes and Co.; Tuel, Inc.; Holiday Kennels; Action Die & Tool; Stovall Well Drilling; Kent Industrial Services, Inc.

For full biographical listings, see the Martindale-Hubbell Law Directory

PETER W. STEKETEE (AV)

660 Cascade West Parkway, S.E., Suite 65, 49546
Telephone: 616-949-6551
Fax: 616-949-8817

For full biographical listings, see the Martindale-Hubbell Law Directory

VARNUM, RIDDERING, SCHMIDT & HOWLETT (AV)

Bridgewater Place, P.O. Box 352, 49501-0352
Telephone: 616-336-6000
800-262-0011
Facsimile: 616-336-7000
Telex: 1561593 VARN
Lansing, Michigan Office: The Victor Center, Suite 810, 210 North Washington Square, 48933.
Telephone: 517-482-6237.
Facsimile: 517-482-6937.
Kalamazoo, Michigan Office: 350 East Michigan Avenue, 49007.
Telephone: 616-382-2300.
Facsimile: 616-382-2382.
Grand Haven, Michigan Office: 321 Washington Street, P.O. Box 288, 49417.
Telephone: 616-846-7100.
Facsimile: 616-846-7101.
Battle Creek, Michigan Office: 4950 West Dickman Road, Suite B-1, 49015.
Telephone: 616-962-7144.
Detroit, Michigan Office: 440 East Congress, Fourth Floor, 48226.
Telephone: 313-961-1600.
Facsimile: 313-961-1636.

MEMBERS OF FIRM

John C. Carlyle (Resident at Grand Haven Office) — Frank G. Dunten
Daniel C. Molhoek — Carl Oosterhouse
Kaplin S. Jones
Scott A. Huizenga

ASSOCIATE

Joseph B. Levan

For Complete List of Firm Personnel, See General Section

For full biographical listings, see the Martindale-Hubbell Law Directory

WARNER, NORCROSS & JUDD (AV)

900 Old Kent Building, 111 Lyon Street, N.W., 49503-2489
Telephone: 616-752-2000
Fax: 616-752-2500
Muskegon, Michigan Office: 400 Terrace Plaza, P.O. Box 900.
Telephone: 616-727-2600.
Fax: 616-727-2699.
Holland, Michigan Office: Curtis Center, Suite 300, 170 College Avenue.
Telephone: 616-396-9800.
Fax: 616-396-3656.

OF COUNSEL

Charles C. Lundstrom

MEMBERS OF FIRM

Thomas R. Winquist — John H. McKendry, Jr. (Resident at Muskegon Office)
George L. Whitfield — Carl W. Dufendach
Jerome M. Smith — Sue O. Conway
Vernon P. Saper — Steven R. Heacock
Roger H. Oetting — Cameron S. DeLong
Stephen R. Kretschman — Jeffrey B. Power
W. Michael Van Haren

Representative Clients: Bissell Inc.; Blodgett Memorial Medical Center; Guardsman Products, Inc.; Haworth, Inc.; Howard Miller Clock Company; Kysor Industrial Corp.; Michigan Bankers Assn.; Old Kent Financial Corp.; Steelcase Inc.; Wolverine World Wide, Inc.

For Complete List of Firm Personnel, See General Section

For full biographical listings, see the Martindale-Hubbell Law Directory

*KALAMAZOO,** Kalamazoo Co.

EARLY, LENNON, PETERS & CROCKER, P.C. (AV)

900 Comerica Building, 49007-4752
Telephone: 616-381-8844
Fax: 616-349-8525

George H. Lennon, III — Robert M. Taylor

Attorneys for: General Motors Corp.; Wal-Mart Stores; Borgess Medical Center; Aetna Insurance: Kemper Group; Medical Protective Co.; Zurich Insurance; AAA; Liberty Mutual; Home Insurance.

For Complete List of Firm Personnel, See General Section

For full biographical listings, see the Martindale-Hubbell Law Directory

Kalamazoo—Continued

HOWARD & HOWARD ATTORNEYS, P.C. (AV)

The Kalamazoo Building, Suite 400, 107 West Michigan Avenue, 49007-3956
Telephone: 616-382-1483
Telecopier: 616-382-1568
Bloomfield Hills, Michigan Office: The Pinehurst Office Center, Suite 101, 1400 North Woodward Avenue.
Telephone: 810-645-1483.
Telecopier: 810-645-1568.
Lansing, Michigan Office: The Phoenix Building, Suite 500, 222 Washington Square North.
Telephone: 517-485-1483.
Telecopier: 517-485-1568.
Peoria, Illinois Office: Howard & Howard, P.C., The Creve Coeur Building, Suite 200, 321 Liberty Street.
Telephone: 309-672-1483.
Telecopier: 309-672-1568.

Eric E. Breisach
Peter J. Livingston
D. Craig Martin

Representative Clients: First of America Bank Corp.; Simpson Paper Company; W.R. Grace & Co.; Stryker Corp.; Kalamazoo Valley Community College.
Local Counsel for: Chrysler Motors Corp.
International Counsel for: Sony Corp.

For Complete List of Firm Personnel, See General Section

For full biographical listings, see the Martindale-Hubbell Law Directory

KREIS, ENDERLE, CALLANDER & HUDGINS, A PROFESSIONAL CORPORATION (AV)

One Moorsbridge, 49002
Telephone: 616-324-3000
Telecopier: 616-324-3010

Russell A. Kreis
C. Reid Hudgins III
Daniel P. Mc Glinn

For Complete List of Firm Personnel, See General Section

For full biographical listings, see the Martindale-Hubbell Law Directory

MILLER, CANFIELD, PADDOCK AND STONE, P.L.C. (AV)

A Professional Limited Liability Company
Founded in 1852 by Sidney Davy Miller
444 West Michigan Avenue, 49007-3752
Telephone: 616-381-7030
Fax: 616-382-0244
Detroit, Michigan Office: 150 West Jefferson, Suite 2500, 48226-4415.
Telephone: 313-963-6420.
Fax: 313-496-7500.
Cable Address: "Stem Detroit."
Ann Arbor, Michigan Office: 101 North Main Street, 7th Floor, 48104-1400.
Telephone: 313-663-2445.
Fax: 313-747-7147.
Bloomfield Hills, Michigan Office: Suite 100, Pinehurst Office Center, 1400 North Woodward, 48303-2014.
Telephone: 313-645-5000.
Fax: 313-645-1917.
Grand Rapids, Michigan Office: 1200 Campau Square Plaza, 99 Monroe, N.W., 49503-2639.
Telephone: 616-454-8656.
Fax: 616-776-6322.
Howell, Michigan Office: 121 South Barnard Street, Suite 4, 48843-2305.
Telephone: 517-546-7600.
Telecopier: 517-546-6974.
Lansing, Michigan Office: One Michigan Avenue, Suite 900, 48933-1609.
Telephone: 517-487-2070.
Fax: 517-374-6304.
Monroe, Michigan Office: The Executive Centre, 214 East Elm Avenue, 48161-2682.
Telephone: 313-243-2000.
Fax: 313-243-0901.
Washington, D.C. Office: 1225 Nineteenth Street, N.W., Suite 400. 20036.
Telephone: 202-429-5575; 785-0600.
Fax: 202-331-1118; 785-1234.
Pensacola, Florida Office: 25 West Cedar, 32501.
Telephone: 904-469-1088.
Fax: 904-432-0677.
St. Petersburg, Florida Office: 100 Second Avenue S., Suite 7045,33701.
Telephone: 813-982-6000.
Fax: 813-892-6002.
Gdansk, Poland Office: Suite 322, Dom Technika Building, Ul. Rajska 6, 80-850.
Telephone: 011-485-831-2808.
Fax: 011-485-831-4719.
Warsaw, Poland Office: Ul. Marszalkowska 82, Suite 561, 00-517.
Telephone: 011-482-623-6457 and 6458.
Fax: 011-482-623-6459.

(See Next Column)

MEMBERS OF FIRM

Eric V. Brown, Jr. (Resident)
Vernon Bennett III (Resident)

Representative Firm Clients: Chrysler Corp.; Comerica, Inc.; City of Detroit, Mich.; Detroit Tigers, Inc.; First of Michigan; Fretter, Inc.; Ford Motor Co.; Ford Motor Credit Co.; Great Lakes Bancorp; Henry Ford Hospital.

For Complete List of Firm Personnel, See General Section

For full biographical listings, see the Martindale-Hubbell Law Directory

LANSING, Ingham Co.

* indicates certain Bar Register subscribers whose principal office is located elsewhere in the state and who have arranged for representation as a part of the state capital listings that follow

*** HONIGMAN MILLER SCHWARTZ AND COHN (AV)**

A Partnership including Professional Corporations
222 North Washington Square, Suite 400, 48933
Telephone: 517-484-8282
Telecopier: 517-484-8286
Detroit, Michigan Office: 2290 First National Building.
Telephone: 313-256-7800.
West Palm Beach, Florida Office: Suite 800 Esperante Building, 222 Lakeview Avenue.
Telephone: 407-838-4500.
Tampa, Florida Office: Suite 350 One Harbour Place, 777 South Harbour Island Boulevard.
Telephone: 813-221-6600.
Orlando, Florida Office: 390 North Orange Avenue, Suite 1300.
Telephone: 407-648-0300.
Houston, Texas Office: 3100 First Interstate Bank Plaza, 1000 Louisiana.
Telephone: 713-650-2600.
Los Angeles, California Office: McNeill Plaza, Suite 820, 15260 Ventura Boulevard, 91403.
Telephone: 818-784-2900.

MEMBERS

Benjamin O. Schwendener, Jr.
Alan M. Valade

For Complete List of Firm Personnel, See General Section

For full biographical listings, see the Martindale-Hubbell Law Directory

HOWARD & HOWARD ATTORNEYS, P.C. (AV)

The Phoenix Building, Suite 500, 222 Washington Square, North, 48933-1817
Telephone: 517-485-1483
Telecopier: 517-485-1568
Kalamazoo, Michigan Office: The Kalamazoo Building, Suite 400, 107 West Michigan Avenue.
Telephone: 616-382-1483.
Telecopier: 616-382-1568.
Bloomfield Hills, Michigan Office: The Pinehurst Office Center, Suite 101, 1400 North Woodward Avenue.
Telephone: 810-645-1483.
Telecopier: 810-645-1568.
Peoria, Illinois Office: Howard & Howard, P.C., The Creve Coeur Building, Suite 200, 321 Liberty Street.
Telephone: 309-672-1483.
Telecopier: 309-672-1568.

Michele LaForest Halloran
Ellen M. Harvath
Patrick R. Van Tiflin

Representative Clients: For Representative Client list, see General Practice, Lansing, MI.

For Complete List of Firm Personnel, See General Section

For full biographical listings, see the Martindale-Hubbell Law Directory

LIVONIA, Wayne Co.

FRIED & ASSOCIATES, P.C. (AV)

32900 5 Mile Road, Suite 4, 48154
Telephone: 313-421-5055
Fax: 313-421-5591

William C. Fried

For full biographical listings, see the Martindale-Hubbell Law Directory

*MIDLAND,** Midland Co.

CURRIE & KENDALL, P.C. (AV)

6024 Eastman Avenue, P.O. Box 1846, 48641-1846
Telephone: 517-839-0300
Fax: 517-832-0077

Gilbert A. Currie (1882-1960)
James A. Kendall
William C. Collins
Thomas L. Ludington
Ramon F. Rolf, Jr.
Daniel J. Cline
Peter A. Poznak
Julia A. Close
Peter J. Kendall
Jeffrey N. Dyer

(See Next Column)

CURRIE & KENDALL P.C., *Midland—Continued*

OF COUNSEL

Gilbert A. Currie
I. Frank Harlow
William D. Schuette

LEGAL SUPPORT PERSONNEL

Barbara J. Byron

Counsel for: Chemical Financial Corp.; Chemical Bank & Trust Co.; Saginaw Valley State University; Northwood University; The Midland Foundation; Elsa U. Pardee Foundation; Rollin M. Gerstacker Foundation; Charles J. Strosacker Foundation.

For full biographical listings, see the Martindale-Hubbell Law Directory

*SAGINAW,** Saginaw Co.

BRAUN KENDRICK FINKBEINER (AV)

8th Floor Second National Bank Building, 48607
Telephone: 517-753-3461
Telecopier: 517-753-3951
Bay City, Michigan Office: 201 Phoenix Building, P.O. Box 2039.
Telephone: 517-895-8505.
Telecopier: 517-895-8437.

MEMBER OF FIRM

Michael H. Allen

BAY CITY, MICHIGAN OFFICE

Gregory T. Demers

Representative Clients: The Dow Chemical Co.; General Motors Corp.; Lobdell Emery Manufacturing Co.; Merrill, Lynch, Inc.; Saginaw General Hospital; Saginaw News; The Wickes Foundation.

For Complete List of Firm Personnel, See General Section

For full biographical listings, see the Martindale-Hubbell Law Directory

SOUTHFIELD, Oakland Co.

DE VINE & KOHN (AV)

29800 Telegraph Road, 48034
Telephone: 810-353-6500

Clifford J. De Vine
Sheldon B. Kohn

For full biographical listings, see the Martindale-Hubbell Law Directory

MYLES B. HOFFERT & ASSOCIATES, P.C. (AV)

3000 Town Center, Suite 2990, 48075-1365
Telephone: 810-355-5600
Facsimile: 810-355-5608

Myles B. Hoffert

Claris K. Cwirko
Frank M. Peraino

LEGAL SUPPORT PERSONNEL

Frederick W. Morgan
Robert A. Eckhardt
Ernest E. Beren (Property Tax Consultant)

Representative Clients: Toys "R" Us, Inc.; Chrysler Realty Corp.; Tamaroff Group of Automotive Cos.; Arnold Lincoln-Mercury, Inc.; Jeffrey Buick-Nissan, Inc.; Aetna Realty; Village Green Management; IBM Corp.; Detroit Edison; Sears.

For full biographical listings, see the Martindale-Hubbell Law Directory

ROBERT B. LABE, P.C. (AV)

260 Franklin Center, 29100 Northwestern Highway, 48034
Telephone: 810-354-3100
Telecopier: 810-351-0487

Robert B. Labe

Reference: NBD Bank, N.A.

For full biographical listings, see the Martindale-Hubbell Law Directory

MADDIN, HAUSER, WARTELL, ROTH, HELLER & PESSES, P.C. (AV)

Third Floor Essex Center, 28400 Northwestern Highway, P.O. Box 215, 48037
Telephone: 810-354-4030, 355-5200
Telefax: 810-354-1422

Milton M. Maddin (1902-1984)
Michael W. Maddin
Mark R. Hauser
C. Robert Wartell
Richard J. Maddin
Richard F. Roth
Harvey R. Heller
Ian D. Pesses
Michael S. Leib
Robert D. Kaplow
William E. Sigler
Stewart C. W. Weiner
Charles M. Lax
Stuart M. Bordman
Steven D. Sallen
Joseph M. Fazio

(See Next Column)

Gregory J. Gamalski
Julie Chenot Mayer
Nathaniel H. Simpson
Ronald A. Sollish
Lisa Schatz Broder
Mark H. Fink
Brian J. Simmons
Gayle L. Landrum
Gary E. Perlmuter
Lowell D. Salesin
Jeffrey B. Hollander

Reference: Comerica Bank.

For full biographical listings, see the Martindale-Hubbell Law Directory

MASON, STEINHARDT, JACOBS & PERLMAN, PROFESSIONAL CORPORATION (AV)

Suite 1500, 4000 Town Center, 48075-1415
Telephone: 810-358-2090
Fax: 810-358-3599

Walter B. Mason, Jr.
Anthony Ilardi, Jr.
Robert G. Schuch

Representative Clients: Citibank, N.A.; City of Dearborn; DeMattia Development Co.; Forest City Enterprises; Michigan Wholesale Drug Assn.; Mortgage Bankers Association of Michigan; Nationwide Insurance Co.; City of Taylor; Union Labor Life Insurance Co.; Yellow Freight Systems, Inc.

For Complete List of Firm Personnel, See General Section

For full biographical listings, see the Martindale-Hubbell Law Directory

RUBENSTEIN PLOTKIN, PROFESSIONAL CORPORATION (AV)

2000 Town Center, Suite 2700, 48075-1318
Telephone: 810-354-3200
FAX: 810-354-3106

Edward L. Haroutunian
Burton E. Isaacs
Jeffrey B. Levine
Marcus Plotkin
Erwin A. Rubenstein
Robert W. Siegel
Allan D. Sobel
David B. Walters
Mark E. Wilson
Neil Zales

Eric Joel Gould
Casimir J. Swastek

OF COUNSEL

Murray Yolles

For full biographical listings, see the Martindale-Hubbell Law Directory

JACK M. SCHULTZ, P.C. (AV)

3000 Town Center, Suite 2990, 48075-1365
Telephone: 810-354-3440
Facsimile: 810-355-5608

Jack M. Schultz

For full biographical listings, see the Martindale-Hubbell Law Directory

SOMMERS, SCHWARTZ, SILVER & SCHWARTZ, P.C. (AV)

2000 Town Center, Suite 900, 48075
Telephone: 810-355-0300
Telecopier: 810-746-4001
Plymouth, Michigan Office: 747 South Main Street.
Telephone: 313-455-4250.

Steven J. Schwartz
Stephen S. Birnkrant
David B. Deutsch

Representative Clients: Foodland Distributors; C.A. Muer Corporation; Vlasic & Company; Nederlander Corporation; Woodland Physicians; Midwest Health Centers, P.C.; Vesco Oil Corporation.

For Complete List of Firm Personnel, See General Section

For full biographical listings, see the Martindale-Hubbell Law Directory

MINNESOTA

*MINNEAPOLIS,** Hennepin Co.

BERNICK AND LIFSON, P.A. (AV)

Suite 1200 The Colonnade, 5500 Wayzata Boulevard, 55416
Telephone: 612-546-1200
FAX: 612-546-1003

Ross A. Sussman
Neal J. Shapiro
Saul A. Bernick
Thomas D. Creighton
Scott Lifson
David K. Nightingale
Paul J. Quast

(See Next Column)

BERNICK AND LIFSON P.A.—*Continued*

Theresa M. Kowalski — Rebecca J. Heltzer

Reference: First Bank N.A., Minneapolis, Minn.

For full biographical listings, see the Martindale-Hubbell Law Directory

LEONARD, STREET AND DEINARD, PROFESSIONAL ASSOCIATION (AV)

Suite 2300, 150 South Fifth Street, 55402
Telephone: 612-335-1500
Telecopier: 612-335-1657

Morris M. Sherman
Stephen R. Litman (P.A.)
Edward M. Moersfelder
David N. Haynes
Angela M. Bohmann
Timothy J. Pabst
Lowell V. Stortz
Thomas P. Sanders

Ronald J. Schultz
Jann M. Eichlersmith
Rosanne Jacuzzi

For Complete List of Firm Personnel, See General Section

For full biographical listings, see the Martindale-Hubbell Law Directory

O'CONNOR & HANNAN (AV)

3800 IDS Center, 80 South Eighth Street, 55402-2254
Telephone: 612-343-1200
Telecopy: 612-343-1256
Washington, D.C. Office: 1919 Pennsylvania Avenue, N.W., Suite 800.
Telephone: 202-887-1400.
Telecopy: 202-466-2198.

MEMBER OF FIRM

John S. Jagiela

WASHINGTON, D.C. OFFICE

Wayne M. Zell *

A List of Representative Clients will be furnished upon request.
*Not admitted in Minn.

For Complete List of Firm Personnel, See General Section

For full biographical listings, see the Martindale-Hubbell Law Directory

PARSINEN BOWMAN & LEVY, A PROFESSIONAL ASSOCIATION (AV)

100 South 5th Street Suite 1100, 55402
Telephone: 612-333-2111
FAX: 612-333-6798

Dennis A. Bowman
John Parsinen
Robert A. Levy
Jack A. Rosberg
John F. Bonner, III
David A. Gotlieb
Karen Ciegler Hansen
Jeffrey C. Robbins
E. Burke Hinds, III
Howard J. Rubin
David A. Orenstein
Diane L. Kroupa
Jeanne K. Stretch
John C. Levy
Joseph M. Sokolowski
Randy B. Evans
Brian R. Martens
Steven R. Katz

Rebecca McDaniel
Ann Marks Sanford
Timothy R. Ring
Robert A. Hill
W. James Vogl, Jr.
Bradley Allen Kletscher
John R. Bedosky
Roben D. Hunter
Jeffrey R. Johnson (Not admitted in MN)

OF COUNSEL

Bruce B. James

For full biographical listings, see the Martindale-Hubbell Law Directory

MISSISSIPPI

*CLARKSDALE,** Coahoma Co.

MERKEL & COCKE, A PROFESSIONAL ASSOCIATION (AV)

30 Delta Avenue, P.O. Box 1388, 38614
Telephone: 601-627-9641
Fax: 601-627-3592

Charles M. Merkel
John H. Cocke
Walter Stephens Cox
Cynthia I. Mitchell
William B. Raiford, III
Jack R. Dodson, Jr.

Reference: United Southern Bank, Clarksdale, Miss.

For full biographical listings, see the Martindale-Hubbell Law Directory

*JACKSON,** Hinds Co.

ALSTON, RUTHERFORD, TARDY & VAN SLYKE (AV)

121 North State Street, P.O. Drawer 1532, 39215-1532
Telephone: 601-948-6882
Fax: 601-948-6902

MEMBERS OF FIRM

Leonard D. Van Slyke, Jr. — William S. Mendenhall

ASSOCIATE

John Howard Shows

Counsel for: E.I. DuPont de Nemours Co.; Prudential Bache-Securities; Mississippi Baptist Foundation; Jostens, Inc.; Trustmark National Bank; Merchants & Farmers Bank; Georgia-Pacific Corp.; Dean Witter Reynolds, Inc.; Transcontinental Gas Pipeline Corp.; Hibernia National Bank.

For Complete List of Firm Personnel, See General Section

For full biographical listings, see the Martindale-Hubbell Law Directory

WATKINS & EAGER (AV)

Suite 300 The Emporium Building, P.O. Box 650, 39205
Telephone: 601-948-6470
Facsimile: (601) 354-3623

MEMBERS OF FIRM

Jamie G. Houston, III
Frank J. Hammond, III
James A. Lowe, III

Representative Clients: Chevron U.S.A. Inc.; Federal Deposit Insurance Corp.; Shell Oil Co.; Trustmark National Bank; Kerr-McGee Chemical Corp.; The Black & Decker Corp.; Blossman Gas, Inc.; Pavco Industries, Inc.; Ham Marine, Inc.; Steelplex, Inc.; Merchants & Marine Bank.

For Complete List of Firm Personnel, See General Section

For full biographical listings, see the Martindale-Hubbell Law Directory

WELLS MARBLE & HURST (AV)

Suite 400, Lamar Life Building, 317 East Capitol Street, P.O. Box 131, 39205-0131
Telephone: 601-355-8321
Telecopier: 601-355-4217

MEMBERS OF FIRM

Joe Jack Hurst — James S. Armstrong

Counsel for: General Motors Corp.; United States Steel Corp.; International Business Machines Corp.; Illinois Central Railroad Co.; Lamar Life Insurance Co.; Metropolitan Life Insurance Co.; Prudential Insurance Company of America; Southern Natural Gas Co.; Trustmark National Bank of Jackson.

For Complete List of Firm Personnel, See General Section

For full biographical listings, see the Martindale-Hubbell Law Directory

MISSOURI

KANSAS CITY, Jackson, Clay & Platte Cos.

BLACKWELL SANDERS MATHENY WEARY & LOMBARDI L.C. (AV)

Suite 1100, Two Pershing Square, 2300 Main Street, 64108
Telephone: 816-274-6800
Telecopier: 816-274-6914
Overland Park, Kansas Office: 40 Corporate Woods, Suite 1200, 9401 Indian Creek Parkway.
Telephone: 913-345-8400.
Telecopier: 913-344-6375.

MEMBERS OF FIRM

David A. Fenley
Winn W. Halverhout
Robert Penninger
Daniel C. Weary
Mark D. Welker
David L. West
John P. Williams

OF COUNSEL

Cornelius E. Lombardi, Jr.

ASSOCIATE

John David Mandelbaum

Representative Clients: Cook Paint and Varnish Co.; Commerce Banchsares, Inc.; Contract Freighters, Inc.; Payless Cashways, Inc.; Puritan-Bennett Corp.; Saint Luke's Hospital; Stanbury Uniforms, Inc.; UtiliCorp United Inc.

For Complete List of Firm Personnel, See General Section

For full biographical listings, see the Martindale-Hubbell Law Directory

Kansas City—Continued

SWANSON, MIDGLEY, GANGWERE, KITCHIN & McLARNEY, L.L.C. (AV)

1500 Commerce Trust Building, 922 Walnut, 64106-1848
Telephone: 816-842-6100
Overland Park, Kansas Office: The NCAA Building, Suite 350, 6201 College Boulevard.
Telephone: 816-842-6100.

George H. Gangwere, Jr.

OF COUNSEL

Daniel V. Hiatt

Counsel for: General Electric Co.; Chrysler Corp.; Conoco, Inc.; Yellow Freight System, Inc.; The Prudential Insurance Co. of America; Metropolitan Life Insurance Co.; National Collegiate Athletic Assn.; Land Title Insurance Co.; Safeway Stores, Inc.; The Lee Apparel Co.

For Complete List of Firm Personnel, See General Section

For full biographical listings, see the Martindale-Hubbell Law Directory

ST. LOUIS, (Independent City)

ARMSTRONG, TEASDALE, SCHLAFLY & DAVIS (AV)

A Partnership including Professional Corporations
One Metropolitan Square, 63102-2740
Telephone: 314-621-5070
Facsimile: 314-621-5065
Twx: 910 761-2246
Cable: ATKV LAW
Kansas City, Missouri Office: 1700 City Center Square. 1100 Main Street, 64105.
Telephone: 816-221-3420.
Facsimile: 816-221-0786.
Belleville, Illinois Office: 23 South First Street, 62220.
Telephone: 618-397-4411.
Olathe, Kansas Office: 100 East Park, 66061.
Telephone: 913-345-0706.

MEMBERS OF FIRM

Edwin S. Baldwin (P.C.)
Robert Lewis Jackson (P.C.)
Frederick O. Hanser (P.C.)
Larry M. Sewell (P.C.)
Peter L. Clark (P.C.)
Philip G. Louis, Jr.
Sally J. McKee

ASSOCIATE

Scott Hunt

Representative Clients: American Bank of St Louis; Anheuser-Busch, Inc;; Blue Cross Health Services, Inc.; Christian Hospitals; Guarantee Electrical Corp.; Gusdorf Corp; Homestake Mining Co.; International Business Machines Corp.; Reliable Life Insurance Co.; Union Electric Company.

For Complete List of Firm Personnel, See General Section

For full biographical listings, see the Martindale-Hubbell Law Directory

KOHN, SHANDS, ELBERT, GIANOULAKIS & GILJUM (AV)

24th Floor, One Mercantile Center, 63101
Telephone: 314-241-3963
Telecopier: 314-241-2509

Joseph P. Giljum

For full biographical listings, see the Martindale-Hubbell Law Directory

LEWIS, RICE & FINGERSH (AV)

A Partnership including Partnerships and Individuals
500 North Broadway, Suite 2000, 63102-2147
Telephone: 314-444-7600
Telecopier: 314-241-6056
Clayton, Missouri Office: Suite 400, 8182 Maryland Avenue.
Telephone: 314-444-7600.
Belleville, Illinois Office: 325 South High Street.
Telephone: 618-234-8636.
Hays, Kansas Office: 201 W. 11th St.
Telephone: 913-625-3997.
Leawood, Kansas Office: Suite 375, 8900 State Line.
Telephone: 913-381-8898.
Kansas City, Missouri Office: 1010 Walnut, Suite 500.
Telephone: 816-421-2500.

RESIDENT PARTNERS

Bernard N. Frank
Lawrence H. Weltman

For Complete List of Firm Personnel, See General Section

For full biographical listings, see the Martindale-Hubbell Law Directory

LOWENHAUPT & CHASNOFF, L.L.C. (AV)

10 South Broadway, Suite 600, 63102-1733
Telephone: 314-241-5950
Telefax: 314-436-2667

(See Next Column)

Charles A. Lowenhaupt
Jerrold D. Rosen

For Complete List of Firm Personnel, See General Section

For full biographical listings, see the Martindale-Hubbell Law Directory

PEPER, MARTIN, JENSEN, MAICHEL AND HETLAGE (AV)

720 Olive Street, Twenty-Fourth Floor, 63101
Telephone: 314-421-3850
Fax: 314-621-4834
Fort Myers, Florida Office: 2080 McGregor Boulevard, Third Floor.
Telephone: 813-337-3850.
Fax: 813-337-0970.
Punta Gorda, Florida Office: 1625 West Marion Avenue, Suite 2.
Telephone: 813-637-1955.
Fax: 813-637-8485.
Naples, Florida Office: 850 Park Shore Drive, Suite 202.
Telephone: 813-261-6525.
Fax: 813-649-1805.
Belleville, Illinois Office: 720 West Main Street, Suite 140.
Telephone: 618-234-9574.
Fax: 618-234-9846.

MEMBERS OF FIRM

Mark R. Leuchtmann
Paul G. Griesemer
Albert S. Rose
Matthew G. Perlow
Raymond S. Kreienkamp

COUNSEL

Warren R. Maichel

ASSOCIATES

Christopher L. Craig
Robert G. Oesch
Ruth A. Streit
Randall S. Thompson

For Complete List of Firm Personnel, See General Section

For full biographical listings, see the Martindale-Hubbell Law Directory

THOMPSON & MITCHELL (AV)

One Mercantile Center, Suite 3300, 63101
Telephone: 314-231-7676
Telecopier: 314-342-1717
Belleville, Illinois Office: 525 West Main Street.
Telephone: 618-277-4700; 314-271-1800.
Telecopier: 618-236-3434.
St. Charles, Missouri Office: 200 North Third Street.
Telephone: 314-946-7717.
Telecopier: 314-946-4938.
Washington, D.C. Office: 700 14th Street, N.W., Suite 900.
Telephone: 202-508-1000.
Telecopier: 202-508-1010.

MEMBERS OF FIRM

William J. McNamara
Millard Backerman
Charles M. Babington III
Joan M. Newman
William J. Falk
Henry A. Bettendorf
Richard L. Lawton
Charles H. Binger

ASSOCIATE

Lisa M. Braun

BELLEVILLE, ILLINOIS OFFICE
RESIDENT MEMBERS OF FIRM

Joseph R. Lowery
Garrett C. Reuter
Mark J. Stegman
Kurt S. Schroeder

Representative Clients: A. P. Green Industries, Inc.; Angelica Corporation; Barry-Wehmiller Company; Contico International, Inc.; Enterprise Rent-A-Car Company; Magna Group, Inc.; Maritz Inc.; Mercantile Bancorporation Inc.; Peabody Coal Co.; United Van Lines, Inc.

For Complete List of Firm Personnel, See General Section

For full biographical listings, see the Martindale-Hubbell Law Directory

MONTANA

*BILLINGS,** Yellowstone Co.

CROWLEY, HAUGHEY, HANSON, TOOLE & DIETRICH (AV)

500 Transwestern II, 490 North 31st Street, P.O. Box 2529, 59103
Telephone: 406-252-3441
Fax: 406-259-4159
Helena, Montana Office: IBM Building, 100 North Park Avenue, Suite 300, 59601.
Telephone: 406-449-4165.
Fax: 406-449-5149.

(See Next Column)

CROWLEY, HAUGHEY, HANSON, TOOLE & DIETRICH—*Continued*

MEMBERS OF FIRM

John M. Dietrich
Myles J. Thomas
David L. Johnson
Terry B. Cosgrove
James P. Sites
Daniel N. McLean
Robert G. Michelotti, Jr.
John R. Alexander
Eric K. Anderson

ASSOCIATE

Scott M. Heard

Representative Clients: AT&T; Pacificorp; General Mills; Billings Clinic; United Grain Corporation; Deaconess Medical Center of Billings; Mid-Rivers Telephone Cooperative; United Parcel Service; Holly Sugar Corporation; MDM Broadcasting, Inc.

For Complete List of Firm Personnel, See General Section

For full biographical listings, see the Martindale-Hubbell Law Directory

*KALISPELL,** Flathead Co.

HASH, O'BRIEN & BARTLETT (AV)

Plaza West, 136 First Avenue, West, P.O. Box 1178, 59901
Telephone: 406-755-6919
Fax: 406-755-6911

MEMBERS OF FIRM

Charles L. Hash
Kenneth E. O'Brien
James C. Bartlett
C. Mark Hash

General Counsel for: Glacier Bank F.S.B.; Budget Finance; Flathead County Title Co.
Representative Clients: Western Surety Co.; Liberty Mutual Insurance Co.; Allstate Insurance Co.; Hillsteads Department Store; Montana Brokers, Inc.
Reference: Glacier Bank F.S.B.

For full biographical listings, see the Martindale-Hubbell Law Directory

NEBRASKA

*GRAND ISLAND,** Hall Co.

THE LEGAL PROFESSIONAL CORPORATION OF TRACY & McQUILLAN (AV)

706 West Koenig Street, 68801-6556
Telephone: 308-382-5154
Fax: 308-382-3242

Howard E. Tracy
Michael J. McQuillan

For full biographical listings, see the Martindale-Hubbell Law Directory

*LINCOLN,** Lancaster Co.

ERICKSON & SEDERSTROM, P.C. (AV)

Suite 400, Cornhusker Plaza, 301 South 13th Street, 68508
Telephone: 402-476-1000
Fax: 402-476-6167
Omaha, Nebraska Office: Regency Westpointe, 10330 Regency Parkway Drive.
Telephone: 402-397-2200.
Fax: 402-390-7137.

Charles Thone
Charles D. Humble
Alan M. Wood
Douglas L. Curry
Mark M. Schorr
Linda W. Rohman
David C. Mussman

Representative Clients: California Public Employees Retirement Plan (CALPERS); Chase Manhattan Leasing Co.; Albertson's, Inc.; Baker's Supermarkets, Inc.; Osco Drug, Inc.; Lincoln General Hospital; Martin Luther Home; Lincoln Electric System.

For full biographical listings, see the Martindale-Hubbell Law Directory

*OMAHA,** Douglas Co.

DWYER, POHREN, WOOD, HEAVEY, GRIMM, GOODALL & LAZER (AV)

A Partnership including Professional Corporations
Suite 400, 8712 West Dodge Road, 68114
Telephone: 402-392-0101
Telefax: 402-392-1011

MEMBERS OF FIRM

Robert V. Dwyer, Jr.
Andrew E. Grimm

Representative Clients: K-Products, Inc.; Bishop Clarkson Memorial Hospital, Omaha, Nebraska; The Community Hospital Association, McCook, Nebraska; Lutheran Community Hospital, Norfolk, Nebraska; Nebraska Hospital Association.

(See Next Column)

For Complete List of Firm Personnel, See General Section

For full biographical listings, see the Martindale-Hubbell Law Directory

ERICKSON & SEDERSTROM, P.C. (AV)

Regency Westpointe, 10330 Regency Parkway Drive, 68114
Telephone: 402-397-2200
Fax: 402-390-7137
Lincoln, Nebraska Office: Suite 400, Cornhusker Plaza, 301 South 13th Street.
Telephone: 402-476-1000.
Fax: 402-476-6167.

Samuel Earle Clark
William T. Foley

Representative Clients: Baker's Supermarkets; Bozell, Inc.; Hicks Construction Co., Inc.; Berkshire Hathaway, Inc.; Immanuel Medical Center; First Data Resources, Inc.; Lincoln General Hospital; Lincoln Electric System; Eli Lilly & Co.; Burkley Envelope Co.

For Complete List of Firm Personnel, See General Section

For full biographical listings, see the Martindale-Hubbell Law Directory

FRASER, STRYKER, VAUGHN, MEUSEY, OLSON, BOYER & BLOCH, P.C. (AV)

500 Energy Plaza, 409 South 17th Street, 68102
Telephone: 402-341-6000
Telecopier: 402-341-8290

Peter J. Vaughn
John K. Boyer
Norman H. Wright
Kenneth W. Sharp

OF COUNSEL

Robert R. Veach

For Complete List of Firm Personnel, See General Section

For full biographical listings, see the Martindale-Hubbell Law Directory

LAUGHLIN, PETERSON & LANG (AV)

11306 Davenport Street, 68154
Telephone: 402-330-1900
Fax: 402-330-0936

MEMBERS OF FIRM

Mark L. Laughlin
James E. Lang

Representative Clients: Andersen Electric Co.; General Electric Capital Corp.; Sears, Roebuck & Co.; Dodge Land Co.; Security Mutual Life Insurance Co. of Lincoln, NE; Century Development Co.

For Complete List of Firm Personnel, See General Section

For full biographical listings, see the Martindale-Hubbell Law Directory

McGILL, GOTSDINER, WORKMAN & LEPP, P.C. (AV)

Suite 500 - First National Plaza, 11404 West Dodge Road, 68154
Telephone: 402-492-9200
Telecopier: 402-492-9222

Stephen T. McGill
Gary M. Gotsdiner
Howard N. Kaplan

Representative Clients: Behlen Mfg. Co.; Bethesda Care Centers; First Data Resources, Inc.; Norwest Bank Nebraska, N.A.

For Complete List of Firm Personnel, See General Section

For full biographical listings, see the Martindale-Hubbell Law Directory

McGRATH, NORTH, MULLIN & KRATZ, P.C. (AV)

Suite 1400, One Central Park Plaza, 68102
Telephone: 402-341-3070
Telecopy: 402-341-0216
Telex: 797122 MNMKOM

John E. North
David L. Hefflinger
Bruce C. Rohde
Jeffrey J. Pirrucello
Randal M. Limbeck
James D. Wegner
Nicholas K. Niemann

Representative Clients: ConAgra, Inc.; Valmont Industries, Inc.; Physicians Mutual Insurance Company; Omaha Airport Authority; American Family Insurance Group; Dow Chemical; Lloyds of London; Mutual of Omaha; The Pacesetter Corporation.

For Complete List of Firm Personnel, See General Section

For full biographical listings, see the Martindale-Hubbell Law Directory

NEVADA

*LAS VEGAS,** Clark Co.

JEROME L. BLUT CHARTERED (AV)
Suite B, 550 East Charleston Boulevard, 89104
Telephone: 702-382-8840
FAX: 702-383-8452

Jerome L. Blut

References: First Interstate Bank of Nevada; Nevada State Bank.

For full biographical listings, see the Martindale-Hubbell Law Directory

*RENO,** Washoe Co.

HALE, LANE, PEEK, DENNISON AND HOWARD (AV)
Porsche Building, 100 West Liberty Street, Tenth Floor, P.O. Box 3237, 89501
Telephone: 702-786-7900
Telefax: 702-786-6179
Las Vegas, Nevada Office: Suite 800, Nevada Financial Center, 2300 West Sahara Avenue, Box 8.
Telephone: 702-362-5118.
Fax: 702-365-6940.

MEMBER OF FIRM
Marilyn L. Skender

ASSOCIATES
James L. Kelly — J. Robert Parke

Representative Clients: Shopping Centers: Moana West Shopping Center. Construction and Development: Trammell Crow Co.; Caughlin Ranch; McKenzie Construction, Inc.; Western Water Development Co.; Falcon Development Corp. General: Puliz Moving & Storage Co.; Scolari's Markets.

For Complete List of Firm Personnel, See General Section

For full biographical listings, see the Martindale-Hubbell Law Directory

MCDONALD, CARANO, WILSON, MCCUNE, BERGIN, FRANKOVICH & HICKS (AV)
241 Ridge Street, 89505
Telephone: 702-322-0635
Telecopier: 702-786-9532
Las Vegas, Nevada Office: Suite 1000, 2300 West Sahara Avenue.
Telephone: 702-873-4100.
Telecopier: 702-873-9966.

MEMBERS OF FIRM
Robert E. Armstrong — John B. Galvin

ASSOCIATES
Scott A. Swain (Resident, Las Vegas Office) — Andrew P. Gordon (Resident, Las Vegas Office)
David F. Grove

Representative Clients: Eldorado Hotel & Casino; Jackpot Enterprises, Inc.; James Hardie (USA), Inc.; Primadonna Resorts, Inc.

For Complete List of Firm Personnel, See General Section

For full biographical listings, see the Martindale-Hubbell Law Directory

NEW HAMPSHIRE

*CONCORD,** Merrimack Co.

ORR & RENO, PROFESSIONAL ASSOCIATION (AV)
One Eagle Square, P.O. Box 3550, 03302-3550
Telephone: 603-224-2381
Fax: 603-224-2318

Charles F. Leahy — Neil F. Castaldo
Mary Susan Leahy

Representative Clients: Beach Aircraft Corporation; Chubb Life America; Fleet Bank; Dartmouth-Hitchcock Medical Center; EnergyNorth, Inc.; National Grange Mutual Co.; New England College; New England Electric System Co.; Newspapers of New England, Inc.; St. Paul's School.

For Complete List of Firm Personnel, See General Section

For full biographical listings, see the Martindale-Hubbell Law Directory

*EXETER,** Rockingham Co.

HOLLAND, DONOVAN, BECKETT & HERMANS, PROFESSIONAL ASSOCIATION (AV)
151 Water Street, P.O. Box 1090, 03833
Telephone: 603-772-5956
Fax: 603-778-1434

(See Next Column)

John W. Perkins (1902-1973) — Robert B. Donovan
Everett P. Holland (1915-1993) — William H. M. Beckett
Stephen G. Hermans

Ronald G. Sutherland

For full biographical listings, see the Martindale-Hubbell Law Directory

NEW JERSEY

ATLANTIC CITY, Atlantic Co.

LEVINE, STALLER, SKLAR, CHAN & BRODSKY, P.A. (AV)
3030 Atlantic Avenue, 08401
Telephone: 609-348-1300
Telecopier: 609-345-2473

Lee A. Levine — Paul T. Chan
Alan C. Staller — Lawrence A. Brodsky
Arthur E. Sklar — Brian J. Cullen
Benjamin Zeltner

Arthur M. Brown — Scott J. Mitnick

Representative Clients: A. G. Edwards & Sons, Inc.; Atlantic Plastic Containers Inc.; The Michaels Development Co., Inc.; Nawas International Travel Services, Inc.; Trump Casino Hotels - Atlantic City, NJ; Interstate Realty Management Company.

For full biographical listings, see the Martindale-Hubbell Law Directory

CHERRY HILL, Camden Co.

EMMANUEL LIEBMAN, CHARTERED A PROFESSIONAL CORPORATION (AV)
409 East Marlton Pike, 08034-2472
Telephone: 609-795-8600
Telecopier: 609-795-6125

Emmanuel Liebman

For full biographical listings, see the Martindale-Hubbell Law Directory

ELMWOOD PARK, Bergen Co.

ANDORA, PALMISANO & GEANEY, A PROFESSIONAL CORPORATION (AV)
303 Molnar Drive, P.O. Box 431, 07407-0431
Telephone: 201-791-0100
Fax: 201-791-8922

Anthony D. Andora — Joseph M. Andresini
John P. Palmisano — Patrick J. Spina
John F. Geaney, Jr. — Melissa A. Muilenburg
Vincent A. Siano — Joseph A. Venti

Representative Client: City of Jersey City.

For full biographical listings, see the Martindale-Hubbell Law Directory

*HACKENSACK,** Bergen Co.

DEENER, FEINGOLD & STERN, A PROFESSIONAL CORPORATION (AV)
2 University Plaza, Suite 602, 07601
Telephone: 201-343-8788
Fax: 201-343-4640

Jerome A. Deener — Cal R. Feingold
Robert A. Stern

Debra T. Hirsch — Anthony M. Vizzoni
David M. Edelblum — James J. Costello, Jr. (Not admitted in NJ)

References: United Jersey Bank; Midlantic Bank; Midland Bank and Trust Co. (Trust Department); Fidelity Bank; Hudson United Bank.

For full biographical listings, see the Martindale-Hubbell Law Directory

DUNN, PASHMAN, SPONZILLI, SWICK & FINNERTY (AV)
411 Hackensack Avenue, 07601
Telephone: 201-489-1500; 845-4000
Fax: 201-489-1512

COUNSEL
Morris Pashman — Murray L. Cole
Paul D. Rosenberg

(See Next Column)

DUNN, PASHMAN, SPONZILLI, SWICK & FINNERTY—*Continued*

MEMBERS OF FIRM

Joseph Dunn
Louis Pashman
John E. Finnerty
Edward G. Sponzilli
Daniel A. Swick
Robert E. Rochford
Warren S. Robins

ASSOCIATES

Nicholas F. Pellitta
Laura S. Kirsch
Danya A. Grunyk
Richard P. Jacobson
Jeffrey M. Shapiro
Deborah L. Ustas
Mark E. Lichtblau
Edward B. Stevenson
Stephen F. Roth

References: United Jersey Bank; Valley National Bank.

For full biographical listings, see the Martindale-Hubbell Law Directory

HEIN, SMITH, BEREZIN, MALOOF & ROGERS (AV)

Court Plaza East, 19 Main Street, 07601-7023
Telephone: 201-487-7400
Telecopier: 201-487-4228

MEMBER OF FIRM

Alan A. Davidson

OF COUNSEL

Seymour A. Smith

For Complete List of Firm Personnel, See General Section

For full biographical listings, see the Martindale-Hubbell Law Directory

LITWIN & HOLSINGER (AV)

Two University Plaza, 07601
Telephone: 201-487-9000
Telecopier: 201-487-9070

MEMBERS OF FIRM

John R. Holsinger
Gerald H. Litwin

OF COUNSEL

Bernard J. Koster (Not admitted in NJ)

For full biographical listings, see the Martindale-Hubbell Law Directory

HADDONFIELD, Camden Co.

KULZER & DIPADOVA, A PROFESSIONAL CORPORATION (AV)

76 Euclid Avenue, 08033
Telephone: 609-795-7744
Telecopier: 609-795-8982

Kevin M. Covert
Arthur A. DiPadova
James B. Evans, Jr.
Glenn A. Henkel
Michael A. Kulzer
Robert H. Williams

James L. Hatzell
Joseph T. Kenney
Donald L. Kingett
George Norton Nager
Ronald M. Warren

OF COUNSEL

Fred C. Chandler, Jr.
John H. Davies
Barbara A. Kulzer

For full biographical listings, see the Martindale-Hubbell Law Directory

*JERSEY CITY,** Hudson Co.

SHEEHY & SHEEHY (AV)

Suite 206, 665 Newark Avenue, 07306
Telephone: 201-795-5500
Fax: 201-795-5172
Toms River, New Jersey Office: 121 Washington Street.
Telephone: 908-505-1919.

MEMBERS OF FIRM

John J. Sheehy
John J. Sheehy
Marian V. Rooney-Sheehy (1926-1984)

References: First Fidelity Bank; Trust Company of New Jersey; Provident Savings.

For full biographical listings, see the Martindale-Hubbell Law Directory

LIVINGSTON, Essex Co.

SKOLOFF & WOLFE (AV)

293 Eisenhower Parkway, 07039
Telephone: 201-992-0900
Fax: 201-992-0301
Morristown, New Jersey Office: 10 Park Place.
Telephone: 201-267-3511.

Saul A. Wolfe
Robert F. Giancaterino
Heather A. Turnbull
Garry J. Roettger

For full biographical listings, see the Martindale-Hubbell Law Directory

MARLTON, Burlington Co.

FLASTER, GREENBERG, WALLENSTEIN, RODERICK, SPIRGEL, ZUCKERMAN, SKINNER & KIRCHNER, P.C. (AV)

Suite 200, Five Greentree Centre, 08053
Telephone: 609-983-7200
Telecopier: 609-983-7877
Philadelphia, Pennsylvania Office: 1710-12 Spruce Street.
Telephone: 215-731-1490.

Richard J. Flaster
Stephen M. Greenberg
Laura B. Wallenstein
Allen P. Fineberg
Markley S. Roderick
Peter R. Spirgel
Alan H. Zuckerman
William S. Skinner
J. Philip Kirchner

E. Richard Dressel
Paul J. Russoniello
Elizabeth J. Hampton
Deborah H. Bjornstad

For full biographical listings, see the Martindale-Hubbell Law Directory

MONTCLAIR, Essex Co.

GARIPPA AND DAVENPORT, A PROFESSIONAL CORPORATION (AV)

66 Park Street, 07042
Telephone: 201-744-1688
Telecopier: 201-744-1641

John E. Garippa
Seth I. Davenport

Philip J. Giannuario
Gregory G. Lotz
Charles J. Harrington, III

For full biographical listings, see the Martindale-Hubbell Law Directory

*MORRISTOWN,** Morris Co.

EDWARDS & ANTHOLIS (AV)

22 Pine Street, 07960-6092
Telephone: 201-540-0050; 800-464-9608
Fax: 201-292-1889

David F. Edwards (1908-1983)
John K. Antholis
James A. Sylvester

ASSOCIATES

Jennie Lee A. O'Donnell
Nancy L. Ruoff

OF COUNSEL

Kary W. Antholis

For full biographical listings, see the Martindale-Hubbell Law Directory

PITNEY, HARDIN, KIPP & SZUCH (AV)

Park Avenue at Morris County, P.O. Box 1945, 07962-1945
Telephone: 201-966-6300
New York City: 212-926-0331
Telex: 642014
Telecopier: 201-966-1550

MEMBERS OF FIRM

Kevin J. O'Donnell
Kenneth J. Norcross
Kathy A. Lawler

COUNSEL

David P. Doyle

Representative Clients: AlliedSignal Inc.; AT&T; Base Ten Systems, Inc.; Exxon Corp.; Ford Motor Co.; Midlantic National Bank; Sony Electronics, Inc.; Union Carbide Corp.; United Parcel Services, Inc.; Warner-Lambert Co.

For Complete List of Firm Personnel, See General Section

For full biographical listings, see the Martindale-Hubbell Law Directory

SHANLEY & FISHER, A PROFESSIONAL CORPORATION (AV)

131 Madison Avenue, 07962-1979
Telephone: 201-285-1000
Telecopier: 1-201-285-1098
Telex: 475-4255 (I.T.T.)
Cable Address: "Shanley"
New York, N.Y. Office: 89th Floor, One World Trade Center.
Telephone: 212-321-1812.
Telecopier: 1-212-466-0569.

John Kandravy
Kevin M. Kilcullen

Joan M. Neri
Stephanie A. Mergel
Edward A. Gramigna, Jr.
Tanya M. Taylor

For Complete List of Firm Personnel, See General Section

For full biographical listings, see the Martindale-Hubbell Law Directory

*NEWARK,** Essex Co.

CARPENTER, BENNETT & MORRISSEY (AV)

(Formerly Carpenter, Gilmour & Dwyer)
Three Gateway Center, 17th Floor, 100 Mulberry Street, 07102-4079
Telephone: 201-622-7711
New York City: 212-943-6530
Telex: 139405
Telecopier: 201-622-5314
EasyLink: 62827845
ABA/net: CARPENTERB

MEMBERS OF FIRM

Laurence Reich
Francis X. O'Brien
Edward F. Day, Jr.
John D. Goldsmith
Jane Andrews

OF COUNSEL

Warren Lloyd Lewis

ASSOCIATES

Hans G. Polak
Douglas S. Witte
Kevin F. Murphy
Dawn M. Felipe

Representative Clients: Texaco Inc.; ITT Corp.; International Flavors & Fragrances Inc.; New Jersey Hospital Association; Star Enterprise; MAN Capital Corp.; MAN Roland, Inc.; Rutgers, The State University of New Jersey.

For Complete List of Firm Personnel, See General Section

For full biographical listings, see the Martindale-Hubbell Law Directory

FOX AND FOX (AV)

570 Broad Street, 07102
Telephone: 201-622-3624
Telecopier: 201-622-6220

MEMBERS OF FIRM

David I. Fox
Arthur D. Grossman
Paul I. Rosenberg
Kenneth H. Fast
Martin Kesselhaut
Dennis J. Alessi
Gabriel H. Halpern
Steven A. Holt
Nancy C. McDonald

OF COUNSEL

Jacob Fox (1898-1992)
Martin S. Fox
Robert J. Rohrberger
Robert S. Catapano-Friedman

ASSOCIATES

Robert P. Donovan
Stacey B. Rosenberg
Susan R. Fox
Virginia S. Ryan
Ronnie Ann Powell
Katherine J. Welsh
Craig S. Gumpel
Brett Alison Rosenberg
Alfred V. Acquaviva
Anthony F. Vitiello

For full biographical listings, see the Martindale-Hubbell Law Directory

GREENBERG DAUBER AND EPSTEIN, A PROFESSIONAL CORPORATION (AV)

Suite 600, One Gateway Center, 07102-5311
Telephone: 201-643-3700
Telecopier: 201-643-1218

Stanley A. Epstein

For Complete List of Firm Personnel, See General Section

For full biographical listings, see the Martindale-Hubbell Law Directory

HELLRING LINDEMAN GOLDSTEIN & SIEGAL (AV)

One Gateway Center, 07102-5386
Telephone: 201-621-9020
Telecopier: 201-621-7406

Jonathan L. Goldstein
Charles Oransky
David N. Narciso

For Complete List of Firm Personnel, See General Section

For full biographical listings, see the Martindale-Hubbell Law Directory

LEVY, EHRLICH & KRONENBERG, A PROFESSIONAL CORPORATION (AV)

60 Park Place, 07102
Telephone: 201-643-0040
Telecopier: 201-596-1781
Hackensack, New Jersey Office: 1 University Plaza, Suite 501, 07601.
Telephone: 301-342-4445.

Ira A. Levy
Alan Ehrlich
Arthur Kronenberg

Representative Clients: Panasonic Co.; Transamerica; General Electric.
Reference: First Fidelity Bank.

For Complete List of Firm Personnel, See General Section

For full biographical listings, see the Martindale-Hubbell Law Directory

MCCARTER & ENGLISH (AV)

Four Gateway Center, 100 Mulberry Street, P.O. Box 652, 07101-0652
Telephone: 201-622-4444
Telecopier: 201-624-7070
Cable Address: "McCarter" Newark
Cherry Hill, New Jersey Office: 1810 Chapel Avenue West.
Telephone: 609-662-8444.
Telecopier: 609-662-6203.
New York, New York Office: Suite 1519, One World Trade Center.
Telephone: 212-466-9018.
Telecopier: 212-432-6568.
Boca Raton, Florida Office: 2255 Glades Road, Suite 319-A.
Telephone: 407-994-6262.
Telecopier: 407-241-0798.
Wilmington, Delaware Office: Mellon Bank Center, 919 Market Street.
Telephone: 302-654-8010.
Telecopier: 302-654-0795.

MEMBERS OF FIRM

John B. Brescher, Jr.
Jeffrey H. Aminoff (Resident Partner, New York, New York Office)
Michael A. Guariglia
David A. Ludgin
Frank E. Ferruggia
Stephen M. Vajtay, Jr.
Mark A. Daniele

OF COUNSEL

Peter C. Aslanides

COUNSEL

Beth Yingling
Gary Duescher

ASSOCIATES

Robert A. Fishbein
Phyllis Gutto
Theresa Borzelli
Malke Borow
Susan A. Feeney
Quedel Principal
John K. Bradley
Susan M. Mello

For Complete List of Firm Personnel, See General Section

For full biographical listings, see the Martindale-Hubbell Law Directory

ROBINSON, ST. JOHN & WAYNE (AV)

Two Penn Plaza East, 07105-2249
Telephone: 201-491-3300
Fax: 201-491-3333
Rochester, New York Office: Robinson, St. John & Curtin. First Federal Plaza.
Telephone: 716-262-6780.
Fax: 716-262-6755.
New York, New York Office: 245 Park Avenue.
Telephone: 212-953-0700.
Fax: 212-880-6555.

MEMBER OF FIRM

John J. Oberdorf

For Complete List of Firm Personnel, See General Section

For full biographical listings, see the Martindale-Hubbell Law Directory

SAIBER SCHLESINGER SATZ & GOLDSTEIN (AV)

One Gateway Center, 13th Floor, 07102-5311
Telephone: 201-622-3333
Telecopier: 201-622-3349

MEMBERS OF FIRM

David M. Satz, Jr.
Bruce I. Goldstein
William F. Maderer
David J. D'Aloia
James H. Aibel
Sean R. Kelly
John L. Conover
Lawrence B. Mink
Michael L. Allen
Michael L. Messer
Jeffrey W. Lorell
Jeffrey M. Schwartz
David J. Satz
Joan M. Schwab
Jennine DiSomma
James H. Forte
Vincent F. Papalia

OF COUNSEL

Samuel S. Saiber
Norman E. Schlesinger

COUNSEL

Andrew Alcorn
Robin B. Horn
Randi Schillinger

ASSOCIATES

Audrey M. Weinstein
Robert B. Nussbaum
Michael J. Geraghty
Jonathan S. Davis
Paul S. DeGiulio
Diana L. Sussman
Deanna M. Beacham
Robert W. Geiger
William S. Gyves
Barry P. Kramer
Susan Rozman
Michelle Viola

LEGAL SUPPORT PERSONNEL

DIRECTOR OF FINANCE AND ADMINISTRATION

Ronald Henry

For full biographical listings, see the Martindale-Hubbell Law Directory

Newark—Continued

SILLS CUMMIS ZUCKERMAN RADIN TISCHMAN EPSTEIN & GROSS, A PROFESSIONAL CORPORATION (AV)

One Riverfront Plaza, 07102-5400
Telephone: 201-643-7000
Fax: 201-643-6500
Telex: 820630 Sillsbeck Nwk
Atlantic City, New Jersey Office: 17 Gordon's Alley.
Telephone: 609-344-2800.
New York, N.Y. Office: 250 Park Avenue.
Telephone: 212-643-7000.

Herbert L. Zuckerman
Lawrence S. Horn
Simon Levin
Alan E. Sherman
Robert J. Alter
Allan C. Bell
Richard J. Sapinski

Nathan E. Arnell
Jay A. Soled

OF COUNSEL

David Beck
Dena L. Wolf

For Complete List of Firm Personnel, See General Section

For full biographical listings, see the Martindale-Hubbell Law Directory

NUTLEY, Essex Co.

FRANCIS J. COSTENBADER (AV)

391 Franklin Avenue, P.O. Box 107, 07110
Telephone: 201-661-5000
Fax: 201-661-0513

Scott Rumana

Representative Clients: Consumer Value Stores (CVS); Melville Corp.; Melville Realty Corp.; Linens 'N Things, Inc.; This End Up Furniture Co., Inc.

For full biographical listings, see the Martindale-Hubbell Law Directory

PRINCETON, Mercer Co.

CONLEY & HAUSHALTER (AV)

Two Princeton Pike Corporate Center, 993 Lenox Drive, CN 5279, Building Two, 08543-5279
Telephone: 609-896-0011
Telecopier: 609-895-0055

PARTNERS

Richard M. Conley
Harry Haushalter

For full biographical listings, see the Martindale-Hubbell Law Directory

ROSELAND, Essex Co.

BRACH, EICHLER, ROSENBERG, SILVER, BERNSTEIN, HAMMER & GLADSTONE, A PROFESSIONAL CORPORATION (AV)

101 Eisenhower Parkway, 07068
Telephone: 201-228-5700
Telecopier: 201-228-7852

Stuart M. Gladstone
Bruce Kleinman
Brian R. Lenker
David J. Ritter

Bruce L. Wolff (Not admitted in NJ)
Frank S. Baldino
Robert C. Mignella
Susan L. Miller
Vicki Sue Hull

OF COUNSEL

Stuart L. Pachman

Representative Clients: Perlmart Shop-Rites; The Kushner Companies; Silverline Building Products; New Community Corporation; Howard Press; Isaac Hazan & Company; Champion Mortgage Company; United Jersey Bank; Valley National Bank; State Bank of South Orange.

For Complete List of Firm Personnel, See General Section

For full biographical listings, see the Martindale-Hubbell Law Directory

GOLDMAN, JACOBSON, KRAMER, FRADKIN & STARR, A PROFESSIONAL CORPORATION (AV)

(Formerly Starr, Weinberg and Fradkin A Professional Corporation)
101 Eisenhower Parkway, P.O. Box 610, 07068
Telephone: 201-228-5888
Telecopier: 201-228-4606

Edwin Fradkin
Bruce E. Goldman
Scott D. Jacobson
Elliot I. Kramer
Andrew P. Fradkin

For full biographical listings, see the Martindale-Hubbell Law Directory

HANNOCH WEISMAN, A PROFESSIONAL CORPORATION (AV)

4 Becker Farm Road, 07068-3788
Telephone: 201-535-5300
New York: 212-732-3262
Telecopier: 201-994-7198
Mailing Address: P.O. Box 1040, Newark, New Jersey, 07101-9819
Washington, D.C. Office: Suite 600, 1150 Seventeenth Street, N.W.
Telephone: 202-296-3432.

Bernard S. Berkowitz
Bernard J. D'Avella, Jr.
Richard S. Finkelstein
Jonathan M. Gross
Gene R. Korf
Stephen P. Lichtstein
Gary Mazart
Carl G. Weisenfeld

Kathleen M. Maher
Rachelle A. Peluso

For Complete List of Firm Personnel, See General Section

For full biographical listings, see the Martindale-Hubbell Law Directory

MARK LEVIN (AV)

5 Becker Farm Road, 4th Floor, 07068
Telephone: 201-740-9299

For full biographical listings, see the Martindale-Hubbell Law Directory

LOWENSTEIN, SANDLER, KOHL, FISHER & BOYLAN, A PROFESSIONAL CORPORATION (AV)

65 Livingston Avenue, 07068
Telephone: 201-992-8700
Telefax: 201-992-5820
Somerville, New Jersey Office: 600 First Avenue. P.O. Box 1113.
Telephone: 201-526-3300.

Benedict M. Kohl
Arnold Fisher
Martin R. Goodman
Kenneth J. Slutsky
John L. Berger

OF COUNSEL

Bonnie K. Levitt

Michael N. Gooen
Sheila Y. Maddox

For Complete List of Firm Personnel, See General Section

For full biographical listings, see the Martindale-Hubbell Law Directory

ORLOFF, LOWENBACH, STIFELMAN & SIEGEL, A PROFESSIONAL CORPORATION (AV)

101 Eisenhower Parkway, 07068
Telephone: 201-622-6200
Telecopier: 201-622-3073

Joel D. Siegel
Frank L. Stifelman
Alan F. Kornstein
Susan Medinets Holzman

James A. Mohoney
Valerie Jacobson Kelleher

For Complete List of Firm Personnel, See General Section

For full biographical listings, see the Martindale-Hubbell Law Directory

WOLFF & SAMSON, P.A. (AV)

280 Corporate Center, 5 Becker Farm Road, 07068
Telephone: 201-740-0500
Fax: 201-740-1407

Joel A. Wolff
David L. Schlossberg

Representative Clients: International Fidelity Insurance Co.; Celentano Brothers, Inc.; Chicago Title Insurance Co.; Hartz Mountain Industries; The Hillier Group; Foster Wheeler Corp.

For Complete List of Firm Personnel, See General Section

For full biographical listings, see the Martindale-Hubbell Law Directory

SECAUCUS, Hudson Co.

ROSENBLUM, WOLF & LLOYD, A PROFESSIONAL CORPORATION (AV)

One Harmon Plaza, 07094
Telephone: 201-330-0220
Fax: 201-863-5472

Leo Rosenblum (1906-1990)
Edward G. Rosenblum
Nathan P. Wolf
John R. Lloyd

Reference: The Bank of New York, formerly National Community Bank.

For full biographical listings, see the Martindale-Hubbell Law Directory

SUMMIT, Union Co.

COOPER ROSE & ENGLISH (AV)

480 Morris Avenue, 07901-1527
Telephone: 908-273-1212
Fax: 908-273-8922
Rumson, New Jersey Office: 20 Bingham Avenue. 07760.
Telephone: 908-741-7777.
Fax: 908-758-1879.

MEMBERS OF FIRM

John W. Cooper
Frederick W. Rose
Jerry Fitzgerald English
Joseph E. Imbriaco
Roger S. Clapp
Arthur H. Garvin, III
Peter M. Burke
Gary F. Danis
John J. DeLaney, Jr.
David G. Hardin

OF COUNSEL

Harrison F. Durand
Russell T. Kerby, Jr.
Ronald J. Tell

ASSOCIATES

Fredi L. Pearlmutter
Kristi Bragg
Stephen R. Geller
Peter W. Ulicny
Thomas J. Sateary
Gianfranco A. Pietrafesa
Donna M. Russo
J. Andrew Kinsey
Jonathan S. Chester
Daniel Jon Kleinman
Holly English
Margaret R. Kalas
Mary T. Zdanowicz
Robert A. Meyers
Richard F. Iglar

Counsel for: Ciba-Geigy Corp.; Witco Corp.; New Jersey American Water Co.; Mikropul Corp.; AT&T Bell Laboratories; Aircast.

For full biographical listings, see the Martindale-Hubbell Law Directory

WESTFIELD, Union Co.

LINDABURY, MCCORMICK & ESTABROOK, A PROFESSIONAL CORPORATION (AV)

53 Cardinal Drive, P.O. Box 2369, 07091
Telephone: 908-233-6800
Fax: 908-233-5078

John R. Blasi
J. Ferd Convery III

COUNSEL

Robert S. Schwartz

OF COUNSEL

Kenneth L. Estabrook

Representative Clients: Adidas America, Inc.; Chilton Memorial Hospital; Elizabeth General Medical Center; Kessler Institute for Rehabilitation; Kuehne Chemical Co., Inc.; Linden Industrial Association; The Morris Museum Foundation; Western Industries, Inc.

For Complete List of Firm Personnel, See General Section

For full biographical listings, see the Martindale-Hubbell Law Directory

WEST ORANGE, Essex Co.

GOLDBERG, MUFSON & SPAR, A PROFESSIONAL CORPORATION (AV)

200 Executive Drive, 07052
Telephone: 201-736-0100
Telecopier: 201-736-0961

Leonard M. Goldberg
Ann Mufson
Michael R. Spar
Kenneth J. Isaacson
Eric W. Olson

OF COUNSEL

Jerome E. Sharfman

For full biographical listings, see the Martindale-Hubbell Law Directory

MELVIN J. WALLERSTEIN, P.A. (AV)

200 Executive Drive Suite 100, 07052
Telephone: 201-731-2500
Fax: 201-731-0163

Melvin J. Wallerstein

LEGAL SUPPORT PERSONNEL

LEGAL ADMINISTRATOR

Charlotte M. Burns

For full biographical listings, see the Martindale-Hubbell Law Directory

ZELLER & STRULOWITZ (AV)

80 Main Street, 07052
Telephone: 201-325-1242
Fax: 201-325-7996

(See Next Column)

MEMBERS OF FIRM

Harvey R. Zeller
Eric A. Strulowitz

For full biographical listings, see the Martindale-Hubbell Law Directory

WOODBRIDGE, Middlesex Co.

GREENBAUM, ROWE, SMITH, RAVIN AND DAVIS (AV)

Metro Corporate Campus I, P.O. Box 5600, 07095-0988
Telephone: 908-549-5600
Cable Address: "Greelaw"
Telecopier: 908-549-1881
ABA Net: 2 529

MEMBERS OF FIRM

Michael A. Backer
Martin L. Lepelstat
Thomas C. Senter
Michael K. Feinberg

ASSOCIATES

Michael F. Bodrato
Kathleen Curran Brown

For Complete List of Firm Personnel, See General Section

For full biographical listings, see the Martindale-Hubbell Law Directory

WILENTZ, GOLDMAN & SPITZER, A PROFESSIONAL CORPORATION (AV)

90 Woodbridge Center Drive Suite 900, Box 10, 07095
Telephone: 908-636-8000
Telecopier: 908-855-6117
Eatontown, New Jersey Office: Meridian Center I, Two Industrial Way West, 07724.
Telephone: 908-493-1000.
Telecopier: 908-493-8387.
New York, New York Office: Wall Street Plaza, 88 Pine Street, 9th Floor, 10005.
Telephone: 212-267-3091.
Telecopier: 212-267-3828.

Charles S. Zucker

Steven P. Marshall
Robert C. Kautz

Representative Clients: Amerada Hess Corp.; Chevron, U.S.A.; Middlesex County Utilities Authority; The Rouse Co.; New Jersey Arts Center at Newark Corp.; Eston Vance Management; Goldman Sachs; Hilton Clothes, Inc.

For Complete List of Firm Personnel, See General Section

For full biographical listings, see the Martindale-Hubbell Law Directory

NEW MEXICO

*ALBUQUERQUE,** Bernalillo Co.

HINKLE, COX, EATON, COFFIELD & HENSLEY (AV)

Suite 800, 500 Marquette, N.W., P.O. Box 2043, 87103
Telephone: 505-768-1500
FAX: 505-768-1529
Roswell, New Mexico Office: Suite 700, United Bank Plaza, P.O. Box 10, 88202.
Telephone: 505-622-6510.
FAX: 505-623-9332.
Midland, Texas Office: 6 Desta Drive, Suite 2800, P.O. Box 3580, 79705.
Telephone: 915-683-4691.
FAX: 915-683-6518.
Amarillo, Texas Office: 1700 Bank One Center. P.O. Box 9238, 79105-9238.
Telephone: 806-372-5569.
FAX: 806-372-9761.
Santa Fe, New Mexico Office: 218 Montezuma, P.O. Box 2068, 87504.
Telephone: 505-982-4554.
FAX: 505-982-8623.
Austin, Texas Office: 401 West 15th Street, Suite 800, 78701.
Telephone: 512-476-7137.
FAX: 512-476-5431.
Associated Office: Hoffman & Stephens, P.C., 401 West 15th Street, Suite 800, 78701.
Telephone: 512-476-5434.
Fax: 512-476-5431.

Fred W. Schwendimann
Julie P. Neerken

Representative Clients: Anadarko Petroleum Corp.; Atlantic Richfield Co.; Bass Enterprises Production Co.; BHP Petroleum; Caroon & Black Management, Inc.; Chevron, USA, Inc.; CIGNA; City of Albuquerque; Coastal Oil & Gas Corp. Co.; Ethicon Inc., A Johnson & Johnson, Co.; Diagnostik; Conoco; Texaco; Presbyterian Healthcare Services.

For Complete List of Firm Personnel, See General Section

For full biographical listings, see the Martindale-Hubbell Law Directory

Albuquerque—Continued

KELLY, RAMMELKAMP, MUEHLENWEG, LUCERO & LEÓN, A PROFESSIONAL ASSOCIATION (AV)

Simms Tower, 400 Gold Avenue S.W., Suite 500, P.O. Box 25127, 87125-5127
Telephone: 505-247-8860
Fax: 505-247-8881

Henry A. Kelly
Robert J. Muehlenweg

Representative Clients: First Bank of Grants; Bank of America, New Mexico; John L. Rust Co. (Caterpillar); Bridgers & Paxton Consulting Engineers, Inc.; Grants State Bank; Basis International, Ltd.; Ponderosa Products, Inc.; Galles Motor Company (Chevrolet and Saturn); Pension Planning Consultants, Inc.; Rogoff, Diamond & Walker Certified Public Accountants.

For Complete List of Firm Personnel, See General Section

For full biographical listings, see the Martindale-Hubbell Law Directory

LAFLIN, LIEUWEN, TUCKER, PICK & HEER, P.A. (AV)

6400 Uptown Boulevard, Suite 600W, 87110
Telephone: 505-883-0679
Fax: 505-883-5834

John D. Laflin
John N. Lieuwen
Patricia Tucker
Daniel E. Pick
John E. Heer, III
Evan S. Hobbs
Linda Q. Sanchez
Janice Dale

References: Sunwest Bank of Albuquerque, N.A. (Trust Dept.); United New Mexico Bank (Trust Dept.); First Security Bank (Trust Dept.).

For full biographical listings, see the Martindale-Hubbell Law Directory

MILLER, STRATVERT, TORGERSON & SCHLENKER, P.A. (AV)

500 Marquette Avenue, N.W., Suite 1100, P.O. Box 25687, 87102
Telephone: 505-842-1950
Facsimile: 505-243-4408
Farmington, New Mexico Office: Suite 300, 300 West Arrington. P.O. Box 869.
Telephone: 505-326-4521.
Facsimile: 505-325-5474.
Las Cruces, New Mexico Office: Suite 300, 277 East Amador. P.O. Drawer 1231.
Telephone: 505-523-2481.
Facsimile: 505-526-2215.
Santa Fe, New Mexico Office: 125 Lincoln Avenue, Suite 221. P.O. Box 1986.
Telephone: 505-989-9614.
Facsimile: 505-989-9857.

Kendall O. Schlenker
Sharon P. Gross
John R. Funk (Resident at Las Cruces Office)

Representative Clients: Aztec Well Servicing Co.; Dennis Cattle Co.; Gurley Motor Co.; Robert H. Weil; Tom Growney Equipment, Inc.; Sunrise Healthcare Corp.; Van Vechten-Lineberry Taos Art Museum; Santa Fe Jazz Foundation; College of Santa Fe.

For Complete List of Firm Personnel, See General Section

For full biographical listings, see the Martindale-Hubbell Law Directory

RODEY, DICKASON, SLOAN, AKIN & ROBB, P.A. (AV)

Albuquerque Plaza, Suite 2200, 201 Third Street, N.W., P.O. Box 1888, 87103-1888
Telephone: 505-765-5900
Fax: 505-768-7395
Santa Fe, New Mexico Office: Suite 101 Marcy Plaza, 123 East Marcy Street, P.O. Box 1357, 87504-1357.
Telephone: 505-984-0100.
Fax: 505-989-9542.

Patricia M. Taylor

COUNSEL

Jeffrey W. Loubet

Representative Clients: Albuquerque Publishing Co.; ASCAP; Associated Aviation Underwriters Co.; Automobile Club Insurance Co.; Avonite, Inc.; Canal Insurance Co.; General Electric Co.; KOAT-TV; Liberty Mutual Insurance Co.; Sandia Corporation.

For Complete List of Firm Personnel, See General Section

For full biographical listings, see the Martindale-Hubbell Law Directory

*CLOVIS,** Curry Co.

TATUM & McDOWELL (AV)

Suite D, Sagebrush Professional Office Complex, 921 East 21st Street, P.O. Drawer 1270, 88101
Telephone: 505-762-7756
Fax: 505-769-1606

(See Next Column)

MEMBER OF FIRM

Edwin B. Tatum

Representative Clients: High Plains Federal Credit Union; Friona Industries Inc.; Valley Rendering Co.; A & M Building Systems Inc.; Citizens Bank of Clovis; American Cattle Feeders, Inc.; Clovis Feedyard, Inc.; Borden's Peanut Co., Inc.
References: Sunwest Bank of Clovis, N.A.; Citizens Bank of Clovis.

For Complete List of Firm Personnel, See General Section

For full biographical listings, see the Martindale-Hubbell Law Directory

*SANTA FE,** Santa Fe Co.

CATRON, CATRON & SAWTELL, A PROFESSIONAL ASSOCIATION (AV)

2006 Botulph Road, P.O. Box 788, 87504-0788
Telephone: 505-982-1947
Telecopier: 505-986-1013

Thomas B. Catron III
John S. Catron
William A. Sawtell, Jr.
Fletcher R. Catron
Forrest S. Smith

LEGAL SUPPORT PERSONNEL

Peggy L. Feldt (Certified Public Accountant)

Attorneys for: Santa Fe Board of Education; American Express Co.; The Santa Fe Opera; Sunwest Bank of Santa Fe; VNS Health Services, Inc.

For Complete List of Firm Personnel, See General Section

For full biographical listings, see the Martindale-Hubbell Law Directory

MONTGOMERY & ANDREWS, PROFESSIONAL ASSOCIATION (AV)

325 Paseo de Peralta, P.O. Box 2307, 87504-2307
Telephone: 505-982-3873
Albuquerque, New Mexico Office: Suite 1300 Albuquerque Plaza, 201 Third Street, N.W., P.O. Box 26927.
Telephone: 505-242-9677.
FAX: 505-243-2542.

Galen M. Buller
Edmund H. Kendrick
David Carroll Johnson

Representative Clients: Burlington Resources, Inc.; El Paso Natural Gas Co.; Mobil Exploration and Producing U.S., Inc.; St. Vincent Hospital; Travelers Insurance Co.; US WEST Communications; Giant Industries, Inc.; Meridian Oil, Inc.

For Complete List of Firm Personnel, See General Section

For full biographical listings, see the Martindale-Hubbell Law Directory

ROSE, KOHL & DAVENPORT, LTD. (AV)

1516 Paseo De Peralta, 87501
Telephone: 505-982-0080
Fax: 505-982-0081

Filmore E. Rose
Bruce R. Kohl
Beth R. Davenport
Robert J. Dodds, III
Marie A. Cioth (Not admitted in NM)

Reference: The First National Bank of Santa Fe.

For full biographical listings, see the Martindale-Hubbell Law Directory

NEW YORK

*ALBANY,** Albany Co.

ISEMAN, CUNNINGHAM, RIESTER & HYDE (AV)

9 Thurlow Terrace, 12203
Telephone: 518-462-3000
Telecopier: 518-462-4199

MEMBERS OF FIRM

Frederick C. Riester
Michael J. Cunningham
Robert Hall Iseman
Carol Ann Hyde
Michael J. McNeil

Brian M. Culnan
Linda J. Clark

For full biographical listings, see the Martindale-Hubbell Law Directory

KOHN, BOOKSTEIN & KARP, P.C. (AV)

Ninety State Street Suite 929, 12207-1888
Telephone: 518-449-8810
Fax: 518-449-1029

Eugene M. Karp

James Blendell

(See Next Column)

KOHN, BOOKSTEIN & KARP P.C., *Albany—Continued*

OF COUNSEL

Karen Martino Valle

Representative Clients: Adirondack Transit Lines, Inc.; Amfast Corp.; Simmons Fastener Corp.; Tagsons Papers, Inc.; Thermo Products, Inc.

For Complete List of Firm Personnel, See General Section

For full biographical listings, see the Martindale-Hubbell Law Directory

*BINGHAMTON,** Broome Co.

HINMAN, HOWARD & KATTELL (AV)

700 Security Mutual Building, 80 Exchange Street, 13901
Telephone: 607-723-5341
Fax: 607-723-6605
Norwich, New York Office: 600 South Broad Street, Suite 200.
Telephone: 607-334-5896.
Fax: 607-336-6240.

COUNSEL

Joseph P. Minnich, Jr.

MEMBERS OF FIRM

C. Addison Keeler, Jr.
Colin T. Naylor, III
Eugene E. Peckham
Wilbur D. Dahlgren

Representative Clients: First-City Division, Chase Lincoln First Bank, N.A.; Binghamton Savings Bank; International Business Machines Corp.; Universal Instruments Corp.; Security Mutual Life Insurance Company of New York; New York Telephone Co.; Travelers Insurance Co.; New York State Electric & Gas Corp.; Exxon Corp.; Columbia Gas System, Inc.

For Complete List of Firm Personnel, See General Section

For full biographical listings, see the Martindale-Hubbell Law Directory

BRONXVILLE, Westchester Co.

GRIFFIN, COOGAN & VENERUSO, P.C. (AV)

51 Pondfield Road, 10708
Telephone: 914-961-1300
Telecopier: 914-961-1476; 914-961-9385

William E. Griffin
James M. Coogan
James J. Veneruso
Robert W. Wolper

Karen J. Walsh
Joseph A. Ruhl
Daniel J. Griffin
Phyllis Knight Marcus
Paul G. Amicucci
Paul V. Greco
Paul R. Herrick

Approved Closing Attorneys: Hudson Valley Bank; Hudson Valley Mortgage Corp.; American Savings and Loan Association.

For full biographical listings, see the Martindale-Hubbell Law Directory

*BUFFALO,** Erie Co.

ALBRECHT, MAGUIRE, HEFFERN & GREGG, P.C. (AV)

2100 Main Place Tower, 14202
Telephone: 716-853-1521
Fax: 716-852-2609

George M. Zimmermann
James M. Beardsley
Raymond H. Barr
Philip John Szabla
Gary J. Gleba

For Complete List of Firm Personnel, See General Section

For full biographical listings, see the Martindale-Hubbell Law Directory

HODGSON, RUSS, ANDREWS, WOODS & GOODYEAR (AV)

A Partnership including Professional Associations
Suite 1800, One M & T Plaza, 14203
Telephone: 716-856-4000
Cable Address: "Magna Carta" Buffalo, N.Y.
Telecopier: 716-849-0349
Albany, New York Office: Three City Square.
Telephone: 518-465-2333.
Telecopier: 518-465-1567.
Rochester, New York Office: 400 East Avenue.
Telephone: 716-454-6950.
Telecopier: 716-454-4698.
Boca Raton, Florida Office: Suite 400, Nations Bank Building, 2000 Glades Road.
Telephone: 407-394-0500.
Telecopier: 305-427-4303.
Mississauga, Ontario, Canada Office: Suite 880, 3 Robert Speck Parkway.
Telephone: 905-566-5061.
Telecopier: 905-566-2049.
New York, New York Office: 330 Madison Avenue, 11th Floor. Telephone 212-297-3370.
Telecopier: 212-972-6521.

(See Next Column)

MEMBERS OF FIRM

(ALPHABETICALLY BY YEAR OF ADMISSION TO BAR)

Richard E. Heath (Boca Raton, Florida Office)
Paul R. Comeau
Todd M. Joseph
Dianne Bennett
Richard F. Campbell
Daniel R. Sharpe
Mark S. Klein
Alice Accola Joseffer
Thomas W. Nelson
Robert D. Plattner (Albany Office)
Richard W. Kaiser
Peter K. Bradley
Carol Anne Fitzsimmons
Christopher L. Doyle

ASSOCIATES

(ALPHABETICALLY BY YEAR OF ADMISSION TO BAR)

Michel Pierre Cassier
Sharon M. Kelly
Wayne J. McChesney
Tim Sawers

Counsel for: Outokumpu American Brass Co.; Baillie Lumber Co., Inc.; Cablesystems Inc.; Delaware North Companies, Inc. Gibraltar Steel; Idex Corp.; Manufacturers & Traders Trust Co.; SKW Alloys Inc.; Tops Markets, Inc.; Tripifoods, Inc..

For Complete List of Firm Personnel, See General Section

For full biographical listings, see the Martindale-Hubbell Law Directory

HURWITZ & FINE, P.C. (AV)

1300 Liberty Building, 14202-3613
Telephone: 716-849-8900
Telecopier: 716-855-0874

Robert P. Fine
Lawrence C. Franco
Lawrence M. Ross

For Complete List of Firm Personnel, See General Section

For full biographical listings, see the Martindale-Hubbell Law Directory

PHILLIPS, LYTLE, HITCHCOCK, BLAINE & HUBER (AV)

(Formerly Kenefick, Letchworth, Baldy, Phillips & Emblidge)
3400 Marine Midland Center, 14203
Telephone: 716-847-8400
Telecopier: 716-852-6100
Jamestown, New York Office: 307 Chase Bank Building, 8 E. Third Street.
Telephone: 716-664-3906.
Telecopier: 716-664-4230.
Rochester, New York Office: 1400 First Federal Plaza.
Telephone: 716-238-2000.
Telecopier: 716-232-3141.
New York, New York Office: 437 Madison Avenue.
Telephone: 212-759-4888.
Telecopier: 212-308-9079.
Fredonia, New York Office: 11 East Main Street.
Telephone: 716-672-2164.
FAX: 716-672-7979.

PARTNERS

Thomas M. Barney
Caroline Hassett Buerk
Thomas R. Burns (Resident, Rochester Office)
Michael C. Foley (Resident, Jamestown Office)
Hugh M. Jones
James A. Locke
Arthur M. Sherwood
John C. Spitzmiller
Paul A. Vick (Resident, Rochester Office)
Robert F. Zogas (Resident, Rochester Office)

General Counsel for: Astronics Corporation; Bryant & Stratton Business Institute; Canisius College; Chase Manhattan Bank, N.A.; Columbus McKinnon Corp.
Local Counsel for: A.O. Smith Corp.; Allied Signal; Bethleham Steel Corp.; Chrysler Motor Corp.; E.I. DuPont deNemours Co., Inc.

For Complete List of Firm Personnel, See General Section

For full biographical listings, see the Martindale-Hubbell Law Directory

EAST MEADOW, Nassau Co.

CERTILMAN BALIN ADLER & HYMAN, LLP (AV)

90 Merrick Avenue, 11554
Telephone: 516-296-7000
Telecopier: 516-296-7111

MEMBERS OF FIRM

Ira J. Adler
Dale Allinson
Herbert M. Balin
Bruce J. Bergman
Michael D. Brofman
Morton L. Certilman
Murray Greenberg
David Z. Herman
Richard Herzbach
M. Allan Hyman
Bernard Hyman
Donna-Marie Korth
Steven J. Kuperschmid
Thomas J. McNamara
Fred S. Skolnik
Louis Soloway
Harold Somer
Howard M. Stein
Brian K. Ziegler

OF COUNSEL

Daniel S. Cohan
Norman J. Levy
Marilyn Price

(See Next Column)

CERTILMAN BALIN ADLER & HYMAN LLP—*Continued*

ASSOCIATES

Howard B. Busch
Scott M. Gerber
Jodi S. Hoffman
Glenn Kleinbaum
Michael C. Manniello
Jaspreet S. Mayall
Stacey R. Miller
Lawrence S. Novak
Kim J. Radbell

For full biographical listings, see the Martindale-Hubbell Law Directory

MASPETH, Queens Co.

EDWARD M. MCGOWAN (AV)

68-15 Borden Avenue, 11378
Telephone: 718-651-7360
Telecopier: 718-446-0796

For full biographical listings, see the Martindale-Hubbell Law Directory

MELVILLE, Suffolk Co.

SPANTON, PARSOFF & SIEGEL, P.C. (AV)

425 Broad Hollow Road, Route 110, 11747
Telephone: 516-777-3200
Fax: 516-777-3204
New York, N.Y. Office: 790 Madison Avenue, 10021.
Telephone: 212-717-5948.

Donald M. Spanton
Neil M. Parsoff
Lawrence A. Siegel

Pamela G. Weiss

OF COUNSEL

Murray D. Schwartz

For full biographical listings, see the Martindale-Hubbell Law Directory

NEW ROCHELLE, Westchester Co.

MCGOVERN, CONNELLY & DAVIDSON (AV)

145 Huguenot Street, P.O. Box 0, 10801
Telephone: 914-632-9300
Telecopier: 914-632-1615

MEMBERS OF FIRM

J. Raymond McGovern (1898-1974)
Frank H. Connelly, Sr. (1907-1989)
Harry G. Davidson (1912-1981)
Frank H. Connelly, Jr.
John A. Vasile
Francis B. Orlando
Margaret M. Fitzpatrick
Scott Weinberger

Representative Clients: Capital Sports Inc.; City of New Rochelle; Halpern-Stillman, Inc.; Marine Midland Bank; Samson Management, Co.; The Rawlplug Company, Inc.; Pace Oldsmobile, Inc.; Flynn Burner Corp.

For full biographical listings, see the Martindale-Hubbell Law Directory

*NEW YORK,** New York Co.

BAKER & BOTTS, L.L.P. (AV)

885 Third Avenue Suite 2000, 10022
Telephone: 212-705-5000
Fax: 212-705-5125
Washington, D.C. Office: The Warner, 1299 Pennsylvania Avenue, N.W.
Telephone: 202-639-7700.
Austin, Texas Office: 1600 San Jacinto Center, 98 San Jacinto Boulevard.
Telephone: 512-322-2500.
Dallas, Texas Office: 2001 Ross Avenue.
Telephone: 214-953-6500.
Houston, Texas Office: One Shell Plaza, 910 Louisiana.
Telephone: 713-229-1234.
Moscow, Russian Federation Office: 10 ul. Pushkinskaya, 103031.
Telephone: 7095/921-5300 (Local); 7095/929-7070 (International).

MEMBER OF FIRM

James A. Hime (Not admitted in NY)

ASSOCIATES

Robert S. Langley, Jr.
Paul A. Manuel

For Complete List of Firm Personnel, See General Section

For full biographical listings, see the Martindale-Hubbell Law Directory

CURTIS, MALLET-PREVOST, COLT & MOSLE (AV)

101 Park Avenue, 10178
Telephone: 212-696-6000
Telecopier: 212-697-1559
Cable Address: "Migniar d New York"
Telex: 12-6811 Migniard; ITT 422127 MGND
Washington, D.C. Office: Suite 1205 L, 1801 K Street, N.W.
Telephone: 202-452-7373.
Telecopier: 202-452-7333.
Telex: ITT 440379 CMPUI.

(See Next Column)

Newark, New Jersey Office: One Gateway Center, Suite 403.
Telephone: 201-622-0605.
Telecopier: 201-622-5646.
Houston, Texas Office: 2 Houston Center, 909 Fannin Street, Suite 3725.
Telephone: 713-759-9555.
Telecopier: 713-759-0712.
Mexico City, D.F., Mexico Office: Torre Chapultepec, Ruben Dario 281, Col. Bosques de Chapultepec, 11530 Mexico, D.F.
Telephone: 525-282-0444.
Telecopier: 525-282-0637.
Paris, France Office: 8 Avenue Victor Hugo.
Telephone: 45-00-99-68.
Telecopier: 45-00-84-06.
London, England Office: Two Throgmorton Avenue, EC2N 2DL.
Telephone: 71-638-7957.
Telecopier: 71-638-5512.
Frankfurt am Main 1 Office: Staufenstrasse 42.
Telephone: 069-971-4420.
Telecopier: 69-17 33 99.

MEMBERS OF FIRM

Alan Berlin
Marco A. Blanco
William L. Bricker, Jr.
William B. Sherman
Robert D. Whoriskey

For Complete List of Firm Personnel, See General Section

For full biographical listings, see the Martindale-Hubbell Law Directory

DEBEVOISE & PLIMPTON (AV)

875 Third Avenue, 10022
Telephone: 212-909-6000
Domestic Telex: 148377 DEBSTEVE NYK
Telecopier: (212) 909-6836
Los Angeles, California Office: 601 South Figueroa Street, Suite 3700, 90017.
Telephone: 213-680-8000.
Telecopier: 213-680-8100.
Washington, D.C. Office: 555 13th Street, N.W., 20004.
Telephone: 202-383-8000.
Telecopier: (202) 383-8118.
Paris, France Office: 21 Avenue George V 75008.
Telephone: (33-1) 40 73 12 12.
Telecopier: (33-1) 47 20 50 82.
Telex: 648141F DPPAR.
London, England Office: 1 Creed Court, 5 Ludgate Hill, EC4M 7AA.
Telephone: (44-171) 329-0779.
Telex: 88 4569 DPLON G.
Telecopier: (44-171) 329-0860.
Budapest, Hungary Office: 1065 Budapest, Révay Köz 2.III/2.
Telephone: (36-1)112-8067.
Telecopier: (36-1) 132-7995.
Hong Kong Office: 13/F Entertainment Building, 30 Queen's Road Central.
Telephone: (852) 2810-7918.
Fax: (852) 2810-9828.

MEMBERS OF FIRM

Bruce D. Haims
Hugh Rowland, Jr. (Resident, London Office)
Jonathan A. Small
Marcus H. Strock
David A. Duff
Robert J. Cubitto
Robert J. Staffaroni
Andrew N. Berg
Burt Rosen
Seth L. Rosen
Lawrence K. Cagney
Gary M. Friedman

OF COUNSEL

Philip S. Winterer

For Complete List of Firm Personnel, See General Section

For full biographical listings, see the Martindale-Hubbell Law Directory

EMMET, MARVIN & MARTIN, LLP (AV)

120 Broadway, 10271
Telephone: 212-238-3000
Cable Address: EMMARRO
Fax: 212-238-3100
Morristown, New Jersey Office: 10 Madison Avenue.
Telephone: 201-538-5600.
Fax: 201-538-6448.

MEMBERS OF FIRM

Thomas B. Fenlon
Thomas F. Noone (P.C.)
Lawrence B. Thompson
William A. Leet
David M. Daly
Peter B. Tisne
Michael C. Johansen
Robert W. Viets
Dennis C. Fleischmann
Eric M. Reuben
Jeffrey S. Chavkin
J. Christopher Eagan
Jesse Dudley B. Kimball
Stephen P. Cerow
Ellen J. Bickal
Edward P. Zujkowski
John P. Uehlinger
Irving C. Apar
Julian A. McQuiston
Maria-Liisa Lydon
Christine B. Cesare
Patrick A. McCartney
Matthew P. D'Amico
Brian D. Obergfell

(See Next Column)

EMMET, MARVIN & MARTIN LLP, *New York—Continued*

OF COUNSEL

Guy B. Capel
Bernard F. Joyce (P.C.)
Richard P. Bourgerie
George H. P. Dwight

ASSOCIATES

Eunice M. O'Neill
Joseph M. Samulski
Sean M. Carlin
Alfred W. J. Marks
Eileen Chin-Bow
John M. Ryan
Francine M. Kors
Wendy E. Kramer
James C. Hughes, IV
Patricia C. Caputo
Bennett E. Josselsohn
Stephen I. Frank
Mildred Quinones
Anthony M. Harvin
Lynn D. Barsamian
Margaret H. Walker
Robert L. Morgan
Sally Shreeves
Michael Fotios Mavrides
Matthew A. Wieland
Eric E. Schneck (Resident, Morristown Office)
Lisa B. Lerner
Elizabeth K. Somers
Steven M. Berg
Michael E. Cavanaugh
Nancy J. Cohen
Peter L. Mancini
Stephen M. Ksenak

For full biographical listings, see the Martindale-Hubbell Law Directory

FEINGOLD & NAPOLI (AV)

1325 Avenue of the Americas, 10019
Telephone: 212-582-8000
Fax: 212-582-8080

Fred Feingold
Mark E. Berg

ASSOCIATES

Louis Vlahos
Edward H. Sedacca

For full biographical listings, see the Martindale-Hubbell Law Directory

HUTTON INGRAM YUZEK GAINEN CARROLL & BERTOLOTTI (AV)

250 Park Avenue, 10177
Telephone: 212-907-9600
Facsimile: 212-907-9681

MEMBERS OF FIRM

Ernest J. Bertolotti
Daniel L. Carroll
Roger Cukras
Larry F. Gainen
G. Thompson Hutton
Samuel W. Ingram, Jr.
Paulette Kendler
Steven Mastbaum
Dean G. Yuzek
David G. Ebert
Shane O'Neill

ASSOCIATES

Warren E. Friss
Patricia Hewitt
Gail A. Buchman
Stuart A. Christie
Beth N. Green
Timish K. Hnateyko
Jeanne F. Pucci
Jane Drummey
Adam L. Sifre
Susan Ann Fennelly
Marc J. Schneider

For full biographical listings, see the Martindale-Hubbell Law Directory

KOSTELANETZ & FINK (AV)

230 Park Avenue, Suite 1140, 10169
Telephone: 212-808-8100
Fax: 212-808-8108

OF COUNSEL

Boris Kostelanetz

MEMBERS OF FIRM

Robert S. Fink
Kevin M. Flynn
Kathryn Keneally
Nora Elizabeth Plesent
Bryan C. Skarlatos
Linda Donahue

For full biographical listings, see the Martindale-Hubbell Law Directory

BUREAU FRANCIS LEFEBVRE (AV)

712 Fifth Avenue, 10019
Telephone: (1.212) 246.80.45
Fax: (1.212) 246.29.51
Paris, France Office: 3, Villa Emile Bergerat, 92522 Neuilly-Sur-Seine, Cedex.
Telephone: (33.1) 47 38 55 00.
Telex: 620971 LEFEB A.
Fax: (33.1) 47 38 55 55.

RESIDENT PARTNERS

Carina Levintoff
Pierre-Sébastien Thill (Not admitted in NY)

RESIDENT ASSOCIATES

Clotilde Fournier
Edouard Milhac (Not admitted in NY)

For full biographical listings, see the Martindale-Hubbell Law Directory

LOEB AND LOEB (AV)

A Partnership including Professional Corporations
345 Park Avenue, 10154-0037
Telephone: 212-407-4000
Facsimile: 212-407-4990
Los Angeles, California Office: Suite 1800, 1000 Wilshire Boulevard, 90017-2475.
Telephone: 213-688-3400.
Cable Address: "Loband LSA".
Telecopier: 213-688-3460; 688-3461; 688-3462.
Century City (Los Angeles), California Office: Suite 2200, 10100 Santa Monica Boulevard, Los Angeles, 90067-4164.
Telephone: 310-282-2000.
Telecopier: 310-282-2191; 282-2192.
Nashville, Tennessee Office: 45 Music Square West, 37203-3205.
Telephone: 615-749-8300.
Facsimile: 615-749-8308.
Rome, Italy Office: Piazza Digione 1, 00197.
Telephone: 011-396-808-8456.
Telecopier: 011-396-674-8223.

MEMBERS OF FIRM

Abraham S. Guterman
Fredric M. Sanders

OF COUNSEL

Arthur A. Segall

ASSOCIATE

Jay Fenster

For Complete List of Firm Personnel, See General Section

For full biographical listings, see the Martindale-Hubbell Law Directory

MALONEY, GERRA, MEHLMAN & KATZ (AV)

Chrysler Building, 405 Lexington Avenue, 10174
Telephone: 212-973-6900
Fax: 212-973-6097

MEMBERS OF FIRM

Ralph A. Gerra, Jr.
Melvin Katz
Thomas J. Maloney
Barry T. Mehlman

ASSOCIATES

Philip H. Sheehan, Jr.
Kenneth J. Zinghini

For full biographical listings, see the Martindale-Hubbell Law Directory

MUDGE ROSE GUTHRIE ALEXANDER & FERDON (AV)

(Mudge, Stern, Baldwin & Todd)
(Caldwell, Trimble & Mitchell)
180 Maiden Lane, 10038
Telephone: 212-510-7000
Cable Address: "Baltuchins, New York"
Telex: 127889 & 703729
Telecopier: 212-248-2655/57
Los Angeles, California Office: 21st Floor, 333 South Grand Avenue, 90071.
Telephone: 213-613-1112.
Telecopier: 213-680-1358.
Washington, D.C. Office: 2121 K Street, N.W., 20037.
Telephone: 202-429-9355.
Telecopier: 202-429-9367.
Telex: MRGA 440264.
Cable Address: "Baltuchins, Washington, DC"
West Palm Beach, Florida Office: Suite 900, 515 North Flagler Drive, 33401.
Telephone: 407-650-8100.
Telecopier: 407-833-1722.
Telex: 514847 MRWPB.
Parsippany, New Jersey Office: Morris Corporate Center Two, Building D, One Upper Pond Road, 07054-1075.
Telephone: 201-335-0004.
Telecopier: 201-402-1593.
European Office: 12, Rue de la Paix, 75002 Paris, France.
Telephone: 42.61.57.71.
Telecopier: 42.61.79.21.
Cable Address: "Baltuchins, Paris".
Tokyo, Japan Office: Infini Akasaka, 8-7-15 Akasaka, Minato-Ku, Tokyo 107, Japan.
Telephone: (03) 3423-3970.
Fax: (03) 3423-3971.

MEMBERS OF FIRM

J. William Dantzler, Jr.
Thomas J. Gormley
Jeffrey L. Piemont
Clayton S. Reynolds

COUNSEL

Richard H. Nicholls

ASSOCIATES

Anthony V. Giancana
Shari Leigh Gordon
John P. Iorillo (Not admitted in NY)
Mark O. Norell
John F. Schaller
Keri Schiowitz
Stephen J. Watson

(See Next Column)

MUDGE ROSE GUTHRIE ALEXANDER & FERDON—*Continued*

For Complete List of Firm Personnel, See General Section

For full biographical listings, see the Martindale-Hubbell Law Directory

PARKER CHAPIN FLATTAU & KLIMPL, L.L.P. (AV)

1211 Avenue of the Americas, 10036
Telephone: 212-704-6000
Telecopier: 212-704-6288
Cable Address: "Lawpark"
Telex: 640347
Great Neck, New York Office: 175 Great Neck Road.
Telephone: 516-482-4422.
Telecopier: 516-482-4469.

MEMBERS OF FIRM

Carol F. Burger
Alan J. Tarr

SENIOR COUNSEL

Irving Rosenzweig

OF COUNSEL

Paul Goldstein

For Complete List of Firm Personnel, See General Section

For full biographical listings, see the Martindale-Hubbell Law Directory

PRERAU & TEITELL

(See White Plains)

STROOCK & STROOCK & LAVAN (AV)

Seven Hanover Square, 10004-2696
Telephone: 212-806-5400
Telecopier: (212) 806-6006
Telexes: Stroock, UT 177693 and Plastroock NYK 177077 (International)
Cable Address: "Plastroock, NYK"
New York Conference Center: 767 Third Avenue, 10017-2023.
Telephones: 212-806-5767; 5768; 5769; 5770.
Telecopier: (212) 421-6234.
Washington, D.C. Office: 1150 Seventeenth Street, N.W., Suite 600, 20036-4652.
Telephone: 202-452-9250.
Telecopier: (202) 421-6234.
Cable Address: "Plastroock, Washington."
Telex: 64238 STROOCK DC; 89401 STROOCK DC.
Los Angeles, California Office: 2029 Century Park East, Floors 16 & 18, 90067-3086.
Telephone: 310-556-5800.
Telecopier: (310) 556-5959.
Cable Address: "Plastroock L.A."
Telex: Plastroock LSA 677190 (Domestic and International).
Miami, Florida Office: 200 South Biscayne Boulevard, Suite 3000, First Union Financial Center, 33131-2385.
Telephone: 305-358-9900.
Telecopier: (305) 789-9302.
Telex: 803133 Stroock Mia (Domestic and International); Broward Line: 527-9900.
Budapest, Hungary Office: East-West Business Center, Rákóczi ut 1-3, H-1088.
Telephone: 011-361-266-9520; 011-361-266-7770.
Telecopier: 001-361-266-9279.

MEMBERS OF FIRM

Micah W. Bloomfield
Charles B. Hochman
Jonathan S. Kusko
Mark A. Levy
Jeffrey D. Uffner

Mayer Greenberg

For Complete List of Firm Personnel, See General Section

For full biographical listings, see the Martindale-Hubbell Law Directory

WINTHROP, STIMSON, PUTNAM & ROBERTS (AV)

One Battery Park Plaza, 10004-1490
Telephone: 212-858-1000
Telex: 62854 WINSTIM
Telefax: 212-858-1500
Stamford, Connecticut Office: Financial Centre, 695 East Main Street, P.O. Box 6760, 06904-6760.
Telephone: 203-348-2300.
Washington, D.C. Office: 1133 Connecticut Avenue, N.W., 20036.
Telephone: 202-775-9800.
Palm Beach, Florida Office: 125 Worth Avenue, 33480.
Telephone: 407-655-7297.
London Office: 2 Throgmorton Avenue, London EC2N 2AP, England.
Telephone: 011-4471-628-4931.
Brussels Office: Rue Du Taciturne 42, B-1040 Brussels, Belgium.
Telephone: 011-322-230-1392.
Tokyo, Japan Office: 608 Atagoyama Bengoshi Building 6-7, Atago 1-chome, Minato-ku, Tokyo 105 Japan.
Telephone: 011-813-3437-9740.

(See Next Column)

Hong Kong Office: 2505 Asia Pacific Finance Tower, Citibank Plaza, 3 Garden Road, Central.
Telephone: 011-852-530-3400.

MEMBERS OF FIRM

William L. Burke
James T. Chudy
Richard G. Cohen
Hugh M. Dougan
Susan P. Serota

COUNSEL

John P. MacMaster

ASSOCIATES

Melissa Goldman
Lori S. Hoberman
David Hubelbank
Michael A. Lehmann
Sarah L. McGill
April P. Tash

For Complete List of Firm Personnel, See General Section

For full biographical listings, see the Martindale-Hubbell Law Directory

*POUGHKEEPSIE,** Dutchess Co.

GUERNSEY BUTTS OSTERTAG & O'LEARY (AV)

75 Washington Street, P.O. Box G, 12602
Telephone: 914-452-1100
FAX: 914-452-0150
Boca Raton, Florida Office: 2424 North Federal Highway, Suite 314.
Telephone: 407-368-3400.

MEMBERS OF FIRM

Robert L. Ostertag
Robert R. Butts
Diane M. O'Leary

OF COUNSEL

Charles A. Butts
David B. Van Kleeck (Not admitted in NY; Resident, Roca Raton, Florida Office)

Representative Clients: Bank of New York Dutchess Division; Vassar College; International Business Machines Corp.
Local Counsel for: John Hancock Mutual Insurance Co.; Connecticut National Bank.

For full biographical listings, see the Martindale-Hubbell Law Directory

TEAHAN & CONSTANTINO (AV)

325 South Road, 12601
Telephone: 914-452-1834
Fax: 914-452-1421
New York, New York Office: 380 Lexington Avenue.
Telephone: 212-986-3925.
Fax: 212-599-2332.
Albany, New York Office: 99 Pine Street, 12207.
Telephone: 518-426-9203.
Fax: 518-426-4655.

MEMBERS OF FIRM

Vincent L. Teahan
James P. Constantino

OF COUNSEL

Gina A. Gulotty

For full biographical listings, see the Martindale-Hubbell Law Directory

*ROCHESTER,** Monroe Co.

HARTER, SECREST & EMERY (AV)

700 Midtown Tower, 14604-2070
Telephone: 716-232-6500
Telecopier: 716-232-2152
Naples, Florida Office: Suite 400, 800 Laurel Oak Drive.
Telephone: 813-598-4444.
Telecopier: 813-598-2781.
Albany, New York Office: One Steuben Place.
Telephone: 518-434-4377.
Telecopier: 518-449-4025.
Syracuse, New York Office: 431 East Fayette Street.
Telephone: 315-474-4000.
Telecopier: 315-474-7789.

MEMBERS OF FIRM

William M. Colby
Michael R. McEvoy

ASSOCIATES

Kenneth A. Marvald
Christopher M. Potash

LEGAL SUPPORT PERSONNEL

Eve M. Peck (Tax Accountant)

For Complete List of Firm Personnel, See General Section

For full biographical listings, see the Martindale-Hubbell Law Directory

SHERRY S. KRAUS (AV)

513 Times Square Building, 45 Exchange Boulevard, 14614
Telephone: 716-262-3360

For full biographical listings, see the Martindale-Hubbell Law Directory

*SYRACUSE,** Onondaga Co.

BOND, SCHOENECK & KING (AV)

18th Floor One Lincoln Center, 13202-1355
Telephone: 315-422-0121
Fax: 315-422-3598
Albany, New York Office: 111 Washington Avenue.
Telephone: 518-462-7421.
Fax: 518-462-7441.
Boca Raton, Florida Office: 5355 Town Center Road, Suite 1002.
Telephone: 407-368-1212.
Fax: 407-338-9955.
Naples, Florida Office: 1167 Third Street South.
Telephone: 813-262-6812.
Fax: 813-262-6908.
Oswego, New York Office: 130 East Second Street.
Telephone: 315-343-9116.
Fax: 315-343-1231.
Overland Park, Kansas Office: 7500 College Boulevard, Suite 910.
Telephone: 913-345-8001.
Fax: 913-345-9017.

MEMBERS OF FIRM

George C. Shattuck
Arthur E. Bongiovanni
James E. Mackin
Gary R. Germain
James P. McDonald (Resident, Boca Raton, Florida Office)
Richard D. Hole
James N. Seeley
Thaddeus J. Lewkowicz
Edwin J. Kelley, Jr.
D. Fred Garner (Resident, Naples, Florida Office)
Brian K. Haynes

ASSOCIATES

Stephen C. Daley
Anne F. Sirota
William M. Burke
Steven J. Ford
Thomas J. Collura (Resident, Albany Office)
Dennis C. Brown

General Counsel for: Syracuse University; Unity Mutual Life Insurance Co.; Manufacturers Association of Central New York.
Regional or Special Counsel for: Newhouse Broadcasting Corp. (WSYR, AM-FM); Syracuse Herald-Post Standard Newspapers.; Miller Brewing Co.; Allied Corp.; General Electric Co.; National Grange.

For Complete List of Firm Personnel, See General Section

For full biographical listings, see the Martindale-Hubbell Law Directory

HANCOCK & ESTABROOK (AV)

Mony Tower 1, P.O. Box 4976, 13221-4976
Telephone: 315-471-3151
Telecopier: 315-471-3167
Albany, New York Office: Suite 505, 125 Wolf Road.
Telephone: 518-458-7660.
Telecopier: 518-458-7731.

MEMBERS OF FIRM

Gerald F. Stack
Jeffrey B. Andrus
Michael L. Corp

ASSOCIATE

Cora A. Alsante

General Counsel for: Marine Midland Bank, (Mid-State Region); Deanco.
Representative Clients: Anheuser-Busch, Inc.; Bristol Laboratories, Division of Bristol-Meyers Squibb; Mutual Benefit Life Insurance Co.; Hartford Insurance Group; Metropolitan Life Insurance Co.; Foremost Insurance Co.

For Complete List of Firm Personnel, See General Section

For full biographical listings, see the Martindale-Hubbell Law Directory

MENTER, RUDIN & TRIVELPIECE, P.C. (AV)

Suite 500, 500 South Salina Street, 13202-3300
Telephone: 315-474-7541
FAX: 315-474-4040
Watertown, New York Office: Suite 316, Woolworth Building, 13601.
Telephone: 315-786-7950.
Fax: 315-786-7852.

A. Solomon Menter (1910-1978)
Stanley R. Rudin
Paul A. Trivelpiece
Gerald J. Mathews
Edward M. Zachary
Peter L. Hubbard
J. Scott Finlay
Antonio E. Caruso
Dale B. Johnson
Jeffrey A. Dove
Mitchell J. Katz
F. Paul Vellano, Jr.
Kevin M. Newman
Addison F. Vars, III

John V. Sheedy
Marcy Robinson Dembs
Douglas J. Mahr
Joseph N. Bulko
Susan K. Tracy
Chaim Judah Jaffe

Representative Clients: Westinghouse Electric Co.; The Chase Manhattan Bank, N.A.; General Motors Acceptance Corp.; Galson Corp.; Edward John Noble Hospital; U.S. Fidelity & Guaranty Co.; Fleet Bank of New York; Sheraton University Hotel; Greater Syracuse Association of Realtors, Inc.; Hydro Development Group, Inc.

(See Next Column)

For full biographical listings, see the Martindale-Hubbell Law Directory

*WHITE PLAINS,** Westchester Co.

DANZIGER & MARKHOFF (AV)

A Partnership including a Professional Corporation
Centroplex-123 Main Street, 10601
Telephone: 914-948-1556
Telecopier: 914-948-1706

Joel Danziger
Harris Markhoff
Ira Langer (P.C.)
Scott M. Sherman
Joshua S. Levine

Anita L. Pomerance
Robert B. Danziger
Michael Markhoff
Susan I. Porter
Susan B. Slater-Jansen
Katherine R. Steiner

LEGAL SUPPORT PERSONNEL

ENROLLED ACTUARIES

William Martin Miller
Aileen T. Palazzo

COUNSEL

Irwin N. Rubin

References: Chase Manhattan Bank, White Plains, N.Y. (Trust Dept.); Bank of New York County Trust Region; Lazard Freres & Co.

For full biographical listings, see the Martindale-Hubbell Law Directory

GREENSPAN & GREENSPAN (AV)

34 South Broadway, 6th Floor, 10601
Telephone: 914-946-2500
Cable Address: "Gadlex"
Telecopier: 914-946-1432

MEMBERS OF FIRM

Leon J. Greenspan
Michael E. Greenspan

For full biographical listings, see the Martindale-Hubbell Law Directory

KURZMAN & EISENBERG (AV)

One North Broadway, 10601
Telephone: 914-285-9800
Fax: 914-285-9855
New York, N.Y. Office: 99 Park Avenue.
Telephone: 212-671-1322.
Hollywood, Florida Office: 2021 Tyler Street.
Telephone: 305-921-5500.

MEMBERS OF FIRM

Robert G. Kurzman
Sam Eisenberg
Lee Harrison Corbin
Robert L. Ecker
Joel S. Lever
Jack S. Older
Alan John Rein
Fred D. Weinstein

OF COUNSEL

Richard A. Danzig
R. Mark Goodman
Stephen R. Levy

For full biographical listings, see the Martindale-Hubbell Law Directory

PRERAU & TEITELL (AV)

50 Main Street, 10606
Telephone: 914-682-9300
Cable Address: "Humanitas"
Telecopier: 914-682-1521

MEMBERS OF FIRM

Sydney Prerau (1900-1968)
Conrad Teitell
Philip T. Temple

ASSOCIATES

Gail D. Resnikoff
Andrea H. Semenuk

For full biographical listings, see the Martindale-Hubbell Law Directory

SMITH, RANSCHT, CONNORS, MUTINO, NORDELL & SIRIGNANO, P.C. (AV)

235 Main Street, 10601
Telephone: 914-946-8800
Telecopier: 914-946-8861
Cable Address: "Smiran" White Plains, New York
Greenwich, Connecticut Office: P.O. Box 4847, 06830-0605.
Telephone: 203-622-6660.

Peter T. Manos (1923-1991)
James P. Connors, Jr.
William F. Ranscht, Jr.
Peter J. Mutino
Michael Nordell
George A. Sirignano, Jr.

OF COUNSEL

Gary E. Bashian
James M. Pollock
Anthony J. Enea

Counsel for: The Corham Artificial Flower Co.; Universal Builders Supply, Inc.; Kalman Floor Co., Inc.; The Walter Karl Companies.

(See Next Column)

SMITH, RANSCHT, CONNORS, MUTINO, NORDELL & SIRIGNANO P.C.—*Continued*

For full biographical listings, see the Martindale-Hubbell Law Directory

NORTH CAROLINA

*CHARLOTTE,** Mecklenburg Co.

BLANCHFIELD AND MOORE, A PROFESSIONAL CORPORATION (AV)

NationsBank Corporate Center, 100 North Tryon Street Suite 2400, 28202
Telephone: 704-377-3788
Telecopier: 704-377-2033

Francis J. Blanchfield, Jr.
William H. Moore, Jr.
Myron L. Moore, III
Hayden D. Brown
Robert T. Duffy
Robert L. Mendenhall

For full biographical listings, see the Martindale-Hubbell Law Directory

CULP ELLIOTT & CARPENTER, P.L.L.C. (AV)

A Partnership including a Professional Association
227 West Trade Street Suite 1500, 28202-1675
Telephone: 704-372-6322
Telefax: 704-372-1474

William R. Culp, Jr., (P.A.)
W. Curtis Elliott, Jr.
John Joseph Carpenter
Margaret R. K. Leinbach
Jonathan E. Gopman
Christopher Hannum
Stefan R. Latorre

For full biographical listings, see the Martindale-Hubbell Law Directory

MOORE & VAN ALLEN, PLLC (AV)

NationsBank Corporate Center, 100 North Tryon Street, Floor 47, 28202-4003
Telephone: 704-331-1000
FAX: 704-331-1159
Durham, North Carolina Office: Suite 800, 2200 West Main Street.
Telephone: 919-286-8000.
Fax: 919-286-8199.
Raleigh, North Carolina Office: One Hannover Square, Suite 1700, P.O. Box 26507.
Telephone: 919-828-4481.
FAX: 919-828-4254.

H. Heath Alexander
R. Michael Childs
Kenneth S. Coe
C. Wells Hall, III
H. Frasier Ives
Neill G. McBryde
John V. McIntosh

DURHAM, NORTH CAROLINA OFFICE

Brian R. Brown
Eugene F. Dauchert, Jr.

RALEIGH, NORTH CAROLINA OFFICE

Joseph D. Joyner, Jr.

For Complete List of Firm Personnel, See General Section

For full biographical listings, see the Martindale-Hubbell Law Directory

SMITH HELMS MULLISS & MOORE, L.L.P. (AV)

227 North Tryon Street, P.O. Box 31247, 28231
Telephone: 704-343-2000
Telecopier: 704-334-8467
Telex: 572460
Greensboro, North Carolina Office: Smith Helms Mulliss & Moore, Suite 1400 First Union Tower, 300 North Greene Street, P.O. Box 21927.
Telephone: 910-378-5200.
Telecopier: 910-379-9558.
Raleigh, North Carolina Office: 316 West Edenton Street, P.O. Box 27525.
Telephone: 919-755-8700.
Telecopier: 919-828-7938.

MEMBERS OF FIRM

Boyd C. Campbell, Jr.
E. Graham McGoogan, Jr.
B. Palmer McArthur, Jr.
Stephen L. Cordell

For Complete List of Firm Personnel, See General Section

For full biographical listings, see the Martindale-Hubbell Law Directory

WOMBLE CARLYLE SANDRIDGE & RICE (AV)

A Professional Limited Liability Company
3300 One First Union Center, 301 S. College Street, 28202-6025
Telephone: 704-331-4900
Telecopy: 704-331-4955
Telex: 853609
Winston-Salem, North Carolina Office: 1600 Southern National Financial Center.
Telephone: 919-721-3600.
Telecopy: 919-721-3660.
Telex: 806498.
Raleigh, North Carolina Office: 2100 First Union Capitol Center, 150 Fayetteville Street Mall, P.O. Box 831.
Telephone: 919-755-2100.
Telecopy: 919-755-2150.
Telex: 806498.
Atlanta, Georgia Office: One Ninety One Peachtree Tower, 191 Peachtree Street N.E., Suite 3250.
Telephone: 404-614-2580.
Fax: 404-614-2595.

MEMBER OF FIRM

James E. Johnson, Jr.

Representative Clients: Childress Klein Properties, Inc.; Food Lion, Inc.; Fieldcrest Cannon, Inc.; J.A. Jones Construction Company; Parkdale Mills, Inc.; Duke Power Company; Bowles Hollowell Conner & Company; ALLTEL Carolina, Inc.; Belk Store Services, Inc.; Philip Holzmann A.G.

For Complete List of Firm Personnel, See General Section

For full biographical listings, see the Martindale-Hubbell Law Directory

*DURHAM,** Durham Co.

WILLIAM V. MCPHERSON, JR. (AV)

Suite 806 University Tower 3100 Tower Boulevard, 27707
Telephone: 919-493-0584
Facsimile: 919-493-0856

For full biographical listings, see the Martindale-Hubbell Law Directory

*GREENSBORO,** Guilford Co.

ADAMS KLEEMEIER HAGAN HANNAH & FOUTS (AV)

North Carolina Trust Center, 301 N. Elm Street, P.O. Box 3463, 27402
Telephone: 910-373-1600
Fax: 910-273-5357

MEMBERS OF FIRM

John A. Kleemeier, Jr. (1911-1973)
William J. Adams, Jr. (1908-1993)
Walter L. Hannah
Daniel W. Fouts
Robert G. Baynes
Joseph W. Moss
Clinton Eudy, Jr.
M. Jay DeVaney
Michael H. Godwin
W. Winburne King III
F. Cooper Brantley
Bruce H. Connors
Charles T. Hagan III
Larry I. Moore III
Elizabeth Dunn White
W. B. Rodman Davis
Thomas W. Brawner
Margaret Shea Burnham
Peter G. Pappas
William M. Wilcox IV
Katherine Bonan McDiarmid
David A. Senter
J. Alexander S. Barrett
Christine L. Myatt

OF COUNSEL

Charles T. Hagan, Jr.
Horace R. Kornegay

ASSOCIATES

Trudy A. Ennis
A. Scott Jackson
Amiel J. Rossabi
James W. Bryan
Betty Pincus Balcomb
Edward L. Bleynat, Jr.
Stephen A. Mayo
Louise Anderson Maultsby
R. Harper Heckman
Dena Beth Langley
David S. Pokela

Representative Clients: NationsBank of North Carolina, N.A.; Hafele America Co.; Duke Power Co.; U.S. Fidelity & Guaranty Co.; Dillard Paper Co.; Carolina Steel Corp.; Electrical South Inc.

For full biographical listings, see the Martindale-Hubbell Law Directory

FORMAN, MARTH, BLACK & ANGLE, P.A. (AV)

235 North Greene Street, P.O. Drawer 2020, 27402-2020
Telephone: 910-378-0172; 272-5591
FAX: 910-378-0015

Richard C. Forman
Paul E. Marth
T. Keith Black
Robert B. Angle, Jr.
Jeffrey S. Iddings

Reference: Wachovia Bank & Trust Co., N.A.; Triad Bank.

For full biographical listings, see the Martindale-Hubbell Law Directory

SCHELL BRAY AYCOCK ABEL & LIVINGSTON L.L.P. (AV)

1500 Renaissance Plaza, 230 North Elm Street, P.O. Box 21847, 27420
Telephone: 910-370-8800
Fax: 910-370-8830

(See Next Column)

SCHELL BRAY AYCOCK ABEL & LIVINGSTON L.L.P., *Greensboro—Continued*

MEMBERS OF FIRM

Braxton Schell
Doris R. Bray
William P. Aycock, II
Michael R. Abel
Paul H. Livingston, Jr.
Kenneth N. Shelton

ASSOCIATES

Barbara R. Christy
Mark Thomas Cain
Dan T. Barker, Jr.
Russell M. Robinson, III
Marshall Todd Jackson

Representative Clients: The Breakers Palm Beach, Inc.; CBP Resources, Inc.; (Carolina By-Products); Cone Mills Corp.; Cornwallis Development Co.; Kenan Transport Co.; Klaussner Furniture Industries, Inc.; North Carolina Trust Co.; Texfi Industries, Inc.; University of North Carolina at Chapel Hill Foundation, Inc.; Vanguard Cellular Systems, Inc.

For Complete List of Firm Personnel, See General Section

For full biographical listings, see the Martindale-Hubbell Law Directory

SMITH HELMS MULLISS & MOORE, L.L.P. (AV)

Suite 1400 First Union Tower, 300 North Greene Street, P.O. Box 21927, 27420
Telephone: 910-378-5200
Telecopier: 910-379-9558
Charlotte, North Carolina Office: Smith Helms Mulliss & Moore, L.L.P., 227 North Tryon Street, P.O. Box 31247.
Telephone: 704-343-2000.
Telecopier: 704-334-8467.
Telex: 572460.
Raleigh, North Carolina Office: Smith Helms Mulliss & Moore, L.L.P., 316 West Edenton Street, P.O. Box 27525.
Telephone: 919-755-8700.
Telecopier: 919-828-7938.

MEMBERS OF FIRM

Carole Watkins Bruce
Mack D. Pridgen, III

For Complete List of Firm Personnel, See General Section
For full biographical listings, see the Martindale-Hubbell Law Directory

TUGGLE DUGGINS & MESCHAN, P.A. (AV)

228 West Market Street, P.O. Box 2888, 27402
Telephone: 910-378-1431
Telecopier: (910) 274-1148

Richard J. Tuggle
James N. Duggins, Jr.
Richard J. Tuggle, Jr.
Henry B. Mangum, Jr.
Barbara C. Ruby
H. Vaughn Ramsey
Bradley L. Jacobs
Michael J. Wenig

Representative Clients: Adaron Group, Inc.; Byrd Food Stores, Inc.; Carolina Hosiery Mills, Inc.; First Union National Bank; Kingsdown, Incorporated; Highland Industries, Inc.; Newman Machine Co., Inc.; Triton Management Co.
Reference: First Union National Bank.

For Complete List of Firm Personnel, See General Section

For full biographical listings, see the Martindale-Hubbell Law Directory

*RALEIGH,** Wake Co.

* indicates certain Bar Register subscribers whose principal office is located elsewhere in the state and who have arranged for representation as a part of the state capital listings that follow

* **SMITH HELMS MULLISS & MOORE, L.L.P.** (AV)

316 West Edenton Street, P.O. Box 27525, 27611-7525
Telephone: 919-755-8700
Telecopier: 919-828-7938
Charlotte, North Carolina Office: 227 North Tryon Street, P.O. Box 31247.
Telephone: 704-343-2000.
Telecopier: 704-334-8467.
Telex: 572460.
Greensboro, North Carolina Office: Smith Helms Mulliss & Moore, Suite 1400 First Union Tower, 300 North Greene Street, P.O. Box 21927.
Telephone: 910-378-5200.
Telecopier: 910-379-9558.

MEMBER OF FIRM

Brad S. Markoff

For Complete List of Firm Personnel, See General Section

For full biographical listings, see the Martindale-Hubbell Law Directory

* **WOMBLE CARLYLE SANDRIDGE & RICE** (AV)

A Professional Limited Liability Company
2100 First Union Capitol Center, 150 Fayetteville Street Mall, P.O. Box 831, 27602
Telephone: 919-755-2100
Telecopy: 919-755-2150
Telex: 806498
Charlotte, North Carolina Office: 3300 One First Union Center, 301 South College Street.
Telephone: 704-331-4900.
Telecopy: 704-331-4955.
Telex: 853609.
Winston-Salem, North Carolina Office: 1600 Southern National Financial Center.
Telephone: 919-721-3600.
Telecopy: 919-721-3660.
Telex: 806498.
Atlanta, Georgia Office: One Ninety One Peachtree Tower, 191 Peachtree Street N.E., Suite 3250.
Telephone: 404-614-2580.
Fax: 404-614-2595.

RESIDENT OF COUNSEL

Jasper L. Cummings, Jr.

Representative Clients: Aetna Casualty and Surety Co., Inc.; AL-SCO/AmeriMark Building Products, Inc.; Aoki Corporation America, Inc.; Empire of Carolina, Inc.; Hackney Brothers, Inc.; Lawyers Mutual Liability Insurance Company of North Carolina; Meredith College; Monk-Austin, Inc.; Regency Park Corporation; Wachovia Bank of North Carolina, N.A.

For Complete List of Firm Personnel, See General Section

For full biographical listings, see the Martindale-Hubbell Law Directory

*WINSTON-SALEM,** Forsyth Co.

MALCOLM E. OSBORN, P.A. (AV)

3639 Kirklees Road, P.O. Box 5192, 27113-5192
Telephone: 910-659-0613
Fax: 910-659-0615

Malcolm E. Osborn

Representative Clients: Blue Ridge Mutual Association, Inc. (Va.); Commercial Life Insurance Company (N.J.); Forethought Life Insurance Company (Ind.); United Family Life Insurance Company (Ga.); United Teacher Associates Insurance Company (Tex.); Heritage Life Insurance Company (N.C.); Preneed Network, Inc. (Fla.).

For full biographical listings, see the Martindale-Hubbell Law Directory

WOMBLE CARLYLE SANDRIDGE & RICE (AV)

A Professional Limited Liability Company
1600 Southern National Financial Center, P.O. Drawer 84, 27102
Telephone: 910-721-3600
Telecopy: 910-721-3660
Telex: 806498
Charlotte, North Carolina Office: 3300 One First Union Center, 301 South College Street.
Telephone: 704-331-4900.
Telecopy: 704-331-4955.
Telex: 853609.
Raleigh, North Carolina Office: 2100 First Union Capitol Center, 150 Fayetteville Street Mall, P.O. Box 831.
Telephone: 919-755-2100.
Telecopy: 919-755-2150.
Telex: 806498.
Atlanta, Georgia Office: One Ninety One Peachtree Tower, 191 Peachtree Street, N.E., Suite 3250.
Telephone: 404-614-2580.
Fax: 404-614-2595.

MEMBERS OF FIRM

Greg L. Smith
W. Preston White, Jr.
Karen M. Wilson

ASSOCIATES

Charles Mark Wiley
Ranlet Shelden Willingham

Representative Clients: Brad Ragan, Inc.; Brenner Companies; Food Lion, Inc.; Hanes Companies, Inc.; North Carolina Baptist Hospitals, Inc.; R.J. Reynolds Tobacco Company; Summit Communications Group, Inc.; Thomasville Furniture Industries, Inc.; Wachovia Corporation; Wake Forest University.

For Complete List of Firm Personnel, See General Section

For full biographical listings, see the Martindale-Hubbell Law Directory

NORTH DAKOTA

*BISMARCK,** Burleigh Co.

FLECK, MATHER & STRUTZ, LTD. (AV)

Sixth Floor, Norwest Bank Building, 400 East Broadway, P.O. Box 2798, 58502
Telephone: 701-223-6585
Telecopier: 701-222-4853

Ernest R. Fleck | John W. Morrison, Jr.

Representative Clients: Amerada Hess Corporation; BHP Petroleum (America's), Inc.; Bechtel Group, Inc.; Chevron USA Inc.; Conoco, Inc.; Koch Industries, Inc.; Occidental Petroleum Services, Inc.; Spiegel, Inc.; True Industries; Western Gas Processors, Ltd.

For Complete List of Firm Personnel, See General Section

For full biographical listings, see the Martindale-Hubbell Law Directory

PEARCE AND DURICK (AV)

314 East Thayer Avenue, P.O. Box 400, 58502
Telephone: 701-223-2890
Fax: 701-223-7865

MEMBER OF FIRM

William P. Pearce

Representative Clients: MDU Resources Group, Inc.; Northwest Airlines; Texaco, Inc.; Shell Oil Co.; Amerada Hess Corp.; IBM; Dupont Inc.; AMOCO; Phillips Petroleum Co.; Conoco, Inc.

For Complete List of Firm Personnel, See General Section

For full biographical listings, see the Martindale-Hubbell Law Directory

TSCHIDER & SMITH (AV)

A Partnership including Professional Corporations
Professional Building - Suite 200, 418 East Rosser Avenue, 58501
Telephone: 701-258-4000
Fax: 701-258-4001

MEMBERS OF FIRM

Morris A. Tschider (P.C.) | Sean O. Smith (P.C.)
David A. Tschider

Representative Clients: Agri Bank, FCB; Farm Credit Services of Mandan, FLCA; Farm Credit Services of Mandan, P.C.A.; Twin City Implement, Inc.; First Bank Bismarck; N.D. Independent Insurance Agents; Western Steel & Plumbing; Froelich Oil Co.; Bismarck Eagles.

For full biographical listings, see the Martindale-Hubbell Law Directory

*FARGO,** Cass Co.

NILLES, HANSEN & DAVIES, LTD. (AV)

1800 Radisson Tower, P.O. Box 2626, 58108
Telephone: 701-237-5544

Russell F. Freeman | Harry M. Pippin

Representative Client: Burlington Northern.

For Complete List of Firm Personnel, See General Section

For full biographical listings, see the Martindale-Hubbell Law Directory

VOGEL, BRANTNER, KELLY, KNUTSON, WEIR & BYE, LTD. (AV)

502 First Avenue North, P.O. Box 1389, 58107
Telephone: 701-237-6983
Facsimile: 701-237-0847

C. Nicholas Vogel | Frank G. Gokey
Maurice G. McCormick | Mart R. Vogel (Retired)

Representative Clients: Associated General Contractors of North Dakota; Clark Equipment Co.; Dakota Hospital; Forum Communications Company; MeritCare Medical Group; Northern Improvement Co.; Dakota Clinic; Gateway Chevrolet, Inc.; West Acres Development Company; Fargo Glass & Paint Company.

For Complete List of Firm Personnel, See General Section

For full biographical listings, see the Martindale-Hubbell Law Directory

OHIO

*AKRON,** Summit Co.

DANIEL G. LAPORTE AND ASSOCIATES (AV)

3250 West Market Street Suite 306, 44333-3321
Telephone: 216-836-5544
Fax: 216-836-2064

(See Next Column)

ASSOCIATE

Christopher M. Van Devere

For full biographical listings, see the Martindale-Hubbell Law Directory

*CINCINNATI,** Hamilton Co.

DINSMORE & SHOHL (AV)

1900 Chemed Center, 255 East Fifth Street, 45202-3172
Telephone: 513-977-8200
FAX: 513-977-8141
Florence, Kentucky Office: Turfway Ridge Office Park, 7300 Turfway Road, Suite 430 41042-1355.
Telephone: 606-283-0515.
FAX: 606-283-6017.
Dayton, Ohio Office: 500 Courthouse Plaza, S.W., 10 N. Ludlow Street, 45402-1834.
Telephone: 513-228-8012.
FAX: 513-461-2543.
Columbus, Ohio Office: NBD Bank Building, Suite 330, 175 South Third Street, 43215-5134.
Telephone: 614-224-7887.
FAX: 614-224-7882.

MEMBERS OF FIRM

Jerome H. Kearns | J. Michael Cooney
William M. Freedman | Edward J. Buechel (Resident, Florence, Kentucky Office)
James H. Stethem
C. Christopher Muth

For Complete List of Firm Personnel, See General Section

For full biographical listings, see the Martindale-Hubbell Law Directory

FROST & JACOBS (AV)

2500 PNC Center, 201 East Fifth Street, P.O. Box 5715, 45201-5715
Telephone: 513-651-6800
Cable Address: "Frostjac"
Telex: 21-4396 F & J CIN
Telecopier: 513-651-6981
Columbus, Ohio Office: One Columbus, 10 West Broad Street.
Telephone: 614-464-1211.
Telecopier: 614-464-1737.
Lexington, Kentucky Office: 1100 Vine Center Tower, 333 West Vine Street.
Telephone: 606-254-1100.
Telecopier: 606-253-2990.
Middletown, Ohio Office: 400 First National Bank Building, 2 North Main Street.
Telephone: 513-422-2001.
Telecopier: 513-422-3010.
Naples, Florida Office: 4001 Tamiami Trail North, Suite 220.
Telephone: 813-261-0582.
Telecopier: 813-261-2083.

MEMBERS OF FIRM

James S. Wachs | Larry H. McMillin
Ronald E. Heinlen | Martin E. Mooney
T. Stephen Phillips | Thomas D. Anthony
Thomas P. Mehnert | Patricia D. Laub
John H. Appel | William C. Strangfeld

SENIOR ATTORNEYS

Barbara F. Applegarth | Douglas D. Thomson

ASSOCIATES

Scott A. Meyer | Christa F. Nordlund
Daniel W. Scharff | Laura A. Ryan
Bernard L. McKay

SENIOR PARTNER

Jerry L. Cowan

OF COUNSEL

Alan R. Vogeler | Joseph J. Connaughton
Verena Smith

Representative Clients: Armco Inc.; Arthur Andersen & Co.; Champion International; Cincinnati Bell Inc.; Cincinnati Milacron Inc.; Federated Department Stores Inc.; Mercy Health Systems; PNC Bank, Ohio, National Association; Sencorp; U.S. Shoe Corp.

For Complete List of Firm Personnel, See General Section

For full biographical listings, see the Martindale-Hubbell Law Directory

KEATING, MUETHING & KLEKAMP (AV)

1800 Provident Tower, One East Fourth Street, 45202
Telephone: 513-579-6400
Facsimile: 513-579-6457

MEMBERS OF FIRM

Joseph P. Rouse | Timothy B. Matthews
J. Neal Gardner | William J. Keating, Jr.
Joseph P. Mellen

(See Next Column)

KEATING, MUETHING & KLEKAMP, *Cincinnati—Continued*

ASSOCIATES

Lisa Wintersheimer Michel | Laura S. Petrie

Representative Clients: American Financial Corporation; BP America Inc.; Chiquita Brands International, Inc.; The Cincinnati Enquirer; Cintas Corporation; Comair Holdings, Inc.; Duke Associates; LSI Industries Inc.; Mosler Inc.; Provident Bankcorp, Inc.

For Complete List of Firm Personnel, See General Section

For full biographical listings, see the Martindale-Hubbell Law Directory

KLAINE, WILEY, HOFFMANN & MEURER A LEGAL PROFESSIONAL ASSOCIATION (AV)

Suite 1850, 105 East Fourth Street, 45202-4080
Telephone: 513-241-0202
Fax: 513-241-9322

Donald L. Wiley | James P. Minutolo

For Complete List of Firm Personnel, See General Section

For full biographical listings, see the Martindale-Hubbell Law Directory

SANTEN & HUGHES A LEGAL PROFESSIONAL ASSOCIATION (AV)

Suite 3100, 312 Walnut Street, 45202
Telephone: 513-721-4450
FAX: 513-721-7644; 721-0109

Harry H. Santen | James P. Wersching

LEGAL SUPPORT PERSONNEL

Karen W. Crane (Corporate Paralegal)
Deborah M. McKinney (Trust/Estate Paralegal)
Karen L. Jansen (Litigation Paralegal)
Bobbie S. Ebbers (Paralegal)

For Complete List of Firm Personnel, See General Section

For full biographical listings, see the Martindale-Hubbell Law Directory

SCHWARTZ, MANES & RUBY A LEGAL PROFESSIONAL ASSOCIATION (AV)

2900 Carew Tower, 441 Vine Street, 45202
Telephone: 513-579-1414
Telecopier: 513-579-1418

Richard M. Schwartz
Dennis L. Manes
Stanley L. Ruby
Scott M. Slovin
Howard L. Richshafer
Michael G. Schwartz

For Complete List of Firm Personnel, See General Section

For full biographical listings, see the Martindale-Hubbell Law Directory

STRAUSS & TROY A LEGAL PROFESSIONAL ASSOCIATION (AV)

2100 PNC Center, 201 East Fifth Street, 45202-4186
Telephone: 513-621-2120
Telecopier: 513-241-8259
Northern Kentucky Office: Suite 1400, 50 East Rivercenter Boulevard, Covington, Kentucky, 41011.
Telephone: 513-621-8900; 513-621-2120.
Telecopier: 513-629-9444.

Mark H. Berliant
Larry A. Neuman
Thomas C. Rink
David A. Groenke
Claudia G. Allen

Marilyn J. Maag
Cynthia A. Fazio
Marshall K. Dosker (Resident, Covington, Kentucky Office)

Representative Clients: PNC Bank, N.A. (Ohio and Kentucky); Corporex Companies, Inc.; Mercantile Stores Company, Inc.; Star Bank, N.A. (Ohio and Kentucky).

For Complete List of Firm Personnel, See General Section

For full biographical listings, see the Martindale-Hubbell Law Directory

THOMPSON, HINE AND FLORY (AV)

312 Walnut Street, 14th Floor, 45202-4029
Telephone: 513-352-6700
Fax: 513-241-4771;
Telex: 938003
Akron, Ohio Office: 50 S. Main Street, Suite 502, 44308-1828.
Telephone: 216-376-8090.
Fax: 216-376-8386.
Cleveland, Ohio Office: 1100 National City Bank Building, 629 Euclid Avenue, 44114-3070.
Telephone: 216-566-5500.
Fax: 216-556-5583.
Telex: 980217.
Cable Address: "Thomflor".

(See Next Column)

Columbus, Ohio Office: One Columbus, 10 West Broad Street, 43215-3435.
Telephone: 614-469-3200.
Fax: 614-469-3361.
Dayton, Ohio Office: 2000 Courthouse Plaza, N.E., 45402-1706.
Telephone: 513-443-6600.
Fax: 513-443-6637; 443-6635.
Palm Beach, Florida Office: 125 Worth Avenue, 33480-4466.
Telephone: 407-833-5900.
Fax: 407-833-5951.
Washington, D.C. Office: 1920 N Street, N.W., 20036-1601.
Telephone: 202-331-8800.
Fax: 202-331-8330.
Telex: 904173.
Cable Address: "Caglaw".
Brussels, Belgium Office: Rue des Chevaliers / Ridderstraat 14 - B.10, B - 1050.
Telephone: 011(32-2) 511-9326.
Fax: 011(-32-2) 513-9206.

MEMBERS OF FIRM

Barbara Schwartz Bromberg
Melvin E. Marmer
Michael H. Neumark

For Complete List of Firm Personnel, See General Section

For full biographical listings, see the Martindale-Hubbell Law Directory

*CLEVELAND,** Cuyahoga Co.

ARTER & HADDEN (AV)

1100 Huntington Building, 925 Euclid Avenue, 44115-1475
Telephone: 216-696-1100
Telex: 98-5384
In Columbus, Ohio: 21st Floor, One Columbus, 10 West Broad Street. 43215-3422.
Telephone: 614-221-3155.
In Washington, D.C.: 1801 K Street, N.W., Suite 400K. 20006-3480.
Telephone: 202-775-7100.
In Dallas, Texas: 1717 Main Street, Suite 4100. 75201-4605.
Telephone: 214-761-2100.
In Los Angeles, California: 700 South Flower Street. 90017-4101.
Telephone: 213-629-9300.
In Irvine, California: Two Park Plaza, Suite 700, Jamboree Center.
Telephone: 714-252-7500.
In Austin, Texas: 100 Congress Avenue, Suite 1800.
Telephone: 512-479-6403.
In San Antonio, Texas: Suite 540, Harte-Hanks Tower, 7710 Jones Maltsberger Road.
Telephone: 210-805-8497.

MEMBERS OF FIRM

Carlton B. Schnell
Robert E. Glaser
Jerome D. Neifach
Edward F. Meyers, Jr.
Michael P. Mahoney
Brian W. FitzSimons
Robert B. Tomaro
Michael F. Harris
Dominic V. Perry
Glen A. Bellinger
Kathy P. Lazar
Bernard J. Smith

RETIRED PARTNERS

Howard M. Kohn
Charles W. Landefeld
Leslie L. Knowlton

OF COUNSEL

John P. Reinartz

ASSOCIATES

Ann H. Womer Benjamin
Susan L. Racey
James K. Warren

For Complete List of Firm Personnel, See General Section

For full biographical listings, see the Martindale-Hubbell Law Directory

BAKER & HOSTETLER (AV)

3200 National City Center, 1900 East Ninth Street, 44114-3485
Telephone: 216-621-0200
Telecopier: 216-696-0740
TWX: 810 421 8375
RCA Telex: 215032
In Columbus, Ohio: Capitol Square, Suite 2100, 65 East State Street.
Telephone: 614-228-1541.
In Denver, Colorado: 303 East 17th Avenue, Suite 1100.
Telephone: 303-861-0600.
In Houston, Texas: 1000 Louisiana, Suite 2000.
Telephone: 713-751-1600.
In Long Beach, California: 300 Oceangate, Suite 620.
Telephone: 310-432-2827.
In Los Angeles, California: 600 Wilshire Boulevard.
Telephone: 213-624-2400.
In Orlando, Florida: SunBank Center, Suite 2300, 200 South Orange Avenue.
Telephone: 407-649-4000.
In Washington, D. C.: Washington Square, Suite 1100, 1050 Connecticut Avenue, N.W.
Telephone: 202-861-1500.
In College Park, Maryland: 9658 Baltimore Boulevard, Suite 206.
Telephone: 301-441-2781.

(See Next Column)

BAKER & HOSTETLER—*Continued*

In Alexandria, Virginia: 437 North Lee Street.
Telephone: 703-549-1294.
In San Francisco, California: One Sansome Street, Suite 2000.
Telephone: 415-951-4705.

PARTNERS

Paul H. Feinberg — David J. Strauss
Edward G. Ptaszek, Jr. — Christopher J. Swift
Hewitt B. Shaw, Jr. — William M. Toomajian
Kenneth F. Snyder — Richard R. Turney

ASSOCIATES

Robert R. Galloway — Alexander J. Szilvas

RETIRED PARTNERS

Sherman Dye — David R. Fullmer

For Complete List of Firm Personnel, See General Section

For full biographical listings, see the Martindale-Hubbell Law Directory

BENESCH, FRIEDLANDER, COPLAN & ARONOFF (AV)

2300 BP America Building, 200 Public Square, 44114-2378
Telephone: 216-363-4500
Telecopier: 216-363-4588
Columbus, Ohio Office: 88 East Broad Street, 43215-3506.
Telephone: 614-223-9300.
Telecopier: 614-223-9330.
Cincinnati, Ohio Office: 2800 Cincinnati Commerce Center, 600 Vine Street, 45202-2409.
Telephone: 713-762-6200.
Telecopier: 513-762-6245.

MEMBERS OF FIRM

Gary B. Bilchik — Allan D. Kleinman
Alan Doris — Kurt J. Smidansky
Gregory L. Hilbrich — Jeffry L. Weiler

ASSOCIATES

Sheila M. Ninneman — Nick D. Shofar
Richard F. Tracanna

COUNSEL

Marvin I. Kelner — Jeffrey A. Perlmuter

COLUMBUS, OHIO
RESIDENT MEMBER
James B. Feibel

COLUMBUS, OHIO
RESIDENT ASSOCIATE
Thomas S. Counts

CINCINNATI, OHIO
RESIDENT MEMBER
Stuart R. Susskind

For Complete List of Firm Personnel, See General Section

For full biographical listings, see the Martindale-Hubbell Law Directory

BERICK, PEARLMAN & MILLS A LEGAL PROFESSIONAL ASSOCIATION (AV)

1350 Eaton Center, 1111 Superior Avenue, 44114-2569
Telephone: 216-861-4900
Automatic Telecopier: 216-861-4929

James H. Berick — William M. Mills
Samuel S. Pearlman — Paul J. Singerman
Osborne Mills, Jr. — Gary S. Desberg
Daniel G. Berick

COUNSEL

Joseph G. Berick — Joan M. Gross

Arthur J. Tassi — Laura D. Nemeth
Edmund G. Kauntz — Robert G. Marischen

Representative Clients: Bakers Furniture, Inc.; Cleveland Browns Football Company, Inc.; The Equitable Life Assurance Society of the United States; The Huntington National Bank; NationsCare, Inc.; Pressco Technology Inc.; Realty ReFund Trust; A. Schulman, Inc.; The Town and Country Trust; The Tranzonic Companies.

For full biographical listings, see the Martindale-Hubbell Law Directory

JONES, DAY, REAVIS & POGUE (AV)

North Point, 901 Lakeside Avenue, 44114
Telephone: 216-586-3939
Cable Address: "Attorneys Cleveland"
Telex: 980389
Telecopier: 216-579-0212
In Columbus, Ohio: 1900 Huntington Center.
Telephone: 614-469-3939.
Cable Address: "Attorneys Columbus."
Telecopier: 614-461-4198.

(See Next Column)

In Atlanta, Georgia: 3500 One Peachtree Center, 303 Peachtree Street, N.E.
Telephone: 404-521-3939.
Cable Address: "Attorneys Atlanta".
Telex: 54-2711.
Telecopier: 404-581-8330.
In Brussels, Belgium: Avenue Louise 480, 7th Floor. B-1050 Brussels.
Telephone: 011-32-2-645-14-11.
Telecopier: 011-32-2-645-14-45.
In Chicago, Illinois: 77 West Wacker.
Telephone: 312-782-3939.
Telecopier: 312-782-8585.
In Dallas, Texas: 2300 Trammell Crow Center, 2001 Ross Avenue.
Telephone: 214-220-3939.
Cable Address: "Attorneys Dallas."
Telex: 730852.
Telecopier: 214-969-5100.
In Frankfurt, Germany: Triton Haus, Bockenheimer Landstrasse 42, 60323 Frankfurt am Main.
Telephone: 49-69-9726-3939.
Telecopier: 49-69-9726-3993.
In Geneva, Switzerland: 20, rue de Candolle.
Telephone: 011-41-22-320-2339.
Telecopier: 011-41-22-320-1232.
In Hong Kong: 1501 One Exchange Square, 8 Connaught Place.
Telephone: 011-852-2526-6895.
Telecopier: 011-852-2810-5787.
In Irvine, California: 2603 Main Street, Suite 900.
Telephone: 714-851-3939.
Telex: 194911 Lawyers LSA.
Telecopier: 714-553-7539.
In London, England: One Mount Street.
Telephone: 011-44-71-493-9361.
Cable Address: "Surgoe London WI."
Telecopier: 011-44-71-493-9666.
In Los Angeles, California: 555 West Fifth Street, Suite 4600.
Telephone: 213-489-3939.
Telex: 181439 UD.
Telecopier: 213-243-2539.
In New York, New York: 599 Lexington Avenue.
Telephone: 212-326-3939.
Cable Address: "JONESDAY NEWYORK."
Telex: 237013 JDRP UR.
Telecopier: 212-755-7306.
In Paris, France: 62, rue du Faubourg Saint-Honore.
Telephone: 011-33-1-44-71-3939.
Cable Address: "Surgoe Paris."
Telex: 290156 Surgoe.
Telecopier: 011-33-1-49-24-0471.
In Pittsburgh, Pennsylvania: 500 Grant Street, 31st Floor.
Telephone: 412-391-3939.
Cable Address: "Attorneys Pittsburgh".
Telecopier: 412-394-7959.
In Riyadh, Saudi Arabia: Law Offices of Saud M.A. Shawwaf, P.O. Box 2700.
Telephones: 011 (966-1) 465-6543, 011 (966-1) 464-8534 or 011 (966-1) 464-8540.
Telex: 401831 SAUCON SJ.
Telecopier: (966-1) 464-8480.
In Taipei, Taiwan: 8th Floor, Tun Hwa South Road, Section 2.
Telephone: 011 (886-2) 704-6808.
Telecopier: 011 (886-2) 704-6791.
In Tokyo, Japan: Toranomon MT Building, 4th Floor, 10-3, Toranomon 3-Chome, Minato-Ku, Tokyo 105, Japan.
Telephone: 011-81-3-3433-3939.
Telecopier: 011-81-3-5401-2725.
In Washington, D.C.: Metropolitan Square, 1450 G Street, N.W.
Telephone: 202-879-3939.
Cable Address: "Attorneys Washington."
Telex: 89-2410 ATTORNEYS WASH.
Telecopier: 202-737-2832.

MEMBERS OF FIRM

Robert B. Nelson — Kenneth G. Hochman
William A. Reale — Jeffrey S. Leavitt
John L. Sterling — Joseph L. Liegl
John R. Cornell — Michael J. Horvitz
Kenneth E. Updegraft, Jr. — John D. Currivan
John C. Duffy, Jr. — Daniel C. Hagen
Carl M. Jenks

SENIOR ATTORNEYS

Charles M. Steines — Kathleen Hohler
Mary Turk-Meena — Mary D. Maloney

ASSOCIATES

Rebecca Holloway Dent — Lisa A. Roberts-Mamone
Ellen E. Halfon — Edward Purnell
Bradley S. Smith

For Complete List of Firm Personnel, See General Section

For full biographical listings, see the Martindale-Hubbell Law Directory

Cleveland—Continued

KADISH & BENDER A LEGAL PROFESSIONAL ASSOCIATION (AV)

2112 East Ohio Building, 44114
Telephone: 216-696-3030
Telecopier: 216-696-3492

Stephen L. Kadish
J. Timothy Bender
Kevin M. Hinkel
David G. Weibel

Aaron H. Bulloff
Joseph P. Alexander
David G. Lambert
William A. Duncan
Mary Beth Duffy
James H. Rownd

For full biographical listings, see the Martindale-Hubbell Law Directory

SPIETH, BELL, MCCURDY & NEWELL CO., L.P.A. (AV)

2000 Huntington Building, 925 Euclid Avenue, 44115-1496
Telephone: 216-696-4700
Telecopier: 216-696-6569; 216-696-2706; 216-696-1052

Patrick J. Amer
John M. Slivka

Representative Clients: Cleveland Cavaliers; Nationwide Advertising Services, Inc.; Independent Steel Co.; Baldwin Wallace College; The Tool-Die Engineering Company.
Representative Labor Relations Clients (Management Only): Parker Hannifin Corp.; Reliance Electric Co.; Brush Wellman Co.

For Complete List of Firm Personnel, See General Section

For full biographical listings, see the Martindale-Hubbell Law Directory

THOMPSON, HINE AND FLORY (AV)

1100 National City Bank Building, 629 Euclid Avenue, 44114-3070
Telephone: 216-566-5500
Fax: 216-566-5583
Telex: 980217
Cable Address: "Thomflor"
Akron, Ohio Office: 50 S. Main Street, Suite 502, 44308-1828.
Telephone: 216-376-8090.
Fax: 216-376-8386.
Cincinnati, Ohio Office: 312 Walnut Street, 14th Floor, 45202-4029.
Telephone: 513-352-6700.
Fax: 513-241-4771.
Telex: 938003.
Columbus, Ohio Office: One Columbus, 10 West Broad Street, 43215-3435.
Telephone: 614-469-3200.
Fax: 614-469-3361.
Dayton, Ohio Office: 2000 Courthouse Plaza, N.E., 45402-1706.
Telephone: 513-443-6600.
Fax: 513-443-6637; 443-6635.
Palm Beach, Florida Office: 125 Worth Avenue, Suite 117, 33480-4466.
Telephone: 407-833-5900.
Fax: 407-833-5951.
Washington, D.C. Office: 1920 N Street, N.W., 20036-1601.
Telephone: 202-331-8800.
Fax: 202-331-8330.
Telex: 904173.
Cable Address: "Caglaw".
Brussels, Belgium Office: Rue des Chevaliers, Ridderstraat 14 - B.10, B - 1050.
Telephone: 011(32-2) 511-9326.
Fax: 011(32-2) 513-9206.

MEMBERS OF FIRM

Malvin E. Bank
Stephen L. Buescher
Donald L. Korb (In Washington, D.C. and Cleveland, Ohio)
Kent L. Mann
Deborah Zider Read
William R. Stewart
Roy L. Turnell

ASSOCIATE

Thomas J. Callahan

For Complete List of Firm Personnel, See General Section

For full biographical listings, see the Martindale-Hubbell Law Directory

ULMER & BERNE (AV)

Ninth Floor, Bond Court Building, 1300 East Ninth Street, 44114-1583
Telephone: 216-621-8400
Telex: 201999 UBLAW
Telecopier: 216-621-7488
Columbus, Ohio Office: 88 East Broad Street, Suite 1980.
Telephone: 614-228-8400.
Telecopier: 614-228-8561.

MEMBERS OF FIRM

Herbert B. Levine
William A. Edwards
Ronald L. Kahn (Chairman, Employee Benefits Group)
John C. Goheen
James A. Goldsmith
Patricia A. Shlonsky

For Complete List of Firm Personnel, See General Section

For full biographical listings, see the Martindale-Hubbell Law Directory

WESTON HURD FALLON PAISLEY & HOWLEY (AV)

2500 Terminal Tower, 50 Public Square, 44113-2241
Telephone: 216-241-6602;
Ohio Toll Free: 800-336-4952
FAX: 216-621-8369

MEMBERS OF FIRM

Lewis T. Barr
Robert P. McManus

For Complete List of Firm Personnel, See General Section

For full biographical listings, see the Martindale-Hubbell Law Directory

ZIEGLER, METZGER & MILLER (AV)

2020 Huntington Building, 44115-1407
Telephone: 216-781-5470
FAX: 216-781-0714

MEMBERS OF FIRM

Robert L. Metzger
William L. Spring
Richard T. Spotz, Jr.

LEGAL SUPPORT PERSONNEL

P. Thomas Austin (Consultant)
Cynthia Moore (Tax Accountant)

For Complete List of Firm Personnel, See General Section

For full biographical listings, see the Martindale-Hubbell Law Directory

*COLUMBUS,** Franklin Co.

* indicates certain Bar Register subscribers whose principal office is located elsewhere in the state and who have arranged for representation as a part of the state capital listings that follow

*** BAKER & HOSTETLER (AV)**

Capitol Square, Suite 2100, 65 East State Street, 43215-4260
Telephone: 614-228-1541
Telecopier: 614-462-2616
In Cleveland, Ohio: 3200 National City Center, 1900 East Ninth Street.
Telephone: 216-621-0200.
In Denver, Colorado: 303 East 17th Avenue, Suite 1100.
Telephone: 202-861-1500.
In Houston, Texas: 1000 Louisiana, Suite 2000.
Telephone: 713-751-1600.
In Long Beach, California: 300 Oceangate, Suite 620.
Telephone: 310-432-2827.
In Los Angeles, California: 600 Wilshire.
Telephone: 213-624-2400.
In Orlando, Florida: SunBank Center, Suite 2300, 200 South Orange Avenue.
Telephone: 407-649-4000.
In Washington, D. C.: Washington Square, Suite 1100, 1050 Connecticut Avenue, N.W.
Telephone: 202-861-1500.
In College Park, Maryland: 9658 Baltimore Boulevard, Suite 301.
Telephone: 301-441-2781.
In Alexandria, Virginia: 437 North Lee Street.
Telephone: 703-549-1294.
In San Francisco, California: One Sansome Street, Suite 2000.
Telephone: 415-951-4705.

PARTNER

Edward J. Bernert

ASSOCIATE

George H. Boerger

For Complete List of Firm Personnel, See General Section

For full biographical listings, see the Martindale-Hubbell Law Directory

BRICKER & ECKLER (AV)

100 South Third Street, 43215-4291
Telephone: 614-227-2300
Telecopy: 614-227-2390
Cleveland, Ohio Office: 600 Superior Avenue East, Suite 800.
Telephone: 216-771-0720. Fax 216-771-7702.

Charles F. Glander
John P. Beavers (Managing Partner)
Marshall L. Lerner
Michael A. Mess
James A. Rutledge
Gordon F. Litt
Mark A. Engel

Jerry O. Allen

OF COUNSEL

Edgar L. Lindley
Christine T. Mesirow

RETIRED

William H. Leighner

Representative Clients: USX Corporation; PPG Industries, Inc.; Ormet Corporation; Consolidated Aluminum Corporation; IBM Corporation; The BF Goodrich Company; Compuserve, Inc.; Electronic Data Systems Corporation; Aristech Chemical Company; American Chemical Society.

(See Next Column)

BRICKER & ECKLER—*Continued*

For Complete List of Firm Personnel, See General Section

For full biographical listings, see the Martindale-Hubbell Law Directory

EISNAUGLE & GRAHAM CO., L.P.A. (AV)

88 East Broad Street, Suite 1220, 43215
Telephone: 614-221-1970

R. William Eisnaugle

Reference: Bank One of Columbus.

For full biographical listings, see the Martindale-Hubbell Law Directory

EMENS, KEGLER, BROWN, HILL & RITTER (AV)

Capitol Square Suite 1800, 65 East State Street, 43215-4294
Telephone: 614-462-5400
Telecopier: 614-464-2634
Cable Address: "Law EKBHR"
Telex: 246671

John F. Allevato
Larry K. Carnahan
Edward C. Hertenstein
Charles J. Kegler
Paul D. Ritter, Jr.

Holly Robinson Fischer

Representative Clients: Abrasive Technology, Inc.; Access Energy Corp.; Donato's Pizza, Inc.; Drug Emporium, Inc.; The Fishel Co.; Spenley Newspapers, Inc.; Warner Cable Communication, Inc.

For Complete List of Firm Personnel, See General Section

For full biographical listings, see the Martindale-Hubbell Law Directory

PORTER, WRIGHT, MORRIS & ARTHUR (AV)

41 South High Street, 43215-6194
Telephone: 614-227-2000; (800-533-2794)
Telex: 6503213584 MCI
Fax: 614-227-2100
Dayton, Ohio Office: One Dayton Centre, One South Main Street, 45402.
Telephones: 513-228-2411; (800-533-4434).
Fax: 513-449-6820.
Cincinnati, Ohio Office: 250 E. Fifth Street, 45202-4166.
Telephones: 513-381-4700; (800-582-5813).
Fax: 513-421-0991.
Cleveland, Ohio Office: 925 Euclid Avenue, 44115-1483.
Telephones: 216-443-9000; (800-824-1980).
Fax: 216-443-9011.
Washington, D.C. Office: 1233 20th Street, N.W., 20036-2395.
Telephones: 202-778-3000; (800-456-7962).
Fax: 202-778-3063.
Naples, Florida Office: 4501 Tamiami Trail North, 33940-3060.
Telephones: 813-263-8898;(800-876-7962).
Fax: 813-436-2990.

MEMBERS OF FIRM
COLUMBUS, OHIO OFFICE

Jon M. Anderson
Richard A. Cheap
Ronald W. Gabriel
Diane K. Goulder
Paul A. Hanke
Elizabeth B. Mayo
Michael T. Radcliffe
David A. Tumen

ASSOCIATES
COLUMBUS, OHIO OFFICE

Joseph R. Irvine
James McArdle Mattimoe

OF COUNSEL
COLUMBUS, OHIO OFFICE

John A. Dunkel

Representative Clients: ChemLawn Services Corp.; Huntington Bancshares Incorporated; Midland Mutual Life Insurance Co.; Red Roof Inns, Inc.; White Castle System, Inc.; Ohio Chamber of Commerce; Harvard Industries, Inc.; DQE, Inc.; Lydall, Inc.

For Complete List of Firm Personnel, See General Section

For full biographical listings, see the Martindale-Hubbell Law Directory

*** THOMPSON, HINE AND FLORY** (AV)

One Columbus, 10 West Broad Street, 43215-3435
Telephone: 614-469-3200
Fax: 614-469-3361
Akron, Ohio Office: 50 S. Main Street, Suite 502, 44308-1828.
Telephone: 216-376-8090.
Fax: 216-376-8386.
Cincinnati, Ohio Office: 312 Walnut Street, 14th Floor, 45202-4029.
Telephone: 513-352-6700.
Fax: 513-241-4771.
Telex: 938003.

(See Next Column)

Cleveland, Ohio Office: 1100 National City Bank Building, 629 Euclid Avenue, 44114-3070.
Telephone: 216-566-5500.
Fax: 216-556-5583.
Telex: 980217.
Cable Address: "Thomflor".
Dayton, Ohio Office: 2000 Courthouse Plaza, N.E., 45402-1706.
Telephone: 513-443-6600.
Fax: 513-443-6637; 443-6635.
Palm Beach, Florida Office: 125 Worth Avenue, 33480-4466.
Telephone: 407-833-5900.
Fax: 407-833-5951.
Washington, D.C. Office: 1920 N Street, N.W., 20036-1601.
Telephone: 202-331-8800.
Fax: 202-331-8330.
Telex: 904173.
Cable Address: "Caglaw".
Brussels, Belgium Office: Rue des Chevaliers / Ridderstraat 14 - B.10, B - 1050.
Telephone: 011(32-2) 511-9326.
Fax: 011(32-2) 513-9206.

MEMBER OF FIRM

Susan A. Petersen

ASSOCIATE

Michael A. Renne

For Complete List of Firm Personnel, See General Section

For full biographical listings, see the Martindale-Hubbell Law Directory

VORYS, SATER, SEYMOUR AND PEASE (AV)

52 East Gay Street, P.O. Box 1008, 43216-1008
Telephone: 614-464-6400
Telex: 241348
Telecopier: 614-464-6350
Cable Address: "Vorysater"
Washington, D.C. Office: Suite 1111, 1828 L Street, N.W., 20036-5104.
Telephone: 202-467-8800.
Telex: 440693.
Telecopier: 202-467-8900.
Cleveland, Ohio Office: 2100 One Cleveland Center, 1375 East Ninth Street, 44114-1724.
Telephone: 216-479-6100.
Telecopier: 216-479-6060.
Cincinnati, Ohio Office: Suite 2100, 221 East Fourth Street, P.O. Box 0236, 45201-0236.
Telephone: 513-723-4000.
Telecopier: 513-723-4056.

MEMBERS OF FIRM

Colborn M. Addison
Richard R. Stedman
Lawrence L. Fisher
George N. Corey
Ronald L. Rowland
John Timothy Young
Raymond D. Anderson
Aaron P. Rosenfeld
Robert G. Dykes
Anker M. Bell
Anthony C. Ciriaco
Richard Heer Oman
Dan L. Jaffe
David A. Swift

Anthony L. Ehler
Mark E. Vannatta
Carol Mahaffey
Eric A. Pierce
Kevin M. Czerwonka
Terren B. Magid

OF COUNSEL

William W. Ellis, Jr.
Kenneth D. Beck
Ruth R. Longenecker (Resident, Cincinnati, Ohio Office)
Benjamin F. Suffron, III

Local Counsel for: Honda of America Mfg., Inc.; R. G. Barry Corporation; Children's Hospital; Wendy's International, Inc.; The Ohio Savings & Loan League; Abbott Laboratories; Dresser Industries, Inc.; GATX Corp.; The Ohio State University; Lennox Industries, Inc.

For Complete List of Firm Personnel, See General Section

For full biographical listings, see the Martindale-Hubbell Law Directory

*DAYTON,** Montgomery Co.

THOMPSON, HINE AND FLORY (AV)

2000 Courthouse Plaza, N.E., 45402-1706
Telephone: 513-443-6600
Fax: 513-443-6637; 443-6635
Akron, Ohio Office: 50 S. Main Street, Suite 502, 44308-1828.
Telephone: 216-376-8090.
Fax: 216-376-8386.
Cincinnati, Ohio Office: 312 Walnut Street, 14th Floor, 45202-4029.
Telephone: 513-352-6700.
Fax: 513-241-4771.
Telex: 938003.
Cleveland, Ohio Office: 1100 National City Bank Building, 629 Euclid Avenue, 44114-3070.
Telephone: 216-566-5500.
Fax: 216-556-5583.
Telex: 980217.
Cable Address: "Thomflor".

(See Next Column)

THOMPSON, HINE AND FLORY, *Dayton—Continued*

Columbus, Ohio Office: One Columbus, 10 West Broad Street, 43215-3435.
Telephone: 614-469-3200.
Fax: 614-469-3361.
Palm Beach, Florida Office: 125 Worth Avenue, 33480-4466.
Telephone: 407-833-5900.
Fax: 407-833-5951.
Washington, D.C. Office: 1920 N Street, N.W., 20036-1601.
Telephone: 202-331-8800.
Fax: 202-331-8330.
Telex: 904173.
Cable Address: "Caglaw".
Brussels, Belgium Office: Rue des Chevaliers / Ridderstraat 14 - B.10, B - 1050.
Telephone: 011(32-2) 511-9326.
Fax: 011(32-2) 513-9206.

MEMBERS OF FIRM

Thomas E. DeBrosse — Francesco A. Ferrante
Bruce R. Lowry

ASSOCIATE

Michael W. McArdle

For Complete List of Firm Personnel, See General Section

For full biographical listings, see the Martindale-Hubbell Law Directory

YOUNG & ALEXANDER CO., L.P.A. (AV)

Suite 100, 367 West Second Street, 45402
Telephone: 513-224-9291
Telecopier: 513-224-9679
Cincinnati, Ohio Office: 110 Boggs Lane, Suite 350.
Telephone: 513-326-5555.
FAX: 513-326-5550.

James M. Brennan

Counsel for: The Children's Medical Center, Dayton, Ohio; The Colonial Stair & Woodwork Co.; The Greater Dayton Area Hospital Assn.; Mike-Sell's Potato Chip Co.; Moorman Pontiac, Inc.
Local Counsel for: Colonial Penn Insurance Co.; John Hancock Mutual Life Insurance Co.; Hertz Corp.; State Farm Insurance Co.

For Complete List of Firm Personnel, See General Section

For full biographical listings, see the Martindale-Hubbell Law Directory

*TOLEDO,** Lucas Co.

EASTMAN & SMITH (AV)

One Seagate, Twenty-Fourth Floor, 43604
Telephone: 419-241-6000
Telecopier: 419-247-1777
Columbus, Ohio Office: 65 East State Street, Suite 1000, 43215.
Telephone: 614-460-3556.
Telecopier: 614-228-5371.

MEMBERS OF FIRM

Frank D. Jacobs — John H. Boggs
Morton Bobowick — Gary M. Harden
Mark C. Abramson

ASSOCIATE

David C. Krock

OF COUNSEL

Gerald P. Moran

Representative Clients: Glass Tech, Inc.; The City of Wauseon; Swanton Local School District; Capital Bank, N.A.; Medicare Equipment Supply Co.; Riverside Hospital; Memorial Hospital; McGruder Hospital; Art Iron, Inc.; Commonwealth Construction Corp.; S & R Equipment Co., Inc.

For Complete List of Firm Personnel, See General Section

For full biographical listings, see the Martindale-Hubbell Law Directory

FULLER & HENRY (AV)

One Seagate Suite 1700, P.O. Box 2088, 43603-2088
Telephone: 419-247-2500
Telecopier: 419-247-2665
Port Clinton, Ohio Office: 125 Jefferson.
Telephone: 419-734-2153.
Telecopier: 419-732-8246.
Columbus, Ohio Office: 2210 Huntington Center, 41 South High Street.
Telephone: 614-228-6611.
Telecopier: 614-228-6623.

MEMBERS OF FIRM

Donald M. Hawkins — James M. Morton, Jr.
Raymond G. Esch — Glenn L. Rambo
David R. Bainbridge

Representative Clients: Brooks Insurance Agency, Inc.; Federal-Mogul Corp.; G.M.P.-Employers Retiree Trust; Harbor Capital Advisors; The National Super Service Co.; Owens-Illinois, Inc.; Millar Elevator Service Corp.; St. Luke's Hospital; The Toledo Edison Co.; Teledyne Industries, Inc.

(See Next Column)

For Complete List of Firm Personnel, See General Section

For full biographical listings, see the Martindale-Hubbell Law Directory

SPENGLER NATHANSON (AV)

608 Madison Avenue, Suite 1000, 43604-1169
Telephone: 419-241-2201
FAX: 419-241-8599

MEMBERS OF FIRM

David A. Katz — Michael J. Berebitsky
Peter N. Kanios

Counsel for: Fifth-Third Bank of Northwestern Ohio, N.A.; Seaway Food Town, Inc.; The University of Toledo; AP Parts; Toledo Board of Education; The Andersons; AVCA Corp.

For Complete List of Firm Personnel, See General Section

For full biographical listings, see the Martindale-Hubbell Law Directory

STOCKWELL & COOPERMAN A LEGAL PROFESSIONAL ASSOCIATION (AV)

Suite 1610, One SeaGate, 43604
Telephone: 419-247-1500
Telecopier: 419-247-1575

John P. Stockwell — Ronald M. Cooperman
Katherine Raup O'Connell

Scott T. Janson

Reference: Fifth Third Bank, Toledo, Ohio.

For full biographical listings, see the Martindale-Hubbell Law Directory

WATKINS, BATES & CAREY (AV)

1200 Fifth Third Center, 608 Madison Avenue, 43604-1157
Telephone: 419-241-2100
Telecopier: 419-241-1960

MEMBERS OF FIRM

William F. Bates — Gary O. Sommer

Counsel for: Flower Hospital; Fostoria Community Hospital; National City Bank; Heidtman Steel Products, Inc.; Nazar Rubber Co.

For Complete List of Firm Personnel, See General Section

For full biographical listings, see the Martindale-Hubbell Law Directory

OKLAHOMA

*LAWTON,** Comanche Co.

O. CHRISTOPHER MEYERS, INC. (AV)

15 N.W. 44th Street, 73505
Telephone: 405-355-0341
Fax: 405-355-0359

O. Christopher Meyers

For full biographical listings, see the Martindale-Hubbell Law Directory

*OKLAHOMA CITY,** Oklahoma Co.

ANDREWS DAVIS LEGG BIXLER MILSTEN & PRICE, A PROFESSIONAL CORPORATION (AV)

500 West Main, 73102
Telephone: 405-272-9241
FAX: 405-235-8786

James F. Davis — Robert B. Milsten
Richard B. Kells, Jr. — Mark H. Price
Timothy M. Larason — Joseph G. Shannonhouse, IV
William H. Whitehill, Jr.

OF COUNSEL

Joseph A. Buckles, II — Keith T. Childers

Representative Clients: CMI Corporation; Grace Petroleum Corporation; Fort Howard Corporation; Petroleum, Inc.; Oklahoma Association of Broadcasters; Crest Discount Foods, Inc.; El Paso Natural Gas Co.; Magic Circle Energy Corp.; Unit Parts Co.; Exxon Co. USA; ANR Production Co.

For Complete List of Firm Personnel, See General Section

For full biographical listings, see the Martindale-Hubbell Law Directory

Oklahoma City—Continued

Crowe & Dunlevy, A Professional Corporation (AV)

1800 Mid-America Tower, 20 North Broadway, 73102-8273
Telephone: 405-235-7700
Fax: 405-239-6651
Tulsa, Oklahoma Office: Crowe & Dunlevy, 500 Kennedy Building, 321 South Boston.
Telephone: 918-592-9800.
Fax: 918-592-9801.
Norman, Oklahoma Office: Crowe & Dunlevy, Luttrell, Pendarvis & Rawlinson, 104 East Eufaula Street.
Telephone: 405-321-7317.
Fax: 405-360-4002.

Allen D. Evans
James H. Holloman, Jr.
Cynda C. Ottaway
Reeder E. Ratliff
Roger A. Stong

Timothy E. Foley

OF COUNSEL

Terry R. Hanna

For Complete List of Firm Personnel, See General Section

For full biographical listings, see the Martindale-Hubbell Law Directory

Hartzog Conger & Cason, A Professional Corporation (AV)

1600 Bank of Oklahoma Plaza, 73102
Telephone: 405-235-7000
Facsimile: 405-235-7329

Larry D. Hartzog
J. William Conger
Len Cason
James C. Prince
Alan Newman
Steven C. Davis
Valerie K. Couch
Mark D. Dickey
Joseph P. Hogsett
John D. Robertson
Kurt M. Rupert
Laura Haag McConnell

Susan B. Shields
Ryan S. Wilson
Melanie J. Jester
Armand Paliotta
Julia Watson
J. Leslie LaReau

OF COUNSEL

Kent F. Frates

For full biographical listings, see the Martindale-Hubbell Law Directory

McAfee & Taft, A Professional Corporation (AV)

Tenth Floor, Two Leadership Square, 73102
Telephone: 405-235-9621
Cable Address: "Oklaw"
TWX: 910-831-3294
Facsimile: (405) 235-0439 (405) 232-2404

Kenneth E. McAfee (1903-1986)
Mark E. Burget
Richard D. Craig
Gary F. Fuller
Frank D. Hill
James Dudley Hyde
Dee A. Replogle, Jr.
John N. Schaefer
Scott W. Sewell
Joel D. Stafford

OF COUNSEL

Richard G. Taft
Eugene Kuntz

Representative Clients: Boatman's First National Bank of Oklahoma; New York Life Insurance Company; Emerson Electric Co.; Merrill Lynch, Pierce, Fenner & Smith Inc.; Arthur Andersen & Co.; Fleming Companies, Inc.; USX Corp.; Amoco Production Company; Ford Motor Company.

For Complete List of Firm Personnel, See General Section

For full biographical listings, see the Martindale-Hubbell Law Directory

Mock, Schwabe, Waldo, Elder, Reeves & Bryant, A Professional Corporation (AV)

Fifteenth Floor, One Leadership Square, 211 North Robinson Avenue, 73102
Telephone: 405-235-5500
Telecopy: 405-235-2875

Randall D. Mock
Steven P. Cole

Representative Clients: Amoco Production Co.; Anson Companies; Liberty Bank & Trust Company of Oklahoma City; Atlantic Richfield Co.; Farm Credit Bank of Wichita; Federal Deposit Insurance Corporation; First Oklahoma Corporation; Holden Energy Corporation; Massachusetts Mutual Life Insurance Co.; Metropolitan Life Insurance Co.

For Complete List of Firm Personnel, See General Section

For full biographical listings, see the Martindale-Hubbell Law Directory

*TULSA,** Tulsa Co.

Conner & Winters, A Professional Corporation (AV)

15 East 5th Street, Suite 2400, 74103-4391
Telephone: 918-586-5711
Fax: 918-586-8982
Oklahoma City, Oklahoma Office: 204 North Robinson, Suite 950, 73102.
Telephone: 405-232-7711.
Facsimile: 405-232-2695.

Martin R. Wing
Douglas M. Rather

Katherine Gallagher Coyle

For Complete List of Firm Personnel, See General Section

For full biographical listings, see the Martindale-Hubbell Law Directory

Eagleton, Eagleton and Harrison, Inc. (AV)

Suite 709, 320 South Boston Avenue, 74103-3727
Telephone: 918-584-0462
Fax: 918-584-3724

E. John Eagleton
James R. Eagleton
Charles D. Harrison

OF COUNSEL

Norma Eagleton

For full biographical listings, see the Martindale-Hubbell Law Directory

Gable & Gotwals (AV)

2000 Bank IV Center, 15 West Sixth Street, 74119-5447
Telephone: 918-582-9201
Facsimile: 918-586-8383

Teresa B. Adwan
Pamela S. Anderson
John R. Barker
David L. Bryant
Gene C. Buzzard
Dennis Clarke Cameron
Timothy A. Carney
Renee DeMoss
Elsie C. Draper
Sidney G. Dunagan
Theodore Q. Eliot
Richard W. Gable
Jeffrey Don Hassell
Patricia Ledvina Himes
Oliver S. Howard
Richard D. Koljack, Jr.
J. Daniel Morgan
Joseph W. Morris
Elizabeth R. Muratet
Richard B. Noulles
Ronald N. Ricketts
John Henry Rule
M. Benjamin Singletary
James M. Sturdivant
Patrick O. Waddel
Michael D. Hall
David Edward Keglovits
Stephen W. Lake
Kari S. McKee
Terry D. Ragsdale
Jeffrey C. Rambach

OF COUNSEL

G. Ellis Gable
Charles P. Gotwals, Jr.

For full biographical listings, see the Martindale-Hubbell Law Directory

James, Potts and Wulfers (AV)

Suite 705, 320 South Boston Avenue, 74103-3712
Telephone: 918-584-0881
FAX: 918-584-4521

MEMBERS OF FIRM

David F. James
Thomas G. Potts
David W. Wulfers

For full biographical listings, see the Martindale-Hubbell Law Directory

Johnson, Allen, Jones & Dornblaser (AV)

900 Petroleum Club Building, 601 South Boulder, 74119
Telephone: 918-584-6644
FAX: 918-584-6645

MEMBERS OF FIRM

Mark H. Allen
W. Thomas Coffman
Kenneth E. Dornblaser
John B. Johnson, Jr.
C. Robert Jones
Richard D. Jones
Randy R. Shorb

ASSOCIATE

Frances F. Hillsman

For full biographical listings, see the Martindale-Hubbell Law Directory

Sneed, Lang, Adams & Barnett, A Professional Corporation (AV)

2300 Williams Center Tower II, Two West Second Street, 74103
Telephone: 918-583-3145
Telecopier: 918-582-0410

(See Next Column)

SNEED, LANG, ADAMS & BARNETT A PROFESSIONAL CORPORATION, *Tulsa—Continued*

James C. Lang
D. Faith Orlowski
Brian S. Gaskill
G. Steven Stidham
Stephen R. McNamara
Thomas E. Black, Jr.
Robbie Emery Burke
C. Raymond Patton, Jr.
Frederick K. Slicker
Richard D. Black
John D. Russell
Jeffrey S. Swyers

OF COUNSEL

James L. Sneed
O. Edwin Adams
Howard G. Barnett, Jr.

Representative Clients: Amoco Production Company; Continental Bank; Deloitte & Touche; Enron Corporation; Halliburton Energy Services; Helmerich & Payne, Inc.; Lehman Brothers, Inc.; Shell Oil Company; Smith Barney, Inc.; State Farm Mutual Automobile Insurance Company.

For full biographical listings, see the Martindale-Hubbell Law Directory

OREGON

*PORTLAND,** Multnomah Co.

BLACK HELTERLINE (AV)

1200 The Bank of California Tower, 707 S.W. Washington Street, 97205
Telephone: 503-224-5560
Telecopier: 503-224-6148

MEMBERS OF FIRM

Clarence H. Greenwood
Robert J. Preston
Richard N. Roskie

ASSOCIATE

Deneen M. Hubertin

COUNSEL

John D. Picco

Representative Clients: Ataka Lumber America, Inc.; The Bank of California, N.A.; E.P. Properties; ESCO Corp.; Georgia-Pacific Corp.; NACCO Materials Handling Group, Inc.; Northwest Copper Works, Inc.; Oregon Potato Company; Pope & Talbot, Inc.; The Sivers Companies.

For Complete List of Firm Personnel, See General Section

For full biographical listings, see the Martindale-Hubbell Law Directory

BURT & VETTERLEIN, P.C. (AV)

Suite 3600 U.S. BanCorp Tower, 111 S.W. Fifth Avenue, 97204-3639
Telephone: 503-223-3600
FAX: 503-274-0778

Robert G. Burt
Eric H. Vetterlein

For full biographical listings, see the Martindale-Hubbell Law Directory

GRENLEY, ROTENBERG EVANS & BRAGG, P.C. (AV)

30th Floor, Pacwest Center, 1211 S.W. Fifth Avenue, 97204
Telephone: 503-241-0570
Facsimile: 503-241-0914

Gary I. Grenley
Stan N. Rotenberg
Lawrence Evans
Michael J. Bragg
Steven D. Adler
Michael S. Evans
Michael C. Zusman
Jeffrey C. Bodie

OF COUNSEL

Sol Siegel
Robert C. Laskowski
Norman A. Rickles

Ann M. Lane

Reference: Key Bank of Oregon.

For full biographical listings, see the Martindale-Hubbell Law Directory

HAGEN, DYE, HIRSCHY & DILORENZO, P.C. (AV)

19th Floor Benj. Franklin Plaza, One S.W. Columbia Street, 97258-2087
Telephone: 503-222-1812
FAX: 503-274-7979

Joseph T. Hagen
Jeffrey L. Dye
John A. Hirschy
John A. DiLorenzo, Jr.
Dana R. Taylor
Mark A. Golding
Kenneth A. Williams

Blanche I. Sommers
Timothy J. Wachter
Annie T. Buell
Adam S. Rittenberg
Michael E. Farnell
John D. Parsons

(See Next Column)

LEGAL SUPPORT PERSONNEL

Carol A. R. Wong
Flora L. Wade

For full biographical listings, see the Martindale-Hubbell Law Directory

HANNA, KERNS & STRADER, A PROFESSIONAL CORPORATION (AV)

300 Hoffman Columbia Plaza, 1300 S.W. Sixth Avenue, 97201
Telephone: 503-273-2700
FAX: 503-273-2712

Harry M. Hanna
Joseph J. Hanna, Jr.
Diane C. Kerns
Timothy R. Strader

Joe F. Yonek
David E. Grein

OF COUNSEL

Jonathan G. Blattmachr (Not admitted in OR)
Peter A. Casciato
Glen R. Kuykendall
Robert J. Woody (Not admitted in OR; Resident, Washington, D.C. Office)

For full biographical listings, see the Martindale-Hubbell Law Directory

SUSSMAN SHANK WAPNICK CAPLAN & STILES (AV)

1000 S.W. Broadway Suite 1400, 97205
Telephone: 503-227-1111
Telecopier: 503-248-0130

ASSOCIATE

William S. Manne

SPECIAL COUNSEL

Aaron Jay Besen
John E. McCormick

For Complete List of Firm Personnel, See General Section

For full biographical listings, see the Martindale-Hubbell Law Directory

ZALUTSKY & KLARQUIST, P.C. (AV)

215 S.W. Washington Street, 3rd Floor, 97204
Telephone: 503-248-0300
FAX: 503-274-8302

Morton H. Zalutsky
Kenneth S. Klarquist, Jr.

References: First Interstate Bank of Oregon (Trust Department); The Bank of California (Trust Department).

For full biographical listings, see the Martindale-Hubbell Law Directory

PENNSYLVANIA

BALA CYNWYD, Montgomery Co.

FURMAN & HALPERN, P.C. (AV)

Suite 612, 401 City Avenue, 19004
Telephone: 610-668-5454
Fax: 610-668-5455
Cherry Hill, New Jersey Office: Suite 245, 411 Route 70 East, 08034.
Telephone: 609-795-4440.
Fax: 609-428-5485.

Barry A. Furman
Mark S. Halpern
Robert S. Levy
Georgeann R. Fusco
Lisanne L. Mikula
Caryn M. DePiano

For full biographical listings, see the Martindale-Hubbell Law Directory

*ERIE,** Erie Co.

MARSH, SPAEDER, BAUR, SPAEDER & SCHAAF (AV)

Suite 300, 300 State Street, 16507
Telephone: 814-456-5301
Fax: 814-456-1112

MEMBERS OF FIRM

Will J. Schaaf
Ritchie T. Marsh
William J. Schaaf
James E. Marsh, Jr.
John P. Eppinger
John C. Brydon
Thomas M. Lent
Francis J. Klemensic
John B. Fessler
Eugene C. Sundberg, Jr.
James R. Fryling

Donald F. Fessler, Jr.
Kurt L. Sundberg

OF COUNSEL

Byron A. Baur

Representative Clients: Aetna Life & Casualty; Borough of Edinboro; Chase Lincoln First Bank, N.A.; Erie Parking Authority; Home Insurance Co.; Marquette Savings Assn.; Motorists Insurance Co.; Northwest Savings

(See Next Column)

MARSH, SPAEDER, BAUR, SPAEDER & SCHAAF—*Continued*

Bank, Pa., S.A.; Ohio Casualty Insurance Co.; Pennsylvania Medical Society Liability Insurance Co.

For Complete List of Firm Personnel, See General Section

For full biographical listings, see the Martindale-Hubbell Law Directory

*HARRISBURG,** Dauphin Co.

BUCHANAN INGERSOLL, PROFESSIONAL CORPORATION (AV)

Vartan Parc, 30 North Third Street, 17101
Telephone: 717-237-4800
Telecopier: 717-233-0852
Pittsburgh, Pennsylvania Office: 5800 USX Tower, 600 Grant Street.
Telephone: 412-562-8800.
Philadelphia, Pennsylvania Office: Two Logan Square, Twelfth Floor, 18th & Arch Streets.
Telephone: 215-665-8700.
Tampa, Florida Office: 101 East Kennedy Boulevard, Suite 1030.
Telephone: 813-222-8180.
North Miami Beach, Florida Office: 19495 Biscayne Boulevard.
Telephone: 305-933-5600.
Lexington, Kentucky Office: 1210 Vine Center Office Tower, 333 West Vine Street.
Telephone: 606-225-5333.
Princeton, New Jersey Office: Buchanan Ingersoll, A Partnership, College Centre, 500 College Road East.
Telephone: 609-452-2666.

Bradley J. Gunnison
Gerald K. Morrison

COUNSEL

Evelyn S. Harris

Arbelyn Elizabeth Wolfe

For Complete List of Firm Personnel, See General Section

For full biographical listings, see the Martindale-Hubbell Law Directory

GOLDBERG, KATZMAN & SHIPMAN, P.C. (AV)

320 Market Street - Strawberry Square, P.O. Box 1268, 17108-1268
Telephone: 717-234-4161
Telecopier: 717-234-6808; 717-234-6810

Ronald M. Katzman
Neil Hendershot
Jesse Jay Cooper
Michael A. Finio

Arnold B. Kogan

Reference: Fulton Bank.

For Complete List of Firm Personnel, See General Section

For full biographical listings, see the Martindale-Hubbell Law Directory

KEEFER, WOOD, ALLEN & RAHAL (AV)

210 Walnut Street, P.O. Box 11963, 17108-1963
Telephone: 717-255-8000
Telecopier: 717-255-8050

MEMBERS OF FIRM

N. David Rahal
Robert L. Weldon
John H. Enos, III
Donna S. Weldon
Jeffrey S. Stokes
Robert R. Church

OF COUNSEL

Samuel C. Harry

ASSOCIATE

Bridget M. Whitley

Representative Clients: ALCOA; American Standard Inc.; Caterpillar, Inc.; CSX Transportation; IBM Corp.; Mellon Bank N.A.; PECO Energy Co.; Philip Morris, Inc.; Rockwell International Corp.; W. R. Grace & Co. - Conn.

For Complete List of Firm Personnel, See General Section

For full biographical listings, see the Martindale-Hubbell Law Directory

McNEES, WALLACE & NURICK (AV)

100 Pine Street, P.O. Box 1166, 17108
Telephone: 717-232-8000
Fax: 717-237-5300

MEMBERS OF FIRM

James L. Fritz
Michael G. Jarman
Richard R. Lefever
John S. Oyler
Timothy J. Pfister
Robert D. Stets
Richard W. Stevenson
David M. Watts, Jr.

Neal S. West

(See Next Column)

ASSOCIATES

David M. Baker
Jonathan C. Berry
Peter F. Kriete
Camille C. Marion
Sharon R. Paxton
Chuong H. Pham

For Complete List of Firm Personnel, See General Section

For full biographical listings, see the Martindale-Hubbell Law Directory

METTE, EVANS & WOODSIDE, A PROFESSIONAL CORPORATION (AV)

3401 North Front Street, P.O. Box 5950, 17110-0950
Telephone: 717-232-5000
Telecopier: 717-236-1816

Howell C. Mette
Peter J. Ressler
Lloyd R. Persun
James A. Ulsh
Glen R. Grell
Elyse E. Rogers

Karen N. Connelly

Counsel for: The B. F. Goodrich Co.; Juniata Valley Financial Corp.; MCI Telecommunications Corp.; Monongahela Power Co.; The Procter and Gamble Paper Products Co.; Community Banks; GTE Products Corp.; Westinghouse Electric; Bell & Howell; Potomac Edison Co.

For Complete List of Firm Personnel, See General Section

For full biographical listings, see the Martindale-Hubbell Law Directory

NAUMAN, SMITH, SHISSLER & HALL (AV)

Eighteenth Floor, 200 North Third Street, P.O. Box 840, 17108-0840
Telephone: 717-236-3010
Telefax: 717-234-1925

MEMBERS OF FIRM

David C. Eaton
Spencer G. Nauman, Jr.
John C. Sullivan
J. Stephen Feinour

Craig J. Staudenmaier

ASSOCIATES

Benjamin Charles Dunlap, Jr.
Stephen J. Keene

OF COUNSEL

Ralph W. Boyles, Jr.

Representative Clients: The W.O. Hickok Mfg. Co.; Delta Dental of Pennsylvania; Mellon Bank, N.A.; PNC Bank, N.A.; General Motors Acceptance Corp.; Chrysler Credit Corp.; Capital Area Tax Collection Bureau; The Greater Harrisburg Foundation; GHF, Inc.; Commonwealth Community Foundations (PA).

For full biographical listings, see the Martindale-Hubbell Law Directory

RHOADS & SINON (AV)

One South Market Square, 12th Floor, P.O. Box 1146, 17108-1146
Telephone: 717-233-5731
Fax: 717-232-1459
Boca Raton, Florida Affiliated Office: Suite 301, 299 West Camino Gardens Boulevard.
Telephone: 407-395-5595.
Fax: 407-395-9497.
Lancaster, Pennsylvania Office: 15 North Lime Street.
Telephone: 717-397-5127.
Fax: 717-397-5267.

MEMBERS OF FIRM

Sherill T. Moyer
John P. Manbeck
Jack F. Hurley, Jr.
Drake D. Nicholas

Lucy E. Kniseley

ASSOCIATE

Lori J. McElroy

For Complete List of Firm Personnel, See General Section

For full biographical listings, see the Martindale-Hubbell Law Directory

*LANCASTER,** Lancaster Co.

APPEL & YOST (AV)

33 North Duke Street, 17602-2886
Telephone: 717-394-0521
Telecopier: 717-299-9781 ABA NET NUMBER 1556
New Holland, Pennsylvania Office: 142 East Main Street.
Telephone: 717-354-4117.
Strasburg, Pennsylvania Office: 39 East Main Street.
Telephone: 717-687-7871.
Quarryville, Pennsylvania Office: 201 East State Street.
Telephone: 717-786-3172.
Ephrata, Pennsylvania Office: 123 East Main Street, 17522.
Telephone: 717-733-2104.

(See Next Column)

APPEL & YOST, *Lancaster—Continued*

MEMBERS OF FIRM

T. Roberts Appel, II
Harry B. Yost
James W. Appel
John L. Sampson
Kenneth H. Howard
William R. Wheatly
William J. Cassidy, Jr.
Greta R. Aul
Matthew G. Guntharp
Peter M. Schannauer

Julia G. Vanasse
Elaine G. Ugolnik
David W. Mersky

OF COUNSEL

Paul F. McKinsey
J. Marlin Shreiner

Counsel for: School Lane Hills, Inc.; Wickersham, Inc. (Construction & Development).

For full biographical listings, see the Martindale-Hubbell Law Directory

LANSDALE, Montgomery Co.

PEARLSTINE/SALKIN ASSOCIATES (AV)

1250 South Broad Street Suite 1000, P.O. Box 431, 19446
Telephone: 215-699-6000
Fax: 215-699-0231

MEMBERS OF FIRM

Philip Salkin
Ronald E. Robinson
Barry Cooperberg
Frederick C. Horn
Marc B. Davis
William R. Wanger
F. Craig La Rocca
Jeffrey T. Sultanik
Neal R. Pearlstine
Wendy G. Rothstein
Alan L. Eisen
Glenn D. Fox

Wilhelm L. Gruszecki
Brian E. Subers
Mark S. Cappuccio
James R. Hall
Michael S. Paul
David J. Draganosky
Lawrence P. Kempner

For full biographical listings, see the Martindale-Hubbell Law Directory

*PHILADELPHIA,** Philadelphia Co.

BALLARD SPAHR ANDREWS & INGERSOLL (AV)

1735 Market Street, 51st Floor, 19103-7599
Telephone: 215-665-8500
Fax: 215-864-8999
Denver, Colorado Office: Seventeenth Street Plaza Building, Suite 2300, 1225 17th Street.
Telephone: 303-292-2400.
Fax: 303-296-3956.
Kaunas, Lithuania Office: Donelaicio g., 71-2, Kaunas 3000.
Telephone: (370-7) 20 56 66.
Fax: (370-7) 20 56 91.
Salt Lake City, Utah Office: One Utah Center, Suite 1200, 201 South Main Street.
Telephone: 801-531-3000.
Fax: 801-531-3001.
Washington, D.C. Office: Suite 900 East, 555 13th Street, N.W.
Telephone: 202-383-8800.
Fax: 202-383-8877; 383-8893.
Baltimore, Maryland Office: 300 East Lombard Street. 19th Floor.
Telephone: 410-528-5600.
Fax: 410-528-5650.
Camden, New Jersey Office: 800 Hudson Square, 5th Floor.
Telephone: 609-541-5577.
Fax: 609-541-8272.

John Marley Bernard
Joel E. Horowitz
Joseph E. Lundy
Louis W. Ricker
Rhonda Resnick Cohen
Michael Lehr
Robert E. McQuiston
Andrew J. Rudolph
Wayne R. Strasbaugh

OF COUNSEL

Robert R. Batt

COUNSEL

Edward Ira Leeds

Barry L. Klein
Kathleen M. Ranalli

For Complete List of Firm Personnel, See General Section

For full biographical listings, see the Martindale-Hubbell Law Directory

BUCHANAN INGERSOLL, PROFESSIONAL CORPORATION (AV)

Two Logan Square Twelfth Floor, 18th & Arch Streets, 19103
Telephone: 215-665-8700
Telecopier: 215-569-2066
Pittsburgh, Pennsylvania Office: 5800 USX Tower, 600 Grant Street.
Telephone: 412-562-8800.
Harrisburg, Pennsylvania Office: Vartan Parc, 30 North Third Street.
Telephone: 717-237-4800.

(See Next Column)

Tampa, Florida Office: 101 East Kennedy Boulevard, Suite 1030.
Telephone: 813-222-8180.
North Miami Beach, Florida Office: 19495 Biscayne Boulevard.
Telephone: 305-933-5600.
Lexington, Kentucky Office: 1210 Vine Center Office Tower, 333 West Vine Street.
Telephone: 606-225-5333.
Princeton, New Jersey Office: Buchanan Ingersoll, A Partnership, College Centre, 500 College Road East.
Telephone: 609-452-2666.

George F. Nagle

For Complete List of Firm Personnel, See General Section

For full biographical listings, see the Martindale-Hubbell Law Directory

DILWORTH, PAXSON, KALISH & KAUFFMAN (AV)

3200 Mellon Bank Center, 1735 Market Street, 19103
Telephone: 215-575-7000
Fax: 215-575-7200
Harrisburg, Pennsylvania Office: 305 N. Front Street, Suite 403.
Telephone: 717-236-4812.
Fax: 717-236-7811.
Plymouth Meeting, Pennsylvania Office: 630 West Germantown Pike, Suite 160.
Telephone: 610-941-4444.
Fax: 610-941-9880.
Westmont, New Jersey Office: 222 Haddon Avenue.
Telephone: 609-854-5150.
Fax: 609-854-2316.
Media, Pennsylvania Office: 606 E. Baltimore Pike.
Telephone: 610-565-4322.
Fax: 610-565-4131.

MEMBERS OF FIRM

Peter J. Picotte, II
Richard M. Segal
Marc A. Feller
John W. Schmehl
Paul W. Baskowsky

ASSOCIATE

Richard L. Fox

For Complete List of Firm Personnel, See General Section

For full biographical listings, see the Martindale-Hubbell Law Directory

DUANE, MORRIS & HECKSCHER (AV)

Suite 4200 One Liberty Place, 19103-7396
Telephone: 215-979-1000
FAX: 215-979-1020
Harrisburg, Pennsylvania Office: 305 North Front Street, 5th Floor, P.O. Box 1003.
Telephone: 717-237-5500.
Fax: 717-232-4015.
Wilmington, Delaware Office: Suite 1500, 1201 Market Street.
Telephone: 302-571-5550.
Fax: 302-571-5560.
New York, N.Y. Office: 112 E. 42nd Street, Suite 2125.
Telephone: 212-499-0410.
Fax: 212-499-0420.
Wayne, Pennsylvania Office 735 Chesterbrook Boulevard, Suite 300.
Telephone: 610-647-3555.
Allentown, Pennsylvania Office: 968 Postal Road, Suite 200.
Telephone: 610-266-3650.
Fax: 610-640-2619.
Cherry Hill, New Jersey Office: 51 Haddonfield Road, Suite 340.
Telephone: 609-488-7300.
Fax: 609-488-7021.

MEMBERS OF FIRM

Sheldon M. Bonovitz
Donald R. Auten
David M. Flynn
Ralph A. Mariani
Steven P. Berman
Frank G. Cooper
Paul J. Schneider
Frederick A. Levy
Neil H. Feinstein
Brian J. Siegel (Resident, Wayne Office)

SPECIAL COUNSEL

Eugene Lowenstein

*Hasday & Margulis, A Professional Corporation

For Complete List of Firm Personnel, See General Section

For full biographical listings, see the Martindale-Hubbell Law Directory

FELLHEIMER EICHEN BRAVERMAN & KASKEY, A PROFESSIONAL CORPORATION (AV)

21st Floor, One Liberty Place, 19103-7334
Telephone: 215-575-3800
FAX: 215-575-3801
Camden, New Jersey Office: 519 Federal Street, Suite 503 Parkade Building, 08103-1147.
Telephone: 609-541-5323.
Fax: 609-541-5370.

(See Next Column)

FELLHEIMER EICHEN BRAVERMAN & KASKEY A PROFESSIONAL CORPORATION—*Continued*

Alan S. Fellheimer
David L. Braverman
Judith Eichen Fellheimer
John E. Kaskey
Kenneth S. Goodkind
Anna Hom
Peter E. Meltzer

Barbara Anisko
Maia R. Caplan
Jeffrey L. Eichen
Michael N. Feder
Jolie G. Kahn
George F. Newton
David B. Spitofsky
W. Thomas Tither, Jr.

For Complete List of Firm Personnel, See General Section

For full biographical listings, see the Martindale-Hubbell Law Directory

FOX, ROTHSCHILD, O'BRIEN & FRANKEL (AV)

10th Floor, 2000 Market Street, 19103-3291
Telephone: 215-299-2000
Cable Address: FROF
Telecopier: 215-299-2150
Exton, Pennsylvania Office: Eagleview Corporate Center, 717 Constitution Drive, Suite 111, P.O. Box 673, 19341-0673.
Telephone: 610-458-2100.
Telecopier: 610-458-2112.
Trenton (Lawrenceville), New Jersey Office: Princeton Pike Corporate Center, 997 Lenox Drive, Building 3, 08648-2311.
Telephone: 609-896-3600.
Telecopier: 609-896-1469.

MEMBERS OF FIRM

Norman Leibovitz
Owen A. Knopping
Stephen P. Weiss
Albert R. Riviezzo (Resident, Exton, Pennsylvania Office)
Mark L. Silow

ASSOCIATE

Kathleen K. Weston

For Complete List of Firm Personnel, See General Section

For full biographical listings, see the Martindale-Hubbell Law Directory

FREEDMAN & ASSOCIATES (AV)

The Widener Building, Seventeenth Floor, One South Penn Square, 19107
Telephone: 215-563-1663
Fax: 215-563-1663

Barbara W. Freedman

ASSOCIATES

Laura J. Lifsey
Susan Bahme Blumenfeld
Donna Hill Prescott

For full biographical listings, see the Martindale-Hubbell Law Directory

KLEHR, HARRISON, HARVEY, BRANZBURG & ELLERS (AV)

1401 Walnut Street, 19102
Telephone: 215-568-6060
Fax: 215-568-6603
Cherry Hill, New Jersey Office: Colwick-Suite 200, 51 Haddonfield Road.
Telephone: 609-486-7900.
Fax: 609-486-4875.
Allentown, Pennsylvania Office: Roma Corporate Center, Suite 501, 1605 North Cedar Crest Boulevard.
Telephone: 215-432-1803.
Fax: 215-433-4031.
Wilmington, Delaware Office: 222 Delaware Avenue, Suite 1101.
Telephone: 302-426-1189.
Fax: 302-426-9193.

MEMBERS OF FIRM

Lawrence J. Arem
Matthew H. Kamens

ASSOCIATES

Keith W. Kaplan
Steven G. Winters

For Complete List of Firm Personnel, See General Section

For full biographical listings, see the Martindale-Hubbell Law Directory

GERALD S. SUSMAN & ASSOCIATES, P.C. (AV)

Suite 432 Benjamin Franklin Business Center, 834 Chestnut Street, 19107
Telephone: 215-440-7500
Fax: 215-440-0188
Cable: Taxlaw
Boca Raton, Florida Office: 1200 N. Federal Highway.
Telephone: 407-368-1888.
West Palm Beach, Florida Office: 1800 S. Australian Boulevard, Suite 205.

Gerald S. Susman

Richard J. Cohen

For full biographical listings, see the Martindale-Hubbell Law Directory

MERVIN M. WILF, LTD. (AV)

3200 Mellon Bank Center, 1735 Market Street, 19103
Telephone: 215-575-7650; 568-4842
Facsimile: 215-575-7652
Boston, Massachusetts Office: 300 Commonwealth Avenue, 02115.
Telephone: 617-437-7981.

Mervin M. Wilf

A list of Representative Clients and References will be furnished upon request.

For full biographical listings, see the Martindale-Hubbell Law Directory

WOLF, BLOCK, SCHORR AND SOLIS-COHEN (AV)

Twelfth Floor, Packard Building, S.E. Corner 15th and Chestnut Streets, 19102-2678
Telephone: 215-977-2000
Cable Address: "WOLBLORR PHA"
TWX: 710-670-1927
Telecopiers: 977-2334; 977-2346
Malvern, Pennsylvania Office: 20 Valley Stream Parkway.
Telephone: 215-889-4900.
Fax: 215-889-4916.
Harrisburg, Pennsylvania Office: 305 North Front Street, Suite 401.
Telephone: 717-237-7160.
Fax: 717-237-7161.

MEMBERS OF FIRM

Charles G. Kopp
Ronald M. Wiener
Ivan I. Light
Arthur A. Zatz
Robert C. Jacobs
Jay A. Dorsch
Jay L. Goldberg
William A. Rosoff
Joseph C. Bright
Dennis L. Cohen
Thomas J. Gallagher, III
John H. Schapiro

For Complete List of Firm Personnel, See General Section

For full biographical listings, see the Martindale-Hubbell Law Directory

*PITTSBURGH,** Allegheny Co.

BUCHANAN INGERSOLL, PROFESSIONAL CORPORATION (AV)

5800 USX Tower, 600 Grant Street, 15219
Telephone: 412-562-8800
Telecopier: 412-562-1041
Philadelphia, Pennsylvania Office: Two Logan Square, Twelfth Floor, 18th & Arch Streets.
Telephone: 215-665-8700.
Harrisburg, Pennsylvania Office: Vartan Parc, 30 North Third Street.
Telephone: 717-237-4800.
Tampa, Florida Office: 101 East Kennedy Boulevard, Suite 1030.
Telephone: 813-222-8180.
North Miami Beach, Florida Office: 19495 Biscayne Boulevard.
Telephone: 305-933-5600.
Lexington, Kentucky Office: 1210 Vine Center Office Tower, 333 West Vine Street.
Telephone: 606-225-5333.
Princeton, New Jersey Office: Buchanan Ingersoll, A Partnership, College Centre, 500 College Road East.
Telephone: 609-452-2666.

Bruce I. Booken
Christopher F. Farrell
Robert A. Johnson
Jack J. Kessler
Robert Y. Kopf, Jr.
Lawrence J. Kuremsky
Francis A. Muracca, II
K. Sidney Neuman
James D. Obermanns
Larry E. Phillips
Jonathan M. Schmerling

SENIOR ATTORNEYS

S. Howard Kline
William H. Morrow
Philip J. Weis

R. Douglas DeNardo
James W. Forsyth
Harrison S. Lauer

For Complete List of Firm Personnel, See General Section

For full biographical listings, see the Martindale-Hubbell Law Directory

DICKIE, MCCAMEY & CHILCOTE, A PROFESSIONAL CORPORATION (AV)

Suite 400, Two PPG Place, 15222-5402
Telephone: 412-281-7272
Fax: 412-392-5367
Wheeling, West Virginia Office: Suite 2002, 1233 Main Street, 26003-2839.
Telephone: 304-233-1022.
Facsimile: 304-233-1026.

Thomas P. Lutz
John W. Lewis, II
George Randal Fox, III

John C. Carlos
Christopher A. Brodman
Robert G. Voinchet, Jr.
James Otis Perry, IV

(See Next Column)

DICKIE, MCCAMEY & CHILCOTE A PROFESSIONAL CORPORATION, *Pittsburgh—Continued*

For Complete List of Firm Personnel, See General Section

For full biographical listings, see the Martindale-Hubbell Law Directory

KLETT LIEBER ROONEY & SCHORLING, A PROFESSIONAL CORPORATION (AV)

40th Floor, One Oxford Centre, 15219-6498
Telephone: 412-392-2000
FAX: 412-392-2128; 412-392-2129
Harrisburg, Pennsylvania Office: 240 North Third Street, Suite 600.
Telephone: 717-231-7700.
Philadelphia, Pennsylvania Office: 28th Floor, One Logan Square.
Telephone: 215-567-7500

SHAREHOLDERS

Jeffrey S. Blum
Richard T. Kennedy
Stanley J. Lehman

SENIOR COUNSEL

Jerome B. Lieber

ASSOCIATES

David R. Berk
Maureen P. Gluntz
Gregg Mitchell Kander

For Complete List of Firm Personnel, See General Section

For full biographical listings, see the Martindale-Hubbell Law Directory

MARCUS & SHAPIRA (AV)

35th Floor, One Oxford Centre, 301 Grant Street, 15219-6401
Telephone: 412-471-3490
Telecopier: 412-391-8758

MEMBERS OF FIRM

Bernard D. Marcus
Daniel H. Shapira
George P. Slesinger
Robert L. Allman, II
Estelle F. Comay
Susan Gromis Flynn
Darlene M. Nowak
Glenn M. Olcerst
Elly Heller-Toig
Sylvester A. Beozzo

OF COUNSEL

John M. Burkoff

SPECIAL COUNSEL

Jane Campbell Moriarty

ASSOCIATES

Scott D. Livingston
Robert M. Barnes
Stephen S. Zubrow
David B. Rodes
Lori E. McMaster
Melody A. Pollock
James F. Rosenberg
Amy M. Gottlieb

For full biographical listings, see the Martindale-Hubbell Law Directory

FRANK MAST & ASSOCIATES (AV)

Chatham Tower Professional Suite 1-R, 15219
Telephone: 412-281-1819
Fax: 412-281-6170

For full biographical listings, see the Martindale-Hubbell Law Directory

TENER, VAN KIRK, WOLF & MOORE (AV)

407 Oliver Building, 15222-2368
Telephone: 412-281-5580

MEMBERS OF FIRM

Alexander C. Tener (1888-1965)
J. R. Van Kirk (1890-1966)
William R. Balph (1908-1979)
Lester K. Wolf
Martin L. Moore, Jr.
Robert B. Shust
Robert B. Wolf
Timothy F. Burke, Jr.
Thomas J. Kessinger

Reference: Pittsburgh National Bank.

For full biographical listings, see the Martindale-Hubbell Law Directory

THORP, REED & ARMSTRONG (AV)

One Riverfront Center, 15222
Telephone: 412-394-7711
Fax: 412-394-2555

MEMBERS OF FIRM

James K. Goldberg
Sidney J. Kelly
Joseph D. Shuman
Keith H. West

For Complete List of Firm Personnel, See General Section

For full biographical listings, see the Martindale-Hubbell Law Directory

VUONO, LAVELLE & GRAY (AV)

2310 Grant Building, 15219
Telephone: 412-471-1800
Fax: 412-471-4477

(See Next Column)

MEMBERS OF FIRM

John A. Vuono
William J. Lavelle
William A. Gray
Mark T. Vuono
Richard R. Wilson

ASSOCIATES

Dennis J. Kusturiss
Christine M. Dolfi
Peter J. Scanlon

Reference: Pittsburgh National Bank.

For full biographical listings, see the Martindale-Hubbell Law Directory

WELLER, WICKS & WALLACE, PROFESSIONAL CORPORATION (AV)

1800 Benedum-Trees Building, 15222
Telephone: 412-471-1751
Fax: 412-471-8117

John S. Weller (1866-1944)
John O. Wicks (1880-1947)
C. L. Wallace (1885-1953)
Henry A. Bergstrom (1911-1993)
J. Murray Egan
Donald W. Shaffer
Henry A. Bergstrom, Jr.
Thomas A. Woodward

Reference: Pittsburgh National Bank.

For full biographical listings, see the Martindale-Hubbell Law Directory

WICK, STREIFF, MEYER, METZ & O'BOYLE, P.C. (AV)

1450 Two Chatham Center, 15219
Telephone: 412-765-1600
Telecopier: 412-261-3783

Henry M. Wick, Jr.
Charles J. Streiff
Carl F. Meyer
LeRoy L. Metz, II
David M. O'Boyle
Vincent P. Szeligo
Patricia J. Liptak-McGrail

Lucille N. Wick
Ronald Joseph Rademacher
Roger A. Isla
Donna Lynn Miller

Reference: PNC Bank.

For full biographical listings, see the Martindale-Hubbell Law Directory

*READING,** Berks Co.

STEVENS & LEE, A PROFESSIONAL CORPORATION (AV)

111 North Sixth Street, P.O. Box 679, 19603
Telephone: 610-478-2000
Fax: 610-376-5610
Wayne, Pennsylvania Office: One Glenhardie Corporate Center, 1275 Drummers Lane, P. O. Box 236.
Telephone: 610-964-1480.
Fax: 610-687-1384.
Lancaster, Pennsylvania Office: One Penn Square, P.O. Box 1594.
Telephone: 717-291-1031.
Fax: 717-394-7726.
Allentown, Pennsylvania Office: 740 North Hamilton Mall, P. O. Box 8838.
Telephone: 610-439-4195.
Fax: 610-439-8415.
Harrisburg, Pennsylvania Office: 208 North Third Street. Suite 310. P.O. Box 12090. 17101.
Telephone: 717-234-1250.
Fax: 717-234-1939.
Philadelphia, Pennsylvania Office: Two Penn Center Plaza, Suite 200.
Telephone: 215-854-6370.
Fax: 215-569-0216.
Wilkes-Barre, Pennsylvania Office: 289 North Main Street.
Telephone: 717-823-6116.
Fax: 717-823-1149.

H. Richard Brooks
R. John MacKoul, Jr.
C. Thomas Work
Ernest J. Choquette
Kenneth R. Dugan

Robert J. Henry
Mark N. Raezer

OF COUNSEL

William R. Lessig, Jr.

For Complete List of Firm Personnel, See General Section

For full biographical listings, see the Martindale-Hubbell Law Directory

*STROUDSBURG,** Monroe Co.

HANNA, YOUNG, UPRIGHT & PAZUHANICH (AV)

800 Main Street, 18360
Telephone: 717-424-9400; 646-2486
Fax: 717-424-9426

MEMBERS OF FIRM

Jerry F. Hanna
Alan Price Young
Kirby G. Upright
Mark P. Pazuhanich

(See Next Column)

HANNA, YOUNG, UPRIGHT & PAZUHANICH—*Continued*

ASSOCIATES

Janet K. Catina | Thomas V. Casale
Nicholas Joseph Masington, III | Ann Marie T. Nasek

For full biographical listings, see the Martindale-Hubbell Law Directory

*WELLSBORO,** Tioga Co.

OWLETT, LEWIS & GINN, P.C. (AV)

One Charles Street, P.O. Box 878, 16901
Telephone: 717-723-1000
Fax: 717-724-6822
Elkland, Pennsylvania Office: 102 East Main Street.
Telephone: 814-258-5148.
Knoxville, Pennsylvania Office: 106 East Main Street.
Telephone: 814-326-4161.

Edwin A. Glover | Edward H. Owlett, III
Edward H. Owlett | Raymond E. Ginn, Jr.
Thomas M. Owlett

Bruce L. Vickery | Judith DeMeester Nichols

OF COUNSEL

John Dean Lewis

Reference: Citizens and Northern Bank.

For full biographical listings, see the Martindale-Hubbell Law Directory

*WEST CHESTER,** Chester Co.

CRAWFORD, WILSON, RYAN & AGULNICK, P.C. (AV)

220 West Gay Street, 19380
Telephone: 610-431-4500
Fax: 610-430-8718
Radnor, Pennsylvania Office: 252 Radnor-Chester Road, P. O. Box 8333, 19087.
Telephone: 215-688-1205.
Fax: 215-688-7802.

Ronald M. Agulnick | Thomas R. Wilson
Fronefield Crawford, Jr. | Kevin J. Ryan

John J. Mahoney | Patricia T. Brennan
Kim Denise Morton | Richard H. Morton
Steven L. Mutart | Patricia J. Kelly
Rita Kathryn Borzillo | Charles W. Tucker

Reference: First National Bank of West Chester.

For full biographical listings, see the Martindale-Hubbell Law Directory

*WILKES-BARRE,** Luzerne Co.

ROSENN, JENKINS & GREENWALD (AV)

15 South Franklin Street, 18711-0075
Telephone: 717-826-5600
Fax: 717-826-5640

MEMBERS OF FIRM

Marshall S. Jacobson | Alan S. Hollander
Murray Ufberg | Gerard M. Musto, Jr.

ASSOCIATE

Carolyn Carr Rhoden

Representative Clients: Allstate Insurance Co.; C-TEC Corporation; Chicago Title Insurance Co.; Franklin First Savings Bank; The Geisinger Medical Center; Guard Insurance Group; The Mays Department Stores Company; Student LoanMarketing Association (Sallie Mae); Subaru of America, Inc.

For Complete List of Firm Personnel, See General Section

For full biographical listings, see the Martindale-Hubbell Law Directory

RHODE ISLAND

*PROVIDENCE,** Providence Co.

EDWARDS & ANGELL (AV)

2700 Hospital Trust Tower, 02903
Telephone: 401-274-9200
Telecopier: 401-276-6611
Cable Address: "Edwangle Providence"
Telex: 952001 "E A PVD"
Boston, Massachusetts Office: 101 Federal Street, 02110.
Telephone: 617-439-444.
Telecopier: 617-439-4170.
New York, New York Office: 750 Lexington Avenue, 10022.
Telephone: 212-308-4411.
Telecopier: 212-308-4844.

(See Next Column)

Palm Beach, Florida Office: 250 Royal Palm Way, 33480.
Telephone: 407-833-7700.
Telecopier: 407-655-8719.
Newark, New Jersey Office: Gateway three, 07120.
Telephone: 201-623-7717.
Telecopier: 201-623-7717.
Hartford, Connecticut Office: 750 Main Street, 14th Floor, 06103.
Telephone: 203-525-5065.
Telecopier: 203-527-4198.
Newport, Rhode Island Office: 130 Bellevue Avenue, 02840.
Telephone: 401-849-7800.
Telecopier: 401-849-7887.

MEMBERS OF FIRM

Alfred S. Lombardi | Philip B. Barr, Jr.
G. Scott Nebergall

COUNSEL

Kenneth L. Levine

For Complete List of Firm Personnel, See General Section

For full biographical listings, see the Martindale-Hubbell Law Directory

LICHT & SEMONOFF (AV)

Fourth Floor, Historic Wayland Building, One Park Row, 02903
Telephone: 401-421-8030
Telecopier: 401-272-9408

MEMBERS OF FIRM

Frank Licht (1916-1987) | Joseph De Angelis
Ralph P. Semonoff (1918-1992) | Richard A. Boren
Jeremiah J. Gorin | Robert B. Berkelhammer
Melvin L. Zurier | Carl I. Freedman
Bruce R. Ruttenberg | Robert D. Fine
Norman G. Orodenker | Susan Leach De Blasio
Nathan W. Chace | Susann G. Mark
George E. Lieberman | Drew P. Kaplan
Richard A. Licht | Patrick A. Guida
Robert N. Huseby, Sr. | Anthony J. Bucci, Jr.
Casby Harrison, III

ASSOCIATES

Susan M. Huntley | Maureen L. Mallon
Glenn R. Friedemann | Jerry H. Elmer
Paul J. Adler | Michael Prescott
Steven C. Sidel

OF COUNSEL

Daniel J. Murray

For Complete List of Firm Personnel, See General Section

For full biographical listings, see the Martindale-Hubbell Law Directory

PLOURDE & LEONARD, LTD. (AV)

One Citizens Plaza Suite 830, 02903
Telephone: 401-453-0550
Fax: 401-421-7806
Boston, Massachusetts Office: 60 Commercial Wharf, 02110.
Telephone: 617-367-2090.

Paul Plourde | Arthur J. Leonard

Richard Bogue | Thomas Moylan
F. Moore McLaughlin, IV | (Not admitted in RI)

For full biographical listings, see the Martindale-Hubbell Law Directory

BRENDAN P. SMITH A PROFESSIONAL CORPORATION (AV)

One Turks Head Place, 02903
Telephone: 401-331-0909
Fax: 401-331-0044

Brendan P. Smith

For full biographical listings, see the Martindale-Hubbell Law Directory

WESTERLY, Washington Co.

THORNTON, THORNTON & THOMSEN (AV)

43 Broad Street, P.O. Box 531, 02891-0531
Telephone: 401-596-4953
Telecopier: 401-596-6659

MEMBERS OF FIRM

William B. Thornton | Matthew H. Thomsen

ASSOCIATES

Marc J. Soss | Pasquale A. Cavaliere (Not admitted in RI)

COUNSEL

James D. Thornton | Chaplin B. Barnes

Approved Attorneys for: Lawyers Title Insurance Corporation of Richmond, Virginia; Commonwealth Land Title Insurance Company; Farm Credit Bank of Springfield.

(See Next Column)

THORNTON, THORNTON & THOMSEN, *Westerly—Continued*

Reference: The Washington Trust Co.

For full biographical listings, see the Martindale-Hubbell Law Directory

SOUTH CAROLINA

*CHARLESTON,** Charleston Co.

EVANS, CARTER, KUNES & BENNETT, P.A. (AV)

151 Meeting Street, Suite 415, P.O. Box 369, 29402-0369
Telephone: 803-577-2300
Telefax: 803-577-2055

George C. Evans
T. Heyward Carter, Jr.
Robert M. Kunes
Edward G. R. Bennett

Charlotte Nancie Quick

For full biographical listings, see the Martindale-Hubbell Law Directory

HAYNSWORTH, MARION, MCKAY & GUÉRARD, L.L.P (AV)

#2 Prioleau Street, P.O. Box 1119, 29402
Telephone: 803-722-7606
Telecopier: 803-723-5263
Columbia, South Carolina Office: Suite 2400 AT&T Building, 1201 Main Street, P.O. Drawer 7157, 29202.
Telephone: 803-765-1818.
Telecopier: 803-765-2399.
Greenville, South Carolina Office: Two Insignia Financial Plaza, 75 Beattie Place, P.O. Box 2048, 29602.
Telephone: 803-240-3200.
Telecopier: 803-240-3300.

MEMBER OF FIRM

Donald Bancroft Meyer

ASSOCIATE

Paul M. Lynch

Counsel for: Fluor-Daniel Corp.; Greenville Hospital System; Baker Hospital; Roper Hospital; Silstar Corp. of America; Santee Cooper; Coward-Hund Construction Co.; Hogan, Mellow and Ladd.

For Complete List of Firm Personnel, See General Section

For full biographical listings, see the Martindale-Hubbell Law Directory

PEARLMAN & PEARLMAN, PROFESSIONAL CORPORATION (AV)

134 Meeting Street, Suite 420, P.O. Box 20519, 29413-0519
Telephone: 803-577-7411
Facsimile: 803-577-7443

Robert B. Pearlman
Gus H. Pearlman

References: Bank of South Carolina; Wachovia Bank Trust Dept.

For full biographical listings, see the Martindale-Hubbell Law Directory

SLOTCHIVER & SLOTCHIVER (AV)

44 State Street, 29401
Telephone: 803-577-6531
Facsimile: 803-577-0261

MEMBERS OF FIRM

Irvin J. Slotchiver
Daniel S. Slotchiver
Stephen M. Slotchiver

For full biographical listings, see the Martindale-Hubbell Law Directory

YOUNG, CLEMENT, RIVERS & TISDALE (AV)

28 Broad Street, P.O. Box 993, 29402
Telephone: 803-577-4000
Fax: 803-724-6600
Columbia, South Carolina Office: 1901 Assembly Street, Suite 300, P.O. Box 8476.
Telephone: 803-799-4000.
Fax: 803-799-7083.
North Charleston , South Carolina Office: 2170 Ashley Phosphate Road, Suite 700, P.O. Box 61509.
Telephone: 803-720-5400.
Fax: 803-724-7796.

MEMBERS OF FIRM

John C. Von Lehe, Jr.
C. Michael Branham

ASSOCIATE

Shawn M. Flanagan

Counsel for: Hoechst Corporation; Jack Eckerd Corp.; Michelin Tire Corporation; NCR Corp.; Peter Kiewit Sons, Inc.; Sonoco Products Corporation; Springs Industries.

(See Next Column)

For Complete List of Firm Personnel, See General Section

For full biographical listings, see the Martindale-Hubbell Law Directory

*COLUMBIA,** Richland Co.

BARNES, ALFORD, STORK & JOHNSON, L.L.P. (AV)

1613 Main Street, P.O. Box 8448, 29202
Telephone: 803-799-1111
Telefax: 803-254-1335

OF COUNSEL

Alan J. Reyner
Roger A. Way, Jr.

Representative Clients: First Union National Bank of South Carolina; Aetna Casualty and Surety Co.; Kline Iron & Steel Co.

For Complete List of Firm Personnel, See General Section

For full biographical listings, see the Martindale-Hubbell Law Directory

THEODORE J. HOPKINS, JR. (AV)

AT&T Building, 1201 Main Street, Suite 2010, P.O. Box 1149, 29201
Telephone: 803-254-1378
Fax: 803-252-0056

NELSON MULLINS RILEY & SCARBOROUGH L.L.P. (AV)

A Registered Limited Liability Partnership including Professional Corporations
Third Floor, Keenan Building, 1330 Lady Street, P.O. Box 11070, 29211
Telephone: 803-799-2000
Telecopy: 803-256-7500; 733-9499
Atlanta, Georgia Office: 1201 Peachtree Street, N.E., P.O. Box 77707.
Telephone: 404-817-6000.
Telecopy: 404-817-6050.
Charleston, South Carolina Office: Suite 500, 151 Meeting Street, P.O. Box 1806.
Telephone: 803-853-5200.
Telecopy: 803-722-8700.
Florence, South Carolina Office: 600 W. Palmetto Street, Suite 200, P.O. Box 5955.
Telephone: 803-662-0019.
Telecopy: 803-662-0491.
Greenville, South Carolina Office: Twenty-Fourth Floor, BB&T Building, 301 North Main Street, P.O. Box 10084.
Telephone: 803-250-2300.
Telecopy: 803-232-2925.
Lexington, South Carolina Office: 334 Old Chapin Road, P.O. Box 729.
Telephone: 803-733-9494; 803-799-200.
Telecopy: 803-957-8226.
Myrtle Beach, South Carolina Office: 2411 N. Oak Street, Founders Centre, Suite 301. P.O. Box 3939.
Telephone: 803-448-3500.
Telecopy: 803-448-3437.

OF COUNSEL

Robert P. Wilkins (Resident, Lexington, SC Office)

MEMBERS OF FIRM

George S. Bailey
John M. Campbell, Jr. (Resident, Greenville, SC Office)
Kenneth A. Janik
Russell Z. Plowden (Resident, Greenville, SC Office)
Thomas F. Moran (Resident, Myrtle Beach, SC Office)

ASSOCIATE

Karen Hudson Thomas

Representative Clients: Bi-Lo, Inc.; BMW, AG; E. I. DuPont de Nemours & Co.; General Motors Corp.; W. R. Grace & Company, Cryovac Division; Hoffmann-LaRoche; The National Bank of South Carolina; NationsBank; Owens-Illinois, Inc.; Southern Bell Telephone & Telegraph Co.; Union Camp Corp.

For Complete List of Firm Personnel, See General Section

For full biographical listings, see the Martindale-Hubbell Law Directory

*GREENVILLE,** Greenville Co.

JAMES R. GILREATH, P.A. (AV)

110 Lavinia Avenue, P.O. Box 2147, 29602
Telephone: 803-242-4727
Telecopier: 803-232-4395

James R. Gilreath

Stephen G. Potts

For full biographical listings, see the Martindale-Hubbell Law Directory

Greenville—Continued

Haynsworth, Marion, McKay & Guérard, L.L.P. (AV)

Two Insignia Financial Plaza, 75 Beattie Place, P.O. Box 2048, 29602
Telephone: 803-240-3200
Telecopier: 803-240-3300
Columbia, South Carolina Office: Suite 2400 A T & T Building, 1201 Main Street, P.O. Drawer 7157, 29202
Telephone: 803-765-1818.
Telecopier: 803-765-2399.
Charleston, South Carolina Office: #2 Prioleau Street, P.O. Box 1119, 29402.
Telephone: 803-722-7606.
Telecopier: 803-723-5263.

MEMBER OF FIRM

David L. McMurray

ASSOCIATE

Arthur Frazier McLean, III

Counsel for: Fluor-Daniel Corp.; Synalloy Corp.; Greenville Hospital System.

For Complete List of Firm Personnel, See General Section

For full biographical listings, see the Martindale-Hubbell Law Directory

Leatherwood Walker Todd & Mann, P.C. (AV)

100 East Coffee Street, P.O. Box 87, 29602
Telephone: 803-242-6440
FAX: 803-233-8461
Spartanburg, South Carolina Office: 1451 East Main Street, P.O. Box 3188.
Telephone: 803-582-4365.
Telefax: 803-583-8961.

J. Richard Kelly
Jack H. Tedards, Jr.
William L. Dennis
Richard L. Few, Jr.

COUNSEL

Johnnie M. Walters

Counsel for: John D. Hollingsworth on Wheels, Inc.; Canal Insurance Co.; Suitt Construction Co.; Platt Saco Lowell Corporation; The Litchfield Company of South Carolina; Textile Hall Corp.
Representative Clients: NationsBank; Cooper Motor Lines, Inc.; Springs Industries, Inc.; American Federal Bank, F.S.B.

For Complete List of Firm Personnel, See General Section

For full biographical listings, see the Martindale-Hubbell Law Directory

Merline & Thomas, P.A. (AV)

665 North Academy Street, P.O. Box 10796, 29603
Telephone: 803-242-4080
Fax: 803-242-5758

David A. Merline
John R. Thomas
David A. Merline, Jr.
Keith G. Meacham

For full biographical listings, see the Martindale-Hubbell Law Directory

Nelson Mullins Riley & Scarborough L.L.P. (AV)

A Registered Limited Liability Partnership including Professional Corporations
Twenty-Fourth Floor, BB&T Building, 301 North Main Street, P.O. Box 10084, 29603
Telephone: 803-250-2300
Telecopy: 803-232-2925
Atlanta, Georgia Office: 1201 Peachtree Street, N.E., P.O. Box 77707.
Telephone: 404-817-6000.
Telecopy: 404-817-6050.
Charleston, South Carolina Office: Suite 500, 151 Meeting Street, P.O. Box 1806.
Telephone: 803-853-5200.
Telecopy: 803-722-8700.
Columbia, South Carolina Office: Third Floor, Keenan Building. 1300 Lady Street. P.O. Box 11070.
Telephone: 803-799-2000.
Telecopy: 803-256-7500; 803-733-9499.
Florence, South Carolina Office: 600 W. Palmetto Street, Suite 200, P.O. Box 5955.
Telephone: 803-662-0019.
Telecopy: 803-662-0491.
Lexington, South Carolina Office: 334 Old Chapin Road, P.O. Box 729.
Telephone: 803-733-9494; 803-799-200.
Telecopy: 803-957-8226.
Myrtle Beach, South Carolina Office: 2411 N. Oak Street, Founders Centre, Suite 301. P.O. Box 3939.
Telephone: 803-448-3500.
Telecopy: 803-448-3437.

(See Next Column)

MEMBERS OF FIRM

John M. Campbell, Jr.
Russell Z. Plowden

Representative Clients: Anderson Memorial Hospital; BMW, AG; First Union National Bank; Jackson Mills, Inc.; Piedmont Olsen, Inc.; Self Memorial Hospital; Stone Manufacturing Co.; Umbro International, J.V.; Varat Enterprises, Inc.; Wangner Systems, Inc.; J.V.

For Complete List of Firm Personnel, See General Section

For full biographical listings, see the Martindale-Hubbell Law Directory

Wyche, Burgess, Freeman & Parham, Professional Association (AV)

44 East Camperdown Way, P.O. Box 728, 29602-0728
Telephone: 803-242-8200
Telecopier: 803-235-8900

C. Thomas Wyche
Cary H. Hall, Jr.
Eric B. Amstutz

Counsel for: Multimedia, Inc.; Delta Woodside Industries, Inc.; Milliken & Company; Ryan's Family Steak Houses, Inc.; St. Francis Hospital; Span-America Medical Systems, Inc.; Carolina First Bank; KEMET Electronics Corp.; Builder Marts of America, Inc.; One Price Clothing, Inc.

For Complete List of Firm Personnel, See General Section

For full biographical listings, see the Martindale-Hubbell Law Directory

HILTON HEAD ISLAND, Beaufort Co.

Bethea, Jordan & Griffin, P.A. (AV)

Suite 400, Shelter Cove Executive Park, 23-B Shelter Cove Lane, P.O. Drawer 3, 29938-5666
Telephone: 803-785-2171
Fax: 803-686-5991

William L. Bethea, Jr.
Michael L. M. Jordan
Cary S. Griffin
Joseph R. Barker
Stephen S. Bird
Marty D. Propst

Stephen E. Carter
Michael E. Cofield
Robert Deeb
Keith M. Parrella (Not admitted in SC)
William R. Phipps
David J. Tigges (Not admitted in SC)

OF COUNSEL

John C. West
John C. West, Jr. (P.A.)

For full biographical listings, see the Martindale-Hubbell Law Directory

Ruth & MacNeille, Professional Association (AV)

The Anchor Bank Building, 11 Pope Avenue, 29938
Telephone: 803-785-4251
Telex: 988944
Telecopier: 803-686-5404

William A. Ruth

References: NationsBank of South Carolina, N.A.; Anchor Bank; South Carolina National Bank; Chicago Title Insurance Corp.; First American Title Insurance Co.

For full biographical listings, see the Martindale-Hubbell Law Directory

SOUTH DAKOTA

*BROOKINGS,** Brookings Co.

Lewayne M. Erickson, P.C. (AV)

517 Sixth Street, 57006-1436
Telephone: 605-692-6158
Fax: 605-692-7734

Lewayne M. Erickson

For full biographical listings, see the Martindale-Hubbell Law Directory

*SIOUX FALLS,** Minnehaha Co.

Davenport, Evans, Hurwitz & Smith (AV)

513 South Main Avenue, P.O. Box 1030, 57101-1030
Telephone: 605-336-2880
Telecopier: 605-335-3639

MEMBERS OF FIRM

David L. Knudson
Catherine A. Tanck

Counsel for: American Society of Composers, Authors and Publishers (A.S.-C.A.P.); Burlington Northern, Inc.; Continental Insurance Cos.; The First National Bank in Sioux Falls; Ford Motor Credit Co.; General Motors Corp.; The St. Paul Cos.; The Travelers.

(See Next Column)

DAVENPORT, EVANS, HURWITZ & SMITH, *Sioux Falls—Continued*

For Complete List of Firm Personnel, See General Section

For full biographical listings, see the Martindale-Hubbell Law Directory

TENNESSEE

*CHATTANOOGA,** Hamilton Co.

BAKER, DONELSON, BEARMAN & CALDWELL (AV)

1800 Republic Centre, 633 Chestnut Street, 37450-1800
Telephone: 615-752-4400
Telecopier: 615-752-4410
Memphis, Tennessee Office: 20th Floor, First Tennessee Building, 165 Madison, 38103.
Telephone: 901-526-2000.
Telecopier: 901-577-2303.
Nashville, Tennessee Office: 1700 Nashville City Center, 511 Union Street, 37219.
Telephone: 615-726-5600.
Telecopier: 615-726-0464.
Knoxville, Tennessee Office: 2200 Riverview Tower, 900 Gay Street, 37901.
Telephone: 615-549-7000.
Telecopier: 615-525-8569.
Huntsville, Tennessee Office: 3 Courthouse Square, 37756.
Telephone: 615-663-2321.
Telecopier: 615-663-2111.
Johnson City, Tennessee Office: Hamilton Bank Building, 207 Mockingbird Lane, 37604.
Telephone: 615-928-0181.
Telecopier: 615-928-5694; 615-928-3654; Kingsport: 615-246-6191.
Washington, D.C. Office: Market Square, 801 Pennsylvania Avenue, N.W., 20004.
Telephone: 202-508-3400.
Telecopier: 202-508-3402.

PARTNERS

Lewis R. Donelson, III
Thomas A. Caldwell
John C. Mooney
David C. Burger
Carl E. Hartley
Louann Prater Smith
Kenneth C. Beckman

ASSOCIATE

Charles D. McDonald

For Complete List of Firm Personnel, See General Section

For full biographical listings, see the Martindale-Hubbell Law Directory

CHAMBLISS & BAHNER (AV)

1000 Tallan Building, Two Union Square, 37402-2500
Telephone: 615-756-3000
Fax: 615-265-9574

MEMBERS OF FIRM

Kirk Snouffer
Martin L. Pierce
Dana B. Perry

ASSOCIATE

George H. Suzich

General Counsel for: McKee Foods Corporation; SCT Yarns, Inc.; Stein Construction Co., Inc.

For Complete List of Firm Personnel, See General Section

For full biographical listings, see the Martindale-Hubbell Law Directory

GEARHISER, PETERS & HORTON (AV)

320 McCallie Avenue, 37402-2007
Telephone: 615-756-5171
Fax: 615-266-1605

MEMBERS OF FIRM

Charles J. Gearhiser
R. Wayne Peters
William H. Horton
Roy C. Maddox, Jr.
Robert L. Lockaby, Jr.
Ralph E. Tallant, Jr.
Terry Atkin Cavett
Sam D. Elliott
Lane C. Avery
Michael A. Anderson
Wade K. Cannon

ASSOCIATE

Robin L. Miller

References: First Tennessee Bank; Pioneer Bank.

For full biographical listings, see the Martindale-Hubbell Law Directory

HUGH F. KENDALL, ATTORNEY, P.C. (AV)

Suite 305, Victorian Gardens, 6918 Shallowford Road, 37421-1783
Telephone: 615-499-9863
Telecopier: 615-894-0682

(See Next Column)

Hugh F. Kendall

For full biographical listings, see the Martindale-Hubbell Law Directory

SHUMACKER & THOMPSON (AV)

Suite 500, First Tennessee Building, 701 Market Street, 37402-4800
Telephone: 615-265-2214
Telecopier: 615-266-1842
Branch Office: Suite 103, One Park Place, 6148 Lee Highway, Chattanooga, Tennessee, 37421-2900.
Telephone: 615-855-1814.
Telecopier: 615-899-1278.

MEMBERS OF FIRM

Ralph Shumacker
Frank M. Thompson
W. Neil Thomas, Jr.
W. Neil Thomas, III
Ronald I. Feldman
Alan L. Cates
Ross I. Schram III
Stephen P. Parish
William Given Colvin
Harold L. North, Jr.
John K. Culpepper
Jeffery V. Curry
Everett L. Hixson, Jr.
Stanley W. Hildebrand
Phillip E. Fleenor
Donna S. Spurlock
James D. Henderson

ASSOCIATE

Char-La Cain Fowler

For Complete List of Firm Personnel, See General Section

For full biographical listings, see the Martindale-Hubbell Law Directory

SPEARS, MOORE, REBMAN & WILLIAMS (AV)

8th Floor Blue Cross Building, 801 Pine Street, 37402
Telephone: 615-756-7000
Facsimile: 615-756-4801

MEMBERS OF FIRM

William L. Taylor, Jr.
Randy Chennault

Counsel for: Pioneer Bank; Chattanooga Gas Co.; South Central Bell Telephone Co.; Tennessee-American Water Co.; Blue Cross and Blue Shield of Tennessee; State Farm Mutual Automobile Insurance Cos.; Nationwide Insurance Co.; Siskin Steel & Supply Co., Inc.; CSX Transportation, Inc.; The McCallie School; Mueller Co.

For Complete List of Firm Personnel, See General Section

For full biographical listings, see the Martindale-Hubbell Law Directory

STOPHEL & STOPHEL, P.C. (AV)

500 Tallan Building, Two Union Square, 37402-2571
Telephone: 615-756-2333
Fax: 615-266-5032

John C. Stophel
Glenn C. Stophel
Barton C. Burns
Wayne E. Thomas
Donald E. Morton
Harry B. Ray

Tracy C. Wooden

Representative Clients: The National Group, Inc.; Electric Systems, Inc.; Graco Children's Products, Inc.; BHY Concrete Finishing, Inc.; Chattanooga Internal Medicine Group, Inc.; Kimsey/Knight Radiology, P.C.

For Complete List of Firm Personnel, See General Section

For full biographical listings, see the Martindale-Hubbell Law Directory

KINGSPORT, Sullivan Co.

HUNTER, SMITH & DAVIS (AV)

1212 North Eastman Road, P.O. Box 3740, 37664
Telephone: 615-378-8800;
Johnson City: 615-282-4186;
Bristol: 615-968-7604
Telecopier: 615-378-8801
Johnson City, Tennessee Office: Suite 500 First American Center, 208 Sunset Drive, 37604.
Telephone: 615-283-6300.
Telecopier: 615-283-6301.

MEMBER OF FIRM

T. Arthur Scott, Jr.

ASSOCIATE

Rodney S. Klein

LEGAL SUPPORT PERSONNEL

James R. Bowles (CPA; CFP)

Representative Clients: Bristol Regional Medical Center; Medical Laundry of Tri-Cities, Inc.; Publix Food Markets, Inc.; Industrial Gas & Supply, Inc.; The Paty Company; Arcata Graphics; Kingsport Power Co.; Moody Dunbar, Inc.; Holston Builders Supply, Inc.

For Complete List of Firm Personnel, See General Section

For full biographical listings, see the Martindale-Hubbell Law Directory

Kingsport—Continued

WILSON, WORLEY, GAMBLE & WARD, P.C. (AV)

Fourth Floor Heritage Federal Building, 110 East Center Street, P.O. Box 1007, 37662-1007
Telephone: 615-246-8181
FAX: 615-246-2831

Donald G. Ward
Michael D. Stice
James W. Holmes

Assistant Division Counsel for: CSX Transportation, Inc.
Local Counsel for: Eastman Chemical Co.; General Motors Corp.; Holston Valley Hospital and Medical Center; United States Fidelity & Guaranty Co.; Eastman Credit Union; Heritage Federal Bank FSB; Vulcan Materials Co.; AFG Industries, Inc.; K mart Corporation.

For Complete List of Firm Personnel, See General Section

For full biographical listings, see the Martindale-Hubbell Law Directory

*KNOXVILLE,** Knox Co.

BAKER, DONELSON, BEARMAN & CALDWELL (AV)

2200 Riverview Tower, 900 Gay Street, 37901
Telephone: 615-549-7000
Telecopier: 615-525-8569
Memphis, Tennessee Office: 20th Floor, First Tennessee Building, 165 Madison, 38103.
Telephone: 901-526-2000.
Telecopier: 901-577-2303.
Nashville, Tennessee Office: 1700 Nashville City Center, 511 Union Street, 37219.
Telephone: 615-726-5600.
Telecopier: 615-726-0464.
Chattanooga, Tennessee Office: 1800 Republic Centre, 633 Chestnut Street, 37450-1800.
Telephone: 615-752-4400.
Telecopier: 615-752-4410.
Huntsville, Tennessee Office: 3 Courthouse Square, 37756.
Telephone: 615-663-2321.
Telecopier: 615-663-2111.
Johnson City, Tennessee Office: Hamilton Bank Building, 207 Mockingbird Lane, 37604.
Telephone: 615-928-0181.
Telecopier: 615-928-5694; 615-928-3654; Kingsport: 615-246-6191.
Washington, D.C. Office: Market Square, 801 Pennsylvania Avenue, N.W., 20004.
Telephone: 202-508-3400.
Telecopier: 202-508-3402.

PARTNER
Edward A. Cox, Jr.
OF COUNSEL
Durward S. Jones

For Complete List of Firm Personnel, See General Section

For full biographical listings, see the Martindale-Hubbell Law Directory

EGERTON, MCAFEE, ARMISTEAD & DAVIS, P.C. (AV)

500 First American National Bank Center, P.O. Box 2047, 37901
Telephone: 615-546-0500
Fax: 615-525-5293

William W. Davis
Joe M. McAfee
Dan W. Holbrook
William E. McClamroch, III

Jonathan D. Reed

Representative Clients: First American National Bank of Knoxville; Home Federal Bank of Tennessee, F.S.B.; Bush Bros. & Co.; Johnson & Galyon Contractors; Baptist Hospital of East Tennessee; Revco D.S., Inc.; White Realty Corp.; Dick Broadcasting, Inc.

For Complete List of Firm Personnel, See General Section

For full biographical listings, see the Martindale-Hubbell Law Directory

GENTRY, TIPTON, KIZER & LITTLE, P.C. (AV)

2610 Plaza Tower, 800 South Gay Street, 37929
Telephone: 615-525-5300
Telecopy: 615-523-7315

Mack A. Gentry
James S. Tipton, Jr.
W. Morris Kizer
Lawrence E. Little
Timothy M. McLemore
Mark Jendrek
Maurice K. Guinn
F. Scott Milligan

For full biographical listings, see the Martindale-Hubbell Law Directory

MCCAMPBELL & YOUNG, A PROFESSIONAL CORPORATION (AV)

2021 Plaza Tower, P.O. Box 550, 37901-0550
Telephone: 615-637-1440
Telecopier: 615-546-9731

(See Next Column)

Herbert H. McCampbell, Jr. (1905-1974)
F. Graham Bartlett (1920-1982)
Robert S. Young
Lindsay Young
Robert S. Marquis
Robert S. Stone
J. Christopher Kirk
Mark K. Williams

Janie C. Porter
Gregory E. Erickson
R. Scott Elmore
Tammy Kaousias
Benét S. Theiss
Allen W. Blevins

Representative Clients: First National Bank of Knoxville Trust Department; First Tennessee Bank National Association Trust Department; Third National Bank Trust Department; The Trust Company of Knoxville.

For full biographical listings, see the Martindale-Hubbell Law Directory

WAGNER, MYERS & SANGER, A PROFESSIONAL CORPORATION (AV)

1801 Plaza Tower, P.O. Box 1308, 37929
Telephone: 615-525-4600
Fax: 615-524-5731

John R. Seymour
William C. Myers, Jr.
M. Douglas Campbell, Jr.

Representative Clients: Carolina Power & Light Co.; Cullman Electric Cooperative; Diversified Energy, Inc.; Fort Sanders Health Systems; Gatliff Coal Company, Inc.; Martin Marietta Energy Systems, Inc.; North American Rayon Corp.; Regal Cinemas, Inc.; Roddy Vending Co.; Skyline Coal Company.

For Complete List of Firm Personnel, See General Section

For full biographical listings, see the Martindale-Hubbell Law Directory

*MEMPHIS,** Shelby Co.

ARMSTRONG ALLEN PREWITT GENTRY JOHNSTON & HOLMES (AV)

80 Monroe Avenue Suite 700, 38103
Telephone: 901-523-8211
Telecopier: 901-524-4936
Jackson, Missippi Office: 1350 One Jackson Place, 188 East Capitol Street.
Telephone: 601-948-8020.
Telecopier: 601-948-8389.

MEMBERS OF FIRM

Joseph Brent Walker
James Rogers Hall, Jr.

For Complete List of Firm Personnel, See General Section

For full biographical listings, see the Martindale-Hubbell Law Directory

BAKER, DONELSON, BEARMAN & CALDWELL (AV)

20th Floor, First Tennessee Building, 165 Madison, 38103
Telephone: 901-526-2000
Telecopier: 901-577-2303
Nashville, Tennessee Office: 1700 Nashville City Center, 511 Union Street, 37219.
Telephone: 615-726-5600.
Telecopier: 615-726-0464.
Knoxville, Tennessee Office: 2200 Riverview Tower, 900 Gay Street, 37901.
Telephone: 615-549-7000.
Telecopier: 615-525-8569.
Chattanooga, Tennessee Office: 1800 Republic Centre, 633 Chestnut Street, 37450-1800.
Telephone: 615-752-4400.
Telecopier: 615-752-4410.
Huntsville, Tennessee Office: 3 Courthouse Square, 37756.
Telephone: 615-663-2321.
Telecopier: 615-663-2111.
Johnson City, Tennessee Office: Hamilton Bank Building, 207 Mockingbird Lane, 37604.
Telephone: 615-928-0181.
Telecopier: 615-928-5694; 615-928-3654; Kingsport: 615-246-6191.
Washington, D.C. Office: Market Square, 801 Pennsylvania Avenue, N.W., 20004.
Telephone: 202-508-3400.
Telecopier: 202-508-3402.

PARTNERS

Lewis R. Donelson, III
Donald A. Malmo
William H.D. Fones, Jr.
William P. Kenworthy
Ben C. Adams, Jr.
Sheila Jordan Cunningham
David T. Popwell

ASSOCIATES

John R. Gregory
Ruth A. Hillis
W. Douglas Sweet

For Complete List of Firm Personnel, See General Section

For full biographical listings, see the Martindale-Hubbell Law Directory

Memphis—Continued

EUGENE BERNSTEIN, SR. (AV)

5050 Poplar, Suite 2410, 38157
Telephone: 901-684-1652
Telecopier: 901-761-5505

For full biographical listings, see the Martindale-Hubbell Law Directory

THE BOGATIN LAW FIRM (AV)

A Partnership including Professional Corporations
(Formerly Bogatin Lawson & Chiapella)
860 Ridge Lake Boulevard, Suite 360, 38120
Telephone: 901-767-1234
Telecopier: 901-767-2803 & 901-767-4010

MEMBERS OF FIRM

G. Patrick Arnoult
Irvin Bogatin (P.C.)
H. Stephen Brown
Susan Callison (P.C.)
Tillman C. Carroll
Matthew P. Cavitch
John André Chiapella (P.C.)
David J. Cocke
Russell J. Hensley
Arlie C. Hooper
Charles M. Key
William H. Lawson, Jr., (P.C.)
David C. Porteous
Arthur E. Quinn
Thaddeus S. Rodda, Jr., (P.C.)

ASSOCIATES

Robert F. Beckmann
James Q. Carr, II
C. William Denton, Jr.
Thomas M. Federico (Not admitted in TN)
James S. King
John F. Murrah

For full biographical listings, see the Martindale-Hubbell Law Directory

MARTIN, TATE, MORROW & MARSTON, P.C. (AV)

The Falls Building, Suite 1100, 22 North Front Street, 38103-1182
Telephone: 901-522-9000
Telecopier: 901-527-3746

S. Shepherd Tate
W. Thomas Hutton
Jeffrey E. Thompson
Robert E. Orians
Harry J. Skefos

For Complete List of Firm Personnel, See General Section

For full biographical listings, see the Martindale-Hubbell Law Directory

WARING COX (AV)

Morgan Keegan Tower, 50 North Front Street, Suite 1300, 38103-1190
Telephone: 901-543-8000
Telecopy: 901-543-8030

MEMBERS OF FIRM

Clayton D. Smith
James J. McMahon
Shellie G. McCain, Jr.
Douglas P. Quay
Herbert B. Wolf, Jr.
William T. Mays, Jr.

ASSOCIATE

Robert C. Starnes

Representative Clients: Federal Express Corp.; Delta Life and Annuity; Vining-Sparks IBG.

For Complete List of Firm Personnel, See General Section

For full biographical listings, see the Martindale-Hubbell Law Directory

*NASHVILLE,** Davidson Co.

BAKER, DONELSON, BEARMAN & CALDWELL (AV)

1700 Nashville City Center, 511 Union Street, 37219
Telephone: 615-726-5600
Telecopier: 615-726-0464
Memphis, Tennessee Office: 20th Floor, First Tennessee Building, 165 Madison, 38103.
Telephone: 901-526-2000.
Telecopier: 901-577-2303.
Knoxville, Tennessee Office: 2200 Riverview Tower, 900 Gay Street, 37901.
Telephone: 615-549-7000.
Telecopier: 615-525-8569.
Chattanooga, Tennessee Office: 1800 Republic Centre, 633 Chestnut Street, 37450-1800.
Telephone: 615-752-4400.
Telecopier: 615-752-4410.
Huntsville, Tennessee Office: 3 Courthouse Square, 37756.
Telephone: 615-663-2321.
Telecopier: 615-663-2111.
Johnson City, Tennessee Office: Hamilton Bank Building, 207 Mockingbird Lane, 37604.
Telephone: 615-928-0181.
Telecopier: 615-928-5694; 615-928-3654; Kingsport: 615-246-6191.
Washington, D.C. Office: Market Square, 801 Pennsylvania Avenue, N.W., 20004.
Telephone: 202-508-3400.
Telecopier: 202-508-3402.

(See Next Column)

PARTNERS

Richard D. Bird
James T. O'Hare
H. Wynne James, III
Douglas A. Walker

ASSOCIATE

Philip Stuart McSween

For Complete List of Firm Personnel, See General Section

For full biographical listings, see the Martindale-Hubbell Law Directory

BASS, BERRY & SIMS (AV)

2700 First American Center, 37238-2700
Telephone: 615-742-6200
Telecopy: 615-742-6293
Knoxville, Tennessee Office: 1700 Riverview Tower, 900 S. Gay Street, P.O. Box 1509, 37901-1509.
Telephone: 615-521-6200.
Telecopy: 615-521-6234.

MEMBERS OF FIRM

W. W. Berry
James C. Gooch
William W. Berry, Jr.
James W. Berry, Jr.
Richard H. Barry
Michael D. Sontag
Paul J. Kardish
K. Gabriel Heiser

Representative Clients: Ingram Industries; Service Merchandise, Inc.; First American Corporation; DeVlieg-Bullard, Inc.; Massey Burch Investment Group; Thomas Nelson. Inc.; CUC International, Inc.

For full biographical listings, see the Martindale-Hubbell Law Directory

HOLTON & HOWARD, A PROFESSIONAL CORPORATION (AV)

424 Church Street, Suite 2700, 37219
Telephone: 615-256-3338
Telecopier: 615-244-2104

Richard D. Holton
Bryan Howard

William E. Blackstone
Scott E. Swartz
K. Coleman Westbrook, Jr.

Reference: Third National Bank in Nashville.

For full biographical listings, see the Martindale-Hubbell Law Directory

KING & BALLOW (AV)

1200 Noel Place, 200 Fourth Avenue, North, 37219
Telephone: 615-259-3456
Fax: 615-254-7907
San Diego, California Office: 2700 Symphony Towers, 750 B Street, 92101.
Telephone: 619-236-9401.
Fax: 619-236-9437.
San Francisco, California Office: 100 First Street, Suite 2700, 94105.
Telephone: 415-541-7803.
Fax: 415-541-7805.

MEMBERS OF FIRM

Frank S. King, Jr.
Robert L. Ballow
R. Eddie Wayland
Larry D. Crabtree
Alan L. Marx
Paul H. Duvall (Resident, San Diego, California Office)
Steven C. Douse
Douglas R. Pierce
Kenneth E. Douthat
Mark E. Hunt

ASSOCIATES

Katheryn M. Millwee
Patrick M. Thomas
R. Brent Ballow

Representative Clients: Capital Cities/ABC, Inc., New York, New York; Garden State Newspapers, Inc., Woodbury, New Jersey; Gaylord Entertainment Company; Ingram Industries, Inc., Nashville, Tennessee; Opryland, Nashville, Tennessee; Parade Magazine, Inc., New York, New York; NationsBank; Pelikan Corporation, Franklin, Tennessee; Sullivan Graphics, Inc., Nashville, Tennessee; Tribune Company, Chicago, Illinois.

For Complete List of Firm Personnel, See General Section

For full biographical listings, see the Martindale-Hubbell Law Directory

MANIER, HEROD, HOLLABAUGH & SMITH, A PROFESSIONAL CORPORATION (AV)

First Union Tower 2200 One Nashville Place, 150 Fourth Avenue North, 37219-2494
Telephone: 615-244-0030
Telecopier: 615-242-4203

Will R. Manier, Jr. (1885-1953)
Larkin E. Crouch (1882-1948)
Vincent L. Fuqua, Jr. (1930-1974)
J. Olin White (1907-1982)
Miller Manier (1897-1986)
William Edward Herod (1917-1992)
Lewis B. Hollabaugh
Don L. Smith
James M. Doran, Jr.
Stephen E. Cox
J. Michael Franks
Randall C. Ferguson
Terry L. Hill
James David Leckrone
Robert C. Evans
Tommy C. Estes

(See Next Column)

MANIER, HEROD, HOLLABAUGH & SMITH A PROFESSIONAL CORPORATION—*Continued*

B. Gail Reese
Michael E. Evans
Laurence M. Papel
John M. Gillum
Gregory L. Cashion
Sam H. Poteet, Jr.
Samuel Arthur Butts III
David J. Deming
Mark S. LeVan
Richard McCallister Smith
Mary Paty Lynn Jetton
H. Rowan Leathers III
Jefferson C. Orr
William L. Penny

Lawrence B. Hammet II
John H. Rowland
Susan C. West
John E. Quinn
John F. Floyd
Paul L. Sprader
Lela M. Hollabaugh
J. Steven Kirkham
T. Richard Travis
Stephanie M. Jennings
Jerry W. Taylor
C. Benton Patton
Kenneth A. Weber
Phillip Robert Newman
Brett A. Oeser

General Counsel for: McKinnon Bridge Co., Inc.

For full biographical listings, see the Martindale-Hubbell Law Directory

TEXAS

*AMARILLO,** Potter Co.

HINKLE, COX, EATON, COFFIELD & HENSLEY (AV)

1700 Bank One Center, P.O. Box 9238, 79105-9238
Telephone: 806-372-5569
FAX: 806-372-9761
Roswell, New Mexico Office: 700 United Bank Plaza, P. O. Box 10, 88202.
Telephone: 505-622-6510.
FAX: 505-623-9332.
Midland, Texas Office: 6 Desta Drive, Suite 2800, P.O. Box 3580, 79702.
Telephone: 915-683-4691.
FAX: 915-683-6518.
Santa Fe, New Mexico Office: 218 Montezuma, P.O. Box 2068, 87504.
Telephone: 505-982-4554.
FAX: 505-982-8623.
Albuquerque, New Mexico Office: Suite 800, 500 Marquette, N.W., P.O. Box 2043, 87102.
Telephone: 505-768-1500.
FAX: 505-768-1529.
Austin, Texas Office: 401 West 15th Street, Suite 800, 78701.
Telephone: 512-476-7137.
FAX: 512-476-5431.
Associated Office: Hoffman & Stephens, P.C., 401 West 15th Street, Suite 800, 78701.
Telephone: 512-476-5434. Fax; 512-476-5431.

RESIDENT PARTNERS

W. H. Brian, Jr.
Thomas E. Hood

Representative Clients: Aerion Industries, Inc.; Amarillo Diagnostic Clinic; Amarillo Federal Credit Union; Amarillo Health Facilities Corp.; Amarillo National Bank; Chrysler Management Corp.; Conoco, Inc.; Federated Insurance; First Interstate Management Co.; Flowers Cattle Co.

For full biographical listings, see the Martindale-Hubbell Law Directory

*AUSTIN,** Travis Co.

JOHN MCDUFF, P.C. A PROFESSIONAL CORPORATION (AV)

100 Congress Avenue Suite 1817, 78701
Telephone: 512-469-6360
Fax: 512-469-5505

John McDuff

For full biographical listings, see the Martindale-Hubbell Law Directory

MCGINNIS, LOCHRIDGE & KILGORE, L.L.P. (AV)

1300 Capitol Center, 919 Congress Avenue, 78701
Telephone: 512-495-6000
Houston, Texas Office: 3200 One Houston Center, 1221 McKinney Street.
Telephone: 713-615-8500.

OF COUNSEL

Denny O. Ingram

RETIRED OF COUNSEL

Morgan Hunter

MEMBERS OF FIRM

Thomas O. Barton
Theresa G. Eilers
Paul J. Wataha

For Complete List of Firm Personnel, See General Section

For full biographical listings, see the Martindale-Hubbell Law Directory

J. SCOTT MORRIS, P.C. (AV)

701 Brazos, Suite 500, 78701
Telephone: 512-320-9039
Facsimile: 512-320-5821

J. Scott Morris

For full biographical listings, see the Martindale-Hubbell Law Directory

*CORPUS CHRISTI,** Nueces Co.

MATTHEWS & BRANSCOMB, A PROFESSIONAL CORPORATION (AV)

802 North Carancahua, Suite 1900, 78470-0700
Telephone: 512-888-9261
Facsimile: 512-888-8504
Austin, Texas Office: 301 Congress Avenue, Suite 2050.
Telephone: 512-305-4400.
Facsimile: 512-305-4413.
San Antonio, Texas Office: One Alamo Center, 106 S. St. Mary's Street, Suite 800.
Telephone: 210-226-4211.
Facsimile: 210-226-0521.
Telex: 51060009283. Cable Code: MBLAW.
Eagle Pass, Texas Office: 675 Main Street.
Telephone: 210-773-6700.
Facsimile: 210-757-4045.
Uvalde, Texas Office: 200 E. Nopal #208.
Telephone: 210-278-4597.
Facsimile: 210-278-4806.
(Associated with Hall, Quintanilla & Alarcon, L.C., Laredo, Texas, under the name of Hall, Quintanilla, Alarcon, Matthews & Branscomb, P.L.L.C.).

Harvie Branscomb, Jr.
Michael W. Stukenberg
Kenton E. McDonald
Gerald E. Thornton, Jr.

For Complete List of Firm Personnel, See General Section

For full biographical listings, see the Martindale-Hubbell Law Directory

*DALLAS,** Dallas Co.

CARRINGTON, COLEMAN, SLOMAN & BLUMENTHAL, L.L.P. (AV)

200 Crescent Court, Suite 1500, 75201
Telephone: 214-855-3000
Telecopy: 214-855-1333

MEMBERS OF FIRM

Robert L. Blumenthal
Ronald M. Weiss
Michael A. Peterson

COUNSEL

Diane W. Bricker

ASSOCIATE

Robert H. Botts, Jr.

For Complete List of Firm Personnel, See General Section

For full biographical listings, see the Martindale-Hubbell Law Directory

GINSBERG AND BRUSILOW, P.C. (AV)

750 Signature Place, 14785 Preston Road, 75240
Telephone: 214-788-1600
Telecopy: 214-702-0662

Michael D. Ginsberg
David E. Brusilow
Michael H. Saks
Paul B. Sander
Terry A. Douglas
Gene F. Stevens
Susan Beilharz
John P. Neihouse
Teresa L. Bishop

OF COUNSEL

Alan J. Harlan

For full biographical listings, see the Martindale-Hubbell Law Directory

GODWIN & CARLTON, A PROFESSIONAL CORPORATION (AV)

Suite 3300, 901 Main Street, 75202-3714
Telephone: 214-939-4400
Telecopier: 214-760-7332
Monterrey, Mexico Correspondent: Quintero y Quintero Abogodos. Martin De Zalva 840-3 Sur Esquinna Con Hidalgo.
Telephone: 44-07-74, 44-07-80, 44-06-56, 44-06-28.
Fax: 83-40-34-54.

James G. Vetter, Jr.
Bob J. Shelton
William F. Pyne

James L. Kissire

For Complete List of Firm Personnel, See General Section

For full biographical listings, see the Martindale-Hubbell Law Directory

Dallas—Continued

HUGHES & LUCE, L.L.P. (AV)

A Registered Limited Liability Partnership including Professional Corporations
1717 Main Street, Suite 2800, 75201
Telephone: 214-939-5500
Fax: 214-939-6100
Telex: 730836
Austin, Texas Office: 111 Congress, Suite 900.
Telephone: 512-482-6800.
Fax: 512-482-6859.
Houston, Texas Office: Three Allen Center, 333 Clay Street, Suite 3800.
Telephone: 713-754-5200.
Fax: 713-754-5206.
Fort Worth, Texas Office: 2421 Westport Parkway, Suite 500A.
Telephone: 817-439-3000.
Fax: 817-439-4222.

MEMBERS OF FIRM

Jeff W. Dorrill
Scott C. Drablos
Jay H. Hebert
Kathryn G. Henkel
Vester T. Hughes, Jr.
Cynthia Morgan Ohlenforst
David L. Sinak

ASSOCIATES

Arthur T. Catterall
Elizabeth R. Turner

STAFF ATTORNEY

Michael L. Kaufman

For Complete List of Firm Personnel, See General Section

For full biographical listings, see the Martindale-Hubbell Law Directory

JACKSON & WALKER, L.L.P. (AV)

901 Main Street, Suite 6000, 75202-3797
Telephone: 214-953-6000
Fax: 214-953-5822
Fort Worth, Texas Office: 777 Main Street, Suite 1800.
Telephone: 817-334-7200.
Fax: 817-334-7290.
Houston, Texas Office: 1100 Louisiana, Suite 4200.
Telephone: 713-752-4200.
Fax: 713-752-4221.
San Antonio, Texas Office: 112 E. Pecan Street, Suite 2100.
Telephone: 210-978-7700.
Fax: 210-978-7790.

MEMBERS OF FIRM

Larry L. Bean
James R. Griffin
R. Thomas Groves, Jr.
William H. Hornberger
William D. Jordan
John J. Klein

OF COUNSEL

W. Orrin Miller
Samuel G. Winstead

ASSOCIATES

Deborah Frome Hare
Robert A. Hawkins
Ann E. Ward

Representative Clients Furnished Upon Request.

For Complete List of Firm Personnel, See General Section

For full biographical listings, see the Martindale-Hubbell Law Directory

MEADOWS, OWENS, COLLIER, REED, COUSINS & BLAU, L.L.P. (AV)

3700 NationsBank Plaza, 901 Main Street, 75202-3792
Telephone: 214-744-3700
Telecopier: 214-747-3732
Wats: 1-800-451-0093

MEMBERS OF FIRM

Charles M. Meadows, Jr.
Rodney J. Owens
Robert Don Collier
David N. Reed
Thomas G. Hineman
William R. Cousins, III
Charles W. Blau
George R. Bedell
Michael E. McCue
Lauren C. LaRue

ASSOCIATES

Joel N. Crouch
Alan K. Davis
Fielder F. Nelms
Patricia King Dorey
Jeffrey C. Adams
Frank E. Sheeder, III
Robert M. Bolton
Michael Todd Welty
Lisa R. Newman

For full biographical listings, see the Martindale-Hubbell Law Directory

NOVAKOV, DAVIDSON & FLYNN, A PROFESSIONAL CORPORATION (AV)

2000 St. Paul Place, 750 North St. Paul, 75201-3286
Telephone: 214-922-9221
Telecopy: 214-969-7557

(See Next Column)

Daniel P. Novakov
Steven D. Erdahl

For Complete List of Firm Personnel, See General Section

For full biographical listings, see the Martindale-Hubbell Law Directory

THOMPSON & KNIGHT, A PROFESSIONAL CORPORATION (AV)

(Attorneys and Counselors)
1700 Pacific Avenue Suite 3300, 75201
Telephone: 214-969-1700
Telecopy: 214-969-1751
Cable Address: "Tomtex"
Telex: 732298
Austin, Texas Office: 1200 San Jacinto Center, 98 San Jacinto Boulevard, 78701.
Telephone: 512-469-6100.
Telecopy: 512-469-6180.
Fort Worth, Texas Office: 801 Cherry Street, Suite 1600, 76102.
Telephone: 817-347-1700.
Telecopy: 817-347-1799.
Houston, Texas Office: 1700 Texas Commerce Tower, 600 Travis, 77002.
Telephone: 713-217-2800.
Telecopy: 713-217-2828.
Monterrey, Mexico Office: Edificio Losoles PD-4, Av. Lázaro Cárdenas No. 2400 Pte., San Pedro Garza Garcia, Nuevo Léon C.P. 66220.
Telephone: (52-8) 363-0096.
Telecopy: (52-8) 363-3067.

SHAREHOLDERS

Margaret S. Alford
Buford P. Berry
Barbara B. Ferguson
Sharon M. Fountain
Dennis J. Grindinger
Russell G. Gully
Thornton Hardie III
James B. Harris
John Michael Holt
Samuel E. Long, Jr.
P. Mike McCullough
Emily A. Parker
Rust E. Reid
James Y. Robb III
David M. Rosenberg
Joe A. Rudberg

ASSOCIATES

Johnny R. Buckles
John R. Cohn
Mary A. McNulty
D'Ana Howard Mikeska
Kirkmichael T. Moore
William R. Mureiko
R. David Wheat
Shelly A. Youree

OF COUNSEL

J. W. Bullion
William E. Collins
Terry L. Simmons

For Complete List of Firm Personnel, See General Section

For full biographical listings, see the Martindale-Hubbell Law Directory

WILSON, WHITE & COPELAND (AV)

2300 Republic Tower II, 325 North St. Paul, 75201-3802
Telephone: 214-742-8422
Telecopier: 214-922-9746

Claude R. Wilson, Jr.
Kemble White
John D. Copeland

ASSOCIATE

S. Cameron Graber

OF COUNSEL

Geo. Garrison Potts

For full biographical listings, see the Martindale-Hubbell Law Directory

*EL PASO,** El Paso Co.

KEMP, SMITH, DUNCAN & HAMMOND, A PROFESSIONAL CORPORATION (AV)

2000 State National Bank Plaza, 79901, P.O. Drawer 2800, 79999
Telephone: 915-533-4424
Fax: 915-546-5360
Albuquerque, New Mexico Office: 500 Marquette, N.W., Suite 1200, P.O. Box 1276.
Telephone: 505-247-2315.
Fax: 505-764-5480.

Robert B. Zaboroski
Roger D. Aksamit
Allan M. Goldfarb

OF COUNSEL

Joseph P. Hammond

Attorneys for: Circle K Corporation; Property Trust of America; Tony Lama Co.; Sun World Corporation.

For Complete List of Firm Personnel, See General Section

For full biographical listings, see the Martindale-Hubbell Law Directory

*FORT WORTH,** Tarrant Co.

CANTEY & HANGER (AV)

A Registered Limited Liability Partnership
2100 Burnett Plaza, 801 Cherry Street, 76102-6899
Telephone: 817-877-2800, Metro Line: 429-3815
Telex: 758631 FAX: 877-2807
Dallas
Dallas, Texas Office: Suite 500, 300 Crescent Court.
Telephone: 214-978-4100.
FAX: 214-978-4150.

MEMBERS OF FIRM

Whitfield J. Collins
Allan Howeth
Harry E. Bartel
Kirk R. Manning
David C. Bakutis
Noel C. Ice

ASSOCIATES

R. Dyann McCully
Joel T. Sawyer
Michael G. Appleman

Represent: General Motors Corp.; Texas-New Mexico Power Co.; Miller Brewing Co.; The Medical Protective Co.; Union Oil Co.; Texas Utilities Electric Co.; NationsBank of Texas, N.A.; Union Pacific Resources; Kimbell Art Foundation; Texas Commerce Bank.

For Complete List of Firm Personnel, See General Section

For full biographical listings, see the Martindale-Hubbell Law Directory

H. ELDRIDGE DICKEY, JR. (AV)

Sundance Courtyard, 115 West Second Street, Suite 204, 76102
Telephone: 817-336-3006
FAX: 817-336-3211

For full biographical listings, see the Martindale-Hubbell Law Directory

MICHENER, LARIMORE, SWINDLE, WHITAKER, FLOWERS, SAWYER, REYNOLDS & CHALK, L.L.P. (AV)

3500 City Center Tower II, 301 Commerce Street, 76102
Telephone: 817-335-4417
Telecopy: 817-335-6935

MEMBERS OF FIRM

John W. Michener, Jr.
Tom L. Larimore
Mack Ed Swindle
Wayne M. Whitaker
H. David Flowers
Jerry K. Sawyer
James G. Reynolds
John Allen Chalk

Thomas S. Brandon, Jr.
Matthew P. McDonald
Clark R. Cowley
Thomas F. Harkins, Jr.
Geno E. Borchardt
John A. Chalk, Jr.
Leslie Combs
Suzanne S. Miskin
Robert G. West
Theresa Brewton Lyons
Jonathan K. Henderson
David R. Childress

OF COUNSEL

Jerry D. Minton

For full biographical listings, see the Martindale-Hubbell Law Directory

THOMPSON & KNIGHT, A PROFESSIONAL CORPORATION (AV)

(Attorneys and Counselors)
801 Cherry Street, Suite 1600, 76102
Telephone: 817-347-1700
Telecopy: 817-347-1799
Dallas, Texas Office: 1700 Pacific Avenue, Suite 3300, 75201.
Telephone: 214-969-1700.
Telecopy: 214-969-1751.
Cable Address: "Tomtex."
Telex: 732298.
Austin, Texas Office: 1200 San Jacinto Center, 98 San Jacinto Boulevard, 78701.
Telephone: 512-469-6100.
Telecopy: 512-469-6180.
Houston, Texas Office: 1700 Texas Commerce Tower, 600 Travis, 77002.
Telephone: 713-217-2800.
Telecopy: 713-217-2828; 713-2882.
Monterrey, Mexico Office: Edificio Losoles PD-4, Av. Lázaro Cárdenas No. 2400 Pte., San Pedro Garza Garcia, Nuevo Léon C.P. 66220.
Telephone: (52-8) 363-0096.
Telecopy: (52-8) 363-3067.

SHAREHOLDERS

R Gordon Appleman

For Complete List of Firm Personnel, See General Section

For full biographical listings, see the Martindale-Hubbell Law Directory

*HOUSTON,** Harris Co.

BAKER & BOTTS, L.L.P. (AV)

One Shell Plaza, 910 Louisiana, 77002
Telephone: 713-229-1234
Cable Address: "Boterlove"
Fax: 713-229-1522
Washington, D.C. Office: The Warner, 1299 Pennsylvania Avenue, N.W.
Telephone: 202-639-7700.
New York, New York Office: 885 Third Avenue, Suite 2000.
Telephone: 212-705-5000.
Austin, Texas Office: 1600 San Jacinto Center, 98 San Jacinto Boulevard.
Telephone: 512-322-2500.
Dallas, Texas Office: 2001 Ross Avenue.
Telephone: 214-953-6500.
Moscow, Russian Federation Office: 10 ul. Pushkinskaya, 103031.
Telephone: 7095/921-5300 (Local); 7095/929-7070 (International).

MEMBERS OF FIRM

William C. Griffith
Stanley C. Beyer
Benjamin G. Wells
John Edward Neslage
James R. Raborn
Gray Jennings
Gregory V. Nelson
Stuart F. Schaffer
Gail Woodson Stewart
Gerard A. Desrochers

ASSOCIATES

Michael P. Bresson
T. Chuck Campbell
Lynne Harkel-Rumford
Laura C. Higley
Richard Allen Husseini
Daniel Harris Kroll
Susan Davenport Letney
Tracee Kennedy Lewis
Lori McFarlin Troutman
Beverly A. Young

For Complete List of Firm Personnel, See General Section

For full biographical listings, see the Martindale-Hubbell Law Directory

THOMAS E. BERRY & ASSOCIATES (AV)

225 Houston Club Building, 811 Rusk Avenue, 77002-2811
Telephone: 713-223-8061
Fax: 713-223-4638

Betty B. Moser
Anne Hardiman
Gary M. Howell

For full biographical listings, see the Martindale-Hubbell Law Directory

VINSON & ELKINS L.L.P. (AV)

2300 First City Tower, 1001 Fannin, 77002-6760
Telephone: 713-758-2222
Fax: 713-758-2346
International Telex: 6868314
Cable Address: Vinelkins
Austin, Texas Office: One American Center, 600 Congress Avenue.
Telephone: 512-495-8400.
Fax: 512-495-8612.
Dallas, Texas Office: 3700 Trammell Crow Center, 2001 Ross Avenue.
Telephone: 214-220-7700.
Fax: 214-220-7716.
Washington, D.C. Office: The Willard Office Building, 1455 Pennsylvania Avenue, N.W.
Telephone: 202-639-6500.
Fax: 202-639-6604.
Cable Address: Vinelkins.
London, England Office: 47 Charles Street, Berkeley Square, London, W1X 7PB, England.
Telephone: 011 (44-171) 491-7236.
Fax: 011 (44-71) 499-5320.
Cable Address: Vinelkins London W.1.
Moscow, Russian Federation Office: 16 Alexey Tolstoy Street, Second Floor, Moscow, 103001 Russian Federation.
Telephone: 011 (70-95) 956-1995.
Telecopy: 011 (70-95) 956-1996.
Mexico City, Mexico Office: Aristóteles 77, 5°Piso, Colonia Chapultepec Polanco, 11560 Mexico, D.F.
Telephone: (52-5) 280-7828.
Fax: (52-5) 280-9223.
Singapore Office: 50 Raffles Place, #19-05 Shell Tower, 0104. U.S. Voice Mailbox: 713-758-3500.
Telephone: (65) 536-8300.
Fax: (65) 536-8311.

Gary P. Amaon
Roger L. Beebe
Brian R. Bloom
Sarah A. Duckers
G. Edward Ellison
George M. Gerachis (U.S. Liaison for Mexico City, Mexico Office)
Steven H. Gerdes
R. Todd Greenwalt
Robert M. Hopson
Carol H. Jewett
Yolanda Chávez Knull
John W. Leggett
John E. Lynch
L. Price Manford
Thomas P. Marinis, Jr.
Edward C. Osterberg, Jr.
Alan J. Robin
Glen A. Rosenbaum

(See Next Column)

VINSON & ELKINS L.L.P., *Houston—Continued*

C. Boone Schwartzel	Eric Viehman
Robert A. Seale, Jr.	Donald F. Wood

HOUSTON OF COUNSEL

Stanley M. Johanson	James D. Penny

ASSOCIATES

Henry Binder	Karey Dubiel Dye
Judith M. Blissard	Bryan W. Lee
Mark A. Bodron	William R. Leighton
Carrie L. Brandon	Tina Kyle Livingston
Dusty Burke	Pamela Hays Stabler
Herman Mallory Caldwell	Jeanne Klinefelter Trippon

For Complete List of Firm Personnel, See General Section

For full biographical listings, see the Martindale-Hubbell Law Directory

*MIDLAND,** Midland Co.

LYNCH, CHAPPELL & ALSUP, A PROFESSIONAL CORPORATION (AV)

The Summit, Suite 700, 300 North Marienfeld, 79701
Telephone: 915-683-3351
Fax: 915-683-2587

Steven C. Lindgren	W. Scott Ryburn

Representative Clients: Tom Brown, Inc.; NationsBank of Texas, N.A.; Parker & Parsley Development Company; Chevron U.S.A. Inc.; Texas National Bank of Midland; Wagner & Brown, Ltd.

For Complete List of Firm Personnel, See General Section

For full biographical listings, see the Martindale-Hubbell Law Directory

*SAN ANTONIO,** Bexar Co.

COX & SMITH INCORPORATED (AV)

112 East Pecan Street, Suite 1800, 78205
Telephone: 210-554-5500
Telecopier: 210-226-8395

William H. Lester, Jr.	Lee S. Garsson

Robert W. Nelson

OF COUNSEL

Jack Guenther

Representative Clients: International Bank of Commerce; Karena Hotels Texas, Inc.; Kinetic Concepts, Inc.; Solo Serve Corporation; Southwest Venture Partnerships.

For Complete List of Firm Personnel, See General Section

For full biographical listings, see the Martindale-Hubbell Law Directory

CROMAN ● GIBBS ● SCHWARTZMAN (AV)

A Partnership including Professional Corporations
5717 Northwest Parkway, 78249
Telephone: 210-691-2999
Fax: 210-691-1939

Earl L. Croman (P.C.)	Larry W. Gibbs (P.C.)

Mark A. Schwartzman

For full biographical listings, see the Martindale-Hubbell Law Directory

MATTHEWS & BRANSCOMB, A PROFESSIONAL CORPORATION (AV)

One Alamo Center, 106 S. St. Mary's Street, Suite 800, 78205
Telephone: 210-226-4211
Facsimile: 210-226-0521
Telex: 5106009283
Cable Code: MBLAW
Austin, Texas Office: 301 Congress Avenue, Suite 2050.
Telephone: 512-305-4400.
Facsimile: 512-305-4413.
Corpus Christi, Texas Office: 802 N. Carancahua, Suite 1900.
Telephone: 512-888-9261.
Facsimile: 512-888-8504.
Eagle Pass, Texas Office: 675 Main Street.
Telephone: 210-773-6700.
Facsimile: 210-757-4045.
Uvalde, Texas Office: 200 E. Nopal #208.
Telephone: 210-278-4597.
Facsimile: 210-278-4806.
(Associated with Hall, Quintanilla & Alarcon, L.C., Laredo, Texas, under the name of Hall, Quintanilla, Alarcon, Matthews & Branscomb, P.L.L.C.)

Richard E. Goldsmith	Farley P. Katz
Charles J. Muller, III	Mary M. Potter
Frank Z. Ruttenberg	Anthony E. Rebollo

Representative Clients: Coca Cola Bottling Company of the Southwest; Concord Oil Co.; Ellison Enterprises, Inc.; H. E. Butt Grocery Co.; Frank B. Hall & Co., Inc.; The Hearst Corp., San Antonio Light Division; San Antonio Gas & Electric Utilities (City Board); Southern Pacific Transportation Co.; Southwest Texas Methodist Hospital.

(See Next Column)

For Complete List of Firm Personnel, See General Section

For full biographical listings, see the Martindale-Hubbell Law Directory

SCHOENBAUM, CURPHY & SCANLAN, P.C. (AV)

NationsBank Plaza, Suite 1775, 300 Convent Street, 78205-3744
Telephone: 210-224-4491
Fax: 210-224-7983

Stanley Schoenbaum	Alfred G. Holcomb
R. James Curphy	Banks M. Smith
William Scanlan, Jr.	R. Bradley Oxford

Darin N. Digby

Patricia Flora Sitchler	Emily Harrison Liljenwall

Susan L. Saeger

For full biographical listings, see the Martindale-Hubbell Law Directory

TEXARKANA, Bowie Co.

PATTON, HALTOM, ROBERTS, McWILLIAMS & GREER, L.L.P. (AV)

A Registered Limited Liability Partnership including Professional Corporations
700 Texarkana National Bank Building, P.O. Box 1928, 75504-1928
Telephone: 903-794-3341
Fax: 903-792-6542; 903-792-0448

William B. Roberts	Fred R. Norton, Jr.

Representative Clients: Allstate Insurance Co.; Aetna Casualty & Surety Co.; Royal Insurance Group; Continental Insurance Group; Ranger/Pan American Insurance Cos.; The Hanover Insurance Group; American Mutual Liability Insurance Co.; American Hardware Mutual Insurance Co.; Kemper Insurance Co.; Texarkana National Bancshares, Inc.

For Complete List of Firm Personnel, See General Section

For full biographical listings, see the Martindale-Hubbell Law Directory

*TYLER,** Smith Co.

ROBERT M. BANDY, P.C. (AV)

NationsBank Plaza Tower, Suite 1122, 75702-7252
Telephone: 903-592-7333
800-374-2263
FAX: 903-592-7751
Dallas, Texas Office: University Tower, Suite 314, 6440 North Central Expressway.
Telephone: 214-480-8220.
Longview, Texas Office: 703 N. Green, 75606.
Telephone: 903-757-7506.
Fax: 903-592-7751.

Robert M. Bandy

William H. Lively, Jr.

For full biographical listings, see the Martindale-Hubbell Law Directory

UTAH

*SALT LAKE CITY,** Salt Lake Co.

CALLISTER, NEBEKER & McCULLOUGH, A PROFESSIONAL CORPORATION (AV)

800 Kennecott Building, 84133
Telephone: 801-530-7300
Telecopier: 801-364-9127

Leland S. McCullough	Charles M. Bennett
Jeffrey N. Clayton	W. Waldan Lloyd

Craig F. McCullough

Douglas K. Cummings

Representative Clients: Zions Bancorporation; WordPerfect Corporation; Novell, Inc.; Sinclair Oil (Little America); Nu Skin International, Inc.; Flying J Inc.

For Complete List of Firm Personnel, See General Section

For full biographical listings, see the Martindale-Hubbell Law Directory

Salt Lake City—Continued

PARSONS BEHLE & LATIMER, A PROFESSIONAL CORPORATION (AV)

One Utah Center, 201 South Main Street, Suite 1800, P.O. Box 45898, 84145-0898
Telephone: 801-532-1234
Telecopy: 801-536-6111

J. Gordon Hansen
Kent W. Winterholler
Kent B. Alderman
Randy M. Grimshaw
Lawrence R. Barusch
Maxwell A. Miller
Robert C. Delahunty
Stuart A. Fredman
Richard M. Marsh
Jo Ann Lippe (Not admitted in UT)
K. C. Jensen
Jeremy E. Wenokur

Representative Clients: Hercules, Inc.; Kennecott Corporation; The Coastal Corporation; Utah Mining Association, Inc.; Wal-Mart Stores, Inc.

For full biographical listings, see the Martindale-Hubbell Law Directory

PRINCE, YEATES & GELDZAHLER (AV)

City Centre I, Suite 900, 175 East 400 South, 84111
Telephone: 801-524-1000
Fax: 801-524-1099
Park City, Utah Office: 614 Main Street, P.O. Box 38.
Telephones: 801-524-1000; 649-7440.

MEMBERS OF FIRM

Robert M. Yeates
John M. Bradley
Geoffrey W. Mangum

Representative Clients: Boyles Bros. Drilling Co.; CrossLand Savings FSB; Marker International/U.S.A.; Norton Co.; Northern Outfitters; Park City Ski Resort.
Labor Matters: Intermountain Retail Health & Welfare, Pension.

For Complete List of Firm Personnel, See General Section

For full biographical listings, see the Martindale-Hubbell Law Directory

RAY, QUINNEY & NEBEKER, A PROFESSIONAL CORPORATION (AV)

Suite 400 Deseret Building, 79 South Main Street, P.O. Box 45385, 84145-0385
Telephone: 801-532-1500
Telecopier: 801-532-7543
Provo, Utah Office: 210 First Security Bank Building, 92 North University Avenue.
Telephone: 801-226-7210.
Telecopier: 801-375-8379.

Alonzo W. Watson, Jr.
Clark P. Giles
Robert M. Graham
Narrvel E. Hall
Herbert C. Livsey
William A. Marshall
Gerald T. Snow
Allen L. Orr
Bruce L. Olson
Lester K. Essig

Sylvia I. Iannucci

Representative Clients: First Security Corporation and banking affiliates; Zions Cooperative Mercantile Institution; Intermountain Power Agency; George S. & Dolores Dore' Eccles Foundation; Morton International; Santa Fe Southern Pacific Corp., its subsidiaries, and Southern Pacific Transportation Co.; Sorenson Development, Inc.; Holy Cross Hospital and Health System; ; John Price Associates, Inc.; Sanders Ranches Inc.

For Complete List of Firm Personnel, See General Section

For full biographical listings, see the Martindale-Hubbell Law Directory

RICHARDS, BRANDT, MILLER & NELSON, A PROFESSIONAL CORPORATION (AV)

Suite 700 50 South Main Street, P.O. Box 2465, 84110
Telephone: 801-531-2000
Fax: 801-532-5506

Robert W. Brandt
Robert W. Miller (1940-1983)
P. Keith Nelson
Gary D. Stott
Robert L. Stevens
David L. Barclay
John L. Young
Brett F. Paulsen
David K. Lauritzen
Lynn S. Davies
Robert G. Gilchrist
Russell C. Fericks
Michael K. Mohrman
Michael N. Emery
Michael P. Zaccheo
Gary L. Johnson
Curtis J. Drake
George T. Naegle
Craig C. Coburn
Lloyd A. Hardcastle

JoAnn E. Carnahan
Brad C. Betebenner
Robert G. Wright
Barbara K. Berrett
Nathan R. Hyde
Christian W. Nelson
Craig Aramaki
Elizabeth A. Hruby-Mills
Bret M. Hanna (Not admitted in UT)

(See Next Column)

OF COUNSEL

William S. Richards
Wallace R. Lauchnor

Reference: Key Bank of Utah.

For full biographical listings, see the Martindale-Hubbell Law Directory

VAN COTT, BAGLEY, CORNWALL & MCCARTHY, A PROFESSIONAL CORPORATION (AV)

Suite 1600, 50 South Main Street, P.O. Box 45340, 84145
Telephone: 801-532-3333
Telex: 453149
Telecopier: 801-534-0058
Ogden, Utah Office: Suite 900, 2404 Washington Boulevard.
Telephone: 801-394-5783.
Park City, Utah Office: 314 Main Street, Suite 205.
Telephone: 801-649-3889.
Reno, Nevada Office: Jeppson & Lee, 100 West Liberty, Suite 990.
Telephone: 702-333-6800.

David E. Salisbury
Stephen D. Swindle
Alan F. Mecham
J. Keith Adams
Richard C. Skeen
Steven D. Woodland
Richard H. Johnson, II
S. Robert Bradley
Gregory N. Barrick
Douglas A. Taggart (Resident, Ogden, Utah Office)

Susan Pierce Lawrence
David E. Sloan

For Complete List of Firm Personnel, See General Section

For full biographical listings, see the Martindale-Hubbell Law Directory

VERMONT

*BURLINGTON,** Chittenden Co.

GRAVEL AND SHEA, A PROFESSIONAL CORPORATION (AV)

Corporate Plaza, 76 St. Paul Street, P.O. Box 369, 05402-0369
Telephone: 802-658-0220
Fax: 802-658-1456

Charles T. Shea
Stephen R. Crampton
William G. Post, Jr.
Peter S. Erly

Stephen P. Magowan

OF COUNSEL

Clarke A. Gravel

SPECIAL COUNSEL

Norman Williams

For Complete List of Firm Personnel, See General Section

For full biographical listings, see the Martindale-Hubbell Law Directory

LISMAN & LISMAN, A PROFESSIONAL CORPORATION (AV)

84 Pine Street, P.O. Box 728, 05402-0728
Telephone: 802-864-5756
Fax: 802-864-3629

Carl H. Lisman
Allen D. Webster
Mary G. Kirkpatrick
E. William Leckerling, III
Douglas K. Riley

Judith Lillian Dillon
Richard W. Kozlowski

OF COUNSEL

Bernard Lisman
Louis Lisman

For full biographical listings, see the Martindale-Hubbell Law Directory

MILLER, EGGLESTON & ROSENBERG, LTD. (AV)

150 South Champlain Street, P.O. Box 1489, 05402-1489
Telephone: 802-864-0880
Telecopier: 802-864-0328

Martin K. Miller
Jon R. Eggleston

Mark A. Saunders

For Complete List of Firm Personnel, See General Section

For full biographical listings, see the Martindale-Hubbell Law Directory

SHEEHEY BRUE GRAY & FURLONG, PROFESSIONAL CORPORATION (AV)

119 South Winooski Avenue, P.O. Box 66, 05402
Telephone: 802-864-9891
Facsimile: 802-864-6815

(See Next Column)

SHEEHEY BRUE GRAY & FURLONG PROFESSIONAL CORPORATION, *Burlington—Continued*

William B. Gray (1942-1994)
David T. Austin
R. Jeffrey Behm
Nordahl L. Brue
Michael G. Furlong
Ralphine Newlin O'Rourke
Donald J. Rendall, Jr.
Christina Schulz
Paul D. Sheehey
Peter H. Zamore

Rebecca L. Owen

Representative Client: Green Mountain Power Corp.

For full biographical listings, see the Martindale-Hubbell Law Directory

VIRGINIA

ALEXANDRIA, (Independent City)

E. MICHAEL PATURIS (AV)

Lee Street Square, 431 North Lee Street, 22314-2301
Telephone: 703-836-2501
Facsimile: 703-836-4487

For full biographical listings, see the Martindale-Hubbell Law Directory

*CHARLOTTESVILLE,** (Ind. City; Seat of Albemarle Co.)

MICHIE, HAMLETT, LOWRY, RASMUSSEN AND TWEEL, P.C. (AV)

Suite 300, 500 Court Square Building, P.O. Box 298, 22902-0298
Telephone: 804-977-3390
Facsimile: 804-295-0681

Thomas J. Michie, Jr.
Leroy R. Hamlett, Jr.
James P. Cox, III

Representative Clients: NationsBank of Virginia, N.A.; Central Telephone Company of Virginia; Virginia Power; Ohio Casualty Co.; Sears Roebuck & Co.; Muhammad Ali; The Mitchie Co.; General Electric Capital Corp.; Bourne Leisure Group, Ltd.; Edgcomb Metals Co.

For Complete List of Firm Personnel, See General Section

For full biographical listings, see the Martindale-Hubbell Law Directory

ROBERT M. MUSSELMAN & ASSOCIATES (AV)

413 7th Street, N.E., P.O. Box 254, 22902
Telephone: 804-977-4500
Fax: 804-293-5727

ASSOCIATES

Carolyn C. Musselman
Douglas E. Little
Rose Marie Downs
Matthew A. Fass

For full biographical listings, see the Martindale-Hubbell Law Directory

*FAIRFAX,** (Ind. City; Seat of Fairfax Co.)

ODIN, FELDMAN & PITTLEMAN, P.C. (AV)

9302 Lee Highway, Suite 1100, 22031
Telephone: 703-218-2100
Facsimile: 703-218-2160

James B. Pittleman
John S. Wisiackas
David J. Brewer
Thomas J. Shaughnessy
David A. Lawrence
Robert A. Hickey
Robert G. Nath
John P. Dedon

Representative Clients: Upper Occoquan Sewage Authority; National Wildlife Federation; The Hair Cuttery; The Bank of the Potomac; Stewart Title and Escrow, Inc.; Software, A.G. of North America, Inc.; Recovermat Technologies, Inc.; Seaward International, Inc.

For Complete List of Firm Personnel, See General Section

For full biographical listings, see the Martindale-Hubbell Law Directory

*HARRISONBURG,** (Ind. City; Seat of Rockingham Co.)

WHARTON, ALDHIZER & WEAVER, P.L.C. (AV)

100 South Mason Street, 22801
Telephone: 703-434-0316
Fax: 703-434-5502

Donald E. Showalter
John W. Flora
Jeffrey G. Lenhart
Phillip C. Stone, Jr.
Mark W. Botkin
David A. Temeles, Jr.

Representative Clients: Bowman Apple Products, Inc.; Bridgewater College; ComSonics, Inc.; Eastern Mennonite College; First Union National Bank of Virginia; Mennonite Board of Missions; Packaging Services, Inc.; Rocco Enterprises, Inc.; Rockingham Memorial Hospital; WLR Foods, Inc.

(See Next Column)

For Complete List of Firm Personnel, See General Section

For full biographical listings, see the Martindale-Hubbell Law Directory

MCLEAN, Fairfax Co.

H. CLAYTON COOK, JR. (AV)

1011 Langley Hill Drive, 22101
Telephone: 703-821-2468
Rapifax: 703-821-2469
Washington, D.C. Office: 2828 Pennsylvania Avenue, N.W. 20007.
Telephone: 202-338-8088.
Rapifax: 202-338-1843.

For full biographical listings, see the Martindale-Hubbell Law Directory

NORFOLK, (Independent City)

VANDEVENTER, BLACK, MEREDITH & MARTIN (AV)

500 World Trade Center, 23510
Telephone: 804-446-8600
Cable Address: "Hughsvan"
Telex: 823-671
Telecopier: 446-8670
North Carolina, Kitty Hawk Office: 6 Juniper Trail.
Telephone: 919-261-5055.
Fax: 919-261-8444.
London, England Office: Suite 692, Level 6, Lloyd's, 1 Lime Street.
Telephone: (071) 623-2081.
Facsimile: (071) 929-0043.
Telex: 987321.

MEMBERS OF FIRM

Walter B. Martin, Jr.
Patrick W. Herman

For Complete List of Firm Personnel, See General Section

For full biographical listings, see the Martindale-Hubbell Law Directory

*RICHMOND,** (Ind. City; Seat of Henrico Co.)

MCGUIRE, WOODS, BATTLE & BOOTHE (AV)

One James Center, 901 East Cary Street, 23219-4030
Telephone: 804-775-1000
Fax: 804-775-1061
Alexandria, Virginia Office: Transpotomac Plaza, Suite 1000, 1199 North Fairfax Street, 22314-1437.
Telephone: 703-739-6200.
Fax: 703-739-6270.
Baltimore, Maryland Office: The Blaustein Building, One North Charles Street, 21201-3793.
Telephone: 410-659-4400.
Fax: 410-659-4599.
Charlottesville, Virginia Office: Court Square Building, P.O. Box 1288, 22902-1288.
Telephone: 804-977-2500.
Fax: 804-980-2222.
Jacksonville, Florida Office: Barnett Center, Suite 2750, 50 North Laura Street, 32202-3635.
Telephone: 904-798-3200.
Fax: 904-798-3207.
McLean, (Tysons Corner) Virginia Office: 8280 Greensboro Drive, Suite 900, Tysons Corner, 22102-3892.
Telephone: 703-712-5000.
Fax: 703-712-5050.
Norfolk, Virginia Office: World Trade Center, Suite 9000, 101 West Main Street, 23510-1655.
Telephone: 804-640-3700.
Fax: 804-640-3701.
Washington, D.C. Office: The Army and Navy Club Building, 1627 Eye Street, N.W., 20006-4007.
Telephone: 202-857-1700.
Fax: 202-857-1737.
Brussels, Belgium Office: 250 Avenue Louise, Ste. 64, 1050.
Telephone: (32 2) 629 42 11.
Fax: (32 2) 629 42 22.
Zürich, Switzerland Office: P.O. Box 4930, Bahnhofstrasse 3, 8022.
Telephone: (41 1) 225 20 00.
Fax: (41 1) 225 20 20.

MEMBERS OF FIRM

Dennis I. Belcher
Jerry L. Bowman (Resident, Norfolk Office)
Lucius H. Bracey, Jr. (Resident, Charlottesville Office)
James D. Bridgeman (Resident, Washington, D.C. Office)
Robert K. Briskin (Resident, Baltimore, Maryland Office)
Thomas F. Dean
Mark Charles Dorigan (Resident, McLean (Tysons Corner) Office)
W. Birch Douglass III
Dennis W. Good, Jr. (Resident, Charlottesville Office)
John S. Graham III (Richmond and Baltimore, Maryland Offices)
Steven D. Kittrell (Resident, Washington, D.C. Office)
John E. McCann (Resident, Baltimore, Maryland Office)
Leigh B. Middleditch, Jr. (Resident, Charlottesville Office)
John Brad O'Grady

(See Next Column)

McGUIRE, WOODS, BATTLE & BOOTHE—*Continued*

MEMBERS OF FIRM (Continued)

David H. Pankey (Resident, Washington, D.C. Office)
Maria L. Payne
Thomas P. Rohman
Frederick L. Russell (Resident, Charlottesville Office)
Arthur P. Scibelli (Resident, McLean (Tysons Corner) Office)
D. French Slaughter III (Resident, Charlottesville Office)
Robert E. Stroud (Resident, Charlottesville Office)
Philip Tierney (Resident, Alexandria Office)
Thomas S. Word, Jr.
Mims Maynard Zabriskie

RETIRED OF COUNSEL

Carle E. Davis
Carrington Williams (Resident, McLean (Tysons Corner) Office)

OF COUNSEL

Lawrence A. Kaufman (Resident, Baltimore, Maryland Office)
Michele A. W. McKinnon
Martin B. Richards

ASSOCIATES

Jeffrey R. Capwell
Robert T. Danforth (Resident Charlottesville Office)
Lisa M. Landry
Francis X. Mellon (Resident, McLean (Tysons Corner) Office)
R. Lisa Mojiri-Azad (Resident, Washington, D.C. Office)
Victoria J. Roberson (Not admitted in VA)
Robert N. Saffelle
Kristen E. Smith (Resident, Charlottesville Office)
Natalie Kaye Wargo

For Complete List of Firm Personnel, See General Section

For full biographical listings, see the Martindale-Hubbell Law Directory

WILLIAMS, MULLEN, CHRISTIAN & DOBBINS, A PROFESSIONAL CORPORATION (AV)

Two James Center, 1021 East Cary Street, P.O. Box 1320, 23210-1320
Telephone: 804-643-1991
Fax: 804-783-6456
Glen Allen, Virginia Office: 4401 Waterfront Drive, Suite 140.
Telephone: 804-965-9168.
Fax: 804-965-0955.
Washington, D.C. Office: 1575 Eye Street, N.W.
Telephone: 202-289-6200.
Fax: 202-289-4126.

David D. Addison
Theodore L. Chandler, Jr.
C. Richard Davis
Randolph H. Lickey
Robert L. Musick, Jr.
Craig L. Rascoe

For Complete List of Firm Personnel, See General Section

For full biographical listings, see the Martindale-Hubbell Law Directory

VIENNA, Fairfax Co.

BORING, PARROTT & PILGER, P.C. (AV)

307 Maple Avenue West, Suite D, 22180-4368
Telephone: 703-281-2161
FAX: 703-281-9464

James L. Boring
M. Bruce Hirshorn

Representative Clients: Balmar, Inc.; Hewlett-Packard Co.; Toshiba America Information Systems, Inc.; King Wholesale, Inc.; FSM Leasing, Inc.; KDI Sylvan Pools, Inc.; Brobst International, Inc.; Telematics, Inc.; Northern Virginia Surgical Associates, P.C.; Rainbow Industries, Inc.

For full biographical listings, see the Martindale-Hubbell Law Directory

PETERSON & BASHA, P.C. (AV)

Tysons Square Office Park, 8214-C Old Courthouse Road, 22182-3855
Telephone: 703-442-3890
Fax: 703-448-1834

Gary G. Peterson
Leigh-Alexandra Basha

Alison K. Markell
Cynthia L. Gausvik
Ki Jun Sung

OF COUNSEL

Daniel J. O'Connell

For full biographical listings, see the Martindale-Hubbell Law Directory

REES, BROOME & DIAZ, P.C. (AV)

Ninth Floor, 8133 Leesburg Pike, 22182
Telephone: 703-790-1911
Telecopier: 703-848-2530

Jonathan J. Broome, Jr.
John F. Boland

For full biographical listings, see the Martindale-Hubbell Law Directory

VIRGINIA BEACH, (Independent City)

CLARK & STANT, P.C. (AV)

One Columbus Center, 23462
Telephone: 804-499-8800
Telecopier: 804-473-0395
Internet: Info @ CLRKNSTNT, COM

Jo Ann Blair-Davis
Stephen W. Burke
Joseph A. DiJulio
Thomas R. Frantz
Robert M. Reed

Robert J. Eveleigh

Counsel For: Tidewater Regional Transit; Virginia Beach General Hospital; Portsmouth General Hospital; Priority Health Plan (HMO); Health First (HMO).
Representative Clients: Central Fidelity Bank; Williamsburg Pottery Factory, Inc.; Bank of Franklin; Miller Oil Company, Inc.; Incendere.

For Complete List of Firm Personnel, See General Section

For full biographical listings, see the Martindale-Hubbell Law Directory

WASHINGTON

*SEATTLE,** King Co.

CHICOINE & HALLETT, P.S. (AV)

Waterfront Place One, Suite 803, 1011 Western Avenue, 98104
Telephone: 206-223-0800
206-467-8170

Robert J. Chicoine
Darrell D. Hallett

Larry N. Johnson
John M. Colvin

For full biographical listings, see the Martindale-Hubbell Law Directory

LANE POWELL SPEARS LUBERSKY (AV)

A Partnership including Professional Corporations
1420 Fifth Avenue, Suite 4100, 98101-2338
Telephone: 206-223-7000
Cable Address: "Embe"
Telex: 32-8808
Telecopier: 206-223-7107
Other Offices at: Mount Vernon and Olympia, Washington; Los Angeles and San Francisco, California; Anchorage, Alaska; Portland, Oregon; London, England.

MEMBERS OF FIRM

Kenyon P. Kellogg
Thomas F. Grohman

OF COUNSEL

G. Keith Grim

Representative Clients: AT&T; Dow Corning Corp.; Fred Hutchinson Cancer Research Center; The Home Depot; Key Bank of Washington; Mitsui & Co., Ltd.; Nordstrom, Inc.; Simpson Investment Co. and Affiliates; Texaco, Inc.; Underwriters at Lloyds, London.

For Complete List of Firm Personnel, See General Section

For full biographical listings, see the Martindale-Hubbell Law Directory

PERKINS COIE (AV)

A Law Partnership including Professional Corporations
Strategic Alliance with Russell & DuMoulin
1201 Third Avenue, 40th Floor, 98101-3099
Telephone: 206-583-8888
Facsimile: 206-583-8500
Cable Address: "Perki ns Seattle."
Telex: 32-0319 PERKINS SEA
Anchorage, Alaska Office: 1029 West Third Avenue, Suite 300.
Telephone: 907-279-8561.
Facsimile: 907-276-3108.
Telex: 32-0319 PERKINS SEA.
Los Angeles, California Office: 1999 Avenue of the Stars, Ninth Floor.
Telephone: 310-788-9900.
Telex: 32-0319 PERKINS SEA.
Facsimile: 310-788-3399.
Washington, D.C. Office: 607 Fourteenth Street, N.W.
Telephone: 202-628-6600.
Facsimile: 202-434-1690.
Telex: 44-0277 PCSO.
Portland, Oregon Office: U.S. Bancorp Tower, Suite 2500, 111 S.W. Fifth Avenue.
Telephone: 503-295-4400.
Facsimile: 503-295-6793.
Telex: 32-0319 PERKINS SEA.

(See Next Column)

PERKINS COIE, *Seattle—Continued*

Bellevue, Washington Office: Suite 1800, One Bellevue Center, 411 - 108th Avenue N.E.
Telephone: 206-453-6980.
Facsimile: 206-453-7350.
Telex: 32-0319 PERKINS SEA.
Spokane, Washington Office: North 221 Wall Street, Suite 600.
Telephone: 509-624-2212.
Facsimile: 509-458-3399.
Telex: 32-0319 PERKINS SEA.
Olympia, Washington Office: 1110 Capitol Way South, Suite 405.
Telephone: 206-956-3300.
Strategic Alliance with Russell & DuMoulin, 1700-1075 West Georgia Street, Vancouver, B.C. V6E 3G2. Telephone: 604-631-3131.
Hong Kong Office: 23rd Floor Asia Pacific Finance Tower, Citibank Plaza, 3 Garden Road.
Telephone: 852-2878-1177.
Facsimile: 852-2524-9988. DX-9230-IC.
London, England Office: 36/38 Cornhill, ECV3 3ND.
Telephone: 071-369-9966.
Facsimile: 071-369-9968.
Taipei, Taiwan Office: 8/F TFIT Tower, 85 Jen AiRoad, Sec. 4,Taipei 106, Taiwan, R.O.C.
Telephone: 886-2-778-1177.
Facsimile: 086-2-777-9898.

PARTNERS/SHAREHOLDERS

George M. Beal II
Kurt Becker
Dori E. Lee Brewer
Graham H. Fernald
Robert Edward Giles (Managing Partner)
James R. Lisbakken
Richard L. Mull

OF COUNSEL

Roland L. Hjorth

RESIDENT ASSOCIATE

Lorri A. Dunsmore

Counsel for: The Boeing Company; Burlington Northern Inc.; Crown Zellerbach Corp.; General Motors Corporation; Puget Sound Power & Light Company; Seattle School District.

For Complete List of Firm Personnel, See General Section

For full biographical listings, see the Martindale-Hubbell Law Directory

SHORT CRESSMAN & BURGESS (AV)

A Partnership including Professional Service Corporations
3000 First Interstate Center, 999 Third Avenue, 98104-4088
Telephone: 206-682-3333
Fax: 206-340-8856

MEMBERS OF FIRM

Robert E. Heaton
Robert J. Shaw
Robert E. Hibbs (P.S.)
Susan Thorbrogger
Ann T. Wilson

Counsel For: West One Bank; Key Bank; U.S. Bank; National Electrical Contractors Assn.

For Complete List of Firm Personnel, See General Section

For full biographical listings, see the Martindale-Hubbell Law Directory

WILLIAMS, KASTNER & GIBBS (AV)

4100 Two Union Square, 601 Union Street, P.O. Box 21926, 98111-3926
Telephone: 206-628-6600
Fax: 206-628-6611
Bellevue, Washington Office: 2000 Skyline Tower, 10900 N.E. Fourth Street, P.O. Box 1800, 98004-5841.
Telephone: 206-462-4700.
Fax: 206-451-0714.
Tacoma, Washington Office: 1000 Financial Center, 1145 Broadway, 98402-3502.
Telephone: 206-593-5620; Seattle: 628-2420.
Fax: 206-593-5625.
Vancouver, Washington Office: First Independent Place, 1220 Main Street, Suite 510.
Telephone: 206-696-0248.
Fax: 206-696-2051.

MEMBER OF FIRM

James W. Minorchio

ASSOCIATES

Pamela A Cairns
Harriet J. Flo

OF COUNSEL

DeWitt Williams
John D. Barline (Tacoma Office)

Representative Clients: Aetna Casulaty & Surety Co.; Atlantic-Richfield Co.; CIGNA; CNA Insurance; Continental Can Company, Inc.; Cushman & Wakefield of Washington, Inc.; General Motors Acceptance Corp.; Loomis Armored, Inc.; Mayne Nickless Incorporated; UNICO Properties, Inc.

For Complete List of Firm Personnel, See General Section

For full biographical listings, see the Martindale-Hubbell Law Directory

WEST VIRGINIA

*CHARLESTON,** Kanawha Co.

JACKSON & KELLY (AV)

1600 Laidley Tower, P.O. Box 553, 25322
Telephone: 304-340-1000
Fax: 304-340-1130
Martinsburg, West Virginia Office: 300 Foxcroft Avenue, P.O. Box 1068.
Telephone: 304-263-8800.
Morgantown, West Virginia Office: 6000 Hampton Center, P.O. Box 619.
Telephone: 304-599-3000.
New Martinsville, West Virginia Office: 256 Russell Avenue, P.O. Box 68.
Telephone: 304-455-1751.
Charles Town, West Virginia Office: 700 East Washington Street, P.O. Box 983.
Telephone: 304-728-6088.
Clarksburg, West Virginia Office: 203 Main Street, P.O. Box 1587.
Telephone: 304-623-3002.
Lexington, Kentucky Office: 175 East Main Street, Suite 500, P.O. Box 2150.
Telephone: 606-255-9500.
Washington, D. C. Office: 2401 Pennsylvania Avenue, N.W., Suite 400.
Telephone: 202-973-0200.
Denver, Colorado Office: Suite 2710, 1660 Lincoln Street.
Telephone: 303-837-0003.

MEMBERS OF FIRM

Louis S. Southworth, II
Thomas G. Freeman, II
Michael D. Foster
Thomas N. McJunkin
Jeffrey J. Yost (Resident, Lexington, Kentucky Office)
David Layva (Martinsburg and Charles Town, West Virginia Offices)

ASSOCIATES

John A. Mairs
Eric H. London (Resident, Morgantown Office)
Anthony J. Ferrise
Robert G. Tweel (Not admitted in WV)

For Complete List of Firm Personnel, See General Section

For full biographical listings, see the Martindale-Hubbell Law Directory

PAYNE, LOEB & RAY (AV)

1210 One Valley Square, 25301
Telephone: 304-342-1141
Fax: 304-342-0691

MEMBERS OF FIRM

Charles W. Loeb
Christopher J. Winton

Counsel for: One Valley Bank, N.A.; Outdoor Advertising Association of West Virginia; Trojan Steel Co.; Thomas, Field & Co.; Kanawha Village Apartments, Inc.; The Eye and Ear Clinic of Charleston, Inc.; Guyan Machinery Co.

For Complete List of Firm Personnel, See General Section

For full biographical listings, see the Martindale-Hubbell Law Directory

*CLARKSBURG,** Harrison Co.

JOHNSON, SIMMERMAN & BROUGHTON, L.C. (AV)

Suite 210, Goff Building, P.O. Box 150, 26301
Telephone: 304-624-6555
Telecopier: 304-623-4933

Charles G. Johnson
Frank E. Simmerman, Jr.
Marcia Allen Broughton

For full biographical listings, see the Martindale-Hubbell Law Directory

McNEER, HIGHLAND & McMUNN (AV)

Empire Building, P.O. Drawer 2040, 26301
Telephone: 304-623-6636
Facsimile: 304-623-3035
Morgantown Office: McNeer, Highland & McMunn, Baker & Armistead, 168 Chancery Row. P.O. Box 1615.
Telephone: 304-292-8473.
Fax: 304-292-1528.
Martinsburg, Office: 1446-1 Edwin Miller Boulevard. P.O. Box 2509.
Telephone: 304-264-4621.
Fax: 304-264-8623.

MEMBERS OF FIRM

C. David McMunn
J. Cecil Jarvis
James A. Varner
George B. Armistead (Resident, Morgantown Office)
Catherine D. Munster
Robert W. Trumble (Resident, Martinsburg Office)
Dennis M. Shreve
Geraldine S. Roberts
Harold M. Sklar
Jeffrey S. Bolyard
Steven R. Bratke
Michael J. Novotny (Resident, Martinsburg Office)

(See Next Column)

McNeer, Highland & McMunn—*Continued*

OF COUNSEL

James E. McNeer
Cecil B. Highland, Jr.
William L. Fury

Representative Clients: One Valley Bank of Clarksburg, National Association; Bruceton Bank; Harrison County Bank; Nationwide Mutual Insurance Cos.; Clarksburg Publishing Co.; C.I.T. Financial Services; State Automobile Mutual Insurance Co.; United Hospital Center, Inc.; West Virginia Coals, Inc.; Swanson Plating Company.

For Complete List of Firm Personnel, See General Section

For full biographical listings, see the Martindale-Hubbell Law Directory

*HUNTINGTON,** Cabell & Wayne Cos.

Frazier & Oxley, L.C. (AV)

The St. James, 401 Tenth Street Mezzanine Level, P.O. Box 2808, 25727
Telephone: 304-697-4370
FAX: Available upon request

William M. Frazier
Leon K. Oxley
W. Michael Frazier

References: The Old National Bank; Commerce Bank, Huntington, N.A.

For full biographical listings, see the Martindale-Hubbell Law Directory

Rife & Daugherty (AV)

Suite 800, Chafin Building, 517 Ninth Street, P.O. Box 542, 25710
Telephone: 304-529-2721; 523-0131

MEMBERS OF FIRM

O. Jennings Rife
David H. Daugherty

References: Banc One West Virginia, Huntington, W. Va.; Commerce Bank of Huntington, Huntington, W. Va.

For full biographical listings, see the Martindale-Hubbell Law Directory

*WHEELING,** Ohio Co.

Schrader, Recht, Byrd, Companion & Gurley (AV)

1000 Hawley Building, 1025 Main Street, P.O. Box 6336, 26003
Telephone: 304-233-3390
Fax: 304-233-2769
Martins Ferry, Ohio Office: 205 North Fifth Street, P.O. Box 309.
Telephone: 614-633-8976.
Fax: 614-633-0400.

PARTNERS

Henry S. Schrader (Retired)
Arthur M. Recht
Ray A. Byrd
James F. Companion
Terence M. Gurley
Frank X. Duff
Teresa Rieman-Camilletti
Yolonda G. Lambert
Patrick S. Casey
Sandra M. Chapman
Daniel P. Fry (Resident, Martins Ferry, Ohio Office)
James P. Mazzone

ASSOCIATES

Sandra K. Law
D. Kevin Coleman
Denise A. Jebbia
Edythe A. Nash
Robert G. McCoid
Denise D. Klug
Thomas E. Johnston

OF COUNSEL

James A. Byrum, Jr.

General Counsel: WesBanco Bank-Elm Grove.
Representative Clients: CIGNA Property and Casualty Cos.; Columbia Gas Transmission Corp.; Commercial Union Assurance Co.; Hazlett, Burt & Watson, Inc.; Stone & Thomas Department Stores; Transamerica Commercial Finance Corp.; Wheeling-Pittsburgh Steel Corp.

For full biographical listings, see the Martindale-Hubbell Law Directory

WISCONSIN

*MILWAUKEE,** Milwaukee Co.

Cook & Franke S.C. (AV)

660 East Mason Street, 53202
Telephone: 414-271-5900
Facsimile: 414-271-2002

Thomas J. Drought
Joseph E. Tierney, Jr.
Margaret T. Lund
Brian R. Wanasek
Victor J. Schultz
Sandra J. Janssen
Ann M. Rieger
Mark J. Maichel

Representative Clients: Wisconsin Electric Power Co.; Kenosha Beef Inc.; Payne & Dolan, Inc.; Bradley Center Corp.; Mr. and Mrs. Lloyd H. Pettit; Super Steel Products Corp.; Seidel Tanning Corp.; Bradley Family Foundation.

(See Next Column)

For Complete List of Firm Personnel, See General Section

For full biographical listings, see the Martindale-Hubbell Law Directory

Davis & Kuelthau, S.C. (AV)

111 East Kilbourn Avenue, Suite 1400, 53202-6613
Telephone: 414-276-0200
Facsimile: 414-276-9369
Cable Address: "Shiplaw"

Daniel J. Minahan
Thomas E. Mountin
Gregory J. Sell

For full biographical listings, see the Martindale-Hubbell Law Directory

Foley & Lardner (AV)

Firstar Center, 777 East Wisconsin Avenue, 53202-5367
Telephone: 414-271-2400
Telex: 26-819 (Foley Lard Mil)
Facsimile: 414-297-4900
Madison, Wisconsin Office: 150 E. Gilman Street, P.O. Box 1497.
Telephone: 608-257-5035.
Facsimile: 608-258-4258.
Chicago, Illinois Office: Suite 3300, One IBM Plaza, 330 N. Wabash Avenue.
Telephone: 312-755-1900.
Facsimile: 312-755-1925.
Washington, D.C. Office: Washington Harbour, Suite 500, 3000 K Street, N.W.
Telephone: 202-672-5300.
Telex: 904136 (Foley Lard Wash).
Facsimile: 202-672-5399.
Annapolis, Maryland Office: Suite 102, 175 Admiral Cochrane Drive.
Telephone: 301-266-8077.
Telex: 899149 (Oldtownpat).
Facsimile: 301-266-8664.
Jacksonville, Florida Office: The Greenleaf Building, 200 Laura Street. P.O. Box 240.
Telephone: 904-359-2000.
Facsimile: 904-359-8700.
Orlando, Florida Office: Suite 1800, 111 North Orange Avenue, P.O. Box 2193.
Telephone: 407-423-7656.
Telex: 441781 (HQ ORL).
Facsimile: 407-648-1743.
Tallahassee, Florida Office: Suite 450, 215 South Monroe Street, P.O. Box 508.
Telephone: 904-222-6100.
Facsimile: 904-224-0496.
Tampa, Florida Offices: Suite 2700, One Hundred Tampa Street, P.O. Box 3391.
Telephones: 813-229-2300; Pinellas County: 813-442-3296.
Facsimile: 813-221-4210.
West Palm Beach, Florida Office: Suite 200, Phillips Point East Tower, 777 South Flagler Drive.
Telephone: 407-655-5050.
Facsimile: 407-655-6925.

PARTNERS

Kevin D. Anderson
Timothy C. Frautschi
Richard S. Gallagher
Marsha E. Huff
Joseph W. Jacobs (Tallahassee, Florida Office)
Jeffrey J. Jones
Wayman C. Lawrence, IV (Madison, Wisconsin Office)
Jere D. McGaffey
Jamshed J. Patel
Thomas G. Ragatz (Madison, Wisconsin Office)
John A. Sanders (Orlando, Florida Office)
Leonard S. Sosnowski (Madison, Wisconsin Office)
Ronald L. Walter

ASSOCIATES

Carl D. Fortner
Vitauts M. Gulbis (Tampa, Florida Office)
Lynette M. Zigman

For Complete List of Firm Personnel, See General Section

For full biographical listings, see the Martindale-Hubbell Law Directory

Gibbs, Roper, Loots & Williams, S.C. (AV)

735 North Water Street, 53202
Telephone: 414-273-7000
Fax: 414-273-7897

Wayne J. Roper
Robert J. Loots
Clay R. Williams
John W. Hein
George A. Evans, Jr.
Thomas P. Guszkowski
Brent E. Gregory
Catherine Mode Eastham

William R. West

For Complete List of Firm Personnel, See General Section

For full biographical listings, see the Martindale-Hubbell Law Directory

Milwaukee—Continued

MEISSNER & TIERNEY, S.C. (AV)

The Milwaukee Center, 111 East Kilbourn Avenue, 19th Floor, 53202-6622
Telephone: 414-273-1300
Facsimile: 414-273-5840

Paul F. Meissner
Joseph E. Tierney III
Thomas J. Nichols
Randal J. Brotherhood

Steven R. Glaser

For full biographical listings, see the Martindale-Hubbell Law Directory

MICHAEL, BEST & FRIEDRICH (AV)

100 East Wisconsin Avenue, 53202-4108
Telephone: 414-271-6560
Telecopier: 414-277-0656
Cable Address: "Mibef"
Madison, Wisconsin Office: One South Pinckney Street, Firstar Plaza, P.O. Box 1806, 53701-1806.
Telephone: 608-257-3501.
Telecopier: 283-2275.
Chicago, Illinois Office: 135 South LaSalle Street, Suite 1610, 60603-4391.
Telephone: 312-845-5800.
Telecopier: 312-845-5828.
Affiliated Law Firm: Edward D. Heffernan, Penthouse One, 1019 19th Street, N.W., Washington, D.C. 20036.
Telephone: 202-331-7444.

PARTNERS

Roy C. LaBudde
Frank J. Pelisek
Robert A. Schnur
Jerome H. Kringel
Robert J. Johannes
Bartlett C. Petersen
Timothy G. Schally
Bret A. Roge

ASSOCIATES

David J. Winkler
Joseph A. Pickart
Richard A. Latta (Resident Associate, Madison, Wisconsin Office)
Sara M. Berman

For Complete List of Firm Personnel, See General Section

For full biographical listings, see the Martindale-Hubbell Law Directory

QUARLES & BRADY (AV)

411 East Wisconsin Avenue, 53202-4497
Telephone: 414-277-5000
Cable Address: "Lawdock"
Fax: 414-271-3552.
TWX: 910-262-3426
Madison, Wisconsin Office: Firstar Plaza, One South Pinckney Street, P.O. Box 2113.
Telephone: 608-251-5000.
Fax: 608-251-9166.
West Palm Beach, Florida Office: 222 Lakeview Avenue, 4th Floor.
Telephone: 407-653-5000.
Fax: 407-653-5333.
Naples, Florida Office: Barnett Center, 4501 Tamiami Trail North.
Telephone: 813-262-5959.
Fax: 813-434-4999.
Phoenix, Arizona Office: One Camelback Building, One East Camelback Road, Suite 400.
Telephone: 602-230-5500.
Fax: 602-230-5598.

MEMBERS OF FIRM

(ALPHABETICALLY BY YEAR OF ADMISSION TO BAR)

Jackson M. Bruce, Jr.
Donald S. Taitelman
John A. Hazelwood
Peter J. Lettenberger
Steven R. Duback
Thomas J. Phillips
Michael J. Conlan
John T. Bannen
Patrick J. Goebel
William D. McEachern (Resident, West Palm Beach, Florida Office)
Paul J. Tilleman
Kimberly Leach Johnson (Resident, Naples, Florida Office)
Thomas A. Simonis
David D. Wilmoth
Michael A. Levey
Elizabeth G. Nowakowski

OF COUNSEL

Roger C. Minahan
Richard R. Teschner
Dale L. Sorden

ASSOCIATES

Jeffrey L. Elverman
Chris K. Gawart

For Complete List of Firm Personnel, See General Section

For full biographical listings, see the Martindale-Hubbell Law Directory

REINHART, BOERNER, VAN DEUREN, NORRIS & RIESELBACH, S.C. (AV)

1000 North Water Street, P.O. Box 92900, 53202-0900
Telephone: 414-298-1000
Facsimile: 414-298-8097
Denver, Colorado Office: One Norwest Center, 1700 Lincoln Street, Suite 3725.
Telephone: 303-831-0909.
Fax: 303-831-4805.
Madison, Wisconsin Office: 7617 Mineral Point Road, 53701-2020.
Telephone: 608-283-7900.
Fax: 608-283-7919.
Washington, D.C. Office: 601 Pennsylvania Avenue, N.W., North Building, Suite 750.
Telephone: 202-393-3636.
Fax: 202-393-0796.

Robert E. Meldman
Gary A. Hollman
Robert E. Dallman
John L. Schliesmann
Anthony J. Handzlik
Timothy A. Nettesheim

Timothy P. Reardon
John R. Austin
Margaret M. Derus
Vincent J. Beres
Wendy J. Keith (Not admitted in WI)

For Complete List of Firm Personnel, See General Section

For full biographical listings, see the Martindale-Hubbell Law Directory

*WAUKESHA,** Waukesha Co.

CRAMER, MULTHAUF & HAMMES (AV)

1601 East Racine Avenue, P.O. Box 558, 53187
Telephone: 414-542-4278
Telecopier: 414-542-4270

MEMBERS OF FIRM

John E. Multhauf
John M. Remmers

Reference: Waukesha State Bank.

For Complete List of Firm Personnel, See General Section

For full biographical listings, see the Martindale-Hubbell Law Directory

WYOMING

*CASPER,** Natrona Co.

BROWN & DREW (AV)

Casper Business Center, Suite 800, 123 West First Street, 82601-2486
Telephone: 307-234-1000
800-877-6755
Telefax: 307-265-8025

MEMBER OF FIRM

John A. Warnick

ASSOCIATE

Drew A. Perkins

Attorneys for: First Interstate Bank of Wyoming, N.A.; Norwest Bank Wyoming, N.A.; The CIT Group/Industrial Financing; Aetna Casualty & Surety Co.; The Doctor's Co.; MEDMARC; WOTCO, Inc.; Chevron USA; Kerr-McGee Corp.; Chicago and NorthWestern Transportation Company.

For Complete List of Firm Personnel, See General Section

For full biographical listings, see the Martindale-Hubbell Law Directory

PUERTO RICO

SAN JUAN, San Juan Dist.

FIDDLER, GONZÁLEZ & RODRÍGUEZ

Chase Manhattan Bank Building (Hato Rey), P.O. Box 363507, 00936-3507
Telephone: 809-753-3113
Telecopier: 809-759-3123

MEMBERS OF FIRM

Salvador E. Casellas
Roberto B. Suárez
Manuel López-Zambrana

Representative Clients: The Chase Manhattan Bank, N.A.; Westinghouse Electric Corp.; Pfizer, Inc.; Merck & Co., Inc.; American Cyanamid Co.; Bacardi Corp.; The Eastman Kodak Co.; Nestle S.A.; United Postal Services; Banco Bilbao Vizcaya, S.A.

For Complete List of Firm Personnel, See General Section

For full biographical listings, see the Martindale-Hubbell Law Directory

San Juan—Continued

GOLDMAN ANTONETTI & CÓRDOVA

American International Plaza Fourteenth & Fifteenth Floors, 250 Muñoz Rivera Avenue (Hato Rey), P.O. Box 70364, 00936-0364
Telephone: 809-759-8000
Telecopiers: 809-767-9333 (Main)
809-767-9177 (Litigation Department)
809-767-8660 (Labor & Corporate Law Departments)
809-767-9325 (Tax & Environmental Law Departments)

MEMBER OF FIRM

Roberto Montalvo Carbia

OF COUNSEL

Max Goldman

ASSOCIATES

Carlos Rodriguez Cintron
Jose E. Franco

Representative Clients: Philip Morris; Borden, Inc.; Xerox Corp.; Crown Cork & Seal Co.; Forest Laboratories; Ferrero, Inc.

For Complete List of Firm Personnel, See General Section

For full biographical listings, see the Martindale-Hubbell Law Directory

MÁRTINEZ ODELL & CALABRIA

Banco Popular Center, 16th Floor, (Hato Rey), P.O. Box 190998, 00919-0998
Telephone: 809-753-8914
Facsimile: 809-753-8402; 809-759-9075; 809-764-5664

MEMBERS OF FIRM

Fred H. Martínez
Jose L. Calabria
Fanny Auz-Patiño
Donald J. Reiser (Not admitted in PR)
Angel S. Ruiz-Rodriguez

OF COUNSEL

Jose R. Cestero
Jose Luis Vila-Perez

ASSOCIATES

Brunilda Rodríguez-Vélez
Gary L. Leonard
Arnaldo A. Mignucci-Giannoni
Waldemar Fabery-Villaespesa

Representative Clients: A.T. & T. Corp.; Pepsi-Cola P.R. Bottling Co.; Banco Popular de Puerto Rico; I.T.T. Financial Corp.; John H. Harland Company of Puerto Rico, Inc.; Lutron Electronics Co., Inc.; Paine Webber, Inc.; Lotus Development Corp.; Western Digital.

For Complete List of Firm Personnel, See General Section

For full biographical listings, see the Martindale-Hubbell Law Directory

O'NEILL & BORGES

10th Floor, Chase Manhattan Bank Building (Hato Rey), 254 Muñoz Rivera Avenue, 00918-1995
Telephone: 809-764-8181
Telecopier: 809-753-8944

MEMBERS OF FIRM

Raymond C. O'Neill
Walter F. Chow
Jaime J. Aponte-Parsi
José R. Cacho
Rosa M. Lázaro-San Miguel
Rosa M. González-Lugo
Pablo Rodríguez-Solá

ASSOCIATES

Eduardo J. Negrón
Néstor R. Nadal-López
Gilberto Maymí

Representative Clients: Coach Leatherware Co.; Fluor Daniel Caribbean; Ford Motor Co.; Hanes Knit Products, Inc.; Monet Jewelers; Margo Nursery Farms, Inc.; The Procter & Gamble Commercial Co.; Sealand Corp.; Zale Corp.

For Complete List of Firm Personnel, See General Section

For full biographical listings, see the Martindale-Hubbell Law Directory

VIRGIN ISLANDS

*CHARLOTTE AMALIE, ST. THOMAS,** St. Thomas

BORNN BORNN HANDY

No. 8 Norre Gade, P.O. Box 1500, 00804
Telephone: 809-774-1400
Fax: 809-774-9607

OF COUNSEL

Joseph M. Erwin (Not admitted in VI)

References: Bank of Nova Scotia; Banco Popular de P.R., St. Thomas, U.S. Virgin Islands.

For Complete List of Firm Personnel, See General Section

For full biographical listings, see the Martindale-Hubbell Law Directory

GRUNERT STOUT BRUCH & MOORE

24-25 Kongensgade, P.O. Box 1030, 00804
Telephone: 809-774-1320
Fax: 809-774-7839

MEMBERS OF FIRM

John E. Stout
Susan Bruch Moorehead
Treston E. Moore

ASSOCIATES

Maryleen Thomas
Richard F. Taylor
H. Kevin Mart (Not admitted in VI)

OF COUNSEL

William L. Blum

For full biographical listings, see the Martindale-Hubbell Law Directory

CANADA ALBERTA

*EDMONTON,** Edmonton Jud. Dist.

PARLEE MCLAWS (AV)

15th Floor Manulife Place, 10180 101st Street, T5J 4K1
Telephone: 403-423-8500
Telecopier: 403-423-2870
Calgary, Alberta Office: 3400, Western Canadian Place, 707 - 8th Avenue, S.W.
Telephone: 403-294-7000.
Telecopier: 403-265-8263.

MEMBERS OF FIRM

C. H. Kerr, Q.C.
M. D. MacDonald
K. F. Bailey, Q.C.
R. B. Davison, Q.C.
F. R. Haldane
P. E. J. Curran
D. G. Finlay
J. K. McFadyen
R. C. Secord
D. L. Kennedy
D. C. Rolf
D. F. Pawlowski
A. A. Garber
R. P. James
D. C. Wintermute
J. L. Cairns
R. A. Newton, Q.C.
T. A. Cockrall, Q.C.
H. D. Montemurro
F. J. Niziol
R. W. Wilson
I. L. MacLachlan
R. O. Langley
R. G. McBean
J. T. Neilson
E. G. Rice
J. F. McGinnis
J. H. H. Hockin
G. W. Jaycock
M. J. K. Nikel
B. J. Curial
S. L. May
M. S. Poretti

ASSOCIATES

C. R. Head
A.W. Slemko
L. H. Hamdon
K.A. Smith
K. D. Fallis-Howell
D. S. Tam
J.W. McClure
F.H. Belzil
R.A. Renz
J.G. Paulson
K. E. Buss
B. L. Andriachuk
P. E. S. J. Kennedy
R. Feraco
R.J. Billingsley
N.B.R. Thompson
P. A. Shenher
I. C. Johnson
K.G. Koshman
D.D. Dubrule
G. T. Lund
W.D. Johnston
G. E. Flemming
K. P. Nayyer

For full biographical listings, see the Martindale-Hubbell Law Directory

CANADA BRITISH COLUMBIA

*VANCOUVER,** Vancouver Co.

BARBEAU & COMPANY (AV)

Toronto Dominion Tower, 700 West Georgia Street, Suite 1450, V7Y 1A1
Telephone: 604-688-4900
Telecopier: 604-688-0649

Jacques Barbeau, Q.C.
Christopher L. T. Falk
Paul S.O. Barbeau

References: Hong Kong Bank of Canada; Laurentian Bank of Canada.

For full biographical listings, see the Martindale-Hubbell Law Directory

Vancouver—Continued

RUSSELL & DUMOULIN (AV)

2100-1075 West Georgia Street, V6E 3G2
Telephone: 604-631-3131
Fax: 604-631-3232
A Member of the national association of Borden DuMoulin Howard Gervais, comprising Russell & DuMoulin, Vancouver, British Columbia; Howard Mackie, Calgary, Alberta; Borden & Elliot, Toronto, Ontario; Mackenzie Gervais, Montreal, Quebec and Borden DuMoulin Howard Gervais, London, England.
Strategic Alliance with Perkins Coie with offices in Seattle, Spokane and Bellevue, Washington; Portland, Oregon; Anchorage, Alaska; Los Angeles, California; Washington, D.C.; Hong Kong and Taipei, Taiwan.
Represented in Hong Kong by Vincent T.K. Cheung, Yap & Co.

MEMBER OF FIRM

Merrill W. Shepard

Representative Clients: Alcan Smelters & Chemicals Ltd.; The Bank of Nova Scotia; Canada Trust Co.; The Canada Life Assurance Co.; Forest Industrial Relations Ltd.; Honda Canada Inc.; IBM Canada Ltd.; Macmillan Bloedel Ltd.; Nissho Iwai Canada Ltd.; The Toronto-Dominion Bank.

For Complete List of Firm Personnel, See General Section

For full biographical listings, see the Martindale-Hubbell Law Directory

THORSTEINSSONS (AV)

27th Floor, Three Bentall Centre, 595 Burrard Street, P.O. Box 49123, V7X 1J2
Telephone: 604-688-1261
Fax: 604-688-4711
Toronto, Ontario Office: P.O. Box 611, BCE Place, 36th Floor, 161 Bay Street, Toronto, Ontario, M5J 2S1.
Telephone: 416-864-0829.
Fax: 416-864-1106.
European Office: 6 Broadgate, London EC2M 2QS, England.
Telephone: 44-71-972-0434.
Fax: 44-71-972-0433.

Warren J. A. Mitchell, Q.C.
Leslie M. Little, Q.C.
Michael J. O'Keefe
A. Barrie Davidson
Ian H. Pitfield
Craig C. Sturrock
James H.G. Roche
Risa E. Levine
Charles E. Beil
W. Jack Millar
Lorne A. Green
Steven M. Cook
John N. Gregory
David G. Thompson
Karen R. Sharlow
John R. Owen
S. Kim Hansen
Douglas J. Powrie
Douglas H. Mathew
Ian J. Gamble
David R. Davies
Terry G. Barnett
David J. Christian
Paul J. Gibney
Malik Z. Talib
Thomas A. Bauer
Thomas M. Boddez
Kerri L. Mooney
David R. Baxter

For full biographical listings, see the Martindale-Hubbell Law Directory

CANADA MANITOBA

*WINNIPEG,** Eastern Jud. Dist.

AIKINS, MACAULAY & THORVALDSON (AV)

Thirtieth Floor, Commodity Exchange Tower, 360 Main Street, R3C 4G1
Telephone: 204-957-0050
Fax: 204-957-0840

MEMBERS OF FIRM

Bryan D. Klein
Frank Lavitt
Anita R. Wortzman
Jacqueline N. Freedman
Joel A. Weinstein
Lisa M. Collins
Carmele N. Peter
Francis J. St.Hilaire

Counsel for: Air Canada; Bank of Montreal; Boeing of Canada; Canada Safeway Limited; Canadian Medical Protective Association; Federal Industries Ltd.; The Great West Life Assurance Company; John Labatt Limited; Winnipeg Free Press; Winnipeg Jets.

For Complete List of Firm Personnel, See General Section

For full biographical listings, see the Martindale-Hubbell Law Directory

CANADA NEW BRUNSWICK

*SAINT JOHN,** Saint John Co.

HANSON, HASHEY (AV)

One Brunswick Square Suite 1212, E2L 4V1
Telephone: 506-652-7771
Telecopier: 506-632-9600
Fredericton, New Brunswick Office: Suite 400, Phoenix Square, Queen Street, P.O. Box 310.
Telephone: 506-453-7771.
Telecopier: 506-453-9600.

J. Ian M. Whitcomb, Q.C. (Resident)

ASSOCIATE

Bruce M. Logan (Resident)

For full biographical listings, see the Martindale-Hubbell Law Directory

CANADA NOVA SCOTIA

*HALIFAX,** Halifax Co.

MCINNES COOPER & ROBERTSON (AV)

1601 Lower Water Street, P.O. Box 730, B3J 2V1
Telephone: 902-425-6500
Fax: 902-425-6350
St. John's, Newfoundland Office: Suite 602, Scotia Centre, 235 Water Street, P.O. Box 547. A1C, 5K8.
Telephone: 709-726-9500.
Fax: 709-726-9550.

Lawrence J. Hayes, Q.C.
Harvey L. Morrison
Karen Oldfield

Attorneys for: Bank of Nova Scotia; Imperial Oil, Limited; Frank B. Hall & Co., Inc. (New York); American Steamship Owners Protection & Indemnity Association, Inc.; Coca-Cola, Ltd.; Scott Worldwide Inc.; Hong Kong Bank of Canada.

For Complete List of Firm Personnel, See General Section

For full biographical listings, see the Martindale-Hubbell Law Directory

CANADA ONTARIO

*TORONTO,** Regional Munic. of York

BORDEN & ELLIOT (AV)

Barristers & Solicitors
Scotia Plaza, 40 King Street West, M5H 3Y4
Telephone: 416-367-6000
Telecopier: 416-367-6749
Internet: @ borden.com
A Member of the national association of Borden DuMoulin Howard Gervais, comprising Borden & Elliot in Toronto, Ontario, Russell & DuMoulin in Vancouver, British Columbia, Howard, Mackie in Calgary, Alberta and Mackenzie Gervais in Montréal, Québec. Borden DuMoulin Howard Gervais also operates an office in London, England.

MEMBER AND ASSOCIATES

Terrance A. Sweeney

For Complete List of Firm Personnel, See General Section

For full biographical listings, see the Martindale-Hubbell Law Directory

DAVIES, WARD & BECK (AV)

44th Floor, 1 First Canadian Place, P.O. Box 63, M5X 1B1
Telephone: 416-863-0900
Fax: 416-863-0871

PARTNERS AND ASSOCIATES

David A. Ward, Q.C.
Maurice Cullity, Q.C.
Brian R. Carr
John A. Zinn
John M. Ulmer
Neal H. Armstrong
Christina H. Medland
Maureen Y. Berry
David W. Smith, Q.C.
Martin J. Rochwerg
Ronald S. Wilson
Timothy G. Youdan
Colin Campbell
K. A. Siobhan Monaghan
R. Ian Crosbie
Geoffrey S. Turner

(See Next Column)

DAVIES, WARD & BECK—*Continued*

For Complete List of Firm Personnel, See General Section

For full biographical listings, see the Martindale-Hubbell Law Directory

McDONALD & HAYDEN (AV)

One Queen Street East Suite 1500, M5C 2Y3
Telephone: 416-364-3100
Telecopier: 416-601-4100

MEMBERS OF FIRM

John G. McDonald, Q.C. (1922-1993)
Lloyd D. Cadsby, Q.C.
Peter Reginald Hayden, Q.C.
David C. Nathanson, Q.C.
Marvin D. Demone
D. H. Jack
David R. Street
Clifford M. Goldlist
Wendy C. Posluns
David H. Goldman
Mark Adilman
Matthew R. Alter
Susan A. Goodeve
Karen Crombie
John D. Brunt
Kevin Cai
Adrienne Parrotta

For full biographical listings, see the Martindale-Hubbell Law Directory

THORSTEINSSONS (AV(T))

P.O. Box 611, BCE Place, 36th Floor, 161 Bay Street, M5J 2S1
Telephone: 416-864-0829
Fax: 416-864-1106
Vancouver, British Columbia Office: 27th Floor, Three Bentall Centre, 595 Burrard Street, P.O. Box 49123, V7X 1J2.
Telephone: 604-688-1261.
Fax: 604-688-4711.
European Office: 6 Broadgate, London EC2M 2QS, England.
Telephone: 44-71-972-0434.
Fax: 44-71-972-0433.

Warren J. A. Mitchell, Q.C.
Michael J. O'Keefe
W. Jack Millar
Lorne A. Green
Steven M. Cook
John N. Gregory
Dennis A. Wyslobicky
John R. Owen
Douglas H. Mathew
Terry G. Barnett
James H.M. Warnock
Robert G. Kreklewetz
Paul J. Gibney
James A. Bodi

For full biographical listings, see the Martindale-Hubbell Law Directory

CANADA QUEBEC

*MONTREAL,** Montreal Dist.

BYERS CASGRAIN (AV)

A Member of McMillan Bull Casgrain
Suite 3900, 1 Place Ville-Marie, H3B 4M7
Telephone: 514-878-8800
Telecopier: 514-866-2241
Cable Address: "Magee"
Telex: 05-24195

John Hurley
Pierre A. Lessard
Gérard Dugré
Guy A. Gagnon
André Morrissette
Constantine Kyres
Jean M. Gagnon
Julie Desrochers

For Complete List of Firm Personnel, See General Section

For full biographical listings, see the Martindale-Hubbell Law Directory

McMASTER MEIGHEN (AV)

A General Partnership
7th Floor, 630 René-Lévesque Boulevard West, H3B 4H7
Telephone: 514-879-1212
Telecopier: 514-878-0605
Cable Address: "Cammerall"
Telex: "Cammerall MTL" 05-268637
Affiliated with Fraser & Beatty in Toronto, North York, Ottawa and Vancouver.

MEMBERS OF FIRM

Brian M. Schneiderman
Francois Morin
Charles P. Marquette
H. John Godber
Marc L. Weinstein

For Complete List of Firm Personnel, See General Section

For full biographical listings, see the Martindale-Hubbell Law Directory

MENDELSOHN ROSENTZVEIG SHACTER (AV)

1000 Sherbrooke Street West, 27th Floor, H3A 3G4
Telephone: 514-987-5000
Telex: 05-27284 Colorlaw
Telecopier: 514-987-1213

MEMBERS OF FIRM AND ASSOCIATES

S. Leon Mendelsohn, Q.C.
Leo Rosentzveig, Q.C.
Manuel Shacter, Q.C.
Jack C. Shayne
William Levitt
Arthur A. Garvis
Max Mendelsohn
Edward E. Aronoff
L. Michael Blumenstein
Monroe A. Charlap
Earl S. Cohen
William Fraiberg
Michael Garonce
Philip S. Garonce, Q.C.
Donald M. Devine
Richard S. Uditsky
Boris P. Stein
Joel Weitzman
Ian R. Rudnikoff
Marc I. Leiter
L. B. Erdle
Frank Zylberberg
Fredric L. Carsley
David L. Rosentzveig
Jules Brossard
Michael Ludwick
Catherine Muraz
Judith G. Shenker
Judie K. Jokinen
Gilles Seguin
Martin Desrosiers
Jean Carrière

ASSOCIATES

Alain Breault
Joelle Sebag
Sharyn W. Gore
Louis Frédérick Côté
Hillel D. Frankel
Sandra Abitan
Dominique Lafleur
Linda Schachter
Roberto Buffone
Emmanuelle Saucier
Arnold Cohen
Isabelle Papillon
Lorne Beiles
Aaron Makovka
Céline Tessier

For full biographical listings, see the Martindale-Hubbell Law Directory

CANADA SASKATCHEWAN

*SASKATOON,** Saskatoon Jud. Centre

McKERCHER, McKERCHER & WHITMORE (AV)

374 Third Avenue, South, S7K 1M5
Telephone: 306-653-2000
Fax: 306-244-7335
Regina, Saskatchewan Office: 1000 - 1783 Hamilton Street.
Telephone: 306-352-7661.
Fax: 306-781-7113.

MEMBERS OF FIRM

Leslie J. Dick Batten
Thomas G. (Casey) Davis

ASSOCIATE

Humphrey Tam

For Complete List of Firm Personnel, See General Section

For full biographical listings, see the Martindale-Hubbell Law Directory

TRADEMARK, COPYRIGHT AND UNFAIR COMPETITION LAW

(See also listings under Patent, Trademark, Copyright and Unfair Competition Law)

ALABAMA

*BIRMINGHAM,** Jefferson Co.

Balch & Bingham (AV)

1710 Sixth Avenue North, P.O. Box 306, 35201
Telephone: 205-251-8100
Facsimile: 205-226-8798
Other Birmingham, Alabama Office: 1901 Sixth Avenue North, 35203.
Telephone: 205-251-8100.
Facsimile: 205-226-8799.
Montgomery, Alabama Office: The Winter Building, 2 Dexter Avenue, 36101.
Telephone: 205-834-6500.
Facsimile: 205-269-3115.
Huntsville, Alabama Office: Suite 810, 200 West Court Square, 35801.
Telephone: 205-551-0171.
Facsimile: 205-551-0174.
Washington, D.C. Office: Suite 800, 1101 Connecticut Avenue, N.W., 20036.
Telephone: 202-296-0387.
Facsimile: 202-452-8180.

MEMBERS OF FIRM

Walter M. Beale, Jr.
Susan B. Bevill
Will Hill Tankersley, Jr.

Counsel for: Alabama Power Co.; Blue Cross and Blue Shield of Alabama; The Boeing Company; Brasfield & Gorrie, Inc.; Compass Bancshares, Inc.; Harbert Corp.; Kimberly-Clark Corp.; Southern Company Services, Inc.; Southern Research Institute; Vesta Insurance Group, Inc.

For Complete List of Firm Personnel, See General Section

For full biographical listings, see the Martindale-Hubbell Law Directory

Bradley, Arant, Rose & White (AV)

1400 Park Place Tower, 2001 Park Place, 35203
Telephone: 205-521-8000
Telex: 494-1324
Facsimile: 205-251-8611, 251-8665, 252-0264
Facsimile (Southtrust Office): 205-251-9915
Huntsville, Alabama Office: 200 Clinton Avenue West, Suite 900.
Telephone: 205-517-5100.
Facsimile: 205-533-5069.

MEMBERS OF FIRM

Thad Gladden Long
Linda A. Friedman
James W. Gewin
Michael R. Pennington

ASSOCIATES

J. David Pugh
Frank M. Caprio (Resident, Huntsville Office)
Michael S. Denniston

Counsel for: SouthTrust Bank of Alabama, National Association; Energen, Corporation (formerly Alagasco, Inc.); Blount, Inc.; Coca-Cola Bottling Company United, Inc.; The New York Times Col; Russell Corp.; Walter Industries, Inc.; ASCAP; Auburn University.

For Complete List of Firm Personnel, See General Section

For full biographical listings, see the Martindale-Hubbell Law Directory

*HUNTSVILLE,** Madison Co.

Balch & Bingham (AV)

Suite 810, 200 West Court Square, P.O. Box 18668, 35804-8668
Telephone: 205-551-0171
Facsimile: 205-551-0174
Birmingham, Alabama Offices: 1710 Sixth Avenue North, 35203.
Telephone: 205-251-8100.
Facsimile: 205-226-8798. 1901 Sixth Avenue North, 35203.
Telephone: 205-251-8100.
Facsimile: 205-226-8799.
Montgomery, Alabama Office: The Winter Building, 2 Dexter Avenue, 36101.
Telephone: 205-834-6500.
Facsimile: 205-269-3115.

(See Next Column)

Washington, D.C. Office: Suite 800, 1101 Connecticut Avenue, N.W., 20036.
Telephone: 202-296-0387.
Facsimile: 202-452-8180.

RESIDENT MEMBER OF FIRM

S. Revelle Gwyn

Counsel for: Alabama Power Co.; Blue Cross and Blue Shield of Alabama; The Boeing Company; Brasfield & Gorrie, Inc.; Compass Bancshares, Inc.; Harbert Corp.; Kimberly-Clark Corp.; Southern Company Services, Inc.; Southern Research Institute; Vesta Insurance Group, Inc.

For Complete List of Firm Personnel, See General Section

For full biographical listings, see the Martindale-Hubbell Law Directory

ARIZONA

*PHOENIX,** Maricopa Co.

Horne, Kaplan and Bistrow, P.C. (AV)

Renaissance Two, 40 North Central, Suite 2800, 85004
Telephone: 602-253-9700
Fax: 602-258-4805

Kimball J. Corson

For full biographical listings, see the Martindale-Hubbell Law Directory

Jennings, Strouss and Salmon, P.L.C. (AV)

A Professional Limited Liability Company
One Renaissance Square, Two North Central, 85004-2393
Telephone: 602-262-5911
Fax: 602-253-3255

Anne L. Kleindienst
Leo L. Miller
Robert E. Coltin

For Complete List of Firm Personnel, See General Section

For full biographical listings, see the Martindale-Hubbell Law Directory

Lewis and Roca (AV)

A Partnership including Professional Corporations
40 North Central Avenue, 85004-4429
Telephone: 602-262-5311
Fax: 602-262-5747
Tucson, Arizona Office: One South Church Avenue, Suite 700.
Telephone: 602-622-2090.
Fax: 602-622-3088.

MEMBERS OF FIRM

Peter D. Baird
Patricia K. Norris
Dale A. Danneman
Thomas H. Campbell
Edward M. Mansfield
James T. Acuff, Jr.
Rosemarie Christofolo

ASSOCIATES

Michael L. Burke
Laura Knoll

OF COUNSEL

Steven Marc Weinberg (Not admitted in AZ)

Representative Clients: Apple Computer; Del Webb Corporation; E & J Gallo Wineries; EMI Records; First Data Corp.; The Frank Lloyd Wright Foundation; Jim Henson Productions; Motion Picture Association of America, Inc.; Next Base, Limited; Nintendo; Skymall, Inc.

For Complete List of Firm Personnel, See General Section

For full biographical listings, see the Martindale-Hubbell Law Directory

Meyer, Hendricks, Victor, Osborn & Maledon, A Professional Association (AV)

2929 North Central Avenue Suite 2100, 85012-2794
Telephone: 602-640-9000
Facsimile: (24 Hrs.) 602-640-9050
Mailing Address: P.O. Box 33449, 85067-3449,

William J. Maledon
David B. Rosenbaum
Don Bivens
G. Murray Snow
Donald M. Peters
Michael A. Lechter
Thomas H. Curzon
Debra A. Hill
Brett L. Dunkelman
Catherine R. Hardwick

Daniel J. Noblitt

Reference: Bank One Arizona, NA.

For Complete List of Firm Personnel, See General Section

For full biographical listings, see the Martindale-Hubbell Law Directory

CALIFORNIA

BEVERLY HILLS, Los Angeles Co.

PAUL D. SUPNIK (AV)

Suite 1200 Wells Fargo Bank Building, 433 North Camden Drive, 90210
Telephone: 310-205-2050
Telex: 292416
Facsimile: 310-205-2011

For full biographical listings, see the Martindale-Hubbell Law Directory

IRVINE, Orange Co.

CALLAHAN & GAUNTLETT (AV)

A Partnership including a Professional Corporation
Suite 800, 18500 Von Karman, 92715
Telephone: 714-553-1155
Fax: 714-553-0784

Daniel J. Callahan (A Professional Corporation)
David A. Gauntlett

ASSOCIATES

Stephen E. Blaine
David A. Stall
J. Craig Williams
Jim P. Mahacek
Leo E. Lundberg, Jr.
Michael J. Sachs
Michael Danton Richardson
Craig E. Lindberg
Edward Susolik
Carol L. Meedon
Andrew A. Smits

OF COUNSEL

Gary L. Hinman
Walt D. Mahaffa
Jose Zorrilla, Jr.
H. Thomas Hicks

For full biographical listings, see the Martindale-Hubbell Law Directory

*LOS ANGELES,** Los Angeles Co.

BAKER & HOSTETLER (AV)

600 Wilshire Boulevard, 90017-3212
Telephone: 213-624-2400
FAX: 213-975-1740
In Cleveland, Ohio, 3200 National City Center, 1900 East Ninth Street. Telephone: 216-621-0200.
In Columbus, Ohio, Capitol Square, Suite 2100, 65 East State Street. Telephone: 614-228-1541.
In Denver, Colorado, 303 East 17th Avenue, Suite 1100. Telephone: 303-861-0600.
In Houston, Texas, 1000 Louisiana, Suite 2000. Telephone: 713-236-0020.
In Long Beach, California: 300 Oceangate, Suite 620. *Telephone:* 310-432-2827.
In Orlando, Florida, SunBank Center, Suite 2300, 200 South Orange Avenue. Telephone: 407-649-4000.
In Washington, D. C., Washington Square, Suite 1100, 1050 Connecticut Avenue, N. W. Telephone: 202-861-1500.
In College Park, Maryland, 9658 Baltimore Boulevard, Suite 206. Telephone: 301-441-2781.
In Alexandria, Virginia, 437 North Lee Street. Telephone: 703-549-1294.
In San Francisco, California: One Sansome Street, Suite 2000. *Telephone:* 415-951-4705.

PARTNER

Anthony M. Keats

ASSOCIATE

Steve W. Ackerman

For Complete List of Firm Personnel, See General Section

For full biographical listings, see the Martindale-Hubbell Law Directory

BERMAN, BLANCHARD, MAUSNER & KINDEM, A LAW CORPORATION (AV)

4727 Wilshire Boulevard, Suite 500, 90010
Telephone: 213-965-1200
Telecopier: 213-965-1919

Laurence M. Berman
Lonnie C. Blanchard, III
Jeffrey N. Mausner
Peter R. Dion-Kindem

Paul A. Hoffman
Eric Levinrad
Cary P. Ocon

For full biographical listings, see the Martindale-Hubbell Law Directory

LANGBERG, LESLIE & GABRIEL (AV)

An Association including a Professional Corporation
2049 Century Park East Suite 3030, 90067
Telephone: 310-286-7700
Telecopier: 310-284-8355

(See Next Column)

Barry B. Langberg (A Professional Corporation)
Jody R. Leslie
Joseph M. Gabriel

Eileen M. Cohn
Deborah Drooz
Richard J. Wynne
Beatrice L. Hoffman
Michael M. Baranov
Beth F. Dumas
Dwayne A. Watts
Mitchell J. Langberg

LEGAL SUPPORT PERSONNEL

PARALEGALS

Patricia Urban
Patricia Ann Essig
Jeanne A. Logé

For full biographical listings, see the Martindale-Hubbell Law Directory

LOEB AND LOEB (AV)

A Partnership including Professional Corporations
Suite 1800, 1000 Wilshire Boulevard, 90017-2475
Telephone: 213-688-3400
Telecopier: 213-688-3460; 688-3461; 688-3462
Century City, California Office: Suite 2200, 10100 Santa Monica Boulevard, Los Angeles, 90067-4164.
Telephone: 310-282-2000.
Telecopier: 310-282-2191; 282-2192.
New York, N.Y. Office: 345 Park Avenue, 10154-0037.
Telephone: 212-407-4000.
Facsimile: 212-407-4990.
Nashville, Tennessee Office: 45 Music Square West, 37203-3205.
Telephone: 615-749-8300;
Facsimile: 615-749-8308.
Rome, Italy Office: Piazza Digione 1, 00197.
Telephone: 011-396-808-8456.
Telecopier: 011-396-674-8223.

MEMBERS OF FIRM

Phillip E. Adler (A P.C.)
David H. Carlin (New York City Office)
Marc A. Chamlin (New York City Office)
Kenneth R. Costello
Martin D. Fern
Ralph Jonas
William J. Marlow (New York City Office)
Charles H. Miller (New York City Office)
Lee N. Steiner (New York City Office)
Robert Thorne (Century City Office)

ASSOCIATES

Maarten B. Kooij (New York City Office)
James D. Taylor (New York City Office)

For Complete List of Firm Personnel, See General Section

For full biographical listings, see the Martindale-Hubbell Law Directory

MCDERMOTT, WILL & EMERY (AV)

A Partnership including Professional Corporations
2049 Century Park East, 90067-3208
Telephone: 310-277-4110
Facsimile: 310-277-4730
Chicago, Illinois Office: 227 West Monroe Street.
Telephone: 312-372-2000.
Telex: 253565 MILAM CGO.
Facsimile: 312-984-7700.
Boston, Massachusetts Office: 75 State Street, Suite 1700.
Telephone: 617-345-5000.
Telex: 951324 MILAM BSN.
Facsimile: 617-345-5077.
Miami, Florida Office: 201 South Biscayne Boulevard.
Telephone: 305-358-3500.
Telex: 441777 LEYES.
Facsimile: 305-347-6500.
Washington, D.C. Office: 1850 K Street, N.W.
Telephone: 202-887-8000.
Telex: 253565 MILAM CGO.
Facsimile: 202-778-8087.
Newport Beach, California Office: 1301 Dove Street, Suite 500.
Telephone: 714-851-0633.
Facsimile: 714-851-9348.
New York, N.Y. Office: 1211 Avenue of the Americas.
Telephone: 212-768-5400.
Facsimile: 212-768-5444.
St. Petersburg, Russia Office: 2/2 Tchaikovsky Street, #517, 191187 St. Petersburg, Russia.
Telephone: (7) (812) 273-9831.
Facsimile: (7) (812) 273-9831.
Vilnius, Lithuania Office: Smetonos 6, 2600 Vilnius, Lithuania.
Telephone: 370 2 61-43-08.
Facsimile: 370 2 22-79-55.
Associated (Independent) Offices:
Brussels, Belgium: Uettwiller Grelon Lippens Dekeyser, 73 avenue Vandendriessche, 1150 Brussels, Belgium.
Telephone: (32) (2) 772-87-50.
Facsimile: (32) (2) 772-87-52.

(See Next Column)

McDERMOTT, WILL & EMERY—*Continued*

London, England: Paisner & Co, Bouverie House, 154 Fleet Street, London EC4A 2DQ, England.
Telephone: (44) (71) 353-0299.
Facsimile: (44) (71) 583-8621.
Paris, France: Uettwiller Grelon Gout Canat & Associes, 68, boulevard de Courcelles, 75017 Paris, France.
Telephone: (33) (1) 48 88 89 00.
Facsimile: (33) (1) 48 88 05 50.

MEMBER OF FIRM

Stephen A. Kroft

*Denotes a lawyer employed by a Professional Corporation which is a member of the Firm

For Complete List of Firm Personnel, See General Section

For full biographical listings, see the Martindale-Hubbell Law Directory

PASADENA, Los Angeles Co.

ROSE & BRUTOCAO (AV)

225 South Lake Avenue, 9th Floor, 91101
Telephone: 818-683-8787; 818-788-8494
Fax: 818-683-0755;
Internet: RobertRose@rbpas.cc mail.compuserve.com
cc: Mail: RBPAS (818) 683-3890

MEMBERS OF FIRM

Robert J. Rose
William J. Brutocao

Christina E. Dickson

Reference: California State Bank (Covina Branch).

For full biographical listings, see the Martindale-Hubbell Law Directory

*SAN DIEGO,** San Diego Co.

FERRIS & BRITTON, A PROFESSIONAL CORPORATION (AV)

1600 First National Bank Center, 401 West A Street, 92101
Telephone: 619-233-3131
Fax: 619-232-9316

Christopher Q. Britton
Michael R. Weinstein

OF COUNSEL

Allan J. Reniche

Representative Clients: Cox Enterprises, Inc.; Total TV, Inc.; Enterprise Rent-A-Car; Exxon.

For Complete List of Firm Personnel, See General Section

For full biographical listings, see the Martindale-Hubbell Law Directory

GRAY CARY WARE & FREIDENRICH, A PROFESSIONAL CORPORATION (AV)

Gray Cary Established in 1927
Ware & Freidenrich Established in 1969
401 "B" Street, Suite 1700, 92101
Telephone: 619-699-2700
Telecopier: 619-236-1048
Palo Alto, California Office: 400 Hamilton Avenue.
Telephone: 415-328-6561.
La Jolla, California Office: Suite 575, 1200 Prospect Street.
Telephone: 619-454-9101.
El Centro, California Office: 1224 State Street, P.O. Box 2890.
Telephone: 619-353-6140.

John Allcock
David E. Monahan
Anthony M. Stiegler
James C. Weseman

Cathy A. Bencivengo
Rodney S. Edmonds
Alexander H. Rogers

Representative Clients: Automobile Club of South California; Bank of America; Brooktree Corp.; C. A. Parr (Agencies), Ltd.; IMED; Pacific Bell; McMillin Development Co.; Scripps Clinic and Research Fdtn.; SeaWorld, Inc.; Underwriters at Lloyds; Wells Fargo Bank.

For Complete List of Firm Personnel, See General Section

For full biographical listings, see the Martindale-Hubbell Law Directory

*SAN FRANCISCO,** San Francisco Co.

ROSEN, BIEN & ASARO (AV)

Eighth Floor, 155 Montgomery Street, 94104
Telephone: 415-433-6830
Fax: 415-433-7104

Sanford Jay Rosen
Michael W. Bien
Andrea G. Asaro

(See Next Column)

Stephen M. Liacouras
Hilary A. Fox
Thomas Nolan
Mary Ann Cryan (Not admitted in CA)
Donna Petrine

For full biographical listings, see the Martindale-Hubbell Law Directory

COLORADO

*DENVER,** Denver Co.

DORR, CARSON, SLOAN & PETERSON, P.C. (AV)

3010 East Sixth Avenue, 80206
Telephone: 303-333-3010
FAX: 303-333-1470

Robert C. Dorr
W. Scott Carson
Jack C. Sloan
Gary H. Peterson
Thomas S. Birney
Stuart Langley

OF COUNSEL

Christopher H. Munch
Steve A. Mains

Representative Clients: Winegard Co.; Ball Corp.; The Gates Rubber Co.; Hewlett Packard; Colorado State University Research Foundation; Colorado Memory Systems, Inc.; Steam Way International; Big Sur Waterbeds; Taco John's International; Micron Technology.

For full biographical listings, see the Martindale-Hubbell Law Directory

DUFFORD & BROWN, P.C. (AV)

1700 Broadway, Suite 1700, 80290-1701
Telephone: 303-861-8013
Facsimile: 303-832-3804

David W. Furgason
Gregory A. Ruegsegger
Edward D. White
Scott J. Mikulecky

Thomas E. J. Hazard

Representative Clients: Starbucks Coffee Company; Louis Vuitton, S.A.

For Complete List of Firm Personnel, See General Section

For full biographical listings, see the Martindale-Hubbell Law Directory

HOLLAND & HART (AV)

Suite 2900, 555 Seventeenth Street, P.O. Box 8749, 80201
Telephone: 303-295-8000
Cable Address: "Holhart Denver"
Telecopier: 303-295-8261
TWX: 910-931-0568
Denver Tech Center, Colorado Office: Suite 1050, 4601 DTC Boulevard.
Telephone: 303-290-1600.
Telecopier: 303-290-1606.
Aspen, Colorado Office: 600 East Main Street.
Telephone: 303-925-3476.
Telecopier: 303-925-9367.
Boulder, Colorado Office: Suite 500, 1050 Walnut.
Telephone: 303-473-2700.
Telecopier: 303-473-2720.
Colorado Springs, Colorado Office: Suite 1000, 90 S. Cascade Avenue.
Telephone: 719-475-7730.
Telex: 82077 SHHTLX.
Telecopier: 719-634-2461.
Washington, D.C. Office: Suite 310, 1001 Pennsylvania Avenue, N.W.
Telephone: 202-638-5500.
Telecopier: 202-737-8998.
Boise, Idaho Office: Suite 1400, West One Plaza, 101 South Capitol Boulevard, P.O. Box 2527.
Telephone: 208-342-5000.
Telecopier: 208-343-8869.
Billings, Montana Office: Suite 1500, First Interstate Center, 401 North 31st Street, P.O. Box 639.
Telephone: 406-252-2166.
Telecopier: 406-252-1669.
Salt Lake City, Utah Office: Suite 880, 111 East Broadway.
Telephone: 801-578-6000.
FAX: 801-578-6010.
Cheyenne, Wyoming Office: Holland & Hart, A Partnership including Professional Corporations, Suite 500, 2020 Carey Avenue, P.O. Box 1347.
Telephone: 307-778-4200.
Telecopier: 307-778-8175.
Jackson, Wyoming Office: Holland & Hart, A Partnership including Professional Corporations, Suite 2, 175 South King Street, P.O. Box 68.
Telephone: 307-739-9741.
Telecopier: 307-739-9744.

(See Next Column)

HOLLAND & HART, *Denver—Continued*

MEMBERS OF FIRM

Ralph F. Crandell
Gary M. Polumbus
Jane Michaels
James E. Hartley
John R. Ley
Gregg I. Anderson
Kevin S. Crandell
William J. Kubida

ASSOCIATES

Carol W. Burton
Donald A. Degnan
Robert H. Kelly
(Not admitted in CO)
Lee R. Osman
John B. Phillips

DENVER TECH CENTER, COLORADO RESIDENT PARTNER

William W. Maywhort

BOULDER, COLORADO PARTNER

Scott Havlick

COLORADO SPRINGS, COLORADO PARTNER

Gary R. Burghart (Resident)

BOISE, IDAHO RESIDENT ASSOCIATES

Kim J. Dockstader
Dana Lieberman Hofstetter

BILLINGS, MONTANA PARTNER

James M. Ragain

CHEYENNE, WYOMING RESIDENT ASSOCIATE

Susan E. Laser-Bair

For Complete List of Firm Personnel, See General Section

For full biographical listings, see the Martindale-Hubbell Law Directory

SHERIDAN ROSS & MCINTOSH, A PROFESSIONAL CORPORATION (AV)

1700 Lincoln Street Suite 3500, 80203
Telephone: 303-863-9700
Facsimile: 303-863-0223

Michael D. McIntosh
David F. Zinger
Lesley Witt Craig
George G. Matava
Thomas R. Marsh
Craig C. Groseth
Michael L. Tompkins
Todd P. Blakely
Gary J. Connell
Susan Pryor Willson
Christopher J. Kulish
Sabrina Crowley Stavish
James L. Johnson
Lewis D. Hansen
Joseph E. Kovarik
Robert R. Brunelli
Kent A. Fischmann
Douglas W. Swartz
John R. Posthumus
Ross E. Breyfogle
Mark H. Snyder
Kevin P. Moran
Bruce A. Kugler
Jeffrey A. Divney
Jed W. Caven
David F. Dockery

OF COUNSEL

Philip H. Sheridan (P.C.)

LEGAL SUPPORT PERSONNEL

TECHNICAL SPECIALISTS

Carol Talkington Verser
Dennis J. Dupray
Nadine C. Chien

PARALEGALS

Cynthia Rapp
Janet E. Balent
Peggy West
Michele McCoy

Representative Clients: Band-It-Houdaille, Inc.; Celestial Seasonings, Inc.; Norgren Co.
Reference: Norwest Bank.

For full biographical listings, see the Martindale-Hubbell Law Directory

CONNECTICUT

FAIRFIELD, Fairfield Co.

PERMAN & GREEN (AV)

425 Post Road, 06430-6232
Telephone: 203-259-1800
Facsimile: 203-255-5170

MEMBER OF FIRM

Clarence A. Green

ASSOCIATES

David M. Warren
(Not admitted in CT)
Albert W. Hilburger
Harry F. Smith
Mark F. Harrington
Thomas L. Tully
David N. Koffsky
Michael J. Tully
(Not admitted in CT)
John J. Goodwin
(Not admitted in CT)

OF COUNSEL

Donald C. Caulfield

For full biographical listings, see the Martindale-Hubbell Law Directory

DISTRICT OF COLUMBIA

WASHINGTON, D.C. Co.

* indicates certain Bar Register subscribers, in cities of comparable size and importance, who maintain an additional office in Washington, D.C. and who have arranged for representation as a part of the Washington, D.C. listings that follow

*** BAKER & BOTTS, L.L.P.** (AV)

A Registered Limited Liability Partnership
The Warner, 1299 Pennsylvania Avenue, N.W., 20004-2400
Telephone: 202-639-7700
Fax: 202-639-7832
Houston, Texas Office: One Shell Plaza, 910 Louisiana.
Telephone: 713-229-1234.
Austin, Texas Office: 1600 San Jacinto Center, 98 San Jacinto Boulevard.
Telephone: 512-322-2500.
Dallas, Texas Office: 2001 Ross Avenue.
Telephone: 214-953-6500.
New York, New York Office: 805 Third Avenue, Suite 2000.
Telephone: 212-705-5000.
Moscow, Russian Federation Office: 10 ul. Pushkinskaya, 103031.
Telephone: 7095/921-5300 (Local); 7501/929-7070 (International).

MEMBERS OF FIRM

Scott F. Partridge
Rodger L. Tate

ASSOCIATES

James B. Arpin
Christopher C. Campbell
James G. Gatto
Jay B. Johnson
Charles B. Lobsenz
James Remenick

For Complete List of Firm Personnel, See General Section

For full biographical listings, see the Martindale-Hubbell Law Directory

BAKER & HOSTETLER (AV)

Washington Square, Suite 1100, 1050 Connecticut Avenue, N.W., 20036-5304
Telephone: 202-861-1500
In Cleveland, Ohio: 3200 National City Center, 1900 East Ninth Street.
Telephone: 216-621-0200.
In Columbus, Ohio: Capitol Square, Suite 2100, 65 East State Street.
Telephone: 614-228-1541.
In Denver, Colorado: 303 East 17th Avenue, Suite 1100.
Telephone: 303-861-0600.
In Houston, Texas: 1000 Louisiana, Suite 2000.
Telephone: 713-751-1600.
In Long Beach, California: 300 Oceangate, Suite 620.
Telephone: 310-432-2827.
In Los Angeles, California: 600 Wilshire Boulevard.
Telephone: 213-624-2400.
In Orlando, Florida: SunBank Center, Suite 2300, 200 South Orange Avenue.
Telephone: 305-841-1111.
In College Park, Maryland: 9658 Baltimore Boulevard, Suite 206.
Telephone: 301-441-2781.
In Alexandria, Virginia: 437 North Lee Street.
Telephone: 703-549-1294.
In San Francisco, California: One Sansome Street, Suite 2000.
Telephone: 415-951-4705.

PARTNER

Belinda Jayne Scrimenti

For Complete List of Firm Personnel, See General Section

For full biographical listings, see the Martindale-Hubbell Law Directory

BANNER, BIRCH, MCKIE & BECKETT (AV)

Eleventh Floor, 1001 G Street, N.W., 20001-4597
Telephone: 202-508-9100
Cable Address: "Bankett"
Telex: 197430 BBMB UT
Facsimile: 202-508-9299; 508-9298; 508-9297

MEMBERS OF FIRM

William W. Beckett
Alan S. Cooper
Joseph M. Potenza
Kathy J. McKnight

ASSOCIATES

Mary Gronlund
Victor W. Marton
(Not admitted in DC)
Eric T. Fingerhut
Richild A. Stewart
Lucille Pratt Nichols

For full biographical listings, see the Martindale-Hubbell Law Directory

Washington—Continued

CUSHMAN DARBY & CUSHMAN, L.L.P. (AV)

1100 New York Avenue, N.W. Ninth Floor, East Tower, 20005
Telephone: 202-861-3000
Telex: 6714627 CUSH;
Telefax G 3/2: 202-822-0944; 202-822-0678; 202-822-0679

Arlon V. Cushman (1892-1950)
John J. Darby (1920-1950)
William Michael Cushman (1925-1964)

MEMBERS OF FIRM

Paul N. Kokulis
Raymond F. Lippitt
Gearry Lloyd Knight, Jr.
Carl G. Love
Edgar H. Martin
William K. West, Jr.
Kevin E. Joyce
Edward M. Prince
Donald B. Deaver
David W. Brinkman
George M. Sirilla
Donald J. Bird
W. Warren Taltavull, III
Susan Tucker Brown
Peter W. Gowdey
Dale S. Lazar
Glenn J. Perry
Kendrew H. Colton
Chris Comuntzis
Richard L. Kirkpatrick
Lawrence Harbin
Wallace G. Walter
Paul E. White, Jr.
Stephen L. Sulzer
Sheldon H. Klein
Michelle N. Lester
Jeffrey A. Simenauer
Robert A. Molan
G. Paul Edgell

ASSOCIATES

Jack S. Barufka (Not admitted in DC)
James D. Berquist
Thomas M. Blasey
William H. Bollman
Gregory P. Brummett (Not admitted in DC)
Marlana Kathryn Chapin
Barry P. Golob
Michael W. Haas (Not admitted in DC)
Adam R. Hess (Not admitted in DC)
Stuart T. F. Huang
David A. Jakopin
Timothy J. Klima
Kevin T. Kramer
Jeffrey Scott Melcher
Mark G. Paulson (Not admitted in DC)
Edward J. Stemberger
Joerg-Uwe Szipl

COUNSEL

Howard D. Doescher
Frederick S. Frei
Lawrence A. Hymo
Allen Kirkpatrick
John P. Moran
Gary J. Rinkerman
Thomas G. Wiseman (Not admitted in DC)

Reference: Sovran Bank/D.C. National, Washington D.C.

For full biographical listings, see the Martindale-Hubbell Law Directory

FINNEGAN, HENDERSON, FARABOW, GARRETT & DUNNER (AV)

Suite 700, 1300 I Street, N.W., 20005-3315
Telephone: 202-408-4000
Cable Address: "Finderbow"
Telex: 440275 ITT; 248740 RCA;
Facsimile: 202-408-4400
Tokyo, Japan Office: Richard V. Burgujian, Gaikokuho Jimu Bengoshi Jimusho, Toranomon No. 45 Mori Building, Third Floor, 1-5, Toranomon 5-chome Minato-Ku.
Telephone: 0081-3-3431-6943.
Facsimile: 0081-3-3431-6945.
Brussels, Belgium Office: Avenue Louise 326, Box 37, 1050.
Telephone: 011-322-646-0353.
Facsimile: 011-322-646-2135.

MEMBERS OF FIRM

Douglas B. Henderson
Ford F. Farabow, Jr.
Arthur S. Garrett
Donald R. Dunner
Tipton D. Jennings IV
Laurence R. Hefter
Michael C. Elmer
John M. Romary
Richard Lee Stroup
David W. Hill
Thomas W. Winland
E. Robert Yoches
Barry W. Graham
Susan Haberman Griffen
Christopher P. Foley
John C. Paul
Griffith B. Price, Jr.
John F. Hornick
Robert D. Litowitz
David M. Kelly

COUNSEL

Arthur J. Levine

ASSOCIATES

Mark S. Sommers
Jeffrey A. Berkowitz (Not admitted in DC)
Carla C. Calcagno
Lisa F. Peller
Randi S. Kremer (Not admitted in DC)
Linda S. Paine-Powell
John R. Alison

Reference: Crestar Bank, N.A., Washington, D.C.

For full biographical listings, see the Martindale-Hubbell Law Directory

LANE, AITKEN & MCCANN (AV)

Watergate Office Building, 2600 Virginia Avenue, N.W., 20037
Telephone: 202-337-5556
Telecopier: 202-337-8073

(See Next Column)

MEMBERS OF FIRM

Richard L. Aitken
Clifton E. McCann
John P. Shannon, Jr.
Laurence J. Marhoefer (Not admitted in DC)
Andrew C. Aitken (Not admitted in DC)

ASSOCIATE

David D'Zurilla

OF COUNSEL

Joseph M. Lane

For full biographical listings, see the Martindale-Hubbell Law Directory

LEWIS & TRATTNER (AV)

Suite 875, 1150 18th Street, N.W., 20036-3816
Telephone: 202-331-1416
800-333-2540
Telecopier: 202-331-1463

MEMBERS OF FIRM

Warren L. Lewis
Stephen M. Trattner

ASSOCIATE

Troy A. Morgan

OF COUNSEL

Jeffrey E. Kolton (Not admitted in DC)

For full biographical listings, see the Martindale-Hubbell Law Directory

*** MCDERMOTT, WILL & EMERY (AV)**

A Partnership including Professional Corporations
1850 K Street, N.W., 20006-2296
Telephone: 202-887-8000
Telex: 253565 MILAM CGO
Facsimile: 202-778-8087
Chicago, Illinois Office: 227 West Monroe Street.
Telephone: 312-372-2000.
Telex: 253565 MILAM CGO.
Facsimile: 312-984-7700.
Boston, Massachusetts Office: 75 State Street, Suite 1700.
Telephone: 617-345-5000.
Telex: 951324 MILAM BSN.
Facsimile: 617-345-5077.
Miami, Florida Office: 201 South Biscayne Boulevard.
Telephone: 305-358-3500.
Telex: 441777 LEYES.
Facsimile: 305-347-6500.
Los Angeles, California Office: 2049 Century Park East.
Telephone: 310-277-4110.
Facsimile: 310-277-4730.
Newport Beach, California Office: 1301 Dove Street, Suite 500.
Telephone: 714-851-0633.
Facsimile: 714-851-9348.
New York, N.Y. Office: 1211 Avenue of the Americas.
Telephone: 212-768-5400.
Facsimile: 212-768-5444.
St. Petersburg, Russia Office: 2/2 Tchaikovsky Street, #517, 191187 St. Petersburg, Russia.
Telephone: (7) (812) 273-9831.
Facsimile: (7) (812) 273-9831.
Tallinn, Estonia Office: Tallinn Business Center, 6 Harju Street, EE0001 Tallinn, Estonia.
Telephone: 372 6 31-05-53.
Facsimile: 372 6 31-05-54.
Vilnius, Lithuania Office: Smetonos 6, 2600 Vilnius, Lithuania.
Telephone: 370 2 61-43-08.
Facsimile: 370 2 22-79-55.
Associated (Independent) Offices:
Brussels, Belgium: Uettwiller Grelon Lippens Dekeyser, 73 avenue Vandendriessche, 1150 Brussels, Belgium.
Telephone: (32) (2) 772-87-50.
Facsimile: (32) (2) 772-87-52.
London, England: Paisner & Co, Bouverie House, 154 Fleet Street, London EC4A 2DQ, England.
Telephone: (44) (71) 353-0299.
Facsimile: (44) (71) 583-8621.
Paris, France: Uettwiller Grelon Gout Canat & Associes, 68, boulevard de Courcelles, 75017 Paris, France.
Telephone: (33) (1) 48 88 89 00.
Facsimile: (33) (1) 48 88 05 50.

MEMBERS OF FIRM

Seth D. Greenstein
Carl W. Schwarz
James H. Sneed

*Denotes a lawyer employed by a Professional Corporation which is a member of the Firm

For Complete List of Firm Personnel, See General Section

For full biographical listings, see the Martindale-Hubbell Law Directory

Washington—Continued

MIDLEN & GUILLOT, CHARTERED (AV)

3238 Prospect Street, N.W., 20007-3214
Telephone: 202-333-1500
Facsimile: 202-333-6852
Internet: MGCG@delphi.com

John H. Midlen, Jr.
Gregory H. Guillot (Not admitted in DC)

For full biographical listings, see the Martindale-Hubbell Law Directory

SHAWN, MANN & NIEDERMAYER, L.L.P. (AV)

1850 M Street, N.W., Suite 280, 20036-5803
Telephone: 202-331-7900
Fax: 202-331-0726

MEMBER OF FIRM

Jeffrey L. Squires

For full biographical listings, see the Martindale-Hubbell Law Directory

*** VENABLE, BAETJER, HOWARD & CIVILETTI** (AV)

A Partnership including Professional Corporations
Suite 1000, 1201 New York Avenue, N.W., 20005
Telephone: 202-962-4800
Fax: 202-962-8300
Baltimore, Maryland Office: Venable, Baetjer and Howard, 1800 Mercantile Bank & Trust Building, 2 Hopkins Plaza.
Telephone: 410-244-7400.
McLean, Virginia Office: Venable, Baetjer and Howard, Suite 400, 2010 Corporate Ridge.
Telephone: 703-760-1600.
Rockville, Maryland Office: Venable, Baetjer and Howard, Suite 500, One Church Street, P. O. Box 1906.
Telephone: 301-217-5600.
Towson, Maryland Office: Venable, Baetjer and Howard, 210 Allegheny Avenue, P. O. Box 5517.
Telephone: 410-494-6200.

MEMBERS OF FIRM

Thomas J. Kenney, Jr. (P.C.) (Not admitted in DC)
Douglas D. Connah, Jr. (P.C.) (Also at Baltimore, Maryland Office)
Kenneth C. Bass, III (Also at McLean, Virginia Office)
Max Stul Oppenheimer (P.C.) (Also at Baltimore and Towson, Maryland Offices)
Edward F. Glynn, Jr.
James R. Myers
Jeffrey D. Knowles
Jeffrey A. Dunn (Also at Baltimore, Maryland Office)
George F. Pappas (Also at Baltimore, Maryland Office)
William D. Coston
William D. Quarles (Also at Towson, Maryland Office)
Jeffrey L. Ihnen
James A. Dunbar (Also at Baltimore, Maryland Office)
Mary E. Pivec (Not admitted in DC; Also at Baltimore, Maryland Office)
Robert J. Bolger, Jr. (Not admitted in DC; Also at Baltimore, Maryland Office)
Paul A. Serini (Not admitted in DC; Also at Baltimore, Maryland Office)
Gary M. Hnath

OF COUNSEL

Fred W. Hathaway

ASSOCIATES

Royal W. Craig (Not admitted in DC)
David W. Goewey
Edward Brendan Magrab (Not admitted in DC)
Barbara L. Waite

For Complete List of Firm Personnel, See General Section

For full biographical listings, see the Martindale-Hubbell Law Directory

FLORIDA

*MIAMI,** Dade Co.

KENNY NACHWALTER SEYMOUR ARNOLD CRITCHLOW & SPECTOR, PROFESSIONAL ASSOCIATION (AV)

1100 Miami Center, 201 South Biscayne Boulevard, 33131-4327
Telephone: 305-373-1000
Facsimile: 305-372-1861
ABA/net: 18338
Rogersville, Tennessee Office: 107 East Main Street, Suite 301, 37857-3347.
Telephone: 615-272-5300.
Facsimile: 615-272-4961.

James J. Kenny
Michael Nachwalter
Richard Alan Arnold
Brian F. Spector
Kevin J. Murray
Harry R. Schafer
David H. Lichter

(See Next Column)

Representative Clients: Cartier, Inc.; Federated Department Stores, Inc.; GTE Directories Corp.; Health Trust, Inc.; Hospital Corporation of America; Macmillan, Inc.; Mont Blanc-Simplo Gmbh.; Pepe (U.K.) Ltd. & Pepe Clothing (U.S.A.), Inc.; Rolex Watch, USA, Inc.

For Complete List of Firm Personnel, See General Section

For full biographical listings, see the Martindale-Hubbell Law Directory

JOHN CYRIL MALLOY (AV)

Suite 1480 701 Buckell Avenue, 33131
Telephone: 305-374-1003

For full biographical listings, see the Martindale-Hubbell Law Directory

MCDERMOTT, WILL & EMERY (AV)

A Partnership including Professional Corporations
201 South Biscayne Boulevard, 33131-4336
Telephone: 305-358-3500
Telex: 441777 LEYES
Facsimile: 305-347-6500
Chicago, Illinois Office: 227 West Monroe Street.
Telephone: 312-372-2000.
Telex: 253565 MILAM CGO.
Facsimile: 312-984-7700.
Boston, Massachusetts Office: 75 State Street, Suite 1700.
Telephone: 617-345-5000.
Telex: 951324 MILAM BSN.
Facsimile: 617-345-5077.
Washington, D.C. Office: 1850 K Street, N.W.
Telephone: 202-887-8000.
Telex: 904261 MILAM CGO.
Facsimile: 202-778-8087.
Los Angeles, California Office: 2049 Century Park East.
Telephone: 310-277-4110.
Facsimile: 310-277-4730.
Newport Beach, California Office: 1301 Dove Street, Suite 500.
Telephone: 714-851-0633.
Facsimile: 714-851-9348.
New York, N.Y. Office: 1211 Avenue of the Americas.
Telephone: 212-768-5400.
Facsimile: 212-768-5444.
St. Petersburg, Russia Office: 2/2 Tchaikovsky Street, #517, 191187 St. Petersburg, Russia.
Telephone: (7) (812) 273-9831.
Facsimile: (7) (812) 273-9831.
Tallinn, Estonia Office: Tallinn Business Center, 6 Harju Street, EE0001 Tallinn, Estonia.
Telephone: 372 6 31-05-53.
Facsimile: 372 6 31-05-54.
Vilnius, Lithuania Office: Smetonos 6, 2600 Vilnius, Lithuania.
Telephone: 370 2 61-43-08.
Facsimile: 370 2 22-79-55.
Associated (Independent) Offices:
Brussels, Belgium: Uettwiller Grelon Lippens Dekeyser, 73 avenue Vandendriessche, 1150 Brussels, Belgium.
Telephone: (32) (2) 772-87-50.
Facsimile: (32) (2) 772-87-52.
London, England: Paisner & Co, Bouverie House, 154 Fleet Street, London EC4A 2DQ, England.
Telephone: (44) (71) 353-0299.
Facsimile: (44) (71) 583-8621.
Paris, France: Uettwiller Grelon Gout Canat & Associes, 68, boulevard de Courcelles, 75017 Paris, France.
Telephone: (33) (1) 48 88 89 00.
Facsimile: (33) (1) 48 88 05 50.

COUNSEL

James A. Gale

Lisa R. Daugherty

For Complete List of Firm Personnel, See General Section

For full biographical listings, see the Martindale-Hubbell Law Directory

MERSHON, SAWYER, JOHNSTON, DUNWODY & COLE (AV)

A Partnership including Professional Associations
Suite 4500 First Union Financial Center, 200 South Biscayne Boulevard, 33131-2387
Telephone: 305-358-5100
Cable Address: "Mercole"
Telex: 515705
Fax: 305-376-8654
Naples, Florida Office: Pelican Bay Corporate Centre, Suite 501, 5551 Ridgewood Drive.
Telephone: 813-598-1055.
Fax: 813-598-1868.
West Palm Beach, Florida Office: 777 South Flagler Drive, Suite 900.
Telephone: 407-659-5990.
Fax: 407-659-6313.

(See Next Column)

MERSHON, SAWYER, JOHNSTON, DUNWODY & COLE—*Continued*

Key West, Florida Office: 3132 North Side Drive, Suite 102.
Telephone: 305-296-1774.
Fax: 305-296-1715
London, England Office: Blake Lodge, Bridge Lane, London SW11 3AD, England.
Telephone: 44-71-978-7748.
Fax: 44-71-350-0156.

MEMBER OF FIRM

William J. Dunaj (P.A.)

Representative Clients: Arvida/JMB Partners; Bankers Trust Co.; Biscayne Kennel Club, Inc.; The Chase Manhattan Bank, N.A.; Lennar Corp.; Reynolds Metals Co.; United States Sugar Corp.; University of Miami.

For Complete List of Firm Personnel, See General Section

For full biographical listings, see the Martindale-Hubbell Law Directory

GEORGIA

*ATLANTA,** Fulton Co.

ALSTON & BIRD (AV)

A Partnership including Professional Corporations
One Atlantic Center, 1201 West Peachtree Street, 30309-3424
Telephone: 404-881-7000
Telecopier: 404-881-7777
Cable Address: AMGRAM GA
Telex: 54-2996
Easylink: 62985848
Washington, D.C. Office: 700 Thirteenth Street, Suite 350 20005-3960.
Telephone: 202-508-3300.
Telecopier: 202-508-3333.

MEMBERS OF FIRM

John K. Train III
William C. Humphreys, Jr.
Peter Kontio
Kevin E. Grady
Peter Q. Bassett
Frank G. Smith III
Martin J. Elgison
H. Stephen Harris, Jr.
Michael P. Kenny
Randall L. Allen

COUNSEL

Janet E. Witt (Not admitted in GA)

ASSOCIATES

Beth E. Kirby
David J. Stewart
James J. Wolfson

Representative Clients: Borden, Inc.; Genuine Parts Company; Houston's Restaurants, Inc.; Printpack, Inc.; Suntory Water Group, Inc.

For Complete List of Firm Personnel, See General Section

For full biographical listings, see the Martindale-Hubbell Law Directory

BONDURANT, MIXSON & ELMORE (AV)

1201 W. Peachtree Street Suite 3900, 30309
Telephone: 404-881-4100
FAX: 404-881-4111

MEMBERS OF FIRM

Emmet J. Bondurant II
Jane E. Fahey
Carolyn R. Gorwitz

Representative Clients: The Aetna Casualty and Surety Company; Bottlers of Coca-Cola, U.S.A.; Brinks Home Security Systems, Inc.; Delta Air Lines, Inc.; Fina Oil and Chemical Company; JMB Realty Corp.; The Paradies Shops, Inc.; Sanifill, Inc.; Trammell Crow Co.

For Complete List of Firm Personnel, See General Section

For full biographical listings, see the Martindale-Hubbell Law Directory

SUTHERLAND, ASBILL & BRENNAN (AV)

999 Peachtree Street, N.E., 30309-3996
Telephone: 404-853-8000
Facsimile: 404-853-8806
Washington, D.C. Office: 1275 Pennsylvania Avenue, N.W., 20004-2404.
Telephone: 202-383-0100.
New York, N.Y. Office: 1270 Avenue of the Americas, 10020-1700.
Telephone: 212-332-3000.
Austin, Texas Office: 111 Congress Avenue, 23rd Floor, 78701-4079.
Telephone: 512-469-3350.

Thomas A. Cox
J. D. Fleming, Jr.
John H. Fleming

COUNSEL OF THE FIRM
IN ATLANTA, GEORGIA

Patricia Bayer Cunningham

(See Next Column)

SPECIAL TRADEMARK AND COPYRIGHT COUNSEL

Paul S. Owens

For Complete List of Firm Personnel, See General Section

For full biographical listings, see the Martindale-Hubbell Law Directory

IDAHO

*BOISE,** Ada Co.

MOFFATT, THOMAS, BARRETT, ROCK & FIELDS, CHARTERED (AV)

First Security Building, 911 West Idaho Street, Suite 300, P.O. Box 829, 83701
Telephone: 208-345-2000
FAX: 208-385-5384
Idaho Falls Office: 525 Park Avenue, Suite 2D, P.O. Box 1367, 83403.
Telephone: 208-522-6700.
FAX: 208-522-5111.
Pocatello, Idaho Office: 1110 Call Creek Drive, P.O. Box 4941, 83201.
Telephone: 208-233-2001.

Paul S. Street
Thomas C. Morris

Representative Clients: BMC West Corporation; Chevron, U.S.A.; First Security Bank of Idaho, N.A.; General Motors Corp.; Idaho Potato Commission; Intermountain Gas Co.; John Alden Life Insurance Co.; Micron, Inc.; Royal Insurance Cos.; St. Luke's Regional Medical Center & Mountain States Tumor Institute.

For Complete List of Firm Personnel, See General Section

For full biographical listings, see the Martindale-Hubbell Law Directory

ILLINOIS

*CHICAGO,** Cook Co.

DICK AND HARRIS (AV)

Suite 3800, 181 West Madison Street, 60602
Telephone: 312-726-4000
Telecopier: 312-726-5834

MEMBERS OF FIRM

Richard Eugene Dick
Richard D. Harris
Max Shaftal
Howard E. Silverman

ASSOCIATES

John S. Pacocha
Douglas B. Teaney
Jody L. Factor
Herbert H. Finn
Jordan A. Sigale
Jordan Herzog

For full biographical listings, see the Martindale-Hubbell Law Directory

GORDON & GLICKSON, P.C. (AV)

36th Floor, 444 North Michigan Avenue, 60611-3903
Telephone: 312-321-1700
FAX: 312-321-9324
Springfield, Illinois Office: 600 South Second Street.
Telephone: 217-789-1040.
FAX: 217-789-1077.

Richard L. Fogel
Scott L. Glickson
Mark L. Gordon
Thomas R. Lamont (Resident, Springfield Office)
Mark A. Luscombe
Diana J. P. McKenzie
Michael E.C. Moss
Stuart Smith
Barry D. Weiss

Gregory T. Riddle (Resident, Springfield Office)
Virginia H. Holden
Randall M. Whitmeyer
Christopher L. Gallinari

For full biographical listings, see the Martindale-Hubbell Law Directory

McDERMOTT, WILL & EMERY (AV)

A Partnership including Professional Corporations
227 West Monroe Street, 60606-5096
Telephone: 312-372-2000
Telex: 253565 Milam CGO
Facsimile: 312-984-7700
Boston, Massachusetts Office: 75 State Street, Suite 1700.
Telephone: 617-345-5000.
Telex: 951324 MILAM BSN.
Facsimile: 617-345-5077.

(See Next Column)

McDERMOTT, WILL & EMERY, *Chicago—Continued*

Miami, Florida Office: 201 South Biscayne Boulevard.
Telephone: 305-358-3500.
Telex: 441777 LEYES.
Facsimile: 305-347-6500.
Washington, D.C. Office: 1850 K Street, N.W.
Telephone: 202-887-8000.
Telex: 253565 MILAM CGO.
Facsimile: 202-778-8087.
Los Angeles, California Office: 2049 Century Park East.
Telephone: 310-277-4110.
Facsimile: 310-277-4730.
Newport Beach, California Office: 1301 Dove Street, Suite 500.
Telephone: 714-851-0633.
Facsimile: 714-851-9348.
New York, N.Y. Office: 1211 Avenue of the Americas.
Telephone: 212-768-5400.
Facsimile: 212-768-5444.
St. Petersburg, Russia Office: 2/2 Tchaikovsky Street, #517, 191187 St. Petersburg, Russia.
Telephone: (7) (812) 273-9831.
Facsimile: (7) (812) 273-9831.
Tallinn, Estonia Office: Tallinn Business Center, 6 Harju Street, EE0001 Tallinn, Estonia.
Telephone: 372 6 31-05-53.
Facsimile: 372 6 31-05-54.
Vilnius, Lithuania Office: Smetonos 6, 2600 Vilnius, Lithuania.
Telephone: 370 2 61-43-08.
Facsimile: 370 2 22-79-55.
Associated (Independent) Offices:
Brussels, Belgium: Uettwiller Grelon Lippens Dekeyser, 73 avenue Vandendriessche, 1150 Brussels, Belgium.
Telephone: (32) (2) 772-87-50.
Facsimile: (32) (2) 772-87-52.
London, England: Paisner & Co, Bouverie House, 154 Fleet Street, London EC4A 2DQ, England.
Telephone: (44) (71) 353-0299.
Facsimile: (44) (71) 583-8621.
Paris, France: Uettwiller Grelon Gout Canat & Associes, 68, boulevard de Courcelles, 75017 Paris, France.
Telephone: (33) (1) 48 88 89 00.
Facsimile: (33) (1) 48 88 05 50.

MEMBERS OF FIRM

Michelle C. Burke
Byron L. Gregory
Steven P. Handler *
David Marx, Jr.
Bruce H. Weitzman *

ASSOCIATES

Paula J. Krasny
Janet A. Marvel

*Denotes a lawyer employed by a Professional Corporation which is a member of the Firm.

For Complete List of Firm Personnel, See General Section

For full biographical listings, see the Martindale-Hubbell Law Directory

PATTISHALL, McAULIFFE, NEWBURY, HILLIARD & GERALDSON (AV)

Suite 5000, 311 South Wacker Drive, 60606
Telephone: 312-554-8000
Facsimile: 312-554-8015
Telex: 27-0500
Washington, D.C. Office: 320 Watergate, Six Hundred 20037.
Telephone: 202-338-1300.
Facsimile: 202-388-9349.
Telex: 89-7453.

MEMBERS OF FIRM

Beverly W. Pattishall
Jeremiah D. McAuliffe
Robert M. Newbury
Benjamin S. Warren III (Resident Partner, Washington, D.C. Office)
Raymond I. Geraldson, Jr.
David Craig Hilliard
Edward G. Wierzbicki
Robert W. Sacoff
Mark V. B. Partridge
Joseph N. Welch II
Mark H. Hellmann
Jean Marie R. Pechette

Daniel D. Frohling
John Thompson Brown
Mary E. Innis
Douglas N. Masters
Brett A. August
Jonathan S. Jennings
John Michael Murphy
Paul R. Garcia
Kimberly White Alcantara
Maxine S. Lans
Nancy L. Clarke

For full biographical listings, see the Martindale-Hubbell Law Directory

*GENEVA,** Kane Co.

SMITH, LANDMEIER & SKAAR, P.C. (AV)

15 North Second Street, 60134
Telephone: 708-232-2880
Fax: 708-232-2889

(See Next Column)

Howard E. Smith, Jr.
Allen L. Landmeier
James D. Skaar

Brian W. Baugh
Vincent J. Elders

References: Firstar Bank, Geneva, N.A., Geneva, Illinois; State Bank of Geneva, Geneva, Illinois.

For full biographical listings, see the Martindale-Hubbell Law Directory

INDIANA

*INDIANAPOLIS,** Marion Co.

ICE MILLER DONADIO & RYAN (AV)

One American Square Box 82001, 46282-0002
Telephone: 317-236-2100
Fax: 317-236-2219

MEMBERS OF FIRM

Jack R. Snyder
Jay G. Taylor
David M. Mattingly
James L. Petersen
Philip A. Whistler
John F. Prescott, Jr.
Lisa Stone Sciscoe

OF COUNSEL

Bradley L. Williams
Roland A. Fuller, III

ASSOCIATES

Bruce W. Longbottom
Dale E. Stackhouse

Counsel For: Biomet, Inc.; Curtis Publishing Co.; Indianapolis Business Journal; Indianapolis Motor Speedway; Integrated Technologies, Inc.; Porsche Ag; K-White Tools, Inc.; Southern Corp.; Subaru-Isuzu Automotive; USA Fund Inc.

For Complete List of Firm Personnel, See General Section

For full biographical listings, see the Martindale-Hubbell Law Directory

KANSAS

*WICHITA,** Sedgwick Co.

FOULSTON & SIEFKIN (AV)

(Formerly Foulston, Siefkin, Powers & Eberhardt)
700 Fourth Financial Center, Broadway at Douglas, 67202
Telephone: 316-267-6371
Facsimile: 316-267-6345
Topeka, Kansas Office: 1515 Bank IV Tower, 534 Kansas Avenue. 66603.
Telephone: 913-233-3600.
FAX: 913-233-1610.
Member: Lex Mundi, A Global Association of Independent Firms

MEMBERS OF FIRM

James D. Oliver
R. Douglas Reagan

For Complete List of Firm Personnel, See General Section

For full biographical listings, see the Martindale-Hubbell Law Directory

KENTUCKY

*LOUISVILLE,** Jefferson Co.

ROACH AND WHEAT (AV)

Suite 800, The Republic Building, 429 West Muhammad Ali Boulevard, 40202-2346
Telephone: 502-585-2040
Facsimile: 502-585-1024

Martin Roach (1938-1988)
Jack A. Wheat

ASSOCIATE

Joel T. Beres

For full biographical listings, see the Martindale-Hubbell Law Directory

SEILLER & HANDMAKER (AV)

2200 Meidinger Tower, 40202
Telephone: 502-584-7400
Telecopier: 502-583-2100
Paris, Kentucky Office: Seiller, Handmaker & Blevins, P.S.C., 1431 South Main Street.
Telephone: 606-987-3980.
Telecopier: 606-987-3982.

(See Next Column)

SEILLER & HANDMAKER—*Continued*

New Albany, Indiana Office: 204 Pearl Street, Suite 200.
Telephone: 812-948-8307.
Telecopier: 812-948-8383.

Edward F. Seiller (1897-1990)

MEMBERS OF FIRM

Stuart Allen Handmaker
Bill V. Seiller
David M. Cantor
Neil C. Bordy
Kyle Anne Citrynell
Maury D. Kommor
Cynthia Compton Stone

ASSOCIATES

Glenn A. Cohen
Pamela M. Greenwell
Tomi Anne Blevins Pulliam (Resident, Paris Office)
Linda Scholle Cowan
Mary Zeller Wing Ceridan
Michael C. Bratcher
John E. Brengle
Patrick R. Holland, II
Edwin Jon Wolfe
Donna F. Townsend
William C. Robinson

OF COUNSEL

Robert S. Frey

For full biographical listings, see the Martindale-Hubbell Law Directory

MARYLAND

*BALTIMORE,** (Independent City)

VENABLE, BAETJER AND HOWARD (AV)

A Partnership including Professional Corporations
1800 Mercantile Bank & Trust Building, 2 Hopkins Plaza, 21201
Telephone: 410-244-7400
Washington, D.C. Office: Venable, Baetjer, Howard & Civiletti. Suite 1000, 1201 New York Avenue, N.W.
Telephone: 202-962-4800.
McLean, Virginia Office: Suite 400, 2010 Corporate Ridge.
Telephone: 703-760-1600.
Rockville, Maryland Office: Suite 500, One Church Street, P. O. Box 1906.
Telephone: 301-217-5600.
Towson, Maryland Office: 210 Allegheny Avenue, P. O. Box 5517.
Telephone: 410-494-6200.

MEMBERS OF FIRM

George Cochran Doub (P.C.)
Thomas J. Kenney, Jr. (P.C.) (Also at Washington, D.C. Office)
Douglas D. Connah, Jr. (P.C.) (Also at Washington, D.C. Office)
Kenneth C. Bass, III (Not admitted in MD; Also at Washington, D.C. and McLean, Virginia Offices)
Max Stul Oppenheimer (P.C.) (Also at Washington, D.C. and Towson, Maryland Offices)
Edward F. Glynn, Jr. (Not admitted in MD; Resident, Washington, D.C. Office)
G. Stewart Webb, Jr.
James R. Myers (Not admitted in MD; Resident, Washington, D.C. Office)
Jeffrey D. Knowles (Not admitted in MD; Resident, Washington, D.C. Office)
F. Dudley Staples, Jr. (Also at Towson, Maryland Office)
Jeffrey A. Dunn (also at Washington, D.C. Office)
George F. Pappas (Also at Washington, D.C. Office)
William D. Coston (Not admitted in MD; Resident, Washington, D.C. Office)
William D. Quarles (Also at Washington, D.C. and Towson, Maryland Offices)
Jeffrey L. Ihnen (Not admitted in MD; Resident, Washington, D. C. Office)
James A. Dunbar (Also at Washington, D.C. Office)
Mary E. Pivec (Also at Washington, D.C. Office)
Robert J. Bolger, Jr. (Also at Washington, D.C. Office)
David J. Heubeck
Paul A. Serini (Also at Washington, D.C. Office)
Gary M. Hnath (Resident, Washington, D.C. Office)

OF COUNSEL

Fred W. Hathaway (Not admitted in MD; Resident, Washington, D.C. Office)

ASSOCIATES

Paul D. Barker, Jr.
Royal W. Craig (Resident, Washington, D.C. Office)
Newton B. Fowler, III
David W. Goewey (Not admitted in MD; Resident, Washington, D.C. Office)
Edward Brendan Magrab (Resident, Washington, D.C. Office)
Vicki Margolis
John T. Prisbe
J. Preston Turner
Barbara L. Waite (Not admitted in MD; Resident, Washington, D.C. Office)

For Complete List of Firm Personnel, See General Section

For full biographical listings, see the Martindale-Hubbell Law Directory

SILVER SPRING, Montgomery Co.

ALEXANDER, GEBHARDT, APONTE & MARKS, L.L.C. (AV)

Lee Plaza-Suite 805, 8601 Georgia Avenue, 20910
Telephone: 301-589-2222
Facsimile: 301-589-2523
Washington, D.C. Office: 1314 Nineteenth Street, N.W., 20036.
Telephone: 202-835-1555.
New York, New York Office: 330 Madison Avenue, 36th Floor.
Telephone: 212-808-0008.
Fax: 212-599-1028.

Koteles Alexander (Not admitted in MD)
James L. Bearden (Not admitted in MD)

Susan C. Lee (Not admitted in MD)

Reference: Riggs National Bank of Washington, D.C.

For full biographical listings, see the Martindale-Hubbell Law Directory

MASSACHUSETTS

*BOSTON,** Suffolk Co.

DIKE, BRONSTEIN, ROBERTS & CUSHMAN (AV)

A Partnership including Professional Corporations
130 Water Street, 02109
Telephone: 617-523-3400
Telex: 200291 STRE UR
Telefax: 617-523-6440; 523-7318
Marlborough, Massachusetts Office: 62 Cotting Avenue. P.O. Box 556.
Telephone: 508-485-7772.
Fax: 508-485-0363.

Sewall P. Bronstein (P.C.)
Donald Brown (P.C.)
Robert L. Goldberg
Robert F. O'Connell
David G. Conlin (P.C.)
George W. Neuner (P.C.)
Ernest V. Linek
Linda M. Buckley
Ronald I. Eisenstein
Henry D. Pahl, Jr.

David S. Resnick
Peter F. Corless
Kevin J. Fournier
Cara Zucker Lowen

OF COUNSEL

Peter J. Manus
John L. Welch
Milton M. Oliver

For full biographical listings, see the Martindale-Hubbell Law Directory

MCDERMOTT, WILL & EMERY (AV)

A Partnership including Professional Corporations
75 State Street, Suite 1700, 02109-1807
Telephone: 617-345-5000
Telex: 951324 MILAM BSN
Facsimile: 617-345-5077
Chicago, Illinois Office: 227 West Monroe Street.
Telephone: 312-372-2000.
Telex: 253565 MILAM CGO.
Facsimile: 312-984-7700.
Miami, Florida Office: 201 South Biscayne Boulevard.
Telephone: 305-358-3500.
Telex: 441777 LEYES.
Facsimile: 305-347-6500.
Washington, D.C. Office: 1850 K Street, N.W.
Telephone: 202-887-8000.
Telex: 253565 MILAM CGO.
Facsimile: 202-778-8087.
Los Angeles, California Office: 2049 Century Park East.
Telephone: 310-277-4110.
Facsimile: 310-277-4730.
Newport Beach, California Office: 1301 Dove Street, Suite 500.
Telephone: 714-851-0633.
Facsimile: 714-851-9348.
New York, N.Y. Office: 1211 Avenue of the Americas.
Telephone: 212-768-5400.
Facsimile: 212-768-5444.
St. Petersburg, Russia Office: 2/2 Tchaikovsky Street, #517, 191187 St. Petersburg, Russia.
Telephone: (7) (812) 273-9831.
Facsimile: (7) (812) 273-9831.
Tallinn, Estonia Office: Tallinn Business Center, 6 Harju Street, EE0001 Tallinn, Estonia.
Telephone: 372 6 31-05-53.
Facsimile: 372 6 31-05-54.
Vilnius, Lithuania Office: Smetonos 6, 2600 Vilnius, Lithuania.
Telephone: 370 2 61-43-08.
Facsimile: 370 2 22-79-55.

(See Next Column)

McDermott, Will & Emery, *Boston—Continued*

Associated (Independent) Offices:
Brussels, Belgium: Uettwiller Grelon Lippens Dekeyser, 73 avenue Vandendriessche, 1150 Brussels, Belgium.
Telephone: (32) (2) 772-87-50.
Facsimile: (32) (2) 772-87-52.
London, England: Paisner & Co, Bouverie House, 154 Fleet Street, London EC4A 2DQ, England.
Telephone: (44) (71) 353-0299.
Facsimile: (44) (71) 583-8621.
Paris, France: Uettwiller Grelon Gout Canat & Associes, 68, Boulevard de Courcelles, 75017 Paris, France.
Telephone: (33) (1) 48 88 89 00.
Facsimile: (33) (1) 48 88 05 50.

MEMBER OF FIRM

James J. Marcellino

For Complete List of Firm Personnel, See General Section

For full biographical listings, see the Martindale-Hubbell Law Directory

Palmer & Dodge (AV)

(Storey Thorndike Palmer & Dodge)
One Beacon Street, 02108
Telephone: 617-573-0100
Telecopier: 617-227-4420
Telex: 951104
Cable Address: "Storeydike," Boston

MEMBER OF FIRM

F. Andrew Anderson

For Complete List of Firm Personnel, See General Section

For full biographical listings, see the Martindale-Hubbell Law Directory

MICHIGAN

*DETROIT,** Wayne Co.

Bodman, Longley & Dahling (AV)

34th Floor 100 Renaissance Center, 48243
Telephone: 313-259-7777
Fax: 313-393-7579
Troy, Michigan Office: Suite 2020, 755 West Big Beaver Road.
Telephone: 810-362-2110.
Ann Arbor, Michigan Office: 110 Miller, Suite 300.
Telephone: 313-761-3780.
Northern Michigan Office: 229 Court Street, P.O. Box 405, Cheboygan.
Telephone: 616-627-4351.

MEMBERS OF FIRM

Randolph S. Perry (Ann Arbor Office)
James J. Walsh
David G. Chardavoyne
Robert G. Brower
Fredrick J. Dindoffer
Susan M. Kornfield (Ann Arbor Office)

Representative Clients: Abitibi Price Group; Archdiocese of Detroit; Comerica Bank; The Detroit Lions, Inc.; Ford Estates; General Motors Corporation; Charles Stewart Mott Foundation; Norfolk Southern Corporation; Panhandle Eastern Corporation; State Farm Mutual Automobile Insurance Company.

For Complete List of Firm Personnel, See General Section

For full biographical listings, see the Martindale-Hubbell Law Directory

Butzel Long, A Professional Corporation (AV)

Suite 900, 150 West Jefferson, 48226
Telephone: 313-225-7000
Telecopier: 313-225-7080
Birmingham, Michigan Office: Suite 200, 32270 Telegraph Road.
Telephone: 810-258-1616.
Telecopier: 810-258-1439.
Lansing, Michigan Office: 118 West Ottawa Street.
Telephone: 517-372-6622.
Telecopier: 517-372-6672.
Ann Arbor, Michigan Office: Suite 400, 121 West Washington.
Telephone: 313-995-3110.
Telecopier: 313-995-1777.
Grosse Pointe Farms, Michigan Office: Suite 260, 21 Kercheval.
Telephone: 313-886-5446.
Telecopier: 313-886-2114.

Richard E. Rassel
Edward M. Kronk
Philip J. Kessler
James E. Stewart
James C. Bruno
James E. Wynne
Leonard M. Niehoff

(See Next Column)

J. Michael Huget
Kenneth H. Adamczyk
Nicholas J. Stasevich

Representative Clients: Bridgestone/Firestone, Inc.; The Detroit News, Inc.; Detroit Diesel Corp.; Kelly Services; Kelsey Hayes Co.; Merrill Lynch & Co., Inc.; Stroh Brewery Co.; Takata Corp.; United Parcel Services of America, Inc.; The University of Michigan.

For Complete List of Firm Personnel, See General Section

For full biographical listings, see the Martindale-Hubbell Law Directory

*GRAND RAPIDS,** Kent Co.

Price, Heneveld, Cooper, DeWitt & Litton (AV)

695 Kenmoor, S.E., P.O. Box 2567, 49501
Telephone: 616-949-9610
Cable Address: "Preld"
Telex: 226-402
Telecopier: 616-957-8196

MEMBERS OF FIRM

Lloyd A. Heneveld
Richard C. Cooper
William W. DeWitt
Randall G. Litton
James A. Mitchell
Daniel Van Dyke
Harold W. Reick
Donald S. Gardner
Thomas M. McKinley
Carl S. Clark
Terence J. Linn
Frederick S. Burkhart

ASSOCIATES

James E. Bartek
Daniel L. Girdwood
Mark E. Bandy
Barry C. Kane

Representative Clients: Amway Corp.; Donnelly Corp.; Dow Chemical Co.; Gerber Products Co.; Kysor Industrial Corp.; L. Perrigo Co.; Prince Corp.; Ralston Purina Co.; Steelcase, Inc.; Wolverine World Wide, Inc.

For full biographical listings, see the Martindale-Hubbell Law Directory

Varnum, Riddering, Schmidt & Howlett (AV)

Bridgewater Place, P.O. Box 352, 49501-0352
Telephone: 616-336-6000
800-262-0011
Facsimile: 616-336-7000
Telex: 1561593 VARN
Lansing, Michigan Office: The Victor Center, Suite 810, 210 North Washington Square, 48933.
Telephone: 517-482-6237.
Facsimile: 517-482-6937.
Kalamazoo, Michigan Office: 350 East Michigan Avenue, 49007.
Telephone: 616-382-2300.
Facsimile: 616-382-2382.
Grand Haven, Michigan Office: 321 Washington Street, P.O. Box 288, 49417.
Telephone: 616-846-7100.
Facsimile: 616-846-7101.
Battle Creek, Michigan Office: 4950 West Dickman Road, Suite B-1, 49015.
Telephone: 616-962-7144.
Detroit, Michigan Office: 440 East Congress, Fourth Floor, 48226.
Telephone: 313-961-1600.
Facsimile: 313-961-1636.

COUNSEL

Peter Visserman

MEMBERS OF FIRM

John E. McGarry
Thomas L. Lockhart
H. Lawrence Smith
Timothy E. Eagle
Joel E. Bair

ASSOCIATES

Richard J. McKenna
Mark A. Davis

Counsel for: Cadillac Rubber & Plastics, Inc.; Cascade Engineering; Herman Miller, Inc.; Neway Anchorlok, Inc.; Smith's Industries; X-Rite, Inc.

For Complete List of Firm Personnel, See General Section

For full biographical listings, see the Martindale-Hubbell Law Directory

MONTANA

*BILLINGS,** Yellowstone Co.

Crowley, Haughey, Hanson, Toole & Dietrich (AV)

500 Transwestern II, 490 North 31st Street, P.O. Box 2529, 59103
Telephone: 406-252-3441
Fax: 406-259-4159
Helena, Montana Office: IBM Building, 100 North Park Avenue, Suite 300, 59601.
Telephone: 406-449-4165.
Fax: 406-449-5149.

(See Next Column)

CROWLEY, HAUGHEY, HANSON, TOOLE & DIETRICH—*Continued*

MEMBERS OF FIRM

Laura A. Mitchell | Mary Scrim

Representative Clients: Montana Power Co.; First Interstate Bank of Commerce; MDU Resources Group, Inc.; Chevron U.S.A., Inc.; Noranda Minerals Corp.; United Parcel Service.
Insurance Clients: Farmers Insurance Group; New York Life Insurance Co.

For Complete List of Firm Personnel, See General Section

For full biographical listings, see the Martindale-Hubbell Law Directory

NEW JERSEY

*HACKENSACK,** Bergen Co.

KLAUBER & JACKSON (AV)

Continental Plaza, 411 Hackensack Avenue, 07601
Telephone: 201-487-5800
Telex: 133521
Fax: 201-343-1684; 343-7544

MEMBERS OF FIRM

Stefan J. Klauber | David A. Jackson

ASSOCIATES

Barbara L. Renda | Lawrence D. Mandel

OF COUNSEL

Jeffrey L. Miller | Herbert H. Waddell

LEGAL SUPPORT PERSONNEL

Thomas E. Anderson

For full biographical listings, see the Martindale-Hubbell Law Directory

*NEWARK,** Essex Co.

McCARTER & ENGLISH (AV)

Four Gateway Center, 100 Mulberry Street, P.O. Box 652, 07101-0652
Telephone: 201-622-4444
Telecopier: 201-624-7070
Cable Address: "McCarter" Newark
Cherry Hill, New Jersey Office: 1810 Chapel Avenue West.
Telephone: 609-662-8444.
Telecopier: 609-662-6203.
New York, New York Office: Suite 1519, One World Trade Center.
Telephone: 212-466-9018.
Telecopier: 212-432-6568.
Boca Raton, Florida Office: 2255 Glades Road, Suite 319-A.
Telephone: 407-994-6262.
Telecopier: 407-241-0798.
Wilmington, Delaware Office: Mellon Bank Center, 919 Market Street.
Telephone: 302-654-8010.
Telecopier: 302-654-0795.

MEMBERS OF FIRM

Charles R. Merrill | John L. McGoldrick
Roslyn S. Harrison

COUNSEL

Robert W. Smith

ASSOCIATES

David W. Opderbeck | Dror Futter

For Complete List of Firm Personnel, See General Section

For full biographical listings, see the Martindale-Hubbell Law Directory

PRINCETON, Mercer Co.

BUCHANAN INGERSOLL (AV)

A Partnership
College Centre, 500 College Road East, 08540-6615
Telephone: 609-452-2666
Telecopier: 609-520-0360
Pittsburgh, Pennsylvania Office: Buchanan Ingersoll, Professional Corporation, 5800 USX Tower, 600 Grant Street.
Telephone: 412-562-8800.
Philadelphia, Pennsylvania Office: Buchanan Ingersoll, Professional Corporation, Two Logan Square, Twelfth Floor, 18th & Arch Streets.
Telephone: 215-665-8700.
Harrisburg, Pennsylvania Office: Buchanan Ingersoll, Professional Corporation, Vartan Parc, 30 North Third Street.
Telephone: 717-237-4800.
Tampa, Florida Office: Buchanan Ingersoll, Professional Corporation, 101 East Kennedy Boulevard, Suite 1030.
Telephone: 813-222-8180.
North Miami Beach, Florida Office: Buchanan Ingersoll, Professional Corporation, 19495 Biscayne Boulevard.
Telephone: 305-933-5600.

(See Next Column)

Lexington, Kentucky Office: Buchanan Ingersoll, Professional Corporation, 1210 Vine Center Office Tower, 333 West Vine Street.
Telephone: 606-225-5333.

Frank S. Chow

For Complete List of Firm Personnel, See General Section

For full biographical listings, see the Martindale-Hubbell Law Directory

MATHEWS, WOODBRIDGE & COLLINS, A PROFESSIONAL CORPORATION (AV)

100 Thanet Circle Suite 306, 08540
Telephone: 609-924-3773
Fax: 609-924-3036
Telex: 642948

H. Hume Mathews (1911-1989) | Jane E. Alexander
Richard C. Woodbridge | Brooks R. Bruneau
Ronald G. Goebel (Retired) | Stuart H. Nissim (Not admitted in NJ)
Bruce M. Collins | Scott N. Bernstein
Robert G. Shepherd | Martha Greenewald Pugh (1913-1992)
Diane F. Dunn

COUNSEL

Dennis J. Helms

OF COUNSEL

Sheila F. Hordon

Representative Clients: Boy Scouts of America; United Jersey Bank.

For full biographical listings, see the Martindale-Hubbell Law Directory

NEW YORK

*NEW YORK,** New York Co.

BRUMBAUGH, GRAVES, DONOHUE & RAYMOND (AV)

30 Rockefeller Plaza, 10112
Telephone: 212-408-2500
Facsimile: 212-765-2519
MCI Mail: 611-1063
Telex: 650 6111063

MEMBERS OF FIRM

Francis J. Hone | Bradley B. Geist
Joseph D. Garon | Russell H. Falconer
Arthur S. Tenser | James J. Maune
Ronald B. Hildreth | John D. Murnane
Thomas R. Nesbitt, Jr. | Henry Y. S. Tang
Robert Neuner | Doreen Leavens Costa
Richard G. Berkley | Robert C. Scheinfeld
Richard S. Clark | Parker H. Bagley
Thomas D. MacBlain | John A. Fogarty, Jr.

OF COUNSEL

Dana M. Raymond | Frank W. Ford, Jr.
Frederick C. Carver

SPECIAL COUNSEL

Peter A. Businger (Not admitted in NY)

ASSOCIATES

Louis S. Sorell | Steven C. Gray
Gary M. Butter | David S. Benyacar
Marta E. Delsignore | Rochelle K. Seide
Dr. Kay-Ellen Smith | Steven R. Gustavson (Not admitted in NY)
Alex L. Yip | Andrew T. Block
Jong H. Lee | Michael J. Doherty
Thomas J. Parker | Paul A. Ragusa
Stephen J. Quigley | Adan Ayala
Neil P. Sirota
David T. Cunningham

For full biographical listings, see the Martindale-Hubbell Law Directory

COOPER & DUNHAM (AV)

1185 Avenue of the Americas, 10036
Telephone: 212-278-0400
Facsimile: 212-391-0525

MEMBERS OF FIRM

Gerald W. Griffin | Lewis H. Eslinger
Christopher C. Dunham | Jay H. Maioli
Ivan S. Kavrukov | Robert B. G. Horowitz
Norman H. Zivin | Donald S. Dowden
Peter D. Murray | Robert D. Katz
John P. White | William E. Pelton
Thomas G. Carulli | Peter J. Phillips
Donna A. Tobin

(See Next Column)

COOPER & DUNHAM, *New York—Continued*

ASSOCIATES

Wendy E. Miller
Richard S. Milner
Robert M. Bauer
Albert Wai-Kit Chan
Matthew J. Golden
Matthew B. Tropper
Lewis J. Kreisler
Jeffrey L. Snow
Jeffrey A. Hovden
Kristina L. Konstas
Robert T. Maldonado
Mark S. Cohen

OF COUNSEL

John N. Cooper
Thomas F. Moran

LEGAL SUPPORT PERSONNEL

SCIENTIFIC ADVISORS

Nathan P. Letts
Elizabeth Ann Bogosian
A. David Joran
Thomas E. Phalen
Adrian Gerard Looney
Keum A. Yoon
Victor DeVito (Patent Agent)

For full biographical listings, see the Martindale-Hubbell Law Directory

DEBEVOISE & PLIMPTON (AV)

875 Third Avenue, 10022
Telephone: 212-909-6000
Domestic Telex: 148377 DEBSTEVE NYK
Telecopier: (212) 909-6836
Los Angeles, California Office: 601 South Figueroa Street, Suite 3700, 90017.
Telephone: 213-680-8000.
Telecopier: 213-680-8100.
Washington, D.C. Office: 555 13th Street, N.W., 20004.
Telephone: 202-383-8000.
Telecopier: (202) 383-8118.
Paris, France Office: 21 Avenue George V 75008.
Telephone: (33-1) 40 73 12 12.
Telecopier: (33-1) 47 20 50 82.
Telex: 648141F DPPAR.
London, England Office: 1 Creed Court, 5 Ludgate Hill, EC4M 7AA.
Telephone: (44-171) 329-0779.
Telex: 88 4569 DPLON G.
Telecopier: (44-171) 329-0860.
Budapest, Hungary Office: 1065 Budapest, Révay Köz 2.III/2.
Telephone: (36-1)112-8067.
Telecopier: (36-1) 132-7995.
Hong Kong Office: 13/F Entertainment Building, 30 Queen's Road Central.
Telephone: (852) 2810-7918.
Fax: (852) 2810-9828.

MEMBERS OF FIRM

Bruce G. Merritt (Los Angeles, California Office)
Bruce P. Keller
John S. Kiernan
Jeffrey P. Cunard (Washington, D.C. Office)

For Complete List of Firm Personnel, See General Section

For full biographical listings, see the Martindale-Hubbell Law Directory

LOEB AND LOEB (AV)

A Partnership including Professional Corporations
345 Park Avenue, 10154-0037
Telephone: 212-407-4000
Facsimile: 212-407-4990
Los Angeles, California Office: Suite 1800, 1000 Wilshire Boulevard, 90017-2475.
Telephone: 213-688-3400.
Cable Address: "Loband LSA".
Telecopier: 213-688-3460; 688-3461; 688-3462.
Century City (Los Angeles), California Office: Suite 2200, 10100 Santa Monica Boulevard, Los Angeles, 90067-4164.
Telephone: 310-282-2000.
Telecopier: 310-282-2191; 282-2192.
Nashville, Tennessee Office: 45 Music Square West, 37203-3205.
Telephone: 615-749-8300.
Facsimile: 615-749-8308.
Rome, Italy Office: Piazza Digione 1, 00197.
Telephone: 011-396-808-8456.
Telecopier: 011-396-674-8223.

MEMBERS OF FIRM

David H. Carlin
Marc A. Chamlin
William J. Marlow
Charles H. Miller
Lee N. Steiner

ASSOCIATES

Maarten B. Kooij
James D. Taylor

For Complete List of Firm Personnel, See General Section

For full biographical listings, see the Martindale-Hubbell Law Directory

McDERMOTT, WILL & EMERY (AV)

A Partnership including Professional Corporations
1211 Avenue of the Americas, 10036-8701
Telephone: 212-768-5400
Facsimile: 212-768-5444
Chicago, Illinois Office: 227 West Monroe Street.
Telephone: 312-372-2000.
Telex: 253565 MILAM CGO.
Facsimile: 312-984-7700.
Boston, Massachusetts Office: 75 State Street, Suite 1700.
Telephone: 617-345-5000.
Telex: 951324 MILAM BSN.
Facsimile: 617-345-5077.
Miami, Florida Office: 201 South Biscayne Boulevard.
Telephone: 305-358-3500.
Telex: 441777 LEYES.
Facsimile: 305-347-6500.
Washington, D.C. Office: 1850 K Street, N.W.
Telephone: 202-887-8000.
Telex: 253565 MILAM CGO.
Facsimile: 202-778-8087.
Los Angeles, California Office: 2049 Century Park East.
Telephone: 310-277-4110.
Facsimile: 310-277-4730.
Newport Beach, California Office: 1301 Dove Street, Suite 500.
Telephone: 714-851-0633.
Facsimile: 714-851-9348.
St. Petersburg, Russia Office: 2/2 Tchaikovsky Street, #517, 191187 St. Petersburg, Russia.
Telephone: (7) (812) 273-9831.
Facsimile: (7) (812) 273-9831.
Vilnius, Lithuania Office: Smetonos 6, 2600 Vilnius, Lithuania.
Telephone: 370 2 61-43-08.
Facsimile: 370 2 22-79-55.
Associated (Independent) Offices:
Brussels, Belgium: Uettwiller Grelon Lippens Dekeyser, 73 avenue Vandendriessche, 1150 Brussels, Belgium.
Telephone: (32) (2) 772-87-50.
Facsimile: (32) (2) 772-87-52.
London, England: Paisner & Co, Bouverie House, 154 Fleet Street, London EC4A 2DQ, England.
Telephone: (44) (71) 353-0299.
Facsimile: (44) (71) 583-8621.
Paris, France: Uettwiller Grelon Gout Canat & Associes, 68, boulevard de Courcelles, 75017 Paris, France.
Telephone: (33) (1) 48 88 89 00.
Facsimile: (33) (1) 48 88 05 50.

MEMBERS OF FIRM

Lawrence I. Fox
Robert A. Weiner

For Complete List of Firm Personnel, See General Section

For full biographical listings, see the Martindale-Hubbell Law Directory

NIMS, HOWES, COLLISON, HANSEN & LACKERT (AV)

605 Third Avenue, Suite 3500, 10158
Telephone: 212-661-9700
Cable Address: "Nims"
Telex: 237665
Facsimile: 212-661-9213

MEMBERS OF FIRM

Oliver P. Howes, Jr.
William R. Hansen
Clark W. Lackert
Karen P. Clancy
Elizabeth Atkins
Thomas H. Curtin
Keith E. Sharkin

OF COUNSEL

Robert E. Isner (1921-1993)
Bert A. Collison
Irving N. Stein
August G. Maron, Jr.
Bruce J. Grossman
Robert P. Schwartz

ASSOCIATES

Robert L. Powley
Steven H. Robinson

For full biographical listings, see the Martindale-Hubbell Law Directory

NOTARO & MICHALOS P.C. (AV)

Suite 6902 Empire State Building, 350 Fifth Avenue, 10118-6985
Telephone: 212-564-0200
Fax: 212-564-0217
Rockland County Office: 100 Dutch Hill Road, Suite 110, Orangeburg, New York, 10962-2100.
Telephone: 914-359-7700.
Fax: 914-359-7798.

Angelo Notaro
Peter C. Michalos

For full biographical listings, see the Martindale-Hubbell Law Directory

New York—Continued

OTTERBOURG, STEINDLER, HOUSTON & ROSEN, P.C. (AV)

230 Park Avenue, 10169
Telephone: 212-661-9100
Cable Address: "Otlerton";
Telecopier: 212-682-6104
Telex: 960916

Kurt J. Wolff
Bernard Beitel

Diane B. Kaplan

For Complete List of Firm Personnel, See General Section

For full biographical listings, see the Martindale-Hubbell Law Directory

PENNIE & EDMONDS (AV)

1155 Avenue of the Americas, 10036
Telephone: 212-790-9090
Telex: (WUI) 66141 PENNIE
Cable Address: "Penangold"
Facsimile: GI/GII/GIII (212) 869-9741
GIII (212) 869-8864
Washington, D.C. Office: 1701 Pennsylvania Avenue, N.W.
Telephone: 202-393-0177.
Facsimile: GI/GII (202) 737-7950; GIII (202) 393-0462.
Menlo Park, California Office: 2730 Sand Hill Road.
Telephone: 415-854-3660.
Facsimile: 415-854-3694.

John C. Pennie (1858-1921)
Dean S. Edmonds (1879-1972)

MEMBERS OF FIRM

S. Leslie Misrock
Harry C. Jones, III
Berj A. Terzian
Gerald J. Flintoft
David Weild, III
Jonathan A. Marshall
Barry D. Rein
Stanton T. Lawrence, III
Charles E. Miller
Francis E. Morris
Gidon D. Stern
John J. Lauter
Brian M. Poissant
Brian D. Coggio
Mercer L. Stockell
Isaac Jarkovsky
Joseph V. Colaianni (Managing Partner, Washington, D.C. Office)
Charles E. McKenney
Philip T. Shannon
John M. Richardson
Rory J. Radding
Robert M. Kunstadt
Stephen J. Harbulak
Donald J. Goodell
James N. Palik
William G. Pecau
Joseph Diamante
Thomas E. Friebel
Laura A. Coruzzi
Jennifer Gordon
Jon R. Stark (Resident, Menlo Park, California Office)
James W. Dabney
Arthur Wineburg (Resident, Washington, D.C. Office)
Paul R. De Stefano (Not admitted in NY; Resident, Menlo Park, California Office)
Allan A. Fanucci
Geraldine F. Baldwin
Victor N. Balancia
Peter D. Vogl
Catherine H. Stockell
John J. Normile, Jr.
Albert P. Halluin

COUNSEL

Constance Golden
Samuel B. Abrams
Marcia H. Sundeen (Resident, Washington, D.C. Office)

ASSOCIATES

Mark A. Farley
Thomas A. Canova
Steven I. Wallach
James G. Markey
Walter E. Stalzer
Paul J. Zegger
Edmond R. Bannon
Bruce J. Barker
Jonathan E. Moskin
Ilene B. Tannen
Adriane M. Antler
Margaret M. Coyne
Darren W. Saunders
Thomas G. Rowan
Wilma F. Triebwasser (Resident, Washington, D.C. Office)
Thomas D. Kohler
Kenneth K. Sharples (Resident, Menlo Park, California Office)
Hope H. Liebke
Scott D. Stimpson
Nancy A. Zoubek
Kent H. Cheng
Ann L. Gisolfi
Lyle Kimms (Not admitted in NY; Resident, Washington, D.C. Office)
Hailing Zhang
Mikhail Lotvin
Scott B. Familant
Brian M. Rothery
Brian D. Siff
Todd A. Wagner
George C. Summerfield, Jr. (Resident, Washington, D.C. Office)
Deborah J. Barnett
John G. de la Rosa
Robert S. Broder
F. Dominic Cerrito
Ronald M. Daignault
Lori S. Gentile
Stephen Michael Patton
William J. Sipio
Laurence Manber
Charles F. Hoyng (Not admitted in NY)
Warren S. Heit (Resident, Menlo Park, California Office)
Barry W. Elledge (Resident, Menlo Park, California Office)
Jacqueline M. Lesser
Michael J. Lyons
Maria E. Pasquale
Melissa Lanni Robertson (Resident, Washington, D.C. Office)
Stephen R. Schaefer
Susan C. Shin
Carol M. Wilhelm

(See Next Column)

ASSOCIATES (Continued)

Sandra A. Bresnick
Alan C. Wong (Resident, Menlo Park, California Office)
Bernard H. Chao (Resident, Menlo Park, California Office)
Laurence Stein (Resident, Washington, D.C. Office)
Louis A. Piccone (Not admitted in NY)
Theresa Stevens Smith (Resident, Washington, D.C. Office)
Linda A. Sasaki (Not admitted in NY)
Daniel Hansburg
Troy R. Lester
H.T. Than
Michael Joel Blum
Bryan W. Butler
Alan Leonard Koller
Lawrence Burton Ebert
Kenneth L. Stein
Christine E. Lehman (Resident, Washington, D.C. Office)
Gianni P. Servodidio
Richard J. Gallagher (Not admitted in NY)
Joyce M. Ferraro
Leslie A. Tilly (Not admitted in NY)
David M. O'Neill
Scott R. Bortner (Resident, Menlo Park, California Office)
Alan Tenenbaum
Rashida A. Karmali
Frederick F. Hadidi (Resident, Menlo Park, California Office)
Kelly D. Talcott
Alan P. Force (Not admitted in NY)
John D. Garretson
Lance K. Ishimoto (Resident, Menlo Park, California Office)
Dwight H. Renfrew, Jr.
Katharine E. Smith
William L. Wang (Resident, Menlo Park, California Office)
Mark R. Scadina (Resident, Menlo Park, California Office)

For full biographical listings, see the Martindale-Hubbell Law Directory

SHACK & SIEGEL, P.C. (AV)

530 Fifth Avenue, 10036
Telephone: 212-782-0700
Fax: 212-730-1964

Charles F. Crames
Pamela E. Flaherty
Paul S. Goodman
Ronald S. Katz
Donald D. Shack
Jeffrey N. Siegel
Jeffrey B. Stone

Paul A. Lucido
Steven M. Lutt
Ruby S. Teich
Keith D. Wellner
Adam F. Wergeles (Not admitted in NY)

For full biographical listings, see the Martindale-Hubbell Law Directory

SUTTON, BASSECHES, MAGIDOFF & AMARAL (AV)

Graybar Building Suite 2310, 420 Lexington Avenue, 10170
Telephone: 212-490-7900
Telefacsimile: 212-370-5559

MEMBERS OF FIRM

Paul J. Sutton
Mark T. Basseches
Barry G. Magidoff
Anthony Amaral, Jr.

SENIOR COUNSEL

Arthur B. Colvin (P.C.)

COUNSEL

David Teschner (Not admitted in NY)
John G. Costa
Steven H. Bazerman
Harold A. Gell (Not admitted in NY)

For full biographical listings, see the Martindale-Hubbell Law Directory

OHIO

*CLEVELAND,** Cuyahoga Co.

BAKER & HOSTETLER (AV)

3200 National City Center, 1900 East Ninth Street, 44114-3485
Telephone: 216-621-0200
Telecopier: 216-696-0740
TWX: 810 421 8375
RCA Telex: 215032
In Columbus, Ohio: Capitol Square, Suite 2100, 65 East State Street.
Telephone: 614-228-1541.
In Denver, Colorado: 303 East 17th Avenue, Suite 1100.
Telephone: 303-861-0600.
In Houston, Texas: 1000 Louisiana, Suite 2000.
Telephone: 713-751-1600.
In Long Beach, California: 300 Oceangate, Suite 620.
Telephone: 310-432-2827.
In Los Angeles, California: 600 Wilshire Boulevard.
Telephone: 213-624-2400.
In Orlando, Florida: SunBank Center, Suite 2300, 200 South Orange Avenue.
Telephone: 407-649-4000.
In Washington, D. C.: Washington Square, Suite 1100, 1050 Connecticut Avenue, N.W.
Telephone: 202-861-1500.
In College Park, Maryland: 9658 Baltimore Boulevard, Suite 206.
Telephone: 301-441-2781.

(See Next Column)

BAKER & HOSTETLER, *Cleveland—Continued*

In Alexandria, Virginia: 437 North Lee Street.
Telephone: 703-549-1294.
In San Francisco, California: One Sansome Street, Suite 2000.
Telephone: 415-951-4705.

PARTNERS

Bruce O. Baumgartner
R. Scott Keller
Raymond Rundelli

ASSOCIATE

Deborah A. Schaff Wilcox

For Complete List of Firm Personnel, See General Section

For full biographical listings, see the Martindale-Hubbell Law Directory

CALFEE, HALTER & GRISWOLD (AV)

Suite 1800, 800 Superior Avenue, 44114-2688
Telephone: 216-622-8200
Telecopier: 216-241-0816
Telex: 980499
Columbus, Ohio Office: 88 East Broad Street, Suite 1500.
Telephone: 614-321-1500.
Telecopier: 614-621-0010.

MEMBERS OF FIRM

Charles B. Lyon
William N. Hogg
John E. Miller, Jr. (Not admitted in OH)
Jeanne E. Longmuir

OF COUNSEL

Lawrence R. Oremland

SENIOR ATTORNEY

Frank C. Manak III

ASSOCIATES

Mary E. Golrick
Kevin P. Hallquist
John S. Cipolla
John A. Kastelic
Chrysso B. Sarkos
James C. Scott
Sean T. Moorhead
Stephen L. McCauley

For Complete List of Firm Personnel, See General Section

For full biographical listings, see the Martindale-Hubbell Law Directory

JANIK & DUNN (AV)

400 Park Plaza Building, 1111 Chester Avenue, 44114
Telephone: 216-781-9700
Fax: 216-781-1250
Brea, California Office: 2601 Saturn Street, Suite 300.
Telephone: 714-572-1101.
Fax: 714-572-1103.

MEMBERS OF FIRM

Steven G. Janik
Theodore M. Dunn, Jr.

ASSOCIATES

Myra Staresina
David L. Mast

For full biographical listings, see the Martindale-Hubbell Law Directory

JONES, DAY, REAVIS & POGUE (AV)

North Point, 901 Lakeside Avenue, 44114
Telephone: 216-586-3939
Cable Address: "Attorneys Cleveland"
Telex: 980389
Telecopier: 216-579-0212
In Columbus, Ohio: 1900 Huntington Center.
Telephone: 614-469-3939.
Cable Address: "Attorneys Columbus."
Telecopier: 614-461-4198.
In Atlanta, Georgia: 3500 One Peachtree Center, 303 Peachtree Street, N.E.
Telephone: 404-521-3939.
Cable Address: "Attorneys Atlanta".
Telex: 54-2711.
Telecopier: 404-581-8330.
In Brussels, Belgium: Avenue Louise 480, 7th Floor. B-1050 Brussels.
Telephone: 011-32-2-645-14-11.
Telecopier: 011-32-2-645-14-45.
In Chicago, Illinois: 77 West Wacker.
Telephone: 312-782-3939.
Telecopier: 312-782-8585.
In Dallas, Texas: 2300 Trammell Crow Center, 2001 Ross Avenue.
Telephone: 214-220-3939.
Cable Address: "Attorneys Dallas."
Telex: 730852.
Telecopier: 214-969-5100.
In Frankfurt, Germany: Triton Haus, Bockenheimer Landstrasse 42, 60323 Frankfurt am Main.
Telephone: 49-69-9726-3939.
Telecopier: 49-69-9726-3993.
In Geneva, Switzerland: 20, rue de Candolle.
Telephone: 011-41-22-320-2339.
Telecopier: 011-41-22-320-1232.

(See Next Column)

In Hong Kong: 1501 One Exchange Square, 8 Connaught Place.
Telephone: 011-852-2526-6895.
Telecopier: 011-852-2810-5787.
In Irvine, California: 2603 Main Street, Suite 900.
Telephone: 714-851-3939.
Telex: 194911 Lawyers LSA.
Telecopier: 714-553-7539.
In London, England: One Mount Street.
Telephone: 011-44-71-493-9361.
Cable Address: "Surgoe London WI."
Telecopier: 011-44-71-493-9666.
In Los Angeles, California: 555 West Fifth Street, Suite 4600.
Telephone: 213-489-3939.
Telex: 181439 UD.
Telecopier: 213-243-2539.
In New York, New York: 599 Lexington Avenue.
Telephone: 212-326-3939.
Cable Address: "JONESDAY NEWYORK."
Telex: 237013 JDRP UR.
Telecopier: 212-755-7306.
In Paris, France: 62, rue du Faubourg Saint-Honore.
Telephone: 011-33-1-44-71-3939.
Cable Address: "Surgoe Paris."
Telex: 290156 Surgoe.
Telecopier: 011-33-1-49-24-0471.
In Pittsburgh, Pennsylvania: 500 Grant Street, 31st Floor.
Telephone: 412-391-3939.
Cable Address: "Attorneys Pittsburgh".
Telecopier: 412-394-7959.
In Riyadh, Saudi Arabia: Law Offices of Saud M.A. Shawwaf, P.O. Box 2700.
Telephones: 011 (966-1) 465-6543, 011 (966-1) 464-8534 or 011 (966-1) 464-8540.
Telex: 401831 SAUCON SJ.
Telecopier: (966-1) 464-8480.
In Taipei, Taiwan: 8th Floor, Tun Hwa South Road, Section 2.
Telephone: 011 (886-2) 704-6808.
Telecopier: 011 (886-2) 704-6791.
In Tokyo, Japan: Toranomon MT Building, 4th Floor, 10-3, Toranomon 3-Chome, Minato-Ku, Tokyo 105, Japan.
Telephone: 011-81-3-3433-3939.
Telecopier: 011-81-3-5401-2725.
In Washington, D.C.: Metropolitan Square, 1450 G Street, N.W.
Telephone: 202-879-3939.
Cable Address: "Attorneys Washington."
Telex: 89-2410 ATTORNEYS WASH.
Telecopier: 202-737-2832.

MEMBERS OF FIRM

Hal D. Cooper
Barry L. Springel
Richard H. Sayler
Regan J. Fay
Kenneth R. Adamo
Robert Conley Kahrl
James L. Wamsley, III
Robert P. Ducatman
Michael W. Vary
Timothy J. O'Hearn

SENIOR ATTORNEYS

H. Duane Switzer
Leozino Agozzino

For Complete List of Firm Personnel, See General Section

For full biographical listings, see the Martindale-Hubbell Law Directory

THOMPSON, HINE AND FLORY (AV)

1100 National City Bank Building, 629 Euclid Avenue, 44114-3070
Telephone: 216-566-5500
Fax: 216-566-5583
Telex: 980217
Cable Address: "Thomflor"
Akron, Ohio Office: 50 S. Main Street, Suite 502, 44308-1828.
Telephone: 216-376-8090.
Fax: 216-376-8386.
Cincinnati, Ohio Office: 312 Walnut Street, 14th Floor, 45202-4029.
Telephone: 513-352-6700.
Fax: 513-241-4771.
Telex: 938003.
Columbus, Ohio Office: One Columbus, 10 West Broad Street, 43215-3435.
Telephone: 614-469-3200.
Fax: 614-469-3361.
Dayton, Ohio Office: 2000 Courthouse Plaza, N.E., 45402-1706.
Telephone: 513-443-6600.
Fax: 513-443-6637; 443-6635.
Palm Beach, Florida Office: 125 Worth Avenue, Suite 117, 33480-4466.
Telephone: 407-833-5900.
Fax: 407-833-5951.
Washington, D.C. Office: 1920 N Street, N.W., 20036-1601.
Telephone: 202-331-8800.
Fax: 202-331-8330.
Telex: 904173.
Cable Address: "Caglaw".
Brussels, Belgium Office: Rue des Chevaliers, Ridderstraat 14 - B.10, B - 1050.
Telephone: 011(32-2) 511-9326.
Fax: 011(32-2) 513-9206.

(See Next Column)

THOMPSON, HINE AND FLORY—*Continued*

MEMBERS OF FIRM

Thomas J. Collin
James B. Niehaus
Thomas F. Zych

SENIOR ATTORNEY

Annette Tucker Sutherland

For Complete List of Firm Personnel, See General Section

For full biographical listings, see the Martindale-Hubbell Law Directory

*COLUMBUS,** Franklin Co.

EMENS, KEGLER, BROWN, HILL & RITTER (AV)

Capitol Square Suite 1800, 65 East State Street, 43215-4294
Telephone: 614-462-5400
Telecopier: 614-464-2634
Cable Address: "Law EKBHR"
Telex: 246671

Gene W. Holliker
S. Martijn Steger

COUNSEL

John L. Gray

Robert G. Schuler
Amy M. Shepherd
Shawnell Williams

Representative Clients: Borden, Inc.; Drug Emporium, Inc.; National Ground Water Association; The Ohio State University; Owens-Corning Fiberglas Corp.; Patrick Petroleum Co.

For Complete List of Firm Personnel, See General Section

For full biographical listings, see the Martindale-Hubbell Law Directory

*DAYTON,** Montgomery Co.

THOMPSON, HINE AND FLORY (AV)

2000 Courthouse Plaza, N.E., 45402-1706
Telephone: 513-443-6600
Fax: 513-443-6637; 443-6635
Akron, Ohio Office: 50 S. Main Street, Suite 502, 44308-1828.
Telephone: 216-376-8090.
Fax: 216-376-8386.
Cincinnati, Ohio Office: 312 Walnut Street, 14th Floor, 45202-4029.
Telephone: 513-352-6700.
Fax: 513-241-4771.
Telex: 938003.
Cleveland, Ohio Office: 1100 National City Bank Building, 629 Euclid Avenue, 44114-3070.
Telephone: 216-566-5500.
Fax: 216-556-5583.
Telex: 980217.
Cable Address: "Thomflor".
Columbus, Ohio Office: One Columbus, 10 West Broad Street, 43215-3435.
Telephone: 614-469-3200.
Fax: 614-469-3361.
Palm Beach, Florida Office: 125 Worth Avenue, 33480-4466.
Telephone: 407-833-5900.
Fax: 407-833-5951.
Washington, D.C. Office: 1920 N Street, N.W., 20036-1601.
Telephone: 202-331-8800.
Fax: 202-331-8330.
Telex: 904173.
Cable Address: "Caglaw".
Brussels, Belgium Office: Rue des Chevaliers / Ridderstraat 14 - B.10, B - 1050.
Telephone: 011(32-2) 511-9326.
Fax: 011(32-2) 513-9206.

MEMBERS OF FIRM

Mark P. Levy
Theodore D. Lienesch
Sue K. McDonnell

For Complete List of Firm Personnel, See General Section

For full biographical listings, see the Martindale-Hubbell Law Directory

OKLAHOMA

*OKLAHOMA CITY,** Oklahoma Co.

ANDREWS DAVIS LEGG BIXLER MILSTEN & PRICE, A PROFESSIONAL CORPORATION (AV)

500 West Main, 73102
Telephone: 405-272-9241
FAX: 405-235-8786

(See Next Column)

John F. Fischer, II
Robert D. Nelon
R. Brown Wallace
William H. Whitehill, Jr.

Representative Clients: Dunkin' Donuts, Inc.; Oklahoma State Medical Assn; Stryker Corp.

For Complete List of Firm Personnel, See General Section

For full biographical listings, see the Martindale-Hubbell Law Directory

*TULSA,** Tulsa Co.

GABLE & GOTWALS (AV)

2000 Bank IV Center, 15 West Sixth Street, 74119-5447
Telephone: 918-582-9201
Facsimile: 918-586-8383

Teresa B. Adwan
Pamela S. Anderson
John R. Barker
David L. Bryant
Gene C. Buzzard
Dennis Clarke Cameron
Timothy A. Carney
Renee DeMoss
Elsie C. Draper
Sidney G. Dunagan
Theodore Q. Eliot
Richard W. Gable
Jeffrey Don Hassell
Patricia Ledvina Himes
Oliver S. Howard
Richard D. Koljack, Jr.
J. Daniel Morgan
Joseph W. Morris
Elizabeth R. Muratet
Richard B. Noulles
Ronald N. Ricketts
John Henry Rule
M. Benjamin Singletary
James M. Sturdivant
Patrick O. Waddel
Michael D. Hall
David Edward Keglovits
Stephen W. Lake
Kari S. McKee
Terry D. Ragsdale
Jeffrey C. Rambach

OF COUNSEL

G. Ellis Gable
Charles P. Gotwals, Jr.

For full biographical listings, see the Martindale-Hubbell Law Directory

PENNSYLVANIA

*PHILADELPHIA,** Philadelphia Co.

CAESAR, RIVISE, BERNSTEIN, COHEN & POKOTILOW, LTD. (AV)

12th Floor, 1635 Market Street, 19103-2212
Telephone: 215-567-2010
Telecopier: 215-751-1142

Alan H. Bernstein
Stanley H. Cohen
Manny D. Pokotilow
Barry A. Stein
Martin L. Faigus
Eric S. Marzluf
Robert S. Silver
Michael J. Berkowitz
Scott M. Slomowitz

OF COUNSEL

Abraham D. Caesar
Max Goldman

For full biographical listings, see the Martindale-Hubbell Law Directory

PAUL & PAUL (AV)

2900 Two Thousand Market Street, 19103
Telephone: 215-568-4900
Cable Address: "Caveat"
Telex: 710-670-1352 Dex
Telecopier: 215-567-5057

MEMBERS OF FIRM

James C. McConnon
John F. McNulty
Alex R. Sluzas

ASSOCIATES

Joseph E. Chovanes
Frank J. Bonini, Jr.
Paul A. Taufer
Craig M. Bell
Alan G. Towner
Gary A. Greene
Joseph A. Tessari

For full biographical listings, see the Martindale-Hubbell Law Directory

*PITTSBURGH,** Allegheny Co.

BUCHANAN INGERSOLL, PROFESSIONAL CORPORATION (AV)

5800 USX Tower, 600 Grant Street, 15219
Telephone: 412-562-8800
Telecopier: 412-562-1041
Philadelphia, Pennsylvania Office: Two Logan Square, Twelfth Floor, 18th & Arch Streets.
Telephone: 215-665-8700.
Harrisburg, Pennsylvania Office: Vartan Parc, 30 North Third Street.
Telephone: 717-237-4800.
Tampa, Florida Office: 101 East Kennedy Boulevard, Suite 1030.
Telephone: 813-222-8180.
North Miami Beach, Florida Office: 19495 Biscayne Boulevard.
Telephone: 305-933-5600.

(See Next Column)

BUCHANAN INGERSOLL PROFESSIONAL CORPORATION, *Pittsburgh—Continued*

Lexington, Kentucky Office: 1210 Vine Center Office Tower, 333 West Vine Street.
Telephone: 606-225-5333.
Princeton, New Jersey Office: Buchanan Ingersoll, A Partnership, College Centre, 500 College Road East.
Telephone: 609-452-2666.

Lynn J. Alstadt
George P. Baier
Paul A. Beck
A. Bruce Bowden
Sheryl Atkinson Clark
Michael L. Dever
Robert G. Devlin
David B. Fawcett III
Pamela A. McCallum
Arthur J. Schwab

SENIOR ATTORNEY

George Raynovich, Jr.

Susan M. Hartman
Robert J. Pugh

For Complete List of Firm Personnel, See General Section

For full biographical listings, see the Martindale-Hubbell Law Directory

VALLEY FORGE, Chester Co.

MICHAEL F. PETOCK (AV)

46 The Commons at Valley Forge, 1220 Valley Forge Road, P.O. Box 856, 19482-0856
Telephone: 610-935-8600; 215-922-5550
Fax: 610-933-9300

For full biographical listings, see the Martindale-Hubbell Law Directory

RATNER & PRESTIA, A PROFESSIONAL CORPORATION (AV)

Suite 400, 500 North Gulph Road, P.O. Box 980, 19482
Telephone: 610-265-6666
Telex: 846169
Telecopy: 610-265-8935

Paul F. Prestia
Allan Ratner
Andrew L. Ney
Kenneth N. Nigon
Kevin R. Casey
Guy T. Donatiello
James Charles Simmons
Viviana Amzel (Not admitted in PA)

Benjamin E. Leace
Lawrence E. Ashery
Christopher R. Lewis
Anthony L. Di Bartolomeo
Steven E Koffs
Allan M. Wheatcraft
Anthony Grillo

For full biographical listings, see the Martindale-Hubbell Law Directory

ZACHARY T. WOBENSMITH, III (AV)

86 The Commons at Valley Forge East, 1288 Valley Forge Road, P.O. Box 750, 19482-0750
Telephone: 610-935-9750
Telecopier: 610-935-0600

For full biographical listings, see the Martindale-Hubbell Law Directory

RHODE ISLAND

*PROVIDENCE,** Providence Co.

EDWARDS & ANGELL (AV)

2700 Hospital Trust Tower, 02903
Telephone: 401-274-9200
Telecopier: 401-276-6611
Cable Address: "Edwangle Providence"
Telex: 952001 "E A PVD"
Boston, Massachusetts Office: 101 Federal Street, 02110.
Telephone: 617-439-444.
Telecopier: 617-439-4170.
New York, New York Office: 750 Lexington Avenue, 10022.
Telephone: 212-308-4411.
Telecopier: 212-308-4844.
Palm Beach, Florida Office: 250 Royal Palm Way, 33480.
Telephone: 407-833-7700.
Telecopier: 407-655-8719.
Newark, New Jersey Office: Gateway three, 07120.
Telephone: 201-623-7717.
Telecopier: 201-623-7717.
Hartford, Connecticut Office: 750 Main Street, 14th Floor, 06103.
Telephone: 203-525-5065.
Telecopier: 203-527-4198.
Newport, Rhode Island Office: 130 Bellevue Avenue, 02840.
Telephone: 401-849-7800.
Telecopier: 401-849-7887.

(See Next Column)

MEMBER OF FIRM

John E. Ottaviani

For Complete List of Firm Personnel, See General Section

For full biographical listings, see the Martindale-Hubbell Law Directory

TENNESSEE

*MEMPHIS,** Shelby Co.

ARMSTRONG ALLEN PREWITT GENTRY JOHNSTON & HOLMES (AV)

80 Monroe Avenue Suite 700, 38103
Telephone: 901-523-8211
Telecopier: 901-524-4936
Jackson, Missippi Office: 1350 One Jackson Place, 188 East Capitol Street.
Telephone: 601-948-8020.
Telecopier: 601-948-8389.

MEMBER OF FIRM

James B. McLaren, Jr.

For Complete List of Firm Personnel, See General Section

For full biographical listings, see the Martindale-Hubbell Law Directory

STREIBICH & SEALE (AV)

Bryton Tower, Suite 101, 1271 Poplar Avenue, 38104
Telephone: 901-722-8188
Fax: 901-278-7126
Cable Address: "Artslaw"

MEMBERS OF FIRM

Harold C. Streibich
William B. Seale

For full biographical listings, see the Martindale-Hubbell Law Directory

*NASHVILLE,** Davidson Co.

BASS, BERRY & SIMS (AV)

2700 First American Center, 37238-2700
Telephone: 615-742-6200
Telecopy: 615-742-6293
Knoxville, Tennessee Office: 1700 Riverview Tower, 900 S. Gay Street, P.O. Box 1509, 37901-1509.
Telephone: 615-521-6200.
Telecopy: 615-521-6234.

MEMBER OF FIRM

Jay S. Bowen

Representative Clients: BMG Music; Warner Brothers Records; Sony Music Entertainment, Inc.; Thomas Nelson, Inc.; First American National Bank; BellSouth Telecommunications, Inc.; Polygram Records, Inc.; Service Merchandise, Inc.; Vanderbilt University; Buntin Advertising.

For full biographical listings, see the Martindale-Hubbell Law Directory

KING & BALLOW (AV)

1200 Noel Place, 200 Fourth Avenue, North, 37219
Telephone: 615-259-3456
Fax: 615-254-7907
San Diego, California Office: 2700 Symphony Towers, 750 B Street, 92101.
Telephone: 619-236-9401.
Fax: 619-236-9437.
San Francisco, California Office: 100 First Street, Suite 2700, 94105.
Telephone: 415-541-7803.
Fax: 415-541-7805.

MEMBERS OF FIRM

Frank S. King, Jr.
Robert L. Ballow
R. Eddie Wayland
Alan L. Marx
Paul H. Duvall (Resident, San Diego, California Office)
Steven C. Douse
Douglas R. Pierce
James P. Thompson
Howard M. Kastrinsky
Kenneth E. Douthat
Mark E. Hunt

ASSOCIATES

Patrick M. Thomas
Elizabeth B. Marney

Representative Clients: August House Publishers, Little Rock, Arkansas; John F. Blair Publishers, Winston-Salem, North Carolina; Cliffie Stone Productions, Los Angeles, California; DC Talk, Nashville, Tennessee; Grant/-Tribune Productions, Los Angeles, California; Hamilton House Entertainment Group, Oklahoma City, Oklahoma; Ideals Publishing Corp., Nashville, Tennessee; Menasha Ridge Press, Inc., Birmingham, Alabama; Opryland Music Group, Nashville, Tennessee; Peachtree Publishers, Atlanta, Georgia; Pelican Publishing, Gretna, Louisiana; Powell Music Group, Nashville, Tennessee.

For Complete List of Firm Personnel, See General Section

For full biographical listings, see the Martindale-Hubbell Law Directory

Nashville—Continued

WYATT, TARRANT & COMBS (AV)

1500 Nashville City Center, 511 Union Street, 37219
Telephone: 615-244-0020
Telecopier: 615-256-1726
Cable Address: "Nashlaw"
Music Row, Office: 29 Music Square East, Nashville, 37203.
Telephone: 615-255-6161.
Telecopier: 615-254-4490.
Louisville, Kentucky Office: Citizens Plaza.
Telephone: 502-589-5235.
Telecopier: 502-589-0309.
Lexington, Kentucky Office: 1700 Lexington Financial Center.
Telephone: 606-233-2012.
Telecopier: 606-259-0649.
Frankfort, Kentucky Office: The Taylor-Scott Building, 311 West Main Street.
Telephone: 502-223-2104.
Telecopier: 502-227-7681.
New Albany, Indiana Office: The Elsby Building, 117 East Spring Street,
Telephone: 812-945-3561.
Telecopier: 812-949-2524.
Hendersonville, Tennessee Office: 313 E. Main Street, Suite 1.
Telephone: 615-822-8822.
Telecopier: 615-824-4684.

MEMBERS OF FIRM

W. Michael Milom (Resident, Music Row Office)
Christian A. Horsnell (Resident, Music Row Office)

COUNSEL

Robin Mitchell Joyce (Resident, Music Row Office)

Representative Clients: Brentwood Music, Inc.; CPL Publishing, Inc.; Morgan Music Group; Ren Corp USA; Thomas Nelson, Inc.

For Complete List of Firm Personnel, See General Section

For full biographical listings, see the Martindale-Hubbell Law Directory

TEXAS

*AUSTIN,** Travis Co.

* indicates certain Bar Register subscribers whose principal office is located elsewhere in the state and who have arranged for representation as a part of the state capital listings that follow

BAKER & BOTTS, L.L.P. (AV)

1600 San Jacinto Center, 98 San Jacinto Boulevard, 78701
Telephone: 512-322-2500
Fax: 512-322-2501
Houston, Texas Office: One Shell Plaza, 910 Louisiana.
Telephone: 713-229-1234.
Dallas, Texas Office: 2001 Ross Avenue.
Telephone: 214-953-6500.
Washington, D.C. Office: The Warner, 1299 Pennsylvania Avenue, N.W.
Telephone: 202-639-7700.
New York, New York Office: 885 Third Avenue, Suite 2000.
Telephone: 212-705-5000.
Moscow, Russian Federation Office: 10 ul. Pushkinskaya, 103031.
Telephone: 7095/921-5300 (Local); 7501/929-7070 (International).

MEMBER OF FIRM

William Noble Hulsey III

ASSOCIATES

Dennis William Braswell
Ann Livingston

For Complete List of Firm Personnel, See General Section

For full biographical listings, see the Martindale-Hubbell Law Directory

*** THOMPSON & KNIGHT, A PROFESSIONAL CORPORATION (AV)**

(Attorneys and Counselors)
1200 San Jacinto Center, 98 San Jacinto Boulevard, 78701
Telephone: 512-469-6100
Telecopy: 512-469-6180
Dallas, Texas Office: 1700 Pacific Avenue, Suite 3300, 75201.
Telephone: 214-969-1700.
Telecopy: 512-969-1751.
Cable Address: "Tomtex."
Telex: 732298.
Fort Worth, Texas Office: 801 Cherry Street, Suite 1600, 76102.
Telephone: 817-347-1700.
Telecopy: 817-347-1799.
Houston, Texas Office: 1700 Texas Commerce Tower, 600 Travis, 77002.
Telephone: 713-217-2800.
Telecopy: 713-217-2828; 713-217-2882.

(See Next Column)

Monterrey, Mexico Office: Edificio Losoles PD-4, Av. Lázaro Cárdenas No. 2400 Pte., San Pedro Garza Garcia, Nuevo Léon C.P. 66220.
Telephone: (52-8) 363-0096.
Telecopy: (52-8) 363-3067.

SHAREHOLDERS

Carrie Parker Tiemann

OF COUNSEL

Richard J. Wieland

For Complete List of Firm Personnel, See General Section

For full biographical listings, see the Martindale-Hubbell Law Directory

*DALLAS,** Dallas Co.

BAKER & BOTTS, L.L.P. (AV)

2001 Ross Avenue, 75201
Telephone: 214-953-6500
Fax: 214-953-6503
Houston, Texas Office: One Shell Plaza, 910 Louisiana.
Telephone: 713-229-1234.
Washington, D.C. Office: The Warner, 1299 Pennsylvania Avenue, N.W.
Telephone: 202-639-7700.
Austin, Texas Office: 1600 San Jacinto Center, 98 San Jacinto Boulevard.
Telephone: 512-322-2500.
New York, New York Office: 885 Third Avenue, Suite 2000.
Telephone: 212-705-5000.
Moscow, Russian Federation Office: 10 ul. Pushkinskaya, 103031.
Telephone: 7095/921-5300 (Local); 7095/929-7070.

MEMBERS OF FIRM

Jerry W. Mills
Robert M. Chiaviello, Jr.

ASSOCIATES

Thomas R. Felger
Charles S. Fish
David Norman Fogg, Sr.
Thomas A. Gigliotti
Wei Wei Jeang
Robert Hugh Johnston III
Kevin J. Meek
Richard J. Moura (Not admitted in TX)

For Complete List of Firm Personnel, See General Section

For full biographical listings, see the Martindale-Hubbell Law Directory

THOMPSON & KNIGHT, A PROFESSIONAL CORPORATION (AV)

(Attorneys and Counselors)
1700 Pacific Avenue Suite 3300, 75201
Telephone: 214-969-1700
Telecopy: 214-969-1751
Cable Address: "Tomtex"
Telex: 732298
Austin, Texas Office: 1200 San Jacinto Center, 98 San Jacinto Boulevard, 78701.
Telephone: 512-469-6100.
Telecopy: 512-469-6180.
Fort Worth, Texas Office: 801 Cherry Street, Suite 1600, 76102.
Telephone: 817-347-1700.
Telecopy: 817-347-1799.
Houston, Texas Office: 1700 Texas Commerce Tower, 600 Travis, 77002.
Telephone: 713-217-2800.
Telecopy: 713-217-2828.
Monterrey, Mexico Office: Edificio Losoles PD-4, Av. Lázaro Cárdenas No. 2400 Pte., San Pedro Garza Garcia, Nuevo Léon C.P. 66220.
Telephone: (52-8) 363-0096.
Telecopy: (52-8) 363-3067.

SHAREHOLDERS

P. Jefferson Ballew
Jane Politz Brandt
Frank Finn
Thornton Hardie III
Gregory S. C. Huffman
Lou H. Jones
Peter A. Lodwick
Schuyler B. Marshall, IV
David E. Morrison
William J. Schuerger
Bruce S. Sostek
Molly Steele
Peter J. Thoma

ASSOCIATES

Beverly Ray Burlingame
Priscilla Lynn Dunckel
Pamela J. Smith

For Complete List of Firm Personnel, See General Section

For full biographical listings, see the Martindale-Hubbell Law Directory

*SAN ANTONIO,** Bexar Co.

MATTHEWS & BRANSCOMB, A PROFESSIONAL CORPORATION (AV)

One Alamo Center, 106 S. St. Mary's Street, Suite 800, 78205
Telephone: 210-226-4211
Facsimile: 210-226-0521
Telex: 5106009283
Cable Code: MBLAW
Austin, Texas Office: 301 Congress Avenue, Suite 2050.
Telephone: 512-305-4400.
Facsimile: 512-305-4413.

(See Next Column)

MATTHEWS & BRANSCOMB A PROFESSIONAL CORPORATION, *San Antonio—Continued*

Corpus Christi, Texas Office: 802 N. Carancahua, Suite 1900.
Telephone: 512-888-9261.
Facsimile: 512-888-8504.
Eagle Pass, Texas Office: 675 Main Street.
Telephone: 210-773-6700.
Facsimile: 210-757-4045.
Uvalde, Texas Office: 200 E. Nopal #208.
Telephone: 210-278-4597.
Facsimile: 210-278-4806.
(Associated with Hall, Quintanilla & Alarcon, L.C., Laredo, Texas, under the name of Hall, Quintanilla, Alarcon, Matthews & Branscomb, P.L.L.C.)

William F. Nowlin (1902-1978)
Harper Macfarlane (1901-1980)
Lionel R. Fuller (1919-1984)
Grady Barrett (1895-1986)
William H. Nowlin (1934-1987)
Wilbur L. Matthews
Patrick H. Swearingen, Jr.
Lewis T. Tarver, Jr.
Richard E. Goldsmith
William H. Robison
John D. Fisch
Jon C. Wood
J. Joe Harris
George P. Parker, Jr.
James M. Doyle, Jr.
C. Michael Montgomery
W. Roger Wilson
Howard P. Newton
Charles J. Muller, III
John McPherson Pinckney, III
Richard C. Danysh
J. Tullos Wells
Charles J. Fitzpatrick
Marshall T. Steves, Jr.
Judith R. Blakeway
James H. Kizziar, Jr.
Frank Z. Ruttenberg
Leslie Selig Byrd
Patrick H. Autry
Farley P. Katz
Dawn Bruner Finlayson
John A. Ferguson, Jr.
Julie B. Adler Koppenheffer
Mary M. Potter
Annalyn G. Smith
Arthur G. Uhl, III
Nancy H. Stumberg
Howard D. Bye
Judy K. Jetelina
Mark A. Phariss
Merritt M. Clements
Robert Shaw-Meadow
Daniel M. Elder
Mark A. Jones
Kay L. Reamey
Timothy H. Bannwolf
Victoria M. García
Anthony E. Rebollo
Steven J. Pugh
Elizabeth H. Chumney
Craig A. Arnold
Inez M. McBride
Kathleen A. Devine
Raquel G. Perez
David L. Doggett
Roberta J. Sharp
Mary Helen Medina

OF COUNSEL

Francis W. Baker
Judson Wood, Jr.

Representative Clients: Coca Cola Bottling Company of the Southwest; Concord Oil Co.; Ellison Enterprises, Inc.; H. E. Butt Grocery Co.; Frank B. Hall & Co., Inc.; The Hearst Corp., San Antonio Light Division; San Antonio Gas & Electric Utilities (City Board); Southern Pacific Transportation Co.; Southwest Texas Methodist Hospital.

For full biographical listings, see the Martindale-Hubbell Law Directory

VIRGINIA

ALEXANDRIA, (Independent City)

BURNS, DOANE, SWECKER & MATHIS (AV)

Suite 100, 699 Prince Street, 22314
Telephone: 703-836-6620
Cable Address: "Patburn"
Telex: Itt 440 580 Bdsm Ale
and Wu 901855 Bdsm Ale Facsimile: 703-836-2021; 703-836-7356; 703-836-3503
Mailing Address: P.O. Box 1404, 22313,
Menlo Park, California Office: 3000 Sand Hill Road, Building 4, Suite 160 94025.
Telephone: 415-854-7400.
Facsimile: 415-854-8275.

MEMBERS OF FIRM

William L. Mathis
Robert S. Swecker
Joseph R. Magnone
Ronald L. Grudziecki (Admitted in District of Columbia; limited admission in Virginia)
George A. Hovanec, Jr.
James A. LaBarre
David D. Reynolds
R. Danny Huntington
Adrienne L. White
William H. Benz (Menlo Park, California Office)

OF COUNSEL

Peter H. Smolka

ASSOCIATE

Christie Baty Heinze

For full biographical listings, see the Martindale-Hubbell Law Directory

*ARLINGTON,** Arlington Co.

HALEY, BADER & POTTS (AV)

4350 North Fairfax Drive, Suite 900, 22203-1633
Telephone: 703-841-0606
FAX: 703-841-2345
INTERNET: haleybp@access.digex.net

MEMBERS OF FIRM

Andrew G. Haley (1904-1966)
Michael H. Bader
William J. Potts, Jr.
Henry A. Solomon
William J. Byrnes
Richard M. Riehl
John Wells King
John M. Pelkey
Lee W. Shubert
John Crigler
Theodore D. Kramer
Melodie A. Virtue
James E. Dunstan
Richard H. Strodel
Benjamin J. Lambiotte

ASSOCIATE

Amelia Logan Brown (Not admitted in VA)

COUNSEL

Kenneth A. Cox (Not admitted in VA)

For full biographical listings, see the Martindale-Hubbell Law Directory

*FAIRFAX,** (Ind. City; Seat of Fairfax Co.)

ODIN, FELDMAN & PITTLEMAN, P.C. (AV)

9302 Lee Highway, Suite 1100, 22031
Telephone: 703-218-2100
Facsimile: 703-218-2160

Dexter S. Odin
Nelson Blitz
Lawrence A. Schultis
Kevin Thomas Oliveira

For Complete List of Firm Personnel, See General Section

For full biographical listings, see the Martindale-Hubbell Law Directory

*RICHMOND,** (Ind. City; Seat of Henrico Co.)

WILLIAMS, MULLEN, CHRISTIAN & DOBBINS, A PROFESSIONAL CORPORATION (AV)

Two James Center, 1021 East Cary Street, P.O. Box 1320, 23210-1320
Telephone: 804-643-1991
Fax: 804-783-6456
Glen Allen, Virginia Office: 4401 Waterfront Drive, Suite 140.
Telephone: 804-965-9168.
Fax: 804-965-0955.
Washington, D.C. Office: 1575 Eye Street, N.W.
Telephone: 202-289-6200.
Fax: 202-289-4126.

Dana D. McDaniel

Henry C. Su
Ian D. Titley

For Complete List of Firm Personnel, See General Section

For full biographical listings, see the Martindale-Hubbell Law Directory

WISCONSIN

*MADISON,** Dane Co.

LATHROP & CLARK (AV)

Suite 1000, 122 West Washington Avenue, P.O. Box 1507, 53701-1507
Telephone: 608-257-7766
Fax: 608-257-1507
Poynette, Wisconsin Office: 111 North Main Street, P.O. Box 128.
Telephone: 608-635-4324.
FAX: 608-635-4690.
Lodi, Wisconsin Office: 108 Lodi Street, P.O. Box 256.
Telephone: 608-592-3877.
FAX: 608-592-5844.
Belleville, Wisconsin Office: 27 West Main.
Telephone: 608-424-3404.

MEMBERS OF FIRM

Theodore J. Long
Shelley J. Safer
Jill Weber Dean

Representative Clients: Olin Corp.; Wickes Companies, Inc.; Hopkins Agricultural Chemical Co.; Metropolitan Life Insurance Co.; Cuna Mutual Insurance Group; Wisconsin Physicians Service Insurance Corp.; TriEnda Corp.; Auto Glass Specialists, Inc.; Highsmith Inc.; Persoft, Inc.

For Complete List of Firm Personnel, See General Section

For full biographical listings, see the Martindale-Hubbell Law Directory

*MILWAUKEE,** Milwaukee Co.

Reinhart, Boerner, Van Deuren, Norris & Rieselbach, S.C. (AV)

1000 North Water Street, P.O. Box 92900, 53202-0900
Telephone: 414-298-1000
Facsimile: 414-298-8097
Denver, Colorado Office: One Norwest Center, 1700 Lincoln Street, Suite 3725.
Telephone: 303-831-0909.
Fax: 303-831-4805.
Madison, Wisconsin Office: 7617 Mineral Point Road, 53701-2020.
Telephone: 608-283-7900.
Fax: 608-283-7919.
Washington, D.C. Office: 601 Pennsylvania Avenue, N.W., North Building, Suite 750.
Telephone: 202-393-3636.
Fax: 202-393-0796.

Michael D. Rechtin — Philip P. Mann

Rodney D. DeKruif — Peter W. Becker
Gerald L. Fellows

For Complete List of Firm Personnel, See General Section

For full biographical listings, see the Martindale-Hubbell Law Directory

PUERTO RICO

SAN JUAN, San Juan Dist.

Fiddler, González & Rodríguez

Chase Manhattan Bank Building (Hato Rey), P.O. Box 363507, 00936-3507
Telephone: 809-753-3113
Telecopier: 809-759-3123

MEMBER OF FIRM
Diego A. Ramos

SENIOR ASSOCIATE
Federico Tilén

Representative Clients: The Chase Manhattan Bank, N.A.; Eastman Kodak Co.; Westinghouse Electric Corp.; Pfizer, Inc.; Merck & Co., Inc.; American Cyanamid Co.; Metropolitan Life Insurance Co.; Bacardi Corp.

For Complete List of Firm Personnel, See General Section

For full biographical listings, see the Martindale-Hubbell Law Directory

Gonzalez & Bennazar

Capital Center Building South Tower - 9th Floor, Arterial Hostos Avenue (Hato Rey), 00918
Telephone: 809-754-9191
Fax: 809-754-9325

MEMBERS OF FIRM
Raul E. González Díaz — A. J. Bennazar-Zequeira

Representative Clients: American Express Travel Related Services Co., Inc.; Mars, Inc.; Wyndham Hotels; BWAC International; Master Foods Interamerica; M & M Mars; G-Tech Corporation; Florida SunShine Beverages; Cervezeria Moctezuma (Mexico); Dos Equis; United Colors of P.R. (Benetton).

For Complete List of Firm Personnel, See General Section

For full biographical listings, see the Martindale-Hubbell Law Directory

O'Neill & Borges

10th Floor, Chase Manhattan Bank Building (Hato Rey), 254 Muñoz Rivera Avenue, 00918-1995
Telephone: 809-764-8181
Telecopier: 809-753-8944

MEMBERS OF FIRM
Walter F. Chow — Jaime J. Aponte-Parsi
Pedro J. Santa-Sánchez — Pablo Rodríguez-Solá

Representative Clients: Anheuser Busch; Best-Foods Caribbean, Inc.; Ford Motor Co.; Hanes Menswear, Inc.; The Procter & Gamble Commercial Co.; Purolator; Seven-Up Bottling Co.; Thomson International Publishing; Tidewater, Inc.; Veryfine Products, Inc.

For Complete List of Firm Personnel, See General Section

For full biographical listings, see the Martindale-Hubbell Law Directory

CANADA BRITISH COLUMBIA

*VANCOUVER,** Vancouver Co.

Russell & DuMoulin (AV)

2100-1075 West Georgia Street, V6E 3G2
Telephone: 604-631-3131
Fax: 604-631-3232
A Member of the national association of Borden DuMoulin Howard Gervais, comprising Russell & DuMoulin, Vancouver, British Columbia; Howard Mackie, Calgary, Alberta; Borden & Elliot, Toronto, Ontario; Mackenzie Gervais, Montreal, Quebec and Borden DuMoulin Howard Gervais, London, England.
Strategic Alliance with Perkins Coie with offices in Seattle, Spokane and Bellevue, Washington; Portland, Oregon; Anchorage, Alaska; Los Angeles, California; Washington, D.C.; Hong Kong and Taipei, Taiwan.
Represented in Hong Kong by Vincent T.K. Cheung, Yap & Co.

ASSOCIATE
Keith E. Spencer

Representative Clients: Alcan Smelters & Chemicals Ltd.; The Bank of Nova Scotia; Canada Trust Co.; The Canada Life Assurance Co.; Forest Industrial Relations Ltd.; Honda Canada Inc.; IBM Canada Ltd.; Macmillan Bloedel Ltd.; Nissho Iwai Canada Ltd.; The Toronto-Dominion Bank.

For Complete List of Firm Personnel, See General Section

For full biographical listings, see the Martindale-Hubbell Law Directory

CANADA ONTARIO

*OTTAWA,** Regional Munic. of Ottawa-Carleton

Bennett Jones Verchere (AV)

Suite 1800, 350 Alberta Street, P.O. Box 25, K1R 1A4
Telephone: (613) 230-4935
Facsimile: (613) 230-3836
Calgary, Alberta Office: 4500 Bankers Hall East. 855-2nd Street S.W.
Telephone: (403) 298-3100.
Facsimile: (403) 265-7219.
Edmonton, Alberta Office: 1000, 10035-105 Street.
Telephone: (403) 421-8133.
Facsimile: (403) 421-7951.
Toronto, Ontario Office: 3400 1 First Canadian Place, P.O. Box 130.
Telephone: (416) 863-1200.
Facsimile: (416) 863-1716.
Montreal, Quebec Office: Suite 1600, 1 Place Ville Marie.
Telephone: (514) 871-1200.
Facsimile: (514) 871-8115.

RESIDENT MEMBER OF FIRM
George Edward Fisk

For Complete List of Firm Personnel, See General Section

For full biographical listings, see the Martindale-Hubbell Law Directory

*TORONTO,** Regional Munic. of York

Fasken Campbell Godfrey (AV)

Toronto-Dominion Centre Toronto-Dominion Bank Tower, P.O. Box 20, M5K 1N6
Telephone: 416-366-8381
Toll Free: 1-800-268-8424 (Ontario & Quebec)
Facsimile: 416-364-7813
The partners and associates of Fasken Campbell Godfrey are also partners and associates of the national and international firm of Fasken Martineau which has offices in Toronto, Montreal, Quebec, Vancouver (Affiliated), London and Brussels.
Montreal, Quebec Office: Martineau Walker, Stock Exchange Tower, Suite 3400, P.O. Box 242. 800 Place-Victoria H4Z 1E9.
Telephone: 514-397-7400. Toll-Free: 1-800-361-6266 (Ontario & Quebec).
Facsimile: 514-397-7600.
Telex: 05-24610 BUOY MTL.
Quebec City, Quebec Office: Martineau Walker, Immeuble Le Saint-Patrick, 140, rue Grande Allée est, bureau 800, G1R 5M8.
Telephone: 418-640-2000. Toll Free: 1-800-463-2827 (Ontario & Quebec).
Facsimile: 418-647-2455.
Vancouver (Affiliated): Davis & Co., 2800 Park Place, 666 Burrard Street, V6C 2Z7.
Telephone: 604-687-9444.
Fax: 604-687-1612.
London, England Office: Fasken Martineau, 10 Arthur Street, 5th Floor, EC4R 9AY.
Telephone: 71-929-2894.
Facsimile: 71-929-3634.

(See Next Column)

FASKEN CAMPBELL GODFREY, *Toronto—Continued*

Brussels, Belgium Office: Fasken Martineau, Avenue Franklin D. Roosevelt, 96 A, 1050, Brussels.
Telephone: 2-640-9796.
Facsimile: 2-640-2779.

MEMBERS

Robert M. Sutherland, Q.C.
James A. Bradshaw, Q.C.
Ronald J. Rolls, Q.C.
Claude R. Thomson, Q.C.
Roger D. Wilson, Q.C.
Rudolph W. Gardner, Q.C.
Donald J. Steadman
J. Michael Robinson, Q.C.
Arthur R. Kitamura
David M. Doubilet
Stephen T. P. Risk
Robert E. Smolkin
Roger R. Elliott, Q.C.
George C. Glover, Jr.
Stephen S. Ruby
John A. Campion
Robert S. Harrison
Kenneth C. Morlock
Esther L. Lenkinski
Walter J. Palmer
Samuel R. Rickett
Donald E. Short
Douglas C. New
Peter L. Roy
D. George Kelly
David G. Stinson
Craig R. Carter
Beryl B. Green
Jeffrey S. Leon
Edward W. Purdy
Peter W. Vair
Colleen Spring Zimmerman
Douglas E. Grundy
Elizabeth J. Johnson
Douglas A. Cannon
Michael N. Melanson
Donald E. Milner
J. David Vincent
Paul R. King
Roxanne E. McCormick
Sheryl E. Seigel
John D. Abraham
Ronald D. Collins
Richard E. Johnston
J. Mark Stinson
Gregory D. Gubitz
Mark S. Hayes
Paul J. Martin
Eric C. Belli-Bivar
Gary S. Fogler
Heather A. Laidlaw
Liana L. Turrin
Peter S. Ascherl
Michael J. MacNaughton
Cathy Singer
John G. Lorito
Robert W. Staley
Norman F. Findlay
Belinda J. James
Ronald N. Robertson, Q.C.
Roger G. Doe, Q.C.
Robert L. Shirriff, Q.C.
Robert B. Tuer, Q.C.
George Tiviluk, Q.C.
Ian MacGregor
John H. Hough, Q.C.
Benjamin J. Hutzel
Richard B. Potter, Q.C.
John T. Morin, Q.C.
Alan M. Schwartz, Q.C. (Managing Partner)
David W. Salomon
Robert W. McDowell
Douglas R. Scott
Robert W. Cosman
Douglas C. Hunt, Q.C.
S. Bruce Blain
Jonathan A. Levin
Mark A. Richardson
Leslie H. Rose
William J. Bies
Brian A. T. O'Byrne
Eleanore A. Cronk
Rand A. Lomas
Joan M. H. Weppler
David N. Corbett
Lorri Kushnir
Ronald J. McCloskey
Constance L. Sugiyama
Philip J. Wolfenden
Anthony F. Baldanza
M. Elena Hoffstein
Allan G. Beach
Jon J. Holmstrom
Barbara Miller
Neal J. Smitheman
Jeffrey A. Kaufman
C. Ian Kyer
Bruce Salvatore
Ronald J. Walker
W. Thomas Barlow
E. Stuart Griffith
Wayne P. J. McArdle
J. Steven Follett
S. Ronald Haber
Nigel P. J. Johnston
Gerald L. R. Ranking
Scott D. Conover
Bryan E. Kelling
David C. Rosenbaum
David G. Allsebrook
Peter A. Downard
Michael J. W. Round
Ruth M. Foster
David Koichi Moritsugu
Steven K. D'Arcy
Ralph J. Glass
Katherine M. Pollock

ASSOCIATES

Ronald W. McInnes
Daniel R. Law
Alan L. W. D'Silva
John M. Elias
Stephen M. Fitterman
Peter J. Pliszka
John S. M. Turner (Resident, London, England)
Jane E. Kelly
Kelley M. McKinnon
W. David Rance
Heidi Visser
Michael Balter
Joel E. Binder
Peter K. Czegledy
David Hausman
Kevin D. Lee
Rahul Erik Saxena
J. Michael Armstrong
Martin K. Denyes
R. Craig Hoskins
Norm D. Kribs
Hugh G. Laurence
A. Thomas Little
Brian P. Dominique
Mark J. Fecenko
B. Lynne Golding
Neil M. Smiley
Linda S. Beairsto
Janne M. Duncan
Kathryn L. Knight
Ralph N. Nero
Christopher J. Staples
John S. Zimmer
Ruby E. Barber
Stephanie Anne Brown
Ed Esposto
Nina N. Hoque
Grant B. Moffat
Richard B. Swan
T. Anthony Ball
Garth J. Foster
C. William Hourigan
Edmond F.B. Lamek
David F. O'Connor

COUNSEL

Hon. John M. Godfrey, Q.C.
D. G. C. Menzel, Q.C.
Jack W. Huckle, Q.C.
Alexander D. T. Givens, Q.C.
Lucien Lamoureux, P.C., Q.C. (Resident, Brussels, Belgium)
Karl J. C. Harries, Q.C.
Fraser M. Fell, Q.C.

For Complete List of Firm Personnel, See General Section

For full biographical listings, see the Martindale-Hubbell Law Directory

TRANSPORTATION LAW

ALABAMA

*BIRMINGHAM,** Jefferson Co.

BRADLEY, ARANT, ROSE & WHITE (AV)

1400 Park Place Tower, 2001 Park Place, 35203
Telephone: 205-521-8000
Telex: 494-1324
Facsimile: 205-251-8611, 251-8665, 252-0264
Facsimile (Southtrust Office): 205-251-9915
Huntsville, Alabama Office: 200 Clinton Avenue West, Suite 900.
Telephone: 205-517-5100.
Facsimile: 205-533-5069.

MEMBERS OF FIRM

Hobart A. McWhorter, Jr.
Joseph B. Mays, Jr.
John D. Watson, III

For Complete List of Firm Personnel, See General Section

For full biographical listings, see the Martindale-Hubbell Law Directory

BURGE & WETTERMARK, P.C. (AV)

2300 SouthTrust Tower, 420 North 20th Street, 35203-3204
Telephone: 205-251-9729; 800-633-3733
Fax: 205-323-0512
Atlanta, Georgia Office: One Atlantic Center, Suite 3250.
Telephone: 505-875-2500; 800-749-8687.
Fax: 404-875-5807.

Frank O. Burge, Jr.
James H. Wettermark
F. Tucker Burge
Courtney Burge Brown
Claire B. Morgan
Michael J. Warshauer (Not admitted in AL)

Monroe D. Barber, Jr.
Van Kirk McCombs, II
James R. Holland, II (Not admitted in AL)

References: AmSouth Bank; First Alabama Bank, Birmingham, Alabama.

For full biographical listings, see the Martindale-Hubbell Law Directory

*MOBILE,** Mobile Co.

MILLER, HAMILTON, SNIDER & ODOM, L.L.C. (AV)

254-256 State Street, P.O. Box 46, 36601
Telephone: 334-432-1414
Telecopier: 334-433-4106
Montgomery, Alabama Office: Suite 802, One Commerce Street.
Telephone: 205-834-5550.
Telecopier: 205-265-4533.
Washington, D.C. Office: Miller, Hamilton, Snider, Odom & Bridgeman, L.L.C., Suite 1150, 1747 Pennsylvania Avenue, N.W.
Telephone: 202-429-9223.
Telecopier: 202-293-2068.

MEMBERS OF FIRM

Lester M. Bridgeman
Louis T. Urbanczyk (Not admitted in AL; Washington, D.C. Office)

Representative Clients: The Colonial BancGroup, Inc.; Colonial Mortgage Co.; Chase Manhattan Bank, N.A.; The Mitchell Co.; Poole Truck Line, Inc.; Brittania Airways, Ltd. (U.K.); Air Europe (Italy); K-Mart Corporation; K & B Alabama Corp.; Ford Consumer Finance Company, Inc.

For Complete List of Firm Personnel, See General Section

For full biographical listings, see the Martindale-Hubbell Law Directory

ARIZONA

*PHOENIX,** Maricopa Co.

FENNEMORE CRAIG, A PROFESSIONAL CORPORATION (AV)

Two North Central, Suite 2200, 85004
Telephone: 602-257-8700
Fax: 602-257-8527
Scottsdale, Arizona Office: 6263 North Scottsdale Road, Suite 290, 85250.
Telephone: 602-257-5400.
Fax: 602-945-4932.
Tucson, Arizona Office: One South Church Avenue, Suite 1030, 85701.
Telephone: 602-624-9312.
Fax: 602-882-7383.

C. Webb Crockett
F. Pendleton Gaines, III

Representative Clients: ASARCO Incorporated; AT&T Communications; Bridgestone/Firestone, Inc.; Catellus Development Corp.; Citibank (Arizona); First Interstate Bank of Arizona; GIANT Industries; Phelps Dodge Corporation; The Atchison, Topeka & Santa Fe Railway, Co.; US WEST Communications.

For Complete List of Firm Personnel, See General Section

For full biographical listings, see the Martindale-Hubbell Law Directory

ARKANSAS

*LITTLE ROCK,** Pulaski Co.

HILBURN, CALHOON, HARPER, PRUNISKI & CALHOUN, LTD. (AV)

P.O. Box 1256, 72203-1256
Telephone: 501-372-0110
FAX: 501-372-2029
North Little Rock, Arkansas Office: Eighth Floor, The Twin City Bank Building, One Riverfront Place, P.O. Box 5551, 72119.
Telephone: 501-372-0110.
FAX: 501-372-2029.

John C. Calhoun, Jr.
Scott E. Daniel

Representative Client: The Twin City Bank.

For Complete List of Firm Personnel, See General Section

For full biographical listings, see the Martindale-Hubbell Law Directory

CALIFORNIA

BEVERLY HILLS, Los Angeles Co.

MILES L. KAVALLER A PROFESSIONAL LAW CORPORATION (AV)

Suite 315, 315 South Beverly Drive, 90212
Telephone: 310-277-2323
Fax: 310-556-2308

Miles L. Kavaller

Reference: City National Bank (6th & Olive Branch).

For full biographical listings, see the Martindale-Hubbell Law Directory

LONG BEACH, Los Angeles Co.

BENNETT & KISTNER (AV)

301 East Ocean Boulevard, Suite 800, 90802
Telephone: 310-435-6675
Fax: 310-437-8375
Riverside, California Office: 3403 Tenth Street, Suite 605, 92501-3676.
Telephone: 909-341-9360.
Fax: 909-341-9362.

Charles J. Bennett
Wayne T. Kistner

ASSOCIATES

Richard R. Bradbury
Mary A. Estante (Resident, Riverside Office)
Todd R. Becker
Karen H. Beckman (Resident, Riverside Office)

Representative Clients: The Hertz Corporation; Thrifty Oil Co.; Golden West Refining Co.; Standard Brands Paint Co.; Mattel, Inc.; Di Salvo Trucking Co.; County of Riverside; Southern California Rapid Transit District.
Reference: First Interstate Bank of California, The Market Place Office, Long Beach, California.

For full biographical listings, see the Martindale-Hubbell Law Directory

Long Beach—Continued

Fisher & Porter, A Law Corporation (AV)

110 Pine Avenue, 11th Floor, P.O. Box 22686, 90801-5686
Telephone: 310-435-5626
Telex: 284549 FPKLAW UR
Fax: 310-432-5399

Gerald M. Fisher
David S. Porter
Therese G. Groff
Michael W. Lodwick
Frank C. Brucculeri

George P. Hassapis
Stephen Chace Bass
Robert M. White, Jr.
Paul J. Rubino
Steven Y. Otera
Jay Russell Sever
Vicki L. Hassman
Linda A. Mancini

OF COUNSEL

Stephen C. Klausen

For full biographical listings, see the Martindale-Hubbell Law Directory

Williams Woolley Cogswell Nakazawa & Russell (AV)

111 West Ocean Boulevard, Suite 2000, 90802-4614
Telephone: 310-495-6000
Telecopier: 310-435-1359
Telex: ITT: 4933872; WU: 984929

MEMBERS OF FIRM

Reed M. Williams
David E. R. Woolley
Forrest R. Cogswell
Alan Nakazawa
Blake W. Larkin
Thomas A. Russell

ASSOCIATES

B. Alexander Moghaddam
Dennis R. Acker

For full biographical listings, see the Martindale-Hubbell Law Directory

*SAN DIEGO,** San Diego Co.

Rice Fowler Booth & Banning (AV)

Emerald - Shapery Center, 402 W. Broadway, Suite 850, 92101
Telephone: 619-230-0030
Telecopier: 619-230-1350
New Orleans, Louisiana Office: 36th Floor, Place St. Charles, 201 St. Charles Avenue, 70130
Telephone: 504-523-2600.
Telecopier: 504-523-2705.
Telex: 9102507910. ELN: 62548910.
London, England Office: Suite 692, Level 6 Lloyd's, 1 Lime Street, London EC3M 7DQ England.
Telephone: 071-327-4222.
Telecopier: 071-929-0043.
San Francisco, California Office: Embarcadero Center West, 275 Battery Street, 27th Floor, 94111.
Telephone: 415-399-9191.
Telecopier: 415-399-9192.
Telex: 451981.
Beijing, China Office: Beijing International Convention Centre, Suite 7024, No. 8 Beichendong Road, Chaoyang District, 100101, P.R.C.
Telephone: (861) 493-4250.
Telecopier: (861) 493-4251.
Bogota, Colombia Office: Avenida Jimenez #4-03 Officina 10-05.
Telephone: (571) 342-1062.
Telecopier: (571) 342-1062.

PARTNERS

William L. Banning
Keith Zakarin
Robert B. Krueger, Jr.

ASSOCIATE

Juan Carlos Dominguez

For full biographical listings, see the Martindale-Hubbell Law Directory

*SAN FRANCISCO,** San Francisco Co.

Rice Fowler Booth & Banning (AV)

Embarcadero Center West, 275 Battery Street, 27th Floor, 94111
Telephone: 415-399-9191
Telecopier: 415-399-9192
Telex: 451981
New Orleans, Louisiana Office: Place St. Charles, 36th Floor, 201 St. Charles Avenue, 70130.
Telephone: 504-523-2600.
Telecopier: 504-523-2705.
Telex: 9102507910. ELN 62548910.
San Diego, California Office: Emerald-Shapery Center, 402 W. Broadway, Suite 850, 92101.
Telephone: 619-230-0030.
Telecopier: 619-230-1350.
London, England Office: Suite 692, Level 6 Lloyd's, 1 Lime Street, London EC3M 7DQ England.
Telephone: 071-327-4222.
Telecopier: 071-929-0043.

(See Next Column)

Beijing, China Office: Beijing International Convention Centre, Suite 7024, No. 8 Beichendong Road, Chaoyang District, 100101, P.R.C.
Telephone: (861) 493-4250.
Telecopier: (861) 493-4251.
Bogota, Colombia Office: Avenida Jimenez #4-03 Oficina 10-05, Bogota, Colombia.
Telephone: (571) 342-1062.
Telecopier: (571) 342-1062.

MEMBERS OF FIRM

Forrest Booth
Kurt L. Micklow
Norman J. Ronneberg, Jr.

ASSOCIATES

Cynthia L. Mitchell
Lynn Haggerty King
Edward M. Bull, III
Kim O. Dincel
Amy Jo Poor
Janice Amenta-Jones
Heidi Loken Benas

For full biographical listings, see the Martindale-Hubbell Law Directory

COLORADO

*DENVER,** Denver Co.

Robert L. Bartholic (AV)

Suite 600, 1600 Broadway, 80202
Telephone: 303-830-0500
Fax: 303-860-7855

OF COUNSEL

Clarence L. Bartholic

Representative Clients: Anschutz Corp.; Denver and Rio Grande Western Railroad Co.; Burlington Northern Railroad Co. and Subsidiaries; American Association of Private Railroad Car Owners, Inc.

For full biographical listings, see the Martindale-Hubbell Law Directory

CONNECTICUT

*NEW HAVEN,** New Haven Co.

Lynch, Traub, Keefe and Errante, A Professional Corporation (AV)

52 Trumbull Street, P.O. Box 1612, 06506
Telephone: 203-787-0275
Fax: 203-782-0278

Stephen I. Traub
Hugh F. Keefe
Steven J. Errante
John J. Keefe, Jr.
Donn A. Swift
Charles E. Tiernan, III
Robert W. Lynch
Richard W. Lynch

Mary Beattie Schairer
John M. Walsh, Jr.
Suzanne L. McAlpine
David J. Vegliante
Christopher M. Licari
David S. Monastersky

OF COUNSEL

William C. Lynch

Local Counsel for: Transport Insurance Co., Dallas, Texas; American Trucking Associations; Roadway Express, Inc., Akron, Ohio; A.R.A. Philadelphia, Penn.; Consolidated Freightways, Menlo Park, California; Ogden Corp.
Labor Counsel: Coca-Cola, U.S.A., Atlanta, Georgia (Private Truck Operation); The Dow Chemical Co.; Cincinnati Milacron.

For full biographical listings, see the Martindale-Hubbell Law Directory

DISTRICT OF COLUMBIA

WASHINGTON, D.C. Co.

* indicates certain Bar Register subscribers, in cities of comparable size and importance, who maintain an additional office in Washington, D.C. and who have arranged for representation as a part of the Washington, D.C. listings that follow

Baker & Hostetler (AV)

Washington Square, Suite 1100, 1050 Connecticut Avenue, N.W., 20036-5304
Telephone: 202-861-1500
In Cleveland, Ohio: 3200 National City Center, 1900 East Ninth Street.
Telephone: 216-621-0200.
In Columbus, Ohio: Capitol Square, Suite 2100, 65 East State Street.
Telephone: 614-228-1541.

(See Next Column)

BAKER & HOSTETLER—*Continued*

In Denver, Colorado: 303 East 17th Avenue, Suite 1100.
Telephone: 303-861-0600.
In Houston, Texas: 1000 Louisiana, Suite 2000.
Telephone: 713-751-1600.
In Long Beach, California: 300 Oceangate, Suite 620.
Telephone: 310-432-2827.
In Los Angeles, California: 600 Wilshire Boulevard.
Telephone: 213-624-2400.
In Orlando, Florida: SunBank Center, Suite 2300, 200 South Orange Avenue.
Telephone: 305-841-1111.
In College Park, Maryland: 9658 Baltimore Boulevard, Suite 206.
Telephone: 301-441-2781.
In Alexandria, Virginia: 437 North Lee Street.
Telephone: 703-549-1294.
In San Francisco, California: One Sansome Street, Suite 2000.
Telephone: 415-951-4705.

PARTNER

Richard A. Hauser

OF COUNSEL

Richard H. Jones

For Complete List of Firm Personnel, See General Section

For full biographical listings, see the Martindale-Hubbell Law Directory

GROVE, JASKIEWICZ AND COBERT (AV)

Suite 400, 1730 M Street, N.W., 20036
Telephone: 202-296-2900
Telecopier: 202-296-1370
Baltimore, Maryland Office: The Park Plaza, 800 North Charles Street, Suite 400.
Telephone: 301-727-7010.

MEMBERS OF FIRM

William J. Grove (1914-1988)
Ronald N. Cobert
Paul H. Lamboley (Not admitted in DC)
Edward J. Kiley
Robert L. Cope
Joseph Michael Roberts
Andrew M. Danas
Andrew M. Whitman (Not admitted in DC)

OF COUNSEL

Leonard A. Jaskiewicz
James F. Flint
Lawrence E. Dubé, Jr.
James K. Jeanblanc
Edmund M. Jaskiewicz

For full biographical listings, see the Martindale-Hubbell Law Directory

HARKINS CUNNINGHAM (AV)

Suite 600, 1300 Nineteenth Street Northwest, 20036-1609
Telephone: 202-973-7600
Facsimile: 202-973-7610
Philadelphia, Pennsylvania Office: 1800 Commerce Square, 2005 Market Street.
Telephone: 215-851-6700.
Facsimile: 215-851-6710.

MEMBERS OF FIRM

John G. Harkins, Jr. (Not admitted in DC)
Paul A. Cunningham

Charles Bramham (Not admitted in DC)
Patricia L. Freeland (Not admitted in DC)
Richard B. Herzog
David A. Hirsh
Eleanor Morris Illoway (Not admitted in DC)
Robert M. Jenkins, III
A. Carl Kaseman, III
Gerald P. Norton
James G. Rafferty
Lloyd R. Ziff (Not admitted in DC)

ASSOCIATES

Elizabeth M. Chachis (Not admitted in DC)
Karin Engstrom Davis (Not admitted in DC)
Stuart L. Fullerton
James M. Guinivan
Neill C. Kling (Not admitted in DC)
Melissa E. Kraras
Joseph L. Lakshmanan
Joel A. Rabinovitz
Steven A. Reed (Not admitted in DC)
Melinda P. Rudolph (Not admitted in DC)
Gay Parks Rainville (Not admitted in DC)

OF COUNSEL

Margaret W. Wiener

For full biographical listings, see the Martindale-Hubbell Law Directory

SHAWN, MANN & NIEDERMAYER, L.L.P. (AV)

1850 M Street, N.W., Suite 280, 20036-5803
Telephone: 202-331-7900
Fax: 202-331-0726

(See Next Column)

MEMBERS OF FIRM

William H. Shawn
Kim D. Mann
Joseph L. Steinfeld, Jr.
Robert B. Walker

For full biographical listings, see the Martindale-Hubbell Law Directory

SLOVER & LOFTUS (AV)

1224 Seventeenth Street, N.W., 20036
Telephone: 202-347-7170
Telecopier: 202-347-3619

William L. Slover
C. Michael Loftus
Donald G. Avery
John H. LeSeur
Kelvin J. Dowd
Robert D. Rosenberg
Frank J. Pergolizzi

Andrew B. Kolesar III
André D. Hollis
Patricia E. Dietrich

For full biographical listings, see the Martindale-Hubbell Law Directory

STEPTOE & JOHNSON (AV)

1330 Connecticut Avenue, N.W., 20036
Telephone: 202-429-3000
Cable Address: "Stepjohn"
Telex: 89-2503
Telecopier: 202-429-3902
Phoenix, Arizona Office: Two Renaissance Square, 40 N. Central Avenue, Suite 2400, 85004.
Telephone: 602-257-5200.
Moscow, Russia Office: Steptoe & Johnson International Affiliate in Moscow. 25 Tsvetnoy Boulevard, Building 3 Moscow, Russia 103051.
Telephone: 011-7-501-929-9700.
Fax: 501-929-9701.

MEMBERS

Richard P. Taylor
Laurence A. Short
Betty Jo Christian
John R. Labovitz
William Karas
Charles G. Cole
Timothy M. Walsh
Samuel M. Sipe, Jr.
Steven Reed
John D. Graubert
David H. Coburn

OF COUNSEL

Robert J. Corber

For Complete List of Firm Personnel, See General Section

For full biographical listings, see the Martindale-Hubbell Law Directory

* THOMPSON, HINE AND FLORY (AV)

1920 N Street, N.W., 20036-1601
Telephone: 202-331-8800
Fax: 202-331-8330
Telex: 904173
Cable Address: "Caglaw"
Akron, Ohio Office: 50 S. Main Street, Suite 502, 44308-1828.
Telephone: 216-376-8090.
Fax: 216-376-8386.
Cincinnati, Ohio Office: 312 Walnut Street, 14th Floor, 45202-4029.
Telephone: 513-352-6700.
Fax: 513-241-4771.
Telex: 938003.
Cleveland, Ohio Office: 1100 National City Bank Building, 629 Euclid Avenue, 44114.
Telephone: 216-566-5500.
Fax: 216-566-5583.
Telex: 980217. Cable Address "Thomflor".
Columbus, Ohio Office: One Columbus, 10 West Broad Street, 43215-34353.
Telephone: 614-469-3200.
Fax: 614-469-3361.
Dayton, Ohio Office: 2000 Courthouse Plaza, N.E., 45402-1706.
Telephone: 513-443-6600.
Fax: 513-443-6637, 513-443-6635.
Palm Beach, Florida Office: 125 Worth Avenue, 33480-4466.
Telephone: 407-833-5900.
Fax: 407-833-5951.
Brussels, Belgium Office: Rue Des Chevaliers, Ridderstraat 14 - B.10, B-1050.
Telephone: 011-32-2-511-9326.
Fax: 011-32-2-513-9206.

MEMBERS OF FIRM

Peter A. Greene (Partner-in-Charge in Washington, D.C.)
Norman J. Philion, III

For Complete List of Firm Personnel, See General Section

For full biographical listings, see the Martindale-Hubbell Law Directory

Washington—Continued

*** VENABLE, BAETJER, HOWARD & CIVILETTI (AV)**

A Partnership including Professional Corporations
Suite 1000, 1201 New York Avenue, N.W., 20005
Telephone: 202-962-4800
Fax: 202-962-8300
Baltimore, Maryland Office: Venable, Baetjer and Howard, 1800 Mercantile Bank & Trust Building, 2 Hopkins Plaza.
Telephone: 410-244-7400.
McLean, Virginia Office: Venable, Baetjer and Howard, Suite 400, 2010 Corporate Ridge.
Telephone: 703-760-1600.
Rockville, Maryland Office: Venable, Baetjer and Howard, Suite 500, One Church Street, P. O. Box 1906.
Telephone: 301-217-5600.
Towson, Maryland Office: Venable, Baetjer and Howard, 210 Allegheny Avenue, P. O. Box 5517.
Telephone: 410-494-6200.

MEMBERS OF FIRM

Jan K. Guben (Not admitted in DC; Also at Baltimore, Maryland Office)
Joe A. Shull
Max Stul Oppenheimer (P.C.) (Also at Baltimore and Towson, Maryland Offices)
Robert G. Ames (Also at Baltimore, Maryland Office)
James K. Archibald (Also at Baltimore and Towson, Maryland Offices)
Judson W. Starr (Also at Baltimore and Towson, Maryland Offices)
James R. Myers
George F. Pappas (Also at Baltimore, Maryland Office)
Paul A. Serini (Not admitted in DC; Also at Baltimore, Maryland Office)

For Complete List of Firm Personnel, See General Section

For full biographical listings, see the Martindale-Hubbell Law Directory

VERNER, LIIPFERT, BERNHARD, MCPHERSON AND HAND, CHARTERED (AV)

901 15th Street, N.W., 20005-2301
Telephone: 202-371-6000
Cable Address: "Verlip"
Telex: 1561792 VERLIP UT
Fax: 202-371-6279
McLean, Virginia Office: Sixth Floor, 8280 Greensboro Drive, 22102.
Telephone: 703-749-6000.
Fax: 703-749-6027.
Houston, Texas Office: 2600 Texas Commerce Tower, 600 Travis, 77002.
Telephone: 713-237-9034.
Fax: 713-237-1216.

Douglas Ochs Adler
Berl Bernhard
Roy G. Bowman
Hopewell H. Darneille, III
William C. Evans
Benjamin H. Flowe, Jr.
Joseph L. Manson, III
Ronald B. Natalie
Russell E. Pommer
Michael J. Roberts

For Complete List of Firm Personnel, See General Section

For full biographical listings, see the Martindale-Hubbell Law Directory

WILMER, CUTLER & PICKERING (AV)

2445 M Street, N.W., 20037-1420
Telephone: 202-663-6000
Facsimile: 202-663-6363
Internet: Law@Wilmer.Com
European Offices:
4 Carlton Gardens, London, SW1Y 5AA, England. Telephone: 011 (4471) 839-4466.
Facsimile: 011 (4471) 839-3537.
Rue de la Loi 15 Wetstraat, B-1040 Brussels, Belgium. Telephone: 011 (322) 231-0903.
Facsimile: 011 (322) 230-4322.
Friedrichstrasse 95, D-10117 Berlin, Germany. Telephone: 011 (4930) 2643-3601.
Facsimile: 011 (4930) 2643-3630.

MEMBERS OF FIRM

James S. Campbell
Dieter G. F. Lange (Not admitted in DC; Resident, European Office, London, England)
Stephen P. Doyle
James S. Venit (Not admitted in DC; Resident, European Office, Brussels, Belgium)
Paul A. von Hehn (Not admitted in DC; Resident, European Office, Brussels, Belgium)

COUNSEL

Lester Nurick
Dr. Andreas Weitbrecht (Not admitted in DC; Resident, European Office, Brussels, Belgium)
Jeffrey N. Shane

(See Next Column)

SPECIAL COUNSEL

John J. Kallaugher (Not admitted in DC; Resident, European Office, London, England)

For Complete List of Firm Personnel, See General Section

For full biographical listings, see the Martindale-Hubbell Law Directory

FLORIDA

*JACKSONVILLE,** Duval Co.

TAYLOR, MOSELEY & JOYNER, P.A. (AV)

501 West Bay Street, 32202
Telephone: 904-356-1306
Cable Address: "Ragland"
Telex: 5-6374
Telecopier: 904-354-0194

Reuben Ragland (1882-1954)
Louis Kurz (1891-1965)
E. Dale Joyner (1943-1993)
Neil C. Taylor
James F. Moseley
Robert E. Warren
Joseph W. Prichard, Jr.
Robert B. Parrish
Andrew J. Knight II
Richard K. Jones
James F. Moseley, Jr.
Phillip A. Buhler
Melanie E. Shepherd
Victor J. Zambetti
Mathew G. Nasrallah

Stanley M. Weston

OF COUNSEL

James E. Williams

Counsel for: CSX Transportation; Britannia Steam Ship Insurance Assn., Ltd.; The West of England Protection & Indemnity Assn. (Luxembourg); Crowley American Transport Services, Inc.; Howard Johnson Co.; United Kingdom Mutal Steamship Assurance Assn., Ltd. (Bermuda); General Food Corp.; The London Steam-Ship Owners' Mutual Insurance Assn., Ltd.

For full biographical listings, see the Martindale-Hubbell Law Directory

NORTH MIAMI BEACH, Dade Co.

BECKHAM & BECKHAM, P.A. (AV)

17071 West Dixie Highway, Suite B, 33160
Telephone: DADE: 305-945-1851; BROWARD: 305-920-9793
Fax: 305-940-8706

Pamela Beckham
Eugene G. Beckham
Robert J. Beckham, Jr.

For full biographical listings, see the Martindale-Hubbell Law Directory

GEORGIA

*ATLANTA,** Fulton Co.

DENNIS, CORRY, PORTER & GRAY (AV)

3300 One Atlanta Plaza, 950 East Paces Ferry Road, P.O. Box 18640, 30326
Telephone: 404-240-6900
Wats: 800-735-0838
Fax: 404-240-6909
Telex: 4611041

MEMBERS OF FIRM

Robert E. Corry, Jr.
R. Clay Porter
William E. Gray, II
James S. Strawinski
Grant B. Smith

OF COUNSEL

Douglas Dennis

ASSOCIATES

Frederick D. Evans, III
Virginia M. Greer
Robert G. Ballard
Matthew J. Jewell
Pamela Jean Gray
Ronald G. Polly, Jr.
Thomas D. Trask
J. Steven Fisher
Stephanie F. Goff
Alison Roberts Solomon
Robert David Schoen
Brian DeVoe Rogers

Representative Clients: Farmers Insurance Group; Roadway Services, Inc.

For full biographical listings, see the Martindale-Hubbell Law Directory

IDAHO

*BOISE,** Ada Co.

MOFFATT, THOMAS, BARRETT, ROCK & FIELDS, CHARTERED (AV)

First Security Building, 911 West Idaho Street, Suite 300, P.O. Box 829, 83701
Telephone: 208-345-2000
FAX: 208-385-5384
Idaho Falls Office: 525 Park Avenue, Suite 2D, P.O. Box 1367, 83403.
Telephone: 208-522-6700.
FAX: 208-522-5111.
Pocatello, Idaho Office: 1110 Call Creek Drive, P.O. Box 4941, 83201.
Telephone: 208-233-2001.

Morgan W. Richards, Jr.

Representative Clients: BMC West Corporation; Chevron, U.S.A.; First Security Bank of Idaho, N.A.; General Motors Corp.; Idaho Potato Commission; Intermountain Gas Co.; John Alden Life Insurance Co.; Micron, Inc.; Royal Insurance Cos.; St. Luke's Regional Medical Center & Mountain States Tumor Institute.

For Complete List of Firm Personnel, See General Section

For full biographical listings, see the Martindale-Hubbell Law Directory

ILLINOIS

*CHICAGO,** Cook Co.

BELGRADE AND O'DONNELL, A PROFESSIONAL CORPORATION (AV)

311 South Wacker Drive, Suite 2770, 60606
Telephone: 312-360-9500
Facsimile: 312-360-9550

Steven B. Belgrade
John A. O'Donnell
George M. Velcich
Kim Richard Kardas
Andrea J. McIntyre
Joseph G. Howard

For full biographical listings, see the Martindale-Hubbell Law Directory

INDIANA

HAMMOND, Lake Co.

ABRAHAMSON, REED & ADLEY (AV)

5231 Hohman Avenue, 46320
Telephone: 219-937-1500
Fax: 219-937-3174

MEMBERS OF FIRM

Harold Abrahamson
Kenneth D. Reed
Michael C. Adley

ASSOCIATES

Scott R. Bilse
Christopher R. Karsten
Joseph L. Curosh

References: Calumet National Bank, Hammond; Mercantile National Bank, Hammond.

For full biographical listings, see the Martindale-Hubbell Law Directory

KANSAS

*TOPEKA,** Shawnee Co.

FOULSTON & SIEFKIN (AV)

(Formerly Foulston, Siefkin, Powers & Eberhardt)
1515 Bank IV Tower, 534 Kansas Avenue, 66603
Telephone: 913-233-3600
FAX: 913-233-1610
Wichita, Kansas Office: 700 Fourth Financial Center, Broadway at Douglas. 67202.
Telephone: 316-267-6371.
Facsimile: 316-267-6345.
Member: Lex Mundi, A Global Association of Independent Firms

SPECIAL COUNSEL

James L. Grimes, Jr.

For full biographical listings, see the Martindale-Hubbell Law Directory

LOUISIANA

*NEW ORLEANS,** Orleans Parish

PULASKI, GIEGER & LABORDE, A PROFESSIONAL LAW CORPORATION (AV)

Suite 4800, One Shell Square, 701 Poydras Street, 70139
Telephone: 504-561-0400
Telecopier: 504-561-1011

Michael T. Pulaski (P.C.)
Ernest P. Gieger, Jr., (P.C.)
Kenneth H. Laborde
Robert W. Maxwell
Keith W. McDaniel
Sharon D. Smith
Gary G. Hebert
Leo R. McAloon, III
J. Jeffrey Raborn
James E. Swinnen
Gina S. Montgomery
Diana L. Tonagel
Katherine B. Hardy
Mary Beth Meyer

For full biographical listings, see the Martindale-Hubbell Law Directory

RICE FOWLER (AV)

Place St. Charles, 36th Floor, 201 St. Charles Avenue, 70130
Telephone: 504-523-2600
Telecopier: 504-523-2705
Telex: 9102507910
ELN 62548910
London, England Office: Suite 692, Level 6 Lloyd's, 1 Lime Street, London EC3M 7DQ England.
Telephone: 071-327-4222.
Telecopier: 071-929-0043.
San Francisco, California Office: Embarcadero Center West, 275 Battery Street, 27th Floor, 94111.
Telephone: 415-399-9191.
Telecopier: 415-399-9192.
Telex: 451981.
San Diego, California Office: Emerald-Shapery Center, 402 W. Broadway, Suite 850, 92101.
Telephone: 619-230-0030.
Telecopier: 619-230-1350.
Beijing, China Office: Beijing International Convention Centre, Suite 7024, No. 8 Beichendong Road, Chaoyang District, 100101, P.R.C.
Telephone: (861) 493-4250.
Telecopier: (861) 493-4251.
Bogota, Colombia Office: Avenida Jimenez #4-03 Oficina 10-05.
Telephone: (571) 342-1062.
Telecopier: (571) 342-1062.

MEMBERS OF FIRM

Winston Edward Rice
George J. Fowler, III
Antonio J. Rodriguez
Thomas H. Kingsmill, III
Paul N. Vance
Delos E. Flint, Jr.
Edward F. LeBreton, III
Docia L. Dalby
Mary Campbell Hubbard
Jon W. Wise
Mat M. Gray, III

OF COUNSEL

T. C. W. Ellis

ASSOCIATES

Mary E. Kerrigan
Susan Molero Vance
Samuel A. Giberga
John F. Billera
D. Roxanne Perkins
Jeffry L. Sanford
Alanson T. Chenault, IV
Cindy T. Matherne
Barry A. Brock
Walter F. Wolf, III
Robert R. Johnston
Virginia R. Quijada
William J. Sommers, Jr.

For full biographical listings, see the Martindale-Hubbell Law Directory

SLATER LAW FIRM, A PROFESSIONAL CORPORATION (AV)

650 Poydras Street Suite 2400, 70130-6101
Telephone: 504-523-7333
Fax: 504-528-1080

Benjamin R. Slater, Jr.
Benjamin R. Slater, III
Mark E. Van Horn
Kevin M. Wheeler

Anne Elise Brown
Donald J. Miester, Jr.

OF COUNSEL

Michael O. Waguespack

Representative Clients: Norfolk Southern Corporation; The Alabama Great Southern Railroad Company; North American Van Lines; New Orleans Steamship Association; Fleet Transport Company, Inc.

For full biographical listings, see the Martindale-Hubbell Law Directory

*SHREVEPORT,** Caddo Parish

BARLOW AND HARDTNER L.C. (AV)

Tenth Floor, Louisiana Tower, 401 Edwards Street, 71101-3289
Telephone: 318-227-1131
Telecopier: 318-227-1141
Mailing Address: P.O. Box 8, Shreveport, Louisiana, 71161-0008

Ray A. Barlow
Malcolm S. Murchison
David R. Taggart
Michael B. Donald

Representative Clients: Kelley Oil Corporation; NorAm Energy Corp. (formerly Arkla, Inc.); NorAm Gas Transmission Company; Central and South West; Panhandle Eastern Corp.; Pennzoil Producing Co.; Johnson Controls, Inc.; Ashland Oil, Inc.; Southwestern Electric Power Company; Brammer Engineering, Inc.

For Complete List of Firm Personnel, See General Section

For full biographical listings, see the Martindale-Hubbell Law Directory

WILKINSON, CARMODY & GILLIAM (AV)

1700 Beck Building, 400 Travis Street, P.O. Box 1707, 71166
Telephone: 318-221-4196
Telecopier: 318-221-3705

MEMBERS OF FIRM

John D. Wilkinson (1867-1929)
William Scott Wilkinson (1895-1985)
Arthur R. Carmody, Jr.
Bobby S. Gilliam
Mark E. Gilliam
Penny D. Sellers
Brian D. Landry

Representative Clients: Farmers Insurance Group; Home Federal Savings & Loan Association of Shreveport; The Kansas City Southern Railway Co.; KTAL-TV; Lincoln National Life Insurance Co.; Mobil Oil Co.; Schumpert Medical Center; Sears, Roebuck & Co.; Southern Pacific Transportation Co.; Southwestern Electric Power Co.

For full biographical listings, see the Martindale-Hubbell Law Directory

MARYLAND

*BALTIMORE,** (Independent City)

THIEBLOT, RYAN, MARTIN & FERGUSON, P.A. (AV)

4th Floor, The World Trade Center, 21202-3091
Telephone: 410-837-1140
Washington, D.C. Line: 202-628-8223
Fax: 410-837-3282

Robert J. Thieblot
Anthony W. Ryan
J. Edward Martin, Jr.
Robert L. Ferguson, Jr.
Bruce R. Miller
Robert D. Harwick, Jr.
Thomas J. Schetelich
Christopher J. Heffernan

M. Brooke Murdock
Anne M. Hrehorovich
Donna Marie Raffaele
Michael N. Russo, Jr.
Jodi K. Ebersole
Hamilton Fisk Tyler
Peter Joseph Basile

Representative Clients: Ford Motor Credit Co.; USF & G Co.; The American Road Insurance Co.; Fidelity Engineering Corp.; The North Charles Street Design Organization; Record Collections, Inc.; Toyota Motor Credit Co.

For full biographical listings, see the Martindale-Hubbell Law Directory

VENABLE, BAETJER AND HOWARD (AV)

A Partnership including Professional Corporations
1800 Mercantile Bank & Trust Building, 2 Hopkins Plaza, 21201
Telephone: 410-244-7400
Washington, D.C. Office: Venable, Baetjer, Howard & Civiletti. Suite 1000, 1201 New York Avenue, N.W.
Telephone: 202-962-4800.
McLean, Virginia Office: Suite 400, 2010 Corporate Ridge.
Telephone: 703-760-1600.
Rockville, Maryland Office: Suite 500, One Church Street, P. O. Box 1906.
Telephone: 301-217-5600.
Towson, Maryland Office: 210 Allegheny Avenue, P. O. Box 5517.
Telephone: 410-494-6200.

MEMBERS OF FIRM

Stanley Mazaroff (P.C.)
Jan K. Guben (Also at Washington, D. C Office)
James D. Wright (P.C.)
John G. Milliken (Not admitted in MD; Also at Washington, D.C. and McLean, Virginia Offices)
Max Stul Oppenheimer (P.C.) (Also at Washington, D.C. and Towson, Maryland Offices)
Joseph C. Wich, Jr. (Resident, Towson, Maryland Office)
Robert G. Ames (Also at Washington, D.C. Office)

(See Next Column)

MEMBERS OF FIRM (Continued)

Richard L. Wasserman (P.C.)
James K. Archibald (Also at Washington, D.C. and Towson, Maryland Offices)
George W. Johnston (P.C.)
Judson W. Starr (Not admitted in MD; Also at Washington, D.C. and Towson, Maryland Offices)
James R. Myers (Not admitted in MD; Resident, Washington, D.C. Office)
Jana Howard Carey (P.C.)
George F. Pappas (Also at Washington, D.C. Office)
Mitchell Kolkin
Paul A. Serini (Also at Washington, D.C. Office)
Kevin L. Shepherd

OF COUNSEL

Emried D. Cole, Jr.

ASSOCIATE

Vicki Margolis

For Complete List of Firm Personnel, See General Section

For full biographical listings, see the Martindale-Hubbell Law Directory

MICHIGAN

*ANN ARBOR,** Washtenaw Co.

MILLER, CANFIELD, PADDOCK AND STONE, P.L.C. (AV)

A Professional Limited Liability Company
Founded in 1852 by Sidney Davy Miller
101 North Main Street, Seventh Floor, 48104-1400
Telephone: 313-663-2445
Fax: 313-747-7147
Detroit, Michigan Office: 150 West Jefferson, Suite 2500, 48226-4415.
Telephone: 313-963-6420.
Fax: 313-496-7500.
Cable Address: "Stem Detroit."
Bloomfield Hills, Michigan Office: Suite 100, Pinehurst Office Center, 1400 North Woodward, 48303-2014.
Telephone: 313-645-5000.
Fax: 313-645-1917.
Grand Rapids, Michigan Office: 1200 Campau Square Plaza, 99 Monroe, N.W., 49503-2639.
Telephone: 616-454-8656.
Fax: 616-776-6322.
Howell, Michigan Office: 121 South Barnard Street, Suite 4, 48843-2305.
Telephone: 517-546-7600.
Telecopier: 517-546-6974.
Kalamazoo, Michigan Office: 444 West Michigan Avenue, 49007-3752.
Telephone: 616-381-7030.
Fax: 616-382-0244.
Lansing, Michigan Office: One Michigan Avenue, Suite 900, 48933-1609.
Telephone: 517-487-2070.
Fax: 517-374-6304.
Monroe, Michigan Office: The Executive Centre, 214 East Elm Avenue, 48161-2682.
Telephone: 313-243-2000.
Fax: 313-243-0901.
Washington, D.C. Office: 1225 Nineteenth Street, N.W., Suite 400. 20036.
Telephone: 202-429-5575; 785-0600.
Fax: 202-331-1118; 785-1234.
Pensacola, Florida Office: 25 West Cedar, 32501.
Telephone: 904-469-1088.
Fax: 904-432-0677.
St. Petersburg, Florida Office: 100 Second Avenue S., Suite 7045, 33701.
Telephone: 813-982-6000.
Fax: 813-892-6002.
Gdansk, Poland Office: Suite 322, Dom Technika Building, Ul. Rajska 6, 80-850.
Telephone: 011-485-831-2808.
Fax: 011-485-831-4719.
Warsaw, Poland Office: Ul. Marszalkowska 82, Suite 561, 00-517.
Telephone: 011-482-623-6457 and 6458.
Fax: 011-482-623-6459.

RESIDENT PARTNER

Robert E. Gilbert

Representative Firm Clients: Chrysler Corp.; Comerica, Inc.; City of Detroit, Mich.; Detroit Tigers, Inc.; First of Michigan; Fretter, Inc.; Ford Motor Co.; Ford Motor Credit Co.; Great Lakes Bancorp; Henry Ford Hospital.

For Complete List of Firm Personnel, See General Section

For full biographical listings, see the Martindale-Hubbell Law Directory

BATTLE CREEK, Calhoun Co.

Varnum, Riddering, Schmidt & Howlett (AV)

4950 West Dickman Road, Suite B-1, 49015
Telephone: 616-962-7144
Grand Rapids, Michigan Office: Bridgewater Place, P.O. Box 352, 49501-0352.
Telephone: 616-336-6000; 800-262-0011.
Facsimile: 616-336-7000.
Telex: 1561593 VARN.
Lansing, Michigan Office: The Victor Center, Suite 810, 201 North Washington Square, 48933.
Telephone: 517-482-6237.
Facsimile: 517-482-6937.
Kalamazoo, Michigan Office: 350 East Michigan Avenue, 49007.
Telephone: 616-382-2300.
Facsimile: 616-382-2382.
Grand Haven, Michigan Office: 321 Washington Street, P.O. Box 288, 49417.
Telephone: 616-846-7100.
Facsimile: 616-846-7101.
Detroit, Michigan Office: 440 East Congress, Fourth Floor, 48226.
Telephone: 313-961-1600.
Facsimile: 313-961-1636.

MEMBER OF FIRM

Carl E. Ver Beek

For full biographical listings, see the Martindale-Hubbell Law Directory

*DETROIT,** Wayne Co.

Butzel Long, A Professional Corporation (AV)

Suite 900, 150 West Jefferson, 48226
Telephone: 313-225-7000
Telecopier: 313-225-7080
Birmingham, Michigan Office: Suite 200, 32270 Telegraph Road.
Telephone: 810-258-1616.
Telecopier: 810-258-1439.
Lansing, Michigan Office: 118 West Ottawa Street.
Telephone: 517-372-6622.
Telecopier: 517-372-6672.
Ann Arbor, Michigan Office: Suite 400, 121 West Washington.
Telephone: 313-995-3110.
Telecopier: 313-995-1777.
Grosse Pointe Farms, Michigan Office: Suite 260, 21 Kercheval.
Telephone: 313-886-5446.
Telecopier: 313-886-2114.

C. Peter Theut
James C. Bruno

Brian J. Miles
Daniel R. W. Rustmann

Representative Clients: Bridgestone/Firestone, Inc.; The Detroit News, Inc.; Detroit Diesel Corp.; Kelly Services; Kelsey Hayes Co.; Merrill Lynch & Co., Inc.; Stroh Brewery Co.; Takata Corp.; United Parcel Services of America, Inc.; The University of Michigan.

For Complete List of Firm Personnel, See General Section

For full biographical listings, see the Martindale-Hubbell Law Directory

Clark, Klein & Beaumont (AV)

1600 First Federal Building, 1001 Woodward Avenue, 48226
Telephone: 313-965-8300
Facsimile: 313-962-4348
Bloomfield Hills Office: 1533 North Woodward Avenue, Suite 220, 48304.
Telephone: 810-258-2900.
Facsimile: 810-258-2949.

MEMBERS OF FIRM

Richard C. Marsh
James E. Baiers

Representative Clients: Leaseway Transportation Corp.; Gra-Bell Truck Line, Inc.; Motor City Cartage Co.; Thompson Transport, Ltd.; Liquid Cargo Lines, Ltd.; Transportation Club of Detroit.

For Complete List of Firm Personnel, See General Section

For full biographical listings, see the Martindale-Hubbell Law Directory

Eames, Wilcox, Mastej, Bryant, Swift & Riddell (AV)

1400 Buhl Building, 48226-3602
Telephone: 313-963-3750
Facsimile: 313-963-8485

MEMBERS OF FIRM

Leonard A. Wilcox, Jr.
Ronald J. Mastej
John W. Bryant
Jerry R. Swift
Neill T. Riddell
Elizabeth Roberto
Kevin N. Summers

ASSOCIATE

Keith M. Aretha

(See Next Column)

OF COUNSEL

Rex Eames
Robert E. Gesell
William B. McIntyre, Jr.

Representative Clients: ABF Freight System, Inc.; ANR Freight System, Inc.; City Transfer Co.; Kingsway Transports Limited; Parker Motor Freight, Inc.; Robinson Cartage Co.; Rogers Cartage Co.; Schneider Transport; Tank Carrier Employers Association of Michigan; TNT Transport Group, Inc.

For full biographical listings, see the Martindale-Hubbell Law Directory

Foster, Meadows & Ballard, P.C. (AV)

3200 Penobscot Building, 48226
Telephone: 313-961-3234
Cable Address: "Foster"
Telex: 23-5823
Facsimile: 313-961-6184

Sparkman D. Foster (1897-1967)
John L. Foster
Charles R. Hrdlicka
Paul D. Galea
Richard A. Dietz
Robert H. Fortunate
Robert G. Lahiff
Camille A. Raffa-Dietz

Michael J. Liddane
Paul A. Kettunen

OF COUNSEL

John F. Langs
John A. Mundell, Jr.

Representative Clients: Burlington Northern Railway; Canadian National Railways; Grand Trunk Western Railroad Co.; Island of Bob-Lo Co.; British Marine Mutual Insurance Association, Ltd.; Brittania Steam-Ship Insurance Association; Japan Ship Owners Mutual Protection & Indemnity Association; Liverpool and London Steamship Protection & Indemnity Association, Ltd.

For full biographical listings, see the Martindale-Hubbell Law Directory

Miller, Canfield, Paddock and Stone, P.L.C. (AV)

A Professional Limited Liability Company
Founded in 1852 by Sidney Davy Miller
150 West Jefferson, Suite 2500, 48226-4415
Telephone: 313-963-6420
Fax: 313-496-7500
Cable Address: "Stem Detroit"
Detroit, Michigan Office: 150 West Jefferson, Suite 2500, 48226-4415.
Telephone: 313-963-6420.
Fax: 313-496-7500.
Cable Address: "Stem Detroit."
Ann Arbor, Michigan Office: 101 North Main Street, 7th Floor, 48104-1400.
Telephone: 313-663-2445.
Fax: 313-747-7147.
Bloomfield Hills, Michigan Office: Suite 100, Pinehurst Office Center, 1400 North Woodward, 48303-2014.
Telephone: 313-645-5000.
Fax: 313-645-1917.
Grand Rapids, Michigan Office: 1200 Campau Square Plaza, 99 Monroe, N.W., 49503-2639.
Telephone: 616-454-8656.
Fax: 616-776-6322.
Howell, Michigan Office: 121 South Barnard Street, Suite 4, 48843-2305.
Telephone: 517-546-7600.
Telecopier: 517-546-6974.
Kalamazoo, Michigan Office: 444 West Michigan Avenue, 49007-3752.
Telephone: 616-381-7030.
Fax: 616-382-0244.
Lansing, Michigan Office: One Michigan Avenue, Suite 900, 48933-1609.
Telephone: 517-487-2070.
Fax: 517-374-6304.
Monroe, Michigan Office: The Executive Centre, 214 East Elm Avenue, 48161-2682.
Telephone: 313-243-2000.
Fax: 313-243-0901.
Washington, D.C. Office: 1225 Nineteenth Street, N.W., Suite 400. 20036.
Telephone: 202-429-5575; 785-0600.
Fax: 202-331-1118; 785-1234.
Pensacola, Florida Office: 25 West Cedar, 32501.
Telephone: 904-469-1088.
Fax: 904-432-0677.
St. Petersburg, Florida Office: 100 Second Avenue S., Suite 7045, 33701.
Telephone: 813-982-6000.
Fax: 813-892-6002.
Gdansk, Poland Office: Suite 322, Dom Technika Building, Ul. Rajska 6, 80-850.
Telephone: 011-485-831-2808.
Fax: 011-485-831-4719.
Warsaw, Poland Office: Ul. Marszalkowska 82, Suite 561, 00-517.
Telephone: 011-482-623-6457 and 6458.
Fax: 011-482-623-6459.

MEMBERS OF FIRM

Leonard D. Givens
John R. Cook (Kalamazoo Office)
Lawrence D. Owen (Lansing Office)
Ronald E. Baylor (Kalamazoo Office)

(See Next Column)

MILLER, CANFIELD, PADDOCK AND STONE P.L.C., *Detroit—Continued*

Representative Firm Clients: Chrysler Corp.; Comerica, Inc.; City of Detroit, Mich.; Detroit Tigers, Inc.; First of Michigan; Fretter, Inc.; Ford Motor Co.; Ford Motor Credit Co.; Great Lakes Bancorp; Henry Ford Hospital.

For Complete List of Firm Personnel, See General Section

For full biographical listings, see the Martindale-Hubbell Law Directory

FARMINGTON HILLS, Oakland Co.

FOSTER, SWIFT, COLLINS & SMITH, P.C. (AV)

32300 Northwestern Highway, Suite 230, 48334
Telephone: 810-851-7500
Fax: 810-851-7504
Lansing, Michigan Office: 313 South Washington Square.
Telephone: 517-371-8100.
Telecopier: 517-371-8200.

James M. Alexander
Robert E. McFarland
Paul J. Millenbach
Kathryn M. Niemer

For full biographical listings, see the Martindale-Hubbell Law Directory

*GRAND RAPIDS,** Kent Co.

WARNER, NORCROSS & JUDD (AV)

900 Old Kent Building, 111 Lyon Street, N.W., 49503-2489
Telephone: 616-752-2000
Fax: 616-752-2500
Muskegon, Michigan Office: 400 Terrace Plaza, P.O. Box 900.
Telephone: 616-727-2600.
Fax: 616-727-2699.
Holland, Michigan Office: Curtis Center, Suite 300, 170 College Avenue.
Telephone: 616-396-9800.
Fax: 616-396-3656.

MEMBER OF FIRM

Edward Malinzak

Representative Clients: Ryder Truck Lines, Inc.; Bernea Trucking Co.; Ron Besteman Transport; Bulkmatic Transport Co.; Bestway Moving Bay Cartage; Davis Motor Express, Inc.; Equity Transportation, Inc.; Graff Trucking Co.; Grand Express Inc.; Lemmen Transportation Co.

For Complete List of Firm Personnel, See General Section

For full biographical listings, see the Martindale-Hubbell Law Directory

WHEELER UPHAM, A PROFESSIONAL CORPORATION (AV)

Second Floor, Trust Building, 40 Pearl Street, N.W., 49503
Telephone: 616-459-7100
Fax: 616-459-6366

Gordon B. Wheeler (1904-1986)
Buford A. Upham (Retired)
Robert H. Gillette
Geoffrey L. Gillis
John M. Roels
Gary A. Maximiuk
Timothy J. Orlebeke
Kenneth E. Tiews
Jack L. Hoffman
Janet C. Baxter
Peter Kladder, III
James M. Shade
Thomas A. Kuiper

Counsel for: Conrail; The Penn Central Corp.; The United Railroad Corp.

For full biographical listings, see the Martindale-Hubbell Law Directory

*KALAMAZOO,** Kalamazoo Co.

MILLER, CANFIELD, PADDOCK AND STONE, P.L.C. (AV)

A Professional Limited Liability Company
Founded in 1852 by Sidney Davy Miller
444 West Michigan Avenue, 49007-3752
Telephone: 616-381-7030
Fax: 616-382-0244
Detroit, Michigan Office: 150 West Jefferson, Suite 2500, 48226-4415.
Telephone: 313-963-6420.
Fax: 313-496-7500.
Cable Address: "Stem Detroit."
Ann Arbor, Michigan Office: 101 North Main Street, 7th Floor, 48104-1400.
Telephone: 313-663-2445.
Fax: 313-747-7147.
Bloomfield Hills, Michigan Office: Suite 100, Pinehurst Office Center, 1400 North Woodward, 48303-2014.
Telephone: 313-645-5000.
Fax: 313-645-1917.
Grand Rapids, Michigan Office: 1200 Campau Square Plaza, 99 Monroe, N.W., 49503-2639.
Telephone: 616-454-8656.
Fax: 616-776-6322.
Howell, Michigan Office: 121 South Barnard Street, Suite 4, 48843-2305.
Telephone: 517-546-7600.
Telecopier: 517-546-6974.
Lansing, Michigan Office: One Michigan Avenue, Suite 900, 48933-1609.
Telephone: 517-487-2070.
Fax: 517-374-6304.

(See Next Column)

Monroe, Michigan Office: The Executive Centre, 214 East Elm Avenue, 48161-2682.
Telephone: 313-243-2000.
Fax: 313-243-0901.
Washington, D.C. Office: 1225 Nineteenth Street, N.W., Suite 400. 20036.
Telephone: 202-429-5575; 785-0600.
Fax: 202-331-1118; 785-1234.
Pensacola, Florida Office: 25 West Cedar, 32501.
Telephone: 904-469-1088.
Fax: 904-432-0677.
St. Petersburg, Florida Office: 100 Second Avenue S., Suite 7045,33701.
Telephone: 813-982-6000.
Fax: 813-892-6002.
Gdansk, Poland Office: Suite 322, Dom Technika Building, UI. Rajska 6, 80-850.
Telephone: 011-485-831-2808.
Fax: 011-485-831-4719.
Warsaw, Poland Office: UI. Marszalkowska 82, Suite 561, 00-517.
Telephone: 011-482-623-6457 and 6458.
Fax: 011-482-623-6459.

MEMBERS OF FIRM

Eric V. Brown, Jr. (Resident)
John R. Cook (Resident)
Ronald E. Baylor (Resident)

Representative Firm Clients: Chrysler Corp.; Comerica, Inc.; City of Detroit, Mich.; Detroit Tigers, Inc.; First of Michigan; Fretter, Inc.; Ford Motor Co.; Ford Motor Credit Co.; Great Lakes Bancorp; Henry Ford Hospital.

For Complete List of Firm Personnel, See General Section

For full biographical listings, see the Martindale-Hubbell Law Directory

LANSING, Ingham Co.

* indicates certain Bar Register subscribers whose principal office is located elsewhere in the state and who have arranged for representation as a part of the state capital listings that follow

FOSTER, SWIFT, COLLINS & SMITH, P.C. (AV)

313 South Washington Square, 48933-2193
Telephone: 517-371-8100
Telecopier: 517-371-8200
Farmington Hills, Michigan Office: 32300 Northwestern Highway, Suite 230.
Telephone: 810-851-7500.
Fax: 810-851-7504.

Robert E. McFarland (Resident, Farmington Hills Office)
Kathryn M. Niemer (Resident, Farmington Hills Office)

Representative Clients: Central Transport, Inc.; Davis Cartage Co.; Pony Express Courier Corp.; Universal Am-Can Ltd.; Michigan Intra-State Motor Tariff Bureau, Inc.; O-J Transport Co.; Troy CAB Co.

For Complete List of Firm Personnel, See General Section

For full biographical listings, see the Martindale-Hubbell Law Directory

* HONIGMAN MILLER SCHWARTZ AND COHN (AV)

A Partnership including Professional Corporations
222 North Washington Square, Suite 400, 48933
Telephone: 517-484-8282
Telecopier: 517-484-8286
Detroit, Michigan Office: 2290 First National Building.
Telephone: 313-256-7800.
West Palm Beach, Florida Office: Suite 800 Esperante Building, 222 Lakeview Avenue.
Telephone: 407-838-4500.
Tampa, Florida Office: Suite 350 One Harbour Place, 777 South Harbour Island Boulevard.
Telephone: 813-221-6600.
Orlando, Florida Office: 390 North Orange Avenue, Suite 1300.
Telephone: 407-648-0300.
Houston, Texas Office: 3100 First Interstate Bank Plaza, 1000 Louisiana.
Telephone: 713-650-2600.
Los Angeles, California Office: McNeill Plaza, Suite 820, 15260 Ventura Boulevard, 91403.
Telephone: 818-784-2900.

MEMBERS

Frederick M. Baker, Jr.
Daniel J. Demlow
Ruth E. Zimmerman

Representative Client: TNT Holland Motor Express, Inc.

For Complete List of Firm Personnel, See General Section

For full biographical listings, see the Martindale-Hubbell Law Directory

*PONTIAC,** Oakland Co.

HACKETT, MAXWELL & PHILLIPS, P.L.L.C. (AV)

The Riker Building, Suite 902, 35 West Huron Street, 48342
Telephone: 810-335-0404
Facsimile: 810-335-0581

(See Next Column)

HACKETT, MAXWELL & PHILLIPS P.L.L.C.—*Continued*

Patrick E. Hackett | Phillip B. Maxwell

Representative Clients: Lake State Railway Co.; Michigan Interstate Railway Co.; CSX Transportation; Michigan Railway Assn.; Norfolk Southern Corp.; Ann Arbor Railroad; North American Van Lines.

For full biographical listings, see the Martindale-Hubbell Law Directory

SOUTHFIELD, Oakland Co.

O'LEARY, O'LEARY, JACOBS, MATTSON, PERRY & MASON, P.C. (AV)

26777 Central Park Boulevard, Suite 275, 48076
Telephone: 810-799-8260

John Patrick O'Leary
Thomas M. O'Leary
John P. Jacobs
Kenneth M. Mattson
C. Kenneth Perry, Jr.
Larry G. Mason
D. Jennifer Andreou
Kevin P. Hanbury
Debra A. Reed

For full biographical listings, see the Martindale-Hubbell Law Directory

TROY, Oakland Co.

MATHESON, PARR, SCHULER, EWALD, ESTER & JOLLY (AV)

2555 Crooks Road, Suite 200, 48084
Telephone: 810-643-7900
Telecopier: 810-643-0417

MEMBERS OF FIRM

Eugene C. Ewald
Robert D. Schuler
John W. Ester

Representative Clients: National Automobile Transporters Labor Division; Brink's Inc.; Expertec, Inc.; Advance Technology, Inc.; Digital Electronic Automation, Inc.; Frito-Lay, Inc.
Reference: Comerica Bank.

For Complete List of Firm Personnel, See General Section

For full biographical listings, see the Martindale-Hubbell Law Directory

MISSISSIPPI

BILOXI, Harrison Co.

BROWN & WATT, P.A. (AV)

115 Main Street, P.O. Box 1377, 39533-1377
Telephone: 601-374-2999
Telecopier: 601-435-7090
Pascagoula, Mississippi Office: 3112 Canty Street, P.O. Box 2220.
Telephone: 601-762-0035.
Fax: 601-762-0299.

Raymond L. Brown
W. Lee Watt
Patrick R. Buchanan
William M. Edwards
A. Kelly Sessoms, III
R. Bradley Prewitt
Alan K. Sudduth

General Counsel For: Mississippi Export Railroad Co.; Pascagoula Municipal Separate School District.
Representative Clients: United States Fidelity & Guaranty Co.; The Travelers Companies; The Home Insurance Co.; CSX Transportation, Inc.; Blue Cross-Blue Shield of Mississippi; Burlington Insurance Co.; Continental Insurance; Deere & Company.

For full biographical listings, see the Martindale-Hubbell Law Directory

*GULFPORT,** Harrison Co.

DUKES, DUKES, KEATING AND FANECA, P.A. (AV)

2308 East Beach Boulevard, P.O. Drawer W, 39501
Telephone: 601-868-1111
FAX: 601-863-2886

Hugh D. Keating
Cy Faneca
William H. Pettey, Jr.

For full biographical listings, see the Martindale-Hubbell Law Directory

*PASCAGOULA,** Jackson Co.

BROWN & WATT, P.A. (AV)

3112 Canty Street, P.O. Box 2220, 39569-2220
Telephone: 601-762-0035
Telecopier: 601-762-0299
Biloxi, Mississippi Office: 115 Main Street, P.O. Box 1377.
Telephone: 601-374-2999.
Fax: 601-435-7090.

(See Next Column)

Raymond L. Brown
W. Lee Watt
Patrick R. Buchanan
William M. Edwards
A. Kelly Sessoms, III
R. Bradley Prewitt
Alan K. Sudduth

General Counsel For: Mississippi Export Railroad Co.; Pascagoula Municipal Separate School District.
Representative Clients: United States Fidelity & Guaranty Co.; The Travelers Companies; The Home Insurance Co.; CSX Transportation, Inc.; Blue Cross-Blue Shield of Mississippi; Burlington Insurance Co.; Continental Insurance; Deere & Company.

For full biographical listings, see the Martindale-Hubbell Law Directory

MISSOURI

KANSAS CITY, Jackson, Clay & Platte Cos.

SWANSON, MIDGLEY, GANGWERE, KITCHIN & MCLARNEY, L.L.C. (AV)

1500 Commerce Trust Building, 922 Walnut, 64106-1848
Telephone: 816-842-6100
Overland Park, Kansas Office: The NCAA Building, Suite 350, 6201 College Boulevard.
Telephone: 816-842-6100.

Richard N. Bien

Counsel for: General Electric Co.; Chrysler Corp.; Conoco, Inc.; Yellow Freight System, Inc.; The Prudential Insurance Co. of America; Metropolitan Life Insurance Co.; National Collegiate Athletic Assn.; Land Title Insurance Co.; Safeway Stores, Inc.; The Lee Apparel Co.

For Complete List of Firm Personnel, See General Section

For full biographical listings, see the Martindale-Hubbell Law Directory

NEW JERSEY

*NEWARK,** Essex Co.

MCCARTER & ENGLISH (AV)

Four Gateway Center, 100 Mulberry Street, P.O. Box 652, 07101-0652
Telephone: 201-622-4444
Telecopier: 201-624-7070
Cable Address: "McCarter" Newark
Cherry Hill, New Jersey Office: 1810 Chapel Avenue West.
Telephone: 609-662-8444.
Telecopier: 609-662-6203.
New York, New York Office: Suite 1519, One World Trade Center.
Telephone: 212-466-9018.
Telecopier: 212-432-6568.
Boca Raton, Florida Office: 2255 Glades Road, Suite 319-A.
Telephone: 407-994-6262.
Telecopier: 407-241-0798.
Wilmington, Delaware Office: Mellon Bank Center, 919 Market Street.
Telephone: 302-654-8010.
Telecopier: 302-654-0795.

MEMBERS OF FIRM

Thomas F. Daly
John L. McGoldrick
James H. Keale

For Complete List of Firm Personnel, See General Section

For full biographical listings, see the Martindale-Hubbell Law Directory

SILLS CUMMIS ZUCKERMAN RADIN TISCHMAN EPSTEIN & GROSS, A PROFESSIONAL CORPORATION (AV)

One Riverfront Plaza, 07102-5400
Telephone: 201-643-7000
Fax: 201-643-6500
Telex: 820630 Sillsbeck Nwk
Atlantic City, New Jersey Office: 17 Gordon's Alley.
Telephone: 609-344-2800.
New York, N.Y. Office: 250 Park Avenue.
Telephone: 212-643-7000.

Clive S. Cummis
Kenneth F. Oettle
Richard J. Schulman (Not admitted in NJ)

Patricia M. Kerins
Paul P. Josephson

OF COUNSEL

Mitchel E. Ostrer

Representative Clients: New England Motor Freight; Gray Line Worldwide Tours; Shortline Bus Company; Westates Airlines; Kiwi Airlines.

(See Next Column)

SILLS CUMMIS ZUCKERMAN RADIN TISCHMAN EPSTEIN & GROSS A PROFESSIONAL CORPORATION, *Newark—Continued*

For Complete List of Firm Personnel, See General Section

For full biographical listings, see the Martindale-Hubbell Law Directory

NEW MEXICO

*SANTA FE,** Santa Fe Co.

JONES, SNEAD, WERTHEIM, RODRIGUEZ & WENTWORTH, P.A. (AV)

215 Lincoln Avenue, P.O. Box 2228, 87504-2228
Telephone: 505-982-0011
Fax: 505-989-6288

O. Russell Jones (1912-1978)
James E. Snead
Jerry Wertheim
Manuel J. Rodriguez
John Wentworth
Arturo L. Jaramillo
Peter V. Culbert
James G. Whitley
Francis J. Mathew

Jerry Todd Wertheim
Carol A. Clifford

LEGAL SUPPORT PERSONNEL

PARALEGALS

Linda A. Zieba

General Counsel for: Charter Bank for Savings, F.S.B.; National Education Association of New Mexico.
Representative Clients: Century Bank, F.S.B.; 3M; Scurlock Permian Corp.; Merchants' Fast Motor Lines; Billy Walker Trucking, Inc.; Centel Cellular, Inc.; Santa Fe Properties, Inc.
Reference: Bank of Santa Fe.

For full biographical listings, see the Martindale-Hubbell Law Directory

NEW YORK

*NEW YORK,** New York Co.

CHALOS & BROWN, P.C. (AV)

300 East 42nd Street, 10017-5982
Telephone: 212-661-5440
Telecopier: 212-697-8999
Telex: 238470 (RCA)
Clifton, New Jersey Office: 1118 Clifton Avenue.
Telephone: 201-779-1116.

Michael G. Chalos
Robert J. Brown
Harry A. Gavalas
Stephan Skoufalos
Thomas M. Russo
Martin F. Casey
Robert J. Seminara

Edward P. Flood
Timothy G. Hourican
Fred G. Wexler
Steven G. Friedberg
George J. Tsimis
Martin F. Marvet
Laurence Curran

References: Citibank, N.A.; Chase Manhattan Bank.

For full biographical listings, see the Martindale-Hubbell Law Directory

WATSON, FARLEY & WILLIAMS (AV)

380 Madison Avenue, 10017
Telephone: 212-922-2200
Telex: 6790626 WFW NY
Fax: 212-922-1512
London, England Office: 15 Appold Street, London EC2A 2HB.
Telephone: (44 71) 814 8000.
Telex: 8955707 WFW LON G.
Fax: (44 71) 814 8141.
Paris, France Office: 19 rue de Marignan, 75008 Paris.
Telephone: (33 1) 45 63 15 15.
Telex: WFW PAR 651096 F.
Fax: (33 1) 45 61 09 01.
Oslo, Norway Office: Beddingen 8, Aker Brygge, 0250 Oslo.
Telephone: (47 22) 83 83 08.
Telex: 79209 WFW N.
Fax: (47 22) 83 83 13.
Athens, Greece Office: Alassia Building, Defteras Merarchias 13, 185-35 Piraeus.
Telephone: (30 1) 422 3660.
Telex: 24 1311 WFW GR.
Fax: (30 1) 422 3664.

(See Next Column)

Moscow, Russia Office: 36 Myaskovskovo Street, Moscow 121019.
Telephone: (7 502) 224 1700 (international only); (7 095) 291 8046/5968.
Fax: (7 502) 224 1701 (international only); (7 095) 202 9027.
Copenhagen, Denmark Office: Lille Kongensgade 20 DK-1074 Copenhagen K.
Telephone: (45 33) 91 33 03.
Fax: (45 33) 91 49 12.

MEMBERS OF FIRM

Derick W. Betts, Jr.
Leo Chang
John E. Nelson II
David N. Osborne
John S. Osborne, Jr.
Alfred E. Yudes, Jr.
Thatcher A. Stone
Joseph G. Braunreuther
Peter S. Smedresman
Philip H. Spector
R. Jay Fortin

For Complete List of Firm Personnel, See General Section

For full biographical listings, see the Martindale-Hubbell Law Directory

OHIO

*COLUMBUS,** Franklin Co.

* indicates certain Bar Register subscribers whose principal office is located elsewhere in the state and who have arranged for representation as a part of the state capital listings that follow

* **BAKER & HOSTETLER** (AV)

Capitol Square, Suite 2100, 65 East State Street, 43215-4260
Telephone: 614-228-1541
Telecopier: 614-462-2616
In Cleveland, Ohio: 3200 National City Center, 1900 East Ninth Street.
Telephone: 216-621-0200.
In Denver, Colorado: 303 East 17th Avenue, Suite 1100.
Telephone: 202-861-1500.
In Houston, Texas: 1000 Louisiana, Suite 2000.
Telephone: 713-751-1600.
In Long Beach, California: 300 Oceangate, Suite 620.
Telephone: 310-432-2827.
In Los Angeles, California: 600 Wilshire.
Telephone: 213-624-2400.
In Orlando, Florida: SunBank Center, Suite 2300, 200 South Orange Avenue.
Telephone: 407-649-4000.
In Washington, D. C.: Washington Square, Suite 1100, 1050 Connecticut Avenue, N.W.
Telephone: 202-861-1500.
In College Park, Maryland: 9658 Baltimore Boulevard, Suite 301.
Telephone: 301-441-2781.
In Alexandria, Virginia: 437 North Lee Street.
Telephone: 703-549-1294.
In San Francisco, California: One Sansome Street, Suite 2000.
Telephone: 415-951-4705.

PARTNERS

A. Charles Tell
David A. Turano

RETIRED PARTNER

John P. McMahon

For Complete List of Firm Personnel, See General Section

For full biographical listings, see the Martindale-Hubbell Law Directory

CLARK, PERDUE, ROBERTS & SCOTT CO., L.P.A. (AV)

471 East Broad Street Suite 1400, 43215
Telephone: 614-469-1400
Fax: 614-469-0900

Dale K. Perdue
Paul O. Scott
Douglas S. Roberts
Edward L. Clark
Glen R. Pritchard
Robert W. Kerpsack, Jr.
D. Andrew List
Brian W. Palmer

For full biographical listings, see the Martindale-Hubbell Law Directory

GAMBLE HARTSHORN ALDEN (AV)

One Livingston Avenue, 43215-5700
Telephone: 614-221-0922
FAX: 614-365-9741

MEMBER OF FIRM

John L. Alden

Theodore F. Claypoole

For full biographical listings, see the Martindale-Hubbell Law Directory

*TOLEDO,** Lucas Co.

DOYLE, LEWIS & WARNER (AV)

202 North Erie Street, P.O. Box 2168, 43603
Telephone: 419-248-1500
Fax: 419-248-2002

MEMBERS OF FIRM

Steven Timonere
Richard F. Ellenberger
Michael E. Hyrne
John A. Borell
Michael A. Bruno

ASSOCIATE

Kevin A. Pituch

OF COUNSEL

Harold A. James

Counsel for: Consolidated Rail Corp.; The Lakefront Dock & Railroad Terminal Co.; Prudential Insurance Co. of America; Equitable Life Assurance Society of the U.S.; Metropolitan Life Insurance Co.; Greyhound Lines; Fireman's Fund Insurance Cos.

For Complete List of Firm Personnel, See General Section

For full biographical listings, see the Martindale-Hubbell Law Directory

OKLAHOMA

*OKLAHOMA CITY,** Oklahoma Co.

ANDREWS DAVIS LEGG BIXLER MILSTEN & PRICE, A PROFESSIONAL CORPORATION (AV)

500 West Main, 73102
Telephone: 405-272-9241
FAX: 405-235-8786

R. Brown Wallace

For Complete List of Firm Personnel, See General Section

For full biographical listings, see the Martindale-Hubbell Law Directory

WILLIAM C. BOSTON & ASSOCIATES (AV)

4005 Northwest Expressway, Suite 600, 73116
Telephone: 405-848-0600
Telefax: 405-848-0655

Scott D. McCreary
William Clayton Boston, III
Eric L. Johnson
KimberLee Kimzey Osby

OF COUNSEL

Joseph T. Brennan (Not admitted in OK)
Donna M. Schmidt (Not admitted in OK)
Willis W. Luttrell (Not admitted in OK)

For full biographical listings, see the Martindale-Hubbell Law Directory

OREGON

*PORTLAND,** Multnomah Co.

COONEY & CREW, P.C. (AV)

Pioneer Tower, Suite 890, 888 S.W. Fifth Avenue, 97204
Telephone: 503-224-7600
FAX: 503-224-6740

Paul A. Cooney
Thomas E. Cooney
Thomas M. Cooney
Brent M. Crew
Michael D. Crew
Kelly T. Hagan
Raymond F. Mensing, Jr.
Robert S. Perkins

LEGAL SUPPORT PERSONNEL

Alma Weber (Paralegal)

For full biographical listings, see the Martindale-Hubbell Law Directory

MARTIN SCHEDLER, P.C. (AV)

Suite 1818, Standard Insurance Center, 900 S.W. Fifth Avenue, 97204
Telephone: 503-228-9641
Fax: 503-228-9642

Martin Schedler

For full biographical listings, see the Martindale-Hubbell Law Directory

PENNSYLVANIA

*HARRISBURG,** Dauphin Co.

MANCKE, WAGNER, HERSHEY AND TULLY (AV)

2233 North Front Street, 17110
Telephone: 717-234-7051
Fax: 717-234-7080

MEMBERS OF FIRM

John B. Mancke
P. Richard Wagner
David E. Hershey
William T. Tully

ASSOCIATE

David R. Breschi

For full biographical listings, see the Martindale-Hubbell Law Directory

McNEES, WALLACE & NURICK (AV)

100 Pine Street, P.O. Box 1166, 17108
Telephone: 717-232-8000
Fax: 717-237-5300

MEMBERS OF FIRM

Terry R. Bossert
William A. Chesnutt
James L. Fritz
Herbert R. Nurick
S. Berne Smith
Lawrence R. Wieder

ASSOCIATE

P. Nicholas Guarneschelli

For Complete List of Firm Personnel, See General Section

For full biographical listings, see the Martindale-Hubbell Law Directory

*PHILADELPHIA,** Philadelphia Co.

LOUIS J. CARTER (AV)

7300 City Line Avenue, 19151-2291
Telephone: 215-879-8665
FAX: 215- 877-0955

For full biographical listings, see the Martindale-Hubbell Law Directory

JOHN GERARD DEVLIN & ASSOCIATES, P.C. (AV)

2100 Fidelity Building, P.O. Box 58908, 19109
Telephone: 215-545-4190
Telefax: 215-564-6732
Allentown, Pennsylvania Office: The Sovereign Building, Executive Suite 103, 609 Hamilton Mall.
Telephone: 215-820-6422.
Westmont, New Jersey Office: 216 Haddon Avenue, Suite 103, 08108.
Telephone: 609-858-1690.
FAX: 609-858-8998.
East Brunswick, New Jersey Office: 190 Route 18, Suite 3000, 08816.
Telephone: 908-214-2621.
Fax: 908-246-2917.

John Gerard Devlin
James B. Corrigan, Jr.
Joseph T. Murphy, Jr.
Louis J. Mairone, Jr.
J. Brian Durkin
Thomas Paschos
Joseph A. Whip, Jr.
Michael Malarick (East Brunswick, N.J. and Westmont, N.J. Offices)
Dora R. Garcia

Representative Clients: Lloyds of London; Commercial Union; John Hancock Property and Casualty Insurance Co.; Sentry Insurance Co.; Wausau Insurance Co.; State Farms Insurance Co.; Hanseco Insurance Co.; American Family Insurance Co.; Liberty Mutual Insurance Co.; Linberg Adjustment Co.

For full biographical listings, see the Martindale-Hubbell Law Directory

GALLAGHER, REILLY AND LACHAT, P.C. (AV)

Suite 1300, 2000 Market Street, 19103
Telephone: 215-299-3000
FAX: 215-299-3010
Pennsauken, New Jersey Office: Kevon Office Center, Suite 130, 2500 McClellan Boulevard, 08109.
Telephone: 609-663-8200.

Stanley S. Frazee, Jr.
Paul F. X. Gallagher
Thomas F. Reilly
Frederick T. Lachat, Jr.
Richard K. Hohn
James Emerson Egbert
Stephen A. Scheuerle
Elizabeth F. Walker

David Scott Morgan
Wilfred T. Mills, Jr.
Maureen Rowan
Charles L. McNabb
Thomas O'Neill
Laurence I. Gross
Sean F. Kennedy
Milica Novakovic
John A. Livingood, Jr.

SPECIAL COUNSEL

Dolores Rocco Kulp

For full biographical listings, see the Martindale-Hubbell Law Directory

Philadelphia—Continued

GERMAN, GALLAGHER & MURTAGH, A PROFESSIONAL CORPORATION (AV)

Fifth Floor, The Bellevue, 200 South Broad Street, 19102
Telephone: 215-545-7700
Telecopier: 215-732-4182
Cherry Hill, New Jersey Office: Suite 643, 1040 North Kings Highway.
Telephone: 609-667-7676.
Lancaster, Pennsylvania Office: 40 East Grant Street.
Telephone: 717-293-8070.

Edward C. German
Michael D. Gallagher
Dean F. Murtagh
Philip A. Ryan
Robert P. Corbin
David P. Rovner
Kathryn A. Dux
Gary R. Gremminger
Kim Plouffe
Jeffrey N. German
John P. Shusted

Kathleen M. Carson
Kevin R. McNulty
Linda Porr Sweeney
Gary H. Hunter
Frank A. Gerolamo, III
Milan K. Mrkobrad
Thomas M. Going
Vincent J. Di Stefano, Jr.
Jack T. Ribble, Jr.
Kimberly J. Keiser
Bernard E. Jude Quinn
Gerald C. Montella
Lisa Beth Zucker
Shelby L. Mattioli
Daniel J. Divis
D. Selaine Belver
Christine L. Davis
Daniel L. Grill
Marta I. Sierra-Epperson
Paul G. Kirk
Aileen R. Thompson
Otis V. Maynard
Gregory S. Capps

For full biographical listings, see the Martindale-Hubbell Law Directory

*PITTSBURGH,** Allegheny Co.

RICHARD J. MILLS & ASSOCIATES (AV)

200 Benedum Trees Building, 223 Fourth Avenue, 15222-1713
Telephone: 412-471-2442
Fax: 412-471-2456

Richard J. Mills

Austin P. Henry
Dale S. Douglas

For full biographical listings, see the Martindale-Hubbell Law Directory

PILLAR AND MULROY, P.C. (AV)

Suite 700, 312 Boulevard of Allies, 15222
Telephone: 412-471-3300
Fax: 412-471-6068

John A. Pillar

Reference: Pittsburgh National Bank.

For full biographical listings, see the Martindale-Hubbell Law Directory

VUONO, LAVELLE & GRAY (AV)

2310 Grant Building, 15219
Telephone: 412-471-1800
Fax: 412-471-4477

MEMBERS OF FIRM

John A. Vuono
William J. Lavelle
William A. Gray
Mark T. Vuono
Richard R. Wilson

ASSOCIATES

Dennis J. Kusturiss
Christine M. Dolfi
Peter J. Scanlon

Reference: Pittsburgh National Bank.

For full biographical listings, see the Martindale-Hubbell Law Directory

WICK, STREIFF, MEYER, METZ & O'BOYLE, P.C. (AV)

1450 Two Chatham Center, 15219
Telephone: 412-765-1600
Telecopier: 412-261-3783

Henry M. Wick, Jr.
Charles J. Streiff
Carl F. Meyer
LeRoy L. Metz, II
David M. O'Boyle
Vincent P. Szeligo
Patricia J. Liptak-McGrail

Lucille N. Wick
Ronald Joseph Rademacher
Roger A. Isla
Donna Lynn Miller

Reference: PNC Bank.

For full biographical listings, see the Martindale-Hubbell Law Directory

TEXAS

*AUSTIN,** Travis Co.

MCGINNIS, LOCHRIDGE & KILGORE, L.L.P. (AV)

1300 Capitol Center, 919 Congress Avenue, 78701
Telephone: 512-495-6000
Houston, Texas Office: 3200 One Houston Center, 1221 McKinney Street.
Telephone: 713-615-8500.

MEMBER OF FIRM

Campbell McGinnis

For Complete List of Firm Personnel, See General Section

For full biographical listings, see the Martindale-Hubbell Law Directory

*DALLAS,** Dallas Co.

CALHOUN & STACY (AV)

5700 NationsBank Plaza, 901 Main Street, 75202-3747
Telephone: 214-748-5000
Telecopier: 214-748-1421
Telex: 211358 CALGUMP UR

Mark Alan Calhoun
David W. Elrod
Steven D. Goldston
Parker Nelson
Roy L. Stacy

ASSOCIATES

Shannon S. Barclay
Robert A. Bragalone
Dennis D. Conder
Jane Elizabeth Diseker
Lawrence I. Fleishman
Thomas C. Jones
Katherine Johnson Knight
V. Paige Pace
Veronika Willard
Michael C. Wright

LEGAL CONSULTANT

Rees T. Bowen, III

For full biographical listings, see the Martindale-Hubbell Law Directory

*SAN ANTONIO,** Bexar Co.

MATTHEWS & BRANSCOMB, A PROFESSIONAL CORPORATION (AV)

One Alamo Center, 106 S. St. Mary's Street, Suite 800, 78205
Telephone: 210-226-4211
Facsimile: 210-226-0521
Telex: 5106009283
Cable Code: MBLAW
Austin, Texas Office: 301 Congress Avenue, Suite 2050.
Telephone: 512-305-4400.
Facsimile: 512-305-4413.
Corpus Christi, Texas Office: 802 N. Carancahua, Suite 1900.
Telephone: 512-888-9261.
Facsimile: 512-888-8504.
Eagle Pass, Texas Office: 675 Main Street.
Telephone: 210-773-6700.
Facsimile: 210-757-4045.
Uvalde, Texas Office: 200 E. Nopal #208.
Telephone: 210-278-4597.
Facsimile: 210-278-4806.
(Associated with Hall, Quintanilla & Alarcon, L.C., Laredo, Texas, under the name of Hall, Quintanilla, Alarcon, Matthews & Branscomb, P.L.L.C.)

Lewis T. Tarver, Jr.
J. Joe Harris
George P. Parker, Jr.
Howard P. Newton
Richard C. Danysh
Marshall T. Steves, Jr.
Howard D. Bye
Merritt M. Clements
Kay L. Reamey

Representative Clients: Coca Cola Bottling Company of the Southwest; Concord Oil Co.; Ellison Enterprises, Inc.; H. E. Butt Grocery Co.; Frank B. Hall & Co., Inc.; The Hearst Corp., San Antonio Light Division; San Antonio Gas & Electric Utilities (City Board); Southern Pacific Transportation Co.; Southwest Texas Methodist Hospital.

For Complete List of Firm Personnel, See General Section

For full biographical listings, see the Martindale-Hubbell Law Directory

VIRGINIA

ALEXANDRIA, (Independent City)

THOMAS, BALLENGER, VOGELMAN AND TURNER, P.C. (AV)

124 South Royal Street, 22314
Telephone: 703-836-3400
Fax: 703-836-3549

(See Next Column)

THOMAS, BALLENGER, VOGELMAN AND TURNER P.C.—*Continued*

John M. Ballenger
Jeffrey A. Vogelman

References: First Union National Bank of Virginia; Burke & Herbert Bank & Trust Co.

For Complete List of Firm Personnel, See General Section

For full biographical listings, see the Martindale-Hubbell Law Directory

*ARLINGTON,** Arlington Co.

JACKSON & JESSUP, P.C. (AV)

3426 North Washington Boulevard, P.O. Box 1240, 22210
Telephone: 703-525-4050
Facsimile: 703-525-4054

William P. Jackson, Jr.
David C. Reeves
John T. Sullivan
John R. Copley

OF COUNSEL

Gerald E. Jessup

Reference: First American Bank.

For full biographical listings, see the Martindale-Hubbell Law Directory

WEST VIRGINIA

*CHARLESTON,** Kanawha Co.

JACKSON & KELLY (AV)

1600 Laidley Tower, P.O. Box 553, 25322
Telephone: 304-340-1000
Fax: 304-340-1130
Martinsburg, West Virginia Office: 300 Foxcroft Avenue, P.O. Box 1068.
Telephone: 304-263-8800.
Morgantown, West Virginia Office: 6000 Hampton Center, P.O. Box 619.
Telephone: 304-599-3000.
New Martinsville, West Virginia Office: 256 Russell Avenue, P.O. Box 68.
Telephone: 304-455-1751.
Charles Town, West Virginia Office: 700 East Washington Street, P.O. Box 983.
Telephone: 304-728-6088.
Clarksburg, West Virginia Office: 203 Main Street, P.O. Box 1587.
Telephone: 304-623-3002.
Lexington, Kentucky Office: 175 East Main Street, Suite 500, P.O. Box 2150.
Telephone: 606-255-9500.
Washington, D. C. Office: 2401 Pennsylvania Avenue, N.W., Suite 400.
Telephone: 202-973-0200.
Denver, Colorado Office: Suite 2710, 1660 Lincoln Street.
Telephone: 303-837-0003.

MEMBERS OF FIRM

Winfield T. Shaffer
Thomas E. Potter
Michael A. Albert
Stephen R. Crislip
Alvin L. Emch
David Allen Barnette
Dennis C. Sauter
Thomas J. Hurney, Jr.
John Philip Melick
William J. Powell
David J. Hardy

ASSOCIATE

Maris E. McCambley

Representative Clients: United Parcel Service; Kanawha Valley Regional Transportation Authority; Central West Virginia Regional Airport Authority; Norfolk & Western Railway Co.; Savage Industries, Inc.; Piper Aviation; Beech Aircraft, Inc.; Overnite Transportation; British Aerospace, Inc.; Lloyds of London.

For Complete List of Firm Personnel, See General Section

For full biographical listings, see the Martindale-Hubbell Law Directory

WISCONSIN

*GREEN BAY,** Brown Co.

SCHOBER & ULATOWSKI, S.C. (AV)

414 East Walnut Street, Suite 150, 54305-1780
Telephone: 414-432-5355
Facsimile: 414-432-5967

Thomas L. Schober

For full biographical listings, see the Martindale-Hubbell Law Directory

PUERTO RICO

SAN JUAN, San Juan Dist.

JIMÉNEZ, GRAFFAM & LAUSELL

Formerly Jiménez & Fusté
Suite 505, Midtown Building, 421 Muñoz Rivera Avenue, Hato Rey, P.O. Box 366104, 00936-6104
Telephone: 809-767-1030; 767-1000; 767-1061; 767-1064
Telefax: 809-751-4068;
Cable: "Nezte"; RCA
Telex: 325-2730

MEMBERS OF FIRM

Nicolás Jiménez
William A. Graffam
Steven C. Lausell
J. Ramón Rivera-Morales
José Juan Torres-Escalera
Raquel M. Dulzaides
Manuel San Juan

ASSOCIATES

Manolo T. Rodríguez-Bird
Patricia Garrity
Carlos E. Bayrón
Isabel J. Vélez-Serrano
Edgardo A. Vega-López

Representative Clients: Crowley Maritime Corp.; Sea-Land Service, Inc.; NYK Line, Inc.; Overnite Transportation Co.; The Britannia Steamship Insurance Association.

For Complete List of Firm Personnel, See General Section

For full biographical listings, see the Martindale-Hubbell Law Directory

CANADA
NEW BRUNSWICK

*SAINT JOHN,** Saint John Co.

CLARK, DRUMMIE & COMPANY (AV)

40 Wellington Row, P.O. Box 6850 Station "A", E2L 4S3
Telephone: 506-633-3800
Telecopier (Automatic): 506-633-3811

MEMBERS OF FIRM

Deno P. Pappas, Q.C.
W. Andrew LeMesurier

Reference: Royal Bank of Canada.

For Complete List of Firm Personnel, See General Section

For full biographical listings, see the Martindale-Hubbell Law Directory

CANADA
NOVA SCOTIA

*HALIFAX,** Halifax Co.

MCINNES COOPER & ROBERTSON (AV)

1601 Lower Water Street, P.O. Box 730, B3J 2V1
Telephone: 902-425-6500
Fax: 902-425-6350
St. John's, Newfoundland Office: Suite 602, Scotia Centre, 235 Water Street, P.O. Box 547. A1C, 5K8.
Telephone: 709-726-9500.
Fax: 709-726-9550.

Reginald A. Cluney, Q.C.
George T. H. Cooper, Q.C.
Wylie Spicer
Harvey L. Morrison
Stewart McInnes, P.C., Q.C.
James E. Gould, Q.C.
John D. Stringer
Thomas E. Hart
Brian G. Johnston

Attorneys for: Bank of Nova Scotia; Imperial Oil, Limited; Frank B. Hall & Co., Inc. (New York); American Steamship Owners Protection & Indemnity Association, Inc.; Coca-Cola, Ltd.; Scott Worldwide Inc.; Hong Kong Bank of Canada.

For Complete List of Firm Personnel, See General Section

For full biographical listings, see the Martindale-Hubbell Law Directory

CANADA
QUEBEC

*MONTREAL,** Montreal Dist.

McMaster Meighen (AV)

A General Partnership
7th Floor, 630 René-Lévesque Boulevard West, H3B 4H7
Telephone: 514-879-1212
Telecopier: 514-878-0605
Cable Address: "Cammerall"
Telex: "Cammerall MTL" 05-268637
Affiliated with Fraser & Beatty in Toronto, North York, Ottawa and Vancouver.

MEMBERS OF FIRM

Sean J. Harrington
P. Jeremy Bolger
Nancy G. Cleman
Jon H. Scott
Nicholas J. Spillane
Peter G. Pamel

COUNSEL

A. Stuart Hyndman, Q.C.

For Complete List of Firm Personnel, See General Section

For full biographical listings, see the Martindale-Hubbell Law Directory